BUTTERWORTHS
SECURITIES & FINANCIAL SERVICES
LAW HANDBOOK

Tenth edition

Consultant Editor

Deborah A Sabalot,
BA, DipLib, MLib, JD (Solicitor),
Professional Associate, Outer Temple Chambers

LexisNexis
® Butterworths

Members of the LexisNexis Group worldwide

United Kingdom	LexisNexis, a Division of Reed Elsevier (UK) Ltd, Halsbury House, 35 Chancery Lane, London, WC2A 1EL, and London House, 20–22 East London Street, Edinburgh EH7 4BQ
Australia	LexisNexis Butterworths, Chatswood, New South Wales
Austria	LexisNexis Verlag ARD Orac GmbH & Co KG, Vienna
Benelux	LexisNexis Benelux, Amsterdam
Canada	LexisNexis Canada, Markham, Ontario
China	LexisNexis China, Beijing and Shanghai
France	LexisNexis SA, Paris
Germany	LexisNexis Deutschland GmbH, Munster
Hong Kong	LexisNexis Hong Kong, Hong Kong
India	LexisNexis India, New Delhi
Italy	Giuffrè Editore, Milan
Japan	LexisNexis Japan, Tokyo
Malaysia	Malayan Law Journal Sdn Bhd, Kuala Lumpur
New Zealand	LexisNexis NZ Ltd, Wellington
Poland	Wydawnictwo Prawnicze LexisNexis Sp, Warsaw
Singapore	LexisNexis Singapore, Singapore
South Africa	LexisNexis Butterworths, Durban
USA	LexisNexis, Dayton, Ohio

© Reed Elsevier (UK) Ltd 2009
Published by LexisNexis

This is a Butterworths title

A CIP Catalogue record for this book is available from the British Library.

ISBN: 978 1 4057 3720 3

Typeset by Columns Design Ltd, Reading, England
Printed in the UK by CPI William Clowes Beccles NR34 7TL

Visit LexisNexis at www.lexisnexis.co.uk

PREFACE

In 1994 when the first edition of the *Financial Services Law Handbook* was published, financial services regulation was a much simpler affair and European materials comprised less than fifty pages of that first edition. Now, the tenth edition sees a change of name to the *Butterworths Securities & Financial Services Law Handbook*, reflecting the changing nature of financial services regulation. Furthermore, the addition of various materials to the Handbook enables it to stand on its own in its field, independent of its sister publication, the *Butterworths Company Law Handbook*.

This tenth edition is, however, coming at a watershed for the financial services industry. After the long bull market, many of the assumptions about the economy and the regulation of the financial services sector have been turned on their head on their head in the past year. As Warren Buffett famously observed, "You only find out who is swimming naked when the tide goes out", and this adage can be applied to politicians and regulators as well.

The credit crunch and its world-wide economic effects, including the uncovering of some notable financial sector frauds, has generated calls for greater regulation of the markets. What is probably required is better, not necessarily more, regulation and a greater emphasis on the harmonisation of regulatory standards as well as the improvement of supervision techniques, both domestically and on an international basis. HM Treasury has taken extraordinary steps to revamp the framework for banks and building societies in financial difficulties to ameliorate some of the problems that arose with the nationalisation of Northern Rock in the form of the Banking Act 2009. The Commission has already outlined its "roadmap" for strengthening the European mandate of national supervisors, and the de Larosiere report and its proposals for the creation of a European system of financial supervisors along the lines of the European Central Bank show that Europe is considering fundamental reform of the regulatory infrastructure. These proposals will, in particular, allow financial supervisory authorities to consider the risk to the wider economic system and take into account financial stability concerns in other Member States when exercising their supervisory duties. The roadmap will also improve the functioning of the EU Committees of Supervisors (Level 3 Committees in the Lamfalussy process) for individual cross-border financial groups, which should also ensure the exchange of information between the home and host country supervisors.

Regulators will, however, be looking more closely in the near to medium term at a range of issues including liquidity requirements, the operation of unregulated sectors and the comprehensiveness of the regulatory regime, the use of leverage and credit policies, and the regulation of credit rating agencies, as well as more general topics such as transparency and the corporate governance of investment firms.

The practical needs of publication deadlines have, as ever, necessitated simply noting some of the prospective changes or providing indications of proposed, but as yet unenacted, measures.

The Handbook is not intended to include the Rules, Regulations and Guidance made by the Financial Services Authority in accordance with its powers under FSMA 2000. The sheer volume of this material, and the rate at which it changes, makes it outside the remit of this work. Transitional Orders relating to FSMA 2000 have not been reproduced in this edition, but a chronological table of statutory instruments made under the Act will, hopefully, help readers to get to grips with the mass of legislation that sits under FSMA 2000.

This volume contains a table showing the updated dates of commencement of FSMA 2000 (including sections and Schedules added to the Act since it received Royal assent in 2000). It also includes extracts from other primary legislation that either affects, or is affected by, FSMA 2000, or which is of particular relevance to the financial services industry; examples being materials in relation to the Proceeds of Crime Act 2002 and anti-money laundering.

The Handbook is divided into six main Parts—

- Part I. Financial Services and Markets Act 2000

- Part II. Other Acts

- Part III. Statutory Instruments

- Part IV. EC materials

- Part V. Other materials

- Appendix (SIs published late February 2009).

Part III (Statutory Instruments) is further divided into sections by function—

- A. FSMA 2000 Commencement Orders

- B. FSMA 2000 Statutory Instruments

- C. Other Statutory Instruments

Section A of the new Part V contains materials issued by the Joint Money Laundering Steering Group (JMLSG) ie, the full Guidance for the UK Financial Sector (Parts I and II), the JMLSG Guidance on Equivalent Jurisdictions and the JMLSG Guidance on Equivalent Markets. Part V, Section B contains the BERR Regulators' Compliance Code.

All material is reproduced chronologically within these Parts. In relation to the statutory and European material, the following points should be noted—

- Material in italics is prospectively repealed/revoked or substituted. The notes provide a detailed explanation of such prospective amendments.

- Material within square brackets is the subject of one or more insertions or substitutions of text. Again, the notes provide full details.

- Modifications of provisions are set out in full in the notes where relevant. In some cases, where modifications or extensions of scope have been made (for example, in relation to the Financial Services and Markets Act 2000 (Regulated Activities) Order 2001), this is noted as a cross-reference to the note at the beginning of that Part or section, etc.

- Where an Act or Statutory Instrument is amending only, it is not included in full, although the notes will provide a summary of the changes. The amendments made by such legislation are fully incorporated into the relevant provisions where they are within the scope of this work.

As with previous editions of the Handbook, this edition provides an up-to-date and readily portable text of FSMA 2000, its associated secondary legislation, as well as relevant other Acts of the UK parliament, and European legislative materials. It is up-to-date to 1 February 2009 though later developments have been noted wherever possible. In particular, this edition includes the Banking Act 2009 and the Payment Services Regulations 2009 both of which were published in mid-February. In addition, a new Appendix was added just a few days before this Handbook went to print and includes the ten statutory instruments made at the end of February under the Banking Act 2009 and the Banking (Special Provisions) Act 2008.

This Handbook is also made available as part of the LexisNexis Butterworths online service and is updated fortnightly on that site.

Deborah A. Sabalot
February 2009.

CONTENTS

PART III STATUTORY INSTRUMENTS

A. FSMA 2000 Commencement Orders

B. FSMA 2000 Statutory Instruments

C. Other Statutory Instruments

PART IV EC MATERIALS

PART V OTHER MATERIALS

A. Joint Money Laundering Steering Group Materials

B. Codes of Practice

APPENDIX

PART I
FINANCIAL SERVICES
AND MARKETS ACT 2000

FINANCIAL SERVICES AND MARKETS ACT 2000

(2000 c 8)

NOTES

This Act is reproduced as amended by the following Acts:

2000	Insolvency Act 2000; Regulation of Investigatory Powers Act 2000.
2001	Criminal Justice and Police Act 2001.
2002	Enterprise Act 2002; Proceeds of Crime Act 2002.
2003	Communications Act 2003.
2004	Civil Partnership Act 2004.
2005	Constitutional Reform Act 2005; Inquiries Act 2005; Gambling Act 2005; Regulation of Financial Services (Land Transactions) Act 2005.
2006	Consumer Credit Act 2006; Companies Act 2006; Investment Exchanges and Clearing Houses Act 2006.
2007	Consumers, Estate Agents and Redress Act 2007; Tribunals, Courts and Enforcement Act 2007.
2008	Dormant Bank and Building Society Accounts Act 2008; Counter-Terrorism Act 2008.
2009	Banking Act 2009.

This Act is reproduced as amended by the following SIs:

2000	Banking Consolidation Directive (Consequential Amendments) Regulations 2000, SI 2000/2952.
2001	Financial Services and Markets Act 2000 (Regulated Activities) Order 2001, SI 2001/544; Limited Liability Partnerships Regulations 2001, SI 2001/1090; Financial Services (EEA Passport Rights) Regulations 2001, SI 2001/1376; Financial Services and Markets Act 2000 (Variation of Threshold Conditions) Order 2001, SI 2001/2507; Public Offers of Securities (Exemptions) Regulations 2001, SI 2001/2955.
2002	Financial Services and Markets Act 2000 (Regulated Activities) (Amendment) Order 2002, SI 2002/682; Electronic Commerce Directive (Financial Services and Markets) Regulations 2002, SI 2002/1775; Financial Services and Markets Act 2000 (Variation of Threshold Conditions) Order 2002, SI 2002/2707.
2003	Insurance Mediation Directive (Miscellaneous Amendments) Regulations 2003, SI 2003/1473; Financial Services and Markets Act 2000 (Regulated Activities) (Amendment) (No 2) Order 2003, SI 2003/1476; Collective Investment Schemes (Miscellaneous Amendments) Regulations 2003, SI 2003/2066.
2004	Life Assurance Consolidation Directive (Consequential Amendments) Regulations 2004, SI 2004/3379.
2005	Financial Services and Markets Act 2000 (Market Abuse) Regulations 2005, SI 2005/381; Prospectus Regulations 2005, SI 2005/1433; Insolvency (Northern Ireland) Order 2005, SI 2005/1455.
2006	Charities and Trustee Investment (Scotland) Act 2005 (Consequential Provisions and Modifications) Order 2006, SI 2006/242; Taxation of Pension Schemes (Consequential Amendments) Order 2006, SI 2006/745; Takeovers Directive (Interim Implementation) Regulations 2006, SI 2006/1183; Financial Services and Markets Act 2000 (Regulated Activities) (Amendment) (No 2) Order 2006, SI 2006/2383; Financial Services and Markets Act 2000 (Markets in Financial Instruments) (Modification of Powers) Regulations 2006, SI 2006/2975; Capital Requirements Regulations 2006, SI 2006/3221.
2007	Financial Services (EEA State) Regulations 2007, SI 2007/108; Financial Services and Markets Act 2000 (Markets in Financial Instruments) Regulations 2007, SI 2007/126; Companies Act 2006 (Commencement No 2, Consequential Amendments, Transitional Provisions and Savings) Order 2007, SI 2007/1093; Regulatory Reform (Financial Services and Markets Act 2000) Order 2007, SI 2007/1973; Companies Act 2006 (Commencement No 3, Consequential Amendments, Transitional Provisions and Savings) Order 2007, SI 2007/2194; Financial Services and Markets Act 2000 (Motor Insurance) Regulations 2007, SI 2007/2403; Reinsurance Directive Regulations 2007, SI 2007/3253.
2008	Companies Act 2006 (Consequential Amendments etc) Order 2008, SI 2008/948; Financial Services and Markets Act 2000 (Market Abuse) Regulations 2008, SI 2008/1439; Financial Services and Markets Act 2000 (Amendments to Part 7) Regulations 2008, SI 2008/1468; Financial Services and Markets Act 2000 (Amendment of section 323) Regulations 2008, SI 2008/1469; Definition of Financial Instrument Order 2008, SI 2008/3053.
2009	Payment Services Regulations 2009.

ARRANGEMENT OF SECTIONS

PART I
THE REGULATOR

PART II
REGULATED AND PROHIBITED ACTIVITIES

The general prohibition

PART III
AUTHORISATION AND EXEMPTION

Authorisation

PART VI
OFFICIAL LISTING

The competent authority

PART I
FSMA 2000

PART XXI
MUTUAL SOCIETIES

Friendly societies

Building societies

Industrial and provident societies and credit unions

Supplemental

PART XXII
AUDITORS AND ACTUARIES

Appointment

Information

Disqualification

Offence

PART XXIII
PUBLIC RECORD, DISCLOSURE OF INFORMATION AND CO-OPERATION

The public record

Disclosure of information

Co-operation

PART XXIV
INSOLVENCY

Interpretation

Voluntary arrangements

Administration orders

PART XXX
SUPPLEMENTAL

SCHEDULES:

An Act to make provision about the regulation of financial services and markets; to provide for the transfer of certain statutory functions relating to building societies, friendly societies, industrial and provident societies and certain other mutual societies; and for connected purposes

[14 June 2000]

NOTES

Commencement: see s 431 at **[457]** and Appendix 1 (Commencement Dates of FSMA 2000) at **[498]**.

Regulatory functions of the Financial Services Authority: the Legislative and Regulatory Reform Act 2006, s 21 imposes a duty on any person exercising a specified regulatory function to have regard to the five principles of good regulation. The principles provide that regulatory activities should be carried out in a way which is transparent, accountable, proportionate and consistent and should be targeted only at cases in which action is needed. Section 22 of the 2006 Act enables a Minister to issue a Code of Practice relating to the exercise of regulatory functions (the "Regulators' Compliance Code"). Section 22 imposes a duty on any person exercising a specified regulatory function to have regard to the Regulators' Compliance Code when determining general policies or principles by reference to which that person exercises those functions. The Legislative and Regulatory Reform (Regulatory Functions) Order 2007, SI 2007/3544, arts 2–4, Schedule, Pt 1 provide that ss 21, 22 of the 2006 Act apply to the regulatory functions of the FSA. The Statutory Code of Practice for Regulators as promulgated by the Department for Business, Enterprise and Regulatory Reform is at **[7101]**.

Limited liability partnerships: ss 215(3), (4), (6), 356, 359(1)–(4), 361–365, 367, 370, and 371 of this Act apply to limited liability partnerships (except where the context otherwise requires and subject to certain modifications); see the Limited Liability Partnerships Regulations 2001, SI 2001/1090, reg 6 at **[3559]**.

Application of Act to certain overseas investment exchanges and clearing houses: see the Companies Act 1989, s 170 at **[1167]**.

Application of Act to payment service providers: see the Payment Services Regulations 2009, SI 2009/209 at **[4387]**. In particular, see Sch 5, Pt 1 to those Regulations ("Application and Modification of the 2000 Act").

Exemption from requirement for contract for sale etc of land to be in writing: a contract regulated under this Act, other than a regulated mortgage contract, a regulated home reversion plan, and a regulated home purchase plan, is exempt from the Law of Property (Miscellaneous Provisions) Act 1989, s 2 (contracts for sale etc of land to be made by writing); see s 2(5) of that Act at **[1150]**.

Transitional provisions and savings: a number of instruments have been made under this Act making various transitional provisions and savings which are not reproduced in this edition. These instruments are listed under the note "Orders" to s 426 and Sch 21.

Transfer of functions – mutual societies: The Financial Services and Markets Act 2000 (Mutual Societies) Order 2001, SI 2001/2617, art 4(2) at **[2456]** (made under ss 334–339, 426, 427, 428(3)) transfers to the Financial Services Authority certain functions which, immediately before 1 December 2001, were functions of: (a) the Chief Registrar of friendly societies, assistant registrars of friendly societies or the central office of the registry of friendly societies; (b) the Friendly Societies Commission; or (c) the Building Societies Commission. Sch 2 to the 2001 Order makes provisions concerning the application of this Act in relation to functions transferred to the Authority by the said art 4(2).

Regulated claims management services: with effect from 23 April 2007 (the day on which the Compensation Act 2006, s 4(1) came into force), a person who provides "regulated claims management services" (i) must be authorised under the 2006 Act to do so, or (ii) be exempted, or (iii) have the benefit of a waiver of the obligation to be authorised, or (iv) be an individual acting otherwise than in the course of business. The Compensation (Regulated Claims Management Services) Order 2006, SI 2006/3319 sets out the kinds of services to be regulated when provided in connection with certain kinds of claim, and this includes claims relating to financial products and services (see art 4(3)(f) of the 2006 Order). The Compensation (Exemptions) Order 2007, SI 2007/209, art 5 exempts a person who is carrying out a regulated claims management service if in providing that service he is carrying on a regulated activity or would be doing so except that he is exempt from the general prohibition under FSMA, or he has the benefit of an exclusion under the Financial Services and Markets Act 2000 (Regulated Activities) Order 2001.

Banking (Special Provisions) Act 2008: various Orders made under the Banking (Special Provisions) Act 2008 apply and modify certain provisions of this Act in relation to the banks that are the subject of the Orders; see:

- the Northern Rock plc Transfer Order 2008, SI 2008/432 at **[4158]**;
- the Northern Rock plc Compensation Scheme Order 2008, SI 2008/718 at **[4149]**;
- the Bradford & Bingley plc Transfer of Securities and Property etc Order 2008, SI 2008/2546 at **[4277]**;
- the Heritable Bank plc Transfer of Certain Rights and Liabilities Order 2008, SI 2008/2644 at **[4272]**;
- the Transfer of Rights and Liabilities to ING Order 2008, SI 2008/2666 at **[4306]**;
- the Kaupthing Singer & Friedlander Limited Transfer of Certain Rights and Liabilities Order 2008, SI 2008/2674 at **[4339]**;
- the Bradford & Bingley plc Compensation Scheme Order 2008, SI 2008/3249 at **[4376]**.

See, in particular, the modifications in those Orders to s 138 of this Act (General rule-making power), s 148 (Modification or waiver of rules), s 155 (Consultation), and s 157 (Guidance).

Offences under this Act:

Generally, see Pt XXVII (ss 397–403) at **[424]** et seq. As to offences committed by bodies corporate etc, see s 400 at **[427]**; as to proceedings for offences, see s 401 at **[428]**; and as to jurisdiction and procedure in respect of offences, see s 403 at **[430]**. See also s 28(9) at **[28]**, as to the illegality or invalidity of agreements.

Standard Scale; Statutory Maximum: there are numerous references to the standard scale and to the statutory maximum throughout this Act (and other legislation contained in this Handbook). The standard scale is the scale

set out in the Criminal Justice Act 1982, s 37(2), but different amounts may be substituted by order under the Magistrates' Courts Act 1980, s 143. The current scale (as substituted by the Criminal Justice Act 1991, s 17(1), as from 1 October 1992) is—
  level 1: £200;
  level 2: £500;
  level 3: £1,000;
  level 4: £2,500; and
  level 5: £5,000.

The statutory maximum is the prescribed sum within the meaning of the Magistrates' Courts Act 1980, s 32. Section 32(9) of the 1980 Act (as amended by the Criminal Justice Act 1991, s 17(2)(c), as from 1 October 1992), provides that the prescribed sum is £5,000, but a different sum may be substituted by order under s 143 of the 1980 Act.

PART I
THE REGULATOR

1   The Financial Services Authority

(1)   The body corporate known as the Financial Services Authority ("the Authority") is to have the functions conferred on it by or under this Act.

(2)   The Authority must comply with the requirements as to its constitution set out in Schedule 1.

(3)   Schedule 1 also makes provision about the status of the Authority and the exercise of certain of its functions.

[(4)   Section 249 of the Banking Act 2009 provides for references to functions of the Authority (whether generally or under this Act) to include references to functions conferred on the Authority by that Act (subject to any order under that section).]

[1]

NOTES
  Sub-s (4): added by the Banking Act 2009, s 249, as from a day to be appointed.
  Note: the FSA is the same corporate entity as the former Securities and Investments Board and later assumed functions under the Banking Act 1985 and exercised other functions on behalf of the Treasury under other financial services legislation.
  The self regulating bodies (the Securities and Futures Authority, the Investment Management Regulatory Organisation and the Personal Investment Authority) established under the Financial Services Act 1986 were constituted as companies limited by guarantee and were wound up on the designated dates specified under the Financial Services and Markets Act 2000 (Transitional Provisions) (Designated Date for The Securities and Futures Authority) Order 2001, SI 2001/2255, and the Financial Services and Markets (Transitional Provisions) (Designated Date for Certain Self-Regulating Organisations) Order 2000, SI 2000/1734.

The Authority's general duties

2   The Authority's general duties

(1)   In discharging its general functions the Authority must, so far as is reasonably possible, act in a way—
  (a)   which is compatible with the regulatory objectives; and
  (b)   which the Authority considers most appropriate for the purpose of meeting those objectives.

(2)   The regulatory objectives are—
  (a)   market confidence;
  (b)   public awareness;
  (c)   the protection of consumers; and
  (d)   the reduction of financial crime.

(3)   In discharging its general functions the Authority must have regard to—
  (a)   the need to use its resources in the most efficient and economic way;
  (b)   the responsibilities of those who manage the affairs of authorised persons;
  (c)   the principle that a burden or restriction which is imposed on a person, or on the carrying on of an activity, should be proportionate to the benefits, considered in general terms, which are expected to result from the imposition of that burden or restriction;
  (d)   the desirability of facilitating innovation in connection with regulated activities;
  (e)   the international character of financial services and markets and the desirability of maintaining the competitive position of the United Kingdom;
  (f)   the need to minimise the adverse effects on competition that may arise from anything done in the discharge of those functions;
  (g)   the desirability of facilitating competition between those who are subject to any form of regulation by the Authority.

(4)   The Authority's general functions are—

    (a)   its function of making rules under this Act (considered as a whole);
    (b)   its function of preparing and issuing codes under this Act (considered as a whole);
    (c)   its functions in relation to the giving of general guidance (considered as a whole); and
    (d)   its function of determining the general policy and principles by reference to which it performs particular functions.

  (5)   "General guidance" has the meaning given in section 158(5).

[2]

The regulatory objectives

3 Market confidence

  (1)   The market confidence objective is: maintaining confidence in the financial system.

  (2)   "The financial system" means the financial system operating in the United Kingdom and includes—
    (a)   financial markets and exchanges;
    (b)   regulated activities; and
    (c)   other activities connected with financial markets and exchanges.

[3]

4 Public awareness

  (1)   The public awareness objective is: promoting public understanding of the financial system.

  (2)   It includes, in particular—
    (a)   promoting awareness of the benefits and risks associated with different kinds of investment or other financial dealing; and
    (b)   the provision of appropriate information and advice.

  (3)   "The financial system" has the same meaning as in section 3.

[4]

5 The protection of consumers

  (1)   The protection of consumers objective is: securing the appropriate degree of protection for consumers.

  (2)   In considering what degree of protection may be appropriate, the Authority must have regard to—
    (a)   the differing degrees of risk involved in different kinds of investment or other transaction;
    (b)   the differing degrees of experience and expertise that different consumers may have in relation to different kinds of regulated activity;
    (c)   the needs that consumers may have for advice and accurate information; and
    (d)   the general principle that consumers should take responsibility for their decisions.

  (3)   "Consumers" means persons—
    (a)   who are consumers for the purposes of section 138; or
    (b)   who, in relation to regulated activities carried on otherwise than by authorised persons, would be consumers for those purposes if the activities were carried on by authorised persons.

[5]

NOTES
Extended definition of "consumer": see the note to s 138 at **[166]**.

---

6 The reduction of financial crime

  (1)   The reduction of financial crime objective is: reducing the extent to which it is possible for a business carried on—
    (a)   by a regulated person, or
    (b)   in contravention of the general prohibition,
to be used for a purpose connected with financial crime.

  (2)   In considering that objective the Authority must, in particular, have regard to the desirability of—
    (a)   regulated persons being aware of the risk of their businesses being used in connection with the commission of financial crime;
    (b)   regulated persons taking appropriate measures (in relation to their administration and employment practices, the conduct of transactions by them and otherwise) to prevent financial crime, facilitate its detection and monitor its incidence;
    (c)   regulated persons devoting adequate resources to the matters mentioned in paragraph (b).

(3)   "Financial crime" includes any offence involving—
(a)   fraud or dishonesty;
(b)   misconduct in, or misuse of information relating to, a financial market; or
(c)   handling the proceeds of crime.

(4)   "Offence" includes an act or omission which would be an offence if it had taken place in the United Kingdom.

(5)   "Regulated person" means an authorised person, a recognised investment exchange or a recognised clearing house.

[6]

NOTES
Note: a "regulated person" for these purposes includes an authorised person, a recognised investment exchange and a recognised clearing house, but the position of exempt persons under s 38 (exemption orders) or s 39 (appointed representatives) is not clear.

Corporate governance

7   Duty of Authority to follow principles of good governance
In managing its affairs, the Authority must have regard to such generally accepted principles of good corporate governance as it is reasonable to regard as applicable to it.

[7]

Arrangements for consulting practitioners and consumers

8   The Authority's general duty to consult
The Authority must make and maintain effective arrangements for consulting practitioners and consumers on the extent to which its general policies and practices are consistent with its general duties under section 2.

[8]

NOTES
See further as to the duty to consult, s 396 at **[423]**.

9   The Practitioner Panel
(1)   Arrangements under section 8 must include the establishment and maintenance of a panel of persons (to be known as "the Practitioner Panel") to represent the interests of practitioners.

(2)   The Authority must appoint one of the members of the Practitioner Panel to be its chairman.

(3)   The Treasury's approval is required for the appointment or dismissal of the chairman.

(4)   The Authority must have regard to any representations made to it by the Practitioner Panel.

(5)   The Authority must appoint to the Practitioner Panel such—
(a)   individuals who are authorised persons,
(b)   persons representing authorised persons,
(c)   persons representing recognised investment exchanges, and
(d)   persons representing recognised clearing houses,
as it considers appropriate.

[9]

NOTES
Note: Information regarding the Practitioner Panel can be obtained through its website at http://www.fs-pp.org.uk.

10   The Consumer Panel
(1)   Arrangements under section 8 must include the establishment and maintenance of a panel of persons (to be known as "the Consumer Panel") to represent the interests of consumers.

(2)   The Authority must appoint one of the members of the Consumer Panel to be its chairman.

(3)   The Treasury's approval is required for the appointment or dismissal of the chairman.

(4)   The Authority must have regard to any representations made to it by the Consumer Panel.

(5)   The Authority must appoint to the Consumer Panel such consumers, or persons representing the interests of consumers, as it considers appropriate.

[(5A)   The Secretary of State may direct the Authority to appoint as a member of the Consumer Panel a person specified by the Secretary of State who—
(a)   is a non-executive member of the National Consumer Council, and
(b)   is nominated for the purposes of this subsection by the National Consumer Council after consultation with the Authority.

(5B) Only one person may, at any time, be a member of the Consumer Panel appointed in accordance with a direction under subsection (5A); but that does not prevent the Authority appointing as a member of the Consumer Panel any person who is also a member of the National Consumer Council.

(5C) A person appointed in accordance with a direction under subsection (5A) ceases to be a member of the Panel on ceasing to be a non-executive member of the National Consumer Council.]

(6) The Authority must secure that the membership of the Consumer Panel is such as to give a fair degree of representation to those who are using, or are or may be contemplating using, services otherwise than in connection with businesses carried on by them.

(7) "Consumers" means persons, other than authorised persons—
    (a)   who are consumers for the purposes of section 138; or
    (b)   who, in relation to regulated activities carried on otherwise than by authorised persons, would be consumers for those purposes if the activities were carried on by authorised persons.

[10]

NOTES
Sub-ss (5A)–(5C): inserted by the Consumers, Estate Agents and Redress Act 2007, s 39, as from 21 December 2007.
Extended definition of "consumer": see the note to s 138 at [166].
Note: Information regarding the Consumer Panel can be obtained through its website at http://www.fs-cp.org.uk.

11 Duty to consider representations by the Panels

(1) This section applies to a representation made, in accordance with arrangements made under section 8, by the Practitioner Panel or by the Consumer Panel.

(2) The Authority must consider the representation.

(3) If the Authority disagrees with a view expressed, or proposal made, in the representation, it must give the Panel a statement in writing of its reasons for disagreeing.

[11]

Reviews

12 Reviews

(1) The Treasury may appoint an independent person to conduct a review of the economy, efficiency and effectiveness with which the Authority has used its resources in discharging its functions.

(2) A review may be limited by the Treasury to such functions of the Authority (however described) as the Treasury may specify in appointing the person to conduct it.

(3) A review is not to be concerned with the merits of the Authority's general policy or principles in pursuing regulatory objectives or in exercising functions under Part VI.

(4) On completion of a review, the person conducting it must make a written report to the Treasury—
    (a)   setting out the result of the review; and
    (b)   making such recommendations (if any) as he considers appropriate.

(5) A copy of the report must be—
    (a)   laid before each House of Parliament; and
    (b)   published in such manner as the Treasury consider appropriate.

(6) Any expenses reasonably incurred in the conduct of a review are to be met by the Treasury out of money provided by Parliament.

(7) "Independent" means appearing to the Treasury to be independent of the Authority.

[12]

13 Right to obtain documents and information

(1) A person conducting a review under section 12—
    (a)   has a right of access at any reasonable time to all such documents as he may reasonably require for purposes of the review; and
    (b)   may require any person holding or accountable for any such document to provide such information and explanation as are reasonably necessary for that purpose.

(2) Subsection (1) applies only to documents in the custody or under the control of the Authority.

(3)   An obligation imposed on a person as a result of the exercise of powers conferred by subsection (1) is enforceable by injunction or, in Scotland, by an order for specific performance under section 45 of the Court of Session Act 1988.

[13]

Inquiries

14   Cases in which the Treasury may arrange independent inquiries

(1)   This section applies in two cases.

(2)   The first is where it appears to the Treasury that—
   (a)   events have occurred in relation to—
      (i)   a collective investment scheme, or
      (ii)   a person who is, or was at the time of the events, carrying on a regulated activity (whether or not as an authorised person),
   which posed or could have posed a grave risk to the financial system or caused or risked causing significant damage to the interests of consumers; and
   (b)   those events might not have occurred, or the risk or damage might have been reduced, but for a serious failure in—
      (i)   the system established by this Act[, or by any previous statutory provision,] for the regulation of such schemes or of such persons and their activities; or
      (ii)   the operation of that system.

(3)   The second is where it appears to the Treasury that—
   (a)   events have occurred in relation to listed securities or an issuer of listed securities which caused or could have caused significant damage to holders of listed securities; and
   (b)   those events might not have occurred but for a serious failure [in—
      (i)   the regulatory system established by Part 6 or by any previous statutory provision concerned with the official listing of securities; or
      (ii)   the operation of that system].

(4)   If the Treasury consider that it is in the public interest that there should be an independent inquiry into the events and the circumstances surrounding them, they may arrange for an inquiry to be held under section 15.

(5)   "Consumers" means persons—
   (a)   who are consumers for the purposes of section 138; or
   (b)   who, in relation to regulated activities carried on otherwise than by authorised persons, would be consumers for those purposes if the activities were carried on by authorised persons.

[(5A)   "Event" does not include any event occurring before 1st December 2001 (but no such limitation applies to the reference in subsection (4) to surrounding circumstances).]

(6)   "The financial system" has the same meaning as in section 3.

(7)   "Listed securities" means anything which has been admitted to the official list under Part VI.

[14]

NOTES
Sub-s (2): words in square brackets inserted by the Inquiries Act 2005, s 46(1), (2), as from 7 June 2005.
Sub-s (3): words in square brackets substituted by the Inquiries Act 2005, s 46(1), (3), as from 7 June 2005.
Sub-s (5A): inserted by the Inquiries Act 2005, s 46(1), (4), as from 7 June 2005.
Extended definition of "consumer": see the note to s 138 at **[166]**.

15   Power to appoint person to hold an inquiry

(1)   If the Treasury decide to arrange for an inquiry to be held under this section, they may appoint such person as they consider appropriate to hold the inquiry.

(2)   The Treasury may, by a direction to the appointed person, control—
   (a)   the scope of the inquiry;
   (b)   the period during which the inquiry is to be held;
   (c)   the conduct of the inquiry; and
   (d)   the making of reports.

(3)   A direction may, in particular—
   (a)   confine the inquiry to particular matters;
   (b)   extend the inquiry to additional matters;
   (c)   require the appointed person to discontinue the inquiry or to take only such steps as are specified in the direction;
   (d)   require the appointed person to make such interim reports as are so specified.

[15]

16 Powers of appointed person and procedure

(1) The person appointed to hold an inquiry under section 15 may—
    (a) obtain such information from such persons and in such manner as he thinks fit;
    (b) make such inquiries as he thinks fit; and
    (c) determine the procedure to be followed in connection with the inquiry.

(2) The appointed person may require any person who, in his opinion, is able to provide any information, or produce any document, which is relevant to the inquiry to provide any such information or produce any such document.

(3) For the purposes of an inquiry, the appointed person has the same powers as the court in respect of the attendance and examination of witnesses (including the examination of witnesses abroad) and in respect of the production of documents.

(4) "Court" means—
    (a) the High Court; or
    (b) in Scotland, the Court of Session.

[16]

17 Conclusion of inquiry

(1) On completion of an inquiry under section 15, the person holding the inquiry must make a written report to the Treasury—
    (a) setting out the result of the inquiry; and
    (b) making such recommendations (if any) as he considers appropriate.

(2) The Treasury may publish the whole, or any part, of the report and may do so in such manner as they consider appropriate.

(3) Subsection (4) applies if the Treasury propose to publish a report but consider that it contains material—
    (a) which relates to the affairs of a particular person whose interests would, in the opinion of the Treasury, be seriously prejudiced by publication of the material; or
    (b) the disclosure of which would be incompatible with an international obligation of the United Kingdom.

(4) The Treasury must ensure that the material is removed before publication.

(5) The Treasury must lay before each House of Parliament a copy of any report or part of a report published under subsection (2).

(6) Any expenses reasonably incurred in holding an inquiry are to be met by the Treasury out of money provided by Parliament.

[17]

18 Obstruction and contempt

(1) If a person ("A")—
    (a) fails to comply with a requirement imposed on him by a person holding an inquiry under section 15, or
    (b) otherwise obstructs such an inquiry,
the person holding the inquiry may certify the matter to the High Court (or, in Scotland, the Court of Session).

(2) The court may enquire into the matter.

(3) If, after hearing—
    (a) any witnesses who may be produced against or on behalf of A, and
    (b) any statement made by or on behalf of A,
the court is satisfied that A would have been in contempt of court if the inquiry had been proceedings before the court, it may deal with him as if he were in contempt.

[18]

PART II
REGULATED AND PROHIBITED ACTIVITIES
The general prohibition

19 The general prohibition

(1) No person may carry on a regulated activity in the United Kingdom, or purport to do so, unless he is—
    (a) an authorised person; or
    (b) an exempt person.

(2) The prohibition is referred to in this Act as the general prohibition.

[19]

Requirement for permission

20   Authorised persons acting without permission

(1)   If an authorised person carries on a regulated activity in the United Kingdom, or purports to do so, otherwise than in accordance with permission—

    (a)   given to him by the Authority under Part IV, or

    (b)   resulting from any other provision of this Act,

he is to be taken to have contravened a requirement imposed on him by the Authority under this Act.

(2)   The contravention does not—

    (a)   make a person guilty of an offence;

    (b)   make any transaction void or unenforceable; or

    (c)   (subject to subsection (3)) give rise to any right of action for breach of statutory duty.

(3)   In prescribed cases the contravention is actionable at the suit of a person who suffers loss as a result of the contravention, subject to the defences and other incidents applying to actions for breach of statutory duty.

[20]

NOTES

Application in relation to interim permissions and interim approvals: see the notes preceding s 40 at **[40]**.

Regulations: the Financial Services and Markets Act 2000 (Rights of Action) Regulations 2001, SI 2001/2256 at **[2375]**.

Financial promotion

21   Restrictions on financial promotion

(1)   A person ("A") must not, in the course of business, communicate an invitation or inducement to engage in investment activity.

(2)   But subsection (1) does not apply if—

    (a)   A is an authorised person; or

    (b)   the content of the communication is approved for the purposes of this section by an authorised person.

(3)   In the case of a communication originating outside the United Kingdom, subsection (1) applies only if the communication is capable of having an effect in the United Kingdom.

(4)   The Treasury may by order specify circumstances in which a person is to be regarded for the purposes of subsection (1) as—

    (a)   acting in the course of business;

    (b)   not acting in the course of business.

(5)   The Treasury may by order specify circumstances (which may include compliance with financial promotion rules) in which subsection (1) does not apply.

(6)   An order under subsection (5) may, in particular, provide that subsection (1) does not apply in relation to communications—

    (a)   of a specified description;

    (b)   originating in a specified country or territory outside the United Kingdom;

    (c)   originating in a country or territory which falls within a specified description of country or territory outside the United Kingdom; or

    (d)   originating outside the United Kingdom.

(7)   The Treasury may by order repeal subsection (3).

(8)   "Engaging in investment activity" means—

    (a)   entering or offering to enter into an agreement the making or performance of which by either party constitutes a controlled activity; or

    (b)   exercising any rights conferred by a controlled investment to acquire, dispose of, underwrite or convert a controlled investment.

(9)   An activity is a controlled activity if—

    (a)   it is an activity of a specified kind or one which falls within a specified class of activity; and

    (b)   it relates to an investment of a specified kind, or to one which falls within a specified class of investment.

(10)   An investment is a controlled investment if it is an investment of a specified kind or one which falls within a specified class of investment.

(11)   Schedule 2 (except paragraph 26) applies for the purposes of subsections (9) and (10) with references to section 22 being read as references to each of those subsections.

(12)   Nothing in Schedule 2, as applied by subsection (11), limits the powers conferred by subsection (9) or (10).

(13)　"Communicate" includes causing a communication to be made.

(14)　"Investment" includes any asset, right or interest.

(15)　"Specified" means specified in an order made by the Treasury.

[21]

NOTES
　Application in relation to interim permissions and interim approvals: see the notes preceding s 40 at **[40]**.
　Orders: the Financial Services and Markets Act 2000 (Miscellaneous Provisions) Order 2001, SI 2001/3650 at **[2643]**; the Financial Services and Markets Act 2000 (Financial Promotion) Order 2005, SI 2005/1529 at **[2757]**.
　Note that the following amending Orders have also been made under this section: the Financial Services and Markets Act 2000 (Financial Promotion and Miscellaneous Amendments) Order 2002, SI 2002/1310; the Financial Services and Markets Act 2000 (Commencement of Mortgage Regulation) (Amendment) Order 2002, SI 2002/1777; the Financial Services and Markets Act 2000 (Promotion of Collective Investment Schemes etc) (Exemptions) (Amendment) Order 2003, SI 2003/2067; the Financial Services and Markets Act 2000 (Financial Promotion and Promotion of Collective Investment Schemes) (Miscellaneous Amendments) Order 2005, SI 2005/270; the Financial Services and Markets Act 2000 (Financial Promotion) (Amendment) Order 2005, SI 2005/3392; the Financial Services and Markets Act 2000 (Financial Promotion) (Amendment) Order 2007, SI 2007/1083; the Financial Services and Markets Act 2000 (Financial Promotion) (Amendment No 2) Order 2007, SI 2007/2615.

Regulated activities

22　The classes of activity and categories of investment

(1)　An activity is a regulated activity for the purposes of this Act if it is an activity of a specified kind which is carried on by way of business and—
　　(a)　relates to an investment of a specified kind; or
　　(b)　in the case of an activity of a kind which is also specified for the purposes of this paragraph, is carried on in relation to property of any kind.

(2)　Schedule 2 makes provision supplementing this section.

(3)　Nothing in Schedule 2 limits the powers conferred by subsection (1).

(4)　"Investment" includes any asset, right or interest.

(5)　"Specified" means specified in an order made by the Treasury.

[22]

NOTES
　Carried on by way of business: as to the meaning of this, see s 419 at **[445]** and the Financial Services and Markets Act 2000 (Carrying on Regulated Activities by way of Business) Order 2001, SI 2001/1177 at **[2206]**.
　Investment of a specified kind: see the Gambling Act 2005, ss 10(2), (3), 38(3) which provides that an order under this section which has the effect that a class of bet becomes or ceases to be a regulated activity may, in particular, include transitional provision relating to the application of the 2005 Act to that class of bet.
　Orders: the Financial Services and Markets Act 2000 (Regulated Activities) Order 2001, SI 2001/544 at **[2010]**.
　Note that the following amending Orders have also been made under this section: the Financial Services and Markets Act 2000 (Regulated Activities) (Amendment) Order 2001, SI 2001/3544; the Financial Services and Markets Act 2000 (Regulated Activities) (Amendment) Order 2002, SI 2002/682; the Financial Services and Markets Act 2000 (Financial Promotion and Miscellaneous Amendments) Order 2002, SI 2002/1310; the Financial Services and Markets Act 2000 (Regulated Activities) (Amendment) (No 2) Order 2002, SI 2002/1776; the Financial Services and Markets Act 2000 (Commencement of Mortgage Regulation) (Amendment) Order 2002, SI 2002/1777; the Financial Services and Markets Act 2000 (Regulated Activities) (Amendment) (No 1) Order 2003, SI 2003/1475 (at **[2698]**); the Financial Services and Markets Act 2000 (Regulated Activities) (Amendment) (No 2) Order 2003, SI 2003/1476 (at **[2704]**); the Financial Services and Markets Act 2000 (Regulated Activities) (Amendment) (No 3) Order 2003, SI 2003/2822; the Financial Services and Markets Act 2000 (Regulated Activities) (Amendment) Order 2004, SI 2004/1610; the Financial Services and Markets Act 2000 (Regulated Activities) (Amendment) (No 2) Order 2004, SI 2004/2737; the Financial Services and Markets Act 2000 (Regulated Activities) (Amendment) Order 2005, SI 2005/593; the Financial Services and Markets Act 2000 (Regulated Activities) (Amendment) (No 2) Order 2005, SI 2005/1518; the Financial Services and Markets Act 2000 (Regulated Activities) (Amendment) Order 2006, SI 2006/1969 (at **[2853]**); the Financial Services and Markets Act 2000 (Regulated Activities) (Amendment) (No 2) Order 2006, SI 2006/2383 (at **[2860]**); the Financial Services and Markets Act 2000 (Regulated Activities) (Amendment No 3) Order 2006, SI 2006/3384; the Financial Services and Markets Act 2000 (Regulated Activities) (Amendment) Order 2007, SI 2007/1339; the Financial Services and Markets Act 2000 (Reinsurance Directive) Order 2007, SI 2007/3254; the Financial Services and Markets Act 2000 (Regulated Activities) (Amendment) (No 2) Order 2007, SI 2007/3510 (at **[2899]**).

Offences

23　Contravention of the general prohibition

(1)　A person who contravenes the general prohibition is guilty of an offence and liable—
　　(a)　on summary conviction, to imprisonment for a term not exceeding six months or a fine not exceeding the statutory maximum, or both;

   (b)   on conviction on indictment, to imprisonment for a term not exceeding two years or a fine, or both.

(2)   In this Act "an authorisation offence" means an offence under this section.

(3)   In proceedings for an authorisation offence it is a defence for the accused to show that he took all reasonable precautions and exercised all due diligence to avoid committing the offence.

[23]

24 False claims to be authorised or exempt

(1)   A person who is neither an authorised person nor, in relation to the regulated activity in question, an exempt person is guilty of an offence if he—
   (a)   describes himself (in whatever terms) as an authorised person;
   (b)   describes himself (in whatever terms) as an exempt person in relation to the regulated activity; or
   (c)   behaves, or otherwise holds himself out, in a manner which indicates (or which is reasonably likely to be understood as indicating) that he is—
       (i)   an authorised person; or
      (ii)   an exempt person in relation to the regulated activity.

(2)   In proceedings for an offence under this section it is a defence for the accused to show that he took all reasonable precautions and exercised all due diligence to avoid committing the offence.

(3)   A person guilty of an offence under this section is liable on summary conviction to imprisonment for a term not exceeding six months or a fine not exceeding level 5 on the standard scale, or both.

(4)   But where the conduct constituting the offence involved or included the public display of any material, the maximum fine for the offence is level 5 on the standard scale multiplied by the number of days for which the display continued.

[24]

25 Contravention of section 21

(1)   A person who contravenes section 21(1) is guilty of an offence and liable—
   (a)   on summary conviction, to imprisonment for a term not exceeding six months or a fine not exceeding the statutory maximum, or both;
   (b)   on conviction on indictment, to imprisonment for a term not exceeding two years or a fine, or both.

(2)   In proceedings for an offence under this section it is a defence for the accused to show—
   (a)   that he believed on reasonable grounds that the content of the communication was prepared, or approved for the purposes of section 21, by an authorised person; or
   (b)   that he took all reasonable precautions and exercised all due diligence to avoid committing the offence.

[25]

NOTES
Application in relation to interim permissions and interim approvals: see the notes preceding s 40 at **[40]**.

Enforceability of agreements

26 Agreements made by unauthorised persons

(1)   An agreement made by a person in the course of carrying on a regulated activity in contravention of the general prohibition is unenforceable against the other party.

(2)   The other party is entitled to recover—
   (a)   any money or other property paid or transferred by him under the agreement; and
   (b)   compensation for any loss sustained by him as a result of having parted with it.

(3)   "Agreement" means an agreement—
   (a)   made after this section comes into force; and
   (b)   the making or performance of which constitutes, or is part of, the regulated activity in question.

(4)   This section does not apply if the regulated activity is accepting deposits.

[26]

NOTES
Application to certain agreements: sub-ss (1), (2) above (and, subject to certain modifications, s 28 below) apply to certain agreements entered into in contravention of the Financial Services Act 1986, s 3 (repealed by the Financial Services and Markets Act 2000 (Consequential Amendments and Repeals) Order 2001, SI 2001/3649, art 3(1)(c)), or the Insurance Companies Act 1982, s 2 (repealed by art 3(1)(b) of that Order) as they apply to an

agreement in contravention of the general prohibition; see the Financial Services and Markets Act 2000 (Transitional Provisions and Savings) (Civil Remedies, Discipline, Criminal Offences etc) (No 2) Order 2001, SI 2001/3083, art 5(1), (3), (4), (6).

27 Agreements made through unauthorised persons

(1) An agreement made by an authorised person ("the provider")—

(a) in the course of carrying on a regulated activity (not in contravention of the general prohibition), but

(b) in consequence of something said or done by another person ("the third party") in the course of a regulated activity carried on by the third party in contravention of the general prohibition,

is unenforceable against the other party.

(2) The other party is entitled to recover—

(a) any money or other property paid or transferred by him under the agreement; and

(b) compensation for any loss sustained by him as a result of having parted with it.

(3) "Agreement" means an agreement—

(a) made after this section comes into force; and

(b) the making or performance of which constitutes, or is part of, the regulated activity in question carried on by the provider.

(4) This section does not apply if the regulated activity is accepting deposits.

[27]

NOTES

Application to certain agreements: sub-ss (1), (2) above (and, subject to certain modifications, s 28 below) apply to certain agreements entered into in contravention of the Financial Services Act 1986, s 3 (repealed by the Financial Services and Markets Act 2000 (Consequential Amendments and Repeals) Order 2001, SI 2001/3649, art 3(1)(c)) as they apply to an agreement in contravention of the general prohibition; see the Financial Services and Markets Act 2000 (Transitional Provisions and Savings) (Civil Remedies, Discipline, Criminal Offences etc) (No 2) Order 2001, SI 2001/3083, art 5(2), (3), (5), (6)

28 Agreements made unenforceable by section 26 or 27

(1) This section applies to an agreement which is unenforceable because of section 26 or 27.

(2) The amount of compensation recoverable as a result of that section is—

(a) the amount agreed by the parties; or

(b) on the application of either party, the amount determined by the court.

(3) If the court is satisfied that it is just and equitable in the circumstances of the case, it may allow—

(a) the agreement to be enforced; or

(b) money and property paid or transferred under the agreement to be retained.

(4) In considering whether to allow the agreement to be enforced or (as the case may be) the money or property paid or transferred under the agreement to be retained the court must—

(a) if the case arises as a result of section 26, have regard to the issue mentioned in subsection (5); or

(b) if the case arises as a result of section 27, have regard to the issue mentioned in subsection (6).

(5) The issue is whether the person carrying on the regulated activity concerned reasonably believed that he was not contravening the general prohibition by making the agreement.

(6) The issue is whether the provider knew that the third party was (in carrying on the regulated activity) contravening the general prohibition.

(7) If the person against whom the agreement is unenforceable—

(a) elects not to perform the agreement, or

(b) as a result of this section, recovers money paid or other property transferred by him under the agreement,

he must repay any money and return any other property received by him under the agreement.

(8) If property transferred under the agreement has passed to a third party, a reference in section 26 or 27 or this section to that property is to be read as a reference to its value at the time of its transfer under the agreement.

(9) The commission of an authorisation offence does not make the agreement concerned illegal or invalid to any greater extent than is provided by section 26 or 27.

[28]

NOTES

Application to certain agreements: see the notes to ss 26 and 27 at [26] and [27].

29   Accepting deposits in breach of general prohibition

(1)   This section applies to an agreement between a person ("the depositor") and another person ("the deposit-taker") made in the course of the carrying on by the deposit-taker of accepting deposits in contravention of the general prohibition.

(2)   If the depositor is not entitled under the agreement to recover without delay any money deposited by him, he may apply to the court for an order directing the deposit-taker to return the money to him.

(3)   The court need not make such an order if it is satisfied that it would not be just and equitable for the money deposited to be returned, having regard to the issue mentioned in subsection (4).

(4)   The issue is whether the deposit-taker reasonably believed that he was not contravening the general prohibition by making the agreement.

(5)   "Agreement" means an agreement—
   (a)   made after this section comes into force; and
   (b)   the making or performance of which constitutes, or is part of, accepting deposits.

[29]

30   Enforceability of agreements resulting from unlawful communications

(1)   In this section—
   "unlawful communication" means a communication in relation to which there has been a contravention of section 21(1);
   "controlled agreement" means an agreement the making or performance of which by either party constitutes a controlled activity for the purposes of that section; and
   "controlled investment" has the same meaning as in section 21.

(2)   If in consequence of an unlawful communication a person enters as a customer into a controlled agreement, it is unenforceable against him and he is entitled to recover—
   (a)   any money or other property paid or transferred by him under the agreement; and
   (b)   compensation for any loss sustained by him as a result of having parted with it.

(3)   If in consequence of an unlawful communication a person exercises any rights conferred by a controlled investment, no obligation to which he is subject as a result of exercising them is enforceable against him and he is entitled to recover—
   (a)   any money or other property paid or transferred by him under the obligation; and
   (b)   compensation for any loss sustained by him as a result of having parted with it.

(4)   But the court may allow—
   (a)   the agreement or obligation to be enforced, or
   (b)   money or property paid or transferred under the agreement or obligation to be retained,
if it is satisfied that it is just and equitable in the circumstances of the case.

(5)   In considering whether to allow the agreement or obligation to be enforced or (as the case may be) the money or property paid or transferred under the agreement to be retained the court must have regard to the issues mentioned in subsections (6) and (7).

(6)   If the applicant made the unlawful communication, the issue is whether he reasonably believed that he was not making such a communication.

(7)   If the applicant did not make the unlawful communication, the issue is whether he knew that the agreement was entered into in consequence of such a communication.

(8)   "Applicant" means the person seeking to enforce the agreement or obligation or retain the money or property paid or transferred.

(9)   Any reference to making a communication includes causing a communication to be made.

(10)   The amount of compensation recoverable as a result of subsection (2) or (3) is—
   (a)   the amount agreed between the parties; or
   (b)   on the application of either party, the amount determined by the court.

(11)   If a person elects not to perform an agreement or an obligation which (by virtue of subsection (2) or (3)) is unenforceable against him, he must repay any money and return any other property received by him under the agreement.

(12)   If (by virtue of subsection (2) or (3)) a person recovers money paid or property transferred by him under an agreement or obligation, he must repay any money and return any other property received by him as a result of exercising the rights in question.

(13)   If any property required to be returned under this section has passed to a third party, references to that property are to be read as references to its value at the time of its receipt by the person required to return it.

[30]

PART III
AUTHORISATION AND EXEMPTION

NOTES

Transitional provisions: see the Financial Services and Markets Act 2000 (Transitional Provisions) (Authorised Persons etc) Order 2001, SI 2001/2636. That Order sets out the transitional arrangements for ensuring that people who have been authorised to carry on particular business under the various regulatory regimes replaced by this Act are treated as authorised persons with the appropriate permission for the purposes of this Act. The regulatory regimes covered by the Order are the Financial Services Act 1986, the Banking Act 1987, the Insurance Companies Act 1982, the Friendly Societies Act 1992, the Building Societies Act 1986, the Banking Coordination (Second Council Directive) Regulations 1992 (SI 1992/3218) and the Investment Services Regulations 1995 (SI 1995/3275).

Authorisation

31 Authorised persons

(1) The following persons are authorised for the purposes of this Act—
  (a) a person who has a Part IV permission to carry on one or more regulated activities;
  (b) an EEA firm qualifying for authorisation under Schedule 3;
  (c) a Treaty firm qualifying for authorisation under Schedule 4;
  (d) a person who is otherwise authorised by a provision of, or made under, this Act.

(2) In this Act "authorised person" means a person who is authorised for the purposes of this Act.

[31]

NOTES

Application in relation to interim permissions and interim approvals: see the notes preceding s 40 at [40].

32 Partnerships and unincorporated associations

(1) If a firm is authorised—
  (a) it is authorised to carry on the regulated activities concerned in the name of the firm; and
  (b) its authorisation is not affected by any change in its membership.

(2) If an authorised firm is dissolved, its authorisation continues to have effect in relation to any [individual or] firm which succeeds to the business of the dissolved firm.

[(3) For the purposes of this section, an individual or firm is to be regarded as succeeding to the business of a dissolved firm only if succession is to the whole or substantially the whole of the business of the former firm.]

(4) "Firm" means—
  (a) a partnership; or
  (b) an unincorporated association of persons.

(5) "Partnership" does not include a partnership which is constituted under the law of any place outside the United Kingdom and is a body corporate.

[32]

NOTES

Para (2): words in square brackets inserted by the Regulatory Reform (Financial Services and Markets Act 2000) Order 2007, SI 2007/1973, arts 2, 3(a), as from 12 July 2007.
Para (3): substituted by SI 2007/1973, arts 2, 3(b), as from 12 July 2007.

Ending of authorisation

33 Withdrawal of authorisation by the Authority

(1) This section applies if—
  (a) an authorised person's Part IV permission is cancelled; and
  (b) as a result, there is no regulated activity for which he has permission.

(2) The Authority must give a direction withdrawing that person's status as an authorised person.

[33]

34 EEA firms

(1) An EEA firm ceases to qualify for authorisation under Part II of Schedule 3 if it ceases to be an EEA firm as a result of—
  (a) having its EEA authorisation withdrawn; or
  (b) ceasing to have an EEA right in circumstances in which EEA authorisation is not required.

(2)   At the request of an EEA firm, the Authority may give a direction cancelling its authorisation under Part II of Schedule 3.

(3)   If an EEA firm has a Part IV permission, it does not cease to be an authorised person merely because it ceases to qualify for authorisation under Part II of Schedule 3.

[34]

NOTES
Note: "EEA firm" is defined in Sch 3, Pt I, para 5, and "EEA right" is defined in Sch 3, Pt I, para 7, both at **[467]**.

35   Treaty firms

(1)   A Treaty firm ceases to qualify for authorisation under Schedule 4 if its home State authorisation is withdrawn.

(2)   At the request of a Treaty firm, the Authority may give a direction cancelling its Schedule 4 authorisation.

(3)   If a Treaty firm has a Part IV permission, it does not cease to be an authorised person merely because it ceases to qualify for authorisation under Schedule 4.

[35]

NOTES
Note: "Treaty firm" is defined in Sch 4, para 1 at **[470]**.

36   Persons authorised as a result of paragraph 1(1) of Schedule 5

(1)   At the request of a person authorised as a result of paragraph 1(1) of Schedule 5, the Authority may give a direction cancelling his authorisation as such a person.

(2)   If a person authorised as a result of paragraph 1(1) of Schedule 5 has a Part IV permission, he does not cease to be an authorised person merely because he ceases to be a person so authorised.

[36]

NOTES
Note: under Sch 5, para 1(1) the operator, trustee or depositary of a collective investment scheme recognised by virtue of s 264 is deemed to be an authorised person (Sch 5, para 1(1), (2)) so far as it is a regulated activity, any activity appropriate to the capacity in which he acts in relation to the scheme, of the kind described in para 8 of Sch 2, or any activity in connection with, or for the purposes of, the scheme or in the case of an authorised OEIC which is an authorised person by virtue of Sch 5, para 1(3) so far as it is a regulated activity, the operation of the scheme or any activity in connection with, or for the purposes of, the operation of the scheme.

Exercise of EEA rights by UK firms

37   Exercise of EEA rights by UK firms

Part III of Schedule 3 makes provision in relation to the exercise outside the United Kingdom of EEA rights by UK firms.

[37]

NOTES
Note: "UK firm" is defined in Sch 3, Pt I, para 10 at **[467]**.

Exemption

38   Exemption orders

(1)   The Treasury may by order ("an exemption order") provide for—
  (a)   specified persons, or
  (b)   persons falling within a specified class,
to be exempt from the general prohibition.

(2)   But a person cannot be an exempt person as a result of an exemption order if he has a Part IV permission.

(3)   An exemption order may provide for an exemption to have effect—
  (a)   in respect of all regulated activities;
  (b)   in respect of one or more specified regulated activities;
  (c)   only in specified circumstances;
  (d)   only in relation to specified functions;
  (e)   subject to conditions.

(4)   "Specified" means specified by the exemption order.

[38]

NOTES
Application in relation to interim permissions and interim approvals: see the notes preceding s 40 at **[40]**.
Orders: the Financial Services and Markets Act 2000 (Exemption) Order 2001, SI 2001/1201 at **[2211]**.
Note that the following amending Orders have also been made under this section: the Financial Services and Markets Act 2000 (Exemption) (Amendment) Order 2001, SI 2001/3623; the Financial Services and Markets Act 2000 (Financial Promotion and Miscellaneous Amendments) Order 2002, SI 2002/1310; the Financial Services and Markets Act 2000 (Exemption) (Amendment) Order 2003, SI 2003/47; the Financial Services and Markets Act 2000 (Exemption) (Amendment) (No 2) Order 2003, SI 2003/1675; the Financial Services and Markets Act 2000 (Exemption) (Amendment) Order 2005, SI 2005/592; the Financial Services and Markets Act 2000 (Exemption) (Amendment) Order 2007, SI 2007/125; the Financial Services and Markets Act 2000 (Exemption) (Amendment No 2) Order 2007, SI 2007/1821; the Financial Services and Markets Act 2000 (Exemption) (Amendment) Order 2008, SI 2008/682; the Financial Services and Markets Act 2000 (Exemption) (Amendment) Order 2009, SI 2009/118; the Financial Services and Markets Act 2000 (Exemption) (Amendment) Order 2009, SI 2009/264.

39 Exemption of appointed representatives

(1) If a person (other than an authorised person)—
   (a) is a party to a contract with an authorised person ("his principal") which—
      (i) permits or requires him to carry on business of a prescribed description, and
      (ii) complies with such requirements as may be prescribed, and
   (b) is someone for whose activities in carrying on the whole or part of that business his principal has accepted responsibility in writing,

he is exempt from the general prohibition in relation to any regulated activity comprised in the carrying on of that business for which his principal has accepted responsibility.

[(1A) But a person is not exempt as a result of subsection (1)—
   (a) if his principal is an investment firm or a credit institution, and
   (b) so far as the business for which his principal has accepted responsibility is investment services business,
unless he is entered on the applicable register.

(1B) The "applicable register" is—
   (a) in the case of a person established in an EEA State (other than the United Kingdom) which permits investment firms authorised by the competent authority of that State to appoint tied agents, the register of tied agents maintained in that State pursuant to Article 23 of the markets in financial instruments directive;
   (b) in the case of a person established in an EEA State which does not permit investment firms authorised as mentioned in paragraph (a) to appoint tied agents—
      (i) if his principal has his relevant office in the United Kingdom, the record maintained by the Authority by virtue of section 347(1)(ha), and
      (ii) if his principal is established in an EEA State (other than the United Kingdom) which permits investment firms authorised by the competent authority of the State to appoint tied agents, the register of tied agents maintained by that State pursuant to Article 23 of the markets in financial instruments directive; and
   (c) in any other case, the record maintained by the Authority by virtue of section 347(1)(ha).]

(2) A person who is exempt as a result of subsection (1) is referred to in this Act as an appointed representative.

(3) The principal of an appointed representative is responsible, to the same extent as if he had expressly permitted it, for anything done or omitted by the representative in carrying on the business for which he has accepted responsibility.

(4) In determining whether an authorised person has complied with a provision contained in or made under this Act, [or with a provision contained in any directly applicable Community regulation made under the markets in financial instruments directive,] anything which a relevant person has done or omitted as respects business for which the authorised person has accepted responsibility is to be treated as having been done or omitted by the authorised person.

(5) "Relevant person" means a person who at the material time is or was an appointed representative by virtue of being a party to a contract with the authorised person.

(6) Nothing in subsection (4) is to cause the knowledge or intentions of an appointed representative to be attributed to his principal for the purpose of determining whether the principal has committed an offence, unless in all the circumstances it is reasonable for them to be attributed to him.

[(7) A person carries on "investment services business" if—
   (a) the business includes providing services or carrying on activities of the kind mentioned in Article 4.1.25 of the markets in financial instruments directive, and
   (b) as a result of providing such services or carrying on such activities he is a tied agent or would be if he were established in an EEA State.

(8)   In this section—
"competent authority" has the meaning given in Article 4.1.22 of the markets in financial instruments directive;
"credit institution" means—

    (a)   a credit institution authorised under the banking consolidation directive, or

    (b)   an institution which would satisfy the requirements for authorisation as a credit institution under that directive if it had its relevant office in an EEA State;

"relevant office" means—

    (a)   in relation to a body corporate, its registered office or, if it has no registered office, its head office, and

    (b)   in relation to a person other than a body corporate, the person's head office.]

[39]

PART I
FSMA 2000

NOTES

Sub-ss (1A), (1B), (7), (8): inserted and added respectively by the Financial Services and Markets Act 2000 (Markets in Financial Instruments) Regulations 2007, SI 2007/126, reg 3(5), Sch 5, paras 1, 2(a), (c), as from 1 April 2007 (certain purposes (see reg 1(2) at **[4051]**)), and as from 1 November 2007 (otherwise).

Sub-s (4): words in square brackets inserted by SI 2007/126, reg 3(5), Sch 5, paras 1, 2(b), as from 1 April 2007 (certain purposes (see reg 1(2) at **[4051]**)), and as from 1 November 2007 (otherwise).

Transitional provisions: see the Financial Services and Markets Act 2000 (Markets in Financial Instruments) Regulations 2007, SI 2007/126, reg 9 at **[4059]** (transitional provision: appointed representatives and tied agents).

Application in relation to interim permissions and interim approvals: see the notes preceding s 40 at **[40]**.

Regulations: the Financial Services and Markets Act 2000 (Appointed Representatives) Regulations 2001, SI 2001/1217 at **[2221]**.

Note that the following amending Regulations have also been made under this section: the Financial Services and Markets Act 2000 (Appointed Representatives) (Amendment) Regulations 2001, SI 2001/2508; the Financial Services and Markets Act 2000 (Appointed Representatives) (Amendment) Regulations 2004, SI 2004/453; the Financial Services and Markets Act 2000 (Appointed Representatives) (Amendment) Regulations 2006, SI 2006/3414; the Financial Services and Markets Act 2000 (Markets in Financial Instruments) (Amendment) Regulations 2007, SI 2007/763.

[39A   Certain tied agents operating outside United Kingdom

(1)   This section applies to an authorised person whose relevant office is in the United Kingdom if—

    (a)   he is a party to a contract with a person (other than an authorised person) who is established—

        (i)   in the United Kingdom, or

        (ii)   in an EEA State which does not permit investment firms authorised by the competent authority of the State to appoint tied agents; and

    (b)   the contract is a relevant contract.

(2)   A contract is a "relevant contract" if it satisfies conditions A to C

(3)   Condition A is that the contract permits or requires the person mentioned in subsection (1)(a) (the "agent") to carry on investment services business.

(4)   Condition B is that either—

    (a)   it is a condition of the contract that such business may only be carried on by the agent in an EEA State other than the United Kingdom; or

    (b)   in a case not falling within paragraph (a), the Authority is satisfied that no such business is, or is likely to be, carried on by the agent in the United Kingdom.

(5)   Condition C is that the business is of a description that, if carried on in the United Kingdom, would be prescribed for the purposes of section 39(1)(a)(i).

(6)   An authorised person to whom this section applies who—

    (a)   enters into or continues to perform a relevant contract with an agent which does not comply with the applicable requirements,

    (b)   enters into or continues to perform a relevant contract without accepting or having accepted responsibility in writing for the agent's activities in carrying on investment services business,

    (c)   enters into a relevant contract with an agent who is not entered on the record maintained by the Authority by virtue of section 347(1)(ha), or

    (d)   continues to perform a relevant contract with an agent when he knows or ought to know that the agent is not entered on that record,

is to be taken for the purposes of this Act to have contravened a requirement imposed on him by or under this Act.

(7)   The "applicable requirements" are the requirements prescribed for the purposes of subsection (1)(a)(ii) of section 39 which have effect in the case of a person to whom subsection (1A) of that section applies.

(8)   A person carries on "investment services business" if—

(a)   his business includes providing services or carrying on activities of the kind mentioned in Article 4.1.25 of the markets in financial instruments directive, and

(b)   as a result of providing such services or carrying on such activities he is a tied agent.

(9)   In this section—

"competent authority" has the meaning given in Article 4.1.22 of the markets in financial instruments directive;

"relevant office" means—

(a)   in relation to a body corporate, its registered office or, if it has no registered office, its head office, and

(b)   in relation to a person other than a body corporate, the person's head office.]

[39A]

NOTES

Commencement: 1 April 2007 (certain purposes); 1 November 2007 (otherwise).

Inserted by the Financial Services and Markets Act 2000 (Markets in Financial Instruments) Regulations 2007, SI 2007/126, reg 3(5), Sch 5, paras 1, 3, as from 1 April 2007 (certain purposes (see reg 1(2) at [4051])), and as from 1 November 2007 (otherwise).

Transitional provisions: see the Financial Services and Markets Act 2000 (Markets in Financial Instruments) Regulations 2007, SI 2007/126, reg 9 at [4059] (transitional provision: appointed representatives and tied agents).

PART IV
PERMISSION TO CARRY ON REGULATED ACTIVITIES

NOTES

Transitional provisions: the Financial Services and Markets Act 2000 (Transitional Provisions) (Authorised Persons etc) Order 2001, SI 2001/2636, Pt II, Chapter I provides that persons who are authorised or exempted from the need for authorisation under provisions of the previous regulatory regimes are treated, as from 1 December 2001, as having permission under Pt IV of this Act to carry on the activities they were lawfully able to carry on immediately before that date by reason of that authorisation or exemption. Pt II of SI 2001/2636 applies to: (a) persons authorised or exempted under the Financial Services Act 1986 (repealed by the Financial Services and Markets Act 2000 (Consequential Amendments and Repeals) Order 2001, SI 2001/3649, art 3(1)(c)); (b) persons authorised under the Banking Act 1987 (repealed by SI 2001/3649, art 3(1)(d)); (c) insurance companies; (d) friendly societies; and (e) building societies.

Pt III of SI 2001/2636 provides that restrictions and prohibitions imposed under provisions of the previous regulatory regimes on authorised persons are to have effect after 1 December 2001 as if they were requirements imposed under s 43 (in relation to persons with a permission under Pt IV of this Act). Pt III of SI 2001/2636 applies to: (a) prohibitions and requirements under the Financial Services Act 1986 (repealed as noted above); (b) restrictions and directions under the Banking Act 1987 (repealed as noted above); (c) directions and requirements under the Insurance Companies Act 1982 (repealed by SI 2001/3649, art 3(1)(b)); (d) conditions and directions under the Friendly Societies Act 1992; (e) conditions and directions under the Building Societies Act 1986; and (f) prohibitions and restrictions under the Banking Coordination (Second Council Directive) Regulations 1992, SI 1992/3218 (revoked by SI 2001/3649, art 3(2)(a)) and the Investment Services Regulations 1995, SI 1995/3275 (revoked by SI 2001/3649, art 3(2)(c)).

See also, the Financial Services and Markets Act 2000 (Permission and Applications) (Credit Unions etc) Order 2002, SI 2002/704 (transitional provisions relating to the expiry, on 2 July 2002, of the transitional exemption of credit unions from the general prohibition imposed by s 19 of this Act (see the Financial Services and Markets Act 2000 (Exemption) Order 2001, SI 2001/1201, art 6 at [2216]).

See also, the Financial Services and Markets Act 2000 (Consequential and Transitional Provisions) (Miscellaneous) (No 2) Order 2001, SI 2001/2659 (transitional provisions in consequence of the Financial Services and Markets Act 2000 (Commencement No 5) Order (SI 2001/2632). That Order brings into force the provisions of the Act relating to (among other things) the making of applications under the Act for permission or authorisation coming into force on 1 December 2001.

Interim permissions and interim approvals: see the Financial Services and Markets Act 2000 (Interim Permissions) Order 2001, SI 2001/3374 at [2502]. This Order conferred an interim permission on certain applicants who applied to the FSA for permission under this Part and whose application was pending on the date when the main provisions of the Act come into force (1 December 2001). The scope of the Order is limited by arts 3–5 to those applicants who were lawfully carrying on the activity which was regulated for the first time under this Act. In order to ensure that their business was not disrupted by the fact that the activity became a regulated activity while their application for permission was pending, an applicant who applied for permission before 31 October 2001 and who opted to benefit from the provisions of this Order had an interim permission to enable him to continue to carry on that activity until his application was determined. The Order does not apply to those who were carrying on an activity which was regulated under previous legislation since they benefited from a Part IV permission conferred by the Financial Services and Markets Act 2000 (Transitional Provisions) (Authorised Persons etc) Order 2001, SI 2001/2636 (see above). See also art 8 of this Order (interim permission lapses at the time when it is superseded by the grant of the application or when the application is withdrawn or refused), and art 9 (which conferred interim approval on people who were working for a person who benefited from interim permission if those people would have needed approval under this Part). Article 12 conferred a power on the Authority to modify the rules and guidance it makes under this Act as it applies to persons with interim permission. Article 13 and the Schedule to the Order provided for the application of provisions in this Part and Part V (and various other provisions of this Act and the Regulated Activities Order) to persons who have interim permission under this Order.

As to interim permissions, interim approvals and the application of this Part and Part V (and various other provisions of this Act) to various activities that have become regulated activities following the amendment of the Regulated Activities Order, see the table below:

Order	Regulated Activity
Financial Services and Markets Act 2000 (Transitional Provisions) (Mortgages) Order 2004, SI 2004/2615 at **[2735]**	Certain mortgage mediation activities
Financial Services and Markets Act 2000 (Regulated Activities) (Amendment) (No 2) Order 2004, SI 2004/2737	Advice on stakeholder products (see the note at **[2085]**)
Financial Services and Markets Act 2000 (Transitional Provisions) (General Insurance Intermediaries) Order 2004, SI 2004/3351 at **[2750]**	Certain general insurance mediation activities
Financial Services and Markets Act 2000 (Regulated Activities) (Amendment) Order 2006, SI 2006/1969 at **[2853]**	Establishing, operating or winding up a personal pension scheme, or activities which relate to the specified investment of rights under a personal pension scheme
Financial Services and Markets Act 2000 (Regulated Activities) (Amendment) (No 2) Order 2006, SI 2006/2383 at **[2860]**	Administering, arranging or advising on regulated home reversion plans or regulated home purchase plans
Financial Services and Markets Act 2000 (Regulated Activities) (Amendment) (No 2) Order 2007, SI 2007/3510 at **[2899]**	Provision of travel insurance in certain circumstances

Investment firms, etc: see the Financial Services and Markets Act 2000 (Markets in Financial Instruments) Regulations 2007, SI 2007/126, reg 4 (at **[4054]**) which requires the FSA to be satisfied that the authorisation requirements of MiFID (as to which see Chapter I of Title II of MiFID (at **[5526]**) and Commission Regulation 1287/2006 (at **[5917]**)) are met before giving permission under this Part to an investment firm (as defined in s 424A) or varying the permission of such a firm. See also regs 4A–4C of the 2007 Regulations (exempt investment firms) at **[4054A]**–**[4054C]**, and reg 9A (transitional provisions) at **[4059A]**.

See also the Financial Services and Markets Act 2000 (Markets in Financial Instruments) Regulations 2007, SI 2007/126, reg 9B at **[4059B]** (transitional provision: operators of alternative trading systems), reg 9C at **[4059C]** (transitional provision for investment firms and credit institutions in relation to options, futures and contracts for differences), reg 9D at **[4059D]** (transitional provision for management companies in relation to options, futures and contracts for differences), and reg 9E at **[4059E]** (transitional provision in relation to client classification).

Application for permission

40   Application for permission

(1)   An application for permission to carry on one or more regulated activities may be made to the Authority by—

    (a)   an individual;
    (b)   a body corporate;
    (c)   a partnership; or
    (d)   an unincorporated association.

(2)   An authorised person may not apply for permission under this section if he has a permission—

    (a)   given to him by the Authority under this Part, or
    (b)   having effect as if so given,

which is in force.

(3)   An EEA firm may not apply for permission under this section to carry on a regulated activity which it is, or would be, entitled to carry on in exercise of an EEA right, whether through a United Kingdom branch or by providing services in the United Kingdom.

(4)   A permission given by the Authority under this Part or having effect as if so given is referred to in this Act as "a Part IV permission".

[40]

NOTES
Interim permissions: see the notes preceding this section.

41   The threshold conditions

(1)   "The threshold conditions", in relation to a regulated activity, means the conditions set out in Schedule 6.

(2) In giving or varying permission, or imposing or varying any requirement, under this Part the Authority must ensure that the person concerned will satisfy, and continue to satisfy, the threshold conditions in relation to all of the regulated activities for which he has or will have permission.

(3) But the duty imposed by subsection (2) does not prevent the Authority, having due regard to that duty, from taking such steps as it considers are necessary, in relation to a particular authorised person, in order to secure its regulatory objective of the protection of consumers.

[41]

Permission

42 Giving permission

(1) "The applicant" means an applicant for permission under section 40.

(2) The Authority may give permission for the applicant to carry on the regulated activity or activities to which his application relates or such of them as may be specified in the permission.

(3) If the applicant—
    (a) in relation to a particular regulated activity, is exempt from the general prohibition as a result of section 39(1) or an order made under section 38(1), but
    (b) has applied for permission in relation to another regulated activity,

the application is to be treated as relating to all the regulated activities which, if permission is given, he will carry on.

(4) If the applicant—
    (a) in relation to a particular regulated activity, is exempt from the general prohibition as a result of section 285(2) or (3), but
    (b) has applied for permission in relation to another regulated activity,

the application is to be treated as relating only to that other regulated activity.

(5) If the applicant—
    (a) is a person to whom, in relation to a particular regulated activity, the general prohibition does not apply as a result of Part XIX, but
    (b) has applied for permission in relation to another regulated activity,

the application is to be treated as relating only to that other regulated activity.

(6) If it gives permission, the Authority must specify the permitted regulated activity or activities, described in such manner as the Authority considers appropriate.

(7) The Authority may—
    (a) incorporate in the description of a regulated activity such limitations (for example as to circumstances in which the activity may, or may not, be carried on) as it considers appropriate;
    (b) specify a narrower or wider description of regulated activity than that to which the application relates;
    (c) give permission for the carrying on of a regulated activity which is not included among those to which the application relates.

[42]

NOTES

Application in relation to interim permissions and interim approvals: see the notes preceding s 40 at **[40]**.

43 Imposition of requirements

(1) A Part IV permission may include such requirements as the Authority considers appropriate.

(2) A requirement may, in particular, be imposed—
    (a) so as to require the person concerned to take specified action; or
    (b) so as to require him to refrain from taking specified action.

(3) A requirement may extend to activities which are not regulated activities.

(4) A requirement may be imposed by reference to the person's relationship with—
    (a) his group; or
    (b) other members of his group.

(5) A requirement expires at the end of such period as the Authority may specify in the permission.

(6) But subsection (5) does not affect the Authority's powers under section 44 or 45.

[43]

NOTES

Application in relation to interim permissions and interim approvals: see the notes preceding s 40 at **[40]**.

Variation and cancellation of Part IV permission

44   Variation etc at request of authorised person

(1)   The Authority may, on the application of an authorised person with a Part IV permission, vary the permission by—

    (a)   adding a regulated activity to those for which it gives permission;

    (b)   removing a regulated activity from those for which it gives permission;

    (c)   varying the description of a regulated activity for which it gives permission;

    (d)   cancelling a requirement imposed under section 43; or

    (e)   varying such a requirement.

(2)   The Authority may, on the application of an authorised person with a Part IV permission, cancel the permission.

(3)   The Authority may refuse an application under this section if it appears to it—

    (a)   that the interests of consumers, or potential consumers, would be adversely affected if the application were to be granted; and

    (b)   that it is desirable in the interests of consumers, or potential consumers, for the application to be refused.

(4)   If, as a result of a variation of a Part IV permission under this section, there are no longer any regulated activities for which the authorised person concerned has permission, the Authority must, once it is satisfied that it is no longer necessary to keep the permission in force, cancel it.

(5)   The Authority's power to vary a Part IV permission under this section extends to including any provision in the permission as varied that could be included if a fresh permission were being given in response to an application under section 40.

[44]

NOTES

    Application in relation to interim permissions and interim approvals: see the notes preceding s 40 at **[40]**.

45   Variation etc on the Authority's own initiative

(1)   The Authority may exercise its power under this section in relation to an authorised person if it appears to it that—

    (a)   he is failing, or is likely to fail, to satisfy the threshold conditions;

    (b)   he has failed, during a period of at least 12 months, to carry on a regulated activity for which he has a Part IV permission; or

    (c)   it is desirable to exercise that power in order to protect the interests of consumers or potential consumers [(whether of the services of the authorised person or of the services of other authorised persons)].

(2)   The Authority's power under this section is the power to vary a Part IV permission in any of the ways mentioned in section 44(1) or to cancel it.

[(2A)   Without prejudice to the generality of subsections (1) and (2), the Authority may, in relation to an authorised person who is an investment firm, exercise its power under this section to cancel the Part IV permission of the firm if it appears to it that—

    (a)   the firm has failed, during a period of at least six months, to carry on a regulated activity which is an investment service or activity for which it has a Part IV permission;

    (b)   the firm obtained the Part IV permission by making a false statement or by other irregular means;

    (c)   the firm no longer satisfies the requirements for authorisation pursuant to Chapter I of Title II of the markets in financial instruments directive, or pursuant to or contained in any Community legislation made under that Chapter, in relation to a regulated activity which is an investment service or activity for which it has a Part IV permission; or

    (d)   the firm has seriously and systematically infringed the operating conditions pursuant to Chapter II of Title II of the markets in financial instruments directive, or pursuant to or contained in any Community legislation made under that Chapter, in relation to a regulated activity which is an investment service or activity for which it has a Part IV permission.

(2B)   For the purposes of subsection (2A) a regulated activity is an investment service or activity if it falls within the definition of "investment services and activities" in section 417(1).]

(3)   If, as a result of a variation of a Part IV permission under this section, there are no longer any regulated activities for which the authorised person concerned has permission, the Authority must, once it is satisfied that it is no longer necessary to keep the permission in force, cancel it.

(4)   The Authority's power to vary a Part IV permission under this section extends to including any provision in the permission as varied that could be included if a fresh permission were being given in response to an application under section 40.

(5)   The Authority's power under this section is referred to in this Part as its own-initiative power.

[45]

NOTES

Sub-s (1): words in square brackets inserted the Banking Act 2009, s 248, as from a day to be appointed.

Sub-ss (2A), (2B): inserted by the Financial Services and Markets Act 2000 (Markets in Financial Instruments) Regulations 2007, SI 2007/126, reg 3(5), Sch 5, paras 1, 4, as from 1 April 2007 (certain purposes (see reg 1(2) at [4051])), and as from 1 November 2007 (otherwise).

46   Variation of permission on acquisition of control

(1)   This section applies if it appears to the Authority that—
- (a)   a person has acquired control over a UK authorised person who has a Part IV permission; but
- (b)   there are no grounds for exercising its own-initiative power.

(2)   If it appears to the Authority that the likely effect of the acquisition of control on the authorised person, or on any of its activities, is uncertain the Authority may vary the authorised person's permission by—
- (a)   imposing a requirement of a kind that could be imposed under section 43 on giving permission; or
- (b)   varying a requirement included in the authorised person's permission under that section.

(3)   Any reference to a person having acquired control is to be read in accordance with Part XII.

[46]

47   Exercise of power in support of overseas regulator

(1)   The Authority's own-initiative power may be exercised in respect of an authorised person at the request of, or for the purpose of assisting, a regulator who is—
- (a)   outside the United Kingdom; and
- (b)   of a prescribed kind.

(2)   Subsection (1) applies whether or not the Authority has powers which are exercisable in relation to the authorised person by virtue of any provision of Part XIII.

(3)   If a request to the Authority for the exercise of its own-initiative power has been made by a regulator who is—
- (a)   outside the United Kingdom,
- (b)   of a prescribed kind, and
- (c)   acting in pursuance of provisions of a prescribed kind,

the Authority must, in deciding whether or not to exercise that power in response to the request, consider whether it is necessary to do so in order to comply with a Community obligation.

(4)   In deciding in any case in which the Authority does not consider that the exercise of its own-initiative power is necessary in order to comply with a Community obligation, it may take into account in particular—
- (a)   whether in the country or territory of the regulator concerned, corresponding assistance would be given to a United Kingdom regulatory authority;
- (b)   whether the case concerns the breach of a law, or other requirement, which has no close parallel in the United Kingdom or involves the assertion of a jurisdiction not recognised by the United Kingdom;
- (c)   the seriousness of the case and its importance to persons in the United Kingdom;
- (d)   whether it is otherwise appropriate in the public interest to give the assistance sought.

(5)   The Authority may decide not to exercise its own-initiative power, in response to a request, unless the regulator concerned undertakes to make such contribution towards the cost of its exercise as the Authority considers appropriate.

(6)   Subsection (5) does not apply if the Authority decides that it is necessary for it to exercise its own-initiative power in order to comply with a Community obligation.

(7)   In subsections (4) and (5) "request" means a request of a kind mentioned in subsection (1).

[47]

NOTES

Regulations: the Financial Services and Markets Act 2000 (Own-initiative Power) (Overseas Regulators) Regulations 2001, SI 2001/2639 at [2484]. Reg 2 at [2485] specifies the kind of overseas regulators whose functions correspond to any of those of the FSA under this Act (including listing) as well as company law regulation and those investigating insider dealing offences. Reg 3 at [2486] specifies the kind of EEA regulators for any EEA provision (or local implementation) and the relevant supervisory authority in Switzerland for Swiss non-life insurance companies.

Community obligation: this term is not defined in this Act but has the meaning given by the European Communities Act 1972, Sch 1, Pt II, which provides ""Community obligation" means any obligation created or arising by or under the Treaties, whether an enforceable Community obligation or not". Note, however, that this definition is prospectively amended (as from a day to be appointed) by the European Union (Amendment) Act 2008, which effectively substitutes "EU" for the word "Community". See also the Interpretation Act 1978, s 5, Sch 1.

PART I
FSMA 2000

48 Prohibitions and restrictions

(1)   This section applies if the Authority—
    (a)   on giving a person a Part IV permission, imposes an assets requirement on him; or
    (b)   varies an authorised person's Part IV permission so as to alter an assets requirement imposed on him or impose such a requirement on him.

(2)   A person on whom an assets requirement is imposed is referred to in this section as "A".

(3)   "Assets requirement" means a requirement under section 43—
    (a)   prohibiting the disposal of, or other dealing with, any of A's assets (whether in the United Kingdom or elsewhere) or restricting such disposals or dealings; or
    (b)   that all or any of A's assets, or all or any assets belonging to consumers but held by A or to his order, must be transferred to and held by a trustee approved by the Authority.

(4)   If the Authority—
    (a)   imposes a requirement of the kind mentioned in subsection (3)(a), and
    (b)   gives notice of the requirement to any institution with whom A keeps an account,
the notice has the effects mentioned in subsection (5).

(5)   Those effects are that—
    (a)   the institution does not act in breach of any contract with A if, having been instructed by A (or on his behalf) to transfer any sum or otherwise make any payment out of A's account, it refuses to do so in the reasonably held belief that complying with the instruction would be incompatible with the requirement; and
    (b)   if the institution complies with such an instruction, it is liable to pay to the Authority an amount equal to the amount transferred from, or otherwise paid out of, A's account in contravention of the requirement.

(6)   If the Authority imposes a requirement of the kind mentioned in subsection (3)(b), no assets held by a person as trustee in accordance with the requirement may, while the requirement is in force, be released or dealt with except with the consent of the Authority.

(7)   If, while a requirement of the kind mentioned in subsection (3)(b) is in force, A creates a charge over any assets of his held in accordance with the requirement, the charge is (to the extent that it confers security over the assets) void against the liquidator and any of A's creditors.

(8)   Assets held by a person as trustee ("T") are to be taken to be held by T in accordance with a requirement mentioned in subsection (3)(b) only if—
    (a)   A has given T written notice that those assets are to be held by T in accordance with the requirement; or
    (b)   they are assets into which assets to which paragraph (a) applies have been transposed by T on the instructions of A.

(9)   A person who contravenes subsection (6) is guilty of an offence and liable on summary conviction to a fine not exceeding level 5 on the standard scale.

(10)   "Charge" includes a mortgage (or in Scotland a security over property).

(11)   Subsections (6) and (8) do not affect any equitable interest or remedy in favour of a person who is a beneficiary of a trust as a result of a requirement of the kind mentioned in subsection (3)(b).

[48]

Connected persons

49 Persons connected with an applicant

(1)   In considering—
    (a)   an application for a Part IV permission, or
    (b)   whether to vary or cancel a Part IV permission,
the Authority may have regard to any person appearing to it to be, or likely to be, in a relationship with the applicant or person given permission which is relevant.

(2)   Before—
    (a)   giving permission in response to an application made by a person who is connected with an EEA firm [(other than an EEA firm falling within paragraph 5(e) of Schedule 3 (insurance and reinsurance intermediaries))], or
    [(b)   varying any permission given by the Authority to such a person, where the effect of the variation is to grant permission for the purposes of a single market directive other than the one for the purposes of which the existing permission was granted,]
the Authority must consult the firm's home state regulator.

[(2A) But subsection (2) does not apply to the extent that the permission relates to—
(a) an insurance mediation activity (within the meaning given by paragraph 2(5) of Schedule 6); or
(b) a regulated activity involving a regulated mortgage contract[, a regulated home reversion plan or a regulated home purchase plan].]

(3) A person ("A") is connected with an EEA firm if—
(a) A is a subsidiary undertaking of the firm; or
(b) A is a subsidiary undertaking of a parent undertaking of the firm.

[49]

NOTES
Sub-s (2): words in square brackets in para (a) inserted by the Financial Services and Markets Act 2000 (Regulated Activities) (Amendment) (No 2) Order 2003, SI 2003/1476, art 20(1), (2), as from 31 October 2004 (in so far as relating to contracts of long-term care insurance), and as from 14 January 2005 (otherwise) (for transitional provisions see arts 22–27 of that Order at **[2706]** et seq); para (b) substituted by the Regulatory Reform (Financial Services and Markets Act 2000) Order 2007, SI 2007/1973, arts 2, 4, as from 12 July 2007.
Sub-s (2A): inserted by the Financial Services and Markets Act 2000 (Regulated Activities) Order 2001, SI 2001/544, art 97, as from 15 July 2004 (see further the note below); words in square brackets inserted by the Financial Services and Markets Act 2000 (Regulated Activities) (Amendment) (No 2) Order 2006, SI 2006/2383, art 28, as from 6 November 2006 (for the purposes of enabling applications to be made for (i) a Pt IV permission, or a variation of a Pt IV permission, in relation to activities of the kind specified by arts 25B, 25C, 53B, 53C, 63B or 63F or, so far as relevant to any such activity, art 64 of the Regulated Activities Order; or (ii) the Authority's approval under s 59 of this Act in relation to any of those activities), and as from 6 April 2007 (otherwise) (for transitional provisions and effect see arts 1, 36–40 of, and the Schedule to, the 2006 Order at **[2861]** et seq).
Note: sub-s (2A) was originally inserted by the Financial Services and Markets Act 2000 (Regulated Activities) (Amendment) (No 2) Order 2003, SI 2003/1476, art 20(1), (3), as from 31 October 2004 (in so far as relating to contracts of long-term care insurance), and as from 14 January 2005 (otherwise), subject to transitional provisions as noted to sub-s (2) above. Article 20(3) of SI 2003/1476 was subsequently revoked by the Financial Services and Markets Act 2000 (Regulated Activities) (Amendment) Order 2004, SI 2004/1610, art 2, as from 15 July 2004. Article 3 of SI 2004/1610 also amended the Financial Services and Markets Act 2000 (Regulated Activities) Order 2001, SI 2001/544 by adding a new art 97 which, in turn, inserted the new sub-s (2A) as noted above.
Note: sub-s (2) above does not apply where the FSA is considering varying the Part IV permission of any person where that person is a member of a financial conglomerate where the FSA is acting in the course of carrying on supplemental supervision for the purposes of any provision (other than Articles 11, 12, 16, 17 or 18(3)) of the Conglomerates Directive (see the Financial Conglomerates and Other Financial Groups Regulations 2004, SI 2004/1862, reg 3(2) at **[2725]**).
Note: "parent undertaking" and "subsidiary undertaking" are defined in s 420 at **[446]**.

Additional permissions

50 Authority's duty to consider other permissions etc

(1) "Additional Part IV permission" means a Part IV permission which is in force in relation to an EEA firm, a Treaty firm or a person authorised as a result of paragraph 1(1) of Schedule 5.

(2) If the Authority is considering whether, and if so how, to exercise its own-initiative power under this Part in relation to an additional Part IV permission, it must take into account—
(a) the home State authorisation of the authorised person concerned;
(b) any relevant directive; and
(c) relevant provisions of the Treaty.

[50]

Procedure

51 Applications under this Part

(1) An application for a Part IV permission must—
(a) contain a statement of the regulated activity or regulated activities which the applicant proposes to carry on and for which he wishes to have permission; and
(b) give the address of a place in the United Kingdom for service on the applicant of any notice or other document which is required or authorised to be served on him under this Act.

(2) An application for the variation of a Part IV permission must contain a statement—
(a) of the desired variation; and
(b) of the regulated activity or regulated activities which the applicant proposes to carry on if his permission is varied.

(3) Any application under this Part must—
(a) be made in such manner as the Authority may direct; and
(b) contain, or be accompanied by, such other information as the Authority may reasonably require.

(4)   At any time after receiving an application and before determining it, the Authority may require the applicant to provide it with such further information as it reasonably considers necessary to enable it to determine the application.

(5)   Different directions may be given, and different requirements imposed, in relation to different applications or categories of application.

(6)   The Authority may require an applicant to provide information which he is required to provide under this section in such form, or to verify it in such a way, as the Authority may direct.

[51]

52 Determination of applications

(1)   An application under this Part must be determined by the Authority before the end of the period of six months beginning with the date on which it received the completed application.

(2)   The Authority may determine an incomplete application if it considers it appropriate to do so; and it must in any event determine such an application within twelve months beginning with the date on which it received the application.

(3)   The applicant may withdraw his application, by giving the Authority written notice, at any time before the Authority determines it.

(4)   If the Authority grants an application for, or for variation of, a Part IV permission, it must give the applicant written notice.

(5)   The notice must state the date from which the permission, or the variation, has effect.

(6)   If the Authority proposes—
  (a)   to give a Part IV permission but to exercise its power under section 42(7)(a) or (b) or 43(1), or
  (b)   to vary a Part IV permission on the application of an authorised person but to exercise its power under any of those provisions (as a result of section 44(5)),
it must give the applicant a warning notice.

(7)   If the Authority proposes to refuse an application made under this Part, it must (unless subsection (8) applies) give the applicant a warning notice.

(8)   This subsection applies if it appears to the Authority that—
  (a)   the applicant is an EEA firm; and
  (b)   the application is made with a view to carrying on a regulated activity in a manner in which the applicant is, or would be, entitled to carry on that activity in the exercise of an EEA right whether through a United Kingdom branch or by providing services in the United Kingdom.

(9)   If the Authority decides—
  (a)   to give a Part IV permission but to exercise its power under section 42(7)(a) or (b) or 43(1),
  (b)   to vary a Part IV permission on the application of an authorised person but to exercise its power under any of those provisions (as a result of section 44(5)), or
  (c)   to refuse an application under this Part,
it must give the applicant a decision notice.

[52]

53 Exercise of own-initiative power: procedure

(1)   This section applies to an exercise of the Authority's own-initiative power to vary an authorised person's Part IV permission.

(2)   A variation takes effect—
  (a)   immediately, if the notice given under subsection (4) states that that is the case;
  (b)   on such date as may be specified in the notice; or
  (c)   if no date is specified in the notice, when the matter to which the notice relates is no longer open to review.

(3)   A variation may be expressed to take effect immediately (or on a specified date) only if the Authority, having regard to the ground on which it is exercising its own-initiative power, reasonably considers that it is necessary for the variation to take effect immediately (or on that date).

(4)   If the Authority proposes to vary the Part IV permission, or varies it with immediate effect, it must give the authorised person written notice.

(5)   The notice must—
  (a)   give details of the variation;
  (b)   state the Authority's reasons for the variation and for its determination as to when the variation takes effect;
  (c)   inform the authorised person that he may make representations to the Authority within such period as may be specified in the notice (whether or not he has referred the matter to the Tribunal);

    (d)   inform him of when the variation takes effect; and

    (e)   inform him of his right to refer the matter to the Tribunal.

(6)   The Authority may extend the period allowed under the notice for making representations.

(7)   If, having considered any representations made by the authorised person, the Authority decides—

    (a)   to vary the permission in the way proposed, or

    (b)   if the permission has been varied, not to rescind the variation,

it must give him written notice.

(8)   If, having considered any representations made by the authorised person, the Authority decides—

    (a)   not to vary the permission in the way proposed,

    (b)   to vary the permission in a different way, or

    (c)   to rescind a variation which has effect,

it must give him written notice.

(9)   A notice given under subsection (7) must inform the authorised person of his right to refer the matter to the Tribunal.

(10)   A notice under subsection (8)(b) must comply with subsection (5).

(11)   If a notice informs a person of his right to refer a matter to the Tribunal, it must give an indication of the procedure on such a reference.

(12)   For the purposes of subsection (2)(c), whether a matter is open to review is to be determined in accordance with section 391(8).

[53]

54 Cancellation of Part IV permission: procedure

(1)   If the Authority proposes to cancel an authorised person's Part IV permission otherwise than at his request, it must give him a warning notice.

(2)   If the Authority decides to cancel an authorised person's Part IV permission otherwise than at his request, it must give him a decision notice.

[54]

References to the Tribunal

55 Right to refer matters to the Tribunal

(1)   An applicant who is aggrieved by the determination of an application made under this Part may refer the matter to the Tribunal.

(2)   An authorised person who is aggrieved by the exercise of the Authority's own-initiative power may refer the matter to the Tribunal.

[55]

PART V
PERFORMANCE OF REGULATED ACTIVITIES

NOTES

Transitional provisions: the Financial Services and Markets Act 2000 (Transitional Provisions) (Authorised Persons etc) Order 2001, SI 2001/2636, Pt VI makes transitional provisions for people working for authorised persons who will be covered by the regime for approved persons in Pt V of the Act after commencement. Where someone is working for an authorised person before commencement in a post for which they would need to be approved under Pt V after commencement, that person is treated has having been approved for the purpose of working in that post. This deemed approval applies unless the person was working before commencement in contravention of certain provisions of the regulatory rules or of rules made by a self-regulating organisation. The Part also carries forward approvals given under the Insurance Companies Act 1982 and the Banking Act 1987 where the person approved did not take up the appointment before commencement.

See also the transitional provisions relating to this Part in the notes relating to interim permissions and interim approvals preceding s 40 at **[40]**.

Prohibition orders

56 Prohibition orders

(1)   Subsection (2) applies if it appears to the Authority that an individual is not a fit and proper person to perform functions in relation to a regulated activity carried on by an authorised person.

(2)   The Authority may make an order ("a prohibition order") prohibiting the individual from performing a specified function, any function falling within a specified description or any function.

(3)   A prohibition order may relate to—

    (a)   a specified regulated activity, any regulated activity falling within a specified description or all regulated activities;

(b)   authorised persons generally or any person within a specified class of authorised person.

(4)   An individual who performs or agrees to perform a function in breach of a prohibition order is guilty of an offence and liable on summary conviction to a fine not exceeding level 5 on the standard scale.

(5)   In proceedings for an offence under subsection (4) it is a defence for the accused to show that he took all reasonable precautions and exercised all due diligence to avoid committing the offence.

(6)   An authorised person must take reasonable care to ensure that no function of his, in relation to the carrying on of a regulated activity, is performed by a person who is prohibited from performing that function by a prohibition order.

(7)   The Authority may, on the application of the individual named in a prohibition order, vary or revoke it.

(8)   This section applies to the performance of functions in relation to a regulated activity carried on by—

(a)   a person who is an exempt person in relation to that activity, and

(b)   a person to whom, as a result of Part XX, the general prohibition does not apply in relation to that activity,

as it applies to the performance of functions in relation to a regulated activity carried on by an authorised person.

(9)   "Specified" means specified in the prohibition order.

[56]

NOTES

Transitional provisions: the Financial Services and Markets Act 2000 (Transitional Provisions) (Authorised Persons etc) Order 2001, SI 2001/2636, art 79 provides that where, on 1 December 2001, a person is the subject of a disqualification direction made under the Financial Services Act 1986, s 59, the direction has effect after that date as a prohibition order made under this section. The 1986 Act is repealed by the Financial Services and Markets Act 2000 (Consequential Amendments and Repeals) Order 2001, SI 2001/3649, art 3(1)(c).

57   Prohibition orders: procedure and right to refer to Tribunal

(1)   If the Authority proposes to make a prohibition order it must give the individual concerned a warning notice.

(2)   The warning notice must set out the terms of the prohibition.

(3)   If the Authority decides to make a prohibition order it must give the individual concerned a decision notice.

(4)   The decision notice must—

(a)   name the individual to whom the prohibition order applies;

(b)   set out the terms of the order; and

(c)   be given to the individual named in the order.

(5)   A person against whom a decision to make a prohibition order is made may refer the matter to the Tribunal.

[57]

58   Applications relating to prohibitions: procedure and right to refer to Tribunal

(1)   This section applies to an application for the variation or revocation of a prohibition order.

(2)   If the Authority decides to grant the application, it must give the applicant written notice of its decision.

(3)   If the Authority proposes to refuse the application, it must give the applicant a warning notice.

(4)   If the Authority decides to refuse the application, it must give the applicant a decision notice.

(5)   If the Authority gives the applicant a decision notice, he may refer the matter to the Tribunal.

[58]

Approval

59   Approval for particular arrangements

(1)   An authorised person ("A") must take reasonable care to ensure that no person performs a controlled function under an arrangement entered into by A in relation to the carrying on by A of a regulated activity, unless the Authority approves the performance by that person of the controlled function to which the arrangement relates.

(2)   An authorised person ("A") must take reasonable care to ensure that no person performs a controlled function under an arrangement entered into by a contractor of A in relation to the carrying on by A of a regulated activity, unless the Authority approves the performance by that person of the controlled function to which the arrangement relates.

(3)   "Controlled function" means a function of a description specified in rules.

(4)   The Authority may specify a description of function under subsection (3) only if, in relation to the carrying on of a regulated activity by an authorised person, it is satisfied that the first, second or third condition is met.

(5)   The first condition is that the function is likely to enable the person responsible for its performance to exercise a significant influence on the conduct of the authorised person's affairs, so far as relating to the regulated activity.

(6)   The second condition is that the function will involve the person performing it in dealing with customers of the authorised person in a manner substantially connected with the carrying on of the regulated activity.

(7)   The third condition is that the function will involve the person performing it in dealing with property of customers of the authorised person in a manner substantially connected with the carrying on of the regulated activity.

(8)   Neither subsection (1) nor subsection (2) applies to an arrangement which allows a person to perform a function if the question of whether he is a fit and proper person to perform the function is reserved under any of the single market directives to an authority in a country or territory outside the United Kingdom.

(9)   In determining whether the first condition is met, the Authority may take into account the likely consequences of a failure to discharge that function properly.

(10)   "Arrangement"—
   (a)   means any kind of arrangement for the performance of a function of A which is entered into by A or any contractor of his with another person; and
   (b)   includes, in particular, that other person's appointment to an office, his becoming a partner or his employment (whether under a contract of service or otherwise).

(11)   "Customer", in relation to an authorised person, means a person who is using, or who is or may be contemplating using, any of the services provided by the authorised person.

[59]

NOTES
   Note: "person" includes both individuals (natural persons) and bodies corporate or unincorporate; see the Interpretation Act 1978, s 5, Sch 1.

60   Applications for approval

(1)   An application for the Authority's approval under section 59 may be made by the authorised person concerned.

(2)   The application must—
   (a)   be made in such manner as the Authority may direct; and
   (b)   contain, or be accompanied by, such information as the Authority may reasonably require.

(3)   At any time after receiving the application and before determining it, the Authority may require the applicant to provide it with such further information as it reasonably considers necessary to enable it to determine the application.

(4)   The Authority may require an applicant to present information which he is required to give under this section in such form, or to verify it in such a way, as the Authority may direct.

(5)   Different directions may be given, and different requirements imposed, in relation to different applications or categories of application.

(6)   "The authorised person concerned" includes a person who has applied for permission under Part IV and will be the authorised person concerned if permission is given.

[60]

NOTES
   The authorised person concerned: as to the meaning of this, see also the Financial Services and Markets Act 2000 (EEA Passport Rights) Regulations 2001, SI 2001/2511, reg 10 at **[2439]**.
   Application in relation to interim permissions and interim approvals: see the notes preceding s 40 at **[40]**.

61   Determination of applications

(1)   The Authority may grant an application made under section 60 only if it is satisfied that the person in respect of whom the application is made ("the candidate") is a fit and proper person to perform the function to which the application relates.

(2)   In deciding that question, the Authority may have regard (among other things) to whether the candidate, or any person who may perform a function on his behalf—
- (a)   has obtained a qualification,
- (b)   has undergone, or is undergoing, training, or
- (c)   possesses a level of competence,

required by general rules in relation to persons performing functions of the kind to which the application relates.

(3)   The Authority must, before the end of the period of three months beginning with the date on which it receives an application made under section 60 ("the period for consideration"), determine whether—
- (a)   to grant the application; or
- (b)   to give a warning notice under section 62(2).

(4)   If the Authority imposes a requirement under section 60(3), the period for consideration stops running on the day on which the requirement is imposed but starts running again—
- (a)   on the day on which the required information is received by the Authority; or
- (b)   if the information is not provided on a single day, on the last of the days on which it is received by the Authority.

(5)   A person who makes an application under section 60 may withdraw his application by giving written notice to the Authority at any time before the Authority determines it, but only with the consent of—
- (a)   the candidate; and
- (b)   the person by whom the candidate is to be retained to perform the function concerned, if not the applicant.

                                                                                              [61]

62   Applications for approval: procedure and right to refer to Tribunal

(1)   If the Authority decides to grant an application made under section 60 ("an application"), it must give written notice of its decision to each of the interested parties.

(2)   If the Authority proposes to refuse an application, it must give a warning notice to each of the interested parties.

(3)   If the Authority decides to refuse an application, it must give a decision notice to each of the interested parties.

(4)   If the Authority decides to refuse an application, each of the interested parties may refer the matter to the Tribunal.

(5)   "The interested parties", in relation to an application, are—
- (a)   the applicant;
- (b)   the person in respect of whom the application is made ("A"); and
- (c)   the person by whom A's services are to be retained, if not the applicant.

                                                                                              [62]

63   Withdrawal of approval

(1)   The Authority may withdraw an approval given under section 59 if it considers that the person in respect of whom it was given is not a fit and proper person to perform the function to which the approval relates.

(2)   When considering whether to withdraw its approval, the Authority may take into account any matter which it could take into account if it were considering an application made under section 60 in respect of the performance of the function to which the approval relates.

(3)   If the Authority proposes to withdraw its approval, it must give each of the interested parties a warning notice.

(4)   If the Authority decides to withdraw its approval, it must give each of the interested parties a decision notice.

(5)   If the Authority decides to withdraw its approval, each of the interested parties may refer the matter to the Tribunal.

(6)   "The interested parties", in relation to an approval, are—
- (a)   the person on whose application it was given ("A");
- (b)   the person in respect of whom it was given ("B"); and
- (c)   the person by whom B's services are retained, if not A.

                                                                                              [63]

Conduct

64   Conduct: statements and codes

(1)   The Authority may issue statements of principle with respect to the conduct expected of approved persons.

(2)   If the Authority issues a statement of principle under subsection (1), it must also issue a code of practice for the purpose of helping to determine whether or not a person's conduct complies with the statement of principle.

(3)   A code issued under subsection (2) may specify—
  (a)   descriptions of conduct which, in the opinion of the Authority, comply with a statement of principle;
  (b)   descriptions of conduct which, in the opinion of the Authority, do not comply with a statement of principle;
  (c)   factors which, in the opinion of the Authority, are to be taken into account in determining whether or not a person's conduct complies with a statement of principle.

(4)   The Authority may at any time alter or replace a statement or code issued under this section.

(5)   If a statement or code is altered or replaced, the altered or replacement statement or code must be issued by the Authority.

(6)   A statement or code issued under this section must be published by the Authority in the way appearing to the Authority to be best calculated to bring it to the attention of the public.

(7)   A code published under this section and in force at the time when any particular conduct takes place may be relied on so far as it tends to establish whether or not that conduct complies with a statement of principle.

(8)   Failure to comply with a statement of principle under this section does not of itself give rise to any right of action by persons affected or affect the validity of any transaction.

(9)   A person is not to be taken to have failed to comply with a statement of principle if he shows that, at the time of the alleged failure, it or its associated code of practice had not been published.

(10)   The Authority must, without delay, give the Treasury a copy of any statement or code which it publishes under this section.

(11)   The power under this section to issue statements of principle and codes of practice—
  (a)   includes power to make different provision in relation to persons, cases or circumstances of different descriptions; and
  (b)   is to be treated for the purposes of section 2(4)(a) as part of the Authority's rule-making functions.

(12)   The Authority may charge a reasonable fee for providing a person with a copy of a statement or code published under this section.

(13)   "Approved person" means a person in relation to whom the Authority has given its approval under section 59.

[64]

65   Statements and codes: procedure

(1)   Before issuing a statement or code under section 64, the Authority must publish a draft of it in the way appearing to the Authority to be best calculated to bring it to the attention of the public.

(2)   The draft must be accompanied by—
  (a)   a cost benefit analysis; and
  (b)   notice that representations about the proposal may be made to the Authority within a specified time.

(3)   Before issuing the proposed statement or code, the Authority must have regard to any representations made to it in accordance with subsection (2)(b).

(4)   If the Authority issues the proposed statement or code it must publish an account, in general terms, of—
  (a)   the representations made to it in accordance with subsection (2)(b); and
  (b)   its response to them.

(5)   If the statement or code differs from the draft published under subsection (1) in a way which is, in the opinion of the Authority, significant—
  (a)   the Authority must (in addition to complying with subsection (4)) publish details of the difference; and
  (b)   those details must be accompanied by a cost benefit analysis.

(6)   Neither subsection (2)(a) nor subsection (5)(b) applies if the Authority considers—
  (a)   that, making the appropriate comparison, there will be no increase in costs; or
  (b)   that, making that comparison, there will be an increase in costs but the increase will be of minimal significance.

(7)   Subsections (1) to (6) do not apply if the Authority considers that the delay involved in complying with them would prejudice the interests of consumers.

(8)   A statement or code must state that it is issued under section 64.

(9)   The Authority may charge a reasonable fee for providing a copy of a draft published under subsection (1).

(10)   This section also applies to a proposal to alter or replace a statement or code.

(11)   "Cost benefit analysis" means an estimate of the costs together with an analysis of the benefits that will arise—
   (a)   if the proposed statement or code is issued; or
   (b)   if subsection (5)(b) applies, from the statement or code that has been issued.

(12)   "The appropriate comparison" means—
   (a)   in relation to subsection (2)(a), a comparison between the overall position if the statement or code is issued and the overall position if it is not issued;
   (b)   in relation to subsection (5)(b), a comparison between the overall position after the issuing of the statement or code and the overall position before it was issued.
                                                                                    [65]

NOTES
Application in relation to interim permissions and interim approvals: see the notes preceding s 40 at **[40]**.

66   Disciplinary powers

(1)   The Authority may take action against a person under this section if—
   (a)   it appears to the Authority that he is guilty of misconduct; and
   (b)   the Authority is satisfied that it is appropriate in all the circumstances to take action against him.

(2)   A person is guilty of misconduct if, while an approved person—
   (a)   he has failed to comply with a statement of principle issued under section 64; or
   (b)   he has been knowingly concerned in a contravention by the relevant authorised person of a requirement imposed on that authorised person by or under this Act [or by any directly applicable Community regulation made under the markets in financial instruments directive].

(3)   If the Authority is entitled to take action under this section against a person, it may—
   (a)   impose a penalty on him of such amount as it considers appropriate; or
   (b)   publish a statement of his misconduct.

(4)   The Authority may not take action under this section after the end of the period of two years beginning with the first day on which the Authority knew of the misconduct, unless proceedings in respect of it against the person concerned were begun before the end of that period.

(5)   For the purposes of subsection (4)—
   (a)   the Authority is to be treated as knowing of misconduct if it has information from which the misconduct can reasonably be inferred; and
   (b)   proceedings against a person in respect of misconduct are to be treated as begun when a warning notice is given to him under section 67(1).

(6)   "Approved person" has the same meaning as in section 64.

(7)   "Relevant authorised person", in relation to an approved person, means the person on whose application approval under section 59 was given.
                                                                                    [66]

NOTES
Sub-s (2): words in square brackets inserted by the Financial Services and Markets Act 2000 (Markets in Financial Instruments) Regulations 2007, SI 2007/126, reg 3(5), Sch 5, paras 1, 5, as from 1 April 2007 (certain purposes (see reg 1(2) at **[4051]**)), and as from 1 November 2007 (otherwise).
As to the power of the Financial Services Authority to take action under this section in relation to persons who were formerly registered individuals (or registered persons) under the rules of a self-regulating organisation, in the case of a failure to comply with, or an act of misconduct or a contravention under, those rules, see the Financial Services and Markets Act 2000 (Transitional Provisions and Savings) (Civil Remedies, Discipline, Criminal Offences etc) (No 2) Order 2001, SI 2001/3083, art 9.

67   Disciplinary measures: procedure and right to refer to Tribunal

(1)   If the Authority proposes to take action against a person under section 66, it must give him a warning notice.

(2)   A warning notice about a proposal to impose a penalty must state the amount of the penalty.

(3)   A warning notice about a proposal to publish a statement must set out the terms of the statement.

(4)   If the Authority decides to take action against a person under section 66, it must give him a decision notice.

(5)   A decision notice about the imposition of a penalty must state the amount of the penalty.

(6)   A decision notice about the publication of a statement must set out the terms of the statement.

(7)   If the Authority decides to take action against a person under section 66, he may refer the matter to the Tribunal.

[67]

68   Publication

After a statement under section 66 is published, the Authority must send a copy of it to the person concerned and to any person to whom a copy of the decision notice was given.

[68]

69   Statement of policy

(1)   The Authority must prepare and issue a statement of its policy with respect to—
    (a)   the imposition of penalties under section 66; and
    (b)   the amount of penalties under that section.

(2)   The Authority's policy in determining what the amount of a penalty should be must include having regard to—
    (a)   the seriousness of the misconduct in question in relation to the nature of the principle or requirement concerned;
    (b)   the extent to which that misconduct was deliberate or reckless; and
    (c)   whether the person on whom the penalty is to be imposed is an individual.

(3)   The Authority may at any time alter or replace a statement issued under this section.

(4)   If a statement issued under this section is altered or replaced, the Authority must issue the altered or replacement statement.

(5)   The Authority must, without delay, give the Treasury a copy of any statement which it publishes under this section.

(6)   A statement issued under this section must be published by the Authority in the way appearing to the Authority to be best calculated to bring it to the attention of the public.

(7)   The Authority may charge a reasonable fee for providing a person with a copy of the statement.

(8)   In exercising, or deciding whether to exercise, its power under section 66 in the case of any particular misconduct, the Authority must have regard to any statement of policy published under this section and in force at the time when the misconduct in question occurred.

[69]

70   Statements of policy: procedure

(1)   Before issuing a statement under section 69, the Authority must publish a draft of the proposed statement in the way appearing to the Authority to be best calculated to bring it to the attention of the public.

(2)   The draft must be accompanied by notice that representations about the proposal may be made to the Authority within a specified time.

(3)   Before issuing the proposed statement, the Authority must have regard to any representations made to it in accordance with subsection (2).

(4)   If the Authority issues the proposed statement it must publish an account, in general terms, of—
    (a)   the representations made to it in accordance with subsection (2); and
    (b)   its response to them.

(5)   If the statement differs from the draft published under subsection (1) in a way which is, in the opinion of the Authority, significant, the Authority must (in addition to complying with subsection (4)) publish details of the difference.

(6)   The Authority may charge a reasonable fee for providing a person with a copy of a draft published under subsection (1).

(7)   This section also applies to a proposal to alter or replace a statement.

[70]

Breach of statutory duty

71   Actions for damages

(1)   A contravention of section 56(6) or 59(1) or (2) is actionable at the suit of a private person who suffers loss as a result of the contravention, subject to the defences and other incidents applying to actions for breach of statutory duty.

(2)   In prescribed cases, a contravention of that kind which would be actionable at the suit of a private person is actionable at the suit of a person who is not a private person, subject to the defences and other incidents applying to actions for breach of statutory duty.

(3)   "Private person" has such meaning as may be prescribed.

[71]

NOTES
Regulations: the Financial Services and Markets Act 2000 (Rights of Action) Regulations 2001, SI 2001/2256 at **[2375]**.

PART VI
OFFICIAL LISTING

NOTES
Transitional provisions: see the Financial Services and Markets Act 2000 (Official Listing of Securities) (Transitional Provisions) Order 2001, SI 2001/2957 which makes transitional provisions in relation to the listing of securities under this Part instead of the Financial Services Act 1986, Pt IV (repealed). The FSA continues to be the competent authority for listing under this Act (as it has been under the 1986 Act since 1 May 2000 by virtue of the Official Listing of Securities (Change of Competent Authority) Regulations 2000 (SI 2000/968)). Securities admitted to the official list prior to commencement continue to be listed after commencement by virtue of s 74(1) of this Act and the definition of "official list" in s 103(1). This Order makes certain further transitional provisions. Many reflect the fact that, while s 142(9) of the 1986 Act permitted securities to be admitted to the official list either in accordance with Part IV of the 1986 Act ("Part IV securities") or else outside the statutory provisions ("non-Part IV securities"), this Act brings all official listing within this Part. Article 3 of the Order provides for listing rules made under the 1986 Act to continue in force but be treated as if made under this Act. Article 4 ensures that applications for listing made before commencement are treated as made under this Act. Article 5 ensures that delivery of a copy of listing particulars or a prospectus to the registrar of companies before commencement can be treated as compliance with s 83(1) of this Act, and carries forward authorisations to omit material from such documentation. By virtue of arts 6 and 7, listing particulars or a prospectus published before commencement are subject to s 81 of this Act (requirement to provide supplementary details of subsequent changes) and ss 150 and 151 of the 1986 Act (obligation to pay compensation for loss arising from misleading particulars). Article 8 provides for a suspension of listing before commencement to be carried forward under this Act. Article 9 carries forward the approval of persons who were approved as sponsors immediately before commencement, or applications for such approval. Articles 10 and 11 provide that, where a sponsor, or an issuer of listed securities or a director of an issuer, was liable to disciplinary action prior to commencement because of a contravention of the old listing rules, the competent authority may take action against it or him in accordance with the relevant provisions of this Act after commencement. If in such a case a referral procedure had previously been begun under the old listing rules, art 12 provides for the committee to whom the matter was referred to continue to hear the case. The committee will then decide whether to issue a decision notice under this Act (without first having to issue a warning notice). This Act confers a right to refer the decision contained in such a decision notice to the Financial Services and Markets Tribunal. Article 13 deals with the situation where, before commencement, a case had reached the subsequent appeal stage under the old listing rules. In such cases the existing appeal body is empowered to continue hearing the appeal, but subject to provisions as to the way in which it considers the case and gives its decision.

The competent authority

72   The competent authority

(1)   On the coming into force of this section, the functions conferred on the competent authority by this Part are to be exercised by the Authority.

(2)   Schedule 7 modifies this Act in its application to the Authority when it acts as the competent authority.

(3)   But provision is made by Schedule 8 allowing some or all of those functions to be transferred by the Treasury so as to be exercisable by another person.

[72]

73   General duty of the competent authority

(1)   In discharging its general functions the competent authority must have regard to—
   (a)   the need to use its resources in the most efficient and economic way;
   (b)   the principle that a burden or restriction which is imposed on a person should be proportionate to the benefits, considered in general terms, which are expected to arise from the imposition of that burden or restriction;
   [(c)   the desirability of facilitating innovation in respect of listed securities and in respect of financial instruments which have otherwise been admitted to trading on a regulated market or for which a request for admission to trading on such a market has been made;]
   (d)   the international character of capital markets and the desirability of maintaining the competitive position of the United Kingdom;
   (e)   the need to minimise the adverse effects on competition of anything done in the discharge of those functions;
   [(f)   the desirability of facilitating competition in relation to listed securities and in relation to

financial instruments which have otherwise been admitted to trading on a regulated market or for which a request for admission to trading on such a market has been made.]

[(1A)   To the extent that those general functions are functions under or relating to transparency rules, subsection (1)(c) and (f) have effect as if the references to a regulated market were references to a market.]

(2)   The competent authority's general functions are—
  (a)   its function of making rules under this Part (considered as a whole);
  (b)   its functions in relation to the giving of general guidance in relation to this Part (considered as a whole);
  (c)   its function of determining the general policy and principles by reference to which it performs particular functions under this Part.

[73]

NOTES
  Sub-s (1): paras (c), (f) substituted by the Financial Services and Markets Act 2000 (Market Abuse) Regulations 2005, SI 2005/381, reg 4, Sch 1, para 1, as from 1 July 2005.
  Sub-s (1A): inserted by the Companies Act 2006, s 1272, Sch 15, Pt 1, paras 1, 2, as from 8 November 2006.

[73A   Part 6 Rules

(1)   The competent authority may make rules ("Part 6 rules") for the purposes of this Part.

(2)   Provisions of Part 6 rules expressed to relate to the official list are referred to in this Part as "listing rules".

(3)   Provisions of Part 6 rules expressed to relate to disclosure of information in respect of financial instruments which have been admitted to trading on a regulated market or for which a request for admission to trading on such a market has been made, are referred to in this Part as "disclosure rules".

[(4)   Provisions of Part 6 rules expressed to relate to transferable securities are referred to in this Part as "prospectus rules".

(5)   In relation to prospectus rules, the purposes of this Part include the purposes of the prospectus directive.]

[(6)   Transparency rules and corporate governance rules are not listing rules, disclosure rules or prospectus rules, but are Part 6 rules.]]

[74]

NOTES
  Commencement: 17 March 2005.
  Inserted by the Financial Services and Markets Act 2000 (Market Abuse) Regulations 2005, SI 2005/381, reg 4, Sch 1, para 2, as from 17 March 2005.
  Sub-ss (4), (5): added by the Prospectus Regulations 2005, SI 2005/1433, reg 2(1), Sch 1, para 1, as from 1 July 2005.
  Sub-s (6): added by the Companies Act 2006, s 1272, Sch 15, Pt 1, paras 1, 3, as from 8 November 2006.

The official list

74   The official list

(1)   The competent authority must maintain the official list.

(2)   The competent authority may admit to the official list such securities and other things as it considers appropriate.

(3)   But—
  (a)   nothing may be admitted to the official list except in accordance with this Part; and
  (b)   the Treasury may by order provide that anything which falls within a description or category specified in the order may not be admitted to the official list.

(4)   ...

(5)   In the following provisions of this Part—
.....
  "listing" means being included in the official list in accordance with this Part.

[75]

NOTES
  Sub-s (4): repealed by the Financial Services and Markets Act 2000 (Market Abuse) Regulations 2005, SI 2005/381, reg 4, Sch 1, para 3, as from 17 March 2005.
  Sub-s (5): definition "security" (omitted) repealed by the Prospectus Regulations 2005, SI 2005/1433, reg 2(1), Sch 1, para 2, as from 1 July 2005.

Note: the Financial Services and Markets Act 2000 (Official Listing of Securities) Regulations 2001, SI 2001/2956 at **[2487]** prescribes certain bodies whose securities may not be considered for listing under this Part.

Listing

75 Applications for listing

(1)   Admission to the official list may be granted only on an application made to the competent authority in such manner as may be required by listing rules.

(2)   No application for listing may be entertained by the competent authority unless it is made by, or with the consent of, the issuer of the securities concerned.

(3)   No application for listing may be entertained by the competent authority in respect of securities which are to be issued by a body of a prescribed kind.

(4)   The competent authority may not grant an application for listing unless it is satisfied that—
  (a)   the requirements of listing rules (so far as they apply to the application), and
  (b)   any other requirements imposed by the authority in relation to the application,
are complied with.

(5)   An application for listing may be refused if, for a reason relating to the issuer, the competent authority considers that granting it would be detrimental to the interests of investors.

(6)   An application for listing securities which are already officially listed in another EEA State may be refused if the issuer has failed to comply with any obligations to which he is subject as a result of that listing.

[76]

NOTES
Regulations: the Financial Services and Markets Act 2000 (Official Listing of Securities) Regulations 2001, SI 2001/2956 at **[2487]**.
Note that the following amending Regulations have also been made under this section: the Financial Services and Markets Act 2000 (Official Listing of Securities) (Amendment) Regulations 2001, SI 2001/3439.

76 Decision on application

(1)   The competent authority must notify the applicant of its decision on an application for listing—
  (a)   before the end of the period of six months beginning with the date on which the application is received; or
  (b)   if within that period the authority has required the applicant to provide further information in connection with the application, before the end of the period of six months beginning with the date on which that information is provided.

(2)   If the competent authority fails to comply with subsection (1), it is to be taken to have decided to refuse the application.

(3)   If the competent authority decides to grant an application for listing, it must give the applicant written notice.

(4)   If the competent authority proposes to refuse an application for listing, it must give the applicant a warning notice.

(5)   If the competent authority decides to refuse an application for listing, it must give the applicant a decision notice.

(6)   If the competent authority decides to refuse an application for listing, the applicant may refer the matter to the Tribunal.

(7)   If securities are admitted to the official list, their admission may not be called in question on the ground that any requirement or condition for their admission has not been complied with.

[77]

77 Discontinuance and suspension of listing

(1)   The competent authority may, in accordance with listing rules, discontinue the listing of any securities if satisfied that there are special circumstances which preclude normal regular dealings in them.

(2)   The competent authority may, in accordance with listing rules, suspend the listing of any securities.

[(2A)   The competent authority may discontinue under subsection (1) or suspend under subsection (2) the listing of any securities on its own initiative or on the application of the issuer of those securities.]

(3)   If securities are suspended under subsection (2) they are to be treated, for the purposes of sections 96 and 99, as still being listed.

(4)   This section applies to securities whenever they were admitted to the official list.

(5)   If the competent authority discontinues or suspends the listing of any securities, [on its own initiative,] the issuer may refer the matter to the Tribunal.

[78]

NOTES
Sub-s (2A): inserted by the Regulatory Reform (Financial Services and Markets Act 2000) Order 2007, SI 2007/1973, arts 2, 5(a), as from 12 July 2007.
Sub-s (5): words in square brackets inserted by SI 2007/1973, arts 2, 5(b), as from 12 July 2007.

78   Discontinuance or suspension: procedure

(1)   A discontinuance or suspension [by the competent authority on its own initiative] takes effect—
- (a)   immediately, if the notice under subsection (2) states that that is the case;
- (b)   in any other case, on such date as may be specified in that notice.

(2)   If [on its own initiative] the competent authority—
- (a)   proposes to discontinue or suspend the listing of securities, or
- (b)   discontinues or suspends the listing of securities with immediate effect,

it must give the issuer of the securities written notice.

(3)   The notice must—
- (a)   give details of the discontinuance or suspension;
- (b)   state the competent authority's reasons for the discontinuance or suspension and for choosing the date on which it took effect or takes effect;
- (c)   inform the issuer of the securities that he may make representations to the competent authority within such period as may be specified in the notice (whether or not he has referred the matter to the Tribunal);
- (d)   inform him of the date on which the discontinuance or suspension took effect or will take effect; and
- (e)   inform him of his right to refer the matter to the Tribunal.

(4)   The competent authority may extend the period within which representations may be made to it.

(5)   If, having considered any representations made by the issuer of the securities, the competent authority decides—
- (a)   to discontinue or suspend the listing of the securities, or
- (b)   if the discontinuance or suspension has taken effect, not to cancel it,

the competent authority must give the issuer of the securities written notice.

(6)   A notice given under subsection (5) must inform the issuer of the securities of his right to refer the matter to the Tribunal.

(7)   If a notice informs a person of his right to refer a matter to the Tribunal, it must give an indication of the procedure on such a reference.

(8)   If the competent authority decides—
- (a)   not to discontinue or suspend the listing of the securities, or
- (b)   if the discontinuance or suspension has taken effect, to cancel it,

the competent authority must give the issuer of the securities written notice.

(9)   The effect of cancelling a discontinuance is that the securities concerned are to be readmitted, without more, to the official list.

(10)   If the competent authority has suspended the listing of securities [on its own initiative] and proposes to refuse an application by the issuer of the securities for the cancellation of the suspension, it must give him a warning notice.

(11)   The competent authority must, having considered any representations made in response to the warning notice—
- (a)   if it decides to refuse the application, give the issuer of the securities a decision notice;
- (b)   if it grants the application, give him written notice of its decision.

(12)   If the competent authority decides to refuse an application for the cancellation of the suspension of listed securities, the applicant may refer the matter to the Tribunal.

(13)   "Discontinuance" means a discontinuance of listing under section 77(1).

(14)   "Suspension" means a suspension of listing under section 77(2).

[79]

NOTES
Sub-ss (1), (2), (10): words in square brackets inserted by the Regulatory Reform (Financial Services and Markets Act 2000) Order 2007, SI 2007/1973, arts 2, 6, as from 12 July 2007.

[78A   Discontinuance or suspension at the request of the issuer: procedure

(1)   A discontinuance or suspension by the competent authority on the application of the issuer of the securities takes effect—
(a)   immediately, if the notice under subsection (2) states that this is the case;
(b)   in any other case, on such date as may be specified in that notice.

(2)   If the competent authority discontinues or suspends the listing of securities on the application of the issuer of the securities it must give him written notice.

(3)   The notice must—
(a)   give details of the discontinuance or suspension;
(b)   inform the issuer of the securities of the date on which the discontinuance or suspension took effect or will take effect; and
(c)   inform the issuer of his right to apply for the cancellation of the suspension.

(4)   If the competent authority proposes to refuse an application by the issuer of the securities for the discontinuance or suspension of the listing of the securities, it must give him a warning notice.

(5)   The competent authority must, having considered any representations made in response to the warning notice, if it decides to refuse the application, give the issuer of the securities a decision notice.

(6)   If the competent authority decides to refuse an application by the issuer of the securities for the discontinuance or suspension of the listing of the securities, the issuer may refer the matter to the Tribunal.

(7)   If the competent authority has suspended the listing of securities on the application of the issuer of the securities and proposes to refuse an application by the issuer for the cancellation of the suspension, it must give him a warning notice.

(8)   The competent authority must, having considered any representations made in response to the warning notice—
(a)   if it decides to refuse the application for the cancellation of the suspension, give the issuer of the securities a decision notice;
(b)   if it grants the application, give him written notice of its decision.

(9)   If the competent authority decides to refuse an application for the cancellation of the suspension of listed securities, the applicant may refer the matter to the Tribunal.

(10)   "Discontinuance" means a discontinuance of listing under section 77(1).

(11)   "Suspension" means a suspension of listing under section 77(2).]

[79A]

NOTES
Commencement: 12 July 2007.
Inserted by the Regulatory Reform (Financial Services and Markets Act 2000) Order 2007, SI 2007/1973, arts 2, 7, as from 12 July 2007.

Listing particulars

79   Listing particulars and other documents

(1)   Listing rules may provide that securities … of a kind specified in the rules may not be admitted to the official list unless—
(a)   listing particulars have been submitted to, and approved by, the competent authority and published; or
(b)   in such cases as may be specified by listing rules, such document (other than listing particulars or a prospectus of a kind required by listing rules) as may be so specified has been published.

(2)   "Listing particulars" means a document in such form and containing such information as may be specified in listing rules.

(3)   For the purposes of this Part, the persons responsible for listing particulars are to be determined in accordance with regulations made by the Treasury.

[(3A)   Listing rules made under subsection (1) may not specify securities of a kind for which an approved prospectus is required as a result of section 85.]

(4)   Nothing in this section affects the competent authority's general power to make listing rules.

[80]

NOTES
Sub-s (1): words omitted repealed by the Prospectus Regulations 2005, SI 2005/1433, reg 2(1), Sch 1, para 3(1), (2), as from 1 July 2005.

Sub-s (3A): inserted by SI 2005/1433, reg 2(1), Sch 1, para 3(1), (3), as from 1 July 2005.
Regulations: the Financial Services and Markets Act 2000 (Official Listing of Securities) Regulations 2001, SI 2001/2956 at **[2487]**.

80 General duty of disclosure in listing particulars

(1)   Listing particulars submitted to the competent authority under section 79 must contain all such information as investors and their professional advisers would reasonably require, and reasonably expect to find there, for the purpose of making an informed assessment of—
  (a)   the assets and liabilities, financial position, profits and losses, and prospects of the issuer of the securities; and
  (b)   the rights attaching to the securities.

(2)   That information is required in addition to any information required by—
  (a)   listing rules, or
  (b)   the competent authority,
as a condition of the admission of the securities to the official list.

(3)   Subsection (1) applies only to information—
  (a)   within the knowledge of any person responsible for the listing particulars; or
  (b)   which it would be reasonable for him to obtain by making enquiries.

(4)   In determining what information subsection (1) requires to be included in listing particulars, regard must be had (in particular) to—
  (a)   the nature of the securities and their issuer;
  (b)   the nature of the persons likely to consider acquiring them;
  (c)   the fact that certain matters may reasonably be expected to be within the knowledge of professional advisers of a kind which persons likely to acquire the securities may reasonably be expected to consult; and
  (d)   any information available to investors or their professional advisers as a result of requirements imposed on the issuer of the securities by a recognised investment exchange, by listing rules or by or under any other enactment.

[81]

81 Supplementary listing particulars

(1)   If at any time after the preparation of listing particulars which have been submitted to the competent authority under section 79 and before the commencement of dealings in the securities concerned following their admission to the official list—
  (a)   there is a significant change affecting any matter contained in those particulars the inclusion of which was required by—
    (i)   section 80,
    (ii)   listing rules, or
    (iii) the competent authority, or
  (b)   a significant new matter arises, the inclusion of information in respect of which would have been so required if it had arisen when the particulars were prepared,
the issuer must, in accordance with listing rules, submit supplementary listing particulars of the change or new matter to the competent authority, for its approval and, if they are approved, publish them.

(2)   "Significant" means significant for the purpose of making an informed assessment of the kind mentioned in section 80(1).

(3)   If the issuer of the securities is not aware of the change or new matter in question, he is not under a duty to comply with subsection (1) unless he is notified of the change or new matter by a person responsible for the listing particulars.

(4)   But it is the duty of any person responsible for those particulars who is aware of such a change or new matter to give notice of it to the issuer.

(5)   Subsection (1) applies also as respects matters contained in any supplementary listing particulars previously published under this section in respect of the securities in question.

[82]

82 Exemptions from disclosure

(1)   The competent authority may authorise the omission from listing particulars of any information, the inclusion of which would otherwise be required by section 80 or 81, on the ground—
  (a)   that its disclosure would be contrary to the public interest;
  (b)   that its disclosure would be seriously detrimental to the issuer; or
  (c)   in the case of securities of a kind specified in listing rules, that its disclosure is unnecessary for persons of the kind who may be expected normally to buy or deal in securities of that kind.

(2)   But—
   (a)   no authority may be granted under subsection (1)(b) in respect of essential information; and
   (b)   no authority granted under subsection (1)(b) extends to any such information.

(3)   The Secretary of State or the Treasury may issue a certificate to the effect that the disclosure of any information (including information that would otherwise have to be included in listing particulars for which they are themselves responsible) would be contrary to the public interest.

(4)   The competent authority is entitled to act on any such certificate in exercising its powers under subsection (1)(a).

(5)   This section does not affect any powers of the competent authority under listing rules made as a result of section 101(2).

(6)   "Essential information" means information which a person considering acquiring securities of the kind in question would be likely to need in order not to be misled about any facts which it is essential for him to know in order to make an informed assessment.

(7)   "Listing particulars" includes supplementary listing particulars.

[83]

83   (*Repealed by the Prospectus Regulations 2005, SI 2005/1433, reg 2(1), Sch 1, para 4, as from 1 July 2005.*)

[Transferable securities: public offers and admission to trading

84   Matters which may be dealt with by prospectus rules
(1)   Prospectus rules may make provision as to—
   (a)   the required form and content of a prospectus (including a summary);
   (b)   the cases in which a summary need not be included in a prospectus;
   (c)   the languages which may be used in a prospectus (including a summary);
   (d)   the determination of the persons responsible for a prospectus;
   (e)   the manner in which applications to the competent authority for the approval of a prospectus are to be made.

(2)   Prospectus rules may also make provision as to—
   (a)   the period of validity of a prospectus;
   (b)   the disclosure of the maximum price or of the criteria or conditions according to which the final offer price is to be determined, if that information is not contained in a prospectus;
   (c)   the disclosure of the amount of the transferable securities which are to be offered to the public or of the criteria or conditions according to which that amount is to be determined, if that information is not contained in a prospectus;
   (d)   the required form and content of other summary documents (including the languages which may be used in such a document);
   (e)   the ways in which a prospectus that has been approved by the competent authority may be made available to the public;
   (f)   the disclosure, publication or other communication of such information as the competent authority may reasonably stipulate;
   (g)   the principles to be observed in relation to advertisements in connection with an offer of transferable securities to the public or admission of transferable securities to trading on a regulated market and the enforcement of those principles;
   (h)   the suspension of trading in transferable securities where continued trading would be detrimental to the interests of investors;
   (i)   elections under section 87 or under Article 2.1(m)(iii) of the prospectus directive as applied for the purposes of this Part by section 102C

(3)   Prospectus rules may also make provision as to—
   (a)   access to the register of investors maintained under section 87R; and
   (b)   the supply of information from that register.

(4)   Prospectus rules may make provision for the purpose of dealing with matters arising out of or related to any provision of the prospectus directive.

(5)   In relation to cases where the home State in relation to an issuer of transferable securities is an EEA State other than the United Kingdom, prospectus rules may make provision for the recognition of elections made in relation to such securities under the law of that State in accordance with Article 1.3 or 2.1(m)(iii) of the prospectus directive.

(6)   In relation to a document relating to transferable securities issued by an issuer incorporated in a non-EEA State and drawn up in accordance with the law of that State, prospectus rules may make provision as to the approval of that document as a prospectus.

PART I
FSMA 2000

(7)   Nothing in this section affects the competent authority's general power to make prospectus rules.]

[84]

NOTES
Commencement: 1 July 2005.
Sections 84–87, 87A–87R substituted (together with the preceding heading) for original ss 84–87, by the Prospectus Regulations 2005, SI 2005/1433, reg 2(1), Sch 1, para 5, as from 1 July 2005.

[85   Prohibition of dealing etc in transferable securities without approved prospectus

(1)   It is unlawful for transferable securities to which this subsection applies to be offered to the public in the United Kingdom unless an approved prospectus has been made available to the public before the offer is made.

(2)   It is unlawful to request the admission of transferable securities to which this subsection applies to trading on a regulated market situated or operating in the United Kingdom unless an approved prospectus has been made available to the public before the request is made.

(3)   A person who contravenes subsection (1) or (2) is guilty of an offence and liable—
   (a)   on summary conviction, to imprisonment for a term not exceeding 3 months or a fine not exceeding the statutory maximum or both;
   (b)   on conviction on indictment, to imprisonment for a term not exceeding 2 years or a fine or both.

(4)   A contravention of subsection (1) or (2) is actionable, at the suit of a person who suffers loss as a result of the contravention, subject to the defences and other incidents applying to actions for breach of statutory duty.

(5)   Subsection (1) applies to all transferable securities other than—
   (a)   those listed in Schedule 11A;
   (b)   such other transferable securities as may be specified in prospectus rules.

(6)   Subsection (2) applies to all transferable securities other than—
   (a)   those listed in Part 1 of Schedule 11A;
   (b)   such other transferable securities as may be specified in prospectus rules.

(7)   "Approved prospectus" means, in relation to transferable securities to which this section applies, a prospectus approved by the competent authority of the home State in relation to the issuer of the securities.]

[85]

NOTES
Commencement: 1 July 2005.
Substituted as noted to s 84 at **[84]**.

[86   Exempt offers to the public

(1)   A person does not contravene section 85(1) if—
   (a)   the offer is made to or directed at qualified investors only;
   (b)   the offer is made to or directed at fewer than 100 persons, other than qualified investors, per EEA State;
   (c)   the minimum consideration which may be paid by any person for transferable securities acquired by him pursuant to the offer is at least 50,000 euros (or an equivalent amount);
   (d)   the transferable securities being offered are denominated in amounts of at least 50,000 euros (or equivalent amounts); or
   (e)   the total consideration for the transferable securities being offered cannot exceed 100,000 euros (or an equivalent amount).

(2)   Where—
   (a)   a person who is not a qualified investor ("the client") has engaged a qualified investor falling within Article 2.1(e)(i) of the prospectus directive to act as his agent, and
   (b)   the terms on which the qualified investor is engaged enable him to make decisions concerning the acceptance of offers of transferable securities on the client's behalf without reference to the client,
an offer made to or directed at the qualified investor is not to be regarded for the purposes of subsection (1) as also having been made to or directed at the client.

(3)   For the purposes of subsection (1)(b), the making of an offer of transferable securities to—
   (a)   trustees of a trust,
   (b)   members of a partnership in their capacity as such, or
   (c)   two or more persons jointly,
is to be treated as the making of an offer to a single person.

(4)   In determining whether subsection (1)(e) is satisfied in relation to an offer ("offer A"), offer A is to be taken together with any other offer of transferable securities of the same class made by the same person which—
- (a)   was open at any time within the period of 12 months ending with the date on which offer A is first made; and
- (b)   had previously satisfied subsection (1)(e).

(5)   For the purposes of this section, an amount (in relation to an amount denominated in euros) is an "equivalent amount" if it is an amount of equal value denominated wholly or partly in another currency or unit of account.

(6)   The equivalent is to be calculated at the latest practicable date before (but in any event not more than 3 working days before) the date on which the offer is first made.

(7)   "Qualified investor" means—
- (a)   an entity falling within Article 2.1(e)(i), (ii) or (iii) of the prospectus directive;
- (b)   an investor registered on the register maintained by the competent authority under section 87R;
- (c)   an investor authorised by an EEA State other than the United Kingdom to be considered as a qualified investor for the purposes of the prospectus directive.]

[86]

NOTES
Commencement: 1 July 2005.
Substituted as noted to s 84 at **[84]**.

[87   Election to have prospectus

(1)   A person who proposes—
- (a)   to issue transferable securities to which this section applies,
- (b)   to offer to the public transferable securities to which this section applies, or
- (c)   to request the admission to a regulated market of transferable securities to which this section applies,

may elect, in accordance with prospectus rules, to have a prospectus in relation to the securities.

(2)   If a person makes such an election, the provisions of this Part and of prospectus rules apply in relation to those transferable securities as if, in relation to an offer of the securities to the public or the admission of the securities to trading on a regulated market, they were transferable securities for which an approved prospectus would be required as a result of section 85.

(3)   Listing rules made under section 79 do not apply to securities which are the subject of an election.

(4)   The transferable securities to which this section applies are those which fall within any of the following paragraphs of Schedule 11A—
- (a)   paragraph 2,
- (b)   paragraph 4,
- (c)   paragraph 8, or
- (d)   paragraph 9,

where the United Kingdom is the home State in relation to the issuer of the securities.]

[87]

NOTES
Commencement: 1 July 2005.
Substituted as noted to s 84 at **[84]**.

[Approval of prospectus

87A   Criteria for approval of prospectus by competent authority

(1)   The competent authority may not approve a prospectus unless it is satisfied that—
- (a)   the United Kingdom is the home State in relation to the issuer of the transferable securities to which it relates,
- (b)   the prospectus contains the necessary information, and
- (c)   all of the other requirements imposed by or in accordance with this Part or the prospectus directive have been complied with (so far as those requirements apply to a prospectus for the transferable securities in question).

(2)   The necessary information is the information necessary to enable investors to make an informed assessment of—
- (a)   the assets and liabilities, financial position, profits and losses, and prospects of the issuer of the transferable securities and of any guarantor; and
- (b)   the rights attaching to the transferable securities.

(3)   The necessary information must be presented in a form which is comprehensible and easy to analyse.

(4)   The necessary information must be prepared having regard to the particular nature of the transferable securities and their issuer.

(5)   The prospectus must include a summary (unless the transferable securities in question are ones in relation to which prospectus rules provide that a summary is not required).

(6)   The summary must, briefly and in non-technical language, convey the essential characteristics of, and risks associated with, the issuer, any guarantor and the transferable securities to which the prospectus relates.

(7)   Where the prospectus for which approval is sought does not include the final offer price or the amount of transferable securities to be offered to the public, the applicant must inform the competent authority in writing of that information as soon as that element is finalised.

(8)   "Prospectus" (except in subsection (5)) includes a supplementary prospectus.]

[88]

NOTES
Commencement: 1 July 2005.
Substituted as noted to s 84 at **[84]**.

[87B   Exemptions from disclosure

(1)   The competent authority may authorise the omission from a prospectus of any information, the inclusion of which would otherwise be required, on the ground—
  (a)   that its disclosure would be contrary to the public interest;
  (b)   that its disclosure would be seriously detrimental to the issuer, provided that the omission would be unlikely to mislead the public with regard to any facts or circumstances which are essential for an informed assessment of the kind mentioned in section 87A(2); or
  (c)   that the information is only of minor importance for a specific offer to the public or admission to trading on a regulated market and unlikely to influence an informed assessment of the kind mentioned in section 87A(2).

(2)   The Secretary of State or the Treasury may issue a certificate to the effect that the disclosure of any information would be contrary to the public interest.

(3)   The competent authority is entitled to act on any such certificate in exercising its powers under subsection (1)(a).

(4)   This section does not affect any powers of the competent authority under prospectus rules.

(5)   "Prospectus" includes a supplementary prospectus.]

[89]

NOTES
Commencement: 1 July 2005.
Substituted as noted to s 84 at **[84]**.

[87C   Consideration of application for approval

(1)   The competent authority must notify the applicant of its decision on an application for approval of a prospectus before the end of the period for consideration.

(2)   The period for consideration—
  (a)   begins with the first working day after the date on which the application is received; but
  (b)   if the competent authority gives a notice under subsection (4), is to be treated as beginning with the first working day after the date on which the notice is complied with.

(3)   The period for consideration is—
  (a)   except in the case of a new issuer, 10 working days; or
  (b)   in that case, 20 working days.

(4)   The competent authority may by notice in writing require a person who has applied for approval of a prospectus to provide—
  (a)   specified documents or documents of a specified description, or
  (b)   specified information or information of a specified description.

(5)   No notice under subsection (4) may be given after the end of the period, beginning with the first working day after the date on which the application is received, of—
  (a)   except in the case of a new issuer, 10 working days; or
  (b)   in that case, 20 working days.

(6)   Subsection (4) applies only to information and documents reasonably required in connection with the exercise by the competent authority of its functions in relation to the application.

(7)   The competent authority may require any information provided under this section to be provided in such form as it may reasonably require.

(8)   The competent authority may require—
  (a)   any information provided, whether in a document or otherwise, to be verified in such manner, or
  (b)   any document produced to be authenticated in such manner,
as it may reasonably require.

(9)   The competent authority must notify the applicant of its decision on an application for approval of a supplementary prospectus before the end of the period of 7 working days beginning with the date on which the application is received; and subsections (4) and (6) to (8) apply to such an application as they apply to an application for approval of a prospectus.

(10)   The competent authority's failure to comply with subsection (1) or (9) does not constitute approval of the application in question.

(11)   "New issuer" means an issuer of transferable securities which—
  (a)   does not have transferable securities admitted to trading on any regulated market; and
  (b)   has not previously offered transferable securities to the public.]

[90]

NOTES
Commencement: 1 July 2005.
Substituted as noted to s 84 at **[84]**.

[87D   Procedure for decision on application for approval

(1)   If the competent authority approves a prospectus, it must give the applicant written notice.

(2)   If the competent authority proposes to refuse to approve a prospectus, it must give the applicant written notice.

(3)   The notice must state the competent authority's reasons for the proposed refusal.

(4)   If the competent authority decides to refuse to approve a prospectus, it must give the applicant written notice.

(5)   The notice must—
  (a)   give the competent authority's reasons for refusing the application; and
  (b)   inform the applicant of his right to refer the matter to the Tribunal.

(6)   If the competent authority refuses to approve a prospectus, the applicant may refer the matter to the Tribunal.

(7)   In this section "prospectus" includes a supplementary prospectus.]

[91]

NOTES
Commencement: 1 July 2005.
Substituted as noted to s 84 at **[84]**.

[Transfer of application for approval of a prospectus

87E   Transfer by competent authority of application for approval

(1)   The competent authority may transfer an application for the approval of a prospectus or a supplementary prospectus to the competent authority of another EEA State ("the transferee authority").

(2)   Before doing so, the competent authority must obtain the agreement of the transferee authority.

(3)   The competent authority must inform the applicant of the transfer within 3 working days beginning with the first working day after the date of the transfer.

(4)   On making a transfer under subsection (1), the competent authority ceases to have functions under this Part in relation to the application transferred.]

[92]

NOTES
Commencement: 1 July 2005.
Substituted as noted to s 84 at **[84]**.

[87F   Transfer to competent authority of application for approval

(1)   Where the competent authority agrees to the transfer to it of an application for the approval of a prospectus made to the competent authority of another EEA State—

    (a)   the United Kingdom is to be treated for the purposes of this Part as the home State in relation to the issuer of the transferable securities to which the prospectus relates, and

    (b)   this Part applies to the application as if it had been made to the competent authority but with the modification in subsection (2).

(2)   Section 87C applies as if the date of the transfer were the date on which the application was received by the competent authority.]

[93]

NOTES
Commencement: 1 July 2005.
Substituted as noted to s 84 at **[84]**.

[Supplementary prospectus

87G   Supplementary prospectus

(1)   Subsection (2) applies if, during the relevant period, there arises or is noted a significant new factor, material mistake or inaccuracy relating to the information included in a prospectus approved by the competent authority.

(2)   The person on whose application the prospectus was approved must, in accordance with prospectus rules, submit a supplementary prospectus containing details of the new factor, mistake or inaccuracy to the competent authority for its approval.

(3)   The relevant period begins when the prospectus is approved and ends—

    (a)   with the closure of the offer of the transferable securities to which the prospectus relates; or

    (b)   when trading in those securities on a regulated market begins.

(4)   "Significant" means significant for the purposes of making an informed assessment of the kind mentioned in section 87A(2).

(5)   Any person responsible for the prospectus who is aware of any new factor, mistake or inaccuracy which may require the submission of a supplementary prospectus in accordance with subsection (2) must give notice of it to—

    (a)   the issuer of the transferable securities to which the prospectus relates, and

    (b)   the person on whose application the prospectus was approved.

(6)   A supplementary prospectus must provide sufficient information to correct any mistake or inaccuracy which gave rise to the need for it.

(7)   Subsection (1) applies also to information contained in any supplementary prospectus published under this section.]

[94]

NOTES
Commencement: 1 July 2005.
Substituted as noted to s 84 at **[84]**.

[Passporting

87H   Prospectus approved in another EEA State

(1)   A prospectus approved by the competent authority of an EEA State other than the United Kingdom is not an approved prospectus for the purposes of section 85 unless that authority has provided the competent authority with—

    (a)   a certificate of approval;

    (b)   a copy of the prospectus as approved; and

    (c)   if requested by the competent authority, a translation of the summary of the prospectus.

(2)   A document is not a certificate of approval unless it states that the prospectus—

    (a)   has been drawn up in accordance with the prospectus directive; and

    (b)   has been approved, in accordance with that directive, by the competent authority providing the certificate.

(3)   A document is not a certificate of approval unless it states whether (and, if so, why) the competent authority providing it authorised, in accordance with the prospectus directive, the omission from the prospectus of information which would otherwise have been required to be included.

(4)   "Prospectus" includes a supplementary prospectus.]

[95]

PART I
FSMA 2000

NOTES
Commencement: 1 July 2005.
Substituted as noted to s 84 at **[84]**.

[87I   Provision of information to host Member State

(1)   The competent authority must, if requested to do so, supply the competent authority of a specified EEA State with—
   (a)   a certificate of approval;
   (b)   a copy of the specified prospectus (as approved by the competent authority); and
   (c)   a translation of the summary of the specified prospectus (if the request states that one has been requested by the other competent authority).

(2)   Only the following may make a request under this section—
   (a)   the issuer of the transferable securities to which the specified prospectus relates;
   (b)   a person who wishes to offer the transferable securities to which the specified prospectus relates to the public in an EEA State other than (or as well as) the United Kingdom;
   (c)   a person requesting the admission of the transferable securities to which the specified prospectus relates to a regulated market situated or operating in an EEA State other than (or as well as) the United Kingdom.

(3)   A certificate of approval must state that the prospectus—
   (a)   has been drawn up in accordance with this Part and the prospectus directive; and
   (b)   has been approved, in accordance with those provisions, by the competent authority.

(4)   A certificate of approval must state whether (and, if so, why) the competent authority authorised, in accordance with section 87B, the omission from the prospectus of information which would otherwise have been required to be included.

(5)   The competent authority must comply with a request under this section—
   (a)   if the prospectus has been approved before the request is made, within 3 working days beginning with the date of the request; or
   (b)   if the request is submitted with an application for the approval of the prospectus, on the first working day after the date on which it approves the prospectus.

(6)   "Prospectus" includes a supplementary prospectus.

(7)   "Specified" means specified in a request made for the purposes of this section.]

[96]

NOTES
Commencement: 1 July 2005.
Substituted as noted to s 84 at **[84]**.

[Transferable securities: powers of competent authority

87J   Requirements imposed as condition of approval

(1)   As a condition of approving a prospectus, the competent authority may by notice in writing—
   (a)   require the inclusion in the prospectus of such supplementary information necessary for investor protection as the competent authority may specify;
   (b)   require a person controlling, or controlled by, the applicant to provide specified information or documents;
   (c)   require an auditor or manager of the applicant to provide specified information or documents;
   (d)   require a financial intermediary commissioned to assist either in carrying out the offer to the public of the transferable securities to which the prospectus relates or in requesting their admission to trading on a regulated market, to provide specified information or documents.

(2)   "Specified" means specified in the notice.

(3)   "Prospectus" includes a supplementary prospectus.]

[97]

NOTES
Commencement: 1 July 2005.
Substituted as noted to s 84 at **[84]**.

[87K   Power to suspend or prohibit offer to the public

(1)   This section applies where a person ("the offeror") has made an offer of transferable securities to the public in the United Kingdom ("the offer").

(2) If the competent authority has reasonable grounds for suspecting that an applicable provision has been infringed, it may—

    (a) require the offeror to suspend the offer for a period not exceeding 10 working days;

    (b) require a person not to advertise the offer, or to take such steps as the authority may specify to suspend any existing advertisement of the offer, for a period not exceeding 10 working days.

(3) If the competent authority has reasonable grounds for suspecting that it is likely that an applicable provision will be infringed, it may require the offeror to withdraw the offer.

(4) If the competent authority finds that an applicable provision has been infringed, it may require the offeror to withdraw the offer.

(5) "An applicable provision" means—

    (a) a provision of this Part,

    (b) a provision contained in prospectus rules,

    (c) any other provision made in accordance with the prospectus directive,

applicable in relation to the offer.]

        [98]

NOTES
Commencement: 1 July 2005.
Substituted as noted to s 84 at **[84]**.

[87L Power to suspend or prohibit admission to trading on a regulated market

(1) This section applies where a person has requested the admission of transferable securities to trading on a regulated market situated or operating in the United Kingdom.

(2) If the competent authority has reasonable grounds for suspecting that an applicable provision has been infringed and the securities have not yet been admitted to trading on the regulated market in question, it may—

    (a) require the person requesting admission to suspend the request for a period not exceeding 10 working days;

    (b) require a person not to advertise the securities to which it relates, or to take such steps as the authority may specify to suspend any existing advertisement in connection with those securities, for a period not exceeding 10 working days.

(3) If the competent authority has reasonable grounds for suspecting that an applicable provision has been infringed and the securities have been admitted to trading on the regulated market in question, it may—

    (a) require the market operator to suspend trading in the securities for a period not exceeding 10 working days;

    (b) require a person not to advertise the securities, or to take such steps as the authority may specify to suspend any existing advertisement in connection with those securities, for a period not exceeding 10 working days.

(4) If the competent authority finds that an applicable provision has been infringed, it may require the market operator to prohibit trading in the securities on the regulated market in question.

(5) "An applicable provision" means—

    (a) a provision of this Part,

    (b) a provision contained in prospectus rules,

    (c) any other provision made in accordance with the prospectus directive,

applicable in relation to the admission of the transferable securities to trading on the regulated market in question.]

        [99]

NOTES
Commencement: 1 July 2005.
Substituted as noted to s 84 at **[84]**.

[87M Public censure of issuer

(1) If the competent authority finds that—

    (a) an issuer of transferable securities,

    (b) a person offering transferable securities to the public, or

    (c) a person requesting the admission of transferable securities to trading on a regulated market,

is failing or has failed to comply with his obligations under an applicable provision, it may publish a statement to that effect.

(2) If the competent authority proposes to publish a statement, it must give the person a warning notice setting out the terms of the proposed statement.

(3)   If, after considering any representations made in response to the warning notice, the competent authority decides to make the proposed statement, it must give the person a decision notice setting out the terms of the statement.

(4)   "An applicable provision" means—

(a)   a provision of this Part,

(b)   a provision contained in prospectus rules,

(c)   any other provision made in accordance with the prospectus directive,

applicable to a prospectus in relation to the transferable securities in question.

(5)   "Prospectus" includes a supplementary prospectus.]

[100]

NOTES
Commencement: 1 July 2005.
Substituted as noted to s 84 at **[84]**.

[87N   Right to refer matters to the Tribunal

(1)   A person to whom a decision notice is given under section 87M may refer the matter to the Tribunal.

(2)   A person to whom a notice is given under section 87O may refer the matter to the Tribunal.]

[101]

NOTES
Commencement: 1 July 2005.
Substituted as noted to s 84 at **[84]**.

[87O   Procedure under sections 87K and 87L

(1)   A requirement under section 87K or 87L takes effect—

(a)   immediately, if the notice under subsection (2) states that that is the case;

(b)   in any other case, on such date as may be specified in that notice.

(2)   If the competent authority—

(a)   proposes to exercise the powers in section 87K or 87L in relation to a person, or

(b)   exercises any of those powers in relation to a person with immediate effect,

it must give that person written notice.

(3)   The notice must—

(a)   give details of the competent authority's action or proposed action;

(b)   state the competent authority's reasons for taking the action in question and choosing the date on which it took effect or takes effect;

(c)   inform the recipient that he may make representations to the competent authority within such period as may be specified by the notice (whether or not he has referred the matter to the Tribunal);

(d)   inform him of the date on which the action took effect or takes effect; and

(e)   inform him of his right to refer the matter to the Tribunal.

(4)   The competent authority may extend the period within which representations may be made to it.

(5)   If, having considered any representations made to it, the competent authority decides to maintain, vary or revoke its earlier decision, it must give written notice to that effect to the person mentioned in subsection (2).

(6)   A notice given under subsection (5) must inform that person, where relevant, of his right to refer the matter to the Tribunal.

(7)   If a notice informs a person of his right to refer a matter to the Tribunal, it must give an indication of the procedure on such a reference.

(8)   If a notice under this section relates to the exercise of the power conferred by section 87L(3), the notice must also be given to the person at whose request the transferable securities were admitted to trading on the regulated market.]

[102]

NOTES
Commencement: 1 July 2005.
Substituted as noted to s 84 at **[84]**.

[87P   Exercise of powers at request of competent authority of another EEA State

(1)   This section applies if—

(a) the competent authority of an EEA State other than the United Kingdom has approved a prospectus,

(b) the transferable securities to which the prospectus relates have been offered to the public in the United Kingdom or their admission to trading on a regulated market has been requested, and

(c) that competent authority makes a request that the competent authority assist it in the performance of its functions under the law of that State in connection with the prospectus directive.

(2) For the purpose of complying with the request mentioned in subsection (1)(c), the powers conferred by sections 87K and 87L may be exercised as if the prospectus were one which had been approved by the competent authority.

(3) Section 87N does not apply to an exercise of those powers as a result of this section.

(4) Section 87O does apply to such an exercise of those powers but with the omission of subsections (3)(e), (6) and (7).]

[103]

NOTES

Commencement: 1 July 2005.
Substituted as noted to s 84 at **[84]**.

[Rights of investors

87Q Right of investor to withdraw

(1) Where a person agrees to buy or subscribe for transferable securities in circumstances where the final offer price or the amount of transferable securities to be offered to the public is not included in the prospectus, he may withdraw his acceptance before the end of the withdrawal period.

(2) The withdrawal period—
(a) begins with the investor's acceptance; and
(b) ends at the end of the second working day after the date on which the competent authority is informed of the information in accordance with section 87A(7).

(3) Subsection (1) does not apply if the prospectus contains—
(a) in the case of the amount of transferable securities to be offered to the public, the criteria or conditions (or both) according to which that element will be determined, or
(b) in the case of price, the criteria or conditions (or both) according to which that element will be determined or the maximum price.

(4) Where a supplementary prospectus has been published and, prior to the publication, a person agreed to buy or subscribe for transferable securities to which it relates, he may withdraw his acceptance before the end of the period of 2 working days beginning with the first working day after the date on which the supplementary prospectus was published.]

[104]

NOTES

Commencement: 1 July 2005.
Substituted as noted to s 84 at **[84]**.

[Registered investors

87R Register of investors

(1) The competent authority must establish and maintain, in accordance with this section and prospectus rules, a register of investors for the purposes of section 86.

(2) An individual may not be entered in the register unless—
(a) he is resident in the United Kingdom; and
(b) he meets at least two of the criteria mentioned in Article 2.2 of the prospectus directive.

(3) A company may not be entered in the register unless—
(a) it falls within the meaning of "small and medium-sized enterprises" in Article 2.1 of the prospectus directive; and
(b) its registered office is in the United Kingdom.

(4) A person who does not fall within subsection (2) or (3) may not be entered in the register.]

[105]

NOTES

Commencement: 1 July 2005.
Substituted as noted to s 84 at **[84]**.

Sponsors

88   Sponsors

(1)   Listing rules may require a person to make arrangements with a sponsor for the performance by the sponsor of such services in relation to him as may be specified in the rules.

(2)   "Sponsor" means a person approved by the competent authority for the purposes of the rules.

(3)   Listing rules made by virtue of subsection (1) may—
  (a)   provide for the competent authority to maintain a list of sponsors;
  (b)   specify services which must be performed by a sponsor;
  (c)   impose requirements on a sponsor in relation to the provision of services or specified services;
  (d)   specify the circumstances in which a person is qualified for being approved as a sponsor.

(4)   If the competent authority proposes—
  (a)   to refuse a person's application for approval as a sponsor, or
  (b)   to cancel a person's approval as a sponsor [otherwise than at his request],
it must give him a warning notice.

(5)   If, after considering any representations made in response to the warning notice, the competent authority decides—
  (a)   to grant the application for approval, or
  (b)   not to cancel the approval,
it must give the person concerned, and any person to whom a copy of the warning notice was given, written notice of its decision.

(6)   If, after considering any representations made in response to the warning notice, the competent authority decides—
  (a)   to refuse to grant the application for approval, or
  (b)   to cancel the approval,
it must give the person concerned a decision notice.

(7)   A person to whom a decision notice is given under this section may refer the matter to the Tribunal.

[106]

NOTES

Sub-s (4): words in square brackets inserted by the Regulatory Reform (Financial Services and Markets Act 2000) Order 2007, SI 2007/1973, arts 2, 9, as from 12 July 2007.

89   Public censure of sponsor

(1)   Listing rules may make provision for the competent authority, if it considers that a sponsor has contravened a requirement imposed on him by rules made as a result of section 88(3)(c), to publish a statement to that effect.

(2)   If the competent authority proposes to publish a statement it must give the sponsor a warning notice setting out the terms of the proposed statement.

(3)   If, after considering any representations made in response to the warning notice, the competent authority decides to make the proposed statement, it must give the sponsor a decision notice setting out the terms of the statement.

(4)   A sponsor to whom a decision notice is given under this section may refer the matter to the Tribunal.

[107]

[Transparency obligations

89A   Transparency rules

(1)   The competent authority may make rules for the purposes of the transparency obligations directive.

(2)   The rules may include provision for dealing with any matters arising out of or related to any provision of the transparency obligations directive.

(3)   The competent authority may also make rules—
  (a)   for the purpose of ensuring that voteholder information in respect of voting shares traded on a UK market other than a regulated market is made public or notified to the competent authority;
  (b)   providing for persons who hold comparable instruments (see section 89F(1)(c)) in respect of voting shares to be treated, in the circumstances specified in the rules, as holding some or all of the voting rights in respect of those shares.

(4)   Rules under this section may, in particular, make provision—
   (a)   specifying how the proportion of—
          (i)   the total voting rights in respect of shares in an issuer, or
          (ii)   the total voting rights in respect of a particular class of shares in an issuer,
   held by a person is to be determined;
   (b)   specifying the circumstances in which, for the purposes of any determination of the voting rights held by a person ("P") in respect of voting shares in an issuer, any voting rights held, or treated by virtue of subsection (3)(b) as held, by another person in respect of voting shares in the issuer are to be regarded as held by P;
   (c)   specifying the nature of the information which must be included in any notification;
   (d)   about the form of any notification;
   (e)   requiring any notification to be given within a specified period;
   (f)   specifying the manner in which any information is to be made public and the period within which it must be made public;
   (g)   specifying circumstances in which any of the requirements imposed by rules under this section does not apply.

(5)   Rules under this section are referred to in this Part as "transparency rules".

(6)   Nothing in sections 89B to 89G affects the generality of the power to make rules under this section.]

[107A]

NOTES
Commencement: 8 November 2006.
Inserted, together with the preceding heading and ss 89B–89G, by the Companies Act 2006, s 1266(1), as from 8 November 2006. See further, the note below.
Section 1266(2) of the 2006 Act provides as follows—

"(2)   The effectiveness for the purposes of section 155 of the Financial Services and Markets Act 2000 (c 8) (consultation on proposed rules) of things done by the Financial Services Authority before this section comes into force with a view to making transparency rules (as defined in the provisions to be inserted in that Act by subsection (1) above) is not affected by the fact that those provisions were not then in force.".

[89B   Provision of voteholder information

(1)   Transparency rules may make provision for voteholder information in respect of voting shares to be notified, in circumstances specified in the rules—
   (a)   to the issuer, or
   (b)   to the public,
or to both.

(2)   Transparency rules may make provision for voteholder information notified to the issuer to be notified at the same time to the competent authority.

(3)   In this Part "voteholder information" in respect of voting shares means information relating to the proportion of voting rights held by a person in respect of the shares.

(4)   Transparency rules may require notification of voteholder information relating to a person—
   (a)   initially, not later than such date as may be specified in the rules for the purposes of the first indent of Article 30.2 of the transparency obligations directive, and
   (b)   subsequently, in accordance with the following provisions.

(5)   Transparency rules under subsection (4)(b) may require notification of voteholder information relating to a person only where there is a notifiable change in the proportion of—
   (a)   the total voting rights in respect of shares in the issuer, or
   (b)   the total voting rights in respect of a particular class of share in the issuer,
held by the person.

(6)   For this purpose there is a "notifiable change" in the proportion of voting rights held by a person when the proportion changes—
   (a)   from being a proportion less than a designated proportion to a proportion equal to or greater than that designated proportion,
   (b)   from being a proportion equal to a designated proportion to a proportion greater or less than that designated proportion, or
   (c)   from being a proportion greater than a designated proportion to a proportion equal to or less than that designated proportion.

(7)   In subsection (6) "designated" means designated by the rules.]

[107B]

[89C Provision of information by issuers of transferable securities

(1) Transparency rules may make provision requiring the issuer of transferable securities, in circumstances specified in the rules—
    (a) to make public information to which this section applies, or
    (b) to notify to the competent authority information to which this section applies,
or to do both.

(2) In the case of every issuer, this section applies to—
    (a) information required by Article 4 of the transparency obligations directive;
    (b) information relating to the rights attached to the transferable securities, including information about the terms and conditions of those securities which could indirectly affect those rights; and
    (c) information about new loan issues and about any guarantee or security in connection with any such issue.

(3) In the case of an issuer of debt securities, this section also applies to information required by Article 5 of the transparency obligations directive.

(4) In the case of an issuer of shares, this section also applies to—
    (a) information required by Article 5 of the transparency obligations directive;
    (b) information required by Article 6 of that directive;
    (c) voteholder information—
        (i) notified to the issuer, or
        (ii) relating to the proportion of voting rights held by the issuer in respect of shares in the issuer;
    (d) information relating to the issuer's capital; and
    (e) information relating to the total number of voting rights in respect of shares or shares of a particular class.]

[107C]

NOTES
Commencement: 8 November 2006.
Inserted as noted to s 89A at **[107A]**.

[89D Notification of voting rights held by issuer

(1) Transparency rules may require notification of voteholder information relating to the proportion of voting rights held by an issuer in respect of voting shares in the issuer—
    (a) initially, not later than such date as may be specified in the rules for the purposes of the second indent of Article 30.2 of the transparency obligations directive, and
    (b) subsequently, in accordance with the following provisions.

(2) Transparency rules under subsection (1)(b) may require notification of voteholder information relating to the proportion of voting rights held by an issuer in respect of voting shares in the issuer only where there is a notifiable change in the proportion of—
    (a) the total voting rights in respect of shares in the issuer, or
    (b) the total voting rights in respect of a particular class of share in the issuer,
held by the issuer.

(3) For this purpose there is a "notifiable change" in the proportion of voting rights held by a person when the proportion changes—
    (a) from being a proportion less than a designated proportion to a proportion equal to or greater than that designated proportion,
    (b) from being a proportion equal to a designated proportion to a proportion greater or less than that designated proportion, or
    (c) from being a proportion greater than a designated proportion to a proportion equal to or less than that designated proportion.

(4) In subsection (3) "designated" means designated by the rules.]

[107D]

NOTES
Commencement: 8 November 2006.
Inserted as noted to s 89A at **[107A]**.

[89E Notification of proposed amendment of issuer's constitution

Transparency rules may make provision requiring an issuer of transferable securities that are admitted to trading on a regulated market to notify a proposed amendment to its constitution—

(a) to the competent authority, and

(b) to the market on which the issuer's securities are admitted,

at times and in circumstances specified in the rules.]

[107E]

NOTES
Commencement: 8 November 2006.
Inserted as noted to s 89A at **[107A]**.

[89F Transparency rules: interpretation etc

(1) For the purposes of sections 89A to 89G—

(a) the voting rights in respect of any voting shares are the voting rights attached to those shares,

(b) a person is to be regarded as holding the voting rights in respect of the shares—

(i) if, by virtue of those shares, he is a shareholder within the meaning of Article 2.1(e) of the transparency obligations directive;

(ii) if, and to the extent that, he is entitled to acquire, dispose of or exercise those voting rights in one or more of the cases mentioned in Article 10(a) to (h) of the transparency obligations directive;

(iii) if he holds, directly or indirectly, a financial instrument which results in an entitlement to acquire the shares and is an Article 13 instrument, and

(c) a person holds a "comparable instrument" in respect of voting shares if he holds, directly or indirectly, a financial instrument in relation to the shares which has similar economic effects to an Article 13 instrument (whether or not the financial instrument results in an entitlement to acquire the shares).

(2) Transparency rules under section 89A(3)(b) may make different provision for different descriptions of comparable instrument.

(3) For the purposes of sections 89A to 89G two or more persons may, at the same time, each be regarded as holding the same voting rights.

(4) In those sections—

"Article 13 instrument" means a financial instrument of a type determined by the European Commission under Article 13.2 of the transparency obligations directive;

["financial instrument" has the meaning given in Article 4.1(17) of Directive 2004/39/EC on markets in financial instruments;]

"UK market" means a market that is situated or operating in the United Kingdom;

"voting shares" means shares of an issuer to which voting rights are attached.]

[107F]

NOTES
Commencement: 8 November 2006.
Inserted as noted to s 89A at **[107A]**.
Sub-s (4): definition "financial instrument" inserted by the Definition of Financial Instrument Order 2008, SI 2008/3053, art 2, as from 31 January 2009.

[89G Transparency rules: other supplementary provisions

(1) Transparency rules may impose the same obligations on a person who has applied for the admission of transferable securities to trading on a regulated market without the issuer's consent as they impose on an issuer of transferable securities.

(2) Transparency rules that require a person to make information public may include provision authorising the competent authority to make the information public in the event that the person fails to do so.

(3) The competent authority may make public any information notified to the authority in accordance with transparency rules.

(4) Transparency rules may make provision by reference to any provision of any rules made by the Panel on Takeovers and Mergers under Part 28 of the Companies Act 2006.

(5) Sections 89A to 89F and this section are without prejudice to any other power conferred by this Part to make Part 6 rules.]

[107G]

NOTES
Commencement: 8 November 2006.
Inserted as noted to s 89A at **[107A]**.

[Power of competent authority to call for information

89H Competent authority's power to call for information

(1) The competent authority may by notice in writing given to a person to whom this section applies require him—
 (a) to provide specified information or information of a specified description, or
 (b) to produce specified documents or documents of a specified description.

(2) This section applies to—
 (a) an issuer in respect of whom transparency rules have effect;
 (b) a voteholder;
 (c) an auditor of—
  (i) an issuer to whom this section applies, or
  (ii) a voteholder;
 (d) a person who controls a voteholder;
 (e) a person controlled by a voteholder;
 (f) a director or other similar officer of an issuer to whom this section applies;
 (g) a director or other similar officer of a voteholder or, where the affairs of a voteholder are managed by its members, a member of the voteholder.

(3) This section applies only to information and documents reasonably required in connection with the exercise by the competent authority of functions conferred on it by or under sections 89A to 89G (transparency rules).

(4) Information or documents required under this section must be provided or produced—
 (a) before the end of such reasonable period as may be specified, and
 (b) at such place as may be specified.

(5) If a person claims a lien on a document, its production under this section does not affect the lien.]

[107H]

NOTES
Commencement: 8 November 2006.
Inserted, together with the preceding heading and ss 89I, 89J, by the Companies Act 2006, s 1267, as from 8 November 2006.

[89I Requirements in connection with call for information

(1) The competent authority may require any information provided under section 89H to be provided in such form as it may reasonably require.

(2) The competent authority may require—
 (a) any information provided, whether in a document or otherwise, to be verified in such manner as it may reasonably require;
 (b) any document produced to be authenticated in such manner as it may reasonably require.

(3) If a document is produced in response to a requirement imposed under section 89H, the competent authority may—
 (a) take copies of or extracts from the document; or
 (b) require the person producing the document, or any relevant person, to provide an explanation of the document.

(4) In subsection (3)(b) "relevant person", in relation to a person who is required to produce a document, means a person who—
 (a) has been or is a director or controller of that person;
 (b) has been or is an auditor of that person;
 (c) has been or is an actuary, accountant or lawyer appointed or instructed by that person; or
 (d) has been or is an employee of that person.

(5) If a person who is required under section 89H to produce a document fails to do so, the competent authority may require him to state, to the best of his knowledge and belief, where the document is.]

[107I]

NOTES
Commencement: 8 November 2006.
Inserted as noted to s 89H at **[107H]**.

[89J Power to call for information: supplementary provisions

(1)   The competent authority may require an issuer to make public any information provided to the authority under section 89H.

(2)   If the issuer fails to comply with a requirement under subsection (1), the competent authority may, after seeking representations from the issuer, make the information public.

(3)   In sections 89H and 89I (power of competent authority to call for information)—
   "control" and "controlled" have the meaning given by subsection (4) below;
   "specified" means specified in the notice;
   "voteholder" means a person who—
      (a)   holds voting rights in respect of any voting shares for the purposes of sections 89A to 89G (transparency rules), or
      (b)   is treated as holding such rights by virtue of rules under section 89A(3)(b).

(4)   For the purposes of those sections a person ("A") controls another person ("B") if—
   (a)   A holds a majority of the voting rights in B,
   (b)   A is a member of B and has the right to appoint or remove a majority of the members of the board of directors (or, if there is no such board, the equivalent management body) of B,
   (c)   A is a member of B and controls alone, pursuant to an agreement with other shareholders or members, a majority of the voting rights in B, or
   (d)   A has the right to exercise, or actually exercises, dominant influence or control over B.

(5)   For the purposes of subsection (4)(b)—
   (a)   any rights of a person controlled by A, and
   (b)   any rights of a person acting on behalf of A or a person controlled by A,
are treated as held by A.]

[107J]

NOTES
   Commencement: 8 November 2006.
   Inserted as noted to s 89H at **[107H]**.

[Powers exercisable in case of infringement of transparency obligation

89K   Public censure of issuer

(1)   If the competent authority finds that an issuer of securities admitted to trading on a regulated market is failing or has failed to comply with an applicable transparency obligation, it may publish a statement to that effect.

(2)   If the competent authority proposes to publish a statement, it must give the issuer a warning notice setting out the terms of the proposed statement.

(3)   If, after considering any representations made in response to the warning notice, the competent authority decides to make the proposed statement, it must give the issuer a decision notice setting out the terms of the statement.

(4)   A notice under this section must inform the issuer of his right to refer the matter to the Tribunal (see section 89N) and give an indication of the procedure on such a reference.

(5)   In this section "transparency obligation" means an obligation under—
   (a)   a provision of transparency rules, or
   (b)   any other provision made in accordance with the transparency obligations directive.

(6)   In relation to an issuer whose home State is a member State other than the United Kingdom, any reference to an applicable transparency obligation must be read subject to section 100A(2).]

[107K]

NOTES
   Commencement: 8 November 2006.
   Inserted, together with the preceding heading and ss 89L–89N, by the Companies Act 2006, s 1268, as from 8 November 2006.

[89L   Power to suspend or prohibit trading of securities

(1)   This section applies to securities admitted to trading on a regulated market.

(2)   If the competent authority has reasonable grounds for suspecting that an applicable transparency obligation has been infringed by an issuer, it may—
   (a)   suspend trading in the securities for a period not exceeding 10 days,
   (b)   prohibit trading in the securities, or
   (c)   make a request to the operator of the market on which the issuer's securities are traded—
      (i)   to suspend trading in the securities for a period not exceeding 10 days, or
      (ii)   to prohibit trading in the securities.

(3)   If the competent authority has reasonable grounds for suspecting that a provision required by the transparency obligations directive has been infringed by a voteholder of an issuer, it may—
  (a)   prohibit trading in the securities, or
  (b)   make a request to the operator of the market on which the issuer's securities are traded to prohibit trading in the securities.

(4)   If the competent authority finds that an applicable transparency obligation has been infringed, it may require the market operator to prohibit trading in the securities.

(5)   In this section "transparency obligation" means an obligation under—
  (a)   a provision contained in transparency rules, or
  (b)   any other provision made in accordance with the transparency obligations directive.

(6)   In relation to an issuer whose home State is a member State other than the United Kingdom, any reference to an applicable transparency obligation must be read subject to section 100A(2).]

[107L]

NOTES
Commencement: 8 November 2006.
Inserted as noted to s 89K at **[107K]**.

[89M   Procedure under section 89L

(1)   A requirement under section 89L takes effect—
  (a)   immediately, if the notice under subsection (2) states that that is the case;
  (b)   in any other case, on such date as may be specified in the notice.

(2)   If the competent authority—
  (a)   proposes to exercise the powers in section 89L in relation to a person, or
  (b)   exercises any of those powers in relation to a person with immediate effect,
it must give that person written notice.

(3)   The notice must—
  (a)   give details of the competent authority's action or proposed action;
  (b)   state the competent authority's reasons for taking the action in question and choosing the date on which it took effect or takes effect;
  (c)   inform the recipient that he may make representations to the competent authority within such period as may be specified by the notice (whether or not he had referred the matter to the Tribunal);
  (d)   inform him of the date on which the action took effect or takes effect;
  (e)   inform him of his right to refer the matter to the Tribunal (see section 89N) and give an indication of the procedure on such a reference.

(4)   The competent authority may extend the period within which representations may be made to it.

(5)   If, having considered any representations made to it, the competent authority decides to maintain, vary or revoke its earlier decision, it must give written notice to that effect to the person mentioned in subsection (2).]

[107M]

NOTES
Commencement: 8 November 2006.
Inserted as noted to s 89K at **[107K]**.

[89N   Right to refer matters to the Tribunal

A person—
  (a)   to whom a decision notice is given under section 89K (public censure), or
  (b)   to whom a notice is given under section 89M (procedure in connection with suspension or prohibition of trading),
may refer the matter to the Tribunal.]

[107N]

NOTES
Commencement: 8 November 2006.
Inserted as noted to s 89K at **[107K]**.

[Corporate governance

89O   Corporate governance rules

(1)   The competent authority may make rules ("corporate governance rules")—
  (a)   for the purpose of implementing, enabling the implementation of or dealing with matters

arising out of or related to, any Community obligation relating to the corporate governance of issuers who have requested or approved admission of their securities to trading on a regulated market;

   (b)   about corporate governance in relation to such issuers for the purpose of implementing, or dealing with matters arising out of or related to, any Community obligation.

  (2)   "Corporate governance", in relation to an issuer, includes—

   (a)   the nature, constitution or functions of the organs of the issuer;
   (b)   the manner in which organs of the issuer conduct themselves;
   (c)   the requirements imposed on organs of the issuer;
   (d)   the relationship between the different organs of the issuer;
   (e)   the relationship between the organs of the issuer and the members of the issuer or holders of the issuer's securities.

  (3)   The burdens and restrictions imposed by rules under this section on foreign-traded issuers must not be greater than the burdens and restrictions imposed on UK-traded issuers by—

   (a)   rules under this section, and
   (b)   listing rules.

  (4)   For this purpose—

"foreign-traded issuer" means an issuer who has requested or approved admission of the issuer's securities to trading on a regulated market situated or operating outside the United Kingdom;

"UK-traded issuer" means an issuer who has requested or approved admission of the issuer's securities to trading on a regulated market situated or operating in the United Kingdom.

  (5)   This section is without prejudice to any other power conferred by this Part to make Part 6 rules.]

                                                                     [107O]

NOTES

Commencement: 8 November 2006.

Inserted, together with the preceding heading, by the Companies Act 2006, s 1269, as from 8 November 2006.

Community obligation: as to the meaning of this, see the note to s 47 at **[47]**.

[Compensation for false or misleading statements etc]

90 [Compensation for statements in listing particulars or prospectus]

  (1)   Any person responsible for listing particulars is liable to pay compensation to a person who has—

   (a)   acquired securities to which the particulars apply; and
   (b)   suffered loss in respect of them as a result of—
       (i)   any untrue or misleading statement in the particulars; or
      (ii)   the omission from the particulars of any matter required to be included by section 80 or 81.

  (2)   Subsection (1) is subject to exemptions provided by Schedule 10.

  (3)   If listing particulars are required to include information about the absence of a particular matter, the omission from the particulars of that information is to be treated as a statement in the listing particulars that there is no such matter.

  (4)   Any person who fails to comply with section 81 is liable to pay compensation to any person who has—

   (a)   acquired securities of the kind in question; and
   (b)   suffered loss in respect of them as a result of the failure.

  (5)   Subsection (4) is subject to exemptions provided by Schedule 10.

  (6)   This section does not affect any liability which may be incurred apart from this section.

  (7)   References in this section to the acquisition by a person of securities include references to his contracting to acquire them or any interest in them.

  (8)   No person shall, by reason of being a promoter of a company or otherwise, incur any liability for failing to disclose information which he would not be required to disclose in listing particulars in respect of a company's securities—

   (a)   if he were responsible for those particulars; or
   (b)   if he is responsible for them, which he is entitled to omit by virtue of section 82.

  (9)   The reference in subsection (8) to a person incurring liability includes a reference to any other person being entitled as against that person to be granted any civil remedy or to rescind or repudiate an agreement.

  (10)   "Listing particulars", in subsection (1) and Schedule 10, includes supplementary listing particulars.

[(11) This section applies in relation to a prospectus as it applies to listing particulars, with the following modifications—
- (a) references in this section or in Schedule 10 to listing particulars, supplementary listing particulars or sections 80, 81 or 82 are to be read, respectively, as references to a prospectus, supplementary prospectus and sections 87A, 87G and 87B;
- (b) references in Schedule 10 to admission to the official list are to be read as references to admission to trading on a regulated market;
- (c) in relation to a prospectus, "securities" means "transferable securities".

(12) A person is not to be subject to civil liability solely on the basis of a summary in a prospectus unless the summary is misleading, inaccurate or inconsistent when read with the rest of the prospectus; and, in this subsection, a summary includes any translation of it.]

[108]

NOTES

The section heading and the heading preceding this section were substituted by the Companies Act 2006, s 1272, Sch 15, Pt 1, paras 1, 4, 5, as from 8 November 2006.

Sub-ss (11), (12): added by the Prospectus Regulations 2005, SI 2005/1433, reg 2(1), Sch 1, para 6(1), (2), as from 1 July 2005.

[90A Compensation for statements in certain publications

(1) The publications to which this section applies are—
- (a) any reports and statements published in response to a requirement imposed by a provision implementing Article 4, 5 or 6 of the transparency obligations directive, and
- (b) any preliminary statement made in advance of a report or statement to be published in response to a requirement imposed by a provision implementing Article 4 of that directive, to the extent that it contains information that it is intended—
   - (i) will appear in the report or statement, and
   - (ii) will be presented in the report or statement in substantially the same form as that in which it is presented in the preliminary statement.

(2) The securities to which this section applies are—
- (a) securities that are traded on a regulated market situated or operating in the United Kingdom, and
- (b) securities that—
   - (i) are traded on a regulated market situated or operating outside the United Kingdom, and
   - (ii) are issued by an issuer for which the United Kingdom is the home Member State within the meaning of Article 2.1(i) of the transparency obligations directive.

(3) The issuer of securities to which this section applies is liable to pay compensation to a person who has—
- (a) acquired such securities issued by it, and
- (b) suffered loss in respect of them as a result of—
   - (i) any untrue or misleading statement in a publication to which this section applies, or
   - (ii) the omission from any such publication of any matter required to be included in it.

(4) The issuer is so liable only if a person discharging managerial responsibilities within the issuer in relation to the publication—
- (a) knew the statement to be untrue or misleading or was reckless as to whether it was untrue or misleading, or
- (b) knew the omission to be dishonest concealment of a material fact.

(5) A loss is not regarded as suffered as a result of the statement or omission in the publication unless the person suffering it acquired the relevant securities—
- (a) in reliance on the information in the publication, and
- (b) at a time when, and in circumstances in which, it was reasonable for him to rely on that information.

(6) Except as mentioned in subsection (8)—
- (a) the issuer is not subject to any other liability than that provided for by this section in respect of loss suffered as a result of reliance by any person on—
   - (i) an untrue or misleading statement in a publication to which this section applies, or
   - (ii) the omission from any such publication of any matter required to be included in it, and
- (b) a person other than the issuer is not subject to any liability, other than to the issuer, in respect of any such loss.

(7)   Any reference in subsection (6) to a person being subject to a liability includes a reference to another person being entitled as against him to be granted any civil remedy or to rescind or repudiate an agreement.

(8)   This section does not affect—
(a)   the powers conferred by section 382 and 384 (powers of the court to make a restitution order and of the Authority to require restitution);
(b)   liability for a civil penalty;
(c)   liability for a criminal offence.

(9)   For the purposes of this section—
(a)   the following are persons "discharging managerial responsibilities" in relation to a publication—
(i)   any director of the issuer (or person occupying the position of director, by whatever name called),
(ii)   in the case of an issuer whose affairs are managed by its members, any member of the issuer,
(iii)   in the case of an issuer that has no persons within sub-paragraph (i) or (ii), any senior executive of the issuer having responsibilities in relation to the publication;
(b)   references to the acquisition by a person of securities include his contracting to acquire them or any interest in them.]

[108A]

NOTES
Commencement: 8 November 2006.
Inserted, together with s 90B, by the Companies Act 2006, s 1270, as from 8 November 2006.
HM Treasury conducted a review of these provisions and issued a consultation paper in July 2008 that proposed the substitution of this section and the insertion of a new Sch 10A dealing with compensation liabilities in connection with published information. Transitional provisions would provide that these provisions would only apply to information first published on or after the commencement date of the amendments. This section (as inserted by the Companies Act 2006) would continue to apply to information first published before that date. See *Extension of the statutory regime for issuer liability* (*July 2008*) at:
http://www.hm-treasury.gov.uk/consult_fullindex.htm.

[90B   Power to make further provision about liability for published information

(1)   The Treasury may by regulations make provision about the liability of issuers of securities traded on a regulated market, and other persons, in respect of information published to holders of securities, to the market or to the public generally.

(2)   Regulations under this section may amend any primary or subordinate legislation, including any provision of, or made under, this Act.]

[108B]

NOTES
Commencement: 8 November 2006.
Inserted as noted to s 90A at **[108A]**.

Penalties

91   [Penalties for breach of Part 6 rules]

[[(1)   If the competent authority considers that—
(a)   an issuer of listed securities, or
(b)   an applicant for listing,
has contravened any provision of listing rules, it may impose on him a penalty of such amount as it considers appropriate.

(1ZA)   If the competent authority considers that—
(a)   an issuer who has requested or approved the admission of a financial instrument to trading on a regulated market,
(b)   a person discharging managerial responsibilities within such an issuer, or
(c)   a person connected with such a person discharging managerial responsibilities,
has contravened any provision of disclosure rules, it may impose on him a penalty of such amount as it considers appropriate.]]

[(1A)   If the competent authority considers that—
(a)   an issuer of transferable securities,
(b)   a person offering transferable securities to the public or requesting their admission to trading on a regulated market,
(c)   an applicant for the approval of a prospectus in relation to transferable securities,
(d)   a person on whom a requirement has been imposed under section 87K or 87L, or
(e)   any other person to whom a provision of the prospectus directive applies,

has contravened a provision of this Part or of prospectus rules, or a provision otherwise made in accordance with the prospectus directive or a requirement imposed on him under such a provision, it may impose on him a penalty of such amount as it considers appropriate.]

[(1B)   If the competent authority considers—
    (a)   that a person has contravened—
        (i)   a provision of transparency rules or a provision otherwise made in accordance with the transparency obligations directive, or
        (ii)   a provision of corporate governance rules, or
    (b)   that a person on whom a requirement has been imposed under section 89L (power to suspend or prohibit trading of securities in case of infringement of applicable transparency obligation), has contravened that requirement,
it may impose on the person a penalty of such amount as it considers appropriate.]

(2)   If, in the case of a contravention [by a person] referred to in subsection [[(1), (1ZA)(a), (1A) or (1B)] ("P")], the competent authority considers that [another person] who was at the material time a director of [P] was knowingly concerned in the contravention, it may impose upon him a penalty of such amount as it considers appropriate.]

(3)   If the competent authority is entitled to impose a penalty on a person under this section in respect of a particular matter it may, instead of imposing a penalty on him in respect of that matter, publish a statement censuring him.

(4)   Nothing in this section prevents the competent authority from taking any other steps which it has power to take under this Part.

(5)   A penalty under this section is payable to the competent authority.

(6)   The competent authority may not take action against a person under this section after the end of the period of two years beginning with the first day on which it knew of the contravention unless proceedings against that person, in respect of the contravention, were begun before the end of that period.

(7)   For the purposes of subsection (6)—
    (a)   the competent authority is to be treated as knowing of a contravention if it has information from which the contravention can reasonably be inferred; and
    (b)   proceedings against a person in respect of a contravention are to be treated as begun when a warning notice is given to him under section 92.

[109]

NOTES
    Section heading: substituted by the Prospectus Regulations 2005, SI 2005/1433, reg 2(1), Sch 1, para 7(1), (4), as from 1 July 2005.
    Sub-s (1): originally substituted (by new sub-s (1) and (2)) by the Financial Services and Markets Act 2000 (Market Abuse) Regulations 2005, SI 2005/381, reg 4, Sch 1, para 4, as from 1 July 2005; further substituted (by new sub-s (1) and (1ZA)) by the Companies Act 2006, s 1272, Sch 15, Pt 1, paras 1, 6(1), (2), as from 8 November 2006.
    Sub-s (1ZA): substituted as noted above.
    Sub-s (1A): inserted by SI 2005/1433, reg 2(1), Sch 1, para 7(1), (2), as from 1 July 2005.
    Sub-s (1B): inserted by the Companies Act 2006, s 1272, Sch 15, Pt 1, paras 1, 6(1), (3), as from 8 November 2006.
    Sub-s (2): substituted as noted above; words "(1), (1ZA)(a), (1A) or (1B)" in square brackets substituted by the Companies Act 2006, s 1272, Sch 15, Pt 1, paras 1, 6(1), (4), as from 8 November 2006; other words in square brackets substituted by SI 2005/1433, reg 2(1), Sch 1, para 6(1), (3), as from 1 July 2005.

92   Procedure

(1)   If the competent authority proposes to take action against a person under section 91, it must give him a warning notice.

(2)   A warning notice about a proposal to impose a penalty must state the amount of the proposed penalty.

(3)   A warning notice about a proposal to publish a statement must set out the terms of the proposed statement.

(4)   If the competent authority decides to take action against a person under section 91, it must give him a decision notice.

(5)   A decision notice about the imposition of a penalty must state the amount of the penalty.

(6)   A decision notice about the publication of a statement must set out the terms of the statement.

(7)   If the competent authority decides to take action against a person under section 91, he may refer the matter to the Tribunal.

[110]

93 Statement of policy

(1) The competent authority must prepare and issue a statement ("its policy statement") of its policy with respect to—
  (a) the imposition of penalties under section 91; and
  (b) the amount of penalties under that section.

(2) The competent authority's policy in determining what the amount of a penalty should be must include having regard to—
  (a) the seriousness of the contravention in question in relation to the nature of the requirement contravened;
  (b) the extent to which that contravention was deliberate or reckless; and
  (c) whether the person on whom the penalty is to be imposed is an individual.

(3) The competent authority may at any time alter or replace its policy statement.

(4) If its policy statement is altered or replaced, the competent authority must issue the altered or replacement statement.

(5) In exercising, or deciding whether to exercise, its power under section 91 in the case of any particular contravention, the competent authority must have regard to any policy statement published under this section and in force at the time when the contravention in question occurred.

(6) The competent authority must publish a statement issued under this section in the way appearing to the competent authority to be best calculated to bring it to the attention of the public.

(7) The competent authority may charge a reasonable fee for providing a person with a copy of the statement.

(8) The competent authority must, without delay, give the Treasury a copy of any policy statement which it publishes under this section.

[111]

94 Statements of policy: procedure

(1) Before issuing a statement under section 93, the competent authority must publish a draft of the proposed statement in the way appearing to the competent authority to be best calculated to bring it to the attention of the public.

(2) The draft must be accompanied by notice that representations about the proposal may be made to the competent authority within a specified time.

(3) Before issuing the proposed statement, the competent authority must have regard to any representations made to it in accordance with subsection (2).

(4) If the competent authority issues the proposed statement it must publish an account, in general terms, of—
  (a) the representations made to it in accordance with subsection (2); and
  (b) its response to them.

(5) If the statement differs from the draft published under subsection (1) in a way which is, in the opinion of the competent authority, significant, the competent authority must (in addition to complying with subsection (4)) publish details of the difference.

(6) The competent authority may charge a reasonable fee for providing a person with a copy of a draft published under subsection (1).

(7) This section also applies to a proposal to alter or replace a statement.

[112]

Competition

95 Competition scrutiny

(1) The Treasury may by order provide for—
  (a) regulating provisions, and
  (b) the practices of the competent authority in exercising its functions under this Part ("practices"),
to be kept under review.

(2) Provision made as a result of subsection (1) must require the person responsible for keeping regulating provisions and practices under review to consider—
  (a) whether any regulating provision or practice has a significantly adverse effect on competition; or
  (b) whether two or more regulating provisions or practices taken together have, or a particular combination of regulating provisions and practices has, such an effect.

(3) An order under this section may include provision corresponding to that made by any provision of Chapter III of Part X.

(4)   Subsection (3) is not to be read as in any way restricting the power conferred by subsection (1).

(5)   Subsections (6) to (8) apply for the purposes of provision made by or under this section.

(6)   Regulating provisions or practices have a significantly adverse effect on competition if—
  (a)   they have, or are intended or likely to have, that effect; or
  (b)   the effect that they have, or are intended or likely to have, is to require or encourage behaviour which has, or is intended or likely to have, a significantly adverse effect on competition.

(7)   If regulating provisions or practices have, or are intended or likely to have, the effect of requiring or encouraging exploitation of the strength of a market position they are to be taken to have, or be intended or be likely to have, an adverse effect on competition.

(8)   In determining whether any of the regulating provisions or practices have, or are intended or likely to have, a particular effect, it may be assumed that the persons to whom the provisions concerned are addressed will act in accordance with them.

(9)   "Regulating provisions" means—
  (a)   [Part 6 rules],
  (b)   general guidance given by the competent authority in connection with its functions under this Part.

                                                                              [113]

NOTES

Sub-s (9): words in square brackets substituted by the Financial Services and Markets Act 2000 (Market Abuse) Regulations 2005, SI 2005/381, reg 4, Sch 1, para 5, as from 1 July 2005.

Miscellaneous

96   Obligations of issuers of listed securities

(1)   Listing rules may—
  (a)   specify requirements to be complied with by issuers of listed securities; and
  (b)   make provision with respect to the action that may be taken by the competent authority in the event of non-compliance.

(2)   If the rules require an issuer to publish information, they may include provision authorising the competent authority to publish it in the event of his failure to do so.

(3)   This section applies whenever the listed securities were admitted to the official list.

                                                                              [114]

[96A   Disclosure of information requirements

(1)   Disclosure rules must include provision specifying the disclosure of information requirements to be complied with by—
  (a)   issuers who have requested or approved admission of their financial instruments to trading on a regulated market in the United Kingdom;
  (b)   persons acting on behalf of or for the account of such issuers;
  (c)   persons discharging managerial responsibilities within an issuer—
    (i)   who is registered in the United Kingdom and who has requested or approved admission of its shares to trading on a regulated market; or
    (ii)   who is not registered in the United Kingdom or any other EEA State but who has requested or approved admission of its shares to trading on a regulated market and who is required to file annual information in relation to the shares in the United Kingdom in accordance with Article 10 of the prospectus directive;
  (d)   persons connected to such persons discharging managerial responsibilities.

(2)   The rules must in particular—
  (a)   require an issuer to publish specified inside information;
  (b)   require an issuer to publish any significant change concerning information it has already published in accordance with paragraph (a);
  (c)   allow an issuer to delay the publication of inside information in specified circumstances;
  (d)   require an issuer (or a person acting on his behalf or for his account) who discloses inside information to a third party to publish that information without delay in specified circumstances;
  (e)   require an issuer (or person acting on his behalf or for his account) to draw up a list of those persons working for him who have access to inside information relating directly or indirectly to that issuer; and
  (f)   require persons discharging managerial responsibilities within an issuer falling within subsection (1)(c)(i) or (ii), and persons connected to such persons discharging

managerial responsibilities, to disclose transactions conducted on their own account in shares of the issuer, or derivatives or any other financial instrument relating to those shares.

(3)   Disclosure rules may make provision with respect to the action that may be taken by the competent authority in respect of non-compliance.]

[115]

NOTES
Commencement: 17 March 2005.
Inserted, together with ss 96B, 96C, by the Financial Services and Markets Act 2000 (Market Abuse) Regulations 2005, SI 2005/381, reg 4, Sch 1, para 6, as from 17 March 2005.

[96B   [Disclosure rules: persons responsible for compliance]

(1)   [For the purposes of the provisions of this Part relating to disclosure rules], a "person discharging managerial responsibilities within an issuer" means—
    (a)   a director of an issuer falling within section 96A(1)(c)(i) or (ii); or
    (b)   a senior executive of such an issuer who—
        (i)   has regular access to inside information relating, directly or indirectly, to the issuer, and
        (ii)   has power to make managerial decisions affecting the future development and business prospects of the issuer.

(2)   A person "connected" with a person discharging managerial responsibilities within an issuer means—
    (a)   a "connected person" within the meaning in section 346 of the Companies Act 1985 (reading that section as if any reference to a director of a company were a reference to a person discharging managerial responsibilities within an issuer);
    (b)   a relative of a person discharging managerial responsibilities within an issuer, who, on the date of the transaction in question, has shared the same household as that person for at least 12 months;
    (c)   a body corporate in which—
        (i)   a person discharging managerial responsibilities within an issuer, or
        (ii)   any person connected with him by virtue of subsection (a) or (b),
    is a director or a senior executive who has the power to make management decisions affecting the future development and business prospects of that body corporate.]

[116]

NOTES
Commencement: 17 March 2005.
Inserted as noted to s 96A at **[115]**.
Section heading: substituted by the Companies Act 2006, s 1272, Sch 15, Pt 1, paras 1, 7(a), as from 8 November 2006.
Sub-s (1): words in square brackets substituted by the Companies Act 2006, s 1272, Sch 15, Pt 1, paras 1, 7(b), as from 8 November 2006.
Note: the repeal of s 346 of, and Sch 13 to, the Companies Act 1985 (meaning of "connected person") does not affect sub-s (2)(a) above; see the Companies Act 2006 (Commencement No 3, Consequential Amendments, Transitional Provisions and Savings) Order 2007, SI 2007/2194, Sch 3, para 50.

[96C   Suspension of trading

(1)   The competent authority may, in accordance with disclosure rules, suspend trading in a financial instrument.

(2)   If the competent authority does so, the issuer of that financial instrument may refer the matter to the Tribunal.

(3)   The provisions relating to suspension of listing of securities in section 78 apply to the suspension of trading in a financial instrument and the references to listing and securities are to be read as references to trading and financial instruments respectively for the purposes of this section.]

[117]

NOTES
Commencement: 17 March 2005.
Inserted as noted to s 96A at **[115]**.

97   Appointment by competent authority of persons to carry out investigations

(1)   Subsection (2) applies if it appears to the competent authority that there are circumstances suggesting that—
    [(a)   there may have been a contravention of—
        (i)   a provision of this Part or of Part 6 rules, or

      (ii)   a provision otherwise made in accordance with the prospectus directive or the transparency obligations directive;

(b)   a person who was at the material time a director of a person mentioned in section 91(1), (1ZA)(a), (1A) or (1B) has been knowingly concerned in a contravention by that person of—

      (i)   a provision of this Part or of Part 6 rules, or

      (ii)   a provision otherwise made in accordance with the prospectus directive or the transparency obligations directive;]

(c)   ...

(d)   there may have been a contravention of section 83, 85[, 87G] or 98.

(2)   The competent authority may appoint one or more competent persons to conduct an investigation on its behalf.

(3)   Part XI applies to an investigation under subsection (2) as if—

(a)   the investigator were appointed under section 167(1);

(b)   references to the investigating authority in relation to him were to the competent authority;

(c)   references to the offences mentioned in section 168 were to those mentioned in subsection (1)(d);

(d)   references to an authorised person were references to the person under investigation.

[118]

NOTES

Sub-s (1): paras (a), (b) substituted by the Companies Act 2006, s 1272, Sch 15, Pt 1, paras 1, 8, as from 8 November 2006; para (c) repealed by the Financial Services and Markets Act 2000 (Market Abuse) Regulations 2005, SI 2005/381, reg 4, Sch 1, para 7, as from 1 July 2005; figure in square brackets in para (d) inserted by the Prospectus Regulations 2005, SI 2005/1433, reg 2(1), Sch 1, para 8, as from 1 July 2005.

98   *(Repealed by the Prospectus Regulations 2005, SI 2005/1433, reg 2(1), Sch 1, para 9, as from 1 July 2005.)*

99 Fees

(1)   Listing rules may require the payment of fees to the competent authority in respect of—

(a)   applications for listing;

(b)   the continued inclusion of securities in the official list;

(c)   applications under section 88 for approval as a sponsor; and

(d)   continued inclusion of sponsors in the list of sponsors.

[(1A)   Disclosure rules may require the payment of fees to the competent authority in respect of the continued admission of financial instruments to trading on a regulated market.]

[(1B)   Prospectus rules may require the payment of fees to the competent authority in respect of—

(a)   applications for approval of a prospectus or a supplementary prospectus;

(b)   applications for inclusion in the register of investors;

(c)   the continued inclusion of investors in that register;

(d)   access to that register.]

[(1C)   Transparency rules may require the payment of fees to the competent authority in respect of the continued admission of financial instruments to trading on a regulated market.]

(2)   In exercising its powers under subsection (1), the competent authority may set such fees as it considers will (taking account of the income it expects as the competent authority) enable it—

(a)   to meet expenses incurred in carrying out its functions under this Part or for any incidental purpose;

(b)   to maintain adequate reserves; and

(c)   in the case of the Authority, to repay the principal of, and pay any interest on, any money which it has borrowed and which has been used for the purpose of meeting expenses incurred in relation to—

      (i)   its assumption of functions from the London Stock Exchange Limited in relation to the official list; and

      (ii)   its assumption of functions under this Part.

(3)   In fixing the amount of any fee which is to be payable to the competent authority, no account is to be taken of any sums which it receives, or expects to receive, by way of penalties imposed by it under this Part.

(4)   Subsection (2)(c) applies whether expenses were incurred before or after the coming into force of this Part.

(5)   Any fee which is owed to the competent authority under any provision made by or under this Part may be recovered as a debt due to it.

[119]

NOTES
   Sub-s (1A): inserted by the Financial Services and Markets Act 2000 (Market Abuse) Regulations 2005, SI 2005/381, reg 4, Sch 1, para 8, as from 1 July 2005.
   Sub-s (1B): inserted by the Prospectus Regulations 2005, SI 2005/1433, reg 2(1), Sch 1, para 10, as from 1 July 2005.
   Sub-s (1C): inserted by the Companies Act 2006, s 1272, Sch 15, Pt 1, paras 1, 9, as from 8 November 2006.

100   Penalties

(1)   In determining its policy with respect to the amount of penalties to be imposed by it under this Part, the competent authority must take no account of the expenses which it incurs, or expects to incur, in discharging its functions under this Part.

(2)   The competent authority must prepare and operate a scheme for ensuring that the amounts paid to it by way of penalties imposed under this Part are applied for the benefit of issuers of securities admitted to the official list[, and issuers who have requested or approved the admission of financial instruments to trading on a regulated market].

(3)   The scheme may, in particular, make different provision with respect to different classes of issuer.

(4)   Up to date details of the scheme must be set out in a document ("the scheme details").

(5)   The scheme details must be published by the competent authority in the way appearing to it to be best calculated to bring them to the attention of the public.

(6)   Before making the scheme, the competent authority must publish a draft of the proposed scheme in the way appearing to it to be best calculated to bring it to the attention of the public.

(7)   The draft must be accompanied by notice that representations about the proposals may be made to the competent authority within a specified time.

(8)   Before making the scheme, the competent authority must have regard to any representations made to it under subsection (7).

(9)   If the competent authority makes the proposed scheme, it must publish an account, in general terms, of—

(a)   the representations made to it in accordance with subsection (7); and

(b)   its response to them.

(10)   If the scheme differs from the draft published under subsection (6) in a way which is, in the opinion of the competent authority, significant the competent authority must (in addition to complying with subsection (9)) publish details of the difference.

(11)   The competent authority must, without delay, give the Treasury a copy of any scheme details published by it.

(12)   The competent authority may charge a reasonable fee for providing a person with a copy of—

(a)   a draft published under subsection (6);

(b)   scheme details.

(13)   Subsections (6) to (10) and (12) apply also to a proposal to alter or replace the scheme.

[120]

NOTES
   Sub-s (2): words in square brackets added by the Financial Services and Markets Act 2000 (Market Abuse) Regulations 2005, SI 2005/381, reg 4, Sch 1, para 9, as from 1 July 2005.

[100A   Exercise of powers where UK is host member state

(1)   This section applies to the exercise by the competent authority of any power under this Part exercisable in case of infringement of—

(a)   a provision of prospectus rules or any other provision made in accordance with the prospectus directive, or

(b)   a provision of transparency rules or any other provision made in accordance with the transparency obligations directive,

in relation to an issuer whose home State is a member State other than the United Kingdom.

(2)   The competent authority may act in such a case only in respect of the infringement of a provision required by the relevant directive.

Any reference to an applicable provision or applicable transparency obligation shall be read accordingly.

(3)   If the authority finds that there has been such an infringement, it must give a notice to that effect to the competent authority of the person's home State requesting it—

(a)   to take all appropriate measures for the purpose of ensuring that the person remedies the situation that has given rise to the notice, and

(b)   to inform the authority of the measures it proposes to take or has taken or the reasons for not taking such measures.

(4)   The authority may not act further unless satisfied—

(a)   that the competent authority of the person's home State has failed or refused to take measures for the purpose mentioned in subsection (3)(a), or

(b)   that the measures taken by that authority have proved inadequate for that purpose.

This does not affect exercise of the powers under section 87K(2), 87L(2) or (3) or 89L(2) or (3) (powers to protect market).

(5)   If the authority is so satisfied, it must, after informing the competent authority of the person's home State, take all appropriate measures to protect investors.

(6)   In such a case the authority must inform the Commission of the measures at the earliest opportunity.]

[120A]

NOTES

Commencement: 8 November 2006.
Inserted by the Companies Act 2006, s 1271, as from 8 November 2006.

101   [Part 6 rules]: general provisions

(1)   [Part 6 rules] may make different provision for different cases.

(2)   [Part 6 rules] may authorise the competent authority to dispense with or modify the application of the rules in particular cases and by reference to any circumstances.

(3)   [Part 6 rules] must be made by an instrument in writing.

(4)   Immediately after an instrument containing [Part 6 rules] is made, it must be printed and made available to the public with or without payment.

(5)   A person is not to be taken to have contravened [any Part 6 rule] if he shows that at the time of the alleged contravention the instrument containing the rule had not been made available as required by subsection (4).

(6)   The production of a printed copy of an instrument purporting to be made by the competent authority on which is endorsed a certificate signed by an officer of the authority authorised by it for that purpose and stating—

(a)   that the instrument was made by the authority,

(b)   that the copy is a true copy of the instrument, and

(c)   that on a specified date the instrument was made available to the public as required by subsection (4),

is evidence (or in Scotland sufficient evidence) of the facts stated in the certificate.

(7)   A certificate purporting to be signed as mentioned in subsection (6) is to be treated as having been properly signed unless the contrary is shown.

(8)   A person who wishes in any legal proceedings to rely on a rule-making instrument may require the Authority to endorse a copy of the instrument with a certificate of the kind mentioned in subsection (6).

[121]

NOTES

Section heading: words in square brackets substituted by virtue of the Financial Services and Markets Act 2000 (Market Abuse) Regulations 2005, SI 2005/381, reg 4, Sch 1, para 10, as from 1 July 2005. Note that SI 2005/381 makes no provision for the section name to be amended, but in consequence of the amendments noted below, it is believed that it should be.

Sub-ss (1)–(5): words in square brackets substituted by SI 2005/381, reg 4, Sch 1, para 10, as from 1 July 2005.

102   Exemption from liability in damages

(1)   Neither the competent authority nor any person who is, or is acting as, a member, officer or member of staff of the competent authority is to be liable in damages for anything done or omitted in the discharge, or purported discharge, of the authority's functions.

(2)   Subsection (1) does not apply—

(a)   if the act or omission is shown to have been in bad faith; or

(b) so as to prevent an award of damages made in respect of an act or omission on the ground that the act or omission was unlawful as a result of section 6(1) of the Human Rights Act 1998.

[122]

[Interpretative provisions

102A Meaning of "securities" etc

(1) This section applies for the purposes of this Part.

(2) "Securities" means (except in section 74(2) and the expression "transferable securities") anything which has been, or may be, admitted to the official list.

(3) "Transferable securities" means anything which is a transferable security for the purposes of [Directive 2004/39/EC of the European Parliament and of the Council on markets in financial instruments], other than money-market instruments for the purposes of that directive which have a maturity of less than 12 months.

[(3A) "Debt securities" has the meaning given in Article 2.1(b) of the transparency obligations directive.]

(4) "Financial instrument" has [(except in section 89F)] the meaning given in Article 1.3 of Directive 2003/6/EC of the European Parliament and of the Council of 28 January 2003 on insider dealing and market manipulation [(as modified by Article 69 of Directive 2004/39/EC on markets in financial instruments)].

(5) "Non-equity transferable securities" means all transferable securities that are not equity securities; and for this purpose "equity securities" has the meaning given in Article 2.1(b) of the prospectus directive.

(6) "Issuer"—
(a) in relation to an offer of transferable securities to the public or admission of transferable securities to trading on a regulated market for which an approved prospectus is required as a result of section 85, means a legal person who issues or proposes to issue the transferable securities in question,
[(aa) in relation to transparency rules, means a legal person whose securities are admitted to trading on a regulated market or whose voting shares are admitted to trading on a UK market other than a regulated market, and in the case of depository receipts representing securities, the issuer is the issuer of the securities represented,]
(b) in relation to anything else which is or may be admitted to the official list, has such meaning as may be prescribed by the Treasury, and
(c) in any other case, means a person who issues financial instruments.]

[123]

NOTES
Commencement: 1 July 2005.
Sections 102A–102C, 103 substituted (together with the preceding heading) for original s 103 by the Prospectus Regulations 2005, SI 2005/1433, reg 2(1), Sch 1, para 11, as from 1 July 2005.
Sub-s (3): words in square brackets substituted by the Companies Act 2006, s 1272, Sch 15, Pt 1, paras 1, 10(1), (3), as from 8 November 2006.
Sub-s (3A): inserted by the Companies Act 2006, s 1272, Sch 15, Pt 1, paras 1, 10(1), (2), as from 8 November 2006.
Sub-s (4): words in square brackets inserted by the Definition of Financial Instrument Order 2008, SI 2008/3053, art 3, as from 31 January 2009.
Sub-s (6): para (aa) inserted by the Companies Act 2006, s 1272, Sch 15, Pt 1, paras 1, 10(1), (4), as from 8 November 2006.

[102B Meaning of "offer of transferable securities to the public" etc

(1) For the purposes of this Part there is an offer of transferable securities to the public if there is a communication to any person which presents sufficient information on—
(a) the transferable securities to be offered, and
(b) the terms on which they are offered,
to enable an investor to decide to buy or subscribe for the securities in question.

(2) For the purposes of this Part, to the extent that an offer of transferable securities is made to a person in the United Kingdom it is an offer of transferable securities to the public in the United Kingdom.

(3) The communication may be made—
(a) in any form;
(b) by any means.

(4) Subsection (1) includes the placing of securities through a financial intermediary.

(5) Subsection (1) does not include a communication in connection with trading on—

(a)   a regulated market;
(b)   a multilateral trading facility; or
(c)   a market prescribed by an order under section 130A(3).

(6)   "Multilateral trading facility" means a multilateral system, operated by an investment firm …) or a market operator, which brings together multiple third-party buying and selling interests in financial instruments in accordance with non-discretionary rules so as to result in a contract.]

[124]

NOTES
Commencement: 1 July 2005.
Substituted as noted to s 102A at **[123]**.
Sub-s (6): words omitted repealed by the Financial Services and Markets Act 2000 (Markets in Financial Instruments) Regulations 2007, SI 2007/126, reg 3(5), Sch 5, paras 1, 6, as from 1 April 2007 (certain purposes (see reg 1(2) at **[4051]**)), and as from 1 November 2007 (otherwise).

[102C   Meaning of "home State" in relation to transferable securities
In this Part, in relation to an issuer of transferable securities, the "home-State" is the EEA State which is the "home Member State" for the purposes of the prospectus directive (which is to be determined in accordance with Article 2.1(m) of that directive).]

[125]

NOTES
Commencement: 1 July 2005.
Substituted as noted to s 102A at **[123]**.

[103   Interpretation of this Part
(1)   In this Part, save where the context otherwise requires—
"disclosure rules" has the meaning given in section 73A;
"inside information" has the meaning given in section 118C;
"listed securities" means anything which has been admitted to the official list;
"listing" has the meaning given in section 74(5);
"listing particulars" has the meaning given in section 79(2);
"listing rules" has the meaning given in section 73A;
"market operator" means a person who manages or operates the business of a regulated market;
"offer of transferable securities to the public" has the meaning given in section 102B;
"the official list" means the list maintained by the competent authority as that list has effect for the time being;
"Part 6 rules" has the meaning given in section 73A;
"the prospectus directive" means Directive 2003/71/EC of the European Parliament and of the Council of 4 November 2003 on the prospectus to be published when securities are offered to the public or admitted to trading;
"prospectus rules" has the meaning given in section 73A;
"regulated market" has the meaning given in [Article 4.1(14) of Directive 2004/39/EC of the European Parliament and of the Council on markets in financial instruments];
"supplementary prospectus" has the meaning given in section 87G;
["the transparency obligations directive" means Directive 2004/109/EC of the European Parliament and of the Council relating to the harmonisation of transparency requirements in relation to information about issuers whose securities are admitted to trading on a regulated market;]
["transparency rules" has the meaning given by section 89A(5);
"voteholder information" has the meaning given by section 89B(3);]
"working day" means any day other that a Saturday, a Sunday, Christmas Day, Good Friday or a day which is a bank holiday under the Banking and Financial Dealings Act 1971 (c 80) in any part of the United Kingdom.

(2)   In relation to any function conferred on the competent authority by this Part, any reference in this Part to the competent authority is to be read as a reference to the person by whom that function is for the time being exercisable.

(3)   If, as a result of an order under Schedule 8, different functions conferred on the competent authority by this Part are exercisable by different persons, the powers conferred by section 91 are exercisable by such person as may be determined in accordance with the provisions of the order.]

[126]

NOTES
Commencement: 1 July 2005.
Substituted as noted to s 102A at **[123]**.
Sub-s (1) is amended as follows:

Words in square brackets in the definition "regulated market" substituted by the Companies Act 2006, s 1272, Sch 15, Pt 1, paras 1, 11(1), (2), as from 1 October 2008.

Definitions "the transparency obligations directive", "transparency rules", and "voteholder information" inserted by the Companies Act 2006, ss 1265, 1272, Sch 15, Pt 1, paras 1, 11(1), (3), as from 8 November 2006.

PART VII
CONTROL OF BUSINESS TRANSFERS

104 Control of business transfers

No insurance business transfer scheme or banking business transfer scheme is to have effect unless an order has been made in relation to it under section 111(1).

[127]

NOTES

Commencement: 1 December 2001 (for the purpose of insurance business transfer schemes); to be appointed (otherwise).

Note: this provision has not been brought into effect in relation to banking business transfer schemes: see the Financial Services and Markets Act 2000 (Commencement No 7) Order 2001, SI 2001/3538 at **[2009]**. Note also that in November 2006 HM Treasury issued a consultation paper entitled *Consultation on amendments to Part VII of FSMA 2000* (*'Control of Business Transfers'*) which proposes certain amendments to Part VII. As noted above, this section has only been partly commenced in that, currently, it only applies in respect of insurance transfers. This means that the legal framework and mechanisms for transfer schemes are only mandatory for insurance transfers, while for banking they are optional. The amendments to the Financial Services and Markets Act 2000 (Control of Business Transfers) (Requirements on Applicants) Regulations 2001, SI 2001/3625 made by the Financial Services and Markets Act 2000 (Reinsurance Directive) Regulations 2007, SI 2007/3255 will, however, apply equally to banking transfer schemes carried out under Part VII and, in the event that this section is one day also commenced in relation to banking transfers, they would become mandatory as they already are for insurance transfer schemes.

105 Insurance business transfer schemes

(1) A scheme is an insurance business transfer scheme if it—
  (a) satisfies one of the conditions set out in subsection (2);
  (b) results in the business transferred being carried on from an establishment of the transferee in an EEA State; and
  (c) is not an excluded scheme.

(2) The conditions are that—
  (a) the whole or part of the business carried on in one or more member States by a UK authorised person who has permission to effect or carry out contracts of insurance ("the authorised person concerned") is to be transferred to another body ("the transferee");
  (b) the whole or part of the business, so far as it consists of reinsurance, carried on in the United Kingdom through an establishment there by an EEA firm [falling within paragraph 5(d) of Schedule 3 and qualifying for authorisation under that Schedule] ("the authorised person concerned") is to be transferred to another body ("the transferee");
  (c) the whole or part of the business carried on in the United Kingdom by an authorised person who is neither a UK authorised person nor an EEA firm but who has permission to effect or carry out contracts of insurance ("the authorised person concerned") is to be transferred to another body ("the transferee").

(3) A scheme is an excluded scheme for the purposes of this section if it falls within any of the following cases:

CASE 1

Where the authorised person concerned is a friendly society.

CASE 2

Where—
  (a) the authorised person concerned is a UK authorised person;
  [(aa) the authorised person concerned is not a reinsurance undertaking (within the meaning of Article 2.1(c) of the reinsurance directive);]
  (b) the business to be transferred under the scheme is business which consists of the effecting or carrying out of contracts of reinsurance in one or more EEA States other than the United Kingdom; and
  (c) the scheme has been approved by a court in an EEA State other than the United Kingdom or by the host state regulator.

CASE 3

Where—
  (a) the authorised person concerned is a UK authorised person;

(b) the business to be transferred under the scheme is carried on in one or more countries or territories (none of which is an EEA State) and does not include policies of insurance ... against risks arising in an EEA State; and

(c) the scheme has been approved by a court in a country or territory other than an EEA State or by the authority responsible for the supervision of that business in a country or territory in which it is carried on.

CASE 4

Where[—

(a) the business to be transferred under the scheme is the whole of the business of the authorised person concerned;]

(b) all the policyholders are controllers of the firm or of firms within the same group as the firm which is the transferee, and

[(c)] all of the policyholders who will be affected by the transfer have consented to it.

[CASE 5

Where—

(a) the business of the authorised person concerned consists solely of the effecting or carrying out of contracts of reinsurance;

(b) the business to be transferred is the whole or part of that business;

(c) the scheme does not fall within Case 4;

(d) all of the policyholders who will be affected by the transfer have consented to it; and

(e) a certificate has been obtained under paragraph 2 of Schedule 12 in relation to the proposed transfer.]

(4) The parties to a scheme which falls within Case 2, [3, 4 or 5] may apply to the court for an order sanctioning the scheme as if it were an insurance business transfer scheme.

[(5) If the scheme involves a compromise or arrangement falling within Part 27 of the Companies Act 2006 (mergers and divisions of public companies), the provisions of that Part (and Part 26 of that Act) apply accordingly but this does not affect the operation of this Part in relation to the scheme.]

(8) "UK authorised person" means a body which is an authorised person and which—

(a) is incorporated in the United Kingdom; or

(b) is an unincorporated association formed under the law of any part of the United Kingdom.

(9) "Establishment" means, in relation to a person, his head office or a branch of his.

[128]

NOTES

Sub-ss (2), (4): words in square brackets substituted by the Reinsurance Directive Regulations 2007, SI 2007/3253, reg 2(1), Sch 1, paras 1, 2(1)(a), (f), as from 10 December 2007.

Sub-s (3): words in square brackets substituted or inserted, and words omitted repealed, by SI 2007/3253, reg 2(1), Sch 1, paras 1, 2(1)(b)–(e), as from 10 December 2007.

Sub-s (5): substituted, for original sub-ss (5)–(7), by the Companies Act 2006 (Consequential Amendments etc) Order 2008, SI 2008/948, art 3(1), Sch 1, Pt 2, para 211(1), as from 6 April 2008.

Transitional provisions: see the Financial Services and Markets Act 2000 (Transitional Provisions and Savings) (Business Transfers) Order 2001, SI 2001/3639. That Order makes savings and transitional provision for applications under the Insurance Companies Act 1982, Sch 2C (repealed) for approval of a transfer of the whole or part of the long term business carried on by an insurance company or approval of the transfer of rights and obligations under contracts of general insurance (including transfers of business to or from members of Lloyd's). In relation to any application that has been made but not determined before 1 December 2001, the relevant provisions of Sch 2C are saved, subject to the general modifications in art 2 of the Order and the specific modifications in arts 3 and 5.

106 Banking business transfer schemes

(1) A scheme is a banking business transfer scheme if it—

(a) satisfies one of the conditions set out in subsection (2);

(b) is one under which the whole or part of the business to be transferred includes the accepting of deposits; and

(c) is not an excluded scheme.

(2) The conditions are that—

(a) the whole or part of the business carried on by a UK authorised person who has permission to accept deposits ("the authorised person concerned") is to be transferred to another body ("the transferee");

(b) the whole or part of the business carried on in the United Kingdom by an authorised person who is not a UK authorised person but who has permission to accept deposits ("the authorised person concerned") is to be transferred to another body which will carry it on in the United Kingdom ("the transferee").

(3)   A scheme is an excluded scheme for the purposes of this section if—
  (a)   the authorised person concerned is a building society or a credit union; or
  [(b)   the scheme is a compromise or arrangement to which Part 27 of the Companies Act 2006 (mergers and divisions of public companies) applies.]

(4)   For the purposes of subsection (2)(a) it is immaterial whether or not the business to be transferred is carried on in the United Kingdom.

(5)   "UK authorised person" has the same meaning as in section 105.

(6)   "Building society" has the meaning given in the Building Societies Act 1986.

(7)   "Credit union" means a credit union within the meaning of—
  (a)   the Credit Unions Act 1979;
  (b)   the Credit Unions (Northern Ireland) Order 1985.

[129]

NOTES
Sub-s (3): para (b) substituted by the Companies Act 2006 (Consequential Amendments etc) Order 2008, SI 2008/948, art 3(1), Sch 1, Pt 2, para 211(2), as from 6 April 2008.

[106A   Reclaim fund business transfer scheme

(1)   A scheme is a reclaim fund business transfer scheme if, under the scheme, the whole or part of the business carried on by a reclaim fund is to be transferred to one or more other reclaim funds.

(2)   "Reclaim fund" has the meaning given by section 5(1) of the Dormant Bank and Building Society Accounts Act 2008.]

[129A]

NOTES
Commencement: to be appointed.
Inserted by the Dormant Bank and Building Society Accounts Act 2008, s 15, Sch 2, para 2 as from a day to be appointed.

107   Application for order sanctioning transfer scheme

(1)   An application may be made to the court for an order sanctioning an insurance business transfer scheme *or a banking business transfer scheme*.

(2)   An application may be made by—
  (a)   the authorised person concerned;
  (b)   the transferee; or
  (c)   both.

(3)   The application must be made—
  (a)   if the authorised person concerned and the transferee are registered or have their head offices in the same jurisdiction, to the court in that jurisdiction;
  (b)   if the authorised person concerned and the transferee are registered or have their head offices in different jurisdictions, to the court in either jurisdiction;
  (c)   if the transferee is not registered in the United Kingdom and does not have his head office there, to the court which has jurisdiction in relation to the authorised person concerned.

(4)   "Court" means—
  (a)   the High Court; or
  (b)   in Scotland, the Court of Session.

[130]

NOTES
Sub-s (1): for the words in italics there are substituted the words ", a banking business transfer scheme or a reclaim fund business transfer scheme" by the Dormant Bank and Building Society Accounts Act 2008, s 15, Sch 2, para 3 as from a day to be appointed.

108   Requirements on applicants

(1)   The Treasury may by regulations impose requirements on applicants under section 107.

(2)   The court may not determine an application under that section if the applicant has failed to comply with a prescribed requirement.

(3)   The regulations may, in particular, include provision—
  (a)   as to the persons to whom, and periods within which, notice of an application must be given;
  (b)   enabling the court to waive a requirement of the regulations in prescribed circumstances.

[131]

NOTES

Regulations: the Financial Services and Markets Act 2000 (Control of Business Transfers) (Requirements on Applicants) Regulations 2001, SI 2001/3625 at **[2517]**.

Note that the following amending Regulations have also been made under this section: the Financial Services and Markets Act 2000 (Reinsurance Directive) Regulations 2007, SI 2007/3255; the Financial Services and Markets Act 2000 (Control of Business Transfers) (Requirements on Applicants) (Amendment) Regulations 2008, SI 2008/1467.

109 Scheme reports

(1)   An application under section 107 in respect of an insurance business transfer scheme must be accompanied by a report on the terms of the scheme ("a scheme report").

(2)   A scheme report may be made only by a person—
  (a)   appearing to the Authority to have the skills necessary to enable him to make a proper report; and
  (b)   nominated or approved for the purpose by the Authority.

(3)   A scheme report must be made in a form approved by the Authority.

[132]

110 Right to participate in proceedings

On an application under section 107, the following are also entitled to be heard—
  (a)   the Authority, and
  (b)   any person (including an employee of the authorised person concerned or of the transferee) who alleges that he would be adversely affected by the carrying out of the scheme.

[133]

111 Sanction of the court for business transfer schemes

(1)   This section sets out the conditions which must be satisfied before the court may make an order under this section sanctioning an insurance business transfer scheme *or a banking business transfer scheme.*

(2)   The court must be satisfied that—
  (a)   [in the case of an insurance business transfer scheme or a banking business transfer scheme,] the appropriate certificates have been obtained (as to which see Parts I and II of Schedule 12);
  [(aa) in the case of a reclaim fund business transfer scheme, the appropriate certificate has been obtained (as to which see Part 2A of that Schedule);]
  (b)   the transferee has the authorisation required (if any) to enable the business, or part, which is to be transferred to be carried on in the place to which it is to be transferred (or will have it before the scheme takes effect).

(3)   The court must consider that, in all the circumstances of the case, it is appropriate to sanction the scheme.

[134]

NOTES

Sub-s (1): for the words in italics there are substituted the words ", a banking business transfer scheme or a reclaim fund business transfer scheme" by the Dormant Bank and Building Society Accounts Act 2008, s 15, Sch 2, para 4(1), (2) as from a day to be appointed.

Sub-s (2): words in square brackets in para (a), and the whole of para (aa), inserted by the Dormant Bank and Building Society Accounts Act 2008, s 15, Sch 2, para 4(1), (3) as from a day to be appointed.

112 Effect of order sanctioning business transfer scheme

(1)   If the court makes an order under section 111(1), it may by that or any subsequent order make such provision (if any) as it thinks fit—
  (a)   for the transfer to the transferee of the whole or any part of the undertaking concerned and of any property or liabilities of the authorised person concerned;
  (b)   for the allotment or appropriation by the transferee of any shares, debentures, policies or other similar interests in the transferee which under the scheme are to be allotted or appropriated to or for any other person;
  (c)   for the continuation by (or against) the transferee of any pending legal proceedings by (or against) the authorised person concerned;
  (d)   with respect to such incidental, consequential and supplementary matters as are, in its opinion, necessary to secure that the scheme is fully and effectively carried out.

(2)   An order under subsection (1)(a) may—
  (a)   transfer property or liabilities whether or not the authorised person concerned otherwise has the capacity to effect the transfer in question;

(b)   make provision in relation to property which was held by the authorised person concerned as trustee;

(c)   make provision as to future or contingent rights or liabilities of the authorised person concerned, including provision as to the construction of instruments (including wills) under which such rights or liabilities may arise;

(d)   make provision as to the consequences of the transfer in relation to any [occupational pension scheme (within the meaning of section 150(5) of the Finance Act 2004)] operated by or on behalf of the authorised person concerned.

[(2A)   Subsection (2)(a) is to be taken to include power to make provision in an order—

(a)   for the transfer of property or liabilities which would not otherwise be capable of being transferred or assigned;

(b)   for a transfer of property or liabilities to take effect as if there were—

(i)   no such requirement to obtain a person's consent or concurrence, and

(ii)   no such contravention, liability or interference with any interest or right,

as there would otherwise be (in the case of a transfer apart from this section) by reason of any provision falling within subsection (2B).

(2B)   A provision falls within this subsection to the extent that it has effect (whether under an enactment or agreement or otherwise) in relation to the terms on which the authorised person concerned is entitled to the property or subject to the liabilities in question.

(2C)   Nothing in subsection (2A) or (2B) is to be read as limiting the scope of subsection (1).]

(3)   If an order under subsection (1) makes provision for the transfer of property or liabilities—

(a)   the property is transferred to and vests in, and

(b)   the liabilities are transferred to and become liabilities of,

the transferee as a result of the order.

(4)   But if any property or liability included in the order is governed by the law of any country or territory outside the United Kingdom, the order may require the authorised person concerned, if the transferee so requires, to take all necessary steps for securing that the transfer to the transferee of the property or liability is fully effective under the law of that country or territory.

(5)   Property transferred as the result of an order under subsection (1) may, if the court so directs, vest in the transferee free from any charge which is (as a result of the scheme) to cease to have effect.

(6)   An order under subsection (1) which makes provision for the transfer of property is to be treated as an instrument of transfer for the purposes of [section 770(1) of the Companies Act 2006] and any other enactment requiring the delivery of an instrument of transfer for the registration of property.

(7)   …

(8)   If the court makes an order under section 111(1) in relation to an insurance business transfer scheme, it may by that or any subsequent order make such provision (if any) as it thinks fit—

(a)   for dealing with the interests of any person who, within such time and in such manner as the court may direct, objects to the scheme;

(b)   for the dissolution, without winding up, of the authorised person concerned;

(c)   for the reduction, on such terms and subject to such conditions (if any) as it thinks fit, of the benefits payable under—

(i)   any description of policy, or

(ii)   policies generally,

entered into by the authorised person concerned and transferred as a result of the scheme.

(9)   If, in the case of an insurance business transfer scheme, the authorised person concerned is not an EEA firm, it is immaterial for the purposes of subsection (1)(a), (c) or (d) or subsection (2), [(2A),] (3) or (4) that the law applicable to any of the contracts of insurance included in the transfer is the law of an EEA State other than the United Kingdom.

(10)   The transferee must, if an insurance or banking business transfer scheme is sanctioned by the court, deposit two office copies of the order made under subsection (1) with the Authority within 10 days of the making of the order.

(11)   But the Authority may extend that period.

(12)   "Property" includes property, rights and powers of any description.

(13)   "Liabilities" includes duties.

(14)   "Shares" and "debentures" have the same meaning as in [the Companies Acts (see sections 540 and 738 of the Companies Act 2006).]

(15)   "Charge" includes a mortgage (or, in Scotland, a security over property).

[135]

NOTES

Sub-s (2): words in square brackets substituted by the Taxation of Pension Schemes (Consequential Amendments) Order 2006, SI 2006/745, art 17, as from 6 April 2006.

Sub-ss (2A)–(2C): inserted by the Financial Services and Markets Act 2000 (Amendments to Part 7) Regulations 2008, SI 2008/1468, reg 2(1), as from 30 June 2008.

Sub-ss (6), (14): words in square brackets substituted by the Companies Act 2006 (Consequential Amendments etc) Order 2008, SI 2008/948, art 3(1), Sch 1, Pt 2, para 211(3)(a), (c), as from 6 April 2008.

Sub-s (7): repealed by SI 2008/948, art 3, Sch 1, Pt 2, para 211(3)(b), Sch 2, as from 6 April 2008.

Sub-s (9): figure in square brackets inserted by SI 2008/1468, reg 2(2), as from 30 June 2008.

Within 10 days: note that any provision of this Act (other than a provision of Part VI) authorising or requiring a person to do anything within a specified number of days must not take into account any day which is a public holiday in any part of the United Kingdom; see s 417(3) at **[443]**.

[112A Rights to terminate etc

(1) Subsection (2) applies where (apart from that subsection) a person would be entitled, in consequence of anything done or likely to be done by or under this Part in connection with an insurance business transfer scheme or a banking business transfer scheme—

    (a) to terminate, modify, acquire or claim an interest or right; or

    (b) to treat an interest or right as terminated or modified.

(2) The entitlement—

    (a) is not enforceable in relation to that interest or right until after an order has been made under section 112(1) in relation to the scheme; and

    (b) is then enforceable in relation to that interest or right only insofar as the order contains provision to that effect.

(3) Nothing in subsection (1) or (2) is to be read as limiting the scope of section 112(1).]

[135A]

NOTES

Commencement: 30 June 2008.

Inserted by the Financial Services and Markets Act 2000 (Amendments to Part 7) Regulations 2008, SI 2008/1468, reg 2(3), as from 30 June 2008.

113 Appointment of actuary in relation to reduction of benefits

(1) This section applies if an order has been made under section 111(1).

(2) The court making the order may, on the application of the Authority, appoint an independent actuary—

    (a) to investigate the business transferred under the scheme; and

    (b) to report to the Authority on any reduction in the benefits payable under policies entered into by the authorised person concerned that, in the opinion of the actuary, ought to be made.

[136]

114 Rights of certain policyholders

(1) This section applies in relation to an insurance business transfer scheme if—

    (a) the authorised person concerned is an authorised person other than an EEA firm qualifying for authorisation under Schedule 3;

    (b) the court has made an order under section 111 in relation to the scheme; and

    (c) an EEA State other than the United Kingdom is, as regards any policy included in the transfer which evidences a contract of insurance [(other than a contract of reinsurance)], the State of the commitment or the EEA State in which the risk is situated ("the EEA State concerned").

(2) The court must direct that notice of the making of the order, or the execution of any instrument, giving effect to the transfer must be published by the transferee in the EEA State concerned.

(3) A notice under subsection (2) must specify such period as the court may direct as the period during which the policyholder may exercise any right which he has to cancel the policy.

(4) The order or instrument mentioned in subsection (2) does not bind the policyholder if—

    (a) the notice required under that subsection is not published; or

    (b) the policyholder cancels the policy during the period specified in the notice given under that subsection.

(5) The law of the EEA State concerned governs—

    (a) whether the policyholder has a right to cancel the policy; and

    (b) the conditions, if any, subject to which any such right may be exercised.

(6) Paragraph 6 of Schedule 12 applies for the purposes of this section as it applies for the purposes of that Schedule.

[137]

NOTES
Sub-s (1): words in square brackets in para (c) inserted by the Reinsurance Directive Regulations 2007, SI 2007/3253, reg 2(1), Sch 1, paras 1, 2(1), (2), as from 10 December 2007.

[114A Notice of transfer of reinsurance contracts

(1) This section applies in relation to an insurance business transfer scheme if—
  (a) the authorised person concerned is an authorised person other than an EEA firm qualifying for authorisation under Schedule 3;
  (b) the court has made an order under section 111 in relation to the scheme; and
  (c) an EEA State other than the United Kingdom is, as regards any policy included in the transfer which evidences a contract of reinsurance, the State in which the establishment of the policyholder to which the policy relates is situated at the date when the contract was entered into ("the EEA State concerned").

(2) The court may direct that notice of the making of the order, or the execution of any instrument, giving effect to the transfer must be published by the transferee in the EEA State concerned.]

[137A]

NOTES
Commencement: 10 December 2007.
Inserted by the Reinsurance Directive Regulations 2007, SI 2007/3253, reg 2(1), Sch 1, paras 1, 2(1), (3), as from 10 December 2007.

Business transfers outside the United Kingdom

115 Certificates for purposes of insurance business transfers overseas

Part III of Schedule 12 makes provision about certificates which the Authority may issue in relation to insurance business transfers taking place outside the United Kingdom.

[138]

116 Effect of insurance business transfers authorised in other EEA States

(1) This section applies if, as a result of an authorised transfer, an EEA firm falling within paragraph 5(d) [or (da)] of Schedule 3 transfers to another body all its rights and obligations under any UK policies.

[(2) This section also applies if, as a result of an authorised transfer, any of the following transfers to another body all its rights and obligations under any UK policies—
  (a) an undertaking authorised in an EEA State other than the United Kingdom under Article 51 of the life assurance consolidation directive;
  (b) an undertaking authorised in an EEA State other than the United Kingdom under Article 23 of the first non-life insurance directive;
  (c) an undertaking, whose head office is not within the EEA, authorised under the law of an EEA State other than the United Kingdom to carry out reinsurance activities in its territory (as mentioned in Article 49 of the reinsurance directive).]

(3) If appropriate notice of the execution of an instrument giving effect to the transfer is published, the instrument has the effect in law—
  (a) of transferring to the transferee all the transferor's rights and obligations under the UK policies to which the instrument applies, and
  (b) if the instrument so provides, of securing the continuation by or against the transferee of any legal proceedings by or against the transferor which relate to those rights and obligations.

(4) No agreement or consent is required before subsection (3) has the effects mentioned.

(5) "Authorised transfer" means—
  (a) in subsection (1), a transfer authorised in the home State of the EEA firm in accordance with—
    [(i) Article 14 of the life assurance consolidation directive; ...]
    (ii) Article 12 of the third non-life directive; [or]
    [(iii) Article 18 of the reinsurance directive; and]
  (b) in subsection (2), a transfer authorised in an EEA State other than the United Kingdom in accordance with—
    [(i) Article 53 of the life assurance consolidation directive; ...]
    (ii) Article 28a of the first non-life directive; [or
    (iii) the provisions in the law of that EEA State which provide for the authorisation of

transfers of all or part of a portfolio of contracts of an undertaking authorised to carry out reinsurance activities in its territory (as mentioned in Article 49 of the reinsurance directive)].

[(6)   "UK policy" means—
   (a)   in the case of an authorised transfer within the meaning of paragraph (a)(i) or (ii) or (b)(i) or (ii) of subsection (5), a policy evidencing a contract of insurance (other than a contract of reinsurance) to which the applicable law is the law of a part of the United Kingdom;
   (b)   in the case of an authorised transfer within the meaning of paragraph (a)(iii) or (b)(iii) of that subsection, a policy evidencing a contract of reinsurance to which the applicable law is the law of a part of the United Kingdom.]

(7)   "Appropriate notice" means—
   (a)   if the UK policy evidences a contract of insurance in relation to which an EEA State other than the United Kingdom is the State of the commitment, notice given in accordance with the law of that State;
   (b)   if the UK policy evidences a contract of insurance where the risk is situated in an EEA State other than the United Kingdom, notice given in accordance with the law of that EEA State;
   (c)   in any other case, notice given in accordance with the applicable law.

(8)   Paragraph 6 of Schedule 12 applies for the purposes of this section as it applies for the purposes of that Schedule.

[139]

NOTES
Sub-s (1): words in square brackets inserted by the Reinsurance Directive Regulations 2007, SI 2007/3253, reg 2(1), Sch 1, paras 1, 2(4)(a), as from 10 December 2007.
Sub-ss (2), (6): substituted by SI 2007/3253, reg 2(1), Sch 1, paras 1, 2(4)(b), (d), as from 10 December 2007.
Sub-s (5): sub-paras (a)(i), (b)(i) substituted the Life Assurance Consolidation Directive (Consequential Amendments) Regulations 2004, SI 2004/3379, reg 6(1), (2)(b), (c), as from 11 January 2005; words omitted from sub-paras (a)(i), (b)(i) repealed, word in square brackets in sub-paras (a)(ii) substituted, and sub-paras (a)(iii) and (b)(iii) (and the word preceding sub-para (b)(iii)) inserted, by SI 2007/3253, reg 2(1), Sch 1, paras 1, 2(4)(c), as from 10 December 2007.

Modifications

117   Power to modify this Part
The Treasury may by regulations—
   (a)   provide for prescribed provisions of this Part to have effect in relation to prescribed cases with such modifications as may be prescribed;
   (b)   make such amendments to any provision of this Part as they consider appropriate for the more effective operation of that or any other provision of this Part.

[140]

NOTES
Regulations: the Financial Services and Markets Act 2000 (Motor Insurance) Regulations 2007, SI 2007/2403 (these Regulations amend this Act and the Financial Services and Markets Act 2000 (Law Applicable to Contracts of Insurance) Regulations 2001, SI 2001/2635 (at **[2472]**)) to change the meaning of "EEA State in which a risk is situated" in certain circumstances in the context of vehicle insurance); the Financial Services and Markets Act 2000 (Amendments to Part 7) Regulations 2008, SI 2008/1468.

PART VIII
PENALTIES FOR MARKET ABUSE

NOTES
Note: this Part, and other provisions of this Act (particularly in Part VI) were amended by Regulations bringing into effect European Parliament and Council Directive 2003/6/EC on insider dealing and market manipulation (market abuse) at **[5430]** et seq. By Article 18 of that Directive (at **[5447]**), Member States were required to bring into force the laws, regulations and administration provisions necessary to comply with the Directive not later than 12 October 2004. The Market Abuse Directive is implemented, in part, by the Financial Services and Markets Act 2000 (Market Abuse) Regulations 2005, SI 2005/381, in part by the Investment Recommendation (Media) Regulations 2005, SI 2005/382, and in part by the FSA using its powers to make rules under this Act. The amendments made by the Financial Services and Markets Act 2000 (Market Abuse) Regulations 2005 came into force on 17 March 2005 for certain purposes and on 1 July 2005 otherwise. The amendments made by those Regulations are noted to the appropriate sections of this Act.

Market abuse

[118 Market abuse

(1)   For the purposes of this Act, market abuse is behaviour (whether by one person alone or by two or more persons jointly or in concert) which—
  (a)   occurs in relation to—
      (i)   qualifying investments admitted to trading on a prescribed market,
      (ii)   qualifying investments in respect of which a request for admission to trading on such a market has been made, or
      (iii)   in the case of subsection (2) or (3) behaviour, investments which are related investments in relation to such qualifying investments, and
  (b)   falls within any one or more of the types of behaviour set out in subsections (2) to (8).

(2)   The first type of behaviour is where an insider deals, or attempts to deal, in a qualifying investment or related investment on the basis of inside information relating to the investment in question.

(3)   The second is where an insider discloses inside information to another person otherwise than in the proper course of the exercise of his employment, profession or duties.

(4)   The third is where the behaviour (not falling within subsection (2) or (3))—
  (a)   is based on information which is not generally available to those using the market but which, if available to a regular user of the market, would be, or would be likely to be, regarded by him as relevant when deciding the terms on which transactions in qualifying investments should be effected, and
  (b)   is likely to be regarded by a regular user of the market as a failure on the part of the person concerned to observe the standard of behaviour reasonably expected of a person in his position in relation to the market.

(5)   The fourth is where the behaviour consists of effecting transactions or orders to trade (otherwise than for legitimate reasons and in conformity with accepted market practices on the relevant market) which—
  (a)   give, or are likely to give, a false or misleading impression as to the supply of, or demand for, or as to the price of, one or more qualifying investments, or
  (b)   secure the price of one or more such investments at an abnormal or artificial level.

(6)   The fifth is where the behaviour consists of effecting transactions or orders to trade which employ fictitious devices or any other form of deception or contrivance.

(7)   The sixth is where the behaviour consists of the dissemination of information by any means which gives, or is likely to give, a false or misleading impression as to a qualifying investment by a person who knew or could reasonably be expected to have known that the information was false or misleading.

(8)   The seventh is where the behaviour (not falling within subsection (5), (6) or (7))—
  (a)   is likely to give a regular user of the market a false or misleading impression as to the supply of, demand for or price or value of, qualifying investments, or
  (b)   would be, or would be likely to be, regarded by a regular user of the market as behaviour that would distort, or would be likely to distort, the market in such an investment,
and the behaviour is likely to be regarded by a regular user of the market as a failure on the part of the person concerned to observe the standard of behaviour reasonably expected of a person in his position in relation to the market.

(9)   Subsections (4) and (8) and the definition of "regular user" in section 130A(3) cease to have effect on [31 December 2009] and subsection (1)(b) is then to be read as no longer referring to those subsections.]

[141]

NOTES
  Commencement: 1 July 2005.
  Substituted, together with ss 118B–118C for original s 118, by the Financial Services and Markets Act 2000 (Market Abuse) Regulations 2005, SI 2005/381, reg 5, Sch 2, para 1, as from 1 July 2005.
  Sub-s (9): words in square brackets substituted by the Financial Services and Markets Act 2000 (Market Abuse) Regulations 2008, SI 2008/1439, reg 3(1), (2), as from 30 June 2008.
  Note: the Financial Services and Markets Act 2000 (Prescribed Markets and Qualifying Investments) Order 2001, SI 2001/996 at [2161] was originally made under s 118(3) but, following the substitution of this section as noted above, now has effect as if made under s 130A(1) at [157].

[118A   Supplementary provision about certain behaviour

(1)   Behaviour is to be taken into account for the purposes of this Part only if it occurs—
  (a)   in the United Kingdom, or
  (b)   in relation to—

      (i)   qualifying investments which are admitted to trading on a prescribed market situated in, or operating in, the United Kingdom,

      (ii)   qualifying investments for which a request for admission to trading on such a prescribed market has been made, or

      (iii) in the case of section 118(2) and (3), investments which are related investments in relation to such qualifying investments.

(2)   For the purposes of subsection (1), as it applies in relation to section 118(4) and (8), a prescribed market accessible electronically in the United Kingdom is to be treated as operating in the United Kingdom.

(3)   For the purposes of section 118(4) and (8), the behaviour that is to be regarded as occurring in relation to qualifying investments includes behaviour which—

    (a)   occurs in relation to anything that is the subject matter, or whose price or value is expressed by reference to the price or value of the qualifying investments, or

    (b)   occurs in relation to investments (whether or not they are qualifying investments) whose subject matter is the qualifying investments.

(4)   For the purposes of section 118(7), the dissemination of information by a person acting in the capacity of a journalist is to be assessed taking into account the codes governing his profession unless he derives, directly or indirectly, any advantage or profits from the dissemination of the information.

(5)   Behaviour does not amount to market abuse for the purposes of this Act if—

    (a)   it conforms with a rule which includes a provision to the effect that behaviour conforming with the rule does not amount to market abuse,

    (b)   it conforms with the relevant provisions of Commission Regulation (EC) No 2273/2003 of 22 December 2003 implementing Directive 2003/6/EC of the European Parliament and of the Council as regards exemptions for buy-back programmes and stabilisation of financial instruments, or

    (c)   it is done by a person acting on behalf of a public authority in pursuit of monetary policies or policies with respect to exchange rates or the management of public debt or foreign exchange reserves.

(6)   Subsections (2) and (3) cease to have effect on [31 December 2009].]

[142]

NOTES

Commencement: 1 July 2005.

Substituted as noted to s 118 at **[141]**.

Sub-s (6): words in square brackets substituted by the Financial Services and Markets Act 2000 (Market Abuse) Regulations 2008, SI 2008/1439, reg 3(1), (3), as from 30 June 2008.

[118B Insiders

For the purposes of this Part an insider is any person who has inside information—

    (a)   as a result of his membership of an administrative, management or supervisory body of an issuer of qualifying investments,

    (b)   as a result of his holding in the capital of an issuer of qualifying investments,

    (c)   as a result of having access to the information through the exercise of his employment, profession or duties,

    (d)   as a result of his criminal activities, or

    (e)   which he has obtained by other means and which he knows, or could reasonably be expected to know, is inside information.]

[143]

NOTES

Commencement: 1 July 2005.

Substituted as noted to s 118 at **[141]**.

[118C Inside information

(1)   This section defines "inside information" for the purposes of this Part.

(2)   In relation to qualifying investments, or related investments, which are not commodity derivatives, inside information is information of a precise nature which—

    (a)   is not generally available,

    (b)   relates, directly or indirectly, to one or more issuers of the qualifying investments or to one or more of the qualifying investments, and

    (c)   would, if generally available, be likely to have a significant effect on the price of the qualifying investments or on the price of related investments.

(3)   In relation to qualifying investments or related investments which are commodity derivatives, inside information is information of a precise nature which—

    (a)   is not generally available,

    (b)   relates, directly or indirectly, to one or more such derivatives, and

    (c)   users of markets on which the derivatives are traded would expect to receive in accordance with any accepted market practices on those markets.

(4)   In relation to a person charged with the execution of orders concerning any qualifying investments or related investments, inside information includes information conveyed by a client and related to the client's pending orders which—

    (a)   is of a precise nature,

    (b)   is not generally available,

    (c)   relates, directly or indirectly, to one or more issuers of qualifying investments or to one or more qualifying investments, and

    (d)   would, if generally available, be likely to have a significant effect on the price of those qualifying investments or the price of related investments.

(5)   Information is precise if it—

    (a)   indicates circumstances that exist or may reasonably be expected to come into existence or an event that has occurred or may reasonably be expected to occur, and

    (b)   is specific enough to enable a conclusion to be drawn as to the possible effect of those circumstances or that event on the price of qualifying investments or related investments.

(6)   Information would be likely to have a significant effect on price if and only if it is information of a kind which a reasonable investor would be likely to use as part of the basis of his investment decisions.

(7)   For the purposes of subsection (3)(c), users of markets on which investments in commodity derivatives are traded are to be treated as expecting to receive information relating directly or indirectly to one or more such derivatives in accordance with any accepted market practices, which is—

    (a)   routinely made available to the users of those markets, or

    (b)   required to be disclosed in accordance with any statutory provision, market rules, or contracts or customs on the relevant underlying commodity market or commodity derivatives market.

(8)   Information which can be obtained by research or analysis conducted by, or on behalf of, users of a market is to be regarded, for the purposes of this Part, as being generally available to them.]

[144]

NOTES

Commencement: 1 July 2005.

Substituted as noted to s 118 at **[141]**.

The code

119 The code

(1)   The Authority must prepare and issue a code containing such provisions as the Authority considers will give appropriate guidance to those determining whether or not behaviour amounts to market abuse.

(2)   The code may among other things specify—

    (a)   descriptions of behaviour that, in the opinion of the Authority, amount to market abuse;

    (b)   descriptions of behaviour that, in the opinion of the Authority, do not amount to market abuse;

    (c)   factors that, in the opinion of the Authority, are to be taken into account in determining whether or not behaviour amounts to market abuse;

    [(d)   descriptions of behaviour that are accepted market practices in relation to one or more specified markets;

    (e)   descriptions of behaviour that are not accepted market practices in relation to one or more specified markets].

[(2A)   In determining, for the purposes of subsections (2)(d) and (2)(e) or otherwise, what are and what are not accepted market practices, the Authority must have regard to the factors and procedures laid down in Articles 2 and 3 respectively of Commission Directive 2004/72/EC of 29 April 2004 implementing Directive 2003/6/EC of the European Parliament and of the Council.]

(3)   The code may make different provision in relation to persons, cases or circumstances of different descriptions.

(4)   The Authority may at any time alter or replace the code.

(5)   If the code is altered or replaced, the altered or replacement code must be issued by the Authority.

(6)   A code issued under this section must be published by the Authority in the way appearing to the Authority to be best calculated to bring it to the attention of the public.

(7)   The Authority must, without delay, give the Treasury a copy of any code published under this section.

(8)   The Authority may charge a reasonable fee for providing a person with a copy of the code.

[145]

NOTES
Sub-s (2): paras (d), (e) added by the Financial Services and Markets Act 2000 (Market Abuse) Regulations 2005, SI 2005/381, reg 5, Sch 2, para 2(1), (2), as from 1 July 2005.
Sub-s (2A): inserted by SI 2005/381, reg 5, Sch 2, para 2(1), (3), as from 1 July 2005.

120   Provisions included in the Authority's code by reference to the City Code

(1)   The Authority may include in a code issued by it under section 119 ("the Authority's code") provision to the effect that in its opinion behaviour conforming with the City Code—
  (a)   does not amount to market abuse;
  (b)   does not amount to market abuse in specified circumstances; or
  (c)   does not amount to market abuse if engaged in by a specified description of person.

(2)   But the Treasury's approval is required before any such provision may be included in the Authority's code.

(3)   If the Authority's code includes provision of a kind authorised by subsection (1), the Authority must keep itself informed of the way in which the Panel on Takeovers and Mergers interprets and administers the relevant provisions of the City Code.

(4)   "City Code" means the City Code on Takeovers and Mergers issued by the Panel as it has effect at the time when the behaviour occurs.

(5)   "Specified" means specified in the Authority's code.

[146]

121   Codes: procedure

(1)   Before issuing a code under section 119, the Authority must publish a draft of the proposed code in the way appearing to the Authority to be best calculated to bring it to the attention of the public.

(2)   The draft must be accompanied by—
  (a)   a cost benefit analysis; and
  (b)   notice that representations about the proposal may be made to the Authority within a specified time.

(3)   Before issuing the proposed code, the Authority must have regard to any representations made to it in accordance with subsection (2)(b).

(4)   If the Authority issues the proposed code it must publish an account, in general terms, of—
  (a)   the representations made to it in accordance with subsection (2)(b); and
  (b)   its response to them.

(5)   If the code differs from the draft published under subsection (1) in a way which is, in the opinion of the Authority, significant—
  (a)   the Authority must (in addition to complying with subsection (4)) publish details of the difference; and
  (b)   those details must be accompanied by a cost benefit analysis.

(6)   Subsections (1) to (5) do not apply if the Authority considers that there is an urgent need to publish the code.

(7)   Neither subsection (2)(a) nor subsection (5)(b) applies if the Authority considers—
  (a)   that, making the appropriate comparison, there will be no increase in costs; or
  (b)   that, making that comparison, there will be an increase in costs but the increase will be of minimal significance.

(8)   The Authority may charge a reasonable fee for providing a person with a copy of a draft published under subsection (1).

(9)   This section also applies to a proposal to alter or replace a code.

(10)   "Cost benefit analysis" means an estimate of the costs together with an analysis of the benefits that will arise—
  (a)   if the proposed code is issued; or
  (b)   if subsection (5)(b) applies, from the code that has been issued.

(11)   "The appropriate comparison" means—
  (a)   in relation to subsection (2)(a), a comparison between the overall position if the code is issued and the overall position if it is not issued;

(b)   in relation to subsection (5)(b), a comparison between the overall position after the issuing of the code and the overall position before it was issued.

[147]

122 Effect of the code

(1)   If a person behaves in a way which is described (in the code in force under section 119 at the time of the behaviour) as behaviour that, in the Authority's opinion, does not amount to market abuse that behaviour of his is to be taken, for the purposes of this Act, as not amounting to market abuse.

(2)   Otherwise, the code in force under section 119 at the time when particular behaviour occurs may be relied on so far as it indicates whether or not that behaviour should be taken to amount to market abuse.

[148]

Power to impose penalties

123 Power to impose penalties in cases of market abuse

(1)   If the Authority is satisfied that a person ("A")—
(a)   is or has engaged in market abuse, or
(b)   by taking or refraining from taking any action has required or encouraged another person or persons to engage in behaviour which, if engaged in by A, would amount to market abuse,
it may impose on him a penalty of such amount as it considers appropriate.

(2)   But the Authority may not impose a penalty on a person if, having considered any representations made to it in response to a warning notice, there are reasonable grounds for it to be satisfied that—
(a)   he believed, on reasonable grounds, that his behaviour did not fall within paragraph (a) or (b) of subsection (1), or
(b)   he took all reasonable precautions and exercised all due diligence to avoid behaving in a way which fell within paragraph (a) or (b) of that subsection.

(3)   If the Authority is entitled to impose a penalty on a person under this section it may, instead of imposing a penalty on him, publish a statement to the effect that he has engaged in market abuse.

[149]

Statement of policy

124 Statement of policy

(1)   The Authority must prepare and issue a statement of its policy with respect to—
(a)   the imposition of penalties under section 123; and
(b)   the amount of penalties under that section.

(2)   The Authority's policy in determining what the amount of a penalty should be must include having regard to—
(a)   whether the behaviour in respect of which the penalty is to be imposed had an adverse effect on the market in question and, if it did, how serious that effect was;
(b)   the extent to which that behaviour was deliberate or reckless; and
(c)   whether the person on whom the penalty is to be imposed is an individual.

(3)   A statement issued under this section must include an indication of the circumstances in which the Authority is to be expected to regard a person as—
(a)   having a reasonable belief that his behaviour did not amount to market abuse; or
(b)   having taken reasonable precautions and exercised due diligence to avoid engaging in market abuse.

(4)   The Authority may at any time alter or replace a statement issued under this section.

(5)   If a statement issued under this section is altered or replaced, the Authority must issue the altered or replacement statement.

(6)   In exercising, or deciding whether to exercise, its power under section 123 in the case of any particular behaviour, the Authority must have regard to any statement published under this section and in force at the time when the behaviour concerned occurred.

(7)   A statement issued under this section must be published by the Authority in the way appearing to the Authority to be best calculated to bring it to the attention of the public.

(8)   The Authority may charge a reasonable fee for providing a person with a copy of a statement published under this section.

(9)   The Authority must, without delay, give the Treasury a copy of any statement which it publishes under this section.

[150]

125   Statement of policy: procedure

(1)   Before issuing a statement of policy under section 124, the Authority must publish a draft of the proposed statement in the way appearing to the Authority to be best calculated to bring it to the attention of the public.

(2)   The draft must be accompanied by notice that representations about the proposal may be made to the Authority within a specified time.

(3)   Before issuing the proposed statement, the Authority must have regard to any representations made to it in accordance with subsection (2).

(4)   If the Authority issues the proposed statement it must publish an account, in general terms, of—
    (a)   the representations made to it in accordance with subsection (2); and
    (b)   its response to them.

(5)   If the statement differs from the draft published under subsection (1) in a way which is, in the opinion of the Authority, significant, the Authority must (in addition to complying with subsection (4)) publish details of the difference.

(6)   The Authority may charge a reasonable fee for providing a person with a copy of a draft published under subsection (1).

(7)   This section also applies to a proposal to alter or replace a statement.

[151]

Procedure

126   Warning notices

(1)   If the Authority proposes to take action against a person under section 123, it must give him a warning notice.

(2)   A warning notice about a proposal to impose a penalty must state the amount of the proposed penalty.

(3)   A warning notice about a proposal to publish a statement must set out the terms of the proposed statement.

[152]

127   Decision notices and right to refer to Tribunal

(1)   If the Authority decides to take action against a person under section 123, it must give him a decision notice.

(2)   A decision notice about the imposition of a penalty must state the amount of the penalty.

(3)   A decision notice about the publication of a statement must set out the terms of the statement.

(4)   If the Authority decides to take action against a person under section 123, that person may refer the matter to the Tribunal.

[153]

Miscellaneous

128   Suspension of investigations

(1)   If the Authority considers it desirable or expedient because of the exercise or possible exercise of a power relating to market abuse, it may direct a recognised investment exchange or recognised clearing house—
    (a)   to terminate, suspend or limit the scope of any inquiry which the exchange or clearing house is conducting under its rules; or
    (b)   not to conduct an inquiry which the exchange or clearing house proposes to conduct under its rules.

(2)   A direction under this section—
    (a)   must be given to the exchange or clearing house concerned by notice in writing; and
    (b)   is enforceable, on the application of the Authority, by injunction or, in Scotland, by an order under section 45 of the Court of Session Act 1988.

(3)   The Authority's powers relating to market abuse are its powers—
    (a)   to impose penalties under section 123; or
    (b)   to appoint a person to conduct an investigation under section 168 in a case falling within subsection (2)(d) of that section.

[154]

129 Power of court to impose penalty in cases of market abuse

(1) The Authority may on an application to the court under section 381 or 383 request the court to consider whether the circumstances are such that a penalty should be imposed on the person to whom the application relates.

(2) The court may, if it considers it appropriate, make an order requiring the person concerned to pay to the Authority a penalty of such amount as it considers appropriate.

[155]

130 Guidance

(1) The Treasury may from time to time issue written guidance for the purpose of helping relevant authorities to determine the action to be taken in cases where behaviour occurs which is behaviour—
  (a) with respect to which the power in section 123 appears to be exercisable; and
  (b) which appears to involve the commission of an offence under section 397 of this Act or Part V of the Criminal Justice Act 1993 (insider dealing).

(2) The Treasury must obtain the consent of the Attorney General and the Secretary of State before issuing any guidance under this section.

(3) In this section "relevant authorities"—
  (a) in relation to England and Wales, means the Secretary of State, the Authority, the Director of the Serious Fraud Office and the Director of Public Prosecutions;
  (b) in relation to Northern Ireland, means the Secretary of State, the Authority, the Director of the Serious Fraud Office and the Director of Public Prosecutions for Northern Ireland.

(4) Subsections (1) to (3) do not apply to Scotland.

(5) In relation to Scotland, the Lord Advocate may from time to time, after consultation with the Treasury, issue written guidance for the purpose of helping the Authority to determine the action to be taken in cases where behaviour mentioned in subsection (1) occurs.

[156]

NOTES
Attorney General: any function of the Attorney General may be exercised by the Solicitor General; see the Law Officers Act 1997, s 1.

[130A Interpretation and supplementary provision

(1) The Treasury may by order specify (whether by name or description)—
  (a) the markets which are prescribed markets for the purposes of specified provisions of this Part, and
  (b) the investments that are qualifying investments in relation to the prescribed markets.

(2) An order may prescribe different investments or descriptions of investment in relation to different markets or descriptions of market.

(3) In this Part—
"accepted market practices" means practices that are reasonably expected in the financial market or markets in question and are accepted by the Authority or, in the case of a market situated in another EEA State, the competent authority of that EEA State within the meaning of Directive 2003/6/EC of the European Parliament and of the Council of 28 January 2003 on insider dealing and market manipulation (market abuse),
"behaviour" includes action or inaction,
"dealing", in relation to an investment, means acquiring or disposing of the investment whether as principal or agent or directly or indirectly, and includes agreeing to acquire or dispose of the investment, and entering into and bringing to an end a contract creating it,
"investment" is to be read with section 22 and Schedule 2,
"regular user", in relation to a particular market, means a reasonable person who regularly deals on that market in investments of the kind in question,
"related investment", in relation to a qualifying investment, means an investment whose price or value depends on the price or value of the qualifying investment.

(4) Any reference in this Act to a person engaged in market abuse is to a person engaged in market abuse either alone or with one or more other persons.]

[157]

NOTES
Commencement: 1 July 2005.
Inserted by the Financial Services and Markets Act 2000 (Market Abuse) Regulations 2005, SI 2005/381, reg 5, Sch 2, para 3, as from 1 July 2005.
Orders: see the note to s 118 at **[141]**.

131 Effect on transactions

The imposition of a penalty under this Part does not make any transaction void or unenforceable.

[158]

[131A Protected Disclosures

(1) A disclosure which satisfies the following three conditions is not to be taken to breach any restriction on the disclosure of information (however imposed).

(2) The first condition is that the information or other matter—
    (a) causes the person making the disclosure (the discloser) to know or suspect, or
    (b) gives him reasonable grounds for knowing or suspecting, that another person has engaged in market abuse.

(3) The second condition is that the information or other matter disclosed came to the discloser in the course of his trade, profession, business or employment.

(4) The third condition is that the disclosure is made to the Authority or to a nominated officer as soon as is practicable after the information or other matter comes to the discloser.

(5) A disclosure to a nominated officer is a disclosure which is made to a person nominated by the discloser's employer to receive disclosures under this section, and is made in the course of the discloser's employment and in accordance with the procedure established by the employer for the purpose.

(6) For the purposes of this section, references to a person's employer include any body, association or organisation (including a voluntary organisation) in connection with whose activities the person exercises a function (whether or not for gain or reward) and references to employment must be construed accordingly.]

[159]

NOTES
Commencement: 1 July 2005.
Inserted by the Financial Services and Markets Act 2000 (Market Abuse) Regulations 2005, SI 2005/381, reg 5, Sch 2, para 4, as from 1 July 2005.

PART IX
HEARINGS AND APPEALS

NOTES
By the Tribunals, Courts and Enforcement Act 2007, Sch 6, Pt 3, the Financial Services and Markets Tribunal is a 'scheduled tribunal' for the purposes of ss 30, 36 of that Act. For the powers of the Lord Chancellor to transfer a function of a scheduled tribunal to the First-tier Tribunal, Upper Tribunal, etc, to abolish the scheduled tribunal and transfer members etc, see ss 30, 31 of the 2007 Act; for powers relating to the transfer of powers to make procedural rules, see s 36 of that Act.
See also the Administrative Justice and Tribunals Council (Listed Tribunals) Order 2007, SI 2007/2951 (made under the Tribunals, Courts and Enforcement Act 2007, Sch 7, para 25(2)). The 2007 Act established the Administrative Justice and Tribunals Council (AJTC) to replace the Council on Tribunals and provides for the AJTC to keep under review, consider and report on matters relating to the listed tribunals. This Order provides that the Financial Services and Markets Tribunal is a listed tribunal for the purposes of the 2007 Act (except for its functions in respect of Northern Ireland).
As to the application of this Part (including Sch 13) to certain appeals to the Financial Services and Markets Tribunal made under the Money Laundering Regulations 2007, SI 2007/2157, see reg 44 of, and Sch 5, Pt 1, para 2 to, those Regulations at **[2877BR]**, **[2877CE]**.
As to the application of this Part to certain appeals under the Banking Act 2009, see s 202 of that Act (at **[1903Y]**).

132 The Financial Services and Markets Tribunal

(1) For the purposes of this Act, there is to be a tribunal known as the Financial Services and Markets Tribunal (but referred to in this Act as "the Tribunal").

(2) The Tribunal is to have the functions conferred on it by or under this Act.

(3) The Lord Chancellor may by rules make such provision as appears to him to be necessary or expedient in respect of the conduct of proceedings before the Tribunal.

(4) Schedule 13 is to have effect as respects the Tribunal and its proceedings (but does not limit the Lord Chancellor's powers under this section).

[160]

NOTES
Note: a reference in this section to this Act includes a reference to the Electronic Commerce Directive (Financial Services and Markets) Regulations 2002, SI 2002/1775; see reg 12(4) of those Regulations at **[2685]**.
Rules: the Financial Services and Markets Tribunal Rules 2001, SI 2001/2476 at **[2389]**.

133 Proceedings: general provision

(1)   A reference to the Tribunal under this Act must be made before the end of—
 (a)   the period of 28 days beginning with the date on which the decision notice or supervisory notice in question is given; or
 (b)   such other period as may be specified in rules made under section 132.

(2)   Subject to rules made under section 132, the Tribunal may allow a reference to be made after the end of that period.

(3)   On a reference the Tribunal may consider any evidence relating to the subject-matter of the reference, whether or not it was available to the Authority at the material time.

(4)   On a reference the Tribunal must determine what (if any) is the appropriate action for the Authority to take in relation to the matter referred to it.

(5)   On determining a reference, the Tribunal must remit the matter to the Authority with such directions (if any) as the Tribunal considers appropriate for giving effect to its determination.

(6)   In determining a reference made as a result of a decision notice, the Tribunal may not direct the Authority to take action which the Authority would not, as a result of section 388(2), have had power to take when giving the decision notice.

(7)   In determining a reference made as a result of a supervisory notice, the Tribunal may not direct the Authority to take action which would have otherwise required the giving of a decision notice.

(8)   The Tribunal may, on determining a reference, make recommendations as to the Authority's regulating provisions or its procedures.

(9)   The Authority must not take the action specified in a decision notice—
 (a)   during the period within which the matter to which the decision notice relates may be referred to the Tribunal; and
 (b)   if the matter is so referred, until the reference, and any appeal against the Tribunal's determination, has been finally disposed of.

(10)   The Authority must act in accordance with the determination of, and any direction given by, the Tribunal.

(11)   An order of the Tribunal may be enforced—
 (a)   as if it were an order of a county court; or
 (b)   in Scotland, as if it were an order of the Court of Session.

(12)   "Supervisory notice" has the same meaning as in section 395.

[161]

NOTES
Note: a reference in this section to this Act includes a reference to the Electronic Commerce Directive (Financial Services and Markets) Regulations 2002, SI 2002/1775; see reg 12(4) of those Regulations at **[2685]**.
Period of 28 days: note that any provision of this Act (other than a provision of Part VI) authorising or requiring a person to do anything within a specified number of days must not take into account any day which is a public holiday in any part of the United Kingdom; see s 417(3) at **[443]**.
References to the Tribunal: may be made under the following provision of this Act: ss 53(7) (read together with s 53(5)), 53(9) (read together with s 53(7)), 55(1), (2), 57(5), 58(5), 62(4), 63(5), 67(7), 76(6), 77(5), 78(3) (read together with ss 78(6) and 78(9)), 87N (in relation to notices given under ss 87K and 87M), 87O (in relation to matters under 87K and 87L), 89(4), 89N (in relation to matters under 89K and 89M), 92(7), 92C(2), 127(4), 185(7), 186(5), 187(4), 197(4) (read together with 197(8)), 200(5)(b), 208(4), 245(2)(b), 252(4), 255(2), 256(5), 259(4) (read together with 259(10)), 260(2)(b), 265(5), 268(4), (7) (read together with 268(10)), 269(3), 271(3)(b), 276(2)(b), 280(2)(b), 281 (read together with 282(4)), 282(6) (read together with 282(8)), 301C(8), 313A(2), 313B(3), 320(4), 321(10), (11), 334(9), 345(5), 386(3), 388(5), 393(9), (11), Sch 3, para 15A(6), Sch 3, para 19(12), Sch 3, para 20(4A), Sch 3, para 22(3)(b).

Legal assistance before the Tribunal

134 Legal assistance scheme

(1)   The Lord Chancellor may by regulations establish a scheme governing the provision of legal assistance in connection with proceedings before the Tribunal.

(2)   If the Lord Chancellor establishes a scheme under subsection (1), it must provide that a person is eligible for assistance only if—
 (a)   he falls within subsection (3); and
 (b)   he fulfils such other criteria (if any) as may be prescribed as a result of section 135(1)(d).

(3)   A person falls within this subsection if he is an individual who has referred a matter to the Tribunal under section 127(4).

(4)   In this Part of this Act "the legal assistance scheme" means any scheme in force under subsection (1).

[162]

NOTES
Regulations: the Financial Services and Markets Tribunal (Legal Assistance) Regulations 2001, SI 2001/3632 at **[2528]**; the Financial Services and Markets Tribunal (Legal Assistance Scheme—Costs) Regulations 2001, SI 2001/3633 at **[2571]**.

135   Provisions of the legal assistance scheme

(1)   The legal assistance scheme may, in particular, make provision as to—
   (a)   the kinds of legal assistance that may be provided;
   (b)   the persons by whom legal assistance may be provided;
   (c)   the manner in which applications for legal assistance are to be made;
   (d)   the criteria on which eligibility for legal assistance is to be determined;
   (e)   the persons or bodies by whom applications are to be determined;
   (f)   appeals against refusals of applications;
   (g)   the revocation or variation of decisions;
   (h)   its administration and the enforcement of its provisions.

(2)   Legal assistance under the legal assistance scheme may be provided subject to conditions or restrictions, including conditions as to the making of contributions by the person to whom it is provided.

[163]

NOTES
Regulations: the Financial Services and Markets Tribunal (Legal Assistance) Regulations 2001, SI 2001/3632 at **[2528]**; the Financial Services and Markets Tribunal (Legal Assistance Scheme—Costs) Regulations 2001, SI 2001/3633 at **[2571]**.

136   Funding of the legal assistance scheme

(1)   The Authority must pay to the Lord Chancellor such sums at such times as he may, from time to time, determine in respect of the anticipated or actual cost of legal assistance provided in connection with proceedings before the Tribunal under the legal assistance scheme.

(2)   In order to enable it to pay any sum which it is obliged to pay under subsection (1), the Authority must make rules requiring the payment to it by authorised persons or any class of authorised person of specified amounts or amounts calculated in a specified way.

(3)   Sums received by the Lord Chancellor under subsection (1) must be paid into the Consolidated Fund.

(4)   The Lord Chancellor must, out of money provided by Parliament fund the cost of legal assistance provided in connection with proceedings before the Tribunal under the legal assistance scheme.

(5)   Subsection (6) applies if, as respects a period determined by the Lord Chancellor, the amount paid to him under subsection (1) as respects that period exceeds the amount he has expended in that period under subsection (4).

(6)   The Lord Chancellor must—
   (a)   repay, out of money provided by Parliament, the excess to the Authority; or
   (b)   take the excess into account on the next occasion on which he makes a determination under subsection (1).

(7)   The Authority must make provision for any sum repaid to it under subsection (6)(a)—
   (a)   to be distributed among—
      (i)   the authorised persons on whom a levy was imposed in the period in question as a result of rules made under subsection (2); or
      (ii)   such of those persons as it may determine;
   (b)   to be applied in order to reduce any amounts which those persons, or such of them as it may determine, are or will be liable to pay to the Authority, whether under rules made under subsection (2) or otherwise; or
   (c)   to be partly so distributed and partly so applied.

(8)   If the Authority considers that it is not practicable to deal with any part of a sum repaid to it under subsection (6)(a) in accordance with provision made by it as a result of subsection (7), it may, with the consent the Lord Chancellor, apply or dispose of that part of that sum in such manner as it considers appropriate.

(9)   "Specified" means specified in the rules.

[164]

Appeals

137 Appeal on a point of law

(1) A party to a reference to the Tribunal may with permission appeal—
    (a) to the Court of Appeal, or
    (b) in Scotland, to the Court of Session,
on a point of law arising from a decision of the Tribunal disposing of the reference.

(2) "Permission" means permission given by the Tribunal or by the Court of Appeal or (in Scotland) the Court of Session.

(3) If, on an appeal under subsection (1), the court considers that the decision of the Tribunal was wrong in law, it may—
    (a) remit the matter to the Tribunal for rehearing and determination by it; or
    (b) itself make a determination.

(4) An appeal may not be brought from a decision of the Court of Appeal under subsection (3) except with the leave of—
    (a) the Court of Appeal; or
    (b) *the House of Lords.*

(5) An appeal lies, with the leave of the Court of Session or the *House of Lords*, from any decision of the Court of Session under this section, and such leave may be given on such terms as to costs, expenses or otherwise as the Court of Session or the *House of Lords* may determine.

(6) Rules made under section 132 may make provision for regulating or prescribing any matters incidental to or consequential on an appeal under this section.

[165]

NOTES

Sub-s (4): para (b) substituted by the Constitutional Reform Act 2005, s 40, Sch 9, Pt 1, para 70(a), as from a day to be appointed, as follows—
"(b) the Supreme Court.".

Sub-s (5): for the words in italics there are substituted the words "Supreme Court" by the Constitutional Reform Act 2005, s 40, Sch 9, Pt 1, para 70(b), as from a day to be appointed.
Rules: see the note to s 132 at **[160]**.

PART X
RULES AND GUIDANCE

CHAPTER I
RULE-MAKING POWERS

138 General rule-making power

(1) The Authority may make such rules applying to authorised persons—
    (a) with respect to the carrying on by them of regulated activities, or
    (b) with respect to the carrying on by them of activities which are not regulated activities,
as appear to it to be necessary or expedient for the purpose of protecting the interests of consumers.

[(1A) The Authority may also make such rules applying to authorised persons who are investment firms or credit institutions, with respect to the provision by them of a relevant ancillary service, as appear to the Authority to be necessary or expedient for the purpose of protecting the interests of consumers.

(1B) "Credit institution" means—
    (a) a credit institution authorised under the banking consolidation directive, or
    (b) an institution which would satisfy the requirements for authorisation as a credit institution under that directive if it had its registered office (or if it does not have a registered office, its head office) in an EEA State.

(1C) "Relevant ancillary service" means any service of a kind mentioned in Section B of Annex I to the markets in financial instruments directive the provision of which does not involve the carrying on of a regulated activity.]

(2) Rules made under this section are referred to in this Act as the Authority's general rules.

(3) The Authority's power to make general rules is not limited by any other power which it has to make regulating provisions.

(4) The Authority's general rules may make provision applying to authorised persons even though there is no relationship between the authorised persons to whom the rules will apply and the persons whose interests will be protected by the rules.

(5) General rules may contain requirements which take into account, in the case of an authorised person who is a member of a group, any activity of another member of the group.

(6)   General rules may not—
- (a)   make provision prohibiting an EEA firm from carrying on, or holding itself out as carrying on, any activity which it has permission conferred by Part II of Schedule 3 to carry on in the United Kingdom;
- (b)   make provision, as respects an EEA firm, about any matter responsibility for which is, under any of the single market directives, reserved to the firm's home state regulator.

(7)   "Consumers" means persons—
- (a)   who use, have used, or are or may be contemplating using, any of the services provided by—
  - (i)   authorised persons in carrying on regulated activities; …
  - [(ia)   authorised persons who are investment firms or credit institutions in providing a relevant ancillary service; or]
  - (ii)   persons acting as appointed representatives;
- (b)   who have rights or interests which are derived from, or are otherwise attributable to, the use of any such services by other persons; or
- (c)   who have rights or interests which may be adversely affected by the use of any such services by persons acting on their behalf or in a fiduciary capacity in relation to them.

(8)   If an authorised person is carrying on a regulated activity in his capacity as a trustee, the persons who are, have been or may be beneficiaries of the trust are to be treated as persons who use, have used or are or may be contemplating using services provided by the authorised person in his carrying on of that activity.

(9)   For the purposes of subsection (7) a person who deals with an authorised person in the course of the authorised person's carrying on of a regulated activity is to be treated as using services provided by the authorised person in carrying on those activities.

[166]

NOTES

Sub-ss (1A)–(1C): inserted by the Financial Services and Markets Act 2000 (Markets in Financial Instruments) (Modification of Powers) Regulations 2006, SI 2006/2975, regs 2, 3(a), as from 6 December 2006, subject to transitional provisions as noted below.

Sub-s (7): word omitted from para (a)(i) repealed, and para (a)(ia) inserted, by SI 2006/2975, regs 2, 3(b), as from 6 December 2006, subject to transitional provisions as noted below.

Transitional provisions: the Financial Services and Markets Act 2000 (Markets in Financial Instruments) (Modification of Powers) Regulations 2006, SI 2006/2975, reg 14 provides as follows—

"14   Transitional provision: rules under sections 138 and 145 of the Act

If, before these Regulations come into force—
- (a)   the Authority has taken any step mentioned in section 155 of the Act in relation to rules proposed to be made under section 138 or 145 of the Act as amended by these Regulations; and
- (b)   that step would have satisfied a requirement of section 155 in relation to those rules had it been taken after these Regulations come into force,

the step shall be treated as having satisfied that requirement of section 155.".

Modification (orders made under the Banking (Special Provisions) Act 2008); various orders made under the 2008 Act make modifications to the Authority's powers under this section so that rules made under them may apply to transfers made under ss 3 or 6 or 8 of the 2008 Act. See the Northern Rock plc Transfer Order 2008, SI 2008/432 at **[4128]**, the Bradford & Bingley plc Transfer of Securities and Property etc Order 2008, SI 2008/2546 at **[4227]**, the Heritable Bank plc Transfer of Certain Rights and Liabilities Order 2008, SI 2008/2644 at **[4272]**, the Transfer of Rights and Liabilities to ING Order 2008, SI 2008/2666 at **[4306]**, and the Kaupthing Singer & Friedlander Limited Transfer of Certain Rights and Liabilities Order 2008, SI 2008/2674 at **[4339]**.

Modification (consumer contract requirements: modification of rule-making power): the power to make rules conferred by this section is to be taken to include a power to make rules applying to unauthorised incoming providers. As a consequence, any reference in sub-ss (4), (5), (7)–(9) above, and in ss 148, 150, 156 of this Act to an authorised person includes a reference to an unauthorised incoming provider, and any reference to a regulated activity includes a reference to an incoming electronic commerce activity; see the Electronic Commerce Directive (Financial Services and Markets) Regulations 2002, SI 2002/1775, reg 3 at **[2676]**.

Modification of the meaning of "Consumers": the definition of "Consumers" in sub-s (7) has been extended by the Financial Services and Markets Act 2000 (Consequential and Transitional Provisions) (Miscellaneous) Order 2001, SI 2001/1821, art 3 (to include users of regulated services before commencement); and by the Financial Services and Markets Act 2000 (Consequential Amendments and Transitional Provisions) (Credit Unions) Order 2002, SI 2002/1501, art 4 (to include customers of credit unions before commencement). This "extended definition" also applies for the purposes of ss 5(3), 10(7), 14(5), 186(6) and 391, but does not apply for the purposes of Sch 4, para 1 (Treaty rights).

Rules: the Industrial Assurance (Premium Receipt Books) Regulations 1948, SI 1948/2770 have effect as if made as rules under this section by virtue of the Industrial Assurance and Friendly Societies Act 1948, s 8(2) (repealed) and the Financial Services and Markets Act 2000 (Transitional Provisions and Savings) (Rules) Order 2001, SI 2001/1534.

139 Miscellaneous ancillary matters

(1) Rules relating to the handling of money held by an authorised person in specified circumstances ("clients' money") may—

(a) make provision which results in that clients' money being held on trust in accordance with the rules;

(b) treat two or more accounts as a single account for specified purposes (which may include the distribution of money held in the accounts);

(c) authorise the retention by the authorised person of interest accruing on the clients' money; and

(d) make provision as to the distribution of such interest which is not to be retained by him.

(2) An institution with which an account is kept in pursuance of rules relating to the handling of clients' money does not incur any liability as constructive trustee if money is wrongfully paid from the account, unless the institution permits the payment—

(a) with knowledge that it is wrongful; or

(b) having deliberately failed to make enquiries in circumstances in which a reasonable and honest person would have done so.

(3) In the application of subsection (1) to Scotland, the reference to money being held on trust is to be read as a reference to its being held as agent for the person who is entitled to call for it to be paid over to him or to be paid on his direction or to have it otherwise credited to him.

(4) Rules may—

(a) confer rights on persons to rescind agreements with, or withdraw offers to, authorised persons within a specified period; and

(b) make provision, in respect of authorised persons and persons exercising those rights, for the restitution of property and the making or recovery of payments where those rights are exercised.

(5) "Rules" means general rules.

(6) "Specified" means specified in the rules.

[**167**]

140 Restriction on managers of [certain collective investment schemes]

[(1) The Authority may make rules prohibiting an authorised person who has permission to act as—

(a) the manager of an authorised unit trust scheme, or

(b) the management company of an authorised UCITS open-ended investment company, from carrying on a specified activity.]

(2) Such rules may specify an activity which is not a regulated activity.

[(3) In this section—

(a) "authorised UCITS open-ended investment company" means an authorised open-ended investment company to which the UCITS directive applies; and

(b) "management company" has the meaning given by Article 1a.2 of the UCITS directive.]

[**168**]

NOTES

Section heading: words in square brackets substituted by the Collective Investment Schemes (Miscellaneous Amendments) Regulations 2003, SI 2003/2066, reg 5(a), as from 13 February 2004.

Sub-s (1): substituted by SI 2003/2066, reg 5(b), as from 13 February 2004.

Sub-s (3): added by SI 2003/2066, reg 5(c), as from 13 February 2004.

Rules made by the Authority under this section and s 141 do not apply to incoming providers to the extent that they specify an activity which is an incoming electronic commerce activity; see the Electronic Commerce Directive (Financial Services and Markets) Regulations 2002, SI 2002/1775, reg 5 at [**2678**].

---

141 Insurance business rules

(1) The Authority may make rules prohibiting an authorised person who has permission to effect or carry out contracts of insurance from carrying on a specified activity.

(2) Such rules may specify an activity which is not a regulated activity.

(3) The Authority may make rules in relation to contracts entered into by an authorised person in the course of carrying on business which consists of the effecting or carrying out of contracts of long-term insurance.

(4) Such rules may, in particular—

(a) restrict the descriptions of property or indices of the value of property by reference to which the benefits under such contracts may be determined;

(b)   make provision, in the interests of the protection of policyholders, for the substitution of one description of property, or index of value, by reference to which the benefits under a contract are to be determined for another such description of property or index.

(5)   Rules made under this section are referred to in this Act as insurance business rules.

[169]

NOTES
Rules made by the Authority: see the note to s 140 at **[169]**.

142   Insurance business: regulations supplementing Authority's rules

(1)   The Treasury may make regulations for the purpose of preventing a person who is not an authorised person but who—
(a)   is a parent undertaking of an authorised person who has permission to effect or carry out contracts of insurance, and
(b)   falls within a prescribed class,
from doing anything to lessen the effectiveness of asset identification rules.

(2)   "Asset identification rules" means rules made by the Authority which require an authorised person who has permission to effect or carry out contracts of insurance to identify assets which belong to him and which are maintained in respect of a particular aspect of his business.

(3)   The regulations may, in particular, include provision—
(a)   prohibiting the payment of dividends;
(b)   prohibiting the creation of charges;
(c)   making charges created in contravention of the regulations void.

(4)   The Treasury may by regulations provide that, in prescribed circumstances, charges created in contravention of asset identification rules are void.

(5)   A person who contravenes regulations under subsection (1) is guilty of an offence and liable on summary conviction to a fine not exceeding level 5 on the standard scale.

(6)   "Charges" includes mortgages (or in Scotland securities over property).

[170]–[171]

143   *(Repealed by the Companies Act 2006, ss 964(1), (2), 1295, Sch 16, as from 6 April 2007.)*

Specific rules

144   Price stabilising rules

(1)   The Authority may make rules ("price stabilising rules") as to—
(a)   the circumstances and manner in which,
(b)   the conditions subject to which, and
(c)   the time when or the period during which,
action may be taken for the purpose of stabilising the price of investments of specified kinds.

(2)   Price stabilising rules—
(a)   are to be made so as to apply only to authorised persons;
(b)   may make different provision in relation to different kinds of investment.

(3)   The Authority may make rules which, for the purposes of section 397(5)(b), treat a person who acts or engages in conduct—
(a)   for the purpose of stabilising the price of investments, and
(b)   in conformity with such provisions corresponding to price stabilising rules and made by a body or authority outside the United Kingdom as may be specified in the rules under this subsection,
as acting, or engaging in that conduct, for that purpose and in conformity with price stabilising rules.

(4)   The Treasury may by order impose limitations on the power to make rules under this section.

(5)   Such an order may, in particular—
(a)   specify the kinds of investment in relation to which price stabilising rules may make provision;
(b)   specify the kinds of investment in relation to which rules made under subsection (3) may make provision;
(c)   provide for price stabilising rules to make provision for action to be taken for the purpose of stabilising the price of investments only in such circumstances as the order may specify;
(d)   provide for price stabilising rules to make provision for action to be taken for that purpose only at such times or during such periods as the order may specify.

(6)   If provisions specified in rules made under subsection (3) are altered, the rules continue to apply to those provisions as altered, but only if before the alteration the Authority has notified the body or authority concerned (and has not withdrawn its notification) that it is satisfied with its consultation procedures.

[(7)   "Consultation procedures" means procedures designed to provide an opportunity for persons likely to be affected by alterations to those provisions to make representations about proposed alterations to any of those provisions.]

[172]

NOTES

Sub-s (7): substituted by the Companies Act 2006, s 964(1), (3), as from 6 April 2007.

145   Financial promotion rules

(1)   The Authority may make rules applying to authorised persons about the communication by them, or their approval of the communication by others, of invitations or inducements—
(a)   to engage in investment activity; or
(b)   to participate in a collective investment scheme.

(2)   Rules under this section may, in particular, make provision about the form and content of communications.

(3)   Subsection (1) applies only to communications which—
(a)   if made by a person other than an authorised person, without the approval of an authorised person, would contravene section 21(1);
(b)   may be made by an authorised person without contravening section 238(1).

[(3A)   But subsection (3) does not prevent the Authority from making rules under subsection (1) in relation to a communication that would not contravene section 21(1) if made by a person other than an authorised person, without the approval of an authorised person, if the conditions set out in subsection (3B) are satisfied.

(3B)   Those conditions are—
(a)   that the communication would not contravene subsection (1) of section 21 because it is a communication to which that subsection does not apply as a result of an order under subsection (5) of that section;
(b)   that the Authority considers that any of the requirements of—
(i)   paragraphs 1 to 8 of Article 19 of the markets in financial instruments directive; or
(ii)   any implementing measure made under paragraph 10 of that Article,
apply to the communication; and
(c)   that the Authority considers that the rules are necessary to secure that the communication satisfies such of the requirements mentioned in paragraph (b) as the Authority considers apply to the communication.]

(4)   "Engage in investment activity" has the same meaning as in section 21.

(5)   The Treasury may by order impose limitations on the power to make rules under this section.

[173]

NOTES

Sub-ss (3A), (3B): inserted by the Financial Services and Markets Act 2000 (Markets in Financial Instruments) (Modification of Powers) Regulations 2006, SI 2006/2975, regs 2, 4, as from 6 December 2006, subject to transitional provisions as noted to s 138 at **[166]**.
Note: The FSA has made a number of legal instruments under this section which are reflected in its Handbook.

146   Money laundering rules

The Authority may make rules in relation to the prevention and detection of money laundering in connection with the carrying on of regulated activities by authorised persons.

[174]

NOTES

Note: From 2001–2005 the FSA made a number of legal instruments under this section which were reflected in its Handbook. However, with effect from 31 August 2006, the FSA has repealed these instruments, and the Money Laundering Sourcebook has been revoked in its entirety.

147   Control of information rules

(1)   The Authority may make rules ("control of information rules") about the disclosure and use of information held by an authorised person ("A").

(2)   Control of information rules may—

(a)   require the withholding of information which A would otherwise have to disclose to a person ("B") for or with whom A does business in the course of carrying on any regulated or other activity;

(b)   specify circumstances in which A may withhold information which he would otherwise have to disclose to B;

(c)   require A not to use for the benefit of B information A holds which A would otherwise have to use in that way;

(d)   specify circumstances in which A may decide not to use for the benefit of B information A holds which A would otherwise have to use in that way.

[175]

NOTES

Note: The FSA has made a number of legal instruments under this section which are reflected in its Handbook.

Modification or waiver

148   Modification or waiver of rules

(1)   ...

[(2)   The Authority may, on the application or with the consent of a person who is subject to rules made by the Authority, direct that all or any of those rules (other than rules made under section 247 (trust scheme rules) or section 248 (scheme particulars rules))—

(a)   are not to apply to that person; or

(b)   are to apply to him with such modifications as may be specified in the direction.]

(3)   An application must be made in such manner as the Authority may direct.

(4)   The Authority may not give a direction unless it is satisfied that—

(a)   compliance by the ... person with the rules, or with the rules as unmodified, would be unduly burdensome or would not achieve the purpose for which the rules were made; and

(b)   the direction would not result in undue risk to persons whose interests the rules are intended to protect.

(5)   A direction may be given subject to conditions.

(6)   Unless it is satisfied that it is inappropriate or unnecessary to do so, a direction must be published by the Authority in such a way as it thinks most suitable for bringing the direction to the attention of—

(a)   those likely to be affected by it; and

(b)   others who may be likely to make an application for a similar direction.

(7)   In deciding whether it is satisfied as mentioned in subsection (6), the Authority must—

(a)   take into account whether the direction relates to a rule contravention of which is actionable in accordance with section 150;

(b)   consider whether its publication would prejudice, to an unreasonable degree, the commercial interests of the ... person concerned or any other member of his immediate group; and

(c)   consider whether its publication would be contrary to an international obligation of the United Kingdom.

(8)   For the purposes of paragraphs (b) and (c) of subsection (7), the Authority must consider whether it would be possible to publish the direction without either of the consequences mentioned in those paragraphs by publishing it without disclosing the identity of the ... person concerned.

(9)   The Authority may—

(a)   revoke a direction; or

(b)   vary it on the application, or with the consent, of the ... person to whom it relates.

(10)   "Direction" means a direction under subsection (2).

(11)   "Immediate group", in relation to [a person] ("A"), means—

(a)   A;

(b)   a parent undertaking of A;

(c)   a subsidiary undertaking of A;

(d)   a subsidiary undertaking of a parent undertaking of A;

(e)   a parent undertaking of a subsidiary undertaking of A.

[176]

NOTES

Sub-s (1): repealed by the Regulatory Reform (Financial Services and Markets Act 2000) Order 2007, SI 2007/1973, arts 2, 10(a), as from 12 July 2007.

Sub-s (2): substituted by SI 2007/1973, arts 2, 10(b), as from 12 July 2007.

Sub-ss (4), (7)–(9): words omitted repealed by SI 2007/1973, arts 2, 10(c), as from 12 July 2007.

Sub-s (11): words in square brackets substituted by SI 2007/1973, arts 2, 10(d), as from 12 July 2007.

Transitional provisions: see the Financial Services and Markets Act 2000 (Transitional Provisions and Savings) (Rules) Order 2001, SI 2001/1534, Pt II, art 8. That Part concerns the power of the FSA to designate rules and legislative provisions which were repealed or lapsed at commencement so that they continue in effect after commencement as if they were rules made by the FSA. Art 8 carries forward any waiver or modification of the pre-commencement provision that was granted before commencement. See also the Financial Services and Markets Act 2000 (Consequential and Transitional Provisions) (Miscellaneous) (No 2) Order 2001, SI 2001/2659, art 3 which makes transitional modifications of certain provisions of this Act (including this one). For example, references to "authorised persons" are treated as referring to persons who will be authorised at commencement.

Modification (orders made under the Banking (Special Provisions) Act 2008); various orders made under the 2008 Act provide that sub-s (2) above applies to the bank that is the subject of that order (a) in the absence of an application by a person subject to rules made by the Authority; and (b) without any requirement for the consent of such a person. Furthermore, sub-s (4) above shall not prevent the Authority from modifying or waiving rules in relation to the bank under this section provided that it is satisfied that the modification or waiver is necessary for the purposes of, to facilitate or in consequence of the transfer. See the Northern Rock plc Transfer Order 2008, SI 2008/432 at **[4128]**, the Bradford & Bingley plc Transfer of Securities and Property etc Order 2008, SI 2008/2546 at **[4227]**, the Heritable Bank plc Transfer of Certain Rights and Liabilities Order 2008, SI 2008/2644 at **[4272]**, the Transfer of Rights and Liabilities to ING Order 2008, SI 2008/2666 at **[4306]**, and the Kaupthing Singer & Friedlander Limited Transfer of Certain Rights and Liabilities Order 2008, SI 2008/2674 at **[4339]**.

Modification (consumer contract requirements: modification of rule-making power): see the note to s 138 at **[166]**.

Application in relation to interim permissions and interim approvals: see the notes preceding s 40 at **[40]**.

Application of this section to financial conglomerates: see the Financial Conglomerates and Other Financial Groups Regulations 2004, SI 2004/1862, reg 4 at **[2726]**.

Application of this section to open-ended investment companies: see the Open-Ended Investment Companies Regulations 2001, SI 2001/1228, reg 7 at **[2244]**.

See also the Capital Requirements Regulations 2006, SI 2006/3221, regs 8, 9 at **[4029]**, **[4030]** (Exercise of functions under this section for the purpose of applying a decision or a joint decision).

Contravention of rules

149 Evidential provisions

(1) If a particular rule so provides, contravention of the rule does not give rise to any of the consequences provided for by other provisions of this Act.

(2) A rule which so provides must also provide—
  (a) that contravention may be relied on as tending to establish contravention of such other rule as may be specified; or
  (b) that compliance may be relied on as tending to establish compliance with such other rule as may be specified.

(3) A rule may include the provision mentioned in subsection (1) only if the Authority considers that it is appropriate for it also to include the provision required by subsection (2).

[177]

NOTES
Transitional provisions: as to the consequences of contravention of continued rules, see the Financial Services and Markets Act 2000 (Transitional Provisions and Savings) (Rules) Order 2001, SI 2001/1534, art 6.

150 Actions for damages

(1) A contravention by an authorised person of a rule is actionable at the suit of a private person who suffers loss as a result of the contravention, subject to the defences and other incidents applying to actions for breach of statutory duty.

(2) If rules so provide, subsection (1) does not apply to contravention of a specified provision of those rules.

(3) In prescribed cases, a contravention of a rule which would be actionable at the suit of a private person is actionable at the suit of a person who is not a private person, subject to the defences and other incidents applying to actions for breach of statutory duty.

(4) In subsections (1) and (3) "rule" does not include—
  (a) [Part 6 rules]; or
  (b) a rule requiring an authorised person to have or maintain financial resources.

(5) "Private person" has such meaning as may be prescribed.

[178]

NOTES
Sub-s (4): words in square brackets substituted by the Financial Services and Markets Act 2000 (Market Abuse) Regulations 2005, SI 2005/381, reg 6, as from 1 July 2005.

Modification (consumer contract requirements: modification of rule-making power): see the note to s 138 at **[166]**.

Regulations: the Financial Services and Markets Act 2000 (Rights of Action) Regulations 2001, SI 2001/2256 at **[2375]**; the Financial Services and Markets Act 2000 (Fourth Motor Insurance Directive) Regulations 2002, SI 2002/2706 at **[2690]**.

151   Limits on effect of contravening rules

(1)   A person is not guilty of an offence by reason of a contravention of a rule made by the Authority.

(2)   No such contravention makes any transaction void or unenforceable.

[179]

NOTES

Note: "Rule" is defined as a rule made by the FSA under this Act; see s 417 at **[443]**.

Procedural provisions

152   Notification of rules to the Treasury

(1)   If the Authority makes any rules, it must give a copy to the Treasury without delay.

(2)   If the Authority alters or revokes any rules, it must give written notice to the Treasury without delay.

(3)   Notice of an alteration must include details of the alteration.

[180]

153   Rule-making instruments

(1)   Any power conferred on the Authority to make rules is exercisable in writing.

(2)   An instrument by which rules are made by the Authority ("a rule-making instrument") must specify the provision under which the rules are made.

(3)   To the extent to which a rule-making instrument does not comply with subsection (2), it is void.

(4)   A rule-making instrument must be published by the Authority in the way appearing to the Authority to be best calculated to bring it to the attention of the public.

(5)   The Authority may charge a reasonable fee for providing a person with a copy of a rule-making instrument.

(6)   A person is not to be taken to have contravened any rule made by the Authority if he shows that at the time of the alleged contravention the rule-making instrument concerned had not been made available in accordance with this section.

[181]

154   Verification of rules

(1)   The production of a printed copy of a rule-making instrument purporting to be made by the Authority—
  (a)   on which is endorsed a certificate signed by a member of the Authority's staff authorised by it for that purpose, and
  (b)   which contains the required statements,
is evidence (or in Scotland sufficient evidence) of the facts stated in the certificate.

(2)   The required statements are—
  (a)   that the instrument was made by the Authority;
  (b)   that the copy is a true copy of the instrument; and
  (c)   that on a specified date the instrument was made available to the public in accordance with section 153(4).

(3)   A certificate purporting to be signed as mentioned in subsection (1) is to be taken to have been properly signed unless the contrary is shown.

(4)   A person who wishes in any legal proceedings to rely on a rule-making instrument may require the Authority to endorse a copy of the instrument with a certificate of the kind mentioned in subsection (1).

[182]

155   Consultation

(1)   If the Authority proposes to make any rules, it must publish a draft of the proposed rules in the way appearing to it to be best calculated to bring them to the attention of the public.

(2)   The draft must be accompanied by—
  (a)   a cost benefit analysis;
  (b)   an explanation of the purpose of the proposed rules;
  (c)   an explanation of the Authority's reasons for believing that making the proposed rules is compatible with its general duties under section 2; and

(d)   notice that representations about the proposals may be made to the Authority within a specified time.

(3)   In the case of a proposal to make rules under a provision mentioned in subsection (9), the draft must also be accompanied by details of the expected expenditure by reference to which the proposal is made.

(4)   Before making the proposed rules, the Authority must have regard to any representations made to it in accordance with subsection (2)(d).

(5)   If the Authority makes the proposed rules, it must publish an account, in general terms, of—
(a)   the representations made to it in accordance with subsection (2)(d); and
(b)   its response to them.

(6)   If the rules differ from the draft published under subsection (1) in a way which is, in the opinion of the Authority, significant—
(a)   the Authority must (in addition to complying with subsection (5)) publish details of the difference; and
(b)   those details must be accompanied by a cost benefit analysis.

(7)   Subsections (1) to (6) do not apply if the Authority considers that the delay involved in complying with them would be prejudicial to the interests of consumers.

(8)   Neither subsection (2)(a) nor subsection (6)(b) applies if the Authority considers—
(a)   that, making the appropriate comparison, there will be no increase in costs; or
(b)   that, making that comparison, there will be an increase in costs but the increase will be of minimal significance.

(9)   Neither subsection (2)(a) nor subsection (6)(b) requires a cost benefit analysis to be carried out in relation to rules made under—
(a)   section 136(2);
(b)   subsection (1) of section 213 as a result of subsection (4) of that section;
(c)   section 234;
(d)   paragraph 17 of Schedule 1.

(10)   "Cost benefit analysis" means an estimate of the costs together with an analysis of the benefits that will arise—
(a)   if the proposed rules are made; or
(b)   if subsection (6) applies, from the rules that have been made.

(11)   "The appropriate comparison" means—
(a)   in relation to subsection (2)(a), a comparison between the overall position if the rules are made and the overall position if they are not made;
(b)   in relation to subsection (6)(b), a comparison between the overall position after the making of the rules and the overall position before they were made.

(12)   The Authority may charge a reasonable fee for providing a person with a copy of a draft published under subsection (1).

[183]

NOTES
Modification (orders made under the Banking (Special Provisions) Act 2008); various orders made under the 2008 Act modify the application of this section in relation to rules made for the purposes of, or to facilitate, or in consequence of, a transfer under ss 3 or 6 or 8 of the 2008 Act. See the Northern Rock plc Transfer Order 2008, SI 2008/432 at **[4128]**, the Bradford & Bingley plc Transfer of Securities and Property etc Order 2008, SI 2008/2546 at **[4227]**, the Heritable Bank plc Transfer of Certain Rights and Liabilities Order 2008, SI 2008/2644 at **[4272]**, the Transfer of Rights and Liabilities to ING Order 2008, SI 2008/2666 at **[4306]**, and the Kaupthing Singer & Friedlander Limited Transfer of Certain Rights and Liabilities Order 2008, SI 2008/2674 at **[4339]**.
Application in relation to interim permissions and interim approvals: see the notes preceding s 40 at **[40]**.
Transitional provisions: see also the Compensation Act 2006 (Contribution for Mesothelioma Claims) Regulations 2006, SI 2006/3259, reg 4 (disapplication of this section in relation to the first occasion that the FSA makes rules or guidance in relation to mesothelioma claims, as from 7 December 2006).
Savings provision: see the Companies Act 2006, s 1266(2) which provides that the effectiveness for the purposes of this section of things done by the FSA before 8 November 2006 with a view to making transparency rules (as defined in ss 89A–89F of this Act as added by s 1266(1)) is not affected by the fact that those provisions were not then in force.

156   General supplementary powers

(1)   Rules made by the Authority may make different provision for different cases and may, in particular, make different provision in respect of different descriptions of authorised person, activity or investment.

(2)   Rules made by the Authority may contain such incidental, supplemental, consequential and transitional provision as the Authority considers appropriate.

[184]

NOTES

Modification (consumer contract requirements: modification of rule-making power): see the note to s 138 at **[166]**.

CHAPTER II
GUIDANCE

157 Guidance

(1)   The Authority may give guidance consisting of such information and advice as it considers appropriate—

  (a)   with respect to the operation of this Act and of any rules made under it;
  (b)   with respect to any matters relating to functions of the Authority;
  (c)   for the purpose of meeting the regulatory objectives;
  (d)   with respect to any other matters about which it appears to the Authority to be desirable to give information or advice.

(2)   The Authority may give financial or other assistance to persons giving information or advice of a kind which the Authority could give under this section.

(3)   If the Authority proposes to give guidance to regulated persons generally, or to a class of regulated person, in relation to rules to which those persons are subject, [subsections (1), (2)(d) and (4) of section 155 apply to the proposed guidance as they apply to proposed rules, unless the Authority considers that the delay in complying with them would be prejudicial to the interests of consumers].

(4)   The Authority may—

  (a)   publish its guidance;
  (b)   offer copies of its published guidance for sale at a reasonable price; and
  (c)   if it gives guidance in response to a request made by any person, make a reasonable charge for that guidance.

(5)   In this Chapter [(except in section 158A)], references to guidance given by the Authority include references to any recommendation made by the Authority to persons generally, to regulated persons generally or to any class of regulated person.

(6)   "Regulated person" means any—

  (a)   authorised person;
  (b)   person who is otherwise subject to rules made by the Authority.

[185]

NOTES

Sub-s (3): words in square brackets substituted by the Regulatory Reform (Financial Services and Markets Act 2000) Order 2007, SI 2007/1973, arts 2, 13, as from 12 July 2007.

Sub-s (5): words in square brackets inserted by the Financial Services and Markets Act 2000 (Markets in Financial Instruments) (Modification of Powers) Regulations 2006, SI 2006/2975, regs 2, 5, as from 6 December 2006.

Modification (orders made under the Banking (Special Provisions) Act 2008); various orders made under the 2008 Act modify the application of this section in relation to guidance made for the purposes of, or to facilitate, or in consequence of, a transfer under ss 3 or 6 or 8 of the 2008 Act. See the Northern Rock plc Transfer Order 2008, SI 2008/432 at **[4128]**, the Bradford & Bingley plc Transfer of Securities and Property etc Order 2008, SI 2008/2546 at **[4227]**, the Heritable Bank plc Transfer of Certain Rights and Liabilities Order 2008, SI 2008/2644 at **[4272]**, the Transfer of Rights and Liabilities to ING Order 2008, SI 2008/2666 at **[4306]**, and the Kaupthing Singer & Friedlander Limited Transfer of Certain Rights and Liabilities Order 2008, SI 2008/2674 at **[4339]**.

Regulated person: for the purposes of sub-s (3) (guidance to regulated persons generally), guidance given to building societies, friendly societies and industrial and provident societies generally or to a class of such societies is to be treated as if given to regulated persons generally or to a class of regulated persons, whether or not those societies would otherwise be "regulated persons" within the meaning of this section; see the Financial Services and Markets Act 2000 (Mutual Societies) Order 2001, SI 2001/2617, Sch 2, para 12 et seq at **[2459]**.

Application in relation to interim permissions and interim approvals: see the notes preceding s 40 at **[40]**.

Transitional provisions: see also the Compensation Act 2006 (Contribution for Mesothelioma Claims) Regulations 2006, SI 206/3259, reg 4 (disapplication of sub-s (3) in relation to the first occasion that the FSA makes rules or guidance in relation to mesothelioma claims, as from 7 December 2006).

158 Notification of guidance to the Treasury

(1)   On giving any general guidance, the Authority must give the Treasury a copy of the guidance without delay.

(2)   If the Authority alters any of its general guidance, it must give written notice to the Treasury without delay.

(3)   The notice must include details of the alteration.

(4)   If the Authority revokes any of its general guidance, it must give written notice to the Treasury without delay.

(5)   "General guidance" means guidance given by the Authority under section 157 which is—
    (a)   given to persons generally, to regulated persons generally or to a class of regulated person;
    (b)   intended to have continuing effect; and
    (c)   given in writing or other legible form.

(6)   "Regulated person" has the same meaning as in section 157.

[186]

NOTES

Regulated person: for the purposes of sub-s (5) (guidance to regulated persons generally), guidance given to building societies, friendly societies and industrial and provident societies generally or to a class of such societies is to be treated as if given to regulated persons generally or to a class of regulated persons, whether or not those societies would otherwise be "regulated persons" within the meaning of this section; see the Financial Services and Markets Act 2000 (Mutual Societies) Order 2001, SI 2001/2617, Sch 2, para 12 et seq at **[2459]**.

[158A   Guidance on outsourcing by investment firms and credit institutions

(1)   Without prejudice to the generality of section 157, the Authority must give guidance in the terms required by Article 15(3) of Commission Directive 2006/73/EC of 10 August 2006 (requirement to publish statement of policy on outsourcing of investment services by investment firms and credit institutions).

(2)   Subsections (1), (2)(b) and (d), (4), (5), (6)(a) and (7) of section 155 apply to guidance which the Authority is required to give under this section as they apply to proposed rules.

(3)   The Authority must publish its guidance under this section.

(4)   The Authority may offer copies of the published guidance for sale at a reasonable price.

(5)   Subsections (1) to (4) of section 158 apply to guidance under this section as they apply to general guidance (as defined by section 158(5)).]

[186A]

NOTES

Commencement: 6 December 2006.

Inserted by the Financial Services and Markets Act 2000 (Markets in Financial Instruments) (Modification of Powers) Regulations 2006, SI 2006/2975, regs 2, 6, as from 6 December 2006, subject to transitional provisions as noted below.

Transitional provisions: the Financial Services and Markets Act 2000 (Markets in Financial Instruments) (Modification of Powers) Regulations 2006, SI 2006/2975, reg 15 provides as follows:

"15   Transitional provision: guidance on outsourcing by investment firms and credit institutions

If, before these Regulations come into force—
    (a)   the Authority has taken any step mentioned in subsection (2) of section 158A of the Act (inserted by these Regulations) in relation to guidance of the sort referred to in subsection (1) of that section; and
    (b)   that step would have satisfied a requirement of section 158A(2) in relation to that guidance had it been taken after these Regulations come into force,

the step shall be treated as having satisfied that requirement."

CHAPTER III
COMPETITION SCRUTINY

159   Interpretation

(1)   In this Chapter—
    ["OFT" means the Office of Fair Trading;]
    "practices", in relation to the Authority, means practices adopted by the Authority in the exercise of functions under this Act;
    "regulating provisions" means any—
        (a)   rules;
        (b)   general guidance (as defined by section 158(5)) [or guidance under section 158A];
        (c)   statement issued by the Authority under section 64;
        (d)   code issued by the Authority under section 64 or 119.

(2)   For the purposes of this Chapter, regulating provisions or practices have a significantly adverse effect on competition if—
    (a)   they have, or are intended or likely to have, that effect; or
    (b)   the effect that they have, or are intended or likely to have, is to require or encourage behaviour which has, or is intended or likely to have, a significantly adverse effect on competition.

(3)   If regulating provisions or practices have, or are intended or likely to have, the effect of requiring or encouraging exploitation of the strength of a market position they are to be taken, for the purposes of this Chapter, to have an adverse effect on competition.

(4)   In determining under this Chapter whether any of the regulating provisions have, or are likely to have, a particular effect, it may be assumed that the persons to whom the provisions concerned are addressed will act in accordance with them.

[187]

NOTES
Sub-s (1): definition in square brackets substituted by the Enterprise Act 2002, s 278(1), Sch 25, para 40(1), (2), as from 1 April 2003; words in square brackets in para (b) of definition "regulating provisions" inserted by the Financial Services and Markets Act 2000 (Markets in Financial Instruments) (Modification of Powers) Regulations 2006, SI 2006/2975, regs 2, 7, as from 6 December 2006.

160   Reports by [OFT]

(1)   The [OFT] must keep the regulating provisions and the Authority's practices under review.

(2)   If at any time the [OFT] considers that—
   (a)   a regulating provision or practice has a significantly adverse effect on competition, or
   (b)   two or more regulating provisions or practices taken together, or a particular combination of regulating provisions and practices, have such an effect,
[the OFT] must make a report to that effect.

(3)   If at any time the [OFT] considers that—
   (a)   a regulating provision or practice does not have a significantly adverse effect on competition, or
   (b)   two or more regulating provisions or practices taken together, or a particular combination of regulating provisions and practices, do not have any such effect,
[the OFT] may make a report to that effect.

(4)   A report under subsection (2) must include details of the adverse effect on competition.

(5)   If the [OFT] makes a report under subsection (2) [the OFT] must—
   (a)   send a copy of it to the Treasury, the Competition Commission and the Authority; and
   (b)   publish it in the way appearing to [it] to be best calculated to bring it to the attention of the public.

(6)   If the [OFT] makes a report under subsection (3)—
   (a)   [the OFT] must send a copy of it to the Treasury, the Competition Commission and the Authority; and
   (b)   [the OFT] may publish it.

(7)   Before publishing a report under this section the [OFT] must, so far as practicable, exclude any matter which relates to the private affairs of a particular individual the publication of which, in the opinion of the [OFT], would or might seriously and prejudicially affect his interests.

(8)   Before publishing such a report the [OFT] must, so far as practicable, exclude any matter which relates to the affairs of a particular body the publication of which, in the opinion of the [OFT], would or might seriously and prejudicially affect its interests.

(9)   Subsections (7) and (8) do not apply in relation to copies of a report which the [OFT] is required to send under subsection (5)(a) or (6)(a).

(10)   For the purposes of the law of defamation, absolute privilege attaches to any report of the [OFT] under this section.

[188]

NOTES
Words in square brackets substituted by the Enterprise Act 2002, s 278(1), Sch 25, para 40(1), (3), as from 1 April 2003.

161   Power of [OFT] to request information

(1)   For the purpose of investigating any matter with a view to its consideration under section 160, the [OFT] may exercise the powers conferred on [it] by this section.

(2)   The [OFT] may by notice in writing require any person to produce to [it] or to a person appointed by [it] for the purpose, at a time and place specified in the notice, any document which—
   (a)   is specified or described in the notice; and
   (b)   is a document in that person's custody or under his control.

(3)   The [OFT] may by notice in writing—
   (a)   require any person carrying on any business to provide [it] with such information as may be specified or described in the notice; and

(b)   specify the time within which, and the manner and form in which, any such information is to be provided.

(4)   A requirement may be imposed under subsection (2) or (3)(a) only in respect of documents or information which relate to any matter relevant to the investigation.

(5)   If a person ("the defaulter") refuses, or otherwise fails, to comply with a notice under this section, the [OFT] may certify that fact in writing to the court and the court may enquire into the case.

(6)   If, after hearing any witness who may be produced against or on behalf of the defaulter and any statement which may be offered in defence, the court is satisfied that the defaulter did not have a reasonable excuse for refusing or otherwise failing to comply with the notice, the court may deal with the defaulter as if he were in contempt.

(7)   "Court" means—
    (a)   the High Court; or
    (b)   in relation to Scotland, the Court of Session.

[189]

NOTES
Words in square brackets substituted by the Enterprise Act 2002, s 278(1), Sch 25, para 40(1), (4), as from 1 April 2003.

162 Consideration by Competition Commission

(1)   If the [OFT]—
    (a)   makes a report under section 160(2), or
    (b)   asks the Commission to consider a report that [the OFT] has made under section 160(3), the Commission must investigate the matter.

(2)   The Commission must then make its own report on the matter unless it considers that, as a result of a change of circumstances, no useful purpose would be served by a report.

(3)   If the Commission decides in accordance with subsection (2) not to make a report, it must make a statement setting out the change of circumstances which resulted in that decision.

(4)   A report made under this section must state the Commission's conclusion as to whether—
    (a)   the regulating provision or practice which is the subject of the report has a significantly adverse effect on competition; or
    (b)   the regulating provisions or practices, or combination of regulating provisions and practices, which are the subject of the report have such an effect.

(5)   A report under this section stating the Commission's conclusion that there is a significantly adverse effect on competition must also—
    (a)   state whether the Commission considers that that effect is justified; and
    (b)   if it states that the Commission considers that it is not justified, state its conclusion as to what action, if any, ought to be taken by the Authority.

(6)   Subsection (7) applies whenever the Commission is considering, for the purposes of this section, whether a particular adverse effect on competition is justified.

(7)   The Commission must ensure, so far as that is reasonably possible, that the conclusion it reaches is compatible with the functions conferred, and obligations imposed, on the Authority by or under this Act.

(8)   A report under this section must contain such an account of the Commission's reasons for its conclusions as is expedient, in the opinion of the Commission, for facilitating proper understanding of them.

(9)   Schedule 14 supplements this section.

(10)   If the Commission makes a report under this section it must send a copy to the Treasury, the Authority and the [OFT].

[190]

NOTES
Sub-ss (1), (10): words in square brackets substituted by the Enterprise Act 2002, s 278(1), Sch 25, para 40(1), (5), as from 1 April 2003.
Investigations by the Competition Commission: for special rules of procedure in connection with investigations by the Competition Commission under this section and s 306 *post*, see the Competition Act 1998, s 45(7), and Sch 7, para 19A, Sch 7A to that Act at [1241]–[1243].

163 Role of the Treasury

(1)   This section applies if the Competition Commission makes a report under section 162(2) which states its conclusion that there is a significantly adverse effect on competition.

(2)   If the Commission's conclusion, as stated in the report, is that the adverse effect on competition is not justified, the Treasury must give a direction to the Authority requiring it to take such action as may be specified in the direction.

(3)   But subsection (2) does not apply if the Treasury consider—
(a)   that, as a result of action taken by the Authority in response to the Commission's report, it is unnecessary for them to give a direction; or
(b)   that the exceptional circumstances of the case make it inappropriate or unnecessary for them to do so.

(4)   In considering the action to be specified in a direction under subsection (2), the Treasury must have regard to any conclusion of the Commission included in the report because of section 162(5)(b).

(5)   Subsection (6) applies if—
(a)   the Commission's conclusion, as stated in its report, is that the adverse effect on competition is justified; but
(b)   the Treasury consider that the exceptional circumstances of the case require them to act.

(6)   The Treasury may give a direction to the Authority requiring it to take such action—
(a)   as they consider to be necessary in the light of the exceptional circumstances of the case; and
(b)   as may be specified in the direction.

(7)   The Authority may not be required as a result of this section to take any action—
(a)   that it would not have power to take in the absence of a direction under this section; or
(b)   that would otherwise be incompatible with any of the functions conferred, or obligations imposed, on it by or under this Act.

(8)   Subsection (9) applies if the Treasury are considering—
(a)   whether subsection (2) applies and, if so, what action is to be specified in a direction under that subsection; or
(b)   whether to give a direction under subsection (6).

(9)   The Treasury must—
(a)   do what they consider appropriate to allow the Authority, and any other person appearing to the Treasury to be affected, an opportunity to make representations; and
(b)   have regard to any such representations.

(10)   If, in reliance on subsection (3)(a) or (b), the Treasury decline to act under subsection (2), they must make a statement to that effect, giving their reasons.

(11)   If the Treasury give a direction under this section they must make a statement giving—
(a)   details of the direction; and
(b)   if the direction is given under subsection (6), their reasons for giving it.

(12)   The Treasury must—
(a)   publish any statement made under this section in the way appearing to them best calculated to bring it to the attention of the public; and
(b)   lay a copy of it before Parliament.

[191]

164   The Competition Act 1998

(1)   The Chapter I prohibition does not apply to an agreement the parties to which consist of or include—
(a)   an authorised person, or
(b)   a person who is otherwise subject to the Authority's regulating provisions,
to the extent to which the agreement consists of provisions the inclusion of which in the agreement is encouraged by any of the Authority's regulating provisions.

(2)   The Chapter I prohibition does not apply to the practices of an authorised person or a person who is otherwise subject to the regulating provisions to the extent to which the practices are encouraged by any of the Authority's regulating provisions.

(3)   The Chapter II prohibition does not apply to conduct of—
(a)   an authorised person, or
(b)   a person who is otherwise subject to the Authority's regulating provisions,
to the extent to which the conduct is encouraged by any of the Authority's regulating provisions.

(4)   "The Chapter I prohibition" means the prohibition imposed by section 2(1) of the Competition Act 1998.

(5)   "The Chapter II prohibition" means the prohibition imposed by section 18(1) of that Act.
[192]

PART XI
INFORMATION GATHERING AND INVESTIGATIONS

Powers to gather information

165 Authority's power to require information

(1)   The Authority may, by notice in writing given to an authorised person, require him—
   (a)   to provide specified information or information of a specified description; or
   (b)   to produce specified documents or documents of a specified description.

(2)   The information or documents must be provided or produced—
   (a)   before the end of such reasonable period as may be specified; and
   (b)   at such place as may be specified.

(3)   An officer who has written authorisation from the Authority to do so may require an authorised person without delay—
   (a)   to provide the officer with specified information or information of a specified description; or
   (b)   to produce to him specified documents or documents of a specified description.

(4)   This section applies only to information and documents reasonably required in connection with the exercise by the Authority of functions conferred on it by or under this Act.

(5)   The Authority may require any information provided under this section to be provided in such form as it may reasonably require.

(6)   The Authority may require—
   (a)   any information provided, whether in a document or otherwise, to be verified in such manner, or
   (b)   any document produced to be authenticated in such manner,
as it may reasonably require.

(7)   The powers conferred by subsections (1) and (3) may also be exercised to impose requirements on—
   (a)   a person who is connected with an authorised person;
   (b)   an operator, trustee or depositary of a scheme recognised under section 270 or 272 who is not an authorised person;
   (c)   a recognised investment exchange or recognised clearing house.

(8)   "Authorised person" includes a person who was at any time an authorised person but who has ceased to be an authorised person.

(9)   "Officer" means an officer of the Authority and includes a member of the Authority's staff or an agent of the Authority.

(10)   "Specified" means—
   (a)   in subsections (1) and (2), specified in the notice; and
   (b)   in subsection (3), specified in the authorisation.

(11)   For the purposes of this section, a person is connected with an authorised person ("A") if he is or has at any relevant time been—
   (a)   a member of A's group;
   (b)   a controller of A;
   (c)   any other member of a partnership of which A is a member; or
   (d)   in relation to A, a person mentioned in Part I of Schedule 15.

[193]

NOTES
Transitional provisions: this section and ss 166, 167 are modified by the Financial Services and Markets Act 2000 (Transitional Provisions and Savings) (Civil Remedies, Discipline, Criminal Offences etc) (No 2) Order 2001, SI 2001/3083, arts 15–17, so that the powers conferred by ss 165–167 are exercisable in respect of any person who was, before 1 December 2001, a regulated person but who is not, and never has been, an authorised person under this Act. See also the Financial Services and Markets Act 2000 (Consequential and Transitional Provisions) (Miscellaneous) (No 2) Order 2001, SI 2001/2659 (modifications of this section (having effect until 1 December 2001) to enable the FSA to exercise its powers under this section in relation to information or documents which are reasonably required in connection with the exercise by it of functions which it has reasonable grounds to believe will be conferred on it by or under the Act or, in the case of persons who are not regulated under existing legislation, functions which will be conferred on the Authority at commencement by the Financial Services and Markets Act 2000 (Transitional Provisions and Savings) (Civil Remedies, Discipline, Criminal Offences etc) Order 2001 (SI 2001/2657)).
Note: any reference in this section, and in ss 166–168 and 176 to an authorised person includes a reference to an unauthorised incoming provider; see the Electronic Commerce Directive (Financial Services and Markets) Regulations 2002, SI 2002/1775, reg 12(3) at **[2685]**.
See also the Banking Act 2009, s 250 (at **[1904W]**) which provides that the FSA shall collect information that it thinks is or may be relevant to the stability of individual financial institutions, or one or more aspects of the financial systems of the UK.

166 Reports by skilled persons

(1)   The Authority may, by notice in writing given to a person to whom subsection (2) applies, require him to provide the Authority with a report on any matter about which the Authority has required or could require the provision of information or production of documents under section 165.

(2)   This subsection applies to—
- (a)   an authorised person ("A"),
- (b)   any other member of A's group,
- (c)   a partnership of which A is a member, or
- (d)   a person who has at any relevant time been a person falling within paragraph (a), (b) or (c),

who is, or was at the relevant time, carrying on a business.

(3)   The Authority may require the report to be in such form as may be specified in the notice.

(4)   The person appointed to make a report required by subsection (1) must be a person—
- (a)   nominated or approved by the Authority; and
- (b)   appearing to the Authority to have the skills necessary to make a report on the matter concerned.

(5)   It is the duty of any person who is providing (or who at any time has provided) services to a person to whom subsection (2) applies in relation to a matter on which a report is required under subsection (1) to give a person appointed to provide such a report all such assistance as the appointed person may reasonably require.

(6)   The obligation imposed by subsection (5) is enforceable, on the application of the Authority, by an injunction or, in Scotland, by an order for specific performance under section 45 of the Court of Session Act 1988.

[194]

NOTES

Transitional provisions: see the note to s 165 at **[193]**.
Authorised person: see the note to s 165 at **[193]**.

Appointment of investigators

167 Appointment of persons to carry out general investigations

(1)   If it appears to the Authority or the Secretary of State ("the investigating authority") that there is good reason for doing so, the investigating authority may appoint one or more competent persons to conduct an investigation on its behalf into—
- (a)   the nature, conduct or state of the business of [a recognised investment exchange or] an authorised person or of an appointed representative;
- (b)   a particular aspect of that business; or
- (c)   the ownership or control of [a recognised investment exchange or] an authorised person.

(2)   If a person appointed under subsection (1) thinks it necessary for the purposes of his investigation, he may also investigate the business of a person who is or has at any relevant time been—
- (a)   a member of the group of which the person under investigation ("A") is part; or
- (b)   a partnership of which A is a member.

(3)   If a person appointed under subsection (1) decides to investigate the business of any person under subsection (2) he must give that person written notice of his decision.

(4)   The power conferred by this section may be exercised in relation to a former authorised person (or appointed representative) but only in relation to—
- (a)   business carried on at any time when he was an authorised person (or appointed representative); or
- (b)   the ownership or control of a former authorised person at any time when he was an authorised person.

(5)   "Business" includes any part of a business even if it does not consist of carrying on regulated activities.

[(6)   References in subsection (1) to a recognised investment exchange do not include references to an overseas investment exchange (as defined by section 313(1)).]

[195]

NOTES

Sub-s (1): words in square brackets inserted by the Financial Services and Markets Act 2000 (Markets in Financial Instruments) Regulations 2007, SI 2007/126, reg 3(5), Sch 5, paras 1, 7(a), as from 1 April 2007 (certain purposes (see reg 1(2) at **[4051]**)), and as from 1 November 2007 (otherwise).

Sub-s (6): added by SI 2007/126, reg 3(5), Sch 5, paras 1, 7(b), as from 1 April 2007 (certain purposes (see reg 1(2) at **[4051]**)), and as from 1 November 2007 (otherwise).

Transitional provisions: see the note to s 165 at **[193]**.
Authorised person: see the note to s 165 at **[193]**.

168 Appointment of persons to carry out investigations in particular cases

(1) Subsection (3) applies if it appears to an investigating authority that there are circumstances suggesting that—

(a) a person may have contravened any regulation made under section 142; or

(b) a person may be guilty of an offence under section 177, 191, 346 or 398(1) or under Schedule 4.

(2) Subsection (3) also applies if it appears to an investigating authority that there are circumstances suggesting that—

(a) an offence under section 24(1) or 397 or under Part V of the Criminal Justice Act 1993 may have been committed;

(b) there may have been a breach of the general prohibition;

(c) there may have been a contravention of section 21 or 238; or

(d) market abuse may have taken place.

(3) The investigating authority may appoint one or more competent persons to conduct an investigation on its behalf.

(4) Subsection (5) applies if it appears to the Authority that there are circumstances suggesting that—

(a) a person may have contravened section 20;

(b) a person may be guilty of an offence under prescribed regulations relating to money laundering;

[(ba) a person may be guilty of an offence under Schedule 7 to the Counter-Terrorism Act 2008 (terrorist financing or money laundering);]

(c) an authorised person may have contravened a rule made by the Authority;

(d) an individual may not be a fit and proper person to perform functions in relation to a regulated activity carried on by an authorised or exempt person;

(e) an individual may have performed or agreed to perform a function in breach of a prohibition order;

(f) an authorised or exempt person may have failed to comply with section 56(6);

(g) an authorised person may have failed to comply with section 59(1) or (2);

(h) a person in relation to whom the Authority has given its approval under section 59 may not be a fit and proper person to perform the function to which that approval relates; ...

(i) a person may be guilty of misconduct for the purposes of section 66[; or

(j) a person may have contravened any provision made by or under this Act for the purpose of implementing the markets in financial instruments directive or by any directly applicable Community regulation made under that directive].

(5) The Authority may appoint one or more competent persons to conduct an investigation on its behalf.

(6) "Investigating authority" means the Authority or the Secretary of State.

[196]

NOTES
Sub-s (4): para (ba) inserted by the Counter-Terrorism Act 2008, s 62, Sch 7, Pt 7, para 33(3), as from 27 November 2008; word omitted from para (h) repealed, and para (j) and the word immediately preceding it inserted, by the Financial Services and Markets Act 2000 (Markets in Financial Instruments) Regulations 2007, SI 2007/126, reg 3(5), Sch 5, paras 1, 8, as from 1 April 2007 (certain purposes (see reg 1(2) at **[4051]**)), and as from 1 November 2007 (otherwise).
Transitional provisions: see the Financial Services and Markets Act 2000 (Transitional Provisions and Savings) (Civil Remedies, Discipline, Criminal Offences etc) (No 2) Order 2001, SI 2001/3083, art 18 which modifies this section so it applies where there are circumstances suggesting that a person has contravened, or committed an offence under, certain enactments, provisions or rules before commencement.
Note: the Money Laundering Regulations 2007, SI 2007/2157 are prescribed for the purposes of sub-s (4)(b) above by reg 1(2) of those Regulations (at **[2877AA]**). The Transfer of Funds (Information on the Payer) Regulations 2007, SI 2007/3298 are also prescribed for the purposes of sub-s (4)(b) above by reg 1(2) of those Regulations (at **[2878]**).
Note: the reference in sub-s (4)(c) above to a rule made by the Authority includes a reference to a requirement imposed by the Authority under the Electronic Commerce Directive (Financial Services and Markets) Regulations 2002, SI 2002/1775; see reg 12(5) of those Regulations at **[2685]**.
Authorised person: see the note to s 165 at **[193]**.
Extension of powers (civil sanctions): where, by virtue of sub-s (4)(b) above, a Minister of the Crown (or the Welsh Ministers) has the power by statutory instrument to make provision creating a criminal offence and the power has been or is being exercised so as to create the offence, then that power is extended so as to include the power to confer on certain persons the power to impose civil sanctions in relation to the offence; see the Regulatory Enforcement and Sanctions Act 2008, s 62, Sch 7
Regulations: the Money Laundering Regulations 2007, SI 2007/2157 at **[2877AA]**; the Transfer of Funds (Information on the Payer) Regulations 2007, SI 2007/3298 at **[2878]**.

Assistance to overseas regulators

169 Investigations etc in support of overseas regulator

(1)   At the request of an overseas regulator, the Authority may—
   (a)   exercise the power conferred by section 165; or
   (b)   appoint one or more competent persons to investigate any matter.

(2)   An investigator has the same powers as an investigator appointed under section 168(3) (as a result of subsection (1) of that section).

(3)   If the request has been made by a competent authority in pursuance of any Community obligation the Authority must, in deciding whether or not to exercise its investigative power, consider whether its exercise is necessary to comply with any such obligation.

(4)   In deciding whether or not to exercise its investigative power, the Authority may take into account in particular—
   (a)   whether in the country or territory of the overseas regulator concerned, corresponding assistance would be given to a United Kingdom regulatory authority;
   (b)   whether the case concerns the breach of a law, or other requirement, which has no close parallel in the United Kingdom or involves the assertion of a jurisdiction not recognised by the United Kingdom;
   (c)   the seriousness of the case and its importance to persons in the United Kingdom;
   (d)   whether it is otherwise appropriate in the public interest to give the assistance sought.

(5)   The Authority may decide that it will not exercise its investigative power unless the overseas regulator undertakes to make such contribution towards the cost of its exercise as the Authority considers appropriate.

(6)   Subsections (4) and (5) do not apply if the Authority considers that the exercise of its investigative power is necessary to comply with a Community obligation.

(7)   If the Authority has appointed an investigator in response to a request from an overseas regulator, it may direct the investigator to permit a representative of that regulator to attend, and take part in, any interview conducted for the purposes of the investigation.

(8)   A direction under subsection (7) is not to be given unless the Authority is satisfied that any information obtained by an overseas regulator as a result of the interview will be subject to safeguards equivalent to those contained in Part XXIII.

(9)   The Authority must prepare a statement of its policy with respect to the conduct of interviews in relation to which a direction under subsection (7) has been given.

(10)   The statement requires the approval of the Treasury.

(11)   If the Treasury approve the statement, the Authority must publish it.

(12)   No direction may be given under subsection (7) before the statement has been published.

(13)   "Overseas regulator" has the same meaning as in section 195.

(14)   "Investigative power" means one of the powers mentioned in subsection (1).

(15)   "Investigator" means a person appointed under subsection (1)(b).

[197]

NOTES

   Community obligation: as to the meaning of this, see the note to s 47 at **[47]**.

Conduct of investigations

170 Investigations: general

(1)   This section applies if an investigating authority appoints one or more competent persons ("investigators") under section 167 or 168(3) or (5) to conduct an investigation on its behalf.

(2)   The investigating authority must give written notice of the appointment of an investigator to the person who is the subject of the investigation ("the person under investigation").

(3)   Subsections (2) and (9) do not apply if—
   (a)   the investigator is appointed as a result of section 168(1) or (4) and the investigating authority believes that the notice required by subsection (2) or (9) would be likely to result in the investigation being frustrated; or
   (b)   the investigator is appointed as a result of subsection (2) of section 168.

(4)   A notice under subsection (2) must—
   (a)   specify the provisions under which, and as a result of which, the investigator was appointed; and
   (b)   state the reason for his appointment.

(5)   Nothing prevents the investigating authority from appointing a person who is a member of its staff as an investigator.

(6)   An investigator must make a report of his investigation to the investigating authority.

(7)   The investigating authority may, by a direction to an investigator, control—
   (a)   the scope of the investigation;
   (b)   the period during which the investigation is to be conducted;
   (c)   the conduct of the investigation; and
   (d)   the reporting of the investigation.

(8)   A direction may, in particular—
   (a)   confine the investigation to particular matters;
   (b)   extend the investigation to additional matters;
   (c)   require the investigator to discontinue the investigation or to take only such steps as are specified in the direction;
   (d)   require the investigator to make such interim reports as are so specified.

(9)   If there is a change in the scope or conduct of the investigation and, in the opinion of the investigating authority, the person subject to investigation is likely to be significantly prejudiced by not being made aware of it, that person must be given written notice of the change.

(10)   "Investigating authority", in relation to an investigator, means—
   (a)   the Authority, if the Authority appointed him;
   (b)   the Secretary of State, if the Secretary of State appointed him.

[198]

171   Powers of persons appointed under section 167

(1)   An investigator may require the person who is the subject of the investigation ("the person under investigation") or any person connected with the person under investigation—
   (a)   to attend before the investigator at a specified time and place and answer questions; or
   (b)   otherwise to provide such information as the investigator may require.

(2)   An investigator may also require any person to produce at a specified time and place any specified documents or documents of a specified description.

(3)   A requirement under subsection (1) or (2) may be imposed only so far as the investigator concerned reasonably considers the question, provision of information or production of the document to be relevant to the purposes of the investigation.

[(3A)   Where the investigation relates to a recognised investment exchange, an investigator has the additional powers conferred by sections 172 and 173 (and for this purpose references in those sections to an investigator are to be read accordingly).]

(4)   For the purposes of this section and section 172, a person is connected with the person under investigation ("A") if he is or has at any relevant time been—
   (a)   a member of A's group;
   (b)   a controller of A;
   (c)   a partnership of which A is a member; or
   (d)   in relation to A, a person mentioned in Part I or II of Schedule 15.

(5)   "Investigator" means a person conducting an investigation under section 167.

(6)   "Specified" means specified in a notice in writing.

[(7)   The reference in subsection (3A) to a recognised investment exchange does not include a reference to an overseas investment exchange (as defined by section 313(1)).]

[199]

NOTES
   Sub-ss (3A), (7): inserted and added respectively by the Financial Services and Markets Act 2000 (Markets in Financial Instruments) Regulations 2007, SI 2007/126, reg 3(5), Sch 5, paras 1, 9, as from 1 April 2007 (certain purposes (see reg 1(2) at [4051])), and as from 1 November 2007 (otherwise).

172   Additional power of persons appointed as a result of section 168(1) or (4)

(1)   An investigator has the powers conferred by section 171.

(2)   An investigator may also require a person who is neither the subject of the investigation ("the person under investigation") nor a person connected with the person under investigation—
   (a)   to attend before the investigator at a specified time and place and answer questions; or
   (b)   otherwise to provide such information as the investigator may require for the purposes of the investigation.

(3)   A requirement may only be imposed under subsection (2) if the investigator is satisfied that the requirement is necessary or expedient for the purposes of the investigation.

(4)   "Investigator" means a person appointed as a result of subsection (1) or (4) of section 168.

(5)   "Specified" means specified in a notice in writing.

[200]

173   Powers of persons appointed as a result of section 168(2)

(1)   Subsections (2) to (4) apply if an investigator considers that any person ("A") is or may be able to give information which is or may be relevant to the investigation.

(2)   The investigator may require A—
  (a)   to attend before him at a specified time and place and answer questions; or
  (b)   otherwise to provide such information as he may require for the purposes of the investigation.

(3)   The investigator may also require A to produce at a specified time and place any specified documents or documents of a specified description which appear to the investigator to relate to any matter relevant to the investigation.

(4)   The investigator may also otherwise require A to give him all assistance in connection with the investigation which A is reasonably able to give.

(5)   "Investigator" means a person appointed under subsection (3) of section 168 (as a result of subsection (2) of that section).

[201]

174   Admissibility of statements made to investigators

(1)   A statement made to an investigator by a person in compliance with an information requirement is admissible in evidence in any proceedings, so long as it also complies with any requirements governing the admissibility of evidence in the circumstances in question.

(2)   But in criminal proceedings in which that person is charged with an offence to which this subsection applies or in proceedings in relation to action to be taken against that person under section 123—
  (a)   no evidence relating to the statement may be adduced, and
  (b)   no question relating to it may be asked,
by or on behalf of the prosecution or (as the case may be) the Authority, unless evidence relating to it is adduced, or a question relating to it is asked, in the proceedings by or on behalf of that person.

(3)   Subsection (2) applies to any offence other than one—
  (a)   under section 177(4) or 398;
  (b)   under section 5 of the Perjury Act 1911 (false statements made otherwise than on oath);
  (c)   under section 44(2) of the Criminal Law (Consolidation)(Scotland) Act 1995 (false statements made otherwise than on oath); or
  (d)   under Article 10 of the Perjury (Northern Ireland) Order 1979.

(4)   "Investigator" means a person appointed under section 167 or 168(3) or (5).

(5)   "Information requirement" means a requirement imposed by an investigator under section 171, 172, 173 or 175.

[202]

175   Information and documents: supplemental provisions

(1)   If the Authority or an investigator has power under this Part to require a person to produce a document but it appears that the document is in the possession of a third person, that power may be exercised in relation to the third person.

(2)   If a document is produced in response to a requirement imposed under this Part, the person to whom it is produced may—
  (a)   take copies or extracts from the document; or
  (b)   require the person producing the document, or any relevant person, to provide an explanation of the document.

(3)   If a person who is required under this Part to produce a document fails to do so, the Authority or an investigator may require him to state, to the best of his knowledge and belief, where the document is.

(4)   A lawyer may be required under this Part to furnish the name and address of his client.

(5)   No person may be required under this Part to disclose information or produce a document in respect of which he owes an obligation of confidence by virtue of carrying on the business of banking unless—
  (a)   he is the person under investigation or a member of that person's group;
  (b)   the person to whom the obligation of confidence is owed is the person under investigation or a member of that person's group;
  (c)   the person to whom the obligation of confidence is owed consents to the disclosure or production; or
  (d)   the imposing on him of a requirement with respect to such information or document has been specifically authorised by the investigating authority.

(6)   If a person claims a lien on a document, its production under this Part does not affect the lien.

(7) "Relevant person", in relation to a person who is required to produce a document, means a person who—

    (a)   has been or is or is proposed to be a director or controller of that person;

    (b)   has been or is an auditor of that person;

    (c)   has been or is an actuary, accountant or lawyer appointed or instructed by that person; or

    (d)   has been or is an employee of that person.

(8) "Investigator" means a person appointed under section 167 or 168(3) or (5).

[203]

176 Entry of premises under warrant

(1) A justice of the peace may issue a warrant under this section if satisfied on information on oath given by or on behalf of the Secretary of State, the Authority or an investigator that there are reasonable grounds for believing that the first, second or third set of conditions is satisfied.

(2) The first set of conditions is—

    (a)   that a person on whom an information requirement has been imposed has failed (wholly or in part) to comply with it; and

    (b)   that on the premises specified in the warrant—

        (i)   there are documents which have been required; or

        (ii)   there is information which has been required.

(3) The second set of conditions is—

    (a)   that the premises specified in the warrant are premises of an authorised person or an appointed representative;

    (b)   that there are on the premises documents or information in relation to which an information requirement could be imposed; and

    (c)   that if such a requirement were to be imposed—

        (i)   it would not be complied with; or

        (ii)   the documents or information to which it related would be removed, tampered with or destroyed.

(4) The third set of conditions is—

    (a)   that an offence mentioned in section 168 for which the maximum sentence on conviction on indictment is two years or more has been (or is being) committed by any person;

    (b)   that there are on the premises specified in the warrant documents or information relevant to whether that offence has been (or is being) committed;

    (c)   that an information requirement could be imposed in relation to those documents or information; and

    (d)   that if such a requirement were to be imposed—

        (i)   it would not be complied with; or

        (ii)   the documents or information to which it related would be removed, tampered with or destroyed.

(5) A warrant under this section shall authorise a constable—

    (a)   to enter the premises specified in the warrant;

    (b)   to search the premises and take possession of any documents or information appearing to be documents or information of a kind in respect of which a warrant under this section was issued ("the relevant kind") or to take, in relation to any such documents or information, any other steps which may appear to be necessary for preserving them or preventing interference with them;

    (c)   to take copies of, or extracts from, any documents or information appearing to be of the relevant kind;

    (d)   to require any person on the premises to provide an explanation of any document or information appearing to be of the relevant kind or to state where it may be found; and

    (e)   to use such force as may be reasonably necessary.

(6) In England and Wales, sections 15(5) to (8) and section 16 of the Police and Criminal Evidence Act 1984 (execution of search warrants and safeguards) apply to warrants issued under this section.

(7) In Northern Ireland, Articles 17(5) to (8) and 18 of the Police and Criminal Evidence (Northern Ireland) Order 1989 apply to warrants issued under this section.

(8) Any document of which possession is taken under this section may be retained—

    (a)   for a period of three months; or

    (b)   if within that period proceedings to which the document is relevant are commenced against any person for any criminal offence, until the conclusion of those proceedings.

(9) In the application of this section to Scotland—

    (a)   for the references to a justice of the peace substitute references to a justice of the peace or a sheriff; and

    (b)   for the references to information on oath substitute references to evidence on oath.

(10) "Investigator" means a person appointed under section 167 or 168(3) or (5).

(11) "Information requirement" means a requirement imposed—
(a) by the Authority under section [87C, 87J,] 165 or 175; or
(b) by an investigator under section 171, 172, 173 or 175.

[204]

NOTES
Sub-s (11): figures in square brackets inserted by the Prospectus Regulations 2005, SI 2005/1433, reg 2(1), Sch 1, para 12, as from 1 July 2005.
Authorised person: see the note to s 165 at **[193]**.
Additional powers of seizure: the power of seizure conferred by sub-s (5) above is a power of seizure to which the Criminal Justice and Police Act 2001, s 50 (additional powers of seizure from premises) applies; see s 50 of, and Sch 1, Pt 1, para 69 to, the 2001 Act at **[1307]**, **[1309]**.
As to the application of this section to building societies and friendly societies, see the Building Societies Act 1986, s 52B, and the Friendly Societies Act 1992, s 62A, respectively.

Offences

177 Offences

(1) If a person other than the investigator ("the defaulter") fails to comply with a requirement imposed on him under this Part the person imposing the requirement may certify that fact in writing to the court.

(2) If the court is satisfied that the defaulter failed without reasonable excuse to comply with the requirement, it may deal with the defaulter (and in the case of a body corporate, any director or officer) as if he were in contempt[; and "officer", in relation to a limited liability partnership, means a member of the limited liability partnership].

(3) A person who knows or suspects that an investigation is being or is likely to be conducted under this Part is guilty of an offence if—
(a) he falsifies, conceals, destroys or otherwise disposes of a document which he knows or suspects is or would be relevant to such an investigation, or
(b) he causes or permits the falsification, concealment, destruction or disposal of such a document,
unless he shows that he had no intention of concealing facts disclosed by the documents from the investigator.

(4) A person who, in purported compliance with a requirement imposed on him under this Part—
(a) provides information which he knows to be false or misleading in a material particular, or
(b) recklessly provides information which is false or misleading in a material particular,
is guilty of an offence.

(5) A person guilty of an offence under subsection (3) or (4) is liable—
(a) on summary conviction, to imprisonment for a term not exceeding six months or a fine not exceeding the statutory maximum, or both;
(b) on conviction on indictment, to imprisonment for a term not exceeding two years or a fine, or both.

(6) Any person who intentionally obstructs the exercise of any rights conferred by a warrant under section 176 is guilty of an offence and liable on summary conviction to imprisonment for a term not exceeding *three months* or a fine not exceeding level 5 on the standard scale, or both.

(7) "Court" means—
(a) the High Court;
(b) in Scotland, the Court of Session.

[205]

NOTES
Sub-s (2): words in square brackets added by the Limited Liability Partnerships Regulations 2001, SI 2001/1090, reg 9, Sch 5, para 21, as from 6 April 2001.
Sub-s (6): for the words in italics there are substituted the words "51 weeks" by the Criminal Justice Act 2003, s 280(2), Sch 26, para 54(1), (2), as from a day to be appointed.

PART XII
CONTROL OVER AUTHORISED PERSONS

NOTES
Transitional provisions: see the Financial Services and Markets Act 2000 (Transitional Provisions) (Controllers) Order 2001, SI 2001/2637 which makes transitional provisions for people who are subject to a regime requiring them to notify a significant shareholding in an authorised person and who will fall within this

Part. The Order deals both with the status after commencement of people who have been approved as shareholder controllers under existing regimes and with partly completed procedures. It also provides that the FSA can exercise its powers under this Act in respect of a person who has failed to comply with obligations under the pre-existing regimes, in circumstances where that person would have been subject to an equivalent obligation under this Part after commencement.

See also s 192 at **[220]** with regard to the Treasury's power to change the definition of "control".

Notice of control

178 Obligation to notify the Authority

(1) If a step which a person proposes to take would result in his acquiring—
  (a) control over a UK authorised person,
  (b) an additional kind of control over a UK authorised person, or
  (c) an increase in a relevant kind of control which he already has over a UK authorised person,

he must notify the Authority of his proposal.

(2) A person who, without himself taking any such step, acquires any such control or additional or increased control must notify the Authority before the end of the period of 14 days beginning with the day on which he first becomes aware that he has acquired it.

(3) A person who is under the duty to notify the Authority imposed by subsection (1) must also give notice to the Authority on acquiring, or increasing, the control in question.

(4) In this Part "UK authorised person" means an authorised person who—
  (a) is a body incorporated in, or an unincorporated association formed under the law of, any part of the United Kingdom; and
  (b) is not a person authorised as a result of paragraph 1 of Schedule 5.

(5) A notice under subsection (1) or (2) is referred to in this Part as "a notice of control".

[206]

NOTES

Period of 14 days: note that any provision of this Act (other than a provision of Part VI) authorising or requiring a person to do anything within a specified number of days must not take into account any day which is a public holiday in any part of the United Kingdom; see s 417(3) at **[443]**.

Acquiring, increasing and reducing control

179 Acquiring control

(1) For the purposes of this Part, a person ("the acquirer") acquires control over a UK authorised person ("A") on first falling within any of the cases in subsection (2).

(2) The cases are where the acquirer—
  (a) holds 10% or more of the shares in A;
  (b) is able to exercise significant influence over the management of A by virtue of his shareholding in A;
  (c) holds 10% or more of the shares in a parent undertaking ("P") of A;
  (d) is able to exercise significant influence over the management of P by virtue of his shareholding in P;
  (e) is entitled to exercise, or control the exercise of, 10% or more of the voting power in A;
  (f) is able to exercise significant influence over the management of A by virtue of his voting power in A;
  (g) is entitled to exercise, or control the exercise of, 10% or more of the voting power in P; or
  (h) is able to exercise significant influence over the management of P by virtue of his voting power in P.

(3) In subsection (2) "the acquirer" means—
  (a) the acquirer;
  (b) any of the acquirer's associates; or
  (c) the acquirer and any of his associates.

(4) For the purposes of this Part, each of the following is to be regarded as a kind of control—
  (a) control arising as a result of the holding of shares in A;
  (b) control arising as a result of the holding of shares in P;
  (c) control arising as a result of the entitlement to exercise, or control the exercise of, voting power in A;
  (d) control arising as a result of the entitlement to exercise, or control the exercise of, voting power in P.

(5) For the purposes of this section and sections 180 and 181, "associate", "shares" and "voting power" have the same meaning as in section 422.

[207]

180 Increasing control

(1)   For the purposes of this Part, a controller of a person ("A") who is a UK authorised person increases his control over A if—

    (a)   the percentage of shares held by the controller in A increases by any of the steps mentioned in subsection (2);

    (b)   the percentage of shares held by the controller in a parent undertaking ("P") of A increases by any of the steps mentioned in subsection (2);

    (c)   the percentage of voting power which the controller is entitled to exercise, or control the exercise of, in A increases by any of the steps mentioned in subsection (2);

    (d)   the percentage of voting power which the controller is entitled to exercise, or control the exercise of, in P increases by any of the steps mentioned in subsection (2); or

    (e)   the controller becomes a parent undertaking of A.

(2)   The steps are—

    (a)   from below 10% to 10% or more but less than 20%;

    (b)   from below 20% to 20% or more but less than 33%;

    (c)   from below 33% to 33% or more but less than 50%;

    (d)   from below 50% to 50% or more.

(3)   In paragraphs (a) to (d) of subsection (1) "the controller" means—

    (a)   the controller;

    (b)   any of the controller's associates; or

    (c)   the controller and any of his associates.

(4)   In the rest of this Part "acquiring control" or "having control" includes—

    (a)   acquiring or having an additional kind of control; or

    (b)   acquiring an increase in a relevant kind of control, or having increased control of a relevant kind.

[208]

181 Reducing control

(1)   For the purposes of this Part, a controller of a person ("A") who is a UK authorised person reduces his control over A if—

    (a)   the percentage of shares held by the controller in A decreases by any of the steps mentioned in subsection (2),

    (b)   the percentage of shares held by the controller in a parent undertaking ("P") of A decreases by any of the steps mentioned in subsection (2),

    (c)   the percentage of voting power which the controller is entitled to exercise, or control the exercise of, in A decreases by any of the steps mentioned in subsection (2),

    (d)   the percentage of voting power which the controller is entitled to exercise, or control the exercise of, in P decreases by any of the steps mentioned in subsection (2), or

    (e)   the controller ceases to be a parent undertaking of A,

unless the controller ceases to have the kind of control concerned over A as a result.

(2)   The steps are—

    (a)   from 50% or more to 33% or more but less than 50%;

    (b)   from 33% or more to 20% or more but less than 33%;

    (c)   from 20% or more to 10% or more but less than 20%;

    (d)   from 10% or more to less than 10%.

(3)   In paragraphs (a) to (d) of subsection (1) "the controller" means—

    (a)   the controller;

    (b)   any of the controller's associates; or

    (c)   the controller and any of his associates.

[209]

Acquiring or increasing control: procedure

182 Notification

(1)   A notice of control must—

    (a)   be given to the Authority in writing; and

    (b)   include such information and be accompanied by such documents as the Authority may reasonably require.

(2)   The Authority may require the person giving a notice of control to provide such additional information or documents as it reasonably considers necessary in order to enable it to determine what action it is to take in response to the notice.

(3)   Different requirements may be imposed in different circumstances.

[210]

183 Duty of Authority in relation to notice of control

(1) The Authority must, before the end of the period of three months beginning with the date on which it receives a notice of control ("the period for consideration"), determine whether—
  (a) to approve of the person concerned having the control to which the notice relates; or
  (b) to serve a warning notice under subsection (3) or section 185(3).

(2) Before doing so, the Authority must comply with such requirements as to consultation with competent authorities outside the United Kingdom as may be prescribed.

(3) If the Authority proposes to give the person concerned a notice of objection under section 186(1), it must give him a warning notice.

[211]

NOTES

Regulations: the Financial Services and Markets Act 2000 (Consultation with Competent Authorities) Regulations 2001, SI 2001/2509 at **[2421]**; the Financial Conglomerates and Other Financial Groups Regulations 2004, SI 2004/1862 at **[2723]**.

Note that the following amending Regulations have also been made under this section: the Collective Investment Schemes (Miscellaneous Amendments) Regulations 2003, SI 2003/2066; the Financial Services and Markets Act 2000 (Reinsurance Directive) Regulations 2007, SI 2007/3255.

184 Approval of acquisition of control

(1) If the Authority decides to approve of the person concerned having the control to which the notice relates it must notify that person of its approval in writing without delay.

(2) If the Authority fails to comply with subsection (1) of section 183 it is to be treated as having given its approval and notified the person concerned at the end of the period fixed by that subsection.

(3) The Authority's approval remains effective only if the person to whom it relates acquires the control in question—
  (a) before the end of such period as may be specified in the notice; or
  (b) if no period is specified, before the end of the period of one year beginning with the date—
    (i) of the notice of approval;
    (ii) on which the Authority is treated as having given approval under subsection (2); or
    (iii) of a decision on a reference to the Tribunal which results in the person concerned receiving approval.

[212]

185 Conditions attached to approval

(1) The Authority's approval under section 184 may be given unconditionally or subject to such conditions as the Authority considers appropriate.

(2) In imposing any conditions, the Authority must have regard to its duty under section 41.

(3) If the Authority proposes to impose conditions on a person it must give him a warning notice.

(4) If the Authority decides to impose conditions on a person it must give him a decision notice.

(5) A person who is subject to a condition imposed under this section may apply to the Authority—
  (a) for the condition to be varied; or
  (b) for the condition to be cancelled.

(6) The Authority may, on its own initiative, cancel a condition imposed under this section.

(7) If the Authority has given its approval to a person subject to a condition, he may refer to the Tribunal—
  (a) the imposition of the condition; or
  (b) the Authority's decision to refuse an application made by him under subsection (5).

[213]

186 Objection to acquisition of control

(1) On considering a notice of control, the Authority may give a decision notice under this section to the person acquiring control ("the acquirer") unless it is satisfied that the approval requirements are met.

(2) The approval requirements are that—
  (a) the acquirer is a fit and proper person to have the control over the authorised person that he has or would have if he acquired the control in question; and
  (b) the interests of consumers would not be threatened by the acquirer's control or by his acquiring that control.

(3)   In deciding whether the approval requirements are met, the Authority must have regard, in relation to the control that the acquirer—

(a)   has over the authorised person concerned ("A"), or

(b)   will have over A if the proposal to which the notice of control relates is carried into effect,

to its duty under section 41 in relation to each regulated activity carried on by A.

(4)   If the Authority gives a notice under this section but considers that the approval requirements would be met if the person to whom a notice is given were to take, or refrain from taking, a particular step, the notice must identify that step.

(5)   A person to whom a notice under this section is given may refer the matter to the Tribunal.

(6)   "Consumers" means persons who are consumers for the purposes of section 138.

[214]

NOTES

Extended definition of "consumer": see the note to s 138 at **[166]**.

---

187   Objection to existing control

(1)   If the Authority is not satisfied that the approval requirements are met, it may give a decision notice under this section to a person if he has failed to comply with a duty to notify imposed by section 178.

(2)   If the failure relates to subsection (1) or (2) of that section, the Authority may (instead of giving a notice under subsection (1)) approve the acquisition of the control in question by the person concerned as if he had given it a notice of control.

(3)   The Authority may also give a decision notice under this section to a person who is a controller of a UK authorised person if the Authority becomes aware of matters as a result of which it is satisfied that—

(a)   the approval requirements are not met with respect to the controller; or

(b)   a condition imposed under section 185 required that person to do (or refrain from doing) a particular thing and the condition has been breached as a result of his failing to do (or doing) that thing.

(4)   A person to whom a notice under this section is given may refer the matter to the Tribunal.

(5)   "Approval requirements" has the same meaning as in section 186.

[215]

NOTES

Note: the Financial Services and Markets Act 2000 (Consultation with Competent Authorities) Regulations 2001, SI 2001/2509, reg 4 at **[2424]** provides that where a notice of control has not been given in respect of such a change of control and the FSA proposes to give a notice of objection under s 187(1) on the basis that it is not satisfied that the appropriate requirements set out in s 186 have been met, the FSA must consult the home state regulator of each EEA firm.

---

188   Notices of objection under section 187: procedure

(1)   If the Authority proposes to give a notice of objection to a person under section 187, it must give him a warning notice.

(2)   Before doing so, the Authority must comply with such requirements as to consultation with competent authorities outside the United Kingdom as may be prescribed.

(3)   If the Authority decides to give a warning notice under this section, it must do so before the end of the period of three months beginning—

(a)   in the case of a notice to be given under section 187(1), with the date on which it became aware of the failure to comply with the duty in question;

(b)   in the case of a notice to be given under section 187(3), with the date on which it became aware of the matters in question.

(4)   The Authority may require the person concerned to provide such additional information or documents as it considers reasonable.

(5)   Different requirements may be imposed in different circumstances.

(6)   In this Part "notice of objection" means a notice under section 186 or 187.

[216]

NOTES

Regulations: the Financial Services and Markets Act 2000 (Consultation with Competent Authorities) Regulations 2001, SI 2001/2509 at **[2421]**; the Financial Conglomerates and Other Financial Groups Regulations 2004, SI 2004/1862 at **[2723]**.

Note that the following amending Regulations have also been made under this section: the Collective Investment Schemes (Miscellaneous Amendments) Regulations 2003, SI 2003/2066; the Financial Services and Markets Act 2000 (Reinsurance Directive) Regulations 2007, SI 2007/3255.

Improperly acquired shares

189 Improperly acquired shares

(1)   The powers conferred by this section are exercisable if a person has acquired, or has continued to hold, any shares in contravention of—
  (a)   a notice of objection; or
  (b)   a condition imposed on the Authority's approval.

(2)   The Authority may by notice in writing served on the person concerned ("a restriction notice") direct that any such shares which are specified in the notice are, until further notice, subject to one or more of the following restrictions—
  (a)   a transfer of (or agreement to transfer) those shares, or in the case of unissued shares any transfer of (or agreement to transfer) the right to be issued with them, is void;
  (b)   no voting rights are to be exercisable in respect of the shares;
  (c)   no further shares are to be issued in right of them or in pursuance of any offer made to their holder;
  (d)   except in a liquidation, no payment is to be made of any sums due from the body corporate on the shares, whether in respect of capital or otherwise.

(3)   The court may, on the application of the Authority, order the sale of any shares to which this section applies and, if they are for the time being subject to any restriction under subsection (2), that they are to cease to be subject to that restriction.

(4)   No order may be made under subsection (3)—
  (a)   until the end of the period within which a reference may be made to the Tribunal in respect of the notice of objection; and
  (b)   if a reference is made, until the matter has been determined or the reference withdrawn.

(5)   If an order has been made under subsection (3), the court may, on the application of the Authority, make such further order relating to the sale or transfer of the shares as it thinks fit.

(6)   If shares are sold in pursuance of an order under this section, the proceeds of sale, less the costs of the sale, must be paid into court for the benefit of the persons beneficially interested in them; and any such person may apply to the court for the whole or part of the proceeds to be paid to him.

(7)   This section applies—
  (a)   in the case of an acquirer falling within section 178(1), to all the shares—
    (i)   in the authorised person which the acquirer has acquired;
    (ii)   which are held by him or an associate of his; and
    (iii)   which were not so held immediately before he became a person with control over the authorised person;
  (b)   in the case of an acquirer falling within section 178(2), to all the shares held by him or an associate of his at the time when he first became aware that he had acquired control over the authorised person; and
  (c)   to all the shares in an undertaking ("C")—
    (i)   which are held by the acquirer or an associate of his, and
    (ii)   which were not so held before he became a person with control in relation to the authorised person,
where C is the undertaking in which shares were acquired by the acquirer (or an associate of his) and, as a result, he became a person with control in relation to that authorised person.

(8)   A copy of the restriction notice must be served on—
  (a)   the authorised person to whose shares it relates; and
  (b)   if it relates to shares held by an associate of that authorised person, on that associate.

(9)   The jurisdiction conferred by this section may be exercised by the High Court and the Court of Session.

[217]

Reducing control: procedure

190 Notification

(1)   If a step which a controller of a UK authorised person proposes to take would result in his—
  (a)   ceasing to have control of a relevant kind over the authorised person, or
  (b)   reducing a relevant kind of control over that person,
he must notify the Authority of his proposal.

(2)   A controller of a UK authorised person who, without himself taking any such step, ceases to have that control or reduces that control must notify the Authority before the end of the period of 14 days beginning with the day on which he first becomes aware that—

(a)   he has ceased to have the control in question; or

(b)   he has reduced that control.

(3)   A person who is under the duty to notify the Authority imposed by subsection (1) must also give a notice to the Authority—

(a)   on ceasing to have the control in question; or

(b)   on reducing that control.

(4)   A notice under this section must—

(a)   be given to the Authority in writing; and

(b)   include details of the extent of the control (if any) which the person concerned will retain (or still retains) over the authorised person concerned.

[218]

PART I
FSMA 2000

NOTES

Period of 14 days: for the purposes of sub-s (2) above note that any provision of this Act (other than a provision of Part VI) authorising or requiring a person to do anything within a specified number of days must not take into account any day which is a public holiday in any part of the United Kingdom; see s 417(3) at **[443]**.

Offences

191   Offences under this Part

(1)   A person who fails to comply with the duty to notify the Authority imposed on him by section 178(1) or 190(1) is guilty of an offence.

(2)   A person who fails to comply with the duty to notify the Authority imposed on him by section 178(2) or 190(2) is guilty of an offence.

(3)   If a person who has given a notice of control to the Authority carries out the proposal to which the notice relates, he is guilty of an offence if—

(a)   the period of three months beginning with the date on which the Authority received the notice is still running; and

(b)   the Authority has not responded to the notice by either giving its approval or giving him a warning notice under section 183(3) or 185(3).

(4)   A person to whom the Authority has given a warning notice under section 183(3) is guilty of an offence if he carries out the proposal to which the notice relates before the Authority has decided whether to give him a notice of objection.

(5)   A person to whom a notice of objection has been given is guilty of an offence if he acquires the control to which the notice applies at a time when the notice is still in force.

(6)   A person guilty of an offence under subsection (1), (2), (3) or (4) is liable on summary conviction to a fine not exceeding level 5 on the standard scale.

(7)   A person guilty of an offence under subsection (5) is liable—

(a)   on summary conviction, to a fine not exceeding the statutory maximum; and

(b)   on conviction on indictment, to imprisonment for a term not exceeding two years or a fine, or both.

(8)   A person guilty of an offence under subsection (5) is also liable on summary conviction to a fine not exceeding one tenth of the statutory maximum for each day on which the offence has continued.

(9)   It is a defence for a person charged with an offence under subsection (1) to show that he had, at the time of the alleged offence, no knowledge of the act or circumstances by virtue of which the duty to notify the Authority arose.

(10)   If a person—

(a)   was under the duty to notify the Authority imposed by section 178(1) or 190(1) but had no knowledge of the act or circumstances by virtue of which that duty arose, but

(b)   subsequently becomes aware of that act or those circumstances,

he must notify the Authority before the end of the period of 14 days beginning with the day on which he first became so aware.

(11)   A person who fails to comply with the duty to notify the Authority imposed by subsection (10) is guilty of an offence and liable, on summary conviction, to a fine not exceeding level 5 on the standard scale.

[219]

NOTES

Period of 14 days: see the note to s 190 at **[218]**.

Miscellaneous

192 Power to change definitions of control etc

The Treasury may by order—

(a) provide for exemptions from the obligations to notify imposed by sections 178 and 190;

(b) amend section 179 by varying, or removing, any of the cases in which a person is treated as having control over a UK authorised person or by adding a case;

(c) amend section 180 by varying, or removing, any of the cases in which a person is treated as increasing control over a UK authorised person or by adding a case;

(d) amend section 181 by varying, or removing, any of the cases in which a person is treated as reducing his control over a UK authorised person or by adding a case;

(e) amend section 422 by varying, or removing, any of the cases in which a person is treated as being a controller of a person or by adding a case.

[220]

NOTES

Orders: the Financial Services and Markets Act 2000 (Controllers) (Exemption) Order 2001, SI 2001/2638 at **[2482]**; the Financial Services and Markets Act 2000 (Controllers) (Exemption) (No 2) Order 2001, SI 2001/3338 at **[2499]**.

Note that the following amending Orders have also been made under this section: the Financial Services and Markets Act 2000 (Regulated Activities) (Amendment) (No 2) Order 2003, SI 2003/1476 at **[2704]**.

PART XIII
INCOMING FIRMS: INTERVENTION BY AUTHORITY

NOTES

Transitional provisions: The Financial Services and Markets Act 2000 (Transitional Provisions) (Authorised Persons etc) Order 2001, SI 2001/2636, Pt III, provides that restrictions and prohibitions imposed under provisions of the previous regulatory regimes on authorised persons are to have effect, as from 1 December 2001, as if they were requirements imposed under s 196 (in relation to persons with a permission under Sch 3 or 4). As to the restrictions and prohibitions to which Pt III of the 2001 Order applies, see the note "Transitional provisions" to Pt IV of this Act. See also the Financial Services and Markets Act 2000 (Consequential and Transitional Provisions) (Miscellaneous) (No 2) Order 2001, SI 2001/2659, art 3(5) which provides that in ss 194–197 the references to an "incoming firm" are to be read as references to any person who is of such a description, and with respect to whom such conditions are met, that (if he is of that description, and if those conditions are met, immediately before commencement) he will, at commencement, be treated as being an "incoming firm" by virtue of SI 2001/2636.

Interpretation

193 Interpretation of this Part

(1) In this Part—

"additional procedure" means the procedure described in section 199;

"incoming firm" means—

(a) an EEA firm which is exercising, or has exercised, its right to carry on a regulated activity in the United Kingdom in accordance with Schedule 3; or

(b) a Treaty firm which is exercising, or has exercised, its right to carry on a regulated activity in the United Kingdom in accordance with Schedule 4; and

"power of intervention" means the power conferred on the Authority by section 196.

(2) In relation to an incoming firm which is an EEA firm, expressions used in this Part and in Schedule 3 have the same meaning in this Part as they have in that Schedule.

[221]

194 General grounds on which power of intervention is exercisable

(1) The Authority may exercise its power of intervention in respect of an incoming firm if it appears to it that—

(a) the firm has contravened, or is likely to contravene, a requirement which is imposed on it by or under this Act (in a case where the Authority is responsible for enforcing compliance in the United Kingdom);

(b) the firm has, in purported compliance with any requirement imposed by or under this Act, knowingly or recklessly given the Authority information which is false or misleading in a material particular; or

(c) it is desirable to exercise the power in order to protect the interests of actual or potential customers.

(2) Subsection (3) applies to an incoming EEA firm falling within sub-paragraph (a) or (b) of paragraph 5 of Schedule 3 which is exercising an EEA right to carry on any Consumer Credit Act business in the United Kingdom.

(3)   The Authority may exercise its power of intervention in respect of the firm if [the Office of Fair Trading] has informed the Authority that—
  (a)   the firm,
  (b)   any of the firm's employees, agents or associates (whether past or present), or
  (c)   if the firm is a body corporate, a controller of the firm or an associate of such a controller,
has done any of the things specified in paragraphs [(a) to (e) of section 25(2A)] of the Consumer Credit Act 1974.

(4)   "Associate", "Consumer Credit Act business" and "controller" have the same meaning as in section 203.

[222]

NOTES
  Sub-s (3): words in first pair of square brackets substituted by the Enterprise Act 2002, s 278(1), Sch 25, para 40(1), (6), as from 1 April 2003; words in second pair of square brackets substituted by the Consumer Credit Act 2006, s 33(7), as from 6 April 2008.
  Note: "customer" is defined in s 59(11) at **[59]**.

[194A   Contravention by relevant EEA firm with UK branch of requirement under markets in financial instruments directive: Authority primarily responsible for securing compliance

(1)   This section applies if—
  (a)   a relevant EEA firm has a branch in the United Kingdom; and
  (b)   the Authority ascertains that the firm has contravened, or is contravening, a requirement falling within subsection (3) (in a case to which Article 62.2 of the markets in financial instruments directive applies).

(2)   "Relevant EEA firm" means an EEA firm falling within paragraph 5(a) or (b) of Schedule 3 which is exercising in the United Kingdom an EEA right deriving from the markets in financial instruments directive.

(3)   A requirement falls within this subsection if it is imposed on the firm—
  (a)   by any provision of or made under this Act which implements the markets in financial instruments directive; or
  (b)   by any directly applicable Community regulation made under that directive.

(4)   The Authority must give the firm written notice which—
  (a)   requires the firm to put an end to the contravention;
  (b)   states that the Authority's power of intervention will become exercisable in relation to the firm if the firm continues the contravention; and
  (c)   indicates any requirements that the Authority proposes to impose on the firm in exercise of its power of intervention in the event of the power becoming exercisable.

(5)   The Authority may exercise its power of intervention in respect of the firm if—
  (a)   a reasonable time has expired since the giving of the notice under subsection (4);
  (b)   the firm has failed to put an end to the contravention within that time; and
  (c)   the Authority has informed the firm's home state regulator of its intention to exercise its power of intervention in respect of the firm.

(6)   Subsection (5) applies whether or not the Authority's power of intervention is also exercisable as a result of section 194.

(7)   If the Authority exercises its power of intervention in respect of a relevant EEA firm by virtue of subsection (5), it must at the earliest opportunity inform the firm's home state regulator and the Commission of—
  (a)   the fact that the Authority has exercised that power in respect of the firm; and
  (b)   any requirements it has imposed on the firm in exercise of the power.]

[222A]

NOTES
  Commencement: 1 April 2007 (certain purposes); 1 November 2007 (otherwise).
  Inserted by the Financial Services and Markets Act 2000 (Markets in Financial Instruments) Regulations 2007, SI 2007/126, reg 3(1), Sch 1, paras 1, 2, as from 1 April 2007 (certain purposes (see reg 1(2) at **[4051]**)), and as from 1 November 2007 (otherwise).

195   Exercise of power in support of overseas regulator

(1)   The Authority may exercise its power of intervention in respect of an incoming firm at the request of, or for the purpose of assisting, an overseas regulator.

(2)   Subsection (1) applies whether or not the Authority's power of intervention is also exercisable as a result of section 194.

(3)   "An overseas regulator" means an authority in a country or territory outside the United Kingdom—
    (a)   which is a home state regulator; or
    (b)   which exercises any function of a kind mentioned in subsection (4).

(4)   The functions are—
    (a)   a function corresponding to any function of the Authority under this Act;
    (b)   a function corresponding to any function exercised by the competent authority under Part VI ...
    (c)   a function corresponding to any function exercised by the Secretary of State under [the Companies Acts (as defined in section 2 of the Companies Act 2006)];
    (d)   a function in connection with—
        (i)   the investigation of conduct of the kind prohibited by Part V of the Criminal Justice Act 1993 (insider dealing); or
        (ii)   the enforcement of rules (whether or not having the force of law) relating to such conduct;
    (e)   a function prescribed by regulations made for the purposes of this subsection which, in the opinion of the Treasury, relates to companies or financial services.

(5)   If—
    (a)   a request to the Authority for the exercise of its power of intervention has been made by a home state regulator in pursuance of a Community obligation, or
    (b)   a home state regulator has notified the Authority that an EEA firm's EEA authorisation has been withdrawn,
the Authority must, in deciding whether or not to exercise its power of intervention, consider whether exercising it is necessary in order to comply with a Community obligation.

(6)   In deciding in any case in which the Authority does not consider that the exercise of its power of intervention is necessary in order to comply with a Community obligation, it may take into account in particular—
    (a)   whether in the country or territory of the overseas regulator concerned, corresponding assistance would be given to a United Kingdom regulatory authority;
    (b)   whether the case concerns the breach of a law, or other requirement, which has no close parallel in the United Kingdom or involves the assertion of a jurisdiction not recognised by the United Kingdom;
    (c)   the seriousness of the case and its importance to persons in the United Kingdom;
    (d)   whether it is otherwise appropriate in the public interest to give the assistance sought.

(7)   The Authority may decide not to exercise its power of intervention, in response to a request, unless the regulator concerned undertakes to make such contribution to the cost of its exercise as the Authority considers appropriate.

(8)   Subsection (7) does not apply if the Authority decides that it is necessary for it to exercise its power of intervention in order to comply with a Community obligation.

[223]

NOTES
Sub-s (4): words omitted from para (b) repealed by the Prospectus Regulations 2005, SI 2005/1433, reg 2(1), Sch 1, para 13, as from 1 July 2005; words in square brackets in para (c) substituted by the Companies Act 2006 (Commencement No 3, Consequential Amendments, Transitional Provisions and Savings) Order 2007, SI 2007/2194, art 10(1), Sch 4, Pt 3, para 92, as from 1 October 2007.
Community obligation: as to the meaning of this, see the note to s 47 at **[47]**.

[195A   Contravention by relevant EEA firm of requirement under markets in financial instruments directive: home state regulator primarily responsible for securing compliance

(1)   This section applies if the Authority has clear and demonstrable grounds for believing that a relevant EEA firm has contravened, or is contravening, a requirement falling within subsection (2) (in a case to which Article 62.1 or 62.3 of the markets in financial instruments directive applies).

(2)   A requirement falls within this subsection if it is imposed on the firm—
    (a)   by or under any provision adopted in the firm's home state for the purpose of implementing the markets in financial instruments directive; or
    (b)   by any directly applicable Community regulation made under that directive.

(3)   The Authority must notify the firm's home state regulator of the situation mentioned in subsection (1).

(4)   The notice under subsection (3) must—
    (a)   request that the home state regulator take all appropriate measures for the purpose of ensuring that the firm puts an end to the contravention;
    (b)   state that the Authority's power of intervention is likely to become exercisable in relation to the firm if the firm continues the contravention; and

(c)   indicate any requirements that the Authority proposes to impose on the firm in exercise of its power of intervention in the event of the power becoming exercisable.

(5)   The Authority may exercise its power of intervention in respect of the firm if—
    (a)   a reasonable time has expired since the giving of the notice under subsection (3); and
    (b)   conditions A to C are satisfied.

(6)   Condition A is that—
    (a)   the firm's home state regulator has failed or refused to take measures for the purpose mentioned in subsection (4)(a); or
    (b)   any measures taken by the home state regulator have proved inadequate for that purpose.

(7)   Condition B is that the firm is acting in a manner which is clearly prejudicial to the interests of investors in the United Kingdom or the orderly functioning of the markets.

(8)   Condition C is that the Authority has informed the firm's home state regulator of its intention to exercise its power of intervention in respect of the firm.

(9)   Subsection (5) applies whether or not the Authority's power of intervention is also exercisable as a result of section 194 or 195.

(10)   If the Authority exercises its power of intervention in respect of a relevant EEA firm by virtue of subsection (5), it must at the earliest opportunity inform the Commission of—
    (a)   the fact that the Authority has exercised that power in respect of the firm; and
    (b)   any requirements it has imposed on the firm in exercise of the power.

(11)   In this section—
"home state", in relation to a relevant EEA firm, means—
    (a)   in the case of a firm which is a body corporate, the EEA State in which the firm has its registered office or, if it has no registered office, its head office; and
    (b)   in any other case, the EEA State in which the firm has its head office;
"relevant EEA firm" has the same meaning as in section 194A.]

[223A]

NOTES

Commencement: 1 April 2007 (certain purposes); 1 November 2007 (otherwise).
Inserted by the Financial Services and Markets Act 2000 (Markets in Financial Instruments) Regulations 2007, SI 2007/126, reg 3(1), Sch 1, paras 1, 3, as from 1 April 2007 (certain purposes (see reg 1(2) at **[4051]**)), and as from 1 November 2007 (otherwise).

---

196   The power of intervention

If the Authority is entitled to exercise its power of intervention in respect of an incoming firm under this Part, it may impose any requirement in relation to the firm which it could impose if—
    (a)   the firm's permission was a Part IV permission; and
    (b)   the Authority was entitled to exercise its power under that Part to vary that permission.

[224]

Exercise of power of intervention

197   Procedure on exercise of power of intervention

(1)   A requirement takes effect—
    (a)   immediately, if the notice given under subsection (3) states that that is the case;
    (b)   on such date as may be specified in the notice; or
    (c)   if no date is specified in the notice, when the matter to which it relates is no longer open to review.

(2)   A requirement may be expressed to take effect immediately (or on a specified date) only if the Authority, having regard to the ground on which it is exercising its power of intervention, considers that it is necessary for the requirement to take effect immediately (or on that date).

(3)   If the Authority proposes to impose a requirement under section 196 on an incoming firm, or imposes such a requirement with immediate effect, it must give the firm written notice.

(4)   The notice must—
    (a)   give details of the requirement;
    (b)   inform the firm of when the requirement takes effect;
    (c)   state the Authority's reasons for imposing the requirement and for its determination as to when the requirement takes effect;
    (d)   inform the firm that it may make representations to the Authority within such period as may be specified in the notice (whether or not it has referred the matter to the Tribunal); and
    (e)   inform it of its right to refer the matter to the Tribunal.

(5)   The Authority may extend the period allowed under the notice for making representations.

(6)   If, having considered any representations made by the firm, the Authority decides—

    (a)   to impose the requirement proposed, or

    (b)   if it has been imposed, not to rescind the requirement,

it must give it written notice.

(7)   If, having considered any representations made by the firm, the Authority decides—

    (a)   not to impose the requirement proposed,

    (b)   to impose a different requirement from that proposed, or

    (c)   to rescind a requirement which has effect,

it must give it written notice.

(8)   A notice given under subsection (6) must inform the firm of its right to refer the matter to the Tribunal.

(9)   A notice under subsection (7)(b) must comply with subsection (4).

(10)   If a notice informs a person of his right to refer a matter to the Tribunal, it must give an indication of the procedure on such a reference.

[225]

198 Power to apply to court for injunction in respect of certain overseas insurance companies

(1)   This section applies if the Authority has received a request made in respect of an incoming EEA firm in accordance with—

    (a)   Article 20.5 of the first non-life insurance directive; ...

    [(b)   Article 37.5 of the life assurance consolidation directive]; [or

    (c)   Article 42.4 of the reinsurance directive].

(2)   The court may, on an application made to it by the Authority with respect to the firm, grant an injunction restraining (or in Scotland an interdict prohibiting) the firm disposing of or otherwise dealing with any of its assets.

(3)   If the court grants an injunction, it may by subsequent orders make provision for such incidental, consequential and supplementary matters as it considers necessary to enable the Authority to perform any of its functions under this Act.

(4)   "The court" means—

    (a)   the High Court; or

    (b)   in Scotland, the Court of Session.

[226]

NOTES

Sub-s (1): word omitted from para (a) repealed, and para (c) (and the word immediately preceding it) inserted, by the Reinsurance Directive Regulations 2007, SI 2007/3253, reg 2(1), Sch 1, paras 1, 3, as from 10 December 2007; para (b) substituted by the Life Assurance Consolidation Directive (Consequential Amendments) Regulations 2004, SI 2004/3379, reg 6(1), (3), as from 11 January 2005.

199 Additional procedure for EEA firms in certain cases

(1)   This section applies if it appears to the Authority that its power of intervention is exercisable in relation to an EEA firm exercising EEA rights in the United Kingdom ("an incoming EEA firm") in respect of the contravention of a relevant requirement.

(2)   A requirement is relevant if—

    (a)   it is imposed by the Authority under this Act; and

    [(b)   as respects its contravention, the single market directive in question provides that a procedure of the kind set out in the following provisions of this section (so far as they are relevant in the firm's case) is to apply].

[(3A)   If the firm falls within paragraph 5(da) of Schedule 3, the Authority must at the same time as it gives notice to the firm under subsection (3) refer its findings to the firm's home state regulator.

(3B)   Subsections (4) to (8) apply to an incoming EEA firm other than a firm falling within paragraph 5(da) of Schedule 3.]

(3)   The Authority must, in writing, require the firm to remedy the situation.

(4)   If the firm fails to comply with the requirement under subsection (3) within a reasonable time, the Authority must give a notice to that effect to the firm's home state regulator requesting it—

    (a)   to take all appropriate measures for the purpose of ensuring that the firm remedies the situation which has given rise to the notice; and

    (b)   to inform the Authority of the measures it proposes to take or has taken or the reasons for not taking such measures.

(5)   Except as mentioned in subsection (6), the Authority may not exercise its power of intervention [before informing the firm's home state regulator and] unless satisfied—

(a)   that the firm's home state regulator has failed or refused to take measures for the purpose mentioned in subsection (4)(a); or

(b)   that the measures taken by the home state regulator have proved inadequate for that purpose.

(6)   If the Authority decides that it should exercise its power of intervention in respect of the incoming EEA firm as a matter of urgency in order to protect the interests of consumers, it may exercise that power—

(a)   before complying with subsections (3) and (4); or

(b)   where it has complied with those subsections, before it is satisfied as mentioned in subsection (5).

(7)   In such a case the Authority must at the earliest opportunity inform the firm's home state regulator and the Commission.

(8)   If—

(a)   the Authority has (by virtue of subsection (6)) exercised its power of intervention before complying with subsections (3) and (4) or before it is satisfied as mentioned in subsection (5), and

(b)   the Commission decides under any of the single market directives [(other than the markets in financial instruments directive)] that the Authority must rescind or vary any requirement imposed in the exercise of its power of intervention,

the Authority must in accordance with the decision rescind or vary the requirement.

[(9)   In the case of a firm falling within paragraph 5(da) of Schedule 3, the Authority may not exercise its power of intervention before informing the firm's home state regulator and unless satisfied—

(a)   that the firm's home state regulator has failed or refused to take all appropriate measures for the purpose of ensuring that the firm remedies the situation which gave rise to the notice under subsection (3); or

(b)   that the measures taken by the home state regulator have proved inadequate for that purpose.]

[227]

NOTES

Sub-s (2): para (b) substituted by the Reinsurance Directive Regulations 2007, SI 2007/3253, reg 2(1), Sch 1, paras 1, 4(a), as from 10 December 2007.

Sub-ss (3A), (3B), (9): inserted and added respectively by SI 2007/3253, reg 2(1), Sch 1, paras 1, 4(b), (d), as from 10 December 2007.

Sub-s (5): words in square brackets inserted by SI 2007/3253, reg 2(1), Sch 1, paras 1, 4(c), as from 10 December 2007.

Sub-s (8): words in square brackets in para (b) inserted by the Financial Services and Markets Act 2000 (Markets in Financial Instruments) Regulations 2007, SI 2007/126, reg 3(1), Sch 1, paras 1, 4, as from 1 April 2007 (certain purposes (see reg 1(2) at **[4051]**)), and as from 1 November 2007 (otherwise).

Supplemental

200   Rescission and variation of requirements

(1)   The Authority may rescind or vary a requirement imposed in exercise of its power of intervention on its own initiative or on the application of the person subject to the requirement.

(2)   The power of the Authority on its own initiative to rescind a requirement is exercisable by written notice given by the Authority to the person concerned, which takes effect on the date specified in the notice.

(3)   Section 197 applies to the exercise of the power of the Authority on its own initiative to vary a requirement as it applies to the imposition of a requirement.

(4)   If the Authority proposes to refuse an application for the variation or rescission of a requirement, it must give the applicant a warning notice.

(5)   If the Authority decides to refuse an application for the variation or rescission of a requirement—

(a)   the Authority must give the applicant a decision notice; and

(b)   that person may refer the matter to the Tribunal.

[228]

201   Effect of certain requirements on other persons

If the Authority, in exercising its power of intervention, imposes on an incoming firm a requirement of a kind mentioned in subsection (3) of section 48, the requirement has the same effect in relation to the firm as it would have in relation to an authorised person if it had been imposed on the authorised person by the Authority acting under section 45.

[229]

202 Contravention of requirement imposed under this Part

   (1)   Contravention of a requirement imposed by the Authority under this Part does not—
     (a)   make a person guilty of an offence;
     (b)   make any transaction void or unenforceable; or
     (c)   (subject to subsection (2)) give rise to any right of action for breach of statutory duty.

   (2)   In prescribed cases the contravention is actionable at the suit of a person who suffers loss as a result of the contravention, subject to the defences and other incidents applying to actions for breach of statutory duty.

[230]

NOTES

   Note: the Financial Services and Markets Act 2000 (Rights of Action) Regulations 2001, SI 2001/2256, regs 3 and 7 (at [2377], [2381]) prescribe those cases where individuals (except when carrying on a regulated activity) may bring an action under these provisions, and those cases where an action could be brought at the suit of a private person or a person acting in a fiduciary or representative capacity on behalf of a private person, provided any remedy would be exclusively for the benefit of that person and could not be effected thought an action brought otherwise than at the suit of the fiduciary or representative.

   Regulations: the Financial Services and Markets Act 2000 (Rights of Action) Regulations 2001, SI 2001/2256 at [2375].

Powers of [Office of Fair Trading]

203 Power to prohibit the carrying on of Consumer Credit Act business

   (1)   If it appears to [the Office of Fair Trading ("the OFT")] that subsection (4) has been, or is likely to be, contravened as respects a consumer credit EEA firm, [it] may by written notice given to the firm impose on the firm a consumer credit prohibition.

   (2)   If it appears to the [OFT] that a restriction imposed under section 204 on an EEA consumer credit firm has not been complied with, [it] may by written notice given to the firm impose a consumer credit prohibition.

   (3)   "Consumer credit prohibition" means a prohibition on carrying on, or purporting to carry on, in the United Kingdom any Consumer Credit Act business which consists of or includes carrying on one or more listed activities.

   (4)   This subsection is contravened as respects a firm if—
     (a)   the firm or any of its employees, agents or associates (whether past or present), or
     (b)   if the firm is a body corporate, any controller of the firm or an associate of any such controller,
does any of the things specified in paragraphs [(a) to (e) of section 25(2A)] of the Consumer Credit Act 1974.

   (5)   A consumer credit prohibition may be absolute or may be imposed—
     (a)   for such period,
     (b)   until the occurrence of such event, or
     (c)   until such conditions are complied with,
as may be specified in the notice given under subsection (1) or (2).

   (6)   Any period, event or condition so specified may be varied by the [OFT] on the application of the firm concerned.

   (7)   A consumer credit prohibition may be withdrawn by written notice served by the [OFT] on the firm concerned, and any such notice takes effect on such date as is specified in the notice.

   (8)   Schedule 16 has effect as respects consumer credit prohibitions and restrictions under section 204.

   (9)   A firm contravening a prohibition under this section is guilty of an offence and liable—
     (a)   on summary conviction, to a fine not exceeding the statutory maximum;
     (b)   on conviction on indictment, to a fine.

   (10)   In this section and section 204—
     "a consumer credit EEA firm" means an EEA firm falling within any of paragraphs (a) to (c) of paragraph 5 of Schedule 3 whose EEA authorisation covers any Consumer Credit Act business;
     "Consumer Credit Act business" means consumer credit business, consumer hire business or ancillary credit business;
     "consumer credit business", "consumer hire business" and "ancillary credit business" have the same meaning as in the Consumer Credit Act 1974;
     "listed activity" means an activity listed in [Annex 1 to the banking consolidation directive] or the Annex to the investment services directive;

"associate" has the same meaning as in section [25(2A)] of the Consumer Credit Act 1974; "controller" has the meaning given by section 189(1) of that Act.

[231]

PART I
FSMA 2000

NOTES

In the heading preceding this section words in square brackets substituted by the Enterprise Act 2002, s 278(1), Sch 25, para 40(1), (7), as from 1 April 2003.

Sub-ss (1), (2), (6), (7): words in square brackets substituted by the Enterprise Act 2002, s 278(1), Sch 25, para 40(1), (7), as from 1 April 2003.

Sub-s (4): words in square brackets substituted by the Consumer Credit Act 2006, s 33(7), as from 6 April 2008.

Sub-s (10): words in square brackets in the definition "listed activity" substituted by the Banking Consolidation Directive (Consequential Amendments) Regulations 2000, SI 2000/2952, reg 8(1), (2), as from 22 November 2000; figure in square brackets in the definition "associate" substituted by the Consumer Credit Act 2006, s 33(8), as from 6 April 2008.

204 Power to restrict the carrying on of Consumer Credit Act business

(1) In this section "restriction" means a direction that a consumer credit EEA firm may not carry on in the United Kingdom, otherwise than in accordance with such condition or conditions as may be specified in the direction, any Consumer Credit Act business which—

(a)   consists of or includes carrying on any listed activity; and

(b)   is specified in the direction.

(2) If it appears to the [OFT] that the situation as respects a consumer credit EEA firm is such that the powers conferred by section 203(1) are exercisable, the [OFT] may, instead of imposing a prohibition, impose such restriction as appears to [it] desirable.

(3) A restriction—

(a)   may be withdrawn, or

(b)   may be varied with the agreement of the firm concerned,

by written notice served by the [OFT] on the firm, and any such notice takes effect on such date as is specified in the notice.

(4) A firm contravening a restriction is guilty of an offence and liable—

(a)   on summary conviction, to a fine not exceeding the statutory maximum;

(b)   on conviction on indictment, to a fine.

[232]

NOTES

Sub-ss (2), (3): words in square brackets substituted by the Enterprise Act 2002, s 278(1), Sch 25, para 40(1), (8), as from 1 April 2003.

PART XIV
DISCIPLINARY MEASURES

NOTES

HM Treasury and the FSA have issued a consultation paper on the Implementation of the Acquisitions Directive which proposes a number of changes to this Part (as well as Chapter 1A of Part 18 (control over recognised investment exchanges) and the definition of controller as set out in s 422). See *Implementation of the Acquisitions Directive: a consultation document* (*September 2008*) at: http://www.hm-treasury.gov.uk/consult_fullindex.htm.

205 Public censure

If the Authority considers that an authorised person has contravened a requirement imposed on him by or under this Act, [or by any directly applicable Community regulation made under the markets in financial instruments directive,] the Authority may publish a statement to that effect.

[233]

NOTES

Words in square brackets inserted by the Financial Services and Markets Act 2000 (Markets in Financial Instruments) Regulations 2007, SI 2007/126, reg 3(5), Sch 5, paras 1, 10, as from 1 April 2007 (certain purposes (see reg 1(2) at **[4051]**)), and as from 1 November 2007 (otherwise).

Transitional provisions: as to the exercise of the power conferred by this section in respect of: (a) certain contraventions of the Financial Services Act 1986 (repealed), before 1 December 2001; and (b) contraventions of the rules of self-regulating organisations before that date, see the Financial Services and Markets Act 2000 (Transitional Provisions and Savings) (Civil Remedies, Discipline, Criminal Offences etc) (No 2) Order 2001, SI 2001/3083, arts 6, 7.

Note: for the purposes of this section a requirement imposed by the FSA under the Electronic Commerce Directive (Financial Services and Markets) Regulations 2002, SI 2002/1775 upon an authorised incoming provider is to be treated as imposed on him by or under this Act; see reg 12(1) of those Regulations at **[2685]**.

206 Financial penalties

(1) If the Authority considers that an authorised person has contravened a requirement imposed on him by or under this Act, [or by any directly applicable Community regulation made under the markets in financial instruments directive,] it may impose on him a penalty, in respect of the contravention, of such amount as it considers appropriate.

(2) The Authority may not in respect of any contravention both require a person to pay a penalty under this section and withdraw his authorisation under section 33.

(3) A penalty under this section is payable to the Authority.

[234]

NOTES

Sub-s (1): words in square brackets inserted by the Financial Services and Markets Act 2000 (Markets in Financial Instruments) Regulations 2007, SI 2007/126, reg 3(5), Sch 5, paras 1, 11, as from 1 April 2007 (certain purposes (see reg 1(2) at **[4051]**)), and as from 1 November 2007 (otherwise).

Transitional provisions: as to the exercise of the power conferred by this section in respect of contraventions of the rules of self-regulating organisations before 1 December 2001, see the Financial Services and Markets Act 2000 (Transitional Provisions and Savings) (Civil Remedies, Discipline, Criminal Offences etc) (No 2) Order 2001, SI 2001/3083, art 8.

Note: for the purposes of this section a requirement imposed by the FSA under the Electronic Commerce Directive (Financial Services and Markets) Regulations 2002, SI 2002/1775 upon an authorised incoming provider is to be treated as imposed on him by or under this Act; see reg 12(1) of those Regulations at **[2685]**.

207 Proposal to take disciplinary measures

(1) If the Authority proposes—
   (a) to publish a statement in respect of an authorised person (under section 205), or
   (b) to impose a penalty on an authorised person (under section 206),
it must give the authorised person a warning notice.

(2) A warning notice about a proposal to publish a statement must set out the terms of the statement.

(3) A warning notice about a proposal to impose a penalty, must state the amount of the penalty.

[235]

NOTES

Note: for the purposes of this section a requirement imposed by the FSA under the Electronic Commerce Directive (Financial Services and Markets) Regulations 2002, SI 2002/1775 upon an authorised incoming provider is to be treated as imposed on him by or under this Act; see reg 12(1) of those Regulations at **[2685]**.

208 Decision notice

(1) If the Authority decides—
   (a) to publish a statement under section 205 (whether or not in the terms proposed), or
   (b) to impose a penalty under section 206 (whether or not of the amount proposed),
it must without delay give the authorised person concerned a decision notice.

(2) In the case of a statement, the decision notice must set out the terms of the statement.

(3) In the case of a penalty, the decision notice must state the amount of the penalty.

(4) If the Authority decides to—
   (a) publish a statement in respect of an authorised person under section 205, or
   (b) impose a penalty on an authorised person under section 206,
the authorised person may refer the matter to the Tribunal.

[236]

NOTES

Note: for the purposes of this section a requirement imposed by the FSA under the Electronic Commerce Directive (Financial Services and Markets) Regulations 2002, SI 2002/1775 upon an authorised incoming provider is to be treated as imposed on him by or under this Act; see reg 12(1) of those Regulations at **[2685]**.

209 Publication

After a statement under section 205 is published, the Authority must send a copy of it to the authorised person and to any person on whom a copy of the decision notice was given under section 393(4).

[237]

PART I
FSMA 2000

NOTES

Note: for the purposes of this section a requirement imposed by the FSA under the Electronic Commerce Directive (Financial Services and Markets) Regulations 2002, SI 2002/1775 upon an authorised incoming provider is to be treated as imposed on him by or under this Act; see reg 12(1) of those Regulations at **[2685]**.

210   Statements of policy

(1)   The Authority must prepare and issue a statement of its policy with respect to—
   (a)   the imposition of penalties under this Part; and
   (b)   the amount of penalties under this Part.

(2)   The Authority's policy in determining what the amount of a penalty should be must include having regard to—
   (a)   the seriousness of the contravention in question in relation to the nature of the requirement contravened;
   (b)   the extent to which that contravention was deliberate or reckless; and
   (c)   whether the person on whom the penalty is to be imposed is an individual.

(3)   The Authority may at any time alter or replace a statement issued under this section.

(4)   If a statement issued under this section is altered or replaced, the Authority must issue the altered or replacement statement.

(5)   The Authority must, without delay, give the Treasury a copy of any statement which it publishes under this section.

(6)   A statement issued under this section must be published by the Authority in the way appearing to the Authority to be best calculated to bring it to the attention of the public.

(7)   In exercising, or deciding whether to exercise, its power under section 206 in the case of any particular contravention, the Authority must have regard to any statement published under this section and in force at the time when the contravention in question occurred.

(8)   The Authority may charge a reasonable fee for providing a person with a copy of the statement.

[238]

211   Statements of policy: procedure

(1)   Before issuing a statement under section 210, the Authority must publish a draft of the proposed statement in the way appearing to the Authority to be best calculated to bring it to the attention of the public.

(2)   The draft must be accompanied by notice that representations about the proposal may be made to the Authority within a specified time.

(3)   Before issuing the proposed statement, the Authority must have regard to any representations made to it in accordance with subsection (2).

(4)   If the Authority issues the proposed statement it must publish an account, in general terms, of—
   (a)   the representations made to it in accordance with subsection (2); and
   (b)   its response to them.

(5)   If the statement differs from the draft published under subsection (1) in a way which is, in the opinion of the Authority, significant, the Authority must (in addition to complying with subsection (4)) publish details of the difference.

(6)   The Authority may charge a reasonable fee for providing a person with a copy of a draft published under subsection (1).

(7)   This section also applies to a proposal to alter or replace a statement.

[239]

PART XV
THE FINANCIAL SERVICES COMPENSATION SCHEME

NOTES

Transitional provisions: see the Financial Services and Markets Act 2000 (Transitional Provisions, Repeals and Savings) (Financial Services Compensation Scheme) Order 2001, SI 2001/2967, which makes transitional provisions in connection with the Financial Services Compensation Scheme. This scheme supersedes eight former compensation schemes; ie, the Policyholders Protection Scheme, the Deposit Protection Scheme, the Building Societies Investor Protection Scheme, the Investor Compensation Scheme, the section 43 Compensation Scheme, the Friendly Societies Protection Scheme, the Personal Investment Authority indemnity scheme, and the arrangements described in the ABI/ICS agreement ("the ABI scheme"). In relation to credit unions, see also the Financial Services and Markets Act 2000 (Consequential Amendments and Transitional Provisions) (Credit Unions) Order 2002, SI 2002/1501, art 5.

The scheme manager

212 The scheme manager

(1)   The Authority must establish a body corporate ("the scheme manager") to exercise the functions conferred on the scheme manager by or under this Part.

(2)   The Authority must take such steps as are necessary to ensure that the scheme manager is, at all times, capable of exercising those functions.

(3)   The constitution of the scheme manager must provide for it to have—
   (a)   a chairman; and
   (b)   a board (which must include the chairman) whose members are the scheme manager's directors.

(4)   The chairman and other members of the board must be persons appointed, and liable to removal from office, by the Authority (acting, in the case of the chairman, with the approval of the Treasury).

(5)   But the terms of their appointment (and in particular those governing removal from office) must be such as to secure their independence from the Authority in the operation of the compensation scheme.

(6)   The scheme manager is not to be regarded as exercising functions on behalf of the Crown.

(7)   The scheme manager's board members, officers and staff are not to be regarded as Crown servants.

[240]

The scheme

213 The compensation scheme

(1)   The Authority must by rules establish a scheme for compensating persons in cases where relevant persons are unable, or are likely to be unable, to satisfy claims against them.

(2)   The rules are to be known as the Financial Services Compensation Scheme (but are referred to in this Act as "the compensation scheme").

(3)   The compensation scheme must, in particular, provide for the scheme manager—
   (a)   to assess and pay compensation, in accordance with the scheme, to claimants in respect of claims made in connection with regulated activities carried on (whether or not with permission) by relevant persons; and
   (b)   to have power to impose levies on authorised persons, or any class of authorised person, for the purpose of meeting its expenses (including in particular expenses incurred, or expected to be incurred, in paying compensation, borrowing or insuring risks).

(4)   The compensation scheme may provide for the scheme manager to have power to impose levies on authorised persons, or any class of authorised person, for the purpose of recovering the cost (whenever incurred) of establishing the scheme.

(5)   In making any provision of the scheme by virtue of subsection (3)(b), the Authority must take account of the desirability of ensuring that the amount of the levies imposed on a particular class of authorised person reflects, so far as practicable, the amount of the claims made, or likely to be made, in respect of that class of person.

(6)   An amount payable to the scheme manager as a result of any provision of the scheme made by virtue of subsection (3)(b) or (4) may be recovered as a debt due to the scheme manager.

(7)   Sections 214 to 217 make further provision about the scheme but are not to be taken as limiting the power conferred on the Authority by subsection (1) [(except where limitations are expressly stated)].

(8)   In those sections "specified" means specified in the scheme.

(9)   In this Part (except in sections 219, 220 or 224) "relevant person" means a person who was—
   (a)   an authorised person at the time the act or omission giving rise to the claim against him took place; or
   (b)   an appointed representative at that time.

(10)   But a person who, at that time—
   (a)   qualified for authorisation under Schedule 3, and
   (b)   fell within a prescribed category,
is not to be regarded as a relevant person in relation to any activities for which he had permission as a result of any provision of, or made under, that Schedule unless he had elected to participate in the scheme in relation to those activities at that time.

[241]

PART I
FSMA 2000

NOTES

Sub-s (7): words in square brackets inserted by the Banking Act 2009, s 170(2), as from a day to be appointed.

Note: membership of the scheme is voluntary for those who qualify for authorisation under Sch 3 to this Act (ie, incoming EEA firms authorised under Sch 3). The compensation scheme may provide that incoming EEA firms can elect to participate in relation to some or all the activities for which it has permission under Sch 3 (see s 214(5)). The Financial Services and Markets Act 2000 (Compensation Scheme: Electing Participants) Regulations 2001, SI 2001/1783, reg 3 (at **[2344]**), as amended, prescribes the categories of firms to which this applies, ie, investment firms, relevant management companies under the UCITS management directive, credit institutions with UK branches, and any insurance intermediary which is not an investment firm or a credit institution. The Financial Services Compensation Scheme provides information including a list of those firms that have voluntarily joined the scheme. See
http://www.fscs.org.uk/consumer/how_to_claim/deposits/eea_firms_that_have_topped_up.

Application in relation to interim permissions and interim approvals: see the notes preceding s 40 at **[40]**.

Regulations: the Financial Services and Markets Act 2000 (Compensation Scheme: Electing Participants) Regulations 2001, SI 2001/1783 at **[2342]**.

Note that the following amending Regulations have also been made under this section: the Collective Investment Schemes (Miscellaneous Amendments) Regulations 2003, SI 2003/2066.

Provisions of the scheme

214   General

(1)   The compensation scheme may, in particular, make provision—

   (a)   as to the circumstances in which a relevant person is to be taken (for the purposes of the scheme) to be unable, or likely to be unable, to satisfy claims made against him;

   (b)   for the establishment of different funds for meeting different kinds of claim;

   (c)   for the imposition of different levies in different cases;

   (d)   limiting the levy payable by a person in respect of a specified period;

   (e)   for repayment of the whole or part of a levy in specified circumstances;

   (f)   for a claim to be entertained only if it is made by a specified kind of claimant;

   (g)   for a claim to be entertained only if it falls within a specified kind of claim;

   (h)   as to the procedure to be followed in making a claim;

   (i)   for the making of interim payments before a claim is finally determined;

   (j)   limiting the amount payable on a claim to a specified maximum amount or a maximum amount calculated in a specified manner;

   (k)   for payment to be made, in specified circumstances, to a person other than the claimant.

[(1A)   Rules by virtue of subsection (1)(h) may, in particular, allow the scheme manager to treat persons who are or may be entitled to claim under the scheme as if they had done so.

(1B)   A reference in any enactment or instrument to a claim or claimant under this Part includes a reference to a deemed claim or claimant in accordance with subsection (1A).

(1C)   Rules by virtue of subsection (1)(j) may, in particular, allow, or be subject to rules which allow, the scheme manager to settle a class of claim by payment of sums fixed without reference to, or by modification of, the normal rules for calculation of maximum entitlement for individual claims.]

(2)   Different provision may be made with respect to different kinds of claim.

(3)   The scheme may provide for the determination and regulation of matters relating to the scheme by the scheme manager.

(4)   The scheme, or particular provisions of the scheme, may be made so as to apply only in relation to—

   (a)   activities carried on,

   (b)   claimants,

   (c)   matters arising, or

   (d)   events occurring,

in specified territories, areas or localities.

(5)   The scheme may provide for a person who—

   (a)   qualifies for authorisation under Schedule 3, and

   (b)   falls within a prescribed category,

to elect to participate in the scheme in relation to some or all of the activities for which he has permission as a result of any provision of, or made under, that Schedule.

(6)   The scheme may provide for the scheme manager to have power—

   (a)   in specified circumstances,

   (b)   but only if the scheme manager is satisfied that the claimant is entitled to receive a payment in respect of his claim—

      (i)   under a scheme which is comparable to the compensation scheme, or

      (ii)   as the result of a guarantee given by a government or other authority, to make a full payment of compensation to the claimant and recover the whole or part of the amount of that payment from the other scheme or under that guarantee.

[242]

NOTES

Sub-ss (1A)–(1C): inserted by the Banking Act 2009, s 174(1), as from a day to be appointed.

Regulations: the Financial Services and Markets Act 2000 (Compensation Scheme: Electing Participants) Regulations 2001, SI 2001/1783 at **[2342]**.

Note that the following amending Regulations have also been made under this section: the Collective Investment Schemes (Miscellaneous Amendments) Regulations 2003, SI 2003/2066.

[214A Contingency funding

(1)   The Treasury may make regulations ("contingency fund regulations") permitting the scheme manager to impose levies under section 213 for the purpose of maintaining contingency funds from which possible expenses may be paid.

(2)   Contingency fund regulations may make provision about the establishment and management of contingency funds; in particular, the regulations may make provision about—

(a)   the number and size of funds;

(b)   the circumstances and timing of their establishment;

(c)   the classes of person from whom contributions to the funds may be levied;

(d)   the amount and timing of payments into and out of funds (which may include provision for different levies for different classes of person);

(e)   refunds;

(f)   the ways in which funds' contents may be invested (including (i) the extent of reliance on section 223A, and (ii) the application of investment income);

(g)   the purposes for which funds may be applied, but only so as to determine whether a fund is to be used (i) for the payment of compensation, (ii) for the purposes of co-operating with a bank liquidator in accordance with section 99 of the Banking Act 2009, or (iii) for contributions under section 214B;

(h)   procedures to be followed in connection with funds, including the keeping of records and the provision of information.

(3)   The compensation scheme may include provision about contingency funds provided that it is not inconsistent with contingency fund regulations.]

[242A]

NOTES

Commencement: to be appointed.

Inserted by the Banking Act 2009, s 170(1), as from a day to be appointed.

[214B Contribution to costs of special resolution regime

(1)   This section applies where—

(a)   a stabilisation power under Part 1 of the Banking Act 2009 has been exercised in respect of a bank, building society or credit union (within the meaning of that Part), and

(b)   the Treasury think that the bank, building society or credit union was, or but for the exercise of the stabilisation power would have become, unable to satisfy claims against it.

(2)   Where this section applies—

(a)   the Treasury may require the scheme manager to make payments in connection with the exercise of the stabilisation power, and

(b)   payments shall be treated as expenditure under the scheme for all purposes (including levies, contingency funds and borrowing).

(3)   The Treasury shall make regulations—

(a)   specifying what expenses the scheme manager may be required to incur under subsection (2),

(b)   providing for independent verification of the nature and amount of expenses incurred in connection with the exercise of the stabilisation power (which may include provision about appointment and payment of an auditor), and

(c)   providing for the method by which amounts to be paid are to be determined.

(4)   The regulations must ensure that payments required do not exceed the amount of compensation that would have been payable under the scheme if the stabilisation power had not been exercised and the bank had been unable to satisfy claims against it; and for that purpose the amount of compensation that would have been payable does not include—

(a)   amounts that would have been likely, at the time when the stabilisation power was exercised, to be recovered by the scheme from the bank, or

(b)   any compensation actually paid to an eligible depositor of the bank.

(5)   The regulations must provide for the appointment of an independent valuer (who may be the person appointed as valuer under section 54 of the Banking Act 2009 in respect of the exercise of the stabilisation power) to calculate the amounts referred to in subsection (4)(a); and the regulations—

- (a)   must provide for the valuer to be appointed by the Treasury or by a person designated by the Treasury,
- (b)   must include provision enabling the valuer to reconsider a decision,
- (c)   must provide a right of appeal to a court or tribunal,
- (d)   must provide for payment of the valuer,
- (e)   may replicate or apply a provision of section 54 or 55, and
- (f)   may apply or include any provision that is or could be made under that section.

(6)   Payments required to be made by the scheme by virtue of section 61 of the Banking Act 2009 (special resolution regime: compensation) shall be treated for the purposes of subsection (4) as if required to be made under this section.

(7)   The regulations may include provision for payments (including payments under those provisions of the Banking Act 2009) to be made—

- (a)   before verification in accordance with subsection (3)(b), and
- (b)   before the calculation of the limit imposed by subsection (4), by reference to estimates of that limit and subject to any necessary later adjustment.

(8)   The regulations may include provision—

- (a)   about timing;
- (b)   about procedures to be followed;
- (c)   for discretionary functions to be exercised by a specified body or by persons of a specified class;
- (d)   about the resolution of disputes (which may include provision conferring jurisdiction on a court or tribunal).

(9)   The compensation scheme may include provision about payments under and levies in connection with this section, provided that it is not inconsistent with this section or regulations under it.]

[242B]

NOTES
Commencement: to be appointed.
Inserted by the Banking Act 2009, s 171(1), as from a day to be appointed.

215   *Rights of the scheme in relevant person's insolvency*

(1)   The compensation scheme may, in particular, make provision—
- *(a)   as to the effect of a payment of compensation under the scheme in relation to rights or obligations arising out of the claim against a relevant person in respect of which the payment was made;*
- *(b)   for conferring on the scheme manager a right of recovery against that person.*

(2)   Such a right of recovery conferred by the scheme does not, in the event of *the relevant person's insolvency*, exceed such right (if any) as the claimant would have had in that event.

(3)   If a person other than the scheme manager [makes an administration application under Schedule B1 to the 1986 Act or [Schedule B1 to] the 1989 Order] in relation to a company or partnership which is a relevant person, the scheme manager has the same rights as are conferred on the Authority by section 362.

[(3A)   In subsection (3) the reference to making an administration application includes a reference to—
- (a)   appointing an administrator under paragraph 14 or 22 of Schedule B1 to the 1986 Act [or paragraph 15 or 23 of Schedule B1 to the 1989 Order], or
- (b)   filing with the court a copy of notice of intention to appoint an administrator under [any] of those paragraphs.]

(4)   If a person other than the scheme manager presents a petition for the winding up of a body which is a relevant person, the scheme manager has the same rights as are conferred on the Authority by section 371.

(5)   If a person other than the scheme manager presents a bankruptcy petition to the court in relation to an individual who, or an entity which, is a relevant person, the scheme manager has the same rights as are conferred on the Authority by section 374.

(6)   Insolvency rules may be made for the purpose of integrating any procedure for which provision is made as a result of subsection (1) into the general procedure on the administration of a company or partnership or on a winding-up, bankruptcy or sequestration.

(7)   "Bankruptcy petition" means a petition to the court—

    (a)   under section 264 of the 1986 Act or Article 238 of the 1989 Order for a bankruptcy order to be made against an individual;

    (b)   under section 5 of the 1985 Act for the sequestration of the estate of an individual; or

    (c)   under section 6 of the 1985 Act for the sequestration of the estate belonging to or held for or jointly by the members of an entity mentioned in subsection (1) of that section.

(8)   "Insolvency rules" are—

    (a)   for England and Wales, rules made under sections 411 and 412 of the 1986 Act;

    (b)   for Scotland, rules made by order by the Treasury, after consultation with the Scottish Ministers, for the purposes of this section; and

    (c)   for Northern Ireland, rules made under Article 359 of the 1989 Order and section 55 of the Judicature (Northern Ireland) Act 1978.

(9)   "The 1985 Act", "the 1986 Act", "the 1989 Order" and "court" have the same meaning as in Part XXIV.

[243]

NOTES

Section heading: for the words in italics there are substituted the words "Rights of the scheme in insolvency" by the Banking Act 2009, s 175(1), (4), as from a day to be appointed.

Sub-s (1): substituted by the Banking Act 2009, s 175(1), (2), as from a day to be appointed, as follows—

"(1)   The compensation scheme may make provision—

    (a)   about the effect of a payment of compensation under the scheme on rights or obligations arising out of matters in connection with which the compensation was paid;

    (b)   giving the scheme manager a right of recovery in respect of those rights or obligations.".

Sub-s (2): for the words in italics there are substituted the words "a person's insolvency" by the Banking Act 2009, s 175(1), (3), as from a day to be appointed.

Sub-s (3): words in first pair of square brackets substituted by the Enterprise Act 2002, s 248(3), Sch 17, paras 53, 54(1), (2), as from 15 September 2003 (for savings and transitional provisions in relation to a petition for an administration order presented before that date, and in relation to special administration regimes (within the meaning of the Enterprise Act 2002, s 249), see the note to the Insolvency Act 1986, s 8 at **[1131]**); words in second pair of square brackets substituted by the Insolvency (Northern Ireland) Order 2005, SI 2005/1455, art 3(3), Sch 2, paras 56, 57(1), (2), as from 27 March 2006.

Sub-s (3A): inserted by the Enterprise Act 2002, s 248(3), Sch 17, paras 53, 54(1), (3), as from 15 September 2003 (subject to savings and transitional provisions as noted above); words in square brackets in para (a) inserted, and word in square brackets in para (b) substituted, by SI 2005/1455, art 3(3), Sch 2, paras 56, 57(1), (3), as from 27 March 2006.

Limited liability partnerships: as to the application of this section to LLPs, see the note at the beginning of this Act.

---

216 Continuity of long-term insurance policies

(1)   The compensation scheme may, in particular, include provision requiring the scheme manager to make arrangements for securing continuity of insurance for policyholders, or policyholders of a specified class, of relevant long-term insurers.

(2)   "Relevant long-term insurers" means relevant persons who—

    (a)   have permission to effect or carry out contracts of long-term insurance; and

    (b)   are unable, or likely to be unable, to satisfy claims made against them.

(3)   The scheme may provide for the scheme manager to take such measures as appear to him to be appropriate—

    (a)   for securing or facilitating the transfer of a relevant long-term insurer's business so far as it consists of the carrying out of contracts of long-term insurance, or of any part of that business, to another authorised person;

    (b)   for securing the issue by another authorised person to the policyholders concerned of policies in substitution for their existing policies.

(4)   The scheme may also provide for the scheme manager to make payments to the policyholders concerned—

    (a)   during any period while he is seeking to make arrangements mentioned in subsection (1);

    (b)   if it appears to him that it is not reasonably practicable to make such arrangements.

(5)   A provision of the scheme made by virtue of section 213(3)(b) may include power to impose levies for the purpose of meeting expenses of the scheme manager incurred in—

    (a)   taking measures as a result of any provision of the scheme made by virtue of subsection (3);

    (b)   making payments as a result of any such provision made by virtue of subsection (4).

[244]

217   Insurers in financial difficulties

(1)   The compensation scheme may, in particular, include provision for the scheme manager to have power to take measures for safeguarding policyholders, or policyholders of a specified class, of relevant insurers.

(2)   "Relevant insurers" means relevant persons who—
   (a)   have permission to effect or carry out contracts of insurance; and
   (b)   are in financial difficulties.

(3)   The measures may include such measures as the scheme manager considers appropriate for—
   (a)   securing or facilitating the transfer of a relevant insurer's business so far as it consists of the carrying out of contracts of insurance, or of any part of that business, to another authorised person;
   (b)   giving assistance to the relevant insurer to enable it to continue to effect or carry out contracts of insurance.

(4)   The scheme may provide—
   (a)   that if measures of a kind mentioned in subsection (3)(a) are to be taken, they should be on terms appearing to the scheme manager to be appropriate, including terms reducing, or deferring payment of, any of the things to which any of those who are eligible policyholders in relation to the relevant insurer are entitled in their capacity as such;
   (b)   that if measures of a kind mentioned in subsection (3)(b) are to be taken, they should be conditional on the reduction of, or the deferment of the payment of, the things to which any of those who are eligible policyholders in relation to the relevant insurer are entitled in their capacity as such;
   (c)   for ensuring that measures of a kind mentioned in subsection (3)(b) do not benefit to any material extent persons who were members of a relevant insurer when it began to be in financial difficulties or who had any responsibility for, or who may have profited from, the circumstances giving rise to its financial difficulties, except in specified circumstances;
   (d)   for requiring the scheme manager to be satisfied that any measures he proposes to take are likely to cost less than it would cost to pay compensation under the scheme if the relevant insurer became unable, or likely to be unable, to satisfy claims made against him.

(5)   The scheme may provide for the Authority to have power—
   (a)   to give such assistance to the scheme manager as it considers appropriate for assisting the scheme manager to determine what measures are practicable or desirable in the case of a particular relevant insurer;
   (b)   to impose constraints on the taking of measures by the scheme manager in the case of a particular relevant insurer;
   (c)   to require the scheme manager to provide it with information about any particular measures which the scheme manager is proposing to take.

(6)   The scheme may include provision for the scheme manager to have power—
   (a)   to make interim payments in respect of eligible policyholders of a relevant insurer;
   (b)   to indemnify any person making payments to eligible policyholders of a relevant insurer.

(7)   A provision of the scheme made by virtue of section 213(3)(b) may include power to impose levies for the purpose of meeting expenses of the scheme manager incurred in—
   (a)   taking measures as a result of any provision of the scheme made by virtue of subsection (1);
   (b)   making payments or giving indemnities as a result of any such provision made by virtue of subsection (6).

(8)   "Financial difficulties" and "eligible policyholders" have such meanings as may be specified.

[245]

Annual report

218   Annual report

(1)   At least once a year, the scheme manager must make a report to the Authority [and the Treasury] on the discharge of its functions.

(2)   The report must—
   (a)   include a statement setting out the value of each of the funds established by the compensation scheme; and
   (b)   comply with any requirements specified in rules made by the Authority [or in contingency fund regulations].

(3)   The scheme manager must publish each report in the way it considers appropriate.

[246]

Information and documents

[218A Authority's power to require information

(1) The Authority may make rules enabling the Authority to require authorised persons to provide information, which may then be made available to the scheme manager by the Authority.

(2) A requirement may be imposed only if the Authority thinks the information is of a kind that may be of use to the scheme manager in connection with functions in respect of the scheme.

(3) A requirement under this section may apply—
    (a) to authorised persons generally or only to specified persons or classes of person;
    (b) to the provision of information at specified periods, in connection with specified events or in other ways.

(4) In addition to requirements under this section, a notice under section 165 may relate to information or documents which the Authority thinks are reasonably required by the scheme manager in connection with the performance of functions in respect of the scheme; and section 165(4) is subject to this subsection.

(5) Rules under subsection (1) shall be prepared, made and treated in the same way as (and may be combined with) the Authority's general rules.]

[246A]

219 Scheme manager's power to require information

(1) The scheme manager may, by notice in writing *given to the relevant person in respect of whom a claim is made under the scheme or to a person otherwise involved, require that person*—
    (a) to provide specified information or information of a specified description; or
    (b) to produce specified documents or documents of a specified description.

[(1A) A requirement may be imposed only—
    (a) on a person (P) against whom a claim has been made under the scheme,
    (b) on a person (P) who is unable or likely to be unable to satisfy claims under the scheme against P,
    (c) on a person ("the Third Party") whom the scheme manager thinks was knowingly involved in matters giving rise to a claim against another person (P) under the scheme, or
    (d) on a person ("the Third Party") whom the scheme manager thinks was knowingly involved in matters giving rise to the actual or likely inability of another person (P) to satisfy claims under the scheme.

(1B) For the purposes of subsection (1A)(b) and (d) whether P is unable or likely to be unable to satisfy claims shall be determined in accordance with provision to be made by the scheme (which may, in particular—
    (a) apply or replicate, with or without modifications, a provision of an enactment;
    (b) confer discretion on a specified person).]

(2) The information or documents must be provided or produced—
    (a) before the end of such reasonable period as may be specified; and
    (b) in the case of information, in such manner or form as may be specified.

(3) This section applies only to information and documents the provision or production of which the scheme manager considers—
    (*a*) *to be necessary for the fair determination of the claim; or*
    (*b*) *to be necessary (or likely to be necessary) for the fair determination of other claims made (or which it expects may be made) in respect of the relevant person concerned.*

[(3A) Where a stabilisation power under Part 1 of the Banking Act 2009 has been exercised in respect of a bank, the scheme manager may by notice in writing require the bank or the Bank of England to provide information that the scheme manager requires for the purpose of applying regulations under section 214B(3) above.]

(4) If a document is produced in response to a requirement imposed under this section, the scheme manager may—
    (a) take copies or extracts from the document; or
    (b) require the person producing the document to provide an explanation of the document.

(5)   If a person who is required under this section to produce a document fails to do so, the scheme manager may require the person to state, to the best of his knowledge and belief, where the document is.

(6)   If *the relevant person* is insolvent, no requirement may be imposed under this section on a person to whom section 220 or 224 applies.

(7)   If a person claims a lien on a document, its production under this Part does not affect the lien.

(8)   *"Relevant person" has the same meaning as in section 224.*

(9)   "Specified" means specified in the notice given under subsection (1).

(10)   *A person is involved in a claim made under the scheme if he was knowingly involved in the act or omission giving rise to the claim.*

[247]

NOTES
Sub-s (1): for the words in italics there are substituted the words "require a person" by the Banking Act 2009, s 176(2), (3), as from a day to be appointed.
Sub-ss (1A), (1B), (3A): inserted by the Banking Act 2009, s 176(2), (4), (6), as from a day to be appointed.
Sub-s (3): for the words in italics there are substituted the words "to be necessary (or likely to be necessary) for the fair determination of claims which have been or may be made against P" by the Banking Act 2009, s 176(2), (5), as from a day to be appointed.
Sub-s (6): for the words in italics there is substituted the letter "P" by the Banking Act 2009, s 176(2), (7), as from a day to be appointed.
Sub-ss (8), (10): repealed by the Banking Act 2009, s 176(2), (8), (9), as from a day to be appointed.

220   Scheme manager's power to inspect information held by liquidator etc

(1)   For the purpose of assisting the scheme manager to discharge its functions in relation to a claim made in respect of an insolvent relevant person, a person to whom this section applies must permit a person authorised by the scheme manager to inspect relevant documents.

(2)   A person inspecting a document under this section may take copies of, or extracts from, the document.

(3)   This section applies to—
(a)   the administrative receiver, administrator, liquidator[, bank liquidator] or trustee in bankruptcy of an insolvent relevant person;
(b)   the permanent trustee, within the meaning of the Bankruptcy (Scotland) Act 1985, on the estate of an insolvent relevant person.

(4)   This section does not apply to a liquidator, administrator or trustee in bankruptcy who is—
(a)   the Official Receiver;
(b)   the Official Receiver for Northern Ireland; or
(c)   the Accountant in Bankruptcy.

(5)   "Relevant person" has the same meaning as in section 224.

[248]

NOTES
Sub-s (3): words in square brackets inserted by the Banking Act 2009, s 123(3), as from a day to be appointed.

221   Powers of court where information required

(1)   If a person ("the defaulter")—
(a)   fails to comply with a requirement imposed under section 219, or
(b)   fails to permit documents to be inspected under section 220,
the scheme manager may certify that fact in writing to the court and the court may enquire into the case.

(2)   If the court is satisfied that the defaulter failed without reasonable excuse to comply with the requirement (or to permit the documents to be inspected), it may deal with the defaulter (and, in the case of a body corporate, any director or officer) as if he were in contempt[; and "officer", in relation to a limited liability partnership, means a member of the limited liability partnership].

(3)   "Court" means—
(a)   the High Court;
(b)   in Scotland, the Court of Session.

[249]

NOTES
Sub-s (2): words in square brackets added by the Limited Liability Partnerships Regulations 2001, SI 2001/1090, reg 9, Sch 5, para 21, as from 6 April 2001.

Miscellaneous

[221A Delegation of functions

(1) The scheme manager may arrange for any of its functions to be discharged on its behalf by another person (a "scheme agent").

(2) Before entering into arrangements the scheme manager must be satisfied that the scheme agent—

    (a) is competent to discharge the function, and

    (b) has been given sufficient directions to enable the agent to take any decisions required in the course of exercising the function in accordance with policy determined by the scheme manager.

(3) Arrangements may include provision for payments to be made by the scheme manager to the scheme agent (which payments are management expenses of the scheme manager).]

[249A]

NOTES

Commencement: to be appointed.
Inserted by the Banking Act 2009, s 179(1), as from a day to be appointed.

222 Statutory immunity

(1) Neither the scheme manager nor any person who is, or is acting as, its board member, officer[, scheme agent] or member of staff is to be liable in damages for anything done or omitted in the discharge, or purported discharge, of the scheme manager's functions.

(2) Subsection (1) does not apply—

    (a) if the act or omission is shown to have been in bad faith; or

    (b) so as to prevent an award of damages made in respect of an act or omission on the ground that the act or omission was unlawful as a result of section 6(1) of the Human Rights Act 1998.

[250]

NOTES

Sub-s (1): words in square brackets inserted by the Banking Act 2009, s 179(2), as from a day to be appointed.

223 Management expenses

(1) The amount which the scheme manager may recover, from the sums levied under the scheme, as management expenses attributable to a particular period may not exceed such amount as may be fixed by the scheme as the limit applicable to that period.

(2) In calculating the amount of any levy to be imposed by the scheme manager, no amount may be included to reflect management expenses unless the limit mentioned in subsection (1) has been fixed by the scheme.

(3) "Management expenses" means expenses incurred, or expected to be incurred, by the scheme manager in connection with its functions under this Act other than those incurred—

    (a) in paying compensation;

    (b) as a result of any provision of the scheme made by virtue of section 216(3) or (4) or 217(1) or (6)[;

    (c) under section 214B].

[251]

NOTES

Sub-s (3): para (c) added by the Banking Act 2009, s 171(2), as from a day to be appointed.

[223A Investing in National Loans Fund

(1) Sums levied for the purpose of maintaining a contingency fund may be paid to the Treasury.

(2) The Treasury may receive sums under subsection (1) and may set terms and conditions of receipts.

(3) Sums received shall be treated as if raised under section 12 of the National Loans Act 1968 (and shall therefore be invested as part of the National Loans Fund).

(4) Interest accruing on the invested sums may be credited to the contingency fund (subject to any terms and conditions set under subsection (2)).

(5) The Treasury shall comply with any request of the scheme manager to arrange for the return of sums for the purpose of making payments out of a contingency fund (subject to any terms and conditions set under subsection (2)).]

[251A]

[223B   Borrowing from National Loans Fund

(1)   The scheme manager may request a loan from the National Loans Fund for the purpose of funding expenses incurred or expected to be incurred under the scheme.

(2)   The Treasury may arrange for money to be paid out of the National Loans Fund in pursuance of a request under subsection (1).

(3)   The Treasury shall determine—
    (a)   the rate of interest on a loan, and
    (b)   other terms and conditions.

(4)   The Treasury may make regulations—
    (a)   about the amounts that may be borrowed under this section;
    (b)   permitting the scheme manager to impose levies under section 213 for the purpose of meeting expenses in connection with loans under this section (and the regulations may have effect despite any provision of this Act);
    (c)   about the classes of person on whom those levies may be imposed;
    (d)   about the amounts and timing of those levies.

(5)   The compensation scheme may include provision about borrowing under this section provided that it is not inconsistent with regulations under this section.]

[251B]

[223C   Payments in error

(1)   Payments made by the scheme manager in error may be provided for in setting a levy by virtue of section 213, 214A, 214B or 223B.

(2)   This section does not apply to payments made in bad faith.]

[251C]

224   Scheme manager's power to inspect documents held by Official Receiver etc

(1)   If, as a result of the insolvency or bankruptcy of a relevant person, any documents have come into the possession of a person to whom this section applies, he must permit any person authorised by the scheme manager to inspect the documents for the purpose of establishing—
    (a)   the identity of persons to whom the scheme manager may be liable to make a payment in accordance with the compensation scheme; or
    (b)   the amount of any payment which the scheme manager may be liable to make.

(2)   A person inspecting a document under this section may take copies or extracts from the document.

(3)   In this section "relevant person" means a person who was—
    (a)   an authorised person at the time the act or omission which may give rise to the liability mentioned in subsection (1)(a) took place; or
    (b)   an appointed representative at that time.

(4)   But a person who, at that time—
    (a)   qualified for authorisation under Schedule 3, and
    (b)   fell within a prescribed category,
is not to be regarded as a relevant person for the purposes of this section in relation to any activities for which he had permission as a result of any provision of, or made under, that Schedule unless he had elected to participate in the scheme in relation to those activities at that time.

(5)   This section applies to—
    (a)   the Official Receiver;
    (b)   the Official Receiver for Northern Ireland; and
    (c)   the Accountant in Bankruptcy.

[252]

NOTES

Regulations: the Financial Services and Markets Act 2000 (Compensation Scheme: Electing Participants) Regulations 2001, SI 2001/1783 at **[2342]**.

Note that the following amending Regulations have also been made under this section: the Collective Investment Schemes (Miscellaneous Amendments) Regulations 2003, SI 2003/2066.

[224A Functions under the Banking Act 2009   A reference in this Part to functions of the scheme manager (including a reference to functions conferred by or under this Part) includes a reference to functions conferred by or under the Banking Act 2009.]

[252A]

NOTES

Commencement: to be appointed.

Inserted by the Banking Act 2009, s 180, as from a day to be appointed.

PART XVI

THE OMBUDSMAN SCHEME

NOTES

Transitional provisions: see the Financial Services and Markets Act 2000 (Transitional Provisions) (Ombudsman Scheme and Complaints Scheme) Order 2001, SI 2001/2326. Arts 2–17 of that Order make transitional provisions in relation to the establishment of the ombudsman scheme by this Part. The Order provides for certain complaints relating to acts or omissions occurring before the commencement of this Part, which fell (or would have fallen) within the scope of one of the "former schemes", to be dealt with under the new scheme, subject to specified modifications set out in arts 4–7. Arts 8–10 make provision for appeals against certain determinations made before commencement under the IMRO scheme, the SFA scheme and the building societies scheme. Art 16 provides that where consultation on rules for the new scheme was undertaken before 19 July 2001, that consultation is to be taken to satisfy the requirements in Sch 17 to this Act to the extent that it would have done so if undertaken after that date. Art 17 provides for liabilities of the former schemes arising from the handling of complaints to become liabilities of the operator of the new scheme. Arts 18–20 are concerned with complaints relating to certain matters occurring before the coming into force of s 19 of this Act. Art 18 empowers the FSA to make arrangements for the investigation of such complaints and supplements the Authority's duty, under Sch 1, paras 7 and 8, to make arrangements for the investigation of complaints relating to the exercise of (or failure to exercise) its functions under the Act. Art 19 makes provision about anticipatory consultation with respect to any "transitional complaints scheme" made under art 18. Art 20 confers exemption from liability in damages on those investigating "transitional complaints" under art 18.

See also the Financial Services and Markets Act 2000 (Transitional Provisions) (Complaints Relating to General Insurance and Mortgages) Order 2004, SI 2004/454 at **[2712]** et seq. The 2004 Order makes further provision in relation to the inclusion of the activities of arranging and advising on regulated mortgage contracts, and insurance mediation activities, as regulated activities for the purposes of this Act. It modifies this Part and provides that certain complaints relating to acts or omissions which would have fallen within the Mortgage Code Arbitration Scheme or the Dispute Resolution Facility established by the General Insurance Standards Council can be dealt with under the new scheme established by this Part.

Disputes relating to mutual societies: nothing in the Friendly Societies Act 1992, s 80(1) (determination of certain disputes by arbitration), or in rules of a kind mentioned in that subsection, prevents any person from having a complaint dealt with under the ombudsman scheme under this Part before, or instead of, arbitration; see s 80(1A) of the 1992 Act. Similarly, nothing in the Industrial and Provident Societies Act 1965, s 60(1) (decision of disputes), or in rules of a kind mentioned in that subsection, prevents any person from having a complaint dealt with under the ombudsman scheme under this Part before, or instead of, determination in the manner directed in the rules; see s 60(1A) of the 1965 Act.

Data protection: personal data processed for the purpose of discharging any function which is conferred by or under this Part on the body established by the FSA for the purposes of this Part are exempt from the subject information provisions in any case to the extent to which the application of those provisions to the data would be likely to prejudice the proper discharge of the function; see the Data Protection Act 1998, s 31 at **[1235]**.

The scheme

225   The scheme and the scheme operator

(1)   This Part provides for a scheme under which certain disputes may be resolved quickly and with minimum formality by an independent person.

(2)   The scheme is to be administered by a body corporate ("the scheme operator").

(3)   The scheme is to be operated under a name chosen by the scheme operator but is referred to in this Act as "the ombudsman scheme".

(4)   Schedule 17 makes provision in connection with the ombudsman scheme and the scheme operator.

[253]

226   Compulsory jurisdiction

(1)   A complaint which relates to an act or omission of a person ("the respondent") in carrying on an activity to which compulsory jurisdiction rules apply is to be dealt with under the ombudsman scheme if the conditions mentioned in subsection (2) are satisfied.

(2)   The conditions are that—

   (a)   the complainant is eligible and wishes to have the complaint dealt with under the scheme;

   (b)   the respondent was an authorised person[, or a payment service provider within the meaning of the Payment Services Regulations 2009,] at the time of the act or omission to which the complaint relates; and

   (c)   the act or omission to which the complaint relates occurred at a time when compulsory jurisdiction rules were in force in relation to the activity in question.

(3)   "Compulsory jurisdiction rules" means rules—

   (a)   made by the Authority for the purposes of this section; and

   (b)   specifying the activities to which they apply.

(4)   Only activities which are regulated activities, or which could be made regulated activities by an order under section 22, may be specified.

(5)   Activities may be specified by reference to specified categories (however described).

(6)   A complainant is eligible, in relation to the compulsory jurisdiction of the ombudsman scheme, if he falls within a class of person specified in the rules as eligible.

(7)   The rules—

   (a)   may include provision for persons other than individuals to be eligible; but

   (b)   may not provide for authorised persons to be eligible except in specified circumstances or in relation to complaints of a specified kind.

(8)   The jurisdiction of the scheme which results from this section is referred to in this Act as the "compulsory jurisdiction".

[254]

NOTES

Sub-s (2): words in square brackets inserted by the Payment Services Regulations 2009, SI 2009/209, reg 126, Sch 6, Pt 1, para 1(1)(a), as from 2 March 2009 (for the full commencement details of the 2009 Regulations, see reg 1 of those Regulations at **[4387]**).

Transitional provisions: see the Financial Services and Markets Act 2000 (Transitional Provisions) (Ombudsman Scheme and Complaints Scheme) Order 2001, SI 2001/2326 in relation to complaints first arising before N2 or relating to acts or omissions occurring before N2. See also the Financial Services and Markets Act 2000 (Transitional Provisions) (Complaints relating to General Insurance and Mortgages) Order 2004, SI 2004/454, art 2 (at **[2713]**) for application of compulsory jurisdiction to a complaint referred to the new scheme on or after the relevant commencement date.

[226A   Consumer credit jurisdiction

(1)   A complaint which relates to an act or omission of a person ("the respondent") is to be dealt with under the ombudsman scheme if the conditions mentioned in subsection (2) are satisfied.

(2)   The conditions are that—

   (a)   the complainant is eligible and wishes to have the complaint dealt with under the scheme;

   (b)   the complaint falls within a description specified in consumer credit rules;

   (c)   at the time of the act or omission the respondent was the licensee under a standard licence or was authorised to carry on an activity by virtue of section 34A of the Consumer Credit Act 1974;

   (d)   the act or omission occurred in the course of a business being carried on by the respondent which was of a type mentioned in subsection (3);

   (e)   at the time of the act or omission that type of business was specified in an order made by the Secretary of State; and

   (f)   the complaint cannot be dealt with under the compulsory jurisdiction.

(3)   The types of business referred to in subsection (2)(d) are—

   (a)   a consumer credit business;

   (b)   a consumer hire business;

   (c)   a business so far as it comprises or relates to credit brokerage;

   (d)   a business so far as it comprises or relates to debt-adjusting;

   (e)   a business so far as it comprises or relates to debt-counselling;

   (f)   a business so far as it comprises or relates to debt-collecting;

   (g)   a business so far as it comprises or relates to debt administration;

   (h)   a business so far as it comprises or relates to the provision of credit information services;

   (i)   a business so far as it comprises or relates to the operation of a credit reference agency.

(4)   A complainant is eligible if—
   (a)   he is—
      (i)   an individual; or
      (ii)   a surety in relation to a security provided to the respondent in connection with the business mentioned in subsection (2)(d); and
   (b)   he falls within a class of person specified in consumer credit rules.

(5)   The approval of the Treasury is required for an order under subsection (2)(e).

(6)   The jurisdiction of the scheme which results from this section is referred to in this Act as the "consumer credit jurisdiction".

(7)   In this Act "consumer credit rules" means rules made by the scheme operator with the approval of the Authority for the purposes of the consumer credit jurisdiction.

(8)   Consumer credit rules under this section may make different provision for different cases.

(9)   Expressions used in the Consumer Credit Act 1974 have the same meaning in this section as they have in that Act.]

[254A]

NOTES
Commencement: 16 June 2006.
Inserted by the Consumer Credit Act 2006, s 59(1), as from 16 June 2006.
Transitional provisions: see the Consumer Credit Act 2006, Sch 3, para 29 which provides that "Section 1 of this Act [ie, substitution of definition of "individual" in the Consumer Credit Act 1974, s 189] shall have no effect for the purposes of section 226A(4)(a) of the 2000 Act in relation to a complaint which relates to an act or omission occurring before the commencement of section 1".
Orders: the Financial Services and Markets Act 2000 (Ombudsman Scheme) (Consumer Credit Jurisdiction) Order 2007, SI 2007/383 at **[2867]**.

227   Voluntary jurisdiction

(1)   A complaint which relates to an act or omission of a person ("the respondent") in carrying on an activity to which voluntary jurisdiction rules apply is to be dealt with under the ombudsman scheme if the conditions mentioned in subsection (2) are satisfied.

(2)   The conditions are that—
   (a)   the complainant is eligible and wishes to have the complaint dealt with under the scheme;
   (b)   at the time of the act or omission to which the complaint relates, the respondent was participating in the scheme;
   (c)   at the time when the complaint is referred under the scheme, the respondent has not withdrawn from the scheme in accordance with its provisions;
   (d)   the act or omission to which the complaint relates occurred at a time when voluntary jurisdiction rules were in force in relation to the activity in question; and
   (e)   the complaint cannot be dealt with under the compulsory jurisdiction [or the consumer credit jurisdiction].

(3)   "Voluntary jurisdiction rules" means rules—
   (a)   made by the scheme operator for the purposes of this section; and
   (b)   specifying the activities to which they apply.

(4)   The only activities which may be specified in the rules are activities which are, or could be, specified in compulsory jurisdiction rules.

(5)   Activities may be specified by reference to specified categories (however described).

(6)   The rules require the Authority's approval.

(7)   A complainant is eligible, in relation to the voluntary jurisdiction of the ombudsman scheme, if he falls within a class of person specified in the rules as eligible.

(8)   The rules may include provision for persons other than individuals to be eligible.

(9)   A person qualifies for participation in the ombudsman scheme if he falls within a class of person specified in the rules in relation to the activity in question.

(10)   Provision may be made in the rules for persons other than authorised persons to participate in the ombudsman scheme.

(11)   The rules may make different provision in relation to complaints arising from different activities.

(12)   The jurisdiction of the scheme which results from this section is referred to in this Act as the "voluntary jurisdiction".

(13)   In such circumstances as may be specified in voluntary jurisdiction rules, a complaint—
   (a)   which relates to an act or omission occurring at a time before the rules came into force, and

(b)   which could have been dealt with under a scheme which has to any extent been replaced by the voluntary jurisdiction,

is to be dealt with under the ombudsman scheme even though paragraph (b) or (d) of subsection (2) would otherwise prevent that.

(14)   In such circumstances as may be specified in voluntary jurisdiction rules, a complaint is to be dealt with under the ombudsman scheme even though—

(a)   paragraph (b) or (d) of subsection (2) would otherwise prevent that, and
(b)   the complaint is not brought within the scheme as a result of subsection (13),

but only if the respondent has agreed that complaints of that kind were to be dealt with under the scheme.

[255]

NOTES

Sub-s (2): words in square brackets inserted by the Consumer Credit Act 2006, s 61(2), as from 16 June 2006.

Determination of complaints

228   Determination under the compulsory jurisdiction

(1)   This section applies only in relation to the compulsory jurisdiction [and to the consumer credit jurisdiction].

(2)   A complaint is to be determined by reference to what is, in the opinion of the ombudsman, fair and reasonable in all the circumstances of the case.

(3)   When the ombudsman has determined a complaint he must give a written statement of his determination to the respondent and to the complainant.

(4)   The statement must—

(a)   give the ombudsman's reasons for his determination;
(b)   be signed by him; and
(c)   require the complainant to notify him in writing, before a date specified in the statement, whether he accepts or rejects the determination.

(5)   If the complainant notifies the ombudsman that he accepts the determination, it is binding on the respondent and the complainant and final.

(6)   If, by the specified date, the complainant has not notified the ombudsman of his acceptance or rejection of the determination he is to be treated as having rejected it.

(7)   The ombudsman must notify the respondent of the outcome.

(8)   A copy of the determination on which appears a certificate signed by an ombudsman is evidence (or in Scotland sufficient evidence) that the determination was made under the scheme.

(9)   Such a certificate purporting to be signed by an ombudsman is to be taken to have been duly signed unless the contrary is shown.

[256]

NOTES

Sub-s (1): words in square brackets inserted by the Consumer Credit Act 2006, s 61(3), as from 16 June 2006.

229   Awards

(1)   This section applies only in relation to the compulsory jurisdiction [and to the consumer credit jurisdiction].

(2)   If a complaint which has been dealt with under the scheme is determined in favour of the complainant, the determination may include—

(a)   an award against the respondent of such amount as the ombudsman considers fair compensation for loss or damage (of a kind falling within subsection (3)) suffered by the complainant ("a money award");
(b)   a direction that the respondent take such steps in relation to the complainant as the ombudsman considers just and appropriate (whether or not a court could order those steps to be taken).

(3)   A money award may compensate for—

(a)   financial loss; or
(b)   any other loss, or any damage, of a specified kind.

(4)   The Authority may specify [for the purposes of the compulsory jurisdiction] the maximum amount which may be regarded as fair compensation for a particular kind of loss or damage specified under subsection (3)(b).

[(4A)   The scheme operator may specify for the purposes of the consumer credit jurisdiction the maximum amount which may be regarded as fair compensation for a particular kind of loss or damage specified under subsection (3)(b).]

(5)   A money award may not exceed the monetary limit; but the ombudsman may, if he considers that fair compensation requires payment of a larger amount, recommend that the respondent pay the complainant the balance.

(6)   The monetary limit is such amount as may be specified.

(7)   Different amounts may be specified in relation to different kinds of complaint.

(8)   A money award—
  (a)   may provide for the amount payable under the award to bear interest at a rate and as from a date specified in the award; and
  (b)   is enforceable by the complainant in accordance with Part III of Schedule 17 [or (as the case may be) Part 3A of that Schedule].

(9)   Compliance with a direction under subsection (2)(b)—
  (a)   is enforceable by an injunction; or
  (b)   in Scotland, is enforceable by an order under section 45 of the Court of Session Act 1988.

(10)   Only the complainant may bring proceedings for an injunction or proceedings for an order.

[(11)   "Specified" means—
  (a)   for the purposes of the compulsory jurisdiction, specified in compulsory jurisdiction rules;
  (b)   for the purposes of the consumer credit jurisdiction, specified in consumer credit rules.

(12)   Consumer credit rules under this section may make different provision for different cases.]

[257]

NOTES

Sub-ss (1), (4), (8): words in square brackets inserted by the Consumer Credit Act 2006, s 61(3), (4), (6), as from 16 June 2006.

Sub-s (4A): inserted by the Consumer Credit Act 2006, s 61(5), as from 16 June 2006.

Sub-ss (11), (12): substituted, for original sub-s (11), by the Consumer Credit Act 2006, s 61(7), as from 16 June 2006.

---

230   Costs

(1)   The scheme operator may by rules ("costs rules") provide for an ombudsman to have power, on determining a complaint under the compulsory jurisdiction [or the consumer credit jurisdiction], to award costs in accordance with the provisions of the rules.

(2)   Costs rules require the approval of the Authority.

(3)   Costs rules may not provide for the making of an award against the complainant in respect of the respondent's costs.

(4)   But they may provide for the making of an award against the complainant in favour of the scheme operator, for the purpose of providing a contribution to resources deployed in dealing with the complaint, if in the opinion of the ombudsman—
  (a)   the complainant's conduct was improper or unreasonable; or
  (b)   the complainant was responsible for an unreasonable delay.

(5)   Costs rules may authorise an ombudsman making an award in accordance with the rules to order that the amount payable under the award bears interest at a rate and as from a date specified in the order.

(6)   An amount due under an award made in favour of the scheme operator is recoverable as a debt due to the scheme operator.

(7)   Any other award made against the respondent is to be treated as a money award for the purposes of paragraph 16 of Schedule 17 [or (as the case may be) paragraph 16D of that Schedule].

[258]

NOTES

Sub-ss (1), (7): words in square brackets inserted by the Consumer Credit Act 2006, s 61(8), as from 16 June 2006.

Information

231   Ombudsman's power to require information

(1)   An ombudsman may, by notice in writing given to a party to a complaint, require that party—
  (a)   to provide specified information or information of a specified description; or

(b)   to produce specified documents or documents of a specified description.

(2)   The information or documents must be provided or produced—
   (a)   before the end of such reasonable period as may be specified; and
   (b)   in the case of information, in such manner or form as may be specified.

(3)   This section applies only to information and documents the production of which the ombudsman considers necessary for the determination of the complaint.

(4)   If a document is produced in response to a requirement imposed under this section, the ombudsman may—
   (a)   take copies or extracts from the document; or
   (b)   require the person producing the document to provide an explanation of the document.

(5)   If a person who is required under this section to produce a document fails to do so, the ombudsman may require him to state, to the best of his knowledge and belief, where the document is.

(6)   If a person claims a lien on a document, its production under this Part does not affect the lien.

(7)   "Specified" means specified in the notice given under subsection (1).

[259]

232   Powers of court where information required

(1)   If a person ("the defaulter") fails to comply with a requirement imposed under section 231, the ombudsman may certify that fact in writing to the court and the court may enquire into the case.

(2)   If the court is satisfied that the defaulter failed without reasonable excuse to comply with the requirement, it may deal with the defaulter (and, in the case of a body corporate, any director or officer) as if he were in contempt[; and "officer", in relation to a limited liability partnership, means a member of the limited liability partnership].

(3)   "Court" means—
   (a)   the High Court;
   (b)   in Scotland, the Court of Session.

[260]

NOTES
Sub-s (2): words in square brackets added by the Limited Liability Partnerships Regulations 2001, SI 2001/1090, reg 9, Sch 5, para 21, as from 6 April 2001.

233   (*Inserts the Data Protection Act 1998, s 31(4A), which provides that the scheme operator is to be one of those persons specified in s 31 of the 1998 Act who is not required to disclose information if that disclosure, obtained when considering a complaint brought under the scheme, would prejudice legal professional privilege (Data Protection Act 1998, s 7, Sch 7, para 10).*)

Funding

234   Industry funding

(1)   For the purpose of funding—
   (a)   the establishment of the ombudsman scheme (whenever any relevant expense is incurred), and
   (b)   its operation in relation to the compulsory jurisdiction,
the Authority may make rules requiring the payment to it or to the scheme operator, by authorised persons or any class of authorised person [or any payment service provider within the meaning of the Payment Services Regulations 2009] of specified amounts (or amounts calculated in a specified way).

(2)   "Specified" means specified in the rules.

[261]

NOTES
Sub-s (1): words in square brackets inserted by the Payment Services Regulations 2009, SI 2009/209, reg 126, Sch 6, Pt 1, para 1(1)(b), as from 2 March 2009 (for the full commencement details of the 2009 Regulations, see reg 1 of those Regulations at **[4387]**).

[234A   Funding by consumer credit licensees etc

(1)   For the purpose of funding—
   (a)   the establishment of the ombudsman scheme so far as it relates to the consumer credit jurisdiction (whenever any relevant expense is incurred), and
   (b)   its operation in relation to the consumer credit jurisdiction,

the scheme operator may from time to time with the approval of the Authority determine a sum which is to be raised by way of contributions under this section.

(2)   A sum determined under subsection (1) may include a component to cover the costs of the collection of contributions to that sum ("collection costs") under this section.

(3)   The scheme operator must notify the OFT of every determination under subsection (1).

(4)   The OFT must give general notice of every determination so notified.

(5)   The OFT may by general notice impose requirements on—
  (a)   licensees to whom this section applies, or
  (b)   persons who make applications to which this section applies,
to pay contributions to the OFT for the purpose of raising sums determined under subsection (1).

(6)   The amount of the contribution payable by a person under such a requirement—
  (a)   shall be the amount specified in or determined under the general notice; and
  (b)   shall be paid before the end of the period or at the time so specified or determined.

(7)   A general notice under subsection (5) may—
  (a)   impose requirements only on descriptions of licensees or applicants specified in the notice;
  (b)   provide for exceptions from any requirement imposed on a description of licensees or applicants;
  (c)   impose different requirements on different descriptions of licensees or applicants;
  (d)   make provision for refunds in specified circumstances.

(8)   Contributions received by the OFT must be paid to the scheme operator.

(9)   As soon as practicable after the end of—
  (a)   each financial year of the scheme operator, or
  (b)   if the OFT and the scheme operator agree that this paragraph is to apply instead of paragraph (a) for the time being, each period agreed by them,
the scheme operator must pay to the OFT an amount representing the extent to which collection costs are covered in accordance with subsection (2) by the total amount of the contributions paid by the OFT to it during the year or (as the case may be) the agreed period.

(10)   Amounts received by the OFT from the scheme operator are to be retained by it for the purpose of meeting its costs.

(11)   The Secretary of State may by order provide that the functions of the OFT under this section are for the time being to be carried out by the scheme operator.

(12)   An order under subsection (11) may provide that while the order is in force this section shall have effect subject to such modifications as may be set out in the order.

(13)   The licensees to whom this section applies are licensees under standard licences which cover to any extent the carrying on of a type of business specified in an order under section 226A(2)(e).

(14)   The applications to which this section applies are applications for—
  (a)   standard licences covering to any extent the carrying on of a business of such a type;
  (b)   the renewal of standard licences on terms covering to any extent the carrying on of a business of such a type.

(15)   Expressions used in the Consumer Credit Act 1974 have the same meaning in this section as they have in that Act.]

[**261A**]

NOTES
  Commencement: 16 June 2006.
  Inserted by the Consumer Credit Act 2006, s 60, as from 16 June 2006.

PART XVII
COLLECTIVE INVESTMENT SCHEMES

NOTES
  Transitional provisions: the Financial Services and Markets Act 2000 (Transitional Provisions) (Authorised Persons etc) Order 2001, SI 2001/2636, Pt V provides that collective investment schemes that were authorised or recognised under the Financial Services Act 1986, Pt I, Chapter VIII immediately before 1 December 2001 are to be treated as from that date as if authorised and recognised under Pt XVII of this Act. Directions imposed on schemes under the 1986 Act have effect, as from 1 December 2001, as directions imposed under Pt XVII of this Act. The 1986 Act was repealed by the Financial Services and Markets Act 2000 (Consequential Amendments and Repeals) Order 2001, SI 2001/3649, art 3(1)(c).

CHAPTER I

INTERPRETATION

235 Collective investment schemes

(1) In this Part "collective investment scheme" means any arrangements with respect to property of any description, including money, the purpose or effect of which is to enable persons taking part in the arrangements (whether by becoming owners of the property or any part of it or otherwise) to participate in or receive profits or income arising from the acquisition, holding, management or disposal of the property or sums paid out of such profits or income.

(2) The arrangements must be such that the persons who are to participate ("participants") do not have day-to-day control over the management of the property, whether or not they have the right to be consulted or to give directions.

(3) The arrangements must also have either or both of the following characteristics—
    (a) the contributions of the participants and the profits or income out of which payments are to be made to them are pooled;
    (b) the property is managed as a whole by or on behalf of the operator of the scheme.

(4) If arrangements provide for such pooling as is mentioned in subsection (3)(a) in relation to separate parts of the property, the arrangements are not to be regarded as constituting a single collective investment scheme unless the participants are entitled to exchange rights in one part for rights in another.

(5) The Treasury may by order provide that arrangements do not amount to a collective investment scheme—
    (a) in specified circumstances; or
    (b) if the arrangements fall within a specified category of arrangement.

[262]

NOTES

Orders: the Financial Services and Markets Act 2000 (Collective Investment Schemes) Order 2001, SI 2001/1062 at **[2202]**; the Financial Services and Markets Act 2000 (Miscellaneous Provisions) Order 2001, SI 2001/3650 at **[2643]**.

Note that the following amending Orders have also been made under this section: the Financial Services and Markets Act 2000 (Collective Investment Schemes) (Amendment) Order 2005, SI 2005/57; the Financial Services and Markets Act 2000 (Collective Investment Schemes) (Amendment) Order 2007, SI 2007/800; the Financial Services and Markets Act 2000 (Collective Investment Schemes) (Amendment) Order 2008, SI 2008/1641; the Financial Services and Markets Act 2000 (Collective Investment Schemes) (Amendment) (No 2) Order 2008, SI 2008/1813.

236 Open-ended investment companies

(1) In this Part "an open-ended investment company" means a collective investment scheme which satisfies both the property condition and the investment condition.

(2) The property condition is that the property belongs beneficially to, and is managed by or on behalf of, a body corporate ("BC") having as its purpose the investment of its funds with the aim of—
    (a) spreading investment risk; and
    (b) giving its members the benefit of the results of the management of those funds by or on behalf of that body.

(3) The investment condition is that, in relation to BC, a reasonable investor would, if he were to participate in the scheme—
    (a) expect that he would be able to realize, within a period appearing to him to be reasonable, his investment in the scheme (represented, at any given time, by the value of shares in, or securities of, BC held by him as a participant in the scheme); and
    (b) be satisfied that his investment would be realized on a basis calculated wholly or mainly by reference to the value of property in respect of which the scheme makes arrangements.

(4) In determining whether the investment condition is satisfied, no account is to be taken of any actual or potential redemption or repurchase of shares or securities under—
    (a) Chapter VII of Part V of the Companies Act 1985;
    (b) Chapter VII of Part VI of the Companies (Northern Ireland) Order 1986;
    (c) corresponding provisions in force in another EEA State; or
    (d) provisions in force in a country or territory other than an EEA state which the Treasury have, by order, designated as corresponding provisions.

(5) The Treasury may by order amend the definition of "an open-ended investment company" for the purposes of this Part.

[263]

237 Other definitions

(1) In this Part "unit trust scheme" means a collective investment scheme under which the property is held on trust for the participants.

(2) In this Part—

"trustee", in relation to a unit trust scheme, means the person holding the property in question on trust for the participants;

"depositary", in relation to—

(a) a collective investment scheme which is constituted by a body incorporated by virtue of regulations under section 262, or

(b) any other collective investment scheme which is not a unit trust scheme,

means any person to whom the property subject to the scheme is entrusted for safekeeping;

"the operator", in relation to a unit trust scheme with a separate trustee, means the manager and in relation to an open-ended investment company, means that company;

"units" means the rights or interests (however described) of the participants in a collective investment scheme.

(3) In this Part—

"an authorised unit trust scheme" means a unit trust scheme which is authorised for the purposes of this Act by an authorisation order in force under section 243;

"an authorised open-ended investment company" means a body incorporated by virtue of regulations under section 262 in respect of which an authorisation order is in force under any provision made in such regulations by virtue of subsection (2)(l) of that section;

"a recognised scheme" means a scheme recognised under section 264, 270 or 272.

[264]

CHAPTER II
RESTRICTIONS ON PROMOTION

238 Restrictions on promotion

(1) An authorised person must not communicate an invitation or inducement to participate in a collective investment scheme.

(2) But that is subject to the following provisions of this section and to section 239.

(3) Subsection (1) applies in the case of a communication originating outside the United Kingdom only if the communication is capable of having an effect in the United Kingdom.

(4) Subsection (1) does not apply in relation to—

(a) an authorised unit trust scheme;

(b) a scheme constituted by an authorised open-ended investment company; or

(c) a recognised scheme.

(5) Subsection (1) does not apply to anything done in accordance with rules made by the Authority for the purpose of exempting from that subsection the promotion otherwise than to the general public of schemes of specified descriptions.

(6) The Treasury may by order specify circumstances in which subsection (1) does not apply.

(7) An order under subsection (6) may, in particular, provide that subsection (1) does not apply in relation to communications—

(a) of a specified description;

(b) originating in a specified country or territory outside the United Kingdom;

(c) originating in a country or territory which falls within a specified description of country or territory outside the United Kingdom; or

(d) originating outside the United Kingdom.

(8) The Treasury may by order repeal subsection (3).

(9) "Communicate" includes causing a communication to be made.

(10) "Promotion otherwise than to the general public" includes promotion in a way designed to reduce, so far as possible, the risk of participation by persons for whom participation would be unsuitable.

(11) "Participate", in relation to a collective investment scheme, means become a participant (within the meaning given by section 235(2)) in the scheme.

[265]

NOTES

Orders: the Financial Services and Markets Act 2000 (Promotion of Collective Investment Schemes) (Exemptions) Order 2001, SI 2001/1060 at **[2166]**.

Note that the following amending Orders have also been made under this section: the Financial Services and Markets Act 2000 (Financial Promotion and Miscellaneous Amendments) Order 2002, SI 2002/1310; the Financial Services and Markets Act 2000 (Promotion of Collective Investment Schemes etc) (Exemptions) (Amendment) Order 2003, SI 2003/2067; the Financial Services and Markets Act 2000 (Financial Promotion and Promotion of Collective Investment Schemes) (Miscellaneous Amendments) Order 2005, SI 2005/270; the Financial Services and Markets Act 2000 (Promotion of Collective Investment Schemes) (Exemptions) (Amendment) Order 2005, SI 2005/1532.

239 Single property schemes

(1) The Treasury may by regulations make provision for exempting single property schemes from section 238(1).

(2) For the purposes of subsection (1) a single property scheme is a scheme which has the characteristics mentioned in subsection (3) and satisfies such other requirements as are prescribed by the regulations conferring the exemption.

(3) The characteristics are—

 (a) that the property subject to the scheme (apart from cash or other assets held for management purposes) consists of—

 (i) a single building (or a single building with ancillary buildings) managed by or on behalf of the operator of the scheme, or

 (ii) a group of adjacent or contiguous buildings managed by him or on his behalf as a single enterprise,

 with or without ancillary land and with or without furniture, fittings or other contents of the building or buildings in question; and

 (b) that the units of the participants in the scheme are either dealt in on a recognised investment exchange or offered on terms such that any agreement for their acquisition is conditional on their admission to dealings on such an exchange.

(4) If regulations are made under subsection (1), the Authority may make rules imposing duties or liabilities on the operator and (if any) the trustee or depositary of a scheme exempted by the regulations.

(5) The rules may include, to such extent as the Authority thinks appropriate, provision for purposes corresponding to those for which provision can be made under section 248 in relation to authorised unit trust schemes.

[266]

240 Restriction on approval of promotion

(1) An authorised person may not approve for the purposes of section 21 the content of a communication relating to a collective investment scheme if he would be prohibited by section 238(1) from effecting the communication himself or from causing it to be communicated.

(2) For the purposes of determining in any case whether there has been a contravention of section 21(1), an approval given in contravention of subsection (1) is to be regarded as not having been given.

[267]

241 Actions for damages

If an authorised person contravenes a requirement imposed on him by section 238 or 240, section 150 applies to the contravention as it applies to a contravention mentioned in that section.

[268]

CHAPTER III
AUTHORISED UNIT TRUST SCHEMES

Applications for authorisation

242 Applications for authorisation of unit trust schemes

(1) Any application for an order declaring a unit trust scheme to be an authorised unit trust scheme must be made to the Authority by the manager and trustee, or proposed manager and trustee, of the scheme.

(2)   The manager and trustee (or proposed manager and trustee) must be different persons.

(3)   The application—
    (a)   must be made in such manner as the Authority may direct; and
    (b)   must contain or be accompanied by such information as the Authority may reasonably require for the purpose of determining the application.

(4)   At any time after receiving an application and before determining it, the Authority may require the applicants to provide it with such further information as it reasonably considers necessary to enable it to determine the application.

(5)   Different directions may be given, and different requirements imposed, in relation to different applications.

(6)   The Authority may require applicants to present information which they are required to give under this section in such form, or to verify it in such a way, as the Authority may direct.

[269]

243   Authorisation orders

(1)   If, on an application under section 242 in respect of a unit trust scheme, the Authority—
    (a)   is satisfied that the scheme complies with the requirements set out in this section,
    (b)   is satisfied that the scheme complies with the requirements of the trust scheme rules, and
    (c)   has been provided with a copy of the trust deed and a certificate signed by a solicitor to the effect that it complies with such of the requirements of this section or those rules as relate to its contents,
the Authority may make an order declaring the scheme to be an authorised unit trust scheme.

(2)   If the Authority makes an order under subsection (1), it must give written notice of the order to the applicant.

(3)   In this Chapter "authorisation order" means an order under subsection (1).

(4)   The manager and the trustee must be persons who are independent of each other.

(5)   The manager and the trustee must each—
    (a)   be a body corporate incorporated in the United Kingdom or another EEA State, and
    (b)   have a place of business in the United Kingdom,
and the affairs of each must be administered in the country in which it is incorporated.

(6)   If the manager is incorporated in another EEA State, the scheme must not be one which satisfies the requirements prescribed for the purposes of section 264.

(7)   The manager and the trustee must each be an authorised person and the manager must have permission to act as manager and the trustee must have permission to act as trustee.

(8)   The name of the scheme must not be undesirable or misleading.

(9)   The purposes of the scheme must be reasonably capable of being successfully carried into effect.

(10)   The participants must be entitled to have their units redeemed in accordance with the scheme at a price—
    (a)   related to the net value of the property to which the units relate; and
    (b)   determined in accordance with the scheme.

(11)   But a scheme is to be treated as complying with subsection (10) if it requires the manager to ensure that a participant is able to sell his units on an investment exchange at a price not significantly different from that mentioned in that subsection.

[270]

NOTES

References to solicitors, etc: a registered European lawyer may provide professional activities by way of legal advice and assistance or legal aid under this Act and references to a solicitor, counsel or legal representative shall be interpreted accordingly: see the European Communities (Lawyer's Practice) Regulations 2000, SI 2000/1119, reg 14, Sch 3, Pt 1 (as amended by the European Communities (Lawyer's Practice) (Amendment) Regulations 2004, SI 2004/1628).

244   Determination of applications

(1)   An application under section 242 must be determined by the Authority before the end of the period of six months beginning with the date on which it receives the completed application.

(2)   The Authority may determine an incomplete application if it considers it appropriate to do so; and it must in any event determine such an application within twelve months beginning with the date on which it first receives the application.

(3)   The applicant may withdraw his application, by giving the Authority written notice, at any time before the Authority determines it.

[271]

Applications refused

245 Procedure when refusing an application

(1)   If the Authority proposes to refuse an application made under section 242 it must give each of the applicants a warning notice.

(2)   If the Authority decides to refuse the application—
    (a)   it must give each of the applicants a decision notice; and
    (b)   either applicant may refer the matter to the Tribunal.

[272]

Certificates

246 Certificates

(1)   If the manager or trustee of a unit trust scheme which complies with the conditions necessary for it to enjoy the rights conferred by any relevant Community instrument so requests, the Authority may issue a certificate to the effect that the scheme complies with those conditions.

(2)   Such a certificate may be issued on the making of an authorisation order in respect of the scheme or at any subsequent time.

[273]

Rules

247 Trust scheme rules

(1)   The Authority may make rules ("trust scheme rules") as to—
    (a)   the constitution, management and operation of authorised unit trust schemes;
    (b)   the powers, duties, rights and liabilities of the manager and trustee of any such scheme;
    (c)   the rights and duties of the participants in any such scheme; and
    (d)   the winding up of any such scheme.

(2)   Trust scheme rules may, in particular, make provision—
    (a)   as to the issue and redemption of the units under the scheme;
    (b)   as to the expenses of the scheme and the means of meeting them;
    (c)   for the appointment, removal, powers and duties of an auditor for the scheme;
    (d)   for restricting or regulating the investment and borrowing powers exercisable in relation to the scheme;
    (e)   requiring the keeping of records with respect to the transactions and financial position of the scheme and for the inspection of those records;
    (f)   requiring the preparation of periodical reports with respect to the scheme and the provision of those reports to the participants and to the Authority; and
    (g)   with respect to the amendment of the scheme.

(3)   Trust scheme rules may make provision as to the contents of the trust deed, including provision requiring any of the matters mentioned in subsection (2) to be dealt with in the deed.

(4)   But trust scheme rules are binding on the manager, trustee and participants independently of the contents of the trust deed and, in the case of the participants, have effect as if contained in it.

(5)   If—
    (a)   a modification is made of the statutory provisions in force in Great Britain or Northern Ireland relating to companies,
    (b)   the modification relates to the rights and duties of persons who hold the beneficial title to any shares in a company without also holding the legal title, and
    (c)   it appears to the Treasury that, for the purpose of assimilating the law relating to authorised unit trust schemes to the law relating to companies as so modified, it is expedient to modify the rule-making powers conferred on the Authority by this section,
the Treasury may by order make such modifications of those powers as they consider appropriate.

[274]

248 Scheme particulars rules

(1)   The Authority may make rules ("scheme particulars rules") requiring the manager of an authorised unit trust scheme—
    (a)   to submit scheme particulars to the Authority; and
    (b)   to publish scheme particulars or make them available to the public on request.

(2)   "Scheme particulars" means particulars in such form, containing such information about the scheme and complying with such requirements, as are specified in scheme particulars rules.

(3)   Scheme particulars rules may require the manager of an authorised unit trust scheme to submit, and to publish or make available, revised or further scheme particulars if there is a significant change affecting any matter—
    (a)   which is contained in scheme particulars previously published or made available; and

(b)   whose inclusion in those particulars was required by the rules.

(4)   Scheme particulars rules may require the manager of an authorised unit trust scheme to submit, and to publish or make available, revised or further scheme particulars if—
  (a)   a significant new matter arises; and
  (b)   the inclusion of information in respect of that matter would have been required in previous particulars if it had arisen when those particulars were prepared.

(5)   Scheme particulars rules may provide for the payment, by the person or persons who in accordance with the rules are treated as responsible for any scheme particulars, of compensation to any qualifying person who has suffered loss as a result of—
  (a)   any untrue or misleading statement in the particulars; or
  (b)   the omission from them of any matter required by the rules to be included.

(6)   "Qualifying person" means a person who—
  (a)   has become or agreed to become a participant in the scheme; or
  (b)   although not being a participant, has a beneficial interest in units in the scheme.

(7)   Scheme particulars rules do not affect any liability which any person may incur apart from the rules.

[275]

249 Disqualification of auditor for breach of trust scheme rules

(1)   If it appears to the Authority that an auditor has failed to comply with a duty imposed on him by trust scheme rules, it may disqualify him from being the auditor for any authorised unit trust scheme or authorised open-ended investment company.

(2)   Subsections (2) to (5) of section 345 have effect in relation to disqualification under subsection (1) as they have effect in relation to disqualification under subsection (1) of that section.

[276]

250 Modification or waiver of rules

(1)   In this section "rules" means—
  (a)   trust scheme rules; or
  (b)   scheme particulars rules.

(2)   The Authority may, on the application or with the consent of any person to whom any rules apply, direct that all or any of the rules—
  (a)   are not to apply to him as respects a particular scheme; or
  (b)   are to apply to him, as respects a particular scheme, with such modifications as may be specified in the direction.

(3)   The Authority may, on the application or with the consent of the manager and trustee of a particular scheme acting jointly, direct that all or any of the rules—
  (a)   are not to apply to the scheme; or
  (b)   are to apply to the scheme with such modifications as may be specified in the direction.

(4)   Subsections (3) to (9) and (11) of section 148 have effect in relation to a direction under subsection (2) as they have effect in relation to a direction under section 148(2) but with the following modifications—
  (a)   ...
  (b)   any reference to the [person] is to be read as a reference to the person mentioned in subsection (2); and
  (c)   subsection (7)(b) is to be read, in relation to a participant of the scheme, as if the word "commercial" were omitted.

(5)   Subsections (3) to (9) and (11) of section 148 have effect in relation to a direction under subsection (3) as they have effect in relation to a direction under section 148(2) but with the following modifications—
  (a)   subsection (4)(a) is to be read as if the words "by the ... person" were omitted;
  (b)   subsections (7)(b) and (11) are to be read as if references to the ... person were references to each of the manager and the trustee of the scheme;
  (c)   subsection (7)(b) is to be read, in relation to a participant of the scheme, as if the word "commercial" were omitted;
  (d)   subsection (8) is to be read as if the reference to the ... person concerned were a reference to the scheme concerned and to its manager and trustee; and
  (e)   subsection (9) is to be read as if the reference to the ... person were a reference to the manager and trustee of the scheme acting jointly.

[277]

NOTES
Sub-s (4): para (a) repealed, and word in square brackets in para (b) substituted, by the Regulatory Reform (Financial Services and Markets Act 2000) Order 2007, SI 2007/1973, arts 2, 11(a), (b), as from 12 July 2007.
Sub-s (5): words omitted repealed by SI 2007/1973, arts 2, 11(c), as from 12 July 2007.

Alterations

251 Alteration of schemes and changes of manager or trustee

(1)   The manager of an authorised unit trust scheme must give written notice to the Authority of any proposal to alter the scheme or to replace its trustee.

(2)   Any notice given in respect of a proposal to alter the scheme involving a change in the trust deed must be accompanied by a certificate signed by a solicitor to the effect that the change will not affect the compliance of the deed with the trust scheme rules.

(3)   The trustee of an authorised unit trust scheme must give written notice to the Authority of any proposal to replace the manager of the scheme.

(4)   Effect is not to be given to any proposal of which notice has been given under subsection (1) or (3) unless—
   (a)   the Authority, by written notice, has given its approval to the proposal; or
   (b)   one month, beginning with the date on which the notice was given, has expired without the manager or trustee having received from the Authority a warning notice under section 252 in respect of the proposal.

(5)   The Authority must not approve a proposal to replace the manager or the trustee of an authorised unit trust scheme unless it is satisfied that, if the proposed replacement is made, the scheme will continue to comply with the requirements of section 243(4) to (7).

[278]

NOTES
References to solicitors, etc: see the note to s 248 at **[270]**.

252 Procedure when refusing approval of change of manager or trustee

(1)   If the Authority proposes to refuse approval of a proposal to replace the trustee or manager of an authorised unit trust scheme, it must give a warning notice to the person by whom notice of the proposal was given under section 251(1) or (3).

(2)   If the Authority proposes to refuse approval of a proposal to alter an authorised unit trust scheme it must give separate warning notices to the manager and the trustee of the scheme.

(3)   To be valid the warning notice must be received by that person before the end of one month beginning with the date on which notice of the proposal was given.

(4)   If, having given a warning notice to a person, the Authority decides to refuse approval—
   (a)   it must give him a decision notice; and
   (b)   he may refer the matter to the Tribunal.

[279]

Exclusion clauses

253 Avoidance of exclusion clauses

Any provision of the trust deed of an authorised unit trust scheme is void in so far as it would have the effect of exempting the manager or trustee from liability for any failure to exercise due care and diligence in the discharge of his functions in respect of the scheme.

[280]

Ending of authorisation

254 Revocation of authorisation order otherwise than by consent

(1)   An authorisation order may be revoked by an order made by the Authority if it appears to the Authority that—
   (a)   one or more of the requirements for the making of the order are no longer satisfied;
   (b)   the manager or trustee of the scheme concerned has contravened a requirement imposed on him by or under this Act;
   (c)   the manager or trustee of the scheme has, in purported compliance with any such requirement, knowingly or recklessly given the Authority information which is false or misleading in a material particular;
   (d)   no regulated activity is being carried on in relation to the scheme and the period of that inactivity began at least twelve months earlier; or
   (e)   none of paragraphs (a) to (d) applies, but it is desirable to revoke the authorisation order in order to protect the interests of participants or potential participants in the scheme.

(2)   For the purposes of subsection (1)(e), the Authority may take into account any matter relating to—
   (a)   the scheme;
   (b)   the manager or trustee;

(c) any person employed by or associated with the manager or trustee in connection with the scheme;
(d) any director of the manager or trustee;
(e) any person exercising influence over the manager or trustee;
(f) any body corporate in the same group as the manager or trustee;
(g) any director of any such body corporate;
(h) any person exercising influence over any such body corporate.

[281]

255 Procedure

(1) If the Authority proposes to make an order under section 254 revoking an authorisation order ("a revoking order"), it must give separate warning notices to the manager and the trustee of the scheme.

(2) If the Authority decides to make a revoking order, it must without delay give each of them a decision notice and either of them may refer the matter to the Tribunal.

[282]

256 Requests for revocation of authorisation order

(1) An authorisation order may be revoked by an order made by the Authority at the request of the manager or trustee of the scheme concerned.

(2) If the Authority makes an order under subsection (1), it must give written notice of the order to the manager and trustee of the scheme concerned.

(3) The Authority may refuse a request to make an order under this section if it considers that—
(a) the public interest requires that any matter concerning the scheme should be investigated before a decision is taken as to whether the authorisation order should be revoked; or
(b) revocation would not be in the interests of the participants or would be incompatible with a Community obligation.

(4) If the Authority proposes to refuse a request under this section, it must give separate warning notices to the manager and the trustee of the scheme.

(5) If the Authority decides to refuse the request, it must without delay give each of them a decision notice and either of them may refer the matter to the Tribunal.

[283]

NOTES
Community obligation: as to the meaning of this, see the note to s 47 at [47].

Powers of intervention

257 Directions

(1) The Authority may give a direction under this section if it appears to the Authority that—
(a) one or more of the requirements for the making of an authorisation order are no longer satisfied;
(b) the manager or trustee of an authorised unit trust scheme has contravened, or is likely to contravene, a requirement imposed on him by or under this Act;
(c) the manager or trustee of such a scheme has, in purported compliance with any such requirement, knowingly or recklessly given the Authority information which is false or misleading in a material particular; or
(d) none of paragraphs (a) to (c) applies, but it is desirable to give a direction in order to protect the interests of participants or potential participants in such a scheme.

(2) A direction under this section may—
(a) require the manager of the scheme to cease the issue or redemption, or both the issue and redemption, of units under the scheme;
(b) require the manager and trustee of the scheme to wind it up.

(3) If the authorisation order is revoked, the revocation does not affect any direction under this section which is then in force.

(4) A direction may be given under this section in relation to a scheme in the case of which the authorisation order has been revoked if a direction under this section was already in force at the time of revocation.

(5) If a person contravenes a direction under this section, section 150 applies to the contravention as it applies to a contravention mentioned in that section.

(6) The Authority may, either on its own initiative or on the application of the manager or trustee of the scheme concerned, revoke or vary a direction given under this section if it appears to the Authority—
(a) in the case of revocation, that it is no longer necessary for the direction to take effect or continue in force;

(b) in the case of variation, that the direction should take effect or continue in force in a different form.

[284]

258 Applications to the court

(1) If the Authority could give a direction under section 257, it may also apply to the court for an order—
    (a) removing the manager or the trustee, or both the manager and the trustee, of the scheme; and
    (b) replacing the person or persons removed with a suitable person or persons nominated by the Authority.

(2) The Authority may nominate a person for the purposes of subsection (1)(b) only if it is satisfied that, if the order was made, the requirements of section 243(4) to (7) would be complied with.

(3) If it appears to the Authority that there is no person it can nominate for the purposes of subsection (1)(b), it may apply to the court for an order—
    (a) removing the manager or the trustee, or both the manager and the trustee, of the scheme; and
    (b) appointing an authorised person to wind up the scheme.

(4) On an application under this section the court may make such order as it thinks fit.

(5) The court may, on the application of the Authority, rescind any such order as is mentioned in subsection (3) and substitute such an order as is mentioned in subsection (1).

(6) The Authority must give written notice of the making of an application under this section to the manager and trustee of the scheme concerned.

(7) The jurisdiction conferred by this section may be exercised by—
    (a) the High Court;
    (b) in Scotland, the Court of Session.

[285]

259 Procedure on giving directions under section 257 and varying them on Authority's own initiative

(1) A direction takes effect—
    (a) immediately, if the notice given under subsection (3) states that that is the case;
    (b) on such date as may be specified in the notice; or
    (c) if no date is specified in the notice, when the matter to which it relates is no longer open to review.

(2) A direction may be expressed to take effect immediately (or on a specified date) only if the Authority, having regard to the ground on which it is exercising its power under section 257, considers that it is necessary for the direction to take effect immediately (or on that date).

(3) If the Authority proposes to give a direction under section 257, or gives such a direction with immediate effect, it must give separate written notice to the manager and the trustee of the scheme concerned.

(4) The notice must—
    (a) give details of the direction;
    (b) inform the person to whom it is given of when the direction takes effect;
    (c) state the Authority's reasons for giving the direction and for its determination as to when the direction takes effect;
    (d) inform the person to whom it is given that he may make representations to the Authority within such period as may be specified in it (whether or not he has referred the matter to the Tribunal); and
    (e) inform him of his right to refer the matter to the Tribunal.

(5) If the direction imposes a requirement under section 257(2)(a), the notice must state that the requirement has effect until—
    (a) a specified date; or
    (b) a further direction.

(6) If the direction imposes a requirement under section 257(2)(b), the scheme must be wound up—
    (a) by a date specified in the notice; or
    (b) if no date is specified, as soon as practicable.

(7) The Authority may extend the period allowed under the notice for making representations.

(8) If, having considered any representations made by a person to whom the notice was given, the Authority decides—
    (a) to give the direction in the way proposed, or

(b)   if it has been given, not to revoke the direction,

it must give separate written notice to the manager and the trustee of the scheme concerned.

(9)   If, having considered any representations made by a person to whom the notice was given, the Authority decides—

(a)   not to give the direction in the way proposed,

(b)   to give the direction in a way other than that proposed, or

(c)   to revoke a direction which has effect,

it must give separate written notice to the manager and the trustee of the scheme concerned.

(10)   A notice given under subsection (8) must inform the person to whom it is given of his right to refer the matter to the Tribunal.

(11)   A notice under subsection (9)(b) must comply with subsection (4).

(12)   If a notice informs a person of his right to refer a matter to the Tribunal, it must give an indication of the procedure on such a reference.

(13)   This section applies to the variation of a direction on the Authority's own initiative as it applies to the giving of a direction.

(14)   For the purposes of subsection (1)(c), whether a matter is open to review is to be determined in accordance with section 391(8).

[286]

260 Procedure: refusal to revoke or vary direction

(1)   If on an application under section 257(6) for a direction to be revoked or varied the Authority proposes—

(a)   to vary the direction otherwise than in accordance with the application, or

(b)   to refuse to revoke or vary the direction,

it must give the applicant a warning notice.

(2)   If the Authority decides to refuse to revoke or vary the direction—

(a)   it must give the applicant a decision notice; and

(b)   the applicant may refer the matter to the Tribunal.

[287]

261 Procedure: revocation of direction and grant of request for variation

(1)   If the Authority decides on its own initiative to revoke a direction under section 257 it must give separate written notices of its decision to the manager and trustee of the scheme.

(2)   If on an application under section 257(6) for a direction to be revoked or varied the Authority decides to revoke the direction or vary it in accordance with the application, it must give the applicant written notice of its decision.

(3)   A notice under this section must specify the date on which the decision takes effect.

(4)   The Authority may publish such information about the revocation or variation, in such way, as it considers appropriate.

[288]

CHAPTER IV
OPEN-ENDED INVESTMENT COMPANIES

262 Open-ended investment companies

(1)   The Treasury may by regulations make provision for—

(a)   facilitating the carrying on of collective investment by means of open-ended investment companies;

(b)   regulating such companies.

(2)   The regulations may, in particular, make provision—

(a)   for the incorporation and registration in Great Britain of bodies corporate;

(b)   for a body incorporated by virtue of the regulations to take such form as may be determined in accordance with the regulations;

(c)   as to the purposes for which such a body may exist, the investments which it may issue and otherwise as to its constitution;

(d)   as to the management and operation of such a body and the management of its property;

(e)   as to the powers, duties, rights and liabilities of such a body and of other persons, including—

(i)   the directors or sole director of such a body;

(ii)   its depositary (if any);

(iii)   its shareholders, and persons who hold the beneficial title to shares in it without holding the legal title;

(iv)   its auditor; and

     (v)   any persons who act or purport to act on its behalf;
- (f)   as to the merger of one or more such bodies and the division of such a body;
- (g)   for the appointment and removal of an auditor for such a body;
- (h)   as to the winding up and dissolution of such a body;
- (i)   for such a body, or any director or depositary of such a body, to be required to comply with directions given by the Authority;
- (j)   enabling the Authority to apply to a court for an order removing and replacing any director or depositary of such a body;
- (k)   for the carrying out of investigations by persons appointed by the Authority or the Secretary of State;
- (l)   corresponding to any provision made in relation to unit trust schemes by Chapter III of this Part.

(3)   Regulations under this section may—
- (a)   impose criminal liability;
- (b)   confer functions on the Authority;
- (c)   in the case of provision made by virtue of subsection (2)(l), authorise the making of rules by the Authority;
- (d)   confer jurisdiction on any court or on the Tribunal;
- (e)   provide for fees to be charged by the Authority in connection with the carrying out of any of its functions under the regulations (including fees payable on a periodical basis);
- (f)   modify, exclude or apply (with or without modifications) any primary or subordinate legislation (including any provision of, or made under, this Act);
- (g)   make consequential amendments, repeals and revocations of any such legislation;
- (h)   modify or exclude any rule of law.

(4)   The provision that may be made by virtue of subsection (3)(f) includes provision extending or adapting any power to make subordinate legislation.

(5)   Regulations under this section may, in particular—
- (a)   revoke the Open-Ended Investment Companies (Investment Companies with Variable Capital) Regulations 1996; and
- (b)   provide for things done under or in accordance with those regulations to be treated as if they had been done under or in accordance with regulations under this section.

[289]

NOTES

Open-Ended Investment Companies (Investment Companies with Variable Capital) Regulations 1996 (SI 1996/2827): revoked, subject to transitional provisions and savings, by the Open-Ended Investment Companies Regulations 2001, SI 2001/1228, reg 85.

Regulations: the Open-Ended Investment Companies Regulations 2001, SI 2001/1228 at **[2238]**.

Note that the following amending Regulations have also been made under this section: the Open-Ended Investment Companies (Amendment) Regulations 2005, SI 2005/923.

263   *(Spent; this section amended the Companies Act 1985, s 716 (s 716 was repealed by the Regulatory Reform (Removal of 20 Member Limit in Partnerships etc) Order 2002, SI 2002/3203, art 2, as from 21 December 2002). This section is also repealed by the Companies Act 2006, s 1295, Sch 16.)*

CHAPTER V
RECOGNISED OVERSEAS SCHEMES
Schemes constituted in other EEA States

264   Schemes constituted in other EEA States

(1)   A collective investment scheme constituted in another EEA State is a recognised scheme if—
- (a)   it satisfies such requirements as are prescribed for the purposes of this section; and
- (b)   not less than two months before inviting persons in the United Kingdom to become participants in the scheme, the operator of the scheme gives notice to the Authority of his intention to do so, specifying the way in which the invitation is to be made.

(2)   But this section does not make the scheme a recognised scheme if within two months of receiving the notice under subsection (1) the Authority notifies—
- (a)   the operator of the scheme, and
- (b)   the authorities of the State in question who are responsible for the authorisation of collective investment schemes,

that the way in which the invitation is to be made does not comply with the law in force in the United Kingdom.

(3)   The notice to be given to the Authority under subsection (1)—

    (a)   must be accompanied by a certificate from the authorities mentioned in subsection (2)(b) to the effect that the scheme complies with the conditions necessary for it to enjoy the rights conferred by any relevant Community instrument;

    (b)   must contain the address of a place in the United Kingdom for the service on the operator of notices or other documents required or authorised to be served on him under this Act; and

    (c)   must contain or be accompanied by such other information and documents as may be prescribed.

(4)   A notice given by the Authority under subsection (2) must—

    (a)   give the reasons for which the Authority considers that the law in force in the United Kingdom will not be complied with; and

    (b)   specify a reasonable period (which may not be less than 28 days) within which any person to whom it is given may make representations to the Authority.

(5)   For the purposes of this section a collective investment scheme is constituted in another EEA State if—

    (a)   it is constituted under the law of that State by a contract or under a trust and is managed by a body corporate incorporated under that law; or

    (b)   it takes the form of an open-ended investment company incorporated under that law.

(6)   The operator of a recognised scheme may give written notice to the Authority that he desires the scheme to be no longer recognised by virtue of this section.

(7)   On the giving of notice under subsection (6), the scheme ceases to be a recognised scheme.

[290]

NOTES

Regulations: the Financial Services and Markets Act 2000 (Collective Investment Schemes Constituted in Other EEA States) Regulations 2001, SI 2001/2383 at **[2385]**.

Note that the following amending Regulations have also been made under this section: the Collective Investment Schemes (Miscellaneous Amendments) Regulations 2003, SI 2003/2066.

265 Representations and references to the Tribunal

(1)   This section applies if any representations are made to the Authority, before the period for making representations has ended, by a person to whom a notice was given by the Authority under section 264(2).

(2)   The Authority must, within a reasonable period, decide in the light of those representations whether or not to withdraw its notice.

(3)   If the Authority withdraws its notice the scheme is a recognised scheme from the date on which the notice is withdrawn.

(4)   If the Authority decides not to withdraw its notice, it must give a decision notice to each person to whom the notice under section 264(2) was given.

(5)   The operator of the scheme to whom the decision notice is given may refer the matter to the Tribunal.

[291]

266 Disapplication of rules

(1)   Apart from—

    (a)   financial promotion rules, and

    (b)   rules under section 283(1),

rules made by the Authority under this Act do not apply to the operator, trustee or depositary of a scheme in relation to the carrying on by him of regulated activities for which he has permission in that capacity.

[(1A)   But subsection (1) does not affect the application of rules to an operator of a scheme if the operator is an EEA firm falling within paragraph 5(f) of Schedule 3 who qualifies for authorisation under that Schedule.]

(2)   "Scheme" means a scheme which is a recognised scheme by virtue of section 264.

[292]

NOTES

Sub-s (1A): inserted by the Collective Investment Schemes (Miscellaneous Amendments) Regulations 2003, SI 2003/2066, reg 9, as from 13 February 2004.

267 Power of Authority to suspend promotion of scheme

(1)   Subsection (2) applies if it appears to the Authority that the operator of a scheme has communicated an invitation or inducement in relation to the scheme in a manner contrary to financial promotion rules.

(2)   The Authority may direct that—

    (a)   the exemption from subsection (1) of section 238 provided by subsection (4)(c) of that section is not to apply in relation to the scheme; and

    (b)   subsection (5) of that section does not apply with respect to things done in relation to the scheme.

(3)   A direction under subsection (2) has effect—

    (a)   for a specified period;

    (b)   until the occurrence of a specified event; or

    (c)   until specified conditions are complied with.

(4)   The Authority may, either on its own initiative or on the application of the operator of the scheme concerned, vary a direction given under subsection (2) if it appears to the Authority that the direction should take effect or continue in force in a different form.

(5)   The Authority may, either on its own initiative or on the application of the operator of the recognised scheme concerned, revoke a direction given under subsection (2) if it appears to the Authority—

    (a)   that the conditions specified in the direction have been complied with; or

    (b)   that it is no longer necessary for the direction to take effect or continue in force.

(6)   If an event is specified, the direction ceases to have effect (unless revoked earlier) on the occurrence of that event.

(7)   For the purposes of this section and sections 268 and 269—

    (a)   the scheme's home State is the EEA State in which the scheme is constituted (within the meaning given by section 264);

    (b)   the competent authorities in the scheme's home State are the authorities in that State who are responsible for the authorisation of collective investment schemes.

(8)   "Scheme" means a scheme which is a recognised scheme by virtue of section 264.

(9)   "Specified", in relation to a direction, means specified in it.

[293]

268   Procedure on giving directions under section 267 and varying them on Authority's own initiative

(1)   A direction under section 267 takes effect—

    (a)   immediately, if the notice given under subsection (3)(a) states that that is the case;

    (b)   on such date as may be specified in the notice; or

    (c)   if no date is specified in the notice, when the matter to which it relates is no longer open to review.

(2)   A direction may be expressed to take effect immediately (or on a specified date) only if the Authority, having regard to its reasons for exercising its power under section 267, considers that it is necessary for the direction to take effect immediately (or on that date).

(3)   If the Authority proposes to give a direction under section 267, or gives such a direction with immediate effect, it must—

    (a)   give the operator of the scheme concerned written notice; and

    (b)   inform the competent authorities in the scheme's home State of its proposal or (as the case may be) of the direction.

(4)   The notice must—

    (a)   give details of the direction;

    (b)   inform the operator of when the direction takes effect;

    (c)   state the Authority's reasons for giving the direction and for its determination as to when the direction takes effect;

    (d)   inform the operator that he may make representations to the Authority within such period as may be specified in it (whether or not he has referred the matter to the Tribunal); and

    (e)   inform him of his right to refer the matter to the Tribunal.

(5)   The Authority may extend the period allowed under the notice for making representations.

(6)   Subsection (7) applies if, having considered any representations made by the operator, the Authority decides—

    (a)   to give the direction in the way proposed, or

    (b)   if it has been given, not to revoke the direction.

(7)   The Authority must—

    (a)   give the operator of the scheme concerned written notice; and

    (b)   inform the competent authorities in the scheme's home State of the direction.

(8)   Subsection (9) applies if, having considered any representations made by a person to whom the notice was given, the Authority decides—

    (a)   not to give the direction in the way proposed,

(b) to give the direction in a way other than that proposed, or

(c) to revoke a direction which has effect.

(9) The Authority must—

(a) give the operator of the scheme concerned written notice; and

(b) inform the competent authorities in the scheme's home State of its decision.

(10) A notice given under subsection (7)(a) must inform the operator of his right to refer the matter to the Tribunal.

(11) A notice under subsection (9)(a) given as a result of subsection (8)(b) must comply with subsection (4).

(12) If a notice informs a person of his right to refer a matter to the Tribunal, it must give an indication of the procedure on such a reference.

(13) This section applies to the variation of a direction on the Authority's own initiative as it applies to the giving of a direction.

(14) For the purposes of subsection (1)(c), whether a matter is open to review is to be determined in accordance with section 391(8).

[294]

269 Procedure on application for variation or revocation of direction

(1) If, on an application under subsection (4) or (5) of section 267, the Authority proposes—

(a) to vary a direction otherwise than in accordance with the application, or

(b) to refuse the application,

it must give the operator of the scheme concerned a warning notice.

(2) If, on such an application, the Authority decides—

(a) to vary a direction otherwise than in accordance with the application, or

(b) to refuse the application,

it must give the operator of the scheme concerned a decision notice.

(3) If the application is refused, the operator of the scheme may refer the matter to the Tribunal.

(4) If, on such an application, the Authority decides to grant the application it must give the operator of the scheme concerned written notice.

(5) If the Authority decides on its own initiative to revoke a direction given under section 267 it must give the operator of the scheme concerned written notice.

(6) The Authority must inform the competent authorities in the scheme's home State of any notice given under this section.

[295]

Schemes authorised in designated countries or territories

270 Schemes authorised in designated countries or territories

(1) A collective investment scheme which is not a recognised scheme by virtue of section 264 but is managed in, and authorised under the law of, a country or territory outside the United Kingdom is a recognised scheme if—

(a) that country or territory is designated for the purposes of this section by an order made by the Treasury;

(b) the scheme is of a class specified by the order;

(c) the operator of the scheme has given written notice to the Authority that he wishes it to be recognised; and

(d) either—

(i) the Authority, by written notice, has given its approval to the scheme's being recognised; or

(ii) two months, beginning with the date on which notice was given under paragraph (c), have expired without the operator receiving a warning notice from the Authority under section 271.

(2) The Treasury may not make an order designating any country or territory for the purposes of this section unless satisfied—

(a) that the law and practice under which relevant collective investment schemes are authorised and supervised in that country or territory affords to investors in the United Kingdom protection at least equivalent to that provided for them by or under this Part in the case of comparable authorised schemes; and

(b) that adequate arrangements exist, or will exist, for co-operation between the authorities of the country or territory responsible for the authorisation and supervision of relevant collective investment schemes and the Authority.

(3) "Relevant collective investment schemes" means collective investment schemes of the class or classes to be specified by the order.

(4)   "Comparable authorised schemes" means whichever of the following the Treasury consider to be the most appropriate, having regard to the class or classes of scheme to be specified by the order—
  (a)   authorised unit trust schemes;
  (b)   authorised open-ended investment companies;
  (c)   both such unit trust schemes and such companies.

(5)   If the Treasury are considering whether to make an order designating a country or territory for the purposes of this section—
  (a)   the Treasury must ask the Authority for a report—
    (i)   on the law and practice of that country or territory in relation to the authorisation and supervision of relevant collective investment schemes,
    (ii)   on any existing or proposed arrangements for co-operation between it and the authorities responsible in that country or territory for the authorisation and supervision of relevant collective investment schemes,
  having regard to the Treasury's need to be satisfied as mentioned in subsection (2);
  (b)   the Authority must provide the Treasury with such a report; and
  (c)   the Treasury must have regard to it in deciding whether to make the order.

(6)   The notice to be given by the operator under subsection (1)(c)—
  (a)   must contain the address of a place in the United Kingdom for the service on the operator of notices or other documents required or authorised to be served on him under this Act; and
  (b)   must contain or be accompanied by such information and documents as may be specified by the Authority.

[296]

NOTES
  Orders: the Financial Services and Markets Act 2000 (Collective Investment Schemes) (Designated Countries and Territories) Order 2003, SI 2003/1181 (which designates Jersey, Guernsey and the Isle of Man). Also, the Financial Services (Designated Countries and Territories) (Overseas Collective Investment Schemes) (Bermuda) Order 1988, SI 1988/2284 (made under FSA 1986, s 87) which continues in force and has effect as if made under sub-s (1)(a) above by virtue of the Financial Services and Markets Act 2000 (Transitional Provisions) (Authorised Persons etc) Order 2001, SI 2001/2636, art 67(1).

271   Procedure

(1)   If the Authority proposes to refuse approval of a scheme's being a recognised scheme by virtue of section 270, it must give the operator of the scheme a warning notice.

(2)   To be valid the warning notice must be received by the operator before the end of two months beginning with the date on which notice was given under section 270(1)(c).

(3)   If, having given a warning notice, the Authority decides to refuse approval—
  (a)   it must give the operator of the scheme a decision notice; and
  (b)   the operator may refer the matter to the Tribunal.

[297]

Individually recognised overseas schemes

272   Individually recognised overseas schemes

(1)   The Authority may, on the application of the operator of a collective investment scheme which—
  (a)   is managed in a country or territory outside the United Kingdom,
  (b)   does not satisfy the requirements prescribed for the purposes of section 264,
  (c)   is not managed in a country or territory designated for the purposes of section 270 or, if it is so managed, is of a class not specified by the designation order, and
  (d)   appears to the Authority to satisfy the requirements set out in the following provisions of this section,
make an order declaring the scheme to be a recognised scheme.

(2)   Adequate protection must be afforded to participants in the scheme.

(3)   The arrangements for the scheme's constitution and management must be adequate.

(4)   The powers and duties of the operator and, if the scheme has a trustee or depositary, of the trustee or depositary must be adequate.

(5)   In deciding whether the matters mentioned in subsection (3) or (4) are adequate, the Authority must have regard to—
  (a)   any rule of law, and
  (b)   any matters which are, or could be, the subject of rules,
applicable in relation to comparable authorised schemes.

(6)   "Comparable authorised schemes" means whichever of the following the Authority considers the most appropriate, having regard to the nature of scheme in respect of which the application is made—
   (a)   authorised unit trust schemes;
   (b)   authorised open-ended investment companies;
   (c)   both such unit trust schemes and such companies.

(7)   The scheme must take the form of an open-ended investment company or (if it does not take that form) the operator must be a body corporate.

(8)   The operator of the scheme must—
   (a)   if an authorised person, have permission to act as operator;
   (b)   if not an authorised person, be a fit and proper person to act as operator.

(9)   The trustee or depositary (if any) of the scheme must—
   (a)   if an authorised person, have permission to act as trustee or depositary;
   (b)   if not an authorised person, be a fit and proper person to act as trustee or depositary.

(10)   The operator and the trustee or depositary (if any) of the scheme must be able and willing to co-operate with the Authority by the sharing of information and in other ways.

(11)   The name of the scheme must not be undesirable or misleading.

(12)   The purposes of the scheme must be reasonably capable of being successfully carried into effect.

(13)   The participants must be entitled to have their units redeemed in accordance with the scheme at a price related to the net value of the property to which the units relate and determined in accordance with the scheme.

(14)   But a scheme is to be treated as complying with subsection (13) if it requires the operator to ensure that a participant is able to sell his units on an investment exchange at a price not significantly different from that mentioned in that subsection.

(15)   Subsection (13) is not to be read as imposing a requirement that the participants must be entitled to have their units redeemed (or sold as mentioned in subsection (14)) immediately following a demand to that effect.

[298]

NOTES
Application in relation to interim permissions and interim approvals: see the notes preceding s 40 at **[40]**.

---

273   Matters that may be taken into account

For the purposes of subsections (8)(b) and (9)(b) of section 272, the Authority may take into account any matter relating to—
   (a)   any person who is or will be employed by or associated with the operator, trustee or depositary in connection with the scheme;
   (b)   any director of the operator, trustee or depositary;
   (c)   any person exercising influence over the operator, trustee or depositary;
   (d)   any body corporate in the same group as the operator, trustee or depositary;
   (e)   any director of any such body corporate;
   (f)   any person exercising influence over any such body corporate.

[299]

274   Applications for recognition of individual schemes

(1)   An application under section 272 for an order declaring a scheme to be a recognised scheme must be made to the Authority by the operator of the scheme.

(2)   The application—
   (a)   must be made in such manner as the Authority may direct;
   (b)   must contain the address of a place in the United Kingdom for the service on the operator of notices or other documents required or authorised to be served on him under this Act;
   (c)   must contain or be accompanied by such information as the Authority may reasonably require for the purpose of determining the application.

(3)   At any time after receiving an application and before determining it, the Authority may require the applicant to provide it with such further information as it reasonably considers necessary to enable it to determine the application.

(4)   Different directions may be given, and different requirements imposed, in relation to different applications.

(5)   The Authority may require an applicant to present information which he is required to give under this section in such form, or to verify it in such a way, as the Authority may direct.

[300]

275   Determination of applications

(1)   An application under section 272 must be determined by the Authority before the end of the period of six months beginning with the date on which it receives the completed application.

(2)   The Authority may determine an incomplete application if it considers it appropriate to do so; and it must in any event determine such an application within twelve months beginning with the date on which it first receives the application.

(3)   If the Authority makes an order under section 272(1), it must give written notice of the order to the applicant.

[301]

276   Procedure when refusing an application

(1)   If the Authority proposes to refuse an application made under section 272 it must give the applicant a warning notice.

(2)   If the Authority decides to refuse the application—
    (a)   it must give the applicant a decision notice; and
    (b)   the applicant may refer the matter to the Tribunal.

[302]

277   Alteration of schemes and changes of operator, trustee or depositary

(1)   The operator of a scheme recognised by virtue of section 272 must give written notice to the Authority of any proposed alteration to the scheme.

(2)   Effect is not to be given to any such proposal unless—
    (a)   the Authority, by written notice, has given its approval to the proposal; or
    (b)   one month, beginning with the date on which notice was given under subsection (1), has expired without the Authority having given written notice to the operator that it has decided to refuse approval.

(3)   At least one month before any replacement of the operator, trustee or depositary of such a scheme, notice of the proposed replacement must be given to the Authority—
    (a)   by the operator, trustee or depositary (as the case may be); or
    (b)   by the person who is to replace him.

[303]

Schemes recognised under sections 270 and 272

278   Rules as to scheme particulars

The Authority may make rules imposing duties or liabilities on the operator of a scheme recognised under section 270 or 272 for purposes corresponding to those for which rules may be made under section 248 in relation to authorised unit trust schemes.

[304]

279   Revocation of recognition

The Authority may direct that a scheme is to cease to be recognised by virtue of section 270 or revoke an order under section 272 if it appears to the Authority—
    (a)   that the operator, trustee or depositary of the scheme has contravened a requirement imposed on him by or under this Act;
    (b)   that the operator, trustee or depositary of the scheme has, in purported compliance with any such requirement, knowingly or recklessly given the Authority information which is false or misleading in a material particular;
    (c)   in the case of an order under section 272, that one or more of the requirements for the making of the order are no longer satisfied; or
    (d)   that none of paragraphs (a) to (c) applies, but it is undesirable in the interests of the participants or potential participants that the scheme should continue to be recognised.

[305]

280   Procedure

(1)   If the Authority proposes to give a direction under section 279 or to make an order under that section revoking a recognition order, it must give a warning notice to the operator and (if any) the trustee or depositary of the scheme.

(2)   If the Authority decides to give a direction or make an order under that section—
    (a)   it must without delay give a decision notice to the operator and (if any) the trustee or depositary of the scheme; and
    (b)   the operator or the trustee or depositary may refer the matter to the Tribunal.

[306]

281   Directions

(1)   In this section a "relevant recognised scheme" means a scheme recognised under section 270 or 272.

(2)   If it appears to the Authority that—

(a)   the operator, trustee or depositary of a relevant recognised scheme has contravened, or is likely to contravene, a requirement imposed on him by or under this Act,

(b)   the operator, trustee or depositary of such a scheme has, in purported compliance with any such requirement, knowingly or recklessly given the Authority information which is false or misleading in a material particular,

(c)   one or more of the requirements for the recognition of a scheme under section 272 are no longer satisfied, or

(d)   none of paragraphs (a) to (c) applies, but the exercise of the power conferred by this section is desirable in order to protect the interests of participants or potential participants in a relevant recognised scheme who are in the United Kingdom,

it may direct that the scheme is not to be a recognised scheme for a specified period or until the occurrence of a specified event or until specified conditions are complied with.

[307]

282 Procedure on giving directions under section 281 and varying them otherwise than as requested

(1)   A direction takes effect—

(a)   immediately, if the notice given under subsection (3) states that that is the case;

(b)   on such date as may be specified in the notice; or

(c)   if no date is specified in the notice, when the matter to which it relates is no longer open to review.

(2)   A direction may be expressed to take effect immediately (or on a specified date) only if the Authority, having regard to the ground on which it is exercising its power under section 281, considers that it is necessary for the direction to take effect immediately (or on that date).

(3)   If the Authority proposes to give a direction under section 281, or gives such a direction with immediate effect, it must give separate written notice to the operator and (if any) the trustee or depositary of the scheme concerned.

(4)   The notice must—

(a)   give details of the direction;

(b)   inform the person to whom it is given of when the direction takes effect;

(c)   state the Authority's reasons for giving the direction and for its determination as to when the direction takes effect;

(d)   inform the person to whom it is given that he may make representations to the Authority within such period as may be specified in it (whether or not he has referred the matter to the Tribunal); and

(e)   inform him of his right to refer the matter to the Tribunal.

(5)   The Authority may extend the period allowed under the notice for making representations.

(6)   If, having considered any representations made by a person to whom the notice was given, the Authority decides—

(a)   to give the direction in the way proposed, or

(b)   if it has been given, not to revoke the direction,

it must give separate written notice to the operator and (if any) the trustee or depositary of the scheme concerned.

(7)   If, having considered any representations made by a person to whom the notice was given, the Authority decides—

(a)   not to give the direction in the way proposed,

(b)   to give the direction in a way other than that proposed, or

(c)   to revoke a direction which has effect,

it must give separate written notice to the operator and (if any) the trustee or depositary of the scheme concerned.

(8)   A notice given under subsection (6) must inform the person to whom it is given of his right to refer the matter to the Tribunal.

(9)   A notice under subsection (7)(b) must comply with subsection (4).

(10)   If a notice informs a person of his right to refer a matter to the Tribunal, it must give an indication of the procedure on such a reference.

(11)   This section applies to the variation of a direction on the Authority's own initiative as it applies to the giving of a direction.

(12)   For the purposes of subsection (1)(c), whether a matter is open to review is to be determined in accordance with section 391(8).

[308]

Facilities and information in UK

283　Facilities and information in UK

(1)　The Authority may make rules requiring operators of recognised schemes to maintain in the United Kingdom, or in such part or parts of it as may be specified, such facilities as the Authority thinks desirable in the interests of participants and as are specified in rules.

(2)　The Authority may by notice in writing require the operator of any recognised scheme to include such explanatory information as is specified in the notice in any communication of his which—

　　(a)　is a communication of an invitation or inducement of a kind mentioned in section 21(1); and

　　(b)　names the scheme.

(3)　In the case of a communication originating outside the United Kingdom, subsection (2) only applies if the communication is capable of having an effect in the United Kingdom.

[309]

CHAPTER VI
INVESTIGATIONS

284　Power to investigate

(1)　An investigating authority may appoint one or more competent persons to investigate on its behalf—

　　(a)　the affairs of, or of the manager or trustee of, any authorised unit trust scheme,

　　(b)　the affairs of, or of the operator, trustee or depositary of, any recognised scheme so far as relating to activities carried on in the United Kingdom, or

　　(c)　the affairs of, or of the operator, trustee or depositary of, any other collective investment scheme except a body incorporated by virtue of regulations under section 262,

if it appears to the investigating authority that it is in the interests of the participants or potential participants to do so or that the matter is of public concern.

(2)　A person appointed under subsection (1) to investigate the affairs of, or of the manager, trustee, operator or depositary of, any scheme (scheme "A"), may also, if he thinks it necessary for the purposes of that investigation, investigate—

　　(a)　the affairs of, or of the manager, trustee, operator or depositary of, any other such scheme as is mentioned in subsection (1) whose manager, trustee, operator or depositary is the same person as the manager, trustee, operator or depositary of scheme A;

　　(b)　the affairs of such other schemes and persons (including bodies incorporated by virtue of regulations under section 262 and the directors and depositaries of such bodies) as may be prescribed.

(3)　If the person appointed to conduct an investigation under this section ("B") considers that a person ("C") is or may be able to give information which is relevant to the investigation, B may require C—

　　(a)　to produce to B any documents in C's possession or under his control which appear to B to be relevant to the investigation,

　　(b)　to attend before B, and

　　(c)　otherwise to give B all assistance in connection with the investigation which C is reasonably able to give,

and it is C's duty to comply with that requirement.

(4)　Subsections (5) to (9) of section 170 apply if an investigating authority appoints a person under this section to conduct an investigation on its behalf as they apply in the case mentioned in subsection (1) of that section.

(5)　Section 174 applies to a statement made by a person in compliance with a requirement imposed under this section as it applies to a statement mentioned in that section.

(6)　Subsections (2) to (4) and (6) of section 175 and section 177 have effect as if this section were contained in Part XI.

(7)　Subsections (1) to (9) of section 176 apply in relation to a person appointed under subsection (1) as if—

　　(a)　references to an investigator were references to a person so appointed;

　　(b)　references to an information requirement were references to a requirement imposed under section 175 or under subsection (3) by a person so appointed;

　　(c)　the premises mentioned in subsection (3)(a) were the premises of a person whose affairs are the subject of an investigation under this section or of an appointed representative of such a person.

(8)   No person may be required under this section to disclose information or produce a document in respect of which he owes an obligation of confidence by virtue of carrying on the business of banking unless subsection (9) or (10) applies.

(9)   This subsection applies if—
  (a)   the person to whom the obligation of confidence is owed consents to the disclosure or production; or
  (b)   the imposing on the person concerned of a requirement with respect to information or a document of a kind mentioned in subsection (8) has been specifically authorised by the investigating authority.

(10)   This subsection applies if the person owing the obligation of confidence or the person to whom it is owed is—
  (a)   the manager, trustee, operator or depositary of any collective investment scheme which is under investigation;
  (b)   the director of a body incorporated by virtue of regulations under section 262 which is under investigation;
  (c)   any other person whose own affairs are under investigation.

(11)   "Investigating authority" means the Authority or the Secretary of State.

[310]

NOTES
The business of banking: this phrase is not defined in this Act and it is not clear whether it applies to all those who have permission or authorisation to accept deposits.

PART XVIII
RECOGNISED INVESTMENT EXCHANGES AND CLEARING HOUSES

CHAPTER I
EXEMPTION

General

285   Exemption for recognised investment exchanges and clearing houses

(1)   In this Act—
  (a)   "recognised investment exchange" means an investment exchange in relation to which a recognition order is in force; and
  (b)   "recognised clearing house" means a clearing house in relation to which a recognition order is in force.

(2)   A recognised investment exchange is exempt from the general prohibition as respects any regulated activity—
  (a)   which is carried on as a part of the exchange's business as an investment exchange; or
  (b)   which is carried on for the purposes of, or in connection with, the provision of clearing services by the exchange.

(3)   A recognised clearing house is exempt from the general prohibition as respects any regulated activity which is carried on for the purposes of, or in connection with, the provision of clearing services by the clearing house.

[311]

286   Qualification for recognition

(1)   The Treasury may make regulations setting out the requirements—
  (a)   which must be satisfied by an investment exchange or clearing house if it is to qualify as a body in respect of which the Authority may make a recognition order under this Part; and
  (b)   which, if a recognition order is made, it must continue to satisfy if it is to remain a recognised body.

(2)   But if regulations contain provision as to the default rules of an investment exchange or clearing house, or as to proceedings taken under such rules by such a body, they require the approval of the Secretary of State.

(3)   "Default rules" means rules of an investment exchange or clearing house which provide for the taking of action in the event of a person's appearing to be unable, or likely to become unable, to meet his obligations in respect of one or more market contracts connected with the exchange or clearing house.

(4)   "Market contract" means—
  (a)   a contract to which Part VII of the Companies Act 1989 applies as a result of section 155 of that Act or a contract to which Part V of the Companies (No 2) (Northern Ireland) Order 1990 applies as a result of Article 80 of that Order; and

(b)　　such other kind of contract as may be prescribed.

[(4A)　If regulations under subsection (1) require an investment exchange to make information available to the public in accordance with—

(a)　Article 29.1 of the markets in financial instruments directive and the Commission Regulation, or

(b)　Article 44.1 of that directive and that Regulation,

the regulations may authorise the Authority to waive the requirement in the circumstances specified in the relevant provisions.

(4B)　The "relevant provisions" for the purposes of subsection (4A) are—

(a)　in a case falling within paragraph (a) of that subsection, Article 29.2 of the markets in financial instruments directive and the Commission Regulation, and

(b)　in a case falling within paragraph (b) of that subsection, Article 44.2 of that directive and that Regulation.

(4C)　If regulations under subsection (1) require an investment exchange to make information available to the public in accordance with—

(a)　Article 30.1 of the markets in financial instruments directive and the Commission Regulation, or

(b)　Article 45.1 of that directive and that Regulation,

the regulations may authorise the Authority to defer the requirement in the circumstances specified, and subject to the requirements contained, in the relevant provisions.

(4D)　The "relevant provisions" for the purposes of subsection (4C) are—

(a)　in a case falling within paragraph (a) of that subsection, Article 30.2 of the markets in financial instruments directive and the Commission Regulation, and

(b)　in a case falling within paragraph (b) of that subsection, Article 45.2 of that directive and that Regulation.

(4E)　"The Commission Regulation" means Commission Regulation 1287/2006 of 10 August 2006.]

(5)　Requirements resulting from this section are referred to in this Part as "recognition requirements".

[(6)　In the case of an investment exchange, requirements resulting from this section are in addition to requirements which must be satisfied by the exchange as a result of section 290(1A) before the Authority may make a recognition order declaring the exchange to be a recognised investment exchange.]

[312]

NOTES

Sub-ss (4A)–(4E): inserted by the Financial Services and Markets Act 2000 (Markets in Financial Instruments) (Modification of Powers) Regulations 2006, SI 2006/2975, regs 2, 8, as from 6 December 2006.

Sub-s (6): added by the Financial Services and Markets Act 2000 (Markets in Financial Instruments) Regulations 2007, SI 2007/126, reg 3(2), Sch 2, paras 1, 2, as from 1 April 2007 (certain purposes (see reg 1(2) at **[4051]**)), and as from 1 November 2007 (otherwise).

Regulations: the Financial Services and Markets Act 2000 (Recognition Requirements for Investment Exchanges and Clearing Houses) Regulations 2001, SI 2001/995 at **[2147]**.

Note that the following amending Regulations have also been made under this section: the Financial Services and Markets Act 2000 (Recognition Requirements for Investment Exchanges and Clearing Houses) (Amendment) Regulations 2006, SI 2006/3386.

Applications for recognition

287　Application by an investment exchange

(1)　Any body corporate or unincorporated association may apply to the Authority for an order declaring it to be a recognised investment exchange for the purposes of this Act.

(2)　The application must be made in such manner as the Authority may direct and must be accompanied by—

(a)　a copy of the applicant's rules;

(b)　a copy of any guidance issued by the applicant;

(c)　the required particulars; and

(d)　such other information as the Authority may reasonably require for the purpose of determining the application.

(3)　The required particulars are—

(a)　particulars of any arrangements which the applicant has made, or proposes to make, for the provision of clearing services in respect of transactions effected on the exchange;

(b)　if the applicant proposes to provide clearing services in respect of transactions other than those effected on the exchange, particulars of the criteria which the applicant will apply when determining to whom it will provide those services[;

(c)   a programme of operations which includes the types of business the applicant proposes to undertake and the applicant's proposed organisational structure;

(d)   such particulars of the persons who effectively direct the business and operations of the exchange as the Authority may reasonably require;

(e)   such particulars of the ownership of the exchange, and in particular of the identity and scale of interests of the persons who are in a position to exercise significant influence over the management of the exchange, whether directly or indirectly, as the Authority may reasonably require].

[(4)   Subsection (3)(c) to (e) does not apply to an application by an overseas applicant.]

[313]

NOTES
Sub-s (3): paras (c)–(e) added by the Financial Services and Markets Act 2000 (Markets in Financial Instruments) Regulations 2007, SI 2007/126, reg 3(2), Sch 2, paras 1, 3(a), as from 1 April 2007 (certain purposes (see reg 1(2) at **[4051]**)), and as from 1 November 2007 (otherwise).
Sub-s (4): added by SI 2007/126, reg 3(2), Sch 2, paras 1, 3(b), as from 1 April 2007 (certain purposes (see reg 1(2) at **[4051]**)), and as from 1 November 2007 (otherwise).
Note: as of the date of publication the recognised investment exchanges are: EDX London Ltd, ICE Futures Europe, LIFFE Administration and Management, London Stock Exchange plc, PLUS Markets plc, the London Metal Exchange Limited, SWX Europe Limited).

288   Application by a clearing house

(1)   Any body corporate or unincorporated association may apply to the Authority for an order declaring it to be a recognised clearing house for the purposes of this Act.

(2)   The application must be made in such manner as the Authority may direct and must be accompanied by—
(a)   a copy of the applicant's rules;
(b)   a copy of any guidance issued by the applicant;
(c)   the required particulars; and
(d)   such other information as the Authority may reasonably require for the purpose of determining the application.

(3)   The required particulars are—
(a)   if the applicant makes, or proposes to make, clearing arrangements with a recognised investment exchange, particulars of those arrangements;
(b)   if the applicant proposes to provide clearing services for persons other than recognised investment exchanges, particulars of the criteria which it will apply when determining to whom it will provide those services.

[314]

NOTES
Note: as at the date of publication the recognised clearing houses are Euroclear UK and Ireland Limited, European Central Counterparty Ltd, ICE Clear Europe Limited, and LCH Clearnet Limited.

289   Applications: supplementary

(1)   At any time after receiving an application and before determining it, the Authority may require the applicant to provide such further information as it reasonably considers necessary to enable it to determine the application.

(2)   Information which the Authority requires in connection with an application must be provided in such form, or verified in such manner, as the Authority may direct.

(3)   Different directions may be given, or requirements imposed, by the Authority with respect to different applications.

[315]

290   Recognition orders

(1)   If it appears to the Authority that the applicant satisfies the recognition requirements applicable in its case, the Authority may make a recognition order declaring the applicant to be—
(a)   a recognised investment exchange, if the application is made under section 287;
(b)   a recognised clearing house, if it is made under section 288.

[(1A)   In the case of an application for an order declaring the applicant to be a recognised investment exchange, the reference in subsection (1) to the recognition requirements applicable in its case includes a reference to requirements contained in any directly applicable Community regulation made under the markets in financial instruments directive.

(1B)   In the case mentioned in subsection (1A), the application must be determined by the Authority before the end of the period of six months beginning with the date on which it receives the completed application.

(1C)   Subsection (1B) does not apply in the case of an application by an overseas applicant.]

(2)   The Treasury's approval of the making of a recognition order is required under section 307.

(3)   In considering an application, the Authority may have regard to any information which it considers is relevant to the application.

(4)   A recognition order must specify a date on which it is to take effect.

(5)   Section 298 has effect in relation to a decision to refuse to make a recognition order—

    (a)   as it has effect in relation to a decision to revoke such an order; and

    (b)   as if references to a recognised body were references to the applicant.

(6)   Subsection (5) does not apply in a case in which the Treasury have failed to give their approval under section 307.

[316]

NOTES

Sub-ss (1A)–(1C): inserted by the Financial Services and Markets Act 2000 (Markets in Financial Instruments) Regulations 2007, SI 2007/126, reg 3(2), Sch 2, paras 1, 4, as from 1 April 2007 (certain purposes (see reg 1(2) at **[4051]**)), and as from 1 November 2007 (otherwise).

[290A   Refusal of recognition on ground of excessive regulatory provision

(1)   The Authority must not make a recognition order if it appears to the Authority that an existing or proposed regulatory provision of the applicant in connection with—

    (a)   the applicant's business as an investment exchange, or

    (b)   the provision by the applicant of clearing services,

imposes or will impose an excessive requirement on the persons affected (directly or indirectly) by it.

(2)   The reference in section 290(1) (making of recognition order) to satisfying the applicable recognition requirements shall be read accordingly.

(3)   Expressions used in subsection (1) above that are defined for the purposes of section 300A (power of Authority to disallow excessive regulatory provision) have the same meaning as in that section.

(4)   The provisions of section 300A(3) and (4) (determination whether regulatory provision excessive) apply for the purposes of this section as for the purposes of section 300A.

(5)   Section 298 has effect in relation to a decision under this section to refuse a recognition order—

    (a)   as it has effect in relation to a decision to revoke such an order, and

    (b)   as if references to a recognised body were references to the applicant.

(6)   This section does not apply to an application for recognition as an overseas investment exchange or overseas clearing house.]

[316A]

NOTES

Commencement: 20 December 2006.

Inserted by the Investment Exchanges and Clearing Houses Act 2006, s 4, as from 20 December 2006.

291   Liability in relation to recognised body's regulatory functions

(1)   A recognised body and its officers and staff are not to be liable in damages for anything done or omitted in the discharge of the recognised body's regulatory functions unless it is shown that the act or omission was in bad faith.

(2)   But subsection (1) does not prevent an award of damages made in respect of an act or omission on the ground that the act or omission was unlawful as a result of section 6(1) of the Human Rights Act 1998.

(3)   "Regulatory functions" means the functions of the recognised body so far as relating to, or to matters arising out of, the obligations to which the body is subject under or by virtue of this Act.

[317]

NOTES

Modification of this section in relation to banks that are the subject of orders made under the Banking (Special Provisions) Act 2008: see the Northern Rock plc Transfer Order 2008, SI 2008/432 at **[4128]**; the Bradford & Bingley plc Transfer of Securities and Property etc Order 2008, SI 2008/2546 at **[4227]**.

292   Overseas investment exchanges and overseas clearing houses

(1)   An application under section 287 or 288 by an overseas applicant must contain the address of a place in the United Kingdom for the service on the applicant of notices or other documents required or authorised to be served on it under this Act.

(2)   If it appears to the Authority that an overseas applicant satisfies the requirements of subsection (3) it may make a recognition order declaring the applicant to be—
   (a)   a recognised investment exchange;
   (b)   a recognised clearing house.

(3)   The requirements are that—
   (a)   investors are afforded protection equivalent to that which they would be afforded if the body concerned were required to comply with recognition requirements[, other than any such requirements which are expressed in regulations under section 286 not to apply for the purposes of this paragraph];
   (b)   there are adequate procedures for dealing with a person who is unable, or likely to become unable, to meet his obligations in respect of one or more market contracts connected with the investment exchange or clearing house;
   (c)   the applicant is able and willing to co-operate with the Authority by the sharing of information and in other ways;
   (d)   adequate arrangements exist for co-operation between the Authority and those responsible for the supervision of the applicant in the country or territory in which the applicant's head office is situated.

(4)   In considering whether it is satisfied as to the requirements mentioned in subsection (3)(a) and (b), the Authority is to have regard to—
   (a)   the relevant law and practice of the country or territory in which the applicant's head office is situated;
   (b)   the rules and practices of the applicant.

(5)   In relation to an overseas applicant and a body or association declared to be a recognised investment exchange or recognised clearing house by a recognition order made by virtue of subsection (2)—
   (a)   the reference in section 313(2) to recognition requirements is to be read as a reference to matters corresponding to the matters in respect of which provision is made in the recognition requirements;
   (b)   sections 296(1) and 297(2) have effect as if the requirements mentioned in section 296(1)(a) and section 297(2)(a) were those of subsection (3)(a), (b), and (c) of this section;
   (c)   section 297(2) has effect as if the grounds on which a recognition order may be revoked under that provision included the ground that in the opinion of the Authority arrangements of the kind mentioned in subsection (3)(d) no longer exist.

[318]

NOTES

Sub-s (3): words in square brackets in para (a) inserted by the Financial Services and Markets Act 2000 (Markets in Financial Instruments) (Modification of Powers) Regulations 2006, SI 2006/2975, regs 2, 9, as from 6 December 2006.

Note: as at the date of publication the recognised overseas investment exchanges are: Cantor Financial Futures Exchange (CFEE), Chicago Board of Trade (CBOT), EUREX (Zurich), ICE Futures US Inc, National Association of Securities Dealers Automated Quotations (NASDAQ), New York Mercantile Exchange Inc (NYMEX Inc), NQLX LLC, Sydney Futures Exchange Limited, The Chicago Mercantile Exchange (CME), the Swiss Stock Exchange (SWX), and US Futures Exchange LLC. The recognised overseas clearing houses are EUREX Clearing AG, SIS x-clear AG, ICE Clear US Limited and The Chicago Mercantile Exchange.

Regulations under section 286: see the final note to that section at **[312]**.

[Publication of information by recognised investment exchange

292A   Publication of information by recognised investment exchange

(1)   A recognised investment exchange must as soon as practicable after a recognition order is made in respect of it publish such particulars of the ownership of the exchange as the Authority may reasonably require.

(2)   The particulars published under subsection (1) must include particulars of the identity and scale of interests of the persons who are in a position to exercise significant influence over the management of the exchange, whether directly or indirectly.

(3)   If an ownership transfer takes place in relation to a recognised investment exchange, the exchange must as soon as practicable after becoming aware of the transfer publish such particulars relating to the transfer as the Authority may reasonably require.

(4)   "Ownership transfer", in relation to an exchange, means a transfer of ownership which gives rise to a change in the persons who are in a position to exercise significant influence over the management of the exchange, whether directly or indirectly.

(5)   A recognised investment exchange must publish such particulars of any decision it makes to suspend or remove a financial instrument from trading on a regulated market operated by it as the Authority may reasonably require.

(6)   The Authority may determine the manner of publication under subsections (1), (3) and (5) and the timing of publication under subsection (5).

(7)   This section does not apply to an overseas investment exchange.]

[318A]

NOTES
  Commencement: 1 April 2007 (certain purposes); 1 November 2007 (otherwise).
  Inserted, together with the preceding heading, by the Financial Services and Markets Act 2000 (Markets in Financial Instruments) Regulations 2007, SI 2007/126, reg 3(2), Sch 2, paras 1, 5, as from 1 April 2007 (certain purposes (see reg 1(2) at **[4051]**)), and as from 1 November 2007 (otherwise).

Supervision

293   Notification requirements

(1)   The Authority may make rules requiring a recognised body to give it—
  (a)   notice of such events relating to the body as may be specified; and
  (b)   such information in respect of those events as may be specified.

(2)   The rules may also require a recognised body to give the Authority, at such times or in respect of such periods as may be specified, such information relating to the body as may be specified.

(3)   An obligation imposed by the rules extends only to a notice or information which the Authority may reasonably require for the exercise of its functions under this Act.

(4)   The rules may require information to be given in a specified form and to be verified in a specified manner.

(5)   If a recognised body—
  (a)   alters or revokes any of its rules or guidance, or
  (b)   makes new rules or issues new guidance,
it must give written notice to the Authority without delay.

(6)   If a recognised investment exchange makes a change—
  (a)   in the arrangements it makes for the provision of clearing services in respect of transactions effected on the exchange, or
  (b)   in the criteria which it applies when determining to whom it will provide clearing services,
it must give written notice to the Authority without delay.

(7)   If a recognised clearing house makes a change—
  (a)   in the recognised investment exchanges for whom it provides clearing services, or
  (b)   in the criteria which it applies when determining to whom (other than recognised investment exchanges) it will provide clearing services,
it must give written notice to the Authority without delay.

(8)   Subsections (5) to (7) do not apply to an overseas investment exchange or an overseas clearing house.

(9)   "Specified" means specified in the Authority's rules.

[319]

[293A   Information: compliance of recognised investment exchanges with directly applicable Community regulations

The Authority may require a recognised investment exchange to give the Authority such information as it reasonably requires in order to satisfy itself that the exchange is complying with any directly applicable Community regulation made under the markets in financial instruments directive.]

[319A]

NOTES
  Commencement: 1 April 2007 (certain purposes); 1 November 2007 (otherwise).
  Inserted by the Financial Services and Markets Act 2000 (Markets in Financial Instruments) Regulations 2007, SI 2007/126, reg 3(2), Sch 2, paras 1, 6, as from 1 April 2007 (certain purposes (see reg 1(2) at **[4051]**)), and as from 1 November 2007 (otherwise).

294   Modification or waiver of rules

(1)   The Authority may, on the application or with the consent of a recognised body, direct that rules made under section 293 or 295—
  (a)   are not to apply to the body; or
  (b)   are to apply to the body with such modifications as may be specified in the direction.

(2)   An application must be made in such manner as the Authority may direct.

(3)   Subsections (4) to (6) apply to a direction given under subsection (1).

(4) The Authority may not give a direction unless it is satisfied that—

(a) compliance by the recognised body with the rules, or with the rules as unmodified, would be unduly burdensome or would not achieve the purpose for which the rules were made; and

(b) the direction would not result in undue risk to persons whose interests the rules are intended to protect.

(5) A direction may be given subject to conditions.

(6) The Authority may—

(a) revoke a direction; or

(b) vary it on the application, or with the consent, of the recognised body to which it relates.

[320]

295 Notification: overseas investment exchanges and overseas clearing houses

(1) At least once a year, every overseas investment exchange and overseas clearing house must provide the Authority with a report.

(2) The report must contain a statement as to whether any events have occurred which are likely—

(a) to affect the Authority's assessment of whether it is satisfied as to the requirements set out in section 292(3); or

(b) to have any effect on competition.

(3) The report must also contain such information as may be specified in rules made by the Authority.

(4) The investment exchange or clearing house must provide the Treasury and the [OFT] with a copy of the report.

[321]

NOTES

Sub-s (4): word in square brackets substituted by the Enterprise Act 2002, s 278(1), Sch 25, para 40(1), (9), as from 1 April 2003.

296 Authority's power to give directions

(1) This section applies if it appears to the Authority that a recognised body—

(a) has failed, or is likely to fail, to satisfy the recognition requirements; or

(b) has failed to comply with any other obligation imposed on it by or under this Act.

[(1A) This section also applies in the case of a recognised body which is a recognised investment exchange if it appears to the Authority that the body has failed, or is likely to fail, to comply with any obligation imposed on it by any directly applicable Community regulation made under the markets in financial instruments directive.]

(2) The Authority may direct the body to take specified steps for the purpose of securing the body's compliance with—

(a) the recognition requirements; or

(b) any obligation of the kind in question.

[(2A) In the case of a recognised investment exchange other than an overseas investment exchange, those steps may include—

(a) the granting to the Authority of access to the premises of the exchange for the purpose of inspecting—

(i) those premises; or

(ii) any documents on the premises which appear to the Authority to be relevant for the purpose mentioned in subsection (2);

(b) the suspension of the carrying on of any regulated activity by the exchange for the period specified in the direction.]

(3) A direction under this section is enforceable, on the application of the Authority, by an injunction or, in Scotland, by an order for specific performance under section 45 of the Court of Session Act 1988.

(4) The fact that a rule made by a recognised body has been altered in response to a direction given by the Authority does not prevent it from being subsequently altered or revoked by the recognised body.

[322]

NOTES

Sub-ss (1A), (2A): inserted by the Financial Services and Markets Act 2000 (Markets in Financial Instruments) Regulations 2007, SI 2007/126, reg 3(2), Sch 2, paras 1, 7, as from 1 April 2007 (certain purposes (see reg 1(2) at [4051])), and as from 1 November 2007 (otherwise).

Application: this section and s 297 apply in relation to a failure by a recognised investment exchange or recognised clearing house to comply with an obligation under the Companies Act 1989, Pt VII, as to a failure to comply with an obligation under this Act; see s 169(2) of the 1989 Act at **[1166]**.

297 Revoking recognition

(1) A recognition order may be revoked by an order made by the Authority at the request, or with the consent, of the recognised body concerned.

(2) If it appears to the Authority that a recognised body—
   (a)   is failing, or has failed, to satisfy the recognition requirements, or
   (b)   is failing, or has failed, to comply with any other obligation imposed on it by or under this Act,
it may make an order revoking the recognition order for that body even though the body does not wish the order to be made.

[(2A) If it appears to the Authority that a recognised body which is a recognised investment exchange—
   (a)   has not carried on the business of an investment exchange during the period of twelve months beginning with the day on which the recognition order took effect in relation to it,
   (b)   has not carried on the business of an investment exchange at any time during the period of six months ending with the relevant day, or
   (c)   has failed, or is likely to fail, to comply with any obligation imposed on it by a directly applicable Community regulation made under the markets in financial instruments directive,
it may make an order revoking the recognition order for that body even though the body does not wish the order to be made.

(2B) The "relevant day", for the purposes of paragraph (b) of subsection (2A), is the day on which the power to make an order under that subsection is exercised.

(2C) Subsection (2A) does not apply to an overseas investment exchange.]

(3) An order under this section ("a revocation order") must specify the date on which it is to take effect.

(4) In the case of a revocation order made under subsection (2) [or (2A)], the specified date must not be earlier than the end of the period of three months beginning with the day on which the order is made.

(5) A revocation order may contain such transitional provisions as the Authority thinks necessary or expedient.

[323]

NOTES

Sub-ss (2A)–(2C): inserted by the Financial Services and Markets Act 2000 (Markets in Financial Instruments) Regulations 2007, SI 2007/126, reg 3(2), Sch 2, paras 1, 8(a), as from 1 April 2007 (certain purposes (see reg 1(2) at **[4051]**)), and as from 1 November 2007 (otherwise).

Sub-s (4): words in square brackets inserted by SI 2007/126, reg 3(2), Sch 2, paras 1, 8(b), as from 1 April 2007 (certain purposes (see reg 1(2) at **[4051]**)), and as from 1 November 2007 (otherwise).

Application: see the note to s 296 at **[322]**.

298 Directions and revocation: procedure

(1) Before giving a direction under section 296, or making a revocation order under section 297(2) [or (2A)], the Authority must—
   (a)   give written notice of its intention to do so to the recognised body concerned;
   (b)   take such steps as it considers reasonably practicable to bring the notice to the attention of members (if any) of that body; and
   (c)   publish the notice in such manner as it thinks appropriate for bringing it to the attention of other persons who are, in its opinion, likely to be affected.

(2) A notice under subsection (1) must—
   (a)   state why the Authority intends to give the direction or make the order; and
   (b)   draw attention to the right to make representations conferred by subsection (3).

(3) Before the end of the period for making representations—
   (a)   the recognised body,
   (b)   any member of that body, and
   (c)   any other person who is likely to be affected by the proposed direction or revocation order,
may make representations to the Authority.

(4) The period for making representations is—
   (a)   two months beginning—

      (i)   with the date on which the notice is served on the recognised body; or

      (ii)   if later, with the date on which the notice is published; or

  (b)   such longer period as the Authority may allow in the particular case.

(5)   In deciding whether to—

  (a)   give a direction, or

  (b)   make a revocation order,

the Authority must have regard to any representations made in accordance with subsection (3).

(6)   When the Authority has decided whether to give a direction under section 296 or to make the proposed revocation order, it must—

  (a)   give the recognised body written notice of its decision; and

  (b)   if it has decided to give a direction or make an order, take such steps as it considers reasonably practicable for bringing its decision to the attention of members of the body or of other persons who are, in the Authority's opinion, likely to be affected.

(7)   If the Authority considers it essential to do so, it may give a direction under section 296—

  (a)   without following the procedure set out in this section; or

  (b)   if the Authority has begun to follow that procedure, regardless of whether the period for making representations has expired.

(8)   If the Authority has, in relation to a particular matter, followed the procedure set out in subsections (1) to (5), it need not follow it again if, in relation to that matter, it decides to take action other than that specified in its notice under subsection (1).

[324]

NOTES

Sub-s (1): words in square brackets inserted by the Financial Services and Markets Act 2000 (Markets in Financial Instruments) Regulations 2007, SI 2007/126, reg 3(2), Sch 2, paras 1, 9, as from 1 April 2007 (certain purposes (see reg 1(2) at **[4051]**)), and as from 1 November 2007 (otherwise).

299 Complaints about recognised bodies

(1)   The Authority must make arrangements for the investigation of any relevant complaint about a recognised body.

(2)   "Relevant complaint" means a complaint which the Authority considers is relevant to the question of whether the body concerned should remain a recognised body.

[325]

300 Extension of functions of Tribunal

(1)   If the Treasury are satisfied that the condition mentioned in subsection (2) is satisfied, they may by order confer functions on the Tribunal with respect to disciplinary proceedings—

  (a)   of one or more investment exchanges in relation to which a recognition order under section 290 is in force or of such investment exchanges generally, or

  (b)   of one or more clearing houses in relation to which a recognition order under that section is in force or of such clearing houses generally.

(2)   The condition is that it is desirable to exercise the power conferred under subsection (1) with a view to ensuring that—

  (a)   decisions taken in disciplinary proceedings with respect to which functions are to be conferred on the Tribunal are consistent with—

      (i)   decisions of the Tribunal in cases arising under Part VIII; and

      (ii)   decisions taken in other disciplinary proceedings with respect to which the Tribunal has functions as a result of an order under this section; or

  (b)   the disciplinary proceedings are in accordance with the Convention rights.

(3)   An order under this section may modify or exclude any provision made by or under this Act with respect to proceedings before the Tribunal.

(4)   "Disciplinary proceedings" means proceedings under the rules of an investment exchange or clearing house in relation to market abuse by persons subject to the rules.

(5)   "The Convention rights" has the meaning given in section 1 of the Human Rights Act 1998.

[326]

[Power to disallow excessive regulatory provision

300A Power of Authority to disallow excessive regulatory provision

(1)   This section applies where a recognised body proposes to make any regulatory provision in connection with its business as an investment exchange or the provision by it of clearing services.

(2)   If it appears to the Authority—

  (a)   that the proposed provision will impose a requirement on persons affected (directly or indirectly) by it, and

(b)   that the requirement is excessive,

the Authority may direct that the proposed provision must not be made.

(3)   A requirement is excessive if—
  (a)   it is not required under Community law or any enactment or rule of law in the United Kingdom, and
  (b)   either—
    (i)   it is not justified as pursuing a reasonable regulatory objective, or
    (ii)   it is disproportionate to the end to be achieved.

(4)   In considering whether a requirement is excessive the Authority must have regard to all the relevant circumstances, including—
  (a)   the effect of existing legal and other requirements,
  (b)   the global character of financial services and markets and the international mobility of activity,
  (c)   the desirability of facilitating innovation, and
  (d)   the impact of the proposed provision on market confidence.

(5)   In this section "requirement" includes any obligation or burden.

(6)   Any provision made in contravention of a direction under this section is of no effect.]

                                                                                    [326A]

NOTES
  Commencement: 20 December 2006.
  Inserted, together with the preceding heading, by the Investment Exchanges and Clearing Houses Act 2006, s 1, as from 20 December 2006. Note that by virtue of s 5(3) of the 2006 Act at **[1736]**, this section (a) does not apply to regulatory provision made before that day, and (b) applies to regulatory provision proposed on or after that day, whenever originally proposed.

[300B   Duty to notify proposal to make regulatory provision

(1)   A recognised body that proposes to make any regulatory provision must give written notice of the proposal to the Authority without delay.

(2)   The Authority may by rules under section 293 (notification requirements)—
  (a)   specify descriptions of regulatory provision in relation to which, or circumstances in which, the duty in subsection (1) above does not apply, or
  (b)   provide that the duty applies only to specified descriptions of regulatory provision or in specified circumstances.

(3)   The Authority may also by rules under that section—
  (a)   make provision as to the form and contents of the notice required, and
  (b)   require the body to provide such information relating to the proposal as may be specified in the rules or as the Authority may reasonably require.]

                                                                                    [326B]

NOTES
  Commencement: 20 December 2006.
  Inserted, together with ss 300C–300E, by the Investment Exchanges and Clearing Houses Act 2006, s 2, as from 20 December 2006. Note that by virtue of s 5(3) of the 2006 Act at **[1736]**, this section (a) does not apply to regulatory provision made before that day, and (b) applies to regulatory provision proposed on or after that day, whenever originally proposed.

[300C   Restriction on making provision before Authority decides whether to act

(1)   Where notice of a proposal to make regulatory provision is required to be given to the Authority under section 300B, the provision must not be made—
  (a)   before that notice is given, or
  (b)   subject to the following provisions of this section, before the end of the initial period.

(2)   The initial period is—
  (a)   the period of 30 days beginning with the day on which the Authority receives notice of the proposal, or
  (b)   if any consultation period announced by the body in relation to the proposal ends after that 30-day period, the end of the consultation period.

(3)   If before the end of the initial period the Authority notifies the body that it is calling in the proposal, the provisions of section 300D (consideration by Authority whether to disallow proposed provision) apply as to when the provision may be made.

(4)   If—
  (a)   before the end of the initial period the Authority notifies the body that it is not calling in the proposal, or

PART I
FSMA 2000

(b)   the initial period ends without the Authority having notified the body that it is calling in the proposal,

the body may then make the proposed provision.

(5)   Any provision made in contravention of this section is of no effect.]

[326C]

NOTES
Commencement: 20 December 2006.
Inserted as noted to s 300B at [326B].

[300D   Consideration by Authority whether to disallow proposed provision

(1)   This section applies where the Authority notifies a recognised body that it is calling in a proposal to make regulatory provision.

(2)   The Authority must publish a notice—
   (a)   giving details of the proposed provision,
   (b)   stating that it has called in the proposal in order to consider whether to disallow it, and
   (c)   specifying a period during which representations with respect to that question may be made to it.

(3)   The Authority may extend the period for making representations.

(4)   The Authority must notify the body of its decision whether to disallow the provision not later than 30 days after the end of the period for making representations, and must publish the decision and the reasons for it.

(5)   The body must not make the provision unless and until—
   (a)   the Authority notifies it of its decision not to disallow it, or
   (b)   the 30-day period specified in subsection (4) ends without the Authority having notified any decision.

(6)   If the Authority notifies the body of its decision to disallow the provision and that decision is questioned in legal proceedings—
   (a)   the body must not make the provision until those proceedings, and any proceedings on appeal, are finally determined,
   (b)   if the Authority's decision is quashed and the matter is remitted to it for reconsideration, the court may give directions as to the period within which the Authority is to complete its reconsideration, and
   (c)   the body must not make the provision until—
      (i)   the Authority notifies it of its decision on reconsideration not to disallow the provision, or
      (ii)   the period specified by the court ends without the Authority having notified any decision.

(7)   Any provision made in contravention of subsection (5) or (6) is of no effect.]

[326D]

NOTES
Commencement: 20 December 2006.
Inserted as noted to s 300B at [326B].

[300E   Power to disallow excessive regulatory provision: supplementary

(1)   In sections 300A to 300D—
   (a)   "regulatory provision" means any rule, guidance, arrangements, policy or practice, and
   (b)   references to making provision shall be read accordingly as including, as the case may require, issuing guidance, entering into arrangements or adopting a policy or practice.

(2)   For the purposes of those sections a variation of a proposal is treated as a new proposal.

(3)   Those sections do not apply to an overseas investment exchange or overseas clearing house.]

[326E]

NOTES
Commencement: 20 December 2006.
Inserted as noted to s 300B at [326B].

Other matters

301   Supervision of certain contracts

(1)   The Secretary of State and the Treasury, acting jointly, may by regulations provide for—
   (a)   Part VII of the Companies Act 1989 (financial markets and insolvency), and

(b)   Part V of the Companies (No 2) (Northern Ireland) Order 1990,

to apply to relevant contracts as it applies to contracts connected with a recognised body.

(2)   "Relevant contracts" means contracts of a prescribed description in relation to which settlement arrangements are provided by a person for the time being included in a list ("the list") maintained by the Authority for the purposes of this section.

(3)   Regulations may be made under this section only if the Secretary of State and the Treasury are satisfied, having regard to the extent to which the relevant contracts concerned are contracts of a kind dealt in by persons supervised by the Authority, that it is appropriate for the arrangements mentioned in subsection (2) to be supervised by the Authority.

(4)   The approval of the Treasury is required for—
    (a)   the conditions set by the Authority for admission to the list; and
    (b)   the arrangements for admission to, and removal from, the list.

(5)   If the Treasury withdraw an approval given by them under subsection (4), all regulations made under this section and then in force are to be treated as suspended.

(6)   But if—
    (a)   the Authority changes the conditions or arrangements (or both), and
    (b)   the Treasury give a fresh approval under subsection (4),

the suspension of the regulations ends on such date as the Treasury may, in giving the fresh approval, specify.

(7)   The Authority must—
    (a)   publish the list as for the time being in force; and
    (b)   provide a certified copy of it to any person who wishes to refer to it in legal proceedings.

(8)   A certified copy of the list is evidence (or in Scotland sufficient evidence) of the contents of the list.

(9)   A copy of the list which purports to be certified by or on behalf of the Authority is to be taken to have been duly certified unless the contrary is shown.

(10)   Regulations under this section may, in relation to a person included in the list—
    (a)   apply (with such exceptions, additions and modifications as appear to the Secretary of State and the Treasury to be necessary or expedient) such provisions of, or made under, this Act as they consider appropriate;
    (b)   provide for the provisions of Part VII of the Companies Act 1989 and Part V of the Companies (No 2)(Northern Ireland) Order 1990 to apply (with such exceptions, additions or modifications as appear to the Secretary of State and the Treasury to be necessary or expedient).

[327]

[CHAPTER 1A
CONTROL OVER RECOGNISED INVESTMENT EXCHANGE

NOTES
  HM Treasury and the FSA have issued a consultation paper on the Implementation of the Acquisitions Directive which proposes a number of changes to this Chapter (as well as Part XII of this Act and the definition of controller as set out in s 422). See *Implementation of the Acquisitions Directive: a consultation document* (*September 2008*) at:
http://www.hm-treasury.gov.uk/consult_fullindex.htm.

Notice of control

301A   Obligation to notify the Authority of acquisition of or increase in control

(1)   If a step which a person proposes to take would result in his acquiring—
    (a)   control over a recognised investment exchange,
    (b)   an additional kind of control over an exchange, or
    (c)   an increase in a relevant kind of control which he already has over an exchange,

he must notify the Authority of his proposal.

(2)   A person who, without himself taking any such step, acquires any such control or additional or increased control must notify the Authority before the end of the period of 14 days beginning with the day on which he first becomes aware that he has acquired it.

(3)   A person who is under the duty to notify the Authority imposed by subsection (1) must also give notice to the Authority on acquiring, or increasing, the control in question.

(4)   A notice under subsection (1) or (2) is referred to in this Chapter as a "notice of control".

(5)   Section 182 applies to a notice of control under this Chapter as it applies to a notice of control under Part 12.

(6)   Nothing in this Chapter applies to an overseas investment exchange.]

[327A]

NOTES
   Commencement: 1 April 2007 (certain purposes); 1 November 2007 (otherwise).
   Chapter 1A (ss 301A–301G) was inserted by the Financial Services and Markets Act 2000 (Markets in Financial Instruments) Regulations 2007, SI 2007/126, reg 3(2), Sch 2, paras 1, 10, as from 1 April 2007 (certain purposes (see reg 1(2) at **[4051]**)), and as from 1 November 2007 (otherwise).

[Acquiring and increasing control

301B   Acquiring and increasing control

(1)   For the purposes of this Chapter, a person ("the acquirer") acquires control over a recognised investment exchange ("E") on first falling within any of the cases in subsection (2).

(2)   The cases are where the acquirer—
   (a)   holds 20% or more of the shares in E;
   (b)   is able to exercise significant influence over the management of E by virtue of his shareholding in E;
   (c)   holds 20% or more shares in a parent undertaking ("P") of E;
   (d)   is able to exercise significant influence over the management of P by virtue of his shareholding in P;
   (e)   is entitled to exercise, or control the exercise of, 20% or more of the voting power in E;
   (f)   is able to exercise significant influence over the management of E by virtue of his voting power in E;
   (g)   is entitled to exercise, or to control the exercise of, 20% or more of the voting power in P; or
   (h)   is able to exercise significant influence over the management of P by virtue of his voting power in P.

(3)   In subsection (2) "the acquirer" means—
   (a)   the acquirer,
   (b)   any of his associates, or
   (c)   the acquirer and any of his associates.

(4)   For the purposes of this Chapter, each of the following is to be regarded as a kind of control—
   (a)   control arising as a result of the holding of shares in E;
   (b)   control arising as a result of the holding of shares in P;
   (c)   control arising as a result of the entitlement to exercise, or control the exercise of, voting power in E;
   (d)   control arising as a result of the entitlement to exercise, or control the exercise of, voting power in P.

(5)   For the purposes of this Chapter, a controller of E increases his control over E if—
   (a)   the percentage of shares held by the controller in E increases by the step mentioned in subsection (6);
   (b)   the percentage of shares held by the controller in P increases by the step mentioned in subsection (6);
   (c)   the percentage of voting power which the controller is entitled to exercise, or control the exercise of, in E increases by the step mentioned in subsection (6);
   (d)   the percentage of voting power which the controller is entitled to exercise, or control the exercise of, in P increases by the step mentioned in subsection (6); or
   (e)   the controller becomes a parent undertaking of E.

(6)   The step is from 20% or more (but less than 50%) to 50% or more.

(7)   In the rest of this Chapter "acquiring control" or "having control" includes—
   (a)   acquiring or having an additional kind of control; or
   (b)   acquiring an increase in a relevant kind of control, or having increased control of a relevant kind.]

[327B]

NOTES
   Commencement: 1 April 2007 (certain purposes); 1 November 2007 (otherwise).
   Inserted as noted to s 301A at **[327A]**.

[Acquiring or increasing control: procedure

301C   Duty of Authority in relation to notice of control

(1)   The Authority must, before the end of the period of three months beginning with the date on which it receives a notice of control, determine whether—

    (a)   to approve of the person concerned having the control to which the notice relates; or

    (b)   to give a warning notice under subsection (7).

(2)   If the Authority decides to approve of the person concerned having the control to which the notice relates it must notify that person of its approval in writing without delay.

(3)   If the Authority fails to comply with subsection (1) it is to be treated as having given its approval and notified the person concerned at the end of the period fixed by that subsection.

(4)   The Authority's approval remains effective only if the person to whom it relates acquires the control in question—

    (a)   before the end of such period as may be specified in the notice of approval under subsection (2); or

    (b)   if no period is specified, before the end of the period of one year beginning with the date—

        (i)   of the notice of approval under subsection (2);

        (ii)   on which the Authority is treated as having given approval under subsection (3); or

        (iii)   of a decision on a reference to the Tribunal which results in the person concerned receiving approval.

(5)   The Authority may give a decision notice under this subsection unless it is satisfied that the approval requirement is met.

(6)   The approval requirement is that the acquisition of control by the person who gave the notice of control does not pose a threat to the sound and prudent management of any financial market operated by the recognised investment exchange.

(7)   If the Authority proposes to give the person concerned a decision notice under subsection (5), it must give him a warning notice.

(8)   A person to whom a decision notice is given under subsection (5) may refer the matter to the Tribunal.]

                                                              [327C]

NOTES

Commencement: 1 April 2007 (certain purposes); 1 November 2007 (otherwise).
Inserted as noted to s 301A at **[327A]**.

[301D   Objection to existing control

(1)   If the Authority is not satisfied that the approval requirement is met, it may give a decision notice under this section to a person if he has failed to comply with a duty to notify imposed by section 301A.

(2)   If the failure relates to subsection (1) or (2) of that section, the Authority may (instead of giving a notice under subsection (1)) approve the acquisition of control in question by the person concerned as if he had given it a notice of control.

(3)   The Authority may also give a decision notice under this section to a person who is a controller of a recognised investment exchange if the Authority becomes aware of matters as a result of which it is satisfied that the approval requirement is not met with respect to the controller.

(4)   If the Authority proposes to give a decision notice under subsection (1) or (3) to a person, it must give him a warning notice before the end of the period of three months beginning—

    (a)   in the case of a notice to be given under subsection (1), with the date on which it became aware of the failure to comply with the duty in question;

    (b)   in the case of a notice to be given under subsection (3), with the date on which it became aware of the matters in question.

(5)   A person to whom a decision notice is given under this section may refer the matter to the Tribunal.

(6)   "Approval requirement" has the same meaning as in section 301C.]

                                                              [327D]

NOTES

Commencement: 1 April 2007 (certain purposes); 1 November 2007 (otherwise).
Inserted as noted to s 301A at **[327A]**.

PART I
FSMA 2000

[Improperly acquired shares

301E Improperly acquired shares

(1)   The powers conferred by this section are exercisable if a person has acquired, or has continued to hold, any shares in contravention of a decision notice given under section 301C(5) or 301D(1) or (3).

(2)   The Authority may by notice in writing given to the person concerned ("a restriction notice") direct that any such shares which are specified in the notice are, until further notice, subject to one or more of the following restrictions—

> (a)   a transfer of (or agreement to transfer) those shares, or in the case of unissued shares any transfer of (or agreement to transfer) the right to be issued with them, is void;
> (b)   no voting rights are to be exercisable in respect of the shares;
> (c)   no further shares are to be issued in right of them or in pursuance of any offer made to their holder;
> (d)   except in a liquidation, no payment is to be made of any sums due from the body corporate on the shares, whether in respect of capital or otherwise.

(3)   The court may, on the application of the Authority, order the sale of any shares to which this section applies and, if they are for the time being subject to any restriction under subsection (2), that they are to cease to be subject to that restriction.

(4)   No order may be made under subsection (3)—

> (a)   until the end of the period within which a reference may be made to the Tribunal in respect of the decision notice in question; and
> (b)   if a reference is made, until the matter has been determined or the reference withdrawn.

(5)   If an order has been made under subsection (3), the court may, on the application of the Authority, make such further order relating to the sale or transfer of the shares as it thinks fit.

(6)   If shares are sold in pursuance of an order under this section, the proceeds of sale, less the costs of the sale, must be paid into court for the benefit of the persons beneficially interested in them; and any such person may apply to the court for the whole or part of the proceeds to be paid to him.

(7)   This section applies—

> (a)   in the case of an acquirer falling within section 301A(1), to all the shares—
>> (i)   in the recognised investment exchange which the acquirer has acquired,
>> (ii)   which are held by him or an associate of his, and
>> (iii)   which were not so held immediately before he became a person having control over the exchange;
> (b)   in the case of an acquirer falling within section 301A(2), to all the shares held by him or an associate of his at the time when he first became aware that he had acquired control over the exchange; and
> (c)   to all the shares in an undertaking ("C")—
>> (i)   which are held by the acquirer or an associate of his, and
>> (ii)   which were not so held before he became a person with control in relation to the exchange,
> where C is the undertaking in which shares were acquired by the acquirer (or an associate of his) and, as a result, he became a person with control in relation to that exchange.

(8)   A copy of the restriction notice must be given to—

> (a)   the recognised investment exchange to whose shares it relates; and
> (b)   if it relates to shares held by an associate of that exchange, that associate.

(9)   The jurisdiction conferred by this section may be exercised by the High Court and the Court of Session.]

[327E]

NOTES

Commencement: 1 April 2007 (certain purposes); 1 November 2007 (otherwise).
Inserted as noted to s 301A at **[327A]**.

[Offences

301F Offences in relation to acquisition of control

(1)   A person who fails to comply with the duty to notify the Authority imposed on him by section 301A(1) is guilty of an offence.

(2)   A person who fails to comply with the duty to notify the Authority imposed on him by section 301A(2) is guilty of an offence.

(3)   If a person who has given a notice of control to the Authority carries out the proposal to which the notice relates, he is guilty of an offence if—

(a) the period of three months beginning with the date on which the Authority received the notice is still running; and

(b) the Authority has not responded to the notice by either giving its approval or giving him a warning notice under section 301C(7).

(4) A person to whom the Authority has given a warning notice under subsection (7) of section 301C is guilty of an offence if he carries out the proposal to which the notice relates before the Authority has decided whether to give him a decision notice under subsection (5) of that section.

(5) A person to whom a decision notice under section 301C(5) or 301D(1) or (3) has been given is guilty of an offence if he acquires or retains the control to which the notice applies at a time when the notice is still in force.

(6) A person guilty of an offence under subsection (1), (2), (3) or (4) is liable on summary conviction to a fine not exceeding level 5 on the standard scale.

(7) A person guilty of an offence under subsection (5) is liable—

(a) on summary conviction, to a fine not exceeding the statutory maximum; and

(b) on conviction on indictment, to imprisonment for a term not exceeding two years, or to a fine, or both.

(8) It is a defence for a person charged with an offence under subsection (1) to show that he had, at the time of the alleged offence, no knowledge of the act or circumstances by virtue of which the duty to notify the Authority arose.

(9) If a person—

(a) was under the duty to notify the Authority imposed by section 301A(1) but had no knowledge of the act or circumstances by virtue of which that duty arose, but

(b) subsequently becomes aware of that act or those circumstances,

he must notify the Authority before the end of the period of 14 days beginning with the day on which he first became so aware.

(10) A person who fails to comply with the duty to notify the Authority imposed by subsection (9) is guilty of an offence and liable, on summary conviction, to a fine not exceeding level 5 on the standard scale.]

[327F]

NOTES

Commencement: 1 April 2007 (certain purposes); 1 November 2007 (otherwise).
Inserted as noted to s 301A at **[327A]**.

[Interpretation

301G   Interpretation of Chapter 1A

In this Chapter—

"associate", "shares" and "voting power" have the same meaning as in section 422;

"controller", in relation to a recognised investment exchange, means a person who falls within any of the cases in section 301B(2);

"notice of control" has the meaning given in section 301A(4).]

[327G]

NOTES

Commencement: 1 April 2007 (certain purposes); 1 November 2007 (otherwise).
Inserted as noted to s 301A at **[327A]**.

CHAPTER II
COMPETITION SCRUTINY

302   Interpretation

(1) In this Chapter and Chapter III—

"practices" means—

(a) in relation to a recognised investment exchange, the practices of the exchange in its capacity as such; and

(b) in relation to a recognised clearing house, the practices of the clearing house in respect of its clearing arrangements;

"regulatory provisions" means—

(a) the rules of an investment exchange or a clearing house;

(b) any guidance issued by an investment exchange or clearing house;

(c) in the case of an investment exchange, the arrangements and criteria mentioned in section [287(3)(a) and (b)];

(d) in the case of a clearing house, the arrangements and criteria mentioned in section 288(3).

(2)   For the purposes of this Chapter, regulatory provisions or practices have a significantly adverse effect on competition if—

(a)   they have, or are intended or likely to have, that effect; or

(b)   the effect that they have, or are intended or likely to have, is to require or encourage behaviour which has, or is intended or likely to have, a significantly adverse effect on competition.

(3)   If regulatory provisions or practices have, or are intended or likely to have, the effect of requiring or encouraging exploitation of the strength of a market position they are to be taken, for the purposes of this Chapter, to have an adverse effect on competition.

(4)   In determining under this Chapter whether any regulatory provisions have, or are intended or likely to have, a particular effect, it may be assumed that persons to whom the provisions concerned are addressed will act in accordance with them.

[328]

NOTES

Sub-s (1): words in square brackets in the definition "regulatory provisions" substituted by the Financial Services and Markets Act 2000 (Markets in Financial Instruments) Regulations 2007, SI 2007/126, reg 3(2), Sch 2, paras 1, 11, as from 1 April 2007 (certain purposes (see reg 1(2) at [4051])), and as from 1 November 2007 (otherwise).

Role of [Office of Fair Trading]

303   Initial report by [OFT]

(1)   The Authority must send to the Treasury and to the [OFT] a copy of any regulatory provisions with which it is provided on an application for recognition under section 287 or 288.

(2)   The Authority must send to the [OFT] such information in its possession as a result of the application for recognition as it considers will assist [the OFT] in discharging [its] functions in connection with the application.

(3)   The [OFT] must issue a report as to whether—

(a)   a regulatory provision of which a copy has been sent to [it] under subsection (1) has a significantly adverse effect on competition; or

(b)   a combination of regulatory provisions so copied to [it] have such an effect.

(4)   If the [OFT's] conclusion is that one or more provisions have a significantly adverse effect on competition, [it] must state [its] reasons for that conclusion.

(5)   When the [OFT] issues a report under subsection (3), [the OFT] must send a copy of it to the Authority, the Competition Commission and the Treasury.

[(6)   In the case of an application for recognition under section 287, the OFT must issue its report under subsection (3) before the end of the period of 12 weeks beginning with the date on which it receives the copy sent to it under subsection (1).

(7)   Subsection (6) does not apply if the application is made by an overseas investment exchange.]

[329]

NOTES

Sub-ss (6), (7): added by the Financial Services and Markets Act 2000 (Markets in Financial Instruments) Regulations 2007, SI 2007/126, reg 3(2), Sch 2, paras 1, 12, as from 1 April 2007 (certain purposes (see reg 1(2) at [4051])), and as from 1 November 2007 (otherwise).

All other words in square brackets (including the words in the heading preceding this section) substituted by the Enterprise Act 2002, s 278(1), Sch 25, para 40(1), (10), as from 1 April 2003.

304   Further reports by [OFT]

(1)   The [OFT] must keep under review the regulatory provisions and practices of recognised bodies.

(2)   If at any time the [OFT] considers that—

(a)   a regulatory provision or practice has a significantly adverse effect on competition, or

(b)   regulatory provisions or practices, or a combination of regulating provisions and practices have such an effect,

[the OFT] must make a report.

(3)   If at any time the [OFT] considers that—

(a)   a regulatory provision or practice does not have a significantly adverse effect on competition, or

(b)   regulatory provisions or practices, or a combination of regulatory provisions and practices do not have any such effect,

[the OFT] may make a report to that effect.

(4)   A report under subsection (2) must contain details of the adverse effect on competition.

(5)   If the [OFT] makes a report under subsection (2), [the OFT] must—
    (a)   send a copy of it to the Treasury, to the Competition Commission and to the Authority; and
    (b)   publish it in the way appearing to [the OFT] to be best calculated to bring it to the attention of the public.

(6)   If the [OFT] makes a report under subsection (3)—
    (a)   [the OFT] must send a copy of it to the Treasury, to the Competition Commission and to the Authority; and
    (b)   [the OFT] may publish it.

(7)   Before publishing a report under this section, the [OFT] must, so far as practicable, exclude any matter which relates to the private affairs of a particular individual the publication of which, in the opinion of the [OFT], would or might seriously and prejudicially affect his interests.

(8)   Before publishing such a report, the [OFT] must exclude any matter which relates to the affairs of a particular body the publication of which, in the opinion of the [OFT], would or might seriously and prejudicially affect its interests.

(9)   Subsections (7) and (8) do not apply to the copy of a report which the [OFT] is required to send to the Treasury, the Competition Commission and the Authority under subsection (5)(a) or (6)(a).

(10)   For the purposes of the law of defamation, absolute privilege attaches to any report of the [OFT] under this section.

[330]

NOTES
  Words in square brackets substituted by the Enterprise Act 2002, s 278(1), Sch 25, para 40(1), (11), as from 1 April 2003.

305   Investigations by [OFT]

(1)   For the purpose of investigating any matter with a view to its consideration under section 303 or 304, the [OFT] may exercise the powers conferred on [it] by this section.

(2)   The [OFT] may by notice in writing require any person to produce to [it] or to a person appointed by [it] for the purpose, at a time and place specified in the notice, any document which—
    (a)   is specified or described in the notice; and
    (b)   is a document in that person's custody or under his control.

(3)   The [OFT] may by notice in writing—
    (a)   require any person carrying on any business to provide [it] with such information as may be specified or described in the notice; and
    (b)   specify the time within which, and the manner and form in which, any such information is to be provided.

(4)   A requirement may be imposed under subsection (2) or (3)(a) only in respect of documents or information which relate to any matter relevant to the investigation.

(5)   If a person ("the defaulter") refuses, or otherwise fails, to comply with a notice under this section, the [OFT] may certify that fact in writing to the court and the court may enquire into the case.

(6)   If, after hearing any witness who may be produced against or on behalf of the defaulter and any statement which may be offered in defence, the court is satisfied that the defaulter did not have a reasonable excuse for refusing or otherwise failing to comply with the notice, the court may deal with the defaulter as if he were in contempt.

(7)   In this section, "the court" means—
    (a)   the High Court; or
    (b)   in Scotland, the Court of Session.

[331]

NOTES
  Words in square brackets substituted by the Enterprise Act 2002, s 278(1), Sch 25, para 40(1), (12), as from 1 April 2003.

Role of Competition Commission

306   Consideration by Competition Commission

(1)   If subsection (2) or (3) applies, the Commission must investigate the matter which is the subject of the [OFT's] report.

(2)   This subsection applies if the [OFT] sends to the Competition Commission a report—

    (a)   issued by [the OFT] under section 303(3) which concludes that one or more regulatory provisions have a significantly adverse effect on competition, or

    (b)   made by [the OFT] under section 304(2).

  (3)   This subsection applies if the [OFT] asks the Commission to consider a report—

    (a)   issued by [the OFT] under section 303(3) which concludes that one or more regulatory provisions do not have a significantly adverse effect on competition, or

    (b)   made by [the OFT] under section 304(3).

  (4)   The Commission must then make its own report on the matter unless it considers that, as a result of a change of circumstances, no useful purpose would be served by a report.

  (5)   If the Commission decides in accordance with subsection (4) not to make a report, it must make a statement setting out the change of circumstances which resulted in that decision.

  (6)   A report made under this section must state the Commission's conclusion as to whether—

    (a)   the regulatory provision or practice which is the subject of the report has a significantly adverse effect on competition, or

    (b)   the regulatory provisions or practices or combination of regulatory provisions and practices which are the subject of the report have such an effect.

  (7)   A report under this section stating the Commission's conclusion that there is a significantly adverse effect on competition must also—

    (a)   state whether the Commission considers that that effect is justified; and

    (b)   if it states that the Commission considers that it is not justified, state its conclusion as to what action, if any, the Treasury ought to direct the Authority to take.

  (8)   Subsection (9) applies whenever the Commission is considering, for the purposes of this section, whether a particular adverse effect on competition is justified.

  (9)   The Commission must ensure, so far as that is reasonably possible, that the conclusion it reaches is compatible with the obligations imposed on the recognised body concerned by or under this Act.

  (10)   A report under this section must contain such an account of the Commission's reasons for its conclusions as is expedient, in the opinion of the Commission, for facilitating proper understanding of them.

  (11)   The provisions of Schedule 14 (except paragraph 2(b)) apply for the purposes of this section as they apply for the purposes of section 162.

  (12)   If the Commission makes a report under this section it must send a copy to the Treasury, the Authority and the [OFT].

  [(13)   Subsection (14) applies if—

    (a)   the case relates to an application for recognition under section 287, other than an application by an overseas applicant; and

    (b)   subsection (2)(a) or (3)(a) of this section applies.

  (14)   The Commission must—

    (a)   make a report under this section, or a statement under subsection (5), before the end of the period of 12 weeks beginning with the date on which it receives a copy of the OFT's report under section 303(3); and

    (b)   if it makes a statement under subsection (5), send a copy to the Authority and the Treasury.]

                                            [332]

NOTES

Sub-ss (13), (14): added by the Financial Services and Markets Act 2000 (Markets in Financial Instruments) Regulations 2007, SI 2007/126, reg 3(2), Sch 2, paras 1, 13, as from 1 April 2007 (certain purposes (see reg 1(2) at [**4051**])), and as from 1 November 2007 (otherwise).

All other words in square brackets substituted by the Enterprise Act 2002, s 278(1), Sch 25, para 40(1), (13), as from 1 April 2003.

Investigations by the Competition Commission: see the note to s 162 at [**190**].

Role of the Treasury

307 Recognition orders: role of the Treasury

  (1)   Subsection (2) applies if, on an application for a recognition order—

    (a)   the [OFT] makes a report under section 303 but does not ask the Competition Commission to consider it under section 306;

    (b)   the Competition Commission concludes—

      (i)   that the applicant's regulatory provisions do not have a significantly adverse effect on competition; or

      (ii)   that if those provisions do have that effect, the effect is justified.

(2)   The Treasury may refuse to approve the making of the recognition order only if they consider that the exceptional circumstances of the case make it inappropriate for them to give their approval.

(3)   Subsection (4) applies if, on an application for a recognition order, the Competition Commission concludes—
(a)   that the applicant's regulatory provisions have a significantly adverse effect on competition; and
(b)   that that effect is not justified.

(4)   The Treasury must refuse to approve the making of the recognition order unless they consider that the exceptional circumstances of the case make it inappropriate for them to refuse their approval.

[(5)   Subsection (6) applies in the case of an application for recognition under section 287, other than an application by an overseas applicant.

(6)   The Treasury must decide whether to approve the application before the end of the period of 10 days beginning with—
(a)   in a case falling within subsection (2)(a) or (3)(a) of section 306, the date on which they receive a copy of the report under that section or, if no such report was made, of the statement under subsection (5) of that section;
(b)   in any other case, the date on which they receive a copy of the report from the OFT under section 303.]

[333]

NOTES
Sub-s (1): word in square brackets substituted by the Enterprise Act 2002, s 278(1), Sch 25, para 40(1), (14)(a), as from 1 April 2003.
Sub-ss (5), (6): added by the Financial Services and Markets Act 2000 (Markets in Financial Instruments) Regulations 2007, SI 2007/126, reg 3(2), Sch 2, paras 1, 14, as from 1 April 2007 (certain purposes (see reg 1(2) at **[4051]**)), and as from 1 November 2007 (otherwise).

308   Directions by the Treasury

(1)   This section applies if the Competition Commission makes a report under section 306(4) (other than a report on an application for a recognition order) which states the Commission's conclusion that there is a significantly adverse effect on competition.

(2)   If the Commission's conclusion, as stated in the report, is that the adverse effect on competition is not justified, the Treasury must give a remedial direction to the Authority.

(3)   But subsection (2) does not apply if the Treasury consider—
(a)   that, as a result of action taken by the Authority or the recognised body concerned in response to the Commission's report, it is unnecessary for them to give a direction; or
(b)   that the exceptional circumstances of the case make it inappropriate or unnecessary for them to do so.

(4)   In considering the action to be specified in a remedial direction, the Treasury must have regard to any conclusion of the Commission included in the report because of section 306(7)(b).

(5)   Subsection (6) applies if—
(a)   the Commission's conclusion, as stated in its report, is that the adverse effect on competition is justified; but
(b)   the Treasury consider that the exceptional circumstances of the case require them to act.

(6)   The Treasury may give a direction to the Authority requiring it to take such action—
(a)   as they consider to be necessary in the light of the exceptional circumstances of the case; and
(b)   as may be specified in the direction.

(7)   If the action specified in a remedial direction is the giving by the Authority of a direction—
(a)   the direction to be given must be compatible with the recognition requirements applicable to the recognised body in relation to which it is given; and
(b)   subsections (3) and (4) of section 296 apply to it as if it were a direction given under that section.

(8)   "Remedial direction" means a direction requiring the Authority—
(a)   to revoke the recognition order for the body concerned; or
(b)   to give such directions to the body concerned as may be specified in it.

[334]

309   Statements by the Treasury

(1)   If, in reliance on subsection (3)(a) or (b) of section 308, the Treasury decline to act under subsection (2) of that section, they must make a statement to that effect, giving their reasons.

(2)   If the Treasury give a direction under section 308 they must make a statement giving—

(a) details of the direction; and

(b) if the direction is given under subsection (6) of that section, their reasons for giving it.

(3) The Treasury must—

(a) publish any statement made under this section in the way appearing to them best calculated to bring it to the attention of the public; and

(b) lay a copy of it before Parliament.

[335]

310 Procedure on exercise of certain powers by the Treasury

(1) Subsection (2) applies if the Treasury are considering—

(a) whether to refuse their approval under section 307;

(b) whether section 308(2) applies; or

(c) whether to give a direction under section 308(6).

(2) The Treasury must—

(a) take such steps as they consider appropriate to allow the exchange or clearing house concerned, and any other person appearing to the Treasury to be affected, an opportunity to make representations—

(i) about any report made by the [OFT] under section 303 or 304 or by the Competition Commission under section 306;

(ii) as to whether, and if so how, the Treasury should exercise their powers under section 307 or 308; and

(b) have regard to any such representations.

[336]

NOTES

Sub-s (2): word in square brackets substituted by the Enterprise Act 2002, s 278(1), Sch 25, para 40(1), (14)(b), as from 1 April 2003.

CHAPTER III
EXCLUSION FROM THE COMPETITION ACT 1998

311 The Chapter I prohibition

(1) The Chapter I prohibition does not apply to an agreement for the constitution of a recognised body to the extent to which the agreement relates to the regulatory provisions of that body.

(2) If the conditions set out in subsection (3) are satisfied, the Chapter I prohibition does not apply to an agreement for the constitution of—

(a) an investment exchange which is not a recognised investment exchange, or

(b) a clearing house which is not a recognised clearing house,

to the extent to which the agreement relates to the regulatory provisions of that body.

(3) The conditions are that—

(a) the body has applied for a recognition order in accordance with the provisions of this Act; and

(b) the application has not been determined.

(4) The Chapter I prohibition does not apply to a recognised body's regulatory provisions.

(5) The Chapter I prohibition does not apply to a decision made by a recognised body to the extent to which the decision relates to any of that body's regulatory provisions or practices.

(6) The Chapter I prohibition does not apply to practices of a recognised body.

(7) The Chapter I prohibition does not apply to an agreement the parties to which consist of or include—

(a) a recognised body, or

(b) a person who is subject to the rules of a recognised body,

to the extent to which the agreement consists of provisions the inclusion of which is required or encouraged by any of the body's regulatory provisions or practices.

(8) If a recognised body's recognition order is revoked, this section is to have effect as if that body had continued to be recognised until the end of the period of six months beginning with the day on which the revocation took effect.

(9) "The Chapter I prohibition" means the prohibition imposed by section 2(1) of the Competition Act 1998.

(10) Expressions used in this section which are also used in Part I of the Competition Act 1998 are to be interpreted in the same way as for the purposes of that Part of that Act.

[337]

312 The Chapter II prohibition

(1) The Chapter II prohibition does not apply to—
  (a) practices of a recognised body;
  (b) the adoption or enforcement of such a body's regulatory provisions;
  (c) any conduct which is engaged in by such a body or by a person who is subject to the rules of such a body to the extent to which it is encouraged or required by the regulatory provisions of the body.

(2) The Chapter II prohibition means the prohibition imposed by section 18(1) of the Competition Act 1998.

[338]

NOTES
  Note: "regulatory provisions" is defined in s 302(1) at **[328]**.

[CHAPTER 3A
PASSPORT RIGHTS

EEA market operators in United Kingdom

312A Exercise of passport rights by EEA market operator

(1) An EEA market operator may, in pursuance of the right under the applicable provision, make arrangements in the United Kingdom to facilitate access to, or use of, a specified regulated market or specified multilateral trading facility operated by it if—
  (a) the operator has given its home state regulator notice of its intention to make such arrangements; and
  (b) the home state regulator has given the Authority notice of the operator's intention.

(2) In making arrangements under subsection (1), the operator is exempt from the general prohibition as respects any regulated activity which is carried on as a part of its business of operating the market or facility in question, or in connection with, or for the purposes of, that business.

(3) "Specified" means specified in the notice referred to in subsection (1)(a).

(4) This section does not apply to an overseas investment exchange.]

[338A]

NOTES
  Commencement: 1 April 2007 (certain purposes); 1 November 2007 (otherwise).
  Chapter 3A (ss 312A–312D) was inserted by the Financial Services and Markets Act 2000 (Markets in Financial Instruments) Regulations 2007, SI 2007/126, reg 3(2), Sch 2, paras 1, 15, as from 1 April 2007 (certain purposes (see reg 1(2) at **[4051]**)), and as from 1 November 2007 (otherwise).
  Transitional provisions: the Financial Services and Markets Act 2000 (Markets in Financial Instruments) Regulations 2007, SI 2007/126, reg 5(1) (at **[4055]**) provides that sub-s (2) above applies to arrangements made on or before 31 October 2007, in the UK, by an EEA market operator to facilitate access to, or use of, a regulated market or multilateral trading facility operated by it as it applies to arrangements under sub-s (1) above.

[312B Removal of passport rights from EEA market operator

(1) The Authority may prohibit an EEA market operator from making or, as the case may be, continuing arrangements in the United Kingdom, in pursuance of the applicable provision, to facilitate access to, or use of, a regulated market or multilateral trading facility operated by the operator if—
  (a) the Authority has clear and demonstrable grounds for believing that the operator has contravened a relevant requirement, and
  (b) the Authority has first complied with subsections (3) to (9).

(2) A requirement is relevant if it is imposed—
  (a) by the operator's home state regulator in the implementation of the markets in financial instruments directive or any Community legislation made under that directive;
  (b) by provision implementing that directive, or any Community legislation made under it, in the operator's home state; or
  (c) by any directly applicable Community regulation made under that directive.

(3) The Authority must notify the operator and its home state regulator of its finding under subsection (1)(a).

(4) The notice to the home state regulator under subsection (3) must—
  (a) request that the home state regulator take all appropriate measures for the purpose of ensuring that the operator puts an end to the contravention; and
  (b) state that the Authority proposes to exercise the power under subsection (1) if the operator continues the contravention.

PART I
FSMA 2000

(5)   The Authority may not exercise the power under subsection (1) unless satisfied—

    (a)   either—

        (i)   that the home state regulator has failed or refused to take measures for the purpose mentioned in subsection (4)(a); or

        (ii)   that the measures taken by the home state regulator have proved inadequate for that purpose; and

    (b)   that the operator is acting in a manner which is clearly prejudicial to the interests of investors in the United Kingdom or the orderly functioning of the financial markets.

(6)   If the Authority is satisfied as mentioned in subsection (5), it must give written notice to—

    (a)   the operator, and

    (b)   the home state regulator,

of its intention to exercise the power under subsection (1).

(7)   A notice under subsection (6) must—

    (a)   state why the Authority intends to exercise its power under subsection (1), and

    (b)   in the case of the notice to the operator, inform the operator that it may make representations to the Authority before the end of the representation period.

(8)   The representation period is—

    (a)   the period of two months beginning with the date on which the notice is given to the operator; or

    (b)   such longer period as the Authority may allow in a particular case.

(9)   If, having considered any representations made by the operator, the Authority decides to exercise the power under subsection (1), it must—

    (a)   notify the operator in writing that it will be prohibited from making or, as the case may be, continuing the arrangements mentioned in that subsection from the date specified in the notice; and

    (b)   notify the home state regulator of the action to be taken in relation to the operator.

(10)   If the Authority exercises the power under subsection (1) it must at the earliest opportunity notify the Commission of the action taken in relation to the operator.

(11)   The exemption conferred on an operator by section 312A(2) ceases to apply if the Authority exercises the power under subsection (1) in relation to the operator.

(12)   The right to make the arrangements mentioned in subsection (1) may be reinstated in relation to the operator (together with the exemption mentioned in subsection (11)) if the Authority is satisfied that the contravention which led to the Authority exercising the power under subsection (1) has been remedied.]

                                                [338B]

NOTES

Commencement: 1 April 2007 (certain purposes); 1 November 2007 (otherwise).
Inserted as noted to s 312A at **[338A]**.

[Recognised investment exchanges operating in EEA States
(other than the United Kingdom)

312C   Exercise of passport rights by recognised investment exchange

(1)   Subject to subsection (4), a recognised investment exchange may, in pursuance of the right under the applicable provision, make arrangements in an EEA State (other than the United Kingdom) to facilitate access to, or use of, a regulated market or multilateral trading facility operated by the exchange ("the relevant arrangements").

(2)   The exchange must give the Authority written notice of its intention to make the relevant arrangements which—

    (a)   describes the arrangements, and

    (b)   identifies the EEA State in which it intends to make them.

(3)   The Authority must, within one month of receiving a notice under subsection (2), send a copy of it to the host state regulator.

(4)   The exchange may not make the relevant arrangements until the Authority has complied with subsection (3).

(5)   Subsection (6) applies if the Authority receives a request for information—

    (a)   under the second sub-paragraph of Article 31.6 of the markets in financial instruments directive (in the case of relevant arrangements relating to a multilateral trading facility), or

    (b)   under the third sub-paragraph of Article 42.6 of that directive (in the case of relevant arrangements relating to a regulated market),

from the host state regulator.

(6)   The Authority must, as soon as reasonably practicable, comply with the request.

(7)   "Host state regulator" means the competent authority (within the meaning of Article 4.1.22 of the markets in financial instruments directive) of the EEA State in which the exchange intends to make, or has made, the relevant arrangements.

(8)   This section does not apply to an overseas investment exchange.]

[338C]

NOTES
Commencement: 1 April 2007 (certain purposes); 1 November 2007 (otherwise).
Inserted as noted to s 312A at **[338A]**.
Transitional provisions: the Financial Services and Markets Act 2000 (Markets in Financial Instruments) Regulations 2007, SI 2007/126, reg 5(2) (at **[4055]**) provides that sub-ss (2), (4) above do not apply in relation to arrangements made by a recognised investment exchange on or before 31 October 2007 in the territory of another EEA State to facilitate access to, or use of, a regulated market or multilateral trading facility operated by it by persons established in that State.

[Interpretation

312D   Interpretation of Chapter 3A

In this Chapter—
  "the applicable provision" means—
    (a)   in the case of arrangements relating to a multilateral trading facility, Article 31.5 of the markets in financial instruments directive; and
    (b)   in the case of arrangements relating to a regulated market, the first sub-paragraph of Article 42.6 of that directive;
  "EEA market operator" means a person who is a market operator (within the meaning of Article 4.1.13 of the markets in financial instruments directive) whose home state is an EEA State other than the United Kingdom;
  "home state", in relation to an EEA market operator, means the EEA State in which it has its registered office, or if it has no registered office, its head office;
  "home state regulator" means the competent authority (within the meaning of Article 4.1.22 of the markets in financial instruments directive) of the EEA State which is the home state in relation to the EEA market operator concerned.]

[338D]

NOTES
Commencement: 1 April 2007 (certain purposes); 1 November 2007 (otherwise).
Inserted as noted to s 312A at **[338A]**.

CHAPTER IV
Interpretation

313   Interpretation of Part XVIII

(1)   In this Part—
  "application" means an application for a recognition order made under section 287 or 288;
  "applicant" means a body corporate or unincorporated association which has applied for a recognition order;
  ["multilateral trading facility" has the meaning given in Article 4.1.15 of the markets in financial instruments directive;]
  ["OFT" means the Office of Fair Trading;]
  "overseas applicant" means a body corporate or association which has neither its head office nor its registered office in the United Kingdom and which has applied for a recognition order;
  "overseas investment exchange" means a body corporate or association which has neither its head office nor its registered office in the United Kingdom and in relation to which a recognition order is in force;
  "overseas clearing house" means a body corporate or association which has neither its head office nor its registered office in the United Kingdom and in relation to which a recognition order is in force;
  "recognised body" means a recognised investment exchange or a recognised clearing house;
  "recognised clearing house" has the meaning given in section 285;
  "recognised investment exchange" has the meaning given in section 285;
  "recognition order" means an order made under section 290 or 292;
  "recognition requirements" has the meaning given by section 286;
  ["regulated market" has the meaning given in Article 4.1.14 of the markets in financial instruments directive;]
  "remedial direction" has the meaning given in section 308(8);

"revocation order" has the meaning given in section 297.

(2)   References in this Part to rules of an investment exchange (or a clearing house) are to rules made, or conditions imposed, by the investment exchange (or the clearing house) with respect to—
(a)   recognition requirements;
(b)   admission of persons to, or their exclusion from the use of, its facilities; or
(c)   matters relating to its constitution.

(3)   References in this Part to guidance issued by an investment exchange are references to guidance issued, or any recommendation made, in writing or other legible form and intended to have continuing effect, by the investment exchange to—
(a)   all or any class of its members or users, or
(b)   persons seeking to become members of the investment exchange or to use its facilities,
with respect to any of the matters mentioned in subsection (2)(a) to (c).

(4)   References in this Part to guidance issued by a clearing house are to guidance issued, or any recommendation made, in writing or other legible form and intended to have continuing effect, by the clearing house to—
(a)   all or any class of its members, or
(b)   persons using or seeking to use its services,
with respect to the provision by it or its members of clearing services.

[339]

NOTES
Sub-s (1): definitions "multilateral trading facility" and "regulated market" inserted by the Financial Services and Markets Act 2000 (Markets in Financial Instruments) Regulations 2007, SI 2007/126, reg 3(2), Sch 2, paras 1, 16, as from 1 April 2007 (certain purposes (see reg 1(2) at **[4051]**)), and as from 1 November 2007 (otherwise); definition "OFT" substituted by the Enterprise Act 2002, s 278(1), Sch 25, para 40(1), (15), as from 1 April 2003.

[PART 18A
SUSPENSION AND REMOVAL OF FINANCIAL INSTRUMENTS
FROM TRADING

313A   Authority's power to require suspension or removal of financial instruments from trading

(1)   The Authority may, for the purpose of protecting—
(a)   the interests of investors, or
(b)   the orderly functioning of the financial markets,
require an institution to suspend or remove a financial instrument from trading.

(2)   If the Authority exercises the power conferred by subsection (1), the institution concerned or, if any, the issuer of the financial instrument concerned may refer the matter to the Tribunal.

(3)   In this section, "trading" includes trading otherwise than on a regulated market or a multilateral trading facility.]

[339A]

NOTES
Commencement: 1 April 2007 (certain purposes); 1 November 2007 (otherwise).
Part 18A (ss 313A–313D) was inserted by the Financial Services and Markets Act 2000 (Markets in Financial Instruments) Regulations 2007, SI 2007/126, reg 3(3), Sch 3, as from 1 April 2007 (certain purposes (see reg 1(2) at **[4051]**)), and as from 1 November 2007 (otherwise).

[313B   Suspension or removal of financial instruments from trading: procedure

(1)   A requirement imposed on an institution under section 313A (a "relevant requirement") takes effect—
(a)   immediately, if the notice given under subsection (2) states that this is the case;
(b)   in any other case, on such date as may be specified in the notice.

(2)   If the Authority proposes to impose a relevant requirement on an institution, or imposes such a requirement with immediate effect, it must give written notice to—
(a)   the institution, and
(b)   if any, the issuer of the financial instrument in question.

(3)   The notice must—
(a)   give details of the relevant requirement;
(b)   state the Authority's reasons for imposing the requirement and choosing the date on which it took effect or takes effect;

    (c)   inform the recipient that he may make representations to the Authority within such period as may be specified by the notice (whether or not he has referred the matter to the Tribunal);

    (d)   inform him of the date on which the requirement took effect or takes effect; and

    (e)   inform him of his right to refer the matter to the Tribunal and give an indication of the procedure on such a reference.

(4)   The Authority may extend the period within which representations may be made to it.

(5)   If, having considered any representations made to it by the institution or any issuer, the Authority decides—

    (a)   to impose the relevant requirement proposed, or

    (b)   if it has been imposed, not to revoke it,

it must give the institution and any issuer written notice.

(6)   If, having considered any representations made to it by the institution or any issuer, the Authority decides—

    (a)   not to impose the relevant requirement proposed, or

    (b)   to revoke a requirement which has been imposed,

it must give the institution and any issuer written notice.

(7)   A notice given under subsection (5) must inform the recipient of his right to refer the matter to the Tribunal.

(8)   Subsections (9) and (10) apply if—

    (a)   the Authority has imposed a relevant requirement on an institution, and

    (b)   the institution or any issuer of the financial instrument in question has applied for the revocation of the requirement.

(9)   If the Authority decides to grant the application, it must give the institution and any issuer written notice of its decision.

(10)   If the Authority proposes to refuse the application, it must give the institution and any issuer a warning notice.

(11)   If, having considered any representations made in response to the warning notice, the Authority decides to refuse the application, it must give the institution and any issuer a decision notice.

(12)   If the Authority gives a decision notice under subsection (11), the recipient may refer the matter to the Tribunal.]

[339B]

NOTES

    Commencement: 1 April 2007 (certain purposes); 1 November 2007 (otherwise).
    Inserted as noted to s 313A at **[339A]**.

[313C Notification in relation to suspension or removal of a financial instrument from trading

(1)   If the Authority exercises the power under section 313A(1) in relation to a financial instrument traded on a regulated market, it must as soon as reasonably practicable—

    (a)   publish its decision in such manner as it considers appropriate, and

    (b)   inform the competent authorities of all other EEA States of its decision.

(2)   If the Authority receives notice from a recognised investment exchange that the exchange has suspended or removed a financial instrument from trading on a regulated market operated by it, the Authority must inform the competent authorities of all other EEA States of the action taken by the exchange.

(3)   Subsections (4) and (5) apply if the Authority receives notice from the competent authority of another EEA State that that authority, pursuant to Article 41.2 of the markets in financial instruments directive—

    (a)   has required the suspension of a financial instrument from trading, or

    (b)   has required the removal of a financial instrument from trading.

(4)   In the case of a notice under subsection (3)(a), the Authority—

    (a)   must require each recognised investment exchange to suspend the instrument from trading on any regulated market operated by the exchange, and

    (b)   must require each institution operating a multilateral trading facility to suspend the instrument from trading on that facility,

unless such a step would be likely to cause significant damage to the interests of investors or the orderly functioning of the financial markets.

(5)   In the case of a notice under subsection (3)(b), the Authority—

PART I
FSMA 2000

(a) must require each recognised investment exchange to remove the instrument from trading on any regulated market operated by the exchange, and

(b) must require each institution operating a multilateral trading facility to remove the instrument from trading on that facility,

unless such a step would be likely to cause significant damage to the interests of investors or the orderly functioning of the financial markets.

(6) "Competent authority" has the meaning given in Article 4.1.22 of the markets in financial instruments directive.]

[339C]

NOTES
Commencement: 1 April 2007 (certain purposes); 1 November 2007 (otherwise).
Inserted as noted to s 313A at **[339A]**.

[313D Interpretation of Part 18A

In this Part—

"financial instrument" has the meaning given in Article 4.1.17 of the markets in financial instruments directive;

"institution" means—

(a) a recognised investment exchange, other than an overseas investment exchange (within the meaning of Part 18);

(b) an investment firm;

(c) a credit institution authorised under the banking consolidation directive, when carrying on investment services and activities; or

(d) an institution which would satisfy the requirements for authorisation as a credit institution under that directive if it had its registered office (or if it does not have a registered office, its head office) in an EEA State,

but does not include an EEA firm qualifying for authorisation under Schedule 3;

"issuer", in relation to a financial instrument, means the person who issued the instrument;

"multilateral trading facility" has the meaning given in Article 4.1.15 of the markets in financial instruments directive;

"regulated market" has the meaning given in Article 4.1.14 of the markets in financial instruments directive.]

[339D]

NOTES
Commencement: 1 April 2007 (certain purposes); 1 November 2007 (otherwise).
Inserted as noted to s 313A at **[339A]**.

PART XIX
LLOYD'S

General

314 Authority's general duty

(1) The Authority must keep itself informed about—

(a) the way in which the Council supervises and regulates the market at Lloyd's; and

(b) the way in which regulated activities are being carried on in that market.

(2) The Authority must keep under review the desirability of exercising—

(a) any of its powers under this Part;

(b) any powers which it has in relation to the Society as a result of section 315.

[340]

The Society

315 The Society: authorisation and permission

(1) The Society is an authorised person.

(2) The Society has permission to carry on a regulated activity of any of the following kinds—

(a) arranging deals in contracts of insurance written at Lloyd's ("the basic market activity");

(b) arranging deals in participation in Lloyd's syndicates ("the secondary market activity"); and

(c) an activity carried on in connection with, or for the purposes of, the basic or secondary market activity.

(3) For the purposes of Part IV, the Society's permission is to be treated as if it had been given on an application for permission under that Part.

(4)   The power conferred on the Authority by section 45 may be exercised in anticipation of the coming into force of the Society's permission (or at any other time).

(5)   The Society is not subject to any requirement of this Act concerning the registered office of a body corporate.

[341]

Power to apply Act to Lloyd's underwriting

316 Direction by Authority

(1)   The general prohibition or (if the general prohibition is not applied under this section) a core provision applies to the carrying on of an insurance market activity by—
  (a)   a member of the Society, or
  (b)   the members of the Society taken together,
only if the Authority so directs.

(2)   A direction given under subsection (1) which applies a core provision is referred to in this Part as "an insurance market direction".

(3)   In subsection (1)—
  "core provision" means a provision of this Act mentioned in section 317; and
  "insurance market activity" means a regulated activity relating to contracts of insurance written at Lloyd's.

(4)   In deciding whether to give a direction under subsection (1), the Authority must have particular regard to—
  (a)   the interests of policyholders and potential policyholders;
  (b)   any failure by the Society to satisfy an obligation to which it is subject as a result of a provision of the law of another EEA State which—
    (i)   gives effect to any of the insurance directives; and
    (ii)   is applicable to an activity carried on in that State by a person to whom this section applies;
  (c)   the need to ensure the effective exercise of the functions which the Authority has in relation to the Society as a result of section 315.

(5)   A direction under subsection (1) must be in writing.

(6)   A direction under subsection (1) applying the general prohibition may apply it in relation to different classes of person.

(7)   An insurance market direction—
  (a)   must specify each core provision, class of person and kind of activity to which it applies;
  (b)   may apply different provisions in relation to different classes of person and different kinds of activity.

(8)   A direction under subsection (1) has effect from the date specified in it, which may not be earlier than the date on which it is made.

(9)   A direction under subsection (1) must be published in the way appearing to the Authority to be best calculated to bring it to the attention of the public.

(10)   The Authority may charge a reasonable fee for providing a person with a copy of the direction.

(11)   The Authority must, without delay, give the Treasury a copy of any direction which it gives under this section.

[342]

317 The core provisions

(1)   The core provisions are Parts V, X, XI, XII, XIV, XV, XVI, XXII and XXIV, sections 384 to 386 and Part XXVI.

(2)   References in an applied core provision to an authorised person are (where necessary) to be read as references to a person in the class to which the insurance market direction applies.

(3)   An insurance market direction may provide that a core provision is to have effect, in relation to persons to whom the provision is applied by the direction, with modifications.

[343]

318 Exercise of powers through Council

(1)   The Authority may give a direction under this subsection to the Council or to the Society (acting through the Council) or to both.

(2)   A direction under subsection (1) is one given to the body concerned—
  (a)   in relation to the exercise of its powers generally with a view to achieving, or in support of, a specified objective; or

(b)   in relation to the exercise of a specified power which it has, whether in a specified manner or with a view to achieving, or in support of, a specified objective.

(3)   "Specified" means specified in the direction.

(4)   A direction under subsection (1) may be given—
    (a)   instead of giving a direction under section 316(1); or
    (b)   if the Authority considers it necessary or expedient to do so, at the same time as, or following, the giving of such a direction.

(5)   A direction may also be given under subsection (1) in respect of underwriting agents as if they were among the persons mentioned in section 316(1).

(6)   A direction under this section—
    (a)   does not, at any time, prevent the exercise by the Authority of any of its powers;
    (b)   must be in writing.

(7)   A direction under subsection (1) must be published in the way appearing to the Authority to be best calculated to bring it to the attention of the public.

(8)   The Authority may charge a reasonable fee for providing a person with a copy of the direction.

(9)   The Authority must, without delay, give the Treasury a copy of any direction which it gives under this section.

[344]

319 Consultation

(1)   Before giving a direction under section 316 or 318, the Authority must publish a draft of the proposed direction.

(2)   The draft must be accompanied by—
    (a)   a cost benefit analysis; and
    (b)   notice that representations about the proposed direction may be made to the Authority within a specified time.

(3)   Before giving the proposed direction, the Authority must have regard to any representations made to it in accordance with subsection (2)(b).

(4)   If the Authority gives the proposed direction it must publish an account, in general terms, of—
    (a)   the representations made to it in accordance with subsection (2)(b); and
    (b)   its response to them.

(5)   If the direction differs from the draft published under subsection (1) in a way which is, in the opinion of the Authority, significant—
    (a)   the Authority must (in addition to complying with subsection (4)) publish details of the difference; and
    (b)   those details must be accompanied by a cost benefit analysis.

(6)   Subsections (1) to (5) do not apply if the Authority considers that the delay involved in complying with them would be prejudicial to the interests of consumers.

(7)   Neither subsection (2)(a) nor subsection (5)(b) applies if the Authority considers—
    (a)   that, making the appropriate comparison, there will be no increase in costs; or
    (b)   that, making that comparison, there will be an increase in costs but the increase will be of minimal significance.

(8)   The Authority may charge a reasonable fee for providing a person with a copy of a draft published under subsection (1).

(9)   When the Authority is required to publish a document under this section it must do so in the way appearing to it to be best calculated to bring it to the attention of the public.

(10)   "Cost benefit analysis" means an estimate of the costs together with an analysis of the benefits that will arise—
    (a)   if the proposed direction is given; or
    (b)   if subsection (5)(b) applies, from the direction that has been given.

(11)   "The appropriate comparison" means—
    (a)   in relation to subsection (2)(a), a comparison between the overall position if the direction is given and the overall position if it is not given;
    (b)   in relation to subsection (5)(b), a comparison between the overall position after the giving of the direction and the overall position before it was given.

[345]

320   Former underwriting members

(1)   A former underwriting member may carry out each contract of insurance that he has underwritten at Lloyd's whether or not he is an authorised person.

(2)   If he is an authorised person, any Part IV permission that he has does not extend to his activities in carrying out any of those contracts.

(3)   The Authority may impose on a former underwriting member such requirements as appear to it to be appropriate for the purpose of protecting policyholders against the risk that he may not be able to meet his liabilities.

(4)   A person on whom a requirement is imposed may refer the matter to the Tribunal.

[346]

321   Requirements imposed under section 320

(1)   A requirement imposed under section 320 takes effect—
   (a)   immediately, if the notice given under subsection (2) states that that is the case;
   (b)   in any other case, on such date as may be specified in that notice.

(2)   If the Authority proposes to impose a requirement on a former underwriting member ("A") under section 320, or imposes such a requirement on him which takes effect immediately, it must give him written notice.

(3)   The notice must—
   (a)   give details of the requirement;
   (b)   state the Authority's reasons for imposing it;
   (c)   inform A that he may make representations to the Authority within such period as may be specified in the notice (whether or not he has referred the matter to the Tribunal);
   (d)   inform him of the date on which the requirement took effect or will take effect; and
   (e)   inform him of his right to refer the matter to the Tribunal.

(4)   The Authority may extend the period allowed under the notice for making representations.

(5)   If, having considered any representations made by A, the Authority decides—
   (a)   to impose the proposed requirement, or
   (b)   if it has been imposed, not to revoke it,
it must give him written notice.

(6)   If the Authority decides—
   (a)   not to impose a proposed requirement, or
   (b)   to revoke a requirement that has been imposed,
it must give A written notice.

(7)   If the Authority decides to grant an application by A for the variation or revocation of a requirement, it must give him written notice of its decision.

(8)   If the Authority proposes to refuse an application by A for the variation or revocation of a requirement it must give him a warning notice.

(9)   If the Authority, having considered any representations made in response to the warning notice, decides to refuse the application, it must give A a decision notice.

(10)   A notice given under—
   (a)   subsection (5), or
   (b)   subsection (9) in the case of a decision to refuse the application,
must inform A of his right to refer the matter to the Tribunal.

(11)   If the Authority decides to refuse an application for a variation or revocation of the requirement, the applicant may refer the matter to the Tribunal.

(12)   If a notice informs a person of his right to refer a matter to the Tribunal, it must give an indication of the procedure on such a reference.

[347]

322   Rules applicable to former underwriting members

(1)   The Authority may make rules imposing such requirements on persons to whom the rules apply as appear to it to be appropriate for protecting policyholders against the risk that those persons may not be able to meet their liabilities.

(2)   The rules may apply to—
   (a)   former underwriting members generally; or
   (b)   to a class of former underwriting member specified in them.

(3)   Section 319 applies to the making of proposed rules under this section as it applies to the giving of a proposed direction under section 316.

(4)   Part X (except sections 152 to 154) does not apply to rules made under this section.

[348]

Transfers of business done at Lloyd's

323   Transfer schemes

The Treasury may by order provide for the application of any provision of Part VII (with or without modification) in relation to schemes for the transfer of the whole or any part of the business carried on by one or more [underwriting members of the Society or by one or more persons who have ceased to be such a member (whether before, on or after 24th December 1996)].

[349]

NOTES
    Words in square brackets substituted by the Financial Services and Markets Act 2000 (Amendment of section 323) Regulations 2008, SI 2008/1469, reg 2, as from 30 June 2008.
    Orders: the Financial Services and Markets Act 2000 (Control of Transfers of Business Done at Lloyd's) Order 2001, SI 2001/3626 at **[2523]**.
    Note that the following amending Orders have also been made under this section: the Financial Services and Markets Act 2000 (Control of Transfers of Business Done at Lloyd's) (Amendment) Order 2008, SI 2008/1725.

Supplemental

324   Interpretation of this Part

(1)   In this Part—
    "arranging deals", in relation to the investments to which this Part applies, has the same meaning as in paragraph 3 of Schedule 2;
    "former underwriting member" means a person ceasing to be an underwriting member of the Society on, or at any time after, 24 December 1996; and
    "participation in Lloyd's syndicates", in relation to the secondary market activity, means the investment described in sub-paragraph (1) of paragraph 21 of Schedule 2.

(2)   A term used in this Part which is defined in Lloyd's Act 1982 has the same meaning as in that Act.

[350]

PART XX
PROVISION OF FINANCIAL SERVICES BY MEMBERS OF THE PROFESSIONS

325   Authority's general duty

(1)   The Authority must keep itself informed about—
    (a)   the way in which designated professional bodies supervise and regulate the carrying on of exempt regulated activities by members of the professions in relation to which they are established;
    (b)   the way in which such members are carrying on exempt regulated activities.

(2)   In this Part—
    "exempt regulated activities" means regulated activities which may, as a result of this Part, be carried on by members of a profession which is supervised and regulated by a designated professional body without breaching the general prohibition; and
    "members", in relation to a profession, means persons who are entitled to practise the profession in question and, in practising it, are subject to the rules of the body designated in relation to that profession, whether or not they are members of that body.

(3)   The Authority must keep under review the desirability of exercising any of its powers under this Part.

(4)   Each designated professional body must co-operate with the Authority, by the sharing of information and in other ways, in order to enable the Authority to perform its functions under this Part.

[351]

326   Designation of professional bodies

(1)   The Treasury may by order designate bodies for the purposes of this Part.

(2)   A body designated under subsection (1) is referred to in this Part as a designated professional body.

(3)   The Treasury may designate a body under subsection (1) only if they are satisfied that—
    (a)   the basic condition, and

PART XXI
MUTUAL SOCIETIES

Friendly societies

334   The Friendly Societies Commission

(1)   The Treasury may by order provide—
  (a)   for any functions of the Friendly Societies Commission to be transferred to the Authority;
  (b)   for any functions of the Friendly Societies Commission which have not been, or are not being, transferred to the Authority to be transferred to the Treasury.

(2)   If the Treasury consider it appropriate to do so, they may by order provide for the Friendly Societies Commission to cease to exist on a day specified in or determined in accordance with the order.

(3)   The enactments relating to friendly societies which are mentioned in Part I of Schedule 18 are amended as set out in that Part.

(4)   Part II of Schedule 18—
  (a)   removes certain restrictions on the ability of incorporated friendly societies to form subsidiaries and control corporate bodies; and
  (b)   makes connected amendments.

[360]

NOTES

Friendly Societies Commission: the Commission was established by the Friendly Societies Act 1992, s 1, Sch 1, as originally enacted. Section 1 of the 1992 Act (together with ss 2–4) was substituted by a new s 1 (functions of the Financial Services Authority in relation to friendly societies), and Sch 1 was repealed by the Financial Services and Markets Act 2000 (Mutual Societies) Order 2001, SI 2001/2617, art 13(1), (2), Sch 3, Pt I, paras 53, 54, 119, Sch 4, subject to transitional provisions and savings in art 13(3) of, and Sch 5, paras 8, 9, 16 to, that Order. Provision for the Commission to cease to exist is made by art 10 of the 2001 Order.

Orders: the Financial Services and Markets Act 2000 (Mutual Societies) Order 2001, SI 2001/2617 at **[2453]**.

335   The Registry of Friendly Societies

(1)   The Treasury may by order provide—
  (a)   for any functions of the Chief Registrar of Friendly Societies, or of an assistant registrar of friendly societies for the central registration area, to be transferred to the Authority;
  (b)   for any of their functions which have not been, or are not being, transferred to the Authority to be transferred to the Treasury.

(2)   The Treasury may by order provide—
  (a)   for any functions of the central office of the registry of friendly societies to be transferred to the Authority;
  (b)   for any functions of that office which have not been, or are not being, transferred to the Authority to be transferred to the Treasury.

(3)   The Treasury may by order provide—
  (a)   for any functions of the assistant registrar of friendly societies for Scotland to be transferred to the Authority;
  (b)   for any functions of the assistant registrar which have not been, or are not being, transferred to the Authority to be transferred to the Treasury.

(4)   If the Treasury consider it appropriate to do so, they may by order provide for—
  (a)   the office of Chief Registrar of Friendly Societies,
  (b)   the office of assistant registrar of friendly societies for the central registration area,
  (c)   the central office, or
  (d)   the office of assistant registrar of friendly societies for Scotland,
to cease to exist on a day specified in or determined in accordance with the order.

[361]

NOTES

The Registry of Friendly Societies: the offices of Chief Registrar of Friendly Societies, Assistant Registrar of Friendly Societies, and Assistant registrar of Friendly Societies for Scotland were continued by the Friendly Societies Act 1974, s 1. That section was repealed by the Financial Services and Markets Act 2000 (Mutual Societies) Order 2001, SI 2001/2617, art 13(1), (2), Sch 3, Pt I, paras 1, 2, Sch 4, subject to transitional provisions and savings in art 13(3), Sch 5, paras 3, 4 thereof. Provision for these offices to cease to exist is made by art 12 of the 2001 Order.

Orders: the Financial Services and Markets Act 2000 (Mutual Societies) Order 2001, SI 2001/2617 at **[2453]**.

Building societies

336 The Building Societies Commission

(1) The Treasury may by order provide—
  (a) for any functions of the Building Societies Commission to be transferred to the Authority;
  (b) for any functions of the Building Societies Commission which have not been, or are not being, transferred to the Authority to be transferred to the Treasury.

(2) If the Treasury consider it appropriate to do so, they may by order provide for the Building Societies Commission to cease to exist on a day specified in or determined in accordance with the order.

(3) The enactments relating to building societies which are mentioned in Part III of Schedule 18 are amended as set out in that Part.

[362]

NOTES
 Building Societies Commission: the Commission was established by the Building Societies Act 1986, s 1, Sch 1, as originally enacted. Section 1 of the 1986 Act (together with ss 2–4) was substituted by a new s 1 (functions of the Financial Services Authority in relation to building societies), and Sch 1 was repealed by the Financial Services and Markets Act 2000 (Mutual Societies) Order 2001, SI 2001/2617, art 13(1), (2), Sch 3, Pt II, paras 131, 132, 199, Sch 4, subject to transitional provisions and savings in art 13(3) of, and Sch 5, paras 17, 18, 27 to, that Order. Provision for the Commission to cease to exist is made by art 9 of the 2001 Order.
 Orders: the Financial Services and Markets Act 2000 (Mutual Societies) Order 2001, SI 2001/2617 at [2453].

337 The Building Societies Investor Protection Board

The Treasury may by order provide for the Building Societies Investor Protection Board to cease to exist on a day specified in or determined in accordance with the order.

[363]

NOTES
 Building Societies Investor Protection Board: the Board was established by the Building Societies Act 1986, s 24, Sch 5 (repealed by the Financial Services and Markets Act 2000 (Mutual Societies) Order 2001, SI 2001/2617, art 13(1), (2), Sch 3, Pt II, paras 131, 139, 202, Sch 4, subject to transitional provisions and savings in art 13(3) of, and Sch 5, paras 17, 19, 29 thereof). Provision for the Board to cease to exist is made by art 11 of the 2001 Order.
 Orders: the Financial Services and Markets Act 2000 (Mutual Societies) Order 2001, SI 2001/2617 at [2453].

Industrial and provident societies and credit unions

338 Industrial and provident societies and credit unions

(1) The Treasury may by order provide for the transfer to the Authority of any functions conferred by—
  (a) the Industrial and Provident Societies Act 1965;
  (b) the Industrial and Provident Societies Act 1967;
  (c) the Friendly and Industrial and Provident Societies Act 1968;
  (d) the Industrial and Provident Societies Act 1975;
  (e) the Industrial and Provident Societies Act 1978;
  (f) the Credit Unions Act 1979.

(2) The Treasury may by order provide for the transfer to the Treasury of any functions under those enactments which have not been, or are not being, transferred to the Authority.

(3) The enactments relating to industrial and provident societies which are mentioned in Part IV of Schedule 18 are amended as set out in that Part.

(4) The enactments relating to credit unions which are mentioned in Part V of Schedule 18 are amended as set out in that Part.

[364]

NOTES
 Note: credit unions in Northern Ireland have not been brought within this Act's regime and remain under the jurisdiction of the Registrar of Friendly Societies in Northern Ireland. A transitional exemption in the Financial Services and Markets Act 2000 (Exemption) Order 2001, SI 2001/1201, art 6 was made permanent in respect of credit unions within the meaning of Credit Unions (Northern Ireland) Order 1985 by the Financial Services and Markets Act 2000 (Exemption) (Amendment) Order 2001, SI 2001/3623, arts 3, 4, which adds a new para 24A to this effect to the Schedule of SI 2001/1201. See FSA Handbook, CRED 1.1.1G for further details.
 Orders: the Financial Services and Markets Act 2000 (Mutual Societies) Order 2001, SI 2001/2617 at [2453].

Supplemental

339 Supplemental provisions

(1)   The additional powers conferred by section 428 on a person making an order under this Act include power for the Treasury, when making an order under section 334, 335, 336 or 338 which transfers functions, to include provision—

(a)   for the transfer of any functions of a member of the body, or servant or agent of the body or person, whose functions are transferred by the order;

(b)   for the transfer of any property, rights or liabilities held, enjoyed or incurred by any person in connection with transferred functions;

(c)   for the carrying on and completion by or under the authority of the person to whom functions are transferred of any proceedings, investigations or other matters commenced, before the order takes effect, by or under the authority of the person from whom the functions are transferred;

(d)   amending any enactment relating to transferred functions in connection with their exercise by, or under the authority of, the person to whom they are transferred;

(e)   for the substitution of the person to whom functions are transferred for the person from whom they are transferred, in any instrument, contract or legal proceedings made or begun before the order takes effect.

(2)   The additional powers conferred by section 428 on a person making an order under this Act include power for the Treasury, when making an order under section 334(2), 335(4), 336(2) or 337, to include provision—

(a)   for the transfer of any property, rights or liabilities held, enjoyed or incurred by any person in connection with the office or body which ceases to have effect as a result of the order;

(b)   for the carrying on and completion by or under the authority of such person as may be specified in the order of any proceedings, investigations or other matters commenced, before the order takes effect, by or under the authority of the person whose office, or the body which, ceases to exist as a result of the order;

(c)   amending any enactment which makes provision with respect to that office or body;

(d)   for the substitution of the Authority, the Treasury or such other body as may be specified in the order in any instrument, contract or legal proceedings made or begun before the order takes effect.

(3)   On or after the making of an order under any of sections 334 to 338 ("the original order"), the Treasury may by order make any incidental, supplemental, consequential or transitional provision which they had power to include in the original order.

(4)   A certificate issued by the Treasury that property vested in a person immediately before an order under this Part takes effect has been transferred as a result of the order is conclusive evidence of the transfer.

(5)   Subsections (1) and (2) are not to be read as affecting in any way the powers conferred by section 428.

[365]

NOTES

Orders: the Financial Services and Markets Act 2000 (Mutual Societies) Order 2001, SI 2001/2617 at **[2453]**; the Financial Services and Markets Act 2000 (Transitional Provisions, Repeals and Savings) (Financial Services Compensation Scheme) Order 2001, SI 2001/2967; the Financial Services and Markets Act 2000 (Consequential Amendments and Savings) (Industrial Assurance) Order 2001, SI 2001/3647.

PART XXII
AUDITORS AND ACTUARIES

Appointment

340 Appointment

(1)   Rules may require an authorised person, or an authorised person falling within a specified class—

(a)   to appoint an auditor, or

(b)   to appoint an actuary,

if he is not already under an obligation to do so imposed by another enactment.

(2)   Rules may require an authorised person, or an authorised person falling within a specified class—

(a)   to produce periodic financial reports; and

(b)   to have them reported on by an auditor or an actuary.

(3)   Rules may impose such other duties on auditors of, or actuaries acting for, authorised persons as may be specified.

PART I
FSMA 2000

(4) Rules under subsection (1) may make provision—
  (a) specifying the manner in which and time within which an auditor or actuary is to be appointed;
  (b) requiring the Authority to be notified of an appointment;
  (c) enabling the Authority to make an appointment if no appointment has been made or notified;
  (d) as to remuneration;
  (e) as to the term of office, removal and resignation of an auditor or actuary.

(5) An auditor or actuary appointed as a result of rules under subsection (1), or on whom duties are imposed by rules under subsection (3)—
  (a) must act in accordance with such provision as may be made by rules; and
  (b) is to have such powers in connection with the discharge of his functions as may be provided by rules.

(6) In subsections (1) to (3) "auditor" or "actuary" means an auditor, or actuary, who satisfies such requirements as to qualifications, experience and other matters (if any) as may be specified.

(7) "Specified" means specified in rules.

[366]

Information

341 Access to books etc

(1) An appointed auditor of, or an appointed actuary acting for, an authorised person—
  (a) has a right of access at all times to the authorised person's books, accounts and vouchers; and
  (b) is entitled to require from the authorised person's officers such information and explanations as he reasonably considers necessary for the performance of his duties as auditor or actuary.

(2) "Appointed" means appointed under or as a result of this Act.

[367]

342 Information given by auditor or actuary to the Authority

(1) This section applies to a person who is, or has been, an auditor of an authorised person appointed under or as a result of a statutory provision.

(2) This section also applies to a person who is, or has been, an actuary acting for an authorised person and appointed under or as a result of a statutory provision.

(3) An auditor or actuary does not contravene any duty to which he is subject merely because he gives to the Authority—
  (a) information on a matter of which he has, or had, become aware in his capacity as auditor of, or actuary acting for, the authorised person, or
  (b) his opinion on such a matter,
if he is acting in good faith and he reasonably believes that the information or opinion is relevant to any functions of the Authority.

(4) Subsection (3) applies whether or not the auditor or actuary is responding to a request from the Authority.

(5) The Treasury may make regulations prescribing circumstances in which an auditor or actuary must communicate matters to the Authority as mentioned in subsection (3).

(6) It is the duty of an auditor or actuary to whom any such regulations apply to communicate a matter to the Authority in the circumstances prescribed by the regulations.

(7) The matters to be communicated to the Authority in accordance with the regulations may include matters relating to persons other than the authorised person concerned.

[368]

NOTES
Regulations: the Financial Services and Markets Act 2000 (Communications by Auditors) Regulations 2001, SI 2001/2587 at **[2451]**; the Financial Services and Markets Act 2000 (Communications by Actuaries) Regulations 2003, SI 2003/1294 at **[2696]**.

343 Information given by auditor or actuary to the Authority: persons with close links

(1) This section applies to a person who—
  (a) is, or has been, an auditor of an authorised person appointed under or as a result of a statutory provision; and
  (b) is, or has been, an auditor of a person ("CL") who has close links with the authorised person.

(2) This section also applies to a person who—

(a)   is, or has been, an actuary acting for an authorised person and appointed under or as a result of a statutory provision; and

(b)   is, or has been, an actuary acting for a person ("CL") who has close links with the authorised person.

(3)   An auditor or actuary does not contravene any duty to which he is subject merely because he gives to the Authority—

(a)   information on a matter concerning the authorised person of which he has, or had, become aware in his capacity as auditor of, or actuary acting for, CL, or

(b)   his opinion on such a matter,

if he is acting in good faith and he reasonably believes that the information or opinion is relevant to any functions of the Authority.

(4)   Subsection (3) applies whether or not the auditor or actuary is responding to a request from the Authority.

(5)   The Treasury may make regulations prescribing circumstances in which an auditor or actuary must communicate matters to the Authority as mentioned in subsection (3).

(6)   It is the duty of an auditor or actuary to whom any such regulations apply to communicate a matter to the Authority in the circumstances prescribed by the regulations.

(7)   The matters to be communicated to the Authority in accordance with the regulations may include matters relating to persons other than the authorised person concerned.

(8)   CL has close links with the authorised person concerned ("A") if CL is—

(a)   a parent undertaking of A;

(b)   a subsidiary undertaking of A;

(c)   a parent undertaking of a subsidiary undertaking of A; or

(d)   a subsidiary undertaking of a parent undertaking of A.

(9)   "Subsidiary undertaking" includes all the instances mentioned in Article 1(1) and (2) of the Seventh Company Law Directive in which an entity may be a subsidiary of an undertaking.

[369]

NOTES
Regulations: the Financial Services and Markets Act 2000 (Communications by Auditors) Regulations 2001, SI 2001/2587 at **[2451]**; the Financial Services and Markets Act 2000 (Communications by Actuaries) Regulations 2003, SI 2003/1294 at **[2696]**.

344   Duty of auditor or actuary resigning etc to give notice

(1)   This section applies to an auditor or actuary to whom section 342 applies.

(2)   He must without delay notify the Authority if he—

(a)   is removed from office by an authorised person;

(b)   resigns before the expiry of his term of office with such a person; or

(c)   is not re-appointed by such a person.

(3)   If he ceases to be an auditor of, or actuary acting for, such a person, he must without delay notify the Authority—

(a)   of any matter connected with his so ceasing which he thinks ought to be drawn to the Authority's attention; or

(b)   that there is no such matter.

[370]

Disqualification

345   Disqualification

(1)   If it appears to the Authority that an auditor or actuary to whom section 342 applies has failed to comply with a duty imposed on him under this Act, it may disqualify him from being the auditor of, or (as the case may be) from acting as an actuary for, any authorised person or any particular class of authorised person.

(2)   If the Authority proposes to disqualify a person under this section it must give him a warning notice.

(3)   If it decides to disqualify him it must give him a decision notice.

(4)   The Authority may remove any disqualification imposed under this section if satisfied that the disqualified person will in future comply with the duty in question.

(5)   A person who has been disqualified under this section may refer the matter to the Tribunal.

[371]

NOTES
Transitional provisions: the Financial Services and Markets Act 2000 (Transitional Provisions) (Authorised Persons etc) Order 2001, SI 2001/2636, art 78 provides for the disqualification under this section of an auditor

who, at 1 December 2001, has been disqualified pursuant to the Financial Services Act 1986, s 111(3) (repealed by the Financial Services and Markets Act 2000 (Consequential Amendments and Repeals) Order 2001, SI 2001/3649, art 3(1)(c)) or the Insurance Companies Act 1982, s 21A(5) (repealed by art 3(1)(b) of that Order).

Modification: the Financial Services and Markets Act 2000 (Transitional Provisions and Savings) (Civil Remedies, Discipline, Criminal Offences etc) (No 2) Order 2001, SI 2001/3083, art 19, provides (as from 1 December 2001 (in accordance with art 1(2)) that this section has effect as if the reference to a duty imposed on an auditor under the Act included a reference to a duty imposed (whether before or, where applicable, after commencement) on an auditor under any of the following enactments: FSA 1986, s 109 (communication by auditor with supervisory authorities); (b) Banking Act 1987, s 47 (communication by auditor with the Authority); (c) Insurance Companies Act 1982, s 21A (communications by auditor with the Treasury or the Secretary of State); (d) Building Societies Act 1986, s 82 (auditors' duties to Commission); (e) Friendly Societies Act 1992, s 79 (auditors' duties to Commission).

Offence

346 Provision of false or misleading information to auditor or actuary

(1)   An authorised person who knowingly or recklessly gives an appointed auditor or actuary information which is false or misleading in a material particular is guilty of an offence and liable—

    (a)   on summary conviction, to imprisonment for a term not exceeding six months or a fine not exceeding the statutory maximum, or both;

    (b)   on conviction on indictment, to imprisonment for a term not exceeding two years or a fine, or both.

(2)   Subsection (1) applies equally to an officer, controller or manager of an authorised person.

(3)   "Appointed" means appointed under or as a result of this Act.

[372]

PART XXIII
PUBLIC RECORD, DISCLOSURE OF INFORMATION
AND CO-OPERATION

The public record

347 The record of authorised persons etc

(1)   The Authority must maintain a record of every—

    (a)   person who appears to the Authority to be an authorised person;
    (b)   authorised unit trust scheme;
    (c)   authorised open-ended investment company;
    (d)   recognised scheme;
    (e)   recognised investment exchange;
    (f)   recognised clearing house;
    (g)   individual to whom a prohibition order relates;
    (h)   approved person; ...
  [(ha) person to whom subsection (2A) applies; and]
    (i)   person falling within such other class (if any) as the Authority may determine.

(2)   The record must include such information as the Authority considers appropriate and at least the following information—

    (a)   in the case of a person appearing to the Authority to be an authorised person—
        (i)   information as to the services which he holds himself out as able to provide; and
       (ii)   any address of which the Authority is aware at which a notice or other document may be served on him;
    (b)   in the case of an authorised unit trust scheme, the name and address of the manager and trustee of the scheme;
    (c)   in the case of an authorised open-ended investment company, the name and address of—
        (i)   the company;
       (ii)   if it has only one director, the director; and
      (iii)   its depositary (if any);
    (d)   in the case of a recognised scheme, the name and address of—
        (i)   the operator of the scheme; and
       (ii)   any representative of the operator in the United Kingdom;
    (e)   in the case of a recognised investment exchange or recognised clearing house, the name and address of the exchange or clearing house;
    (f)   in the case of an individual to whom a prohibition order relates—
        (i)   his name; and
       (ii)   details of the effect of the order;
    (g)   in the case of a person who is an approved person—
        (i)   his name;
       (ii)   the name of the relevant authorised person;

    (iii) if the approved person is performing a controlled function under an arrangement with a contractor of the relevant authorised person, the name of the contractor.

[(2A) This subsection applies to—
  (a) an appointed representative to whom subsection (1A) of section 39 applies for whom the applicable register (as defined by subsection (1B) of that section) is the record maintained by virtue of subsection (1)(ha) above;
  (b) a person mentioned in subsection (1)(a) of section 39A if—
    (i) the contract with an authorised person to which he is party complies with the applicable requirements (as defined by subsection (7) of that section), and
    (ii) the authorised person has accepted responsibility in writing for the person's activities in carrying on investment services business (as defined by subsection (8) of that section); and
  (c) any person not falling within paragraph (a) or (b) in respect of whom the Authority considers that a record must be maintained for the purpose of securing compliance with Article 23.3 of the markets in financial instruments directive (registration of tied agents).]

(3) If it appears to the Authority that a person in respect of whom there is an entry in the record as a result of one of the paragraphs of subsection (1) has ceased to be a person to whom that paragraph applies, the Authority may remove the entry from the record.

(4) But if the Authority decides not to remove the entry, it must—
  (a) make a note to that effect in the record; and
  (b) state why it considers that the person has ceased to be a person to whom that paragraph applies.

(5) The Authority must—
  (a) make the record available for inspection by members of the public in a legible form at such times and in such place or places as the Authority may determine; and
  (b) provide a certified copy of the record, or any part of it, to any person who asks for it—
    (i) on payment of the fee (if any) fixed by the Authority; and
    (ii) in a form (either written or electronic) in which it is legible to the person asking for it.

(6) The Authority may—
  (a) publish the record, or any part of it;
  (b) exploit commercially the information contained in the record, or any part of that information.

(7) "Authorised unit trust scheme", "authorised open-ended investment company" and "recognised scheme" have the same meaning as in Part XVII, and associated expressions are to be read accordingly.

(8) "Approved person" means a person in relation to whom the Authority has given its approval under section 59 and "controlled function" and "arrangement" have the same meaning as in that section.

(9) "Relevant authorised person" has the meaning given in section 66.

[373]

NOTES
  Sub-s (1): word omitted from para (h) repealed, and para (ha) inserted, by the Financial Services and Markets Act 2000 (Markets in Financial Instruments) Regulations 2007, SI 2007/126, reg 3(5), Sch 5, paras 1, 12(a), (b), as from 1 April 2007 (certain purposes (see reg 1(2) at **[4051]**)), and as from 1 November 2007 (otherwise).
  Sub-s (2A): inserted by SI 2007/126, reg 3(5), Sch 5, paras 1, 12(c), as from 1 April 2007 (certain purposes (see reg 1(2) at **[4051]**)), and as from 1 November 2007 (otherwise).
  Application in relation to interim permissions and interim approvals: see the notes preceding s 40 at **[40]**.

Disclosure of information

348 Restrictions on disclosure of confidential information by Authority etc

(1) Confidential information must not be disclosed by a primary recipient, or by any person obtaining the information directly or indirectly from a primary recipient, without the consent of—
  (a) the person from whom the primary recipient obtained the information; and
  (b) if different, the person to whom it relates.

(2) In this Part "confidential information" means information which—
  (a) relates to the business or other affairs of any person;
  (b) was received by the primary recipient for the purposes of, or in the discharge of, any functions of the Authority, the competent authority for the purposes of Part VI or the Secretary of State under any provision made by or under this Act; and
  (c) is not prevented from being confidential information by subsection (4).

(3)   It is immaterial for the purposes of subsection (2) whether or not the information was received—

(a)   by virtue of a requirement to provide it imposed by or under this Act;

(b)   for other purposes as well as purposes mentioned in that subsection.

(4)   Information is not confidential information if—

(a)   it has been made available to the public by virtue of being disclosed in any circumstances in which, or for any purposes for which, disclosure is not precluded by this section; or

(b)   it is in the form of a summary or collection of information so framed that it is not possible to ascertain from it information relating to any particular person.

(5)   Each of the following is a primary recipient for the purposes of this Part—

(a)   the Authority;

(b)   any person exercising functions conferred by Part VI on the competent authority;

(c)   the Secretary of State;

(d)   a person appointed to make a report under section 166;

(e)   any person who is or has been employed by a person mentioned in paragraphs (a) to (c);

(f)   any auditor or expert instructed by a person mentioned in those paragraphs.

(6)   In subsection (5)(f) "expert" includes—

(a)   a competent person appointed by the competent authority under section 97;

(b)   a competent person appointed by the Authority or the Secretary of State to conduct an investigation under Part XI;

(c)   any body or person appointed under paragraph 6 of Schedule 1 to perform a function on behalf of the Authority.

[374]

NOTES

Note: "primary recipient" includes the Bank of England for the purposes of the Financial Services and Markets Act 2000 (Confidential Information) (Bank of England) (Consequential Provisions) Order 2001, SI 2001/3648, art 3(4) at **[2637]**, and any person upon whom functions are conferred by, or under, the Financial Services and Markets Act 2000 (Disclosure of Confidential Information) (Amendment) (No 2) Regulations 2003, SI 2003/2174, with effect from 23 August 2003.

Information relating to mutual societies: the following information is to be treated as confidential information for the purposes of this section and ss 349–353: (a) certain information relating to the business or other affairs of a building society or other body (see the Building Societies Act 1986, s 53A (disclosure of information)); (b) certain information relating to the business or other affairs of a friendly society, a registered branch of a friendly society or any other person (see the Friendly Societies Act 1992, s 63A (disclosure of information)).

Modification: the Takeovers Directive (Interim Implementation) Regulations 2006, SI 2006/1183, reg 18(1), (2), provided that this section did not apply to: (a) the disclosure by specified authorities of confidential information disclosed to it by the FSA in reliance on sub-s (1) of this section; and (b) the disclosure of such information by a person obtaining it directly or indirectly from such an authority (with effect from 20 May 2006). This regulation was revoked by the Companies Act 2006 (Commencement No 2, Consequential Amendments, Transitional Provisions and Savings) Order 2007, SI 2007/1093, art 7, Sch 5 (with effect from 6 April 2007) however, the revocation of the Regulations does not affect the operation of Part 5 in relation to a takeover offer where the date of the offer was before 6 April 2007 (Sch 6, para 2) or the continued operation of reg 8(2)(b) in respect of offences committed prior to that date (Sch 6, para 3).

349   Exceptions from section 348

(1)   Section 348 does not prevent a disclosure of confidential information which is—

(a)   made for the purpose of facilitating the carrying out of a public function; and

(b)   permitted by regulations made by the Treasury under this section.

(2)   The regulations may, in particular, make provision permitting the disclosure of confidential information or of confidential information of a prescribed kind—

(a)   by prescribed recipients, or recipients of a prescribed description, to any person for the purpose of enabling or assisting the recipient to discharge prescribed public functions;

(b)   by prescribed recipients, or recipients of a prescribed description, to prescribed persons, or persons of prescribed descriptions, for the purpose of enabling or assisting those persons to discharge prescribed public functions;

(c)   by the Authority to the Treasury or the Secretary of State for any purpose;

(d)   by any recipient if the disclosure is with a view to or in connection with prescribed proceedings.

(3)   The regulations may also include provision—

(a)   making any permission to disclose confidential information subject to conditions (which may relate to the obtaining of consents or any other matter);

(b)   restricting the uses to which confidential information disclosed under the regulations may be put.

[(3A)   Section 348 does not apply to—

(a) the disclosure by a recipient to which subsection (3B) applies of confidential information disclosed to it by the Authority in reliance on subsection (1);
(b) the disclosure of such information by a person obtaining it directly or indirectly from a recipient to which subsection (3B) applies.

(3B) This subsection applies to—
(a) the Panel on Takeovers and Mergers;
(b) an authority designated as a supervisory authority for the purposes of Article 4.1 of the Takeovers Directive;
(c) any other person or body that exercises public functions, under legislation in an EEA State other than the United Kingdom, that are similar to the Authority's functions or those of the Panel on Takeovers and Mergers.]

(4) In relation to confidential information, each of the following is a "recipient"—
(a) a primary recipient;
(b) a person obtaining the information directly or indirectly from a primary recipient.

(5) "Public functions" includes—
(a) functions conferred by or in accordance with any provision contained in any enactment or subordinate legislation;
(b) functions conferred by or in accordance with any provision contained in the Community Treaties or any Community instrument;
(c) similar functions conferred on persons by or under provisions having effect as part of the law of a country or territory outside the United Kingdom;
(d) functions exercisable in relation to prescribed disciplinary proceedings.

(6) "Enactment" includes—
(a) an Act of the Scottish Parliament;
(b) Northern Ireland legislation.

(7) "Subordinate legislation" has the meaning given in the Interpretation Act 1978 and also includes an instrument made under an Act of the Scottish Parliament or under Northern Ireland legislation.

[(8) ...]

[375]

NOTES
Sub-ss (3A), (3B): inserted by the Companies Act 2006, s 964(1), (4), as from 6 April 2007.
Sub-s (8): added by the Takeovers Directive (Interim Implementation) Regulations 2006, SI 2006/1183, reg 18(3), (5), as from 20 May 2006; repealed by the Companies Act 2006 (Commencement No 2, Consequential Amendments, Transitional Provisions and Savings) Order 2007, SI 2007/1093, art 7, Sch 5, as from 6 April 2007.
Transitional provisions: in relation to the Financial Services and Markets Act 2000 (Disclosure of Confidential Information) Regulations 2001, SI 2001/2188, see the Financial Services and Markets Act 2000 (Consequential and Transitional Provisions) (Miscellaneous) (No 2) Order 2001, SI 2001/2659, art 7, which makes transitional modifications of the 2001 Regulations in relation to exemptions from restrictions on disclosure.
Information relating to mutual societies: see the note to s 348 at **[374]**.
Regulations: the Financial Services and Markets Act 2000 (Disclosure of Confidential Information) Regulations 2001, SI 2001/2188 at **[2350]**; the Electronic Commerce Directive (Financial Services and Markets) Regulations 2002, SI 2002/1775 at **[2674]**.
Note that the following amending Regulations have also been made under this section: the Financial Services and Markets Act 2000 (Disclosure of Confidential Information) (Amendment) Regulations 2001, SI 2001/3437; the Financial Services and Markets Act 2000 (Disclosure of Confidential Information) (Amendment) (No 2) Regulations 2001, SI 2001/3624; the Financial Services and Markets Act 2000 (Disclosure of Confidential Information) (Amendment) Regulations 2003, SI 2003/693; the Insurance Mediation Directive (Miscellaneous Amendments) Regulations 2003, SI 2003/1473; the Collective Investment Schemes (Miscellaneous Amendments) Regulations 2003, SI 2003/2066; the Financial Services and Markets Act 2000 (Disclosure of Confidential Information) (Amendment) (No 2) Regulations 2003, SI 2003/2174; the Financial Services and Markets Act 2000 (Disclosure of Confidential Information) (Amendment) (No 3) Regulations 2003, SI 2003/2817; the Financial Services and Markets Act 2000 (Disclosure of Confidential Information) (Amendment) Regulations 2005, SI 2005/3071; the Financial Services and Markets Act 2000 (Disclosure of Confidential Information) (Amendment) Regulations 2006, SI 2006/3413; the Financial Services and Markets Act 2000 (Markets in Financial Instruments) (Amendment) Regulations 2007, SI 2007/763; the Financial Services and Markets Act 2000 (Reinsurance Directive) Regulations 2007, SI 2007/3255.

350 Disclosure of information by the Inland Revenue

(1) No obligation as to secrecy imposed by statute or otherwise prevents the disclosure of Revenue information to—
(a) the Authority, or
(b) the Secretary of State,
if the disclosure is made for the purpose of assisting in the investigation of a matter under section 168 or with a view to the appointment of an investigator under that section.

(2)   A disclosure may only be made under subsection (1) by or under the authority of the Commissioners of Inland Revenue.

(3)   Section 348 does not apply to Revenue information.

(4)   Information obtained as a result of subsection (1) may not be used except—
  (a)   for the purpose of deciding whether to appoint an investigator under section 168;
  (b)   in the conduct of an investigation under section 168;
  (c)   in criminal proceedings brought against a person under this Act or the Criminal Justice Act 1993 as a result of an investigation under section 168;
  (d)   for the purpose of taking action under this Act against a person as a result of an investigation under section 168;
  (e)   in proceedings before the Tribunal as a result of action taken as mentioned in paragraph (d).

(5)   Information obtained as a result of subsection (1) may not be disclosed except—
  (a)   by or under the authority of the Commissioners of Inland Revenue;
  (b)   in proceedings mentioned in subsection (4)(c) or (e) or with a view to their institution.

(6)   Subsection (5) does not prevent the disclosure of information obtained as a result of subsection (1) to a person to whom it could have been disclosed under subsection (1).

(7)   "Revenue information" means information held by a person which it would be an offence under section 182 of the Finance Act 1989 for him to disclose.

                                                                                                                                  [376]

NOTES
  Information relating to mutual societies: see the note to s 348 at **[374]**.
  Commissioners of Inland Revenue: a reference to the Commissioners of Inland Revenue is now to be taken as a reference to the Commissioners for Her Majesty's Revenue and Customs; see the Commissioners for Revenue and Customs Act 2005, s 50(1), (7).
  Application: the Commissioners for Her Majesty's Revenue and Customs may supply information in accordance with this section only if the information was obtained or is held in the exercise of a function relating to matters to which the Commissioners for Revenue and Customs Act 2005, s 7 applies; see s 17(6) of, and Sch 2, Pt 2, para 18 to, that Act

351   Competition information

  (1)–(3)   ...

  (4)   Section 348 does not apply to competition information.

  (5)   "Competition information" means information which—
  (a)   relates to the affairs of a particular individual or body;
  (b)   is not otherwise in the public domain; and
  (c)   was obtained under or by virtue of a competition provision.

  (6)   "Competition provision" means any provision of—
  (a)   an order made under section 95;
  (b)   Chapter III of Part X; or
  (c)   Chapter II of Part XVIII.

  (7)   ...

                                                                                                                                  [377]

NOTES
  Sub-ss (1)–(3), (7): repealed by the Enterprise Act 2002, ss 247(k), 278(2), Sch 26, as from 20 June 2003.
  Information relating to mutual societies: see the note to s 348 at **[374]**.

352   Offences

  (1)   A person who discloses information in contravention of section 348 or 350(5) is guilty of an offence.

  (2)   A person guilty of an offence under subsection (1) is liable—
  (a)   on summary conviction, to imprisonment for a term not exceeding three months or a fine not exceeding the statutory maximum, or both;
  (b)   on conviction on indictment, to imprisonment for a term not exceeding two years or a fine, or both.

  (3)   A person is guilty of an offence if, in contravention of any provision of regulations made under section 349, he uses information which has been disclosed to him in accordance with the regulations.

  (4)   A person is guilty of an offence if, in contravention of subsection (4) of section 350, he uses information which has been disclosed to him in accordance with that section.

(5)   A person guilty of an offence under subsection (3) or (4) is liable on summary conviction to imprisonment for a term not exceeding *three months* or a fine not exceeding level 5 on the standard scale, or both.

(6)   In proceedings for an offence under this section it is a defence for the accused to prove—
- (a)   that he did not know and had no reason to suspect that the information was confidential information or that it had been disclosed in accordance with section 350;
- (b)   that he took all reasonable precautions and exercised all due diligence to avoid committing the offence.

[378]

NOTES

Sub-s (5): for the words in italics there are substituted the words "51 weeks" by the Criminal Justice Act 2003, s 280(2), Sch 26, para 54(1), (3), as from a day to be appointed.

Information relating to mutual societies: see the note to s 348 at **[374]**.

353   Removal of other restrictions on disclosure

(1)   The Treasury may make regulations permitting the disclosure of any information, or of information of a prescribed kind—
- (a)   by prescribed persons for the purpose of assisting or enabling them to discharge prescribed functions under this Act or any rules or regulations made under it;
- (b)   by prescribed persons, or persons of a prescribed description, to the Authority for the purpose of assisting or enabling the Authority to discharge prescribed functions;
- [(c)   by the scheme operator to the Office of Fair Trading for the purpose of assisting or enabling that Office to discharge prescribed functions under the Consumer Credit Act 1974].

(2)   Regulations under this section may not make any provision in relation to the disclosure of confidential information by primary recipients or by any person obtaining confidential information directly or indirectly from a primary recipient.

(3)   If a person discloses any information as permitted by regulations under this section the disclosure is not to be taken as a contravention of any duty to which he is subject.

[379]

NOTES

Sub-s (1): para (c) inserted by the Consumer Credit Act 2006, s 61(9), as from 16 June 2006.

Information relating to mutual societies: see the note to s 348 at **[374]**.

Regulations: the Financial Services and Markets Act 2000 (Disclosure of Information by Prescribed Persons) Regulations 2001, SI 2001/1857 at **[2346]**.

Note that the following amending Regulations have also been made under this section: the Financial Services and Markets Act 2000 (Disclosure of Information by Prescribed Persons) (Amendment) Regulations 2005, SI 2005/272.

Co-operation

354   Authority's duty to co-operate with others

(1)   The Authority must take such steps as it considers appropriate to co-operate with other persons (whether in the United Kingdom or elsewhere) who have functions—
- (a)   similar to those of the Authority; or
- (b)   in relation to the prevention or detection of financial crime.

[(1A)   The Authority must take such steps as it considers appropriate to co-operate with—
- (a)   the Panel on Takeovers and Mergers;
- (b)   an authority designated as a supervisory authority for the purposes of Article 4.1 of the Takeovers Directive;
- (c)   any other person or body that exercises functions of a public nature, under legislation in any country or territory outside the United Kingdom, that appear to the Authority to be similar to those of the Panel on Takeovers and Mergers.]

(2)   Co-operation may include the sharing of information which the Authority is not prevented from disclosing.

(3)   "Financial crime" has the same meaning as in section 6.

[380]

NOTES

Sub-s (1A): inserted by the Companies Act 2006, s 964(1), (5), as from 6 April 2007.

PART XXIV
INSOLVENCY

Interpretation

355 Interpretation of this Part

(1)　In this Part—
"the 1985 Act" means the Bankruptcy (Scotland) Act 1985;
"the 1986 Act" means the Insolvency Act 1986;
"the 1989 Order" means the Insolvency (Northern Ireland) Order 1989;
"body" means a body of persons—
    (a)　over which the court has jurisdiction under any provision of, or made under, the 1986 Act (or the 1989 Order); but
    (b)　which is not a building society, a friendly society or an industrial and provident society; and
"court" means—
    (a)　the court having jurisdiction for the purposes of the 1985 Act or the 1986 Act; or
    (b)　in Northern Ireland, the High Court.

(2)　In this Part "insurer" has such meaning as may be specified in an order made by the Treasury.

[381]

NOTES
Orders: the Financial Services and Markets Act 2000 (Insolvency) (Definition of "Insurer") Order 2001, SI 2001/2634 at **[2470]**; the Financial Services and Markets Act 2000 (Administration Orders Relating to Insurers) Order 2002, SI 2002/1242 at **[2669]**.

Voluntary arrangements

356 Authority's powers to participate in proceedings: company voluntary arrangements

[(1)　Where a voluntary arrangement has effect under Part I of the 1986 Act in respect of a company or insolvent partnership which is an authorised person, the Authority may apply to the court under section 6 or 7 of that Act.

(2)　Where a voluntary arrangement has been approved under Part II of the 1989 Order in respect of a company or insolvent partnership which is an authorised person, the Authority may apply to the court under Article 19 or 20 of that Order.]

(3)　If a person other than the Authority makes an application to the court in relation to the company or insolvent partnership under [any] of those provisions, the Authority is entitled to be heard at any hearing relating to the application.

[382]

NOTES
Sub-ss (1), (2): substituted by the Insolvency Act 2000, s 15(3)(a), (b), as from 1 January 2003.
Sub-s (3): word in square brackets substituted by the Insolvency Act 2000, s 15(3)(c), as from 1 January 2003.
Limited liability partnerships: as to the application of this section to LLPs, see the note at the beginning of this Act.

357 Authority's powers to participate in proceedings: individual voluntary arrangements

(1)　The Authority is entitled to be heard on an application by an individual who is an authorised person under section 253 of the 1986 Act (or Article 227 of the 1989 Order).

(2)　Subsections (3) to (6) apply if such an order is made on the application of such a person.

(3)　A person appointed for the purpose by the Authority is entitled to attend any meeting of creditors of the debtor summoned under section 257 of the 1986 Act (or Article 231 of the 1989 Order).

(4)　Notice of the result of a meeting so summoned is to be given to the Authority by the chairman of the meeting.

(5)　The Authority may apply to the court—
    (a)　under section 262 of the 1986 Act (or Article 236 of the 1989 Order); or
    (b)　under section 263 of the 1986 Act (or Article 237 of the 1989 Order).

(6)　If a person other than the Authority makes an application to the court under any provision mentioned in subsection (5), the Authority is entitled to be heard at any hearing relating to the application.

[383]

358   Authority's powers to participate in proceedings: trust deeds for creditors in Scotland

(1)   This section applies where a trust deed has been granted by or on behalf of a debtor who is an authorised person.

(2)   The trustee must, as soon as practicable after he becomes aware that the debtor is an authorised person, send to the Authority—

    (a)   in every case, a copy of the trust deed;

    (b)   where any other document or information is sent to every creditor known to the trustee in pursuance of paragraph 5(1)(c) of Schedule 5 to the 1985 Act, a copy of such document or information.

(3)   Paragraph 7 of that Schedule applies to the Authority as if it were a qualified creditor who has not been sent a copy of the notice as mentioned in paragraph 5(1)(c) of the Schedule.

(4)   The Authority must be given the same notice as the creditors of any meeting of creditors held in relation to the trust deed.

(5)   A person appointed for the purpose by the Authority is entitled to attend and participate in (but not to vote at) any such meeting of creditors as if the Authority were a creditor under the deed.

(6)   This section does not affect any right the Authority has as a creditor of a debtor who is an authorised person.

(7)   Expressions used in this section and in the 1985 Act have the same meaning in this section as in that Act.

[384]

Administration orders

[359   Administration order

(1)   The Authority may make an administration application under Schedule B1 to the 1986 Act [or Schedule B1 to the 1989 Order] in relation to a company or insolvent partnership which—

    (a)   is or has been an authorised person,

    (b)   is or has been an appointed representative, or

    (c)   is carrying on or has carried on a regulated activity in contravention of the general prohibition.

(2)   Subsection (3) applies in relation to an administration application made (or a petition presented) by the Authority by virtue of this section.

(3)   Any of the following shall be treated for the purpose of paragraph 11(a) of Schedule B1 to the 1986 Act [or paragraph 12(a) of Schedule B1 to the 1989 Order] as unable to pay its debts—

    (a)   a company or partnership in default on an obligation to pay a sum due and payable under an agreement, *and*

    (b)   an authorised deposit taker in default on an obligation to pay a sum due and payable in respect of a relevant deposit[, and

    (c)   an authorised reclaim fund in default on an obligation to pay a sum payable as a result of a claim made by virtue of section 1(2)(b) or 2(2)(b) of the Dormant Bank and Building Society Accounts Act 2008].

(4)   In this section—

    "agreement" means an agreement the making or performance of which constitutes or is part of a regulated activity carried on by the company or partnership,

    "authorised deposit taker" means a person with a Part IV permission to accept deposits (but not a person who has a Part IV permission to accept deposits only for the purpose of carrying on another regulated activity in accordance with that permission),

    ["authorised reclaim fund" means a reclaim fund within the meaning given by section 5(1) of the Dormant Bank and Building Society Accounts Act 2008 that is authorised for the purposes of this Act;]

    "company" means a company—

        (a)   in respect of which an administrator may be appointed under Schedule B1 to the 1986 Act, or

        [(b)   in respect of which an administrator may be appointed under Schedule B1 to the 1989 Order,] and

    "relevant deposit" shall, ignoring any restriction on the meaning of deposit arising from the identity of the person making the deposit, be construed in accordance with—

        (a)   section 22,

        (b)   any relevant order under that section, and

        (c)   Schedule 2.

(5)   The definition of "authorised deposit taker" in subsection (4) shall be construed in accordance with—

(a) section 22,
(b) any relevant order under that section, and
(c) Schedule 2.]

[385]

NOTES
Substituted by the Enterprise Act 2002, s 248(3), Sch 17, paras 53, 55, as from 15 September 2003 (for savings and transitional provisions in relation to a petition for an administration order presented before that date, and in relation to special administration regimes (within the meaning of the Enterprise Act 2002, s 249), see the note to the Insolvency Act 1986, s 8 at **[1131]**).
Sub-s (1): words in square brackets substituted by the Insolvency (Northern Ireland) Order 2005, SI 2005/1455, art 3(3), Sch 2, paras 56, 58(1), (2), as from 27 March 2006.
Sub-s (3): first words in square brackets substituted by the Insolvency (Northern Ireland) Order 2005, SI 2005/1455, art 3(3), Sch 2, paras 56, 58(1), (3), as from 27 March 2006; word in italics in para (a) repealed, and para (c) and the word immediately preceding it added, by the Dormant Bank and Building Society Accounts Act 2008, s 15, Sch 2, para 6(1), (2), as from a day to be appointed.
Sub-s (4): definition "authorised reclaim fund" inserted by the Dormant Bank and Building Society Accounts Act 2008, s 15, Sch 2, para 6(1), (3), as from a day to be appointed; words in square brackets in definition "company" substituted by the Insolvency (Northern Ireland) Order 2005, SI 2005/1455, art 3(3), Sch 2, paras 56, 58(1), (4), as from 27 March 2006.
Limited liability partnerships: as to the application of this section to LLPs, see the note at the beginning of this Act.

360 Insurers

(1) The Treasury may by order provide that such provisions of Part II of the 1986 Act (or Part III of the 1989 Order) as may be specified are to apply in relation to insurers with such modifications as may be specified.

(2) An order under this section—
    (a) may provide that such provisions of this Part as may be specified are to apply in relation to the administration of insurers in accordance with the order with such modifications as may be specified; and
    (b) requires the consent of the Secretary of State.

(3) "Specified" means specified in the order.

[386]

NOTES
Orders: the Financial Services and Markets Act 2000 (Administration Orders Relating to Insurers) Order 2002, SI 2002/1242 at **[2669]**; the Financial Services and Markets Act 2000 (Administration Orders Relating to Insurers) (Northern Ireland) Order 2005, SI 2005/1644 (revoked by SI 2007/846 as from 6 April 2007, subject to savings in relation to cases where a petition for an administration order was presented before that date); the Financial Services and Markets Act 2000 (Administration Orders Relating to Insurers) (Northern Ireland) Order 2007, SI 2007/846.
Note that the following amending Orders have also been made under this section: the Financial Services and Markets Act 2000 (Administration Orders Relating to Insurers) (Amendment) Order 2003, SI 2003/2134; the Financial Services and Markets Act 2000 (Transitional Provisions, Repeals and Savings) (Financial Services Compensation Scheme) (Amendment) Order 2004, SI 2004/952.

[361 Administrator's duty to report to Authority

(1) This section applies where a company or partnership is—
    (a) in administration within the meaning of Schedule B1 to the 1986 Act, or
    [(b) in administration within the meaning of Schedule B1 to the 1989 Order].

(2) If the administrator thinks that the company or partnership is carrying on or has carried on a regulated activity in contravention of the general prohibition, he must report to the Authority without delay.

(3) Subsection (2) does not apply where the administration arises out of an administration order made on an application made or petition presented by the Authority.]

[387]

NOTES
Substituted by the Enterprise Act 2002, s 248(3), Sch 17, paras 53, 56, as from 15 September 2003 (for savings and transitional provisions in relation to a petition for an administration order presented before that date, and in relation to special administration regimes (within the meaning of the Enterprise Act 2002, s 249), see the note to the Insolvency Act 1986, s 8 at **[1131]**).
Sub-s (1): para (b) substituted by the Insolvency (Northern Ireland) Order 2005, SI 2005/1455, art 3(3), Sch 2, paras 56, 59, as from 27 March 2006.
Limited liability partnerships: as to the application of this section to LLPs, see the note at the beginning of this Act.

362 Authority's powers to participate in proceedings

(1) This section applies if a person other than the Authority [makes an administration application under Schedule B1 to the 1986 Act] [or Schedule B1 to the 1989 Order] in relation to a company or partnership which—

    (a) is, or has been, an authorised person;

    (b) is, or has been, an appointed representative; or

    (c) is carrying on, or has carried on, a regulated activity in contravention of the general prohibition.

[(1A) This section also applies in relation to—

    (a) the appointment under paragraph 14 or 22 of Schedule B1 to the 1986 Act [or paragraph 15 or 23 of Schedule B1 to the 1989 Order] of an administrator of a company of a kind described in subsection (1)(a) to (c), or

    (b) the filing with the court of a copy of notice of intention to appoint an administrator under [any] of those paragraphs.]

(2) The Authority is entitled to be heard—

    (a) at the hearing of the [administration application ...]; and

    (b) at any other hearing of the court in relation to the company or partnership under Part II of the 1986 Act (or Part III of the 1989 Order).

(3) Any notice or other document required to be sent to a creditor of the company or partnership must also be sent to the Authority.

[(4) The Authority may apply to the court under paragraph 74 of Schedule B1 to the 1986 Act [or paragraph 75 of Schedule B1 to the 1989 Order].

(4A) In respect of an application under subsection (4)—

    (a) paragraph 74(1)(a) and (b) shall have effect as if for the words "harm the interests of the applicant (whether alone or in common with some or all other members or creditors)" there were substituted the words "harm the interests of some or all members or creditors", and

    [(b) paragraph 75(1)(a) and (b) of Schedule B1 to the 1989 Order shall have effect as if for the words "harm the interests of the applicant (whether alone or in common with some or all other members or creditors)" there were substituted the words "harm the interests of some or all members or creditors".]]

(5) A person appointed for the purpose by the Authority is entitled—

    (a) to attend any meeting of creditors of the company or partnership summoned under any enactment;

    (b) to attend any meeting of a committee established under [paragraph 57 of Schedule B1 to the 1986 Act] [or paragraph 58 of Schedule B1 to the 1989 Order]; and

    (c) to make representations as to any matter for decision at such a meeting.

(6) If, during the course of the administration of a company, a compromise or arrangement is proposed between the company and its creditors, or any class of them, the Authority may apply to the court under [section 896 or 899 of the Companies Act 2006].

[388]

NOTES

Sub-s (1): words in first pair of square brackets substituted by the Enterprise Act 2002, s 248(3), Sch 17, paras 53, 57(a), as from 15 September 2003 (for savings and transitional provisions in relation to a petition for an administration order presented before that date, and in relation to special administration regimes (within the meaning of the Enterprise Act 2002, s 249), see the note to the Insolvency Act 1986, s 8 at **[1131]**); words in second pair of square brackets substituted by the Insolvency (Northern Ireland) Order 2005, SI 2005/1455, art 3(3), Sch 2, paras 56, 60(1), (2), as from 27 March 2006.

Sub-s (1A): inserted by the Enterprise Act 2002, s 248(3), Sch 17, paras 53, 57(b), as from 15 September 2003 (subject to savings and transitional provisions as noted above); words in square brackets in para (a) inserted, and word in square brackets in para (b) substituted, by SI 2005/1455, art 3(3), Sch 2, paras 56, 60(1), (3), as from 27 March 2006.

Sub-s (2): words in square brackets substituted by the Enterprise Act 2002, s 248(3), Sch 17, paras 53, 57(c), as from 15 September 2003 (subject to savings and transitional provisions as noted above); words omitted repealed by SI 2005/1455, arts 3(3), 31, Sch 2, paras 56, 60(1), (4), Sch 9, as from 27 March 2006.

Sub-s (4): substituted, together with sub-s (4A) for original sub-s (4), by the Enterprise Act 2002, s 248(3), Sch 17, paras 53, 57(d), as from 15 September 2003 (subject to savings and transitional provisions as noted above); words in square brackets substituted by SI 2005/1455, art 3(3), Sch 2, paras 56, 60(1), (5), as from 27 March 2006.

Sub-s (4A): substituted as noted above; para (b) substituted by SI 2005/1455, art 3(3), Sch 2, paras 56, 60(1), (6), as from 27 March 2006.

Sub-s (5): words in first pair of square brackets substituted by the Enterprise Act 2002, s 248(3), Sch 17, paras 53, 57(e), as from 15 September 2003 (subject to savings and transitional provisions as noted above); words in second pair of square brackets substituted by SI 2005/1455, art 3(3), Sch 2, paras 56, 60(1), (7), as from 27 March 2006.

Sub-s (6): words in square brackets substituted by the Companies Act 2006 (Consequential Amendments etc) Order 2008, SI 2008/948, art 3(1), Sch 1, Pt 2, para 211(4), as from 6 April 2008.

Limited liability partnerships: as to the application of this section to LLPs, see the note at the beginning of this Act.

[362A Administrator appointed by company or directors

(1) This section applies in relation to a company of a kind described in section 362(1)(a) to (c).

(2) An administrator of the company may not be appointed under paragraph 22 of Schedule B1 to the 1986 Act [or paragraph 23 of Schedule B1 to the 1989 Order] without the consent of the Authority.

(3) Consent under subsection (2)—
  (a) must be in writing, and
  (b) must be filed with the court along with the notice of intention to appoint under paragraph 27 of [Schedule B1 to the 1986 Act or paragraph 28 of Schedule B1 to the 1989 Order].

(4) In a case where no notice of intention to appoint is required—
  (a) subsection (3)(b) shall not apply, but
  (b) consent under subsection (2) must accompany the notice of appointment filed under paragraph 29 of [Schedule B1 to the 1986 Act or paragraph 30 of Schedule B1 to the 1989 Order].]

[389]

NOTES

Inserted by the Enterprise Act 2002, s 248(3), Sch 17, paras 53, 58, as from 15 September 2003 (for savings and transitional provisions in relation to a petition for an administration order presented before that date, and in relation to special administration regimes (within the meaning of the Enterprise Act 2002, s 249), see the note to the Insolvency Act 1986, s 8 at **[1131]**).

Sub-s (2): words in square brackets inserted by the Insolvency (Northern Ireland) Order 2005, SI 2005/1455, art 3(3), Sch 2, paras 56, 61(1), (2), as from 27 March 2006.

Sub-ss (3), (4): words in square brackets substituted by the SI 2005/1455, art 3(3), Sch 2, paras 56, 61(1), (3), (4), as from 27 March 2006.

Limited liability partnerships: by virtue of the Limited Liability Partnership Regulations 2001, SI 2001/1090, reg 6, this section is applied to companies of a kind described in s 362(1)(a)–(c) which would include limited liability partnerships with modifications.

Receivership

363 Authority's powers to participate in proceedings

(1) This section applies if a receiver has been appointed in relation to a company which—
  (a) is, or has been, an authorised person;
  (b) is, or has been, an appointed representative; or
  (c) is carrying on, or has carried on, a regulated activity in contravention of the general prohibition.

(2) The Authority is entitled to be heard on an application made under section 35 or 63 of the 1986 Act (or Article 45 of the 1989 Order).

(3) The Authority is entitled to make an application under section 41(1)(a) or 69(1)(a) of the 1986 Act (or Article 51(1)(a) of the 1989 Order).

(4) A report under section 48(1) or 67(1) of the 1986 Act (or Article 58(1) of the 1989 Order) must be sent by the person making it to the Authority.

(5) A person appointed for the purpose by the Authority is entitled—
  (a) to attend any meeting of creditors of the company summoned under any enactment;
  (b) to attend any meeting of a committee established under section 49 or 68 of the 1986 Act (or Article 59 of the 1989 Order); and
  (c) to make representations as to any matter for decision at such a meeting.

[390]

NOTES

Limited liability partnerships: as to the application of this section to LLPs, see the note at the beginning of this Act.

364 Receiver's duty to report to Authority

If—
  (a) a receiver has been appointed in relation to a company, and

(b)　it appears to the receiver that the company is carrying on, or has carried on, a regulated activity in contravention of the general prohibition,

the receiver must report the matter to the Authority without delay.

[391]

PART I
FSMA 2000

NOTES

Limited liability partnerships: as to the application of this section to LLPs, see the note at the beginning of this Act.

Voluntary winding up

365　Authority's powers to participate in proceedings

(1)　This section applies in relation to a company which—
　(a)　is being wound up voluntarily;
　(b)　is an authorised person; and
　(c)　is not an insurer effecting or carrying out contracts of long-term insurance.

(2)　The Authority may apply to the court under section 112 of the 1986 Act (or Article 98 of the 1989 Order) in respect of the company.

(3)　The Authority is entitled to be heard at any hearing of the court in relation to the voluntary winding up of the company.

(4)　Any notice or other document required to be sent to a creditor of the company must also be sent to the Authority.

(5)　A person appointed for the purpose by the Authority is entitled—
　(a)　to attend any meeting of creditors of the company summoned under any enactment;
　(b)　to attend any meeting of a committee established under section 101 of the 1986 Act (or Article 87 of the 1989 Order); and
　(c)　to make representations as to any matter for decision at such a meeting.

(6)　The voluntary winding up of the company does not bar the right of the Authority to have it wound up by the court.

(7)　If, during the course of the winding up of the company, a compromise or arrangement is proposed between the company and its creditors, or any class of them, the Authority may apply to the court under [section 896 or 899 of the Companies Act 2006].

[392]

NOTES

Sub-s (7): words in square brackets substituted by the Companies Act 2006 (Consequential Amendments etc) Order 2008, SI 2008/948, art 3(1), Sch 1, Pt 2, para 211(4), as from 6 April 2008.

Limited liability partnerships: as to the application of this section to LLPs, see the note at the beginning of this Act.

366　Insurers effecting or carrying out long-term contracts or insurance

(1)　An insurer effecting or carrying out contracts of long-term insurance may not be wound up voluntarily without the consent of the Authority.

(2)　If notice of a general meeting of such an insurer is given, specifying the intention to propose a resolution for voluntary winding up of the insurer, a director of the insurer must notify the Authority as soon as practicable after he becomes aware of it.

(3)　A person who fails to comply with subsection (2) is guilty of an offence and liable on summary conviction to a fine not exceeding level 5 on the standard scale.

[(4)　A winding up resolution may not be passed—
　(a)　as a written resolution (in accordance with Chapter 2 of Part 13 of the Companies Act 2006), or
　(b)　at a meeting called in accordance with section 307(4) to (6) or 337(2) of that Act (agreement of members to calling of meeting at short notice).]

(5)　A copy of a winding-up resolution forwarded to the registrar of companies in accordance with [section 30 of the Companies Act 2006] must be accompanied by a certificate issued by the Authority stating that it consents to the voluntary winding up of the insurer.

(6)　If subsection (5) is complied with, the voluntary winding up is to be treated as having commenced at the time the resolution was passed.

(7)　If subsection (5) is not complied with, the resolution has no effect.

(8)　"Winding-up resolution" means a resolution for voluntary winding up of an insurer effecting or carrying out contracts of long-term insurance.

[393]

NOTES
Sub-s (4): substituted by the Companies Act 2006 (Commencement No 3, Consequential Amendments, Transitional Provisions and Savings) Order 2007, SI 2007/2194, art 10(1), Sch 4, Pt 3, para 93(1), (2), as from 1 October 2007.
Sub-s (5): words in square brackets substituted by SI 2007/2194, art 10(1), Sch 4, Pt 3, para 93(1), (3), as from 1 October 2007.

Winding up by the court

367 Winding-up petitions

(1)   The Authority may present a petition to the court for the winding up of a body which—
   (a)   is, or has been, an authorised person;
   (b)   is, or has been, an appointed representative; or
   (c)   is carrying on, or has carried on, a regulated activity in contravention of the general prohibition.

(2)   In subsection (1) "body" includes any partnership.

(3)   On such a petition, the court may wind up the body if—
   (a)   the body is unable to pay its debts within the meaning of section 123 or 221 of the 1986 Act (or Article 103 or 185 of the 1989 Order); or
   (b)   the court is of the opinion that it is just and equitable that it should be wound up.

(4)   If a body is in default on an obligation to pay a sum due and payable under an agreement, it is to be treated for the purpose of subsection (3)(a) as unable to pay its debts.

(5)   "Agreement" means an agreement the making or performance of which constitutes or is part of a regulated activity carried on by the body concerned.

(6)   Subsection (7) applies if a petition is presented under subsection (1) for the winding up of a partnership—
   (a)   on the ground mentioned in subsection (3)(b); or
   (b)   in Scotland, on a ground mentioned in subsection (3)(a) or (b).

(7)   The court has jurisdiction, and the 1986 Act (or the 1989 Order) has effect, as if the partnership were an unregistered company as defined by section 220 of that Act (or Article 184 of that Order).

[394]

NOTES
Transitional provisions: as to the application of this section to a body that had been an authorised institution within the meaning of the Banking Act 1987 (repealed by the Financial Services and Markets Act 2000 (Consequential Amendments and Repeals) Order 2001, SI 2001/3649, art 3(1)(d)), or which, before 1 December 2001, contravened s 3 of the 1987 Act (restriction on acceptance of deposits), see the Financial Services and Markets Act 2000 (Transitional Provisions and Savings) (Civil Remedies, Discipline, Criminal Offences etc) (No 2) Order 2001, SI 2001/3083, art 12.
Limited liability partnerships: as to the application of this section to LLPs, see the note at the beginning of this Act.

368 Winding-up petitions: EEA and Treaty firms

The Authority may not present a petition to the court under section 367 for the winding up of—
   (a)   an EEA firm which qualifies for authorisation under Schedule 3, or
   (b)   a Treaty firm which qualifies for authorisation under Schedule 4,

unless it has been asked to do so by the home state regulator of the firm concerned.

[395]

369 Insurers: service of petition etc on Authority

(1)   If a person other than the Authority presents a petition for the winding up of an authorised person with permission to effect or carry out contracts of insurance, the petitioner must serve a copy of the petition on the Authority.

(2)   If a person other than the Authority applies to have a provisional liquidator appointed under section 135 of the 1986 Act (or Article 115 of the 1989 Order) in respect of an authorised person with permission to effect or carry out contracts of insurance, the applicant must serve a copy of the application on the Authority.

[396]

[369A Reclaim funds: service of petition etc on Authority

(1)   If a person other than the Authority presents a petition for the winding up of an authorised reclaim fund, the petitioner must serve a copy of the petition on the Authority.

(2)   If a person other than the Authority applies to have a provisional liquidator appointed under section 135 of the 1986 Act (or Article 115 of the 1989 Order) in respect of an authorised reclaim fund, the applicant must serve a copy of the application on the Authority.

(3)   In this section "authorised reclaim fund" means a reclaim fund within the meaning given by section 5(1) of the Dormant Bank and Building Society Accounts Act 2008 that is authorised for the purposes of this Act.]

[396A]

NOTES
Commencement: to be appointed.
Inserted by the Dormant Bank and Building Society Accounts Act 2008, s 15, Sch 2, para 7, as from a day to be appointed.

370   Liquidator's duty to report to Authority

If—
(a)   a company is being wound up voluntarily or a body is being wound up on a petition presented by a person other than the Authority, and
(b)   it appears to the liquidator that the company or body is carrying on, or has carried on, a regulated activity in contravention of the general prohibition,
the liquidator must report the matter to the Authority without delay.

[397]

NOTES
Limited liability partnerships: as to the application of this section to LLPs, see the note at the beginning of this Act.

371   Authority's powers to participate in proceedings

(1)   This section applies if a person other than the Authority presents a petition for the winding up of a body which—
(a)   is, or has been, an authorised person;
(b)   is, or has been, an appointed representative; or
(c)   is carrying on, or has carried on, a regulated activity in contravention of the general prohibition.

(2)   The Authority is entitled to be heard—
(a)   at the hearing of the petition; and
(b)   at any other hearing of the court in relation to the body under or by virtue of Part IV or V of the 1986 Act (or Part V or VI of the 1989 Order).

(3)   Any notice or other document required to be sent to a creditor of the body must also be sent to the Authority.

(4)   A person appointed for the purpose by the Authority is entitled—
(a)   to attend any meeting of creditors of the body;
(b)   to attend any meeting of a committee established for the purposes of Part IV or V of the 1986 Act under section 101 of that Act or under section 141 or 142 of that Act;
(c)   to attend any meeting of a committee established for the purposes of Part V or VI of the 1989 Order under Article 87 of that Order or under Article 120 of that Order; and
(d)   to make representations as to any matter for decision at such a meeting.

(5)   If, during the course of the winding up of a company, a compromise or arrangement is proposed between the company and its creditors, or any class of them, the Authority may apply to the court under [section 896 or 899 of the Companies Act 2006].

[398]

NOTES
Sub-s (5): words in square brackets substituted by the Companies Act 2006 (Consequential Amendments etc) Order 2008, SI 2008/948, art 3(1), Sch 1, Pt 2, para 211(4), as from 6 April 2008.
Limited liability partnerships: as to the application of this section to LLPs, see the note at the beginning of this Act.

Bankruptcy

372   Petitions

(1)   The Authority may present a petition to the court—
(a)   under section 264 of the 1986 Act (or Article 238 of the 1989 Order) for a bankruptcy order to be made against an individual; or
(b)   under section 5 of the 1985 Act for the sequestration of the estate of an individual.

(2)   But such a petition may be presented only on the ground that—

(a)   the individual appears to be unable to pay a regulated activity debt; or

(b)   the individual appears to have no reasonable prospect of being able to pay a regulated activity debt.

(3)   An individual appears to be unable to pay a regulated activity debt if he is in default on an obligation to pay a sum due and payable under an agreement.

(4)   An individual appears to have no reasonable prospect of being able to pay a regulated activity debt if—

(a)   the Authority has served on him a demand requiring him to establish to the satisfaction of the Authority that there is a reasonable prospect that he will be able to pay a sum payable under an agreement when it falls due;

(b)   at least three weeks have elapsed since the demand was served; and

(c)   the demand has been neither complied with nor set aside in accordance with rules.

(5)   A demand made under subsection (4)(a) is to be treated for the purposes of the 1986 Act (or the 1989 Order) as if it were a statutory demand under section 268 of that Act (or Article 242 of that Order).

(6)   For the purposes of a petition presented in accordance with subsection (1)(b)—

(a)   the Authority is to be treated as a qualified creditor; and

(b)   a ground mentioned in subsection (2) constitutes apparent insolvency.

(7)   "Individual" means an individual—

(a)   who is, or has been, an authorised person; or

(b)   who is carrying on, or has carried on, a regulated activity in contravention of the general prohibition.

(8)   "Agreement" means an agreement the making or performance of which constitutes or is part of a regulated activity carried on by the individual concerned.

(9)   "Rules" means—

(a)   in England and Wales, rules made under section 412 of the 1986 Act;

(b)   in Scotland, rules made by order by the Treasury, after consultation with the Scottish Ministers, for the purposes of this section; and

(c)   in Northern Ireland, rules made under Article 359 of the 1989 Order.

[399]

_____

NOTES

Rules: the Bankruptcy (Financial Services and Markets Act 2000) (Scotland) Rules 2001, SI 2001/3591 at **[2516]**.

_____

373   Insolvency practitioner's duty to report to Authority

(1)   If—

(a)   a bankruptcy order or sequestration award is in force in relation to an individual by virtue of a petition presented by a person other than the Authority, and

(b)   it appears to the insolvency practitioner that the individual is carrying on, or has carried on, a regulated activity in contravention of the general prohibition,

the insolvency practitioner must report the matter to the Authority without delay.

(2)   "Bankruptcy order" means a bankruptcy order under Part IX of the 1986 Act (or Part IX of the 1989 Order).

(3)   "Sequestration award" means an award of sequestration under section 12 of the 1985 Act.

(4)   "Individual" includes an entity mentioned in section 374(1)(c).

[400]

374   Authority's powers to participate in proceedings

(1)   This section applies if a person other than the Authority presents a petition to the court—

(a)   under section 264 of the 1986 Act (or Article 238 of the 1989 Order) for a bankruptcy order to be made against an individual;

(b)   under section 5 of the 1985 Act for the sequestration of the estate of an individual; or

(c)   under section 6 of the 1985 Act for the sequestration of the estate belonging to or held for or jointly by the members of an entity mentioned in subsection (1) of that section.

(2)   The Authority is entitled to be heard—

(a)   at the hearing of the petition; and

(b)   at any other hearing in relation to the individual or entity under—

(i)   Part IX of the 1986 Act;

(ii)   Part IX of the 1989 Order; or

(iii)   the 1985 Act.

(3)   A copy of the report prepared under section 274 of the 1986 Act (or Article 248 of the 1989 Order) must also be sent to the Authority.

(4)   A person appointed for the purpose by the Authority is entitled—
- (a)   to attend any meeting of creditors of the individual or entity;
- (b)   to attend any meeting of a committee established under section 301 of the 1986 Act (or Article 274 of the 1989 Order);
- (c)   to attend any meeting of commissioners held under paragraph 17 or 18 of Schedule 6 to the 1985 Act; and
- (d)   to make representations as to any matter for decision at such a meeting.

(5)   "Individual" means an individual who—
- (a)   is, or has been, an authorised person; or
- (b)   is carrying on, or has carried on, a regulated activity in contravention of the general prohibition.

(6)   "Entity" means an entity which—
- (a)   is, or has been, an authorised person; or
- (b)   is carrying on, or has carried on, a regulated activity in contravention of the general prohibition.

[401]

Provisions against debt avoidance

375   Authority's right to apply for an order

(1)   The Authority may apply for an order under section 423 of the 1986 Act (or Article 367 of the 1989 Order) in relation to a debtor if—
- (a)   at the time the transaction at an undervalue was entered into, the debtor was carrying on a regulated activity (whether or not in contravention of the general prohibition); and
- (b)   a victim of the transaction is or was party to an agreement entered into with the debtor, the making or performance of which constituted or was part of a regulated activity carried on by the debtor.

(2)   An application made under this section is to be treated as made on behalf of every victim of the transaction to whom subsection (1)(b) applies.

(3)   Expressions which are given a meaning in Part XVI of the 1986 Act (or Article 367, 368 or 369 of the 1989 Order) have the same meaning when used in this section.

[402]

Supplemental provisions concerning insurers

376   Continuation of contracts of long-term insurance where insurer in liquidation

(1)   This section applies in relation to the winding up of an insurer which effects or carries out contracts of long-term insurance.

(2)   Unless the court otherwise orders, the liquidator must carry on the insurer's business so far as it consists of carrying out the insurer's contracts of long-term insurance with a view to its being transferred as a going concern to a person who may lawfully carry out those contracts.

(3)   In carrying on the business, the liquidator—
- (a)   may agree to the variation of any contracts of insurance in existence when the winding up order is made; but
- (b)   must not effect any new contracts of insurance.

(4)   If the liquidator is satisfied that the interests of the creditors in respect of liabilities of the insurer attributable to contracts of long-term insurance effected by it require the appointment of a special manager, he may apply to the court.

(5)   On such an application, the court may appoint a special manager to act during such time as the court may direct.

(6)   The special manager is to have such powers, including any of the powers of a receiver or manager, as the court may direct.

(7)   Section 177(5) of the 1986 Act (or Article 151(5) of the 1989 Order) applies to a special manager appointed under subsection (5) as it applies to a special manager appointed under section 177 of the 1986 Act (or Article 151 of the 1989 Order).

(8)   If the court thinks fit, it may reduce the value of one or more of the contracts of long-term insurance effected by the insurer.

(9)   Any reduction is to be on such terms and subject to such conditions (if any) as the court thinks fit.

(10)   The court may, on the application of an official, appoint an independent actuary to investigate the insurer's business so far as it consists of carrying out its contracts of long-term insurance and to report to the official—
- (a)   on the desirability or otherwise of that part of the insurer's business being continued; and

(b)   on any reduction in the contracts of long-term insurance effected by the insurer that may be necessary for successful continuation of that part of the insurer's business.

(11)   "Official" means—
(a)   the liquidator;
(b)   a special manager appointed under subsection (5); or
(c)   the Authority.

(12)   The liquidator may make an application in the name of the insurer and on its behalf under Part VII without obtaining the permission that would otherwise be required by section 167 of, and Schedule 4 to, the 1986 Act (or Article 142 of, and Schedule 2 to, the 1989 Order).

[403]

377   Reducing the value of contracts instead of winding up

(1)   This section applies in relation to an insurer which has been proved to be unable to pay its debts.

(2)   If the court thinks fit, it may reduce the value of one or more of the insurer's contracts instead of making a winding up order.

(3)   Any reduction is to be on such terms and subject to such conditions (if any) as the court thinks fit.

[404]

NOTES
EEA insurers: this section does not apply in relation to an EEA insurer; see the Insurers (Reorganisation and Winding Up) Regulations 2004, SI 2004/353, reg 4 at **[3839]**.

378   Treatment of assets on winding up

(1)   The Treasury may by regulations provide for the treatment of the assets of an insurer on its winding up.

(2)   The regulations may, in particular, provide for—
(a)   assets representing a particular part of the insurer's business to be available only for meeting liabilities attributable to that part of the insurer's business;
(b)   separate general meetings of the creditors to be held in respect of liabilities attributable to a particular part of the insurer's business.

[405]

379   Winding-up rules

(1)   Winding-up rules may include provision—
(a)   for determining the amount of the liabilities of an insurer to policyholders of any class or description for the purpose of proof in a winding up; and
(b)   generally for carrying into effect the provisions of this Part with respect to the winding up of insurers.

(2)   Winding-up rules may, in particular, make provision for all or any of the following matters—
(a)   the identification of assets and liabilities;
(b)   the apportionment, between assets of different classes or descriptions, of—
(i)   the costs, charges and expenses of the winding up; and
(ii)   any debts of the insurer of a specified class or description;
(c)   the determination of the amount of liabilities of a specified description;
(d)   the application of assets for meeting liabilities of a specified description;
(e)   the application of assets representing any excess of a specified description.

(3)   "Specified" means specified in winding-up rules.

(4)   "Winding-up rules" means rules made under section 411 of the 1986 Act (or Article 359 of the 1989 Order).

(5)   Nothing in this section affects the power to make winding-up rules under the 1986 Act or the 1989 Order.

[406]

NOTES
Rules: the Insurers (Winding Up) Rules 2001, SI 2001/3635 at **[2596]**; the Insurers (Winding Up) (Scotland) Rules 2001, SI 2001/4040.

PART XXV
INJUNCTIONS AND RESTITUTION

Injunctions

380   Injunctions

(1)   If, on the application of the Authority or the Secretary of State, the court is satisfied—
   (a)   that there is a reasonable likelihood that any person will contravene a relevant requirement, or
   (b)   that any person has contravened a relevant requirement and that there is a reasonable likelihood that the contravention will continue or be repeated,

the court may make an order restraining (or in Scotland an interdict prohibiting) the contravention.

(2)   If on the application of the Authority or the Secretary of State the court is satisfied—
   (a)   that any person has contravened a relevant requirement, and
   (b)   that there are steps which could be taken for remedying the contravention,

the court may make an order requiring that person, and any other person who appears to have been knowingly concerned in the contravention, to take such steps as the court may direct to remedy it.

(3)   If, on the application of the Authority or the Secretary of State, the court is satisfied that any person may have—
   (a)   contravened a relevant requirement, or
   (b)   been knowingly concerned in the contravention of such a requirement,

it may make an order restraining (or in Scotland an interdict prohibiting) him from disposing of, or otherwise dealing with, any assets of his which it is satisfied he is reasonably likely to dispose of or otherwise deal with.

(4)   The jurisdiction conferred by this section is exercisable by the High Court and the Court of Session.

(5)   In subsection (2), references to remedying a contravention include references to mitigating its effect.

(6)   "Relevant requirement"—
   (a)   in relation to an application by the Authority, means a requirement—
      (i)   which is imposed by or under this Act [or by any directly applicable Community regulation made under the markets in financial instruments directive]; or
      (ii)   which is imposed by or under any other Act and whose contravention constitutes an offence which the Authority has power to prosecute under this Act;
   (b)   in relation to an application by the Secretary of State, means a requirement which is imposed by or under this Act and whose contravention constitutes an offence which the Secretary of State has power to prosecute under this Act.

(7)   In the application of subsection (6) to Scotland—
   (a)   in paragraph (a)(ii) for "which the Authority has power to prosecute under this Act" substitute "mentioned in paragraph (a) or (b) of section 402(1)"; and
   (b)   in paragraph (b) omit "which the Secretary of State has power to prosecute under this Act".

[407]

NOTES

Sub-s (6): words in square brackets inserted by the Financial Services and Markets Act 2000 (Markets in Financial Instruments) Regulations 2007, SI 2007/126, reg 3(5), Sch 5, paras 1, 13, as from 1 April 2007 (certain purposes (see reg 1(2) at **[4051]**)), and as from 1 November 2007 (otherwise).

Transitional provisions: any requirement, condition or prohibition imposed before 1 December 2001 by or under certain specified provisions is to be treated as a relevant requirement for the purposes of sub-s (2) above, and any restriction or requirement imposed by or under certain other provisions is to be treated as a relevant requirement for the purposes of sub-s (3)(a) above; see, in general, the Financial Services and Markets Act 2000 (Transitional Provisions and Savings) (Civil Remedies, Discipline, Criminal Offences etc) (No 2) Order 2001, SI 2001/3083, arts 2, 4. The specified provisions for the purposes of sub-ss (2), (3)(a) are listed in arts 2(3), 4(3) of the 2001 Order.

Note: for the purposes of this section a requirement imposed by the FSA under the Electronic Commerce Directive (Financial Services and Markets) Regulations 2002, SI 2002/1775 upon an incoming provider is to be treated as imposed on him by or under this Act; see reg 12(2) of those Regulations at **[2685]**.

---

381   Injunctions in cases of market abuse

(1)   If, on the application of the Authority, the court is satisfied—
   (a)   that there is a reasonable likelihood that any person will engage in market abuse, or
   (b)   that any person is or has engaged in market abuse and that there is a reasonable likelihood that the market abuse will continue or be repeated,

the court may make an order restraining (or in Scotland an interdict prohibiting) the market abuse.

(2)   If on the application of the Authority the court is satisfied—

    (a)   that any person is or has engaged in market abuse, and

    (b)   that there are steps which could be taken for remedying the market abuse,

the court may make an order requiring him to take such steps as the court may direct to remedy it.

    (3)   Subsection (4) applies if, on the application of the Authority, the court is satisfied that any person—

    (a)   may be engaged in market abuse; or

    (b)   may have been engaged in market abuse.

    (4)   The court make an order restraining (or in Scotland an interdict prohibiting) the person concerned from disposing of, or otherwise dealing with, any assets of his which it is satisfied that he is reasonably likely to dispose of, or otherwise deal with.

    (5)   The jurisdiction conferred by this section is exercisable by the High Court and the Court of Session.

    (6)   In subsection (2), references to remedying any market abuse include references to mitigating its effect.

[408]

Restitution orders

382   Restitution orders

    (1)   The court may, on the application of the Authority or the Secretary of State, make an order under subsection (2) if it is satisfied that a person has contravened a relevant requirement, or been knowingly concerned in the contravention of such a requirement, and—

    (a)   that profits have accrued to him as a result of the contravention; or

    (b)   that one or more persons have suffered loss or been otherwise adversely affected as a result of the contravention.

    (2)   The court may order the person concerned to pay to the Authority such sum as appears to the court to be just having regard—

    (a)   in a case within paragraph (a) of subsection (1), to the profits appearing to the court to have accrued;

    (b)   in a case within paragraph (b) of that subsection, to the extent of the loss or other adverse effect;

    (c)   in a case within both of those paragraphs, to the profits appearing to the court to have accrued and to the extent of the loss or other adverse effect.

    (3)   Any amount paid to the Authority in pursuance of an order under subsection (2) must be paid by it to such qualifying person or distributed by it among such qualifying persons as the court may direct.

    (4)   On an application under subsection (1) the court may require the person concerned to supply it with such accounts or other information as it may require for any one or more of the following purposes—

    (a)   establishing whether any and, if so, what profits have accrued to him as mentioned in paragraph (a) of that subsection;

    (b)   establishing whether any person or persons have suffered any loss or adverse effect as mentioned in paragraph (b) of that subsection and, if so, the extent of that loss or adverse effect; and

    (c)   determining how any amounts are to be paid or distributed under subsection (3).

    (5)   The court may require any accounts or other information supplied under subsection (4) to be verified in such manner as it may direct.

    (6)   The jurisdiction conferred by this section is exercisable by the High Court and the Court of Session.

    (7)   Nothing in this section affects the right of any person other than the Authority or the Secretary of State to bring proceedings in respect of the matters to which this section applies.

    (8)   "Qualifying person" means a person appearing to the court to be someone—

    (a)   to whom the profits mentioned in subsection (1)(a) are attributable; or

    (b)   who has suffered the loss or adverse effect mentioned in subsection (1)(b).

    (9)   "Relevant requirement"—

    (a)   in relation to an application by the Authority, means a requirement—

        (i)   which is imposed by or under this Act [or by any directly applicable Community regulation made under the markets in financial instruments directive]; or

        (ii)   which is imposed by or under any other Act and whose contravention constitutes an offence which the Authority has power to prosecute under this Act;

    (b)   in relation to an application by the Secretary of State, means a requirement which is imposed by or under this Act and whose contravention constitutes an offence which the Secretary of State has power to prosecute under this Act.

(10)   In the application of subsection (9) to Scotland—
    (a)   in paragraph (a)(ii) for "which the Authority has power to prosecute under this Act" substitute "mentioned in paragraph (a) or (b) of section 402(1); and
    (b)   in paragraph (b) omit "which the Secretary of State has power to prosecute under this Act".

[409]

NOTES

Sub-s (9): words in square brackets inserted by the Financial Services and Markets Act 2000 (Markets in Financial Instruments) Regulations 2007, SI 2007/126, reg 3(5), Sch 5, paras 1, 14, as from 1 April 2007 (certain purposes (see reg 1(2) at **[4051]**)), and as from 1 November 2007 (otherwise).

Transitional provisions: any requirement, condition or prohibition imposed before 1 December 2001 by or under certain specified provisions is to be treated as a relevant requirement for the purposes of this section; see the Financial Services and Markets Act 2000 (Transitional Provisions and Savings) (Civil Remedies, Discipline, Criminal Offences etc) (No 2) Order 2001, SI 2001/3083, art 2. The specified provisions are listed in art 2(3) of the 2001 Order.

Note: for the purposes of this section a requirement imposed by the FSA under the Electronic Commerce Directive (Financial Services and Markets) Regulations 2002, SI 2002/1775 upon an incoming provider is to be treated as imposed on him by or under this Act; see reg 12(2) of those Regulations at **[2685]**.

383   Restitution orders in cases of market abuse

(1)   The court may, on the application of the Authority, make an order under subsection (4) if it is satisfied that a person ("the person concerned")—
    (a)   has engaged in market abuse, or
    (b)   by taking or refraining from taking any action has required or encouraged another person or persons to engage in behaviour which, if engaged in by the person concerned, would amount to market abuse,
and the condition mentioned in subsection (2) is fulfilled.

(2)   The condition is—
    (a)   that profits have accrued to the person concerned as a result; or
    (b)   that one or more persons have suffered loss or been otherwise adversely affected as a result.

(3)   But the court may not make an order under subsection (4) if it is satisfied that—
    (a)   the person concerned believed, on reasonable grounds, that his behaviour did not fall within paragraph (a) or (b) of subsection (1); or
    (b)   he took all reasonable precautions and exercised all due diligence to avoid behaving in a way which fell within paragraph (a) or (b) of subsection (1).

(4)   The court may order the person concerned to pay to the Authority such sum as appears to the court to be just having regard—
    (a)   in a case within paragraph (a) of subsection (2), to the profits appearing to the court to have accrued;
    (b)   in a case within paragraph (b) of that subsection, to the extent of the loss or other adverse effect;
    (c)   in a case within both of those paragraphs, to the profits appearing to the court to have accrued and to the extent of the loss or other adverse effect.

(5)   Any amount paid to the Authority in pursuance of an order under subsection (4) must be paid by it to such qualifying person or distributed by it among such qualifying persons as the court may direct.

(6)   On an application under subsection (1) the court may require the person concerned to supply it with such accounts or other information as it may require for any one or more of the following purposes—
    (a)   establishing whether any and, if so, what profits have accrued to him as mentioned in subsection (2)(a);
    (b)   establishing whether any person or persons have suffered any loss or adverse effect as mentioned in subsection (2)(b) and, if so, the extent of that loss or adverse effect; and
    (c)   determining how any amounts are to be paid or distributed under subsection (5).

(7)   The court may require any accounts or other information supplied under subsection (6) to be verified in such manner as it may direct.

(8)   The jurisdiction conferred by this section is exercisable by the High Court and the Court of Session.

(9)   Nothing in this section affects the right of any person other than the Authority to bring proceedings in respect of the matters to which this section applies.

(10)   "Qualifying person" means a person appearing to the court to be someone—
    (a)   to whom the profits mentioned in paragraph (a) of subsection (2) are attributable; or

(b)   who has suffered the loss or adverse effect mentioned in paragraph (b) of that subsection.

[410]

Restitution required by Authority

384   Power of Authority to require restitution

(1)   The Authority may exercise the power in subsection (5) if it is satisfied that an authorised person ("the person concerned") has contravened a relevant requirement, or been knowingly concerned in the contravention of such a requirement, and—
   (a)   that profits have accrued to him as a result of the contravention; or
   (b)   that one or more persons have suffered loss or been otherwise adversely affected as a result of the contravention.

(2)   The Authority may exercise the power in subsection (5) if it is satisfied that a person ("the person concerned")—
   (a)   has engaged in market abuse, or
   (b)   by taking or refraining from taking any action has required or encouraged another person or persons to engage in behaviour which, if engaged in by the person concerned, would amount to market abuse,
and the condition mentioned in subsection (3) is fulfilled,

(3)   The condition is—
   (a)   that profits have accrued to the person concerned as a result of the market abuse; or
   (b)   that one or more persons have suffered loss or been otherwise adversely affected as a result of the market abuse.

(4)   But the Authority may not exercise that power as a result of subsection (2) if, having considered any representations made to it in response to a warning notice, there are reasonable grounds for it to be satisfied that—
   (a)   the person concerned believed, on reasonable grounds, that his behaviour did not fall within paragraph (a) or (b) of that subsection; or
   (b)   he took all reasonable precautions and exercised all due diligence to avoid behaving in a way which fell within paragraph (a) or (b) of that subsection.

(5)   The power referred to in subsections (1) and (2) is a power to require the person concerned, in accordance with such arrangements as the Authority considers appropriate, to pay to the appropriate person or distribute among the appropriate persons such amount as appears to the Authority to be just having regard—
   (a)   in a case within paragraph (a) of subsection (1) or (3), to the profits appearing to the Authority to have accrued;
   (b)   in a case within paragraph (b) of subsection (1) or (3), to the extent of the loss or other adverse effect;
   (c)   in a case within paragraphs (a) and (b) of subsection (1) or (3), to the profits appearing to the Authority to have accrued and to the extent of the loss or other adverse effect.

(6)   "Appropriate person" means a person appearing to the Authority to be someone—
   (a)   to whom the profits mentioned in paragraph (a) of subsection (1) or (3) are attributable; or
   (b)   who has suffered the loss or adverse effect mentioned in paragraph (b) of subsection (1) or (3).

(7)   "Relevant requirement" means—
   (a)   a requirement imposed by or under this Act [or by any directly applicable Community regulation made under the markets in financial instruments directive]; and
   (b)   a requirement which is imposed by or under any other Act and whose contravention constitutes an offence in relation to which this Act confers power to prosecute on the Authority.

(8)   In the application of subsection (7) to Scotland, in paragraph (b) for "in relation to which this Act confers power to prosecute on the Authority" substitute "mentioned in paragraph (a) or (b) of section 402(1)".

[411]

NOTES

Sub-s (7): words in square brackets inserted by the Financial Services and Markets Act 2000 (Markets in Financial Instruments) Regulations 2007, SI 2007/126, reg 3(5), Sch 5, paras 1, 15, as from 1 April 2007 (certain purposes (see reg 1(2) at [4051])), and as from 1 November 2007 (otherwise).

Transitional provisions: as to the power of the Authority under sub-s (5) in relation to certain conduct before 1 December 2001, see the Financial Services and Markets Act 2000 (Transitional Provisions and Savings) (Civil Remedies, Discipline, Criminal Offences etc) (No 2) Order 2001, SI 2001/3083, art 3.

Note: for the purposes of this section a requirement imposed by the FSA under the Electronic Commerce Directive (Financial Services and Markets) Regulations 2002, SI 2002/1775 upon an authorised incoming provider is to be treated as imposed on him by or under this Act; see reg 12(1) of those Regulations at **[2685]**.

385   Warning notices

(1)   If the Authority proposes to exercise the power under section 384(5) in relation to a person, it must give him a warning notice.

(2)   A warning notice under this section must specify the amount which the Authority proposes to require the person concerned to pay or distribute as mentioned in section 384(5).

[412]

386   Decision notices

(1)   If the Authority decides to exercise the power under section 384(5), it must give a decision notice to the person in relation to whom the power is exercised.

(2)   The decision notice must—
   (a)   state the amount that he is to pay or distribute as mentioned in section 384(5);
   (b)   identify the person or persons to whom that amount is to be paid or among whom that amount is to be distributed; and
   (c)   state the arrangements in accordance with which the payment or distribution is to be made.

(3)   If the Authority decides to exercise the power under section 384(5), the person in relation to whom it is exercised may refer the matter to the Tribunal.

[413]

PART XXVI
NOTICES

Warning notices

387   Warning notices

(1)   A warning notice must—
   (a)   state the action which the Authority proposes to take;
   (b)   be in writing;
   (c)   give reasons for the proposed action;
   (d)   state whether section 394 applies; and
   (e)   if that section applies, describe its effect and state whether any secondary material exists to which the person concerned must be allowed access under it.

(2)   The warning notice must specify a reasonable period (which may not be less than 28 days) within which the person to whom it is given may make representations to the Authority.

(3)   The Authority may extend the period specified in the notice.

(4)   The Authority must then decide, within a reasonable period, whether to give the person concerned a decision notice.

[414]

NOTES
   Note: "secondary material" is defined in s 394(6) at **[421]**.
   Not be less than 28 days: note that any provision of this Act (other than a provision of Part VI) authorising or requiring a person to do anything within a specified number of days must not take into account any day which is a public holiday in any part of the United Kingdom; see s 417(3) at **[443]**.

Decision notices

388   Decision notices

(1)   A decision notice must—
   (a)   be in writing;
   (b)   give the Authority's reasons for the decision to take the action to which the notice relates;
   (c)   state whether section 394 applies;
   (d)   if that section applies, describe its effect and state whether any secondary material exists to which the person concerned must be allowed access under it; and
   (e)   give an indication of—
      (i)   any right to have the matter referred to the Tribunal which is given by this Act; and
      (ii)   the procedure on such a reference.

(2)   If the decision notice was preceded by a warning notice, the action to which the decision notice relates must be action under the same Part as the action proposed in the warning notice.

(3) The Authority may, before it takes the action to which a decision notice ("the original notice") relates, give the person concerned a further decision notice which relates to different action in respect of the same matter.

(4) The Authority may give a further decision notice as a result of subsection (3) only if the person to whom the original notice was given consents.

(5) If the person to whom a decision notice is given under subsection (3) had the right to refer the matter to which the original decision notice related to the Tribunal, he has that right as respects the decision notice under subsection (3).

[415]

Conclusion of proceedings

389 Notices of discontinuance

(1) If the Authority decides not to take—
   (a) the action proposed in a warning notice, or
   (b) the action to which a decision notice relates,
it must give a notice of discontinuance to the person to whom the warning notice or decision notice was given.

(2) But subsection (1) does not apply if the discontinuance of the proceedings concerned results in the granting of an application made by the person to whom the warning or decision notice was given.

(3) A notice of discontinuance must identify the proceedings which are being discontinued.

[416]

390 Final notices

(1) If the Authority has given a person a decision notice and the matter was not referred to the Tribunal within the period mentioned in section 133(1), the Authority must, on taking the action to which the decision notice relates, give the person concerned and any person to whom the decision notice was copied a final notice.

(2) If the Authority has given a person a decision notice and the matter was referred to the Tribunal, the Authority must, on taking action in accordance with any directions given by—
   (a) the Tribunal, or
   (b) the court under section 137,
give that person and any person to whom the decision notice was copied a final notice.

(3) A final notice about a statement must—
   (a) set out the terms of the statement;
   (b) give details of the manner in which, and the date on which, the statement will be published.

(4) A final notice about an order must—
   (a) set out the terms of the order;
   (b) state the date from which the order has effect.

(5) A final notice about a penalty must—
   (a) state the amount of the penalty;
   (b) state the manner in which, and the period within which, the penalty is to be paid;
   (c) give details of the way in which the penalty will be recovered if it is not paid by the date stated in the notice.

(6) A final notice about a requirement to make a payment or distribution in accordance with section 384(5) must state—
   (a) the persons to whom,
   (b) the manner in which, and
   (c) the period within which,
it must be made.

(7) In any other case, the final notice must—
   (a) give details of the action being taken;
   (b) state the date on which the action is to be taken.

(8) The period stated under subsection (5)(b) or (6)(c) may not be less than 14 days beginning with the date on which the final notice is given.

(9) If all or any of the amount of a penalty payable under a final notice is outstanding at the end of the period stated under subsection (5)(b), the Authority may recover the outstanding amount as a debt due to it.

(10)   If all or any of a required payment or distribution has not been made at the end of a period stated in a final notice under subsection (6)(c), the obligation to make the payment is enforceable, on the application of the Authority, by injunction or, in Scotland, by an order under section 45 of the Court of Session Act 1988.

[417]

NOTES
   Not be less than 14 days: note that any provision of this Act (other than a provision of Part VI) authorising or requiring a person to do anything within a specified number of days must not take into account any day which is a public holiday in any part of the United Kingdom; see s 417(3) at **[443]**.

Publication

391   Publication

(1)   Neither the Authority nor a person to whom a warning notice or decision notice is given or copied may publish the notice or any details concerning it.

(2)   A notice of discontinuance must state that, if the person to whom the notice is given consents, the Authority may publish such information as it considers appropriate about the matter to which the discontinued proceedings related.

(3)   A copy of a notice of discontinuance must be accompanied by a statement that, if the person to whom the notice is copied consents, the Authority may publish such information as it considers appropriate about the matter to which the discontinued proceedings related, so far as relevant to that person.

(4)   The Authority must publish such information about the matter to which a final notice relates as it considers appropriate.

(5)   When a supervisory notice takes effect, the Authority must publish such information about the matter to which the notice relates as it considers appropriate.

(6)   But the Authority may not publish information under this section if publication of it would, in its opinion, be unfair to the person with respect to whom the action was taken or prejudicial to the interests of consumers.

(7)   Information is to be published under this section in such manner as the Authority considers appropriate.

(8)   For the purposes of determining when a supervisory notice takes effect, a matter to which the notice relates is open to review if—
   (a)   the period during which any person may refer the matter to the Tribunal is still running;
   (b)   the matter has been referred to the Tribunal but has not been dealt with;
   (c)   the matter has been referred to the Tribunal and dealt with but the period during which an appeal may be brought against the Tribunal's decision is still running; or
   (d)   such an appeal has been brought but has not been determined.

(9)   "Notice of discontinuance" means a notice given under section 389.

(10)   "Supervisory notice" has the same meaning as in section 395.

(11)   "Consumers" means persons who are consumers for the purposes of section 138.

[418]

NOTES
   Extended definition of "consumer": see the note to s 138 at **[166]**.

Third party rights and access to evidence

392   Application of sections 393 and 394

Sections 393 and 394 apply to—
   (a)   a warning notice given in accordance with section 54(1), 57(1), 63(3), 67(1), 88(4)(b), 89(2), 92(1), 126(1), 207(1), 255(1), 280(1), 331(1), 345(2) (whether as a result of subsection (1) of that section or section 249(1))[, 385(1) or 412B(4) or (8)];
   (b)   a decision notice given in accordance with section 54(2), 57(3), 63(4), 67(4), 88(6)(b), 89(3), 92(4), 127(1), 208(1), 255(2), 280(2), 331(3), 345(3) (whether as a result of subsection (1) of that section or section 249(1))[, 386(1) or 412B(5) or (9)].

[419]

NOTES
   Words in square brackets substituted by the Financial Services and Markets Act 2000 (Markets in Financial Instruments) Regulations 2007, SI 2007/126, reg 3(5), Sch 5, paras 1, 16, as from 1 April 2007 (certain purposes (see reg 1(2) at **[4051]**)), and as from 1 November 2007 (otherwise).

393 Third party rights

(1)   If any of the reasons contained in a warning notice to which this section applies relates to a matter which—

(a)   identifies a person ("the third party") other than the person to whom the notice is given, and

(b)   in the opinion of the Authority, is prejudicial to the third party,

a copy of the notice must be given to the third party.

(2)   Subsection (1) does not require a copy to be given to the third party if the Authority—

(a)   has given him a separate warning notice in relation to the same matter; or

(b)   gives him such a notice at the same time as it gives the warning notice which identifies him.

(3)   The notice copied to a third party under subsection (1) must specify a reasonable period (which may not be less than 28 days) within which he may make representations to the Authority.

(4)   If any of the reasons contained in a decision notice to which this section applies relates to a matter which—

(a)   identifies a person ("the third party") other than the person to whom the decision notice is given, and

(b)   in the opinion of the Authority, is prejudicial to the third party,

a copy of the notice must be given to the third party.

(5)   If the decision notice was preceded by a warning notice, a copy of the decision notice must (unless it has been given under subsection (4)) be given to each person to whom the warning notice was copied.

(6)   Subsection (4) does not require a copy to be given to the third party if the Authority—

(a)   has given him a separate decision notice in relation to the same matter; or

(b)   gives him such a notice at the same time as it gives the decision notice which identifies him.

(7)   Neither subsection (1) nor subsection (4) requires a copy of a notice to be given to a third party if the Authority considers it impracticable to do so.

(8)   Subsections (9) to (11) apply if the person to whom a decision notice is given has a right to refer the matter to the Tribunal.

(9)   A person to whom a copy of the notice is given under this section may refer to the Tribunal—

(a)   the decision in question, so far as it is based on a reason of the kind mentioned in subsection (4); or

(b)   any opinion expressed by the Authority in relation to him.

(10)   The copy must be accompanied by an indication of the third party's right to make a reference under subsection (9) and of the procedure on such a reference.

(11)   A person who alleges that a copy of the notice should have been given to him, but was not, may refer to the Tribunal the alleged failure and—

(a)   the decision in question, so far as it is based on a reason of the kind mentioned in subsection (4); or

(b)   any opinion expressed by the Authority in relation to him.

(12)   Section 394 applies to a third party as it applies to the person to whom the notice to which this section applies was given, in so far as the material which the Authority must disclose under that section relates to the matter which identifies the third party.

(13)   A copy of a notice given to a third party under this section must be accompanied by a description of the effect of section 394 as it applies to him.

(14)   Any person to whom a warning notice or decision notice was copied under this section must be given a copy of a notice of discontinuance applicable to the proceedings to which the warning notice or decision notice related.

[420]

394 Access to Authority material

(1)   If the Authority gives a person ("A") a notice to which this section applies, it must—

(a)   allow him access to the material on which it relied in taking the decision which gave rise to the obligation to give the notice;

(b)   allow him access to any secondary material which, in the opinion of the Authority, might undermine that decision.

(2)   But the Authority does not have to allow A access to material under subsection (1) if the material is excluded material or it—

(a)   relates to a case involving a person other than A; and

  (b)   was taken into account by the Authority in A's case only for purposes of comparison
         with other cases.

  (3)   The Authority may refuse A access to particular material which it would otherwise have to
allow him access to if, in its opinion, allowing him access to the material—
  (a)   would not be in the public interest; or
  (b)   would not be fair, having regard to—
         (i)   the likely significance of the material to A in relation to the matter in respect of
                which he has been given a notice to which this section applies; and
         (ii)   the potential prejudice to the commercial interests of a person other than A which
                would be caused by the material's disclosure.

  (4)   If the Authority does not allow A access to material because it is excluded material
consisting of a protected item, it must give A written notice of—
  (a)   the existence of the protected item; and
  (b)   the Authority's decision not to allow him access to it.

  (5)   If the Authority refuses under subsection (3) to allow A access to material, it must give him
written notice of—
  (a)   the refusal; and
  (b)   the reasons for it.

  (6)   "Secondary material" means material, other than material falling within paragraph (a) of
subsection (1) which—
  (a)   was considered by the Authority in reaching the decision mentioned in that paragraph; or
  (b)   was obtained by the Authority in connection with the matter to which the notice to
         which this section applies relates but which was not considered by it in reaching that
         decision.

  (7)   "Excluded material" means material which—
  [(a)   is material the disclosure of which for the purposes of or in connection with any legal
         proceedings is prohibited by section 17 of the Regulation of Investigatory Powers
         Act 2000; or]
  (c)   is a protected item (as defined in section 413).

                                                                                          [421]

NOTES
   Sub-s (7): para (a) substituted, for original paras (a), (b), by the Regulation of Investigatory Powers Act 2000,
s 82(1), Sch 4, para 11, as from 2 October 2000.

The Authority's procedures

395   The Authority's procedures

  (1)   The Authority must determine the procedure that it proposes to follow in relation to the
giving of—
  (a)   supervisory notices; and
  (b)   warning notices and decision notices.

  (2)   That procedure must be designed to secure, among other things, that the decision which
gives rise to the obligation to give any such notice is taken by a person not directly involved in
establishing the evidence on which that decision is based.

  (3)   But the procedure may permit a decision which gives rise to an obligation to give a
supervisory notice to be taken by a person other than a person mentioned in subsection (2) if—
  (a)   the Authority considers that, in the particular case, it is necessary in order to protect the
         interests of consumers; and
  (b)   the person taking the decision is of a level of seniority laid down by the procedure.

  (4)   A level of seniority laid down by the procedure for the purposes of subsection (3)(b) must
be appropriate to the importance of the decision.

  (5)   The Authority must issue a statement of the procedure.

  (6)   The statement must be published in the way appearing to the Authority to be best calculated
to bring it to the attention of the public.

  (7)   The Authority may charge a reasonable fee for providing a person with a copy of the
statement.

  (8)   The Authority must, without delay, give the Treasury a copy of any statement which it
issues under this section.

  (9)   When giving a supervisory notice, or a warning notice or decision notice, the Authority
must follow its stated procedure.

  (10)   If the Authority changes the procedure in a material way, it must publish a revised
statement.

(11)   The Authority's failure in a particular case to follow its procedure as set out in the latest published statement does not affect the validity of a notice given in that case.

(12)   But subsection (11) does not prevent the Tribunal from taking into account any such failure in considering a matter referred to it.

(13)   "Supervisory notice" means a notice given in accordance with section—
   (a)   53(4), (7) or (8)(b);
   (b)   78(2) or (5);
   [(bza) 78A(2) or (8)(b);]
   [(ba) 96C;]
   [(bb) 87O(2) or (5);]
   (c)   197(3), (6) or (7)(b);
   (d)   259(3), (8) or (9)(b);
   (e)   268(3), (7)(a) or (9)(a) (as a result of subsection (8)(b));
   (f)   282(3), (6) or (7)(b);
   (g)   321(2) or (5).

[422]

NOTES
   Sub-s (13): para (bza) inserted by the Regulatory Reform (Financial Services and Markets Act 2000) Order 2007, SI 2007/1973, arts 2, 8, as from 12 July 2007; para (ba) inserted by the Financial Services and Markets Act 2000 (Market Abuse) Regulations 2005, SI 2005/381, reg 7, as from 1 July 2005; para (bb) inserted by the Prospectus Regulations 2005, SI 2005/1433, reg 2(1), Sch 1, para 14, as from 1 July 2005.
   Open-Ended Investment Companies: this section has effect as if sub-s (13) included a reference to a notice given in accordance with the Open-Ended Investment Companies Regulations 2001, SI 2001/1228, reg 27(3), (8) or (9)(b); see reg 27(15) of the 2001 Regulations at [2264].

396   Statements under section 395: consultation

(1)   Before issuing a statement of procedure under section 395, the Authority must publish a draft of the proposed statement in the way appearing to the Authority to be best calculated to bring it to the attention of the public.

(2)   The draft must be accompanied by notice that representations about the proposal may be made to the Authority within a specified time.

(3)   Before issuing the proposed statement of procedure, the Authority must have regard to any representations made to it in accordance with subsection (2).

(4)   If the Authority issues the proposed statement of procedure it must publish an account, in general terms, of—
   (a)   the representations made to it in accordance with subsection (2); and
   (b)   its response to them.

(5)   If the statement of procedure differs from the draft published under subsection (1) in a way which is, in the opinion of the Authority, significant, the Authority must (in addition to complying with subsection (4)) publish details of the difference.

(6)   The Authority may charge a reasonable fee for providing a person with a copy of a draft published under subsection (1).

(7)   This section also applies to a proposal to revise a statement of policy.

[423]

PART XXVII
OFFENCES

Miscellaneous offences

397   Misleading statements and practices

(1)   This subsection applies to a person who—
   (a)   makes a statement, promise or forecast which he knows to be misleading, false or deceptive in a material particular;
   (b)   dishonestly conceals any material facts whether in connection with a statement, promise or forecast made by him or otherwise; or
   (c)   recklessly makes (dishonestly or otherwise) a statement, promise or forecast which is misleading, false or deceptive in a material particular.

(2)   A person to whom subsection (1) applies is guilty of an offence if he makes the statement, promise or forecast or conceals the facts for the purpose of inducing, or is reckless as to whether it may induce, another person (whether or not the person to whom the statement, promise or forecast is made)—
   (a)   to enter or offer to enter into, or to refrain from entering or offering to enter into, a relevant agreement; or

(b)   to exercise, or refrain from exercising, any rights conferred by a relevant investment.

(3)   Any person who does any act or engages in any course of conduct which creates a false or misleading impression as to the market in or the price or value of any relevant investments is guilty of an offence if he does so for the purpose of creating that impression and of thereby inducing another person to acquire, dispose of, subscribe for or underwrite those investments or to refrain from doing so or to exercise, or refrain from exercising, any rights conferred by those investments.

(4)   In proceedings for an offence under subsection (2) brought against a person to whom subsection (1) applies as a result of paragraph (a) of that subsection, it is a defence for him to show that the statement, promise or forecast was made in conformity with[—

    (a)   price stabilising rules;

    (b)   control of information rules; or

    (c)   the relevant provisions of Commission Regulation (EC) No 2273/2003 of 22 December 2003 implementing Directive 2003/6/EC of the European Parliament and of the Council as regards exemptions for buy-back programmes and stabilisation of financial instruments].

(5)   In proceedings brought against any person for an offence under subsection (3) it is a defence for him to show—

    (a)   that he reasonably believed that his act or conduct would not create an impression that was false or misleading as to the matters mentioned in that subsection;

    (b)   that he acted or engaged in the conduct—

        (i)   for the purpose of stabilising the price of investments; and

        (ii)   in conformity with price stabilising rules; ...

    (c)   that he acted or engaged in the conduct in conformity with control of information rules[; or

    (d)   that he acted or engaged in the conduct in conformity with the relevant provisions of Commission Regulation (EC) No 2273/2003 of 22 December 2003 implementing Directive 2003/6/EC of the European Parliament and of the Council as regards exemptions for buy-back programmes and stabilisation of financial instruments].

(6)   Subsections (1) and (2) do not apply unless—

    (a)   the statement, promise or forecast is made in or from, or the facts are concealed in or from, the United Kingdom or arrangements are made in or from the United Kingdom for the statement, promise or forecast to be made or the facts to be concealed;

    (b)   the person on whom the inducement is intended to or may have effect is in the United Kingdom; or

    (c)   the agreement is or would be entered into or the rights are or would be exercised in the United Kingdom.

(7)   Subsection (3) does not apply unless—

    (a)   the act is done, or the course of conduct is engaged in, in the United Kingdom; or

    (b)   the false or misleading impression is created there.

(8)   A person guilty of an offence under this section is liable—

    (a)   on summary conviction, to imprisonment for a term not exceeding six months or a fine not exceeding the statutory maximum, or both;

    (b)   on conviction on indictment, to imprisonment for a term not exceeding seven years or a fine, or both.

(9)   "Relevant agreement" means an agreement—

    (a)   the entering into or performance of which by either party constitutes an activity of a specified kind or one which falls within a specified class of activity; and

    (b)   which relates to a relevant investment.

(10)   "Relevant investment" means an investment of a specified kind or one which falls within a prescribed class of investment.

(11)   Schedule 2 (except paragraphs 25 and 26) applies for the purposes of subsections (9) and (10) with references to section 22 being read as references to each of those subsections.

(12)   Nothing in Schedule 2, as applied by subsection (11), limits the power conferred by subsection (9) or (10).

(13)   "Investment" includes any asset, right or interest.

(14)   "Specified" means specified in an order made by the Treasury.

[424]

NOTES

Sub-s (4): words in square brackets substituted by the Financial Services and Markets Act 2000 (Market Abuse) Regulations 2005, SI 2005/381, reg 8(1), (2), as from 17 March 2005.

Sub-s (5): word omitted from para (b) repealed, and para (d) and the word immediately preceding it added, by SI 2005/381, reg 8(1), (3), as from 17 March 2005. Note that in the Queen's Printer's copy of SI 2008/381 the new paragraph inserted into this subsection is actually designated as para (a). It is assumed that this is an error as it specifically says that the new paragraph should be inserted after para (c), and a para (a) obviously already exists.

Orders: the Financial Services and Markets Act 2000 (Misleading Statements and Practices) Order 2001, SI 2001/3645 at **[2631]**.

Note that the following amending Orders have also been made under this section: the Financial Services and Markets Act 2000 (Commencement of Mortgage Regulation) (Amendment) Order 2002, SI 2002/1777; the Financial Services and Markets Act 2000 (Misleading Statements and Practices) (Amendment) Order 2003, SI 2003/1474.

398 Misleading the Authority: residual cases

(1) A person who, in purported compliance with any requirement imposed by or under this Act, knowingly or recklessly gives the Authority information which is false or misleading in a material particular is guilty of an offence.

(2) Subsection (1) applies only to a requirement in relation to which no other provision of this Act creates an offence in connection with the giving of information.

(3) A person guilty of an offence under this section is liable—
  (a) on summary conviction, to a fine not exceeding the statutory maximum;
  (b) on conviction on indictment, to a fine.

[425]

NOTES
Note: for the purposes of this section a requirement imposed by the FSA under the Electronic Commerce Directive (Financial Services and Markets) Regulations 2002, SI 2002/1775 upon an incoming provider is to be treated as imposed on him by or under this Act; see reg 12(2) of those Regulations at **[2685]**.

399 Misleading [the OFT]

Section 44 of the Competition Act 1998 (offences connected with the provision of false or misleading information) applies in relation to any function of [the Office of Fair Trading] under this Act as if it were a function under Part I of that Act.

[426]

NOTES
Words in square brackets substituted by the Enterprise Act 2002, s 278(1), Sch 25, para 40(1), (16), as from 1 April 2003.

Bodies corporate and partnerships

400 Offences by bodies corporate etc

(1) If an offence under this Act committed by a body corporate is shown—
  (a) to have been committed with the consent or connivance of an officer, or
  (b) to be attributable to any neglect on his part,
the officer as well as the body corporate is guilty of the offence and liable to be proceeded against and punished accordingly.

(2) If the affairs of a body corporate are managed by its members, subsection (1) applies in relation to the acts and defaults of a member in connection with his functions of management as if he were a director of the body.

(3) If an offence under this Act committed by a partnership is shown—
  (a) to have been committed with the consent or connivance of a partner, or
  (b) to be attributable to any neglect on his part,
the partner as well as the partnership is guilty of the offence and liable to be proceeded against and punished accordingly.

(4) In subsection (3) "partner" includes a person purporting to act as a partner.

(5) "Officer", in relation to a body corporate, means—
  (a) a director, member of the committee of management, chief executive, manager, secretary or other similar officer of the body, or a person purporting to act in any such capacity; and
  (b) an individual who is a controller of the body.

(6) If an offence under this Act committed by an unincorporated association (other than a partnership) is shown—
  (a) to have been committed with the consent or connivance of an officer of the association or a member of its governing body, or
  (b) to be attributable to any neglect on the part of such an officer or member,
that officer or member as well as the association is guilty of the offence and liable to be proceeded against and punished accordingly.

(7) Regulations may provide for the application of any provision of this section, with such modifications as the Treasury consider appropriate, to a body corporate or unincorporated association formed or recognised under the law of a territory outside the United Kingdom.

[427]

Institution of proceedings

401 Proceedings for offences

(1) In this section "offence" means an offence under this Act or subordinate legislation made under this Act.

(2) Proceedings for an offence may be instituted in England and Wales only—
  (a) by the Authority or the Secretary of State; or
  (b) by or with the consent of the Director of Public Prosecutions.

(3) Proceedings for an offence may be instituted in Northern Ireland only—
  (a) by the Authority or the Secretary of State; or
  (b) by or with the consent of the Director of Public Prosecutions for Northern Ireland.

(4) Except in Scotland, proceedings for an offence under section 203 may also be instituted by [the Office of Fair Trading].

(5) In exercising its power to institute proceedings for an offence, the Authority must comply with any conditions or restrictions imposed in writing by the Treasury.

(6) Conditions or restrictions may be imposed under subsection (5) in relation to—
  (a) proceedings generally; or
  (b) such proceedings, or categories of proceedings, as the Treasury may direct.

[428]

NOTES
Sub-s (4):words in square brackets substituted by the Enterprise Act 2002, s 278(1), Sch 25, para 40(1), (17), as from 1 April 2003.
Transitional provisions: this section and s 403 have effect as if offences committed before 1 December 2001 under certain provisions (the Insurance Companies Act 1982, the Financial Services Act 1986, the Banking Act 1987, and certain related provisions) were an offence under this Act; see the Financial Services and Markets Act 2000 (Transitional Provisions and Savings) (Civil Remedies, Discipline, Criminal Offences etc) (No 2) Order 2001, SI 2001/3083, art 13. The 1982, 1986 and 1987 Acts were repealed by the Financial Services and Markets Act 2000 (Consequential Amendments and Repeals) Order 2001, SI 2001/3649, art 3(1)(b)–(d).

402 Power of the Authority to institute proceedings for certain other offences

(1) Except in Scotland, the Authority may institute proceedings for an offence under—
  (a) Part V of the Criminal Justice Act 1993 (insider dealing); ...
  (b) prescribed regulations relating to money laundering; [or
  (c) Schedule 7 to the Counter-Terrorism Act 2008 (terrorist financing or money laundering)].

(2) In exercising its power to institute proceedings for any such offence, the Authority must comply with any conditions or restrictions imposed in writing by the Treasury.

(3) Conditions or restrictions may be imposed under subsection (2) in relation to—
  (a) proceedings generally; or
  (b) such proceedings, or categories of proceedings, as the Treasury may direct.

[429]

NOTES
Para (1): word omitted repealed, and para (c) (and the word immediately preceding it) inserted, by the Counter-Terrorism Act 2008, s62, Sch 7, Pt 7, para 33(4), as from 27 November 2008.
Note: the Money Laundering Regulations 2007, SI 2007/2157 are prescribed for the purposes of sub-s (1)(b) above by reg 1(2) of those Regulations (at **[2877AA]**). The Transfer of Funds (Information on the Payer) Regulations 2007, SI 2007/3298 are also prescribed for the purposes of sub-s (1)(b) above by reg 1(2) of those Regulations (at **[2878]**).
Regulations: the Money Laundering Regulations 2007, SI 2007/2157 at **[2877AA]**; the Transfer of Funds (Information on the Payer) Regulations 2007, SI 2007/3298 at **[2878]**.

403 Jurisdiction and procedure in respect of offences

(1) A fine imposed on an unincorporated association on its conviction of an offence is to be paid out of the funds of the association.

(2) Proceedings for an offence alleged to have been committed by an unincorporated association must be brought in the name of the association (and not in that of any of its members).

(3) Rules of court relating to the service of documents are to have effect as if the association were a body corporate.

(4)   In proceedings for an offence brought against an unincorporated association—
  (a)   section 33 of the Criminal Justice Act 1925 and Schedule 3 to the Magistrates' Courts Act 1980 (procedure) apply as they do in relation to a body corporate;
  (b)   section 70 of the Criminal Procedure (Scotland) Act 1995 (procedure) applies as if the association were a body corporate;
  (c)   section 18 of the Criminal Justice (Northern Ireland) Act 1945 and Schedule 4 to the Magistrates' Courts (Northern Ireland) Order 1981 (procedure) apply as they do in relation to a body corporate.

(5)   Summary proceedings for an offence may be taken—
  (a)   against a body corporate or unincorporated association at any place at which it has a place of business;
  (b)   against an individual at any place where he is for the time being.

(6)   Subsection (5) does not affect any jurisdiction exercisable apart from this section.

(7)   "Offence" means an offence under this Act.

[430]

NOTES
Transitional provisions: See the note to s 401 at [428].

PART XXVIII
MISCELLANEOUS
Schemes for reviewing past business

404   Schemes for reviewing past business

(1)   Subsection (2) applies if the Treasury are satisfied that there is evidence suggesting—
  (a)   that there has been a widespread or regular failure on the part of authorised persons to comply with rules relating to a particular kind of activity; and
  (b)   that, as a result, private persons have suffered (or will suffer) loss in respect of which authorised persons are (or will be) liable to make payments ("compensation payments").

(2)   The Treasury may by order ("a scheme order") authorise the Authority to establish and operate a scheme for—
  (a)   determining the nature and extent of the failure;
  (b)   establishing the liability of authorised persons to make compensation payments; and
  (c)   determining the amounts payable by way of compensation payments.

(3)   An authorised scheme must be made so as to comply with specified requirements.

(4)   A scheme order may be made only if—
  (a)   the Authority has given the Treasury a report about the alleged failure and asked them to make a scheme order;
  (b)   the report contains details of the scheme which the Authority propose to make; and
  (c)   the Treasury are satisfied that the proposed scheme is an appropriate way of dealing with the failure.

(5)   A scheme order may provide for specified provisions of or made under this Act to apply in relation to any provision of, or determination made under, the resulting authorised scheme subject to such modifications (if any) as may be specified.

(6)   For the purposes of this Act, failure on the part of an authorised person to comply with any provision of an authorised scheme is to be treated (subject to any provision made by the scheme order concerned) as a failure on his part to comply with rules.

(7)   The Treasury may prescribe circumstances in which loss suffered by a person ("A") acting in a fiduciary or other prescribed capacity is to be treated, for the purposes of an authorised scheme, as suffered by a private person in relation to whom A was acting in that capacity.

(8)   This section applies whenever the failure in question occurred.

(9)   "Authorised scheme" means a scheme authorised by a scheme order.

(10)   "Private person" has such meaning as may be prescribed.

(11)   "Specified" means specified in a scheme order.

[431]

NOTES
Comply with rules: "Rule" is defined as a rule made by the FSA under this Act; see s 417 at [443].
"Private person": as at publication, no Regulations have been made under sub-s (10). It is not clear whether the definition of "private person" for this section will be the same as may be specified for the purposes of other provisions of this Act; see, for example, s 71 at [71], and the Financial Services and Markets Act 2000 (Rights of Action) Regulations 2001, SI 2001/2256, reg 3 at [2377] (made under s 71(2), (3)).

Transitional provisions: certain transitional provisions were made concerning the pensions mis-selling and FSAVC reviews conducted under FSA 1986 to treat them as a scheme made under this Act; see the Financial Services and Markets Act 2000 (Transitional Provisions) (Reviews of Pensions Business) Order 2001, SI 2001/2512.

Third countries

405 Directions

(1) For the purpose of implementing a third country decision, the Treasury may direct the Authority to—

(a) refuse an application for permission under Part IV made by a body incorporated in, or formed under the law of, any part of the United Kingdom;

(b) defer its decision on such an application either indefinitely or for such period as may be specified in the direction;

(c) give a notice of objection to a person who has served a notice of control to the effect that he proposes to acquire a 50% stake in a UK authorised person; or

(d) give a notice of objection to a person who has acquired a 50% stake in a UK authorised person without having served the required notice of control.

(2) A direction may also be given in relation to—

(a) any person falling within a class specified in the direction;

(b) future applications, notices of control or acquisitions.

(3) The Treasury may revoke a direction at any time.

(4) But revocation does not affect anything done in accordance with the direction before it was revoked.

(5) "Third country decision" means a decision of the Council or the Commission under—

[(a) Article 15(3) of the markets in financial instruments directive;]

(b) ...

(c) Article 29b(4) of the first non-life insurance directive; or

[(d) Article 59(4) of the life assurance consolidation directive.]

[432]

NOTES

Sub-s (5): para (a) substituted by the Financial Services and Markets Act 2000 (Markets in Financial Instruments) Regulations 2007, SI 2007/126, reg 3(5), Sch 5, paras 1, 17, as from 1 April 2007 (certain purposes (see reg 1(2) at **[4051]**)), and as from 1 November 2007 (otherwise); para (b) repealed by the Capital Requirements Regulations 2006, SI 2006/3221, reg 29(1), Sch 3, para 1, as from 1 January 2007; para (d) substituted by the Life Assurance Consolidation Directive (Consequential Amendments) Regulations 2004, SI 2004/3379, reg 6(1), (4), as from 11 January 2005.

406 Interpretation of section 405

(1) For the purposes of section 405, a person ("the acquirer") acquires a 50% stake in a UK authorised person ("A") on first falling within any of the cases set out in subsection (2).

(2) The cases are where the acquirer—

(a) holds 50% or more of the shares in A;

(b) holds 50% or more of the shares in a parent undertaking ("P") of A;

(c) is entitled to exercise, or control the exercise of, 50% or more of the voting power in A; or

(d) is entitled to exercise, or control the exercise of, 50% or more of the voting power in P.

(3) In subsection (2) "the acquirer" means—

(a) the acquirer;

(b) any of the acquirer's associates; or

(c) the acquirer and any of his associates.

(4) "Associate", "shares" and "voting power" have the same meaning as in section 422.

[433]

407 Consequences of a direction under section 405

(1) If the Authority refuses an application for permission as a result of a direction under section 405(1)(a)—

(a) subsections (7) to (9) of section 52 do not apply in relation to the refusal; but

(b) the Authority must notify the applicant of the refusal and the reasons for it.

(2) If the Authority defers its decision on an application for permission as a result of a direction under section 405(1)(b)—

(a) the time limit for determining the application mentioned in section 52(1) or (2) stops running on the day of the deferral and starts running again (if at all) on the day the period specified in the direction (if any) ends or the day the direction is revoked; and

   (b)   the Authority must notify the applicant of the deferral and the reasons for it.

(3)   If the Authority gives a notice of objection to a person as a result of a direction under section 405(1)(c) or (d)—

   (a)   sections 189 and 191 have effect as if the notice was a notice of objection within the meaning of Part XII; and

   (b)   the Authority must state in the notice the reasons for it.

[434]

408 EFTA firms

(1)   If a third country decision has been taken, the Treasury may make a determination in relation to an EFTA firm which is a subsidiary undertaking of a parent undertaking which is governed by the law of the country to which the decision relates.

(2)   "Determination" means a determination that the firm concerned does not qualify for authorisation under Schedule 3 even if it satisfies the conditions in paragraph 13 or 14 of that Schedule.

(3)   A determination may also be made in relation to any firm falling within a class specified in the determination.

(4)   The Treasury may withdraw a determination at any time.

(5)   But withdrawal does not affect anything done in accordance with the determination before it was withdrawn.

(6)   If the Treasury make a determination in respect of a particular firm, or withdraw such a determination, they must give written notice to that firm.

(7)   The Treasury must publish notice of any determination (or the withdrawal of any determination)—

   (a)   in such a way as they think most suitable for bringing the determination (or withdrawal) to the attention of those likely to be affected by it; and

   (b)   on, or as soon as practicable after, the date of the determination (or withdrawal).

(8)   "EFTA firm" means a firm, institution or undertaking which—

   (a)   is an EEA firm as a result of paragraph 5(a), (b) or (d) of Schedule 3; and

   (b)   is incorporated in, or formed under the law of, an EEA State which is not a member State.

(9)   "Third country decision" has the same meaning as in section 405.

[435]

409 Gibraltar

(1)   The Treasury may by order—

   (a)   modify Schedule 3 so as to provide for Gibraltar firms of a specified description to qualify for authorisation under that Schedule in specified circumstances;

   (b)   modify Schedule 3 so as to make provision in relation to the exercise by UK firms of rights under the law of Gibraltar which correspond to EEA rights;

   (c)   modify Schedule 4 so as to provide for Gibraltar firms of a specified description to qualify for authorisation under that Schedule in specified circumstances;

   (d)   modify section 264 so as to make provision in relation to collective investment schemes constituted under the law of Gibraltar;

   (e)   provide for the Authority to be able to give notice under section 264(2) on grounds relating to the law of Gibraltar;

   (f)   provide for this Act to apply to a Gibraltar recognised scheme as if the scheme were a scheme recognised under section 264.

(2)   The fact that a firm may qualify for authorisation under Schedule 3 as a result of an order under subsection (1) does not prevent it from applying for a Part IV permission.

(3)   "Gibraltar firm" means a firm which has its head office in Gibraltar or is otherwise connected with Gibraltar.

(4)   "Gibraltar recognised scheme" means a collective investment scheme—

   (a)   constituted in an EEA State other than the United Kingdom, and

   (b)   recognised in Gibraltar under provisions which appear to the Treasury to give effect to the provisions of a relevant Community instrument.

(5)   "Specified" means specified in the order.

(6)   "UK firm" and "EEA right" have the same meaning as in Schedule 3.

[436]

NOTES

Orders: the Financial Services and Markets Act 2000 (Gibraltar) Order 2001, SI 2001/3084 at **[2495]**.

Note that the following amending Orders have also been made under this section: the Financial Services and Markets Act 2000 (Gibraltar) (Amendment) Order 2005, SI 2005/1; the Financial Services and Markets Act 2000 (Gibraltar) (Amendment) Order 2006, SI 2006/1805; the Financial Services and Markets Act 2000 (Reinsurance Directive) Order 2007 SI 2007/3254.

International obligations

410 International obligations

(1) If it appears to the Treasury that any action proposed to be taken by a relevant person would be incompatible with Community obligations or any other international obligations of the United Kingdom, they may direct that person not to take that action.

(2) If it appears to the Treasury that any action which a relevant person has power to take is required for the purpose of implementing any such obligations, they may direct that person to take that action.

(3) A direction under this section—
  (a) may include such supplemental or incidental requirements as the Treasury consider necessary or expedient; and
  (b) is enforceable, on an application made by the Treasury, by injunction or, in Scotland, by an order for specific performance under section 45 of the Court of Session Act 1988.

(4) "Relevant person" means—
  (a) the Authority;
  (b) any person exercising functions conferred by Part VI on the competent authority;
  (c) any recognised investment exchange (other than one which is an overseas investment exchange);
  (d) any recognised clearing house (other than one which is an overseas clearing house);
  (e) a person included in the list maintained under section 301; or
  (f) the scheme operator of the ombudsman scheme.

[437]

NOTES

Community obligation: as to the meaning of this, see the note to s 47 at **[47]**.

---

411 (*Sub-s (1) repealed by the Financial Services and Markets Act 2000 (Consequential Amendments) (Taxes) Order 2001, SI 2001/3629, art 109, Schedule, as from 1 December 2001; sub-s (2) inserts the Income and Corporations Taxes Act 1988, ss 76A, 76B.*)

Gaming contracts

412 Gaming contracts

(1) No contract to which this section applies is void or unenforceable because of—
  (a) ... Article 170 of the Betting, Gaming, Lotteries and Amusements (Northern Ireland) Order 1985; or
  (b) ...

(2) This section applies to a contract if—
  (a) it is entered into by either or each party by way of business;
  (b) the entering into or performance of it by either party constitutes an activity of a specified kind or one which falls within a specified class of activity; and
  (c) it relates to an investment of a specified kind or one which falls within a specified class of investment.

(3) Part II of Schedule 2 applies for the purposes of subsection (2)(c), with the references to section 22 being read as references to that subsection.

(4) Nothing in Part II of Schedule 2, as applied by subsection (3), limits the power conferred by subsection (2)(c).

(5) "Investment" includes any asset, right or interest.

(6) "Specified" means specified in an order made by the Treasury.

[438]

NOTES

Sub-s (1): words omitted from para (a), and the whole of para (b), repealed by the Gambling Act 2005, ss 334(1)(e), 356, (2), Sch 17, as from 1 September 2007. Note that s 334(2) of the 2005 Act specifically provides that the repeal of the words in sub-s (1) above does not permit enforcement of a right which is created, or which emanates from an agreement made, before 1 September 2007.

Orders: the Financial Services and Markets Act 2000 (Gaming Contracts) Order 2001, SI 2001/2510 at **[2428]**.

[Trade-matching and reporting systems

412A Approval and monitoring of trade-matching and reporting systems

(1) A relevant system is an approved relevant system if it is approved by the Authority under subsection (2) for the purposes of Article 25.5 of the markets in financial instruments directive; and references in this section and section 412B to an "approved relevant system" are to be read accordingly.

(2) The Authority must approve a relevant system if, on an application by the operator of the system, it is satisfied that the arrangements established by the system for reporting transactions comply with Article 12(1) of Commission Regulation 1287/2006 of 10 August 2006 ("the Regulation").

(3) Section 51(3) and (4) applies to an application under this section as it applies to an application under Part 4.

(4) If, at any time after approving a relevant system under subsection (2), the Authority is not satisfied as mentioned in that subsection, it may suspend or withdraw the approval.

(5) The Authority must keep under review the arrangements established by an approved relevant system for reporting transactions for the purpose of ensuring that the arrangements comply with Article 12(1) of the Regulation; and for the purposes of this subsection the Authority must have regard to information provided to it under subsections (6) and (7).

(6) The operator of an approved relevant system must make reports to the Authority at specified intervals containing specified information relating to—
   (a)   the system,
   (b)   the reports made by the system in accordance with Article 25 of the markets in financial instruments directive and the Regulation, and
   (c)   the transactions to which those reports relate.

"Specified" means specified by the Authority.

(7) The Authority may by written notice require the operator of an approved relevant system to provide such additional information as may be specified in the notice, by such reasonable time as may be so specified, about any of the matters mentioned in subsection (6).

(8) The recipient of a notice under subsection (7) must provide the information by the time specified in the notice.

(9) In this section and section 412B, "relevant system" means a trade-matching or reporting system of a kind described in Article 12 of the Regulation.]

[438A]

NOTES
   Commencement: 1 April 2007 (certain purposes); 1 November 2007 (otherwise).
   Inserted, together with the preceding heading and s 412B, by the Financial Services and Markets Act 2000 (Markets in Financial Instruments) Regulations 2007, SI 2007/126, reg 3(5), Sch 5, paras 1, 18, as from 1 April 2007 (certain purposes (see reg 1(2) at [4051])), and as from 1 November 2007 (otherwise).

[412B Procedure for approval and suspension or withdrawal of approval

(1) If the Authority approves a relevant system, it must give the operator of the system written notice specifying the date from which the approval has effect.

(2) If the Authority proposes to refuse to approve a relevant system, it must give the operator of the system a warning notice.

(3) If the Authority decides to refuse to approve a relevant system, it must give the operator of the system a decision notice.

(4) If the Authority proposes to suspend or withdraw its approval in relation to an approved relevant system, it must give the operator of the system a warning notice.

(5) If the Authority decides to suspend or withdraw its approval in relation to an approved relevant system, it must give the operator of the system a decision notice specifying the date from which the suspension or withdrawal is to take effect.

(6) Subsections (7) to (9) apply if—
   (a)   the Authority has suspended its approval in relation to an approved relevant system, and
   (b)   the operator of the system has applied for the suspension to be cancelled.

(7) The Authority must grant the application if it is satisfied as mentioned in section 412A(2); and in such a case the Authority must give written notice to the operator that the suspension is to be cancelled from the date specified in the notice.

(8) If the Authority proposes to refuse the application, it must give the operator a warning notice.

(9) If the Authority decides to refuse the application, it must give the operator a decision notice.

(10)   A person who receives a decision notice under subsection (3), (5) or (9) may refer the matter to the Tribunal.]

[438B]

NOTES
Commencement: 1 April 2007 (certain purposes); 1 November 2007 (otherwise).
Inserted as noted to s 412A at **[438A]**.

Limitation on powers to require documents

413   Protected items

(1)   A person may not be required under this Act to produce, disclose or permit the inspection of protected items.

(2)   "Protected items" means—
   (a)   communications between a professional legal adviser and his client or any person representing his client which fall within subsection (3);
   (b)   communications between a professional legal adviser, his client or any person representing his client and any other person which fall within subsection (3) (as a result of paragraph (b) of that subsection);
   (c)   items which—
      (i)   are enclosed with, or referred to in, such communications;
      (ii)   fall within subsection (3); and
      (iii)   are in the possession of a person entitled to possession of them.

(3)   A communication or item falls within this subsection if it is made—
   (a)   in connection with the giving of legal advice to the client; or
   (b)   in connection with, or in contemplation of, legal proceedings and for the purposes of those proceedings.

(4)   A communication or item is not a protected item if it is held with the intention of furthering a criminal purpose.

[439]

Service of notices

414   Service of notices

(1)   The Treasury may by regulations make provision with respect to the procedure to be followed, or rules to be applied, when a provision of or made under this Act requires a notice, direction or document of any kind to be given or authorises the imposition of a requirement.

(2)   The regulations may, in particular, make provision—
   (a)   as to the manner in which a document must be given;
   (b)   as to the address to which a document must be sent;
   (c)   requiring, or allowing, a document to be sent electronically;
   (d)   for treating a document as having been given, or as having been received, on a date or at a time determined in accordance with the regulations;
   (e)   as to what must, or may, be done if the person to whom a document is required to be given is not an individual;
   (f)   as to what must, or may, be done if the intended recipient of a document is outside the United Kingdom.

(3)   Subsection (1) applies however the obligation to give a document is expressed (and so, in particular, includes a provision which requires a document to be served or sent).

(4)   Section 7 of the Interpretation Act 1978 (service of notice by post) has effect in relation to provisions made by or under this Act subject to any provision made by regulations under this section.

[440]

NOTES
Regulations: the Financial Services and Markets Act 2000 (Service of Notices) Regulations 2001, SI 2001/1420 at **[2331]**; the Electronic Commerce Directive (Financial Services and Markets) Regulations 2002, SI 2002/1775 at **[2674]**.
Note that the following amending Regulations have also been made under this section: the Financial Services and Markets Act 2000 (Service of Notices) (Amendment) Regulations 2005, SI 2005/274.

Jurisdiction

415   Jurisdiction in civil proceedings

(1)   Proceedings arising out of any act or omission (or proposed act or omission) of—
   (a)   the Authority,

(b)   the competent authority for the purposes of Part VI,

(c)   the scheme manager, or

(d)   the scheme operator,

in the discharge or purported discharge of any of its functions under this Act may be brought before the High Court or the Court of Session.

(2)   The jurisdiction conferred by subsection (1) is in addition to any other jurisdiction exercisable by those courts.

[441]

Removal of certain unnecessary provisions

416 Provisions relating to industrial assurance and certain other enactments

(1)   The following enactments are to cease to have effect—

(a)   the Industrial Assurance Act 1923;

(b)   the Industrial Assurance and Friendly Societies Act 1948;

(c)   the Insurance Brokers (Registration) Act 1977.

(2)   The Industrial Assurance (Northern Ireland) Order 1979 is revoked.

(3)   The following bodies are to cease to exist—

(a)   the Insurance Brokers Registration Council;

(b)   the Policyholders Protection Board;

(c)   the Deposit Protection Board;

(d)   the Board of Banking Supervision.

(4)   If the Treasury consider that, as a consequence of any provision of this section, it is appropriate to do so, they may by order make any provision of a kind that they could make under this Act (and in particular any provision of a kind mentioned in section 339) with respect to anything done by or under any provision of Part XXI.

(5)   Subsection (4) is not to be read as affecting in any way any other power conferred on the Treasury by this Act.

[442]

NOTES

Insurance Brokers Registration Act 1977: repealed by this Act.

Orders: the Financial Services and Markets Act 2000 (Dissolution of the Insurance Brokers Registration Council) (Consequential Provisions) Order 2001, SI 2001/1283 at **[2330]**; the Financial Services and Markets Act 2000 (Transitional Provisions, Repeals and Savings) (Financial Services Compensation Scheme) Order 2001, SI 2001/2967; the Financial Services and Markets Act 2000 (Consequential Amendments and Savings) (Industrial Assurance) Order 2001, SI 2001/3647.

Note that the following amending Orders have also been made under this section: the Financial Services and Markets Act 2000 (Consequential Amendments) Order 2002, SI 2002/1555.

PART XXIX
INTERPRETATION

417 Definitions

(1)   In this Act—

"appointed representative" has the meaning given in section 39(2);

"auditors and actuaries rules" means rules made under section 340;

"authorisation offence" has the meaning given in section 23(2);

"authorised open-ended investment company" has the meaning given in section 237(3);

"authorised person" has the meaning given in section 31(2);

"the Authority" means the Financial Services Authority;

"body corporate" includes a body corporate constituted under the law of a country or territory outside the United Kingdom;

"chief executive"—

(a)   in relation to a body corporate whose principal place of business is within the United Kingdom, means an employee of that body who, alone or jointly with one or more others, is responsible under the immediate authority of the directors, for the conduct of the whole of the business of that body; and

(b)   in relation to a body corporate whose principal place of business is outside the United Kingdom, means the person who, alone or jointly with one or more others, is responsible for the conduct of its business within the United Kingdom;

["claim", in relation to the Financial Services Compensation Scheme under Part XV, is to be construed in accordance with section 214(1B);]

"collective investment scheme" has the meaning given in section 235;

"the Commission" means the European Commission (except in provisions relating to the Competition Commission);

"the compensation scheme" has the meaning given in section 213(2);

"control of information rules" has the meaning given in section 147(1);

"director", in relation to a body corporate, includes—

    (a)   a person occupying in relation to it the position of a director (by whatever name called); and

    (b)   a person in accordance with whose directions or instructions (not being advice given in a professional capacity) the directors of that body are accustomed to act;

"documents" includes information recorded in any form and, in relation to information recorded otherwise than in legible form, references to its production include references to producing a copy of the information in legible form[, or in a form from which it can readily be produced in visible and legible form];

["electronic commerce directive" means Directive 2000/31/EC of the European Parliament and the Council of 8 June 2000 on certain legal aspects of information society services, in particular electronic commerce, in the Internal Market (Directive on electronic commerce);]

"exempt person", in relation to a regulated activity, means a person who is exempt from the general prohibition in relation to that activity as a result of an exemption order made under section 38(1) or as a result of section 39(1) or 285(2) or (3);

"financial promotion rules" means rules made under section 145;

"friendly society" means an incorporated or registered friendly society;

"general prohibition" has the meaning given in section 19(2);

"general rules" has the meaning given in section 138(2);

"incorporated friendly society" means a society incorporated under the Friendly Societies Act 1992;

"industrial and provident society" means a society registered or deemed to be registered under the Industrial and Provident Societies Act 1965 or the Industrial and Provident Societies Act (Northern Ireland) 1969;

["information society service" means an information society service within the meaning of Article 2(a) of the electronic commerce directive;]

["investment services and activities" has the meaning given in Article 4.1.2 of the markets in financial instruments directive, read with—

    (a)   Chapter VI of Commission Regulation 1287/2006 of 10 August 2006, and

    (b)   Article 52 of Commission Directive 2006/73/EC of 10 August 2006;]

"market abuse" has the meaning given in section 118;

"Minister of the Crown" has the same meaning as in the Ministers of the Crown Act 1975;

"money laundering rules" means rules made under section 146;

"notice of control" [(except in Chapter 1A of Part 18)] has the meaning given in section 178(5);

"the ombudsman scheme" has the meaning given in section 225(3);

"open-ended investment company" has the meaning given in section 236;

"Part IV permission" has the meaning given in section 40(4);

"partnership" includes a partnership constituted under the law of a country or territory outside the United Kingdom;

"prescribed" (where not otherwise defined) means prescribed in regulations made by the Treasury;

"price stabilising rules" means rules made under section 144;

"private company" has the meaning given in section 1(3) of the Companies Act 1985 or in Article 12(3) of the Companies (Northern Ireland) Order 1986;

"prohibition order" has the meaning given in section 56(2);

"recognised clearing house" and "recognised investment exchange" have the meaning given in section 285;

"registered friendly society" means a society which is—

    (a)   a friendly society within the meaning of section 7(1)(a) of the Friendly Societies Act 1974; and

    (b)   registered within the meaning of that Act;

"regulated activity" has the meaning given in section 22;

"regulating provisions" has the meaning given in section 159(1);

"regulatory objectives" means the objectives mentioned in section 2;

"regulatory provisions" has the meaning given in section 302;

"rule" means a rule made by the Authority under this Act;

"rule-making instrument" has the meaning given in section 153;

"the scheme manager" has the meaning given in section 212(1);

"the scheme operator" has the meaning given in section 225(2);

"scheme particulars rules" has the meaning given in section 248(1);

"Seventh Company Law Directive" means the European Council Seventh Company Law Directive of 13 June 1983 on consolidated accounts (No 83/349/EEC);

["Takeovers Directive" means Directive 2004/25/EC of the European Parliament and of the Council;]

"threshold conditions", in relation to a regulated activity, has the meaning given in section 41;

"the Treaty" means the treaty establishing the European Community;

"trust scheme rules" has the meaning given in section 247(1);

"UK authorised person" has the meaning given in section 178(4); and

"unit trust scheme" has the meaning given in section 237.

(2)　In the application of this Act to Scotland, references to a matter being actionable at the suit of a person are to be read as references to the matter being actionable at the instance of that person.

(3)　For the purposes of any provision of this Act [(other than a provision of Part 6)] authorising or requiring a person to do anything within a specified number of days no account is to be taken of any day which is a public holiday in any part of the United Kingdom.

[(4)　For the purposes of this Act—

(a)　an information society service is provided from an EEA State if it is provided from an establishment in that State;

(b)　an establishment, in connection with an information society service, is the place at which the provider of the service (being a national of an EEA State or a company or firm as mentioned in Article 48 of the Treaty) effectively pursues an economic activity for an indefinite period;

(c)　the presence or use in a particular place of equipment or other technical means of providing an information society service does not, of itself, constitute that place as an establishment of the kind mentioned in paragraph (b);

(d)　where it cannot be determined from which of a number of establishments a given information society service is provided, that service is to be regarded as provided from the establishment where the provider has the centre of his activities relating to the service.]

[443]

NOTES

Sub-s (1) is amended as follows:

Definition "claim" inserted by the Banking Act 2009, s 174(2), as from a day to be appointed.

Words in square brackets in definition "documents" inserted by the Criminal Justice and Police Act 2001, s 70, Sch 2, Pt 2, para 16(1), (2)(f), as from 1 April 2003.

Definitions "electronic commerce directive" and "information society service" inserted by the Electronic Commerce Directive (Financial Services and Markets) Regulations 2002, SI 2002/1775, reg 13(1), (2)(a), (b), as from 21 August 2002.

Definition "investment services and activities" inserted, and words in square brackets in definition "notice of control" inserted, by the Financial Services and Markets Act 2000 (Markets in Financial Instruments) Regulations 2007, SI 2007/126, reg 3(5), Sch 5, paras 1, 19, as from 1 April 2007 (certain purposes (see reg 1(2) at [4051])), and as from 1 November 2007 (otherwise).

Definition "Takeovers Directive" inserted by the Companies Act 2006, s 964(1), (6), as from 6 April 2007.

Sub-s (3): words in square brackets inserted by the Prospectus Regulations 2005, SI 2005/1433, reg 2(1), Sch 1, para 15, as from 1 July 2005.

Sub-s (4): added by SI 2002/1775, reg 13(1), (2)(c), as from 21 August 2002.

Seventh Company Law Directive (83/349/EEC): OJ L193 18.7.1983 p 1.

Companies Act 1985, s 1(3): repealed by the Companies Act 2006 (as from 1 October 2009) and prospectively replaced by s 4(1)–(3) of the 2006 Act.

418　Carrying on regulated activities in the United Kingdom

(1)　In the [five] cases described in this section, a person who—

(a)　is carrying on a regulated activity, but

(b)　would not otherwise be regarded as carrying it on in the United Kingdom,

is, for the purposes of this Act, to be regarded as carrying it on in the United Kingdom.

(2)　The first case is where—

(a)　his registered office (or if he does not have a registered office his head office) is in the United Kingdom;

(b)　he is entitled to exercise rights under a single market directive as a UK firm; and

(c)　he is carrying on in another EEA State a regulated activity to which that directive applies.

(3)　The second case is where—

(a)　his registered office (or if he does not have a registered office his head office) is in the United Kingdom;

(b)　he is the manager of a scheme which is entitled to enjoy the rights conferred by an instrument which is a relevant Community instrument for the purposes of section 264; and

(c)　persons in another EEA State are invited to become participants in the scheme.

(4)　The third case is where—

(a)　his registered office (or if he does not have a registered office his head office) is in the United Kingdom;

(b)   the day-to-day management of the carrying on of the regulated activity is the responsibility of—
    (i)   his registered office (or head office); or
    (ii)   another establishment maintained by him in the United Kingdom.

(5)   The fourth case is where—
    (a)   his head office is not in the United Kingdom; but
    (b)   the activity is carried on from an establishment maintained by him in the United Kingdom.

[(5A)   The fifth case is any other case where the activity—
    (a)   consists of the provision of an information society service to a person or persons in one or more EEA States; and
    (b)   is carried on from an establishment in the United Kingdom.]

(6)   For the purposes of subsections (2) to [(5A)] it is irrelevant where the person with whom the activity is carried on is situated.

[444]

NOTES
Sub-s (1): word in square brackets substituted by the Electronic Commerce Directive (Financial Services and Markets) Regulations 2002, SI 2002/1775, reg 13(1), (3)(a), as from 21 August 2002.
Sub-s (5A): inserted by SI 2002/1775, reg 13(1), (3)(b), as from 21 August 2002.
Sub-s (6): number in square brackets substituted by SI 2002/1775, reg 13(1), (3)(c), as from 21 August 2002.

419   Carrying on regulated activities by way of business

(1)   The Treasury may by order make provision—
    (a)   as to the circumstances in which a person who would otherwise not be regarded as carrying on a regulated activity by way of business is to be regarded as doing so;
    (b)   as to the circumstances in which a person who would otherwise be regarded as carrying on a regulated activity by way of business is to be regarded as not doing so.

(2)   An order under subsection (1) may be made so as to apply—
    (a)   generally in relation to all regulated activities;
    (b)   in relation to a specified category of regulated activity; or
    (c)   in relation to a particular regulated activity.

(3)   An order under subsection (1) may be made so as to apply—
    (a)   for the purposes of all provisions;
    (b)   for a specified group of provisions; or
    (c)   for a specified provision.

(4)   "Provision" means a provision of, or made under, this Act.

(5)   Nothing in this section is to be read as affecting the provisions of section 428(3).

[445]

NOTES
Orders: the Financial Services and Markets Act 2000 (Carrying on Regulated Activities by Way of Business) Order 2001, SI 2001/1177 at [2206].
Note that the following amending Orders have also been made under this section: the Financial Services and Markets Act 2000 (Carrying on Regulated Activities by Way of Business) (Amendment) Order 2005, SI 2005/922.

420   Parent and subsidiary undertaking

(1)   In this Act, except in relation to an incorporated friendly society, "parent undertaking" and "subsidiary undertaking" have the same meaning as in [the Companies Acts (see section 1162 of, and Schedule 7 to, the Companies Act 2006)].

(2)   But—
    (a)   "parent undertaking" also includes an individual who would be a parent undertaking for the purposes of those provisions if he were taken to be an undertaking (and "subsidiary undertaking" is to be read accordingly);
    (b)   "subsidiary undertaking" also includes, in relation to a body incorporated in or formed under the law of an EEA State other than the United Kingdom, an undertaking which is a subsidiary undertaking within the meaning of any rule of law in force in that State for purposes connected with implementation of the Seventh Company Law Directive (and "parent undertaking" is to be read accordingly).

(3)   In this Act "subsidiary undertaking", in relation to an incorporated friendly society, means a body corporate of which the society has control within the meaning of section 13(9)(a) or (aa) of the Friendly Societies Act 1992 (and "parent undertaking" is to be read accordingly).

[446]

NOTES
Sub-s (1): words in square brackets substituted by the Companies Act 2006 (Consequential Amendments etc)
Order 2008, SI 2008/948, art 3(1), Sch 1, Pt 2, para 212(1), as from 6 April 2008.

421 Group

(1)   In this Act "group", in relation to a person ("A"), means A and any person who is—
- (a)   a parent undertaking of A;
- (b)   a subsidiary undertaking of A;
- (c)   a subsidiary undertaking of a parent undertaking of A;
- (d)   a parent undertaking of a subsidiary undertaking of A;
- (e)   an undertaking in which A or an undertaking mentioned in paragraph (a), (b), (c) or (d) has a participating interest;
- (f)   if A or an undertaking mentioned in paragraph (a) or (d) is a building society, an associated undertaking of the society; or
- (g)   if A or an undertaking mentioned in paragraph (a) or (d) is an incorporated friendly society, a body corporate of which the society has joint control (within the meaning of section 13(9)(c) or (cc) of the Friendly Societies Act 1992).

(2)   "Participating interest" [has the meaning given in section 421A]; but also includes an interest held by an individual which would be a participating interest for the purposes of those provisions if he were taken to be an undertaking.

(3)   "Associated undertaking" has the meaning given in section 119(1) of the Building Societies Act 1986.

[447]

NOTES
Sub-s (2): words in square brackets substituted by the Companies Act 2006 (Consequential Amendments etc)
Order 2008, SI 2008/948, art 3(1), Sch 1, Pt 2, para 212(2), as from 6 April 2008.

[421A   Meaning of "participating interest"

(1)   In section 421 a "participating interest" means an interest held by an undertaking in the shares of another undertaking which it holds on a long-term basis for the purpose of securing a contribution to its activities by the exercise of control or influence arising from or related to that interest.

(2)   A holding of 20% or more of the shares of an undertaking is presumed to be a participating interest unless the contrary is shown.

(3)   The reference in subsection (1) to an interest in shares includes—
- (a)   an interest which is convertible into an interest in shares, and
- (b)   an option to acquire shares or any such interest;

And an interest or option falls within paragraph (a) or (b) notwithstanding that the shares to which it relates are, until the conversion or the exercise of the option, unissued.

(4)   For the purposes of this section an interest held on behalf of an undertaking shall be treated as held by it.

(5)   In this section "undertaking" has the same meaning as in the Companies Acts (see section 1161(1) of the Companies Act 2006).]

[447A]

NOTES
Commencement: 6 April 2008.
Inserted by the Companies Act 2006 (Consequential Amendments etc) Order 2008, SI 2008/948, art 3(1), Sch 1, Pt 2, para 212(3), as from 6 April 2008.

422 Controller

(1)   In this Act[, except in Chapter 1A of Part 18,] "controller", in relation to an undertaking ("A"), means a person who falls within any of the cases in subsection (2).

(2)   The cases are where the person—
- (a)   holds 10% or more of the shares in A;
- (b)   is able to exercise significant influence over the management of A by virtue of his shareholding in A;
- (c)   holds 10% or more of the shares in a parent undertaking ("P") of A;
- (d)   is able to exercise significant influence over the management of P by virtue of his shareholding in P;
- (e)   is entitled to exercise, or control the exercise of, 10% or more of the voting power in A;

(f) is able to exercise significant influence over the management of A by virtue of his voting power in A;

(g) is entitled to exercise, or control the exercise of, 10% or more of the voting power in P; or

(h) is able to exercise significant influence over the management of P by virtue of his voting power in P.

(3) In subsection (2) "the person" means—

 (a) the person;

 (b) any of the person's associates; or

 (c) the person and any of his associates.

(4) "Associate", in relation to a person ("H") holding shares in an undertaking ("C") or entitled to exercise or control the exercise of voting power in relation to another undertaking ("D"), means—

 (a) the spouse [or civil partner] of H;

 (b) a child or stepchild of H (if under 18);

 (c) the trustee of any settlement under which H has a life interest in possession (or in Scotland a life interest);

 (d) an undertaking of which H is a director;

 (e) a person who is an employee or partner of H;

 (f) if H is an undertaking—

  (i) a director of H;

  (ii) a subsidiary undertaking of H;

  (iii) a director or employee of such a subsidiary undertaking; and

 (g) if H has with any other person an agreement or arrangement with respect to the acquisition, holding or disposal of shares or other interests in C or D or under which they undertake to act together in exercising their voting power in relation to C or D, that other person.

(5) "Settlement", in subsection (4)(c), includes any disposition or arrangement under which property is held on trust (or subject to a comparable obligation).

(6) "Shares"—

 (a) in relation to an undertaking with a share capital, means allotted shares;

 (b) in relation to an undertaking with capital but no share capital, means rights to share in the capital of the undertaking;

 (c) in relation to an undertaking without capital, means interests—

  (i) conferring any right to share in the profits, or liability to contribute to the losses, of the undertaking; or

  (ii) giving rise to an obligation to contribute to the debts or expenses of the undertaking in the event of a winding up.

(7) "Voting power", in relation to an undertaking which does not have general meetings at which matters are decided by the exercise of voting rights, means the right under the constitution of the undertaking to direct the overall policy of the undertaking or alter the terms of its constitution.

[448]

NOTES

Sub-s (1): words in square brackets inserted by the Financial Services and Markets Act 2000 (Markets in Financial Instruments) Regulations 2007, SI 2007/126, reg 3(5), Sch 5, paras 1, 20, as from 1 April 2007 (certain purposes (see reg 1(2) at **[4051]**)), and as from 1 November 2007 (otherwise).

Sub-s (4): words in square brackets inserted by the Civil Partnership Act 2004, s 261(1), Sch 27, para 165, as from 5 December 2005.

Stepchild: as to the extended meaning of this to include equivalent relationships arising under civil partnership, see the Civil Partnership Act 2004, ss 246, 247, Sch 21.

HM Treasury and the FSA have issued a consultation paper on the Implementation of the Acquisitions Directive which proposes certain changes to the definition of controller as set out in this section (as well as to Part XII and Part 18, Chapter 1A of this Act). See *Implementation of the Acquisitions Directive: a consultation document (September 2008)* at:
http://www.hm-treasury.gov.uk/consult_fullindex.htm.

423 Manager

(1) In this Act, except in relation to a unit trust scheme or a registered friendly society, "manager" means an employee who—

 (a) under the immediate authority of his employer is responsible, either alone or jointly with one or more other persons, for the conduct of his employer's business; or

 (b) under the immediate authority of his employer or of a person who is a manager by virtue of paragraph (a) exercises managerial functions or is responsible for maintaining accounts or other records of his employer.

(2) If the employer is not an individual, references in subsection (1) to the authority of the employer are references to the authority—

    (a)   in the case of a body corporate, of the directors;
    (b)   in the case of a partnership, of the partners; and
    (c)   in the case of an unincorporated association, of its officers or the members of its governing body.

    (3)   "Manager", in relation to a body corporate, means a person (other than an employee of the body) who is appointed by the body to manage any part of its business and includes an employee of the body corporate (other than the chief executive) who, under the immediate authority of a director or chief executive of the body corporate, exercises managerial functions or is responsible for maintaining accounts or other records of the body corporate.

[449]

424 Insurance

    (1)   In this Act, references to—
    (a)   contracts of insurance,
    (b)   reinsurance,
    (c)   contracts of long-term insurance,
    (d)   contracts of general insurance,
are to be read with section 22 and Schedule 2.

    (2)   In this Act "policy" and "policyholder", in relation to a contract of insurance, have such meaning as the Treasury may by order specify.

    (3)   The law applicable to a contract of insurance, the effecting of which constitutes the carrying on of a regulated activity, is to be determined, if it is of a prescribed description, in accordance with regulations made by the Treasury.

[450]

NOTES

Orders: the Financial Services and Markets Act 2000 (Meaning of "Policy" and "Policyholder") Order 2001, SI 2001/2361 at **[2382]**.

Regulations: the Financial Services and Markets Act 2000 (Law Applicable to Contracts of Insurance) Regulations 2001, SI 2001/2635 at **[2472]**.

Note that the following amending Regulations have also been made under this section: the Financial Services and Markets Act 2000 (Law Applicable to Contracts of Insurance) (Amendment) Regulations 2001, SI 2001/3542; the Financial Services and Markets Act 2000 (Motor Insurance) Regulations 2007, SI 2007/2403.

[424A Investment firm

    (1)   In this Act, "investment firm" has the meaning given in Article 4.1.1 of the markets in financial instruments directive.

    (2)   Subsection (1) is subject to subsections (3) to (5).

    [(3)   References in this Act to an "investment firm" include references to a person who would be an investment firm (within the meaning of Article 4.1.1 of the markets in financial instruments directive) if—
    (a)   in the case of a body corporate, his registered office or, if he has no registered office, his head office, and
    (b)   in the case of a person other than a body corporate, his head office,
were in an EEA State.]

    (4)   But subsection (3) does not apply if the person in question is one to whom the markets in financial instruments directive would not apply by virtue of Article 2 of that directive.

    (5)   References in this Act to an "investment firm" do not include references to—
    (a)   a person to whom the markets in financial instruments directive does not apply by virtue of Article 2 of the directive; or
    (b)   a person whose home Member State (within the meaning of Article 4.1.20 of the markets in financial instruments directive) is an EEA State and to whom, by reason of the fact that the State has given effect to Article 3 of that directive, that directive does not apply by virtue of that Article.]

[450A]

NOTES

Commencement: 6 December 2006.

Inserted by the Financial Services and Markets Act 2000 (Markets in Financial Instruments) (Modification of Powers) Regulations 2006, SI 2006/2975, regs 2, 10, as from 6 December 2006.

Sub-s (3): substituted by the Financial Services and Markets Act 2000 (Markets in Financial Instruments) Regulations 2007, SI 2007/126, reg 3(5), Sch 5, paras 1, 21, as from 1 April 2007 (certain purposes (see reg 1(2) at **[4051]**)), and as from 1 November 2007 (otherwise).

425 Expressions relating to authorisation elsewhere in the single market

    (1)   In this Act—

[(a) "banking consolidation directive", ["life assurance consolidation directive",] "EEA authorisation", "EEA firm", "EEA right", "EEA State", ... , "first non-life insurance directive", "insurance directives", ["reinsurance directive",] "insurance mediation directive", ... ["markets in financial instruments directive",] "single market directives"[, " tied agent"] and "UCITS directive" have the meaning given in Schedule 3; and]

(b) "home state regulator", in relation to an EEA firm, has the meaning given in Schedule 3.

(2) In this Act—

(a) "home state authorisation" has the meaning given in Schedule 4;

(b) "Treaty firm" has the meaning given in Schedule 4; and

(c) "home state regulator", in relation to a Treaty firm, has the meaning given in Schedule 4.

[451]

PART I
FSMA 2000

NOTES

Sub-s (1) is amended as follows:

Para (a) substituted by the Collective Investment Schemes (Miscellaneous Amendments) Regulations 2003, SI 2003/2066, reg 2(1), as from 13 February 2004.

Words in first pair of square brackets in para (a) inserted, and first words omitted from that paragraph repealed, by the Life Assurance Consolidation Directive (Consequential Amendments) Regulations 2004, SI 2004/3379, reg 6(1), (5), as from 11 January 2005.

Words in second pair of square brackets in para (a) inserted by the Reinsurance Directive Regulations 2007, SI 2007/3253, reg 2(1), Sch 1, paras 1, 5, as from 10 December 2007.

Words in third pair of square brackets in para (a) inserted by the Financial Services and Markets Act 2000 (Markets in Financial Instruments) (Modification of Powers) Regulations 2006, SI 2006/2975, regs 2, 11, as from 6 December 2006.

Second words omitted from para (a) repealed, and words in final pair of square brackets in that paragraph inserted, by the Financial Services and Markets Act 2000 (Markets in Financial Instruments) Regulations 2007, SI 2007/126, reg 3(5), Sch 5, paras 1, 22, as from 1 April 2007 (certain purposes (see reg 1(2) at **[4051]**)), and as from 1 November 2007 (otherwise).

Note: following the substitution of sub-s (1)(a) by SI 2003/2066 (as noted above), the amendment made by the Insurance Mediation Directive (Miscellaneous Amendments) Regulations 2003, SI 2003/1473 reg 2(1), which was to come into force on 14 January 2005, was rendered redundant.

PART XXX
SUPPLEMENTAL

426 Consequential and supplementary provision

(1) A Minister of the Crown may by order make such incidental, consequential, transitional or supplemental provision as he considers necessary or expedient for the general purposes, or any particular purpose, of this Act or in consequence of any provision made by or under this Act or for giving full effect to this Act or any such provision.

(2) An order under subsection (1) may, in particular, make provision—

(a) for enabling any person by whom any powers will become exercisable, on a date set by or under this Act, by virtue of any provision made by or under this Act to take before that date any steps which are necessary as a preliminary to the exercise of those powers;

(b) for applying (with or without modifications) or amending, repealing or revoking any provision of or made under an Act passed before this Act or in the same Session;

(c) dissolving any body corporate established by any Act passed, or instrument made, before the passing of this Act;

(d) for making savings, or additional savings, from the effect of any repeal or revocation made by or under this Act.

(3) Amendments made under this section are additional, and without prejudice, to those made by or under any other provision of this Act.

(4) No other provision of this Act restricts the powers conferred by this section.

[452]

NOTES

Modification: this section shall have effect as if the provisions referred to in sub-s (2)(b) above included the provisions of the Criminal Justice and Police Act 2001, Pt 2: see Sch 2, Pt 2, para 26 to the 2001 Act.

Regulations: the Financial Services and Markets Act 2000 (Recognition Requirements for Investment Exchanges and Clearing Houses) Regulations 2001, SI 2001/995 at **[2147]**; the Financial Services and Markets Act 2000 (Disclosure of Confidential Information) Regulations 2001, SI 2001/2188 at **[2350]**; the Financial Services and Markets Act 2000 (EEA Passport Rights) Regulations 2001, SI 2001/2511 at **[2430]**.

Orders: the Financial Services and Markets Act 2000 (Regulated Activities) Order 2001, SI 2001/544 at **[2010]**; the Financial Services and Markets Act 2000 (Transitional Provisions and Savings) (Rules) Order 2001, SI 2001/1534; the Financial Services and Markets Act 2000 (Consequential and Transitional Provisions) (Miscellaneous) Order 2001, SI 2001/1821; the Financial Services and Markets Act 2000 (Transitional Provisions) (Ombudsman Scheme and Complaints Scheme) Order 2001, SI 2001/2326; the Financial Services and Markets Act 2000 (Transitional Provisions) (Reviews of Pensions Business) Order 2001, SI 2001/2512; the Financial Services and Markets Act 2000 (Mutual Societies) Order 2001, SI 2001/2617 at **[2453]**; the Financial Services and Markets Act 2000 (Transitional Provisions) (Authorised Persons etc) Order 2001, SI 2001/2636;

the Financial Services and Markets Act 2000 (Transitional Provisions) (Controllers) Order 2001, SI 2001/2637; the Financial Services and Markets Act 2000 (Consequential and Transitional Provisions) (Miscellaneous) (No 2) Order 2001, SI 2001/2659; the Financial Services and Markets Act 2000 (Official Listing of Securities) (Transitional Provisions) Order 2001, SI 2001/2957; the Financial Services and Markets Act 2000 (Consequential Amendments) (Pre-Commencement Modifications) Order 2001, SI 2001/2966; the Financial Services and Markets Act 2000 (Transitional Provisions, Repeals and Savings) (Financial Services Compensation Scheme) Order 2001, SI 2001/2967; the Financial Services and Markets Act 2000 (Transitional Provisions and Savings) (Civil Remedies, Discipline, Criminal Offences etc) (No 2) Order 2001, SI 2001/3083; the Financial Services and Markets Act 2000 (Interim Permissions) Order 2001, SI 2001/3374 at **[2502]**; the Financial Services and Markets Act 2000 (Dissolution of the Board of Banking Supervision) (Transitional Provisions) Order 2001, SI 2001/3582; the Financial Services and Markets Act 2000 (Transitional Provisions) (Partly Completed Procedures) Order 2001, SI 2001/3592; the Financial Services and Markets Act 2000 (Disclosure of Confidential Information) (Amendment) (No 2) Regulations 2001, SI 2001/3624; the Financial Services and Markets Act 2000 (Consequential Amendments) (Taxes) Order 2001, SI 2001/3629; the Financial Services and Markets Act 2000 (Transitional Provisions and Savings) (Business Transfers) Order 2001, SI 2001/3639; the Financial Services and Markets Act 2000 (Savings, Modifications and Consequential Provisions) (Rehabilitation of Offenders) (Scotland) Order 2001, SI 2001/3640; the Financial Services and Markets Act 2000 (Transitional Provisions and Savings) (Information Requirements and Investigations) Order 2001, SI 2001/3646; the Financial Services and Markets Act 2000 (Consequential Amendments and Savings) (Industrial Assurance) Order 2001, SI 2001/3647; the Financial Services and Markets Act 2000 (Confidential Information) (Bank of England) (Consequential Provisions) Order 2001, SI 2001/3648 at **[2635]**; the Financial Services and Markets Act 2000 (Consequential Amendments and Repeals) Order 2001, SI 2001/3649; the Financial Services and Markets Act 2000 (Miscellaneous Provisions) Order 2001, SI 2001/3650 at **[2643]**; the Financial Services and Markets Act 2000 (Scope of Permission Notices) Order 2001, SI 2001/3771 at **[2662]**; the Financial Services and Markets Act 2000 (Consequential Amendments) (No 2) Order 2001, SI 2001/3801; the Financial Services and Markets Act 2000 (Permission and Applications) (Credit Unions etc) Order 2002, SI 2002/704; the Financial Services and Markets Act 2000 (Administration Orders Relating to Insurers) Order 2002, SI 2002/1242 at **[2669]**; the Financial Services and Markets Act 2000 (Consequential Amendments) (Taxes) Order 2002, SI 2002/1409; the Financial Services and Markets Act 2000 (Consequential Amendments and Transitional Provisions) (Credit Unions) Order 2002, SI 2002/1501; the Financial Services and Markets Act 2000 (Consequential Amendments) Order 2002, SI 2002/1555; the Financial Services and Markets Act 2000 (Collective Investment Schemes) (Designated Countries and Territories) Order 2003, SI 2003/1181 at **[2692]**; the Financial Services and Markets Act 2000 (Regulated Activities) (Amendment) (No 1) Order 2003, SI 2003/1475 at **[2698]**; the Financial Services and Markets Act 2000 (Regulated Activities) (Amendment) (No 2) Order 2003, SI 2003/1476 at **[2704]**; the Financial Services and Markets Act 2000 (Administration Orders Relating to Insurers) (Amendment) Order 2003, SI 2003/2134; the Financial Services and Markets Act 2000 (Consequential Amendments) Order 2004, SI 2004/355; the Financial Services and Markets Act 2000 (Transitional Provisions) (Complaints Relating to General Insurance and Mortgages) Order 2004, SI 2004/454 at **[2712]**; the Financial Services and Markets Act 2000 (Transitional Provisions, Repeals and Savings) (Financial Services Compensation Scheme) (Amendment) Order 2004, SI 2004/952; the Financial Services and Markets Act 2000 (Transitional Provisions) (Complaints Relating to General Insurance and Mortgages) (Amendment) Order 2004, SI 2004/1609; the Financial Services and Markets Act 2000 (Transitional Provisions) (Mortgages) Order 2004, SI 2004/2615 at **[2735]**; the Financial Services and Markets Act 2000 (Transitional Provisions) (General Insurance Intermediaries) Order 2004, SI 2004/3351 at **[2750]**; the Financial Services and Markets Act 2000 (Consequential Amendments) Order 2005, SI 2005/2967; the Financial Services and Markets Act 2000 (Regulated Activities) (Amendment) Order 2006, SI 2006/1969 at **[2853]**; the Financial Services and Markets Act 2000 (Regulated Activities) (Amendment) (No 2) Order 2006, SI 2006/2383 at **[2860]**; the Lloyd's Sourcebook (Finance Act 1993 and Finance Act 1994) (Amendment) Order 2006, SI 2006/3273; the Financial Services and Markets Act 2000 (Administration Orders Relating to Insurers) (Northern Ireland) Order 2007, SI 2007/846; the Financial Services and Markets Act 2000 (Regulated Activities) (Amendment) (No 2) Order 2007, SI 2007/3510 (at **[2899]**); the Financial Services and Markets Act 2000 (Consequential Amendments) Order 2008, SI 2008/733; the Financial Services and Markets Act 2000 (Consequential Amendments) (Taxes) Order 2008, SI 2008/2673.

427 Transitional provisions

(1) Subsections (2) and (3) apply to an order under section 426 which makes transitional provisions or savings.

(2) The order may, in particular—

(a) if it makes provision about the authorisation and permission of persons who before commencement were entitled to carry on any activities, also include provision for such persons not to be treated as having any authorisation or permission (whether on an application to the Authority or otherwise);

(b) make provision enabling the Authority to require persons of such descriptions as it may direct to re-apply for permissions having effect by virtue of the order;

(c) make provision for the continuation as rules of such provisions (including primary and subordinate legislation) as may be designated in accordance with the order by the Authority, including provision for the modification by the Authority of provisions designated;

(d) make provision about the effect of requirements imposed, liabilities incurred and any other things done before commencement, including provision for and about investigations, penalties and the taking or continuing of any other action in respect of contraventions;

(e) make provision for the continuation of disciplinary and other proceedings begun before commencement, including provision about the decisions available to bodies before which such proceedings take place and the effect of their decisions;

(f)   make provision as regards the Authority's obligation to maintain a record under section 347 as respects persons in relation to whom provision is made by the order.

(3)   The order may—

(a)   confer functions on the Treasury, the Secretary of State, the Authority, the scheme manager, the scheme operator, members of the panel established under paragraph 4 of Schedule 17, the Competition Commission or [the Office of Fair Trading];

(b)   confer jurisdiction on the Tribunal;

(c)   provide for fees to be charged in connection with the carrying out of functions conferred under the order;

(d)   modify, exclude or apply (with or without modifications) any primary or subordinate legislation (including any provision of, or made under, this Act).

(4)   In subsection (2) "commencement" means the commencement of such provisions of this Act as may be specified by the order.

[453]

NOTES

Sub-s (3):words in square brackets substituted by the Enterprise Act 2002, s 278(1), Sch 25, para 40(1), (18), as from 1 April 2003.

Note: in accordance with the Financial Services and Markets Act 2000 (Transitional Provisions) (Mortgages) Order 2004, SI 2004/2615 and the Financial Services and Markets Act 2000 (Transitional Provisions) (General Insurance Intermediaries) Order 2004, SI 2004/3351, certain firms carrying on regulated mortgage business and insurance mediation business whose applications for permission were still pending prior to the relevant dates on which these activities became regulated activities received interim permission or interim approval to carry on these regulated activities. Generally, firms with interim permission or approval were subject to FSA's rules as well as its supervisory jurisdiction and its associated sanctions and enforcement regime. Such firms were not, however, covered by the Financial Services Compensation Scheme. Interim permission or interim approval continued until the firm's application was determined and permission granted, or until the applicant withdrew their application, or until the Financial Services Tribunal confirmed the FSA's decision to refuse the application for permission. In any event, interim permission and interim approval ended on 31 October 2005 for regulated mortgage firms and on 14 January 2006 for insurance mediation activities and after this date no firms have interim permission to carry on these activities. See also the Financial Services and Markets Act 2000 (Regulated Activities) (Amendment) Order 2006, SI 2006/1969 at **[2853]** (interim permissions and interim approvals relating to the activity of establishing, operating or winding up a personal pension scheme, or which relate to the specified investment of rights under a personal pension scheme), the Financial Services and Markets Act 2000 (Regulated Activities) (Amendment) (No 2) Order 2006, SI 2006/2383 at **[2860]** (interim permissions and interim approvals relating to the activity of administering, arranging or advising on regulated home reversion plans or regulated home purchase plans), and the Financial Services and Markets Act 2000 (Regulated Activities) (Amendment) (No 2) Order 2007, SI 2007/3510 at **[2899]** (interim permissions, interim approvals relating to the provision of travel insurance (where a contract of insurance is linked to (a) travel to an event organised by the travel provider where the person seeking insurance is not an individual or a business with a group annual turnover of less than £1,000,000; or (b) the hire of a vehicle) where such provision will become a regulated activity on 1 January 2009 following the amendments made by this Order to the Regulated Activities Order (SI 2001/544).

An Order under section 426: see the notes to s 426 at **[452]**.

428   Regulations and orders

(1)   Any power to make an order which is conferred on a Minister of the Crown by this Act and any power to make regulations which is conferred by this Act is exercisable by statutory instrument.

(2)   The Lord Chancellor's power to make rules under section 132 is exercisable by statutory instrument.

(3)   Any statutory instrument made under this Act may—

(a)   contain such incidental, supplemental, consequential and transitional provision as the person making it considers appropriate; and

(b)   make different provision for different cases.

[454]

429   Parliamentary control of statutory instruments

(1)   No order is to be made under—

(a)   section 144(4), 192(b) or (e), 236(5), 404 or 419, or

(b)   paragraph 1 of Schedule 8,

unless a draft of the order has been laid before Parliament and approved by a resolution of each House.

(2)   No regulations are to be made under section [90B[, 214A, 214B] or] 262 unless a draft of the regulations has been laid before Parliament and approved by a resolution of each House.

(3)   An order to which, if it is made, subsection (4) or (5) will apply is not to be made unless a draft of the order has been laid before Parliament and approved by a resolution of each House.

(4) This subsection applies to an order under section 21 if—

(a) it is the first order to be made, or to contain provisions made, under section 21(4);

(b) it varies an order made under section 21(4) so as to make section 21(1) apply in circumstances in which it did not previously apply;

(c) it is the first order to be made, or to contain provision made, under section 21(5);

(d) it varies a previous order made under section 21(5) so as to make section 21(1) apply in circumstances in which it did not, as a result of that previous order, apply;

(e) it is the first order to be made, or to contain provisions made, under section 21(9) or (10);

(f) it adds one or more activities to those that are controlled activities for the purposes of section 21; or

(g) it adds one or more investments to those which are controlled investments for the purposes of section 21.

(5) This subsection applies to an order under section 38 if—

(a) it is the first order to be made, or to contain provisions made, under that section; or

(b) it contains provisions restricting or removing an exemption provided by an earlier order made under that section.

(6) An order containing a provision to which, if the order is made, subsection (7) will apply is not to be made unless a draft of the order has been laid before Parliament and approved by a resolution of each House.

(7) This subsection applies to a provision contained in an order if—

(a) it is the first to be made in the exercise of the power conferred by subsection (1) of section 326 or it removes a body from those for the time being designated under that subsection; or

(b) it is the first to be made in the exercise of the power conferred by subsection (6) of section 327 or it adds a description of regulated activity or investment to those for the time being specified for the purposes of that subsection.

(8) Any other statutory instrument made under this Act, apart from one made under section 431(2) or to which paragraph 26 of Schedule 2 applies, shall be subject to annulment in pursuance of a resolution of either House of Parliament.

[455]

NOTES

Sub-s (2): words in first (outer) pair of square brackets inserted by the Companies Act 2006, s 1272, Sch 15, Pt 1, paras 1, 12, as from 8 November 2006; words in second (inner) pair of square brackets inserted by the Banking Act 2009, s 178, as from a day to be appointed.

430 Extent

(1) This Act, except Chapter IV of Part XVII, extends to Northern Ireland.

(2) Except where Her Majesty by Order in Council provides otherwise, the extent of any amendment or repeal made by or under this Act is the same as the extent of the provision amended or repealed.

(3) Her Majesty may by Order in Council provide for any provision of or made under this Act relating to a matter which is the subject of other legislation which extends to any of the Channel Islands or the Isle of Man to extend there with such modifications (if any) as may be specified in the Order.

[456]

431 Commencement

(1) The following provisions come into force on the passing of this Act—

(a) this section;

(b) sections 428, 430 and 433;

(c) paragraphs 1 and 2 of Schedule 21.

(2) The other provisions of this Act come into force on such day as the Treasury may by order appoint; and different days may be appointed for different purposes.

[457]

NOTES

Orders: the Financial Services and Markets Act 2000 (Commencement No 1) Order 2001, SI 2001/516 at [**2001**]; the Financial Services and Markets Act 2000 (Commencement No 2) Order 2001, SI 2001/1282 at [**2002**]; the Financial Services and Markets Act 2000 (Commencement No 3) Order 2001, SI 2001/1820 at [**2003**]; the Financial Services and Markets Act 2000 (Commencement No 4 and Transitional Provision) Order 2001, SI 2001/2364 at [**2004**]; the Financial Services and Markets Act 2000 (Commencement No 5) Order 2001, SI 2001/2632 at [**2007**]; the Financial Services and Markets Act 2000 (Commencement No 6) Order 2001, SI 2001/3436 at [**2008**]; the Financial Services and Markets Act 2000 (Commencement No 7) Order 2001, SI 2001/3538 at [**2009**].

432 Minor and consequential amendments, transitional provisions and repeals

(1)   Schedule 20 makes minor and consequential amendments.

(2)   Schedule 21 makes transitional provisions.

(3)   The enactments set out in Schedule 22 are repealed.

[458]

433 Short title

This Act may be cited as the Financial Services and Markets Act 2000.

[459]

SCHEDULES

SCHEDULE 1
THE FINANCIAL SERVICES AUTHORITY
Section 1

_____

NOTES

Note: the functions of the FSA under the Transfer of Funds (Information on the Payer) Regulations 2007, SI 2007/3298 shall be treated for the purposes of Parts 1, 2 and 4 of this Schedule as functions conferred on the Authority under that Act; see reg 4(4) of the 2007 Regulations at **[2881]**. Also, the functions of the FSA under the Counter-Terrorism Act 2008, Sch 7 shall be treated for the purposes of Parts 1, 2 and 4 of this Schedule as functions conferred on the Authority under that Act; see Sch 7, para 41 at **[1821]**.

_____

PART I
GENERAL

Interpretation

1.—(1)   In this Schedule—
"the 1985 Act" means the Companies Act 1985;
"non-executive committee" means the committee maintained under paragraph 3;
"functions", in relation to the Authority, means functions conferred on the Authority by or under any provision of this Act.

(2)   For the purposes of this Schedule, the following are the Authority's legislative functions—
(a)   making rules;
(b)   issuing codes under section 64 or 119;
(c)   issuing statements under section 64, 69, 124 or 210;
(d)   giving directions under section 316, 318 or 328;
(e)   issuing general guidance (as defined by section 158(5)) [or guidance under section 158A].

Constitution

2.—(1)   The constitution of the Authority must continue to provide for the Authority to have—
(a)   a chairman; and
(b)   a governing body.

(2)   The governing body must include the chairman.

(3)   The chairman and other members of the governing body must be appointed, and be liable to removal from office, by the Treasury.

(4)   The validity of any act of the Authority is not affected—
(a)   by a vacancy in the office of chairman; or
(b)   by a defect in the appointment of a person as a member of the governing body or as chairman.

Non-executive members of the governing body

3.—(1)   The Authority must secure—
(a)   that the majority of the members of its governing body are non-executive members; and
(b)   that a committee of its governing body, consisting solely of the non-executive members, is set up and maintained for the purposes of discharging the functions conferred on the committee by this Schedule.

(2)   The members of the non-executive committee are to be appointed by the Authority.

(3)   The non-executive committee is to have a chairman appointed by the Treasury from among its members.

Functions of the non-executive committee

4.—(1)   In this paragraph "the committee" means the non-executive committee.

(2)   The non-executive functions are functions of the Authority but must be discharged by the committee.

(3)   The non-executive functions are—
- (a)   keeping under review the question whether the Authority is, in discharging its functions in accordance with decisions of its governing body, using its resources in the most efficient and economic way;
- (b)   keeping under review the question whether the Authority's internal financial controls secure the proper conduct of its financial affairs; and
- (c)   determining the remuneration of—
  - (i)   the chairman of the Authority's governing body; and
  - (ii)   the executive members of that body.

(4)   The function mentioned in sub-paragraph (3)(b) and those mentioned in sub-paragraph (3)(c) may be discharged on behalf of the committee by a sub-committee.

(5)   Any sub-committee of the committee—
- (a)   must have as its chairman the chairman of the committee; but
- (b)   may include persons other than members of the committee.

(6)   The committee must prepare a report on the discharge of its functions for inclusion in the Authority's annual report to the Treasury under paragraph 10.

(7)   The committee's report must relate to the same period as that covered by the Authority's report.

Arrangements for discharging functions

5.—(1)   The Authority may make arrangements for any of its functions to be discharged by a committee, sub-committee, officer or member of staff of the Authority.

[(2)   But—
- (a)   in exercising the legislative functions mentioned in paragraph 1(2)(a) to (d), the Authority must act through its governing body; and
- (b)   the legislative function mentioned in paragraph 1(2)(e) may not be discharged by an officer or member of staff of the Authority.]

(3)   Sub-paragraph (1) does not apply to the non-executive functions.

Monitoring and enforcement

6.—(1)   The Authority must maintain arrangements designed to enable it to determine whether persons on whom requirements are imposed by or under this Act[, or by any directly applicable Community regulation made under the markets in financial instruments directive,] are complying with them.

(2)   Those arrangements may provide for functions to be performed on behalf of the Authority by any body or person who, in its opinion, is competent to perform them.

(3)   The Authority must also maintain arrangements for enforcing the provisions of, or made under, this Act [or of any directly applicable Community regulation made under the markets in financial instruments directive].

(4)   Sub-paragraph (2) does not affect the Authority's duty under sub-paragraph (1).

Arrangements for the investigation of complaints

7.—(1)   The Authority must—
- (a)   make arrangements ("the complaints scheme") for the investigation of complaints arising in connection with the exercise of, or failure to exercise, any of its functions (other than its legislative functions); and
- (b)   appoint an independent person ("the investigator") to be responsible for the conduct of investigations in accordance with the complaints scheme.

(2)   The complaints scheme must be designed so that, as far as reasonably practicable, complaints are investigated quickly.

(3)   The Treasury's approval is required for the appointment or dismissal of the investigator.

(4)   The terms and conditions on which the investigator is appointed must be such as, in the opinion of the Authority, are reasonably designed to secure—
- (a)   that he will be free at all times to act independently of the Authority; and
- (b)   that complaints will be investigated under the complaints scheme without favouring the Authority.

(5)   Before making the complaints scheme, the Authority must publish a draft of the proposed scheme in the way appearing to the Authority best calculated to bring it to the attention of the public.

(6)   The draft must be accompanied by notice that representations about it may be made to the Authority within a specified time.

(7)   Before making the proposed complaints scheme, the Authority must have regard to any representations made to it in accordance with sub-paragraph (6).

(8)   If the Authority makes the proposed complaints scheme, it must publish an account, in general terms, of—

(a)   the representations made to it in accordance with sub-paragraph (6); and

(b)   its response to them.

(9)   If the complaints scheme differs from the draft published under sub-paragraph (5) in a way which is, in the opinion of the Authority, significant the Authority must (in addition to complying with sub-paragraph (8)) publish details of the difference.

(10)   The Authority must publish up-to-date details of the complaints scheme including, in particular, details of—

(a)   the provision made under paragraph 8(5); and

(b)   the powers which the investigator has to investigate a complaint.

(11)   Those details must be published in the way appearing to the Authority to be best calculated to bring them to the attention of the public.

(12)   The Authority must, without delay, give the Treasury a copy of any details published by it under this paragraph.

(13)   The Authority may charge a reasonable fee for providing a person with a copy of—

(a)   a draft published under sub-paragraph (5);

(b)   details published under sub-paragraph (10).

(14)   Sub-paragraphs (5) to (9) and (13)(a) also apply to a proposal to alter or replace the complaints scheme.

Investigation of complaints

8.—(1)   The Authority is not obliged to investigate a complaint in accordance with the complaints scheme which it reasonably considers would be more appropriately dealt with in another way (for example by referring the matter to the Tribunal or by the institution of other legal proceedings).

(2)   The complaints scheme must provide—

(a)   for reference to the investigator of any complaint which the Authority is investigating; and

(b)   for him—

(i)   to have the means to conduct a full investigation of the complaint;

(ii)   to report on the result of his investigation to the Authority and the complainant; and

(iii)   to be able to publish his report (or any part of it) if he considers that it (or the part) ought to be brought to the attention of the public.

(3)   If the Authority has decided not to investigate a complaint, it must notify the investigator.

(4)   If the investigator considers that a complaint of which he has been notified under sub-paragraph (3) ought to be investigated, he may proceed as if the complaint had been referred to him under the complaints scheme.

(5)   The complaints scheme must confer on the investigator the power to recommend, if he thinks it appropriate, that the Authority—

(a)   makes a compensatory payment to the complainant,

(b)   remedies the matter complained of,

or takes both of those steps.

(6)   The complaints scheme must require the Authority, in a case where the investigator—

(a)   has reported that a complaint is well-founded, or

(b)   has criticised the Authority in his report,

to inform the investigator and the complainant of the steps which it proposes to take in response to the report.

(7)   The investigator may require the Authority to publish the whole or a specified part of the response.

(8)   The investigator may appoint a person to conduct the investigation on his behalf but subject to his direction.

(9)   Neither an officer nor an employee of the Authority may be appointed under sub-paragraph (8).

(10)   Sub-paragraph (2) is not to be taken as preventing the Authority from making arrangements for the initial investigation of a complaint to be conducted by the Authority.

Records

9. The Authority must maintain satisfactory arrangements for—
  (a) recording decisions made in the exercise of its functions; and
  (b) the safe-keeping of those records which it considers ought to be preserved.

Annual report

10.—(1) At least once a year the Authority must make a report to the Treasury on—
  (a) the discharge of its functions;
  (b) the extent to which, in its opinion, the regulatory objectives have been met;
  (c) its consideration of the matters mentioned in section 2(3); and
  (d) such other matters as the Treasury may from time to time direct.

  (2) The report must be accompanied by—
  (a) the report prepared by the non-executive committee under paragraph 4(6); and
  (b) such other reports or information, prepared by such persons, as the Treasury may from time to time direct.

  (3) The Treasury must lay before Parliament a copy of each report received by them under this paragraph.

  (4) The Treasury may—
  (a) require the Authority to comply with any provisions of [the Companies Act 2006] about accounts and their audit which would not otherwise apply to it; or
  (b) direct that any such provision of that Act is to apply to the Authority with such modifications as are specified in the direction.

  (5) Compliance with any requirement imposed under sub-paragraph (4)(a) or (b) is enforceable by injunction or, in Scotland, an order under section 45(b) of the Court of Session Act 1988.

  (6) Proceedings under sub-paragraph (5) may be brought only by the Treasury.

Annual public meeting

11.—(1) Not later than three months after making a report under paragraph 10, the Authority must hold a public meeting ("the annual meeting") for the purposes of enabling that report to be considered.

  (2) The Authority must organise the annual meeting so as to allow—
  (a) a general discussion of the contents of the report which is being considered; and
  (b) a reasonable opportunity for those attending the meeting to put questions to the Authority about the way in which it discharged, or failed to discharge, its functions during the period to which the report relates.

  (3) But otherwise the annual meeting is to be organised and conducted in such a way as the Authority considers appropriate.

  (4) The Authority must give reasonable notice of its annual meeting.

  (5) That notice must—
  (a) give details of the time and place at which the meeting is to be held;
  (b) set out the proposed agenda for the meeting;
  (c) indicate the proposed duration of the meeting;
  (d) give details of the Authority's arrangements for enabling persons to attend; and
  (e) be published by the Authority in the way appearing to it to be most suitable for bringing the notice to the attention of the public.

  (6) If the Authority proposes to alter any of the arrangements which have been included in the notice given under sub-paragraph (4) it must—
  (a) give reasonable notice of the alteration; and
  (b) publish that notice in the way appearing to the Authority to be best calculated to bring it to the attention of the public.

Report of annual meeting

12. Not later than one month after its annual meeting, the Authority must publish a report of the proceedings of the meeting.

[460]

NOTES
  Para 1: words in square brackets in sub-para (2)(e) inserted by the Financial Services and Markets Act 2000 (Markets in Financial Instruments) (Modification of Powers) Regulations 2006, SI 2006/2975, regs 2, 12, as from 6 December 2006.
  Para 5: sub-para (2) substituted by the Regulatory Reform (Financial Services and Markets Act 2000) Order 2007, SI 2007/1973, arts 2, 14, as from 12 July 2007.

Para 6: words in square brackets inserted by the Financial Services and Markets Act 2000 (Markets in Financial Instruments) Regulations 2007, SI 2007/126, reg 3(5), Sch 5, paras 1, 23, as from 1 April 2007 (certain purposes (see reg 1(2) at **[4051]**)), and as from 1 November 2007 (otherwise).

Para 10: words in square brackets substituted (for the original words "the 1985 Act") by the Companies Act 2006 (Consequential Amendments etc) Order 2008, SI 2008/948, art 3(1), Sch 1, Pt 2, para 213, as from 6 April 2008 (for savings see art 6(4) of the 2008 Order which provides that where by virtue of any transitional provision, a provision of the Companies Act 2006 has effect only (a) on or after a specified date, or (b) in relation to matters occurring or arising on or after a specified date, any amendment substituting or inserting a reference to that provision has effect correspondingly).

Transitional provisions: see the Financial Services and Markets Act 2000 (Transitional Provisions and Savings) (Rules) Order 2001, SI 2001/1534, art 4(7), the Financial Services and Markets Act 2000 (Transitional Provisions) (Reviews of Pensions Business) Order 2001, SI 2001/2512, and the Financial Services and Markets Act 2000 (Interim Permissions) Order 2001, SI 2001/3374, art 12(3) at **[2513]**. Note also that the reference to the Authority's functions includes its functions as a designated agency under the Financial Services Act 1986 (repealed by the Financial Services and Markets Act 2000 (Consequential Amendments and Repeals) Order 2001, SI 2001/3649, art 3(1)(c)) and the reference to the Authority's legislative functions includes its functions of issuing statements of principle, rules, regulations and codes of practice under that Act; see the Financial Services and Markets Act 2000 (Consequential and Transitional Provisions) (Miscellaneous) Order 2001, SI 2001/1821, art 2(1)(b), (c).

Note: for the purposes of para 6 a requirement imposed by the FSA under the Electronic Commerce Directive (Financial Services and Markets) Regulations 2002, SI 2002/1775 upon an incoming provider is to be treated as imposed on him by or under this Act; see reg 12(2) of those Regulations at **[2685]**.

Note: FSA 1986, s 190 was repealed by the Data Protection Act 1998, s 74(2), Sch 16, Pt I, as from 1 March 2000. Section 31(1) of the 1998 Act provides that personal data processed for the purposes of discharging functions to which that subsection applies are exempt from the subject information provisions in any case to the extent to which the application of those provisions to the data would be likely to prejudice the proper discharge of those functions.

PART II
STATUS

13.   In relation to any of its functions—
(a)   the Authority is not to be regarded as acting on behalf of the Crown; and
(b)   its members, officers and staff are not to be regarded as Crown servants.

Exemption from requirement of "limited" in Authority's name

14.   The Authority is to continue to be exempt from the requirements of the 1985 Act relating to the use of "limited" as part of its name.

15.   If the Secretary of State is satisfied that any action taken by the Authority makes it inappropriate for the exemption given by paragraph 14 to continue he may, after consulting the Treasury, give a direction removing it.

[461]

NOTES
Transitional provisions: see the note to Pt I of this Schedule at **[460]**.
1985 Act: ie, the Companies Act 1985 which is mostly repealed by the Companies Act 2006.

PART III
PENALTIES AND FEES

Penalties

16.—(1)   In determining its policy with respect to the amounts of penalties to be imposed by it under this Act, the Authority must take no account of the expenses which it incurs, or expects to incur, in discharging its functions.

(2)   The Authority must prepare and operate a scheme for ensuring that the amounts paid to the Authority by way of penalties imposed under this Act are applied for the benefit of authorised persons.

(3)   The scheme may, in particular, make different provision with respect to different classes of authorised person.

(4)   Up to date details of the scheme must be set out in a document ("the scheme details").

(5)   The scheme details must be published by the Authority in the way appearing to it to be best calculated to bring them to the attention of the public.

(6)   Before making the scheme, the Authority must publish a draft of the proposed scheme in the way appearing to the Authority to be best calculated to bring it to the attention of the public.

(7)   The draft must be accompanied by notice that representations about the proposals may be made to the Authority within a specified time.

(8)   Before making the scheme, the Authority must have regard to any representations made to it in accordance with sub-paragraph (7).

(9)   If the Authority makes the proposed scheme, it must publish an account, in general terms, of—
- (a)   the representations made to it in accordance with sub-paragraph (7); and
- (b)   its response to them.

(10)   If the scheme differs from the draft published under sub-paragraph (6) in a way which is, in the opinion of the Authority, significant the Authority must (in addition to complying with sub-paragraph (9)) publish details of the difference.

(11)   The Authority must, without delay, give the Treasury a copy of any scheme details published by it.

(12)   The Authority may charge a reasonable fee for providing a person with a copy of—
- (a)   a draft published under sub-paragraph (6);
- (b)   scheme details.

(13)   Sub-paragraphs (6) to (10) and (12)(a) also apply to a proposal to alter or replace the complaints scheme.

Fees

17.—(1)   The Authority may make rules providing for the payment to it of such fees, in connection with the discharge of any of its functions under or as a result of this Act, as it considers will (taking account of its expected income from fees and charges provided for by any other provision of this Act) enable it—
- (a)   to meet expenses incurred in carrying out its functions or for any incidental purpose;
- (b)   to repay the principal of, and pay any interest on, any money which it has borrowed and which has been used for the purpose of meeting expenses incurred in relation to its assumption of functions under this Act or the Bank of England Act 1998; and
- (c)   to maintain adequate reserves.

(2)   In fixing the amount of any fee which is to be payable to the Authority, no account is to be taken of any sums which the Authority receives, or expects to receive, by way of penalties imposed by it under this Act.

(3)   Sub-paragraph (1)(b) applies whether expenses were incurred before or after the coming into force of this Act or the Bank of England Act 1998.

(4)   Any fee which is owed to the Authority under any provision made by or under this Act may be recovered as a debt due to the Authority.

Services for which fees may not be charged

18.   The power conferred by paragraph 17 may not be used to require—
- (a)   a fee to be paid in respect of the discharge of any of the Authority's functions under paragraphs 13, 14, 19 or 20 of Schedule 3; or
- (b)   a fee to be paid by any person whose application for approval under section 59 has been granted.

[462]

NOTES

Transitional provisions: see the note to Pt I of this Schedule at [460].

PART IV
MISCELLANEOUS

Exemption from liability in damages

19.—(1)   Neither the Authority nor any person who is, or is acting as, a member, officer or member of staff of the Authority is to be liable in damages for anything done or omitted in the discharge, or purported discharge, of the Authority's functions.

(2)   Neither the investigator appointed under paragraph 7 nor a person appointed to conduct an investigation on his behalf under paragraph 8(8) is to be liable in damages for anything done or omitted in the discharge, or purported discharge, of his functions in relation to the investigation of a complaint.

(3)   Neither sub-paragraph (1) nor sub-paragraph (2) applies—
- (a)   if the act or omission is shown to have been in bad faith; or
- (b)   so as to prevent an award of damages made in respect of an act or omission on the ground that the act or omission was unlawful as a result of section 6(1) of the Human Rights Act 1998.

[19A.   For the purposes of this Act anything done by an accredited financial investigator within the meaning of the Proceeds of Crime Act 2002 who is—
- (a)   a member of the staff of the Authority, or

(b)   a person appointed by the Authority under section 97, 167 or 168 to conduct an investigation,

must be treated as done in the exercise or discharge of a function of the Authority.]

20, 21. ...

[463]

PART I
FSMA 2000

NOTES

Para 19A: inserted by the Proceeds of Crime Act 2002, s 456, Sch 11, para 38, as from 24 February 2003.

Paras 20, 21: amend the House of Commons Disqualification Act 1975, Sch 1, Pt III and the Northern Ireland Assembly Disqualification Act 1975, Sch 1, Pt III.

Transitional provisions: see the note to Pt I of this Schedule at **[460]**.

SCHEDULE 2
REGULATED ACTIVITIES

Section 22(2)

NOTES

The regulated activities for the purposes of s 22 of this Act are set out in the Financial Services and Markets Act 2000 (Regulated Activities) Order 2001, SI 2001/544 at **[2010]**.

PART I
REGULATED ACTIVITIES
General

1.   The matters with respect to which provision may be made under section 22(1) in respect of activities include, in particular, those described in general terms in this Part of this Schedule.

Dealing in investments

2.—(1)   Buying, selling, subscribing for or underwriting investments or offering or agreeing to do so, either as a principal or as an agent.

(2)   In the case of an investment which is a contract of insurance, that includes carrying out the contract.

Arranging deals in investments

3.   Making, or offering or agreeing to make—
(a)   arrangements with a view to another person buying, selling, subscribing for or underwriting a particular investment;
(b)   arrangements with a view to a person who participates in the arrangements buying, selling, subscribing for or underwriting investments.

Deposit taking

4.   Accepting deposits.

Safekeeping and administration of assets

5.—(1)   Safeguarding and administering assets belonging to another which consist of or include investments or offering or agreeing to do so.

(2)   Arranging for the safeguarding and administration of assets belonging to another, or offering or agreeing to do so.

Managing investments

6.   Managing, or offering or agreeing to manage, assets belonging to another person where—
(a)   the assets consist of or include investments; or
(b)   the arrangements for their management are such that the assets may consist of or include investments at the discretion of the person managing or offering or agreeing to manage them.

Investment advice

7.   Giving or offering or agreeing to give advice to persons on—
(a)   buying, selling, subscribing for or underwriting an investment; or
(b)   exercising any right conferred by an investment to acquire, dispose of, underwrite or convert an investment.

Establishing collective investment schemes

8.   Establishing, operating or winding up a collective investment scheme, including acting as—
    (a)   trustee of a unit trust scheme;
    (b)   depositary of a collective investment scheme other than a unit trust scheme; or
    (c)   sole director of a body incorporated by virtue of regulations under section 262.

Using computer-based systems for giving investment instructions

9.—(1)   Sending on behalf of another person instructions relating to an investment by means of a computer-based system which enables investments to be transferred without a written instrument.

(2)   Offering or agreeing to send such instructions by such means on behalf of another person.

(3)   Causing such instructions to be sent by such means on behalf of another person.

(4)   Offering or agreeing to cause such instructions to be sent by such means on behalf of another person.

[464]

NOTES
    Part heading: for the words in italics there are substituted the words "Regulated activities: general" by the Dormant Bank and Building Society Accounts Act 2008, s 15, Sch 2, para 1(1), (2), as from a day to be appointed.

[PART 1A
REGULATED ACTIVITIES: RECLAIM FUNDS

Activities of reclaim funds

9A.—(1)   The matters with respect to which provision may be made under section 22(1) in respect of activities include, in particular, any of the activities of a reclaim fund.

(2)   "Reclaim fund" has the meaning given by section 5(1) of the Dormant Bank and Building Society Accounts Act 2008.]

[464A]

NOTES
    Commencement: to be appointed.
    Inserted by the Dormant Bank and Building Society Accounts Act 2008, s 15, Sch 2, para 1(1), (3), as from a day to be appointed.

PART II
INVESTMENTS

General

10.   The matters with respect to which provision may be made under section 22(1) in respect of investments include, in particular, those described in general terms in this Part of this Schedule.

Securities

11.—(1)   Shares or stock in the share capital of a company.

(2)   "Company" includes—
    (a)   any body corporate (wherever incorporated), and
    (b)   any unincorporated body constituted under the law of a country or territory outside the United Kingdom,
other than an open-ended investment company.

Instruments creating or acknowledging indebtedness

12.   Any of the following—
    (a)   debentures;
    (b)   debenture stock;
    (c)   loan stock;
    (d)   bonds;
    (e)   certificates of deposit;
    (f)   any other instruments creating or acknowledging a present or future indebtedness.

Government and public securities

13.—(1)   Loan stock, bonds and other instruments—
    (a)   creating or acknowledging indebtedness; and
    (b)   issued by or on behalf of a government, local authority or public authority.

(2)   "Government, local authority or public authority" means—
  (a)   the government of the United Kingdom, of Northern Ireland, or of any country or territory outside the United Kingdom;
  (b)   a local authority in the United Kingdom or elsewhere;
  (c)   any international organisation the members of which include the United Kingdom or another member State.

Instruments giving entitlement to investments

14.—(1)   Warrants or other instruments entitling the holder to subscribe for any investment.

(2)   It is immaterial whether the investment is in existence or identifiable.

Certificates representing securities

15.   Certificates or other instruments which confer contractual or property rights—
  (a)   in respect of any investment held by someone other than the person on whom the rights are conferred by the certificate or other instrument; and
  (b)   the transfer of which may be effected without requiring the consent of that person.

Units in collective investment schemes

16.—(1)   Shares in or securities of an open-ended investment company.

(2)   Any right to participate in a collective investment scheme.

Options

17.   Options to acquire or dispose of property.

Futures

18.   Rights under a contract for the sale of a commodity or property of any other description under which delivery is to be made at a future date.

Contracts for differences

19.   Rights under—
  (a)   a contract for differences; or
  (b)   any other contract the purpose or pretended purpose of which is to secure a profit or avoid a loss by reference to fluctuations in—
    (i)   the value or price of property of any description; or
    (ii)   an index or other factor designated for that purpose in the contract.

Contracts of insurance

20.   Rights under a contract of insurance, including rights under contracts falling within head C of Schedule 2 to the Friendly Societies Act 1992.

Participation in Lloyd's syndicates

21.—(1)   The underwriting capacity of a Lloyd's syndicate.

(2)   A person's membership (or prospective membership) of a Lloyd's syndicate.

Deposits

22.   Rights under any contract under which a sum of money (whether or not denominated in a currency) is paid on terms under which it will be repaid, with or without interest or a premium, and either on demand or at a time or in circumstances agreed by or on behalf of the person making the payment and the person receiving it.

Loans secured on land

23.—(1)   Rights under any contract under which—
  (a)   one person provides another with credit; and
  (b)   the obligation of the borrower to repay is secured on land.

(2)   "Credit" includes any cash loan or other financial accommodation.

(3)   "Cash" includes money in any form.

[Other finance arrangements involving land

23A.—(1)   Rights under any arrangement for the provision of finance under which the person providing the finance either—
  (a)   acquires a major interest in land from the person to whom the finance is provided, or

(b)   disposes of a major interest in land to that person,

as part of the arrangement.

(2)   References in sub-paragraph (1) to a "major interest" in land are to—

    (a)   in relation to land in England or Wales—

        (i)   an estate in fee simple absolute, or

        (ii)   a term of years absolute,

whether subsisting at law or in equity;

    (b)   in relation to land in Scotland—

        (i)   the interest of an owner of land, or

        (ii)   the tenant's right over or interest in a property subject to a lease;

    (c)   in relation to land in Northern Ireland—

        (i)   any freehold estate, or

        (ii)   any leasehold estate,

whether subsisting at law or in equity.

(3)   It is immaterial for the purposes of sub-paragraph (1) whether either party acquires or (as the case may be) disposes of the interest in land—

    (a)   directly, or

    (b)   indirectly.]

Rights in investments

24.   Any right or interest in anything which is an investment as a result of any other provision made under section 22(1).

[465]

NOTES

Para 23A: inserted by the Regulation of Financial Services (Land Transactions) Act 2005, s 1, as from 19 February 2006.

Modifications to para 12(e): (i) a reference to a certificate of deposit includes a reference to uncertificated units of an eligible debt security where the issue of those units corresponds, in accordance with the current terms of issue of the security, to the issue of a certificate of deposit which is a certificate of deposit for the purposes of that enactment; (ii) a reference to an amount stated in a certificate of deposit includes a reference to a principal amount stated in, or determined in accordance with, the current terms of issue of an eligible debt security of the kind referred to in (i) above; see the Uncertificated Securities (Amendment) (Eligible Debt Securities) Regulations 2003, SI 2003/1633, reg 15, Sch 2, para 6 (as from 24 June 2003).

Modifications to para 12(f): the reference to securities, instruments or investments creating or acknowledging indebtedness (or creating or acknowledging a present or future indebtedness) includes a reference to uncertificated units of eligible debt securities; see the Uncertificated Securities (Amendment) (Eligible Debt Securities) Regulations 2003, SI 2003/1633, reg 15, Sch 2, para 8 (as from 24 June 2003).

PART III
SUPPLEMENTAL PROVISIONS

The order-making power

25.—(1)   An order under section 22(1) may—

    (a)   provide for exemptions;

    (b)   confer powers on the Treasury or the Authority;

    (c)   authorise the making of regulations or other instruments by the Treasury for purposes of, or connected with, any relevant provision;

    (d)   authorise the making of rules or other instruments by the Authority for purposes of, or connected with, any relevant provision;

    (e)   make provision in respect of any information or document which, in the opinion of the Treasury or the Authority, is relevant for purposes of, or connected with, any relevant provision;

    (f)   make such consequential, transitional or supplemental provision as the Treasury consider appropriate for purposes of, or connected with, any relevant provision.

(2)   Provision made as a result of sub-paragraph (1)(f) may amend any primary or subordinate legislation, including any provision of, or made under, this Act.

(3)   "Relevant provision" means any provision—

    (a)   of section 22 or this Schedule; or

    (b)   made under that section or this Schedule.

Parliamentary control

26.—(1)   This paragraph applies to the first order made under section 22(1).

(2)   This paragraph also applies to any subsequent order made under section 22(1) which contains a statement by the Treasury that, in their opinion, the effect (or one of the effects) of the proposed order would be that an activity which is not a regulated activity would become a regulated activity.

(3)   An order to which this paragraph applies—
(a)   must be laid before Parliament after being made; and
(b)   ceases to have effect at the end of the relevant period unless before the end of that period the order is approved by a resolution of each House of Parliament (but without that affecting anything done under the order or the power to make a new order).

(4)   "Relevant period" means a period of twenty-eight days beginning with the day on which the order is made.

(5)   In calculating the relevant period no account is to be taken of any time during which Parliament is dissolved or prorogued or during which both Houses are adjourned for more than four days.

Interpretation

27.—(1)   In this Schedule—
"buying" includes acquiring for valuable consideration;
"offering" includes inviting to treat;
"property" includes currency of the United Kingdom or any other country or territory; and
"selling" includes disposing for valuable consideration.

(2)   In sub-paragraph (1) "disposing" includes—
(a)   in the case of an investment consisting of rights under a contract—
(i)   surrendering, assigning or converting those rights; or
(ii)   assuming the corresponding liabilities under the contract;
(b)   in the case of an investment consisting of rights under other arrangements, assuming the corresponding liabilities under the contract or arrangements;
(c)   in the case of any other investment, issuing or creating the investment or granting the rights or interests of which it consists.

(3)   In this Schedule references to an instrument include references to any record (whether or not in the form of a document).

[466]

NOTES
Orders: as to Orders made under para 25 above (ie, Orders under section 22(1)), see that section at **[22]**.

SCHEDULE 3
EEA PASSPORT RIGHTS

Sections 31(1)(b) and 37

NOTES
Transitional provisions: the Financial Services and Markets Act 2000 (Transitional Provisions) (Authorised Persons etc) Order 2001, SI 2001/2636, Pt II, Chapter II, provides that EEA firms with "passports" before 1 December 2001 under the Insurance Companies Act 1982, the Banking Coordination (Second Council Directive) Regulations 1992, SI 1992/3218, or the Investment Services Regulations 1995, SI 1995/3275, are to be treated after that date as having complied with the procedures in this Schedule. In relation to UK firms with "passports" before 1 December 2001, see art 77 of the 2001 Order. The 1982 Act was repealed, and SI 1992/3218 and SI 1995/3275 were revoked, by the Financial Services and Markets Act 2000 (Consequential Amendments and Repeals) Order 2001, SI 2001/3649, art 3(1)(b), (2)(a), (c).

PART I
DEFINED TERMS

The single market directives

1.   "The single market directives" means—
[(a)   the banking consolidation directive;]
(c)   the insurance directives; ...
[(ca)   the reinsurance directive;]
(d)   the [markets in financial instruments directive][; ...
(e)   the insurance mediation directive][; and
(f)   the UCITS directive.]

The banking [consolidation directive]

[2.   The banking consolidation directive" means Directive 2006/48/EC of the European Parliament and of the Council of 14 June 2006 relating to the taking up and pursuit of the business of credit institutions.]

The insurance directives

3.—(1)   "The insurance directives" means the first, second and third non-life insurance directives and the [life assurance consolidation directive].

(2)   "First non-life insurance directive" means the Council Directive of 24 July 1973 on the co-ordination of laws, regulations and administrative provisions relating to the taking up and pursuit of the business of direct insurance other than life assurance (No 73/239/EEC).

(3)   "Second non-life insurance directive" means the Council Directive of 22 June 1988 on the co-ordination of laws, etc, and laying down provisions to facilitate the effective exercise of freedom to provide services and amending Directive 73/239/EEC (No 88/357/EEC).

(4)   "Third non-life insurance directive" means the Council Directive of 18 June 1992 on the co-ordination of laws, etc, and amending Directives 73/239/EEC and 88/357/EEC (No 92/49/EEC).

[(8)   "Life assurance consolidation directive" means Directive 2002/83/EC of the European Parliament and of the Council of 5th November 2002 concerning life assurance.]

[The reinsurance directive

3A.   "The reinsurance directive" means Directive 2005/68/EC of the European Parliament and of the Council of 16 November 2005 on reinsurance and amending Council Directives 73/239/EEC, 92/49/EEC as well as Directives 98/78/EC and 2002/83/EC.]

...

4.   ...

[The insurance mediation directive

4A.   "The insurance mediation directive" means the European Parliament and Council Directive of 9th December 2002 on insurance mediation (No 2002/92/EC).]

[The UCITS directive

4B.   "The UCITS directive" means the Council Directive of 20 December 1985 on the coordination of laws, regulations and administrative provisions relating to undertakings for collective investment in transferable securities (No 85/611/EEC).]

[The markets in financial instruments directive

4C.   "The markets in financial instruments directive" means Directive 2004/39/EC of the European Parliament and of the Council of 21 April 2004 on markets in financial instruments.]

EEA firm

5.   "EEA firm" means any of the following if it does not have its [relevant office] in the United Kingdom—
- (a)   an investment firm (as defined in [Article 4.1.1 of the markets in financial instruments directive]) which is authorised (within the meaning of [Article 5]) by its home state regulator;
- [(b)   a credit institution (as defined in Article 4.1 of the banking consolidation directive) which is authorised (within the meaning of Article 4.2) by its home state regulator,
- (c)   a financial institution (as defined in Article 4.5 of the banking consolidation directive) which is a subsidiary of the kind mentioned in Article 24 and which fulfils the conditions in that Article;]
- (d)   an undertaking pursuing the activity of direct insurance (within the meaning of [Article 2 of the life assurance consolidation directive or Article 1 of the first non-life insurance directive]) which has received authorisation under [Article 4 of the life assurance consolidation directive or Article 6 of the first non-life insurance directive] from its home state regulator[; ...
- [(da)   an undertaking pursuing the activity of reinsurance (within the meaning of Article 2.1(a) of the reinsurance directive) which has received authorisation under (or is deemed to be authorised in accordance with) Article 3 of the reinsurance directive from its home state regulator;]
- (e)   an insurance intermediary (as defined in Article 2.5 of the insurance mediation directive), or a reinsurance intermediary (as defined in Article 2.6) which is registered with its home state regulator under Article 3][; or

(f)   a management company (as defined in Article 1a.2 of the UCITS directive) which is authorised (within the meaning of Article 5) by its home state regulator.]

[5A.   In paragraph 5, "relevant office" means—
   (a)   in relation to a firm falling within sub-paragraph (e) of that paragraph which has a registered office, its registered office;
   (b)   in relation to any other firm, its head office.]

EEA authorisation

[6.   "EEA authorisation" means—
   (a)   in relation to an EEA firm falling within paragraph 5(e), registration with its home state regulator under Article 3 of the insurance mediation directive;
   (b)   in relation to any other EEA firm, authorisation granted to an EEA firm by its home state regulator for the purpose of the relevant single market directive.]

EEA right

7.   "EEA right" means the entitlement of a person to establish a branch, or provide services, in an EEA State other than that in which he has his [relevant office]—
   (a)   in accordance with the Treaty as applied in the EEA; and
   (b)   subject to the conditions of the relevant single market directive.

[7A.   In paragraph 7, "relevant office" means—
   (a)   in relation to a person who has a registered office and whose entitlement is subject to the conditions of the insurance mediation directive, his registered office;
   (b)   in relation to any other person, his head office.]

EEA State

[8.   "EEA State" has the meaning given by Schedule 1 to the Interpretation Act 1978.]

Home state regulator

9.   "Home state regulator" means the competent authority (within the meaning of the relevant single market directive) of an EEA State (other than the United Kingdom) in relation to the EEA firm concerned.

UK firm

10.   "UK firm" means a person whose [relevant office] is in the UK and who has an EEA right to carry on activity in an EEA State other than the United Kingdom.

[10A.   In paragraph 10, "relevant office" means—
   (a)   in relation to a firm whose EEA right derives from the insurance mediation directive and which has a registered office, its registered office;
   (b)   in relation to any other firm, its head office.]

[UK investment firm

10B.   "UK investment firm" means a UK firm—
   (a)   which is an investment firm, and
   (b)   whose EEA right derives from the markets in financial instruments directive.]

11.   "Host state regulator" means the competent authority (within the meaning of the relevant single market directive) of an EEA State (other than the United Kingdom) in relation to a UK firm's exercise of EEA rights there.

[Tied agent

11A.   "Tied agent" has the meaning given in Article 4.1.25 of the markets in financial instruments directive.]

                                                                                                      [467]

NOTES

Para 1 is amended as follows:

Sub-para (a) substituted, for original sub-paras (a), (b), by the Banking Consolidation Directive (Consequential Amendments) Regulations 2000, SI 2000/2952, reg 8(1), (5)(a), as from 22 November 2000.

Word omitted from sub-para (c) repealed, and sub-para (e) and the word immediately preceding it inserted, by the Insurance Mediation Directive (Miscellaneous Amendments) Regulations 2003, SI 2003/1473, reg 2(2)(a), as from 14 January 2005.

Sub-para (ca) inserted by the Reinsurance Directive Regulations 2007, SI 2007/3253, reg 2(1), Sch 1, paras 1, 6(a), as from 10 December 2007.

Words in square brackets in sub-para (d) substituted by the Financial Services and Markets Act 2000 (Markets in Financial Instruments) Regulations 2007, SI 2007/126, reg 3(4), Sch 4, paras 1, 2, as from 1 April 2007 (certain purposes (see reg 1(2) at **[4051]**)), and as from 1 November 2007 (otherwise).

Word omitted from sub-para (d) repealed, and sub-para (f) and the word immediately preceding it inserted, by the Collective Investment Schemes (Miscellaneous Amendments) Regulations 2003, SI 2003/2066, reg 2(2)(a), as from 13 February 2004.

Para 2: substituted by the Capital Requirements Regulations 2006, SI 2006/3221, reg 29(1), Sch 3, para 2(1), (2), as from 1 January 2007; words in square brackets in the heading preceding para 2 substituted by virtue of SI 2000/2952, reg 8(1), (5)(b), as from 22 November 2000.

Para 3: words in square brackets in sub-para (1) substituted, and sub-para (8) substituted for the original sub-paras (5)–(7), by the Life Assurance Consolidation Directive (Consequential Amendments) Regulations 2004, SI 2004/3379, reg 6(1), (6)(a), as from 11 January 2005.

Para 3A: inserted by SI 2007/3253, reg 2(1), Sch 1, paras 1, 6(b), as from 10 December 2007.

Para 4: repealed by SI 2007/126, reg 3(4), Sch 4, paras 1, 3, as from 1 April 2007 (certain purposes (see reg 1(2) at [4051])), and as from 1 November 2007 (otherwise).

Paras 4A, 5A, 7A, 10A: inserted by SI 2003/1473, reg 2(2)(b), (d), (g), (i), as from 14 January 2005.

Para 4B: inserted by SI 2003/2066, reg 2(2)(b), as from 13 February 2004.

Para 4C: inserted by the Financial Services and Markets Act 2000 (Markets in Financial Instruments) (Modification of Powers) Regulations 2006, SI 2006/2975, regs 2, 13, as from 6 December 2006.

Para 5 is amended as follows:

Words in first pair of square brackets substituted, and sub-para (e) and the word immediately preceding it inserted, by SI 2003/1473, reg 2(2)(c), as from 14 January 2005.

Words in square brackets in sub-para (a) substituted by SI 2007/126, reg 3(4), Sch 4, paras 1, 4, as from 1 April 2007 (certain purposes (see reg 1(2) at [4051])), and as from 1 November 2007 (otherwise).

Sub-paras (b), (c) substituted by SI 2006/3221, reg 29(1), Sch 3, para 2(1), (3), as from 1 January 2007.

Words in square brackets in sub-para (d) substituted by SI 2004/3379, reg 6(1), (6)(b), as from 11 January 2005.

Word omitted from sub-para (d) repealed, and sub-para (f) and the word immediately preceding it inserted, by SI 2003/2066, reg 2(2)(c), as from 13 February 2004.

Sub-para (da) inserted by SI 2007/3253, reg 2(1), Sch 1, paras 1, 6(c), as from 10 December 2007.

Para 6: substituted by SI 2003/1473, reg 2(2)(e), as from 14 January 2005.

Paras 7, 10: words in square brackets substituted by SI 2003/1473, reg 2(2)(f), (h), as from 14 January 2005.

Para 8: substituted by the Financial Services (EEA State) Regulations 2007, SI 2007/108, reg 2, as from 13 February 2007.

Paras 10B, 11A: inserted by SI 2007/126, reg 3(4), Sch 4, paras 1, 5, 6, as from 1 April 2007 (certain purposes (see reg 1(2) at [4051])), and as from 1 November 2007 (otherwise).

EEA firm: (para 5): Regulations made under the Income Tax (Trading and Other Income) Act 2005, s 694, may provide that an EEA firm of the kind mentioned in para 5(a)–(c) of this Schedule that qualifies for authorisation under para 12 *post* may only be an individual investment plan manager if certain requirements specified in those Regulations are met; see ss 697, 698 of the 2005 Act.

PART II
EXERCISE OF PASSPORT RIGHTS BY EEA FIRMS
Firms qualifying for authorisation

12.—(1)   Once an EEA firm which is seeking to establish a branch in the United Kingdom in exercise of an EEA right satisfies the establishment conditions, it qualifies for authorisation.

(2)   Once an EEA firm which is seeking to provide services in the United Kingdom in exercise of an EEA right satisfies the service conditions, it qualifies for authorisation.

[(3)   If an EEA firm falling within paragraph 5(a) is seeking to use a tied agent established in the United Kingdom in connection with the exercise of an EEA right deriving from the markets in financial instruments directive, this Part of this Schedule applies as if the firm were seeking to establish a branch in the United Kingdom.

(4)   But if—
   (a)   an EEA firm already qualifies for authorisation by virtue of sub-paragraph (1); and
   (b)   the EEA right which it is exercising derives from the markets in financial instruments directive,
sub-paragraph (3) does not require the firm to satisfy the establishment conditions in respect of its use of the tied agent in question.]

[(5)   An EEA firm which falls within paragraph 5(da) which establishes a branch in the United Kingdom, or provides services in the United Kingdom, in exercise of an EEA right qualifies for authorisation.

(6)   Sub-paragraphs (1) and (2) do not apply to an EEA firm falling within paragraph 5(da).]

Establishment

13.—(1)   [If the firm falls within paragraph 5(a), (b), [(c), (d) or (f)],] The establishment conditions are that—
   (a)   the Authority has received notice ("a consent notice") from the firm's home state regulator that it has given the firm consent to establish a branch in the United Kingdom;
   (b)   the consent notice—
      (i)   is given in accordance with the relevant single market directive;
      (ii)   identifies the activities to which consent relates; and

(iii)   includes such other information as may be prescribed; ...

[(ba) in the case of a firm falling within paragraph 5(a), the Authority has given the firm notice for the purposes of this paragraph or two months have elapsed beginning with the date when the home state regulator gave the consent notice; and"]

(c)   [in the case of a firm falling within paragraph 5(b), (c), (d) or (f),] the firm has been informed of the applicable provisions or two months have elapsed beginning with the date when the Authority received the consent notice.

[(1A) If the firm falls within paragraph 5(e), the establishment conditions are that—

(a)   the firm has given its home state regulator notice of its intention to establish a branch in the United Kingdom;

(b)   the Authority has received notice ("a regulator's notice") from the firm's home state regulator that the firm intends to establish a branch in the United Kingdom;

(c)   the firm's home state regulator has informed the firm that the regulator's notice has been sent to the Authority; and

(d)   one month has elapsed beginning with the date on which the firm's home state regulator informed the firm that the regulator's notice has been sent to the Authority.]

(2)   If the Authority has received a consent notice, it must—

(a)   prepare for the firm's supervision;

(b)   [except if the firm falls within paragraph 5(a),] notify the firm of the applicable provisions (if any); and

(c)   if the firm falls within paragraph 5(d), notify its home state regulator of the applicable provisions (if any).

(3)   A notice under sub-paragraph (2)(b) or (c) must be given before the end of the period of two months beginning with the day on which the Authority received the consent notice.

(4)   For the purposes of this paragraph—

"applicable provisions" means the host state rules with which the firm is required to comply when carrying on a permitted activity through a branch in the United Kingdom;

"host state rules" means rules—

(a)   made in accordance with the relevant single market directive; and

(b)   which are the responsibility of the United Kingdom (both as to implementation and as to supervision of compliance) in accordance with that directive; and

"permitted activity" means an activity identified in the consent notice [or regulator's notice, as the case may be].

Services

14.—(1) The service conditions are that—

(a)   the firm has given its home state regulator notice of its intention to provide services in the United Kingdom ("a notice of intention");

(b)   if the firm falls within [paragraph 5(a), [(d), (e) or (f)]], the Authority has received notice ("a regulator's notice") from the firm's home state regulator containing such information as may be prescribed; ...

[(ba) if the firm falls within paragraph 5(b) and is seeking to provide services in exercise of the right under Article 31.5 of the markets in financial instruments directive, the Authority has received notice ("a regulator's notice") from the firm's home state regulator stating that the firm intends to exercise that right in the United Kingdom;]

(c)   if the firm falls within [paragraph 5(d) or (e)], its home state regulator has informed it that the regulator's notice has been sent to the Authority[; and

(d)   if the firm falls within paragraph 5(e), one month has elapsed beginning with the date on which the firm's home state regulator informed the firm that the regulator's notice has been sent to the Authority].

(2)   If the Authority has received a regulator's notice or, where none is required by sub-paragraph (1), has been informed of the firm's intention to provide services in the United Kingdom, it must[, unless the firm falls within paragraph 5(e),]—

(a)   prepare for the firm's supervision; and

(b)   notify the firm of the applicable provisions (if any).

[(2A) Sub-paragraph (2)(b) does not apply in the case of a firm falling within paragraph 5(a).]

(3)   A notice under sub-paragraph (2)(b) must be given before the end of the period of two months beginning on the day on which the Authority received the regulator's notice, or was informed of the firm's intention.

(4)   For the purposes of this paragraph—

"applicable provisions" means the host state rules with which the firm is required to comply when carrying on a permitted activity by providing services in the United Kingdom;

"host state rules" means rules—

(a)   made in accordance with the relevant single market directive; and

(b) which are the responsibility of the United Kingdom (both as to implementation and as to supervision of compliance) in accordance with that directive; and

"permitted activity" means an activity identified in—

(a) the regulator's notice; or

(b) where none is required by sub-paragraph (1), the notice of intention.

Grant of permission

15.—(1) On qualifying for authorisation as a result of [paragraph 12(1), (2) or (3)], a firm has, in respect of each permitted activity which is a regulated activity, permission to carry it on through its United Kingdom branch (if it satisfies the establishment conditions) or by providing services in the United Kingdom (if it satisfies the service conditions).

[(1A) Sub-paragraph (1) is to be read subject to paragraph 15A(3).]

(2) The permission is to be treated as being on terms equivalent to those appearing from the consent notice, regulator's notice or notice of intention.

(3) Sections [21 and 39(1)] of the Consumer Credit Act 1974 (business requiring a licence under that Act) do not apply in relation to the carrying on of a permitted activity which is Consumer Credit Act business by a firm which qualifies for authorisation as a result of paragraph 12, unless [the Office of Fair Trading] has exercised the power conferred on [it] by section 203 in relation to the firm.

(4) "Consumer Credit Act business" has the same meaning as in section 203.

[(5) A firm which qualifies for authorisation as a result of paragraph 12(5) has, in respect of each permitted activity which is a regulated activity, permission to carry it on through its United Kingdom branch or by providing services in the United Kingdom.

(6) The permission is to be treated as being on terms equivalent to those appearing in the authorisation granted to the firm under Article 3 of the reinsurance directive by its home state regulator ("its home authorisation").

(7) For the purposes of sub-paragraph (5), "permitted activity" means an activity which the firm is permitted to carry on under its home authorisation.]

[*Power to Restrict Permission of Management Companies*

15A.—(1) Sub-paragraph (2) applies if—

(a) a firm falling within paragraph 5(f) qualifies for authorisation as a result of paragraph 12(1) (establishment conditions satisfied); but

(b) the Authority determines that the way in which the firm intends to invite persons in the United Kingdom to become participants in any collective investment scheme which that firm manages does not comply with the law in force in the United Kingdom.

(2) The Authority may give a notice to the firm and the firm's home state regulator of the Authority's determination under sub-paragraph (1)(b).

(3) Paragraph 15(1) does not give a firm to which the Authority has given (and not withdrawn) a notice under sub-paragraph (2) permission to carry on through the firm's United Kingdom branch the regulated activity of dealing in units in the collective investment schemes which the firm manages.

(4) Any notice given under sub-paragraph (2) must be given before the end of the period of two months beginning with the day on which the Authority received the consent notice.

(5) Sections 264(4) and 265(1), (2) and (4) apply to a notice given under sub-paragraph (2) as they apply to a notice given by the Authority under section 264(2).

(6) If a decision notice is given to the firm under section 265(4), by virtue of sub-paragraph (5), the firm may refer the matter to the Tribunal.

(7) In sub-paragraph (3)—

(a) "units" has the meaning given by section 237(2); and

(b) the reference to "dealing in" units in a collective investment scheme must be read with—

(i) section 22;

(ii) any relevant order under that section; and

(iii) Schedule 2.]

Effect of carrying on regulated activity when not qualified for authorisation

16.—(1) This paragraph applies to an EEA firm which is not qualified for authorisation under paragraph 12.

(2) Section 26 does not apply to an agreement entered into by the firm.

(3)   Section 27 does not apply to an agreement in relation to which the firm is a third party for the purposes of that section.

(4)   Section 29 does not apply to an agreement in relation to which the firm is the deposit-taker.

Continuing regulation of EEA firms

17.   Regulations may—
    (a)   modify any provision of this Act which is an applicable provision (within the meaning of paragraph 13 or 14) in its application to an EEA firm qualifying for authorisation;
    (b)   make provision as to any change (or proposed change) of a prescribed kind relating to an EEA firm or to an activity that it carries on in the United Kingdom and as to the procedure to be followed in relation to such cases;
    (c)   provide that the Authority may treat an EEA firm's notification that it is to cease to carry on regulated activity in the United Kingdom as a request for cancellation of its qualification for authorisation under this Schedule.

Giving up right to authorisation

18.   Regulations may provide that in prescribed circumstances an EEA firm falling within paragraph 5(c) may, on following the prescribed procedure—
    (a)   have its qualification for authorisation under this Schedule cancelled; and
    (b)   seek to become an authorised person by applying for a Part IV permission.

[468]

NOTES

Para 12: sub-paras (3), (4) added by the Financial Services and Markets Act 2000 (Markets in Financial Instruments) Regulations 2007, SI 2007/126, reg 3(4), Sch 4, paras 1, 7, as from 1 April 2007 (certain purposes (see reg 1(2) at **[4051]**)), and as from 1 November 2007 (otherwise); sub-paras (5), (6) added by the Reinsurance Directive Regulations 2007, SI 2007/3253, reg 2(1), Sch 1, paras 1, 6(d), as from 10 December 2007.

Para 13 is amended as follows:

Words in first (outer) pair of square brackets in sub-para (1), words in square brackets in sub-para (4), and the whole of sub-para (1A), inserted by the Insurance Mediation Directive (Miscellaneous Amendments) Regulations 2003, SI 2003/1473, reg 3, as from 14 January 2005.

Words in second (inner) pair of square brackets in sub-para (1) substituted by the Collective Investment Schemes (Miscellaneous Amendments) Regulations 2003, SI 2003/2066, reg 3(1)(a), as from 13 February 2004.

Word omitted from sub-para (1)(b)(iii) repealed, and sub-para (1)(ba) and the words in square brackets in sub-paras (1)(c), (2)(b) inserted, by SI 2007/126, reg 3(4), Sch 4, paras 1, 8, as from 1 April 2007 (certain purposes (see reg 1(2) at **[4051]**)), and as from 1 November 2007 (otherwise).

Para 14: words in first (outer) pair of square brackets in sub-para (1)(b) substituted, and word omitted from that paragraph repealed, by SI 2003/1473, reg 4(1), (2)(a), (b), as from 14 January 2005; words in second (inner) pair of square brackets in sub-para (1)(b) substituted by SI 2003/2066, reg 3(1)(b), as from 13 February 2004; sub-paras (1)(ba), (2A) inserted by SI 2007/126, reg 3(4), Sch 4, paras 1, 9, as from 1 April 2007 (certain purposes (see reg 1(2) at **[4051]**)), and as from 1 November 2007 (otherwise); words in square brackets in sub-para (1)(c) substituted, sub-para (1)(iii) and the word immediately preceding it inserted, and words in square brackets in sub-para (2) inserted, by SI 2003/1473, reg 4(1), (2)(c), (d), (3), as from 14 January 2005.

Para 15: words in square brackets in sub-para (1) substituted, and sub-paras (5)–(7) added, by SI 2007/3253, reg 2(1), Sch 1, paras 1, 6(e), as from 10 December 2007; sub-para (1A) inserted by SI 2003/2066, reg 3(1)(c), as from 13 February 2004; words in first pair of square brackets in sub-para (3) substituted by the Consumer Credit Act 2006, s 33(9), as from 6 April 2008; other words in square brackets in sub-para (3) substituted by the Enterprise Act 2002, s 278(1), Sch 25, para 40(1), (19)(a), as from 1 April 2003.

Para 15A: inserted by SI 2003/2066, reg 3(1)(d), as from 13 February 2004.

Transitional provisions: see the Financial Services and Markets Act 2000 (Markets in Financial Instruments) Regulations 2007, SI 2007/126, reg 6 at **[4056]** (transitional and saving provisions: EEA firms), and reg 6A at **[4056A]** (transitional provisions: EEA investment firms exercising passport rights under the investment services directive).

Establishment (para 13): see further the Financial Services and Markets Act 2000 (EEA Passport Rights) Regulations 2001, SI 2001/2511, reg 2 at **[2431]**.

Services (para 14): see further the Financial Services and Markets Act 2000 (EEA Passport Rights) Regulations 2001, SI 2001/2511, reg 3 at **[2432]**.

See also the note "EEA firm" to Pt I of this Schedule at **[460]**.

Regulations: the Financial Services and Markets Act 2000 (EEA Passport Rights) Regulations 2001, SI 2001/2511 at **[2430]**.

Note that the following amending Regulations have also been made under this Part: the Electronic Money (Miscellaneous Amendments) Regulations 2002, SI 2002/765; the Insurance Mediation Directive (Miscellaneous Amendments) Regulations 2003, SI 2003/1473; the Collective Investment Schemes (Miscellaneous Amendments) Regulations 2003, SI 2003/2066; the Financial Services and Markets Act 2000 (EEA Passport Rights) (Amendment) Regulations 2006, SI 2006/3385.

PART III
EXERCISE OF PASSPORT RIGHTS BY UK FIRMS

Establishment

19.—(1)   [Subject to [sub-paragraphs (5ZA) and (5A)],] A UK firm may not exercise an EEA right to establish a branch unless three conditions are satisfied.

(2)   The first is that the firm has given the Authority, in the specified way, notice of its intention to establish a branch ("a notice of intention") which—

(a)   identifies the activities which it seeks to carry on through the branch; and

(b)   includes such other information as may be specified.

(3)   [Subject to sub-paragraph (5B), the] activities identified in a notice of intention may include activities which are not regulated activities.

(4)   The second is that the Authority has given notice in specified terms ("a consent notice") to the host state regulator.

[(5)   The third is—

(a)   if the EEA right in question derives from the insurance mediation directive, that one month has elapsed beginning with the date on which the firm received notice, in accordance with sub-paragraph (11), that the Authority has given a consent notice;

(b)   in any other case, that either—

(i)   the host state regulator has notified the firm (or, where the EEA right in question derives from any of the insurance directives, the Authority) of the applicable provisions; or

(ii)   two months have elapsed beginning with the date on which the Authority gave the consent notice.]

[(5ZA)   This paragraph does not apply to a UK firm having an EEA right which is subject to the conditions of the reinsurance directive.]

[(5A)   If—

(a)   the EEA right in question derives from the insurance mediation directive, and

(b)   the EEA State in which the firm intends to establish a branch has not notified the Commission, in accordance with Article 6(2) of that directive, of its wish to be informed of the intention of any UK firm to establish a branch in its territory,

the second and third conditions do not apply (and so the firm may establish the branch to which its notice of intention relates as soon as the first condition is satisfied).]

[(5B)   If the firm is a UK investment firm, a notice of intention may not include ancillary services unless such services are to be provided in connection with the carrying on of one or more investment services and activities.

(5C)   In sub-paragraph (5B) "ancillary services" has the meaning given in Article 4.1.3 of the markets in financial instruments directive.]

(6)   If the firm's EEA right derives from [the banking consolidation directive, [the UCITS directive or, in the case of a credit institution authorised under the banking consolidation directive, the markets in financial instruments directive]] and the first condition is satisfied, the Authority must give a consent notice to the host state regulator unless it has reason to doubt the adequacy of the firm's resources or its administrative structure.

(7)   If the firm's EEA right derives from any of the insurance directives and the first condition is satisfied, the Authority must give a consent notice unless it has reason—

(a)   to doubt the adequacy of the firm's resources or its administrative structure, or

(b)   to question the reputation, qualifications or experience of the directors or managers of the firm or the person proposed as the branch's authorised agent for the purposes of those directives,

in relation to the business to be conducted through the proposed branch.

[(7A)   If—

(a)   the firm's EEA right derives from the insurance mediation directive,

(b)   the first condition is satisfied, and

(c)   the second condition applies,

the Authority must give a consent notice, and must do so within one month beginning with the date on which it received the firm's notice of intention.]

[(7B)   If the firm is a UK investment firm and the first condition is satisfied, the Authority must give a consent notice to the host state regulator within three months beginning with the date on which it received the firm's notice of intention unless the Authority has reason to doubt the adequacy of the firm's resources or its administrative structure.]

(8)   If the Authority proposes to refuse to give a consent notice it must give the firm concerned a warning notice.

(9) If the firm's EEA right derives from any of the insurance directives and the host state regulator has notified it of the applicable provisions, the Authority must inform the firm of those provisions.

(10) Rules may specify the procedure to be followed by the Authority in exercising its functions under this paragraph.

(11) If the Authority gives a consent notice it must give written notice that it has done so to the firm concerned.

(12) If the Authority decides to refuse to give a consent notice—
    (a) it must, [within the relevant period], give the person who gave that notice a decision notice to that effect; and
    (b) that person may refer the matter to the Tribunal.

[(12A) In sub-paragraph (12), "the relevant period" means—
    (a) if the firm's EEA right derives from the UCITS directive, two months beginning with the date on which the Authority received the notice of intention;
    (b) in any other case, three months beginning with that date.]

(13) In this paragraph, "applicable provisions" means the host state rules with which the firm will be required to comply when conducting business through the proposed branch in the EEA State concerned.

(14) In sub-paragraph (13), "host state rules" means rules—
    (a) made in accordance with the relevant single market directive; and
    (b) which are the responsibility of the EEA State concerned (both as to implementation and as to supervision of compliance) in accordance with that directive.

(15) "Specified" means specified in rules.

Services

20.—(1) [Subject to sub-paragraph (4D),] a UK firm may not exercise an EEA right to provide services unless the firm has given the Authority, in the specified way, notice of its intention to provide services ("a notice of intention") which—
    (a) identifies the activities which it seeks to carry out by way of provision of services; and
    (b) includes such other information as may be specified.

(2) [Subject to sub-paragraph (2A), the] activities identified in a notice of intention may include activities which are not regulated activities.

[(2A) If the firm is a UK investment firm, a notice of intention may not include ancillary services unless such services are to be provided in connection with the carrying on of one or more investment services and activities.

(2B) In sub-paragraph (2A) "ancillary services" has the meaning given in Article 4.1.3 of the markets in financial instruments directive.]

(3) If the firm's EEA right derives from [the banking consolidation directive, the [markets in financial instruments directive] or the UCITS directive], the Authority must, within one month of receiving a notice of intention, send a copy of it to the host state regulator [with such other information as may be specified].

[(3A) If the firm's EEA right derives from any of the insurance directives, the Authority must, within one month of receiving the notice of intention—
    (a) give notice in specified terms ("a consent notice") to the host state regulator; or
    (b) give written notice to the firm of—
        (i) its refusal to give a consent notice; and
        (ii) its reasons for that refusal.]

[(3B) If the firm's EEA right derives from the insurance mediation directive and the EEA State in which the firm intends to provide services has notified the Commission, in accordance with Article 6(2) of that directive, of its wish to be informed of the intention of any UK firm to provide services in its territory—
    (a) the Authority must, within one month of receiving the notice of intention, send a copy of it to the host state regulator;
    (b) the Authority, when it sends the copy in accordance with sub-paragraph (a), must give written notice to the firm concerned that it has done so; and
    (c) the firm concerned must not provide the services to which its notice of intention relates until one month, beginning with the date on which it receives the notice under sub-paragraph (b), has elapsed.]

(4) When the Authority sends the copy under sub-paragraph (3) [or gives a consent notice], it must give written notice to the firm concerned.

[(4A) If the firm is given notice under sub-paragraph (3A)(b), it may refer the matter to the Tribunal.

(4B)   If the firm's EEA right derives from any of the insurance directives [or from the markets in financial instruments directive], it must not provide the services to which its notice of intention relates until it has received written notice under sub-paragraph (4).

[(4BA)   If the firm's EEA right derives from the markets in financial instruments directive, the Authority must comply as soon as reasonably practicable with a request for information under the second sub-paragraph of Article 31.6 of that directive from the host state regulator.]

(4C)   Rules may specify the procedure to be followed by the Authority under this paragraph.]

[(4D)   This paragraph does not apply to a UK firm having an EEA right which is subject to the conditions of the reinsurance directive.]

(5)   …

(6)   "Specified" means specified in rules.

[Tied agents

20A.—(1)   If a UK investment firm is seeking to use a tied agent established in an EEA State (other than the United Kingdom) in connection with the exercise of an EEA right deriving from the markets in financial instruments directive, this Part of this Schedule applies as if the firm were seeking to establish a branch in that State.

(2)   But if—
  (a)   a UK investment firm has already established a branch in an EEA State other than the United Kingdom in accordance with paragraph 19; and
  (b)   the EEA right which it is exercising derives from the markets in financial instruments directive,

paragraph 19 does not apply in respect of its use of the tied agent in question.]

Offence relating to exercise of passport rights

21.—(1)   If a UK firm which is not an authorised person contravenes the prohibition imposed by—
  (a)   sub-paragraph (1) of paragraph 19, or
  (b)   [sub-paragraph (1), (3B)(c) or (4B)] of paragraph 20,
it is guilty of an offence.

(2)   A firm guilty of an offence under sub-paragraph (1) is liable—
  (a)   on summary conviction, to a fine not exceeding the statutory maximum; or
  (b)   on conviction on indictment, to a fine.

(3)   In proceedings for an offence under sub-paragraph (1), it is a defence for the firm to show that it took all reasonable precautions and exercised all due diligence to avoid committing the offence.

Continuing regulation of UK firms

22.—(1)   Regulations may make such provision as the Treasury consider appropriate in relation to a UK firm's exercise of EEA rights, and may in particular provide for the application (with or without modification) of any provision of, or made under, this Act in relation to an activity of a UK firm.

(2)   Regulations may—
  (a)   make provision as to any change (or proposed change) of a prescribed kind relating to a UK firm or to an activity that it carries on and as to the procedure to be followed in relation to such cases;
  (b)   make provision with respect to the consequences of the firm's failure to comply with a provision of the regulations.

(3)   Where a provision of the kind mentioned in sub-paragraph (2) requires the Authority's consent to a change (or proposed change)—
  (a)   consent may be refused only on prescribed grounds; and
  (b)   if the Authority decides to refuse consent, the firm concerned may refer the matter to the Tribunal.

23.—(1)   [Sub-paragraphs (2) and (2A) apply] if a UK firm—
  (a)   has a Part IV permission; and
  (b)   is exercising an EEA right to carry on any Consumer Credit Act business in an EEA State other than the United Kingdom.

(2)   The Authority may exercise its power under section 45 in respect of the firm if [the Office of Fair Trading] has informed the Authority that—
  (a)   the firm,
  (b)   any of the firm's employees, agents or associates (whether past or present), or
  (c)   if the firm is a body corporate, a controller of the firm or an associate of such a controller,

has done any of the things specified in paragraphs [(a) to (e) of section 25(2A)] of the Consumer Credit Act 1974.

[(2A)   The Authority may also exercise its power under section 45 in respect of the firm if the Office of Fair Trading has informed the Authority that it has concerns about any of the following—
- (a)   the firm's skills, knowledge and experience in relation to Consumer Credit Act businesses;
- (b)   such skills, knowledge and experience of other persons who are participating in any Consumer Credit Act business being carried on by the firm;
- (c)   practices and procedures that the firm is implementing in connection with any such business.]

(3)   "Associate", "Consumer Credit Act business" and "controller" have the same meaning as in section 203.

24.—(1)   Sub-paragraph (2) applies if a UK firm—
- (a)   is not required to have a Part IV permission in relation to the business which it is carrying on; and
- (b)   is exercising the right conferred by [[Article 24] of the banking consolidation directive] to carry on that business in an EEA State other than the United Kingdom.

(2)   If requested to do so by the host state regulator in the EEA State in which the UK firm's business is being carried on, the Authority may impose any requirement in relation to the firm which it could impose if—
- (a)   the firm had a Part IV permission in relation to the business which it is carrying on; and
- (b)   the Authority was entitled to exercise its power under that Part to vary that permission.

[Information to be included in the public record]

25.   The Authority must include in the record that it maintains under section 347 in relation to any UK firm whose EEA right derives from the insurance mediation directive information as to each EEA State in which the UK firm, in accordance with such a right—
- (a)   has established a branch; or
- (b)   is providing services.]

[469]

NOTES

Para 19 is amended as follows:
Words in first (outer) pair of square brackets in sub-para (1), and the whole of sub-paras (5A), (7A) inserted, and sub-para (5) substituted, by the Insurance Mediation Directive (Miscellaneous Amendments) Regulations 2003, SI 2003/1473, reg 5, as from 14 January 2005.
Words in second (inner) pair of square brackets in sub-para (1) substituted, and sub-para (5ZA) inserted, by the Reinsurance Directive Regulations 2007, SI 2007/3253, reg 2(1), Sch 1, paras 1, 6(f), (g), as from 10 December 2007.
Words in square brackets in sub-para (3), and words in second (inner) pair of square brackets in sub-para (6) substituted, and sub-paras (5B), (5C), (7B) inserted, by the Financial Services and Markets Act 2000 (Markets in Financial Instruments) Regulations 2007, SI 2007/126, reg 3(4), Sch 4, paras 1, 10, as from 1 April 2007 (certain purposes (see reg 1(2) at **[4051]**)), and as from 1 November 2007 (otherwise) (for transitional provisions, see the note below).
Words in first (outer) pair of square brackets in sub-para (6) and words in square brackets in sub-para (12) substituted, and sub-para (12A) inserted, by the Collective Investment Schemes (Miscellaneous Amendments) Regulations 2003, SI 2003/2066, reg 4(1)(a), as from 13 February 2004.
Para 20 is amended as follows:
Words in square brackets in sub-para (1), and sub-para (4D), inserted by SI 2007/3253, reg 2(1), Sch 1, paras 1, 6(h), (i), as from 10 December 2007.
Words in square brackets in sub-para (2), and words in second (inner) pair of square brackets in sub-para (3), substituted, sub-paras (2A), (2B), (4BA) inserted, and words in square brackets in sub-para (4B) inserted, by SI 2007/126, reg 3(4), Sch 4, paras 1, 11, as from 1 April 2007 (certain purposes (see reg 1(2) at **[4051]**)), and as from 1 November 2007 (otherwise).
Words in first (outer) pair of square brackets in sub-para (3) substituted, and words in third pair of square brackets in that paragraph added, by SI 2003/2066, reg 4(1)(b), as from 13 February 2004.
Sub-paras (3A), (4A)–(4C) inserted, words in square brackets in sub-para (4) inserted, and sub-para (5) repealed, by the Financial Services (EEA Passport Rights) Regulations 2001, SI 2001/1376, reg 2(1)–(5), as from 30 April 2001; sub-para (3B) inserted by SI 2003/1473, reg 6(1), as from 14 January 2005.
Para 20A: inserted by SI 2007/126, reg 3(4), Sch 4, paras 1, 12, as from 1 April 2007 (certain purposes (see reg 1(2) at **[4051]**)), and as from 1 November 2007 (otherwise).
Para 21: words in square brackets substituted by SI 2003/1473, reg 6(2), as from 14 January 2005.
Para 23: words in square brackets in sub-para (1), and words in second pair of square brackets in sub-para (2) substituted, and sub-para (2A) inserted, by the Consumer Credit Act 2006, s 33(10)–(12), as from 6 April 2008; words in first pair of square brackets in sub-para (2) substituted by the Enterprise Act 2002, s 278(1), Sch 25, para 40(1), (19)(b), as from 1 April 2003.
Para 24: words in first (outer) pair of square brackets substituted by the Banking Consolidation Directive (Consequential Amendments) Regulations 2000, SI 2000/2952, reg 8(1), (5)(f), as from 22 November 2000; words in second (inner) pair of square brackets substituted by the Capital Requirements Regulations 2006, SI 2006/3221, reg 29(1), Sch 3, para 2(1), (4), as from 1 January 2007.
Para 25: inserted, together with preceding heading, by SI 2003/1473, reg 7, as from 14 January 2005.

Transitional provisions: see the Financial Services and Markets Act 2000 (Markets in Financial Instruments) Regulations 2007, SI 2007/126, reg 7 at **[4057]** (transitional provisions: UK investment firms exercising passport rights under the investment services directive), reg 7A at **[4057A]** (transitional provision: investment research and financial analysis), and reg 8 at **[4058]** (additional saving provision: UK investment firms).

Exercise of passport rights by UK firms: see further the Financial Services and Markets Act 2000 (EEA Passport Rights) Regulations 2001, SI 2001/2511, Pt III (regs 11–18) at **[2440]** et seq.

Regulations: the Financial Services and Markets Act 2000 (EEA Passport Rights) Regulations 2001, SI 2001/2511 at **[2430]**.

Note that the following amending Regulations have also been made under this Part: the Collective Investment Schemes (Miscellaneous Amendments) Regulations 2003, SI 2003/2066; the Financial Services and Markets Act 2000 (EEA Passport Rights) (Amendment) Regulations 2006, SI 2006/3385; the Financial Services and Markets Act 2000 (Markets in Financial Instruments) (Amendment) Regulations 2007, SI 2007/763.

SCHEDULE 4
TREATY RIGHTS

Section 31(1)(c)

NOTES

Transitional provisions: the Financial Services and Markets Act 2000 (Transitional Provisions) (Authorised Persons etc) Order 2001, SI 2001/2636, Pt II, Chapter III provides that treaty firms authorised before 1 December 2001 under the Financial Services Act 1986, s 31 and certain treaty firms which were authorised insurance companies before that date are to be treated after 1 December 2001 as having complied with the procedures of this Schedule. The 1986 Act was repealed by the Financial Services and Markets Act 2000 (Consequential Amendments and Repeals) Order 2001, SI 2001/3649, art 3(1)(c).

Definitions

1. In this Schedule—
   "consumers" means persons who are consumers for the purposes of section 138;
   "Treaty firm" means a person—
      (a) whose head office is situated in an EEA State (its "home state") other than the United Kingdom; and
      (b) which is recognised under the law of that State as its national; and
   "home state regulator", in relation to a Treaty firm, means the competent authority of the firm's home state for the purpose of its home state authorisation (as to which see paragraph 3(1)(a)).

Firms qualifying for authorisation

2. Once a Treaty firm which is seeking to carry on a regulated activity satisfies the conditions set out in paragraph 3(1), it qualifies for authorisation.

Exercise of Treaty rights

3.—(1) The conditions are that—
   (a) the firm has received authorisation ("home state authorisation") under the law of its home state to carry on the regulated activity in question ("the permitted activity");
   (b) the relevant provisions of the law of the firm's home state—
      (i) afford equivalent protection; or
      (ii) satisfy the conditions laid down by a Community instrument for the co-ordination or approximation of laws, regulations or administrative provisions of member States relating to the carrying on of that activity; and
   (c) the firm has no EEA right to carry on that activity in the manner in which it is seeking to carry it on.

(2) A firm is not to be regarded as having home state authorisation unless its home state regulator has so informed the Authority in writing.

(3) Provisions afford equivalent protection if, in relation to the firm's carrying on of the permitted activity, they afford consumers protection which is at least equivalent to that afforded by or under this Act in relation to that activity.

(4) A certificate issued by the Treasury that the provisions of the law of a particular EEA State afford equivalent protection in relation to the activities specified in the certificate is conclusive evidence of that fact.

Permission

4.—(1) On qualifying for authorisation under this Schedule, a Treaty firm has permission to carry on each permitted activity through its United Kingdom branch or by providing services in the United Kingdom.

(2) The permission is to be treated as being on terms equivalent to those to which the firm's home state authorisation is subject.

(3)   If, on qualifying for authorisation under this Schedule, a firm has a Part IV permission which includes permission to carry on a permitted activity, the Authority must give a direction cancelling the permission so far as it relates to that activity.

(4)   The Authority need not give a direction under sub-paragraph (3) if it considers that there are good reasons for not doing so.

Notice to Authority

5.—(1)   Sub-paragraph (2) applies to a Treaty firm which—
- (a)   qualifies for authorisation under this Schedule, but
- (b)   is not carrying on in the United Kingdom the regulated activity, or any of the regulated activities, which it has permission to carry on there.

(2)   At least seven days before it begins to carry on such a regulated activity, the firm must give the Authority written notice of its intention to do so.

(3)   If a Treaty firm to which sub-paragraph (2) applies has given notice under that sub-paragraph, it need not give such a notice if it again becomes a firm to which that sub-paragraph applies.

(4)   Subsections (1), (3) and (6) of section 51 apply to a notice under sub-paragraph (2) as they apply to an application for a Part IV permission.

Offences

6.—(1)   A person who contravenes paragraph 5(2) is guilty of an offence.

(2)   In proceedings against a person for an offence under sub-paragraph (1) it is a defence for him to show that he took all reasonable precautions and exercised all due diligence to avoid committing the offence.

(3)   A person is guilty of an offence if in, or in connection with, a notice given by him under paragraph 5(2) he—
- (a)   provides information which he knows to be false or misleading in a material particular; or
- (b)   recklessly provides information which is false or misleading in a material particular.

(4)   A person guilty of an offence under this paragraph is liable—
- (a)   on summary conviction, to a fine not exceeding the statutory maximum;
- (b)   on conviction on indictment, to a fine.

[470]

NOTES

Qualifies for authorisation (para 2): regulations made under the Income Tax (Trading and Other Income) Act 2005, s 694, may provide that a firm which is an authorised person as a result of qualifying for authorisation under para 2 of this Schedule may only be a plan manager if certain requirements specified in those regulations are met; see ss 697, 698 of the 2005 Act.

SCHEDULE 5
PERSONS CONCERNED IN COLLECTIVE INVESTMENT SCHEMES
Section 36

Authorisation

1.—(1)   A person who for the time being is an operator, trustee or depositary of a recognised collective investment scheme is an authorised person.

(2)   "Recognised" means recognised by virtue of section 264.

(3)   An authorised open-ended investment company is an authorised person.

[(4)   A body—
- (a)   incorporated by virtue of regulations made under section 1 of the Open-Ended Investment Companies Act (Northern Ireland) 2002 in respect of which an authorisation order is in force, and
- (b)   to which the UCITS directive applies,

is an authorised person.

(5)   "Authorisation order" means an order made under (or having effect as made under) any provision of those regulations which is made by virtue of section 1(2)(1) of that Act (provision corresponding to Chapter 3 of Part 17 of the Act).]

Permission

2.—(1)   A person authorised as a result of paragraph 1(1) has permission to carry on, so far as it is a regulated activity—

(a) any activity, appropriate to the capacity in which he acts in relation to the scheme, of the kind described in paragraph 8 of Schedule 2;

(b) any activity in connection with, or for the purposes of, the scheme.

(2) A person authorised as a result of paragraph 1(3) [or (4)] has permission to carry on, so far as it is a regulated activity—

(a) the operation of the scheme;

(b) any activity in connection with, or for the purposes of, the operation of the scheme.

[471]

NOTES

Para 1: sub-paras (4), (5) added by the Collective Investment Schemes (Miscellaneous Amendments) Regulations 2003, SI 2003/2066, reg 10(a), as from 13 February 2004.

Para 2: words in square brackets inserted by SI 2003/2066, reg 10(b), as from 13 February 2004.

SCHEDULE 6
THRESHOLD CONDITIONS

Section 41

PART I
PART IV PERMISSION

Legal status

1.—(1) If the regulated activity concerned is the effecting or carrying out of contracts of insurance the authorised person must be a body corporate [(other than a limited liability partnership)], a registered friendly society or a member of Lloyd's.

(2) If the person concerned appears to the Authority to be seeking to carry on, or to be carrying on, a regulated activity constituting accepting deposits [or issuing electronic money], it must be—

(a) a body corporate; or

(b) a partnership.

Location of offices

2.—(1) [Subject to [sub-paragraphs (2A) and (3)],] If the person concerned is a body corporate constituted under the law of any part of the United Kingdom—

(a) its head office, and

(b) if it has a registered office, that office,

must be in the United Kingdom.

(2) If the person concerned has its head office in the United Kingdom but is not a body corporate, it must carry on business in the United Kingdom.

[(2A) If—

(a) the regulated activity concerned is any of the investment services and activities, and

(b) the person concerned is a body corporate with no registered office,

sub-paragraph (2B) applies in place of sub-paragraph (1).

(2B) If the person concerned has its head office in the United Kingdom, it must carry on business in the United Kingdom.]

[(3) If the regulated activity concerned is an insurance mediation activity, sub-paragraph (1) does not apply.

(4) If the regulated activity concerned is an insurance mediation activity, the person concerned—

(a) if he is a body corporate constituted under the law of any part of the United Kingdom, must have its registered office, or if it has no registered office, its head office, in the United Kingdom;

(b) if he is a natural person, is to be treated for the purposes of sub-paragraph (2), as having his head office in the United Kingdom if his residence is situated there.

(5) "Insurance mediation activity" means any of the following activities—

(a) dealing in rights under a contract of insurance as agent;

(b) arranging deals in rights under a contract of insurance;

(c) assisting in the administration and performance of a contract of insurance;

(d) advising on buying or selling rights under a contract of insurance;

(e) agreeing to do any of the activities specified in sub-paragraph (a) to (d).

(6) Paragraph (5) must be read with—

(a) section 22;

(b) any relevant order under that section; and

(c) Schedule 2.]

[Appointment of claims representatives

2A.—(1)   If it appears to the Authority that—

    (a)   the regulated activity that the person concerned is carrying on, or is seeking to carry on, is the effecting or carrying out of contracts of insurance, and

    (b)   contracts of insurance against damage arising out of or in connection with the use of motor vehicles on land (other than carrier's liability) are being, or will be, effected or carried out by the person concerned,

that person must have a claims representative in each EEA State other than the United Kingdom.

(2)   For the purposes of sub-paragraph (1)(b), contracts of reinsurance are to be disregarded.

(3)   A claims representative is a person with responsibility for handling and settling claims arising from accidents of the kind mentioned in Article 1(2) of the fourth motor insurance directive.

(4)   In this paragraph "fourth motor insurance directive" means Directive 2000/26/EC of the European Parliament and of the Council of 16th May 2000 on the approximation of the laws of the Member States relating to insurance against civil liability in respect of the use of motor vehicles and amending Council Directives 73/239/EEC and 88/357/EEC.]

Close links

3.—(1)   If the person concerned ("A") has close links with another person ("CL") the Authority must be satisfied—

    (a)   that those links are not likely to prevent the Authority's effective supervision of A; and

    (b)   if it appears to the Authority that CL is subject to the laws, regulations or administrative provisions of a territory which is not an EEA State ("the foreign provisions"), that neither the foreign provisions, nor any deficiency in their enforcement, would prevent the Authority's effective supervision of A.

(2)   A has close links with CL if—

    (a)   CL is a parent undertaking of A;

    (b)   CL is a subsidiary undertaking of A;

    (c)   CL is a parent undertaking of a subsidiary undertaking of A;

    (d)   CL is a subsidiary undertaking of a parent undertaking of A;

    (e)   CL owns or controls 20% or more of the voting rights or capital of A; or

    (f)   A owns or controls 20% or more of the voting rights or capital of CL.

(3)   "Subsidiary undertaking" includes all the instances mentioned in Article 1(1) and (2) of the Seventh Company Law Directive in which an entity may be a subsidiary of an undertaking.

Adequate resources

4.—(1)   The resources of the person concerned must, in the opinion of the Authority, be adequate in relation to the regulated activities that he seeks to carry on, or carries on.

(2)   In reaching that opinion, the Authority may—

    (a)   take into account the person's membership of a group and any effect which that membership may have; and

    (b)   have regard to—

        (i)   the provision he makes and, if he is a member of a group, which other members of the group make in respect of liabilities (including contingent and future liabilities); and

        (ii)   the means by which he manages and, if he is a member of a group, which other members of the group manage the incidence of risk in connection with his business.

Suitability

5.   The person concerned must satisfy the Authority that he is a fit and proper person having regard to all the circumstances, including—

    (a)   his connection with any person;

    (b)   the nature of any regulated activity that he carries on or seeks to carry on; and

    (c)   the need to ensure that his affairs are conducted soundly and prudently.

[472]

NOTES

Para 1: words in first pair of square brackets inserted by the Financial Services and Markets Act 2000 (Variation of Threshold Conditions) Order 2001, SI 2001/2507, art 2, as from 3 September 2001; words in second pair of square brackets inserted by the Financial Services and Markets Act 2000 (Regulated Activities) (Amendment) Order 2002, SI 2002/682, art 8, as from 27 April 2002.

Para 2: words in first (outer) pair of square brackets in sub-para (1), and the whole of sub-paras (3)–(6) inserted by the Financial Services and Markets Act 2000 (Regulated Activities) (Amendment) (No 2) Order 2003, SI 2003/1476, art 19, as from 31 October 2004 (in so far as relating to contracts of long-term care insurance), and as from 14 January 2005 (otherwise) (for transitional provisions see arts 22–27 of that Order at

[2706] et seq); words in second (inner) pair of square brackets in sub-para (1) substituted, and sub-paras (2A), (2B) inserted, by the Financial Services and Markets Act 2000 (Markets in Financial Instruments) Regulations 2007, SI 2007/126, reg 3(5), Sch 5, paras 1, 24, as from 1 April 2007 (certain purposes (see reg 1(2) at [4051])), and as from 1 November 2007 (otherwise).

Para 2A: inserted by the Financial Services and Markets Act 2000 (Variation of Threshold Conditions) Order 2002, SI 2002/2707, art 2, as from 19 January 2003.

Swiss general insurance companies: the conditions in paras 4, 5 have been removed in relation to a Swiss general insurance company; see the Financial Services and Markets Act 2000 (Variation of Threshold Conditions) Order 2001, SI 2001/2507, art 3(3) (as substituted by the Financial Services and Markets Act 2000 (Variation of Threshold Conditions) (Amendment) Order 2005, SI 2005/680). For additional conditions imposed on such a company see the Note for SI 2001/2507 at [2420].

PART II
AUTHORISATION

Authorisation under Schedule 3

6.   In relation to an EEA firm qualifying for authorisation under Schedule 3, the conditions set out in paragraphs 1 and 3 to 5 apply, so far as relevant, to—

(a)   an application for permission under Part IV;
(b)   exercise of the Authority's own-initiative power under section 45 in relation to a Part IV permission.

Authorisation under Schedule 4

7.   In relation to a person who qualifies for authorisation under Schedule 4, the conditions set out in paragraphs 1 and 3 to 5 apply, so far as relevant, to—

(a)   an application for an additional permission;
(b)   the exercise of the Authority's own-initiative power under section 45 in relation to additional permission.

[473]

PART III
ADDITIONAL CONDITIONS

8.—(1)   If this paragraph applies to the person concerned, he must, for the purposes of such provisions of this Act as may be specified, satisfy specified additional conditions.

(2)   This paragraph applies to a person who—

(a)   has his head office outside the EEA; and
(b)   appears to the Authority to be seeking to carry on a regulated activity relating to insurance business.

(3)   "Specified" means specified in, or in accordance with, an order made by the Treasury.

9.   The Treasury may by order—

(a)   vary or remove any of the conditions set out in Parts I and II;
(b)   add to those conditions.

[474]

NOTES

Orders: the Financial Services and Markets Act 2000 (Variation of Threshold Conditions) Order 2001, SI 2001/2507 at [2420].

Note that the following amending Orders have also been made under this Part: the Financial Services and Markets Act 2000 (Variation of Threshold Conditions) Order 2002, SI 2002/2707; the Financial Services and Markets Act 2000 (Variation of Threshold Conditions) (Amendment) Order 2005, SI 2005/680.

SCHEDULE 7
THE AUTHORITY AS COMPETENT AUTHORITY FOR PART VI
Section 72(2)

General

1.   This Act applies in relation to the Authority when it is exercising functions under Part VI as the competent authority subject to the following modifications.

The Authority's general functions

2.   In section 2—

(a)   subsection (4)(a) does not apply to [Part 6 rules];
(b)   subsection (4)(c) does not apply to general guidance given in relation to Part VI; and
(c)   subsection (4)(d) does not apply to functions under Part VI.

PART I
FSMA 2000

Duty to consult

3.   Section 8 does not apply.

Rules

4.—(1)   Sections 149, 153, 154 and 156 do not apply.

(2)   Section 155 has effect as if—
  (a)   the reference in subsection (2)(c) to the general duties of the Authority under section 2 were a reference to its duty under section 73; and
  (b)   section 99 were included in the provisions referred to in subsection (9).

Statements of policy

5.—(1)   Paragraph 5 of Schedule 1 has effect as if the requirement to act through the Authority's governing body applied also to the exercise of its functions of publishing statements under section 93.

(2)   Paragraph 1 of Schedule 1 has effect as if section 93 were included in the provisions referred to in sub-paragraph (2)(d).

Penalties

6.   Paragraph 16 of Schedule 1 does not apply in relation to penalties under Part VI (for which separate provision is made by section 100).

Fees

7.   Paragraph 17 of Schedule 1 does not apply in relation to fees payable under Part VI (for which separate provision is made by section 99).

Exemption from liability in damages

8.   Schedule 1 has effect as if—
  (a)   sub-paragraph (1) of paragraph 19 were omitted (similar provision being made in relation to the competent authority by section 102); and
  (b)   for the words from the beginning to "(a)" in sub-paragraph (3) of that paragraph, there were substituted "Sub-paragraph (2) does not apply".

[475]

NOTES
  Para 2: words in square brackets in sub-para (a) substituted by the Financial Services and Markets Act 2000 (Market Abuse) Regulations 2005, SI 2005/381, reg 4, Sch 1, para 12, as from 1 July 2005.

SCHEDULE 8
TRANSFER OF FUNCTIONS UNDER PART VI
Section 72(3)

The power to transfer

1.—(1)   The Treasury may by order provide for any function conferred on the competent authority which is exercisable for the time being by a particular person to be transferred so as to be exercisable by another person.

(2)   An order may be made under this paragraph only if—
  (a)   the person from whom the relevant functions are to be transferred has agreed in writing that the order should be made;
  (b)   the Treasury are satisfied that the manner in which, or efficiency with which, the functions are discharged would be significantly improved if they were transferred to the transferee; or
  (c)   the Treasury are satisfied that it is otherwise in the public interest that the order should be made.

Supplemental

2.—(1)   An order under this Schedule does not affect anything previously done by any person ("the previous authority") in the exercise of functions which are transferred by the order to another person ("the new authority").

(2)   Such an order may, in particular, include provision—
  (a)   modifying or excluding any provision of Part VI, IX or XXVI in its application to any such functions;
  (b)   for reviews similar to that made, in relation to the Authority, by section 12;

(c)   imposing on the new authority requirements similar to those imposed, in relation to the Authority, by sections 152, 155 and 354;

(d)   as to the giving of guidance by the new authority;

(e)   for the delegation by the new authority of the exercise of functions under Part VI and as to the consequences of delegation;

(f)   for the transfer of any property, rights or liabilities relating to any such functions from the previous authority to the new authority;

(g)   for the carrying on and completion by the new authority of anything in the process of being done by the previous authority when the order takes effect;

(h)   for the substitution of the new authority for the previous authority in any instrument, contract or legal proceedings;

(i)   for the transfer of persons employed by the previous authority to the new authority and as to the terms on which they are to transfer;

(j)   making such amendments to any primary or subordinate legislation (including any provision of, or made under, this Act) as the Treasury consider appropriate in consequence of the transfer of functions effected by the order.

(3)   Nothing in this paragraph is to be taken as restricting the powers conferred by section 428.

3.   If the Treasury have made an order under paragraph 1 ("the transfer order") they may, by a separate order made under this paragraph, make any provision of a kind that could have been included in the transfer order.

[476]

(Sch 9 repealed by the Prospectus Regulations 2005, SI 2005/1433, reg 2(1), Sch 1, para 16, as from 1 July 2005.)

SCHEDULE 10
COMPENSATION: EXEMPTIONS
Section 90(2) and (5)

Statements believed to be true

1.—(1)   In this paragraph "statement" means—

(a)   any untrue or misleading statement in listing particulars; or

(b)   the omission from listing particulars of any matter required to be included by section 80 or 81.

(2)   A person does not incur any liability under section 90(1) for loss caused by a statement if he satisfies the court that, at the time when the listing particulars were submitted to the competent authority, he reasonably believed (having made such enquiries, if any, as were reasonable) that—

(a)   the statement was true and not misleading, or

(b)   the matter whose omission caused the loss was properly omitted,

and that one or more of the conditions set out in sub-paragraph (3) are satisfied.

(3)   The conditions are that—

(a)   he continued in his belief until the time when the securities in question were acquired;

(b)   they were acquired before it was reasonably practicable to bring a correction to the attention of persons likely to acquire them;

(c)   before the securities were acquired, he had taken all such steps as it was reasonable for him to have taken to secure that a correction was brought to the attention of those persons;

(d)   he continued in his belief until after the commencement of dealings in the securities following their admission to the official list and they were acquired after such a lapse of time that he ought in the circumstances to be reasonably excused.

Statements by experts

2.—(1)   In this paragraph "statement" means a statement included in listing particulars which—

(a)   purports to be made by, or on the authority of, another person as an expert; and

(b)   is stated to be included in the listing particulars with that other person's consent.

(2)   A person does not incur any liability under section 90(1) for loss in respect of any securities caused by a statement if he satisfies the court that, at the time when the listing particulars were submitted to the competent authority, he reasonably believed that the other person—

(a)   was competent to make or authorise the statement, and

(b)   had consented to its inclusion in the form and context in which it was included,

and that one or more of the conditions set out in sub-paragraph (3) are satisfied.

(3)   The conditions are that—

(a)   he continued in his belief until the time when the securities were acquired;

(b)   they were acquired before it was reasonably practicable to bring the fact that the expert was not competent, or had not consented, to the attention of persons likely to acquire the securities in question;

(c)   before the securities were acquired he had taken all such steps as it was reasonable for him to have taken to secure that that fact was brought to the attention of those persons;

(d)   he continued in his belief until after the commencement of dealings in the securities following their admission to the official list and they were acquired after such a lapse of time that he ought in the circumstances to be reasonably excused.

PART I
FSMA 2000

Corrections of statements

3.—(1)   In this paragraph "statement" has the same meaning as in paragraph 1.

(2)   A person does not incur liability under section 90(1) for loss caused by a statement if he satisfies the court—

(a)   that before the securities in question were acquired, a correction had been published in a manner calculated to bring it to the attention of persons likely to acquire the securities; or

(b)   that he took all such steps as it was reasonable for him to take to secure such publication and reasonably believed that it had taken place before the securities were acquired.

(3)   Nothing in this paragraph is to be taken as affecting paragraph 1.

Corrections of statements by experts

4.—(1)   In this paragraph "statement" has the same meaning as in paragraph 2.

(2)   A person does not incur liability under section 90(1) for loss caused by a statement if he satisfies the court—

(a)   that before the securities in question were acquired, the fact that the expert was not competent or had not consented had been published in a manner calculated to bring it to the attention of persons likely to acquire the securities; or

(b)   that he took all such steps as it was reasonable for him to take to secure such publication and reasonably believed that it had taken place before the securities were acquired.

(3)   Nothing in this paragraph is to be taken as affecting paragraph 2.

Official statements

5.   A person does not incur any liability under section 90(1) for loss resulting from—

(a)   a statement made by an official person which is included in the listing particulars, or

(b)   a statement contained in a public official document which is included in the listing particulars,

if he satisfies the court that the statement is accurately and fairly reproduced.

False or misleading information known about

6.   A person does not incur any liability under section 90(1) or (4) if he satisfies the court that the person suffering the loss acquired the securities in question with knowledge—

(a)   that the statement was false or misleading,

(b)   of the omitted matter, or

(c)   of the change or new matter,

as the case may be.

Belief that supplementary listing particulars not called for

7.   A person does not incur any liability under section 90(4) if he satisfies the court that he reasonably believed that the change or new matter in question was not such as to call for supplementary listing particulars.

Meaning of "expert"

8.   "Expert" includes any engineer, valuer, accountant or other person whose profession, qualifications or experience give authority to a statement made by him.

[477]

(Sch 11 repealed by the Prospectus Regulations 2005, SI 2005/1433, reg 2(1), Sch 1, para 16, as from 1 July 2005.)

[SCHEDULE 11A
TRANSFERABLE SECURITIES
Section 85(5)(a)

PART 1

1.   Units (within the meaning in section 237(2)) in an open-ended collective investment scheme.

2.   Non-equity transferable securities issued by
   (a)   the government of an EEA State;
   (b)   a local or regional authority of an EEA State;
   (c)   a public international body of which an EEA State is a member;
   (d)   the European Central Bank;
   (e)   the central bank of an EEA State.

3.   Shares in the share capital of the central bank of an EEA State.

4.   Transferable securities unconditionally and irrevocably guaranteed by the government, or a local or regional authority, of an EEA State.

5.—(1)   Non-equity transferable securities, issued in a continuous or repeated manner by a credit institution, which satisfy the conditions in sub-paragraph (2).

   (2)   The conditions are that the transferable securities—
   (a)   are not subordinated, convertible or exchangeable;
   (b)   do not give a right to subscribe to or acquire other types of securities and are not linked to a derivative instrument;
   (c)   materialise reception of repayable deposits; and
   (d)   are covered by a deposit guarantee under directive 94/19/EC of the European Parliament and of the Council on deposit-guarantee schemes.

6.   Non-fungible shares of capital—
   (a)   the main purpose of which is to provide the holder with a right to occupy any immoveable property, and
   (b)   which cannot be sold without that right being given up.]

[478]

NOTES
   Commencement: 1 July 2005.
   Inserted by the Prospectus Regulations 2005, SI 2005/1433, reg 2(2), Sch 2, as from 1 July 2005.

[PART 2

7.—(1)   Transferable securities issued by a body specified in sub-paragraph (2) if, and only if, the proceeds of the offer of the transferable securities to the public will be used solely for the purposes of the issuer's objectives.

   (2)   The bodies are
   (a)   a charity within the meaning of—
      (i)   section 96(1) of the Charities Act 1993 (c 10), or
      (ii)   section 35 of the Charities Act (Northern Ireland) 1964 (c 33 (NI));
   [(b)   a body entered in the Scottish Charity Register;]
   (c)   a housing association within the meaning of—
      (i)   section 5(1) of the Housing Act 1985 (c 68),
      (ii)   section 1 of the Housing Associations Act 1985 (c 69), or
      (iii)   Article 3 of the Housing (Northern Ireland) Order 1992 (SI 1992/1725 (NI 15));
   (d)   an industrial and provident society registered in accordance with—
      (i)   section 1(2)(b) of the Industrial and Provident Societies Act 1965 (c 12), or
      (ii)   section 1(2)(b) of the Industrial and Provident Societies Act (Northern Ireland) 1969 (c 24 (NI));
   (e)   a non-profit making association or body recognised by an EEA State with objectives similar to those of a body falling within any of sub-paragraphs (a) to (d).

8.—(1)   Non-equity transferable securities, issued in a continuous or repeated manner by a credit institution, which satisfy the conditions in sub-paragraph (2).

   (2)   The conditions are—
   (a)   that the total consideration of the offer is less than 50,000,000 euros (or an equivalent amount); and
   (b)   those mentioned in paragraph 5(2)(a) and (b).

   (3)   In determining whether sub-paragraph (2)(a) is satisfied in relation to an offer ("offer A"), offer A is to be taken together with any other offer of transferable securities of the same class made by the same person which—

    (a)   was open at any time within the period of 12 months ending with the date on which offer A is first made; and

    (b)   had previously satisfied sub-paragraph (2)(a).

    (4)   For the purposes of this paragraph, an amount (in relation to an amount denominated in euros) is an "equivalent amount" if it is an amount of equal value denominated wholly or partly in another currency or unit of account.

    (5)   The equivalent is to be calculated at the latest practicable date before (but in any event not more than 3 working days before) the date on which the offer is first made.

    (6)   "Credit institution" means a credit institution as defined in [Article 4(1)(a)] of the banking consolidation directive.

9.—(1)   Transferable securities included in an offer where the total consideration of the offer is less than 2,500,000 euros (or an equivalent amount).

    (2)   Sub-paragraphs (3) to (5) of paragraph 8 apply for the purposes of this paragraph but with the references in sub-paragraph (3) to "sub-paragraph (2)(a)" being read as references to "paragraph 9(1)".]

[479]

NOTES

  Commencement: 1 July 2005.

  Inserted by the Prospectus Regulations 2005, SI 2005/1433, reg 2(2), Sch 2, as from 1 July 2005.

  Para 7: sub-para (2)(b) substituted by the Charities and Trustee Investment (Scotland) Act 2005 (Consequential Provisions and Modifications) Order 2006, SI 2006/242, art 5, Schedule, Pt 1, para 7, as from 1 April 2006.

  Para 8: words in square brackets in sub-para (6) substituted by the Capital Requirements Regulations 2006, SI 2006/3221, reg 29(1), Sch 3, para 3, as from 1 January 2007.

SCHEDULE 12
TRANSFER SCHEMES: CERTIFICATES

Sections 111(2) and 115

PART I
INSURANCE BUSINESS TRANSFER SCHEMES

1.—(1)   For the purposes of section 111(2) the appropriate certificates, in relation to an insurance business transfer scheme, are—

    (a)   a certificate under paragraph 2;

    (b)   if sub-paragraph (2) applies, a certificate under paragraph 3;

    (c)   if sub-paragraph (3) applies, a certificate under paragraph 4;

    (d)   if sub-paragraph (4) applies, a certificate under paragraph 5;

    [(e)   if sub-paragraph (5) applies, the certificates under paragraph 5A].

    (2)   This sub-paragraph applies if—

    (a)   the authorised person concerned is a UK authorised person which has received authorisation under [Article 4 of the life assurance consolidation directive or Article 6] of the first non-life insurance directive from the Authority; and

    (b)   the establishment from which the business is to be transferred under the proposed insurance business transfer scheme is in an EEA State other than the United Kingdom.

    (3)   This sub-paragraph applies if—

    (a)   the authorised person concerned has received authorisation under [Article 4 [or Article 51] of the life assurance consolidation directive] from the Authority;

    (b)   the proposed transfer relates to business which consists of the effecting or carrying out of contracts of long-term insurance; and

    (c)   as regards any policy which is included in the proposed transfer and which evidences a contract of insurance (other than reinsurance), an EEA State other than the United Kingdom is the State of the commitment.

    (4)   This sub-paragraph applies if—

    (a)   the authorised person concerned has received authorisation under Article 6 [or Article 23] of the first non-life insurance directive from the Authority;

    (b)   the business to which the proposed insurance business transfer scheme relates is business which consists of the effecting or carrying out of contracts of general insurance; and

    (c)   as regards any policy which is included in the proposed transfer and which evidences a contract of insurance (other than reinsurance), the risk is situated in an EEA State other than the United Kingdom.

    [(5)   This sub-paragraph applies if—

(a)   the authorised person concerned has received authorisation under Article 23 of the first non-life insurance directive or Article 51 of the life assurance consolidation directive from the Authority; and

(b)   the proposed transfer is to a branch or agency, in an EEA State other than the United Kingdom, authorised under the same Article.]

Certificates as to margin of solvency

2.—(1)   A certificate under this paragraph is to be given—

(a)   by the relevant authority; or

(b)   in a case in which there is no relevant authority, by the Authority.

(2)   A certificate given under sub-paragraph (1)(a) is one certifying that, taking the proposed transfer into account—

(a)   the transferee possesses, or will possess before the scheme takes effect, the necessary margin of solvency; or

(b)   there is no necessary margin of solvency applicable to the transferee.

(3)   A certificate under sub-paragraph (1)(b) is one certifying that the Authority has received from the authority which it considers to be the authority responsible for supervising persons who effect or carry out contracts of insurance in the place to which the business is to be transferred that, taking the proposed transfer into account—

(a)   the transferee possesses or will possess before the scheme takes effect the margin of solvency required under the law applicable in that place; or

(b)   there is no such margin of solvency applicable to the transferee.

(4)   "Necessary margin of solvency" means the margin of solvency required in relation to the transferee, taking the proposed transfer into account, under the law which it is the responsibility of the relevant authority to apply.

(5)   "Margin of solvency" means the excess of the value of the assets of the transferee over the amount of its liabilities.

(6)   "Relevant authority" means—

(a)   if the transferee is an EEA firm falling within paragraph 5(d) [or (da)] of Schedule 3, its home state regulator;

[(aa) if the transferee is a non-EEA branch, the competent authorities of the EEA State in which the transferee is situated or, where appropriate, the competent authorities of an EEA State which supervises the state of solvency of the entire business of the transferee's agencies and branches within the EEA in accordance with Article 26 of the first non-life insurance directive or Article 56 of the life assurance consolidation directive;]

(b)   if the transferee is a Swiss general insurer, the authority responsible in Switzerland for supervising persons who effect or carry out contracts of insurance;

(c)   if the transferee is an authorised person not falling within [paragraph (a), (aa) or (b), the Authority.

(7)   In sub-paragraph (6), any reference to a transferee of a particular description includes a reference to a transferee who will be of that description if the proposed scheme takes effect.

[(7A)   "Competent authorities" has the same meaning as in the insurance directives.]

(8)   "Swiss general insurer" means a body—

(a)   whose head office is in Switzerland;

(b)   which has permission to carry on regulated activities consisting of the effecting and carrying out of contracts of general insurance; and

(c)   whose permission is not restricted to the effecting or carrying out of contracts of reinsurance.

[(9)   "Non-EEA branch" means a branch or agency which has received authorisation under Article 23 of the first non-life insurance directive or Article 51 of the life assurance consolidation directive.]

Certificates as to consent

3.   A certificate under this paragraph is one given by the Authority and certifying that the host State regulator has been notified of the proposed scheme and that—

(a)   that regulator has responded to the notification; or

(b)   that it has not responded but the period of three months beginning with the notification has elapsed.

Certificates as to long-term business

4.   A certificate under this paragraph is one given by the Authority and certifying that the authority responsible for supervising persons who effect or carry out contracts of insurance in the State of the commitment has been notified of the proposed scheme and that—

    (a)   that authority has consented to the proposed scheme; or
    (b)   the period of three months beginning with the notification has elapsed and that authority has not refused its consent.

Certificates as to general business

5.   A certificate under this paragraph is one given by the Authority and certifying that the authority responsible for supervising persons who effect or carry out contracts of insurance in the EEA State in which the risk is situated has been notified of the proposed scheme and that—
    (a)   that authority has consented to the proposed scheme; or
    (b)   the period of three months beginning with the notification has elapsed and that authority has not refused its consent.

[Certificates as to legality and as to consent

5A.—(1)   The certificates under this paragraph are to be given—
    (a)   in the case of the certificate under sub-paragraph (2), by the Authority;
    (b)   in the case of the certificate under sub-paragraph (3), by the relevant authority.

(2)   A certificate given under this sub-paragraph is one certifying that the relevant authority has been notified of the proposed scheme and that—
    (a)   the relevant authority has consented to the proposed scheme; or
    (b)   the period of three months beginning with the notification has elapsed and that relevant authority has not refused its consent.

(3)   A certificate given under this sub-paragraph is one certifying that the law of the EEA State in which the transferee is set up permits such a transfer.

(4)   "Relevant authority" means the competent authorities (within the meaning of the insurance directives) of the EEA State in which the transferee is set up.]

Interpretation of Part I

6.—(1)   "State of the commitment", in relation to a commitment entered into at any date, means—
    (a)   if the policyholder is an individual, the State in which he had his habitual residence at that date;
    (b)   if the policyholder is not an individual, the State in which the establishment of the policyholder to which the commitment relates was situated at that date.

(2)   "Commitment" means a commitment represented by contracts of insurance of a prescribed class.

(3)   References to the EEA State in which a risk is situated are—
    (a)   if the insurance relates to a building or to a building and its contents (so far as the contents are covered by the same policy), to the EEA State in which the building is situated;
    (b)   if the insurance relates to a vehicle of any type, to the EEA State of registration;
    (c)   in the case of policies of a duration of four months or less covering travel or holiday risks (whatever the class concerned), to the EEA State in which the policyholder took out the policy;
    (d)   in a case not covered by paragraphs (a) to (c)—
        (i)   if the policyholder is an individual, to the EEA State in which he has his habitual residence at the date when the contract is entered into; and
        (ii)   otherwise, to the EEA State in which the establishment of the policyholder to which the policy relates is situated at that date.

[(4)   If the insurance relates to a vehicle dispatched from one EEA State to another, in respect of the period of 30 days beginning with the day on which the purchaser accepts delivery a reference to the EEA State in which a risk is situated is a reference to the State of destination (and not, as provided by sub-paragraph (3)(b), to the State of registration).]

                                                  [480]

NOTES

    Para 1: sub-para (1)(e), words in second (inner) pair of square brackets in sub-para (3)(a), words in square brackets in sub-para (4)(a), and sub-para (5) inserted by the Reinsurance Directive Regulations 2007, SI 2007/3253, reg 2(1), Sch 1, paras 1, 2(5)(a)–(d), as from 10 December 2007; words in square brackets in sub-para (2)(a) and words in first (outer) pair of square brackets in sub-para (3)(a) substituted by the Life Assurance Consolidation Directive (Consequential Amendments) Regulations 2004, SI 2004/3379, reg 6(1), (7)(a), as from 11 January 2005.
    Para 2: words in square brackets in sub-para (6)(a), sub-para (6)(aa), and sub-paras (7A), (9) inserted, and words in square brackets in sub-para (6)(c) substituted, by SI 2007/3253, reg 2(1), Sch 1, paras 1, 2(5)(e), as from 10 December 2007.
    Para 5A: inserted by SI 2007/3253, reg 2(1), Sch 1, paras 1, 2(5)(f), as from 10 December 2007.
    Para 6: sub-para (4) added by the Financial Services and Markets Act 2000 (Motor Insurance) Regulations 2007, SI 2007/2403, reg 2, as from 5 September 2007.

Regulations: the Financial Services and Markets Act 2000 (Control of Business Transfers) (Requirements on Applicants) Regulations 2001, SI 2001/3625 at **[2517]** (made under para 6).

PART II
BANKING BUSINESS TRANSFER SCHEMES

7.—(1)   For the purposes of section 111(2) the appropriate certificates, in relation to a banking business transfer scheme, are—
  (a)   a certificate under paragraph 8; and
  (b)   if sub-paragraph (2) applies, a certificate under paragraph 9.

   (2)   This sub-paragraph applies if the authorised person concerned or the transferee is an EEA firm falling within paragraph 5(b) of Schedule 3.

Certificates as to financial resources

8.—(1)   A certificate under this paragraph is one given by the relevant authority and certifying that, taking the proposed transfer into account, the transferee possesses, or will possess before the scheme takes effect, adequate financial resources.

   (2)   "Relevant authority" means—
  (a)   if the transferee is a person with a Part IV permission or with permission under Schedule 4, the Authority;
  (b)   if the transferee is an EEA firm falling within paragraph 5(b) of Schedule 3, its home state regulator;
  (c)   if the transferee does not fall within paragraph (a) or (b), the authority responsible for the supervision of the transferee's business in the place in which the transferee has its head office.

   (3)   In sub-paragraph (2), any reference to a transferee of a particular description of person includes a reference to a transferee who will be of that description if the proposed banking business transfer scheme takes effect.

Certificates as to consent of home state regulator

9.   A certificate under this paragraph is one given by the Authority and certifying that the home State regulator of the authorised person concerned or of the transferee has been notified of the proposed scheme and that—
  (a)   the home State regulator has responded to the notification; or
  (b)   the period of three months beginning with the notification has elapsed.

[481]

[PART 2A
RECLAIM FUND BUSINESS TRANSFER SCHEMES

Certificate as to financial resources

9A.   For the purposes of section 111(2) the appropriate certificate, in relation to a reclaim fund business transfer scheme, is a certificate given by the Authority certifying that, taking the proposed transfer into account, the transferee possesses, or will possess before the scheme takes effect, adequate financial resources.]

[481A]

NOTES
   Commencement: to be appointed.
   Inserted by the Dormant Bank and Building Society Accounts Act 2008, s 15, Sch 2, para 5, as from a day to be appointed.

PART III
INSURANCE BUSINESS TRANSFERS EFFECTED OUTSIDE THE UNITED KINGDOM

10.—(1)   This paragraph applies to a proposal to execute under provisions corresponding to Part VII in a country or territory other than the United Kingdom an instrument transferring all the rights and obligations of the transferor under general or long-term insurance policies, or under such descriptions of such policies as may be specified in the instrument, to the transferee if any of the conditions in sub-paragraphs (2), (3) or (4) is met in relation to it.

   (2)   The transferor is an EEA firm falling within paragraph 5(d) [or (da)] of Schedule 3 and the transferee is an authorised person whose margin of solvency is supervised by the Authority.

   (3)   The transferor is a company authorised in an EEA State other than the United Kingdom under [Article 51 of the life assurance consolidation directive], or Article 23 of the first non-life

insurance directive and the transferee is a UK authorised person which has received authorisation under [Article 4 of the life assurance consolidation directive or Article 6 of the first non-life insurance directive].

(4)   The transferor is a Swiss general insurer and the transferee is a UK authorised person which has received authorisation under [Article 4 of the life assurance consolidation directive or Article 6 of the first non-life insurance directive].

(5)   In relation to a proposed transfer to which this paragraph applies, the Authority may, if it is satisfied that the transferee possesses the necessary margin of solvency, issue a certificate to that effect.

(6)   "Necessary margin of solvency" means the margin of solvency which the transferee, taking the proposed transfer into account, is required by the Authority to maintain.

(7)   "Swiss general insurer" has the same meaning as in paragraph 2.

(8)   "General policy" means a policy evidencing a contract which, if it had been effected by the transferee, would have constituted the carrying on of a regulated activity consisting of the effecting of contracts of general insurance.

(9)   "Long-term policy" means a policy evidencing a contract which, if it had been effected by the transferee, would have constituted the carrying on of a regulated activity consisting of the effecting of contracts of long-term insurance.

[482]

NOTES

Para 10: words in square brackets in sub-para (2) inserted by the Reinsurance Directive Regulations 2007, SI 2007/3253, reg 2(1), Sch 1, paras 1, 2(5)(g), as from 10 December 2007; other words in square brackets substituted by the Life Assurance Consolidation Directive (Consequential Amendments) Regulations 2004, SI 2004/3379, reg 6(1), (7)(b), (c), as from 11 January 2005.

SCHEDULE 13
THE FINANCIAL SERVICES AND MARKETS TRIBUNAL

Section 132(4)

NOTES

Application: see the note preceding s 132 at **[160]**.

PART I
GENERAL

Interpretation

1.   In this Schedule—
   "panel of chairmen" means the panel established under paragraph 3(1);
   "lay panel" means the panel established under paragraph 3(4);
   "rules" means rules made by the Lord Chancellor under section 132.

[483]

PART II
THE TRIBUNAL

President

2.—(1)   The Lord Chancellor must appoint one of the members of the panel of chairmen to preside over the discharge of the Tribunal's functions.

(2)   The member so appointed is to be known as the President of the Financial Services and Markets Tribunal (but is referred to in this Act as "the President").

(3)   The Lord Chancellor may appoint one of the members of the panel of chairmen to be Deputy President.

(4)   The Deputy President is to have such functions in relation to the Tribunal as the President may assign to him.

(5)   The Lord Chancellor may not appoint a person to be the President or Deputy President unless that person—
   [(a)   satisfies the judicial-appointment eligibility condition on a 7-year basis;]
   (b)   is an advocate or solicitor in Scotland of at least [7] years' standing; or
   (c)   is—
      (i)   a member of the Bar of Northern Ireland of at least [7] years' standing; or
      (ii)   a *solicitor of the Supreme Court of Northern Ireland* of at least [7] years' standing.

(6)   If the President (or Deputy President) ceases to be a member of the panel of chairmen, he also ceases to be the President (or Deputy President).

(7)   The functions of the President may, if he is absent or is otherwise unable to act, be discharged—

    (a)   by the Deputy President; or

    (b)   if there is no Deputy President or he too is absent or otherwise unable to act, by a person appointed for that purpose from the panel of chairmen by the Lord Chancellor.

[(8)   The Lord Chancellor may appoint a person under sub-paragraph (7)(b) only after consulting the following—

    (a)   the Lord Chief Justice of England and Wales;

    (b)   the Lord President of the Court of Session;

    (c)   the Lord Chief Justice of Northern Ireland.

(9)   The Lord Chief Justice of England and Wales may nominate a judicial office holder (as defined in section 109(4) of the Constitutional Reform Act 2005) to exercise his functions under this paragraph.

(10)   The Lord President of the Court of Session may nominate a judge of the Court of Session who is a member of the First or Second Division of the Inner House of that Court to exercise his functions under this paragraph.

(11)   The Lord Chief Justice of Northern Ireland may nominate any of the following to exercise his functions under this paragraph—

    (a)   the holder of one of the offices listed in Schedule 1 to the Justice (Northern Ireland) Act 2002;

    (b)   a Lord Justice of Appeal (as defined in section 88 of that Act).]

Panels

3.—(1)   The Lord Chancellor must appoint a panel of persons for the purposes of serving as chairmen of the Tribunal.

(2)   A person is qualified for membership of the panel of chairmen if—

    [(a)   he satisfies the judicial-appointment eligibility condition on a 5-year basis;]

    (b)   he is an advocate or solicitor in Scotland of at least [5] years' standing; or

    (c)   he is—

        (i)   a member of the Bar of Northern Ireland of at least [5] years' standing; or

        (ii)   a *solicitor of the Supreme Court of Northern Ireland* of at least [5] years' standing.

(3)   The panel of chairmen must include at least one member who is a person of the kind mentioned in sub-paragraph (2)(b).

(4)   The Lord Chancellor must also appoint a panel of persons who appear to him to be qualified by experience or otherwise to deal with matters of the kind that may be referred to the Tribunal.

Terms of office etc

4.—(1)   Subject to the provisions of this Schedule, each member of the panel of chairmen and the lay panel is to hold and vacate office in accordance with the terms of his appointment.

(2)   The Lord Chancellor may remove a member of either panel (including the President) on the ground of incapacity or misbehaviour.

[(2A)   The Lord Chancellor may remove a person under sub-paragraph (2) only with the concurrence of the appropriate senior judge.

(2B)   The appropriate senior judge is the Lord Chief Justice of England and Wales, unless—

    (a)   the person to be removed exercises functions wholly or mainly in Scotland, in which case it is the Lord President of the Court of Session, or

    (b)   the person to be removed exercises functions wholly or mainly in Northern Ireland, in which case it is the Lord Chief Justice of Northern Ireland.]

(3)   A member of either panel—

    (a)   may at any time resign office by notice in writing to the Lord Chancellor;

    (b)   is eligible for re-appointment if he ceases to hold office.

Remuneration and expenses

5.   The Lord Chancellor may pay to any person, in respect of his service—

    (a)   as a member of the Tribunal (including service as the President or Deputy President), or

    (b)   as a person appointed under paragraph 7(4),

such remuneration and allowances as he may determine.

Staff

6.—(1)　The Lord Chancellor may appoint such staff for the Tribunal as he may determine.

(2)　The remuneration of the Tribunal's staff is to be defrayed by the Lord Chancellor.

(3)　Such expenses of the Tribunal as the Lord Chancellor may determine are to be defrayed by the Lord Chancellor.

[484]

NOTES

Para 2 is amended as follows:

Sub-para (5)(a) substituted by the Tribunals, Courts and Enforcement Act 2007, s 50(6), Sch 10, Pt 1, para 34(1), (2)(a), as from 21 July 2008 (for transitional provisions in relation to on-going appointment processes, see SI 2008/1653, arts 3, 4).

Number "7" in square brackets in each of sub-paras (5)(b), (c)(i) and (ii) substituted by the Tribunals, Courts and Enforcement Act 2007, s 50(6), Sch 10, Pt 1, para 34(1), (2)(b), as from 21 July 2008 (for transitional provisions in relation to on-going appointment processes, see SI 2008/1653, arts 3, 4).

For the words "solicitor of the Supreme Court of Northern Ireland" in italics in sub-para (5)(c)(ii) there are substituted the words "solicitor of the Court of Judicature of Northern Ireland" by the Constitutional Reform Act 2005, s 59(5), Sch 11, Pt 3, para 5, as from a day to be appointed.

Sub-paras (8)–(11) added by the Constitutional Reform Act 2005, s 15, Sch 4, Pt 1, para 286(1), (2), as from 3 April 2006.

Para 3 is amended as follows:

Sub-para (2)(a) substituted by the Tribunals, Courts and Enforcement Act 2007, s 50(6), Sch 10, Pt 1, para 34(1), (3)(a), as from 21 July 2008 (for transitional provisions in relation to on-going appointment processes, see SI 2008/1653, arts 3, 4).

Number "5" in square brackets in each of sub-paras (2)(b), (c)(i) and (ii) substituted by the Tribunals, Courts and Enforcement Act 2007, s 50(6), Sch 10, Pt 1, para 34(1), (3)(b), as from 21 July 2008 (for transitional provisions in relation to on-going appointment processes, see SI 2008/1653, arts 3, 4).

For the words "solicitor of the Supreme Court of Northern Ireland" in italics in sub-para (2)(c)(ii) there are substituted the words "solicitor of the Court of Judicature of Northern Ireland" by the Constitutional Reform Act 2005, s 59(5), Sch 11, Pt 3, para 5, as from a day to be appointed.

Para 4: sub-paras (2A), (2B) inserted by the Constitutional Reform Act 2005, s 15, Sch 4, Pt 1, para 286(1), (3), as from 3 April 2006.

PART III
CONSTITUTION OF TRIBUNAL

7.—(1)　On a reference to the Tribunal, the persons to act as members of the Tribunal for the purposes of the reference are to be selected from the panel of chairmen or the lay panel in accordance with arrangements made by the President for the purposes of this paragraph ("the standing arrangements").

(2)　The standing arrangements must provide for at least one member to be selected from the panel of chairmen.

(3)　If while a reference is being dealt with, a person serving as member of the Tribunal in respect of the reference becomes unable to act, the reference may be dealt with by—

    (a)　the other members selected in respect of that reference; or

    (b)　if it is being dealt with by a single member, such other member of the panel of chairmen as may be selected in accordance with the standing arrangements for the purposes of the reference.

(4)　If it appears to the Tribunal that a matter before it involves a question of fact of special difficulty, it may appoint one or more experts to provide assistance.

[485]

PART IV
TRIBUNAL PROCEDURE

8.　For the purpose of dealing with references, or any matter preliminary or incidental to a reference, the Tribunal must sit at such times and in such place or places as the Lord Chancellor may[, after consulting the President of the Financial Services and Markets Tribunal,] direct.

9.　Rules made by the Lord Chancellor under section 132 may, in particular, include provision—

    (a)　as to the manner in which references are to be instituted;

    (b)　for the holding of hearings in private in such circumstances as may be specified in the rules;

    (c)　as to the persons who may appear on behalf of the parties;

    (d)　for a member of the panel of chairmen to hear and determine interlocutory matters arising on a reference;

    (e)　for the suspension of decisions of the Authority which have taken effect;

    (f)　as to the withdrawal of references;

    (g)　as to the registration, publication and proof of decisions and orders.

Practice directions

10.   The President of the Tribunal may give directions as to the practice and procedure to be followed by the Tribunal in relation to references to it.

Evidence

11.—(1)   The Tribunal may by summons require any person to attend, at such time and place as is specified in the summons, to give evidence or to produce any document in his custody or under his control which the Tribunal considers it necessary to examine.

(2)   The Tribunal may—
    (a)   take evidence on oath and for that purpose administer oaths; or
    (b)   instead of administering an oath, require the person examined to make and subscribe a declaration of the truth of the matters in respect of which he is examined.

(3)   A person who without reasonable excuse—
    (a)   refuses or fails—
        (i)   to attend following the issue of a summons by the Tribunal, or
        (ii)   to give evidence, or
    (b)   alters, suppresses, conceals or destroys, or refuses to produce a document which he may be required to produce for the purposes of proceedings before the Tribunal,
is guilty of an offence.

(4)   A person guilty of an offence under sub-paragraph (3)(a) is liable on summary conviction to a fine not exceeding the statutory maximum.

(5)   A person guilty of an offence under sub-paragraph (3)(b) is liable—
    (a)   on summary conviction, to a fine not exceeding the statutory maximum;
    (b)   on conviction on indictment, to imprisonment for a term not exceeding two years or a fine or both.

Decisions of Tribunal

12.—(1)   A decision of the Tribunal may be taken by a majority.

(2)   The decision must—
    (a)   state whether it was unanimous or taken by a majority;
    (b)   be recorded in a document which—
        (i)   contains a statement of the reasons for the decision; and
        (ii)   is signed and dated by the member of the panel of chairmen dealing with the reference.

(3)   The Tribunal must—
    (a)   inform each party of its decision; and
    (b)   as soon as reasonably practicable, send to each party and, if different, to any authorised person concerned, a copy of the document mentioned in sub-paragraph (2).

(4)   The Tribunal must send the Treasury a copy of its decision.

Costs

13.—(1)   If the Tribunal considers that a party to any proceedings on a reference has acted vexatiously, frivolously or unreasonably it may order that party to pay to another party to the proceedings the whole or part of the costs or expenses incurred by the other party in connection with the proceedings.

(2)   If, in any proceedings on a reference, the Tribunal considers that a decision of the Authority which is the subject of the reference was unreasonable it may order the Authority to pay to another party to the proceedings the whole or part of the costs or expenses incurred by the other party in connection with the proceedings.

[486]

NOTES
  Para 8: words in square brackets inserted by the Constitutional Reform Act 2005, s 15, Sch 4, Pt 1, para 286(1), (4), as from 3 April 2006.
  Rules: as to Rules made under para 9 above (ie, Rules made by the Lord Chancellor under section 132), see that section at **[160]**.

SCHEDULE 14
ROLE OF THE COMPETITION COMMISSION

Section 162

PART I
FSMA 2000

Provision of information by Treasury

1.—(1)   The Treasury's powers under this paragraph are to be exercised only for the purpose of assisting the Commission in carrying out an investigation under section 162.

(2)   The Treasury may give to the Commission—
   (a)   any information in their possession which relates to matters falling within the scope of the investigation; and
   (b)   other assistance in relation to any such matters.

(3)   In carrying out an investigation under section 162, the Commission must have regard to any information given to it under this paragraph.

Consideration of matters arising on a report

2.   In considering any matter arising from a report made by the [OFT] under section 160, the Commission must have regard to—
   (a)   any representations made to [the Commission] in connection with the matter by any person appearing to the Commission to have a substantial interest in the matter; and
   (b)   any cost benefit analysis prepared by the Authority (at any time) in connection with the regulatory provision or practice, or any of the regulatory provisions or practices, which are the subject of the report.

[Investigations under section 162: application of Enterprise Act 2002

2A.—(1)   The following sections of Part 3 of the Enterprise Act 2002 shall apply, with the modifications mentioned in sub-paragraphs (2) and (3), for the purposes of any investigation by the Commission under section 162 of this Act as they apply for the purposes of references under that Part—
   (a)   section 109 (attendance of witnesses and production of documents etc);
   (b)   section 110 (enforcement of powers under section 109: general);
   (c)   section 111 (penalties);
   (d)   section 112 (penalties: main procedural requirements);
   (e)   section 113 (payments and interest by instalments);
   (f)   section 114 (appeals in relation to penalties);
   (g)   section 115 (recovery of penalties); and
   (h)   section 116 (statement of policy).

(2)   Section 110 shall, in its application by virtue of sub-paragraph (1), have effect as if—
   (a)   subsection (2) were omitted; and
   (b)   in subsection (9) the words from "or section" to "section 65(3))" were omitted.

(3)   Section 111(5)(b) shall, in its application by virtue of sub-paragraph (1), have effect as if for sub-paragraph (ii) there were substituted—
   "(ii)   if earlier, the day on which the report of the Commission on the investigation concerned is made or, if the Commission decides not to make a report, the day on which the Commission makes the statement required by section 162(3) of the Financial Services and Markets Act 2000."

(4)   Section 117 of the Enterprise Act 2002 (false or misleading information) shall apply in relation to functions of the Commission in connection with an investigation under section 162 of this Act as it applies in relation to its functions under Part 3 of that Act but as if, in subsections (1)(a) and (2), the words ["the OFT, OFCOM,"] and "or the Secretary of State" were omitted.

(5)   Provisions of Part 3 of the Enterprise Act 2002 which have effect for the purposes of sections 109 to 117 of that Act (including, in particular, provisions relating to offences and the making of orders) shall, for the purposes of the application of those sections by virtue of sub-paragraph (1) or (4) above, have effect in relation to those sections as applied by virtue of those sub-paragraphs.

(6)   Accordingly, corresponding provisions of this Act shall not have effect in relation to those sections as applied by virtue of those sub-paragraphs.

Section 162: modification of Schedule 7 to the Competition Act 1998

2B.   For the purposes of its application in relation to the function of the Commission of deciding in accordance with section 162(2) of this Act not to make a report, paragraph 15(7) of Schedule 7 to the Competition Act 1998 (power of the Chairman to act on his own while a group is being constituted) has effect as if, after paragraph (a), there were inserted

   "; or
   (aa)   in the case of an investigation under section 162 of the Financial Services and

Markets Act 2000, decide not to make a report in accordance with subsection (2) of that section (decision not to make a report where no useful purpose would be served).".

Reports under section 162: further provision

2C.—(1) For the purposes of section 163 of this Act, a conclusion contained in a report of the Commission is to be disregarded if the conclusion is not that of at least two-thirds of the members of the group constituted in connection with the investigation concerned in pursuance of paragraph 15 of Schedule 7 to the Competition Act 1998.

(2) If a member of a group so constituted disagrees with any conclusions contained in a report made under section 162 of this Act as the conclusions of the Commission, the report shall, if the member so wishes, include a statement of his disagreement and of his reasons for disagreeing.

(3) For the purposes of the law relating to defamation, absolute privilege attaches to any report made by the Commission under section 162.]

...

3. ...

Publication of reports

4.—(1) If the Commission makes a report under section 162, it must publish it in such a way as appears to it to be best calculated to bring it to the attention of the public.

(2) Before publishing the report the Commission must, so far as practicable, exclude any matter which relates to the private affairs of a particular individual the publication of which, in the opinion of the Commission, would or might seriously and prejudicially affect his interests.

(3) Before publishing the report the Commission must, so far as practicable, also exclude any matter which relates to the affairs of a particular body the publication of which, in the opinion of the Commission, would or might seriously and prejudicially affect its interests.

(4) Sub-paragraphs (2) and (3) do not apply in relation to copies of a report which the Commission is required to send under section 162(10).

[487]

NOTES

Para 2: words in square brackets substituted by the Enterprise Act 2002, s 278(1), Sch 25, para 40(1), (20)(a), as from 1 April 2003.

Paras 2A–2C: inserted by the Enterprise Act 2002, s 278(1), Sch 25, para 40(1), (20)(b), as from 20 June 2003, except in relation to any investigation commenced before that date under ss 162 or 306 of this Act; words in square brackets in para 2A(4) substituted by the Communications Act 2003, s 389, Sch 16, para 5, as from 29 December 2003.

Para 3: repealed by the Enterprise Act 2002, s 278, Sch 25, para 40(1), (20)(c), Sch 26, as from 20 June 2003, except in relation to any investigation commenced before that date under ss 162 or 306 of this Act.

SCHEDULE 15
INFORMATION AND INVESTIGATIONS: CONNECTED PERSONS
Sections 165(11) and 171(4)

PART I
RULES FOR SPECIFIC BODIES

Corporate bodies

1. If the authorised person ("BC") is a body corporate, a person who is or has been—
   (a) an officer or manager of BC or of a parent undertaking of BC;
   (b) an employee of BC;
   (c) an agent of BC or of a parent undertaking of BC.

Partnerships

2. If the authorised person ("PP") is a partnership, a person who is or has been a member, manager, employee or agent of PP.

Unincorporated associations

3. If the authorised person ("UA") is an unincorporated association of persons which is neither a partnership nor an unincorporated friendly society, a person who is or has been an officer, manager, employee or agent of UA.

Friendly societies

4.—(1)   If the authorised person ("FS") is a friendly society, a person who is or has been an officer, manager or employee of FS.

(2)   In relation to FS, "officer" and "manager" have the same meaning as in section 119(1) of the Friendly Societies Act 1992.

Building societies

5.—(1)   If the authorised person ("BS") is a building society, a person who is or has been an officer or employee of BS.

(2)   In relation to BS, "officer" has the same meaning as it has in section 119(1) of the Building Societies Act 1986.

Individuals

6.   If the authorised person ("IP") is an individual, a person who is or has been an employee or agent of IP.

Application to sections 171 and 172

7.   For the purposes of sections 171 and 172, if the person under investigation is not an authorised person the references in this Part of this Schedule to an authorised person are to be taken to be references to the person under investigation.

[488]

PART II
ADDITIONAL RULES

8.   A person who is, or at the relevant time was, the partner, manager, employee, agent, appointed representative, banker, auditor, actuary or solicitor of—
   (a)   the person under investigation ("A");
   (b)   a parent undertaking of A;
   (c)   a subsidiary undertaking of A;
   (d)   a subsidiary undertaking of a parent undertaking of A; or
   (e)   a parent undertaking of a subsidiary undertaking of A.

[489]

SCHEDULE 16
PROHIBITIONS AND RESTRICTIONS IMPOSED BY [OFFICE OF FAIR TRADING]
Section 203(8)

Preliminary

1.   In this Schedule—
   "appeal period" has the same meaning as in the Consumer Credit Act 1974;
   "prohibition" means a consumer credit prohibition under section 203;
   "restriction" means a restriction under section 204.

Notice of prohibition or restriction

2.—(1)   This paragraph applies if the [OFT] proposes, in relation to a firm—
   (a)   to impose a prohibition;
   (b)   to impose a restriction; or
   (c)   to vary a restriction otherwise than with the agreement of the firm.

(2)   The [OFT] must by notice—
   (a)   inform the firm of [its] proposal, stating [its] reasons; and
   (b)   invite the firm to submit representations in accordance with paragraph 4.

(3)   If [the OFT] imposes the prohibition or restriction or varies the restriction, the [OFT] may give directions authorising the firm to carry into effect agreements made before the coming into force of the prohibition, restriction or variation.

(4)   A prohibition, restriction or variation is not to come into force before the end of the appeal period.

(5)   If the [OFT] imposes a prohibition or restriction or varies a restriction, [the OFT] must serve a copy of the prohibition, restriction or variation—
   (a)   on the Authority; and
   (b)   on the firm's home state regulator.

Application to revoke prohibition or restriction

3.—(1) This paragraph applies if the [OFT] proposes to refuse an application made by a firm for the revocation of a prohibition or restriction.

(2) The [OFT] must by notice—
(a) inform the firm of the proposed refusal, stating [its] reasons; and
(b) invite the firm to submit representations in accordance with paragraph 4.

Representations to [OFT]

4.—(1) If this paragraph applies to an invitation to submit representations, the [OFT] must invite the firm, within 21 days after the notice containing the invitation is given to it or such longer period as [the OFT] may allow—
(a) to submit its representations in writing to [the OFT]; and
(b) to give notice to [the OFT], if the firm thinks fit, that it wishes to make representations orally.

(2) If notice is given under sub-paragraph (1)(b), the [OFT] must arrange for the oral representations to be heard.

(3) The [OFT] must give the firm notice of [its] determination.

Appeals

5. Section 41 of the Consumer Credit Act 1974 (appeals to the Secretary of State) has effect as if—
(a) the following determinations were mentioned in column 1 of the table set out at the end of that section—
(i) imposition of a prohibition or restriction or the variation of a restriction; and
(ii) refusal of an application for the revocation of a prohibition or restriction; and
(b) the firm concerned were mentioned in column 2 of that table in relation to those determinations.

[490]

NOTES
Words in square brackets substituted by the Enterprise Act 2002, s 278(1), Sch 25, para 40(1), (21), as from 1 April 2003.
Within 21 days: note that any provision of this Act (other than a provision of Part VI) authorising or requiring a person to do anything within a specified number of days must not take into account any day which is a public holiday in any part of the United Kingdom; see s 417(3) at **[443]**.

SCHEDULE 17
THE OMBUDSMAN SCHEME

Section 225(4)

NOTES
Transitional provisions: see the notes preceding s 225 at **[253]**.

PART I
GENERAL

Interpretation

1. In this Schedule—
"ombudsman" means a person who is a member of the panel; and
"the panel" means the panel established under paragraph 4.

[491]

PART II
THE SCHEME OPERATOR

Establishment by the Authority

2.—(1) The Authority must establish a body corporate to exercise the functions conferred on the scheme operator by or under this Act.

(2) The Authority must take such steps as are necessary to ensure that the scheme operator is, at all times, capable of exercising those functions.

Constitution

3.—(1) The constitution of the scheme operator must provide for it to have—
(a) a chairman; and

(b)   a board (which must include the chairman) whose members are the scheme operator's directors.

(2)   The chairman and other members of the board must be persons appointed, and liable to removal from office, by the Authority (acting, in the case of the chairman, with the approval of the Treasury).

(3)   But the terms of their appointment (and in particular those governing removal from office) must be such as to secure their independence from the Authority in the operation of the scheme.

(4)   The function of making voluntary jurisdiction rules under section 227[, the function of making consumer credit rules, the function of making determinations under section 234A(1)] and the functions conferred by paragraphs 4, 5, 7, 9 or 14 may be exercised only by the board.

(5)   The validity of any act of the scheme operator is unaffected by—
  (a)   a vacancy in the office of chairman; or
  (b)   a defect in the appointment of a person as chairman or as a member of the board.

The panel of ombudsmen

4.—(1)   The scheme operator must appoint and maintain a panel of persons, appearing to it to have appropriate qualifications and experience, to act as ombudsmen for the purposes of the scheme.

(2)   A person's appointment to the panel is to be on such terms (including terms as to the duration and termination of his appointment and as to remuneration) as the scheme operator considers—
  (a)   consistent with the independence of the person appointed; and
  (b)   otherwise appropriate.

The Chief Ombudsman

5.—(1)   The scheme operator must appoint one member of the panel to act as Chief Ombudsman.

(2)   The Chief Ombudsman is to be appointed on such terms (including terms as to the duration and termination of his appointment) as the scheme operator considers appropriate.

Status

6.—(1)   The scheme operator is not to be regarded as exercising functions on behalf of the Crown.

(2)   The scheme operator's board members, officers and staff are not to be regarded as Crown servants.

(3)   Appointment as Chief Ombudsman or to the panel or as a deputy ombudsman does not confer the status of Crown servant.

Annual reports

7.—(1)   At least once a year—
  (a)   the scheme operator must make a report to the Authority on the discharge of its functions; and
  (b)   the Chief Ombudsman must make a report to the Authority on the discharge of his functions.

(2)   Each report must distinguish between functions in relation to the scheme's compulsory jurisdiction[, functions in relation to its consumer credit jurisdiction] and functions in relation to its voluntary jurisdiction.

(3)   Each report must also comply with any requirements specified in rules made by the Authority.

(4)   The scheme operator must publish each report in the way it considers appropriate.

Guidance

8.   The scheme operator may publish guidance consisting of such information and advice as it considers appropriate and may charge for it or distribute it free of charge.

Budget

9.—(1)   The scheme operator must, before the start of each of its financial years, adopt an annual budget which has been approved by the Authority.

(2)   The scheme operator may, with the approval of the Authority, vary the budget for a financial year at any time after its adoption.

(3)   The annual budget must include an indication of—
  (a)   the distribution of resources deployed in the operation of the scheme, and

(b) the amounts of income of the scheme operator arising or expected to arise from the operation of the scheme,

distinguishing between the scheme's compulsory[, consumer credit] and voluntary jurisdiction.

Exemption from liability in damages

10.—(1) No person is to be liable in damages for anything done or omitted in the discharge, or purported discharge, of any functions under this Act in relation to the compulsory jurisdiction [or to the consumer credit jurisdiction].

(2) Sub-paragraph (1) does not apply—

(a) if the act or omission is shown to have been in bad faith; or

(b) so as to prevent an award of damages made in respect of an act or omission on the ground that the act or omission was unlawful as a result of section 6(1) of the Human Rights Act 1998.

Privilege

11. For the purposes of the law relating to defamation, proceedings in relation to a complaint which is subject to the compulsory jurisdiction [or to the consumer credit jurisdiction] are to be treated as if they were proceedings before a court.

[492]

NOTES

Paras 3, 7, 9–11: words in square brackets inserted by the Consumer Credit Act 2006, s 61(10), as from 16 June 2006.

Para 9(3) above did not apply to the scheme operator's first budget (ie, its budget for the financial year during which 18 June 2001 occurs); see the Financial Services and Markets Act 2000 (Consequential and Transitional Provisions) (Miscellaneous) Order 2001, SI 2001/1821, art 4.

PART III
THE COMPULSORY JURISDICTION

Introduction

12. This Part of this Schedule applies only in relation to the compulsory jurisdiction.

Authority's procedural rules

13.—(1) The Authority must make rules providing that a complaint is not to be entertained unless the complainant has referred it under the ombudsman scheme before the applicable time limit (determined in accordance with the rules) has expired.

(2) The rules may provide that an ombudsman may extend that time limit in specified circumstances.

(3) The Authority may make rules providing that a complaint is not to be entertained (except in specified circumstances) if the complainant has not previously communicated its substance to the respondent and given him a reasonable opportunity to deal with it.

(4) The Authority may make rules requiring an authorised person[, or a payment service provider within the meaning of the Payment Services Regulations 2009,] who may become subject to the compulsory jurisdiction as a respondent to establish such procedures as the Authority considers appropriate for the resolution of complaints which—

(a) may be referred to the scheme; and

(b) arise out of activity to which the Authority's powers under Part X do not apply.

The scheme operator's rules

14.—(1) The scheme operator must make rules, to be known as "scheme rules", which are to set out the procedure for reference of complaints and for their investigation, consideration and determination by an ombudsman.

(2) Scheme rules may, among other things—

(a) specify matters which are to be taken into account in determining whether an act or omission was fair and reasonable;

(b) provide that a complaint may, in specified circumstances, be dismissed without consideration of its merits;

(c) provide for the reference of a complaint, in specified circumstances and with the consent of the complainant, to another body with a view to its being determined by that body instead of by an ombudsman;

(d) make provision as to the evidence which may be required or admitted, the extent to which it should be oral or written and the consequences of a person's failure to produce any information or document which he has been required (under section 231 or otherwise) to produce;

  (e)   allow an ombudsman to fix time limits for any aspect of the proceedings and to extend a time limit;

  (f)   provide for certain things in relation to the reference, investigation or consideration (but not determination) of a complaint to be done by a member of the scheme operator's staff instead of by an ombudsman;

  (g)   make different provision in relation to different kinds of complaint.

(3)   The circumstances specified under sub-paragraph (2)(b) may include the following—

  (a)   the ombudsman considers the complaint frivolous or vexatious;

  (b)   legal proceedings have been brought concerning the subject-matter of the complaint and the ombudsman considers that the complaint is best dealt with in those proceedings; or

  (c)   the ombudsman is satisfied that there are other compelling reasons why it is inappropriate for the complaint to be dealt with under the ombudsman scheme.

(4)   If the scheme operator proposes to make any scheme rules it must publish a draft of the proposed rules in the way appearing to it to be best calculated to bring them to the attention of persons appearing to it to be likely to be affected.

(5)   The draft must be accompanied by a statement that representations about the proposals may be made to the scheme operator within a time specified in the statement.

(6)   Before making the proposed scheme rules, the scheme operator must have regard to any representations made to it under sub-paragraph (5).

(7)   The consent of the Authority is required before any scheme rules may be made.

Fees

15.—(1)   Scheme rules may require a respondent to pay to the scheme operator such fees as may be specified in the rules.

(2)   The rules may, among other things—

  (a)   provide for the scheme operator to reduce or waive a fee in a particular case;

  (b)   set different fees for different stages of the proceedings on a complaint;

  (c)   provide for fees to be refunded in specified circumstances;

  (d)   make different provision for different kinds of complaint.

Enforcement of money awards

16.   A money award, including interest, which has been registered in accordance with scheme rules may—

  (a)   if a county court so orders in England and Wales, be recovered *by execution issued from the county court* (or otherwise) as if it were payable under an order of that court;

  (b)   be enforced in Northern Ireland as a money judgment under the Judgments Enforcement (Northern Ireland) Order 1981;

  (c)   be enforced in Scotland by the sheriff, as if it were a judgment or order of the sheriff and whether or not the sheriff could himself have granted such judgment or order.

[493]

NOTES

  Para 13: words in square brackets in sub-para (4) inserted by the Payment Services Regulations 2009, SI 2009/209, reg 126, Sch 6, Pt 1, para 1(2), as from 2 March 2009 (for the full commencement details of the 2009 Regulations, see reg 1 of those Regulations at **[4387]**).

  Para 16: for the words in italics in sub-para (a) there are substituted the words "under section 85 of the County Courts Act 1984" by the Tribunals, Courts and Enforcement Act 2007, s 62(3), Sch 13, para 134, as from a day to be appointed.

[PART 3A
THE CONSUMER CREDIT JURISDICTION

Introduction

16A.   This Part of this Schedule applies only in relation to the consumer credit jurisdiction.

Procedure for complaints etc

16B.—(1)   Consumer credit rules—

  (a)   must provide that a complaint is not to be entertained unless the complainant has referred it under the ombudsman scheme before the applicable time limit (determined in accordance with the rules) has expired;

  (b)   may provide that an ombudsman may extend that time limit in specified circumstances;

(c)   may provide that a complaint is not to be entertained (except in specified circumstances) if the complainant has not previously communicated its substance to the respondent and given him a reasonable opportunity to deal with it;

(d)   may make provision about the procedure for the reference of complaints and for their investigation, consideration and determination by an ombudsman.

(2)   Sub-paragraphs (2) and (3) of paragraph 14 apply in relation to consumer credit rules under sub-paragraph (1) of this paragraph as they apply in relation to scheme rules under that paragraph.

(3)   Consumer credit rules may require persons falling within sub-paragraph (6) to establish such procedures as the scheme operator considers appropriate for the resolution of complaints which may be referred to the scheme.

(4)   Consumer credit rules under sub-paragraph (3) may make different provision in relation to persons of different descriptions or to complaints of different descriptions.

(5)   Consumer credit rules under sub-paragraph (3) may authorise the scheme operator to dispense with or modify the application of such rules in particular cases where the scheme operator—

(a)   considers it appropriate to do so; and

(b)   is satisfied that the specified conditions (if any) are met.

(6)   A person falls within this sub-paragraph if he is licensed by a standard licence (within the meaning of the Consumer Credit Act 1974) to carry on to any extent a business of a type specified in an order under section 226A(2)(e) of this Act.

Fees

16C.—(1)   Consumer credit rules may require a respondent to pay to the scheme operator such fees as may be specified in the rules.

(2)   Sub-paragraph (2) of paragraph 15 applies in relation to consumer credit rules under this paragraph as it applies in relation to scheme rules under that paragraph.

Enforcement of money awards

16D.   A money award, including interest, which has been registered in accordance with consumer credit rules may—

(a)   if a county court so orders in England and Wales, be recovered by execution issued from the county court (or otherwise) as if it were payable under an order of that court;

(b)   be enforced in Northern Ireland as a money judgment under the Judgments Enforcement (Northern Ireland) Order 1981;

(c)   be enforced in Scotland as if it were a decree of the sheriff and whether or not the sheriff could himself have granted such a decree.

Procedure for consumer credit rules

16E.—(1)   If the scheme operator makes any consumer credit rules, it must give a copy of them to the Authority without delay.

(2)   If the scheme operator revokes any such rules, it must give written notice to the Authority without delay.

(3)   The power to make such rules is exercisable in writing.

(4)   Immediately after the making of such rules, the scheme operator must arrange for them to be printed and made available to the public.

(5)   The scheme operator may charge a reasonable fee for providing a person with a copy of any such rules.

Verification of consumer credit rules

16F.—(1)   The production of a printed copy of consumer credit rules purporting to be made by the scheme operator—

(a)   on which there is endorsed a certificate signed by a member of the scheme operator's staff authorised by the scheme operator for that purpose, and

(b)   which contains the required statements,

is evidence (or in Scotland sufficient evidence) of the facts stated in the certificate.

(2)   The required statements are—

(a)   that the rules were made by the scheme operator;

(b)   that the copy is a true copy of the rules; and

(c)   that on a specified date the rules were made available to the public in accordance with paragraph 16E(4).

(3)   A certificate purporting to be signed as mentioned in sub-paragraph (1) is to be taken to have been duly signed unless the contrary is shown.

Consultation

16G.—(1)   If the scheme operator proposes to make consumer credit rules, it must publish a draft of the proposed rules in the way appearing to it to be best calculated to bring the draft to the attention of the public.

(2)   The draft must be accompanied by—
   (a)   an explanation of the proposed rules; and
   (b)   a statement that representations about the proposals may be made to the scheme operator within a specified time.

(3)   Before making any consumer credit rules, the scheme operator must have regard to any representations made to it in accordance with sub-paragraph (2)(b).

(4)   If consumer credit rules made by the scheme operator differ from the draft published under sub-paragraph (1) in a way which the scheme operator considers significant, the scheme operator must publish a statement of the difference.]

[493A]

NOTES
Commencement: 16 June 2006.
Inserted by the Consumer Credit Act 2006, s 59(2), Sch 2, as from 16 June 2006.

PART IV
THE VOLUNTARY JURISDICTION

Introduction

17.   This Part of this Schedule applies only in relation to the voluntary jurisdiction.

Terms of reference to the scheme

18.—(1)   Complaints are to be dealt with and determined under the voluntary jurisdiction on standard terms fixed by the scheme operator with the approval of the Authority.

(2)   Different standard terms may be fixed with respect to different matters or in relation to different cases.

(3)   The standard terms may, in particular—
   (a)   require the making of payments to the scheme operator by participants in the scheme of such amounts, and at such times, as may be determined by the scheme operator;
   (b)   make provision as to the award of costs on the determination of a complaint.

(4)   The scheme operator may not vary any of the standard terms or add or remove terms without the approval of the Authority.

(5)   The standard terms may include provision to the effect that (unless acting in bad faith) none of the following is to be liable in damages for anything done or omitted in the discharge or purported discharge of functions in connection with the voluntary jurisdiction—
   (a)   the scheme operator;
   (b)   any member of its governing body;
   (c)   any member of its staff;
   (d)   any person acting as an ombudsman for the purposes of the scheme.

Delegation by and to other schemes

19.—(1)   The scheme operator may make arrangements with a relevant body—
   (a)   for the exercise by that body of any part of the voluntary jurisdiction of the ombudsman scheme on behalf of the scheme; or
   (b)   for the exercise by the scheme of any function of that body as if it were part of the voluntary jurisdiction of the scheme.

(2)   A "relevant body" is one which the scheme operator is satisfied—
   (a)   is responsible for the operation of a broadly comparable scheme (whether or not established by statute) for the resolution of disputes; and
   (b)   in the case of arrangements under sub-paragraph (1)(a), will exercise the jurisdiction in question in a way compatible with the requirements imposed by or under this Act in relation to complaints of the kind concerned.

(3)   Such arrangements require the approval of the Authority.

Voluntary jurisdiction rules: procedure

20.—(1)   If the scheme operator makes voluntary jurisdiction rules, it must give a copy to the Authority without delay.

(2)   If the scheme operator revokes any such rules, it must give written notice to the Authority without delay.

(3)   The power to make voluntary jurisdiction rules is exercisable in writing.

(4)   Immediately after making voluntary jurisdiction rules, the scheme operator must arrange for them to be printed and made available to the public.

(5)   The scheme operator may charge a reasonable fee for providing a person with a copy of any voluntary jurisdiction rules.

Verification of the rules

21.—(1)   The production of a printed copy of voluntary jurisdiction rules purporting to be made by the scheme operator—
  (a)   on which is endorsed a certificate signed by a member of the scheme operator's staff authorised by the scheme operator for that purpose, and
  (b)   which contains the required statements,
is evidence (or in Scotland sufficient evidence) of the facts stated in the certificate.

(2)   The required statements are—
  (a)   that the rules were made by the scheme operator;
  (b)   that the copy is a true copy of the rules; and
  (c)   that on a specified date the rules were made available to the public in accordance with paragraph 20(4).

(3)   A certificate purporting to be signed as mentioned in sub-paragraph (1) is to be taken to have been duly signed unless the contrary is shown.

Consultation

22.—(1)   If the scheme operator proposes to make voluntary jurisdiction rules, it must publish a draft of the proposed rules in the way appearing to it to be best calculated to bring them to the attention of the public.

(2)   The draft must be accompanied by—
  (a)   an explanation of the proposed rules; and
  (b)   a statement that representations about the proposals may be made to the scheme operator within a specified time.

(3)   Before making any voluntary jurisdiction rules, the scheme operator must have regard to any representations made to it in accordance with sub-paragraph (2)(b).

(4)   If voluntary jurisdiction rules made by the scheme operator differ from the draft published under sub-paragraph (1) in a way which the scheme operator considers significant, the scheme operator must publish a statement of the difference.

[494]

SCHEDULE 18
MUTUALS

Sections 334, 336 and 338

(Sch 18, Pt I repeals the Friendly Societies Act 1974, ss 4, 10, 31–36A, 37(1), (1A), (7A)–(9), 38–50, and amends the Friendly Societies Act 1974, ss 7, 11, 99(4).)

PART II
FRIENDLY SOCIETIES: SUBSIDIARIES AND CONTROLLED BODIES

Interpretation

9.   In this Part of this Schedule—
  "the 1992 Act" means the Friendly Societies Act 1992; and
  "section 13" means section 13 of that Act.

10–15.   ...

References in other enactments

16.   References in any provision of, or made under, any enactment to subsidiaries of, or bodies jointly controlled by, an incorporated friendly society are to be read as including references to bodies which are such subsidiaries or bodies as a result of any provision of this Part of this Schedule.

[495]

NOTES

Paras 10–15: amend the Friendly Societies Act 1992; ss 13, 52, Sch 8, and repeal Sch 7 to that Act.

PART I
FSMA 2000

(Sch 18, Pt III repeals the Building Societies Act 1986, s 9, Sch 3; Sch 18, Pt IV repeals the Industrial and Provident Societies Act 1965, ss 8, 70; Sch 18, Pt IV repeals the Credit Unions Act 1979, ss 6(2)–(6), 11(2)–(6), 11B–11D, 12(4), (5), 14(2), (3), (5), (6), 28(2); Sch 19 repealed by the Enterprise Act 2002, ss 247(k), 278(2), Sch 26, as from 20 June 2003; Sch 20 contains minor and consequential amendments to legislation not reproduced in this Handbook.)

SCHEDULE 21
TRANSITIONAL PROVISIONS AND SAVINGS

Section 432(2)

Self-regulating organisations

1.—(1) No new application under section 9 of the 1986 Act (application for recognition) may be entertained.

(2) No outstanding application made under that section before the passing of this Act may continue to be entertained.

(3) After the date which is the designated date for a recognised self-regulating organisation—
  (a) the recognition order for that organisation may not be revoked under section 11 of the 1986 Act (revocation of recognition);
  (b) no application may be made to the court under section 12 of the 1986 Act (compliance orders) with respect to that organisation.

(4) The powers conferred by section 13 of the 1986 Act (alteration of rules for protection of investors) may not be exercised.

(5) "Designated date" means such date as the Treasury may by order designate.

(6) Sub-paragraph (3) does not apply to a recognised self-regulating organisation in respect of which a notice of intention to revoke its recognition order was given under section 11(3) of the 1986 Act before the passing of this Act if that notice has not been withdrawn.

(7) Expenditure incurred by the Authority in connection with the winding up of any body which was, immediately before the passing of this Act, a recognised self-regulating organisation is to be treated as having been incurred in connection with the discharge by the Authority of functions under this Act.

(8) "Recognised self-regulating organisation" means an organisation which, immediately before the passing of this Act, was such an organisation for the purposes of the 1986 Act.

(9) "The 1986 Act" means the Financial Services Act 1986.

Self-regulating organisations for friendly societies

2.—(1) No new application under paragraph 2 of Schedule 11 to the 1986 Act (application for recognition) may be entertained.

(2) No outstanding application made under that paragraph before the passing of this Act may continue to be entertained.

(3) After the date which is the designated date for a recognised self-regulating organisation for friendly societies—
  (a) the recognition order for that organisation may not be revoked under paragraph 5 of Schedule 11 to the 1986 Act (revocation of recognition);
  (b) no application may be made to the court under paragraph 6 of that Schedule (compliance orders) with respect to that organisation.

(4) "Designated date" means such date as the Treasury may by order designate.

(5) Sub-paragraph (3) does not apply to a recognised self-regulating organisation for friendly societies in respect of which a notice of intention to revoke its recognition order was given under section 11(3) of the 1986 Act (as applied by paragraph 5(2) of that Schedule) before the passing of this Act if that notice has not been withdrawn.

(6) Expenditure incurred by the Authority in connection with the winding up of any body which was, immediately before the passing of this Act, a recognised self-regulating organisation for friendly societies is to be treated as having been incurred in connection with the discharge by the Authority of functions under this Act.

(7) "Recognised self-regulating organisation for friendly societies" means an organisation which, immediately before the passing of this Act, was such an organisation for the purposes of the 1986 Act.

(8) "The 1986 Act" means the Financial Services Act 1986.

NOTES

Financial Services Act 1986: repealed by the Financial Services and Markets Act 2000 (Consequential Amendments and Repeals) Order 2001, SI 2001/3649, art 3(1)(c).

Orders: the Financial Services and Markets (Transitional Provisions) (Designated Date for Certain Self-Regulating Organisations) Order 2000, SI 2000/1734, art 2, provides that for the purposes of paras 1, 2 of this Schedule, 25 July 2000 shall be the designated date for the Personal Investment Authority Limited and the Investment Management Regulatory Organisation Limited; the Financial Services and Markets (Transitional Provisions) (Designated Date for The Securities and Futures Authority) Order 2001, SI 2001/2255, art 2, provides that for the purposes of para 1(5) of this Schedule, 13 July 2001 shall be the designated date for the Securities and Futures Authority Limited.

SCHEDULE 22
REPEALS

Section 432(3)

Chapter	Short title	Extent of repeal
1923 c 8	The Industrial Assurance Act 1923.	The whole Act.
1948 c 39	The Industrial Assurance and Friendly Societies Act 1948.	The whole Act.
1965 c 12	The Industrial and Provident Societies Act 1965.	Section 8.
		Section 70.
1974 c 46	The Friendly Societies Act 1974.	Section 4.
		Section 10.
		In section 11, from "and where" to "that society".
		In section 99(4), "in the central registration area".
1975 c 24	The House of Commons Disqualification Act 1975.	In Schedule 1, in Part III, "Any member of the Financial Services Tribunal in receipt of remuneration".
1975 c 25	The Northern Ireland Assembly Disqualification Act 1975.	In Schedule 1, in Part III, "Any member of the Financial Services Tribunal in receipt of remuneration".
1977 c 46	The Insurance Brokers (Registration) Act 1977.	The whole Act.
1979 c 34	The Credit Unions Act 1979.	Section 6(2) to (6).
		Section 11(2) and (6).
		Sections 11B, 11C and 11D.
		Section 12(4) and (5).
		In section 14, subsections (2), (3), (5) and (6).
		Section 28(2).
1986 c 53	The Building Societies Act 1986.	Section 9.
		Schedule 3.
1988 c 1	The Income and Corporation Taxes Act 1988.	In section 76, in subsection (8), the definitions of "the 1986 Act", "authorised person", "investment business", "investor", "investor protection scheme", "prescribed" and "recognised self-regulating organisation".
1991 c 31	The Finance Act 1991.	In section 47, subsections (1), (2) and (4).

Chapter	Short title	Extent of repeal
1992 c 40	The Friendly Societies Act 1992.	In section 13, subsections (2) to (5), (8) and (11).
		Sections 31 to 36.
		In section 37, subsections (1), (1A) and (7A) to (9).
		Sections 38 to 50.
		In section 52, subsection (2)(d) and, in subsection (5), the words from "or where" to the end.
		Schedule 7.
		In Schedule 8, paragraph 3(2).
1993 c 8	The Judicial Pensions and Retirement Act 1993.	In Schedule 5, "Member of the Financial Services Tribunal appointed by the Lord Chancellor".

Appendix 1

COMMENCEMENT DATES OF THE FINANCIAL SERVICES AND MARKETS ACT 2000

Abbreviations: the following abbreviations are used in this table:
— RA: Royal assent (ie, 14 June 2000)
— CO No 1: the Financial Services and Markets Act 2000 (Commencement No 1) Order 2001, SI 2001/516
— CO No 2: the Financial Services and Markets Act 2000 (Commencement No 2) Order 2001, SI 2001/1282
— CO No 3: the Financial Services and Markets Act 2000 (Commencement No 3) Order 2001, SI 2001/1820
— CO No 4: the Financial Services and Markets Act 2000 (Commencement No 4 and Transitional Provisions) Order 2001, SI 2001/2364[1]
— CO No 5: the Financial Services and Markets Act 2000 (Commencement No 5) Order 2001, SI 2001/2632
— CO No 6: the Financial Services and Markets Act 2000 (Commencement No 6) Order 2001, SI 2001/3436
— CO No 7: the Financial Services and Markets Act 2000 (Commencement No 7) Order 2001, SI 2001/3538

All commencement orders were made under s 431 of this Act at [**457**].

Subsequent amendment of this Act: the insertion, substitution or repeal of a *whole* section or Schedule is noted in the table below. Other amendments (ie, where the amendments are at less than provision level) are not noted.

Transitional provisions etc: only CO No 4 contained transitional provisions (as to which see footnote 1 below). Transitional provisions and savings in connection with the insertion, substitution and repeal of provisions in this Act are not noted in the table below. For details, see the provision concerned in Part I of this Handbook.

Part I: The Regulator	
1–11	18 Jun 2001 (CO No 3)
12–18	1 Dec 2001 (CO No 7)
Part II: Regulated and Prohibited Activities	
19	1 Dec 2001 (CO No 7)
20	25 Feb 2001 (sub-s (3) for the purpose of making orders or regulations) (CO No 1); 1 Dec 2001 (otherwise) (CO No 7)
21	25 Feb 2001 (for the purpose of making orders or regulations) (CO No 1); 1 Dec 2001 (otherwise) (CO No 7)
22	25 Feb 2001 (CO No 1)
23–30	1 Dec 2001 (CO No 7)
Part III: Authorisation and Exemption	
31	1 Dec 2001 (sub-ss (1)(a), (d), (2)) (CO No 7); see Schs 3, 4 below (sub-s (1)(b), (c))
32–36	1 Dec 2001 (CO No 7)
37	See Sch 3 below
38	25 Feb 2001 (CO No 1)
39	25 Feb 2001 (sub-s (1) for the purpose of making orders or regulations) (CO No 1); 1 Dec 2001 (otherwise) (CO No 7)
39A	1 Apr 2007 (certain purposes); 1 Nov 2007 (otherwise)[3]
Part IV: Permission to Carry on Regulated Activities	
40	3 Sep 2001 (CO No 5)
41	25 Feb 2001 (sub-s (1)) (CO No 1); 3 Sep 2001 (sub-ss (2), (3)) (CO No 5)

Part IV: Permission to Carry on Regulated Activities

42, 43	3 Sep 2001 (for the purposes of permissions coming into force not sooner than the day on which s 19 of this Act comes into force, and applications for such permissions); 1 Dec 2001 (otherwise) (CO No 7)
44–46	3 Sep 2001 (for the purposes of variations or cancellations taking effect not sooner than the day on which s 19 of this Act comes into force, and applications for such variations or cancellations) (CO No 5); 1 Dec 2001 (otherwise) (CO No 7)
47	25 Feb 2001 (sub-ss (1), (3) for the purpose of making orders or regulations) (CO No 1); 3 Sep 2001 (for the purposes of variations or cancellations taking effect not sooner than the day on which s 19 of this Act comes into force, and applications for such variations or cancellations) (CO No 5); 1 Dec 2001 (otherwise) (CO No 7)
48–50	3 Sep 2001 (CO No 5)
51	18 Jun 2001 (for the purpose of giving directions or imposing requirements as mentioned in sub-s (3)) (CO No 3); 3 Sep 2001 (otherwise) (CO No 5)
52	3 Sep 2001 (CO No 5)
53, 54	3 Sep 2001 (for the purposes of variations and cancellations taking effect not sooner than the day on which s 19 of this Act comes into force) (CO No 5); 1 Dec 2001 (otherwise) (CO No 7)
55	3 Sep 2001 (CO No 5)

Part V: Performance of Regulated Activities

56–58	3 Sep 2001 (for the purposes of prohibition orders coming into force not sooner than the day on which s 19 of this Act comes into force) (CO No 5); 1 Dec 2001 (otherwise) (CO No 7)
59	18 Jun 2001 (for the purpose of making rules) (CO No 3); 3 Sep 2001 (for the purposes of approvals coming into force not sooner than the day on which s 19 of this Act comes into force, and applications for such approvals) (CO No 5); 1 Dec 2001 (otherwise) (CO No 7)
60	18 Jun 2001 (for the purpose of giving directions or imposing requirements as mentioned in sub-s (2) or (4)) (CO No 3); 3 Sep 2001 (for the purposes of approvals coming into force not sooner than the day on which s 19 of this Act comes into force, and applications for such approvals) (CO No 5); 1 Dec 2001 (otherwise) (CO No 7)
61–63	3 Sep 2001 (for the purposes of approvals coming into force not sooner than the day on which s 19 of this Act comes into force, and applications for such approvals) (CO No 5); 1 Dec 2001 (otherwise) (CO No 7)
64, 65	18 Jun 2001 (CO No 3)
66–68	1 Dec 2001 (CO No 7)
69, 70	18 Jun 2001 (CO No 3)
71	25 Feb 2001 (sub-ss (2), (3) for the purpose of making orders or regulations) (CO No 1); 1 Dec 2001 (otherwise) (CO No 7)

Part VI: Official Listing

72, 73	18 Jun 2001 (CO No 3)
73A	17 Mar 2005[4]
74	18 Jun 2001 (sub-ss (4), (5)) (CO No 3); 1 Dec 2001 (otherwise) (CO No 7)
75	25 Feb 2001 (sub-s (3) for the purpose of making orders or regulations) (CO No 1); 18 Jun 2001 (sub-s (1) for the purpose of making listing rules) (CO No 3); 1 Dec 2001 (otherwise) (CO No 7)
76	1 Dec 2001 (CO No 7)
77	18 Jun 2001 (sub-ss (1), (2), (4) for the purpose of making listing rules) (CO No 3); 1 Dec 2001 (otherwise) (CO No 7)
78	1 Dec 2001 (CO No 7)
78A	12 Jul 2007[5]

Part VI: Official Listing

79	25 Feb 2001 (sub-s (3)) (CO No 1); 18 Jun 2001 (otherwise) (CO No 3)
80	1 Dec 2001 (CO No 7)
81	18 Jun 2001 (sub-ss (1), (5) for the purpose of making listing rules) (CO No 3); 1 Dec 2001 otherwise) (CO No 7)
82	18 Jun 2001 (sub-ss (1), (5), (7) for the purpose of making listing rules) (CO No 3); 1 Dec 2001 (otherwise) (CO No 7)
83	*Repealed by SI 2005/1433 (as from 1 Jul 2005)*
84–87R	1 Jul 2005[6]
88	18 Jun 2001 (sub-ss (1)–(3)) (CO No 3); 1 Dec 2001 (otherwise) (CO No 7)
89	18 Jun 2001 (sub-s (1)) (CO No 3); 1 Dec 2001 (otherwise) (CO No 7)
89A–89O	8 Nov 2006[7]
90	1 Dec 2001 (CO No 7)
90A, 90B	8 Nov 2006[7]
91, 92	1 Dec 2001 (CO No 7)
93, 94	18 Jun 2001 (CO No 3)
95	1 Dec 2001 (CO No 7)
96	18 Jun 2001 (CO No 3)
96A–96C	17 Mar 2005[4]
97	1 Dec 2001 (CO No 7)
98	*Repealed by SI 2005/1433 (as from 1 Jul 2005)*
99, 100	18 Jun 2001 (CO No 3)
100A	8 Nov 2006[7]
101, 102	18 Jun 2001 (CO No 3)
102A–102C, 103	1 Jul 2005[8]

Part VII: Control of Business Transfers

104	1 Dec 2001 (for the purpose of insurance business transfer schemes only) (CO No 7); not in force (otherwise)
105, 106	1 Dec 2001 (CO No 7)
106A	Not in force[9]
107	1 Dec 2001 (CO No 7)
108	25 Feb 2001 (for the purpose of making orders or regulations) (CO No 1); 1 Dec 2001 (otherwise) (CO No 7)
109, 110	1 Dec 2001 (CO No 7)
111	25 Feb 2001 (sub-s (2) for the purpose of introducing Sch 12, Pt I to the extent brought into force by CO No 1) (CO No 1); 1 Dec 2001 (otherwise) (CO No 7)
112	1 Dec 2001 (CO No 7)
112A	30 Jun 2008[10]
113, 114	1 Dec 2001 (CO No 7)
114A	10 Dec 2007[11]
115–117	1 Dec 2001 (CO No 7)

Part VIII: Penalties for Market Abuse

118–118C	1 Jul 2005[12]
119–121	18 Jun 2001 (CO No 3)
122, 123	1 Dec 2001 (CO No 7)
124, 125	18 Jun 2001 (CO No 3)
126–130	1 Dec 2001 (CO No 7)

Part VIII: Penalties for Market Abuse

130A	1 Jul 2005[4]
131	1 Dec 2001 (CO No 7)
131A	1 Jul 2005[4]

Part IX: Hearings and Appeals

132	25 Feb 2001 (sub-s (1) for the purpose of the definition "the Tribunal" and sub-s (3)) (CO No 1); 3 Sep 2001 (sub-s (1) otherwise and sub-s (2)) (CO No 5); see Sch 13 below (sub-s (4))
133	3 Sep 2001 (CO No 5)
134, 135	25 Feb 2001 (CO No 1)
136	18 Jun 2001 (for the purpose of making rules) (CO No 3); 3 Sep 2001 (otherwise) (CO No 5)
137	25 Feb 2001 (sub-s (6)) (CO No 1); 3 Sep 2001 (otherwise) (CO No 5)

Part X: Rules and Guidance

138–141	18 Jun 2001 (CO No 3)
142	25 Feb 2001 (sub-ss (1)–(4), (6)) (CO No 1); 1 Dec 2001 (otherwise) (CO No 7)
143	*Repealed by the Companies Act 2006 (as from 6 Apr 2007)*
144	25 Feb 2001 (sub-ss (4), (5)) (CO No 1); 18 Jun 2001 (otherwise) (CO No 3)
145	25 Feb 2001 (sub-s (5)) (CO No 1); 18 Jun 2001 (otherwise) (CO No 3)
146, 147	18 Jun 2001 (CO No 3)
148	18 Jun 2001 (for the purpose of giving directions as mentioned in sub-s (3)) (CO No 3); 3 Sep 2001 (otherwise) (CO No 5)
149	18 Jun 2001 (CO No 3)
150	25 Feb 2001 (sub-ss (3)–(5) for the purpose of making orders or regulations) (CO No 1); 18 Jun 2001 (for the purpose of making rules) (CO No 3); 1 Dec 2001 (otherwise) (CO No 7)
151	1 Dec 2001 (CO No 7)
152–158	18 Jun 2001 (CO No 3)
158A	6 Dec 2006[13]
159–164	18 Jun 2001 (CO No 3)

Part XI: Information Gathering and Investigations

165–167	3 Sep 2001 (CO No 5)
168	25 Feb 2001 (sub-s (4)(b) for the purpose of making orders or regulations) (CO No 1); 3 Sep 2001 (otherwise) (CO No 5)
169	18 Jun 2001 (for the purpose of preparing a statement of policy as mentioned in sub-s (9)) (CO No 3); 3 Sep 2001 (otherwise) (CO No 5)
170–177	3 Sep 2001 (CO No 5)

Part XII: Control Over Authorised Persons

178–181	1 Dec 2001 (CO No 7)
182	18 Jun 2001 (for the purpose of imposing requirements as mentioned in sub-s (1)(b)) (CO No 3); 1 Dec 2001 (otherwise) (CO No 7)
183	25 Feb 2001 (sub-s (2) for the purpose of making orders or regulations) (CO No 1); 1 Dec 2001 (otherwise) (CO No 7)
184–187	1 Dec 2001 (CO No 7)
188	25 Feb 2001 (sub-s (2) for the purpose of making orders or regulations) (CO No 1); 1 Dec 2001 (otherwise) (CO No 7)
189–191	1 Dec 2001 (CO No 7)
192	25 Feb 2001 (para (a)) (CO No 1); 1 Dec 2001 (otherwise) (CO No 7)

Part XIII: Incoming Firms: Intervention by Authority

193	3 Sep 2001 (CO No 5)
194	3 Sep 2001 (for the purposes of requirements (as mentioned in s 196) taking effect not sooner than the day on which s 19 of this Act comes into force) (CO No 5); 1 Dec 2001 (otherwise) (CO No 7)
194A	1 Apr 2007 (certain purposes); 1 Nov 2007 (otherwise)[3]
195	3 Sep 2001 (for the purposes of requirements (as mentioned in s 196) taking effect not sooner than the day on which s 19 of this Act comes into force) (CO No 5); 1 Dec 2001 (otherwise) (CO No 7)
195A	1 Apr 2007 (certain purposes); 1 Nov 2007 (otherwise)[3]
196, 197	3 Sep 2001 (for the purposes of requirements (as mentioned in s 196) taking effect not sooner than the day on which s 19 of this Act comes into force) (CO No 5); 1 Dec 2001 (otherwise) (CO No 7)
198	1 Dec 2001 (CO No 7)
199	3 Sep 2001 (for the purposes of requirements (as mentioned in s 196) taking effect not sooner than the day on which s 19 of this Act comes into force) (CO No 5); 1 Dec 2001 (otherwise) (CO No 7)
200, 201	3 Sep 2001 (CO No 5)
202	25 Feb 2001 (sub-s (2) for the purpose of making orders or regulations) (CO No 1); 3 Sep 2001 (otherwise) (CO No 5)
203, 204	1 Dec 2001 (CO No 7)

Part XIV: Disciplinary Measures

205–209	1 Dec 2001 (CO No 7)
210, 211	18 Jun 2001 (CO No 3)

Part XV: The Financial Services Compensation Scheme

212	18 Jun 2001 (CO No 3)
213	25 Feb 2001 (sub-s (10) for the purpose of making orders or regulations) (CO No 1); 18 Jun 2001 (otherwise) (CO No 3)
214	25 Feb 2001 (sub-s (5) for the purpose of making orders or regulations) (CO No 1); 18 Jun 2001 (otherwise) (CO No 3)
214A, 214B	Not in force[21]
215	25 Feb 2001 (sub-ss (6), (8), (9)) (CO No 1); 18 Jun 2001 (otherwise) (CO No 3)
216–218	18 Jun 2001 (CO No 3)
218A	Not in force[21]
219–221	1 Dec 2001 (CO No 7)
221A	Not in force[21]
222	18 Jun 2001 (CO No 3)
223	18 Jun 2001 (for the purpose of fixing an amount by the scheme as mentioned in sub-s (1)) (CO No 3); 1 Dec 2001 (otherwise) (CO No 7)
223A–223C	Not in force[21]
224	25 Feb 2001 (sub-s (4) for the purpose of making orders or regulations) (CO No 1); 1 Dec 2001 (otherwise) (CO No 7)
224A	Not in force[21]

Part XVI: The Ombudsman Scheme

225	18 Jun 2001 (CO No 3)
226	18 Jun 2001 (for the purpose of the making of rules by the Authority and the scheme operator) (CO No 3); 1 Dec 2001 (otherwise) (CO No 7)
226A	16 Jun 2006[14]
227	18 Jun 2001 (for the purpose of the making of rules by the Authority and the scheme operator) (CO No 3); 1 Dec 2001 (otherwise) (CO No 7)

Part XVI: The Ombudsman Scheme

228	1 Dec 2001 (CO No 7)
229	18 Jun 2001 (for the purpose of the making of rules by the Authority and the scheme operator) (CO No 3); 1 Dec 2001 (otherwise) (CO No 7)
230	18 Jun 2001 (CO No 3)
231–233	1 Dec 2001 (CO No 7)
234	18 Jun 2001 (CO No 3)
234A	16 Jun 2006[14]

Part XVII: Collective Investment Schemes

235–237	25 Feb 2001 (CO No 1)
238	25 Feb 2001 (for the purpose of making orders or regulations) (CO No 1); 18 Jun 2001 (for the purpose of making rules) (CO No 3); 1 Dec 2001 (otherwise) (CO No 7)
239	25 Feb 2001 (sub-ss (1)–(3)) (CO No 1); 18 Jun 2001 (otherwise) (CO No 3)
240, 241	1 Dec 2001 (CO No 7)
242	18 Jun 2001 (for the purpose of giving directions or imposing requirements as mentioned in sub-s (3)) (CO No 3); 3 Sep 2001 (for the purposes of authorisation orders coming into force not sooner than the day on which s 19 of this Act comes into force) (CO No 5); 1 Dec 2001 (otherwise) (CO No 7)
243–245	3 Sep 2001 (for the purposes of authorisation orders coming into force not sooner than the day on which s 19 of this Act comes into force) (CO No 5); 1 Dec 2001 (otherwise) (CO No 7)
246	3 Sep 2001 (for the purposes of certificates coming into force not sooner than the day on which s 19 of this Act comes into force) (CO No 5); 1 Dec 2001 (otherwise) (CO No 7)
247, 248	18 Jun 2001 (CO No 3)
249	1 Dec 2001 (CO No 7)
250	3 Sep 2001 (CO No 5)
251	3 Sep 2001 (sub-ss (1)–(3), (4)(a), (5) for the purposes of the giving of notice of any proposal to alter a scheme, or to replace its trustee or manager, not sooner than the day on which s 19 of this Act comes into force, and the giving of approval to any such proposal) (CO No 5); 1 Dec 2001 (otherwise) (CO No 7)
252	3 Sep 2001 (for the purposes of the giving of notice of any proposal to alter a scheme, or to replace its trustee or manager, not sooner than the day on which s 19 of this Act comes into force, and the giving of approval to any such proposal) (CO No 5); 1 Dec 2001 (otherwise) (CO No 7)
253	1 Dec 2001 (CO No 7)
254–256	3 Sep 2001 (CO No 5)
257	3 Sep 2001 (for the purposes of directions coming into force not sooner than the day on which s 19 of this Act comes into force) (CO No 5); 1 Dec 2001 (otherwise) (CO No 7)
258	1 Dec 2001 (CO No 7)
259–261	3 Sep 2001 (for the purposes of directions coming into force not sooner than the day on which s 19 of this Act comes into force) (CO No 5); 1 Dec 2001 (otherwise) (CO No 7)
262	25 Feb 2001 (CO No 1)
263	*Spent*[15]
264	25 Feb 2001 (sub-ss (1), (3)(c) for the purpose of making orders or regulations) (CO No 1); 3 Sep 2001 (for the purposes of (a) the giving of notice under sub-s (1) of intention to make invitations not sooner than the day on which s 19 of this Act comes into force; and (b) the giving of notice under sub-ss (2) or (6)) (CO No 5); 1 Dec 2001 (otherwise) (CO No 7)
265	3 Sep 2001 (sub-ss (1), (2), (4), (5)) (CO No 5); 1 Dec 2001 (otherwise) (CO No 7)

Part XVII: Collective Investment Schemes

266	18 Jun 2001 (CO No 3)
267–269	1 Dec 2001 (CO No 7)
270	25 Feb 2001 (for the purpose of making orders or regulations) (CO No 1); 3 Sep 2001 (for the purposes of (a) the giving of notices under sub-s (1)(c); and (b) the giving of notice of approval under sub-s (1)(d)(i) coming into force not sooner than the day on which s 19 of this Act comes into force) (CO No 5); 1 Dec 2001 (otherwise) (CO No 7)
271	3 Sep 2001 (sub-ss (1), (3)) (CO No 5); 1 Dec 2001 (otherwise) (CO No 7)
272, 273	3 Sep 2001 (for the purposes of orders (and applications for orders) coming into force not sooner than the day on which s 19 of this Act comes into force) (CO No 5); 1 Dec 2001 (otherwise) (CO No 7)
274	18 Jun 2001 (for the purpose of giving directions or imposing requirements as mentioned in sub-s (2)) (CO No 3); 3 Sep 2001 (for the purposes of orders (and applications for orders) coming into force not sooner than the day on which s 19 of this Act comes into force) (CO No 5); 1 Dec 2001 (otherwise) (CO No 7)
275, 276	3 Sep 2001 (for the purposes of orders (and applications for orders) coming into force not sooner than the day on which s 19 of this Act comes into force) (CO No 5); 1 Dec 2001 (otherwise) (CO No 7)
277	3 Sep 2001 (sub-ss (1), (2)(a), (3)) (for the purposes of (a) the giving of notice under sub-s (1) of any proposal to alter a scheme not sooner than the day on which s 19 of this Act comes into force, and the giving of approval to any such proposal; and (b) the giving of notice under sub-s (3) of any proposal to replace an operator, trustee or depositary not sooner than the day on which s 19 of this Act comes into force) (CO No 5); 1 Dec 2001 (otherwise) (CO No 7)
278	18 Jun 2001 (CO No 3)
279–282	3 Sep 2001 (CO No 5)
283	18 Jun 2001 (sub-s (1)) (CO No 3); 1 Dec 2001 (otherwise) (CO No 7)
284	25 Feb 2001 (sub-s (2) for the purpose of making orders or regulations) (CO No 1); 1 Dec 2001 (otherwise) (CO No 7)

Part XVIII: Recognised Investment Exchanges and Clearing Houses

285	1 Dec 2001 (CO No 7)
286	25 Feb 2001 (CO No 1)
287, 288	18 Jun 2001 (for the purpose of giving directions or imposing requirements as mentioned in sub-s (2)) (CO No 3); 3 Sep 2001 (otherwise) (CO No 5)
289	3 Sep 2001 (CO No 5)
290	3 Sep 2001 (for the purposes of recognition orders coming into force not sooner than the day on which s 19 of this Act comes into force) (CO No 5); 1 Dec 2001 (otherwise) (CO No 7)
290A	20 Dec 2006[16]
291	1 Dec 2001 (CO No 7)
292	3 Sep 2001 (sub-s (1) and sub-ss (2)–(5) for the purposes of recognition orders coming into force not sooner than the day on which s 19 of this Act comes into force) (CO No 5); 1 Dec 2001 (otherwise) (CO No 7)
292A	1 Apr 2007 (certain purposes); 1 Nov 2007 (otherwise)[3]
293	18 Jun 2001 (for the purpose of making rules) (CO No 3); 1 Dec 2001 (otherwise) (CO No 7)
293A	1 Apr 2007 (certain purposes); 1 Nov 2007 (otherwise)[3]
294	18 Jun 2001 (for the purpose of giving directions as mentioned in sub-s (2)) (CO No 3); 3 Sep 2001 (otherwise) (CO No 5)
295	18 Jun 2001 (for the purpose of making rules) (CO No 3); 1 Dec 2001 (otherwise) (CO No 7)
296	1 Dec 2001 (CO No 7)
297	3 Sep 2001 (CO No 5)

Part XVIII: Recognised Investment Exchanges and Clearing Houses

298	3 Sep 2001 (for the purposes of revocation orders under s 297) (CO No 5); 1 Dec 2001 (otherwise) (CO No 7)
299	18 Jun 2001 (CO No 3)
300	1 Dec 2001 (CO No 7)
300A–300E	20 Dec 2006[16]
301	1 Dec 2001 (CO No 7)
301A–301G	1 Apr 2007 (certain purposes); 1 Nov 2007 (otherwise)[3]
302, 303	3 Sep 2001 (CO No 5)
304	1 Dec 2001 (CO No 7)
305	3 Sep 2001 (for the purposes of s 303) (CO No 5); 1 Dec 2001 (otherwise) (CO No 7)
306	3 Sep 2001 (for the purposes of reports issued by the Director under s 303) (CO No 5); 1 Dec 2001 (otherwise) (CO No 7)
307	3 Sep 2001 (CO No 5)
308, 309	1 Dec 2001 (CO No 7)
310	3 Sep 2001 (for the purposes of s 307) (CO No 5); 1 Dec 2001 (otherwise) (CO No 7)
311, 312	3 Sep 2001 (CO No 5)
312A–312D	1 Apr 2007 (certain purposes); 1 Nov 2007 (otherwise)[3]
313	25 Feb 2001 (CO No 1)

Part 18A: Suspension and Removal of Financial Instruments from Trading

313A–313D	1 Apr 2007 (certain purposes); 1 Nov 2007 (otherwise)[3]

Part XIX: Lloyd's

314	3 Sep 2001 (CO No 5)
315	3 Sep 2001 (sub-ss (3)–(5)) (CO No 5); 1 Dec 2001 (otherwise) (CO No 7)
316	18 Jun 2001 (for the purpose of giving directions as mentioned in sub-s (1) coming into force not sooner than the day on which s 19 of the Act comes into force) (CO No 3); 1 Dec 2001 (otherwise) (CO No 7)
317	18 Jun 2001 (CO No 3)
318	18 Jun 2001 (for the purpose of giving directions as mentioned in sub-s (1) coming into force not sooner than the day on which s 19 of the Act comes into force) (CO No 3); 1 Dec 2001 (otherwise) (CO No 7)
319	18 Jun 2001 (CO No 3)
320	3 Sep 2001 (sub-ss (3), (4) for the purposes of requirements taking effect not sooner than the day on which s 19 of this Act comes into force) (CO No 5); 1 Dec 2001 (otherwise) (CO No 7)
321	3 Sep 2001 (for the purposes of requirements taking effect not sooner than the day on which s 19 of this Act comes into force) (CO No 5); 1 Dec 2001 (otherwise) (CO No 7)
322	18 Jun 2001 (for the purpose of making rules coming into force not sooner than the day on which s 19 of the Act comes into force) (CO No 3); 1 Dec 2001 (otherwise) (CO No 7)
323, 324	18 Jun 2001 (CO No 3)

Part XX: Provision of Financial Services by Members of the Professions

325	3 Sep 2001 (sub-s (4)) (CO No 5); 1 Dec 2001 (otherwise) (CO No 7)
326	25 Feb 2001 (CO No 1)
327	25 Feb 2001 (sub-s (6) for the purpose of making orders or regulations) (CO No 1); 1 Dec 2001 (otherwise) (CO No 7)
328–331	3 Sep 2001 (CO No 5)
332	18 Jun 2001 (CO No 3)

Part XX: Provision of Financial Services by Members of the Professions

333	1 Dec 2001 (CO No 7)

Part XXI: Mutual Societies

334	25 Feb 2001 (sub-ss (1), (2)) (CO No 1); 1 Dec 2001 (otherwise) (CO No 7)
335	25 Feb 2001 (CO No 1)
336	25 Feb 2001 (sub-ss (1), (2)) (CO No 1); 1 Dec 2001 (otherwise) (CO No 7)
337	25 Feb 2001 (CO No 1)
338	25 Feb 2001 (sub-ss (1), (2)) (CO No 1); 1 Dec 2001 (otherwise) (CO No 7)
339	25 Feb 2001 (CO No 1)

Part XXII: Auditors and Actuaries

340	18 Jun 2001 (CO No 3)
341	1 Dec 2001 (CO No 7)
342	25 Feb 2001 (sub-s (5)) (CO No 1); 1 Dec 2001 (otherwise) (CO No 7)
343	25 Feb 2001 (sub-s (5)) (CO No 1); 1 Dec 2001 (otherwise) (CO No 7)
344–346	1 Dec 2001 (CO No 7)

Part XXIII: Public Record, Disclosure of Information and Co-operation

347	1 Dec 2001 except as follows: (i) 1 May 2002 (sub-ss (1), (2) for the purpose of requiring the Authority to maintain a record of persons who appear to the Authority to be authorised persons who are EEA firms or Treaty firms); (ii) 1 Aug 2002 (sub-ss (1), (2) for the purpose of requiring the Authority to maintain a record of persons who appear to it to be authorised persons who were, immediately before 1 Dec 2001, authorised under FSA 1986 by virtue of holding a certificate issued for the purposes of Pt I of that Act by a recognised professional body (within the meaning of that Act)); 1 Dec 2002 (sub-ss (1), (2) for the purpose of requiring the Authority to maintain a record of approved persons) (CO No 7)
348	18 Jun 2001 (CO No 3)
349	25 Feb 2001 (for the purpose of making orders or regulations) (CO No 1); 18 Jun 2001 (otherwise) (CO No 3)
350	18 Jun 2001 (sub-ss (3), (7)) (CO No 3); 3 Sep 2001 (otherwise) (CO No 5)
351	25 Feb 2001 (sub-s (7)) (CO No 1); 18 Jun 2001 (otherwise) (CO No 3)
352	18 Jun 2001 (for the purpose of any contravention of s 348) (CO No 3); 3 Sep 2001 (otherwise) (CO No 5)
353	25 Feb 2001 (CO No 1)
354	3 Sep 2001 (CO No 5)

Part XXIV: Insolvency

355	20 Jul 2001 (CO No 5)
356–358	1 Dec 2001 (CO No 7)
359	15 Sep 2003[17]
360	20 Jul 2001 (CO No 5)
361	15 Sep 2003[17]
362	1 Dec 2001 (CO No 7)
362A	15 Sep 2003[20]
363–369	1 Dec 2001 (CO No 7)
369A	Not in force[9]
370, 371	1 Dec 2001 (CO No 7)
372	20 Jul 2001 (for the purpose of making rules[2]) (CO No 5); 1 Dec 2001 (otherwise) (CO No 7)
373–377	1 Dec 2001 (CO No 7)
378, 379	20 Jul 2001 (CO No 5)

Part XXV: Injunctions and Restitution

380	18 Jun 2001 (CO No 3)
381	1 Dec 2001 (CO No 7)
382	18 Jun 2001 (CO No 3)
383–386	1 Dec 2001 (CO No 7)

Part XXVI: Notices

387–394	3 Sep 2001 (CO No 5)
395, 396	18 Jun 2001 (CO No 3)

Part XXVII: Offences

397	25 Feb 2001 (sub-ss (9)–14)) (CO No 1); 1 Dec 2001 (otherwise) (CO No 7)
398–401	18 Jun 2001 (CO No 3)
402	25 Feb 2001 (sub-s (1)(b) for the purpose of making orders or regulations) (CO No 1); 19 Oct 2001 (sub-s (1)(b), (2), (3) for the purposes of proceedings for offences under prescribed regulations relating to money laundering) (CO No 6); 1 Dec 2001 (otherwise) (CO No 7)
403	18 Jun 2001 (CO No 3)

Part XXVIII: Miscellaneous

404	1 Dec 2001 (CO No 7)
405	3 Sep 2001 (sub-ss (1)(a), (b), (2)–(5)) (CO No 5); 1 Dec 2001 (otherwise) (CO No 7)
406	1 Dec 2001 (CO No 7)
407	3 Sep 2001 (sub-ss (1), (2)) (CO No 5); 1 Dec 2001 (otherwise) (CO No 7)
408	3 Sep 2001 (for the purposes of determinations coming into force not sooner than the day on which s 19 of this Act comes into force) (CO No 5); 1 Dec 2001 (otherwise) (CO No 7)
409	25 Feb 2001 (CO No 1)
410	18 Jun 2001 (CO No 3)
411	1 Dec 2001 (CO No 7)
412	25 Feb 2001 (for the purpose of making orders or regulations) (CO No 1); 1 Dec 2001 (otherwise) (CO No 7)
412A, 412B	1 Apr 2007 (certain purposes); 1 Nov 2007 (otherwise)[3]
413	3 Sep 2001 (CO No 5)
414	25 Feb 2001 (sub-ss (1)–(3)) (CO No 1); 18 Jun 2001 (otherwise) (CO No 3)
415	18 Jun 2001 (CO No 3)
416	25 Feb 2001 (sub-ss (4), (5)) (CO No 1); 30 Apr 2001 (sub-ss (1)(c), (3)(a)) (CO No 2); 1 Dec 2001 (sub-ss (1)(a), (b), (2), (3)(d)) (CO No 7); 2 Mar 2002 (otherwise) (CO No 7)

Part XXIX: Interpretation

417	25 Feb 2001 (CO No 1)
418	3 Sep 2001 (CO No 5)
419–421	25 Feb 2001 (CO No 1)
421A	6 Apr 2008[18]
422, 423	25 Feb 2001 (CO No 1)
424	25 Feb 2001 (sub-ss (1), (2) and sub-s (3) for the purpose of making orders or regulations) (CO No 1); 1 Dec 2001 (otherwise) (CO No 7)
424A	6 Dec 2006[13]
425	25 Feb 2001 (CO No 1)

Part XXX: Supplemental

426, 427	25 Feb 2001 (CO No 1)
428	14 Jun 2000 (RA)
429	25 Feb 2001 (CO No 1)
430, 431	14 Jun 2000 (RA)
432	See Sch 20 below (sub-s (1)); see Sch 21 below (sub-s (2)); see Sch 22 below (sub-s (3))
433	14 Jun 2000 (RA)

Schedules

Sch 1	18 Jun 2001 (paras 1–6, 9–21) (CO No 3); 19 Jul 2001 (paras 7, 8 for the purpose of enabling the Authority to make the complaints scheme and appoint the investigator) (CO No 4); 3 Sep 2001 (otherwise) (CO No 5)
Sch 2	25 Feb 2001 (Parts I, II, III) (CO No 1); not in force (Pt 1A)[9]
Sch 3	25 Feb 2001 (for the purpose of making orders or regulations) (CO No 1); 18 Jun 2001 (for the purpose of making rules) (CO No 3); 3 Sep 2001 (para 19 for the purposes of the giving of notice under sub-para (2) of intention to establish a branch not sooner than the day on which s 19 of this Act comes into force; para 20 for the purposes of the giving of notice under sub-para (1) of intention to provide services not sooner than the day on which s 19 of this Act comes into force) (CO No 5); 1 Dec 2001 (otherwise) (CO No 7)
Sch 4	3 Sep 2001 (as follows: (i) para 1; (ii) para 3 for the purposes of issuing certificates under sub-para (4); (iii) para 5 for the purposes of giving notice under sub-para (2) of intention to carry on regulated activities not sooner than the day on which s 19 of this Act comes into force) (CO No 5); 1 Dec 2001 (otherwise) (CO No 7)
Sch 5	1 Dec 2001 (CO No 7)
Sch 6	25 Feb 2001 (paras 8, 9 for the purpose of making orders or regulations) (CO No 1); 3 Sep 2001 (otherwise) (CO No 5)
Schs 7, 8	18 Jun 2001 (CO No 3)
Sch 9	*Repealed by SI 2005/1433 (as from 1 Jul 2005)*
Sch 10	1 Dec 2001 (CO No 7)
Sch 11	*Repealed by SI 2005/1433 (as from 1 Jul 2005)*
Sch 11A	1 Jul 2005[19]
Sch 12	Original Pts I, III, III came into force on 1 Dec 2001 (with the exception of para 6(2) (in Pt II) which came into force on 25 Feb 2001) (see CO No 1 and CO No 7); not in force (Pt 2A)[9]
Sch 13	25 Feb 2001 (para 9) (CO No 1); 3 Sep 2001 (otherwise) (CO No 5)
Sch 14	18 Jun 2001 (CO No 3)
Sch 15	3 Sep 2001 (CO No 5)
Sch 16	1 Dec 2001 (CO No 7)
Sch 17	18 Jun 2001 (Pts I, II, III, IV) (CO No 3); 16 Jun 2006 (Pt 3A)[14]
Sch 18	1 Dec 2001 (Pt I–IV) (CO No 7); 2 Jul 2002 (Pt V) (CO No 7)
Sch 19	*Repealed by the Enterprise Act 2002 (as from 20 Jun 2003)*
Sch 20	3 Jul 2001 (para 6) (CO No 4)[1]; 3 Sep 2001 (paras 1(b), 2(b), 3, 7(1), (2), (3)(b)) (CO No 5); 1 Dec 2001 (otherwise) (CO No 7)
Sch 21	14 Jun 2000 (RA)
Sch 22	30 Apr 2001 (repeal of Insurance Brokers (Registration) Act 1977) (CO No 2); 1 Dec 2001 (otherwise, except repeals in Credit Unions Act 1979) (CO No 7); 2 Jul 2002 (repeals in Credit Unions Act 1979) (CO No 7)

NOTES

1   This Order contains transitional provisions in relation to the Financial Services Tribunal. Article 3 provides as follows: "Notwithstanding paragraph 6 of Schedule 20 to the Act, Schedule 1 to the Tribunals and Inquiries Act 1992 (tribunals under supervision of the Council on Tribunals) is to be treated as if it still contained the existing entry relating to financial services and paragraph 18 (which refers to the Financial Services Tribunal established under section 96 of the Financial Services Act 1986), for as long as that Tribunal retains functions conferred by or under any enactment". See the Tribunals and Inquiries Act 1992, Sch 1 at **[1214]**.

2   Note that SI 2001/2632, art 2(1) provides that "20th July 2001 is the day appointed for the coming into force of the provisions of the Act listed in Part 1 of the Schedule to this Order, for all purposes". However, Part 1 of the Schedule to that Order provides that s 372 comes into force on that date only "for the purpose of making rules". It is thought that the intention was to bring that section into force for the purpose of making rules only.

3   Inserted by SI 2007/126.

4   Inserted by SI 2005/381.

5   Inserted by SI 2007/1973.

6   Sections 84–87R substituted for original ss 84–87 by SI 2005/1433.

7   Inserted by the Companies Act 2006.

8   Sections 102A–102C, 103 substituted for original s 103 by SI 2005/1433.

9   Inserted by the Dormant Bank and Building Society Accounts Act 2008.

10   Inserted by SI 2008/1468.

11   Inserted by SI 2007/3253.

12   Sections 118–118C substituted for original s 118 by SI 2005/381.

13   Inserted by SI 2006/2975.

14   Inserted by the Consumer Credit Act 2006.

15   This section is spent. It amended the Companies Act 1985, s 716 but that section was repealed by SI 2002/3203, as from 21 December 2002. This section is also repealed by the Companies Act 2006.

16   Inserted by the Investment Exchanges and Clearing Houses Act 2006.

17   Substituted by the Enterprise Act 2002.

18   Inserted by SI 2008/948.

19   Inserted by SI 2005/1433.

20   Inserted by the Enterprise Act 2002.

21   Inserted by the Banking Act 2009.

PART I
FSMA 2000

[498]–[1000]

PART II
OTHER ACTS

GAMING ACT 1845 (NOTE)

(8 & 9 Vict c 109)

NOTES

Prior to 1 September 2007 most of this Act had been repealed by a combination of the Statute Law Revision Act 1875, the Betting and Gaming Act 1960, the Billiards (Abolition of Restrictions) Act 1987, and the Statute Law Revision Act 1875. The remaining sections (ie, ss 17 and 18) were repealed by the Gambling Act 2005, ss 42(6), 334(1)(c), 356, Sch 17, as from 1 September 2007. Note that s 334(2) of the 2005 Act specifically provides that the repeal of s 18 (voiding of gaming contracts) does not permit enforcement of a right which is created, or which emanates from an agreement made, before 1 September 2007.

[1001]

GAMING ACT 1892 (NOTE)

(8 & 9 Vict c 9)

NOTES

This Act was repealed by the Gambling Act 2005, ss 334(1)(d), 356(3)(e), (4), Sch 17, as from 1 September 2007. Note that s 334(2) of the 2005 Act specifically provides that the repeal of s 1 (voiding of promise to repay) does not permit enforcement of a right which is created, or which emanates from an agreement made, before 1 September 2007.

[1002]–[1003]

LIMITED PARTNERSHIPS ACT 1907

(1907 c 24)

NOTES

This Act is reproduced as amended by: the Companies (Consolidation) Act 1908; the Perjury Act 1911; the Statute Law Revision Act 1927; the Perjury Act (Northern Ireland) 1946; the Decimal Currency Act 1969; the Finance Act 1973; the Banking Act 1979; the Companies Act 2006; the Finance (Miscellaneous Provisions) (Northern Ireland) Order 1973, SI 1973/1323; the Regulatory Reform (Removal of 20 Member Limit in Partnerships etc) Order 2002, SI 2002/3203.

Application of the Banking Act 2009: s 132 of the Banking Act 2009 (at **[1901W]**) provides that the Lord Chancellor may, by order made with the concurrence of the Secretary of State and the Lord Chief Justice, modify provisions of Part 2 of the 2009 Act (bank insolvency) in their application to partnerships. See also s 163 of the 2009 Act (at **[1902X]**) which makes the same provision with regard to the application of Part 3 of that Act (bank administration). Similar provision is made with regard to Scottish partnerships by ss 133 and 164 respectively.

As to the repeal of this Act in relation to Northern Ireland, see the Companies Act 2006, s 1286(2).

ARRANGEMENT OF SECTIONS

An Act to establish Limited Partnership

[28 August 1907]

1 Short title

This Act may be cited for all purposes as the Limited Partnerships Act 1907.

[1003]

2 *(Repealed by the Statute Law Revision Act 1927.)*

3 Interpretation of terms

In the construction of this Act the following words and expressions shall have the meanings respectively assigned to them in this section, unless there be something in the subject or context repugnant to such construction—

"Firm," "firm name," and "business" have the same meanings as in the Partnership Act 1890;

"General partner" shall mean any partner who is not a limited partner as defined by this Act.

[1003A]

4 Definition and constitution of limited partnership

(1)   ... Limited partnerships may be formed in the manner and subject to the conditions by this Act provided.

(2)   A limited partnership ... must consist of one or more persons called general partners, who shall be liable for all debts and obligations of the firm, and one or more persons to be called limited partners, who shall at the time of entering into such partnership contribute thereto a sum or sums as capital or property valued at a stated amount, and who shall not be liable for the debts or obligations of the firm beyond the amount so contributed.

(3)   A limited partner shall not during the continuance of the partnership, either directly or indirectly, draw out or receive back any part of his contribution, and if he does so draw out or receive back any such part shall be liable for the debts and obligations of the firm up to the amount so drawn out or received back.

(4)   A body corporate may be a limited partner.

[1003B]

NOTES

Sub-s (1): words omitted repealed by the Statute Law Revision Act 1927, as from 22 December 1927.

Sub-s (2): words omitted repealed by a combination of the Banking Act 1979, ss 46(b), 51(2), Sch 7, as from 19 February 1982, the Regulatory Reform (Removal of 20 Member Limit in Partnerships etc) Order 2002, SI 2002/3203, art 3, as from 21 December 2002, and the Partnerships etc (Removal of Twenty Member Limit) (Northern Ireland) Order 2003, SI 2003/2904, arts 3(1), 4, Schedule, as from 13 January 2004.

Note: the Regulatory Reform (Removal of 20 Member Limit in Partnerships etc) Order 2002, SI 2002/3203 reforms the law relating to the maximum limit of 20 on the numbers of persons who can be members of partnerships (including limited partnerships), and of certain companies or associations. It does so by repealing CA 1985, ss 716, 717 and amending sub-s (2) above, thereby removing the maximum limits on the number of members in a partnership or limited partnership, company or association.

5 Registration of limited partnership required

Every limited partnership must be registered as such in accordance with the provisions of this Act, or in default thereof it shall be deemed to be a general partnership, and every limited partner shall be deemed to be a general partner.

[1003C]

6 Modifications of general law in case of limited partnerships

(1)   A limited partner shall not take part in the management of the partnership business, and shall not have power to bind the firm—

Provided that a limited partner may by himself or his agent at any time inspect the books of the firm and examine into the state and prospects of the partnership business, and may advise with the partners thereon.

If a limited partner takes part in the management of the partnership business he shall be liable for all debts and obligations of the firm incurred while he so takes part in the management as though he were a general partner.

(2)   A limited partnership shall not be dissolved by the death or bankruptcy of a limited partner, and the lunacy of a limited partner shall not be a ground for dissolution of the partnership by the court unless the lunatic's share cannot be otherwise ascertained and realised.

(3)   In the event of the dissolution of a limited partnership its affairs shall be wound up by the general partners unless the court otherwise orders.

(4)   ...

(5)   Subject to any agreement expressed or implied between the partners—

(a)   Any difference arising as to ordinary matters connected with the partnership business may be decided by a majority of the general partners;

(b)   A limited partner may, with the consent of the general partners, assign his share in the partnership, and upon such an assignment the assignee shall become a limited partner with all the rights of the assignor;

(c)   The other partners shall not be entitled to dissolve the partnership by reason of any limited partner suffering his share to be charged for his separate debt;

(d)   A person may be introduced as a partner without the consent of the existing limited partners;

(e)   A limited partner shall not be entitled to dissolve the partnership by notice.

[1003D]

NOTES

Sub-s (4): repealed by the Companies (Consolidation) Act 1908, s 286, Sch 6, Pt I, as from 21 December 1908.

---

7 Law as to private partnerships to apply where not excluded by this Act

Subject to the provisions of this Act, the Partnership Act 1890 and the rules of equity and of common law applicable to partnerships, except so far as they are inconsistent with the express provisions of the last-mentioned Act, shall apply to limited partnerships.

[1003E]

8 Manner and particulars of registration

The registration of a limited partnership shall be effected by sending by post or delivering to the registrar at the register office in that part of the United Kingdom in which the principal place of business of the limited partnership is situated or proposed to be situated a statement signed by the partners containing the following particulars—

(a)   The firm name;

(b)   The general nature of the business;

(c)   The principal place of business;

(d)   The full name of each of the partners;

(e)   The term, if any, for which the partnership is entered into, and the date of its commencement;

(f)   A statement that the partnership is limited, and the description of every limited partner as such;

(g)   The sum contributed by each limited partner, and whether paid in cash or how otherwise.

[1003F]

9 Registration of changes in partnerships

(1)   If during the continuance of a limited partnership any change is made or occurs in—

(a)   the firm name,

(b)   the general nature of the business,

(c)   the principal place of business,

(d)   the partners or the name of any partner,

(e)   the term or character of the partnership,

(f)   the sum contributed by any limited partner,

(g)   the liability of any partner by reason of his becoming a limited instead of a general partner or a general instead of a limited partner,

a statement, signed by the firm, specifying the nature of the change shall within seven days be sent by post or delivered to the registrar at the register office in that part of the United Kingdom in which the partnership is registered.

(2)   If default is made in compliance with the requirements of this section each of the general partners shall, on conviction under the Summary Jurisdiction Acts, be liable to a fine not exceeding one pound for each day during which the default continues.

[1003G]

10 Advertisement in Gazette of statement of general partner becoming a limited partner and of assignment of share of limited partner

(1)   Notice of any arrangement or transaction under which any person will cease to be a general partner in any firm, and will become a limited partner in that firm, or under which the share of a limited partner in a firm will be assigned to any person, shall be forthwith advertised in the Gazette, and until notice of the arrangement or transaction is so advertised the arrangement or transaction shall, for the purposes of this Act, be deemed to be of no effect.

(2)   For the purposes of this section, the expression "the Gazette" means—

In the case of a limited partnership registered in England, the London Gazette.

In the case of a limited partnership registered in Scotland, the Edinburgh Gazette.

In the case of a limited partnership registered in Ireland, the Dublin Gazette.

[1003H]

NOTES

Dublin Gazette: this should now be construed as a reference to the Belfast Gazette: see the General Adaptation of Enactments (Northern Ireland) Order 1921, SR & O 1921/1804.

11, 12 *(S 11 repealed by the Finance Act 1973, s 59(7), Sch 22, Pt V and the Finance (Miscellaneous Provisions) (Northern Ireland) Order 1973, SI 1973/1323, art 10(1), Sch 4, as from 1 August 1973; s 12 repealed by the Perjury Act 1911, s 17, Schedule and the Perjury Act (Northern Ireland) 1946, s 16(3), Schedule, as from 1 January 1912.)*

13 Registrar to file statement and issue certificate of registration

On receiving any statement made in pursuance of this Act the registrar shall cause the same to be filed, and he shall send by post to the firm from whom such statement shall have been received a certificate of the registration thereof.

[1003I]

14 Register and index to be kept

At each of the register offices herein-after referred to the registrar shall keep, in proper books to be provided for the purpose, a register and an index of all the limited partnerships registered as aforesaid, and of all the statements registered in relation to such partnerships.

[1003J]

15 Registrar of joint stock companies to be registrar under Act

The registrar of joint stock companies shall be the registrar of limited partnerships, and the several offices for the registration of joint stock companies in London, Edinburgh, and Dublin shall be the offices for the registration of limited partnerships carrying on business within those parts of the United Kingdom in which they are respectively situated.

[1003K]

16 Inspection of statements registered

(1) Any person may inspect the statements filed by the registrar in the register offices aforesaid ... and any person may require a certificate of the registration of any limited partnership, or a copy of or extract from any registered statement, to be certified by the registrar ...

(2) A certificate of registration or a copy of or extract from any statement registered under this Act, if duly certified to be a true copy under the hand of the registrar or one of the assistant registrars (whom it shall not be necessary to prove to be the registrar or assistant registrar) shall, in all legal proceedings, civil or criminal, and in all cases whatsoever be received in evidence.

[1003L]

NOTES

Sub-s (1): words omitted repealed by the Companies Act 2006, ss 1063(7)(a), 1295, Sch 16, as from 6 April 2007 (for transitional provisions see the note below).

Transitional provisions: the Companies Act 2006 (Commencement No 1, Transitional Provisions and Savings) Order 2006, SI 2006/3428, Sch 5, para 6(2) provides as follows—

(2) Notwithstanding the coming into force of the repeals in section 16 of the Limited Partnerships Act 1907 and the repeal of section 17(a) of that Act, the fees appointed under the said section 16 and having effect immediately before 6th April 2007 shall continue to be payable, and the rules in force under the said section 17(a) immediately before 6th April 2007 shall continue to have effect.

The fees were previously as follows—
- inspecting the statements filed by the registrar: such fee as may be appointed by the Board of Trade, not exceeding 5p;
- certificate of registration of any limited partnership: such fee as may be appointed by the Board of Trade, not exceeding 10p;
- copy of, or extract from, any registered statement (certified by the registrar): such fee as may be appointed by the Board of Trade, not exceeding 2p for each folio of seventy-two words, or in Scotland for each sheet of two hundred words.

Note also that SI 2006/3428, art 4(4) provides that the commencement of CA 2006, s 1063 does not extend to Northern Ireland.

17 Power to Board of Trade to make rules

The Board of Trade may make rules ... concerning any of the following matters:—
  (a) ...
  (b) The duties or additional duties to be performed by the registrar for the purposes of this Act;
  (c) The performance by assistant registrars and other officers of acts by this Act required to be done by the registrar;
  (d) The forms to be used for the purposes of this Act;

(e) Generally, the conduct and regulation of registration under this Act and any matters incidental thereto.

[1003M]

NOTES

Words omitted repealed by the Companies Act 2006, ss 1063(7)(b), 1295, Sch 16, as from 6 April 2007 (for transitional provisions see the note to s 16 at **[1003L]**).

Rules: the Limited Partnerships Rules 1907, SR & O 1907/1020.

THEFT ACT 1968

(1968 c 60)

NOTES

This Act is reproduced as amended by: the Northern Ireland Constitution Act 1973; the Criminal Justice Act 1991; the Theft (Amendment) Act 1996; the Fraud Act 2006; the Financial Services and Markets Act 2000 (Consequential Amendments and Repeals) Order 2001, SI 2001/3649; the Postal Services Act 2000 (Consequential Modifications) Order 2003, SI 2003/2908.

ARRANGEMENT OF SECTIONS

Definition of "Theft"

An Act to revise the law of England and Wales as to theft and similar or associated offences, and in connection therewith to make provision as to criminal proceedings by one party to a marriage against the other, and to make certain amendments extending beyond England and Wales in the Post Office Act 1953 and other enactments; and for other purposes connected therewith

[26 July 1968]

Definition of "Theft"

1 Basic definition of theft

(1) A person is guilty of theft if he dishonestly appropriates property belonging to another with the intention of permanently depriving the other of it; and "thief" and "steal" shall be construed accordingly.

(2) It is immaterial whether the appropriation is made with a view to gain, or is made for the thief's own benefit.

(3) The five following sections of this Act shall have effect as regards the interpretation and operation of this section (and, except as otherwise provided by this Act, shall apply only for purposes of this section).

[1004]

2 "Dishonestly"

(1) A person's appropriation of property belonging to another is not to be regarded as dishonest—

(a) if he appropriates the property in the belief that he has in law the right to deprive the other of it, on behalf of himself or of a third person; or

(b) if he appropriates the property in the belief that he would have the other's consent if the other knew of the appropriation and the circumstances of it; or

(c) (except where the property came to him as trustee or personal representative) if he appropriates the property in the belief that the person to whom the property belongs cannot be discovered by taking reasonable steps.

(2) A person's appropriation of property belonging to another may be dishonest notwithstanding that he is willing to pay for the property.

[1005]

3 "Appropriates"

(1) Any assumption by a person of the rights of an owner amounts to an appropriation, and this includes, where he has come by the property (innocently or not) without stealing it, any later assumption of a right to it by keeping or dealing with it as owner.

(2) Where property or a right or interest in property is or purports to be transferred for value to a person acting in good faith, no later assumption by him of rights which he believed himself to be acquiring shall, by reason of any defect in the transferor's title, amount to theft of the property.

[1006]

4 "Property"

(1) "Property" includes money and all other property, real or personal, including things in action and other intangible property.

(2) A person cannot steal land, or things forming part of land and severed from it by him or by his directions, except in the following cases, that is to say—

(a) when he is a trustee or personal representative, or is authorised by power of attorney, or as liquidator of a company, or otherwise, to sell or dispose of land belonging to another, and he appropriates the land or anything forming part of it by dealing with it in breach of the confidence reposed in him; or

(b) when he is not in possession of the land and appropriates anything forming part of the land by severing it or causing it to be severed, or after it has been severed; or

(c) when, being in possession of the land under a tenancy, he appropriates the whole or part of any fixture or structure let to be used with the land.

For purposes of this subsection "land" does not include incorporeal hereditaments; "tenancy" means a tenancy for years or any less period and includes an agreement for such a tenancy, but a person who after the end of a tenancy remains in possession as statutory tenant or otherwise is to be treated as having possession under the tenancy, and "let" shall be construed accordingly.

(3) A person who picks mushrooms growing wild on any land, or who picks flowers, fruit or foliage from a plant wild on any land, does not (although not in possession of the land) steal what he picks, unless he does it for reward or for sale or other commercial purpose.

For purposes of this subsection "mushroom" includes any fungus, and "plant" includes any shrub or tree.

(4) Wild creatures, tamed or untamed, shall be regarded as property; but a person cannot steal a wild creature not tamed nor ordinarily kept in captivity, or the carcase of any such creature, unless either it has been reduced into possession by or on behalf of another person and possession of it has not since been lost or abandoned, or another person is in course of reducing it into possession.

[1007]

5 "Belonging to another"

(1) Property shall be regarded as belonging to any person having possession or control of it, or having in it any proprietary right or interest (not being an equitable interest arising only from an agreement to transfer or grant an interest).

(2) Where property is subject to a trust, the persons to whom it belongs shall be regarded as including any person having a right to enforce the trust, and an intention to defeat the trust shall be regarded accordingly as an intention to deprive of the property any person having that right.

(3) Where a person receives property from or on account of another, and is under an obligation to the other to retain and deal with that property or its proceeds in a particular way, the property or proceeds shall be regarded (as against him) as belonging to the other.

(4) Where a person gets property by another's mistake, and is under an obligation to make restoration (in whole or in part) of the property or its proceeds or of the value thereof, then to the extent of that obligation the property or proceeds shall be regarded (as against him) as belonging to the person entitled to restoration, and an intention not to make restoration shall be regarded accordingly as an intention to deprive that person of the property or proceeds.

(5) Property of a corporation sole shall be regarded as belonging to the corporation notwithstanding a vacancy in the corporation.

[1008]

6 "With the intention of permanently depriving the other of it"

(1) A person appropriating property belonging to another without meaning the other permanently to lose the thing itself is nevertheless to be regarded as having the intention of permanently depriving the other of it if his intention is to treat the thing as his own to dispose of regardless of the other's rights; and a borrowing or lending of it may amount to so treating it if, but only if, the borrowing or lending is for a period and in circumstances making it equivalent to an outright taking or disposal.

(2) Without prejudice to the generality of subsection (1) above, where a person, having possession or control (lawfully or not) of property belonging to another, parts with the property under a condition as to its return which he may not be able to perform, this (if done for purposes of his own and without the other's authority) amounts to treating the property as his own to dispose of regardless of the other's rights.

[1009]

Theft, Robbery, Burglary, etc

7 Theft

A person guilty of theft shall on conviction on indictment be liable to imprisonment for a term not exceeding [seven years].

[1010]–[1013]

NOTES
Words in square brackets substituted by the Criminal Justice Act 1991, s 26(1).

8–14, 15, 15A, 15B, 16 (Ss 8–14 (*robbery, burglary, taking vehicles, abstracting electricity, etc, outside the scope of this work*); s 15 (*Obtaining property by deception*), s 15A (*Obtaining a money transfer by deception*), s 15B (*Section 15A: supplementary*), and s 16 (*Obtaining pecuniary advantage by deception*) repealed by the Fraud Act 2006, s 14(1), (3), Sch 1, paras 1(a), 3, Sch 3, as from 15 January 2007 (for savings and transitional provisions in relation to any liability, investigation, legal proceeding or penalty for, or in respect of, any offence partly committed before that date, see Sch 2, para 3 to the 2006 Act at* **[1503]**).)

17 False accounting

(1) Where a person dishonestly, with a view to gain for himself or another or with intent to cause loss to another,—

(a)   destroys, defaces, conceals or falsifies any account or any record or document made or required for any accounting purpose; or

(b)   in furnishing information for any purpose produces or makes use of any account, or any such record or document as aforesaid, which to his knowledge is or may be misleading, false or deceptive in a material particular;

he shall, on conviction on indictment, be liable to imprisonment for a term not exceeding seven years.

(2) For purposes of this section a person who makes or concurs in making in an account or other document an entry which is or may be misleading, false or deceptive in a material particular, or who omits or concurs in omitting a material particular from an account or other document, is to be treated as falsifying the account or document.

[1014]

NOTES
Serious crime prevention orders: a court may make a serious crime prevention order under the Serious Crime Act 2007, ss 1, 19 if it is satisfied that a person has been involved in serious crime, and it has reasonable grounds to believe that the order would protect the public by preventing, restricting or disrupting involvement by the person in serious crime. By virtue of s 2 of, and Sch 1, the 2007 Act, the offence under this section is a serious crime.

18 Liability of company officers for certain offences by company

(1) Where an offence committed by a body corporate under section … 17 of this Act is proved to have been committed with the consent or connivance of any director, manager, secretary or other similar officer of the body corporate, or any person who was purporting to act in any such capacity, he as well as the body corporate shall be guilty of that offence, and shall be liable to be proceeded against and punished accordingly.

(2)   Where the affairs of a body corporate are managed by its members, this section shall apply in relation to the acts and defaults of a member in connection with his functions of management as if he were a director of the body corporate.

[1015]

NOTES
  Sub-s (1): words omitted repealed by the Fraud Act 2006, s 14(1), (3), Sch 1, para 4, Sch 3, as from 15 January 2007.

19   False statements by company directors, etc

(1)   Where an officer of a body corporate or unincorporated association (or person purporting to act as such), with intent to deceive members or creditors of the body corporate or association about its affairs, publishes or concurs in publishing a written statement or account which to his knowledge is or may be misleading, false or deceptive in a material particular, he shall on conviction on indictment be liable to imprisonment for a term not exceeding seven years.

(2)   For purposes of this section a person who has entered into a security for the benefit of a body corporate or association is to be treated as a creditor of it.

(3)   Where the affairs of a body corporate or association are managed by its members, this section shall apply to any statement which a member publishes or concurs in publishing in connection with his functions of management as if he were an officer of the body corporate or association.

[1016]

20   Suppression, etc of documents

(1)   A person who dishonestly, with a view to gain for himself or another or with intent to cause loss to another, destroys, defaces or conceals any valuable security, any will or other testamentary document or any original document of or belonging to, or filed or deposited in, any court of justice or any government department shall on conviction on indictment be liable to imprisonment for a term not exceeding seven years.

(2)   ...

(3)   For purposes of this section ... "valuable security" means any document creating, transferring, surrendering or releasing any right to, in or over property, or authorising the payment of money or delivery of any property, or evidencing the creation, transfer, surrender or release of any such right, or the payment of money or delivery of any property, or the satisfaction of any obligation.

[1017]

NOTES
  Sub-s (2): repealed by the Fraud Act 2006, s 14(1), (3), Sch 1, para 1(a)(iv), Sch 3, as from 15 January 2007 (for savings and transitional provisions in relation to any liability, investigation, legal proceeding or penalty for, or in respect of, any offence partly committed before that date, see Sch 2, para 3 to the 2006 Act at **[1503]**).
  Sub-s (3): words omitted repealed by the Fraud Act 2006, s 14(1), (3), Sch 1, para 5, Sch 3, as from 15 January 2007.

21   Blackmail

(1)   A person is guilty of blackmail if, with a view to gain for himself or another or with intent to cause loss to another, he makes any unwarranted demand with menaces; and for this purpose a demand with menaces is unwarranted unless the person making it does so in the belief—
  (a)   that he has reasonable grounds for making the demand; and
  (b)   that the use of the menaces is a proper means of reinforcing the demand.

(2)   The nature of the act or omission demanded is immaterial, and it is also immaterial whether the menaces relate to action to be taken by the person making the demand.

(3)   A person guilty of blackmail shall on conviction on indictment be liable to imprisonment for a term not exceeding fourteen years.

[1018]

NOTES
  Serious crime prevention orders: a court may make a serious crime prevention order under the Serious Crime Act 2007, ss 1, 19 if it is satisfied that a person has been involved in serious crime, and it has reasonable grounds to believe that the order would protect the public by preventing, restricting or disrupting involvement by the person in serious crime. By virtue of s 2 of, and Sch 1, the 2007 Act, the offence under this section is a serious crime.

22–33   (Ss 22–33 (*offences relating to stolen goods, possession of house breaking implements, enforcement, etc*) *outside the scope of this work.*)

Supplementary

34 Interpretation

(1) Sections 4(1) and 5(1) of this Act shall apply generally for purposes of this Act as they apply for purposes of section 1.

(2) For purposes of this Act—

(a) "gain" and "loss" are to be construed as extending only to gain or loss in money or other property, but as extending to any such gain or loss whether temporary or permanent; and—

(i) "gain" includes a gain by keeping what one has, as well as a gain by getting what one has not; and

(ii) "loss" includes a loss by not getting what one might get, as well as a loss by parting with what one has;

(b) "goods", except in so far as the context otherwise requires, includes money and every other description of property except land, and includes things severed from the land by stealing[; and

(c) "mail bag" and "postal packet" have the meanings given by section 125(1) of the Postal Services Act 2000].

[1018A]

NOTES
Sub-s (2): para (c) and the word immediately preceding it inserted by the Postal Services Act 2000 (Consequential Modifications) Order 2003, SI 2003/2908, art 3(1), Sch 1, para 1, as from 12 November 2003 (except in relation to offences committed before that date).

35 Commencement and transitional provisions

(1) This Act shall come into force on the 1st January 1969 and, save as otherwise provided by this Act, shall have effect only in relation to offences wholly or partly committed on or after that date.

(2), (3) *(Outside the scope of this work.)*

[1019]

36 Short title, and general provisions as to Scotland and Northern Ireland

(1) This Act may be cited as the Theft Act 1968.

(2) ...

(3) This Act does not extend to Scotland or, ... to Northern Ireland, except as regards any amendment or repeal which in accordance with section 33 above is to extend to Scotland or Northern Ireland.

[1020]

NOTES
Sub s (2): repealed by the Northern Ireland Constitution Act 1973, s 41(1), Sch 6, Pt I.
Sub-s (3): words omitted repealed by the Northern Ireland Constitution Act 1973, s 41(1), Sch 6, Pt I.

(Sch 1 (offences of taking, etc, deer or fish), Sch 2 (minor and consequential amendments), Sch 3 (repeals) outside the scope of this work.)

STOCK EXCHANGE (COMPLETION OF BARGAINS) ACT 1976

(1976 c 47)

NOTES
This Act is reproduced as amended by: the Companies Consolidation (Consequential Provisions) Act 1985; the Financial Services Act 1986; the Financial Services and Markets Act 2000 (Consequential Amendments and Repeals) Order 2001, SI 2001/3649.

An Act to amend and clarify the law relating to the transfer of securities and to companies, trustees and personal representatives with a view to simplifying the activities connected with the periodic completion of bargains made on stock exchanges; and for purposes connected therewith
[12 October 1976]

1–4 *(Repealed by the Companies Consolidation (Consequential Provisions) Act 1985, s 29, Sch 1.)*

5 Acquisition and disposal of securities by trustees and personal representatives

[(1)]   A trustee or personal representative shall not be chargeable with breach of trust or, as the case may be, with default in administering the estate by reason only of the fact that—
- (a)   he has, for the purpose of acquiring securities which he has power to acquire in connection with the trust or estate, paid for the securities under arrangements which provide for them to be transferred to him from [a financial institution] but not to be so transferred until after payment of the price; or
- (b)   he has, for the purpose of disposing of securities which he has power to dispose of in connection with the trust or estate, transferred the securities to [such a [financial institution]] under arrangements which provide that the price is not to be paid to him until after the transfer is made

...

[(2)   "Financial institution" means—
- (a)   a recognised clearing house acting in relation to a recognised investment exchange; or
- (b)   a nominee of—
  - (i)   a recognised clearing house acting in that way; or
  - (ii)   a recognised investment exchange.

(3)   No person may be a nominee for the purposes of this section unless he is a person designated for those purposes in the rules of the recognised investment exchange in question.

(4)   Expressions used in subsections (2) and (3) have the same meaning as in the Part 18 of the Financial Services and Markets Act 2000.]

[1021]

NOTES
Sub-s (1): numbered as such, and words in second (outer) pair of square brackets substituted, by the Financial Services Act 1986, s 194(1), (2); words in first and third (inner) pairs of square brackets substituted, and words omitted repealed, by the Financial Services and Markets Act 2000 (Consequential Amendments and Repeals) Order 2001, SI 2001/3649, art 289(1)–(4), as from 1 December 2001.
Sub-ss (2)–(4): substituted for original sub-s (2) (as added by FSA 1986, s 194(1), (2)) by SI 2001/3649, art 289(1), (5), as from 1 December 2001.

6 Forms for transfer of securities

(1)   ...

(2)   The subsection (5) inserted in the said section 3 by the preceding subsection shall extend to Northern Ireland in accordance with the provisions of section 5(1) and (2) of the said Act of 1963.

[1022]

NOTES
Sub-s (1): adds the Stock Transfer Act 1963, s 3(5).
Said section 3; said Act of 1963: the Stock Transfer Act 1963, s 3, and the Stock Transfer Act 1963 respectively.

7 Short title, interpretation, commencement and extent

(1)   This Act may be cited as the Stock Exchange (Completion of Bargains) Act 1976.

(2), (3)   ...

(4)   This Act shall come into force on such date as the Secretary of State may appoint by an order made by statutory instrument.

(5)   Except as provided by section 6(2) of this Act, this Act does not extend to Northern Ireland.

[1023]

NOTES
Sub-s (2): repealed by the Financial Services Act 1986, s 212(3), Sch 17, Pt I.
Sub-s (3): repealed by the Companies Consolidation (Consequential Provisions) Act 1985, ss 29, 30, Schs 1, 2.
Orders: the Stock Exchange (Completion of Bargains) Act 1976 (Commencement) Order 1979, SI 1979/55 (bringing this Act into force on 12 February 1979).

COMPETITION ACT 1980

(1980 c 21)

NOTES

Only provisions of this Act relevant to Financial Services law are reproduced. Provisions not reproduced are not annotated.

This Act is reproduced as amended by: the London Regional Transport Act 1984; the Companies Consolidation (Consequential Provisions) Act 1985; the Transport Act 1985; the Water Act 1989; the Companies Act 1989; the Railways Act 1993; Local Government etc (Scotland) Act 1994; the Competition Act 1998; the Enterprise Act 2002; the Water Industry (Scotland) Act 2002; the Communications Act 2003; the Agricultural Marketing (Northern Ireland) Order 1982, SI 1982/1080; the Environment Act 1995 (Consequential Amendments) Regulations 1996, SI 1996/593; the Transport for London (Consequential Provisions) Order 2003, SI 2003/1615; the Water Industry (Scotland) Act 2002 (Consequential Modifications) Order 2004, SI 2004/1822.

ARRANGEMENT OF SECTIONS

Further references and investigations

An Act to abolish the Price Commission; to make provision for the control of anti-competitive practices in the supply and acquisition of goods and the supply and securing of services; to provide for references of certain public bodies and other persons to the Monopolies and Mergers Commission; to provide for the investigation of prices and charges by the Director General of Fair Trading; to provide for the making of grants to certain bodies; to amend and provide for the amendment of the Fair Trading Act 1973; to make amendments with respect to the Restrictive Trade Practices Act 1976; to repeal the remaining provisions of the Counter-Inflation Act 1973; and for purposes connected therewith

[3 April 1980]

Further references and investigations

11   References of public bodies and certain other persons to the Commission

(1)   The Secretary of State may at any time refer to the Commission any question relating to—

   (a)   the efficiency and costs of, [or]

   (b)   the service provided by, ...

   (c)   ...

a person falling within subsection (3) below and specified in the reference, including any question whether, in relation to a matter falling within [paragraph (a) or (b)] above, the person is pursuing a course of conduct which operates against the public interest.

(2)   ...

(3)   The persons referred to in subsection (1) above are—

   (a)   any body corporate—

      (i)   which supplies goods or services by way of business,

      (ii)   the affairs of which are managed by its members, and

      (iii)   the members of which hold office as such by virtue of their appointment to that or another office by a Minister under any enactment; or

   [(aa)   any publicly owned railway company, within the meaning of the Railways Act 1993, which supplies network services or station services, within the meaning of Part I of that Act; or]

   [(b)   any person (not falling within paragraph (a) above) who provides in Northern Ireland a bus service within the meaning of section 14 of the Finance Act (Northern Ireland) 1966; or]

   [(bb)   any person who provides a railway passenger service in pursuance of an agreement entered into by Transport for London or any of its subsidiaries (within the meaning of the Greater London Authority Act 1999) by virtue of section 156(2) or (3) of the Greater London Authority Act 1999;] or]

   [(c)   the [Environment Agency];] or

   [(ca)   Scottish water;]

[(cc)   ...]
(d)   any board administering a scheme under the Agricultural Marketing Act 1958 [or the Agricultural Marketing (Northern Ireland) Order 1982]; or
(e)   any body corporate with a statutory duty to promote and assist the maintenance and development of the efficient supply of any goods or services by a body falling within paragraphs (a) to (d) above; or
(f)   any subsidiary, within the meaning of [section 736 of] the [Companies Act 1985], of a body falling within paragraphs (a) to (e) above.

(4)   The Secretary of State may by order exclude from subsection (3)(b) [or (bb)] above persons of such descriptions as may be specified in the order.

(5)   No question concerning a person falling within subsection (3)(b) [or (bb)] above or a subsidiary of a body falling within [either of those paragraphs] may be referred to the Commission under this section unless it relates to the carriage of passengers by the person or, as the case may be, the subsidiary.

(6)   The Secretary of State may at any time by notice given to the Commission vary a reference under this section.

(7)   On making a reference under this section or on varying such a reference under subsection (6) above the Secretary of State shall arrange for the reference or, as the case may be, the variation to be published in such manner as he considers most suitable for bringing it to the attention of persons who in his opinion would be affected by it or be likely to have an interest in it.

(8)   On a reference under this section the Commission shall investigate and report on any question referred to them but shall exclude from their investigation and report consideration of—
(a)   any question relating to the appropriateness of any financial obligations or guidance as to financial objectives (however expressed) imposed on or given to the person in question by or under any enactment, or otherwise by a Minister; ...
(b)   ...

[(9), (9A)   ...]

(10)   A report of the Commission on a reference under this section shall be made to the Secretary of State and shall state, with reasons, the conclusions of the Commission with respect to any question referred to them and, where the Commission conclude that the person specified in the reference is pursuing a course of conduct which operates against the public interest, the report may include recommendations as to what action (if any) should be taken by the person for the purpose of remedying or preventing what the Commission consider are the adverse effects of that course of conduct.

(11)   In this section "Minister" includes a Northern Ireland department and the head of such a department.

[1023A]

NOTES

Sub-s (1): word in first pair of square brackets inserted, para (c) (and the word immediately preceding it) repealed, and words in second pair of square brackets substituted, by the Enterprise Act 2002, s 278(1), Sch 25, para 10(1), (2)(a), (10), as from 20 June 2003.

Sub-s (2): repealed by the Enterprise Act 2002, s 278, Sch 25, para 10(1), (2)(b), (10), Sch 26, as from 20 June 2003.

Sub-s (3): para (aa) inserted by the Railways Act 1993, s 152, Sch 12, para 12(1); para (b) substituted by the Transport Act 1985, s 114(1); para (bb) inserted by the London Regional Transport Act 1984, s 71(3)(a), Sch 6, para 15, and substituted by the Transport for London (Consequential Provisions) Order 2003, SI 2003/1615, art 2, Sch 1, Pt 1, para 6, as from 15 July 2003; para (c) substituted by the Water Act 1989, s 190(1), Sch 25, para 59(1); words in square brackets in para (c) substituted by the Environment Act 1995 (Consequential Amendments) Regulations 1996, SI 1996/593, reg 2, Sch 1; para (ca) inserted by the Water Industry (Scotland) Act 2002 (Consequential Modifications) Order 2004, SI 2004/1822, art 2, Schedule, Pt 1, para 10, as from 14 July 2004; para (cc) inserted by the Local Government etc (Scotland) Act 1994, s 72, and repealed by the Water Industry (Scotland) Act 2002, s 71(2), Sch 7, para 10, as from 1 April 2002; words in square brackets in para (d) substituted by the Agricultural Marketing (Northern Ireland) Order 1982, SI 1982/1080, art 46, Schs 8, 9; words in first pair of square brackets in para (f) inserted by the Companies Act 1989, s 144(4), Sch 18, para 22; words in second pair of square brackets in para (f) substituted by the Companies Consolidation (Consequential Provisions) Act 1985, s 30, Sch 2.

Sub-s (4): words in square brackets inserted by the London Regional Transport Act 1984, s 71(3)(a), Sch 6, para 15.

Sub-s (5): words in first pair of square brackets inserted, and words in second pair of square brackets substituted, by the London Regional Transport Act 1984, s 71(3)(a), Sch 6, para 15.

Sub-s (8): para (b) (and the word immediately preceding it) repealed by the Competition Act 1998, s 74(1), (3), Sch 12, para 4(2), Sch 14, Pt I, as from 1 March 2000.

Sub-ss (9), (9A): substituted for original sub-s (9) by the Competition Act 1998, s 74(1), Sch 12, para 4(3), as from 1 April 1999, and repealed by the Enterprise Act 2002, s 278, Sch 25, para 10(1), (2)(b), (10), Sch 26, as from 20 June 2003.

Rules of procedure: for special rules of procedure in connection with references to the Competition Commission under this section, see the Competition Act 1998, Sch 7, Pt II, para 19A, Sch 7A at [122], [124].

Ministers of the Crown, etc: the Enterprise Act 2002, Sch 25, para 10(10) provides that for the purposes of the Scotland Act 1998, the amendments made by Sch 25, para 10(1)–(9) to that Act (including the amendments made to this section) shall be taken to be pre-commencement enactments within the meaning of the 1998 Act; references to a Minister of the Crown should be construed accordingly.

[11A   References under section 11: time-limits

(1)   Every reference under section 11 above shall specify a period (not longer than six months beginning with the date of the reference) within which a report on the reference is to be made.

(2)   A report of the Commission on a reference under section 11 above shall not have effect (and no action shall be taken in relation to it under section 12 below) unless the report is made before the end of the period specified in the reference or such further period (if any) as may be allowed by the Secretary of State under subsection (3) below.

(3)   The Secretary of State may, if he has received representations on the subject from the Commission and is satisfied that there are special reasons why the report cannot be made within the period specified in the reference, extend that period by no more than three months.

(4)   No more than one extension is possible under subsection (3) above in relation to the same reference.

(5)   The Secretary of State shall publish any extension made by him under subsection (3) above in such manner as he considers most suitable for bringing it to the attention of persons who in his opinion would be affected by it or be likely to have an interest in it.]

[1023B]

NOTES
Inserted, together with ss 11B–11D, by the Enterprise Act 2002, s 278(1), Sch 25, para 10(1), (3), (10), as from 20 June 2003.
Ministers of the Crown, etc: see the note to s 11 at **[1023A]**.

[11B   References under section 11: powers of investigation and penalties

(1)   The following sections of Part 3 of the Enterprise Act 2002 shall apply, with the modifications mentioned in subsections (2) and (3) below, for the purposes of references under section 11 above as they apply for the purposes of references under that Part—
  (a)   section 109 (attendance of witnesses and production of documents etc);
  (b)   section 110 (enforcement of powers under section 109: general);
  (c)   section 111 (penalties);
  (d)   section 112 (penalties: main procedural requirements);
  (e)   section 113 (payments and interest by instalments);
  (f)   section 114 (appeals in relation to penalties);
  (g)   section 115 (recovery of penalties); and
  (h)   section 116 (statement of policy).

(2)   Section 110 shall, in its application by virtue of subsection (1) above, have effect as if—
  (a)   subsection (2) were omitted;
  (b)   in subsection (4), for the word "publication" there were substituted "laying before both Houses of Parliament"; and
  (c)   in subsection (9) the words from "or section" to "section 65(3))" were omitted.

(3)   Section 111(5)(b)(ii) shall, in its application by virtue of subsection (1) above, have effect as if—
  (a)   for the words "published (or, in the case of a report under section 50 or 65, given)" there were substituted "made";
  (b)   for the words "published (or given)", in both places where they appear, there were substituted "made"; and
  (c)   the words "by this Part" were omitted.]

[1023C]

NOTES
Inserted as noted to s 11A at **[1023B]**.
Ministers of the Crown, etc: see the note to s 11 at **[1023A]**.

[11C   References under section 11: further supplementary provisions

(1)   Section 117 of the Enterprise Act 2002 (false or misleading information) shall apply in relation to functions under this Act as it applies in relation to functions under Part 3 of that Act but as if, in subsections (1)(a) and (2), the words ["the OFT, OFCOM,"] were omitted.

(2)   Section 125 of the Enterprise Act 2002 (offences by bodies corporate) shall apply for the purposes of this Act as it applies for the purposes of Part 3 of that Act.

(3)   For the purposes of section 12 below, a conclusion contained in a report of the Commission is to be disregarded if the conclusion is not that of at least two-thirds of the members of the group constituted in connection with the reference concerned in pursuance of paragraph 15 of Schedule 7 to the Competition Act 1998.]

[1023D]

NOTES
Inserted as noted to s 11A at **[1023B]**.
Sub-s (1): words in square brackets substituted by the Communications Act 2003, s 389(1), Sch 16, para 1, as from 29 December 2003.
Ministers of the Crown, etc: see the note to s 11 at **[1023A]**.

[11D   Interim orders

(1)   Subsection (2) below applies where, in the circumstances specified in subsection (1) of section 12 below, the Secretary of State has under consideration the making of an order under subsection (5) of that section.

(2)   The Secretary of State may by order, for the purpose of preventing pre-emptive action—
  (a)   prohibit or restrict the doing of things which the Secretary of State considers would constitute pre-emptive action;
  (b)   impose on any person concerned obligations as to the carrying on of any activities or the safeguarding of any assets;
  (c)   provide for the carrying on of any activities or the safeguarding of any assets either by the appointment of a person to conduct or supervise the conduct of any activities (on such terms and with such powers as may be specified or described in the order) or in any other manner;
  (d)   do anything which may be done by virtue of paragraph 19 of Schedule 8 to the Enterprise Act 2002 (information powers).

(3)   An order under this section shall come into force at such time as is determined by or under the order.

(4)   An order under this section shall, if it has not previously ceased to be in force, cease to be in force on the making of the order under section 12(5) below or (as the case may be) on the making of the decision not to make such an order.

(5)   The Secretary of State shall publish any decision made by him not to make an order under section 12(5) below in such manner as he considers most suitable for bringing it to the attention of persons who in his opinion would be affected by it or be likely to have an interest in it.

(6)   The Secretary of State shall, as soon as reasonably practicable, consider any representations received by him in relation to varying or revoking an order under this section.

(7)   The following provisions of Part 3 of the Enterprise Act 2002 shall apply in relation to orders under this section as they apply in relation to orders under paragraph 2 of Schedule 7 to that Act—
  (a)   section 86(2) and (3) (enforcement orders: general provisions);
  (b)   section 87 (delegated power of directions); and
  (c)   section 94(1) to (5), (8) and (9) (rights to enforce orders).

(8)   In this section "pre-emptive action" means action which might impede the making of an order under section 12(5) below.]

[1024]

NOTES
Inserted as noted to s 11A at **[1023B]**.
Ministers of the Crown, etc: see the note to s 11 at **[1023A]**.

12   Orders following report under section 11

(1)   This section applies where a report of the Commission on a reference under section 11 above concludes that the person specified in the reference is pursuing a course of conduct which operates against the public interest.

(2)   If it appears to the Secretary of State that any other Minister has functions directly relating to the person specified in the reference or, in the case of a reference only concerning the activities of the person in a part of the United Kingdom, functions directly relating to the person in respect of his activities in that part, he shall send a copy of the report of the Commission on the reference to that Minister; and in subsection (3) below "the relevant Minister" means—
  (a)   in a case where it appears to the Secretary of State that any Minister (including himself) has such functions, that Minister, and
  (b)   in a case where it appears to the Secretary of State that no Minister has such functions, the Secretary of State.

(3)   If—

    (a)   the relevant Minister considers it appropriate for the purpose of remedying or preventing what he considers are the adverse effects of the course of conduct specified in the report of the Commission as operating against the public interest, and

    (b)   the person specified in the reference does not fall within paragraph (d) of section 11(3) above and is not a subsidiary of a body falling within that paragraph,

he may by order direct the person to prepare within such time, if any, as may be specified in the order a plan for remedying or preventing such of those effects as are so specified; but where there is more than one relevant Minister no such order shall be made except by all the relevant Ministers acting jointly and where none of the relevant Ministers is the Secretary of State no such order shall be made except after consultation with him.

(4)   It shall be the duty of a person to whom a direction is given under subsection (3) above to prepare such a plan as is mentioned in that subsection and to send a copy of that plan to the Minister or Ministers by whom the order containing the direction was made who shall lay it before Parliament; and, in a case where the plan involves the use by a body of its powers in relation to any subsidiary within the meaning of [section 736 of] the [Companies Act 1985], the plan shall specify the manner in which the body proposes using those powers.

(5)   Whether or not an order has been or may be made under subsection (3) above, the Secretary of State may, if he considers it appropriate for the purpose of remedying or preventing what he considers are the adverse effects of the course of conduct specified in the report of the Commission as operating against the public interest, [make an order under this subsection].

[(5A)   An order under subsection (5) above may contain anything permitted by Schedule 8 to the Enterprise Act 2002, except paragraphs 8, 13 and 14 of that Schedule.

(5B)   An order under subsection (5) above shall come into force at such time as is determined by or under the order.]

[(6)   The following provisions of Part 3 of the Enterprise Act 2002 shall apply in relation to orders under subsection (5) above as they apply in relation to orders under paragraph 11 of Schedule 7 to that Act—

    (a)   section 86(2) and (3) (enforcement orders: general provisions);

    (b)   section 87 (delegated power of directions);

    (c)   section 88 (contents of certain enforcement orders);

    (d)   section 94(1) to (5), (8) and (9) (rights to enforce orders); and

    (e)   Schedule 10 (procedural requirements for orders).

(7)   The Secretary of State shall publish any decision made by him to dispense with the requirements of Schedule 10 to the Enterprise Act 2002 as applied by subsection (6) above; and shall do so in such manner as he considers most suitable for bringing the decision to the attention of persons who in his opinion would be affected by it or be likely to have an interest in it.]

[1024A]

NOTES

Sub-s (4): words in first pair of square brackets inserted by the Companies Act 1989, s 144(4), Sch 18, para 22; words in second pair of square brackets substituted by the Companies Consolidation (Consequential Provisions) Act 1985, s 30, Sch 2.

Sub-s (5): words in square brackets substituted by the Enterprise Act 2002, s 278(1), Sch 25, para 10(1), (4)(a), (10), as from 20 June 2003.

Sub-ss (5A), (5B): inserted by the Enterprise Act 2002, s 278(1), Sch 25, para 10(1), (4)(b), (10), as from 20 June 2003.

Sub-ss (6), (7): substituted, for original sub-s (6), by the Enterprise Act 2002, s 278(1), Sch 25, para 10(1), (4)(c), (10), as from 20 June 2003.

Ministers of the Crown, etc: see the note to s 11 at **[1023A]**.

Supplementary

33   Short title, interpretation, repeals, commencement and extent

(1)   This Act may be cited as the Competition Act 1980.

[(2)   Unless the context otherwise requires, in this Act "Minister" includes a government department and the following expressions shall have the same meanings as they have in Part 3 of the Enterprise Act 2002—

"business"

"the Commission"

"enactment"

"goods"

"services"

"supply (in relation to the supply of goods)"

"the supply of services".]

(3), (4)   ...

(5)   This Act shall come into operation on such day as the Secretary of State may by order appoint, and different days may be so appointed for different provisions and for different purposes.

(6), (7)   (*Outside the scope of this work.*)

(8)   This Act extends to Northern Ireland.

[1025]

NOTES
Sub-s (2): substituted by the Enterprise Act 2002, s 278(1), Sch 25, para 10(1), (9), (10), as from 20 June 2003.
Sub-ss (3), (4): repealed by the Competition Act 1998, s 74(1), (3), Sch 12, para 4(15)(b), Sch 14, Pt I, as from 1 March 2000.
Orders: the Competition Act 1980 (Commencement No 1) Order 1980, SI 1980/497; the Competition Act 1980 (Commencement No 2) Order 1980, SI 1980/978.

POLICE AND CRIMINAL EVIDENCE ACT 1984

(1984 c 60)

NOTES
Only provisions of this Act relevant to Financial Services law are reproduced. Provisions not reproduced are not annotated.
This Act is reproduced as amended by: the Access to Justice Act 1999; the Courts Act 2003; the Criminal Justice Act 2003; the Serious Organised Crime and Police Act 2005; the Serious Organised Crime and Police Act 2005 (Amendment) Order 2005, SI 2005/3496.

An Act to make further provision in relation to the powers and duties of the police, persons in police detention, criminal evidence, police discipline and complaints against the police; to provide for arrangements for obtaining the views of the community on policing and for a rank of deputy chief constable; to amend the law relating to the Police Federations and Police Forces and Police Cadets in Scotland; and for connected purposes

[31 October 1984]

PART II
POWERS OF ENTRY, SEARCH AND SEIZURE

NOTES
Powers of seizure: the powers of seizure conferred by this Part are powers to which the Criminal Justice and Police Act 2001, s 50 apply (additional powers of seizure from premises); see s 50 of, and Sch 1, Pt 1, para 1 to, that Act at [1307], [1309].
Modification in relation to money laundering investigations, etc: as to the application with modifications of, inter alia, ss 15, 16 of this Act to search and seizure warrants sought under the Proceeds of Crime Act 2002, s 352 for the purposes of a confiscation investigation or a money laundering investigation and powers of seizure under them, see the Proceeds of Crime Act 2002 (Application of Police and Criminal Evidence Act 1984 and Police and Criminal Evidence (Northern Ireland) Order 1989) Order 2003, SI 2003/174 at [3711] et seq.
Application to officers of Revenue and Customs: as to the application with modifications of, inter alia, ss 15, 16 of this Act to relevant investigations conducted by officers of Revenue and Customs and to persons detained by such officers, see the Police and Criminal Evidence Act 1984 (Application to Revenue and Customs) Order 2007, SI 2007/3175.

Search warrants

15   Search warrants—safeguards

(1)–(4)   (*Outside the scope of this work.*)

(5)   A warrant shall authorise an entry on one occasion only [unless it specifies that it authorises multiple entries].

[(5A)   If it specifies that it authorises multiple entries, it must also specify whether the number of entries authorised is unlimited, or limited to a specified maximum.]

(6)   A warrant—
  (a)   shall specify—
    (i)   the name of the person who applies for it;
    (ii)   the date on which it is issued;
    (iii)   the enactment under which it is issued; and
    (iv)   each set of premises to be searched, or (in the case of an all premises warrant) the

person who is in occupation or control of premises to be searched, together with
any premises under his occupation or control which can be specified and which
are to be searched; and]
   (b)   shall identify, so far as is practicable, the articles or persons to be sought.

[(7)   Two copies shall be made of a [warrant] which specifies only one set of premises and does
not authorise multiple entries; and as many copies as are reasonably required may be made of any
other kind of warrant.]

(8)   The copies shall be clearly certified as copies.

[1026]

NOTES
   Sub-s (5): words in square brackets added by the Serious Organised Crime and Police Act 2005, s 114(1), (5),
as from 1 January 2006.
   Sub-s (5A): inserted by the Serious Organised Crime and Police Act 2005, s 114(1), (6), as from 1 January
2006.
   Sub-s (6): para (a)(iv) substituted by the Serious Organised Crime and Police Act 2005, s 113(1), (8), as from
1 January 2006.
   Sub-s (7): substituted by the Serious Organised Crime and Police Act 2005, s 114(1), (7), as from 1 January
2006; word in square brackets substituted by the Serious Organised Crime and Police Act 2005 (Amendment)
Order 2005, SI 2005/3496, art 7(1), (3), as from 1 January 2006.

16 Execution of warrants
   (1)   A warrant to enter and search premises may be executed by any constable.
   (2)   Such a warrant may authorise persons to accompany any constable who is executing it.
   [(2A)   A person so authorised has the same powers as the constable whom he accompanies in
respect of—
   (a)   the execution of the warrant, and
   (b)   the seizure of anything to which the warrant relates.
   (2B)   But he may exercise those powers only in the company, and under the supervision, of a
constable.]
   (3)   Entry and search under a warrant must be within [three months] from the date of its issue.
   [(3A)   If the warrant is an all premises warrant, no premises which are not specified in it may be
entered or searched unless a police officer of at least the rank of inspector has in writing authorised
them to be entered.]
   [(3B)   No premises may be entered or searched for the second or any subsequent time under a
warrant which authorises multiple entries unless a police officer of at least the rank of inspector has
in writing authorised that entry to those premises.]
   (4)   Entry and search under a warrant must be at a reasonable hour unless it appears to the
constable executing it that the purpose of a search may be frustrated on an entry at a reasonable
hour.
   (5)   Where the occupier of premises which are to be entered and searched is present at the time
when a constable seeks to execute a warrant to enter and search them, the constable—
   (a)   shall identify himself to the occupier and, if not in uniform, shall produce to him
documentary evidence that he is a constable;
   (b)   shall produce the warrant to him; and
   (c)   shall supply him with a copy of it.
   (6)   Where—
   (a)   the occupier of such premises is not present at the time when a constable seeks to
execute such a warrant; but
   (b)   some other person who appears to the constable to be in charge of the premises is
present,
subsection (5) above shall have effect as if any reference to the occupier were a reference to that
other person.
   (7)   If there is no person present who appears to the constable to be in charge of the premises, he
shall leave a copy of the warrant in a prominent place on the premises.
   (8)   A search under a warrant may only be a search to the extent required for the purpose for
which the warrant was issued.
   (9)   A constable executing a warrant shall make an endorsement on it stating—
   (a)   whether the articles or persons sought were found; and
   (b)   whether any articles were seized, other than articles which were sought,
[and, unless the warrant is a ... warrant specifying one set of premises only, he shall do so separately
in respect of each set of premises entered and searched, which he shall in each case state in the
endorsement.]

[(10) A warrant shall be returned to the appropriate person mentioned in subsection (10A) below—
  (a) when it has been executed; or
  (b) in the case of a specific premises warrant which has not been executed, or an all premises warrant, or any warrant authorising multiple entries, upon the expiry of the period of three months referred to in subsection (3) above or sooner.
  (10A) The appropriate person is—
  (a) if the warrant was issued by a justice of the peace, the designated officer for the local justice area in which the justice was acting when he issued the warrant;
  (b) if it was issued by a judge, the appropriate officer of the court from which he issued it.]

(11) A warrant which is returned under subsection (10) above shall be retained for 12 months from its return—
  (a) by the [designated officer for the local justice area], if it was returned under paragraph (i) of that subsection; and
  (b) by the appropriate officer, if it was returned under paragraph (ii).

(12) If during the period for which a warrant is to be retained the occupier of [premises] to which it relates asks to inspect it, he shall be allowed to do so.

[1027]

NOTES
  Sub-ss (2A), (2B): inserted by the Criminal Justice Act 2003, s 2, as from 20 January 2004.
  Sub-ss (3), (12): words in square brackets substituted by the Serious Organised Crime and Police Act 2005, ss 113(1), (9)(c), 114(1), (8)(a), as from 1 January 2006.
  Sub-ss (3A), (3B): inserted by the Serious Organised Crime and Police Act 2005, ss 113(1), (9)(a), 114(1), (8)(b), as from 1 January 2006.
  Sub-s (9): words in square brackets inserted by the Serious Organised Crime and Police Act 2005, s 113(1), (9)(b), as from 1 January 2006; words omitted repealed by the Serious Organised Crime and Police Act 2005 (Amendment) Order 2005, SI 2005/3496, art 8, as from 1 January 2006.
  Sub-ss (10), (10A): substituted, for original sub-s (10), by the Serious Organised Crime and Police Act 2005, s 114(1), (8)(c), as from 1 January 2006.
  Sub-s (11): words in square brackets substituted by the Courts Act 2003, s 109(1), Sch 8, para 281, as from 1 April 2005.
  Staff of SOCA: this section is modified in relation to a member of the staff of the Serious Organised Crime Agency designated as having the powers of a constable under the Serious Organised Crime and Police Act 2005, s 43(1)(a), by the Serious Organised Crime and Police Act 2005 (Application and Modification of Certain Enactments to Designated Staff of SOCA) Order 2006, SI 2006/987, art 3, Sch 1, para 4, as follows—
  4.—(1) In section 16(3A) and (3B) (execution of warrants) for the words "police officer of at least the rank of inspector" there is substituted "designated person of at least grade 3".
  (2) In section 16(5)(a) for the words ", if not in uniform, shall produce to him documentary evidence that he is a constable" there is substituted "shall produce to him documentary evidence that he is a designated person".

PART XI
MISCELLANEOUS AND SUPPLEMENTARY

120 Extent

(1) Subject to the following provisions of this section, this Act extends to England and Wales only.

(2)–(11) *(Outside the scope of this work.)*

[1028]

121 Commencement

(1) This Act, except section 120 above, this section and section 122 below, shall come into operation on such day as the Secretary of State may by order made by statutory instrument appoint, and different days may be so appointed for different provisions and for different purposes.

(2), (3) *(Outside the scope of this work.)*

(4) An order under this section may make such transitional provision as appears to the Secretary of State to be necessary or expedient in connection with the provisions thereby brought into operation.

[1029]

NOTES
  Orders: various Orders have been made under this section bringing provisions of this Act into force on various dates.

122   Short title

This Act may be cited as the Police and Criminal Evidence Act 1984.

COMPANIES ACT 1985 (NOTE)

(1985 c 6)

NOTES

Of the provisions reproduced in the ninth edition of the Financial Services Law Handbook, only s 1 (Mode of forming incorporated company) and ss 746, 747 are still in force (as to which, see below). The other provisions have been repealed as follows:

- Section 183 (Transfer and registration) was repealed by the Companies Act 2006, s 1295, Sch 16, as from 6 April 2008.
- Sections 221–262A and Sch 10A (Part VII: Accounts and Audit) were repealed by the Companies Act 2006, s 1295, Sch 16, as from 6 April 2008, subject to savings in relation to accounts and reports for financial years beginning before that date and in relation to their application to LLPs (for details see the Companies Act 2006 (Commencement No 5, Transitional Provisions and Savings) Order 2007, SI 2007/3495, art 12, Sch 4, Pt 1, paras 6–9, 12(1), (2)).
- Sections 378 (Extraordinary and special resolutions) and 381A (Written resolutions of private companies) were repealed by the Companies Act 2006, s 1295, Sch 16, as from 1 October 2007, subject to a variety of savings in relation to resolutions given or circulated (etc) before that date (for details see the Companies Act 2006 (Commencement No 3, Consequential Amendments, Transitional Provisions and Savings) Order 2007, SI 2007/2194, Sch 3, paras 22–40).
- Sections 425–427A (Part XIII: Arrangements and Reconstructions) were repealed by the Companies Act 2006, s 1295, Sch 16, as from 6 April 2008, subject to certain savings in relation to orders of the court made before that date (for details see SI 2007/3495, Sch 4, Pt 1, para 36).
- Sections 428–430F (Part XIIIA: Takeover Offers) were repealed by the Companies Act 2006, s 1295, Sch 16, as from 6 April 2007, subject to savings in relation to a takeover offer where the date of the offer was before that date (for details and further provision, see the Companies Act 2006 (Commencement No 2, Consequential Amendments, Transitional Provisions and Savings) Order 2007, SI 2007/1093, Sch 6, para 1 and the Takeovers Directive (Interim Implementation) Regulations 2006, SI 2006/1183).
- Sections 742A (Meaning of "offer to the public"), 742B (Meaning of "banking company"), and 742C (Meaning of "insurance company" and "authorised insurance company") were repealed by the Companies Act 2006, s 1295, Sch 16, as from 6 April 2008.

Sections 746 (Commencement) and 747 (Citation) are not reproduced. Section 1 (as amended by the Companies (Single Member Private Limited Companies) Regulations 1992, SI 1992/1699, reg 2(1)(b), Schedule, para 1) provides as follows—

"1   Mode of forming incorporated company

(1)   Any two or more persons associated for a lawful purpose may, by subscribing their names to a memorandum of association and otherwise complying with the requirements of this Act in respect of registration, form an incorporated company, with or without limited liability.

(2)   A company so formed may be either—
  (a)   a company having the liability of its members limited by the memorandum to the amount, if any, unpaid on the shares respectively held by them ("a company limited by shares");
  (b)   a company having the liability of its members limited by the memorandum to such amount as the members may respectively thereby undertake to contribute to the assets of the company in the event of its being wound up ("a company limited by guarantee"); or
  (c)   a company not having any limit on the liability of its members ("an unlimited company").

(3)   A "public company" is a company limited by shares or limited by guarantee and having a share capital, being a company—
  (a)   the memorandum of which states that it is to be a public company, and
  (b)   in relation to which the provisions of this Act or the former Companies Acts as to the registration or re-registration of a company as a public company have been complied with on or after 22nd December 1980;

and a "private company" is a company that is not a public company.

[(3A)   Notwithstanding subsection (1), one person may, for a lawful purpose, by subscribing his name to a memorandum of association and otherwise complying with the requirements of this Act in respect of registration, form an incorporated company being a private company limited by shares or by guarantee.]

(4)   With effect from 22nd December 1980, a company cannot be formed as, or become, a company limited by guarantee with a share capital.".

Section 1 will be repealed as from 1 October 2009 – see the Companies Act 2006 (Commencement No 8, Transitional Provisions and Savings) Order 2008, SI 2008/2860. For transitional provisions and savings in relation to the commencement of ss 7–16 of the 2006 Act (company formation) and the repeal of s 1, see Sch 2, para 2 to that Order.

The Companies Act 2006 is at **[1504]** et seq.

INSOLVENCY ACT 1986

(1986 c 45)

NOTES

Only provisions of this Act relevant to Financial Services law are reproduced. Provisions not reproduced are not annotated.

This Act is reproduced as amended by: the Criminal Justice Act 1988; the Companies Act 1989; the Insolvency Act 2000; the Enterprise Act 2002; the Courts Act 2003; the Companies (Audit, Investigations and Community Enterprise) Act 2004; the Constitutional Reform Act 2005; the Tribunals, Courts and Enforcement Act 2007; the Banking Act 2009; the Financial Services and Markets Act 2000 (Consequential Amendments and Repeals) Order 2001, SI 2001/3649; the Insolvency Act 1986 (Amendment) Regulations 2002, SI 2002/1037; the Insolvency Act 1986 (Amendment) (No 2) Regulations 2002, SI 2002/1240; the Financial Services and Markets Act 2000 (Consequential Amendments) Order 2002, SI 2002/1555; the Insolvency Act 1986 (Amendment) (No 3) Regulations 2002, SI 2002/1990; the Enterprise Act 2002 (Insolvency) Order 2003, SI 2003/2096; the Enterprise Act 2002 (Insolvency) Order 2004, SI 2004/2312; the European Public Limited-Liability Company Regulations 2004, SI 2004/2326; the Insolvency Act 1986 (Amendment) Regulations 2005, SI 2005/879; the Companies Act 2006 (Commencement No 3, Consequential Amendments, Transitional Provisions and Savings) Order 2007, SI 2007/2194; the Companies (Cross-Border Mergers) Regulations 2007, SI 2007/2974; the Companies Act 2006 (Consequential Amendments etc) Order 2008, SI 2008/948; the Companies (Trading Disclosures) (Insolvency) Regulations 2008, SI 2008/1897.

ARRANGEMENT OF SECTIONS

THE FIRST GROUP OF PARTS
COMPANY INSOLVENCY; COMPANIES WINDING UP

PART II
ADMINISTRATION

PART III
RECEIVERSHIP

CHAPTER VI
WINDING UP BY THE COURT

Grounds and effect of winding-up petition

THE SECOND GROUP OF PARTS
INSOLVENCY OF INDIVIDUALS; BANKRUPTCY

PART IX
BANKRUPTCY

CHAPTER I
BANKRUPTCY PETITIONS; BANKRUPTCY ORDERS

Preliminary

THE THIRD GROUP OF PARTS
MISCELLANEOUS MATTERS BEARING ON BOTH COMPANY AND INDIVIDUAL INSOLVENCY; GENERAL INTERPRETATION; FINAL PROVISIONS

PART XV
SUBORDINATE LEGISLATION

General insolvency rules

PART XIX
FINAL PROVISIONS

SCHEDULES:

An Act to consolidate the enactments relating to company insolvency and winding up (including the winding up of companies that are not insolvent, and of unregistered companies); enactments relating to the insolvency and bankruptcy of individuals; and other enactments bearing on those two subject matters, including the functions and qualification of insolvency practitioners, the public administration of insolvency, the penalisation and redress of malpractice and wrongdoing, and the avoidance of certain transactions at an undervalue

[25 July 1986]

NOTES
Commencement:
This Act came into force on 29 December 1986 by virtue of s 443 and the Insolvency Act 1985 (Commencement No 5) Order 1986, SI 1986/1924.
Application of this Act:
This Act is applied, with certain modifications, to various types of business and financial sectors, etc, as follows:
Banks: as to the application of certain provisions of this Act to particular banks, see the Banking (Special Provisions) Act 2008 (at **[1758]**) and the Orders made under it. As to the application of this Act to banks generally, see the Banking Act 2009 (at **[1822]**) and see, in particular Part 2 of that Act (bank insolvency) and Part 3 (bank administration).
Former authorised institutions: see the Banks (Former Authorised Institutions) (Insolvency) Order 2006, SI 2006/3107 as to the application of this Act to any company within the meaning of s 735(1) of the Companies Act 1985 that (a) has a liability in respect of a deposit which it accepted in accordance with the Banking Act 1979 or Banking Act 1987, but (b) does not have permission under Part IV of the Financial Services and Markets Act 2000 to accept deposits.
British insolvency law (as defined in Article 2 of the UNCITRAL Model Law as set out in Schedule 1 to the Cross-Border Insolvency Regulations 2006, SI 2006/1030) and Part III of the Insolvency Act 1986 shall apply with such modifications as the context requires for the purpose of giving effect to the provisions of the 2006 Regulations; see reg 2 of the 2006 Regulations.
Agricultural marketing boards: see the Agricultural Marketing Act 1958, s 3(3), Sch 2, para 4.
Industrial and provident societies: see the Industrial and Provident Societies Act 1965, s 55 (see also the note 'Non companies' below).
Building societies: see the Building Societies Act 1986, ss 90, 90A, 90B, Schs 15, 15A.
Recognised investment exchanges and clearing houses, etc: see the Companies Act 1989, s 182 at **[1178]**.
European Economic Interest Groupings: see the European Economic Interest Grouping Regulations 1989, SI 1989/638.
Friendly societies: see the Friendly Societies Act 1992, s 23, Sch 10 (see also the note 'Non companies' below).
Insolvent partnerships: see the Insolvent Partnerships Order 1994, SI 1994/2421.
Limited liability partnerships: see the Limited Liability Partnerships (Scotland) Regulations 2001, SSI 2001/128, and the Limited Liability Partnerships Regulations 2001, SI 2001/1090 at **[3554]**.
Open-ended investment companies: see the Open-Ended Investment Companies Regulations 2001, SI 2001/1228, reg 31 at **[2268]**.
Companies incorporated outside Great Britain: see the Enterprise Act 2002, s 254.
Energy licensees: see the Energy Act 2004, ss 154–171, Schs 20, 21, and the Energy Administration Rules 2005, SI 2005/2483.
Insurers: see the Insurers (Reorganisation and Winding Up) Regulations 2004, SI 2004/353 at **[3836]**.
EEA credit institutions: see the Credit Institutions (Reorganisation and Winding up) Regulations 2004, SI 2004/1045.
Societas Europaea: see the European Public Limited-Liability Company Regulations 2004, SI 2004/2326.
European Grouping of Territorial Cooperation: see the European Grouping of Territorial Cooperation Regulations 2007, SI 2007/1949.
Non-companies: the Enterprise Act 2002, s 255 provides that the Treasury may with the concurrence of the Secretary of State by order provide for a company arrangement or administration provision to apply (ie, Pts I, II) in relation to (a) a society registered under the Industrial and Provident Societies Act 1965; (b) a society registered under the Friendly Societies Act 1974, s 7(1)(b), (c), (d), (e) or (f); (c) a friendly society within the meaning of the Friendly Societies Act 1992; (d) an unregistered friendly society.
Miscellaneous:
Modification: the provisions of this Act, except s 413 and Sch 7, are applied, with modifications, in relation to a "recognised body" under the Administration of Justice Act 1985, s 9, by the Solicitors' Incorporated Practices Order 1991, SI 1991/2684, arts 2–5, Sch 1, as amended by SI 2001/645.
Registrar of companies: as to the contracting out of certain functions of the registrar of companies in relation to Scotland conferred by or under this Act, see the Contracting Out (Functions in relation to the Registration of Companies) Order 1995, SI 1995/1013, art 4, Sch 2.
Official Receiver: as to the contracting out of functions of the Official Receiver conferred by or under this Act, see the Contracting Out (Functions of the Official Receiver) Order 1995, SI 1995/1386.
Proceeds of crime: if an order for the winding up of a company is made or it passes a resolution for its voluntary winding up, the functions of the liquidator (or any provisional liquidator) are not exercisable in relation to property deemed to be the proceeds of crime; see, generally, the Proceeds of Crime Act 2002, Pt 9 (ss 417–434).

See the Serious Crime Act 2007, ss 27, 29 in relation to the power of the Director of Public Prosecutions, the Director of Revenue and Customs Prosecutions and the Director of the Serious Fraud Office to present a petition to the court for the winding up of a company, partnership (etc) where the company, partnership (etc) has been convicted of an offence under s 25 of that Act (offence of failing to comply with serious crime prevention order) and the Director concerned considers that it would be in the public interest for the company, partnership (etc) to be wound up.

Companies Act: references in this Act to the Companies Act are to the Companies Act 1985.

THE FIRST GROUP OF PARTS
COMPANY INSOLVENCY; COMPANIES WINDING UP

[PART II
ADMINISTRATION

8 Administration

Schedule B1 to this Act (which makes provision about the administration of companies) shall have effect.]

[1131]

NOTES
The original Pt II of this Act (ss 8–27) was substituted by a new Pt II (s 8 only) by the Enterprise Act 2002, s 248(1), as from 15 September 2003, subject to savings and transitional provisions as set out below.
Transitional provisions:
See the Enterprise Act 2002 (Commencement No 4 and Transitional Provisions and Savings) Order 2003, SI 2003/2093, art 3 for transitional provisions in relation to petitions for an administration order presented before 15 September 2003.
See also, the Enterprise Act 2002, Sch 17, para 1 which provides that in any instrument made before s 248(1)–(3) of the 2002 Act comes into force: (a) a reference to the making of an administration order shall be treated as including a reference to the appointment of an administrator under Sch B1, para 14 or 22 to this Act (as inserted by s 248(2) of the 2002 Act), and (b) a reference to making an application for an administration order by petition shall be treated as including a reference to making an administration application under that Schedule, appointing an administrator under para 14 or 22 of that Schedule or giving notice under para 15 or 26 of that Schedule.
Savings in relation to special administration regimes:
The substitution of this Part by s 248(1) of the Enterprise Act 2002 has no effect in relation to special administration regimes within the meaning of s 249 of that Act; see s 249(1), (2) (as amended by the Water Act 2003) which provides as follows—

"249 Special administration regimes
(1) Section 248 shall have no effect in relation to—
    (a) a company holding an appointment under Chapter I of Part II of the Water Industry Act 1991 (c 56) (water and sewerage undertakers),
    [(aa) a qualifying licensed water supplier within the meaning of subsection (6) of section 23 of the Water Industry Act 1991 (meaning and effect of special administration order),]
    (b) a protected railway company within the meaning of section 59 of the Railways Act 1993 (c 43) (railway administration order) (including that section as it has effect by virtue of section 19 of the Channel Tunnel Rail Link Act 1996 (c 61) (administration)),
    (c) a licence company within the meaning of section 26 of the Transport Act 2000 (c 38) (air traffic services),
    (d) a public-private partnership company within the meaning of section 210 of the Greater London Authority Act 1999 (c 29) (public-private partnership agreement), or
    (e) a building society within the meaning of section 119 of the Building Societies Act 1986 (c 53) (interpretation).
(2) A reference in an Act listed in subsection (1) to a provision of Part II of the Insolvency Act 1986 (or to a provision which has effect in relation to a provision of that Part of that Act) shall, in so far as it relates to a company or society listed in subsection (1), continue to have effect as if it referred to Part II as it had effect immediately before the coming into force of section 248.".

See also the Companies Act 2006 (Consequential Amendments etc) Order 2008, SI 2008/948, art 3(1), Sch 1, Pt 2, para 101, which (as from 6 April 2008) provides as follows—
    "101.—(1) Part 2 of the Insolvency Act 1986 (administration) as it has effect by virtue of—
    (a) section 249(1) of the Enterprise Act 2002 (special administration regimes), or
    (b) article 3(2) or (3) of the Enterprise Act 2002 (Commencement No 4 and Transitional Provisions and Savings) Order 2003 (other purposes),
(that is, without the amendments made by the Enterprise Act 2002) is amended as follows.
    (2) In section 8(3), for paragraph (c) substitute—
        "(c) the sanctioning under Part 26 of the Companies Act 2006 of a compromise or arrangement between the company and its creditors or members; and".
    (3) In section 27(3)(a) for "section 425 of the Companies Act" substitute "Part 26 of the Companies Act 2006".".

As to special administration regimes, see also the Energy Act 2004, Pt 3, Chapter 3 (in particular, s 159 of, and Sch 20 to, that Act).

PART IV
WINDING UP OF COMPANIES REGISTERED UNDER THE COMPANIES ACTS

CHAPTER VI
WINDING UP BY THE COURT

Grounds and effect of winding-up petition

[124A   Petition for winding up on grounds of public interest

(1)   Where it appears to the Secretary of State from—

   (a)   any report made or information obtained under Part XIV [(except section 448A)] of the Companies Act 1985 (company investigations, &c.),

   [(b)   any report made by inspectors under—

      (i)   section 167, 168, 169 or 284 of the Financial Services and Markets Act 2000, or

      (ii)   where the company is an open-ended investment company (within the meaning of that Act), regulations made as a result of section 262(2)(k) of that Act;

   (bb)   any information or documents obtained under section 165, 171, 172, 173 or 175 of that Act,]

   (c)   any information obtained under section 2 of the Criminal Justice Act 1987 or section 52 of the Criminal Justice (Scotland) Act 1987 (fraud investigations), or

   (d)   any information obtained under section 83 of the Companies Act 1989 (powers exercisable for purpose of assisting overseas regulatory authorities),

that it is expedient in the public interest that a company should be wound up, he may present a petition for it to be wound up if the court thinks it just and equitable for it to be so.

(2)   This section does not apply if the company is already being wound up by the court.]

[1132]–[1133]

NOTES

Inserted by the Companies Act 1989, s 60(3), as from 21 February 1990.

Sub-s (1): words in square brackets in para (a) inserted by the Companies (Audit, Investigations and Community Enterprise) Act 2004, s 25, Sch 2, Pt 3, para 27, as from 6 April 2005 (for transitional provisions see the Companies (Audit, Investigations and Community Enterprise) Act 2004 (Commencement) and Companies Act 1989 (Commencement No 18) Order 2004, SI 2004/3322, art 13); paras (b), (bb) substituted, for original para (b), by the Financial Services and Markets Act 2000 (Consequential Amendments and Repeals) Order 2001, SI 2001/3649, art 305, as from 1 December 2001.

THE SECOND GROUP OF PARTS
INSOLVENCY OF INDIVIDUALS; BANKRUPTCY

PART IX
BANKRUPTCY

CHAPTER I
BANKRUPTCY PETITIONS; BANKRUPTCY ORDERS

Preliminary

264   Who may present a bankruptcy petition

(1)   A petition for a bankruptcy order to be made against an individual may be presented to the court in accordance with the following provisions of this Part—

   (a)   by one of the individual's creditors or jointly by more than one of them,

   (b)   by the individual himself,

   [(ba)   by a temporary administrator (within the meaning of Article 38 of the EC Regulation),

   (bb)   by a liquidator (within the meaning of Article 2(b) of the EC Regulation) appointed in proceedings by virtue of Article 3(1) of the EC Regulation,]

   (c)   by the supervisor of, or any person (other than the individual) who is for the time being bound by, a voluntary arrangement proposed by the individual and approved under Part VIII, *or*

   (d)   *where a criminal bankruptcy order has been made against the individual, by the Official Petitioner or by any person specified in the order in pursuance of section 39(3)(b) of the Powers of Criminal Courts Act 1973.*

(2)   Subject to those provisions, the court may make a bankruptcy order on any such petition.

[1134]

NOTES

Sub-s (1): paras (ba), (bb) inserted by the Insolvency Act 1986 (Amendment) (No 2) Regulations 2002, SI 2002/1240, regs 3, 13, as from 31 May 2002; para (d) and word immediately preceding it repealed by the Criminal Justice Act 1988, s 170(2), Sch 16, as from a day to be appointed.

THE THIRD GROUP OF PARTS
MISCELLANEOUS MATTERS BEARING ON BOTH COMPANY AND INDIVIDUAL
INSOLVENCY; GENERAL INTERPRETATION; FINAL PROVISIONS

PART XV
SUBORDINATE LEGISLATION

General insolvency rules

411 Company insolvency rules

(1) Rules may be made—
- (a) in relation to England and Wales, by the Lord Chancellor with the concurrence of the Secretary of State [and, in the case of rules that affect court procedure, with the concurrence of the Lord Chief Justice], or
- (b) in relation to Scotland, by the Secretary of State,

for the purpose of giving effect to Parts I to VII of this Act [or the EC Regulation].

[(1A) Rules may also be made for the purpose of giving effect to Part 2 of the Banking Act 2009 (bank insolvency orders); and rules for that purpose shall be made—
- (a) in relation to England and Wales, by the Lord Chancellor with the concurrence of—
  - (i) the Treasury, and
  - (ii) in the case of rules that affect court procedure, the Lord Chief Justice, or
- (b) in relation to Scotland, by the Treasury.]

[(1B) Rules may also be made for the purpose of giving effect to Part 3 of the Banking Act 2009 (bank administration); and rules for that purpose shall be made—
- (a) in relation to England and Wales, by the Lord Chancellor with the concurrence of—
  - (i) the Treasury, and
  - (ii) in the case of rules that affect court procedure, the Lord Chief Justice, or
- (b) in relation to Scotland, by the Treasury.]

(2) Without prejudice to the generality of subsection (1), [(1A)] [or (1B)] or to any provision of those Parts by virtue of which rules under this section may be made with respect to any matter, rules under this section may contain—
- (a) any such provision as is specified in Schedule 8 to this Act or corresponds to provision contained immediately before the coming into force of section 106 of the Insolvency Act 1985 in rules made, or having effect as if made, under section 663(1) or (2) of the Companies Act (old winding-up rules), and
- (b) such incidental, supplemental and transitional provisions as may appear to the Lord Chancellor or, as the case may be, the Secretary of State [or the Treasury] necessary or expedient.

[(2A) For the purposes of subsection (2), a reference in Schedule 8 to this Act to doing anything under or for the purposes of a provision of this Act includes a reference to doing anything under or for the purposes of the EC Regulation (in so far as the provision of this Act relates to a matter to which the EC Regulation applies).

(2B) Rules under this section for the purpose of giving effect to the EC Regulation may not create an offence of a kind referred to in paragraph 1(1)(d) of Schedule 2 to the European Communities Act 1972.]

[(2C) For the purposes of subsection (2), a reference in Schedule 8 to this Act to doing anything under or for the purposes of a provision of this Act includes a reference to doing anything under or for the purposes of Part 2 of the Banking Act 2009.]

[(2D) For the purposes of subsection (2), a reference in Schedule 8 to this Act to doing anything under or for the purposes of a provision of this Act includes a reference to doing anything under or for the purposes of Part 3 of the Banking Act 2009.]

(3) In Schedule 8 to this Act "liquidator" includes a provisional liquidator [or bank liquidator] [or administrator]; and references above in this section to Parts I to VII of this Act [or Part 2 [or 3] of the Banking Act 2009] are to be read as including [the Companies Acts] so far as relating to, and to matters connected with or arising out of, the insolvency or winding up of companies.

(4) Rules under this section shall be made by statutory instrument subject to annulment in pursuance of a resolution of either House of Parliament.

(5) Regulations made by the Secretary of State [or the Treasury] under a power conferred by rules under this section shall be made by statutory instrument and, after being made, shall be laid before each House of Parliament.

(6) Nothing in this section prejudices any power to make rules of court.

[(7) The Lord Chief Justice may nominate a judicial office holder (as defined in section 109(4) of the Constitutional Reform Act 2005) to exercise his functions under this section.]

[1135]

NOTES

Sub-s (1): words in square brackets in para (a) inserted by the Constitutional Reform Act 2005, s 15, Sch 4, Pt 1, paras 185, 188(1), (2), as from 3 April 2006; words in second pair of square brackets inserted by the Insolvency Act 1986 (Amendment) Regulations 2002, SI 2002/1037, regs 2, 3(1), as from 3 May 2002.

Sub-ss (1A), (1B), (2C), (2D): inserted by the Banking Act 2009, ss 125(1), (2), (4), 160(1), (2), (4), as from a day to be appointed.

Sub-ss (2), (5): words in square brackets inserted by the Banking Act 2009, ss 125(1), (3), (6), 160(1), (3), as from a day to be appointed.

Sub-ss (2A), (2B): inserted by SI 2002/1037, regs 2, 3(2), as from 3 May 2002.

Sub-s (3): words in the final pair of square brackets substituted by the Companies Act 2006 (Commencement No 3, Consequential Amendments, Transitional Provisions and Savings) Order 2007, SI 2007/2194, art 10(1), Sch 4, Pt 3, para 44, as from 1 October 2007; all other words in square brackets inserted by the Banking Act 2009, ss 125(1), (5). 160(1), (5), as from a day to be appointed.

Sub-s (7): added by the Constitutional Reform Act 2005, s 15, Sch 4, Pt 1, paras 185, 188(1), (3), as from 3 April 2006.

Rules: the Insolvency (Scotland) Rules 1986, SI 1986/1915; the Insurance Companies (Winding-up) (Scotland) Rules 1986, SI 1986/1918; the Insolvency Rules 1986, SI 1986/1925; the Companies (Unfair Prejudice Applications) Proceedings Rules 1986, SI 1986/2000; the Insolvent Companies (Disqualification of Unfit Directors) Proceedings Rules 1987, SI 1987/2023; the Insolvent Companies (Reports on Conduct of Directors) Rules 1996, SI 1996/1909; the Insolvent Companies (Reports on Conduct of Directors) (Scotland) Rules 1996, SI 1996/1910; the Railway Administration Order Rules 2001, SI 2001/3352, the Insurers (Winding up) Rules 2001, SI 2001/3635; the Insurers (Winding Up) (Scotland) Rules 2001, SI 2001/4040; the Energy Administration Rules 2005, SI 2005/2483; the Energy Administration (Scotland) Rules 2006, SI 2006/772; the PPP Administration Order Rules 2007, SI 2007/3141.

Regulations: the Insolvency Regulations 1994, SI 1994/2507.

See also the Banking Act 2009, ss 125(8), 160(6) which provide that s 313(2) of this Act (duty to consult Insolvency Rules Committee) shall not apply to the first set of rules made in reliance on ss 125, 160 (which amend this section as noted above).

412 Individual insolvency rules (England and Wales)

(1)   The Lord Chancellor may, with the concurrence of the Secretary of State [and, in the case of rules that affect court procedure, with the concurrence of the Lord Chief Justice], make rules for the purpose of giving effect to *Parts VIII to XI* of this Act [or the EC Regulation].

(2)   Without prejudice to the generality of subsection (1), or to any provision of those Parts by virtue of which rules under this section may be made with respect to any matter, rules under this section may contain—

(a)   any such provision as is specified in Schedule 9 to this Act or corresponds to provision contained immediately before the appointed day in rules made under section 132 of the Bankruptcy Act 1914; and

(b)   such incidental, supplemental and transitional provisions as may appear to the Lord Chancellor necessary or expedient.

[(2A)   For the purposes of subsection (2), a reference in Schedule 9 to this Act to doing anything under or for the purposes of a provision of this Act includes a reference to doing anything under or for the purposes of the EC Regulation (in so far as the provision of this Act relates to a matter to which the EC Regulation applies).

(2B)   Rules under this section for the purpose of giving effect to the EC Regulation may not create an offence of a kind referred to in paragraph 1(1)(d) of Schedule 2 to the European Communities Act 1972.]

(3)   Rules under this section shall be made by statutory instrument subject to annulment in pursuance of a resolution of either House of Parliament.

(4)   Regulations made by the Secretary of State under a power conferred by rules under this section shall be made by statutory instrument and, after being made, shall be laid before each House of Parliament.

(5)   Nothing in this section prejudices any power to make rules of court.

[(6)   The Lord Chief Justice may nominate a judicial office holder (as defined in section 109(4) of the Constitutional Reform Act 2005) to exercise his functions under this section.]

[1136]

NOTES

Sub-s (1): words in first pair of square brackets inserted by the Constitutional Reform Act 2005, s 15, Sch 4, Pt 1, paras 185, 189(1), (2), as from 3 April 2006 (note that para 189(2) does not specify that this amendment is to subsection (1) but that is believed to be the case); for the words in italics there are substituted the words "Parts 7A to 11" by the Tribunals, Courts and Enforcement Act 2007, s 108(3), Sch 20, Pt 1, para 8, as from a day to be appointed; words in second pair of square brackets inserted by the Insolvency Act 1986 (Amendment) Regulations 2002, SI 2002/1037, regs 2, 3(3), as from 3 May 2002.

Sub-ss (2A), (2B): inserted by SI 2002/1037, regs 2, 3(4), as from 3 May 2002.

Sub-s (6): added by the Constitutional Reform Act 2005, s 15, Sch 4, Pt 1, paras 185, 189(1), (3), as from 3 April 2006.

Rules: the Insolvency Rules 1986, SI 1986/1925; the Bankruptcy (Financial Services and Markets Act 2000) Rules 2001, SI 2001/3634.
Regulations: the Insolvency Regulations 1994, SI 1994/2507.

PART XIX
FINAL PROVISIONS

443 Commencement

This Act comes into force on the day appointed under section 236(2) of the Insolvency Act 1985 for the coming into force of Part III of that Act (individual insolvency and bankruptcy), immediately after that Part of that Act comes into force for England and Wales.

[1137]

NOTES
The Insolvency Act 1985, Pt III came into force on 29 December 1986: see SI 1986/1924, art 3.

444 Citation

This Act may be cited as the Insolvency Act 1986.

[1138]

SCHEDULES

[SCHEDULE A1
MORATORIUM WHERE DIRECTORS PROPOSE VOLUNTARY ARRANGEMENT

PART I
INTRODUCTORY

Interpretation

1. In this Schedule—
"the beginning of the moratorium" has the meaning given by paragraph 8(1),
"the date of filing" means the date on which the documents for the time being referred to in paragraph 7(1) are filed or lodged with the court,
"hire-purchase agreement" includes a conditional sale agreement, a chattel leasing agreement and a retention of title agreement,
"market contract" and "market charge" have the meanings given by Part VII of the Companies Act 1989,

.....

"moratorium" means a moratorium under section 1A,
"the nominee" includes any person for the time being carrying out the functions of a nominee under this Schedule,

.....

"the settlement finality regulations" means the Financial Markets and Insolvency (Settlement Finality) Regulations 1999,
"system-charge" has the meaning given by the Financial Markets and Insolvency Regulations 1996.

Eligible companies

2.—(1) A company is eligible for a moratorium if it meets the requirements of paragraph 3, unless—
(a) it is excluded from being eligible by virtue of paragraph 4, or
(b) it falls within sub-paragraph (2).

(2) A company falls within this sub-paragraph if—
[(a) it effects or carries out contracts of insurance, but is not exempt from the general prohibition, within the meaning of section 19 of the Financial Services and Markets Act 2000, in relation to that activity,
(b) it has permission under Part IV of that Act to accept deposits,
(bb) it has a liability in respect of a deposit which it accepted in accordance with the Banking Act 1979 (c 37) or 1987 (c 22),]
(c) it is a party to a market contract ... or any of its property is subject to a market charge ... or a system-charge, or
(d) it is a participant (within the meaning of the settlement finality regulations) or any of its property is subject to a collateral security charge (within the meaning of those regulations).

[(3) Paragraphs (a), (b) and (bb) of sub-paragraph (2) must be read with—
(a) section 22 of the Financial Services and Markets Act 2000;

(b)   any relevant order under that section; and
(c)   Schedule 2 to that Act.]

3.—(1)   A company meets the requirements of this paragraph if the qualifying conditions are met—
   (a)   in the year ending with the date of filing, or
   (b)   in the financial year of the company which ended last before that date.

(2)   For the purposes of sub-paragraph (1)—
   (a)   the qualifying conditions are met by a company in a period if, in that period, it satisfies two or more of the requirements for being a small company specified for the time being in [section 382(3) of the Companies Act 2006], and
   (b)   a company's financial year is to be determined in accordance with that Act.

(3)   [Section 382(4), (5) and (6)] of that Act apply for the purposes of this paragraph as they apply for the purposes of that section.

[(4)   A company does not meet the requirements of this paragraph if it is a [parent company] of a group of companies which does not qualify as a small group or a medium-sized group [in relation to] the financial year of the company which ended last before the date of filing.

[(5)   For the purposes of sub-paragraph (4)—
   (a)   "group" has the same meaning as in Part 15 of the Companies Act 2006 (see section 474(1) of that Act); and
   (b)   a group qualifies as small in relation to a financial year if it so qualifies under section 383(2) to (7) of that Act, and qualifies as medium-sized in relation to a financial year if it so qualifies under section 466(2) to (7) of that Act.]]

4.—(1)   A company is excluded from being eligible for a moratorium if, on the date of filing—
  [(a)   the company is in administration,]
  (b)   the company is being wound up,
  (c)   there is an administrative receiver of the company,
  (d)   a voluntary arrangement has effect in relation to the company,
  (e)   there is a provisional liquidator of the company,
  (f)   a moratorium has been in force for the company at any time during the period of 12 months ending with the date of filing and—
    (i)   no voluntary arrangement had effect at the time at which the moratorium came to an end, or
    (ii)   a voluntary arrangement which had effect at any time in that period has come to an end prematurely,
  [(fa)   an administrator appointed under paragraph 22 of Schedule B1 has held office in the period of 12 months ending with the date of filing,] or
  (g)   a voluntary arrangement in relation to the company which had effect in pursuance of a proposal under section 1(3) has come to an end prematurely and, during the period of 12 months ending with the date of filing, an order under section 5(3)(a) has been made.

(2)   Sub-paragraph (1)(b) does not apply to a company which, by reason of a winding-up order made after the date of filing, is treated as being wound up on that date.

[Capital market arrangement

4A.   A company is also excluded from being eligible for a moratorium if, on the date of filing, it is a party to an agreement which is or forms part of a capital market arrangement under which—
    (i)   a party has incurred, or when the agreement was entered into was expected to incur, a debt of at least £10 million under the arrangement, and
    (ii)   the arrangement involves the issue of a capital market investment.

Public private partnership

4B.   A company is also excluded from being eligible for a moratorium if, on the date of filing, it is a project company of a project which—
    (i)   is a public-private partnership project, and
    (ii)   includes step-in rights.

Liability under an arrangement

4C.—(1)   A company is also excluded from being eligible for a moratorium if, on the date of filing, it has incurred a liability under an agreement of £10 million or more.

(2)   Where the liability in sub-paragraph (1) is a contingent liability under or by virtue of a guarantee or an indemnity or security provided on behalf of another person, the amount of that liability is the full amount of the liability in relation to which the guarantee, indemnity or security is provided.

(3)   In this paragraph—
   (a)   the reference to "liability" includes a present or future liability whether, in either case, it is certain or contingent,

(b) the reference to "liability" includes a reference to a liability to be paid wholly or partly in foreign currency (in which case the sterling equivalent shall be calculated as at the time when the liability is incurred).

Interpretation of capital market arrangement

4D.—(1) For the purposes of paragraph 4A an arrangement is a capital market arrangement if—
    (a) it involves a grant of security to a person holding it as trustee for a person who holds a capital market investment issued by a party to the arrangement, or
    (b) at least one party guarantees the performance of obligations of another party, or
    (c) at least one party provides security in respect of the performance of obligations of another party, or
    (d) the arrangement involves an investment of a kind described in articles 83 to 85 of the Financial Services and Markets Act 2000 (Regulated Activities) Order 2001 (SI 2001/544) (options, futures and contracts for differences).

(2) For the purposes of sub-paragraph (1)—
    (a) a reference to holding as trustee includes a reference to holding as nominee or agent,
    (b) a reference to holding for a person who holds a capital market investment includes a reference to holding for a number of persons at least one of whom holds a capital market investment, and
    (c) a person holds a capital market investment if he has a legal or beneficial interest in it.

(3) In paragraph 4A, 4C, 4J and this paragraph—
"agreement" includes an agreement or undertaking effected by—
    (a) contract,
    (b) deed, or
    (c) any other instrument intended to have effect in accordance with the law of England and Wales, Scotland or another jurisdiction, and
"party" to an arrangement includes a party to an agreement which—
    (a) forms part of the arrangement,
    (b) provides for the raising of finance as part of the arrangement, or
    (c) is necessary for the purposes of implementing the arrangement.

Capital market investment

4E.—(1) For the purposes of paragraphs 4A and 4D, an investment is a capital market investment if—
    (a) it is within article 77 of the Financial Services and Markets Act 2000 (Regulated Activities) Order 2001 (SI 2001/544) (debt instruments) and
    (b) it is rated, listed or traded or designed to be rated, listed or traded.

(2) In sub-paragraph (1)—
"listed" means admitted to the official list within the meaning given by section 103(1) of the Financial Services and Markets Act 2000 (c 8) (interpretation),
"rated" means rated for the purposes of investment by an internationally recognised rating agency,
"traded" means admitted to trading on a market established under the rules of a recognised investment exchange or on a foreign market.

(3) In sub-paragraph (2)—
"foreign market" has the same meaning as "relevant market" in article 67(2) of the Financial Services and Markets Act 2000 (Financial Promotion) Order 2001 (SI 2001/1335) (foreign markets),
"recognised investment exchange" has the meaning given by section 285 of the Financial Services and Markets Act 2000 (recognised investment exchange).

4F.—(1) For the purposes of paragraphs 4A and 4D an investment is also a capital market investment if it consists of a bond or commercial paper issued to one or more of the following—
    (a) an investment professional within the meaning of article 19(5) of the Financial Services and Markets Act 2000 (Financial Promotion) Order 2001,
    (b) a person who is, when the agreement mentioned in paragraph 4A is entered into, a certified high net worth individual in relation to a communication within the meaning of article 48(2) of that order,
    (c) a person to whom article 49(2) of that order applies (high net worth company, &c.),
    (d) a person who is, when the agreement mentioned in paragraph 4A is entered into, a certified sophisticated investor in relation to a communication within the meaning of article 50(1) of that order, and
    (e) a person in a State other than the United Kingdom who under the law of that State is not prohibited from investing in bonds or commercial paper.

(2) For the purposes of sub-paragraph (1)—

(a)   in applying article 19(5) of the Financial Services and Markets Act 2000 (Financial Promotion) Order 2001 for the purposes of sub-paragraph (1)(a)—
    (i)   in article 19(5)(b), ignore the words after "exempt person",
    (ii)   in article 19(5)(c)(i), for the words from "the controlled activity" to the end substitute "a controlled activity", and
    (iii) in article 19(5)(e) ignore the words from "where the communication" to the end, and
(b)   in applying article 49(2) of that order for the purposes of sub-paragraph (1)(c), ignore article 49(2)(e).

(3)   In sub-paragraph (1)—
"bond" shall be construed in accordance with article 77 of the Financial Services and Markets Act 2000 (Regulated Activities) Order 2001 (SI 2001/544), and
"commercial paper" has the meaning given by article 9(3) of that order.

Debt

4G.   The debt of at least £10 million referred to in paragraph 4A—
(a)   may be incurred at any time during the life of the capital market arrangement, and
(b)   may be expressed wholly or partly in a foreign currency (in which case the sterling equivalent shall be calculated as at the time when the arrangement is entered into).

Interpretation of project company

4H.—(1)   For the purposes of paragraph 4B a company is a "project company" of a project if—
(a)   it holds property for the purpose of the project,
(b)   it has sole or principal responsibility under an agreement for carrying out all or part of the project,
(c)   it is one of a number of companies which together carry out the project,
(d)   it has the purpose of supplying finance to enable the project to be carried out, or
(e)   it is the holding company of a company within any of paragraphs (a) to (d).

(2)   But a company is not a "project company" of a project if—
(a)   it performs a function within sub-paragraph (1)(a) to (d) or is within sub-paragraph (1)(e), but
(b)   it also performs a function which is not—
    (i)   within sub-paragraph (1)(a) to (d),
    (ii)   related to a function within sub-paragraph (1)(a) to (d), or
    (iii) related to the project.

(3)   For the purposes of this paragraph a company carries out all or part of a project whether or not it acts wholly or partly through agents.

Public-private partnership project

4I.—(1)   In paragraph 4B "public-private partnership project" means a project—
(a)   the resources for which are provided partly by one or more public bodies and partly by one or more private persons, or
(b)   which is designed wholly or mainly for the purpose of assisting a public body to discharge a function.

(2)   In sub-paragraph (1) "resources" includes—
(a)   funds (including payment for the provision of services or facilities),
(b)   assets,
(c)   professional skill,
(d)   the grant of a concession or franchise, and
(e)   any other commercial resource.

(3)   In sub-paragraph (1) "public body" means—
(a)   a body which exercises public functions,
(b)   a body specified for the purposes of this paragraph by the Secretary of State, and
(c)   a body within a class specified for the purposes of this paragraph by the Secretary of State.

(4)   A specification under sub-paragraph (3) may be—
(a)   general, or
(b)   for the purpose of the application of paragraph 4B to a specified case.

Step-in rights

4J.—(1)   For the purposes of paragraph 4B a project has "step-in rights" if a person who provides finance in connection with the project has a conditional entitlement under an agreement to—
    (i)   assume sole or principal responsibility under an agreement for carrying out all or part of the project, or
    (ii)   make arrangements for carrying out all or part of the project.

PART II
OTHER ACTS

(2) In sub-paragraph (1) a reference to the provision of finance includes a reference to the provision of an indemnity.

"Person"

4K. For the purposes of paragraphs 4A to 4J, a reference to a person includes a reference to a partnership or another unincorporated group of persons.]

5. The Secretary of State may by regulations modify the qualifications for eligibility of a company for a moratorium.]

[1139]

NOTES

Inserted by the Insolvency Act 2000, s 1, Sch 1, paras 1, 4, as from 11 May 2001 (in part), and 1 January 2003 (otherwise).

Para 1: definitions omitted repealed by virtue of the Financial Services and Markets Act 2000 (Consequential Amendments) Order 2002, SI 2002/1555, art 28(1), (2), as from 3 July 2002.

Para 2: sub-paras (2)(a)–(bb) substituted for original sub-paras (a), (b), words omitted from sub-para (2)(c) repealed, and sub-para (3) added, by virtue of SI 2002/1555, arts 28(1), (3), 29, as from 3 July 2002.

Para 3 is amended as follows:

Words in square brackets in sub-para (2) substituted (for the original words "section 247(3) of the Companies Act 1985") by the Companies Act 2006 (Consequential Amendments etc) Order 2008, SI 2008/948, art 3(1), Sch 1, Pt 2, para 99(1), (2), as from 6 April 2008; for transitional provisions and savings see the note below.

Words in square brackets in sub-para (3) substituted (for the original words "Subsections (4), (5) and (6) of section 247") by SI 2008/948, art 3(1), Sch 1, Pt 2, para 99(1), (3), as from 6 April 2008; for transitional provisions and savings see the note below.

Sub-paras (4), (5) added by the Insolvency Act 1986 (Amendment) (No 3) Regulations 2002, SI 2002/1990, reg 3(1), (2), as from 1 January 2003 (being the day on which the Insolvency Act 2000, s 1 comes into force for the purpose of giving effect to para 4 of this Schedule; see reg 2 of the 2002 Regulations).

Words in square brackets in sub-para (4) substituted (for the original words "holding company" and "in respect of" respectively) by SI 2008/948, art 3(1), Sch 1, Pt 2, para 99(1), (4), as from 6 April 2008; for transitional provisions and savings see the note below.

Sub-para (5) substituted by SI 2008/948, art 3(1), Sch 1, Pt 2, para 99(1), (5), as from 6 April 2008; for transitional provisions and savings see the note below. The original sub-para read as follows—

"(5) For the purposes of sub-paragraph (4) "group" has the meaning given by section 262 of the Companies Act 1985 (c 6) (definitions for Part VII) and a group qualifies as small or medium-sized if it qualifies as such under section 249 of the Companies Act 1985 (qualification of group as small or medium-sized).".

Para 4: sub-para (1)(a) substituted, and sub-para (1)(fa) inserted, by the Enterprise Act 2002, s 248(3), Sch 17, paras 9, 37(1), (2), as from 15 September 2003 (for savings and transitional provisions in relation to a petition for an administration order presented before that date, and in relation to special administration regimes (within the meaning of the Enterprise Act 2002, s 249), see the note to s 8 at **[1131]**).

Paras 4A–4K: inserted by SI 2002/1990, reg 3(1), (3), as from 1 January 2003.

Transitional provisions and savings: the Companies Act 2006 (Consequential Amendments etc) Order 2008, SI 2008/948, Sch 1, Pt 2, para 99(6) provides that the amendments made by para 99 as noted above apply only in relation to periods, or parts of periods, falling on or after 6 April 2008. See also art 6(4) of the 2008 Order which provides that where by virtue of any transitional provision, a provision of the Companies Act 2006 has effect only (a) on or after a specified date, or (b) in relation to matters occurring or arising on or after a specified date, any amendment substituting or inserting a reference to that provision has effect correspondingly).

Modification: a reference to commercial paper in this Schedule includes a reference to uncertificated units of an eligible debt security where the issue of the units corresponds, in accordance with the current terms of issue of the security, to the issue of commercial paper within the meaning of the Financial Services and Markets Act 2000 (Regulated Activities) Order 2001, SI 2001/544, art 9(3); see the Uncertificated Securities (Amendment) (Eligible Debt Securities) Regulations 2003, SI 2003/1633, reg 15, Sch 2, para 7 (as from 24 June 2003).

Banking Act 1987, Insurance Companies Act 1982: repealed by the Financial Services and Markets Act 2000 (Consequential Amendments and Repeals) Order 2001, SI 2001/3649, art 3(1)(b), (d), as from 1 December 2001.

Financial Services and Markets Act 2000 (Financial Promotion) Order 2001, SI 2001/1335: revoked and replaced by the Financial Services and Markets Act 2000 (Financial Promotion) Order 2005, SI 2005/1529.

Regulations: the Insolvency Act 1986 (Amendment) (No 3) Regulations 2002, SI 2002/1990.

[PART II
OBTAINING A MORATORIUM

Nominee's statement

6.—(1) Where the directors of a company wish to obtain a moratorium, they shall submit to the nominee—

(a) a document setting out the terms of the proposed voluntary arrangement,

(b) a statement of the company's affairs containing—

(i) such particulars of its creditors and of its debts and other liabilities and of its assets as may be prescribed, and

(ii) such other information as may be prescribed, and

(c) any other information necessary to enable the nominee to comply with sub-paragraph (2) which he requests from them.

(2) The nominee shall submit to the directors a statement in the prescribed form indicating whether or not, in his opinion—

(a)   the proposed voluntary arrangement has a reasonable prospect of being approved and implemented,

(b)   the company is likely to have sufficient funds available to it during the proposed moratorium to enable it to carry on its business, and

(c)   meetings of the company and its creditors should be summoned to consider the proposed voluntary arrangement.

(3)   In forming his opinion on the matters mentioned in sub-paragraph (2), the nominee is entitled to rely on the information submitted to him under sub-paragraph (1) unless he has reason to doubt its accuracy.

(4)   The reference in sub-paragraph (2)(b) to the company's business is to that business as the company proposes to carry it on during the moratorium.

Documents to be submitted to court

7.—(1)   To obtain a moratorium the directors of a company must file (in Scotland, lodge) with the court—

(a)   a document setting out the terms of the proposed voluntary arrangement,

(b)   a statement of the company's affairs containing—

  (i)   such particulars of its creditors and of its debts and other liabilities and of its assets as may be prescribed, and

  (ii)   such other information as may be prescribed,

(c)   a statement that the company is eligible for a moratorium,

(d)   a statement from the nominee that he has given his consent to act, and

(e)   a statement from the nominee that, in his opinion—

  (i)   the proposed voluntary arrangement has a reasonable prospect of being approved and implemented,

  (ii)   the company is likely to have sufficient funds available to it during the proposed moratorium to enable it to carry on its business, and

  (iii)   meetings of the company and its creditors should be summoned to consider the proposed voluntary arrangement.

(2)   Each of the statements mentioned in sub-paragraph (1)(b) to (e), except so far as it contains the particulars referred to in paragraph (b)(i), must be in the prescribed form.

(3)   The reference in sub-paragraph (1)(e)(ii) to the company's business is to that business as the company proposes to carry it on during the moratorium.

(4)   The Secretary of State may by regulations modify the requirements of this paragraph as to the documents required to be filed (in Scotland, lodged) with the court in order to obtain a moratorium.

Duration of moratorium

8.—(1)   A moratorium comes into force when the documents for the time being referred to in paragraph 7(1) are filed or lodged with the court and references in this Schedule to "the beginning of the moratorium" shall be construed accordingly.

(2)   A moratorium ends at the end of the day on which the meetings summoned under paragraph 29(1) are first held (or, if the meetings are held on different days, the later of those days), unless it is extended under paragraph 32.

(3)   If either of those meetings has not first met before the end of the period of 28 days beginning with the day on which the moratorium comes into force, the moratorium ends at the end of the day on which those meetings were to be held (or, if those meetings were summoned to be held on different days, the later of those days), unless it is extended under paragraph 32.

(4)   If the nominee fails to summon either meeting within the period required by paragraph 29(1), the moratorium ends at the end of the last day of that period.

(5)   If the moratorium is extended (or further extended) under paragraph 32, it ends at the end of the day to which it is extended (or further extended).

(6)   Sub-paragraphs (2) to (5) do not apply if the moratorium comes to an end before the time concerned by virtue of—

(a)   paragraph 25(4) (effect of withdrawal by nominee of consent to act),

(b)   an order under paragraph 26(3), 27(3) or 40 (challenge of actions of nominee or directors), or

(c)   a decision of one or both of the meetings summoned under paragraph 29.

(7)   If the moratorium has not previously come to an end in accordance with sub-paragraphs (2) to (6), it ends at the end of the day on which a decision under paragraph 31 to approve a voluntary arrangement takes effect under paragraph 36.

(8)   The Secretary of State may by order increase or reduce the period for the time being specified in sub-paragraph (3).

Notification of beginning of moratorium

9.—(1)   When a moratorium comes into force, the directors shall notify the nominee of that fact forthwith.

(2)   If the directors without reasonable excuse fail to comply with sub-paragraph (1), each of them is liable to imprisonment or a fine, or both.

10.—(1)   When a moratorium comes into force, the nominee shall, in accordance with the rules—
    (a)   advertise that fact forthwith, and
    (b)   notify the registrar of companies, the company and any petitioning creditor of the company of whose claim he is aware of that fact.

(2)   In sub-paragraph (1)(b), "petitioning creditor" means a creditor by whom a winding-up petition has been presented before the beginning of the moratorium, as long as the petition has not been dismissed or withdrawn.

(3)   If the nominee without reasonable excuse fails to comply with sub-paragraph (1)(a) or (b), he is liable to a fine.

Notification of end of moratorium

11.—(1)   When a moratorium comes to an end, the nominee shall, in accordance with the rules—
    (a)   advertise that fact forthwith, and
    (b)   notify the court, the registrar of companies, the company and any creditor of the company of whose claim he is aware of that fact.

(2)   If the nominee without reasonable excuse fails to comply with sub-paragraph (1)(a) or (b), he is liable to a fine.]

[1140]

NOTES
Inserted by the Insolvency Act 2000, s 1, Sch 1, paras 1, 4, as from 1 January 2003.

[PART III
EFFECTS OF MORATORIUM]

Effect on creditors, etc

12.—(1)   During the period for which a moratorium is in force for a company—
    (a)   no petition may be presented for the winding up of the company,
    (b)   no meeting of the company may be called or requisitioned except with the consent of the nominee or the leave of the court and subject (where the court gives leave) to such terms as the court may impose,
    (c)   no resolution may be passed or order made for the winding up of the company,
    [(d)   no administration application may be made in respect of the company,
    (da)   no administrator of the company may be appointed under paragraph 14 or 22 of Schedule B1,]
    (e)   no administrative receiver of the company may be appointed,
    (f)   no landlord or other person to whom rent is payable may exercise any right of forfeiture by peaceable re-entry in relation to premises let to the company in respect of a failure by the company to comply with any term or condition of its tenancy of such premises, except with the leave of the court and subject to such terms as the court may impose,
    (g)   no other steps may be taken to enforce any security over the company's property, or to repossess goods in the company's possession under any hire-purchase agreement, except with the leave of the court and subject to such terms as the court may impose, and
    (h)   no other proceedings and no execution or other legal process may be commenced or continued, and no distress may be levied, against the company or its property except with the leave of the court and subject to such terms as the court may impose.

(2)   Where a petition, other than an excepted petition, for the winding up of the company has been presented before the beginning of the moratorium, section 127 shall not apply in relation to any disposition of property, transfer of shares or alteration in status made during the moratorium or at a time mentioned in paragraph 37(5)(a).

(3)   In the application of sub-paragraph (1)(h) to Scotland, the reference to execution being commenced or continued includes a reference to diligence being carried out or continued, and the reference to distress being levied is omitted.

(4)   Paragraph (a) of sub-paragraph (1) does not apply to an excepted petition and, where such a petition has been presented before the beginning of the moratorium or is presented during the moratorium, paragraphs (b) and (c) of that sub-paragraph do not apply in relation to proceedings on the petition.

(5)   For the purposes of this paragraph, "excepted petition" means a petition under—

(a)   section 124A [or 124B] of this Act,
(b)   section 72 of the Financial Services Act 1986 on the ground mentioned in subsection (1)(b) of that section, or
(c)   section 92 of the Banking Act 1987 on the ground mentioned in subsection (1)(b) of that section;
[(d)   section 367 of the Financial Services and Markets Act 2000 on the ground mentioned in subsection (3)(b) of that section.]

13.—(1)   This paragraph applies where there is an uncrystallised floating charge on the property of a company for which a moratorium is in force.

(2)   If the conditions for the holder of the charge to give a notice having the effect mentioned in sub-paragraph (4) are met at any time, the notice may not be given at that time but may instead be given as soon as practicable after the moratorium has come to an end.

(3)   If any other event occurs at any time which (apart from this sub-paragraph) would have the effect mentioned in sub-paragraph (4), then—
(a)   the event shall not have the effect in question at that time, but
(b)   if notice of the event is given to the company by the holder of the charge as soon as is practicable after the moratorium has come to an end, the event is to be treated as if it had occurred when the notice was given.

(4)   The effect referred to in sub-paragraphs (2) and (3) is—
(a)   causing the crystallisation of the floating charge, or
(b)   causing the imposition, by virtue of provision in the instrument creating the charge, of any restriction on the disposal of any property of the company.

(5)   Application may not be made for leave under paragraph 12(1)(g) or (h) with a view to obtaining—
(a)   the crystallisation of the floating charge, or
(b)   the imposition, by virtue of provision in the instrument creating the charge, of any restriction on the disposal of any property of the company.

14.   Security granted by a company at a time when a moratorium is in force in relation to the company may only be enforced if, at that time, there were reasonable grounds for believing that it would benefit the company.

Effect on company

15.—(1)   Paragraphs 16 to 23 apply in relation to a company for which a moratorium is in force.

(2)   The fact that a company enters into a transaction in contravention of any of paragraphs 16 to 22 does not—
(a)   make the transaction void, or
(b)   make it to any extent unenforceable against the company.

Company invoices, etc

16.—[(1)   Every invoice, order for goods or services, business letter or order form (whether in hard copy, electronic or any other form) issued by or on behalf of the company, and all the company's websites, must also contain the nominee's name and a statement that the moratorium is in force for the company.]

(2)   If default is made in complying with sub-paragraph (1), the company and (subject to sub-paragraph (3)) any officer of the company is liable to a fine.

(3)   An officer of the company is only liable under sub-paragraph (2) if, without reasonable excuse, he authorises or permits the default.

Obtaining credit during moratorium

17.—(1)   The company may not obtain credit to the extent of £250 or more from a person who has not been informed that a moratorium is in force in relation to the company.

(2)   The reference to the company obtaining credit includes the following cases—
(a)   where goods are bailed (in Scotland, hired) to the company under a hire-purchase agreement, or agreed to be sold to the company under a conditional sale agreement, and
(b)   where the company is paid in advance (whether in money or otherwise) for the supply of goods or services.

(3)   Where the company obtains credit in contravention of sub-paragraph (1)—
(a)   the company is liable to a fine, and
(b)   if any officer of the company knowingly and wilfully authorised or permitted the contravention, he is liable to imprisonment or a fine, or both.

(4)   The money sum specified in sub-paragraph (1) is subject to increase or reduction by order under section 417A in Part XV.

Disposals and payments

18.—(1) Subject to sub-paragraph (2), the company may only dispose of any of its property if—

(a) there are reasonable grounds for believing that the disposal will benefit the company, and

(b) the disposal is approved by the committee established under paragraph 35(1) or, where there is no such committee, by the nominee.

(2) Sub-paragraph (1) does not apply to a disposal made in the ordinary way of the company's business.

(3) If the company makes a disposal in contravention of sub-paragraph (1) otherwise than in pursuance of an order of the court—

(a) the company is liable to a fine, and

(b) if any officer of the company authorised or permitted the contravention, without reasonable excuse, he is liable to imprisonment or a fine, or both.

19.—(1) Subject to sub-paragraph (2), the company may only make any payment in respect of any debt or other liability of the company in existence before the beginning of the moratorium if—

(a) there are reasonable grounds for believing that the payment will benefit the company, and

(b) the payment is approved by the committee established under paragraph 35(1) or, where there is no such committee, by the nominee.

(2) Sub-paragraph (1) does not apply to a payment required by paragraph 20(6).

(3) If the company makes a payment in contravention of sub-paragraph (1) otherwise than in pursuance of an order of the court—

(a) the company is liable to a fine, and

(b) if any officer of the company authorised or permitted the contravention, without reasonable excuse, he is liable to imprisonment or a fine, or both.

Disposal of charged property, etc

20.—(1) This paragraph applies where—

(a) any property of the company is subject to a security, or

(b) any goods are in the possession of the company under a hire-purchase agreement.

(2) If the holder of the security consents, or the court gives leave, the company may dispose of the property as if it were not subject to the security.

(3) If the owner of the goods consents, or the court gives leave, the company may dispose of the goods as if all rights of the owner under the hire-purchase agreement were vested in the company.

(4) Where property subject to a security which, as created, was a floating charge is disposed of under sub-paragraph (2), the holder of the security has the same priority in respect of any property of the company directly or indirectly representing the property disposed of as he would have had in respect of the property subject to the security.

(5) Sub-paragraph (6) applies to the disposal under sub-paragraph (2) or (as the case may be) sub-paragraph (3) of—

(a) any property subject to a security other than a security which, as created, was a floating charge, or

(b) any goods in the possession of the company under a hire-purchase agreement.

(6) It shall be a condition of any consent or leave under sub-paragraph (2) or (as the case may be) sub-paragraph (3) that—

(a) the net proceeds of the disposal, and

(b) where those proceeds are less than such amount as may be agreed, or determined by the court, to be the net amount which would be realised on a sale of the property or goods in the open market by a willing vendor, such sums as may be required to make good the deficiency,

shall be applied towards discharging the sums secured by the security or payable under the hire-purchase agreement.

(7) Where a condition imposed in pursuance of sub-paragraph (6) relates to two or more securities, that condition requires—

(a) the net proceeds of the disposal, and

(b) where paragraph (b) of sub-paragraph (6) applies, the sums mentioned in that paragraph,

to be applied towards discharging the sums secured by those securities in the order of their priorities.

(8) Where the court gives leave for a disposal under sub-paragraph (2) or (3), the directors shall, within 14 days after leave is given, send an office copy of the order giving leave to the registrar of companies.

(9) If the directors without reasonable excuse fail to comply with sub-paragraph (8), they are liable to a fine.

21.—(1) Where property is disposed of under paragraph 20 in its application to Scotland, the company shall grant to the disponee an appropriate document of transfer or conveyance of the property, and
  (a) that document, or
  (b) where any recording, intimation or registration of the document is a legal requirement for completion of title to the property, that recording, intimation or registration,

has the effect of disencumbering the property of, or (as the case may be) freeing the property from, the security.

  (2) Where goods in the possession of the company under a hire-purchase agreement are disposed of under paragraph 20 in its application to Scotland, the disposal has the effect of extinguishing, as against the disponee, all rights of the owner of the goods under the agreement.

22.—(1) If the company—
  (a) without any consent or leave under paragraph 20, disposes of any of its property which is subject to a security otherwise than in accordance with the terms of the security,
  (b) without any consent or leave under paragraph 20, disposes of any goods in the possession of the company under a hire-purchase agreement otherwise than in accordance with the terms of the agreement, or
  (c) fails to comply with any requirement imposed by paragraph 20 or 21,

it is liable to a fine.

  (2) If any officer of the company, without reasonable excuse, authorises or permits any such disposal or failure to comply, he is liable to imprisonment or a fine, or both.

Market contracts, etc.

23.—(1) If the company enters into any transaction to which this paragraph applies—
  (a) the company is liable to a fine, and
  (b) if any officer of the company, without reasonable excuse, authorised or permitted the company to enter into the transaction, he is liable to imprisonment or a fine, or both.

  (2) A company enters into a transaction to which this paragraph applies if it—
  (a) enters into a market contract, …
  (b) gives a transfer order,
  (c) grants a market charge … or a system-charge, or
  (d) provides any collateral security.

  (3) The fact that a company enters into a transaction in contravention of this paragraph does not—
  (a) make the transaction void, or
  (b) make it to any extent unenforceable by or against the company.

  (4) Where during the moratorium a company enters into a transaction to which this paragraph applies, nothing done by or in pursuance of the transaction is to be treated as done in contravention of paragraphs 12(1)(g), 14 or 16 to 22.

  (5) Paragraph 20 does not apply in relation to any property which is subject to a market charge, … a system-charge or a collateral security charge.

  (6) In this paragraph, "transfer order", "collateral security" and "collateral security charge" have the same meanings as in the settlement finality regulations.]

[1141]

NOTES

    Inserted by the Insolvency Act 2000, s 1, Sch 1, paras 1, 4, as from 1 January 2003.
    Para 12: sub-paras (1)(d), (da) substituted, for original sub-para (1)(d), by the Enterprise Act 2002, s 248(3), Sch 17, paras 9, 37(1), (3), as from 15 September 2003 (for savings and transitional provisions in relation to a petition for an administration order presented before that date, and in relation to special administration regimes (within the meaning of the Enterprise Act 2002, s 249), see the note to s 8 at **[1131]**); words in square brackets in sub-para (5)(a) inserted by the European Public Limited-Liability Company Regulations 2004, SI 2004/2326, reg 73(4)(b), as from 8 October 2004; sub-para (5)(d) inserted by virtue of the Financial Services and Markets Act 2000 (Consequential Amendments) Order 2002, SI 2002/1555, art 30, as from 3 July 2002.
    Para 16: sub-para (1) substituted by the Companies (Trading Disclosures) (Insolvency) Regulations 2008, SI 2008/1897, reg 3(1), as from 1 October 2008.
    Para 23: words omitted from sub-paras (2), (5) repealed by virtue of SI 2002/1555, art 28(1), (4), as from 3 July 2002.
    Financial collateral arrangements: see the Financial Collateral Arrangements (No 2) Regulations 2003, SI 2003/3226, reg 8(5) at **[3824]** with regard to the disapplication of paras 12(1)(g), 20 in relation to such arrangements.
    Banking Act 1987, Financial Services Act 1986,: repealed by the Financial Services and Markets Act 2000 (Consequential Amendments and Repeals) Order 2001, SI 2001/3649, art 3(1)(c), (d), as from 1 December 2001.

[PART IV
NOMINEES

Monitoring of company's activities

24.—(1)   During a moratorium, the nominee shall monitor the company's affairs for the purpose of forming an opinion as to whether—
    (a)   the proposed voluntary arrangement or, if he has received notice of proposed modifications under paragraph 31(7), the proposed arrangement with those modifications has a reasonable prospect of being approved and implemented, and
    (b)   the company is likely to have sufficient funds available to it during the remainder of the moratorium to enable it to continue to carry on its business.

(2)   The directors shall submit to the nominee any information necessary to enable him to comply with sub-paragraph (1) which he requests from them.

(3)   In forming his opinion on the matters mentioned in sub-paragraph (1), the nominee is entitled to rely on the information submitted to him under sub-paragraph (2) unless he has reason to doubt its accuracy.

(4)   The reference in sub-paragraph (1)(b) to the company's business is to that business as the company proposes to carry it on during the remainder of the moratorium.

Withdrawal of consent to act

25.—(1)   The nominee may only withdraw his consent to act in the circumstances mentioned in this paragraph.

(2)   The nominee must withdraw his consent to act if, at any time during a moratorium—
    (a)   he forms the opinion that—
        (i)   the proposed voluntary arrangement or, if he has received notice of proposed modifications under paragraph 31(7), the proposed arrangement with those modifications no longer has a reasonable prospect of being approved or implemented, or
        (ii)   the company will not have sufficient funds available to it during the remainder of the moratorium to enable it to continue to carry on its business,
    (b)   he becomes aware that, on the date of filing, the company was not eligible for a moratorium, or
    (c)   the directors fail to comply with their duty under paragraph 24(2).

(3)   The reference in sub-paragraph (2)(a)(ii) to the company's business is to that business as the company proposes to carry it on during the remainder of the moratorium.

(4)   If the nominee withdraws his consent to act, the moratorium comes to an end.

(5)   If the nominee withdraws his consent to act he must, in accordance with the rules, notify the court, the registrar of companies, the company and any creditor of the company of whose claim he is aware of his withdrawal and the reason for it.

(6)   If the nominee without reasonable excuse fails to comply with sub-paragraph (5), he is liable to a fine.

Challenge of nominee's actions, etc

26.—(1)   If any creditor, director or member of the company, or any other person affected by a moratorium, is dissatisfied by any act, omission or decision of the nominee during the moratorium, he may apply to the court.

(2)   An application under sub-paragraph (1) may be made during the moratorium or after it has ended.

(3)   On an application under sub-paragraph (1) the court may—
    (a)   confirm, reverse or modify any act or decision of the nominee,
    (b)   give him directions, or
    (c)   make such other order as it thinks fit.

(4)   An order under sub-paragraph (3) may (among other things) bring the moratorium to an end and make such consequential provision as the court thinks fit.

27.—(1)   Where there are reasonable grounds for believing that—
    (a)   as a result of any act, omission or decision of the nominee during the moratorium, the company has suffered loss, but
    (b)   the company does not intend to pursue any claim it may have against the nominee,
any creditor of the company may apply to the court.

(2)   An application under sub-paragraph (1) may be made during the moratorium or after it has ended.

(3)   On an application under sub-paragraph (1) the court may—

    (a)   order the company to pursue any claim against the nominee,

    (b)   authorise any creditor to pursue such a claim in the name of the company, or

    (c)   make such other order with respect to such a claim as it thinks fit,

unless the court is satisfied that the act, omission or decision of the nominee was in all the circumstances reasonable.

    (4)   An order under sub-paragraph (3) may (among other things)—

    (a)   impose conditions on any authority given to pursue a claim,

    (b)   direct the company to assist in the pursuit of a claim,

    (c)   make directions with respect to the distribution of anything received as a result of the pursuit of a claim,

    (d)   bring the moratorium to an end and make such consequential provision as the court thinks fit.

    (5)   On an application under sub-paragraph (1) the court shall have regard to the interests of the members and creditors of the company generally.

Replacement of nominee by court

28.—(1)   The court may—

    (a)   on an application made by the directors in a case where the nominee has failed to comply with any duty imposed on him under this Schedule or has died, or

    (b)   on an application made by the directors or the nominee in a case where it is impracticable or inappropriate for the nominee to continue to act as such,

direct that the nominee be replaced as such by another person qualified to act as an insolvency practitioner, or authorised to act as nominee, in relation to the voluntary arrangement.

    (2)   A person may only be appointed as a replacement nominee under this paragraph if he submits to the court a statement indicating his consent to act.]

                                                                    [1142]

NOTES

    Inserted by the Insolvency Act 2000, s 1, Sch 1, paras 1, 4, as from 1 January 2003.

[PART V
CONSIDERATION AND IMPLEMENTATION OF VOLUNTARY ARRANGEMENT

Summoning of meetings

29.—(1)   Where a moratorium is in force, the nominee shall summon meetings of the company and its creditors for such a time, date (within the period for the time being specified in paragraph 8(3)) and place as he thinks fit.

    (2)   The persons to be summoned to a creditors' meeting under this paragraph are every creditor of the company of whose claim the nominee is aware.

Conduct of meetings

30.—(1)   Subject to the provisions of paragraphs 31 to 35, the meetings summoned under paragraph 29 shall be conducted in accordance with the rules.

    (2)   A meeting so summoned may resolve that it be adjourned (or further adjourned).

    (3)   After the conclusion of either meeting in accordance with the rules, the chairman of the meeting shall report the result of the meeting to the court, and, immediately after reporting to the court, shall give notice of the result of the meeting to such persons as may be prescribed.

Approval of voluntary arrangement

31.—(1)   The meetings summoned under paragraph 29 shall decide whether to approve the proposed voluntary arrangement (with or without modifications).

    (2)   The modifications may include one conferring the functions proposed to be conferred on the nominee on another person qualified to act as an insolvency practitioner, or authorised to act as nominee, in relation to the voluntary arrangement.

    (3)   The modifications shall not include one by virtue of which the proposal ceases to be a proposal such as is mentioned in section 1.

    (4)   A meeting summoned under paragraph 29 shall not approve any proposal or modification which affects the right of a secured creditor of the company to enforce his security, except with the concurrence of the creditor concerned.

    (5)   Subject to sub-paragraph (6), a meeting so summoned shall not approve any proposal or modification under which—

(a) any preferential debt of the company is to be paid otherwise than in priority to such of its debts as are not preferential debts, or

(b) a preferential creditor of the company is to be paid an amount in respect of a preferential debt that bears to that debt a smaller proportion than is borne to another preferential debt by the amount that is to be paid in respect of that other debt.

(6) The meeting may approve such a proposal or modification with the concurrence of the preferential creditor concerned.

(7) The directors of the company may, before the beginning of the period of seven days which ends with the meetings (or either of them) summoned under paragraph 29 being held, give notice to the nominee of any modifications of the proposal for which the directors intend to seek the approval of those meetings.

(8) References in this paragraph to preferential debts and preferential creditors are to be read in accordance with section 386 in Part XII of this Act.

Extension of moratorium

32.—(1) Subject to sub-paragraph (2), a meeting summoned under paragraph 29 which resolves that it be adjourned (or further adjourned) may resolve that the moratorium be extended (or further extended), with or without conditions.

(2) The moratorium may not be extended (or further extended) to a day later than the end of the period of two months which begins—

(a) where both meetings summoned under paragraph 29 are first held on the same day, with that day,

(b) in any other case, with the day on which the later of those meetings is first held.

(3) At any meeting where it is proposed to extend (or further extend) the moratorium, before a decision is taken with respect to that proposal, the nominee shall inform the meeting—

(a) of what he has done in order to comply with his duty under paragraph 24 and the cost of his actions for the company, and

(b) of what he intends to do to continue to comply with that duty if the moratorium is extended (or further extended) and the expected cost of his actions for the company.

(4) Where, in accordance with sub-paragraph (3)(b), the nominee informs a meeting of the expected cost of his intended actions, the meeting shall resolve whether or not to approve that expected cost.

(5) If a decision not to approve the expected cost of the nominee's intended actions has effect under paragraph 36, the moratorium comes to an end.

(6) A meeting may resolve that a moratorium which has been extended (or further extended) be brought to an end before the end of the period of the extension (or further extension).

(7) The Secretary of State may by order increase or reduce the period for the time being specified in sub-paragraph (2).

33.—(1) The conditions which may be imposed when a moratorium is extended (or further extended) include a requirement that the nominee be replaced as such by another person qualified to act as an insolvency practitioner, or authorised to act as nominee, in relation to the voluntary arrangement.

(2) A person may only be appointed as a replacement nominee by virtue of sub-paragraph (1) if he submits to the court a statement indicating his consent to act.

(3) At any meeting where it is proposed to appoint a replacement nominee as a condition of extending (or further extending) the moratorium—

(a) the duty imposed by paragraph 32(3)(b) on the nominee shall instead be imposed on the person proposed as the replacement nominee, and

(b) paragraphs 32(4) and (5) and 36(1)(e) apply as if the references to the nominee were to that person.

34.—(1) If a decision to extend, or further extend, the moratorium takes effect under paragraph 36, the nominee shall, in accordance with the rules, notify the registrar of companies and the court.

(2) If the moratorium is extended, or further extended, by virtue of an order under paragraph 36(5), the nominee shall, in accordance with the rules, send an office copy of the order to the registrar of companies.

(3) If the nominee without reasonable excuse fails to comply with this paragraph, he is liable to a fine.

Moratorium committee

35.—(1) A meeting summoned under paragraph 29 which resolves that the moratorium be extended (or further extended) may, with the consent of the nominee, resolve that a committee be established to exercise the functions conferred on it by the meeting.

(2) The meeting may not so resolve unless it has approved an estimate of the expenses to be incurred by the committee in the exercise of the proposed functions.

(3) Any expenses, not exceeding the amount of the estimate, incurred by the committee in the exercise of its functions shall be reimbursed by the nominee.

(4) The committee shall cease to exist when the moratorium comes to an end.

Effectiveness of decisions

36.—(1) Sub-paragraph (2) applies to references to one of the following decisions having effect, that is, a decision, under paragraph 31, 32 or 35, with respect to—
- (a) the approval of a proposed voluntary arrangement,
- (b) the extension (or further extension) of a moratorium,
- (c) the bringing of a moratorium to an end,
- (d) the establishment of a committee, or
- (e) the approval of the expected cost of a nominee's intended actions.

(2) The decision has effect if, in accordance with the rules—
- (a) it has been taken by both meetings summoned under paragraph 29, or
- (b) (subject to any order made under sub-paragraph (5)) it has been taken by the creditors' meeting summoned under that paragraph.

(3) If a decision taken by the creditors' meeting under any of paragraphs 31, 32 or 35 with respect to any of the matters mentioned in sub-paragraph (1) differs from one so taken by the company meeting with respect to that matter, a member of the company may apply to the court.

(4) An application under sub-paragraph (3) shall not be made after the end of the period of 28 days beginning with—
- (a) the day on which the decision was taken by the creditors' meeting, or
- (b) where the decision of the company meeting was taken on a later day, that day.

(5) On an application under sub-paragraph (3), the court may—
- (a) order the decision of the company meeting to have effect instead of the decision of the creditors' meeting, or
- (b) make such other order as it thinks fit.

Effect of approval of voluntary arrangement

37.—(1) This paragraph applies where a decision approving a voluntary arrangement has effect under paragraph 36.

(2) The approved voluntary arrangement—
- (a) takes effect as if made by the company at the creditors' meeting, and
- (b) binds every person who in accordance with the rules—
  - (i) was entitled to vote at that meeting (whether or not he was present or represented at it), or
  - (ii) would have been so entitled if he had had notice of it,
as if he were a party to the voluntary arrangement.

(3) If—
- (a) when the arrangement ceases to have effect any amount payable under the arrangement to a person bound by virtue of sub-paragraph (2)(b)(ii) has not been paid, and
- (b) the arrangement did not come to an end prematurely,
the company shall at that time become liable to pay to that person the amount payable under the arrangement.

(4) Where a petition for the winding up of the company, other than an excepted petition within the meaning of paragraph 12, was presented before the beginning of the moratorium, the court shall dismiss the petition.

(5) The court shall not dismiss a petition under sub-paragraph (4)—
- (a) at any time before the end of the period of 28 days beginning with the first day on which each of the reports of the meetings required by paragraph 30(3) has been made to the court, or
- (b) at any time when an application under paragraph 38 or an appeal in respect of such an application is pending, or at any time in the period within which such an appeal may be brought.

PART II
OTHER ACTS

Challenge of decisions

38.—(1) Subject to the following provisions of this paragraph, any of the persons mentioned in sub-paragraph (2) may apply to the court on one or both of the following grounds—

(a) that a voluntary arrangement approved at one or both of the meetings summoned under paragraph 29 and which has taken effect unfairly prejudices the interests of a creditor, member or contributory of the company,

(b) that there has been some material irregularity at or in relation to either of those meetings.

(2) The persons who may apply under this paragraph are—

(a) a person entitled, in accordance with the rules, to vote at either of the meetings,

(b) a person who would have been entitled, in accordance with the rules, to vote at the creditors' meeting if he had had notice of it, and

(c) the nominee.

(3) An application under this paragraph shall not be made—

(a) after the end of the period of 28 days beginning with the first day on which each of the reports required by paragraph 30(3) has been made to the court, or

(b) in the case of a person who was not given notice of the creditors' meeting, after the end of the period of 28 days beginning with the day on which he became aware that the meeting had taken place,

but (subject to that) an application made by a person within sub-paragraph (2)(b) on the ground that the arrangement prejudices his interests may be made after the arrangement has ceased to have effect, unless it came to an end prematurely.

(4) Where on an application under this paragraph the court is satisfied as to either of the grounds mentioned in sub-paragraph (1), it may do any of the following—

(a) revoke or suspend—

(i) any decision approving the voluntary arrangement which has effect under paragraph 36, or

(ii) in a case falling within sub-paragraph (1)(b), any decision taken by the meeting in question which has effect under that paragraph,

(b) give a direction to any person—

(i) for the summoning of further meetings to consider any revised proposal for a voluntary arrangement which the directors may make, or

(ii) in a case falling within sub-paragraph (1)(b), for the summoning of a further company or (as the case may be) creditors' meeting to reconsider the original proposal.

(5) Where at any time after giving a direction under sub-paragraph (4)(b)(i) the court is satisfied that the directors do not intend to submit a revised proposal, the court shall revoke the direction and revoke or suspend any decision approving the voluntary arrangement which has effect under paragraph 36.

(6) Where the court gives a direction under sub-paragraph (4)(b), it may also give a direction continuing or, as the case may require, renewing, for such period as may be specified in the direction, the effect of the moratorium.

(7) Sub-paragraph (8) applies in a case where the court, on an application under this paragraph—

(a) gives a direction under sub-paragraph (4)(b), or

(b) revokes or suspends a decision under sub-paragraph (4)(a) or (5).

(8) In such a case, the court may give such supplemental directions as it thinks fit and, in particular, directions with respect to—

(a) things done under the voluntary arrangement since it took effect, and

(b) such things done since that time as could not have been done if a moratorium had been in force in relation to the company when they were done.

(9) Except in pursuance of the preceding provisions of this paragraph, a decision taken at a meeting summoned under paragraph 29 is not invalidated by any irregularity at or in relation to the meeting.

Implementation of voluntary arrangement

39.—(1) This paragraph applies where a voluntary arrangement approved by one or both of the meetings summoned under paragraph 29 has taken effect.

(2) The person who is for the time being carrying out in relation to the voluntary arrangement the functions conferred—

(a) by virtue of the approval of the arrangement, on the nominee, or

(b) by virtue of paragraph 31(2), on a person other than the nominee,

shall be known as the supervisor of the voluntary arrangement.

(3)   If any of the company's creditors or any other person is dissatisfied by any act, omission or decision of the supervisor, he may apply to the court.

(4)   On an application under sub-paragraph (3) the court may—
(a)   confirm, reverse or modify any act or decision of the supervisor,
(b)   give him directions, or
(c)   make such other order as it thinks fit.

(5)   The supervisor—
(a)   may apply to the court for directions in relation to any particular matter arising under the voluntary arrangement, and
(b)   is included among the persons who may apply to the court for the winding up of the company or for an administration order to be made in relation to it.

(6)   The court may, whenever—
(a)   it is expedient to appoint a person to carry out the functions of the supervisor, and
(b)   it is inexpedient, difficult or impracticable for an appointment to be made without the assistance of the court,
make an order appointing a person who is qualified to act as an insolvency practitioner, or authorised to act as supervisor, in relation to the voluntary arrangement, either in substitution for the existing supervisor or to fill a vacancy.

(7)   The power conferred by sub-paragraph (6) is exercisable so as to increase the number of persons exercising the functions of supervisor or, where there is more than one person exercising those functions, so as to replace one or more of those persons.]

[1143]

NOTES
Inserted by the Insolvency Act 2000, s 1, Sch 1, paras 1, 4, as from 1 January 2003.

[PART VI
MISCELLANEOUS
Challenge of directors' actions

40.—(1)   This paragraph applies in relation to acts or omissions of the directors of a company during a moratorium.

(2)   A creditor or member of the company may apply to the court for an order under this paragraph on the ground—
(a)   that the company's affairs, business and property are being or have been managed by the directors in a manner which is unfairly prejudicial to the interests of its creditors or members generally, or of some part of its creditors or members (including at least the petitioner), or
(b)   that any actual or proposed act or omission of the directors is or would be so prejudicial.

(3)   An application for an order under this paragraph may be made during or after the moratorium.

(4)   On an application for an order under this paragraph the court may—
(a)   make such order as it thinks fit for giving relief in respect of the matters complained of,
(b)   adjourn the hearing conditionally or unconditionally, or
(c)   make an interim order or any other order that it thinks fit.

(5)   An order under this paragraph may in particular—
(a)   regulate the management by the directors of the company's affairs, business and property during the remainder of the moratorium,
(b)   require the directors to refrain from doing or continuing an act complained of by the petitioner, or to do an act which the petitioner has complained they have omitted to do,
(c)   require the summoning of a meeting of creditors or members for the purpose of considering such matters as the court may direct,
(d)   bring the moratorium to an end and make such consequential provision as the court thinks fit.

(6)   In making an order under this paragraph the court shall have regard to the need to safeguard the interests of persons who have dealt with the company in good faith and for value.

[(7)   Sub-paragraph (8) applies where—
[(a)   the appointment of an administrator has effect in relation to the company and that appointment was in pursuance of—
(i)   an administration application made, or
(ii)   a notice of intention to appoint filed,
before the moratorium came into force, or]
(b)   the company is being wound up in pursuance of a petition presented before the moratorium came into force.

(8)   No application for an order under this paragraph may be made by a creditor or member of the company; but such an application may be made instead by the administrator or (as the case may be) the liquidator.]

Offences

41.—(1)   This paragraph applies where a moratorium has been obtained for a company.

(2)   If, within the period of 12 months ending with the day on which the moratorium came into force, a person who was at the time an officer of the company—
- (a)   did any of the things mentioned in paragraphs (a) to (f) of sub-paragraph (4), or
- (b)   was privy to the doing by others of any of the things mentioned in paragraphs (c), (d) and (e) of that sub-paragraph,

he is to be treated as having committed an offence at that time.

(3)   If, at any time during the moratorium, a person who is an officer of the company—
- (a)   does any of the things mentioned in paragraphs (a) to (f) of sub-paragraph (4), or
- (b)   is privy to the doing by others of any of the things mentioned in paragraphs (c), (d) and (e) of that sub-paragraph,

he commits an offence.

(4)   Those things are—
- (a)   concealing any part of the company's property to the value of £500 or more, or concealing any debt due to or from the company, or
- (b)   fraudulently removing any part of the company's property to the value of £500 or more, or
- (c)   concealing, destroying, mutilating or falsifying any book or paper affecting or relating to the company's property or affairs, or
- (d)   making any false entry in any book or paper affecting or relating to the company's property or affairs, or
- (e)   fraudulently parting with, altering or making any omission in any document affecting or relating to the company's property or affairs, or
- (f)   pawning, pledging or disposing of any property of the company which has been obtained on credit and has not been paid for (unless the pawning, pledging or disposal was in the ordinary way of the company's business).

(5)   For the purposes of this paragraph, "officer" includes a shadow director.

(6)   It is a defence—
- (a)   for a person charged under sub-paragraph (2) or (3) in respect of the things mentioned in paragraph (a) or (f) of sub-paragraph (4) to prove that he had no intent to defraud, and
- (b)   for a person charged under sub-paragraph (2) or (3) in respect of the things mentioned in paragraph (c) or (d) of sub-paragraph (4) to prove that he had no intent to conceal the state of affairs of the company or to defeat the law.

(7)   Where a person pawns, pledges or disposes of any property of a company in circumstances which amount to an offence under sub-paragraph (2) or (3), every person who takes in pawn or pledge, or otherwise receives, the property knowing it to be pawned, pledged or disposed of in circumstances which—
- (a)   would, if a moratorium were obtained for the company within the period of 12 months beginning with the day on which the pawning, pledging or disposal took place, amount to an offence under sub-paragraph (2), or
- (b)   amount to an offence under sub-paragraph (3),

commits an offence.

(8)   A person guilty of an offence under this paragraph is liable to imprisonment or a fine, or both.

(9)   The money sums specified in paragraphs (a) and (b) of sub-paragraph (4) are subject to increase or reduction by order under section 417A in Part XV.

42.—(1)   If, for the purpose of obtaining a moratorium, or an extension of a moratorium, for a company, a person who is an officer of the company—
- (a)   makes any false representation, or
- (b)   fraudulently does, or omits to do, anything,

he commits an offence.

(2)   Sub-paragraph (1) applies even if no moratorium or extension is obtained.

(3)   For the purposes of this paragraph, "officer" includes a shadow director.

(4)   A person guilty of an offence under this paragraph is liable to imprisonment or a fine, or both.

Void provisions in floating charge documents

43.—(1) A provision in an instrument creating a floating charge is void if it provides for—

  (a) obtaining a moratorium, or

  (b) anything done with a view to obtaining a moratorium (including any preliminary decision or investigation),

to be an event causing the floating charge to crystallise or causing restrictions which would not otherwise apply to be imposed on the disposal of property by the company or a ground for the appointment of a receiver.

(2) In sub-paragraph (1), "receiver" includes a manager and a person who is appointed both receiver and manager.

Functions of the Financial Services Authority

44.—(1) This Schedule has effect in relation to a moratorium for a regulated company with the modifications in sub-paragraphs (2) to (16) below.

(2) Any notice or other document required by virtue of this Schedule to be sent to a creditor of a regulated company must also be sent to the Authority.

(3) The Authority is entitled to be heard on any application to the court for leave under paragraph 20(2) or 20(3) (disposal of charged property, etc).

(4) Where paragraph 26(1) (challenge of nominee's actions, etc) applies, the persons who may apply to the court include the Authority.

(5) If a person other than the Authority applies to the court under that paragraph, the Authority is entitled to be heard on the application.

(6) Where paragraph 27(1) (challenge of nominee's actions, etc) applies, the persons who may apply to the court include the Authority.

(7) If a person other than the Authority applies to the court under that paragraph, the Authority is entitled to be heard on the application.

(8) The persons to be summoned to a creditors' meeting under paragraph 29 include the Authority.

(9) A person appointed for the purpose by the Authority is entitled to attend and participate in (but not to vote at)—

  (a) any creditors' meeting summoned under that paragraph,

  (b) any meeting of a committee established under paragraph 35 (moratorium committee).

(10) The Authority is entitled to be heard on any application under paragraph 36(3) (effectiveness of decisions).

(11) Where paragraph 38(1) (challenge of decisions) applies, the persons who may apply to the court include the Authority.

(12) If a person other than the Authority applies to the court under that paragraph, the Authority is entitled to be heard on the application.

(13) Where paragraph 39(3) (implementation of voluntary arrangement) applies, the persons who may apply to the court include the Authority.

(14) If a person other than the Authority applies to the court under that paragraph, the Authority is entitled to be heard on the application.

(15) Where paragraph 40(2) (challenge of directors' actions) applies, the persons who may apply to the court include the Authority.

(16) If a person other than the Authority applies to the court under that paragraph, the Authority is entitled to be heard on the application.

(17) This paragraph does not prejudice any right the Authority has (apart from this paragraph) as a creditor of a regulated company.

(18) In this paragraph—

  "the Authority" means the Financial Services Authority, and

  "regulated company" means a company which—

  (a) is, or has been, an authorised person within the meaning given by section 31 of the Financial Services and Markets Act 2000,

  (b) is, or has been, an appointed representative within the meaning given by section 39 of that Act, or

  (c) is carrying on, or has carried on, a regulated activity, within the meaning given by section 22 of that Act, in contravention of the general prohibition within the meaning given by section 19 of that Act.

Subordinate legislation

45.—(1)   Regulations or an order made by the Secretary of State under this Schedule may make different provision for different cases.

(2)   Regulations so made may make such consequential, incidental, supplemental and transitional provision as may appear to the Secretary of State necessary or expedient.

(3)   Any power of the Secretary of State to make regulations under this Schedule may be exercised by amending or repealing any enactment contained in this Act (including one contained in this Schedule) or contained in the Company Directors Disqualification Act 1986.

(4)   Regulations (except regulations under paragraph 5) or an order made by the Secretary of State under this Schedule shall be made by statutory instrument subject to annulment in pursuance of a resolution of either House of Parliament.

(5)   Regulations under paragraph 5 of this Schedule are to be made by statutory instrument and shall only be made if a draft containing the regulations has been laid before and approved by resolution of each House of Parliament.]

[1144]

NOTES
Inserted by the Insolvency Act 2000, s 1, Sch 1, paras 1, 4, as from 11 May 2001 (para 45(1)–(3), (5)), and as from 1 January 2003 (otherwise).
Para 40: sub-paras (7), (8) substituted, for original sub-para (7), by the Enterprise Act 2002, s 248(3), Sch 17, paras 9, 37(1), (4), as from 15 September 2003 (for savings and transitional provisions in relation to a petition for an administration order presented before that date, and in relation to special administration regimes (within the meaning of the Enterprise Act 2002, s 249), see the note to s 8 at **[1131]**); sub-para (7)(a) further substituted by the Enterprise Act 2002 (Insolvency) Order 2004, SI 2004/2312, art 2, as from 15 October 2004.

[SCHEDULE B1
ADMINISTRATION

Section 8

ARRANGEMENT OF SCHEDULE

NATURE OF ADMINISTRATION

Administration

1.—(1)   For the purposes of this Act "administrator" of a company means a person appointed under this Schedule to manage the company's affairs, business and property.

(2)   For the purposes of this Act—

(a)   a company is "in administration" while the appointment of an administrator of the company has effect,

(b)   a company "enters administration" when the appointment of an administrator takes effect,

(c)   a company ceases to be in administration when the appointment of an administrator of the company ceases to have effect in accordance with this Schedule, and

(d)   a company does not cease to be in administration merely because an administrator vacates office (by reason of resignation, death or otherwise) or is removed from office.

2.   A person may be appointed as administrator of a company—

(a)   by administration order of the court under paragraph 10,

(b)   by the holder of a floating charge under paragraph 14, or
(c)   by the company or its directors under paragraph 22.

Purpose of administration

3.—(1)   The administrator of a company must perform his functions with the objective of—
(a)   rescuing the company as a going concern, or
(b)   achieving a better result for the company's creditors as a whole than would be likely if the company were wound up (without first being in administration), or
(c)   realising property in order to make a distribution to one or more secured or preferential creditors.

(2)   Subject to sub-paragraph (4), the administrator of a company must perform his functions in the interests of the company's creditors as a whole.

(3)   The administrator must perform his functions with the objective specified in sub-paragraph (1)(a) unless he thinks either—
(a)   that it is not reasonably practicable to achieve that objective, or
(b)   that the objective specified in sub-paragraph (1)(b) would achieve a better result for the company's creditors as a whole.

(4)   The administrator may perform his functions with the objective specified in sub-paragraph (1)(c) only if—
(a)   he thinks that it is not reasonably practicable to achieve either of the objectives specified in sub-paragraph (1)(a) and (b), and
(b)   he does not unnecessarily harm the interests of the creditors of the company as a whole.

4.   The administrator of a company must perform his functions as quickly and efficiently as is reasonably practicable.

Status of administrator

5.   An administrator is an officer of the court (whether or not he is appointed by the court).

General restrictions

6.   A person may be appointed as administrator of a company only if he is qualified to act as an insolvency practitioner in relation to the company.

7.   A person may not be appointed as administrator of a company which is in administration (subject to the provisions of paragraphs 90 to 97 and 100 to 103 about replacement and additional administrators).

8.—(1)   A person may not be appointed as administrator of a company which is in liquidation by virtue of—
(a)   a resolution for voluntary winding up, or
(b)   a winding-up order.

(2)   Sub-paragraph (1)(a) is subject to paragraph 38.

(3)   Sub-paragraph (1)(b) is subject to paragraphs 37 and 38.

9.—(1)   A person may not be appointed as administrator of a company which—
(a)   has a liability in respect of a deposit which it accepted in accordance with the Banking Act 1979 (c 37) or 1987 (c 22), but
(b)   is not an authorised deposit taker.

(2)   A person may not be appointed as administrator of a company which effects or carries out contracts of insurance.

(3)   But sub-paragraph (2) does not apply to a company which—
(a)   is exempt from the general prohibition in relation to effecting or carrying out contracts of insurance, or
(b)   is an authorised deposit taker effecting or carrying out contracts of insurance in the course of a banking business.

(4)   In this paragraph—
"authorised deposit taker" means a person with permission under Part IV of the Financial Services and Markets Act 2000 (c 8) to accept deposits, and
"the general prohibition" has the meaning given by section 19 of that Act.

(5)   This paragraph shall be construed in accordance with—
(a)   section 22 of the Financial Services and Markets Act 2000 (classes of regulated activity and categories of investment),
(b)   any relevant order under that section, and
(c)   Schedule 2 to that Act (regulated activities).

PART II
OTHER ACTS

APPOINTMENT OF ADMINISTRATOR BY COURT

Administration order

10.   An administration order is an order appointing a person as the administrator of a company.

Conditions for making order

11.   The court may make an administration order in relation to a company only if satisfied—
    (a)   that the company is or is likely to become unable to pay its debts, and
    (b)   that the administration order is reasonably likely to achieve the purpose of administration.

Administration application

12.—(1)   An application to the court for an administration order in respect of a company (an "administration application") may be made only by—
    (a)   the company,
    (b)   the directors of the company,
    (c)   one or more creditors of the company,
    (d)   the [designated officer] for a magistrates' court in the exercise of the power conferred by section 87A of the Magistrates' Courts Act 1980 (c 43) (fine imposed on company), or
    (e)   a combination of persons listed in paragraphs (a) to (d).

(2)   As soon as is reasonably practicable after the making of an administration application the applicant shall notify—
    (a)   any person who has appointed an administrative receiver of the company,
    (b)   any person who is or may be entitled to appoint an administrative receiver of the company,
    (c)   any person who is or may be entitled to appoint an administrator of the company under paragraph 14, and
    (d)   such other persons as may be prescribed.

(3)   An administration application may not be withdrawn without the permission of the court.

(4)   In sub-paragraph (1) "creditor" includes a contingent creditor and a prospective creditor.

[(5)   Sub-paragraph (1) is without prejudice to section 7(4)(b).]

Powers of court

13.—(1)   On hearing an administration application the court may—
    (a)   make the administration order sought;
    (b)   dismiss the application;
    (c)   adjourn the hearing conditionally or unconditionally;
    (d)   make an interim order;
    (e)   treat the application as a winding-up petition and make any order which the court could make under section 125;
    (f)   make any other order which the court thinks appropriate.

(2)   An appointment of an administrator by administration order takes effect—
    (a)   at a time appointed by the order, or
    (b)   where no time is appointed by the order, when the order is made.

(3)   An interim order under sub-paragraph (1)(d) may, in particular—
    (a)   restrict the exercise of a power of the directors or the company;
    (b)   make provision conferring a discretion on the court or on a person qualified to act as an insolvency practitioner in relation to the company.

(4)   This paragraph is subject to paragraph 39.

APPOINTMENT OF ADMINISTRATOR BY HOLDER OF FLOATING CHARGE

Power to appoint

14.—(1)   The holder of a qualifying floating charge in respect of a company's property may appoint an administrator of the company.

(2)   For the purposes of sub-paragraph (1) a floating charge qualifies if created by an instrument which—
    (a)   states that this paragraph applies to the floating charge,
    (b)   purports to empower the holder of the floating charge to appoint an administrator of the company,
    (c)   purports to empower the holder of the floating charge to make an appointment which would be the appointment of an administrative receiver within the meaning given by section 29(2), or

(d)   purports to empower the holder of a floating charge in Scotland to appoint a receiver who on appointment would be an administrative receiver.

(3)   For the purposes of sub-paragraph (1) a person is the holder of a qualifying floating charge in respect of a company's property if he holds one or more debentures of the company secured—

    (a)   by a qualifying floating charge which relates to the whole or substantially the whole of the company's property,

    (b)   by a number of qualifying floating charges which together relate to the whole or substantially the whole of the company's property, or

    (c)   by charges and other forms of security which together relate to the whole or substantially the whole of the company's property and at least one of which is a qualifying floating charge.

Restrictions on power to appoint

15.—(1)   A person may not appoint an administrator under paragraph 14 unless—

    (a)   he has given at least two business days' written notice to the holder of any prior floating charge which satisfies paragraph 14(2), or

    (b)   the holder of any prior floating charge which satisfies paragraph 14(2) has consented in writing to the making of the appointment.

(2)   One floating charge is prior to another for the purposes of this paragraph if—

    (a)   it was created first, or

    (b)   it is to be treated as having priority in accordance with an agreement to which the holder of each floating charge was party.

(3)   Sub-paragraph (2) shall have effect in relation to Scotland as if the following were substituted for paragraph (a)—

    "(a)   it has priority of ranking in accordance with section 464(4)(b) of the Companies Act 1985 (c 6),

16.   An administrator may not be appointed under paragraph 14 while a floating charge on which the appointment relies is not enforceable.

17.   An administrator of a company may not be appointed under paragraph 14 if—

    (a)   a provisional liquidator of the company has been appointed under section 135, or

    (b)   an administrative receiver of the company is in office.

Notice of appointment

18.—(1)   A person who appoints an administrator of a company under paragraph 14 shall file with the court—

    (a)   a notice of appointment, and

    (b)   such other documents as may be prescribed.

(2)   The notice of appointment must include a statutory declaration by or on behalf of the person who makes the appointment—

    (a)   that the person is the holder of a qualifying floating charge in respect of the company's property,

    (b)   that each floating charge relied on in making the appointment is (or was) enforceable on the date of the appointment, and

    (c)   that the appointment is in accordance with this Schedule.

(3)   The notice of appointment must identify the administrator and must be accompanied by a statement by the administrator—

    (a)   that he consents to the appointment,

    (b)   that in his opinion the purpose of administration is reasonably likely to be achieved, and

    (c)   giving such other information and opinions as may be prescribed.

(4)   For the purpose of a statement under sub-paragraph (3) an administrator may rely on information supplied by directors of the company (unless he has reason to doubt its accuracy).

(5)   The notice of appointment and any document accompanying it must be in the prescribed form.

(6)   A statutory declaration under sub-paragraph (2) must be made during the prescribed period.

(7)   A person commits an offence if in a statutory declaration under sub-paragraph (2) he makes a statement—

    (a)   which is false, and

    (b)   which he does not reasonably believe to be true.

Commencement of appointment

19.   The appointment of an administrator under paragraph 14 takes effect when the requirements of paragraph 18 are satisfied.

20. A person who appoints an administrator under paragraph 14—
   (a) shall notify the administrator and such other persons as may be prescribed as soon as is reasonably practicable after the requirements of paragraph 18 are satisfied, and
   (b) commits an offence if he fails without reasonable excuse to comply with paragraph (a).

Invalid appointment: indemnity

21.—(1) This paragraph applies where—
   (a) a person purports to appoint an administrator under paragraph 14, and
   (b) the appointment is discovered to be invalid.

   (2) The court may order the person who purported to make the appointment to indemnify the person appointed against liability which arises solely by reason of the appointment's invalidity.

APPOINTMENT OF ADMINISTRATOR BY COMPANY OR DIRECTORS

Power to appoint

22.—(1) A company may appoint an administrator.

   (2) The directors of a company may appoint an administrator.

Restrictions on power to appoint

23.—(1) This paragraph applies where an administrator of a company is appointed—
   (a) under paragraph 22, or
   (b) on an administration application made by the company or its directors.

   (2) An administrator of the company may not be appointed under paragraph 22 during the period of 12 months beginning with the date on which the appointment referred to in sub-paragraph (1) ceases to have effect.

24.—(1) If a moratorium for a company under Schedule A1 ends on a date when no voluntary arrangement is in force in respect of the company, this paragraph applies for the period of 12 months beginning with that date.

   (2) This paragraph also applies for the period of 12 months beginning with the date on which a voluntary arrangement in respect of a company ends if—
   (a) the arrangement was made during a moratorium for the company under Schedule A1, and
   (b) the arrangement ends prematurely (within the meaning of section 7B).

   (3) While this paragraph applies, an administrator of the company may not be appointed under paragraph 22.

25. An administrator of a company may not be appointed under paragraph 22 if—
   (a) a petition for the winding up of the company has been presented and is not yet disposed of,
   (b) an administration application has been made and is not yet disposed of, or
   (c) an administrative receiver of the company is in office.

Notice of intention to appoint

26.—(1) A person who proposes to make an appointment under paragraph 22 shall give at least five business days' written notice to—
   (a) any person who is or may be entitled to appoint an administrative receiver of the company, and
   (b) any person who is or may be entitled to appoint an administrator of the company under paragraph 14.

   (2) A person who proposes to make an appointment under paragraph 22 shall also give such notice as may be prescribed to such other persons as may be prescribed.

   (3) A notice under this paragraph must—
   (a) identify the proposed administrator, and
   (b) be in the prescribed form.

27.—(1) A person who gives notice of intention to appoint under paragraph 26 shall file with the court as soon as is reasonably practicable a copy of—
   (a) the notice, and
   (b) any document accompanying it.

   (2) The copy filed under sub-paragraph (1) must be accompanied by a statutory declaration made by or on behalf of the person who proposes to make the appointment—
   (a) that the company is or is likely to become unable to pay its debts,
   (b) that the company is not in liquidation, and

(c)   that, so far as the person making the statement is able to ascertain, the appointment is not prevented by paragraphs 23 to 25, and

(d)   to such additional effect, and giving such information, as may be prescribed.

(3)   A statutory declaration under sub-paragraph (2) must—

(a)   be in the prescribed form, and

(b)   be made during the prescribed period.

(4)   A person commits an offence if in a statutory declaration under sub-paragraph (2) he makes a statement—

(a)   which is false, and

(b)   which he does not reasonably believe to be true.

28.—(1)   An appointment may not be made under paragraph 22 unless the person who makes the appointment has complied with any requirement of paragraphs 26 and 27 and—

(a)   the period of notice specified in paragraph 26(1) has expired, or

(b)   each person to whom notice has been given under paragraph 26(1) has consented in writing to the making of the appointment.

(2)   An appointment may not be made under paragraph 22 after the period of ten business days beginning with the date on which the notice of intention to appoint is filed under paragraph 27(1).

Notice of appointment

29.—(1)   A person who appoints an administrator of a company under paragraph 22 shall file with the court—

(a)   a notice of appointment, and

(b)   such other documents as may be prescribed.

(2)   The notice of appointment must include a statutory declaration by or on behalf of the person who makes the appointment—

(a)   that the person is entitled to make an appointment under paragraph 22,

(b)   that the appointment is in accordance with this Schedule, and

(c)   that, so far as the person making the statement is able to ascertain, the statements made and information given in the statutory declaration filed with the notice of intention to appoint remain accurate.

(3)   The notice of appointment must identify the administrator and must be accompanied by a statement by the administrator—

(a)   that he consents to the appointment,

(b)   that in his opinion the purpose of administration is reasonably likely to be achieved, and

(c)   giving such other information and opinions as may be prescribed.

(4)   For the purpose of a statement under sub-paragraph (3) an administrator may rely on information supplied by directors of the company (unless he has reason to doubt its accuracy).

(5)   The notice of appointment and any document accompanying it must be in the prescribed form.

(6)   A statutory declaration under sub-paragraph (2) must be made during the prescribed period.

(7)   A person commits an offence if in a statutory declaration under sub-paragraph (2) he makes a statement—

(a)   which is false, and

(b)   which he does not reasonably believe to be true.

30.   In a case in which no person is entitled to notice of intention to appoint under paragraph 26(1) (and paragraph 28 therefore does not apply)—

(a)   the statutory declaration accompanying the notice of appointment must include the statements and information required under paragraph 27(2), and

(b)   paragraph 29(2)(c) shall not apply.

Commencement of appointment

31.   The appointment of an administrator under paragraph 22 takes effect when the requirements of paragraph 29 are satisfied.

32.   A person who appoints an administrator under paragraph 22—

(a)   shall notify the administrator and such other persons as may be prescribed as soon as is reasonably practicable after the requirements of paragraph 29 are satisfied, and

(b)   commits an offence if he fails without reasonable excuse to comply with paragraph (a).

33.   If before the requirements of paragraph 29 are satisfied the company enters administration by virtue of an administration order or an appointment under paragraph 14—

(a)   the appointment under paragraph 22 shall not take effect, and

(b)   paragraph 32 shall not apply.

Invalid appointment: indemnity

34.—(1) This paragraph applies where—
  (a) a person purports to appoint an administrator under paragraph 22, and
  (b) the appointment is discovered to be invalid.

(2) The court may order the person who purported to make the appointment to indemnify the person appointed against liability which arises solely by reason of the appointment's invalidity.

ADMINISTRATION APPLICATION—SPECIAL CASES

Application by holder of floating charge

35.—(1) This paragraph applies where an administration application in respect of a company—
  (a) is made by the holder of a qualifying floating charge in respect of the company's property, and
  (b) includes a statement that the application is made in reliance on this paragraph.

(2) The court may make an administration order—
  (a) whether or not satisfied that the company is or is likely to become unable to pay its debts, but
  (b) only if satisfied that the applicant could appoint an administrator under paragraph 14.

Intervention by holder of floating charge

36.—(1) This paragraph applies where—
  (a) an administration application in respect of a company is made by a person who is not the holder of a qualifying floating charge in respect of the company's property, and
  (b) the holder of a qualifying floating charge in respect of the company's property applies to the court to have a specified person appointed as administrator (and not the person specified by the administration applicant).

(2) The court shall grant an application under sub-paragraph (1)(b) unless the court thinks it right to refuse the application because of the particular circumstances of the case.

Application where company in liquidation

37.—(1) This paragraph applies where the holder of a qualifying floating charge in respect of a company's property could appoint an administrator under paragraph 14 but for paragraph 8(1)(b).

(2) The holder of the qualifying floating charge may make an administration application.

(3) If the court makes an administration order on hearing an application made by virtue of sub-paragraph (2)—
  (a) the court shall discharge the winding-up order,
  (b) the court shall make provision for such matters as may be prescribed,
  (c) the court may make other consequential provision,
  (d) the court shall specify which of the powers under this Schedule are to be exercisable by the administrator, and
  (e) this Schedule shall have effect with such modifications as the court may specify.

38.—(1) The liquidator of a company may make an administration application.

(2) If the court makes an administration order on hearing an application made by virtue of sub-paragraph (1)—
  (a) the court shall discharge any winding-up order in respect of the company,
  (b) the court shall make provision for such matters as may be prescribed,
  (c) the court may make other consequential provision,
  (d) the court shall specify which of the powers under this Schedule are to be exercisable by the administrator, and
  (e) this Schedule shall have effect with such modifications as the court may specify.

Effect of administrative receivership

39.—(1) Where there is an administrative receiver of a company the court must dismiss an administration application in respect of the company unless—
  (a) the person by or on behalf of whom the receiver was appointed consents to the making of the administration order,
  (b) the court thinks that the security by virtue of which the receiver was appointed would be liable to be released or discharged under sections 238 to 240 (transaction at undervalue and preference) if an administration order were made,
  (c) the court thinks that the security by virtue of which the receiver was appointed would be avoided under section 245 (avoidance of floating charge) if an administration order were made, or

    (d)   the court thinks that the security by virtue of which the receiver was appointed would be challengeable under section 242 (gratuitous alienations) or 243 (unfair preferences) or under any rule of law in Scotland.

(2)   Sub-paragraph (1) applies whether the administrative receiver is appointed before or after the making of the administration application.

EFFECT OF ADMINISTRATION

Dismissal of pending winding-up petition

40.—(1)   A petition for the winding up of a company—
    (a)   shall be dismissed on the making of an administration order in respect of the company, and
    (b)   shall be suspended while the company is in administration following an appointment under paragraph 14.

(2)   Sub-paragraph (1)(b) does not apply to a petition presented under—
    (a)   section 124A (public interest),
    [(aa)   section 124B (SEs),] or
    (b)   section 367 of the Financial Services and Markets Act 2000 (c 8) (petition by Financial Services Authority).

(3)   Where an administrator becomes aware that a petition was presented under a provision referred to in sub-paragraph (2) before his appointment, he shall apply to the court for directions under paragraph 63.

Dismissal of administrative or other receiver

41.—(1)   When an administration order takes effect in respect of a company any administrative receiver of the company shall vacate office.

(2)   Where a company is in administration, any receiver of part of the company's property shall vacate office if the administrator requires him to.

(3)   Where an administrative receiver or receiver vacates office under sub-paragraph (1) or (2)—
    (a)   his remuneration shall be charged on and paid out of any property of the company which was in his custody or under his control immediately before he vacated office, and
    (b)   he need not take any further steps under section 40 or 59.

(4)   In the application of sub-paragraph (3)(a)—
    (a)   "remuneration" includes expenses properly incurred and any indemnity to which the administrative receiver or receiver is entitled out of the assets of the company,
    (b)   the charge imposed takes priority over security held by the person by whom or on whose behalf the administrative receiver or receiver was appointed, and
    (c)   the provision for payment is subject to paragraph 43.

Moratorium on insolvency proceedings

42.—(1)   This paragraph applies to a company in administration.

(2)   No resolution may be passed for the winding up of the company.

(3)   No order may be made for the winding up of the company.

(4)   Sub-paragraph (3) does not apply to an order made on a petition presented under—
    (a)   section 124A (public interest),
    [(aa)   section 124B (SEs),] or
    (b)   section 367 of the Financial Services and Markets Act 2000 (c 8) (petition by Financial Services Authority).

(5)   If a petition presented under a provision referred to in sub-paragraph (4) comes to the attention of the administrator, he shall apply to the court for directions under paragraph 63.

Moratorium on other legal process

43.—(1)   This paragraph applies to a company in administration.

(2)   No step may be taken to enforce security over the company's property except—
    (a)   with the consent of the administrator, or
    (b)   with the permission of the court.

(3)   No step may be taken to repossess goods in the company's possession under a hire-purchase agreement except—
    (a)   with the consent of the administrator, or
    (b)   with the permission of the court.

(4)   A landlord may not exercise a right of forfeiture by peaceable re-entry in relation to premises let to the company except—

    (a)   with the consent of the administrator, or
    (b)   with the permission of the court.

    (5)   In Scotland, a landlord may not exercise a right of irritancy in relation to premises let to the company except—
    (a)   with the consent of the administrator, or
    (b)   with the permission of the court.

    (6)   No legal process (including legal proceedings, execution, distress and diligence) may be instituted or continued against the company or property of the company except—
    (a)   with the consent of the administrator, or
    (b)   with the permission of the court.

    [(6A)   An administrative receiver of the company may not be appointed.]

    (7)   Where the court gives permission for a transaction under this paragraph it may impose a condition on or a requirement in connection with the transaction.

    (8)   In this paragraph "landlord" includes a person to whom rent is payable.

Interim moratorium

44.—(1)   This paragraph applies where an administration application in respect of a company has been made and—
    (a)   the application has not yet been granted or dismissed, or
    (b)   the application has been granted but the administration order has not yet taken effect.

    (2)   This paragraph also applies from the time when a copy of notice of intention to appoint an administrator under paragraph 14 is filed with the court until—
    (a)   the appointment of the administrator takes effect, or
    (b)   the period of five business days beginning with the date of filing expires without an administrator having been appointed.

    (3)   Sub-paragraph (2) has effect in relation to a notice of intention to appoint only if it is in the prescribed form.

    (4)   This paragraph also applies from the time when a copy of notice of intention to appoint an administrator is filed with the court under paragraph 27(1) until—
    (a)   the appointment of the administrator takes effect, or
    (b)   the period specified in paragraph 28(2) expires without an administrator having been appointed.

    (5)   The provisions of paragraphs 42 and 43 shall apply (ignoring any reference to the consent of the administrator).

    (6)   If there is an administrative receiver of the company when the administration application is made, the provisions of paragraphs 42 and 43 shall not begin to apply by virtue of this paragraph until the person by or on behalf of whom the receiver was appointed consents to the making of the administration order.

    (7)   This paragraph does not prevent or require the permission of the court for—
    (a)   the presentation of a petition for the winding up of the company under a provision mentioned in paragraph 42(4),
    (b)   the appointment of an administrator under paragraph 14,
    (c)   the appointment of an administrative receiver of the company, or
    (d)   the carrying out by an administrative receiver (whenever appointed) of his functions.

Publicity

[45.—(1)   While a company is in administration, every business document issued by or on behalf of the company or the administrator, and all the company's websites, must state—
    (a)   the name of the administrator, and
    (b)   that the affairs, business and property of the company are being managed by the administrator.

    (2)   Any of the following persons commits an offence if without reasonable excuse the person authorises or permits a contravention of sub-paragraph (1)—
    (a)   the administrator,
    (b)   an officer of the company, and
    (c)   the company.

    (3)   In sub-paragraph (1) "business document" means—
    (a)   an invoice,
    (b)   an order for goods or services,
    (c)   a business letter, and
    (d)   an order form,
whether in hard copy, electronic or any other form.]

PROCESS OF ADMINISTRATION

Announcement of administrator's appointment

46.—(1) This paragraph applies where a person becomes the administrator of a company.

(2) As soon as is reasonably practicable the administrator shall—
  (a) send a notice of his appointment to the company, and
  (b) publish a notice of his appointment in the prescribed manner.

(3) As soon as is reasonably practicable the administrator shall—
  (a) obtain a list of the company's creditors, and
  (b) send a notice of his appointment to each creditor of whose claim and address he is aware.

(4) The administrator shall send a notice of his appointment to the registrar of companies before the end of the period of 7 days beginning with the date specified in sub-paragraph (6).

(5) The administrator shall send a notice of his appointment to such persons as may be prescribed before the end of the prescribed period beginning with the date specified in sub-paragraph (6).

(6) The date for the purpose of sub-paragraphs (4) and (5) is—
  (a) in the case of an administrator appointed by administration order, the date of the order,
  (b) in the case of an administrator appointed under paragraph 14, the date on which he receives notice under paragraph 20, and
  (c) in the case of an administrator appointed under paragraph 22, the date on which he receives notice under paragraph 32.

(7) The court may direct that sub-paragraph (3)(b) or (5)—
  (a) shall not apply, or
  (b) shall apply with the substitution of a different period.

(8) A notice under this paragraph must—
  (a) contain the prescribed information, and
  (b) be in the prescribed form.

(9) An administrator commits an offence if he fails without reasonable excuse to comply with a requirement of this paragraph.

Statement of company's affairs

47.—(1) As soon as is reasonably practicable after appointment the administrator of a company shall by notice in the prescribed form require one or more relevant persons to provide the administrator with a statement of the affairs of the company.

(2) The statement must—
  (a) be verified by a statement of truth in accordance with Civil Procedure Rules,
  (b) be in the prescribed form,
  (c) give particulars of the company's property, debts and liabilities,
  (d) give the names and addresses of the company's creditors,
  (e) specify the security held by each creditor,
  (f) give the date on which each security was granted, and
  (g) contain such other information as may be prescribed.

(3) In sub-paragraph (1) "relevant person" means—
  (a) a person who is or has been an officer of the company,
  (b) a person who took part in the formation of the company during the period of one year ending with the date on which the company enters administration,
  (c) a person employed by the company during that period, and
  (d) a person who is or has been during that period an officer or employee of a company which is or has been during that year an officer of the company.

(4) For the purpose of sub-paragraph (3) a reference to employment is a reference to employment through a contract of employment or a contract for services.

(5) In Scotland, a statement of affairs under sub-paragraph (1) must be a statutory declaration made in accordance with the Statutory Declarations Act 1835 (c 62) (and sub-paragraph (2)(a) shall not apply).

48.—(1) A person required to submit a statement of affairs must do so before the end of the period of 11 days beginning with the day on which he receives notice of the requirement.

(2) The administrator may—
  (a) revoke a requirement under paragraph 47(1), or
  (b) extend the period specified in sub-paragraph (1) (whether before or after expiry).

(3) If the administrator refuses a request to act under sub-paragraph (2)—
  (a) the person whose request is refused may apply to the court, and

(b)   the court may take action of a kind specified in sub-paragraph (2).

(4)   A person commits an offence if he fails without reasonable excuse to comply with a requirement under paragraph 47(1).

Administrator's proposals

49.—(1)   The administrator of a company shall make a statement setting out proposals for achieving the purpose of administration.

(2)   A statement under sub-paragraph (1) must, in particular—
  (a)   deal with such matters as may be prescribed, and
  (b)   where applicable, explain why the administrator thinks that the objective mentioned in paragraph 3(1)(a) or (b) cannot be achieved.

(3)   Proposals under this paragraph may include—
  (a)   a proposal for a voluntary arrangement under Part I of this Act (although this paragraph is without prejudice to section 4(3));
  (b)   a proposal for a compromise or arrangement to be sanctioned under [Part 26 of the Companies Act 2006 (arrangements and reconstructions)].

(4)   The administrator shall send a copy of the statement of his proposals—
  (a)   to the registrar of companies,
  (b)   to every creditor of the company of whose claim and address he is aware, and
  (c)   to every member of the company of whose address he is aware.

(5)   The administrator shall comply with sub-paragraph (4)—
  (a)   as soon as is reasonably practicable after the company enters administration, and
  (b)   in any event, before the end of the period of eight weeks beginning with the day on which the company enters administration.

(6)   The administrator shall be taken to comply with sub-paragraph (4)(c) if he publishes in the prescribed manner a notice undertaking to provide a copy of the statement of proposals free of charge to any member of the company who applies in writing to a specified address.

(7)   An administrator commits an offence if he fails without reasonable excuse to comply with sub-paragraph (5).

(8)   A period specified in this paragraph may be varied in accordance with paragraph 107.

Creditors' meeting

50.—(1)   In this Schedule "creditors' meeting" means a meeting of creditors of a company summoned by the administrator—
  (a)   in the prescribed manner, and
  (b)   giving the prescribed period of notice to every creditor of the company of whose claim and address he is aware.

(2)   A period prescribed under sub-paragraph (1)(b) may be varied in accordance with paragraph 107.

(3)   A creditors' meeting shall be conducted in accordance with the rules.

Requirement for initial creditors' meeting

51.—(1)   Each copy of an administrator's statement of proposals sent to a creditor under paragraph 49(4)(b) must be accompanied by an invitation to a creditors' meeting (an "initial creditors' meeting").

(2)   The date set for an initial creditors' meeting must be—
  (a)   as soon as is reasonably practicable after the company enters administration, and
  (b)   in any event, within the period of ten weeks beginning with the date on which the company enters administration.

(3)   An administrator shall present a copy of his statement of proposals to an initial creditors' meeting.

(4)   A period specified in this paragraph may be varied in accordance with paragraph 107.

(5)   An administrator commits an offence if he fails without reasonable excuse to comply with a requirement of this paragraph.

52.—(1)   Paragraph 51(1) shall not apply where the statement of proposals states that the administrator thinks—
  (a)   that the company has sufficient property to enable each creditor of the company to be paid in full,
  (b)   that the company has insufficient property to enable a distribution to be made to unsecured creditors other than by virtue of section 176A(2)(a), or
  (c)   that neither of the objectives specified in paragraph 3(1)(a) and (b) can be achieved.

(2) But the administrator shall summon an initial creditors' meeting if it is requested—
  (a) by creditors of the company whose debts amount to at least 10% of the total debts of the company,
  (b) in the prescribed manner, and
  (c) in the prescribed period.

(3) A meeting requested under sub-paragraph (2) must be summoned for a date in the prescribed period.

(4) The period prescribed under sub-paragraph (3) may be varied in accordance with paragraph 107.

Business and result of initial creditors' meeting

53.—(1) An initial creditors' meeting to which an administrator's proposals are presented shall consider them and may—
  (a) approve them without modification, or
  (b) approve them with modification to which the administrator consents.

(2) After the conclusion of an initial creditors' meeting the administrator shall as soon as is reasonably practicable report any decision taken to—
  (a) the court,
  (b) the registrar of companies, and
  (c) such other persons as may be prescribed.

(3) An administrator commits an offence if he fails without reasonable excuse to comply with sub-paragraph (2).

Revision of administrator's proposals

54.—(1) This paragraph applies where—
  (a) an administrator's proposals have been approved (with or without modification) at an initial creditors' meeting,
  (b) the administrator proposes a revision to the proposals, and
  (c) the administrator thinks that the proposed revision is substantial.

(2) The administrator shall—
  (a) summon a creditors' meeting,
  (b) send a statement in the prescribed form of the proposed revision with the notice of the meeting sent to each creditor,
  (c) send a copy of the statement, within the prescribed period, to each member of the company of whose address he is aware, and
  (d) present a copy of the statement to the meeting.

(3) The administrator shall be taken to have complied with sub-paragraph (2)(c) if he publishes a notice undertaking to provide a copy of the statement free of charge to any member of the company who applies in writing to a specified address.

(4) A notice under sub-paragraph (3) must be published—
  (a) in the prescribed manner, and
  (b) within the prescribed period.

(5) A creditors' meeting to which a proposed revision is presented shall consider it and may—
  (a) approve it without modification, or
  (b) approve it with modification to which the administrator consents.

(6) After the conclusion of a creditors' meeting the administrator shall as soon as is reasonably practicable report any decision taken to—
  (a) the court,
  (b) the registrar of companies, and
  (c) such other persons as may be prescribed.

(7) An administrator commits an offence if he fails without reasonable excuse to comply with sub-paragraph (6).

Failure to obtain approval of administrator's proposals

55.—(1) This paragraph applies where an administrator reports to the court that—
  (a) an initial creditors' meeting has failed to approve the administrator's proposals presented to it, or
  (b) a creditors' meeting has failed to approve a revision of the administrator's proposals presented to it.

(2) The court may—
  (a) provide that the appointment of an administrator shall cease to have effect from a specified time;
  (b) adjourn the hearing conditionally or unconditionally;

(c)   make an interim order;

(d)   make an order on a petition for winding up suspended by virtue of paragraph 40(1)(b);

(e)   make any other order (including an order making consequential provision) that the court thinks appropriate.

Further creditors' meetings

56.—(1)   The administrator of a company shall summon a creditors' meeting if—

(a)   it is requested in the prescribed manner by creditors of the company whose debts amount to at least 10% of the total debts of the company, or

(b)   he is directed by the court to summon a creditors' meeting.

(2)   An administrator commits an offence if he fails without reasonable excuse to summon a creditors' meeting as required by this paragraph.

Creditors' committee

57.—(1)   A creditors' meeting may establish a creditors' committee.

(2)   A creditors' committee shall carry out functions conferred on it by or under this Act.

(3)   A creditors' committee may require the administrator—

(a)   to attend on the committee at any reasonable time of which he is given at least seven days' notice, and

(b)   to provide the committee with information about the exercise of his functions.

Correspondence instead of creditors' meeting

58.—(1)   Anything which is required or permitted by or under this Schedule to be done at a creditors' meeting may be done by correspondence between the administrator and creditors—

(a)   in accordance with the rules, and

(b)   subject to any prescribed condition.

(2)   A reference in this Schedule to anything done at a creditors' meeting includes a reference to anything done in the course of correspondence in reliance on sub-paragraph (1).

(3)   A requirement to hold a creditors' meeting is satisfied by conducting correspondence in accordance with this paragraph.

FUNCTIONS OF ADMINISTRATOR

General powers

59.—(1)   The administrator of a company may do anything necessary or expedient for the management of the affairs, business and property of the company.

(2)   A provision of this Schedule which expressly permits the administrator to do a specified thing is without prejudice to the generality of sub-paragraph (1).

(3)   A person who deals with the administrator of a company in good faith and for value need not inquire whether the administrator is acting within his powers.

60.   The administrator of a company has the powers specified in Schedule 1 to this Act.

61.   The administrator of a company—

(a)   may remove a director of the company, and

(b)   may appoint a director of the company (whether or not to fill a vacancy).

62.   The administrator of a company may call a meeting of members or creditors of the company.

63.   The administrator of a company may apply to the court for directions in connection with his functions.

64.—(1)   A company in administration or an officer of a company in administration may not exercise a management power without the consent of the administrator.

(2)   For the purpose of sub-paragraph (1)—

(a)   "management power" means a power which could be exercised so as to interfere with the exercise of the administrator's powers,

(b)   it is immaterial whether the power is conferred by an enactment or an instrument, and

(c)   consent may be general or specific.

Distribution

65.—(1)   The administrator of a company may make a distribution to a creditor of the company.

(2)   Section 175 shall apply in relation to a distribution under this paragraph as it applies in relation to a winding up.

(3)   A payment may not be made by way of distribution under this paragraph to a creditor of the company who is neither secured nor preferential unless the court gives permission.

66. The administrator of a company may make a payment otherwise than in accordance with paragraph 65 or paragraph 13 of Schedule 1 if he thinks it likely to assist achievement of the purpose of administration.

General duties

67. The administrator of a company shall on his appointment take custody or control of all the property to which he thinks the company is entitled.

68.—(1) Subject to sub-paragraph (2), the administrator of a company shall manage its affairs, business and property in accordance with—

 (a) any proposals approved under paragraph 53,

 (b) any revision of those proposals which is made by him and which he does not consider substantial, and

 (c) any revision of those proposals approved under paragraph 54.

(2) If the court gives directions to the administrator of a company in connection with any aspect of his management of the company's affairs, business or property, the administrator shall comply with the directions.

(3) The court may give directions under sub-paragraph (2) only if—

 (a) no proposals have been approved under paragraph 53,

 (b) the directions are consistent with any proposals or revision approved under paragraph 53 or 54,

 (c) the court thinks the directions are required in order to reflect a change in circumstances since the approval of proposals or a revision under paragraph 53 or 54, or

 (d) the court thinks the directions are desirable because of a misunderstanding about proposals or a revision approved under paragraph 53 or 54.

Administrator as agent of company

69. In exercising his functions under this Schedule the administrator of a company acts as its agent.

Charged property: floating charge

70.—(1) The administrator of a company may dispose of or take action relating to property which is subject to a floating charge as if it were not subject to the charge.

(2) Where property is disposed of in reliance on sub-paragraph (1) the holder of the floating charge shall have the same priority in respect of acquired property as he had in respect of the property disposed of.

(3) In sub-paragraph (2) "acquired property" means property of the company which directly or indirectly represents the property disposed of.

Charged property: non-floating charge

71.—(1) The court may by order enable the administrator of a company to dispose of property which is subject to a security (other than a floating charge) as if it were not subject to the security.

(2) An order under sub-paragraph (1) may be made only—

 (a) on the application of the administrator, and

 (b) where the court thinks that disposal of the property would be likely to promote the purpose of administration in respect of the company.

(3) An order under this paragraph is subject to the condition that there be applied towards discharging the sums secured by the security—

 (a) the net proceeds of disposal of the property, and

 (b) any additional money required to be added to the net proceeds so as to produce the amount determined by the court as the net amount which would be realised on a sale of the property at market value.

(4) If an order under this paragraph relates to more than one security, application of money under sub-paragraph (3) shall be in the order of the priorities of the securities.

(5) An administrator who makes a successful application for an order under this paragraph shall send a copy of the order to the registrar of companies before the end of the period of 14 days starting with the date of the order.

(6) An administrator commits an offence if he fails to comply with sub-paragraph (5) without reasonable excuse.

Hire-purchase property

72.—(1)   The court may by order enable the administrator of a company to dispose of goods which are in the possession of the company under a hire-purchase agreement as if all the rights of the owner under the agreement were vested in the company.

(2)   An order under sub-paragraph (1) may be made only—
  (a)   on the application of the administrator, and
  (b)   where the court thinks that disposal of the goods would be likely to promote the purpose of administration in respect of the company.

(3)   An order under this paragraph is subject to the condition that there be applied towards discharging the sums payable under the hire-purchase agreement—
  (a)   the net proceeds of disposal of the goods, and
  (b)   any additional money required to be added to the net proceeds so as to produce the amount determined by the court as the net amount which would be realised on a sale of the goods at market value.

(4)   An administrator who makes a successful application for an order under this paragraph shall send a copy of the order to the registrar of companies before the end of the period of 14 days starting with the date of the order.

(5)   An administrator commits an offence if he fails without reasonable excuse to comply with sub-paragraph (4).

Protection for secured or preferential creditor

73.—(1)   An administrator's statement of proposals under paragraph 49 may not include any action which—
  (a)   affects the right of a secured creditor of the company to enforce his security,
  (b)   would result in a preferential debt of the company being paid otherwise than in priority to its non-preferential debts, or
  (c)   would result in one preferential creditor of the company being paid a smaller proportion of his debt than another.

(2)   Sub-paragraph (1) does not apply to—
  (a)   action to which the relevant creditor consents,
  (b)   a proposal for a voluntary arrangement under Part I of this Act (although this sub-paragraph is without prejudice to section 4(3)), ...
  (c)   a proposal for a compromise or arrangement to be sanctioned under [Part 26 of the Companies Act 2006 (arrangements and reconstructions)]; [or
  (d)   a proposal for a cross-border merger within the meaning of regulation 2 of the Companies (Cross-Border Mergers) Regulations 2007].

(3)   The reference to a statement of proposals in sub-paragraph (1) includes a reference to a statement as revised or modified.

Challenge to administrator's conduct of company

74.—(1)   A creditor or member of a company in administration may apply to the court claiming that—
  (a)   the administrator is acting or has acted so as unfairly to harm the interests of the applicant (whether alone or in common with some or all other members or creditors), or
  (b)   the administrator proposes to act in a way which would unfairly harm the interests of the applicant (whether alone or in common with some or all other members or creditors).

(2)   A creditor or member of a company in administration may apply to the court claiming that the administrator is not performing his functions as quickly or as efficiently as is reasonably practicable.

(3)   The court may—
  (a)   grant relief;
  (b)   dismiss the application;
  (c)   adjourn the hearing conditionally or unconditionally;
  (d)   make an interim order;
  (e)   make any other order it thinks appropriate.

(4)   In particular, an order under this paragraph may—
  (a)   regulate the administrator's exercise of his functions;
  (b)   require the administrator to do or not do a specified thing;
  (c)   require a creditors' meeting to be held for a specified purpose;
  (d)   provide for the appointment of an administrator to cease to have effect;
  (e)   make consequential provision.

(5)   An order may be made on a claim under sub-paragraph (1) whether or not the action complained of—

(a)   is within the administrator's powers under this Schedule;
(b)   was taken in reliance on an order under paragraph 71 or 72.

(6)   An order may not be made under this paragraph if it would impede or prevent the implementation of—
(a)   a voluntary arrangement approved under Part I,
(b)   a compromise or arrangement sanctioned under [Part 26 of the Companies Act 2006 (arrangements and reconstructions)], ...
[(ba) a cross-border merger within the meaning of regulation 2 of the Companies (Cross-Border Mergers) Regulations 2007, or].
(c)   proposals or a revision approved under paragraph 53 or 54 more than 28 days before the day on which the application for the order under this paragraph is made.

Misfeasance

75.—(1)   The court may examine the conduct of a person who—
(a)   is or purports to be the administrator of a company, or
(b)   has been or has purported to be the administrator of a company.

(2)   An examination under this paragraph may be held only on the application of—
(a)   the official receiver,
(b)   the administrator of the company,
(c)   the liquidator of the company,
(d)   a creditor of the company, or
(e)   a contributory of the company.

(3)   An application under sub-paragraph (2) must allege that the administrator—
(a)   has misapplied or retained money or other property of the company,
(b)   has become accountable for money or other property of the company,
(c)   has breached a fiduciary or other duty in relation to the company, or
(d)   has been guilty of misfeasance.

(4)   On an examination under this paragraph into a person's conduct the court may order him—
(a)   to repay, restore or account for money or property;
(b)   to pay interest;
(c)   to contribute a sum to the company's property by way of compensation for breach of duty or misfeasance.

(5)   In sub-paragraph (3) "administrator" includes a person who purports or has purported to be a company's administrator.

(6)   An application under sub-paragraph (2) may be made in respect of an administrator who has been discharged under paragraph 98 only with the permission of the court.

ENDING ADMINISTRATION

Automatic end of administration

76.—(1)   The appointment of an administrator shall cease to have effect at the end of the period of one year beginning with the date on which it takes effect.

(2)   But—
(a)   on the application of an administrator the court may by order extend his term of office for a specified period, and
(b)   an administrator's term of office may be extended for a specified period not exceeding six months by consent.

77.—(1)   An order of the court under paragraph 76—
(a)   may be made in respect of an administrator whose term of office has already been extended by order or by consent, but
(b)   may not be made after the expiry of the administrator's term of office.

(2)   Where an order is made under paragraph 76 the administrator shall as soon as is reasonably practicable notify the registrar of companies.

(3)   An administrator who fails without reasonable excuse to comply with sub-paragraph (2) commits an offence.

78.—(1)   In paragraph 76(2)(b) "consent" means consent of—
(a)   each secured creditor of the company, and
(b)   if the company has unsecured debts, creditors whose debts amount to more than 50% of the company's unsecured debts, disregarding debts of any creditor who does not respond to an invitation to give or withhold consent.

(2)   But where the administrator has made a statement under paragraph 52(1)(b) "consent" means—
(a)   consent of each secured creditor of the company, or

(b)   if the administrator thinks that a distribution may be made to preferential creditors, consent of—

     (i)   each secured creditor of the company, and

    (ii)   preferential creditors whose debts amount to more than 50% of the preferential debts of the company, disregarding debts of any creditor who does not respond to an invitation to give or withhold consent.

(3)   Consent for the purposes of paragraph 76(2)(b) may be—

(a)   written, or

(b)   signified at a creditors' meeting.

(4)   An administrator's term of office—

(a)   may be extended by consent only once,

(b)   may not be extended by consent after extension by order of the court, and

(c)   may not be extended by consent after expiry.

(5)   Where an administrator's term of office is extended by consent he shall as soon as is reasonably practicable—

(a)   file notice of the extension with the court, and

(b)   notify the registrar of companies.

(6)   An administrator who fails without reasonable excuse to comply with sub-paragraph (5) commits an offence.

Court ending administration on application of administrator

79.—(1)   On the application of the administrator of a company the court may provide for the appointment of an administrator of the company to cease to have effect from a specified time.

(2)   The administrator of a company shall make an application under this paragraph if—

(a)   he thinks the purpose of administration cannot be achieved in relation to the company,

(b)   he thinks the company should not have entered administration, or

(c)   a creditors' meeting requires him to make an application under this paragraph.

(3)   The administrator of a company shall make an application under this paragraph if—

(a)   the administration is pursuant to an administration order, and

(b)   the administrator thinks that the purpose of administration has been sufficiently achieved in relation to the company.

(4)   On an application under this paragraph the court may—

(a)   adjourn the hearing conditionally or unconditionally;

(b)   dismiss the application;

(c)   make an interim order;

(d)   make any order it thinks appropriate (whether in addition to, in consequence of or instead of the order applied for).

Termination of administration where objective achieved

80.—(1)   This paragraph applies where an administrator of a company is appointed under paragraph 14 or 22.

(2)   If the administrator thinks that the purpose of administration has been sufficiently achieved in relation to the company he may file a notice in the prescribed form—

(a)   with the court, and

(b)   with the registrar of companies.

(3)   The administrator's appointment shall cease to have effect when the requirements of sub-paragraph (2) are satisfied.

(4)   Where the administrator files a notice he shall within the prescribed period send a copy to every creditor of the company of whose claim and address he is aware.

(5)   The rules may provide that the administrator is taken to have complied with sub-paragraph (4) if before the end of the prescribed period he publishes in the prescribed manner a notice undertaking to provide a copy of the notice under sub-paragraph (2) to any creditor of the company who applies in writing to a specified address.

(6)   An administrator who fails without reasonable excuse to comply with sub-paragraph (4) commits an offence.

Court ending administration on application of creditor

81.—(1)   On the application of a creditor of a company the court may provide for the appointment of an administrator of the company to cease to have effect at a specified time.

(2)   An application under this paragraph must allege an improper motive—

(a) in the case of an administrator appointed by administration order, on the part of the applicant for the order, or

(b) in any other case, on the part of the person who appointed the administrator.

(3) On an application under this paragraph the court may—

(a) adjourn the hearing conditionally or unconditionally;

(b) dismiss the application;

(c) make an interim order;

(d) make any order it thinks appropriate (whether in addition to, in consequence of or instead of the order applied for).

Public interest winding-up

82.—(1) This paragraph applies where a winding-up order is made for the winding up of a company in administration on a petition presented under—

(a) section 124A (public interest),

[(aa) section 124B (SEs),] or

(b) section 367 of the Financial Services and Markets Act 2000 (c 8) (petition by Financial Services Authority).

(2) This paragraph also applies where a provisional liquidator of a company in administration is appointed following the presentation of a petition under any of the provisions listed in sub-paragraph (1).

(3) The court shall order—

(a) that the appointment of the administrator shall cease to have effect, or

(b) that the appointment of the administrator shall continue to have effect.

(4) If the court makes an order under sub-paragraph (3)(b) it may also—

(a) specify which of the powers under this Schedule are to be exercisable by the administrator, and

(b) order that this Schedule shall have effect in relation to the administrator with specified modifications.

Moving from administration to creditors' voluntary liquidation

83.—(1) This paragraph applies in England and Wales where the administrator of a company thinks—

(a) that the total amount which each secured creditor of the company is likely to receive has been paid to him or set aside for him, and

(b) that a distribution will be made to unsecured creditors of the company (if there are any).

(2) This paragraph applies in Scotland where the administrator of a company thinks—

(a) that each secured creditor of the company will receive payment in respect of his debt, and

(b) that a distribution will be made to unsecured creditors (if there are any).

(3) The administrator may send to the registrar of companies a notice that this paragraph applies.

(4) On receipt of a notice under sub-paragraph (3) the registrar shall register it.

(5) If an administrator sends a notice under sub-paragraph (3) he shall as soon as is reasonably practicable—

(a) file a copy of the notice with the court, and

(b) send a copy of the notice to each creditor of whose claim and address he is aware.

(6) On the registration of a notice under sub-paragraph (3)—

(a) the appointment of an administrator in respect of the company shall cease to have effect, and

(b) the company shall be wound up as if a resolution for voluntary winding up under section 84 were passed on the day on which the notice is registered.

(7) The liquidator for the purposes of the winding up shall be—

(a) a person nominated by the creditors of the company in the prescribed manner and within the prescribed period, or

(b) if no person is nominated under paragraph (a), the administrator.

(8) In the application of Part IV to a winding up by virtue of this paragraph—

(a) section 85 shall not apply,

(b) section 86 shall apply as if the reference to the time of the passing of the resolution for voluntary winding up were a reference to the beginning of the date of registration of the notice under sub-paragraph (3),

(c) section 89 does not apply,

(d) sections 98, 99 and 100 shall not apply,

(e) section 129 shall apply as if the reference to the time of the passing of the resolution for voluntary winding up were a reference to the beginning of the date of registration of the notice under sub-paragraph (3), and

(f) any creditors' committee which is in existence immediately before the company ceases to be in administration shall continue in existence after that time as if appointed as a liquidation committee under section 101.

Moving from administration to dissolution

84.—(1) If the administrator of a company thinks that the company has no property which might permit a distribution to its creditors, he shall send a notice to that effect to the registrar of companies.

(2) The court may on the application of the administrator of a company disapply sub-paragraph (1) in respect of the company.

(3) On receipt of a notice under sub-paragraph (1) the registrar shall register it.

(4) On the registration of a notice in respect of a company under sub-paragraph (1) the appointment of an administrator of the company shall cease to have effect.

(5) If an administrator sends a notice under sub-paragraph (1) he shall as soon as is reasonably practicable—
   (a) file a copy of the notice with the court, and
   (b) send a copy of the notice to each creditor of whose claim and address he is aware.

(6) At the end of the period of three months beginning with the date of registration of a notice in respect of a company under sub-paragraph (1) the company is deemed to be dissolved.

(7) On an application in respect of a company by the administrator or another interested person the court may—
   (a) extend the period specified in sub-paragraph (6),
   (b) suspend that period, or
   (c) disapply sub-paragraph (6).

(8) Where an order is made under sub-paragraph (7) in respect of a company the administrator shall as soon as is reasonably practicable notify the registrar of companies.

(9) An administrator commits an offence if he fails without reasonable excuse to comply with sub-paragraph (5).

Discharge of administration order where administration ends

85.—(1) This paragraph applies where—
   (a) the court makes an order under this Schedule providing for the appointment of an administrator of a company to cease to have effect, and
   (b) the administrator was appointed by administration order.

(2) The court shall discharge the administration order.

Notice to Companies Registrar where administration ends

86.—(1) This paragraph applies where the court makes an order under this Schedule providing for the appointment of an administrator to cease to have effect.

(2) The administrator shall send a copy of the order to the registrar of companies within the period of 14 days beginning with the date of the order.

(3) An administrator who fails without reasonable excuse to comply with sub-paragraph (2) commits an offence.

REPLACING ADMINISTRATOR

Resignation of administrator

87.—(1) An administrator may resign only in prescribed circumstances.

(2) Where an administrator may resign he may do so only—
   (a) in the case of an administrator appointed by administration order, by notice in writing to the court,
   (b) in the case of an administrator appointed under paragraph 14, by notice in writing to the [holder of the floating charge by virtue of which the appointment was made],
   (c) in the case of an administrator appointed under paragraph 22(1), by notice in writing to the company, or
   (d) in the case of an administrator appointed under paragraph 22(2), by notice in writing to the directors of the company.

Removal of administrator from office

88. The court may by order remove an administrator from office.

Administrator ceasing to be qualified

89.—(1) The administrator of a company shall vacate office if he ceases to be qualified to act as an insolvency practitioner in relation to the company.

(2) Where an administrator vacates office by virtue of sub-paragraph (1) he shall give notice in writing—

    (a) in the case of an administrator appointed by administration order, to the court,

    (b) in the case of an administrator appointed under paragraph 14, to the [holder of the floating charge by virtue of which the appointment was made],

    (c) in the case of an administrator appointed under paragraph 22(1), to the company, or

    (d) in the case of an administrator appointed under paragraph 22(2), to the directors of the company.

(3) An administrator who fails without reasonable excuse to comply with sub-paragraph (2) commits an offence.

Supplying vacancy in office of administrator

90. Paragraphs 91 to 95 apply where an administrator—

    (a) dies,

    (b) resigns,

    (c) is removed from office under paragraph 88, or

    (d) vacates office under paragraph 89.

91.—(1) Where the administrator was appointed by administration order, the court may replace the administrator on an application under this sub-paragraph made by—

    (a) a creditors' committee of the company,

    (b) the company,

    (c) the directors of the company,

    (d) one or more creditors of the company, or

    (e) where more than one person was appointed to act jointly or concurrently as the administrator, any of those persons who remains in office.

(2) But an application may be made in reliance on sub-paragraph (1)(b) to (d) only where—

    (a) there is no creditors' committee of the company,

    (b) the court is satisfied that the creditors' committee or a remaining administrator is not taking reasonable steps to make a replacement, or

    (c) the court is satisfied that for another reason it is right for the application to be made.

92. Where the administrator was appointed under paragraph 14 the holder of the floating charge by virtue of which the appointment was made may replace the administrator.

93.—(1) Where the administrator was appointed under paragraph 22(1) by the company it may replace the administrator.

(2) A replacement under this paragraph may be made only—

    (a) with the consent of each person who is the holder of a qualifying floating charge in respect of the company's property, or

    (b) where consent is withheld, with the permission of the court.

94.—(1) Where the administrator was appointed under paragraph 22(2) the directors of the company may replace the administrator.

(2) A replacement under this paragraph may be made only—

    (a) with the consent of each person who is the holder of a qualifying floating charge in respect of the company's property, or

    (b) where consent is withheld, with the permission of the court.

95. The court may replace an administrator on the application of a person listed in paragraph 91(1) if the court—

    (a) is satisfied that a person who is entitled to replace the administrator under any of paragraphs 92 to 94 is not taking reasonable steps to make a replacement, or

    (b) that for another reason it is right for the court to make the replacement.

Substitution of administrator: competing floating charge-holder

96.—(1) This paragraph applies where an administrator of a company is appointed under paragraph 14 by the holder of a qualifying floating charge in respect of the company's property.

(2) The holder of a prior qualifying floating charge in respect of the company's property may apply to the court for the administrator to be replaced by an administrator nominated by the holder of the prior floating charge.

(3)   One floating charge is prior to another for the purposes of this paragraph if—
    (a)   it was created first, or
    (b)   it is to be treated as having priority in accordance with an agreement to which the holder of each floating charge was party.

(4)   Sub-paragraph (3) shall have effect in relation to Scotland as if the following were substituted for paragraph (a)—
        "(a)   it has priority of ranking in accordance with section 464(4)(b) of the Companies Act 1985 (c 6),

Substitution of administrator appointed by company or directors: creditors' meeting

97.—(1)   This paragraph applies where—
    (a)   an administrator of a company is appointed by a company or directors under paragraph 22, and
    (b)   there is no holder of a qualifying floating charge in respect of the company's property.

(2)   A creditors' meeting may replace the administrator.

(3)   A creditors' meeting may act under sub-paragraph (2) only if the new administrator's written consent to act is presented to the meeting before the replacement is made.

Vacation of office: discharge from liability

98.—(1)   Where a person ceases to be the administrator of a company (whether because he vacates office by reason of resignation, death or otherwise, because he is removed from office or because his appointment ceases to have effect) he is discharged from liability in respect of any action of his as administrator.

(2)   The discharge provided by sub-paragraph (1) takes effect—
    (a)   in the case of an administrator who dies, on the filing with the court of notice of his death,
    (b)   in the case of an administrator appointed under paragraph 14 or 22, at a time appointed by resolution of the creditors' committee or, if there is no committee, by resolution of the creditors, or
    (c)   in any case, at a time specified by the court.

(3)   For the purpose of the application of sub-paragraph (2)(b) in a case where the administrator has made a statement under paragraph 52(1)(b), a resolution shall be taken as passed if (and only if) passed with the approval of—
    (a)   each secured creditor of the company, or
    (b)   if the administrator has made a distribution to preferential creditors or thinks that a distribution may be made to preferential creditors—
        (i)   each secured creditor of the company, and
        (ii)   preferential creditors whose debts amount to more than 50% of the preferential debts of the company, disregarding debts of any creditor who does not respond to an invitation to give or withhold approval.

(4)   Discharge—
    (a)   applies to liability accrued before the discharge takes effect, and
    (b)   does not prevent the exercise of the court's powers under paragraph 75.

Vacation of office: charges and liabilities

99.—(1)   This paragraph applies where a person ceases to be the administrator of a company (whether because he vacates office by reason of resignation, death or otherwise, because he is removed from office or because his appointment ceases to have effect).

(2)   In this paragraph—
"the former administrator" means the person referred to in sub-paragraph (1), and
"cessation" means the time when he ceases to be the company's administrator.

(3)   The former administrator's remuneration and expenses shall be—
    (a)   charged on and payable out of property of which he had custody or control immediately before cessation, and
    (b)   payable in priority to any security to which paragraph 70 applies.

(4)   A sum payable in respect of a debt or liability arising out of a contract entered into by the former administrator or a predecessor before cessation shall be—
    (a)   charged on and payable out of property of which the former administrator had custody or control immediately before cessation, and
    (b)   payable in priority to any charge arising under sub-paragraph (3).

(5)   Sub-paragraph (4) shall apply to a liability arising under a contract of employment which was adopted by the former administrator or a predecessor before cessation; and for that purpose—

(a) action taken within the period of 14 days after an administrator's appointment shall not be taken to amount or contribute to the adoption of a contract,

(b) no account shall be taken of a liability which arises, or in so far as it arises, by reference to anything which is done or which occurs before the adoption of the contract of employment, and

(c) no account shall be taken of a liability to make a payment other than wages or salary.

(6) In sub-paragraph (5)(c) "wages or salary" includes—

(a) a sum payable in respect of a period of holiday (for which purpose the sum shall be treated as relating to the period by reference to which the entitlement to holiday accrued),

(b) a sum payable in respect of a period of absence through illness or other good cause,

(c) a sum payable in lieu of holiday,

(d) in respect of a period, a sum which would be treated as earnings for that period for the purposes of an enactment about social security, and

(e) a contribution to an occupational pension scheme.

GENERAL

Joint and concurrent administrators

100.—(1) In this Schedule—

(a) a reference to the appointment of an administrator of a company includes a reference to the appointment of a number of persons to act jointly or concurrently as the administrator of a company, and

(b) a reference to the appointment of a person as administrator of a company includes a reference to the appointment of a person as one of a number of persons to act jointly or concurrently as the administrator of a company.

(2) The appointment of a number of persons to act as administrator of a company must specify—

(a) which functions (if any) are to be exercised by the persons appointed acting jointly, and

(b) which functions (if any) are to be exercised by any or all of the persons appointed.

101.—(1) This paragraph applies where two or more persons are appointed to act jointly as the administrator of a company.

(2) A reference to the administrator of the company is a reference to those persons acting jointly.

(3) But a reference to the administrator of a company in paragraphs 87 to 99 of this Schedule is a reference to any or all of the persons appointed to act jointly.

(4) Where an offence of omission is committed by the administrator, each of the persons appointed to act jointly—

(a) commits the offence, and

(b) may be proceeded against and punished individually.

(5) The reference in paragraph 45(1)(a) to the name of the administrator is a reference to the name of each of the persons appointed to act jointly.

(6) Where persons are appointed to act jointly in respect of only some of the functions of the administrator of a company, this paragraph applies only in relation to those functions.

102.—(1) This paragraph applies where two or more persons are appointed to act concurrently as the administrator of a company.

(2) A reference to the administrator of a company in this Schedule is a reference to any of the persons appointed (or any combination of them).

103.—(1) Where a company is in administration, a person may be appointed to act as administrator jointly or concurrently with the person or persons acting as the administrator of the company.

(2) Where a company entered administration by administration order, an appointment under sub-paragraph (1) must be made by the court on the application of—

(a) a person or group listed in paragraph 12(1)(a) to (e), or

(b) the person or persons acting as the administrator of the company.

(3) Where a company entered administration by virtue of an appointment under paragraph 14, an appointment under sub-paragraph (1) must be made by—

(a) the holder of the floating charge by virtue of which the appointment was made, or

(b) the court on the application of the person or persons acting as the administrator of the company.

(4) Where a company entered administration by virtue of an appointment under paragraph 22(1), an appointment under sub-paragraph (1) above must be made either by the court on the application of the person or persons acting as the administrator of the company or—

(a)   by the company, and
(b)   with the consent of each person who is the holder of a qualifying floating charge in respect of the company's property or, where consent is withheld, with the permission of the court.

(5)   Where a company entered administration by virtue of an appointment under paragraph 22(2), an appointment under sub-paragraph (1) must be made either by the court on the application of the person or persons acting as the administrator of the company or—
(a)   by the directors of the company, and
(b)   with the consent of each person who is the holder of a qualifying floating charge in respect of the company's property or, where consent is withheld, with the permission of the court.

(6)   An appointment under sub-paragraph (1) may be made only with the consent of the person or persons acting as the administrator of the company.

Presumption of validity

104.   An act of the administrator of a company is valid in spite of a defect in his appointment or qualification.

Majority decision of directors

105.   A reference in this Schedule to something done by the directors of a company includes a reference to the same thing done by a majority of the directors of a company.

Penalties

106.—(1)   A person who is guilty of an offence under this Schedule is liable to a fine (in accordance with section 430 and Schedule 10).

(2)   A person who is guilty of an offence under any of the following paragraphs of this Schedule is liable to a daily default fine (in accordance with section 430 and Schedule 10)—
(a)   paragraph 20,
(b)   paragraph 32,
(c)   paragraph 46,
(d)   paragraph 48,
(e)   paragraph 49,
(f)   paragraph 51,
(g)   paragraph 53,
(h)   paragraph 54,
(i)   paragraph 56,
(j)   paragraph 71,
(k)   paragraph 72,
(l)   paragraph 77,
(m)   paragraph 78,
(n)   paragraph 80,
(o)   paragraph 84,
(p)   paragraph 86, and
(q)   paragraph 89.

Extension of time limit

107.—(1)   Where a provision of this Schedule provides that a period may be varied in accordance with this paragraph, the period may be varied in respect of a company—
(a)   by the court, and
(b)   on the application of the administrator.

(2)   A time period may be extended in respect of a company under this paragraph—
(a)   more than once, and
(b)   after expiry.

108.—(1)   A period specified in paragraph 49(5), 50(1)(b) or 51(2) may be varied in respect of a company by the administrator with consent.

(2)   In sub-paragraph (1) "consent" means consent of—
(a)   each secured creditor of the company, and
(b)   if the company has unsecured debts, creditors whose debts amount to more than 50% of the company's unsecured debts, disregarding debts of any creditor who does not respond to an invitation to give or withhold consent.

(3)   But where the administrator has made a statement under paragraph 52(1)(b) "consent" means—
(a)   consent of each secured creditor of the company, or

(b)   if the administrator thinks that a distribution may be made to preferential creditors, consent of—
     (i)   each secured creditor of the company, and
     (ii)   preferential creditors whose debts amount to more than 50% of the total preferential debts of the company, disregarding debts of any creditor who does not respond to an invitation to give or withhold consent.

(4)   Consent for the purposes of sub-paragraph (1) may be—
     (a)   written, or
     (b)   signified at a creditors' meeting.

(5)   The power to extend under sub-paragraph (1)—
     (a)   may be exercised in respect of a period only once,
     (b)   may not be used to extend a period by more than 28 days,
     (c)   may not be used to extend a period which has been extended by the court, and
     (d)   may not be used to extend a period after expiry.

109.   Where a period is extended under paragraph 107 or 108, a reference to the period shall be taken as a reference to the period as extended.

Amendment of provision about time

110.—(1)   The Secretary of State may by order amend a provision of this Schedule which—
     (a)   requires anything to be done within a specified period of time,
     (b)   prevents anything from being done after a specified time, or
     (c)   requires a specified minimum period of notice to be given.

(2)   An order under this paragraph—
     (a)   must be made by statutory instrument, and
     (b)   shall be subject to annulment in pursuance of a resolution of either House of Parliament.

Interpretation

111.—(1)   In this Schedule—
"administrative receiver" has the meaning given by section 251,
"administrator" has the meaning given by paragraph 1 and, where the context requires, includes a reference to a former administrator,
        .....
"correspondence" includes correspondence by telephonic or other electronic means,
"creditors' meeting" has the meaning given by paragraph 50,
"enters administration" has the meaning given by paragraph 1,
"floating charge" means a charge which is a floating charge on its creation,
"in administration" has the meaning given by paragraph 1,
"hire-purchase agreement" includes a conditional sale agreement, a chattel leasing agreement and a retention of title agreement,
"holder of a qualifying floating charge" in respect of a company's property has the meaning given by paragraph 14,
"market value" means the amount which would be realised on a sale of property in the open market by a willing vendor,
"the purpose of administration" means an objective specified in paragraph 3, and
"unable to pay its debts" has the meaning given by section 123.

[(1A)   In this Schedule, "company" means—
     (a)   a company within the meaning of section 735(1) of the Companies Act 1985,
     (b)   a company incorporated in an EEA State other than the United Kingdom, or
     (c)   a company not incorporated in an EEA State but having its centre of main interests in a member State other than Denmark.

(1B)   In sub-paragraph (1A), in relation to a company, "centre of main interests" has the same meaning as in the EC Regulation and, in the absence of proof to the contrary, is presumed to be the place of its registered office (within the meaning of that Regulation).]

(2)   A reference in this Schedule to a thing in writing includes a reference to a thing in electronic form.

(3)   In this Schedule a reference to action includes a reference to inaction.

[Non-UK companies

111A.   A company incorporated outside the United Kingdom that has a principal place of business in Northern Ireland may not enter administration under this Schedule unless it also has a principal place of business in England and Wales or Scotland (or both in England and Wales and in Scotland).]

Scotland

112.   In the application of this Schedule to Scotland—
   (a)   a reference to filing with the court is a reference to lodging in court, and
   (b)   a reference to a charge is a reference to a right in security.

113.   Where property in Scotland is disposed of under paragraph 70 or 71, the administrator shall grant to the disponee an appropriate document of transfer or conveyance of the property, and—
   (a)   that document, or
   (b)   recording, intimation or registration of that document (where recording, intimation or registration of the document is a legal requirement for completion of title to the property),

has the effect of disencumbering the property of or, as the case may be, freeing the property from, the security.

114.   In Scotland, where goods in the possession of a company under a hire-purchase agreement are disposed of under paragraph 72, the disposal has the effect of extinguishing as against the disponee all rights of the owner of the goods under the agreement.

115.—(1)   In Scotland, the administrator of a company may make, in or towards the satisfaction of the debt secured by the floating charge, a payment to the holder of a floating charge which has attached to the property subject to the charge.

   (2)   In Scotland, where the administrator thinks that the company has insufficient property to enable a distribution to be made to unsecured creditors other than by virtue of section 176A(2)(a), he may file a notice to that effect with the registrar of companies.

   (3)   On delivery of the notice to the registrar of companies, any floating charge granted by the company shall, unless it has already so attached, attach to the property which is subject to the charge and that attachment shall have effect as if each floating charge is a fixed security over the property to which it has attached.

116.   In Scotland, the administrator in making any payment in accordance with paragraph 115 shall make such payment subject to the rights of any of the following categories of persons (which rights shall, except to the extent provided in any instrument, have the following order of priority)—
   (a)   the holder of any fixed security which is over property subject to the floating charge and which ranks prior to, or pari passu with, the floating charge,
   (b)   creditors in respect of all liabilities and expenses incurred by or on behalf of the administrator,
   (c)   the administrator in respect of his liabilities, expenses and remuneration and any indemnity to which he is entitled out of the property of the company,
   (d)   the preferential creditors entitled to payment in accordance with paragraph 65,
   (e)   the holder of the floating charge in accordance with the priority of that charge in relation to any other floating charge which has attached, and
   (f)   the holder of a fixed security, other than one referred to in paragraph (a), which is over property subject to the floating charge.]

[1145]

NOTES
   Inserted by the Enterprise Act 2002, s 248(2), Sch 16, as from 15 September 2003 (for savings and transitional provisions in relation to a petition for an administration order presented before that date, and in relation to special administration regimes (within the meaning of the Enterprise Act 2002, s 249), see the note to s 8 at **[1131]**).
   Para 12: words in square brackets in sub-para (1)(d) substituted by the Courts Act 2003, s 109(1), Sch 8, para 299, as from 1 April 2005; sub-para (5) added by the Enterprise Act 2002 (Insolvency) Order 2003, SI 2003/2096, arts 2(1), (2), 6, as from 15 September 2003, except in relation to any case where a petition for an administration order was presented before that date.
   Para 40: sub-para (2)(aa) inserted by the European Public Limited-Liability Company Regulations 2004, SI 2004/2326, reg 73(4)(c), as from 8 October 2004.
   Para 42: sub-para (4)(aa) inserted by SI 2004/2326, reg 73(4)(c), as from 8 October 2004.
   Para 43: sub-para (6A) inserted by SI 2003/2096, art 2(1), (3), as from 15 September 2003, except in relation to any case where a petition for an administration order was presented before that date.
   Para 45: substituted by the Companies (Trading Disclosures) (Insolvency) Regulations 2008, SI 2008/1897, reg 4(1), as from 1 October 2008.
   Para 49: words in square brackets substituted by the Companies Act 2006 (Consequential Amendments etc) Order 2008, SI 2008/948, art 3(1), Sch 1, Pt 2, para 100(a), as from 6 April 2008.
   Para 73: word omitted from sub-para (2)(b) repealed, and sub-para (2)(d) (and the word immediately preceding it) added, by the Companies (Cross-Border Mergers) Regulations 2007, SI 2007/2974, reg 65(1)–(3), as from 15 December 2007; words in square brackets in sub-para (2)(c) substituted by SI 2008/948, art 3(1), Sch 1, Pt 2, para 100(a), as from 6 April 2008.
   Para 74: word omitted from sub-para (6)(b) repealed, and sub-para (6)(ba) added, by SI 2007/2974, reg 65(1), (4), (5), as from 15 December 2007; words in square brackets in sub-para (6)(b) substituted by SI 2008/948, art 3(1), Sch 1, Pt 2, para 100(b), as from 6 April 2008.
   Para 82: sub-para (1)(aa) inserted by SI 2004/2326, reg 73(4)(c), as from 8 October 2004.

Paras 87, 89: words in square brackets in sub-para (2)(b) substituted by SI 2003/2096, art 2(1), (4), (5), as from 15 September 2003, except in relation to any case where a petition for an administration order was presented before that date.

Para 111: definition "company" in sub-para (1) (omitted) repealed, and sub-paras (1A), (1B) inserted, by the Insolvency Act 1986 (Amendment) Regulations 2005, SI 2005/879, reg 2(1), (4)(a), (b), as from 13 April 2005, except in relation to the appointment of an administrator under Part II that took effect before that date.

Para 111A: inserted by SI 2005/879, reg 2(1), (4)(c), as from 13 April 2005, except in relation to the appointment of an administrator under Part II that took effect before that date.

Financial collateral arrangements: see the Financial Collateral Arrangements (No 2) Regulations 2003, SI 2003/3226, reg 8(1), (2) at **[3824]** with regard to the disapplication of paras 41(2), 43(2), 70, 71, in relation to such arrangements.

BUILDING SOCIETIES ACT 1986

(1986 c 53)

NOTES

Only provisions of this Act relevant to Financial Services law are reproduced. Provisions not reproduced are not annotated.

This Act is reproduced as amended by: the Financial Services and Markets Act 2000 (Mutual Societies) Order 2001, SI 2001/2617.

Application of the Banking Act 2009: as to the application of Part 1 of the 2009 Act (Special Resolution Regime) to building societies, see s 84 of that Act (at **[1900E]**). Note also that the Treasury may, by order, apply Part 2 of that Act (bank insolvency) and Part 3 (bank administration) to building societies (see ss 130 and 158 respectively at **[1901U]** and **[1902V]**). See also s 251 (at **[1904X]**) which provides that the Treasury may by order modify this Act for the purpose of facilitating, or in connection with, the provision of financial assistance to building societies by (a) itself, (b) the Bank of England, (c) another central bank of a Member State of the EEA, or (d) the European Central Bank.

An Act to make fresh provision with respect to building societies and further provision with respect to conveyancing services

[25 July 1986]

[PART I
FUNCTIONS OF THE AUTHORITY

1   Functions of the Financial Services Authority in relation to building societies

(1)   The Financial Services Authority ("the Authority") has the following functions under this Act in relation to building societies—

    (a)   to secure that the principal purpose of building societies remains that of making loans which are secured on residential property and are funded substantially by their members;

    (b)   to administer the system of regulation of building societies provided for by or under this Act; and

    (c)   to advise and make recommendations to the Treasury and other government departments on any matter relating to building societies.

(2)   The Authority also has, in relation to such societies, the other functions conferred on it by or under this Act or any other enactment.]

[1146]

NOTES

The original Part I (ss 1–4) was substituted by a new Part I (s 1 only) by the Financial Services and Markets Act 2000 (Mutual Societies) Order 2001, SI 2001/2617, art 13(1), Sch 3, Pt II, paras 131, 132, as from 1 December 2001; for transitional provisions in relation to the functions, etc, of the Building Societies Commission, see art 13(3) of, and Sch 5, paras 17, 18 to, the 2001 Order.

Note: the FSA's functions under this section are amended with regard to a building society that is receiving "relevant financial assistance" within the meaning of the Banking (Special Provisions) Act 2008; see the Building Societies (Financial Assistance) Order 2008, SI 2008/1427.

PART XI
MISCELLANEOUS AND SUPPLEMENTARY AND CONVEYANCING SERVICES

General

125   Short title

This Act may be cited as the Building Societies Act 1986.

[1147]

FINANCE ACT 1989

(1989 c 26)

NOTES

Only provisions of this Act relevant to Financial Services law are reproduced. Provisions not reproduced are not annotated.

This Act is reproduced as amended by: the Government of Wales Act 1998; the Social Security Contributions (Transfer of Functions, etc) Act 1999; the Tax Credits Act 1999; the Employment Act 2002; the Tax Credits Act 2002; the Child Trust Funds Act 2004; the Statute Law (Repeals) Act 2004; the Public Services Ombudsman (Wales) Act 2005; the Commissioners for Revenue and Customs Act 2005; the Work and Families Act 2006; the Income Tax Act 2007; the Scottish Public Services Ombudsman Act 2002 (Consequential Provisions and Modifications) Order 2004, SI 2004/1823; the Transfer of Tribunal Functions and Revenue and Customs Appeals Order 2009.

An Act to grant certain duties, to alter other duties, and to amend the law relating to the National Debt and the Public Revenue, and to make further provision in connection with Finance

[27 July 1989]

PART III
MISCELLANEOUS AND GENERAL

Miscellaneous

182 Disclosure of information

(1)   A person who discloses any information which he holds or has held in the exercise of tax functions[, tax credit functions][, child trust fund functions] [or social security functions] is guilty of an offence if it is information about any matter relevant, for the purposes of [any of those functions—

    (a)   to tax or duty in the case of any identifiable person,

    [(aa) to a tax credit in respect of any identifiable person,]

    [(ab) to a child trust fund of any identifiable person,]

    (b)   to contributions payable by or in respect of any identifiable person, or

    (c)   to statutory sick pay[, statutory maternity pay, statutory paternity pay or statutory adoption pay] in respect of any identifiable person.]

(2)   In this section "tax functions" means functions relating to tax or duty—

    (a)   of the Commissioners, the Board and their officers,

    (b)   of any person carrying out the administrative work of *any tribunal mentioned in subsection (3) below,* and

    (c)   of any other person providing, or employed in the provision of, services to any person mentioned in paragraph (a) or (b) above.

[(2ZA)   In this section "tax credit functions" means the functions relating to tax credits—

    (a)   of the Board,

    (b)   of any person carrying out the administrative work of the *General Commissioners or the Special Commissioners,* and

    (c)   of any other person providing, or employed in the provision of, services to the Board or to any person mentioned in paragraph (b) above.]

[(2ZB)   In this section "child trust fund functions" means the functions relating to child trust funds—

    (a)   of the Board and their officers,

    (b)   of any person carrying out the administrative work of the *General Commissioners or the Special Commissioners,* or

    (c)   of any person providing, or employed in the provision of, services to the Board or any person mentioned in paragraph (b) above.]

[(2A)   In this section "social security functions" means—

    (a)   the functions relating to contributions, [child benefit, guardian's allowance,] statutory sick pay[, statutory maternity pay, statutory paternity pay or statutory adoption pay]—

        (i)   of the Board and their officers,

        (ii)   of any person carrying out the administrative work of the *General Commissioners or the Special Commissioners,* and

        (iii) of any other person providing, or employed in the provision of, services to any person mentioned in sub-paragraph (i) or (ii) above, and

    (b)   the functions under Part III of the Pension Schemes Act 1993 or Part III of the Pension Schemes (Northern Ireland) Act 1993 of the Board and their officers and any other person providing, or employed in the provision of, services to the Board or their officers.]

(3)   The tribunals referred to in subsection (2)(b) above are—
   (a)   the General Commissioners and the Special Commissioners,
   (b)   any value added tax tribunal,
   (c)   ...
   (d)   any tribunal established under section 463 of the Taxes Act 1970 or section 706 of the Taxes Act 1988 [or section 704 of the Income Tax Act 2007].

(4)   A person who discloses any information which—
   (a)   he holds or has held in the exercise of functions—
      (i)   of the Comptroller and Auditor General and any member of the staff of the National Audit Office,...
      (ii)   of the Parliamentary Commissioner for Administration and his officers,
      [(iii)   of the Auditor General for Wales and any member of his staff,...
      [(iv)   of the Public Services Ombudsman for Wales and any member of his staff, or]
      [(v)   of the Scottish Public Services Ombudsman and any member of his staff,]
   (b)   is, or is derived from, information which was held by any person in the exercise of tax functions[, tax credit functions][, child trust fund functions] [or social security functions], and
   (c)   is information about any matter relevant, for the purposes of [tax functions[, tax credit functions][, child trust fund functions] or social security functions—
      (i)   to tax or duty in the case of any identifiable person,
      [(ia)   to a tax credit in respect of any identifiable person,]
      [(ib)   to a child trust fund of any identifiable person,]
      (ii)   to contributions payable by or in respect of any identifiable person, or
      (iii)   to [child benefit, guardian's allowance,] statutory sick pay[, statutory maternity pay, statutory paternity pay or statutory adoption pay] in respect of any identifiable person]
is guilty of an offence.

(5)   Subsections (1) and (4) above do not apply to any disclosure of information—
   (a)   with lawful authority,
   (b)   with the consent of any person in whose case the information is about a matter relevant to tax or duty[, to a tax credit or to a child trust fund] [or to contributions, statutory sick pay[, statutory maternity pay, statutory paternity pay or statutory adoption pay]], or
   (c)   which has been lawfully made available to the public before the disclosure is made.

(6)   For the purposes of this section a disclosure of any information is made with lawful authority if, and only if, it is made—
   (a)   by a Crown servant in accordance with his official duty,
   (b)   by any other person for the purposes of the function in the exercise of which he holds the information and without contravening any restriction duly imposed by the person responsible,
   (c)   to, or in accordance with an authorisation duly given by, the person responsible,
   (d)   in pursuance of any enactment or of any order of a court, or
   (e)   in connection with the institution of or otherwise for the purposes of any proceedings relating to any matter within the general responsibility of the Commissioners or, as the case requires, the Board,
and in this subsection, "the person responsible" means the Commissioners, the Board, the Comptroller[, the Parliamentary Commissioner, the Auditor General for Wales[, [the Public Services Ombudsman for Wales] or the Scottish Public Services Ombudsman],] as the case requires.

(7)   It is a defence for a person charged with an offence under this section to prove that at the time of the alleged offence—
   (a)   he believed that he had lawful authority to make the disclosure in question and had not reasonable cause to believe otherwise, or
   (b)   he believed that the information in question had been lawfully made available to the public before the disclosure was made and had no reasonable cause to believe otherwise.

(8)   A person guilty of an offence under this section is liable—
   (a)   on conviction on indictment, to imprisonment for a term not exceeding two years or a fine or both, and
   (b)   on summary conviction, to imprisonment for a term not exceeding six months or a fine not exceeding the statutory maximum or both.

(9)   No prosecution for an offence under this section shall be instituted in England and Wales or in Northern Ireland except—
   (a)   by the Commissioners or the Board, as the case requires, or
   (b)   by or with the consent of the Director of Public Prosecutions or, in Northern Ireland, the Director of Public Prosecutions for Northern Ireland.

(10)   In this section—
"the Board" means the Commissioners of Inland Revenue,

["child trust fund" has the same meaning as in the Child Trust Funds Act 2004,]

"the Commissioners" means the Commissioners of Customs and Excise,

["contributions" means contributions under Part I of the Social Security Contributions and Benefits Act 1992 or Part I of the Social Security Contributions and Benefits (Northern Ireland) Act 1992;]

"Crown servant" has the same meaning as in the Official Secrets Act 1989,

["tax credit" means a tax credit under the Tax Credits Act 2002,] and

"tax or duty" means any tax or duty within the general responsibility of the Commissioners or the Board.

[(10A)   In this section, in relation to the disclosure of information "identifiable person" means a person whose identity is specified in the disclosure or can be deduced from it.

(11)   In this section—
    (a)   references to the Comptroller and Auditor General include the Comptroller and Auditor General for Northern Ireland,
    (b)   references to the National Audit Office include the Northern Ireland Audit Office, and
    (c)   references to the Parliamentary Commissioner for Administration include the Health Service Commissioner for England, ..., the Northern Ireland Parliamentary Commissioner for Administration and the Northern Ireland Commissioner for Complaints.

[(11A)   In this section, references to statutory paternity pay or statutory adoption pay include statutory pay under Northern Ireland legislation corresponding to Part 12ZA or Part 12ZB of the Social Security Contributions and Benefits Act 1992 (c 4).]

(12)   This section shall come into force on the repeal of section 2 of the Official Secrets Act 1911.

[1148]

NOTES

Sub-s (1) is amended as follows:

Words ", tax credit functions" inserted by the Tax Credits Act 1999, s 12(1), (2)(a), as from 5 October 1999, and continued in force by the Tax Credits Act 2002, s 59, Sch 5, para 11(1), (2)(a).

Words ", child trust fund functions" in square brackets, and the whole of para (ab), inserted by the Child Trust Funds Act 2004, s 18(1), (2), as from 1 January 2005.

Words "or social security functions" inserted by the Social Security Contributions (Transfer of Functions, etc) Act 1999, s 6, Sch 6, para 9(1), (2)(a), as from 1 April 1999.

Words from "any of those functions" to the end of para (c) substituted by the Social Security Contributions (Transfer of Functions, etc) Act 1999, s 6, Sch 6, para 9(1), (2)(b), as from 1 April 1999.

Para (aa) inserted by the Tax Credits Act 1999, s 12(1), (2)(b), as from 5 October 1999, and substituted by the Tax Credits Act 2002, s 59, Sch 5, para 11(1), (2)(b), as from 1 August 2002.

Words in square brackets in para (c) substituted by the Employment Act 2002, s 53, Sch 7, para 1(1), (2)(a), as from 8 December 2002.

Sub-s (2): for the words in italics in para (b) there are substituted the words "the First-tier Tribunal or Upper Tribunal" by the Transfer of Tribunal Functions and Revenue and Customs Appeals Order 2009, SI 2009/56, art 3, Sch 1, para 167(a), as from 1 April 2009.

Sub-s (2ZA): substituted (for sub-s (2AA) as inserted by the Tax Credits Act 1999, s 12(1), (3)) by the Tax Credits Act 2002, s 59, Sch 5, para 11(1), (3), as from 1 August 2002; for the words in italics in para (b) there are substituted the words "the First-tier Tribunal or Upper Tribunal" by SI 2009/56, art 3, Sch 1, para 167(b), as from 1 April 2009.

Sub-s (2ZB): inserted by the Child Trust Funds Act 2004, s 18(1), (3), as from 1 January 2005. Note that s 24(1)(c) of the 2004 Act provides that, until such date that may be appointed by Order, sub-s (2ZB) has effect subject to s 24(4). That subsection provides "The reference to the General Commissioners or the Special Commissioners in section 182(2ZB) of the Finance Act 1989 is to an appeal tribunal". For the words in italics in para (b) there are substituted the words "First-tier Tribunal or an appeal tribunal constituted under Chapter 1 of Part 2 of the Social Security (Northern Ireland) Order 1998" by SI 2009/56, art 3, Sch 1, para 167(c), as from 1 April 2009.

Sub-s (2A): inserted by the Social Security Contributions (Transfer of Functions, etc) Act 1999, s 6, Sch 6, para 9(1), (3), as from 1 April 1999; words in first pair of square brackets in para (a) inserted by the Tax Credits Act 2002, s 59, Sch 5, para 11(1), (4), as from 1 April 2003; words in second pair of square brackets in para (a) substituted by the Employment Act 2002, s 53, Sch 7, para 1(1), (2)(b), as from 8 December 2002; for the words in italics in para (a)(ii) there are substituted the words "the First-tier Tribunal or Upper Tribunal" by SI 2009/56, art 3, Sch 1, para 167(d), as from 1 April 2009.

Sub-s (3): repealed by SI 2009/56, art 3, Sch 1, para 167(e), as from 1 April 2009; previously it had been amended as follows: para (c) repealed by the Statute Law (Repeals) Act 2004, as from 22 July 2004; words in square brackets in para (d) inserted by the Income Tax Act 2007, s 1027, Sch 1, Pt 2, para 282, as from 6 April 2007 (and have effect, for the purposes of income tax for the year 2007–08 and subsequent tax years, and for the purposes of corporation tax for accounting periods ending after 5 April 2007; for transitional provisions and savings see Sch 2 to the 2007 Act).

Sub-s (4) is amended as follows:

Word omitted from para (a)(i) repealed, and paras (a)(iii), (iv) inserted, by the Government of Wales Act 1998, ss 125, 152, Sch 12, para 31(2), Sch 18, Pt I, as from 1 February 1999.

Word omitted from para (a)(iii) repealed, and para (a)(v) inserted, by the Scottish Public Services Ombudsman Act 2002 (Consequential Provisions and Modifications) Order 2004, SI 2004/1823, art 10(a), (b), as from 14 July 2004.

Finance Act 1989, s 188 **[1149]**

Para (a)(iv) substituted by the Public Services Ombudsman (Wales) Act 2005, s 39, Sch 6, para 22(a), as from a 1 April 2006 (for transitional provisions in connection with complaints made before and after that date, see SI 2005/2800).

Words in first pair of square brackets in para (b) inserted by the Tax Credits Act 1999, s 12(1), (4)(a), as from 5 October 1999, and continued in force by the Tax Credits Act 2002, s 59, Sch 5, para 11(1), (5)(a).

Words in second pair of square brackets in para (b) inserted by the Child Trust Funds Act 2004, s 18(1), (4)(a), as from 1 January 2005.

Words in third pair of square brackets in para (b) inserted by the Social Security Contributions (Transfer of Functions, etc) Act 1999, s 6, Sch 6, para 9(1), (4)(a), as from 1 April 1999.

In para (c) words from "tax functions" to the end of sub-para (iii) substituted by the Social Security Contributions (Transfer of Functions, etc) Act 1999, s 6, Sch 6, para 9(1), (4)(b), as from 1 April 1999.

Words ", tax credit functions" in para (c) inserted by the Tax Credits Act 1999, s 12(1), (4)(a), as from 5 October 1999, and continued in force by the Tax Credits Act 2002, s 59, Sch 5, para 11(1), (5)(b).

Words ", child trust fund functions" in para (c) inserted by the Child Trust Funds Act 2004, s 18(1), (4)(a), as from 1 January 2005.

Para (c)(ia) inserted by the Tax Credits Act 1999, s 12(1), (4)(b), as from 5 October 1999, and continued in force by the Tax Credits Act 2002, s 59, Sch 5, para 11(1), (5)(c).

Para (c)(ib) inserted by the Child Trust Funds Act 2004, s 18(1), (4)(b), as from 1 January 2005.

Words in first pair of square brackets in para (c)(iii) inserted by the Tax Credits Act 2002, Sch 5, para 11(1), (5)(d), as from 1 April 2003.

Words in second pair of square brackets in para (c)(iii) substituted by the Employment Act 2002, s 53, Sch 7, para 1(1), (2)(c), as from 8 December 2002.

Sub-s (5) is amended as follows:

Words in first pair of square brackets in para (b) originally inserted by the Tax Credits Act 1999, s 12(1), (5), as from 5 October 1999, subsequently substituted by the Tax Credits Act 2002, s 59, Sch 5, para 11(1), (6), as from 1 August 2002, and subsequently further substituted by the Child Trust Funds Act 2004, s 18(1), (5), as from 1 January 2005.

Words in second (outer) pair of square brackets in para (b) inserted by the Social Security Contributions (Transfer of Functions, etc) Act 1999, s 6, Sch 6, para 9(1), (5), as from 1 April 1999.

Words in third (inner) pair of square brackets in para (b) substituted by the Employment Act 2002, s 53, Sch 7, para 1(1), (2)(d), as from 8 December 2002.

Sub-s (6): words in first (outer) pair of square brackets substituted by the Government of Wales Act 1998, s 125, Sch 12, para 31(3), as from 1 February 1999; words in second (inner) pair of square brackets substituted by the Public Services Ombudsman (Wales) Act 2005, s 39, Sch 6, para 22(b), as from 1 April 2006 (for transitional provisions in connection with complaints made before and after that date, see SI 2005/2800); words in third (inner) pair of square brackets substituted by SI 2004/1823, art 10(c), as from 14 July 2004.

Sub-s (10): definition "child trust fund" inserted by the Child Trust Funds Act 2004, s 18(1), (6), as from 1 January 2005; definition "contributions" inserted by the Social Security Contributions (Transfer of Functions, etc) Act 1999, s 6, Sch 6, para 9(1), (6), as from 1 April 1999; definition "tax credit" inserted by the Tax Credits Act 2002, s 59, Sch 5, para 11(1), (7), as from 1 August 2002.

Sub-s (10A): inserted by Commissioners for Revenue and Customs Act 2005, s 50, Sch 4, para 39, as from 18 April 2005.

Sub-s (11): words omitted from para (c) repealed by a combination of by the Public Services Ombudsman (Wales) Act 2005, s 39, Sch 6, para 22(c), as from 1 April 2006 (for transitional provisions in connection with complaints made before and after that date, see SI 2005/2800), and by SI 2004/1823, art 10(d), as from 14 July 2004.

Sub-s (11A): inserted by the Employment Act 2002, s 53, Sch 7, para 1(1), (3), as from 8 December 2002.

Note that this section is also prospectively amended by the Work and Families Act 2006, s 11, Sch 1, para 2, as from a day to be appointed, as follows—

"In section 182 of the Finance Act 1989 (disclosure of information), in each of the following provisions—
    (a)   subsection (1)(c),
    (b)   subsection (2A)(a),
    (c)   subsection (4)(c)(iii),
    (d)   subsection (5)(b), and
    (e)   subsection (11A),
for "statutory paternity pay" substitute "ordinary statutory paternity pay, additional statutory paternity pay".".

Commissioners of Inland Revenue; Commissioners of Customs and Excise: references to the Commissioners of Inland Revenue and the Commissioners of Customs and Excise are now to be taken as a reference to the Commissioners for Her Majesty's Revenue and Customs; see the Commissioners for Revenue and Customs Act 2005, s 50(1), (7).

188   Short title

This Act may be cited as the Finance Act 1989.

[1149]

PART II
OTHER ACTS

LAW OF PROPERTY (MISCELLANEOUS PROVISIONS) ACT 1989

(1989 c 34)

NOTES
This Act is reproduced as amended by: the Trusts of Land and Appointment of Trustees Act 1996; the Financial Services and Markets Act 2000 (Consequential Amendments and Repeals) Order 2001, SI 2001/3649; the Financial Services and Markets Act 2000 (Regulated Activities) (Amendment) (No 2) Order 2006, SI 2006/2383.

An Act to make new provision with respect to deeds and their execution and contracts for the sale or other disposition of interests in land; and to abolish the rule of law known as the rule in Bain v Fothergill

[27 July 1989]

1   ((*Deeds and their execution*) outside the scope of this work.)

2   Contracts for sale etc of land to be made by signed writing

(1)   A contract for the sale or other disposition of an interest in land can only be made in writing and only by incorporating all the terms which the parties have expressly agreed in one document or, where contracts are exchanged, in each.

(2)   The terms may be incorporated in a document either by being set out in it or by reference to some other document.

(3)   The document incorporating the terms or, where contracts are exchanged, one of the documents incorporating them (but not necessarily the same one) must be signed by or on behalf of each party to the contract.

(4)   Where a contract for the sale or other disposition of an interest in land satisfies the conditions of this section by reason only of the rectification of one or more documents in pursuance of an order of a court, the contract shall come into being, or be deemed to have come into being, at such time as may be specified in the order.

(5)   This section does not apply in relation to—
   (a)   a contract to grant such a lease as is mentioned in section 54(2) of the Law Property Act 1925 (short leases);
   (b)   a contract made in the course of a public auction; or
   [(c)   a contract regulated under the Financial Services and Markets Act 2000, other than a regulated mortgage contract[, a regulated home reversion plan or a regulated home purchase plan];]
and nothing in this section affects the creation or operation of resulting, implied or constructive trusts.

(6)   In this section—
   "disposition" has the same meaning as in the Law of Property Act 1925;
   "interest in land" means any estate, interest or charge in or over land …
   ["regulated mortgage contract"[, "regulated home reversion plan" and "regulated home purchase plan"] must be read with—
   (a)   section 22 of the Financial Services and Markets Act 2000,
   (b)   any relevant order under that section, and
   (c)   Schedule 22 to that Act].

(7)   Nothing in this section shall apply in relation to contracts made before this section comes into force.

(8)   …

[1150]

NOTES
Sub-s (5): para (c) substituted by the Financial Services and Markets Act 2000 (Consequential Amendments and Repeals) Order 2001, SI 2001/3649, art 317(1), (2), as from 1 December 2001; words in square brackets in para (c) inserted by the Financial Services and Markets Act 2000 (Regulated Activities) (Amendment) (No 2) Order 2006, SI 2006/2383, art 27(a), as from 6 April 2007 (for the full commencement details of SI 2006/2383, see art 1 of that Order at [2860]).
Sub-s (6): words "or in or over the proceeds of sale of land" which are omitted from the definition "interest in land" were repealed by the Trusts of Land and Appointment of Trustees Act 1996, s 25(2), Sch 4 (for savings in relation to the abolition of the doctrine of conversion, see ss 3, 18(3), 25(5) of the 1996 Act); definition "regulated mortgage contract" inserted by SI 2001/3649, art 317(1), (3), as from 1 December 2001, and words in square brackets in that definition inserted by the Financial Services and Markets Act 2000 (Regulated Activities) (Amendment) (No 2) Order 2006, SI 2006/2383, art 27(b), as from 6 April 2007 (for the full commencement details of SI 2006/2383, see art 1 of that Order at [2860]).
Sub-s (8): repeals the Law of Property Act 1925, s 40.

3, 4   (*S 3 (Abolition of rule in Bain v Fothergill), s 4 (repeals) outside the scope of this work.*)

5   Commencement

(1), (2)   (*Outside the scope of this work.*)

(3)   The provisions of this Act to which this subsection applies shall come into force at the end of the period of two months beginning with the day on which this Act is passed.

(4)   The provisions of this Act to which subsection (3) above applies are—
   (a)   sections 2 and 3 above; and
   (b)   (*outside the scope of this work*).

[1151]

NOTES
Orders: the Law of Property (Miscellaneous Provisions) Act 1989 (Commencement) Order 1990, SI 1990/1175.

6   Citation

(1)   This Act may be cited as the Law of Property (Miscellaneous Provisions) Act 1989.

(2)   This Act extends to England and Wales only.

[1152]

(*Schs 1, 2 (Consequential amendments and repeals) outside the scope of this work.*)

COMPANIES ACT 1989

(1989 c 40)

NOTES
This Act is reproduced as amended by: the Bank of England Act 1998; the Enterprise Act 2002; the Companies Act 2006; the Tribunals, Courts and Enforcement Act 2007; the Financial Markets and Insolvency Regulations 1991, SI 1991/880; the Transfer of Functions (Financial Services) Order 1992, SI 1992/1315; the Financial Markets and Insolvency Regulations 1998, SI 1998/1748; the Financial Services and Markets Act 2000 (Consequential Amendments and Repeals) Order 2001, SI 2001/3649; the Civil Jurisdiction and Judgments Order 2001, SI 2001/3929; the Financial Services and Markets Act 2000 (Regulated Activities) (Amendment No 3) Order 2006, SI 2006/3384; the Civil Jurisdiction and Judgments Regulations 2007, SI 2007/1655.

ARRANGEMENT OF SECTIONS

PART VII
FINANCIAL MARKETS AND INSOLVENCY

Introduction

PART II / OTHER ACTS

PART X
MISCELLANEOUS AND GENERAL PROVISIONS

General

An Act to amend the law relating to company accounts; to make new provision with respect to the persons eligible for appointment as company auditors; to amend the Companies Act 1985 and certain other enactments with respect to investigations and powers to obtain information and to confer new powers exercisable to assist overseas regulatory authorities; to make new provision with respect to the registration of company charges and otherwise to amend the law relating to companies; to amend the Fair Trading Act 1973; to enable provision to be made for the payment of fees in connection with the exercise by the Secretary of State, the Director General of Fair Trading and the Monopolies and Mergers Commission of their functions under Part V of that Act; to make provision for safeguarding the operation of certain financial markets; to amend the Financial Services Act 1986; to enable provision to be made for the recording and transfer of title to securities without a written instrument; to amend the Company Directors Disqualification Act 1986, the Company Securities (Insider Dealing) Act 1985, the Policyholders Protection Act 1975 and the law relating to building societies; and for connected purposes

[16 November 1989]

1–153   ((*Pts I–VI*) *outside the scope of this work.*)

PART VII
FINANCIAL MARKETS AND INSOLVENCY

NOTES

Transfer of functions: by the Transfer of Functions (Financial Services) Order 1992, SI 1992/1315, art 2(1)(c), the functions of the Secretary of State under this Part of this Act are transferred to the Treasury. However, by art 4 of, and Sch 2, para 7 to, that Order, the functions of the Secretary of State under ss 158(4), (5), 160(5), 170 (other than the function under s 170(1) of approving an overseas investment exchange) 171–174, 181, 185, and so much of his functions under s 186 as relate to any function under the aforementioned provisions, are to be exercisable jointly by the Secretary of State and the Treasury.

Introduction

154 Introduction

This Part has effect for the purposes of safeguarding the operation of certain financial markets by provisions with respect to—

    (a)   the insolvency, winding up or default of a person party to transactions in the market (sections 155 to 172),

    (b) the effectiveness or enforcement of certain charges given to secure obligations in connection with such transactions (sections 173 to 176), and (c)	rights and remedies in relation to certain property provided as cover for margin in relation to such transactions or subject to such a charge (sections 177 to 181).

[1153]

Recognised investment exchanges and clearing houses

155 Market contracts

(1)	This Part applies to the following descriptions of contract connected with a recognised investment exchange or recognised clearing house.

The contracts are referred to in this Part as "market contracts".

[(2)	Except as provided in subsection (2A), in relation to a recognised investment exchange this Part applies to—

(a)	contracts entered into by a member or designated non-member of the exchange [with a person other than the exchange] which are either
	(i)	contracts made on the exchange or an exchange to whose undertaking the exchange has succeeded whether by amalgamation, merger or otherwise; or
	(ii)	contracts in the making of which the member or designated non-member was subject to the rules of the exchange or of an exchange to whose undertaking the exchange has succeeded whether by amalgamation, merger or otherwise; and

[(b)	contracts entered into by the exchange with its members for the purpose of enabling the rights and liabilities of that member under transactions in investments to be settled.]

A "designated non-member" means a person in respect of whom action may be taken under the default rules of the exchange but who is not a member of the exchange.

(2A)	This Part does not apply to contracts falling within paragraph (a) of subsection (2) above where the exchange in question is a recognised overseas investment exchange.]

[(3)	In relation to a recognised clearing house, this Part applies to contracts entered into by the clearing house with a member of the clearing house for the purpose of enabling the rights and liabilities of that member under transactions in investments to be settled.]

(4)	The Secretary of State may by regulations make further provision as to the contracts to be treated as "market contracts", for the purposes of this Part, in relation to a recognised investment exchange or recognised clearing house.

(5)	The regulations may add to, amend or repeal the provisions of subsections (2) and (3) above.

[1154]

NOTES

Sub-s (2): substituted, together with sub-s (2A), for original sub-s (2) by the Financial Markets and Insolvency Regulations 1991, SI 1991/880, reg 3, as from 25 April 1991; words in first pair of square brackets inserted, and para (b) substituted, by the Financial Markets and Insolvency Regulations 1998, SI 1998/1748, reg 3, as from 11 August 1998.

Sub-s (2A): substituted as noted above.

Sub-s (3): substituted by SI 1998/1748, reg 4, as from 11 August 1998.

HM Treasury has issued a consultation document *Modernising the insolvency protections for the operation of financial markets – proposals to reform Part 7 of the 1989 Companies Act (July 2008)* to consider changes to Part VII of the 1989 Act which modifies general insolvency law to provide systemic protection for certain financial markets in the event that one of their participants defaults. The Treasury is also considering a specific insolvency procedures for investment firms along the lines of the US Securities Investor Protection Act 1970. See: http://www.hm-treasury.gov.uk/consult_fullindex.htm.

Regulations: the Financial Markets and Insolvency Regulations 1991, SI 1991/880 at **[3515A]**; the Financial Markets and Insolvency Regulations 1998, SI 1998/1748.

156	(*Repealed by the Financial Services and Markets Act 2000 (Consequential Amendments and Repeals) Order 2001, SI 2001/3649, art 75(e), as from 1 December 2001).*)

157 Change in default rules

(1)	A recognised UK investment exchange or recognised UK clearing house shall give the [Authority] at least 14 days' notice of any proposal to amend, revoke or add to its default rules; and the [Authority] may within 14 days from receipt of the notice direct the exchange or clearing house not to proceed with the proposal, in whole or in part.

(2)	A direction under this section may be varied or revoked.

(3)	Any amendment or revocation of, or addition to, the default rules of an exchange or clearing house in breach of a direction under this section is ineffective.

[1155]

PART II
OTHER ACTS

NOTES
Sub-s (1): words in square brackets substituted by the Financial Services and Markets Act 2000 (Consequential Amendments and Repeals) Order 2001, SI 2001/3649, art 79, as from 1 December 2001.

158 Modifications of the law of insolvency

(1) The general law of insolvency has effect in relation to market contracts, and action taken under the rules of a recognised investment exchange or recognised clearing house with respect to such contracts, subject to the provisions of sections 159 to 165.

(2) So far as those provisions relate to insolvency proceedings in respect of a person other than a defaulter, they apply in relation to—

(a) proceedings in respect of a member or designated non-member of a recognised investment exchange or a member of a recognised clearing house, and

(b) proceedings in respect of a party to a market contract begun after a recognised investment exchange or recognised clearing house has taken action under its default rules in relation to a person party to the contract as principal,

but not in relation to any other insolvency proceedings, notwithstanding that rights or liabilities arising from market contracts fall to be dealt with in the proceedings.

(3) The reference in subsection (2)(b) to the beginning of insolvency proceedings is to—

(a) the presentation of a bankruptcy petition or a petition for sequestration of a person's estate, or

[(b) the application for an administration order or the presentation of a winding-up petition or the passing of a resolution for voluntary winding up,]

(c) the appointment of an administrative receiver.

[(3A) In subsection (3)(b) the reference to an application for an administration order shall be taken to include a reference to—

(a) in a case where an administrator is appointed under paragraph 14 or 22 of Schedule B1 to the Insolvency Act 1986 (appointment by floating charge holder, company or directors) following filing with the court of a copy of a notice of intention to appoint under that paragraph, the filing of the copy of the notice, and

(b) in a case where an administrator is appointed under either of those paragraphs without a copy of a notice of intention to appoint having been filed with the court, the appointment of the administrator.]

(4) The Secretary of State may make further provision by regulations modifying the law of insolvency in relation to the matters mentioned in subsection (1).

(5) The regulations may add to, amend or repeal the provisions mentioned in subsection (1), and any other provision of this Part as it applies for the purposes of those provisions, or provide that those provisions have effect subject to such additions, exceptions or adaptations as are specified in the regulations.

[1156]

NOTES
Sub-s (3): para (b) substituted by the Enterprise Act 2002, s 248(3), Sch 17, paras 43, 44(a), as from 15 September 2003 (for savings and transitional provisions in relation to a petition for an administration order presented before that date, and in relation to special administration regimes (within the meaning of the Enterprise Act 2002, s 249), see the note to the Insolvency Act 1986, s 8 at [1131]).
Sub-s (3A): inserted by the Enterprise Act 2002, s 248(3), Sch 17, paras 43, 44(b), as from 15 September 2003 (subject to savings and transitional provisions as noted above).
Regulations: the Financial Markets and Insolvency Regulations 1991, SI 1991/880 at [3515A].

159 Proceedings of exchange or clearing house take precedence over insolvency procedures

(1) None of the following shall be regarded as to any extent invalid at law on the ground of inconsistency with the law relating to the distribution of the assets of a person on bankruptcy, winding up or sequestration, or in the administration of an insolvent estate—

(a) a market contract,

(b) the default rules of a recognised investment exchange or recognised clearing house,

(c) the rules of a recognised investment exchange or recognised clearing house as to the settlement of market contracts not dealt with under its default rules.

(2) The powers of a relevant office-holder in his capacity as such, and the powers of the court under the Insolvency Act 1986 or the Bankruptcy (Scotland) Act 1985 shall not be exercised in such a way as to prevent or interfere with—

(a) the settlement in accordance with the rules of a recognised investment exchange or recognised clearing house of a market contract not dealt with under its default rules, or

(b) any action taken under the default rules of such an exchange or clearing house.

This does not prevent a relevant office-holder from afterwards seeking to recover any amount under section 163(4) or 164(4) or prevent the court from afterwards making any such order or decree as is mentioned in section 165(1) or (2) (but subject to subsections (3) and (4) of that section).

(3) Nothing in the following provisions of this Part shall be construed as affecting the generality of the above provisions.

(4) A debt or other liability arising out of a market contract which is the subject of default proceedings may not be proved in a winding up or bankruptcy, or in Scotland claimed in a winding up or sequestration, until the completion of the default proceedings.

A debt or other liability which by virtue of this subsection may not be proved or claimed shall not be taken into account for the purposes of any set-off until the completion of the default proceedings.

[(4A) However, prior to the completion of default proceedings—

(a) where it appears to the chairman of the meeting of creditors that a sum will be certified under section 162(1) to be payable, subsection (4) shall not prevent any proof or claim including or consisting of an estimate of that sum which has been lodged or, in Scotland, submitted, from being admitted or, in Scotland, accepted, for the purpose only of determining the entitlement of a creditor to vote at a meeting of creditors; and

(b) a creditor whose claim or proof has been lodged and admitted or, in Scotland, submitted and accepted, for the purpose of determining the entitlement of a creditor to vote at a meeting of creditors and which has not been subsequently wholly withdrawn, disallowed or rejected, is eligible as a creditor to be a member of a liquidation committee or, in bankruptcy proceedings in England and Wales, a creditors' committee.]

(5) For the purposes of [subsections (4) and (4A)] the default proceedings shall be taken to be completed in relation to a person when a report is made under section 162 stating the sum (if any) certified to be due to or from him.

[1157]

NOTES

Sub-s (4A): inserted by the Financial Markets and Insolvency Regulations 1991, SI 1991/880, reg 4(1), (2), as from 25 April 1991.

Sub-s (5): words in square brackets substituted by SI 1991/880, reg 4(1), (3), as from 25 April 1991.

160 Duty to give assistance for purposes of default proceedings

(1) It is the duty of—

(a) any person who has or had control of any assets of a defaulter, and

(b) any person who has or had control of any documents of or relating to a defaulter,

to give a recognised investment exchange or recognised clearing house such assistance as it may reasonably require for the purposes of its default proceedings.

This applies notwithstanding any duty of that person under the enactments relating to insolvency.

(2) A person shall not under this section be required to provide any information or produce any document which he would be entitled to refuse to provide or produce on grounds of legal professional privilege in proceedings in the High Court or on grounds of confidentiality as between client and professional legal adviser in proceedings in the Court of Session.

(3) Where original documents are supplied in pursuance of this section, the exchange or clearing house shall return them forthwith after the completion of the relevant default proceedings, and shall in the meantime allow reasonable access to them to the person by whom they were supplied and to any person who would be entitled to have access to them if they were still in the control of the person by whom they were supplied.

(4) The expenses of a relevant office-holder in giving assistance under this section are recoverable as part of the expenses incurred by him in the discharge of his duties; and he shall not be required under this section to take any action which involves expenses which cannot be so recovered, unless the exchange or clearing house undertakes to meet them.

There shall be treated as expenses of his such reasonable sums as he may determine in respect of time spent in giving the assistance [and for the purpose of determining the priority in which his expenses are payable out of the assets, sums in respect of time spent shall be treated as his remuneration and other sums shall be treated as his disbursements or, in Scotland, outlays].

(5) The Secretary of State may by regulations make further provision as to the duties of persons to give assistance to a recognised investment exchange or recognised clearing house for the purposes of its default proceedings, and the duties of the exchange or clearing house with respect to information supplied to it.

The regulations may add to, amend or repeal the provisions of subsections (1) to (4) above.

(6) In this section "document" includes information recorded in any form.

NOTES
Sub-s (4): words in square brackets added by the Financial Markets and Insolvency Regulations 1991, SI 1991/880, reg 5, as from 25 April 1991.
Regulations: the Financial Markets and Insolvency Regulations 1991, SI 1991/880 at **[3515A]**.

161 Supplementary provisions as to default proceedings

(1)   If the court is satisfied on an application by a relevant office-holder that a party to a market contract with a defaulter intends to dissipate or apply his assets so as to prevent the officer-holder recovering such sums as may become due upon the completion of the default proceedings, the court may grant such interlocutory relief (in Scotland, such interim order) as it thinks fit.

(2)   A liquidator or trustee of a defaulter or, in Scotland, a permanent trustee on the sequestrated estate of the defaulter shall not—

    (a)   declare or pay any dividend to the creditors, or

    (b)   return any capital to contributories,

unless he has retained what he reasonably considers to be an adequate reserve in respect of any claims arising as a result of the default proceedings of the exchange or clearing house concerned.

(3)   The court may on an application by a relevant office-holder make such order as it thinks fit altering or dispensing from compliance with such of the duties of his office as are affected by the fact that default proceedings are pending or could be taken, or have been or could have been taken.

(4)   Nothing in [section 126, 128, 130, 185 or 285 of, or paragraph 42 or 43 (including paragraph 43(6) as applied by paragraph 44) of Schedule B1 to, the Insolvency Act 1986] (which restrict the taking of certain legal proceedings and other steps), and nothing in any rule of law in Scotland to the like effect as the said section 285, in the Bankruptcy (Scotland) Act 1985 or in the Debtors (Scotland) Act 1987 as to the effect of sequestration, shall affect any action taken by an exchange or clearing house for the purpose of its default proceedings.

[1159]

NOTES
Sub-s (4): words in square brackets substituted by the Enterprise Act 2002, s 248(3), Sch 17, paras 43, 45, as from 15 September 2003 (for savings and transitional provisions in relation to a petition for an administration order presented before that date, and in relation to special administration regimes (within the meaning of the Enterprise Act 2002, s 249), see the note to the Insolvency Act 1986, s 8 at **[1131]**).

162 Duty to report on completion of default proceedings

(1)   [Subject to subsection (1A),] a recognised investment exchange or recognised clearing house shall, on the completion of proceedings under its default rules, report to the [Authority] on its proceedings stating in respect of each creditor or debtor the sum certified by them to be payable from or to the defaulter or, as the case may be, the fact that no sum is payable.

[(1A)   A recognised overseas investment exchange or recognised overseas clearing house shall not be subject to the obligation under subsection (1) unless it has been notified by the [Authority] that a report is required for the purpose of insolvency proceedings in any part of the United Kingdom.]

(2)   The exchange or clearing house may make a single report or may make reports from time to time as proceedings are completed with respect to the transactions affecting particular persons.

(3)   The exchange or clearing house shall supply a copy of every report under this section to the defaulter and to any relevant office-holder acting in relation to him or his estate.

(4)   When a report under this section is received by the [Authority, it] shall publish notice of that fact in such manner as [it] thinks appropriate for bringing [the report] to the attention of creditors and debtors of the defaulter.

(5)   An exchange or clearing house shall make available for inspection by a creditor or debtor of the defaulter so much of any report by it under this section as relates to the sum (if any) certified to be due to or from him or to the method by which that sum was determined.

(6)   Any such person may require the exchange or clearing house, on payment of such reasonable fee as the exchange or clearing house may determine, to provide him with a copy of any part of a report which he is entitled to inspect.

[1160]

NOTES
Sub-s (1): words in first pair of square brackets inserted by the Financial Markets and Insolvency Regulations 1991, SI 1991/880, reg 6(1), (2), as from 25 April 1991; word in second pair of square brackets substituted by the Financial Services and Markets Act 2000 (Consequential Amendments and Repeals) Order 2001, SI 2001/3649, art 80(1), (2), as from 1 December 2001.
Sub-s (1A): inserted by SI 1991/880, reg 6(1), (3), as from 25 April 1991; word in square brackets substituted by SI 2001/3649, art 80(1), (3), as from 1 December 2001.
Sub-s (4): words in square brackets substituted by SI 2001/3649, art 80(1), (4), as from 1 December 2001.

163   Net sum payable on completion of default proceedings

(1)   The following provisions apply with respect to the net sum certified by a recognised investment exchange or recognised clearing house, upon proceedings under its default rules being duly completed in accordance with this Part, to be payable by or to a defaulter.

(2)   If, in England and Wales, a bankruptcy or winding-up order has been made, or a resolution for voluntary winding up has been passed, the debt—

    (a)   is provable in the bankruptcy or winding up or, as the case may be, is payable to the relevant officer-holder, and

    (b)   shall be taken into account, where appropriate, under section 323 of the Insolvency Act 1986 (mutual dealings and set-off) or the corresponding provision applicable in the case of winding up,

in the same way as a debt due before the commencement of the bankruptcy, the date on which the body corporate goes into liquidation (within the meaning of section 247 of the Insolvency Act 1986) or, in the case of a partnership, the date of the winding-up order.

(3)   If, in Scotland, an award of sequestration or a winding-up order has been made, or a resolution for voluntary winding up has been passed, the debt—

    (a)   may be claimed in the sequestration or winding up or, as the case may be, is payable to the relevant office-holder, and

    (b)   shall be taken into account for the purposes of any rule of law relating to set-off applicable in sequestration or winding up,

in the same way as a debt due before the date of sequestration (within the meaning of section 73(1) of the Bankruptcy (Scotland) Act 1985) or the commencement of the winding up (within the meaning of section 129 of the Insolvency Act 1986).

(4)   However, where (or to the extent that) a sum is taken into account by virtue of subsection (2)(b) or (3)(b) which arises from a contract entered into at a time when the creditor had notice—

    (a)   that a bankruptcy petition or, in Scotland, a petition for sequestration was pending, or

    (b)   that a meeting of creditors had been summoned under section 98 of the Insolvency Act 1986 or that a winding-up petition was pending,

the value of any profit to him arising from the sum being so taken into account (or being so taken into account to that extent) is recoverable from him by the relevant office-holder unless the court directs otherwise.

(5)   Subsection (4) does not apply in relation to a sum arising from a contract effected under the default rules of a recognised investment exchange or recognised clearing house.

(6)   Any sum recoverable by virtue of subsection (4) ranks for priority, in the event of the insolvency of the person from whom it is due, immediately before preferential or, in Scotland, preferred debts.

[1161]

164   Disclaimer of property, rescission of contracts, &c

(1)   Sections 178, 186, 315 and 345 of the Insolvency Act 1986 (power to disclaim onerous property and court's power to order rescission of contracts, &c) do not apply in relation to—

    (a)   a market contract, or

    (b)   a contract effected by the exchange or clearing house for the purpose of realising property provided as margin in relation to market contracts.

In the application of this subsection in Scotland, the reference to sections 178, 315 and 345 shall be construed as a reference to any rule of law having the like effect as those sections.

(2)   In Scotland, a permanent trustee on the sequestrated estate of a defaulter or a liquidator is bound by any market contract to which that defaulter is a party and by any contract as is mentioned in subsection (1)(b) above notwithstanding section 42 of the Bankruptcy (Scotland) Act 1985 or any rule of law to the like effect applying in liquidations.

(3)   Sections 127 and 284 of the Insolvency Act 1986 (avoidance of property dispositions effected after commencement of winding up or presentation of bankruptcy petition), and section 32(8) of the Bankruptcy (Scotland) Act 1985 (effect of dealing with debtor relating to estate vested in permanent trustee) do not apply to—

    (a)   a market contract, or any disposition of property in pursuance of such a contract,

    (b)   the provision of margin in relation to market contracts,

    (c)   a contract effected by the exchange or clearing house for the purpose of realising property provided as margin in relation to a market contract, or any disposition of property in pursuance of such a contract, or

    (d)   any disposition of property in accordance with the rules of the exchange or clearing house as to the application of property provided as margin.

PART II
OTHER ACTS

(4)   However, where—

(a)   a market contract is entered into by a person who has notice that a petition has been presented for the winding up or bankruptcy or sequestration of the estate of the other party to the contract, or

(b)   margin in relation to a market contract is accepted by a person who has notice that such a petition has been presented in relation to the person by whom or on whose behalf the margin is provided,

the value of any profit to him arising from the contract or, as the case may be, the amount or value of the margin is recoverable from him by the relevant office-holder unless the court directs otherwise.

(5)   Subsection (4)(a) does not apply where the person entering into the contract is a recognised investment exchange or recognised clearing house acting in accordance with its rules, or where the contract is effected under the default rules of such an exchange or clearing house; but subsection (4)(b) applies in relation to the provision of margin in relation to such a contract.

(6)   Any sum recoverable by virtue of subsection (4) ranks for priority, in the event of the insolvency of the person from whom it is due, immediately before preferential or, in Scotland, preferred debts.

[1162]

165   Adjustment of prior transactions

(1)   No order shall be made in relation to a transaction to which this section applies under—

(a)   section 238 or 339 of the Insolvency Act 1986 (transactions at an undervalue),

(b)   section 239 or 340 of that Act (preferences), or

(c)   section 423 of that Act (transactions defrauding creditors).

(2)   As respects Scotland, no decree shall be granted in relation to any such transaction—

(a)   under section 34 or 36 of the Bankruptcy (Scotland) Act 1985 or section 242 or 243 of the Insolvency Act 1986 (gratuitous alienations and unfair preferences), or

(b)   at common law on grounds of gratuitous alienations or fraudulent preferences.

(3)   This section applies to—

(a)   a market contract to which a recognised investment exchange or recognised clearing house is a party or which is entered into under its default rules, and

(b)   a disposition of property in pursuance of such a market contract.

(4)   Where margin is provided in relation to a market contract and (by virtue of subsection (3)(a) or otherwise) no such order or decree as is mentioned in subsection (1) or (2) has been, or could be, made in relation to that contract, this section applies to—

(a)   the provision of the margin,

(b)   any contract effected by the exchange or clearing house in question for the purpose of realising the property provided as margin, and

(c)   any disposition of property in accordance with the rules of the exchange or clearing house as to the application of property provided as margin.

[1163]

166   Powers of Secretary of State to give directions

(1)   The powers conferred by this section are exercisable in relation to a recognised UK investment exchange or recognised UK clearing house.

(2)   Where in any case an exchange or clearing house has not taken action under its default rules—

(a)   if it appears to the [Authority] that it could take action, he may direct it to do so, and

(b)   if it appears to the [Authority] that it is proposing to take or may take action, [the Authority] may direct it not to do so.

(3)   Before giving such a direction the [Authority] shall consult the exchange or clearing house in question; and [it] shall not give a direction unless [it] is satisfied, in the light of that consultation—

(a)   in the case of a direction to take action, that failure to take action would involve undue risk to investors or other participants in the market, or

(b)   in the case of a direction not to take action, that the taking of action would be premature or otherwise undesirable in the interests of investors or other participants in the market.

(4)   A direction shall specify the grounds on which it is given.

(5)   A direction not to take action may be expressed to have effect until the giving of a further direction (which may be a direction to take action or simply revoking the earlier direction).

(6)   No direction shall be given not to take action if, in relation to the person in question—

(a)   a bankruptcy order or an award of sequestration of his estate has been made, or an interim receiver or interim trustee has been appointed, or

(b) a winding up order has been made, a resolution for voluntary winding up has been passed or an administrator, administrative receiver or provisional liquidator has been appointed;

and any previous direction not to take action shall cease to have effect on the making or passing of any such order, award or appointment.

(7) Where an exchange or clearing house has taken or been directed to take action under its default rules, the [Authority] may direct it to do or not to do such things (being things which it has power to do under its default rules) as are specified in the direction.

The [Authority] shall not give such a direction unless [it is satisfied that the direction] will not impede or frustrate the proper and efficient conduct of the default proceedings.

(8) A direction under this section is enforceable, on the application of the [Authority], by injunction or, in Scotland, by an order under section 45 of the Court of Session Act 1988; and where an exchange or clearing house has not complied with a direction, the court may make such order as it thinks fit for restoring the position to what it would have been if the direction had been complied with.

[1164]

NOTES

Sub-ss (2), (3), (7), (8): words in square brackets substituted by the Financial Services and Markets Act 2000 (Consequential Amendments and Repeals) Order 2001, SI 2001/3649, art 81, as from 1 December 2001.

In consequence of these amendments it is thought that the heading to this section should refer to the powers of the Authority.

---

167 Application to determine whether default proceedings to be taken

(1) Where there has been made or passed in relation to a member or designated non-member of a recognised investment exchange or a member of a recognised clearing house—
    (a) a bankruptcy order or an award of sequestration of his estate, or an order appointing an interim receiver of his property, or
    (b) an administration or winding up order, a resolution for voluntary winding up or an order appointing a provisional liquidator,

and the exchange or clearing house has not taken action under its default rules in consequence of the order, award or resolution or the matters giving rise to it, a relevant office-holder appointed by, or in consequence of or in connection with, the order, award or resolution may apply to the [Authority].

[(1A) In subsection (1) a reference to an administration order shall be taken to include a reference to the appointment of an administrator under—
    (a) paragraph 14 of Schedule B1 to the Insolvency Act 1986 (c 45) (appointment by holder of qualifying floating charge), or
    (b) paragraph 22 of that Schedule (appointment by company or directors).]

(2) The application shall specify the exchange or clearing house concerned and the grounds on which it is made.

(3) On receipt of the application the [Authority] shall notify the exchange or clearing house, and unless within three business days after the day on which the notice is received the exchange or clearing house—
    (a) takes action under its default rules, or
    (b) notifies the [Authority] that it proposes to do so forthwith,

then, subject as follows, the provisions of sections 158 to 165 above do not apply in relation to market contracts to which the member or designated non-member in question is a party or to anything done by the exchange or clearing house for the purposes of, or in connection with, the settlement of any such contract.

For this purpose a "business day" means any day which is not a Saturday or Sunday, Christmas Day, Good Friday or a bank holiday in any part of the United Kingdom under the Banking and Financial Dealings Act 1971.

(4) The provisions of sections 158 to 165 are not disapplied if before the end of the period mentioned in subsection (3) the [Authority] gives the exchange or clearing house a direction under section 166(2)(a) (direction to take action under default rules).

No such direction may be given after the end of that period.

(5) If the exchange or clearing house notifies the [Authority] that it proposes to take action under its default rules forthwith, it shall do so; and that duty is enforceable, on the application of the [Authority], by injunction or, in Scotland, by an order under section 45 of the Court of Session Act 1988.

[1165]

Sub-ss (1), (3)–(5): words in square brackets substituted by the Financial Services and Markets Act 2000 (Consequential Amendments and Repeals) Order 2001, SI 2001/3649, art 82, as from 1 December 2001.

Sub-s (1A): inserted by the Enterprise Act 2002, s 248(3), Sch 17, paras 43, 46, as from 15 September 2003 (for savings and transitional provisions in relation to a petition for an administration order presented before that date, and in relation to special administration regimes (within the meaning of the Enterprise Act 2002, s 249), see the note to the Insolvency Act 1986, s 8 at **[1131]**).

168 *(Repealed by the Financial Services and Markets Act 2000 (Consequential Amendments and Repeals) Order 2001, SI 2001/3649, art 75(f), as from 1 December 2001.)*

169 Supplementary provisions

(1) ...

(2) [Sections 296 and 297 of the Financial Services and Markets Act 2000 apply] in relation to a failure by a recognised investment exchange or recognised clearing house to comply with an obligation under this Part as to a failure to comply with an obligation under that Act.

(3) Where the recognition of an investment exchange or clearing house is revoked under the [Financial Services and Markets Act 2000, the appropriate authority] may, before or after the revocation order, give such directions as [it] thinks fit with respect to the continued application of the provisions of this Part, with such exceptions, additions and adaptations as may be specified in the direction, in relation to cases where a relevant event of any description specified in the directions occurred before the revocation order takes effect.

[(3A) "The appropriate authority" means—
  (a) in the case of an overseas investment exchange or clearing house, the Treasury; and
  (b) in the case of a UK investment exchange or clearing house, the Authority.]

(4) ...

(5) [Regulations under section 414 of the Financial Services and Markets Act 2000 (service of notices) may make provision] in relation to a notice, direction or other document required or authorised by or under this Part to be given to or served on any person other than the [Treasury or the Authority].

[1166]

Sub-s (1): repealed by the Financial Services and Markets Act 2000 (Consequential Amendments and Repeals) Order 2001, SI 2001/3649, art 75(g), as from 1 December 2001.

Sub-ss (2), (3), (5): words in square brackets substituted by SI 2001/3649, art 83(1)–(3), (5), as from 1 December 2001.

Sub-s (3A): inserted by SI 2001/3649, art 83(1), (4), as from 1 December 2001.

Sub-s (4): repealed (without having been brought into force) by SI 2001/3649, art 75(g), as from 1 December 2001.

Other exchanges and clearing houses

170 Certain overseas exchanges and clearing houses

(1) The Secretary of State [and the Treasury] may by regulations provide that this Part applies in relation to contracts connected with an overseas investment exchange or clearing house which is approved by [the Treasury] in accordance with such procedures as may be specified in the regulations, as satisfying such requirements as may be so specified, as it applies in relation to contracts connected with a recognised investment exchange or clearing house.

(2) The [Treasury] shall not approve an overseas investment exchange or clearing house unless [they are] satisfied—
  (a) that the rules and practices of the body, together with the law of the country in which the body's head office is situated, provide adequate procedures for dealing with the default of persons party to contracts connected with the body, and
  (b) that it is otherwise appropriate to approve the body.

(3) The reference in subsection (2)(a) to default is to a person being unable to meet his obligations.

(4) The regulations may apply in relation to the approval of a body under this section such of the provisions of the [Financial Services and Markets Act 2000] as the Secretary of State considers appropriate.

(5) The Secretary of State may make regulations which, in relation to a body which is so approved—
  (a) apply such of the provisions of the [Financial Services and Markets Act 2000] as the Secretary of State considers appropriate, and

(b)   provide that the provisions of this Part apply with such exceptions, additions and adaptations as appear to the Secretary of State to be necessary or expedient;

and different provision may be made with respect to different bodies or descriptions of body.

(6)   Where the regulations apply any provisions of the [Financial Services and Markets Act 2000], they may provide that those provisions apply with such exceptions, additions and adaptations as appear to the Secretary of State to be necessary or expedient.

[1167]

NOTES

Commencement: 25 March 1991 (certain purposes); to be appointed (otherwise). See the note below.

Sub-s (1): words in first pair of square brackets inserted, and words in second pair of square brackets substituted, by the Financial Services and Markets Act 2000 (Consequential Amendments and Repeals) Order 2001, SI 2001/3649, art 84(1), (2), as from 1 December 2001.

Sub-ss (2), (4)–(6): words in square brackets substituted by SI 2001/3649, art 84(1), (3), (4), as from 1 December 2001.

Note: the Companies Act 1989 (Commencement No 9 and Saving and Transitional Provisions) Order 1991, SI 1991/488 brought into force Part VII of this Act in so far as necessary to make regulations under ss 155(4), (5), 158(4), (5), 160(5), 173(4), (5), 174(2)–(4), 185, 186, and Sch 21, para 2(3). No further Order has been made commencing this section for other purposes.

171   (*Repealed by the Financial Services and Markets Act 2000 (Consequential Amendments and Repeals) Order 2001, SI 2001/3649, art 75(h), as from 1 December 2001.*)

172   Settlement arrangements provided by the Bank of England

(1)   The Secretary of State may by regulations provide that this Part applies to contracts of any specified description in relation to which settlement arrangements are provided by the Bank of England, as it applies to contracts connected with a recognised investment exchange or recognised clearing house.

(2)   Regulations under this section may provide that the provisions of this Part apply with such exceptions, additions and adaptations as appear to the Secretary of State to be necessary or expedient.

(3)   Before making any regulations under this section, the Secretary of State [and the Treasury shall consult] the Bank of England.

[1168]

NOTES

Commencement: 25 March 1991 (certain purposes); to be appointed (otherwise). See the note to s 170 at **[1167]**.

Sub-s (3): words in square brackets substituted by the Transfer of Functions (Financial Services) Order 1992, SI 1992/1315, art 10(1), Sch 4, para 13, as from 7 June 1992.

Market charges

173   Market charges

(1)   In this Part "market charge" means a charge whether fixed or floating, granted—

(a)   in favour of a recognised investment exchange, for the purpose of securing debts or liabilities arising in connection with the settlement of market contracts,

[(aa) in favour of The Stock Exchange, for the purpose of securing debts or liabilities arising in connection with short term certificates;]

(b)   in favour of a recognised clearing house, for the purpose of securing debts or liabilities arising in connection with their ensuring the performance of market contracts, or

(c)   in favour of a person who agrees to make payments as a result of the transfer [or allotment] of specified securities made through the medium of a computer-based system established by the Bank of England and The Stock Exchange, for the purpose of securing debts or liabilities of the transferee [or allottee] arising in connection therewith.

(2)   Where a charge is granted partly for purposes specified in subsection (1)(a), [(aa),] (b) or (c) and partly for other purposes, it is a "market charge" so far as it has effect for the specified purposes.

(3)   [In subsection (1)—

"short term certificate" means an instrument issued by The Stock Exchange undertaking to procure the transfer of property of a value and description specified in the instrument to or to the order of the person to whom the instrument is issued or his endorsee or to a person acting on behalf of either of them and also undertaking to make appropriate payments in cash, in the event that the obligation to procure the transfer of property cannot be discharged in whole or in part;]

"specified securities" means securities for the time being specified in the list in Schedule 1 to the Stock Transfer Act 1982, and includes any right to such securities; and "transfer", in relation to any such securities or right, means a transfer of the beneficial interest.

(4)   The Secretary of State may by regulations make further provision as to the charges granted in favour of any such person as is mentioned in subsection (1)(a), (b) or (c) which are to be treated as "market charges" for the purposes of this Part; and the regulations may add to, amend or repeal the provisions of subsections (1) to (3) above.

(5)   The regulations may provide that a charge shall or shall not be treated as a market charge if or to the extent that it secures obligations of a specified description, is a charge over property of a specified description or contains provisions of a specified description.

(6)   Before making regulations under this section in relation to charges granted in favour of a person within subsection (1)(c), the Secretary of State [and the Treasury shall consult] the Bank of England.

[1169]

NOTES
Sub-s (1): para (aa), and words in square brackets in para (c), inserted by the Financial Markets and Insolvency Regulations 1991, SI 1991/880, reg 9(a), (b), as from 25 April 1991.
Sub-s (2): words in square brackets inserted by SI 1991/880, reg 9(c), as from 25 April 1991.
Sub-s (3): words in square brackets substituted by SI 1991/880, reg 9(d), as from 25 April 1991.
Sub-s (6): words in square brackets substituted by the Transfer of Functions (Financial Services) Order 1992, SI 1992/1315, art 10(1), Sch 4, para 13, as from 7 June 1992.
Regulations: the Financial Markets and Insolvency Regulations 1991, SI 1991/880 at **[3515A]**; the Financial Markets and Insolvency (CGO Service) Regulations 1999, SI 1999/1209.

174 Modifications of the law of insolvency

(1)   The general law of insolvency has effect in relation to market charges and action taken in enforcing them subject to the provisions of section 175.

(2)   The Secretary of State may by regulations make further provision modifying the law of insolvency in relation to the matters mentioned in subsection (1).

(3)   The regulations may add to, amend or repeal the provisions mentioned in subsection (1), and any other provision of this Part as it applies for the purposes of those provisions, or provide that those provisions have effect with such exceptions, additions or adaptations as are specified in the regulations.

(4)   The regulations may make different provision for cases defined by reference to the nature of the charge, the nature of the property subject to it, the circumstances, nature or extent of the obligations secured by it or any other relevant factor.

(5)   Before making regulations under this section in relation to charges granted in favour of a person within section 173(1)(c), the Secretary of State [and the Treasury shall consult] the Bank of England.

[1170]

NOTES
Sub-s (5): words in square brackets substituted by the Transfer of Functions (Financial Services) Order 1992, SI 1992/1315, art 10(1), Sch 4, para 13, as from 7 June 1992.
Regulations: the Financial Markets and Insolvency Regulations 1991, SI 1991/880 at **[3515A]**; the Financial Markets and Insolvency (CGO Service) Regulations 1999, SI 1999/1209.

175 Administration orders, &c

[(1)   The following provisions of Schedule B1 to the Insolvency Act 1986 (administration) do not apply in relation to a market charge—
   (a)   paragraph 43(2) and (3) (restriction on enforcement of security or repossession of goods) (including that provision as applied by paragraph 44 (interim moratorium)), and
   (b)   paragraphs 70, 71 and 72 (power of administrator to deal with charged or hire-purchase property).

(1A)   Paragraph 41(2) of that Schedule (receiver to vacate office at request of administrator) does not apply to a receiver appointed under a market charge.]

(2)   However, where a market charge falls to be enforced after [the occurrence of an event to which subsection (2A) applies], and there exists another charge over some or all of the same property ranking in priority to or *pari passu* with the market charge [on the application of any person interested], the court may order that there shall be taken after enforcement of the market charge such steps as the court may direct for the purpose of ensuring that the chargee under the other charge is not prejudiced by the enforcement of the market charge.

[(2A)   This subsection applies to—
   (a)   making an administration application under paragraph 12 of Schedule B1 to the Insolvency Act 1986,

(b)   appointing an administrator under paragraph 14 or 22 of that Schedule (appointment by floating charge holder, company or directors),

(c)   filing with the court a copy of notice of intention to appoint an administrator under either of those paragraphs.]

(3)   The following provisions of the Insolvency Act 1986 (which relate to the powers of receivers) do not apply in relation to a market charge—

(a)   section 43 (power of administrative receiver to dispose of charged property), and

(b)   section 61 (power of receiver in Scotland to dispose of an interest in property).

(4)   Sections 127 and 284 of the Insolvency Act 1986 (avoidance of property dispositions effected after commencement of winding up or presentation of bankruptcy petition), and section 32(8) of the Bankruptcy (Scotland) Act 1985 (effect of dealing with debtor relating to estate vested in permanent trustee), do not apply to a disposition of property as a result of which the property becomes subject to a market charge or any transaction pursuant to which that disposition is made.

(5)   However, if a person (other than the chargee under the market charge) who is party to a disposition mentioned in subsection (4) has notice at the time of the disposition that a petition has been presented for the winding up or bankruptcy or sequestration of the estate of the party making the disposition, the value of any profit to him arising from the disposition is recoverable from him by the relevant office-holder unless the court directs otherwise.

(6)   Any sum recoverable by virtue of subsection (5) ranks for priority, in the event of the insolvency of the person from whom it is due, immediately before preferential or, in Scotland, preferred debts.

(7)   In a case falling within both subsection (4) above (as a disposition of property as a result of which the property becomes subject to a market charge) and section 164(3) (as the provision of margin in relation to a market contract), section 164(4) applies with respect to the recovery of the amount or value of the margin and subsection (5) above does not apply.

                                                        [1171]

NOTES

Sub-ss (1), (1A): substituted, for original sub-s (1), by the Enterprise Act 2002, s 248(3), Sch 17, paras 43, 47(1), (2), as from 15 September 2003 (for savings and transitional provisions in relation to a petition for an administration order presented before that date, and in relation to special administration regimes (within the meaning of the Enterprise Act 2002, s 249), see the note to the Insolvency Act 1986, s 8 at **[1131]**).

Sub-s (2): words in first pair of square brackets substituted by the Enterprise Act 2002, s 248(3), Sch 17, paras 43, 47(1), (3), as from 15 September 2003 (subject to savings and transitional provisions as noted above); words in second pair of square brackets inserted by the Financial Markets and Insolvency Regulations 1991, SI 1991/880, reg 18, as from 25 April 1991.

Sub-s (2A): inserted by the Enterprise Act 2002, s 248(3), Sch 17, paras 43, 47(1), (4), as from 15 September 2003 (subject to savings and transitional provisions as noted above).

176 Power to make provision about certain other charges

(1)   The Secretary of State may by regulations provide that the general law of insolvency has effect in relation to charges of such descriptions as may be specified in the regulations, and action taken in enforcing them, subject to such provisions as may be specified in the regulations.

(2)   The regulations may specify any description of charge granted in favour of—

(a)   a body approved under section 170 (certain overseas exchanges and clearing houses),

(b)   a person included in the list maintained by the [... Authority] for the purposes of [section 301 of the Financial Services and Markets Act 2000] (certain money market institutions),

(c)   the Bank of England,

[(d)   a person who has permission under Part 4 of the Financial Services and Markets Act 2000 to carry on a relevant regulated activity, or

(e)   an international securities self-regulating organisation approved for the purposes of an order made under section 22 of the Financial Services and Markets Act 2000,]

for the purpose of securing debts or liabilities arising in connection with or as a result of the settlement of contracts or the transfer of assets, rights or interests on a financial market.

(3)   The regulations may specify any description of charge granted for that purpose in favour of any other person in connection with exchange facilities or clearing services provided by a recognised investment exchange or recognised clearing house or by any such body, person, authority or organisation as is mentioned in subsection (2).

(4)   Where a charge is granted partly for the purpose specified in subsection (2) and partly for other purposes, the power conferred by this section is exercisable in relation to the charge so far as it has effect for that purpose.

(5)   The regulations may—

(a)   make the same or similar provision in relation to the charges to which they apply as is made by or under sections 174 and 175 in relation to market charges, or

(b)   apply any of those provisions with such exceptions, additions or adaptations as are specified in the regulations.

[(6)   Before making regulations under this section relating to a description of charges defined by reference to their being granted in favour of a person included in the list maintained by the …Authority for the purposes of [section 301 of the Financial Services and Markets Act 2000], or in connection with exchange facilities or clearing services provided by a person included in that list, the Secretary of State and the Treasury shall consult the Authority and the Bank of England.

(6A)   Before making regulations under this section relating to a description of charges defined by reference to their being granted in favour of the Bank of England, or in connection with settlement arrangements provided by the Bank, the Secretary of State and the Treasury shall consult the Bank.]

(7)   Regulations under this section may provide that they apply or do not apply to a charge if or to the extent that it secures obligations of a specified description, is a charge over property of a specified description or contains provisions of a specified description.

[(8)   For the purposes of subsection (2)(d), "relevant regulated activity" means—
(a)   dealing in investments as principal or as agent;
(b)   arranging deals in investments;
[(ba) operating a multilateral trading facility;]
(c)   managing investments;
(d)   safeguarding and administering investments;
(e)   sending dematerialised instructions; or
(f)   establishing etc a collective investment scheme.

(9)   Subsection (8) must be read with—
(a)   section 22 of the Financial Services and Markets Act 2000;
(b)   any relevant order under that section; and
(c)   Schedule 2 to that Act.]

[1172]

NOTES

Sub-s (2) is amended as follows:

Words in first pair of square brackets in para (b) substituted by the Bank of England Act 1998, s 23(1), Sch 5, Pt III, paras 46, 48(1), (2), as from 1 June 1998.

Words omitted from para (b) repealed, and words in second pair of square brackets substituted, by the Financial Services and Markets Act 2000 (Consequential Amendments and Repeals) Order 2001, SI 2001/3649, art 85(1), (2), as from 1 December 2001. Note that the sidenote to the Financial Services and Markets Act 2000, s 301 is "supervision of certain contracts" and not "certain money market institutions" as stated in sub-s (2)(b) above, therefore it is thought that the words "certain money market institutions" should be deleted from the text of this subsection.

Paras (d), (e) substituted by SI 2001/3649, art 85(1), (3), as from 1 December 2001.

Sub-s (6): substituted, together with sub-s (6A), for original sub-s (6), by the Bank of England Act 1998, s 23(1), Sch 5, Pt III, paras 46, 48(1), (3), as from 1 June 1998; words omitted repealed, and words in square brackets substituted, by SI 2001/3649, art 85(1), (4), as from 1 December 2001.

Sub-s (6A): substituted as noted above.

Sub-s (8): added, together with sub-s (9), by SI 2001/3649, art 85(1), (5), as from 1 December 2001; para (ba) inserted by the Financial Services and Markets Act 2000 (Regulated Activities) (Amendment No 3) Order 2006, SI 2006/3384, art 32, as from 1 November 2007 (for the full commencement details of SI 2006/3384, see the Note for that Order at **[2866A]**).

Sub-s (9): added as noted above.

Market property

177   Application of margin not affected by certain other interests

(1)   The following provisions have effect with respect to the application by a recognised investment exchange or recognised clearing house of property (other than land) held by the exchange or clearing house as margin in relation to a market contract.

(2)   So far as necessary to enable the property to be applied in accordance with the rules of the exchange or clearing house, it may be so applied notwithstanding any prior equitable interest or right, or any right or remedy arising from a breach of fiduciary duty, unless the exchange or clearing house had notice of the interest, right or breach of duty at the time the property was provided as margin.

(3)   No right or remedy arising subsequently to the property being provided as margin may be enforced so as to prevent or interfere with the application of the property by the exchange or clearing house in accordance with its rules.

(4)   Where an exchange or clearing house has power by virtue of the above provisions to apply property notwithstanding an interest, right or remedy, a person to whom the exchange or clearing house disposes of the property in accordance with its rules takes free from that interest, right or remedy.

[1173]

178   Priority of floating market charge over subsequent charges

(1)   The Secretary of State may by regulations provide that a market charge which is a floating charge has priority over a charge subsequently created or arising, including a fixed charge.

(2)   The regulations may make different provision for cases defined, as regards the market charge or the subsequent charge, by reference to the description of charge, its terms, the circumstances in which it is created or arises, the nature of the charge, the person in favour of whom it is granted or arises or any other relevant factor.

[1174]

NOTES

Commencement: 25 March 1991 (certain purposes); not in force (otherwise). See the note to s 170 at **[1167]**.

179   Priority of market charge over unpaid vendor's lien

Where property subject to an unpaid vendor's lien becomes subject to a market charge, the charge has priority over the lien unless the chargee had actual notice of the lien at the time the property became subject to the charge.

[1175]

180   Proceedings against market property by unsecured creditors

(1)   Where property (other than land) is held by a recognised investment exchange or recognised clearing house as margin in relation to market contracts or is subject to a market charge, no execution or other legal process for the enforcement of a judgment or order may be commenced or continued, and no distress may be levied, [and no power to use the procedure in Schedule 12 to the Tribunals, Courts and Enforcement Act 2007 (taking control of goods) may be exercised,] against the property by a person not seeking to enforce any interest in or security over the property, except with the consent of—

    (a)   in the case of property provided as cover for margin, the investment exchange or clearing house in question, or

    (b)   in the case of property subject to a market charge, the person in whose favour the charge was granted.

(2)   Where consent is given the proceedings may be commenced or continued notwithstanding any provision of the Insolvency Act 1986 or the Bankruptcy (Scotland) Act 1985.

(3)   Where by virtue of this section a person would not be entitled to enforce a judgment or order against any property, any injunction or other remedy granted with a view to facilitating the enforcement of any such judgment or order shall not extend to that property.

(4)   In the application of this section to Scotland, the reference to execution being commenced or continued includes a reference to diligence being carried out or continued, and the reference to distress being levied shall be omitted.

[1176]

NOTES

Sub-s (1): words in square brackets inserted by the Tribunals, Courts and Enforcement Act 2007, s 62(3), Sch 13, para 91, as from a day to be appointed.

181   Power to apply provisions to other cases

(1)   [A power to which this subsection applies includes the] power to apply sections 177 to 180 to any description of property provided as cover for margin in relation to contracts in relation to which the power is exercised or, as the case may be, property subject to charges in relation to which the power is exercised.

(2)   The regulations may provide that those sections apply with such exceptions, additions and adaptations as may be specified in the regulations.

[(3)   Subsection (1) applies to the powers of the Secretary of State and the Treasury to act jointly under—

    (a)   sections 170, 172 and 176 of this Act; and

    (b)   section 301 of the Financial Services and Markets Act 2000 (supervision of certain contracts).]

[1177]

PART II
OTHER ACTS

Supplementary provisions

182 Powers of court in relation to certain proceedings begun before commencement

(1) The powers conferred by this section are exercisable by the court where insolvency proceedings in respect of—

(a) a member of a recognised investment exchange or a recognised clearing house, or

(b) a person by whom a market charge has been granted,

are begun on or after 22nd December 1988 and before the commencement of this section.

That person is referred to in this section as "the relevant person".

(2) For the purposes of this section "insolvency proceedings" means proceedings under Part II, IV, V or IX of the Insolvency Act 1986 (administration, winding up and bankruptcy) or under the Bankruptcy (Scotland) Act 1985; and references in this section to the beginning of such proceedings are to—

(a) the presentation of a petition on which an administration order, winding-up order, bankruptcy order or award of sequestration is made, or

(b) the passing of a resolution for voluntary winding up.

(3) This section applies in relation to—

(a) in England and Wales, the administration of the insolvent estate of a deceased person, and

(b) in Scotland, the administration by a judicial factor appointed under section 11A of the Judicial Factors (Scotland) Act 1889 of the insolvent estate of a deceased person,

as it applies in relation to insolvency proceedings.

In such a case references to the beginning of the proceedings shall be construed as references to the death of the relevant person.

(4) The court may on an application made, within three months after the commencement of this section, by—

(a) a recognised investment exchange or recognised clearing house, or

(b) a person in whose favour a market charge has been granted,

make such order as it thinks fit for achieving, except so far as assets of the relevant person have been distributed before the making of the application, the same result as if the provisions of Schedule 22 had come into force on 22nd December 1988.

(5) The provisions of that Schedule ("the relevant provisions") reproduce the effect of certain provisions of this Part as they appeared in the Bill for this Act as introduced into the House of Lords and published on that date.

(6) The court may in particular—

(a) require the relevant person or a relevant office-holder—

(i) to return property provided as cover for margin or which was subject to a market charge, or to pay to the applicant or any other person the proceeds of realisation of such property, or

(ii) to pay to the applicant or any other person such amount as the court estimates would have been payable to that person if the relevant provisions had come into force on 22nd December 1988 and market contracts had been settled in accordance with the rules of the recognised investment exchange or recognised clearing house, or a proportion of that amount if the property of the relevant person or relevant office-holder is not sufficient to meet the amount in full;

(b) provide that contracts, rules and dispositions shall be treated as not having been void;

(c) modify the functions of a relevant office-holder, or the duties of the applicant or any other person, in relation to the insolvency proceedings, or indemnify any such person in respect of acts or omissions which would have been proper if the relevant provisions had been in force;

(d) provide that conduct which constituted an offence be treated as not having done so;

(e) dismiss proceedings which could not have been brought if the relevant provisions had come into force on 22nd December 1988, and reverse the effect of any order of a court which could not, or would not, have been made if those provisions had come into force on that date.

(7) An order under this section shall not be made against a relevant office-holder if the effect would be that his remuneration, costs and expenses could not be met.

183 Insolvency proceedings in other jurisdictions

(1) The references to insolvency law in section 426 of the Insolvency Act 1986 (co-operation with courts exercising insolvency jurisdiction in other jurisdictions) include, in relation to a part of the United Kingdom, the provisions made by or under this Part and, in relation to a relevant country or territory within the meaning of that section, so much of the law of that country or territory as corresponds to any provisions made by or under this Part.

(2) A court shall not, in pursuance of that section or any other enactment or rule of law, recognise or give effect to—

(a) any order of a court exercising jurisdiction in relation to insolvency law in a country or territory outside the United Kingdom, or

(b) any act of a person appointed in such a country or territory to discharge any functions under insolvency law,

in so far as the making of the order or the doing of the act would be prohibited in the case of a court in the United Kingdom or a relevant office-holder by provisions made by or under this Part.

(3) Subsection (2) does not affect the recognition or enforcement of a judgment required to be recognised or enforced under or by virtue of the Civil Jurisdiction and Judgments Act 1982 [or Council Regulation (EC) No 44/2001 of 22nd December 2000 on jurisdiction and the recognition and enforcement of judgments in civil and commercial matters][, as amended from time to time and as applied by the Agreement made on 19th October 2005 between the European Community and the Kingdom of Denmark on jurisdiction and the recognition and enforcement of judgments in civil and commercial matters (OJ No L299 16.11.2005 at p 62)].

[1179]

NOTES

Sub-s (3): words in first pair of square brackets added by the Civil Jurisdiction and Judgments Order 2001, SI 2001/3929, art 5, Sch 3, para 21, as from 1 March 2002; words in second pair of square brackets added by the Civil Jurisdiction and Judgments Regulations 2007, SI 2007/1655, reg 5, Schedule, Pt 1, para 15, as from 1 July 2007.

184 Indemnity for certain acts, &c

(1) Where a relevant office-holder takes any action in relation to property of a defaulter which is liable to be dealt with in accordance with the default rules of a recognised investment exchange or recognised clearing house, and believes and has reasonable grounds for believing that he is entitled to take that action, he is not liable to any person in respect of any loss or damage resulting from his action except in so far as the loss or damage is caused by the office-holder's own negligence.

(2) Any failure by a recognised investment exchange or recognised clearing house to comply with its own rules in respect of any matter shall not prevent that matter being treated for the purposes of this Part as done in accordance with those rules so long as the failure does not substantially affect the rights of any person entitled to require compliance with the rules.

(3) No recognised investment exchange or recognised clearing house, nor any officer or servant or member of the governing body of a recognised investment exchange or recognised clearing house, shall be liable in damages for anything done or omitted in the discharge or purported discharge of any functions to which this subsection applies unless the act or omission is shown to have been in bad faith.

(4) The functions to which subsection (3) applies are the functions of the exchange or clearing house so far as relating to, or to matters arising out of—

(a) its default rules, or

(b) any obligations to which it is subject by virtue of this Part.

(5) No person [to whom the exercise of any function of a recognised investment exchange or recognised clearing house is delegated under its default rules], nor any officer or servant of such a person, shall be liable in damages for anything done or omitted in the discharge or purported discharge of those functions unless the act or omission is shown to have been in bad faith.

[1180]

NOTES

Sub-s (5): words in square brackets substituted by the Financial Services and Markets Act 2000 (Consequential Amendments and Repeals) Order 2001, SI 2001/3649, art 87, as from 1 December 2001.

185 Power to make further provision by regulations

(1) The Secretary of State may by regulations make such further provision as appears to him necessary or expedient for the purposes of this Part.

(2) Provision may, in particular, be made—

(a) for integrating the provisions of this Part with the general law of insolvency, and

(b)   for adapting the provisions of this Part in their application to overseas investment exchanges and clearing houses.

(3)   Regulations under this section may add to, amend or repeal any of the provisions of this Part or provide that those provisions have effect subject to such additions, exceptions or adaptations as are specified in the regulations.

[(4)   References in this section to the provisions of this Part include any provision made under section 301 of the Financial Services and Markets Act 2000.]

[1181]

NOTES

Sub-s (4): added by the Financial Services and Markets Act 2000 (Consequential Amendments and Repeals) Order 2001, SI 2001/3649, art 88, as from 1 December 2001.

Regulations: the Financial Markets and Insolvency Regulations 1991, SI 1991/880 at **[3515A]**; the Financial Markets and Insolvency Regulations 1996, SI 1996/1469 at **[3526A]**; the Financial Markets and Insolvency Regulations 1998, SI 1998/1748; the Financial Markets and Insolvency (CGO Service) Regulations 1999, SI 1999/1209.

186 Supplementary provisions as to regulations

(1)   Regulations under this Part may make different provision for different cases and may contain such incidental, transitional and other supplementary provisions as appear to the Secretary of State to be necessary or expedient.

(2)   Regulations under this Part shall be made by statutory instrument which shall be subject to annulment in pursuance of a resolution of either House of Parliament.

[1182]

NOTES

Regulations: the Financial Markets and Insolvency Regulations 1996, SI 1996/1469 at **[3526A]**; the Financial Markets and Insolvency Regulations 1998, SI 1998/1748; the Financial Markets and Insolvency (CGO Service) Regulations 1999, SI 1999/1209.

187 Construction of references to parties to market contracts

(1)   Where a person enters into market contracts in more than one capacity, the provisions of this Part apply (subject as follows) as if the contracts entered into in each different capacity were entered into by different persons.

(2)   References in this Part to a market contract to which a person is a party include (subject as follows, and unless the context otherwise requires) contracts to which he is party as agent.

(3)   The Secretary of State may by regulations—
    (a)   modify or exclude the operation of subsections (1) and (2), and
    (b)   make provision as to the circumstances in which a person is to be regarded for the purposes of those provisions as acting in different capacities.

[1183]

NOTES

Regulations: the Financial Markets and Insolvency Regulations 1991, SI 1991/880 at **[3515A]**.

188 Meaning of "default rules" and related expressions

(1)   In this Part "default rules" means rules of a recognised investment exchange or recognised clearing house which provide for the taking of action in the event of a person appearing to be unable, or likely to become unable, to meet his obligations in respect of one or more market contracts connected with the exchange or clearing house.

(2)   References in this Part to a "defaulter" are to a person in respect of whom action has been taken by a recognised investment exchange or recognised clearing house under its default rules, whether by declaring him to be a defaulter or otherwise; and references in this Part to "default" shall be construed accordingly.

(3)   In this Part "default proceedings" means proceedings taken by a recognised investment exchange or recognised clearing house under its default rules.

(4)   If an exchange or clearing house takes action under its default rules in respect of a person, all subsequent proceedings under its rules for the purposes of or in connection with the settlement of market contracts to which the defaulter is a party shall be treated as done under its default rules.

[1184]

189 Meaning of "relevant office-holder"

(1)   The following are relevant office-holders for the purposes of this Part—
    (a)   the official receiver,

(b)   any person acting in relation to a company as its liquidator, provisional liquidator, administrator or administrative receiver,

(c)   any person acting in relation to an individual (or, in Scotland, any debtor within the meaning of the Bankruptcy (Scotland) Act 1985) as his trustee in bankruptcy or interim receiver of his property or as permanent or interim trustee in the sequestration of his estate,

(d)   any person acting as administrator of an insolvent estate of a deceased person.

(2)   In subsection (1)(b) "company" means any company, society, association, partnership or other body which may be wound up under the Insolvency Act 1986.

[1185]

190 Minor definitions

(1)   In this Part—

"administrative receiver" has the meaning given by section 251 of the Insolvency Act 1986;

["the Authority" means the Financial Services Authority;]

"charge" means any form of security, including a mortgage and, in Scotland, a heritable security;

.....

"interim trustee" and "permanent trustee" have the same meaning as in the Bankruptcy (Scotland) Act 1985;

.....

"overseas", in relation to an investment exchange or clearing house, means having its head office outside the United Kingdom;

["recognised clearing house" and "recognised investment exchange" have the same meaning as in the Financial Services and Markets Act 2000;]

.....

"set-off", in relation to Scotland, includes compensation;

["The Stock Exchange" means the London Stock Exchange Limited;]

"UK", in relation to an investment exchange or clearing house, means having its head office in the United Kingdom.

(2)   References in this Part to settlement in relation to a market contract are to the discharge of the rights and liabilities of the parties to the contract, whether by performance, compromise or otherwise.

(3)   In this Part the expressions "margin" and "cover for margin" have the same meaning.

(4)   ...

(5)   For the purposes of this Part a person shall be taken to have notice of a matter if he deliberately failed to make enquiries as to that matter in circumstances in which a reasonable and honest person would have done so.

This does not apply for the purposes of a provision requiring "actual notice".

(6)   References in this Part to the law of insolvency include references to every provision made by or under the Insolvency Act 1986 or the Bankruptcy (Scotland) Act 1985; and in relation to a building society references to insolvency law or to any provision of the Insolvency Act 1986 are to that law or provision as modified by the Building Societies Act 1986.

(7)   In relation to Scotland, references in this Part—

(a)   to sequestration include references to the administration by a judicial factor of the insolvent estate of a deceased person, and

(b)   to an interim or permanent trustee include references to a judicial factor on the insolvent estate of a deceased person,

unless the context otherwise requires.

[1186]

NOTES

Sub-s (1): definitions "the Authority", "recognised clearing house" and "recognised investment exchange" inserted, definitions "clearing house", "investment" and "investment exchange" and "recognised" (omitted) repealed, and definition "The Stock Exchange" substituted, by the Financial Services and Markets Act 2000 (Consequential Amendments and Repeals) Order 2001, SI 2001/3649, art 89(1)–(5), as from 1 December 2001.

Sub-s (4): repealed by SI 2001/3649, art 89(1), (6), as from 1 December 2001.

191 Index of defined expressions

The following Table shows provisions defining or otherwise explaining expressions used in this Part (other than provisions defining or explaining an expression used only in the same section or paragraph)—

administrative receiver	section 190(1)
[the Authority	section 190(1)]
charge	section 190(1)
...	...
cover for margin	section 190(3)
default rules (and related expressions)	section 188
designated non-member	section 155(2)
...	...
insolvency law (and similar expressions)	section 190(6)
interim trustee	section 190(1) and (7)(b)
...	...
...	...
margin	section 190(3)
market charge	section 173
market contract	section 155
notice	section 190(5)
overseas (in relation to an investment exchange or clearing house)	section 190(1)
party (in relation to a market contract)	section 187
permanent trustee	section 190(1) and (7)(b)
...	...
[recognised clearing house and recognised investment exchange	section 190(1)]
relevant office-holder	section 189
sequestration	section 190(7)(a)
set off (in relation to Scotland)	section 190(1)
settlement and related expressions (in relation to a market contract)	section 190(2)
The Stock Exchange	section 190(1)
trustee, interim or permanent (in relation to Scotland)	section 190(7)(b)
UK (in relation to an investment exchange or clearing house)	section 190(1).

[1187]

NOTES

Entries relating to "clearing house", "ensuring the performance of a transaction", "investment," "investment exchange" and "recognised" (omitted) repealed, and entries relating to "the Authority" and "recognised clearing house and recognised investment exchange" inserted, by the Financial Services and Markets Act 2000 (Consequential Amendments and Repeals) Order 2001, SI 2001/3649, art 89(7), as from 1 December 2001.

192–207 (Ss 192–206 (Pt VIII: Amendments of FSA 1986): ss 192–197 repealed by the Financial Services and Markets Act 2000 (Consequential Amendments and Repeals) Order 2001, SI 2001/3649, art 75(i), as from 1 December 2001; ss 198, 199 repealed by the Public Offers of Securities Regulations 1995, SI 1995/1537, reg 17, Sch 2, Pt II, para 10, as from 19 June 1995; s 200 repealed in part by SI 2001/3649, art 75(j), as from 1 December 2001 and the reminder of the section is effectively spent (it amended the Civil Jurisdiction and Judgments Act 1982 by inserting a reference to FSA 1986, s 188 into Sch 5 to the 1982 Act – that reference has now been superseded by a reference to FSMA 2000, s 415); ss 201–206 repealed by SI 2001/3649, art 75(k), as from 1 December 2001. S 207 (Pt IX: Transfer of Securities) repealed by the Companies Act 2006, s 1295, Sch 16, as from 6 April 2008. Note that by virtue of the Companies Act 2006, s 1297 (continuity of law) the Uncertificated Securities Regulations 2001, SI 2001/3755 (at **[3581]**) and the

Uncertificated Securities (Amendment) (Eligible Debt Securities) Regulations 2003, SI 2003/1633 which were made under this section now have effect as if made under ss 783, 784(3), 785 and 788 of the 2006 Act.)

PART X

MISCELLANEOUS AND GENERAL PROVISIONS

208–214   *(S 208 adds the Company Directors Disqualification Act 1986, s 21(4); s 209 repealed by the Criminal Justice Act 1993, s 79(14), Sch 6, Pt I; s 210 spent; s 211 amends the Building Societies Act 1986, s 104, Sch 15 and inserts the Company Directors Disqualification Act 1986, s 22A; s 212 introduces Sch 24 to this Act (repeals); s 213 (Northern Ireland) outside the scope of this work; s 214 repealed by the Financial Services and Markets Act 2000 (Consequential Amendments and Repeals) Order 2001, SI 2001/3649, art 75(m), as from 1 December 2001.)*

215   Commencement and transitional provisions

(1)   The following provisions of this Act come into force on Royal Assent—
  (a)   in Part V (amendments of company law), section 141 (application to declare dissolution of company void);
  (b)   in Part VI (mergers)—
      (i)   sections 147 to 150, and
      (ii)   paragraphs 2 to 12, 14 to 16, 18 to 20, 22 to 25 of Schedule 20, and section 153 so far as relating to those paragraphs;
  (c)   in Part VIII (amendments of the Financial Services Act 1986), section 202 (offers of short-dated debentures);
  (d)   in Part X (miscellaneous and general provisions), the repeals made by Schedule 24 in sections 71, 74, 88 and 89 of, and Schedule 9 to, the Fair Trading Act 1973, and section 212 so far as relating to those repeals.

(2)   The other provisions of this Act come into force on such day as the Secretary of State may appoint by order made by statutory instrument; and different days may be appointed for different provisions and different purposes.

(3)   An order bringing into force any provision may contain such transitional provisions and savings as appear to the Secretary of State to be necessary or expedient.

(4)   The Secretary of State may also by order under this section amend any enactment which refers to the commencement of a provision brought into force by the order so as to substitute a reference to the actual date on which it comes into force.

[1189]

NOTES
    Transfer of functions: by the Transfer of Functions (Financial Services) Order 1992, SI 1992/1315, art 2(2)(c), certain functions of the Secretary of State under sub-ss (2)–(4) above are transferred to the Treasury.
    Financial Services Act 1986: repealed by the Financial Services and Markets Act 2000 (Consequential Amendments and Repeals) Order 2001, SI 2001/3649, art 3(1)(c), as from 1 December 2001.
    Orders: the Companies Act 1989 (Commencement No 1) Order 1990, SI 1990/98; the Companies Act 1989 (Commencement No 2) Order 1990, SI 1990/142; the Companies Act 1989 (Commencement No 3, Transitional Provisions and Transfer of Functions under the Financial Services Act 1986) Order 1990, SI 1990/354; the Companies Act 1989 (Commencement No 4, Transitional and Saving Provisions) Order 1990, SI 1990/355; the Companies Act 1989 (Commencement No 5 and Transitional and Saving Provisions) Order 1990, SI 1990/713; the Companies Act 1989 (Commencement No 6 and Transitional and Savings Provisions) Order 1990, SI 1990/1392; the Companies Act 1989 (Commencement No 7, Transitional and Saving Provisions) Order 1990, SI 1990/1707; the Companies Act 1989 (Commencement No 8 and Transitional and Saving Provisions) Order 1990, SI 1990/2569; the Companies Act 1989 (Commencement No 9 and Saving and Transitional Provisions) Order 1991, SI 1991/488; the Companies Act 1989 (Commencement No 10 and Saving Provisions) Order 1991, SI 1991/878; the Companies Act 1989 (Commencement No 11) Order 1991, SI 1991/1452; the Companies Act 1989 (Commencement No 12 and Transitional Provision) Order 1991, SI 1991/1996; the Companies Act 1989 (Commencement No 13) Order 1991, SI 1991/2173; the Companies Act 1989 (Commencement No 14 and Transitional Provision) Order 1991, SI 1991/2945; the Companies Act 1989 (Commencement No 15 and Transitional and Savings Provisions) Order 1995, SI 1995/1352; the Companies Act 1989 (Commencement No 16) Order 1995, SI 1995/1591; the Companies Act 1989 (Commencement No 17) Order 1998, SI 1998/1747; the Companies (Audit, Investigations and Community Enterprise) Act 2004 (Commencement) and Companies Act 1989 (Commencement No 18) Order 2004, SI 2004/3322.

216   Short title

This Act may be cited as the Companies Act 1989.

[1190]

(Schs 1–24 outside the scope of this work.)

FRIENDLY SOCIETIES ACT 1992

(1992 c 40)

NOTES
Only provisions of this Act relevant to Financial Services law are reproduced. Provisions not reproduced are not annotated.
This Act is reproduced as amended by: the Financial Services and Markets Act 2000; the Friendly Societies Act 1992 (Amendment) Regulations 1994, SI 1994/1984; the Financial Services and Markets Act 2000 (Mutual Societies) Order 2001, SI 2001/2617; the Financial Services and Markets Act 2000 (Consequential Amendments and Repeals) Order 2001, SI 2001/3649; the Life Assurance Consolidation Directive (Consequential Amendments) Regulations 2004, SI 2004/3379; the Friendly Societies Act 1992 (International Accounting Standards and Other Accounting Amendments) Order 2005, SI 2005/2211; the Friendly Societies Act 1992 (Accounts, Audit and EEA State Amendments) Order 2008, SI 2008/1144.

An Act to make further provision for friendly societies; to provide for the cessation of registration under the Friendly Societies Act 1974; to make provision about disputes involving friendly societies or other bodies registered under the Friendly Societies Act 1974 and about the functions of the Chief Registrar of friendly societies; and for connected purposes

[16 March 1992]

PART II
INCORPORATED FRIENDLY SOCIETIES

Constitution and purposes of incorporated friendly societies

13 Control of subsidiaries and other bodies corporate

(1)   (*Outside the scope of this work.*)

(2)–(5)   ...

(6), (7)   (*Outside the scope of this work.*)

(8)   ...

(9)   For the purposes of this Act—

  (a)   an incorporated friendly society has control of a body corporate if the society—
    (i)   holds a majority of the voting rights in it; or
    (ii)   is a member of it and has the right to appoint or remove a majority of its board of directors; or
    (iii)   is a member of it and controls alone, pursuant to an agreement with other shareholders or members, a majority of the voting rights in it;

  [(aa)   an incorporated friendly society also has control of a body corporate if the body corporate is itself a body controlled in one of the ways mentioned in paragraph (a)(i), (ii) or (iii) by a body corporate of which the society has control;]

  (b)   a body corporate is a subsidiary of an incorporated friendly society if the society has control of it;

  (c)   an incorporated friendly society has joint control of a body corporate if, in pursuance of an agreement or other arrangement between them, the society and another person—
    (i)   hold a majority of the voting rights in that body; or
    (ii)   are members of it and together have the right to appoint or remove a majority of its board of directors; or
    (iii)   are members of it and alone control, pursuant to an agreement with other shareholders or members, a majority of the voting rights in it;

  [(cc)   an incorporated friendly society also has joint control of a body corporate if—
    (i)   a subsidiary of the society has joint control of the body corporate in a way mentioned in paragraph (c)(i), (ii) or (iii);
    (ii)   a body corporate of which the society has joint control has joint control of the body corporate in such a way; or
    (iii)   the body corporate is controlled in a way mentioned in paragraph (a)(i), (ii) or (iii) by a body corporate of which the society has joint control;]

  (d)   a body corporate is a body jointly controlled by an incorporated friendly society if the society has joint control of it;

and a society acquires joint control whenever any of the conditions mentioned in paragraph (c) [or (cc)] above are satisfied with respect to a body corporate, notwithstanding that it may already be a subsidiary of the society.

(10)   (*Outside the scope of this work.*)

(11)   ...

[1191]

NOTES
   Sub-ss (2)–(5), (8), (11): repealed by the Financial Services and Markets Act 2000, ss 334(4), 432(3), Sch 18, Pt II, para 10(1), (2)(a), Sch 22, as from 1 December 2001.
   Sub-s (9): paras (aa), (cc), and words in final pair of square brackets, inserted by the Financial Services and Markets Act 2000, s 334(4), Sch 18, Pt II, paras 11–13, as from 1 December 2001.

PART X
GENERAL AND SUPPLEMENTARY
Interpretation

119   General interpretation

(1)   In this Act, unless the context otherwise requires—
   "the 1974 Act" means the Friendly Societies Act 1974;
   "actuary" means an actuary possessing [such qualifications, if any, as may be specified in rules made by the Authority under section 340 of the Financial Services and Markets Act 2000 (and subsections (3) to (6) of that section apply in relation to an actuary appointed by virtue of any provision of this Act as they apply in relation to an actuary appointed in compliance with such rules)];
   "annuities on human life" does not include superannuation allowances and annuities payable out of any fund applicable solely to the relief and maintenance of persons engaged or who have been engaged in any particular profession, trade or employment, or of the dependants of such persons;
   ["the Authority" means the Financial Services Authority;]
   "appointed actuary" means the actuary appointed [in accordance with rules made under section 340 of the Financial Services and Markets Act 2000];
   "the appropriate actuary" means—
   (a)   if the society is under [a duty imposed by rules made by the Authority under section 340 of the Financial Services and Markets Act 2000], the society's appointed actuary; and
   (b)   if it is not under [such a] duty, an actuary appointed to perform the function in question;

   .....
   .....
   .....

   "committee of management" means the committee of management or other directing body of a society or branch;
   ["the life assurance consolidation Directive" means Directive 2002/83/EC of the European Parliament and of the Council of 5th November 2002 concerning life assurance;]
   "contract of insurance" includes any contract the effecting of which constitutes the carrying on of insurance business by virtue of section 117 above;
   ["controller" has the meaning given by section 55A above;]
   "the court" except in relation to the winding-up of an incorporated friendly society, means—
   (a)   in the case of a body whose registered office is situated in England and Wales or in Northern Ireland, the county court for the district in which the office is situated;
   (b)   in the case of a body whose registered office is situated in Scotland, the sheriff in whose jurisdiction the office is situated;
   and, in relation to the winding-up of an incorporated friendly society, means the court which has jurisdiction under the applicable winding-up legislation to wind-up the society;

   .....
   [.....
   ["EEA State" has the meaning given by Schedule 1 to the Interpretation Act 1978 (c 30);]
   "EFTA State" means an EEA State which is not a member State;]
   "financial year" is to be construed in accordance with section 118;
   "the first general insurance Directive" means Council Directive 73/239/EEC of 24th July 1973 on the coordination of laws, regulations and administrative provisions relating to the taking up and pursuit of the business of direct insurance other than life assurance;

   .....
   ["the general insurance Directives" means the first general insurance Directive, the second general insurance Directive and the third general insurance Directive as amended, and such other Directives as make provision with respect to the business of direct insurance other than life assurance;]
   "group business" is to be construed in accordance with section 11 above;
   "jointly controlled body" is to be construed in accordance with section 13 above;

   .....

["manager", in relation to a friendly society to which section 37(2) or (3) above applies, means any person (other than an employee of a society) appointed by the society to manage any part of its insurance business, or any employee of the society (other than a chief executive) who, under the immediate authority of a member of the committee of management or chief executive of the society—
    (a)   exercises managerial functions, or is responsible for maintaining accounts or other records of the society; and
    (b)   is not a person whose functions relate exclusively to business conducted from a place of business which is not in a member State;]

"memorandum" has the meaning given by paragraph 4(3) of Schedule 3 to this Act;

"modifications", in relation to enactments, includes additions, omissions and amendments [and cognate expressions are to be construed accordingly];

"non-insurance business" means business falling within head C of Schedule 2 to this Act;

"notice" means written notice and "notice to" a person means notice given to that person, and "notify" shall be construed accordingly;

[.....]

"officer" means—
    (a)   in relation to a registered friendly society or a registered branch—
        (i)   a trustee;
        (ii)   the treasurer, secretary and chief executive (however described);
        (iii)   a member of the committee of management; and
        (iv)   a person appointed by the society or branch to sue or be sued on its behalf; or
    (b)   in relation to an incorporated friendly society, a member of the committee of management, the chief executive (however described) and the secretary;

"the public file", in relation to a friendly society, means the file relating to the society which the [Authority] is required to maintain under section 104 above;

"registered address", in relation to a member of an incorporated friendly society, has the meaning given by paragraph 14(6) of Schedule 3 to this Act;

"the second general insurance Directive" means Council Directive 88/357/EEC of 22nd June 1988 on the coordination of laws, regulations and administrative provisions relating to direct insurance other than life assurance and laying down provisions to facilitate the effective exercise of freedom to provide services and amending Directive 73/239/EEC;

.....

"special resolution" has the meaning given by paragraph 7 of Schedule 12 to this Act;

"subscription" includes any premium or other sum (however described) payable, in respect of the provision of benefits, by (or on behalf of) a member of a friendly society under the rules of the society;

"subsidiary" is to be construed in accordance with section 13 above;

["supervisory authority", in relation to an EEA State other than the United Kingdom, means the authority responsible in that State for supervising [persons whose business consists of effecting or carrying out contracts of insurance];

"the third general insurance Directive" means Council Directive 92/49/EEC of 18th June 1992 on the coordination of laws, regulations and administrative provisions relating to direct insurance other than life assurance and amending Directives 73/239/EEC and 88/357/EEC;

.....

[(1AA), (1A)–(1D)], (2), [(3)] (*Outside the scope of this work.*)

[1192]

NOTES

Sub-s (1) is amended as follows:

In definition "actuary" words in square brackets substituted by the Financial Services and Markets Act 2000 (Mutual Societies) Order 2001, SI 2001/2617, art 13(1), Sch 3, Pt I, paras 53, 115(a)(i), as from 1 December 2001.

Definition "the Authority" inserted by SI 2001/2617, art 13(1), Sch 3, Pt I, paras 53, 115(a)(ii), as from 1 December 2001.

In definition "appointed actuary" words in square brackets substituted by SI 2001/2617, art 13(1), Sch 3, Pt I, paras 53, 115(a)(iii), as from 1 December 2001.

In definition "appropriate actuary" words in square brackets substituted by SI 2001/2617, art 13(1), Sch 3, Pt I, paras 53, 115(a)(iv), as from 1 December 2001.

Definition "central office" (omitted) repealed by SI 2001/2617, art 13(1), (2), Sch 3, Pt I, paras 53, 115(a)(v), Sch 4, as from 1 December 2001.

Definition "the Chief Registrar" (omitted) repealed by SI 2001/2617, art 13(1), (2), Sch 3, Pt I, paras 53, 115(a)(v), Sch 4, as from 1 December 2001.

Definition "collecting society" (omitted) repealed by SI 2001/2617, art 13(1), (2), Sch 3, Pt I, paras 53, 115(a)(v), Sch 4, as from 1 December 2001.

Definition "the Commission" (omitted) repealed by SI 2001/2617, art 13(1), (2), Sch 3, Pt I, paras 53, 115(a)(v), Sch 4, as from 1 December 2001.

Definition "the life assurance consolidation Directive" inserted by the Life Assurance Consolidation Directive (Consequential Amendments) Regulations 2004, SI 2004/3379, reg 3(1), (3)(a), as from 11 January 2005.

SCHEDULES:

An Act to consolidate the Tribunals and Inquiries Act 1971 and certain other enactments relating to tribunals and inquiries

[16 July 1992]

1–4

    (*Ss 1–4 (the Council on Tribunals and their functions) repealed by the Tribunals, Courts and Enforcement Act 2007, ss 45(2), 146, Sch 23, Pt 1, as from 1 November 2007. As to the abolition (as from 1 November 2007) of the Council on Tribunals and the Scottish Committee of the Council on Tribunals, and the establishment of the Administrative Justice and Tribunals Council, see ss 44, 45(1), (2) of the 2007 Act. See also s 45(3) of that Act in relation to the transfer of the property, rights and liabilities of the Council and the Committee to the Administrative Justice and Tribunals Council.*)

Composition and procedure of tribunals and inquiries

5 Recommendations of Council as to appointment of members of tribunals

    (*1*) *Subject to section 6 but without prejudice to the generality of section 1(1)(a), the Council may make to the appropriate Minister general recommendations as to the making of appointments to membership of any tribunals mentioned in Schedule 1 or of panels constituted for the purposes of any such tribunals; and (without prejudice to any statutory provisions having effect with respect to such appointments) the appropriate Minister shall have regard to recommendations under this section.*

    (*2*) *In this section "the appropriate Minister", in relation to appointments of any description, means the Minister making the appointments or, if they are not made by a Minister, the Minister in charge of the government department concerned with the tribunals in question.*

    (*3*) *The following provisions shall have effect as respects any tribunal specified in Part II of Schedule 1—*
    (*a*) *the Council shall not make any recommendations under this section until—*
        (*i*) *they have referred the matter of the recommendations for consideration, and report to the Council, by the Scottish Committee, and*
        (*ii*) *they have considered the report of that Committee,*
    (*b*) *without prejudice to the generality of section 4(5), the Scottish Committee may of its own motion propose any such general recommendations as expedient to be made by the Council to the appropriate Minister, and*
    (*c*) *if the Council—*
        (*i*) *in making recommendations under this section on any matter which they have referred to the Scottish Committee or on which that Committee has made proposals, do not adopt the report or proposals of that Committee without modification, or*
        (*ii*) *do not make recommendations on matters on which the Scottish Committee has made proposals to the Council,*
    the Scottish Committee may submit its report or proposals to the [Scottish Ministers].

[1199]

NOTES
  Repealed by the Tribunals, Courts and Enforcement Act 2007, ss 48(1), 146, Sch 8, paras 23, 24, Sch 23, Pt 1, as from a day to be appointed.
  Sub-s (3): words in square brackets substituted by the Scotland Act 1998 (Cross-Border Public Authorities) (Adaptation of Functions etc) Order 1999, SI 1999/1747, art 3, Sch 9, para 2(1), (2), as from 1 July 1999.

6 Appointment of chairmen of certain tribunals

    (*1*) *The chairman, or any person appointed to act as chairman, of any of the tribunals to which this subsection applies shall (without prejudice to any statutory provisions as to qualifications) be selected by the appropriate authority from a panel of persons appointed by the Lord Chancellor.*

(2)   *Members of panels constituted under this section shall hold and vacate office under the terms of the instruments under which they are appointed, but may resign office by notice in writing to the Lord Chancellor; and any such member who ceases to hold office shall be eligible for re-appointment.*

(3)   *Subsection (1) applies to any tribunal specified in [paragraph 7(b) or 38(a)] of Schedule 1.*

(4)   *In relation to the tribunals specified in paragraph 41(a), (b) and (c) of Schedule 1, this section has effect subject to sections 41 (social security appeal tribunals), 43 (disability appeal tribunals) and 50 (medical appeal tribunals) of the Social Security Administration Act 1992.*

(5)   The person or persons constituting any tribunal specified in paragraph 31 of Schedule 1 shall be appointed by the Lord Chancellor, and where such a tribunal consists of more than one person the Lord Chancellor shall designate which of them is to be the chairman.

(6)   *In this section, "the appropriate authority" means the Minister who apart from this Act would be empowered to appoint or select the chairman, person to act as chairman, members or member of the tribunal in question.*

(7)   *A panel may be constituted under this section for the purposes either of a single tribunal or of two or more tribunals, whether or not of the same description.*

(8)   In relation to any of the tribunals referred to in this section which sits in Scotland, this section shall have effect with the substitution for any reference to the Lord Chancellor of a reference to the Lord President of the Court of Session.

(9)   ...

[1200]

NOTES

Sub-ss (1)–(3): repealed by the Tribunals, Courts and Enforcement Act 2007, ss 48(1), 146, Sch 8, paras 23, 25, Sch 23, Pt 1, as from 3 November 2008 (in so far as relating to paragraph 7(b) of Schedule 1 to the Tribunals and Inquiries Act 1992 (see SI 2008/2696, art 5)), and as from a day to be appointed (otherwise); words in square brackets in sub-s (3) substituted by the Social Security Act 1998, s 86, Sch 7, para 118(1), partly as from 1 June 1999, 18 October 1999, and 29 November 1999 (see SI 1999/1510, SI 1999/2860, SI 1999/3178).

Sub-s (4): repealed by the Social Security Act 1998, s 86, Sch 7, para 118(2), Sch 8, as from 18 October 1999 (for certain purposes), as from 29 November 1999 (for certain purposes), and as from a day to be appointed (otherwise) (see SI 1999/2860, SI 1999/3178).

Sub-ss (6), (7): repealed by the Tribunals, Courts and Enforcement Act 2007, s 146, Sch 23, Pt 1, as from a day to be appointed.

Sub-s (9): repealed by the Constitutional Reform Act 2005, ss 15, 146, Sch 4, Pt 1, paras 223, 224, Sch 18, Pt 2, as from 3 April 2006.

7   Concurrence required for removal of members of certain tribunals

(1)   Subject to subsection (2), the power of a Minister ... to terminate a person's membership of any tribunal specified in Schedule 1, or of a panel constituted for the purposes of any such tribunal, shall be exercisable only with the consent of—

(a)   the Lord Chancellor [(unless he is the Minister terminating the person's membership), the Lord Chief Justice of England and Wales,], the Lord President of the Court of Session and the Lord Chief Justice of Northern Ireland, if the tribunal sits in all parts of the United Kingdom;

(b)   the Lord Chancellor [(unless he is the Minister terminating the person's membership), the Lord Chief Justice of England and Wales,] and the Lord President of the Court of Session, if the tribunal sits in all parts of Great Britain;

(c)   the Lord Chancellor [(unless he is the Minister terminating the person's membership), the Lord Chief Justice of England and Wales,] and the Lord Chief Justice of Northern Ireland, if the tribunal sits both in England and Wales and in Northern Ireland;

(d)   the Lord Chancellor [(unless he is the Minister terminating the person's membership) and the Lord Chief Justice of England and Wales], if the tribunal does not sit outside England and Wales;

(e)   the Lord President of the Court of Session, if the tribunal sits only in Scotland;

(f)   the Lord Chief Justice of Northern Ireland, if the tribunal sits only in Northern Ireland.

(2)   This section does not apply to any tribunal specified in paragraph 3 ...12, 14, [15(f),] 17, 18 [...] 26, 33(a), [33AA,] [...] 34, 35 ... (e) [(i), (j), (k) or (l)], 36(a), [36A[...],] 39(b), 40, [48 or 56(a)] [or 57A] of Schedule 1.

(3)   ...

[1201]

NOTES

Sub-s (1): words omitted repealed, and words in square brackets inserted, by the Constitutional Reform Act 2005, ss 15, 146, Sch 4, Pt 1, paras 223, 225, Sch 18, Pt 2, as from 3 April 2006.

Sub-s (2) is amended as follows:

First figure omitted repealed by the Financial Services and Markets Act 2000 (Consequential Amendments and Repeals) Order 2001, SI 2001/3649, art 334, as from 1 December 2001.

Figure "15(f)" in square brackets inserted by the School Standards and Framework Act 1998, s 25(4), Sch 5, para 10(1), as from 1 October 1998.

Second figure omitted originally inserted by the Tribunals and Inquiries (Friendly Societies) Order 1993, SI 1993/3258, art 2(a), as from 1 February 1994, and repealed by SI 2001/3649, art 334, as from 1 December 2001.

Figure "33AA" in square brackets inserted by the National Lottery Act 1998, s 1(5), Sch 1, para 12(1), (2)(a), as from 1 April 1999.

Third figure omitted originally inserted by the National Lottery etc Act 1993, s 3(2), Sch 2, para 8(1), as from 25 October 1993, and repealed by the National Lottery Act 1998, ss 1(5), 26, Sch 1, para 12(1), (2)(b), Sch 5, Pt I, as from 1 April 1999.

Fourth words omitted repealed by the Pensions Act 1995, ss 151, 177, Sch 5, para 16(2), Sch 7, Pt III, as from 6 April 1997.

Words "(i), (j), (k) or (l)" in square brackets substituted by the Pensions Act 2004, s 319, Sch 12, para 8(1), (2), as from 10 February 2005.

Figure "36A," in square brackets inserted by the Police and Magistrates' Courts Act 1994, s 44, Sch 5, Pt II, para 39 and the Police Act 1996, s 103, Sch 7, para 45.

Words omitted following the figure "36A," originally inserted by the Police Act 1997, s 134(1), Sch 9, para 69, as from 1 April 1998; and repealed by the Serious Organised Crime and Police Act 2005, ss 59, 174, Sch 4, paras 60, 61, Sch 17, Pt 2, as from 1 April 2006.

Words "48 or 56(a)" in square brackets substituted by the Social Security Act 1998, s 86(1), Sch 7, para 119, as from 18 October 1999.

Words "or 57A" in square brackets substituted by the Police and Magistrates' Courts Act 1994, s 44, Sch 5, Pt II, para 39.

Sub-s (3): repealed by the Asylum and Immigration (Treatment of Claimants, etc) Act 2004, ss 26(7), 47, Sch 2, Pt 1, para 7(1), (2), Sch 4, as from 4 April 2005 (subject to transitional provisions in relation to pending appeals made to an adjudicator before that date and in relation to further appeals and applications in such cases in SI 2005/565).

---

8   Procedural rules for tribunals

(1)   The power of a Minister, the Lord President of the Court of Session, the Commissioners of Inland Revenue or the Foreign Compensation Commission to make, approve, confirm or concur in procedural rules for any tribunal specified in Schedule 1 shall be exercisable only after consultation with the Council.

[(1A)   Subsection (1) does not apply with respect to any procedural rules made or to be made by the Tribunal Procedure Committee.]

(2)   ...

(3)   The Council shall consult the Scottish Committee in relation to the exercise of their functions under this section [with respect to any tribunal specified in Part 2 of Schedule 1].

(4)   In this section "procedural rules" includes any statutory provision relating to the procedure of the tribunal in question.

[1202]

NOTES

Repealed by the Tribunals, Courts and Enforcement Act 2007, ss 48(1), 146, Sch 8, paras 23, 27, Sch 23, Pt 1, as from 21 July 2008 (in so far as relating to the powers of a Minister), and as from a day to be appointed (otherwise).

Sub-s (1A): inserted by the Tribunals, Courts and Enforcement Act 2007, s 48(1), Sch 8, paras 23, 26, as from a day to be appointed.

Sub-s (2): repealed by the Financial Services and Markets Act 2000 (Consequential Amendments and Repeals) Order 2001, SI 2001/3649, art 335(1), (2), as from 1 December 2001.

Sub-s (3): words in square brackets substituted by SI 2001/3649, art 335(1), (3), as from 1 December 2001.

Commissioners of Inland Revenue: a reference to the Commissioners of Inland Revenue is now to be taken as a reference to the Commissioners for Her Majesty's Revenue and Customs; see the Commissioners for Revenue and Customs Act 2005, s 50(1), (7).

---

9   Procedure in connection with statutory inquiries

(1)   The Lord Chancellor, after consultation with the Council, may make rules regulating the procedure to be followed in connection with statutory inquiries held by or on behalf of Ministers; and different provision may be made by any such rules in relation to different classes of such inquiries.

(2)   Any rules made by the Lord Chancellor under this section shall have effect, in relation to any statutory inquiry, subject to the provisions of the enactment under which the inquiry is held, and of any rules or regulations made under that enactment.

(3)   Subject to subsection (2), rules made under this section may regulate procedure in connection with matters preparatory to such statutory inquiries as are mentioned in subsection (1), and in connection with matters subsequent to such inquiries, as well as in connection with the conduct of proceedings at such inquiries.

[(3A) The Council, in exercising their functions under this section in relation to inquiries to be held in Wales, shall consult with the Welsh Committee.]

(4) In the application of this section to inquiries held in Scotland—
  (a) for any reference to the Lord Chancellor there shall be substituted a reference to the [Secretary of State], and
  (b) the Council, in exercising their functions under this section in relation to rules to be made by the [Secretary of State], shall consult with the Scottish Committee.

[(5) For the purposes of the application of this section to Scotland, the expression "statutory inquiry" in subsections (1) to (3) is not to be construed as including an inquiry held under section 265 of, or paragraph 6 of Schedule 4 to, the Town and Country Planning (Scotland) Act 1997 (c 8).]

[1203]

NOTES

Sub-s (3A): inserted by the Tribunals, Courts and Enforcement Act 2007, s 48(1), Sch 8, paras 23, 28, as from 3 November 2008.

Sub-s (4): words in square brackets substituted by virtue of the Transfer of Functions (Lord Advocate and Secretary of State) Order 1999, SI 1999/678, arts 2(1), 7(4), Schedule, as from 19 May 1999.

Sub-s (5): added by the Planning etc (Scotland) Act 2006, s 52(2), as from a day to be appointed.

Transfer of functions: functions under this section are transferred, in so far as they are exercisable in or as regards Scotland, to the Scottish Ministers, by the Scotland Act 1998 (Transfer of Functions to the Scottish Ministers etc) Order 1999, SI 1999/1750, art 2, Sch 1.

Rules: Rules made under this section are outside the scope of this work.

Judicial control of tribunals etc

10 Reasons to be given for decisions of tribunals and Ministers

(1) Subject to the provisions of this section and of section 14, where—
  (a) any tribunal specified in Schedule 1 gives any decision, or
  (b) any Minister notifies any decision taken by him—
    (i) after a statutory inquiry has been held by him or on his behalf, or
    (ii) in a case in which a person concerned could (whether by objecting or otherwise) have required a statutory inquiry to be so held,

it shall be the duty of the tribunal or Minister to furnish a statement, either written or oral, of the reasons for the decision if requested, on or before the giving or notification of the decision, to state the reasons.

(2) The statement referred to in subsection (1) may be refused, or the specification of the reasons restricted, on grounds of national security.

(3) A tribunal or Minister may refuse to furnish a statement under subsection (1) to a person not primarily concerned with the decision if of the opinion that to furnish it would be contrary to the interests of any person primarily concerned.

(4) Subsection (1) does not apply to any decision taken by a Minister after the holding by him or on his behalf of an inquiry or hearing which is a statutory inquiry by virtue only of an order made under section 16(2) unless the order contains a direction that this section is to apply in relation to any inquiry or hearing to which the order applies.

(5) Subsection (1) does not apply—
  (a) to decisions in respect of which any statutory provision has effect, apart from this section, as to the giving of reasons,
  (b) to decisions of a Minister in connection with the preparation, making, approval, confirmation, or concurrence in regulations, rules or byelaws, or orders or schemes of a legislative and not executive character, ...
  [(ba)], (c) ...

(6) Any statement of the reasons for a decision referred to in paragraph (a) or (b) of subsection (1), whether given in pursuance of that subsection or of any other statutory provision, shall be taken to form part of the decision and accordingly to be incorporated in the record.

(7) If, after consultation with the Council, it appears to the Lord Chancellor and the [Secretary of State] that it is expedient that—
  (a) decisions of any particular tribunal or any description of such decisions, or
  (b) any description of decisions of a Minister,

should be excluded from the operation of subsection (1) on the ground that the subject-matter of such decisions, or the circumstances in which they are made, make the giving of reasons unnecessary or impracticable, the Lord Chancellor and the [Secretary of State] may by order direct that subsection (1) shall not apply to such decisions.

(8) Where an order relating to any decisions has been made under subsection (7), the Lord Chancellor and the [Secretary of State] may, by a subsequent order made after consultation with the Council, revoke or vary the earlier order so that subsection (1) applies to any of those decisions.

[1204]

NOTES

Sub-s (5): para (ba) inserted, and para (c) repealed, by the Pensions Act 1995, ss 122, 151, 177, Sch 3, para 21(b), Sch 5, para 16(1), (3), Sch 7, Pt III, as from 1 April 1997; para (ba) (and the word immediately preceding it) repealed by the Pensions Act 2004, s 320, Sch 13, Pt 1, as from 1 September 2005.

Sub-ss (7), (8): words in square brackets substituted by virtue of the Transfer of Functions (Lord Advocate and Secretary of State) Order 1999, SI 1999/678, arts 2(1), 7(4), Schedule, as from 19 May 1999.

Functions under this section: functions under sub-ss (7) and (8) are transferred, in so far as they are exercisable in or as regards Scotland, to the Scottish Ministers, by the Scotland Act 1998 (Transfer of Functions to the Scottish Ministers etc) Order 1999, SI 1999/1750, art 2, Sch 1.

11 Appeals from certain tribunals

(1) Subject to subsection (2), if any party to proceedings before any tribunal specified in paragraph 8, [15(a) or (d)], 16 … 24, 26, 31, 33(b), 37, [40A,] […], 44 or 45 of Schedule 1 is dissatisfied in point of law with a decision of the tribunal he may, according as rules of court may provide, either appeal from the tribunal to the High Court or require the tribunal to state and sign a case for the opinion of the High Court.

(2) [This section] shall not apply in relation to
    [(a) proceedings before [employment tribunals] which arise under or by virtue of any of the enactments mentioned in [section 21(1) of the [Employment Tribunals Act 1996]][; or
    (b) proceedings under section 20 of the Abolition of Feudal Tenure etc (Scotland) Act 2000 (asp 5) (reallotment of real burden)].

(3) Rules of court made with respect to all or any of the tribunals referred to in subsection (1) may provide for authorising or requiring a tribunal, in the course of proceedings before it, to state, in the form of a special case for the decision of the High Court, any question of law arising in the proceedings; and a decision of the High Court on a case stated by virtue of this subsection shall be deemed to be a judgment of the Court within the meaning of section 16 of the *Supreme Court Act 1981* (jurisdiction of Court of Appeal to hear and determine appeals from judgments of the High Court).

(4) In relation to proceedings in the High Court or the Court of Appeal brought by virtue of this section, the power to make rules of court shall include power to make rules prescribing the powers of the High Court or the Court of Appeal with respect to—
    (a) the giving of any decision which might have been given by the tribunal;
    (b) the remitting of the matter with the opinion or direction of the court for re-hearing and determination by the tribunal;
    (c) the giving of directions to the tribunal;
and different provisions may be made for different tribunals.

(5) An appeal to the Court of Appeal shall not be brought by virtue of this section except with the leave of the High Court or the Court of Appeal.

(6) *Subsection (1) shall apply to a decision of the Secretary of State on an appeal under section 41 of the Consumer Credit Act 1974 from a determination of [the Office of Fair Trading] as it applies to a decision of any of the tribunals mentioned in that subsection, but with the substitution for the reference to a party to proceedings of a reference to any person who had a right to appeal to the Secretary of State (whether or not he has exercised that right); and accordingly references in subsections (1) and (4) to a tribunal shall be construed, in relation to such an appeal, as references to the Secretary of State.*

(7) The following provisions shall have effect for the application of this section to Scotland—
    (a) in relation to any proceedings in Scotland of any of the tribunals referred to in the preceding provisions of this section, *or on an appeal under section 41 of the Consumer Credit Act 1974 by a company registered in Scotland* or by any other person whose principal or prospective principal place of business in the United Kingdom is in Scotland, this section shall have effect with the following modifications—
        (i) for references to the High Court or the Court of Appeal there shall be substituted references to the Court of Session,
        (ii) in subsection (3) for "in the form of a special case for the decision of the High Court" there shall be substituted "a case for the opinion of the Court of Session on" and the words from "and a decision" to the end of the subsection shall be omitted, and
        (iii) subsection (5) shall be omitted,
    (b) this section shall apply, with the modifications specified in paragraph (a)—

    (i)   to proceedings before any such tribunal as is specified in paragraph 51, 56(b), 59 or 63 of Schedule 1, and

    (ii)   subject to paragraph (c) below, to proceedings before the Lands Tribunal for Scotland,

as it applies to proceedings before the tribunals referred to in subsection (1);

(c)   subsection (1) shall not apply in relation to proceedings before the Lands Tribunal for Scotland which arise under section 1(3A) of the Lands Tribunal Act 1949 (jurisdiction of the tribunal in valuation matters);

(d)   an appeal shall lie, with the leave of the Court of Session or the *House of Lords*, from any decision of the Court of Session under this section, and such leave may be given on such terms as to costs or otherwise as the Court of Session or the *House of Lords* may determine.

(8)   In relation to any proceedings in Northern Ireland of any of the tribunals referred to in subsection (1) *and in relation to a decision of the Secretary of State on an appeal under section 41 of the Consumer Credit Act 1974 by a company registered in Northern Ireland or by any other person whose principal or prospective principal place of business in the United Kingdom is in Northern Ireland*, this section shall have effect with the following modifications—

(a)   in subsection (3), for the words from the beginning to "provide" there shall be substituted "Rules may be made under section 55 of the Judicature (Northern Ireland) Act 1978 providing", and for "section 16 of the *Supreme Court Act 1981*" there shall be substituted "section 35 of the Judicature (Northern Ireland) Act 1978";

(b)   in subsection (4), for "the power to make rules of court shall include power to make rules" there shall be substituted "rules may be made under section 55 of the Judicature (Northern Ireland) Act 1978";

(c)   at the beginning of subsection (5), there shall be inserted "Rules made under section 55 of the Judicature (Northern Ireland) Act 1978, relating to such proceedings as are mentioned in subsection (4), shall provide that the appeal shall be heard, or as the case may be, the decision of the High Court shall be given, by a single judge, but".

(9)   Her Majesty may by Order in Council direct that all or any of the provisions of this section, so far as it relates to proceedings in the Isle of Man or any of the Channel Islands of the tribunal specified in paragraph 45 of Schedule 1, shall extend to the Isle of Man or to any of the Channel Islands subject to such modifications as may be specified in the Order.

(10)   In this section "decision" includes any direction or order, and references to the giving of a decision shall be construed accordingly.

[1205]

NOTES

Sub-s (1) is amended as follows:

Words in first pair of square brackets substituted by the Special Educational Needs and Disability Act 2001, s 42(1), Sch 8, Pt 2, paras 19, 20(a), as from 1 September 2002.

First figure omitted repealed by the Financial Services and Markets Act 2000 (Consequential Amendments and Repeals) Order 2001, SI 2001/3649, art 336, as from 1 December 2001.

Figure "40A" in square brackets inserted by the Sea Fish (Conservation) Act 1992, s 9, as from 17 December 1992.

Figure "40B" (omitted) originally inserted by the Special Educational Needs and Disability Act 2001, s 42(1), Sch 8, Pt 2, paras 19, 20(b), as from 1 September 2002, and repealed by the Transfer of Tribunal Functions Order 2008, SI 2008/2833, art 9(1), Sch 3, paras 105, 106, as from 3 November 2008, subject to savings in Sch 4, para 7(2) to that Order which provide that sub-s (1) above continues to apply to any decision given by the Special Educational Needs and Disability Tribunal or the Special Educational Needs Tribunal for Wales before that date as if the amendments to it in Schedule 3 had not been made.

Sub-s (2): words in first pair of square brackets substituted by the Employment Rights Act 1996, s 240, Sch 1, para 57, as from 22 August 1996; para (a) numbered as such, and para (b) and the word immediately preceding it inserted, by the Abolition of Feudal Tenure etc (Scotland) Act 2000, s 22, as from 1 November 2003; in para (a) words in first and third (inner) pairs of square brackets substituted by the Employment Rights (Dispute Resolution) Act 1998, s 1(2)(b), (c), as from 1 August 1998; words in second (outer) pair of square brackets substituted by the Employment Tribunals Act 1996, s 43, Sch 1, para 9(1), (2), as from 22 August 1996.

Sub-s (3): for the words in italics there are substituted the words "Senior Courts Act 1981" by the Constitutional Reform Act 2005, s 59(5), Sch 11, Pt 1, para 1(2), as from a day to be appointed.

Sub-s (6): repealed by the Consumer Credit Act 2006, s 70, Sch 4, as from 6 April 2008, subject to transitional provisions as noted below; words in square brackets substituted by the Enterprise Act 2002, s 278(1), Sch 25, para 27(1), (2), as from 1 April 2003.

Sub-s (7): first words in italics repealed by the Consumer Credit Act 2006, s 70, Sch 4, as from 6 April 2008, subject to transitional provisions as noted below; for the other words in italics there are substituted the words "Supreme Court" by the Constitutional Reform Act 2005, s 40, Sch 9, Pt 1, para 59, as from a day to be appointed.

Sub-s (8): first words in italics repealed by the Consumer Credit Act 2006, s 70, Sch 4, as from 6 April 2008, subject to transitional provisions as noted below; for the second words in italics there are substituted the words "Senior Courts Act 1981" by the Constitutional Reform Act 2005, s 59(5), Sch 11, Pt 1, para 1(2), as from a day to be appointed.

Transitional provisions: Sch 3, para 27 to the Consumer Credit Act 2006 provides that the repeals made to this section by that Act have no effect in relation to determinations of the OFT made before the commencement of s 56 of the 2006 Act (ie, 6 April 2008).

Orders in Council: Orders in Council made under this section are outside the scope of this work.

12 Supervisory functions of superior courts not excluded by Acts passed before 1st August 1958

(1)   As respects England and Wales—
  (a)   any provision in an Act passed before 1st August 1958 that any order or determination shall not be called into question in any court, or
  (b)   any provision in such an Act which by similar words excludes any of the powers of the High Court,

shall not have effect so as to prevent the removal of the proceedings into the High Court by order of certiorari or to prejudice the powers of the High Court to make orders of mandamus.

(2)   As respects Scotland—
  (a)   any provision in an Act passed before 1st August 1958 that any order or determination shall not be called into question in any court, or
  (b)   any provision in such an Act which by similar words excludes any jurisdiction which the Court of Session would otherwise have to entertain an application for reduction or suspension of any order or determination, or otherwise to consider the validity of any order or determination,

shall not have effect so as to prevent the exercise of any such jurisdiction.

(3)   Nothing in this section shall apply—
  (a)   to any order or determination of a court of law, or
  (b)   where an Act makes special provision for application to the High Court or the Court of Session within a time limited by the Act.

[1206]

Supplementary provisions

13 Power to apply Act to additional tribunals and to repeal or amend certain provisions

(1)   The Lord Chancellor and the [Secretary of State] may by order amend Part I or Part II of Schedule 1 by adding to that Part any such tribunals, other than any of the ordinary courts of law, as may be provided by the order.

(2)   *The Lord Chancellor and the [Secretary of State] may by order make provision, as respects any tribunal for the time being specified in Schedule 1, not being a tribunal mentioned in section 6, for amending that section so as to apply any of the provisions of that section to the tribunal or for providing for the appointment by the Lord Chancellor, the Lord President of the Court of Session or the Lord Chief Justice of Northern Ireland of the chairman of the tribunal and of any person to be appointed to act as chairman.*

(3)   The Lord Chancellor and the [Secretary of State] may by order amend section 11 so as to apply that section to any tribunal for the time being specified in Schedule 1.

(4)   Any order under subsection (1), (2) or (3) may make any such adaptations of the provisions of this Act as may be necessary or expedient in consequence of the order.

(5)   The Lord Chancellor and the [Secretary of State] may by order—
  (a)   repeal or amend section 7(3) of this Act or any of paragraphs 5 ... , 9, 13, 16, 20, 22, 23, 24, 29, 30, 32, 35(a) ... , 37, 39(c), 43, 44, 47, 49, 51, 54, 55, 56(d), 57(a), 58, 59 and 63 of Schedule 1;
  (b)   ...
  (c)   repeal ... the reference in section 14(1) to paragraph 20 of Schedule 1;
  (d)   repeal the references in section 11 to any of paragraphs 16, 24, 37, 44, 51, 59 and 63 of Schedule 1; and
  (e)   repeal the references in paragraphs 21 and 53 of Schedule 1 to sections 16, 17B and 25 of the Forestry Act 1967.

(6)   Nothing in this section authorises the making of an order with respect to a tribunal having jurisdiction only over matters with respect to which the Parliament of Northern Ireland had power to make laws.

[1207]

NOTES

Sub-ss (1), (3): words in square brackets substituted by virtue of the Transfer of Functions (Lord Advocate and Secretary of State) Order 1999, SI 1999/678, arts 2(1), 7(4), Schedule, as from 19 May 1999.

Sub-s (2): repealed by the Tribunals, Courts and Enforcement Act 2007, s 146, Sch 23, Pt 1, as from a day to be appointed; words in square brackets substituted by virtue of SI 1999/678, arts 2(1), 7(4), Schedule, as from 19 May 1999.

Sub-s (5): words in square brackets substituted by virtue of SI 1999/678, arts 2(1), 7(4), Schedule, as from 19 May 1999; first words omitted from para (a) repealed by the Financial Services and Markets Act 2000 (Consequential Amendments and Repeals) Order 2001, SI 2001/3649, art 337, as from 1 December 2001; second words omitted from para (a) repealed by the Pensions Act 1995, ss 151, 177, Sch 5, para 16(1), (4), Sch 7, Pt III, as from 6 April 1997; para (b) repealed by the Social Security Act 1998, s 86, Sch 7, para 120(b), Sch 8, as from 29 November 1999; words omitted from para (c) repealed by the Tribunals, Courts and Enforcement Act 2007, s 146, Sch 23, Pt 1, as from 1 November 2007.

Note that the Social Security Act 1998, s 86, Sch 7, para 120(a) provides for sub-s (5)(a) above to be amended by substituting "35(d)" for the words "35(a) and (d)". In the light of the existing amendment of sub-s (5)(a) by the Pensions Act 1995, it is believed that the amendment by the Social Security Act 1998, Sch 7, para 120(a) is a drafting error.

Functions under this section: functions under this section are transferred, in so far as they are exercisable in or as regards Scotland, to the Scottish Ministers, by the Scotland Act 1998 (Transfer of Functions to the Scottish Ministers etc) Order 1999, SI 1999/1750, art 2, Sch 1.

Orders: Orders made under this section are outside the scope of this work.

14 Restricted application of Act in relation to certain tribunals

(1) References in this Act to *the working or a decision of, or procedural rules for,—*
    (a) any tribunals specified in paragraph 14(a), 20, 33, 34, 39(a) or (b), 40, 48, 56 or 60 of Schedule 1,
    (b) [the Office of Fair Trading] referred to in paragraph 17 of Schedule 1, or
    (c) the Controller of Plant Variety Rights referred to in paragraph 36(a) of Schedule 1,

do not include references to their *working, decisions or procedure* in the exercise of executive functions.

[(1A) *In this Act—*
    (a) *references to the working of the Pensions Regulator referred to in paragraph 35(i) of Schedule 1 are references to its working so far as relating to the exercise of its regulatory functions (within the meaning of section 93(2) of the Pensions Act 2004) or any corresponding function conferred by a provision in force in Northern Ireland, and*
    (b) *references to procedural rules for the Pensions Regulator are references to regulations under paragraph 19 of Schedule 1 to that Act (Secretary of State's powers to make regulations in respect of Regulator's procedure) so far as they relate to the procedure to be followed when exercising those functions.]*

(2) ...

(3) For the purposes of this Act, the functions of the Civil Aviation Authority referred to in paragraph 3 of Schedule 1 are to be taken to be confined to those prescribed for the purposes of section 7(2) of the Civil Aviation Act 1982.

[1208]

NOTES

Sub-s (1): for the first words in italics there are substituted the words "a decision of", and for the second words in italics there are substituted the word "decisions", by the Tribunals, Courts and Enforcement Act 2007, s 48(1), Sch 8, paras 23, 29, as from a day to be appointed; words in square brackets substituted by the Enterprise Act 2002, s 278(1), Sch 25, para 27(1), (3), as from 1 April 2003.

Sub-s (1A): inserted by the Pensions Act 1995, s 122, Sch 3, para 21(c), as from 6 April 1997; substituted by the Pensions Act 2004, s 319, Sch 12, para 8(1), (3), as from 10 February 2005; repealed by the Tribunals, Courts and Enforcement Act 2007, s 146, Sch 23, Pt 1, as from a day to be appointed.

Sub-s (2): repealed by the Pensions Act 1995, ss 151, 177, Sch 5, para 16(1), (5), Sch 7, Pt III, as from 6 April 1997.

15 Rules and orders

Any power of the Lord Chancellor and the Lord Advocate or either of them to make rules or orders under this Act shall be exercisable by statutory instrument subject to annulment in pursuance of a resolution of either House of Parliament.

[1209]

16 Interpretation

(1) In this Act, except where the context otherwise requires—
    "decision", *"procedural rules" and "working"*, in relation to a tribunal, shall be construed subject to section 14,
    ["Council" means the Administrative Justice and Tribunals Council,]
    ["enactment" includes an Act of the Scottish Parliament,]
    "Minister" includes [the [Welsh Ministers] and] any Board presided over by a Minister,
    ["Scottish Committee" means the Scottish Committee of the Administrative Justice and Tribunals Council,]
    "statutory inquiry" means—
        (a) an inquiry or hearing held or to be held in pursuance of a duty imposed by any statutory provision, or

Entry relating to Friendly Societies (para 21A): inserted by the Tribunals and Inquiries (Friendly Societies) Order 1993, SI 1993/3258, art 3; repealed by SI 2001/3649, art 338, as from 1 December 2001.

Entry relating to National Savings Bank and National Savings Stock Register (para 33B): inserted by Tribunals and Inquiries (Friendly Societies) Order 1993, SI 1993/3258, art 3, and repealed by the Finance (No 2) Act 2005, s 70, Sch 11, Pt 5, as from 1 September 2005.

Entry relating to Pensions (para 35): sub-para (d) repealed by the Pensions Act 1995, ss 151, 177, Sch 5, para 16(6), Sch 7, Pt III, as from 6 April 1997; in sub-para (e) words in first pair of square brackets substituted by the Pensions Schemes Act 1993, s 190, Sch 8, para 44(b), words in second pair of square brackets substituted by the Pensions Act 1995, s 157(12); sub-paras (g), (h) added by the Pensions Act 1995, s 122, Sch 3, para 21(d), and repealed by the Pensions Act 2004, s 320, Sch 13, Pt 1, as from 6 April 2005 (in relation to para (g)), and as from 1 September 2005 (in relation to para (h)); sub-paras (i)–(l) added by the Pensions Act 2004, s 319, Sch 12, para 8(1), (4), as from 10 February 2005.

(Pt II (Tribunals under supervision of Scottish committee) outside the scope of this work.)

SCHEDULE 2
TRANSITORY PROVISIONS

Section 17

Transitory modifications of sections 6 and 7 and Schedule 1

1.   ...
2.   If—
     (a)   no date has been appointed before the commencement of this Act as the date on which paragraph 2 of Schedule 18 to the Courts and Legal Services Act 1990 is to come into force, or
     (b)   a date has been appointed which is later than the commencement of this Act,
paragraph 10 of Schedule 1 shall be omitted until the appointed day.
3.   ...
4.   In paragraphs 1, 2 and 3 "the appointed day" means
     (a)   in the case mentioned in paragraph [1(a) or 2(a)], such day as may be appointed by the Secretary of State for the purposes of the paragraph concerned by order made by statutory instrument, and
     (b)   in the case mentioned in paragraph [1(b) or 2(b)], the day appointed as the day on which the provision mentioned in paragraph [1(a) or 2(a)] (as the case may be) is to come into force.

Application of section 6 in relation to persons appointed before 1st January 1959

5.   ...

[1215]

NOTES

Para 1: repealed by the Criminal Injuries Compensation Act 1995, s 12(7), Schedule, as from 8 November 1995.

Para 3: repealed by the Social Security Act 1998, s 86, Sch 7, para 122(1), Sch 8, as from 1 June 1999.

Para 4: words in square brackets substituted by the Social Security Act 1998, s 86, Sch 7, para 122(2), as from 1 June 1999.

Para 5: repealed by the Statute Law (Repeals) Act 1998, as from 19 November 1998.

(Sch 3 in so far as unrepealed, makes amendments to legislation outside the scope of this work.)

SCHEDULE 4
REPEALS

Section 18(2)

PART I
ENACTMENTS REPEALED

Chapter	Short title	Extent of Repeal
1971 c 62	The Tribunals and Inquiries Act 1971	The whole Act
1972 c 11	The Superannuation Act 1972	In Schedule 6, paragraph 91
1972 c 58	The National Health Service (Scotland) Act 1972	In Schedule 6, paragraph 152

Chapter	Short title	Extent of Repeal
1973 c 32	The National Health Service Reorganisation Act 1973	In Schedule 4, paragraph 134
1973 c 38	The Social Security Act 1973	Section 66(4) and (9)
1974 c 39	The Consumer Credit Act 1974	Sections 3 and 42
1975 c 18	The Social Security (Consequential Provisions) Act 1975	In Schedule 2, paragraph 46
1975 c 68	The Industry Act 1975	In Schedule 3, paragraph 10
1976 c 35	The Police Pensions Act 1976	In Schedule 2, paragraph 9
1977 c 3	The Aircraft and Shipbuilding Industries Act 1977	Section 42(10)
1977 c 49	The National Health Service Act 1977	In Schedule 15, paragraph 53
1978 c 23	The Judicature (Northern Ireland) Act 1978	In Schedule 5, in Part II, the entry relating to the Tribunals and Inquiries Act 1971
1978 c 29	The National Health Service (Scotland) Act 1978	In Schedule 16, paragraph 35
1978 c 44	The Employment Protection (Consolidation) Act 1978	In Schedule 16, paragraph 11
1979 c 38	The Estate Agents Act 1979	Section 24(1)
1980 c 20	The Education Act 1980	Section 7(6)
1980 c 44	The Education (Scotland) Act 1980	Section 28E(7)
1981 c 54	The Supreme Court Act 1981	In Schedule 5, the entry relating to the Tribunals and Inquiries Act 1971
1982 c 10	The Industrial Training Act 1982	In Schedule 3, paragraph 2
1982 c 16	The Civil Aviation Act 1982	Section 7(3)
1982 c 45	The Civic Government (Scotland) Act 1982	Section 18(11)
1983 c 20	The Mental Health Act 1983	In Schedule 4, paragraph 29
1983 c 41	The Health and Social Services and Social Security Adjudications Act 1983	In Schedule 9, in Part I, paragraphs 10, 11 and 15
1984 c 23	The Registered Homes Act 1984	In Schedule 1, paragraph 5
1984 c 31	The Rating and Valuation (Amendment) (Scotland) Act 1984	In Schedule 2, paragraph 12
1984 c 35	The Data Protection Act 1984	In Schedule 2, paragraph 13
1985 c 17	The Reserve Forces (Safeguard of Employment) Act 1985.	In Schedule 4, paragraph 3.
1985 c 65	The Insolvency Act 1985	In Schedule 1, paragraph 5
1985 c 67	The Transport Act 1985	In Schedule 2, in Part II, paragraph 2
		In Schedule 7, paragraph 15
1986 c 5	The Agricultural Holdings Act 1986	In Schedule 14, paragraph 49
1986 c 39	The Patents, Designs and Marks Act 1986	In Schedule 2, in Part I, paragraph 1(2)(d)
1986 c 45	The Insolvency Act 1986	In Schedule 14, the entry relating to the Tribunals and Inquiries Act 1971
1986 c 53	The Building Societies Act 1986	In section 48(3), the words "after consultation with the Council on Tribunals"
1986 c 60	The Financial Services Act 1986	In Schedule 6, paragraph 6

Chapter	Short title	Extent of Repeal
1987 c 22	The Banking Act 1987	In section 30, in subsection (3), the words "after consultation with the Council on Tribunals" and, in subsection (4), the words from "after consultation" onwards
		In Schedule 6, paragraph 4
1988 c 33	The Criminal Justice Act 1988	In Schedule 15, paragraph 37
1988 c 40	The Education Reform Act 1988	In Schedule 12, in Part I, paragraph 12
1988 c 41	The Local Government Finance Act 1988	In Schedule 12, in Part III, paragraph 41
1988 c 48	The Copyright, Designs and Patents Act 1988	In Schedule 7, paragraph 14
1989 c 39	The Self-Governing Schools etc (Scotland) Act 1989	In Schedule 10, paragraph 4
1989 c 41	The Children Act 1989	In Schedule 13, paragraph 30
1990 c 16	The Food Safety Act 1990	In Schedule 3, paragraph 14
1990 c 27	The Social Security Act 1990	Section 12(2)
1990 c 41	The Courts and Legal Services Act 1990	In Schedule 18, paragraph 2
1991 c 21	The Disability Living Allowance and Disability Working Allowance Act 1991	In Schedule 2, paragraph 2(1)
1991 c 40	The Road Traffic Act 1991	In Schedule 7, paragraph 1
1991 c 48	The Child Support Act 1991	In Schedule 5, paragraph 1
1992 c 6	The Social Security (Consequential Provisions) Act 1992	In Schedule 2, paragraphs 8 and 9
1992 c 14	The Local Government Finance Act 1992	In Schedule 13, paragraph 31
1992 c 38	The Education (Schools) Act 1992	In Schedule 4, paragraphs 2 and 3

[1216]

NOTES

Supreme Court Act 1981: see the Constitutional Reform Act 2005, s 59(5), Sch 11, Pt 1, para 1(2), which provides that the "Supreme Court Act 1981" shall be renamed the "Senior Courts Act 1981".

PART II
INSTRUMENTS REVOKED

Number	Title
SI 1972/1210	The Tribunals and Inquiries (Value Added Tax Tribunals) Order 1972
SI 1974/1478	The Tribunals and Inquiries (Industrial Training Levy Exemption Referees) Order 1974
SI 1974/1964	The Tribunals and Inquiries (Misuse of Drugs Tribunals) Order 1974
SI 1975/1404	The Tribunals and Inquiries (Valuation Appeal Committees) Order 1975
SI 1979/659	The Tribunals and Inquiries (Vaccine Damage Tribunals) Order 1979
SI 1984/1094	The Tribunals and Inquiries (Dairy Produce Quota Tribunals) Order 1984
SI 1984/1247	The Tribunals and Inquiries (Foreign Compensation Commission) Order 1984
SI 1991/2699	The Tribunals and Inquiries (Specified Tribunals) Order 1991

PART II
OTHER ACTS

CRIMINAL JUSTICE ACT 1993

(1993 c 36)

NOTES

This Act is reproduced as amended by: the Drug Trafficking Act 1994; the Northern Ireland Act 1998; the Extradition Act 2003; the Financial Services and Markets Act 2000 (Consequential Amendments and Repeals) Order 2001, SI 2001/3649; the Financial Services and Markets Act 2000 (Market Abuse) Regulations 2005, SI 2005/381.

ARRANGEMENT OF SECTIONS

PART V
INSIDER DEALING

The offence of insider dealing

Interpretation

Miscellaneous

PART VII
SUPPLEMENTARY

SCHEDULES:

An Act to make provision about the jurisdiction of courts in England and Wales in relation to certain offences of dishonesty and blackmail; to amend the law about drug trafficking offences and to implement provisions of the Community Council Directive No 91/308/EEC; to amend Part VI of the Criminal Justice Act 1988; to make provision with respect to the financing of terrorism, the proceeds of terrorist-related activities and the investigation of terrorist activities; to amend Part I of the Criminal Justice Act 1991; to implement provisions of the Community Council Directive No 89/592/EEC and to amend and restate the law about insider dealing in securities; to provide for certain offences created by the Banking Coordination (Second Council Directive) Regulations 1992 to be punishable in the same way as offences under sections 39, 40 and 41 of the Banking Act 1987 and to enable regulations implementing Article 15 of the Community Council Directive No 89/646/EEC and Articles 3, 6 and 7 of the Community Council Directive No 92/30/EEC to create offences punishable in that way; to make provision with respect to the penalty for causing death by dangerous driving or causing death by careless driving while under the influence of drink or drugs; to make it an offence to assist in or induce certain conduct which for the purposes of, or in connection with, the provisions of Community law is unlawful in another member State; to provide for the introduction of safeguards in connection with the return of persons under backing of warrants arrangements; to amend the Criminal Procedure (Scotland) Act 1975 and Part I of the Prisoners and Criminal Proceedings (Scotland) Act 1993; and for connected purposes

[27 July 1993]

PART V
INSIDER DEALING
The offence of insider dealing

52　The offence

(1)　An individual who has information as an insider is guilty of insider dealing if, in the circumstances mentioned in subsection (3), he deals in securities that are price-affected securities in relation to the information.

(2)　An individual who has information as an insider is also guilty of insider dealing if—

(a)　he encourages another person to deal in securities that are (whether or not that other knows it) price-affected securities in relation to the information, knowing or having reasonable cause to believe that the dealing would take place in the circumstances mentioned in subsection (3); or

(b)　he discloses the information, otherwise than in the proper performance of the functions of his employment, office or profession, to another person.

(3)　The circumstances referred to above are that the acquisition or disposal in question occurs on a regulated market, or that the person dealing relies on a professional intermediary or is himself acting as a professional intermediary.

(4)　This section has effect subject to section 53.

[1218]

53　Defences

(1)　An individual is not guilty of insider dealing by virtue of dealing in securities if he shows—

(a)　that he did not at the time expect the dealing to result in a profit attributable to the fact that the information in question was price-sensitive information in relation to the securities, or

(b)　that at the time he believed on reasonable grounds that the information had been disclosed widely enough to ensure that none of those taking part in the dealing would be prejudiced by not having the information, or

(c)　that he would have done what he did even if he had not had the information.

(2)　An individual is not guilty of insider dealing by virtue of encouraging another person to deal in securities if he shows—

(a)　that he did not at the time expect the dealing to result in a profit attributable to the fact that the information in question was price-sensitive information in relation to the securities, or

(b)　that at the time he believed on reasonable grounds that the information had been or would be disclosed widely enough to ensure that none of those taking part in the dealing would be prejudiced by not having the information, or

(c)　that he would have done what he did even if he had not had the information.

(3)　An individual is not guilty of insider dealing by virtue of a disclosure of information if he shows—

(a)　that he did not at the time expect any person, because of the disclosure, to deal in securities in the circumstances mentioned in subsection (3) of section 52; or

(b)　that, although he had such an expectation at the time, he did not expect the dealing to result in a profit attributable to the fact that the information was price-sensitive information in relation to the securities.

(4)　Schedule 1 (special defences) shall have effect.

(5)　The Treasury may by order amend Schedule 1.

(6)　In this section references to a profit include references to the avoidance of a loss.

[1219]

Interpretation

54　Securities to which Part V applies

(1)　This Part applies to any security which—

(a)　falls within any paragraph of Schedule 2; and

(b)　satisfies any conditions applying to it under an order made by the Treasury for the purposes of this subsection;

and in the provisions of this Part (other than that Schedule) any reference to a security is a reference to a security to which this Part applies.

(2)　The Treasury may by order amend Schedule 2.

[1220]

NOTES
Orders: the Insider Dealing (Securities and Regulated Markets) Order 1994, SI 1994/187 at **[3516]**.

55 "Dealing" in securities

(1)   For the purposes of this Part, a person deals in securities if—
   (a)   he acquires or disposes of the securities (whether as principal or agent); or
   (b)   he procures, directly or indirectly, an acquisition or disposal of the securities by any other person.

(2)   For the purposes of this Part, "acquire", in relation to a security, includes—
   (a)   agreeing to acquire the security; and
   (b)   entering into a contract which creates the security.

(3)   For the purposes of this Part, "dispose", in relation to a security, includes—
   (a)   agreeing to dispose of the security; and
   (b)   bringing to an end a contract which created the security.

(4)   For the purposes of subsection (1), a person procures an acquisition or disposal of a security if the security is acquired or disposed of by a person who is—
   (a)   his agent,
   (b)   his nominee, or
   (c)   a person who is acting at his direction,
in relation to the acquisition or disposal.

(5)   Subsection (4) is not exhaustive as to the circumstances in which one person may be regarded as procuring an acquisition or disposal of securities by another.

[1221]

56 "Inside information", etc

(1)   For the purposes of this section and section 57, "inside information" means information which—
   (a)   relates to particular securities or to a particular issuer of securities or to particular issuers of securities and not to securities generally or to issuers of securities generally;
   (b)   is specific or precise;
   (c)   has not been made public; and
   (d)   if it were made public would be likely to have a significant effect on the price of any securities.

(2)   For the purposes of this Part, securities are "price-affected securities" in relation to inside information, and inside information is "price-sensitive information" in relation to securities, if and only if the information would, if made public, be likely to have a significant effect on the price of the securities.

(3)   For the purposes of this section "price" includes value.

[1222]

57 "Insiders"

(1)   For the purposes of this Part, a person has information as an insider if and only if—
   (a)   it is, and he knows that it is, inside information, and
   (b)   he has it, and knows that he has it, from an inside source.

(2)   For the purposes of subsection (1), a person has information from an inside source if and only if—
   (a)   he has it through—
      (i)   being a director, employee or shareholder of an issuer of securities; or
      (ii)   having access to the information by virtue of his employment, office or profession; or
   (b)   the direct or indirect source of his information is a person within paragraph (a).

[1223]

58 Information "made public"

(1)   For the purposes of section 56, "made public", in relation to information, shall be construed in accordance with the following provisions of this section; but those provisions are not exhaustive as to the meaning of that expression.

(2)   Information is made public if—
   (a)   it is published in accordance with the rules of a regulated market for the purpose of informing investors and their professional advisers;
   (b)   it is contained in records which by virtue of any enactment are open to inspection by the public;
   (c)   it can be readily acquired by those likely to deal in any securities—

        (i)   to which the information relates, or

        (ii)   of an issuer to which the information relates; or

  (d)   it is derived from information which has been made public.

(3)   Information may be treated as made public even though—

  (a)   it can be acquired only by persons exercising diligence or expertise;

  (b)   it is communicated to a section of the public and not to the public at large;

  (c)   it can be acquired only by observation;

  (d)   it is communicated only on payment of a fee; or

  (e)   it is published only outside the United Kingdom.

[1224]

59 "Professional intermediary"

(1)   For the purposes of this Part, a "professional intermediary" is a person—

  (a)   who carries on a business consisting of an activity mentioned in subsection (2) and who holds himself out to the public or any section of the public (including a section of the public constituted by persons such as himself) as willing to engage in any such business; or

  (b)   who is employed by a person falling within paragraph (a) to carry out any such activity.

(2)   The activities referred to in subsection (1) are—

  (a)   acquiring or disposing of securities (whether as principal or agent); or

  (b)   acting as an intermediary between persons taking part in any dealing in securities.

(3)   A person is not to be treated as carrying on a business consisting of an activity mentioned in subsection (2)—

  (a)   if the activity in question is merely incidental to some other activity not falling within subsection (2); or

  (b)   merely because he occasionally conducts one of those activities.

(4)   For the purposes of section 52, a person dealing in securities relies on a professional intermediary if and only if a person who is acting as a professional intermediary carries out an activity mentioned in subsection (2) in relation to that dealing.

[1225]

60 Other interpretation provisions

(1)   For the purposes of this Part, "regulated market" means any market, however operated, which, by an order made by the Treasury, is identified (whether by name or by reference to criteria prescribed by the order) as a regulated market for the purposes of this Part.

(2)   For the purposes of this Part an "issuer", in relation to any securities, means any company, public sector body or individual by which or by whom the securities have been or are to be issued.

(3)   For the purposes of this Part—

  (a)   "company" means any body (whether or not incorporated and wherever incorporated or constituted) which is not a public sector body; and

  (b)   "public sector body" means—

        (i)   the government of the United Kingdom, of Northern Ireland or of any country or territory outside the United Kingdom;

        (ii)   a local authority in the United Kingdom or elsewhere;

        (iii) any international organisation the members of which include the United Kingdom or another member state;

        (iv) the Bank of England; or

        (v)   the central bank of any sovereign State.

(4)   For the purposes of this Part, information shall be treated as relating to an issuer of securities which is a company not only where it is about the company but also where it may affect the company's business prospects.

[1226]

NOTES

Orders: the Insider Dealing (Securities and Regulated Markets) Order 1994, SI 1994/187 at **[3516]**.

Miscellaneous

61 Penalties and prosecution

(1)   An individual guilty of insider dealing shall be liable—

  (a)   on summary conviction, to a fine not exceeding the statutory maximum or imprisonment for a term not exceeding six months or to both; or

  (b)   on conviction on indictment, to a fine or imprisonment for a term not exceeding seven years or to both.

(2)   Proceedings for offences under this Part shall not be instituted in England and Wales except by or with the consent of—

    (a)   the Secretary of State; or

    (b)   the Director of Public Prosecutions.

(3)   In relation to proceedings in Northern Ireland for offences under this Part, subsection (2) shall have effect as if the reference to the Director of Public Prosecutions were a reference to the Director of Public Prosecutions for Northern Ireland.

                                                                            [1227]

62   Territorial scope of offence of insider dealing

(1)   An individual is not guilty of an offence falling within subsection (1) of section 52 unless—

    (a)   he was within the United Kingdom at the time when he is alleged to have done any act constituting or forming part of the alleged dealing;

    (b)   the regulated market on which the dealing is alleged to have occurred is one which, by an order made by the Treasury, is identified (whether by name or by reference to criteria prescribed by the order) as being, for the purposes of this Part, regulated in the United Kingdom; or

    (c)   the professional intermediary was within the United Kingdom at the time when he is alleged to have done anything by means of which the offence is alleged to have been committed.

(2)   An individual is not guilty of an offence falling within subsection (2) of section 52 unless—

    (a)   he was within the United Kingdom at the time when he is alleged to have disclosed the information or encouraged the dealing; or

    (b)   the alleged recipient of the information or encouragement was within the United Kingdom at the time when he is alleged to have received the information or encouragement.

                                                                            [1228]

NOTES

Orders: the Insider Dealing (Securities and Regulated Markets) Order 1994, SI 1994/187 at **[3516]**.

63   Limits on section 52

(1)   Section 52 does not apply to anything done by an individual acting on behalf of a public sector body in pursuit of monetary policies or policies with respect to exchange rates or the management of public debt or foreign exchange reserves.

(2)   No contract shall be void or unenforceable by reason only of section 52.

                                                                            [1229]

64   Orders

(1)   Any power under this Part to make an order shall be exercisable by statutory instrument.

(2)   No order shall be made under this Part unless a draft of it has been laid before and approved by a resolution of each House of Parliament.

(3)   An order under this Part—

    (a)   may make different provision for different cases; and

    (b)   may contain such incidental, supplemental and transitional provisions as the Treasury consider expedient.

                                                                            [1230]

65–77   ((*Pt VI*) *outside the scope of this work.*)

PART VII

SUPPLEMENTARY

78   Commencement etc

(1)   Sections 70 and 71 shall come into force at the end of the period of two months beginning with the day on which this Act is passed.

(2)   Sections 68, 69, 75, 76 and 79(1) to (12), paragraph 2 of Schedule 5 and, in so far as relating to the Criminal Procedure (Scotland) Act 1975, and the Prisoners and Criminal Proceedings (Scotland) Act 1993, Schedule 6, shall come into force on the passing of this Act.

(3)   The other provisions of this Act shall come into force on such day as may be appointed by the Secretary of State by an order made by statutory instrument.

(4)   Different days may be appointed under subsection (3) for different provisions and different purposes.

(5), (6)   (*Outside the scope of this work.*)

(7)   ...

(8), (9)   (*Outside the scope of this work.*)

(10)   An order under subsection (3) may contain such transitional provisions and savings as the Secretary of State considers appropriate.

(11), (12)   (*Outside the scope of this work.*)

[1231]

NOTES

Sub-s (7): repealed by the Drug Trafficking Act 1994, s 67(1), Sch 3, as from 3 February 1995.

Orders: the Criminal Justice Act 1993 (Commencement No 1) Order 1993, SI 1993/1968; the Criminal Justice Act 1993 (Commencement No 2 Transitional Provisions and Savings) (Scotland) Order 1993, SI 1993/2035; the Criminal Justice Act 1993 (Commencement No 3) Order 1993, SI 1993/2734; the Criminal Justice Act 1993 (Commencement No 4) Order 1994, SI 1994/71; the Criminal Justice Act 1993 (Commencement No 5) Order 1994, SI 1994/242; the Criminal Justice Act 1993 (Commencement No 6) Order 1994, SI 1994/700; the Criminal Justice Act 1993 (Commencement No 7) Order 1994, SI 1994/1951; the Criminal Justice Act 1993 (Commencement No 8) Order 1995, SI 1995/43; the Criminal Justice Act 1993 (Commencement No 9) Order 1995, SI 1995/1958; the Criminal Justice Act 1993 (Commencement No 10) Order 1999, SI 1999/1189; the Criminal Justice Act 1993 (Commencement No 11) Order 1999, SI 1999/1499.

79   Short title, extent etc

(1)   This Act may be cited as the Criminal Justice Act 1993.

(2)   The following provisions of this Act extend to the United Kingdom—
Part V;
sections 21(1) and (3)(h), 23, ... , 45 to 51, 70 to 72, 77, 78 and this section;
Schedules 1 and 2; and
paragraphs 4, ... and 6 of Schedule 4.

(3)–(14)   (*In so far as still in force, outside the scope of this work.*)

[1232]

NOTES

Sub-s (2): words omitted repealed by the Drug Trafficking Act 1994, ss 65(1), 67(1), Sch 1, para 30(1)–(3), Sch 3.

SCHEDULES

SCHEDULE 1
SPECIAL DEFENCES

Section 53(4)

Market makers

1.—(1)   An individual is not guilty of insider dealing by virtue of dealing in securities or encouraging another person to deal if he shows that he acted in good faith in the course of—
    (a)   his business as a market maker, or
    (b)   his employment in the business of a market maker.

(2)   A market maker is a person who—
    (a)   holds himself out at all normal times in compliance with the rules of a regulated market or an approved organisation as willing to acquire or dispose of securities; and
    (b)   is recognised as doing so under those rules.

(3)   In this paragraph "approved organisation" means an international securities self-regulating organisation approved [by the Treasury under any relevant order under section 22 of the Financial Services and Markets Act 2000].

Market information

2.—(1)   An individual is not guilty of insider dealing by virtue of dealing in securities or encouraging another person to deal if he shows that—
    (a)   the information which he had as an insider was market information; and
    (b)   it was reasonable for an individual in his position to have acted as he did despite having that information as an insider at the time.

(2)   In determining whether it is reasonable for an individual to do any act despite having market information at the time, there shall, in particular, be taken into account—
    (a)   the content of the information;
    (b)   the circumstances in which he first had the information and in what capacity; and
    (c)   the capacity in which he now acts.

3.   An individual is not guilty of insider dealing by virtue of dealing in securities or encouraging another person to deal if he shows—
    (a)   that he acted—
        (i)   in connection with an acquisition or disposal which was under consideration or the subject of negotiation, or in the course of a series of such acquisitions or disposals; and
        (ii)   with a view to facilitating the accomplishment of the acquisition or disposal or the series of acquisitions or disposals; and
    (b)   that the information which he had as an insider was market information arising directly out of his involvement in the acquisition or disposal or series of acquisitions or disposals.

4.   For the purposes of paragraphs 2 and 3 market information is information consisting of one or more of the following facts—
    (a)   that securities of a particular kind have been or are to be acquired or disposed of, or that their acquisition or disposal is under consideration or the subject of negotiation;
    (b)   that securities of a particular kind have not been or are not to be acquired or disposed of;
    (c)   the number of securities acquired or disposed of or to be acquired or disposed of or whose acquisition or disposal is under consideration or the subject of negotiation;
    (d)   the price (or range of prices) at which securities have been or are to be acquired or disposed of or the price (or range of prices) at which the securities whose acquisition or disposal is under consideration or the subject of negotiation may be acquired or disposed of;
    (e)   the identity of the persons involved or likely to be involved in any capacity in an acquisition or disposal.

Price stabilisation

5.—(1)   An individual is not guilty of insider dealing by virtue of dealing in securities or encouraging another person to deal if he shows that he acted in conformity with the price stabilisation rules [or with the relevant provisions of Commission Regulation (EC) No 2273/2003 of 22 December 2003 implementing Directive 2003/6/EC of the European Parliament and of the Council as regards exemptions for buy-back programmes and stabilisation of financial instruments].

[(2)   "Price stabilisation rules" means rules made under section 144(1) of the Financial Services and Markets Act 2000.]

[1233]

NOTES
   Para 1: words in square brackets in sub-para (3) substituted by the Financial Services and Markets Act 2000 (Consequential Amendments and Repeals) Order 2001, SI 2001/3649, art 341(1), (2), as from 1 December 2001.
   Para 5: words in square brackets in sub-para (1) added by the Financial Services and Markets Act 2000 (Market Abuse) Regulations 2005, SI 2005/381, reg 3, as from 17 March 2005; sub-para (2) substituted by SI 2001/3649, art 341(1), (3), as from 1 December 2001.

SCHEDULE 2
SECURITIES

Section 54

Shares

1.   Shares and stock in the share capital of a company ("shares").

Debt securities

2.   Any instrument creating or acknowledging indebtedness which is issued by a company or public sector body, including, in particular, debentures, debenture stock, loan stock, bonds and certificates of deposit ("debt securities").

Warrants

3.   Any right (whether conferred by warrant or otherwise) to subscribe for shares or debt securities ("warrants").

Depositary receipts

4.—(1)   The rights under any depositary receipt.

(2)   For the purposes of sub-paragraph (1) a "depositary receipt" means a certificate or other record (whether or not in the form of a document)—
    (a)   which is issued by or on behalf of a person who holds any relevant securities of a particular issuer; and

(b)   which acknowledges that another person is entitled to rights in relation to the relevant securities or relevant securities of the same kind.

(3)   In sub-paragraph (2) "relevant securities" means shares, debt securities and warrants.

Options

5.   Any option to acquire or dispose of any security falling within any other paragraph of this Schedule.

Futures

6.—(1)   Rights under a contract for the acquisition or disposal of relevant securities under which delivery is to be made at a future date and at a price agreed when the contract is made.

(2)   In sub-paragraph (1)—
(a)   the references to a future date and to a price agreed when the contract is made include references to a date and a price determined in accordance with terms of the contract; and
(b)   "relevant securities" means any security falling within any other paragraph of this Schedule.

Contracts for differences

7.—(1)   Rights under a contract which does not provide for the delivery of securities but whose purpose or pretended purpose is to secure a profit or avoid a loss by reference to fluctuations in—
(a)   a share index or other similar factor connected with relevant securities;
(b)   the price of particular relevant securities; or
(c)   the interest rate offered on money placed on deposit.

(2)   In sub-paragraph (1) "relevant securities" means any security falling within any other paragraph of this Schedule.

[1234]

NOTES
Modification: the reference in para 2 to securities, instruments or investments creating or acknowledging indebtedness (or creating or acknowledging a present or future indebtedness) includes a reference to uncertificated units of eligible debt securities; see the Uncertificated Securities (Amendment) (Eligible Debt Securities) Regulations 2003, SI 2003/1633, reg 15, Sch 2, para 8 (as from 24 June 2003).

(Schs 3–5, in so far as unrepealed, amend various Acts that are outside the scope of this work; Sch 6 contains repeals and revocations only.)

BANK OF ENGLAND ACT 1998 (NOTE)

(1998 c 11)

NOTES
The Bank of England Act 1998 (the 1998 Act) came into force on 1 June 1998 and sets out the constitution of the Bank of England. Certain other statutes regulate the operations of the Bank including the Bank of England Act 1694 (the 1694 Act), the Charter of the Bank of England 1694 (the 1694 Charter), the Bank Charter Act 1844 (the 1844 Act), the Bank of England Act 1946 (the 1946 Act), the Charter of the Bank of England 1998 (the 1998 Charter). In addition, there are various orders made under the 1998 Act including—
- the Bank of England Act 1998 (Commencement) Order 1998 (SI 1998/1120),
- the Bank of England Act 1998 (Consequential Amendments of Subordinate Legislation) Order 1998 (SI 1998/1129),
- the Cash Ratio Deposits (Eligible Liabilities) Order 1998 (SI 1998/1130),
- the Bank of England (Information Powers) Order 1998 (SI 1998/1270),
- the Cash Ratio Deposits (Value Bands and Ratios) Order 2008 (SI 2008/1344) which replaces earlier orders of the same name (ie, the Cash Ratio Deposits (Value Bands and Ratios) Order 2004, SI 2004/1270, and the Cash Ratio Deposits (Value Bands and Ratios) Order 1998, SI 1998/1269).

The constitution of the Bank therefore now comprises—
- the 1694 Act, which provides for the incorporation of the Bank,
- the 1694 Charter, insofar as it incorporates the Bank, constitutes its capital stock and authorises it to have a common seal, to hold land and other property, and to sue and be sued,
- the 1844 Act, which provides for the separation of the issue and banking departments,
- the 1946 Act (but only to the extent of keeping in force certain amended provisions relating to the Bank's power to request certain information from and make recommendations to bankers, and, if so authorised by the Treasury, to issue directions to any banker for the purpose of securing that effect is given to any such request or recommendation),
- the 1998 Charter which, apart from continuing the 1694 Charter, contains provisions relating to the transfer of capital stock and the declaration required of Governors and Directors, and

- the 1998 Act, which deals with the constitution and functions of Court and the MPC, reporting, funding and related matters.

The 1998 Act will, however, be amended in several respects by the Banking Bill which is currently going through Parliament. This Bill contains provisions that will include:
- Formalising and strengthening the Bank of England's role in maintaining the UK's financial stability by giving the Bank a statutory financial stability objective, establishing a Financial Stability Committee and providing the Bank of England with additional financial stability tools, such as formal oversight of payment systems and a key role in the SRR.
- Making certain amendments to the composition and operation of the Governors and the Court of the Bank of England.
- Enabling the Bank of England to lend in a more effective manner, including by allowing short-term non-disclosure of liquidity assistance by the Bank of England.
- Enabling the FSA to collect information from banks in difficulty and removing any impediments to them sharing it with the Bank of England or HM Treasury, where relevant to maintaining financial stability and with the Financial Services Compensation Scheme (FSCS) to assist it carrying out its functions.
- The introduction of a 'special resolution regime' to allow the authorities (HM Treasury, Bank of England and FSA) to intervene when a bank gets into severe difficulties. This includes the introduction of two new insolvency regimes for banks.
- Make changes to the Financial Services Compensation Scheme framework set out in the Financial Services and Markets Act 2000 to allow improvements to facilitate faster pay out.
- Strengthening the arrangements underpinning banknote issuance by commercial banks in Scotland and Northern Ireland.

Various amendments are made to this Act by the Banking Act 2009 (at **[1822]** et seq). See, in particular, s 238 of the 2009 Act which inserts new ss 2A–2C ("the financial stability objective") and other amendments made by ss 239–243 relating to the court of directors and the tenure of the Governor and Deputy Governor. See also s 244 of the 2009 Act (immunity of the Bank of England in its capacity as a monetary authority) and s 246 (Bank's power to disclose information relating to the financial stability of individual financial institutions or the financial systems of the UK).

[1234A]

DATA PROTECTION ACT 1998

(1998 c 29)

NOTES

Only provisions of this Act relevant to Financial Services law are reproduced. Provisions not reproduced are not annotated.

This Act is reproduced as amended by: the Financial Services and Markets Act 2000; the Enterprise Act 2002; the Health and Social Care (Community Health and Standards) Act 2003; the Companies (Audit, Investigations and Community Enterprise) Act 2004; the Public Services Ombudsman (Wales) Act 2005; the Education and Inspections Act 2006; the NHS Redress Act 2006; the Local Government and Public Involvement in Health Act 2007; the Legal Services Act 2007; the Secretary of State for Constitutional Affairs Order 2003, SI 2003/1887; the Scottish Public Services Ombudsman Act 2002 (Consequential Provisions and Modifications) Order 2004, SI 2004/1823; the Enterprise Act 2002 (Amendment) Regulations 2006, SI 2006/3363.

An Act to make new provision for the regulation of the processing of information relating to individuals, including the obtaining, holding, use or disclosure of such information

[16 July 1998]

31 Regulatory activity

(1) Personal data processed for the purposes of discharging functions to which this subsection applies are exempt from the subject information provisions in any case to the extent to which the application of those provisions to the data would be likely to prejudice the proper discharge of those functions.

(2) Subsection (1) applies to any relevant function which is designed—

    (a)   for protecting members of the public against—

        (i)   financial loss due to dishonesty, malpractice or other seriously improper conduct by, or the unfitness or incompetence of, persons concerned in the provision of banking, insurance, investment or other financial services or in the management of bodies corporate,

        (ii)   financial loss due to the conduct of discharged or undischarged bankrupts, or

        (iii)   dishonesty, malpractice or other seriously improper conduct by, or the unfitness or incompetence of, persons authorised to carry on any profession or other activity,

    (b)   for protecting charities [or community interest companies] against misconduct or mismanagement (whether by trustees[, directors] or other persons) in their administration,

(c)   for protecting the property of charities [or community interest companies] from loss or misapplication,

(d)   for the recovery of the property of charities [or community interest companies],

(e)   for securing the health, safety and welfare of persons at work, or

(f)   for protecting persons other than persons at work against risk to health or safety arising out of or in connection with the actions of persons at work.

(3)   In subsection (2) "relevant function" means—

    (a)   any function conferred on any person by or under any enactment,

    (b)   any function of the Crown, a Minister of the Crown or a government department, or

    (c)   any other function which is of a public nature and is exercised in the public interest.

(4)   Personal data processed for the purpose of discharging any function which—

    (a)   is conferred by or under any enactment on—

        (i)   the Parliamentary Commissioner for Administration,

        (ii)   the Commission for Local Administration in England ... ,

        (iii)   the Health Service Commissioner for England ... ,

        [(iv)   the Public Services Ombudsman for Wales,]

        (v)   the Assembly Ombudsman for Northern Ireland, ...

        (vi)   the Northern Ireland Commissioner for Complaints, [or]

        [(vii)   the Scottish Public Services Ombudsman, and]

    (b)   is designed for protecting members of the public against—

        (i)   maladministration by public bodies,

        (ii)   failures in services provided by public bodies, or

        (iii)   a failure of a public body to provide a service which it was a function of the body to provide,

are exempt from the subject information provisions in any case to the extent to which the application of those provisions to the data would be likely to prejudice the proper discharge of that function.

[(4A)   Personal data processed for the purpose of discharging any function which is conferred by or under Part XVI of the Financial Services and Markets Act 2000 on the body established by the Financial Services Authority for the purposes of that Part are exempt from the subject information provisions in any case to the extent to which the application of those provisions to the data would be likely to prejudice the proper discharge of the function.]

[(4B)   Personal data processed for the purposes of discharging any function of the Legal Services Board are exempt from the subject information provisions in any case to the extent to which the application of those provisions to the data would be likely to prejudice the proper discharge of the function.]

[(4C)   Personal data processed for the purposes of the function of considering a complaint under the scheme established under Part 6 of the Legal Services Act 2007 (legal complaints) are exempt from the subject information provisions in any case to the extent to which the application of those provisions to the data would be likely to prejudice the proper discharge of the function.]

(5)   Personal data processed for the purpose of discharging any function which—

    (a)   is conferred by or under any enactment on [the Office of Fair Trading], and

    (b)   is designed—

        (i)   for protecting members of the public against conduct which may adversely affect their interests by persons carrying on a business,

        (ii)   for regulating agreements or conduct which have as their object or effect the prevention, restriction or distortion of competition in connection with any commercial activity, or

        (iii)   for regulating conduct on the part of one or more undertakings which amounts to the abuse of a dominant position in a market,

are exempt from the subject information provisions in any case to the extent to which the application of those provisions to the data would be likely to prejudice the proper discharge of that function.

[(5A)   Personal data processed by a CPC enforcer for the purpose of discharging any function conferred on such a body by or under the CPC Regulation are exempt from the subject information provisions in any case to the extent to which the application of those provisions to the data would be likely to prejudice the proper discharge of that function.

(5B)   In subsection (5A)—

    (a)   "CPC enforcer" has the meaning given to it in section 213(5A) of the Enterprise Act 2002 but does not include the Office of Fair Trading;

    (b)   "CPC Regulation" has the meaning given to it in section 235A of that Act.]

[(6)   Personal data processed for the purpose of the function of considering a complaint under [section 14 of the NHS Redress Act 2006,] section 113(1) or (2) or 114(1) or (3) of the Health and Social Care (Community Health and Standards) Act 2003, or section 24D, 26, ... or 26ZB of the

Children Act 1989, are exempt from the subject information provisions in any case to the extent to which the application of those provisions to the data would be likely to prejudice the proper discharge of that function.]

[(7) Personal data processed for the purpose of discharging any function which is conferred by or under Part 3 of the Local Government Act 2000 on—
  (a) the monitoring officer of a relevant authority,
  (b) an ethical standards officer, or
  (c) the Public Services Ombudsman for Wales,

are exempt from the subject information provisions in any case to the extent to which the application of those provisions to the data would be likely to prejudice the proper discharge of that function.

  (8) In subsection (7)—
  (a) "relevant authority" has the meaning given by section 49(6) of the Local Government Act 2000, and
  (b) any reference to the monitoring officer of a relevant authority, or to an ethical standards officer, has the same meaning as in Part 3 of that Act.]

[1235]

NOTES
Sub-s (2): words in square brackets inserted by the Companies (Audit, Investigations and Community Enterprise) Act 2004, s 59(3), as from 1 July 2005.
Sub-s (4): amended by the Scottish Public Services Ombudsman Act 2002 (Consequential Provisions and Modifications) Order 2004, SI 2004/1823, art 19, as from 14 July 2004, and the Public Services Ombudsman (Wales) Act 2005, s 39, Sch 6, para 60, Sch 7, as from 1 April 2006 (for transitional provisions in relation to the Public Services Ombudsman for Wales, see SI 2005/2800).
Sub-s (4A): inserted by the Financial Services and Markets Act 2000, s 233, as from 1 December 2001.
Sub-ss (4B), (4C): inserted by the Legal Services Act 2007, ss 153, 170, as from a day to be appointed.
Sub-s (5): words in square brackets in para (a) substituted by the Enterprise Act 2002, s 278(1), Sch 25, para 37, as from 1 April 2003.
Sub-ss (5A), (5B): inserted by the Enterprise Act 2002 (Amendment) Regulations 2006, SI 2006/3363, reg 29, as from 8 January 2007.
Sub-s (6): added by the Health and Social Care (Community Health and Standards) Act 2003, s 119, as from 1 June 2004; words in square brackets inserted by the NHS Redress Act 2006, s 14(10), as from a day to be appointed; figure omitted repealed by the Education and Inspections Act 2006, ss 157, 184, Sch 14, para 32, Sch 18, Pt 5, as from 1 April 2007.
Sub-ss (7), (8): added by the Local Government and Public Involvement in Health Act 2007, s 200, as from 1 April 2008.

75 Short title, commencement and extent
  (1) This Act may be cited as the Data Protection Act 1998.
  (2) The following provisions of this Act—
  (a)–(d) (*Outside the scope of this work*),
  (e) this section,
  (f)–(i) (*Outside the scope of this work*),
shall come into force on the day on which this Act is passed.

  (3) The remaining provisions of this Act shall come into force on such day as the [Secretary of State] may by order appoint; and different days may be appointed for different purposes.

(4), (4A), (5), (6) (*Outside the scope of this work.*)

[1236]

NOTES
Sub-s (3): words in square brackets substituted by the Secretary of State for Constitutional Affairs Order 2003, SI 2003/1887, art 9, Sch 2, para 9(1)(a), as from 19 August 2003.
Note that by virtue of sub-ss (5), (6) above, this Act applies to the whole of the UK.
Orders: the Data Protection Act 1998 (Commencement) Order 2000, SI 2000/183; the Data Protection Act 1998 (Commencement No 2) Order 2008, SI 2008/1592.

COMPETITION ACT 1998

(1998 c 41)

NOTES
Only provisions of this Act relevant to Financial Services law are reproduced. Provisions not reproduced are not annotated.

This Act is reproduced as amended by: the Utilities Act 2000; the Enterprise Act 2002; the Communications Act 2003; the Water Act 2003; the Competition Act 1998 and Other Enactments (Amendment) Regulations 2004, SI 2004/1261; the Water Services etc (Scotland) Act 2005 (Consequential Provisions and Modifications) Order 2005, SI 2005/3172.

ARRANGEMENT OF SECTIONS

PART I
COMPETITION

CHAPTER I
AGREEMENTS

The Prohibition

CHAPTER II
ABUSE OF DOMINANT POSITION

The prohibition

CHAPTER III
INVESTIGATION AND ENFORCEMENT

Offences

PART IV
SUPPLEMENTAL AND TRANSITIONAL

SCHEDULES:

An Act to make provision about competition and the abuse of a dominant position in the market; to confer powers in relation to investigations conducted in connection with [Article 81 or 82] of the treaty establishing the European Community; to amend the Fair Trading Act 1973 in relation to information which may be required in connection with investigations under that Act; to make provision with respect to the meaning of "supply of services" in the Fair Trading Act 1973; and for connected purposes

[9 November 1998]

NOTES

Words in square brackets in the long title substituted by the Competition Act 1998 and Other Enactments (Amendment) Regulations 2004, SI 2004/1261, Sch 1, para 1, as from 1 May 2004.

PART I
COMPETITION

NOTES

Sectoral regulators: certain functions of the OFT under this Part are exercisable concurrently with various sectoral regulators; ie—

(i) the OFT shall exercise its functions under this Part (other than ss 31D(1)–(6), 38(1)–(6) and 51) concurrently with the Office of Rail Regulation in so far as relating to (a) agreements, decisions or concerted practices of the kind mentioned in s 2(1) of this Act; (b) conduct of the kind mentioned in s 18(1) of this Act; (c) agreements, decisions or concerted practices of the kind mentioned in Article 81(1) of the treaty establishing the European Community, or (d) conduct which amounts to abuse of the kind mentioned in Article 82 of the treaty establishing the European Community, and which relate to the supply of services relating to railways (see the Railways Act 1993, s 67(3));

(ii) the OFT shall exercise its functions under this Part (other than ss 31D(1)–(6), 38(1)–(6) and 51) concurrently with the Office of Communications (OFCOM) in so far as relating to (a) agreements, decisions or concerted practices of the kind mentioned in s 2(1) of this Act; (b) conduct of the kind mentioned in s 18(1) of this Act; (c) agreements, decisions or concerted practices of the kind mentioned in Article 81(1) of the treaty establishing the European Community, or (d) conduct which amounts to abuse of the kind mentioned in Article 82 of the treaty establishing the European Community, and which relate to activities connected with communication matters (see the Communications Act 2003, s 371(1), (2));

(iii) the OFT shall exercise its functions under this Part (other than ss 31D(1)–(6), 38(1)–(6) and 51) concurrently with the Gas and Electricity Markets Authority in so far as relating to (a) agreements, decisions or concerted practices of the kind mentioned in s 2(1) of this Act; (b) conduct of the kind mentioned in s 18(1) of this Act; (c) agreements, decisions or concerted practices of the kind mentioned in Article 81(1) of the treaty establishing the European Community, or (d) conduct which amounts to abuse of the kind mentioned in Article 82 of the treaty establishing the European Community, and which relate to the supply (etc) of gas to any premises and ancillary matters (see the Gas Act 1986, s 36A(3));

(iv) the OFT shall exercise its functions under this Part (other than ss 31D(1)–(6), 38(1)–(6) and 51) concurrently with the Gas and Electricity Markets Authority in so far as relating to (a) agreements, decisions or concerted practices of the kind mentioned in s 2(1) of this Act; (b) conduct of the kind mentioned in s 18(1) of this Act; (c) agreements, decisions or concerted practices of the kind mentioned in Article 81(1) of the treaty establishing the European Community, or (d) conduct which amounts to abuse of the kind mentioned in Article 82 of the treaty establishing the European Community, and which relate to commercial activities connected with the generation, transmission or supply of electricity or the use of electricity interconnectors (see the Electricity Act 1989, s 43(3));

(v) the OFT shall exercise its functions under this Part (other than ss 31D(1)–(6), 38(1)–(6) and 51) concurrently with the Water Services Regulation Authority in so far as relating to (a) agreements, decisions or concerted practices of the kind mentioned in s 2(1) of this Act; (b) conduct of the kind mentioned in s 18(1) of this Act; (c) agreements, decisions or concerted practices of the kind mentioned in Article 81(1) of the treaty establishing the European Community, or (d) conduct which amounts to abuse of the kind mentioned in Article 82 of the treaty establishing the European Community, and which relate to commercial activities connected with the supply of water or securing a supply of water or with the provision or securing of sewerage services (see the Water Industry Act 1991, s 31(3));

(vi) the OFT shall exercise its functions under this Part (other than ss 31D(1)–(6), 38(1)–(6) and 51) concurrently with the Civil Aviation Authority in so far as relating to (a) agreements, decisions or concerted practices of the kind mentioned in s 2(1) of this Act, (b) conduct of the kind mentioned in s 18(1) of this Act, (c) agreements, decisions or concerted practices of the kind mentioned in Article 81(1) of the treaty establishing the European Community, or (d) conduct which amounts to abuse of the kind mentioned in Article 82 of the treaty establishing the European Community, and which relate to the supply of air traffic services (see the Transport Act 2000, s 86(3)).

Accordingly (and by virtue of the Railways Act 1993, 67(3A), the Communications Act 2003, s 371(3), the Gas Act 1986, s 36A(3A), the Electricity Act 1989, s 43(3A), the Water Industry Act 1991, s 31(4A), and the Transport Act 2000, s 86(4)), references in this Part (other than in the ss 31D(1)–(6), 38(1)–(6), 51, 52(6), (8), 54, and where the context otherwise requires) to the OFT shall, in so far as is necessary for the purposes of, or in connection with the concurrent exercise of functions, be construed as including references to the appropriate sectoral regulator.

CHAPTER I
AGREEMENTS

The prohibition

2 Agreements etc preventing, restricting or distorting competition

(1) Subject to section 3, agreements between undertakings, decisions by associations of undertakings or concerted practices which—

(a) may affect trade within the United Kingdom, and

(b) have as their object or effect the prevention, restriction or distortion of competition within the United Kingdom,

are prohibited unless they are exempt in accordance with the provisions of this Part.

(2)–(8) (*Outside the scope of this work.*)

[1237]

CHAPTER II
ABUSE OF DOMINANT POSITION

The prohibition

18 Abuse of dominant position

(1) Subject to section 19, any conduct on the part of one or more undertakings which amounts to the abuse of a dominant position in a market is prohibited if it may affect trade within the United Kingdom.

(1) Subject to section 19, any conduct on the part of one or more undertakings which amounts to the abuse of a dominant position in a market is prohibited if it may affect trade within the United Kingdom.

(2) Conduct may, in particular, constitute such an abuse if it consists in—

(a) directly or indirectly imposing unfair purchase or selling prices or other unfair trading conditions;

(b)   limiting production, markets or technical development to the prejudice of consumers;

(c)   applying dissimilar conditions to equivalent transactions with other trading parties, thereby placing them at a competitive disadvantage;

(d)   making the conclusion of contracts subject to acceptance by the other parties of supplementary obligations which, by their nature or according to commercial usage, have no connection with the subject of the contracts.

(3)   In this section—

"dominant position" means a dominant position within the United Kingdom; and "the United Kingdom" means the United Kingdom or any part of it.

(4)   The prohibition imposed by subsection (1) is referred to in this Act as "the Chapter II prohibition".

[1238]

Offences

44   False or misleading information

(1)   If information is provided by a person to the [OFT] in connection with any function of the [OFT] under this Part, that person is guilty of an offence if—

(a)   the information is false or misleading in a material particular, and

(b)   he knows that it is or is reckless as to whether it is.

(2)   A person who—

(a)   provides any information to another person, knowing the information to be false or misleading in a material particular, or

(b)   recklessly provides any information to another person which is false or misleading in a material particular,

knowing that the information is to be used for the purpose of providing information to the [OFT] in connection with any of [its] functions under this Part, is guilty of an offence.

(3)   A person guilty of an offence under this section is liable—

(a)   on summary conviction, to a fine not exceeding the statutory maximum;

(b)   on conviction on indictment, to imprisonment for a term not exceeding two years or to a fine or to both.

[1239]

NOTES

Sub-ss (1), (2): words in square brackets substituted by the Enterprise Act 2002, s 278(1), Sch 25, para 38(1), (34), as from 1 April 2003.

PART IV
SUPPLEMENTAL AND TRANSITIONAL

76   Short title, commencement and extent

(1)   This Act may be cited as the Competition Act 1998.

(2)   (*Outside the scope of this work.*)

(3)   The other provisions of this Act come into force on such day as the Secretary of State may by order appoint; and different days may be appointed for different purposes.

(4)   This Act extends to Northern Ireland.

[1240]

NOTES

Orders: the commencement orders relevant to the provisions of this Act reproduced here are the Competition Act 1998 (Commencement No 3) Order 1999, SI 1999/505, and the Competition Act 1998 (Commencement No 5) Order 2000, SI 2000/344.

SCHEDULES

SCHEDULE 7
THE COMPETITION COMMISSION

Section 45(7)

PART I
GENERAL

Interpretation

1.   In this Schedule—

"the 1973 Act" means the Fair Trading Act 1973;

.....

"Chairman" means the chairman of the Commission;
"the Commission" means the Competition Commission;
"Council" has the meaning given in paragraph 5;
"general functions" means any functions of the Commission other than functions—
    (a)   ...
    (b)   which are to be discharged by the Council;
"member" means a member of the Commission;
"newspaper merger reference" means a [reference under section 45 of the Enterprise Act 2002 which specifies a newspaper public interest consideration (within the meaning of paragraph 20A of Schedule 8 to that Act) or a reference under section 62 of that Act which specifies a consideration specified in section 58(2A) or (2B) of that Act];
["newspaper panel member" means a member of the panel maintained under paragraph 22;]

.....

"reporting panel member" means a member appointed under paragraph 2(1)(b);
"secretary" means the secretary of the Commission appointed under paragraph 9; and
"specialist panel member" means a member appointed under any of the provisions mentioned in paragraph 2(1)(d).

Membership of the Commission

2.—(1)   The Commission is to consist of—
    (a)   ...
    (b)   members appointed by the Secretary of State to form a panel for the purposes of the Commission's general functions;
    (c)   [the members of] the panel maintained under paragraph 22;
    (d)   members appointed by the Secretary of State under or by virtue of—
        (i)   ...;
        [(ii)   section 104 of the Utilities Act 2000;]
        [(iii)   section 194(1) of the Communications Act 2003;]
        (iv)   Article 15(9) of the Electricity (Northern Ireland) Order 1992;
    [(e)   one or members appointed by the Secretary of State to serve on the Council].

[(1A)   A person may not be, at the same time, a member of the Commission and a member of the Tribunal.]

(2)   A person who is appointed as a member of a kind mentioned in one of paragraphs [(aa)] to (c) of sub-paragraph (3) may also be appointed as a member of either or both of the other kinds mentioned in those paragraphs.

(3)   The kinds of member are—
    (a)   ...
    [(aa) a newspaper panel member;]
    (b)   a reporting panel member;
    (c)   a specialist panel member.

(4)   ...

(5)   The validity of the Commission's proceedings is not affected by a defect in the appointment of a member.

Chairman and deputy chairmen

3.—(1)   The Commission is to have a chairman appointed by the Secretary of State from among the reporting panel members.

(2)   The Secretary of State may appoint one or more of the reporting panel members to act as deputy chairman.

(3)   The Chairman, and any deputy chairman, may resign that office at any time by notice in writing addressed to the Secretary of State.

(4)   If the Chairman (or a deputy chairman) ceases to be a member he also ceases to be Chairman (or a deputy chairman).

(5)   If the Chairman is absent or otherwise unable to act, or there is no chairman, any of his functions may be performed—
    (a)   if there is one deputy chairman, by him;
    (b)   if there is more than one—
        (i)   by the deputy chairman designated by the Secretary of State; or
        (ii)   if no such designation has been made, by the deputy chairman designated by the deputy chairmen;
    (c)   if there is no deputy chairman able to act—
        (i)   by the member designated by the Secretary of State; or

        (ii)   if no such designation has been made, by the member designated by the Commission.

4.   ...

The Council

5.—(1)   The Commission is to have a ... board to be known as the Competition Commission Council (but referred to in this Schedule as "the Council").

   (2)   The Council is to consist of—
      (a)   the Chairman [and any deputy chairmen of the Commission];
      (b)   ...
   [(bb) the member or members appointed under paragraph 2(1)(e);]
      (c)   such other members as the Secretary of State may appoint; and
      (d)   the secretary.

   (3)   In exercising its functions under paragraphs 3 and 7 to 12 ... the Commission is to act through the Council.

   [(3A)   Without prejudice to the question whether any other functions of the Commission are to be so discharged, the functions of the Commission under sections 106, 116, and 171 of the Enterprise Act 2002 (and under section 116 as applied for the purposes of references under Part 4 of that Act by section 176 of that Act) are to be discharged by the Council.]

   (4)   The Council may determine its own procedure including, in particular, its quorum.

   (5)   The Chairman (and any person acting as Chairman) is to have a casting vote on any question being decided by the Council.

Term of office

6.—(1)   Subject to the provisions of this Schedule, each member is to hold and vacate office in accordance with the terms of his appointment.

   (2)   A person is not to be appointed as a member for more than [eight years (but this does not prevent a re-appointment for the purpose only of continuing to act as a member of a group selected under paragraph 15 before the end of his term of office)].

   (3)   Any member may at any time resign by notice in writing addressed to the Secretary of State.

   (4)   The Secretary of State may remove a member on the ground of incapacity or misbehaviour.

   (5)   ...

Expenses, remuneration and pensions

7.—(1)   The Secretary of State shall pay to the Commission such sums as he considers appropriate to enable it to perform its functions.

   (2)   The Commission may pay, or make provision for paying, to or in respect of each member such salaries or other remuneration and such pensions, allowances, fees, expenses or gratuities as the Secretary of State may determine.

   (3)   If a person ceases to be a member otherwise than on the expiry of his term of office and it appears to the Secretary of State that there are special circumstances which make it right for him to receive compensation, the Commission may make a payment to him of such amount as the Secretary of State may determine.

   (4)   ...

[7A.   The Commission may publish advice and information in relation to any matter connected with the exercise of its functions.]

The Commission's powers

8.   Subject to the provisions of this Schedule, the Commission has power to do anything (except borrow money)—
      (a)   calculated to facilitate the discharge of its functions; or
      (b)   incidental or conducive to the discharge of its functions.

Staff

9.—(1)   The Commission is to have a secretary, appointed by the Secretary of State on such terms and conditions of service as he considers appropriate.

   (2)   ...

   (3)   Before appointing a person to be secretary, the Secretary of State must consult the Chairman ...

(4)   Subject to obtaining the approval of [the Secretary of State as to numbers and terms and conditions of service] the Commission may appoint such staff as it thinks appropriate.

Procedure

10.   ...

Application of seal and proof of instruments

11.—(1)   The application of the seal of the Commission must be authenticated by the signature of the secretary or of some other person authorised for the purpose.

(2)   Sub-paragraph (1) does not apply in relation to any document which is or is to be signed in accordance with the law of Scotland.

(3)   A document purporting to be duly executed under the seal of the Commission—
    (a)   is to be received in evidence; and
    (b)   is to be taken to have been so executed unless the contrary is proved.

Accounts

12.—(1)   The Commission must—
    (a)   keep proper accounts and proper records in relation to its accounts;
    (b)   prepare a statement of accounts in respect of each of its financial years; and
    (c)   send copies of the statement to the Secretary of State and to the Comptroller and Auditor General before the end of the month of August next following the financial year to which the statement relates.

(2)   The statement of accounts must comply with any directions given by the Secretary of State with the approval of the Treasury as to—
    (a)   the information to be contained in it,
    (b)   the manner in which the information contained in it is to be presented, or
    (c)   the methods and principles according to which the statement is to be prepared,
and must contain such additional information as the Secretary of State may with the approval of the Treasury require to be provided for informing Parliament.

(3)   The Comptroller and Auditor General must—
    (a)   examine, certify and report on each statement received by him as a result of this paragraph; and
    (b)   lay copies of each statement and of his report before each House of Parliament.

(4)   In this paragraph "financial year" means the period beginning with the date on which the Commission is established and ending with March 31st next, and each successive period of twelve months.

[Annual reports

12A.—(1)   The Commission shall make to the Secretary of State a report for each financial year on its activities during the year.

(2)   The annual report must be made before the end of August next following the financial year to which it relates.

(3)   The Secretary of State shall lay a copy of the annual report before Parliament and arrange for the report to be published.]

Status

13.—(1)   The Commission is not to be regarded as the servant or agent of the Crown or as enjoying any status, privilege or immunity of the Crown.

(2)   The Commission's property is not to be regarded as property of, or held on behalf of, the Crown.

[1241]

NOTES
    Para 1: definitions "appeal panel member" and "President" (omitted), and para (a) of definition "general functions" repealed, and definition "newspaper panel member" inserted, by the Enterprise Act 2002, ss 21, 185, 278(2), Sch 5, paras 1, 7(1), (2), Sch 11, paras 1, 2, Sch 26, as from 1 April 2003; in definition "newspaper merger reference" words in square brackets substituted by the Communications Act 2003, s 388, as from 29 December 2003.
    Para 2: sub-paras (1)(a), (3)(a), (4) repealed, words in square brackets in sub-paras (1)(c), (2) substituted, and sub-paras (1)(e), (1A), (3)(aa) inserted, by the Enterprise Act 2002, ss 21, 185, 278(2), Sch 5, paras 1, 7(1), (3), Sch 11, paras 1, 3, Sch 26, as from 1 April 2003; sub-para (1)(d)(i) repealed by the Water Act 2003, s 101, Sch 7, Pt 2, para 32(1), (3), Sch 9, Pt 3, as from 1 April 2004; sub-para (1)(d)(ii) substituted by the Utilities Act 2000, s 104(3), as from 16 May 2001; sub-para (1)(d)(iii) substituted by the Communications Act 2003, s 406(1),

Sch 17, para 153(1), (2), as from 25 July 2003 (certain purposes) and as from 29 December 2003 (otherwise) (note that s 406(7) of, and Sch 19 to, the 2003 Act, also purport to repeal para 2(1)(d)(iii)).

Para 4: repealed by the Enterprise Act 2002, ss 21, 278(2), Sch 5, paras 1, 7(1), (4), Sch 26, as from 1 April 2003.

Para 5: words omitted from sub-paras (1), (3), and the whole of sub-para (2)(b) repealed, and words in square brackets in sub-para (2)(a), and sub-para (2)(bb) inserted, by the Enterprise Act 2002, ss 21, 185, 278(2), Sch 5, paras 1, 7(1), (5), Sch 11, paras 1, 4(a)–(c), Sch 26, as from 1 April 2003; sub-para (3A) inserted by s 185 of, and Sch 11, paras 1, 4(d) to, the 2002 Act, as from 20 June 2003.

Para 6: words in square brackets in sub-para (2) substituted, and sub-para (5) repealed, by the Enterprise Act 2002, ss 185, 278(2), Sch 11, paras 1, 5, Sch 26, as from 1 April 2003, except in relation to the re-appointment as a member of any person who is a member on that date.

Para 7: sub-para (4) repealed by the Enterprise Act 2002, ss 185, 278(2), Sch 11, paras 1, 6, Sch 26, as from 1 April 2003.

Para 7A: inserted by the Enterprise Act 2002, s 185, Sch 11, paras 1, 7, as from 1 April 2003.

Para 9: sub-para (2), and words omitted from sub-para (3) repealed, and words in square brackets in sub-para (4) substituted, by the Enterprise Act 2002, ss 185, 278(2), Sch 11, paras 1, 8, Sch 26, as from 1 April 2003.

Para 10: repealed by the Enterprise Act 2002, ss 185, 278(2), Sch 11, paras 1, 9, Sch 26, as from 20 June 2003.

Para 12A: inserted by the Enterprise Act 2002, s 186, as from 1 April 2003.

Transitional provisions: for transitional provisions in relation to the constitution, etc, of the Competition Appeal Tribunal, see the Enterprise Act 2002, Sch 24, paras 7–12.

PART II
PERFORMANCE OF THE COMMISSION'S GENERAL FUNCTIONS

Interpretation

14.   In this Part of this Schedule "group" means a group selected under paragraph 15.

Discharge of certain functions by groups

15.—(1)   Except where sub-paragraph (7) [or (8)] gives the Chairman power to act on his own, any general function of the Commission must be performed through a group selected for the purpose by the Chairman.

(2)   The group must consist of at least three persons one of whom may be the Chairman.

(3)   In selecting the members of the group, the Chairman must comply with any requirement as to its constitution imposed by any enactment applying to specialist panel members.

(4)   If the functions to be performed through the group relate to a newspaper merger reference, the group must, subject to sub-paragraph (5), consist of such reporting panel members as the Chairman may select.

[(5)   The Chairman must select one or more newspaper panel members to be members of the group dealing with functions relating to a newspaper merger reference and, if he selects at least three such members, the group may consist entirely of those members.]

(6)   Subject to sub-paragraphs (2) to (5), a group must consist of reporting panel members or specialist panel members selected by the Chairman.

(7)   While a group is being constituted to perform a particular general function of the Commission, the Chairman may—

   (a)   take such steps (falling within that general function) as he considers appropriate to facilitate the work of the group when it has been constituted; ...

   (b)   ...

[(8)   The Chairman may exercise the power conferred by section 37(1), 48(1) or 64(1) of the Enterprise Act 2002 while a group is being constituted to perform a relevant general function of the Commission or, when it has been so constituted, before it has held its first meeting.]

Chairmen of groups

16.   The Chairman must appoint one of the members of a group to act as the chairman of the group.

Replacement of member of group

17.—(1)   If, during the proceedings of a group—

   (a)   a member of the group ceases to be a member of the Commission,

   (b)   the Chairman is satisfied that a member of the group will be unable for a substantial period to perform his duties as a member of the group, or

   (c)   it appears to the Chairman that because of a particular interest of a member of the group it is inappropriate for him to remain in the group,

the Chairman may appoint a replacement.

(2)   The Chairman may also at any time appoint any reporting panel member to be an additional member of a group.

Attendance of other members

18.—(1)   At the invitation of the chairman of a group, any reporting panel member who is not a member of the group may attend meetings or otherwise take part in the proceedings of the group.

(2)   But any person attending in response to such an invitation may not—
  (a)   vote in any proceedings of the group; or
  (b)   have a statement of his dissent from a conclusion of the group included in a report made by them.

(3)   Nothing in sub-paragraph (1) is to be taken to prevent a group, or a member of a group, from consulting any member of the Commission with respect to any matter or question with which the group is concerned.

Procedure

19.—(1)   Subject to any special or general directions given by the Secretary of State, each group may determine its own procedure.

(2)   Each group may, in particular, determine its quorum and determine—
  (a)   the extent, if any, to which persons interested or claiming to be interested in the subject-matter of the reference are allowed—
      (i)   to be present or to be heard, either by themselves or by their representatives;
      (ii)   to cross-examine witnesses; or
      (iii)   otherwise to take part; and
  (b)   the extent, if any, to which sittings of the group are to be held in public.

(3)   In determining its procedure a group must have regard to any guidance issued by the Chairman.

(4)   Before issuing any guidance for the purposes of this paragraph the Chairman must consult the members of the Commission.

[(5)   This paragraph does not apply to groups for which rules must be made under paragraph 19A.]

[19A.—(1)   The Chairman must make rules of procedure in relation to merger reference groups, market reference groups and special reference groups.

(2)   Schedule 7A makes further provision about rules made under this paragraph but is not to be taken as restricting the Chairman's powers under this section.

(3)   The Chairman must publish rules made under this paragraph in such manner as he considers appropriate for the purpose of bringing them to the attention of those likely to be affected by them.

(4)   The Chairman must consult the members of the Commission and such other persons as he considers appropriate before making rules under this paragraph.

(5)   Rules under this paragraph may—
  (a)   make different provision for different cases or different purposes;
  (b)   be varied or revoked by subsequent rules made under this paragraph.

(6)   Subject to rules made under this paragraph, each merger reference group and special reference group may determine its own procedure.

(7)   In determining how to proceed in accordance with rules made under this paragraph and in determining its procedure under sub-paragraph (6), a group must have regard to any guidance issued by the Chairman.

(8)   Before issuing any guidance for the purposes of this paragraph the Chairman shall consult the members of the Commission and such other persons as he considers appropriate.

(9)   In this paragraph and in Schedule 7A—
  "market reference group" means any group constituted in connection with a reference under section 126 or 127 of the Enterprise Act 2002 (including that section as it has effect by virtue of another enactment);
  "merger reference group" means any group constituted in connection with a reference under … section 32 of the Water Industry Act 1991 (c 56) or section 21, 32, 44 or 61 of the Enterprise Act 2002; and
  "special reference group" means any group constituted with a reference or (in the case of the Financial Services and Markets Act 2000 (c 8)) an investigation under—
      (a)   section 11 of the Competition Act 1980 (c 21);
      (b)   …
      (c)   section 43 of the Airports Act 1986 (c 31);
      (d)   section 24 or 41E of the Gas Act 1986 (c 44);
      (e)   section 12 or 56C of the Electricity Act 1989 (c 29);
      (f)   …
      (g)   section 12[, 14 or 17K] of the Water Industry Act 1991 (c 56);
      (h)   article 15 of the Electricity (Northern Ireland) Order 1992 (SI 1992/231 (NI 1));

(i)   section 13 of, or Schedule 4A to, the Railways Act 1993 (c 43);
(j)   article 34 of the Airports (Northern Ireland) Order 1994 (SI 1994/426 (NI 1));
(k)   article 15 of the Gas (Northern Ireland) Order 1996 (SI 1996/275 (NI 2));
(l)   section 15 of the Postal Services Act 2000 (c 26);
(m)   section 162 or 306 of the Financial Services and Markets Act 2000; ...
(n)   section 12 of the Transport Act 2000 (c 38);
[(o)   section 193 of the Communications Act 2003][; or
(p)   article 3 of the Water Services etc (Scotland) Act 2005 (Consequential Provisions and Modifications) Order 2005].]

Effect of exercise of functions by group

20.—(1)   Subject to [sub-paragraphs (2) to (9)], anything done by or in relation to a group in, or in connection with, the performance of functions to be performed by the group is to have the same effect as if done by or in relation to the Commission.

[(2)   For the purposes of Part 3 of the Enterprise Act 2002 (mergers) any decision of a group under section 34(1) or 35(1) of that Act (questions to be decided on non-public interest merger references) that there is an anti-competitive outcome is to be treated as a decision under that section that there is not an anti-competitive outcome if the decision is not that of at least two-thirds of the members of the group.

(3)   For the purposes of Part 3 of the Act of 2002, if the decision is not that of at least two-thirds of the members of the group—
(a)   any decision of a group under section 46 of that Act (questions to be decided on public interest merger references) that a relevant merger situation has been created is to be treated as a decision under that section that no such situation has been created;
(b)   any decision of a group under section 46 of that Act that the creation of a relevant merger situation has resulted, or may be expected to result, in a substantial lessening of competition within any market or markets in the United Kingdom for goods or services is to be treated as a decision under that section that the creation of that situation has not resulted, or may be expected not to result, in such a substantial lessening of competition;
(c)   any decision of a group under section 46 of that Act that arrangements are in progress or in contemplation which, if carried into effect, will result in the creation of a relevant merger situation is to be treated as a decision under that section that no such arrangements are in progress or in contemplation; and
(d)   any decision of a group under section 46 of that Act that the creation of such a situation as is mentioned in paragraph (c) may be expected to result in a substantial lessening of competition within any market or markets in the United Kingdom for goods or services is to be treated as a decision under that section that the creation of that situation may be expected not to result in such a substantial lessening of competition.

(4)   For the purposes of Part 3 of the Act of 2002, if the decision is not that of at least two-thirds of the members of the group—
(a)   any decision of a group under section 62 of that Act (questions to be decided on special public interest merger references) that a special merger situation has been created is to be treated as a decision under that section that no such situation has been created; and
(b)   any decision of a group under section 62 of that Act that arrangements are in progress or in contemplation which, if carried into effect, will result in the creation of a special merger situation is to be treated as a decision under that section that no such arrangements are in progress or in contemplation.

(5)   For the purposes of Part 4 of the Act of 2002 (market investigations), if the decision is not that of at least two-thirds of the members of the group, any decision of a group under section 129 or 136 (questions to be decided on market investigation references) that a feature, or combination of features, of a relevant market prevents, restricts or distorts competition in connection with the supply or acquisition of any goods or services in the United Kingdom or a part of the United Kingdom is to be treated as a decision that the feature or (as the case may be) combination of features does not prevent, restrict or distort such competition.

(6)   Accordingly, for the purposes of Part 4 of the Act of 2002, a group is to be treated as having decided under section 129 or 136 that there is no adverse effect on competition if—
(a)   one or more than one decision of the group is to be treated as mentioned in sub-paragraph (5); and
(b)   there is no other relevant decision of the group.

(7)   In sub-paragraph (6) "relevant decision" means a decision which is not to be treated as mentioned in sub-paragraph (5) and which is that a feature, or combination of features, of a relevant market prevents, restricts or distorts competition in connection with the supply or acquisition of any goods or services in the United Kingdom or a part of the United Kingdom.

(8)   Expressions used in sub-paragraphs (2) to (7) shall be construed in accordance with Part 3 or (as the case may be) 4 of the Act of 2002.

(9)   Sub-paragraph (1) is also subject to specific provision made by or under other enactments about decisions which are not decisions of at least two-thirds of the members of a group.]

Casting votes

21.   The chairman of a group is to have a casting vote on any question to be decided by the group.

Newspaper merger references

22.   [There are to be members of the Commission appointed by the Secretary of State to form a panel of persons available] for selection as members of a group constituted in connection with a newspaper merger reference.

[1242]

NOTES
Para 15: words in square brackets in sub-para (1), and sub-para (8) inserted, sub-para (7)(b) and the word immediately preceding it repealed, and sub-para (5) substituted, by the Enterprise Act 2002, ss 185, 278(2), Sch 11, paras 1, 10, Sch 26 (these amendments came into effect on 1 April 2003 (sub-para (5)), 20 June 2003 (sub-paras (1), (8)), and 20 June 2003 (sub-para (7) certain purposes) and 29 December 2004 (sub-para (7) otherwise)).
Para 19: sub-para (5) inserted by the Enterprise Act 2002, s 187(2), as from 20 June 2003.
Para 19A was inserted by the Enterprise Act 2002, s 187(3), as from 20 June 2003, and sub-para (9) of that paragraph has been amended as follows:
Words omitted from definition "merger reference group" repealed by the Communications Act 2003, s 406, Sch 19, as from 29 December 2003.
In definition "special reference group" paras (b), (f), and the word omitted from the end of para (m), repealed by the Communications Act 2003, s 406, Sch 19, as from 29 December 2003.
In definition "special reference group" words in square brackets in para (g) substituted by the Water Act 2003, s 101(1), Sch 8, para 54, as from 1 December 2005.
In definition "special reference group" para (o) added by the Communications Act 2003, s 406, Sch 17, para 153(1), (3), as from 25 July 2003 (certain purposes) and as from 29 December 2003 (otherwise).
In definition "special reference group" para (p) (and the word immediately preceding it) added by the Water Services etc (Scotland) Act 2005 (Consequential Provisions and Modifications) Order 2005, SI 2005/3172, art 11, Schedule, Pt 1, para 3(a), as from 11 November 2005.
Para 20: words in square brackets in sub-para (1) substituted, and sub-paras (2)–(9) substituted for original sub-para (2), by the Enterprise Act 2002, s 185, Sch 11, paras 1, 11, as from 20 June 2003.
Para 22: words in square brackets substituted by the Enterprise Act 2002, ss 185, Sch 11, paras 1, 12, as from 1 April 2003.

[SCHEDULE 7A
THE COMPETITION COMMISSION: PROCEDURAL RULES FOR MERGERS AND
MARKET REFERENCES ETC
Schedule 7, para 19A

1.   In this Schedule—
"market investigation" means an investigation carried out by a market reference group in connection with a reference under section 131 or 132 of the Enterprise Act 2002 (including that section as it has effect by virtue of another enactment);
"market reference group" has the meaning given by paragraph 19A(9) of Schedule 7 to this Act;
"merger investigation" means an investigation carried out by a merger reference group in connection with a reference under *section 59 of the Fair Trading Act 1973 (c 41)*, section 32 of the Water Industry Act 1991 (c 56) or section 22, 33, 45 or 62 of the Act of 2002;
"merger reference group" has the meaning given by paragraph 19A(9) of Schedule 7 to this Act;
"relevant group" means a market reference group, merger reference group or special reference group;
"special investigation" means an investigation carried out by a special reference group—
    (a)   in connection with a reference under a provision mentioned in any of paragraphs (a) to (l) [and (n) to (p)] of the definition of "special reference group" in paragraph 19A(9) of Schedule 7 to this Act; or
    (b)   under a provision mentioned in paragraph (m) of that definition; and
"special reference group" has the meaning given by paragraph 19A(9) of Schedule 7 to this Act.

2.   Rules may make provision—
    (a)   for particular stages of a merger investigation, a market investigation or a special investigation to be dealt with in accordance with a timetable and for the revision of that timetable;
    (b)   as to the documents and information which must be given to a relevant group in connection with a merger investigation, a market investigation or a special investigation;
    (c)   as to the documents or information which a relevant group must give to other persons in connection with such an investigation.

3.   Rules made by virtue of paragraph 2(a) and (b) may, in particular, enable or require a relevant group to disregard documents or information given after a particular date.

4.   Rules made by virtue of paragraph 2(c) may, in particular, make provision for the notification or publication of, and for consultation about, provisional findings of a relevant group.

5.   Rules may make provision as to the quorum of relevant groups.

6.   Rules may make provision—
   (a)   as to the extent (if any) to which persons interested or claiming to be interested in a matter under consideration which is specified or described in the rules are allowed—
      (i)   to be (either by themselves or by their representatives) present before a relevant group or heard by that group;
      (ii)   to cross-examine witnesses; or
      (iii) otherwise to take part;
   (b)   as to the extent (if any) to which sittings of a relevant group are to be held in public; and
   (c)   generally in connection with any matters permitted by rules made under paragraph (a) or (b) (including, in particular, provision for a record of any hearings).

7.   Rules may make provision for—
   (a)   the notification or publication of information in relation to merger investigations, market investigations or special investigations;
   (b)   consultation about such investigations.]

[1243]

NOTES
  Inserted by the Enterprise Act 2002, s 187(4), Sch 12, as from 20 June 2003.
  Para 1: words omitted from definition "merger investigation" repealed by the Communications Act 2003, s 406, Sch 19, as from 29 December 2003; words in square brackets in para (a) of definition "special investigation" substituted by the Water Services etc (Scotland) Act 2005 (Consequential Provisions and Modifications) Order 2005, SI 2005/3172, art 11, Schedule, Pt 1, para 3(b), as from 11 November 2005.

HUMAN RIGHTS ACT 1998

(1998 c 42)

NOTES
  Only provisions of this Act relevant to Financial Services law are reproduced. Provisions not reproduced are not annotated.
  This Act is reproduced as amended by: the Secretary of State for Constitutional Affairs Order 2003, SI 2003/1887; the Human Rights Act 1998 (Amendment) Order 2004, SI 2004/1574.

An Act to give further effect to rights and freedoms guaranteed under the European Convention on Human Rights; to make provision with respect to holders of certain judicial offices who become judges of the European Court of Human Rights; and for connected purposes

[9 November 1998]

Introduction

1   The Convention Rights

(1)   In this Act "the Convention rights" means the rights and fundamental freedoms set out in—
   (a)   Articles 2 to 12 and 14 of the Convention,
   (b)   Articles 1 to 3 of the First Protocol, and
   (c)   [Article 1 of the Thirteenth Protocol],
as read with Articles 16 to 18 of the Convention.

(2)   Those Articles are to have effect for the purposes of this Act subject to any designated derogation or reservation (as to which see sections 14 and 15).

(3)   The Articles are set out in Schedule 1.

(4)   The [Secretary of State] may by order make such amendments to this Act as he considers appropriate to reflect the effect, in relation to the United Kingdom, of a protocol.

(5)   In subsection (4) "protocol" means a protocol to the Convention—
   (a)   which the United Kingdom has ratified; or
   (b)   which the United Kingdom has signed with a view to ratification.

(6)   No amendment may be made by an order under subsection (4) so as to come into force before the protocol concerned is in force in relation to the United Kingdom.

[1244]

NOTES
Sub-s (1): words in square brackets in para (c) substituted by the Human Rights Act 1998 (Amendment) Order 2004, SI 2004/1574, art 2(1), as from 22 June 2004.
Sub-s (4): words in square brackets substituted by the Secretary of State for Constitutional Affairs Order 2003, SI 2003/1887, art 9, Sch 2, para 10, as from 19 August 2003.
Orders: the Human Rights Act 1998 (Amendment) Order 2004, SI 2004/1574.

Public authorities

6   Acts of public authorities

(1)   It is unlawful for a public authority to act in a way which is incompatible with a Convention right.

(2)   Subsection (1) does not apply to an act if—
   (a)   as the result of one or more provisions of primary legislation, the authority could not have acted differently; or
   (b)   in the case of one or more provisions of, or made under, primary legislation which cannot be read or given effect in a way which is compatible with the Convention rights, the authority was acting so as to give effect to or enforce those provisions.

(3)   In this section "public authority" includes—
   (a)   a court or tribunal, and
   (b)   any person certain of whose functions are functions of a public nature,

but does not include either House of Parliament or a person exercising functions in connection with proceedings in Parliament.

(4)–(6)   *(Outside the scope of this work.)*

[1245]

Supplemental

22   Short title, commencement, application and extent

(1)   This Act may be cited as the Human Rights Act 1998.

(2)   Sections 18, 20 and 21(5) and this section come into force on the passing of this Act.

(3)   The other provisions of this Act come into force on such day as the Secretary of State may by order appoint; and different days may be appointed for different purposes.

(4)   *(Outside the scope of this work.)*

(5)   This Act binds the Crown.

(6)   This Act extends to Northern Ireland.

(7)   *(Outside the scope of this work.)*

[1246]

NOTES
Orders: the Human Rights Act 1998 (Commencement) Order 1998, SI 1998/2882; the Human Rights Act 1998 (Commencement No 2) Order 2000, SI 2000/1851.

TERRORISM ACT 2000

(2000 c 11)

NOTES
Only provisions of this Act relevant to Financial Services law are reproduced. Provisions not reproduced are not annotated.
  This Act is reproduced as amended by: the Police (Northern Ireland) Act 2000; the Anti-terrorism, Crime and Security Act 2001; the Enterprise Act 2002; the Justice (Northern Ireland) Act 2002; the Land Registration Act 2002; the Courts Act 2003; the Crime (International Co-operation) Act 2003; the Criminal Justice Act 2003; the Railways and Transport Safety Act 2003; the Pensions Act 2004; the Justice (Northern Ireland) Act 2004; the Commissioners for Revenue and Customs Act 2005; the Serious Organised Crime and Police Act 2005; the Constitutional Reform Act 2005; the Terrorism (Northern Ireland) Act 2006; the Terrorism Act 2006; the Fraud Act 2006; the Bankruptcy and Diligence etc (Scotland) Act 2007; the Counter-Terrorism Act 2008; the Banking Consolidation Directive (Consequential Amendments) Regulations 2000, SI 2000/2952; the Financial Services and Markets Act 2000 (Consequential Amendments and Repeals) Order 2001, SI 2001/3649; the Terrorism Act 2000 (Continuance of Part VII) Order 2003, SI 2003/427; the Firearms (Northern Ireland) Order 2004, SI 2004/702; the British Transport Police (Transitional and Consequential Provisions) Order 2004, SI 2004/1573; the Life Assurance Consolidation Directive (Consequential Amendments) Regulations 2004, SI 2004/3379; the Capital Requirements Regulations 2006, SI 2006/3221; the Financial Services and Markets Act 2000 (Regulated Activities) (Amendment No 3) Order 2006, SI 2006/3384; the Terrorism Act 2000

(Business in the Regulated Sector and Supervisory Authorities) Order 2007, SI 2007/3288; the Terrorism Act 2000 and Proceeds of Crime Act 2002 (Amendment) Regulations 2007, SI 2007/3398; the Companies Act 2006 (Consequential Amendments etc) Order 2008, SI 2008/948.

ARRANGEMENT OF SECTIONS

PART I
INTRODUCTORY

PART III
TERRORIST PROPERTY

Offences

PART IV
TERRORIST INVESTIGATIONS

Information and evidence

PART VI
MISCELLANEOUS

Terrorist bombing and finance offences

PART VIII
GENERAL

SCHEDULES

PART II
OTHER ACTS

An Act to make provision about terrorism; and to make temporary provision for Northern Ireland about the prosecution and punishment of certain offences, the preservation of peace and the maintenance of order

[20 July 2000]

PART I
INTRODUCTORY

1 Terrorism: interpretation

(1) In this Act "terrorism" means the use or threat of action where—
- (a)   the action falls within subsection (2),
- (b)   the use or threat is designed to influence the government [or an international governmental organisation] or to intimidate the public or a section of the public, and
- (c)   the use or threat is made for the purpose of advancing a political, religious[, racial] or ideological cause.

(2) Action falls within this subsection if it—
- (a)   involves serious violence against a person,
- (b)   involves serious damage to property,
- (c)   endangers a person's life, other than that of the person committing the action,
- (d)   creates a serious risk to the health or safety of the public or a section of the public, or
- (e)   is designed seriously to interfere with or seriously to disrupt an electronic system.

(3) The use or threat of action falling within subsection (2) which involves the use of firearms or explosives is terrorism whether or not subsection (1)(b) is satisfied.

(4) In this section—
- (a)   "action" includes action outside the United Kingdom,
- (b)   a reference to any person or to property is a reference to any person, or to property, wherever situated,
- (c)   a reference to the public includes a reference to the public of a country other than the United Kingdom, and
- (d)   "the government" means the government of the United Kingdom, of a Part of the United Kingdom or of a country other than the United Kingdom.

(5) In this Act a reference to action taken for the purposes of terrorism includes a reference to action taken for the benefit of a proscribed organisation.

[1247]

NOTES

Sub-s (1): words in square brackets in para (b) inserted by the Terrorism Act 2006, s 34(a), as from 13 April 2006; word in square brackets in para (c) inserted by the Counter-Terrorism Act 2008, s 75, as from 16 February 2009.

PART III
TERRORIST PROPERTY

Offences

18 Money laundering

(1) A person commits an offence if he enters into or becomes concerned in an arrangement which facilitates the retention or control by or on behalf of another person of terrorist property—
- (a)   by concealment,
- (b)   by removal from the jurisdiction,
- (c)   by transfer to nominees, or
- (d)   in any other way.

(2) It is a defence for a person charged with an offence under subsection (1) to prove that he did not know and had no reasonable cause to suspect that the arrangement related to terrorist property.

[1248]

NOTES

Post-charge questioning and jurisdiction to try offences: see further the Counter-Terrorism Act 2008, ss 22–24, 27 in relation to post-charge questioning for an offence under this section. See also s 28 of that Act which provides that such an offence may be tried anywhere in the UK.

Notification requirements: Part 4 of the Counter-Terrorism Act 2008 imposes notification requirements on persons dealt with in respect of certain offences (including an offence under this section). These require a person to whom that Part applies to give to the police certain information such as date of birth, national insurance number, etc.

19 Disclosure of information: duty

(1) This section applies where a person—
  (a) believes or suspects that another person has committed an offence under any of sections 15 to 18, and
  (b) bases his belief or suspicion on information which [comes to his attention—
    (i) in the course of a trade, profession or business, or
    (ii) in the course of his employment (whether or not in the course of a trade, profession or business).]

[(1A)   But this section does not apply if the information came to the person in the course of a business in the regulated sector.]

(2) The person commits an offence if he does not disclose to a constable as soon as is reasonably practicable—
  (a) his belief or suspicion, and
  (b) the information on which it is based.

(3) It is a defence for a person charged with an offence under subsection (2) to prove that he had a reasonable excuse for not making the disclosure.

(4) Where—
  (a) a person is in employment,
  (b) his employer has established a procedure for the making of disclosures of the matters specified in subsection (2), and
  (c) he is charged with an offence under that subsection,
it is a defence for him to prove that he disclosed the matters specified in that subsection in accordance with the procedure.

(5) Subsection (2) does not require disclosure by a professional legal adviser of—
  (a) information which he obtains in privileged circumstances, or
  (b) a belief or suspicion based on information which he obtains in privileged circumstances.

(6) For the purpose of subsection (5) information is obtained by an adviser in privileged circumstances if it comes to him, otherwise than with a view to furthering a criminal purpose—
  (a) from a client or a client's representative, in connection with the provision of legal advice by the adviser to the client,
  (b) from a person seeking legal advice from the adviser, or from the person's representative, or
  (c) from any person, for the purpose of actual or contemplated legal proceedings.

(7) For the purposes of subsection (1)(a) a person shall be treated as having committed an offence under one of sections 15 to 18 if—
  (a) he has taken an action or been in possession of a thing, and
  (b) he would have committed an offence under one of those sections if he had been in the United Kingdom at the time when he took the action or was in possession of the thing.

[(7A)   The reference to a business in the regulated sector must be construed in accordance with Schedule 3A.

(7B)   The reference to a constable includes a reference to a [member of the staff of the Serious Organised Crime Agency] authorised for the purposes of this section by the Director General of [that Agency].]

(8) A person guilty of an offence under this section shall be liable—
  (a) on conviction on indictment, to imprisonment for a term not exceeding five years, to a fine or to both, or
  (b) on summary conviction, to imprisonment for a term not exceeding six months, or to a fine not exceeding the statutory maximum or to both.

[1249]

NOTES
   Sub-s (1): words in square brackets substituted by the Counter-Terrorism Act 2008, s 77(1), (2), as from 16 February 2009.
   Sub-s (1A): inserted by the Anti-terrorism, Crime and Security Act 2001, s 3, Sch 2, Pt 3, para 5(1), (3), as from 20 December 2001.
   Sub-s (7A): inserted, together with sub-s (7B), by the Anti-terrorism, Crime and Security Act 2001, s 3, Sch 2, Pt 3, para 5(1), (4), as from 20 December 2001.
   Sub-s (7B): inserted as noted above; words in square brackets substituted by the Serious Organised Crime and Police Act 2005, s 59, Sch 4, paras 125, 126, as from 1 April 2006.

Note the Terrorism Act 2000 (Crown Servants and Regulators) Regulations 2001, SI 2001/192, reg 4, which, following its amendment by the Financial Services and Markets Act 2000 (Consequential Amendments) Order 2002, SI 2002/1555 (on 3 July 2002), provides that this section shall not apply to the following persons, being persons who are, in the opinion of the Secretary of State, performing or connected with the performance of regulatory, supervisory, investigative or registration functions of a public nature, namely—
— the Bank of England;
— the Financial Services Authority;
— a designated professional body within the meaning of section 326(2) of the Financial Services and Markets Act 2000;
— the Council of Lloyds;
— the Registrar of Credit Unions for Northern Ireland;
— the Assistant Registrar of Credit Unions for Northern Ireland, and
— any person who is employed by, or otherwise engaged in, the service of any person referred to above for the purpose of performing such functions.

Post-charge questioning and jurisdiction to try offences: see further the Counter-Terrorism Act 2008, ss 22–24, 27 in relation to post-charge questioning for an offence under this section. See also s 28 of that Act which provides that such an offence may be tried anywhere in the UK.

20 Disclosure of information: permission

(1)   A person may disclose to a constable—
(a)   a suspicion or belief that any money or other property is terrorist property or is derived from terrorist property;
(b)   any matter on which the suspicion or belief is based.

(2)   A person may make a disclosure to a constable in the circumstances mentioned in section 19(1) and (2).

(3)   Subsections (1) and (2) shall have effect notwithstanding any restriction on the disclosure of information imposed by statute or otherwise.

(4)   Where—
(a)   a person is in employment, and
(b)   his employer has established a procedure for the making of disclosures of the kinds mentioned in subsection (1) and section 19(2),
subsections (1) and (2) shall have effect in relation to that person as if any reference to disclosure to a constable included a reference to disclosure in accordance with the procedure.

[(5)   References to a constable include references to a [member of the staff of the Serious Organised Crime Agency] authorised for the purposes of this section by the Director General of [that Agency].]

[1250]

NOTES
Sub-s (5): added by the Anti-terrorism, Crime and Security Act 2001, s 3, Sch 2, Pt 3, para 5(1), (5), as from 20 December 2001; words in square brackets substituted by the Serious Organised Crime and Police Act 2005, s 59, Sch 4, paras 125, 127, as from 1 April 2006.

21 Cooperation with police

(1)   A person does not commit an offence under any of sections 15 to 18 if he is acting with the express consent of a constable.

(2)   Subject to subsections (3) and (4), a person does not commit an offence under any of sections 15 to 18 by involvement in a transaction or arrangement relating to money or other property if he discloses to a constable—
(a)   his suspicion or belief that the money or other property is terrorist property, and
(b)   the information on which his suspicion or belief is based.

(3)   Subsection (2) applies only where a person makes a disclosure—
(a)   after he becomes concerned in the transaction concerned,
(b)   on his own initiative, and
(c)   as soon as is reasonably practicable.

(4)   Subsection (2) does not apply to a person if—
(a)   a constable forbids him to continue his involvement in the transaction or arrangement to which the disclosure relates, and
(b)   he continues his involvement.

(5)   It is a defence for a person charged with an offence under any of sections 15(2) and (3) and 16 to 18 to prove that—
(a)   he intended to make a disclosure of the kind mentioned in subsections (2) and (3), and
(b)   there is reasonable excuse for his failure to do so.

(6)   Where—
(a)   a person is in employment, and

(b)   his employer has established a procedure for the making of disclosures of the same kind as may be made to a constable under subsection (2),

this section shall have effect in relation to that person as if any reference to disclosure to a constable included a reference to disclosure in accordance with the procedure.

(7)   A reference in this section to a transaction or arrangement relating to money or other property includes a reference to use or possession.

[1251]

[21ZA   Arrangements with prior consent

(1)   A person does not commit an offence under any of sections 15 to 18 by involvement in a transaction or an arrangement relating to money or other property if, before becoming involved, the person—

     (a)   discloses to an authorised officer the person's suspicion or belief that the money or other property is terrorist property and the information on which the suspicion or belief is based, and

     (b)   has the authorised officer's consent to becoming involved in the transaction or arrangement.

(2)   A person is treated as having an authorised officer's consent if before the end of the notice period the person does not receive notice from an authorised officer that consent is refused.

(3)   The notice period is the period of 7 working days starting with the first working day after the person makes the disclosure.

(4)   A working day is a day other than a Saturday, a Sunday, Christmas Day, Good Friday or a day that is a bank holiday under the Banking and Financial Dealings Act 1971 (c 80) in the part of the United Kingdom in which the person is when making the disclosure.

(5)   In this section "authorised officer" means a member of the staff of the Serious Organised Crime Agency authorised for the purposes of this section by the Director General of that Agency.

(6)   The reference in this section to a transaction or arrangement relating to money or other property includes a reference to use or possession.]

[1251A]

NOTES
Commencement: 26 December 2007.
Inserted, together with ss 21ZB, 21ZC, by the Terrorism Act 2000 and Proceeds of Crime Act 2002 (Amendment) Regulations 2007, SI 2007/3398, reg 2, Sch 1, paras 1, 2, as from 26 December 2007.

[21ZB   Disclosure after entering into arrangements

(1)   A person does not commit an offence under any of sections 15 to 18 by involvement in a transaction or an arrangement relating to money or other property if, after becoming involved, the person discloses to an authorised officer—

     (a)   the person's suspicion or belief that the money or other property is terrorist property, and

     (b)   the information on which the suspicion or belief is based.

(2)   This section applies only where—

     (a)   there is a reasonable excuse for the person's failure to make the disclosure before becoming involved in the transaction or arrangement, and

     (b)   the disclosure is made on the person's own initiative and as soon as it is reasonably practicable for the person to make it.

(3)   This section does not apply to a person if—

     (a)   an authorised officer forbids the person to continue involvement in the transaction or arrangement to which the disclosure relates, and

     (b)   the person continues that involvement.

(4)   In this section "authorised officer" means a member of the staff of the Serious Organised Crime Agency authorised for the purposes of this section by the Director General of that Agency.

(5)   The reference in this section to a transaction or arrangement relating to money or other property includes a reference to use or possession.]

[1251B]

NOTES
Commencement: 26 December 2007.
Inserted as noted to s 21ZA at **[1251A]**.

21ZC   Reasonable excuse for failure to disclose

It is a defence for a person charged with an offence under any of sections 15 to 18 to prove that—

(a)   the person intended to make a disclosure of the kind mentioned in section 21ZA or 21ZB, and

(b)   there is a reasonable excuse for the person's failure to do so.]

[1251C]

NOTES
Commencement: 26 December 2007.
Inserted as noted to s 21ZA at **[1251A]**.

[21A   Failure to disclose: regulated sector

(1)   A person commits an offence if each of the following three conditions is satisfied.

(2)   The first condition is that he—
   (a)   knows or suspects, or
   (b)   has reasonable grounds for knowing or suspecting,
that another person has committed [or attempted to commit] an offence under any of sections 15 to 18.

(3)   The second condition is that the information or other matter—
   (a)   on which his knowledge or suspicion is based, or
   (b)   which gives reasonable grounds for such knowledge or suspicion,
came to him in the course of a business in the regulated sector.

(4)   The third condition is that he does not disclose the information or other matter to a constable or a nominated officer as soon as is practicable after it comes to him.

(5)   But a person does not commit an offence under this section if—
   (a)   he has a reasonable excuse for not disclosing the information or other matter;
   (b)   he is a professional legal adviser [or relevant professional adviser] and the information or other matter came to him in privileged circumstances[; or
   (c)   subsection (5A) applies to him.]

[(5A)   This subsection applies to a person if—
   (a)   the person is employed by, or is in partnership with, a professional legal adviser or relevant professional adviser to provide the adviser with assistance or support,
   (b)   the information or other matter comes to the person in connection with the provision of such assistance or support, and
   (c)   the information or other matter came to the adviser in privileged circumstances.]

(6)   In deciding whether a person committed an offence under this section the court must consider whether he followed any relevant guidance which was at the time concerned—
   (a)   issued by a supervisory authority or any other appropriate body,
   (b)   approved by the Treasury, and
   (c)   published in a manner it approved as appropriate in its opinion to bring the guidance to the attention of persons likely to be affected by it.

(7)   A disclosure to a nominated officer is a disclosure which—
   (a)   is made to a person nominated by the alleged offender's employer to receive disclosures under this section, and
   (b)   is made in the course of the alleged offender's employment and in accordance with the procedure established by the employer for the purpose.

(8)   Information or other matter comes to a professional legal adviser [or relevant professional adviser] in privileged circumstances if it is communicated or given to him—
   (a)   by (or by a representative of) a client of his in connection with the giving by the adviser of legal advice to the client,
   (b)   by (or by a representative of) a person seeking legal advice from the adviser, or
   (c)   by a person in connection with legal proceedings or contemplated legal proceedings.

(9)   But subsection (8) does not apply to information or other matter which is communicated or given with a view to furthering a criminal purpose.

(10)   Schedule 3A has effect for the purpose of determining what is—
   (a)   a business in the regulated sector;
   (b)   a supervisory authority.

(11)   For the purposes of subsection (2) a person is to be taken to have committed an offence there mentioned if—
   (a)   he has taken an action or been in possession of a thing, and
   (b)   he would have committed the offence if he had been in the United Kingdom at the time when he took the action or was in possession of the thing.

(12)   A person guilty of an offence under this section is liable—
   (a)   on conviction on indictment, to imprisonment for a term not exceeding five years or to a fine or to both;

(b)   on summary conviction, to imprisonment for a term not exceeding six months or to a fine not exceeding the statutory maximum or to both.

(13)   An appropriate body is any body which regulates or is representative of any trade, profession, business or employment carried on by the alleged offender.

(14)   The reference to a constable includes a reference to a [member of the staff of the Serious Organised Crime Agency]authorised for the purposes of this section by the Director General of [that Agency].]

[(15)   In this section "relevant professional adviser" means an accountant, auditor or tax adviser who is a member of a professional body which is established for accountants, auditors or tax advisers (as the case may be) and which makes provision for—

(a)   testing the competence of those seeking admission to membership of such a body as a condition for such admission; and

(b)   imposing and maintaining professional and ethical standards for its members, as well as imposing sanctions for non-compliance with those standards.]

[1252]

NOTES

Inserted by the Anti-terrorism, Crime and Security Act 2001, s 3, Sch 2, Pt 3, para 5(1), (2), as from 20 December 2001.

Sub-ss (2), (5), (8): words in square brackets inserted by the Terrorism Act 2000 and Proceeds of Crime Act 2002 (Amendment) Regulations 2007, SI 2007/3398, reg 2, Sch 1, paras 1, 3(1)–(3), (5), as from 26 December 2007.

Sub-ss (5A), (15): inserted and added respectively by SI 2007/3398, reg 2, Sch 1, paras 1, 3(1), (4), (6), as from 26 December 2007.

Sub-s (14): words in square brackets substituted by the Serious Organised Crime and Police Act 2005, s 59, Sch 4, paras 125, 128, as from 1 April 2006.

Post-charge questioning and jurisdiction to try offences: see further the Counter-Terrorism Act 2008, ss 22–24, 27 in relation to post-charge questioning for an offence under this section. See also s 28 of that Act which provides that such an offence may be tried anywhere in the UK.

[21B   Protected disclosures

(1)   A disclosure which satisfies the following three conditions is not to be taken to breach any restriction on the disclosure of information (however imposed).

(2)   The first condition is that the information or other matter disclosed came to the person making the disclosure (the discloser) in the course of a business in the regulated sector.

(3)   The second condition is that the information or other matter—

(a)   causes the discloser to know or suspect, or

(b)   gives him reasonable grounds for knowing or suspecting,

that another person has committed [or attempted to commit] an offence under any of sections 15 to 18.

(4)   The third condition is that the disclosure is made to a constable or a nominated officer as soon as is practicable after the information or other matter comes to the discloser.

(5)   A disclosure to a nominated officer is a disclosure which—

(a)   is made to a person nominated by the discloser's employer to receive disclosures under this section, and

(b)   is made in the course of the discloser's employment and in accordance with the procedure established by the employer for the purpose.

(6)   The reference to a business in the regulated sector must be construed in accordance with Schedule 3A.

(7)   The reference to a constable includes a reference to a [member of the staff of the Serious Organised Crime Agency] authorised for the purposes of this section by the Director General of [that Agency].]

[1253]

NOTES

Inserted by the Anti-terrorism, Crime and Security Act 2001, s 3, Sch 2, Pt 3, para 5(1), (2), as from 20 December 2001.

Sub-s (3): words in square brackets inserted by the Terrorism Act 2000 and Proceeds of Crime Act 2002 (Amendment) Regulations 2007, SI 2007/3398, reg 2, Sch 1, paras 1, 4, as from 26 December 2007.

Sub-s (7): words in square brackets substituted by the Serious Organised Crime and Police Act 2005, s 59, Sch 4, paras 125, 129, as from 1 April 2006.

PART II
OTHER ACTS

[21C   Disclosures to SOCA

(1)   Where a disclosure is made under a provision of this Part to a constable, the constable must disclose it in full as soon as practicable after it has been made to a member of staff of the Serious Organised Crime Agency authorised for the purposes of that provision by the Director General of that Agency.

(2)   Where a disclosure is made under section 21 (cooperation with police) to a constable, the constable must disclose it in full as soon as practicable after it has been made to a member of staff of the Serious Organised Crime Agency authorised for the purposes of this subsection by the Director General of that Agency.]

[1253A]

NOTES
Commencement: 26 December 2007.
Inserted, together with ss 21D–21H, by the Terrorism Act 2000 and Proceeds of Crime Act 2002 (Amendment) Regulations 2007, SI 2007/3398, reg 2, Sch 1, paras 1, 5, as from 26 December 2007.

[21D   Tipping off: regulated sector

(1)   A person commits an offence if—
  (a)   the person discloses any matter within subsection (2);
  (b)   the disclosure is likely to prejudice any investigation that might be conducted following the disclosure referred to in that subsection; and
  (c)   the information on which the disclosure is based came to the person in the course of a business in the regulated sector.

(2)   The matters are that the person or another person has made a disclosure under a provision of this Part—
  (a)   to a constable,
  (b)   in accordance with a procedure established by that person's employer for the making of disclosures under that provision,
  (c)   to a nominated officer, or
  (d)   to a member of staff of the Serious Organised Crime Agency authorised for the purposes of that provision by the Director General of that Agency,
of information that came to that person in the course of a business in the regulated sector.

(3)   A person commits an offence if—
  (a)   the person discloses that an investigation into allegations that an offence under this Part has been committed is being contemplated or is being carried out;
  (b)   the disclosure is likely to prejudice that investigation; and
  (c)   the information on which the disclosure is based came to the person in the course of a business in the regulated sector.

(4)   A person guilty of an offence under this section is liable—
  (a)   on summary conviction to imprisonment for a term not exceeding three months, or to a fine not exceeding level 5 on the standard scale, or to both;
  (b)   on conviction on indictment to imprisonment for a term not exceeding two years, or to a fine, or to both.

(5)   This section is subject to—
  (a)   section 21E (disclosures within an undertaking or group etc),
  (b)   section 21F (other permitted disclosures between institutions etc), and
  (c)   section 21G (other permitted disclosures etc).]

[1253B]

NOTES
Commencement: 26 December 2007.
Inserted as noted to s 21C at **[1253A]**.
Post-charge questioning and jurisdiction to try offences: see further the Counter-Terrorism Act 2008, ss 22–24, 27 in relation to post-charge questioning for an offence under this section. See also s 28 of that Act which provides that such an offence may be tried anywhere in the UK.

[21E   Disclosures within an undertaking or group etc

(1)   An employee, officer or partner of an undertaking does not commit an offence under section 21D if the disclosure is to an employee, officer or partner of the same undertaking.

(2)   A person does not commit an offence under section 21D in respect of a disclosure by a credit institution or a financial institution if—
  (a)   the disclosure is to a credit institution or a financial institution,
  (b)   the institution to whom the disclosure is made is situated in an EEA State or in a country or territory imposing equivalent money laundering requirements, and

    (c)   both the institution making the disclosure and the institution to whom it is made belong to the same group.

    (3)   In subsection (2) "group" has the same meaning as in Directive 2002/87/EC of the European Parliament and of the Council of 16th December 2002 on the supplementary supervision of credit institutions, insurance undertakings and investment firms in a financial conglomerate.

    (4)   A professional legal adviser or a relevant professional adviser does not commit an offence under section 21D if—

    (a)   the disclosure is to a professional legal adviser or a relevant professional adviser,

    (b)   both the person making the disclosure and the person to whom it is made carry on business in an EEA state or in a country or territory imposing equivalent money laundering requirements, and

    (c)   those persons perform their professional activities within different undertakings that share common ownership, management or control.]

[1253C]

NOTES
Commencement: 26 December 2007.
Inserted as noted to s 21C at **[1253A]**.

[21F   Other permitted disclosures between institutions etc

    (1)   This section applies to a disclosure—

    (a)   by a credit institution to another credit institution,

    (b)   by a financial institution to another financial institution,

    (c)   by a professional legal adviser to another professional legal adviser, or

    (d)   by a relevant professional adviser of a particular kind to another relevant professional adviser of the same kind.

    (2)   A person does not commit an offence under section 21D in respect of a disclosure to which this section applies if—

    (a)   the disclosure relates to—

        (i)   a client or former client of the institution or adviser making the disclosure and the institution or adviser to whom it is made,

        (ii)   a transaction involving them both, or

        (iii)   the provision of a service involving them both;

    (b)   the disclosure is for the purpose only of preventing an offence under this Part of this Act;

    (c)   the institution or adviser to whom the disclosure is made is situated in an EEA State or in a country or territory imposing equivalent money laundering requirements; and

    (d)   the institution or adviser making the disclosure and the institution or adviser to whom it is made are subject to equivalent duties of professional confidentiality and the protection of personal data (within the meaning of section 1 of the Data Protection Act 1998).]

[1253D]

NOTES
Commencement: 26 December 2007.
Inserted as noted to s 21C at **[1253A]**.

[21G   Other permitted disclosures etc

    (1)   A person does not commit an offence under section 21D if the disclosure is—

    (a)   to the authority that is the supervisory authority for that person by virtue of the Money Laundering Regulations 2007 (SI 2007/2157); or

    (b)   for the purpose of—

        (i)   the detection, investigation or prosecution of a criminal offence (whether in the United Kingdom or elsewhere),

        (ii)   an investigation under the Proceeds of Crime Act 2002, or

        (iii)   the enforcement of any order of a court under that Act.

    (2)   A professional legal adviser or a relevant professional adviser does not commit an offence under section 21D if the disclosure—

    (a)   is to the adviser's client, and

    (b)   is made for the purpose of dissuading the client from engaging in conduct amounting to an offence.

    (3)   A person does not commit an offence under section 21D(1) if the person does not know or suspect that the disclosure is likely to have the effect mentioned in section 21D(1)(b).

    (4)   A person does not commit an offence under section 21D(3) if the person does not know or suspect that the disclosure is likely to have the effect mentioned in section 21D(3)(b).]

[1253E]

PART II
OTHER ACTS

NOTES
Commencement: 26 December 2007.
Inserted as noted to s 21C at **[1253A]**.

[21H Interpretation of sections 21D to 21G

(1) The references in sections 21D to 21G—
    (a)   to a business in the regulated sector, and
    (b)   to a supervisory authority,
are to be construed in accordance with Schedule 3A.

(2) In those sections—
"credit institution" has the same meaning as in Schedule 3A;
"financial institution" means an undertaking that carries on a business in the regulated sector by virtue of any of paragraphs (b) to (i) of paragraph 1(1) of that Schedule.

(3) References in those sections to a disclosure by or to a credit institution or a financial institution include disclosure by or to an employee, officer or partner of the institution acting on its behalf.

(4) For the purposes of those sections a country or territory imposes "equivalent money laundering requirements" if it imposes requirements equivalent to those laid down in Directive 2005/60/EC of the European Parliament and of the Council of 26th October 2005 on the prevention of the use of the financial system for the purpose of money laundering and terrorist financing.

(5) In those sections "relevant professional adviser" means an accountant, auditor or tax adviser who is a member of a professional body which is established for accountants, auditors or tax advisers (as the case may be) and which makes provision for—
    (a)   testing the competence of those seeking admission to membership of such a body as a condition for such admission; and
    (b)   imposing and maintaining professional and ethical standards for its members, as well as imposing sanctions for non-compliance with those standards.]

[1253F]

NOTES
Commencement: 26 December 2007.
Inserted as noted to s 21C at **[1253A]**.

22 Penalties

A person guilty of an offence under any of sections 15 to 18 shall be liable—
    (a)   on conviction on indictment, to imprisonment for a term not exceeding 14 years, to a fine or to both, or
    (b)   on summary conviction, to imprisonment for a term not exceeding six months, to a fine not exceeding the statutory maximum or to both.

[1254]

[22A Meaning of "employment"

In sections 19 to 21B—
    (a)   "employment" means any employment (whether paid or unpaid) and includes—
        (i)   work under a contract for services or as an office-holder,
        (ii)   work experience provided pursuant to a training course or programme or in the course of training for employment, and
        (iii)   voluntary work;
    (b)   "employer" has a corresponding meaning.]

[1254A]

NOTES
Commencement: 16 February 2009.
Inserted by the Counter-Terrorism Act 2008, s 77(1), (3), as from 16 February 2009.
Note that s 77(4) of the 2008 Act provides that in so far as this insertion extends any provision of ss 19–21B of this Act involving belief or suspicion to cases to which that provision did not previously apply, that provision applies where the belief or suspicion is held after s 77(3) comes into force even if based on information that came to the person's attention before that subsection was in force. In any such case, ss 19(2), 21(3) and 21A(4) of this Act (duty to make disclosure as soon as is reasonably practicable) are to be read as requiring the person to act as soon as is reasonably practicable after s 77(3) comes into force.

23 Forfeiture

(1) The court by or before which a person is convicted of an offence under any of sections 15 to 18 may make a forfeiture order in accordance with the provisions of this section.

(2)   Where a person is convicted of an offence under section 15(1) or (2) or 16 the court may order the forfeiture of any money or other property—

(a)   which, at the time of the offence, he had in his possession or under his control, and

(b)   which, at that time, he intended should be used, or had reasonable cause to suspect might be used, for the purposes of terrorism.

(3)   Where a person is convicted of an offence under section 15(3) the court may order the forfeiture of any money or other property—

(a)   which, at the time of the offence, he had in his possession or under his control, and

(b)   which, at that time, he knew or had reasonable cause to suspect would or might be used for the purposes of terrorism.

(4)   Where a person is convicted of an offence under section 17 the court may order the forfeiture of the money or other property—

(a)   to which the arrangement in question related, and

(b)   which, at the time of the offence, he knew or had reasonable cause to suspect would or might be used for the purposes of terrorism.

(5)   Where a person is convicted of an offence under section 18 the court may order the forfeiture of the money or other property to which the arrangement in question related.

(6)   Where a person is convicted of an offence under any of sections 15 to 18, the court may order the forfeiture of any money or other property which wholly or partly, and directly or indirectly, is received by any person as a payment or other reward in connection with the commission of the offence.

(7)   Where a person other than the convicted person claims to be the owner of or otherwise interested in anything which can be forfeited by an order under this section, the court shall give him an opportunity to be heard before making an order.

(8)   A court in Scotland shall not make an order under this section except on the application of the prosecutor—

(a)   in proceedings on indictment, when he moves for sentence, and

(b)   in summary proceedings, before the court convicts the accused,

and for the purposes of any appeal or review, an order under this section made by a court in Scotland is a sentence.

(9)   Schedule 4 (which makes further provision in relation to forfeiture orders under this section) shall have effect.

[1255]

NOTES

Substituted by the Counter-Terrorism Act 2008, s 34, as from a day to be appointed, as follows—

"*Forfeiture*

23   Forfeiture: terrorist property offences

(1)   The court by or before which a person is convicted of an offence under any of sections 15 to 18 may make a forfeiture order in accordance with the provisions of this section.

(2)   Where a person is convicted of an offence under section 15(1) or (2) or 16, the court may order the forfeiture of any money or other property which, at the time of the offence, the person had in their possession or under their control and which—

(a)   had been used for the purposes of terrorism, or

(b)   they intended should be used, or had reasonable cause to suspect might be used, for those purposes.

(3)   Where a person is convicted of an offence under section 15(3) the court may order the forfeiture of any money or other property which, at the time of the offence, the person had in their possession or under their control and which—

(a)   had been used for the purposes of terrorism, or

(b)   which, at that time, they knew or had reasonable cause to suspect would or might be used for those purposes.

(4)   Where a person is convicted of an offence under section 17 or 18 the court may order the forfeiture of any money or other property which, at the time of the offence, the person had in their possession or under their control and which—

(a)   had been used for the purposes of terrorism, or

(b)   was, at that time, intended by them to be used for those purposes.

(5)   Where a person is convicted of an offence under section 17 the court may order the forfeiture of the money or other property to which the arrangement in question related, and which—

(a)   had been used for the purposes of terrorism, or

(b)   at the time of the offence, the person knew or had reasonable cause to suspect would or might be used for those purposes.

(6)   Where a person is convicted of an offence under section 18 the court may order the forfeiture of the money or other property to which the arrangement in question related.

(7)   Where a person is convicted of an offence under any of sections 15 to 18, the court may order the forfeiture of any money or other property which wholly or partly, and directly or indirectly, is received by any person as a payment or other reward in connection with the commission of the offence.".

See further, the Proceeds of Crime Act 2002, s 13, which provides that a court in England and Wales must take account of a confiscation order made under s 6 of the 2002 Act before making a forfeiture order under this section. See also, in relation to Scotland, s 97 of the 2002 Act and, in relation to Northern Ireland, s 163 of that Act.

[23A Forfeiture: other terrorism offences and offences with a terrorist connection

(1) The court by or before which a person is convicted of an offence to which this section applies may order the forfeiture of any money or other property in relation to which the following conditions are met—
  (a) that it was, at the time of the offence, in the possession or control of the person convicted; and
  (b) that—
      (i) it had been used for the purposes of terrorism,
      (ii) it was intended by that person that it should be used for the purposes of terrorism, or
      (iii) the court believes that it will be used for the purposes of terrorism unless forfeited.

(2) This section applies to an offence under—
  (a) any of the following provisions of this Act—
      section 54 (weapons training);
      section 57, 58 or 58A (possessing things and collecting information for the purposes of terrorism);
      section 59, 60 or 61 (inciting terrorism outside the United Kingdom);
  (b) any of the following provisions of Part 1 of the Terrorism Act 2006 (c 11)—
      section 2 (dissemination of terrorist publications);
      section 5 (preparation of terrorist acts);
      section 6 (training for terrorism);
      sections 9 to 11 (offences involving radioactive devices or materials).

(3) This section applies to any ancillary offence (as defined in section 94 of the Counter-Terrorism Act 2008) in relation to an offence listed in subsection (2).

(4) This section also applies to an offence specified in Schedule 2 to the Counter-Terrorism Act 2008 (offences where terrorist connection to be considered) as to which—
  (a) in England and Wales, the court dealing with the offence has determined, in accordance with section 30 of that Act, that the offence has a terrorist connection;
  (b) in Scotland, it has been proved, in accordance with section 31 of that Act, that the offence has a terrorist connection.

(5) The Secretary of State may by order amend subsection (2).

(6) An order adding an offence to subsection (2) applies only in relation to offences committed after the order comes into force.]

[1255A]

NOTES
Commencement: to be appointed.
Inserted by the Counter-Terrorism Act 2008, s 35(1), as from a day to be appointed.

[23B Forfeiture: supplementary provisions

(1) Before making an order under section 23 or 23A, a court must give an opportunity to be heard to any person, other than the convicted person, who claims to be the owner or otherwise interested in anything which can be forfeited under that section.

(2) In considering whether to make an order under section 23 or 23A in respect of any property, a court shall have regard to—
  (a) the value of the property, and
  (b) the likely financial and other effects on the convicted person of the making of the order (taken together with any other order that the court contemplates making).

(3) A court in Scotland must not make an order under section 23 or 23A except on the application of the prosecutor—
  (a) in proceedings on indictment, when the prosecutor moves for sentence, and
  (b) in summary proceedings, before the court sentences the accused;
and for the purposes of any appeal or review, an order under either of those sections made by a court in Scotland is a sentence.

(4) Schedule 4 makes further provision in relation to forfeiture orders under section 23 or 23A.]

[1255B]

NOTES
Commencement: to be appointed.
Inserted by the Counter-Terrorism Act 2008, s 36, as from a day to be appointed.

PART IV
TERRORIST INVESTIGATIONS

Information and evidence

38 Financial information

Schedule 6 (financial information) shall have effect.

[1256]

[38A Account monitoring orders

Schedule 6A (account monitoring orders) shall have effect.]

[1257]

NOTES
Inserted by the Anti-terrorism, Crime and Security Act 2001, s 3, Sch 2, Pt 1, para 1(1), (2), as from 20 December 2001.

PART VI
MISCELLANEOUS

Terrorist bombing and finance offences

63 Terrorist finance: jurisdiction

(1) If—
    (a) a person does anything outside the United Kingdom, and
    (b) his action would have constituted the commission of an offence under any of sections 15 to 18 if it had been done in the United Kingdom,
he shall be guilty of the offence.

(2) For the purposes of subsection (1)(b), section 18(1)(b) shall be read as if for "the jurisdiction" there were substituted "a jurisdiction".

[1258]–[1260A]

(Pt VII (Northern Ireland): certain sections in Pt VII (ie, ss 65, 103) were reproduced in previous editions of this Handbook. By virtue of s 112 of this Act (as originally enacted) Pt VII would expire on 18 February 2002 unless continued in force for a specified period not exceeding twelve months. Various Orders were made under s 112 section extending the operation of Pt VIII to 18 February 2006, and the Terrorism (Northern Ireland) Act 2006, s 1, further provided that Pt VII shall continue in force until 31 July 2007. No provision was made to extend the operation of this Part beyond 31 July 2007 and, accordingly, this Part (including Sch 9 to this Act) ceased to have effect on that date.)

PART VIII
GENERAL

120A *(S 120A of this Act (as inserted by the Terrorism Act 2006, s 37(3), as from 13 April 2006) made, inter alia, further provision with regard to s 103. Following the expiry of that section (see the note above) s 120A is now outside the scope of this work.)*

121 Interpretation

In this Act—
    "act" and "action" include omission,
    "article" includes substance and any other thing,

             .....

    ["customs officer" means an officer of Revenue and Customs,]
    "dwelling" means a building or part of a building used as a dwelling, and a vehicle which is habitually stationary and which is used as a dwelling,
    "explosive" means—
        (a) an article or substance manufactured for the purpose of producing a practical effect by explosion,
        (b) materials for making an article or substance within paragraph (a),
        (c) anything used or intended to be used for causing or assisting in causing an explosion, and

PART II
OTHER ACTS

(d)   a part of anything within paragraph (a) or (c),

"firearm" includes an air gun or air pistol,

"immigration officer" means a person appointed as an immigration officer under paragraph 1 of Schedule 2 to the Immigration Act 1971,

"the Islands" means the Channel Islands and the Isle of Man,

"organisation" includes any association or combination of persons,

[.....]

"premises"[, except in section 63D,] includes any place and in particular includes—

    (a)   a vehicle,

    (b)   an offshore installation within the meaning given in section 44 of the Petroleum Act 1998, and

    (c)   a tent or moveable structure,

"property" includes property wherever situated and whether real or personal, heritable or moveable, and things in action and other intangible or incorporeal property,

"public place" means a place to which members of the public have or are permitted to have access, whether or not for payment,

"road" has the same meaning as in the Road Traffic Act 1988 (in relation to England and Wales), the Roads (Scotland) Act 1984 (in relation to Scotland) and the Road Traffic Regulation (Northern Ireland) Order 1997 (in relation to Northern Ireland), and includes part of a road, and

"vehicle", except in sections 48 to 52 and Schedule 7, includes an aircraft, hovercraft, train or vessel.

[1261]

NOTES

Definition "British Transport Police Force" (omitted) originally inserted by the Anti-terrorism, Crime and Security Act 2001, s 101, Sch 7, para 29, as from 14 December 2001, and repealed by virtue of the Railways and Transport Safety Act 2003, s 73, Sch 5, para 4, as from 1 July 2004.

Definition "customs officer" substituted by the Commissioners for Revenue and Customs Act 2005, s 50, Sch 4, para 78, as from 18 April 2005.

Definition "policed premises" (omitted) originally inserted by the Anti-terrorism, Crime and Security Act 2001, s 101, Sch 7, para 32, as from 14 December 2001, and repealed by the British Transport Police (Transitional and Consequential Provisions) Order 2004, SI 2004/1573, art 12(6)(d), as from 1 July 2004.

In definition "premises" words in square brackets inserted by the Crime (International Co-operation) Act 2003, s 91(1), Sch 5, paras 75, 76, as from 26 April 2004.

128 Commencement

The preceding provisions of this Act, apart from sections 2(1)(b) and (2) and 118 and Schedule 1, shall come into force in accordance with provision made by the Secretary of State by order.

[1262]

NOTES

Orders: the Terrorism Act 2000 (Commencement No 1) Order 2000, SI 2000/2800; the Terrorism Act 2000 (Commencement No 2) Order 2000, SI 2000/2944; the Terrorism Act 2000 (Commencement No 3) Order 2001, SI 2001/421.

130 Extent

(1)   Subject to subsections (2) to (6), this Act extends to the whole of the United Kingdom.

(2)   *(Outside the scope of this work.)*

(3)   The following shall extend to Northern Ireland only—

    (a)   *(outside the scope of this work)*;

    (b)   Part VII.

(4)–(6)   *(Outside the scope of this work.)*

[1263]

131 Short title

This Act may be cited as the Terrorism Act 2000.

[1264]

SCHEDULES

[SCHEDULE 3A
REGULATED SECTOR AND SUPERVISORY AUTHORITIES

[PART 1
REGULATED SECTOR

Business in the Regulated Sector

1.—(1)   A business is in the regulated sector to the extent that it consists of—
   (a)   the acceptance by a credit institution of deposits or other repayable funds from the public, or the granting by a credit institution of credits for its own account;
   (b)   the carrying on of one or more of the activities listed in points 2 to 12 and 14 of Annex 1 to the Banking Consolidation Directive by an undertaking other than—
      (i)   a credit institution; or
      (ii)   an undertaking whose only listed activity is trading for own account in one or more of the products listed in point 7 of Annex 1 to the Banking Consolidation Directive and which does not act on behalf of a customer (that is, a third party which is not a member of the same group as the undertaking);
   (c)   the carrying on of activities covered by the Life Assurance Consolidation Directive by an insurance company authorised in accordance with that Directive;
   (d)   the provision of investment services or the performance of investment activities by a person (other than a person falling within Article 2 of the Markets in Financial Instruments Directive) whose regular occupation or business is the provision to other persons of an investment service or the performance of an investment activity on a professional basis;
   (e)   the marketing or other offering of units or shares by a collective investment undertaking;
   (f)   the activities of an insurance intermediary as defined in Article 2(5) of the Insurance Mediation Directive, other than a tied insurance intermediary as mentioned in Article 2(7) of that Directive, in respect of contracts of long-term insurance within the meaning given by article 3(1) of, and Part II of Schedule 1 to, the Financial Services and Markets Act 2000 (Regulated Activities) Order 2001;
   (g)   the carrying on of any of the activities mentioned in paragraphs (b) to (f) by a branch located in an EEA State of a person referred to in those paragraphs (or of an equivalent person in any other State), wherever its head office is located;
   (h)   the activities of the National Savings Bank;
   (i)   any activity carried on for the purpose of raising money authorised to be raised under the National Loans Act 1968 under the auspices of the Director of Savings;
   [(j)   the carrying on of statutory audit work within the meaning of section 1210 of the Companies Act 2006 (meaning of "statutory auditor" etc) by any firm or individual who is a statutory auditor within the meaning of Part 42 of that Act (statutory auditors);]
   (k)   the activities of a person appointed to act as an insolvency practitioner within the meaning of section 388 of the Insolvency Act 1986 (meaning of "act as insolvency practitioner") or article 3 of the Insolvency (Northern Ireland) Order 1989;
   (l)   the provision to other persons of accountancy services by a firm or sole practitioner who by way of business provides such services to other persons;
   (m)   the provision of advice about the tax affairs of other persons by a firm or sole practitioner who by way of business provides advice about the tax affairs of other persons;
   (n)   the participation in financial or real property transactions concerning—
      (i)   the buying and selling of real property (or, in Scotland, heritable property) or business entities;
      (ii)   the managing of client money, securities or other assets;
      (iii)   the opening or management of bank, savings or securities accounts;
      (iv)   the organisation of contributions necessary for the creation, operation or management of companies;
      (v)   the creation, operation or management of trusts, companies or similar structures,
   by a firm or sole practitioner who by way of business provides legal or notarial services to other persons;
   (o)   the provision to other persons by way of business by a firm or sole practitioner of any of the services mentioned in sub-paragraph (4);
   (p)   the carrying on of estate agency work (within the meaning given by section 1 of the Estate Agents Act 1979 (estate agency work)) by a firm or a sole practitioner who carries on, or whose employees carry on, such work;
   (q)   the trading in goods (including dealing as an auctioneer) whenever a transaction involves the receipt of a payment or payments in cash of at least 15,000 euros in total, whether the transaction is executed in a single operation or in several operations which appear to be linked, by a firm or sole trader who by way of business trades in goods;

PART II
OTHER ACTS

    (r)   operating a casino under a casino operating licence (within the meaning given by section 65(2) of the Gambling Act 2005 (nature of licence)).

(2) For the purposes of sub-paragraph (1)(a) and (b) "credit institution" means—
    (a)   a credit institution as defined in Article 4(1)(a) of the Banking Consolidation Directive; or
    (b)   a branch (within the meaning of Article 4(3) of that Directive) located in an EEA state of an institution falling within paragraph (a) (or of an equivalent institution in any other State) wherever its head office is located.

(3) For the purposes of sub-paragraph (1)(n) a person participates in a transaction by assisting in the planning or execution of the transaction or otherwise acting for or on behalf of a client in the transaction.

(4) The services referred to in sub-paragraph (1)(o) are—
    (a)   forming companies or other legal persons;
    (b)   acting, or arranging for another person to act—
        (i)   as a director or secretary of a company;
        (ii)   as a partner of a partnership; or
        (iii)   in a similar position in relation to other legal persons;
    (c)   providing a registered office, business address, correspondence or administrative address or other related services for a company, partnership or any other legal person or arrangement;
    (d)   acting, or arranging for another person to act, as—
        (i)   a trustee of an express trust or similar legal arrangement; or
        (ii)   a nominee shareholder for a person other than a company whose securities are listed on a regulated market.

(5) For the purposes of sub-paragraph (4)(d) "regulated market"—
    (a)   in relation to any EEA State, has the meaning given by point 14 of Article 4(1) of the Markets in Financial Instruments Directive; and
    (b)   in relation to any other State, means a regulated financial market which subjects companies whose securities are admitted to trading to disclosure obligations which are contained in international standards and are equivalent to the specified disclosure obligations.

(6) For the purposes of sub-paragraph (5) "the specified disclosure obligations" means disclosure requirements consistent with—
    (a)   Article 6(1) to (4) of Directive 2003/6/EC of the European Parliament and of the Council of 28th January 2003 on insider dealing and market manipulation;
    (b)   Articles 3, 5, 7, 8, 10, 14 and 16 of Directive 2003/71/EC of the European Parliament and of the Council of 4th November 2003 on the prospectuses to be published when securities are offered to the public or admitted to trading;
    (c)   Articles 4 to 6, 14, 16 to 19 and 30 of Directive 2004/109/EC of the European Parliament and of the Council of 15th December 2004 relating to the harmonisation of transparency requirements in relation to information about issuers whose securities are admitted to trading on a regulated market; or
    (d)   Community legislation made under the provisions mentioned in paragraphs (a) to (c).

(7) For the purposes of sub-paragraph (1)(j) and (l) to (q) "firm" means any entity, whether or not a legal person, that is not an individual and includes a body corporate and a partnership or other unincorporated association.

(8) For the purposes of sub-paragraph (1)(q) "cash" means notes, coins or travellers' cheques in any currency.

Excluded Activities

2.—(1) A business is not in the regulated sector to the extent that it consists of—
    (a)   the issuing of withdrawable share capital within the limit set by section 6 of the Industrial and Provident Societies Act 1965 (maximum shareholding in society), or the acceptance of deposits from the public within the limit set by section 7(3) of that Act (carrying on of banking by societies), by a society registered under that Act;
    (b)   the issuing of withdrawable share capital within the limit set by section 6 of the Industrial and Provident Societies Act (Northern Ireland) 1969 (maximum shareholding in society), or the acceptance of deposits from the public within the limit set by section 7(3) of that Act (carrying on of banking by societies), by a society registered under that Act;
    (c)   the carrying on of any activity in respect of which a person who is (or falls within a class of persons) specified in any of paragraphs 2 to 23, 25 to 38 or 40 to 49 of the Schedule to the Financial Services and Markets Act 2000 (Exemption) Order 2001 is exempt;
    (d)   the exercise of the functions specified in section 45 of the Financial Services Act 1986

(miscellaneous exemptions) by a person who was an exempted person for the purposes of that section immediately before its repeal;

(e) the engaging in financial activity which fulfils all of the conditions set out in paragraphs (a) to (g) of sub-paragraph (3) of this paragraph by a person whose main activity is that of a high value dealer; or

(f) the preparation of a home information pack (within the meaning of Part 5 of the Housing Act 2004 (home information packs)) or a document or information for inclusion in a home information pack.

(2) For the purposes of sub-paragraph (1)(e) a "high value dealer" means a person mentioned in paragraph 1(1)(q) when carrying on the activities mentioned in that paragraph.

(3) A business is not in the regulated sector to the extent that it consists of financial activity if—

(a) the person's total annual turnover in respect of the financial activity does not exceed £64,000;

(b) the financial activity is limited in relation to any customer to no more than one transaction exceeding 1,000 euros, whether the transaction is carried out in a single operation, or a series of operations which appear to be linked;

(c) the financial activity does not exceed 5% of the person's total annual turnover;

(d) the financial activity is ancillary to the person's main activity and directly related to that activity;

(e) the financial activity is not the transmission or remittance of money (or any representation of monetary value) by any means;

(f) the main activity of the person carrying on the financial activity is not an activity mentioned in paragraph 1(1)(a) to (p) or (r); and

(g) the financial activity is provided only to customers of the person's main activity and is not offered to the public.

(4) A business is not in the regulated sector if it is carried on by—

(a) the Auditor General for Scotland;

(b) the Auditor General for Wales;

(c) the Bank of England;

(d) the Comptroller and Auditor General;

(e) the Comptroller and Auditor General for Northern Ireland;

(f) the Official Solicitor to the Supreme Court, when acting as trustee in his official capacity; or

(g) the Treasury Solicitor.

Interpretation

3.—(1) In this Part—

"the Banking Consolidation Directive" means directive 2006/48/EC of the European Parliament and of the Council of 14th June 2006 relating to the taking up and pursuit of the business of credit institutions;

"the Insurance Mediation Directive" means directive 2002/92/EC of the European Parliament and of the Council of 9th December 2002 on insurance mediation;

"the Life Assurance Consolidation Directive" means directive 2002/83/EC of the European Parliament and of the Council of 5th November 2002 concerning life assurance; and

"the Markets in Financial Instruments Directive" means directive 2004/39/EC of the European Parliament and of the Council of 12th April 2004 on markets in financial instruments.

(2) In this Part references to amounts in euros include references to equivalent amounts in another currency.

(3) Terms used in this Part and in the Banking Consolidation Directive or the Markets in Financial Instruments Directive have the same meaning in this Part as in those Directives.]]

[1265]

NOTES

Commencement: 15 December 2007.

Inserted by the Anti-terrorism, Crime and Security Act 2001, s 3, Sch 2, Pt 3, para 5(1), (6), as from 20 December 2001.

Substituted by the Terrorism Act 2000 (Business in the Regulated Sector and Supervisory Authorities) Order 2007, SI 2007/3288, art 2, as from 15 December 2007.

Para 1: sub-para (1)(j) substituted by the Companies Act 2006 (Consequential Amendments etc) Order 2008, SI 2008/948, art 3(1), Sch 1, Pt 1, para 25, as from 6 April 2008 (for savings see art 6(4) of the 2008 Order which provides that where by virtue of any transitional provision, a provision of the Companies Act 2006 has effect only (a) on or after a specified date, or (b) in relation to matters occurring or arising on or after a specified date, any amendment substituting or inserting a reference to that provision has effect correspondingly). The original sub-paragraph read as follows—

"(j)   the provision of audit services by a person who is eligible for appointment as a company auditor under section 25 of the Companies Act 1989 (eligibility for appointment) or article 28 of the Companies (Northern Ireland) Order 1990;".

[PART 2
SUPERVISORY AUTHORITIES

4.—(1)   The following bodies are supervisory authorities—
(a)   the Commissioners for Her Majesty's Revenue and Customs;
(b)   the Department of Enterprise, Trade and Investment in Northern Ireland;
(c)   the Financial Services Authority;
(d)   the Gambling Commission;
(e)   the Office of Fair Trading;
(f)   the Secretary of State; and
(g)   the professional bodies listed in sub-paragraph (2).

(2)   The professional bodies referred to in sub-paragraph (1)(g) are—
(a)   the Association of Accounting Technicians;
(b)   the Association of Chartered Certified Accountants;
(c)   the Association of International Accountants;
(d)   the Association of Taxation Technicians;
(e)   the Chartered Institute of Management Accountants;
(f)   the Chartered Institute of Public Finance and Accountancy;
(g)   the Chartered Institute of Taxation;
(h)   the Council for Licensed Conveyancers;
(i)   the Faculty of Advocates;
(j)   the Faculty Office of the Archbishop of Canterbury;
(k)   the General Council of the Bar;
(l)   the General Council of the Bar of Northern Ireland;
(m)   the Insolvency Practitioners Association;
(n)   the Institute of Certified Bookkeepers;
(o)   the Institute of Chartered Accountants in England and Wales;
(p)   the Institute of Chartered Accountants in Ireland;
(q)   the Institute of Chartered Accountants of Scotland;
(r)   the Institute of Financial Accountants;
(s)   the International Association of Book-keepers;
(t)   the Law Society;
(u)   the Law Society for Northern Ireland; and
(v)   the Law Society of Scotland.]

[1266]

NOTES
Inserted as noted to Part 1 at **[1265]**.
Substituted by the Terrorism Act 2000 (Business in the Regulated Sector and Supervisory Authorities) Order 2007, SI 2007/3288, art 2, as from 15 December 2007.

[PART 3
POWER TO AMEND

5.—(1)   The Treasury may by order amend Part 1 or 2 of this Schedule.

(2)   An order under sub-paragraph (1) must be made by statutory instrument subject to annulment in pursuance of a resolution of either House of Parliament.]

[1267]

NOTES
Inserted as noted to Part 1 at **[1265]**.
Orders: the Terrorism Act 2000 (Business in the Regulated Sector and Supervisory Authorities) Order 2007, SI 2007/3288 (which supersedes all other amending SIs made under para 5).

SCHEDULE 4
FORFEITURE ORDERS

Section 23

PART I
ENGLAND AND WALES

Interpretation

1.   In this Part of this Schedule—

"forfeiture order" means an order made by a court in England and Wales under section 23 [or 23A], and

"forfeited property" means the money or other property to which a forfeiture order applies;

["relevant offence" means—

    (a)   an offence under any of sections 15 to 18,

    (b)   an offence to which section 23A applies, or

    (c)   in relation to a restraint order, any offence specified in Schedule 2 to the Counter-Terrorism Act 2008 (offences where terrorist connection to be considered)].

Implementation of forfeiture orders

2.—(1)   Where a court in England and Wales makes a forfeiture order it may make such other provision as appears to it to be necessary for giving effect to the order, and in particular it may—

    (a)   require any of the forfeited property to be paid or handed over to the proper officer or to a constable designated for the purpose by the chief officer of police of a police force specified in the order;

    (b)   direct any of the forfeited property other than money or land to be sold or otherwise disposed of in such manner as the court may direct and the proceeds (if any) to be paid to the proper officer;

    (c)   appoint a receiver to take possession, subject to such conditions and exceptions as may be specified by the court, of any of the forfeited property, to realise it in such manner as the court may direct and to pay the proceeds to the proper officer;

    (d)   direct a specified part of any forfeited money, or of the proceeds of the sale, disposal or realisation of any forfeited property, to be paid by the proper officer to a specified person falling within *section 23(7)*.

(2)   A forfeiture order shall not come into force until there is no further possibility of it being varied, or set aside, on appeal (disregarding any power of a court to grant leave to appeal out of time).

(3)   In sub-paragraph (1)(b) and (d) a reference to the proceeds of the sale, disposal or realisation of property is a reference to the proceeds after deduction of the costs of sale, disposal or realisation.

(4)   Section 140 of the Magistrates' Courts Act 1980 (disposal of non-pecuniary forfeitures) shall not apply.

3.—(1)   A receiver appointed under paragraph 2 shall be entitled to be paid his remuneration and expenses by the proper officer out of the proceeds of the property realised by the receiver and paid to the proper officer under paragraph 2(1)(c).

(2)   If and so far as those proceeds are insufficient, the receiver shall be entitled to be paid his remuneration and expenses by the prosecutor.

(3)   A receiver appointed under paragraph 2 shall not be liable to any person in respect of any loss or damage resulting from action—

    (a)   which he takes in relation to property which is not forfeited property, but which he reasonably believes to be forfeited property,

    (b)   which he would be entitled to take if the property were forfeited property, and

    (c)   which he reasonably believes that he is entitled to take because of his belief that the property is forfeited property.

(4)   Sub-paragraph (3) does not apply in so far as the loss or damage is caused by the receiver's negligence.

4.—(1)   In paragraphs 2 and 3 "the proper officer" means—

    (a)   where the forfeiture order is made by a magistrates' court, the [designated officer] for that court,

    (b)   where the forfeiture order is made by the Crown Court and the defendant was committed to the Crown Court by a magistrates' court, the [designated officer] for the magistrates' court, and

    (c)   where the forfeiture order is made by the Crown Court and the proceedings were instituted by a bill of indictment preferred by virtue of section 2(2)(b) of the Administration of Justice (Miscellaneous Provisions) Act 1933, the [designated officer] for the magistrates' court for the place where the trial took place.

(2)   The proper officer shall issue a certificate in respect of a forfeiture order if an application is made by—

    (a)   the prosecutor in the proceedings in which the forfeiture order was made,

    (b)   the defendant in those proceedings, or

    (c)   a person whom the court heard under *section 23(7)* before making the order.

(3)   The certificate shall state the extent (if any) to which, at the date of the certificate, effect has been given to the forfeiture order.

[Application of proceeds to compensate victims

4A.—(1)   Where a court makes a forfeiture order in a case where—
   (a)   the offender has been convicted of an offence that has resulted in a person suffering personal injury, loss or damage, or
   (b)   any such offence is taken into consideration by the court in determining sentence,
the court may also order that an amount not exceeding a sum specified by the court is to be paid to that person out of the proceeds of the forfeiture.

(2)   For this purpose the proceeds of the forfeiture means the aggregate amount of—
   (a)   any forfeited money, and
   (b)   the proceeds of the sale, disposal or realisation of any forfeited property, after deduction of the costs of the sale, disposal or realisation,
reduced by the amount of any payment under paragraph 2(1)(d) or 3(1).

(3)   The court may make an order under this paragraph only if it is satisfied that but for the inadequacy of the offender's means it would have made a compensation order under section 130 of the Powers of Criminal Courts (Sentencing) Act 2000 under which the offender would have been required to pay compensation of an amount not less than the specified amount.]

Restraint orders

5.—(1)   The High Court may make a restraint order under this paragraph where—
   (a)   proceedings have been instituted in England and Wales for *an offence under any of sections 15 to 18*,
   (b)   the proceedings have not been concluded,
   (c)   an application for a restraint order is made to the High Court by the prosecutor, and
   (d)   a forfeiture order has been made, or it appears to the High Court that a forfeiture order may be made, in the proceedings for the offence.

[(2)   The High Court may also make a restraint order under this paragraph where—
   (a)   a criminal investigation has been started in England and Wales with regard to *an offence under any of sections 15 to 18*,
   (b)   an application for a restraint order is made to the High Court by the person who the High Court is satisfied will have the conduct of any proceedings for the offence, and
   (c)   it appears to the High Court that a forfeiture order may be made in any proceedings for the offence.]

(3)   A restraint order prohibits a person to whom notice of it is given, subject to any conditions and exceptions specified in the order, from dealing with property in respect of which a forfeiture order has been or could be made in [any proceedings] referred to in sub-paragraph (1) or (2).

(4)   An application for a restraint order may be made to a judge in chambers without notice.

(5)   In this paragraph a reference to dealing with property includes a reference to removing the property from Great Britain.

[(6)   In this paragraph "criminal investigation" means an investigation which police officers or other persons have a duty to conduct with a view to it being ascertained whether a person should be charged with an offence.]

6.—(1)   A restraint order shall provide for notice of it to be given to any person affected by the order.

(2)   A restraint order may be discharged or varied by the High Court on the application of a person affected by it.

[(3)   A restraint order made under paragraph 5(1) shall in particular be discharged on an application under sub-paragraph (2) if the proceedings for the offence have been concluded.

(4)   A restraint order made under paragraph 5(2) shall in particular be discharged on an application under sub-paragraph (2)—
   (a)   if no proceedings in respect of *offences under any of sections 15 to 18* are instituted within such time as the High Court considers reasonable, and
   (b)   if all proceedings in respect of *offences under any of sections 15 to 18* have been concluded.]

7.—(1)   A constable may seize any property subject to a restraint order for the purpose of preventing it from being removed from Great Britain.

(2)   Property seized under this paragraph shall be dealt with in accordance with the High Court's directions.

8.—(1)   The Land Charges Act 1972 and the [Land Registration Act 2002]—
   (a)   shall apply in relation to restraint orders as they apply in relation to orders affecting land made by the court for the purpose of enforcing judgments or recognizances[, except that no notice may be entered in the register of title under the Land Registration Act 2002 in respect of such orders], and

(b)   shall apply in relation to applications for restraint orders as they apply in relation to other pending land actions.

(2), (3)   ...

Compensation

9.—(1)   This paragraph applies where a restraint order is discharged under [paragraph 6(4)(a)].

(2)   This paragraph also applies where a forfeiture order or a restraint order is made in or in relation to proceedings for *an offence under any of sections 15 to 18* which—
- (a)   do not result in conviction for *an offence under any of those sections,*
- (b)   result in conviction for *an offence under any of those sections* in respect of which the person convicted is subsequently pardoned by Her Majesty, or
- (c)   result in conviction for *an offence under any of those sections* which is subsequently quashed.

(3)   A person who had an interest in any property which was subject to the order may apply to the High Court for compensation.

(4)   The High Court may order compensation to be paid to the applicant if satisfied—
- (a)   that there was a serious default on the part of a person concerned in the investigation or prosecution of the offence,
- (b)   that the person in default was or was acting as a member of a police force, or was a member of the Crown Prosecution Service or was acting on behalf of the Service,
- (c)   that the applicant has suffered loss in consequence of anything done in relation to the property by or in pursuance of the forfeiture order or restraint order, and
- (d)   that, having regard to all the circumstances, it is appropriate to order compensation to be paid.

(5)   The High Court shall not order compensation to be paid where it appears to it that proceedings for the offence would have been instituted even if the serious default had not occurred.

(6)   Compensation payable under this paragraph shall be paid—
- (a)   where the person in default was or was acting as a member of a police force, out of the police fund out of which the expenses of that police force are met, and
- (b)   where the person in default was a member of the Crown Prosecution Service, or was acting on behalf of the Service, by the Director of Public Prosecutions.

10.—(1)   This paragraph applies where—
- (a)   a forfeiture order or a restraint order is made in or in relation to proceedings for *an offence under any of sections 15 to 18,* and
- (b)   the proceedings result in a conviction which is subsequently quashed on an appeal under section 7(2) or (5).

(2)   A person who had an interest in any property which was subject to the order may apply to the High Court for compensation.

(3)   The High Court may order compensation to be paid to the applicant if satisfied—
- (a)   that the applicant has suffered loss in consequence of anything done in relation to the property by or in pursuance of the forfeiture order or restraint order, and
- (b)   that, having regard to all the circumstances, it is appropriate to order compensation to be paid.

(4)   Compensation payable under this paragraph shall be paid by the Secretary of State.

Proceedings for an offence: timing

11.—(1)   For the purposes of this Part of this Schedule proceedings for an offence are instituted—
- (a)   when a justice of the peace issues a summons or warrant under section 1 of the Magistrates' Courts Act 1980 in respect of the offence;
- [(aa)   when a public prosecutor issues a written charge and requisition in respect of the offence;]
- (b)   when a person is charged with the offence after being taken into custody without a warrant;
- (c)   when a bill of indictment charging a person with the offence is preferred by virtue of section 2(2)(b) of the Administration of Justice (Miscellaneous Provisions) Act 1933.

(2)   Where the application of sub-paragraph (1) would result in there being more than one time for the institution of proceedings they shall be taken to be instituted at the earliest of those times.

[(2A)   In sub-paragraph (1) "public prosecutor", "requisition" and "written charge" have the same meaning as in section 29 of the Criminal Justice Act 2003.

(3)   For the purposes of this Part of this Schedule proceedings are concluded—
- (a)   when a forfeiture order has been made in those proceedings and effect has been given to it in respect of all the forfeited property, or

    (b)   when no forfeiture order has been made in those proceedings and there is no further possibility of one being made as a result of an appeal (disregarding any power of a court to grant leave to appeal out of time).

[Domestic and overseas freezing orders

11A.—(1)   This paragraph has effect for the purposes of paragraphs 11B to 11G.

(2)   The relevant Framework Decision means the Framework Decision on the execution in the European Union of orders freezing property or evidence adopted by the Council of the European Union on 22nd July 2003.

(3)   A listed offence means—
    (a)   an offence described in Article 3(2) of the relevant Framework Decision, or
    (b)   a prescribed offence or an offence of a prescribed description.

(4)   An order under sub-paragraph (3)(b) which, for the purposes of paragraph 11D, prescribes an offence or a description of offences may require that the conduct which constitutes the offence or offences would, if it occurred in a part of the United Kingdom, constitute an offence in that part.

(5)   Specified information, in relation to a certificate under paragraph 11B or 11D, means—
    (a)   any information required to be given by the form of certificate annexed to the relevant Framework Decision, or
    (b)   any prescribed information.

(6)   In this paragraph, "prescribed" means prescribed by an order made by the Secretary of State.

(7)   A participating country means—
    (a)   a country other than the United Kingdom which is a member State on a day appointed for the commencement of Schedule 4 to the Crime (International Co-operation) Act 2003, and
    (b)   any other member State designated by an order made by the Secretary of State.

(8)   "Country" includes territory.

(9)   Section 14(2)(a) applies for the purposes of determining what are the proceeds of the commission of an offence.

Domestic freezing orders: certification

11B.—(1)   If any of the property to which an application for a restraint order relates is property in a participating country, the applicant may ask the High Court to make a certificate under this paragraph.

(2)   The High Court may make a certificate under this paragraph if—
    (a)   it makes a restraint order in relation to property in the participating country, and
    (b)   it is satisfied that there is a good arguable case that the property is likely to be used for the purposes of a listed offence or is the proceeds of the commission of a listed offence.

(3)   A certificate under this paragraph is a certificate which—
    (a)   is made for the purposes of the relevant Framework Decision, and
    (b)   gives the specified information.

(4)   If the High Court makes a certificate under this paragraph—
    (a)   the restraint order must provide for notice of the certificate to be given to the person affected by it, and
    (b)   paragraph 6(2) to (4) applies to the certificate as it applies to the restraint order.

Sending domestic freezing orders

11C.—(1)   If a certificate is made under paragraph 11B, the restraint order and the certificate are to be sent to the Secretary of State for forwarding to—
    (a)   a court exercising jurisdiction in the place where the property is situated, or
    (b)   any authority recognised by the government of the participating country as the appropriate authority for receiving orders of that kind.

(2)   The restraint order and the certificate must be accompanied by a forfeiture order, unless the certificate indicates when the court expects a forfeiture order to be sent.

(3)   The certificate must include a translation of it into an appropriate language of the participating country (if that language is not English).

(4)   The certificate must be signed by or on behalf of the court and must include a statement as to the accuracy of the information given in it.

The signature may be an electronic signature.

(5)   If the restraint order and the certificate are not accompanied by a forfeiture order, but a forfeiture order is subsequently made, it is to be sent to the Secretary of State for forwarding as mentioned in sub-paragraph (1).

Overseas freezing orders

11D.—(1)   Paragraph 11E applies where an overseas freezing order made by an appropriate court or authority in a participating country is received by the Secretary of State from the court or authority which made or confirmed the order.

(2)   An overseas freezing order is an order prohibiting dealing with property—
   (a)   which is in the United Kingdom,
   (b)   which the appropriate court or authority considers is likely to be used for the purposes of a listed offence or is the proceeds of the commission of such an offence, and
   (c)   in respect of which an order has been or may be made by a court exercising criminal jurisdiction in the participating country for the forfeiture of the property,
and in respect of which the following requirements of this paragraph are met.

(3)   The action which the appropriate court or authority considered would constitute or, as the case may be, constituted the listed offence is action done as an act of terrorism or for the purposes of terrorism.

(4)   The order must relate to—
   (a)   criminal proceedings instituted in the participating country, or
   (b)   a criminal investigation being carried on there.

(5)   The order must be accompanied by a certificate which gives the specified information; but a certificate may be treated as giving any specified information which is not given in it if the Secretary of State has the information in question.

(6)   The certificate must—
   (a)   be signed by or on behalf of the court or authority which made or confirmed the order,
   (b)   include a statement as to the accuracy of the information given in it,
   (c)   if it is not in English, include a translation of it into English (or, if appropriate, Welsh).
The signature may be an electronic signature.

(7)   The order must be accompanied by an order made by a court exercising criminal jurisdiction in that country for the forfeiture of the property, unless the certificate indicates when such an order is expected to be sent.

(8)   An appropriate court or authority in a participating country in relation to an overseas freezing order is—
   (a)   a court exercising criminal jurisdiction in the country,
   (b)   a prosecuting authority in the country,
   (c)   any other authority in the country which appears to the Secretary of State to have the function of making such orders.

(9)   References in paragraphs 11E to 11G to an overseas freezing order include its accompanying certificate.

Enforcement of overseas freezing orders

11E.—(1)   Where this paragraph applies the Secretary of State must send a copy of the overseas freezing order to the High Court and to the Director of Public Prosecutions.

(2)   The court is to consider the overseas freezing order on its own initiative within a period prescribed by rules of court.

(3)   Before giving effect to the overseas freezing order, the court must give the Director an opportunity to be heard.

(4)   The court may decide not to give effect to the overseas freezing order only if, in its opinion, giving effect to it would be incompatible with any of the Convention rights (within the meaning of the Human Rights Act 1998).

11F.   The High Court may postpone giving effect to an overseas freezing order in respect of any property—
   (a)   in order to avoid prejudicing a criminal investigation which is taking place in the United Kingdom, or
   (b)   if, under an order made by a court in criminal proceedings in the United Kingdom, the property may not be dealt with.

11G.—(1)   Where the High Court decides to give effect to an overseas freezing order, it must—
   (a)   register the order in that court,
   (b)   provide for notice of the registration to be given to any person affected by it.

(2)   For the purpose of enforcing an overseas freezing order registered in the High Court, the order is to have effect as if it were an order made by that court.

(3)   Paragraph 7 applies to an overseas freezing order registered in the High Court as it applies to a restraint order under paragraph 5.

(4)   The High Court may cancel the registration of the order, or vary the property to which the order applies, on an application by the Director of Public Prosecutions or any other person affected by it, if or to the extent that—
  (a)   the court is of the opinion mentioned in paragraph 11E(4), or
  (b)   the court is of the opinion that the order has ceased to have effect in the participating country.

(5)   Her Majesty may by Order in Council make further provision for the enforcement in England and Wales of registered overseas freezing orders.

(6)   An Order in Council under this paragraph—
  (a)   may make different provision for different cases,
  (b)   is not to be made unless a draft of it has been laid before and approved by resolution of each House of Parliament.]

Enforcement of orders made elsewhere in the British Islands

12.   In the following provisions of this Part of this Schedule—
  "a Scottish order" means—
  (a)   an order made in Scotland under section 23 [or 23A] ("a Scottish forfeiture order"),
  (b)   an order made under paragraph 18 ("a Scottish restraint order"), or
  (c)   an order made under any other provision of Part II of this Schedule in relation to a Scottish forfeiture or restraint order;
  "a Northern Ireland order" means—
  (a)   an order made in Northern Ireland under section 23 [or 23A] ("a Northern Ireland forfeiture order"),
  (b)   an order made under paragraph 33 ("a Northern Ireland restraint order"), or
  (c)   an order made under any other provision of Part III of this Schedule in relation to a Northern Ireland forfeiture or restraint order;
  "an Islands order" means an order made in any of the Islands under a provision of the law of that Island corresponding to—
  (a)   section 23 [or 23A] ("an Islands forfeiture order"),
  (b)   paragraph 5 ("an Islands restraint order"), or
  (c)   any other provision of this Part of this Schedule.

13.—(1)   Subject to the provisions of this paragraph, a Scottish, Northern Ireland or Islands order shall have effect in the law of England and Wales.

(2)   But such an order shall be enforced in England and Wales only in accordance with—
  (a)   the provisions of this paragraph, and
  (b)   any provision made by rules of court as to the manner in which, and the conditions subject to which, such orders are to be enforced there.

(3)   On an application made to it in accordance with rules of court for registration of a Scottish, Northern Ireland or Islands order, the High Court shall direct that the order shall, in accordance with such rules, be registered in that court.

(4)   Rules of court shall also make provision—
  (a)   for cancelling or varying the registration of a Scottish, Northern Ireland or Islands forfeiture order when effect has been given to it, whether in England and Wales or elsewhere, in respect of all or, as the case may be, part of the money or other property to which the order applies;
  (b)   for cancelling or varying the registration of a Scottish, Northern Ireland or Islands restraint order which has been discharged or varied by the court by which it was made.

(5)   If a Scottish, Northern Ireland or Islands forfeiture order is registered under this paragraph the High Court shall have, in relation to that order, the same powers as a court has under paragraph 2(1) to give effect to a forfeiture order made by it and—
  (a)   paragraph 3 shall apply accordingly,
  (b)   any functions of [the designated officer for a magistrates' court] shall be exercised by the appropriate officer of the High Court, and
  (c)   after making any payment required by virtue of paragraph 2(1)(d) or 3, the balance of any sums received by the appropriate officer of the High Court by virtue of an order made under this sub-paragraph shall be paid by him to the Secretary of State.

(6)   If a Scottish, Northern Ireland or Islands restraint order is registered under this paragraph—
  (a)   paragraphs 7 and 8 shall apply as they apply to a restraint order under paragraph 5, and
  (b)   the High Court shall have power to make an order under section 33 of the *Supreme*

Court Act 1981 (extended power to order inspection of property, &c) in relation to proceedings brought or likely to be brought for a Scottish, Northern Ireland or Islands restraint order as if those proceedings had been brought or were likely to be brought in the High Court.

(7)   In addition, if a Scottish, Northern Ireland or Islands order is registered under this paragraph—

(a)   the High Court shall have, in relation to its enforcement, the same power as if the order had originally been made in the High Court,

(b)   proceedings for or with respect to its enforcement may be taken as if the order had originally been made in the High Court, and

(c)   proceedings for or with respect to contravention of such an order, whether before or after such registration, may be taken as if the order had originally been made in the High Court.

(8)   The High Court may also make such orders or do otherwise as seems to it appropriate for the purpose of—

(a)   assisting the achievement in England and Wales of the purposes of a Scottish, Northern Ireland or Islands order, or

(b)   assisting a receiver or other person directed by a Scottish, Northern Ireland or Islands order to sell or otherwise dispose of property.

(9)   The following documents shall be received in evidence in England and Wales without further proof—

(a)   a document purporting to be a copy of a Scottish, Northern Ireland or Islands order and to be certified as such by a proper officer of the court by which it was made, and

(b)   a document purporting to be a certificate for purposes corresponding to those of paragraph 4(2) and (3) and to be certified by a proper officer of the court concerned.

Enforcement of orders made in designated countries

14.—(1)   Her Majesty may by Order in Council make provision for the purpose of enabling the enforcement in England and Wales of external orders.

(2)   An "external order" means an order [(other than an overseas freezing order within the meaning of paragraph 11D)]—

(a)   which is made in a country or territory designated for the purposes of this paragraph by the Order in Council, and

(b)   which makes relevant provision.

(3)   "Relevant provision" means—

(a)   provision for the forfeiture of terrorist property ("an external forfeiture order"), or

(b)   provision prohibiting dealing with property which is subject to an external forfeiture order or in respect of which such an order could be made in proceedings which have been or are to be instituted in the designated country or territory ("an external restraint order").

(4)   An Order in Council under this paragraph may, in particular, include provision—

(a)   which, for the purpose of facilitating the enforcement of any external order that may be made, has effect at times before there is an external order to be enforced;

(b)   for matters corresponding to those for which provision is made by, or can be made under, paragraph 13(1) to (8) in relation to the orders to which that paragraph applies;

(c)   for the proof of any matter relevant for the purposes of anything falling to be done in pursuance of the Order in Council.

(5)   An Order in Council under this paragraph may also make provision with respect to anything falling to be done on behalf of the United Kingdom in a designated country or territory in relation to proceedings in that country or territory for or in connection with the making of an external order.

(6)   An Order in Council under this paragraph—

(a)   may make different provision for different cases, and

(b)   shall not be made unless a draft of it has been laid before and approved by resolution of each House of Parliament.

[1268]

NOTES

Para 1: words in square brackets in definition "forfeiture order" inserted, and definition "relevant offence" inserted, by the Counter-Terrorism Act 2008, s 39, Sch 3, para 5(1), (2), as from a day to be appointed.

Para 2: for the words in italics in sub-para (1)(d) there are substituted the words "section 23B(1)" by the Counter-Terrorism Act 2008, s 39, Sch 3, para 5(1), (3), as from a day to be appointed.

Para 4: words in square brackets in sub-para (1) substituted by the Courts Act 2003, s 109(1), Sch 8, para 388(1), (2), as from 1 April 2005; for the words in italics in sub-para (2)(c) there are substituted the words "section 23B(1)" by the Counter-Terrorism Act 2008, s 39, Sch 3, para 5(1), (4), as from a day to be appointed.

Para 4A: inserted by the Counter-Terrorism Act 2008, s 37(1), as from a day to be appointed.

Para 5: for the words in italics in sub-paras (1)(a), (2)(a) there are substituted the words "a relevant offence" by the Counter-Terrorism Act 2008, s 39, Sch 3, para 5(1), (5), as from a day to be appointed; sub-para (2) and words in square brackets in sub-para (3) substituted, and sub-para (6) added, by the Anti-terrorism, Crime and Security Act 2001, s 3, Sch 2, Pt 2, para 2(1)–(4), as from 20 December 2001.

Para 6: sub-paras (3), (4) substituted, for original sub-para (3), by the Anti-terrorism, Crime and Security Act 2001, s 3, Sch 2, Pt 2, para 2(1), (5), as from 20 December 2001; for the words in italics in sub-paras (4)(a), (b) there are substituted the words "relevant offences" by the Counter-Terrorism Act 2008, s 39, Sch 3, para 5(1), (6), as from a day to be appointed.

Para 8: words in first pair of square brackets in sub-para (1) substituted, words in second pair of square brackets inserted, and sub-paras (2), (3) repealed, by the Land Registration Act 2002, ss 133, 135, Sch 11, para 38, Sch 13, as from 13 October 2003.

Para 9 is amended as follows:

The heading "Compensation" is repealed by the Counter-Terrorism Act 2008, s 39, Sch 3, para 5(1), (7), as from a day to be appointed.

Words in square brackets in sub-para (1) substituted by the Anti-terrorism, Crime and Security Act 2001, s 3, Sch 2, Pt 2, para 2(1), (7), as from 20 December 2001.

For the words in italics in sub-para (2) (in all 4 places) there are substituted the words "a relevant offence" by the Counter-Terrorism Act 2008, s 39, Sch 3, para 5(1), (8), as from a day to be appointed.

Para 10: for the words in italics in sub-para (1)(a) there are substituted the words "a relevant offence" by the Counter-Terrorism Act 2008, s 39, Sch 3, para 5(1), (9), as from a day to be appointed.

Para 11: sub-paras (1)(aa), (2A) inserted by the Criminal Justice Act 2003, s 331, Sch 36, Pt 2, para 14, as from a day to be appointed.

Paras 11A–11G: inserted by the Crime (International Co-operation) Act 2003, s 90, Sch 4, paras 1, 3, as from a day to be appointed.

Para 12: words "or 23A" in square brackets (in each place they occur) inserted by the Counter-Terrorism Act 2008, s 39, Sch 3, para 5(1), (10), as from a day to be appointed.

Para 13: words in square brackets in sub-para (5)(b) substituted by the Courts Act 2003, s 109(1), Sch 8, para 388(1), (3), as from 1 April 2005; for the words in italics in sub-para (6)(b) there are substituted the words "Senior Courts Act 1981" by the Constitutional Reform Act 2005, s 59(5), Sch 11, Pt 1, para 1(2), as from a day to be appointed.

Para 14: words in square brackets in sub-para (2) inserted by the Crime (International Co-operation) Act 2003, s 90, Sch 4, paras 1, 4, as from a day to be appointed.

Orders: the Terrorism Act 2000 (Enforcement of External Orders) Order 2001, SI 2001/3927.

PART II
SCOTLAND

Implementation of forfeiture orders

15.   In this Part of this Schedule—

"forfeiture order" means an order made by a court in Scotland under section 23 [or 23A], and "forfeited property" means the money or other property to which a forfeiture order applies; ["relevant offence" means—

    (a)   an offence under any of sections 15 to 18,
    (b)   an offence to which section 23A applies, or
    (c)   in relation to a restraint order, any offence specified in Schedule 2 to the Counter-Terrorism Act 2008 (offences where terrorist connection to be considered)].

16.—(1)   Where a court in Scotland makes a forfeiture order it may make such other provision as appears to it to be necessary for giving effect to the order, and in particular it may—

    (a)   direct any of the forfeited property other than money or land to be sold or otherwise disposed of in such manner as the court may direct;
    (b)   appoint an administrator to take possession, subject to such conditions and exceptions as may be specified by the court, of any of the forfeited property and to realise it in such manner as the court may direct;
    (c)   direct a specified part of any forfeited money, or of the proceeds of the sale, disposal or realisation of any forfeited property, to be paid to a specified person falling within *section 23(7)*.

(2)   A forfeiture order shall not come into force so long as an appeal is pending against the order or against the conviction on which it was made; and for this purpose where an appeal is competent but has not been brought it shall be treated as pending until the expiry of a period of fourteen days from the date when the order was made.

(3)   Any balance remaining after making any payment required under sub-paragraph (1)(c) or paragraph 17 shall be treated for the purposes of section 211(5) of the Criminal Procedure (Scotland) Act 1995 (fines payable to the Treasury) as if it were a fine imposed in the High Court of Justiciary.

(4)   The clerk of court shall, on the application of—

    (a)   the prosecutor in the proceedings in which a forfeiture order is made,
    (b)   the accused in those proceedings, or
    (c)   a person whom the court heard under *section 23(7)* before making the order,

certify in writing the extent (if any) to which, at the date of the certificate, effect has been given to the order in respect of the money or other property to which it applies.

(5)   In sub-paragraph (1) references to the proceeds of the sale, disposal or realisation of property are references to the proceeds after deduction of the costs of sale, disposal or realisation.

Administrators

17.—(1)   The Court of Session may by rules of court prescribe the powers and duties of an administrator appointed under paragraph 16.

(2)   An administrator appointed under paragraph 16 shall be entitled to be paid his remuneration and expenses out of the proceeds of the property realised by him or, if and so far as those proceeds are insufficient, by the Lord Advocate.

(3)   The accountant of court shall supervise an administrator appointed under paragraph 16 in the exercise of the powers conferred, and discharge of the duties imposed, on him under or by virtue of that paragraph.

(4)   An administrator appointed under paragraph 16 shall not be liable to any person in respect of any loss or damage resulting from action—

  (a)   which he takes in relation to property which is not forfeited property, but which he reasonably believes to be forfeited property,

  (b)   which he would be entitled to take if the property were forfeited property, and

  (c)   which he takes reasonably believing that he is entitled to take because of his belief that the property is forfeited property.

(5)   Sub-paragraph (4) does not apply in so far as the loss or damage is caused by the administrator's negligence.

[Application of proceeds to compensate victims

17A.—(1)   Where a court makes a forfeiture order in a case where—

  (a)   the offender has been convicted of an offence that has resulted in a person suffering personal injury, loss or damage, or

  (b)   any such offence is taken into consideration by the court in determining sentence,

the court may also order that an amount not exceeding a sum specified by the court is to be paid to that person out of the proceeds of the forfeiture.

(2)   For this purpose the proceeds of the forfeiture means the aggregate amount of—

  (a)   any forfeited money, and

  (b)   the proceeds of the sale, disposal or realisation of any forfeited property, after deduction of the costs of the sale, disposal or realisation,

reduced by the amount of any payment under paragraph 16(1)(c) or 17(2).

(3)   The court may make an order under this paragraph only if it is satisfied that but for the inadequacy of the offender's means it would have made a compensation order under section 249 of the Criminal Procedure (Scotland) Act 1995 under which the offender would have been required to pay compensation of an amount not less than the specified amount.]

Restraint orders

18.—(1)   The Court of Session, on an application made by the Lord Advocate, may make a restraint order under this paragraph where—

  (a)   proceedings have been instituted in Scotland for *an offence under any of sections 15 to 18*,

  (b)   the proceedings have not been concluded, and

  (c)   a forfeiture order has been made, or it appears to the court that a forfeiture order may be made, in the proceedings for the offence.

  [(2)   The Court of Session may also make a restraint order on such an application where—

  (a)   a criminal investigation has been instituted in Scotland with regard to *an offence under any of sections 15 to 18*, and

  (b)   it appears to the Court of Session that a forfeiture order may be made in any proceedings for the offence.]

(3)   A restraint order prohibits a person to whom notice of it is given, subject to any conditions and exceptions specified in the order, from dealing with property in respect of which a forfeiture order has been or could be made in [any proceedings] referred to in sub-paragraph (1) or (2).

(4)   An application for a restraint order may be made ex parte in chambers.

(5)   For the purposes of this paragraph, dealing with property includes removing the property from Great Britain.

[(6)   In this paragraph "criminal investigation" means an investigation which police officers or other persons have a duty to conduct with a view to it being ascertained whether a person should be charged with an offence.]

19.—(1)   A restraint order shall provide for notice of it to be given to any person affected by the order.

(2)   A restraint order may be recalled or varied by the Court of Session on the application of any person affected by it.

[(3)   A restraint order made under paragraph 18(1) shall in particular be recalled on an application under sub-paragraph (2) if the proceedings for the offence have been concluded.

(3A)   A restraint order made under paragraph 18(2) shall in particular be discharged on an application under sub-paragraph (2)—
    (a)   if no proceedings in respect of *offences under any of sections 15 to 18* are instituted within such time as the Court of Session considers reasonable, and
    (b)   if all proceedings in respect of *offences under any of sections 15 to 18* have been concluded.]

(4)   When proceedings for the offence are concluded the Lord Advocate shall forthwith apply to the Court for recall of the order.

20.—(1)   A constable may seize any property subject to a restraint order for the purpose of preventing it from being removed from Great Britain.

(2)   Property seized under this paragraph shall be dealt with in accordance with the Court's directions.

21.—(1)   On the application of the Lord Advocate, the Court of Session may, in respect of heritable property in Scotland affected by a restraint order (whether such property generally or particular such property) grant warrant for inhibition against any person interdicted by the order.

(2)   Subject to this Part of this Schedule, a warrant under sub-paragraph (1)—
    (a)   shall have effect as if granted on the dependence of an action for debt at the instance of the Lord Advocate against the person and may be executed, recalled, loosed or restricted accordingly;
    (b)   *shall have the effect of letters of inhibition and* shall forthwith be registered by the Lord Advocate in the register of inhibitions *and adjudications*.

(3)   Section 155 of the Titles to Land Consolidation (Scotland) Act 1868 (effective date of inhibition) shall apply in relation to an inhibition for which warrant has been granted under sub-paragraph (2)(a) *as that section applies to an inhibition by separate letters or contained in a summons*.

(4)   The execution of an inhibition under sub-paragraph (2) in respect of property shall not prejudice the exercise of an administrator's powers under or for the purposes of this Part of this Schedule in respect of that property.

(5)   No inhibition executed under sub-paragraph (2) shall have effect once, or in so far as, the restraint order affecting the property in respect of which the warrant for the inhibition has been granted has ceased to have effect in respect of that property, and the Lord Advocate shall—
    (a)   apply for the recall, or as the case may be restriction, of the inhibition or arrestment accordingly; and
    (b)   ensure that recall, or restriction, of an inhibition on such application is reflected in the register of inhibitions *and adjudications*.

22.—(1)   On the application of the Lord Advocate, the court may, in respect of moveable property affected by a restraint order (whether such property generally or particular such property), grant warrant for arrestment if the property would be arrestable if the person entitled to it were a debtor.

(2)   A warrant under sub-paragraph (1) shall have effect as if granted on the dependence of an action for debt at the instance of the Lord Advocate against the person and may be executed, recalled, loosed or restricted accordingly.

(3)   The execution of an arrestment under sub-paragraph (2) in respect of property shall not prejudice the exercise of an administrator's powers under or for the purposes of this Part of this Schedule in respect of that property.

(4)   No arrestment executed under sub-paragraph (2) shall have effect once, or in so far as, the restraint order affecting the property in respect of which the warrant for such arrestment has been granted has ceased to have effect in respect of that property; and the Lord Advocate shall apply to the court for an order recalling, or as the case may be, restricting the arrestment accordingly.

Compensation

23.—(1)   This paragraph applies where a restraint order is recalled under paragraph [19(3A)(a)].

(2)   This paragraph also applies where a forfeiture order or a restraint order is made in or in relation to proceedings for *an offence under any of sections 15 to 18* which—
- (a)   do not result in conviction for *an offence under any of those sections,*
- (b)   result in conviction for *an offence under any of those sections* in respect of which the person convicted is subsequently pardoned by Her Majesty, or
- (c)   result in conviction for *an offence under any of those sections* which is subsequently quashed.

(3)   A person who had an interest in any property which was subject to the order may apply to the Court of Session for compensation.

(4)   The Court of Session may order compensation to be paid to the applicant if it is satisfied—
- (a)   that there was a serious default on the part of a person concerned in the investigation or prosecution of the offence,
- (b)   that the person in default was a constable of a police force or a constable acting with the powers of such a constable, or was a procurator fiscal or was acting on behalf of the Lord Advocate,
- (c)   that the applicant has suffered loss in consequence of anything done in relation to the property by or in pursuance of the forfeiture order or the restraint order, and
- (d)   having regard to all the circumstances, it is appropriate to order compensation to be paid.

(5)   The Court of Session shall not order compensation to be paid where it appears to it that the proceedings for the offence would have been instituted even if the serious default had not occurred.

(6)   Compensation payable under this paragraph shall be paid—
- (a)   where the person in default was a constable of a police force, out of the police fund out of which the expenses of that police force are met;
- (b)   where the person in default was a constable other than is mentioned in paragraph (a) above, but with the powers of such a constable, by the body under whose authority he acts; and
- (c)   where the person in default was a procurator fiscal or was acting on behalf of the Lord Advocate, by the Lord Advocate.

(7)   This paragraph is without prejudice to any right which may otherwise exist to institute proceedings in respect of delictual liability disclosed by such circumstances as are mentioned in paragraphs (a) to (c) of sub-paragraph (2).

24.—(1)   This paragraph applies where—
- (a)   a forfeiture order or a restraint order is made in or in relation to proceedings for *an offence under any of sections 15 to 18*, and
- (b)   the proceedings result in a conviction which is subsequently quashed on an appeal under section 7(2) or (5) as applied by section 8(1).

(2)   A person who had an interest in any property which was subject to the order may apply to the Court of Session for compensation.

(3)   The Court of Session may order compensation to be paid to the applicant if satisfied—
- (a)   that the applicant has suffered loss in consequence of anything done in relation to the property by or in pursuance of the forfeiture order or restraint order, and
- (b)   that, having regard to all the circumstances, it is appropriate to order compensation to be paid.

(4)   Compensation payable under this paragraph shall be paid by the Secretary of State.

Proceedings for an offence: timing

25.—(1)   For the purposes of this Part of this Schedule proceedings for an offence are instituted—
- (a)   when a person is arrested for the offence,
- (b)   when a warrant to arrest or cite a person is granted,
- (c)   when an indictment or complaint is served on a person in respect of the offence.

(2)   Where the application of sub-paragraph (1) would result in there being more than one time for the institution of proceedings they shall be taken to be instituted at the earliest of those times.

(3)   For the purposes of this Part of this Schedule proceedings are concluded—
- (a)   when a forfeiture order has been made in those proceedings and effect has been given to it in respect of all the money or other property to which it applies, or
- (b)   when (disregarding any power of a court to extend the period within which an appeal may be made) there is no further possibility of a forfeiture order being made in the proceedings.

[Domestic and overseas freezing orders

25A.—(1)   This paragraph has effect for the purposes of paragraphs 25B to 25G.

(2) The relevant Framework Decision means the Framework Decision on the execution in the European Union of orders freezing property or evidence adopted by the Council of the European Union on 22nd July 2003.

(3) A listed offence means—
- (a) an offence described in Article 3(2) of the relevant Framework Decision, or
- (b) a prescribed offence or an offence of a prescribed description.

(4) An order under sub-paragraph (3)(b) which, for the purposes of paragraph 25D, prescribes an offence or a description of offences may require that the conduct which constitutes the offence or offences would, if it occurred in a part of the United Kingdom, constitute an offence in that part.

(5) Specified information, in relation to a certificate under paragraph 25B or 25D, means—
- (a) any information required to be given by the form of certificate annexed to the relevant Framework Decision, or
- (b) any prescribed information.

(6) In this paragraph, "prescribed" means prescribed by an order made by the Secretary of State.

(7) A participating country means—
- (a) a country other than the United Kingdom which is a member State on a day appointed for the commencement of Schedule 4 to the Crime (International Co-operation) Act 2003, and
- (b) any other member State designated by an order made by the Secretary of State.

(8) "Country" includes territory.

(9) Section 14(2)(a) applies for the purposes of determining what are the proceeds of the commission of an offence.

Domestic freezing orders: certification

25B.—(1) If any of the property to which an application for a restraint order relates is property in a participating country, the applicant may ask the Court of Session to make a certificate under this paragraph.

(2) The Court of Session may make a certificate under this paragraph if—
- (a) it makes a restraint order in relation to property in the participating country, and
- (b) it is satisfied that there is a good arguable case that the property is likely to be used for the purposes of a listed offence or is the proceeds of the commission of a listed offence.

(3) A certificate under this paragraph is a certificate which—
- (a) is made for the purposes of the relevant Framework Decision, and
- (b) gives the specified information.

(4) If the Court of Session makes a certificate under this paragraph—
- (a) the restraint order must provide for notice of the certificate to be given to the person affected by it, and
- (b) paragraph 19(2) to (4) applies to the certificate as it applies to the restraint order.

Sending domestic freezing orders

25C.—(1) If a certificate is made under paragraph 25B, the restraint order and the certificate are to be sent to the Lord Advocate for forwarding to—
- (a) a court exercising jurisdiction in the place where the property is situated, or
- (b) any authority recognised by the government of the participating country as the appropriate authority for receiving orders of that kind.

(2) The restraint order and the certificate must be accompanied by a forfeiture order, unless the certificate indicates when the court expects a forfeiture order to be sent.

(3) The certificate must include a translation of it into an appropriate language of the participating country (if that language is not English).

(4) The certificate must be signed by or on behalf of the court and must include a statement as to the accuracy of the information given in it.

The signature may be an electronic signature.

(5) If the restraint order and the certificate are not accompanied by a forfeiture order, but a forfeiture order is subsequently made, it is to be sent to the Lord Advocate for forwarding as mentioned in sub-paragraph (1).

Overseas freezing orders

25D.—(1) Paragraph 25E applies where an overseas freezing order made by an appropriate court or authority in a participating country is received by the Secretary of State from the court or authority which made or confirmed the order.

(2)   An overseas freezing order is an order prohibiting dealing with property—
    (a)   which is in the United Kingdom,
    (b)   which the appropriate court or authority considers is likely to be used for the purposes of a listed offence or is the proceeds of the commission of such an offence, and
    (c)   in respect of which an order has been or may be made by a court exercising criminal jurisdiction in the participating country for the forfeiture of the property,
and in respect of which the following requirements of this paragraph are met.

(3)   The action which the appropriate court or authority considered would constitute or, as the case may be, constituted the listed offence is action done as an act of terrorism or for the purposes of terrorism.

(4)   The order must relate to—
    (a)   criminal proceedings instituted in the participating country, or
    (b)   a criminal investigation being carried on there.

(5)   The order must be accompanied by a certificate which gives the specified information; but a certificate may be treated as giving any specified information which is not given in it if the Secretary of State has the information in question.

(6)   The certificate must—
    (a)   be signed by or on behalf of the court or authority which made or confirmed the order,
    (b)   include a statement as to the accuracy of the information given in it,
    (c)   if it is not in English, include a translation of it into English.
The signature may be an electronic signature.

(7)   The order must be accompanied by an order made by a court exercising criminal jurisdiction in that country for the forfeiture of the property, unless the certificate indicates when such an order is expected to be sent.

(8)   An appropriate court or authority in a participating country in relation to an overseas freezing order is—
    (a)   a court exercising criminal jurisdiction in the country,
    (b)   a prosecuting authority in the country,
    (c)   any other authority in the country which appears to the Secretary of State to have the function of making such orders.

(9)   References in paragraphs 25E to 25G to an overseas freezing order include its accompanying certificate.

Enforcement of overseas freezing orders

25E.—(1)   Where this paragraph applies the Secretary of State must send a copy of the overseas freezing order to the Court of Session and to the Lord Advocate.

(2)   The court is to consider the overseas freezing order on its own initiative within a period prescribed by rules of court.

(3)   Before giving effect to the overseas freezing order, the court must give the Lord Advocate an opportunity to be heard.

(4)   The court may decide not to give effect to the overseas freezing order only if, in its opinion, giving effect to it would be incompatible with any of the Convention rights (within the meaning of the Human Rights Act 1998).

25F.   The Court of Session may postpone giving effect to an overseas freezing order in respect of any property—
    (a)   in order to avoid prejudicing a criminal investigation which is taking place in the United Kingdom, or
    (b)   if, under an order made by a court in criminal proceedings in the United Kingdom, the property may not be dealt with.

25G.—(1)   Where the Court of Session decides to give effect to an overseas freezing order, the Deputy Principal Clerk of Session must—
    (a)   register the order in the Books of Council and Session,
    (b)   provide for notice of the registration to be given to any person affected by it.

(2)   For the purpose of enforcing an overseas freezing order registered in the Books of Council and Session, the order is to have effect as if it were an order made by the Court of Session.

(3)   Paragraphs 20 and 21 apply to an overseas freezing order registered in the Books of Council and Session as they apply to a restraint order under paragraph 18.

(4)   The Court of Session may cancel the registration of the order, or vary the property to which the order applies, on an application by the Lord Advocate or any other person affected by it, if or to the extent that—
    (a)   the court is of the opinion mentioned in paragraph 25E(4), or

PART II
OTHER ACTS

(b)   the court is of the opinion that the order has ceased to have effect in the participating country.

(5)   Her Majesty may by Order in Council make further provision for the enforcement in Scotland of registered overseas freezing orders.

(6)   An Order in Council under this paragraph—
(a)   may make different provision for different cases,
(b)   is not to be made unless a draft of it has been laid before and approved by resolution of each House of Parliament.]

Enforcement of orders made elsewhere in the British Islands

26.   In the following provisions of this Part of this Schedule—
"an England and Wales order" means—
(a)   an order made in England and Wales under section 23 [or 23A] ("an England and Wales forfeiture order"),
(b)   an order made under paragraph 5 ("an England and Wales restraint order"), or
(c)   an order made under any other provision of Part I of this Schedule in relation to an England and Wales forfeiture or restraint order;
"a Northern Ireland order" means—
(a)   an order made in Northern Ireland under section 23 [or 23A] ("a Northern Ireland forfeiture order"),
(b)   an order made under paragraph 33 ("a Northern Ireland restraint order"), or
(c)   an order made under any other provision of Part III of this Schedule in relation to a Northern Ireland forfeiture or restraint order;
"an Islands order" means an order made in any of the Islands under a provision of the law of that Island corresponding to—
(a)   section 23 [or 23A] ("an Islands forfeiture order"),
(b)   paragraph 18 ("an Islands restraint order"), or
(c)   any other provision of this Part of this Schedule.

27.—(1)   Subject to the provisions of this paragraph, an England and Wales order, Northern Ireland order or Islands order shall have effect in the law of Scotland.

(2)   But such an order shall be enforced in Scotland only in accordance with—
(a)   the provisions of this paragraph, and
(b)   any provision made by rules of court as to the manner in which, and the conditions subject to which, such orders are to be enforced there.

(3)   On an application made to it in accordance with rules of court for registration of an England and Wales order, Northern Ireland order or Islands order, the Court of Session shall direct that the order shall, in accordance with such rules, be registered in that court.

(4)   Rules of court shall also make provision—
(a)   for cancelling or varying the registration of an England and Wales, Northern Ireland or Islands forfeiture order when effect has been given to it, whether in Scotland or elsewhere, in respect of all or, as the case may be, part of the money or other property to which the order applies,
(b)   for cancelling or varying the registration of an England and Wales, Northern Ireland or Islands restraint order which has been discharged or varied by the court by which it was made.

(5)   If an England and Wales, Northern Ireland or Islands forfeiture order is registered under this paragraph the Court of Session shall have, in relation to that order, the same powers as a court has under paragraph 16(1) above in relation to a forfeiture order made by it and paragraphs 16(3) to (5) and 17 apply accordingly.

(6)   If an England and Wales, Northern Ireland or Islands forfeiture order is registered under this paragraph—
(a)   paragraphs 20 and 21 above shall apply as they apply to a restraint order, and
(b)   the Court of Session shall have the like power to make an order under section 1 of the Administration of Justice (Scotland) Act 1972 (extended power to order inspection of documents, &c) in relation to proceedings brought or likely to be brought for an England and Wales, Northern Ireland or Islands restraint order as if those proceedings had been brought or were likely to be brought in the Court of Session.

(7)   In addition, if an England and Wales order, Northern Ireland order or Islands order is registered under this paragraph—
(a)   the Court of Session shall have, in relation to its enforcement, the same power,
(b)   proceedings for or with respect to its enforcement may be taken, and
(c)   proceedings for or with respect to any contravention of such an order (whether before or after such registration) may be taken,
as if the order had originally been made in the Court of Session.

(8)   The Court of Session may also make such orders or do otherwise as seems to it appropriate for the purpose of—
- (a)   assisting the achievement in Scotland of the purposes of an England and Wales order, Northern Ireland order or Islands order, or
- (b)   assisting any receiver or other person directed by any such order to sell or otherwise dispose of property.

(9)   The following documents shall, in Scotland, be sufficient evidence of their contents—
- (a)   a document purporting to be a copy of an England and Wales order, Northern Ireland order or Islands order and to be certified as such by a proper officer of the court by which it was made, and
- (b)   a document purporting to be a certificate for purposes corresponding to those of paragraph 16(4) and to be certified by a proper officer of the court concerned.

(10)   Nothing in any England and Wales order, Northern Ireland order or Islands order prejudices any enactment or rule of law in respect of the recording of deeds relating to heritable property in Scotland or the registration of interests in such property.

Enforcement of orders made in designated countries

28.—(1)   Her Majesty may by Order in Council make provision for the purpose of enabling the enforcement in Scotland of external orders.

(2)   An "external order" means an order [(other than an overseas freezing order within the meaning of paragraph 25D)]—
- (a)   which is made in a country or territory designated for the purposes of this paragraph by the Order in Council, and
- (b)   which makes relevant provision.

(3)   "Relevant provision" means—
- (a)   provision for the forfeiture of terrorist property ("an external forfeiture order"); or
- (b)   provision prohibiting dealing with property which is subject to an external forfeiture order or in respect of which such an order could be made in proceedings which have been or are to be instituted in the designated country or territory ("an external restraint order").

(4)   An Order in Council under this paragraph may, in particular, include provision—
- (a)   which, for the purpose of facilitating the enforcement of any external order that may be made, has effect at times before there is an external order to be enforced,
- (b)   for matters corresponding to those for which provision is made by, or can be made under, paragraph 27(1) to (8) in relation to the orders to which that paragraph applies, and
- (c)   for the proof of any matter relevant for the purposes of anything falling to be done in pursuance of the Order in Council.

(5)   An Order in Council under this paragraph may also make provision with respect to anything falling to be done on behalf of the United Kingdom in a designated country or territory in relation to proceedings in that country or territory for or in connection with the making of an external order.

(6)   An Order under this paragraph—
- (a)   may make different provision for different cases, and
- (b)   shall not be made unless a draft of it has been laid before and approved by resolution of each House of Parliament.

[1269]

NOTES

Para 15: words in square brackets in definition "forfeiture order" inserted, and definition "relevant offence" inserted, by the Counter-Terrorism Act 2008, s 39, Sch 3, para 5(1), (11), as from a day to be appointed.

Para 16: for the words in italics in sub-paras (1)(c), (4)(c) there are substituted the words "section 23B(1)" by the Counter-Terrorism Act 2008, s 39, Sch 3, para 5(1), (12), as from a day to be appointed.

Para 17A: inserted by the Counter-Terrorism Act 2008, s 37(2), as from a day to be appointed.

Para 18: for the words in italics in sub-paras (1)(a), (2)(a) there are substituted the words "a relevant offence" by the Counter-Terrorism Act 2008, s 39, Sch 3, para 5(1), (13), as from a day to be appointed; sub-para (2) and words in square brackets in sub-para (3) substituted, and sub-para (6) added, by the Anti-terrorism, Crime and Security Act 2001, s 3, Sch 2, Pt 2, para 3(1)–(4), as from 20 December 2001.

Para 19: sub-paras (3), (3A) substituted, for original sub-para (3), by the Anti-terrorism, Crime and Security Act 2001, s 3, Sch 2, Pt 2, para 3(1), (5), as from 20 December 2001; for the words in italics in sub-paras (3A)(a), (b) there are substituted the words "relevant offences" by the Counter-Terrorism Act 2008, s 39, Sch 3, para 5(1), (14), as from a day to be appointed.

Para 21: words in italics in sub-paras (2)(b), (3), (5)(b) repealed by the Bankruptcy and Diligence etc (Scotland) Act 2007, s 226, Sch 6, Pt 1, as from a day to be appointed.

Para 23 is amended as follows:

The heading "Compensation" is repealed by the Counter-Terrorism Act 2008, s 39, Sch 3, para 5(1), (15), as from a day to be appointed.

Words in square brackets in sub-para (1) substituted by the Anti-terrorism, Crime and Security Act 2001, s 3, Sch 2, Pt 2, para 3(1), (6), as from 20 December 2001.

For the words in italics in sub-para (2) (in all 4 places) there are substituted the words "a relevant offence" by the Counter-Terrorism Act 2008, s 39, Sch 3, para 5(1), (16), as from a day to be appointed.

Para 24: for the words in italics in sub-para (1)(a) there are substituted the words "a relevant offence" by the Counter-Terrorism Act 2008, s 39, Sch 3, para 5(1), (17), as from a day to be appointed.

Paras 25A–25G: inserted by the Crime (International Co-operation) Act 2003, s 90, Sch 4, paras 1, 5, as from a day to be appointed.

Para 26: words "or 23A" in square brackets (in each place they occur) inserted by the Counter-Terrorism Act 2008, s 39, Sch 3, para 5(1), (18), as from a day to be appointed.

Para 28: words in square brackets in sub-para (2) inserted by the Crime (International Co-operation) Act 2003, s 90, Sch 4, paras 1, 6, as from a day to be appointed.

Orders: the Terrorism Act 2000 (Enforcement of External Orders) Order 2001, SI 2001/3927; the Act of Sederunt (Rules of the Court of Session Amendment No 6) (Terrorism Act 2000) 2001, SSI 2001/494.

PART III
NORTHERN IRELAND

Interpretation

29.   In this Part of this Schedule—
   "forfeiture order" means an order made by a court in Northern Ireland under section 23 [or 23A], and
   "forfeited property" means the money or other property to which a forfeiture order applies;
   ["relevant offence" means—
       (a)   an offence under any of sections 15 to 18, or
       (b)   an offence to which section 23A applies].

Implementation of forfeiture orders

30.—(1)   Where a court in Northern Ireland makes a forfeiture order it may make such other provision as appears to it to be necessary for giving effect to the order, and in particular it may—
   (a)   require any of the forfeited property to be paid or handed over to the proper officer or to a [member of the Police Service of Northern Ireland] designated for the purpose by the Chief Constable;
   (b)   direct any of the forfeited property other than money or land to be sold or otherwise disposed of in such manner as the court may direct and the proceeds (if any) to be paid to the proper officer;
   (c)   appoint a receiver to take possession, subject to such conditions and exceptions as may be specified by the court, of any of the forfeited property, to realise it in such manner as the court may direct and to pay the proceeds to the proper officer;
   (d)   direct a specified part of any forfeited money, or of the proceeds of the sale, disposal or realisation of any forfeited property, to be paid by the proper officer to a specified person falling within *section 23(7)*.

(2)   A forfeiture order shall not come into force until there is no further possibility of it being varied, or set aside, on appeal (disregarding any power of a court to grant leave to appeal out of time).

(3)   In sub-paragraph (1)(b) and (d) a reference to the proceeds of the sale, disposal or realisation of property is a reference to the proceeds after deduction of the costs of sale, disposal or realisation.

(4)   Article 58 of the Magistrates' Courts (Northern Ireland) Order 1981 (disposal of non-pecuniary forfeitures) shall not apply.

31.—(1)   A receiver appointed under paragraph 30 shall be entitled to be paid his remuneration and expenses by the proper officer out of the proceeds of the property realised by the receiver and paid to the proper officer under paragraph 30(1)(c).

(2)   If and so far as those proceeds are insufficient, the receiver shall be entitled to be paid his remuneration and expenses by the prosecutor.

(3)   A receiver appointed under paragraph 30 shall not be liable to any person in respect of any loss or damage resulting from action—
   (a)   which he takes in relation to property which is not forfeited property, but which he reasonably believes to be forfeited property,
   (b)   which he would be entitled to take if the property were forfeited property, and
   (c)   which he reasonably believes that he is entitled to take because of his belief that the property is forfeited property.

(4)   Sub-paragraph (3) does not apply in so far as the loss or damage is caused by the receiver's negligence.

32.—(1)   In paragraphs 30 and 31 "the proper officer" means—

     (a)   where the forfeiture order is made by a court of summary jurisdiction, the clerk of petty sessions, and

     (b)   where the forfeiture order is made by the Crown Court, the appropriate officer of the Crown Court.

    (2)   The proper officer shall issue a certificate in respect of a forfeiture order if an application is made by—

     (a)   the prosecutor in the proceedings in which the forfeiture order was made,

     (b)   the defendant in those proceedings, or

     (c)   a person whom the court heard under section 23(7) before making the order.

    (3)   The certificate shall state the extent (if any) to which, at the date of the certificate, effect has been given to the forfeiture order.

    (4)   Any balance in the hands of the proper officer after making any payment required under paragraph 30(1)(d) or 31 shall be treated for the purposes of section 20 of the Administration of Justice (Northern Ireland) Act 1954 (application of fines, &c) as if it were a fine.

[Application of proceeds to compensate victims

32A.—(1)   Where a court makes a forfeiture order in a case where—

     (a)   the offender has been convicted of an offence that has resulted in a person suffering personal injury, loss or damage, or

     (b)   any such offence is taken into consideration by the court in determining sentence,

the court may also order that an amount not exceeding a sum specified by the court is to be paid to that person out of the proceeds of the forfeiture.

    (2)   For this purpose the proceeds of the forfeiture means the aggregate amount of—

     (a)   any forfeited money, and

     (b)   the proceeds of the sale, disposal or realisation of any forfeited property, after deduction of the costs of the sale, disposal or realisation,

reduced by the amount of any payment under paragraph 30(1)(d) or 31(1).

    (3)   The court may make an order under this paragraph only if it is satisfied that but for the inadequacy of the offender's means it would have made a compensation order under Article 14 of the Criminal Justice (Northern Ireland) Order 1994 under which the offender would have been required to pay compensation of an amount not less than the specified amount.]

Restraint orders

33.—(1)   The High Court may make a restraint order under this paragraph where—

     (a)   proceedings have been instituted in Northern Ireland for *an offence under any of sections 15 to 18*,

     (b)   the proceedings have not been concluded,

     (c)   an application for a restraint order is made to the High Court by the prosecutor, and

     (d)   a forfeiture order has been made, or it appears to the High Court that a forfeiture order may be made, in the proceedings for the offence.

    [(2)   The High Court may also make a restraint order under this paragraph where—

     (a)   a criminal investigation has been started in Northern Ireland with regard to *an offence under any of sections 15 to 18*,

     (b)   an application for a restraint order is made to the High Court by the person who the High Court is satisfied will have the conduct of any proceedings for the offence, and

     (c)   it appears to the High Court that a forfeiture order may be made in any proceedings for the offence.]

    (3)   A restraint order prohibits a person to whom notice of it is given, subject to any conditions and exceptions specified in the order, from dealing with property in respect of which a forfeiture order has been or could be made in [any proceedings] referred to in sub-paragraph (1) or (2).

    (4)   An application for a restraint order may be made to a judge in chambers without notice.

    (5)   For the purposes of this paragraph a reference to dealing with property includes a reference to removing the property from Northern Ireland.

    [(6)   In this paragraph "criminal investigation" means an investigation which police officers or other persons have a duty to conduct with a view to it being ascertained whether a person should be charged with an offence.]

34.—(1)   A restraint order shall provide for notice of it to be given to any person affected by the order.

    (2)   A restraint order may be discharged or varied by the High Court on the application of a person affected by it.

    [(3)   A restraint order made under paragraph 33(1) shall in particular be discharged on an application under sub-paragraph (2) if the proceedings for the offence have been concluded.

(4) A restraint order made under paragraph 33(2) shall in particular be discharged on an application under sub-paragraph (2)—
- (a) if no proceedings in respect of *offences under any of sections 15 to 18* are instituted within such time as the High Court considers reasonable, and
- (b) if all proceedings in respect of *offences under any of sections 15 to 18* have been concluded.]

35.—(1) A constable may seize any property subject to a restraint order for the purpose of preventing it from being removed from Northern Ireland.

(2) Property seized under this paragraph shall be dealt with in accordance with the High Court's directions.

36. ...

37.—(1) A person commits an offence if he contravenes a restraint order.

(2) It is a defence for a person charged with an offence under this paragraph to prove that he had a reasonable excuse for the contravention.

(3) A person guilty of an offence under this paragraph shall be liable—
- (a) on conviction on indictment, to imprisonment for a term not exceeding 14 years, to a fine or to both, or
- (b) on summary conviction, to imprisonment for a term not exceeding six months, to a fine not exceeding the statutory maximum, or to both.

(4) Nothing in this paragraph shall be taken to prejudice any power of the High Court to deal with the contravention of a restraint order as a contempt of court.

38.—(1) The prosecutor shall be treated for the purposes of section 66 of the Land Registration Act (Northern Ireland) 1970 (cautions) as a person interested in respect of any registered land to which a restraint order or an application for such an order relates.

(2) On the application of the prosecutor, the Registrar of Titles shall, in respect of any registered land to which a restraint order or an application for such an order relates, make an entry inhibiting any dealing with the land without the consent of the High Court.

(3) Subsections (2) and (4) of section 67 of the Land Registration Act (Northern Ireland) 1970 (inhibitions) shall apply to an entry made on the application of the prosecutor under sub-paragraph (2) as they apply to an entry made on the application of any person interested in the registered land under subsection (1) of that section.

(4) In this paragraph—
"registered land" has the meaning assigned to it by section 45(1)(a) of the Interpretation Act (Northern Ireland) 1954,
"Registrar of Titles" and "entry" have the same meanings as in the Land Registration Act (Northern Ireland) 1970, and
"prosecutor" in a case where a restraint order is made under paragraph 33(2) or an application for such an order is made, means the person who the High Court is satisfied has or will have the conduct of [any proceedings for *an offence under any of sections 15 to 18*].

Compensation

39.—(1) This paragraph applies where a restraint order is discharged under [paragraph 34(4)(a)].

(2) This paragraph also apples where a forfeiture order or a restraint order is made in or in relation to proceedings for *an offence under any of sections 15 to 18* which—
- (a) do not result in conviction for *an offence under any of those sections*,
- (b) result in conviction for *an offence under any of those sections* in respect of which the person convicted is subsequently pardoned by Her Majesty, or
- (c) result in a conviction for *an offence under any of those sections* which is subsequently quashed.

(3) A person who had an interest in any property which was subject to the order may apply to the High Court for compensation.

(4) The High Court may order compensation to be paid to the applicant if satisfied—
- (a) that there was a serious default on the part of a person concerned in the investigation or prosecution of the offence,
- (b) that the person in default was or was acting as a [member of the Police Service of Northern Ireland], or was a [member of staff of the Public Prosecution Service for Northern Ireland],
- (c) that the applicant has suffered loss in consequence of anything done in relation to the property by or in pursuance of the forfeiture order or restraint order, and
- (d) that, having regard to all the circumstances, it is appropriate to order compensation to be paid.

(5)   The High Court shall not order compensation to be paid where it appears to it that proceedings for the offence would have been instituted even if the serious default had not occurred.

(6)   Compensation payable under this paragraph shall be paid—
- (a)   where the person in default was or was acting as a [member of the Police Service of Northern Ireland], out of funds put at the disposal of the Chief Constable under section 10(5) of the Police (Northern Ireland) Act 1998, and
- (b)   where the person in default was a [member of staff of the Public Prosecution Service for Northern Ireland], by the Director of Public Prosecutions for Northern Ireland.

40.—(1)   This paragraph applies where—
- (a)   a forfeiture order or a restraint order is made in or in relation to proceedings for *an offence under any of sections 15 to 18*, and
- (b)   the proceedings result in a conviction which is subsequently quashed on an appeal under section 7(2) or (5), as applied by section 8(2).

(2)   A person who had an interest in any property which was subject to the order may apply to the High Court for compensation.

(3)   The High Court may order compensation to be paid to the applicant if satisfied—
- (a)   that the applicant has suffered loss in consequence of anything done in relation to the property by or in pursuance of the forfeiture order or restraint order, and
- (b)   that, having regard to all the circumstances, it is appropriate to order compensation to be paid.

(4)   Compensation payable under this paragraph shall be paid by the Secretary of State.

Proceedings for an offence: timing

41.—(1)   For the purposes of this Part of this Schedule proceedings for an offence are instituted—
- (a)   when a summons or warrant is issued under Article 20 of the Magistrates' Courts (Northern Ireland) Order 1981 in respect of the offence;
- (b)   when a person is charged with the offence after being taken into custody without a warrant;
- (c)   when an indictment charging a person with the offence is presented under section 2(2)(c), (e) or (f) of the Grand Jury (Abolition) Act (Northern Ireland) 1969.

(2)   Where the application of sub-paragraph (1) would result in there being more than one time for the institution of proceedings they shall be taken to be instituted at the earliest of those times.

(3)   For the purposes of this Part of this Schedule proceedings are concluded—
- (a)   when a forfeiture order has been made in those proceedings and effect has been given to it in respect of all the forfeited property, or
- (b)   when no forfeiture order has been made in those proceedings and there is no further possibility of one being made as a result of an appeal (disregarding any power of a court to grant leave to appeal out of time).

[Domestic and overseas freezing orders

41A.—(1)   This paragraph has effect for the purposes of paragraphs 41B to 41G.

(2)   The relevant Framework Decision means the Framework Decision on the execution in the European Union of orders freezing property or evidence adopted by the Council of the European Union on 22nd July 2003.

(3)   A listed offence means—
- (a)   an offence described in Article 3(2) of the relevant Framework Decision, or
- (b)   a prescribed offence or an offence of a prescribed description.

(4)   An order under sub-paragraph (3)(b) which, for the purposes of paragraph 41D, prescribes an offence or a description of offences may require that the conduct which constitutes the offence or offences would, if it occurred in a part of the United Kingdom, constitute an offence in that part.

(5)   Specified information, in relation to a certificate under paragraph 41B or 41D, means—
- (a)   any information required to be given by the form of certificate annexed to the relevant Framework Decision, or
- (b)   any prescribed information.

(6)   In this paragraph, "prescribed" means prescribed by an order made by the Secretary of State.

(7)   A participating country means—
- (a)   a country other than the United Kingdom which is a member State on a day appointed for the commencement of Schedule 4 to the Crime (International Co-operation) Act 2003, and
- (b)   any other member State designated by an order made by the Secretary of State.

(8)   "Country" includes territory.

(9)   Section 14(2)(a) applies for the purposes of determining what are the proceeds of the commission of an offence.

Domestic freezing orders: certification

41B.—(1)   If any of the property to which an application for a restraint order relates is property in a participating country, the applicant may ask the High Court to make a certificate under this paragraph.

(2)   The High Court may make a certificate under this paragraph if—
 (a)   it makes a restraint order in relation to property in the participating country, and
 (b)   it is satisfied that there is a good arguable case that the property is likely to be used for the purposes of a listed offence or is the proceeds of the commission of a listed offence.

(3)   A certificate under this paragraph is a certificate which—
 (a)   is made for the purposes of the relevant Framework Decision, and
 (b)   gives the specified information.

(4)   If the High Court makes a certificate under this paragraph—
 (a)   the restraint order must provide for notice of the certificate to be given to the person affected by it, and
 (b)   paragraph 34(2) to (4) applies to the certificate as it applies to the restraint order.

Sending domestic freezing orders

41C.—(1)   If a certificate is made under paragraph 41B, the restraint order and the certificate are to be sent to the Secretary of State for forwarding to—
 (a)   a court exercising jurisdiction in the place where the property is situated, or
 (b)   any authority recognised by the government of the participating country as the appropriate authority for receiving orders of that kind.

(2)   The restraint order and the certificate must be accompanied by a forfeiture order, unless the certificate indicates when the court expects a forfeiture order to be sent.

(3)   The certificate must include a translation of it into an appropriate language of the participating country (if that language is not English).

(4)   The certificate must be signed by or on behalf of the court and must include a statement as to the accuracy of the information given in it.

The signature may be an electronic signature.

(5)   If the restraint order and the certificate are not accompanied by a forfeiture order, but a forfeiture order is subsequently made, it is to be sent to the Secretary of State for forwarding as mentioned in sub-paragraph (1).

Overseas freezing orders

41D.—(1)   Paragraph 41E applies where an overseas freezing order made by an appropriate court or authority in a participating country is received by the Secretary of State from the court or authority which made or confirmed the order.

(2)   An overseas freezing order is an order prohibiting dealing with property—
 (a)   which is in the United Kingdom,
 (b)   which the appropriate court or authority considers is likely to be used for the purposes of a listed offence or is the proceeds of the commission of such an offence, and
 (c)   in respect of which an order has been or may be made by a court exercising criminal jurisdiction in the participating country for the forfeiture of the property,
and in respect of which the following requirements of this paragraph are met.

(3)   The action which the appropriate court or authority considered would constitute or, as the case may be, constituted the listed offence is action done as an act of terrorism or for the purposes of terrorism.

(4)   The order must relate to—
 (a)   criminal proceedings instituted in the participating country, or
 (b)   a criminal investigation being carried on there.

(5)   The order must be accompanied by a certificate which gives the specified information; but a certificate may be treated as giving any specified information which is not given in it if the Secretary of State has the information in question.

(6)   The certificate must—
 (a)   be signed by or on behalf of the court or authority which made or confirmed the order,
 (b)   include a statement as to the accuracy of the information given in it,
 (c)   if it is not in English, include a translation of it into English.

The signature may be an electronic signature.

(7) The order must be accompanied by an order made by a court exercising criminal jurisdiction in that country for the forfeiture of the property, unless the certificate indicates when such an order is expected to be sent.

(8) An appropriate court or authority in a participating country in relation to an overseas freezing order is—

    (a) a court exercising criminal jurisdiction in the country,

    (b) a prosecuting authority in the country,

    (c) any other authority in the country which appears to the Secretary of State to have the function of making such orders.

(9) References in paragraphs 41E to 41G to an overseas freezing order include its accompanying certificate.

Enforcement of overseas freezing orders

41E.—(1) Where this paragraph applies the Secretary of State must send a copy of the overseas freezing order to the High Court and to the Director of Public Prosecutions for Northern Ireland.

(2) The court is to consider the overseas freezing order on its own initiative within a period prescribed by rules of court.

(3) Before giving effect to the overseas freezing order, the court must give the Director an opportunity to be heard.

(4) The court may decide not to give effect to the overseas freezing order only if, in its opinion, giving effect to it would be incompatible with any of the Convention rights (within the meaning of the Human Rights Act 1998).

41F. The High Court may postpone giving effect to an overseas freezing order in respect of any property—

    (a) in order to avoid prejudicing a criminal investigation which is taking place in the United Kingdom, or

    (b) if, under an order made by a court in criminal proceedings in the United Kingdom, the property may not be dealt with.

41G.—(1) Where the High Court decides to give effect to an overseas freezing order, it must—

    (a) register the order in that court,

    (b) provide for notice of the registration to be given to any person affected by it.

(2) For the purpose of enforcing an overseas freezing order registered in the High Court, the order is to have effect as if it were an order made by that court.

(3) Paragraph 35 applies to an overseas freezing order registered in the High Court as it applies to a restraint order under paragraph 33.

(4) The High Court may cancel the registration of the order, or vary the property to which the order applies, on an application by the Director of Public Prosecutions for Northern Ireland or any other person affected by it, if or to the extent that—

    (a) the court is of the opinion mentioned in paragraph 41E(4), or

    (b) the court is of the opinion that the order has ceased to have effect in the participating country.

(5) Her Majesty may by Order in Council make further provision for the enforcement in Northern Ireland of registered overseas freezing orders.

(6) An Order in Council under this paragraph—

    (a) may make different provision for different cases,

    (b) is not to be made unless a draft of it has been laid before and approved by resolution of each House of Parliament.]

Enforcement of orders made elsewhere in the British Islands

42. In the following provisions of this Part of this Schedule— "an England and Wales order" means—

    (a) an order made in England and Wales under section 23 [or 23A] ("an England and Wales forfeiture order"),

    (b) an order made under paragraph 5 ("an England and Wales restraint order"), or

    (c) an order made under any other provision of Part I of this Schedule in relation to an England and Wales forfeiture or restraint order;

"a Scottish order" means—

    (a) an order made in Scotland under section 23 [or 23A] ("a Scottish forfeiture order"),

    (b) an order made under paragraph 18 ("a Scottish restraint order"), or

    (c) an order made under any other provision of Part II of this Schedule in relation to a Scottish forfeiture or restraint order;

"an Islands order" means an order made in any of the Islands under a provision of the law of that Island corresponding to—

(a)   section 23 [or 23A] ("an Islands forfeiture order"),
(b)   paragraph 33 ("an Islands restraint order"), or
(c)   any other provision of this Part of this Schedule.

43.—(1)   Subject to the provisions of this paragraph, an England and Wales, Scottish or Islands order shall have effect in the law of Northern Ireland.

(2)   But such an order shall be enforced in Northern Ireland only in accordance with—

(a)   the provisions of this paragraph, and
(b)   any provision made by rules of court as to the manner in which, and the conditions subject to which, such orders are to be enforced there.

(3)   On an application made to it in accordance with rules of court for registration of an England and Wales, Scottish or Islands order, the High Court shall direct that the order shall, in accordance with such rules, be registered in that court.

(4)   Rules of court shall also make provision—

(a)   for cancelling or varying the registration of an England and Wales, Scottish or Islands forfeiture order when effect has been given to it, whether in Northern Ireland or elsewhere, in respect of all or, as the case may be, part of the money or other property to which the order applies;
(b)   for cancelling or varying the registration of an England and Wales, Scottish or Islands restraint order which has been discharged or varied by the court by which it was made.

(5)   If an England and Wales, Scottish or Islands forfeiture order is registered under this paragraph the High Court shall have, in relation to that order, the same powers as a court has under paragraph 30(1) to give effect to a forfeiture order made by it and—

(a)   paragraph 31 shall apply accordingly,
(b)   any functions of the clerk of petty sessions or the appropriate officer of the Crown Court shall be exercised by the appropriate officer of the High Court, and
(c)   after making any payment required by virtue of paragraph 30(1)(d) or 31, the balance of any sums received by the appropriate officer of the High Court by virtue of an order made under this sub-paragraph shall be paid into the Consolidated Fund.

(6)   If an England and Wales, Scottish or Islands restraint order is registered under this paragraph—

(a)   paragraphs 35 and 38 shall apply as they apply to a restraint order under paragraph 33, and
(b)   the High Court shall have the like power to make an order under section 21 of the Administration of Justice Act 1969 (extended power to order inspection of property, &c) in relation to proceedings brought or likely to be brought for an England and Wales, Scottish or Islands restraint order as if those proceedings had been brought or were likely to be brought in the High Court.

(7)   In addition, if an England and Wales, Scottish or Islands order is registered under this paragraph—

(a)   the High Court shall have, in relation to its enforcement, the same power as if the order had originally been made in the High Court,
(b)   proceedings for or with respect to its enforcement may be taken as if the order had originally been made in the High Court, and
(c)   proceedings for or with respect to any contravention of such an order, whether before or after such registration, may be taken as if the order had originally been made in the High Court.

(8)   The High Court may also make such orders or do otherwise as seems to it appropriate for the purpose of—

(a)   assisting the achievement in Northern Ireland of the purposes of an England and Wales, Scottish or Islands order, or
(b)   assisting any receiver or other person directed by any such order to sell or otherwise dispose of property.

(9)   The following documents shall be received in evidence in Northern Ireland without further proof—

(a)   a document purporting to be a copy of an England and Wales, Scottish or Islands order and to be certified as such by a proper officer of the court by which it was made, and
(b)   a document purporting to be a certificate for purposes corresponding to those of paragraph 32(2) and (3) and to be certified by a proper officer of the court concerned.

Enforcement of orders made in designated countries

44.—(1)   Her Majesty may by Order in Council make provision for the purpose of enabling the enforcement in Northern Ireland of external orders.

(2)   An "external order" means an order [(other than an overseas freezing order within the meaning of paragraph 41D)]—
- (a)   which is made in a country or territory designated for the purposes of this paragraph by the Order in Council, and
- (b)   which makes relevant provision.

(3)   "Relevant provision" means—
- (a)   provision for the forfeiture of terrorist property ("an external forfeiture order"), or
- (b)   provision prohibiting dealing with property which is subject to an external forfeiture order or in respect of which such an order could be made in proceedings which have been or are to be instituted in the designated country or territory ("an external restraint order").

(4)   An Order in Council under this paragraph may, in particular, include provision—
- (a)   which, for the purpose of facilitating the enforcement of any external order that may be made, has effect at times before there is an external order to be enforced;
- (b)   for matters corresponding to those for which provision is made by, or can be made under, paragraph 43(1) to (8) in relation to the orders to which that paragraph applies;
- (c)   for the proof of any matter relevant for the purposes of anything falling to be done in pursuance of the Order in Council.

(5)   An Order in Council under this paragraph may also make provision with respect to anything falling to be done on behalf of the United Kingdom in a designated country or territory in relation to proceedings in that country or territory for or in connection with the making of an external order.

(6)   An Order in Council under this paragraph—
- (a)   may make different provision for different cases, and
- (b)   shall not be made unless a draft of it has been laid before and approved by resolution of each House of Parliament.

[1270]

NOTES

Para 29: words in square brackets in definition "forfeiture order" inserted, and definition "relevant offence" inserted, by the Counter-Terrorism Act 2008, s 39, Sch 3, para 5(1), (19), as from a day to be appointed.

Para 30: words in square brackets in sub-para (1)(a) substituted by the Police (Northern Ireland) Act 2000, s 78(2)(c), as from 4 November 2001; for the words in italics in sub-para (1)(d) there are substituted the words "section 23B(1)" by the Counter-Terrorism Act 2008, s 39, Sch 3, para 5(1), (20), as from a day to be appointed.

Para 32: for the words in italics in sub-para (2)(c) there are substituted the words "section 23B(1)" by the Counter-Terrorism Act 2008, s 39, Sch 3, para 5(1), (21), as from a day to be appointed.

Para 32A: inserted by the Counter-Terrorism Act 2008, s 37(3), as from a day to be appointed.

Para 33: for the words in italics in sub-paras (1)(a), (2)(a) there are substituted the words "a relevant offence" by the Counter-Terrorism Act 2008, s 39, Sch 3, para 5(1), (22), as from a day to be appointed; sub-para (2) and words in square brackets in sub-para (3) substituted, and sub-para (6) added, by the Anti-terrorism, Crime and Security Act 2001, s 3, Sch 2, Pt 2, para 4(1)–(4), as from 20 December 2001.

Para 34: sub-paras (3), (4) substituted, for original sub-para (3), by the Anti-terrorism, Crime and Security Act 2001, s 3, Sch 2, Pt 2, para 4(1), (5), as from 20 December 2001; for the words in italics in sub-paras (4)(a), (b) there are substituted the words "relevant offences" by the Counter-Terrorism Act 2008, s 39, Sch 3, para 5(1), (23), as from a day to be appointed.

Para 36: repealed by the Terrorism Act 2000 (Continuance of Part VII) Order 2003, SI 2003/427, art 2(2)(b), as from 19 February 2003, and by the Terrorism (Northern Ireland) Act 2006, s 5(2), Schedule, as from 18 February 2006.

Para 38: words in square brackets in sub-para (4) of the definition "prosecutor" substituted by the Anti-terrorism, Crime and Security Act 2001, s 3, Sch 2, Pt 2, para 4(1), (6), as from 20 December 2001; for the words in italics in that paragraph there are substituted the words "a relevant offence" by the Counter-Terrorism Act 2008, s 39, Sch 3, para 5(1), (24), as from a day to be appointed.

Para 39 is amended as follows:

The heading "Compensation" is repealed by the Counter-Terrorism Act 2008, s 39, Sch 3, para 5(1), (25), as from a day to be appointed.

Words in square brackets in sub-para (1) substituted by the Anti-terrorism, Crime and Security Act 2001, s 3, Sch 2, Pt 2, para 4(1), (7), as from 20 December 2001.

For the words in italics in sub-para (2) (in all 4 places) there are substituted the words "a relevant offence" by the Counter-Terrorism Act 2008, s 39, Sch 3, para 5(1), (26), as from a day to be appointed.

Words in first pair of square brackets in sub-paras (4), (6) substituted by the Police (Northern Ireland) Act 2000, s 78(2)(c), as from 4 November 2001; words in second pair of square brackets in those sub-paragraphs substituted by the Justice (Northern Ireland) Act 2002, s 85, Sch 12, para 80, as from 13 June 2005.

Para 40: for the words in italics in sub-para (1)(a) there are substituted the words "a relevant offence" by the Counter-Terrorism Act 2008, s 39, Sch 3, para 5(1), (27), as from a day to be appointed.

Paras 41A–41G: inserted by the Crime (International Co-operation) Act 2003, s 90, Sch 4, paras 1, 7, as from a day to be appointed.

Para 42: words "or 23A" in square brackets (in each place they occur) inserted by the Counter-Terrorism Act 2008, s 39, Sch 3, para 5(1), (28), as from a day to be appointed.

Para 44: words in square brackets in sub-para (2) inserted by the Crime (International Co-operation) Act 2003, s 90, Sch 4, paras 1, 8, as from a day to be appointed.

Orders: the Terrorism Act 2000 (Enforcement of External Orders) Order 2001, SI 2001/3927.

PART IV
INSOLVENCY: UNITED KINGDOM PROVISIONS

General

45.   In this Part of this Schedule—
   "ancillary order" means an order made in connection with a forfeiture, other than the forfeiture order,
   "forfeiture order" means—
   (a)   an order made in England and Wales, Scotland or Northern Ireland under section 23 [or 23A],
   (b)   an Islands forfeiture order within the meaning given in paragraph 12, 26 or 42, or
   (c)   an external forfeiture order which is enforceable in England and Wales, Scotland or Northern Ireland by virtue of an Order in Council made under paragraph 14, 28 or 44,
   "forfeited property" means the money or other property to which a forfeiture order applies, and
   "restraint order" means—
   (a)   an order made under paragraph 5, 18 or 33,
   (b)   an Islands restraint order within the meaning given in paragraph 12, 26 or 42, or
   (c)   an external restraint order which is enforceable in England and Wales, Scotland or Northern Ireland by virtue of an Order in Council made under paragraph 14, 28 or 44 [or an order which is enforceable in England and Wales, Scotland or Northern Ireland by virtue of paragraph 11G, 25G or 41G].

Protection of creditors against forfeiture

46.—(1)   During the period of six months beginning with the making of a forfeiture order, the following shall not be finally disposed of under this Schedule—
   (a)   the money to which the order applies, and
   (b)   the money which represents any property to which the order applies.

   (2)   For the purposes of this paragraph money is finally disposed of under this Schedule when—
   (a)   in England and Wales, it is paid to the Lord Chancellor in accordance with [section 38 of the Courts Act 2003 (application of receipts of designated officers)] or to the Secretary of State in accordance with paragraph 13(5)(c),
   (b)   in Scotland, it is paid to the Treasury in accordance with section 211(5) of the Criminal Procedure (Scotland) Act 1995 (as modified by paragraph 16(3)), or
   (c)   in Northern Ireland, it is paid into the Consolidated Fund in accordance with paragraph 32(4) or 43(5)(c).

47.—(1)   This paragraph applies where—
   (a)   before or after a forfeiture order is made, the commencement of an insolvency occurs in qualifying insolvency proceedings,
   (b)   an insolvency practitioner would, but for the forfeiture order, exercise a function in those proceedings in relation to property to which the forfeiture order applies, and
   (c)   he gives written notice to the relevant officer of the matters referred to in paragraphs (a) and (b) before the end of the period of six months beginning with the making of the forfeiture order.

   (2)   Sub-paragraph (3) shall apply to—
   (a)   the property in relation to which the insolvency practitioner would, but for the forfeiture order, exercise a function as described in sub-paragraph (1)(b), and
   (b)   the proceeds of sale of that property.

   (3)   The property—
   (a)   shall cease to be subject to the forfeiture order and any ancillary order, and
   (b)   shall be dealt with in the insolvency proceedings as if the forfeiture order had never been made.

   (4)   But—
   (a)   the property to which sub-paragraph (3) applies is the balance remaining after the relevant officer has exercised his powers under paragraph 50(1), and
   (b)   sub-paragraph (3) shall not take effect in respect of property in relation to which the relevant officer, or any person acting in pursuance of an ancillary order, has incurred obligations until those obligations have been discharged.

   (5)   In this paragraph "the commencement of an insolvency" means—
   (a)   the making of a bankruptcy order,
   (b)   the award of sequestration,
   (c)   in England and Wales or in Northern Ireland, in the case of the insolvent estate of a deceased person, the making of an insolvency administration order, or

(d) in the case of a company, the passing of a resolution for its winding up, or where no such resolution has been passed, the making of an order by the court for the winding up of the company.

48.—(1) Where by virtue of paragraph 47(3) property falls to be dealt with in insolvency proceedings, the Secretary of State shall be taken to be a creditor in those proceedings to the amount or value of the property.

(2) Except in a sequestration, his debt—
(a) shall rank after the debts of all other creditors, and
(b) shall not be paid until they have been paid in full with interest under the relevant provision.

(3) In sub-paragraph (2)(b) the "relevant provision" means—
(a) in relation to the winding up of a company in England and Wales or Scotland, section 189(2) of the Insolvency Act 1986,
(b) in relation to a bankruptcy in England and Wales, section 328(4) of that Act,
(c) in relation to the winding up of a company in Northern Ireland, Article 160(2) of the Insolvency (Northern Ireland) Order 1989, and
(d) in relation to a bankruptcy in Northern Ireland, Article 300(4) of that Order.

(4) In a sequestration, his debt shall rank after all of the debts mentioned in section 51(1) of the Bankruptcy (Scotland) Act 1985 and shall not be paid until they have been paid in full.

(5) Sub-paragraphs (2) to (4) apply notwithstanding any provision contained in or made under any other enactment.

49.—(1) This paragraph applies to property which ceased to be subject to a forfeiture order by virtue of paragraph 47(3) in consequence of the making of a bankruptcy order or an award of sequestration.

(2) The property shall again become subject to the forfeiture order and, if applicable, any ancillary order if—
(a) the bankruptcy order is annulled, or
(b) the award of sequestration is recalled or reduced.

(3) Where the property is money or has been converted into money—
(a) the relevant court shall make an order specifying property comprised in the estate of the bankrupt or debtor to the amount or value of the property, and
(b) the specified property shall become subject to the forfeiture order, and any applicable ancillary order, in place of the property.

(4) In sub-paragraph (3) the "relevant court" means—
(a) the court which ordered the annulment of the bankruptcy, or
(b) the court which recalled or reduced the award of sequestration.

Expenses incurred in connection with forfeiture

50.—(1) Where money or other property falls to be dealt with in accordance with paragraph 47(3), the relevant officer may—
(a) deduct allowable forfeiture expenses from that money;
(b) retain so much of that property as he considers necessary for the purpose of realising it and deducting allowable forfeiture expenses from the proceeds of realisation.

(2) Where property is delivered up in pursuance of paragraph 47(3) and the relevant officer has not made provision under sub-paragraph (1) for all the allowable forfeiture expenses then—
(a) a person who has incurred allowable forfeiture expenses for which provision has not been made shall have a claim to their value in the insolvency proceedings, and
(b) the expenses in question shall be treated for the purposes of the insolvency proceedings as if they were expenses of those proceedings.

(3) In this paragraph "allowable forfeiture expenses"—
(a) means expenses incurred in relation to the forfeited property by the relevant officer,
(b) means expenses incurred in relation to the forfeited property by a receiver, administrator or other person appointed by the relevant officer,
(c) means expenses incurred in relation to the forfeited property by any person appointed or directed to deal with any property under paragraph 16, and
(d) includes sums paid or required to be paid under paragraph 2(1)(d), 16(1)(c) or 30(1)(d).

Protection of insolvency practitioners

51.—(1) This paragraph applies where an insolvency practitioner seizes or disposes of property which is subject to a forfeiture order or a restraint order and—
(a) he reasonably believes that he is entitled to do so in the exercise of his functions, and
(b) he would be so entitled if the property were not subject to a forfeiture order or a restraint order.

(2)   The insolvency practitioner shall not be liable to any person in respect of any loss or damage resulting from the seizure or disposal except in so far as the loss or damage is caused by his negligence.

(3)   The insolvency practitioner shall have a lien on the property seized or the proceeds of its sale—

(a)   for such of his expenses as were incurred in connection with the insolvency proceedings in relation to which the seizure or disposal purported to take place, and

(b)   for so much of his remuneration as may be reasonably assigned for his acting in connection with those proceedings.

(4)   Sub-paragraphs (1) to (3) are without prejudice to the generality of any provision contained in the Insolvency Act 1986 or the Bankruptcy (Scotland) Act 1985 or any other Act or the Insolvency (Northern Ireland) Order 1989.

(5)   In this paragraph "insolvency practitioner", in any part of the United Kingdom, means a person acting as an insolvency practitioner in that or any other part of the United Kingdom.

(6)   For the purpose of sub-paragraph (5) any question whether a person is acting as an insolvency practitioner in England and Wales or in Scotland shall be determined in accordance with section 388 of the Insolvency Act 1986, except that—

(a)   the reference in section 388(2)(a) to a permanent or interim trustee in the sequestration of a debtor's estate shall be taken to include a reference to a trustee in sequestration,

(b)   section 388(5) shall be disregarded, and

(c)   the expression shall also include the Official Receiver acting as receiver or manager of property.

(7)   For the purpose of sub-paragraph (5) any question whether a person is acting as an insolvency practitioner in Northern Ireland shall be determined in accordance with Article 3 of the Insolvency (Northern Ireland) Order 1989, except that—

(a)   Article 3(5) shall be disregarded, and

(b)   the expression shall also include the Official Receiver acting as receiver or manager of property.

Insolvency practitioners in the Islands and designated countries

52.—(1)   An order may be made under this paragraph to secure that an Islands or external insolvency practitioner has the same rights under this Part of this Schedule in relation to—

(a)   property situated in England and Wales,

(b)   property situated in Scotland, or

(c)   property situated in Northern Ireland,

as he would have if he were an insolvency practitioner in that part of the United Kingdom.

(2)   The Secretary of State may make an order—

(a)   under sub-paragraph (1)(a) with the concurrence of the Lord Chancellor;

(b)   under sub-paragraph (1)(b).

(3)   An order under sub-paragraph (1)(c)—

(a)   may be made by the Department of Enterprise, Trade and Investment in Northern Ireland,

(b)   shall be a statutory rule for the purposes of the Statutory Rules (Northern Ireland) Order 1979, and

(c)   shall be subject to negative resolution within the meaning of section 41(6) of the Interpretation (Northern Ireland) Act 1954.

(4)   An order under this paragraph may, in particular, include—

(a)   provision which modifies the rights under this Part of this Schedule which are to be conferred under the order;

(b)   provision as to the manner in which the rights conferred under the order are to be exercised;

(c)   provision as to the conditions subject to which those rights are to be exercised, including the obtaining of leave from a court;

(d)   provision for empowering a court granting such leave to impose such conditions as it thinks fit.

(5)   An order under this paragraph may make different provision for different purposes.

(6)   In this paragraph—

"Islands or external insolvency practitioner" means a person exercising under the insolvency law of a relevant country or territory functions corresponding to those exercised by insolvency practitioners under the insolvency law of any part of the United Kingdom,

"insolvency law" has the same meaning as in section 426(10) of the Insolvency Act 1986, except that the reference to a relevant country or territory shall be construed in accordance with this paragraph, and

"relevant country or territory" means—
  (a) any of the Channel Islands,
  (b) the Isle of Man, or
  (c) any country or territory designated as mentioned in paragraph 14, 28 or 44.

Interpretation

53.—(1) In this Part of this Schedule (other than in paragraph 51) "insolvency practitioner" means a person acting in any qualifying insolvency proceedings in any part of the United Kingdom as—
  (a) a liquidator of a company or partnership,
  (b) a trustee in bankruptcy,
  (c) the permanent or interim trustee on the debtor's estate,
  (d) an administrator of the insolvent estate of a deceased person, or
  (e) a receiver or manager of any property.

  (2) In this Part of this Schedule "qualifying insolvency proceedings" means—
  (a) any proceedings under the Insolvency Act 1986 or the Insolvency (Northern Ireland) Order 1989 for the winding up of a company or an unregistered company and includes any voluntary winding up of a company under Part IV of that Act or Part V of that Order,
  (b) any proceedings in England and Wales or Northern Ireland under or by virtue of section 420 of the Insolvency Act 1986 or Article 364 of the Insolvency (Northern Ireland) Order 1989 for the winding up of an insolvent partnership,
  (c) any proceedings in bankruptcy or, in Scotland, any sequestration of a debtor's estate, or
  (d) any proceedings in England and Wales or in Northern Ireland under or by virtue of section 421 of the Insolvency Act 1986 or Article 365 of the Insolvency (Northern Ireland) Order 1989 in relation to the insolvent estate of a deceased person.

  (3) In this Part of this Schedule "the relevant officer" means in England and Wales and in Northern Ireland—
  (a) where the forfeiture order in question is made by a court in England and Wales, the proper officer within the meaning given in paragraph 4,
  (b) where the forfeiture order in question is made by a court in Northern Ireland, the proper officer within the meaning given in paragraph 32, and
  (c) in any other case, the appropriate officer of the High Court.

  (4) In this Part of this Schedule "the relevant officer" means in Scotland—
  (a) where the forfeiture order in question is made by a court in Scotland, the clerk of the court,
  (b) in any other case, the Principal Clerk of Session and Justiciary.

  (5) In this Part of this Schedule references to the proceeds of sale or realisation of property are references to the proceeds after deduction of the costs of sale or realisation.

[1271]

NOTES
  Para 45: words in square brackets in para (a) of the definition "forfeiture order" inserted by the Counter-Terrorism Act 2008, s 39, Sch 3, para 5(1), (29), as from a day to be appointed; words in square brackets in para (c) of the definition "restraint order" inserted by the Crime (International Co-operation) Act 2003, s 90, Sch 4, paras 1, 9, as from a day to be appointed.
  Para 46: words in square brackets in sub-para (2)(a) substituted by the Courts Act 2003, s 109(1), Sch 8, para 388(1), (4), as from 1 April 2005.

SCHEDULE 6
FINANCIAL INFORMATION
Section 38

Orders

1.—(1) Where an order has been made under this paragraph in relation to a terrorist investigation, a constable named in the order may require a financial institution [to which the order applies] to provide customer information for the purposes of the investigation.

  [(1A) The order may provide that it applies to—
  (a) all financial institutions,
  (b) a particular description, or particular descriptions, of financial institutions, or
  (c) a particular financial institution or particular financial institutions.]

  (2) The information shall be provided—
  (a) in such manner and within such time as the constable may specify, and
  (b) notwithstanding any restriction on the disclosure of information imposed by statute or otherwise.

  (3) An institution which fails to comply with a requirement under this paragraph shall be guilty of an offence.

PART II OTHER ACTS

(4)   It is a defence for an institution charged with an offence under sub-paragraph (3) to prove—
  (a)   that the information required was not in the institution's possession, or
  (b)   that it was not reasonably practicable for the institution to comply with the requirement.

(5)   An institution guilty of an offence under sub-paragraph (3) shall be liable on summary conviction to a fine not exceeding level 5 on the standard scale.

Procedure

2.   An order under paragraph 1 may be made only on the application of—
  (a)   in England and Wales or Northern Ireland, a police officer of at least the rank of superintendent, or
  (b)   in Scotland, the procurator fiscal.

3.   An order under paragraph 1 may be made only by—
  (a)   in England and Wales, a Circuit judge [or a District Judge (Magistrates' Courts)],
  (b)   in Scotland, the sheriff, or
  (c)   in Northern Ireland, a [Crown Court judge].

4.—(1)   [Criminal Procedure Rules] may make provision about the procedure for an application under paragraph 1.

(2)   The High Court of Justiciary may, by Act of Adjournal, make provision about the procedure for an application under paragraph 1.

[(3)   Crown Court Rules may make provision about the procedure for an application under paragraph 1.]

Criteria for making order

5.   An order under paragraph 1 may be made only if the person making it is satisfied that—
  (a)   the order is sought for the purposes of a terrorist investigation,
  (b)   the tracing of terrorist property is desirable for the purposes of the investigation, and
  (c)   the order will enhance the effectiveness of the investigation.

Financial institution

6.—(1)   In this Schedule "financial institution" means—
  [(a)   a person who has permission under Part 4 of the Financial Services and Markets Act 2000 to accept deposits,]
  (b)   ...
  (c)   a credit union (within the meaning of the Credit Unions Act 1979 or the Credit Unions (Northern Ireland) Order 1985),
  [(d)   a person carrying on a relevant regulated activity,]
  (e)   the National Savings Bank,
  (f)   a person who carries out an activity for the purposes of raising money authorised to be raised under the National Loans Act 1968 under the auspices of the Director of National Savings,
  (g)   a European institution carrying on a home regulated activity (within the meaning of [Directive 2006/48/EC of the European Parliament and of the Council of 14 June 2006] relating to the taking up and pursuit of the business of credit institutions),
  (h)   a person carrying out an activity specified in any of points 1 to 12 and 14 of [Annex 1] to that Directive, and
  (i)   a person who carries on an insurance business in accordance with an authorisation pursuant to [Article 4 or 51 of Directive 2002/83/EC of the European Parliament and of the Council of 5th November 2002 concerning life assurance].

[(1A)   For the purposes of sub-paragraph (1)(d), a relevant regulated activity means—
  (a)   dealing in investments as principal or as agent,
  (b)   arranging deals in investments,
  [(ba)   operating a multilateral trading facility,]
  (c)   managing investments,
  (d)   safeguarding and administering investments,
  (e)   sending dematerialised instructions,
  (f)   establishing etc collective investment schemes,
  (g)   advising on investments.

(1B)   Sub-paragraphs (1)(a) and (1A) must be read with—
  (a)   section 22 of the Financial Services and Markets Act 2000;
  (b)   any relevant order under that section; and
  (c)   Schedule 2 to that Act.]

(2)   The Secretary of State may by order provide for a class of person—
  (a)   to be a financial institution for the purposes of this Schedule, or
  (b)   to cease to be a financial institution for the purposes of this Schedule.

(3)   An institution which ceases to be a financial institution for the purposes of this Schedule (whether by virtue of sub-paragraph (2)(b) or otherwise) shall continue to be treated as a financial institution for the purposes of any requirement under paragraph 1 to provide customer information which relates to a time when the institution was a financial institution.

Customer information

7.—(1)   In this Schedule "customer information" means (subject to sub-paragraph (3))—
   (a)   information whether a business relationship exists or existed between a financial institution and a particular person ("a customer"),
   (b)   a customer's account number,
   (c)   a customer's full name,
   (d)   a customer's date of birth,
   (e)   a customer's address or former address,
   (f)   the date on which a business relationship between a financial institution and a customer begins or ends,
   (g)   any evidence of a customer's identity obtained by a financial institution in pursuance of or for the purposes of any legislation relating to money laundering, and
   (h)   the identity of a person sharing an account with a customer.

   (2)   For the purposes of this Schedule there is a business relationship between a financial institution and a person if (and only if)—
   (a)   there is an arrangement between them designed to facilitate the carrying out of frequent or regular transactions between them, and
   (b)   the total amount of payments to be made in the course of the arrangement is neither known nor capable of being ascertained when the arrangement is made.

   (3)   The Secretary of State may by order provide for a class of information—
   (a)   to be customer information for the purposes of this Schedule, or
   (b)   to cease to be customer information for the purposes of this Schedule.

Offence by body corporate, &c

8.—(1)   This paragraph applies where an offence under paragraph 1(3) is committed by an institution and it is proved that the offence—
   (a)   was committed with the consent or connivance of an officer of the institution, or
   (b)   was attributable to neglect on the part of an officer of the institution.

   (2)   The officer, as well as the institution, shall be guilty of the offence.

   (3)   Where an individual is convicted of an offence under paragraph 1(3) by virtue of this paragraph, he shall be liable on summary conviction to—
   (a)   imprisonment for a term not exceeding six months,
   (b)   a fine not exceeding level 5 on the standard scale, or
   (c)   both.

   (4)   In the case of an institution which is a body corporate, in this paragraph "officer" includes—
   (a)   a director, manager or secretary,
   (b)   a person purporting to act as a director, manager or secretary, and
   (c)   if the affairs of the body are managed by its members, a member.

   (5)   In the case of an institution which is a partnership, in this paragraph "officer" means a partner.

   (6)   In the case of an institution which is an unincorporated association (other than a partnership), in this paragraph "officer" means a person concerned in the management or control of the association.

Self-incrimination

9.—(1)   Customer information provided by a financial institution under this Schedule shall not be admissible in evidence in criminal proceedings against the institution or any of its officers or employees.

   (2)   Sub-paragraph (1) shall not apply in relation to proceedings for an offence under paragraph 1(3) (including proceedings brought by virtue of paragraph 8).

[1272]

NOTES
   Para 1: words in square brackets in sub-para (1), and sub-para (1A), inserted by the Anti-terrorism, Crime and Security Act 2001, s 3, Sch 2, Pt 4, para 6, as from 20 December 2001.
   Para 3: words in square brackets in sub-para (a) inserted by the Courts Act 2003, s 65, Sch 4, para 10, as from a day to be appointed (see further the note below); words in square brackets in sub-para (c) substituted by the Anti-terrorism, Crime and Security Act 2001, s 121(1), (4), as from 7 July 2002.

Para 4: words in square brackets in sub-para (1) substituted, and sub-para (3) added, by the Courts Act 2003, s 109(1), Sch 8, para 390, as from 1 September 2004 (except in relation to the operation of this Schedule in relation to rules of court other than Criminal Procedure Rules during the period between that date and the coming into force of the first Criminal Procedure Rules made under the Courts Act 2003, s 69: see SI 2004/2066, art 3).

Para 6: sub-paras (1)(a), (d) substituted, sub-para (1)(b) repealed, and sub-paras (1A), (1B) inserted, by the Financial Services and Markets Act 2000 (Consequential Amendments and Repeals) Order 2001, SI 2001/3649, art 361, as from 1 December 2001; words in square brackets in sub-para (1)(g) substituted by the Capital Requirements Regulations 2006, SI 2006/3221, reg 29(2), Sch 4, para 6(1), (3), as from 1 January 2007; words in square brackets in sub-para (1)(h) substituted by the Banking Consolidation Directive (Consequential Amendments) Regulations 2000, SI 2000/2952, reg 9, as from 22 November 2000; words in square brackets in sub-para (1)(i) substituted by the Life Assurance Consolidation Directive (Consequential Amendments) Regulations 2004, SI 2004/3379, reg 7, as from 11 January 2005; sub-para (1A)(ba) inserted by the Financial Services and Markets Act 2000 (Regulated Activities) (Amendment No 3) Order 2006, SI 2006/3384, art 33, as from 1 November 2007 (for the full commencement details of SI 2006/3384, see the Note for that Order at [2866A]).

Note: the Courts Act 2003 (Commencement No 10) Order 2005, SI 2005/910 brings s 65 of the Courts Act 2003 into force on 1 April 2005; it does not, however, specifically provide that Sch 4 shall also come into force on that date and it is believed that the intention was not to commence Sch 4 on that date.

Post-charge questioning and jurisdiction to try offences: see further the Counter-Terrorism Act 2008, ss 22–24, 27 in relation to post-charge questioning for an offence under para 1. See also s 28 of that Act which provides that such an offence may be tried anywhere in the UK.

[SCHEDULE 6A
ACCOUNT MONITORING ORDERS

1 Introduction

(1)   This paragraph applies for the purposes of this Schedule.

(2)   A judge is—
    (a)   a *Circuit judge* in England and Wales;
    (b)   the sheriff, in Scotland;
    (c)   a Crown Court judge, in Northern Ireland.

(3)   The court is—
    (a)   the Crown Court, in England and Wales or Northern Ireland;
    (b)   the sheriff, in Scotland.

(4)   An appropriate officer is—
    (a)   a police officer, in England and Wales or Northern Ireland;
    (b)   the procurator fiscal, in Scotland.

(5)   "Financial institution" has the same meaning as in Schedule 6.

2 Account monitoring orders

(1)   A judge may, on an application made to him by an appropriate officer, make an account monitoring order if he is satisfied that—
    (a)   the order is sought for the purposes of a terrorist investigation,
    (b)   the tracing of terrorist property is desirable for the purposes of the investigation, and
    (c)   the order will enhance the effectiveness of the investigation.

(2)   The application for an account monitoring order must state that the order is sought against the financial institution specified in the application in relation to information which—
    (a)   relates to an account or accounts held at the institution by the person specified in the application (whether solely or jointly with another), and
    (b)   is of the description so specified.

(3)   The application for an account monitoring order may specify information relating to—
    (a)   all accounts held by the person specified in the application for the order at the financial institution so specified,
    (b)   a particular description, or particular descriptions, of accounts so held, or
    (c)   a particular account, or particular accounts, so held.

(4)   An account monitoring order is an order that the financial institution specified in the application for the order must—
    (a)   for the period specified in the order,
    (b)   in the manner so specified,
    (c)   at or by the time or times so specified, and
    (d)   at the place or places so specified,
provide information of the description specified in the application to an appropriate officer.

(5)   The period stated in an account monitoring order must not exceed the period of 90 days beginning with the day on which the order is made.

3 Applications

(1) An application for an account monitoring order may be made ex parte to a judge in chambers.

(2) The description of information specified in an application for an account monitoring order may be varied by the person who made the application.

(3) If the application was made by a police officer, the description of information specified in it may be varied by a different police officer.

4 Discharge or variation

(1) An application to discharge or vary an account monitoring order may be made to the court by—
   (a) the person who applied for the order;
   (b) any person affected by the order.

(2) If the application for the account monitoring order was made by a police officer, an application to discharge or vary the order may be made by a different police officer.

(3) The court—
   (a) may discharge the order;
   (b) may vary the order.

5 Rules of court

(1) Rules of court may make provision as to the practice and procedure to be followed in connection with proceedings relating to account monitoring orders.

(2) In Scotland, rules of court shall, without prejudice to section 305 of the Criminal Procedure (Scotland) Act 1995 (c 46), be made by Act of Adjournal.

6 Effect of orders

(1) In England and Wales and Northern Ireland, an account monitoring order has effect as if it were an order of the court.

(2) An account monitoring order has effect in spite of any restriction on the disclosure of information (however imposed).

7 Statements

(1) A statement made by a financial institution in response to an account monitoring order may not be used in evidence against it in criminal proceedings.

(2) But sub-paragraph (1) does not apply—
   (a) in the case of proceedings for contempt of court;
   (b) in the case of proceedings under section 23 where the financial institution has been convicted of an offence under any of sections 15 to 18;
   (c) on a prosecution for an offence where, in giving evidence, the financial institution makes a statement inconsistent with the statement mentioned in sub-paragraph (1).

(3) A statement may not be used by virtue of sub-paragraph (2)(c) against a financial institution unless—
   (a) evidence relating to it is adduced, or
   (b) a question relating to it is asked,
by or on behalf of the financial institution in the proceedings arising out of the prosecution.]

[1273]

NOTES
Inserted by the Anti-terrorism, Crime and Security Act 2001, s 3, Sch 2, Pt 1, para 1(1), (3), as from 20 December 2001.
Para 1: for the words in italics in sub-para (a) there are substituted the words "a Circuit judge or a District Judge (Magistrates' Courts)," by the Courts Act 2003, s 65, Sch 4, para 11, as from a day to be appointed (see further the note below).
Note: the Courts Act 2003 (Commencement No 10) Order 2005, SI 2005/910 brings s 65 of the Courts Act 2003 into force on 1 April 2005; it does not, however, specifically provide that Sch 4 shall also come into force on that date and it is believed that the intention was not to commence Sch 4 on that date.

(Sch 9 (Scheduled Offences): as to the expiry of this Schedule,
see the note following s 63 at **[1258]**.)

LIMITED LIABILITY PARTNERSHIPS ACT 2000

(2000 c 12)

NOTES
This Act is reproduced as amended by: the Companies (Audit, Investigations and Community Enterprise) Act 2004; the Companies Act 2006; the Income Tax Act 2007; the Open-Ended Investment Companies Regulations 2001, SI 2001/1228; the Limited Liability Partnerships (Particulars of Usual Residential Address) (Confidentiality Orders) Regulations 2002, SI 2002/915.
Application of the Banking Act 2009: s 132 of the Banking Act 2009 (at **[1901W]**) provides that the Lord Chancellor may, by order made with the concurrence of the Secretary of State and the Lord Chief Justice, modify provisions of Part 2 of the 2009 Act (bank insolvency) in their application to partnerships. See also s 163 of the 2009 Act (at **[1902X]**) which makes the same provision with regard to the application of Part 3 of that Act (bank administration). Similar provision is made with regard to Scottish partnerships by ss 133 and 164 respectively.
Fees: for fees prescribed under this Act see the Limited Liability Partnerships (Fees) Regulations 2004, SI 2004/2620 (made under the Companies Act 1985, s 708 as applied to LLPs by reg 4 of, and Sch 2 to, the Limited Liability Partnerships Regulations 2001, SI 2001/1090).

ARRANGEMENT OF SECTIONS

Introductory

An Act to make provision for limited liability partnerships

[20 July 2000]

Introductory

1 Limited liability partnerships

(1)   There shall be a new form of legal entity to be known as a limited liability partnership.

(2)   A limited liability partnership is a body corporate (with legal personality separate from that of its members) which is formed by being incorporated under this Act; and—

    (a)   in the following provisions of this Act (except in the phrase "oversea limited liability partnership"), and

    (b)   in any other enactment (except where provision is made to the contrary or the context otherwise requires),

references to a limited liability partnership are to such a body corporate.

(3)   A limited liability partnership has unlimited capacity.

(4)   The members of a limited liability partnership have such liability to contribute to its assets in the event of its being wound up as is provided for by virtue of this Act.

(5)   Accordingly, except as far as otherwise provided by this Act or any other enactment, the law relating to partnerships does not apply to a limited liability partnership.

(6)   The Schedule (which makes provision about the names and registered offices of limited liability partnerships) has effect.

[1274]

Incorporation

2   Incorporation document etc

(1)   For a limited liability partnership to be incorporated—

   (a)   two or more persons associated for carrying on a lawful business with a view to profit must have subscribed their names to an incorporation document,

   (b)   there must have been delivered to the registrar either the incorporation document or a copy authenticated in a manner approved by him, and

   (c)   there must have been so delivered a statement in a form approved by the registrar, made by either a solicitor engaged in the formation of the limited liability partnership or anyone who subscribed his name to the incorporation document, that the requirement imposed by paragraph (a) has been complied with.

(2)   The incorporation document must—

   (a)   be in a form approved by the registrar (or as near to such a form as circumstances allow),

   (b)   state the name of the limited liability partnership,

   (c)   state whether the registered office of the limited liability partnership is to be situated in England and Wales, in Wales or in Scotland,

   (d)   state the address of that registered office,

   (e)   state the name and address of each of the persons who are to be members of the limited liability partnership on incorporation, and

   (f)   either specify which of those persons are to be designated members or state that every person who from time to time is a member of the limited liability partnership is a designated member.

[(2A)   Where a confidentiality order, made under section 723B of the Companies Act 1985 as applied to a limited liability partnerships, is in force in respect of any individual named as a member of a limited liability partnership under subsection (2) that subsection shall have effect as if the reference to the address of the individual were a reference to the address for the time being notified by him under the Limited Liability Partnerships (Particulars of Usual Residential Address) (Confidentiality Orders) Regulations 2002 to any limited liability partnership of which he is a member or if he is not such a member either the address specified in his application for a confidentiality order or the address last notified by him under such a confidentiality order as the case may be.

(2B)   Where the incorporation document or a copy of such delivered under this section includes an address specified in reliance on subsection (2A) there shall be delivered with it or the copy of it a statement in a form approved by the registrar containing particulars of the usual residential address of the member whose address is so specified.]

(3)   If a person makes a false statement under subsection (1)(c) which he—

   (a)   knows to be false, or

   (b)   does not believe to be true,

he commits an offence.

(4)   A person guilty of an offence under subsection (3) is liable—

   (a)   on summary conviction, to imprisonment for a period not exceeding six months or a fine not exceeding the statutory maximum, or to both, or

   (b)   on conviction on indictment, to imprisonment for a period not exceeding two years or a fine, or to both.

[1275]

NOTES

Sub-ss (2A), (2B): inserted by the Limited Liability Partnerships (Particulars of Usual Residential Address) (Confidentiality Orders) Regulations 2002, SI 2002/915, reg 16, Sch 2, para 1, as from 2 April 2002.

3   Incorporation by registration

(1)   When the requirements imposed by paragraphs (b) and (c) of subsection (1) of section 2 have been complied with, the registrar shall retain the incorporation document or copy delivered to him and, unless the requirement imposed by paragraph (a) of that subsection has not been complied with, he shall—

   (a)   register the incorporation document or copy, and

(b)   give a certificate that the limited liability partnership is incorporated by the name specified in the incorporation document.

(2)   The registrar may accept the statement delivered under paragraph (c) of subsection (1) of section 2 as sufficient evidence that the requirement imposed by paragraph (a) of that subsection has been complied with.

(3)   The certificate shall either be signed by the registrar or be authenticated by his official seal.

(4)   The certificate is conclusive evidence that the requirements of section 2 are complied with and that the limited liability partnership is incorporated by the name specified in the incorporation document.

[1276]

Membership

4 Members

(1)   On the incorporation of a limited liability partnership its members are the persons who subscribed their names to the incorporation document (other than any who have died or been dissolved).

(2)   Any other person may become a member of a limited liability partnership by and in accordance with an agreement with the existing members.

(3)   A person may cease to be a member of a limited liability partnership (as well as by death or dissolution) in accordance with an agreement with the other members or, in the absence of agreement with the other members as to cessation of membership, by giving reasonable notice to the other members.

(4)   A member of a limited liability partnership shall not be regarded for any purpose as employed by the limited liability partnership unless, if he and the other members were partners in a partnership, he would be regarded for that purpose as employed by the partnership.

[1276A]

5 Relationship of members etc

(1)   Except as far as otherwise provided by this Act or any other enactment, the mutual rights and duties of the members of a limited liability partnership, and the mutual rights and duties of a limited liability partnership and its members, shall be governed—
(a)   by agreement between the members, or between the limited liability partnership and its members, or
(b)   in the absence of agreement as to any matter, by any provision made in relation to that matter by regulations under section 15(c).

(2)   An agreement made before the incorporation of a limited liability partnership between the persons who subscribe their names to the incorporation document may impose obligations on the limited liability partnership (to take effect at any time after its incorporation).

[1276B]

6 Members as agents

(1)   Every member of a limited liability partnership is the agent of the limited liability partnership.

(2)   But a limited liability partnership is not bound by anything done by a member in dealing with a person if—
(a)   the member in fact has no authority to act for the limited liability partnership by doing that thing, and
(b)   the person knows that he has no authority or does not know or believe him to be a member of the limited liability partnership.

(3)   Where a person has ceased to be a member of a limited liability partnership, the former member is to be regarded (in relation to any person dealing with the limited liability partnership) as still being a member of the limited liability partnership unless—
(a)   the person has notice that the former member has ceased to be a member of the limited liability partnership, or
(b)   notice that the former member has ceased to be a member of the limited liability partnership has been delivered to the registrar.

(4)   Where a member of a limited liability partnership is liable to any person (other than another member of the limited liability partnership) as a result of a wrongful act or omission of his in the course of the business of the limited liability partnership or with its authority, the limited liability partnership is liable to the same extent as the member.

[1276C]

7 Ex-members

(1)   This section applies where a member of a limited liability partnership has either ceased to be a member or—

   (a)   has died,

   (b)   has become bankrupt or had his estate sequestrated or has been wound up,

   (c)   has granted a trust deed for the benefit of his creditors, or

   (d)   has assigned the whole or any part of his share in the limited liability partnership (absolutely or by way of charge or security).

(2)   In such an event the former member or—

   (a)   his personal representative,

   (b)   his trustee in bankruptcy or permanent or interim trustee (within the meaning of the Bankruptcy (Scotland) Act 1985) or liquidator,

   (c)   his trustee under the trust deed for the benefit of his creditors, or

   (d)   his assignee,

may not interfere in the management or administration of any business or affairs of the limited liability partnership.

(3)   But subsection (2) does not affect any right to receive an amount from the limited liability partnership in that event.

[1276D]

8 Designated members

(1)   If the incorporation document specifies who are to be designated members—

   (a)   they are designated members on incorporation, and

   (b)   any member may become a designated member by and in accordance with an agreement with the other members,

and a member may cease to be a designated member in accordance with an agreement with the other members.

(2)   But if there would otherwise be no designated members, or only one, every member is a designated member.

(3)   If the incorporation document states that every person who from time to time is a member of the limited liability partnership is a designated member, every member is a designated member.

(4)   A limited liability partnership may at any time deliver to the registrar—

   (a)   notice that specified members are to be designated members, or

   (b)   notice that every person who from time to time is a member of the limited liability partnership is a designated member,

and, once it is delivered, subsection (1) (apart from paragraph (a)) and subsection (2), or subsection (3), shall have effect as if that were stated in the incorporation document.

(5)   A notice delivered under subsection (4)—

   (a)   shall be in a form approved by the registrar, and

   (b)   shall be signed by a designated member of the limited liability partnership or authenticated in a manner approved by the registrar.

(6)   A person ceases to be a designated member if he ceases to be a member.

[1276E]

9 Registration of membership changes

(1)   A limited liability partnership must ensure that—

   (a)   where a person becomes or ceases to be a member or designated member, notice is delivered to the registrar within fourteen days, and

   (b)   where there is any change in the name or address of a member, notice is delivered to the registrar within 28 days.

(2)   Where all the members from time to time of a limited liability partnership are designated members, subsection (1)(a) does not require notice that a person has become or ceased to be a designated member as well as a member.

(3)   A notice delivered under subsection (1)—

   (a)   shall be in a form approved by the registrar, and

   (b)   shall be signed by a designated member of the limited liability partnership or authenticated in a manner approved by the registrar,

and, if it relates to a person becoming a member or designated member, shall contain a statement that he consents to becoming a member or designated member signed by him or authenticated in a manner approved by the registrar.

[(3A)   Where a confidentiality order under section 723B of the Companies Act 1985 as applied to limited liability partnerships is made in respect of an existing member, the limited liability partnership must ensure that there is delivered within 28 days to the registrar notice in a form approved by the registrar containing the address for the time being notified to it by the member under the Limited Liability Partnerships (Particulars of Usual Residential Address) (Confidentiality Orders) Regulations 2002.

(3B)   Where such a confidentiality order is in force in respect of a member the requirement in subsection (1)(b) to notify a change in the address of a member shall be read in relation to that member as a requirement to deliver to the registrar, within 28 days, notice of—

(a)   any change in the usual residential address of that member; and

(b)   any change in the address for the time being notified to the limited liability partnership by the member under the Limited Liability Partnerships (Particulars of Usual Residential Address) (Confidentiality Orders) Regulations 2002,

and the registrar may approve different forms for the notification of each kind of address.]

(4)   If a limited liability partnership fails to comply with subsection (1), the partnership and every designated member commits an offence.

(5)   But it is a defence for a designated member charged with an offence under subsection (4) to prove that he took all reasonable steps for securing that subsection (1) was complied with.

(6)   A person guilty of an offence under subsection (4) is liable on summary conviction to a fine not exceeding level 5 on the standard scale.

[1276F]

NOTES
Sub-ss (3A), (3B): inserted by the Limited Liability Partnerships (Particulars of Usual Residential Address) (Confidentiality Orders) Regulations 2002, SI 2002/915, reg 16, Sch 2, para 1, as from 2 April 2002.

Taxation

10, 11   (*S 10 amends the Income and Corporation Taxes Act 1988 and the Taxation of Chargeable Gains Act 1992, and is repealed in part by the Income Tax Act 2007, s 1031, Sch 3; s 11 amends the Inheritance Tax Act 1984.*)

12   Stamp duty

(1)   Stamp duty shall not be chargeable on an instrument by which property is conveyed or transferred by a person to a limited liability partnership in connection with its incorporation within the period of one year beginning with the date of incorporation if the following two conditions are satisfied.

(2)   The first condition is that at the relevant time the person—

(a)   is a partner in a partnership comprised of all the persons who are or are to be members of the limited liability partnership (and no-one else), or

(b)   holds the property conveyed or transferred as nominee or bare trustee for one or more of the partners in such a partnership.

(3)   The second condition is that—

(a)   the proportions of the property conveyed or transferred to which the persons mentioned in subsection (2)(a) are entitled immediately after the conveyance or transfer are the same as those to which they were entitled at the relevant time, or

(b)   none of the differences in those proportions has arisen as part of a scheme or arrangement of which the main purpose, or one of the main purposes, is avoidance of liability to any duty or tax.

(4)   For the purposes of subsection (2) a person holds property as bare trustee for a partner if the partner has the exclusive right (subject only to satisfying any outstanding charge, lien or other right of the trustee to resort to the property for payment of duty, taxes, costs or other outgoings) to direct how the property shall be dealt with.

(5)   In this section "the relevant time" means—

(a)   if the person who conveyed or transferred the property to the limited liability partnership acquired the property after its incorporation, immediately after he acquired the property, and

(b)   in any other case, immediately before its incorporation.

(6)   An instrument in respect of which stamp duty is not chargeable by virtue of subsection (1) shall not be taken to be duly stamped unless—

(a)   it has, in accordance with section 12 of the Stamp Act 1891, been stamped with a particular stamp denoting that it is not chargeable with any duty or that it is duly stamped, or

(b)   it is stamped with the duty to which it would be liable apart from that subsection.

[1276G]

13 (*Amends the Social Security Contributions and Benefits Act 1992 and the Social Security Contributions and Benefits (Northern Ireland) Act 1992.*)

Regulations

14 Insolvency and winding up

(1)   Regulations shall make provision about the insolvency and winding up of limited liability partnerships by applying or incorporating, with such modifications as appear appropriate, Parts I to IV, VI and VII of the Insolvency Act 1986.

(2)   Regulations may make other provision about the insolvency and winding up of limited liability partnerships, and provision about the insolvency and winding up of oversea limited liability partnerships, by—

(a)   applying or incorporating, with such modifications as appear appropriate, any law relating to the insolvency or winding up of companies or other corporations which would not otherwise have effect in relation to them, or

(b)   providing for any law relating to the insolvency or winding up of companies or other corporations which would otherwise have effect in relation to them not to apply to them or to apply to them with such modifications as appear appropriate.

(3)   In this Act "oversea limited liability partnership" means a body incorporated or otherwise established outside Great Britain and having such connection with Great Britain, and such other features, as regulations may prescribe.

[1276H]

NOTES

Regulations: the Limited Liability Partnerships (Scotland) Regulations 2001, SSI 2001/128 at **[3572A]**; the Limited Liability Partnerships Regulations 2001, SI 2001/1090 at **[3554]**.

15 Application of company law etc

Regulations may make provision about limited liability partnerships and oversea limited liability partnerships (not being provision about insolvency or winding up) by—

(a)   applying or incorporating, with such modifications as appear appropriate, any law relating to companies or other corporations which would not otherwise have effect in relation to them,

(b)   providing for any law relating to companies or other corporations which would otherwise have effect in relation to them not to apply to them or to apply to them with such modifications as appear appropriate, or

(c)   applying or incorporating, with such modifications as appear appropriate, any law relating to partnerships.

[1276I]

NOTES

Regulations: the Limited Liability Partnerships (Scotland) Regulations 2001, SSI 2001/128 at **[3572A]**; the Limited Liability Partnerships Regulations 2001, SI 2001/1090 at **[3554]**; the Limited Liability Partnerships (No 2) Regulations 2002, SI 2002/913 at **[3638B]**; the Companies (Registrar, Languages and Trading Disclosures) Regulations 2006, SI 2006/3429; the Companies (Late Filing Penalties) and Limited Liability Partnerships (Filing Periods and Late Filing Penalties) Regulations 2008, SI 2008/497; the Limited Liability Partnerships (Accounts and Audit) (Application of Companies Act 2006) Regulations 2008, SI 2008/1911 at **[4169]**; the Small Limited Liability Partnerships (Accounts) Regulations 2008, SI 2008/1912; the Large and Medium-sized Limited Liability Partnerships (Accounts) Regulations 2008, SI 2008/1913.

16 Consequential amendments

(1)   Regulations may make in any enactment such amendments or repeals as appear appropriate in consequence of this Act or regulations made under it.

(2)   The regulations may, in particular, make amendments and repeals affecting companies or other corporations or partnerships.

[1276J]

NOTES

Regulations: the Limited Liability Partnerships (Scotland) Regulations 2001, SSI 2001/128 at **[3572A]**; the Limited Liability Partnerships Regulations 2001, SI 2001/1090 at **[3554]**; the Limited Liability Partnerships (No 2) Regulations 2002, SI 2002/913 at **[3638B]**.

17 General

(1)   In this Act "regulations" means regulations made by the Secretary of State by statutory instrument.

(2)   Regulations under this Act may in particular—

(a)   make provisions for dealing with non-compliance with any of the regulations (including the creation of criminal offences),

(b)   impose fees (which shall be paid into the Consolidated Fund), and

(c)   provide for the exercise of functions by persons prescribed by the regulations.

(3)   Regulations under this Act may—

(a)   contain any appropriate consequential, incidental, supplementary or transitional provisions or savings, and

(b)   make different provision for different purposes.

(4)   No regulations to which this subsection applies shall be made unless a draft of the statutory instrument containing the regulations (whether or not together with other provisions) has been laid before, and approved by a resolution of, each House of Parliament.

(5)   Subsection (4) applies to—

(a)   regulations under section 14(2) not consisting entirely of the application or incorporation (with or without modifications) of provisions contained in or made under the Insolvency Act 1986,

(b)   regulations under section 15 not consisting entirely of the application or incorporation (with or without modifications) of provisions contained in or made under Part I, Chapter VIII of Part V, Part VII, Parts XI to XIII, Parts XVI to XVIII, Part XX or Parts XXIV to XXVI of the Companies Act 1985,

(c)   regulations under section 14 or 15 making provision about oversea limited liability partnerships, and

(d)   regulations under section 16.

(6)   A statutory instrument containing regulations under this Act shall (unless a draft of it has been approved by a resolution of each House of Parliament) be subject to annulment in pursuance of a resolution of either House of Parliament.

[1276K]

Supplementary

18 Interpretation

In this Act—

"address", in relation to a member of a limited liability partnership, means—

(a)   if an individual, his usual residential address, and

(b)   if a corporation or Scottish firm, its registered or principal office,

"business" includes every trade, profession and occupation,

"designated member" shall be construed in accordance with section 8,

"enactment" includes subordinate legislation (within the meaning of the Interpretation Act 1978),

"incorporation document" shall be construed in accordance with section 2,

"limited liability partnership" has the meaning given by section 1(2),

"member" shall be construed in accordance with section 4,

"modifications" includes additions and omissions,

"name", in relation to a member of a limited liability partnership, means—

(a)   if an individual, his forename and surname (or, in the case of a peer or other person usually known by a title, his title instead of or in addition to either or both his forename and surname), and

(b)   if a corporation or Scottish firm, its corporate or firm name,

"oversea limited liability partnership" has the meaning given by section 14(3),

"the registrar" means—

(a)   if the registered office of the limited liability partnership is, or is to be, situated in England and Wales or in Wales, the registrar or other officer performing under the Companies Act 1985 the duty of registration of companies in England and Wales, and

(b)   if its registered office is, or is to be, situated in Scotland, the registrar or other officer performing under that Act the duty of registration of companies in Scotland, and

"regulations" has the meaning given by section 17(1).

[1276L]

19 Commencement, extent and short title

(1)   The preceding provisions of this Act shall come into force on such day as the Secretary of State may by order made by statutory instrument appoint; and different days may be appointed for different purposes.

(2)   The Secretary of State may by order made by statutory instrument make any transitional provisions and savings which appear appropriate in connection with the coming into force of any provision of this Act.

(3) For the purposes of the Scotland Act 1998 this Act shall be taken to be a pre-commencement enactment within the meaning of that Act.

(4) Apart from sections 10 to 13 (and this section), this Act does not extend to Northern Ireland.

(5) This Act may be cited as the Limited Liability Partnerships Act 2000.

[1276M]

NOTES

Orders: the Limited Liability Partnerships Act 2000 (Commencement) Order 2000, SI 2000/3316 (bringing this Act (with the exception of this section which came into force on Royal assent) into force on 6 April 2001).

SCHEDULE
NAMES AND REGISTERED OFFICES
Section 1

PART I
NAMES

1. ...

Name to indicate status

2.—(1) The name of a limited liability partnership must end with—
  (a) the expression "limited liability partnership", or
  (b) the abbreviation "llp" or "LLP".

(2) But if the incorporation document for a limited liability partnership states that the registered office is to be situated in Wales, its name must end with—
  (a) one of the expressions "limited liability partnership" and "partneriaeth atebolrwydd cyfyngedig", or
  (b) one of the abbreviations "llp", "LLP", "pac" and "PAC".

Registration of names

3.—(1) A limited liability partnership shall not be registered by a name—
  (a) which includes, otherwise than at the end of the name, either of the expressions "limited liability partnership" and "partneriaeth atebolrwydd cyfyngedig" or any of the abbreviations "llp", "LLP", "pac" and "PAC",
  (b) which is the same as a name appearing in the index kept under section 714(1) of the Companies Act 1985,
  (c) the use of which by the limited liability partnership would in the opinion of the Secretary of State constitute a criminal offence, or
  (d) which in the opinion of the Secretary of State is offensive.

(2) Except with the approval of the Secretary of State, a limited liability partnership shall not be registered by a name which—
  (a) in the opinion of the Secretary of State would be likely to give the impression that it is connected in any way with Her Majesty's Government or with any local authority, or
  (b) includes any word or expression for the time being specified in regulations under section 29 of the Companies Act 1985 (names needing approval),

and in paragraph (a) "local authority" means any local authority within the meaning of the Local Government Act 1972 or the Local Government etc (Scotland) Act 1994, the Common Council of the City of London or the Council of the Isles of Scilly.

Change of name

4.—(1) A limited liability partnership may change its name at any time.

(2) Where a limited liability partnership has been registered by a name which—
  (a) is the same as or, in the opinion of the Secretary of State, too like a name appearing at the time of registration in the index kept under section 714(1) of the Companies Act 1985, or
  (b) is the same as or, in the opinion of the Secretary of State, too like a name which should have appeared in the index at that time,

the Secretary of State may within twelve months of that time in writing direct the limited liability partnership to change its name within such period as he may specify.

(3) If it appears to the Secretary of State—
  (a) that misleading information has been given for the purpose of the registration of a limited liability partnership by a particular name, or
  (b) that undertakings or assurances have been given for that purpose and have not been fulfilled,

he may, within five years of the date of its registration by that name, in writing direct the limited liability partnership to change its name within such period as he may specify.

(4)   If in the Secretary of State's opinion the name by which a limited liability partnership is registered gives so misleading an indication of the nature of its activities as to be likely to cause harm to the public, he may in writing direct the limited liability partnership to change its name within such period as he may specify.

(5)   But the limited liability partnership may, within three weeks from the date of the direction apply to the court to set it aside and the court may set the direction aside or confirm it and, if it confirms it, shall specify the period within which it must be complied with.

(6)   In sub-paragraph (5) "the court" means—
    (a)   if the registered office of the limited liability partnership is situated in England and Wales or in Wales, the High Court, and
    (b)   if it is situated in Scotland, the Court of Session.

(7)   Where a direction has been given under sub-paragraph (2), (3) or (4) specifying a period within which a limited liability partnership is to change its name, the Secretary of State may at any time before that period ends extend it by a further direction in writing.

(8)   If a limited liability partnership fails to comply with a direction under this paragraph—
    (a)   the limited liability partnership, and
    (b)   any designated member in default,
commits an offence.

(9)   A person guilty of an offence under sub-paragraph (8) is liable on summary conviction to a fine not exceeding level 3 on the standard scale.

Notification of change of name

5.—(1)   Where a limited liability partnership changes its name it shall deliver notice of the change to the registrar.

(2)   A notice delivered under sub-paragraph (1)—
    (a)   shall be in a form approved by the registrar, and
    (b)   shall be signed by a designated member of the limited liability partnership or authenticated in a manner approved by the registrar.

(3)   Where the registrar receives a notice under sub-paragraph (2) he shall (unless the new name is one by which a limited liability partnership may not be registered)—
    (a)   enter the new name in the index kept under section 714(1) of the Companies Act 1985, and
    (b)   issue a certificate of the change of name.

(4)   The change of name has effect from the date on which the certificate is issued.

Effect of change of name

6.   A change of name by a limited liability partnership does not—
    (a)   affect any of its rights or duties,
    (b)   render defective any legal proceedings by or against it,
and any legal proceedings that might have been commenced or continued against it by its former name may be commenced or continued against it by its new name.

Improper use of "limited liability partnership" etc

7.—(1)   If any person carries on a business under a name or title which includes as the last words—
    (a)   the expression "limited liability partnership" or "partneriaeth atebolrwydd cyfyngedig", or
    (b)   any contraction or imitation of either of those expressions,
that person, unless a limited liability partnership or oversea limited liability partnership, commits an offence.

(2)   A person guilty of an offence under sub-paragraph (1) is liable on summary conviction to a fine not exceeding level 3 on the standard scale.

Similarity of names

8.   In determining for the purposes of this Part whether one name is the same as another there are to be disregarded—
    (1)   the definite article as the first word of the name,
    (2)   any of the following (or their Welsh equivalents or abbreviations of them or their Welsh equivalents) at the end of the name—
        "limited liability partnership",

"company",
"and company",
"company limited"
"and company limited",
"limited",
"unlimited",
"public limited company", ...
["community interest company",
"community interest public limited company",]
"investment company with variable capital", and
["open-ended investment company", and]

 (3) type and case of letters, accents, spaces between letters and punctuation marks,
and "and" and "&" are to be taken as the same.

[1276N]

NOTES
 Para 1: amends CA 1985, s 714(1) and is repealed by the Companies Act 2006, s 1295, Sch 16, as from 1 October 2009.
 Para 8: word omitted from entry "public limited company" repealed, and entry "open-ended investment company" inserted, by the Open-Ended Investment Companies Regulations 2001, SI 2001/1228, reg 84, Sch 7, para 11, as from 1 December 2001; entries "community interest company" and "community interest public limited company" inserted by the Companies (Audit, Investigations and Community Enterprise) Act 2004, s 33, Sch 6, para 10, as from 1 July 2005.

PART II
REGISTERED OFFICES

Situation of registered office

9.—(1) A limited liability partnership shall—
 (a) at all times have a registered office situated in England and Wales or in Wales, or
 (b) at all times have a registered office situated in Scotland,
to which communications and notices may be addressed.

 (2) On the incorporation of a limited liability partnership the situation of its registered office shall be that stated in the incorporation document.

 (3) Where the registered office of a limited liability partnership is situated in Wales, but the incorporation document does not state that it is to be situated in Wales (as opposed to England and Wales), the limited liability partnership may deliver notice to the registrar stating that its registered office is to be situated in Wales.

 (4) A notice delivered under sub-paragraph (3)—
 (a) shall be in a form approved by the registrar, and
 (b) shall be signed by a designated member of the limited liability partnership or authenticated in a manner approved by the registrar.

Change of registered office

10.—(1) A limited liability partnership may change its registered office by delivering notice of the change to the registrar.

 (2) A notice delivered under sub-paragraph (1)—
 (a) shall be in a form approved by the registrar, and
 (b) shall be signed by a designated member of the limited liability partnership or authenticated in a manner approved by the registrar.

[1276O]

REGULATION OF INVESTIGATORY POWERS ACT 2000

(2000 c 23)

NOTES
 Only provisions of this Act relevant to Financial Services law are reproduced. Provisions not reproduced are not annotated.
 This Act is reproduced as amended by: the Communications Act 2003; the Inquiries Act 2005; the Serious Organised Crime and Police Act 2005; the Prevention of Terrorism Act 2005; the Armed Forces Act 2006; the Wireless Telegraphy Act 2006; the Counter-Terrorism Act 2008; the Postal Services Act 2000 (Consequential Modifications No 1) Order 2001, SI 2001/1149; the Police, Public Order and Criminal Justice (Scotland) Act 2006 (Consequential Provisions and Modifications) Order 2007, SI 2007/1098.

An Act to make provision for and about the interception of communications, the acquisition and disclosure of data relating to communications, the carrying out of surveillance, the use of covert human intelligence sources and the acquisition of the means by which electronic data protected by encryption or passwords may be decrypted or accessed; to provide for Commissioners and a tribunal with functions and jurisdiction in relation to those matters, to entries on and interferences with property or with wireless telegraphy and to the carrying out of their functions by the Security Service, the Secret Intelligence Service and the Government Communications Headquarters; and for connected purposes

[28 July 2000]

PART 1
COMMUNICATIONS

CHAPTER I
INTERCEPTION

Restrictions on use of intercepted material etc

17 Exclusion of matters from legal proceedings

(1)   Subject to section 18, no evidence shall be adduced, question asked, assertion or disclosure made or other thing done in, for the purposes of or in connection with any legal proceedings [or Inquiries Act proceedings] which (in any manner)—

(a)   discloses, in circumstances from which its origin in anything falling within subsection (2) may be inferred, any of the contents of an intercepted communication or any related communications data; or

(b)   tends (apart from any such disclosure) to suggest that anything falling within subsection (2) has or may have occurred or be going to occur.

(2)   The following fall within this subsection—

(a)   conduct by a person falling within subsection (3) that was or would be an offence under section 1(1) or (2) of this Act or under section 1 of the Interception of Communications Act 1985;

(b)   a breach by the Secretary of State of his duty under section 1(4) of this Act;

(c)   the issue of an interception warrant or of a warrant under the Interception of Communications Act 1985;

(d)   the making of an application by any person for an interception warrant, or for a warrant under that Act;

(e)   the imposition of any requirement on any person to provide assistance with giving effect to an interception warrant.

(3)   The persons referred to in subsection (2)(a) are—

(a)   any person to whom a warrant under this Chapter may be addressed;

(b)   any person holding office under the Crown;

[(c)   any member of the staff of the Serious Organised Crime Agency;].

[(ca)   any member of the Scottish Crime and Drug Enforcement Agency;]

(e)   any person employed by or for the purposes of a police force;

(f)   any person providing a postal service or employed for the purposes of any business of providing such a service; and

(g)   any person providing a public telecommunications service or employed for the purposes of any business of providing such a service.

(4)   [In this section—

"Inquiries Act proceedings" means proceedings of an inquiry under the Inquiries Act 2005;

"intercepted communications" means"] any communication intercepted in the course of its transmission by means of a postal service or telecommunication system.

[1277]

NOTES

Sub-s (1): words in square brackets inserted by the Inquiries Act 2005, s 48, Sch 2, Pt 1, para 20(1), (2), as from 7 June 2005.

Sub-s (3): para (c) substituted, for original paras (c), (d), by the Serious Organised Crime and Police Act 2005, s 59, Sch 4, paras 131, 133, as from 1 April 2006 (except in relation to conduct by any member of the National Criminal Intelligence Service or the National Crime Squad which took place before that date); para (ca) inserted by the Police, Public Order and Criminal Justice (Scotland) Act 2006 (Consequential Provisions and Modifications) Order 2007, SI 2007/1098, art 6, Schedule, Pt 1, para 4(1), (3), as from 1 April 2007.

Sub-s (4): words in square brackets substituted by the Inquiries Act 2005, s 48, Sch 2, Pt 1, para 20(1), (2), as from 7 June 2005.

18 Exceptions to section 17

(1)   Section 17(1) shall not apply in relation to—

(a)   any proceedings for a relevant offence;
(b)   any civil proceedings under section 11(8);
(c)   any proceedings before the Tribunal;
(d)   any proceedings on an appeal or review for which provision is made by an order under section 67(8);
[(da) any control order proceedings (within the meaning of the Prevention of Terrorism Act 2005) or any proceedings arising out of such proceedings;]
[(db) any financial restrictions proceedings as defined in section 65 of the Counter-Terrorism Act 2008, or any proceedings arising out of such proceedings;]
(e)   any proceedings before the Special Immigration Appeals Commission or any proceedings arising out of proceedings before that Commission; or
(f)   any proceedings before the Proscribed Organisations Appeal Commission or any proceedings arising out of proceedings before that Commission.

(2)   Subsection (1) shall not, by virtue of [paragraphs (da) to (f)], authorise the disclosure of anything—
[(za) in the case of any proceedings falling within paragraph (da) to—
    (i)   a person who, within the meaning of the Schedule to the Prevention of Terrorism Act 2005, is or was a relevant party to the control order proceedings; or
    (ii)   any person who for the purposes of any proceedings so falling (but otherwise than by virtue of an appointment under paragraph 7 of that Schedule) represents a person falling within sub-paragraph (i);]
[(zb) in the case of proceedings falling within paragraph (db), to—
    (i)   a person, other than the Treasury, who is or was a party to the proceedings, or
    (ii)   any person who for the purposes of the proceedings (but otherwise than by virtue of appointment as a special advocate) represents a person falling within sub-paragraph (i);]
(a)   in the case of any proceedings falling within paragraph (e), to—
    (i)   the appellant to the Special Immigration Appeals Commission; or
    (ii)   any person who for the purposes of any proceedings so falling (but otherwise than by virtue of an appointment under section 6 of the Special Immigration Appeals Commission Act 1997) represents that appellant; or
(b)   in the case of proceedings falling within paragraph (f), to—
    (i)   the applicant to the Proscribed Organisations Appeal Commission;
    (ii)   the organisation concerned (if different);
    (iii) any person designated under paragraph 6 of Schedule 3 to the Terrorism Act 2000 to conduct proceedings so falling on behalf of that organisation; or
    (iv)   any person who for the purposes of any proceedings so falling (but otherwise than by virtue of an appointment under paragraph 7 of that Schedule) represents that applicant or that organisation.

(3)   Section 17(1) shall not prohibit anything done in, for the purposes of, or in connection with, so much of any legal proceedings as relates to the fairness or unfairness of a dismissal on the grounds of any conduct constituting an offence under section 1(1) or (2), 11(7) or 19 of this Act, or section 1 of the Interception of Communications Act 1985.

(4)   Section 17(1)(a) shall not prohibit the disclosure of any of the contents of a communication if the interception of that communication was lawful by virtue of section 1(5)(c), 3 or 4.

(5)   Where any disclosure is proposed to be or has been made on the grounds that it is authorised by subsection (4), section 17(1) shall not prohibit the doing of anything in, or for the purposes of, so much of any ... proceedings as relates to the question whether that disclosure is or was so authorised.

(6)   Section 17(1)(b) shall not prohibit the doing of anything that discloses any conduct of a person for which he has been convicted of an offence under section 1(1) or (2), 11(7) or 19 of this Act, or section 1 of the Interception of Communications Act 1985.

(7)   Nothing in section 17(1) shall prohibit any such disclosure of any information that continues to be available for disclosure as is confined to—
(a)   a disclosure to a person conducting a criminal prosecution for the purpose only of enabling that person to determine what is required of him by his duty to secure the fairness of the prosecution; ...
(b)   a disclosure to a relevant judge in a case in which that judge has ordered the disclosure to be made to him alone[; or
[(c)   a disclosure to the panel of an inquiry held under the Inquiries Act 2005 or to a person appointed as counsel to such an inquiry where, in the course of the inquiry, the panel has ordered the disclosure to be made to the panel alone or (as the case may be) to the panel and the person appointed as counsel to the inquiry]].

(8)   A relevant judge shall not order a disclosure under subsection (7)(b) except where he is satisfied that the exceptional circumstances of the case make the disclosure essential in the interests of justice.

[(8A)   The panel of an inquiry shall not order a disclosure under subsection (7)(c) except where it is satisfied that the exceptional circumstances of the case make the disclosure essential to enable the inquiry to fulfil its terms of reference.]

(9)   Subject to subsection (10), where in any criminal proceedings—
  (a)   a relevant judge does order a disclosure under subsection (7)(b), and
  (b)   in consequence of that disclosure he is of the opinion that there are exceptional circumstances requiring him to do so,

he may direct the person conducting the prosecution to make for the purposes of the proceedings any such admission of fact as that judge thinks essential in the interests of justice.

(10)   Nothing in any direction under subsection (9) shall authorise or require anything to be done in contravention of section 17(1).

(11)   In this section "a relevant judge" means—
  (a)   any judge of the High Court or of the Crown Court or any Circuit judge;
  (b)   any judge of the High Court of Justiciary or any sheriff;
  (c)   *in relation to a court-martial, the judge advocate appointed in relation to that court-martial under section 84B of the Army Act 1955, section 84B of the Air Force Act 1955 or section 53B of the Naval Discipline Act 1957; or*
  (d)   any person holding any such judicial office as entitles him to exercise the jurisdiction of a judge falling within paragraph (a) or (b).

(12)   In this section "relevant offence" means—
  (a)   an offence under any provision of this Act;
  (b)   an offence under section 1 of the Interception of Communications Act 1985;
  (c)   an offence under [section 47 or 48 of the Wireless Telegraphy Act 2006];
  (d)   an offence under ... [section 83 or 84 of the Postal Services Act 2000];
  (e)   ...
  (f)   an offence under section 4 of the Official Secrets Act 1989 relating to any such information, document or article as is mentioned in subsection (3)(a) of that section;
  (g)   an offence under section 1 or 2 of the Official Secrets Act 1911 relating to any sketch, plan, model, article, note, document or information which incorporates or relates to the contents of any intercepted communication or any related communications data or tends to suggest as mentioned in section 17(1)(b) of this Act;
  (h)   perjury committed in the course of any proceedings mentioned in subsection (1) or (3) of this section;
  (i)   attempting or conspiring to commit, or aiding, abetting, counselling or procuring the commission of, an offence falling within any of the preceding paragraphs; and
  (j)   contempt of court committed in the course of, or in relation to, any proceedings mentioned in subsection (1) or (3) of this section.

(13)   In subsection (12) "intercepted communication" has the same meaning as in section 17.

[1277A]

NOTES

Sub-s (1): para (da) inserted by the Prevention of Terrorism Act 2005, s 11(5), Schedule, para 9(1), (2), as from 11 March 2005; para (db) inserted by the Counter-Terrorism Act 2008, s 69(1), (2), as from 27 November 2008.

Sub-s (2): words in first pair of square brackets substituted, and para (za) inserted, by the Prevention of Terrorism Act 2005, s 11(5), Schedule, para 9(1), (3), (4), as from 11 March 2005; para (zb) inserted by the Counter-Terrorism Act 2008, s 69(1), (3), as from 27 November 2008.

Sub-s (5): word omitted repealed by the Inquiries Act 2005, ss 48(1), 49(2), Sch 2, Pt 1, para 21(1), (2), Sch 3, as from 7 June 2005.

Sub-s (7): word omitted from para (a) repealed, and para (c) and the word immediately preceding it inserted, by the Inquiries Act 2005, ss 48(1), 49(2), Sch 2, Pt 1, para 21(1), (3), Sch 3, as from 7 June 2005; para (c) subsequently substituted by the Counter-Terrorism Act 2008, s 74(1), as from 16 February 2009 (for transitional provisions see the note below).

Sub-s (8A): inserted by the Inquiries Act 2005, s 48(1), Sch 2, Pt 1, para 21(1), (4), as from 7 June 2005.

Sub-s (11): para (c) substituted by the Armed Forces Act 2006, s 378(1), Sch 16, para 169, as from a day to be appointed, as follows—

  "(c)   in relation to proceedings before the Court Martial, the judge advocate for those proceedings; or".

Sub-s (12): words in square brackets in para (c) substituted by the Wireless Telegraphy Act 2006, s 123, Sch 7, paras 21, 23, as from 8 February 2007; words omitted from para (d) repealed, and words in square brackets in that paragraph substituted, by the Postal Services Act 2000 (Consequential Modifications No 1) Order 2001, SI 2001/1149, art 3, Sch 1, para 135(1), (2), Sch 2, as from 26 March 2001; para (e) repealed by the Communications Act 2003, s 406(7), Sch 19, as from 25 July 2003 (certain purposes), and as from 29 December 2003 (otherwise).

Transitional provisions: the Counter-Terrorism Act 2008, s 74(2), (3) provide that the substitution of sub-s (7)(c) as noted above has effect in relation to inquiries under the Inquiries Act 2005 that have begun, but have not come to an end, before the day on which s 18 of the 2008 Act comes into force as well as to such inquiries beginning or on after that day. Furthermore, s 14 of the Inquiries Act 2005 (end of inquiry) has effect for determining when an inquiry under that Act comes to an end for those purposes.

PART V
MISCELLANEOUS AND SUPPLEMENTAL

Supplemental

83 Short title, commencement and extent

(1)   This Act may be cited as the Regulation of Investigatory Powers Act 2000.

(2)   The provisions of this Act, other than this section, shall come into force on such day as the Secretary of State may by order appoint; and different days may be appointed under this subsection for different purposes.

(3)   This Act extends to Northern Ireland.

[1278]

NOTES
 Orders: various commencement orders have been made under this section; the commencement order relevant to the provisions of this Act reproduced here is the Regulation of Investigatory Powers Act 2000 (Commencement No 1 and Transitional Provisions) Order 2000, SI 2000/2543.

ANTI-TERRORISM, CRIME AND SECURITY ACT 2001

(2001 c 24)

NOTES
 Only provisions of this Act relevant to Financial Services law are reproduced. Provisions not reproduced are not annotated.
 This Act is reproduced as amended by: the British Overseas Territories Act 2002; the Criminal Justice Act 2003; the Terrorism Act 2006; the Armed Forces Act 2006; the Counter-Terrorism Act 2008.

ARRANGEMENT OF SECTIONS
PART 1
TERRORIST PROPERTY

PART 2
FREEZING ORDERS

Orders

Interpretation

Orders: procedure etc

Miscellaneous

PART 3
DISCLOSURE OF INFORMATION

An Act to amend the Terrorism Act 2000; to make further provision about terrorism and security; to provide for the freezing of assets; to make provision about immigration and asylum; to amend or extend the criminal law and powers for preventing crime and enforcing that law; to make provision about the control of pathogens and toxins; to provide for the retention of communications data; to provide for implementation of Title VI of the Treaty on European Union; and for connected purposes

[14 December 2001]

PART 1
TERRORIST PROPERTY

1   Forfeiture of terrorist cash

(1)   Schedule 1 (which makes provision for enabling cash which—
    (a)   is intended to be used for the purposes of terrorism,
    (b)   consists of resources of an organisation which is a proscribed organisation, or
    (c)   is, or represents, property obtained through terrorism,

to be forfeited in civil proceedings before a magistrates' court or (in Scotland) the sheriff) is to have effect.

(2)   The powers conferred by Schedule 1 are exercisable in relation to any cash whether or not any proceedings have been brought for an offence in connection with the cash.

(3)   Expressions used in this section have the same meaning as in Schedule 1.

(4)   Sections 24 to 31 of the Terrorism Act 2000 (c 11) (seizure of terrorist cash) are to cease to have effect.

(5)   An order under section 127 bringing Schedule 1 into force may make any modifications of any code of practice then in operation under Schedule 14 to the Terrorism Act 2000 (exercise of officers' powers) which the Secretary of State thinks necessary or expedient.

[1279]

PART 2
FREEZING ORDERS

NOTES

As to the right of any person affected by a decision of the Treasury under this Part to apply to the High Court (or, in Scotland, the Court of Session) to set aside that decision, see the Counter-Terrorism Act 2008, s 63 et seq.

Orders

4   Power to make order

(1)   The Treasury may make a freezing order if the following two conditions are satisfied.

(2)   The first condition is that the Treasury reasonably believe that—
    (a)   action to the detriment of the United Kingdom's economy (or part of it) has been or is likely to be taken by a person or persons, or
    (b)   action constituting a threat to the life or property of one or more nationals of the United Kingdom or residents of the United Kingdom has been or is likely to be taken by a person or persons.

(3) If one person is believed to have taken or to be likely to take the action the second condition is that the person is—
- (a) the government of a country or territory outside the United Kingdom, or
- (b) a resident of a country or territory outside the United Kingdom.

(4) If two or more persons are believed to have taken or to be likely to take the action the second condition is that each of them falls within paragraph (a) or (b) of subsection (3); and different persons may fall within different paragraphs.

[1280]

NOTES
Orders: the Landsbanki Freezing Order 2008, SI 2008/2668 at **[4325]**.

5 Contents of order

(1) A freezing order is an order which prohibits persons from making funds available to or for the benefit of a person or persons specified in the order.

(2) The order must provide that these are the persons who are prohibited—
- (a) all persons in the United Kingdom, and
- (b) all persons elsewhere who are nationals of the United Kingdom or are bodies incorporated under the law of any part of the United Kingdom or are Scottish partnerships.

(3) The order may specify the following (and only the following) as the person or persons to whom or for whose benefit funds are not to be made available—
- (a) the person or persons reasonably believed by the Treasury to have taken or to be likely to take the action referred to in section 4;
- (b) any person the Treasury reasonably believe has provided or is likely to provide assistance (directly or indirectly) to that person or any of those persons.

(4) A person may be specified under subsection (3) by—
- (a) being named in the order, or
- (b) falling within a description of persons set out in the order.

(5) The description must be such that a reasonable person would know whether he fell within it.

(6) Funds are financial assets and economic benefits of any kind.

[1281]

6 Contents: further provisions

Schedule 3 contains further provisions about the contents of freezing orders.

[1282]

7 Review of order

The Treasury must keep a freezing order under review.

[1283]

8 Duration of order

A freezing order ceases to have effect at the end of the period of 2 years starting with the day on which it is made.

[1284]

Interpretation

9 Nationals and residents

(1) A national of the United Kingdom is an individual who is—
- (a) a British citizen, a [British overseas territories citizen], a British National (Overseas) or a British Overseas citizen
- (b) a person who under the British Nationality Act 1981 (c 61) is a British subject, or
- (c) a British protected person within the meaning of that Act.

(2) A resident of the United Kingdom is—
- (a) an individual who is ordinarily resident in the United Kingdom,
- (b) a body incorporated under the law of any part of the United Kingdom, or
- (c) a Scottish partnership.

(3) A resident of a country or territory outside the United Kingdom is—
- (a) an individual who is ordinarily resident in such a country or territory, or
- (b) a body incorporated under the law of such a country or territory.

(4) For the purposes of subsection (3)(b) a branch situated in a country or territory outside the United Kingdom of—
- (a) a body incorporated under the law of any part of the United Kingdom, or

(b)   a Scottish partnership,

is to be treated as a body incorporated under the law of the country or territory where the branch is situated.

(5)   This section applies for the purposes of this Part.

[1285]

NOTES
Sub-s (1): words in square brackets in para (a) substituted by virtue of the British Overseas Territories Act 2002, s 2(3), as from 26 February 2002.

Orders: procedure etc

10   Procedure for making freezing orders

(1)   A power to make a freezing order is exercisable by statutory instrument.

(2)   A freezing order—
   (a)   must be laid before Parliament after being made;
   (b)   ceases to have effect at the end of the relevant period unless before the end of that period the order is approved by a resolution of each House of Parliament (but without that affecting anything done under the order or the power to make a new order).

(3)   The relevant period is a period of 28 days starting with the day on which the order is made.

(4)   In calculating the relevant period no account is to be taken of any time during which Parliament is dissolved or prorogued or during which both Houses are adjourned for more than 4 days.

(5)   If the Treasury propose to make a freezing order in the belief that the condition in section 4(2)(b) is satisfied, they must not make the order unless they consult the Secretary of State.

[1286]

11   Procedure for making certain amending orders

(1)   This section applies if—
   (a)   a freezing order is made specifying by description (rather than by name) the person or persons to whom or for whose benefit funds are not to be made available,
   (b)   it is proposed to make a further order which amends the freezing order only so as to make it specify by name the person or persons (or any of the persons) to whom or for whose benefit funds are not to be made available, and
   (c)   the Treasury reasonably believe that the person or persons named fall within the description contained in the freezing order and the further order contains a statement of the Treasury's belief.

(2)   This section also applies if—
   (a)   a freezing order is made specifying by name the person or persons to whom or for whose benefit funds are not to be made available,
   (b)   it is proposed to make a further order which amends the freezing order only so as to make it specify by name a further person or further persons to whom or for whose benefit funds are not to be made available, and
   (c)   the Treasury reasonably believe that the further person or persons fall within the same description as the person or persons specified in the freezing order and the further order contains a statement of the Treasury's belief.

(3)   This section also applies if—
   (a)   a freezing order is made, and
   (b)   it is proposed to make a further order which amends the freezing order only so as to make it specify (whether by name or description) fewer persons to whom or for whose benefit funds are not to be made available.

(4)   If this section applies, a statutory instrument containing the further order is subject to annulment in pursuance of a resolution of either House of Parliament.

[1287]

12   Procedure for revoking orders

A statutory instrument containing an order revoking a freezing order (without re-enacting it) is subject to annulment in pursuance of a resolution of either House of Parliament.

[1288]

13   De-hybridisation

If apart from this section an order under this Part would be treated for the purposes of the standing orders of either House of Parliament as a hybrid instrument, it is to proceed in that House as if it were not such an instrument.

[1289]

533   *Anti-terrorism, Crime and Security Act 2001, s 17*   **[1293]**

14   Orders: supplementary

(1)   Where this Part confers a power to make provision, different provision may be made for different purposes.

(2)   An order under this Part may include supplementary, incidental, saving or transitional provisions.

(3)   Nothing in this Part affects the generality of subsection (2).

Orders: the Landsbanki Freezing Order 2008, SI 2008/2668 at **[4325]**.

15   The Crown

(1)   A freezing order binds the Crown, subject to the following provisions of this section.

(2)   No contravention by the Crown of a provision of a freezing order makes the Crown criminally liable; but the High Court or in Scotland the Court of Session may, on the application of a person appearing to the Court to have an interest, declare unlawful any act or omission of the Crown which constitutes such a contravention.

(3)   Nothing in this section affects Her Majesty in her private capacity; and this is to be construed as if section 38(3) of the Crown Proceedings Act 1947 (c 44) (meaning of Her Majesty in her private capacity) were contained in this Act.

(1)   These provisions shall cease to have effect—

    (a)   section 2 of the Emergency Laws (Re-enactments and Repeals) Act 1964 (c 60) (Treasury's power to prohibit action on certain orders as to gold etc);

    (b)   section 55 of the Finance Act 1968 (c 44) (meaning of security in section 2 of 1964 Act).

(2)   Subsection (1) does not affect a reference which—

    (a)   is to a provision referred to in that subsection, and

    (b)   is contained in a provision made under an Act.

DISCLOSURE OF INFORMATION

17   Extension of existing disclosure powers

(1)   This section applies to the provisions listed in Schedule 4, so far as they authorise the disclosure of information.

(2)   Each of the provisions to which this section applies shall have effect, in relation to the disclosure of information by or on behalf of a public authority, as if the purposes for which the disclosure of information is authorised by that provision included each of the following—

    (a)   the purposes of any criminal investigation whatever which is being or may be carried out, whether in the United Kingdom or elsewhere;

    (b)   the purposes of any criminal proceedings whatever which have been or may be initiated, whether in the United Kingdom or elsewhere;

    (c)   the purposes of the initiation or bringing to an end of any such investigation or proceedings;

    (d)   the purpose of facilitating a determination of whether any such investigation or proceedings should be initiated or brought to an end.

(3)   The Treasury may by order made by statutory instrument add any provision contained in any subordinate legislation to the provisions to which this section applies.

(4)   The Treasury shall not make an order under subsection (3) unless a draft of it has been laid before Parliament and approved by a resolution of each House.

(5)   No disclosure of information shall be made by virtue of this section unless the public authority by which the disclosure is made is satisfied that the making of the disclosure is proportionate to what is sought to be achieved by it.

(6)   Nothing in this section shall be taken to prejudice any power to disclose information which exists apart from this section.

(7)   The information that may be disclosed by virtue of this section includes information obtained before the commencement of this section.

PART II
OTHER ACTS

18 Restriction on disclosure of information for overseas purposes

(1)   Subject to subsections (2) and (3), the Secretary of State may give a direction which—
   (a)   specifies any overseas proceedings or any description of overseas proceedings; and
   (b)   prohibits the making of any relevant disclosure for the purposes of those proceedings or, as the case may be, of proceedings of that description.

(2)   In subsection (1) the reference, in relation to a direction, to a relevant disclosure is a reference to a disclosure authorised by any of the provisions to which section 17 applies which—
   (a)   is made for a purpose mentioned in subsection (2)(a) to (d) of that section; and
   (b)   is a disclosure of any such information as is described in the direction.

(3)   The Secretary of State shall not give a direction under this section unless it appears to him that the overseas proceedings in question, or that overseas proceedings of the description in question, relate or would relate—
   (a)   to a matter in respect of which it would be more appropriate for any jurisdiction or investigation to be exercised or carried out by a court or other authority of the United Kingdom, or of a particular part of the United Kingdom;
   (b)   to a matter in respect of which it would be more appropriate for any jurisdiction or investigation to be exercised or carried out by a court or other authority of a third country; or
   (c)   to a matter that would fall within paragraph (a) or (b)—
      (i)   if it were appropriate for there to be any exercise of jurisdiction or investigation at all; and
      (ii) if (where one does not exist) a court or other authority with the necessary jurisdiction or functions existed in the United Kingdom, in the part of the United Kingdom in question or, as the case may be, in the third country in question.

(4)   A direction under this section shall not have the effect of prohibiting—
   (a)   the making of any disclosure by a Minister of the Crown or by the Treasury; or
   (b)   the making of any disclosure in pursuance of a Community obligation.

(5)   A direction under this section—
   (a)   may prohibit the making of disclosures absolutely or in such cases, or subject to such conditions as to consent or otherwise, as may be specified in it; and
   (b)   must be published or otherwise issued by the Secretary of State in such manner as he considers appropriate for bringing it to the attention of persons likely to be affected by it.

(6)   A person who, knowing of any direction under this section, discloses any information in contravention of that direction shall be guilty of an offence and liable—
   (a)   on conviction on indictment, to imprisonment for a term not exceeding two years or to a fine or to both;
   (b)   on summary conviction, to imprisonment for a term not exceeding three months or to a fine not exceeding the statutory maximum or to both.

(7)   The following are overseas proceedings for the purposes of this section—
   (a)   criminal proceedings which are taking place, or will or may take place, in a country or territory outside the United Kingdom;
   (b)   a criminal investigation which is being, or will or may be, conducted by an authority of any such country or territory.

(8)   References in this section, in relation to any proceedings or investigation, to a third country are references to any country or territory outside the United Kingdom which is not the country or territory where the proceedings are taking place, or will or may take place or, as the case may be, is not the country or territory of the authority which is conducting the investigation, or which will or may conduct it.

(9)   In this section "court" includes a tribunal of any description.

[1294]

19 Disclosure of information held by revenue departments

(1)   This section applies to information which is held by or on behalf of the Commissioners of Inland Revenue or by or on behalf of the Commissioners of Customs and Excise, including information obtained before the coming into force of this section.

(2)   No obligation of secrecy imposed by statute or otherwise prevents the disclosure, in accordance with the following provisions of this section, of information to which this section applies if the disclosure is made—
   (a)   ...
   (b)   for the purposes of any criminal investigation whatever which is being or may be carried out, whether in the United Kingdom or elsewhere;
   (c)   for the purposes of any criminal proceedings whatever which have been or may be initiated, whether in the United Kingdom or elsewhere;

   (d)   for the purposes of the initiation or bringing to an end of any such investigation or proceedings; or

   (e)   for the purpose of facilitating a determination of whether any such investigation or proceedings should be initiated or brought to an end.

(3)   No disclosure of information to which this section applies shall be made by virtue of this section unless the person by whom the disclosure is made is satisfied that the making of the disclosure is proportionate to what is sought to be achieved by it.

(4)   Information to which this section applies shall not be disclosed by virtue of this section except by the Commissioners by or on whose behalf it is held or with their authority.

(5)   Information obtained by means of a disclosure authorised by subsection (2) shall not be further disclosed except—

   (a)   for a purpose mentioned in that subsection; and

   (b)   with the consent of the Commissioners by whom or with whose authority it was initially disclosed;

and information so obtained otherwise than by or on behalf of any of the intelligence services shall not be further disclosed (with or without such consent) to any of those services, or to any person acting on behalf of any of those services, except for a purpose mentioned in paragraphs (b) to (e) of that subsection.

(6)   A consent for the purposes of subsection (5) may be given either in relation to a particular disclosure or in relation to disclosures made in such circumstances as may be specified or described in the consent.

(7)   Nothing in this section authorises the making of any disclosure which is prohibited by any provision of the Data Protection Act 1998 (c 29).

(8)   References in this section to information which is held on behalf of the Commissioners of Inland Revenue or of the Commissioners of Customs and Excise include references to information which—

   (a)   is held by a person who provides services to the Commissioners of Inland Revenue or, as the case may be, to the Commissioners of Customs and Excise; and

   (b)   is held by that person in connection with the provision of those services.

(9)   In this section "intelligence service" has the same meaning as in the Regulation of Investigatory Powers Act 2000 (c 23).

(10)   Nothing in this section shall be taken to prejudice any power to disclose information which exists apart from this section.

[1295]

NOTES

Sub-s (2): para (a) repealed by the Counter-Terrorism Act 2008, ss 20, 99, Sch 1, para 1, Sch 9, Pt 2, as from 24 December 2008.

Commissioners of Inland Revenue; Commissioners of Customs and Excise: references to the Commissioners of Inland Revenue and the Commissioners of Customs and Excise are now to be taken as a reference to the Commissioners for Her Majesty's Revenue and Customs; see the Commissioners for Revenue and Customs Act 2005, s 50(1), (7).

Note: the Counter-Terrorism Act 2008 (Commencement No 1) Order 2008, SI 2008/3296 (which commences ss 19–21 of, and Sch 1 to, the 2008 Act) contains a drafting error in that it purports to bring those provisions into force "on the day after the day on which [the Act] is made". The Home Office have confirmed that those provisions should have been commenced on the day after the commencement order itself was made (ie, on 24 December 2008) and have indicated that a correction slip will be issued to this effect.

20   Interpretation of Part 3

(1)   In this Part—

"criminal investigation" means an investigation of any criminal conduct, including an investigation of alleged or suspected criminal conduct and an investigation of whether criminal conduct has taken place;

"information" includes—

   (a)   documents; and

   (b)   in relation to a disclosure authorised by a provision to which section 17 applies, anything that falls to be treated as information for the purposes of that provision;

"public authority" has the same meaning as in section 6 of the Human Rights Act 1998 (c 42); and

"subordinate legislation" has the same meaning as in the Interpretation Act 1978 (c 30).

(2)   Proceedings outside the United Kingdom shall not be taken to be criminal proceedings for the purposes of this Part unless the conduct with which the defendant in those proceedings is charged is criminal conduct or conduct which, to a substantial extent, consists of criminal conduct.

(3)   In this section—

"conduct" includes acts, omissions and statements; and

"criminal conduct" means any conduct which—

    (a)   constitutes one or more criminal offences under the law of a part of the United Kingdom; or

    (b)   is, or corresponds to, conduct which, if it all took place in a particular part of the United Kingdom, would constitute one or more offences under the law of that part of the United Kingdom.

[1296]

PART 14
SUPPLEMENTAL

127 Commencement

(1)   Except as provided in subsections (2) to (4), this Act comes into force on such day as the Secretary of State may appoint by order.

(2)–(4)   (*Outside the scope of this work.*)

(5)   Different days may be appointed for different provisions and for different purposes.

(6)   An order under this section—

    (a)   must be made by statutory instrument, and

    (b)   may contain incidental, supplemental, consequential or transitional provision.

[1297]

NOTES

Orders: the Anti-terrorism, Crime and Security Act 2001 (Commencement No 1 and Consequential Provisions) Order 2001, SI 2001/4019; the Anti-terrorism, Crime and Security Act 2001 (Commencement No 2) (Scotland) Order 2001, SI 2001/4104; the Anti-terrorism, Crime and Security Act 2001 (Commencement No 3) Order 2002, SI 2002/228; the Anti-terrorism, Crime and Security Act 2001 (Commencement No 4) Order 2002, SI 2002/1279; the Anti-terrorism, Crime and Security Act 2001 (Commencement No 5) Order 2002, SI 2002/1558.

128 Extent

(1)   The following provisions do not extend to Scotland—

    (a)   Part 5,

    (b)   Part 12,

    (c)   in Part 6 of Schedule 8, the repeals in the Criminal Justice and Police Order Act 1994 and in the Crime and Disorder Act 1998.

(2)   The following provisions do not extend to Northern Ireland—

    (a)   section 76,

    (b)   section 100.

(3)   Except as provided in subsections (1) and (2), an amendment, repeal or revocation in this Act has the same extent as the enactment amended, repealed or revoked.

[1298]

129 Short title

This Act may be cited as the Anti-terrorism, Crime and Security Act 2001.

[1299]

SCHEDULES

SCHEDULE 1
FORFEITURE OF TERRORIST CASH

Section 1

PART 1
INTRODUCTORY

1 Terrorist cash

(1)   This Schedule applies to cash ("terrorist cash") which—

    (a)   is within subsection (1)(a) or (b) of section 1, or

    (b)   is property earmarked as terrorist property.

(2)   "Cash" means—

    (a)   coins and notes in any currency,

    (b)   postal orders,

    (c)   cheques of any kind, including travellers' cheques,

    (d)   bankers' drafts,

    (e)   bearer bonds and bearer shares,

found at any place in the United Kingdom.

(3)   Cash also includes any kind of monetary instrument which is found at any place in the United Kingdom, if the instrument is specified by the Secretary of State by order.

(4)   The power to make an order under sub-paragraph (3) is exercisable by statutory instrument, which is subject to annulment in pursuance of a resolution of either House of Parliament.

[1300]

PART 2
SEIZURE AND DETENTION

2   Seizure of cash

(1)   An authorised officer may seize any cash if he has reasonable grounds for suspecting that it is terrorist cash.

(2)   An authorised officer may also seize cash part of which he has reasonable grounds for suspecting to be terrorist cash if it is not reasonably practicable to seize only that part.

3   Detention of seized cash

(1)   While the authorised officer continues to have reasonable grounds for his suspicion, cash seized under this Schedule may be detained initially for a period of 48 hours.

[(1A)   In determining the period of 48 hours specified in sub-paragraph (1) there shall be disregarded—
   (a)   any Saturday or Sunday;
   (b)   Christmas Day;
   (c)   Good Friday;
   (d)   any day that is a bank holiday under the Banking and Financial Dealings Act 1971 in the part of the United Kingdom in which the cash is seized;
   (e)   any day prescribed under section 8(2) of the Criminal Procedure (Scotland) Act 1995 as a court holiday in the sheriff court district in which the cash is seized.]

(2)   The period for which the cash or any part of it may be detained may be extended by an order made by a magistrates' court or (in Scotland) the sheriff; but the order may not authorise the detention of any of the cash—
   (a)   beyond the end of the period of three months beginning with the date of the order, and
   (b)   in the case of any further order under this paragraph, beyond the end of the period of two years beginning with the date of the first order.

(3)   A justice of the peace may also exercise the power of a magistrates' court to make the first order under sub-paragraph (2) extending the period.

[(3A)   An application to a justice of the peace or the sheriff for an order under sub-paragraph (2) making the first extension of the period—
   (a)   may be made and heard without notice of the application or hearing having been given to any of the persons affected by the application or to the legal representative of such a person, and
   (b)   may be heard and determined in private in the absence of persons so affected and of their legal representatives.]

(4)   An order under sub-paragraph (2) must provide for notice to be given to persons affected by it.

(5)   An application for an order under sub-paragraph (2)—
   (a)   in relation to England and Wales and Northern Ireland, may be made by the Commissioners of Customs and Excise or an authorised officer,
   (b)   in relation to Scotland, may be made by a procurator fiscal,
and the court, sheriff or justice may make the order if satisfied, in relation to any cash to be further detained, that one of the following conditions is met.

(6)   The first condition is that there are reasonable grounds for suspecting that the cash is intended to be used for the purposes of terrorism and that either—
   (a)   its continued detention is justified while its intended use is further investigated or consideration is given to bringing (in the United Kingdom or elsewhere) proceedings against any person for an offence with which the cash is connected, or
   (b)   proceedings against any person for an offence with which the cash is connected have been started and have not been concluded.

(7)   The second condition is that there are reasonable grounds for suspecting that the cash consists of resources of an organisation which is a proscribed organisation and that either—
   (a)   its continued detention is justified while investigation is made into whether or not it consists of such resources or consideration is given to bringing (in the United Kingdom or elsewhere) proceedings against any person for an offence with which the cash is connected, or

PART II
OTHER ACTS

(b)   proceedings against any person for an offence with which the cash is connected have been started and have not been concluded.

(8)   The third condition is that there are reasonable grounds for suspecting that the cash is property earmarked as terrorist property and that either—

(a)   its continued detention is justified while its derivation is further investigated or consideration is given to bringing (in the United Kingdom or elsewhere) proceedings against any person for an offence with which the cash is connected, or

(b)   proceedings against any person for an offence with which the cash is connected have been started and have not been concluded.

4   Payment of detained cash into an account

(1)   If cash is detained under this Schedule for more than 48 hours [(determined in accordance with paragraph 3(1A))], it is to be held in an interest-bearing account and the interest accruing on it is to be added to it on its forfeiture or release.

(2)   In the case of cash seized under paragraph 2(2), the authorised officer must, on paying it into the account, release so much of the cash then held in the account as is not attributable to terrorist cash.

(3)   Sub-paragraph (1) does not apply if the cash is required as evidence of an offence or evidence in proceedings under this Schedule.

5   Release of detained cash

(1)   This paragraph applies while any cash is detained under this Schedule.

(2)   A magistrates' court or (in Scotland) the sheriff may direct the release of the whole or any part of the cash if satisfied, on an application by the person from whom it was seized, that the conditions in paragraph 3 for the detention of cash are no longer met in relation to the cash to be released.

(3)   A authorised officer or (in Scotland) a procurator fiscal may, after notifying the magistrates' court, sheriff or justice under whose order cash is being detained, release the whole or any part of it if satisfied that the detention of the cash to be released is no longer justified.

(4)   But cash is not to be released—

(a)   if an application for its forfeiture under paragraph 6, or for its release under paragraph 9, is made, until any proceedings in pursuance of the application (including any proceedings on appeal) are concluded,

(b)   if (in the United Kingdom or elsewhere) proceedings are started against any person for an offence with which the cash is connected, until the proceedings are concluded.

[1301]

PART 3
FORFEITURE

6   Forfeiture

(1)   While cash is detained under this Schedule, an application for the forfeiture of the whole or any part of it may be made—

(a)   to a magistrates' court by the Commissioners of Customs and Excise or an authorised officer,

(b)   (in Scotland) to the sheriff by the Scottish Ministers.

(2)   The court or sheriff may order the forfeiture of the cash or any part of it if satisfied that the cash or part is terrorist cash.

(3)   In the case of property earmarked as terrorist property which belongs to joint tenants one of whom is an excepted joint owner, the order may not apply to so much of it as the court or sheriff thinks is attributable to the excepted joint owner's share.

(4)   An excepted joint owner is a joint tenant who obtained the property in circumstances in which it would not (as against him) be earmarked; and references to his share of the earmarked property are to so much of the property as would have been his if the joint tenancy had been severed.

[7   Appeal against decision in forfeiture proceedings

(1)   A party to proceedings for an order under paragraph 6 ("a forfeiture order") who is aggrieved by a forfeiture order made in the proceedings or by the decision of the court or sheriff not to make a forfeiture order may appeal—

    (a)   in England and Wales, to the Crown Court;

    (b)   in Scotland, to the sheriff principal;

    (c)   in Northern Ireland, to a county court.

(2)   The appeal must be brought before the end of the period of 30 days beginning with the date on which the order is made or, as the case may be, the decision is given.

This is subject to paragraph 7A (extended time for appealing in certain cases of deproscription).

(3)   The court or sheriff principal hearing the appeal may make any order that appears to the court or sheriff principal to be appropriate.

(4)   If an appeal against a forfeiture order is upheld, the court or sheriff principal may order the release of the cash.

7A   Extended time for appealing in certain cases where deproscription order made

(1)   This paragraph applies where—

    (a)   a successful application for a forfeiture order relies (wholly or partly) on the fact that an organisation is proscribed,

    (b)   an application under section 4 of the Terrorism Act 2000 for a deproscription order in respect of the organisation is refused by the Secretary of State,

    (c)   the forfeited cash is seized under this Schedule on or after the date of the refusal of that application,

    (d)   an appeal against that refusal is allowed under section 5 of that Act,

    (e)   a deproscription order is made accordingly, and

    (f)   if the order is made in reliance on section 123(5) of that Act, a resolution is passed by each House of Parliament under section 123(5)(b).

(2)   Where this paragraph applies, an appeal under paragraph 7 above against the forfeiture order may be brought at any time before the end of the period of 30 days beginning with the date on which the deproscription order comes into force.

(3)   In this paragraph a "deproscription order" means an order under section 3(3)(b) or (8) of the Terrorism Act 2000.]

8   Application of forfeited cash

(1)   Cash forfeited under this Schedule, and any accrued interest on it—

    (a)   if forfeited by a magistrates' court in England and Wales or Northern Ireland, is to be paid into the Consolidated Fund,

    (b)   if forfeited by the sheriff, is to be paid into the Scottish Consolidated Fund.

(2)   But it is not to be paid in—

    (a)   before the end of the period within which an appeal under paragraph 7 may be made, or

    (b)   if a person appeals under that paragraph, before the appeal is determined or otherwise disposed of.

[1302]

NOTES

Paras 7, 7A: substituted, for the original para 7, by the Counter-Terrorism Act 2008, s 84, as from 16 February 2009 (this amendment applies where the order or decision of the court or sheriff against which the appeal is brought is made or given after that date).

Commissioners of Customs and Excise: a reference to the Commissioners of Customs and Excise is now to be taken as a reference to the Commissioners for Her Majesty's Revenue and Customs; see the Commissioners for Revenue and Customs Act 2005, s 50(1), (7).

PART 4
MISCELLANEOUS

9   Victims

(1)   A person who claims that any cash detained under this Schedule, or any part of it, belongs to him may apply to a magistrates' court or (in Scotland) the sheriff for the cash or part to be released to him.

(2)   The application may be made in the course of proceedings under paragraph 3 or 6 or at any other time.

(3)   If it appears to the court or sheriff concerned that—

    (a)   the applicant was deprived of the cash claimed, or of property which it represents, by criminal conduct,

(b)   the property he was deprived of was not, immediately before he was deprived of it, property obtained by or in return for criminal conduct and nor did it then represent such property, and

(c)   the cash claimed belongs to him,

the court or sheriff may order the cash to be released to the applicant.

10   Compensation

(1)   If no forfeiture order is made in respect of any cash detained under this Schedule, the person to whom the cash belongs or from whom it was seized may make an application to the magistrates' court or (in Scotland) the sheriff for compensation.

(2)   If, for any period after the initial detention of the cash for 48 hours [(determined in accordance with paragraph 3(1A))], the cash was not held in an interest-bearing account while detained, the court or sheriff may order an amount of compensation to be paid to the applicant.

(3)   The amount of compensation to be paid under sub-paragraph (2) is the amount the court or sheriff thinks would have been earned in interest in the period in question if the cash had been held in an interest-bearing account.

(4)   If the court or sheriff is satisfied that, taking account of any interest to be paid under this Schedule or any amount to be paid under sub-paragraph (2), the applicant has suffered loss as a result of the detention of the cash and that the circumstances are exceptional, the court or sheriff may order compensation (or additional compensation) to be paid to him.

(5)   The amount of compensation to be paid under sub-paragraph (4) is the amount the court or sheriff thinks reasonable, having regard to the loss suffered and any other relevant circumstances.

(6)   If the cash was seized by a customs officer, the compensation is to be paid by the Commissioners of Customs and Excise.

(7)   If the cash was seized by a constable, the compensation is to be paid as follows—

(a)   in the case of a constable of a police force in England and Wales, it is to be paid out of the police fund from which the expenses of the police force are met,

(b)   in the case of a constable of a police force in Scotland, it is to be paid by the police authority or joint police board for the police area for which that force is maintained,

(c)   in the case of a police officer within the meaning of the Police (Northern Ireland) Act 2000 (c 32), it is to be paid out of money provided by the Chief Constable.

(8)   If the cash was seized by an immigration officer, the compensation is to be paid by the Secretary of State.

(9)   If a forfeiture order is made in respect only of a part of any cash detained under this Schedule, this paragraph has effect in relation to the other part.

(10)   This paragraph does not apply if the court or sheriff makes an order under paragraph 9.

[1303]

NOTES

Para 10: words in square brackets inserted by the Counter-Terrorism Act 2008, s 83(1), (3), (4), as from 16 February 2009 (in relation to cash seized after that date).

Commissioners of Customs and Excise: a reference to the Commissioners of Customs and Excise is now to be taken as a reference to the Commissioners for Her Majesty's Revenue and Customs; see the Commissioners for Revenue and Customs Act 2005, s 50(1), (7).

PART 5
PROPERTY EARMARKED AS TERRORIST PROPERTY

11   Property obtained through terrorism

(1)   A person obtains property through terrorism if he obtains property by or in return for acts of terrorism, or acts carried out for the purposes of terrorism.

(2)   In deciding whether any property was obtained through terrorism—

(a)   it is immaterial whether or not any money, goods or services were provided in order to put the person in question in a position to carry out the acts,

(b)   it is not necessary to show that the act was of a particular kind if it is shown that the property was obtained through acts of one of a number of kinds, each of which would have been an act of terrorism, or an act carried out for the purposes of terrorism.

12   Property earmarked as terrorist property

(1)   Property obtained through terrorism is earmarked as terrorist property.

(2)   But if property obtained through terrorism has been disposed of (since it was so obtained), it is earmarked as terrorist property only if it is held by a person into whose hands it may be followed.

(3)   Earmarked property obtained through terrorism may be followed into the hands of a person obtaining it on a disposal by—
  (a)   the person who obtained the property through terrorism, or
  (b)   a person into whose hands it may (by virtue of this sub-paragraph) be followed.

13   Tracing property

(1)   Where property obtained through terrorism ("the original property") is or has been earmarked as terrorist property, property which represents the original property is also earmarked.

(2)   If a person enters into a transaction by which—
  (a)   he disposes of earmarked property, whether the original property or property which (by virtue of this Part) represents the original property, and
  (b)   he obtains other property in place of it,
the other property represents the original property.

(3)   If a person disposes of earmarked property which represents the original property, the property may be followed into the hands of the person who obtains it (and it continues to represent the original property).

14   Mixing property

(1)   Sub-paragraph (2) applies if a person's property which is earmarked as terrorist property is mixed with other property (whether his property or another's).

(2)   The portion of the mixed property which is attributable to the property earmarked as terrorist property represents the property obtained through terrorism.

(3)   Property earmarked as terrorist property is mixed with other property if (for example) it is used—
  (a)   to increase funds held in a bank account,
  (b)   in part payment for the acquisition of an asset,
  (c)   for the restoration or improvement of land,
  (d)   by a person holding a leasehold interest in the property to acquire the freehold.

15   Accruing profits

(1)   This paragraph applies where a person who has property earmarked as terrorist property obtains further property consisting of profits accruing in respect of the earmarked property.

(2)   The further property is to be treated as representing the property obtained through terrorism.

16   General exceptions

(1)   If—
  (a)   a person disposes of property earmarked as terrorist property, and
  (b)   the person who obtains it on the disposal does so in good faith, for value and without notice that it was earmarked,
the property may not be followed into that person's hands and, accordingly, it ceases to be earmarked.

(2)   If—
  (a)   in pursuance of a judgment in civil proceedings (whether in the United Kingdom or elsewhere), the defendant makes a payment to the claimant or the claimant otherwise obtains property from the defendant,
  (b)   the claimant's claim is based on the defendant's criminal conduct, and
  (c)   apart from this sub-paragraph, the sum received, or the property obtained, by the claimant would be earmarked as terrorist property,
the property ceases to be earmarked.

In relation to Scotland, "claimant" and "defendant" are to be read as "pursuer" and "defender"; and, in relation to Northern Ireland, "claimant" is to be read as "plaintiff".

(3)   If—
  (a)   a payment is made to a person in pursuance of a compensation order under Article 14 of the Criminal Justice (Northern Ireland) Order 1994 (SI 1994/2795 (NI 15)), section 249 of the Criminal Procedure (Scotland) Act 1995 (c 46) or section 130 of the Powers of Criminal Courts (Sentencing) Act 2000 (c 6), [or in pursuance of a service compensation order under the Armed Forces Act 2006,] and
  (b)   apart from this sub-paragraph, the sum received would be earmarked as terrorist property,
the property ceases to be earmarked.

(4)   If—
  (a)   a payment is made to a person in pursuance of a restitution order under section 27 of the

Theft Act (Northern Ireland) 1969 (c 16 (NI)) or section 148(2) of the Powers of Criminal Courts (Sentencing) Act 2000 or a person otherwise obtains any property in pursuance of such an order, and

(b)   apart from this sub-paragraph, the sum received, or the property obtained, would be earmarked as terrorist property,

the property ceases to be earmarked.

(5)   If—

(a)   in pursuance of an order made by the court under section 382(3) or 383(5) of the Financial Services and Markets Act 2000 (c 8) (restitution orders), an amount is paid to or distributed among any persons in accordance with the court's directions, and

(b)   apart from this sub-paragraph, the sum received by them would be earmarked as terrorist property,

the property ceases to be earmarked.

(6)   If—

(a)   in pursuance of a requirement of the Financial Services Authority under section 384(5) of the Financial Services and Markets Act 2000 (c 8) (power of authority to require restitution), an amount is paid to or distributed among any persons, and

(b)   apart from this sub-paragraph, the sum received by them would be earmarked as terrorist property,

the property ceases to be earmarked.

(7)   Where—

(a)   a person enters into a transaction to which paragraph 13(2) applies, and

(b)   the disposal is one to which sub-paragraph (1) applies,

this paragraph does not affect the question whether (by virtue of paragraph 13(2)) any property obtained on the transaction in place of the property disposed of is earmarked.

[1304]

NOTES

Para 16: words in square brackets in sub-para (3)(a) inserted by the Armed Forces Act 2006, s 378(1), Sch 16, para 196, as from a day to be appointed.

PART 6
INTERPRETATION

17   Property

(1)   Property is all property wherever situated and includes—

(a)   money,

(b)   all forms of property, real or personal, heritable or moveable,

(c)   things in action and other intangible or incorporeal property.

(2)   Any reference to a person's property (whether expressed as a reference to the property he holds or otherwise) is to be read as follows.

(3)   In relation to land, it is a reference to any interest which he holds in the land.

(4)   In relation to property other than land, it is a reference—

(a)   to the property (if it belongs to him), or

(b)   to any other interest which he holds in the property.

18   Obtaining and disposing of property

(1)   References to a person disposing of his property include a reference—

(a)   to his disposing of a part of it, or

(b)   to his granting an interest in it,

(or to both); and references to the property disposed of are to any property obtained on the disposal.

(2)   If a person grants an interest in property of his which is earmarked as terrorist property, the question whether the interest is also earmarked is to be determined in the same manner as it is on any other disposal of earmarked property.

(3)   A person who makes a payment to another is to be treated as making a disposal of his property to the other, whatever form the payment takes.

(4)   Where a person's property passes to another under a will or intestacy or by operation of law, it is to be treated as disposed of by him to the other.

(5)   A person is only to be treated as having obtained his property for value in a case where he gave unexecuted consideration if the consideration has become executed consideration.

19 General interpretation

(1) In this Schedule—

"authorised officer" means a constable, a customs officer or an immigration officer,

"cash" has the meaning given by paragraph 1,

"constable", in relation to Northern Ireland, means a police officer within the meaning of the Police (Northern Ireland) Act 2000 (c 32),

"criminal conduct" means conduct which constitutes an offence in any part of the United Kingdom, or would constitute an offence in any part of the United Kingdom if it occurred there,

"customs officer" means an officer commissioned by the Commissioners of Customs and Excise under section 6(3) of the Customs and Excise Management Act 1979 (c 2),

"forfeiture order" has the meaning given by paragraph 7,

"immigration officer" means a person appointed as an immigration officer under paragraph 1 of Schedule 2 to the Immigration Act 1971 (c 77),

"interest", in relation to land—

(a) in the case of land in England and Wales or Northern Ireland, means any legal estate and any equitable interest or power,

(b) in the case of land in Scotland, means any estate, interest, servitude or other heritable right in or over land, including a heritable security,

"interest", in relation to property other than land, includes any right (including a right to possession of the property),

"part", in relation to property, includes a portion,

"property obtained through terrorism" has the meaning given by paragraph 11,

"property earmarked as terrorist property" is to be read in accordance with Part 5,

"proscribed organisation" has the same meaning as in the Terrorism Act 2000 (c 11),

"terrorism" has the same meaning as in the Terrorism Act 2000,

"terrorist cash" has the meaning given by paragraph 1,

"value" means market value.

(2) Paragraphs 17 and 18 and the following provisions apply for the purposes of this Schedule.

(3) For the purpose of deciding whether or not property was earmarked as terrorist property at any time (including times before commencement), it is to be assumed that this Schedule was in force at that and any other relevant time.

(4) References to anything done or intended to be done for the purposes of terrorism include anything done or intended to be done for the benefit of a proscribed organisation.

(5) An organisation's resources include any cash which is applied or made available, or is to be applied or made available, for use by the organisation.

(6) Proceedings against any person for an offence are concluded when—

(a) the person is convicted or acquitted,

(b) the prosecution is discontinued or, in Scotland, the trial diet is deserted simpliciter, or

(c) the jury is discharged without a finding [otherwise than in circumstances where the proceedings are continued without a jury].

[1305]

NOTES

Para 19: words in square brackets in sub-para (6)(c) added by the Criminal Justice Act 2003, s 331, Sch 36, Pt 4, para 77, as from 24 July 2006 (in relation to England and Wales), as from 8 January 2007 (in relation to Northern Ireland), and as from a day to be appointed (in relation to Scotland).

Commissioners of Customs and Excise: a reference to the Commissioners of Customs and Excise is now to be taken as a reference to the Commissioners for Her Majesty's Revenue and Customs; see the Commissioners for Revenue and Customs Act 2005, s 50(1), (7).

Customs and Excise Management Act 1979, s 6: repealed by the Commissioners for Revenue and Customs Act 2005, s 52(2), Sch 5.

SCHEDULE 3
FREEZING ORDERS

Section 6

1 Interpretation

References in this Schedule to a person specified in a freezing order as a person to whom or for whose benefit funds are not to be made available are to be read in accordance with section 5(4).

2 Funds

A freezing order may include provision that funds include gold, cash, deposits, securities (such as stocks, shares and debentures) and such other matters as the order may specify.

3   Making funds available

(1)   A freezing order must include provision as to the meaning (in relation to funds) of making available to or for the benefit of a person.

(2)   In particular, an order may provide that the expression includes—

(a)   allowing a person to withdraw from an account;

(b)   honouring a cheque payable to a person;

(c)   crediting a person's account with interest;

(d)   releasing documents of title (such as share certificates) held on a person's behalf;

(e)   making available the proceeds of realisation of a person's property;

(f)   making a payment to or for a person's benefit (for instance, under a contract or as a gift or under any enactment such as the enactments relating to social security);

(g)   such other acts as the order may specify.

4   Licences

(1)   A freezing order must include—

(a)   provision for the granting of licences authorising funds to be made available;

(b)   provision that a prohibition under the order is not to apply if funds are made available in accordance with a licence.

(2)   In particular, an order may provide—

(a)   that a licence may be granted generally or to a specified person or persons or description of persons;

(b)   that a licence may authorise funds to be made available to or for the benefit of persons generally or a specified person or persons or description of persons;

(c)   that a licence may authorise funds to be made available generally or for specified purposes;

(d)   that a licence may be granted in relation to funds generally or to funds of a specified description;

(e)   for a licence to be granted in pursuance of an application or without an application being made;

(f)   for the form and manner in which applications for licences are to be made;

(g)   for licences to be granted by the Treasury or a person authorised by the Treasury;

(h)   for the form in which licences are to be granted;

(i)   for licences to be granted subject to conditions;

(j)   for licences to be of a defined or indefinite duration;

(k)   for the charging of a fee to cover the administrative costs of granting a licence;

(l)   for the variation and revocation of licences.

5   Information and documents

(1)   A freezing order may include provision that a person—

(a)   must provide information if required to do so and it is reasonably needed for the purpose of ascertaining whether an offence under the order has been committed;

(b)   must produce a document if required to do so and it is reasonably needed for that purpose.

(2)   In particular, an order may include—

(a)   provision that a requirement to provide information or to produce a document may be made by the Treasury or a person authorised by the Treasury;

(b)   provision that information must be provided, and a document must be produced, within a reasonable period specified in the order and at a place specified by the person requiring it;

(c)   provision that the provision of information is not to be taken to breach any restriction on the disclosure of information (however imposed);

(d)   provision restricting the use to which information or a document may be put and the circumstances in which it may be disclosed;

(e)   provision that a requirement to provide information or produce a document does not apply to privileged information or a privileged document;

(f)   provision that information is privileged if the person would be entitled to refuse to provide it on grounds of legal professional privilege in proceedings in the High Court or (in Scotland) on grounds of confidentiality of communications in proceedings in the Court of Session;

(g)   provision that a document is privileged if the person would be entitled to refuse to produce it on grounds of legal professional privilege in proceedings in the High Court or (in Scotland) on grounds of confidentiality of communications in proceedings in the Court of Session;

(h)   provision that information or a document held with the intention of furthering a criminal purpose is not privileged.

6　Disclosure of information

(1)　A freezing order may include provision requiring a person to disclose information as mentioned below if the following three conditions are satisfied.

(2)　The first condition is that the person required to disclose is specified or falls within a description specified in the order.

(3)　The second condition is that the person required to disclose knows or suspects, or has grounds for knowing or suspecting, that a person specified in the freezing order as a person to whom or for whose benefit funds are not to be made available—

　(a)　is a customer of his or has been a customer of his at any time since the freezing order came into force, or

　(b)　is a person with whom he has dealings in the course of his business or has had such dealings at any time since the freezing order came into force.

(4)　The third condition is that the information—

　(a)　on which the knowledge or suspicion of the person required to disclose is based, or

　(b)　which gives grounds for his knowledge or suspicion,

came to him in the course of a business in the regulated sector.

(5)　The freezing order may require the person required to disclose to make a disclosure to the Treasury of that information as soon as is practicable after it comes to him.

(6)　The freezing order may include—

　(a)　provision that Schedule 3A to the Terrorism Act 2000 (c 11) is to have effect for the purpose of determining what is a business in the regulated sector;

　(b)　provision that the disclosure of information is not to be taken to breach any restriction on the disclosure of information (however imposed);

　(c)　provision restricting the use to which information may be put and the circumstances in which it may be disclosed by the Treasury;

　(d)　provision that the requirement to disclose information does not apply to privileged information;

　(e)　provision that information is privileged if the person would be entitled to refuse to disclose it on grounds of legal professional privilege in proceedings in the High Court or (in Scotland) on grounds of confidentiality of communications in proceedings in the Court of Session;

　(f)　provision that information held with the intention of furthering a criminal purpose is not privileged.

7　Offences

(1)　A freezing order may include any of the provisions set out in this paragraph.

(2)　A person commits an offence if he fails to comply with a prohibition imposed by the order.

(3)　A person commits an offence if he engages in an activity knowing or intending that it will enable or facilitate the commission by another person of an offence under a provision included under sub-paragraph (2).

(4)　A person commits an offence if—

　(a)　he fails without reasonable excuse to provide information, or to produce a document, in response to a requirement made under the order;

　(b)　he provides information, or produces a document, which he knows is false in a material particular in response to such a requirement or with a view to obtaining a licence under the order;

　(c)　he recklessly provides information, or produces a document, which is false in a material particular in response to such a requirement or with a view to obtaining a licence under the order;

　(d)　he fails without reasonable excuse to disclose information as required by a provision included under paragraph 6.

(5)　A person does not commit an offence under a provision included under sub-paragraph (2) or (3) if he proves that he did not know and had no reason to suppose that the person to whom or for whose benefit funds were made available, or were to be made available, was the person (or one of the persons) specified in the freezing order as a person to whom or for whose benefit funds are not to be made available.

(6)　A person guilty of an offence under a provision included under sub-paragraph (2) or (3) is liable—

　(a)　on summary conviction, to imprisonment for a term not exceeding 6 months or to a fine not exceeding the statutory maximum or to both;

　(b)　on conviction on indictment, to imprisonment for a term not exceeding 2 years or to a fine or to both.

(7)   A person guilty of an offence under a provision included under sub-paragraph (4) is liable on summary conviction to imprisonment for a term not exceeding 6 months or to a fine not exceeding level 5 on the standard scale or to both.

8   Offences: procedure

(1)   A freezing order may include any of the provisions set out in this paragraph.

(2)   Proceedings for an offence under the order are not to be instituted in England and Wales except by or with the consent of the Treasury or the Director of Public Prosecutions.

(3)   Proceedings for an offence under the order are not to be instituted in Northern Ireland except by or with the consent of the Treasury or the Director of Public Prosecutions for Northern Ireland.

(4)   Despite anything in section 127(1) of the Magistrates' Courts Act 1980 (c 43) (information to be laid within 6 months of offence) an information relating to an offence under the order which is triable by a magistrates' court in England and Wales may be so tried if it is laid at any time in the period of one year starting with the date of the commission of the offence.

(5)   In Scotland summary proceedings for an offence under the order may be commenced at any time in the period of one year starting with the date of the commission of the offence.

(6)   In its application to an offence under the order Article 19(1)(a) of the Magistrates' Courts (Northern Ireland) Order 1981 (SI 1981/1675 (NI 26)) (time limit within which complaint charging offence must be made) is to have effect as if the reference to six months were a reference to twelve months.

9   Offences by bodies corporate etc

(1)   A freezing order may include any of the provisions set out in this paragraph.

(2)   If an offence under the order—
    (a)   is committed by a body corporate, and
    (b)   is proved to have been committed with the consent or connivance of an officer, or to be attributable to any neglect on his part,
he as well as the body corporate is guilty of the offence and liable to be proceeded against and punished accordingly.

(3)   These are officers of a body corporate—
    (a)   a director, manager, secretary or other similar officer of the body;
    (b)   any person purporting to act in any such capacity.

(4)   If the affairs of a body corporate are managed by its members sub-paragraph (2) applies in relation to the acts and defaults of a member in connection with his functions of management as if he were an officer of the body.

(5)   If an offence under the order—
    (a)   is committed by a Scottish partnership, and
    (b)   is proved to have been committed with the consent or connivance of a partner, or to be attributable to any neglect on his part,
he as well as the partnership is guilty of the offence and liable to be proceeded against and punished accordingly.

10   Compensation

(1)   A freezing order may include provision for the award of compensation to or on behalf of a person on the grounds that he has suffered loss as a result of—
    (a)   the order;
    (b)   the fact that a licence has not been granted under the order;
    (c)   the fact that a licence under the order has been granted on particular terms rather than others;
    (d)   the fact that a licence under the order has been varied or revoked.

(2)   In particular, the order may include—
    (a)   provision about the person who may make a claim for an award;
    (b)   provision about the person to whom a claim for an award is to be made (which may be provision that it is to be made to the High Court or, in Scotland, the Court of Session);
    (c)   provision about the procedure for making and deciding a claim;
    (d)   provision that no compensation is to be awarded unless the claimant has behaved reasonably (which may include provision requiring him to mitigate his loss, for instance by applying for a licence);
    (e)   provision that compensation must be awarded in specified circumstances or may be awarded in specified circumstances (which may include provision that the circumstances involve negligence or other fault);
    (f)   provision about the amount that may be awarded;

(g)   provision about who is to pay any compensation awarded (which may include provision that it is to be paid or reimbursed by the Treasury);

(h)   provision about how compensation is to be paid (which may include provision for payment to a person other than the claimant).

11 Treasury's duty to give reasons

[(1)]   A freezing order must include provision that if—

(a)   a person is specified in the order as a person to whom or for whose benefit funds are not to be made available, and

(b)   he makes a written request to the Treasury to give him the reason why he is so specified,

as soon as is practicable the Treasury must give the person the reason in writing.

[(2)   Sub-paragraph (1) does not apply if, or to the extent that, particulars of the reason would not be required to be disclosed to the applicant in proceedings to set aside the freezing order.]

[1306]

NOTES

Para 11: sub-para (1) numbered as such, and sub-para (2) added, by the Counter-Terrorism Act 2008, s 70, as from 27 November 2009.

See also the note following the Part II heading *ante*.

Orders: the Landsbanki Freezing Order 2008, SI 2008/2668 at **[4325]**.

CRIMINAL JUSTICE AND POLICE ACT 2001

(2001 c 16)

NOTES

Only provisions of this Act relevant to Financial Services law are reproduced. Provisions not reproduced are not annotated.

This Act is reproduced as amended by: the Proceeds of Crime Act 2002; the Money Laundering Regulations 2007, SI 2007/2157.

An Act to make provision for combatting crime and disorder; to make provision about the disclosure of information relating to criminal matters and about powers of search and seizure; to amend the Police and Criminal Evidence Act 1984, the Police and Criminal Evidence (Northern Ireland) Order 1989 and the Terrorism Act 2000; to make provision about the police, the National Criminal Intelligence Service and the National Crime Squad; to make provision about the powers of the courts in relation to criminal matters; and for connected purposes

[11 May 2001]

PART 2
POWERS OF SEIZURE

Additional powers of seizure

50 Additional powers of seizure from premises

(1)   Where—

(a)   a person who is lawfully on any premises finds anything on those premises that he has reasonable grounds for believing may be or may contain something for which he is authorised to search on those premises,

(b)   a power of seizure to which this section applies or the power conferred by subsection (2) would entitle him, if he found it, to seize whatever it is that he has grounds for believing that thing to be or to contain, and

(c)   in all the circumstances, it is not reasonably practicable for it to be determined, on those premises—

     (i)   whether what he has found is something that he is entitled to seize, or

     (ii)   the extent to which what he has found contains something that he is entitled to seize,

that person's powers of seizure shall include power under this section to seize so much of what he has found as it is necessary to remove from the premises to enable that to be determined.

(2)   Where—

(a)   a person who is lawfully on any premises finds anything on those premises ("the seizable property") which he would be entitled to seize but for its being comprised in something else that he has (apart from this subsection) no power to seize,

(b)   the power under which that person would have power to seize the seizable property is a power to which this section applies, and

(c)   in all the circumstances it is not reasonably practicable for the seizable property to be separated, on those premises, from that in which it is comprised,

that person's powers of seizure shall include power under this section to seize both the seizable property and that from which it is not reasonably practicable to separate it.

(3)   The factors to be taken into account in considering, for the purposes of this section, whether or not it is reasonably practicable on particular premises for something to be determined, or for something to be separated from something else, shall be confined to the following—

(a)   how long it would take to carry out the determination or separation on those premises;

(b)   the number of persons that would be required to carry out that determination or separation on those premises within a reasonable period;

(c)   whether the determination or separation would (or would if carried out on those premises) involve damage to property;

(d)   the apparatus or equipment that it would be necessary or appropriate to use for the carrying out of the determination or separation; and

(e)   in the case of separation, whether the separation—

(i)   would be likely, or

(ii)   if carried out by the only means that are reasonably practicable on those premises, would be likely,

to prejudice the use of some or all of the separated seizable property for a purpose for which something seized under the power in question is capable of being used.

(4)   Section 19(6) of the 1984 Act and Article 21(6) of the Police and Criminal Evidence (Northern Ireland) Order 1989 (SI 1989/1341 (NI 12)) (powers of seizure not to include power to seize anything that a person has reasonable grounds for believing is legally privileged) shall not apply to the power of seizure conferred by subsection (2).

(5)   This section applies to each of the powers of seizure specified in Part 1 of Schedule 1.

(6)   Without prejudice to any power conferred by this section to take a copy of any document, nothing in this section, so far as it has effect by reference to the power to take copies of documents under section 28(2)(b) of the Competition Act 1998 (c 41), shall be taken to confer any power to seize any document.

[1307]

NOTES

1984 Act: ie, the Police and Criminal Evidence Act 1984.

PART 6
MISCELLANEOUS AND SUPPLEMENTAL

Supplemental

138 Short title, commencement and extent

(1)   This Act may be cited as the Criminal Justice and Police Act 2001.

(2)   The provisions of this Act, other than this section and sections 42 and 43, 81 to 85, 109, 116(7) and 119(7), shall come into force on such day as the Secretary of State may by order made by statutory instrument appoint; and different days may be appointed under this subsection for different purposes.

(3)   An order under subsection (2) may contain such savings as the Secretary of State thinks fit.

(4)   (*Outside the scope of this work.*)

(5)   Subject to subsections (6) to (12), this Act extends to England and Wales only.

(6)   The following provisions of this Act extend to the United Kingdom—

(a)   (*outside the scope of this work;*)

(b)   Part 2;

(c)–(e) (*outside the scope of this work;*)

(f)   section 136 and this section.

(7)–(12)   (*Outside the scope of this work.*)

[1308]

NOTES

Orders: various commencement orders have been made under this section; the commencement order relevant to the provisions of this Act reproduced in this work is the Criminal Justice and Police Act 2001 (Commencement No 9) Order 2003, SI 2003/708.

SCHEDULES

SCHEDULE 1
POWERS OF SEIZURE

Sections 50, 51 & 55

PART 1
POWERS TO WHICH SECTION 50 APPLIES

Police and Criminal Evidence Act 1984 (c 60)

1. Each of the powers of seizure conferred by the provisions of Part 2 or 3 of the 1984 Act (police powers of entry, search and seizure).

Financial Services and Markets Act 2000 (c 8)

69. The power of seizure conferred by section 176(5) of the Financial Services and Markets Act 2000 (seizure of documents or information not supplied in compliance with a requirement etc).

[Proceeds of Crime Act 2002 (c 29)

73A. The power of seizure conferred by section 352(4) of the Proceeds of Crime Act 2002 (seizure of material likely to be of substantial value to certain investigations).]

[73C. The power of seizure conferred by sections 17 and 22 of the Crime (International Co-operation) Act 2003 (seizure of evidence relevant to overseas investigation or offence).

[The Money Laundering Regulations 2007

73J. The power of seizure conferred by regulation 39(6) of the Money Laundering Regulations 2007 (entry to premises under warrant).]

[The Transfer of Funds (Information on the Payer) Regulations 2007

73K. The power of seizure conferred by regulation 9(6) of the Transfer of Funds (Information on the Payer) Regulations 2007 (entry to premises under warrant).]

[1309]

NOTES
  Commencement: 1 April 2003 (with the exception of paras 35, 42, 67); 1 June 2004 (paras 42, 67); 8 October 2005 (para 35).
  Only entries relevant to this work are reproduced.
  Para 73A: added by the Proceeds of Crime Act 2002, s 456, Sch 11, para 40(1), (6), as from 24 February 2003.
  Para 73C: added by the Crime (International Co-operation) Act 2003, s 26(3)(b).
  Para 73J: added by the Money Laundering Regulations 2007, SI 2007/2157, reg 51, Sch 6, para 3, as from 15 December 2007.
  Para 73K: added by the Transfer of Funds (Information on the Payer) Regulations 2007, SI 2007/3298, reg 19, Sch 3, para 3, as from 15 December 2007.

PROCEEDS OF CRIME ACT 2002

(2002 c 29)

NOTES
  Only provisions of this Act relevant to Financial Services law are reproduced. Provisions not reproduced are not annotated.
  This Act is reproduced as amended by: the Crime (International Co-operation) Act 2003; the Commissioners for Revenue and Customs Act 2005; the Serious Organised Crime and Police Act 2005; the Serious Crime Act 2007; the Proceeds of Crime Act 2002 and Money Laundering Regulations 2003 (Amendment) Order 2006, SI 2006/308; the Proceeds of Crime Act 2002 (Business in the Regulated Sector and Supervisory Authorities) Order 2007, SI 2007/3287; the Terrorism Act 2000 and Proceeds of Crime Act 2002 (Amendment) Regulations 2007, SI 2007/3398.

ARRANGEMENT OF SECTIONS

PART 7
MONEY LAUNDERING

Offences

An Act to establish the Assets Recovery Agency and make provision about the appointment of its Director and his functions (including Revenue functions), to provide for confiscation orders in relation to persons who benefit from criminal conduct and for restraint orders to prohibit dealing with property, to allow the recovery of property which is or represents property obtained through unlawful conduct or which is intended to be used in unlawful conduct, to make provision about money laundering, to make provision about investigations relating to benefit from criminal conduct or to property which is or represents property obtained through unlawful conduct or to money laundering, to make provision to give effect to overseas requests and orders made where property is found or believed to be obtained through criminal conduct, and for connected purposes

[24 July 2002]

PART 7
MONEY LAUNDERING

Offences

327 Concealing etc

(1)   A person commits an offence if he—
   (a)   conceals criminal property;
   (b)   disguises criminal property;
   (c)   converts criminal property;
   (d)   transfers criminal property;
   (e)   removes criminal property from England and Wales or from Scotland or from Northern Ireland.

(2)   But a person does not commit such an offence if—
   (a)   he makes an authorised disclosure under section 338 and (if the disclosure is made before he does the act mentioned in subsection (1)) he has the appropriate consent;
   (b)   he intended to make such a disclosure but had a reasonable excuse for not doing so;
   (c)   the act he does is done in carrying out a function he has relating to the enforcement of any provision of this Act or of any other enactment relating to criminal conduct or benefit from criminal conduct.

[(2A)   Nor does a person commit an offence under subsection (1) if—
   (a)   he knows, or believes on reasonable grounds, that the relevant criminal conduct occurred in a particular country or territory outside the United Kingdom, and
   (b)   the relevant criminal conduct—
        (i)   was not, at the time it occurred, unlawful under the criminal law then applying in that country or territory, and
        (ii)   is not of a description prescribed by an order made by the Secretary of State.

(2B)   In subsection (2A) "the relevant criminal conduct" is the criminal conduct by reference to which the property concerned is criminal property.]

[(2C)   A deposit-taking body that does an act mentioned in paragraph (c) or (d) of subsection (1) does not commit an offence under that subsection if—
   (a)   it does the act in operating an account maintained with it, and
   (b)   the value of the criminal property concerned is less than the threshold amount determined under section 339A for the act.]

(3)   Concealing or disguising criminal property includes concealing or disguising its nature, source, location, disposition, movement or ownership or any rights with respect to it.

[1310]

NOTES

Sub-ss (2A), (2B): inserted by the Serious Organised Crime and Police Act 2005, s 102(1), (2), as from 15 May 2006.

Sub-s (2C): inserted by the Serious Organised Crime and Police Act 2005, s 103(1), (2), as from 1 July 2005.

Transitional provisions: for transitional provisions in relation to the operation of the new principal money laundering offences (ie, those contained in ss 327–329 of this Act) where the conduct in question began before 24 February 2003, see the Proceeds of Crime Act 2002 (Commencement No 4, Transitional Provisions and Savings) Order 2003, SI 2003/120, art 3 at **[3697]**.

Serious crime prevention orders: a court may make a serious crime prevention order under the Serious Crime Act 2007, ss 1 or 19 if it is satisfied that a person has been involved in serious crime, and it has reasonable grounds to believe that the order would protect the public by preventing, restricting or disrupting involvement by the person in serious crime. By virtue of s 2 of, and Sch 1 to, the 2007 Act, the offence under this section (and ss 328, 329) is a serious crime.

Orders: the Proceeds of Crime Act 2002 (Money Laundering: Exceptions to Overseas Conduct Defence) Order 2006, SI 2006/1070 at **[3981]**.

328 Arrangements

(1)   A person commits an offence if he enters into or becomes concerned in an arrangement which he knows or suspects facilitates (by whatever means) the acquisition, retention, use or control of criminal property by or on behalf of another person.

(2)   But a person does not commit such an offence if—
  (a)   he makes an authorised disclosure under section 338 and (if the disclosure is made before he does the act mentioned in subsection (1)) he has the appropriate consent;
  (b)   he intended to make such a disclosure but had a reasonable excuse for not doing so;
  (c)   the act he does is done in carrying out a function he has relating to the enforcement of any provision of this Act or of any other enactment relating to criminal conduct or benefit from criminal conduct.

[(3)   Nor does a person commit an offence under subsection (1) if—
  (a)   he knows, or believes on reasonable grounds, that the relevant criminal conduct occurred in a particular country or territory outside the United Kingdom, and
  (b)   the relevant criminal conduct—
    (i)   was not, at the time it occurred, unlawful under the criminal law then applying in that country or territory, and
    (ii)   is not of a description prescribed by an order made by the Secretary of State.

(4)   In subsection (3) "the relevant criminal conduct" is the criminal conduct by reference to which the property concerned is criminal property.]

[(5)   A deposit-taking body that does an act mentioned in subsection (1) does not commit an offence under that subsection if—
  (a)   it does the act in operating an account maintained with it, and
  (b)   the arrangement facilitates the acquisition, retention, use or control of criminal property of a value that is less than the threshold amount determined under section 339A for the act.]

[1311]

NOTES
Sub-ss (3), (4): added by the Serious Organised Crime and Police Act 2005, s 102(1), (3), as from 15 May 2006.
Sub-s (5): added by the Serious Organised Crime and Police Act 2005, s 103(1), (3), as from 1 July 2005.
Transitional provisions: see the note to s 327 at **[1310]**.
Serious crime prevention orders: see the note to s 327 at **[1310]**.
Orders: the Proceeds of Crime Act 2002 (Money Laundering: Exceptions to Overseas Conduct Defence) Order 2006, SI 2006/1070 at **[3981]**.

329   Acquisition, use and possession
(1)   A person commits an offence if he—
  (a)   acquires criminal property;
  (b)   uses criminal property;
  (c)   has possession of criminal property.

(2)   But a person does not commit such an offence if—
  (a)   he makes an authorised disclosure under section 338 and (if the disclosure is made before he does the act mentioned in subsection (1)) he has the appropriate consent;
  (b)   he intended to make such a disclosure but had a reasonable excuse for not doing so;
  (c)   he acquired or used or had possession of the property for adequate consideration;
  (d)   the act he does is done in carrying out a function he has relating to the enforcement of any provision of this Act or of any other enactment relating to criminal conduct or benefit from criminal conduct.

[(2A)   Nor does a person commit an offence under subsection (1) if—
  (a)   he knows, or believes on reasonable grounds, that the relevant criminal conduct occurred in a particular country or territory outside the United Kingdom, and
  (b)   the relevant criminal conduct—
    (i)   was not, at the time it occurred, unlawful under the criminal law then applying in that country or territory, and
    (ii)   is not of a description prescribed by an order made by the Secretary of State.

(2B)   In subsection (2A) "the relevant criminal conduct" is the criminal conduct by reference to which the property concerned is criminal property.]

[(2C)   A deposit-taking body that does an act mentioned in subsection (1) does not commit an offence under that subsection if—
  (a)   it does the act in operating an account maintained with it, and
  (b)   the value of the criminal property concerned is less than the threshold amount determined under section 339A for the act.]

(3)   For the purposes of this section—
  (a)   a person acquires property for inadequate consideration if the value of the consideration is significantly less than the value of the property;
  (b)   a person uses or has possession of property for inadequate consideration if the value of the consideration is significantly less than the value of the use or possession;

(c)   the provision by a person of goods or services which he knows or suspects may help another to carry out criminal conduct is not consideration.

[1312]

NOTES

Sub-ss (2A), (2B): inserted by the Serious Organised Crime and Police Act 2005, s 102(1), (4), as from 15 May 2006.

Sub-s (2C): inserted by the Serious Organised Crime and Police Act 2005, s 103(1), (4), as from 1 July 2005.

Transitional provisions: see the note to s 327 at **[1310]**.

Serious crime prevention orders: see the note to s 327 at **[1310]**.

Orders: the Proceeds of Crime Act 2002 (Money Laundering: Exceptions to Overseas Conduct Defence) Order 2006, SI 2006/1070 at **[3981]**.

330   Failure to disclose: regulated sector

(1)   A person commits an offence if [the conditions in subsections (2) to (4) are satisfied].

(2)   The first condition is that he—
  (a)   knows or suspects, or
  (b)   has reasonable grounds for knowing or suspecting,

that another person is engaged in money laundering.

(3)   The second condition is that the information or other matter—
  (a)   on which his knowledge or suspicion is based, or
  (b)   which gives reasonable grounds for such knowledge or suspicion,

came to him in the course of a business in the regulated sector.

[(3A)   The third condition is—
  (a)   that he can identify the other person mentioned in subsection (2) or the whereabouts of any of the laundered property, or
  (b)   that he believes, or it is reasonable to expect him to believe, that the information or other matter mentioned in subsection (3) will or may assist in identifying that other person or the whereabouts of any of the laundered property.

(4)   The fourth condition is that he does not make the required disclosure to—
  (a)   a nominated officer, or
  (b)   a person authorised for the purposes of this Part by the Director General of [SOCA],

as soon as is practicable after the information or other matter mentioned in subsection (3) comes to him.

(5)   The required disclosure is a disclosure of—
  (a)   the identity of the other person mentioned in subsection (2), if he knows it,
  (b)   the whereabouts of the laundered property, so far as he knows it, and
  (c)   the information or other matter mentioned in subsection (3).

(5A)   The laundered property is the property forming the subject-matter of the money laundering that he knows or suspects, or has reasonable grounds for knowing or suspecting, that other person to be engaged in.

(6)   But he does not commit an offence under this section if—
  (a)   he has a reasonable excuse for not making the required disclosure,
  (b)   he is a professional legal adviser [or ... relevant professional adviser] and—
      (i)   if he knows either of the things mentioned in subsection (5)(a) and (b), he knows the thing because of information or other matter that came to him in privileged circumstances, or
      (ii)   the information or other matter mentioned in subsection (3) came to him in privileged circumstances, or
  (c)   subsection (7) [or (7B)] applies to him.]

(7)   This subsection applies to a person if—
  (a)   he does not know or suspect that another person is engaged in money laundering, and
  (b)   he has not been provided by his employer with such training as is specified by the Secretary of State by order for the purposes of this section.

[(7A)   Nor does a person commit an offence under this section if—
  (a)   he knows, or believes on reasonable grounds, that the money laundering is occurring in a particular country or territory outside the United Kingdom, and
  (b)   the money laundering—
      (i)   is not unlawful under the criminal law applying in that country or territory, and
      (ii)   is not of a description prescribed in an order made by the Secretary of State.]

[(7B)   This subsection applies to a person if—
  (a)   he is employed by, or is in partnership with, a professional legal adviser or a relevant professional adviser to provide the adviser with assistance or support,

(b) the information or other matter mentioned in subsection (3) comes to the person in connection with the provision of such assistance or support, and

(c) the information or other matter came to the adviser in privileged circumstances.]

(8) In deciding whether a person committed an offence under this section the court must consider whether he followed any relevant guidance which was at the time concerned—

(a) issued by a supervisory authority or any other appropriate body,

(b) approved by the Treasury, and

(c) published in a manner it approved as appropriate in its opinion to bring the guidance to the attention of persons likely to be affected by it.

(9) A disclosure to a nominated officer is a disclosure which—

(a) is made to a person nominated by the alleged offender's employer to receive disclosures under this section, and

(b) is made in the course of the alleged offender's employment ...

[(9A) But a disclosure which satisfies paragraphs (a) and (b) of subsection (9) is not to be taken as a disclosure to a nominated officer if the person making the disclosure—

(a) is a professional legal adviser [or ... relevant professional adviser],

(b) makes it for the purpose of obtaining advice about making a disclosure under this section, and

(c) does not intend it to be a disclosure under this section.]

(10) Information or other matter comes to a professional legal adviser [or ... relevant professional adviser] in privileged circumstances if it is communicated or given to him—

(a) by (or by a representative of) a client of his in connection with the giving by the adviser of legal advice to the client,

(b) by (or by a representative of) a person seeking legal advice from the adviser, or

(c) by a person in connection with legal proceedings or contemplated legal proceedings.

(11) But subsection (10) does not apply to information or other matter which is communicated or given with the intention of furthering a criminal purpose.

(12) Schedule 9 has effect for the purpose of determining what is—

(a) a business in the regulated sector;

(b) a supervisory authority.

(13) An appropriate body is any body which regulates or is representative of any trade, profession, business or employment carried on by the alleged offender.

[(14) A relevant professional adviser is an accountant, auditor or tax adviser who is a member of a professional body which is established for accountants, auditors or tax advisers (as the case may be) and which makes provision for—

(a) testing the competence of those seeking admission to membership of such a body as a condition for such admission; and

(b) imposing and maintaining professional and ethical standards for its members, as well as imposing sanctions for non-compliance with those standards.]

[1313]

NOTES

Sub-s (1): words in square brackets substituted by the Serious Organised Crime and Police Act 2005, s 104(1), (2), as from 1 July 2005.

Sub-ss (3A), (5), (5A): substituted together with sub-ss (4), (6), for original sub-ss (4)–(6), by the Serious Organised Crime and Police Act 2005, s 104(1), (3), as from 1 July 2005.

Sub-s (4): substituted as noted above; word in square brackets substituted by the Serious Crime Act 2007, s 74(2), Sch 8, Pt 6, paras 121, 126, as from 1 April 2008 (for transitional provisions in relation to the transfer of functions from the Assets Recovery Agency to SOCA and the National Policing Improvement Agency, see the Serious Crime Act 2007 (Commencement No 2 and Transitional and Transitory Provisions and Savings) Order 2008, SI 2008/755, art 3).

Sub-s (6): substituted as noted above; words in square brackets inserted by the Proceeds of Crime Act 2002 and Money Laundering Regulations 2003 (Amendment) Order 2006, SI 2006/308, art 2(1)–(3), as from 21 February 2006; word omitted repealed by the Terrorism Act 2000 and Proceeds of Crime Act 2002 (Amendment) Regulations 2007, SI 2007/3398, reg 3, Sch 2, paras 1, 2, as from 26 December 2007.

Sub-s (7A): inserted by the Serious Organised Crime and Police Act 2005, s 102(1), (5), as from 15 May 2006.

Sub-ss (7B), (14): inserted and added respectively by SI 2006/308, art 2(1), (4), (5), as from 21 February 2006.

Sub-s (9): words omitted from para (b) repealed by the Serious Organised Crime and Police Act 2005, ss 105(1), (2), 174, Sch 17, Pt 2, as from 1 July 2005.

Sub-s (9A): inserted by the Serious Organised Crime and Police Act 2005, s 106(1), (2), as from 1 July 2005; words in square brackets inserted by SI 2006/308, art 2(1), (2), as from 21 February 2006; word omitted repealed by SI 2007/3398, reg 3, Sch 2, paras 1, 2, as from 26 December 2007.

Sub-s (10): words in square brackets inserted by SI 2006/308, art 2(1), (2), as from 21 February 2006; word omitted repealed by SI 2007/3398, reg 3, Sch 2, paras 1, 2, as from 26 December 2007.

Transitional provisions: for transitional provisions in relation to the operation of the new failure to disclose offences (ie, those contained in ss 330–332 of this Act) where the information or other matter on which knowledge or suspicion of money laundering is based came to a person before 24 February 2003, see the Proceeds of Crime Act 2002 (Commencement No 4, Transitional Provisions and Savings) Order 2003, SI 2003/120, art 4 at **[3695]**.

Orders: the Proceeds of Crime Act 2002 (Failure to Disclose Money Laundering: Specified Training) Order 2003, SI 2003/171 at **[3702]** (which provides that, as from 15 December 2007, the training specified for the purposes of this section is the training required to be provided under the Money Laundering Regulations 2007, SI 2007/2157, reg 21 at **[2877AU]**).

331 Failure to disclose: nominated officers in the regulated sector

(1)   A person nominated to receive disclosures under section 330 commits an offence if the conditions in subsections (2) to (4) are satisfied.

(2)   The first condition is that he—
    (a)   knows or suspects, or
    (b)   has reasonable grounds for knowing or suspecting,
that another person is engaged in money laundering.

(3)   The second condition is that the information or other matter—
    (a)   on which his knowledge or suspicion is based, or
    (b)   which gives reasonable grounds for such knowledge or suspicion,
came to him in consequence of a disclosure made under section 330.

[(3A)   The third condition is—
    (a)   that he knows the identity of the other person mentioned in subsection (2), or the whereabouts of any of the laundered property, in consequence of a disclosure made under section 330,
    (b)   that that other person, or the whereabouts of any of the laundered property, can be identified from the information or other matter mentioned in subsection (3), or
    (c)   that he believes, or it is reasonable to expect him to believe, that the information or other matter will or may assist in identifying that other person or the whereabouts of any of the laundered property.

(4)   The fourth condition is that he does not make the required disclosure to a person authorised for the purposes of this Part by the Director General of [SOCA] as soon as is practicable after the information or other matter mentioned in subsection (3) comes to him.

(5)   The required disclosure is a disclosure of—
    (a)   the identity of the other person mentioned in subsection (2), if disclosed to him under section 330,
    (b)   the whereabouts of the laundered property, so far as disclosed to him under section 330, and
    (c)   the information or other matter mentioned in subsection (3).

(5A)   The laundered property is the property forming the subject-matter of the money laundering that he knows or suspects, or has reasonable grounds for knowing or suspecting, that other person to be engaged in.

(6)   But he does not commit an offence under this section if he has a reasonable excuse for not making the required disclosure.]

[(6A)   Nor does a person commit an offence under this section if—
    (a)   he knows, or believes on reasonable grounds, that the money laundering is occurring in a particular country or territory outside the United Kingdom, and
    (b)   the money laundering—
        (i)   is not unlawful under the criminal law applying in that country or territory, and
        (ii)   is not of a description prescribed in an order made by the Secretary of State.]

(7)   In deciding whether a person committed an offence under this section the court must consider whether he followed any relevant guidance which was at the time concerned—
    (a)   issued by a supervisory authority or any other appropriate body,
    (b)   approved by the Treasury, and
    (c)   published in a manner it approved as appropriate in its opinion to bring the guidance to the attention of persons likely to be affected by it.

(8)   Schedule 9 has effect for the purpose of determining what is a supervisory authority.

(9)   An appropriate body is a body which regulates or is representative of a trade, profession, business or employment.

[1314]

NOTES

Sub-ss (3A), (5), (5A), (6): substituted, together with sub-s (4), for original sub-ss (4)–(6), by the Serious Organised Crime and Police Act 2005, s 104(1), (4), as from 1 July 2005.

Sub-s (4): substituted as noted above; word in square brackets substituted by the Serious Crime Act 2007, s 74(2), Sch 8, Pt 6, paras 121, 127, as from 1 April 2008 (for transitional provisions in relation to the transfer of functions from the Assets Recovery Agency to SOCA and the National Policing Improvement Agency, see the Serious Crime Act 2007 (Commencement No 2 and Transitional and Transitory Provisions and Savings) Order 2008, SI 2008/755, art 3).

    Sub-s (6A): inserted by the Serious Organised Crime and Police Act 2005, s 102(1), (6), as from 15 May 2006.
    Transitional provisions: see the transitional provisions notes to s 330 at **[1313]**.

332   Failure to disclose: other nominated officers

    (1)   A person nominated to receive disclosures under section 337 or 338 commits an offence if the conditions in subsections (2) to (4) are satisfied.

    (2)   The first condition is that he knows or suspects that another person is engaged in money laundering.

    (3)   The second condition is that the information or other matter on which his knowledge or suspicion is based came to him in consequence of a disclosure made under [the applicable section].

    [(3A)   The third condition is—
      (a)   that he knows the identity of the other person mentioned in subsection (2), or the whereabouts of any of the laundered property, in consequence of a disclosure made under the applicable section,
      (b)   that that other person, or the whereabouts of any of the laundered property, can be identified from the information or other matter mentioned in subsection (3), or
      (c)   that he believes, or it is reasonable to expect him to believe, that the information or other matter will or may assist in identifying that other person or the whereabouts of any of the laundered property.

    (4)   The fourth condition is that he does not make the required disclosure to a person authorised for the purposes of this Part by the Director General of [SOCA] as soon as is practicable after the information or other matter mentioned in subsection (3) comes to him.

    (5)   The required disclosure is a disclosure of—
      (a)   the identity of the other person mentioned in subsection (2), if disclosed to him under the applicable section,
      (b)   the whereabouts of the laundered property, so far as disclosed to him under the applicable section, and
      (c)   the information or other matter mentioned in subsection (3).

    (5A)   The laundered property is the property forming the subject-matter of the money laundering that he knows or suspects that other person to be engaged in.

    (5B)   The applicable section is section 337 or, as the case may be, section 338.

    (6)   But he does not commit an offence under this section if he has a reasonable excuse for not making the required disclosure.]

    [(7)   Nor does a person commit an offence under this section if—
      (a)   he knows, or believes on reasonable grounds, that the money laundering is occurring in a particular country or territory outside the United Kingdom, and
      (b)   the money laundering—
        (i)   is not unlawful under the criminal law applying in that country or territory, and
        (ii)   is not of a description prescribed in an order made by the Secretary of State.]

[1315]–[1316]

NOTES
    Sub-s (3): words in square brackets substituted by the Serious Organised Crime and Police Act 2005, s 104(1), (5), as from 1 July 2005.
    Sub-ss (3A), (5), (5A), (6): substituted, together with sub-s (4), for original sub-ss (4)–(6), by the Serious Organised Crime and Police Act 2005, s 104(1), (6), as from 1 July 2005.
    Sub-s (4): substituted as noted above; word in square brackets substituted by the Serious Crime Act 2007, s 74(2), Sch 8, Pt 6, paras 121, 128, as from 1 April 2008 (for transitional provisions in relation to the transfer of functions from the Assets Recovery Agency to SOCA and the National Policing Improvement Agency, see the Serious Crime Act 2007 (Commencement No 2 and Transitional and Transitory Provisions and Savings) Order 2008, SI 2008/755, art 3).
    Sub-s (7): added by the Serious Organised Crime and Police Act 2005, s 102(1), (7), as from 15 May 2006.
    Transitional provisions: see the transitional provisions notes to s 330 at **[1313]**.

333   (*Repealed by the Terrorism Act 2000 and Proceeds of Crime Act 2002 (Amendment) Regulations 2007, SI 2007/3398, reg 3, Sch 2, paras 1, 3, as from 26 December 2007.*)

[333A   Tipping off: regulated sector

    (1)   A person commits an offence if—
      (a)   the person discloses any matter within subsection (2);
      (b)   the disclosure is likely to prejudice any investigation that might be conducted following the disclosure referred to in that subsection; and

  (c) the information on which the disclosure is based came to the person in the course of a business in the regulated sector.

 (2) The matters are that the person or another person has made a disclosure under this Part—
  (a) to a constable,
  (b) to an officer of Revenue and Customs,
  (c) to a nominated officer, or
  (d) to a member of staff of the Serious Organised Crime Agency authorised for the purposes of this Part by the Director General of that Agency,
of information that came to that person in the course of a business in the regulated sector.

 (3) A person commits an offence if—
  (a) the person discloses that an investigation into allegations that an offence under this Part has been committed is being contemplated or is being carried out;
  (b) the disclosure is likely to prejudice that investigation; and
  (c) the information on which the disclosure is based came to the person in the course of a business in the regulated sector.

 (4) A person guilty of an offence under this section is liable—
  (a) on summary conviction to imprisonment for a term not exceeding three months, or to a fine not exceeding level 5 on the standard scale, or to both;
  (b) on conviction on indictment to imprisonment for a term not exceeding two years, or to a fine, or to both.

 (5) This section is subject to—
  (a) section 333B (disclosures within an undertaking or group etc),
  (b) section 333C (other permitted disclosures between institutions etc), and
  (c) section 333D (other permitted disclosures etc).]

                   [1316A]

NOTES
Commencement: 26 December 2007.
Inserted, together with ss 333B–333E, by the Terrorism Act 2000 and Proceeds of Crime Act 2002 (Amendment) Regulations 2007, SI 2007/3398, reg 3, Sch 2, paras 1, 4, as from 26 December 2007.

[333B Disclosures within an undertaking or group etc

 (1) An employee, officer or partner of an undertaking does not commit an offence under section 333A if the disclosure is to an employee, officer or partner of the same undertaking.

 (2) A person does not commit an offence under section 333A in respect of a disclosure by a credit institution or a financial institution if—
  (a) the disclosure is to a credit institution or a financial institution,
  (b) the institution to whom the disclosure is made is situated in an EEA State or in a country or territory imposing equivalent money laundering requirements, and
  (c) both the institution making the disclosure and the institution to whom it is made belong to the same group.

 (3) In subsection (2) "group" has the same meaning as in Directive 2002/87/EC of the European Parliament and of the Council of 16th December 2002 on the supplementary supervision of credit institutions, insurance undertakings and investment firms in a financial conglomerate.

 (4) A professional legal adviser or a relevant professional adviser does not commit an offence under section 333A if—
  (a) the disclosure is to professional legal adviser or a relevant professional adviser,
  (b) both the person making the disclosure and the person to whom it is made carry on business in an EEA State or in a country or territory imposing equivalent money laundering requirements, and
  (c) those persons perform their professional activities within different undertakings that share common ownership, management or control.]

                   [1316B]

NOTES
Commencement: 26 December 2007.
Inserted as noted to s 333A at **[1316A]**.

[333C Other permitted disclosures between institutions etc

 (1) This section applies to a disclosure—
  (a) by a credit institution to another credit institution,
  (b) by a financial institution to another financial institution,
  (c) by a professional legal adviser to another professional legal adviser, or
  (d) by a relevant professional adviser of a particular kind to another relevant professional adviser of the same kind.

(2)   A person does not commit an offence under section 333A in respect of a disclosure to which this section applies if—
  (a)   the disclosure relates to—
    (i)   a client or former client of the institution or adviser making the disclosure and the institution or adviser to whom it is made,
    (ii)   a transaction involving them both, or
    (iii)   the provision of a service involving them both;
  (b)   the disclosure is for the purpose only of preventing an offence under this Part of this Act;
  (c)   the institution or adviser to whom the disclosure is made is situated in an EEA State or in a country or territory imposing equivalent money laundering requirements; and
  (d)   the institution or adviser making the disclosure and the institution or adviser to whom it is made are subject to equivalent duties of professional confidentiality and the protection of personal data (within the meaning of section 1 of the Data Protection Act 1998).]

[1316C]

NOTES
Commencement: 26 December 2007.
Inserted as noted to s 333A at **[1316A]**.

[333D   Other permitted disclosures etc

(1)   A person does not commit an offence under section 333A if the disclosure is—
  (a)   to the authority that is the supervisory authority for that person by virtue of the Money Laundering Regulations 2007 (SI 2007/2157); or
  (b)   for the purpose of—
    (i)   the detection, investigation or prosecution of a criminal offence (whether in the United Kingdom or elsewhere),
    (ii)   an investigation under this Act, or
    (iii)   the enforcement of any order of a court under this Act.

(2)   A professional legal adviser or a relevant professional adviser does not commit an offence under section 333A if the disclosure—
  (a)   is to the adviser's client, and
  (b)   is made for the purpose of dissuading the client from engaging in conduct amounting to an offence.

(3)   A person does not commit an offence under section 333A(1) if the person does not know or suspect that the disclosure is likely to have the effect mentioned in section 333A(1)(b).

(4)   A person does not commit an offence under section 333A(3) if the person does not know or suspect that the disclosure is likely to have the effect mentioned in section 333A(3)(b).]

[1316D]

NOTES
Commencement: 26 December 2007.
Inserted as noted to s 333A at **[1316A]**.

[333E   Interpretation of sections 333A to 333D

(1)   For the purposes of sections 333A to 333D, Schedule 9 has effect for determining—
  (a)   what is a business in the regulated sector, and
  (b)   what is a supervisory authority.

(2)   In those sections—
  "credit institution" has the same meaning as in Schedule 9;
  "financial institution" means an undertaking that carries on a business in the regulated sector by virtue of any of paragraphs (b) to (i) of paragraph 1(1) of that Schedule.

(3)   References in those sections to a disclosure by or to a credit institution or a financial institution include disclosure by or to an employee, officer or partner of the institution acting on its behalf.

(4)   For the purposes of those sections a country or territory imposes "equivalent money laundering requirements" if it imposes requirements equivalent to those laid down in Directive 2005/60/EC of the European Parliament and of the Council of 26th October 2005 on the prevention of the use of the financial system for the purpose of money laundering and terrorist financing.

(5)   In those sections "relevant professional adviser" means an accountant, auditor or tax adviser who is a member of a professional body which is established for accountants, auditors or tax advisers (as the case may be) and which makes provision for—
  (a)   testing the competence of those seeking admission to membership of such a body as a condition for such admission; and

(b) imposing and maintaining professional and ethical standards for its members, as well as imposing sanctions for non-compliance with those standards.]

[1316E]

NOTES
Commencement: 26 December 2007.
Inserted as noted to s 333A at **[1316A]**.

334 Penalties

(1) A person guilty of an offence under section 327, 328 or 329 is liable—
   (a) on summary conviction, to imprisonment for a term not exceeding six months or to a fine not exceeding the statutory maximum or to both, or
   (b) on conviction on indictment, to imprisonment for a term not exceeding 14 years or to a fine or to both.

(2) A person guilty of an offence under section 330, 331, [or 332] is liable—
   (a) on summary conviction, to imprisonment for a term not exceeding six months or to a fine not exceeding the statutory maximum or to both, or
   (b) on conviction on indictment, to imprisonment for a term not exceeding five years or to a fine or to both.

[(3) A person guilty of an offence under section 339(1A) is liable on summary conviction to a fine not exceeding level 5 on the standard scale.]

[1317]

NOTES
Sub-s (2): words in square brackets substituted by the Terrorism Act 2000 and Proceeds of Crime Act 2002 (Amendment) Regulations 2007, SI 2007/3398, reg 3, Sch 2, paras 1, 5, as from 26 December 2007.
Sub-s (3): added by the Serious Organised Crime and Police Act 2005, s 105(1), (3), as from 1 July 2005.

Consent

335 Appropriate consent

(1) The appropriate consent is—
   (a) the consent of a nominated officer to do a prohibited act if an authorised disclosure is made to the nominated officer;
   (b) the consent of a constable to do a prohibited act if an authorised disclosure is made to a constable;
   (c) the consent of a customs officer to do a prohibited act if an authorised disclosure is made to a customs officer.

(2) A person must be treated as having the appropriate consent if—
   (a) he makes an authorised disclosure to a constable or a customs officer, and
   (b) the condition in subsection (3) or the condition in subsection (4) is satisfied.

(3) The condition is that before the end of the notice period he does not receive notice from a constable or customs officer that consent to the doing of the act is refused.

(4) The condition is that—
   (a) before the end of the notice period he receives notice from a constable or customs officer that consent to the doing of the act is refused, and
   (b) the moratorium period has expired.

(5) The notice period is the period of seven working days starting with the first working day after the person makes the disclosure.

(6) The moratorium period is the period of 31 days starting with the day on which the person receives notice that consent to the doing of the act is refused.

(7) A working day is a day other than a Saturday, a Sunday, Christmas Day, Good Friday or a day which is a bank holiday under the Banking and Financial Dealings Act 1971 (c 80) in the part of the United Kingdom in which the person is when he makes the disclosure.

(8) References to a prohibited act are to an act mentioned in section 327(1), 328(1) or 329(1) (as the case may be).

(9) A nominated officer is a person nominated to receive disclosures under section 338.

(10) Subsections (1) to (4) apply for the purposes of this Part.

[1318]

336 Nominated officer: consent

(1) A nominated officer must not give the appropriate consent to the doing of a prohibited act unless the condition in subsection (2), the condition in subsection (3) or the condition in subsection (4) is satisfied.

(2)   The condition is that—
(a)   he makes a disclosure that property is criminal property to a person authorised for the purposes of this Part by [the Director General of [SOCA]], and
(b)   such a person gives consent to the doing of the act.

(3)   The condition is that—
(a)   he makes a disclosure that property is criminal property to a person authorised for the purposes of this Part by [the Director General of [SOCA]], and
(b)   before the end of the notice period he does not receive notice from such a person that consent to the doing of the act is refused.

(4)   The condition is that—
(a)   he makes a disclosure that property is criminal property to a person authorised for the purposes of this Part by [the Director General of [SOCA]],
(b)   before the end of the notice period he receives notice from such a person that consent to the doing of the act is refused, and
(c)   the moratorium period has expired.

(5)   A person who is a nominated officer commits an offence if—
(a)   he gives consent to a prohibited act in circumstances where none of the conditions in subsections (2), (3) and (4) is satisfied, and
(b)   he knows or suspects that the act is a prohibited act.

(6)   A person guilty of such an offence is liable—
(a)   on summary conviction, to imprisonment for a term not exceeding six months or to a fine not exceeding the statutory maximum or to both, or
(b)   on conviction on indictment, to imprisonment for a term not exceeding five years or to a fine or to both.

(7)   The notice period is the period of seven working days starting with the first working day after the nominated officer makes the disclosure.

(8)   The moratorium period is the period of 31 days starting with the day on which the nominated officer is given notice that consent to the doing of the act is refused.

(9)   A working day is a day other than a Saturday, a Sunday, Christmas Day, Good Friday or a day which is a bank holiday under the Banking and Financial Dealings Act 1971 (c 80) in the part of the United Kingdom in which the nominated officer is when he gives the appropriate consent.

(10)   References to a prohibited act are to an act mentioned in section 327(1), 328(1) or 329(1) (as the case may be).

(11)   A nominated officer is a person nominated to receive disclosures under section 338.

[1319]

NOTES
  Sub-ss (2)–(4): words in first (outer) pair of square brackets substituted by the Serious Organised Crime and Police Act 2005, s 59, Sch 4, paras 168, 173, as from 1 April 2006; word in second (inner) pair of square brackets substituted by the Serious Crime Act 2007, s 74(2), Sch 8, Pt 6, paras 121, 129, as from 1 April 2008 (for transitional provisions in relation to the transfer of functions from the Assets Recovery Agency to SOCA and the National Policing Improvement Agency, see the Serious Crime Act 2007 (Commencement No 2 and Transitional and Transitory Provisions and Savings) Order 2008, SI 2008/755, art 3).

Disclosures

337   Protected disclosures

(1)   A disclosure which satisfies the following three conditions is not to be taken to breach any restriction on the disclosure of information (however imposed).

(2)   The first condition is that the information or other matter disclosed came to the person making the disclosure (the discloser) in the course of his trade, profession, business or employment.

(3)   The second condition is that the information or other matter—
(a)   causes the discloser to know or suspect, or
(b)   gives him reasonable grounds for knowing or suspecting,
that another person is engaged in money laundering.

(4)   The third condition is that the disclosure is made to a constable, a customs officer or a nominated officer as soon as is practicable after the information or other matter comes to the discloser.

[(4A)   Where a disclosure consists of a disclosure protected under subsection (1) and a disclosure of either or both of—
(a)   the identity of the other person mentioned in subsection (3), and
(b)   the whereabouts of property forming the subject-matter of the money laundering that the discloser knows or suspects, or has reasonable grounds for knowing or suspecting, that other person to be engaged in,

the disclosure of the thing mentioned in paragraph (a) or (b) (as well as the disclosure protected under subsection (1)) is not to be taken to breach any restriction on the disclosure of information (however imposed).]

(5)   A disclosure to a nominated officer is a disclosure which—
    (a)   is made to a person nominated by the discloser's employer to receive disclosures under [section 330 or] this section, and
    (b)   is made in the course of the discloser's employment …

[1320]

NOTES

Sub-s (4A): inserted by the Serious Organised Crime and Police Act 2005, s 104(1), (7), as from 1 July 2005.
Sub-s (5): words in square brackets in para (a) inserted, and words omitted from para (b) repealed, by the Serious Organised Crime and Police Act 2005, ss 105(1), (2), 106(1), (3), 174, Sch 17, Pt 2, as from 1 July 2005.

338   Authorised disclosures

(1)   For the purposes of this Part a disclosure is authorised if—
    (a)   it is a disclosure to a constable, a customs officer or a nominated officer by the alleged offender that property is criminal property,
    (b)   … and
    (c)   the first[, second or third] condition set out below is satisfied.

(2)   The first condition is that the disclosure is made before the alleged offender does the prohibited act.

[(2A)   The second condition is that—
    (a)   the disclosure is made while the alleged offender is doing the prohibited act,
    (b)   he began to do the act at a time when, because he did not then know or suspect that the property constituted or represented a person's benefit from criminal conduct, the act was not a prohibited act, and
    (c)   the disclosure is made on his own initiative and as soon as is practicable after he first knows or suspects that the property constitutes or represents a person's benefit from criminal conduct.]

(3)   The [third] condition is that—
    (a)   the disclosure is made after the alleged offender does the prohibited act,
    (b)   [he has a reasonable excuse] for his failure to make the disclosure before he did the act, and
    (c)   the disclosure is made on his own initiative and as soon as it is practicable for him to make it.

(4)   An authorised disclosure is not to be taken to breach any restriction on the disclosure of information (however imposed).

(5)   A disclosure to a nominated officer is a disclosure which—
    (a)   is made to a person nominated by the alleged offender's employer to receive authorised disclosures, and
    (b)   is made in the course of the alleged offender's employment …

(6)   References to the prohibited act are to an act mentioned in section 327(1), 328(1) or 329(1) (as the case may be).

[1321]

NOTES

Sub-s (1): words omitted from para (b) repealed, and words in square brackets in para (c) substituted, by the Serious Organised Crime and Police Act 2005, ss 105(1), (4), 106(1), (4), 174, Sch 17, Pt 2, as from 1 July 2005.
Sub-s (2A): inserted by the Serious Organised Crime and Police Act 2005, s 106(1), (5), as from 1 July 2005.
Sub-s (3): word in first pair of square brackets substituted by the Serious Organised Crime and Police Act 2005, s 106(1), (6), as from 1 July 2005; words in second pair of square brackets substituted by the Terrorism Act 2000 and Proceeds of Crime Act 2002 (Amendment) Regulations 2007, SI 2007/3398, reg 3, Sch 2, paras 1, 6, as from 26 December 2007.
Sub-s (5): words omitted from para (b) repealed by the Serious Organised Crime and Police Act 2005, ss 105(1), (2), 174, Sch 17, Pt 2, as from 1 July 2005.

339   Form and manner of disclosures

(1)   The Secretary of State may by order prescribe the form and manner in which a disclosure under section 330, 331, 332 or 338 must be made.

[(1A)   A person commits an offence if he makes a disclosure under section 330, 331, 332 or 338 otherwise than in the form prescribed under subsection (1) or otherwise than in the manner so prescribed.

(1B)   But a person does not commit an offence under subsection (1A) if he has a reasonable excuse for making the disclosure otherwise than in the form prescribed under subsection (1) or (as the case may be) otherwise than in the manner so prescribed.

(2)   The power under subsection (1) to prescribe the form in which a disclosure must be made includes power to provide for the form to include a request to a person making a disclosure that the person provide information specified or described in the form if he has not provided it in making the disclosure.

(3)   Where under subsection (2) a request is included in a form prescribed under subsection (1), the form must—
- (a)   state that there is no obligation to comply with the request, and
- (b)   explain the protection conferred by subsection (4) on a person who complies with the request.]

(4)   A disclosure made in pursuance of a request under subsection (2) is not to be taken to breach any restriction on the disclosure of information (however imposed).

(5), (6)   …

(7)   Subsection (2) does not apply to a disclosure made to a nominated officer.

[1322]

NOTES

Sub-ss (1A)–(3): substituted, for original sub-ss (2), (3), by the Serious Organised Crime and Police Act 2005, s 105(1), (5), as from 1 July 2005.

Sub-ss (5), (6): repealed by the Serious Organised Crime and Police Act 2005, s 174, Sch 17, Pt 2, as from 1 July 2005.

[339ZA Disclosures to SOCA

Where a disclosure is made under this Part to a constable or an officer of Revenue and Customs, the constable or officer of Revenue and Customs must disclose it in full to a person authorised for the purposes of this Part by the Director General of the Serious Organised Crime Agency as soon as practicable after it has been made.]

[1322A]

NOTES

Commencement: 26 December 2007.

Inserted by the Terrorism Act 2000 and Proceeds of Crime Act 2002 (Amendment) Regulations 2007, SI 2007/3398, reg 3, Sch 2, paras 1, 7, as from 26 December 2007.

[Threshold amounts

339A   Threshold amounts

(1)   This section applies for the purposes of sections 327(2C), 328(5) and 329(2C).

(2)   The threshold amount for acts done by a deposit-taking body in operating an account is £250 unless a higher amount is specified under the following provisions of this section (in which event it is that higher amount).

(3)   An officer of Revenue and Customs, or a constable, may specify the threshold amount for acts done by a deposit-taking body in operating an account—
- (a)   when he gives consent, or gives notice refusing consent, to the deposit-taking body's doing of an act mentioned in section 327(1), 328(1) or 329(1) in opening, or operating, the account or a related account, or
- (b)   on a request from the deposit-taking body.

(4)   Where the threshold amount for acts done in operating an account is specified under subsection (3) or this subsection, an officer of Revenue and Customs, or a constable, may vary the amount (whether on a request from the deposit-taking body or otherwise) by specifying a different amount.

(5)   Different threshold amounts may be specified under subsections (3) and (4) for different acts done in operating the same account.

(6)   The amount specified under subsection (3) or (4) as the threshold amount for acts done in operating an account must, when specified, not be less than the amount specified in subsection (2).

(7)   The Secretary of State may by order vary the amount for the time being specified in subsection (2).

(8)   For the purposes of this section, an account is related to another if each is maintained with the same deposit-taking body and there is a person who, in relation to each account, is the person or one of the persons entitled to instruct the body as respects the operation of the account.]

[1323]

NOTES
Commencement: 1 July 2005.
Inserted, together with the preceding heading, by the Serious Organised Crime and Police Act 2005, s 103(1), (5), as from 1 July 2005.

Interpretation

340 Interpretation

(1)   This section applies for the purposes of this Part.

(2)   Criminal conduct is conduct which—
(a)   constitutes an offence in any part of the United Kingdom, or
(b)   would constitute an offence in any part of the United Kingdom if it occurred there.

(3)   Property is criminal property if—
(a)   it constitutes a person's benefit from criminal conduct or it represents such a benefit (in whole or part and whether directly or indirectly), and
(b)   the alleged offender knows or suspects that it constitutes or represents such a benefit.

(4)   It is immaterial—
(a)   who carried out the conduct;
(b)   who benefited from it;
(c)   whether the conduct occurred before or after the passing of this Act.

(5)   A person benefits from conduct if he obtains property as a result of or in connection with the conduct.

(6)   If a person obtains a pecuniary advantage as a result of or in connection with conduct, he is to be taken to obtain as a result of or in connection with the conduct a sum of money equal to the value of the pecuniary advantage.

(7)   References to property or a pecuniary advantage obtained in connection with conduct include references to property or a pecuniary advantage obtained in both that connection and some other.

(8)   If a person benefits from conduct his benefit is the property obtained as a result of or in connection with the conduct.

(9)   Property is all property wherever situated and includes—
(a)   money;
(b)   all forms of property, real or personal, heritable or moveable;
(c)   things in action and other intangible or incorporeal property.

(10)   The following rules apply in relation to property—
(a)   property is obtained by a person if he obtains an interest in it;
(b)   references to an interest, in relation to land in England and Wales or Northern Ireland, are to any legal estate or equitable interest or power;
(c)   references to an interest, in relation to land in Scotland, are to any estate, interest, servitude or other heritable right in or over land, including a heritable security;
(d)   references to an interest, in relation to property other than land, include references to a right (including a right to possession).

(11)   Money laundering is an act which—
(a)   constitutes an offence under section 327, 328 or 329,
(b)   constitutes an attempt, conspiracy or incitement to commit an offence specified in paragraph (a),
(c)   constitutes aiding, abetting, counselling or procuring the commission of an offence specified in paragraph (a), or
(d)   would constitute an offence specified in paragraph (a), (b) or (c) if done in the United Kingdom.

(12)   For the purposes of a disclosure to a nominated officer—
(a)   references to a person's employer include any body, association or organisation (including a voluntary organisation) in connection with whose activities the person exercises a function (whether or not for gain or reward), and
(b)   references to employment must be construed accordingly.

(13)   References to a constable include references to a person authorised for the purposes of this Part by [the Director General of [SOCA]].

[(14)   "Deposit-taking body" means—
(a)   a business which engages in the activity of accepting deposits, or
(b)   the National Savings Bank.]

**PART II
OTHER ACTS**

NOTES

Sub-s (13): words in first (outer) pair of square brackets substituted by the Serious Organised Crime and Police Act 2005, s 59, Sch 4, paras 168, 174, as from 1 April 2006; word in second (inner) pair of square brackets substituted by the Serious Crime Act 2007, s 74(2), Sch 8, Pt 6, paras 121, 129, as from 1 April 2008 (for transitional provisions in relation to the transfer of functions from the Assets Recovery Agency to SOCA and the National Policing Improvement Agency, see the Serious Crime Act 2007 (Commencement No 2 and Transitional and Transitory Provisions and Savings) Order 2008, SI 2008/755, art 3).

Sub-s (14): added by the Serious Organised Crime and Police Act 2005, s 103(1), (6), as from 1 July 2005.

Attempt, conspiracy or incitement to commit an offence: see the Serious Crime Act 2007, s 63(1), (2), Sch 6, Pt 1, para 44 which provides that any reference however expressed to (or to conduct amounting to) the offence abolished by s 59 of the 2007 Act (abolition of common law offence of inciting the commission of another offence) has effect as a reference to (or to conduct amounting to) the offences of encouraging or assisting the commission of an offence.

PART 8
INVESTIGATIONS

NOTES

Enforcement in other parts of the UK: see the Proceeds of Crime Act 2002 (Investigations in different parts of the United Kingdom) Order 2003, SI 2003/425 at **[3740]**, which makes provision for orders and warrants made or issued under this Part in one part of the United Kingdom to be enforced in another part of the United Kingdom.

CHAPTER 1
INTRODUCTION

341 Investigations

(1)   For the purposes of this Part a confiscation investigation is an investigation into—
   (a)   whether a person has benefited from his criminal conduct, or
   (b)   the extent or whereabouts of his benefit from his criminal conduct.

(2)   For the purposes of this Part a civil recovery investigation is an investigation into—
   (a)   whether property is recoverable property or associated property,
   (b)   who holds the property, or
   (c)   its extent or whereabouts.

(3)   But an investigation is not a civil recovery investigation if—
   (a)   proceedings for a recovery order have been started in respect of the property in question,
   (b)   an interim receiving order applies to the property in question,
   (c)   an interim administration order applies to the property in question, or
   (d)   the property in question is detained under section 295.

[(3A)   For the purposes of this Part a detained cash investigation is—
   (a)   an investigation for the purposes of Chapter 3 of Part 5 into the derivation of cash detained under section 295 or a part of such cash, or
   (b)   an investigation for the purposes of Chapter 3 of Part 5 into whether cash detained under section 295, or a part of such cash, is intended by any person to be used in unlawful conduct.]

(4)   For the purposes of this Part a money laundering investigation is an investigation into whether a person has committed a money laundering offence.

[1325]

NOTES

Sub-s (3A): inserted by the Serious Crime Act 2007, s 75(1), as from 6 April 2008.

342 Offences of prejudicing investigation

(1)   This section applies if a person knows or suspects that an appropriate officer or (in Scotland) a proper person is acting (or proposing to act) in connection with a confiscation investigation, a civil recovery investigation[, a detained cash investigation] or a money laundering investigation which is being or is about to be conducted.

(2)   The person commits an offence if—
   (a)   he makes a disclosure which is likely to prejudice the investigation, or
   (b)   he falsifies, conceals, destroys or otherwise disposes of, or causes or permits the falsification, concealment, destruction or disposal of, documents which are relevant to the investigation.

(3)   A person does not commit an offence under subsection (2)(a) if—
   (a)   he does not know or suspect that the disclosure is likely to prejudice the investigation,
   (b)   the disclosure is made in the exercise of a function under this Act or any other enactment

relating to criminal conduct or benefit from criminal conduct or in compliance with a requirement imposed under or by virtue of this Act, or

[(ba) the disclosure is of a matter within section 333A(2) or (3)(a) (money laundering: tipping off) and the information on which the disclosure is based came to the person in the course of a business in the regulated sector,]

(c) he is a professional legal adviser and the disclosure falls within subsection (4).

(4) A disclosure falls within this subsection if it is a disclosure—

(a) to (or to a representative of) a client of the professional legal adviser in connection with the giving by the adviser of legal advice to the client, or

(b) to any person in connection with legal proceedings or contemplated legal proceedings.

(5) But a disclosure does not fall within subsection (4) if it is made with the intention of furthering a criminal purpose.

(6) A person does not commit an offence under subsection (2)(b) if—

(a) he does not know or suspect that the documents are relevant to the investigation, or

(b) he does not intend to conceal any facts disclosed by the documents from any appropriate officer or (in Scotland) proper person carrying out the investigation.

(7) A person guilty of an offence under subsection (2) is liable—

(a) on summary conviction, to imprisonment for a term not exceeding six months or to a fine not exceeding the statutory maximum or to both, or

(b) on conviction on indictment, to imprisonment for a term not exceeding five years or to a fine or to both.

(8) For the purposes of this section—

(a) "appropriate officer" must be construed in accordance with section 378;

(b) "proper person" must be construed in accordance with section 412;

[(c) Schedule 9 has effect for determining what is a business in the regulated sector].

[1326]

NOTES

Sub-s (1): words in square brackets inserted by the Serious Crime Act 2007, s 77, Sch 10, paras 1, 2, as from a 6 April 2008.

Sub-s (3): para (ba) inserted by the Terrorism Act 2000 and Proceeds of Crime Act 2002 (Amendment) Regulations 2007, SI 2007/3398, reg 3, Sch 2, paras 1, 8(1), (2), as from 26 December 2007.

Sub-s (8): para (c) added by SI 2007/3398, reg 3, Sch 2, paras 1, 8(1), (3), as from 26 December 2007.

Transitional provisions: this section shall not have effect where the conduct constituting an offence began before 24 February 2003 and ended on or after that date; see the Proceeds of Crime Act 2002 (Commencement No 4, Transitional Provisions and Savings) Order 2003, SI 2003/120, art 5 at **[3699]**.

CHAPTER 2
ENGLAND AND WALES AND NORTHERN IRELAND
Judges and courts

343 Judges

(1) In this Chapter references to a judge in relation to an application must be construed in accordance with this section.

(2) In relation to an application for the purposes of a confiscation investigation or a money laundering investigation a judge is—

(a) in England and Wales, a judge entitled to exercise the jurisdiction of the Crown Court;

(b) in Northern Ireland, a Crown Court judge.

(3) In relation to an application for the purposes of a civil recovery investigation [or a detained cash investigation] a judge is a judge of the High Court.

[1327]

NOTES

Sub-s (3): words in square brackets inserted by the Serious Crime Act 2007, s 77, Sch 10, paras 1, 3, as from a 6 April 2008.

344 Courts

In this Chapter references to the court are to—

(a) the Crown Court, in relation to an order for the purposes of a confiscation investigation or a money laundering investigation;

(b) the High Court, in relation to an order for the purposes of a civil recovery investigation [or a detained cash investigation].

[1328]

NOTES

Words in square brackets in para (b) inserted by the Serious Crime Act 2007, s 77, Sch 10, paras 1, 4, as from 6 April 2008.

Production orders

345 Production orders

(1)   A judge may, on an application made to him by an appropriate officer, make a production order if he is satisfied that each of the requirements for the making of the order is fulfilled.

(2)   The application for a production order must state that—
- (a)   a person specified in the application is subject to a confiscation investigation or a money laundering investigation, or
- (b)   property specified in the application is subject to a civil recovery investigation [or a detained cash investigation].

(3)   The application must also state that—
- (a)   the order is sought for the purposes of the investigation;
- (b)   the order is sought in relation to material, or material of a description, specified in the application;
- (c)   a person specified in the application appears to be in possession or control of the material.

(4)   A production order is an order either—
- (a)   requiring the person the application for the order specifies as appearing to be in possession or control of material to produce it to an appropriate officer for him to take away, or
- (b)   requiring that person to give an appropriate officer access to the material,

within the period stated in the order.

(5)   The period stated in a production order must be a period of seven days beginning with the day on which the order is made, unless it appears to the judge by whom the order is made that a longer or shorter period would be appropriate in the particular circumstances.

[1329]

NOTES

Sub-s (2): words in square brackets inserted by the Serious Crime Act 2007, s 75(2), as from 6 April 2008.

346 Requirements for making of production order

(1)   These are the requirements for the making of a production order.

(2)   There must be reasonable grounds for suspecting that—
- (a)   in the case of a confiscation investigation, the person the application for the order specifies as being subject to the investigation has benefited from his criminal conduct;
- (b)   in the case of a civil recovery investigation, the property the application for the order specifies as being subject to the investigation is recoverable property or associated property;
- [(ba)   in the case of a detained cash investigation into the derivation of cash, the property the application for the order specifies as being subject to the investigation, or a part of it, is recoverable property;
- (bb)   in the case of a detained cash investigation into the intended use of cash, the property the application for the order specifies as being subject to the investigation, or a part of it, is intended by any person to be used in unlawful conduct;]
- (c)   in the case of a money laundering investigation, the person the application for the order specifies as being subject to the investigation has committed a money laundering offence.

(3)   There must be reasonable grounds for believing that the person the application specifies as appearing to be in possession or control of the material so specified is in possession or control of it.

(4)   There must be reasonable grounds for believing that the material is likely to be of substantial value (whether or not by itself) to the investigation for the purposes of which the order is sought.

(5)   There must be reasonable grounds for believing that it is in the public interest for the material to be produced or for access to it to be given, having regard to—
- (a)   the benefit likely to accrue to the investigation if the material is obtained;
- (b)   the circumstances under which the person the application specifies as appearing to be in possession or control of the material holds it.

[1330]

NOTES
Sub-s (2): paras (ba), (bb) inserted by the Serious Crime Act 2007, s 75(3), as from 6 April 2008.

347 Order to grant entry

(1) This section applies if a judge makes a production order requiring a person to give an appropriate officer access to material on any premises.

(2) The judge may, on an application made to him by an appropriate officer and specifying the premises, make an order to grant entry in relation to the premises.

(3) An order to grant entry is an order requiring any person who appears to an appropriate officer to be entitled to grant entry to the premises to allow him to enter the premises to obtain access to the material.

[1331]

348 Further provisions

(1) A production order does not require a person to produce, or give access to, privileged material.

(2) Privileged material is any material which the person would be entitled to refuse to produce on grounds of legal professional privilege in proceedings in the High Court.

(3) A production order does not require a person to produce, or give access to, excluded material.

(4) A production order has effect in spite of any restriction on the disclosure of information (however imposed).

(5) An appropriate officer may take copies of any material which is produced, or to which access is given, in compliance with a production order.

(6) Material produced in compliance with a production order may be retained for so long as it is necessary to retain it (as opposed to copies of it) in connection with the investigation for the purposes of which the order was made.

(7) But if an appropriate officer has reasonable grounds for believing that—
   (a) the material may need to be produced for the purposes of any legal proceedings, and
   (b) it might otherwise be unavailable for those purposes,
it may be retained until the proceedings are concluded.

[1332]

349 Computer information

(1) This section applies if any of the material specified in an application for a production order consists of information contained in a computer.

(2) If the order is an order requiring a person to produce the material to an appropriate officer for him to take away, it has effect as an order to produce the material in a form in which it can be taken away by him and in which it is visible and legible.

(3) If the order is an order requiring a person to give an appropriate officer access to the material, it has effect as an order to give him access to the material in a form in which it is visible and legible.

[1333]

350 Government departments

(1) A production order may be made in relation to material in the possession or control of an authorised government department.

(2) An order so made may require any officer of the department (whether named in the order or not) who may for the time being be in possession or control of the material to comply with it.

(3) An order containing such a requirement must be served as if the proceedings were civil proceedings against the department.

(4) If an order contains such a requirement—
   (a) the person on whom it is served must take all reasonable steps to bring it to the attention of the officer concerned;
   (b) any other officer of the department who is in receipt of the order must also take all reasonable steps to bring it to the attention of the officer concerned.

(5) If the order is not brought to the attention of the officer concerned within the period stated in the order (in pursuance of section 345(4)) the person on whom it is served must report the reasons for the failure to—
   (a) a judge entitled to exercise the jurisdiction of the Crown Court or (in Northern Ireland) a Crown Court judge, in the case of an order made for the purposes of a confiscation investigation or a money laundering investigation;

(b)		a High Court judge, in the case of an order made for the purposes of a civil recovery investigation [or a detained cash investigation].

(6)		An authorised government department is a government department, or a Northern Ireland department, which is an authorised department for the purposes of the Crown Proceedings Act 1947 (c 44).

[1334]

NOTES
Sub-s (5): words in square brackets inserted by the Serious Crime Act 2007, s 77, Sch 10, paras 1, 5, as from 6 April 2008.

351 Supplementary

(1)		An application for a production order or an order to grant entry may be made ex parte to a judge in chambers.

(2)		Rules of court may make provision as to the practice and procedure to be followed in connection with proceedings relating to production orders and orders to grant entry.

(3)		An application to discharge or vary a production order or an order to grant entry may be made to the court by—
	(a)		the person who applied for the order;
	(b)		any person affected by the order.

(4)		The court—
	(a)		may discharge the order;
	(b)		may vary the order.

(5)		If an accredited financial investigator, [a member of SOCA's staff,] a constable or a customs officer applies for a production order or an order to grant entry, an application to discharge or vary the order need not be by the same accredited financial investigator, [member of SOCA's staff,] constable or customs officer.

(6)		References to a person who applied for a production order or an order to grant entry must be construed accordingly.

(7)		Production orders and orders to grant entry have effect as if they were orders of the court.

(8)		Subsections (2) to (7) do not apply to orders made in England and Wales for the purposes of a civil recovery investigation [or a detained cash investigation].

[1335]

NOTES
Sub-s (5): words in square brackets inserted by the Serious Crime Act 2007, s 74(2), Sch 8, Pt 4, paras 103, 104, as from 1 April 2008 (for transitional provisions in relation to the transfer of functions from the Assets Recovery Agency to SOCA and the National Policing Improvement Agency, see the Serious Crime Act 2007 (Commencement No 2 and Transitional and Transitory Provisions and Savings) Order 2008, SI 2008/755, art 3).
Sub-s (8): words in square brackets inserted by the Serious Crime Act 2007, s 77, Sch 10, paras 1, 6, as from 6 April 2008.
Rules: the Crown Court (Amendment) Rules 2003, SI 2003/422 (these Rules amend the Crown Court Rules 1982 in consequence of the enactment of this Act. Part 8 of the Act deals with investigations into the proceeds of crime and makes provision for applications to be made to Crown Court judges for various orders and warrants).

Search and seizure warrants

352 Search and seizure warrants

(1)		A judge may, on an application made to him by an appropriate officer, issue a search and seizure warrant if he is satisfied that either of the requirements for the issuing of the warrant is fulfilled.

(2)		The application for a search and seizure warrant must state that—
	(a)		a person specified in the application is subject to a confiscation investigation or a money laundering investigation, or
	(b)		property specified in the application is subject to a civil recovery investigation [or a detained cash investigation].

(3)		The application must also state—
	(a)		that the warrant is sought for the purposes of the investigation;
	(b)		that the warrant is sought in relation to the premises specified in the application;
	(c)		that the warrant is sought in relation to material specified in the application, or that there are reasonable grounds for believing that there is material falling within section 353(6), (7)[, (7A), (7B)] or (8) on the premises.

(4)		A search and seizure warrant is a warrant authorising an appropriate person—
	(a)		to enter and search the premises specified in the application for the warrant, and

(b)   to seize and retain any material found there which is likely to be of substantial value (whether or not by itself) to the investigation for the purposes of which the application is made.

(5)   An appropriate person is—
   (a)   a constable[, an accredited financial investigator] or a customs officer, if the warrant is sought for the purposes of a confiscation investigation or a money laundering investigation;
   (b)   a [member of SOCA's staff or of the staff of the relevant Director], if the warrant is sought for the purposes of a civil recovery investigation;
  [(c)   a constable[, an accredited financial investigator] or an officer of Revenue and Customs, if the warrant is sought for the purposes of a detained cash investigation].

[(5A)   In this Part "relevant Director"—
   (a)   in relation to England and Wales, means the Director of Public Prosecutions, the Director of Revenue and Customs Prosecutions or the Director of the Serious Fraud Office; and
   (b)   in relation to Northern Ireland, means the Director of the Serious Fraud Office or the Director of Public Prosecutions for Northern Ireland.]

(6)   The requirements for the issue of a search and seizure warrant are—
   (a)   that a production order made in relation to material has not been complied with and there are reasonable grounds for believing that the material is on the premises specified in the application for the warrant, or
   (b)   that section 353 is satisfied in relation to the warrant.

[(7)   The reference in paragraph (a) or (c) of subsection (5) to an accredited financial investigator is a reference to an accredited financial investigator who falls within a description specified in an order made for the purposes of that paragraph by the Secretary of State under section 453.]

[1336]

NOTES

Sub-s (2): words in square brackets inserted by the Serious Crime Act 2007, s 76(1), as from 6 April 2008.

Sub-s (3): words in square brackets in para (c) inserted by the Serious Crime Act 2007, s 77, Sch 10, paras 1, 7(1), (2), as from 6 April 2008.

Sub-s (5): words in square brackets in para (a) inserted by the Serious Crime Act 2007, s 80(1)(a), as from 6 April 2008; words in square brackets in para (b) substituted by the Serious Crime Act 2007, s 74(2), Sch 8, Pt 4, paras 103, 105(1), (2), as from 1 April 2008 (for transitional provisions in relation to the transfer of functions from the Assets Recovery Agency to SOCA and the National Policing Improvement Agency, see the Serious Crime Act 2007 (Commencement No 2 and Transitional and Transitory Provisions and Savings) Order 2008, SI 2008/755, art 3); para (c) is inserted by s 77 of, and Sch 10, para 7(1), (3) to, the 2007 Act, as from 6 April 2008, and the words in square brackets in that paragraph are inserted by s 80(1)(b) of that Act, as from the same date.

Sub-s (5A): inserted by the Serious Crime Act 2007, s 74(2), Sch 8, Pt 4, paras 103, 105(1), (3), as from 1 April 2008 (for transitional provisions in relation to the transfer of functions from the Assets Recovery Agency to SOCA and the National Policing Improvement Agency, see SI 2008/755, art 3).

Sub-s (7): added by the Serious Crime Act 2007, s 80(2), as from 6 April 2008.

Transitional provisions: for transitional provisions in relation to a search and seizure warrant issued under this section before 1 April 2008 on an application made by the Director of the Assets Recovery Agency, see the Serious Crime Act 2007 (Commencement No 2 and Transitional and Transitory Provisions and Savings) Order 2008, SI 2008/755, art 8.

Powers of seizure: the powers of seizure conferred by sub-s (4) are powers to which the Criminal Justice and Police Act 2001, s 50 apply (additional powers of seizure from premises); see s 50 of, and Sch 1, Pt 1, para 73A to, that Act.

353   Requirements where production order not available

(1)   This section is satisfied in relation to a search and seizure warrant if—
   (a)   subsection (2) applies, and
   (b)   either the first or the second set of conditions is complied with.

(2)   This subsection applies if there are reasonable grounds for suspecting that—
   (a)   in the case of a confiscation investigation, the person specified in the application for the warrant has benefited from his criminal conduct;
   (b)   in the case of a civil recovery investigation, the property specified in the application for the warrant is recoverable property or associated property;
  [(ba)   in the case of a detained cash investigation into the derivation of cash, the property specified in the application for the warrant, or a part of it, is recoverable property;
  (bb)   in the case of a detained cash investigation into the intended use of cash, the property specified in the application for the warrant, or a part of it, is intended by any person to be used in unlawful conduct;]
   (c)   in the case of a money laundering investigation, the person specified in the application for the warrant has committed a money laundering offence.

(3)   The first set of conditions is that there are reasonable grounds for believing that—
  (a)   any material on the premises specified in the application for the warrant is likely to be of substantial value (whether or not by itself) to the investigation for the purposes of which the warrant is sought,
  (b)   it is in the public interest for the material to be obtained, having regard to the benefit likely to accrue to the investigation if the material is obtained, and
  (c)   it would not be appropriate to make a production order for any one or more of the reasons in subsection (4).

(4)   The reasons are—
  (a)   that it is not practicable to communicate with any person against whom the production order could be made;
  (b)   that it is not practicable to communicate with any person who would be required to comply with an order to grant entry to the premises;
  (c)   that the investigation might be seriously prejudiced unless an appropriate person is able to secure immediate access to the material.

(5)   The second set of conditions is that—
  (a)   there are reasonable grounds for believing that there is material on the premises specified in the application for the warrant and that the material falls within subsection (6), (7)[, (7A), (7B)] or (8),
  (b)   there are reasonable grounds for believing that it is in the public interest for the material to be obtained, having regard to the benefit likely to accrue to the investigation if the material is obtained, and
  (c)   any one or more of the requirements in subsection (9) is met.

(6)   In the case of a confiscation investigation, material falls within this subsection if it cannot be identified at the time of the application but it—
  (a)   relates to the person specified in the application, the question whether he has benefited from his criminal conduct or any question as to the extent or whereabouts of his benefit from his criminal conduct, and
  (b)   is likely to be of substantial value (whether or not by itself) to the investigation for the purposes of which the warrant is sought.

(7)   In the case of a civil recovery investigation, material falls within this subsection if it cannot be identified at the time of the application but it—
  (a)   relates to the property specified in the application, the question whether it is recoverable property or associated property, the question as to who holds any such property, any question as to whether the person who appears to hold any such property holds other property which is recoverable property, or any question as to the extent or whereabouts of any property mentioned in this paragraph, and
  (b)   is likely to be of substantial value (whether or not by itself) to the investigation for the purposes of which the warrant is sought.

[(7A)   In the case of a detained cash investigation into the derivation of cash, material falls within this subsection if it cannot be identified at the time of the application but it—
  (a)   relates to the property specified in the application, the question whether the property, or a part of it, is recoverable property or any other question as to its derivation, and
  (b)   is likely to be of substantial value (whether or not by itself) to the investigation for the purposes of which the warrant is sought.

(7B)   In the case of a detained cash investigation into the intended use of cash, material falls within this subsection if it cannot be identified at the time of the application but it—
  (a)   relates to the property specified in the application or the question whether the property, or a part of it, is intended by any person to be used in unlawful conduct, and
  (b)   is likely to be of substantial value (whether or not by itself) to the investigation for the purposes of which the warrant is sought.]

(8)   In the case of a money laundering investigation, material falls within this subsection if it cannot be identified at the time of the application but it—
  (a)   relates to the person specified in the application or the question whether he has committed a money laundering offence, and
  (b)   is likely to be of substantial value (whether or not by itself) to the investigation for the purposes of which the warrant is sought.

(9)   The requirements are—
  (a)   that it is not practicable to communicate with any person entitled to grant entry to the premises;
  (b)   that entry to the premises will not be granted unless a warrant is produced;
  (c)   that the investigation might be seriously prejudiced unless an appropriate person arriving at the premises is able to secure immediate entry to them.

(10)   An appropriate person is—

(a)   a constable[, an accredited financial investigator] or a customs officer, if the warrant is sought for the purposes of a confiscation investigation or a money laundering investigation;

(b)   a member of [SOCA's staff or of the staff of the relevant Director], if the warrant is sought for the purposes of a civil recovery investigation;

[(c)   a constable[, an accredited financial investigator] or an officer of Revenue and Customs, if the warrant is sought for the purposes of a detained cash investigation].

[(11)   The reference in paragraph (a) or (c) of subsection (10) to an accredited financial investigator is a reference to an accredited financial investigator who falls within a description specified in an order made for the purposes of that paragraph by the Secretary of State under section 453.]

[1337]

NOTES

Sub-s (2): paras (ba), (bb) inserted by the Serious Crime Act 2007, s 76(2), as from 6 April 2008.

Sub-s (5): words in square brackets in para (a) inserted by the Serious Crime Act 2007, s 77, Sch 10, paras 1, 8(1), (2), as from 6 April 2008.

Sub-ss (7A), (7B), (11): inserted and added respectively by the Serious Crime Act 2007, ss 76(3), 80(4), as from 6 April 2008.

Sub-s (10): words in square brackets in para (a) inserted by the Serious Crime Act 2007, s 80(3)(a), as from 6 April 2008; words in square brackets in para (b) substituted by the Serious Crime Act 2007, s 74(2), Sch 8, Pt 4, paras 103, 106, as from 1 April 2008 (for transitional provisions in relation to the transfer of functions from the Assets Recovery Agency to SOCA and the National Policing Improvement Agency, see the Serious Crime Act 2007 (Commencement No 2 and Transitional and Transitory Provisions and Savings) Order 2008, SI 2008/755, art 3); para (c) is inserted by s 77 of, and Sch 10, para 8(1), (3) to, the 2007 Act, as from 6 April 2008, and the words in square brackets in that paragraph are inserted by s 80(3)(b) of that Act, as from the same date.

354 Further provisions: general

(1)   A search and seizure warrant does not confer the right to seize privileged material.

(2)   Privileged material is any material which a person would be entitled to refuse to produce on grounds of legal professional privilege in proceedings in the High Court.

(3)   A search and seizure warrant does not confer the right to seize excluded material.

[1338]

355 Further provisions: confiscation and money laundering

(1)   This section applies to—
   (a)   search and seizure warrants sought for the purposes of a confiscation investigation or a money laundering investigation, and
   (b)   powers of seizure under them.

(2)   In relation to such warrants and powers, the Secretary of State may make an order which applies the provisions to which subsections (3) and (4) apply subject to any specified modifications.

(3)   This subsection applies to the following provisions of the Police and Criminal Evidence Act 1984 (c 60)—
   (a)   section 15 (search warrants – safeguards);
   (b)   section 16 (execution of warrants);
   (c)   section 21 (access and copying);
   (d)   section 22 (retention).

(4)   This subsection applies to the following provisions of the Police and Criminal Evidence (Northern Ireland) Order 1989 (SI 1989/1341 (NI 12))—
   (a)   Article 17 (search warrants -safeguards);
   (b)   Article 18 (execution of warrants);
   (c)   Article 23 (access and copying);
   (d)   Article 24 (retention).

[1339]

NOTES

Orders: the Proceeds of Crime Act 2002 (Application of Police and Criminal Evidence Act 1984 and Police and Criminal Evidence (Northern Ireland) Order 1989) Order 2003, SI 2003/174 at [3711] (which applies, with specified modifications, certain provisions of the Police and Criminal Evidence Act 1984 and the Police and Criminal Evidence (Northern Ireland) Order 1989 to search and seizure warrants sought under s 352 of this Act for the purposes of a confiscation investigation or a money laundering investigation, and powers of seizure under them).

356 Further provisions: civil recovery [and detained cash]

(1)   This section applies to search and seizure warrants sought for the purposes of civil recovery investigations [or detained cash investigations].

(2)   An application for a warrant may be made ex parte to a judge in chambers.

(3)   A warrant may be issued subject to conditions.

(4)   A warrant continues in force until the end of the period of one month starting with the day on which it is issued.

(5)   A warrant authorises the person it names to require any information which is held in a computer and is accessible from the premises specified in the application for the warrant, and which the named person believes relates to any matter relevant to the investigation, to be produced in a form—
   (a)   in which it can be taken away, and
   (b)   in which it is visible and legible.

(6)   ...

(7)   A warrant may include provision authorising a person who is exercising powers under it to do other things which—
   (a)   are specified in the warrant, and
   (b)   need to be done in order to give effect to it.

(8)   Copies may be taken of any material seized under a warrant.

(9)   Material seized under a warrant may be retained for so long as it is necessary to retain it (as opposed to copies of it) in connection with the investigation for the purposes of which the warrant was issued.

(10)   But [if the appropriate person has reasonable] grounds for believing that—
   (a)   the material may need to be produced for the purposes of any legal proceedings, and
   (b)   it might otherwise be unavailable for those purposes,
it may be retained until the proceedings are concluded.

[(11)   The appropriate person is—
   (a)   [an appropriate officer], if the warrant was issued for the purposes of a civil recovery investigation;
   (b)   a constable[, an accredited financial investigator] or an officer of Revenue and Customs, if the warrant was issued for the purposes of a detained cash investigation.]

[(12)   The reference in paragraph (b) of subsection (11) to an accredited financial investigator is a reference to an accredited financial investigator who falls within a description specified in an order made for the purposes of that paragraph by the Secretary of State under section 453.]

[1340]

NOTES

Section heading, sub-s (1): words in square brackets inserted by the Serious Crime Act 2007, s 77, Sch 10, paras 1, 9(1)–(3), as from 6 April 2008.
Sub-s (6): repealed by the Serious Crime Act 2007, ss 74(2), 92, Sch 8, Pt 4, paras 103, 107(1), (2), Sch 14, as from 1 April 2008 (for transitional provisions in relation to the transfer of functions from the Assets Recovery Agency to SOCA and the National Policing Improvement Agency, see the Serious Crime Act 2007 (Commencement No 2 and Transitional and Transitory Provisions and Savings) Order 2008, SI 2008/755, art 3).
Sub-s (11): words in square brackets substituted by the Serious Crime Act 2007, s 77, Sch 10, paras 1, 9(1), (5), as from 6 April 2008.
Sub-s (11): added by the Serious Crime Act 2007, s 77, Sch 10, paras 1, 9(1), (6), as from 6 April 2008; words in first pair of square brackets substituted by the Serious Crime Act 2007, s 74(2), Sch 8, Pt 4, paras 103, 107(1), (3), as from 1 April 2008 (for transitional provisions in relation to the transfer of functions from the Assets Recovery Agency to SOCA and the National Policing Improvement Agency, see the Serious Crime Act 2007 (Commencement No 2 and Transitional and Transitory Provisions and Savings) Order 2008, SI 2008/755, art 3); words in second pair of square brackets inserted by s 80(5) of the 2007 Act, as from 6 April 2008.
Sub-s (12): added by the Serious Crime Act 2007, s 80(6), as from 6 April 2008.
Transitional provisions: for transitional provisions in relation to any written authority given before 1 April 2008 by the Director under sub-s (6) above, see the Serious Crime Act 2007 (Commencement No 2 and Transitional and Transitory Provisions and Savings) Order 2008, SI 2008/755, art 8.

Disclosure orders

357   Disclosure orders

(1)   A judge may, on an application made to him by [an appropriate officer], make a disclosure order if he is satisfied that each of the requirements for the making of the order is fulfilled.

(2)   No application for a disclosure order may be made in relation to a [detained cash investigation or a] money laundering investigation.

[(2A)   The relevant authority may only make an application for a disclosure order in relation to a confiscation investigation if the relevant authority is in receipt of a request to do so from an appropriate officer.]

(3)   The application for a disclosure order must state that—

(a)   a person specified in the application is subject to a confiscation investigation which is being carried out by [an appropriate officer] and the order is sought for the purposes of the investigation, or

(b)   property specified in the application is subject to a civil recovery investigation and the order is sought for the purposes of the investigation.

(4)   A disclosure order is an order authorising [an appropriate officer] to give to any person [the appropriate officer] considers has relevant information notice in writing requiring him to do, with respect to any matter relevant to the investigation for the purposes of which the order is sought, any or all of the following—

(a)   answer questions, either at a time specified in the notice or at once, at a place so specified;

(b)   provide information specified in the notice, by a time and in a manner so specified;

(c)   produce documents, or documents of a description, specified in the notice, either at or by a time so specified or at once, and in a manner so specified.

(5)   Relevant information is information (whether or not contained in a document) which [the appropriate officer concerned] considers to be relevant to the investigation.

(6)   A person is not bound to comply with a requirement imposed by a notice given under a disclosure order unless evidence of authority to give the notice is produced to him.

[(7)   In this Part "relevant authority" means—

(a)   in relation to a confiscation investigation, a prosecutor; and

(b)   in relation to a civil recovery investigation, a member of SOCA's staff or the relevant Director.

(8)   For the purposes of subsection (7)(a) a prosecutor is—

(a)   in relation to a confiscation investigation carried out by a member of SOCA's staff, the relevant Director or any specified person;

(b)   in relation to a confiscation investigation carried out by an accredited financial investigator, the Director of Public Prosecutions, the Director of Public Prosecutions for Northern Ireland or any specified person;

(c)   in relation to a confiscation investigation carried out by a constable, the Director of Public Prosecutions, the Director of Public Prosecutions for Northern Ireland, the Director of the Serious Fraud Office or any specified person; and

(d)   in relation to a confiscation investigation carried out by an officer of Revenue and Customs, the Director of Revenue and Customs Prosecutions, the Director of Public Prosecutions for Northern Ireland or any specified person.

(9)   In subsection (8) "specified person" means any person specified, or falling within a description specified, by an order of the Secretary of State.]

[1341]

NOTES

Sub-ss (1), (3)–(5): words in square brackets substituted by the Serious Crime Act 2007, s 74(2), Sch 8, Pt 4, paras 103, 108(1), (2), (4)–(6), as from 1 April 2008 (for transitional provisions in relation to the transfer of functions from the Assets Recovery Agency to SOCA and the National Policing Improvement Agency, see the Serious Crime Act 2007 (Commencement No 2 and Transitional and Transitory Provisions and Savings) Order 2008, SI 2008/755, art 3).

Sub-s (2): words in square brackets inserted by the Serious Crime Act 2007, s 77, Sch 10, paras 1, 10, as from 6 April 2008.

Sub-ss (2A), (7)–(9): inserted and added respectively by the Serious Crime Act 2007, s 74(2), Sch 8, Pt 4, paras 103, 108(1), (3), (7), as from 1 April 2008 (for transitional provisions in relation to the transfer of functions from the Assets Recovery Agency to SOCA and the National Policing Improvement Agency, see SI 2008/755, art 3).

Transitional provisions: for transitional provisions in relation to disclosure orders, see the Serious Crime Act 2007 (Commencement No 2 and Transitional and Transitory Provisions and Savings) Order 2008, SI 2008/755, art 9.

---

358 Requirements for making of disclosure order

(1)   These are the requirements for the making of a disclosure order.

(2)   There must be reasonable grounds for suspecting that—

(a)   in the case of a confiscation investigation, the person specified in the application for the order has benefited from his criminal conduct;

(b)   in the case of a civil recovery investigation, the property specified in the application for the order is recoverable property or associated property.

(3)   There must be reasonable grounds for believing that information which may be provided in compliance with a requirement imposed under the order is likely to be of substantial value (whether or not by itself) to the investigation for the purposes of which the order is sought.

(4)   There must be reasonable grounds for believing that it is in the public interest for the information to be provided, having regard to the benefit likely to accrue to the investigation if the information is obtained.

[1342]

359   Offences

(1)   A person commits an offence if without reasonable excuse he fails to comply with a requirement imposed on him under a disclosure order.

(2)   A person guilty of an offence under subsection (1) is liable on summary conviction to—
  (a)   imprisonment for a term not exceeding six months,
  (b)   a fine not exceeding level 5 on the standard scale, or
  (c)   both.

(3)   A person commits an offence if, in purported compliance with a requirement imposed on him under a disclosure order, he—
  (a)   makes a statement which he knows to be false or misleading in a material particular, or
  (b)   recklessly makes a statement which is false or misleading in a material particular.

(4)   A person guilty of an offence under subsection (3) is liable—
  (a)   on summary conviction, to imprisonment for a term not exceeding six months or to a fine not exceeding the statutory maximum or to both, or
  (b)   on conviction on indictment, to imprisonment for a term not exceeding two years or to a fine or to both.

[1343]

360   Statements

(1)   A statement made by a person in response to a requirement imposed on him under a disclosure order may not be used in evidence against him in criminal proceedings.

(2)   But subsection (1) does not apply—
  (a)   in the case of proceedings under Part 2 or 4,
  (b)   on a prosecution for an offence under section 359(1) or (3),
  (c)   on a prosecution for an offence under section 5 of the Perjury Act 1911 (c 6) or Article 10 of the Perjury (Northern Ireland) Order 1979 (SI 1979/1714 (NI 19)) (false statements), or
  (d)   on a prosecution for some other offence where, in giving evidence, the person makes a statement inconsistent with the statement mentioned in subsection (1).

(3)   A statement may not be used by virtue of subsection (2)(d) against a person unless—
  (a)   evidence relating to it is adduced, or
  (b)   a question relating to it is asked,
by him or on his behalf in the proceedings arising out of the prosecution.

[1344]

361   Further provisions

(1)   A disclosure order does not confer the right to require a person to answer any privileged question, provide any privileged information or produce any privileged document, except that a lawyer may be required to provide the name and address of a client of his.

(2)   A privileged question is a question which the person would be entitled to refuse to answer on grounds of legal professional privilege in proceedings in the High Court.

(3)   Privileged information is any information which the person would be entitled to refuse to provide on grounds of legal professional privilege in proceedings in the High Court.

(4)   Privileged material is any material which the person would be entitled to refuse to produce on grounds of legal professional privilege in proceedings in the High Court.

(5)   A disclosure order does not confer the right to require a person to produce excluded material.

(6)   A disclosure order has effect in spite of any restriction on the disclosure of information (however imposed).

(7)   [An appropriate officer] may take copies of any documents produced in compliance with a requirement to produce them which is imposed under a disclosure order.

(8)   Documents so produced may be retained for so long as it is necessary to retain them (as opposed to a copy of them) in connection with the investigation for the purposes of which the order was made.

(9)   But if [an appropriate officer] has reasonable grounds for believing that—
  (a)   the documents may need to be produced for the purposes of any legal proceedings, and

(b) they might otherwise be unavailable for those purposes,

they may be retained until the proceedings are concluded.

[1345]

NOTES

Sub-ss (7), (9): words in square brackets substituted by the Serious Crime Act 2007, s 74(2), Sch 8, Pt 4, paras 103, 109, as from 1 April 2008 (for transitional provisions in relation to the transfer of functions from the Assets Recovery Agency to SOCA and the National Policing Improvement Agency, see the Serious Crime Act 2007 (Commencement No 2 and Transitional and Transitory Provisions and Savings) Order 2008, SI 2008/755, art 3).

362 Supplementary

(1) An application for a disclosure order may be made ex parte to a judge in chambers.

(2) Rules of court may make provision as to the practice and procedure to be followed in connection with proceedings relating to disclosure orders.

(3) An application to discharge or vary a disclosure order may be made to the court by—
    (a) the [person who applied for the order];
    (b) any person affected by the order.

(4) The court—
    (a) may discharge the order;
    (b) may vary the order.

[(4A) If a member of SOCA's staff or a person falling within a description of persons specified by virtue of section 357(9) applies for a disclosure order, an application to discharge or vary the order need not be by the same member of SOCA's staff or (as the case may be) the same person falling within that description.

(4B) References to a person who applied for a disclosure order must be construed accordingly.]

(5) Subsections (2) to [(4B)] do not apply to orders made in England and Wales for the purposes of a civil recovery investigation.

[1346]

NOTES

Sub-ss (3), (5): words in square brackets substituted by the Serious Crime Act 2007, s 74(2), Sch 8, Pt 4, paras 103, 110(1), (2), (4), as from 1 April 2008 (for transitional provisions in relation to the transfer of functions from the Assets Recovery Agency to SOCA and the National Policing Improvement Agency, see the Serious Crime Act 2007 (Commencement No 2 and Transitional and Transitory Provisions and Savings) Order 2008, SI 2008/755, art 3).

Sub-ss (4A), (4B): inserted by the Serious Crime Act 2007, s 74(2), Sch 8, Pt 4, paras 103, 110(1), (3), as from 1 April 2008 (for transitional provisions in relation to the transfer of functions from the Assets Recovery Agency to SOCA and the National Policing Improvement Agency, see SI 2008/755, art 3).

Rules: the Crown Court (Amendment) Rules 2003, SI 2003/422 (see the note to s 351 at **[1335]**).

Customer information orders

363 Customer information orders

(1) A judge may, on an application made to him by an appropriate officer, make a customer information order if he is satisfied that each of the requirements for the making of the order is fulfilled.

[(1A) No application for a customer information order may be made in relation to a detained cash investigation.]

(2) The application for a customer information order must state that—
    (a) a person specified in the application is subject to a confiscation investigation or a money laundering investigation, or
    (b) property specified in the application is subject to a civil recovery investigation and a person specified in the application appears to hold the property.

(3) The application must also state that—
    (a) the order is sought for the purposes of the investigation;
    (b) the order is sought against the financial institution or financial institutions specified in the application.

(4) An application for a customer information order may specify—
    (a) all financial institutions,
    (b) a particular description, or particular descriptions, of financial institutions, or
    (c) a particular financial institution or particular financial institutions.

(5) A customer information order is an order that a financial institution covered by the application for the order must, on being required to do so by notice in writing given by an appropriate officer, provide any such customer information as it has relating to the person specified in the application.

(6) A financial institution which is required to provide information under a customer information order must provide the information to an appropriate officer in such manner, and at or by such time, as an appropriate officer requires.

(7) If a financial institution on which a requirement is imposed by a notice given under a customer information order requires the production of evidence of authority to give the notice, it is not bound to comply with the requirement unless evidence of the authority has been produced to it.

[1347]

NOTES
Sub-s (1A): inserted by the Serious Crime Act 2007, s 77, Sch 10, paras 1, 11, as from 6 April 2008.

364 Meaning of customer information

(1) "Customer information", in relation to a person and a financial institution, is information whether the person holds, or has held, an account or accounts at the financial institution (whether solely or jointly with another) and (if so) information as to—
  (a) the matters specified in subsection (2) if the person is an individual;
  (b) the matters specified in subsection (3) if the person is a company or limited liability partnership or a similar body incorporated or otherwise established outside the United Kingdom.

(2) The matters referred to in subsection (1)(a) are—
  (a) the account number or numbers;
  (b) the person's full name;
  (c) his date of birth;
  (d) his most recent address and any previous addresses;
  (e) the date or dates on which he began to hold the account or accounts and, if he has ceased to hold the account or any of the accounts, the date or dates on which he did so;
  (f) such evidence of his identity as was obtained by the financial institution under or for the purposes of any legislation relating to money laundering;
  (g) the full name, date of birth and most recent address, and any previous addresses, of any person who holds, or has held, an account at the financial institution jointly with him;
  (h) the account number or numbers of any other account or accounts held at the financial institution to which he is a signatory and details of the person holding the other account or accounts.

(3) The matters referred to in subsection (1)(b) are—
  (a) the account number or numbers;
  (b) the person's full name;
  (c) a description of any business which the person carries on;
  (d) the country or territory in which it is incorporated or otherwise established and any number allocated to it under the Companies Act 1985 (c 6) or the Companies (Northern Ireland) Order 1986 (SI 1986/ 1032 (NI 6)) or corresponding legislation of any country or territory outside the United Kingdom;
  (e) any number assigned to it for the purposes of value added tax in the United Kingdom;
  (f) its registered office, and any previous registered offices, under the Companies Act 1985 or the Companies (Northern Ireland) Order 1986 (SI 1986/1032 (NI 6)) or anything similar under corresponding legislation of any country or territory outside the United Kingdom;
  (g) its registered office, and any previous registered offices, under the Limited Liability Partnerships Act 2000 (c 12) or anything similar under corresponding legislation of any country or territory outside Great Britain;
  (h) the date or dates on which it began to hold the account or accounts and, if it has ceased to hold the account or any of the accounts, the date or dates on which it did so;
  (i) such evidence of its identity as was obtained by the financial institution under or for the purposes of any legislation relating to money laundering;
  (j) the full name, date of birth and most recent address and any previous addresses of any person who is a signatory to the account or any of the accounts.

(4) The Secretary of State may by order provide for information of a description specified in the order—
  (a) to be customer information, or
  (b) no longer to be customer information.

(5) Money laundering is an act which—

(a)   constitutes an offence under section 327, 328 or 329 of this Act or section 18 of the Terrorism Act 2000 (c 11), or

[(aa) constitutes an offence specified in section 415(1A) of this Act,]

(b)   would constitute an offence specified in paragraph (a) [or (aa)] if done in the United Kingdom.

[1348]

NOTES

Sub-s (5): para (aa) and the words in square brackets in para (b) inserted by the Serious Organised Crime and Police Act 2005, s 107(1), (2), as from 1 July 2005.

Note: amendments made in relation to Northern Ireland only by the Criminal Justice (Northern Ireland) Order 2005, SI 2005/1965 are not reproduced.

365   Requirements for making of customer information order

(1)   These are the requirements for the making of a customer information order.

(2)   In the case of a confiscation investigation, there must be reasonable grounds for suspecting that the person specified in the application for the order has benefited from his criminal conduct.

(3)   In the case of a civil recovery investigation, there must be reasonable grounds for suspecting that—

(a)   the property specified in the application for the order is recoverable property or associated property;

(b)   the person specified in the application holds all or some of the property.

(4)   In the case of a money laundering investigation, there must be reasonable grounds for suspecting that the person specified in the application for the order has committed a money laundering offence.

(5)   In the case of any investigation, there must be reasonable grounds for believing that customer information which may be provided in compliance with the order is likely to be of substantial value (whether or not by itself) to the investigation for the purposes of which the order is sought.

(6)   In the case of any investigation, there must be reasonable grounds for believing that it is in the public interest for the customer information to be provided, having regard to the benefit likely to accrue to the investigation if the information is obtained.

[1349]

366   Offences

(1)   A financial institution commits an offence if without reasonable excuse it fails to comply with a requirement imposed on it under a customer information order.

(2)   A financial institution guilty of an offence under subsection (1) is liable on summary conviction to a fine not exceeding level 5 on the standard scale.

(3)   A financial institution commits an offence if, in purported compliance with a customer information order, it—

(a)   makes a statement which it knows to be false or misleading in a material particular, or

(b)   recklessly makes a statement which is false or misleading in a material particular.

(4)   A financial institution guilty of an offence under subsection (3) is liable—

(a)   on summary conviction, to a fine not exceeding the statutory maximum, or

(b)   on conviction on indictment, to a fine.

[1350]

367   Statements

(1)   A statement made by a financial institution in response to a customer information order may not be used in evidence against it in criminal proceedings.

(2)   But subsection (1) does not apply—

(a)   in the case of proceedings under Part 2 or 4,

(b)   on a prosecution for an offence under section 366(1) or (3), or

(c)   on a prosecution for some other offence where, in giving evidence, the financial institution makes a statement inconsistent with the statement mentioned in subsection (1).

(3)   A statement may not be used by virtue of subsection (2)(c) against a financial institution unless—

(a)   evidence relating to it is adduced, or

(b)   a question relating to it is asked,

by or on behalf of the financial institution in the proceedings arising out of the prosecution.

[1351]

368 Disclosure of information

A customer information order has effect in spite of any restriction on the disclosure of information (however imposed).

[1352]

369 Supplementary

(1) An application for a customer information order may be made ex parte to a judge in chambers.

(2) Rules of court may make provision as to the practice and procedure to be followed in connection with proceedings relating to customer information orders.

(3) An application to discharge or vary a customer information order may be made to the court by—
  (a) the person who applied for the order;
  (b) any person affected by the order.

(4) The court—
  (a) may discharge the order;
  (b) may vary the order.

(5) If an accredited financial investigator, [a member of SOCA's staff,] a constable or a customs officer applies for a customer information order, an application to discharge or vary the order need not be by the same accredited financial investigator, [member of SOCA's staff,] constable or customs officer.

(6) References to a person who applied for a customer information order must be construed accordingly.

(7) An accredited financial investigator, [a member of SOCA's staff,] a constable or a customs officer may not make an application for a customer information order or an application to vary such an order unless he is a senior appropriate officer or he is authorised to do so by a senior appropriate officer.

(8) Subsections (2) to (6) do not apply to orders made in England and Wales for the purposes of a civil recovery investigation.

[1353]

NOTES

Sub-ss (5), (7): words in square brackets inserted by the Serious Crime Act 2007, s 74(2), Sch 8, Pt 4, paras 103, 111, as from 1 April 2008 (for transitional provisions in relation to the transfer of functions from the Assets Recovery Agency to SOCA and the National Policing Improvement Agency, see the Serious Crime Act 2007 (Commencement No 2 and Transitional and Transitory Provisions and Savings) Order 2008, SI 2008/755, art 3).

Rules: the Crown Court (Amendment) Rules 2003, SI 2003/422 (see the note to s 351 at **[1335]**).

Account monitoring orders

370 Account monitoring orders

(1) A judge may, on an application made to him by an appropriate officer, make an account monitoring order if he is satisfied that each of the requirements for the making of the order is fulfilled.

[(1A) No application for an account monitoring order may be made in relation to a detained cash investigation.]

(2) The application for an account monitoring order must state that—
  (a) a person specified in the application is subject to a confiscation investigation or a money laundering investigation, or
  (b) property specified in the application is subject to a civil recovery investigation and a person specified in the application appears to hold the property.

(3) The application must also state that—
  (a) the order is sought for the purposes of the investigation;
  (b) the order is sought against the financial institution specified in the application in relation to account information of the description so specified.

(4) Account information is information relating to an account or accounts held at the financial institution specified in the application by the person so specified (whether solely or jointly with another).

(5) The application for an account monitoring order may specify information relating to—
  (a) all accounts held by the person specified in the application for the order at the financial institution so specified,
  (b) a particular description, or particular descriptions, of accounts so held, or
  (c) a particular account, or particular accounts, so held.

PART II
OTHER ACTS

(6)   An account monitoring order is an order that the financial institution specified in the application for the order must, for the period stated in the order, provide account information of the description specified in the order to an appropriate officer in the manner, and at or by the time or times, stated in the order.

(7)   The period stated in an account monitoring order must not exceed the period of 90 days beginning with the day on which the order is made.

[1354]

NOTES

Sub-s (1A): inserted by the Serious Crime Act 2007, s 77, Sch 10, paras 1, 12, as from 6 April 2008.

371   Requirements for making of account monitoring order

(1)   These are the requirements for the making of an account monitoring order.

(2)   In the case of a confiscation investigation, there must be reasonable grounds for suspecting that the person specified in the application for the order has benefited from his criminal conduct.

(3)   In the case of a civil recovery investigation, there must be reasonable grounds for suspecting that—
  (a)   the property specified in the application for the order is recoverable property or associated property;
  (b)   the person specified in the application holds all or some of the property.

(4)   In the case of a money laundering investigation, there must be reasonable grounds for suspecting that the person specified in the application for the order has committed a money laundering offence.

(5)   In the case of any investigation, there must be reasonable grounds for believing that account information which may be provided in compliance with the order is likely to be of substantial value (whether or not by itself) to the investigation for the purposes of which the order is sought.

(6)   In the case of any investigation, there must be reasonable grounds for believing that it is in the public interest for the account information to be provided, having regard to the benefit likely to accrue to the investigation if the information is obtained.

[1355]

372   Statements

(1)   A statement made by a financial institution in response to an account monitoring order may not be used in evidence against it in criminal proceedings.

(2)   But subsection (1) does not apply—
  (a)   in the case of proceedings under Part 2 or 4,
  (b)   in the case of proceedings for contempt of court, or
  (c)   on a prosecution for an offence where, in giving evidence, the financial institution makes a statement inconsistent with the statement mentioned in subsection (1).

(3)   A statement may not be used by virtue of subsection (2)(c) against a financial institution unless—
  (a)   evidence relating to it is adduced, or
  (b)   a question relating to it is asked,

by or on behalf of the financial institution in the proceedings arising out of the prosecution.

[1356]

373   Applications

An application for an account monitoring order may be made ex parte to a judge in chambers.

[1357]

374   Disclosure of information

An account monitoring order has effect in spite of any restriction on the disclosure of information (however imposed).

[1358]

375   Supplementary

(1)   Rules of court may make provision as to the practice and procedure to be followed in connection with proceedings relating to account monitoring orders.

(2)   An application to discharge or vary an account monitoring order may be made to the court by—
  (a)   the person who applied for the order;
  (b)   any person affected by the order.

(3)   The court—
  (a)   may discharge the order;

(b)   may vary the order.

(4)   If an accredited financial investigator, [a member of SOCA's staff,] a constable or a customs officer applies for an account monitoring order, an application to discharge or vary the order need not be by the same accredited financial investigator, [member of SOCA's staff,] constable or customs officer.

(5)   References to a person who applied for an account monitoring order must be construed accordingly.

(6)   Account monitoring orders have effect as if they were orders of the court.

(7)   This section does not apply to orders made in England and Wales for the purposes of a civil recovery investigation.

[1359]–[1360]

NOTES

Sub-s (4): words in square brackets inserted by the Serious Crime Act 2007, s 74(2), Sch 8, Pt 4, paras 103, 112, as from 1 April 2008 (for transitional provisions in relation to the transfer of functions from the Assets Recovery Agency to SOCA and the National Policing Improvement Agency, see the Serious Crime Act 2007 (Commencement No 2 and Transitional and Transitory Provisions and Savings) Order 2008, SI 2008/755, art 3).

Rules: the Crown Court (Amendment) Rules 2003, SI 2003/422 (see the note to s 351 at **[1335]**).

376   (*Repealed by the Serious Crime Act 2007, ss 74(2), 92, Sch 8, Pt 4, paras 103, 113, Sch 14, as from 1 April 2008, except in relation to confiscation investigations begun before 1 April 2008 and carried on by SOCA on or after that date. For transitional provisions in relation to the transfer of functions from the Assets Recovery Agency to SOCA and the National Policing Improvement Agency, and in relation to confiscation investigations begun before 1 April 2008, see the Serious Crime Act 2007 (Commencement No 2 and Transitional and Transitory Provisions and Savings) Order 2008, SI 2008/755, arts 3, 10.*)

Code of practice

377   Code of practice [of Secretary of State etc]

(1)   The Secretary of State must prepare a code of practice as to the exercise by all of the following of functions they have under this Chapter—
    (a)   [the Director General of SOCA];
    (b)   [other members of SOCA's staff];
    (c)   accredited financial investigators;
    (d)   constables;
    (e)   customs officers.

(2)   After preparing a draft of the code the Secretary of State—
    (a)   must publish the draft;
    (b)   must consider any representations made to him about the draft;
    (c)   may amend the draft accordingly.

(3)   After the Secretary of State has proceeded under subsection (2) he must lay the code before Parliament.

(4)   When he has done so the Secretary of State may bring the code into operation on such day as he may appoint by order.

(5)   A person specified in subsection (1)(a) to (e) must comply with a code of practice which is in operation under this section in the exercise of any function he has under this Chapter.

(6)   If such a person fails to comply with any provision of such a code of practice he is not by reason only of that failure liable in any criminal or civil proceedings.

(7)   But the code of practice is admissible in evidence in such proceedings and a court may take account of any failure to comply with its provisions in determining any question in the proceedings.

(8)   The Secretary of State may from time to time revise a code previously brought into operation under this section; and the preceding provisions of this section apply to a revised code as they apply to the code as first prepared.

(9)   The following provisions do not apply to an appropriate officer [or the relevant authority] in the exercise of any function [either] has under this Chapter—
    (a)   section 67(9) of the Police and Criminal Evidence Act 1984 (c 60) (application of codes of practice under that Act to persons other than police officers);
    (b)   Article 66(8) of the Police and Criminal Evidence (Northern Ireland) Order 1989 (SI 1989/1341 (NI 12)) (which makes similar provision for Northern Ireland).

[1361]

PART II
OTHER ACTS

NOTES
Section heading: words in square brackets inserted the Serious Crime Act 2007, s 74(2), Sch 8, Pt 4, paras 103, 114(1), (2), as from 1 April 2008 (for transitional provisions in relation to the transfer of functions from the Assets Recovery Agency to SOCA and the National Policing Improvement Agency, see the Serious Crime Act 2007 (Commencement No 2 and Transitional and Transitory Provisions and Savings) Order 2008, SI 2008/755, art 3).
Sub-s (1): words in square brackets substituted by the Serious Crime Act 2007, s 74(2), Sch 8, Pt 4, paras 103, 114(1), (3), as from 1 April 2008 (for transitional provisions in relation to the transfer of functions from the Assets Recovery Agency to SOCA and the National Policing Improvement Agency, see SI 2008/755, art 3).
Sub-s (9): words in first pair of square brackets inserted, and words in second pair of square brackets substituted, by the Serious Crime Act 2007, s 74(2), Sch 8, Pt 4, paras 103, 114(1), (4), as from 1 April 2008 (for transitional provisions in relation to the transfer of functions from the Assets Recovery Agency to SOCA and the National Policing Improvement Agency, see SI 2008/755, art 3).
Orders: the Proceeds of Crime Act 2002 (Investigations in England, Wales and Northern Ireland: Code of Practice) Order 2008, SI 2008/946 at **[4156]**. This Order brings into operation on 1 April 2008 the revised code of practice made pursuant to this section as to the exercise of functions under Chapter 2 of Part 8 of this Act. It replaces the Proceeds of Crime Act 2002 (Investigations in England, Wales and Northern Ireland: Code of Practice) Order 2003, SI 2003/334.

[377A   Code of practice of Attorney General or Advocate General for Northern Ireland
(1)   The Attorney General must prepare a code of practice as to—
   (a)   the exercise by the Director of Public Prosecutions, the Director of Revenue and Customs Prosecutions and the Director of the Serious Fraud Office of functions they have under this Chapter; and
   (b)   the exercise by any other person, who is the relevant authority by virtue of section 357(9) in relation to a confiscation investigation, of functions he has under this Chapter in relation to England and Wales as the relevant authority.

(2)   The Advocate General for Northern Ireland must prepare a code of practice as to—
   (a)   the exercise by the Director of Public Prosecutions for Northern Ireland of functions he has under this Chapter; and
   (b)   the exercise by any other person, who is the relevant authority by virtue of section 357(9) in relation to a confiscation investigation, of functions he has under this Chapter in relation to Northern Ireland as the relevant authority.

(3)   After preparing a draft of the code the Attorney General or (as the case may be) the Advocate General for Northern Ireland—
   (a)   must publish the draft;
   (b)   must consider any representations made to him about the draft;
   (c)   may amend the draft accordingly.

(4)   After the Attorney General or the Advocate General for Northern Ireland has proceeded under subsection (3) he must lay the code before Parliament.

(5)   When the code has been so laid the Attorney General or (as the case may be) the Advocate General for Northern Ireland may bring the code into operation on such day as he may appoint by order.

(6)   A person specified in subsection (1)(a) or (b) or (2)(a) or (b) must comply with a code of practice which is in operation under this section in the exercise of any function he has under this Chapter to which the code relates.

(7)   If such a person fails to comply with any provision of such a code of practice the person is not by reason only of that failure liable in any criminal or civil proceedings.

(8)   But the code of practice is admissible in evidence in such proceedings and a court may take account of any failure to comply with its provisions in determining any question in the proceedings.

(9)   The Attorney General or (as the case may be) the Advocate General for Northern Ireland may from time to time revise a code previously brought into operation under this section; and the preceding provisions of this section apply to a revised code as they apply to the code as first prepared.

(10)   In this section references to the Advocate General for Northern Ireland are to be read, before the coming into force of section 27(1) of the Justice (Northern Ireland) Act 2002 (c 26), as references to the Attorney General for Northern Ireland.]

[1361A]

NOTES
Commencement: 1 March 2008 (sub-ss (1)–(5), (10)); 1 April 2008 (otherwise).
Inserted by the Serious Crime Act 2007, s 74(2), Sch 8, Pt 4, paras 103, 115, as from 1 March 2008 (in so far as relating to sub-ss (1)–(5), (10)), and as from 1 April 2008 (otherwise); for transitional provisions in relation to the transfer of functions from the Assets Recovery Agency to SOCA and the National Policing Improvement Agency, see the Serious Crime Act 2007 (Commencement No 2 and Transitional and Transitory Provisions and Savings) Order 2008, SI 2008/755, art 3.

Orders: the Proceeds of Crime Act 2002 (Investigative Powers of Prosecutors in England, Wales and Northern Ireland: Code of Practice) Order 2008, SI 2008/1978 (at **[4226A]**), which provides that the code of practice entitled "Code of Practice issued under section 377A of the Proceeds of Crime Act 2002" which was laid before Parliament on 18 June 2008 shall come into operation on 22 July 2008.

Interpretation

378　Officers

(1)　In relation to a confiscation investigation these are appropriate officers—
    (a)　[a member of SOCA's staff];
    (b)　an accredited financial investigator;
    (c)　a constable;
    (d)　a customs officer.

(2)　In relation to a confiscation investigation these are senior appropriate officers—
    (a)　[a senior member of SOCA's staff];
    (b)　a police officer who is not below the rank of superintendent;
    (c)　a customs officer who is not below such grade as is designated by the Commissioners of Customs and Excise as equivalent to that rank;
    (d)　an accredited financial investigator who falls within a description specified in an order made for the purposes of this paragraph by the Secretary of State under section 453.

(3)　In relation to a civil recovery investigation[—
    (a)　a member of SOCA's staff or the relevant Director is an appropriate officer;
    (b)　a senior member of SOCA's staff is a senior appropriate officer.]

[(3A)　In relation to a detained cash investigation these are appropriate officers—
    (a)　a constable;
    [(ab)　an accredited financial investigator;]
    (b)　an officer of Revenue and Customs.]

[(3B)　The reference in paragraph (ab) of subsection (3A) to an accredited financial investigator is a reference to an accredited financial investigator who falls within a description specified in an order made for the purposes of that paragraph by the Secretary of State under section 453.]

(4)　In relation to a money laundering investigation these are appropriate officers—
    (a)　an accredited financial investigator;
    (b)　a constable;
    (c)　a customs officer.

(5)　For the purposes of section 342, in relation to a money laundering investigation a person authorised for the purposes of money laundering investigations by [the Director General of [SOCA]] is also an appropriate officer.

(6)　In relation to a money laundering investigation these are senior appropriate officers—
    (a)　a police officer who is not below the rank of superintendent;
    (b)　a customs officer who is not below such grade as is designated by the Commissioners of Customs and Excise as equivalent to that rank;
    (c)　an accredited financial investigator who falls within a description specified in an order made for the purposes of this paragraph by the Secretary of State under section 453.

(7)　…

[(8)　For the purposes of this Part a senior member of SOCA's staff is—
    (a)　the Director General of SOCA; or
    (b)　any member of SOCA's staff authorised by the Director General (whether generally or specifically) for this purpose.]

[1362]

PART II
OTHER ACTS

NOTES

Sub-ss (1)–(3): words in square brackets substituted by the Serious Crime Act 2007, s 74(2), Sch 8, Pt 4, paras 103, 116(1), (2)–(4), as from 1 April 2008 (for transitional provisions in relation to the transfer of functions from the Assets Recovery Agency to SOCA and the National Policing Improvement Agency, see the Serious Crime Act 2007 (Commencement No 2 and Transitional and Transitory Provisions and Savings) Order 2008, SI 2008/755, art 3).

Sub-s (3A): inserted by the Serious Crime Act 2007, s 77, Sch 10, paras 1, 13, as from 6 April 2008; para (ab) inserted by s 80(7) of that Act, as from the same date.

Sub-s (3B): inserted by the Serious Crime Act 2007, s 80(8), as from 6 April 2008.

Sub-s (5): words in first (outer) pair of square brackets substituted by the Serious Organised Crime and Police Act 2005, s 59, Sch 4, paras 168, 175, as from 1 April 2006; words in second (inner) pair of square brackets substituted by the Serious Crime Act 2007, s 74(2), Sch 8, Pt 4, paras 103, 116(1), (5), as from 1 April 2008 (for transitional provisions in relation to the transfer of functions from the Assets Recovery Agency to SOCA and the National Policing Improvement Agency, see SI 2008/755, art 3).

Sub-s (7): repealed by the Serious Crime Act 2007, ss 74(2), 92, Sch 8, Pt 4, paras 103, 116(1), (6), Sch 14, as from 1 April 2008 (for transitional provisions in relation to the transfer of functions from the Assets Recovery Agency to SOCA and the National Policing Improvement Agency, see SI 2008/755, art 3).

Sub-s (8): added by the Serious Crime Act 2007, s 74(2), Sch 8, Pt 4, paras 103, 116(1), (7), as from 1 April 2008 (for transitional provisions in relation to the transfer of functions from the Assets Recovery Agency to SOCA and the National Policing Improvement Agency, see SI 2008/755, art 3).

Commissioners of Customs and Excise: a reference to the Commissioners of Customs and Excise is now to be taken as a reference to the Commissioners for Her Majesty's Revenue and Customs; see the Commissioners for Revenue and Customs Act 2005, s 50(1), (7).

379 Miscellaneous

"Document", "excluded material" and "premises" have the same meanings as in the Police and Criminal Evidence Act 1984 (c 60) or (in relation to Northern Ireland) the Police and Criminal Evidence (Northern Ireland) Order 1989 (SI 1989/1341 (NI 12)).

[1363]

CHAPTER 4
INTERPRETATION

413 Criminal conduct

(1) Criminal conduct is conduct which—
    (a) constitutes an offence in any part of the United Kingdom, or
    (b) would constitute an offence in any part of the United Kingdom if it occurred there.

(2) A person benefits from conduct if he obtains property or a pecuniary advantage as a result of or in connection with the conduct.

(3) References to property or a pecuniary advantage obtained in connection with conduct include references to property or a pecuniary advantage obtained in both that connection and some other.

(4) If a person benefits from conduct his benefit is the property or pecuniary advantage obtained as a result of or in connection with the conduct.

(5) It is immaterial—
    (a) whether conduct occurred before or after the passing of this Act, and
    (b) whether property or a pecuniary advantage constituting a benefit from conduct was obtained before or after the passing of this Act.

[1364]

414 Property

(1) Property is all property wherever situated and includes—
    (a) money;
    (b) all forms of property, real or personal, heritable or moveable;
    (c) things in action and other intangible or incorporeal property.

(2) "Recoverable property" and "associated property" have the same meanings as in Part 5.

(3) The following rules apply in relation to property—
    (a) property is obtained by a person if he obtains an interest in it;
    (b) references to an interest, in relation to land in England and Wales or Northern Ireland, are to any legal estate or equitable interest or power;
    (c) references to an interest, in relation to land in Scotland, are to any estate, interest, servitude or other heritable right in or over land, including a heritable security;
    (d) references to an interest, in relation to property other than land, include references to a right (including a right to possession).

[1365]

415 Money laundering offences

(1) An offence under section 327, 328 or 329 is a money laundering offence.

[(1A) Each of the following is a money laundering offence—
    (a) an offence under section 93A, 93B or 93C of the Criminal Justice Act 1988;
    (b) an offence under section 49, 50 or 51 of the Drug Trafficking Act 1994;
    (c) an offence under section 37 or 38 of the Criminal Law (Consolidation) (Scotland) Act 1995;
    (d) an offence under article 45, 46 or 47 of the Proceeds of Crime (Northern Ireland) Order 1996.]

(2) Each of the following is a money laundering offence—
    (a) an attempt, conspiracy or incitement to commit an offence specified in subsection (1);
    (b) aiding, abetting, counselling or procuring the commission of an offence specified in subsection (1).

[1366]

NOTES

Sub-s (1A): inserted by the Serious Organised Crime and Police Act 2005, s 107(1), (4), as from 1 July 2005.

Attempt, conspiracy or incitement to commit an offence: see the Serious Crime Act 2007, s 63(1), (2), Sch 6, Pt 1, para 44 which provides that any reference however expressed to (or to conduct amounting to) the offence abolished by s 59 of the 2007 Act (abolition of common law offence of inciting the commission of another offence) has effect as a reference to (or to conduct amounting to) the offences of encouraging or assisting the commission of an offence.

Criminal Justice Act 1988, ss 93A, 93B, 93C; Drug Trafficking Act 1994, ss 49, 50, 51; Criminal Law (Consolidation) (Scotland) Act 1995, ss 37, 38: repealed by ss 456, 457 of, and Sch 11, paras 17, 25, Sch 12 to, this Act.

416 Other interpretative provisions

(1) These expressions are to be construed in accordance with these provisions of this Part—
     civil recovery investigation: section 341(2) and (3)
     confiscation investigation: section 341(1)
     [detained cash investigation: section 341(3A)]
     money laundering investigation: section 341(4).

(2) In the application of this Part to England and Wales and Northern Ireland, these expressions are to be construed in accordance with these provisions of this Part—
     account information: section 370(4)
     account monitoring order: section 370(6)
     appropriate officer: section 378
     customer information: section 364
     customer information order: section 363(5)
     disclosure order: section 357(4)
     document: section 379
     order to grant entry: section 347(3)
     production order: section 345(4)
     [relevant authority: section 357(7) to (9)
     relevant Director: section 352(5A)]
     search and seizure warrant: section 352(4)
     senior appropriate officer: section 378.
     [senior member of SOCA's staff: section 378(8)]

(3) In the application of this Part to Scotland, these expressions are to be construed in accordance with these provisions of this Part—
     account information: section 404(5)
     account monitoring order: section 404(7)
     customer information: section 398
     customer information order: section 397(6)
     disclosure order: section 391(4)
     production order: section 380(5)
     proper person: section 412
     search warrant: section 387(4).

(4) "Financial institution" means a person carrying on a business in the regulated sector.

(5) But a person who ceases to carry on a business in the regulated sector (whether by virtue of paragraph 5 of Schedule 9 or otherwise) is to continue to be treated as a financial institution for the purposes of any requirement under—
     (a)   a customer information order, or
     (b)   an account monitoring order,
to provide information which relates to a time when the person was a financial institution.

(6) References to a business in the regulated sector must be construed in accordance with Schedule 9.

(7) "Recovery order", "interim receiving order" and "interim administration order" have the same meanings as in Part 5.

[(7A) "Unlawful conduct" has the meaning given by section 241.]

(8) References to notice in writing include references to notice given by electronic means.

(9) This section and sections 413 to 415 apply for the purposes of this Part.

[1367]

PART II
OTHER ACTS

NOTES

Sub-s (1): words in square brackets inserted by the Serious Crime Act 2007, s 77, Sch 10, paras 1, 24(1), (2), as from 6 April 2008.

Sub-s (2): words in square brackets inserted by the Serious Crime Act 2007, s 74(2), Sch 8, Pt 4, paras 103, 117, as from 1 April 2008 (for transitional provisions in relation to the transfer of functions from the Assets Recovery Agency to SOCA and the National Policing Improvement Agency, see the Serious Crime Act 2007 (Commencement No 2 and Transitional and Transitory Provisions and Savings) Order 2008, SI 2008/755, art 3).

Sub-s (7A): inserted by the Serious Crime Act 2007, s 77, Sch 10, paras 1, 24(1), (3), as from 6 April 2008.

PART 10

INFORMATION

England and Wales and Northern Ireland

[435 Use of information by certain Directors

(1)   Information obtained by or on behalf of the Director in connection with the exercise of any of his functions under, or in relation to, Part 5 or 8 may be used by him in connection with his exercise of any of his other functions (whether under, or in relation to, either Part, another Part of this Act or otherwise).

(2)   Information obtained by or on behalf of the Director in connection with the exercise of any of his functions (whether under, or in relation to, this Act or otherwise) which are not functions under, or in relation to, Part 5 or 8 may be used by him in connection with his exercise of any of his functions under, or in relation to, Part 5 or 8.

(3)   This section applies to information obtained before the coming into force of the section as well as to information obtained after the coming into force of the section.

(4)   In this section "the Director" means—
   (a)   the Director of Public Prosecutions;
   (b)   the Director of the Serious Fraud Office; or
   (c)   the Director of Public Prosecutions for Northern Ireland.]

[1368]

NOTES
Commencement: 1 April 2008.
Substituted by the Serious Crime Act 2007, s 74(2), Sch 8, Pt 6, paras 121, 131, as from 1 April 2008 (for transitional provisions in relation to the transfer of functions from the Assets Recovery Agency to SOCA and the National Policing Improvement Agency, see the Serious Crime Act 2007 (Commencement No 2 and Transitional and Transitory Provisions and Savings) Order 2008, SI 2008/755, art 3).

436   Disclosure of information to [certain Directors]

(1)   Information which is held by or on behalf of a permitted person (whether it was obtained before or after the coming into force of [subsection (10)]) may be disclosed to the Director for the purpose of the exercise by the Director of his functions [under, or in relation to, Part 5 or 8].

(2)   A disclosure under this section is not to be taken to breach any restriction on the disclosure of information (however imposed).

(3)   But nothing in this section authorises the making of a disclosure—
   (a)   which contravenes the Data Protection Act 1998 (c 29);
   (b)   which is prohibited by Part 1 of the Regulation of Investigatory Powers Act 2000 (c 23).

(4)   This section does not affect a power to disclose which exists apart from this section.

(5)   These are permitted persons—
   (a)   a constable;
   [(b)   ...]
   (d)   the Director of the Serious Fraud Office;
   (e)   the Commissioners of Inland Revenue;
   (f)   the Commissioners of Customs and Excise;
   (g)   the Director of Public Prosecutions;
   [(ga) ...]
   (h)   the Director of Public Prosecutions for Northern Ireland.

(6)   The Secretary of State may by order designate as permitted persons other persons who exercise functions which he believes are of a public nature.

(7)   But an order under subsection (6) must specify the functions in respect of which the designation is made.

(8)   Information must not be disclosed under this section on behalf of the Commissioners of Inland Revenue or on behalf of the Commissioners of Customs and Excise unless the Commissioners concerned authorise the disclosure.

(9)   The power to authorise a disclosure under subsection (8) may be delegated (either generally or for a specified purpose)—
   (a)   in the case of the Commissioners of Inland Revenue, to an officer of the Board of Inland Revenue;
   (b)   in the case of the Commissioners of Customs and Excise, to a customs officer.

[(10)   In this section "the Director" has the same meaning as in section 435.]

[1369]

NOTES

Section heading: words in square brackets substituted by the Serious Crime Act 2007, s 74(2), Sch 8, Pt 6, paras 121, 132(1), (2), as from 1 April 2008 (for transitional provisions in relation to the transfer of functions from the Assets Recovery Agency to SOCA and the National Policing Improvement Agency, see the Serious Crime Act 2007 (Commencement No 2 and Transitional and Transitory Provisions and Savings) Order 2008, SI 2008/755, art 3).

Sub-s (1): words in first pair of square brackets substituted, and words in second pair of square brackets inserted, by the Serious Crime Act 2007, s 74(2), Sch 8, Pt 6, paras 121, 132(1), (3), as from 1 April 2008 (for transitional provisions in relation to the transfer of functions from the Assets Recovery Agency to SOCA and the National Policing Improvement Agency, see SI 2008/755, art 3).

Sub-s (5): para (b) substituted, for original paras (b), (c), by the Serious Organised Crime and Police Act 2005, s 59, Sch 4, paras 168, 176, as from 1 April 2006; para (ga) inserted by the Commissioners for Revenue and Customs Act 2005, s 50, Sch 4, para 98, as from 18 April 2005; paras (b), (ga) repealed by the Serious Crime Act 2007, ss 74(2), 92, Sch 8, Pt 6, paras 121, 132(1), (4), Sch 14, as from 1 April 2008 (for transitional provisions in relation to the transfer of functions from the Assets Recovery Agency to SOCA and the National Policing Improvement Agency, see SI 2008/755, art 3).

Sub-s (10): added by the Serious Crime Act 2007, s 74(2), Sch 8, Pt 6, paras 121, 132(1), (5), as from 1 April 2008 (for transitional provisions in relation to the transfer of functions from the Assets Recovery Agency to SOCA and the National Policing Improvement Agency, see SI 2008/755, art 3).

Commissioners of Inland Revenue; Commissioners of Customs and Excise: references to the Commissioners of Inland Revenue and the Commissioners of Customs and Excise are now to be taken as a reference to the Commissioners for Her Majesty's Revenue and Customs; see the Commissioners for Revenue and Customs Act 2005, s 50(1), (7). See also s 50(2) of that Act (references to officers of the Board of Inland Revenue and customs officers to be construed as a reference to officers of Revenue and Customs).

Orders: the Proceeds of Crime Act 2002 (Disclosure of Information) Order 2008, SI 2008/1909 at **[4164]**.

437 Further disclosure

(1) Subsection (2) applies to information obtained under section 436 from the Commissioners of Inland Revenue or from the Commissioners of Customs and Excise or from a person acting on behalf of either of them.

(2) Such information must not be further disclosed except—
  (a) for a purpose connected with the exercise of the Director's functions [under, or in relation to, Part 5 or 8], and
  (b) with the consent of the Commissioners concerned.

(3) Consent under subsection (2) may be given—
  (a) in relation to a particular disclosure;
  (b) in relation to disclosures made in circumstances specified or described in the consent.

(4) The power to consent to further disclosure under subsection (2)(b) may be delegated (either generally or for a specified purpose)—
  (a) in the case of the Commissioners of Inland Revenue, to an officer of the Board of Inland Revenue;
  (b) in the case of the Commissioners of Customs and Excise, to a customs officer.

(5) Subsection (6) applies to information obtained under section 436 from a permitted person other than the Commissioners of Inland Revenue or the Commissioners of Customs and Excise or a person acting on behalf of either of them.

(6) A permitted person who discloses such information to the Director may make the disclosure subject to such conditions as to further disclosure by the Director as the permitted person thinks appropriate; and the information must not be further disclosed in contravention of the conditions.

[(7) In this section "the Director" has the same meaning as in section 435.]

[1370]

NOTES

Sub-s (2): words in square brackets inserted by the Serious Crime Act 2007, s 74(2), Sch 8, Pt 6, paras 121, 133(1), (2), as from 1 April 2008 (for transitional provisions in relation to the transfer of functions from the Assets Recovery Agency to SOCA and the National Policing Improvement Agency, see the Serious Crime Act 2007 (Commencement No 2 and Transitional and Transitory Provisions and Savings) Order 2008, SI 2008/755, art 3).

Sub-s (7): added by the Serious Crime Act 2007, s 74(2), Sch 8, Pt 6, paras 121, 133(1), (3), as from 1 April 2008 (for transitional provisions in relation to the transfer of functions from the Assets Recovery Agency to SOCA and the National Policing Improvement Agency, see SI 2008/755, art 3).

Commissioners of Inland Revenue; Commissioners of Customs and Excise, etc: see the note to s 436 at **[1369]**.

438 Disclosure of information by [certain Directors]

(1) Information obtained by or on behalf of the Director in connection with the exercise of any of his functions [under, or in relation to, Part 5 or 8] may be disclosed by him if the disclosure is for the purposes of any of the following—

(a)   any criminal investigation which is being or may be carried out, whether in the United Kingdom or elsewhere;

(b)   any criminal proceedings which have been or may be started, whether in the United Kingdom or elsewhere;

(c)   the exercise of the Director's functions [under, or in relation to, Part 5 or 8];

(d)   the exercise by the prosecutor of functions under Parts 2, 3 and 4;

(e)   the exercise by the Scottish Ministers of their functions under Part 5;

(f)   the exercise by a customs officer[, an accredited financial investigator] or a constable of his functions under Chapter 3 of Part 5;

[(fa)   the exercise of any functions of SOCA, another Director or the Director of Revenue and Customs Prosecutions under, or in relation to, Part 5 or 8;]

(g)   safeguarding national security;

(h)   investigations or proceedings outside the United Kingdom which have led or may lead to the making of an external order within the meaning of section 447;

(i)   the exercise of a designated function.

(2)–(4)   ...

(5)   If the Director makes a disclosure of information for a purpose specified in subsection (1) he may make any further disclosure of the information by the person to whom he discloses it subject to such conditions as he thinks fit.

(6)   Such a person must not further disclose the information in contravention of the conditions.

(7)   A disclosure under this section is not to be taken to breach any restriction on the disclosure of information (however imposed).

(8)   But nothing in this section authorises the making of a disclosure—

(a)   which contravenes the Data Protection Act 1998 (c 29);

(b)   which is prohibited by Part 1 of the Regulation of Investigatory Powers Act 2000 (c 23).

[(8A)   This section does not affect a power to disclose which exists apart from this section.]

(8B)   This section applies to information obtained before the coming into force of subsection (10) as well as to information obtained after the coming into force of that subsection.]

(9)   A designated function is a function which the Secretary of State thinks is a function of a public nature and which he designates by order.

[(10)   In this section "the Director" has the same meaning as in section 435.]

[1371]

NOTES

Section heading: words in square brackets substituted by the Serious Crime Act 2007, s 74(2), Sch 8, Pt 6, paras 121, 134(1), (2), as from 1 April 2008 (for transitional provisions in relation to the transfer of functions from the Assets Recovery Agency to SOCA and the National Policing Improvement Agency, see the Serious Crime Act 2007 (Commencement No 2 and Transitional and Transitory Provisions and Savings) Order 2008, SI 2008/755, art 3).

Sub-s (1): words in first pair of square brackets, words in square brackets in para (c), and para (fa), inserted by the Serious Crime Act 2007, s 74(2), Sch 8, Pt 6, paras 121, 134(1), (3), as from 1 April 2008 (for transitional provisions in relation to the transfer of functions from the Assets Recovery Agency to SOCA and the National Policing Improvement Agency, see SI 2008/755, art 3); words in square brackets in para (f) inserted by s 79 of, and Sch 11, para 14 to, the 2007 Act, as from 6 April 2008.

Sub-ss (2)–(4): repealed by the Serious Crime Act 2007, ss 74(2), 92, Sch 8, Pt 6, paras 121, 134(1), (4), Sch 14, as from 1 April 2008 (for transitional provisions in relation to the transfer of functions from the Assets Recovery Agency to SOCA and the National Policing Improvement Agency, see SI 2008/755, art 3).

Sub-ss (8A), (8B), (10): inserted and added respectively by the Serious Crime Act 2007, s 74(2), Sch 8, Pt 6, paras 121, 134(1), (5), (6), as from 1 April 2008 (for transitional provisions in relation to the transfer of functions from the Assets Recovery Agency to SOCA and the National Policing Improvement Agency, see SI 2008/755, art 3).

Commissioners of Inland Revenue: a reference to the Commissioners of Inland Revenue is now to be taken as a reference to the Commissioners for Her Majesty's Revenue and Customs; see the Commissioners for Revenue and Customs Act 2005, s 50(1), (7).

Orders: the Proceeds of Crime Act 2002 (Disclosure of Information) Order 2008, SI 2008/1909 at [4164].

Overseas purposes

442   Restriction on disclosure for overseas purposes

(1)   Section 18 of the Anti-terrorism, Crime and Security Act 2001 (c 24) (restrictions on disclosure of information for overseas purposes) applies to a disclosure of information authorised by section 438(1)(a) or (b) or 441(2)(a) or (b).

(2)   In the application of section 18 of the Anti-terrorism, Crime and Security Act 2001 by virtue of subsection (1) section 20 of that Act must be ignored and the following subsection is substituted for subsection (2) of section 18 of that Act—

"(2)   In subsection (1) the reference, in relation to a direction, to a relevant disclosure is a reference to a disclosure which—

    (a)   is made for a purpose authorised by section 438(1)(a) or (b) or 441(2)(a) or (b) of the Proceeds of Crime Act 2002, and

    (b)   is of any such information as is described in the direction.".

[1372]

PART 11
CO-OPERATION

443 Enforcement in different parts of the United Kingdom

(1)   Her Majesty may by Order in Council make provision—

    (a)   for an order made by a court under Part 2 to be enforced in Scotland or Northern Ireland;

    (b)   for an order made by a court under Part 3 to be enforced in England and Wales or Northern Ireland;

    (c)   for an order made by a court under Part 4 to be enforced in England and Wales or Scotland;

    (d)   for an order made under Part 8 in one part of the United Kingdom to be enforced in another part;

    (e)   for a warrant issued under Part 8 in one part of the United Kingdom to be executed in another part.

(2)   Her Majesty may by Order in Council make provision—

    (a)   for a function of a receiver appointed in pursuance of Part 2 to be exercisable in Scotland or Northern Ireland;

    (b)   for a function of an administrator appointed in pursuance of Part 3 to be exercisable in England and Wales or Northern Ireland;

    (c)   for a function of a receiver appointed in pursuance of Part 4 to be exercisable in England and Wales or Scotland.

(3)   An Order under this section may include—

    (a)   provision conferring and imposing functions on the prosecutor[, SOCA and the relevant Director];

    (b)   provision about the registration of orders and warrants;

    (c)   provision allowing directions to be given in one part of the United Kingdom about the enforcement there of an order made or warrant issued in another part;

    (d)   provision about the authentication in one part of the United Kingdom of an order made or warrant issued in another part.

(4)   An Order under this section may—

    (a)   amend an enactment;

    (b)   apply an enactment (with or without modifications).

[(5)   In this section "relevant Director" has the meaning given by section 352(5A).]

[1373]

NOTES

Sub-s (3): words in square brackets substituted by the Serious Crime Act 2007, s 74(2), Sch 8, Pt 6, paras 121, 137(1), (2), as from 1 April 2008 (for transitional provisions in relation to the transfer of functions from the Assets Recovery Agency to SOCA and the National Policing Improvement Agency, see the Serious Crime Act 2007 (Commencement No 2 and Transitional and Transitory Provisions and Savings) Order 2008, SI 2008/755, art 3).

Sub-s (5): added by the Serious Crime Act 2007, s 74(2), Sch 8, Pt 6, paras 121, 137(1), (3), as from 1 April 2008 (for transitional provisions in relation to the transfer of functions from the Assets Recovery Agency to SOCA and the National Policing Improvement Agency, see SI 2008/755, art 3).

Orders: the Proceeds of Crime Act 2002 (Enforcement in different parts of the United Kingdom) Order 2002, SI 2002/3133 at [3663]; the Proceeds of Crime Act 2002 (Investigations in different parts of the United Kingdom) Order 2003, SI 2003/425 at [3740].

444 External requests and orders

(1)   Her Majesty may by Order in Council—

    (a)   make provision for a prohibition on dealing with property which is the subject of an external request;

    (b)   make provision for the realisation of property for the purpose of giving effect to an external order.

(2)   An Order under this section may include provision which (subject to any specified modifications) corresponds to any provision of Part 2, 3 or 4 or Part 5 except Chapter 3.

(3)   An Order under this section may include—

    [(a)   provision about the functions of any of the listed persons in relation to external requests and orders;]

    (b)   provision about the registration of external orders;

    (c)   provision about the authentication of any judgment or order of an overseas court, and of any other document connected with such a judgment or order or any proceedings relating to it;

    (d)   provision about evidence (including evidence required to establish whether proceedings have been started or are likely to be started in an overseas court);

    (e)   provision to secure that any person affected by the implementation of an external request or the enforcement of an external order has an opportunity to make representations to a court in the part of the United Kingdom where the request is being implemented or the order is being enforced.

[(4)   For the purposes of subsection (3)(a) "the listed persons" are—

    (a)   the Secretary of State;

    (b)   the Lord Advocate;

    (c)   the Scottish Ministers;

    (d)   [SOCA];

    (e)   the Director of Public Prosecutions;

    (f)   the Director of Public Prosecutions for Northern Ireland;

    (g)   the Director of the Serious Fraud Office; and

    (h)   the Director of Revenue and Customs Prosecutions.]

[1374]

NOTES

Sub-s (3): para (a) substituted by the Serious Organised Crime and Police Act 2005, s 108(1), (2), as from 1 July 2005.

Sub-s (4): added by the Serious Organised Crime and Police Act 2005, s 108(1), (3), as from 1 July 2005; word in square brackets substituted by the Serious Crime Act 2007, s 74(2), Sch 8, Pt 6, paras 121, 138, as from 1 April 2008 (for transitional provisions in relation to the transfer of functions from the Assets Recovery Agency to SOCA and the National Policing Improvement Agency, see the Serious Crime Act 2007 (Commencement No 2 and Transitional and Transitory Provisions and Savings) Order 2008, SI 2008/755, art 3).

Transitional provisions: see also SI 2008/755, art 11 which provides that any modifications made by an Order in Council under this section which correspond to modifications made by the Serious Crime Act 2007, Sch 8 are to be treated as subject to transitional, transitory or saving provisions which correspond to those to which the modifications made by Sch 8 to the 2007 Act are subject by virtue of that Order

Orders: the Proceeds of Crime Act 2002 (External Requests and Orders) Order 2005, SI 2005/3181 at **[3980AA]**.

445 External investigations

(1)   Her Majesty may by Order in Council make—

    (a)   provision to enable orders equivalent to those under Part 8 to be made, and warrants equivalent to those under Part 8 to be issued, for the purposes of an external investigation;

    (b)   provision creating offences in relation to external investigations which are equivalent to offences created by Part 8.

(2)   An Order under this section may include—

    (a)   provision corresponding to any provision of Part 8 (subject to any specified modifications);

    (b)   provision about the functions of the Secretary of State, the Lord Advocate, the Scottish Ministers, [SOCA, the Director of Public Prosecutions, the Director of Public Prosecutions for Northern Ireland, the Director of Revenue and Customs Prosecutions], the Director of the Serious Fraud Office, constables and customs officers;

    (c)   provision about evidence (including evidence required to establish whether an investigation is being carried out in a country or territory outside the United Kingdom).

(3)   But an Order under this section must not provide for a disclosure order to be made for the purposes of an external investigation into whether a money laundering offence has been committed.

[1375]

NOTES

Sub-s (2): words in square brackets substituted by the Serious Crime Act 2007, s 74(2), Sch 8, Pt 6, paras 121, 139, as from 1 April 2008 (for transitional provisions in relation to the transfer of functions from the Assets Recovery Agency to SOCA and the National Policing Improvement Agency, see the Serious Crime Act 2007 (Commencement No 2 and Transitional and Transitory Provisions and Savings) Order 2008, SI 2008/755, art 3).

446 Rules of court

Rules of court may make such provision as is necessary or expedient to give effect to an Order in Council made under this Part (including provision about the exercise of functions of a judge conferred or imposed by the Order).

[1376]

447 Interpretation

(1)   An external request is a request by an overseas authority to prohibit dealing with relevant property which is identified in the request.

(2)   An external order is an order which—
   (a)   is made by an overseas court where property is found or believed to have been obtained as a result of or in connection with criminal conduct, and
   (b)   is for the recovery of specified property or a specified sum of money.

(3)   An external investigation is an investigation by an overseas authority into—
   (a)   whether property has been obtained as a result of or in connection with criminal conduct, ...
   [(aa) the extent or whereabouts of property obtained as a result of or in connection with criminal conduct, or]
   (b)   whether a money laundering offence has been committed.

(4)   Property is all property wherever situated and includes—
   (a)   money;
   (b)   all forms of property, real or personal, heritable or moveable;
   (c)   things in action and other intangible or incorporeal property.

(5)   Property is obtained by a person if he obtains an interest in it.

(6)   References to an interest, in relation to property other than land, include references to a right (including a right to possession).

(7)   Property is relevant property if there are reasonable grounds to believe that it may be needed to satisfy an external order which has been or which may be made.

(8)   Criminal conduct is conduct which—
   (a)   constitutes an offence in any part of the United Kingdom, or
   (b)   would constitute an offence in any part of the United Kingdom if it occurred there.

(9)   A money laundering offence is conduct carried out in a country or territory outside the United Kingdom and which if carried out in the United Kingdom would constitute any of the following offences—
   (a)   an offence under section 327, 328 or 329;
   (b)   an attempt, conspiracy or incitement to commit an offence specified in paragraph (a);
   (c)   aiding, abetting, counselling or procuring the commission of an offence specified in paragraph (a).

(10)   An overseas court is a court of a country or territory outside the United Kingdom.

(11)   An overseas authority is an authority which has responsibility in a country or territory outside the United Kingdom—
   (a)   for making a request to an authority in another country or territory (including the United Kingdom) to prohibit dealing with relevant property,
   (b)   for carrying out an investigation into whether property has been obtained as a result of or in connection with criminal conduct, or
   (c)   for carrying out an investigation into whether a money laundering offence has been committed.

(12)   This section applies for the purposes of this Part.

[1377]

PART II
OTHER ACTS

NOTES

Sub-s (3): word omitted from para (a) repealed, and para (aa) inserted, by the Serious Organised Crime and Police Act 2005, ss 108(1), (4), 174, Sch 17, Pt 2, as from 1 July 2005.

Attempt, conspiracy or incitement to commit an offence: see the Serious Crime Act 2007, s 63(1), (2), Sch 6, Pt 1, para 44 which provides that any reference however expressed to (or to conduct amounting to) the offence abolished by s 59 of the 2007 Act (abolition of common law offence of inciting the commission of another offence) has effect as a reference to (or to conduct amounting to) the offences of encouraging or assisting the commission of an offence.

PART 12
MISCELLANEOUS AND GENERAL

General

458 Commencement

(1)   The preceding provisions of this Act (except the provisions specified in subsection (3)) come into force in accordance with provision made by the Secretary of State by order.

(2)   But no order may be made which includes provision for the commencement of Part 5, 8 or 10 unless the Secretary of State has consulted the Scottish Ministers.

(3)   The following provisions come into force in accordance with provision made by the Scottish Ministers by order after consultation with the Secretary of State—
    (a)   Part 3;
    (b)   this Part, to the extent that it relates to Part 3.

[1378]

NOTES
    Orders: the Proceeds of Crime Act 2002 (Commencement No 1 and Savings) Order 2002, SI 2002/3015; the Proceeds of Crime Act 2002 (Commencement No 2) Order 2002, SI 2002/3055; the Proceeds of Crime Act 2002 (Commencement No 3) Order 2002, SI 2002/3145; the Proceeds of Crime Act 2002 (Commencement No 4, Transitional Provisions and Savings) Order 2003, SI 2003/120 at **[3695]** (bringing most of the provisions reproduced here into force on 24 February 2003); the Proceeds of Crime Act 2002 (Commencement No 5, Transitional Provisions, Savings and Amendment) Order 2003, SI 2003/333 (bringing the remaining provisions reproduced here into force on 24 March 2003); the Proceeds of Crime Act 2002 (Commencement No 5) (Amendment of Transitional Provisions) Order 2003, SI 2003/531; the Proceeds of Crime Act 2002 (Commencement No 6, Transitional Provisions and Savings) (Scotland) Order 2003, SSI 2003/210.

461   Extent

(1)   Part 2 extends to England and Wales only.

(2)   In Part 8, Chapter 2 extends to England and Wales and Northern Ireland only.

(3)   These provisions extend to Scotland only—
    (a)   Part 3;
    (b)   in Part 8, Chapter 3.

(4)   Part 4 extends to Northern Ireland only.

(5)   The amendments in Schedule 11 have the same extent as the provisions amended.

(6)   The repeals and revocations in Schedule 12 have the same extent as the provisions repealed or revoked.

[1379]

462   Short title

This Act may be cited as the Proceeds of Crime Act 2002.

[1380]

SCHEDULES

SCHEDULE 9
REGULATED SECTOR AND SUPERVISORY AUTHORITIES
Section 330

[PART 1
REGULATED SECTOR

Business in the Regulated Sector

1.—(1)   A business is in the regulated sector to the extent that it consists of—
    (a)   the acceptance by a credit institution of deposits or other repayable funds from the public, or the granting by a credit institution of credits for its own account;
    (b)   the carrying on of one or more of the activities listed in points 2 to 12 and 14 of Annex 1 to the Banking Consolidation Directive by an undertaking other than—
        (i)   a credit institution; or
        (ii)   an undertaking whose only listed activity is trading for own account in one or more of the products listed in point 7 of Annex 1 to the Banking Consolidation Directive and which does not act on behalf of a customer (that is, a third party which is not a member of the same group as the undertaking);
    (c)   the carrying on of activities covered by the Life Assurance Consolidation Directive by an insurance company authorised in accordance with that Directive;
    (d)   the provision of investment services or the performance of investment activities by a person (other than a person falling within Article 2 of the Markets in Financial Instruments Directive) whose regular occupation or business is the provision to other persons of an investment service or the performance of an investment activity on a professional basis;
    (e)   the marketing or other offering of units or shares by a collective investment undertaking;
    (f)   the activities of an insurance intermediary as defined in Article 2(5) of the Insurance Mediation Directive, other than a tied insurance intermediary as mentioned in Article 2(7) of that Directive, in respect of contracts of long-term insurance within the meaning given by article 3(1) of, and Part II of Schedule 1 to, the Financial Services and Markets Act 2000 (Regulated Activities) Order 2001;
    (g)   the carrying on of any of the activities mentioned in paragraphs (b) to (f) by a branch

located in an EEA State of a person referred to in those paragraphs (or of an equivalent person in any other State), wherever its head office is located;

(h)   the activities of the National Savings Bank;

(i)   any activity carried on for the purpose of raising money authorised to be raised under the National Loans Act 1968 under the auspices of the Director of Savings;

(j)   the carrying on of statutory audit work within the meaning of section 1210 of the Companies Act 2006 (meaning of "statutory auditor" etc) by any firm or individual who is a statutory auditor within the meaning of Part 42 of that Act (statutory auditors);

(k)   the activities of a person appointed to act as an insolvency practitioner within the meaning of section 388 of the Insolvency Act 1986 (meaning of "act as insolvency practitioner") or article 3 of the Insolvency (Northern Ireland) Order 1989;

(l)   the provision to other persons of accountancy services by a firm or sole practitioner who by way of business provides such services to other persons;

(m)   the provision of advice about the tax affairs of other persons by a firm or sole practitioner who by way of business provides advice about the tax affairs of other persons;

(n)   the participation in financial or real property transactions concerning—
(i)   the buying and selling of real property (or, in Scotland, heritable property) or business entities;
(ii)   the managing of client money, securities or other assets;
(iii)   the opening or management of bank, savings or securities accounts;
(iv)   the organisation of contributions necessary for the creation, operation or management of companies; or
(v)   the creation, operation or management of trusts, companies or similar structures,
by a firm or sole practitioner who by way of business provides legal or notarial services to other persons;

(o)   the provision to other persons by way of business by a firm or sole practitioner of any of the services mentioned in sub-paragraph (4);

(p)   the carrying on of estate agency work (within the meaning given by section 1 of the Estate Agents Act 1979 (estate agency work)) by a firm or a sole practitioner who carries on, or whose employees carry on, such work;

(q)   the trading in goods (including dealing as an auctioneer) whenever a transaction involves the receipt of a payment or payments in cash of at least 15,000 euros in total, whether the transaction is executed in a single operation or in several operations which appear to be linked, by a firm or sole trader who by way of business trades in goods;

(r)   operating a casino under a casino operating licence (within the meaning given by section 65(2) of the Gambling Act 2005 (nature of licence)).

(2)   For the purposes of sub-paragraph (1)(a) and (b) "credit institution" means—
(a)   a credit institution as defined in Article 4(1)(a) of the Banking Consolidation Directive; or
(b)   a branch (within the meaning of Article 4(3) of that Directive) located in an EEA state of an institution falling within paragraph (a) (or of an equivalent institution in any other State) wherever its head office is located.

(3)   For the purposes of sub-paragraph (1)(n) a person participates in a transaction by assisting in the planning or execution of the transaction or otherwise acting for or on behalf of a client in the transaction.

(4)   The services referred to in sub-paragraph (1)(o) are—
(a)   forming companies or other legal persons;
(b)   acting, or arranging for another person to act—
(i)   as a director or secretary of a company;
(ii)   as a partner of a partnership; or
(iii)   in a similar position in relation to other legal persons;
(c)   providing a registered office, business address, correspondence or administrative address or other related services for a company, partnership or any other legal person or arrangement;
(d)   acting, or arranging for another person to act, as—
(i)   a trustee of an express trust or similar legal arrangement; or
(ii)   a nominee shareholder for a person other than a company whose securities are listed on a regulated market.

(5)   For the purposes of sub-paragraph (4)(d) "regulated market"—
(a)   in relation to any EEA State, has the meaning given by point 14 of Article 4(1) of the Markets in Financial Instruments Directive; and
(b)   in relation to any other State, means a regulated financial market which subjects companies whose securities are admitted to trading to disclosure obligations which are contained in international standards and are equivalent to the specified disclosure obligations.

(6)   For the purposes of sub-paragraph (5) "the specified disclosure obligations" means disclosure requirements consistent with—

- (a)   Article 6(1) to (4) of Directive 2003/6/EC of the European Parliament and of the Council of 28th January 2003 on insider dealing and market manipulation;
- (b)   Articles 3, 5, 7, 8, 10, 14 and 16 of Directive 2003/71/EC of the European Parliament and of the Council of 4th November 2003 on the prospectuses to be published when securities are offered to the public or admitted to trading;
- (c)   Articles 4 to 6, 14, 16 to 19 and 30 of Directive 2004/109/EC of the European Parliament and of the Council of 15th December 2004 relating to the harmonisation of transparency requirements in relation to information about issuers whose securities are admitted to trading on a regulated market; or
- (d)   Community legislation made under the provisions mentioned in paragraphs (a) to (c).

(7)   For the purposes of sub-paragraph (1)(j) and (l) to (q) "firm" means any entity, whether or not a legal person, that is not an individual and includes a body corporate and a partnership or other unincorporated association.

(8)   For the purposes of sub-paragraph (1)(q) "cash" means notes, coins or travellers' cheques in any currency.

Excluded Activities

2.—(1)   A business is not in the regulated sector to the extent that it consists of—

- (a)   the issuing of withdrawable share capital within the limit set by section 6 of the Industrial and Provident Societies Act 1965 (maximum shareholding in society), or the acceptance of deposits from the public within the limit set by section 7(3) of that Act (carrying on of banking by societies), by a society registered under that Act;
- (b)   the issuing of withdrawable share capital within the limit set by section 6 of the Industrial and Provident Societies Act (Northern Ireland) 1969 (maximum shareholding in society), or the acceptance of deposits from the public within the limit set by section 7(3) of that Act (carrying on of banking by societies), by a society registered under that Act;
- (c)   the carrying on of any activity in respect of which a person who is (or falls within a class of persons) specified in any of paragraphs 2 to 23, 25 to 38 or 40 to 49 of the Schedule to the Financial Services and Markets Act 2000 (Exemption) Order 2001 is exempt;
- (d)   the exercise of the functions specified in section 45 of the Financial Services Act 1986 (miscellaneous exemptions) by a person who was an exempted person for the purposes of that section immediately before its repeal;
- (e)   the engaging in financial activity which fulfils all of the conditions set out in paragraphs (a) to (g) of sub-paragraph (3) of this paragraph by a person whose main activity is that of a high value dealer; or
- (f)   the preparation of a home information pack (within the meaning of Part 5 of the Housing Act 2004 (home information packs)) or a document or information for inclusion in a home information pack.

(2)   For the purposes of sub-paragraph (1)(e) a "high value dealer" means a person mentioned in paragraph 1(1)(q) when carrying on the activities mentioned in that paragraph.

(3)   A business is not in the regulated sector to the extent that it consists of financial activity if—

- (a)   the person's total annual turnover in respect of the financial activity does not exceed £64,000;
- (b)   the financial activity is limited in relation to any customer to no more than one transaction exceeding 1,000 euros, whether the transaction is carried out in a single operation, or a series of operations which appear to be linked;
- (c)   the financial activity does not exceed 5% of the person's total annual turnover;
- (d)   the financial activity is ancillary to the person's main activity and directly related to that activity;
- (e)   the financial activity is not the transmission or remittance of money (or any representation of monetary value) by any means;
- (f)   the main activity of the person carrying on the financial activity is not an activity mentioned in paragraph 1(1)(a) to (p) or (r); and
- (g)   the financial activity is provided only to customers of the person's main activity and is not offered to the public.

(4)   A business is not in the regulated sector if it is carried on by—

- (a)   the Auditor General for Scotland;
- (b)   the Auditor General for Wales;
- (c)   the Bank of England;
- (d)   the Comptroller and Auditor General;
- (e)   the Comptroller and Auditor General for Northern Ireland;

(f)   the Official Solicitor to the Supreme Court, when acting as trustee in his official capacity; or

(g)   the Treasury Solicitor.

Interpretation

3.—(1)   In this Part—

"the Banking Consolidation Directive" means directive 2006/48/EC of the European Parliament and of the Council of 14th June 2006 relating to the taking up and pursuit of the business of credit institutions;

"the Insurance Mediation Directive" means directive 2002/92/EC of the European Parliament and of the Council of 9th December 2002 on insurance mediation;

"the Life Assurance Consolidation Directive" means directive 2002/83/EC of the European Parliament and of the Council of 5th November 2002 concerning life assurance; and

"the Markets in Financial Instruments Directive" means directive 2004/39/EC of the European Parliament and of the Council of 12th April 2004 on markets in financial instruments.

(2)   In this Part references to amounts in euros include references to equivalent amounts in another currency.

(3)   Terms used in this Part and in the Banking Consolidation Directive or the Markets in Financial Instruments Directive have the same meaning in this Part as in those Directives.]

[1381]

NOTES

Commencement: 15 December 2007.

Substituted by the Proceeds of Crime Act 2002 (Business in the Regulated Sector and Supervisory Authorities) Order 2007, SI 2007/3287, art 2, as from 15 December 2007.

[PART 2
SUPERVISORY AUTHORITIES

4.—(1)   The following bodies are supervisory authorities—

(a)   the Commissioners for Her Majesty's Revenue and Customs;

(b)   the Department of Enterprise, Trade and Investment in Northern Ireland;

(c)   the Financial Services Authority;

(d)   the Gambling Commission;

(e)   the Office of Fair Trading;

(f)   the Secretary of State; and

(g)   the professional bodies listed in sub-paragraph (2).

(2)   The professional bodies referred to in sub-paragraph (1)(g) are—

(a)   the Association of Accounting Technicians;

(b)   the Association of Chartered Certified Accountants;

(c)   the Association of International Accountants;

(d)   the Association of Taxation Technicians;

(e)   the Chartered Institute of Management Accountants;

(f)   the Chartered Institute of Public Finance and Accountancy;

(g)   the Chartered Institute of Taxation;

(h)   the Council for Licensed Conveyancers;

(i)   the Faculty of Advocates;

(j)   the Faculty Office of the Archbishop of Canterbury;

(k)   the General Council of the Bar;

(l)   the General Council of the Bar of Northern Ireland;

(m)   the Insolvency Practitioners Association;

(n)   the Institute of Certified Bookkeepers;

(o)   the Institute of Chartered Accountants in England and Wales;

(p)   the Institute of Chartered Accountants in Ireland;

(q)   the Institute of Chartered Accountants of Scotland;

(r)   the Institute of Financial Accountants;

(s)   the International Association of Book-keepers;

(t)   the Law Society;

(u)   the Law Society for Northern Ireland; and

(v)   the Law Society of Scotland.]

[1382]

NOTES

Commencement: 15 December 2007.

Substituted by the Proceeds of Crime Act 2002 (Business in the Regulated Sector and Supervisory Authorities) Order 2007, SI 2007/3287, art 2, as from 15 December 2007.

PART 3
POWER TO AMEND

5.   The Treasury may by order amend Part 1 or 2 of this Schedule.

[1383]

NOTES
Orders: the Proceeds of Crime Act 2002 (Business in the Regulated Sector and Supervisory Authorities) Order 2007, SI 2007/3287 (which supersedes all other amending SIs made under para 5).

ENTERPRISE ACT 2002

(2002 c 40)

NOTES
Only provisions of this Act relevant to Financial Services law are reproduced. Provisions not reproduced are not annotated.
   This Act is reproduced as amended by: the Communications Act 2003; the Railways and Transport Safety Act 2003; the Water Act 2003; the Railways Act 2005; the EC Merger Control (Consequential Amendments) Regulations 2004, SI 2004/1079; the Railways Infrastructure (Access, Management and Licensing of Railway Undertakings) Regulations (Northern Ireland) 2005, SR 2005/537; the Water and Sewerage Services (Northern Ireland) Order 2006, SI 2006/3336; the Enterprise Act 2002 (Specification of Additional Section 58 Consideration) Order 2008, SI 2008/2645.

ARRANGEMENT OF SECTIONS

PART 1
THE OFFICE OF FAIR TRADING

Establishment of OFT

General functions of OFT

PART 4
MARKET INVESTIGATIONS

CHAPTER 1
MARKET INVESTIGATION REFERENCES

Making of references

Determination of references

CHAPTER 2
PUBLIC INTEREST CASES

Intervention notices

Intervention notices under section 139(1)

Establish and provide for the functions of the Office of Fair Trading, the Competition Appeal Tribunal and the Competition Service; to make provision about mergers and market structures and conduct; to amend the constitution and functions of the Competition Commission; to create an offence for those entering into certain anti-competitive agreements; to provide for the disqualification of directors of companies engaging in certain anti-competitive practices; to make other provision about competition law; to amend the law relating to the protection of the collective interests of consumers; to make further provision about the disclosure of information obtained under competition and consumer legislation; to amend the Insolvency Act 1986 and make other provision about insolvency; and for connected purposes

[7 November 2002]

PART 1
THE OFFICE OF FAIR TRADING
Establishment of OFT

1   The Office of Fair Trading

(1)   There shall be a body corporate to be known as the Office of Fair Trading (in this Act referred to as "the OFT").

(2)   The functions of the OFT are carried out on behalf of the Crown.

(3)   Schedule 1 (which makes further provision about the OFT) has effect.

(4)   In managing its affairs the OFT shall have regard, in addition to any relevant general guidance as to the governance of public bodies, to such generally accepted principles of good corporate governance as it is reasonable to regard as applicable to the OFT.

[1384]

2   The Director General of Fair Trading

(1)   The functions of the Director General of Fair Trading (in this Act referred to as "the Director"), and his property, rights and liabilities, are transferred to the OFT.

(2)   The office of the Director is abolished.

(3)   Any enactment, instrument or other document passed or made before the commencement of subsection (1) which refers to the Director shall have effect, so far as necessary for the purposes of or in consequence of anything being transferred, as if any reference to the Director were a reference to the OFT.

[1385]

3   Annual plan

(1)   The OFT shall, before each financial year, publish a document (the "annual plan") containing a statement of its main objectives and priorities for the year.

(2)   The OFT shall for the purposes of public consultation publish a document containing proposals for its annual plan at least two months before publishing the annual plan for any year.

(3)   The OFT shall lay before Parliament a copy of each document published under subsection (2) and each annual plan.

[1386]

4   Annual and other reports

(1)   The OFT shall, as soon as practicable after the end of each financial year, make to the Secretary of State a report (the "annual report") on its activities and performance during that year.

(2)   The annual report for each year shall include—

(a)   a general survey of developments in respect of matters relating to the OFT's functions;

(b)   an assessment of the extent to which the OFT's main objectives and priorities for the year (as set out in the annual plan) have been met;

    (c)   a summary of the significant decisions, investigations or other activities made or carried out by the OFT during the year;

    (d)   a summary of the allocation of the OFT's financial resources to its various activities during the year; and

    (e)   an assessment of the OFT's performance and practices in relation to its enforcement functions.

(3)   The OFT shall lay a copy of each annual report before Parliament and arrange for the report to be published.

(4)   The OFT may—

    (a)   prepare other reports in respect of matters relating to any of its functions; and

    (b)   arrange for any such report to be published.

[1387]

General functions of OFT

5 Acquisition of information etc

(1)   The OFT has the function of obtaining, compiling and keeping under review information about matters relating to the carrying out of its functions.

(2)   That function is to be carried out with a view to (among other things) ensuring that the OFT has sufficient information to take informed decisions and to carry out its other functions effectively.

(3)   In carrying out that function the OFT may carry out, commission or support (financially or otherwise) research.

[1388]

6 Provision of information etc to the public

(1)   The OFT has the function of—

    (a)   making the public aware of the ways in which competition may benefit consumers in, and the economy of, the United Kingdom; and

    (b)   giving information or advice in respect of matters relating to any of its functions to the public.

(2)   In carrying out those functions the OFT may—

    (a)   publish educational materials or carry out other educational activities; or

    (b)   support (financially or otherwise) the carrying out by others of such activities or the provision by others of information or advice.

[1389]

7 Provision of information and advice to Ministers etc

(1)   The OFT has the function of—

    (a)   making proposals, or

    (b)   giving other information or advice,

on matters relating to any of its functions to any Minister of the Crown or other public authority (including proposals, information or advice as to any aspect of the law or a proposed change in the law).

(2)   A Minister of the Crown may request the OFT to make proposals or give other information or advice on any matter relating to any of its functions; and the OFT shall, so far as is reasonably practicable and consistent with its other functions, comply with the request.

[1390]

8 Promoting good consumer practice

(1)   The OFT has the function of promoting good practice in the carrying out of activities which may affect the economic interests of consumers in the United Kingdom.

(2)   In carrying out that function the OFT may (without prejudice to the generality of subsection (1)) make arrangements for approving consumer codes and may, in accordance with the arrangements, give its approval to or withdraw its approval from any consumer code.

(3)   Any such arrangements must specify the criteria to be applied by the OFT in determining whether to give approval to or withdraw approval from a consumer code.

(4)   Any such arrangements may in particular—

    (a)   specify descriptions of consumer code which may be the subject of an application to the OFT for approval (and any such description may be framed by reference to any feature of a consumer code, including the persons who are, or are to be, subject to the code, the manner in which it is, or is to be, operated and the persons responsible for its operation); and

    (b)   provide for the use in accordance with the arrangements of an official symbol intended to signify that a consumer code is approved by the OFT.

PART II
OTHER ACTS

(5)   The OFT shall publish any arrangements under subsection (2) in such manner it considers appropriate.

(6)   In this section "consumer code" means a code of practice or other document (however described) intended, with a view to safeguarding or promoting the interests of consumers, to regulate by any means the conduct of persons engaged in the supply of goods or services to consumers (or the conduct of their employees or representatives).

[1391]

PART 4
MARKET INVESTIGATIONS

CHAPTER 1
MARKET INVESTIGATION REFERENCES

Making of references

131   Power of OFT to make references

(1)   The OFT may, subject to subsection (4), make a reference to the Commission if the OFT has reasonable grounds for suspecting that any feature, or combination of features, of a market in the United Kingdom for goods or services prevents, restricts or distorts competition in connection with the supply or acquisition of any goods or services in the United Kingdom or a part of the United Kingdom.

(2)   For the purposes of this Part any reference to a feature of a market in the United Kingdom for goods or services shall be construed as a reference to—
  (a)   the structure of the market concerned or any aspect of that structure;
  (b)   any conduct (whether or not in the market concerned) of one or more than one person who supplies or acquires goods or services in the market concerned; or
  (c)   any conduct relating to the market concerned of customers of any person who supplies or acquires goods or services.

(3)   In subsection (2) "conduct" includes any failure to act (whether or not intentional) and any other unintentional conduct.

(4)   No reference shall be made under this section if—
  (a)   the making of the reference is prevented by section 156(1); or
  (b)   a reference has been made under section 132 in relation to the same matter but has not been finally determined.

(5)   References in this Part to a market investigation reference being finally determined shall be construed in accordance with section 183(3) to (6).

(6)   In this Part—
  "market in the United Kingdom" includes—
      (a)   so far as it operates in the United Kingdom or a part of the United Kingdom, any market which operates there and in another country or territory or in a part of another country or territory; and
      (b)   any market which operates only in a part of the United Kingdom;
  "market investigation reference" means a reference under this section or section 132;

and references to a market for goods or services include references to a market for goods and services.

[1392]

132   Ministerial power to make references

(1)   Subsection (3) applies where, in relation to any goods or services, the appropriate Minister is not satisfied with a decision of the OFT not to make a reference under section 131.

(2)   Subsection (3) also applies where, in relation to any goods or services, the appropriate Minister—
  (a)   has brought to the attention of the OFT information which the appropriate Minister considers to be relevant to the question of whether the OFT should make a reference under section 131; but
  (b)   is not satisfied that the OFT will decide, within such period as the appropriate Minister considers to be reasonable, whether to make such a reference.

(3)   The appropriate Minister may, subject to subsection (4), make a reference to the Commission if he has reasonable grounds for suspecting that any feature, or combination of features, of a market in the United Kingdom for goods or services prevents, restricts or distorts competition in connection with the supply or acquisition of any goods or services in the United Kingdom or a part of the United Kingdom.

(4)   No reference shall be made under this section if the making of the reference is prevented by section 156(1).

(5)   In this Part "the appropriate Minister" means—
- (a)   the Secretary of State; or
- (b)   the Secretary of State and one or more than one other Minister of the Crown acting jointly.

[1393]

133   Contents of references

(1)   A market investigation reference shall, in particular, specify—
- (a)   the enactment under which it is made;
- (b)   the date on which it is made; and
- (c)   the description of goods or services to which the feature or combination of features concerned relates.

(2)   A market investigation reference may be framed so as to require the Commission to confine its investigation into the effects of features of markets in the United Kingdom for goods or services of a description specified in the reference to the effects of features of such of those markets as exist in connection with—
- (a)   a supply, of a description specified in the reference, of the goods or services concerned; or
- (b)   an acquisition, of a description specified in the reference, of the goods or services concerned.

(3)   A description of the kind mentioned in subsection (2)(a) or (b) may, in particular, be by reference to—
- (a)   the place where the goods or services are supplied or acquired; or
- (b)   the persons by or to whom they are supplied or by or from whom they are acquired.

[1394]

Determination of references

134   Questions to be decided on market investigation references

(1)   The Commission shall, on a market investigation reference, decide whether any feature, or combination of features, of each relevant market prevents, restricts or distorts competition in connection with the supply or acquisition of any goods or services in the United Kingdom or a part of the United Kingdom.

(2)   For the purposes of this Part, in relation to a market investigation reference, there is an adverse effect on competition if any feature, or combination of features, of a relevant market prevents, restricts or distorts competition in connection with the supply or acquisition of any goods or services in the United Kingdom or a part of the United Kingdom.

(3)   In subsections (1) and (2) "relevant market" means—
- (a)   in the case of subsection (2) so far as it applies in connection with a possible reference, a market in the United Kingdom—
  - (i)   for goods or services of a description to be specified in the reference; and
  - (ii)   which would not be excluded from investigation by virtue of section 133(2); and
- (b)   in any other case, a market in the United Kingdom—
  - (i)   for goods or services of a description specified in the reference concerned; and
  - (ii)   which is not excluded from investigation by virtue of section 133(2).

(4)   The Commission shall, if it has decided on a market investigation reference that there is an adverse effect on competition, decide the following additional questions—
- (a)   whether action should be taken by it under section 138 for the purpose of remedying, mitigating or preventing the adverse effect on competition concerned or any detrimental effect on customers so far as it has resulted from, or may be expected to result from, the adverse effect on competition;
- (b)   whether it should recommend the taking of action by others for the purpose of remedying, mitigating or preventing the adverse effect on competition concerned or any detrimental effect on customers so far as it has resulted from, or may be expected to result from, the adverse effect on competition; and
- (c)   in either case, if action should be taken, what action should be taken and what is to be remedied, mitigated or prevented.

(5)   For the purposes of this Part, in relation to a market investigation reference, there is a detrimental effect on customers if there is a detrimental effect on customers or future customers in the form of—
- (a)   higher prices, lower quality or less choice of goods or services in any market in the United Kingdom (whether or not the market to which the feature or features concerned relate); or

(b)   less innovation in relation to such goods or services.

(6)   In deciding the questions mentioned in subsection (4), the Commission shall, in particular, have regard to the need to achieve as comprehensive a solution as is reasonable and practicable to the adverse effect on competition and any detrimental effects on customers so far as resulting from the adverse effect on competition.

(7)   In deciding the questions mentioned in subsection (4), the Commission may, in particular, have regard to the effect of any action on any relevant customer benefits of the feature or features of the market concerned.

(8)   For the purposes of this Part a benefit is a relevant customer benefit of a feature or features of a market if—

    (a)   it is a benefit to customers or future customers in the form of—

        (i)   lower prices, higher quality or greater choice of goods or services in any market in the United Kingdom (whether or not the market to which the feature or features concerned relate); or

        (ii) greater innovation in relation to such goods or services; and

    (b)   the Commission, the Secretary of State or (as the case may be) the OFT believes that—

        (i)   the benefit has accrued as a result (whether wholly or partly) of the feature or features concerned or may be expected to accrue within a reasonable period as a result (whether wholly or partly) of that feature or those features; and

        (ii) the benefit was, or is, unlikely to accrue without the feature or features concerned.

[1395]

135 Variation of market investigation references

(1)   The OFT or (as the case may be) the appropriate Minister may at any time vary a market investigation reference made by it or (as the case may be) him.

(2)   The OFT or (as the case may be) the appropriate Minister shall consult the Commission before varying any such reference.

(3)   Subsection (2) shall not apply if the Commission has requested the variation concerned.

(4)   No variation under this section shall be capable of altering the period permitted by section 137 within which the report of the Commission under section 136 is to be prepared and published or (as the case may be) the period permitted by section 144 within which the report of the Commission under section 142 is to be prepared and published or given.

[1396]

136 Investigations and reports on market investigation references

(1)   The Commission shall prepare and publish a report on a market investigation reference within the period permitted by section 137.

(2)   The report shall, in particular, contain—

    (a)   the decisions of the Commission on the questions which it is required to answer by virtue of section 134;

    (b)   its reasons for its decisions; and

    (c)   such information as the Commission considers appropriate for facilitating a proper understanding of those questions and of its reasons for its decisions.

(3)   The Commission shall carry out such investigations as it considers appropriate for the purposes of preparing a report under this section.

(4)   The Commission shall, at the same time as a report under this section is published—

    (a)   in the case of a reference under section 131, give it to the OFT; and

    (b)   in the case of a reference under section 132, give it to the appropriate Minister and give a copy of it to the OFT.

(5)   Where a reference has been made by the OFT under section 131 or by the appropriate Minister under section 132 in circumstances in which a reference could have been made by a relevant sectoral regulator under section 131 as it has effect by virtue of a relevant sectoral enactment, the Commission shall, at the same time as the report under this section is published, give a copy of it to the relevant sectoral regulator concerned.

(6)   Where a reference has been made by a relevant sectoral regulator under section 131 as it has effect by virtue of a relevant sectoral enactment, the Commission shall, at the same time as the report under this section is published, give a copy of it to the OFT.

(7)   In this Part "relevant sectoral enactment" means—

    (a)   ...

    (b)   in relation to the Gas and Electricity Markets Authority, section 36A of the Gas Act 1986 (c 44) or (as the case may be) section 43 of the Electricity Act 1989 (c 29);

    (c)   in relation to [the Water Services Regulation Authority], section 31 of the Water Industry Act 1991 (c 56);

    (d)   ...

(e)   in relation to [the Office of Rail Regulation], section 67 of the Railways Act 1993 (c 43);
(f)   ...
(g)   in relation to the Civil Aviation Authority, section 86 of the Transport Act 2000 (c 38);
[(h)   in relation to the Office of Communications, sections 370 and 371 of the Communications Act 2003];
[(h)   in relation to the Northern Ireland Authority for Utility Regulation, Article 46 of the Electricity (Northern Ireland) Order 1992, Article 23 of the Gas (Northern Ireland) Order 1996 or Article 29 of the Water and Sewerage Services (Northern Ireland) Order 2006].

(8)   In this Part "relevant sectoral regulator" means ... the Gas and Electricity Markets Authority, [the Water Services Regulation Authority], ... , [the Office of Rail Regulation], ... [, the Civil Aviation Authority or the Office of Communications] [or the Northern Ireland Authority for Utility Regulation].

(9)   The Secretary of State may by order modify subsection (7) or (8).

[1397]

NOTES
Sub-s (7) is amended as follows:
Para (a) repealed, and first para (h) added, by the Communications Act 2003, s 406(1), (7), Sch 17, para 174(1), (4)(a), Sch 19, as from 25 July 2003 (certain purposes), and as from 29 December 2003 (otherwise).
Words in square brackets in para (c) substituted by the Water Act 2003, s 101(1), Sch 7, Pt 2, para 36(1), (2), as from 1 April 2006.
Paras (d), (f) repealed, and second para (h) inserted, by the Water and Sewerage Services (Northern Ireland) Order 2006, SI 2006/3336, art 308, Sch 12, para 46(1), Sch 13, as from 1 April 2007.
Words in square brackets in para (e) substituted by the Railways and Transport Safety Act 2003, s 16(5), Sch 2, Pt 2, para 19(u), as from 5 July 2004.
Sub-s (8) is amended as follows:
First words omitted repealed, and words in the penultimate pair of square brackets substituted, by the Communications Act 2003, s 406(7), Sch 19(1), as from 25 July 2003 (certain purposes) and as from 29 December 2003 (otherwise).
Words in first pair of square brackets substituted by the Water Act 2003, s 101(1), Sch 7, Pt 2, para 36(1), (2), as from 1 April 2006.
Second and third words omitted repealed, and words in final pair of square brackets inserted, by SI 2006/3336, art 308, Sch 12, para 46(2), Sch 13, as from 1 April 2007.
Words in second pair of square brackets substituted by the Railways and Transport Safety Act 2003, s 16(5), Sch 2, Pt 2, para 19(u), as from 5 July 2004.

137 Time-limits for market investigations and reports

(1)   The Commission shall prepare and publish its report under section 136 within the period of two years beginning with the date of the market investigation reference concerned.

(2)   Subsection (1) is subject to section 151(3) and (5).

(3)   The Secretary of State may by order amend subsection (1) so as to alter the period of two years mentioned in that subsection or any period for the time being mentioned in that subsection in substitution for that period.

(4)   No alteration shall be made by virtue of subsection (3) which results in the period for the time being mentioned in subsection (1) exceeding two years.

(5)   An order under subsection (3) shall not affect any period of time within which the Commission is under a duty to prepare and publish its report under section 136 in relation to a market investigation reference if the Commission is already under that duty in relation to that reference when the order is made.

(6)   Before making an order under subsection (3) the Secretary of State shall consult the Commission and such other persons as he considers appropriate.

(7)   References in this Part to the date of a market investigation reference shall be construed as references to the date specified in the reference as the date on which it is made.

[1398]

138 Duty to remedy adverse effects

(1)   Subsection (2) applies where a report of the Commission has been prepared and published under section 136 within the period permitted by section 137 and contains the decision that there is one or more than one adverse effect on competition.

(2)   The Commission shall, in relation to each adverse effect on competition, take such action under section 159 or 161 as it considers to be reasonable and practicable—
(a)   to remedy, mitigate or prevent the adverse effect on competition concerned; and
(b)   to remedy, mitigate or prevent any detrimental effects on customers so far as they have resulted from, or may be expected to result from, the adverse effect on competition.

(3)   The decisions of the Commission under subsection (2) shall be consistent with its decisions as included in its report by virtue of section 134(4) unless there has been a material change of circumstances since the preparation of the report or the Commission otherwise has a special reason for deciding differently.

(4)   In making a decision under subsection (2), the Commission shall, in particular, have regard to the need to achieve as comprehensive a solution as is reasonable and practicable to the adverse effect on competition concerned and any detrimental effects on customers so far as resulting from the adverse effect on competition.

(5)   In making a decision under subsection (2), the Commission may, in particular, have regard to the effect of any action on any relevant customer benefits of the feature or features of the market concerned.

(6)   The Commission shall take no action under subsection (2) to remedy, mitigate or prevent any detrimental effect on customers so far as it may be expected to result from the adverse effect on competition concerned if—
(a)   no detrimental effect on customers has resulted from the adverse effect on competition; and
(b)   the adverse effect on competition is not being remedied, mitigated or prevented.

[1399]

CHAPTER 2
PUBLIC INTEREST CASES

Intervention notices

139 Public interest intervention by Secretary of State

(1)   The Secretary of State may give a notice to the Commission if—
(a)   a market investigation reference has been made to the Commission;
(b)   no more than four months has passed since the date of the reference;
(c)   the reference is not finally determined; and
(d)   the Secretary of State believes that it is or may be the case that one or more than one public interest consideration is relevant to the case.

(2)   The Secretary of State may give a notice to the OFT if—
(a)   the OFT is considering whether to accept—
(i)   an undertaking under section 154 instead of making a reference under section 131; or
(ii)   an undertaking varying or superseding any such undertaking;
(b)   the OFT has published a notice under section 155(1) or (4); and
(c)   the Secretary of State believes that it is or may be the case that one or more than one public interest consideration is relevant to the case.

(3)   In this Part "intervention notice" means a notice under subsection (1) or (2).

(4)   No more than one intervention notice shall be given under subsection (1) in relation to the same market investigation reference and no more than one intervention notice shall be given under subsection (2) in relation to the same proposed undertaking or in relation to proposed undertakings which do not differ from each other in any material respect.

(5)   For the purposes of this Part a public interest consideration is a consideration which, at the time of the giving of the intervention notice concerned, is specified in section 153 or is not so specified but, in the opinion of the Secretary of State, ought to be so specified.

(6)   Where the Secretary of State has given an intervention notice mentioning a public interest consideration which, at that time, is not finalised, he shall, as soon as practicable, take such action as is within his power to ensure that it is finalised.

(7)   For the purposes of this Part a public interest consideration is finalised if—
(a)   it is specified in section 153 otherwise than by virtue of an order under subsection (3) of that section; or
(b)   it is specified in that section by virtue of an order under subsection (3) of that section and the order providing for it to be so specified has been laid before, and approved by, Parliament in accordance with subsection (6) of section 181 and within the period mentioned in that subsection.

[1400]

Intervention notices under section 139(1)

140 Intervention notices under section 139(1)

(1)   An intervention notice under section 139(1) shall state—
(a)   the market investigation reference concerned;
(b)   the date of the market investigation reference concerned;

   (c)   the public interest consideration or considerations which are, or may be, relevant to the case; and

   (d)   where any public interest consideration concerned is not finalised, the proposed timetable for finalising it.

(2)   Where the Secretary of State believes that it is or may be the case that two or more public interest considerations are relevant to the case, he may decide not to mention in the intervention notice such of those considerations as he considers appropriate.

(3)   The Secretary of State may at any time revoke an intervention notice which has been given under section 139(1) and which is in force.

(4)   An intervention notice under section 139(1) shall come into force when it is given and shall cease to be in force when the matter to which it relates is finally determined under this Chapter.

(5)   For the purposes of subsection (4) a matter to which an intervention notice under section 139(1) relates is finally determined under this Chapter if—

   (a)   the period permitted by section 144 for the preparation of the report of the Commission under section 142 and for action to be taken in relation to it under section 143(1) or (3) has expired and no such report has been so prepared or no such action has been taken;

   (b)   the Commission decides under section 145(1) to terminate its investigation;

   (c)   the report of the Commission has been prepared under section 142 and published under section 143(1) within the period permitted by section 144;

   (d)   the Secretary of State fails to make and publish a decision under subsection (2) of section 146 within the period required by subsection (3) of that section;

   (e)   the Secretary of State decides under section 146(2) that no eligible public interest consideration is relevant;

   (f)   the Secretary of State decides under section 147(2) neither to accept an undertaking under section 159 nor to make an order under section 161;

   (g)   the Secretary of State accepts an undertaking under section 159 or makes an order under section 161; or

   (h)   the Secretary of State decides to revoke the intervention notice concerned.

(6)   For the purposes of subsections (4) and (5) the time when a matter to which an intervention notice under section 139(1) relates is finally determined under this Chapter is—

   (a)   in a case falling within subsection (5)(a) or (d), the expiry of the period concerned;

   (b)   in a case falling within subsection (5)(b), (e), (f) or (h), the making of the decision concerned;

   (c)   in a case falling within subsection (5)(c), the publication of the report concerned; and

   (d)   in a case falling within subsection (5)(g), the acceptance of the undertaking concerned or (as the case may be) the making of the order concerned.

(7)   In subsection (6)(d) the reference to the acceptance of the undertaking concerned or the making of the order concerned shall, in a case where the enforcement action under section 147(2) involves the acceptance of a group of undertakings, the making of a group of orders or the acceptance and making of a group of undertakings and orders, be treated as a reference to the acceptance or making of the last undertaking or order in the group; but undertakings or orders which vary, supersede or revoke earlier undertakings or orders shall be disregarded for the purposes of subsections (5)(g) and (6)(d).

        [1401]

141   Questions to be decided by Commission

(1)   This section applies where an intervention notice under section 139(1) is in force in relation to a market investigation reference.

(2)   The Commission shall decide whether any feature, or combination of features, of each relevant market (within the meaning given by section 134(3)) prevents, restricts or distorts competition in connection with the supply or acquisition of any goods or services in the United Kingdom or a part of the United Kingdom.

(3)   The Commission shall, if it has decided that there is an adverse effect on competition, decide the following additional questions—

   (a)   whether action should be taken by the Secretary of State under section 147 for the purpose of remedying, mitigating or preventing the adverse effect on competition concerned or any detrimental effect on customers so far as it has resulted from, or may be expected to result from, the adverse effect on competition;

   (b)   whether the Commission should recommend the taking of other action by the Secretary of State or action by persons other than itself and the Secretary of State for the purpose of remedying, mitigating or preventing the adverse effect on competition concerned or any detrimental effect on customers so far as it has resulted from, or may be expected to result from, the adverse effect on competition; and

   (c)   in either case, if action should be taken, what action should be taken and what is to be remedied, mitigated or prevented.

(4)   The Commission shall, if it has decided that there is an adverse effect on competition, also decide separately the following questions (on the assumption that it is proceeding as mentioned in section 148(1))—
  (a)   whether action should be taken by it under section 138 for the purpose of remedying, mitigating or preventing the adverse effect on competition concerned or any detrimental effect on customers so far as it has resulted from, or may be expected to result from, the adverse effect on competition;
  (b)   whether the Commission should recommend the taking of action by other persons for the purpose of remedying, mitigating or preventing the adverse effect on competition concerned or any detrimental effect on customers so far as it has resulted from, or may be expected to result from, the adverse effect on competition; and
  (c)   in either case, if action should be taken, what action should be taken and what is to be remedied, mitigated or prevented.

(5)   In deciding the questions mentioned in subsections (3) and (4), the Commission shall, in particular, have regard to the need to achieve as comprehensive a solution as is reasonable and practicable to the adverse effect on competition concerned and any detrimental effects on customers so far as resulting from the adverse effect on competition.

(6)   In deciding the questions mentioned in subsections (3) and (4), the Commission may, in particular, have regard to the effect of any action on any relevant customer benefits of the feature or features of the market concerned.

[1402]

142   Investigations and reports by Commission

(1)   Where an intervention notice under section 139(1) is in force in relation to a market investigation reference, the Commission shall prepare a report on the reference and take action in relation to it under section 143(1) or (3) within the period permitted by section 144.

(2)   The report shall, in particular, contain—
  (a)   the decisions of the Commission on the questions which it is required to answer by virtue of section 141;
  (b)   its reasons for its decisions; and
  (c)   such information as the Commission considers appropriate for facilitating a proper understanding of those questions and of its reasons for its decisions.

(3)   The Commission shall carry out such investigations as it considers appropriate for the purposes of preparing a report under this section.

[1403]

143   Publication etc of reports of Commission

(1)   The Commission shall publish a report under section 142 if it contains—
  (a)   the decision of the Commission that there is no adverse effect on competition; or
  (b)   the decisions of the Commission that there is one or more than one adverse effect on competition but, on the question mentioned in section 141(4)(a) and in relation to each adverse effect on competition, that no action should be taken by it.

(2)   The Commission shall, at the same time as the report is published under subsection (1)—
  (a)   in the case of a reference under section 131, give it to the OFT; and
  (b)   in the case of a reference under section 132, give it to the appropriate Minister and give a copy of it to the OFT.

(3)   Where a report under section 142 contains the decisions of the Commission that there is one or more than one adverse effect on competition and, on the question mentioned in section 141(4)(a) and in relation to at least one such adverse effect, that action should be taken by it, the Commission shall give the report to the Secretary of State.

(4)   The Secretary of State shall publish, no later than publication of his decision under section 146(2) in relation to the case, a report of the Commission given to him under subsection (3) and not required to be published by virtue of section 148(2).

(5)   The Secretary of State shall, at the same time as a report of the Commission given to him under subsection (3) is published under subsection (4), give a copy of it—
  (a)   in the case of a reference under section 131, to the OFT; and
  (b)   in the case of a reference under section 132, to any other Minister of the Crown who made the reference and to the OFT.

(6)   Where a reference has been made by the OFT under section 131 or by the appropriate Minister under section 132 in circumstances in which a reference could have been made by a relevant sectoral regulator under section 131 as it has effect by virtue of a relevant sectoral enactment, the relevant authority shall, at the same time as the report under section 142 is published under subsection (1) or (4), give a copy of it to the relevant sectoral regulator concerned.

(7) Where a reference has been made by a relevant sectoral regulator under section 131 as it has effect by virtue of a relevant sectoral enactment, the relevant authority shall, at the same time as the report under section 142 is published under subsection (1) or (4), give a copy of it to the OFT.

(8) In subsections (6) and (7) "the relevant authority" means—
  (a) in the case of a report published under subsection (1), the Commission; and
  (b) in the case of a report published under subsection (4), the Secretary of State.

[1404]

144 Time-limits for investigations and reports: Part 4

(1) The Commission shall, within the period of two years beginning with the date of the reference, prepare its report under section 142 and publish it under subsection (1) of section 143 or (as the case may be) give it to the Secretary of State under subsection (3) of that section.

(2) The Secretary of State may by order amend subsection (1) so as to alter the period of two years mentioned in that subsection or any period for the time being mentioned in that subsection in substitution for that period.

(3) No alteration shall be made by virtue of subsection (2) which results in the period for the time being mentioned in subsection (1) exceeding two years.

(4) An order under subsection (2) shall not affect any period of time within which, in relation to a market investigation reference, the Commission is under a duty to prepare its report under section 142 and take action in relation to it under section 143(1) or (3) if the Commission is already under that duty in relation to that reference when the order is made.

(5) Before making an order under subsection (2) the Secretary of State shall consult the Commission and such other persons as he considers appropriate.

[1405]

145 Restrictions where public interest considerations not finalised: Part 4

(1) The Commission shall terminate its investigation under section 142 if—
  (a) the intervention notice concerned mentions a public interest consideration which was not finalised on the giving of that notice or public interest considerations which, at that time, were not finalised;
  (b) no other public interest consideration is mentioned in the notice;
  (c) at least 24 weeks has elapsed since the giving of the notice; and
  (d) the public interest consideration mentioned in the notice has not been finalised within that period of 24 weeks or (as the case may be) none of the public interest considerations mentioned in the notice has been finalised within that period of 24 weeks.

(2) Where the intervention notice concerned mentions a public interest consideration which is not finalised on the giving of the notice, the Commission shall not give its report under section 142 to the Secretary of State in accordance with section 143(3) unless the period of 24 weeks beginning with the giving of the intervention notice concerned has expired or the public interest consideration concerned has been finalised.

(3) The Commission shall, in reporting on any of the questions mentioned in section 141(3), disregard any public interest consideration which has not been finalised before the giving of the report.

(4) The Commission shall, in reporting on any of the questions mentioned in section 141(3), disregard any public interest consideration which was not finalised on the giving of the intervention notice concerned and has not been finalised within the period of 24 weeks beginning with the giving of the notice concerned.

(5) Subsections (1) to (4) are without prejudice to the power of the Commission to carry out investigations in relation to any public interest consideration to which it might be able to have regard in its report.

[1406]

146 Decision of Secretary of State

(1) Subsection (2) applies where the Secretary of State has received a report of the Commission which—
  (a) has been prepared under section 142;
  (b) contains the decisions that there is one or more than one adverse effect on competition and, on the question mentioned in section 141(4)(a) and in relation to at least one such adverse effect, that action should be taken by it; and
  (c) has been given to the Secretary of State as required by section 143(3).

(2) The Secretary of State shall decide whether—
  (a) any eligible public interest consideration is relevant; or
  (b) any eligible public interest considerations are relevant;

to any action which is mentioned in the report by virtue of section 141(4)(a) and (c) and which the Commission should take for the purpose of remedying, mitigating or preventing any adverse effect on competition concerned or any detrimental effect on customers so far as it has resulted or may be expected to result from any adverse effect on competition.

(3)   The Secretary of State shall make and publish his decision under subsection (2) within the period of 90 days beginning with the receipt of the report of the Commission under section 142.

(4)   In this section "eligible public interest consideration" means a public interest consideration which—
-   (a)   was mentioned in the intervention notice concerned; and
-   (b)   was not disregarded by the Commission for the purposes of its report under section 142.

[1407]

147   Remedial action by Secretary of State

(1)   Subsection (2) applies where the Secretary of State—
-   (a)   has decided under subsection (2) of section 146 within the period required by subsection (3) of that section that an eligible public interest consideration is relevant as mentioned in subsection (2) of that section or eligible public interest considerations are so relevant; and
-   (b)   has published his decision within the period required by subsection (3) of that section.

(2)   The Secretary of State may, in relation to any adverse effect on competition identified in the report concerned, take such action under section 159 or 161 as he considers to be—
-   (a)   reasonable and practicable—
    -   (i)   to remedy, mitigate or prevent the adverse effect on competition concerned; or
    -   (ii)   to remedy, mitigate or prevent any detrimental effect on customers so far as it has resulted from, or may be expected to result from, the adverse effect on competition; and
-   (b)   appropriate in the light of the eligible public interest consideration concerned or (as the case may be) the eligible public interest considerations concerned.

(3)   In making a decision under subsection (2), the Secretary of State shall, in particular, have regard to—
-   (a)   the need to achieve as comprehensive a solution as is reasonable and practicable to the adverse effect on competition concerned and any detrimental effects on customers so far as resulting from the adverse effect on competition; and
-   (b)   the report of the Commission under section 142.

(4)   In having regard by virtue of subsection (3) to the report of the Commission under section 142, the Secretary of State shall not challenge the decision of the Commission contained in the report that there is one or more than one adverse effect on competition.

(5)   In making a decision under subsection (2), the Secretary of State may, in particular, have regard to the effect of any action on any relevant customer benefits of the feature or features of the market concerned.

(6)   The Secretary of State shall take no action under subsection (2) to remedy, mitigate or prevent any detrimental effect on customers so far as it may be expected to result from the adverse effect on competition concerned if—
-   (a)   no detrimental effect on customers has resulted from the adverse effect on competition; and
-   (b)   the adverse effect on competition is not being remedied, mitigated or prevented.

(7)   In this section "eligible public interest consideration" has the same meaning as in section 146.

[1408]

148   Reversion of the matter to the Commission

(1)   If—
-   (a)   the Secretary of State fails to make and publish his decision under subsection (2) of section 146 within the period required by subsection (3) of that section; or
-   (b)   the Secretary of State decides that no eligible public interest consideration is relevant as mentioned in subsection (2) of that section;

the Commission shall proceed under section 138 as if the report had been prepared and published under section 136 within the period permitted by section 137.

(2)   The Commission shall publish the report which has been prepared by it under section 142 (if still unpublished) as soon as it becomes able to proceed by virtue of subsection (1).

(3)   The Commission shall, at the same time as its report is published under subsection (2), give a copy of it—
-   (a)   in the case of a reference under section 131, to the OFT; and

(b)   in the case of a reference under section 132, to any Minister of the Crown who made the reference (other than the Secretary of State) and to the OFT.

(4)   Where a reference has been made by the OFT under section 131 or by the appropriate Minister under section 132 in circumstances in which a reference could have been made by a relevant sectoral regulator under section 131 as it has effect by virtue of a relevant sectoral enactment, the Commission shall, at the same time as its report is published under subsection (2), give a copy of it to the relevant sectoral regulator concerned.

(5)   Where a reference has been made by a relevant sectoral regulator under section 131 as it has effect by virtue of a relevant sectoral enactment, the Commission shall, at the same time as its report is published under subsection (2), give a copy of it to the OFT.

(6)   In relation to proceedings by virtue of subsection (1), the reference in section 138(3) to decisions of the Commission included in its report by virtue of section 134(4) shall be construed as a reference to decisions which were included in the report of the Commission by virtue of section 141(4).

(7)   Where the Commission, in proceeding by virtue of subsection (1), intends to proceed in a way which is not consistent with its decisions as included in its report by virtue of section 141(4), it shall not so proceed without the consent of the Secretary of State.

(8)   The Secretary of State shall not withhold his consent under subsection (7) unless he believes that the proposed alternative way of proceeding will operate against the public interest.

(9)   For the purposes of subsection (8) a proposed alternative way of proceeding will operate against the public interest only if any eligible public interest consideration or considerations outweigh the considerations which have led the Commission to propose proceeding in that way.

(10)   In deciding whether to withhold his consent under subsection (7), the Secretary of State shall accept the Commission's view of what, if the only relevant consideration were how to remedy, mitigate or prevent the adverse effect on competition concerned or any detrimental effect on customers so far as resulting from the adverse effect on competition, would be the most appropriate way to proceed.

(11)   In this section "eligible public interest consideration" has the same meaning as in section 146.

[1409]

Intervention notices under section 139(2)

149   Intervention notices under section 139(2)

(1)   An intervention notice under section 139(2) shall state—
(a)   the proposed undertaking which may be accepted by the OFT;
(b)   the notice under section 155(1) or (4);
(c)   the public interest consideration or considerations which are, or may be, relevant to the case; and
(d)   where any public interest consideration concerned is not finalised, the proposed timetable for finalising it.

(2)   Where the Secretary of State believes that it is or may be the case that two or more public interest considerations are relevant to the case, he may decide not to mention in the intervention notice such of those considerations as he considers appropriate.

(3)   The Secretary of State may at any time revoke an intervention notice which has been given under section 139(2) and which is in force.

(4)   An intervention notice under section 139(2) shall come into force when it is given and shall cease to be in force on the occurrence of any of the events mentioned in subsection (5).

(5)   The events are—
(a)   the acceptance by the OFT with the consent of the Secretary of State of an undertaking which is the same as the proposed undertaking mentioned in the intervention notice by virtue of subsection (1)(a) or which does not differ from it in any material respect;
(b)   the decision of the OFT to proceed neither with the proposed undertaking mentioned in the intervention notice by virtue of subsection (1)(a) nor a proposed undertaking which does not differ from it in any material respect; or
(c)   the decision of the Secretary of State to revoke the intervention notice concerned.

[1410]

150   Power of veto of Secretary of State

(1)   Where an intervention notice under section 139(2) is in force, the OFT shall not, without the consent of the Secretary of State, accept the proposed undertaking concerned or a proposed undertaking which does not differ from it in any material respect.

(2)   The Secretary of State shall withhold his consent if he believes that it is or may be the case that the proposed undertaking will, if accepted, operate against the public interest.

(3)   For the purposes of subsection (2) a proposed undertaking will, if accepted, operate against the public interest only if any public interest consideration which is mentioned in the intervention notice concerned and has been finalised, or any public interest considerations which are so mentioned and have been finalised, outweigh the considerations which have led the OFT to propose accepting the undertaking.

(4)   In making his decision under subsection (2) the Secretary of State shall accept the OFT's view of what undertakings, if the only relevant consideration were how to remedy, mitigate or prevent the adverse effect on competition concerned or any detrimental effect on customers so far as resulting from the adverse effect on competition, would be most appropriate.

(5)   Where a public interest consideration which is mentioned in the intervention notice concerned is not finalised on the giving of the notice, the Secretary of State shall not make his decision as to whether to give his consent under this section before—
(a)   the end of the period of 24 weeks beginning with the giving of the intervention notice; or
(b)   if earlier, the date on which the public interest consideration concerned has been finalised.

(6)   Subject to subsections (2) to (5), the Secretary of State shall not withhold his consent under this section.

[1411]

Other

151   Further interaction of intervention notices with general procedure

(1)   Where an intervention notice under section 139(1) comes into force in relation to a market investigation reference, sections 134(1), (4), (6) and (7), 136(1) to (6), 137(1) to (6) and 138 shall cease to apply in relation to that reference.

(2)   Where the Secretary of State revokes an intervention notice which has been given under section 139(1), the Commission shall instead proceed under sections 134 and 136 to 138.

(3)   Where the Commission is proceeding by virtue of subsection (2), the period within which the Commission shall prepare and publish its report under section 136 shall be extended by an additional period of 20 days.

(4)   Where the Commission terminates its investigation under section 145(1), the Commission shall proceed under sections 134 and 136 to 138.

(5)   Where the Commission is proceeding by virtue of subsection (4), the period within which the Commission shall prepare and publish its report under section 136 shall be extended by an additional period of 20 days.

(6)   In determining the period of 20 days mentioned in subsection (3) or (5) no account shall be taken of—
(a)   Saturday, Sunday, Good Friday and Christmas Day; and
(b)   any day which is a bank holiday in England and Wales.

[1412]

152   Certain duties of OFT and Commission

(1)   The OFT shall, in considering whether to make a reference under section 131, bring to the attention of the Secretary of State any case which it believes raises any consideration specified in section 153 unless it believes that the Secretary of State would consider any such consideration immaterial in the context of the particular case.

(2)   The Commission shall, in investigating any reference made to it under section 131 or 132 within the previous four months, bring to the attention of the Secretary of State any case which it believes raises any consideration specified in section 153 unless it believes that the Secretary of State would consider any such consideration immaterial in the context of the particular case.

(3)   The OFT and the Commission shall bring to the attention of the Secretary of State any representations about exercising his power under section 153(3) which have been made to the OFT or (as the case may be) the Commission.

[1413]

153   Specified considerations: Part 4

(1)   The interests of national security are specified in this section.

(2)   In subsection (1) "national security" includes public security; and in this subsection "public security" has the same meaning as in article [21(4) of Council Regulation (EC) No 139/2004 of 20th January 2004 on the control of concentrations between undertakings].

(3)   The Secretary of State may by order modify this section for the purpose of specifying in this section a new consideration or removing or amending any consideration which is for the time being specified in this section.

(4)   An order under this section may apply in relation to cases under consideration by the OFT, by the Secretary of State, by the appropriate Minister (other than the Secretary of State acting alone) or by the Commission before the making of the order as well as cases under consideration on or after the making of the order.

[1414]

NOTES
Sub-s (2): words in square brackets substituted by the EC Merger Control (Consequential Amendments) Regulations 2004, SI 2004/1079, reg 2, Schedule, para 2(1), (27), as from 1 May 2004.

CHAPTER 3
ENFORCEMENT

Undertakings and orders

154   Undertakings in lieu of market investigation references

(1)   Subsection (2) applies if the OFT considers that it has the power to make a reference under section 131 and otherwise intends to make such a reference.

(2)   The OFT may, instead of making such a reference and for the purpose of remedying, mitigating or preventing—
(a)   any adverse effect on competition concerned; or
(b)   any detrimental effect on customers so far as it has resulted from, or may be expected to result from, the adverse effect on competition;
accept, from such persons as it considers appropriate, undertakings to take such action as it considers appropriate.

(3)   In proceeding under subsection (2), the OFT shall, in particular, have regard to the need to achieve as comprehensive a solution as is reasonable and practicable to the adverse effect on competition concerned and any detrimental effects on customers so far as resulting from the adverse effect on competition.

(4)   In proceeding under subsection (2), the OFT may, in particular, have regard to the effect of any action on any relevant customer benefits of the feature or features of the market concerned.

(5)   The OFT shall take no action under subsection (2) to remedy, mitigate or prevent any detrimental effect on customers so far as it may be expected to result from the adverse effect on competition concerned if—
(a)   no detrimental effect on customers has resulted from the adverse effect on competition; and
(b)   the adverse effect on competition is not being remedied, mitigated or prevented.

(6)   An undertaking under this section—
(a)   shall come into force when accepted;
(b)   may be varied or superseded by another undertaking; and
(c)   may be released by the OFT.

(7)   The OFT shall, as soon as reasonably practicable, consider any representations received by it in relation to varying or releasing an undertaking under this section.

(8)   This section is subject to sections 150 and 155.

[1415]

155   Undertakings in lieu: procedural requirements

(1)   Before accepting an undertaking under section 154 (other than an undertaking under that section which varies an undertaking under that section but not in any material respect), the OFT shall—
(a)   publish notice of the proposed undertaking; and
(b)   consider any representations made in accordance with the notice and not withdrawn.

(2)   A notice under subsection (1) shall state—
(a)   that the OFT proposes to accept the undertaking;
(b)   the purpose and effect of the undertaking;
(c)   the situation that the undertaking is seeking to deal with;
(d)   any other facts which the OFT considers justify the acceptance of the undertaking;
(e)   a means of gaining access to an accurate version of the proposed undertaking at all reasonable times; and
(f)   the period (not less than 15 days starting with the date of publication of the notice) within which representations may be made in relation to the proposed undertaking.

(3)   The matters to be included in a notice under subsection (1) by virtue of subsection (2) shall, in particular, include—
  (a)   the terms of the reference under section 131 which the OFT considers that it has power to make and which it otherwise intends to make; and
  (b)   the adverse effect on competition, and any detrimental effect on customers so far as resulting from the adverse effect on competition, which the OFT has identified.

(4)   The OFT shall not accept the undertaking with modifications unless it—
  (a)   publishes notice of the proposed modifications; and
  (b)   considers any representations made in accordance with the notice and not withdrawn.

(5)   A notice under subsection (4) shall state—
  (a)   the proposed modifications;
  (b)   the reasons for them; and
  (c)   the period (not less than 7 days starting with the date of the publication of the notice under subsection (4)) within which representations may be made in relation to the proposed modifications.

(6)   If, after publishing notice under subsection (1) or (4), the OFT decides—
  (a)   not to accept the undertaking concerned; and
  (b)   not to proceed by virtue of subsection (8) or (9);
it shall publish notice of that decision.

(7)   As soon as practicable after accepting an undertaking to which this section applies, the OFT shall—
  (a)   serve a copy of the undertaking on any person by whom it is given; and
  (b)   publish the undertaking.

(8)   The requirements of subsection (4) (and those of subsection (1)) shall not apply if the OFT—
  (a)   has already published notice under subsection (1) but not subsection (4) in relation to the proposed undertaking; and
  (b)   considers that the modifications which are now being proposed are not material in any respect.

(9)   The requirements of subsection (4) (and those of subsection (1)) shall not apply if the OFT—
  (a)   has already published notice under subsections (1) and (4) in relation to the matter concerned; and
  (b)   considers that the further modifications which are now being proposed do not differ in any material respect from the modifications in relation to which notice was last given under subsection (4).

(10)   Paragraphs 6 to 8 (but not paragraph 9) of Schedule 10 (procedural requirements before terminating undertakings) shall apply in relation to the proposed release of undertakings under section 154 (other than in connection with accepting an undertaking under that section which varies or supersedes an undertaking under that section) as they apply in relation to the proposed release of undertakings under section 73.

[1416]

156   Effect of undertakings under section 154

(1)   No market investigation reference shall be made by the OFT or the appropriate Minister in relation to any feature, or combination of features, of a market in the United Kingdom for goods or services if—
  (a)   the OFT has accepted an undertaking or group of undertakings under section 154 within the previous 12 months; and
  (b)   the goods or services to which the undertaking or group of undertakings relates are of the same description as the goods or services to which the feature, or combination of features, relates.

(2)   Subsection (1) does not prevent the making of a market investigation reference if—
  (a)   the OFT considers that any undertaking concerned has been breached and has given notice of that fact to the person responsible for giving the undertaking; or
  (b)   the person responsible for giving any undertaking concerned supplied, in connection with the matter, information to the OFT which was false or misleading in a material respect.

[1417]

157   Interim undertakings: Part 4

(1)   Subsection (2) applies where—
  (a)   a market investigation reference has been made;
  (b)   a report has been published under section 136 within the period permitted by section 137

or (as the case may be) a report prepared under section 142 and given to the Secretary of State under section 143(3) within the period permitted by section 144 has been published; and

(c) the market investigation reference concerned is not finally determined.

(2) The relevant authority may, for the purpose of preventing pre-emptive action, accept, from such persons as the relevant authority considers appropriate, undertakings to take such action as the relevant authority considers appropriate.

(3) An undertaking under this section—
(a) shall come into force when accepted;
(b) may be varied or superseded by another undertaking; and
(c) may be released by the relevant authority.

(4) An undertaking under this section shall, if it has not previously ceased to be in force, cease to be in force when the market investigation reference is finally determined.

(5) The relevant authority shall, as soon as reasonably practicable, consider any representations received by the relevant authority in relation to varying or releasing an undertaking under this section.

(6) In this section and section 158—
"pre-emptive action" means action which might impede the taking of any action under section 138(2) or (as the case may be) 147(2) in relation to the market investigation reference concerned; and
"the relevant authority" means—
(a) where an intervention notice is in force in relation to the market investigation reference, the Secretary of State;
(b) in any other case, the Commission.

[1418]

158 Interim orders: Part 4

(1) Subsection (2) applies where—
(a) a market investigation reference has been made;
(b) a report has been published under section 136 within the period permitted by section 137 or (as the case may be) a report prepared under section 142 and given to the Secretary of State under section 143(3) within the period permitted by section 144 has been published; and
(c) the market investigation reference concerned is not finally determined.

(2) The relevant authority may by order, for the purpose of preventing pre-emptive action—
(a) prohibit or restrict the doing of things which the relevant authority considers would constitute pre-emptive action;
(b) impose on any person concerned obligations as to the carrying on of any activities or the safeguarding of any assets;
(c) provide for the carrying on of any activities or the safeguarding of any assets either by the appointment of a person to conduct or supervise the conduct of any activities (on such terms and with such powers as may be specified or described in the order) or in any other manner;
(d) do anything which may be done by virtue of paragraph 19 of Schedule 8.

(3) An order under this section—
(a) shall come into force at such time as is determined by or under the order; and
(b) may be varied or revoked by another order.

(4) An order under this section shall, if it has not previously ceased to be in force, cease to be in force when the market investigation reference is finally determined.

(5) The relevant authority shall, as soon as reasonably practicable, consider any representations received by the relevant authority in relation to varying or revoking an order under this section.

[1419]

159 Final undertakings: Part 4

(1) The Commission may, in accordance with section 138, accept, from such persons as it considers appropriate, undertakings to take action specified or described in the undertakings.

(2) The Secretary of State may, in accordance with section 147, accept, from such persons as he considers appropriate, undertakings to take action specified or described in the undertakings.

(3) An undertaking under this section shall come into force when accepted.

(4) An undertaking under subsection (1) or (2) may be varied or superseded by another undertaking under that subsection.

(5) An undertaking under subsection (1) may be released by the Commission and an undertaking under subsection (2) may be released by the Secretary of State.

(6)   The Commission or (as the case may be) the Secretary of State shall, as soon as reasonably practicable, consider any representations received by it or (as the case may be) him in relation to varying or releasing an undertaking under this section.

[1420]

160   Order-making power where final undertakings not fulfilled: Part 4

(1)   Subsection (2) applies where the relevant authority considers that—
  (a)   an undertaking accepted by the relevant authority under section 159 has not been, is not being or will not be fulfilled; or
  (b)   in relation to an undertaking accepted by the relevant authority under that section, information which was false or misleading in a material respect was given to the relevant authority or the OFT by the person giving the undertaking before the relevant authority decided to accept the undertaking.

(2)   The relevant authority may, for any of the purposes mentioned in section 138(2) or (as the case may be) 147(2), make an order under this section.

(3)   Subsections (3) to (6) of section 138 or (as the case may be) 147 shall apply for the purposes of subsection (2) above as they apply for the purposes of that section.

(4)   An order under this section may contain—
  (a)   anything permitted by Schedule 8; and
  (b)   such supplementary, consequential or incidental provision as the relevant authority considers appropriate.

(5)   An order under this section—
  (a)   shall come into force at such time as is determined by or under the order;
  (b)   may contain provision which is different from the provision contained in the undertaking concerned; and
  (c)   may be varied or revoked by another order.

(6)   No order shall be varied or revoked under this section unless the OFT advises that such a variation or revocation is appropriate by reason of a change of circumstances.

(7)   In this section "the relevant authority" means—
  (a)   in the case of an undertaking accepted under section 159 by the Commission, the Commission; and
  (b)   in the case of an undertaking accepted under that section by the Secretary of State, the Secretary of State.

[1421]

161   Final orders: Part 4

(1)   The Commission may, in accordance with section 138, make an order under this section.

(2)   The Secretary of State may, in accordance with section 147, make an order under this section.

(3)   An order under this section may contain—
  (a)   anything permitted by Schedule 8; and
  (b)   such supplementary, consequential or incidental provision as the person making it considers appropriate.

(4)   An order under this section—
  (a)   shall come into force at such time as is determined by or under the order; and
  (b)   may be varied or revoked by another order.

(5)   No order shall be varied or revoked under this section unless the OFT advises that such a variation or revocation is appropriate by reason of a change of circumstances.

[1422]

Enforcement functions of OFT

162   Duty of OFT to monitor undertakings and orders: Part 4

(1)   The OFT shall keep under review the carrying out of any enforcement undertaking or any enforcement order.

(2)   The OFT shall, in particular, from time to time consider—
  (a)   whether an enforcement undertaking or enforcement order has been or is being complied with;
  (b)   whether, by reason of any change of circumstances, an enforcement undertaking is no longer appropriate and—
      (i)   one or more of the parties to it can be released from it; or
      (ii)   it needs to be varied or to be superseded by a new enforcement undertaking; and
  (c)   whether, by reason of any change of circumstances, an enforcement order is no longer appropriate and needs to be varied or revoked.

(3)   The OFT shall give the Commission or (as the case may be) the Secretary of State such advice as it considers appropriate in relation to—
  (a)   any possible variation or release by the Commission or (as the case may be) the Secretary of State of an enforcement undertaking accepted by it or (as the case may be) him;
  (b)   any possible new enforcement undertaking to be accepted by the Commission or (as the case may be) the Secretary of State so as to supersede another enforcement undertaking given to the Commission or (as the case may be) the Secretary of State;
  (c)   any possible variation or revocation by the Commission or (as the case may be) the Secretary of State of an enforcement order made by the Commission or (as the case may be) the Secretary of State;
  (d)   any possible enforcement undertaking to be accepted by the Commission or (as the case may be) the Secretary of State instead of an enforcement order or any possible enforcement order to be made by the Commission or (as the case may be) the Secretary of State instead of an enforcement undertaking; or
  (e)   the enforcement by virtue of section 167(6) to (8) of any enforcement undertaking or enforcement order.

(4)   The OFT shall take such action as it considers appropriate in relation to—
  (a)   any possible variation or release by it of an undertaking accepted by it under section 154;
  (b)   any possible new undertaking to be accepted by it under section 154 so as to supersede another undertaking given to it under that section; or
  (c)   the enforcement by it by virtue of section 167(6) of any enforcement undertaking or enforcement order.

(5)   The OFT shall keep under review the effectiveness of enforcement undertakings accepted under this Part and enforcement orders made under this Part.

(6)   The OFT shall, whenever requested to do so by the Secretary of State and otherwise from time to time, prepare a report of its findings under subsection (5).

(7)   The OFT shall—
  (a)   give any report prepared by it under subsection (6) to the Commission;
  (b)   give a copy of the report to the Secretary of State; and
  (c)   publish the report.

(8)   In this Part—
  "enforcement order" means an order made under section 158, 160 or 161; and
  "enforcement undertaking" means an undertaking accepted under section 154, 157 or 159.

[1423]

163   Further role of OFT in relation to undertakings and orders: Part 4

(1)   Subsections (2) and (3) apply where the Commission or the Secretary of State (in this section "the relevant authority") is considering whether to accept undertakings under section 157 or 159.

(2)   The relevant authority may require the OFT to consult with such persons as the relevant authority considers appropriate with a view to discovering whether they will offer undertakings which the relevant authority would be prepared to accept under section 157 or (as the case may be) 159.

(3)   The relevant authority may require the OFT to report to the relevant authority on the outcome of the OFT's consultations within such period as the relevant authority may require.

(4)   A report under subsection (3) shall, in particular, contain advice from the OFT as to whether any undertakings offered should be accepted by the relevant authority under section 157 or (as the case may be) 159.

(5)   The powers conferred on the relevant authority by subsections (1) to (4) are without prejudice to the power of the relevant authority to consult the persons concerned itself.

(6)   If asked by the relevant authority for advice in relation to the taking of enforcement action (whether or not by way of undertakings) in a particular case, the OFT shall give such advice as it considers appropriate.

[1424]

Supplementary

164   Enforcement undertakings and orders under this Part: general provisions

(1)   The provision which may be contained in an enforcement undertaking is not limited to the provision which is permitted by Schedule 8.

(2)   The following enactments in Part 3 shall apply in relation to enforcement orders under this Part as they apply in relation to enforcement orders under that Part—

    (a)   section 86(1) to (5) (enforcement orders: general provisions); and

    (b)   section 87 (power of directions conferred by enforcement order).

  (3)   An enforcement order under section 160 or 161 or any explanatory material accompanying the order shall state—

    (a)   the actions that the persons or description of persons to whom the order is addressed must do or (as the case may be) refrain from doing;

    (b)   the date on which the order comes into force;

    (c)   the possible consequences of not complying with the order; and

    (d)   the section of this Part under which a review can be sought in relation to the order.

[1425]

165 Procedural requirements for certain undertakings and orders: Part 4

Schedule 10 (procedural requirements for certain undertakings and orders), other than paragraph 9 of that Schedule, shall apply in relation to undertakings under section 159 and orders under section 160 or 161 as it applies in relation to undertakings under section 82 and orders under section 83 or 84.

[1426]

166 Register of undertakings and orders: Part 4

  (1)   The OFT shall compile and maintain a register for the purposes of this Part.

  (2)   The register shall be kept in such form as the OFT considers appropriate.

  (3)   The OFT shall ensure that the following matters are entered in the register—

    (a)   the provisions of any enforcement undertaking accepted by virtue of this Part (whether by the OFT, the Commission, the Secretary of State or a relevant sectoral regulator);

    (b)   the provisions of any enforcement order made by virtue of this Part (whether by the Commission, the Secretary of State or a relevant sectoral regulator); and

    (c)   the details of any variation, release or revocation of such an undertaking or order.

  (4)   The duty in subsection (3) does not extend to anything of which the OFT is unaware.

  (5)   The Commission, the Secretary of State and any relevant sectoral regulator shall inform the OFT of any matters which are to be included in the register by virtue of subsection (3) and which relate to enforcement undertakings accepted by them or enforcement orders made by them.

  (6)   The OFT shall ensure that the contents of the register are available to the public—

    (a)   during (as a minimum) such hours as may be specified in an order made by the Secretary of State; and

    (b)   subject to such reasonable fees (if any) as the OFT may determine.

  (7)   If requested by any person to do so and subject to such reasonable fees (if any) as the OFT may determine, the OFT shall supply the person concerned with a copy (certified to be true) of the register or of an extract from it.

[1427]

NOTES

  Orders: the OFT Registers of Undertakings and Orders (Available Hours) Order 2003, SI 2003/1373 (which provides that the OFT shall ensure that the contents of the register are available to the public (as a minimum) between the hours of 10.00 am and 4.00 pm on any working day).

---

167 Rights to enforce undertakings and orders under this Part

  (1)   This section applies to any enforcement undertaking or enforcement order.

  (2)   Any person to whom such an undertaking or order relates shall have a duty to comply with it.

  (3)   The duty shall be owed to any person who may be affected by a contravention of the undertaking or (as the case may be) order.

  (4)   Any breach of the duty which causes such a person to sustain loss or damage shall be actionable by him.

  (5)   In any proceedings brought under subsection (4) against a person to whom an enforcement undertaking or enforcement order relates it shall be a defence for that person to show that he took all reasonable steps and exercised all due diligence to avoid contravening the undertaking or (as the case may be) order.

  (6)   Compliance with an enforcement undertaking or an enforcement order shall also be enforceable by civil proceedings brought by the OFT for an injunction or for interdict or for any other appropriate relief or remedy.

  (7)   Compliance with an undertaking accepted under section 157 or 159, or an order under section 158, 160 or 161, shall also be enforceable by civil proceedings brought by the relevant authority for an injunction or for interdict or for any other appropriate relief or remedy.

(8)   In subsection (7) "the relevant authority" means—

  (a)   in the case of an undertaking accepted by the Commission or an order made by the Commission, the Commission; and

  (b)   in the case of an undertaking accepted by the Secretary of State or an order made by the Secretary of State, the Secretary of State.

(9)   Subsections (6) to (8) shall not prejudice any right that a person may have by virtue of subsection (4) to bring civil proceedings for contravention or apprehended contravention of an enforcement undertaking or an enforcement order.

[1428]

CHAPTER 4
SUPPLEMENTARY

Regulated markets

168   Regulated markets

(1)   Subsection (2) applies where the Commission or the Secretary of State is considering for the purposes of this Part whether relevant action would be reasonable and practicable for the purpose of remedying, mitigating or preventing an adverse effect on competition or any detrimental effect on customers so far as resulting from such an effect.

(2)   The Commission or (as the case may be) the Secretary of State shall, in deciding whether such action would be reasonable and practicable, have regard to the relevant statutory functions of the sectoral regulator concerned.

(3)   In this section "relevant action" means—

  (a)   ...

  (b)   modifying conditions in force under Part 4 of the Airports Act 1986 (c 31) other than any conditions imposed or modified in pursuance of section 40(3) or (4) of that Act;

  (c)   modifying the conditions of a licence granted under section 7 or 7A of the Gas Act 1986 (c 44);

  (d)   modifying the conditions of a licence granted under section 6 of the Electricity Act 1989 (c 29);

  (e)   modifying networking arrangements (within the meaning given by [section 290 of the Communications Act 2003]);

  (f)   modifying the conditions of a company's appointment under Chapter 1 of Part 2 of the Water Industry Act 1991 (c 56);

  [(ff)   modifying the conditions of a licence granted under Chapter 1A of Part 2 of the Act of 1991 or modifying the terms and conditions of an agreement under section 66D of that Act;]

  (g)   modifying the conditions of a licence granted under article 10 of the Electricity (Northern Ireland) Order 1992 (SI 1992/231 (NI 1));

  (h)   modifying the conditions of a licence granted under section 8 of the Railways Act 1993 (c 43);

  [(hh)   modifying the conditions of a SNRP issued pursuant to the Railways Infrastructure (Access, Management and Licensing of Railway Undertakings) Regulations (Northern Ireland) 2005;]

  (i)   modifying an access agreement (within the meaning given by section 83(1) of the Act of 1993) or a franchise agreement (within the meaning given by section 23(3) of that Act);

  (j)   modifying conditions in force under Part 4 of the Airports (Northern Ireland) Order 1994 (SI 1994/426 (NI 1)) other than any conditions imposed or modified in pursuance of article 40(3) or (4) of that Order;

  (k)   modifying the conditions of a licence granted under article 8 of the Gas (Northern Ireland) Order 1996 (SI 1996/275 (NI 2));

  (l)   modifying the conditions of a licence granted under section 11 of the Postal Services Act 2000 (c 26); or

  (m)   modifying the conditions of a licence granted under section 5 of the Transport Act 2000 (c 38);

  [(n)   modifying the conditions of a company's appointment under Chapter I of Part III of the Water and Sewerage Services (Northern Ireland) Order 2006].

(4)   In this section "relevant statutory functions" means—

  (a)   ...

  (b)   in relation to conditions in force under Part 4 of the Airports Act 1986 (c 31) other than any conditions imposed or modified in pursuance of section 40(3) or (4) of that Act, the duties of the Civil Aviation Authority under section 39(2) and (3) of that Act;

  (c)   in relation to any licence granted under section 7 or 7A of the Gas Act 1986 (c 44), the objectives and duties of the Gas and Electricity Markets Authority under section 4AA and 4AB(2) of that Act;

   (d)   in relation to any licence granted under section 6 of the Electricity Act 1989 (c 29), the objectives and duties of the Gas and Electricity Markets Authority under section 3A and 3B(2) of that Act;

   [(e)   in relation to any networking arrangements (within the meaning given by section 290 of the Communications Act 2003), the duty of the Office of Communications under subsection (1) of section 3 of that Act to secure the matters mentioned in subsection (2)(c) of that section;]

   (f)   in relation to a company's appointment under Chapter 1 of Part 2 of the Water Industry Act 1991 (c 56), the duties of [the Water Services Regulation Authority] under section 2 of that Act;

   [(ff) in relation to a licence granted under Chapter 1A of Part 2 of the Act of 1991 or an agreement under section 66D of that Act, the duties of the Authority under section 2 of that Act or under that section and section 66D of that Act (as the case may be);]

   (g)   in relation to any licence granted under article 10 of the Electricity (Northern Ireland) Order 1992 (SI 1992/231 (NI 1)), the duty of the Director General of Electricity Supply for Northern Ireland under article 6 of that Order;

   (h)   in relation to any licence granted under section 8 of the Railways Act 1993 (c 43) ... the duties of [the Office of Rail Regulation] under section 4 of that Act;

   [(hh) in relation to a SNRP issued pursuant to the Railways Infrastructure (Access, Management and Licensing of Railway Undertakings) Regulations (Northern Ireland) 2005 where none of the conditions of the SNRP relate to consumer protection, the duties of the Department for Regional Development under regulation 36 of those Regulations;]

   (i)   ...

   (j)   in relation to any access agreement (within the meaning given by section 83(1) of the Act of 1993), the duties of [the Office of Rail Regulation] under section 4 of the Act of 1993;

   (k)   in relation to any franchise agreement (within the meaning given by section 23(3) of the Act of 1993), the duties of the [Secretary of State, the Scottish Ministers and the National Assembly for Wales under section 4 of the Act of 1993];

   (l)   in relation to conditions in force under Part 4 of the Airports (Northern Ireland) Order 1994 (SI 1994/426 (NI 1)) other than any conditions imposed or modified in pursuance of article 40(3) or (4) of that Order, the duties of the Civil Aviation Authority under article 30(2) and (3) of that Order;

   (m)   in relation to any licence granted under article 8 of the Gas (Northern Ireland) Order 1996 (SI 1996/275 (NI 2)), the duties of the Director General of Gas for Northern Ireland under article 5 of that Order;

   (n)   in relation to any licence granted under section 11 of the Postal Services Act 2000 (c 26), the duties of the Postal Services Commission under sections 3 and 5 of that Act; and

   (o)   in relation to any licence granted under section 5 of the Transport Act 2000, the duties of the Civil Aviation Authority under section 87 of that Act;

   [(p)   in relation to a company's appointment under Chapter I of Part III of the Water and Sewerage Services (Northern Ireland) Order 2006, the duties of the Northern Ireland Authority for Utility Regulation under Article 6 of that Order].

(5)   In this section "sectoral regulator" means—

   (a)   the Civil Aviation Authority;

   [(b)   the Northern Ireland Authority for Utility Regulation;]

   (d)   ...

   [(e)   the Water Services Regulation Authority;]

   (f)   the Gas and Electricity Markets Authority;

   [(g)   the Office of Communications;]

   (h)   the Postal Services Commission;

   (i)   [the Office of Rail Regulation]; ...

   [(j)   the Secretary of State;

   (k)   the Scottish Ministers; or

   (l)   the National Assembly for Wales].

(6)   Subsection (7) applies where the Commission or the Secretary of State is considering for the purposes of this Part whether modifying the conditions of a licence granted under section 7 or 7A of the Gas Act 1986 (c 44) or section 6 of the Electricity Act 1989 (c 29) would be reasonable and practicable for the purpose of remedying, mitigating or preventing an adverse effect on competition or any detrimental effect on customers so far as resulting from such an effect.

(7)   The Commission or (as the case may be) the Secretary of State may, in deciding whether modifying the conditions of such a licence would be reasonable and practicable, have regard to those matters to which the Gas and Electricity Markets Authority may have regard by virtue of section 4AA(4) of the Act of 1986 or (as the case may be) section 3A(4) of the Act of 1989.

(8)   The Secretary of State may by order modify subsection (3), (4), (5), (6) or (7).

(9)　Part 2 of Schedule 9 (which makes provision for functions under this Part to be exercisable by various sectoral regulators) shall have effect.

[1429]

NOTES

Sub-s (3) is amended as follows:

Para (a) repealed by the Communications Act 2003, s 406(7), Sch 19(1), as from 25 July 2003 (certain purposes) and as from 29 December 2003 (otherwise).

Words in square brackets in para (e) substituted by the Communications Act 2003, s 406(1), Sch 17, para 174(1), (5)(a), as from 29 December 2003.

Para (ff) inserted by the Water Act 2003, s 101(1), Sch 8, para 55(1), (2)(a), as from 1 December 2005.

Para (hh) inserted by the Railways Infrastructure (Access, Management and Licensing of Railway Undertakings) Regulations (Northern Ireland) 2005, SR 2005/537, reg 45, Sch 5, para 4(a), as from 3 January 2006.

Para (n) inserted by the Water and Sewerage Services (Northern Ireland) Order 2006, SI 2006/3336, art 308(1), Sch 12, para 46(3), as from 1 April 2007.

Sub-s (4) is amended as follows:

Para (a) repealed by the Communications Act 2003, s 406(7), Sch 19(1), as from 25 July 2003 (certain purposes) and as from 29 December 2003 (otherwise).

Para (e) substituted by the Communications Act 2003, s 406(1), Sch 17, para 174(1), (5)(b), as from 29 December 2003.

Words in square brackets in para (f) substituted by the Water Act 2003, s 101(1), Sch 7, Pt 2, para 36(1), (3)(a), as from 1 April 2006.

Para (ff) added by the Water Act 2003, s 101(1), Sch 8, para 55(1), (2)(b), as from 1 December 2005.

Words omitted from para (h) repealed by the Railways Act 2005, s 59(1), (6), Sch 12, para 18(1), (2)(a), Sch 13, Pt 1, as from 24 July 2005; words in square brackets in para (h) substituted by the Railways and Transport Safety Act 2003, s 16(5), Sch 2, Pt 2, para 19(u), as from 5 July 2004.

Para (hh) inserted by the Railways Infrastructure (Access, Management and Licensing of Railway Undertakings) Regulations (Northern Ireland) 2005, SR 2005/537, reg 45, Sch 5, para 4(b), as from 3 January 2006.

Para (i) repealed by the Railways Act 2005, s 59(1), (6), Sch 12, para 18(1), (2)(b), Sch 13, Pt 1, as from 24 July 2005.

Words in square brackets in para (j) substituted by the Railways and Transport Safety Act 2003, s 16(5), Sch 2, Pt 2, para 19(u), as from 5 July 2004.

Words in square brackets in para (k) substituted by the Railways Act 2005, s 59(1), Sch 12, para 18(1), (2)(c), as from 24 July 2005 (except in so far as it relates to the transfer of functions from the Strategic Rail Authority to the Scottish Ministers), and as from 16 October 2005 (otherwise).

Para (p) inserted by the Water and Sewerage Services (Northern Ireland) Order 2006, SI 2006/3336, art 308(1), Sch 12, para 46(4), as from 1 April 2007.

Sub-s (5) is amended as follows:

Para (b) substituted, for original paras (b), (c), by the Water and Sewerage Services (Northern Ireland) Order 2006, SI 2006/3336, art 308(1), Sch 12, para 46(5), as from 1 April 2007.

Para (d) repealed by the Communications Act 2003, s 406(7), Sch 19(1), as from 25 July 2003 (certain purposes) and as from 29 December 2003 (otherwise).

Para (e) substituted by the Water Act 2003, s 101(1), Sch 7, Pt 2, para 36(1), (3)(b), as from 1 April 2006.

Para (g) substituted by the Communications Act 2003, s 406(1), Sch 17, para 174(1), (5)(c), as from 29 December 2003.

Words in square brackets in para (i) substituted by the Railways and Transport Safety Act 2003, s 16(5), Sch 2, Pt 2, para 19(u), as from 5 July 2004; word omitted repealed by the Railways Act 2005, s 59(6), Sch 13, Pt 1, as from 16 October 2005 (in relation to England, Scotland and Wales), and by the Railways Infrastructure (Access, Management and Licensing of Railway Undertakings) Regulations (Northern Ireland) 2005, SR 2005/537, reg 45, Sch 5, para 4(c)(i), as from 3 January 2006 (in relation to Northern Ireland).

Paras (j)–(l) substituted, for original para (j), by the Railways Act 2005, s 59(1), Sch 12, para 18(1), (3), as from 24 July 2005 (except in so far as it relates to the transfer of functions from the Strategic Rail Authority to the Scottish Ministers), and as from 16 October 2005 (otherwise) (in relation to England, Scotland and Wales). Note that a corresponding amendment has been made by SR 2005/537, reg 45, Sch 5, para 4(c) in relation to Northern Ireland which added the following para (k) after the original para (j)—

"(k)　the Department for Regional Development".

PART II
OTHER ACTS

Consultation, information and publicity

169　Certain duties of relevant authorities to consult: Part 4

(1)　Subsection (2) applies where the relevant authority is proposing to make a relevant decision in a way which the relevant authority considers is likely to have a substantial impact on the interests of any person.

(2)　The relevant authority shall, so far as practicable, consult that person about what is proposed before making that decision.

(3)　In consulting the person concerned, the relevant authority shall, so far as practicable, give the reasons of the relevant authority for the proposed decision.

(4)　In considering what is practicable for the purposes of this section the relevant authority shall, in particular, have regard to—

(a)　any restrictions imposed by any timetable for making the decision; and

(b)　any need to keep what is proposed, or the reasons for it, confidential.

(5)   The duty under this section shall not apply in relation to the making of any decision so far as particular provision is made elsewhere by virtue of this Part for consultation before the making of that decision.

(6)   In this section—

"the relevant authority" means the OFT, the appropriate Minister or the Commission; and

"relevant decision" means—

    (a)   in the case of the OFT, any decision by the OFT—

        (i)   as to whether to make a reference under section 131 or accept undertakings under section 154 instead of making such a reference; or

        (ii)   to vary under section 135 such a reference;

    (b)   in the case of the appropriate Minister, any decision by the appropriate Minister—

        (i)   as to whether to make a reference under section 132; or

        (ii)   to vary under section 135 such a reference; and

    (c)   in the case of the Commission, any decision on the questions mentioned in section 134 or 141.

[1430]

170   General information duties

(1)   The OFT shall give the Commission—

    (a)   such information in its possession as the Commission may reasonably require to enable the Commission to carry out its functions under this Part; and

    (b)   any other assistance which the Commission may reasonably require for the purpose of assisting it in carrying out its functions under this Part and which it is within the power of the OFT to give.

(2)   The OFT shall give the Commission any information in its possession which has not been requested by the Commission but which, in the opinion of the OFT, would be appropriate to give to the Commission for the purpose of assisting it in carrying out its functions under this Part.

(3)   The OFT and the Commission shall give the Secretary of State or the appropriate Minister so far as he is not the Secretary of State acting alone—

    (a)   such information in their possession as the Secretary of State or (as the case may be) the appropriate Minister concerned may by direction reasonably require to enable him to carry out his functions under this Part; and

    (b)   any other assistance which the Secretary of State or (as the case may be) the appropriate Minister concerned may by direction reasonably require for the purpose of assisting him in carrying out his functions under this Part and which it is within the power of the OFT or (as the case may be) the Commission to give.

(4)   The OFT shall give the Secretary of State or the appropriate Minister so far as he is not the Secretary of State acting alone any information in its possession which has not been requested by the Secretary of State or (as the case may be) the appropriate Minister concerned but which, in the opinion of the OFT, would be appropriate to give to the Secretary of State or (as the case may be) the appropriate Minister concerned for the purpose of assisting him in carrying out his functions under this Part.

(5)   The Commission shall have regard to any information given to it under subsection (1) or (2); and the Secretary of State or (as the case may be) the appropriate Minister concerned shall have regard to any information given to him under subsection (3) or (4).

(6)   Any direction given under subsection (3)—

    (a)   shall be in writing; and

    (b)   may be varied or revoked by a subsequent direction.

[1431]

171   Advice and information: Part 4

(1)   As soon as reasonably practicable after the passing of this Act, the OFT shall prepare and publish general advice and information about the making of references by it under section 131.

(2)   The OFT may at any time publish revised, or new, advice or information.

(3)   As soon as reasonably practicable after the passing of this Act, the Commission shall prepare and publish general advice and information about the consideration by it of market investigation references and the way in which relevant customer benefits may affect the taking of enforcement action in relation to such references.

(4)   The Commission may at any time publish revised, or new, advice or information.

(5)   Advice and information published under this section shall be prepared with a view to—

    (a)   explaining relevant provisions of this Part to persons who are likely to be affected by them; and

    (b)   indicating how the OFT or (as the case may be) the Commission expects such provisions to operate.

(6)   Advice and information published by virtue of subsection (1) or (3) shall include such advice and information about the effect of Community law, and anything done under or in accordance with it, on the provisions of this Part as the OFT or (as the case may be) the Commission considers appropriate.

(7)   Advice (or information) published by virtue of subsection (1) or (3) may include advice (or information) about the factors which the OFT or (as the case may be) the Commission may take into account in considering whether, and if so how, to exercise a function conferred by this Part.

(8)   Any advice or information published by the OFT or the Commission under this section shall be published in such manner as the OFT or (as the case may be) the Commission considers appropriate.

(9)   In preparing any advice or information under this section, the OFT shall consult the Commission and such other persons as it considers appropriate.

(10)   In preparing any advice or information under this section, the Commission shall consult the OFT and such other persons as it considers appropriate.

(11)   In this section "Community law" means—
  (a)   all the rights, powers, liabilities, obligations and restrictions from time to time created or arising by or under the Community Treaties; and
  (b)   all the remedies and procedures from time to time provided for by or under the Community Treaties.

[1432]

172   Further publicity requirements: Part 4

(1)   The OFT shall publish—
  (a)   any reference made by it under section 131;
  (b)   any variation made by it under section 135 of a reference under section 131;
  (c)   any decision of a kind mentioned in section 149(5)(b); and
  (d)   such information as it considers appropriate about any decision made by it under section 152(1) to bring a case to the attention of the Secretary of State.

(2)   The Commission shall publish—
  (a)   any decision made by it under section 138(2) neither to accept an undertaking under section 159 nor to make an order under section 161;
  (b)   any decision made by it that there has been a material change of circumstances as mentioned in section 138(3) or there is another special reason as mentioned in that section;
  (c)   any termination under section 145(1) of an investigation by it;
  (d)   such information as it considers appropriate about any decision made by it under section 152(2) to bring a case to the attention of the Secretary of State;
  (e)   any enforcement undertaking accepted by it under section 157;
  (f)   any enforcement order made by it under section 158; and
  (g)   any variation, release or revocation of such an undertaking or order.

(3)   The Secretary of State shall publish—
  (a)   any reference made by him under section 132;
  (b)   any variation made by him under section 135 of a reference under section 132;
  (c)   any intervention notice given by him;
  (d)   any decision made by him to revoke such a notice;
  (e)   any decision made by him under section 147(2) neither to accept an undertaking under section 159 nor to make an order under section 161;
  (f)   any enforcement undertaking accepted by him under section 157;
  (g)   any variation or release of such an undertaking; and
  (h)   any direction given by him under section 170(3) in connection with the exercise by him of his functions under section 132(3).

(4)   The appropriate Minister (other than the Secretary of State acting alone) shall publish—
  (a)   any reference made by him under section 132;
  (b)   any variation made by him under section 135 of a reference under section 132; and
  (c)   any direction given by him under section 170(3) in connection with the exercise by him of his functions under section 132(3).

(5)   Where any person is under an obligation by virtue of subsection (1), (2), (3) or (4) to publish the result of any action taken by that person or any decision made by that person, the person concerned shall, subject to subsections (6) and (7), also publish that person's reasons for the action concerned or (as the case may be) the decision concerned.

(6)   Such reasons need not, if it is not reasonably practicable to do so, be published at the same time as the result of the action concerned or (as the case may be) as the decision concerned.

(7)   Subsections (5) and (6) shall not apply in relation to any case falling within subsection (1)(d) or (2)(d).

(8)   The Secretary of State shall publish his reasons for—
   (a)   any decision made by him under section 146(2); or
   (b)   any decision to make an order under section 153(3) or vary or revoke such an order.

(9)   Such reasons may be published after—
   (a)   in the case of subsection (8)(a), the publication of the decision concerned; and
   (b)   in the case of subsection (8)(b), the making of the order or of the variation or revocation;
if it is not reasonably practicable to publish them at the same time as the publication of the decision or (as the case may be) the making of the order or variation or revocation.

(10)   Where the Secretary of State has decided under section 147(2) to accept an undertaking under section 159 or to make an order under section 161, he shall (after the acceptance of the undertaking or (as the case may be) the making of the order) lay details of his decision and his reasons for it, and the Commission's report under section 142, before each House of Parliament.

[1433]

173   Defamation: Part 4

For the purposes of the law relating to defamation, absolute privilege attaches to any advice, guidance, notice or direction given, or decision or report made, by the OFT, by the Secretary of State, by the appropriate Minister (other than the Secretary of State acting alone) or by the Commission in the exercise of any of their functions under this Part.

[1434]

Investigation powers

174   Investigation powers of OFT

(1)   The OFT may exercise any of the powers in subsections (3) to (5) for the purpose of assisting it in deciding whether to make a reference under section 131 or to accept undertakings under section 154 instead of making such a reference.

(2)   The OFT shall not exercise any of the powers in subsections (3) to (5) for the purpose of assisting it as mentioned in subsection (1) unless it already believes that it has power to make such a reference.

(3)   The OFT may give notice to any person requiring him—
   (a)   to attend at a time and place specified in the notice; and
   (b)   to give evidence to the OFT or a person nominated by the OFT for the purpose.

(4)   The OFT may give notice to any person requiring him—
   (a)   to produce any documents which—
      (i)   are specified or described in the notice, or fall within a category of document which is specified or described in the notice; and
      (ii)   are in that person's custody or under his control; and
   (b)   to produce them at a time and place so specified and to a person so specified.

(5)   The OFT may give notice to any person who carries on any business requiring him—
   (a)   to supply to the OFT such estimates, forecasts, returns or other information as may be specified or described in the notice; and
   (b)   to supply it at a time and place, and in a form and manner, so specified and to a person so specified.

(6)   A notice under this section shall include information about the possible consequences of not complying with the notice.

(7)   The person to whom any document is produced in accordance with a notice under this section may, for the purpose mentioned in subsection (1), copy the document so produced.

(8)   No person shall be required under this section—
   (a)   to give any evidence or produce any documents which he could not be compelled to give or produce in civil proceedings before the court; or
   (b)   to supply any information which he could not be compelled to supply in evidence in such proceedings.

(9)   No person shall be required, in compliance with a notice under this section, to go more than 10 miles from his place of residence unless his necessary travelling expenses are paid or offered to him.

(10)   Any reference in this section to the production of a document includes a reference to the production of a legible and intelligible copy of information recorded otherwise than in legible form.

(11)   In this section "the court" means—
   (a)   in relation to England and Wales or Northern Ireland, the High Court; and
   (b)   in relation to Scotland, the Court of Session.

[1435]

175 Enforcement of powers under section 174: offences

(1)   A person commits an offence if he, intentionally and without reasonable excuse, fails to comply with any requirement of a notice under section 174.

(2)   A person commits an offence if he intentionally and without reasonable excuse alters, suppresses or destroys any document which he has been required to produce by a notice under section 174.

(3)   A person who commits an offence under subsection (1) or (2) shall be liable—
  (a)   on summary conviction, to a fine not exceeding the statutory maximum;
  (b)   on conviction on indictment, to imprisonment for a term not exceeding two years or to a fine or to both.

(4)   A person commits an offence if he intentionally obstructs or delays—
  (a)   the OFT in the exercise of its powers under section 174; or
  (b)   any person in the exercise of his powers under subsection (7) of that section.

(5)   A person who commits an offence under subsection (4) shall be liable—
  (a)   on summary conviction, to a fine not exceeding the statutory maximum;
  (b)   on conviction on indictment, to a fine.

[1436]

176 Investigation powers of the Commission

(1)   The following sections in Part 3 shall apply, with the modifications mentioned in subsections (2) and (3) below, for the purposes of references under this Part as they apply for the purposes of references under that Part—
  (a)   section 109 (attendance of witnesses and production of documents etc);
  (b)   section 110 (enforcement of powers under section 109: general);
  (c)   section 111 (penalties);
  (d)   section 112 (penalties: main procedural requirements);
  (e)   section 113 (payments and interest by instalments);
  (f)   section 114 (appeals in relation to penalties);
  (g)   section 115 (recovery of penalties); and
  (h)   section 116 (statement of policy).

(2)   Section 110 shall, in its application by virtue of subsection (1) above, have effect as if—
  (a)   subsection (2) were omitted; and
  (b)   in subsection (9) the words from "or section" to "section 65(3))" were omitted.

(3)   Section 111(5)(b)(ii) shall, in its application by virtue of subsection (1) above, have effect as if—
  (a)   for the words "section 50 or 65, given" there were substituted "section 142, published or given under section 143(1) or (3)"; and
  (b)   for the words "(or given)", in both places where they appear, there were substituted "(or published or given)".

[1437]

Reports

177 Excisions from reports: Part 4

(1)   Subsection (2) applies where the Secretary of State is under a duty to publish a report of the Commission under section 142.

(2)   The Secretary of State may exclude a matter from the report if he considers that publication of the matter would be inappropriate.

(3)   In deciding what is inappropriate for the purposes of subsection (2) the Secretary of State shall have regard to the considerations mentioned in section 244.

(4)   The Commission shall advise the Secretary of State as to the matters (if any) which it considers should be excluded by him under subsection (2).

(5)   References in sections 136(4) to (6), 143(2) and (5) to (7), 148(3) to (5) and 172(10) to the giving or laying of a report of the Commission shall be construed as references to the giving or laying of the report as published.

[1438]

178 Minority reports of Commission: Part 4

(1)   Subsection (2) applies where, on a market investigation reference, a member of a group constituted in connection with the reference in pursuance of paragraph 15 of Schedule 7 to the Competition Act 1998 (c 41), disagrees with any decisions contained in the report of the Commission under this Part as the decisions of the Commission.

(2)   The report shall, if the member so wishes, include a statement of his disagreement and of his reasons for disagreeing.

[1439]

Other

179   Review of decisions under Part 4

(1)   Any person aggrieved by a decision of the OFT, the appropriate Minister, the Secretary of State or the Commission in connection with a reference or possible reference under this Part may apply to the Competition Appeal Tribunal for a review of that decision.

(2)   For this purpose "decision"—
   (a)   does not include a decision to impose a penalty under section 110(1) or (3) as applied by section 176; but
   (b)   includes a failure to take a decision permitted or required by this Part in connection with a reference or possible reference.

(3)   Except in so far as a direction to the contrary is given by the Competition Appeal Tribunal, the effect of the decision is not suspended by reason of the making of the application.

(4)   In determining such an application the Competition Appeal Tribunal shall apply the same principles as would be applied by a court on an application for judicial review.

(5)   The Competition Appeal Tribunal may—
   (a)   dismiss the application or quash the whole or part of the decision to which it relates; and
   (b)   where it quashes the whole or part of that decision, refer the matter back to the original decision maker with a direction to reconsider and make a new decision in accordance with the ruling of the Competition Appeal Tribunal.

(6)   An appeal lies on any point of law arising from a decision of the Competition Appeal Tribunal under this section to the appropriate court.

(7)   An appeal under subsection (6) requires the permission of the Tribunal or the appropriate court.

(8)   In this section—
   "the appropriate court" means the Court of Appeal or, in the case of Tribunal proceedings in Scotland, the Court of Session; and
   "Tribunal rules" has the meaning given by section 15(1).

[1440]

180   Offences

(1)   Sections 117 (false or misleading information) and 125 (offences by bodies corporate) shall apply, with the modifications mentioned in subsection (2) below, for the purposes of this Part as they apply for the purposes of Part 3.

(2)   Section 117 shall, in its application by virtue of subsection (1) above, have effect as if references to the Secretary of State included references to the appropriate Minister so far as he is not the Secretary of State acting alone [and as if the references to OFCOM were omitted].

[1441]

NOTES

Sub-s (2): words in square brackets added by the Communications Act 2003, s 389(1), Sch 16, para 26, as from 29 December 2003.

---

181   Orders under Part 4

(1)   Any power of the Secretary of State to make an order under this Part shall be exercisable by statutory instrument.

(2)   Any power of the Secretary of State to make an order under this Part—
   (a)   may be exercised so as to make different provision for different cases or different purposes;
   (b)   includes power to make such incidental, supplementary, consequential, transitory, transitional or saving provision as the Secretary of State considers appropriate.

(3)   The power of the Secretary of State under section 136(9), 137(3), 144(2), 153(3) or 168(8) as extended by subsection (2) above may be exercised by modifying any enactment comprised in or made under this Act, or any other enactment.

(4)   An order made by the Secretary of State under section 137(3), 144(2), 158, 160 or 161, or under section 111(4) or (6) or 114(3)(b) or (4)(b) as applied by section 176, shall be subject to annulment in pursuance of a resolution of either House of Parliament.

(5) No order shall be made by the Secretary of State under section 136(9) or 168(8), or section 128(6) as applied by section 183(2), unless a draft of it has been laid before, and approved by a resolution of, each House of Parliament.

(6) An order made by the Secretary of State under section 153(3) shall be laid before Parliament after being made and shall cease to have effect unless approved, within the period of 28 days beginning with the day on which it is made, by a resolution of each House of Parliament.

(7) In calculating the period of 28 days mentioned in subsection (6), no account shall be taken of any time during which Parliament is dissolved or prorogued or during which both Houses are adjourned for more than four days.

(8) If an order made by the Secretary of State ceases to have effect by virtue of subsection (6), any modification made by it of an enactment is repealed (and the previous enactment revived) but without prejudice to the validity of anything done in connection with that modification before the order ceased to have effect and without prejudice to the making of a new order.

(9) If, apart from this subsection, an order made by the Secretary of State under section 153(3) would be treated for the purposes of the standing orders of either House of Parliament as a hybrid instrument, it shall proceed in that House as if it were not such an instrument.

(10) References in this section to an order made under this Part include references to an order made under section 111(4) or (6) or 114(3)(b) or (4)(b) as applied by section 176 and an order made under section 128(6) as applied by section 183(2).

[1442]

182 Service of documents: Part 4
Section 126 shall apply for the purposes of this Part as it applies for the purposes of Part 3.

[1443]

183 Interpretation: Part 4
(1) In this Part, unless the context otherwise requires—
    "action" includes omission; and references to the taking of action include references to refraining from action;
    "business" includes a professional practice and includes any other undertaking which is carried on for gain or reward or which is an undertaking in the course of which goods or services are supplied otherwise than free of charge;
    "change of circumstances" includes any discovery that information has been supplied which is false or misleading in a material respect;
    "consumer" means any person who is—
        (a) a person to whom goods are or are sought to be supplied (whether by way of sale or otherwise) in the course of a business carried on by the person supplying or seeking to supply them; or
        (b) a person for whom services are or are sought to be supplied in the course of a business carried on by the person supplying or seeking to supply them;
    and who does not receive or seek to receive the goods or services in the course of a business carried on by him;
    "customer" includes a customer who is not a consumer;
    "enactment" includes an Act of the Scottish Parliament, Northern Ireland legislation and an enactment comprised in subordinate legislation, and includes an enactment whenever passed or made;
    "goods" includes buildings and other structures, and also includes ships, aircraft and hovercraft;
    "Minister of the Crown" means the holder of an office in Her Majesty's Government in the United Kingdom and includes the Treasury;
    "modify" includes amend or repeal;
    "notice" means notice in writing;
    "subordinate legislation" has the same meaning as in the Interpretation Act 1978 (c 30) and also includes an instrument made under an Act of the Scottish Parliament and an instrument made under Northern Ireland legislation; and
    "supply", in relation to the supply of goods, includes supply by way of sale, lease, hire or hire-purchase, and, in relation to buildings or other structures, includes the construction of them by a person for another person.

(2) Sections 127(1)(b) and (4) to (6) and 128 shall apply for the purposes of this Part as they apply for the purposes of Part 3.

(3) For the purposes of this Part a market investigation reference is finally determined if—
    (a) where no intervention notice under section 139(1) has been given in relation to it—
        (i) the period permitted by section 137 for preparing and publishing a report under section 136 has expired and no such report has been prepared and published;

(ii)   such a report has been prepared and published within the period permitted by section 137 and contains the decision that there is no adverse effect on competition;

(iii)   the Commission has decided under section 138(2) neither to accept undertakings under section 159 nor to make an order under section 161; or

(iv)   the Commission has accepted an undertaking under section 159 or made an order under section 161;

(b)   where an intervention notice under section 139(1) has been given in relation to it—

(i)   the period permitted by section 144 for the preparation of the report of the Commission under section 142 and for action to be taken in relation to it under section 143(1) or (3) has expired while the intervention notice is still in force and no such report has been so prepared or no such action has been taken;

(ii)   the Commission has terminated under section 145(1) its investigation and the reference is finally determined under paragraph (a) above (disregarding the fact that the notice was given);

(iii)   the report of the Commission has been prepared under section 142 and published under section 143(1) within the period permitted by section 144;

(iv)   the intervention notice was revoked and the reference is finally determined under paragraph (a) above (disregarding the fact that the notice was given);

(v)   the Secretary of State has failed to make and publish a decision under subsection (2) of section 146 within the period permitted by subsection (3) of that section and the reference is finally determined under paragraph (a) above (disregarding the fact that the notice was given);

(vi)   the Secretary of State has decided under section 146(2) that no eligible public interest consideration is relevant and the reference is finally determined under paragraph (a) above (disregarding the fact that the notice was given);

(vii)   the Secretary of State has decided under 146(2) that a public interest consideration is relevant but has decided under section 147(2) neither to accept an undertaking under section 159 nor to make an order under section 161; or

(viii)   the Secretary of State has decided under section 146(2) that a public interest consideration is relevant and has accepted an undertaking under section 159 or made an order under section 161.

(4)   For the purposes of this Part the time when a market investigation reference is finally determined is—

(a)   in a case falling within subsection (3)(a)(i) or (b)(i), the expiry of the time concerned;

(b)   in a case falling within subsection (3)(a)(ii) or (b)(iii), the publication of the report;

(c)   in a case falling within subsection (3)(a)(iv) or (b)(viii), the acceptance of the undertaking concerned or (as the case may be) the making of the order concerned; and

(d)   in any other case, the making of the decision or last decision concerned or the taking of the action concerned.

(5)   The references in subsection (4) to subsections (3)(a)(i), (ii) and (iv) include those enactments as applied by subsection (3)(b)(ii), (iv), (v) or (vi).

(6)   In subsection (4)(c) the reference to the acceptance of the undertaking concerned or the making of the order concerned shall, in a case where the enforcement action concerned involves the acceptance of a group of undertakings, the making of a group of orders or the acceptance and making of a group of undertakings and orders, be treated as a reference to the acceptance or making of the last undertaking or order in the group; but undertakings or orders which vary, supersede or revoke earlier undertakings or orders shall be disregarded for the purposes of subsections (3)(a)(iv) and (b)(viii) and (4)(c).

(7)   Any duty to publish which is imposed on a person by this Part shall, unless the context otherwise requires, be construed as a duty on that person to publish in such manner as that person considers appropriate for the purpose of bringing the matter concerned to the attention of those likely to be affected by it.

[1444]

184   Index of defined expressions: Part 4

In this Part, the expressions listed in the left-hand column have the meaning given by, or are to be interpreted in accordance with, the provisions listed in the right-hand column.

Expression	Provision of this Act
Action (and the taking of action)	Section 183(1)
Adverse effect on competition	Section 134(2)

Expression	Provision of this Act
Appropriate Minister	Section 132(5)
Business	Section 183(1)
Change of circumstances	Section 183(1)
The Commission	Section 273
Consumer	Section 183(1)
Customer	Section 183(1)
Date of market investigation reference	Section 137(7)
Detrimental effect on customers	Section 134(5)
Enactment	Section 183(1)
Enforcement order	Section 162(8)
Enforcement undertaking	Section 162(8)
Feature of a market	Section 131(2)
Final determination of market investigation reference	Section 183(3) to (6)
Goods	Section 183(1)
Intervention notice	Section 139(3)
Market for goods or services	Section 131(6)
Market in the United Kingdom	Section 131(6)
Market investigation reference	Section 131(6)
Minister of the Crown	Section 183(1)
Modify	Section 183(1)
Notice	Section 183(1)
The OFT	Section 273
Public interest consideration	Section 139(5)
Public interest consideration being finalised	Section 139(7)
Publish	Section 183(7)
Relevant customer benefit	Section 134(8)
Relevant sectoral enactment	Section 136(7)
Relevant sectoral regulator	Section 136(8)
Reports of the Commission	Section 177(5)
Subordinate legislation	Section 183(1)
Supply (in relation to the supply of goods)	Section 183(1)
The supply of services (and a market for services etc)	Section 183(2)

[1445]

PART 11

SUPPLEMENTARY

279 Commencement

The preceding provisions of this Act shall come into force on such day as the Secretary of State may by order made by statutory instrument appoint; and different days may be appointed for different purposes.

[1446]

280 Extent

(1)　Sections 256 to 265, 267, 269 and 272 extend only to England and Wales.

(2)　Sections 204, 248 to 255 and 270 extend only to England and Wales and Scotland (but subsection (3) of section 415A as inserted by section 270 extends only to England and Wales).

(3)　Any other modifications by this Act of an enactment have the same extent as the enactment being modified.

(4)　Otherwise, this Act extends to England and Wales, Scotland and Northern Ireland.

[1447]

281　Short title

This Act may be cited as the Enterprise Act 2002.

[1448]

SCHEDULES

SCHEDULE 1
THE OFFICE OF FAIR TRADING

Section 1

Membership

1.—(1)　The OFT shall consist of a chairman and no fewer than four other members, appointed by the Secretary of State.

(2)　The Secretary of State shall consult the chairman before appointing any other member.

Terms of appointment, remuneration, pensions etc

2.—(1)　Subject to this Schedule, the chairman and other members shall hold and vacate office in accordance with the terms of their respective appointments.

(2)　The terms of appointment of the chairman and other members shall be determined by the Secretary of State.

3.—(1)　An appointment of a person to hold office as chairman or other member shall be for a term not exceeding five years.

(2)　A person holding office as chairman or other member—
  (a)　may resign that office by giving notice in writing to the Secretary of State; and
  (b)　may be removed from office by the Secretary of State on the ground of incapacity or misbehaviour.

(3)　A previous appointment as chairman or other member does not affect a person's eligibility for appointment to either office.

4.—(1)　The OFT shall pay to the chairman and other members such remuneration, and such travelling and other allowances, as may be determined by the Secretary of State.

(2)　The OFT shall, if required to do so by the Secretary of State—
  (a)　pay such pension, allowances or gratuities as may be determined by the Secretary of State to or in respect of a person who holds or has held office as chairman or other member; or
  (b)　make such payments as may be so determined towards provision for the payment of a pension, allowances or gratuities to or in respect of such a person.

(3)　If, where any person ceases to hold office as chairman or other member, the Secretary of State determines that there are special circumstances which make it right that he should receive compensation, the OFT shall pay to him such amount by way of compensation as the Secretary of State may determine.

Staff

5.—(1)　The Secretary of State shall, after consulting the chairman, appoint a person (who may, subject to sub-paragraph (2), also be a member of the OFT) to act as chief executive of the OFT on such terms and conditions as the Secretary of State may think appropriate.

(2)　A person appointed as chief executive after the end of the transitional period may not at the same time be chairman.

(3)　In sub-paragraph (2) "the transitional period" means the period of two years beginning with the day on which this paragraph comes into force.

6.　The OFT may, with the approval of the Minister for the Civil Service as to numbers and terms and conditions of service, appoint such other staff as it may determine.

Membership of committees or sub-committees of OFT

7.   The members of a committee or sub-committee of the OFT may include persons who are not members of the OFT (and a sub-committee may include persons who are not members of the committee which established it).

Proceedings etc

8.—(1)   The OFT may regulate its own procedure (including quorum).

(2)   The OFT shall consult the Secretary of State before making or revising its rules and procedures for dealing with conflicts of interest.

(3)   The OFT shall from time to time publish a summary of its rules and procedures for dealing with conflicts of interest.

9.   The validity of anything done by the OFT is not affected by a vacancy among its members or by a defect in the appointment of a member.

10.—(1)   The application of the seal of the OFT shall be authenticated by the signature of—
    (a)   any member; or
    (b)   some other person who has been authorised for that purpose by the OFT, whether generally or specially.

(2)   Sub-paragraph (1) does not apply in relation to any document which is, or is to be, signed in accordance with the law of Scotland.

11.   A document purporting to be duly executed under the seal of the OFT, or signed on its behalf, shall be received in evidence and, unless the contrary is proved, be taken to be so executed or signed.

Performance of functions

12.—(1)   Anything authorised or required to be done by the OFT (including exercising the power under this paragraph) may be done by—
    (a)   any member or employee of the OFT who is authorised for that purpose by the OFT, whether generally or specially;
    (b)   any committee of the OFT which has been so authorised.

(2)   Sub-paragraph (1)(b) does not apply to a committee whose members include any person who is not a member or employee of the OFT.

Supplementary powers

13.   The OFT has power to do anything which is calculated to facilitate, or is conducive or incidental to, the performance of its functions.

14–16.   …

[1449]

NOTES

Paras 14–16: amend the Parliamentary Commissioner Act 1967, Sch 2, the House of Commons Disqualification Act 1975, Sch 1, Pt II, and the Northern Ireland Assembly Disqualification Act 1975, Sch 1, Pt II.

SCHEDULE 8
PROVISION THAT MAY BE CONTAINED IN CERTAIN ENFORCEMENT ORDERS
Section 86(4)

Introductory

1.   This Schedule applies in relation to such orders, and to such extent, as is provided by this Part and Part 4 and any other enactment; and references in this Schedule to an order shall be construed accordingly.

General restrictions on conduct

2.—(1)   An order may—
    (a)   prohibit the making or performance of an agreement;
    (b)   require any party to an agreement to terminate the agreement.

(2)   An order made by virtue of sub-paragraph (1) shall not—
    (a)   prohibit the making or performance of; or
    (b)   require any person to terminate,

an agreement so far as, if made, the agreement would relate, or (as the case may be) so far as the agreement relates, to the terms and conditions of employment of any workers or to the physical conditions in which any workers are required to work.

3.—(1)   An order may prohibit the withholding from any person of—
  (a)   any goods or services;
  (b)   any orders for any such goods or services.

  (2)   References in sub-paragraph (1) to withholding include references to—
  (a)   agreeing or threatening to withhold; and
  (b)   procuring others to withhold or to agree or threaten to withhold.

4.   An order may prohibit requiring as a condition of the supply of goods or services to any person—
  (a)   the buying of any goods;
  (b)   the making of any payment in respect of services other than the goods or services supplied;
  (c)   the doing of any other such matter or the refraining from doing anything mentioned in paragraph (a) or (b) or any other such matter.

5.   An order may prohibit—
  (a)   discrimination between persons in the prices charged for goods or services;
  (b)   anything which the relevant authority considers to be such discrimination;
  (c)   procuring others to do anything which is such discrimination or which the relevant authority considers to be such discrimination.

6.   An order may prohibit—
  (a)   giving, or agreeing to give in other ways, any preference in respect of the supply of goods or services or in respect of the giving of orders for goods or services;
  (b)   giving, or agreeing to give in other ways, anything which the relevant authority considers to be a preference in respect of the supply of goods or services or in respect of the giving of orders for goods or services;
  (c)   procuring others to do anything mentioned in paragraph (a) or (b).

7.   An order may prohibit—
  (a)   charging, for goods or services supplied, prices differing from those in any published list or notification;
  (b)   doing anything which the relevant authority considers to be charging such prices.

8.—(1)   An order may regulate the prices to be charged for any goods or services.

  (2)   No order shall be made by virtue of sub-paragraph (1) unless the relevant report in relation to the matter concerned identifies the prices charged for the goods or services as requiring remedial action.

  (3)   In this paragraph "the relevant report" means the report of the Commission which is required by the enactment concerned before an order can be made under this Schedule.

9.   An order may prohibit the exercise of any right to vote exercisable by virtue of the holding of any shares, stock or securities.

General obligations to be performed

10.—(1)   An order may require a person to supply goods or services or to do anything which the relevant authority considers appropriate to facilitate the provision of goods or services.

  (2)   An order may require a person who is supplying, or is to supply, goods or services to supply such goods or services to a particular standard or in a particular manner or to do anything which the relevant authority considers appropriate to facilitate the provision of such goods or services to that standard or in that manner.

11.   An order may require any activities to be carried on separately from any other activities.

Acquisitions and divisions

12.—(1)   An order may prohibit or restrict—
  (a)   the acquisition by any person of the whole or part of the undertaking or assets of another person's business;
  (b)   the doing of anything which will or may result in two or more bodies corporate becoming interconnected bodies corporate.

  (2)   An order may require that if—
  (a)   an acquisition of the kind mentioned in sub-paragraph (1)(a) is made; or
  (b)   anything is done which results in two or more bodies corporate becoming interconnected bodies corporate;

the persons concerned or any of them shall observe any prohibitions or restrictions imposed by or under the order.

  (3)   This paragraph shall also apply to any result consisting in two or more enterprises ceasing to be distinct enterprises (other than any result consisting in two or more bodies corporate becoming interconnected bodies corporate).

13.—(1) An order may provide for—
- (a) the division of any business (whether by the sale of any part of the undertaking or assets or otherwise);
- (b) the division of any group of interconnected bodies corporate.

(2) For the purposes of sub-paragraph (1)(a) all the activities carried on by way of business by any one person or by any two or more interconnected bodies corporate may be treated as a single business.

(3) An order made by virtue of this paragraph may contain such provision as the relevant authority considers appropriate to effect or take account of the division, including, in particular, provision as to—
- (a) the transfer or creation of property, rights, liabilities or obligations;
- (b) the number of persons to whom the property, rights, liabilities or obligations are to be transferred or in whom they are to be vested;
- (c) the time within which the property, rights, liabilities or obligations are to be transferred or vested;
- (d) the adjustment of contracts (whether by discharge or reduction of any liability or obligation or otherwise);
- (e) the creation, allotment, surrender or cancellation of any shares, stock or securities;
- (f) the formation or winding up of any company or other body of persons corporate or unincorporate;
- (g) the amendment of the memorandum and articles or other instruments regulating any such company or other body of persons;
- (h) the extent to which, and the circumstances in which, provisions of the order affecting a company or other body of persons corporate or unincorporate in its share capital, constitution or other matters may be altered by the company or other body of persons concerned;
- (i) the registration of the order under any enactment by a company or other body of persons corporate or unincorporate which is affected by it as mentioned in paragraph (h);
- (j) the continuation, with any necessary change of parties, of any legal proceedings;
- (k) the approval by the relevant authority or another person of anything required by virtue of the order to be done or of any person to whom anything is to be transferred, or in whom anything is to be vested, by virtue of the order; or
- (l) the appointment of trustees or other persons to do anything on behalf of another person which is required of that person by virtue of the order or to monitor the doing by that person of any such thing.

14. The references in paragraph 13 to the division of a business as mentioned in sub-paragraph (1)(a) of that paragraph shall, in the case of an order under section 75, 83, 84, 160 or 161, or an order under paragraph 5, 10 or 11 of Schedule 7, be construed as including references to the separation, by the sale of any part of any undertaking or assets concerned or other means, of enterprises which are under common control (within the meaning of section 26) otherwise than by reason of their being enterprises of interconnected bodies corporate.

Supply and publication of information

15.—(1) An order may require a person supplying goods or services to publish a list of prices or otherwise notify prices.

(2) An order made by virtue of this paragraph may also require or prohibit the publication or other notification of further information.

16. An order may prohibit any person from notifying (whether by publication or otherwise) to persons supplying goods or services prices recommended or suggested as appropriate to be charged by those persons for those goods or services.

17.—(1) An order may require a person supplying goods or services to publish—
- (a) accounting information in relation to the supply of the goods or services;
- (b) information in relation to the quantities of goods or services supplied;
- (c) information in relation to the geographical areas in which they are supplied.

(2) In sub-paragraph (1) "accounting information", in relation to a supply of goods or services, means information as to—
- (a) the costs of the supply, including fixed costs and overheads;
- (b) the manner in which fixed costs and overheads are calculated and apportioned for accounting purposes of the supplier; and
- (c) the income attributable to the supply.

18. An order made by virtue of paragraph 15 or 17 may provide for the manner in which information is to be published or otherwise notified.

19. An order may—
- (a) require any person to supply information to the relevant authority;

(b) where the OFT is not the relevant authority, require any person to supply information to the OFT;

(c) provide for the publication, by the person who has received information by virtue of paragraph (a) or (b), of that information.

National security

20.—(1) An order may make such provision as the person making the order considers to be appropriate in the interests of national security (within the meaning of section 58(1)).

(2) Such provision may, in particular, include provision requiring a person to do, or not to do, particular things.

[Newspaper mergers

20A.—(1) This paragraph applies in relation to any order—

(a) which is to be made following the giving of—
  (i) an intervention notice which mentions a newspaper public interest consideration;
  (ii) an intervention notice which mentions any other media public interest consideration in relation to a relevant merger situation in which one of the enterprises ceasing to be distinct is a newspaper enterprise;
  (iii) a special intervention notice which mentions a consideration specified in section 58(2A) or (2B); or
  (iv) a special intervention notice which, in relation to a special merger situation in which one of the enterprises ceasing to be distinct is a newspaper enterprise, mentions a consideration specified in section 58(2C); and
(b) to which the consideration concerned is still relevant.

(2) The order may make such provision as the person making the order considers to be appropriate in all circumstances of the case.

(3) Such provision may, in particular, include provision requiring a person to do, or not to do, particular things.

(4) Provision made by virtue of this paragraph may, in particular, include provision—

(a) altering the constitution of a body corporate (whether in connection with the appointment of directors, the establishment of an editorial board or otherwise);
(b) requiring the agreement of the relevant authority or another person before the taking of particular action (including the appointment or dismissal of an editor, journalists or directors or acting as a shadow director);
(c) attaching conditions to the operation of a newspaper;
(d) prohibiting consultation or co-operation between subsidiaries.

(5) In this paragraph "newspaper public interest consideration" means a media public interest consideration other than one which is such a consideration—

(a) by virtue of section 58(2C); or
(b) by virtue of having been, in the opinion of the Secretary of State, concerned with broadcasting and a consideration that ought to have been specified in section 58.

(6) This paragraph is without prejudice to the operation of the other paragraphs of this Schedule in relation to the order concerned.]

[Maintaining the stability of the UK financial system

20B.—(1) This paragraph applies for the purposes of a relevant order under paragraph 5, 10 or 11 of Schedule 7 (enforcement orders in cases relating to the stability of the UK financial system) but not for any other purposes of Part 3 or 4 or any other enactment.

(2) The order may make such provision as the person making the order considers to be appropriate in the interest of maintaining the stability of the UK financial system.

(3) Such provision may, in particular, include provision requiring a person to do, or not to do, particular things.

(4) This paragraph is without prejudice to the operation of the other paragraphs of this Schedule in relation to the order.

(5) In this paragraph "relevant order" means an order—

(a) which is to be made following the giving of an intervention notice or special intervention notice which mentions the consideration specified in section 58(2D) (including, in the case of a notice given before the consideration was so specified, an intervention notice which mentions the consideration as a consideration which ought to be specified in section 58); and
(b) to which the consideration is still relevant.]

Supplementary

21.—(1)   An order, as well as making provision in relation to all cases to which it may extend, may make provision in relation to—

(a)   those cases subject to specified exceptions; or

(b)   any particular case or class of case.

(2)   An order may, in relation to the cases in relation to which it applies, make the full provision which may be made by it or any less provision (whether by way of exception or otherwise).

(3)   An order may make provision for matters to be determined under the order.

(4)   An order may—

(a)   make different provision for different cases or classes of case or different purposes;

(b)   make such transitional, transitory or saving provision as the person making it considers appropriate.

22.—(1)   An order which may prohibit the doing of anything (or the refraining from doing anything) may in particular by virtue of paragraph 21(2) prohibit the doing of that thing (or the refraining from doing of it) except to such extent and in such circumstances as may be provided by or under the order.

(2)   Any such order may, in particular, prohibit the doing of that thing (or the refraining from doing of it)—

(a)   without the agreement of the relevant authority or another person; or

(b)   by or in relation to a person who has not been approved by the relevant authority or another person.

Interpretation

23.   References in this Schedule to the notification of prices or other information are not limited to the notification in writing of prices or other information.

24.   In this Schedule "the relevant authority" means—

(a)   in the case of an order to be made by the OFT, the OFT;

(b)   in the case of an order to be made by the Commission, the Commission; and

(c)   in the case of an order to be made by the Secretary of State, the Secretary of State.

[1450]–[1458]

NOTES

Para 20A: inserted by the Communications Act 2003, s 387, as from 29 December 2003.

Para 20B: inserted by the Enterprise Act 2002 (Specification of Additional Section 58 Consideration) Order 2008, SI 2008/2645, art 4, as from 24 October 2008. Note that art 1(2) of the 2008 Order provides as follows—

"(2)   This Order shall apply in relation to cases under consideration by the OFT, OFCOM, the Commission or the Secretary of State before the making of this Order as well as cases under consideration on or after the making of this Order.".

CIVIL PARTNERSHIP ACT 2004

(2004 c 33)

NOTES

Only provisions of this Act relevant to Financial Services law are reproduced. Provisions not reproduced are not annotated. By virtue of s 262 (not reproduced) Pt 1 extends to the whole of the United Kingdom.

As of 1 February 2009, this Act (as reproduced here) had not been amended.

An Act to make provision for and in connection with civil partnership

[18 November 2004]

PART 1
INTRODUCTION

1   Civil partnership

(1)   A civil partnership is a relationship between two people of the same sex ("civil partners")—

(a)   which is formed when they register as civil partners of each other—

(i)   in England or Wales (under Part 2),

(ii)   in Scotland (under Part 3),

(iii)   in Northern Ireland (under Part 4), or

(iv)   outside the United Kingdom under an Order in Council made under Chapter 1 of Part 5 (registration at British consulates etc or by armed forces personnel), or

(b)   which they are treated under Chapter 2 of Part 5 as having formed (at the time determined under that Chapter) by virtue of having registered an overseas relationship.

(2)   Subsection (1) is subject to the provisions of this Act under or by virtue of which a civil partnership is void.

(3)   A civil partnership ends only on death, dissolution or annulment.

(4)   The references in subsection (3) to dissolution and annulment are to dissolution and annulment having effect under or recognised in accordance with this Act.

(5)   References in this Act to an overseas relationship are to be read in accordance with Chapter 2 of Part 5.

[1459]

NOTES
Commencement: 5 December 2005.

PART 8
SUPPLEMENTARY

263 Commencement

(1)   Part 1 comes into force in accordance with provision made by order by the Secretary of State, after consulting the Scottish Ministers and the Department of Finance and Personnel.

(2)–(11)   (*Outside the scope of this work.*)

[1460]

NOTES
Commencement: 18 November 2004.
Orders: various commencement orders have been made under this section; the order relevant to the provisions of this Act reproduced here is the Civil Partnership Act 2004 (Commencement No 2) Order 2005, SI 2005/3175.

264 Short title

This Act may be cited as the Civil Partnership Act 2004.

[1461]

NOTES
Commencement: 18 November 2004.

INQUIRIES ACT 2005

(2005 c 12)

NOTES
Only provisions of this Act relevant to Financial Services law are reproduced. Provisions not reproduced are not annotated.
This Act is reproduced as amended by: the Government of Wales Act 2006.

ARRANGEMENT OF SECTIONS

Constitution of inquiry

An Act to make provision about the holding of inquiries

[7 April 2005]

Constitution of inquiry

1   Power to establish inquiry

(1)   A Minister may cause an inquiry to be held under this Act in relation to a case where it appears to him that—

    (a)   particular events have caused, or are capable of causing, public concern, or

    (b)   there is public concern that particular events may have occurred.

(2)   In this Act "Minister" means—

    (a)   a United Kingdom Minister;

    (b)   the Scottish Ministers;

    [(ba) the Welsh Ministers;]

    (c)   a Northern Ireland Minister;

...

(3)   References in this Act to an inquiry, except where the context requires otherwise, are to an inquiry under this Act.

[1462]

NOTES

    Commencement: 7 June 2005.

    Sub-s (2): para (ba) inserted, and words omitted repealed, by the Government of Wales Act 2006, s 160(1), Sch 10, paras 89, 90, as from 25 May 2007.

2   No determination of liability

(1)   An inquiry panel is not to rule on, and has no power to determine, any person's civil or criminal liability.

(2)   But an inquiry panel is not to be inhibited in the discharge of its functions by any likelihood of liability being inferred from facts that it determines or recommendations that it makes.

[1463]

NOTES

    Commencement: 7 June 2005.

3   The inquiry panel

(1)   An inquiry is to be undertaken either—

    (a)   by a chairman alone, or

    (b)   by a chairman with one or more other members.

(2)   References in this Act to an inquiry panel are to the chairman and any other member or members.

[1464]

NOTES

    Commencement: 7 June 2005.

4   Appointment of inquiry panel

(1)   Each member of an inquiry panel is to be appointed by the Minister by an instrument in writing.

(2)   The instrument appointing the chairman must state that the inquiry is to be held under this Act.

(3)   Before appointing a member to the inquiry panel (otherwise than as chairman) the Minister must consult the person he has appointed, or proposes to appoint, as chairman.

[1465]

NOTES
Commencement: 7 June 2005.

5 Setting-up date and terms of reference

(1) In the instrument under section 4 appointing the chairman, or by a notice given to him within a reasonable time afterwards, the Minister must—
    (a)   specify the date that is to be the setting-up date for the purposes of this Act; and
    (b)   before that date—
        (i)   set out the terms of reference of the inquiry;
        (ii)   state whether or not the Minister proposes to appoint other members to the inquiry panel, and if so how many.

(2) An inquiry must not begin considering evidence before the setting-up date.

(3) The Minister may at any time after setting out the terms of reference under this section amend them if he considers that the public interest so requires.

(4) Before setting out or amending the terms of reference the Minister must consult the person he proposes to appoint, or has appointed, as chairman.

(5) Functions conferred by this Act on an inquiry panel, or a member of an inquiry panel, are exercisable only within the inquiry's terms of reference.

(6) In this Act "terms of reference", in relation to an inquiry under this Act, means—
    (a)   the matters to which the inquiry relates;
    (b)   any particular matters as to which the inquiry panel is to determine the facts;
    (c)   whether the inquiry panel is to make recommendations;
    (d)   any other matters relating to the scope of the inquiry that the Minister may specify.

[1466]

NOTES
Commencement: 7 June 2005.

6 Minister's duty to inform Parliament or Assembly

(1) A Minister who proposes to cause an inquiry to be held, or who has already done so without making a statement under this section, must as soon as is reasonably practicable make a statement to that effect to the relevant Parliament or Assembly.

(2) A statement under subsection (1) must state—
    (a)   who is to be, or has been, appointed as chairman of the inquiry;
    (b)   whether the Minister has appointed, or proposes to appoint, any other members to the inquiry panel, and if so how many;
    (c)   what are to be, or are, the inquiry's terms of reference.

(3) Where the terms of reference of an inquiry are amended under section 5(3), the Minister must, as soon as is reasonably practicable, make a statement to the relevant Parliament or Assembly setting out the amended terms of reference.

(4) A statement under this section may be oral or written.

[1467]

NOTES
Commencement: 7 June 2005.

7 Further appointments to inquiry panel

(1) The Minister may at any time (whether before the setting-up date or during the course of the inquiry) appoint a member to the inquiry panel—
    (a)   to fill a vacancy that has arisen in the panel (including a vacancy in the position of chairman), or
    (b)   to increase the number of members of the panel.

(2) The power to appoint a member under subsection (1)(b) is exercisable only—
    (a)   in accordance with a proposal under section 5(1)(b)(ii), or
    (b)   with the consent of the chairman.

(3) The power to appoint a replacement chairman may be exercised by appointing a person who is already a member of the inquiry panel.

[1468]

NOTES
Commencement: 7 June 2005.

8   Suitability of inquiry panel

(1)   In appointing a member of the inquiry panel, the Minister must have regard—

    (a)   to the need to ensure that the inquiry panel (considered as a whole) has the necessary expertise to undertake the inquiry;

    (b)   in the case of an inquiry panel consisting of a chairman and one or more other members, to the need for balance (considered against the background of the terms of reference) in the composition of the panel.

(2)   For the purposes of subsection (1)(a) the Minister may have regard to the assistance that may be provided to the inquiry panel by any assessor whom the Minister proposes to appoint, or has appointed, under section 11.

[1469]

NOTES

    Commencement: 7 June 2005.

9   Requirement of impartiality

(1)   The Minister must not appoint a person as a member of the inquiry panel if it appears to the Minister that the person has—

    (a)   a direct interest in the matters to which the inquiry relates, or

    (b)   a close association with an interested party,

unless, despite the person's interest or association, his appointment could not reasonably be regarded as affecting the impartiality of the inquiry panel.

(2)   Before a person is appointed as a member of an inquiry panel he must notify the Minister of any matters that, having regard to subsection (1), could affect his eligibility for appointment.

(3)   If at any time (whether before the setting-up date or during the course of the inquiry) a member of the inquiry panel becomes aware that he has an interest or association falling within paragraph (a) or (b) of subsection (1), he must notify the Minister.

(4)   A member of the inquiry panel must not, during the course of the inquiry, undertake any activity that could reasonably be regarded as affecting his suitability to serve as such.

[1470]

NOTES

    Commencement: 7 June 2005.

10   Appointment of judge as panel member

(1)   If the Minister proposes to appoint as a member of an inquiry panel a particular person who is a judge of a description specified in the first column of the following table, he must first consult the person specified in the second column.

Description of judge	*Person to be consulted*
Lord of Appeal in Ordinary	The senior Lord of Appeal in Ordinary
Judge of the Supreme Court of England and Wales, or Circuit judge	The Lord Chief Justice of England and Wales
Judge of the Court of Session, sheriff principal or sheriff	The Lord President of the Court of Session
Judge of the Supreme Court of Northern Ireland, or county court judge in Northern Ireland	The Lord Chief Justice of Northern Ireland

(2)   In this section "sheriff principal" and "sheriff" have the same meaning as in the Sheriff Courts (Scotland) Act 1971 (c 58).

[1471]

NOTES

    Commencement: 7 June 2005.

    Supreme Court of England and Wales: the Constitutional Reform Act 2005, s 59(1) provides that (as from a ay to be appointed) the Supreme Court of England and Wales is renamed the Senior Courts of England and Wale.

11   Assessors

(1)   One or more persons may be appointed to act as assessors to assist the inquiry panel.

(2)   The power to appoint assessors is exercisable—

(a)   before the setting-up date, by the Minister;

(b)   during the course of the inquiry, by the chairman (whether or not the Minister has appointed assessors).

(3)   Before exercising his powers under subsection (2)(a) the Minister must consult the person he proposes to appoint, or has appointed, as chairman.

(4)   A person may be appointed as an assessor only if it appears to the Minister or the chairman (as the case requires) that he has expertise that makes him a suitable person to provide assistance to the inquiry panel.

(5)   The chairman may at any time terminate the appointment of an assessor, but only with the consent of the Minister in the case of an assessor appointed by the Minister.

[1472]

NOTES
Commencement: 7 June 2005.

12   Duration of appointment of members of inquiry panel

(1)   Subject to the following provisions of this section, a member of an inquiry panel remains a member until the inquiry comes to an end (or until his death if he dies before then).

(2)   A member of an inquiry panel may at any time resign his appointment by notice to the Minister.

(3)   The Minister may at any time by notice terminate the appointment of a member of an inquiry panel—

(a)   on the ground that, by reason of physical or mental illness or for any other reason, the member is unable to carry out the duties of a member of the inquiry panel;

(b)   on the ground that the member has failed to comply with any duty imposed on him by this Act;

(c)   on the ground that the member has—

(i)   a direct interest in the matters to which the inquiry relates, or

(ii)   a close association with an interested party,

such that his membership of the inquiry panel could reasonably be regarded as affecting its impartiality;

(d)   on the ground that the member has, since his appointment, been guilty of any misconduct that makes him unsuited to membership of the inquiry panel.

(4)   In determining whether subsection (3)(a) applies in a case where the inability to carry out the duties is likely to be temporary, the Minister may have regard to the likely duration of the inquiry.

(5)   The Minister may not terminate a member's appointment under subsection (3)(c) if the Minister was aware of the interest or association in question when appointing him.

(6)   Before exercising his powers under subsection (3) in relation to a member other than the chairman, the Minister must consult the chairman.

(7)   Before exercising his powers under subsection (3) in relation to any member of the inquiry panel, the Minister must—

(a)   inform the member of the proposed decision and of the reasons for it, and take into account any representations made by the member in response, and

(b)   if the member so requests, consult the other members of the inquiry panel (to the extent that no obligation to consult them arises under subsection (6)).

[1473]

NOTES
Commencement: 7 June 2005.

13   Power to suspend inquiry

(1)   The Minister may at any time, by notice to the chairman, suspend an inquiry for such period as appears to him to be necessary to allow for—

(a)   the completion of any other investigation relating to any of the matters to which the inquiry relates, or

(b)   the determination of any civil or criminal proceedings (including proceedings before a disciplinary tribunal) arising out of any of those matters.

(2)   The power conferred by subsection (1) may be exercised whether or not the investigation or proceedings have begun.

(3)   Before exercising that power the Minister must consult the chairman.

(4)   A notice under subsection (1) may suspend the inquiry until a specified day, until the happening of a specified event or until the giving by the Minister of a further notice to the chairman.

(5)   Where the Minister gives a notice under subsection (1) he must—
 (a)   set out in the notice his reasons for suspending the inquiry;
 (b)   lay a copy of the notice, as soon as is reasonably practicable, before the relevant Parliament or Assembly.

(6)   A member of an inquiry panel may not exercise the powers conferred by this Act during any period of suspension; but the duties imposed on a member of an inquiry panel by section 9(3) and (4) continue during any such period.

(7)   In this section "period of suspension" means the period beginning with the receipt by the chairman of the notice under subsection (1) and ending with whichever of the following is applicable—
 (a)   the day referred to in subsection (4);
 (b)   the happening of the event referred to in that subsection;
 (c)   the receipt by the chairman of the further notice under that subsection.

[1474]

NOTES
Commencement: 7 June 2005.

14   End of inquiry

(1)   For the purposes of this Act an inquiry comes to an end—
 (a)   on the date, after the delivery of the report of the inquiry, on which the chairman notifies the Minister that the inquiry has fulfilled its terms of reference, or
 (b)   on any earlier date specified in a notice given to the chairman by the Minister.

(2)   The date specified in a notice under subsection (1)(b) may not be earlier than the date on which the notice is sent.

(3)   Before exercising his power under subsection (1)(b) the Minister must consult the chairman.

(4)   Where the Minister gives a notice under subsection (1)(b) he must—
 (a)   set out in the notice his reasons for bringing the inquiry to an end;
 (b)   lay a copy of the notice, as soon as is reasonably practicable, before the relevant Parliament or Assembly.

[1475]

NOTES
Commencement: 7 June 2005.

Inquiry proceedings

23   Risk of damage to the economy

(1)   This section applies where it is submitted to an inquiry panel, on behalf of the Crown, the Financial Services Authority or the Bank of England, that there is information held by any person which, in order to avoid a risk of damage to the economy, ought not to be revealed.

(2)   The panel must not permit or require the information to be revealed, or cause it to be revealed, unless satisfied that the public interest in the information being revealed outweighs the public interest in avoiding a risk of damage to the economy.

(3)   In making a decision under this section the panel must take account of any restriction notice given under section 19 or any restriction order that the chairman has made or proposes to make under that section.

(4)   In this section—
 "damage to the economy" means damage to the economic interests of the United Kingdom or of any part of the United Kingdom;
 "revealed" means revealed to anyone who is not a member of the inquiry panel.

(5)   This section does not prevent the inquiry panel from communicating any information in confidence to the Minister.

(6)   This section does not affect the rules of law referred to in section 22(2).

[1476]

NOTES
Commencement: 7 June 2005.

Final provisions

51 Commencement

(1) The preceding provisions of this Act come into force on such day as the Lord Chancellor may appoint by order made by statutory instrument.

(2) Before making an order under this section the Lord Chancellor must consult the Scottish Ministers, the [Welsh Ministers] and the First Minister and deputy First Minister.

(3) An order under this section—

(a) may include any transitory, transitional or saving provision that the Secretary of State considers necessary or expedient;

(b) may appoint different days for different purposes.

[1477]

NOTES
Commencement: 7 April 2005.
Sub-s (2): words in square brackets substituted by the Government of Wales Act 2006, s 160(1), Sch 10, paras 89, 97, as from 25 May 2007.
Orders: the Inquiries Act 2005 (Commencement) Order 2005, SI 2005/1432 (which brings this Act, in so far as it didn't come into force on Royal assent, into force on 7 June 2005).

52 Extent

This Act extends to the whole of the United Kingdom.

[1478]

NOTES
Commencement: 7 April 2005.

53 Short title

This Act may be cited as the Inquiries Act 2005.

[1479]

NOTES
Commencement: 7 April 2005.

GAMBLING ACT 2005

(2005 c 19)

NOTES
Only provisions of this Act relevant to Financial Services law are reproduced. Provisions not reproduced are not annotated.
This Act is reproduced as amended by: the Serious Crime Act 2007; the Gambling Act 2005 (Amendment of Schedule 6) Order 2007, SI 2007/2101.
See Financial Markets Law Committee, Issue 138: *Legal assessment of the potential problems for financial markets arising from the Gambling Act 2005 (October 2008)* in relation to certain difficulties with the interpretation of the Act in relation to financial services. Available on the Financial Markets Law Committee website at: http://www.fmlc.org/.

ARRANGEMENT OF SECTIONS

PART 1
INTERPRETATION OF KEY CONCEPTS

Betting

PART 2
THE GAMBLING COMMISSION

PART 18
MISCELLANEOUS AND GENERAL

Miscellaneous

An Act to make provision about gambling

[7 April 2005]

PART 1
INTERPRETATION OF KEY CONCEPTS

Betting

9 Betting: general

(1) In this Act "betting" means making or accepting a bet on—
  (a)   the outcome of a race, competition or other event or process,
  (b)   the likelihood of anything occurring or not occurring, or
  (c)   whether anything is or is not true.

(2) A transaction that relates to the outcome of a race, competition or other event or process may be a bet within the meaning of subsection (1) despite the facts that—
  (a)   the race, competition, event or process has already occurred or been completed, and
  (b)   one party to the transaction knows the outcome.

(3) A transaction that relates to the likelihood of anything occurring or not occurring may be a bet within the meaning of subsection (1) despite the facts that—
  (a)   the thing has already occurred or failed to occur, and
  (b)   one party to the transaction knows that the thing has already occurred or failed to occur.
[1480]

NOTES
  Commencement: 1 October 2005.

10 Spread bets, &c

(1) For the purposes of section 9(1) "bet" does not include a bet the making or accepting of which is a regulated activity within the meaning of section 22 of the Financial Services and Markets Act 2000 (c 8).

(2) An order under section 22 of that Act which has the effect that a class of bet becomes or ceases to be a regulated activity may, in particular, include transitional provision relating to the application of this Act to that class of bet.

(3) This section is subject to section 38(3).
[1481]

NOTES
  Commencement: 1 October 2005 (sub-ss (1), (2)); 1 September 2007 (otherwise).
  Note: s 38(3) provides that an Order under subsection (1) of that section may apply s 37(1) of this Act (offence of carrying on certain gambling activities on premises without the appropriate licence, etc) to betting of the kind referred to in subsection (1) above.

PART 2
THE GAMBLING COMMISSION

NOTES
  Note: s 20 of this Act establishes the Gambling Commission, and s 21 transfers the functions, rights and liabilities of the Gaming Board for Great Britain to the Gambling Commission.

30 Other exchange of information

(1) The Commission may provide information received by it in the exercise of its functions to any of the persons or bodies listed in Schedule 6—
  (a)   for use in the exercise of the person's or body's functions, or
  (b)   for the purpose of a function of the Commission.

(2)   Any of the persons or bodies listed in Part 1 or 2 of Schedule 6 may provide to the Commission, for use in the exercise of its functions, information received by the person or body in the exercise of his or its functions.

(3)   The Commission may provide information received by it in the exercise of its functions to the Comptroller and Auditor General for use in the exercise of his functions under Part 2 of the National Audit Act 1983 (c 44).

(4)   The Commission may provide information received by it in the exercise of its functions to a person if the provision is for the purpose of—
(a)   a criminal investigation (whether in the United Kingdom or elsewhere), or
(b)   criminal proceedings (whether in the United Kingdom or elsewhere).

(5)   Note 2 to Schedule 6 shall not apply to the provision of information under subsection (3).

(6)   Provision of information in reliance on this section may be subject to conditions (whether as to use, storage, disposal or otherwise).

(7)   The Commission may charge a fee for the provision of information under subsection (1)(a).

(8)   This section is subject to section 352.

[1482]

NOTES
Commencement: 1 October 2005.
Note: s 352 of this Act (data protection) provides that nothing in this Act authorises a disclosure which contravenes the Data Protection Act 1998.

PART 18
MISCELLANEOUS AND GENERAL

Miscellaneous

350   Exchange of information

(1)   A person or body listed in Part 1 of Schedule 6 may provide information to any other person or body so listed for use in the exercise of a function under this Act.

(2)   A person or body listed in Part 1 of Schedule 6 may provide information obtained in the course of the exercise of a function under this Act to Her Majesty's Commissioners of Customs and Excise for use in the exercise of any function.

(3)   Provision of information in reliance on this section may be subject to conditions (whether as to use, storage, disposal or otherwise).

[1483]

NOTES
Commencement: 1 January 2007.

General

358   Commencement

(1)   The preceding provisions of this Act shall come into force in accordance with provision made by the Secretary of State by order.

(2)   An order under subsection (1) may (without prejudice to the generality of section 355(1))—
(a)   bring only specified provisions into force;
(b)   bring different provisions into force at different times;
(c)   bring a provision into force for a specified purpose only;
(d)   bring a provision into force at different times for different purposes;
(e)   in particular, bring Part 2 into force only for specified preliminary purposes relating to the establishment of the Commission (which may include the assumption of functions of the Gaming Board for Great Britain pending the commencement of repeals made by this Act);
(f)   in particular, bring a provision of this Act into force for the purpose of enabling an advance application for a licence or permit to be made, considered and determined;
(g)   in particular, bring an offence or other provision of this Act into force only in relation to gambling of a specified class or in specified circumstances;
(h)   include transitional provision modifying the application of a provision of this Act pending the commencement of, or pending the doing of anything under, a provision of another enactment.

(3)–(6)   (*Outside the scope of this work.*)

[1484]

NOTES
Commencement: 7 April 2005.
Orders: various commencement orders have been made under this section; the orders relevant to the provisions of this Act reproduced here are the Gambling Act 2005 (Commencement No 2 and Transitional Provisions) Order 2005, SI 2005/2455 and the Gambling Act 2005 (Commencement No 6 and Transitional Provisions) Order 2006, SI 2006/3272.

361 Extent

(1) The following provisions of this Act extend to England and Wales, Scotland and Northern Ireland—
    (a)   section 43,
    (b)   section 331, and
    (c)   section 340 (and the related entry in Schedule 17).

(2) The other provisions of this Act shall extend only to—
    (a)   England and Wales, and
    (b)   Scotland.

(3) (*Outside the scope of this work.*)

[1485]

NOTES
Commencement: 7 April 2005.

362 Short title

This Act may be cited as the Gambling Act 2005.

[1486]

NOTES
Commencement: 7 April 2005.

SCHEDULE 6
EXCHANGE OF INFORMATION: PERSONS AND BODIES
Sections 30 and 350

PART 2
ENFORCEMENT AND REGULATORY BODIES

...

The Charity Commission

The Financial Services Authority

[The Horserace Betting Levy Board]

...

...

The Occupational Pensions Regulatory Authority

The Office of Fair Trading

The Serious Fraud Office.

[The Serious Organised Crime Agency.]

[1487]

NOTES
Commencement: 1 October 2005.
Entry "The Horserace Betting Levy Board" inserted by the Gambling Act 2005 (Amendment of Schedule 6) Order 2007, SI 2007/2101, art 2(a), as from 20 July 2007.
Entries omitted repealed, and entry "The Serious Organised Crime Agency" inserted, by the Serious Crime Act 2007, ss 74(2), 92, Sch 8, Pt 7, para 176, Sch 14, as from 1 April 2008 (for transitional provisions in relation to the transfer of functions from the Assets Recovery Agency to SOCA and the National Policing Improvement Agency, see the Serious Crime Act 2007 (Commencement No 2 and Transitional and Transitory Provisions and Savings) Order 2008, SI 2008/755, art 3).

REGULATION OF FINANCIAL SERVICES (LAND TRANSACTIONS) ACT 2005 (NOTE)

(2005 c 24)

NOTES

This Act received Royal assent on 19 December 2005 and came into force on 19 February 2006. The purpose of the Act is to enable activities relating to financial arrangements involving the acquisition or disposal of land to be specified as regulated activities under s 22 of FSMA 2000, and hence to be brought under FSA regulation. Section 1 of the Act amends FSMA 2000, Sch 2, Pt II (at **[465]**) to add financial arrangements where the finance provider either (i) acquires a major interest in land from the person being provided with finance, or (ii) disposes of a major interest in land to the person being provided with finance. "Major interest" means a freehold or leasehold interest and is defined separately for England and Wales, Scotland and Northern Ireland to take account of the different property laws in the three jurisdictions. The transfer of the major interest in land can be made either directly between the finance provider and the person being provided with finance or via an intermediary. The amendment of Schedule 2 is, in broad terms, consistent with the approach taken in the existing provisions of Schedule 2. The definition of home reversion schemes and Ijara products, and the description of activities to be regulated in connection with them, would be described in detail in the order which it is intended to make under section 22 of FSMA 2000. However, the breadth of the amendment in section 1 would also allow other financial arrangements involving the acquisition or disposal of land to be brought under FSA regulation, if it became appropriate to do so in the future (for example, for new products which may emerge in the market).

[1488]

FRAUD ACT 2006

(2006 c 35)

NOTES

This Act is reproduced as amended by: the Companies Act 2006 (Commencement No 3, Consequential Amendments, Transitional Provisions and Savings) Order 2007, SI 2007/2194.

ARRANGEMENT OF SECTIONS

Fraud

An Act to make provision for, and in connection with, criminal liability for fraud and obtaining services dishonestly

[8 November 2006]

Fraud

1 Fraud

(1)   A person is guilty of fraud if he is in breach of any of the sections listed in subsection (2) (which provide for different ways of committing the offence).

    (2)   The sections are—
        (a)   section 2 (fraud by false representation),
        (b)   section 3 (fraud by failing to disclose information), and
        (c)   section 4 (fraud by abuse of position).

    (3)   A person who is guilty of fraud is liable—
        (a)   on summary conviction, to imprisonment for a term not exceeding 12 months or to a fine not exceeding the statutory maximum (or to both);
        (b)   on conviction on indictment, to imprisonment for a term not exceeding 10 years or to a fine (or to both).

    (4)   Subsection (3)(a) applies in relation to Northern Ireland as if the reference to 12 months were a reference to 6 months.

[1489]

NOTES
Commencement: 15 January 2007.
Serious crime prevention orders: a court may make a serious crime prevention order under the Serious Crime Act 2007, ss 1, 19 if it is satisfied that a person has been involved in serious crime, and it has reasonable grounds to believe that the order would protect the public by preventing, restricting or disrupting involvement by the person in serious crime. By virtue of s 2 of, and Sch 1, para 7(2) to, the 2007 Act, the offence under this section (and ss 6, 7, 9, 11) is a serious crime. Note also that by virtue paras 7(3), 23(3) of that Schedule, the common law offence of conspiracy to defraud is also a serious offence for these purposes.

2 Fraud by false representation

    (1)   A person is in breach of this section if he—
        (a)   dishonestly makes a false representation, and
        (b)   intends, by making the representation—
            (i)   to make a gain for himself or another, or
            (ii)   to cause loss to another or to expose another to a risk of loss.

    (2)   A representation is false if—
        (a)   it is untrue or misleading, and
        (b)   the person making it knows that it is, or might be, untrue or misleading.

    (3)   "Representation" means any representation as to fact or law, including a representation as to the state of mind of—
        (a)   the person making the representation, or
        (b)   any other person.

    (4)   A representation may be express or implied.

    (5)   For the purposes of this section a representation may be regarded as made if it (or anything implying it) is submitted in any form to any system or device designed to receive, convey or respond to communications (with or without human intervention).

[1490]

NOTES
Commencement: 15 January 2007.

3 Fraud by failing to disclose information

A person is in breach of this section if he—
        (a)   dishonestly fails to disclose to another person information which he is under a legal duty to disclose, and
        (b)   intends, by failing to disclose the information—
            (i)   to make a gain for himself or another, or
            (ii)   to cause loss to another or to expose another to a risk of loss.

[1491]

NOTES
Commencement: 15 January 2007.

4 Fraud by abuse of position

    (1)   A person is in breach of this section if he—
        (a)   occupies a position in which he is expected to safeguard, or not to act against, the financial interests of another person,
        (b)   dishonestly abuses that position, and
        (c)   intends, by means of the abuse of that position—
            (i)   to make a gain for himself or another, or
            (ii)   to cause loss to another or to expose another to a risk of loss.

(2)   A person may be regarded as having abused his position even though his conduct consisted of an omission rather than an act.

[1492]

NOTES
Commencement: 15 January 2007.

5 "Gain" and "loss"

(1)   The references to gain and loss in sections 2 to 4 are to be read in accordance with this section.

(2)   "Gain" and "loss"—
- (a)   extend only to gain or loss in money or other property;
- (b)   include any such gain or loss whether temporary or permanent;

and "property" means any property whether real or personal (including things in action and other intangible property).

(3)   "Gain" includes a gain by keeping what one has, as well as a gain by getting what one does not have.

(4)   "Loss" includes a loss by not getting what one might get, as well as a loss by parting with what one has.

[1493]

NOTES
Commencement: 15 January 2007.

6 Possession etc of articles for use in frauds

(1)   A person is guilty of an offence if he has in his possession or under his control any article for use in the course of or in connection with any fraud.

(2)   A person guilty of an offence under this section is liable—
- (a)   on summary conviction, to imprisonment for a term not exceeding 12 months or to a fine not exceeding the statutory maximum (or to both);
- (b)   on conviction on indictment, to imprisonment for a term not exceeding 5 years or to a fine (or to both).

(3)   Subsection (2)(a) applies in relation to Northern Ireland as if the reference to 12 months were a reference to 6 months.

[1494]

NOTES
Commencement: 15 January 2007.
Serious crime prevention orders: see the note to s 1 at **[1489]**.

7 Making or supplying articles for use in frauds

(1)   A person is guilty of an offence if he makes, adapts, supplies or offers to supply any article—
- (a)   knowing that it is designed or adapted for use in the course of or in connection with fraud, or
- (b)   intending it to be used to commit, or assist in the commission of, fraud.

(2)   A person guilty of an offence under this section is liable—
- (a)   on summary conviction, to imprisonment for a term not exceeding 12 months or to a fine not exceeding the statutory maximum (or to both);
- (b)   on conviction on indictment, to imprisonment for a term not exceeding 10 years or to a fine (or to both).

(3)   Subsection (2)(a) applies in relation to Northern Ireland as if the reference to 12 months were a reference to 6 months.

[1495]

NOTES
Commencement: 15 January 2007.
Serious crime prevention orders: see the note to s 1 at **[1489]**.

8 "Article"

(1)   For the purposes of—
- (a)   sections 6 and 7, and
- (b)   the provisions listed in subsection (2), so far as they relate to articles for use in the course of or in connection with fraud,

"article" includes any program or data held in electronic form.

(2)   The provisions are—
   (a)   section 1(7)(b) of the Police and Criminal Evidence Act 1984 (c 60),
   (b)   section 2(8)(b) of the Armed Forces Act 2001 (c 19), and
   (c)   Article 3(7)(b) of the Police and Criminal Evidence (Northern Ireland) Order 1989 (SI 1989/1341 (NI 12));

(meaning of "prohibited articles" for the purposes of stop and search powers).

[1496]

NOTES
Commencement: 15 January 2007.

9   Participating in fraudulent business carried on by sole trader etc

(1)   A person is guilty of an offence if he is knowingly a party to the carrying on of a business to which this section applies.

(2)   This section applies to a business which is carried on—
   (a)   by a person who is outside the reach of [section 993 of the Companies Act 2006] (offence of fraudulent trading), and
   (b)   with intent to defraud creditors of any person or for any other fraudulent purpose.

(3)   The following are within the reach of [that section]—
   (a)   a company (within the meaning of [the Companies Act 1985 or the Companies (Northern Ireland) Order 1986]);
   (b)   a person to whom that section applies (with or without adaptations or modifications) as if the person were a company;
   (c)   a person exempted from the application of that section.

(4)   ...

(5)   "Fraudulent purpose" has the same meaning as in [that section].

(6)   A person guilty of an offence under this section is liable—
   (a)   on summary conviction, to imprisonment for a term not exceeding 12 months or to a fine not exceeding the statutory maximum (or to both);
   (b)   on conviction on indictment, to imprisonment for a term not exceeding 10 years or to a fine (or to both).

(7)   Subsection (6)(a) applies in relation to Northern Ireland as if the reference to 12 months were a reference to 6 months.

[1497]

NOTES
Commencement: 15 January 2007.
Sub-s (2): words in square brackets substituted (for the original words "section 458 of the Companies Act 1985 (c 6) or Article 451 of the Companies (Northern Ireland) Order 1986 (SI 1986/1032) (NI 6))") by the Companies Act 2006 (Commencement No 3, Consequential Amendments, Transitional Provisions and Savings) Order 2007, SI 2007/2194, art 10(1), Sch 4, Pt 3, para 111(1), (2), (6), as from 1 October 2007 (for transitional provisions see the note below). Note that para 111(2) of Sch 4 to the 2007 Order actually provides "for "section 458 of the Companies Act 1985 or Article 451 of the Companies (Northern Ireland) Order 1986" substitute "section 993 of the Companies Act 2006"". It is believed that this is an error as this would leave the words "(SI 1986/1032) (NI 6))" following "section 993 of the Companies Act 2006".
Sub-s (3): words in first pair of square brackets substituted (for the original words "section 458 of the 1985 Act"), and words in second pair of square brackets substituted (for the original words "that Act"), by SI 2007/2194, art 10(1), Sch 4, Pt 3, para 111(1), (3), (6), as from 1 October 2007 (for transitional provisions see the note below).
Sub-s (4): repealed by SI 2007/2194, art 10(1), (3), Sch 4, Pt 3, para 111(1), (4), (6), Sch 5, as from 1 October 2007 (for transitional provisions see the note below). This subsection previously read as follows—

"(4)   The following are within the reach of Article 451 of the 1986 Order—
   (a)   a company (within the meaning of that Order);
   (b)   a person to whom that Article applies (with or without adaptations or modifications) as if the person were a company;
   (c)   a person exempted from the application of that Article.".

Sub-s (5): words in square brackets substituted (for the original words "section 458 of the 1985 Act or Article 451 of the 1986 Order") by SI 2007/2194, art 10(1), (3), Sch 4, Pt 3, para 111(1), (5), (6), Sch 5, as from 1 October 2007 (for transitional provisions see the note below).
Transitional provisions: the Companies Act 2006 (Commencement No 3, Consequential Amendments, Transitional Provisions and Savings) Order 2007, SI 2007/2194, Sch 4, Pt 3, para 111(6) provides as follows—

"(6)   These amendments apply to an offence if any act, omission or other event (including any result of one or more acts or omissions) proof of which is required for conviction of the offence occurs on or after 1st October 2007.".

Serious crime prevention orders: see the note to s 1 at **[1489]**.

10 (*Amends the Companies Act 1985, Sch 24, and the Companies* (*Northern Ireland*) *Order 1986, Sch 23.*)

Obtaining services dishonestly

11 Obtaining services dishonestly

(1) A person is guilty of an offence under this section if he obtains services for himself or another—

    (a)   by a dishonest act, and

    (b)   in breach of subsection (2).

(2) A person obtains services in breach of this subsection if—

    (a)   they are made available on the basis that payment has been, is being or will be made for or in respect of them,

    (b)   he obtains them without any payment having been made for or in respect of them or without payment having been made in full, and

    (c)   when he obtains them, he knows—

        (i)   that they are being made available on the basis described in paragraph (a), or

        (ii)   that they might be,

but intends that payment will not be made, or will not be made in full.

(3) A person guilty of an offence under this section is liable—

    (a)   on summary conviction, to imprisonment for a term not exceeding 12 months or to a fine not exceeding the statutory maximum (or to both);

    (b)   on conviction on indictment, to imprisonment for a term not exceeding 5 years or to a fine (or to both).

(4) Subsection (3)(a) applies in relation to Northern Ireland as if the reference to 12 months were a reference to 6 months.

[1498]

NOTES

Commencement: 15 January 2007.

Serious crime prevention orders: see the note to s 1 at **[1489]**.

Supplementary

12 Liability of company officers for offences by company

(1) Subsection (2) applies if an offence under this Act is committed by a body corporate.

(2) If the offence is proved to have been committed with the consent or connivance of—

    (a)   a director, manager, secretary or other similar officer of the body corporate, or

    (b)   a person who was purporting to act in any such capacity,

he (as well as the body corporate) is guilty of the offence and liable to be proceeded against and punished accordingly.

(3) If the affairs of a body corporate are managed by its members, subsection (2) applies in relation to the acts and defaults of a member in connection with his functions of management as if he were a director of the body corporate.

[1499]

NOTES

Commencement: 15 January 2007.

13 Evidence

(1) A person is not to be excused from—

    (a)   answering any question put to him in proceedings relating to property, or

    (b)   complying with any order made in proceedings relating to property,

on the ground that doing so may incriminate him or his spouse or civil partner of an offence under this Act or a related offence.

(2) But, in proceedings for an offence under this Act or a related offence, a statement or admission made by the person in—

    (a)   answering such a question, or

    (b)   complying with such an order,

is not admissible in evidence against him or (unless they married or became civil partners after the making of the statement or admission) his spouse or civil partner.

(3) "Proceedings relating to property" means any proceedings for—

    (a)   the recovery or administration of any property,

    (b)   the execution of a trust, or

    (c)   an account of any property or dealings with property, and "property" means money or other property whether real or personal (including things in action and other intangible property).

(4)   "Related offence" means—

    (a)   conspiracy to defraud;

    (b)   any other offence involving any form of fraudulent conduct or purpose.

[1500]

NOTES

   Commencement: 15 January 2007.

14   (*Introduces Sch 1 (minor and consequential amendments), Sch 2 (transitional provisions and savings), and Sch 3 (repeals and revocations).*)

15   Commencement and extent

   (1)   This Act (except this section and section 16) comes into force on such day as the Secretary of State may appoint by an order made by statutory instrument; and different days may be appointed for different purposes.

   (2)   Subject to subsection (3), sections 1 to 9 and 11 to 13 extend to England and Wales and Northern Ireland only.

   (3)   Section 8, so far as it relates to the Armed Forces Act 2001 (c 19), extends to any place to which that Act extends.

   (4)   Any amendment in section 10 or Schedule 1, and any related provision in section 14 or Schedule 2 or 3, extends to any place to which the provision which is the subject of the amendment extends.

[1501]

NOTES

   Commencement: 8 November 2006.

   Orders: the Fraud Act 2006 (Commencement) Order 2006, SI 2006/3200.

16   Short title

This Act may be cited as the Fraud Act 2006.

[1502]

NOTES

   Commencement: 8 November 2006.

SCHEDULES

(*Sch 1: para 1 repeals the Theft Act 1968, ss 15, 15A, 16, 20(2) (the deception offences); paras 2–38 contain minor and consequential amendments which, in so far as relevant to this work, are incorporated at the appropriate place.*)

SCHEDULE 2
TRANSITIONAL PROVISIONS AND SAVINGS

Section 14(2)

Maximum term of imprisonment for offences under this Act

1.   In relation to an offence committed before the commencement of section 154(1) of the Criminal Justice Act 2003 (c 44), the references to 12 months in sections 1(3)(a), 6(2)(a), 7(2)(a), 9(6)(a) and 11(3)(a) are to be read as references to 6 months.

Increase in penalty for fraudulent trading

2.   Section 10 does not affect the penalty for any offence committed before that section comes into force.

Abolition of deception offences

3.—(1)   Paragraph 1 of Schedule 1 does not affect any liability, investigation, legal proceeding or penalty for or in respect of any offence partly committed before the commencement of that paragraph.

   (2)   An offence is partly committed before the commencement of paragraph 1 of Schedule 1 if—

    (a)   a relevant event occurs before its commencement, and

    (b)   another relevant event occurs on or after its commencement.

(3) "Relevant event", in relation to an offence, means any act, omission or other event (including any result of one or more acts or omissions) proof of which is required for conviction of the offence.

Scope of offences relating to stolen goods under the Theft Act 1968 (c 60)

4. Nothing in paragraph 6 of Schedule 1 affects the operation of section 24 of the Theft Act 1968 in relation to goods obtained in the circumstances described in section 15(1) of that Act where the obtaining is the result of a deception made before the commencement of that paragraph.

Dishonestly retaining a wrongful credit under the Theft Act 1968

5. Nothing in paragraph 7 of Schedule 1 affects the operation of section 24A(7) and (8) of the Theft Act 1968 in relation to credits falling within section 24A(3) or (4) of that Act and made before the commencement of that paragraph.

6–11. (*Outside the scope of this work.*)

[1503]

NOTES

Commencement: 15 January 2007.

(*Sch 3 (repeals and revocations) omitted.*)

COMPANIES ACT 2006

(2006 c 46)

NOTES

Only provisions of this Act relevant to Financial Services law are reproduced. Provisions not reproduced are not annotated.

Commencement: the commencement of this Act is provided for by s 1300 at **[1732]**. See also the Orders made under that section.

Interpretation of provisions in this Act: the Companies Act 2006 (Commencement No 1, Transitional Provisions and Savings) Order 2006, SI 2006/3428, art 6 provides as set out below. Note that the same provision is also made by the Companies Act 2006 (Commencement No 2, Consequential Amendments, Transitional Provisions and Savings) Order 2007, SI 2007/1093, art 4, the Companies Act 2006 (Commencement No 3, Consequential Amendments, Transitional Provisions and Savings) Order 2007, SI 2007/2194, art 7, the Companies Act 2006 (Commencement No 4 and Commencement No 3 (Amendment)) Order 2007, SI 2007/2607, art 3, the Companies Act 2006 (Commencement No 5, Transitional Provisions and Savings) Order 2007, SI 2007/3495, art 7, and the Companies Act 2006 (Commencement No 7, Transitional Provisions and Savings) Order 2008, SI 2008/1886, art 6:

"6 Interpretation of provisions brought into force

Where an expression in a provision brought into force by this Order (or in an adaptation made by this Order of such a provision)—

    (a)   is defined in the 1985 Act or the 1986 Order ("the old definition"); and

    (b)   is defined in the Companies Act 2006 by another provision that is not yet in force for the purposes of the provision brought into force ("the new definition"),

the expression has, for the purposes of the provision brought into force (or the adaptation), the meaning given by the old definition until the new definition is brought into force for the purposes of that provision.".

The provisions of this Act included in this work are reproduced as amended by: the Legal Services Act 2007; the Companies (EEA State) Regulations 2007, SI 2007/732; the Government of Wales Act 2006 (Consequential Modifications and Transitional Provisions) Order 2007, SI 2007/1388; the Markets in Financial Instruments Directive (Consequential Amendments) Regulations 2007, SI 2007/2932; the Statutory Auditors and Third Country Auditors Regulations 2007, SI 2007/3494; the Companies Act 2006 (Amendment) (Accounts and Reports) Regulations 2008, SI 2008/393; the Insurance Accounts Directive (Miscellaneous Insurance Undertakings) Regulations 2008, SI 2008/565; the Bank Accounts Directive (Miscellaneous Banks) Regulations 2008, SI 2008/567; the Companies Act 2006 (Consequential Amendments etc) Order 2008, SI 2008/948; the Consumer Protection from Unfair Trading Regulations 2008, SI 2008/1277; the Insurance Accounts Directive (Lloyd's Syndicate and Aggregate Accounts) Regulations 2008, SI 2008/1950; the Companies Act 2006 (Annual Return and Service Addresses) Regulations 2008, SI 2008/3000; the Companies Act 2006 (Amendment of Schedule 2) Order 2009, SI 2009/202.

Application to limited liability partnerships: as to the application of this Act to LLPs, see the Limited Liability Partnerships (Accounts and Audit) (Application of Companies Act 2006) Regulations 2008, SI 2008/1911 at **[4169]**. Note also that separate Regulations (ie, the Small Limited Liability Partnerships (Accounts) Regulations 2008, SI 2008/1912, and the Large and Medium-sized Limited Liability Partnerships (Accounts) Regulations 2008, SI 2008/1913) apply provisions on the form and content of accounts to LLPs.

Application to unregistered companies: as to the application of certain parts of this Act to unregistered companies (including Part 28 Takeovers etc), see the Companies Acts (Unregistered Companies) Regulations 2007, SI 2007/318 (made under s 1043 of this Act).

Application to insurance undertakings: as to the application of the accounts and audit provisions of this Act to specified insurance undertakings, see the Insurance Accounts Directive (Miscellaneous Insurance

Undertakings) Regulations 2008, SI 2008/565. See also, the Insurance Accounts Directive (Lloyd's Syndicate and Aggregate Accounts) Regulations 2008, SI 2008/1950.

Application to banks: as to the application of the accounts and audit provisions of this Act to specified banks, see the Bank Accounts Directive (Miscellaneous Banks) Regulations 2008, SI 2008/567. As to the application of certain provisions of this Act to particular banks, see the Banking (Special Provisions) Act 2008 (at **[1758]**) and the Orders made under it.

Application to partnerships: as to the application of the accounts and audit provisions of this Act to partnerships, see the Partnerships (Accounts) Regulations 2008, SI 2008/569.

Civil Procedure Rules: the Civil Procedure Rules 1998, SI 1998/3132, rule 49 (as amended), states that those Rules apply to proceedings under this Act subject to the provisions of the relevant practice direction which applies to those proceedings.

CHAPTER 3
A COMPANY'S FINANCIAL YEAR

CHAPTER 4
ANNUAL ACCOUNTS

General

Individual accounts

Group accounts: small companies

Group accounts: other companies

Group accounts: general

Information to be given in notes to the accounts

Approval and signing of accounts

CHAPTER 5
DIRECTORS' REPORT

Directors' report

CHAPTER 6
QUOTED COMPANIES: DIRECTORS' REMUNERATION REPORT

CHAPTER 7
PUBLICATION OF ACCOUNTS AND REPORTS

Duty to circulate copies of accounts and reports

PART II
OTHER ACTS

PART II
OTHER ACTS

PART 26
ARRANGEMENTS AND RECONSTRUCTIONS

Application of this Part

Meeting of creditors or members

Court sanction for compromise or arrangement

Reconstructions and amalgamations

Obligations of company with respect to articles etc

PART 28
TAKEOVERS ETC

CHAPTER 1
THE TAKEOVER PANEL

The Panel and its rules

Information

CHAPTER 2
IMPEDIMENTS TO TAKEOVERS

Opting in and opting out

Consequences of opting in

Supplementary

CHAPTER 3
"SQUEEZE-OUT" AND "SELL-OUT"

Takeover offers

"Squeeze-out"

"Sell-out"

An Act to reform company law and restate the greater part of the enactments relating to companies; to make other provision relating to companies and other forms of business organisation; to make provision about directors' disqualification, business names, auditors and actuaries; to amend Part 9 of the Enterprise Act 2002; and for connected purposes

[8 November 2006]

PART 1
GENERAL INTRODUCTORY PROVISIONS

Companies and Companies Acts

1 Companies

(1) In the Companies Acts, unless the context otherwise requires—
"company" means a company formed and registered under this Act, that is—
  (a) a company so formed and registered after the commencement of this Part, or
  (b) a company that immediately before the commencement of this Part—
    (i) was formed and registered under the Companies Act 1985 (c 6) or the Companies (Northern Ireland) Order 1986 (SI 1986/1032 (NI 6)), or
    (ii) was an existing company for the purposes of that Act or that Order,
    (which is to be treated on commencement as if formed and registered under this Act).

(2) Certain provisions of the Companies Acts apply to—
  (a) companies registered, but not formed, under this Act (see Chapter 1 of Part 33), and
  (b) bodies incorporated in the United Kingdom but not registered under this Act (see Chapter 2 of that Part).

(3) For provisions applying to companies incorporated outside the United Kingdom, see Part 34 (overseas companies).

[1503A]

NOTES
Commencement: 1 October 2009.
Transitional provisions: as to the definition of "company" see further the transitional provisions note to s 7 at **[1503G]**.

2 The Companies Acts

(1) In this Act "the Companies Acts" means—
  (a) the company law provisions of this Act,
  (b) Part 2 of the Companies (Audit, Investigations and Community Enterprise) Act 2004 (c 27) (community interest companies), and
  (c) the provisions of the Companies Act 1985 (c 6) and the Companies Consolidation (Consequential Provisions) Act 1985 (c 9) that remain in force.

(2) The company law provisions of this Act are—
  (a) the provisions of Parts 1 to 39 of this Act, and
  (b) the provisions of Parts 45 to 47 of this Act so far as they apply for the purposes of those Parts.

[1503B]

NOTES

Commencement: 1 January 2007 (certain purposes); 20 January 2007 (certain purposes); 6 April 2007 (otherwise) (see the note below).

Commencement (transitional adaptations): art 5 of the Companies Act 2006 (Commencement No 1, Transitional Provisions and Savings) Order 2006, SI 2006/3428 provides that the provisions brought into force by arts 2–4 of 2006 Order shall have effect subject to any transitional adaptations specified in Sch 1 to that Order. Schedule 1, para 1 to the Order provides as follows (note that this paragraph is revoked by the Companies Act 2006 (Commencement No 8, Transitional Provisions and Savings) Order 2008, SI 2008/2860, art 6, as from 1 October 2009 (subject to any relevant transitional provision or saving in Sch 2 to that Order))—

"1.—(1)   Section 2 (the Companies Acts) has effect with the following adaptation.

(2)   For subsection (1)(c) substitute—

"(c) the provisions of the Companies Acts as defined in section 744 of the Companies Act 1985, and the Companies Orders as defined in Article 2(3) of the Companies (Northern Ireland) Order 1986, that remain in force.".".

Commencement (transitional adaptations): art 3 of the Companies Act 2006 (Commencement No 2, Consequential Amendments, Transitional Provisions and Savings) Order 2007, SI 2007/1093 provides that the provisions brought into force by art 2 of 2007 Order shall have effect subject to any transitional adaptations specified in Sch 1 to that Order. Schedule 1, para 1 to the Order provides as follows (note that this paragraph is revoked by the Companies Act 2006 (Commencement No 8, Transitional Provisions and Savings) Order 2008, SI 2008/2860, art 6, as from 1 October 2009 (subject to any relevant transitional provision or saving in Sch 2 to that Order))—

"1.—(1)   Section 2 (the Companies Acts) has effect with the following adaptation.

(2)   For subsection (1)(c) substitute—

"(c) the provisions of the Companies Acts as defined in section 744 of the Companies Act 1985, and the Companies Orders as defined in Article 2(3) of the Companies (Northern Ireland) Order 1986, that remain in force"".

Commencement (note): the Companies Act 2006 (Commencement No 1, Transitional Provisions and Savings) Order 2006, SI 2006/3428, arts 2(2), 3(2) provide that this section shall come into force on 1 January 2007 and 20 January 2007 respectively so far as is necessary for the purposes of the provisions of this Act brought into force on those dates by arts 2(1), 3(1) of that Order.

Types of company

3   Limited and unlimited companies

(1)   A company is a "limited company" if the liability of its members is limited by its constitution.

It may be limited by shares or limited by guarantee.

(2)   If their liability is limited to the amount, if any, unpaid on the shares held by them, the company is "limited by shares".

(3)   If their liability is limited to such amount as the members undertake to contribute to the assets of the company in the event of its being wound up, the company is "limited by guarantee".

(4)   If there is no limit on the liability of its members, the company is an "unlimited company".

[1503C]

NOTES

Commencement: 1 October 2009.

4   Private and public companies

(1)   A "private company" is any company that is not a public company.

(2)   A "public company" is a company limited by shares or limited by guarantee and having a share capital—

(a)   whose certificate of incorporation states that it is a public company, and

(b)   in relation to which the requirements of this Act, or the former Companies Acts, as to registration or re-registration as a public company have been complied with on or after the relevant date.

(3)   For the purposes of subsection (2)(b) the relevant date is—

(a)   in relation to registration or re-registration in Great Britain, 22nd December 1980;

(b)   in relation to registration or re-registration in Northern Ireland, 1st July 1983.

(4)   For the two major differences between private and public companies, see Part 20.

[1503D]

NOTES

Commencement: 1 October 2009.

5 Companies limited by guarantee and having share capital

(1) A company cannot be formed as, or become, a company limited by guarantee with a share capital.

(2) Provision to this effect has been in force—
  (a) in Great Britain since 22nd December 1980, and
  (b) in Northern Ireland since 1st July 1983.

(3) Any provision in the constitution of a company limited by guarantee that purports to divide the company's undertaking into shares or interests is a provision for a share capital.

This applies whether or not the nominal value or number of the shares or interests is specified by the provision.

[1503E]

NOTES
Commencement: 1 October 2009.

6 Community interest companies

(1) In accordance with Part 2 of the Companies (Audit, Investigations and Community Enterprise) Act 2004 (c 27)—
  (a) a company limited by shares or a company limited by guarantee and not having a share capital may be formed as or become a community interest company, and
  (b) a company limited by guarantee and having a share capital may become a community interest company.

(2) The other provisions of the Companies Acts have effect subject to that Part.

[1503F]

NOTES
Commencement: 1 October 2009.

PART 2

COMPANY FORMATION

General

7 Method of forming company

(1) A company is formed under this Act by one or more persons—
  (a) subscribing their names to a memorandum of association (see section 8), and
  (b) complying with the requirements of this Act as to registration (see sections 9 to 13).

(2) A company may not be so formed for an unlawful purpose.

[1503G]

NOTES
Commencement: 1 October 2009.
Commencement (transitional provisions): Sch 2, para 2 to the Companies Act 2006 (Commencement No 8, Transitional Provisions and Savings) Order 2008, SI 2008/2860 provides as follows—

"Company formation (ss 7 to 16)

2.—(1) Sections 7 to 16 of the Companies Act 2006 (company formation) apply to applications for registration received by the registrar on or after 1st October 2009.

(2) Any application for registration under those provisions received by the registrar before that date shall not be entertained.

(3) The corresponding provisions of the 1985 Act or 1986 Order continue to apply to an application for registration if—
  (a) it is received by the registrar, and
  (b) the requirements as to registration are met in relation to it,
before 1st October 2009.

(4) Any application for registration under that Act or Order in relation to which the requirements as to registration are not met before that date shall be treated as withdrawn.

(5) For the purposes of section 1297(3) of the Companies Act 2006 (continuity of the law) as it applies to treat a company formed and registered under Part 1 of the 1985 Act or Part 2 of the 1986 Order as if formed and registered under the corresponding provisions of the Companies Act 2006, the registration of a company on an application to which sub-paragraph (3) above applies is to be regarded as in force and effective immediately before the commencement of Part 1 of the Companies Act 2006.

(6) In the definition of "company" in section 1 of the Companies Act 2006—
  (a) the reference to a company formed and registered after the commencement of Part 1 of that Act shall be read as a reference to a company formed and registered on an application to which sub-paragraph (1) above applies, and

(b)   the reference to a company formed and registered under the 1985 Act or 1986 Order immediately before the commencement of Part 1 of the Companies Act 2006 includes a company formed and registered on an application to which sub-paragraph (3) above applies.".

8 Memorandum of association

(1)   A memorandum of association is a memorandum stating that the subscribers—
    (a)   wish to form a company under this Act, and
    (b)   agree to become members of the company and, in the case of a company that is to have a share capital, to take at least one share each.

(2)   The memorandum must be in the prescribed form and must be authenticated by each subscriber.

[1503H]

NOTES
Commencement: 20 January 2007 (for the purpose of enabling the exercise of powers to make Orders or Regulations by statutory instrument); 1 October 2009 (otherwise).
Commencement (transitional provisions): see the note to s 7 at **[1503G]**.
Regulations: the Companies (Registration) Regulations 2008, SI 2008/3014.

PART 8
A COMPANY'S MEMBERS

CHAPTER 4
PROHIBITION ON SUBSIDIARY BEING MEMBER OF ITS HOLDING COMPANY

General prohibition

136 Prohibition on subsidiary being a member of its holding company

(1)   Except as provided by this Chapter—
    (a)   a body corporate cannot be a member of a company that is its holding company, and
    (b)   any allotment or transfer of shares in a company to its subsidiary is void.

(2)   The exceptions are provided for in—
section 138 (subsidiary acting as personal representative or trustee), and
section 141 (subsidiary acting as authorised dealer in securities).

[1504]

NOTES
Commencement: 1 October 2009.

Subsidiary acting as dealer in securities

141 Subsidiary acting as authorised dealer in securities

(1)   The prohibition in section 136 (prohibition on subsidiary being a member of its holding company) does not apply where the shares are held by the subsidiary in the ordinary course of its business as an intermediary.

(2)   For this purpose a person is an intermediary if he—
    (a)   carries on a bona fide business of dealing in securities,
    (b)   is a member of or has access to a regulated market, and
    (c)   does not carry on an excluded business.

(3)   The following are excluded businesses—
    (a)   a business that consists wholly or mainly in the making or managing of investments;
    (b)   a business that consists wholly or mainly in, or is carried on wholly or mainly for the purposes of, providing services to persons who are connected with the person carrying on the business;
    (c)   a business that consists in insurance business;
    (d)   a business that consists in managing or acting as trustee in relation to a pension scheme, or that is carried on by the manager or trustee of such a scheme in connection with or for the purposes of the scheme;
    (e)   a business that consists in operating or acting as trustee in relation to a collective investment scheme, or that is carried on by the operator or trustee of such a scheme in connection with and for the purposes of the scheme.

(4)   For the purposes of this section—
    (a)   the question whether a person is connected with another shall be determined in accordance with section 839 of the Income and Corporation Taxes Act 1988 (c 1);
    (b)   "collective investment scheme" has the meaning given in section 235 of the Financial Services and Markets Act 2000 (c 8);

(c)   "insurance business" means business that consists in the effecting or carrying out of contracts of insurance;

(d)   "securities" includes—

(i)   options,

(ii)   futures, and

(iii) contracts for differences,

and rights or interests in those investments;

(e)   "trustee" and "the operator" in relation to a collective investment scheme shall be construed in accordance with section 237(2) of the Financial Services and Markets Act 2000 (c 8).

(5)   Expressions used in this section that are also used in the provisions regulating activities under the Financial Services and Markets Act 2000 have the same meaning here as they do in those provisions.

See section 22 of that Act, orders made under that section and Schedule 2 to that Act.

[1505]

NOTES

Commencement: 1 October 2009.

142   Protection of third parties in other cases where subsidiary acting as dealer in securities

(1)   This section applies where—

(a)   a subsidiary that is a dealer in securities has purportedly acquired shares in its holding company in contravention of the prohibition in section 136, and

(b)   a person acting in good faith has agreed, for value and without notice of the contravention, to acquire shares in the holding company—

(i)   from the subsidiary, or

(ii)   from someone who has purportedly acquired the shares after their disposal by the subsidiary.

(2)   A transfer to that person of the shares mentioned in subsection (1)(a) has the same effect as it would have had if their original acquisition by the subsidiary had not been in contravention of the prohibition.

[1506]

NOTES

Commencement: 1 October 2009.

PART 15
ACCOUNTS AND REPORTS

CHAPTER 1
INTRODUCTION

General

380   Scheme of this Part

(1)   The requirements of this Part as to accounts and reports apply in relation to each financial year of a company.

(2)   In certain respects different provisions apply to different kinds of company.

(3)   The main distinctions for this purpose are—

(a)   between companies subject to the small companies regime (see section 381) and companies that are not subject to that regime; and

(b)   between quoted companies (see section 385) and companies that are not quoted.

(4)   In this Part, where provisions do not apply to all kinds of company—

(a)   provisions applying to companies subject to the small companies regime appear before the provisions applying to other companies,

(b)   provisions applying to private companies appear before the provisions applying to public companies, and

(c)   provisions applying to quoted companies appear after the provisions applying to other companies.

[1507]

NOTES

Commencement: 6 April 2008.

Commencement (transitional provisions): Sch 4, Pt 1, paras 6–8 to the Companies Act 2006 (Commencement No 5, Transitional Provisions and Savings) Order 2007, SI 2007/3495 provide as follows—

"*Accounts and reports (ss 380 to 389, 393 to 416, 418 to 462 and 464 to 474)*

6.—(1)   Sections 380 to 389, 393 to 416, 418 to 462 and 464 to 474 of the Companies Act 2006 (accounts and reports) apply to accounts and reports for financial years beginning on or after 6th April 2008.

(2)   The corresponding provisions of the 1985 Act or the 1986 Order continue to apply to accounts and reports for financial years beginning before that date.

7.   Any question whether—
    (a)   for the purposes of section 382, 383, 384(3) or 467(3) of the Companies Act 2006 a company or group qualified as small in a financial year beginning before 6th April 2008, or
    (b)   for the purposes of section 465 or 466 of that Act a company or group qualified as medium-sized in any such financial year,

is to be determined by reference to the corresponding provisions of the 1985 Act or the 1986 Order.

8.   Until section 1068(1) of the Companies Act 2006 comes into force, the notice referred to in section 392 of that Act (notice of alteration of accounting reference date) must be given in the form prescribed for the purposes of section 225(1) of the 1985 Act or Article 233(1) of the 1986 Order.".

Companies subject to the small companies regime

381   Companies subject to the small companies regime

The small companies regime … applies to a company for a financial year in relation to which the company—
    (a)   qualifies as small (see sections 382 and 383), and
    (b)   is not excluded from the regime (see section 384).

[1508]

NOTES
Commencement: 6 April 2008.
Commencement (transitional provisions): see the note to s 380 at **[1507]**.
Words omitted repealed by the Companies Act 2006 (Amendment) (Accounts and Reports) Regulations 2008, SI 2008/393, reg 6(1), as from 6 April 2008, in relation to financial years beginning on or after that date.

382   Companies qualifying as small: general

(1)   A company qualifies as small in relation to its first financial year if the qualifying conditions are met in that year.

(2)   A company qualifies as small in relation to a subsequent financial year—
    (a)   if the qualifying conditions are met in that year and the preceding financial year;
    (b)   if the qualifying conditions are met in that year and the company qualified as small in relation to the preceding financial year;
    (c)   if the qualifying conditions were met in the preceding financial year and the company qualified as small in relation to that year.

(3)   The qualifying conditions are met by a company in a year in which it satisfies two or more of the following requirements—

1 Turnover	[Not more than £6.5 million]
2 Balance sheet total	[Not more than £3.26 million]
3 Number of employees	Not more than 50

(4)   For a period that is a company's financial year but not in fact a year the maximum figures for turnover must be proportionately adjusted.

(5)   The balance sheet total means the aggregate of the amounts shown as assets in the company's balance sheet.

(6)   The number of employees means the average number of persons employed by the company in the year, determined as follows—

    (a)   find for each month in the financial year the number of persons employed under contracts of service by the company in that month (whether throughout the month or not),
    (b)   add together the monthly totals, and
    (c)   divide by the number of months in the financial year.

(7)   This section is subject to section 383 (companies qualifying as small: parent companies).

[1509]

NOTES
Commencement: 6 April 2008.
Commencement (transitional provisions): see the note to s 380 at **[1507]**.

Sub-s (3): words in square brackets substituted by the Companies Act 2006 (Amendment) (Accounts and Reports) Regulations 2008, SI 2008/393, reg 3(1), as from 6 April 2008, in relation to financial years beginning on or after that date. See further reg 2(3) of the 2008 Regulations which provides as follows—

"(3)   In determining whether a company or group qualifies as small or medium-sized under section 382(2), 383(3), 465(2) or 466(3) of the 2006 Act (qualification in relation to subsequent financial year by reference to circumstances in preceding financial years) in relation to a financial year ending on or after 6th April 2008, the company or group shall be treated as having qualified as small or medium-sized (as the case may be) in any previous financial year in which it would have so qualified if amendments to the same effect as those made by these Regulations had been in force.".

383   Companies qualifying as small: parent companies

(1)   A parent company qualifies as a small company in relation to a financial year only if the group headed by it qualifies as a small group.

(2)   A group qualifies as small in relation to the parent company's first financial year if the qualifying conditions are met in that year.

(3)   A group qualifies as small in relation to a subsequent financial year of the parent company—

    (a)   if the qualifying conditions are met in that year and the preceding financial year;

    (b)   if the qualifying conditions are met in that year and the group qualified as small in relation to the preceding financial year;

    (c)   if the qualifying conditions were met in the preceding financial year and the group qualified as small in relation to that year.

(4)   The qualifying conditions are met by a group in a year in which it satisfies two or more of the following requirements—

1. Aggregate turnover	[Not more than £6.5 million net (or £7.8 million gross)]
2. Aggregate balance sheet total	[Not more than £3.26 million net (or £3.9 million gross)]
3. Aggregate number of employees	Not more than 50

(5)   The aggregate figures are ascertained by aggregating the relevant figures determined in accordance with section 382 for each member of the group.

(6)   In relation to the aggregate figures for turnover and balance sheet total—

"net" means after any set-offs and other adjustments made to eliminate group transactions—

    (a)   in the case of Companies Act accounts, in accordance with regulations under section 404,

    (b)   in the case of IAS accounts, in accordance with international accounting standards; and

"gross" means without those set-offs and other adjustments.

A company may satisfy any relevant requirement on the basis of either the net or the gross figure.

(7)   The figures for each subsidiary undertaking shall be those included in its individual accounts for the relevant financial year, that is—

    (a)   if its financial year ends with that of the parent company, that financial year, and

    (b)   if not, its financial year ending last before the end of the financial year of the parent company.

If those figures cannot be obtained without disproportionate expense or undue delay, the latest available figures shall be taken.

[1510]

NOTES

Commencement: 6 April 2008.

Commencement (transitional provisions): see the note to s 380 at **[1507]**.

Sub-s (4): words in square brackets substituted by the Companies Act 2006 (Amendment) (Accounts and Reports) Regulations 2008, SI 2008/393, reg 3(2), as from 6 April 2008, in relation to financial years beginning on or after that date. See further the note to s 382 at **[1509]**.

384   Companies excluded from the small companies regime

(1)   The small companies regime does not apply to a company that is, or was at any time within the financial year to which the accounts relate—

    (a)   a public company,

    (b)   a company that—

(i)   is an authorised insurance company, a banking company, an e- money issuer, [a MiFID investment firm] or a UCITS management company, or

(ii)   carries on insurance market activity, or

(c)   a member of an ineligible group.

(2)   A group is ineligible if any of its members is—

(a)   a public company,

(b)   a body corporate (other than a company) whose shares are admitted to trading on a regulated market in an EEA State,

(c)   a person (other than a small company) who has permission under Part 4 of the Financial Services and Markets Act 2000 (c 8) to carry on a regulated activity,

(d)   a small company that is an authorised insurance company, a banking company, an e-money issuer, [a MiFID investment firm] or a UCITS management company, or

(e)   a person who carries on insurance market activity.

(3)   A company is a small company for the purposes of subsection (2) if it qualified as small in relation to its last financial year ending on or before the end of the financial year to which the accounts relate.

[1511]

NOTES
Commencement: 6 April 2008.
Commencement (transitional provisions): see the note to s 380 at **[1507]**.
Sub-ss (1), (2): words in square brackets substituted by the Markets in Financial Instruments Directive (Consequential Amendments) Regulations 2007, SI 2007/2932, reg 3(1), (2), as from 1 November 2007.

Quoted and unquoted companies

385 Quoted and unquoted companies

(1)   For the purposes of this Part a company is a quoted company in relation to a financial year if it is a quoted company immediately before the end of the accounting reference period by reference to which that financial year was determined.

(2)   A "quoted company" means a company whose equity share capital—

(a)   has been included in the official list in accordance with the provisions of Part 6 of the Financial Services and Markets Act 2000 (c 8), or

(b)   is officially listed in an EEA State, or

(c)   is admitted to dealing on either the New York Stock Exchange or the exchange known as Nasdaq.

In paragraph (a) "the official list" has the meaning given by section 103(1) of the Financial Services and Markets Act 2000.

(3)   An "unquoted company" means a company that is not a quoted company.

(4)   The Secretary of State may by regulations amend or replace the provisions of subsections (1) to (2) so as to limit or extend the application of some or all of the provisions of this Part that are expressed to apply to quoted companies.

(5)   Regulations under this section extending the application of any such provision of this Part are subject to affirmative resolution procedure.

(6)   Any other regulations under this section are subject to negative resolution procedure.

[1512]

NOTES
Commencement: 20 January 2007 (for the purpose of enabling the exercise of powers to make Orders or Regulations by statutory instrument); 1 October 2007 (certain purposes); 6 April 2008 (otherwise) (see the note below).
Commencement (transitional provisions): see the note to s 380 at **[1507]**.
Commencement (note): the Companies Act 2006 (Commencement No 3, Consequential Amendments, Transitional Provisions and Savings) Order 2007, SI 2007/2194, art 2(3) provides that this section shall come into force on 1 October 2007 so far as is necessary for the purposes of the provisions of this Act brought into force on that date by art 2(1), (2) of that Order.

CHAPTER 2
ACCOUNTING RECORDS

386 Duty to keep accounting records

(1)   Every company must keep adequate accounting records.

(2)   Adequate accounting records means records that are sufficient—

(a)   to show and explain the company's transactions,

(b)   to disclose with reasonable accuracy, at any time, the financial position of the company at that time, and (c)　to enable the directors to ensure that any accounts required to be prepared comply with the requirements of this Act (and, where applicable, of Article 4 of the IAS Regulation).

(3)　Accounting records must, in particular, contain—
  (a)　entries from day to day of all sums of money received and expended by the company and the matters in respect of which the receipt and expenditure takes place, and
  (b)　a record of the assets and liabilities of the company.

(4)　If the company's business involves dealing in goods, the accounting records must contain—
  (a)　statements of stock held by the company at the end of each financial year of the company,
  (b)　all statements of stocktakings from which any statement of stock as is mentioned in paragraph (a) has been or is to be prepared, and
  (c)　except in the case of goods sold by way of ordinary retail trade, statements of all goods sold and purchased, showing the goods and the buyers and sellers in sufficient detail to enable all these to be identified.

(5)　A parent company that has a subsidiary undertaking in relation to which the above requirements do not apply must take reasonable steps to secure that the undertaking keeps such accounting records as to enable the directors of the parent company to ensure that any accounts required to be prepared under this Part comply with the requirements of this Act (and, where applicable, of Article 4 of the IAS Regulation).

[1513]

NOTES
Commencement: 6 April 2008.
Commencement (transitional provisions): see the note to s 380 at **[1507]**.

387　Duty to keep accounting records: offence

(1)　If a company fails to comply with any provision of section 386 (duty to keep accounting records), an offence is committed by every officer of the company who is in default.

(2)　It is a defence for a person charged with such an offence to show that he acted honestly and that in the circumstances in which the company's business was carried on the default was excusable.

(3)　A person guilty of an offence under this section is liable—
  (a)　on conviction on indictment, to imprisonment for a term not exceeding two years or a fine (or both);
  (b)　on summary conviction—
    (i)　in England and Wales, to imprisonment for a term not exceeding twelve months or to a fine not exceeding the statutory maximum (or both);
    (ii)　in Scotland or Northern Ireland, to imprisonment for a term not exceeding six months, or to a fine not exceeding the statutory maximum (or both).

[1514]

NOTES
Commencement: 6 April 2008.
Commencement (transitional provisions): see the note to s 380 at **[1507]**.
Imprisonment for a term not exceeding twelve months: see further s 1131 of this Act which provides as follows—

"1131　Imprisonment on summary conviction in England and Wales: transitory provision

(1)　This section applies to any provision of the Companies Acts that provides that a person guilty of an offence is liable on summary conviction in England and Wales to imprisonment for a term not exceeding twelve months.

(2)　In relation to an offence committed before the commencement of section 154(1) of the Criminal Justice Act 2003 (c 44), for "twelve months" substitute "six months".".

Note that by virtue of s 2 of this Act, "the Companies Acts" means (i) the company law provisions of this Act (ie, Parts 1–39, and Parts 45–47 in so far as they apply for the purposes of those Parts); (ii) the Companies (Audit, Investigations and Community Enterprise) Act 2004, Pt 2; (iii) the provisions of the Companies Act 1985 and the Companies Consolidation (Consequential Provisions) Act 1985 that remain in force.

388　Where and for how long records to be kept

(1)　A company's accounting records—
  (a)　must be kept at its registered office or such other place as the directors think fit, and
  (b)　must at all times be open to inspection by the company's officers.

(2)　If accounting records are kept at a place outside the United Kingdom, accounts and returns with respect to the business dealt with in the accounting records so kept must be sent to, and kept at, a place in the United Kingdom, and must at all times be open to such inspection.

(3)　The accounts and returns to be sent to the United Kingdom must be such as to—

(a) disclose with reasonable accuracy the financial position of the business in question at intervals of not more than six months, and

(b) enable the directors to ensure that the accounts required to be prepared under this Part comply with the requirements of this Act (and, where applicable, of Article 4 of the IAS Regulation).

(4) Accounting records that a company is required by section 386 to keep must be preserved by it—

(a) in the case of a private company, for three years from the date on which they are made;

(b) in the case of a public company, for six years from the date on which they are made.

(5) Subsection (4) is subject to any provision contained in rules made under section 411 of the Insolvency Act 1986 (c 45) (company insolvency rules) or Article 359 of the Insolvency (Northern Ireland) Order 1989 (SI 1989/2405 (NI 19)).

[1515]

NOTES

Commencement: 6 April 2008.
Commencement (transitional provisions): see the note to s 380 at **[1507]**.

389 Where and for how long records to be kept: offences

(1) If a company fails to comply with any provision of subsections (1) to (3) of section 388 (requirements as to keeping of accounting records), an offence is committed by every officer of the company who is in default.

(2) It is a defence for a person charged with such an offence to show that he acted honestly and that in the circumstances in which the company's business was carried on the default was excusable.

(3) An officer of a company commits an offence if he—

(a) fails to take all reasonable steps for securing compliance by the company with subsection (4) of that section (period for which records to be preserved), or

(b) intentionally causes any default by the company under that subsection.

(4) A person guilty of an offence under this section is liable—

(a) on conviction on indictment, to imprisonment for a term not exceeding two years or a fine (or both);

(b) on summary conviction—

   (i) in England and Wales, to imprisonment for a term not exceeding twelve months or to a fine not exceeding the statutory maximum (or both);

   (ii) in Scotland or Northern Ireland, to imprisonment for a term not exceeding six months, or to a fine not exceeding the statutory maximum (or both).

[1516]

NOTES

Commencement: 6 April 2008.
Commencement (transitional provisions): see the note to s 380 at **[1507]**.
Imprisonment for a term not exceeding twelve months: see the note to s 387 at **[1514]**.

CHAPTER 3
A COMPANY'S FINANCIAL YEAR

390 A company's financial year

(1) A company's financial year is determined as follows.

(2) Its first financial year—

(a) begins with the first day of its first accounting reference period, and

(b) ends with the last day of that period or such other date, not more than seven days before or after the end of that period, as the directors may determine.

(3) Subsequent financial years—

(a) begin with the day immediately following the end of the company's previous financial year, and

(b) end with the last day of its next accounting reference period or such other date, not more than seven days before or after the end of that period, as the directors may determine.

(4) In relation to an undertaking that is not a company, references in this Act to its financial year are to any period in respect of which a profit and loss account of the undertaking is required to be made up (by its constitution or by the law under which it is established), whether that period is a year or not.

(5) The directors of a parent company must secure that, except where in their opinion there are good reasons against it, the financial year of each of its subsidiary undertakings coincides with the company's own financial year.

[1517]

NOTES
Commencement: 6 April 2008.

391 Accounting reference periods and accounting reference date

(1) A company's accounting reference periods are determined according to its accounting reference date in each calendar year.

(2) The accounting reference date of a company incorporated in Great Britain before 1st April 1996 is—
   (a) the date specified by notice to the registrar in accordance with section 224(2) of the Companies Act 1985 (c 6) (notice specifying accounting reference date given within nine months of incorporation), or
   (b) failing such notice—
      (i) in the case of a company incorporated before 1st April 1990, 31st March, and
      (ii) in the case of a company incorporated on or after 1st April 1990, the last day of the month in which the anniversary of its incorporation falls.

(3) The accounting reference date of a company incorporated in Northern Ireland before 22nd August 1997 is—
   (a) the date specified by notice to the registrar in accordance with article 232(2) of the Companies (Northern Ireland) Order 1986 (SI 1986/1032 (NI 6)) (notice specifying accounting reference date given within nine months of incorporation), or
   (b) failing such notice—
      (i) in the case of a company incorporated before the coming into operation of Article 5 of the Companies (Northern Ireland) Order 1990 (SI 1990/593 (NI 5)), 31st March, and
      (ii) in the case of a company incorporated after the coming into operation of that Article, the last day of the month in which the anniversary of its incorporation falls.

(4) The accounting reference date of a company incorporated—
   (a) in Great Britain on or after 1st April 1996 and before the commencement of this Act,
   (b) in Northern Ireland on or after 22nd August 1997 and before the commencement of this Act, or
   (c) after the commencement of this Act,
is the last day of the month in which the anniversary of its incorporation falls.

(5) A company's first accounting reference period is the period of more than six months, but not more than 18 months, beginning with the date of its incorporation and ending with its accounting reference date.

(6) Its subsequent accounting reference periods are successive periods of twelve months beginning immediately after the end of the previous accounting reference period and ending with its accounting reference date.

(7) This section has effect subject to the provisions of section 392 (alteration of accounting reference date).

[1518]

NOTES
Commencement: 6 April 2008.

392 Alteration of accounting reference date

(1) A company may by notice given to the registrar specify a new accounting reference date having effect in relation to—
   (a) the company's current accounting reference period and subsequent periods, or
   (b) the company's previous accounting reference period and subsequent periods.

A company's "previous accounting reference period" means the one immediately preceding its current accounting reference period.

(2) The notice must state whether the current or previous accounting reference period—
   (a) is to be shortened, so as to come to an end on the first occasion on which the new accounting reference date falls or fell after the beginning of the period, or
   (b) is to be extended, so as to come to an end on the second occasion on which that date falls or fell after the beginning of the period.

(3)   A notice extending a company's current or previous accounting reference period is not effective if given less than five years after the end of an earlier accounting reference period of the company that was extended under this section.

This does not apply—
 (a)   to a notice given by a company that is a subsidiary undertaking or parent undertaking of another EEA undertaking if the new accounting reference date coincides with that of the other EEA undertaking or, where that undertaking is not a company, with the last day of its financial year, or
 (b)   where the company is in administration under Part 2 of the Insolvency Act 1986 (c 45) or Part 3 of the Insolvency (Northern Ireland) Order 1989 (SI 1989/2405 (NI 19)), or
 (c)   where the Secretary of State directs that it should not apply, which he may do with respect to a notice that has been given or that may be given.

(4)   A notice under this section may not be given in respect of a previous accounting reference period if the period for filing accounts and reports for the financial year determined by reference to that accounting reference period has already expired.

(5)   An accounting reference period may not be extended so as to exceed 18 months and a notice under this section is ineffective if the current or previous accounting reference period as extended in accordance with the notice would exceed that limit.

This does not apply where the company is in administration under Part 2 of the Insolvency Act 1986 (c 45) or Part 3 of the Insolvency (Northern Ireland) Order 1989 (SI 1989/2405 (NI 19)).

(6)   In this section "EEA undertaking" means an undertaking established under the law of any part of the United Kingdom or the law of any other EEA State.

[1519]

NOTES
Commencement: 6 April 2008.
Commencement (transitional provisions): see the note to s 380 at **[1507]**.

CHAPTER 4
ANNUAL ACCOUNTS
General

393   Accounts to give true and fair view
(1)   The directors of a company must not approve accounts for the purposes of this Chapter unless they are satisfied that they give a true and fair view of the assets, liabilities, financial position and profit or loss—
 (a)   in the case of the company's individual accounts, of the company;
 (b)   in the case of the company's group accounts, of the undertakings included in the consolidation as a whole, so far as concerns members of the company.

(2)   The auditor of a company in carrying out his functions under this Act in relation to the company's annual accounts must have regard to the directors' duty under subsection (1).

[1520]

NOTES
Commencement: 6 April 2008.
Commencement (transitional provisions): see the note to s 380 at **[1507]**.

Individual accounts

394   Duty to prepare individual accounts
The directors of every company must prepare accounts for the company for each of its financial years.

Those accounts are referred to as the company's "individual accounts".

[1521]

NOTES
Commencement: 6 April 2008.
Commencement (transitional provisions): see the note to s 380 at **[1507]**.

395   Individual accounts: applicable accounting framework
(1)   A company's individual accounts may be prepared—
 (a)   in accordance with section 396 ("Companies Act individual accounts"), or
 (b)   in accordance with international accounting standards ("IAS individual accounts").

This is subject to the following provisions of this section and to section 407 (consistency of financial reporting within group).

(2)　The individual accounts of a company that is a charity must be Companies Act individual accounts.

(3)　After the first financial year in which the directors of a company prepare IAS individual accounts ("the first IAS year"), all subsequent individual accounts of the company must be prepared in accordance with international accounting standards unless there is a relevant change of circumstance.

(4)　There is a relevant change of circumstance if, at any time during or after the first IAS year—

(a)　the company becomes a subsidiary undertaking of another undertaking that does not prepare IAS individual accounts,

[(aa)　the company ceases to be a subsidiary undertaking,]

(b)　the company ceases to be a company with securities admitted to trading on a regulated market in an EEA State, or

(c)　a parent undertaking of the company ceases to be an undertaking with securities admitted to trading on a regulated market in an EEA State.

(5)　If, having changed to preparing Companies Act individual accounts following a relevant change of circumstance, the directors again prepare IAS individual accounts for the company, subsections (3) and (4) apply again as if the first financial year for which such accounts are again prepared were the first IAS year.

[1522]

NOTES

　Commencement: 6 April 2008.

　Commencement (transitional provisions): see the note to s 380 at **[1507]**.

　Sub-s (4): para (aa) inserted by the Companies Act 2006 (Amendment) (Accounts and Reports) Regulations 2008, SI 2008/393, reg 9, as from 6 April 2008, in relation to financial years beginning on or after that date.

396　Companies Act individual accounts

(1)　Companies Act individual accounts must comprise—

(a)　a balance sheet as at the last day of the financial year, and

(b)　a profit and loss account.

(2)　The accounts must—

(a)　in the case of the balance sheet, give a true and fair view of the state of affairs of the company as at the end of the financial year, and

(b)　in the case of the profit and loss account, give a true and fair view of the profit or loss of the company for the financial year.

(3)　The accounts must comply with provision made by the Secretary of State by regulations as to—

(a)　the form and content of the balance sheet and profit and loss account, and

(b)　additional information to be provided by way of notes to the accounts.

(4)　If compliance with the regulations, and any other provision made by or under this Act as to the matters to be included in a company's individual accounts or in notes to those accounts, would not be sufficient to give a true and fair view, the necessary additional information must be given in the accounts or in a note to them.

(5)　If in special circumstances compliance with any of those provisions is inconsistent with the requirement to give a true and fair view, the directors must depart from that provision to the extent necessary to give a true and fair view.

　Particulars of any such departure, the reasons for it and its effect must be given in a note to the accounts.

[1523]

NOTES

　Commencement: 20 January 2007 (for the purpose of enabling the exercise of powers to make Orders or Regulations by statutory instrument); 6 April 2008 (otherwise).

　Commencement (transitional provisions): see the note to s 380 at **[1507]**.

　Regulations: the Small Companies and Groups (Accounts and Directors' Report) Regulations 2008, SI 2008/409. These Regulations specify the form and content of the accounts and directors' report of companies subject to the small companies regime under Part 15 of this Act. The Regulations replace provisions previously contained in the Schedules to Part VII of the Companies Act 1985, and in the Schedules to Part VIII of the Companies (Northern Ireland) Order 1986 (SI 1986/1032). The Regulations come into force on 6 April 2008, and apply in relation to financial years beginning on or after that date. The corresponding provisions of the 1985 Act or the 1986 Order continue to apply to accounts and directors' reports for financial years beginning before that date.

The Large and Medium-sized Companies and Groups (Accounts and Reports) Regulations 2008, SI 2008/410. These Regulations specify the form and content of the accounts and reports of companies under Part 15 of this Act (other than those subject to the small companies regime). The Regulations replace provisions previously contained in the Schedules to Part VII of the Companies Act 1985, and in the Schedules to Part VIII of the Companies (Northern Ireland) Order 1986 (SI 1986/1032). The Regulations come into force on 6 April 2008 and, with one exception, apply to financial years beginning on or after that date. The corresponding provisions of the 1985 Act or the 1986 Order continue to apply to accounts and reports for financial years beginning before that date. The new disclosure required by Sch 8, para 4 to the Regulations applies in relation to financial years beginning on or after 6 April 2009.

397 IAS individual accounts

Where the directors of a company prepare IAS individual accounts, they must state in the notes to the accounts that the accounts have been prepared in accordance with international accounting standards.

[1524]

NOTES
Commencement: 6 April 2008.
Commencement (transitional provisions): see the note to s 380 at **[1507]**.

Group accounts: small companies

398 Option to prepare group accounts

If at the end of a financial year a company subject to the small companies regime is a parent company the directors, as well as preparing individual accounts for the year, may prepare group accounts for the year.

[1525]

NOTES
Commencement: 6 April 2008.
Commencement (transitional provisions): see the note to s 380 at **[1507]**.

Group accounts: other companies

399 Duty to prepare group accounts

(1) This section applies to companies that are not subject to the small companies regime.

(2) If at the end of a financial year the company is a parent company the directors, as well as preparing individual accounts for the year, must prepare group accounts for the year unless the company is exempt from that requirement.

(3) There are exemptions under—
    section 400 (company included in EEA accounts of larger group),
    section 401 (company included in non-EEA accounts of larger group), and
    section 402 (company none of whose subsidiary undertakings need be included in the consolidation).

(4) A company to which this section applies but which is exempt from the requirement to prepare group accounts, may do so.

[1526]

NOTES
Commencement: 6 April 2008.
Commencement (transitional provisions): see the note to s 380 at **[1507]**.

400 Exemption for company included in EEA group accounts of larger group

(1) A company is exempt from the requirement to prepare group accounts if it is itself a subsidiary undertaking and its immediate parent undertaking is established under the law of an EEA State, in the following cases—
    (a) where the company is a wholly-owned subsidiary of that parent undertaking;
    (b) where that parent undertaking holds more than 50% of the allotted shares in the company and notice requesting the preparation of group accounts has not been served on the company by shareholders holding in aggregate—
        (i) more than half of the remaining allotted shares in the company, or
        (ii) 5% of the total allotted shares in the company.
    Such notice must be served not later than six months after the end of the financial year before that to which it relates.

(2) Exemption is conditional upon compliance with all of the following conditions—

(a)   the company must be included in consolidated accounts for a larger group drawn up to the same date, or to an earlier date in the same financial year, by a parent undertaking established under the law of an EEA State;

(b)   those accounts must be drawn up and audited, and that parent undertaking's annual report must be drawn up, according to that law—
      (i)   in accordance with the provisions of the Seventh Directive (83/ 349/EEC) (as modified, where relevant, by the provisions of the Bank Accounts Directive (86/635/EEC) or the Insurance Accounts Directive (91/674/EEC)), or
      (ii)   in accordance with international accounting standards;

(c)   the company must disclose in its individual accounts that it is exempt from the obligation to prepare and deliver group accounts;

(d)   the company must state in its individual accounts the name of the parent undertaking that draws up the group accounts referred to above and—
      (i)   if it is incorporated outside the United Kingdom, the country in which it is incorporated, or
      (ii)   if it is unincorporated, the address of its principal place of business;

(e)   the company must deliver to the registrar, within the period for filing its accounts and reports for the financial year in question, copies of—
      (i)   those group accounts, and
      (ii)   the parent undertaking's annual report,
together with the auditor's report on them;

(f)   any requirement of Part 35 of this Act as to the delivery to the registrar of a certified translation into English must be met in relation to any document comprised in the accounts and reports delivered in accordance with paragraph (e).

(3)   For the purposes of subsection (1)(b) shares held by a wholly-owned subsidiary of the parent undertaking, or held on behalf of the parent undertaking or a wholly-owned subsidiary, shall be attributed to the parent undertaking.

(4)   The exemption does not apply to a company any of whose securities are admitted to trading on a regulated market in an EEA State.

(5)   Shares held by directors of a company for the purpose of complying with any share qualification requirement shall be disregarded in determining for the purposes of this section whether the company is a wholly-owned subsidiary.

(6)   In subsection (4) "securities" includes—
(a)   shares and stock,
(b)   debentures, including debenture stock, loan stock, bonds, certificates of deposit and other instruments creating or acknowledging indebtedness,
(c)   warrants or other instruments entitling the holder to subscribe for securities falling within paragraph (a) or (b), and
(d)   certificates or other instruments that confer—
      (i)   property rights in respect of a security falling within paragraph (a), (b) or (c),
      (ii)   any right to acquire, dispose of, underwrite or convert a security, being a right to which the holder would be entitled if he held any such security to which the certificate or other instrument relates, or
      (iii) a contractual right (other than an option) to acquire any such security otherwise than by subscription.

[1527]

NOTES
Commencement: 6 April 2008.
Commencement (transitional provisions): see the note to s 380 at **[1507]**.

401   Exemption for company included in non-EEA group accounts of larger group

(1)   A company is exempt from the requirement to prepare group accounts if it is itself a subsidiary undertaking and its parent undertaking is not established under the law of an EEA State, in the following cases—
(a)   where the company is a wholly-owned subsidiary of that parent undertaking;
(b)   where that parent undertaking holds more than 50% of the allotted shares in the company and notice requesting the preparation of group accounts has not been served on the company by shareholders holding in aggregate—
      (i)   more than half of the remaining allotted shares in the company, or
      (ii)   5% of the total allotted shares in the company.

Such notice must be served not later than six months after the end of the financial year before that to which it relates.

(2)   Exemption is conditional upon compliance with all of the following conditions—

(a)   the company and all of its subsidiary undertakings must be included in consolidated
      accounts for a larger group drawn up to the same date, or to an earlier date in the same
      financial year, by a parent undertaking;
(b)   those accounts and, where appropriate, the group's annual report, must be drawn up—
      (i)   in accordance with the provisions of the Seventh Directive (83/ 349/EEC) (as
            modified, where relevant, by the provisions of the Bank Accounts Directive
            (86/635/EEC) or the Insurance Accounts Directive (91/674/EEC)), or
      (ii) in a manner equivalent to consolidated accounts and consolidated annual reports
            so drawn up;
(c)   the group accounts must be audited by one or more persons authorised to audit accounts
      under the law under which the parent undertaking which draws them up is established;
(d)   the company must disclose in its individual accounts that it is exempt from the
      obligation to prepare and deliver group accounts;
(e)   the company must state in its individual accounts the name of the parent undertaking
      which draws up the group accounts referred to above and—
      (i)   if it is incorporated outside the United Kingdom, the country in which it is
            incorporated, or
      (ii) if it is unincorporated, the address of its principal place of business;
(f)   the company must deliver to the registrar, within the period for filing its accounts and
      reports for the financial year in question, copies of—
      (i)   the group accounts, and
      (ii) where appropriate, the consolidated annual report,
together with the auditor's report on them;
(g)   any requirement of Part 35 of this Act as to the delivery to the registrar of a certified
      translation into English must be met in relation to any document comprised in the
      accounts and reports delivered in accordance with paragraph (f).

(3)   For the purposes of subsection (1)(b), shares held by a wholly-owned subsidiary of the
parent undertaking, or held on behalf of the parent undertaking or a wholly-owned subsidiary, are
attributed to the parent undertaking.

(4)   The exemption does not apply to a company any of whose securities are admitted to trading
on a regulated market in an EEA State.

(5)   Shares held by directors of a company for the purpose of complying with any share
qualification requirement shall be disregarded in determining for the purposes of this section
whether the company is a wholly-owned subsidiary.

(6)   In subsection (4) "securities" includes—
(a)   shares and stock,
(b)   debentures, including debenture stock, loan stock, bonds, certificates of deposit and
      other instruments creating or acknowledging indebtedness,
(c)   warrants or other instruments entitling the holder to subscribe for securities falling
      within paragraph (a) or (b), and
(d)   certificates or other instruments that confer—
      (i)   property rights in respect of a security falling within paragraph (a), (b) or (c),
      (ii) any right to acquire, dispose of, underwrite or convert a security, being a right to
            which the holder would be entitled if he held any such security to which the
            certificate or other instrument relates, or
      (iii) a contractual right (other than an option) to acquire any such security otherwise
            than by subscription.

[1528]

NOTES
Commencement: 6 April 2008.
Commencement (transitional provisions): see the note to s 380 at **[1507]**.

402   Exemption if no subsidiary undertakings need be included in the consolidation
A parent company is exempt from the requirement to prepare group accounts if under section 405 all
of its subsidiary undertakings could be excluded from consolidation in Companies Act group
accounts.

[1529]

NOTES
Commencement: 6 April 2008.
Commencement (transitional provisions): see the note to s 380 at **[1507]**.

Group accounts: general

403 Group accounts: applicable accounting framework

(1) The group accounts of certain parent companies are required by Article 4 of the IAS Regulation to be prepared in accordance with international accounting standards ("IAS group accounts").

(2) The group accounts of other companies may be prepared—
  (a) in accordance with section 404 ("Companies Act group accounts"), or
  (b) in accordance with international accounting standards ("IAS group accounts").

This is subject to the following provisions of this section.

(3) The group accounts of a parent company that is a charity must be Companies Act group accounts.

(4) After the first financial year in which the directors of a parent company prepare IAS group accounts ("the first IAS year"), all subsequent group accounts of the company must be prepared in accordance with international accounting standards unless there is a relevant change of circumstance.

(5) There is a relevant change of circumstance if, at any time during or after the first IAS year—
  (a) the company becomes a subsidiary undertaking of another undertaking that does not prepare IAS group accounts,
  (b) the company ceases to be a company with securities admitted to trading on a regulated market in an EEA State, or
  (c) a parent undertaking of the company ceases to be an undertaking with securities admitted to trading on a regulated market in an EEA State.

(6) If, having changed to preparing Companies Act group accounts following a relevant change of circumstance, the directors again prepare IAS group accounts for the company, subsections (4) and (5) apply again as if the first financial year for which such accounts are again prepared were the first IAS year.

                                                           [1530]

NOTES

Commencement: 6 April 2008.

Commencement (transitional provisions): see the note to s 380 at **[1507]**.

404 Companies Act group accounts

(1) Companies Act group accounts must comprise—
  (a) a consolidated balance sheet dealing with the state of affairs of the parent company and its subsidiary undertakings, and
  (b) a consolidated profit and loss account dealing with the profit or loss of the parent company and its subsidiary undertakings.

(2) The accounts must give a true and fair view of the state of affairs as at the end of the financial year, and the profit or loss for the financial year, of the undertakings included in the consolidation as a whole, so far as concerns members of the company.

(3) The accounts must comply with provision made by the Secretary of State by regulations as to—
  (a) the form and content of the consolidated balance sheet and consolidated profit and loss account, and
  (b) additional information to be provided by way of notes to the accounts.

(4) If compliance with the regulations, and any other provision made by or under this Act as to the matters to be included in a company's group accounts or in notes to those accounts, would not be sufficient to give a true and fair view, the necessary additional information must be given in the accounts or in a note to them.

(5) If in special circumstances compliance with any of those provisions is inconsistent with the requirement to give a true and fair view, the directors must depart from that provision to the extent necessary to give a true and fair view.

Particulars of any such departure, the reasons for it and its effect must be given in a note to the accounts.

                                                             [1531]

NOTES

Commencement: 20 January 2007 (for the purpose of enabling the exercise of powers to make Orders or Regulations by statutory instrument); 6 April 2008 (otherwise).

Commencement (transitional provisions): see the note to s 380 at **[1507]**.

Regulations: the Small Companies and Groups (Accounts and Directors' Report) Regulations 2008, SI 2008/409; the Large and Medium-sized Companies and Groups (Accounts and Reports) Regulations 2008, SI 2008/410 (see the notes to s 396 at **[1523]**).

405 Companies Act group accounts: subsidiary undertakings included in the consolidation

(1)   Where a parent company prepares Companies Act group accounts, all the subsidiary undertakings of the company must be included in the consolidation, subject to the following exceptions.

(2)   A subsidiary undertaking may be excluded from consolidation if its inclusion is not material for the purpose of giving a true and fair view (but two or more undertakings may be excluded only if they are not material taken together).

(3)   A subsidiary undertaking may be excluded from consolidation where—
  (a)   severe long-term restrictions substantially hinder the exercise of the rights of the parent company over the assets or management of that undertaking, or
  (b)   the information necessary for the preparation of group accounts cannot be obtained without disproportionate expense or undue delay, or
  (c)   the interest of the parent company is held exclusively with a view to subsequent resale.

(4)   The reference in subsection (3)(a) to the rights of the parent company and the reference in subsection (3)(c) to the interest of the parent company are, respectively, to rights and interests held by or attributed to the company for the purposes of the definition of "parent undertaking" (see section 1162) in the absence of which it would not be the parent company.

[1532]

NOTES
  Commencement: 6 April 2008.
  Commencement (transitional provisions): see the note to s 380 at **[1507]**.

406 IAS group accounts

Where the directors of a company prepare IAS group accounts, they must state in the notes to those accounts that the accounts have been prepared in accordance with international accounting standards.

[1533]

NOTES
  Commencement: 6 April 2008.
  Commencement (transitional provisions): see the note to s 380 at **[1507]**.

407 Consistency of financial reporting within group

(1)   The directors of a parent company must secure that the individual accounts of—
  (a)   the parent company, and
  (b)   each of its subsidiary undertakings,
are all prepared using the same financial reporting framework, except to the extent that in their opinion there are good reasons for not doing so.

(2)   Subsection (1) does not apply if the directors do not prepare group accounts for the parent company.

(3)   Subsection (1) only applies to accounts of subsidiary undertakings that are required to be prepared under this Part.

(4)   Subsection (1) does not require accounts of undertakings that are charities to be prepared using the same financial reporting framework as accounts of undertakings which are not charities.

(5)   Subsection (1)(a) does not apply where the directors of a parent company prepare IAS group accounts and IAS individual accounts.

[1534]

NOTES
  Commencement: 6 April 2008.
  Commencement (transitional provisions): see the note to s 380 at **[1507]**.

408 Individual profit and loss account where group accounts prepared

(1)   This section applies where—
  (a)   a company prepares group accounts in accordance with this Act, and
  (b)   the notes to the company's individual balance sheet show the company's profit or loss for the financial year determined in accordance with this Act.

(2)   [The company's individual profit and loss account] need not contain the information specified in section 411 (information about employee numbers and costs).

(3) The company's individual profit and loss account must be approved in accordance with section 414(1) (approval by directors) but may be omitted from the company's annual accounts for the purposes of the other provisions of the Companies Acts.

(4) The exemption conferred by this section is conditional upon its being disclosed in the company's annual accounts that the exemption applies.

[1535]

NOTES
Commencement: 6 April 2008.
Commencement (transitional provisions): see the note to s 380 at **[1507]**.
Sub-s (2): words in square brackets substituted by the Companies Act 2006 (Amendment) (Accounts and Reports) Regulations 2008, SI 2008/393, reg 10, as from 6 April 2008, in relation to financial years beginning on or after that date.

Information to be given in notes to the accounts

409 Information about related undertakings

(1) The Secretary of State may make provision by regulations requiring information about related undertakings to be given in notes to a company's annual accounts.

(2) The regulations—
  (a) may make different provision according to whether or not the company prepares group accounts, and
  (b) may specify the descriptions of undertaking in relation to which they apply, and make different provision in relation to different descriptions of related undertaking.

(3) The regulations may provide that information need not be disclosed with respect to an undertaking that—
  (a) is established under the law of a country outside the United Kingdom, or
  (b) carries on business outside the United Kingdom,
if the following conditions are met.

(4) The conditions are—
  (a) that in the opinion of the directors of the company the disclosure would be seriously prejudicial to the business of—
    (i) that undertaking,
    (ii) the company,
    (iii) any of the company's subsidiary undertakings, or
    (iv) any other undertaking which is included in the consolidation;
  (b) that the Secretary of State agrees that the information need not be disclosed.

(5) Where advantage is taken of any such exemption, that fact must be stated in a note to the company's annual accounts.

[1536]

NOTES
Commencement: 20 January 2007 (for the purpose of enabling the exercise of powers to make Orders or Regulations by statutory instrument); 6 April 2008 (otherwise).
Commencement (transitional provisions): see the note to s 380 at **[1507]**.
Regulations: the Small Companies and Groups (Accounts and Directors' Report) Regulations 2008, SI 2008/409; the Large and Medium-sized Companies and Groups (Accounts and Reports) Regulations 2008, SI 2008/410 (see the notes to s 396 at **[1523]**).

410 Information about related undertakings: alternative compliance

(1) This section applies where the directors of a company are of the opinion that the number of undertakings in respect of which the company is required to disclose information under any provision of regulations under section 409 (related undertakings) is such that compliance with that provision would result in information of excessive length being given in notes to the company's annual accounts.

(2) The information need only be given in respect of—
  (a) the undertakings whose results or financial position, in the opinion of the directors, principally affected the figures shown in the company's annual accounts, and
  (b) where the company prepares group accounts, undertakings excluded from consolidation under section 405(3) (undertakings excluded on grounds other than materiality).

(3) If advantage is taken of subsection (2)—
  (a) there must be included in the notes to the company's annual accounts a statement that the information is given only with respect to such undertakings as are mentioned in that subsection, and
  (b) the full information (both that which is disclosed in the notes to the accounts and that which is not) must be annexed to the company's next annual return.

For this purpose the "next annual return" means that next delivered to the registrar after the accounts in question have been approved under section 414.

(4)   If a company fails to comply with subsection (3)(b), an offence is committed by—
  (a)   the company, and
  (b)   every officer of the company who is in default.

(5)   A person guilty of an offence under subsection (4) is liable on summary conviction to a fine not exceeding level 3 on the standard scale and, for continued contravention, a daily default fine not exceeding one-tenth of level 3 on the standard scale.

[1537]

NOTES
  Commencement: 6 April 2008.
  Commencement (transitional provisions): see the note to s 380 at **[1507]**.

[410A   Information about off-balance sheet arrangements

(1)   In the case of a company that is not subject to the small companies regime, if in any financial year—
  (a)   the company is or has been party to arrangements that are not reflected in its balance sheet, and
  (b)   at the balance sheet date the risks or benefits arising from those arrangements are material,
the information required by this section must be given in notes to the company's annual accounts.

(2)   The information required is—
  (a)   the nature and business purpose of the arrangements, and
  (b)   the financial impact of the arrangements on the company.

(3)   The information need only be given to the extent necessary for enabling the financial position of the company to be assessed.

(4)   If the company qualifies as medium-sized in relation to the financial year (see sections 465 to 467) it need not comply with subsection (2)(b).

(5)   This section applies in relation to group accounts as if the undertakings included in the consolidation were a single company.]

[1537A]

NOTES
  Commencement: 6 April 2008.
  Inserted by the Companies Act 2006 (Amendment) (Accounts and Reports) Regulations 2008, SI 2008/393, reg 8, as from 6 April 2008, in relation to financial years beginning on or after that date.

411   Information about employee numbers and costs

(1)   In the case of a company not subject to the small companies regime, the following information with respect to the employees of the company must be given in notes to the company's annual accounts—
  (a)   the average number of persons employed by the company in the financial year, and
  (b)   the average number of persons so employed within each category of persons employed by the company.

(2)   The categories by reference to which the number required to be disclosed by subsection (1)(b) is to be determined must be such as the directors may select having regard to the manner in which the company's activities are organised.

(3)   The average number required by subsection (1)(a) or (b) is determined by dividing the relevant annual number by the number of months in the financial year.

(4)   The relevant annual number is determined by ascertaining for each month in the financial year—
  (a)   for the purposes of subsection (1)(a), the number of persons employed under contracts of service by the company in that month (whether throughout the month or not);
  (b)   for the purposes of subsection (1)(b), the number of persons in the category in question of persons so employed;
and adding together all the monthly numbers.

(5)   In respect of all persons employed by the company during the financial year who are taken into account in determining the relevant annual number for the purposes of subsection (1)(a) there must also be stated the aggregate amounts respectively of—
  (a)   wages and salaries paid or payable in respect of that year to those persons;
  (b)   social security costs incurred by the company on their behalf; and
  (c)   other pension costs so incurred.

This does not apply in so far as those amounts, or any of them, are stated elsewhere in the company's accounts.

(6)　In subsection (5)—

"pension costs" includes any costs incurred by the company in respect of—

(a)　any pension scheme established for the purpose of providing pensions for persons currently or formerly employed by the company,

(b)　any sums set aside for the future payment of pensions directly by the company to current or former employees, and

(c)　any pensions paid directly to such persons without having first been set aside;

"social security costs" means any contributions by the company to any state social security or pension scheme, fund or arrangement.

[(7)　This section applies in relation to group accounts as if the undertakings included in the consolidation were a single company.]

[1538]

NOTES

Commencement: 6 April 2008.

Commencement (transitional provisions): see the note to s 380 at **[1507]**.

Sub-s (7): substituted by the Companies Act 2006 (Amendment) (Accounts and Reports) Regulations 2008, SI 2008/393, reg 11, as from 6 April 2008, in relation to financial years beginning on or after that date.

412　Information about directors' benefits: remuneration

(1)　The Secretary of State may make provision by regulations requiring information to be given in notes to a company's annual accounts about directors' remuneration.

(2)　The matters about which information may be required include—

(a)　gains made by directors on the exercise of share options;

(b)　benefits received or receivable by directors under long-term incentive schemes;

(c)　payments for loss of office (as defined in section 215);

(d)　benefits receivable, and contributions for the purpose of providing benefits, in respect of past services of a person as director or in any other capacity while director;

(e)　consideration paid to or receivable by third parties for making available the services of a person as director or in any other capacity while director.

(3)　Without prejudice to the generality of subsection (1), regulations under this section may make any such provision as was made immediately before the commencement of this Part by Part 1 of Schedule 6 to the Companies Act 1985 (c 6).

(4)　For the purposes of this section, and regulations made under it, amounts paid to or receivable by—

(a)　a person connected with a director, or

(b)　a body corporate controlled by a director,

are treated as paid to or receivable by the director.

The expressions "connected with" and "controlled by" in this subsection have the same meaning as in Part 10 (company directors).

(5)　It is the duty of—

(a)　any director of a company, and

(b)　any person who is or has at any time in the preceding five years been a director of the company,

to give notice to the company of such matters relating to himself as may be necessary for the purposes of regulations under this section.

(6)　A person who makes default in complying with subsection (5) commits an offence and is liable on summary conviction to a fine not exceeding level 3 on the standard scale.

[1539]

NOTES

Commencement: 20 January 2007 (for the purpose of enabling the exercise of powers to make Orders or Regulations by statutory instrument); 6 April 2008 (otherwise).

Commencement (transitional provisions): see the note to s 380 at **[1507]**.

Regulations: the Small Companies and Groups (Accounts and Directors' Report) Regulations 2008, SI 2008/409; the Large and Medium-sized Companies and Groups (Accounts and Reports) Regulations 2008, SI 2008/410 (see the notes to s 396 at **[1523]**).

413　Information about directors' benefits: advances, credit and guarantees

(1)　In the case of a company that does not prepare group accounts, details of—

(a)　advances and credits granted by the company to its directors, and

(b)　guarantees of any kind entered into by the company on behalf of its directors,

must be shown in the notes to its individual accounts.

(2)   In the case of a parent company that prepares group accounts, details of—
   (a)   advances and credits granted to the directors of the parent company, by that company or by any of its subsidiary undertakings, and
   (b)   guarantees of any kind entered into on behalf of the directors of the parent company, by that company or by any of its subsidiary undertakings,
must be shown in the notes to the group accounts.

(3)   The details required of an advance or credit are—
   (a)   its amount,
   (b)   an indication of the interest rate,
   (c)   its main conditions, and
   (d)   any amounts repaid.

(4)   The details required of a guarantee are—
   (a)   its main terms,
   (b)   the amount of the maximum liability that may be incurred by the company (or its subsidiary), and
   (c)   any amount paid and any liability incurred by the company (or its subsidiary) for the purpose of fulfilling the guarantee (including any loss incurred by reason of enforcement of the guarantee).

(5)   There must also be stated in the notes to the accounts the totals—
   (a)   of amounts stated under subsection (3)(a),
   (b)   of amounts stated under subsection (3)(d),
   (c)   of amounts stated under subsection (4)(b), and
   (d)   of amounts stated under subsection (4)(c).

(6)   References in this section to the directors of a company are to the persons who were a director at any time in the financial year to which the accounts relate.

(7)   The requirements of this section apply in relation to every advance, credit or guarantee subsisting at any time in the financial year to which the accounts relate—
   (a)   whenever it was entered into,
   (b)   whether or not the person concerned was a director of the company in question at the time it was entered into, and
   (c)   in the case of an advance, credit or guarantee involving a subsidiary undertaking of that company, whether or not that undertaking was such a subsidiary undertaking at the time it was entered into.

(8)   Banking companies and the holding companies of credit institutions need only state the details required by subsections (3)(a) and (4)(b).

[1540]

NOTES
Commencement: 6 April 2008.
Commencement (transitional provisions): see the note to s 380 at **[1507]**.

Approval and signing of accounts

414   Approval and signing of accounts

(1)   A company's annual accounts must be approved by the board of directors and signed on behalf of the board by a director of the company.

(2)   The signature must be on the company's balance sheet.

(3)   If the accounts are prepared in accordance with the provisions applicable to companies subject to the small companies regime, the balance sheet must contain a statement to that effect in a prominent position above the signature.

(4)   If annual accounts are approved that do not comply with the requirements of this Act (and, where applicable, of Article 4 of the IAS Regulation), every director of the company who—
   (a)   knew that they did not comply, or was reckless as to whether they complied, and
   (b)   failed to take reasonable steps to secure compliance with those requirements or, as the case may be, to prevent the accounts from being approved,
commits an offence.

(5)   A person guilty of an offence under this section is liable—
   (a)   on conviction on indictment, to a fine;
   (b)   on summary conviction, to a fine not exceeding the statutory maximum.

[1541]

NOTES
Commencement: 6 April 2008.
Commencement (transitional provisions): see the note to s 380 at **[1507]**.

CHAPTER 5
DIRECTORS' REPORT

Directors' report

415 Duty to prepare directors' report

(1) The directors of a company must prepare a directors' report for each financial year of the company.

(2) For a financial year in which—
(a) the company is a parent company, and
(b) the directors of the company prepare group accounts,

the directors' report must be a consolidated report (a "group directors' report") relating to the undertakings included in the consolidation.

(3) A group directors' report may, where appropriate, give greater emphasis to the matters that are significant to the undertakings included in the consolidation, taken as a whole.

(4) In the case of failure to comply with the requirement to prepare a directors' report, an offence is committed by every person who—
(a) was a director of the company immediately before the end of the period for filing accounts and reports for the financial year in question, and
(b) failed to take all reasonable steps for securing compliance with that requirement.

(5) A person guilty of an offence under this section is liable—
(a) on conviction on indictment, to a fine;
(b) on summary conviction, to a fine not exceeding the statutory maximum.

[1542]

NOTES

Commencement: 6 April 2008.
Commencement (transitional provisions): see the note to s 380 at [1507].
Transfer of money held in dormant bank accounts: where (a) directors of a company that is a bank are required by sub-s (1) above to prepare a report for a particular financial year, and (b) in that year the company made transfers in relation to which the Dormant Bank and Building Society Accounts Act 2008, s 2 applied (transfer of balances to charities, with proportion to reclaim fund) the report must identify each of the charities concerned and specify the amount transferred to each of them. See s 13 of the 2008 Act at [1789].

[415A Directors' report: small companies exemption

(1) A company is entitled to small companies exemption in relation to the directors' report for a financial year if—
(a) it is entitled to prepare accounts for the year in accordance with the small companies regime, or
(b) it would be so entitled but for being or having been a member of an ineligible group.

(2) The exemption is relevant to—
section 416(3) (contents of report: statement of amount recommended by way of dividend),
section 417 (contents of report: business review), and
sections 444 to 446 (filing obligations of different descriptions of company).]

[1542A]

NOTES

Commencement: 6 April 2008.
Inserted by the Companies Act 2006 (Amendment) (Accounts and Reports) Regulations 2008, SI 2008/393, reg 6(2), as from 6 April 2008, in relation to financial years beginning on or after that date.

416 Contents of directors' report: general

(1) The directors' report for a financial year must state—
(a) the names of the persons who, at any time during the financial year, were directors of the company, and
(b) the principal activities of the company in the course of the year.

(2) In relation to a group directors' report subsection (1)(b) has effect as if the reference to the company was to the undertakings included in the consolidation.

(3) Except in the case of a company [entitled to the small companies exemption], the report must state the amount (if any) that the directors recommend should be paid by way of dividend.

(4) The Secretary of State may make provision by regulations as to other matters that must be disclosed in a directors' report.

Without prejudice to the generality of this power, the regulations may make any such provision as was formerly made by Schedule 7 to the Companies Act 1985.

[1543]

NOTES
Commencement: 20 January 2007 (for the purpose of enabling the exercise of powers to make Orders or Regulations by statutory instrument); 6 April 2008 (otherwise).
Commencement (transitional provisions): see the note to s 380 at **[1507]**.
Sub-s (3): words in square brackets substituted by the Companies Act 2006 (Amendment) (Accounts and Reports) Regulations 2008, SI 2008/393, reg 6(3), as from 6 April 2008, in relation to financial years beginning on or after that date.
Regulations: the Small Companies and Groups (Accounts and Directors' Report) Regulations 2008, SI 2008/409; the Large and Medium-sized Companies and Groups (Accounts and Reports) Regulations 2008, SI 2008/410 (see the notes to s 396 at **[1523]**).

417   Contents of directors' report: business review

(1)   Unless the company is [entitled to the small companies exemption], the directors' report must contain a business review.

(2)   The purpose of the business review is to inform members of the company and help them assess how the directors have performed their duty under section 172 (duty to promote the success of the company).

(3)   The business review must contain—
  (a)   a fair review of the company's business, and
  (b)   a description of the principal risks and uncertainties facing the company.

(4)   The review required is a balanced and comprehensive analysis of—
  (a)   the development and performance of the company's business during the financial year, and
  (b)   the position of the company's business at the end of that year,
consistent with the size and complexity of the business.

(5)   In the case of a quoted company the business review must, to the extent necessary for an understanding of the development, performance or position of the company's business, include—
  (a)   the main trends and factors likely to affect the future development, performance and position of the company's business; and
  (b)   information about—
    (i)   environmental matters (including the impact of the company's business on the environment),
    (ii)   the company's employees, and
    (iii) social and community issues,
  including information about any policies of the company in relation to those matters and the effectiveness of those policies; and
  (c)   subject to subsection (11), information about persons with whom the company has contractual or other arrangements which are essential to the business of the company.
If the review does not contain information of each kind mentioned in paragraphs (b)(i), (ii) and (iii) and (c), it must state which of those kinds of information it does not contain.

(6)   The review must, to the extent necessary for an understanding of the development, performance or position of the company's business, include—
  (a)   analysis using financial key performance indicators, and
  (b)   where appropriate, analysis using other key performance indicators, including information relating to environmental matters and employee matters.
"Key performance indicators" means factors by reference to which the development, performance or position of the company's business can be measured effectively.

(7)   Where a company qualifies as medium-sized in relation to a financial year (see sections 465 to 467), the directors' report for the year need not comply with the requirements of subsection (6) so far as they relate to non-financial information.

(8)   The review must, where appropriate, include references to, and additional explanations of, amounts included in the company's annual accounts.

(9)   In relation to a group directors' report this section has effect as if the references to the company were references to the undertakings included in the consolidation.

(10)   Nothing in this section requires the disclosure of information about impending developments or matters in the course of negotiation if the disclosure would, in the opinion of the directors, be seriously prejudicial to the interests of the company.

(11)   Nothing in subsection (5)(c) requires the disclosure of information about a person if the disclosure would, in the opinion of the directors, be seriously prejudicial to that person and contrary to the public interest.

NOTES

Commencement: 1 October 2007 (for transitional provisions etc see the note below).

Commencement (transitional provisions): Sch 3, para 43 to the Companies Act 2006 (Commencement No 3, Consequential Amendments, Transitional Provisions and Savings) Order 2007, SI 2007/2194 provides as follows—

"43   Contents of directors' report: business review (s 417)

(1)   Section 417 of the Companies Act 2006 (contents of directors' report: business review) applies to directors' reports for financial years beginning on or after 1st October 2007.

(2)   Sections 234(1)(a), 234ZZB, 246(4)(a) and 246A(2A) of the 1985 Act or Articles 242(1), 242ZZB, 254(4)(a) and 254A(2A) of the 1986 Order continue to apply to directors' reports for financial years beginning before that date.".

Commencement (transitional adaptations): art 6 of the Companies Act 2006 (Commencement No 3, Consequential Amendments, Transitional Provisions and Savings) Order 2007, SI 2007/2194 provides that the provisions brought into force by that Order shall have effect subject to any transitional adaptations specified in Sch 1 to that Order. Schedule 1, para 16 to the Order provides as follows (but note that para 16 is revoked by the Companies Act 2006 (Commencement No 5, Transitional Provisions and Savings) Order 2007, SI 2007/3495, art 10(1)(b), as from 6 April 2008 (subject to the same transitional provisions and savings as apply, in accordance with Sch 4 to that Order, in relation to the repeal of the provisions of the 1985 Act referred to in the adaptation))—

"16   Contents of directors' report: business review (s 417)

(1)   Section 417 (contents of directors' report: business review) has effect with the following adaptations.

(2)   For subsection (1) substitute—

"(1)   Unless the company is entitled to small companies exemption in relation to the directors' report, the report must contain a business review.

(1A)   A company is entitled to small companies exemption in relation to the directors' report for a financial year if it—
   (a)   qualifies as small in relation to that year under Part 7 of the Companies Act 1985 or Part 8 of the Companies (Northern Ireland) Order 1986, and
   (b)   is not, and was not at any time within that year, an ineligible company as defined in section 247A(1B) of that Act or Article 255A(1B) of that Order.".

(3)   For subsection (7) substitute—

"(7)   Where a company—
   (a)   qualifies as medium-sized in relation to a financial year under Part 7 of the Companies Act 1985 or Part 8 of the Companies (Northern Ireland) Order 1986, and
   (b)   is not, and was not at any time within that year, an ineligible company as defined in section 247A(1B) of that Act or Article 255A(1B) of that Order,

the directors' report for the year need not comply with the requirements of subsection (6) so far as they relate to non-financial information.".".

Sub-s (1): words in square brackets by the Companies Act 2006 (Amendment) (Accounts and Reports) Regulations 2008, SI 2008/393, reg 6(4), as from 6 April 2008, in relation to financial years beginning on or after that date.

418   Contents of directors' report: statement as to disclosure to auditors

(1)   This section applies to a company unless—
   (a)   it is exempt for the financial year in question from the requirements of Part 16 as to audit of accounts, and
   (b)   the directors take advantage of that exemption.

(2)   The directors' report must contain a statement to the effect that, in the case of each of the persons who are directors at the time the report is approved—
   (a)   so far as the director is aware, there is no relevant audit information of which the company's auditor is unaware, and
   (b)   he has taken all the steps that he ought to have taken as a director in order to make himself aware of any relevant audit information and to establish that the company's auditor is aware of that information.

(3)   "Relevant audit information" means information needed by the company's auditor in connection with preparing his report.

(4)   A director is regarded as having taken all the steps that he ought to have taken as a director in order to do the things mentioned in subsection (2)(b) if he has—
   (a)   made such enquiries of his fellow directors and of the company's auditors for that purpose, and
   (b)   taken such other steps (if any) for that purpose,

as are required by his duty as a director of the company to exercise reasonable care, skill and diligence.

(5)   Where a directors' report containing the statement required by this section is approved but the statement is false, every director of the company who—

(a) knew that the statement was false, or was reckless as to whether it was false, and

(b) failed to take reasonable steps to prevent the report from being approved,

commits an offence.

(6) A person guilty of an offence under subsection (5) is liable—

(a) on conviction on indictment, to imprisonment for a term not exceeding two years or a fine (or both);

(b) on summary conviction—

(i) in England and Wales, to imprisonment for a term not exceeding twelve months or to a fine not exceeding the statutory maximum (or both);

(ii) in Scotland or Northern Ireland, to imprisonment for a term not exceeding six months, or to a fine not exceeding the statutory maximum (or both).

[1545]

NOTES

Commencement: 6 April 2008.

Commencement (transitional provisions): see the note to s 380 at **[1507]**.

Imprisonment for a term not exceeding twelve months: see the note to s 387 at **[1514]**.

419 Approval and signing of directors' report

(1) The directors' report must be approved by the board of directors and signed on behalf of the board by a director or the secretary of the company.

(2) [If in preparing the report advantage is taken of the small companies exemption,] it must contain a statement to that effect in a prominent position above the signature.

(3) If a directors' report is approved that does not comply with the requirements of this Act, every director of the company who—

(a) knew that it did not comply, or was reckless as to whether it complied, and

(b) failed to take reasonable steps to secure compliance with those requirements or, as the case may be, to prevent the report from being approved,

commits an offence.

(4) A person guilty of an offence under this section is liable—

(a) on conviction on indictment, to a fine;

(b) on summary conviction, to a fine not exceeding the statutory maximum.

[1546]

NOTES

Commencement: 6 April 2008.

Commencement (transitional provisions): see the note to s 380 at **[1507]**.

Sub-s (2): words in square brackets substituted by the Companies Act 2006 (Amendment) (Accounts and Reports) Regulations 2008, SI 2008/393, reg 6(5), as from 6 April 2008, in relation to financial years beginning on or after that date.

CHAPTER 6
QUOTED COMPANIES: DIRECTORS' REMUNERATION REPORT

420 Duty to prepare directors' remuneration report

(1) The directors of a quoted company must prepare a directors' remuneration report for each financial year of the company.

(2) In the case of failure to comply with the requirement to prepare a directors' remuneration report, every person who—

(a) was a director of the company immediately before the end of the period for filing accounts and reports for the financial year in question, and

(b) failed to take all reasonable steps for securing compliance with that requirement,

commits an offence.

(3) A person guilty of an offence under this section is liable—

(a) on conviction on indictment, to a fine;

(b) on summary conviction, to a fine not exceeding the statutory maximum.

[1547]

NOTES

Commencement: 6 April 2008.

Commencement (transitional provisions): see the note to s 380 at **[1507]**.

421 Contents of directors' remuneration report

(1) The Secretary of State may make provision by regulations as to—

(a)   the information that must be contained in a directors' remuneration report,
(b)   how information is to be set out in the report, and
(c)   what is to be the auditable part of the report.

(2)   Without prejudice to the generality of this power, the regulations may make any such provision as was made, immediately before the commencement of this Part, by Schedule 7A to the Companies Act 1985 (c 6).

(3)   It is the duty of—
(a)   any director of a company, and
(b)   any person who is or has at any time in the preceding five years been a director of the company,
to give notice to the company of such matters relating to himself as may be necessary for the purposes of regulations under this section.

(4)   A person who makes default in complying with subsection (3) commits an offence and is liable on summary conviction to a fine not exceeding level 3 on the standard scale.

[1548]

NOTES
Commencement: 20 January 2007 (for the purpose of enabling the exercise of powers to make Orders or Regulations by statutory instrument); 6 April 2008 (otherwise).
Commencement (transitional provisions): see the note to s 380 at **[1507]**.
Regulations: the Large and Medium-sized Companies and Groups (Accounts and Reports) Regulations 2008, SI 2008/410 (see the note to s 396 at **[1523]**).

422   Approval and signing of directors' remuneration report

(1)   The directors' remuneration report must be approved by the board of directors and signed on behalf of the board by a director or the secretary of the company.

(2)   If a directors' remuneration report is approved that does not comply with the requirements of this Act, every director of the company who—
(a)   knew that it did not comply, or was reckless as to whether it complied, and
(b)   failed to take reasonable steps to secure compliance with those requirements or, as the case may be, to prevent the report from being approved,
commits an offence.

(3)   A person guilty of an offence under this section is liable—
(a)   on conviction on indictment, to a fine;
(b)   on summary conviction, to a fine not exceeding the statutory maximum.

[1549]

NOTES
Commencement: 6 April 2008.
Commencement (transitional provisions): see the note to s 380 at **[1507]**.

CHAPTER 7
PUBLICATION OF ACCOUNTS AND REPORTS

Duty to circulate copies of accounts and reports

423   Duty to circulate copies of annual accounts and reports

(1)   Every company must send a copy of its annual accounts and reports for each financial year to—
(a)   every member of the company,
(b)   every holder of the company's debentures, and
(c)   every person who is entitled to receive notice of general meetings.

(2)   Copies need not be sent to a person for whom the company does not have a current address.

(3)   A company has a "current address" for a person if—
(a)   an address has been notified to the company by the person as one at which documents may be sent to him, and
(b)   the company has no reason to believe that documents sent to him at that address will not reach him.

(4)   In the case of a company not having a share capital, copies need not be sent to anyone who is not entitled to receive notices of general meetings of the company.

(5)   Where copies are sent out over a period of days, references in the Companies Acts to the day on which copies are sent out shall be read as references to the last day of that period.

(6) This section has effect subject to section 426 (option to provide summary financial statement).

[1550]

NOTES
Commencement: 6 April 2008.
Commencement (transitional provisions): see the note to s 380 at [1507].

424 Time allowed for sending out copies of accounts and reports

(1) The time allowed for sending out copies of the company's annual accounts and reports is as follows.

(2) A private company must comply with section 423 not later than—
    (a) the end of the period for filing accounts and reports, or
    (b) if earlier, the date on which it actually delivers its accounts and reports to the registrar.

(3) A public company must comply with section 423 at least 21 days before the date of the relevant accounts meeting.

(4) If in the case of a public company copies are sent out later than is required by subsection (3), they shall, despite that, be deemed to have been duly sent if it is so agreed by all the members entitled to attend and vote at the relevant accounts meeting.

(5) Whether the time allowed is that for a private company or a public company is determined by reference to the company's status immediately before the end of the accounting reference period by reference to which the financial year for the accounts in question was determined.

(6) In this section the "relevant accounts meeting" means the accounts meeting of the company at which the accounts and reports in question are to be laid.

[1551]

NOTES
Commencement: 6 April 2008.
Commencement (transitional provisions): see the note to s 380 at [1507].

425 Default in sending out copies of accounts and reports: offences

(1) If default is made in complying with section 423 or 424, an offence is committed by—
    (a) the company, and
    (b) every officer of the company who is in default.

(2) A person guilty of an offence under this section is liable—
    (a) on conviction on indictment, to a fine;
    (b) on summary conviction, to a fine not exceeding the statutory maximum.

[1552]

NOTES
Commencement: 6 April 2008.
Commencement (transitional provisions): see the note to s 380 at [1507].

Option to provide summary financial statement

426 Option to provide summary financial statement

(1) A company may—
    (a) in such cases as may be specified by regulations made by the Secretary of State, and
    (b) provided any conditions so specified are complied with,
provide a summary financial statement instead of copies of the accounts and reports required to be sent out in accordance with section 423.

(2) Copies of those accounts and reports must, however, be sent to any person entitled to be sent them in accordance with that section and who wishes to receive them.

(3) The Secretary of State may make provision by regulations as to the manner in which it is to be ascertained, whether before or after a person becomes entitled to be sent a copy of those accounts and reports, whether he wishes to receive them.

(4) A summary financial statement must comply with the requirements of—
section 427 (form and contents of summary financial statement: unquoted companies), or
section 428 (form and contents of summary financial statement: quoted companies).

(5)   This section applies to copies of accounts and reports required to be sent out by virtue of section 146 to a person nominated to enjoy information rights as it applies to copies of accounts and reports required to be sent out in accordance with section 423 to a member of the company.

(6)   Regulations under this section are subject to negative resolution procedure.

[1553]

NOTES

Commencement: 20 January 2007 (for the purpose of enabling the exercise of powers to make Orders or Regulations by statutory instrument); 6 April 2008 (otherwise).

Commencement (transitional provisions): see the note to s 380 at **[1507]**.

Regulations: the Companies (Summary Financial Statement) Regulations 2008, SI 2008/374. These Regulations concern the summary financial statements which companies may send out in place of their full accounts and reports under ss 426–428 of this Act. They come into force on 6 April 2008 and apply in relation to companies' financial years beginning on or after that date. They revoke and replace the Companies (Summary Financial Statement) Regulations 1995, SI 1995/2092 (which were made under the corresponding provisions of the Companies Act 1985), and the Companies (Summary Financial Statement) Regulations (Northern Ireland) 1996, SR 1996/179.

427   Form and contents of summary financial statement: unquoted companies

(1)   A summary financial statement by a company that is not a quoted company must—
   (a)   be derived from the company's annual accounts, and
   (b)   be prepared in accordance with this section and regulations made under it.

(2)   The summary financial statement must be in such form, and contain such information, as the Secretary of State may specify by regulations.

The regulations may require the statement to include information derived from the directors' report.

(3)   Nothing in this section or regulations made under it prevents a company from including in a summary financial statement additional information derived from the company's annual accounts or the directors' report.

(4)   The summary financial statement must—
   (a)   state that it is only a summary of information derived from the company's annual accounts;
   (b)   state whether it contains additional information derived from the directors' report and, if so, that it does not contain the full text of that report;
   (c)   state how a person entitled to them can obtain a full copy of the company's annual accounts and the directors' report;
   (d)   contain a statement by the company's auditor of his opinion as to whether the summary financial statement—
     (i)   is consistent with the company's annual accounts and, where information derived from the directors' report is included in the statement, with that report, and
     (ii)   complies with the requirements of this section and regulations made under it;
   (e)   state whether the auditor's report on the annual accounts was unqualified or qualified and, if it was qualified, set out the report in full together with any further material needed to understand the qualification;
   (f)   state whether, in that report, the auditor's statement under section 496 (whether directors' report consistent with accounts) was qualified or unqualified and, if it was qualified, set out the qualified statement in full together with any further material needed to understand the qualification;
   (g)   state whether that auditor's report contained a statement under—
     (i)   section 498(2)(a) or (b) (accounting records or returns inadequate or accounts not agreeing with records and returns), or
     (ii)   section 498(3) (failure to obtain necessary information and explanations),
and if so, set out the statement in full.

(5)   Regulations under this section may provide that any specified material may, instead of being included in the summary financial statement, be sent separately at the same time as the statement.

(6)   Regulations under this section are subject to negative resolution procedure.

[1554]

NOTES

Commencement: 20 January 2007 (for the purpose of enabling the exercise of powers to make Orders or Regulations by statutory instrument); 6 April 2008 (otherwise).

Commencement (transitional provisions): see the note to s 380 at **[1507]**.

Regulations: the Companies (Summary Financial Statement) Regulations 2008, SI 2008/374 (see the note to s 426 at **[1553]**).

428 Form and contents of summary financial statement: quoted companies

(1) A summary financial statement by a quoted company must—
   (a) be derived from the company's annual accounts and the directors' remuneration report, and
   (b) be prepared in accordance with this section and regulations made under it.

(2) The summary financial statement must be in such form, and contain such information, as the Secretary of State may specify by regulations.

The regulations may require the statement to include information derived from the directors' report.

(3) Nothing in this section or regulations made under it prevents a company from including in a summary financial statement additional information derived from the company's annual accounts, the directors' remuneration report or the directors' report.

(4) The summary financial statement must—
   (a) state that it is only a summary of information derived from the company's annual accounts and the directors' remuneration report;
   (b) state whether it contains additional information derived from the directors' report and, if so, that it does not contain the full text of that report;
   (c) state how a person entitled to them can obtain a full copy of the company's annual accounts, the directors' remuneration report or the directors' report;
   (d) contain a statement by the company's auditor of his opinion as to whether the summary financial statement—
      (i) is consistent with the company's annual accounts and the directors' remuneration report and, where information derived from the directors' report is included in the statement, with that report, and
      (ii) complies with the requirements of this section and regulations made under it;
   (e) state whether the auditor's report on the annual accounts and the auditable part of the directors' remuneration report was unqualified or qualified and, if it was qualified, set out the report in full together with any further material needed to understand the qualification;
   (f) state whether that auditor's report contained a statement under—
      (i) section 498(2) (accounting records or returns inadequate or accounts or directors' remuneration report not agreeing with records and returns), or
      (ii) section 498(3) (failure to obtain necessary information and explanations),
      and if so, set out the statement in full;
   (g) state whether, in that report, the auditor's statement under section 496 (whether directors' report consistent with accounts) was qualified or unqualified and, if it was qualified, set out the qualified statement in full together with any further material needed to understand the qualification.

(5) Regulations under this section may provide that any specified material may, instead of being included in the summary financial statement, be sent separately at the same time as the statement.

(6) Regulations under this section are subject to negative resolution procedure.

[1555]

NOTES
Commencement: 20 January 2007 (for the purpose of enabling the exercise of powers to make Orders or Regulations by statutory instrument); 6 April 2008 (otherwise).
Commencement (transitional provisions): see the note to s 380 at **[1507]**.
Regulations: the Companies (Summary Financial Statement) Regulations 2008, SI 2008/374 (see the note to s 426 at **[1553]**).

429 Summary financial statements: offences

(1) If default is made in complying with any provision of section 426, 427 or 428, or of regulations under any of those sections, an offence is committed by—
   (a) the company, and
   (b) every officer of the company who is in default.

(2) A person guilty of an offence under this section is liable on summary conviction to a fine not exceeding level 3 on the standard scale.

[1556]

NOTES
Commencement: 6 April 2008.
Commencement (transitional provisions): see the note to s 380 at **[1507]**.

Quoted companies: requirements as to website publication

430   Quoted companies: annual accounts and reports to be made available on website

(1)   A quoted company must ensure that its annual accounts and reports—
   (a)   are made available on a website, and
   (b)   remain so available until the annual accounts and reports for the company's next financial year are made available in accordance with this section.

(2)   The annual accounts and reports must be made available on a website that—
   (a)   is maintained by or on behalf of the company, and
   (b)   identifies the company in question.

(3)   Access to the annual accounts and reports on the website, and the ability to obtain a hard copy of the annual accounts and reports from the website, must not be—
   (a)   conditional on the payment of a fee, or
   (b)   otherwise restricted, except so far as necessary to comply with any enactment or regulatory requirement (in the United Kingdom or elsewhere).

(4)   The annual accounts and reports—
   (a)   must be made available as soon as reasonably practicable, and
   (b)   must be kept available throughout the period specified in subsection (1)(b).

(5)   A failure to make the annual accounts and reports available on a website throughout that period is disregarded if—
   (a)   the annual accounts and reports are made available on the website for part of that period, and
   (b)   the failure is wholly attributable to circumstances that it would not be reasonable to have expected the company to prevent or avoid.

(6)   In the event of default in complying with this section, an offence is committed by every officer of the company who is in default.

(7)   A person guilty of an offence under subsection (6) is liable on summary conviction to a fine not exceeding level 3 on the standard scale.

[1557]

NOTES
Commencement: 6 April 2008.
Commencement (transitional provisions): see the note to s 380 at **[1507]**.

Right of member or debenture holder to demand copies of accounts and reports

431   Right of member or debenture holder to copies of accounts and reports: unquoted companies

(1)   A member of, or holder of debentures of, an unquoted company is entitled to be provided, on demand and without charge, with a copy of—
   (a)   the company's last annual accounts,
   (b)   the last directors' report, and
   (c)   the auditor's report on those accounts (including the statement on that report).

(2)   The entitlement under this section is to a single copy of those documents, but that is in addition to any copy to which a person may be entitled under section 423.

(3)   If a demand made under this section is not complied with within seven days of receipt by the company, an offence is committed by—
   (a)   the company, and
   (b)   every officer of the company who is in default.

(4)   A person guilty of an offence under this section is liable on summary conviction to a fine not exceeding level 3 on the standard scale and, for continued contravention, a daily default fine not exceeding one-tenth of level 3 on the standard scale.

[1558]

NOTES
Commencement: 6 April 2008.
Commencement (transitional provisions): see the note to s 380 at **[1507]**.

432   Right of member or debenture holder to copies of accounts and reports: quoted companies

(1)   A member of, or holder of debentures of, a quoted company is entitled to be provided, on demand and without charge, with a copy of—
   (a)   the company's last annual accounts,
   (b)   the last directors' remuneration report,

(c) the last directors' report, and

(d) the auditor's report on those accounts (including the report on the directors' remuneration report and on the directors' report).

(2) The entitlement under this section is to a single copy of those documents, but that is in addition to any copy to which a person may be entitled under section 423.

(3) If a demand made under this section is not complied with within seven days of receipt by the company, an offence is committed by—

(a) the company, and

(b) every officer of the company who is in default.

(4) A person guilty of an offence under this section is liable on summary conviction to a fine not exceeding level 3 on the standard scale and, for continued contravention, a daily default fine not exceeding one-tenth of level 3 on the standard scale.

[1559]

NOTES

Commencement: 6 April 2008.

Commencement (transitional provisions): see the note to s 380 at **[1507]**.

Requirements in connection with publication of accounts and reports

433 Name of signatory to be stated in published copies of accounts and reports

(1) Every copy of a document to which this section applies that is published by or on behalf of the company must state the name of the person who signed it on behalf of the board.

(2) In the case of an unquoted company, this section applies to copies of—

(a) the company's balance sheet, and

(b) the directors' report.

(3) In the case of a quoted company, this section applies to copies of—

(a) the company's balance sheet,

(b) the directors' remuneration report, and

(c) the directors' report.

(4) If a copy is published without the required statement of the signatory's name, an offence is committed by—

(a) the company, and

(b) every officer of the company who is in default.

(5) A person guilty of an offence under this section is liable on summary conviction to a fine not exceeding level 3 on the standard scale.

[1560]

NOTES

Commencement: 6 April 2008.

Commencement (transitional provisions): see the note to s 380 at **[1507]**.

434 Requirements in connection with publication of statutory accounts

(1) If a company publishes any of its statutory accounts, they must be accompanied by the auditor's report on those accounts (unless the company is exempt from audit and the directors have taken advantage of that exemption).

(2) A company that prepares statutory group accounts for a financial year must not publish its statutory individual accounts for that year without also publishing with them its statutory group accounts.

(3) A company's "statutory accounts" are its accounts for a financial year as required to be delivered to the registrar under section 441.

(4) If a company contravenes any provision of this section, an offence is committed by—

(a) the company, and

(b) every officer of the company who is in default.

(5) A person guilty of an offence under this section is liable on summary conviction to a fine not exceeding level 3 on the standard scale.

(6) This section does not apply in relation to the provision by a company of a summary financial statement (see section 426).

[1561]

NOTES

Commencement: 6 April 2008.

Commencement (transitional provisions): see the note to s 380 at **[1507]**.

435   Requirements in connection with publication of non-statutory accounts

(1)   If a company publishes non-statutory accounts, it must publish with them a statement indicating—

    (a)   that they are not the company's statutory accounts,

    (b)   whether statutory accounts dealing with any financial year with which the non-statutory accounts purport to deal have been delivered to the registrar, and

    (c)   whether an auditor's report has been made on the company's statutory accounts for any such financial year, and if so whether the report—

        (i)   was qualified or unqualified, or included a reference to any matters to which the auditor drew attention by way of emphasis without qualifying the report, or

        (ii)   contained a statement under section 498(2) (accounting records or returns inadequate or accounts or directors' remuneration report not agreeing with records and returns), or section 498(3) (failure to obtain necessary information and explanations).

(2)   The company must not publish with non-statutory accounts the auditor's report on the company's statutory accounts.

(3)   References in this section to the publication by a company of "non-statutory accounts" are to the publication of—

    (a)   any balance sheet or profit and loss account relating to, or purporting to deal with, a financial year of the company, or

    (b)   an account in any form purporting to be a balance sheet or profit and loss account for a group headed by the company relating to, or purporting to deal with, a financial year of the company,

otherwise than as part of the company's statutory accounts.

(4)   In subsection (3)(b) "a group headed by the company" means a group consisting of the company and any other undertaking (regardless of whether it is a subsidiary undertaking of the company) other than a parent undertaking of the company.

(5)   If a company contravenes any provision of this section, an offence is committed by—

    (a)   the company, and

    (b)   every officer of the company who is in default.

(6)   A person guilty of an offence under this section is liable on summary conviction to a fine not exceeding level 3 on the standard scale.

(7)   This section does not apply in relation to the provision by a company of a summary financial statement (see section 426).

                                                                  [1562]

NOTES

Commencement: 6 April 2008.

Commencement (transitional provisions): see the note to s 380 at **[1507]**.

436   Meaning of "publication" in relation to accounts and reports

(1)   This section has effect for the purposes of—

section 433 (name of signatory to be stated in published copies of accounts and reports),

section 434 (requirements in connection with publication of statutory accounts), and

section 435 (requirements in connection with publication of non-statutory accounts).

(2)   For the purposes of those sections a company is regarded as publishing a document if it publishes, issues or circulates it or otherwise makes it available for public inspection in a manner calculated to invite members of the public generally, or any class of members of the public, to read it.

                                                                 [1563]

NOTES

Commencement: 6 April 2008.

Commencement (transitional provisions): see the note to s 380 at **[1507]**.

CHAPTER 8
PUBLIC COMPANIES: LAYING OF ACCOUNTS AND REPORTS BEFORE GENERAL MEETING

437   Public companies: laying of accounts and reports before general meeting

(1)   The directors of a public company must lay before the company in general meeting copies of its annual accounts and reports.

(2)   This section must be complied with not later than the end of the period for filing the accounts and reports in question.

(3)   In the Companies Acts "accounts meeting", in relation to a public company, means a general meeting of the company at which the company's annual accounts and reports are (or are to be) laid in accordance with this section.

[1564]

NOTES
Commencement: 6 April 2008.
Commencement (transitional provisions): see the note to s 380 at **[1507]**.

438   Public companies: offence of failure to lay accounts and reports

(1)   If the requirements of section 437 (public companies: laying of accounts and reports before general meeting) are not complied with before the end of the period allowed, every person who immediately before the end of that period was a director of the company commits an offence.

(2)   It is a defence for a person charged with such an offence to prove that he took all reasonable steps for securing that those requirements would be complied with before the end of that period.

(3)   It is not a defence to prove that the documents in question were not in fact prepared as required by this Part.

(4)   A person guilty of an offence under this section is liable on summary conviction to a fine not exceeding level 5 on the standard scale and, for continued contravention, a daily default fine not exceeding one-tenth of level 5 on the standard scale.

[1565]

NOTES
Commencement: 6 April 2008.
Commencement (transitional provisions): see the note to s 380 at **[1507]**.

CHAPTER 9
QUOTED COMPANIES: MEMBERS' APPROVAL OF DIRECTORS'
REMUNERATION REPORT

439   Quoted companies: members' approval of directors' remuneration report

(1)   A quoted company must, prior to the accounts meeting, give to the members of the company entitled to be sent notice of the meeting notice of the intention to move at the meeting, as an ordinary resolution, a resolution approving the directors' remuneration report for the financial year.

(2)   The notice may be given in any manner permitted for the service on the member of notice of the meeting.

(3)   The business that may be dealt with at the accounts meeting includes the resolution.

This is so notwithstanding any default in complying with subsection (1) or (2).

(4)   The existing directors must ensure that the resolution is put to the vote of the meeting.

(5)   No entitlement of a person to remuneration is made conditional on the resolution being passed by reason only of the provision made by this section.

(6)   In this section—
"the accounts meeting" means the general meeting of the company before which the company's annual accounts for the financial year are to be laid; and
"existing director" means a person who is a director of the company immediately before that meeting.

[1566]

NOTES
Commencement: 6 April 2008.
Commencement (transitional provisions): see the note to s 380 at **[1507]**.

440   Quoted companies: offences in connection with procedure for approval

(1)   In the event of default in complying with section 439(1) (notice to be given of resolution for approval of directors' remuneration report), an offence is committed by every officer of the company who is in default.

(2)   If the resolution is not put to the vote of the accounts meeting, an offence is committed by each existing director.

(3)   It is a defence for a person charged with an offence under subsection (2) to prove that he took all reasonable steps for securing that the resolution was put to the vote of the meeting.

(4)   A person guilty of an offence under this section is liable on summary conviction to a fine not exceeding level 3 on the standard scale.

(5)   In this section—
"the accounts meeting" means the general meeting of the company before which the company's annual accounts for the financial year are to be laid; and
"existing director" means a person who is a director of the company immediately before that meeting.

[1567]

NOTES
Commencement: 6 April 2008.
Commencement (transitional provisions): see the note to s 380 at **[1507]**.

CHAPTER 10
FILING OF ACCOUNTS AND REPORTS
Duty to file accounts and reports

441   Duty to file accounts and reports with the registrar

(1)   The directors of a company must deliver to the registrar for each financial year the accounts and reports required by—
section 444 (filing obligations of companies subject to small companies regime),
[section 444A (filing obligations of companies entitled to small companies exemption in relation to directors' report),]
section 445 (filing obligations of medium-sized companies),
section 446 (filing obligations of unquoted companies), or
section 447 (filing obligations of quoted companies).

(2)   This is subject to section 448 (unlimited companies exempt from filing obligations).

[1568]

NOTES
Commencement: 6 April 2008.
Commencement (transitional provisions): see the note to s 380 at **[1507]**.
Entry in square brackets inserted by the Companies Act 2006 (Amendment) (Accounts and Reports) Regulations 2008, SI 2008/393, reg 6(6), as from 6 April 2008, in relation to financial years beginning on or after that date.

442   Period allowed for filing accounts

(1)   This section specifies the period allowed for the directors of a company to comply with their obligation under section 441 to deliver accounts and reports for a financial year to the registrar.
This is referred to in the Companies Acts as the "period for filing" those accounts and reports.

(2)   The period is—
(a)   for a private company, nine months after the end of the relevant accounting reference period, and
(b)   for a public company, six months after the end of that period.
This is subject to the following provisions of this section.

(3)   If the relevant accounting reference period is the company's first and is a period of more than twelve months, the period is—
(a)   nine months or six months, as the case may be, from the first anniversary of the incorporation of the company, or
(b)   three months after the end of the accounting reference period,
whichever last expires.

(4)   If the relevant accounting reference period is treated as shortened by virtue of a notice given by the company under section 392 (alteration of accounting reference date), the period is—
(a)   that applicable in accordance with the above provisions, or
(b)   three months from the date of the notice under that section,
whichever last expires.

(5)   If for any special reason the Secretary of State thinks fit he may, on an application made before the expiry of the period otherwise allowed, by notice in writing to a company extend that period by such further period as may be specified in the notice.

(6)   Whether the period allowed is that for a private company or a public company is determined by reference to the company's status immediately before the end of the relevant accounting reference period.

(7)   In this section "the relevant accounting reference period" means the accounting reference period by reference to which the financial year for the accounts in question was determined.

[1569]

NOTES
Commencement: 6 April 2008.
Commencement (transitional provisions): see the note to s 380 at **[1507]**.

443 Calculation of period allowed

(1)   This section applies for the purposes of calculating the period for filing a company's accounts and reports which is expressed as a specified number of months from a specified date or after the end of a specified previous period.

(2)   Subject to the following provisions, the period ends with the date in the appropriate month corresponding to the specified date or the last day of the specified previous period.

(3)   If the specified date, or the last day of the specified previous period, is the last day of a month, the period ends with the last day of the appropriate month (whether or not that is the corresponding date).

(4)   If—
    (a)   the specified date, or the last day of the specified previous period, is not the last day of a month but is the 29th or 30th, and
    (b)   the appropriate month is February,
the period ends with the last day of February.

(5)   "The appropriate month" means the month that is the specified number of months after the month in which the specified date, or the end of the specified previous period, falls.

[1570]

NOTES
Commencement: 6 April 2008.
Commencement (transitional provisions): see the note to s 380 at **[1507]**.
Limited Liability Partnerships: this section is applied to LLPs (in relation to accounts and auditors' reports for financial years beginning on or after 6 April 2008) and modified in its application so that, in sub-s (1), for the words "the period for filing a company's reports and accounts" there are substituted the words "the period allowed for delivering the accounts and the auditor's report"; see the Companies (Late Filing Penalties) and Limited Liability Partnerships (Filing Periods and Late Filing Penalties) Regulations 2008, SI 2008/497, reg 6(1) and Schedule, Pt 1.

Filing obligations of different descriptions of company

444 Filing obligations of companies subject to small companies regime

(1)   The directors of a company subject to the small companies regime—
    (a)   must deliver to the registrar for each financial year a copy of a balance sheet drawn up as at the last day of that year, and
    (b)   may also deliver to the registrar—
        (i)   a copy of the company's profit and loss account for that year, and
        (ii)   a copy of the directors' report for that year.

(2)   The directors must also deliver to the registrar a copy of the auditor's report on [the accounts (and any directors' report) that it delivers].

This does not apply if the company is exempt from audit and the directors have taken advantage of that exemption.

(3)   The copies of accounts and reports delivered to the registrar must be copies of the company's annual accounts and reports, except that where the company prepares Companies Act accounts—
    (a)   the directors may deliver to the registrar a copy of a balance sheet drawn up in accordance with regulations made by the Secretary of State, and
    (b)   there may be omitted from the copy profit and loss account delivered to the registrar such items as may be specified by the regulations.

These are referred to in this Part as "abbreviated accounts".

(4)   If abbreviated accounts are delivered to the registrar the obligation to deliver a copy of the auditor's report on the accounts is to deliver a copy of the special auditor's report required by section 449.

(5)   Where the directors of a company subject to the small companies regime deliver to the registrar IAS accounts, or Companies Act accounts that are not abbreviated accounts, and in accordance with this section—
    (a)   do not deliver to the registrar a copy of the company's profit and loss account, or
    (b)   do not deliver to the registrar a copy of the directors' report,
the copy of the balance sheet delivered to the registrar must contain in a prominent position a statement that the company's annual accounts and reports have been delivered in accordance with the provisions applicable to companies subject to the small companies regime.

(6)   The copies of the balance sheet and any directors' report delivered to the registrar under this section must state the name of the person who signed it on behalf of the board.

(7)   The copy of the auditor's report delivered to the registrar under this section must—
    (a)   state the name of the auditor and (where the auditor is a firm) the name of the person who signed it as senior statutory auditor, or
    (b)   if the conditions in section 506 (circumstances in which names may be omitted) are met, state that a resolution has been passed and notified to the Secretary of State in accordance with that section.

[1571]

NOTES
Commencement: 20 January 2007 (for the purpose of enabling the exercise of powers to make Orders or Regulations by statutory instrument); 6 April 2008 (otherwise).
Commencement (transitional provisions): see the note to s 380 at **[1507]**.
Commencement (transitional adaptations): art 6 of the Companies Act 2006 (Commencement No 5, Transitional Provisions and Savings) Order 2007, SI 2007/3495 provides that the provisions brought into force by arts 3 and 5 of that Order shall have effect subject to any transitional adaptations specified in Sch 1 to that Order. Schedule 1, Pt 1, para 6 to the Order provides as follows (note that this paragraph is revoked by the Companies Act 2006 (Commencement No 8, Transitional Provisions and Savings) Order 2008, SI 2008/2860, art 6, as from 1 October 2009 (subject to any relevant transitional provision or saving in Sch 2 to that Order))—

"Authentication of accounts and reports filed with registrar (ss 444 to 447 and 449)
6.—(1)   Section 444 (filing obligations of companies subject to the small companies regime) has effect with the following adaptations.
(2)   For subsection (6) substitute—
"(6)   The copy of the balance sheet delivered to the registrar under this section must—
    (a)   state the name of the person who signed it on behalf of the board under section 414, and
    (b)   be signed on behalf of the board by a director of the company.
(6A)   The copy of the directors' report delivered to the registrar under this section must—
    (a)   state the name of the person who signed it on behalf of the board under section 419, and
    (b)   be signed on behalf of the board by a director or the secretary of the company.".
(3)   For subsection (7) substitute—
"(7)   The copy of the auditor's report delivered to the registrar under this section must—
    (a)   state the name of the auditor and (where the auditor is a firm) the name of the person who signed it as senior statutory auditor, and
    (b)   be signed by the auditor or (where the auditor is a firm) in the name of the firm by a person authorised to sign on its behalf,
or, if the conditions in section 506 (circumstances in which names may be omitted) are met, state that a resolution has been passed and notified to the Secretary of State in accordance with that section.".".

Sub-s (2): words in square brackets substituted by the Companies Act 2006 (Amendment) (Accounts and Reports) Regulations 2008, SI 2008/393, reg 12, as from 6 April 2008, in relation to financial years beginning on or after that date.
Regulations: the Small Companies and Groups (Accounts and Directors' Report) Regulations 2008, SI 2008/409 (see the note to s 396 at **[1523]**).

[444A   Filing obligations of companies entitled to small companies exemption in relation to directors' report

(1)   The directors of a company that is entitled to small companies exemption in relation to the directors' report for a financial year—
    (a)   must deliver to the registrar a copy of the company's annual accounts for that year, and
    (b)   may also deliver to the registrar a copy of the directors' report.

(2)   The directors must also deliver to the registrar a copy of the auditor's report on the accounts (and any directors' report) that it delivers.

This does not apply if the company is exempt from audit and the directors have taken advantage of that exception.

(3)   The copies of the balance sheet and directors' report delivered to the registrar under this section must state the name of the person who signed it on behalf of the board.

(4)   The copy of the auditor's report delivered to the registrar under this section must—
    (a)   state the name of the auditor and (where the auditor is a firm) the name of the person who signed it as senior statutory auditor, and
    (b)   be signed by the auditor or (where the auditor is a firm) in the name of the firm by a person authorised to sign on its behalf,
or, if the conditions in section 506 (circumstances in which names may be omitted) are met, state that a resolution has been passed and notified to the Secretary of State in accordance with that section.

(5) This section does not apply to companies within section 444 (filing obligations of companies subject to the small companies regime).]

[1571A]

NOTES
Commencement: 6 April 2008.
Inserted by the Companies Act 2006 (Amendment) (Accounts and Reports) Regulations 2008, SI 2008/393, reg 6(7), as from 6 April 2008, in relation to financial years beginning on or after that date.

445 Filing obligations of medium-sized companies

(1) The directors of a company that qualifies as a medium-sized company in relation to a financial year (see sections 465 to 467) must deliver to the registrar a copy of—
  (a) the company's annual accounts, and
  (b) the directors' report.

(2) They must also deliver to the registrar a copy of the auditor's report on those accounts (and on the directors' report).

This does not apply if the company is exempt from audit and the directors have taken advantage of that exemption.

(3) Where the company prepares Companies Act accounts, the directors may deliver to the registrar a copy of the company's annual accounts for the financial year—
  (a) that includes a profit and loss account in which items are combined in accordance with regulations made by the Secretary of State, and
  (b) that does not contain items whose omission is authorised by the regulations.

These are referred to in this Part as "abbreviated accounts".

(4) If abbreviated accounts are delivered to the registrar the obligation to deliver a copy of the auditor's report on the accounts is to deliver a copy of the special auditor's report required by section 449.

(5) The copies of the balance sheet and directors' report delivered to the registrar under this section must state the name of the person who signed it on behalf of the board.

(6) The copy of the auditor's report delivered to the registrar under this section must—
  (a) state the name of the auditor and (where the auditor is a firm) the name of the person who signed it as senior statutory auditor, or
  (b) if the conditions in section 506 (circumstances in which names may be omitted) are met, state that a resolution has been passed and notified to the Secretary of State in accordance with that section.

[(7) This section does not apply to companies within—
  (a) section 444 (filing obligations of companies subject to the small companies regime), or
  (b) section 444A (filing obligations of companies entitled to small companies exemption in relation to directors' report).]

[1572]

NOTES
Commencement: 20 January 2007 (for the purpose of enabling the exercise of powers to make Orders or Regulations by statutory instrument); 6 April 2008 (otherwise).
Commencement (transitional provisions): see the note to s 380 at [1507].
Commencement (transitional adaptations): art 6 of the Companies Act 2006 (Commencement No 5, Transitional Provisions and Savings) Order 2007, SI 2007/3495 provides that the provisions brought into force by arts 3 and 5 of that Order shall have effect subject to any transitional adaptations specified in Sch 1 to that Order. Schedule 1, Pt 1, para 7 to the Order provides as follows (note that this paragraph is revoked by the Companies Act 2006 (Commencement No 8, Transitional Provisions and Savings) Order 2008, SI 2008/2860, art 6, as from 1 October 2009 (subject to any relevant transitional provision or saving in Sch 2 to that Order))—

"7.—(1)   Section 445 (filing obligations of medium-sized companies) has effect with the following adaptations.

(2)   For subsection (5) substitute—

"(5)   The copy of the balance sheet delivered to the registrar under this section must—
    (a) state the name of the person who signed it on behalf of the board under section 414, and
    (b) be signed on behalf of the board by a director of the company.

(5A)   The copy of the directors' report delivered to the registrar under this section must—
    (a) state the name of the person who signed it on behalf of the board under section 419, and
    (b) be signed on behalf of the board by a director or the secretary of the company.".

(3)   For subsection (6) substitute—

"(6)   The copy of the auditor's report delivered to the registrar under this section must—
    (a) state the name of the auditor and (where the auditor is a firm) the name of the person who signed it as senior statutory auditor, and
    (b) be signed by the auditor or (where the auditor is a firm) in the name of the firm by a person authorised to sign on its behalf,

or, if the conditions in section 506 (circumstances in which names may be omitted) are met, state that a resolution has been passed and notified to the Secretary of State in accordance with that section.".".

Sub-s (7): substituted by the Companies Act 2006 (Amendment) (Accounts and Reports) Regulations 2008, SI 2008/393, reg 6(8), as from 6 April 2008, in relation to financial years beginning on or after that date.
Regulations: the Large and Medium-sized Companies and Groups (Accounts and Reports) Regulations 2008, SI 2008/410 (see the note to s 396 at **[1523]**).

446   Filing obligations of unquoted companies

(1)   The directors of an unquoted company must deliver to the registrar for each financial year of the company a copy of—
   (a)   the company's annual accounts, and
   (b)   the directors' report.

(2)   The directors must also deliver to the registrar a copy of the auditor's report on those accounts (and the directors' report).

This does not apply if the company is exempt from audit and the directors have taken advantage of that exemption.

(3)   The copies of the balance sheet and directors' report delivered to the registrar under this section must state the name of the person who signed it on behalf of the board.

(4)   The copy of the auditor's report delivered to the registrar under this section must—
   (a)   state the name of the auditor and (where the auditor is a firm) the name of the person who signed it as senior statutory auditor, or
   (b)   if the conditions in section 506 (circumstances in which names may be omitted) are met, state that a resolution has been passed and notified to the Secretary of State in accordance with that section.

(5)   This section does not apply to companies within—
   (a)   section 444 (filing obligations of companies subject to the small companies regime), ...
   [(aa)   section 444A (filing obligations of companies entitled to small companies exemption in relation to directors' report), or]
   (b)   section 445 (filing obligations of medium-sized companies).

[1573]

NOTES
Commencement: 6 April 2008.
Commencement (transitional provisions): see the note to s 380 at **[1507]**.
Commencement (transitional adaptations): art 6 of the Companies Act 2006 (Commencement No 5, Transitional Provisions and Savings) Order 2007, SI 2007/3495 provides that the provisions brought into force by arts 3 and 5 of that Order shall have effect subject to any transitional adaptations specified in Sch 1 to that Order. Schedule 1, Pt 1, para 8 to the Order provides as follows (note that this paragraph is revoked by the Companies Act 2006 (Commencement No 8, Transitional Provisions and Savings) Order 2008, SI 2008/2860, art 6, as from 1 October 2009 (subject to any relevant transitional provision or saving in Sch 2 to that Order))—

"8.—(1)   Section 446 (filing obligations of unquoted companies) has effect with the following adaptations.

(2)   For subsection (3) substitute—

"(3)   The copy of the balance sheet delivered to the registrar under this section must—
   (a)   state the name of the person who signed it on behalf of the board under section 414, and
   (b)   be signed on behalf of the board by a director of the company.

(3A)   The copy of the directors' report delivered to the registrar under this section must—
   (a)   state the name of the person who signed it on behalf of the board under section 419, and
   (b)   be signed on behalf of the board by a director or the secretary of the company.".

(3)   For subsection (4) substitute—

"(4)   The copy of the auditor's report delivered to the registrar under this section must—
   (a)   state the name of the auditor and (where the auditor is a firm) the name of the person who signed it as senior statutory auditor, and
   (b)   be signed by the auditor or (where the auditor is a firm) in the name of the firm by a person authorised to sign on its behalf,

or, if the conditions in section 506 (circumstances in which names may be omitted) are met, state that a resolution has been passed and notified to the Secretary of State in accordance with that section.".".

Sub-s (5): word omitted from para (a) repealed, and para (aa) inserted, by the Companies Act 2006 (Amendment) (Accounts and Reports) Regulations 2008, SI 2008/393, reg 6(9), as from 6 April 2008, in relation to financial years beginning on or after that date.

447   Filing obligations of quoted companies

(1)   The directors of a quoted company must deliver to the registrar for each financial year of the company a copy of—
   (a)   the company's annual accounts,
   (b)   the directors' remuneration report, and
   (c)   the directors' report.

(2)   They must also deliver a copy of the auditor's report on those accounts (and on the directors' remuneration report and the directors' report).

(3)   The copies of the balance sheet, the directors' remuneration report and the directors' report delivered to the registrar under this section must state the name of the person who signed it on behalf of the board.

(4)   The copy of the auditor's report delivered to the registrar under this section must—
(a)   state the name of the auditor and (where the auditor is a firm) the name of the person who signed it as senior statutory auditor, or
(b)   if the conditions in section 506 (circumstances in which names may be omitted) are met, state that a resolution has been passed and notified to the Secretary of State in accordance with that section.

[1574]

NOTES
Commencement: 6 April 2008.
Commencement (transitional provisions): see the note to s 380 at [1507].
Commencement (transitional adaptations): art 6 of the Companies Act 2006 (Commencement No 5, Transitional Provisions and Savings) Order 2007, SI 2007/3495 provides that the provisions brought into force by arts 3 and 5 of that Order shall have effect subject to any transitional adaptations specified in Sch 1 to that Order. Schedule 1, Pt 1, para 9 to the Order provides as follows (note that this paragraph is revoked by the Companies Act 2006 (Commencement No 8, Transitional Provisions and Savings) Order 2008, SI 2008/2860, art 6, as from 1 October 2009 (subject to any relevant transitional provision or saving in Sch 2 to that Order))—

"9.—(1)   Section 447 (filing obligations of quoted companies) has effect with the following adaptations.

(2)   For subsection (3) substitute—

"(3)   The copy of the balance sheet delivered to the registrar under this section must—
(a)   state the name of the person who signed it on behalf of the board under section 414, and
(b)   be signed on behalf of the board by a director of the company.

(3A)   The copy of the directors' remuneration report delivered to the registrar under this section must—
(a)   state the name of the person who signed it on behalf of the board under section 422, and
(b)   be signed on behalf of the board by a director or the secretary of the company.

(3B)   The copy of the directors' report delivered to the registrar under this section must—
(a)   state the name of the person who signed it on behalf of the board under section 419, and
(b)   be signed on behalf of the board by a director or the secretary of the company.".

(3)   For subsection (4) substitute—

"(4)   The copy of the auditor's report delivered to the registrar under this section must—
(a)   state the name of the auditor and (where the auditor is a firm) the name of the person who signed it as senior statutory auditor, and
(b)   be signed by the auditor or (where the auditor is a firm) in the name of the firm by a person authorised to sign on its behalf,

or, if the conditions in section 506 (circumstances in which names may be omitted) are met, state that a resolution has been passed and notified to the Secretary of State in accordance with that section.".".

448   Unlimited companies exempt from obligation to file accounts

(1)   The directors of an unlimited company are not required to deliver accounts and reports to the registrar in respect of a financial year if the following conditions are met.

(2)   The conditions are that at no time during the relevant accounting reference period—
(a)   has the company been, to its knowledge, a subsidiary undertaking of an undertaking which was then limited, or
(b)   have there been, to its knowledge, exercisable by or on behalf of two or more undertakings which were then limited, rights which if exercisable by one of them would have made the company a subsidiary undertaking of it, or
(c)   has the company been a parent company of an undertaking which was then limited.

The references above to an undertaking being limited at a particular time are to an undertaking (under whatever law established) the liability of whose members is at that time limited.

(3)   The exemption conferred by this section does not apply if—
(a)   the company is a banking or insurance company or the parent company of a banking or insurance group, or
[(b)   each of the members of the company is—
(i)   a limited company,
(ii)   another unlimited company each of whose members is a limited company, or
(iii)   a Scottish partnership each of whose members is a limited company.]

[The references in paragraph (b) to a limited company, another unlimited company or a Scottish partnership include a comparable undertaking incorporated in or formed under the law of a country or territory outside the United Kingdom.]

(4)   Where a company is exempt by virtue of this section from the obligation to deliver accounts—

(a)   section 434(3) (requirements in connection with publication of statutory accounts: meaning of "statutory accounts") has effect with the substitution for the words "as required to be delivered to the registrar under section 441" of the words "as prepared in accordance with this Part and approved by the board of directors"; and

(b)   section 435(1)(b) (requirements in connection with publication of non-statutory accounts: statement whether statutory accounts delivered) has effect with the substitution for the words from "whether statutory accounts" to "have been delivered to the registrar" of the words "that the company is exempt from the requirement to deliver statutory accounts".

(5)   In this section the "relevant accounting reference period", in relation to a financial year, means the accounting reference period by reference to which that financial year was determined.

[1575]

NOTES
Commencement: 6 April 2008.
Commencement (transitional provisions): see the note to s 380 at **[1507]**.
Sub-s (3): para (b) substituted, and final words in square brackets inserted, by the Companies Act 2006 (Amendment) (Accounts and Reports) Regulations 2008, SI 2008/393, reg 13, as from 6 April 2008, in relation to financial years beginning on or after that date.

Requirements where abbreviated accounts delivered

449   Special auditor's report where abbreviated accounts delivered

(1)   This section applies where—
(a)   the directors of a company deliver abbreviated accounts to the registrar, and
(b)   the company is not exempt from audit (or the directors have not taken advantage of any such exemption).

(2)   The directors must also deliver to the registrar a copy of a special report of the company's auditor stating that in his opinion—
(a)   the company is entitled to deliver abbreviated accounts in accordance with the section in question, and
(b)   the abbreviated accounts to be delivered are properly prepared in accordance with regulations under that section.

(3)   The auditor's report on the company's annual accounts need not be delivered, but—
(a)   if that report was qualified, the special report must set out that report in full together with any further material necessary to understand the qualification, and
(b)   if that report contained a statement under—
    (i)   section 498(2)(a) or (b) (accounts, records or returns inadequate or accounts not agreeing with records and returns), or
    (ii)   section 498(3) (failure to obtain necessary information and explanations),
the special report must set out that statement in full.

(4)   The provisions of—
sections 503 to 506 (signature of auditor's report), and
sections 507 to 509 (offences in connection with auditor's report),
apply to a special report under this section as they apply to an auditor's report on the company's annual accounts prepared under Part 16.

(5)   If abbreviated accounts are delivered to the registrar, the references in section 434 or 435 (requirements in connection with publication of accounts) to the auditor's report on the company's annual accounts shall be read as references to the special auditor's report required by this section.

[1576]

NOTES
Commencement: 6 April 2008.
Commencement (transitional provisions): see the note to s 380 at **[1507]**.
Commencement (transitional adaptations): art 6 of the Companies Act 2006 (Commencement No 5, Transitional Provisions and Savings) Order 2007, SI 2007/3495 provides that the provisions brought into force by arts 3 and 5 of that Order shall have effect subject to any transitional adaptations specified in Sch 1 to that Order. Schedule 1, Pt 1, para 10 to the Order provides as follows (note that this paragraph is revoked by the Companies Act 2006 (Commencement No 8, Transitional Provisions and Savings) Order 2008, SI 2008/2860, art 6, as from 1 October 2009 (subject to any relevant transitional provision or saving in Sch 2 to that Order))—

"10.—(1)   Section 449 (special auditor's report where abbreviated accounts delivered) has effect with the following adaptation.

(2)   After subsection (4) insert—

"(4A)   The copy of the special report delivered to the registrar under this section must—
(a)   be signed by the auditor or (where the auditor is a firm) in the name of the firm by a person authorised to sign on its behalf, or

(b)   if the conditions in section 506 (circumstances in which names may be omitted) are met, state that a resolution has been passed and notified to the Secretary of State in accordance with that section.".".

450   Approval and signing of abbreviated accounts

(1)   Abbreviated accounts must be approved by the board of directors and signed on behalf of the board by a director of the company.

(2)   The signature must be on the balance sheet.

(3)   The balance sheet must contain in a prominent position above the signature a statement to the effect that it is prepared in accordance with the special provisions of this Act relating (as the case may be) to companies subject to the small companies regime or to medium-sized companies.

(4)   If abbreviated accounts are approved that do not comply with the requirements of regulations under the relevant section, every director of the company who—
(a)   knew that they did not comply, or was reckless as to whether they complied, and
(b)   failed to take reasonable steps to prevent them from being approved,
commits an offence.

(5)   A person guilty of an offence under subsection (4) is liable—
(a)   on conviction on indictment, to a fine;
(b)   on summary conviction, to a fine not exceeding the statutory maximum.

[1577]

NOTES
Commencement: 6 April 2008.
Commencement (transitional provisions): see the note to s 380 at **[1507]**.

Failure to file accounts and reports

451   Default in filing accounts and reports: offences

(1)   If the requirements of section 441 (duty to file accounts and reports) are not complied with in relation to a company's accounts and reports for a financial year before the end of the period for filing those accounts and reports, every person who immediately before the end of that period was a director of the company commits an offence.

(2)   It is a defence for a person charged with such an offence to prove that he took all reasonable steps for securing that those requirements would be complied with before the end of that period.

(3)   It is not a defence to prove that the documents in question were not in fact prepared as required by this Part.

(4)   A person guilty of an offence under this section is liable on summary conviction to a fine not exceeding level 5 on the standard scale and, for continued contravention, a daily default fine not exceeding one-tenth of level 5 on the standard scale.

[1578]

NOTES
Commencement: 6 April 2008.
Commencement (transitional provisions): see the note to s 380 at **[1507]**.

452   Default in filing accounts and reports: court order

(1)   If—
(a)   the requirements of section 441 (duty to file accounts and reports) are not complied with in relation to a company's accounts and reports for a financial year before the end of the period for filing those accounts and reports, and
(b)   the directors of the company fail to make good the default within 14 days after the service of a notice on them requiring compliance,
the court may, on the application of any member or creditor of the company or of the registrar, make an order directing the directors (or any of them) to make good the default within such time as may be specified in the order.

(2)   The court's order may provide that all costs (in Scotland, expenses) of and incidental to the application are to be borne by the directors.

[1579]

NOTES
Commencement: 6 April 2008.
Commencement (transitional provisions): see the note to s 380 at **[1507]**.

453 Civil penalty for failure to file accounts and reports

(1) Where the requirements of section 441 are not complied with in relation to a company's accounts and reports for a financial year before the end of the period for filing those accounts and reports, the company is liable to a civil penalty.

This is in addition to any liability of the directors under section 451.

(2) The amount of the penalty shall be determined in accordance with regulations made by the Secretary of State by reference to—

   (a) the length of the period between the end of the period for filing the accounts and reports in question and the day on which the requirements are complied with, and

   (b) whether the company is a private or public company.

(3) The penalty may be recovered by the registrar and is to be paid into the Consolidated Fund.

(4) It is not a defence in proceedings under this section to prove that the documents in question were not in fact prepared as required by this Part.

(5) Regulations under this section having the effect of increasing the penalty payable in any case are subject to affirmative resolution procedure. Otherwise, the regulations are subject to negative resolution procedure.

[1580]

NOTES
Commencement: 20 January 2007 (for the purpose of enabling the exercise of powers to make Orders or Regulations by statutory instrument); 6 April 2008 (otherwise).
Commencement (transitional provisions): see the note to s 380 at **[1507]**.
Regulations: the Companies (Late Filing Penalties) and Limited Liability Partnerships (Filing Periods and Late Filing Penalties) Regulations 2008, SI 2008/497.

CHAPTER 11
REVISION OF DEFECTIVE ACCOUNTS AND REPORTS
Voluntary revision

454 Voluntary revision of accounts etc

(1) If it appears to the directors of a company that—

   (a) the company's annual accounts,

   (b) the directors' remuneration report or the directors' report, or

   (c) a summary financial statement of the company,

did not comply with the requirements of this Act (or, where applicable, of Article 4 of the IAS Regulation), they may prepare revised accounts or a revised report or statement.

(2) Where copies of the previous accounts or report have been sent out to members, delivered to the registrar or (in the case of a public company) laid before the company in general meeting, the revisions must be confined to—

   (a) the correction of those respects in which the previous accounts or report did not comply with the requirements of this Act (or, where applicable, of Article 4 of the IAS Regulation), and

   (b) the making of any necessary consequential alterations.

(3) The Secretary of State may make provision by regulations as to the application of the provisions of this Act in relation to—

   (a) revised annual accounts,

   (b) a revised directors' remuneration report or directors' report, or

   (c) a revised summary financial statement.

(4) The regulations may, in particular—

   (a) make different provision according to whether the previous accounts, report or statement are replaced or are supplemented by a document indicating the corrections to be made;

   (b) make provision with respect to the functions of the company's auditor in relation to the revised accounts, report or statement;

   (c) require the directors to take such steps as may be specified in the regulations where the previous accounts or report have been—

     (i) sent out to members and others under section 423,

     (ii) laid before the company in general meeting, or

     (iii) delivered to the registrar,

or where a summary financial statement containing information derived from the previous accounts or report has been sent to members under section 426;

   (d) apply the provisions of this Act (including those creating criminal offences) subject to such additions, exceptions and modifications as are specified in the regulations.

(5) Regulations under this section are subject to negative resolution procedure.

[1581]

NOTES
Commencement: 20 January 2007 (for the purpose of enabling the exercise of powers to make Orders or Regulations by statutory instrument); 6 April 2008 (otherwise).
Commencement (transitional provisions): see the note to s 380 at **[1507]**.
Regulations: the Companies (Revision of Defective Accounts and Reports) Regulations 2008, SI 2008/373. These Regulations set out how the provisions of this Act are to apply to revised annual accounts, directors' reports, directors' remuneration reports and summary financial statements prepared under this section. They come into force on 6 April 2008 and apply in relation to companies' financial years beginning on or after that date. They revoke and replace (subject to transitional provisions) the Companies (Revision of Defective Accounts and Report) Regulations 1990, SI 1990/2570 (which were made under the Companies Act 1985), and the Companies (Revision of Defective Accounts and Report) Regulations (Northern Ireland) 1991, SR 1991/268.

Secretary of State's notice

455 Secretary of State's notice in respect of accounts or reports

(1) This section applies where—
   (a) copies of a company's annual accounts or directors' report have been sent out under section 423, or
   (b) a copy of a company's annual accounts or directors' report has been delivered to the registrar or (in the case of a public company) laid before the company in general meeting,

and it appears to the Secretary of State that there is, or may be, a question whether the accounts or report comply with the requirements of this Act (or, where applicable, of Article 4 of the IAS Regulation).

(2) The Secretary of State may give notice to the directors of the company indicating the respects in which it appears that such a question arises or may arise.

(3) The notice must specify a period of not less than one month for the directors to give an explanation of the accounts or report or prepare revised accounts or a revised report.

(4) If at the end of the specified period, or such longer period as the Secretary of State may allow, it appears to the Secretary of State that the directors have not—
   (a) given a satisfactory explanation of the accounts or report, or
   (b) revised the accounts or report so as to comply with the requirements of this Act (or, where applicable, of Article 4 of the IAS Regulation),
the Secretary of State may apply to the court.

(5) The provisions of this section apply equally to revised annual accounts and revised directors' reports, in which case they have effect as if the references to revised accounts or reports were references to further revised accounts or reports.

[1582]

NOTES
Commencement: 6 April 2008.
Commencement (transitional provisions): see the note to s 380 at **[1507]**.

Application to court

456 Application to court in respect of defective accounts or reports

(1) An application may be made to the court—
   (a) by the Secretary of State, after having complied with section 455, or
   (b) by a person authorised by the Secretary of State for the purposes of this section,

for a declaration (in Scotland, a declarator) that the annual accounts of a company do not comply, or a directors' report does not comply, with the requirements of this Act (or, where applicable, of Article 4 of the IAS Regulation) and for an order requiring the directors of the company to prepare revised accounts or a revised report.

(2) Notice of the application, together with a general statement of the matters at issue in the proceedings, shall be given by the applicant to the registrar for registration.

(3) If the court orders the preparation of revised accounts, it may give directions as to—
   (a) the auditing of the accounts,
   (b) the revision of any directors' remuneration report, directors' report or summary financial statement, and
   (c) the taking of steps by the directors to bring the making of the order to the notice of persons likely to rely on the previous accounts,
and such other matters as the court thinks fit.

(4) If the court orders the preparation of a revised directors' report it may give directions as to—
   (a) the review of the report by the auditors,

(b)   the revision of any summary financial statement,
(c)   the taking of steps by the directors to bring the making of the order to the notice of persons likely to rely on the previous report, and
(d)   such other matters as the court thinks fit.

(5)   If the court finds that the accounts or report did not comply with the requirements of this Act (or, where applicable, of Article 4 of the IAS Regulation) it may order that all or part of—
(a)   the costs (in Scotland, expenses) of and incidental to the application, and
(b)   any reasonable expenses incurred by the company in connection with or in consequence of the preparation of revised accounts or a revised report,
are to be borne by such of the directors as were party to the approval of the defective accounts or report.

For this purpose every director of the company at the time of the approval of the accounts or report shall be taken to have been a party to the approval unless he shows that he took all reasonable steps to prevent that approval.

(6)   Where the court makes an order under subsection (5) it shall have regard to whether the directors party to the approval of the defective accounts or report knew or ought to have known that the accounts or report did not comply with the requirements of this Act (or, where applicable, of Article 4 of the IAS Regulation), and it may exclude one or more directors from the order or order the payment of different amounts by different directors.

(7)   On the conclusion of proceedings on an application under this section, the applicant must send to the registrar for registration a copy of the court order or, as the case may be, give notice to the registrar that the application has failed or been withdrawn.

(8)   The provisions of this section apply equally to revised annual accounts and revised directors' reports, in which case they have effect as if the references to revised accounts or reports were references to further revised accounts or reports.

[1583]

NOTES
Commencement: 6 April 2008.
Commencement (transitional provisions): see the note to s 380 at **[1507]**.

457   Other persons authorised to apply to the court

(1)   The Secretary of State may by order (an "authorisation order") authorise for the purposes of section 456 any person appearing to him—
(a)   to have an interest in, and to have satisfactory procedures directed to securing, compliance by companies with the requirements of this Act (or, where applicable, of Article 4 of the IAS Regulation) relating to accounts and directors' reports,
(b)   to have satisfactory procedures for receiving and investigating complaints about companies' annual accounts and directors' reports, and
(c)   otherwise to be a fit and proper person to be authorised.

(2)   A person may be authorised generally or in respect of particular classes of case, and different persons may be authorised in respect of different classes of case.

(3)   The Secretary of State may refuse to authorise a person if he considers that his authorisation is unnecessary having regard to the fact that there are one or more other persons who have been or are likely to be authorised.

(4)   If the authorised person is an unincorporated association, proceedings brought in, or in connection with, the exercise of any function by the association as an authorised person may be brought by or against the association in the name of a body corporate whose constitution provides for the establishment of the association.

(5)   An authorisation order may contain such requirements or other provisions relating to the exercise of functions by the authorised person as appear to the Secretary of State to be appropriate.

No such order is to be made unless it appears to the Secretary of State that the person would, if authorised, exercise his functions as an authorised person in accordance with the provisions proposed.

(6)   Where authorisation is revoked, the revoking order may make such provision as the Secretary of State thinks fit with respect to pending proceedings.

(7)   An order under this section is subject to negative resolution procedure.

[1584]

NOTES
Commencement: 20 January 2007 (for the purpose of enabling the exercise of powers to make Orders or Regulations by statutory instrument); 6 April 2008 (otherwise).
Commencement (transitional provisions): see the note to s 380 at **[1507]**.

Orders: the Companies (Defective Accounts and Directors' Reports) (Authorised Person) and Supervision of Accounts and Reports (Prescribed Body) Order 2008, SI 2008/623. Article 2 of this Order authorises the Financial Reporting Review Panel established under the articles of association of The Financial Reporting Council Limited for the purposes of s 456 of this Act. For transitional provisions in relation to proceedings under the Companies Act 1985, s 245B pending at 6 April 2008, see art 6 of the Order.

458 Disclosure of information by tax authorities

(1) The Commissioners for Her Majesty's Revenue and Customs may disclose information to a person authorised under section 457 for the purpose of facilitating—

    (a)   the taking of steps by that person to discover whether there are grounds for an application to the court under section 456 (application in respect of defective accounts etc), or

    (b)   a decision by the authorised person whether to make such an application.

(2) This section applies despite any statutory or other restriction on the disclosure of information.

Provided that, in the case of personal data within the meaning of the Data Protection Act 1998 (c 29), information is not to be disclosed in contravention of that Act.

(3) Information disclosed to an authorised person under this section—

    (a)   may not be used except in or in connection with—

        (i)   taking steps to discover whether there are grounds for an application to the court under section 456, or

        (ii)   deciding whether or not to make such an application,

or in, or in connection with, proceedings on such an application; and

    (b)   must not be further disclosed except—

        (i)   to the person to whom the information relates, or

        (ii)   in, or in connection with, proceedings on any such application to the court.

(4) A person who contravenes subsection (3) commits an offence unless—

    (a)   he did not know, and had no reason to suspect, that the information had been disclosed under this section, or

    (b)   he took all reasonable steps and exercised all due diligence to avoid the commission of the offence.

(5) A person guilty of an offence under subsection (4) is liable—

    (a)   on conviction on indictment, to imprisonment for a term not exceeding two years or a fine (or both);

    (b)   on summary conviction—

        (i)   in England and Wales, to imprisonment for a term not exceeding twelve months or to a fine not exceeding the statutory maximum (or both);

        (ii)   in Scotland or Northern Ireland, to imprisonment for a term not exceeding six months, or to a fine not exceeding the statutory maximum (or both).

[(6) Where an offence under this section is committed by a body corporate, every officer of the body who is in default also commits the offence.

For this purpose—

    (a)   any person who purports to act as director, manager or secretary of the body is treated as an officer of the body, and

    (b)   if the body is a company, any shadow director is treated as an officer of the company.]

[1585]

NOTES

Commencement: 6 April 2008.
Commencement (transitional provisions): see the note to s 380 at **[1507]**.
Sub-s (6): added by the Companies Act 2006 (Consequential Amendments etc) Order 2008, SI 2008/948, art 3(1), Sch 1, Pt 2, para 244, as from 6 April 2008.
Imprisonment for a term not exceeding twelve months: see the note to s 387 at **[1514]**.

Power of authorised person to require documents etc

459 Power of authorised person to require documents, information and explanations

(1) This section applies where it appears to a person who is authorised under section 457 that there is, or may be, a question whether a company's annual accounts or directors' report comply with the requirements of this Act (or, where applicable, of Article 4 of the IAS Regulation).

(2) The authorised person may require any of the persons mentioned in subsection (3) to produce any document, or to provide him with any information or explanations, that he may reasonably require for the purpose of—

    (a)   discovering whether there are grounds for an application to the court under section 456, or

    (b)   deciding whether to make such an application.

  (3) Those persons are—

    (a)   the company;

    (b)   any officer, employee, or auditor of the company;

    (c)   any persons who fell within paragraph (b) at a time to which the document or information required by the authorised person relates.

  (4) If a person fails to comply with such a requirement, the authorised person may apply to the court.

  (5) If it appears to the court that the person has failed to comply with a requirement under subsection (2), it may order the person to take such steps as it directs for securing that the documents are produced or the information or explanations are provided.

  (6) A statement made by a person in response to a requirement under subsection (2) or an order under subsection (5) may not be used in evidence against him in any criminal proceedings.

  (7) Nothing in this section compels any person to disclose documents or information in respect of which a claim to legal professional privilege (in Scotland, to confidentiality of communications) could be maintained in legal proceedings.

  (8) In this section "document" includes information recorded in any form.

[1586]

NOTES

Commencement: 6 April 2008.

Commencement (transitional provisions): see the note to s 380 at **[1507]**.

460 Restrictions on disclosure of information obtained under compulsory powers

  (1) This section applies to information (in whatever form) obtained in pursuance of a requirement or order under section 459 (power of authorised person to require documents etc) that relates to the private affairs of an individual or to any particular business.

  (2) No such information may, during the lifetime of that individual or so long as that business continues to be carried on, be disclosed without the consent of that individual or the person for the time being carrying on that business.

  (3) This does not apply—

    (a)   to disclosure permitted by section 461 (permitted disclosure of information obtained under compulsory powers), or

    (b)   to the disclosure of information that is or has been available to the public from another source.

  (4) A person who discloses information in contravention of this section commits an offence, unless—

    (a)   he did not know, and had no reason to suspect, that the information had been disclosed under section 459, or

    (b)   he took all reasonable steps and exercised all due diligence to avoid the commission of the offence.

  (5) A person guilty of an offence under this section is liable—

    (a)   on conviction on indictment, to imprisonment for a term not exceeding two years or a fine (or both);

    (b)   on summary conviction—

        (i)   in England and Wales, to imprisonment for a term not exceeding twelve months or to a fine not exceeding the statutory maximum (or both);

       (ii)   in Scotland or Northern Ireland, to imprisonment for a term not exceeding six months, or to a fine not exceeding the statutory maximum (or both).

  [(6) Where an offence under this section is committed by a body corporate, every officer of the body who is in default also commits the offence.

  For this purpose—

    (a)   any person who purports to act as director, manager or secretary of the body is treated as an officer of the body, and

    (b)   if the body is a company, any shadow director is treated as an officer of the company.]

[1587]

NOTES

Commencement: 6 April 2008.

Commencement (transitional provisions): see the note to s 380 at **[1507]**.

Sub-s (6): added by the Companies Act 2006 (Consequential Amendments etc) Order 2008, SI 2008/948, art 3(1), Sch 1, Pt 2, para 245, as from 6 April 2008.

Imprisonment for a term not exceeding twelve months: see the note to s 387 at **[1514]**.

PART II
OTHER ACTS

461 Permitted disclosure of information obtained under compulsory powers

(1)   The prohibition in section 460 of the disclosure of information obtained in pursuance of a requirement or order under section 459 (power of authorised person to require documents etc) that relates to the private affairs of an individual or to any particular business has effect subject to the following exceptions.

(2)   It does not apply to the disclosure of information for the purpose of facilitating the carrying out by the authorised person of his functions under section 456.

(3)   It does not apply to disclosure to—
  (a)   the Secretary of State,
  (b)   the Department of Enterprise, Trade and Investment for Northern Ireland,
  (c)   the Treasury,
  (d)   the Bank of England,
  (e)   the Financial Services Authority, or
  (f)   the Commissioners for Her Majesty's Revenue and Customs.

(4)   It does not apply to disclosure—
  (a)   for the purpose of assisting a body designated by an order under [section 1252] (delegation of functions of the Secretary of State) to exercise its functions under [Part 42];
  (b)   with a view to the institution of, or otherwise for the purposes of, disciplinary proceedings relating to the performance by an accountant or auditor of his professional duties;
  (c)   for the purpose of enabling or assisting the Secretary of State or the Treasury to exercise any of their functions under any of the following—
    (i)   the Companies Acts,
    (ii)   Part 5 of the Criminal Justice Act 1993 (c 36) (insider dealing),
    (iii)   the Insolvency Act 1986 (c 45) or the Insolvency (Northern Ireland) Order 1989 (SI 1989/2405 (NI 19)),
    (iv)   the Company Directors Disqualification Act 1986 (c 46) or the Company Directors Disqualification (Northern Ireland) Order 2002 (SI 2002/3150 (NI 4)),
    (v)   the Financial Services and Markets Act 2000 (c 8);
  (d)   for the purpose of enabling or assisting the Department of Enterprise, Trade and Investment for Northern Ireland to exercise any powers conferred on it by the enactments relating to companies, directors' disqualification or insolvency;
  (e)   for the purpose of enabling or assisting the Bank of England to exercise its functions;
  (f)   for the purpose of enabling or assisting the Commissioners for Her Majesty's Revenue and Customs to exercise their functions;
  (g)   for the purpose of enabling or assisting the Financial Services Authority to exercise its functions under any of the following—
    (i)   the legislation relating to friendly societies or to industrial and provident societies,
    (ii)   the Building Societies Act 1986 (c 53),
    (iii)   Part 7 of the Companies Act 1989 (c 40),
    (iv)   the Financial Services and Markets Act 2000; or
  (h)   in pursuance of any Community obligation.

(5)   It does not apply to disclosure to a body exercising functions of a public nature under legislation in any country or territory outside the United Kingdom that appear to the authorised person to be similar to his functions under section 456 for the purpose of enabling or assisting that body to exercise those functions.

(6)   In determining whether to disclose information to a body in accordance with subsection (5), the authorised person must have regard to the following considerations—
  (a)   whether the use which the body is likely to make of the information is sufficiently important to justify making the disclosure;
  (b)   whether the body has adequate arrangements to prevent the information from being used or further disclosed other than—
    (i)   for the purposes of carrying out the functions mentioned in that subsection, or
    (ii)   for other purposes substantially similar to those for which information disclosed to the authorised person could be used or further disclosed.

(7)   Nothing in this section authorises the making of a disclosure in contravention of the Data Protection Act 1998 (c 29).

[1588]

NOTES
Commencement: 6 April 2008.
Commencement (transitional provisions): see the note to s 380 at **[1507]**.

Sub-s (4): words in square brackets substituted by the Companies Act 2006 (Consequential Amendments etc) Order 2008, SI 2008/948, art 3(1), Sch 1, Pt 2, para 246, as from 6 April 2008.

462　Power to amend categories of permitted disclosure

(1)　The Secretary of State may by order amend section 461(3), (4) and (5).

(2)　An order under this section must not—

(a)　amend subsection (3) of that section (UK public authorities) by specifying a person unless the person exercises functions of a public nature (whether or not he exercises any other function);

(b)　amend subsection (4) of that section (purposes for which disclosure permitted) by adding or modifying a description of disclosure unless the purpose for which the disclosure is permitted is likely to facilitate the exercise of a function of a public nature;

(c)　amend subsection (5) of that section (overseas regulatory authorities) so as to have the effect of permitting disclosures to be made to a body other than one that exercises functions of a public nature in a country or territory outside the United Kingdom.

(3)　An order under this section is subject to negative resolution procedure.

[1589]

NOTES

Commencement: 20 January 2007 (for the purpose of enabling the exercise of powers to make Orders or Regulations by statutory instrument); 6 April 2008 (otherwise).

Commencement (transitional provisions): see the note to s 380 at **[1507]**.

CHAPTER 12
SUPPLEMENTARY PROVISIONS
Liability for false or misleading statements in reports

463　Liability for false or misleading statements in reports

(1)　The reports to which this section applies are—

(a)　the directors' report,

(b)　the directors' remuneration report, and

(c)　a summary financial statement so far as it is derived from either of those reports.

(2)　A director of a company is liable to compensate the company for any loss suffered by it as a result of—

(a)　any untrue or misleading statement in a report to which this section applies, or

(b)　the omission from a report to which this section applies of anything required to be included in it.

(3)　He is so liable only if—

(a)　he knew the statement to be untrue or misleading or was reckless as to whether it was untrue or misleading, or

(b)　he knew the omission to be dishonest concealment of a material fact.

(4)　No person shall be subject to any liability to a person other than the company resulting from reliance, by that person or another, on information in a report to which this section applies.

(5)　The reference in subsection (4) to a person being subject to a liability includes a reference to another person being entitled as against him to be granted any civil remedy or to rescind or repudiate an agreement.

(6)　This section does not affect—

(a)　liability for a civil penalty, or

(b)　liability for a criminal offence.

[1590]

NOTES

Commencement: 20 January 2007.

Commencement (transitional provisions): the Companies Act 2006 (Commencement No 1, Transitional Provisions and Savings) Order 2006, SI 2006/3428, Sch 5, Pt 2, para 3 provides that this section does not apply to a directors' report, directors' remuneration report or summary financial statement first sent to members and others under CA 1985, ss 238 or 251 (or Arts 246 or 259 of the 1986 Northern Ireland Order) before 20 January 2007.

Accounting and reporting standards

464　Accounting standards

(1)　In this Part "accounting standards" means statements of standard accounting practice issued by such body or bodies as may be prescribed by regulations.

(2) References in this Part to accounting standards applicable to a company's annual accounts are to such standards as are, in accordance with their terms, relevant to the company's circumstances and to the accounts.

(3) Regulations under this section may contain such transitional and other supplementary and incidental provisions as appear to the Secretary of State to be appropriate.

[1591]

NOTES
Commencement: 20 January 2007 (for the purpose of enabling the exercise of powers to make Orders or Regulations by statutory instrument); 6 April 2008 (otherwise).
Commencement (transitional provisions): see the note to s 380 at **[1507]**.
Orders: the Accounting Standards (Prescribed Body) Regulations 2008, SI 2008/651. Article 2 of that Order prescribes the body known as the Accounting Standards Board established under the articles of association of the Financial Reporting Council Limited for the purposes of this section. See also art 4 (transitional provisions), which provides that statements of standard accounting practice which immediately before 6 April 2008 have been issued and not withdrawn by the former body known as the Accounting Standards Board for the purposes of the Companies Act 1985, s 256 or the Companies (Northern Ireland) Order 1986, art 264 shall be treated, on and after that date, as statements of standard accounting practice issued by the Accounting Standards Board for the purposes of this section.

Companies qualifying as medium-sized

465 Companies qualifying as medium-sized: general

(1) A company qualifies as medium-sized in relation to its first financial year if the qualifying conditions are met in that year.

(2) A company qualifies as medium-sized in relation to a subsequent financial year—
    (a) if the qualifying conditions are met in that year and the preceding financial year;
    (b) if the qualifying conditions are met in that year and the company qualified as medium-sized in relation to the preceding financial year;
    (c) if the qualifying conditions were met in the preceding financial year and the company qualified as medium-sized in relation to that year.

(3) The qualifying conditions are met by a company in a year in which it satisfies two or more of the following requirements—

1 Turnover	[Not more than £25.9 million]
2 Balance sheet total	[Not more than £12.9 million]
3 Number of employees	Not more than 250

(4) For a period that is a company's financial year but not in fact a year the maximum figures for turnover must be proportionately adjusted.

(5) The balance sheet total means the aggregate of the amounts shown as assets in the company's balance sheet.

(6) The number of employees means the average number of persons employed by the company in the year, determined as follows—

    (a) find for each month in the financial year the number of persons employed under contracts of service by the company in that month (whether throughout the month or not),
    (b) add together the monthly totals, and
    (c) divide by the number of months in the financial year.

(7) This section is subject to section 466 (companies qualifying as medium-sized: parent companies).

[1592]

NOTES
Commencement: 6 April 2008.
Commencement (transitional provisions): see the note to s 380 at **[1507]**.
Sub-s (3): words in square brackets substituted by the Companies Act 2006 (Amendment) (Accounts and Reports) Regulations 2008, SI 2008/393, reg 4(1), as from 6 April 2008, in relation to financial years beginning on or after that date. See further the note to s 382 at **[1509]**.

466 Companies qualifying as medium-sized: parent companies

(1) A parent company qualifies as a medium-sized company in relation to a financial year only if the group headed by it qualifies as a medium-sized group.

(2)   A group qualifies as medium-sized in relation to the parent company's first financial year if the qualifying conditions are met in that year.

(3)   A group qualifies as medium-sized in relation to a subsequent financial year of the parent company—

    (a)   if the qualifying conditions are met in that year and the preceding financial year;

    (b)   if the qualifying conditions are met in that year and the group qualified as medium-sized in relation to the preceding financial year;

    (c)   if the qualifying conditions were met in the preceding financial year and the group qualified as medium-sized in relation to that year.

(4)   The qualifying conditions are met by a group in a year in which it satisfies two or more of the following requirements—

1 Aggregate turnover	[Not more than £25.9 million net (or £31.1 million gross)]
2 Aggregate balance sheet total	[Not more than £12.9 million net (or £15.5 million gross)]
3 Aggregate number of employees	Not more than 250

(5)   The aggregate figures are ascertained by aggregating the relevant figures determined in accordance with section 465 for each member of the group.

(6)   In relation to the aggregate figures for turnover and balance sheet total—

"net" means after any set-offs and other adjustments made to eliminate group transactions—

    (a)   in the case of Companies Act accounts, in accordance with regulations under section 404,

    (b)   in the case of IAS accounts, in accordance with international accounting standards; and

"gross" means without those set-offs and other adjustments.

A company may satisfy any relevant requirement on the basis of either the net or the gross figure.

(7)   The figures for each subsidiary undertaking shall be those included in its individual accounts for the relevant financial year, that is—

    (a)   if its financial year ends with that of the parent company, that financial year, and

    (b)   if not, its financial year ending last before the end of the financial year of the parent company.

If those figures cannot be obtained without disproportionate expense or undue delay, the latest available figures shall be taken.

[1593]

NOTES

Commencement: 6 April 2008.

Commencement (transitional provisions): see the note to s 380 at **[1507]**.

Sub-s (4): words in square brackets substituted by the Companies Act 2006 (Amendment) (Accounts and Reports) Regulations 2008, SI 2008/393, reg 4(2), as from 6 April 2008, in relation to financial years beginning on or after that date. See further the note to s 382 at **[1509]**.

467   Companies excluded from being treated as medium-sized

(1)   A company is not entitled to take advantage of any of the provisions of this Part relating to companies qualifying as medium-sized if it was at any time within the financial year in question—

    (a)   a public company,

    (b)   a company that—

        (i)   has permission under Part 4 of the Financial Services and Markets Act 2000 (c 8) to carry on a regulated activity, or

        (ii)   carries on insurance market activity, or

    (c)   a member of an ineligible group.

(2)   A group is ineligible if any of its members is—

    (a)   a public company,

    (b)   a body corporate (other than a company) whose shares are admitted to trading on a regulated market,

    (c)   a person (other than a small company) who has permission under Part 4 of the Financial Services and Markets Act 2000 to carry on a regulated activity,

    (d)   a small company that is an authorised insurance company, a banking company, an e-money issuer, [a MiFID investment firm] or a UCITS management company, or

    (e)   a person who carries on insurance market activity.

(3)   A company is a small company for the purposes of subsection (2) if it qualified as small in relation to its last financial year ending on or before the end of the financial year in question.

[(4)   This section does not prevent a company from taking advantage of section 417(7) (business review: non-financial information) by reason only of its having been a member of an ineligible group at any time within the financial year in question.]

[1594]

NOTES
Commencement: 6 April 2008.
Commencement (transitional provisions): see the note to s 380 at **[1507]**.
Sub-s (2): words in square brackets in para (d) substituted by the Markets in Financial Instruments Directive (Consequential Amendments) Regulations 2007, SI 2007/2932, reg 3(1), (3), as from 1 November 2007.
Sub-s (4): added by the Companies Act 2006 (Amendment) (Accounts and Reports) Regulations 2008, SI 2008/393, reg 7, as from 6 April 2008, in relation to financial years beginning on or after that date.

General power to make further provision about accounts and reports

468   General power to make further provision about accounts and reports

(1)   The Secretary of State may make provision by regulations about—
(a)   the accounts and reports that companies are required to prepare;
(b)   the categories of companies required to prepare accounts and reports of any description;
(c)   the form and content of the accounts and reports that companies are required to prepare;
(d)   the obligations of companies and others as regards—
  (i)   the approval of accounts and reports,
  (ii)   the sending of accounts and reports to members and others,
  (iii)   the laying of accounts and reports before the company in general meeting,
  (iv)   the delivery of copies of accounts and reports to the registrar, and
  (v)   the publication of accounts and reports.

(2)   The regulations may amend this Part by adding, altering or repealing provisions.

(3)   But they must not amend (other than consequentially)—
(a)   section 393 (accounts to give true and fair view), or
(b)   the provisions of Chapter 11 (revision of defective accounts and reports).

(4)   The regulations may create criminal offences in cases corresponding to those in which an offence is created by an existing provision of this Part.

The maximum penalty for any such offence may not be greater than is provided in relation to an offence under the existing provision.

(5)   The regulations may provide for civil penalties in circumstances corresponding to those within section 453(1) (civil penalty for failure to file accounts and reports).

The provisions of section 453(2) to (5) apply in relation to any such penalty.

[1595]

NOTES
Commencement: 20 January 2007 (for the purpose of enabling the exercise of powers to make Orders or Regulations by statutory instrument); 6 April 2008 (otherwise).
Commencement (transitional provisions): see the note to s 380 at **[1507]**.
Regulations: the Companies Act 2006 (Amendment) (Accounts and Reports) Regulations 2008, SI 2008/393. These Regulations amend various provisions in Parts 15 and 16 of this Act.

Other supplementary provisions

469   Preparation and filing of accounts in euros

(1)   The amounts set out in the annual accounts of a company may also be shown in the same accounts translated into euros.

(2)   When complying with section 441 (duty to file accounts and reports), the directors of a company may deliver to the registrar an additional copy of the company's annual accounts in which the amounts have been translated into euros.

(3)   In both cases—
(a)   the amounts must have been translated at the exchange rate prevailing on the date to which the balance sheet is made up, and
(b)   that rate must be disclosed in the notes to the accounts.

(4)   For the purposes of sections 434 and 435 (requirements in connection with published accounts) any additional copy of the company's annual accounts delivered to the registrar under subsection (2) above shall be treated as statutory accounts of the company.

In the case of such a copy, references in those sections to the auditor's report on the company's annual accounts shall be read as references to the auditor's report on the annual accounts of which it is a copy.

[1596]

NOTES
Commencement: 6 April 2008.
Commencement (transitional provisions): see the note to s 380 at **[1507]**.

470 Power to apply provisions to banking partnerships

(1) The Secretary of State may by regulations apply to banking partnerships, subject to such exceptions, adaptations and modifications as he considers appropriate, the provisions of this Part (and of regulations made under this Part) applying to banking companies.

(2) A "banking partnership" means a partnership which has permission under Part 4 of the Financial Services and Markets Act 2000 (c 8).

But a partnership is not a banking partnership if it has permission to accept deposits only for the purpose of carrying on another regulated activity in accordance with that permission.

(3) Expressions used in this section that are also used in the provisions regulating activities under the Financial Services and Markets Act 2000 have the same meaning here as they do in those provisions.

See section 22 of that Act, orders made under that section and Schedule 2 to that Act.

(4) Regulations under this section are subject to affirmative resolution procedure.

[1597]

NOTES
Commencement: 20 January 2007 (for the purpose of enabling the exercise of powers to make Orders or Regulations by statutory instrument); 6 April 2008 (otherwise).
Commencement (transitional provisions): see the note to s 380 at **[1507]**.

471 Meaning of "annual accounts" and related expressions

(1) In this Part a company's "annual accounts", in relation to a financial year, means—
  (a) the company's individual accounts for that year (see section 394), and
  (b) any group accounts prepared by the company for that year (see sections 398 and 399).

This is subject to section 408 (option to omit individual profit and loss account from annual accounts where information given in group accounts).

(2) In the case of an unquoted company, its "annual accounts and reports" for a financial year are—
  (a) its annual accounts,
  (b) the directors' report, and
  (c) the auditor's report on those accounts and the directors' report (unless the company is exempt from audit).

(3) In the case of a quoted company, its "annual accounts and reports" for a financial year are—
  (a) its annual accounts,
  (b) the directors' remuneration report,
  (c) the directors' report, and
  (d) the auditor's report on those accounts, on the auditable part of the directors' remuneration report and on the directors' report.

[1598]

NOTES
Commencement: 6 April 2008.
Commencement (transitional provisions): see the note to s 380 at **[1507]**.

472 Notes to the accounts

(1) Information required by this Part to be given in notes to a company's annual accounts may be contained in the accounts or in a separate document annexed to the accounts.

(2) References in this Part to a company's annual accounts, or to a balance sheet or profit and loss account, include notes to the accounts giving information which is required by any provision of this Act or international accounting standards, and required or allowed by any such provision to be given in a note to company accounts.

[1599]

NOTES
Commencement: 6 April 2008.
Commencement (transitional provisions): see the note to s 380 at **[1507]**.

473 Parliamentary procedure for certain regulations under this Part

(1)   This section applies to regulations under the following provisions of this Part—
section 396 (Companies Act individual accounts),
section 404 (Companies Act group accounts),
section 409 (information about related undertakings),
section 412 (information about directors' benefits: remuneration, pensions and compensation for loss of office),
section 416 (contents of directors' report: general),
section 421 (contents of directors' remuneration report),
section 444 (filing obligations of companies subject to small companies regime),
section 445 (filing obligations of medium-sized companies),
section 468 (general power to make further provision about accounts and reports).

(2)   Any such regulations may make consequential amendments or repeals in other provisions of this Act, or in other enactments.

(3)   Regulations that—
(a)   restrict the classes of company which have the benefit of any exemption, exception or special provision,
(b)   require additional matter to be included in a document of any class, or
(c)   otherwise render the requirements of this Part more onerous,
are subject to affirmative resolution procedure.

(4)   Otherwise, the regulations are subject to negative resolution procedure.

[1600]

NOTES
Commencement: 20 January 2007 (for the purpose of enabling the exercise of powers to make Orders or Regulations by statutory instrument); 6 April 2008 (otherwise).
Commencement (transitional provisions): see the note to s 380 at **[1507]**.
As to Regulations made under the sections listed in sub-s (1), see the notes to those sections *ante*.

474 Minor definitions

(1)   In this Part—
"e-money issuer" means a person who has permission under Part 4 of the Financial Services and Markets Act 2000 (c 8) to carry on the activity of issuing electronic money within the meaning of article 9B of the Financial Services and Markets Act 2000 (Regulated Activities) Order 2001 (SI 2001/544);
"group" means a parent undertaking and its subsidiary undertakings;
"IAS Regulation" means EC Regulation No 1606/2002 of the European Parliament and of the Council of 19 July 2002 on the application of international accounting standards;
"included in the consolidation", in relation to group accounts, or "included in consolidated group accounts", means that the undertaking is included in the accounts by the method of full (and not proportional) consolidation, and references to an undertaking excluded from consolidation shall be construed accordingly;
"international accounting standards" means the international accounting standards, within the meaning of the IAS Regulation, adopted from time to time by the European Commission in accordance with that Regulation;

.....

["MiFID investment firm" means an investment firm within the meaning of Article 4.1.1 of Directive 2004/39/EC of the European Parliament and of the Council of 21 April 2004 on markets in financial instruments, other than—
(a)   a company to which that Directive does not apply by virtue of Article 2 of that Directive,
(b)   a company which is an exempt investment firm within the meaning of regulation 4A(3) of the Financial Services and Markets Act 2000 (Markets in Financial Instruments) Regulations 2007, and
(c)   any other company which fulfils all the requirements set out in regulation 4C(3) of those Regulations;]
"profit and loss account", in relation to a company that prepares IAS accounts, includes an income statement or other equivalent financial statement required to be prepared by international accounting standards;

"regulated activity" has the meaning given in section 22 of the Financial Services and Markets Act 2000, except that it does not include activities of the kind specified in any of the following provisions of the Financial Services and Markets Act 2000 (Regulated Activities) Order 2001 (SI 2001/544)—
- (a)　article 25A (arranging regulated mortgage contracts),
- (b)　article 25B (arranging regulated home reversion plans),
- (c)　article 25C (arranging regulated home purchase plans),
- (d)　article 39A (assisting administration and performance of a contract of insurance),
- (e)　article 53A (advising on regulated mortgage contracts),
- (f)　article 53B (advising on regulated home reversion plans),
- (g)　article 53C (advising on regulated home purchase plans),
- (h)　article 21 (dealing as agent), article 25 (arranging deals in investments) or article 53 (advising on investments) where the activity concerns relevant investments that are not contractually based investments (within the meaning of article 3 of that Order), or
- (i)　article 64 (agreeing to carry on a regulated activity of the kind mentioned in paragraphs (a) to (h));

"turnover", in relation to a company, means the amounts derived from the provision of goods and services falling within the company's ordinary activities, after deduction of—
- (a)　trade discounts,
- (b)　value added tax, and
- (c)　any other taxes based on the amounts so derived;

"UCITS management company" has the meaning given by the Glossary forming part of the Handbook made by the Financial Services Authority under the Financial Services and Markets Act 2000 (c 8).

(2)　In the case of an undertaking not trading for profit, any reference in this Part to a profit and loss account is to an income and expenditure account. References to profit and loss and, in relation to group accounts, to a consolidated profit and loss account shall be construed accordingly.

[1601]

NOTES

Commencement: 6 April 2008.
Commencement (transitional provisions): see the note to s 380 at **[1507]**.
Sub-s (1): definition "ISD investment firm" (omitted) revoked, and definition "MiFID investment firm" inserted, by the Markets in Financial Instruments Directive (Consequential Amendments) Regulations 2007, SI 2007/2932, reg 3(4), as from 1 November 2007.

PART 16
AUDIT

CHAPTER 1
REQUIREMENT FOR AUDITED ACCOUNTS

Requirement for audited accounts

475　Requirement for audited accounts

(1)　A company's annual accounts for a financial year must be audited in accordance with this Part unless the company—
- (a)　is exempt from audit under—
  section 477 (small companies), or
  section 480 (dormant companies);
  or
- (b)　is exempt from the requirements of this Part under section 482 (non- profit-making companies subject to public sector audit).

(2)　A company is not entitled to any such exemption unless its balance sheet contains a statement by the directors to that effect.

(3)　A company is not entitled to exemption under any of the provisions mentioned in subsection (1)(a) unless its balance sheet contains a statement by the directors to the effect that—
- (a)　the members have not required the company to obtain an audit of its accounts for the year in question in accordance with section 476, and
- (b)　the directors acknowledge their responsibilities for complying with the requirements of this Act with respect to accounting records and the preparation of accounts.

(4)　The statement required by subsection (2) or (3) must appear on the balance sheet above the signature required by section 414.

[1602]

NOTES
Commencement: 6 April 2008.
Commencement (transitional provisions): Sch 4, Pt 1, para 9 to the Companies Act 2006 (Commencement No 5, Transitional Provisions and Savings) Order 2007, SI 2007/3495 provides as follows—

"9.—(1)   In Chapter 1 of Part 16 of the Companies Act 2006 (requirement for audited accounts)—
    (a)   sections 475 to 481 (general provisions) apply to accounts for financial years beginning on or after 6th April 2008;
    (b)   sections 482 and 483 (companies subject to public sector audit) apply to accounts for financial years beginning on or after 1st April 2008;
    (c)   section 484 (general power of amendment by regulations) applies accordingly.

(2)   Sections 235(1), 249A(1), (3) and (6) to (7), 249AA and 249B of the 1985 Act or Articles 243(1), 257A(1), (3) and (6) to (7), 257AA and 257B of the 1986 Order continue to apply to accounts for financial years beginning before 6th April 2008.

(3)   In section 482 of the Companies Act 2006 (non-profit-making companies subject to public sector audit) as it applies in relation to accounts for financial years beginning on or after 1st April 2008 and before 6th April 2008, the reference to the requirements of Part 16 of that Act shall be read as a reference to the requirements of Part 7 of the 1985 Act or Part 8 of the 1986 Order.".

476   Right of members to require audit

(1)   The members of a company that would otherwise be entitled to exemption from audit under any of the provisions mentioned in section 475(1)(a) may by notice under this section require it to obtain an audit of its accounts for a financial year.

(2)   The notice must be given by—
    (a)   members representing not less in total than 10% in nominal value of the company's issued share capital, or any class of it, or
    (b)   if the company does not have a share capital, not less than 10% in number of the members of the company.

(3)   The notice may not be given before the financial year to which it relates and must be given not later than one month before the end of that year.

[1603]

NOTES
Commencement: 6 April 2008.
Commencement (transitional provisions): see the note to s 475 at **[1602]**.

Exemption from audit: small companies

477   Small companies: conditions for exemption from audit

(1)   A company that meets the following conditions in respect of a financial year is exempt from the requirements of this Act relating to the audit of accounts for that year.

(2)   The conditions are—
    (a)   that the company qualifies as a small company in relation to that year,
    (b)   that its turnover in that year is [not more than £6.5 million], and
    (c)   that its balance sheet total for that year is [not more than £3.26 million].

(3)   For a period which is a company's financial year but not in fact a year the maximum figure for turnover shall be proportionately adjusted.

(4)   For the purposes of this section—
    (a)   whether a company qualifies as a small company shall be determined in accordance with section 382(1) to (6), and
    (b)   "balance sheet total" has the same meaning as in that section.

(5)   This section has effect subject to—
section 475(2) and (3) (requirements as to statements to be contained in balance sheet),
section 476 (right of members to require audit),
section 478 (companies excluded from small companies exemption), and
section 479 (availability of small companies exemption in case of group company).

[1604]

NOTES
Commencement: 6 April 2008.
Commencement (transitional provisions): see the note to s 475 at **[1602]**.
Sub-s (2): words in square brackets substituted by the Companies Act 2006 (Amendment) (Accounts and Reports) Regulations 2008, SI 2008/393, reg 5(1), as from 6 April 2008, in relation to financial years beginning on or after that date.

478   Companies excluded from small companies exemption

A company is not entitled to the exemption conferred by section 477 (small companies) if it was at any time within the financial year in question—

   (a)   a public company,

   (b)   a company that—

         (i)   is an authorised insurance company, a banking company, an e- money issuer, [a MiFID investment firm] or a UCITS management company, or

        (ii)   carries on insurance market activity, or

   (c)   a special register body as defined in section 117(1) of the Trade Union and Labour Relations (Consolidation) Act 1992 (c 52) or an employers' association as defined in section 122 of that Act or Article 4 of the Industrial Relations (Northern Ireland) Order 1992 (SI 1992/807 (NI 5)).

[1605]

NOTES

  Commencement: 6 April 2008.

  Commencement (transitional provisions): see the note to s 475 at **[1602]**.

  Words in square brackets in para (b)(i) substituted by the Markets in Financial Instruments Directive (Consequential Amendments) Regulations 2007, SI 2007/2932, reg 3(5), as from 1 November 2007.

479   Availability of small companies exemption in case of group company

  (1)   A company is not entitled to the exemption conferred by section 477 (small companies) in respect of a financial year during any part of which it was a group company unless—

   (a)   the conditions specified in subsection (2) below are met, or

   (b)   subsection (3) applies.

  (2)   The conditions are—

   (a)   that the group—

         (i)   qualifies as a small group in relation to that financial year, and

        (ii)   was not at any time in that year an ineligible group;

   (b)   that the group's aggregate turnover in that year is [not more than £6.5 million net (or £7.8 million gross)];

   (c)   that the group's aggregate balance sheet total for that year is [not more than £3.26 million net (or £3.9 million gross)].

  (3)   A company is not excluded by subsection (1) if, throughout the whole of the period or periods during the financial year when it was a group company, it was both a subsidiary undertaking and dormant.

  (4)   In this section—

   (a)   "group company" means a company that is a parent company or a subsidiary undertaking, and

   (b)   "the group", in relation to a group company, means that company together with all its associated undertakings.

For this purpose undertakings are associated if one is a subsidiary undertaking of the other or both are subsidiary undertakings of a third undertaking.

  (5)   For the purposes of this section—

   (a)   whether a group qualifies as small shall be determined in accordance with section 383 (companies qualifying as small: parent companies);

   (b)   "ineligible group" has the meaning given by section 384(2) and (3);

   (c)   a group's aggregate turnover and aggregate balance sheet total shall be determined as for the purposes of section 383;

   (d)   "net" and "gross" have the same meaning as in that section;

   (e)   a company may meet any relevant requirement on the basis of either the gross or the net figure.

  (6)   The provisions mentioned in subsection (5) apply for the purposes of this section as if all the bodies corporate in the group were companies.

[1606]

NOTES

  Commencement: 6 April 2008.

  Commencement (transitional provisions): see the note to s 475 at **[1602]**.

  Sub-s (2): words in square brackets substituted by the Companies Act 2006 (Amendment) (Accounts and Reports) Regulations 2008, SI 2008/393, reg 5(2), as from 6 April 2008, in relation to financial years beginning on or after that date.

PART II
OTHER ACTS

Exemption from audit: dormant companies

480 Dormant companies: conditions for exemption from audit

(1)   A company is exempt from the requirements of this Act relating to the audit of accounts in respect of a financial year if—
    (a)   it has been dormant since its formation, or
    (b)   it has been dormant since the end of the previous financial year and the following conditions are met.

(2)   The conditions are that the company—
    (a)   as regards its individual accounts for the financial year in question—
        (i)   is entitled to prepare accounts in accordance with the small companies regime (see sections 381 to 384), or
        (ii) would be so entitled but for having been a public company or a member of an ineligible group, and
    (b)   is not required to prepare group accounts for that year.

(3)   This section has effect subject to—
section 475(2) and (3) (requirements as to statements to be contained in balance sheet),
section 476 (right of members to require audit), and
section 481 (companies excluded from dormant companies exemption).

[1607]

NOTES
Commencement: 6 April 2008.
Commencement (transitional provisions): see the note to s 475 at **[1602]**.

481 Companies excluded from dormant companies exemption

A company is not entitled to the exemption conferred by section 480 (dormant companies) if it was at any time within the financial year in question a company that—
    (a)   is an authorised insurance company, a banking company, an e-money issuer, [a MiFID investment firm] or a UCITS management company, or
    (b)   carries on insurance market activity.

[1608]

NOTES
Commencement: 6 April 2008.
Commencement (transitional provisions): see the note to s 475 at **[1602]**.
Words in square brackets in para (a) substituted by the Markets in Financial Instruments Directive (Consequential Amendments) Regulations 2007, SI 2007/2932, reg 3(6), as from 1 November 2007.

Companies subject to public sector audit

482 Non-profit-making companies subject to public sector audit

(1)   The requirements of this Part as to audit of accounts do not apply to a company for a financial year if it is non-profit-making and its accounts—
    (a)   are subject to audit—
        (i)   by the Comptroller and Auditor General by virtue of an order under section 25(6) of the Government Resources and Accounts Act 2000 (c 20), or
        (ii) by the Auditor General for Wales by virtue of section 96, or an order under section 144, of the Government of Wales Act 1998 (c 38);
    (b)   are accounts—
        (i)   in relation to which section 21 of the Public Finance and Accountability (Scotland) Act 2000 (asp 1) (audit of accounts: Auditor General for Scotland) applies, or
        (ii) that are subject to audit by the Auditor General for Scotland by virtue of an order under section 483 (Scottish public sector companies: audit by Auditor General for Scotland); or
    (c)   are subject to audit by the Comptroller and Auditor General for Northern Ireland by virtue of an order under Article 5(3) of the Audit and Accountability (Northern Ireland) Order 2003 (SI 2003/418 (NI 5)).

(2)   In the case of a company that is a parent company or a subsidiary undertaking, subsection (1) applies only if every group undertaking is non-profit-making.

(3)   In this section "non-profit-making" has the same meaning as in Article 48 of the Treaty establishing the European Community.

(4)   This section has effect subject to section 475(2) (balance sheet to contain statement that company entitled to exemption under this section).

[1609]

NOTES
Commencement: 6 April 2008.
Commencement (transitional provisions): see the note to s 475 at **[1602]**.

483   Scottish public sector companies: audit by Auditor General for Scotland

(1)   The Scottish Ministers may by order provide for the accounts of a company having its registered office in Scotland to be audited by the Auditor General for Scotland.

(2)   An order under subsection (1) may be made in relation to a company only if it appears to the Scottish Ministers that the company—
    (a)   exercises in or as regards Scotland functions of a public nature none of which relate to reserved matters (within the meaning of the Scotland Act 1998 (c 46)), or
    (b)   is entirely or substantially funded from a body having accounts falling within paragraph (a) or (b) of subsection (3).

(3)   Those accounts are—
    (a)   accounts in relation to which section 21 of the Public Finance and Accountability (Scotland) Act 2000 (asp 1) (audit of accounts: Auditor General for Scotland) applies,
    (b)   accounts which are subject to audit by the Auditor General for Scotland by virtue of an order under this section.

(4)   An order under subsection (1) may make such supplementary or consequential provision (including provision amending an enactment) as the Scottish Ministers think expedient.

(5)   An order under subsection (1) shall not be made unless a draft of the statutory instrument containing it has been laid before, and approved by resolution of, the Scottish Parliament.

[1610]

NOTES
Commencement: 20 January 2007 (for the purpose of enabling the exercise of powers to make Orders or Regulations by statutory instrument); 6 April 2008 (otherwise).
Commencement (transitional provisions): see the note to s 475 at **[1602]**.
Orders: the Companies Act 2006 (Scottish public sector companies to be audited by the Auditor General for Scotland) Order 2008, SSI 2008/144. This Order provides that certain companies with registered offices in Scotland are to have their accounts audited by the Auditor General for Scotland. This means that in terms of s 475 of the 2006 Act, these companies will be exempt from the auditing of company accounts requirements of Part 16. The companies subject to this Order are non-profit making public sector companies, which appear to Scottish Ministers to carry out functions of a public nature or are funded by bodies audited by the Auditor General for Scotland.

General power of amendment by regulations

484   General power of amendment by regulations

(1)   The Secretary of State may by regulations amend this Chapter or section 539 (minor definitions) so far as applying to this Chapter by adding, altering or repealing provisions.

(2)   The regulations may make consequential amendments or repeals in other provisions of this Act, or in other enactments.

(3)   Regulations under this section imposing new requirements, or rendering existing requirements more onerous, are subject to affirmative resolution procedure.

(4)   Other regulations under this section are subject to negative resolution procedure.

[1611]

NOTES
Commencement: 20 January 2007 (for the purpose of enabling the exercise of powers to make Orders or Regulations by statutory instrument); 6 April 2008 (otherwise).
Commencement (transitional provisions): see the note to s 475 at **[1602]**.
Regulations: the Companies Act 2006 (Amendment) (Accounts and Reports) Regulations 2008, SI 2008/393. These Regulations amend various provisions in Parts 15 and 16 of this Act.

CHAPTER 2
APPOINTMENT OF AUDITORS

Private companies

485   Appointment of auditors of private company: general

(1)   An auditor or auditors of a private company must be appointed for each financial year of the company, unless the directors reasonably resolve otherwise on the ground that audited accounts are unlikely to be required.

(2)   For each financial year for which an auditor or auditors is or are to be appointed (other than the company's first financial year), the appointment must be made before the end of the period of 28 days beginning with—

    (a)   the end of the time allowed for sending out copies of the company's annual accounts and reports for the previous financial year (see section 424), or

    (b)   if earlier, the day on which copies of the company's annual accounts and reports for the previous financial year are sent out under section 423.

This is the "period for appointing auditors".

(3)   The directors may appoint an auditor or auditors of the company—

    (a)   at any time before the company's first period for appointing auditors,

    (b)   following a period during which the company (being exempt from audit) did not have any auditor, at any time before the company's next period for appointing auditors, or

    (c)   to fill a casual vacancy in the office of auditor.

(4)   The members may appoint an auditor or auditors by ordinary resolution—

    (a)   during a period for appointing auditors,

    (b)   if the company should have appointed an auditor or auditors during a period for appointing auditors but failed to do so, or

    (c)   where the directors had power to appoint under subsection (3) but have failed to make an appointment.

(5)   An auditor or auditors of a private company may only be appointed—

    (a)   in accordance with this section, or

    (b)   in accordance with section 486 (default power of Secretary of State).

This is without prejudice to any deemed re-appointment under section 487.

[1612]

NOTES

Commencement: 1 October 2007 (for transitional provisions see the note below).

Commencement (transitional provisions): Sch 3, paras 44, 45 to the Companies Act 2006 (Commencement No 3, Consequential Amendments, Transitional Provisions and Savings) Order 2007, SI 2007/2194 provide as follows—

"Appointment of auditors of private companies (ss 485 to 488)

44.—(1)   Sections 485 to 488 of the Companies Act 2006 (appointment of auditors of private companies) apply in relation to appointments for financial years beginning on or after 1st October 2007.

(2)   Sections 384 to 388A of the 1985 Act or Articles 392 to 396A of the 1986 Order continue to apply in relation to appointments for financial years beginning before that date.

(3)   Where—

    (a)   a private company has elected under section 386 of the 1985 Act or Article 394 of the 1986 Order to dispense with the annual appointment of auditors, and

    (b)   the election is in force immediately before 1st October 2007,

section 487(2)(a) of the Companies Act 2006 (no deemed reappointment of auditors appointed by directors) does not prevent the deemed reappointment under that subsection of auditors first appointed before 1st October 2007.

45.—(1)   This paragraph applies where immediately before 1st October 2007 a resolution of a private company under section 390A of the 1985 Act or Article 398A of the 1986 Order (remuneration of auditors) was in force and was expressed (in whatever terms) to continue to have effect so long as a resolution under section 386 of that Act or Article 394 of that Order (election to dispense with annual appointment of auditors) continued in force.

(2)   The repeal of section 386 of the 1985 Act or Article 394 of the 1986 Order does not affect the continued operation of the resolution, which shall continue to have effect until—

    (a)   it is revoked or superseded by a further resolution,

    (b)   the auditors to which it applies cease to hold office, or

    (c)   it otherwise ceases to have effect in accordance with its terms.".

Commencement (transitional adaptations): art 6 of the Companies Act 2006 (Commencement No 3, Consequential Amendments, Transitional Provisions and Savings) Order 2007, SI 2007/2194 provides that the provisions brought into force by that Order shall have effect subject to any transitional adaptations specified in Sch 1 to that Order. Schedule 1, para 17 to the Order provides as follows (but note that para 17 is revoked by the Companies Act 2006 (Commencement No 5, Transitional Provisions and Savings) Order 2007, SI 2007/3495, art 10(1), (3), as from 6 April 2008 (subject to the same transitional provisions and savings as apply, in accordance with Sch 4 to that Order, in relation to the repeal of the provisions of the 1985 Act referred to in the adaptation))—

"17   Appointment of auditors of private company (ss 485 to 488)

(1)   Section 485 (appointment of auditors of private companies: general) has effect with the following adaptations.

(2)   For paragraph (a) of subsection (2) substitute—

    "(a)   the end of the period allowed for delivering accounts and reports under section 244 of the Companies Act 1985 or Article 252 of the Companies (Northern Ireland) Order 1986, or".

(3)   In paragraph (b) of subsection (2), for "section 423" substitute "section 238 of the Companies Act 1985 or Article 246 of the Companies (Northern Ireland) Order 1986".".

486   Appointment of auditors of private company: default power of Secretary of State

(1)   If a private company fails to appoint an auditor or auditors in accordance with section 485, the Secretary of State may appoint one or more persons to fill the vacancy.

(2)   Where subsection (2) of that section applies and the company fails to make the necessary appointment before the end of the period for appointing auditors, the company must within one week of the end of that period give notice to the Secretary of State of his power having become exercisable.

(3)   If a company fails to give the notice required by this section, an offence is committed by—
(a)   the company, and
(b)   every officer of the company who is in default.

(4)   A person guilty of an offence under this section is liable on summary conviction to a fine not exceeding level 3 on the standard scale and, for continued contravention, a daily default fine not exceeding one-tenth of level 3 on the standard scale.

[1613]

NOTES
Commencement: 1 October 2007.
Commencement (transitional provisions): see the note to s 485 at **[1612]**.

487   Term of office of auditors of private company

(1)   An auditor or auditors of a private company hold office in accordance with the terms of their appointment, subject to the requirements that—
(a)   they do not take office until any previous auditor or auditors cease to hold office, and
(b)   they cease to hold office at the end of the next period for appointing auditors unless re-appointed.

(2)   Where no auditor has been appointed by the end of the next period for appointing auditors, any auditor in office immediately before that time is deemed to be re-appointed at that time, unless—
(a)   he was appointed by the directors, or
(b)   the company's articles require actual re-appointment, or
(c)   the deemed re-appointment is prevented by the members under section 488, or
(d)   the members have resolved that he should not be re-appointed, or
(e)   the directors have resolved that no auditor or auditors should be appointed for the financial year in question.

(3)   This is without prejudice to the provisions of this Part as to removal and resignation of auditors.

(4)   No account shall be taken of any loss of the opportunity of deemed re- appointment under this section in ascertaining the amount of any compensation or damages payable to an auditor on his ceasing to hold office for any reason.

[1614]

NOTES
Commencement: 1 October 2007.
Commencement (transitional provisions): see the note to s 485 at **[1612]**.
Commencement (transitional adaptations): art 6 of the Companies Act 2006 (Commencement No 3, Consequential Amendments, Transitional Provisions and Savings) Order 2007, SI 2007/2194 provides that the provisions brought into force by that Order shall have effect subject to any transitional adaptations specified in Sch 1 to that Order. Schedule 1, para 18 to the Order provides as follows (but note that para 18 is revoked by the Companies Act 2006 (Commencement No 5, Transitional Provisions and Savings) Order 2007, SI 2007/3495, art 10(1), (3), as from 6 April 2008 (subject to the same transitional provisions and savings as apply, in accordance with Sch 4 to that Order, in relation to the repeal of the provisions of the 1985 Act referred to in the adaptation))—
"18.—(1)   Section 487 (term of office of auditors of private company) has effect with the following adaptation.
(2)   In subsection (3) for "the provisions of this Part" substitute "the provisions of Chapter 5 of Part 11 of the Companies Act 1985 or Chapter 5 of Part 12 of the Companies (Northern Ireland) Order 1986".".

488   Prevention by members of deemed re-appointment of auditor

(1)   An auditor of a private company is not deemed to be re-appointed under section 487(2) if the company has received notices under this section from members representing at least the requisite percentage of the total voting rights of all members who would be entitled to vote on a resolution that the auditor should not be re-appointed.

PART II
OTHER ACTS

(2)   The "requisite percentage" is 5%, or such lower percentage as is specified for this purpose in the company's articles.

(3)   A notice under this section—
    (a)   may be in hard copy or electronic form,
    (b)   must be authenticated by the person or persons giving it, and
    (c)   must be received by the company before the end of the accounting reference period immediately preceding the time when the deemed re- appointment would have effect.

[1615]

NOTES
Commencement: 1 October 2007.
Commencement (transitional provisions): see the note to s 485 at **[1612]**.

Public companies

489   Appointment of auditors of public company: general

(1)   An auditor or auditors of a public company must be appointed for each financial year of the company, unless the directors reasonably resolve otherwise on the ground that audited accounts are unlikely to be required.

(2)   For each financial year for which an auditor or auditors is or are to be appointed (other than the company's first financial year), the appointment must be made before the end of the accounts meeting of the company at which the company's annual accounts and reports for the previous financial year are laid.

(3)   The directors may appoint an auditor or auditors of the company—
    (a)   at any time before the company's first accounts meeting;
    (b)   following a period during which the company (being exempt from audit) did not have any auditor, at any time before the company's next accounts meeting;
    (c)   to fill a casual vacancy in the office of auditor.

(4)   The members may appoint an auditor or auditors by ordinary resolution—
    (a)   at an accounts meeting;
    (b)   if the company should have appointed an auditor or auditors at an accounts meeting but failed to do so;
    (c)   where the directors had power to appoint under subsection (3) but have failed to make an appointment.

(5)   An auditor or auditors of a public company may only be appointed—
    (a)   in accordance with this section, or
    (b)   in accordance with section 490 (default power of Secretary of State).

[1616]

NOTES
Commencement: 6 April 2008.
Commencement (transitional provisions): Sch 4, Pt 1, paras 10, 11 to the Companies Act 2006 (Commencement No 5, Transitional Provisions and Savings) Order 2007, SI 2007/3495 provide as follows—
    "10.—(1)   In Chapter 2 of Part 16 of that Act (appointment of auditors)—
        (a)   sections 489 and 490 (appointment of auditors by public companies) apply to appointments for financial years beginning on or after 6th April 2008;
        (b)   section 491 (term of office of auditors of public company) applies to auditors appointed for financial years beginning on or after that date.

(2)   Sections 384, 385, 387 and 388(1), (3) and (4) of the 1985 Act or Articles 392, 393, 395 and 396(1), (3) and (4) of the 1986 Order continue to apply to appointments by public companies for financial years beginning before that date.

11.—(1)   In that Chapter, the following provisions apply to auditors appointed for financial years beginning on or after 6th April 2008—
    section 492 (fixing of auditor's remuneration),
    section 493 (disclosure of terms of audit appointment), and
    section 494 (disclosure of services provided by auditor or associated and related remuneration).

(2)   Sections 390A and 390B of the 1985 Act or Articles 398A and 398B of the 1986 Order continue to apply to auditors appointed for financial years beginning before that date.

(3)   The repeal of section 390A of the 1985 Act and Article 398A of the 1986 Order (remuneration of auditors) does not affect the operation of any such resolution as is mentioned in paragraph 45 of Schedule 3 to the Companies Act 2006 (Commencement No 3, Consequential Amendments, Transitional Provisions and Savings) Order 2007.".

490   Appointment of auditors of public company: default power of Secretary of State

(1)   If a public company fails to appoint an auditor or auditors in accordance with section 489, the Secretary of State may appoint one or more persons to fill the vacancy.

(2)　Where subsection (2) of that section applies and the company fails to make the necessary appointment before the end of the accounts meeting, the company must within one week of the end of that meeting give notice to the Secretary of State of his power having become exercisable.

(3)　If a company fails to give the notice required by this section, an offence is committed by—
    (a)　the company, and
    (b)　every officer of the company who is in default.

(4)　A person guilty of an offence under this section is liable on summary conviction to a fine not exceeding level 3 on the standard scale and, for continued contravention, a daily default fine not exceeding one-tenth of level 3 on the standard scale.

[1617]

NOTES
Commencement: 6 April 2008.
Commencement (transitional provisions): see the note to s 489 at **[1616]**.

491　Term of office of auditors of public company

(1)　The auditor or auditors of a public company hold office in accordance with the terms of their appointment, subject to the requirements that—
    (a)　they do not take office until the previous auditor or auditors have ceased to hold office, and
    (b)　they cease to hold office at the conclusion of the accounts meeting next following their appointment, unless re-appointed.

(2)　This is without prejudice to the provisions of this Part as to removal and resignation of auditors.

[1618]

NOTES
Commencement: 6 April 2008.
Commencement (transitional provisions): see the note to s 489 at **[1616]**.

General provisions

492　Fixing of auditor's remuneration

(1)　The remuneration of an auditor appointed by the members of a company must be fixed by the members by ordinary resolution or in such manner as the members may by ordinary resolution determine.

(2)　The remuneration of an auditor appointed by the directors of a company must be fixed by the directors.

(3)　The remuneration of an auditor appointed by the Secretary of State must be fixed by the Secretary of State.

(4)　For the purposes of this section "remuneration" includes sums paid in respect of expenses.

(5)　This section applies in relation to benefits in kind as to payments of money.

[1619]

NOTES
Commencement: 6 April 2008.
Commencement (transitional provisions): see the note to s 489 at **[1616]**.

493　Disclosure of terms of audit appointment

(1)　The Secretary of State may make provision by regulations for securing the disclosure of the terms on which a company's auditor is appointed, remunerated or performs his duties.

Nothing in the following provisions of this section affects the generality of this power.

(2)　The regulations may—
    (a)　require disclosure of—
        (i)　a copy of any terms that are in writing, and
        (ii)　a written memorandum setting out any terms that are not in writing;
    (b)　require disclosure to be at such times, in such places and by such means as are specified in the regulations;
    (c)　require the place and means of disclosure to be stated—
        (i)　in a note to the company's annual accounts (in the case of its individual accounts) or in such manner as is specified in the regulations (in the case of group accounts),
        (ii)　in the directors' report, or
        (iii)　in the auditor's report on the company's annual accounts.

(3)   The provisions of this section apply to a variation of the terms mentioned in subsection (1) as they apply to the original terms.

(4)   Regulations under this section are subject to affirmative resolution procedure.

[1620]

NOTES
Commencement: 20 January 2007 (for the purpose of enabling the exercise of powers to make Orders or Regulations by statutory instrument); 6 April 2008 (otherwise).
Commencement (transitional provisions): see the note to s 489 at **[1616]**.

494   Disclosure of services provided by auditor or associates and related remuneration

(1)   The Secretary of State may make provision by regulations for securing the disclosure of—
   (a)   the nature of any services provided for a company by the company's auditor (whether in his capacity as auditor or otherwise) or by his associates;
   (b)   the amount of any remuneration received or receivable by a company's auditor, or his associates, in respect of any such services.

Nothing in the following provisions of this section affects the generality of this power.

(2)   The regulations may provide—
   (a)   for disclosure of the nature of any services provided to be made by reference to any class or description of services specified in the regulations (or any combination of services, however described);
   (b)   for the disclosure of amounts of remuneration received or receivable in respect of services of any class or description specified in the regulations (or any combination of services, however described);
   (c)   for the disclosure of separate amounts so received or receivable by the company's auditor or any of his associates, or of aggregate amounts so received or receivable by all or any of those persons.

(3)   The regulations may—
   (a)   provide that "remuneration" includes sums paid in respect of expenses;
   (b)   apply to benefits in kind as well as to payments of money, and require the disclosure of the nature of any such benefits and their estimated money value;
   (c)   apply to services provided for associates of a company as well as to those provided for a company;
   (d)   define "associate" in relation to an auditor and a company respectively.

(4)   The regulations may provide that any disclosure required by the regulations is to be made—
   (a)   in a note to the company's annual accounts (in the case of its individual accounts) or in such manner as is specified in the regulations (in the case of group accounts),
   (b)   in the directors' report, or
   (c)   in the auditor's report on the company's annual accounts.

(5)   If the regulations provide that any such disclosure is to be made as mentioned in subsection (4)(a) or (b), the regulations may require the auditor to supply the directors of the company with any information necessary to enable the disclosure to be made.

(6)   Regulations under this section are subject to negative resolution procedure.

[1621]

NOTES
Commencement: 20 January 2007 (for the purpose of enabling the exercise of powers to make Orders or Regulations by statutory instrument); 6 April 2008 (otherwise).
Commencement (transitional provisions): see the note to s 489 at **[1616]**.
Regulations: the Companies (Disclosure of Auditor Remuneration and Liability Limitation Agreements) Regulations 2008, SI 2008/489. These Regulations provide for companies to disclose fees receivable by their auditors and their auditors' associates' (in relation to the accounts of a company for any financial year beginning on or after 6 April 2008), and also to disclose liability limitation agreements that they make with their auditors (as from 6 April 2008). Disclosure must be in a note to the company's annual accounts.

CHAPTER 3
FUNCTIONS OF AUDITOR

Auditor's report

495   Auditor's report on company's annual accounts

(1)   A company's auditor must make a report to the company's members on all annual accounts of the company of which copies are, during his tenure of office—
   (a)   in the case of a private company, to be sent out to members under section 423;
   (b)   in the case of a public company, to be laid before the company in general meeting under section 437.

(2) The auditor's report must include—
(a) an introduction identifying the annual accounts that are the subject of the audit and the financial reporting framework that has been applied in their preparation, and
(b) a description of the scope of the audit identifying the auditing standards in accordance with which the audit was conducted.

(3) The report must state clearly whether, in the auditor's opinion, the annual accounts—
(a) give a true and fair view—
(i) in the case of an individual balance sheet, of the state of affairs of the company as at the end of the financial year,
(ii) in the case of an individual profit and loss account, of the profit or loss of the company for the financial year,
(iii) in the case of group accounts, of the state of affairs as at the end of the financial year and of the profit or loss for the financial year of the undertakings included in the consolidation as a whole, so far as concerns members of the company;
(b) have been properly prepared in accordance with the relevant financial reporting framework; and
(c) have been prepared in accordance with the requirements of this Act (and, where applicable, Article 4 of the IAS Regulation).

Expressions used in this subsection that are defined for the purposes of Part 15 (see section 474) have the same meaning as in that Part.

(4) The auditor's report—
(a) must be either unqualified or qualified, and
(b) must include a reference to any matters to which the auditor wishes to draw attention by way of emphasis without qualifying the report.

[1622]

NOTES
Commencement: 6 April 2008.
Commencement (transitional provisions): Sch 4, Pt 1, para 12 to the Companies Act 2006 (Commencement No 5, Transitional Provisions and Savings) Order 2007, SI 2007/3495 provides as follows—
"12.—(1) In Chapter 3 of Part 16 of that Act (functions of auditor)—
(a) sections 495 to 498 (auditor's report and duties of auditor) apply to auditors' reports on accounts or reports for financial years beginning on or after 6th April 2008;
(b) sections 499 to 501 (rights of auditors) apply to auditors appointed for financial years beginning on or after that date;
(c) sections 503 to 509 (signature of auditor's report and offences in connection with auditor's report) apply to auditors' reports on accounts or reports for financial years beginning on or after that date.
(2) Sections 235 to 237, 389A and 389B of the 1985 Act or Articles 243 to 245, 397A and 397B of the 1986 Order continue to apply as regards financial years beginning before that date.
(3) Section 502 of the Companies Act 2006 (auditor's rights in relation to resolutions and meetings) applies to auditors appointed on or after 6th April 2008.
(4) Section 390 of the 1985 Act or Article 398 of the 1986 Order continues to apply to auditors appointed before that date.".

496 Auditor's report on directors' report

The auditor must state in his report on the company's annual accounts whether in his opinion the information given in the directors' report for the financial year for which the accounts are prepared is consistent with those accounts.

[1623]

NOTES
Commencement: 6 April 2008.
Commencement (transitional provisions): see the note to s 495 at **[1622]**.

497 Auditor's report on auditable part of directors' remuneration report

(1) If the company is a quoted company, the auditor, in his report on the company's annual accounts for the financial year, must—
(a) report to the company's members on the auditable part of the directors' remuneration report, and
(b) state whether in his opinion that part of the directors' remuneration report has been properly prepared in accordance with this Act.

(2) For the purposes of this Part, "the auditable part" of a directors' remuneration report is the part identified as such by regulations under section 421.

[1624]

NOTES
Commencement: 6 April 2008.
Commencement (transitional provisions): see the note to s 495 at **[1622]**.

Duties and rights of auditors

498 Duties of auditor

(1)   A company's auditor, in preparing his report, must carry out such investigations as will enable him to form an opinion as to—

    (a)   whether adequate accounting records have been kept by the company and returns adequate for their audit have been received from branches not visited by him, and

    (b)   whether the company's individual accounts are in agreement with the accounting records and returns, and

    (c)   in the case of a quoted company, whether the auditable part of the company's directors' remuneration report is in agreement with the accounting records and returns.

(2)   If the auditor is of the opinion—

    (a)   that adequate accounting records have not been kept, or that returns adequate for their audit have not been received from branches not visited by him, or

    (b)   that the company's individual accounts are not in agreement with the accounting records and returns, or

    (c)   in the case of a quoted company, that the auditable part of its directors' remuneration report is not in agreement with the accounting records and returns,

the auditor shall state that fact in his report.

(3)   If the auditor fails to obtain all the information and explanations which, to the best of his knowledge and belief, are necessary for the purposes of his audit, he shall state that fact in his report.

(4)   If—

    (a)   the requirements of regulations under section 412 (disclosure of directors' benefits: remuneration, pensions and compensation for loss of office) are not complied with in the annual accounts, or

    (b)   in the case of a quoted company, the requirements of regulations under section 421 as to information forming the auditable part of the directors' remuneration report are not complied with in that report,

the auditor must include in his report, so far as he is reasonably able to do so, a statement giving the required particulars.

[(5)   If the directors of the company—

    (a)   have prepared accounts in accordance with the small companies regime, or

    (b)   have taken advantage of small companies exemption in preparing the directors' report,

and in the auditor's opinion they were not entitled to do so, the auditor shall state that fact in his report.]

[1625]

NOTES
Commencement: 6 April 2008.
Commencement (transitional provisions): see the note to s 495 at **[1622]**.
Sub-s (5): substituted by the Companies Act 2006 (Amendment) (Accounts and Reports) Regulations 2008, SI 2008/393, reg 6(10), as from 6 April 2008, in relation to financial years beginning on or after that date.

499 Auditor's general right to information

(1)   An auditor of a company—

    (a)   has a right of access at all times to the company's books, accounts and vouchers (in whatever form they are held), and

    (b)   may require any of the following persons to provide him with such information or explanations as he thinks necessary for the performance of his duties as auditor.

(2)   Those persons are—

    (a)   any officer or employee of the company;

    (b)   any person holding or accountable for any of the company's books, accounts or vouchers;

    (c)   any subsidiary undertaking of the company which is a body corporate incorporated in the United Kingdom;

    (d)   any officer, employee or auditor of any such subsidiary undertaking or any person holding or accountable for any books, accounts or vouchers of any such subsidiary undertaking;

    (e)   any person who fell within any of paragraphs (a) to (d) at a time to which the information or explanations required by the auditor relates or relate.

(3)   A statement made by a person in response to a requirement under this section may not be used in evidence against him in criminal proceedings except proceedings for an offence under section 501.

(4)   Nothing in this section compels a person to disclose information in respect of which a claim to legal professional privilege (in Scotland, to confidentiality of communications) could be maintained in legal proceedings.

[1626]

NOTES

Commencement: 6 April 2008.

Commencement (transitional provisions): see the note to s 495 at **[1622]**.

500   Auditor's right to information from overseas subsidiaries

(1)   Where a parent company has a subsidiary undertaking that is not a body corporate incorporated in the United Kingdom, the auditor of the parent company may require it to obtain from any of the following persons such information or explanations as he may reasonably require for the purposes of his duties as auditor.

(2)   Those persons are—
   (a)   the undertaking;
   (b)   any officer, employee or auditor of the undertaking;
   (c)   any person holding or accountable for any of the undertaking's books, accounts or vouchers;
   (d)   any person who fell within paragraph (b) or (c) at a time to which the information or explanations relates or relate.

(3)   If so required, the parent company must take all such steps as are reasonably open to it to obtain the information or explanations from the person concerned.

(4)   A statement made by a person in response to a requirement under this section may not be used in evidence against him in criminal proceedings except proceedings for an offence under section 501.

(5)   Nothing in this section compels a person to disclose information in respect of which a claim to legal professional privilege (in Scotland, to confidentiality of communications) could be maintained in legal proceedings.

[1627]

NOTES

Commencement: 6 April 2008.

Commencement (transitional provisions): see the note to s 495 at **[1622]**.

501   Auditor's rights to information: offences

(1)   A person commits an offence who knowingly or recklessly makes to an auditor of a company a statement (oral or written) that—
   (a)   conveys or purports to convey any information or explanations which the auditor requires, or is entitled to require, under section 499, and
   (b)   is misleading, false or deceptive in a material particular.

(2)   A person guilty of an offence under subsection (1) is liable—
   (a)   on conviction on indictment, to imprisonment for a term not exceeding two years or a fine (or both);
   (b)   on summary conviction—
      (i)   in England and Wales, to imprisonment for a term not exceeding twelve months or to a fine not exceeding the statutory maximum (or both);
      (ii)   in Scotland or Northern Ireland, to imprisonment for a term not exceeding six months or to a fine not exceeding the statutory maximum (or both).

(3)   A person who fails to comply with a requirement under section 499 without delay commits an offence unless it was not reasonably practicable for him to provide the required information or explanations.

(4)   If a parent company fails to comply with section 500, an offence is committed by—
   (a)   the company, and
   (b)   every officer of the company who is in default.

(5)   A person guilty of an offence under subsection (3) or (4) is liable on summary conviction to a fine not exceeding level 3 on the standard scale.

(6)   Nothing in this section affects any right of an auditor to apply for an injunction (in Scotland, an interdict or an order for specific performance) to enforce any of his rights under section 499 or 500.

[1628]

NOTES
Commencement: 6 April 2008.
Commencement (transitional provisions): see the note to s 495 at [1622].
Imprisonment for a term not exceeding twelve months: see the note to s 387 at [1514].

502   Auditor's rights in relation to resolutions and meetings

(1)   In relation to a written resolution proposed to be agreed to by a private company, the company's auditor is entitled to receive all such communications relating to the resolution as, by virtue of any provision of Chapter 2 of Part 13 of this Act, are required to be supplied to a member of the company.

(2)   A company's auditor is entitled—
(a)   to receive all notices of, and other communications relating to, any general meeting which a member of the company is entitled to receive,
(b)   to attend any general meeting of the company, and
(c)   to be heard at any general meeting which he attends on any part of the business of the meeting which concerns him as auditor.

(3)   Where the auditor is a firm, the right to attend or be heard at a meeting is exercisable by an individual authorised by the firm in writing to act as its representative at the meeting.

[1629]

NOTES
Commencement: 6 April 2008.
Commencement (transitional provisions): see the note to s 495 at [1622].

Signature of auditor's report

503   Signature of auditor's report

(1)   The auditor's report must state the name of the auditor and be signed and dated.

(2)   Where the auditor is an individual, the report must be signed by him.

(3)   Where the auditor is a firm, the report must be signed by the senior statutory auditor in his own name, for and on behalf of the auditor.

[1630]

NOTES
Commencement: 6 April 2008.
Commencement (transitional provisions): see the note to s 495 at [1622].

504   Senior statutory auditor

(1)   The senior statutory auditor means the individual identified by the firm as senior statutory auditor in relation to the audit in accordance with—
(a)   standards issued by the European Commission, or
(b)   if there is no applicable standard so issued, any relevant guidance issued by—
(i)   the Secretary of State, or
(ii)   a body appointed by order of the Secretary of State.

(2)   The person identified as senior statutory auditor must be eligible for appointment as auditor of the company in question (see Chapter 2 of Part 42 of this Act).

(3)   The senior statutory auditor is not, by reason of being named or identified as senior statutory auditor or by reason of his having signed the auditor's report, subject to any civil liability to which he would not otherwise be subject.

(4)   An order appointing a body for the purpose of subsection (1)(b)(ii) is subject to negative resolution procedure.

[1631]

NOTES
Commencement: 20 January 2007 (for the purpose of enabling the exercise of powers to make Orders or Regulations by statutory instrument); 6 April 2008 (otherwise).
Commencement (transitional provisions): see the note to s 495 at [1622].
Orders: the Statutory Auditors (Delegation of Functions etc) Order 2008, SI 2008/496. This Order transfers most of the functions of the Secretary of State under Part 42 to the Professional Oversight Board. It revokes and replaces the Companies Act 1989 (Delegation) Order 2005, SI 2005/2337, as from 6 April 2008, except in relation to functions relating to appointments of company auditors for any financial year beginning before that

date. Note that art 11 of that Order provides that the body known as the Auditing Practices Board established under the articles of association of the Financial Reporting Council Limited is appointed for the purposes of sub-s (1)(b)(ii) above.

505   Names to be stated in published copies of auditor's report

(1)   Every copy of the auditor's report that is published by or on behalf of the company must—
- (a)   state the name of the auditor and (where the auditor is a firm) the name of the person who signed it as senior statutory auditor, or
- (b)   if the conditions in section 506 (circumstances in which names may be omitted) are met, state that a resolution has been passed and notified to the Secretary of State in accordance with that section.

(2)   For the purposes of this section a company is regarded as publishing the report if it publishes, issues or circulates it or otherwise makes it available for public inspection in a manner calculated to invite members of the public generally, or any class of members of the public, to read it.

(3)   If a copy of the auditor's report is published without the statement required by this section, an offence is committed by—
- (a)   the company, and
- (b)   every officer of the company who is in default.

(4)   A person guilty of an offence under this section is liable on summary conviction to a fine not exceeding level 3 on the standard scale.

[1632]

NOTES
Commencement: 6 April 2008.
Commencement (transitional provisions): see the note to s 495 at **[1622]**.

506   Circumstances in which names may be omitted

(1)   The auditor's name and, where the auditor is a firm, the name of the person who signed the report as senior statutory auditor, may be omitted from—
- (a)   published copies of the report, and
- (b)   the copy of the report delivered to the registrar under Chapter 10 of Part 15 (filing of accounts and reports),
if the following conditions are met.

(2)   The conditions are that the company—
- (a)   considering on reasonable grounds that statement of the name would create or be likely to create a serious risk that the auditor or senior statutory auditor, or any other person, would be subject to violence or intimidation, has resolved that the name should not be stated, and
- (b)   has given notice of the resolution to the Secretary of State, stating—
  - (i)   the name and registered number of the company,
  - (ii)   the financial year of the company to which the report relates, and
  - (iii) the name of the auditor and (where the auditor is a firm) the name of the person who signed the report as senior statutory auditor.

[1633]

NOTES
Commencement: 6 April 2008.
Commencement (transitional provisions): see the note to s 495 at **[1622]**.

Offences in connection with auditor's report

507   Offences in connection with auditor's report

(1)   A person to whom this section applies commits an offence if he knowingly or recklessly causes a report under section 495 (auditor's report on company's annual accounts) to include any matter that is misleading, false or deceptive in a material particular.

(2)   A person to whom this section applies commits an offence if he knowingly or recklessly causes such a report to omit a statement required by—
- (a)   section 498(2)(b) (statement that company's accounts do not agree with accounting records and returns),
- (b)   section 498(3) (statement that necessary information and explanations not obtained), or
- (c)   section 498(5) (statement that directors wrongly took advantage of exemption from obligation to prepare group accounts).

(3)   This section applies to—

(a) where the auditor is an individual, that individual and any employee or agent of his who is eligible for appointment as auditor of the company;

(b) where the auditor is a firm, any director, member, employee or agent of the firm who is eligible for appointment as auditor of the company.

(4) A person guilty of an offence under this section is liable—

(a) on conviction on indictment, to a fine;

(b) on summary conviction, to a fine not exceeding the statutory maximum.

[1634]

NOTES

Commencement: 6 April 2008.

Commencement (transitional provisions): see the note to s 495 at [1622].

508 Guidance for regulatory and prosecuting authorities: England, Wales and Northern Ireland

(1) The Secretary of State may issue guidance for the purpose of helping relevant regulatory and prosecuting authorities to determine how they should carry out their functions in cases where behaviour occurs that—

(a) appears to involve the commission of an offence under section 507 (offences in connection with auditor's report), and

(b) has been, is being or may be investigated pursuant to arrangements—

(i) under paragraph 15 of Schedule 10 (investigation of complaints against auditors and supervisory bodies), or

(ii) of a kind mentioned in paragraph 24 of that Schedule (independent investigation for disciplinary purposes of public interest cases).

(2) The Secretary of State must obtain the consent of the Attorney General before issuing any such guidance.

(3) In this section "relevant regulatory and prosecuting authorities" means—

(a) supervisory bodies within the meaning of Part 42 of this Act,

(b) bodies to which the Secretary of State may make grants under section 16(1) of the Companies (Audit, Investigations and Community Enterprise) Act 2004 (c 27) (bodies concerned with accounting standards etc),

(c) the Director of the Serious Fraud Office,

(d) the Director of Public Prosecutions or the Director of Public Prosecutions for Northern Ireland, and

(e) the Secretary of State.

(4) This section does not apply to Scotland.

[1635]

NOTES

Commencement: 6 April 2008.

Commencement (transitional provisions): see the note to s 495 at [1622].

509 Guidance for regulatory authorities: Scotland

(1) The Lord Advocate may issue guidance for the purpose of helping relevant regulatory authorities to determine how they should carry out their functions in cases where behaviour occurs that—

(a) appears to involve the commission of an offence under section 507 (offences in connection with auditor's report), and

(b) has been, is being or may be investigated pursuant to arrangements—

(i) under paragraph 15 of Schedule 10 (investigation of complaints against auditors and supervisory bodies), or

(ii) of a kind mentioned in paragraph 24 of that Schedule (independent investigation for disciplinary purposes of public interest cases).

(2) The Lord Advocate must consult the Secretary of State before issuing any such guidance.

(3) In this section "relevant regulatory authorities" means—

(a) supervisory bodies within the meaning of Part 42 of this Act,

(b) bodies to which the Secretary of State may make grants under section 16(1) of the Companies (Audit, Investigations and Community Enterprise) Act 2004 (c 27) (bodies concerned with accounting standards etc), and

(c) the Secretary of State.

(4) This section applies only to Scotland.

[1636]

NOTES
Commencement: 6 April 2008.
Commencement (transitional provisions): see the note to s 495 at **[1622]**.

CHAPTER 4
REMOVAL, RESIGNATION, ETC OF AUDITORS
Removal of auditor

510 Resolution removing auditor from office

(1)   The members of a company may remove an auditor from office at any time.

(2)   This power is exercisable only—
   (a)   by ordinary resolution at a meeting, and
   (b)   in accordance with section 511 (special notice of resolution to remove auditor).

(3)   Nothing in this section is to be taken as depriving the person removed of compensation or damages payable to him in respect of the termination—
   (a)   of his appointment as auditor, or
   (b)   of any appointment terminating with that as auditor.

(4)   An auditor may not be removed from office before the expiration of his term of office except by resolution under this section.

[1637]

NOTES
Commencement: 6 April 2008.
Commencement (transitional provisions): Sch 4, Pt 1, paras 13–17 to the Companies Act 2006 (Commencement No 5, Transitional Provisions and Savings) Order 2007, SI 2007/3495 (as amended by the Companies Act 2006 (Commencement No 7, Transitional Provisions and Savings) Order 2008, SI 2008/1886, art 8, as from 11 August 2008) provide as follows—

"13.—(1)   In Chapter 4 of Part 16 of that Act (removal, resignation, etc of auditors), sections 510 to 513 (removal of auditor) apply where notice of the intended resolution is given to the company on or after 6th April 2008.

(2)   Sections 391 and 391A of the 1985 Act or Articles 399 and 399A of the 1986 Order continue to apply where notice of the intended resolution is given to the company before that date.

(3)   Until section 1068(1) of the Companies Act 2006 comes into force, the notice referred to in section 512(1) (notice to registrar of resolution removing auditor from office) must be in the form prescribed for the purposes of section 391(2) of the 1985 Act or Article 399(2) of the 1986 Order.

(4)   In section 513 (rights of auditor removed from office) as it applies in relation to an auditor appointed before 6th April 2008, the reference to rights under section 502(2) shall be read as a reference to rights under section 390(1) of the 1985 Act or Article 398(1) of the 1986 Order.

14.—(1)   In that Chapter, sections 514 and 515 (failure to re-appoint auditor) apply to appointments for financial years beginning on or after 6th April 2008.

(2)   Section 391A of the 1985 Act or Article 399A of the 1986 Order continues to apply to appointments for financial years beginning before that date.

15.—(1)   In that Chapter, sections 516 to 518 (resignation of auditor) apply to resignations occurring on or after 6th April 2008.

(2)   Sections 392 and 392A of the 1985 Act or Articles 400 and 400A of the 1986 Order continue to apply to resignations occurring before that date.

[(3)   In section 518 (rights of resigning auditor) as it applies in relation to an auditor appointed before 6th April 2008, the reference to rights under section 502(2) shall be read as a reference to rights under section 390(1) of the 1985 Act or Article 398(1) of the 1986 Order.]

16.—(1)   In that Chapter, sections 519 to 525 (statement by auditor ceasing to hold office) apply where the auditor ceases to hold office on or after 6th April 2008.

(2)   Sections 394 and 394A of the 1985 Act or Articles 401A and 401B of the 1986 Order continue to apply where the auditor ceases to hold office before that date.

17.—(1)   In that Chapter, section 526 (effect of casual vacancies) applies where the vacancy occurs on or after 6th April 2008.

(2)   Section 388(2) of the 1985 Act or Article 396(2) of the 1986 Order continues to apply where the vacancy occurred before that date.".

511 Special notice required for resolution removing auditor from office

(1)   Special notice is required for a resolution at a general meeting of a company removing an auditor from office.

(2)   On receipt of notice of such an intended resolution the company must immediately send a copy of it to the auditor proposed to be removed.

(3)   The auditor proposed to be removed may make with respect to the intended resolution representations in writing to the company (not exceeding a reasonable length) and request their notification to members of the company.

(4)   The company must (unless the representations are received by it too late for it to do so)—
   (a)   in any notice of the resolution given to members of the company, state the fact of the representations having been made, and
   (b)   send a copy of the representations to every member of the company to whom notice of the meeting is or has been sent.

(5)   If a copy of any such representations is not sent out as required because received too late or because of the company's default, the auditor may (without prejudice to his right to be heard orally) require that the representations be read out at the meeting.

(6)   Copies of the representations need not be sent out and the representations need not be read at the meeting if, on the application either of the company or of any other person claiming to be aggrieved, the court is satisfied that the auditor is using the provisions of this section to secure needless publicity for defamatory matter.

The court may order the company's costs (in Scotland, expenses) on the application to be paid in whole or in part by the auditor, notwithstanding that he is not a party to the application.

[1638]

NOTES
Commencement: 6 April 2008.
Commencement (transitional provisions): see the note to s 510 at **[1637]**.

512   Notice to registrar of resolution removing auditor from office

(1)   Where a resolution is passed under section 510 (resolution removing auditor from office), the company must give notice of that fact to the registrar within 14 days.

(2)   If a company fails to give the notice required by this section, an offence is committed by—
   (a)   the company, and
   (b)   every officer of it who is in default.

(3)   A person guilty of an offence under this section is liable on summary conviction to a fine not exceeding level 3 on the standard scale and, for continued contravention, a daily default fine not exceeding one-tenth of level 3 on the standard scale.

[1639]

NOTES
Commencement: 6 April 2008.
Commencement (transitional provisions): see the note to s 510 at **[1637]**.

513   Rights of auditor who has been removed from office

(1)   An auditor who has been removed by resolution under section 510 has, notwithstanding his removal, the rights conferred by section 502(2) in relation to any general meeting of the company—
   (a)   at which his term of office would otherwise have expired, or
   (b)   at which it is proposed to fill the vacancy caused by his removal.

(2)   In such a case the references in that section to matters concerning the auditor as auditor shall be construed as references to matters concerning him as a former auditor.

[1640]

NOTES
Commencement: 6 April 2008.
Commencement (transitional provisions): see the note to s 510 at **[1637]**.

Failure to re-appoint auditor

514   Failure to re-appoint auditor: special procedure required for written resolution

(1)   This section applies where a resolution is proposed as a written resolution of a private company whose effect would be to appoint a person as auditor in place of a person (the "outgoing auditor") whose term of office has expired, or is to expire, at the end of the period for appointing auditors.

(2)   The following provisions apply if—
   (a)   no period for appointing auditors has ended since the outgoing auditor ceased to hold office, or
   (b)   such a period has ended and an auditor or auditors should have been appointed but were not.

(3)   The company must send a copy of the proposed resolution to the person proposed to be appointed and to the outgoing auditor.

(4)   The outgoing auditor may, within 14 days after receiving the notice, make with respect to the proposed resolution representations in writing to the company (not exceeding a reasonable length) and request their circulation to members of the company.

(5)   The company must circulate the representations together with the copy or copies of the resolution circulated in accordance with section 291 (resolution proposed by directors) or section 293 (resolution proposed by members).

(6)   Where subsection (5) applies—
  (a)   the period allowed under section 293(3) for service of copies of the proposed resolution is 28 days instead of 21 days, and
  (b)   the provisions of section 293(5) and (6) (offences) apply in relation to a failure to comply with that subsection as in relation to a default in complying with that section.

(7)   Copies of the representations need not be circulated if, on the application either of the company or of any other person claiming to be aggrieved, the court is satisfied that the auditor is using the provisions of this section to secure needless publicity for defamatory matter.

The court may order the company's costs (in Scotland, expenses) on the application to be paid in whole or in part by the auditor, notwithstanding that he is not a party to the application.

(8)   If any requirement of this section is not complied with, the resolution is ineffective.

[1641]

NOTES

Commencement: 6 April 2008.
Commencement (transitional provisions): see the note to s 510 at **[1637]**.

---

515   Failure to re-appoint auditor: special notice required for resolution at general meeting

(1)   This section applies to a resolution at a general meeting of a company whose effect would be to appoint a person as auditor in place of a person (the "outgoing auditor") whose term of office has ended, or is to end—
  (a)   in the case of a private company, at the end of the period for appointing auditors;
  (b)   in the case of a public company, at the end of the next accounts meeting.

(2)   Special notice is required of such a resolution if—
  (a)   in the case of a private company—
    (i)   no period for appointing auditors has ended since the outgoing auditor ceased to hold office, or
    (ii)   such a period has ended and an auditor or auditors should have been appointed but were not;
  (b)   in the case of a public company—
    (i)   there has been no accounts meeting of the company since the outgoing auditor ceased to hold office, or
    (ii)   there has been an accounts meeting at which an auditor or auditors should have been appointed but were not.

(3)   On receipt of notice of such an intended resolution the company shall forthwith send a copy of it to the person proposed to be appointed and to the outgoing auditor.

(4)   The outgoing auditor may make with respect to the intended resolution representations in writing to the company (not exceeding a reasonable length) and request their notification to members of the company.

(5)   The company must (unless the representations are received by it too late for it to do so)—
  (a)   in any notice of the resolution given to members of the company, state the fact of the representations having been made, and
  (b)   send a copy of the representations to every member of the company to whom notice of the meeting is or has been sent.

(6)   If a copy of any such representations is not sent out as required because received too late or because of the company's default, the outgoing auditor may (without prejudice to his right to be heard orally) require that the representations be read out at the meeting.

(7)   Copies of the representations need not be sent out and the representations need not be read at the meeting if, on the application either of the company or of any other person claiming to be aggrieved, the court is satisfied that the auditor is using the provisions of this section to secure needless publicity for defamatory matter.

The court may order the company's costs (in Scotland, expenses) on the application to be paid in whole or in part by the outgoing auditor, notwithstanding that he is not a party to the application.

[1642]

NOTES

Commencement: 6 April 2008.

Commencement (transitional provisions): see the note to s 510 at **[1637]**.

Resignation of auditor

516 Resignation of auditor

(1)   An auditor of a company may resign his office by depositing a notice in writing to that effect at the company's registered office.

(2)   The notice is not effective unless it is accompanied by the statement required by section 519.

(3)   An effective notice of resignation operates to bring the auditor's term of office to an end as of the date on which the notice is deposited or on such later date as may be specified in it.

[1643]

NOTES

Commencement: 6 April 2008.

Commencement (transitional provisions): see the note to s 510 at **[1637]**.

517   Notice to registrar of resignation of auditor

(1)   Where an auditor resigns the company must within 14 days of the deposit of a notice of resignation send a copy of the notice to the registrar of companies.

(2)   If default is made in complying with this section, an offence is committed by—
   (a)   the company, and
   (b)   every officer of the company who is in default.

(3)   A person guilty of an offence under this section is liable—
   (a)   on conviction on indictment, to a fine;
   (b)   on summary conviction, to a fine not exceeding the statutory maximum and, for continued contravention, a daily default fine not exceeding one-tenth of the statutory maximum.

[1644]

NOTES

Commencement: 6 April 2008.

Commencement (transitional provisions): see the note to s 510 at **[1637]**.

518   Rights of resigning auditor

(1)   This section applies where an auditor's notice of resignation is accompanied by a statement of the circumstances connected with his resignation (see section 519).

(2)   He may deposit with the notice a signed requisition calling on the directors of the company forthwith duly to convene a general meeting of the company for the purpose of receiving and considering such explanation of the circumstances connected with his resignation as he may wish to place before the meeting.

(3)   He may request the company to circulate to its members—
   (a)   before the meeting convened on his requisition, or
   (b)   before any general meeting at which his term of office would otherwise have expired or at which it is proposed to fill the vacancy caused by his resignation,
a statement in writing (not exceeding a reasonable length) of the circumstances connected with his resignation.

(4)   The company must (unless the statement is received too late for it to comply)—
   (a)   in any notice of the meeting given to members of the company, state the fact of the statement having been made, and
   (b)   send a copy of the statement to every member of the company to whom notice of the meeting is or has been sent.

(5)   The directors must within 21 days from the date of the deposit of a requisition under this section proceed duly to convene a meeting for a day not more than 28 days after the date on which the notice convening the meeting is given.

(6)   If default is made in complying with subsection (5), every director who failed to take all reasonable steps to secure that a meeting was convened commits an offence.

(7)   A person guilty of an offence under this section is liable—
   (a)   on conviction on indictment, to a fine;
   (b)   on summary conviction to a fine not exceeding the statutory maximum.

(8)   If a copy of the statement mentioned above is not sent out as required because received too late or because of the company's default, the auditor may (without prejudice to his right to be heard orally) require that the statement be read out at the meeting.

(9)   Copies of a statement need not be sent out and the statement need not be read out at the meeting if, on the application either of the company or of any other person who claims to be aggrieved, the court is satisfied that the auditor is using the provisions of this section to secure needless publicity for defamatory matter.

The court may order the company's costs (in Scotland, expenses) on such an application to be paid in whole or in part by the auditor, notwithstanding that he is not a party to the application.

(10)   An auditor who has resigned has, notwithstanding his resignation, the rights conferred by section 502(2) in relation to any such general meeting of the company as is mentioned in subsection (3)(a) or (b) above.

In such a case the references in that section to matters concerning the auditor as auditor shall be construed as references to matters concerning him as a former auditor.

[1645]

NOTES
Commencement: 6 April 2008.
Commencement (transitional provisions): see the note to s 510 at **[1637]**.

Statement by auditor on ceasing to hold office

519   Statement by auditor to be deposited with company

(1)   Where an auditor of an unquoted company ceases for any reason to hold office, he must deposit at the company's registered office a statement of the circumstances connected with his ceasing to hold office, unless he considers that there are no circumstances in connection with his ceasing to hold office that need to be brought to the attention of members or creditors of the company.

(2)   If he considers that there are no circumstances in connection with his ceasing to hold office that need to be brought to the attention of members or creditors of the company, he must deposit at the company's registered office a statement to that effect.

(3)   Where an auditor of a quoted company ceases for any reason to hold office, he must deposit at the company's registered office a statement of the circumstances connected with his ceasing to hold office.

(4)   The statement required by this section must be deposited—
    (a)   in the case of resignation, along with the notice of resignation;
    (b)   in the case of failure to seek re-appointment, not less than 14 days before the end of the time allowed for next appointing an auditor;
    (c)   in any other case, not later than the end of the period of 14 days beginning with the date on which he ceases to hold office.

(5)   A person ceasing to hold office as auditor who fails to comply with this section commits an offence.

(6)   In proceedings for such an offence it is a defence for the person charged to show that he took all reasonable steps and exercised all due diligence to avoid the commission of the offence.

(7)   A person guilty of an offence under this section is liable—
    (a)   on conviction on indictment, to a fine;
    (b)   on summary conviction, to a fine not exceeding the statutory maximum.

[(8)   Where an offence under this section is committed by a body corporate, every officer of the body who is in default also commits the offence.

For this purpose—
    (a)   any person who purports to act as director, manager or secretary of the body is treated as an officer of the body, and
    (b)   if the body is a company, any shadow director is treated as an officer of the company.]

[1646]

NOTES
Commencement: 6 April 2008.
Commencement (transitional provisions): see the note to s 510 at **[1637]**.
Sub-s (8): added by the Companies Act 2006 (Consequential Amendments etc) Order 2008, SI 2008/948, art 3(1), Sch 1, Pt 2, para 247, as from 6 April 2008.

520   Company's duties in relation to statement

(1)   This section applies where the statement deposited under section 519 states the circumstances connected with the auditor's ceasing to hold office.

(2)   The company must within 14 days of the deposit of the statement either—
  (a)   send a copy of it to every person who under section 423 is entitled to be sent copies of the accounts, or
  (b)   apply to the court.

(3)   If it applies to the court, the company must notify the auditor of the application.

(4)   If the court is satisfied that the auditor is using the provisions of section 519 to secure needless publicity for defamatory matter—
  (a)   it shall direct that copies of the statement need not be sent out, and
  (b)   it may further order the company's costs (in Scotland, expenses) on the application to be paid in whole or in part by the auditor, even if he is not a party to the application.

The company must within 14 days of the court's decision send to the persons mentioned in subsection (2)(a) a statement setting out the effect of the order.

(5)   If no such direction is made the company must send copies of the statement to the persons mentioned in subsection (2)(a) within 14 days of the court's decision or, as the case may be, of the discontinuance of the proceedings.

(6)   In the event of default in complying with this section an offence is committed by every officer of the company who is in default.

(7)   In proceedings for such an offence it is a defence for the person charged to show that he took all reasonable steps and exercised all due diligence to avoid the commission of the offence.

(8)   A person guilty of an offence under this section is liable—
  (a)   on conviction on indictment, to a fine;
  (b)   on summary conviction, to a fine not exceeding the statutory maximum.

[1647]

NOTES
Commencement: 6 April 2008.
Commencement (transitional provisions): see the note to s 510 at **[1637]**.

521   Copy of statement to be sent to registrar

(1)   Unless within 21 days beginning with the day on which he deposited the statement under section 519 the auditor receives notice of an application to the court under section 520, he must within a further seven days send a copy of the statement to the registrar.

(2)   If an application to the court is made under section 520 and the auditor subsequently receives notice under subsection (5) of that section, he must within seven days of receiving the notice send a copy of the statement to the registrar.

(3)   An auditor who fails to comply with subsection (1) or (2) commits an offence.

(4)   In proceedings for such an offence it is a defence for the person charged to show that he took all reasonable steps and exercised all due diligence to avoid the commission of the offence.

(5)   A person guilty of an offence under this section is liable—
  (a)   on conviction on indictment, to a fine;
  (b)   on summary conviction, to a fine not exceeding the statutory maximum.

[(6)   Where an offence under this section is committed by a body corporate, every officer of the body who is in default also commits the offence.

For this purpose—
  (a)   any person who purports to act as director, manager or secretary of the body is treated as an officer of the body, and
  (b)   if the body is a company, any shadow director is treated as an officer of the company.]

[1648]

NOTES
Commencement: 6 April 2008.
Commencement (transitional provisions): see the note to s 510 at **[1637]**.
Sub-s (6): added by the Companies Act 2006 (Consequential Amendments etc) Order 2008, SI 2008/948, art 3(1), Sch 1, Pt 2, para 248, as from 6 April 2008.

522   Duty of auditor to notify appropriate audit authority

(1)   Where—
  (a)   in the case of a major audit, an auditor ceases for any reason to hold office, or
  (b)   in the case of an audit that is not a major audit, an auditor ceases to hold office before the end of his term of office,
the auditor ceasing to hold office must notify the appropriate audit authority.

(2)   The notice must—

(a) inform the appropriate audit authority that he has ceased to hold office, and
(b) be accompanied by a copy of the statement deposited by him at the company's registered office in accordance with section 519.

(3) If the statement so deposited is to the effect that he considers that there are no circumstances in connection with his ceasing to hold office that need to be brought to the attention of members or creditors of the company, the notice must also be accompanied by a statement of the reasons for his ceasing to hold office.

(4) The auditor must comply with this section—
(a) in the case of a major audit, at the same time as he deposits a statement at the company's registered office in accordance with section 519;
(b) in the case of an audit that is not a major audit, at such time (not being earlier than the time mentioned in paragraph (a)) as the appropriate audit authority may require.

(5) A person ceasing to hold office as auditor who fails to comply with this section commits an offence.

(6) If that person is a firm an offence is committed by—
(a) the firm, and
(b) every officer of the firm who is in default.

(7) In proceedings for an offence under this section it is a defence for the person charged to show that he took all reasonable steps and exercised all due diligence to avoid the commission of the offence.

(8) A person guilty of an offence under this section is liable—
(a) on conviction on indictment, to a fine;
(b) on summary conviction, to a fine not exceeding the statutory maximum.

[1649]

NOTES
Commencement: 6 April 2008.
Commencement (transitional provisions): see the note to s 510 at **[1637]**.

523 Duty of company to notify appropriate audit authority

(1) Where an auditor ceases to hold office before the end of his term of office, the company must notify the appropriate audit authority.

(2) The notice must—
(a) inform the appropriate audit authority that the auditor has ceased to hold office, and
(b) be accompanied by—
(i) a statement by the company of the reasons for his ceasing to hold office, or
(ii) if the copy of the statement deposited by the auditor at the company's registered office in accordance with section 519 contains a statement of circumstances in connection with his ceasing to hold office that need to be brought to the attention of members or creditors of the company, a copy of that statement.

(3) The company must give notice under this section not later than 14 days after the date on which the auditor's statement is deposited at the company's registered office in accordance with section 519.

(4) If a company fails to comply with this section, an offence is committed by—
(a) the company, and
(b) every officer of the company who is in default.

(5) In proceedings for such an offence it is a defence for the person charged to show that he took all reasonable steps and exercised all due diligence to avoid the commission of the offence.

(6) A person guilty of an offence under this section is liable—
(a) on conviction on indictment, to a fine;
(b) on summary conviction, to a fine not exceeding the statutory maximum.

[1650]

NOTES
Commencement: 6 April 2008.
Commencement (transitional provisions): see the note to s 510 at **[1637]**.

524 Information to be given to accounting authorities

(1) The appropriate audit authority on receiving notice under section 522 or 523 of an auditor's ceasing to hold office—
(a) must inform the accounting authorities, and
(b) may if it thinks fit forward to those authorities a copy of the statement or statements accompanying the notice.

(2)   The accounting authorities are—

    (a)   the Secretary of State, and

    (b)   any person authorised by the Secretary of State for the purposes of section 456 (revision of defective accounts: persons authorised to apply to court).

(3)   If either of the accounting authorities is also the appropriate audit authority it is only necessary to comply with this section as regards any other accounting authority.

(4)   If the court has made an order under section 520(4) directing that copies of the statement need not be sent out by the company, sections 460 and 461 (restriction on further disclosure) apply in relation to the copies sent to the accounting authorities as they apply to information obtained under section 459 (power to require documents etc).

[1651]

NOTES

Commencement: 6 April 2008.
Commencement (transitional provisions): see the note to s 510 at **[1637]**.

525   Meaning of "appropriate audit authority" and "major audit"

(1)   In sections 522, 523 and 524 "appropriate audit authority" means—

    (a)   in the case of a major audit [(other than one conducted by an Auditor General)]—

        (i)   the Secretary of State, or

        (ii)   if the Secretary of State has delegated functions under section 1252 to a body whose functions include receiving the notice in question, that body;

    (b)   in the case of an audit [(other than one conducted by an Auditor General)] that is not a major audit, the relevant supervisory body;

    [(c)   in the case of an audit conducted by an Auditor General, the Independent Supervisor.]

["Supervisory body" and "Independent Supervisor" have the same meaning] as in Part 42 (statutory auditors) (see [sections 1217 and 1228]).

(2)   In sections 522 and this section "major audit" means a statutory audit conducted in respect of—

    (a)   a company any of whose securities have been admitted to the official list (within the meaning of Part 6 of the Financial Services and Markets Act 2000 (c 8)), or

    (b)   any other person in whose financial condition there is a major public interest.

(3)   In determining whether an audit is a major audit within subsection (2)(b), regard shall be had to any guidance issued by any of the authorities mentioned in subsection (1).

[1652]

NOTES

Commencement: 6 April 2008.
Commencement (transitional provisions): see the note to s 510 at **[1637]**.
Sub-s (1): words in square brackets in paras (a), (b), and the whole of para (c) inserted, and fourth and final words in square brackets substituted, by the Statutory Auditors and Third Country Auditors Regulations 2007, SI 2007/3494, reg 41, as from 6 April 2008.
As to the delegation of the Secretary of State's functions to the Professional Oversight Board (for the purposes of sub-s (1)(a)(ii) above): see the Statutory Auditors (Delegation of Functions etc) Order 2008, SI 2008/496, art 5.

Supplementary

526   Effect of casual vacancies

If an auditor ceases to hold office for any reason, any surviving or continuing auditor or auditors may continue to act.

[1653]

NOTES

Commencement: 6 April 2008.
Commencement (transitional provisions): see the note to s 510 at **[1637]**.

CHAPTER 5
QUOTED COMPANIES: RIGHT OF MEMBERS TO RAISE AUDIT CONCERNS AT
ACCOUNTS MEETING

527   Members' power to require website publication of audit concerns

(1)   The members of a quoted company may require the company to publish on a website a statement setting out any matter relating to—

    (a)   the audit of the company's accounts (including the auditor's report and the conduct of the audit) that are to be laid before the next accounts meeting, or

(b)   any circumstances connected with an auditor of the company ceasing to hold office since the previous accounts meeting,

that the members propose to raise at the next accounts meeting of the company.

(2)   A company is required to do so once it has received requests to that effect from—
  (a)   members representing at least 5% of the total voting rights of all the members who have a relevant right to vote (excluding any voting rights attached to any shares in the company held as treasury shares), or
  (b)   at least 100 members who have a relevant right to vote and hold shares in the company on which there has been paid up an average sum, per member, of at least £100.

See also section 153 (exercise of rights where shares held on behalf of others).

(3)   In subsection (2) a "relevant right to vote" means a right to vote at the accounts meeting.

(4)   A request—
  (a)   may be sent to the company in hard copy or electronic form,
  (b)   must identify the statement to which it relates,
  (c)   must be authenticated by the person or persons making it, and
  (d)   must be received by the company at least one week before the meeting to which it relates.

(5)   A quoted company is not required to place on a website a statement under this section if, on an application by the company or another person who claims to be aggrieved, the court is satisfied that the rights conferred by this section are being abused.

(6)   The court may order the members requesting website publication to pay the whole or part of the company's costs (in Scotland, expenses) on such an application, even if they are not parties to the application.

[1654]

NOTES
Commencement: 6 April 2008.
Commencement (transitional provisions): Sch 4, Pt 1, para 18 to the Companies Act 2006 (Commencement No 5, Transitional Provisions and Savings) Order 2007, SI 2007/3495 provides as follows—

"18.   In Chapter 5 of Part 16 of that Act (quoted companies: right of members to raise audit concerns at accounts meeting), in section 527 (members' powers to require website publication of audit concerns)—
  (a)   subsection (1)(a) (matters relating to audit of company's accounts) applies to accounts for financial years beginning on or after 6th April 2008, and
  (b)   subsection (1)(b) (matters relating to circumstances connected with an auditor of the company) applies to auditors appointed for financial years beginning on or after that date.".

---

528   Requirements as to website availability

(1)   The following provisions apply for the purposes of section 527 (website publication of members' statement of audit concerns).

(2)   The information must be made available on a website that—
  (a)   is maintained by or on behalf of the company, and
  (b)   identifies the company in question.

(3)   Access to the information on the website, and the ability to obtain a hard copy of the information from the website, must not be conditional on the payment of a fee or otherwise restricted.

(4)   The statement—
  (a)   must be made available within three working days of the company being required to publish it on a website, and
  (b)   must be kept available until after the meeting to which it relates.

(5)   A failure to make information available on a website throughout the period specified in subsection (4)(b) is disregarded if—
  (a)   the information is made available on the website for part of that period, and
  (b)   the failure is wholly attributable to circumstances that it would not be reasonable to have expected the company to prevent or avoid.

[1655]

NOTES
Commencement: 6 April 2008.

---

529   Website publication: company's supplementary duties

(1)   A quoted company must in the notice it gives of the accounts meeting draw attention to—
  (a)   the possibility of a statement being placed on a website in pursuance of members' requests under section 527, and
  (b)   the effect of the following provisions of this section.

(2)   A company may not require the members requesting website publication to pay its expenses in complying with that section or section 528 (requirements in connection with website publication).

(3)   Where a company is required to place a statement on a website under section 527 it must forward the statement to the company's auditor not later than the time when it makes the statement available on the website.

(4)   The business which may be dealt with at the accounts meeting includes any statement that the company has been required under section 527 to publish on a website.

[1656]

NOTES
Commencement: 6 April 2008.

530   Website publication: offences

(1)   In the event of default in complying with
   (a)   section 528 (requirements as to website publication), or
   (b)   section 529 (companies' supplementary duties in relation to request for website publication),

an offence is committed by every officer of the company who is in default.

(2)   A person guilty of an offence under this section is liable—
   (a)   on conviction on indictment, to a fine;
   (b)   on summary conviction, to a fine not exceeding the statutory maximum.

[1657]

NOTES
Commencement: 6 April 2008.

531   Meaning of "quoted company"

(1)   For the purposes of this Chapter a company is a quoted company if it is a quoted company in accordance with section 385 (quoted and unquoted companies for the purposes of Part 15) in relation to the financial year to which the accounts to be laid at the next accounts meeting relate.

(2)   The provisions of subsections (4) to (6) of that section (power to amend definition by regulations) apply in relation to the provisions of this Chapter as in relation to the provisions of that Part.

[1658]

NOTES
Commencement: 6 April 2008.

CHAPTER 6
AUDITORS' LIABILITY
Voidness of provisions protecting auditors from liability

532   Voidness of provisions protecting auditors from liability

(1)   This section applies to any provision—
   (a)   for exempting an auditor of a company (to any extent) from any liability that would otherwise attach to him in connection with any negligence, default, breach of duty or breach of trust in relation to the company occurring in the course of the audit of accounts, or
   (b)   by which a company directly or indirectly provides an indemnity (to any extent) for an auditor of the company, or of an associated company, against any liability attaching to him in connection with any negligence, default, breach of duty or breach of trust in relation to the company of which he is auditor occurring in the course of the audit of accounts.

(2)   Any such provision is void, except as permitted by—
   (a)   section 533 (indemnity for costs of successfully defending proceedings), or
   (b)   sections 534 to 536 (liability limitation agreements).

(3)   This section applies to any provision, whether contained in a company's articles or in any contract with the company or otherwise.

(4)   For the purposes of this section companies are associated if one is a subsidiary of the other or both are subsidiaries of the same body corporate.

[1659]

PART II
OTHER ACTS

NOTES
  Commencement: 6 April 2008.

Indemnity for costs of defending proceedings

533 Indemnity for costs of successfully defending proceedings

Section 532 (general voidness of provisions protecting auditors from liability) does not prevent a company from indemnifying an auditor against any liability incurred by him—
  (a)   in defending proceedings (whether civil or criminal) in which judgment is given in his favour or he is acquitted, or
  (b)   in connection with an application under section 1157 (power of court to grant relief in case of honest and reasonable conduct) in which relief is granted to him by the court.
[1660]

NOTES
  Commencement: 6 April 2008.
  Commencement (transitional adaptations): the transitional adaptations of this section contained in the Companies Act 2006 (Commencement No 5, Transitional Provisions and Savings) Order 2007, SI 2007/3495, Sch 1, Pt 1, para 11 were revoked by art 10(2) of that Order, as from 1 October 2008.

Liability limitation agreements

534 Liability limitation agreements

  (1)   A "liability limitation agreement" is an agreement that purports to limit the amount of a liability owed to a company by its auditor in respect of any negligence, default, breach of duty or breach of trust, occurring in the course of the audit of accounts, of which the auditor may be guilty in relation to the company.

  (2)   Section 532 (general voidness of provisions protecting auditors from liability) does not affect the validity of a liability limitation agreement that—
  (a)   complies with section 535 (terms of liability limitation agreement) and of any regulations under that section, and
  (b)   is authorised by the members of the company (see section 536).

  (3)   Such an agreement—
  (a)   is effective to the extent provided by section 537, and
  (b)   is not subject—
      (i)   in England and Wales or Northern Ireland, to section 2(2) or 3(2)(a) of the Unfair Contract Terms Act 1977 (c 50);
      (ii) in Scotland, to section 16(1)(b) or 17(1)(a) of that Act.
[1661]

NOTES
  Commencement: 6 April 2008.

535 Terms of liability limitation agreement

  (1)   A liability limitation agreement—
  (a)   must not apply in respect of acts or omissions occurring in the course of the audit of accounts for more than one financial year, and
  (b)   must specify the financial year in relation to which it applies.

  (2)   The Secretary of State may by regulations—
  (a)   require liability limitation agreements to contain specified provisions or provisions of a specified description;
  (b)   prohibit liability limitation agreements from containing specified provisions or provisions of a specified description.
"Specified" here means specified in the regulations.

  (3)   Without prejudice to the generality of the power conferred by subsection (2), that power may be exercised with a view to preventing adverse effects on competition.

  (4)   Subject to the preceding provisions of this section, it is immaterial how a liability limitation agreement is framed.

  In particular, the limit on the amount of the auditor's liability need not be a sum of money, or a formula, specified in the agreement.

  (5)   Regulations under this section are subject to negative resolution procedure.
[1662]

NOTES
Commencement: 20 January 2007 (for the purpose of enabling the exercise of powers to make Orders or Regulations by statutory instrument); 6 April 2008 (otherwise).

536 Authorisation of agreement by members of the company

(1)   A liability limitation agreement is authorised by the members of the company if it has been authorised under this section and that authorisation has not been withdrawn.

(2)   A liability limitation agreement between a private company and its auditor may be authorised—
    (a)   by the company passing a resolution, before it enters into the agreement, waiving the need for approval,
    (b)   by the company passing a resolution, before it enters into the agreement, approving the agreement's principal terms, or
    (c)   by the company passing a resolution, after it enters into the agreement, approving the agreement.

(3)   A liability limitation agreement between a public company and its auditor may be authorised—
    (a)   by the company passing a resolution in general meeting, before it enters into the agreement, approving the agreement's principal terms, or
    (b)   by the company passing a resolution in general meeting, after it enters into the agreement, approving the agreement.

(4)   The "principal terms" of an agreement are terms specifying, or relevant to the determination of—
    (a)   the kind (or kinds) of acts or omissions covered,
    (b)   the financial year to which the agreement relates, or
    (c)   the limit to which the auditor's liability is subject.

(5)   Authorisation under this section may be withdrawn by the company passing an ordinary resolution to that effect—
    (a)   at any time before the company enters into the agreement, or
    (b)   if the company has already entered into the agreement, before the beginning of the financial year to which the agreement relates.

Paragraph (b) has effect notwithstanding anything in the agreement.

[1663]

NOTES
Commencement: 6 April 2008.
Commencement (transitional provisions): Sch 4, Pt 1, para 19 to the Companies Act 2006 (Commencement No 5, Transitional Provisions and Savings) Order 2007, SI 2007/3495 provides as follows—
"19.   A resolution passed before 6th April 2008 authorising a liability limitation agreement is effective for the purposes of section 536 (authorisation of agreement by members of company) if it complies with the requirements of that section.".

537 Effect of liability limitation agreement

(1)   A liability limitation agreement is not effective to limit the auditor's liability to less than such amount as is fair and reasonable in all the circumstances of the case having regard (in particular) to—
    (a)   the auditor's responsibilities under this Part,
    (b)   the nature and purpose of the auditor's contractual obligations to the company, and
    (c)   the professional standards expected of him.

(2)   A liability limitation agreement that purports to limit the auditor's liability to less than the amount mentioned in subsection (1) shall have effect as if it limited his liability to that amount.

(3)   In determining what is fair and reasonable in all the circumstances of the case no account is to be taken of—
    (a)   matters arising after the loss or damage in question has been incurred, or
    (b)   matters (whenever arising) affecting the possibility of recovering compensation from other persons liable in respect of the same loss or damage.

[1664]

NOTES
Commencement: 6 April 2008.

538 Disclosure of agreement by company

(1)   A company which has entered into a liability limitation agreement must make such disclosure in connection with the agreement as the Secretary of State may require by regulations.

(2)   The regulations may provide, in particular, that any disclosure required by the regulations shall be made—

(a)   in a note to the company's annual accounts (in the case of its individual accounts) or in such manner as is specified in the regulations (in the case of group accounts), or

(b)   in the directors' report.

(3)   Regulations under this section are subject to negative resolution procedure.

[1665]

NOTES

Commencement: 20 January 2007 (for the purpose of enabling the exercise of powers to make Orders or Regulations by statutory instrument); 6 April 2008 (otherwise).

Regulations: the Companies (Disclosure of Auditor Remuneration and Liability Limitation Agreements) Regulations 2008, SI 2008/489 (see the note to s 494 at **[1621]**).

CHAPTER 7
SUPPLEMENTARY PROVISIONS

539   Minor definitions

In this Part—

"e-money issuer" means a person who has permission under Part 4 of the Financial Services and Markets Act 2000 (c 8) to carry on the activity of issuing electronic money within the meaning of article 9B of the Financial Services and Markets Act 2000 (Regulated Activities) Order 2001 (SI 2001/544);

.....

["MiFID investment firm" means an investment firm within the meaning of Article 4.1.1 of Directive 2004/39/EC of the European Parliament and of the Council of 21 April 2004 on markets in financial instruments, other than—

(a)   a company to which that Directive does not apply by virtue of Article 2 of that Directive,

(b)   a company which is an exempt investment firm within the meaning of regulation 4A(3) of the Financial Services and Markets Act 2000 (Markets in Financial Instruments) Regulations 2007, and

(c)   any other company which fulfils all the requirements set out in regulation 4C(3) of those Regulations;]

"qualified", in relation to an auditor's report (or a statement contained in an auditor's report), means that the report or statement does not state the auditor's unqualified opinion that the accounts have been properly prepared in accordance with this Act or, in the case of an undertaking not required to prepare accounts in accordance with this Act, under any corresponding legislation under which it is required to prepare accounts;

"turnover", in relation to a company, means the amounts derived from the provision of goods and services falling within the company's ordinary activities, after deduction of—

(a)   trade discounts,

(b)   value added tax, and

(c)   any other taxes based on the amounts so derived;

"UCITS management company" has the meaning given by the Glossary forming part of the Handbook made by the Financial Services Authority under the Financial Services and Markets Act 2000.

[1666]

NOTES

Commencement: 6 April 2008.

Definition "ISD investment firm" (omitted) revoked, and definition "MiFID investment firm" inserted, by the Markets in Financial Instruments Directive (Consequential Amendments) Regulations 2007, SI 2007/2932, reg 3(7), as from 1 November 2007.

PART 17
A COMPANY'S SHARE CAPITAL

CHAPTER 1
SHARES AND SHARE CAPITAL OF A COMPANY

Shares

544   Transferability of shares

(1)   The shares or other interest of any member in a company are transferable in accordance with the company's articles.

(2)   This is subject to—

(a)   the Stock Transfer Act 1963 (c 18) or the Stock Transfer Act (Northern Ireland) 1963 (c 24 (NI)) (which enables securities of certain descriptions to be transferred by a simplified process), and

(b)   regulations under Chapter 2 of Part 21 of this Act (which enable title to securities to be evidenced and transferred without a written instrument).

(3)   See Part 21 of this Act generally as regards share transfers.

[1666ZA]

NOTES
Commencement: 6 April 2008.

PART 20
PRIVATE AND PUBLIC COMPANIES

CHAPTER 1
PROHIBITION OF PUBLIC OFFERS BY PRIVATE COMPANIES

755   Prohibition of public offers by private company

(1)   A private company limited by shares or limited by guarantee and having a share capital must not—

(a)   offer to the public any securities of the company, or

(b)   allot or agree to allot any securities of the company with a view to their being offered to the public.

(2)   Unless the contrary is proved, an allotment or agreement to allot securities is presumed to be made with a view to their being offered to the public if an offer of the securities (or any of them) to the public is made—

(a)   within six months after the allotment or agreement to allot, or

(b)   before the receipt by the company of the whole of the consideration to be received by it in respect of the securities.

(3)   A company does not contravene this section if—

(a)   it acts in good faith in pursuance of arrangements under which it is to re-register as a public company before the securities are allotted, or

(b)   as part of the terms of the offer it undertakes to re-register as a public company within a specified period, and that undertaking is complied with.

(4)   The specified period for the purposes of subsection (3)(b) must be a period ending not later than six months after the day on which the offer is made (or, in the case of an offer made on different days, first made).

(5)   In this Chapter "securities" means shares or debentures.

[1666A]

NOTES
Commencement: 6 April 2008.
Commencement (transitional provisions): Sch 4, Pt 1, para 24 to the Companies Act 2006 (Commencement No 5, Transitional Provisions and Savings) Order 2007, SI 2007/3495 provides as follows—

"Prohibition of public offers by private companies (ss 755 to 759)

24.—(1)   Sections 755 and 756 of the Companies Act 2006 (prohibition of public offers by private companies) apply to offers made on or after 6th April 2008.

(2)   Section 81 of the 1985 Act or Article 91 of the 1986 Order continues to apply to offers made before that date.".

756   Meaning of "offer to the public"

(1)   This section explains what is meant in this Chapter by an offer of securities to the public.

(2)   An offer to the public includes an offer to any section of the public, however selected.

(3)   An offer is not regarded as an offer to the public if it can properly be regarded, in all the circumstances, as—

(a)   not being calculated to result, directly or indirectly, in securities of the company becoming available to persons other than those receiving the offer, or

(b)   otherwise being a private concern of the person receiving it and the person making it.

(4)   An offer is to be regarded (unless the contrary is proved) as being a private concern of the person receiving it and the person making it if—

(a)   it is made to a person already connected with the company and, where it is made on terms allowing that person to renounce his rights, the rights may only be renounced in favour of another person already connected with the company; or

    (b)   it is an offer to subscribe for securities to be held under an employees' share scheme and, where it is made on terms allowing that person to renounce his rights, the rights may only be renounced in favour of—

        (i)   another person entitled to hold securities under the scheme, or

        (ii)   a person already connected with the company.

  (5)   For the purposes of this section "person already connected with the company" means—

    (a)   an existing member or employee of the company,

    (b)   a member of the family of a person who is or was a member or employee of the company,

    (c)   the widow or widower, or surviving civil partner, of a person who was a member or employee of the company,

    (d)   an existing debenture holder of the company, or

    (e)   a trustee (acting in his capacity as such) of a trust of which the principal beneficiary is a person within any of paragraphs (a) to (d).

  (6)   For the purposes of subsection (5)(b) the members of a person's family are the person's spouse or civil partner and children (including step-children) and their descendants.

[1667]

NOTES

Commencement: 6 April 2008.

Commencement (transitional provisions): see the note to s 755 at **[1666A]**.

757 Enforcement of prohibition: order restraining proposed contravention

  (1)   If it appears to the court—

    (a)   on an application under this section, or

    (b)   in proceedings under Part 30 (protection of members against unfair prejudice),

that a company is proposing to act in contravention of section 755 (prohibition of public offers by private companies), the court shall make an order under this section.

  (2)   An order under this section is an order restraining the company from contravening that section.

  (3)   An application for an order under this section may be made by—

    (a)   a member or creditor of the company, or

    (b)   the Secretary of State.

[1667A]

NOTES

Commencement: 6 April 2008.

With regard to proceedings under this section, see further the Companies (Authorised Minimum) Regulations 2008, SI 2008/729, reg 6 (Determination of exchange rates by the court in certain proceedings).

758 Enforcement of prohibition: orders available to the court after contravention

  (1)   This section applies if it appears to the court—

    (a)   on an application under this section, or

    (b)   in proceedings under Part 30 (protection of members against unfair prejudice),

that a company has acted in contravention of section 755 (prohibition of public offers by private companies).

  (2)   The court must make an order requiring the company to re-register as a public company unless it appears to the court—

    (a)   that the company does not meet the requirements for re-registration as a public company, and

    (b)   that it is impractical or undesirable to require it to take steps to do so.

  (3)   If it does not make an order for re-registration, the court may make either or both of the following—

    (a)   a remedial order (see section 759), or

    (b)   an order for the compulsory winding up of the company.

  (4)   An application under this section may be made by—

    (a)   a member of the company who—

        (i)   was a member at the time the offer was made (or, if the offer was made over a period, at any time during that period), or

        (ii)   became a member as a result of the offer,

    (b)   a creditor of the company who was a creditor at the time the offer was made (or, if the offer was made over a period, at any time during that period), or

    (c)   the Secretary of State.

[1667B]

NOTES
Commencement: 6 April 2008.
Commencement (transitional provisions): Sch 4, Pt 1, para 25 to the Companies Act 2006 (Commencement No 5, Transitional Provisions and Savings) Order 2007, SI 2007/3495 provides as follows—

"25. Sections 758 and 759 of the Companies Act 2006 (enforcement of prohibition: orders after contravention) apply to offers made on or after 6th April 2008.".

With regard to proceedings under this section, see further the Companies (Authorised Minimum) Regulations 2008, SI 2008/729, reg 6 (Determination of exchange rates by the court in certain proceedings).

759 Enforcement of prohibition: remedial order

(1) A "remedial order" is an order for the purpose of putting a person affected by anything done in contravention of section 755 (prohibition of public offers by private company) in the position he would have been in if it had not been done.

(2) The following provisions are without prejudice to the generality of the power to make such an order.

(3) Where a private company has—
(a) allotted securities pursuant to an offer to the public, or
(b) allotted or agreed to allot securities with a view to their being offered to the public,

a remedial order may require any person knowingly concerned in the contravention of section 755 to offer to purchase any of those securities at such price and on such other terms as the court thinks fit.

(4) A remedial order may be made—
(a) against any person knowingly concerned in the contravention, whether or not an officer of the company;
(b) notwithstanding anything in the company's constitution (which includes, for this purpose, the terms on which any securities of the company are allotted or held);
(c) whether or not the holder of the securities subject to the order is the person to whom the company allotted or agreed to allot them.

(5) Where a remedial order is made against the company itself, the court may provide for the reduction of the company's capital accordingly.

[1667C]

NOTES
Commencement: 6 April 2008.
Commencement (transitional provisions): see the note to s 758 at **[1667B]**.

760 Validity of allotment etc not affected

Nothing in this Chapter affects the validity of any allotment or sale of securities or of any agreement to allot or sell securities.

[1667D]

NOTES
Commencement: 6 April 2008.

CHAPTER 2
MINIMUM SHARE CAPITAL REQUIREMENT FOR PUBLIC COMPANIES

761 Public company: requirement as to minimum share capital

(1) A company that is a public company (otherwise than by virtue of re-registration as a public company) must not do business or exercise any borrowing powers unless the registrar has issued it with a certificate under this section (a "trading certificate").

(2) The registrar shall issue a trading certificate if, on an application made in accordance with section 762, he is satisfied that the nominal value of the company's allotted share capital is not less than the authorised minimum.

(3) For this purpose a share allotted in pursuance of an employees' share scheme shall not be taken into account unless paid up as to—
(a) at least one-quarter of the nominal value of the share, and
(b) the whole of any premium on the share.

(4) A trading certificate has effect from the date on which it is issued and is conclusive evidence that the company is entitled to do business and exercise any borrowing powers.

[1667E]

NOTES
Commencement: 6 April 2008.

Commencement (transitional provisions): Sch 4, Pt 1, para 26 to the Companies Act 2006 (Commencement No 5, Transitional Provisions and Savings) Order 2007, SI 2007/3495 provides as follows—

"Minimum share capital requirement for public companies (ss 761 to 767)

26.   A certificate issued under section 117 of the 1985 Act or Article 127 of the 1986 Order (public company share capital requirements) has effect on and after 6th April 2008 as if issued under section 761 of the Companies Act 2006.".

762   Procedure for obtaining certificate

(1)   An application for a certificate under section 761 must—

    (a)   state that the nominal value of the company's allotted share capital is not less than the authorised minimum,

    (b)   specify the amount, or estimated amount, of the company's preliminary expenses,

    (c)   specify any amount or benefit paid or given, or intended to be paid or given, to any promoter of the company, and the consideration for the payment or benefit, and

    (d)   be accompanied by a statement of compliance.

(2)   The statement of compliance is a statement that the company meets the requirements for the issue of a certificate under section 761.

(3)   The registrar may accept the statement of compliance as sufficient evidence of the matters stated in it.

                                                          [1667F]

NOTES

Commencement: 6 April 2008.

Commencement (transitional provisions): Sch 4, Pt 1, paras 27, 28 to the Companies Act 2006 (Commencement No 5, Transitional Provisions and Savings) Order 2007, SI 2007/3495 provide as follows—

"27.—(1)   Section 762 of the Companies Act 2006 (procedure for obtaining trading certificate) applies to applications made on or after 6th April 2008.

(2)   Section 117(1) to (5) and (7A) of the 1985 Act or Article 127(1) to (5) and (7A) of the 1986 Order continue to apply to applications made before 6th April 2008.

(3)   An application is treated as made before 6th April 2008 if—

    (a)   a statutory declaration is delivered to the registrar in accordance with section 117(2) of the 1985 Act or Article 127(2) of the 1986 Order, and

    (b)   the declaration was signed before that date.

28.—(1)   Until section 1068(1) of the Companies Act 2006 comes into force—

    (a)   an application under section 762 of that Act must be in the form prescribed for the purposes of section 117(2) of the 1985 Act or Article 127(2) of the 1986 Order;

    (b)   the statement and information required by section 762(1)(a) to (c) must be provided on the form prescribed for the statutory declaration required by section 117(3) of the 1985 Act or Article 127(3) of the 1986 Order (but not in the form of a statutory declaration and disregarding so much of the form as requires other information);

    (c)   a company seeking to satisfy the minimum share capital requirement in euros may adapt the form accordingly; and

    (d)   the form must be signed by a director or by the company secretary.

(2)   A form completed in accordance with sub-paragraph (1) is treated as the statement of compliance required by section 762(1)(d) and (2).

(3)   By adapting the form as mentioned in paragraph (1)(c) the applicant is treated as electing that euros shall be the currency by reference to which it is determined whether the requirement mentioned in section 765(1) is met.

(4)   By not so adapting the form the applicant is treated as electing that sterling shall be that currency.

(5)   Sub-paragraphs (1)(c), (3) and (4) above also apply in relation to the form prescribed for the purposes of section 43(3) of the 1985 Act or Article 53(3) of the 1986 Order (re-registration or private company as public) where a company seeks to satisfy the minimum share capital requirement in section 45(2)(a) of that Act or Article 55(2)(a) of that Order in euros.".

763   The authorised minimum

(1)   "The authorised minimum", in relation to the nominal value of a public company's allotted share capital is—

    (a)   £50,000, or

    (b)   the prescribed euro equivalent.

(2)   The Secretary of State may by order prescribe the amount in euros that is for the time being to be treated as equivalent to the sterling amount of the authorised minimum.

(3)   This power may be exercised from time to time as appears to the Secretary of State to be appropriate.

(4)   The amount prescribed shall be determined by applying an appropriate spot rate of exchange to the sterling amount and rounding to the nearest 100 euros.

(5)   An order under this section is subject to negative resolution procedure.

(6)   This section has effect subject to any exercise of the power conferred by section 764 (power to alter authorised minimum).

[1667G]

NOTES
Commencement: 20 January 2007 (for the purpose of enabling the exercise of powers to make Orders or Regulations by statutory instrument); 6 April 2008 (otherwise).
Regulations: the Companies (Authorised Minimum) Regulations 2008, SI 2008/729 (reg 2 of which prescribes €65,600 as the equivalent amount for the purposes of sub-s (2)).

764   Power to alter authorised minimum

(1)   The Secretary of State may by order—
  (a)   alter the sterling amount of the authorised minimum, and
  (b)   make a corresponding alteration of the prescribed euro equivalent.

(2)   The amount of the prescribed euro equivalent shall be determined by applying an appropriate spot rate of exchange to the sterling amount and rounding to the nearest 100 euros.

(3)   An order under this section that increases the authorised minimum may—
  (a)   require a public company having an allotted share capital of which the nominal value is less than the amount specified in the order to—
      (i)   increase that value to not less than that amount, or
      (ii)   re-register as a private company;
  (b)   make provision in connection with any such requirement for any of the matters for which provision is made by this Act relating to—
      (i)   a company's registration, re-registration or change of name,
      (ii)   payment for shares comprised in a company's share capital, and
      (iii)   offers to the public of shares in or debentures of a company,
including provision as to the consequences (in criminal law or otherwise) of a failure to comply with any requirement of the order;
  (c)   provide for any provision of the order to come into force on different days for different purposes.

(4)   An order under this section is subject to affirmative resolution procedure.

[1667H]

NOTES
Commencement: 20 January 2007 (for the purpose of enabling the exercise of powers to make Orders or Regulations by statutory instrument); 6 April 2008 (otherwise).

765   Authorised minimum: application of initial requirement

(1)   The initial requirement for a public company to have allotted share capital of a nominal value not less than the authorised minimum, that is—
  (a)   the requirement in section 761(2) for the issue of a trading certificate, or
  (b)   the requirement in section 91(1)(a) for re-registration as a public company,
must be met either by reference to allotted share capital denominated in sterling or by reference to allotted share capital denominated in euros (but not partly in one and partly in the other).

(2)   Whether the requirement is met is determined in the first case by reference to the sterling amount and in the second case by reference to the prescribed euro equivalent.

(3)   No account is to be taken of any allotted share capital of the company denominated in a currency other than sterling or, as the case may be, euros.

(4)   If the company could meet the requirement either by reference to share capital denominated in sterling or by reference to share capital denominated in euros, it must elect in its application for a trading certificate or, as the case may be, for re-registration as a public company which is to be the currency by reference to which the matter is determined.

[1667I]

NOTES
Commencement: 6 April 2008.
Commencement (transitional adaptations): art 6 of the Companies Act 2006 (Commencement No 5, Transitional Provisions and Savings) Order 2007, SI 2007/3495 provides that the provisions brought into force by arts 3 and 5 of that Order shall have effect subject to any transitional adaptations specified in Sch 1 to that Order. Schedule 1, Pt 1, para 12 to the Order provides as follows (note that this paragraph is revoked by the Companies Act 2006 (Commencement No 8, Transitional Provisions and Savings) Order 2008, SI 2008/2860, art 6, as from 1 October 2009 (subject to any relevant transitional provision or saving in Sch 2 to that Order))—

"Authorised minimum: application of initial requirement (s 765)

12.—(1)   Section 765 (minimum share capital requirement for public companies: application of initial requirement) has effect with the following adaptation.

(2)   In subsection (1)(b) for "section 91(1)(a)" substitute "section 45(2)(a) of the Companies Act 1985 or Article 55(2)(a) of the Companies (Northern Ireland) Order 1986".".

766   Authorised minimum: application where shares denominated in different currencies etc

(1)   The Secretary of State may make provision by regulations as to the application of the authorised minimum in relation to a public company that—

(a)   has shares denominated in more than one currency,

(b)   redenominates the whole or part of its allotted share capital, or

(c)   allots new shares.

(2)   The regulations may make provision as to the currencies, exchange rates and dates by reference to which it is to be determined whether the nominal value of the company's allotted share capital is less than the authorised minimum.

(3)   The regulations may provide that where—

(a)   a company has redenominated the whole or part of its allotted share capital, and

(b)   the effect of the redenomination is that the nominal value of the company's allotted share capital is less than the authorised minimum,

the company must re-register as a private company.

(4)   Regulations under subsection (3) may make provision corresponding to any provision made by sections 664 to 667 (re-registration as private company in consequence of cancellation of shares).

(5)   Any regulations under this section have effect subject to section 765 (authorised minimum: application of initial requirement).

(6)   Regulations under this section are subject to negative resolution procedure.

[1667J]

NOTES

Commencement: 20 January 2007 (for the purpose of enabling the exercise of powers to make Orders or Regulations by statutory instrument); 6 April 2008 (otherwise).

Commencement (transitional adaptations): art 6 of the Companies Act 2006 (Commencement No 5, Transitional Provisions and Savings) Order 2007, SI 2007/3495 provides that the provisions brought into force by arts 3 and 5 of that Order shall have effect subject to any transitional adaptations specified in Sch 1 to that Order. Schedule 1, Pt 1, para 13 to the Order provides as follows (note that this paragraph is revoked by the Companies Act 2006 (Commencement No 8, Transitional Provisions and Savings) Order 2008, SI 2008/2860, art 6, as from 1 October 2009 (subject to any relevant transitional provision or saving in Sch 2 to that Order))—

"Authorised minimum: application where shares denominated in
different currencies etc (s 766)

13.—(1)   Section 766 (authorised minimum: application where shares denominated in different currencies etc) has effect with the following adaptation.

(2)   In subsection (4) for "sections 664 to 667" substitute "sections 147 to 149 of the Companies Act 1985 or Articles 157 to 159 of the Companies (Northern Ireland) Order 1986".".

Regulations: the Companies (Authorised Minimum) Regulations 2008, SI 2008/729.

767   Consequences of doing business etc without a trading certificate

(1)   If a company does business or exercises any borrowing powers in contravention of section 761, an offence is committed by—

(a)   the company, and

(b)   every officer of the company who is in default.

(2)   A person guilty of an offence under subsection (1) is liable—

(a)   on conviction on indictment, to a fine;

(b)   on summary conviction, to a fine not exceeding the statutory maximum.

(3)   A contravention of section 761 does not affect the validity of a transaction entered into by the company, but if a company—

(a)   enters into a transaction in contravention of that section, and

(b)   fails to comply with its obligations in connection with the transaction within 21 days from being called on to do so,

the directors of the company are jointly and severally liable to indemnify any other party to the transaction in respect of any loss or damage suffered by him by reason of the company's failure to comply with its obligations.

(4)   The directors who are so liable are those who were directors at the time the company entered into the transaction.

[1667K]

NOTES

Commencement: 6 April 2008.

Commencement (transitional provisions): Sch 4, Pt 1, para 29 to the Companies Act 2006 (Commencement No 5, Transitional Provisions and Savings) Order 2007, SI 2007/3495 provides as follows—

"29.—(1)   Section 767 of the Companies Act 2006 (consequences of doing business etc without a trading certificate) applies in relation to things done on or after 6th April 2008.

(2)   Section 117(6), (7) and (8) of the 1985 Act or Article 127(6), (7) and (8) of the 1986 Order continue to apply in relation to things done before that date.".

PART 21
CERTIFICATION AND TRANSFER OF SECURITIES

CHAPTER 1
CERTIFICATION AND TRANSFER OF SECURITIES: GENERAL

Share certificates

768   Share certificate to be evidence of title

(1)   In the case of a company registered in England and Wales or Northern Ireland, a certificate under the common seal of the company specifying any shares held by a member is prima facie evidence of his title to the shares.

(2)   In the case of a company registered in Scotland—
    (a)   a certificate under the common seal of the company specifying any shares held by a member, or
    (b)   a certificate specifying any shares held by a member and subscribed by the company in accordance with the Requirements of Writing (Scotland) Act 1995 (c 7),
is sufficient evidence, unless the contrary is shown, of his title to the shares.

[1667L]

NOTES
Commencement: 6 April 2008.

Issue of certificates etc on allotment

769   Duty of company as to issue of certificates etc on allotment

(1)   A company must, within two months after the allotment of any of its shares, debentures or debenture stock, complete and have ready for delivery—
    (a)   the certificates of the shares allotted,
    (b)   the debentures allotted, or
    (c)   the certificates of the debenture stock allotted.

(2)   Subsection (1) does not apply—
    (a)   if the conditions of issue of the shares, debentures or debenture stock provide otherwise,
    (b)   in the case of allotment to a financial institution (see section 778), or
    (c)   in the case of an allotment of shares if, following the allotment, the company has issued a share warrant in respect of the shares (see section 779).

(3)   If default is made in complying with subsection (1) an offence is committed by every officer of the company who is in default.

(4)   A person guilty of an offence under subsection (3) is liable on summary conviction to a fine not exceeding level 3 on the standard scale and, for continued contravention, a daily default fine not exceeding one-tenth of level 3 on the standard scale.

[1667M]

NOTES
Commencement: 6 April 2008.

Transfer of securities

770   Registration of transfer

(1)   A company may not register a transfer of shares in or debentures of the company unless—
    (a)   a proper instrument of transfer has been delivered to it, or
    (b)   the transfer—
        (i)   is an exempt transfer within the Stock Transfer Act 1982 (c 41), or
        (ii)   is in accordance with regulations under Chapter 2 of this Part.

(2)   Subsection (1) does not affect any power of the company to register as shareholder or debenture holder a person to whom the right to any shares in or debentures of the company has been transmitted by operation of law.

[1668]

NOTES
Commencement: 6 April 2008.

771 Procedure on transfer being lodged

(1) When a transfer of shares in or debentures of a company has been lodged with the company, the company must either—

(a) register the transfer, or

(b) give the transferee notice of refusal to register the transfer, together with its reasons for the refusal,

as soon as practicable and in any event within two months after the date on which the transfer is lodged with it.

(2) If the company refuses to register the transfer, it must provide the transferee with such further information about the reasons for the refusal as the transferee may reasonably request.

This does not include copies of minutes of meetings of directors.

(3) If a company fails to comply with this section, an offence is committed by—

(a) the company, and

(b) every officer of the company who is in default.

(4) A person guilty of an offence under this section is liable on summary conviction to a fine not exceeding level 3 on the standard scale and, for continued contravention, a daily default fine not exceeding one-tenth of level 3 on the standard scale.

(5) This section does not apply—

(a) in relation to a transfer of shares if the company has issued a share warrant in respect of the shares (see section 779);

(b) in relation to the transmission of shares or debentures by operation of law.

[1668A]

NOTES
Commencement: 6 April 2008.
Commencement (transitional provisions): Sch 4, Pt 1, para 30 to the Companies Act 2006 (Commencement No 5, Transitional Provisions and Savings) Order 2007, SI 2007/3495 provides as follows—

"Certification and transfer of securities (ss 769 to 782)"

30. Section 771 of the Companies Act 2006 (procedure on transfer being lodged) applies to transfers lodged with the company on or after 6th April 2008.".

772 Transfer of shares on application of transferor

On the application of the transferor of any share or interest in a company, the company shall enter in its register of members the name of the transferee in the same manner and subject to the same conditions as if the application for the entry were made by the transferee.

[1668B]

NOTES
Commencement: 6 April 2008.

773 Execution of share transfer by personal representative

An instrument of transfer of the share or other interest of a deceased member of a company—

(a) may be made by his personal representative although the personal representative is not himself a member of the company, and

(b) is as effective as if the personal representative had been such a member at the time of the execution of the instrument.

[1668C]

NOTES
Commencement: 6 April 2008.

774 Evidence of grant of probate etc

The production to a company of any document that is by law sufficient evidence of the grant of—

(a) probate of the will of a deceased person,

(b) letters of administration of the estate of a deceased person, or

(c) confirmation as executor of a deceased person,

shall be accepted by the company as sufficient evidence of the grant.

[1668D]

775 Certification of instrument of transfer

(1)   The certification by a company of an instrument of transfer of any shares in, or debentures of, the company is to be taken as a representation by the company to any person acting on the faith of the certification that there have been produced to the company such documents as on their face show a prima facie title to the shares or debentures in the transferor named in the instrument.

(2)   The certification is not to be taken as a representation that the transferor has any title to the shares or debentures.

(3)   Where a person acts on the faith of a false certification by a company made negligently, the company is under the same liability to him as if the certification had been made fraudulently.

(4)   For the purposes of this section—
  (a)   an instrument of transfer is certificated if it bears the words "certificate lodged" (or words to the like effect);
  (b)   the certification of an instrument of transfer is made by a company if—
    (i)   the person issuing the instrument is a person authorised to issue certificated instruments of transfer on the company's behalf, and
    (ii)   the certification is signed by a person authorised to certificate transfers on the company's behalf or by an officer or employee either of the company or of a body corporate so authorised;
  (c)   a certification is treated as signed by a person if—
    (i)   it purports to be authenticated by his signature or initials (whether handwritten or not), and
    (ii)   it is not shown that the signature or initials was or were placed there neither by himself nor by a person authorised to use the signature or initials for the purpose of certificating transfers on the company's behalf.

[1668E]

Issue of certificates etc on transfer

776 Duty of company as to issue of certificates etc on transfer

(1)   A company must, within two months after the date on which a transfer of any of its shares, debentures or debenture stock is lodged with the company, complete and have ready for delivery—
  (a)   the certificates of the shares transferred,
  (b)   the debentures transferred, or
  (c)   the certificates of the debenture stock transferred.

(2)   For this purpose a "transfer" means—
  (a)   a transfer duly stamped and otherwise valid, or
  (b)   an exempt transfer within the Stock Transfer Act 1982 (c 41),

but does not include a transfer that the company is for any reason entitled to refuse to register and does not register.

(3)   Subsection (1) does not apply—
  (a)   if the conditions of issue of the shares, debentures or debenture stock provide otherwise,
  (b)   in the case of a transfer to a financial institution (see section 778), or
  (c)   in the case of a transfer of shares if, following the transfer, the company has issued a share warrant in respect of the shares (see section 779).

(4)   Subsection (1) has effect subject to section 777 (cases where the Stock Transfer Act 1982 applies).

(5)   If default is made in complying with subsection (1) an offence is committed by every officer of the company who is in default.

(6)   A person guilty of an offence under this section is liable on summary conviction to a fine not exceeding level 3 on the standard scale and, for continued contravention, a daily default fine not exceeding one-tenth of level 3 on the standard scale.

[1668F]

777   Issue of certificates etc: cases within the Stock Transfer Act 1982

(1)   Section 776(1) (duty of company as to issue of certificates etc on transfer) does not apply in the case of a transfer to a person where, by virtue of regulations under section 3 of the Stock Transfer Act 1982, he is not entitled to a certificate or other document of or evidencing title in respect of the securities transferred.

(2)   But if in such a case the transferee—
     (a)   subsequently becomes entitled to such a certificate or other document by virtue of any provision of those regulations, and
     (b)   gives notice in writing of that fact to the company,

section 776 (duty to company as to issue of certificates etc) has effect as if the reference in subsection (1) of that section to the date of the lodging of the transfer were a reference to the date of the notice.

[1668G]

NOTES
Commencement: 6 April 2008.

Issue of certificates etc on allotment or transfer to financial institution

778   Issue of certificates etc: allotment or transfer to financial institution

(1)   A company—
     (a)   of which shares or debentures are allotted to a financial institution,
     (b)   of which debenture stock is allotted to a financial institution, or
     (c)   with which a transfer for transferring shares, debentures or debenture stock to a financial institution is lodged,

is not required in consequence of that allotment or transfer to comply with section 769(1) or 776(1) (duty of company as to issue of certificates etc).

(2)   A "financial institution" means—
     (a)   a recognised clearing house acting in relation to a recognised investment exchange, or
     (b)   a nominee of—
         (i)   a recognised clearing house acting in that way, or
         (ii)   a recognised investment exchange,
     designated for the purposes of this section in the rules of the recognised investment exchange in question.

(3)   Expressions used in subsection (2) have the same meaning as in Part 18 of the Financial Services and Markets Act 2000 (c 8).

[1668H]

NOTES
Commencement: 6 April 2008.

Share warrants

779   Issue and effect of share warrant to bearer

(1)   A company limited by shares may, if so authorised by its articles, issue with respect to any fully paid shares a warrant (a "share warrant") stating that the bearer of the warrant is entitled to the shares specified in it.

(2)   A share warrant issued under the company's common seal or (in the case of a company registered in Scotland) subscribed in accordance with the Requirements of Writing (Scotland) Act 1995 (c 7) entitles the bearer to the shares specified in it and the shares may be transferred by delivery of the warrant.

(3)   A company that issues a share warrant may, if so authorised by its articles, provide (by coupons or otherwise) for the payment of the future dividends on the shares included in the warrant.

[1668I]

NOTES
Commencement: 6 April 2008.

780   Duty of company as to issue of certificates on surrender of share warrant

(1)   A company must, within two months of the surrender of a share warrant for cancellation, complete and have ready for delivery the certificates of the shares specified in the warrant.

(2)   Subsection (1) does not apply if the company's articles provide otherwise.

(3)   If default is made in complying with subsection (1) an offence is committed by every officer of the company who is in default.

PART II
OTHER ACTS

(4)   A person guilty of an offence under subsection (3) is liable on summary conviction to a fine not exceeding level 3 on the standard scale and, for continued contravention, a daily default fine not exceeding one-tenth of level 3 on the standard scale.

[1668J]

NOTES
Commencement: 6 April 2008.
Commencement (transitional provisions): Sch 4, Pt 1, para 31 to the Companies Act 2006 (Commencement No 5, Transitional Provisions and Savings) Order 2007, SI 2007/3495 provides as follows—
"31.   Section 780 of the Companies Act 2006 (duty of company as to issue of certificates on surrender of share warrant) applies to share warrants surrendered on or after 6th April 2008.".

781   Offences in connection with share warrants (Scotland)

(1)   If in Scotland a person—
   (a)   with intent to defraud, forges or alters, or offers, utters, disposes of, or puts off, knowing the same to be forged or altered, any share warrant or coupon, or any document purporting to be a share warrant or coupon issued in pursuance of this Act, or
   (b)   by means of any such forged or altered share warrant, coupon or document—
      (i)   demands or endeavours to obtain or receive any share or interest in a company under this Act, or
      (ii)   demands or endeavours to receive any dividend or money payment in respect of any such share or interest,
   knowing the warrant, coupon or document to be forged or altered,
he commits an offence.

(2)   If in Scotland a person without lawful authority or excuse (of which proof lies on him)—
   (a)   engraves or makes on any plate, wood, stone, or other material, any share warrant or coupon purporting to be—
      (i)   a share warrant or coupon issued or made by any particular company in pursuance of this Act, or
      (ii)   a blank share warrant or coupon so issued or made, or
      (iii)   a part of such a share warrant or coupon, or
   (b)   uses any such plate, wood, stone, or other material, for the making or printing of any such share warrant or coupon, or of any such blank share warrant or coupon or of any part of such a share warrant or coupon, or
   (c)   knowingly has in his custody or possession any such plate, wood, stone, or other material,
he commits an offence.

(3)   A person guilty of an offence under subsection (1) is liable on summary conviction to imprisonment for a term not exceeding six months or to a fine not exceeding level 5 on the standard scale (or both).

(4)   A person guilty of an offence under subsection (2) is liable—
   (a)   on conviction on indictment, to imprisonment for a term not exceeding seven years or a fine (or both);
   (b)   on summary conviction, to imprisonment for a term not exceeding six months or a fine not exceeding the statutory maximum (or both).

[1668K]

NOTES
Commencement: 6 April 2008.

Supplementary provisions

782   Issue of certificates etc: court order to make good default

(1)   If a company on which a notice has been served requiring it to make good any default in complying with—
   (a)   section 769(1) (duty of company as to issue of certificates etc on allotment),
   (b)   section 776(1) (duty of company as to issue of certificates etc on transfer), or
   (c)   section 780(1) (duty of company as to issue of certificates etc on surrender of share warrant),
fails to make good the default within ten days after service of the notice, the person entitled to have the certificates or the debentures delivered to him may apply to the court.

(2)   The court may on such an application make an order directing the company and any officer of it to make good the default within such time as may be specified in the order.

(3)   The order may provide that all costs (in Scotland, expenses) of and incidental to the application are to be borne by the company or by an officer of it responsible for the default.

[1668L]

NOTES
Commencement: 6 April 2008.

CHAPTER 2
EVIDENCING AND TRANSFER OF TITLE TO SECURITIES WITHOUT
WRITTEN INSTRUMENT

Introductory

783   Scope of this Chapter

In this Chapter—
(a)   "securities" means shares, debentures, debenture stock, loan stock, bonds, units of a collective investment scheme within the meaning of the Financial Services and Markets Act 2000 (c 8) and other securities of any description;
(b)   references to title to securities include any legal or equitable interest in securities;
(c)   references to a transfer of title include a transfer by way of security;
(d)   references to transfer without a written instrument include, in relation to bearer securities, transfer without delivery.

[1668M]

NOTES
Commencement: 6 April 2008.

784   Power to make regulations

(1)   The power to make regulations under this Chapter is exercisable by the Treasury and the Secretary of State, either jointly or concurrently.

(2)   References in this Chapter to the authority having power to make regulations shall accordingly be read as references to both or either of them, as the case may require.

(3)   Regulations under this Chapter are subject to affirmative resolution procedure.

[1668N]

NOTES
Commencement: 20 January 2007 (for the purpose of enabling the exercise of powers to make Orders or Regulations by statutory instrument); 6 April 2008 (otherwise).
Regulations: by virtue of s 1297 of this Act (continuity of law) the Uncertificated Securities Regulations 2001, SI 2001/3755 (at **[3581]**) have effect as if made under this section.

Powers exercisable

785   Provision enabling procedures for evidencing and transferring title

(1)   Provision may be made by regulations for enabling title to securities to be evidenced and transferred without a written instrument.

(2)   The regulations may make provision—
(a)   for procedures for recording and transferring title to securities, and
(b)   for the regulation of those procedures and the persons responsible for or involved in their operation.

(3)   The regulations must contain such safeguards as appear to the authority making the regulations appropriate for the protection of investors and for ensuring that competition is not restricted, distorted or prevented.

(4)   The regulations may, for the purpose of enabling or facilitating the operation of the procedures provided for by the regulations, make provision with respect to the rights and obligations of persons in relation to securities dealt with under the procedures.

(5)   The regulations may include provision for the purpose of giving effect to—
(a)   the transmission of title to securities by operation of law;
(b)   any restriction on the transfer of title to securities arising by virtue of the provisions of any enactment or instrument, court order or agreement;
(c)   any power conferred by any such provision on a person to deal with securities on behalf of the person entitled.

(6)   The regulations may make provision with respect to the persons responsible for the operation of the procedures provided for by the regulations—
(a)   as to the consequences of their insolvency or incapacity, or

    (b)   as to the transfer from them to other persons of their functions in relation to those
procedures.

[1668O]

NOTES
Commencement: 20 January 2007 (for the purpose of enabling the exercise of powers to make Orders or
Regulations by statutory instrument); 6 April 2008 (otherwise).
Regulations: by virtue of s 1297 of this Act (continuity of law) the Uncertificated Securities Regulations 2001,
SI 2001/3755 (at **[3581]**) have effect as if made under this section.

786 Provision enabling or requiring arrangements to be adopted

(1)   Regulations under this Chapter may make provision—
    (a)   enabling the members of a company or of any designated class of companies to adopt,
by ordinary resolution, arrangements under which title to securities is required to be
evidenced or transferred (or both) without a written instrument; or
    (b)   requiring companies, or any designated class of companies, to adopt such arrangements.

(2)   The regulations may make such provision—
    (a)   in respect of all securities issued by a company, or
    (b)   in respect of all securities of a specified description.

(3)   The arrangements provided for by regulations making such provision as is mentioned in
subsection (1)—
    (a)   must not be such that a person who but for the arrangements would be entitled to have
his name entered in the company's register of members ceases to be so entitled, and
    (b)   must be such that a person who but for the arrangements would be entitled to exercise
any rights in respect of the securities continues to be able effectively to control the
exercise of those rights.

(4)   The regulations may—
    (a)   prohibit the issue of any certificate by the company in respect of the issue or transfer of
securities,
    (b)   require the provision by the company to holders of securities of statements (at specified
intervals or on specified occasions) of the securities held in their name, and
    (c)   make provision as to the matters of which any such certificate or statement is, or is not,
evidence.

(5)   In this section—
    (a)   references to a designated class of companies are to a class designated in the regulations
or by order under section 787; and
    (b)   "specified" means specified in the regulations.

[1668P]

NOTES
Commencement: 20 January 2007 (for the purpose of enabling the exercise of powers to make Orders or
Regulations by statutory instrument); 6 April 2008 (otherwise).

787 Provision enabling or requiring arrangements to be adopted: order-making powers

(1)   The authority having power to make regulations under this Chapter may by order—
    (a)   designate classes of companies for the purposes of section 786 (provision enabling or
requiring arrangements to be adopted);
    (b)   provide that, in relation to securities of a specified description—
        (i)   in a designated class of companies, or
        (ii)   in a specified company or class of companies,
specified provisions of regulations made under this Chapter by virtue of that section either do
not apply or apply subject to specified modifications.

(2)   In subsection (1) "specified" means specified in the order.

(3)   An order under this section is subject to negative resolution procedure.

[1668Q]

NOTES
Commencement: 20 January 2007 (for the purpose of enabling the exercise of powers to make Orders or
Regulations by statutory instrument); 6 April 2008 (otherwise).

Supplementary

788 Provision that may be included in regulations

Regulations under this Chapter may—
    (a)   modify or exclude any provision of any enactment or instrument, or any rule of law;

    (b)   apply, with such modifications as may be appropriate, the provisions of any enactment or instrument (including provisions creating criminal offences);

    (c)   require the payment of fees, or enable persons to require the payment of fees, of such amounts as may be specified in the regulations or determined in accordance with them;

    (d)   empower the authority making the regulations to delegate to any person willing and able to discharge them any functions of the authority under the regulations.

[1668R]

NOTES

    Commencement: 20 January 2007 (for the purpose of enabling the exercise of powers to make Orders or Regulations by statutory instrument); 6 April 2008 (otherwise).

    Regulations: by virtue of s 1297 of this Act (continuity of law) the Uncertificated Securities Regulations 2001, SI 2001/3755 (at **[3581]**) have effect as if made under this section.

789   Duty to consult

Before making—

    (a)   regulations under this Chapter, or

    (b)   any order under section 787,

the authority having power to make regulations under this Chapter must carry out such consultation as appears to it to be appropriate.

[1668S]

NOTES

    Commencement: 20 January 2007 (for the purpose of enabling the exercise of powers to make Orders or Regulations by statutory instrument); 6 April 2008 (otherwise).

790   Resolutions to be forwarded to registrar

Chapter 3 of Part 3 (resolutions affecting a company's constitution) applies to a resolution passed by virtue of regulations under this Chapter.

[1668T]

NOTES

    Commencement: 6 April 2008.

PART 22
INFORMATION ABOUT INTERESTS IN A COMPANY'S SHARES

Introductory

791   Companies to which this Part applies

This Part applies only to public companies.

[1668U]

NOTES

    Commencement: 20 January 2007.

792   Shares to which this Part applies

    (1)   References in this Part to a company's shares are to the company's issued shares of a class carrying rights to vote in all circumstances at general meetings of the company (including any shares held as treasury shares).

    (2)   The temporary suspension of voting rights in respect of any shares does not affect the application of this Part in relation to interests in those or any other shares.

[1668V]

NOTES

    Commencement: 20 January 2007.

Notice requiring information about interests in shares

793   Notice by company requiring information about interests in its shares

    (1)   A public company may give notice under this section to any person whom the company knows or has reasonable cause to believe—

    (a)   to be interested in the company's shares, or

    (b)   to have been so interested at any time during the three years immediately preceding the date on which the notice is issued.

    (2)   The notice may require the person—

(a)   to confirm that fact or (as the case may be) to state whether or not it is the case, and
(b)   if he holds, or has during that time held, any such interest, to give such further information as may be required in accordance with the following provisions of this section.

(3)   The notice may require the person to whom it is addressed to give particulars of his own present or past interest in the company's shares (held by him at any time during the three year period mentioned in subsection (1)(b)).

(4)   The notice may require the person to whom it is addressed, where—
(a)   his interest is a present interest and another interest in the shares subsists, or
(b)   another interest in the shares subsisted during that three year period at a time when his interest subsisted,
to give, so far as lies within his knowledge, such particulars with respect to that other interest as may be required by the notice.

(5)   The particulars referred to in subsections (3) and (4) include—
(a)   the identity of persons interested in the shares in question, and
(b)   whether persons interested in the same shares are or were parties to—
    (i)   an agreement to which section 824 applies (certain share acquisition agreements), or
    (ii)   an agreement or arrangement relating to the exercise of any rights conferred by the holding of the shares.

(6)   The notice may require the person to whom it is addressed, where his interest is a past interest, to give (so far as lies within his knowledge) particulars of the identity of the person who held that interest immediately upon his ceasing to hold it.

(7)   The information required by the notice must be given within such reasonable time as may be specified in the notice.

[1668W]

NOTES
Commencement: 20 January 2007.

794   Notice requiring information: order imposing restrictions on shares
(1)   Where—
(a)   a notice under section 793 (notice requiring information about interests in company's shares) is served by a company on a person who is or was interested in shares in the company, and
(b)   that person fails to give the company the information required by the notice within the time specified in it,
the company may apply to the court for an order directing that the shares in question be subject to restrictions.
For the effect of such an order see section 797.

(2)   If the court is satisfied that such an order may unfairly affect the rights of third parties in respect of the shares, the court may, for the purpose of protecting those rights and subject to such terms as it thinks fit, direct that such acts by such persons or descriptions of persons and for such purposes as may be set out in the order shall not constitute a breach of the restrictions.

(3)   On an application under this section the court may make an interim order. Any such order may be made unconditionally or on such terms as the court thinks fit.

(4)   Sections 798 to 802 make further provision about orders under this section.

[1668X]

NOTES
Commencement: 20 January 2007.

795   Notice requiring information: offences
(1)   A person who—
(a)   fails to comply with a notice under section 793 (notice requiring information about interests in company's shares), or
(b)   in purported compliance with such a notice—
    (i)   makes a statement that he knows to be false in a material particular, or
    (ii)   recklessly makes a statement that is false in a material particular,
commits an offence.

(2)   A person does not commit an offence under subsection (1)(a) if he proves that the requirement to give information was frivolous or vexatious.

(3) A person guilty of an offence under this section is liable—
    (a) on conviction on indictment, to imprisonment for a term not exceeding two years or a fine (or both);
    (b) on summary conviction—
        (i) in England and Wales, to imprisonment for a term not exceeding twelve months or to a fine not exceeding the statutory maximum (or both);
        (ii) in Scotland or Northern Ireland, to imprisonment for a term not exceeding six months, or to a fine not exceeding the statutory maximum (or both).

[1668Y]

NOTES
Commencement: 20 January 2007.
Imprisonment for a term not exceeding twelve months: see the note to s 387 at **[1514]**.

796 Notice requiring information: persons exempted from obligation to comply

(1) A person is not obliged to comply with a notice under section 793 (notice requiring information about interests in company's shares) if he is for the time being exempted by the Secretary of State from the operation of that section.

(2) The Secretary of State must not grant any such exemption unless—
    (a) he has consulted the Governor of the Bank of England, and
    (b) he (the Secretary of State) is satisfied that, having regard to any undertaking given by the person in question with respect to any interest held or to be held by him in any shares, there are special reasons why that person should not be subject to the obligations imposed by that section.

[1668Z]

NOTES
Commencement: 20 January 2007.

Orders imposing restrictions on shares

797 Consequences of order imposing restrictions

(1) The effect of an order under section 794 that shares are subject to restrictions is as follows—
    (a) any transfer of the shares is void;
    (b) no voting rights are exercisable in respect of the shares;
    (c) no further shares may be issued in right of the shares or in pursuance of an offer made to their holder;
    (d) except in a liquidation, no payment may be made of sums due from the company on the shares, whether in respect of capital or otherwise.

(2) Where shares are subject to the restriction in subsection (1)(a), an agreement to transfer the shares is void.

This does not apply to an agreement to transfer the shares on the making of an order under section 800 made by virtue of subsection (3)(b) (removal of restrictions in case of court-approved transfer).

(3) Where shares are subject to the restriction in subsection (1)(c) or (d), an agreement to transfer any right to be issued with other shares in right of those shares, or to receive any payment on them (otherwise than in a liquidation), is void.

This does not apply to an agreement to transfer any such right on the making of an order under section 800 made by virtue of subsection (3)(b) (removal of restrictions in case of court-approved transfer).

(4) The provisions of this section are subject—
    (a) to any directions under section 794(2) or section 799(3) (directions for protection of third parties), and
    (b) in the case of an interim order under section 794(3), to the terms of the order.

[1669]

NOTES
Commencement: 20 January 2007.

798 Penalty for attempted evasion of restrictions

(1) This section applies where shares are subject to restrictions by virtue of an order under section 794.

(2) A person commits an offence if he—
    (a) exercises or purports to exercise any right—

      (i)   to dispose of shares that to his knowledge, are for the time being subject to restrictions, or

      (ii) to dispose of any right to be issued with any such shares, or

(b)   votes in respect of any such shares (whether as holder or proxy), or appoints a proxy to vote in respect of them, or

(c)   being the holder of any such shares, fails to notify of their being subject to those restrictions a person whom he does not know to be aware of that fact but does know to be entitled (apart from the restrictions) to vote in respect of those shares whether as holder or as proxy, or

(d)   being the holder of any such shares, or being entitled to a right to be issued with other shares in right of them, or to receive any payment on them (otherwise than in a liquidation), enters into an agreement which is void under section 797(2) or (3).

(3)   If shares in a company are issued in contravention of the restrictions, an offence is committed by—

    (a)   the company, and

    (b)   every officer of the company who is in default.

(4)   A person guilty of an offence under this section is liable—

    (a)   on conviction on indictment, to a fine;

    (b)   on summary conviction, to a fine not exceeding the statutory maximum.

(5)   The provisions of this section are subject—

    (a)   to any directions under—

        section 794(2) (directions for protection of third parties), or

        section 799 or 800 (relaxation or removal of restrictions), and

    (b)   in the case of an interim order under section 794(3), to the terms of the order.

[1669A]

NOTES

Commencement: 20 January 2007.

799 Relaxation of restrictions

(1)   An application may be made to the court on the ground that an order directing that shares shall be subject to restrictions unfairly affects the rights of third parties in respect of the shares.

(2)   An application for an order under this section may be made by the company or by any person aggrieved.

(3)   If the court is satisfied that the application is well-founded, it may, for the purpose of protecting the rights of third parties in respect of the shares, and subject to such terms as it thinks fit, direct that such acts by such persons or descriptions of persons and for such purposes as may be set out in the order do not constitute a breach of the restrictions.

[1669B]

NOTES

Commencement: 20 January 2007.

800 Removal of restrictions

(1)   An application may be made to the court for an order directing that the shares shall cease to be subject to restrictions.

(2)   An application for an order under this section may be made by the company or by any person aggrieved.

(3)   The court must not make an order under this section unless—

    (a)   it is satisfied that the relevant facts about the shares have been disclosed to the company and no unfair advantage has accrued to any person as a result of the earlier failure to make that disclosure, or

    (b)   the shares are to be transferred for valuable consideration and the court approves the transfer.

(4)   An order under this section made by virtue of subsection (3)(b) may continue, in whole or in part, the restrictions mentioned in section 797(1)(c) and (d) (restrictions on issue of further shares or making of payments) so far as they relate to a right acquired or offer made before the transfer.

(5)   Where any restrictions continue in force under subsection (4)—

    (a)   an application may be made under this section for an order directing that the shares shall cease to be subject to those restrictions, and

    (b)   subsection (3) does not apply in relation to the making of such an order.

[1669C]

801   Order for sale of shares

(1)   The court may order that the shares subject to restrictions be sold, subject to the court's approval as to the sale.

(2)   An application for an order under subsection (1) may only be made by the company.

(3)   Where the court has made an order under this section, it may make such further order relating to the sale or transfer of the shares as it thinks fit.

(4)   An application for an order under subsection (3) may be made—
  (a)   by the company,
  (b)   by the person appointed by or in pursuance of the order to effect the sale, or
  (c)   by any person interested in the shares.

(5)   On making an order under subsection (1) or (3) the court may order that the applicant's costs (in Scotland, expenses) be paid out of the proceeds of sale.

[1669D]

802   Application of proceeds of sale under court order

(1)   Where shares are sold in pursuance of an order of the court under section 801, the proceeds of the sale, less the costs of the sale, must be paid into court for the benefit of the persons who are beneficially interested in the shares.

(2)   A person who is beneficially interested in the shares may apply to the court for the whole or part of those proceeds to be paid to him.

(3)   On such an application the court shall order the payment to the applicant of—
  (a)   the whole of the proceeds of sale together with any interest on them, or
  (b)   if another person had a beneficial interest in the shares at the time of their sale, such proportion of the proceeds and interest as the value of the applicant's interest in the shares bears to the total value of the shares.

This is subject to the following qualification.

(4)   If the court has ordered under section 801(5) that the costs (in Scotland, expenses) of an applicant under that section are to be paid out of the proceeds of sale, the applicant is entitled to payment of his costs (or expenses) out of those proceeds before any person interested in the shares receives any part of those proceeds.

[1669E]

Power of members to require company to act

803   Power of members to require company to act

(1)   The members of a company may require it to exercise its powers under section 793 (notice requiring information about interests in shares).

(2)   A company is required to do so once it has received requests (to the same effect) from members of the company holding at least 10% of such of the paid-up capital of the company as carries a right to vote at general meetings of the company (excluding any voting rights attached to any shares in the company held as treasury shares).

(3)   A request—
  (a)   may be in hard copy form or in electronic form,
  (b)   must—
    (i)   state that the company is requested to exercise its powers under section 793,
    (ii)   specify the manner in which the company is requested to act, and
    (iii) give reasonable grounds for requiring the company to exercise those powers in the manner specified, and
  (c)   must be authenticated by the person or persons making it.

[1669F]

804 Duty of company to comply with requirement

(1)   A company that is required under section 803 to exercise its powers under section 793 (notice requiring information about interests in company's shares) must exercise those powers in the manner specified in the requests.

(2)   If default is made in complying with subsection (1) an offence is committed by every officer of the company who is in default.

(3)   A person guilty of an offence under this section is liable—
   (a)   on conviction on indictment, to a fine;
   (b)   on summary conviction, to a fine not exceeding the statutory maximum.

[1669G]

NOTES
Commencement: 20 January 2007.

---

805 Report to members on outcome of investigation

(1)   On the conclusion of an investigation carried out by a company in pursuance of a requirement under section 803 the company must cause a report of the information received in pursuance of the investigation to be prepared.

The report must be made available for inspection within a reasonable period (not more than 15 days) after the conclusion of the investigation.

(2)   Where—
   (a)   a company undertakes an investigation in pursuance of a requirement under section 803, and
   (b)   the investigation is not concluded within three months after the date on which the company became subject to the requirement,
the company must cause to be prepared in respect of that period, and in respect of each succeeding period of three months ending before the conclusion of the investigation, an interim report of the information received during that period in pursuance of the investigation.

(3)   Each such report must be made available for inspection within a reasonable period (not more than 15 days) after the end of the period to which it relates.

(4)   The reports must be retained by the company for at least six years from the date on which they are first made available for inspection and must be kept available for inspection during that time—
   (a)   at the company's registered office, or
   (b)   at a place specified in regulations under section 1136.

(5)   The company must give notice to the registrar—
   (a)   of the place at which the reports are kept available for inspection, and
   (b)   of any change in that place,
unless they have at all times been kept at the company's registered office.

(6)   The company must within three days of making any report prepared under this section available for inspection, notify the members who made the requests under section 803 where the report is so available.

(7)   For the purposes of this section an investigation carried out by a company in pursuance of a requirement under section 803 is concluded when—
   (a)   the company has made all such inquiries as are necessary or expedient for the purposes of the requirement, and
   (b)   in the case of each such inquiry—
     (i)   a response has been received by the company, or
     (ii)   the time allowed for a response has elapsed.

[1669H]

NOTES
Commencement: 20 January 2007.

---

806 Report to members: offences

(1)   If default is made for 14 days in complying with section 805(5) (notice to registrar of place at which reports made available for inspection) an offence is committed by—
   (a)   the company, and
   (b)   every officer of the company who is in default.

(2)   A person guilty of an offence under subsection (1) is liable on summary conviction to a fine not exceeding level 3 on the standard scale and, for continued contravention, a daily default fine not exceeding one-tenth of level 3 on the standard scale.

(3) If default is made in complying with any other provision of section 805 (report to members on outcome of investigation), an offence is committed by every officer of the company who is in default.

(4) A person guilty of an offence under subsection (3) is liable—
  (a) on conviction on indictment, to a fine;
  (b) on summary conviction, to a fine not exceeding the statutory maximum.

[1669I]

NOTES
  Commencement: 20 January 2007.

807 Right to inspect and request copy of reports

(1) Any report prepared under section 805 must be open to inspection by any person without charge.

(2) Any person is entitled, on request and on payment of such fee as may be prescribed, to be provided with a copy of any such report or any part of it. The copy must be provided within ten days after the request is received by the company.

(3) If an inspection required under subsection (1) is refused, or default is made in complying with subsection (2), an offence is committed by—
  (a) the company, and
  (b) every officer of the company who is in default.

(4) A person guilty of an offence under this section is liable on summary conviction to a fine not exceeding level 3 on the standard scale and, for continued contravention, a daily default fine not exceeding one-tenth of level 3 on the standard scale.

(5) In the case of any such refusal or default the court may by order compel an immediate inspection or, as the case may be, direct that the copy required be sent to the person requiring it.

[1669J]

NOTES
  Commencement: 20 January 2007.
  Regulations: the Companies (Fees for Inspection and Copying of Company Records) Regulations 2007, SI 2007/2612.

Register of interests disclosed

808 Register of interests disclosed

(1) The company must keep a register of information received by it in pursuance of a requirement imposed under section 793 (notice requiring information about interests in company's shares).

(2) A company which receives any such information must, within three days of the receipt, enter in the register—
  (a) the fact that the requirement was imposed and the date on which it was imposed, and
  (b) the information received in pursuance of the requirement.

(3) The information must be entered against the name of the present holder of the shares in question or, if there is no present holder or the present holder is not known, against the name of the person holding the interest.

(4) The register must be made up so that the entries against the names entered in it appear in chronological order.

(5) If default is made in complying with this section an offence is committed by—
  (a) the company, and
  (b) every officer of the company who is in default.

(6) A person guilty of an offence under this section is liable on summary conviction to a fine not exceeding level 3 on the standard scale and, for continued contravention, a daily default fine not exceeding one-tenth of level 3 on the standard scale.

(7) The company is not by virtue of anything done for the purposes of this section affected with notice of, or put upon inquiry as to, the rights of any person in relation to any shares.

[1669K]

NOTES
  Commencement: 20 January 2007.
  Commencement (transitional provisions): the Companies Act 2006 (Commencement No 1, Transitional Provisions and Savings) Order 2006, SI 2006/3428, Sch 5, Pt 2, para 2 (as amended by the Companies Act 2006 (Commencement No 5, Transitional Provisions and Savings) Order 2007, SI 2007/3495, art 11, Sch 5, para 1, as from 14 January 2008) provides as follows—

"2   Information about interests in a company's shares

(1)   The repeal of sections 198 to 210 and 220 of the 1985 Act or Articles 206 to 218 and 228 of the 1986 Order (obligation to disclose acquisitions and disposals of interests in shares) does not affect any obligation to which a person became subject under section 198 of that Act or Article 206 of that Order before 20th January 2007.

(2)   The repeal of sections 212 to 220 of the 1985 Act or Articles 220 to 228 of the 1986 Order (power of public company to require disclosure of interests in shares) does not affect the operation of those provisions in relation to a notice issued by a company under section 212 of the 1985 Act or Article 220 of the 1986 Order before 20th January 2007.

(3)   On and after 20th January 2007 any separate part of a register kept by a company under section 213 of the 1985 Act or Article 221 of the 1986 Order (register of interests disclosed in response to requirement by company) shall continue to be kept by the company and shall be treated as a register kept under and for the purposes of section 808 of the Companies Act 2006.

(4)   Until regulations under section 1136 of the Companies Act 2006 (regulations about where certain company records are to be kept available for inspection) [come into force] specifying a place for the purposes of section 809(1)(b) of that Act—

   (a)   the register kept under section 808 of that Act (register of interests disclosed) may be kept by a company at any place where its register of members is kept; and
   (b)   no notice need be given to the registrar of companies under section 809(2) of that Act.".

809   Register to be kept available for inspection

(1)   The register kept under section 808 (register of interests disclosed) must be kept available for inspection—

   (a)   at the company's registered office, or
   (b)   at a place specified in regulations under section 1136.

(2)   A company must give notice to the registrar of companies of the place where the register is kept available for inspection and of any change in that place.

(3)   No such notice is required if the register has at all times been kept available for inspection at the company's registered office.

(4)   If default is made in complying with subsection (1), or a company makes default for 14 days in complying with subsection (2), an offence is committed by—

   (a)   the company, and
   (b)   every officer of the company who is in default.

(5)   A person guilty of an offence under this section is liable on summary conviction to a fine not exceeding level 3 on the standard scale and, for continued contravention, a daily default fine not exceeding one-tenth of level 3 on the standard scale.

[1669L]

NOTES

Commencement: 20 January 2007.
Commencement (transitional provisions): see the note to s 808 at **[1669K]**.

810   Associated index

(1)   Unless the register kept under section 808 (register of interests disclosed) is kept in such a form as itself to constitute an index, the company must keep an index of the names entered in it.

(2)   The company must make any necessary entry or alteration in the index within ten days after the date on which any entry or alteration is made in the register.

(3)   The index must contain, in respect of each name, a sufficient indication to enable the information entered against it to be readily found.

(4)   The index must be at all times kept available for inspection at the same place as the register.

(5)   If default is made in complying with this section, an offence is committed by—

   (a)   the company, and
   (b)   every officer of the company who is in default.

(6)   A person guilty of an offence under this section is liable on summary conviction to a fine not exceeding level 3 on the standard scale and, for continued contravention, a daily default fine not exceeding one-tenth of level 3 on the standard scale.

[1669M]

NOTES

Commencement: 20 January 2007.

811   Rights to inspect and require copy of entries

(1)   The register required to be kept under section 808 (register of interests disclosed), and any associated index, must be open to inspection by any person without charge.

(2)   Any person is entitled, on request and on payment of such fee as may be prescribed, to be provided with a copy of any entry in the register.

(3)   A person seeking to exercise either of the rights conferred by this section must make a request to the company to that effect.

(4)   The request must contain the following information—
    (a)   in the case of an individual, his name and address;
    (b)   in the case of an organisation, the name and address of an individual responsible for making the request on behalf of the organisation;
    (c)   the purpose for which the information is to be used; and
    (d)   whether the information will be disclosed to any other person, and if so—
        (i)   where that person is an individual, his name and address,
        (ii)   where that person is an organisation, the name and address of an individual responsible for receiving the information on its behalf, and
        (iii)   the purpose for which the information is to be used by that person.

[1669N]

NOTES

Commencement: 20 January 2007 (sub-ss (1)–(3)); 6 April 2008 (otherwise).

Commencement (transitional provisions): Sch 4, Pt 1, para 32 to the Companies Act 2006 (Commencement No 5, Transitional Provisions and Savings) Order 2007, SI 2007/3495 provides as follows—

> *"Request to inspect a company's register of interests disclosed*
> *(ss 811(4), 812 and 814)*

32.   Sections 811(4), 812 and 814 of the Companies Act 2006 (inspection of register of interests disclosed: further provision about requests) apply to requests under section 811 of that Act made on or after 6th April 2008.".

Regulations: the Companies (Fees for Inspection and Copying of Company Records) Regulations 2007, SI 2007/2612.

812   Court supervision of purpose for which rights may be exercised

(1)   Where a company receives a request under section 811 (register of interests disclosed: right to inspect and require copy), it must—
    (a)   comply with the request if it is satisfied that it is made for a proper purpose, and
    (b)   refuse the request if it is not so satisfied.

(2)   If the company refuses the request, it must inform the person making the request, stating the reason why it is not satisfied.

(3)   A person whose request is refused may apply to the court.

(4)   If an application is made to the court—
    (a)   the person who made the request must notify the company, and
    (b)   the company must use its best endeavours to notify any persons whose details would be disclosed if the company were required to comply with the request.

(5)   If the court is not satisfied that the inspection or copy is sought for a proper purpose, it shall direct the company not to comply with the request.

(6)   If the court makes such a direction and it appears to the court that the company is or may be subject to other requests made for a similar purpose (whether made by the same person or different persons), it may direct that the company is not to comply with any such request.

The order must contain such provision as appears to the court appropriate to identify the requests to which it applies.

(7)   If the court does not direct the company not to comply with the request, the company must comply with the request immediately upon the court giving its decision or, as the case may be, the proceedings being discontinued.

[1669O]

NOTES

Commencement: 6 April 2008.

Commencement (transitional provisions): see the note to s 811 at **[1669N]**.

813   Register of interests disclosed: refusal of inspection or default in providing copy

(1)   If an inspection required under section 811 (register of interests disclosed: right to inspect and require copy) is refused or default is made in providing a copy required under that section, otherwise than in accordance with an order of the court, an offence is committed by—
    (a)   the company, and
    (b)   every officer of the company who is in default.

(2) A person guilty of an offence under this section is liable on summary conviction to a fine not exceeding level 3 on the standard scale and, for continued contravention, a daily default fine not exceeding one-tenth of level 3 on the standard scale.

(3) In the case of any such refusal or default the court may by order compel an immediate inspection or, as the case may be, direct that the copy required be sent to the person requesting it.

[1669P]

NOTES
Commencement: 20 January 2007.
Commencement (transitional adaptations): the transitional adaptations of this section contained in the Companies Act 2006 (Commencement No 1, Transitional Provisions and Savings) Order 2006, SI 2006/3428, Sch 1, para 2 were revoked by the Companies Act 2006 (Commencement No 5, Transitional Provisions and Savings) Order 2007, SI 2007/3495, art 10(2), as from 1 October 2008.

814 Register of interests disclosed: offences in connection with request for or disclosure of information

(1) It is an offence for a person knowingly or recklessly to make in a request under section 811 (register of interests disclosed: right to inspect or require copy) a statement that is misleading, false or deceptive in a material particular.

(2) It is an offence for a person in possession of information obtained by exercise of either of the rights conferred by that section—
  (a) to do anything that results in the information being disclosed to another person, or
  (b) to fail to do anything with the result that the information is disclosed to another person,
knowing, or having reason to suspect, that person may use the information for a purpose that is not a proper purpose.

(3) A person guilty of an offence under this section is liable—
  (a) on conviction on indictment, to imprisonment for a term not exceeding two years or a fine (or both);
  (b) on summary conviction—
    (i) in England and Wales, to imprisonment for a term not exceeding twelve months or to a fine not exceeding the statutory maximum (or both);
    (ii) in Scotland or Northern Ireland, to imprisonment for a term not exceeding six months, or to a fine not exceeding the statutory maximum (or both).

[1669Q]

NOTES
Commencement: 6 April 2008.
Commencement (transitional provisions): see the note to s 811 at **[1669N]**.
Imprisonment for a term not exceeding twelve months: see the note to s 387 at **[1514]**.

815 Entries not to be removed from register

(1) Entries in the register kept under section 808 (register of interests disclosed) must not be deleted except in accordance with—
  section 816 (old entries), or
  section 817 (incorrect entry relating to third party).

(2) If an entry is deleted in contravention of subsection (1), the company must restore it as soon as reasonably practicable.

(3) If default is made in complying with subsection (1) or (2), an offence is committed by—
  (a) the company, and
  (b) every officer of the company who is in default.

(4) A person guilty of an offence under this section is liable on summary conviction to a fine not exceeding level 3 on the standard scale and, for continued contravention of subsection (2), a daily default fine not exceeding one-tenth of level 3 on the standard scale.

[1669R]

NOTES
Commencement: 20 January 2007.

816 Removal of entries from register: old entries

A company may remove an entry from the register kept under section 808 (register of interests disclosed) if more than six years have elapsed since the entry was made.

[1669S]

NOTES
Commencement: 20 January 2007.

817 Removal of entries from register: incorrect entry relating to third party

(1) This section applies where in pursuance of an obligation imposed by a notice under section 793 (notice requiring information about interests in company's shares) a person gives to a company the name and address of another person as being interested in shares in the company.

(2) That other person may apply to the company for the removal of the entry from the register.

(3) If the company is satisfied that the information in pursuance of which the entry was made is incorrect, it shall remove the entry.

(4) If an application under subsection (3) is refused, the applicant may apply to the court for an order directing the company to remove the entry in question from the register.

The court may make such an order if it thinks fit.

[1669T]

NOTES
Commencement: 20 January 2007.

818 Adjustment of entry relating to share acquisition agreement

(1) If a person who is identified in the register kept by a company under section 808 (register of interests disclosed) as being a party to an agreement to which section 824 applies (certain share acquisition agreements) ceases to be a party to the agreement, he may apply to the company for the inclusion of that information in the register.

(2) If the company is satisfied that he has ceased to be a party to the agreement, it shall record that information (if not already recorded) in every place where his name appears in the register as a party to the agreement.

(3) If an application under this section is refused (otherwise than on the ground that the information has already been recorded), the applicant may apply to the court for an order directing the company to include the information in question in the register.

The court may make such an order if it thinks fit.

[1669U]

NOTES
Commencement: 20 January 2007.

819 Duty of company ceasing to be public company

(1) If a company ceases to be a public company, it must continue to keep any register kept under section 808 (register of interests disclosed), and any associated index, until the end of the period of six years after it ceased to be such a company.

(2) If default is made in complying with this section, an offence is committed by—
 (a) the company, and
 (b) every officer of the company who is in default.

(3) A person guilty of an offence under this section is liable on summary conviction to a fine not exceeding level 3 on the standard scale and, for continued contravention, a daily default fine not exceeding one-tenth of level 3 on the standard scale.

[1669V]

NOTES
Commencement: 20 January 2007.

Meaning of interest in shares

820 Interest in shares: general

(1) This section applies to determine for the purposes of this Part whether a person has an interest in shares.

(2) In this Part—
 (a) a reference to an interest in shares includes an interest of any kind whatsoever in the shares, and
 (b) any restraints or restrictions to which the exercise of any right attached to the interest is or may be subject shall be disregarded.

(3) Where an interest in shares is comprised in property held on trust, every beneficiary of the trust is treated as having an interest in the shares.

(4) A person is treated as having an interest in shares if—
 (a) he enters into a contract to acquire them, or
 (b) not being the registered holder, he is entitled—

(i)   to exercise any right conferred by the holding of the shares, or

(ii) to control the exercise of any such right.

(5)   For the purposes of subsection (4)(b) a person is entitled to exercise or control the exercise of a right conferred by the holding of shares if he—

(a)   has a right (whether subject to conditions or not) the exercise of which would make him so entitled, or

(b)   is under an obligation (whether subject to conditions or not) the fulfilment of which would make him so entitled.

(6)   A person is treated as having an interest in shares if—

(a)   he has a right to call for delivery of the shares to himself or to his order, or

(b)   he has a right to acquire an interest in shares or is under an obligation to take an interest in shares.

This applies whether the right or obligation is conditional or absolute.

(7)   Persons having a joint interest are treated as each having that interest.

(8)   It is immaterial that shares in which a person has an interest are unidentifiable.

[1669W]

NOTES
Commencement: 20 January 2007.

821   Interest in shares: right to subscribe for shares

(1)   Section 793 (notice by company requiring information about interests in its shares) applies in relation to a person who has, or previously had, or is or was entitled to acquire, a right to subscribe for shares in the company as it applies in relation to a person who is or was interested in shares in that company.

(2)   References in that section to an interest in shares shall be read accordingly.

[1669X]

NOTES
Commencement: 20 January 2007.

822   Interest in shares: family interests

(1)   For the purposes of this Part a person is taken to be interested in shares in which—

(a)   his spouse or civil partner, or

(b)   any infant child or step-child of his,

is interested.

(2)   In relation to Scotland "infant" means a person under the age of 18 years.

[1669Y]

NOTES
Commencement: 20 January 2007.

823   Interest in shares: corporate interests

(1)   For the purposes of this Part a person is taken to be interested in shares if a body corporate is interested in them and—

(a)   the body or its directors are accustomed to act in accordance with his directions or instructions, or

(b)   he is entitled to exercise or control the exercise of one-third or more of the voting power at general meetings of the body.

(2)   For the purposes of this section a person is treated as entitled to exercise or control the exercise of voting power if—

(a)   another body corporate is entitled to exercise or control the exercise of that voting power, and

(b)   he is entitled to exercise or control the exercise of one-third or more of the voting power at general meetings of that body corporate.

(3)   For the purposes of this section a person is treated as entitled to exercise or control the exercise of voting power if—

(a)   he has a right (whether or not subject to conditions) the exercise of which would make him so entitled, or

(b)   he is under an obligation (whether or not subject to conditions) the fulfilment of which would make him so entitled.

[1669Z]

NOTES
Commencement: 20 January 2007.

824   Interest in shares: agreement to acquire interests in a particular company

(1)   For the purposes of this Part an interest in shares may arise from an agreement between two or more persons that includes provision for the acquisition by any one or more of them of interests in shares of a particular public company (the "target company" for that agreement).

(2)   This section applies to such an agreement if—
  (a)   the agreement includes provision imposing obligations or restrictions on any one or more of the parties to it with respect to their use, retention or disposal of their interests in the shares of the target company acquired in pursuance of the agreement (whether or not together with any other interests of theirs in the company's shares to which the agreement relates), and
  (b)   an interest in the target company's shares is in fact acquired by any of the parties in pursuance of the agreement.

(3)   The reference in subsection (2) to the use of interests in shares in the target company is to the exercise of any rights or of any control or influence arising from those interests (including the right to enter into an agreement for the exercise, or for control of the exercise, of any of those rights by another person).

(4)   Once an interest in shares in the target company has been acquired in pursuance of the agreement, this section continues to apply to the agreement so long as the agreement continues to include provisions of any description mentioned in subsection (2).

This applies irrespective of—
  (a)   whether or not any further acquisitions of interests in the company's shares take place in pursuance of the agreement;
  (b)   any change in the persons who are for the time being parties to it;
  (c)   any variation of the agreement.

References in this subsection to the agreement include any agreement having effect (whether directly or indirectly) in substitution for the original agreement.

(5)   In this section—
  (a)   "agreement" includes any agreement or arrangement, and
  (b)   references to provisions of an agreement include—
    (i)   undertakings, expectations or understandings operative under an arrangement, and
    (ii)   any provision whether express or implied and whether absolute or not.

References elsewhere in this Part to an agreement to which this section applies have a corresponding meaning.

(6)   This section does not apply—
  (a)   to an agreement that is not legally binding unless it involves mutuality in the undertakings, expectations or understandings of the parties to it; or
  (b)   to an agreement to underwrite or sub-underwrite an offer of shares in a company, provided the agreement is confined to that purpose and any matters incidental to it.

[1670]

NOTES
Commencement: 20 January 2007.

825   Extent of obligation in case of share acquisition agreement

(1)   For the purposes of this Part each party to an agreement to which section 824 applies is treated as interested in all shares in the target company in which any other party to the agreement is interested apart from the agreement (whether or not the interest of the other party was acquired, or includes any interest that was acquired, in pursuance of the agreement).

(2)   For those purposes an interest of a party to such an agreement in shares in the target company is an interest apart from the agreement if he is interested in those shares otherwise than by virtue of the application of section 824 (and this section) in relation to the agreement.

(3)   Accordingly, any such interest of the person (apart from the agreement) includes for those purposes any interest treated as his under section 822 or 823 (family or corporate interests) or by the application of section 824 (and this section) in relation to any other agreement with respect to shares in the target company to which he is a party.

(4)   A notification with respect to his interest in shares in the target company made to the company under this Part by a person who is for the time being a party to an agreement to which section 824 applies must—

PART II
OTHER ACTS

(a)   state that the person making the notification is a party to such an agreement,

(b)   include the names and (so far as known to him) the addresses of the other parties to the agreement, identifying them as such, and

(c)   state whether or not any of the shares to which the notification relates are shares in which he is interested by virtue of section 824 (and this section) and, if so, the number of those shares.

[1670A]

NOTES
Commencement: 20 January 2007.

Other supplementary provisions

826   Information protected from wider disclosure

(1)   Information in respect of which a company is for the time being entitled to any exemption conferred by regulations under section 409(3) (information about related undertakings to be given in notes to accounts: exemption where disclosure harmful to company's business)—

(a)   must not be included in a report under section 805 (report to members on outcome of investigation), and

(b)   must not be made available under section 811 (right to inspect and request copy of entries).

(2)   Where any such information is omitted from a report under section 805, that fact must be stated in the report.

[1670B]

NOTES
Commencement: 20 January 2007.
Commencement (transitional adaptations): art 5 of the Companies Act 2006 (Commencement No 1, Transitional Provisions and Savings) Order 2006, SI 2006/3428 provides that the provisions brought into force by arts 2–4 of 2006 Order shall have effect subject to any transitional adaptations specified in Sch 1 to that Order. Schedule 1, para 3 to the Order provides as follows (note, however, that this paragraph was revoked by the Companies Act 2006 (Commencement No 5, Transitional Provisions and Savings) Order 2007, SI 2007/3495, art 10(1), (3), as from 6 April 2008 (subject to any transitional provisions and savings as apply, in accordance with Sch 4 to that Order, in relation to the repeal of the provisions of the 1985 Act referred to in the adaptation; see art 10))—
"3.—(1)   Section 826 (information about interests in a company's shares protected from wider disclosure) has effect with the following adaptation.
(2)   In subsection (1) for "regulations under section 409(3)" substitute "section 231(3) of the Companies Act 1985 or Article 239(3) of the Companies (Northern Ireland) Order 1986".".

827   Reckoning of periods for fulfilling obligations

Where the period allowed by any provision of this Part for fulfilling an obligation is expressed as a number of days, any day that is not a working day shall be disregarded in reckoning that period.

[1670C]

NOTES
Commencement: 20 January 2007.

828   Power to make further provision by regulations

(1)   The Secretary of State may by regulations amend—

(a)   the definition of shares to which this Part applies (section 792),

(b)   the provisions as to notice by a company requiring information about interests in its shares (section 793), and

(c)   the provisions as to what is taken to be an interest in shares (sections 820 and 821).

(2)   The regulations may amend, repeal or replace those provisions and make such other consequential amendments or repeals of provisions of this Part as appear to the Secretary of State to be appropriate.

(3)   Regulations under this section are subject to affirmative resolution procedure.

[1670D]

NOTES
Commencement: 20 January 2007.

PART 26
ARRANGEMENTS AND RECONSTRUCTIONS
Application of this Part

895   Application of this Part

(1)   The provisions of this Part apply where a compromise or arrangement is proposed between a company and—

    (a)   its creditors, or any class of them, or

    (b)   its members, or any class of them.

(2)   In this Part—

"arrangement" includes a reorganisation of the company's share capital by the consolidation of shares of different classes or by the division of shares into shares of different classes, or by both of those methods; and "company"—

    (a)   in section 900 (powers of court to facilitate reconstruction or amalgamation) means a company within the meaning of this Act, and

    (b)   elsewhere in this Part means any company liable to be wound up under the Insolvency Act 1986 (c 45) or the Insolvency (Northern Ireland) Order 1989 (SI 1989/2405 (NI 19)).

(3)   The provisions of this Part have effect subject to Part 27 (mergers and divisions of public companies) where that Part applies (see sections 902 and 903).

                                                      [1670E]

NOTES

Commencement: 6 April 2008.

Meeting of creditors or members

896   Court order for holding of meeting

(1)   The court may, on an application under this section, order a meeting of the creditors or class of creditors, or of the members of the company or class of members (as the case may be), to be summoned in such manner as the court directs.

(2)   An application under this section may be made by—

    (a)   the company,

    (b)   any creditor or member of the company,

    [(c)   if the company is being wound up, the liquidator, or

    (d)   if the company is in administration, the administrator.]

[(3)   Section 323 (representation of corporations at meetings) applies to a meeting of creditors under this section as to a meeting of the company (references to a member of the company being read as references to a creditor).]

                                                      [1670F]

NOTES

Commencement: 6 April 2008.

Sub-s (2): paras (c), (d) substituted (for the original para (c) (and the word "or" preceding it)) by the Companies Act 2006 (Consequential Amendments etc) Order 2008, SI 2008/948, art 3(1), Sch 1, Pt 2, para 249(1), (2), as from 6 April 2008.

Sub-s (3): added by SI 2008/948, art 3(1), Sch 1, Pt 2, para 249(1), (3), as from 6 April 2008.

897   Statement to be circulated or made available

(1)   Where a meeting is summoned under section 896—

    (a)   every notice summoning the meeting that is sent to a creditor or member must be accompanied by a statement complying with this section, and

    (b)   every notice summoning the meeting that is given by advertisement must either—

        (i)   include such a statement, or

        (ii)   state where and how creditors or members entitled to attend the meeting may obtain copies of such a statement.

(2)   The statement must—

    (a)   explain the effect of the compromise or arrangement, and

    (b)   in particular, state—

        (i)   any material interests of the directors of the company (whether as directors or as members or as creditors of the company or otherwise), and

        (ii)   the effect on those interests of the compromise or arrangement, in so far as it is different from the effect on the like interests of other persons.

(3)   Where the compromise or arrangement affects the rights of debenture holders of the company, the statement must give the like explanation as respects the trustees of any deed for securing the issue of the debentures as it is required to give as respects the company's directors.

(4)   Where a notice given by advertisement states that copies of an explanatory statement can be obtained by creditors or members entitled to attend the meeting, every such creditor or member is entitled, on making application in the manner indicated by the notice, to be provided by the company with a copy of the statement free of charge.

(5)   If a company makes default in complying with any requirement of this section, an offence is committed by—
   (a)   the company, and
   (b)   every officer of the company who is in default.

This is subject to subsection (7) below.

(6)   For this purpose the following are treated as officers of the company—
   (a)   a liquidator or administrator of the company, and
   (b)   a trustee of a deed for securing the issue of debentures of the company.

(7)   A person is not guilty of an offence under this section if he shows that the default was due to the refusal of a director or trustee for debenture holders to supply the necessary particulars of his interests.

(8)   A person guilty of an offence under this section is liable—
   (a)   on conviction on indictment, to a fine;
   (b)   on summary conviction, to a fine not exceeding the statutory maximum.

                                                                                    [1671]

NOTES
Commencement: 6 April 2008.

898   Duty of directors and trustees to provide information

(1)   It is the duty of—
   (a)   any director of the company, and
   (b)   any trustee for its debenture holders,
to give notice to the company of such matters relating to himself as may be necessary for the purposes of section 897 (explanatory statement to be circulated or made available).

(2)   Any person who makes default in complying with this section commits an offence.

(3)   A person guilty of an offence under this section is liable on summary conviction to a fine not exceeding level 3 on the standard scale.

                                                                                    [1672]

NOTES
Commencement: 6 April 2008.

Court sanction for compromise or arrangement

899   Court sanction for compromise or arrangement

(1)   If a majority in number representing 75% in value of the creditors or class of creditors or members or class of members (as the case may be), present and voting either in person or by proxy at the meeting summoned under section 896, agree a compromise or arrangement, the court may, on an application under this section, sanction the compromise or arrangement.

(2)   An application under this section may be made by—
   (a)   the company,
   (b)   any creditor or member of the company,
   [(c)   if the company is being wound up, the liquidator, or
   (d)   if the company is in administration, the administrator.]

(3)   A compromise or agreement sanctioned by the court is binding on—
   (a)   all creditors or the class of creditors or on the members or class of members (as the case may be), and
   (b)   the company or, in the case of a company in the course of being wound up, the liquidator and contributories of the company.

(4)   The court's order has no effect until a copy of it has been delivered to the registrar.

[(5)   Section 323 (representation of corporations at meetings) applies to a meeting of creditors under this section as to a meeting of the company (references to a member of the company being read as references to a creditor).]

                                                                                    [1673]

NOTES
Commencement: 6 April 2008.
Sub-s (2): paras (c), (d) substituted (for the original para (c) (and the word "or" preceding it)) by the
Companies Act 2006 (Consequential Amendments etc) Order 2008, SI 2008/948, art 3(1), Sch 1, Pt 2,
para 250(1), (2), as from 6 April 2008.
Sub-s (5): added by SI 2008/948, art 3(1), Sch 1, Pt 2, para 250(1), (3), as from 6 April 2008.

Reconstructions and amalgamations

900   Powers of court to facilitate reconstruction or amalgamation

(1)   This section applies where application is made to the court under section 899 to sanction a
compromise or arrangement and it is shown that—
  (a)   the compromise or arrangement is proposed for the purposes of, or in connection with, a
        scheme for the reconstruction of any company or companies, or the amalgamation of
        any two or more companies, and
  (b)   under the scheme the whole or any part of the undertaking or the property of any
        company concerned in the scheme ("a transferor company") is to be transferred to
        another company ("the transferee company").

(2)   The court may, either by the order sanctioning the compromise or arrangement or by a
subsequent order, make provision for all or any of the following matters—
  (a)   the transfer to the transferee company of the whole or any part of the undertaking and of
        the property or liabilities of any transferor company;
  (b)   the allotting or appropriation by the transferee company of any shares, debentures,
        policies or other like interests in that company which under the compromise or
        arrangement are to be allotted or appropriated by that company to or for any person;
  (c)   the continuation by or against the transferee company of any legal proceedings pending
        by or against any transferor company;
  (d)   the dissolution, without winding up, of any transferor company;
  (e)   the provision to be made for any persons who, within such time and in such manner as
        the court directs, dissent from the compromise or arrangement;
  (f)   such incidental, consequential and supplemental matters as are necessary to secure that
        the reconstruction or amalgamation is fully and effectively carried out.

(3)   If an order under this section provides for the transfer of property or liabilities—
  (a)   the property is by virtue of the order transferred to, and vests in, the transferee company,
        and
  (b)   the liabilities are, by virtue of the order, transferred to and become liabilities of that
        company.

(4)   The property (if the order so directs) vests freed from any charge that is by virtue of the
compromise or arrangement to cease to have effect.

(5)   In this section—
"property" includes property, rights and powers of every description; and
"liabilities" includes duties.

(6)   Every company in relation to which an order is made under this section must cause a copy
of the order to be delivered to the registrar within seven days after its making.

(7)   If default is made in complying with subsection (6) an offence is committed by—
  (a)   the company, and
  (b)   every officer of the company who is in default.

(8)   A person guilty of an offence under subsection (7) is liable on summary conviction to a fine
not exceeding level 3 on the standard scale and, for continued contravention, a daily default fine not
exceeding one-tenth of level 3 on the standard scale.

[1674]

NOTES
Commencement: 6 April 2008.

Obligations of company with respect to articles etc

901   Obligations of company with respect to articles etc

(1)   This section applies—
  (a)   to any order under section 899 (order sanctioning compromise or arrangement), and
  (b)   to any order under section 900 (order facilitating reconstruction or amalgamation) that
        alters the company's constitution.

(2)   If the order amends—
  (a)   the company's articles, or

(b) any resolution or agreement to which Chapter 3 of Part 3 applies (resolution or agreement affecting a company's constitution),

the copy of the order delivered to the registrar by the company under section 899(4) or section 900(6) must be accompanied by a copy of the company's articles, or the resolution or agreement in question, as amended.

(3) Every copy of the company's articles issued by the company after the order is made must be accompanied by a copy of the order, unless the effect of the order has been incorporated into the articles by amendment.

(4) In this section—
(a) references to the effect of the order include the effect of the compromise or arrangement to which the order relates; and
(b) in the case of a company not having articles, references to its articles shall be read as references to the instrument constituting the company or defining its constitution.

(5) If a company makes default in complying with this section an offence is committed by—
(a) the company, and
(b) every officer of the company who is in default.

(6) A person guilty of an offence under this section is liable on summary conviction to a fine not exceeding level 3 on the standard scale.

[1675]

NOTES
Commencement: 6 April 2008.
Commencement (transitional provisions): Sch 4, Pt 1, para 36 to the Companies Act 2006 (Commencement No 5, Transitional Provisions and Savings) Order 2007, SI 2007/3495 provides as follows—

"Arrangements and reconstructions (ss 896 to 901)

36.—(1) Section 901 of the Companies Act 2006 (obligations of company with respect to articles etc) applies to orders of the court made on or after 6th April 2008, including orders made under section 425(2) or 427 of the 1985 Act or 418(2) or 420 of the 1986 Order.

(2) Section 425(3) and (4) of the 1985 Act or Article 418(3) and (4) of the 1986 Order continues to apply to orders made before that date.".

PART 28
TAKEOVERS ETC

NOTES
The Takeovers Directive (Directive 2004/25/EC of the European Parliament and of the Council of 21 April 2004 on Takeover Bids) had to be implemented by 20 May 2006 and, as this Act had not completed Parliamentary passage by that date, this was achieved by means of the Takeovers Directive (Interim Implementation) Regulations 2006, SI 2006/1183 (see the note at **[3983]**). The 2006 Regulations were revoked by the Companies Act 2006 (Commencement No 2, Consequential Amendments, Transitional Provisions and Savings) Order 2007, SI 2007/1093, art 7, Sch 5, as from 6 April 2007 (the same date as this Part came into force). The revocation of SI 2006/1183 is subject to certain savings contained in Sch 6, paras 2, 3 to the 2007 Order.

Application to unregistered companies: the Companies Acts (Unregistered Companies) Regulations 2007, SI 2007/318 provides that Chapter 2 of this Part, and Chapter 3 of this Part (in so far as relating to the offeree company only if it has voting shares admitted to trading on a regulated market) apply to unregistered companies.

CHAPTER 1
THE TAKEOVER PANEL
The Panel and its rules

942 The Panel

(1) The body known as the Panel on Takeovers and Mergers ("the Panel") is to have the functions conferred on it by or under this Chapter.

(2) The Panel may do anything that it considers necessary or expedient for the purposes of, or in connection with, its functions.

(3) The Panel may make arrangements for any of its functions to be discharged by—
(a) a committee or sub-committee of the Panel, or
(b) an officer or member of staff of the Panel, or a person acting as such.

This is subject to section 943(4) and (5).

[1676]

NOTES
Commencement: 6 April 2007.

943   Rules

(1)   The Panel must make rules giving effect to Articles 3.1, 4.2, 5, 6.1 to 6.3, 7 to 9 and 13 of the Takeovers Directive.

(2)   Rules made by the Panel may also make other provision—
- (a)   for or in connection with the regulation of—
  - (i)   takeover bids,
  - (ii)   merger transactions, and
  - (iii)   transactions (not falling within sub-paragraph (i) or (ii)) that have or may have, directly or indirectly, an effect on the ownership or control of companies;
- (b)   for or in connection with the regulation of things done in consequence of, or otherwise in relation to, any such bid or transaction;
- (c)   about cases where—
  - (i)   any such bid or transaction is, or has been, contemplated or apprehended, or
  - (ii)   an announcement is made denying that any such bid or transaction is intended.

(3)   The provision that may be made under subsection (2) includes, in particular, provision for a matter that is, or is similar to, a matter provided for by the Panel in the City Code on Takeovers and Mergers as it had effect immediately before the passing of this Act.

(4)   In relation to rules made by virtue of section 957 (fees and charges), functions under this section may be discharged either by the Panel itself or by a committee of the Panel (but not otherwise).

(5)   In relation to rules of any other description, the Panel must discharge its functions under this section by a committee of the Panel.

(6)   Section 1 (meaning of "company") does not apply for the purposes of this section.

(7)   In this section "takeover bid" includes a takeover bid within the meaning of the Takeovers Directive.

(8)   In this Chapter "the Takeovers Directive" means Directive 2004/25/EC of the European Parliament and of the Council.

(9)   A reference to rules in the following provisions of this Chapter is to rules under this section.

                                                              [1677]

NOTES

Commencement: 6 April 2007.

Commencement (transitional adaptations): art 3 of the Companies Act 2006 (Commencement No 2, Consequential Amendments, Transitional Provisions and Savings) Order 2007, SI 2007/1093 provides that the provisions brought into force by art 2 of 2007 Order shall have effect subject to any transitional adaptations specified in Sch 1 to that Order. Schedule 1, para 2 to the Order provides as follows (note that this paragraph is revoked by the Companies Act 2006 (Commencement No 8, Transitional Provisions and Savings) Order 2008, SI 2008/2860, art 6, as from 1 October 2009 (subject to any relevant transitional provision or saving in Sch 2 to that Order))—

"2.—(1)   Section 943 (power of Takeover Panel to make rules) has effect with the following adaptation.

(2)   For subsection (6) substitute—

"(6)   Section 735(1) of the Companies Act 1985 and Article 2(3) of the Companies (Northern Ireland) Order 1986 (meaning of "company") do not apply for the purposes of this section.""

As to Rules made by the Takeover Panel under this section, see:
http:/www.thetakeoverpanel.org.uk/new/

944   Further provisions about rules

(1)   Rules may—
- (a)   make different provision for different purposes;
- (b)   make provision subject to exceptions or exemptions;
- (c)   contain incidental, supplemental, consequential or transitional provision;
- (d)   authorise the Panel to dispense with or modify the application of rules in particular cases and by reference to any circumstances.

Rules made by virtue of paragraph (d) must require the Panel to give reasons for acting as mentioned in that paragraph.

(2)   Rules must be made by an instrument in writing.

(3)   Immediately after an instrument containing rules is made, the text must be made available to the public, with or without payment, in whatever way the Panel thinks appropriate.

(4)   A person is not to be taken to have contravened a rule if he shows that at the time of the alleged contravention the text of the rule had not been made available as required by subsection (3).

(5)   The production of a printed copy of an instrument purporting to be made by the Panel on which is endorsed a certificate signed by an officer of the Panel authorised by it for that purpose and stating—

    (a)   that the instrument was made by the Panel,

    (b)   that the copy is a true copy of the instrument, and

    (c)   that on a specified date the text of the instrument was made available to the public as required by subsection (3),

is evidence (or in Scotland sufficient evidence) of the facts stated in the certificate.

    (6)   A certificate purporting to be signed as mentioned in subsection (5) is to be treated as having been properly signed unless the contrary is shown.

    (7)   A person who wishes in any legal proceedings to rely on an instrument by which rules are made may require the Panel to endorse a copy of the instrument with a certificate of the kind mentioned in subsection (5).

[1678]

NOTES

Commencement: 6 April 2007.

945 Rulings

    (1)   The Panel may give rulings on the interpretation, application or effect of rules.

    (2)   To the extent and in the circumstances specified in rules, and subject to any review or appeal, a ruling has binding effect.

[1679]

NOTES

Commencement: 6 April 2007.

946 Directions

Rules may contain provision conferring power on the Panel to give any direction that appears to the Panel to be necessary in order—

    (a)   to restrain a person from acting (or continuing to act) in breach of rules;

    (b)   to restrain a person from doing (or continuing to do) a particular thing, pending determination of whether that or any other conduct of his is or would be a breach of rules;

    (c)   otherwise to secure compliance with rules.

[1680]

NOTES

Commencement: 6 April 2007.

Information

947 Power to require documents and information

    (1)   The Panel may by notice in writing require a person—

    (a)   to produce any documents that are specified or described in the notice;

    (b)   to provide, in the form and manner specified in the notice, such information as may be specified or described in the notice.

    (2)   A requirement under subsection (1) must be complied with—

    (a)   at a place specified in the notice, and

    (b)   before the end of such reasonable period as may be so specified.

    (3)   This section applies only to documents and information reasonably required in connection with the exercise by the Panel of its functions.

    (4)   The Panel may require—

    (a)   any document produced to be authenticated, or

    (b)   any information provided (whether in a document or otherwise) to be verified,

in such manner as it may reasonably require.

    (5)   The Panel may authorise a person to exercise any of its powers under this section.

    (6)   A person exercising a power by virtue of subsection (5) must, if required to do so, produce evidence of his authority to exercise the power.

    (7)   The production of a document in pursuance of this section does not affect any lien that a person has on the document.

    (8)   The Panel may take copies of or extracts from a document produced in pursuance of this section.

    (9)   A reference in this section to the production of a document includes a reference to the production of—

    (a)   a hard copy of information recorded otherwise than in hard copy form, or

(b)   information in a form from which a hard copy can be readily obtained.

(10)   A person is not required by this section to disclose documents or information in respect of which a claim to legal professional privilege (in Scotland, to confidentiality of communications) could be maintained in legal proceedings.

[1681]

NOTES

Commencement: 6 April 2007.

948   Restrictions on disclosure

(1)   This section applies to information (in whatever form)—

    (a)   relating to the private affairs of an individual, or

    (b)   relating to any particular business,

that is provided to the Panel in connection with the exercise of its functions.

(2)   No such information may, during the lifetime of the individual or so long as the business continues to be carried on, be disclosed without the consent of that individual or (as the case may be) the person for the time being carrying on that business.

(3)   Subsection (2) does not apply to any disclosure of information that—

    (a)   is made for the purpose of facilitating the carrying out by the Panel of any of its functions,

    (b)   is made to a person specified in Part 1 of Schedule 2,

    (c)   is of a description specified in Part 2 of that Schedule, or

    (d)   is made in accordance with Part 3 of that Schedule.

(4)   The Secretary of State may amend Schedule 2 by order subject to negative resolution procedure.

(5)   An order under subsection (4) must not—

    (a)   amend Part 1 of Schedule 2 by specifying a person unless the person exercises functions of a public nature (whether or not he exercises any other function);

    (b)   amend Part 2 of Schedule 2 by adding or modifying a description of disclosure unless the purpose for which the disclosure is permitted is likely to facilitate the exercise of a function of a public nature;

    (c)   amend Part 3 of Schedule 2 so as to have the effect of permitting disclosures to be made to a body other than one that exercises functions of a public nature in a country or territory outside the United Kingdom.

(6)   Subsection (2) does not apply to—

    (a)   the disclosure by an authority within subsection (7) of information disclosed to it by the Panel in reliance on subsection (3);

    (b)   the disclosure of such information by anyone who has obtained it directly or indirectly from an authority within subsection (7).

(7)   The authorities within this subsection are—

    (a)   the Financial Services Authority;

    (b)   an authority designated as a supervisory authority for the purposes of Article 4.1 of the Takeovers Directive;

    (c)   any other person or body that exercises functions of a public nature, under legislation in an EEA State other than the United Kingdom, that are similar to the Panel's functions or those of the Financial Services Authority.

(8)   This section does not prohibit the disclosure of information if the information is or has been available to the public from any other source.

(9)   Nothing in this section authorises the making of a disclosure in contravention of the Data Protection Act 1998 (c 29).

[1682]

NOTES

Commencement: 20 January 2007 (for the purpose of enabling the exercise of powers to make Orders or Regulations by statutory instrument); 6 April 2007 (otherwise).

Orders: the Companies Act 2006 (Amendment of Schedule 2) Order 2009, SI 2009/202.

949   Offence of disclosure in contravention of section 948

(1)   A person who discloses information in contravention of section 948 is guilty of an offence, unless—

    (a)   he did not know, and had no reason to suspect, that the information had been provided as mentioned in section 948(1), or

    (b)   he took all reasonable steps and exercised all due diligence to avoid the commission of the offence.

(2)   A person guilty of an offence under this section is liable—
- (a)   on conviction on indictment, to imprisonment for a term not exceeding two years or a fine (or both);
- (b)   on summary conviction—
  - (i)   in England and Wales, to imprisonment for a term not exceeding twelve months or to a fine not exceeding the statutory maximum (or both);
  - (ii)   in Scotland or Northern Ireland, to imprisonment for a term not exceeding six months, or to a fine not exceeding the statutory maximum (or both).

(3)   Where a company or other body corporate commits an offence under this section, an offence is also committed by every officer of the company or other body corporate who is in default.

[1683]

NOTES
Commencement: 6 April 2007.
Imprisonment for a term not exceeding twelve months: see the note to s 387 at **[1514]**.

Co-operation

950   Panel's duty of co-operation

(1)   The Panel must take such steps as it considers appropriate to co-operate with—
- (a)   the Financial Services Authority;
- (b)   an authority designated as a supervisory authority for the purposes of Article 4.1 of the Takeovers Directive;
- (c)   any other person or body that exercises functions of a public nature, under legislation in any country or territory outside the United Kingdom, that appear to the Panel to be similar to its own functions or those of the Financial Services Authority.

(2)   Co-operation may include the sharing of information that the Panel is not prevented from disclosing.

[1684]

NOTES
Commencement: 6 April 2007.

Hearings and appeals

951   Hearings and appeals

(1)   Rules must provide for a decision of the Panel to be subject to review by a committee of the Panel (the "Hearings Committee") at the instance of such persons affected by the decision as are specified in the rules.

(2)   Rules may also confer other functions on the Hearings Committee.

(3)   Rules must provide for there to be a right of appeal against a decision of the Hearings Committee to an independent tribunal (the "Takeover Appeal Board") in such circumstances and subject to such conditions as are specified in the rules.

(4)   Rules may contain—
- (a)   provision as to matters of procedure in relation to proceedings before the Hearings Committee (including provision imposing time limits);
- (b)   provision about evidence in such proceedings;
- (c)   provision as to the powers of the Hearings Committee dealing with a matter referred to it;
- (d)   provision about enforcement of decisions of the Hearings Committee and the Takeover Appeal Board.

(5)   Rules must contain provision—
- (a)   requiring the Panel, when acting in relation to any proceedings before the Hearings Committee or the Takeover Appeal Board, to do so by an officer or member of staff of the Panel (or a person acting as such);
- (b)   preventing a person who is or has been a member of the committee mentioned in section 943(5) from being a member of the Hearings Committee or the Takeover Appeal Board;
- (c)   preventing a person who is a member of the committee mentioned in section 943(5), of the Hearings Committee or of the Takeover Appeal Board from acting as mentioned in paragraph (a).

[1685]

NOTES
Commencement: 6 April 2007.

Contravention of rules etc

952   Sanctions

(1)   Rules may contain provision conferring power on the Panel to impose sanctions on a person who has—
  (a)   acted in breach of rules, or
  (b)   failed to comply with a direction given by virtue of section 946.

(2)   Subsection (3) applies where rules made by virtue of subsection (1) confer power on the Panel to impose a sanction of a kind not provided for by the City Code on Takeovers and Mergers as it had effect immediately before the passing of this Act.

(3)   The Panel must prepare a statement (a "policy statement") of its policy with respect to—
  (a)   the imposition of the sanction in question, and
  (b)   where the sanction is in the nature of a financial penalty, the amount of the penalty that may be imposed.

An element of the policy must be that, in making a decision about any such matter, the Panel has regard to the factors mentioned in subsection (4).

(4)   The factors are—
  (a)   the seriousness of the breach or failure in question in relation to the nature of the rule or direction contravened;
  (b)   the extent to which the breach or failure was deliberate or reckless;
  (c)   whether the person on whom the sanction is to be imposed is an individual.

(5)   The Panel may at any time revise a policy statement.

(6)   The Panel must prepare a draft of any proposed policy statement (or revised policy statement) and consult such persons about the draft as the Panel considers appropriate.

(7)   The Panel must publish, in whatever way it considers appropriate, any policy statement (or revised policy statement) that it prepares.

(8)   In exercising, or deciding whether to exercise, its power to impose a sanction within subsection (2) in the case of any particular breach or failure, the Panel must have regard to any relevant policy statement published and in force at the time when the breach or failure occurred.

[1686]

NOTES
Commencement: 6 April 2007.

953   Failure to comply with rules about bid documentation

(1)   This section applies where a takeover bid is made for a company that has securities carrying voting rights admitted to trading on a regulated market in the United Kingdom.

(2)   Where an offer document published in respect of the bid does not comply with offer document rules, an offence is committed by—
  (a)   the person making the bid, and
  (b)   where the person making the bid is a body of persons, any director, officer or member of that body who caused the document to be published.

(3)   A person commits an offence under subsection (2) only if—
  (a)   he knew that the offer document did not comply, or was reckless as to whether it complied, and
  (b)   he failed to take all reasonable steps to secure that it did comply.

(4)   Where a response document published in respect of the bid does not comply with response document rules, an offence is committed by any director or other officer of the company referred to in subsection (1) who—
  (a)   knew that the response document did not comply, or was reckless as to whether it complied, and
  (b)   failed to take all reasonable steps to secure that it did comply.

(5)   Where an offence is committed under subsection (2)(b) or (4) by a company or other body corporate ("the relevant body")—
  (a)   subsection (2)(b) has effect as if the reference to a director, officer or member of the person making the bid included a reference to a director, officer or member of the relevant body;
  (b)   subsection (4) has effect as if the reference to a director or other officer of the company referred to in subsection (1) included a reference to a director, officer or member of the relevant body.

(6)   A person guilty of an offence under this section is liable—
  (a)   on conviction on indictment, to a fine;
  (b)   on summary conviction, to a fine not exceeding the statutory maximum.

(7)   Nothing in this section affects any power of the Panel in relation to the enforcement of its rules.

(8)   Section 1 (meaning of "company") does not apply for the purposes of this section.

(9)   In this section—

"designated" means designated in rules;

"offer document" means a document required to be published by rules giving effect to Article 6.2 of the Takeovers Directive;

"offer document rules" means rules designated as rules that give effect to Article 6.3 of that Directive;

"response document" means a document required to be published by rules giving effect to Article 9.5 of that Directive;

"response document rules" means rules designated as rules that give effect to the first sentence of Article 9.5 of that Directive;

"securities" means shares or debentures;

"takeover bid" has the same meaning as in that Directive;

"voting rights" means rights to vote at general meetings of the company in question, including rights that arise only in certain circumstances.

[1687]

NOTES
Commencement: 6 April 2007.
Commencement (transitional adaptations): art 3 of the Companies Act 2006 (Commencement No 2, Consequential Amendments, Transitional Provisions and Savings) Order 2007, SI 2007/1093 provides that the provisions brought into force by art 2 of 2007 Order shall have effect subject to any transitional adaptations specified in Sch 1 to that Order. Schedule 1, para 3 to the Order provides as follows (note that this paragraph is revoked by the Companies Act 2006 (Commencement No 8, Transitional Provisions and Savings) Order 2008, SI 2008/2860, art 6, as from 1 October 2009 (subject to any relevant transitional provision or saving in Sch 2 to that Order))—

"3.—(1)   Section 953 (failure to comply with rules about bid documentation) has effect with the following adaptation.

(2)   For subsection (8) substitute—

"(8)   Section 735(1) of the Companies Act 1985 and Article 2(3) of the Companies (Northern Ireland) Order 1986 (meaning of "company") do not apply for the purposes of this section."."

954   Compensation

(1)   Rules may confer power on the Panel to order a person to pay such compensation as it thinks just and reasonable if he is in breach of a rule the effect of which is to require the payment of money.

(2)   Rules made by virtue of this section may include provision for the payment of interest (including compound interest).

[1688]

NOTES
Commencement: 6 April 2007.

955   Enforcement by the court

(1)   If, on the application of the Panel, the court is satisfied—

(a)   that there is a reasonable likelihood that a person will contravene a rule-based requirement, or

(b)   that a person has contravened a rule-based requirement or a disclosure requirement,

the court may make any order it thinks fit to secure compliance with the requirement.

(2)   In subsection (1) "the court" means the High Court or, in Scotland, the Court of Session.

(3)   Except as provided by subsection (1), no person—

(a)   has a right to seek an injunction, or

(b)   in Scotland, has title or interest to seek an interdict or an order for specific performance,

to prevent a person from contravening (or continuing to contravene) a rule- based requirement or a disclosure requirement.

(4)   In this section—

"contravene" includes fail to comply;

"disclosure requirement" means a requirement imposed under section 947;

"rule-based requirement" means a requirement imposed by or under rules.

[1689]

NOTES
Commencement: 6 April 2007.

956 No action for breach of statutory duty etc

(1) Contravention of a rule-based requirement or a disclosure requirement does not give rise to any right of action for breach of statutory duty.

(2) Contravention of a rule-based requirement does not make any transaction void or unenforceable or (subject to any provision made by rules) affect the validity of any other thing.

(3) In this section—
  (a) "contravention" includes failure to comply;
  (b) "disclosure requirement" and "rule-based requirement" have the same meaning as in section 955.

[1690]

NOTES

Commencement: 6 April 2007.

Funding

957 Fees and charges

(1) Rules may provide for fees or charges to be payable to the Panel for the purpose of meeting any part of its expenses.

(2) A reference in this section or section 958 to expenses of the Panel is to any expenses that have been or are to be incurred by the Panel in, or in connection with, the discharge of its functions, including in particular—
  (a) payments in respect of the expenses of the Takeover Appeal Board;
  (b) the cost of repaying the principal of, and of paying any interest on, any money borrowed by the Panel;
  (c) the cost of maintaining adequate reserves.

[1691]

NOTES

Commencement: 6 April 2007.

958 Levy

(1) For the purpose of meeting any part of the expenses of the Panel, the Secretary of State may by regulations provide for a levy to be payable to the Panel—
  (a) by specified persons or bodies, or persons or bodies of a specified description, or
  (b) on transactions, of a specified description, in securities on specified markets.

In this subsection "specified" means specified in the regulations.

(2) The power to specify (or to specify descriptions of) persons or bodies must be exercised in such a way that the levy is payable only by persons or bodies that appear to the Secretary of State—
  (a) to be capable of being directly affected by the exercise of any of the functions of the Panel, or
  (b) otherwise to have a substantial interest in the exercise of any of those functions.

(3) Regulations under this section may in particular—
  (a) specify the rate of the levy and the period in respect of which it is payable at that rate;
  (b) make provision as to the times when, and the manner in which, payments are to be made in respect of the levy.

(4) In determining the rate of the levy payable in respect of a particular period, the Secretary of State—
  (a) must take into account any other income received or expected by the Panel in respect of that period;
  (b) may take into account estimated as well as actual expenses of the Panel in respect of that period.

(5) The Panel must—
  (a) keep proper accounts in respect of any amounts of levy received by virtue of this section;
  (b) prepare, in relation to each period in respect of which any such amounts are received, a statement of account relating to those amounts in such form and manner as is specified in the regulations.

Those accounts must be audited, and the statement certified, by persons appointed by the Secretary of State.

(6) Regulations under this section—
  (a) are subject to affirmative resolution procedure if subsection (7) applies to them;
  (b) otherwise, are subject to negative resolution procedure.

(7) This subsection applies to—

PART II
OTHER ACTS

(a) the first regulations under this section;

(b) any other regulations under this section that would result in a change in the persons or bodies by whom, or the transactions on which, the levy is payable.

(8) If a draft of an instrument containing regulations under this section would, apart from this subsection, be treated for the purposes of the Standing Orders of either House of Parliament as a hybrid instrument, it is to proceed in that House as if it were not such an instrument.

[1692]

NOTES
Commencement: 20 January 2007 (for the purpose of enabling the exercise of powers to make Orders or Regulations by statutory instrument); 6 April 2007 (otherwise).

959 Recovery of fees, charges or levy

An amount payable by any person or body by virtue of section 957 or 958 is a debt due from that person or body to the Panel, and is recoverable accordingly.

[1693]

NOTES
Commencement: 6 April 2007.

Miscellaneous and supplementary

960 Panel as party to proceedings

The Panel is capable (despite being an unincorporated body) of—

(a) bringing proceedings under this Chapter in its own name;

(b) bringing or defending any other proceedings in its own name.

[1694]

NOTES
Commencement: 6 April 2007.

961 Exemption from liability in damages

(1) Neither the Panel, nor any person within subsection (2), is to be liable in damages for anything done (or omitted to be done) in, or in connection with, the discharge or purported discharge of the Panel's functions.

(2) A person is within this subsection if—

(a) he is (or is acting as) a member, officer or member of staff of the Panel, or

(b) he is a person authorised under section 947(5).

(3) Subsection (1) does not apply—

(a) if the act or omission is shown to have been in bad faith, or

(b) so as to prevent an award of damages in respect of the act or omission on the ground that it was unlawful as a result of section 6(1) of the Human Rights Act 1998 (c 42) (acts of public authorities incompatible with Convention rights).

[1695]

NOTES
Commencement: 6 April 2007.

962 Privilege against self-incrimination

(1) A statement made by a person in response to—

(a) a requirement under section 947(1), or

(b) an order made by the court under section 955 to secure compliance with such a requirement,

may not be used against him in criminal proceedings in which he is charged with an offence to which this subsection applies.

(2) Subsection (1) applies to any offence other than an offence under one of the following provisions (which concern false statements made otherwise than on oath)—

(a) section 5 of the Perjury Act 1911 (c 6);

(b) section 44(2) of the Criminal Law (Consolidation) (Scotland) Act 1995 (c 39);

(c) Article 10 of the Perjury (Northern Ireland) Order 1979 (SI 1979/1714 (NI 19)).

[1696]

NOTES
Commencement: 6 April 2007.

963 Annual reports

(1)   After the end of each financial year the Panel must publish a report.

(2)   The report must—
   (a)   set out how the Panel's functions were discharged in the year in question;
   (b)   include the Panel's accounts for that year;
   (c)   mention any matters the Panel considers to be of relevance to the discharge of its functions.

[1697]

NOTES
Commencement: 6 April 2007.

964   (*Amends the Financial Services and Markets Act 2000, ss 144, 349, 354, 417 at* **[172]**, **[375]**, **[380]**, **[443]**, *and repeals s 143 of the 2000 Act.*)

965 Power to extend to Isle of Man and Channel Islands

Her Majesty may by Order in Council direct that any of the provisions of this Chapter extend, with such modifications as may be specified in the Order, to the Isle of Man or any of the Channel Islands.

[1698]

NOTES
Commencement: 20 January 2007 (for the purpose of enabling the exercise of powers to make Orders or Regulations by statutory instrument); 6 April 2007 (otherwise).
Orders: the Companies Act 2006 (Extension of Takeover Panel Provisions) (Isle of Man) Order 2008, SI 2008/3122 (this Order (which comes into force on 1 March 2009) extends the provisions of this Chapter to the Isle of Man with certain modifications. Its purpose is to place on a statutory footing the role of the Panel on Takeovers and Mergers ("the Takeovers Panel") in supervising relevant takeovers involving Isle of Man companies. The modifications in the Schedule reflect differences in the legal system and governmental and regulatory structures of the Isle of Man, and make necessary consequential amendments to the Financial Services Act 2008 (an Act of Tynwald). Among other things, the modifications impose a duty on the Island's Financial Supervision Commission to co-operate with the Takeover Panel. The modifications also provide for the exchange of information about takeovers (subject to appropriate safeguards) between: (i) the Takeover Panel and those with regulatory, registry, prosecution and disciplinary functions on the Isle of Man in relation to companies and their officers; and (ii) those Manx authorities and corresponding bodies elsewhere).

PART II
OTHER ACTS

CHAPTER 2
IMPEDIMENTS TO TAKEOVERS

Opting in and opting out

966 Opting in and opting out

(1)   A company may by special resolution (an "opting-in resolution") opt in for the purposes of this Chapter if the following three conditions are met in relation to the company.

(2)   The first condition is that the company has voting shares admitted to trading on a regulated market.

(3)   The second condition is that—
   (a)   the company's articles of association—
      (i)   do not contain any such restrictions as are mentioned in Article 11 of the Takeovers Directive, or
      (ii)   if they do contain any such restrictions, provide for the restrictions not to apply at a time when, or in circumstances in which, they would be disapplied by that Article,
   and
   (b)   those articles do not contain any other provision which would be incompatible with that Article.

(4)   The third condition is that—
   (a)   no shares conferring special rights in the company are held by—
      (i)   a minister,
      (ii)   a nominee of, or any other person acting on behalf of, a minister, or
      (iii)   a company directly or indirectly controlled by a minister,
   and
   (b)   no such rights are exercisable by or on behalf of a minister under any enactment.

(5)   A company may revoke an opting-in resolution by a further special resolution (an "opting-out resolution").

(6)   For the purposes of subsection (3), a reference in Article 11 of the Takeovers Directive to Article 7.1 or 9 of that Directive is to be read as referring to rules under section 943(1) giving effect to the relevant Article.

(7)   In subsection (4) "minister" means—
  (a)   the holder of an office in Her Majesty's Government in the United Kingdom;
  (b)   the Scottish Ministers;
  (c)   a Minister within the meaning given by section 7(3) of the Northern Ireland Act 1998 (c 47);
  [(d)   the Welsh Ministers;]

and for the purposes of that subsection "minister" also includes the Treasury, the Board of Trade [and] the Defence Council ...

(8)   The Secretary of State may by order subject to negative resolution procedure provide that subsection (4) applies in relation to a specified person or body that exercises functions of a public nature as it applies in relation to a minister. "Specified" means specified in the order.

[1699]

NOTES
Commencement: 20 January 2007 (for the purpose of enabling the exercise of powers to make Orders or Regulations by statutory instrument); 6 April 2007 (otherwise).
Sub-s (7): para (d) inserted, word in second pair of square brackets inserted, and words omitted repealed, by the Government of Wales Act 2006 (Consequential Modifications and Transitional Provisions) Order 2007, SI 2007/1388, art 3, Sch 1, para 142, as from 2 May 2007.

967   Further provision about opting-in and opting-out resolutions

(1)   An opting-in resolution or an opting-out resolution must specify the date from which it is to have effect (the "effective date").

(2)   The effective date of an opting-in resolution may not be earlier than the date on which the resolution is passed.

(3)   The second and third conditions in section 966 must be met at the time when an opting-in resolution is passed, but the first one does not need to be met until the effective date.

(4)   An opting-in resolution passed before the time when voting shares of the company are admitted to trading on a regulated market complies with the requirement in subsection (1) if, instead of specifying a particular date, it provides for the resolution to have effect from that time.

(5)   An opting-in resolution passed before the commencement of this section complies with the requirement in subsection (1) if, instead of specifying a particular date, it provides for the resolution to have effect from that commencement.

(6)   The effective date of an opting-out resolution may not be earlier than the first anniversary of the date on which a copy of the opting-in resolution was forwarded to the registrar.

(7)   Where a company has passed an opting-in resolution, any alteration of its articles of association that would prevent the second condition in section 966 from being met is of no effect until the effective date of an opting-out resolution passed by the company.

[1700]

NOTES
Commencement: 6 April 2007.

Consequences of opting in

968   Effect on contractual restrictions

(1)   The following provisions have effect where a takeover bid is made for an opted-in company.

(2)   An agreement to which this section applies is invalid in so far as it places any restriction—
  (a)   on the transfer to the offeror, or at his direction to another person, of shares in the company during the offer period;
  (b)   on the transfer to any person of shares in the company at a time during the offer period when the offeror holds shares amounting to not less than 75% in value of all the voting shares in the company;
  (c)   on rights to vote at a general meeting of the company that decides whether to take any action which might result in the frustration of the bid;
  (d)   on rights to vote at a general meeting of the company that—
      (i)   is the first such meeting to be held after the end of the offer period, and
      (ii)   is held at a time when the offeror holds shares amounting to not less than 75% in value of all the voting shares in the company.

(3)   This section applies to an agreement—

(a)   entered into between a person holding shares in the company and another such person on or after 21st April 2004, or

(b)   entered into at any time between such a person and the company,

and it applies to such an agreement even if the law applicable to the agreement (apart from this section) is not the law of a part of the United Kingdom.

(4)   The reference in subsection (2)(c) to rights to vote at a general meeting of the company that decides whether to take any action which might result in the frustration of the bid includes a reference to rights to vote on a written resolution concerned with that question.

(5)   For the purposes of subsection (2)(c), action which might result in the frustration of a bid is any action of that kind specified in rules under section 943(1) giving effect to Article 9 of the Takeovers Directive.

(6)   If a person suffers loss as a result of any act or omission that would (but for this section) be a breach of an agreement to which this section applies, he is entitled to compensation, of such amount as the court considers just and equitable, from any person who would (but for this section) be liable to him for committing or inducing the breach.

(7)   In subsection (6) "the court" means the High Court or, in Scotland, the Court of Session.

(8)   A reference in this section to voting shares in the company does not include—
(a)   debentures, or
(b)   shares that, under the company's articles of association, do not normally carry rights to vote at its general meetings (for example, shares carrying rights to vote that, under those articles, arise only where specified pecuniary advantages are not provided).

[1701]

NOTES
Commencement: 6 April 2007.
Commencement (transitional adaptations): the transitional adaptations of this section contained in the Companies Act 2006 (Commencement No 2, Consequential Amendments, Transitional Provisions and Savings) Order 2007, SI 2007/1093, Sch 1, para 4 were revoked by the Companies Act 2006 (Commencement No 3, Consequential Amendments, Transitional Provisions and Savings) Order 2007, SI 2007/2194, art 11(b), as from 1 October 2007.

969   Power of offeror to require general meeting to be called

(1)   Where a takeover bid is made for an opted-in company, the offeror may by making a request to the directors of the company require them to call a general meeting of the company if, at the date at which the request is made, he holds shares amounting to not less than 75% in value of all the voting shares in the company.

(2)   The reference in subsection (1) to voting shares in the company does not include—
(a)   debentures, or
(b)   shares that, under the company's articles of association, do not normally carry rights to vote at its general meetings (for example, shares carrying rights to vote that, under those articles, arise only where specified pecuniary advantages are not provided).

(3)   Sections 303 to 305 (members' power to require general meetings to be called) apply as they would do if subsection (1) above were substituted for subsections (1) to (3) of section 303, and with any other necessary modifications.

[1702]

NOTES
Commencement: 6 April 2007.

Supplementary

970   Communication of decisions

(1)   A company that has passed an opting-in resolution or an opting-out resolution must notify—
(a)   the Panel, and
(b)   where the company—
    (i)   has voting shares admitted to trading on a regulated market in an EEA State other than the United Kingdom, or
    (ii)   has requested such admission,
the authority designated by that state as the supervisory authority for the purposes of Article 4.1 of the Takeovers Directive.

(2)   Notification must be given within 15 days after the resolution is passed and, if any admission or request such as is mentioned in subsection (1)(b) occurs at a later time, within 15 days after that time.

(3)   If a company fails to comply with this section, an offence is committed by—

(a)   the company, and
(b)   every officer of it who is in default.

(4)   A person guilty of an offence under this section is liable on summary conviction to a fine not exceeding level 3 on the standard scale and, for continued contravention, a daily default fine not exceeding one-tenth of level 3 on the standard scale.

[1703]

NOTES
Commencement: 6 April 2007.

971   Interpretation of this Chapter

(1)   In this Chapter—
    "offeror" and "takeover bid" have the same meaning as in the Takeovers Directive;
    "offer period", in relation to a takeover bid, means the time allowed for acceptance of the bid by—
        (a)   rules under section 943(1) giving effect to Article 7.1 of the Takeovers Directive, or
        (b)   where the rules giving effect to that Article which apply to the bid are those of an EEA State other than the United Kingdom, those rules;
    "opted-in company" means a company in relation to which—
        (a)   an opting-in resolution has effect, and
        (b)   the conditions in section 966(2) and (4) continue to be met;
    "opting-in resolution" has the meaning given by section 966(1);
    "opting-out resolution" has the meaning given by section 966(5);
    "the Takeovers Directive" means Directive 2004/25/EC of the European Parliament and of the Council;
    "voting rights" means rights to vote at general meetings of the company in question, including rights that arise only in certain circumstances;
    "voting shares" means shares carrying voting rights.

(2)   For the purposes of this Chapter—
    (a)   securities of a company are treated as shares in the company if they are convertible into or entitle the holder to subscribe for such shares;
    (b)   debentures issued by a company are treated as shares in the company if they carry voting rights.

[1704]

NOTES
Commencement: 6 April 2007.

972   Transitory provision

(1)   Where a takeover bid is made for an opted-in company, section 368 of the Companies Act 1985 (c 6) (extraordinary general meeting on members' requisition) and section 378 of that Act (extraordinary and special resolutions) have effect as follows until their repeal by this Act.

(2)   Section 368 has effect as if a members' requisition included a requisition of a person who—
    (a)   is the offeror in relation to the takeover bid, and
    (b)   holds at the date of the deposit of the requisition shares amounting to not less than 75% in value of all the voting shares in the company.

(3)   In relation to a general meeting of the company that—
    (a)   is the first such meeting to be held after the end of the offer period, and
    (b)   is held at a time when the offeror holds shares amounting to not less than 75% in value of all the voting shares in the company,
section 378(2) (meaning of "special resolution") has effect as if "14 days' notice" were substituted for "21 days' notice".

(4)   A reference in this section to voting shares in the company does not include—
    (a)   debentures, or
    (b)   shares that, under the company's articles of association, do not normally carry rights to vote at its general meetings (for example, shares carrying rights to vote that, under those articles, arise only where specified pecuniary advantages are not provided).

[1705]

NOTES
Commencement: 6 April 2007.

973 Power to extend to Isle of Man and Channel Islands

Her Majesty may by Order in Council direct that any of the provisions of this Chapter extend, with such modifications as may be specified in the Order, to the Isle of Man or any of the Channel Islands.

[1706]

NOTES
Commencement: 20 January 2007 (for the purpose of enabling the exercise of powers to make Orders or Regulations by statutory instrument); 6 April 2007 (otherwise).

CHAPTER 3
"SQUEEZE-OUT" AND "SELL-OUT"
Takeover offers

974 Meaning of "takeover offer"

(1)   For the purposes of this Chapter an offer to acquire shares in a company is a "takeover offer" if the following two conditions are satisfied in relation to the offer.

(2)   The first condition is that it is an offer to acquire—
   (a)   all the shares in a company, or
   (b)   where there is more than one class of shares in a company, all the shares of one or more classes,
other than shares that at the date of the offer are already held by the offeror. Section 975 contains provision supplementing this subsection.

(3)   The second condition is that the terms of the offer are the same—
   (a)   in relation to all the shares to which the offer relates, or
   (b)   where the shares to which the offer relates include shares of different classes, in relation to all the shares of each class.

Section 976 contains provision treating this condition as satisfied in certain circumstances.

(4)   In subsections (1) to (3) "shares" means shares, other than relevant treasury shares, that have been allotted on the date of the offer (but see subsection (5)).

(5)   A takeover offer may include among the shares to which it relates—
   (a)   all or any shares that are allotted after the date of the offer but before a specified date;
   (b)   all or any relevant treasury shares that cease to be held as treasury shares before a specified date;
   (c)   all or any other relevant treasury shares.

(6)   In this section—
   "relevant treasury shares" means shares that—
      (a)   are held by the company as treasury shares on the date of the offer, or
      (b)   become shares held by the company as treasury shares after that date but before a specified date;
   "specified date" means a date specified in or determined in accordance with the terms of the offer.

(7)   Where the terms of an offer make provision for their revision and for acceptances on the previous terms to be treated as acceptances on the revised terms, then, if the terms of the offer are revised in accordance with that provision—
   (a)   the revision is not to be regarded for the purposes of this Chapter as the making of a fresh offer, and
   (b)   references in this Chapter to the date of the offer are accordingly to be read as references to the date of the original offer.

[1707]

NOTES
Commencement: 6 April 2007.

975 Shares already held by the offeror etc

(1)   The reference in section 974(2) to shares already held by the offeror includes a reference to shares that he has contracted to acquire, whether unconditionally or subject to conditions being met.

This is subject to subsection (2).

(2)   The reference in section 974(2) to shares already held by the offeror does not include a reference to shares that are the subject of a contract—
   (a)   intended to secure that the holder of the shares will accept the offer when it is made, and
   (b)   entered into—
      (i)   by deed and for no consideration,

(ii)   for consideration of negligible value, or

(iii)   for consideration consisting of a promise by the offeror to make the offer.

(3)   In relation to Scotland, this section applies as if the words "by deed and" in subsection (2)(b)(i) were omitted.

(4)   The condition in section 974(2) is treated as satisfied where—

(a)   the offer does not extend to shares that associates of the offeror hold or have contracted to acquire (whether unconditionally or subject to conditions being met), and

(b)   the condition would be satisfied if the offer did extend to those shares.

(For further provision about such shares, see section 977(2)).

[1708]

NOTES

Commencement: 6 April 2007.

976 Cases where offer treated as being on same terms

(1)   The condition in section 974(3) (terms of offer to be the same for all shares or all shares of particular classes) is treated as satisfied where subsection (2) or (3) below applies.

(2)   This subsection applies where—

(a)   shares carry an entitlement to a particular dividend which other shares of the same class, by reason of being allotted later, do not carry,

(b)   there is a difference in the value of consideration offered for the shares allotted earlier as against that offered for those allotted later,

(c)   that difference merely reflects the difference in entitlement to the dividend, and

(d)   the condition in section 974(3) would be satisfied but for that difference.

(3)   This subsection applies where—

(a)   the law of a country or territory outside the United Kingdom—

(i)   precludes an offer of consideration in the form, or any of the forms, specified in the terms of the offer ("the specified form"), or

(ii)   precludes it except after compliance by the offeror with conditions with which he is unable to comply or which he regards as unduly onerous,

(b)   the persons to whom an offer of consideration in the specified form is precluded are able to receive consideration in another form that is of substantially equivalent value, and

(c)   the condition in section 974(3) would be satisfied but for the fact that an offer of consideration in the specified form to those persons is precluded.

[1709]

NOTES

Commencement: 6 April 2007.

977 Shares to which an offer relates

(1)   Where a takeover offer is made and, during the period beginning with the date of the offer and ending when the offer can no longer be accepted, the offeror—

(a)   acquires or unconditionally contracts to acquire any of the shares to which the offer relates, but

(b)   does not do so by virtue of acceptances of the offer,

those shares are treated for the purposes of this Chapter as excluded from those to which the offer relates.

(2)   For the purposes of this Chapter shares that an associate of the offeror holds or has contracted to acquire, whether at the date of the offer or subsequently, are not treated as shares to which the offer relates, even if the offer extends to such shares.

In this subsection "contracted" means contracted unconditionally or subject to conditions being met.

(3)   This section is subject to section 979(8) and (9).

[1710]

NOTES

Commencement: 6 April 2007.

978 Effect of impossibility etc of communicating or accepting offer

(1)   Where there are holders of shares in a company to whom an offer to acquire shares in the company is not communicated, that does not prevent the offer from being a takeover offer for the purposes of this Chapter if—

(a)   those shareholders have no registered address in the United Kingdom,

(b)   the offer was not communicated to those shareholders in order not to contravene the law of a country or territory outside the United Kingdom, and

(c)   either—
    (i)   the offer is published in the Gazette, or
    (ii)   the offer can be inspected, or a copy of it obtained, at a place in an EEA State or on a website, and a notice is published in the Gazette specifying the address of that place or website.

(2)   Where an offer is made to acquire shares in a company and there are persons for whom, by reason of the law of a country or territory outside the United Kingdom, it is impossible to accept the offer, or more difficult to do so, that does not prevent the offer from being a takeover offer for the purposes of this Chapter.

(3)   It is not to be inferred—
(a)   that an offer which is not communicated to every holder of shares in the company cannot be a takeover offer for the purposes of this Chapter unless the requirements of paragraphs (a) to (c) of subsection (1) are met, or
(b)   that an offer which is impossible, or more difficult, for certain persons to accept cannot be a takeover offer for those purposes unless the reason for the impossibility or difficulty is the one mentioned in subsection (2).

[1711]

NOTES
Commencement: 6 April 2007.

"Squeeze-out"

979   Right of offeror to buy out minority shareholder

(1)   Subsection (2) applies in a case where a takeover offer does not relate to shares of different classes.

(2)   If the offeror has, by virtue of acceptances of the offer, acquired or unconditionally contracted to acquire—
(a)   not less than 90% in value of the shares to which the offer relates, and
(b)   in a case where the shares to which the offer relates are voting shares, not less than 90% of the voting rights carried by those shares,

he may give notice to the holder of any shares to which the offer relates which the offeror has not acquired or unconditionally contracted to acquire that he desires to acquire those shares.

(3)   Subsection (4) applies in a case where a takeover offer relates to shares of different classes.

(4)   If the offeror has, by virtue of acceptances of the offer, acquired or unconditionally contracted to acquire—
(a)   not less than 90% in value of the shares of any class to which the offer relates, and
(b)   in a case where the shares of that class are voting shares, not less than 90% of the voting rights carried by those shares,

he may give notice to the holder of any shares of that class to which the offer relates which the offeror has not acquired or unconditionally contracted to acquire that he desires to acquire those shares.

(5)   In the case of a takeover offer which includes among the shares to which it relates—
(a)   shares that are allotted after the date of the offer, or
(b)   relevant treasury shares (within the meaning of section 974) that cease to be held as treasury shares after the date of the offer,

the offeror's entitlement to give a notice under subsection (2) or (4) on any particular date shall be determined as if the shares to which the offer relates did not include any allotted, or ceasing to be held as treasury shares, on or after that date.

(6)   Subsection (7) applies where—
(a)   the requirements for the giving of a notice under subsection (2) or (4) are satisfied, and
(b)   there are shares in the company which the offeror, or an associate of his, has contracted to acquire subject to conditions being met, and in relation to which the contract has not become unconditional.

(7)   The offeror's entitlement to give a notice under subsection (2) or (4) shall be determined as if—
(a)   the shares to which the offer relates included shares falling within paragraph (b) of subsection (6), and
(b)   in relation to shares falling within that paragraph, the words "by virtue of acceptances of the offer" in subsection (2) or (4) were omitted.

(8)   Where—
(a)   a takeover offer is made,

(b)   during the period beginning with the date of the offer and ending when the offer can no
       longer be accepted, the offeror—
       (i)   acquires or unconditionally contracts to acquire any of the shares to which the
              offer relates, but
       (ii)   does not do so by virtue of acceptances of the offer, and
(c)   subsection (10) applies,

then for the purposes of this section those shares are not excluded by section 977(1) from those to
which the offer relates, and the offeror is treated as having acquired or contracted to acquire them by
virtue of acceptances of the offer.

(9)   Where—
(a)   a takeover offer is made,
(b)   during the period beginning with the date of the offer and ending when the offer can no
       longer be accepted, an associate of the offeror acquires or unconditionally contracts to
       acquire any of the shares to which the offer relates, and
(c)   subsection (10) applies,

then for the purposes of this section those shares are not excluded by section 977(2) from those to
which the offer relates.

(10)   This subsection applies if—
(a)   at the time the shares are acquired or contracted to be acquired as mentioned in
       subsection (8) or (9) (as the case may be), the value of the consideration for which they
       are acquired or contracted to be acquired ("the acquisition consideration") does not
       exceed the value of the consideration specified in the terms of the offer, or
(b)   those terms are subsequently revised so that when the revision is announced the value of
       the acquisition consideration, at the time mentioned in paragraph (a), no longer exceeds
       the value of the consideration specified in those terms.

                                                                                        [1712]

NOTES
Commencement: 6 April 2007.

980 Further provision about notices given under section 979

(1)   A notice under section 979 must be given in the prescribed manner.

(2)   No notice may be given under section 979(2) or (4) after the end of—
(a)   the period of three months beginning with the day after the last day on which the offer
       can be accepted, or
(b)   the period of six months beginning with the date of the offer, where that period ends
       earlier and the offer is one to which subsection (3) below applies.

(3)   This subsection applies to an offer if the time allowed for acceptance of the offer is not
governed by rules under section 943(1) that give effect to Article 7 of the Takeovers Directive.

In this subsection "the Takeovers Directive" has the same meaning as in section 943.

(4)   At the time when the offeror first gives a notice under section 979 in relation to an offer, he
must send to the company—
(a)   a copy of the notice, and
(b)   a statutory declaration by him in the prescribed form, stating that the conditions for the
       giving of the notice are satisfied.

(5)   Where the offeror is a company (whether or not a company within the meaning of this Act)
the statutory declaration must be signed by a director.

(6)   A person commits an offence if—
(a)   he fails to send a copy of a notice or a statutory declaration as required by subsection (4),
       or
(b)   he makes such a declaration for the purposes of that subsection knowing it to be false or
       without having reasonable grounds for believing it to be true.

(7)   It is a defence for a person charged with an offence for failing to send a copy of a notice as
required by subsection (4) to prove that he took reasonable steps for securing compliance with that
subsection.

(8)   A person guilty of an offence under this section is liable—
(a)   on conviction on indictment, to imprisonment for a term not exceeding two years or a
       fine (or both);
(b)   on summary conviction—
       (i)   in England and Wales, to imprisonment for a term not exceeding twelve months
              or to a fine not exceeding the statutory maximum (or both) and, for continued
              contravention, a daily default fine not exceeding one-fiftieth of the statutory
              maximum;

(ii) in Scotland or Northern Ireland, to imprisonment for a term not exceeding six months, or to a fine not exceeding the statutory maximum (or both) and, for continued contravention, a daily default fine not exceeding one-fiftieth of the statutory maximum.

[1713]

NOTES

Commencement: 20 January 2007 (for the purpose of enabling the exercise of powers to make Orders or Regulations by statutory instrument); 6 April 2007 (otherwise).

Imprisonment for a term not exceeding twelve months: see the note to s 387 at **[1514]**.

981　Effect of notice under section 979

(1) Subject to section 986 (applications to the court), this section applies where the offeror gives a shareholder a notice under section 979.

(2) The offeror is entitled and bound to acquire the shares to which the notice relates on the terms of the offer.

(3) Where the terms of an offer are such as to give the shareholder a choice of consideration, the notice must give particulars of the choice and state—
   (a) that the shareholder may, within six weeks from the date of the notice, indicate his choice by a written communication sent to the offeror at an address specified in the notice, and
   (b) which consideration specified in the offer will apply if he does not indicate a choice.

The reference in subsection (2) to the terms of the offer is to be read accordingly.

(4) Subsection (3) applies whether or not any time-limit or other conditions applicable to the choice under the terms of the offer can still be complied with.

(5) If the consideration offered to or (as the case may be) chosen by the shareholder—
   (a) is not cash and the offeror is no longer able to provide it, or
   (b) was to have been provided by a third party who is no longer bound or able to provide it,

the consideration is to be taken to consist of an amount of cash, payable by the offeror, which at the date of the notice is equivalent to the consideration offered or (as the case may be) chosen.

(6) At the end of six weeks from the date of the notice the offeror must immediately—
   (a) send a copy of the notice to the company, and
   (b) pay or transfer to the company the consideration for the shares to which the notice relates.

Where the consideration consists of shares or securities to be allotted by the offeror, the reference in paragraph (b) to the transfer of the consideration is to be read as a reference to the allotment of the shares or securities to the company.

(7) If the shares to which the notice relates are registered, the copy of the notice sent to the company under subsection (6)(a) must be accompanied by an instrument of transfer executed on behalf of the holder of the shares by a person appointed by the offeror.

On receipt of that instrument the company must register the offeror as the holder of those shares.

(8) If the shares to which the notice relates are transferable by the delivery of warrants or other instruments, the copy of the notice sent to the company under subsection (6)(a) must be accompanied by a statement to that effect. On receipt of that statement the company must issue the offeror with warrants or other instruments in respect of the shares, and those already in issue in respect of the shares become void.

(9) The company must hold any money or other consideration received by it under subsection (6)(b) on trust for the person who, before the offeror acquired them, was entitled to the shares in respect of which the money or other consideration was received.

Section 982 contains further provision about how the company should deal with such money or other consideration.

[1714]

NOTES

Commencement: 6 April 2007.

982　Further provision about consideration held on trust under section 981(9)

(1) This section applies where an offeror pays or transfers consideration to the company under section 981(6).

(2) The company must pay into a separate bank account that complies with subsection (3)—
   (a) any money it receives under paragraph (b) of section 981(6), and
   (b) any dividend or other sum accruing from any other consideration it receives under that paragraph.

(3)   A bank account complies with this subsection if the balance on the account—
   (a)   bears interest at an appropriate rate, and
   (b)   can be withdrawn by such notice (if any) as is appropriate.

(4)   If—
   (a)   the person entitled to the consideration held on trust by virtue of section 981(9) cannot be found, and
   (b)   subsection (5) applies,
the consideration (together with any interest, dividend or other benefit that has accrued from it) must be paid into court.

(5)   This subsection applies where—
   (a)   reasonable enquiries have been made at reasonable intervals to find the person, and
   (b)   twelve years have elapsed since the consideration was received, or the company is wound up.

(6)   In relation to a company registered in Scotland, subsections (7) and (8) apply instead of subsection (4).

(7)   If the person entitled to the consideration held on trust by virtue of section 981(9) cannot be found and subsection (5) applies—
   (a)   the trust terminates,
   (b)   the company or (if the company is wound up) the liquidator must sell any consideration other than cash and any benefit other than cash that has accrued from the consideration, and
   (c)   a sum representing—
      (i)   the consideration so far as it is cash,
      (ii)   the proceeds of any sale under paragraph (b), and
      (iii)   any interest, dividend or other benefit that has accrued from the consideration,
must be deposited in the name of the Accountant of Court in a separate bank account complying with subsection (3) and the receipt for the deposit must be transmitted to the Accountant of Court.

(8)   Section 58 of the Bankruptcy (Scotland) Act 1985 (c 66) (so far as consistent with this Act) applies (with any necessary modifications) to sums deposited under subsection (7) as it applies to sums deposited under section 57(1)(a) of that Act.

(9)   The expenses of any such enquiries as are mentioned in subsection (5) may be paid out of the money or other property held on trust for the person to whom the enquiry relates.

[1715]

NOTES
Commencement: 6 April 2007.

"Sell-out"

983   Right of minority shareholder to be bought out by offeror

(1)   Subsections (2) and (3) apply in a case where a takeover offer relates to all the shares in a company.

For this purpose a takeover offer relates to all the shares in a company if it is an offer to acquire all the shares in the company within the meaning of section 974.

(2)   The holder of any voting shares to which the offer relates who has not accepted the offer may require the offeror to acquire those shares if, at any time before the end of the period within which the offer can be accepted—
   (a)   the offeror has by virtue of acceptances of the offer acquired or unconditionally contracted to acquire some (but not all) of the shares to which the offer relates, and
   (b)   those shares, with or without any other shares in the company which he has acquired or contracted to acquire (whether unconditionally or subject to conditions being met)—
      (i)   amount to not less than 90% in value of all the voting shares in the company (or would do so but for section 990(1)), and
      (ii)   carry not less than 90% of the voting rights in the company (or would do so but for section 990(1)).

(3)   The holder of any non-voting shares to which the offer relates who has not accepted the offer may require the offeror to acquire those shares if, at any time before the end of the period within which the offer can be accepted—
   (a)   the offeror has by virtue of acceptances of the offer acquired or unconditionally contracted to acquire some (but not all) of the shares to which the offer relates, and
   (b)   those shares, with or without any other shares in the company which he has acquired or

contracted to acquire (whether unconditionally or subject to conditions being met), amount to not less than 90% in value of all the shares in the company (or would do so but for section 990(1)).

(4)   If a takeover offer relates to shares of one or more classes and at any time before the end of the period within which the offer can be accepted—

(a)   the offeror has by virtue of acceptances of the offer acquired or unconditionally contracted to acquire some (but not all) of the shares of any class to which the offer relates, and

(b)   those shares, with or without any other shares of that class which he has acquired or contracted to acquire (whether unconditionally or subject to conditions being met)—

(i)   amount to not less than 90% in value of all the shares of that class, and

(ii)   in a case where the shares of that class are voting shares, carry not less than 90% of the voting rights carried by the shares of that class,

the holder of any shares of that class to which the offer relates who has not accepted the offer may require the offeror to acquire those shares.

(5)   For the purposes of subsections (2) to (4), in calculating 90% of the value of any shares, shares held by the company as treasury shares are to be treated as having been acquired by the offeror.

(6)   Subsection (7) applies where—

(a)   a shareholder exercises rights conferred on him by subsection (2), (3) or (4),

(b)   at the time when he does so, there are shares in the company which the offeror has contracted to acquire subject to conditions being met, and in relation to which the contract has not become unconditional, and

(c)   the requirement imposed by subsection (2)(b), (3)(b) or (4)(b) (as the case may be) would not be satisfied if those shares were not taken into account.

(7)   The shareholder is treated for the purposes of section 985 as not having exercised his rights under this section unless the requirement imposed by paragraph (b) of subsection (2), (3) or (4) (as the case may be) would be satisfied if—

(a)   the reference in that paragraph to other shares in the company which the offeror has contracted to acquire unconditionally or subject to conditions being met were a reference to such shares which he has unconditionally contracted to acquire, and

(b)   the reference in that subsection to the period within which the offer can be accepted were a reference to the period referred to in section 984(2).

(8)   A reference in subsection (2)(b), (3)(b), (4)(b), (6) or (7) to shares which the offeror has acquired or contracted to acquire includes a reference to shares which an associate of his has acquired or contracted to acquire.

[1716]

NOTES

Commencement: 6 April 2007.

---

984   Further provision about rights conferred by section 983

(1)   Rights conferred on a shareholder by subsection (2), (3) or (4) of section 983 are exercisable by a written communication addressed to the offeror.

(2)   Rights conferred on a shareholder by subsection (2), (3) or (4) of that section are not exercisable after the end of the period of three months from—

(a)   the end of the period within which the offer can be accepted, or

(b)   if later, the date of the notice that must be given under subsection (3) below.

(3)   Within one month of the time specified in subsection (2), (3) or (4) (as the case may be) of that section, the offeror must give any shareholder who has not accepted the offer notice in the prescribed manner of—

(a)   the rights that are exercisable by the shareholder under that subsection, and

(b)   the period within which the rights are exercisable.

If the notice is given before the end of the period within which the offer can be accepted, it must state that the offer is still open for acceptance.

(4)   Subsection (3) does not apply if the offeror has given the shareholder a notice in respect of the shares in question under section 979.

(5)   An offeror who fails to comply with subsection (3) commits an offence.

If the offeror is a company, every officer of that company who is in default or to whose neglect the failure is attributable also commits an offence.

(6)   If an offeror other than a company is charged with an offence for failing to comply with subsection (3), it is a defence for him to prove that he took all reasonable steps for securing compliance with that subsection.

(7)   A person guilty of an offence under this section is liable—
  (a)   on conviction on indictment, to a fine;
  (b)   on summary conviction, to a fine not exceeding the statutory maximum and, for continued contravention, a daily default fine not exceeding one-fiftieth of the statutory maximum.

[1717]

NOTES
Commencement: 20 January 2007 (for the purpose of enabling the exercise of powers to make Orders or Regulations by statutory instrument); 6 April 2007 (otherwise).
2007, SI 2007/318.

985   Effect of requirement under section 983

(1)   Subject to section 986, this section applies where a shareholder exercises his rights under section 983 in respect of any shares held by him.

(2)   The offeror is entitled and bound to acquire those shares on the terms of the offer or on such other terms as may be agreed.

(3)   Where the terms of an offer are such as to give the shareholder a choice of consideration—
  (a)   the shareholder may indicate his choice when requiring the offeror to acquire the shares, and
  (b)   the notice given to the shareholder under section 984(3)—
    (i)   must give particulars of the choice and of the rights conferred by this subsection, and
    (ii)   may state which consideration specified in the offer will apply if he does not indicate a choice.

The reference in subsection (2) to the terms of the offer is to be read accordingly.

(4)   Subsection (3) applies whether or not any time-limit or other conditions applicable to the choice under the terms of the offer can still be complied with.

(5)   If the consideration offered to or (as the case may be) chosen by the shareholder—
  (a)   is not cash and the offeror is no longer able to provide it, or
  (b)   was to have been provided by a third party who is no longer bound or able to provide it,

the consideration is to be taken to consist of an amount of cash, payable by the offeror, which at the date when the shareholder requires the offeror to acquire the shares is equivalent to the consideration offered or (as the case may be) chosen.

[1718]

NOTES
Commencement: 6 April 2007.

Supplementary

986   Applications to the court

(1)   Where a notice is given under section 979 to a shareholder the court may, on an application made by him, order—
  (a)   that the offeror is not entitled and bound to acquire the shares to which the notice relates, or
  (b)   that the terms on which the offeror is entitled and bound to acquire the shares shall be such as the court thinks fit.

(2)   An application under subsection (1) must be made within six weeks from the date on which the notice referred to in that subsection was given.

If an application to the court under subsection (1) is pending at the end of that period, section 981(6) does not have effect until the application has been disposed of.

(3)   Where a shareholder exercises his rights under section 983 in respect of any shares held by him, the court may, on an application made by him or the offeror, order that the terms on which the offeror is entitled and bound to acquire the shares shall be such as the court thinks fit.

(4)   On an application under subsection (1) or (3)—
  (a)   the court may not require consideration of a higher value than that specified in the terms of the offer ("the offer value") to be given for the shares to which the application relates unless the holder of the shares shows that the offer value would be unfair;
  (b)   the court may not require consideration of a lower value than the offer value to be given for the shares.

(5)   No order for costs or expenses may be made against a shareholder making an application under subsection (1) or (3) unless the court considers that—
  (a)   the application was unnecessary, improper or vexatious,

(b) there has been unreasonable delay in making the application, or

(c) there has been unreasonable conduct on the shareholder's part in conducting the proceedings on the application.

(6) A shareholder who has made an application under subsection (1) or (3) must give notice of the application to the offeror.

(7) An offeror who is given notice of an application under subsection (1) or (3) must give a copy of the notice to—

(a) any person (other than the applicant) to whom a notice has been given under section 979;

(b) any person who has exercised his rights under section 983.

(8) An offeror who makes an application under subsection (3) must give notice of the application to—

(a) any person to whom a notice has been given under section 979;

(b) any person who has exercised his rights under section 983.

(9) Where a takeover offer has not been accepted to the extent necessary for entitling the offeror to give notices under subsection (2) or (4) of section 979 the court may, on an application made by him, make an order authorising him to give notices under that subsection if it is satisfied that—

(a) the offeror has after reasonable enquiry been unable to trace one or more of the persons holding shares to which the offer relates,

(b) the requirements of that subsection would have been met if the person, or all the persons, mentioned in paragraph (a) above had accepted the offer, and

(c) the consideration offered is fair and reasonable.

This is subject to subsection (10).

(10) The court may not make an order under subsection (9) unless it considers that it is just and equitable to do so having regard, in particular, to the number of shareholders who have been traced but who have not accepted the offer.

[1719]

NOTES

Commencement: 6 April 2007.

987 Joint offers

(1) In the case of a takeover offer made by two or more persons jointly, this Chapter has effect as follows.

(2) The conditions for the exercise of the rights conferred by section 979 are satisfied—

(a) in the case of acquisitions by virtue of acceptances of the offer, by the joint offerors acquiring or unconditionally contracting to acquire the necessary shares jointly;

(b) in other cases, by the joint offerors acquiring or unconditionally contracting to acquire the necessary shares either jointly or separately.

(3) The conditions for the exercise of the rights conferred by section 983 are satisfied—

(a) in the case of acquisitions by virtue of acceptances of the offer, by the joint offerors acquiring or unconditionally contracting to acquire the necessary shares jointly;

(b) in other cases, by the joint offerors acquiring or contracting (whether unconditionally or subject to conditions being met) to acquire the necessary shares either jointly or separately.

(4) Subject to the following provisions, the rights and obligations of the offeror under sections 979 to 985 are respectively joint rights and joint and several obligations of the joint offerors.

(5) A provision of sections 979 to 986 that requires or authorises a notice or other document to be given or sent by or to the joint offerors is complied with if the notice or document is given or sent by or to any of them (but see subsection (6)).

(6) The statutory declaration required by section 980(4) must be made by all of the joint offerors and, where one or more of them is a company, signed by a director of that company.

(7) In sections 974 to 977, 979(9), 981(6), 983(8) and 988 references to the offeror are to be read as references to the joint offerors or any of them.

(8) In section 981(7) and (8) references to the offeror are to be read as references to the joint offerors or such of them as they may determine.

(9) In sections 981(5)(a) and 985(5)(a) references to the offeror being no longer able to provide the relevant consideration are to be read as references to none of the joint offerors being able to do so.

(10)   In section 986 references to the offeror are to be read as references to the joint offerors, except that—
    (a)   an application under subsection (3) or (9) may be made by any of them, and
    (b)   the reference in subsection (9)(a) to the offeror having been unable to trace one or more of the persons holding shares is to be read as a reference to none of the offerors having been able to do so.

[1720]

NOTES
Commencement: 6 April 2007.

Interpretation

988 Associates

(1)   In this Chapter "associate", in relation to an offeror, means—
    (a)   a nominee of the offeror,
    (b)   a holding company, subsidiary or fellow subsidiary of the offeror or a nominee of such a holding company, subsidiary or fellow subsidiary,
    (c)   a body corporate in which the offeror is substantially interested,
    (d)   a person who is, or is a nominee of, a party to a share acquisition agreement with the offeror, or
    (e)   (where the offeror is an individual) his spouse or civil partner and any minor child or step-child of his.

(2)   For the purposes of subsection (1)(b) a company is a fellow subsidiary of another body corporate if both are subsidiaries of the same body corporate but neither is a subsidiary of the other.

(3)   For the purposes of subsection (1)(c) an offeror has a substantial interest in a body corporate if—
    (a)   the body or its directors are accustomed to act in accordance with his directions or instructions, or
    (b)   he is entitled to exercise or control the exercise of one-third or more of the voting power at general meetings of the body.

Subsections (2) and (3) of section 823 (which contain provision about when a person is treated as entitled to exercise or control the exercise of voting power) apply for the purposes of this subsection as they apply for the purposes of that section.

(4)   For the purposes of subsection (1)(d) an agreement is a share acquisition agreement if—
    (a)   it is an agreement for the acquisition of, or of an interest in, shares to which the offer relates,
    (b)   it includes provisions imposing obligations or restrictions on any one or more of the parties to it with respect to their use, retention or disposal of such shares, or their interests in such shares, acquired in pursuance of the agreement (whether or not together with any other shares to which the offer relates or any other interests of theirs in such shares), and
    (c)   it is not an excluded agreement (see subsection (5)).

(5)   An agreement is an "excluded agreement"—
    (a)   if it is not legally binding, unless it involves mutuality in the undertakings, expectations or understandings of the parties to it, or
    (b)   if it is an agreement to underwrite or sub-underwrite an offer of shares in a company, provided the agreement is confined to that purpose and any matters incidental to it.

(6)   The reference in subsection (4)(b) to the use of interests in shares is to the exercise of any rights or of any control or influence arising from those interests (including the right to enter into an agreement for the exercise, or for control of the exercise, of any of those rights by another person).

(7)   In this section—
    (a)   "agreement" includes any agreement or arrangement;
    (b)   references to provisions of an agreement include—
        (i)   undertakings, expectations or understandings operative under an arrangement, and
        (ii)   any provision whether express or implied and whether absolute or not.

[1721]

NOTES
Commencement: 6 April 2007.

989 Convertible securities

(1)   For the purposes of this Chapter securities of a company are treated as shares in the company if they are convertible into or entitle the holder to subscribe for such shares.

References to the holder of shares or a shareholder are to be read accordingly.

(2)   Subsection (1) is not to be read as requiring any securities to be treated—

(a)   as shares of the same class as those into which they are convertible or for which the holder is entitled to subscribe, or

(b)   as shares of the same class as other securities by reason only that the shares into which they are convertible or for which the holder is entitled to subscribe are of the same class.

[1722]

NOTES
Commencement: 6 April 2007.

990   Debentures carrying voting rights

(1)   For the purposes of this Chapter debentures issued by a company to which subsection (2) applies are treated as shares in the company if they carry voting rights.

(2)   This subsection applies to a company that has voting shares, or debentures carrying voting rights, which are admitted to trading on a regulated market.

(3)   In this Chapter, in relation to debentures treated as shares by virtue of subsection (1)—

(a)   references to the holder of shares or a shareholder are to be read accordingly;

(b)   references to shares being allotted are to be read as references to debentures being issued.

[1723]

NOTES
Commencement: 6 April 2007.

991   Interpretation

(1)   In this Chapter—

"the company" means the company whose shares are the subject of a takeover offer;

"date of the offer" means—

(a)   where the offer is published, the date of publication;

(b)   where the offer is not published, or where any notices of the offer are given before the date of publication, the date when notices of the offer (or the first such notices) are given;

and references to the date of the offer are to be read in accordance with section 974(7) (revision of offer terms) where that applies;

"non-voting shares" means shares that are not voting shares;

"offeror" means (subject to section 987) the person making a takeover offer;

"voting rights" means rights to vote at general meetings of the company, including rights that arise only in certain circumstances;

"voting shares" means shares carrying voting rights.

(2)   For the purposes of this Chapter a person contracts unconditionally to acquire shares if his entitlement under the contract to acquire them is not (or is no longer) subject to conditions or if all conditions to which it was subject have been met.

A reference to a contract becoming unconditional is to be read accordingly.

[1724]

NOTES
Commencement: 6 April 2007.

992   (*Inserts the Companies Act 1985, Sch 7, Pt VII, and amends ss 234ZZA and 251, in relation to directors' reports for financial years beginning on or after 20 May 2006 (all repealed by virtue of this Act as from 6 April 2008, subject to savings in relation to financial years beginning before that date*).)

PART 38
COMPANIES: INTERPRETATION
Meaning of "UK-registered company"

1158   Meaning of "UK-registered company"

In the Companies Acts "UK-registered company" means a company registered under this Act.

The expression does not include an overseas company that has registered particulars under section 1046.

[1724A]

NOTES
Commencement: 1 October 2007 (certain purposes); 1 November 2007 (certain purposes); 1 October 2009 (otherwise) (see the note below).

Commencement (transitional adaptations): art 6 of the Companies Act 2006 (Commencement No 3, Consequential Amendments, Transitional Provisions and Savings) Order 2007, SI 2007/2194 provides that the provisions brought into force by that Order shall have effect subject to any transitional adaptations specified in Sch 1 to that Order. Schedule 1, para 21 to the Order provides as follows (note that this paragraph is revoked by the Companies Act 2006 (Commencement No 8, Transitional Provisions and Savings) Order 2008, SI 2008/2860, art 6, as from 1 October 2009 (subject to any relevant transitional provision or saving in Sch 2 to that Order))—

"21 Meaning of "UK-registered company" (s 1158)

    (1)   Section 1158 (meaning of "UK-registered company") has effect with the following adaptations.

    (2)   For "a company registered under this Act" substitute "a company within the meaning of the Companies Act 1985 or the Companies (Northern Ireland) Order 1986 or a company registered under section 680 of that Act or Article 629 of that Order.".

    (3)   For "an overseas company that has registered particulars under section 1046" substitute "an oversea company within the meaning of that Act or a Part 23 company within the meaning of that Order".".

Commencement (note): the Companies Act 2006 (Commencement No 3, Consequential Amendments, Transitional Provisions and Savings) Order 2007, SI 2007/2194, arts 2(3) and 3(2) provide that this section shall come into force on 1 October 2007 and 1 November 2007 so far as is necessary for the purposes of the provisions of this Act brought into force on those dates by arts 2(1), (2) and 3(2) of that Order respectively.

Meaning of "subsidiary" and related expressions

1159 Meaning of "subsidiary" etc

    (1)   A company is a "subsidiary" of another company, its "holding company", if that other company—

        (a)   holds a majority of the voting rights in it, or

        (b)   is a member of it and has the right to appoint or remove a majority of its board of directors, or

        (c)   is a member of it and controls alone, pursuant to an agreement with other members, a majority of the voting rights in it,

or if it is a subsidiary of a company that is itself a subsidiary of that other company.

    (2)   A company is a "wholly-owned subsidiary" of another company if it has no members except that other and that other's wholly-owned subsidiaries or persons acting on behalf of that other or its wholly-owned subsidiaries.

    (3)   Schedule 6 contains provisions explaining expressions used in this section and otherwise supplementing this section.

    (4)   In this section and that Schedule "company" includes any body corporate.

[1725]

NOTES
Commencement: 6 April 2008 (so far as necessary for the purposes of ss 1209–1241, 1245–1264, and Schs 10, 11, 13, 14 (statutory auditors)); 1 October 2009 (otherwise).

1160 Meaning of "subsidiary" etc: power to amend

    (1)   The Secretary of State may by regulations amend the provisions of section 1159 (meaning of "subsidiary" etc) and Schedule 6 (meaning of "subsidiary" etc: supplementary provisions) so as to alter the meaning of the expressions "subsidiary", "holding company" or "wholly-owned subsidiary".

    (2)   Regulations under this section are subject to negative resolution procedure.

    (3)   Any amendment made by regulations under this section does not apply for the purposes of enactments outside the Companies Acts unless the regulations so provide.

    (4)   So much of section 23(3) of the Interpretation Act 1978 (c 30) as applies section 17(2)(a) of that Act (effect of repeal and re-enactment) to deeds, instruments and documents other than enactments does not apply in relation to any repeal and re-enactment effected by regulations under this section.

[1726]

NOTES
Commencement: 20 January 2007 (for the purpose of enabling the exercise of powers to make Orders or Regulations by statutory instrument); 6 April 2008 (so far as necessary for the purposes of ss 1209–1241, 1245–1264, and Schs 10, 11, 13, 14 (statutory auditors)); 1 October 2009 (otherwise).

Meaning of "undertaking" and related expressions

1161   Meaning of "undertaking" and related expressions

(1)   In the Companies Acts "undertaking" means—

    (a)   a body corporate or partnership, or

    (b)   an unincorporated association carrying on a trade or business, with or without a view to profit.

(2)   In the Companies Acts references to shares—

    (a)   in relation to an undertaking with capital but no share capital, are to rights to share in the capital of the undertaking; and

    (b)   in relation to an undertaking without capital, are to interests—

        (i)   conferring any right to share in the profits or liability to contribute to the losses of the undertaking, or

        (ii)   giving rise to an obligation to contribute to the debts or expenses of the undertaking in the event of a winding up.

(3)   Other expressions appropriate to companies shall be construed, in relation to an undertaking which is not a company, as references to the corresponding persons, officers, documents or organs, as the case may be, appropriate to undertakings of that description.

This is subject to provision in any specific context providing for the translation of such expressions.

(4)   References in the Companies Acts to "fellow subsidiary undertakings" are to undertakings which are subsidiary undertakings of the same parent undertaking but are not parent undertakings or subsidiary undertakings of each other.

(5)   In the Companies Acts "group undertaking", in relation to an undertaking, means an undertaking which is—

    (a)   a parent undertaking or subsidiary undertaking of that undertaking, or

    (b)   a subsidiary undertaking of any parent undertaking of that undertaking.

[1727]

NOTES

Commencement: 6 April 2008.

1162   Parent and subsidiary undertakings

(1)   This section (together with Schedule 7) defines "parent undertaking" and "subsidiary undertaking" for the purposes of the Companies Acts.

(2)   An undertaking is a parent undertaking in relation to another undertaking, a subsidiary undertaking, if—

    (a)   it holds a majority of the voting rights in the undertaking, or

    (b)   it is a member of the undertaking and has the right to appoint or remove a majority of its board of directors, or

    (c)   it has the right to exercise a dominant influence over the undertaking—

        (i)   by virtue of provisions contained in the undertaking's articles, or

        (ii)   by virtue of a control contract, or

    (d)   it is a member of the undertaking and controls alone, pursuant to an agreement with other shareholders or members, a majority of the voting rights in the undertaking.

(3)   For the purposes of subsection (2) an undertaking shall be treated as a member of another undertaking—

    (a)   if any of its subsidiary undertakings is a member of that undertaking; or

    (b)   if any shares in that other undertaking are held by a person acting on behalf of the undertaking or any of its subsidiary undertakings.

(4)   An undertaking is also a parent undertaking in relation to another undertaking, a subsidiary undertaking, if—

    (a)   it has the power to exercise, or actually exercises, dominant influence or control over it, or

    (b)   it and the subsidiary undertaking are managed on a unified basis.

(5)   A parent undertaking shall be treated as the parent undertaking of undertakings in relation to which any of its subsidiary undertakings are, or are to be treated as, parent undertakings; and references to its subsidiary undertakings shall be construed accordingly.

(6)   Schedule 7 contains provisions explaining expressions used in this section and otherwise supplementing this section.

(7)   In this section and that Schedule references to shares, in relation to an undertaking, are to allotted shares.

[1728]

NOTES
Commencement: 6 April 2008.

Other definitions

1163 "Non-cash asset"

(1) In the Companies Acts "non-cash asset" means any property or interest in property, other than cash.

For this purpose "cash" includes foreign currency.

(2) A reference to the transfer or acquisition of a non-cash asset includes—
   (a) the creation or extinction of an estate or interest in, or a right over, any property, and
   (b) the discharge of a liability of any person, other than a liability for a liquidated sum.

[1728A]

NOTES
Commencement: 1 October 2009.

1164 Meaning of "banking company" and "banking group"

(1) This section defines "banking company" and "banking group" for the purposes of the Companies Acts.

(2) "Banking company" means a person who has permission under Part 4 of the Financial Services and Markets Act 2000 (c 8) to accept deposits, other than—
   (a) a person who is not a company, and
   (b) a person who has such permission only for the purpose of carrying on another regulated activity in accordance with permission under that Part.

(3) The definition in subsection (2) must be read with section 22 of that Act, any relevant order under that section and Schedule 2 to that Act.

(4) References to a banking group are to a group where the parent company is a banking company or where—
   (a) the parent company's principal subsidiary undertakings are wholly or mainly credit institutions, and
   (b) the parent company does not itself carry on any material business apart from the acquisition, management and disposal of interests in subsidiary undertakings.

"Group" here means a parent undertaking and its subsidiary undertakings.

(5) For the purposes of subsection (4)—
   (a) a parent company's principal subsidiary undertakings are the subsidiary undertakings of the company whose results or financial position would principally affect the figures shown in the group accounts, and
   (b) the management of interests in subsidiary undertakings includes the provision of services to such undertakings.

[1728B]

NOTES
Commencement: 6 April 2008.

1165 Meaning of "insurance company" and related expressions

(1) This section defines "insurance company", "authorised insurance company", "insurance group" and "insurance market activity" for the purposes of the Companies Acts.

(2) An "authorised insurance company" means a person (whether incorporated or not) who has permission under Part 4 of the Financial Services and Markets Act 2000 (c 8) to effect or carry out contracts of insurance.

(3) An "insurance company" means—
   (a) an authorised insurance company, or
   (b) any other person (whether incorporated or not) who—
     (i) carries on insurance market activity, or
     (ii) may effect or carry out contracts of insurance under which the benefits provided by that person are exclusively or primarily benefits in kind in the event of accident to or breakdown of a vehicle.

(4) Neither expression includes a friendly society within the meaning of the Friendly Societies Act 1992 (c 40).

(5) References to an insurance group are to a group where the parent company is an insurance company or where—

(a)　the parent company's principal subsidiary undertakings are wholly or mainly insurance companies, and

(b)　the parent company does not itself carry on any material business apart from the acquisition, management and disposal of interests in subsidiary undertakings.

"Group" here means a parent undertaking and its subsidiary undertakings.

(6)　For the purposes of subsection (5)—

(a)　a parent company's principal subsidiary undertakings are the subsidiary undertakings of the company whose results or financial position would principally affect the figures shown in the group accounts, and

(b)　the management of interests in subsidiary undertakings includes the provision of services to such undertakings.

(7)　"Insurance market activity" has the meaning given in section 316(3) of the Financial Services and Markets Act 2000.

(8)　References in this section to contracts of insurance and to the effecting or carrying out of such contracts must be read with section 22 of that Act, any relevant order under that section and Schedule 2 to that Act.

[1729]

NOTES
Commencement: 6 April 2008.

1166　"Employees' share scheme"

For the purposes of the Companies Acts an employees' share scheme is a scheme for encouraging or facilitating the holding of shares in or debentures of a company by or for the benefit of—

(a)　the bona fide employees or former employees of—

(i)　the company,

(ii)　any subsidiary of the company, or

(iii)　the company's holding company or any subsidiary of the company's holding company, or

(b)　the spouses, civil partners, surviving spouses, surviving civil partners, or minor children or step-children of such employees or former employees.

[1729A]

NOTES
Commencement: 1 October 2009.

1170　Meaning of "EEA State" and related expressions

In the Companies Acts—

["EEA State" has the meaning given by Schedule 1 to the Interpretation Act 1978;]

"EEA company" and "EEA undertaking" mean a company or undertaking governed by the law of an EEA State.

[1729B]

NOTES
Commencement: 6 April 2007.
Definition "EEA State" substituted by the Companies (EEA State) Regulations 2007, SI 2007/732, reg 3, as from 9 March 2007.

1171　The former Companies Acts

In the Companies Acts—

"the former Companies Acts" means—

(a)　the Joint Stock Companies Acts, the Companies Act 1862 (c 89), the Companies (Consolidation) Act 1908 (c 69), the Companies Act 1929 (c 23), the Companies Act (Northern Ireland) 1932 (c 7 (NI)), the Companies Acts 1948 to 1983, the Companies Act (Northern Ireland) 1960 (c 22 (NI)), the Companies (Northern Ireland) Order 1986 (SI 1986/1032 (NI 6)) and the Companies Consolidation (Consequential Provisions) (Northern Ireland) Order 1986 (SI 1986/1035 (NI 9)), and

(b)　the provisions of the Companies Act 1985 (c 6) and the Companies Consolidation (Consequential Provisions) Act 1985 (c 9) that are no longer in force;

"the Joint Stock Companies Acts" means the Joint Stock Companies Act 1856 (c 47), the Joint Stock Companies Acts 1856, 1857 (20 & 21 Vict c 14), the Joint Stock Banking Companies

Act 1857 (c 49), and the Act to enable Joint Stock Banking Companies to be formed on the principle of limited liability (1858 c 91), but does not include the Joint Stock Companies Act 1844 (c 110).

[1729C]

NOTES
Commencement: 1 October 2009.

1173 Minor definitions: general

(1) In the Companies Acts—
"body corporate" and "corporation" include a body incorporated outside the United Kingdom, but do not include—
    (a)   a corporation sole, or
    (b)   a partnership that, whether or not a legal person, is not regarded as a body corporate under the law by which it is governed;
"credit institution" means a credit institution as defined in Article 4.1(a) of Directive 2006/48/EC of the European Parliament and of the Council relating to the taking up and pursuit of the business of credit institutions;
"financial institution" means a financial institution within the meaning of Article 1.1 of the Council Directive on the obligations of branches established in a Member State of credit and financial institutions having their head offices outside that Member State regarding the publication of annual accounting documents (the Bank Branches Directive, 89/117/EEC);
"firm" means any entity, whether or not a legal person, that is not an individual and includes a body corporate, a corporation sole and a partnership or other unincorporated association;
"the Gazette" means—
    (a)   as respects companies registered in England and Wales, the London Gazette,
    (b)   as respects companies registered in Scotland, the Edinburgh Gazette, and
    (c)   as respects companies registered in Northern Ireland, the Belfast Gazette;
"hire-purchase agreement" has the same meaning as in the Consumer Credit Act 1974 (c 39);
"officer", in relation to a body corporate, includes a director, manager or secretary;
"parent company" means a company that is a parent undertaking (see section 1162 and Schedule 7);
"regulated activity" has the meaning given in section 22 of the Financial Services and Markets Act 2000 (c 8);
"regulated market" has the same meaning as in Directive 2004/39/EC of the European Parliament and of the Council on markets in financial instruments (see Article 4.1(14));
"working day", in relation to a company, means a day that is not a Saturday or Sunday, Christmas Day, Good Friday or any day that is a bank holiday under the Banking and Financial Dealings Act 1971 (c 80) in the part of the United Kingdom where the company is registered.

(2) In relation to an EEA State that has not implemented Directive 2004/39/EC of the European Parliament and of the Council on markets in financial instruments, the following definition of "regulated market" has effect in place of that in subsection (1)—
"regulated market" has the same meaning as it has in Council Directive 93/22/EEC on investment services in the securities field.

[1729D]

NOTES
Commencement: 1 January 2007 (certain purposes); 20 January 2007 (certain purposes); 6 April 2007 (certain purposes); 1 October 2007 (certain purposes); 1 November 2007 (certain purposes); 6 April 2008 (certain purposes); 1 October 2008 (certain purposes); 1 October 2009 (otherwise) (see the notes below).
Commencement (note): the Companies Act 2006 (Commencement No 1, Transitional Provisions and Savings) Order 2006, SI 2006/3428, art 2(2) provides that the definitions "the Gazette" and "working day" shall come into force on 1 January 2007 so far as is necessary for the purposes of the provisions of this Act brought into force on that date by art 2(1) of that Order.
Commencement (note): the Companies Act 2006 (Commencement No 1, Transitional Provisions and Savings) Order 2006, SI 2006/3428, art 3(2) provides that the definition "working day" shall come into force on 20 January 2007 so far as is necessary for the purposes of the provisions of this Act brought into force on that date by art 3(1) of that Order.
Commencement (note): the Companies Act 2006 (Commencement No 2, Consequential Amendments, Transitional Provisions and Savings) Order 2007, SI 2007/1093, art 2(2) provides that the definitions "body corporate", "the Gazette" and "regulated market" shall come into force on 6 April 2007 so far as is necessary for the purposes of the provisions of this Act brought into force on that date by art 2(1) of that Order.
Commencement (note): the Companies Act 2006 (Commencement No 3, Consequential Amendments, Transitional Provisions and Savings) Order 2007, SI 2007/2194, art 2(3) provides that the definitions of "body corporate" (and "corporation"), "firm" and "working day" shall come into force on 1 October 2007 so far as is necessary for the purposes of the provisions of this Act brought into force on that date by art 2(1), (2) of that Order.
Commencement (note): the Companies Act 2006 (Commencement No 3, Consequential Amendments, Transitional Provisions and Savings) Order 2007, SI 2007/2194, art 3(2) provides that the definition of "body

corporate" shall come into force on 1 November 2007 so far as is necessary for the purposes of the provisions of this Act brought into force on that date by art 3(1) of that Order.

Commencement (note): the Companies Act 2006 (Commencement No 5, Transitional Provisions and Savings) Order 2007, SI 2007/3495, art 3(1)(t) provides that the definitions of "credit institution" and "working day" shall come into force on 6 April 2008.

Commencement (note): the Companies Act 2006 (Commencement No 5, Transitional Provisions and Savings) Order 2007, SI 2007/3495, art 3(3) provides that the definitions of "body corporate" (and "corporation"), "firm", "the Gazette", "parent company" and "regulated market" shall come into force on 6 April 2008 so far as is necessary for the purposes of the provisions of this Act brought into force on that date by art 3(1)(a)–(t), (2) of that Order. Article 5(3) of that Order further provides that the definitions of "body corporate" (and "corporation"), "firm" and "officer" shall come into force on 1 October 2008 so far as is necessary for the purposes of the provisions of this Act brought into force on that date by art 5(1)(a)–(f) of that Order .

PART 42
STATUTORY AUDITORS

NOTES

Transfer of functions: as to the transfer of the functions of the Secretary of State under this Part to the Professional Oversight Board, see the Statutory Auditors (Delegation of Functions etc) Order 2008, SI 2008/496, art 4.

CHAPTER 1
INTRODUCTORY

1209   Main purposes of Part

The main purposes of this Part are—
    (a)   to secure that only persons who are properly supervised and appropriately qualified are appointed as statutory auditors, and
    (b)   to secure that audits by persons so appointed are carried out properly, with integrity and with a proper degree of independence.

[1729DA]

NOTES

Commencement: 6 April 2008.

1210   Meaning of "statutory auditor" etc

    (1)   In this Part "statutory auditor" means—
    (a)   a person appointed as auditor under Part 16 of this Act,
    (b)   a person appointed as auditor under section 77 of or Schedule 11 to the Building Societies Act 1986 (c 53),
    (c)   a person appointed as auditor of an insurer that is a friendly society under section 72 of or Schedule 14 to the Friendly Societies Act 1992 (c 40),
    (d)   …
    [(e)   a person appointed as auditor for the purposes of regulation 5 of the Insurance Accounts Directive (Lloyd's Syndicate and Aggregate Accounts) Regulations 2008 or appointed to report on the "aggregate accounts" within the meaning of those Regulations,]
    [(f)   a person appointed as auditor of an insurance undertaking for the purposes of the Insurance Accounts Directive (Miscellaneous Insurance Undertakings) Regulations 2008,]
    [(g)   a person appointed as auditor of a bank for the purposes of the Bank Accounts Directive (Miscellaneous Banks) Regulations 2008,]
    (h)   a person appointed as auditor of a prescribed person under a prescribed enactment authorising or requiring the appointment;
and the expressions "statutory audit" and "statutory audit work" are to be construed accordingly.

    (2)   In this Part "audited person" means the person in respect of whom a statutory audit is conducted.

    (3)   In subsection (1)—
    "bank" means a person who—
        (a)   is a credit institution within the meaning given by Article 4.1(a) of Directive 2006/48/EC of the European Parliament and of the Council relating to the taking up and pursuit of the business of credit institutions, and
        (b)   is a company or a firm as defined in Article 48 of the Treaty establishing the European Community;
    "friendly society" means a friendly society within the meaning of the Friendly Societies Act 1992 (c 40);

"insurer" means a person who is an insurance undertaking within the meaning given by Article 2.1 of Council Directive 1991/674/EEC on the annual accounts and consolidated accounts of insurance undertakings;

"prescribed" means prescribed, or of a description prescribed, by order made by the Secretary of State for the purposes of subsection (1)(h).

(4)   An order under this section is subject to negative resolution procedure.

[1729DB]

NOTES
Commencement: 20 January 2007 (for the purpose of enabling the exercise of powers to make Orders or Regulations by statutory instrument); 6 April 2008 (otherwise).
Sub-s (1) is amended as follows:
Para (d) repealed, and para (f) substituted by the Insurance Accounts Directive (Miscellaneous Insurance Undertakings) Regulations 2008, SI 2008/565, reg 15, as from 6 April 2008, in relation to insurance undertakings' financial years beginning on or after that date, and auditors appointed in respect of those financial years.
Para (e) substituted by the Insurance Accounts Directive (Lloyd's Syndicate and Aggregate Accounts) Regulations 2008, SI 2008/1950, reg 31, as from 15 August 2008, in relation to financial years beginning on or after 1 January 2009. The paragraph previously read as follows—
"(e)   a person appointed as auditor for the purposes of regulation 3 of the Insurance Accounts Directive (Lloyd's Syndicate and Aggregate Accounts) Regulations 2004 (SI 2004/3219) or appointed to report on the "aggregate accounts" within the meaning of those Regulations,".

Para (g) substituted by the Bank Accounts Directive (Miscellaneous Banks) Regulations 2008, SI 2008/567, reg 14, as from 6 April 2008, in relation to qualifying banks' financial years beginning on or after that date, and auditors appointed in respect of those financial years.
Sub-s (3): definition "industrial and provident society" (omitted) repealed by SI 2008/565, reg 15, as from 6 April 2008, in relation to insurance undertakings' financial years beginning on or after that date, and auditors appointed in respect of those financial years.
Regulations: the Partnerships (Accounts) Regulations 2008, SI 2008/569; the Limited Liability Partnerships (Accounts and Audit) (Application of Companies Act 2006) Regulations 2008, SI 2008/1911 at **[4169]** (reg 48 of which provides that for the purposes of sub-s (1)(h) an LLP is a prescribed person, and Pt 16 of this Act (as applied to LLPs) is a prescribed enactment).

1211   Eligibility for appointment as a statutory auditor: overview

A person is eligible for appointment as a statutory auditor only if the person is so eligible—
(a)   by virtue of Chapter 2 (individuals and firms), or
(b)   by virtue of Chapter 3 (Comptroller and Auditor General, etc).

[1729DC]

NOTES
Commencement: 6 April 2008.

CHAPTER 2
INDIVIDUALS AND FIRMS

Eligibility for appointment

1212   Individuals and firms: eligibility for appointment as a statutory auditor

(1)   An individual or firm is eligible for appointment as a statutory auditor if the individual or firm—
(a)   is a member of a recognised supervisory body, and
(b)   is eligible for appointment under the rules of that body.

(2)   In the cases to which section 1222 applies (individuals retaining only 1967 Act authorisation) a person's eligibility for appointment as a statutory auditor is restricted as mentioned in that section.

[1729DD]

NOTES
Commencement: 6 April 2008.
Commencement (transitional provisions): the Companies Act 2006 (Commencement No 5, Transitional Provisions and Savings) Order 2007, SI 2007/3495, Sch 4, Pt 1, paras 37–42 (as amended by the Companies Act 2006 (Commencement No 6, Saving and Commencement Nos 3 and 5 (Amendment)) Order 2008, SI 2008/674, art 5, Sch 3, para 6(1), (4), as from 6 April 2008) provide as follows—

"Statutory auditors (ss 1209 to 1241 and 1245 to 1264)

37.—(1)   The following provisions of Chapter 2 of Part 42 of the Companies Act 2006 (statutory auditors: individuals and firms) apply to the appointment of auditors for financial years beginning on or after 6th April 2008—
(a)   sections 1212 and 1213 (eligibility for appointment);
(b)   sections 1214 and 1215 (independence requirement);

(c) section 1216 (effect of appointment of partnership).

(2) Sections 25 to 28 of the Companies Act 1989 or Articles 28 to 31 of the Companies (Northern Ireland) Order 1990 continue to apply to auditors appointed for financial years beginning before that date.

38.—(1) The following provisions of that Chapter apply in relation to the supervision and qualification of auditors appointed for financial years beginning on or after 6th April 2008—
    (a) sections 1217 and 1218 and Schedule 10 (supervisory bodies);
    (b) sections 1219 to 1222 and Schedule 11 (professional qualifications and qualifying bodies).

(2) Sections 30 to 34 and 48 of, and Schedules 11 and 12 to, the Companies Act 1989 or Articles 33 to 36 and 50 of, and Schedules 11 and 12 to, the Companies (Northern Ireland) Order 1990 continue to apply in relation to the supervision and qualification of auditors appointed for financial years beginning before that date.

(3) Any declaration by the Secretary of State in force under section 33 of the Companies Act 1989 or [by the Department of Enterprise, Trade and Investment in force under] Article 36 of the Companies (Northern Ireland) Order 1990 (approval of overseas qualifications) immediately before 6th April 2008 continues in force on and after that date as if made under section 1221 of the Companies Act 2006.".

39. The repeal of sections 37 and 38 of the Companies Act 1989 (information to be provided to the Secretary of State) or Articles 39 and 40 of the Companies (Northern Ireland) Order 1990 (information to be provided to the Department of Enterprise, Trade and Investment) does not affect the operation of those provisions in relation to functions exercised under Part 2 of that Act or Part 3 of that Order on or after 6th April 2008.

40.—(1) Section 1226(2) of the Companies Act 2006 (eligibility of Auditor General for appointment as statutory auditor) applies to appointment as a statutory auditor for financial years beginning on or after 1st April 2008.

(2) Sections 1229 and 1230 (supervision of Auditors General by the Independent Supervisor) apply accordingly.

41.—(1) The following provisions of Chapter 6 of Part 42 of the Companies Act 2006 (statutory auditors: supplementary and general provisions) apply to auditors, supervisory bodies or qualifying bodies to whom Chapters 2 to 5 of that Part apply—
    (a) sections 1248 and 1249 (second audits);
    (b) section 1250 (false and misleading statements);
    (c) section 1251 (fees);
    (d) section 1254 (directions to comply with international obligations);
    (e) sections 1255 to 1257 (general provisions about offences);
    (f) sections 1258 and 1259 (notices etc).

(2) Sections 29, 40 to 45 and 49 of the Companies Act 1989 or Articles 32, 42 to 47 and 51 of the Companies (Northern Ireland) Order 1990 continue to apply to auditors, supervisory bodies or qualifying bodies to whom sections 25 to 28 and 30 to 39 of that Act or Articles 28 to 31 and 33 to 41 of that Order apply.

(3) The repeal of sections 52 to 54 of the Companies Act 1989 or Articles 54 to 56 of the Companies (Northern Ireland) Order 1990 (definitions) does not affect the operation of those provisions for the purposes of interpreting provisions of that Act or that Order that continue to apply on or after 6th April 2008.

42.—(1) The repeal of sections 46 and 46A of, and Schedule 13 to, the Companies Act 1989 (delegation of functions of Secretary of State) does not affect the operation of those provisions in relation to functions exercised under Part 2 of that Act on or after 6th April 2008.

(2) The repeal of Articles 48 and 48A of, and Schedule 13 to, the Companies (Northern Ireland) Order 1990 (delegation of functions of Department of Enterprise, Trade and Investment) does not affect the operation of those provisions in relation to functions exercised under Part 3 of that Order on or after 6th April 2008.".

1213 Effect of ineligibility

(1) No person may act as statutory auditor of an audited person if he is ineligible for appointment as a statutory auditor.

(2) If at any time during his term of office a statutory auditor becomes ineligible for appointment as a statutory auditor, he must immediately—
    (a) resign his office (with immediate effect), and
    (b) give notice in writing to the audited person that he has resigned by reason of his becoming ineligible for appointment.

(3) A person is guilty of an offence if—
    (a) he acts as a statutory auditor in contravention of subsection (1), or
    (b) he fails to give the notice mentioned in paragraph (b) of subsection (2) in accordance with that subsection.

(4) A person guilty of an offence under subsection (3) is liable—
    (a) on conviction on indictment, to a fine;
    (b) on summary conviction, to a fine not exceeding the statutory maximum.

(5) A person is guilty of an offence if—
    (a) he has been convicted of an offence under subsection (3)(a) or this subsection, and
    (b) he continues to act as a statutory auditor in contravention of subsection (1) after the conviction.

(6) A person is guilty of an offence if—

(a) he has been convicted of an offence under subsection (3)(b) or this subsection, and
(b) he continues, after the conviction, to fail to give the notice mentioned in subsection (2)(b).

(7) A person guilty of an offence under subsection (5) or (6) is liable—
(a) on conviction on indictment, to a fine;
(b) on summary conviction, to a fine not exceeding one-tenth of the statutory maximum for each day on which the act or the failure continues.

(8) In proceedings against a person for an offence under this section it is a defence for him to show that he did not know and had no reason to believe that he was, or had become, ineligible for appointment as a statutory auditor.

[1729DE]

NOTES
Commencement: 6 April 2008.
Commencement (transitional provisions): see the note to s 1212 at **[1729DD]**.

Independence requirement

1214 Independence requirement

(1) A person may not act as statutory auditor of an audited person if one or more of subsections (2), (3) and (4) apply to him.

(2) This subsection applies if the person is—
(a) an officer or employee of the audited person, or
(b) a partner or employee of such a person, or a partnership of which such a person is a partner.

(3) This subsection applies if the person is—
(a) an officer or employee of an associated undertaking of the audited person, or
(b) a partner or employee of such a person, or a partnership of which such a person is a partner.

(4) This subsection applies if there exists, between—
(a) the person or an associate of his, and
(b) the audited person or an associated undertaking of the audited person,
a connection of any such description as may be specified by regulations made by the Secretary of State.

(5) An auditor of an audited person is not to be regarded as an officer or employee of the person for the purposes of subsections (2) and (3).

(6) In this section "associated undertaking", in relation to an audited person, means—
(a) a parent undertaking or subsidiary undertaking of the audited person, or
(b) a subsidiary undertaking of a parent undertaking of the audited person.

(7) Regulations under subsection (4) are subject to negative resolution procedure.

[1729DF]

NOTES
Commencement: 20 January 2007 (for the purpose of enabling the exercise of powers to make Orders or Regulations by statutory instrument); 6 April 2008 (otherwise).
Commencement (transitional provisions): see the note to s 1212 at **[1729DD]**.

1215 Effect of lack of independence

(1) If at any time during his term of office a statutory auditor becomes prohibited from acting by section 1214(1), he must immediately—
(a) resign his office (with immediate effect), and
(b) give notice in writing to the audited person that he has resigned by reason of his lack of independence.

(2) A person is guilty of an offence if—
(a) he acts as a statutory auditor in contravention of section 1214(1), or
(b) he fails to give the notice mentioned in paragraph (b) of subsection (1) in accordance with that subsection.

(3) A person guilty of an offence under subsection (2) is liable—
(a) on conviction on indictment, to a fine;
(b) on summary conviction, to a fine not exceeding the statutory maximum.

(4) A person is guilty of an offence if—
(a) he has been convicted of an offence under subsection (2)(a) or this subsection, and
(b) he continues to act as a statutory auditor in contravention of section 1214(1) after the conviction.

(5) A person is guilty of an offence if—
(a) he has been convicted of an offence under subsection (2)(b) or this subsection, and
(b) after the conviction, he continues to fail to give the notice mentioned in subsection (1)(b).

(6) A person guilty of an offence under subsection (4) or (5) is liable—
(a) on conviction on indictment, to a fine;
(b) on summary conviction, to a fine not exceeding one-tenth of the statutory maximum for each day on which the act or the failure continues.

(7) In proceedings against a person for an offence under this section it is a defence for him to show that he did not know and had no reason to believe that he was, or had become, prohibited from acting as statutory auditor of the audited person by section 1214(1).

[1729DG]

NOTES
Commencement: 6 April 2008.
Commencement (transitional provisions): see the note to s 1212 at **[1729DD]**.

Effect of appointment of a partnership

1216 Effect of appointment of a partnership

(1) This section applies where a partnership constituted under the law of—
(a) England and Wales,
(b) Northern Ireland, or
(c) any other country or territory in which a partnership is not a legal person,
is by virtue of this Chapter appointed as statutory auditor of an audited person.

(2) Unless a contrary intention appears, the appointment is an appointment of the partnership as such and not of the partners.

(3) Where the partnership ceases, the appointment is to be treated as extending to—
(a) any appropriate partnership which succeeds to the practice of that partnership, or
(b) any other appropriate person who succeeds to that practice having previously carried it on in partnership.

(4) For the purposes of subsection (3)—
(a) a partnership is to be regarded as succeeding to the practice of another partnership only if the members of the successor partnership are substantially the same as those of the former partnership, and
(b) a partnership or other person is to be regarded as succeeding to the practice of a partnership only if it or he succeeds to the whole or substantially the whole of the business of the former partnership.

(5) Where the partnership ceases and the appointment is not treated under subsection (3) as extending to any partnership or other person, the appointment may with the consent of the audited person be treated as extending to an appropriate partnership, or other appropriate person, who succeeds to—
(a) the business of the former partnership, or
(b) such part of it as is agreed by the audited person is to be treated as comprising the appointment.

(6) For the purposes of this section, a partnership or other person is "appropriate" if it or he—
(a) is eligible for appointment as a statutory auditor by virtue of this Chapter, and
(b) is not prohibited by section 1214(1) from acting as statutory auditor of the audited person.

[1729DH]

NOTES
Commencement: 6 April 2008.
Commencement (transitional provisions): see the note to s 1212 at **[1729DD]**.
See also the Companies Act 2006 (Consequential Amendments etc) Order 2008, SI 2008/948, art 5 which provides as follows—

5 Eligibility for appointment as statutory auditor: effect of appointing partnership

(1) Section 1216 of the Companies Act 2006 (effect of appointing partnership) applies in relation to any statutory appointment where eligibility for the appointment depends on eligibility for appointment as a statutory auditor under Part 42 of that Act.

(2) In subsection (6)(b) of that section as it applies by virtue of this article, the reference to being prohibited by virtue of section 1214(1) of that Act from acting as statutory auditor shall be read as including a reference to being prohibited or disqualified from acting, or ineligible or disqualified for appointment, on the ground of lack of independence (of any description) by virtue of any other enactment applying in relation to the appointment.

(3)   For the purposes of this article a "statutory appointment" means an appointment in pursuance of an enactment authorising or requiring the making of the appointment.

(4)   This article applies only where that enactment was passed or made before 6th April 2008.

Supervisory bodies

1217   Supervisory bodies

(1)   In this Part a "supervisory body" means a body established in the United Kingdom (whether a body corporate or an unincorporated association) which maintains and enforces rules as to—

    (a)   the eligibility of persons for appointment as a statutory auditor, and

    (b)   the conduct of statutory audit work,

which are binding on persons seeking appointment or acting as a statutory auditor ... because they are members of that body ...

[(1A)   The rules referred to in paragraphs 9(3)(b) (confidentiality of information) and 10C(3)(a) and (b) (bar on appointment as director or other officer) of Schedule 10 must also be binding on persons who—

    (a)   have sought appointment or acted as a statutory auditor, and

    (b)   have been members of the body at any time after the commencement of this Part.]

(2)   In this Part references to the members of a supervisory body are to the persons who, whether or not members of the body, are subject to its rules in seeking appointment or acting as a statutory auditor.

(3)   In this Part references to the rules of a supervisory body are to the rules (whether or not laid down by the body itself) which the body has power to enforce and which are relevant for the purposes of this Part.

This includes rules relating to the admission or expulsion of members of the body, so far as relevant for the purposes of this Part.

(4)   Schedule 10 has effect with respect to the recognition of supervisory bodies for the purposes of this Part.

[1729DI]

NOTES

    Commencement: 6 April 2008.
    Commencement (transitional provisions): see the note to s 1212 at **[1729DD]**.
    Sub-s (1): words omitted repealed by the Statutory Auditors and Third Country Auditors Regulations 2007, SI 2007/3494, reg 4(1), (2), as from 6 April 2008.
    Sub-s (1A): inserted by SI 2007/3494, reg 4(1), (3), as from 6 April 2008.

1218   Exemption from liability for damages

(1)   No person within subsection (2) is to be liable in damages for anything done or omitted in the discharge or purported discharge of functions to which this subsection applies.

(2)   The persons within this subsection are—

    (a)   any recognised supervisory body,

    (b)   any officer or employee of a recognised supervisory body, and

    (c)   any member of the governing body of a recognised supervisory body.

(3)   Subsection (1) applies to the functions of a recognised supervisory body so far as relating to, or to matters arising out of, any of the following—

    (a)   rules, practices, powers and arrangements of the body to which the requirements of Part 2 of Schedule 10 apply;

    (b)   the obligations with which paragraph 20 of that Schedule requires the body to comply;

    (c)   any guidance issued by the body;

    (d)   the obligations imposed on the body by or by virtue of this Part.

(4)   The reference in subsection (3)(c) to guidance issued by a recognised supervisory body is a reference to any guidance or recommendation which is—

    (a)   issued or made by it to all or any class of its members or persons seeking to become members, and

    (b)   relevant for the purposes of this Part,

including any guidance or recommendation relating to the admission or expulsion of members of the body, so far as relevant for the purposes of this Part.

(5)   Subsection (1) does not apply—

    (a)   if the act or omission is shown to have been in bad faith, or

    (b)   so as to prevent an award of damages in respect of the act or omission on the ground that it was unlawful as a result of section 6(1) of the Human Rights Act 1998 (c 42) (acts of public authorities incompatible with Convention rights).

[1729DJ]

NOTES

Commencement: 6 April 2008.

Commencement (transitional provisions): see the note to s 1212 at **[1729DD]**.

Professional qualifications

1219 Appropriate qualifications

(1)   A person holds an appropriate qualification for the purposes of this Chapter if and only if—

(a)   he holds a recognised professional qualification obtained in the United Kingdom,

(b)   immediately before the commencement of this Chapter, he—

     (i)   held an appropriate qualification for the purposes of Part 2 of the Companies Act 1989 (c 40) (eligibility for appointment as company auditor) by virtue of section 31(1)(a) or (c) of that Act, or

     (ii)   was treated as holding an appropriate qualification for those purposes by virtue of section 31(2), (3) or (4) of that Act,

(c)   immediately before the commencement of this Chapter, he—

     (i)   held an appropriate qualification for the purposes of Part III of the Companies (Northern Ireland) Order 1990 (SI 1990/593 (NI 5)) by virtue of Article 34(1)(a) or (c) of that Order, or

     (ii)   was treated as holding an appropriate qualification for those purposes by virtue of Article 34(2), (3) or (4) of that Order,

(d)   he is within subsection (2), [or]

(e)   ...

(f)   subject to any direction under section 1221(5), he is regarded for the purposes of this Chapter as holding an approved [third country] qualification.

(2)   A person is within this subsection if—

(a)   before 1st January 1990, he began a course of study or practical training leading to a professional qualification in accountancy offered by a body established in the United Kingdom,

(b)   he obtained that qualification on or after 1st January 1990 and before 1st January 1996, and

(c)   the Secretary of State approves his qualification as an appropriate qualification for the purposes of this Chapter.

(3)   The Secretary of State may approve a qualification under subsection (2)(c) only if he is satisfied that, at the time the qualification was awarded, the body concerned had adequate arrangements to ensure that the qualification was awarded only to persons educated and trained to a standard equivalent to that required, at that time, in the case of a recognised professional qualification under Part 2 of the Companies Act 1989 (c 40) (eligibility for appointment as company auditor).

[1729DK]

NOTES

Commencement: 6 April 2008.

Commencement (transitional provisions): see the note to s 1212 at **[1729DD]**.

Sub-s (1): word in square brackets in para (d) inserted, para (e) repealed, and words in square brackets in para (f) substituted, by the Statutory Auditors and Third Country Auditors Regulations 2007, SI 2007/3494, reg 5, as from 6 April 2008.

1220 Qualifying bodies and recognised professional qualifications

(1)   In this Part a "qualifying body" means a body established in the United Kingdom (whether a body corporate or an unincorporated association) which offers a professional qualification in accountancy.

(2)   In this Part references to the rules of a qualifying body are to the rules (whether or not laid down by the body itself) which the body has power to enforce and which are relevant for the purposes of this Part.

This includes, so far as so relevant, rules relating to—

(a)   admission to or expulsion from a course of study leading to a qualification,

(b)   the award or deprivation of a qualification, or

(c)   the approval of a person for the purposes of giving practical training or the withdrawal of such approval.

(3)   Schedule 11 has effect with respect to the recognition for the purposes of this Part of a professional qualification offered by a qualifying body.

[1729DL]

NOTES
Commencement: 6 April 2008.
Commencement (transitional provisions): see the note to s 1212 at **[1729DD]**.

1221 Approval of [third country] qualifications

(1)   The Secretary of State may declare that the following are to be regarded for the purposes of this Chapter as holding an approved [third country] qualification—

(a)   persons who are qualified to audit accounts under the law of a specified [third country], or

(b)   persons who hold a specified professional qualification in accountancy obtained in a specified [third country].

[(1A)   A declaration under subsection (1)(a) or (b) must be expressed to be subject to the requirement that any person to whom the declaration relates must pass an aptitude test in accordance with subsection (7A), unless an aptitude test is not required (see subsection (7B)).]

(2)   A declaration under subsection (1)(b) may be expressed to be subject to the satisfaction of any specified requirement or requirements.

(3)   The Secretary of State may make a declaration under subsection (1) only if he is satisfied that—

(a)   in the case of a declaration under subsection (1)(a), the fact that the persons in question are qualified to audit accounts under the law of the specified [third country], or

(b)   in the case of a declaration under subsection (1)(b), the specified professional qualification taken with any requirement or requirements to be specified under subsection (2),

affords an assurance of professional competence equivalent to that afforded by a recognised professional qualification.

(4)   The Secretary of State may make a declaration under subsection (1) only if he is satisfied that the treatment that the persons who are the subject of the declaration will receive as a result of it is comparable to the treatment which is, or is likely to be, afforded in the specified [third country] or a part of it to—

(a)   in the case of a declaration under subsection (1)(a), some or all persons who are eligible to be appointed as a statutory auditor, and

(b)   in the case of a declaration under subsection (1)(b), some or all persons who hold a corresponding recognised professional qualification.

(5)   The Secretary of State may direct that persons holding an approved [third country] qualification are not to be treated as holding an appropriate qualification for the purposes of this Chapter unless they hold such additional educational qualifications as the Secretary of State may specify for the purpose of ensuring that such persons have an adequate knowledge of the law and practice in the United Kingdom relevant to the audit of accounts.

(6)   The Secretary of State may give different directions in relation to different approved [third country] qualifications.

(7)   The Secretary of State may, if he thinks fit, having regard to the considerations mentioned in subsections (3) and (4), withdraw a declaration under subsection (1) in relation to—

(a)   persons becoming qualified to audit accounts under the law of the specified [third country] after such date as he may specify, or

(b)   persons obtaining the specified professional qualification after such date as he may specify.

[(7A)   An aptitude test required for the purposes of subsection (1A)—

(a)   must test the person's knowledge of subjects—

(i)   that are covered by a recognised professional qualification,

(ii)   that are not covered by the professional qualification already held by the person, and

(iii)   the knowledge of which is essential for the pursuit of the profession of statutory auditor;

(b)   may test the person's knowledge of rules of professional conduct;

(c)   must not test the person's knowledge of any other matters.

(7B)   No aptitude test is required for the purposes of subsection (1A) if the subjects that are covered by a recognised professional qualification and the knowledge of which is essential for the pursuit of the profession of statutory auditor are covered by the professional qualification already held by the person.]

(8)   The Secretary of State may, if he thinks fit, having regard to the considerations mentioned in subsections (3) and (4), vary or revoke a requirement specified under subsection (2) from such date as he may specify.

(9) ...

[1729DM]

NOTES
Commencement: 6 April 2008.
Commencement (transitional provisions): see the note to s 1212 at **[1729DD]**.
Section heading, sub-ss (1), (3)–(7): words in square brackets substituted by the Statutory Auditors and Third Country Auditors Regulations 2007, SI 2007/3494, reg 6(1)–(3), as from 6 April 2008.
Sub-ss (1A), (7A), (7B): inserted by SI 2007/3494, reg 6(1), (4), (5), as from 6 April 2008.
Sub-s (9): repealed by SI 2007/3494, reg 6(1), (6), as from 6 April 2008.

1222 Eligibility of individuals retaining only 1967 Act authorisation

(1) A person whose only appropriate qualification is based on his retention of an authorisation originally granted by the Board of Trade or the Secretary of State under section 13(1) of the Companies Act 1967 (c 81) is eligible only for appointment as auditor of an unquoted company.

(2) A company is "unquoted" if, at the time of the person's appointment, neither the company, nor any parent undertaking of which it is a subsidiary undertaking, is a quoted company within the meaning of section 385(2).

(3) References to a person eligible for appointment as a statutory auditor by virtue of this Part in enactments relating to eligibility for appointment as auditor of a person other than a company do not include a person to whom this section applies.

[1729DN]

NOTES
Commencement: 6 April 2008.
Commencement (transitional provisions): see the note to s 1212 at **[1729DD]**.

Information

1223 Matters to be notified to the Secretary of State

(1) The Secretary of State may require a recognised supervisory body or a recognised qualifying body—
   (a) to notify him immediately of the occurrence of such events as he may specify in writing and to give him such information in respect of those events as is so specified;
   (b) to give him, at such times or in respect of such periods as he may specify in writing, such information as is so specified.

(2) The notices and information required to be given must be such as the Secretary of State may reasonably require for the exercise of his functions under this Part.

(3) The Secretary of State may require information given under this section to be given in a specified form or verified in a specified manner.

(4) Any notice or information required to be given under this section must be given in writing unless the Secretary of State specifies or approves some other manner.

[1729DO]

NOTES
Commencement: 6 April 2008.

[1223A Notification of matters relevant to other EEA States

(1) A recognised supervisory body must notify the Secretary of State of—
   (a) any withdrawal of a notifiable person's eligibility for appointment as a statutory auditor; and
   (b) the reasons for the withdrawal.

(2) A recognised supervisory body must also notify the Secretary of State of any reasonable grounds it has for suspecting that—
   (a) a person has contravened the law of the United Kingdom, or any other EEA State or part of an EEA State, implementing the Audit Directive, and
   (b) the act or omission constituting that contravention took place on the territory of an EEA State other than the United Kingdom.

(3) In this section "notifiable person" means a member of the recognised supervisory body in question—
   (a) who is also an EEA auditor; and
   (b) in respect of whom the EEA competent authority is not the recognised supervisory body itself.]

[1729DP]

NOTES
Commencement: 6 April 2008.
Inserted by the Statutory Auditors and Third Country Auditors Regulations 2007, SI 2007/3494, reg 7, as from 6 April 2008.

1224 The Secretary of State's power to call for information

(1) The Secretary of State may by notice in writing require a person within subsection (2) to give him such information as he may reasonably require for the exercise of his functions under this Part.

(2) The persons within this subsection are—
  (a)   any recognised supervisory body,
  (b)   any recognised qualifying body, and
  (c)   any person eligible for appointment as a statutory auditor by virtue of this Chapter.

(3) The Secretary of State may require that any information which he requires under this section is to be given within such reasonable time and verified in such manner as he may specify.

[1729DQ]

NOTES
Commencement: 6 April 2008.

[1224A Restrictions on disclosure

(1) This section applies to information (in whatever form)—
  (a)   relating to the private affairs of an individual, or
  (b)   relating to any particular business,
that is provided to a body to which this section applies in connection with the exercise of its functions under this Part or sections 522 to 524 (notification to appropriate audit authority of resignation or removal of auditor).

(2) This section applies to—
  (a)   a recognised supervisory body,
  (b)   a recognised qualifying body,
  (c)   a body performing functions for the purposes of arrangements within paragraph 23(1) (independent monitoring of certain audits) or paragraph 24(1) (independent investigation of public interest cases) of Schedule 10,
  (d)   the Independent Supervisor,
  (e)   the Secretary of State, and
  (f)   a body designated by the Secretary of State under section 1252 (delegation of the Secretary of State's functions).

(3) No such information may, during the lifetime of the individual or so long as the business continues to be carried on, be disclosed without the consent of that individual or (as the case may be) the person for the time being carrying on that business.

(4) Subsection (3) does not apply to any disclosure of information that—
  (a)   is made for the purpose of facilitating the carrying out by the body of any of its functions,
  (b)   is made to a person specified in Part 1 of Schedule 11A,
  (c)   is of a description specified in Part 2 of that Schedule, or
  (d)   is made in accordance with Part 3 of that Schedule.

(5) Subsection (3) does not apply to—
  (a)   the disclosure by an EEA competent authority of information disclosed to it by the body in reliance on subsection (4);
  (b)   the disclosure of such information by anyone who has obtained it directly or indirectly from an EEA competent authority.

(6) This section does not prohibit the disclosure of information if the information is or has been available to the public from any other source.

(7) Nothing in this section authorises the making of a disclosure in contravention of the Data Protection Act 1998.]

[1729DR]

NOTES
Commencement: 6 April 2008.
Inserted by the Statutory Auditors and Third Country Auditors Regulations 2007, SI 2007/3494, reg 8(1), (3), as from 6 April 2008, in relation to information that is provided to a body on or after that date.

[1224B   Offence of disclosure in contravention of section 1224A

(1)   A person who discloses information in contravention of section 1224A (restrictions on disclosure) is guilty of an offence, unless—

    (a)   he did not know, and had no reason to suspect, that the information had been provided as mentioned in section 1224A(1), or

    (b)   he took all reasonable steps and exercised all due diligence to avoid the commission of the offence.

(2)   A person guilty of an offence under this section is liable—

    (a)   on conviction on indictment, to imprisonment for a term not exceeding two years or a fine (or both);

    (b)   on summary conviction—

        (i)   in Scotland, to imprisonment for a term not exceeding 12 months or to a fine not exceeding the statutory maximum, or to both;

        (ii)   in England and Wales or Northern Ireland, to imprisonment for a term not exceeding three months or to a fine not exceeding the statutory maximum, or to both.]

[1729DS]

NOTES
Commencement: 6 April 2008.
Inserted by the Statutory Auditors and Third Country Auditors Regulations 2007, SI 2007/3494, reg 8(1), as from 6 April 2008.

Enforcement

1225   Compliance orders

(1)   If at any time it appears to the Secretary of State—

    (a)   in the case of a recognised supervisory body, that any requirement of Schedule 10 is not satisfied,

    (b)   in the case of a recognised professional qualification, that any requirement of Schedule 11 is not satisfied, or

    (c)   that a recognised supervisory body or a recognised qualifying body has failed to comply with an obligation to which it is subject under or by virtue of this Part,

he may, instead of revoking the relevant recognition order, make an application to the court under this section.

(2)   If on an application under this section the court decides that the requirement in question is not satisfied or, as the case may be, that the body has failed to comply with the obligation in question, it may order the body to take such steps as the court directs for securing that the requirement is satisfied or that the obligation is complied with.

(3)   In this section "the court" means the High Court or, in Scotland, the Court of Session.

[1729DT]

NOTES
Commencement: 6 April 2008.

CHAPTER 3
AUDITORS GENERAL

Eligibility for appointment

1226   Auditors General: eligibility for appointment as a statutory auditor

(1)   In this Part "Auditor General" means—

    (a)   the Comptroller and Auditor General,

    (b)   the Auditor General for Scotland,

    (c)   the Auditor General for Wales, or

    (d)   the Comptroller and Auditor General for Northern Ireland.

(2)   An Auditor General is eligible for appointment as a statutory auditor.

(3)   Subsection (2) is subject to any suspension notice having effect under section 1234 (notices suspending eligibility for appointment as a statutory auditor).

[1729DU]

NOTES
Commencement: 6 April 2008.
Commencement (transitional provisions): see the note to s 1212 at **[1729DD]**.

Conduct of audits

1227 Individuals responsible for audit work on behalf of Auditors General

An Auditor General must secure that each individual responsible for statutory audit work on behalf of that Auditor General is eligible for appointment as a statutory auditor by virtue of Chapter 2.

[1729DV]

NOTES
Commencement: 6 April 2008.

The Independent Supervisor

1228 Appointment of the Independent Supervisor

(1) The Secretary of State must appoint a body ("the Independent Supervisor") to discharge the function mentioned in section 1229(1) ("the supervision function").

(2) An appointment under this section must be made by order.

(3) The order has the effect of making the body appointed under subsection (1) designated under section 5 of the Freedom of Information Act 2000 (c 36) (further powers to designate public authorities).

(4) A body may be appointed under this section only if it is a body corporate or an unincorporated association which appears to the Secretary of State—
    (a)   to be willing and able to discharge the supervision function, and
    (b)   to have arrangements in place relating to the discharge of that function which are such as to be likely to ensure that the conditions in subsection (5) are met.

(5) The conditions are—
    (a)   that the supervision function will be exercised effectively, and
    (b)   where the order is to contain any requirements or other provisions specified under subsection (6), that that function will be exercised in accordance with any such requirements or provisions.

(6) An order under this section may contain such requirements or other provisions relating to the exercise of the supervision function by the Independent Supervisor as appear to the Secretary of State to be appropriate.

(7) An order under this section is subject to negative resolution procedure.

[1729DW]

NOTES
Commencement: 20 January 2007 (for the purpose of enabling the exercise of powers to make Orders or Regulations by statutory instrument); 6 April 2008 (otherwise).
Orders: the Independent Supervisor Appointment Order 2007, SI 2007/3534. This Order provides that the body known as the Professional Oversight Board, established under the articles of association of The Financial Reporting Council Limited, is appointed for the purposes of this section to discharge the supervision function (as from 6 April 2008).

Supervision of Auditors General

1229 Supervision of Auditors General by the Independent Supervisor

(1) The Independent Supervisor must supervise the performance by each Auditor General of his functions as a statutory auditor.

[(2) The Independent Supervisor must discharge that duty by—
    (a)   establishing supervision arrangements itself, or
    (b)   entering into supervision arrangements with one or more bodies.

(2A) If the Independent Supervisor enters into supervision arrangements with one or more bodies, it must oversee the effective operation of those supervision arrangements.]

(3) For this purpose "supervision arrangements" are arrangements [established by the Independent Supervisor or] entered into by the Independent Supervisor with a body, for the purposes of this section, in accordance with which [the Independent Supervisor or] the body does … the following—
    (a)   determines standards relating to professional integrity and independence which must be applied by an Auditor General in statutory audit work;
    (b)   determines technical standards which must be applied by an Auditor General in statutory audit work and the manner in which those standards are to be applied in practice;
    (c)   monitors the performance of statutory audits carried out by an Auditor General;
    (d)   investigates any matter arising from the performance by an Auditor General of a statutory audit;
    (e)   holds disciplinary hearings in respect of an Auditor General which appear to be desirable following the conclusion of such investigations;

(f) decides whether (and, if so, what) disciplinary action should be taken against an Auditor General to whom such a hearing related.

[(3A) The requirements of paragraphs 9 to 10A and 12 to 15 of Schedule 10 (requirements for recognition of a supervisory body) apply in relation to supervision arrangements as they apply in relation to the rules, practices and arrangements of supervisory bodies.]

(4) The Independent Supervisor may enter into supervision arrangements with a body despite any relationship that may exist between the Independent Supervisor and that body.

(5) The Independent Supervisor must notify each Auditor General in writing of any supervision arrangements that it [establishes or] enters into under this section.

[(5A) The Independent Supervisor must, at least once in every calendar year, deliver to the Secretary of State a summary of the results of any inspections conducted for the purposes of subsection (3)(c).]

(6) Supervision arrangements within subsection (3)(f) may, in particular, provide for the payment by an Auditor General of a fine to any person.

(7) Any fine received by the Independent Supervisor under supervision arrangements is to be paid into the Consolidated Fund.

[1729DX]

NOTES

Commencement: 6 April 2008.
Commencement (transitional provisions): see the note to s 1212 at **[1729DD]**.
Sub-ss (2), (2A): substituted, for original sub-s (2), by the Statutory Auditors and Third Country Auditors Regulations 2007, SI 2007/3494, reg 9(1), (2), as from 6 April 2008.
Sub-s (3): words in square brackets inserted, and words omitted repealed, by SI 2007/3494, reg 9(1), (3), as from 6 April 2008.
Sub-ss (3A), (5A): inserted by SI 2007/3494, reg 9(1), (4), (6), as from 6 April 2008.
Sub-s (5): words in square brackets inserted by SI 2007/3494, reg 9(1), (5), as from 6 April 2008.
As to the duty of the Independent Supervisor to consult with the Auditors General (and such other persons as seem to it to be appropriate) before establishing or entering into a supervision arrangement for the purposes of this section, see the Independent Supervisor Appointment Order 2007, SI 2007/3534, art 6.

1230 Duties of Auditors General in relation to supervision arrangements

(1) Each Auditor General must—
    (a) comply with any standards of the kind mentioned in subsection (3)(a) or (b) of section 1229 determined under the supervision arrangements,
    (b) take such steps as may be reasonably required of that Auditor General to enable his performance of statutory audits to be monitored by means of inspections carried out under the supervision arrangements, and
    (c) comply with any decision of the kind mentioned in subsection (3)(f) of that section made under the supervision arrangements.

[(2) Each Auditor General must—
    (a) if the Independent Supervisor has established supervision arrangements, pay to the Independent Supervisor;
    (b) if the Independent Supervisor has entered into supervision arrangements with a body, pay to that body,
such proportion of the costs incurred by the Independent Supervisor or body for the purposes of the arrangements as the Independent Supervisor may notify to him in writing.]

(3) Expenditure under subsection (2) is—
    (a) in the case of expenditure of the Comptroller and Auditor General, to be regarded as expenditure of the National Audit Office for the purposes of section 4(1) of the National Audit Act 1983 (c 44);
    (b) in the case of expenditure of the Comptroller and Auditor General for Northern Ireland, to be regarded as expenditure of the Northern Ireland Audit Office for the purposes of Article 6(1) of the Audit (Northern Ireland) Order 1987 (SI 1987/460 (NI 5)).

(4) In this section "the supervision arrangements" means the arrangements [established or] entered into under section 1229.

[1729DY]

NOTES

Commencement: 6 April 2008.
Commencement (transitional provisions): see the note to s 1212 at **[1729DD]**.
Sub-s (2): substituted by the Statutory Auditors and Third Country Auditors Regulations 2007, SI 2007/3494, reg 10(1), (2), as from 6 April 2008.
Sub-s (4): words in square brackets inserted by SI 2007/3494, reg 10(1), (3), as from 6 April 2008.

PART II
OTHER ACTS

Reporting requirement

1231 Reports by the Independent Supervisor

(1)   The Independent Supervisor must, at least once in each calendar year, prepare a report on the discharge of its functions.

(2)   The Independent Supervisor must give a copy of each report prepared under subsection (1) to—

(a)   the Secretary of State;

(b)   the First Minister in Scotland;

(c)   the First Minister and the deputy First Minister in Northern Ireland;

(d)   the Assembly First Secretary in Wales.

(3)   The Secretary of State must lay before each House of Parliament a copy of each report received by him under subsection (2)(a).

(4)   In relation to a calendar year during which an appointment of a body as the Independent Supervisor is made or revoked by an order under section 1228, this section applies with such modifications as may be specified in the order.

[1729DZ]

NOTES

Commencement: 20 January 2007 (for the purpose of enabling the exercise of powers to make Orders or Regulations by statutory instrument); 6 April 2008 (otherwise).

As to the content of reports under this section, see the Independent Supervisor Appointment Order 2007, SI 2007/3534, art 4.

Information

1232 Matters to be notified to the Independent Supervisor

(1)   The Independent Supervisor may require an Auditor General—

(a)   to notify the Independent Supervisor immediately of the occurrence of such events as it may specify in writing and to give it such information in respect of those events as is so specified;

(b)   to give the Independent Supervisor, at such times or in respect of such periods as it may specify in writing, such information as is so specified.

(2)   The notices and information required to be given must be such as the Independent Supervisor may reasonably require for the exercise of the functions conferred on it by or by virtue of this Part.

(3)   The Independent Supervisor may require information given under this section to be given in a specified form or verified in a specified manner.

(4)   Any notice or information required to be given under this section must be given in writing unless the Independent Supervisor specifies or approves some other manner.

[1729EA]

NOTES

Commencement: 6 April 2008.

1233 The Independent Supervisor's power to call for information

(1)   The Independent Supervisor may by notice in writing require an Auditor General to give it such information as it may reasonably require for the exercise of the functions conferred on it by or by virtue of this Part.

(2)   The Independent Supervisor may require that any information which it requires under this section is to be given within such reasonable time and verified in such manner as it may specify.

[1729EB]

NOTES

Commencement: 6 April 2008.

Enforcement

1234 Suspension notices

(1)   The Independent Supervisor may issue—

(a)   a notice (a "suspension notice") suspending an Auditor General's eligibility for appointment as a statutory auditor in relation to all persons, or any specified person or persons, indefinitely or until a date specified in the notice;

(b)   a notice amending or revoking a suspension notice previously issued to an Auditor General.

(2) In determining whether it is appropriate to issue a notice under subsection (1), the Independent Supervisor must have regard to—
(a) the Auditor General's performance of the obligations imposed on him by or by virtue of this Part, and
(b) the Auditor General's performance of his functions as a statutory auditor.

(3) A notice under subsection (1) must—
(a) be in writing, and
(b) state the date on which it takes effect (which must be after the period of three months beginning with the date on which it is issued).

(4) Before issuing a notice under subsection (1), the Independent Supervisor must—
(a) give written notice of its intention to do so to the Auditor General, and
(b) publish the notice mentioned in paragraph (a) in such manner as it thinks appropriate for bringing it to the attention of any other persons who are likely to be affected.

(5) A notice under subsection (4) must—
(a) state the reasons for which the Independent Supervisor proposes to act, and
(b) give particulars of the rights conferred by subsection (6).

(6) A person within subsection (7) may, within the period of three months beginning with the date of service or publication of the notice under subsection (4) or such longer period as the Independent Supervisor may allow, make written representations to the Independent Supervisor and, if desired, oral representations to a person appointed for that purpose by the Independent Supervisor.

(7) The persons within this subsection are—
(a) the Auditor General, and
(b) any other person who appears to the Independent Supervisor to be affected.

(8) The Independent Supervisor must have regard to any representations made in accordance with subsection (6) in determining—
(a) whether to issue a notice under subsection (1), and
(b) the terms of any such notice.

(9) If in any case the Independent Supervisor considers it appropriate to do so in the public interest it may issue a notice under subsection (1), without regard to the restriction in subsection (3)(b), even if—
(a) no notice has been given or published under subsection (4), or
(b) the period of time for making representations in pursuance of such a notice has not expired.

(10) On issuing a notice under subsection (1), the Independent Supervisor must—
(a) give a copy of the notice to the Auditor General, and
(b) publish the notice in such manner as it thinks appropriate for bringing it to the attention of persons likely to be affected.

(11) In this section "specified" means specified in, or of a description specified in, the suspension notice in question.

[1729EC]

NOTES
Commencement: 6 April 2008.

1235 Effect of suspension notices

(1) An Auditor General must not act as a statutory auditor at any time when a suspension notice issued to him in respect of the audited person has effect.

(2) If at any time during an Auditor General's term of office as a statutory auditor a suspension notice issued to him in respect of the audited person takes effect, he must immediately—
(a) resign his office (with immediate effect), and
(b) give notice in writing to the audited person that he has resigned by reason of his becoming ineligible for appointment.

(3) A suspension notice does not make an Auditor General ineligible for appointment as a statutory auditor for the purposes of section 1213 (effect of ineligibility: criminal offences).

[1729ED]

NOTES
Commencement: 6 April 2008.

1236 Compliance orders

(1) If at any time it appears to the Independent Supervisor that an Auditor General has failed to comply with an obligation imposed on him by or by virtue of this Part, the Independent Supervisor may make an application to the court under this section.

(2)   If on an application under this section the court decides that the Auditor General has failed to comply with the obligation in question, it may order the Auditor General to take such steps as the court directs for securing that the obligation is complied with.

(3)   In this section "the court" means the High Court or, in Scotland, the Court of Session.

[1729EE]

NOTES
Commencement: 6 April 2008.

Proceedings

1237   Proceedings involving the Independent Supervisor

(1)   If the Independent Supervisor is an unincorporated association, any relevant proceedings may be brought by or against it in the name of any body corporate whose constitution provides for the establishment of the body.

(2)   For this purpose "relevant proceedings" means proceedings brought in or in connection with the exercise of any function by the body as the Independent Supervisor.

(3)   Where an appointment under section 1228 is revoked, the revoking order may make such provision as the Secretary of State thinks fit with respect to pending proceedings.

[1729EF]

NOTES
Commencement: 20 January 2007 (for the purpose of enabling the exercise of powers to make Orders or Regulations by statutory instrument); 6 April 2008 (otherwise).

1238   (*Inserts the Companies (Audit, Investigations and Community Enterprise) Act 2004, s 16(2)(ka)*.)

CHAPTER 4
THE REGISTER OF AUDITORS ETC

1239   The register of auditors

(1)   The Secretary of State must make regulations requiring the keeping of a register of—
   (a)   the persons eligible for appointment as a statutory auditor, and
   (b)   third country auditors (see Chapter 5) who apply to be registered in the specified manner and in relation to whom specified requirements are met.

(2)   The regulations must require each person's entry in the register to contain—
   (a)   his name and address,
   (b)   in the case of an individual eligible for appointment as a statutory auditor, the specified information relating to any firm on whose behalf he is responsible for statutory audit work,
   (c)   in the case of a firm eligible for appointment as a statutory auditor, the specified information relating to the individuals responsible for statutory audit work on its behalf,
   (d)   in the case of an individual or firm eligible for appointment as a statutory auditor by virtue of Chapter 2, the name of the relevant supervisory body, ...
   (e)   in the case of a firm eligible for appointment as a statutory auditor by virtue of Chapter 2 ... , the information mentioned in subsection (3), [and
   (f)   in the case of a third country auditor which is a firm, the name and address of each person who is—
       (i)   an owner or shareholder of the firm, or
       (ii)   a member of the firm's administrative or management body],
and may require each person's entry to contain other specified information.

(3)   The information referred to in subsection (2)(e) is—
   (a)   in relation to a body corporate, except where paragraph (b) applies, the name and address of each person who is a director of the body or holds any shares in it;
   (b)   in relation to a limited liability partnership, the name and address of each member of the partnership;
   (c)   in relation to a corporation sole, the name and address of the individual for the time being holding the office by the name of which he is the corporation sole;
   (d)   in relation to a partnership, the name and address of each partner.

(4)   The regulations may provide that different parts of the register are to be kept by different persons.

(5)   The regulations may impose such obligations as the Secretary of State thinks fit on—
   (a)   recognised supervisory bodies,

    (b)   any body designated by order under section 1252 (delegation of Secretary of State's functions),

    (c)   persons eligible for appointment as a statutory auditor,

    (d)   third country auditors,

    (e)   any person with whom arrangements are made by one or more recognised supervisory bodies, or by any body designated by order under section 1252, with respect to the keeping of the register, or

    (f)   the Independent Supervisor appointed under section 1228.

  (6)   The regulations may include—

    (a)   provision requiring that specified entries in the register be open to inspection at times and places specified or determined in accordance with the regulations;

    (b)   provision enabling a person to require a certified copy of specified entries in the register;

    (c)   provision authorising the charging of fees for inspection, or the provision of copies, of such reasonable amount as may be specified or determined in accordance with the regulations.

  (7)   The Secretary of State may direct in writing that the requirements imposed by the regulations … , or such of those requirements as are specified in the direction, are not to apply, in whole or in part, in relation to a particular registered third country auditor or class of registered third country auditors.

  (8)   The obligations imposed by regulations under this section on such persons as are mentioned in subsection (5)(b) or (e) are enforceable on the application of the Secretary of State by injunction or, in Scotland, by an order under section 45 of the Court of Session Act 1988 (c 36).

  (9)   In this section "specified" means specified by regulations under this section.

  (10)   Regulations under this section are subject to negative resolution procedure.

[1729EG]

NOTES

  Commencement: 20 January 2007 (for the purpose of enabling the exercise of powers to make Orders or Regulations by statutory instrument); 6 April 2008 (otherwise).

  Sub-s (2): words omitted from paras (d), (e) repealed, and para (f) (and the word immediately preceding it) inserted, by the Statutory Auditors and Third Country Auditors Regulations 2007, SI 2007/3494, reg 30(1)–(4), as from 6 April 2008.

  Sub-s (7): words omitted repealed by SI 2007/3494, reg 30(1), (5), as from 6 April 2008.

  Regulations: the Statutory Auditors and Third Country Auditors Regulations 2007, SI 2007/3494.

  Note that the following amending Regulations have also been made under this section: the Statutory Auditors and Third Country Auditors (Amendment) Regulations 2008, SI 2008/499; the Statutory Auditors and Third Country Auditors (Amendment) (No 2) Regulations 2008, SI 2008/2639.

1240 Information to be made available to public

  (1)   The Secretary of State may make regulations requiring a person eligible for appointment as a statutory auditor, or a member of a specified class of such persons, to keep and make available to the public specified information, including information regarding—

    (a)   the person's ownership and governance,

    (b)   the person's internal controls with respect to the quality and independence of its audit work,

    (c)   the person's turnover, and

    (d)   the audited persons of whom the person has acted as statutory auditor.

  (2)   Regulations under this section may—

    (a)   impose such obligations as the Secretary of State thinks fit on persons eligible for appointment as a statutory auditor;

    (b)   require the information to be made available to the public in a specified manner.

  (3)   In this section "specified" means specified by regulations under this section.

  (4)   Regulations under this section are subject to negative resolution procedure.

[1729EH]

NOTES

  Commencement: 20 January 2007 (for the purpose of enabling the exercise of powers to make Orders or Regulations by statutory instrument); 6 April 2008 (otherwise).

CHAPTER 5
REGISTERED THIRD COUNTRY AUDITORS

Introductory

1241 [Meaning of "registered third country auditor" and "UK-traded non-EEA company"]

(1)   In this Part—

.....

"registered third country auditor" means a third country auditor who is entered in the register kept in accordance with regulations under section 1239(1).

(2)   [In this Part "UK-traded non-EEA company" means a body corporate—]
  (a)   which is incorporated or formed under the law of [a third country],
  (b)   whose transferable securities are admitted to trading on a regulated market situated or operating in the United Kingdom, and
  (c)   which has not been excluded, or is not of a description of bodies corporate which has been excluded, from this definition by an order made by the Secretary of State.

(3)   For this purpose—
"regulated market" has the meaning given by Article 4.1(14) of Directive 2004/39/EC of the European Parliament and of the Council on markets in financial instruments;
"transferable securities" has the meaning given by Article 4.1(18) of that Directive.

(4)   An order under this section is subject to negative resolution procedure.

[1729EI]

NOTES

Commencement: 20 January 2007 (for the purpose of enabling the exercise of powers to make Orders or Regulations by statutory instrument); 6 April 2008 (otherwise).

Section heading: substituted by the Statutory Auditors and Third Country Auditors Regulations 2007, SI 2007/3494, reg 31(1), (2), as from 6 April 2008.

Sub-s (1): definition "third country auditor" (omitted) repealed by SI 2007/3494, reg 31(1), (3), as from 6 April 2008.

Sub-s (2): words in square brackets substituted by SI 2007/3494, reg 31(1), (4), as from 6 April 2008.

UK-traded non-EEA company: see further the Statutory Auditors and Third Country Auditors Regulations 2007, SI 2007/3494, reg 43 which provides as follows—

"43   Exclusion of large debt securities issuer from definition of "UK-traded non-EEA company"

(1)   A large debt securities issuer is excluded from the definition of "UK-traded non-EEA company" for the purposes of Part 42 of the Companies Act 2006 (see section 1241(2)).

(2)   In paragraph (1) "large debt securities issuer" means a body corporate whose only issued transferable securities admitted to trading on a regulated market are debt securities, the denomination per unit of which is not less than—
  (a)   50,000 euros, or
  (b)   in the case of debt securities denominated in a currency other than euros, a sum equivalent at the date of issue to 50,000 euros.

(3)   In paragraph (2)—
"debt securities" has the same meaning as in Article 2.1(b) of Directive 2004/109/EC of the European Parliament and of the Council on the harmonisation of transparency requirements in relation to information about issuers whose securities are admitted to trading on a regulated market and amending Directive 2001/34/EC(a);
"transferable securities" and "regulated market" have the same meaning as in section 1241(3) of the Companies Act 2006.".

Regulations: the Statutory Auditors and Third Country Auditors Regulations 2007, SI 2007/3494.

Duties

1242   Duties of registered third country auditors

(1)   A registered third country auditor [who audits the accounts of a UK-traded non-EEA company] must participate in—
  (a)   arrangements within paragraph 1 of Schedule 12 (arrangements for independent monitoring of audits …), and
  (b)   arrangements within paragraph 2 of that Schedule (arrangements for independent investigation for disciplinary purposes of public interest cases).

(2)   A registered third country auditor must—
  (a)   take such steps as may be reasonably required of it to enable its performance of [audits of accounts of UK-traded non-EEA companies] to be monitored by means of inspections carried out under the arrangements mentioned in subsection (1)(a), and
  (b)   comply with any decision as to disciplinary action to be taken against it made under the arrangements mentioned in subsection (1)(b).

(3)   Schedule 12 makes further provision with respect to the arrangements in which registered third country auditors are required to participate.

(4)   The Secretary of State may direct in writing that subsections (1) to (3) are not to apply, in whole or in part, in relation to a particular registered third country auditor or class of registered third country auditors.

[1729EJ]

NOTES
Commencement: 29 June 2008.
Commencement (transitional provisions): Sch 4, Pt 2, para 45 to the Companies Act 2006 (Commencement No 5, Transitional Provisions and Savings) Order 2007, SI 2007/3495 provides as follows—
"45.   Sections 1242 to 1244 of, and Schedule 12 to, the Companies Act 2006 (duties of third country auditors: information to be supplied by third country auditors) apply to third country auditors appointed for financial years beginning on or after 29th June 2008.".

Sub-s (1): words in square brackets inserted, and words omitted repealed, by the Statutory Auditors and Third Country Auditors Regulations 2007, SI 2007/3494, reg 32(1), (2), as from 29 June 2008.
Sub-s (2): words in square brackets substituted by SI 2007/3494, reg 32(1), (3), as from 29 June 2008.

Information

1243   Matters to be notified to the Secretary of State

(1)   The Secretary of State may require a registered third country auditor—
  (a)   to notify him immediately of the occurrence of such events as he may specify in writing and to give him such information in respect of those events as is so specified;
  (b)   to give him, at such times or in respect of such periods as he may specify in writing, such information as is so specified.

(2)   The notices and information required to be given must be such as the Secretary of State may reasonably require for the exercise of his functions under this Part.

(3)   The Secretary of State may require information given under this section to be given in a specified form or verified in a specified manner.

(4)   Any notice or information required to be given under this section must be given in writing unless the Secretary of State specifies or approves some other manner.

[1729EK]

NOTES
Commencement: 29 June 2008.
Commencement (transitional provisions): see the note to s 1242 at **[1729EJ]**.

1244   The Secretary of State's power to call for information

(1)   The Secretary of State may by notice in writing require a registered third country auditor to give him such information as he may reasonably require for the exercise of his functions under this Part.

(2)   The Secretary of State may require that any information which he requires under this section is to be given within such reasonable time and verified in such manner as he may specify.

[1729EL]

NOTES
Commencement: 29 June 2008.
Commencement (transitional provisions): see the note to s 1242 at **[1729EJ]**.

Enforcement

1245   Compliance orders

(1)   If at any time it appears to the Secretary of State that a registered third country auditor has failed to comply with an obligation imposed on him by or by virtue of this Part, the Secretary of State may make an application to the court under this section.

(2)   If on an application under this section the court decides that the auditor has failed to comply with the obligation in question, it may order the auditor to take such steps as the court directs for securing that the obligation is complied with.

(3)   In this section "the court" means the High Court or, in Scotland, the Court of Session.

[1729EM]

NOTES
Commencement: 6 April 2008.

1246 Removal of third country auditors from the register of auditors

(1)   The Secretary of State may, by regulations, confer on the person keeping the register in accordance with regulations under section 1239(1) power to remove a third country auditor from the register.

(2)   Regulations under this section must require the person keeping the register, in determining whether to remove a third country auditor from the register, to have regard to the auditor's compliance with obligations imposed on him by or by virtue of this Part.

(3)   Where provision is made under section 1239(4) (different parts of the register to be kept by different persons), references in this section to the person keeping the register are to the person keeping that part of the register which relates to third country auditors.

(4)   Regulations under this section are subject to negative resolution procedure.

[1729EN]

NOTES

Commencement: 20 January 2007 (for the purpose of enabling the exercise of powers to make Orders or Regulations by statutory instrument); 6 April 2008 (otherwise).

Regulations: the Statutory Auditors and Third Country Auditors Regulations 2007, SI 2007/3494.

Note that the following amending Regulations have also been made under this section: the Statutory Auditors and Third Country Auditors (Amendment) (No 2) Regulations 2008, SI 2008/2639.

1247   (*Inserts the Companies (Audit, Investigations and Community Enterprise) Act 2004, s 16(2)(kb).*)

CHAPTER 6
SUPPLEMENTARY AND GENERAL

Power to require second company audit

1248 Secretary of State's power to require second audit of a company

(1)   This section applies where a person appointed as statutory auditor of a company was not an appropriate person for any part of the period during which the audit was conducted.

(2)   The Secretary of State may direct the company concerned to retain an appropriate person—
   (a)   to conduct a second audit of the relevant accounts, or
   (b)   to review the first audit and to report (giving his reasons) whether a second audit is needed.

(3)   For the purposes of subsections (1) and (2) a person is "appropriate" if he—
   (a)   is eligible for appointment as a statutory auditor or, if the person is an Auditor General, for appointment as statutory auditor of the company, and
   (b)   is not prohibited by section 1214(1) (independence requirement) from acting as statutory auditor of the company.

(4)   The Secretary of State must send a copy of a direction under subsection (2) to the registrar of companies.

(5)   The company is guilty of an offence if—
   (a)   it fails to comply with a direction under subsection (2) within the period of 21 days beginning with the date on which it is given, or
   (b)   it has been convicted of a previous offence under this subsection and the failure to comply with the direction which led to the conviction continues after the conviction.

(6)   The company must—
   (a)   send a copy of a report under subsection (2)(b) to the registrar of companies, and
   (b)   if the report states that a second audit is needed, take such steps as are necessary for the carrying out of that audit.

(7)   The company is guilty of an offence if—
   (a)   it fails to send a copy of a report under subsection (2)(b) to the registrar within the period of 21 days beginning with the date on which it receives it,
   (b)   in a case within subsection (6)(b), it fails to take the steps mentioned immediately it receives the report, or
   (c)   it has been convicted of a previous offence under this subsection and the failure to send a copy of the report, or take the steps, which led to the conviction continues after the conviction.

(8)   A company guilty of an offence under this section is liable on summary conviction—
   (a)   in a case within subsection (5)(a) or (7)(a) or (b), to a fine not exceeding level 5 on the standard scale, and
   (b)   in a case within subsection (5)(b) or (7)(c), to a fine not exceeding one-tenth of level 5 on the standard scale for each day on which the failure continues.

(9)   In this section "registrar of companies" has the meaning given by section 1060.

[1729EO]

NOTES
Commencement: 6 April 2008.
Commencement (transitional provisions): see the note to s 1212 at **[1729DD]**.

1249   Supplementary provision about second audits

(1)   If a person accepts an appointment, or continues to act, as statutory auditor of a company at a time when he knows he is not an appropriate person, the company may recover from him any costs incurred by it in complying with the requirements of section 1248.

For this purpose "appropriate" is to be construed in accordance with subsection (3) of that section.

(2)   Where a second audit is carried out under section 1248, any statutory or other provision applying in relation to the first audit applies also, in so far as practicable, in relation to the second audit.

(3)   A direction under section 1248(2) is, on the application of the Secretary of State, enforceable by injunction or, in Scotland, by an order under section 45 of the Court of Session Act 1988 (c 36).

[1729EP]

NOTES
Commencement: 6 April 2008.
Commencement (transitional provisions): see the note to s 1212 at **[1729DD]**.

False and misleading statements

1250   Misleading, false and deceptive statements

(1)   A person is guilty of an offence if—
  (a)   for the purposes of or in connection with any application under this Part, or
  (b)   in purported compliance with any requirement imposed on him by or by virtue of this Part,
he knowingly or recklessly furnishes information which is misleading, false or deceptive in a material particular.

(2)   It is an offence for a person whose name does not appear on the register of auditors kept under regulations under section 1239 in an entry made under subsection (1)(a) of that section to describe himself as a registered auditor or so to hold himself out as to indicate, or be reasonably understood to indicate, that he is a registered auditor.

(3)   It is an offence for a person whose name does not appear on the register of auditors kept under regulations under that section in an entry made under subsection (1)(b) of that section to describe himself as a registered third country auditor or so to hold himself out as to indicate, or be reasonably understood to indicate, that he is a registered third country auditor.

(4)   It is an offence for a body which is not a recognised supervisory body or a recognised qualifying body to describe itself as so recognised or so to describe itself or hold itself out as to indicate, or be reasonably understood to indicate, that it is so recognised.

(5)   A person guilty of an offence under subsection (1) is liable—
  (a)   on conviction on indictment, to imprisonment for a term not exceeding two years or to a fine (or both);
  (b)   on summary conviction—
    (i)   in England and Wales, to imprisonment for a term not exceeding twelve months or to a fine not exceeding the statutory maximum (or both),
    (ii)   in Scotland or Northern Ireland, to imprisonment for a term not exceeding six months or to a fine not exceeding the statutory maximum (or both).
In relation to an offence committed before the commencement of section 154(1) of the Criminal Justice Act 2003 (c 44), for "twelve months" in paragraph (b)(i) substitute "six months".

(6)   Subject to subsection (7), a person guilty of an offence under subsection (2), (3) or (4) is liable on summary conviction—
  (a)   in England and Wales, to imprisonment for a term not exceeding 51 weeks or to a fine not exceeding level 5 on the standard scale (or both),
  (b)   in Scotland or Northern Ireland, to imprisonment for a term not exceeding six months or to a fine not exceeding level 5 on the standard scale (or both).
In relation to an offence committed before the commencement of section 281(5) of the Criminal Justice Act 2003, for "51 weeks" in paragraph (a) substitute "six months".

(7)   Where a contravention of subsection (2), (3) or (4) involves a public display of the offending description, the maximum fine that may be imposed is an amount equal to level 5 on the standard scale multiplied by the number of days for which the display has continued.

(8)   It is a defence for a person charged with an offence under subsection (2), (3) or (4) to show that he took all reasonable precautions and exercised all due diligence to avoid the commission of the offence.

[1729EQ]

NOTES
Commencement: 6 April 2008.
Commencement (transitional provisions): see the note to s 1212 at **[1729DD]**.

Fees

1251   Fees

(1)   An applicant for a recognition order under this Part must pay such fee in respect of his application as the Secretary of State may by regulations prescribe; and no application is to be regarded as duly made unless this subsection is complied with.

(2)   The Secretary of State may by regulations prescribe periodical fees to be paid by—
   (a)   every recognised supervisory body,
   (b)   every recognised qualifying body,
   (c)   every Auditor General, and
   (d)   every registered third country auditor.

(3)   Fees received by the Secretary of State by virtue of this Part are to be paid into the Consolidated Fund.

(4)   Regulations under this section are subject to negative resolution procedure.

[1729ER]

NOTES
Commencement: 20 January 2007 (for the purpose of enabling the exercise of powers to make Orders or Regulations by statutory instrument); 6 April 2008 (otherwise).
Commencement (transitional provisions): see the note to s 1212 at **[1729DD]**.

[Duty of Secretary of State to Report on Inspections]

1251A   Duty of the Secretary of State to report on inspections

The Secretary of State must, at least once in every calendar year, publish a report containing a summary of the results of inspections that are delivered to him—
   (a)   by the Independent Supervisor under section 1229(5A);
   (b)   by a recognised supervisory body under paragraph 13(9) of Schedule 10.]

[1729ES]

NOTES
Commencement: 6 April 2008.
Inserted, together with the preceding heading, by the Statutory Auditors and Third Country Auditors Regulations 2007, SI 2007/3494, reg 11, as from 6 April 2008.

Delegation of Secretary of State's functions

1252   Delegation of the Secretary of State's functions

(1)   The Secretary of State may make an order under this section (a "delegation order") for the purpose of enabling functions of the Secretary of State under this Part to be exercised by a body designated by the order.

(2)   The body designated by a delegation order may be either—
   (a)   a body corporate which is established by the order, or
   (b)   subject to section 1253, a body (whether a body corporate or an unincorporated association) which is already in existence ("an existing body").

(3)   A delegation order has the effect of making the body designated by the order designated under section 5 of the Freedom of Information Act 2000 (c 36) (further powers to designate public authorities).

(4)   A delegation order has the effect of transferring to the body designated by it all functions of the Secretary of State under this Part—
   (a)   subject to such exceptions and reservations as may be specified in the order, and
   (b)   except—
      (i)   his functions in relation to the body itself, and
      (ii)   his functions under section 1228 (appointment of Independent Supervisor).

(5)   A delegation order may confer on the body designated by it such other functions supplementary or incidental to those transferred as appear to the Secretary of State to be appropriate.

(6)   Any transfer of functions under the following provisions must be subject to the reservation that the functions remain exercisable concurrently by the Secretary of State—
  (a)   section 1224 (power to call for information from recognised bodies etc);
  (b)   section 1244 (power to call for information from registered third country auditors);
  (c)   section 1254 (directions to comply with international obligations).

(7)   Any transfer of—
  (a)   the function of refusing to make a declaration under section 1221(1) (approval of *overseas* qualifications) on the grounds referred to in section 1221(4) (lack of comparable treatment), or
  (b)   the function of withdrawing such a declaration under section 1221(7) on those grounds,
must be subject to the reservation that the function is exercisable only with the consent of the Secretary of State.

(8)   A delegation order may be amended or, if it appears to the Secretary of State that it is no longer in the public interest that the order should remain in force, revoked by a further order under this section.

(9)   Where functions are transferred or resumed, the Secretary of State may by order confer or, as the case may be, take away such other functions supplementary or incidental to those transferred or resumed as appear to him to be appropriate.

(10)   Where a delegation order is made, Schedule 13 has effect with respect to—
  (a)   the status of the body designated by the order in exercising functions of the Secretary of State under this Part,
  (b)   the constitution and proceedings of the body where it is established by the order,
  (c)   the exercise by the body of certain functions transferred to it, and
  (d)   other supplementary matters.

(11)   An order under this section which has the effect of transferring or resuming any functions is subject to affirmative resolution procedure.

(12)   Any other order under this section is subject to negative resolution procedure.

[1729ET]

NOTES
Commencement: 20 January 2007 (for the purpose of enabling the exercise of powers to make Orders or Regulations by statutory instrument); 6 April 2008 (otherwise).
Sub-s (7): words in square brackets substituted by the Statutory Auditors and Third Country Auditors Regulations 2007, SI 2007/3494, reg 12, as from 6 April 2008.
Orders: the Statutory Auditors (Delegation of Functions etc) Order 2008, SI 2008/496 (this Order transfers most of the functions of the Secretary of State under this Part to the Professional Oversight Board).

1253 Delegation of functions to an existing body

(1)   The Secretary of State's power to make a delegation order under section 1252 which designates an existing body is exercisable in accordance with this section.

(2)   The Secretary of State may make such a delegation order if it appears to him that—
  (a)   the body is able and willing to exercise the functions that would be transferred by the order, and
  (b)   the body has arrangements in place relating to the exercise of those functions which are such as to be likely to ensure that the conditions in subsection (3) are met.

(3)   The conditions are—
  (a)   that the functions in question will be exercised effectively, and
  (b)   where the delegation order is to contain any requirements or other provisions specified under subsection (4), that those functions will be exercised in accordance with any such requirements or provisions.

(4)   The delegation order may contain such requirements or other provision relating to the exercise of the functions by the designated body as appear to the Secretary of State to be appropriate.

(5)   An existing body—
  (a)   may be designated by a delegation order under section 1252, and
  (b)   may accordingly exercise functions of the Secretary of State in pursuance of the order,
despite any involvement of the body in the exercise of any functions under arrangements within [paragraph 21 to 22B, 23(1) or 24(1) of Schedule 10] or paragraph 1 or 2 of Schedule 12.

[1729EU]

NOTES
Commencement: 20 January 2007 (for the purpose of enabling the exercise of powers to make Orders or Regulations by statutory instrument); 6 April 2008 (otherwise).
Sub-s (5): words in square brackets substituted by the Statutory Auditors and Third Country Auditors Regulations 2007, SI 2007/3494, reg 13, as from 6 April 2008.
Orders: the Statutory Auditors (Delegation of Functions etc) Order 2008, SI 2008/496.

[Cooperation with Foreign Competent Authorities

1253A Requests to foreign competent authorities

The Secretary of State may request from an EEA competent authority or a third country competent authority such assistance, information or investigation as he may reasonably require in connection with the exercise of his functions under this Part.]

[1729EV]

NOTES
Commencement: 6 April 2008.
Inserted, together with the preceding heading and ss 1253B, 1253C, by the Statutory Auditors and Third Country Auditors Regulations 2007, SI 2007/3494, reg 14(1), as from 6 April 2008.

[1253B Requests from EEA competent authorities

(1)   The Secretary of State must take all necessary steps to—
   (a)   ensure that an investigation is carried out, or
   (b)   provide any other assistance or information,
if requested to do so by an EEA competent authority in accordance with Article 36 of the Audit Directive (cooperation between Member State authorities).

(2)   Within 28 days following the date on which he receives the request, the Secretary of State must—
   (a)   provide the assistance or information required by the EEA competent authority under subsection (1)(b), or
   (b)   notify the EEA competent authority which made the request of the reasons why he has not done so.

(3)   But the Secretary of State need not take steps to comply with a request under subsection (1) if—
   (a)   he considers that complying with the request may prejudice the sovereignty, security or public order of the United Kingdom;
   (b)   legal proceedings have been brought in the United Kingdom (whether continuing or not) in relation to the persons and matters to which the request relates; or
   (c)   disciplinary action has been taken by a recognised supervisory body in relation to the persons and matters to which the request relates.]

[1729EW]

NOTES
Commencement: 6 April 2008.
Inserted as noted to s 1253A at **[1729EV]**. By virtue of reg 14(2) of the 2007 Regulations, this section applies only to investigations, assistance or information relating to auditors appointed for financial years beginning on or after 6 April 2008.

[1253C Notification to competent authorities of other EEA States

(1)   The Secretary of State must notify the relevant EEA competent authority if he receives notice from a recognised supervisory body under section 1223A(1) (notification of withdrawal of eligibility for appointment) of the withdrawal of a person's eligibility for appointment as a statutory auditor.

(2)   In subsection (1) "the relevant EEA competent authority" means the EEA competent authority which has approved the person concerned in accordance with the Audit Directive to carry out audits of annual accounts or consolidated accounts required by Community law.

(3)   The notification under subsection (1) must include the name of the person concerned and the reasons for the withdrawal of his eligibility for appointment as statutory auditor.

(4)   The Secretary of State must notify the relevant EEA competent authority if he has reasonable grounds for suspecting that—
   (a)   a person has contravened the law of the United Kingdom, or any other EEA State or part of an EEA State, implementing the Audit Directive, and
   (b)   the act or omission constituting that contravention took place on the territory of an EEA State other than the United Kingdom.,

(5)   In subsection (4) "the relevant EEA competent authority" means the EEA competent authority for the EEA State in which the suspected contravention took place.

(6)   The notification under subsection (4) must include the name of the person concerned and the grounds for the Secretary of State's suspicion.]

[1729EX]

NOTES
Commencement: 6 April 2008.
Inserted as noted to s 1253A at **[1729EV]**.

[Transfer of Papers to Third Countries

1253D   Restriction on transfer of audit working papers to third countries

Audit working papers must not be transferred to a third country competent authority by any person other than a statutory auditor acting in accordance with rules imposed under paragraph 16A of Schedule 10 (transfer of papers to third countries).]

[1729EY]

NOTES
Commencement: 6 April 2008.
Inserted, together with the preceding heading and ss 1253E, 1253F, by the Statutory Auditors and Third Country Auditors Regulations 2007, SI 2007/3494, reg 15(1), as from 6 April 2008. By virtue of reg 15(2) of the 2007 Regulations, this section only applies to working papers for audits conducted by auditors appointed for financial years beginning on or after 6 April 2008.

[1253E   Working arrangements for transfer of papers

(1)   The Secretary of State may enter into arrangements with a third country competent authority relating to the transfer of audit working papers—
   (a)   from the third country competent authority or third country auditors regulated by that authority to the Secretary of State; and
   (b)   from statutory auditors to the third country competent authority.

(2)   The arrangements must provide that—
   (a)   the Secretary of State has the rights and duties referred to in subsections (3) to (5) in relation to papers he requests from the third country competent authority or third country auditors, and
   (b)   the third country competent authority has comparable rights and duties in relation to papers it requests from statutory auditors.

(3)   Any request by the Secretary of State for audit working papers from the third country competent authority or a third country auditor must be accompanied by a statement explaining the reasons for the request.

(4)   The Secretary of State may use the audit working papers he receives in response to a request only in connection with—
   (a)   quality assurance functions which meet requirements equivalent to those of Article 29 of the Audit Directive (quality assurance),
   (b)   investigation or disciplinary functions which meet requirements equivalent to those of Article 30 of the Audit Directive (investigations and penalties), or
   (c)   public oversight functions which meet requirements equivalent to those of Article 32 of the Audit Directive (principles of public oversight).

(5)   The Secretary of State, a person exercising the functions of the Secretary of State and persons employed in discharging those functions must be subject to obligations of professional secrecy in relation to audit papers supplied to the Secretary of State by a third country competent authority or a third country auditor.]

[1729EZ]

NOTES
Commencement: 6 April 2008.
Inserted as noted to s 1253D at **[1729EY]**. By virtue of reg 15(2) of the 2007 Regulations, this section only applies to working papers for audits conducted by auditors appointed for financial years beginning on or after 6 April 2008.

[1253F   Publication of working arrangements

If the Secretary of State enters into working arrangements in accordance with section 1253E, he must publish on a website without undue delay—

   (a)   the name of the third country competent authority with which he has entered into such
          arrangements, and
   (b)   the country or territory in which it is established.]

                                                                                    [1729FA]

NOTES
Commencement: 6 April 2008.
Inserted as noted to s 1253D at **[1729EY]**.

                              International obligations

1254   Directions to comply with international obligations

   (1)   If it appears to the Secretary of State—
   (a)   that any action proposed to be taken by a recognised supervisory body or a recognised
          qualifying body, [the Independent Supervisor] or a body designated by order under
          section 1252, would be incompatible with Community obligations or any other
          international obligations of the United Kingdom, or
   (b)   that any action which that body has power to take is required for the purpose of
          implementing any such obligations,

he may direct the body not to take or, as the case may be, to take the action in question.

   (2)   A direction may include such supplementary or incidental requirements as the Secretary of
State thinks necessary or expedient.

   (3)   A direction under this section given to [the Independent Supervisor or] a body designated
by order under section 1252 is enforceable on the application of the Secretary of State by injunction
or, in Scotland, by an order under section 45 of the Court of Session Act 1988 (c 36).

                                                                                    [1729FB]

NOTES
Commencement: 6 April 2008.
Commencement (transitional provisions): see the note to s 1212 at **[1729DD]**.
Sub-ss (1), (3): words in square brackets inserted by the Statutory Auditors and Third Country Auditors
Regulations 2007, SI 2007/3494, reg 16, as from 6 April 2008.

                         General provision relating to offences

1255   Offences by bodies corporate, partnerships and unincorporated associations

   (1)   Where an offence under this Part committed by a body corporate is proved to have been
committed with the consent or connivance of, or to be attributable to any neglect on the part of, an
officer of the body, or a person purporting to act in any such capacity, he as well as the body
corporate is guilty of the offence and liable to be proceeded against and punished accordingly.

   (2)   Where an offence under this Part committed by a partnership is proved to have been
committed with the consent or connivance of, or to be attributable to any neglect on the part of, a
partner, he as well as the partnership is guilty of the offence and liable to be proceeded against and
punished accordingly.

   (3)   Where an offence under this Part committed by an unincorporated association (other than a
partnership) is proved to have been committed with the consent or connivance of, or to be
attributable to any neglect on the part of, any officer of the association or any member of its
governing body, he as well as the association is guilty of the offence and liable to be proceeded
against and punished accordingly.

                                                                                    [1729FC]

NOTES
Commencement: 6 April 2008.
Commencement (transitional provisions): see the note to s 1212 at **[1729DD]**.

1256   Time limits for prosecution of offences

   (1)   An information relating to an offence under this Part which is triable by a magistrates' court
in England and Wales may be so tried if it is laid at any time within the period of twelve months
beginning with the date on which evidence sufficient in the opinion of the Director of Public
Prosecutions or the Secretary of State to justify the proceedings comes to his knowledge.

   (2)   Proceedings in Scotland for an offence under this Part may be commenced at any time
within the period of twelve months beginning with the date on which evidence sufficient in the
Lord Advocate's opinion to justify proceedings came to his knowledge or, where such evidence was
reported to him by the Secretary of State, within the period of twelve months beginning with the
date on which it came to the knowledge of the Secretary of State.

(3)   For the purposes of subsection (2) proceedings are to be deemed to be commenced on the date on which a warrant to apprehend or cite the accused is granted, if the warrant is executed without undue delay.

(4)   A complaint charging an offence under this Part which is triable by a magistrates' court in Northern Ireland may be so tried if it is made at any time within the period of twelve months beginning with the date on which evidence sufficient in the opinion of the Director of Public Prosecutions for Northern Ireland or the Secretary of State to justify the proceedings comes to his knowledge.

(5)   This section does not authorise—
(a)   in the case of proceedings in England and Wales, the trial of an information laid,
(b)   in the case of proceedings in Scotland, the commencement of proceedings, or
(c)   in the case of proceedings in Northern Ireland, the trial of a complaint made,
more than three years after the commission of the offence.

(6)   For the purposes of this section a certificate of the Director of Public Prosecutions, the Lord Advocate, the Director of Public Prosecutions for Northern Ireland or the Secretary of State as to the date on which such evidence as is referred to above came to his knowledge is conclusive evidence.

(7)   Nothing in this section affects proceedings within the time limits prescribed by section 127(1) of the Magistrates' Courts Act 1980 (c 43), section 331 of the Criminal Procedure (Scotland) Act 1975 or Article 19 of the Magistrates' Courts (Northern Ireland) Order 1981 (SI 1981/1675 (NI 26)) (the usual time limits for criminal proceedings).

[1729FD]

NOTES
Commencement: 6 April 2008.
Commencement (transitional provisions): see the note to s 1212 at **[1729DD]**.
Note: following the transfer of functions of most of the Secretary of State's functions under this Part (see further the note at the beginning of this Part) the references in sub-ss (1), (2), (4) and (6) above to the Secretary of State have effect as references to the Secretary of State or the Professional Oversight Board; see the Statutory Auditors (Delegation of Functions etc) Order 2008, SI 2008/496, art 10.

1257   Jurisdiction and procedure in respect of offences

(1)   Summary proceedings for an offence under this Part may, without prejudice to any jurisdiction exercisable apart from this section, be taken—
(a)   against a body corporate or unincorporated association at any place at which it has a place of business, and
(b)   against an individual at any place where he is for the time being.

(2)   Proceedings for an offence alleged to have been committed under this Part by an unincorporated association must be brought in the name of the association (and not in that of any of its members), and for the purposes of any such proceedings any rules of court relating to the service of documents apply as in relation to a body corporate.

(3)   Section 33 of the Criminal Justice Act 1925 (c 86) and Schedule 3 to the Magistrates' Courts Act 1980 (c 43) (procedure on charge of offence against a corporation) apply in a case in which an unincorporated association is charged in England and Wales with an offence under this Part as they apply in the case of a corporation.

(4)   Section 18 of the Criminal Justice Act (Northern Ireland) 1945 (c 15 (NI)) and Article 166 and Schedule 4 to the Magistrates' Courts (Northern Ireland) Order 1981 (SI 1981/1675 (NI 26)) (procedure on charge of offence against a corporation) apply in a case in which an unincorporated association is charged in Northern Ireland with an offence under this Part as they apply in the case of a corporation.

(5)   In relation to proceedings on indictment in Scotland for an offence alleged to have been committed under this Part by an unincorporated association, section 70 of the Criminal Procedure (Scotland) Act 1995 (proceedings on indictment against bodies corporate) applies as if the association were a body corporate.

(6)   A fine imposed on an unincorporated association on its conviction of such an offence must be paid out of the funds of the association.

[1729FE]

NOTES
Commencement: 6 April 2008.
Commencement (transitional provisions): see the note to s 1212 at **[1729DD]**.

Notices etc

1258 Service of notices

(1) This section has effect in relation to any notice, direction or other document required or authorised by or by virtue of this Part to be given to or served on any person other than the Secretary of State.

(2) Any such document may be given to or served on the person in question—

    (a) by delivering it to him,

    (b) by leaving it at his proper address, or

    (c) by sending it by post to him at that address.

(3) Any such document may—

    (a) in the case of a body corporate, be given to or served on an officer of that body;

    (b) in the case of a partnership, be given to or served on any partner;

    (c) in the case of an unincorporated association other than a partnership, be given to or served on any member of the governing body of that association.

(4) For the purposes of this section and section 7 of the Interpretation Act 1978 (c 30) (service of documents by post) in its application to this section, the proper address of any person is his last known address (whether of his residence or of a place where he carries on business or is employed) and also—

    (a) in the case of a person who is eligible under the rules of a recognised supervisory body for appointment as a statutory auditor and who does not have a place of business in the United Kingdom, the address of that body;

    (b) in the case of a body corporate or an officer of that body, the address of the registered or principal office of that body in the United Kingdom;

    (c) in the case of an unincorporated association other than a partnership or a member of its governing body, its principal office in the United Kingdom.

[1729FF]

NOTES

Commencement: 6 April 2008.

Commencement (transitional provisions): see the note to s 1212 at **[1729DD]**.

1259 Documents in electronic form

(1) This section applies where—

    (a) section 1258 authorises the giving or sending of a notice, direction or other document by its delivery to a particular person ("the recipient"), and

    (b) the notice, direction or other document is transmitted to the recipient—

        (i) by means of an electronic communications network, or

        (ii) by other means but in a form that requires the use of apparatus by the recipient to render it intelligible.

(2) The transmission has effect for the purposes of this Part as a delivery of the notice, direction or other document to the recipient, but only if the recipient has indicated to the person making the transmission his willingness to receive the notice, direction or other document in the form and manner used.

(3) An indication to a person for the purposes of subsection (2)—

    (a) must be given to the person in such manner as he may require,

    (b) may be a general indication or an indication that is limited to notices, directions or other documents of a particular description,

    (c) must state the address to be used,

    (d) must be accompanied by such other information as the person requires for the making of the transmission, and

    (e) may be modified or withdrawn at any time by a notice given to the person in such manner as he may require.

(4) In this section "electronic communications network" has the same meaning as in the Communications Act 2003 (c 21).

[1729FG]

NOTES

Commencement: 6 April 2008.

Commencement (transitional provisions): see the note to s 1212 at **[1729DD]**.

Interpretation

1260   Meaning of "associate"

(1)   In this Part "associate", in relation to a person, is to be construed as follows.

(2)   In relation to an individual, "associate" means—
    (a)   that individual's spouse, civil partner or minor child or step-child,
    (b)   any body corporate of which that individual is a director, and
    (c)   any employee or partner of that individual.

(3)   In relation to a body corporate, "associate" means—
    (a)   any body corporate of which that body is a director,
    (b)   any body corporate in the same group as that body, and
    (c)   any employee or partner of that body or of any body corporate in the same group.

(4)   In relation to a partnership constituted under the law of Scotland, or any other country or territory in which a partnership is a legal person, "associate" means—
    (a)   any body corporate of which that partnership is a director,
    (b)   any employee of or partner in that partnership, and
    (c)   any person who is an associate of a partner in that partnership.

(5)   In relation to a partnership constituted under the law of England and Wales or Northern Ireland, or the law of any other country or territory in which a partnership is not a legal person, "associate" means any person who is an associate of any of the partners.

(6)   In subsections (2)(b), (3)(a) and (4)(a), in the case of a body corporate which is a limited liability partnership, "director" is to be read as "member".

[1729FH]

NOTES
Commencement: 6 April 2008.

1261   Minor definitions

(1)   In this Part, unless a contrary intention appears—
"address" means—
    (a)   in relation to an individual, his usual residential or business address;
    (b)   in relation to a firm, its registered or principal office in the United Kingdom;
["the Audit Directive" means Directive 2006/43/EC of the European Parliament and of the Council on statutory audits of annual accounts and consolidated accounts, amending Council Directives 78/660/EEC and 83/349/EEC and repealing Council Directive 84/253/EEC, as amended at any time before 1st January 2009;]
["audit working papers" means any documents which—
    (a)   are or have been held by a statutory auditor or a third country auditor, and
    (b)   are related to the conduct of an audit conducted by that auditor;]
"company" means any company or other body the accounts of which must be audited in accordance with Part 16;
"director", in relation to a body corporate, includes any person occupying in relation to it the position of a director (by whatever name called) and any person in accordance with whose directions or instructions (not being advice given in a professional capacity) the directors of the body are accustomed to act;
["EEA auditor" means an individual who is approved in accordance with the Audit Directive by an EEA competent authority to carry out audits of annual accounts or consolidated accounts required by Community law;]
["EEA competent authority" means a competent authority within the meaning of Article 2.10 of the Audit Directive of an EEA State other than the United Kingdom;]
"firm" means any entity, whether or not a legal person, which is not an individual and includes a body corporate, a corporation sole and a partnership or other unincorporated association;
"group", in relation to a body corporate, means the body corporate, any other body corporate which is its holding company or subsidiary and any other body corporate which is a subsidiary of that holding company;
"holding company" and "subsidiary" are to be read in accordance with section 1159 and Schedule 6;
"officer", in relation to a body corporate, includes a director, a manager, a secretary or, where the affairs of the body are managed by its members, a member;
"parent undertaking" and "subsidiary undertaking" are to be read in accordance with section 1162 and Schedule 7;
["third country" means a country or territory that is not an EEA State or part of an EEA State;]
["third country auditor" means a person, other than a person eligible for appointment as a statutory auditor, who is eligible to conduct audits of the accounts of bodies corporate incorporated or formed under the law of a third country in accordance with the law of that country;]

["third country competent authority" means a body established in a third country exercising functions related to the regulation or oversight of auditors.]

(2)   For the purposes of this Part a body is to be regarded as "established in the United Kingdom" if and only if—

> (a)   it is incorporated or formed under the law of the United Kingdom or a part of the United Kingdom, or
>
> (b)   its central management and control are exercised in the United Kingdom;

and any reference to a qualification "obtained in the United Kingdom" is to a qualification obtained from such a body.

[(2A)   For the purposes of this Part, Gibraltar shall be treated as if it were an EEA State.]

(3)   The Secretary of State may by regulations make such modifications of this Part as appear to him to be necessary or appropriate for the purposes of its application in relation to any firm, or description of firm, which is not a body corporate or a partnership.

(4)   Regulations under subsection (3) are subject to negative resolution procedure.

[1729FI]

NOTES

Commencement: 20 January 2007 (for the purpose of enabling the exercise of powers to make Orders or Regulations by statutory instrument); 6 April 2008 (otherwise).

Sub-s (1): definitions in square brackets inserted by the Statutory Auditors and Third Country Auditors Regulations 2007, SI 2007/3494, reg 1(1), (2), as from 6 April 2008.

Sub-s (2A): inserted by SI 2007/3494, reg 1(1), (3), as from 6 April 2008.

1262   Index of defined expressions

The following Table shows provisions defining or otherwise explaining expressions used in this Part (other than provisions defining or explaining an expression used only in the same section)—

Expression	Provision
address	section 1261(1)
appropriate qualification	section 1219
associate	section 1260
[Audit Directive	section 1261(1)]
audited person	section 1210(2)
Auditor General	section 1226(1)
[audit working papers	section 1261(1)]
company	section 1261(1)
delegation order	section 1252(1)
director (of a body corporate)	section 1261(1)
[EEA auditor	section 1261(1)]
[EEA competent authority	section 1261(1)]
enactment	section 1293
established in the United Kingdom	section 1261(2)
firm	section 1261(1)
group (in relation to a body corporate)	section 1261(1)
holding company	section 1261(1)
main purposes of this Part	section 1209
member (of a supervisory body)	section 1217(2)
obtained in the United Kingdom	section 1261(2)
officer	section 1261(1)
parent undertaking	section 1261(1)
qualifying body	section 1220(1)
recognised, in relation to a professional qualification	section 1220(3) and Schedule 11

Expression	Provision
recognised, in relation to a qualifying body	paragraph 1(2) of Schedule 11
recognised, in relation to a supervisory body	section 1217(4) and Schedule 10
registered third country auditor	section 1241(1)
rules of a qualifying body	section 1220(2)
rules of a supervisory body	section 1217(3)
statutory auditor, statutory audit and statutory audit work	section 1210(1)
subsidiary	section 1261(1)
supervisory body	section 1217(1)
subsidiary undertaking	section 1261(1)
[third country	section 1261(1)]
third country auditor ...	[section 1261(1)]
[third country competent authority	section 1261(1)]
[UK traded non EEA company	section 1241(2)]

[1729FJ]

NOTES
Commencement: 6 April 2008.
Entries in square brackets inserted by the Statutory Auditors and Third Country Auditors Regulations 2007, SI 2007/3494, reg 3(1), (2), as from 6 April 2008.
Words omitted from column 1 of the antepenultimate entry repealed, and words in square brackets in column 2 of that entry substituted, by SI 2007/3494, reg 3(1), (3), as from 6 April 2008.

Miscellaneous and general

1263   Power to make provision in consequence of changes affecting accountancy bodies

(1)   The Secretary of State may by regulations make such amendments of enactments as appear to him to be necessary or expedient in consequence of any change of name, merger or transfer of engagements affecting—
   (a)   a recognised supervisory body or recognised qualifying body, or
   (b)   a body of accountants referred to in, or approved, authorised or otherwise recognised for the purposes of, any other enactment.

(2)   Regulations under this section are subject to negative resolution procedure.

[1729FK]

NOTES
Commencement: 20 January 2007 (for the purpose of enabling the exercise of powers to make Orders or Regulations by statutory instrument); 6 April 2008 (otherwise).

1264   *(Introduces Sch 14 (consequential amendments.))*

PART 43
TRANSPARENCY OBLIGATIONS AND RELATED MATTERS

NOTES
This Part (ss 1265–1273 and Sch 15) mainly contains amendments. It came into force on 8 November 2006 (except in so far as relating to the amendment in Sch 15, para 11(2) to the definition of "regulated market" in s 103 of the 2000 Act, for which purposes it came into force on 1 October 2008).
•   Section 1265 (The transparency obligations directive) amends FSMA 2000, s 103 at **[126]**.
•   Section 1266 (Transparency rules) provides as follows. Section 1266(1) inserts FSMA 2000, ss 89A–89G at **[107A]** et seq. Section 1266(2) provides that the effectiveness for the purposes of s 155 of the 2000 Act (consultation on proposed rules) of things done by the FSA before s 1266 comes into force with a view to making transparency rules is not affected by the fact that those provisions were not then in force.
•   Section 1267 (Competent authority's power to call for information) inserts FSMA 2000, ss 89H–89J at **[107H]** et seq.
•   Section 1268 (Powers exercisable in case of infringement of transparency obligation) inserts FSMA 2000, ss 89K–89K at **[107K]** et seq.
•   Section 1269 (Corporate governance rules) inserts FSMA 2000, s 89O at **[107O]**.
•   Section 1270 (Liability for false or misleading statements in certain publications) inserts FSMA 2000, ss 90A, 90B at **[108A]** et seq.

- Section 1271 (Exercise of powers where UK is host member State) inserts FSMA 2000, s 100A at **[120A]**.
- Section 1272 (Transparency obligations and related matters: minor and consequential amendments) introduces Sch 15 to this Act (as to which see below).
- Section 1273 (Corporate governance regulations) is set out after this note.
- Schedule 15, Part 1 amends FSMA 2000, ss 73, 73A, 90 (and the preceding heading), 91, 96B, 97, 99, 102A, 103, 429 at **[73]**, **[74]**, **[108]**, **[109]**, **[116]**, **[118]**, **[119]**, **[123]**, **[126]**, **[455]**.
- Schedule 15, Part 2 amends the Companies (Audit, Investigations and Community Enterprise) Act 2004, ss 14, 15.

Other matters

1273 Corporate governance regulations

(1) The Secretary of State may make regulations—

    (a) for the purpose of implementing, enabling the implementation of or dealing with matters arising out of or related to, any Community obligation relating to the corporate governance of issuers who have requested or approved admission of their securities to trading on a regulated market;

    (b) about corporate governance in relation to such issuers for the purpose of implementing, or dealing with matters arising out of or related to, any Community obligation.

(2) "Corporate governance", in relation to an issuer, includes—

    (a) the nature, constitution or functions of the organs of the issuer;

    (b) the manner in which organs of the issuer conduct themselves;

    (c) the requirements imposed on organs of the issuer;

    (d) the relationship between different organs of the issuer;

    (e) the relationship between the organs of the issuer and the members of the issuer or holders of the issuer's securities.

(3) The regulations may—

    (a) make provision by reference to any specified code on corporate governance that may be issued from time to time by a specified body;

    (b) create new criminal offences (subject to subsection (4));

    (c) make provision excluding liability in damages in respect of things done or omitted for the purposes of, or in connection with, the carrying on, or purported carrying on, of any specified activities.

"Specified" here means specified in the regulations.

(4) The regulations may not create a criminal offence punishable by a greater penalty than—

    (a) on indictment, a fine;

    (b) on summary conviction, a fine not exceeding the statutory maximum or (if calculated on a daily basis) £100 a day.

(5) Regulations under this section are subject to negative resolution procedure.

(6) In this section "issuer", "securities" and "regulated market" have the same meaning as in Part 6 of the Financial Services and Markets Act 2000 (c 8).

[1729FL]

NOTES
Commencement: 8 November 2006.

PART 46
GENERAL SUPPLEMENTARY PROVISIONS

NOTES
Application of this Part to unregistered companies: see the Companies Acts (Unregistered Companies) Regulations 2007, SI 2007/318.

Consequential and transitional provisions

1297 Continuity of the law

(1) This section applies where any provision of this Act re-enacts (with or without modification) an enactment repealed by this Act.

(2) The repeal and re-enactment does not affect the continuity of the law.

(3) Anything done (including subordinate legislation made), or having effect as if done, under or for the purposes of the repealed provision that could have been done under or for the purposes of the corresponding provision of this Act, if in force or effective immediately before the commencement of that corresponding provision, has effect thereafter as if done under or for the purposes of that corresponding provision.

(4)   Any reference (express or implied) in this Act or any other enactment, instrument or document to a provision of this Act shall be construed (so far as the context permits) as including, as respects times, circumstances or purposes in relation to which the corresponding repealed provision had effect, a reference to that corresponding provision.

(5)   Any reference (express or implied) in any enactment, instrument or document to a repealed provision shall be construed (so far as the context permits), as respects times, circumstances and purposes in relation to which the corresponding provision of this Act has effect, as being or (according to the context) including a reference to the corresponding provision of this Act.

(6)   This section has effect subject to any specific transitional provision or saving contained in this Act.

(7)   References in this section to this Act include subordinate legislation made under this Act.

(8)   In this section "subordinate legislation" has the same meaning as in the Interpretation Act 1978 (c 30).

[1729FM]

NOTES
Commencement: 8 November 2006.
General saving for existing companies etc: the Companies Act 2006 (Commencement No 8, Transitional Provisions and Savings) Order 2008, SI 2008/2860, Sch 2, para 1(2), (3) provides as follows—

"(2)   Section 1297(3) of the Companies Act 2006 (continuity of the law: things done under old law to be treated as done under the corresponding provision of the new law) applies—
- (a)   in relation to a company to which section 675(1) of the 1985 Act or Article 625(1) of the 1986 Order applied (application of Act or Order to companies formed and registered under earlier companies legislation) as if the company had been formed and registered under Part 1 of the 1985 Act or Part 2 of the 1986 Order;
- (b)   in relation to a company to which section 676(1) of the 1985 Act or Article 626(1) of the 1986 Order applied (application of Act or Order to companies registered but not formed under earlier companies legislation) as if the company had been registered under Chapter 2 of Part 22 of the 1985 Act or Chapter 2 of Part 22 of the 1986 Order;
- (c)   in relation to a company to which section 677(1) of the 1985 Act or Article 627(1) of the 1986 Order applied (application of Act or Order to companies re-registered under earlier companies legislation) as if the company had been re-registered under Part 2 of the 1985 Act or Part 3 of the 1986 Order.

(3)   Nothing in this paragraph or in section 1297(3) of the Companies Act 2006 shall be read as affecting any reference to the date on which a company was registered or re-registered.".

Note: the Companies Act 2006 (Commencement No 2, Consequential Amendments, Transitional Provisions and Savings) Order 2007, SI 2007/1093, art 10 provides as follows (note that by virtue of art 1(2) "the Interim Regulations" means the Takeovers Directive (Interim Implementation) Regulations 2006)—

"10.   Section 1297 of the Companies Act 2006 (continuity of the law) has effect as if, for the purpose of section 1297(1), the Interim Regulations were an enactment repealed and re-enacted by that Act.".

See also the Companies Act 2006 (Commencement No 3, Consequential Amendments, Transitional Provisions and Savings) Order 2007, SI 2007/2194, art 12(1), the Companies Act 2006 (Commencement No 5, Transitional Provisions and Savings) Order 2007, SI 2007/3495, art 12(2), the Companies Act 2006 (Commencement No 6, Saving and Commencement Nos 3 and 5 (Amendment)) Order 2008, SI 2008/674, art 6(2), and the Companies Act 2006 (Consequential Amendments etc) Order 2008, SI 2008/948, art 12 which provide that the amendments and repeals made by those Orders do not affect the operation of this section.

PART 47
FINAL PROVISIONS

NOTES
Application of this Part to unregistered companies: see the Companies Acts (Unregistered Companies) Regulations 2007, SI 2007/318.

1298   Short title

The short title of this Act is the Companies Act 2006.

[1730]

NOTES
Commencement: 8 November 2006.

1299   Extent

Except as otherwise provided (or the context otherwise requires), the provisions of this Act extend to the whole of the United Kingdom.

[1731]

1300 Commencement

(1)   The following provisions come into force on the day this Act is passed—
  (a)   Part 43 (transparency obligations and related matters), except the amendment in paragraph 11(2) of Schedule 15 of the definition of "regulated market" in Part 6 of the Financial Services and Markets Act 2000 (c 8),
  (b)   in Part 44 (miscellaneous provisions)—
    section 1274 (grants to bodies concerned with actuarial standards etc), and
    section 1276 (application of provisions to Scotland and Northern Ireland),
  (c)   Part 46 (general supplementary provisions), except section 1295 and Schedule 16 (repeals), and
  (d)   this Part.

(2)   The other provisions of this Act come into force on such day as may be appointed by order of the Secretary of State or the Treasury.

[1732]

SCHEDULES

SCHEDULE 2
SPECIFIED PERSONS, DESCRIPTIONS OF DISCLOSURES ETC FOR THE PURPOSES OF SECTION 948

Section 948

PART 1
SPECIFIED PERSONS

1.   The Secretary of State.

2.   The Department of Enterprise, Trade and Investment for Northern Ireland.

3.   The Treasury.

[3A.   The Treasury of the Isle of Man.]

4.   The Bank of England.

5.   The Financial Services Authority.

[5A.   The Financial Supervision Commission of the Isle of Man.]

6.   The Commissioners for Her Majesty's Revenue and Customs.

7.   The Lord Advocate.

[7A.   The Attorney General of the Isle of Man.]

8.   The Director of Public Prosecutions.

9.   The Director of Public Prosecutions for Northern Ireland.

10.   A constable.

11.   A procurator fiscal.

12.   The Scottish Ministers.

[12A.   The members and officers of each of the Departments constituted by section 1(1) of the Government Departments Act 1987 (an Act of Tynwald: c 13).

"Member" has the same meaning as it has by virtue of section 7(1) of that Act.]

[1732A]

Paras 3A, 5A, 7A, 12A: inserted by the Companies Act 2006 (Amendment of Schedule 2) Order 2009, SI 2009/202, art 2, Schedule, para 1, as from 1 March 2009.

PART 2
SPECIFIED DESCRIPTIONS OF DISCLOSURES

13. A disclosure for the purpose of enabling or assisting a person authorised under section 457 of this Act (persons authorised to apply to court) to exercise his functions.

Until the coming into force of section 457, the reference to that section is to be read as a reference to section 245C of the Companies Act 1985 (c 6).

14. A disclosure for the purpose of enabling or assisting an inspector appointed under Part 14 of the Companies Act 1985 (investigation of companies and their affairs, etc) to exercise his functions.

[14A. A disclosure for the purpose of enabling or assisting an inspector appointed by the High Court of the Isle of Man under the enactments relating to companies to exercise the functions of the inspector.]

15. A disclosure for the purpose of enabling or assisting a person authorised under section 447 of the Companies Act 1985 (power to require production of documents) or section 84 of the Companies Act 1989 (c 40) (exercise of powers by officer etc) to exercise his functions.

16. A disclosure for the purpose of enabling or assisting a person appointed under section 167 of the Financial Services and Markets Act 2000 (c 8) (general investigations) to conduct an investigation to exercise his functions.

17. A disclosure for the purpose of enabling or assisting a person appointed under section 168 of the Financial Services and Markets Act 2000 (investigations in particular cases) to conduct an investigation to exercise his functions.

18. A disclosure for the purpose of enabling or assisting a person appointed under section 169(1)(b) of the Financial Services and Markets Act 2000 (investigation in support of overseas regulator) to conduct an investigation to exercise his functions.

19. A disclosure for the purpose of enabling or assisting the body corporate responsible for administering the scheme referred to in section 225 of the Financial Services and Markets Act 2000 (the ombudsman scheme) to exercise its functions.

20. A disclosure for the purpose of enabling or assisting a person appointed under paragraph 4 (the panel of ombudsmen) or 5 (the Chief Ombudsman) of Schedule 17 to the Financial Services and Markets Act 2000 to exercise his functions.

21. A disclosure for the purpose of enabling or assisting a person appointed under regulations made under section 262(1) and (2)(k) of the Financial Services and Markets Act 2000 (investigations into open-ended investment companies) to conduct an investigation to exercise his functions.

22. A disclosure for the purpose of enabling or assisting a person appointed under section 284 of the Financial Services and Markets Act 2000 (investigations into affairs of certain collective investment schemes) to conduct an investigation to exercise his functions.

[22A. A disclosure for the purpose of enabling or assisting a person conducting an investigation under—
    (a)   section 16 of the Collective Investment Schemes Act 2008 (an Act of Tynwald: c 7);
    (b)   Schedule 2 to the Financial Services Act 2008 (an Act of Tynwald: c 8); or
    (c)   Schedule 5 to the Insurance Act 2008 (an Act of Tynwald: c 16),
to exercise that person's functions.]

23. A disclosure for the purpose of enabling or assisting the investigator appointed under paragraph 7 of Schedule 1 to the Financial Services and Markets Act 2000 (arrangements for investigation of complaints) to exercise his functions.

24. A disclosure for the purpose of enabling or assisting a person appointed by the Treasury to hold an inquiry into matters relating to financial services (including an inquiry under section 15 of the Financial Services and Markets Act 2000 (c 8)) to exercise his functions.

25. A disclosure for the purpose of enabling or assisting the Secretary of State or the Treasury to exercise any of their functions under any of the following—
    (a)   the Companies Acts;
    (b)   Part 5 of the Criminal Justice Act 1993 (c 36) (insider dealing);
    (c)   the Insolvency Act 1986 (c 45);
    (d)   the Company Directors Disqualification Act 1986 (c 46);
    (e)   Part 42 of this Act (statutory auditors);
    (f)   Part 3 (investigations and powers to obtain information) or 7 (financial markets and insolvency) of the Companies Act 1989 (c 40);
    (g)   the Financial Services and Markets Act 2000.

Until the coming into force of Part 42 of this Act, the reference to it in paragraph (e) is to be read as a reference to Part 2 of the Companies Act 1989.

[25A.   A disclosure for the purpose of enabling or assisting the Financial Supervision Commission of the Isle of Man to exercise any of its functions.

25B.   A disclosure for the purpose of enabling or assisting an auditor of a permitted person (within the meaning of the Financial Services Act 2008 (an Act of Tynwald)) to exercise the auditor's functions.]

26.   A disclosure for the purpose of enabling or assisting the Scottish Ministers to exercise their functions under the enactments relating to insolvency.

27.   A disclosure for the purpose of enabling or assisting the Department of Enterprise, Trade and Investment for Northern Ireland to exercise any powers conferred on it by the enactments relating to companies or insolvency.

[27A.   A disclosure for the purpose of enabling or assisting the Treasury of the Isle of Man to exercise its functions under the enactments relating to companies, insurance companies or insolvency.]

28.   A disclosure for the purpose of enabling or assisting a person appointed or authorised by the Department of Enterprise, Trade and Investment for Northern Ireland under the enactments relating to companies or insolvency to exercise his functions.

29.   A disclosure for the purpose of enabling or assisting the Pensions Regulator to exercise the functions conferred on it by or by virtue of any of the following—
   (a)   the Pension Schemes Act 1993 (c 48);
   (b)   the Pensions Act 1995 (c 26);
   (c)   the Welfare Reform and Pensions Act 1999 (c 30);
   (d)   the Pensions Act 2004 (c 35);
   (e)   any enactment in force in Northern Ireland corresponding to any of those enactments.

[29A.   A disclosure for the purpose of enabling or assisting—
   (a)   the Insurance and Pensions Authority of the Isle of Man; or
   (b)   the Retirement Benefits Schemes Supervisor of the Isle of Man,
to exercise its functions under the Retirement Benefits Schemes Act 2000 (an Act of Tynwald: c 14).]

30.   A disclosure for the purpose of enabling or assisting the Board of the Pension Protection Fund to exercise the functions conferred on it by or by virtue of Part 2 of the Pensions Act 2004 or any enactment in force in Northern Ireland corresponding to that Part.

31.   A disclosure for the purpose of enabling or assisting—
   (a)   the Bank of England,
   (b)   the European Central Bank, or
   (c)   the central bank of any country or territory outside the United Kingdom,
to exercise its functions.

32.   A disclosure for the purpose of enabling or assisting the Commissioners for Her Majesty's Revenue and Customs to exercise their functions.

[32A.   A disclosure for the purpose of enabling or assisting the Assessor of Income Tax to exercise the Assessor's functions under enactments of the Isle of Man relating to income tax.]

33.   A disclosure for the purpose of enabling or assisting organs of the Society of Lloyd's (being organs constituted by or under the Lloyd's Act 1982 (c xiv)) to exercise their functions under or by virtue of the Lloyd's Acts 1871 to 1982.

34.   A disclosure for the purpose of enabling or assisting the Office of Fair Trading to exercise its functions under any of the following—
   (a)   the Fair Trading Act 1973 (c 41);
   (b)   the Consumer Credit Act 1974 (c 39);
   (c)   the Estate Agents Act 1979 (c 38);
   (d)   the Competition Act 1980 (c 21);
   (e)   the Competition Act 1998 (c 41);
   (f)   the Financial Services and Markets Act 2000 (c 8);
   (g)   the Enterprise Act 2002 (c 40);
   (h)   ...
   (i)   the Unfair Terms in Consumer Contracts Regulations 1999 (SI 1999/2083);
   [(j)   the Business Protection from Misleading Marketing Regulations 2008;
   (k)   the Consumer Protection from Unfair Trading Regulations 2008].

35.   A disclosure for the purpose of enabling or assisting the Competition Commission to exercise its functions under any of the following—
   (a)   the Fair Trading Act 1973;
   (b)   the Competition Act 1980;

(c)   the Competition Act 1998;
(d)   the Enterprise Act 2002.

36.   A disclosure with a view to the institution of, or otherwise for the purposes of, proceedings before the Competition Appeal Tribunal.

37.   A disclosure for the purpose of enabling or assisting an enforcer under Part 8 of the Enterprise Act 2002 (enforcement of consumer legislation) to exercise its functions under that Part.

38.   A disclosure for the purpose of enabling or assisting the Charity Commission to exercise its functions.

39.   A disclosure for the purpose of enabling or assisting the Attorney General [or the Attorney General of the Isle of Man] to exercise his functions in connection with charities.

40.   A disclosure for the purpose of enabling or assisting the National Lottery Commission to exercise its functions under sections 5 to 10 (licensing) and 15 (power of Secretary of State to require information) of the National Lottery etc Act 1993 (c 39).

41.   A disclosure by the National Lottery Commission to the National Audit Office for the purpose of enabling or assisting the Comptroller and Auditor General to carry out an examination under Part 2 of the National Audit Act 1983 (c 44) into the economy, effectiveness and efficiency with which the National Lottery Commission has used its resources in discharging its functions under sections 5 to 10 of the National Lottery etc Act 1993.

42.   A disclosure for the purpose of enabling or assisting a qualifying body under the Unfair Terms in Consumer Contracts Regulations 1999 (SI 1999/ 2083) to exercise its functions under those Regulations.

43.   A disclosure for the purpose of enabling or assisting an enforcement authority under the Consumer Protection (Distance Selling) Regulations 2000 (SI 2000/2334) to exercise its functions under those Regulations.

44.   A disclosure for the purpose of enabling or assisting an enforcement authority under the Financial Services (Distance Marketing) Regulations 2004 (SI 2004/2095) to exercise its functions under those Regulations.

45.   A disclosure for the purpose of enabling or assisting a local weights and measures authority in England and Wales to exercise its functions under section 230(2) of the Enterprise Act 2002 (c 40) (notice of intention to prosecute, etc).

46.   A disclosure for the purpose of enabling or assisting the Financial Services Authority to exercise its functions under any of the following—
(a)   the legislation relating to friendly societies or to industrial and provident societies;
(b)   the Building Societies Act 1986 (c 53);
(c)   Part 7 of the Companies Act 1989 (c 40) (financial markets and insolvency);
(d)   the Financial Services and Markets Act 2000 (c 8).

47.   A disclosure for the purpose of enabling or assisting the competent authority for the purposes of Part 6 of the Financial Services and Markets Act 2000 (official listing) to exercise its functions under that Part.

48.   A disclosure for the purpose of enabling or assisting a body corporate established in accordance with section 212(1) of the Financial Services and Markets Act 2000 (compensation scheme manager) to exercise its functions.

[48A.   A disclosure for the purpose of enabling or assisting the body administering a scheme under section 25 of the Financial Services Act 2008 (an Act of Tynwald) (compensation schemes) to exercise its functions under the scheme.]

49.   A disclosure for the purpose of enabling or assisting a recognised investment exchange or a recognised clearing house to exercise its functions as such.

    "Recognised investment exchange" and "recognised clearing house" have the same meaning as in section 285 of the Financial Services and Markets Act 2000.

50.   A disclosure for the purpose of enabling or assisting a person approved under the Uncertificated Securities Regulations 2001 (SI 2001/3755) as an operator of a relevant system (within the meaning of those regulations) to exercise his functions.

51.   A disclosure for the purpose of enabling or assisting a body designated under section 326(1) of the Financial Services and Markets Act 2000 (designated professional bodies) to exercise its functions in its capacity as a body designated under that section.

52.   A disclosure with a view to the institution of, or otherwise for the purposes of, civil proceedings arising under or by virtue of the Financial Services and Markets Act 2000.

[52A.   A disclosure with a view to the institution of, or otherwise for the purposes of, civil proceedings arising under or by virtue of the Financial Services Act 2008 (an Act of Tynwald).]

PART II
OTHER ACTS

53. A disclosure for the purpose of enabling or assisting a body designated by order under section 1252 of this Act (delegation of functions of Secretary of State) to exercise its functions under Part 42 of this Act (statutory auditors).

Until the coming into force of that Part, the references to section 1252 and Part 42 are to be read as references to section 46 of the Companies Act 1989 (c 40) and Part 2 of that Act respectively.

54. A disclosure for the purpose of enabling or assisting a recognised supervisory or qualifying body, within the meaning of Part 42 of this Act, to exercise its functions as such.

Until the coming into force of that Part, the reference to it is to be read as a reference to Part 2 of the Companies Act 1989.

55. A disclosure for the purpose of enabling or assisting an official receiver (including the Accountant in Bankruptcy in Scotland and the Official Assignee in Northern Ireland) to exercise his functions under the enactments relating to insolvency.

[55A. A disclosure for the purpose of enabling or assisting an official receiver appointed in the Isle of Man to exercise the official receiver's functions under the enactments relating to insolvency.]

56. A disclosure for the purpose of enabling or assisting the Insolvency Practitioners Tribunal to exercise its functions under the Insolvency Act 1986 (c 45).

57. A disclosure for the purpose of enabling or assisting a body that is for the time being a recognised professional body for the purposes of section 391 of the Insolvency Act 1986 (recognised professional bodies) to exercise its functions as such.

58. A disclosure for the purpose of enabling or assisting an overseas regulatory authority to exercise its regulatory functions.

"Overseas regulatory authority" and "regulatory functions" have the same meaning as in section 82 of the Companies Act 1989.

59. A disclosure for the purpose of enabling or assisting the Regulator of Community Interest Companies to exercise functions under the Companies (Audit, Investigations and Community Enterprise) Act 2004 (c 27).

60. A disclosure with a view to the institution of, or otherwise for the purposes of, criminal proceedings.

61. A disclosure for the purpose of enabling or assisting a person authorised by the Secretary of State under Part 2, 3 or 4 of the Proceeds of Crime Act 2002 (c 29) to exercise his functions.

62. A disclosure with a view to the institution of, or otherwise for the purposes of, proceedings on an application under section 6, 7 or 8 of the Company Directors Disqualification Act 1986 (c 46) (disqualification for unfitness).

63. A disclosure with a view to the institution of, or otherwise for the purposes of, proceedings before the Financial Services and Markets Tribunal.

64. A disclosure for the purposes of proceedings before the Financial Services Tribunal by virtue of the Financial Services and Markets Act 2000 (Transitional Provisions) (Partly Completed Procedures) Order 2001 (SI 2001/3592).

65. A disclosure for the purposes of proceedings before the Pensions Regulator Tribunal.

66. A disclosure for the purpose of enabling or assisting a body appointed under section 14 of the Companies (Audit, Investigations and Community Enterprise) Act 2004 (supervision of periodic accounts and reports of issuers of listed securities) to exercise functions mentioned in subsection (2) of that section.

67. A disclosure with a view to the institution of, or otherwise for the purposes of, disciplinary proceedings relating to the performance by a *solicitor, barrister, advocate*, foreign lawyer, auditor, accountant, valuer or actuary of his professional duties.

"*Foreign lawyer*" *has the meaning given by section 89(9) of the Courts and Legal Services Act 1990 (c 41)*.

68. A disclosure with a view to the institution of, or otherwise for the purposes of, disciplinary proceedings relating to the performance by a public servant of his duties.

"Public servant" means an officer or employee of the Crown or of any public or other authority for the time being designated for the purposes of this paragraph by the Secretary of State by order subject to negative resolution procedure.

69. A disclosure for the purpose of the provision of a summary or collection of information framed in such a way as not to enable the identity of any person to whom the information relates to be ascertained.

70. A disclosure in pursuance of any Community obligation.

[1732B]

NOTES

Commencement: 20 January 2007 (for the purpose of enabling the exercise of powers to make Orders or Regulations by statutory instrument); 6 April 2007 (otherwise).

Paras 14A, 22A, 25A, 25B, 27A, 29A, 32A, 48A, 52A, 55A: inserted by the Companies Act 2006 (Amendment of Schedule 2) Order 2009, SI 2009/202, art 2, Schedule, para 2(a)–(f), (h)–(j), as from 1 March 2009.

Para 34: sub-para (h) repealed, and sub-paras (j), (k) added, by the Consumer Protection from Unfair Trading Regulations 2008, SI 2008/1277, reg 30(1), (3), Sch 2, Pt 1, para 75, Sch 4, Pt 1, as from 26 May 2008.

Para 39: words in square brackets inserted by SI 2009/202, art 2, Schedule, para 2(g), as from 1 March 2009.

Para 67: for the first words in italics there are substituted the words "relevant lawyer", and for the second words in italics there are substituted the following words, by the Legal Services Act 2007, s 208, Sch 21, para 156, as from a day to be appointed—

"In this paragraph—

"foreign lawyer" means a person (other than a relevant lawyer) who is a foreign lawyer within the meaning of section 89(9) of the Courts and Legal Services Act 1990;

"relevant lawyer" means—

(a) a person who, for the purposes of the Legal Services Act 2007, is an authorised person in relation to an activity which constitutes a reserved legal activity (within the meaning of that Act),

(b) a solicitor or barrister in Northern Ireland, or

(c) a solicitor or advocate in Scotland.".

PART 3
OVERSEAS REGULATORY BODIES

71.   A disclosure is made in accordance with this Part of this Schedule if—

(a) it is made to a person or body within paragraph 72, and

(b) it is made for the purpose of enabling or assisting that person or body to exercise the functions mentioned in that paragraph.

72.   The persons or bodies that are within this paragraph are those exercising functions of a public nature, under legislation in any country or territory outside the United Kingdom, that appear to the Panel to be similar to its own functions or those of the Financial Services Authority.

73.   In determining whether to disclose information to a person or body in accordance with this Part of this Schedule, the Panel must have regard to the following considerations—

(a) whether the use that the person or body is likely to make of the information is sufficiently important to justify making the disclosure;

(b) whether the person or body has adequate arrangements to prevent the information from being used or further disclosed otherwise than for the purposes of carrying out the functions mentioned in paragraph 72 or any other purposes substantially similar to those for which information disclosed to the Panel could be used or further disclosed.

[1732C]

NOTES

Commencement: 6 April 2007.

SCHEDULE 6
MEANING OF "SUBSIDIARY" ETC: SUPPLEMENTARY PROVISIONS
Section 1159

Introduction

1.   The provisions of this Part of this Schedule explain expressions used in section 1159 (meaning of "subsidiary" etc) and otherwise supplement that section.

Voting rights in a company

2.   In section 1159(1)(a) and (c) the references to the voting rights in a company are to the rights conferred on shareholders in respect of their shares or, in the case of a company not having a share capital, on members, to vote at general meetings of the company on all, or substantially all, matters.

Right to appoint or remove a majority of the directors

3.—(1)   In section 1159(1)(b) the reference to the right to appoint or remove a majority of the board of directors is to the right to appoint or remove directors holding a majority of the voting rights at meetings of the board on all, or substantially all, matters.

(2)   A company shall be treated as having the right to appoint to a directorship if—

(a) a person's appointment to it follows necessarily from his appointment as director of the company, or

(b) the directorship is held by the company itself.

(3)   A right to appoint or remove which is exercisable only with the consent or concurrence of another person shall be left out of account unless no other person has a right to appoint or, as the case may be, remove in relation to that directorship.

Rights exercisable only in certain circumstances or temporarily incapable of exercise

4.—(1)   Rights which are exercisable only in certain circumstances shall be taken into account only—

  (a)   when the circumstances have arisen, and for so long as they continue to obtain, or
  (b)   when the circumstances are within the control of the person having the rights.

(2)   Rights which are normally exercisable but are temporarily incapable of exercise shall continue to be taken into account.

Rights held by one person on behalf of another

5.   Rights held by a person in a fiduciary capacity shall be treated as not held by him.

6.—(1)   Rights held by a person as nominee for another shall be treated as held by the other.

(2)   Rights shall be regarded as held as nominee for another if they are exercisable only on his instructions or with his consent or concurrence.

Rights attached to shares held by way of security

7.   Rights attached to shares held by way of security shall be treated as held by the person providing the security—

  (a)   where apart from the right to exercise them for the purpose of preserving the value of the security, or of realising it, the rights are exercisable only in accordance with his instructions, and
  (b)   where the shares are held in connection with the granting of loans as part of normal business activities and apart from the right to exercise them for the purpose of preserving the value of the security, or of realising it, the rights are exercisable only in his interests.

Rights attributed to holding company

8.—(1)   Rights shall be treated as held by a holding company if they are held by any of its subsidiary companies.

(2)   Nothing in paragraph 6 or 7 shall be construed as requiring rights held by a holding company to be treated as held by any of its subsidiaries.

(3)   For the purposes of paragraph 7 rights shall be treated as being exercisable in accordance with the instructions or in the interests of a company if they are exercisable in accordance with the instructions of or, as the case may be, in the interests of—

  (a)   any subsidiary or holding company of that company, or
  (b)   any subsidiary of a holding company of that company.

Disregard of certain rights

9.   The voting rights in a company shall be reduced by any rights held by the company itself.

Supplementary

10.   References in any provision of paragraphs 5 to 9 to rights held by a person include rights falling to be treated as held by him by virtue of any other provision of those paragraphs but not rights which by virtue of any such provision are to be treated as not held by him.

[1733]

NOTES

Commencement: 6 April 2008 (so far as necessary for the purposes of ss 1209–1241, 1245–1264, and Schs 10, 11, 13, 14 (statutory auditors)); 1 October 2009 (otherwise).

SCHEDULE 7
PARENT AND SUBSIDIARY UNDERTAKINGS: SUPPLEMENTARY PROVISIONS
Section 1162

Introduction

1.   The provisions of this Schedule explain expressions used in section 1162 (parent and subsidiary undertakings) and otherwise supplement that section.

Voting rights in an undertaking

2.—(1) In section 1162(2)(a) and (d) the references to the voting rights in an undertaking are to the rights conferred on shareholders in respect of their shares or, in the case of an undertaking not having a share capital, on members, to vote at general meetings of the undertaking on all, or substantially all, matters.

(2) In relation to an undertaking which does not have general meetings at which matters are decided by the exercise of voting rights the references to holding a majority of the voting rights in the undertaking shall be construed as references to having the right under the constitution of the undertaking to direct the overall policy of the undertaking or to alter the terms of its constitution.

Right to appoint or remove a majority of the directors

3.—(1) In section 1162(2)(b) the reference to the right to appoint or remove a majority of the board of directors is to the right to appoint or remove directors holding a majority of the voting rights at meetings of the board on all, or substantially all, matters.

(2) An undertaking shall be treated as having the right to appoint to a directorship if—
   (a)   a person's appointment to it follows necessarily from his appointment as director of the undertaking, or
   (b)   the directorship is held by the undertaking itself.

(3) A right to appoint or remove which is exercisable only with the consent or concurrence of another person shall be left out of account unless no other person has a right to appoint or, as the case may be, remove in relation to that directorship.

Right to exercise dominant influence

4.—(1) For the purposes of section 1162(2)(c) an undertaking shall not be regarded as having the right to exercise a dominant influence over another undertaking unless it has a right to give directions with respect to the operating and financial policies of that other undertaking which its directors are obliged to comply with whether or not they are for the benefit of that other undertaking.

(2) A "control contract" means a contract in writing conferring such a right which—
   (a)   is of a kind authorised by the articles of the undertaking in relation to which the right is exercisable, and
   (b)   is permitted by the law under which that undertaking is established.

(3) This paragraph shall not be read as affecting the construction of section 1162(4)(a).

Rights exercisable only in certain circumstances or temporarily incapable of exercise

5.—(1) Rights which are exercisable only in certain circumstances shall be taken into account only—
   (a)   when the circumstances have arisen, and for so long as they continue to obtain, or
   (b)   when the circumstances are within the control of the person having the rights.

(2) Rights which are normally exercisable but are temporarily incapable of exercise shall continue to be taken into account.

Rights held by one person on behalf of another

6.   Rights held by a person in a fiduciary capacity shall be treated as not held by him.

7.—(1) Rights held by a person as nominee for another shall be treated as held by the other.

(2) Rights shall be regarded as held as nominee for another if they are exercisable only on his instructions or with his consent or concurrence.

Rights attached to shares held by way of security

8.   Rights attached to shares held by way of security shall be treated as held by the person providing the security—
   (a)   where apart from the right to exercise them for the purpose of preserving the value of the security, or of realising it, the rights are exercisable only in accordance with his instructions, and
   (b)   where the shares are held in connection with the granting of loans as part of normal business activities and apart from the right to exercise them for the purpose of preserving the value of the security, or of realising it, the rights are exercisable only in his interests.

Rights attributed to parent undertaking

9.—(1) Rights shall be treated as held by a parent undertaking if they are held by any of its subsidiary undertakings.

(2)   Nothing in paragraph 7 or 8 shall be construed as requiring rights held by a parent undertaking to be treated as held by any of its subsidiary undertakings.

(3)   For the purposes of paragraph 8 rights shall be treated as being exercisable in accordance with the instructions or in the interests of an undertaking if they are exercisable in accordance with the instructions of or, as the case may be, in the interests of any group undertaking.

Disregard of certain rights

10.   The voting rights in an undertaking shall be reduced by any rights held by the undertaking itself.

Supplementary

11.   References in any provision of paragraphs 6 to 10 to rights held by a person include rights falling to be treated as held by him by virtue of any other provision of those paragraphs but not rights which by virtue of any such provision are to be treated as not held by him.

[1733A]

NOTES
Commencement: 6 April 2008.

SCHEDULE 8
INDEX OF DEFINED EXPRESSIONS
Section 1174

abbreviated accounts (in Part 15)	sections 444(4) and 445(3)
accounting reference date and accounting reference period	section 391
accounting standards (in Part 15)	section 464
accounts meeting	section 437(3)
acquisition, in relation to a non-cash asset	section 1163(2)
address	
— generally in the Companies Acts	section 1142
— in the company communications provisions	section 1148(1)
affirmative resolution procedure, in relation to regulations and orders	section 1290
allotment (time of)	section 558
allotment of equity securities (in Chapter 3 of Part 17)	section 560(2)
allotted share capital and allotted shares	section 546(1)(b) and (2)
annual accounts (in Part 15)	section 471
annual accounts and reports (in Part 15)	section 471
annual general meeting	section 336
annual return	section 854
appropriate audit authority (in sections 522, 523 and 524)	section 525(1)
appropriate rate of interest	
— in Chapter 5 of Part 17	section 592
— in Chapter 6 of Part 17	section 609
approval after being made, in relation to regulations and orders	section 1291
arrangement	
— in Chapter 7 of Part 17	section 616(1)
— in Part 26	section 895(2)

articles	section 18
associate (in Chapter 3 of Part 28)	section 988
associated bodies corporate and associated company (in Part 10)	section 256
authenticated, in relation to a document or information sent or supplied to a company	section 1146
authorised group, of members of a company (in Part 14)	section 370(3)
authorised insurance company	section 1165(2)
authorised minimum (in relation to share capital of public company)	section 763
available profits (in Chapter 5 of Part 18)	sections 711 and 712
banking company and banking group	section 1164
body corporate	section 1173(1)
called-up share capital	section 547
capital redemption reserve	section 733
capitalisation in relation to a company's profits (in Part 23)	section 853(3)
cash (in relation to paying up or allotting shares)	section 583
cause of action, in relation to derivative proceedings (in Chapter 2 of Part 11)	section 265(7)
certified translation (in Part 35)	section 1107
charge (in Chapter 1 of Part 25)	section 861(5)
circulation date, in relation to a written resolution (in Part 13)	section 290
class of shares	section 629
the Companies Acts	section 2
Companies Act accounts	sections 395(1)(a) and 403(2)(a)
Companies Act group accounts	section 403(2)(a)
Companies Act individual accounts	section 395(1)(a)
companies involved in the division (in Part 27)	section 919(2)
company	
— generally in the Companies Acts	section 1
— in Chapter 7 of Part 17	section 616(1)
— in Chapter 1 of Part 25	section 861(5)
— in Chapter 2 of Part 25	section 879(6)
— in Part 26	section 895(2)
— in Chapter 3 of Part 28	section 991(1)
— in the company communications provisions	section 1148(1)
the company communications provisions	section 1143
the company law provisions of this Act	section 2(2)
company records (in Part 37)	section 1134
connected with, in relation to a director (in Part 10)	sections 252 to 254
constitution, of a company	
— generally in the Companies Acts	section 17
— in Part 10	section 257

enactment	section 1293
equity securities (in Chapter 3 of Part 17)	section 560(1)
equity share capital	section 548
equity shares (in Chapter 7 of Part 17)	section 616(1)
existing company (in Part 27)	section 902(2)
fellow subsidiary undertakings	section 1161(4)
financial assistance (in Chapter 2 of Part 18)	section 677
financial institution	section 1173(1)
financial year, of a company	section 390
firm	section 1173(1)
fixed assets (in Part 23)	section 853
the former Companies Acts	section 1171
the Gazette	section 1173(1)
group (in Part 15)	section 474(1)
group undertaking	section 1161(5)
hard copy form and hard copy	
— generally in the Companies Acts	section 1168(2)
— in relation to communications to a company	Part 2 of Schedule 4
— in relation to communications by a company	Part 2 of Schedule 5
hire-purchase agreement	section 1173(1)
holder of shares (in Chapter 3 of Part 17)	section 574
holding company	section 1159 (and see section 1160 and Schedule 6)
IAS accounts	sections 395(1)(b) and 403(1) and (2)(b)
IAS group accounts	section 403(1) and (2)(b)
IAS individual accounts	section 395(1)(b)
IAS Regulation (in Part 15)	section 474(1)
included in the consolidation, in relation to group accounts (in Part 15)	section 474(1)
individual accounts	section 394
information rights (in Part 9)	section 146(3)
insurance company	section 1165(3)
insurance group	section 1165(5)
insurance market activity	section 1165(7)
interest in shares (for the purposes of Part 22)	sections 820 to 825
international accounting standards (in Part 15)	section 474(1)
investment company (in Part 23)	section 833
…	…
issued share capital and issued shares	section 546(1)(a) and (2)
the issuing company (in Chapter 7 of Part 17)	section 610(6)
the Joint Stock Companies Acts	section 1171
liabilities (in Part 27)	section 941
liability, references to incurring, reducing or discharging (in Chapter 2 of Part 18)	section 683(2)
limited by guarantee	section 3(3)
limited by shares	section 3(2)

the Panel (in Part 28)	section 942
parent company	section 1173(1)
parent undertaking	section 1162 (and see Schedule 7)
payment for loss of office (in Chapter 4 of Part 10)	section 215
pension scheme (in Chapter 1 of Part 18)	section 675
period for appointing auditors, in relation to a private company	section 485(2)
period for filing, in relation to accounts and reports for a financial year	section 442
permissible capital payment (in Chapter 5 of Part 18)	section 710
political donation (in Part 14)	section 364
political expenditure (in Part 14)	section 365
political organisation (in Part 14)	section 363(2)
prescribed	section 1167
private company	section 4
profit and loss account (in Part 15)	section 474(1) and (2)
profits and losses (in Part 23)	section 853(2)
profits available for distribution (for the purposes of Part 23)	section 830(2)
property (in Part 27)	section 941
protected information (in Chapter 8 of Part 10)	section 240
provision for entrenchment, in relation to a company's articles	section 22
public company	section 4
publication, in relation to accounts and reports (in sections 433 to 435)	section 436
qualified, in relation to an auditor's report etc (in Part 16)	section 539
qualifying shares (in Chapter 6 of Part 18)	section 724(2)
qualifying third party indemnity provision (in Chapter 7 of Part 10)	section 234
qualifying pension scheme indemnity provision (in Chapter 7 of Part 10)	section 235
quasi-loan (in Chapter 4 of Part 10)	section 199
quoted company	
— in Part 13	section 361
— in Part 15	section 385
— in Chapter 5 of Part 16	section 531 (and section 385)
realised profits and losses (in Part 23)	section 853(4)
redeemable shares	section 684(1)
redenominate	section 622(1)
redenomination reserve	section 628
the register	section 1080
register of charges, kept by registrar	
— in England and Wales and Northern Ireland	section 869
— in Scotland	section 885

subsidiary	section 1159 (and see section 1160 and Schedule 6)
subsidiary undertaking	section 1162 (and see Schedule 7)
summary financial statement	section 426
takeover bid (in Chapter 2 of Part 28)	section 971(1)
takeover offer (in Chapter 3 of Part 28)	section 974
the Takeovers Directive	
— in Chapter 1 of Part 28	section 943(8)
— in Chapter 2 of Part 28	section 971(1)
[traded company (in Part 24)	section 855(4)]
trading certificate	section 761(1)
transfer, in relation to a non-cash asset	section 1163(2)
treasury shares	section 724(5)
turnover	
— in Part 15	section 474(1)
— in Part 16	section 539
UCITS management company	
— in Part 15	section 474(1)
— in Part 16	section 539
UK-registered company	section 1158
uncalled share capital	section 547
unconditional, in relation to a contract to acquire shares (in Chapter 3 of Part 28)	section 991(2)
undistributable reserves	section 831(4)
undertaking	section 1161(1)
unique identifier	section 1082
unlimited company	section 3
unquoted company (in Part 15)	section 385
voting rights	
— in Chapter 2 of Part 28	section 971(1)
— in Chapter 3 of Part 28	section 991(1)
— in section 1159 and Schedule 6	paragraph 2 of Schedule 6
— in section 1162 and Schedule 7	paragraph 2 of Schedule 7
voting shares	
— in Chapter 2 of Part 28	section 971(1)
— in Chapter 3 of Part 28	section 991(1)
website, communication by a company by means of	Part 4 of Schedule 5
Welsh company	section 88
wholly-owned subsidiary	section 1159(2) (and see section 1160 and Schedule 6)
working day, in relation to a company	section 1173(1)
written resolution	section 288

[1734]

NOTES
  Commencement: 1 October 2009.
  Entry "ISD investment firm" (omitted) repealed, and entry "MiFID investment firm" inserted, by the Markets in Financial Instruments Directive (Consequential Amendments) Regulations 2007, SI 2007/2932, reg 3(8), as from 1 November 2007.

Entries "non-traded company (in Part 24)", "return period (in Part 24)", and "traded company (in Part 24)" inserted by the Companies Act 2006 (Annual Return and Service Addresses) Regulations 2008, SI 2008/3000, reg 9, as from 1 October 2009 (in relation to annual returns made up to that date or a later date).

Entry "small companies exemption (in relation to directors' report)" inserted by the Companies Act 2006 (Amendment) (Accounts and Reports) Regulations 2008, SI 2008/393, reg 6(11), as from 6 April 2008, in relation to financial years beginning on or after that date.

Words in square brackets in the entry "small companies regime" substituted by SI 2008/393, reg 6(12), as from 6 April 2008, in relation to financial years beginning on or after that date.

SCHEDULE 10
RECOGNISED SUPERVISORY BODIES

Section 1217

PART 1
GRANT AND REVOCATION OF RECOGNITION OF A SUPERVISORY BODY

Application for recognition of supervisory body

1.—(1) A supervisory body may apply to the Secretary of State for an order declaring it to be a recognised supervisory body for the purposes of this Part of this Act ("a recognition order").

(2) Any such application must be—
  (a) made in such manner as the Secretary of State may direct, and
  (b) accompanied by such information as the Secretary of State may reasonably require for the purpose of determining the application.

(3) At any time after receiving an application and before determining it the Secretary of State may require the applicant to furnish additional information.

(4) The directions and requirements given or imposed under sub-paragraphs (2) and (3) may differ as between different applications.

(5) The Secretary of State may require any information to be furnished under this paragraph to be in such form or verified in such manner as he may specify.

(6) Every application must be accompanied by—
  (a) a copy of the applicant's rules, and
  (b) a copy of any guidance issued by the applicant in writing.

(7) The reference in sub-paragraph (6)(b) to guidance issued by the applicant is a reference to any guidance or recommendation—
  (a) issued or made by it to all or any class of its members or persons seeking to become members,
  (b) relevant for the purposes of this Part, and
  (c) intended to have continuing effect,
including any guidance or recommendation relating to the admission or expulsion of members of the body, so far as relevant for the purposes of this Part.

Grant and refusal of recognition

2.—(1) The Secretary of State may, on an application duly made in accordance with paragraph 1 and after being furnished with all such information as he may require under that paragraph, make or refuse to make a recognition order in respect of the applicant.

(2) The Secretary of State may make a recognition order only if it appears to him, from the information furnished by the body and having regard to any other information in his possession, that the requirements of Part 2 of this Schedule are satisfied in the case of that body.

(3) The Secretary of State may refuse to make a recognition order in respect of a body if he considers that its recognition is unnecessary having regard to the existence of one or more other bodies which—
  (a) maintain and enforce rules as to the appointment and conduct of statutory auditors, and
  (b) have been or are likely to be recognised.

(4) Where the Secretary of State refuses an application for a recognition order he must give the applicant a written notice to that effect—
  (a) specifying which requirements, in the opinion of the Secretary of State, are not satisfied, or
  (b) stating that the application is refused on the ground mentioned in sub-paragraph (3).

(5) A recognition order must state the date on which it takes effect.

Revocation of recognition

3.—(1) A recognition order may be revoked by a further order made by the Secretary of State if at any time it appears to him—

(a)   that any requirement of Part 2 of this Schedule is not satisfied in the case of the body to which the recognition order relates ("the recognised body"),

(b)   that the body has failed to comply with any obligation imposed on it by or by virtue of this Part of this Act, or

(c)   that the continued recognition of the body is undesirable having regard to the existence of one or more other bodies which have been or are to be recognised.

(2)   An order revoking a recognition order must state the date on which it takes effect, which must be after the period of three months beginning with the date on which the revocation order is made.

(3)   Before revoking a recognition order the Secretary of State must—

(a)   give written notice of his intention to do so to the recognised body,

(b)   take such steps as he considers reasonably practicable for bringing the notice to the attention of the members of the body, and

(c)   publish the notice in such manner as he thinks appropriate for bringing it to the attention of any other persons who are in his opinion likely to be affected.

(4)   A notice under sub-paragraph (3) must—

(a)   state the reasons for which the Secretary of State proposes to act, and

(b)   give particulars of the rights conferred by sub-paragraph (5).

(5)   A person within sub-paragraph (6) may, within the period of three months beginning with the date of service or publication of the notice under sub-paragraph (3) or such longer period as the Secretary of State may allow, make written representations to the Secretary of State and, if desired, oral representations to a person appointed for that purpose by the Secretary of State.

(6)   The persons within this sub-paragraph are—

(a)   the recognised body on which a notice is served under sub-paragraph (3),

(b)   any member of the body, and

(c)   any other person who appears to the Secretary of State to be affected.

(7)   The Secretary of State must have regard to any representations made in accordance with sub-paragraph (5) in determining whether to revoke the recognition order.

(8)   If in any case the Secretary of State considers it essential to do so in the public interest he may revoke a recognition order without regard to the restriction imposed by sub-paragraph (2), even if—

(a)   no notice has been given or published under sub-paragraph (3), or

(b)   the period of time for making representations in pursuance of such a notice has not expired.

(9)   An order revoking a recognition order may contain such transitional provision as the Secretary of State thinks necessary or expedient.

(10)   A recognition order may be revoked at the request or with the consent of the recognised body and any such revocation is not subject to—

(a)   the restrictions imposed by sub-paragraphs (1) and (2), or

(b)   the requirements of sub-paragraphs (3) to (5) and (7).

(11)   On making an order revoking a recognition order in respect of a body the Secretary of State must—

(a)   give written notice of the making of the order to the body,

(b)   take such steps as he considers reasonably practicable for bringing the making of the order to the attention of the members of the body, and

(c)   publish a notice of the making of the order in such manner as he thinks appropriate for bringing it to the attention of any other persons who are in his opinion likely to be affected.

Transitional provision

4.   A recognition order made and not revoked under—

(a)   paragraph 2(1) of Schedule 11 to the Companies Act 1989 (c 40), or

(b)   paragraph 2(1) of Schedule 11 to the Companies (Northern Ireland) Order 1990 (SI 1990/593 (NI 5)),

before the commencement of this Chapter of this Part of this Act is to have effect after the commencement of this Chapter as a recognition order made under paragraph 2(1) of this Schedule.

Orders not statutory instruments

5.   Orders under this Part of this Schedule shall not be made by statutory instrument.

[1734A]

PART II
OTHER ACTS

NOTES
Commencement: 6 April 2008.
Commencement (transitional provisions): see the note to s 1212 at **[1729DD]**.

PART 2
REQUIREMENTS FOR RECOGNITION OF A SUPERVISORY BODY

Holding of appropriate qualification

6.—(1)   The body must have rules to the effect that a person is not eligible for appointment as a statutory auditor unless—

(a)   in the case of an individual [other than an EEA auditor], he holds an appropriate qualification,

[(aa)   in the case of an individual who is an EEA auditor—

(i)   he holds an appropriate qualification,

(ii)   he has been authorised on or before 5 April 2008 to practise the profession of company auditor pursuant to the European Communities (Recognition of Professional Qualifications) (First General System) Regulations 2005 (SI 2005/18) and has fulfilled any requirements imposed pursuant to regulation 6 of those Regulations, or

(iii)   he has passed an aptitude test in accordance with sub-paragraph (2), unless an aptitude test is not required (see sub-paragraph (2A)).]

(b)   in the case of a firm—

(i)   each individual responsible for statutory audit work on behalf of the firm is eligible for appointment as a statutory auditor, and

(ii)   the firm is controlled by qualified persons (see paragraph 7 below).

[(2)   The aptitude test—

(a)   must test the person's knowledge of subjects—

(i)   that are covered by a recognised professional qualification,

(ii)   that are not covered by the professional qualification already held by the person, and

(iii)   the knowledge of which is essential for the pursuit of the profession of statutory auditor;

(b)   may test the person's knowledge of rules of professional conduct;

(c)   must not test the person's knowledge of any other matters.

(2A)   No aptitude test is required if the subjects that are covered by a recognised professional qualification and the knowledge of which is essential for the pursuit of the profession of statutory auditor are covered by the professional qualification already held by the person.]

(3)   A firm which has ceased to comply with the conditions mentioned in sub-paragraph (1)(b) may be permitted to remain eligible for appointment as a statutory auditor for a period of not more than three months.

7.—(1)   This paragraph explains what is meant in paragraph 6(1)(b) by a firm being "controlled by qualified persons".

(2)   In this paragraph references to a person being qualified are—

(a)   in relation to an individual, to his holding—

(i)   an appropriate qualification, or

(ii)   a corresponding qualification to audit accounts under the law of [an EEA State], or part of [an EEA State], other than the United Kingdom;

(b)   in relation to a firm, to its—

(i)   being eligible for appointment as a statutory auditor, or

(ii)   being eligible for a corresponding appointment as an auditor under the law of [an EEA State], or part of [an EEA State], other than the United Kingdom.

(3)   A firm is to be treated as controlled by qualified persons if, and only if—

(a)   a majority of the members of the firm are qualified persons, and

(b)   where the firm's affairs are managed by a board of directors, committee or other management body, a majority of that body are qualified persons or, if the body consists of two persons only, at least one of them is a qualified person.

(4)   A majority of the members of a firm means—

(a)   where under the firm's constitution matters are decided upon by the exercise of voting rights, members holding a majority of the rights to vote on all, or substantially all, matters;

(b)   in any other case, members having such rights under the constitution of the firm as enable them to direct its overall policy or alter its constitution.

(5)   A majority of the members of the management body of a firm means—

(a)   where matters are decided at meetings of the management body by the exercise of voting rights, members holding a majority of the rights to vote on all, or substantially all, matters at such meetings;

(b)   in any other case, members having such rights under the constitution of the firm as enable them to direct its overall policy or alter its constitution.

(6)   Paragraphs 5 to 11 of Schedule 7 to this Act (rights to be taken into account and attribution of rights) apply for the purposes of this paragraph.

Auditors to be fit and proper persons

8.—(1)   The body must have adequate rules and practices designed to ensure that the persons eligible under its rules for appointment as a statutory auditor are fit and proper persons to be so appointed.

(2)   The matters which the body may take into account for this purpose in relation to a person must include—

(a)   any matter relating to any person who is or will be employed by or associated with him for the purposes of or in connection with statutory audit work;

(b)   in the case of a body corporate, any matter relating to—
   (i)   any director or controller of the body,
   (ii)   any other body corporate in the same group, or
   (iii) any director or controller of any such other body; and

(c)   in the case of a partnership, any matter relating to—
   (i)   any of the partners,
   (ii)   any director or controller of any of the partners,
   (iii) any body corporate in the same group as any of the partners, or
   (iv)   any director or controller of any such other body.

(3)   Where the person is a limited liability partnership, in sub-paragraph (2)(b) "director" is to be read as "member".

(4)   In sub-paragraph (2)(b) and (c) "controller", in relation to a body corporate, means a person who either alone or with an associate or associates is entitled to exercise or control the exercise of 15% or more of the rights to vote on all, or substantially all, matters at general meetings of the body or another body corporate of which it is a subsidiary.

Professional integrity and independence

9.—(1)   The body must have adequate rules and practices designed to ensure that—

(a)   statutory audit work is conducted properly and with integrity, …

(b)   persons are not appointed as statutory auditors in circumstances in which they have an interest likely to conflict with the proper conduct of the audit,

[(c)   persons appointed as statutory auditors take steps to safeguard their independence from any significant threats to it,

(d)   persons appointed as statutory auditors record any such threats and the steps taken to safeguard the proper conduct of the audit from them, and

(e)   remuneration received or receivable by a statutory auditor in respect of statutory audit work is not—
   (i)   influenced or determined by the statutory auditor providing other services to the audited person, or
   (ii)   on a contingent fee basis.]

(2)   The body must participate in arrangements within paragraph 21, and the rules and practices mentioned in sub-paragraph (1) must include provision requiring compliance with any standards for the time being determined under such arrangements.

[(3)   The body must also have adequate rules and practices designed to ensure that—

(a)   no firm is eligible under its rules for appointment as a statutory auditor unless the firm has arrangements to prevent any person from being able to exert any influence over the way in which a statutory audit is conducted in circumstances in which that influence would be likely to affect the independence or integrity of the audit;

(b)   any rule of law relating to the confidentiality of information received in the course of statutory audit work by persons appointed as statutory auditors is complied with; and

(c)   a person ceasing to hold office as a statutory auditor makes available to his successor in that office all relevant information which he holds in relation to that office.]

[(4)   The rules referred to in sub-paragraph (3)(b) (confidentiality of information) must apply to persons who are no longer members of the body as they apply to members and any fine imposed in the enforcement of those rules shall be recoverable by the body as a debt due to it from the person obliged to pay it.]

Technical standards

10.—(1)   The body must have rules and practices as to—
    (a)   the technical standards to be applied in statutory audit work, and
    (b)   the manner in which those standards are to be applied in practice.

(2)   The body must participate in arrangements within paragraph 22, and the rules and practices mentioned in sub-paragraph (1) must include provision requiring compliance with any standards for the time being determined under such arrangements.

[Technical standards for group audits

10A.—(1)   The body must have rules and practices as to technical standards ensuring that group auditors—
    (a)   review for the purposes of a group audit the audit work conducted by other persons, and
    (b)   record that review.

(2)   The body must participate in arrangements within paragraph 22, and the rules and practices mentioned in sub-paragraph (1) must include provision requiring compliance with any standards for the time being determined under such arrangements.

(3)   The body must also have rules and practices ensuring that group auditors—
    (a)   retain copies of any documents necessary for the purposes of the review that they have received from third country auditors who are not covered by working arrangements under section 1253E, or
    (b)   agree with those third country auditors proper and unrestricted access to those documents on request.

(4)   The body's rules and practices must ensure that group auditors make those documents available on request to—
    (a)   the body;
    (b)   any other body with which the body has entered into arrangements for the purposes of paragraph 23 or 24 (independent arrangements for monitoring and investigation);
    (c)   the Secretary of State.

(5)   The body may provide that the rules and practices referred to in sub-paragraphs (3) and (4) do not apply if, after taking all reasonable steps, a group auditor is unable to obtain the copies of the documents or the access to the documents necessary for the review.

(6)   If the body does so provide, its rules and practices must ensure that the group auditor records—
    (a)   the steps taken to obtain copies of or access to those documents,
    (b)   the reasons why the copies or access could not be obtained, and
    (c)   any evidence of those steps or those reasons.

(7)   In this paragraph—
    "group auditor" means a person appointed as statutory auditor to conduct an audit of group accounts;
    "group" has the same meaning as in Part 15 of this Act (see section 474).]

[Public interest entity reporting requirements

10B.—(1)   The body must have adequate rules and practices designed to ensure that persons appointed as statutory auditors of public interest entities report to the entity's audit committee (if it has one) at least once in each calendar year at any time during which they hold the office of statutory auditor.

(2)   The report must include—
    (a)   a statement in writing confirming the person's independence from the public interest entity;
    (b)   a description of any services provided by the person to the public interest entity other than in his capacity as statutory auditor;
    (c)   a description of any significant threats to the person's independence;
    (d)   an explanation of the steps taken by the person to safeguard his independence from those threats;
    (e)   a description of any material weaknesses arising from the statutory audit in the public interest entity's internal control in relation to the preparation of accounts; and
    (f)   any other significant matters arising from the statutory audit.

(3)   The body must participate in arrangements within paragraph 22A (arrangements for setting standards), and the rules and practices mentioned in sub-paragraph (1) must include provision requiring compliance with any standards for the time being determined under such arrangements.

(4)   In this paragraph, "audit committee" means a body which performs the functions referred to in Article 41.2 of the Audit Directive or equivalent functions.

Public interest entity independence requirements

10C.—(1)   The body must have adequate rules and practices designed to ensure that—
   (a)   an individual does not accept an appointment by a public interest entity as statutory auditor if—
      (i)   he has been the statutory auditor of the entity for a continuous period of more than seven years, and
      (ii)   less than two years have passed since he was last the statutory auditor of the entity;
   (b)   where a firm has been appointed by a public interest entity as statutory auditor, an individual may not be a key audit partner if—
      (i)   he has been a key audit partner in relation to audits of the entity for a continuous period of more than seven years, and
      (ii)   less than two years have passed since he was last the key audit partner in relation to an audit of the entity.

(2)   The body must participate in arrangements within paragraph 22B (arrangements for setting standards), and the rules and practices mentioned in sub-paragraph (1) must include provision requiring compliance with any standards for the time being determined under such arrangements.

(3)   The body must also have adequate rules and practices designed to ensure that—
   (a)   an individual who has been appointed by a public interest entity as statutory auditor may not be appointed as a director or other officer of the entity during a period of two years commencing on the date on which his appointment as statutory auditor ended;
   (b)   a key audit partner of a firm which has been appointed by a public interest entity as statutory auditor may not be appointed as a director or other officer of the entity during a period of two years commencing on the date on which his work as key audit partner ended.

(4)   The rules referred to in sub-paragraph (3) must apply to persons who are no longer members of the body as they apply to members and any fine imposed in the enforcement of those rules shall be recoverable by the body as a debt due to it from the person obliged to pay it.

(5)   An auditor of a public interest entity is not to be regarded as an officer of the entity for the purposes of sub-paragraph (3)(a) and (b).

(6)   For the purposes of this paragraph—
   (a)   a "key audit partner" is an individual identified by a firm appointed as statutory auditor as being primarily responsible for the statutory audit; and
   (b)   a key audit partner of a firm appointed as statutory auditor of a parent undertaking or a material subsidiary undertaking of a public interest entity is to be treated as if he were a key audit partner of the firm appointed as statutory auditor of the public interest entity.]

Procedures for maintaining competence

11.   The body must have rules and practices designed to ensure that persons eligible under its rules for appointment as a statutory auditor continue to maintain an appropriate level of competence in the conduct of statutory audits.

Monitoring and enforcement

12.—[(1)   The body must—
   (a)   have adequate resources for the effective monitoring and enforcement of compliance with its rules, and
   (b)   ensure that those resources may not be influenced improperly by the persons monitored.

(1A)   The body must—
   (a)   have adequate arrangements for the effective monitoring and enforcement of compliance with its rules, and
   (b)   ensure that those arrangements operate independently of the persons monitored.]

(2)   The arrangements for monitoring may make provision for that function to be performed on behalf of the body (and without affecting its responsibility) by any other body or person who is able and willing to perform it.

[(3)   The arrangements for enforcement must include provision for—
   (a)   sanctions which include—
      (i)   the withdrawal of eligibility for appointment as a statutory auditor; and
      (ii)   any other disciplinary measures necessary to ensure the effective enforcement of the body's rules; and
   (b)   the body making available to the public information relating to steps it has taken to ensure the effective enforcement of its rules.]

[Monitoring of audits

13.—(1)   The body must—
- (a)   in the case of members of the body who do not perform any statutory audit functions in respect of major audits, have adequate arrangements for enabling the performance by its members of statutory audit functions to be monitored by means of inspections;
- (b)   in the case of members of the body who perform any statutory audit functions in respect of major audits, participate in arrangements within paragraph 23(1); and
- (c)   have rules designed to ensure that members of the body take such steps as may reasonably be required of them to enable their performance of any statutory audit functions to be monitored by means of inspections.

(2)   Any monitoring of members of the body under the arrangements within paragraph 23(1) is to be regarded (so far as their performance of statutory audit functions in respect of major audits is concerned) as monitoring of compliance with the body's rules for the purposes of paragraph 12(1) and (1A).

(3)   The arrangements referred to in sub-paragraph (1)(a) must include an inspection which is conducted in relation to each person eligible for appointment as a statutory auditor at least once every six years.

(4)   The inspection must be conducted by persons who—
- (a)   have an appropriate professional education;
- (b)   have experience of—
  - (i)   statutory audit work, or
  - (ii)   equivalent work on the audit of accounts under the law of an EEA State, or part of an EEA State, other than the United Kingdom;
- (c)   have received adequate training in the conduct of inspections;
- (d)   do not have any interests likely to conflict with the proper conduct of the inspection.

(5)   The inspection must review one or more statutory audits in which the person to whom the inspection relates has participated.

(6)   The inspection must include an assessment of—
- (a)   the person's compliance with the body's rules established for the purposes of paragraphs 9 (professional integrity and independence), 10 (technical standards), 10A (technical standards for group audits) and 10C (public interest entity independence requirements);
- (b)   the resources allocated by the person to statutory audit work;
- (c)   in the case of an inspection in relation to a firm, its internal quality control system;
- (d)   the remuneration received by the person in respect of statutory audit work.

(7)   An inspection conducted in relation to a firm may be treated as an inspection of all individuals responsible for statutory audit work on behalf of that firm, if the firm has a common quality assurance policy with which each such individual is required to comply.

(8)   The main conclusions of the inspection must be recorded in a report which is made available to—
- (a)   the person to whom the inspection relates, and
- (b)   the body.

(9)   The body must, at least once in every calendar year, deliver to the Secretary of State a summary of the results of inspections conducted under this paragraph.

(10)   In this paragraph—
"major audit" means a statutory audit conducted in respect of—
- (a)   a public interest entity, or
- (b)   any other person in whose financial condition there is a major public interest;
"statutory audit function" means any function performed as a statutory auditor.]

Membership, eligibility and discipline

14.   The rules and practices of the body relating to—
- (a)   the admission and expulsion of members,
- (b)   the grant and withdrawal of eligibility for appointment as a statutory auditor, and
- (c)   the discipline it exercises over its members,

must be fair and reasonable and include adequate provision for appeals.

Investigation of complaints

15.—(1)   The body must have effective arrangements for the investigation of complaints against—
- (a)   persons who are eligible under its rules for appointment as a statutory auditor, and
- (b)   the body in respect of matters arising out of its functions as a supervisory body.

(2)   The arrangements mentioned in sub-paragraph (1) may make provision for the whole or part of that function to be performed by and to be the responsibility of a body or person independent of the body itself.

Independent investigation for disciplinary purposes of public interest cases

16.—(1)   The body must—
   (a)   participate in arrangements within paragraph 24(1), and
   (b)   have rules and practices designed to ensure that, where the designated persons have decided that any particular disciplinary action should be taken against a member of the body following the conclusion of an investigation under such arrangements, that decision is to be treated as if it were a decision made by the body in disciplinary proceedings against the member.

(2)   In sub-paragraph (1) "the designated persons" means the persons who, under the arrangements, have the function of deciding whether (and if so, what) disciplinary action should be taken against a member of the body in the light of an investigation carried out under the arrangements.

[Transfer of papers to third countries

16A.—(1)   The body must have adequate rules and practices designed to ensure that persons eligible under its rules for appointment as a statutory auditor deliver audit working papers to a third country competent authority only if—
   (a)   the authority has entered into arrangements with the Secretary of State in accordance with section 1253E (working arrangements); and
   (b)   the following four conditions are met.

(2)   The first condition is that the competent authority has requested the audit working papers for the purposes of an investigation.

(3)   The second condition is that the competent authority has given to the Secretary of State notice of its request.

(4)   The third condition is that the papers relate to the audit of a body which—
   (a)   has issued securities in the country or territory in which the competent authority is established, or
   (b)   forms part of a group issuing statutory consolidated accounts in that country or territory.

(5)   The fourth condition is that no legal proceedings have been brought (whether continuing or not) in relation to the auditor or audit to which the working papers relate.

(6)   The body must also have adequate rules and practices designed to ensure that a person eligible under its rules for appointment as a statutory auditor may refuse to deliver audit working papers to a third country competent authority if the Secretary of State certifies that the delivery of the papers would adversely affect the sovereignty, security or public order of the United Kingdom.]

Meeting of claims arising out of audit work

17.—(1)   The body must have adequate rules or arrangements designed to ensure that persons eligible under its rules for appointment as a statutory auditor take such steps as may reasonably be expected of them to secure that they are able to meet claims against them arising out of statutory audit work.

(2)   This may be achieved by professional indemnity insurance or other appropriate arrangements.

Register of auditors and other information to be made available

18.   The body must have rules requiring persons eligible under its rules for appointment as a statutory auditor to comply with any obligations imposed on them by—
   (a)   requirements under section 1224 (Secretary of State's power to call for information);
   (b)   regulations under section 1239 (the register of auditors);
   (c)   regulations under section 1240 (information to be made available to the public).

Taking account of costs of compliance

19.   The body must have satisfactory arrangements for taking account, in framing its rules, of the cost to those to whom the rules would apply of complying with those rules and any other controls to which they are subject.

Promotion and maintenance of standards

20.   The body must be able and willing—
   (a)   to promote and maintain high standards of integrity in the conduct of statutory audit work, and

(b) to co-operate, by the sharing of information and otherwise, with the Secretary of State and any other authority, body or person having responsibility in the United Kingdom for the qualification, supervision or regulation of auditors.

[Interpretation

20A. In this Part of this Schedule—
"public interest entity" means an issuer—
    (a) whose transferable securities are admitted to trading on a regulated market; and
    (b) the audit of which is a statutory audit (see section 1210(1));
"issuer" and "regulated market" have the same meaning as in Part 6 of the Financial Services and Markets Act 2000 (see sections 102A to 103); and
"transferable securities" means anything which is a transferable security for the purposes of Directive 2004/39/EC of the European Parliament and of the Council on markets in financial instruments.]

[1734B]

NOTES
Commencement: 6 April 2008.
Commencement (transitional provisions): see the note to s 1212 at **[1729DD]**.
Para 6: sub-para (1)(aa), and the words in square brackets in sub-para (1)(a) inserted, and sub-paras (2), (2A) substituted (for original sub-para (2)), by the Statutory Auditors and Third Country Auditors Regulations 2007, SI 2007/3494, reg 17, as from 6 April 2008.
Para 7: words in square brackets substituted by SI 2007/3494, reg 18, as from 6 April 2008.
Para 9: word omitted from sub-para (1)(a) repealed, sub-paras (1)(c)–(e) inserted, and sub-paras (3), (4) substituted, by SI 2007/3494, reg 19, as from 6 April 2008.
Paras 10A–10C, 16A, 20A: inserted by SI 2007/3494, regs 20, 21, 24, 25, as from 6 April 2008.
Para 12: sub-paras (1), (1A) substituted (for original sub-para (1)), and sub-para (3) added, by SI 2007/3494, reg 22, as from 6 April 2008.
Para 13: substituted by SI 2007/3494, reg 23, as from 6 April 2008.

PART 3
ARRANGEMENTS IN WHICH RECOGNISED SUPERVISORY BODIES ARE REQUIRED TO PARTICIPATE

Arrangements for setting standards relating to professional integrity and independence

21. The arrangements referred to in paragraph 9(2) are appropriate arrangements—
    (a) for the determining of standards for the purposes of the rules and practices mentioned in paragraph 9(1), and
    (b) for ensuring that the determination of those standards is done independently of the body.

Arrangements for setting technical standards

22. The arrangements referred to in [paragraphs 10(2) and 10A(2)] are appropriate arrangements—
    (a) for the determining of standards for the purposes of the rules and practices mentioned in [paragraphs 10(1) and 10A(1) respectively], and
    (b) for ensuring that the determination of those standards is done independently of the body.

[Arrangements for setting standards relating to public interest entity reporting requirements

22A. The arrangements referred to in paragraph 10B(3) are appropriate arrangements—
    (a) for the determining of standards for the purposes of the rules and practices mentioned in paragraph 10B(1), and
    (b) for ensuring that the determination of those standards is done independently of the body.

Arrangements for setting standards relating to public interest entity independence requirements

22B. The arrangements referred to in paragraph 10C(2) are appropriate arrangements—
    (a) for the determining of standards for the purposes of the rules and practices mentioned in paragraph 10C(1), and
    (b) for ensuring that the determination of those standards is done independently of the body.]

Arrangements for independent monitoring of audits of listed companies and other major bodies

23.—(1) The arrangements referred to in [paragraph 13(1)(b)] are appropriate arrangements—
    (a) for enabling the performance by members of the body of statutory audit functions in respect of major audits to be monitored by means of inspections carried out under the arrangements, and

(b)   for ensuring that the carrying out of such monitoring and inspections is done independently of the body.

[(1A)   Subject to sub-paragraph (1C), the arrangements referred to in sub-paragraph (1) must include provision for an inspection conducted in relation to each person eligible for appointment as a statutory auditor at least once every three years.

(1B)   Sub-paragraphs (4) to (9) of paragraph 13 apply in relation to inspections under sub-paragraph (1A) as they apply in relation to inspections under that paragraph.

(1C)   The arrangements referred to in sub-paragraph (1) may provide that the body performing the inspections may decide that all or part of the inspection referred to in sub-paragraph (1A) is not required in the case of a member of a supervisory body who performs statutory audit functions in respect of ten or fewer major audits per year.

(1D)   If—
(a)   the arrangements make the provision referred to in sub-paragraph (1C), and
(b)   the body performing the inspections decides that all of an inspection is not required in relation to a member,
the supervisory body must ensure that the arrangements referred to in paragraph 13(1)(a) apply in relation to that member, subject to the modification specified in sub-paragraph (1F).

(1E)   If—
(a)   the arrangements make the provision referred to in sub-paragraph (1C), and
(b)   the body performing the inspections decides that part of an inspection is not required in relation to a member,
the supervisory body must ensure that the arrangements referred to in paragraph 13(1)(a) apply in relation to that part of the inspection of that member, subject to the modification specified in sub-paragraph (1F).

(1F)   For the purposes of sub-paragraphs (1D) and (1E), paragraph 13(3) applies with the substitution of "three years" for "six years".]

(2)   In this paragraph "major audit" and "statutory audit function" have the same meaning as in paragraph 13.

Arrangements for independent investigation for disciplinary purposes of public interest cases

24.—(1)   The arrangements referred to in paragraph 16(1) are appropriate arrangements—
(a)   for the carrying out of investigations into public interest cases arising in connection with the performance of statutory audit functions by members of the body,
(b)   for the holding of disciplinary hearings relating to members of the body which appear to be desirable following the conclusion of such investigations,
(c)   for requiring such hearings to be held in public except where the interests of justice otherwise require,
(d)   for the persons before whom such hearings have taken place to decide whether (and, if so, what) disciplinary action should be taken against the members to whom the hearings related, and
(e)   for ensuring that the carrying out of those investigations, the holding of those hearings and the taking of those decisions are done independently of the body.

(2)   In this paragraph—
"public interest cases" means matters which raise or appear to raise important issues affecting the public interest;
"statutory audit function" means any function performed as a statutory auditor.

Supplementary: arrangements to operate independently of body

25.—(1)   This paragraph applies for the purposes of—
(a)   paragraph 21(b),
(b)   paragraph 22(b),
(c)   paragraph 23(1)(b), or
(d)   paragraph 24(1)(e).

(2)   Arrangements are not to be regarded as appropriate for the purpose of ensuring that a thing is done independently of the body unless they are designed to ensure that the body—
(a)   will have no involvement in the appointment or selection of any of the persons who are to be responsible for doing that thing, and
(b)   will not otherwise be involved in the doing of that thing.

(3)   Sub-paragraph (2) imposes a minimum requirement and does not preclude the possibility that additional criteria may need to be satisfied in order for the arrangements to be regarded as appropriate for the purpose in question.

Supplementary: funding of arrangements

26.   The body must pay any of the costs of maintaining any arrangements within paragraph 21, 22, 23 or 24 which the arrangements provide are to be paid by it.

Supplementary: scope of arrangement

27.   Arrangements may qualify as arrangements within any of paragraphs 21, 22, 23 and 24 even though the matters for which they provide are more extensive in any respect than those mentioned in the applicable paragraph.

[1734C]

NOTES
Commencement: 6 April 2008.
Commencement (transitional provisions): see the note to s 1212 at **[1729DD]**.
Para 22: words in square brackets substituted by the Statutory Auditors and Third Country Auditors Regulations 2007, SI 2007/3494, reg 26, as from 6 April 2008.
Paras 22A, 22B: inserted by SI 2007/3494, reg 27, as from 6 April 2008.
Para 23: words in first pair of square brackets substituted, and sub-paras (1A)–(1F) inserted, by SI 2007/3494, reg 28, as from 6 April 2008.

SCHEDULE 11
RECOGNISED PROFESSIONAL QUALIFICATIONS

Section 1220

PART 1
GRANT AND REVOCATION OF RECOGNITION OF A PROFESSIONAL QUALIFICATION

Application for recognition of professional qualification

1.—(1)   A qualifying body may apply to the Secretary of State for an order declaring a qualification offered by it to be a recognised professional qualification for the purposes of this Part of this Act ("a recognition order").

(2)   In this Part of this Act "a recognised qualifying body" means a qualifying body offering a recognised professional qualification.

(3)   Any application must be—
   (a)   made in such manner as the Secretary of State may direct, and
   (b)   accompanied by such information as the Secretary of State may reasonably require for the purpose of determining the application.

(4)   At any time after receiving an application and before determining it the Secretary of State may require the applicant to furnish additional information.

(5)   The directions and requirements given or imposed under sub-paragraphs (3) and (4) may differ as between different applications.

(6)   The Secretary of State may require any information to be furnished under this paragraph to be in such form or verified in such manner as he may specify.

(7)   In the case of examination standards, the verification required may include independent moderation of the examinations over such a period as the Secretary of State considers necessary.

(8)   Every application must be accompanied by—
   (a)   a copy of the applicant's rules, and
   (b)   a copy of any guidance issued by the applicant in writing.

(9)   The reference in sub-paragraph (8)(b) to guidance issued by the applicant is a reference to any guidance or recommendation—
   (a)   issued or made by it to all or any class of persons holding or seeking to hold a qualification, or approved or seeking to be approved by the body for the purposes of giving practical training,
   (b)   relevant for the purposes of this Part of this Act, and
   (c)   intended to have continuing effect,
including any guidance or recommendation relating to a matter within sub-paragraph (10).

(10)   The matters within this sub-paragraph are—
   (a)   admission to or expulsion from a course of study leading to a qualification,
   (b)   the award or deprivation of a qualification, and
   (c)   the approval of a person for the purposes of giving practical training or the withdrawal of such an approval,
so far as relevant for the purposes of this Part of this Act.

Grant and refusal of recognition

2.—(1) The Secretary of State may, on an application duly made in accordance with paragraph 1 and after being furnished with all such information as he may require under that paragraph, make or refuse to make a recognition order in respect of the qualification in relation to which the application was made.

(2) The Secretary of State may make a recognition order only if it appears to him, from the information furnished by the applicant and having regard to any other information in his possession, that the requirements of Part 2 of this Schedule are satisfied in relation to the qualification.

(3) Where the Secretary of State refuses an application for a recognition order he must give the applicant a written notice to that effect specifying which requirements, in his opinion, are not satisfied.

(4) A recognition order must state the date on which it takes effect.

Revocation of recognition

3.—(1) A recognition order may be revoked by a further order made by the Secretary of State if at any time it appears to him—

    (a)   that any requirement of Part 2 of this Schedule is not satisfied in relation to the qualification to which the recognition order relates, or

    (b)   that the qualifying body has failed to comply with any obligation imposed on it by or by virtue of this Part of this Act.

(2) An order revoking a recognition order must state the date on which it takes effect, which must be after the period of three months beginning with the date on which the revocation order is made.

(3) Before revoking a recognition order the Secretary of State must—

    (a)   give written notice of his intention to do so to the qualifying body,

    (b)   take such steps as he considers reasonably practicable for bringing the notice to the attention of persons holding the qualification or in the course of studying for it, and

    (c)   publish the notice in such manner as he thinks appropriate for bringing it to the attention of any other persons who are in his opinion likely to be affected.

(4) A notice under sub-paragraph (3) must—

    (a)   state the reasons for which the Secretary of State proposes to act, and

    (b)   give particulars of the rights conferred by sub-paragraph (5).

(5) A person within sub-paragraph (6) may, within the period of three months beginning with the date of service or publication or such longer period as the Secretary of State may allow, make written representations to the Secretary of State and, if desired, oral representations to a person appointed for that purpose by the Secretary of State.

(6) The persons within this sub-paragraph are—

    (a)   the qualifying body on which a notice is served under sub-paragraph (3),

    (b)   any person holding the qualification or in the course of studying for it, and

    (c)   any other person who appears to the Secretary of State to be affected.

(7) The Secretary of State must have regard to any representations made in accordance with sub-paragraph (5) in determining whether to revoke the recognition order.

(8) If in any case the Secretary of State considers it essential to do so in the public interest he may revoke a recognition order without regard to the restriction imposed by sub-paragraph (2), even if—

    (a)   no notice has been given or published under sub-paragraph (3), or

    (b)   the period of time for making representations in pursuance of such a notice has not expired.

(9) An order revoking a recognition order may contain such transitional provision as the Secretary of State thinks necessary or expedient.

(10) A recognition order may be revoked at the request or with the consent of the qualifying body and any such revocation is not subject to—

    (a)   the restrictions imposed by sub-paragraphs (1) and (2), or

    (b)   the requirements of sub-paragraphs (3) to (5) and (7).

(11) On making an order revoking a recognition order the Secretary of State must—

    (a)   give written notice of the making of the order to the qualifying body,

    (b)   take such steps as he considers reasonably practicable for bringing the making of the order to the attention of persons holding the qualification or in the course of studying for it, and

    (c)   publish a notice of the making of the order in such manner as he thinks appropriate for bringing it to the attention of any other persons who are in his opinion likely to be affected.

PART II
OTHER ACTS

Transitional provision

4.   A recognition order made and not revoked under—
   (a)   paragraph 2(1) of Schedule 12 to the Companies Act 1989 (c 40), or
   (b)   paragraph 2(1) of Schedule 12 to the Companies (Northern Ireland) Order 1990 (SI 1990/593 (NI 5)),

before the commencement of this Chapter of this Part of this Act is to have effect after the commencement of this Chapter as a recognition order made under paragraph 2(1) of this Schedule.

Orders not statutory instruments

5.   Orders under this Part of this Schedule shall not be made by statutory instrument.

[1734D]

NOTES
   Commencement: 20 January 2007 (for the purpose of enabling the exercise of powers to make Orders or Regulations by statutory instrument); 6 April 2008 (otherwise).
   Commencement (transitional provisions): see the note to s 1212 at **[1729DD]**.

PART 2
REQUIREMENTS FOR RECOGNITION OF A PROFESSIONAL QUALIFICATION

Entry requirements

6.—(1)   The qualification must only be open to persons who—
   (a)   have attained university entrance level, or
   (b)   have a sufficient period of professional experience.

   (2)   In relation to a person who has not been admitted to a university or other similar establishment in the United Kingdom, "attaining university entrance level" means—
   (a)   being educated to such a standard as would entitle him to be considered for such admission on the basis of—
      (i)   academic or professional qualifications obtained in the United Kingdom and recognised by the Secretary of State to be of an appropriate standard, or
      (ii)   academic or professional qualifications obtained outside the United Kingdom which the Secretary of State considers to be of an equivalent standard, or
   (b)   being assessed, on the basis of written tests of a kind appearing to the Secretary of State to be adequate for the purpose (with or without oral examination), as of such a standard of ability as would entitle him to be considered for such admission.

   (3)   The assessment, tests and oral examination referred to in sub-paragraph (2)(b) may be conducted by—
   (a)   the qualifying body, or
   (b)   some other body approved by the Secretary of State.

   (4)   The reference in sub-paragraph (1)(b) to "a sufficient period of professional experience" is to not less than seven years' experience in a professional capacity in the fields of finance, law and accountancy.

Requirement for theoretical instruction or professional experience

7.—(1)   The qualification must be restricted to persons who—
   (a)   have completed a course of theoretical instruction in the subjects prescribed for the purposes of paragraph 8, or
   (b)   have a sufficient period of professional experience.

   (2)   The reference in sub-paragraph (1)(b) to "a sufficient period of professional experience" is to not less than seven years' experience in a professional capacity in the fields of finance, law and accountancy.

Examination

8.—(1)   The qualification must be restricted to persons who have passed an examination (at least part of which is in writing) testing—
   (a)   theoretical knowledge of the subjects prescribed for the purposes of this paragraph by regulations made by the Secretary of State, and
   (b)   ability to apply that knowledge in practice,
and requiring a standard of attainment at least equivalent to that required to obtain a degree from a university or similar establishment in the United Kingdom.

   (2)   The qualification may be awarded to a person without his theoretical knowledge of a subject being tested by examination if he has passed a university or other examination of equivalent standard in that subject or holds a university degree or equivalent qualification in it.

(3)   The qualification may be awarded to a person without his ability to apply his theoretical knowledge of a subject in practice being tested by examination if he has received practical training in that subject which is attested by an examination or diploma recognised by the Secretary of State for the purposes of this paragraph.

(4)   Regulations under this paragraph are subject to negative resolution procedure.

Practical training

9.—(1)   The qualification must be restricted to persons who have completed at least three years' practical training of which—

    (a)   part was spent being trained in statutory audit work, and
    (b)   a substantial part was spent being trained in statutory audit work or other audit work of a description approved by the Secretary of State as being similar to statutory audit work.

(2)   For the purpose of sub-paragraph (1) "statutory audit work" includes the work of a person appointed as the auditor of a person under the law of a country or territory outside the United Kingdom where it appears to the Secretary of State that the law and practice with respect to the audit of accounts is similar to that in the United Kingdom.

(3)   The training must be given by persons approved by the body offering the qualification as persons whom the body is satisfied, in the light of undertakings given by them and the supervision to which they are subject (whether by the body itself or some other body or organisation), will provide adequate training.

(4)   At least two-thirds of the training must be given by a person—

    (a)   eligible for appointment as a statutory auditor, or
    (b)   eligible for a corresponding appointment as an auditor under the law of [an EEA State], or part of [an EEA State], other than the United Kingdom.

Supplementary provision with respect to a sufficient period of professional experience

10.—(1)   Periods of theoretical instruction in the fields of finance, law and accountancy may be deducted from the required period of professional experience, provided the instruction—

    (a)   lasted at least one year, and
    (b)   is attested by an examination recognised by the Secretary of State for the purposes of this paragraph;

but the period of professional experience may not be so reduced by more than four years.

(2)   The period of professional experience together with the practical training required in the case of persons satisfying the requirement in paragraph 7 by virtue of having a sufficient period of professional experience must not be shorter than the course of theoretical instruction referred to in that paragraph and the practical training required in the case of persons satisfying the requirement of that paragraph by virtue of having completed such a course.

The body offering the qualification

11.—(1)   The body offering the qualification must have—

    (a)   rules and arrangements adequate to ensure compliance with the requirements of paragraphs 6 to 10, and
    (b)   adequate arrangements for the effective monitoring of its continued compliance with those requirements.

(2)   The arrangements must include arrangements for monitoring—

    (a)   the standard of the body's examinations, and
    (b)   the adequacy of the practical training given by the persons approved by it for that purpose.

[1734E]

PART II OTHER ACTS

NOTES

    Commencement: 20 January 2007 (for the purpose of enabling the exercise of powers to make Orders or Regulations by statutory instrument); 6 April 2008 (otherwise).

    Commencement (transitional provisions): see the note to s 1212 at **[1729DD]**.

    Para 9: words in square brackets in sub-para (4)(b) substituted by the Statutory Auditors and Third Country Auditors Regulations 2007, SI 2007/3494, reg 44, as from 6 April 2008.

    Regulations: the Statutory Auditors and Third Country Auditors Regulations 2007, SI 2007/3494.

[SCHEDULE 11A
SPECIFIED PERSONS, DESCRIPTIONS, DISCLOSURES ETC FOR THE PURPOSES OF
SECTION 1224A

PART 1
SPECIFIED PERSONS

1. The Secretary of State.

2. The Department of Enterprise, Trade and Investment for Northern Ireland.

3. The Treasury.

4. The Bank of England.

5. The Financial Services Authority.

6. The Commissioners for Her Majesty's Revenue and Customs.

7. The Lord Advocate.

8. The Director of Public Prosecutions.

9. The Director of Public Prosecutions for Northern Ireland.

10. A constable.

11. A procurator fiscal.

12. The Scottish Ministers.

13. A body designated by the Secretary of State under section 1252 (delegation of the Secretary of State's functions).

14. A recognised supervisory body.

15. A recognised qualifying body.

16. A body with which a recognised supervisory body is participating in arrangements for the purposes of paragraph 23 (independent monitoring of audits) or 24 (independent investigation for disciplinary purposes) of Schedule 10 to this Act.

17. The Independent Supervisor.]

[1734F]

NOTES
Commencement: 6 April 2008.
Inserted by the Statutory Auditors and Third Country Auditors Regulations 2007, SI 2007/3494, reg 10(2), Schedule, as from 6 April 2008.

[PART 2
SPECIFIED DESCRIPTIONS OF DISCLOSURES

18. A disclosure for the purpose of enabling or assisting a person authorised under section 457 of this Act (persons authorised to apply to court) to exercise his functions.

19. A disclosure for the purpose of enabling or assisting an inspector appointed under Part 14 of the Companies Act 1985 (investigation of companies and their affairs, etc) to exercise his functions.

20. A disclosure for the purpose of enabling or assisting a person authorised under section 447 of the Companies Act 1985 (power to require production of documents) or section 84 of the Companies Act 1989 (c 40) (exercise of powers by officer etc) to exercise his functions.

21. A disclosure for the purpose of enabling or assisting a person appointed under section 167 of the Financial Services and Markets Act 2000 (c 8) (general investigations) to conduct an investigation to exercise his functions.

22. A disclosure for the purpose of enabling or assisting a person appointed under section 168 of the Financial Services and Markets Act 2000 (investigations in particular cases) to conduct an investigation to exercise his functions.

23. A disclosure for the purpose of enabling or assisting a person appointed under section 169(1)(b) of the Financial Services and Markets Act 2000 (investigation in support of overseas regulator) to conduct an investigation to exercise his functions.

24. A disclosure for the purpose of enabling or assisting the body corporate responsible for administering the scheme referred to in section 225 of the Financial Services and Markets Act 2000 (the ombudsman scheme) to exercise its functions.

25. A disclosure for the purpose of enabling or assisting a person appointed under paragraph 4 (the panel of ombudsmen) or 5 (the Chief Ombudsman) of Schedule 17 to the Financial Services and Markets Act 2000 to exercise his functions.

26.   A disclosure for the purpose of enabling or assisting a person appointed under regulations made under section 262(1) and (2)(k) of the Financial Services and Markets Act 2000 (investigations into open-ended investment companies) to conduct an investigation to exercise his functions.

27.   A disclosure for the purpose of enabling or assisting a person appointed under section 284 of the Financial Services and Markets Act 2000 (investigations into affairs of certain collective investment schemes) to conduct an investigation to exercise his functions.

28.   A disclosure for the purpose of enabling or assisting the investigator appointed under paragraph 7 of Schedule 1 to the Financial Services and Markets Act 2000 (arrangements for investigation of complaints) to exercise his functions.

29.   A disclosure for the purpose of enabling or assisting a person appointed by the Treasury to hold an inquiry into matters relating to financial services (including an inquiry under section 15 of the Financial Services and Markets Act 2000 (c 8)) to exercise his functions.

30.   A disclosure for the purpose of enabling or assisting the Secretary of State or the Treasury to exercise any of their functions under any of the following—
   (a)   the Companies Acts;
   (b)   Part 5 of the Criminal Justice Act 1993 (c 36) (insider dealing);
   (c)   the Insolvency Act 1986 (c 45);
   (d)   the Company Directors Disqualification Act 1986 (c 46);
   (e)   Part 42 of this Act (statutory auditors)
   (f)   Part 3 (investigations and powers to obtain information) or 7 (financial markets and insolvency) of the Companies Act 1989 (c 40);
   (g)   the Financial Services and Markets Act 2000.

31.   A disclosure for the purpose of enabling or assisting the Scottish Ministers to exercise their functions under the enactments relating to insolvency.

32.   A disclosure for the purpose of enabling or assisting the Department of Enterprise, Trade and Investment for Northern Ireland to exercise any powers conferred on it by the enactments relating to companies or insolvency.

33.   A disclosure for the purpose of enabling or assisting a person appointed or authorised by the Department of Enterprise, Trade and Investment for Northern Ireland under the enactments relating to companies or insolvency to exercise his functions.

34.   A disclosure for the purpose of enabling or assisting the Pensions Regulator to exercise the functions conferred on it by or by virtue of any of the following—
   (a)   the Pension Schemes Act 1993 (c 48);
   (b)   the Pensions Act 1995 (c 26);
   (c)   the Welfare Reform and Pensions Act 1999 (c 30);
   (d)   the Pensions Act 2004 (c 35);
   (e)   any enactment in force in Northern Ireland corresponding to any of those enactments.

35.   A disclosure for the purpose of enabling or assisting the Board of the Pension Protection Fund to exercise the functions conferred on it by or by virtue of Part 2 of the Pensions Act 2004 or any enactment in force in Northern Ireland corresponding to that Part.

36.   A disclosure for the purpose of enabling or assisting—
   (a)   the Bank of England,
   (b)   the European Central Bank, or
   (c)   the central bank of any country or territory outside the United Kingdom, to exercise its functions.

37.   A disclosure for the purpose of enabling or assisting the Commissioners for Her Majesty's Revenue and Customs to exercise their functions.

38.   A disclosure for the purpose of enabling or assisting organs of the Society of Lloyd's (being organs constituted by or under the Lloyd's Act 1982 (c xiv)) to exercise their functions under or by virtue of the Lloyd's Acts 1871 to 1982.

39.   A disclosure for the purpose of enabling or assisting the Office of Fair Trading to exercise its functions under any of the following—
   (a)   the Fair Trading Act 1973 (c 41);
   (b)   the Consumer Credit Act 1974 (c 39);
   (c)   the Estate Agents Act 1979 (c 38);
   (d)   the Competition Act 1980 (c 21);
   (e)   the Competition Act 1998 (c 41);
   (f)   the Financial Services and Markets Act 2000 (c 8);
   (g)   the Enterprise Act 2002 (c 40);
   (h)   the Control of Misleading Advertisements Regulations 1988 (SI 1988/915);
   (i)   the Unfair Terms in Consumer Contracts Regulations 1999 (SI 1999/2083).

PART II
OTHER ACTS

40.   A disclosure for the purpose of enabling or assisting the Competition Commission to exercise its functions under any of the following—
   (a)   the Fair Trading Act 1973;
   (b)   the Competition Act 1980;
   (c)   the Competition Act 1998;
   (d)   the Enterprise Act 2002.

41.   A disclosure with a view to the institution of, or otherwise for the purposes of, proceedings before the Competition Appeal Tribunal.

42.   A disclosure for the purpose of enabling or assisting an enforcer under Part 8 of the Enterprise Act 2002 (enforcement of consumer legislation) to exercise its functions under that Part.

43.   A disclosure for the purpose of enabling or assisting the Takeover Panel to perform any of its functions under Part 28 of this Act (takeovers etc).

44.   A disclosure for the purpose of enabling or assisting the Charity Commission to exercise its functions.

45.   A disclosure for the purpose of enabling or assisting the Attorney General to exercise his functions in connection with charities.

46.   A disclosure for the purpose of enabling or assisting the National Lottery Commission to exercise its functions under sections 5 to 10 (licensing) and 15 (power of Secretary of State to require information) of the National Lottery etc Act 1993 (c 39).

47.   A disclosure by the National Lottery Commission to the National Audit Office for the purpose of enabling or assisting the Comptroller and Auditor General to carry out an examination under Part 2 of the National Audit Act 1983 (c 44) into the economy, effectiveness and efficiency with which the National Lottery Commission has used its resources in discharging its functions under sections 5 to 10 of the National Lottery etc Act 1993.

48.   A disclosure for the purpose of enabling or assisting a qualifying body under the Unfair Terms in Consumer Contracts Regulations 1999 (SI 1999/2083) to exercise its functions under those Regulations.

49.   A disclosure for the purpose of enabling or assisting an enforcement authority under the Consumer Protection (Distance Selling) Regulations 2000 (SI 2000/2334) to exercise its functions under those Regulations.

50.   A disclosure for the purpose of enabling or assisting an enforcement authority under the Financial Services (Distance Marketing) Regulations 2004 (SI 2004/2095) to exercise its functions under those Regulations.

51.   A disclosure for the purpose of enabling or assisting a local weights and measures authority in England and Wales to exercise its functions under section 230(2) of the Enterprise Act 2002 (c 40) (notice of intention to prosecute, etc).

52.   A disclosure for the purpose of enabling or assisting the Financial Services Authority to exercise its functions under any of the following—
   (a)   the legislation relating to friendly societies or to industrial and provident societies;
   (b)   the Building Societies Act 1986 (c 53);
   (c)   Part 7 of the Companies Act 1989 (c 40) (financial markets and insolvency);
   (d)   the Financial Services and Markets Act 2000 (c 8).

53.   A disclosure for the purpose of enabling or assisting the competent authority for the purposes of Part 6 of the Financial Services and Markets Act 2000 (official listing) to exercise its functions under that Part.

54.   A disclosure for the purpose of enabling or assisting a body corporate established in accordance with section 212(1) of the Financial Services and Markets Act 2000 (compensation scheme manager) to exercise its functions.

55.   A disclosure for the purpose of enabling or assisting a recognised investment exchange or a recognised clearing house to exercise its functions as such.

   "Recognised investment exchange" and "recognised clearing house" have the same meaning as in section 285 of the Financial Services and Markets Act 2000.

56.   A disclosure for the purpose of enabling or assisting a person approved under the Uncertificated Securities Regulations 2001 (SI 2001/3755) as an operator of a relevant system (within the meaning of those regulations) to exercise his functions.

57.   A disclosure for the purpose of enabling or assisting a body designated under section 326(1) of the Financial Services and Markets Act 2000 (designated professional bodies) to exercise its functions in its capacity as a body designated under that section.

58.   A disclosure with a view to the institution of, or otherwise for the purposes of, civil proceedings arising under or by virtue of the Financial Services and Markets Act 2000.

59. A disclosure for the purpose of enabling or assisting a body designated by order under section 1252 of this Act (delegation of functions of Secretary of State) to exercise its functions under Part 42 of this Act (statutory auditors).

60. A disclosure for the purpose of enabling or assisting a recognised supervisory or qualifying body, within the meaning of Part 42 of this Act, to exercise its functions as such.

61. A disclosure for the purpose of making available to an audited person information relating to a statutory audit of that person's accounts.

62. A disclosure for the purpose of making available to the public information relating to monitoring or inspections carried out under arrangements within paragraph 23(1) of Schedule 10 to this Act (arrangements for independent monitoring of audits of listed companies and other major bodies), provided such information does not identify any audited person.

63. A disclosure for the purpose of enabling or assisting an official receiver (including the Accountant in Bankruptcy in Scotland and the Official Assignee in Northern Ireland) to exercise his functions under the enactments relating to insolvency.

64. A disclosure for the purpose of enabling or assisting the Insolvency Practitioners Tribunal to exercise its functions under the Insolvency Act 1986 (c 45).

65. A disclosure for the purpose of enabling or assisting a body that is for the time being a recognised professional body for the purposes of section 391 of the Insolvency Act 1986 (recognised professional bodies) to exercise its functions as such.

66. A disclosure for the purpose of enabling or assisting an overseas regulatory authority to exercise its regulatory functions.

"Overseas regulatory authority" and "regulatory functions" have the same meaning as in section 82 of the Companies Act 1989.

67. A disclosure for the purpose of enabling or assisting the Regulator of Community Interest Companies to exercise functions under the Companies (Audit, Investigations and Community Enterprise) Act 2004 (c 27).

68. A disclosure with a view to the institution of, or otherwise for the purposes of, criminal proceedings.

69. A disclosure for the purpose of enabling or assisting a person authorised by the Secretary of State under Part 2, 3 or 4 of the Proceeds of Crime Act 2002 (c 29) to exercise his functions.

70. A disclosure with a view to the institution of, or otherwise for the purposes of, proceedings on an application under section 6, 7 or 8 of the Company Directors Disqualification Act 1986 (c 46) (disqualification for unfitness).

71. A disclosure with a view to the institution of, or otherwise for the purposes of, proceedings before the Financial Services and Markets Tribunal.

72. A disclosure for the purposes of proceedings before the Financial Services Tribunal by virtue of the Financial Services and Markets Act 2000 (Transitional Provisions) (Partly Completed Procedures) Order 2001 (SI 2001/3592).

73. A disclosure for the purposes of proceedings before the Pensions Regulator Tribunal.

74. A disclosure for the purpose of enabling or assisting a body appointed under section 14 of the Companies (Audit, Investigations and Community Enterprise) Act 2004 (supervision of periodic accounts and reports of issuers of listed securities) to exercise functions mentioned in subsection (2) of that section.

75. A disclosure with a view to the institution of, or otherwise for the purposes of, disciplinary proceedings relating to the performance by a relevant lawyer, foreign lawyer, auditor, accountant, valuer or actuary of his professional duties.

In this paragraph—
  "foreign lawyer" means a person (other than a relevant lawyer) who is a foreign lawyer within the meaning of section 89(9) of the Courts and Legal Services Act 1990;
  "relevant lawyer" means—
      (a)   a person who, for the purposes of the Legal Services Act 2007, is an authorised person in relation to an activity which constitutes a reserved legal activity (within the meaning of that Act),
      (b)   a solicitor or barrister in Northern Ireland, or
      (c)   a solicitor or advocate in Scotland.

76. A disclosure with a view to the institution of, or otherwise for the purposes of, disciplinary proceedings relating to the performance by a public servant of his duties.

"Public servant" means an officer or employee of the Crown.

77.   A disclosure for the purpose of the provision of a summary or collection of information framed in such a way as not to enable the identity of any person to whom the information relates to be ascertained.

78.   A disclosure in pursuance of any Community obligation.]

[1734G]

NOTES
   Commencement: 6 April 2008.
   Inserted by the Statutory Auditors and Third Country Auditors Regulations 2007, SI 2007/3494, reg 10(2), Schedule, as from 6 April 2008.

[PART 3
OVERSEAS REGULATORY BODIES

79.   A disclosure is made in accordance with this Part of this Schedule if it is made to an EEA competent authority in accordance with section 1253B (requests from EEA competent authorities).

80.   A disclosure is made in accordance with this Part of this Schedule if it is—
   (a)   a transfer of audit working papers to a third country competent authority in accordance with rules imposed under paragraph 16A of Schedule 10 (transfer of papers to third countries), or
   (b)   a disclosure other than a transfer of audit working papers made to a third country competent authority for the purpose of enabling or assisting the authority to exercise its functions.]

[1734H]

NOTES
   Commencement: 6 April 2008.
   Inserted by the Statutory Auditors and Third Country Auditors Regulations 2007, SI 2007/3494, reg 10(2), Schedule, as from 6 April 2008.

SCHEDULE 12
ARRANGEMENTS IN WHICH REGISTERED THIRD COUNTRY AUDITORS ARE
REQUIRED TO PARTICIPATE
Section 1242

Arrangements for independent monitoring of audits of [UK-traded non-EEA companies]

1.—(1)   The arrangements referred to in section 1242(1)(a) are appropriate arrangements—
   (a)   for enabling the performance by the registered third country auditor of [functions related to the audit of UK-traded non-EEA companies] to be monitored by means of inspections carried out under the arrangements, and
   (b)   for ensuring that the carrying out of such monitoring and inspections is done independently of the registered third country auditor.

   (2)   ...

Arrangements for independent investigations for disciplinary purposes

2.—(1)   The arrangements referred to in section 1242(1)(b) are appropriate arrangements—
   (a)   for the carrying out of investigations into matters arising in connection with the performance of [functions related to the audit of UK-traded non-EEA companies] by the registered third country auditor,
   (b)   for the holding of disciplinary hearings relating to the registered third country auditor which appear to be desirable following the conclusion of such investigations,
   (c)   for requiring such hearings to be held in public except where the interests of justice otherwise require,
   (d)   for the persons before whom such hearings have taken place to decide whether (and, if so, what) disciplinary action should be taken against the registered third country auditor, and
   (e)   for ensuring that the carrying out of those investigations, the holding of those hearings and the taking of those decisions are done independently of the registered third country auditor.

   (2)   In this paragraph—
      "disciplinary action" includes the imposition of a fine; and
                                    .....

Supplementary: arrangements to operate independently of third country auditor

3.—(1)   This paragraph applies for the purposes of—

    (a)   paragraph 1(1)(b), or

    (b)   paragraph 2(1)(e).

    (2)   Arrangements are not to be regarded as appropriate for the purpose of ensuring that a thing is done independently of the registered third country auditor unless they are designed to ensure that the registered third country auditor—

    (a)   will have no involvement in the appointment or selection of any of the persons who are to be responsible for doing that thing, and

    (b)   will not otherwise be involved in the doing of that thing.

    (3)   Sub-paragraph (2) imposes a minimum requirement and does not preclude the possibility that additional criteria may need to be satisfied in order for the arrangements to be regarded as appropriate for the purpose in question.

Supplementary: funding of arrangements

4.—(1)   The registered third country auditor must pay any of the costs of maintaining any relevant arrangements which the arrangements provide are to be paid by it.

    (2)   For this purpose "relevant arrangements" are arrangements within paragraph 1 or 2 in which the registered third country auditor is obliged to participate.

Supplementary: scope of arrangements

5.   Arrangements may qualify as arrangements within either of paragraphs 1 and 2 even though the matters for which they provide are more extensive in any respect than those mentioned in the applicable paragraph.

Specification of particular arrangements by the Secretary of State

6.—(1)   If there exist two or more sets of arrangements within paragraph 1 or within paragraph 2, the obligation of a registered third country auditor under section 1242(1)(a) or (b), as the case may be, is to participate in such set of arrangements as the Secretary of State may by order specify.

    (2)   An order under sub-paragraph (1) is subject to negative resolution procedure.

[1734I]

NOTES

    Commencement: 20 January 2007 (for the purpose of enabling the exercise of powers to make Orders or Regulations by statutory instrument); 29 June 2008 (otherwise).

    Commencement (transitional provisions): see the note to s 1242 at **[1729EJ]**.

    Para 1: words in square brackets in sub-para (1)(a) and in the heading preceding this paragraph substituted, and sub-para (2) repealed, by the Statutory Auditors and Third Country Auditors Regulations 2007, SI 2007/3494, reg 33(1)–(3), as from 29 June 2008.

    Para 2: words in square brackets in sub-para (1)(a) substituted, and definition omitted from sub-para (2) repealed, by SI 2007/3494, reg 33(1), (4), as from 29 June 2008.

SCHEDULE 13
SUPPLEMENTARY PROVISIONS WITH RESPECT TO DELEGATION ORDER
Section 1252

Operation of this Schedule

1.—(1)   This Schedule has effect in relation to a body designated by a delegation order under section 1252 as follows—

    (a)   paragraphs 2 to 12 have effect in relation to the body where it is established by the order;

    (b)   paragraphs 2 and 6 to 11 have effect in relation to the body where it is an existing body;

    (c)   paragraph 13 has effect in relation to the body where it is an existing body that is an unincorporated association.

    (2)   In their operation in accordance with sub-paragraph (1)(b), paragraphs 2 and 6 apply only in relation to—

    (a)   things done by or in relation to the body in or in connection with the exercise of functions transferred to it by the delegation order, and

    (b)   functions of the body which are functions so transferred.

    (3)   Any power conferred by this Schedule to make provision by order is a power to make provision by an order under section 1252.

Status

2.   The body is not to be regarded as acting on behalf of the Crown and its members, officers and employees are not to be regarded as Crown servants.

Name, members and chairman

3.—(1)   The body is to be known by such name as may be specified in the delegation order.

(2)   The body is to consist of such persons (not being less than eight) as the Secretary of State may appoint after such consultation as he thinks appropriate.

(3)   The chairman of the body is to be such person as the Secretary of State may appoint from among its members.

(4)   The Secretary of State may make provision by order as to—
   (a)   the terms on which the members of the body are to hold and vacate office;
   (b)   the terms on which a person appointed as chairman is to hold and vacate the office of chairman.

Financial provisions

4.—(1)   The body must pay to its chairman and members such remuneration, and such allowances in respect of expenses properly incurred by them in the performance of their duties, as the Secretary of State may determine.

(2)   As regards any chairman or member in whose case the Secretary of State so determines, the body must pay or make provision for the payment of—
   (a)   such pension, allowance or gratuity to or in respect of that person on his retirement or death, or
   (b)   such contributions or other payment towards the provision of such a pension, allowance or gratuity,
as the Secretary of State may determine.

(3)   Where—
   (a)   a person ceases to be a member of the body otherwise than on the expiry of his term of office, and
   (b)   it appears to the Secretary of State that there are special circumstances which make it right for that person to receive compensation,
the body must make a payment to him by way of compensation of such amount as the Secretary of State may determine.

Proceedings

5.—(1)   The delegation order may contain such provision as the Secretary of State considers appropriate with respect to the proceedings of the body.

(2)   The delegation order may, in particular—
   (a)   authorise the body to discharge any functions by means of committees consisting wholly or partly of members of the body;
   (b)   provide that the validity of proceedings of the body, or of any such committee, is not affected by any vacancy among the members or any defect in the appointment of any member.

Fees

6.—(1)   The body may retain fees payable to it.

(2)   The fees must be applied for—
   (a)   meeting the expenses of the body in discharging its functions, and
   (b)   any purposes incidental to those functions.

(3)   Those expenses include any expenses incurred by the body on such staff, accommodation, services and other facilities as appear to it to be necessary or expedient for the proper performance of its functions.

(4)   In prescribing the amount of fees in the exercise of the functions transferred to it the body must prescribe such fees as appear to it sufficient to defray those expenses, taking one year with another.

(5)   Any exercise by the body of the power to prescribe fees requires the approval of the Secretary of State.

(6)   The Secretary of State may, after consultation with the body, by order vary or revoke any regulations prescribing fees made by the body.

Legislative functions

7.—(1)   Regulations or an order made by the body in the exercise of the functions transferred to it must be made by instrument in writing, but not by statutory instrument.

(2)   The instrument must specify the provision of this Part of this Act under which it is made.

(3)   The Secretary of State may by order impose such requirements as he thinks necessary or expedient as to the circumstances and manner in which the body must consult on any regulations or order it proposes to make.

(4)   Nothing in this Part applies to make regulations or an order made by the body subject to negative resolution procedure or affirmative resolution procedure.

8.—(1)   Immediately after an instrument is made it must be printed and made available to the public with or without payment.

(2)   A person is not to be taken to have contravened any regulation or order if he shows that at the time of the alleged contravention the instrument containing the regulation or order had not been made available as required by this paragraph.

9.—(1)   The production of a printed copy of an instrument purporting to be made by the body on which is endorsed a certificate signed by an officer of the body authorised by it for the purpose and stating—

(a)   that the instrument was made by the body,

(b)   that the copy is a true copy of the instrument, and

(c)   that on a specified date the instrument was made available to the public as required by paragraph 8,

is evidence (or, in Scotland, sufficient evidence) of the facts stated in the certificate.

(2)   A certificate purporting to be signed as mentioned in sub-paragraph (1) is to be deemed to have been duly signed unless the contrary is shown.

(3)   Any person wishing in any legal proceedings to cite an instrument made by the body may require the body to cause a copy of it to be endorsed with such a certificate as is mentioned in this paragraph.

Report and accounts

10.—(1)   The body must, at least once in each calendar year for which the delegation order is in force, make a report to the Secretary of State on—

(a)   the discharge of the functions transferred to it, and

(b)   such other matters as the Secretary of State may by order require.

(2)   The delegation order may modify sub-paragraph (1) as it has effect in relation to the calendar year in which the order comes into force or is revoked.

(3)   The Secretary of State must lay before Parliament copies of each report received by him under this paragraph.

(4)   The following provisions of this paragraph apply as follows—

(a)   sub-paragraphs (5) and (6) apply only where the body is established by the order, and

(b)   sub-paragraphs (7) and (8) apply only where the body is an existing body.

(5)   The Secretary of State may, with the consent of the Treasury, give directions to the body with respect to its accounts and the audit of its accounts.

(6)   A person may only be appointed as auditor of the body if he is eligible for appointment as a statutory auditor.

(7)   Unless the body is a company to which section 394 (duty to prepare individual company accounts) applies, the Secretary of State may, with the consent of the Treasury, give directions to the body with respect to its accounts and the audit of its accounts.

(8)   Whether or not the body is a company to which section 394 applies, the Secretary of State may direct that any provisions of this Act specified in the directions are to apply to the body, with or without any modifications so specified.

Other supplementary provisions

11.—(1)   The transfer of a function to a body designated by a delegation order does not affect anything previously done in the exercise of the function transferred; and the resumption of a function so transferred does not affect anything previously done in exercise of the function resumed.

(2)   The Secretary of State may by order make such transitional and other supplementary provision as he thinks necessary or expedient in relation to the transfer or resumption of a function.

(3)   The provision that may be made in connection with the transfer of a function includes, in particular, provision—

(a)   for modifying or excluding any provision of this Part of this Act in its application to the function transferred;

(b)   for applying to the body designated by the delegation order, in connection with the function transferred, any provision applying to the Secretary of State which is contained in or made under any other enactment;

(c)   for the transfer of any property, rights or liabilities from the Secretary of State to that body;

(d)   for the carrying on and completion by that body of anything in the process of being done by the Secretary of State when the order takes effect;

(e)   for the substitution of that body for the Secretary of State in any instrument, contract or legal proceedings.

(4)   The provision that may be made in connection with the resumption of a function includes, in particular, provision—

(a)   for the transfer of any property, rights or liabilities from that body to the Secretary of State;

(b)   for the carrying on and completion by the Secretary of State of anything in the process of being done by that body when the order takes effect;

(c)   for the substitution of the Secretary of State for that body in any instrument, contract or legal proceedings.

12.   Where a delegation order is revoked, the Secretary of State may by order make provision—

(a)   for the payment of compensation to persons ceasing to be employed by the body established by the delegation order;

(b)   as to the winding up and dissolution of the body.

13.—(1)   This paragraph applies where the body is an unincorporated association.

(2)   Any relevant proceedings may be brought by or against the body in the name of any body corporate whose constitution provides for the establishment of the body.

(3)   In sub-paragraph (2) "relevant proceedings" means proceedings brought in or in connection with the exercise of any transferred function.

(4)   In relation to proceedings brought as mentioned in sub-paragraph (2), any reference in paragraph 11(3)(e) or (4)(c) to the body replacing or being replaced by the Secretary of State in any legal proceedings is to be read with the appropriate modifications.

[1734J]

NOTES

Commencement: 20 January 2007 (for the purpose of enabling the exercise of powers to make Orders or Regulations by statutory instrument); 6 April 2008 (otherwise).

Orders: the Statutory Auditors (Delegation of Functions etc) Order 2008, SI 2008/496.

(Sch 14 (Statutory Auditors: Consequential Amendments) amends the Companies (Audit, Investigations and Community Enterprise) Act 2004, s 16.)

INVESTMENT EXCHANGES AND CLEARING HOUSES ACT 2006 (NOTE)

(2006 c 55)

NOTES

Section 1 (Power of FSA to disallow excessive regulatory provision) and s 2 (Procedural and other supplementary provisions) of this Act insert the Financial Services and Markets Act 2000, ss 300A–300E at **[326A]** et seq. Section 3 (Interim power to give directions about notification) ceased to have effect on 19 December 2007 by virtue of sub-s (8) of that section (ie, 12 months after the passing of this Act). Section 4 (Consequential amendment of grounds for refusing recognition) inserts the Financial Services and Markets Act 2000, s 290A at **[316A]**. Section 5 (Short title and commencement) provides that the Act comes into force on 20 December 2006, and that ss 300A–300E (as inserted by ss 1,2) do not apply to regulatory provision made before 20 December 2006, and apply to regulatory provision proposed on or after that day, whenever originally proposed.

As of 1 February 2009, this Act had not been amended.

[1735]

TRIBUNALS, COURTS AND ENFORCEMENT ACT 2007

(2007 c 15)

NOTES

As of 1 February 2009, this Act (as reproduced here) had not been amended.

ARRANGEMENT OF SECTIONS

PART 1
TRIBUNALS AND INQUIRIES

CHAPTER 2
FIRST-TIER TRIBUNAL AND UPPER TRIBUNAL

Establishment

An Act to make provision about tribunals and inquiries; to establish an Administrative Justice and Tribunals Council; to amend the law relating to judicial appointments and appointments to the Law Commission; to amend the law relating to the enforcement of judgments and debts; to make further provision about the management and relief of debt; to make provision protecting cultural objects from seizure or forfeiture in certain circumstances; to amend the law relating to the taking of possession of land affected by compulsory purchase; to alter the powers of the High Court in judicial review applications; and for connected purposes

[19 July 2007]

PART 1
TRIBUNALS AND INQUIRIES

CHAPTER 2
FIRST-TIER TRIBUNAL AND UPPER TRIBUNAL

Establishment

3   The First-tier Tribunal and the Upper Tribunal

(1)   There is to be a tribunal, known as the First-tier Tribunal, for the purpose of exercising the functions conferred on it under or by virtue of this Act or any other Act.

(2)   There is to be a tribunal, known as the Upper Tribunal, for the purpose of exercising the functions conferred on it under or by virtue of this Act or any other Act.

(3)   Each of the First-tier Tribunal, and the Upper Tribunal, is to consist of its judges and other members.

(4)   The Senior President of Tribunals is to preside over both of the First-tier Tribunal and the Upper Tribunal.

(5)   The Upper Tribunal is to be a superior court of record.

[1736]

NOTES
Commencement: 3 November 2008.

Members and composition of tribunals

5   Judges and other members of the Upper Tribunal

(1)   A person is a judge of the Upper Tribunal if the person—
   (a)   is the Senior President of Tribunals,
   (b)   is a judge of the Upper Tribunal by virtue of appointment under paragraph 1(1) of Schedule 3,
   (c)   is a transferred-in judge of the Upper Tribunal (see section 31(2)),
   (d)   is a member of the Asylum and Immigration Tribunal appointed under paragraph 2(1)(a) to (d) of Schedule 4 to the Nationality, Immigration and Asylum Act 2002 (c 41) (legally qualified members) who—
      (i)   is the President or a Deputy President of that tribunal, or
      (ii)   has the title Senior Immigration Judge but is neither the President nor a Deputy President of that tribunal,
   (e)   is the Chief Social Security Commissioner, or any other Social Security Commissioner, appointed under section 50(1) of the Social Security Administration (Northern Ireland) Act 1992 (c 8),
   (f)   is a Social Security Commissioner appointed under section 50(2) of that Act (deputy Commissioners),
   (g)   is within section 6(1),
   (h)   is a deputy judge of the Upper Tribunal (whether under paragraph 7 of Schedule 3 or under section 31(2)), or
   (i)   is a Chamber President or a Deputy Chamber President, whether of a chamber of the Upper Tribunal or of a chamber of the First-tier Tribunal, and does not fall within any of paragraphs (a) to (h).

(2)   A person is one of the other members of the Upper Tribunal if the person—
   (a)   is a member of the Upper Tribunal by virtue of appointment under paragraph 2(1) of Schedule 3,
   (b)   is a transferred-in other member of the Upper Tribunal (see section 31(2)),
   (c)   is a member of the Employment Appeal Tribunal appointed under section 22(1)(c) of the Employment Tribunals Act 1996 (c 17), or
   (d)   is a member of the Asylum and Immigration Tribunal appointed under paragraph 2(1)(e) of Schedule 4 to the Nationality, Immigration and Asylum Act 2002 (members other than "legally qualified members").

(3)   Schedule 3—
   contains provision for the appointment of persons to be judges (including deputy judges), or other members, of the Upper Tribunal, and
   makes further provision in connection with judges and other members of the Upper Tribunal.

[1737]

NOTES
Commencement: 3 November 2008.

6   Certain judges who are also judges of First-tier Tribunal and Upper Tribunal

(1)   A person is within this subsection (and so, by virtue of sections 4(1)(c) and 5(1)(g), is a judge of the First-tier Tribunal and of the Upper Tribunal) if the person—
   (a)   is an ordinary judge of the Court of Appeal in England and Wales (including the vice-president, if any, of either division of that Court),
   (b)   is a Lord Justice of Appeal in Northern Ireland,
   (c)   is a judge of the Court of Session,
   (d)   is a puisne judge of the High Court in England and Wales or Northern Ireland,
   (e)   is a circuit judge,
   (f)   is a sheriff in Scotland,
   (g)   is a county court judge in Northern Ireland,

    (h)   is a district judge in England and Wales or Northern Ireland, or

    (i)   is a District Judge (Magistrates' Courts).

(2)   References in subsection (1)(c) to (i) to office-holders do not include deputies or temporary office-holders.

[1738]

NOTES
    Commencement: 3 November 2008.

Review of decisions and appeals

10 Review of decision of Upper Tribunal

(1)   The Upper Tribunal may review a decision made by it on a matter in a case, other than a decision that is an excluded decision for the purposes of section 13(1) (but see subsection (7)).

(2)   The Upper Tribunal's power under subsection (1) in relation to a decision is exercisable—

    (a)   of its own initiative, or

    (b)   on application by a person who for the purposes of section 13(2) has a right of appeal in respect of the decision.

(3)   Tribunal Procedure Rules may—

    (a)   provide that the Upper Tribunal may not under subsection (1) review (whether of its own initiative or on application under subsection (2)(b)) a decision of a description specified for the purposes of this paragraph in Tribunal Procedure Rules;

    (b)   provide that the Upper Tribunal's power under subsection (1) to review a decision of a description specified for the purposes of this paragraph in Tribunal Procedure Rules is exercisable only of the tribunal's own initiative;

    (c)   provide that an application under subsection (2)(b) that is of a description specified for the purposes of this paragraph in Tribunal Procedure Rules may be made only on grounds specified for the purposes of this paragraph in Tribunal Procedure Rules;

    (d)   provide, in relation to a decision of a description specified for the purposes of this paragraph in Tribunal Procedure Rules, that the Upper Tribunal's power under subsection (1) to review the decision of its own initiative is exercisable only on grounds specified for the purposes of this paragraph in Tribunal Procedure Rules.

(4)   Where the Upper Tribunal has under subsection (1) reviewed a decision, the Upper Tribunal may in the light of the review do any of the following—

    (a)   correct accidental errors in the decision or in a record of the decision;

    (b)   amend reasons given for the decision;

    (c)   set the decision aside.

(5)   Where under subsection (4)(c) the Upper Tribunal sets a decision aside, the Upper Tribunal must re-decide the matter concerned.

(6)   Where the Upper Tribunal is acting under subsection (5), it may make such findings of fact as it considers appropriate.

(7)   This section has effect as if a decision under subsection (4)(c) to set aside an earlier decision were not an excluded decision for the purposes of section 13(1), but the Upper Tribunal's only power in the light of a review under subsection (1) of a decision under subsection (4)(c) is the power under subsection (4)(a).

(8)   A decision of the Upper Tribunal may not be reviewed under subsection (1) more than once, and once the Upper Tribunal has decided that an earlier decision should not be reviewed under subsection (1) it may not then decide to review that earlier decision under that subsection.

(9)   Where under this section a decision is set aside and the matter concerned is then re-decided, the decision set aside and the decision made in re-deciding the matter are for the purposes of subsection (8) to be taken to be different decisions.

[1739]

NOTES
    Commencement: 19 September 2007 (sub-s (3)); 3 November 2008 (otherwise).

13 Right to appeal to Court of Appeal etc

(1)   For the purposes of subsection (2), the reference to a right of appeal is to a right to appeal to the relevant appellate court on any point of law arising from a decision made by the Upper Tribunal other than an excluded decision.

(2)   Any party to a case has a right of appeal, subject to subsection (14).

(3)   That right may be exercised only with permission (or, in Northern Ireland, leave).

(4)   Permission (or leave) may be given by—

(a)   the Upper Tribunal, or
(b)   the relevant appellate court,

on an application by the party.

(5)   An application may be made under subsection (4) to the relevant appellate court only if permission (or leave) has been refused by the Upper Tribunal.

(6)   The Lord Chancellor may, as respects an application under subsection (4) that falls within subsection (7) and for which the relevant appellate court is the Court of Appeal in England and Wales or the Court of Appeal in Northern Ireland, by order make provision for permission (or leave) not to be granted on the application unless the Upper Tribunal or (as the case may be) the relevant appellate court considers—

(a)   that the proposed appeal would raise some important point of principle or practice, or
(b)   that there is some other compelling reason for the relevant appellate court to hear the appeal.

(7)   An application falls within this subsection if the application is for permission (or leave) to appeal from any decision of the Upper Tribunal on an appeal under section 11.

(8)   For the purposes of subsection (1), an "excluded decision" is—

(a)   any decision of the Upper Tribunal on an appeal under section 28(4) or (6) of the Data Protection Act 1998 (c 29) (appeals against national security certificate),
(b)   any decision of the Upper Tribunal on an appeal under section 60(1) or (4) of the Freedom of Information Act 2000 (c 36) (appeals against national security certificate),
(c)   any decision of the Upper Tribunal on an application under section 11(4)(b) (application for permission or leave to appeal),
(d)   a decision of the Upper Tribunal under section 10—
       (i)   to review, or not to review, an earlier decision of the tribunal,
       (ii)   to take no action, or not to take any particular action, in the light of a review of an earlier decision of the tribunal, or
       (iii) to set aside an earlier decision of the tribunal,
(e)   a decision of the Upper Tribunal that is set aside under section 10 (including a decision set aside after proceedings on an appeal under this section have been begun), or
(f)   any decision of the Upper Tribunal that is of a description specified in an order made by the Lord Chancellor.

(9)   A description may be specified under subsection (8)(f) only if—

(a)   in the case of a decision of that description, there is a right to appeal to a court from the decision and that right is, or includes, something other than a right (however expressed) to appeal on any point of law arising from the decision, or
(b)   decisions of that description are made in carrying out a function transferred under section 30 and prior to the transfer of the function under section 30(1) there was no right to appeal from decisions of that description.

(10)   Where—

(a)   an order under subsection (8)(f) specifies a description of decisions, and
(b)   decisions of that description are made in carrying out a function transferred under section 30,

the order must be framed so as to come into force no later than the time when the transfer under section 30 of the function takes effect (but power to revoke the order continues to be exercisable after that time, and power to amend the order continues to be exercisable after that time for the purpose of narrowing the description for the time being specified).

(11)   Before the Upper Tribunal decides an application made to it under subsection (4), the Upper Tribunal must specify the court that is to be the relevant appellate court as respects the proposed appeal.

(12)   The court to be specified under subsection (11) in relation to a proposed appeal is whichever of the following courts appears to the Upper Tribunal to be the most appropriate—

(a)   the Court of Appeal in England and Wales;
(b)   the Court of Session;
(c)   the Court of Appeal in Northern Ireland.

(13)   In this section except subsection (11), "the relevant appellate court", as respects an appeal, means the court specified as respects that appeal by the Upper Tribunal under subsection (11).

(14)   The Lord Chancellor may by order make provision for a person to be treated as being, or to be treated as not being, a party to a case for the purposes of subsection (2).

(15)   Rules of court may make provision as to the time within which an application under subsection (4) to the relevant appellate court must be made.

[1740]

NOTES

Commencement: 19 September 2007 (sub-ss (6), (8)(f), (9), (10), (14), (15)); 3 November 2008 (otherwise).
Orders: the Appeals from the Upper Tribunal to the Court of Appeal Order 2008, SI 2008/2834.

14   Proceedings on appeal to Court of Appeal etc

(1)   Subsection (2) applies if the relevant appellate court, in deciding an appeal under section 13, finds that the making of the decision concerned involved the making of an error on a point of law.

(2)   The relevant appellate court—

    (a)   may (but need not) set aside the decision of the Upper Tribunal, and

    (b)   if it does, must either—

        (i)   remit the case to the Upper Tribunal or, where the decision of the Upper Tribunal was on an appeal or reference from another tribunal or some other person, to the Upper Tribunal or that other tribunal or person, with directions for its reconsideration, or

        (ii)   re-make the decision.

(3)   In acting under subsection (2)(b)(i), the relevant appellate court may also—

    (a)   direct that the persons who are chosen to reconsider the case are not to be the same as those who—

        (i)   where the case is remitted to the Upper Tribunal, made the decision of the Upper Tribunal that has been set aside, or

        (ii)   where the case is remitted to another tribunal or person, made the decision in respect of which the appeal or reference to the Upper Tribunal was made;

    (b)   give procedural directions in connection with the reconsideration of the case by the Upper Tribunal or other tribunal or person.

(4)   In acting under subsection (2)(b)(ii), the relevant appellate court—

    (a)   may make any decision which the Upper Tribunal could make if the Upper Tribunal were re-making the decision or (as the case may be) which the other tribunal or person could make if that other tribunal or person were re-making the decision, and

    (b)   may make such findings of fact as it considers appropriate.

(5)   Where—

    (a)   under subsection (2)(b)(i) the relevant appellate court remits a case to the Upper Tribunal, and

    (b)   the decision set aside under subsection (2)(a) was made by the Upper Tribunal on an appeal or reference from another tribunal or some other person,

the Upper Tribunal may (instead of reconsidering the case itself) remit the case to that other tribunal or person, with the directions given by the relevant appellate court for its reconsideration.

(6)   In acting under subsection (5), the Upper Tribunal may also—

    (a)   direct that the persons who are chosen to reconsider the case are not to be the same as those who made the decision in respect of which the appeal or reference to the Upper Tribunal was made;

    (b)   give procedural directions in connection with the reconsideration of the case by the other tribunal or person.

(7)   In this section "the relevant appellate court", as respects an appeal under section 13, means the court specified as respects that appeal by the Upper Tribunal under section 13(11).

[1741]

NOTES

Commencement: 3 November 2008.

Miscellaneous

22   Tribunal Procedure Rules

(1)   There are to be rules, to be called "Tribunal Procedure Rules", governing—

    (a)   the practice and procedure to be followed in the First-tier Tribunal, and

    (b)   the practice and procedure to be followed in the Upper Tribunal.

(2)   Tribunal Procedure Rules are to be made by the Tribunal Procedure Committee.

(3)   In Schedule 5—

Part 1 makes further provision about the content of Tribunal Procedure Rules,

Part 2 makes provision about the membership of the Tribunal Procedure Committee,

Part 3 makes provision about the making of Tribunal Procedure Rules by the Committee, and

Part 4 confers power to amend legislation in connection with Tribunal Procedure Rules.

(4)   Power to make Tribunal Procedure Rules is to be exercised with a view to securing—

**PART II
OTHER ACTS**

(a)   that, in proceedings before the First-tier Tribunal and Upper Tribunal, justice is done,
(b)   that the tribunal system is accessible and fair,
(c)   that proceedings before the First-tier Tribunal or Upper Tribunal are handled quickly and efficiently,
(d)   that the rules are both simple and simply expressed, and
(e)   that the rules where appropriate confer on members of the First-tier Tribunal, or Upper Tribunal, responsibility for ensuring that proceedings before the tribunal are handled quickly and efficiently.

(5)   In subsection (4)(b) "the tribunal system" means the system for deciding matters within the jurisdiction of the First-tier Tribunal or the Upper Tribunal.

[1742]

NOTES
Commencement: 19 September 2007.
Rules: the Tribunal Procedure (Upper Tribunal) Rules 2008, SI 2008/2698. Note that Part 1 of this Act establishes a new tribunal structure comprising a First-tier Tribunal and an Upper Tribunal. Appeal functions of existing tribunals are being transferred to this structure and assigned to chambers within the new tribunals. Other Rules made under this section govern the practice and procedure to be followed in the First-tier Tribunal in proceedings which have been allocated to a particular Chamber, and are outside the scope of this work.

23 Practice directions

(1)   The Senior President of Tribunals may give directions—
(a)   as to the practice and procedure of the First-tier Tribunal;
(b)   as to the practice and procedure of the Upper Tribunal.

(2)   A Chamber President may give directions as to the practice and procedure of the chamber over which he presides.

(3)   A power under this section to give directions includes—
(a)   power to vary or revoke directions made in exercise of the power, and
(b)   power to make different provision for different purposes (including different provision for different areas).

(4)   Directions under subsection (1) may not be given without the approval of the Lord Chancellor.

(5)   Directions under subsection (2) may not be given without the approval of—
(a)   the Senior President of Tribunals, and
(b)   the Lord Chancellor.

(6)   Subsections (4) and (5)(b) do not apply to directions to the extent that they consist of guidance about any of the following—
(a)   the application or interpretation of the law;
(b)   the making of decisions by members of the First-tier Tribunal or Upper Tribunal.

(7)   Subsections (4) and (5)(b) do not apply to directions to the extent that they consist of criteria for determining which members of the First-tier Tribunal or Upper Tribunal may be chosen to decide particular categories of matter; but the directions may, to that extent, be given only after consulting the Lord Chancellor.

[1743]

NOTES
Commencement: 3 November 2008.

24 Mediation

(1)   A person exercising power to make Tribunal Procedure Rules or give practice directions must, when making provision in relation to mediation, have regard to the following principles—
(a)   mediation of matters in dispute between parties to proceedings is to take place only by agreement between those parties;
(b)   where parties to proceedings fail to mediate, or where mediation between parties to proceedings fails to resolve disputed matters, the failure is not to affect the outcome of the proceedings.

(2)   Practice directions may provide for members to act as mediators in relation to disputed matters in a case that is the subject of proceedings.

(3)   The provision that may be made by virtue of subsection (2) includes provision for a member to act as a mediator in relation to disputed matters in a case even though the member has been chosen to decide matters in the case.

(4)   Once a member has begun to act as a mediator in relation to a disputed matter in a case that is the subject of proceedings, the member may decide matters in the case only with the consent of the parties.

(5)   Staff appointed under section 40(1) may, subject to their terms of appointment, act as mediators in relation to disputed matters in a case that is the subject of proceedings.

(6)   In this section—
"member" means a judge or other member of the First-tier Tribunal or a judge or other member of the Upper Tribunal;
"practice direction" means a direction under section 23(1) or (2);
"proceedings" means proceedings before the First-tier Tribunal or proceedings before the Upper Tribunal.

[1744]

NOTES
Commencement: 3 November 2008.

25   Supplementary powers of Upper Tribunal

(1)   In relation to the matters mentioned in subsection (2), the Upper Tribunal—
(a)   has, in England and Wales or in Northern Ireland, the same powers, rights, privileges and authority as the High Court, and
(b)   has, in Scotland, the same powers, rights, privileges and authority as the Court of Session.

(2)   The matters are—
(a)   the attendance and examination of witnesses,
(b)   the production and inspection of documents, and
(c)   all other matters incidental to the Upper Tribunal's functions.

(3)   Subsection (1) shall not be taken—
(a)   to limit any power to make Tribunal Procedure Rules;
(b)   to be limited by anything in Tribunal Procedure Rules other than an express limitation.

(4)   A power, right, privilege or authority conferred in a territory by subsection (1) is available for purposes of proceedings in the Upper Tribunal that take place outside that territory (as well as for purposes of proceedings in the tribunal that take place within that territory).

[1745]

NOTES
Commencement: 3 November 2008.

26   First-tier Tribunal and Upper Tribunal: sitting places

Each of the First-tier Tribunal and the Upper Tribunal may decide a case—
(a)   in England and Wales,
(b)   in Scotland, or
(c)   in Northern Ireland,
even though the case arises under the law of a territory other than the one in which the case is decided.

[1746]

NOTES
Commencement: 3 November 2008.

28   Assessors

(1)   If it appears to the First-tier Tribunal or the Upper Tribunal that a matter before it requires special expertise not otherwise available to it, it may direct that in dealing with that matter it shall have the assistance of a person or persons appearing to it to have relevant knowledge or experience.

(2)   The remuneration of a person who gives assistance to either tribunal as mentioned in subsection (1) shall be determined and paid by the Lord Chancellor.

(3)   The Lord Chancellor may—
(a)   establish panels of persons from which either tribunal may (but need not) select persons to give it assistance as mentioned in subsection (1);
(b)   under paragraph (a) establish different panels for different purposes;
(c)   after carrying out such consultation as he considers appropriate, appoint persons to a panel established under paragraph (a);
(d)   remove a person from such a panel.

[1747]

NOTES
Commencement: 3 November 2008.

CHAPTER 5
OVERSIGHT OF ADMINISTRATIVE JUSTICE SYSTEM, TRIBUNALS AND INQUIRIES

44   The Administrative Justice and Tribunals Council

(1)   There is to be a council to be known as the Administrative Justice and Tribunals Council.

(2)   In Schedule 7—
Part 1 makes provision about membership and committees of the Council,
Part 2 makes provision about functions of the Council,
Part 3 requires the Council to be consulted before procedural rules for certain tribunals are made, confirmed etc, and
Part 4 contains interpretative provisions.

[1748]

NOTES
Commencement: 1 November 2007.

45   Abolition of the Council on Tribunals

(1)   The following are abolished—
(a)   the Council on Tribunals, and
(b)   the Scottish Committee of the Council on Tribunals.

(2)   In consequence of subsection (1), sections 1 to 4 of the Tribunals and Inquiries Act 1992 (c 53) cease to have effect.

(3)   The Lord Chancellor may by order transfer to the Administrative Justice and Tribunals Council the property, rights and liabilities of—
(a)   the Council on Tribunals;
(b)   the Scottish Committee of the Council on Tribunals.

[1749]

NOTES
Commencement: 19 September 2007 (sub-s (3)); 1 November 2007 (otherwise).

PART 8
GENERAL

147   Extent

(1)   Parts 1, 2 and 6 and this Part extend to England and Wales, Scotland and Northern Ireland.

(2)–(5)   (*Outside the scope of this work.*)

[1750]

NOTES
Commencement: 19 July 2007.

148   Commencement

(1)–(4)   (*Outside the scope of this work.*)

(5)   The remaining provisions of this Act, except sections 53, 55, 56, 57, 145, 147, 149, this section and Schedule 11, come into force in accordance with provision made by the Lord Chancellor by order.

(6)   An order under this section may make different provision for different purposes.

(7)   The power to make an order under this section is exercisable by statutory instrument.

[1751]

NOTES
Commencement: 19 July 2007.
Orders: the Tribunals, Courts and Enforcement Act 2007 (Commencement No 1) Order 2007, SI 2007/2709; the Tribunals, Courts and Enforcement Act 2007 (Commencement No 2) Order 2007, SI 2007/3613; the Tribunals, Courts and Enforcement Act 2007 (Commencement No 3) Order 2008, SI 2008/749; the Tribunals, Courts and Enforcement Act 2007 (Commencement) (Scotland) Order 2008, SSI 2008/150; the Tribunals, Courts and Enforcement Act 2007 (Commencement No 4) Order 2008, SI 2008/1158; the Tribunals, Courts and Enforcement Act 2007 (Commencement No 5 and Transitional Provisions) Order 2008, SI 2008/1653; the Tribunals, Courts and Enforcement Act 2007 (Commencement No 6 and Transitional Provisions) Order 2008, SI 2008/2696.

149   Short title

This Act may be cited as the Tribunals, Courts and Enforcement Act 2007.

[1752]

NOTES
  Commencement: 19 July 2007.

SCHEDULES

SCHEDULE 5
PROCEDURE IN FIRST-TIER TRIBUNAL AND UPPER TRIBUNAL
Section 22

PART 1
TRIBUNAL PROCEDURE RULES

Introductory

1.—(1)   This Part of this Schedule makes further provision about the content of Tribunal Procedure Rules.

(2)   The generality of section 22(1) is not to be taken to be prejudiced by—
  (a)   the following paragraphs of this Part of this Schedule, or
  (b)   any other provision (including future provision) authorising or requiring the making of provision by Tribunal Procedure Rules.

(3)   In the following paragraphs of this Part of this Schedule "Rules" means Tribunal Procedure Rules.

Concurrent functions

2.   Rules may make provision as to who is to decide, or as to how to decide, which of the First-tier Tribunal and Upper Tribunal is to exercise, in relation to any particular matter, a function that is exercisable by the two tribunals on the basis that the question as to which of them is to exercise the function is to be determined by, or under, Rules.

Delegation of functions to staff

3.—(1)   Rules may provide for functions—
  (a)   of the First-tier Tribunal, or
  (b)   of the Upper Tribunal,
to be exercised by staff appointed under section 40(1).

(2)   In making provision of the kind mentioned in sub-paragraph (1) in relation to a function, Rules may (in particular)—
  (a)   provide for the function to be exercisable by a member of staff only if the member of staff is, or is of a description, specified in exercise of a discretion conferred by Rules;
  (b)   provide for the function to be exercisable by a member of staff only if the member of staff is approved, or is of a description approved, for the purpose by a person specified in Rules.

Time limits

4.   Rules may make provision for time limits as respects initiating, or taking any step in, proceedings before the First-tier Tribunal or the Upper Tribunal.

Repeat applications

5.   Rules may make provision restricting the making of fresh applications where a previous application in relation to the same matter has been made.

Tribunal acting of its own initiative

6.   Rules may make provision about the circumstances in which the First-tier Tribunal, or the Upper Tribunal, may exercise its powers of its own initiative.

Hearings

7.   Rules may—
  (a)   make provision for dealing with matters without a hearing;
  (b)   make provision as respects allowing or requiring a hearing to be in private or as respects allowing or requiring a hearing to be in public.

Proceedings without notice

8.   Rules may make provision for proceedings to take place, in circumstances described in Rules, at the request of one party even though the other, or another, party has had no notice.

Representation

9.   Rules may make provision conferring additional rights of audience before the First-tier Tribunal or the Upper Tribunal.

Evidence, witnesses and attendance

10.—(1)   Rules may make provision about evidence (including evidence on oath and administration of oaths).

(2)   Rules may modify any rules of evidence provided for elsewhere, so far as they would apply to proceedings before the First-tier Tribunal or Upper Tribunal.

(3)   Rules may make provision, where the First-tier Tribunal has required a person—
   (a)   to attend at any place for the purpose of giving evidence,
   (b)   otherwise to make himself available to give evidence,
   (c)   to swear an oath in connection with the giving of evidence,
   (d)   to give evidence as a witness,
   (e)   to produce a document, or
   (f)   to facilitate the inspection of a document or any other thing (including any premises),

for the Upper Tribunal to deal with non-compliance with the requirement as though the requirement had been imposed by the Upper Tribunal.

(4)   Rules may make provision for the payment of expenses and allowances to persons giving evidence, producing documents, attending proceedings or required to attend proceedings.

Use of information

11.—(1)   Rules may make provision for the disclosure or non-disclosure of information received during the course of proceedings before the First-tier Tribunal or Upper Tribunal.

(2)   Rules may make provision for imposing reporting restrictions in circumstances described in Rules.

Costs and expenses

12.—(1)   Rules may make provision for regulating matters relating to costs, or (in Scotland) expenses, of proceedings before the First-tier Tribunal or Upper Tribunal.

(2)   The provision mentioned in sub-paragraph (1) includes (in particular)—
   (a)   provision prescribing scales of costs or expenses;
   (b)   provision for enabling costs to undergo detailed assessment in England and Wales by a county court or the High Court;
   (c)   provision for taxation in Scotland of accounts of expenses by an Auditor of Court;
   (d)   provision for enabling costs to be taxed in Northern Ireland in a county court or the High Court;
   (e)   provision for costs or expenses—
       (i)   not to be allowed in respect of items of a description specified in Rules;
       (ii) not to be allowed in proceedings of a description so specified;
   (f)   provision for other exceptions to either or both of subsections (1) and (2) of section 29.

Set-off and interest

13.—(1)   Rules may make provision for a party to proceedings to deduct, from amounts payable by him, amounts payable to him.

(2)   Rules may make provision for interest on sums awarded (including provision conferring a discretion or provision in accordance with which interest is to be calculated).

Arbitration

14.   Rules may provide for Part 1 of the Arbitration Act 1996 (c 23) (which extends to England and Wales, and Northern Ireland, but not Scotland) not to apply, or not to apply except so far as is specified in Rules, where the First-tier Tribunal, or Upper Tribunal, acts as arbitrator.

Correction of errors and setting-aside of decisions on procedural grounds

15.—(1)   Rules may make provision for the correction of accidental errors in a decision or record of a decision.

(2)   Rules may make provision for the setting aside of a decision in proceedings before the First-tier Tribunal or Upper Tribunal—
   (a)   where a document relating to the proceedings was not sent to, or was not received at an appropriate time by, a party to the proceedings or a party's representative,
   (b)   where a document relating to the proceedings was not sent to the First-tier Tribunal or Upper Tribunal at an appropriate time,

(c)   where a party to the proceedings, or a party's representative, was not present at a hearing related to the proceedings, or

(d)   where there has been any other procedural irregularity in the proceedings.

(3)   Sub-paragraphs (1) and (2) shall not be taken to prejudice, or to be prejudiced by, any power to correct errors or set aside decisions that is exercisable apart from rules made by virtue of those sub-paragraphs.

Ancillary powers

16.   Rules may confer on the First-tier Tribunal, or the Upper Tribunal, such ancillary powers as are necessary for the proper discharge of its functions.

Rules may refer to practice directions

17.   Rules may, instead of providing for any matter, refer to provision made or to be made about that matter by directions under section 23.

Presumptions

18.   Rules may make provision in the form of presumptions (including, in particular, presumptions as to service or notification).

Differential provision

19.   Rules may make different provision for different purposes or different areas.

[1753]

NOTES
   Commencement: 19 September 2007.
   Rules: the Tribunal Procedure (Upper Tribunal) Rules 2008, SI 2008/2698. Note that Part 1 of this Act establishes a new tribunal structure comprising a First-tier Tribunal and an Upper Tribunal. Appeal functions of existing tribunals are being transferred to this structure and assigned to chambers within the new tribunals. Other Rules made under this Schedule govern the practice and procedure to be followed in the First-tier Tribunal in proceedings which have been allocated to a particular Chamber, and are outside the scope of this work.

PART 2
TRIBUNAL PROCEDURE COMMITTEE

Membership

20.   The Tribunal Procedure Committee is to consist of—

(a)   the Senior President of Tribunals or a person nominated by him,

(b)   the persons currently appointed by the Lord Chancellor under paragraph 21,

(c)   the persons currently appointed by the Lord Chief Justice of England and Wales under paragraph 22,

(d)   the person currently appointed by the Lord President of the Court of Session under paragraph 23, and

(e)   any person currently appointed under paragraph 24 at the request of the Senior President of Tribunals.

Lord Chancellor's appointees

21.—(1)   The Lord Chancellor must appoint—

(a)   three persons each of whom must be a person with experience of—

(i)   practice in tribunals, or

(ii)   advising persons involved in tribunal proceedings, and

(b)   one person nominated by the Administrative Justice and Tribunals Council.

(2)   Before making an appointment under sub-paragraph (1), the Lord Chancellor must consult the Lord Chief Justice of England and Wales.

(3)   Until the Administrative Justice and Tribunals Council first has ten members appointed under paragraph 1(2) of Schedule 7, the reference to that council in sub-paragraph (1)(b) is to be read as a reference to the Council on Tribunals; and if, when the Administrative Justice and Tribunals Council first has ten members so appointed, the person appointed under sub-paragraph (1)(b) is a nominee of the Council on Tribunals, that person ceases to be a member of the Tribunal Procedure Committee at that time.

Lord Chief Justice's appointees

22.—(1)   The Lord Chief Justice of England and Wales must appoint—

(a)   one of the judges of the First-tier Tribunal,

(b)   one of the judges of the Upper Tribunal, and

(c) one person who is a member of the First-tier Tribunal, or is a member of the Upper Tribunal, but is not a judge of the First-tier Tribunal and is not a judge of the Upper Tribunal.

(2) Before making an appointment under sub-paragraph (1), the Lord Chief Justice of England and Wales must consult the Lord Chancellor.

Lord President's appointee

23.—(1) The Lord President of the Court of Session must appoint one person with experience in and knowledge of the Scottish legal system.

(2) Before making an appointment under sub-paragraph (1), the Lord President of the Court of Session must consult the Lord Chancellor.

Persons appointed at request of Senior President of Tribunals

24.—(1) At the request of the Senior President of Tribunals, an appropriate senior judge may appoint a person or persons with experience in and knowledge of—
   (a) a particular issue, or
   (b) a particular subject area in relation to which the First-tier Tribunal or the Upper Tribunal has, or is likely to have, jurisdiction,
for the purpose of assisting the Committee with regard to that issue or subject area.

(2) In sub-paragraph (1) "an appropriate senior judge" means any of—
   (a) the Lord Chief Justice of England and Wales,
   (b) the Lord President of the Court of Session, and
   (c) the Lord Chief Justice of Northern Ireland.

(3) The total number of persons appointed at any time under sub-paragraph (1) must not exceed four.

(4) Before making an appointment under sub-paragraph (1), the person making the appointment must consult the Lord Chancellor.

(5) The terms of appointment of a person appointed under sub-paragraph (1) may (in particular) authorise him to act as a member of the Committee only in relation to matters specified by those terms.

Power to amend paragraphs 20 to 24

25.—(1) The Lord Chancellor may by order—
   (a) amend any of paragraphs 20, 21(1), 22(1), 23(1) and 24(1), and
   (b) make consequential amendments in any other provision of paragraphs 21 to 24 or in paragraph 28(7).

(2) The making of an order under this paragraph—
   (a) requires the concurrence of the Lord Chief Justice of England and Wales,
   (b) if the order amends paragraph 23(1), requires also the concurrence of the Lord President of the Court of Session, and
   (c) if the order amends paragraph 24(1), requires also the concurrence of the Lord President of the Court of Session and the Lord Chief Justice of Northern Ireland.

Committee members' expenses

26. The Lord Chancellor may reimburse members of the Tribunal Procedure Committee their travelling and out-of-pocket expenses.

[1754]

NOTES

Commencement: 19 September 2007.

Rules: as to First-tier Tribunal Rules, see the note to Part 1 of this Schedule at **[1753]**.

PART 3
MAKING OF TRIBUNAL PROCEDURE RULES BY TRIBUNAL PROCEDURE COMMITTEE

Meaning of "Rules" and "the Committee"

27. In the following provisions of this Part of this Schedule—
   "the Committee" means the Tribunal Procedure Committee;
   "Rules" means Tribunal Procedure Rules.

Process for making Rules

28.—(1) Before the Committee makes Rules, the Committee must—

    (a)   consult such persons (including such of the Chamber Presidents) as it considers appropriate,

    (b)   consult the Lord President of the Court of Session if the Rules contain provision relating to proceedings in Scotland, and

    (c)   meet (unless it is inexpedient to do so).

  (2)   Rules made by the Committee must be—

    (a)   signed by a majority of the members of the Committee, and

    (b)   submitted to the Lord Chancellor.

  (3)   The Lord Chancellor may allow or disallow Rules so made.

  (4)   If the Lord Chancellor disallows Rules so made, he must give the Committee written reasons for doing so.

  (5)   Rules so made and allowed—

    (a)   come into force on such day as the Lord Chancellor directs, and

    (b)   are to be contained in a statutory instrument to which the Statutory Instruments Act 1946 (c 36) applies as if the instrument contained rules made by a Minister of the Crown.

  (6)   A statutory instrument containing Rules made by the Committee is subject to annulment in pursuance of a resolution of either House of Parliament.

  (7)   In the case of a member of the Committee appointed under paragraph 24, the terms of his appointment may (in particular) provide that, for the purposes of sub-paragraph (2)(a), he is to count as a member of the Committee only in relation to matters specified in those terms.

Power of Lord Chancellor to require Rules to be made

29.—(1)   This paragraph applies if the Lord Chancellor gives the Committee written notice that he thinks it is expedient for Rules to include provision that would achieve a purpose specified in the notice.

  (2)   The Committee must make such Rules, in accordance with paragraph 28, as it considers necessary to achieve the specified purpose.

  (3)   Those Rules must be made—

    (a)   within such period as may be specified by the Lord Chancellor in the notice, or

    (b)   if no period is so specified, within a reasonable period after the Lord Chancellor gives the notice to the Committee.

[1755]

NOTES

Commencement: 19 September 2007.

Rules: as to First-tier Tribunal Rules, see the note to Part 1 of this Schedule at **[1753]**.

PART 4
POWER TO AMEND LEGISLATION IN CONNECTION WITH TRIBUNAL PROCEDURE RULES

Lord Chancellor's power

30.—(1)   The Lord Chancellor may by order amend, repeal or revoke any enactment to the extent he considers necessary or desirable—

    (a)   in order to facilitate the making of Tribunal Procedure Rules, or

    (b)   in consequence of—

        (i)   section 22,

        (ii)   Part 1 or 3 of this Schedule, or

        (iii)   Tribunal Procedure Rules.

  (2)   In this paragraph "enactment" means any enactment whenever passed or made, including an enactment comprised in subordinate legislation (within the meaning of the Interpretation Act 1978 (c 30)).

[1756]

NOTES

Commencement: 19 September 2007.

Orders: the Tribunals, Courts and Enforcement Act 2007 (Transitional and Consequential Provisions) Order 2008, SI 2008/2683; the Transfer of Tribunal Functions Order 2008, SI 2008/2833.

Rules: as to First-tier Tribunal Rules, see the note to Part 1 of this Schedule at **[1753]**.

PART II
OTHER ACTS

BUILDING SOCIETIES (FUNDING) AND MUTUAL SOCIETIES (TRANSFERS) ACT 2007 (NOTE)

(2007 c 26)

NOTES

This Act amends certain provisions of the Building Societies Act 1986 and provides for the transfer of the whole of the business of subsidiaries of one mutual society to another or the transfers of part of the funds of the transferor or the mutual society of which the transferee is a subsidiary (the holding mutual) to be distributed in consideration of the transfer among the members of the transferor, the holding mutual, or both the transferor and the holding mutual. It also amends certain funding limits in respect of building societies as well as the powers of the Treasury to alter priorities on the dissolution and winding up of a building society.

HM Treasury has issued a consultation paper, *The Building Societies (Funding) and Mutual Societies (Transfers) Act 2007: a consultation (September 2008)* which seeks views on proposals to amend building society law to enable building societies to borrow a greater proportion (up to 75 per cent) of their funding from the wholesale markets (section 1). Also, to amend the law so that, in the event of a building society insolvency, members' shares would rank equally with liabilities to creditors (section 2), and to make it easier for a mutual society to transfer its business to the subsidiary of another mutual society (sections 3 and 4). See: http://www.hm-treasury.gov.uk/consult_fullindex.htm.

[1757]

BANKING (SPECIAL PROVISIONS) ACT 2008

NOTES

As of 1 February 2009, this Act had not been amended.

See the Banking Act 2009, s 262 (at **[1905F]**) which provides that the Treasury may by order repeal this Act. Note: certain statutory instruments were made under this Act after the main body of this Handbook had been typeset. They are included in the Appendix to this work.

(2008 c 2)

ARRANGEMENT OF SECTIONS

Introduction

SCHEDULES

An Act to make provision to enable the Treasury in certain circumstances to make an order relating to the transfer of securities issued by, or of property, rights or liabilities belonging to, an authorised deposit-taker; to make further provision in relation to building societies; and for connected purposes

[21 February 2008]

Introduction

1 Meaning of "authorised UK deposit-taker"

(1)   In this Act "authorised UK deposit-taker" means a UK undertaking that under Part 4 of FSMA 2000 has permission to accept deposits.

(2)   That expression does not, however, include such an undertaking with permission to accept deposits only for the purposes of, or in the course of, an activity other than accepting deposits.

[1758]

NOTES

Commencement: 21 February 2008.

2 Cases where Treasury's powers are exercisable

(1)   The power of the Treasury to make an order under—
   (a)   section 3 (transfer of securities issued by an authorised UK deposit-taker), or
   (b)   section 6 (transfer of property, rights and liabilities of an authorised UK deposit-taker),
is exercisable in relation to an authorised UK deposit-taker if (and only if) it appears to the Treasury to be desirable to make the order for either or both of the following purposes.

This is subject to subsection (7).

(2)   The purposes are—
   (a)   maintaining the stability of the UK financial system in circumstances where the Treasury consider that there would be a serious threat to its stability if the order were not made;
   (b)   protecting the public interest in circumstances where financial assistance has been provided by the Treasury to the deposit-taker for the purpose of maintaining the stability of the UK financial system.

(3)   The reference in subsection (2)(b) to the provision of financial assistance by the Treasury to the deposit-taker includes—
   (a)   any case where the Bank of England has provided financial assistance to the deposit-taker and—
      (i)   the Treasury have assumed a liability in respect of the assistance,
      (ii)   the liability is of a kind of which the Treasury are expected to give relevant notice, and
      (iii)   the Treasury have given relevant notice of the liability;
   (b)   any case where the Chancellor of the Exchequer has announced that the Treasury (whether acting alone or with the Bank of England) would, if necessary, put in place relevant guarantee arrangements in relation to the deposit-taker (as well as any case where any such arrangements have been put in place, whether or not following such an announcement).

(4)   For the purposes of subsection (3) the Treasury give "relevant notice" of a liability if—
   (a)   they lay a Minute before the House of Commons containing information about the liability, or
   (b)   they give written notice containing such information to the person who chairs the House of Commons Committee of Public Accounts and the person who chairs the House of Commons Treasury Committee.

(5)   It is immaterial whether the notice or announcement mentioned in subsection (3) is given or made before or after the passing of this Act.

(6)   In this Act "relevant guarantee arrangements", in relation to any authorised UK deposit-taker, means any guarantee arrangements for protecting some or all of the depositors or other creditors of the deposit-taker.

(7)   Where an order has been made under section 3 or 6 in relation to any authorised UK deposit-taker, subsection (1) does not apply in relation to any subsequent exercise of the power to make an order under either of those sections in relation to that deposit-taker.

(8)   The power of the Treasury to make an order under section 3 or 6 in relation to an authorised UK deposit-taker may not be exercised after the end of the period of one year beginning with the day on which this Act is passed.

(9)   Subsection (8) does not affect the continuation in force or effect of any order made or other thing done by virtue of either of those sections before the end of that period.

(10)   In this section "the UK financial system" means the financial system in the United Kingdom.

(11)   Section 13 of the National Audit Act 1983 (c 44) (interpretation of references to Committee of Public Accounts) applies for the purposes of this section, but as if—

    (a)   the references in that section to that Act were to this Act, and

    (b)   the references in that section to the House of Commons Committee of Public Accounts included the House of Commons Treasury Committee.

[1759]

NOTES

Commencement: 21 February 2008.

Transfer of securities

3 Transfer of securities

(1)   The Treasury may, in relation to all or any securities of a specified description that have been issued by an authorised UK deposit-taker, by order make provision for or in connection with, or in consequence of, the transfer of the securities to any of the following—

    (a)   the Bank of England;

    (b)   a nominee of the Treasury;

    (c)   a company wholly owned by the Bank of England or the Treasury;

    (d)   any body corporate not within paragraph (c).

(2)   Schedule 1 specifies particular kinds of provisions that may be included in an order under this section.

(3)   Where an order providing for the transfer of any securities has been made under this section, the power to make an order under this section may be subsequently exercised so as to make provision in connection with, or in consequence of, the transfer (including provision of a kind specified in Schedule 1) even though the order does not itself provide for the transfer of any securities.

(4)   Where an order under this section or section 6 ("the initial order") has been made in relation to an authorised UK deposit-taker, the power to make an order under this section may be subsequently exercised in relation to that deposit-taker whether or not any transfer of securities provided for by the order is to the person to whom any transfer was made by or under the initial order.

(5)   For the purposes of this section any provision made by an order under this section in relation to any transaction or event taking place while securities transferred by such an order are held by a person within subsection (1)(a), (b) or (c) is to be regarded as provision made in consequence of the transfer.

[1760]

NOTES

Commencement: 21 February 2008.

Orders: the Northern Rock plc Transfer Order 2008, SI 2008/432 at **[4128]**; the Bradford & Bingley plc Transfer of Securities and Property etc Order 2008, SI 2008/2546 at **[4227]**.

4 Extinguishment of subscription rights

(1)   This section applies where the Treasury make, or have made, an order under section 3 providing for the transfer of securities issued by an authorised UK deposit-taker.

(2)   The Treasury may by order make provision for or in connection with, or in consequence of, the extinguishment of rights of any specified description to subscribe for, or otherwise acquire, securities of—

    (a)   the deposit-taker, or

    (b)   any of its subsidiary undertakings.

(3)   Subsection (2) applies whether the rights have been granted by the deposit-taker or otherwise.

(4)   Where an order providing for the extinguishment of any rights has been made under this section, the power to make an order under this section may be subsequently exercised so as to make

provision in connection with, or in consequence of, the extinguishment of those rights even though the order does not itself provide for any rights to be extinguished.

[1761]

NOTES
Commencement: 21 February 2008.
Orders: the Northern Rock plc Transfer Order 2008, SI 2008/432 at **[4128]**; the Bradford & Bingley plc Transfer of Securities and Property etc Order 2008, SI 2008/2546 at **[4227]**.

5 Compensation etc for securities transferred etc

(1) The Treasury must by order—

(a) in relation to an order under section 3 that transfers securities only to the public sector, make a scheme for determining the amount of any compensation payable by the Treasury to persons who held the securities immediately before they were so transferred;

(b) in relation to an order under section 3 that transfers securities only to a private sector body, make provision for determining the amount of any consideration payable by the body to persons who held the securities immediately before they were so transferred;

(c) in relation to an order under section 3 that transfers securities both to the public sector and a private sector body, make provision for determining—

(i) the amount of any compensation payable by the Treasury, and

(ii) the amount of any consideration payable by the private sector body concerned,

to persons who held the securities immediately before they were so transferred.

(2) The Treasury must by order make provision for determining the amount of any compensation payable to persons whose rights are extinguished by virtue of an order under section 4 (a "section 4 order") and—

(a) in any case where the section 4 order is made in consequence of an order under section 3 that transfers securities only to the public sector, the order must provide for any compensation to be payable by the Treasury;

(b) in any case where the section 4 order is made in consequence of an order under section 3 that transfers securities only to a private sector body, the order must provide for any compensation to be payable by the private sector body concerned;

(c) in any case where the section 4 order is made in consequence of an order under section 3 that transfers securities both to the public sector and a private sector body, the order must make provision for determining the amount of any compensation payable by the Treasury or the private sector body concerned (or both).

(3) An order under this section may also make provision for extending provisions of the order, in any specified circumstances, to persons otherwise affected by any provision made in an order under section 3 or 4.

(4) In determining the amount of any compensation payable by the Treasury by virtue of any provision in an order under this section, it must be assumed—

(a) that all financial assistance provided by the Bank of England or the Treasury to the deposit-taker in question has been withdrawn (whether by the making of a demand for repayment or otherwise), and

(b) that no financial assistance would in future be provided by the Bank of England or the Treasury to the deposit-taker in question (apart from ordinary market assistance offered by the Bank of England subject to its usual terms).

(5) For the purposes of subsection (4)—

(a) the references to the provision of financial assistance by the Treasury to the deposit-taker include any case where the Chancellor of the Exchequer announces that the Treasury (whether acting alone or with the Bank of England) would, if necessary, put in place relevant guarantee arrangements in relation to the deposit-taker (as well as any case where any such arrangements are put in place, whether or not following such an announcement);

(b) "ordinary market assistance" means assistance provided as part of the Bank's standing facilities in the sterling money markets or as part of the Bank's open market operations in those markets.

(6) It is immaterial whether the announcement mentioned in subsection (5)(a) is made before or after the passing of this Act.

(7) In this section—

(a) any reference to any transfer of securities to the public sector is a reference to the transfer of any securities to any person within paragraphs (a) to (c) of subsection (1) of section 3;

(b) any reference to any transfer of securities to a private sector body is a reference to the transfer of any securities to any body corporate within paragraph (d) of that subsection.

(8)   An order under subsection (1) or (2) must be made within the period of 3 months beginning with—

  (a)   the day on which the order under section 3 is made (in the case of an order under subsection (1)), or

  (b)   the day on which the order under section 4 is made (in the case of an order under subsection (2)).

(9)   But nothing in subsection (8) prevents the making, at any time after the end of that period, of a second or subsequent order under this section in relation to the order under section 3 or 4.

                                                                                                      [1762]

NOTES
  Commencement: 21 February 2008.
  Orders: the Northern Rock plc Compensation Scheme Order 2008, SI 2008/718 at **[4149]**; the Bradford & Bingley plc Compensation Scheme Order 2008, SI 2008/3249 at **[4376]**.

Transfer of property etc

6   Transfer of property, rights and liabilities

(1)   The Treasury may by order make provision for or in connection with, or in consequence of, the transfer of property, rights and liabilities of an authorised UK deposit-taker to either (or each) of the following—

  (a)   a company wholly owned by the Bank of England or the Treasury;

  (b)   a body corporate not within paragraph (a).

(2)   An order under this section may define the property, rights and liabilities to be transferred in one or more of the following ways—

  (a)   by specifying or describing the property, rights and liabilities in question;

  (b)   by referring to all the property, rights and liabilities comprised in the whole or a specified part of the deposit-taker's business;

  (c)   by identifying the manner in which the property, rights and liabilities to be transferred are to be determined.

(3)   Schedule 2 specifies particular kinds of provisions that may be included in an order under this section.

(4)   Where an order providing for the transfer of any property, rights or liabilities has been made under this section, the power to make an order under this section may be subsequently exercised so as to make provision in connection with, or in consequence of, the transfer (including provision of a kind specified in Schedule 2) even though the order does not itself provide for the transfer of any property, rights or liabilities.

(5)   Where an order under this section or section 3 ("the initial order") has been made in relation to an authorised UK deposit-taker, the power to make an order under this section may be subsequently exercised in relation to that deposit-taker whether or not any transfer of property, rights or liabilities provided for by the order is to the person to whom any transfer was made by or under the initial order.

(6)   A second or subsequent order made under this section in relation to an authorised UK deposit-taker may make provision for any of the property, rights or liabilities transferred by or under a previous order under this section to be transferred back to the deposit-taker.

(7)   The provisions of this section and Schedule 2 apply for the purposes of subsection (6) with any necessary modifications.

(8)   For the purposes of this section any provision made by an order under this section in relation to any transaction or event taking place while property, rights or liabilities transferred by or under such an order are held by a company within subsection (1)(a) is to be regarded as provision made in consequence of the transfer.

                                                                                                      [1763]

NOTES
  Commencement: 21 February 2008.
  Orders: the Heritable Bank plc Transfer of Certain Rights and Liabilities Order 2008, SI 2008/2644 at **[4272]**; the Transfer of Rights and Liabilities to ING Order 2008, SI 2008/2666 at **[4306]**; the Kaupthing Singer & Friedlander Limited Transfer of Certain Rights and Liabilities Order 2008, SI 2008/2674 at **[4339]**.

7   Compensation etc for property etc transferred

(1)   The Treasury must by order make provision—

  (a)   in relation to an order under section 6 providing for the transfer of property, rights or liabilities to a company within subsection (1)(a) of that section, for determining the amount of any compensation payable by the Treasury to the authorised UK deposit-taker concerned;

(b)   in relation to an order under section 6 providing for the transfer of property, rights or liabilities to any other body, for determining the amount of any consideration payable by the transferee to the authorised UK deposit-taker concerned.

(2)   An order under this section may also make provision for extending provisions of the order, in any specified circumstances, to persons otherwise affected by any provision made in an order under section 6.

(3)   In determining the amount of any compensation payable by the Treasury by virtue of any provision in an order under this section, it must be assumed—

(a)   that all financial assistance provided by the Bank of England or the Treasury to the deposit-taker in question has been withdrawn (whether by the making of a demand for repayment or otherwise), and

(b)   that no financial assistance would in future be provided by the Bank of England or the Treasury to the deposit-taker in question (apart from ordinary market assistance offered by the Bank of England subject to its usual terms).

(4)   For the purposes of subsection (3)—

(a)   the references to the provision of financial assistance by the Treasury to the deposit-taker include any case where the Chancellor of the Exchequer announces that the Treasury (whether acting alone or with the Bank of England) would, if necessary, put in place relevant guarantee arrangements in relation to the deposit-taker (as well as any case where any such arrangements are put in place, whether or not following such an announcement);

(b)   "ordinary market assistance" means assistance provided as part of the Bank's standing facilities in the sterling money markets or as part of the Bank's open market operations in those markets.

(5)   It is immaterial whether the announcement mentioned in subsection (4)(a) is made before or after the passing of this Act.

(6)   An order under this section must be made within the period of 3 months beginning with the day on which the order under section 6 is made.

(7)   But nothing in subsection (6) prevents the making, at any time after the end of that period, of a second or subsequent order under this section in relation to the order under section 6.

[1764]

NOTES

Commencement: 21 February 2008.

Orders: the Kaupthing Singer & Friedlander Limited (Determination of Compensation) Order 2008, SI 2008/3250 at **[4383]**; the Heritable Bank plc (Determination of Compensation) Order 2008, SI 2008/3251 at **[4385]**.

Further transfers

8   Further transfers following transfer to public sector

(1)   Subsection (2) applies where any securities issued by an authorised UK deposit-taker have been transferred to a person within section 3(1)(a) to (c) by an order under section 3.

(2)   In such a case the Treasury may by order make provision for or in connection with, or in consequence of, the transfer to a specified person of any of the following—

(a)   any of the securities transferred as mentioned in subsection (1);

(b)   any securities issued by the deposit-taker at any time after the transfer mentioned in that subsection;

(c)   any of the property, rights and liabilities of the deposit-taker;

(d)   any of the property, rights and liabilities of any UK undertaking which is a subsidiary undertaking of the deposit-taker;

(e)   where the securities so transferred were transferred to a company within section 3(1)(c)—

(i)   any securities issued by the company;

(ii)   any property, rights and liabilities of the company.

(3)   Subsection (4) applies where any property, rights or liabilities have been transferred to a company within section 6(1)(a) ("the company") by or under an order under section 6.

(4)   In such a case the Treasury may by order make provision for or in connection with, or in consequence of, the transfer to a specified person of any of the following—

(a)   any property, rights and liabilities of the company;

(b)   any property, rights and liabilities of any UK undertaking which is a subsidiary undertaking of the company;

(c)   any securities issued by the company.

(5)   The following provisions apply in relation to an order under subsection (2) or (4) with any necessary modifications—

(a)   sections 3(2) to (4) and 4, together with Schedule 1, so apply in relation to an order making provision for or in connection with, or in consequence of, the transfer of any securities;

(b)   section 6(2) to (5), together with Schedule 2, so apply in relation to an order making provision for or in connection with, or in consequence of, the transfer of any property, rights or liabilities.

(6)   The Treasury may by order make provision, in relation to any description of order under subsection (2) or (4), for determining the amount of any consideration payable by the transferee in respect of any securities, or any property, rights and liabilities, transferred by or under any such order under that subsection.

(7)   A person to whom anything is transferred by or under an order under section 3 or 6 is not to be regarded as precluded by subsection (2) or (4) from making any contractual or other disposition of, or relating to, anything falling within those subsections.

[1765]

NOTES

Commencement: 21 February 2008.

Orders: the Bradford & Bingley plc Transfer of Securities and Property etc Order 2008, SI 2008/2546 at **[4227]**; the Transfer of Rights and Liabilities to ING Order 2008, SI 2008/2666 at **[4306]**; the Kaupthing Singer & Friedlander Limited Transfer of Certain Rights and Liabilities Order 2008, SI 2008/2674 at **[4339]**.

Supplementary

9 Supplementary provision about compensation schemes etc

(1)   An order under section 5, 7 or 8(6) may in particular make provision—

(a)   for the manner in which any compensation or consideration is to be assessed, including provision as to methods of calculation, valuation dates and matters to be taken into, or left out of, account in making valuations;

(b)   for the assessment to be made by an independent valuer appointed by the Treasury;

(c)   as to the procedure in relation to the assessment of any compensation or consideration, including provision enabling any such valuer to make rules as to that procedure;

(d)   for decisions relating to the assessment of any compensation or consideration to be reconsidered by the person who made those decisions (including any such provision as to procedure as is mentioned in paragraph (c));

(e)   for enabling persons to apply for decisions relating to the assessment of any compensation or consideration to be reviewed by the Financial Services and Markets Tribunal or a tribunal appointed by the Treasury for the purposes of the order;

(f)   as to the powers of a relevant tribunal (that is to say, the Financial Services and Markets Tribunal or a tribunal appointed by the Treasury for the purposes of the order);

(g)   as to the procedure for applying for any review to a relevant tribunal, including provision enabling the tribunal to make rules as to that procedure;

(h)   as to remuneration and expenses of any independent valuer, or of any tribunal, appointed by the Treasury for the purposes of the order;

(i)   as to the appointment of any staff of any such valuer (including provision as to their terms and conditions of employment and as to their pensions, allowances or gratuities).

(2)   The provision that may be made by virtue of subsection (1)(a) includes the making of assumptions as to any matter, including in particular the making of one or more of the following assumptions about the authorised UK deposit-taker in question—

(a)   that it is unable to continue as a going concern;

(b)   that it is in administration;

(c)   that it is being wound up.

(3)   Subsection (1)(a) is subject to sections 5(4) and 7(3), but those subsections do not—

(a)   prevent the inclusion of provision requiring the making of the assumptions mentioned in those subsections in any case where they are not required to be made by either of those subsections; or

(b)   otherwise restrict the provision that may be made by virtue of subsection (1)(a).

(4)   In subsection (1)(a) the reference to valuation dates includes—

(a)   valuation dates falling before the day on which this Act is passed; and

(b)   valuation dates falling before the day on which the relevant event takes place.

(5)   In subsection (1)(e)—

(a)   the reference to persons includes the Treasury; and

(b)   the reference to decisions relating to the assessment of any compensation or consideration includes decisions following any such reconsideration as is mentioned in subsection (1)(d).

(6)   The provision that may be made by virtue of subsection (1)(f)—

(a)   includes provision enabling a relevant tribunal, where satisfied that the decision in question was not a reasonable decision, to send the matter back to the person who made the decision for reconsideration in accordance with such directions (if any) as it considers appropriate; but

(b) does not include provision enabling a relevant tribunal to substitute its own decision for that of the person who made the decision.

(7) The power of any valuer or tribunal to make provision as to procedure by virtue of subsection (1)(c), (d) or (g) includes power to make different provision for different cases or circumstances.

(8) In this section "the relevant event" means the transfer or (as the case may be) extinguishment of rights made by or under the order to which the order mentioned in subsection (1) relates.

[1766]

NOTES
Commencement: 21 February 2008.
See also the Banking Act 2009, s 237 (Compensation: valuer) which provides that without prejudice to the generality of s 12 of this Act, it is declared that the power under this section to make provision for the appointment of a valuer includes power to replicate, or to make provision of a kind that may be made under, s 55(1)–(3) of the 2009 Act (see **[1904L]**).
An order under section 5, 7 or 8(6): see those sections *ante*.

10 Tax consequences

(1) The Treasury may by regulations make provision for or in connection with varying the way in which any relevant tax would, apart from the regulations, have effect in relation to, or in connection with, any of the following—

(a) anything done for the purpose of, in relation to, or by or under or in consequence of, a relevant order;

(b) any securities, or any property, rights or liabilities, which are transferred, extinguished or otherwise affected by any provision made by or under a relevant order;

(c) any securities issued by, or any property, rights or liabilities of, any transferee which have not been transferred by or under a relevant order;

(d) any securities issued by, or any property, rights or liabilities of, any relevant institution which have not been so transferred.

(2) The provision that may be made by the regulations includes provision for or in connection with any of the following—

(a) a tax provision not to apply, or to apply with modifications, in prescribed cases or circumstances;

(b) anything done to have or not to have a specified consequence for the purposes of a tax provision in prescribed cases or circumstances;

(c) any securities, or any property, rights or liabilities, to be treated in a specified way for the purposes of a tax provision in prescribed cases or circumstances (whether or not affected by any provision made by or under a relevant order);

(d) the withdrawal of relief (whether or not granted by virtue of the regulations), and the charging of any relevant tax, in prescribed cases or circumstances;

(e) requiring or enabling the Treasury to determine, or to specify the method to be used for determining, anything (including amounts or values, or times or periods of time) which needs to be determined for the purposes of any tax provision (whether or not modified by the regulations) as it applies in relation to, or in connection with, any of the matters mentioned in subsection (1)(a) to (d).

(3) In this section—

"prescribed" means prescribed by or determined in accordance with regulations under this section;

"relevant institution" means any body in relation to which a relevant order is made;

"relevant order" means an order under section 3, 4, 6 or 8;

"relevant tax" means corporation tax, income tax, capital gains tax, stamp duty, stamp duty reserve tax and stamp duty land tax;

"tax provision" means any enactment relating to any relevant tax;

"transferee" means any person to whom any securities, or any property, rights or liabilities, are transferred by or under a relevant order.

[1767]

NOTES
Commencement: 21 February 2008.

Building societies

11 Modification of legislation applying in relation to building societies

(1) The Treasury may by order make such modifications of the Building Societies Act 1986 (c 53) as they consider appropriate for or in connection with facilitating the provision of relevant financial assistance by the Bank of England to building societies.

(2) In this section "relevant financial assistance" means any financial assistance provided for the purpose of maintaining the stability of the financial system in the United Kingdom.

(3) An order under this section may in particular make provision for or in connection with modifying the operation of any of the following—

(a) sections 5, 6 and 7 of, and Schedule 2 to, the Building Societies Act 1986 (c 53) (establishment, constitution and powers, the lending limit and the funding limit);

(b) any other provision of that Act which might otherwise prevent any relevant financial assistance from being provided by the Bank of England to building societies or affect the amount of any such assistance;

(c) sections 8, 9A and 9B of the Building Societies Act 1986 (restrictions on raising funds and borrowing, on transactions involving derivative instruments etc and on creation of floating charges);

(d) any other provision of that Act which might otherwise prevent building societies from entering into any transaction in connection with the provision of financial assistance by the Bank of England to building societies;

(e) sections 90 and 90A of, and Schedules 15 and 15A to, that Act (application of companies winding up legislation and other companies insolvency legislation to building societies).

(4) An order under this section may in particular disapply (to such extent as is specified) any specified statutory provision.

(5) In this section "building society" means a building society incorporated (or deemed to be incorporated) under the Building Societies Act 1986.

[1768]

NOTES
Commencement: 21 February 2008.
Orders: the Building Societies (Financial Assistance) Order 2008, SI 2008/1427.

General

12 Consequential and supplementary provision

(1) The Treasury may by order make—

(a) such supplementary, incidental or consequential provision, or

(b) such transitory, transitional or saving provision,

as they consider appropriate for the general purposes, or any particular purposes, of this Act or in consequence of any provision made by or under this Act, or for giving full effect to this Act or any such provision.

(2) An order under this section may in particular—

(a) disapply (to such extent as is specified) any specified statutory provision or rule of law;

(b) provide for any specified statutory provision to apply (whether or not it would otherwise apply) with specified modifications;

(c) make provision for or in connection with any of the matters mentioned in subsection (3).

(3) Those matters are—

(a) imposing a moratorium on the commencement or continuation of proceedings or other legal processes of any specified description in relation to any body or property of any such description;

(b) providing exceptions from any provision made in pursuance of paragraph (a), whether framed by reference to—

(i) the leave of the court or the consent of the Treasury or the Bank of England, or

(ii) instruments or transactions of specified descriptions,

or otherwise;

(c) the dissolution of any relevant deposit-taker or of any UK undertaking which is a subsidiary undertaking of any relevant deposit-taker;

(d) exempting directors of any relevant deposit-taker, or of any group undertaking of any relevant deposit-taker, from liability in connection with acts or omissions in relation to the deposit-taker or undertaking;

(e) the payment of any compensation by the Treasury to persons affected by an order under this section.

(4)   An order under this section may, in connection with the payment of any such compensation, make provision for any matter for which provision is or may be made by or under section 5, 7 or 9.

(5)   In this section "relevant deposit-taker" means any authorised UK deposit-taker in relation to which an order is being, or has been, made under section 3 or 6.

[1769]

NOTES
Commencement: 21 February 2008.
Orders: the Northern Rock plc Transfer Order 2008, SI 2008/432 at **[4128]**; the Northern Rock plc Compensation Scheme Order 2008, SI 2008/718 at **[4149]**; the Building Societies (Financial Assistance) Order 2008, SI 2008/1427; the Bradford & Bingley plc Transfer of Securities and Property etc Order 2008, SI 2008/2546 at **[4227]**; the Heritable Bank plc Transfer of Certain Rights and Liabilities Order 2008, SI 2008/2644 at **[4272]**; the Transfer of Rights and Liabilities to ING Order 2008, SI 2008/2666 at **[4306]**; the Kaupthing Singer & Friedlander Limited Transfer of Certain Rights and Liabilities Order 2008, SI 2008/2674 at **[4339]**; the Bradford & Bingley plc Compensation Scheme Order 2008, SI 2008/3249 at **[4376]**.

13   Orders and regulations: general

(1)   Orders and regulations under this Act are to be made by statutory instrument.

(2)   Such orders and regulations—
   (a)   may make different provision for different cases or circumstances;
   (b)   may make such supplementary, incidental, consequential, transitory, transitional or saving provision as the Treasury consider appropriate.

(3)   A statutory instrument which contains an order under section 5, 7, 8(6) or 11 (whether alone or with other provision) may not be made unless a draft of the instrument has been laid before, and approved by a resolution of, each House of Parliament.

(4)   If a statutory instrument to which subsection (3) applies would, apart from this subsection, be treated as a hybrid instrument for the purposes of the Standing Orders of either House of Parliament, it is to proceed in that House as if it were not such an instrument.

(5)   A statutory instrument containing an order under this Act to which subsection (3) does not apply is subject to annulment in pursuance of a resolution of either House of Parliament.

(6)   A statutory instrument containing regulations under section 10 is subject to annulment in pursuance of a resolution of the House of Commons.

(7)   Nothing in any provision of this Act that authorises the making of any order or regulations, or the making of any particular kind of provision by any order or regulations, affects the generality of any other such provision of this Act.

[1770]

NOTES
Commencement: 21 February 2008.

14   Orders and regulations: retrospective provisions

(1)   Subsections (2) and (3) apply to any order made under section 3, 4, 6 or 12 (a "relevant order").

(2)   A relevant order may—
   (a)   provide for any provision made by the order to have retrospective effect as from any appropriate time or any specified later time;
   (b)   make provision for or in connection with, or in consequence of, nullifying the effect of transactions or events taking place after the time in question.

(3)   "Appropriate time", in relation to a relevant order, means—
   (a)   the specified time on the date of a statement published by the Treasury of their intention to make an order that would have the same general effect as the relevant order;
   (b)   the specified time on the date on which any transfer was effected by or under a previous relevant order.

(4)   It is immaterial whether the statement mentioned in subsection (3)(a) is published before or after the passing of this Act.

(5)   Regulations under section 10 may provide for any of their provisions to have retrospective effect as from any time which is not earlier than 3 months before the day on which this Act is passed.

[1771]

NOTES
Commencement: 21 February 2008.

15 Interpretation

(1)   In this Act—

"authorised UK deposit-taker" has the meaning given by section 1;

"body corporate" includes a body incorporated outside the United Kingdom, but does not include the Bank of England;

"company" means a company within the meaning of section 1 of the Companies Act 2006 (c 46);

"director", in relation to a body corporate whose affairs are managed by its members, means a member of the body corporate;

"enactment" includes—

(a)   an enactment comprised in subordinate legislation within the meaning of the Interpretation Act 1978 (c 30),

(b)   an enactment contained in, or in an instrument made under, an Act of the Scottish Parliament, and

(c)   an enactment contained in, or in an instrument made under, Northern Ireland legislation within the meaning of the Interpretation Act 1978;

"financial assistance", in relation to any person, includes—

(a)   assistance provided by way of loan, guarantee or indemnity,

(b)   assistance provided by way of any transaction which equates, in substance, to a transaction for lending money at interest (such as a transaction involving the sale and repurchase of securities or other assets), and

(c)   assistance falling within paragraph (a) or (b) provided indirectly to or otherwise for the benefit of the person (including the provision of assistance within paragraph (a) or (b) to any group undertaking of that person),

whether provided in pursuance of an agreement or otherwise and whether provided before or after the passing of this Act;

"FSMA 2000" means the Financial Services and Markets Act 2000 (c 8);

"group undertaking" has the meaning given by section 1161 of the Companies Act 2006;

"indemnity" includes any undertaking or other arrangement entered into for the purpose of indemnifying any person or for any similar purpose;

"liabilities" includes obligations;

"modifications" includes omissions, additions and alterations, and "modify" has a corresponding meaning;

"pension scheme" means a scheme or other arrangements for the provision of benefits to or in respect of people—

(a)   on retirement,

(b)   on death,

(c)   on having reached a particular age,

(d)   on the onset of any serious ill-health or incapacity, or

(e)   in similar circumstances;

"relevant guarantee arrangements", in relation to any authorised UK deposit-taker, has the meaning given by section 2(6);

"securities" includes—

(a)   shares and stock,

(b)   debentures, including debenture stock, loan stock, bonds, certificates of deposit and other instruments creating or acknowledging indebtedness, and

(c)   warrants or other instruments entitling the holder to subscribe for, or otherwise acquire, securities falling within paragraph (a) or (b),

and see also subsection (2);

"specified", in relation to any order or regulations under this Act, means specified in the order or regulations;

"statutory provision" means any provision made by or under an enactment (whenever passed or made);

"subsidiary undertaking" has the meaning given by section 1162 of the Companies Act 2006 (c 46);

"UK undertaking" means an undertaking which is incorporated in, or formed under the law of any part of, the United Kingdom;

"undertaking" has the meaning given by section 1161 of the Companies Act 2006 (except in the definition of "indemnity");

"wholly owned", in relation to the Bank of England or the Treasury, is to be construed in accordance with subsection (6);

"wholly-owned subsidiary" has the meaning given by section 1159 of the Companies Act 2006.

(2)   In this Act any reference (however expressed) to securities issued by any authorised UK deposit-taker includes a reference to rights granted by the deposit-taker which form part of its own funds for the purposes of Section 1 of Chapter 2 of Title V of the Banking Consolidation Directive (and which would not otherwise be securities by virtue of subsection (1)).

(3)　In subsection (2) "the Banking Consolidation Directive" means Directive 2006/48/EC of the European Parliament and of the Council of 14 June 2006 relating to the taking up and pursuit of the business of credit institutions (recast).

(4)　For the purposes of this Act any undertaking that was an authorised UK deposit-taker immediately before the making of the first order under section 3 or 6 in relation to the undertaking is to be regarded as continuing to be an authorised UK deposit-taker, whether or not it would be one apart from this subsection.

(5)　For the purposes of this Act any reference (however expressed) to an undertaking which is—

(a)　a group undertaking of an authorised UK deposit-taker, or

(b)　a subsidiary undertaking of an authorised UK deposit-taker,

includes, in relation to any time after the making of the first order under section 3 or 6 in relation to the deposit-taker ("the relevant time"), a reference to an undertaking which was a group or subsidiary undertaking of the deposit-taker immediately before the making of that order but is not one at the relevant time.

(6)　For the purposes of this Act—

(a)　a company is to be regarded as wholly owned by the Bank of England at any time if at that time—

(i)　it is a company of which no person other than the Bank or a nominee of the Bank is a member, or

(ii)　it is a wholly-owned subsidiary of a company within sub-paragraph (i); and

(b)　a company is to be regarded as wholly owned by the Treasury at any time if at that time—

(i)　it is a company of which no person other than a nominee of the Treasury is a member, or

(ii)　it is a wholly-owned subsidiary of a company within sub-paragraph (i).

(7)　This subsection makes transitional provision for the purposes of this Act in relation to expressions defined by subsection (1) by reference to provisions of the Companies Act 2006 (c 46) ("the 2006 Act")—

(a)　in relation to any time before the commencement of section 1 of the 2006 Act, "company" means a company within the meaning of the Companies Act 1985 (c 6) ("the 1985 Act") or the Companies (Northern Ireland) Order 1986 (SI 1986/1032 (NI 6)) ("the 1986 Order");

(b)　in relation to any time before the commencement of section 1159 of the 2006 Act, "wholly-owned subsidiary" has the meaning given by section 736 of the 1985 Act or Article 4 of the 1986 Order;

(c)　in relation to any time before the commencement of sections 1161 and 1162 of the 2006 Act, "group undertaking", "subsidiary undertaking" and "undertaking" have the meanings given by sections 258 and 259 of the 1985 Act or Articles 266 and 267 of the 1986 Order.

[1772]

NOTES

Commencement: 21 February 2008.

16　Financial provision

(1)　There is to be paid out of money provided by Parliament—

(a)　any expenditure incurred by the Treasury in connection with the provision of financial assistance to any authorised UK deposit-taker in relation to which an order is made under section 3 or 6;

(b)　any expenditure incurred by the Treasury in connection with the provision of financial assistance to any person to whom any transfer is made under this Act;

(c)　any expenditure incurred by the Treasury in connection with the giving of any relevant indemnity or the putting in place of relevant guarantee arrangements in relation to any particular authorised UK deposit-taker; and

(d)　any other expenditure incurred by the Treasury by virtue of this Act.

(2)　In subsection (1)(c) "relevant indemnity" means any indemnity given to—

(a)　directors of any authorised UK deposit-taker in relation to which an order is made under section 3 or 6,

(b)　directors of any body to which any transfer is made under this Act,

(c)　directors of any body which is a group undertaking of any body to which any transfer is made under this Act,

(d)　the Bank of England in respect of, or in connection with, any financial assistance provided by it to any body within any of paragraphs (a) to (c), or

    (e)   any person appointed by the Treasury as an independent valuer for the purposes of any order made under this Act.

(3)   It is immaterial whether the indemnity or arrangements mentioned in subsection (1) are given or put in place before or after the passing of this Act.

[1773]

NOTES
Commencement: 21 February 2008.

17 Short title, commencement and extent

(1)   This Act may be cited as the Banking (Special Provisions) Act 2008.

(2)   This Act comes into force on the day on which it is passed.

(3)   This Act extends to England and Wales, Scotland and Northern Ireland.

[1774]

NOTES
Commencement: 21 February 2008.

SCHEDULES

SCHEDULE 1
TRANSFER ORDERS UNDER SECTION 3

Section 3

1 Provisions relating to securities transferred: general

(1)   An order under section 3 may make provision—
    (a)   for securities to be transferred free from all trusts, liabilities and incumbrances;
    (b)   for any transfer of securities to take effect despite—
        (i)   the absence of any required consent or concurrence to or with the transfer,
        (ii)   any other restriction relating to the transfer of the securities, or
        (iii)   the absence of the delivery of any instrument representing securities transferable by delivery (a "bearer instrument");
    (c)   for the delivery of any such instruments to a specified person, and the issue to the transferee of instruments representing such securities;
    (d)   for the transferee to be entitled to be entered in any register of securities without the need for delivery of any instrument of transfer;
    (e)   for requiring the person maintaining any such register to register the transferee in the register;
    (f)   for the transferee to be, as from the transfer date, entitled, or subject, to rights, privileges, advantages and liabilities arising from or relating to transferred securities, whether or not the transferee has been so registered or any bearer instrument representing the transferred securities has been delivered to the transferee;
    (g)   for deeming the transferee for any specified purposes to be the holder of the transferred securities at a time when the transferee has yet to be so registered or any such instrument has yet to be so delivered;
    (h)   for securing that rights of holders of securities, and rights relating to securities that are held by persons other than—
        (i)   the holders of the securities, or
        (ii)   the transferee,
    cease to be exercisable by the holders of the securities or (as the case may be) such other persons;
    (i)   for requiring distributions or other relevant amounts payable by the relevant deposit-taker on or after the transfer date to be paid into the Consolidated Fund.

(2)   Sub-paragraph (1)(h) applies to—
    (a)   securities issued by the relevant deposit-taker (whether or not transferred by an order under section 3), or
    (b)   securities issued by any of its group undertakings;
and, in relation to any transferred securities, any references in that provision to holders of securities are to former holders of them.

2 Conversion of form in which securities held etc

(1)   An order under section 3 may make provision—
    (a)   for securities held in one form to be converted, in the specified manner, from that form into another specified form;
    (b)   for converting a specified class of securities into securities of another specified class;

(c)   for matters consequential on any such conversion as is mentioned in paragraph (a) or (b).

(2)   Sub-paragraph (1) applies to securities issued by the relevant deposit-taker, whether or not transferred by an order under section 3.

3 Delisting of securities

(1)   An order under section 3 may make provision for discontinuing the listing of securities issued by the relevant deposit-taker (whether or not the securities have been transferred by such an order).

(2)   In this paragraph "listing" has the meaning given by section 74(5) of FSMA 2000.

4 Alteration of terms of securities or contracts etc

(1)   An order under section 3 may make provision for varying or nullifying the terms, or the effect of terms, of—

(a)   securities issued by the relevant deposit-taker (whether or not transferred by such an order),

(b)   securities issued by any of its group undertakings, or

(c)   other relevant instruments.

(2)   The provision that may be made by virtue of sub-paragraph (1) includes provision—

(a)   for securing that transactions or events of any specified description have or do not have (directly or indirectly) such consequences as are specified, or are to be treated in the specified manner for any specified purposes;

(b)   for discharging persons from further performance of obligations under relevant instruments, and for dealing with the consequences of persons being so discharged.

(3)   In this paragraph "relevant instrument" means any agreement, licence or other instrument to or by which any of the following is a party or bound—

(a)   the relevant deposit-taker,

(b)   any of its group undertakings, or

(c)   any person having a specified connection with the relevant deposit-taker or any of its group undertakings (whether framed by reference to a sale of assets by one to the other, or otherwise).

5 Creation of new rights etc

An order under section 3 may make provision for the creation of new rights and liabilities as between the relevant deposit-taker and any of its group undertakings.

6 Rights etc under pension schemes

(1)   An order under section 3 may make provision—

(a)   as to the consequences of any transfer, by such an order, in relation to any pension scheme;

(b)   in relation to any property, rights and liabilities of any relevant occupational pension scheme.

(2)   Such an order may—

(a)   modify any such rights and liabilities;

(b)   apportion any such rights and liabilities between different persons;

(c)   provide for property of, or accrued rights in, any relevant occupational pension scheme to be transferred to another occupational pension scheme without the consent of any person.

(3)   Provision made in pursuance of this paragraph may be made by means of modifications of a relevant occupational pension scheme or otherwise.

(4)   In this paragraph—

"occupational pension scheme" has the meaning given by section 150(5) of the Finance Act 2004 (c 12);

"relevant occupational pension scheme" means an occupational pension scheme in relation to which—

(a)   the relevant deposit-taker, or

(b)   any of its group undertakings,

is or has been an employer.

7 Provisions relating to directors of relevant deposit-taker etc

(1)   An order under section 3 may make provision enabling the Treasury—

(a)   to remove or appoint directors of the relevant deposit-taker or any of its group undertakings;

(b)   to determine, by agreement with persons so appointed by the Treasury, their remuneration and the other terms and conditions of their service contracts;

(c) to terminate, or vary the terms and conditions of, the service contracts of persons who (however appointed) are directors of the relevant deposit-taker or any of its group undertakings.

(2) An order under section 3 may provide for anything done by the Treasury in accordance with provision made by virtue of sub-paragraph (1) to be treated as done by the relevant deposit-taker.

(3) In this paragraph "service contract" has the meaning given by section 227 of the Companies Act 2006 (c 46).

8 Supplementary provisions

(1) An order under section 3 may make provision—
  (a) for agreements made or other things done by or in relation to former holders of transferred securities to be treated as made or done by or in relation to the transferee;
  (b) for references to such persons in instruments or documents to have effect with specified modifications;
  (c) for anything that relates to anything transferred by an order under section 3, and is in the process of being done by or in relation to any such person immediately before it is transferred, to be continued by or in relation to the transferee.

(2) An order under section 3 may require former holders of transferred securities to provide the transferee with such information and other assistance as is specified.

(3) An order under section 3 may make provision for disputes as to specified matters arising under or by virtue of an order under that section to be determined in the specified manner.

9 Interpretation

(1) In this Schedule—
  "distributions or other relevant amounts" includes dividends, payments of interest, principal or capital, premiums and other payments arising in connection with securities transferred by an order under section 3;
  "former holder", in relation to transferred securities, means a person holding the securities before the transfer date;
  "the relevant deposit-taker", in relation to an order under section 3, means the authorised UK deposit-taker in relation to which the order is made;
  "remuneration" includes any benefit in kind;
  "register of securities" means a register of members or any other register of the holders of securities;
  "specified purposes" include the purposes of any specified statutory provision;
  "the transferee" means the person to whom securities are transferred by an order under section 3;
  "the transfer date" means (subject to sub-paragraph (2)) the date on which such a transfer takes place.

(2) If an order under section 3 provides for any transfer to take place at a particular time on a particular date, then in relation to that transfer, references to the transfer date are to that time on that date.

[1775]

NOTES
Commencement: 21 February 2008.
As to Orders under section 3, see that section *ante*.

SCHEDULE 2
TRANSFER ORDERS UNDER SECTION 6
Section 6

1 Property, rights and liabilities that may be transferred by or under order

The property, rights and liabilities that may be transferred by or under an order under section 6 include—
  (a) property, rights and liabilities that would not be capable of being assigned or otherwise transferred by the relevant deposit-taker;
  (b) property, rights and liabilities acquired or incurred in the period between the making of the order and the transfer date;
  (c) rights and liabilities arising on or after the transfer date in respect of matters occurring before that date;
  (d) rights and liabilities under any pension scheme or under any other arrangement for the payment of pensions, allowances and gratuities;
  (e) property situated outside the United Kingdom and rights and liabilities under the law of a place outside the United Kingdom;
  (f) rights and liabilities under an enactment or Community instrument.

2   Provisions relating to property, rights and liabilities transferred

(1)   An order under section 6 may make provision—

   (a)   for any transfer of any interests or rights to take effect despite the absence of any required consent or concurrence to or with the transfer;

   (b)   for any transfer of any interests or rights to take effect as if—

      (i)   no associated liability existed in respect of any failure to comply with any other requirement, and

      (ii)   there were no associated interference with the interests or rights;

   (c)   for securing that in any specified circumstances—

      (i)   a person is not entitled to terminate, modify, acquire or claim an interest or right (or to treat an interest or right as terminated or modified) until it is transferred by or under the order, and

      (ii)   the entitlement is subsequently either not enforceable or enforceable only to the specified extent;

   (d)   for rights and liabilities—

      (i)   to be transferred so as to be enforceable by or against both the transferee and the transferor, and

      (ii)   where they are so enforceable, to be enforceable in different or modified respects by or against each of those persons;

   (e)   for interests, rights or liabilities of third parties in relation to anything to which an order under section 6 relates to be modified in the specified manner, including provision—

      (i)   for securing that transactions or events of any specified description do or do not have (directly or indirectly) such consequences as are specified, or are to be treated in the specified manner for any specified purposes;

      (ii)   for persons to be discharged from the further performance of contracts and for dealing with the consequences of persons being so discharged;

   (f)   for the manner in which—

      (i)   any property held in trust by the relevant deposit-taker before the transfer date (whether as sole or joint trustee) is to be held on or after that date, and

      (ii)   any powers, provisions and liabilities relating to any such property are to be exercisable or to have effect on or after that date;

   (g)   for excluding from the transfer specified property, rights and liabilities comprised in the relevant deposit-taker's business or a specified part of it;

   (h)   for the creation of rights, liabilities or interests in relation to property, rights or liabilities transferred from or retained by the relevant deposit-taker;

   (i)   for dealing with cases where securities of a subsidiary undertaking are transferred by or under the order;

   (j)   for enabling the relevant deposit-taker and the transferee (in accordance with the order) to agree on any modification of the order, so long as the order could originally have been made with that modification in accordance with the relevant provisions of this Act;

   (k)   for apportioning liabilities in respect of any tax or duty (in the United Kingdom or elsewhere) between the relevant deposit-taker and the transferee.

(2)   In sub-paragraph (1)(b) "associated liability" and "associated interference" mean respectively any liability or interference that would otherwise exist by virtue of any provision (of an enactment or agreement or otherwise) having effect in relation to the terms on which the relevant deposit-taker is entitled, or subject, to anything to which the transfer relates.

(3)   In sub-paragraph (1)(e) "third parties" means persons other than the relevant deposit-taker or the transferee under an order under section 6.

3   Creation of new rights etc

An order under section 6 may make provision for the creation of new rights and liabilities as between the relevant deposit-taker and any of its group undertakings.

4   Rights etc under pension schemes

(1)   An order under section 6 may make provision—

   (a)   as to the consequences of any transfer, by or under such an order, in relation to any pension scheme;

   (b)   in relation to any property, rights and liabilities of any relevant occupational pension scheme.

(2)   Such an order may—

   (a)   modify any such rights and liabilities;

   (b)   apportion any such rights and liabilities between different persons;

   (c)   provide for property of, or accrued rights in, any relevant occupational pension scheme to be transferred to another occupational pension scheme without the consent of any person.

(3)   Provision made in pursuance of this paragraph may be made by means of modifications of a relevant occupational pension scheme or otherwise.

PART II
OTHER ACTS

(4)   In this paragraph—

"occupational pension scheme" has the meaning given by section 150(5) of the Finance Act 2004 (c 12);

"relevant occupational pension scheme" means an occupational pension scheme in relation to which—

    (a)   the relevant deposit-taker, or

    (b)   any of its group undertakings,

is or has been an employer.

5   Foreign property etc

(1)   An order under section 6 may make provision—

  (a)   for requiring or authorising the relevant deposit-taker or the transferee to take any specified steps—

    (i)   for securing the vesting in the transferee under the relevant foreign law of foreign property or foreign rights or liabilities, or

    (ii)   pending any such vesting of such property, rights or liabilities, or

    (iii)   otherwise in relation to such property, rights or liabilities;

  (b)   for the payment by a specified person of expenses incurred in connection with such property, rights or liabilities.

(2)   In this paragraph—

  (a)   "foreign law" means the law of a place outside the United Kingdom; and

  (b)   "foreign property" and "foreign rights or liabilities" mean respectively property and rights and liabilities as respects which an issue arising in any proceedings would be determined (in accordance with the rules of private international law) by reference to foreign law.

6   Authorisations and permissions etc

(1)   An order under section 6 may make provision for securing that, if on the transfer date the transferee satisfies the specified conditions, it is to be treated for the specified period—

  (a)   as an authorised person in relation to any specified regulated activities carried on by the relevant deposit-taker before that date, or

  (b)   as an authorised person who has a Part IV permission granted by the Financial Services Authority to carry on any such activities.

(2)   Where an order makes provision in accordance with sub-paragraph (1)(b), it may provide that any decision by the Financial Services Authority of a specified description is to have the effect of varying or cancelling (to any specified extent) the Part IV permission which the transferee is to be treated as having by virtue of that provision.

(3)   An order under section 6 may make provision—

  (a)   for securing that licences, permissions or approvals—

    (i)   relating to anything transferred by or under the order, and

    (ii)   in force or effective immediately before the transfer date,

  are to continue in force or in effect as from that date;

  (b)   for apportioning (by means of making modifications of the instruments concerned or otherwise) responsibility between the relevant deposit-taker and the transferee as regards compliance with requirements of licences, permissions or approvals.

(4)   In this paragraph "authorised person", "Part IV permission" and "regulated activities" have the same meanings as in FSMA 2000.

7   Supplementary provisions

(1)   An order under section 6 may make provision—

  (a)   for the transferee to be treated for any purpose connected with the transfer as the same person in law as the relevant deposit-taker;

  (b)   for agreements made or other things done by or in relation to any relevant deposit-taker to be treated as made or done by or in relation to the transferee;

  (c)   for references in instruments or documents to the relevant deposit-taker, to any combination of bodies that includes that deposit-taker, or to any officer or employee of that deposit-taker, to have effect with specified modifications;

  (d)   for securing continuity of employment in the case of contracts of employment transferred by or under the order;

  (e)   for anything (including legal proceedings) that relates to anything transferred by or under the order, and is in the process of being done by or in relation to the relevant deposit-taker immediately before it is transferred, to be continued by or in relation to the transferee.

(2)   In sub-paragraph (1)(b), (c) and (e) any reference to the relevant deposit-taker includes a reference to any of its group undertakings.

(3)   An order under section 6 may require the relevant deposit-taker to provide the transferee with such information and other assistance as is specified.

(4)   An order under section 6 may make provision for disputes as to specified matters arising under or by virtue of an order under that section to be determined in the specified manner.

8 Interpretation

(1)   In this Schedule—
"the relevant deposit-taker", in relation to an order under section 6, means the authorised UK deposit-taker in relation to which the order is made;
"specified purposes" include the purposes of any specified statutory provision;
"the transferee" means the person to whom property, rights or liabilities are transferred by or under an order under section 6;
"the transfer date" means (subject to sub-paragraph (2)) the date on which such a transfer takes place.

(2)   If provision is made by or under an order under section 6 for any transfer to take place at a particular time on a particular date, then in relation to that transfer—
(a)   references to the transfer date are to that time on that date; and
(b)   references to things occurring before or on or after the transfer date are references to things occurring before or at or after that time on that date.

(3)   In this Schedule any reference to anything transferred by or under a particular order under section 6 includes a reference to anything transferred by or under any other order under that section.

[1776]

NOTES
Commencement: 21 February 2008.
As to Orders under section 6, see that section *ante*.

DORMANT BANK AND BUILDING SOCIETY ACCOUNTS ACT 2008

(2008 c 31)

NOTES
As of 1 February 2009, this Act had not been amended.

ARRANGEMENT OF SECTIONS

PART 1
TRANSFER OF BALANCES IN DORMANT ACCOUNTS

An Act to make provision for, and in connection with, using money from dormant bank and building society accounts for social or environmental purposes

[26 November 2008]

PART 1
TRANSFER OF BALANCES IN DORMANT ACCOUNTS

The general scheme

1 Transfer of balances to reclaim fund

(1) This section applies where—

    (a) a bank or building society transfers to an authorised reclaim fund the balance of a dormant account that a person ("the customer") holds with it, and

    (b) the reclaim fund consents to the transfer.

(2) After the transfer—

    (a) the customer no longer has any right against the bank or building society to payment of the balance, but

    (b) the customer has against the reclaim fund whatever right to payment of the balance the customer would have against the bank or building society if the transfer had not happened.

(3)   The reference in subsection (1) to an account that a person holds is to be read as including an account held by a deceased individual immediately before his or her death.

In such a case, a reference in subsection (2) to the customer is to be read as a reference to the person to whom the right to payment of the balance has passed.

[1777]

NOTES
  Commencement: to be appointed.

Alternative scheme for smaller institutions

2   Transfer of balances to charities, with proportion to reclaim fund

(1)   This section applies where—
  (a)   a smaller bank or building society transfers to an authorised reclaim fund an agreed proportion of the balance of a dormant account that a person ("the customer") holds with it,
  (b)   the bank or building society transfers the remainder of that balance to one or more charities,
  (c)   the charity, or each of the charities, either—
      (i)   is a charity that the bank or building society considers to have a special connection with it, or
      (ii) undertakes to apply the money in question for the benefit of members of communities that are local to the branches of the bank or building society,
  (d)   the reclaim fund consents to the transfer to it, and
  (e)   the charity, or each of the charities, consents to the transfer to it.

(2)   After the transfers—
  (a)   the customer no longer has any right against the bank or building society to payment of the balance, but
  (b)   the customer has against the reclaim fund whatever right to payment of the balance the customer would have against the bank or building society if the transfers had not happened.

(3)   The reference in subsection (1) to an account that a person holds is to be read as including an account held by a deceased individual immediately before his or her death.

In such a case, a reference in subsection (2) to the customer is to be read as a reference to the person to whom the right to payment of the balance has passed.

(4)   In subsection (1) "agreed proportion" means a proportion agreed between the bank or building society and the reclaim fund.

In agreeing that proportion, the reclaim fund must take account of the need for the fund to have access at any given time to enough money to enable it to meet whatever repayment claims it is prudent to anticipate.

(5)   For the purposes of this section—
  (a)   "repayment claim" means a claim made by virtue of subsection (2)(b);
  (b)   a "smaller" bank or building society is one that meets the assets-limit condition (see section 3);
  (c)   a charity has a "special connection" with a bank if (and only if) the purpose, or any of the main purposes, of the charity is to benefit members of communities that are local to the branches of the bank;
  (d)   a charity has a "special connection" with a building society if (and only if) the purpose, or any of the main purposes, of the charity—
      (i)   is to benefit members of communities that are local to the branches of the building society, or
      (ii) is especially consonant with any particular purposes that the building society has.

(6)   The reference in subsection (5)(d)(ii) to particular purposes does not include the purpose mentioned in section 5(1)(a) of the Building Societies Act 1986 (c 53) (making loans that are secured on residential property and substantially funded by members).

[1778]

NOTES
  Commencement: to be appointed.

3   The assets-limit condition

(1)   A bank or building society meets the assets-limit condition if the aggregate of the amounts shown in its balance sheet as assets on the last day of the latest financial year for which it has prepared accounts is less than £7,000 million.

(2)   In relation to a bank or building society that was a member of a group on the day referred to in subsection (1), that subsection has effect as if the aggregate of the amounts shown in its balance sheet as assets on that day also included the aggregate of the amounts shown in each group member's balance sheet as assets—

    (a)   on that day, or

    (b)   (in the case of a group member whose financial year did not end on that day) on the last day of its latest financial year to end before that day.

(3)   Where a balance sheet for a particular day shows amounts in a currency other than sterling, for the purposes of this section the amounts are to be converted into sterling at the London closing exchange rate for that currency and that day.

(4)   The Treasury may by order amend the figure in subsection (1).

(5)   An order under this section is subject to annulment in pursuance of a resolution of either House of Parliament.

[1779]

NOTES

Commencement: to be appointed.

Shareholding members of building societies

4   Effect of balance transfer on membership rights

(1)   This section applies where a person ("the member") holds a share in a building society represented by an account with the society, and either—

    (a)   a transfer is made to a reclaim fund with the result that section 1 applies in relation to the account, or

    (b)   transfers are made to a reclaim fund and one or more charities with the result that section 2 applies in relation to the account.

(2)   After the transfer or transfers the member is to be treated as having whatever share in the building society the member would have if the transfer or transfers had not happened (and accordingly as having whatever rights, including distribution rights, a holder of that share would have as such).

(3)   In subsection (2) "distribution rights" means rights to any distribution arising as mentioned in section 96 (amalgamation or transfer of engagements) or 100 (transfer of business) of the Building Societies Act 1986.

(4)   Subsection (2) ceases to apply where the balance of the account is paid out following a claim made by virtue of section 1(2)(b) or 2(2)(b).

(5)   But where the balance of the account is paid out following such a claim and, as soon as reasonably practical, the money is—

    (a)   paid back into the account, or

    (b)   paid into another share account with the building society in the member's name,

subsection (2) continues to apply until the account is credited with the money.

(6)   Where, after the transfer or transfers referred to in subsection (1), the building society is succeeded by another building society as a result of an amalgamation or transfer of engagements, a reference in subsection (2) or (5) to the building society is to be read, in relation to any time after the amalgamation or transfer of engagements, as a reference to the successor building society (or to the successor building society of the successor, in relation to any time after a subsequent amalgamation or transfer; and so on).

[1780]

NOTES

Commencement: to be appointed.

Reclaim funds

5   Functions etc of a reclaim fund

(1)   A "reclaim fund" is a company the objects of which are restricted by its articles of association to the following—

    (a)   the meeting of repayment claims;

    (b)   the management of dormant account funds in such a way as to enable the company to meet whatever repayment claims it is prudent to anticipate;

    (c)   the transfer of money to the body or bodies for the time being specified in section 16(1), subject to the need for the company—

        (i)   to have access at any given time to enough money to meet whatever repayment claims it is prudent to anticipate,

        (ii)   to comply with any requirement with regard to its financial resources that is imposed on it by or under any enactment, and

        (iii)   to defray its expenses;

    (d)   objects that are incidental or conducive to, or otherwise connected with, any of the above (including in particular the prudent investment of dormant account funds).

(2)   Schedule 1 makes further provision about provision that must be made in the articles of association of a reclaim fund.

(3)   An alteration by a reclaim fund of its articles of association is ineffective if it would result in—

    (a)   the company ceasing to have objects restricted to those mentioned in subsection (1);

    (b)   the company's articles of association not containing any provision that they are required to make under Schedule 1.

(4)   The Treasury may give a direction to a reclaim fund requiring it—

    (a)   to give effect to any specified object that it has, or

    (b)   to comply with any specified obligation or prohibition imposed on it by a provision that its articles of association are required to make under Schedule 1.

        "Specified" means specified in the direction.

(5)   The Treasury shall lay before Parliament a copy of any direction given under subsection (4).

(6)   In this section—

        "company" has the meaning given by section 1(1) of the Companies Act 2006 (c 46);

        "dormant account funds" means money paid to a reclaim fund by banks and by building societies in respect of dormant accounts;

        "repayment claims" means claims made by virtue of section 1(2)(b) or 2(2)(b).

[1781]

NOTES

Commencement: to be appointed.

Interpretation etc

6   Interpretation of Part 1

In this Part—

        "account" has the meaning given by section 9;

        "authorised", in relation to a reclaim fund, means authorised for the purposes of the Financial Services and Markets Act 2000 (c 8);

        "balance" has the meaning given by section 8;

        "bank" has the meaning given by section 7;

        "building society" means a building society incorporated (or deemed to be incorporated) under the Building Societies Act 1986 (c 53);

        "charity" means a body, or the trustees of a trust, established for charitable purposes only;

        "dormant" has the meaning given by section 10;

        "financial year"—

        (a)   in relation to a company (other than a building society) within the meaning of the Companies Act 2006, has the meaning given in section 390(1) to (3) of that Act;

        (b)   in relation to an undertaking that is not a company within the meaning of that Act (and is not a building society), has the meaning given in section 390(4) of that Act;

        (c)   in relation to a building society, has the meaning given in section 117 of the Building Societies Act 1986;

        "group" means a parent undertaking and its subsidiary undertakings;

        "parent undertaking" and "subsidiary undertaking" have the same meaning as in the Companies Act 2006 (see section 1162 of that Act);

        "reclaim fund" has the meaning given by section 5(1).

[1782]

NOTES

Commencement: to be appointed.

7   "Bank"

(1)   Subject to subsection (4), "bank" means an authorised deposit-taker that has its head office, or one or more branches, in the United Kingdom.

(2)   In subsection (1) "authorised deposit-taker" means—

    (a)   a person who under Part 4 of FSMA 2000 has permission to accept deposits;

    (b)   an EEA firm of the kind mentioned in paragraph 5(b) of Schedule 3 to FSMA 2000 that has permission under paragraph 15 of that Schedule (as a result of qualifying for authorisation under paragraph 12(1) of that Schedule) to accept deposits.

(3)   A reference in subsection (2) to a person or firm with permission to accept deposits does not include a person or firm with permission to do so only for the purposes of, or in the course of, an activity other than accepting deposits.

(4)   "Bank" does not include—
    (a)   a building society;
    (b)   a person who is specified, or is within a class of persons specified, by an order under section 38 of FSMA 2000 (exemption orders);
    (c)   a credit union;
    (d)   a friendly society.

(5)   In this section—
    "credit union" has the same meaning as in the Credit Unions Act 1979 (c 34) (see section 1(1) of that Act);
    "friendly society" has the same meaning as in the Friendly Societies Act 1992 (c 40) (see section 116 of that Act);
    "FSMA 2000" means the Financial Services and Markets Act 2000 (c 8).

[1783]

NOTES
Commencement: to be appointed.

8 "Balance"

(1)   The balance of a person's account at any particular time is the amount owing to the person in respect of the account at that time, after the appropriate adjustments have been made for such things as interest due and fees and charges payable.

(2)   In relation to a time after a transfer has been made as mentioned in section 1(1) or transfers have been made as mentioned in section 2(1), the adjustments referred to in subsection (1) above include those that would fall to be made but for the transfer or transfers.

[1784]

NOTES
Commencement: to be appointed.

9 "Account"

(1)   "Account" means an account that has at all times consisted only of money.

(2)   A reference in this Part to an account held with a bank or building society is to an account provided by the bank or building society as part of its activity of accepting deposits.

(3)   In relation to a building society, "account" includes an account representing shares in the society, other than—
    (a)   preferential shares, or
    (b)   deferred shares within the meaning given in section 119(1) of the Building Societies Act 1986 (c 53).

[1785]

NOTES
Commencement: to be appointed.

10 "Dormant"

(1)   An account is "dormant" at a particular time if—
    (a)   the account has been open throughout the period of 15 years ending at that time, but
    (b)   during that period no transactions have been carried out in relation to the account by or on the instructions of the holder of the account.

(2)   But an account is to be treated as not dormant if at any time during that period—
    (a)   the bank or building society in question was under instructions from the holder of the account not to communicate with that person about the account, or
    (b)   under the terms of the account—
        (i)   withdrawals were prevented, or
        (ii)   there was a penalty or other disincentive for making withdrawals in all circumstances.

(3)   For the purposes of subsection (1) an account is to be treated as remaining open where it is closed otherwise than on the instructions of the holder of the account.

(4)   For the purposes of subsection (2)(b)(i) withdrawals are prevented if they are prevented except as permitted by provision made under subsection (4)(d) of section 3 of the Child Trust Funds Act 2004 (c 6) (requirements to be satisfied by child trust funds).

(5)   The Treasury may by order amend the figure in subsection (1)(a).

(6)   An order under this section may not be made unless a draft of the statutory instrument containing it has been laid before, and approved by a resolution of, each House of Parliament.

[1786]

NOTES
Commencement: to be appointed.

Supplemental

11   Customer's rights preserved on insolvency etc of bank or building society

(1)   Where after a person has acquired a right to payment under section 1(2)(b) or 2(2)(b)—
  (a)   the bank or building society in question is dissolved or wound up, or
  (b)   for any other reason the liability that the bank or building society would have to the person (but for the transfer referred to in section 1(1) or the transfers referred to in section 2(1)) is extinguished or reduced,

the dissolution, winding-up, extinguishment or reduction is to be disregarded for the purposes of section 1(2)(b) or 2(2)(b).

(2)   Subsection (1)(b) does not apply to an extinguishment of liability by prescription under the law of Scotland.

[1787]

NOTES
Commencement: to be appointed.

12   Disclosure of information

No obligation as to secrecy or other restriction on disclosure (however imposed) prevents a bank or building society from giving to an authorised reclaim fund information needed by the fund to enable it to deal with claims made by virtue of section 1(2)(b) or 2(2)(b).

[1788]

NOTES
Commencement: to be appointed.

13   Banks making transfers under section 2: information in directors' reports

(1)   Where—
  (a)   the directors of a company that is a bank are required by section 415(1) of the Companies Act 2006 (c 46) to prepare a report for a particular financial year, and
  (b)   in that year the company made transfers in relation to which section 2 applied,

the report must identify each of the charities concerned and specify the amount transferred to each of them.

(2)   The requirements of subsection (1) are to be treated for the purposes of the Companies Act 2006 (c 46) as requirements of that Act.

[1789]

NOTES
Commencement: to be appointed.

14   Review and report to Parliament

(1)   The Treasury shall carry out a review of—
  (a)   the operation of this Part, and
  (b)   the effectiveness of the efforts made by financial institutions to secure that those entitled to money in inactive accounts are made aware of the fact.

(2)   In reviewing the operation of this Part the Treasury shall in particular consider—
  (a)   how many banks and building societies have transferred balances as mentioned in section 1(1) or 2(1);
  (b)   how much money has been transferred and how promptly;
  (c)   how effective have been the arrangements for meeting claims made by virtue of section 1(2)(b) or 2(2)(b).

But the review shall not consider the activities of a reclaim fund in so far as they are regulated activities for the purposes of the Financial Services and Markets Act 2000 (c 8).

PART II
OTHER ACTS

(3)   The Treasury shall make arrangements to enable anyone with an interest in any aspect of the review to make representations, and shall consider all representations received.

(4)   The Treasury shall set out the results and conclusions of the review in a report and lay it before Parliament.

(5)   The report must be laid within three years from the date when a reclaim fund is first authorised.

[1790]

NOTES
Commencement: to be appointed.

Amendments

15   Amendments to the Financial Services and Markets Act 2000

The Financial Services and Markets Act 2000 is amended as set out in Schedule 2.

[1791]

NOTES
Commencement: to be appointed.

PART 2

DISTRIBUTION OF MONEY UNDER THE GENERAL SCHEME

The distribution system: general

16   Distribution of dormant account money by Big Lottery Fund

(1)   Subject to the provisions of this Part, the Big Lottery Fund shall distribute dormant account money for meeting expenditure that has a social or environmental purpose.

(2)   In this Part "dormant account money" means money transferred to the Big Lottery Fund by a reclaim fund in pursuance of the object mentioned in section 5(1)(c), and also includes the proceeds of such money invested under—
    (a)   paragraph 20(1) of Schedule 4A to the National Lottery etc Act 1993 (c 39), or
    (b)   arrangements made under section 25(1).

(3)   The Fund may make grants or loans, or make or enter into other arrangements, for the purpose of complying with subsection (1).

(4)   A grant or loan may be subject to conditions (which may, in particular, include conditions as to repayment with interest).

(5)   For the purposes of this Part, distributing money for meeting expenditure of a particular description includes distributing money for the purpose of establishing, or contributing to, endowments (including permanent endowments) in connection with expenditure of that description.

(6)   Schedule 3 makes further provision about the functions of the Fund in relation to dormant account money.

[1792]

NOTES
Commencement: to be appointed.

17   Apportionment of dormant account money

(1)   The apportionable income of the Big Lottery Fund in each financial year is to be apportioned as follows and distributed accordingly—
    (a)   a prescribed percentage for meeting expenditure in relation to England;
    (b)   a prescribed percentage for meeting expenditure in relation to Wales;
    (c)   a prescribed percentage for meeting expenditure in relation to Scotland;
    (d)   a prescribed percentage for meeting expenditure in relation to Northern Ireland.

The four percentages must add up to 100%.

(2)   Expenditure within paragraphs (a), (b), (c) and (d) of subsection (1) is referred to in this Part as English expenditure, Welsh expenditure, Scottish expenditure and Northern Ireland expenditure respectively.

(3)   For the purposes of this section, the apportionable income of the Big Lottery Fund for a given financial year is—

$$A - B - C$$

where—
    A is the amount of dormant account money received by the Fund in the year;

B is the amount of the expenses defrayed in the year under subsections (1) and (2) of
section 26;

C is the amount paid in the year under subsection (3)(b) of that section.

(4)   In this section "prescribed" means prescribed by an order made by the Secretary of State.

(5)   Before making an order under this section the Secretary of State shall consult—
(a)   the Welsh Ministers;
(b)   the Scottish Ministers;
(c)   the Department of Finance and Personnel in Northern Ireland;
(d)   the Big Lottery Fund;
(e)   such other persons (if any) as the Secretary of State thinks appropriate.

(6)   An order under this section may not be made unless a draft of the statutory instrument
containing it has been laid before, and approved by a resolution of, each House of Parliament.

[1793]

NOTES
Commencement: to be appointed.

Distribution for England, Wales, Scotland and Northern Ireland

18 Distribution of money for meeting English expenditure

(1)   A distribution of dormant account money for meeting English expenditure must be—
(a)   made for meeting expenditure on or connected with the provision of services, facilities
or opportunities to meet the needs of young people,
(b)   made for meeting expenditure on or connected with—
(i)   the development of individuals' ability to manage their finances, or
(ii)   the improvement of access to personal financial services,

or
(c)   made to a social investment wholesaler.

(2)   In this section—
"social investment wholesaler" means a body that exists to assist or enable other bodies to give
financial or other support to third sector organisations;
"third sector organisation" means an organisation that exists wholly or mainly to provide
benefits for society or the environment.

[1794]

NOTES
Commencement: to be appointed.

---

19 Distribution of money for meeting Welsh expenditure

(1)   The Welsh Ministers may by order made by statutory instrument make provision restricting
the purposes for which, or the kinds of person to which, a distribution of dormant account money for
meeting Welsh expenditure may be made.

(2)   Before making an order under this section the Welsh Ministers shall consult the Big Lottery
Fund and such other persons (if any) as they think appropriate.

(3)   An order under this section may not be made unless a draft of the statutory instrument
containing it has been laid before, and approved by a resolution of, the National Assembly
for Wales.

[1795]

NOTES
Commencement: to be appointed.

---

20 Distribution of money for meeting Scottish expenditure

(1)   The Scottish Ministers may by order made by statutory instrument make provision
restricting the purposes for which, or the kinds of person to which, a distribution of dormant account
money for meeting Scottish expenditure may be made.

(2)   Before making an order under this section the Scottish Ministers shall consult the Big
Lottery Fund and such other persons (if any) as they think appropriate.

(3)   An order under this section may not be made unless a draft of the statutory instrument
containing it has been laid before, and approved by a resolution of, the Scottish Parliament.

[1796]

NOTES
Commencement: to be appointed.

---

21 Distribution of money for meeting Northern Ireland expenditure

(1) The Department of Finance and Personnel in Northern Ireland may by order make provision restricting the purposes for which, or the kinds of person to which, a distribution of dormant account money for meeting Northern Ireland expenditure may be made.

(2) Before making an order under this section the Department of Finance and Personnel shall consult the Big Lottery Fund and such other persons (if any) as the Department thinks appropriate.

(3) The power to make an order under this section is exercisable by statutory rule for the purposes of the Statutory Rules (Northern Ireland) Order 1979 (SI 1979/1573 (NI 12)).

(4) An order under this section may not be made unless a draft of it has been laid before, and approved by a resolution of, the Northern Ireland Assembly.

[1797]

NOTES
Commencement: to be appointed.

Powers of Secretary of State or appropriate national authority

22 Directions to Big Lottery Fund

(1) In exercising any of its functions under this Act the Big Lottery Fund shall comply with any direction given to it under this section.

(2) Subject to subsection (5), the power to give a direction under this section is exercisable by the Secretary of State.

(3) A direction under this section may, in particular—
(a) specify matters to be taken into account in determining the persons to whom the Fund distributes money;
(b) specify purposes for which (or matters to be taken into account in determining the purposes for which) the Fund may or may not distribute money;
(c) relate to the process used to determine what payments to make;
(d) relate to—
    (i) the terms and conditions on which the Fund makes grants or loans, or
    (ii) other arrangements under section 16(3).

(4) A direction under this section may, in particular—
(a) relate to arrangements under section 25;
(b) relate to the management and control of money received by the Fund;
(c) relate to the employment of staff;
(d) relate to the form of accounts or methods and principles for the preparation of accounts;
(e) in so far as it relates to a matter specified in paragraphs (a) to (d)—
    (i) relate to the persons to whom or the terms on which the Fund delegates functions;
    (ii) require the Fund to obtain the Secretary of State's consent before taking action of a specified kind;
    (iii) require the Fund to provide information to the Secretary of State.

(5) A direction under this section may not be given by the Secretary of State in relation to Welsh, Scottish or Northern Ireland expenditure, but—
(a) may be given by the Welsh Ministers in relation to Welsh expenditure;
(b) may be given by the Scottish Ministers in relation to Scottish expenditure;
(c) may be given by the Department of Finance and Personnel in Northern Ireland in relation to Northern Ireland expenditure.

This subsection does not apply to a direction given by virtue only of subsection (4).

(6) A direction under this section may not be inconsistent with—
(a) section 16(1), or
(b) section 18 or an order under section 19, 20 or 21 (whichever is applicable).

(7) Any minister, ministers or department proposing to give a direction under this section must consult the Big Lottery Fund before doing so.

(8) The power of the Fund to appoint staff under paragraph 6 of Schedule 4A to the National Lottery etc Act 1993 (c 39), or to make payments under paragraph 18 of that Schedule (remuneration etc), has effect subject to any directions under subsection (4)(c).

[1798]

NOTES
Commencement: to be appointed.

23 Power to prohibit distribution in certain cases

(1)   The Secretary of State may by order prohibit the Big Lottery Fund from distributing dormant account money to a person specified in the order if the Secretary of State considers that the Fund is able (whether directly or indirectly) to control or materially to influence the policy of that person in carrying on any undertaking or performing any functions.

(2)   Before making an order under this section that—
   (a)   relates to Welsh expenditure, Scottish expenditure or Northern Ireland expenditure, or
   (b)   would otherwise be likely, in the opinion of the Secretary of State, to affect persons in Wales, Scotland or Northern Ireland,
the Secretary of State shall consult the Welsh Ministers, the Scottish Ministers or the Department of Finance and Personnel in Northern Ireland (as appropriate).

(3)   An order under this section is subject to annulment in pursuance of a resolution of either House of Parliament.

(4)   The Secretary of State may require the Fund to provide such information as is needed for the purpose of exercising his or her powers under this section.

[1799]

NOTES
   Commencement: to be appointed.

24 Power to add or remove distributors

(1)   The Secretary of State may by order amend this Act so that functions exercisable by the body or bodies currently specified in section 16(1) are exercisable instead by the body or bodies specified there as a result of the order.

(2)   The Secretary of State may exercise the power conferred by subsection (1) so as to remove from section 16(1) a body that has contravened or failed to comply with a requirement or prohibition imposed on it by or under section 22 or 23.

This is not to be read as limiting subsection (1).

(3)   An order under this section may—
   (a)   make consequential amendments to this Act;
   (b)   make transitional or supplemental provision (including provision amending this Act).

(4)   Where two or more bodies are specified in section 16(1) as a result of an order under this section, the order must provide that any amount transferred by a reclaim fund in pursuance of the object mentioned in section 5(1)(c) is to be apportioned between those bodies in the percentages specified in the order.

(5)   Functions conferred on a body as a result of an order under this section are exercisable notwithstanding anything to the contrary in any enactment or instrument relating to the functions of the body.

(6)   Before making an order under this section the Secretary of State shall consult—
   (a)   the Welsh Ministers;
   (b)   the Scottish Ministers;
   (c)   the Department of Finance and Personnel in Northern Ireland.

(7)   An order under this section may not be made unless a draft of the statutory instrument containing it has been laid before, and approved by a resolution of, each House of Parliament.

[1800]

NOTES
   Commencement: to be appointed.

Supplemental

25 Power of Big Lottery Fund to enter into arrangements

(1)   The Big Lottery Fund may enter into arrangements with a body or person (including a reclaim fund) for money that may be or has been paid to the Big Lottery Fund to be held or invested, on its behalf, by that body or person.

(2)   The Big Lottery Fund may enter into arrangements with a reclaim fund for payments that the Big Lottery Fund is required to make under section 26(3), (6), (8) or (10) to be made on its behalf by the reclaim fund.

[1801]

NOTES
   Commencement: to be appointed.

PART II
OTHER ACTS

26 Expenses

(1)   The Big Lottery Fund may defray out of dormant account money any expenses incurred by it in consequence of this Act.

(2)   Where the Fund makes an appointment under paragraph 5 of Schedule 3 it may defray out of dormant account money any expenses incurred by the appointee in consequence of the appointment.

(3)   At such times as the Secretary of State determines to be appropriate, the Big Lottery Fund shall pay into the Consolidated Fund, out of dormant account money received by it, such amounts as the Secretary of State determines to be appropriate for defraying—
(a)   expenses incurred or to be incurred by the Secretary of State in respect of the giving of directions under section 22 in relation to English expenditure, and
(b)   any other expenses incurred or to be incurred by the Secretary of State under this Act.

(4)   Amounts paid under subsection (3)(a) are to be paid out of money apportioned under section 17 for meeting English expenditure.

(5)   For the purposes of this section, a direction under section 22 is not to be regarded as a direction given in relation to English expenditure if it is given by virtue only of subsection (4) of that section.

(6)   At such times as the Welsh Ministers determine to be appropriate, the Big Lottery Fund shall pay to those ministers, out of money apportioned under section 17 for meeting Welsh expenditure, such amounts as they determine to be appropriate for defraying expenses incurred or to be incurred by them under this Act.

(7)   The power of the Treasury under section 120(3) of the Government of Wales Act 2006 (c 32) to designate descriptions of sums received by the Welsh Ministers (with the result that they become payable to the Secretary of State) is not exercisable in relation to amounts payable to those Ministers under subsection (6) above.

(8)   At such times as the Scottish Ministers determine to be appropriate, the Big Lottery Fund shall pay into the Scottish Consolidated Fund, out of money apportioned under section 17 for meeting Scottish expenditure, such amounts as those ministers determine to be appropriate for defraying expenses incurred or to be incurred by them under this Act.

(9)   The power of the Treasury under section 64(5) of the Scotland Act 1998 (c 46) to designate descriptions of receipts payable into the Scottish Consolidated Fund (with the result that they become payable to the Secretary of State) is not exercisable in relation to amounts payable into that Fund under subsection (8) above.

(10)   At such times as the Department of Finance and Personnel in Northern Ireland determines to be appropriate, the Big Lottery Fund shall pay into the Consolidated Fund of Northern Ireland, out of money apportioned under section 17 for meeting Northern Ireland expenditure, such amounts as that Department determines to be appropriate for defraying expenses incurred or to be incurred by that Department under this Act.

[1802]

NOTES
Commencement: to be appointed.

Interpretation

27   Interpretation of Part 2

(1)   In this Part—
"dormant account money" has the meaning given by section 16(2);
"English expenditure", "Welsh expenditure", "Scottish expenditure" and "Northern Ireland expenditure" have the meaning given by section 17(2);
"financial year" means a period of 12 months ending with 31 March;
"reclaim fund" has the meaning given by section 5(1).

(2)   A reference in this Part to the distribution of money is to be read as including a reference to making or entering into arrangements in accordance with section 16(3), and related expressions are to be read accordingly.

See also section 16(5).

[1803]

NOTES
Commencement: to be appointed.

PART 3
FINAL PROVISIONS

28 Orders

A power of the Treasury or the Secretary of State to make an order under this Act is exercisable by statutory instrument.

[1804]

NOTES
Commencement: 26 November 2008.

29 Directions

(1)   A direction under this Act must be given in writing.

(2)   A direction under this Act may be varied or revoked by a subsequent direction.

[1805]

NOTES
Commencement: 26 November 2008.

30 Extent

This Act extends to England and Wales, Scotland and Northern Ireland.

[1806]

NOTES
Commencement: 26 November 2008.

31 Commencement

(1)   Parts 1 and 2 come into force in accordance with provision made by order of the Treasury.

(2)   An order under this section—
    (a)   may make different provision for different purposes;
    (b)   may make transitional or saving provision.

[1807]

NOTES
Commencement: 26 November 2008.

32 Short title

This Act may be cited as the Dormant Bank and Building Society Accounts Act 2008.

[1808]

NOTES
Commencement: 26 November 2008.

SCHEDULES

SCHEDULE 1
PROVISION TO BE MADE IN ARTICLES OF ASSOCIATION OF RECLAIM FUND
Section 5

Expenses

1.—(1)   The articles of association of a reclaim fund must make provision—
    (a)   allowing it to defray its expenses out of its income, but
    (b)   preventing the defraying of expenses that are unreasonable, or to the extent that they are unreasonable.

(2)   For the purposes of this paragraph "expenses" includes, in particular, the costs of—
    (a)   paying fees or remuneration to any member, officer, employee or other person for services provided to the reclaim fund in connection with the carrying out of its functions;
    (b)   reimbursing any person incurring costs in relation to services provided in connection with the formation of the fund.

PART II
OTHER ACTS

No distribution to members

2. The articles of association of a reclaim fund must make provision preventing a distribution, including a distribution on winding up, of any of its income or assets to its members (except as allowed for by provision made by virtue of paragraph 1).

Publication of information

3.—(1) The articles of association of a reclaim fund must make provision requiring it to publish, as soon as possible after the end of each financial year of the fund—
    (a) its annual accounts and reports for that year (within the meaning given by section 471 of the Companies Act 2006 (c 46));
    (b) the name of each bank and building society that transferred money to the fund in that year and the amount transferred by each one;
    (c) the name of each bank and building society in respect of whose accounts payments were made from the fund in that year following repayment claims and, in relation to each of those banks and building societies, the total of the payments made;
    (d) the total amount transferred in that year to the body or bodies for the time being specified in section 16(1).

  (2) For the purposes of sub-paragraph (1)(c)—
    (a) "repayment claims" means claims made by virtue of section 1(2)(b) or 2(2)(b);
    (b) where an account was previously operated by a bank or building society as part of a business currently carried on by another bank or building society ("the successor"), the account is treated as that of the successor.

[1809]

NOTES
    Commencement: to be appointed.

(Sch 2 inserts the Financial Services and Markets Act 2000, ss 106A, 369A, Sch 2, Pt 1A, Sch 12, Pt 2A, and amends 107, 111, 359, Sch 2, Pt I (see that Act at [1] et seq.)

SCHEDULE 3
FURTHER PROVISION ABOUT THE FUNCTIONS OF THE BIG LOTTERY FUND
Section 16

PART 1
STRATEGIC PLANS

Strategic plans for England

1.—(1) If the Secretary of State instructs it to do so, the Big Lottery Fund shall—
    (a) prepare and adopt a strategic plan for England,
    (b) review and modify any such plan that it has adopted, or
    (c) replace any such plan that it has adopted by preparing and adopting another.

  (2) In this paragraph "strategic plan for England" means a statement containing the Fund's policies for the distribution of dormant account money for meeting English expenditure.

  (3) A strategic plan for England must include—
    (a) a statement of any directions given to the Fund under section 22 by the Secretary of State, other than directions given by virtue only of subsection (4) of that section;
    (b) a statement of the Fund's assessment of the needs in England that the Fund has power to deal with, in whole or in part, by distributing dormant account money;
    (c) a statement of the Fund's priorities in dealing with those needs by the distribution of dormant account money.

  (4) A strategic plan for England must be such as to demonstrate how the Fund is complying with any directions to which sub-paragraph (3)(a) applies.

  (5) Before adopting a strategic plan for England, the Fund shall—
    (a) consult such other bodies as it thinks fit for the purpose of identifying the needs mentioned in sub-paragraph (3)(b) and formulating the policies to be adopted for dealing with those needs;
    (b) prepare a draft of the proposed plan;
    (c) send a copy of the draft to the Secretary of State;
    (d) after consultation with the Secretary of State, make such modifications to the draft as it considers necessary or expedient.

  (6) Where the Fund adopts a strategic plan for England—
    (a) the Fund shall send copies of the document containing the plan to the Secretary of State;
    (b) the Secretary of State shall lay a copy of the document before each House of Parliament.

Strategic plans for Wales

2.—(1)   If the Welsh Ministers instruct it to do so, the Big Lottery Fund shall—
- (a)   prepare and adopt a strategic plan for Wales,
- (b)   review and modify any such plan that it has adopted, or
- (c)   replace any such plan that it has adopted by preparing and adopting another.

(2)   In this paragraph "strategic plan for Wales" means a statement containing the Fund's policies for the distribution of dormant account money for meeting Welsh expenditure.

(3)   A strategic plan for Wales must include—
- (a)   a statement of any directions under section 22 given to the Fund by the Welsh Ministers;
- (b)   a statement of the Fund's assessment of the needs in Wales that the Fund has power to deal with, in whole or in part, by distributing dormant account money;
- (c)   a statement of the Fund's priorities in dealing with those needs by the distribution of dormant account money.

(4)   A strategic plan for Wales must be such as to demonstrate how the Fund is complying with any directions to which sub-paragraph (3)(a) applies.

(5)   Before adopting a strategic plan for Wales, the Fund shall—
- (a)   consult such other bodies as it thinks fit for the purpose of identifying the needs mentioned in sub-paragraph (3)(b) and formulating the policies to be adopted for dealing with those needs;
- (b)   prepare a draft of the proposed plan;
- (c)   send a copy of the draft to the Welsh Ministers;
- (d)   after consultation with the Welsh Ministers, make such modifications to the draft as it considers necessary or expedient.

(6)   Where the Fund adopts a strategic plan for Wales—
- (a)   the Fund shall send copies of the document containing the plan to the Welsh Ministers;
- (b)   the Welsh Ministers shall lay a copy of the document before the National Assembly for Wales.

Strategic plans for Scotland

3.—(1)   If the Scottish Ministers instruct it to do so, the Big Lottery Fund shall—
- (a)   prepare and adopt a strategic plan for Scotland,
- (b)   review and modify any such plan that it has adopted, or
- (c)   replace any such plan that it has adopted by preparing and adopting another.

(2)   In this paragraph "strategic plan for Scotland" means a statement containing the Fund's policies for the distribution of dormant account money for meeting Scottish expenditure.

(3)   A strategic plan for Scotland must include—
- (a)   a statement of any directions under section 22 given to the Fund by the Scottish Ministers;
- (b)   a statement of the Fund's assessment of the needs in Scotland that the Fund has power to deal with, in whole or in part, by distributing dormant account money;
- (c)   a statement of the Fund's priorities in dealing with those needs by the distribution of dormant account money.

(4)   A strategic plan for Scotland must be such as to demonstrate how the Fund is complying with any directions to which sub-paragraph (3)(a) applies.

(5)   Before adopting a strategic plan for Scotland, the Fund shall—
- (a)   consult such other bodies as it thinks fit for the purpose of identifying the needs mentioned in sub-paragraph (3)(b) and formulating the policies to be adopted for dealing with those needs;
- (b)   prepare a draft of the proposed plan;
- (c)   send a copy of the draft to the Scottish Ministers;
- (d)   after consultation with the Scottish Ministers, make such modifications to the draft as it considers necessary or expedient.

(6)   Where the Fund adopts a strategic plan for Scotland—
- (a)   the Fund shall send copies of the document containing the plan to the Scottish Ministers;
- (b)   the Scottish Ministers shall lay a copy of the document before the Scottish Parliament.

Strategic plans for Northern Ireland

4.—(1)   If instructed to do so by the Department of Finance and Personnel in Northern Ireland ("the Department"), the Big Lottery Fund shall—
- (a)   prepare and adopt a strategic plan for Northern Ireland,
- (b)   review and modify any such plan that it has adopted, or
- (c)   replace any such plan that it has adopted by preparing and adopting another.

(2)   In this paragraph "strategic plan for Northern Ireland" means a statement containing the Fund's policies for the distribution of dormant account money for meeting Northern Ireland expenditure.

(3)   A strategic plan for Northern Ireland must include—
  (a)   a statement of any directions under section 22 given to the Fund by the Department;
  (b)   a statement of the Fund's assessment of the needs in Northern Ireland that the Fund has power to deal with, in whole or in part, by distributing dormant account money;
  (c)   a statement of the Fund's priorities in dealing with those needs by the distribution of dormant account money.

(4)   A strategic plan for Northern Ireland must be such as to demonstrate how the Fund is complying with any directions to which sub-paragraph (3)(a) applies.

(5)   Before adopting a strategic plan for Northern Ireland, the Fund shall—
  (a)   consult such other bodies as it thinks fit for the purpose of identifying the needs mentioned in sub-paragraph (3)(b) and formulating the policies to be adopted for dealing with those needs;
  (b)   prepare a draft of the proposed plan;
  (c)   send a copy of the draft to the Department;
  (d)   after consultation with the Department, make such modifications to the draft as it considers necessary or expedient.

(6)   Where the Fund adopts a strategic plan for Northern Ireland—
  (a)   the Fund shall send copies of the document containing the plan to the Department;
  (b)   the Department shall lay a copy of the document before the Northern Ireland Assembly.

[1810]

NOTES
Commencement: to be appointed.

PART 2
DELEGATION ETC

Delegation to other bodies or persons, or to committees

5.—(1)   The Big Lottery Fund may appoint any other body or person to exercise on its behalf any of its dormant account functions—
  (a)   in any particular case, or
  (b)   in cases of any particular description.

(2)   The persons who may be appointed by the Fund under sub-paragraph (1) include a member, employee or committee of the Fund.

(3)   The following bodies may accept an appointment under this paragraph (in addition to any that may do so apart from this sub-paragraph)—
  (a)   a body that distributes money under section 25(1) of the National Lottery etc Act 1993 (c 39);
  (b)   a charity or a charitable, benevolent or philanthropic institution;
  (c)   a body established by or under an enactment;
  (d)   a body established by Royal Charter.

(4)   A body appointed by virtue of sub-paragraph (1) to exercise a function on behalf of the Fund may itself appoint any of its members or employees, or a committee, to exercise the function in its place, but only if—
  (a)   the terms of the appointment so permit, and
  (b)   the body has power apart from this paragraph to appoint a member or (as the case may be) an employee or committee of the body to exercise some or all of its functions.

(5)   The Fund may establish a committee for the purpose of exercising on its behalf any of its dormant account functions.

(6)   A body falling within any paragraph of sub-paragraph (3) may establish a committee for the purpose of exercising on behalf of the Fund any of the Fund's dormant account functions.

(7)   A committee established under sub-paragraph (6)—
  (a)   must consist of or include one or more members, or one or more employees, of the body establishing the committee, but
  (b)   may include persons who are neither members nor employees of that body.

Interpretation of paragraph 5

6.—(1)   In paragraph 5—
  "charity" means a body, or the trustees of a trust, established for charitable purposes only;

"charitable, benevolent or philanthropic institution" means a body, or the trustees of a trust, that is established—
  (a)   for charitable purposes (whether or not those purposes are charitable within the meaning of any rule of law),
  (b)   for benevolent purposes, or
  (c)   for philanthropic purposes,
and is not a charity;
"dormant account functions" means functions relating to, or connected with, the distribution of dormant account money (including the function of making decisions as to the persons to whom distributions are to be made).

(2)   For the purposes of paragraph 5—
  (a)   the trustees of a trust are to be regarded as a body;
  (b)   a reference to a member of a body, in the case of a body of trustees, is to be read as a reference to any of the trustees.

(3)   A reference in paragraph 5 to a member of a body includes the chairman or deputy chairman of the body (or the holder of any corresponding office in relation to it).

Provision supplementing paragraph 5
7.—(1)   The Big Lottery Fund may make payments in respect of expenditure (which may include expenditure of a capital nature) of a body or person to whom it delegates a function under paragraph 5(1).

(2)   Paragraph 5(5) is not to be read as preventing the Fund from—
  (a)   establishing a committee otherwise than in accordance with that provision, or
  (b)   authorising a committee (whether or not established in accordance with that provision) to exercise a function of the Fund.

(3)   A power conferred on a body by paragraph 5 is so conferred—
  (a)   to the extent that the body would not have the power apart from that paragraph, and
  (b)   notwithstanding anything to the contrary in any enactment or instrument relating to the functions of the body.

New functions for existing devolved expenditure committees
8.—(1)   The functions of the committee established under paragraph 7(1)(a) of Schedule 4A to the National Lottery etc Act 1993 (c 39) are to include exercising the functions of the Big Lottery Fund under this Act in relation to English expenditure.

(2)   The functions of the committee established under paragraph 7(1)(b) of that Schedule are to include exercising the functions of the Fund under this Act in relation to Welsh expenditure.

(3)   The functions of the committee established under paragraph 7(1)(c) of that Schedule are to include exercising the functions of the Fund under this Act in relation to Scottish expenditure.

(4)   The functions of the committee established under paragraph 7(1)(d) of that Schedule are to include exercising the functions of the Fund under this Act in relation to Northern Ireland expenditure.

[1811]

NOTES
Commencement: to be appointed.

PART 3
REPORTS AND ACCOUNTS

Annual reports
9.—(1)   As soon as possible after the end of every financial year, the Big Lottery Fund shall prepare a report on the exercise during that year of its functions under this Act.

(2)   The report shall set out any directions given to the Fund under section 22 that had effect during the financial year to which the report relates.

(3)   The report shall set out the Fund's policy and practice in relation to the principle that dormant account money should be used to fund projects, or aspects of projects, for which funds would be unlikely to be made available by—
  (a)   a Government department,
  (b)   the Welsh Ministers,
  (c)   the Scottish Ministers, or
  (d)   a Northern Ireland department.

(4)   Every report under this paragraph shall be—

(a) given by the Fund to the Secretary of State and laid by him or her before Parliament;
(b) given by the Fund to the Welsh Ministers and laid by them before the National Assembly for Wales;
(c) given by the Fund to the Scottish Ministers and laid by them before the Scottish Parliament;
(d) given by the Fund to the Department of Finance and Personnel in Northern Ireland and laid by that Department before the Northern Ireland Assembly.

Accounts

10.—(1) The Big Lottery Fund shall—
  (a) keep proper accounting records relating to the exercise of its functions under this Act, and
  (b) prepare in respect of each financial year a statement of accounts relating to the exercise of those functions.

(2) The Fund shall send a copy of a statement under sub-paragraph (1)(b)—
  (a) to the Secretary of State;
  (b) to the Welsh Ministers;
  (c) to the Scottish Ministers;
  (d) to the Department of Finance and Personnel in Northern Ireland;
  (e) to the Comptroller and Auditor General.

(3) A copy of a statement must be sent under sub-paragraph (2) within such period, beginning with the end of the financial year to which the statement relates, as the Secretary of State may direct.

(4) The Comptroller and Auditor General shall—
  (a) examine, certify and report on a statement received under this paragraph;
  (b) lay a copy of the statement and the report on it before Parliament, before the National Assembly for Wales, before the Scottish Parliament and before the Northern Ireland Assembly.

11. (*Amends the National Lottery etc Act 1993, Sch 4A* (*outside the scope of this work*).)

[1812]

NOTES

Commencement: to be appointed.

PART 4
MISCELLANEOUS POWERS

Power to solicit applications

12.—(1) The Big Lottery Fund has power to solicit applications from other bodies or persons for dormant account money.

(2) In determining whether a decision of the Fund concerning its distribution of dormant account money was unlawful, it is immaterial whether or not the Fund, or any person acting on its behalf, solicited an application from a body or person for such money.

Power to consult

13. In determining how to distribute dormant account money the Big Lottery Fund may—
  (a) consult any person;
  (b) take account of opinions expressed to it or information submitted to it.

Power to publish information etc

14.—(1) The Big Lottery Fund may make or participate in arrangements for—
  (a) publishing information relating to the effect of a provision of this Act;
  (b) publishing information relating to the distribution of dormant account money or the expenditure of dormant account money that has been distributed;
  (c) encouraging participation in activities relating to the distribution of dormant account money.

(2) The reference in section 25E of the National Lottery etc Act 1993 (distribution of funds: publicity) to a body which distributes money under section 25(1) of that Act is to be read as including the Big Lottery Fund in its capacity as distributor of dormant account money.

Power to give advice

15. The Big Lottery Fund may give advice about—
  (a) the distribution of dormant account money;

(b)   inviting, making or considering applications for grants and loans out of dormant account money;

(c)   the use of dormant account money that has been distributed.

[1813]

NOTES

Commencement: to be appointed.

COUNTER-TERRORISM ACT 2008

(2008 c 28)

NOTES

As of 1 February 2009, this Act as reproduced here had not been amended.

An Act to confer further powers to gather and share information for counter-terrorism and other purposes; to make further provision about the detention and questioning of terrorist suspects and the prosecution and punishment of terrorist offences; to impose notification requirements on persons convicted of such offences; to confer further powers to act against terrorist financing, money laundering and certain other activities; to provide for review of certain Treasury decisions and about evidence in, and other matters connected with, review proceedings; to amend the law relating to inquiries; to amend the definition of "terrorism"; to amend the enactments relating to terrorist offences, control orders and the forfeiture of terrorist cash; to provide for recovering the costs of policing at certain gas facilities; to amend provisions about the appointment of special advocates in Northern Ireland; and for connected purposes

[26 November 2008]

NOTES

Only Schedule 7 to this Act is reproduced here although the amendments made by this Act to other enactments (the Anti-terrorism, Crime and Security Act 2001, the Regulation of Investigatory Powers Act 2000, and the Terrorism Act 2000) have been taken in at the appropriate place. Other provisions of this Act are not annotated. Schedule 7 is introduced by s 62 of this Act which merely provides that "Schedule 7 makes provision conferring powers on the Treasury to act against terrorist financing, money laundering and certain other activities". By virtue of s 100(2) of this Act, Sch 7 comes into force on 27 November 2008, and by virtue of s 101 it applies to the whole of the UK.

SCHEDULE 7
TERRORIST FINANCING AND MONEY LAUNDERING

Section 62

NOTES

As to the right of any person affected by a decision of the Treasury under this Schedule (except para 8 or 28(6)) to apply to the High Court (or, in Scotland, the Court of Session) to set aside that decision, see s 63 et seq of the 2008 Act.

PART 1
CONDITIONS FOR GIVING A DIRECTION

Conditions for giving a direction

1.—(1)   The Treasury may give a direction under this Schedule if one or more of the following conditions is met in relation to a country.

(2)   The first condition is that the Financial Action Task Force has advised that measures should be taken in relation to the country because of the risk of terrorist financing or money laundering activities being carried on—

(a)   in the country,

(b)   by the government of the country, or

(c)   by persons resident or incorporated in the country.

(3)   The second condition is that the Treasury reasonably believe that there is a risk that terrorist financing or money laundering activities are being carried on—

(a)   in the country,

(b)   by the government of the country, or

(c)   by persons resident or incorporated in the country,

and that this poses a significant risk to the national interests of the United Kingdom.

(4) The third condition is that the Treasury reasonably believe that—
  (a) the development or production of nuclear, radiological, biological or chemical weapons in the country, or
  (b) the doing in the country of anything that facilitates the development or production of any such weapons,
poses a significant risk to the national interests of the United Kingdom.

(5) The power to give a direction is not exercisable in relation to an EEA state.

Main definitions

2.—(1) "Terrorist financing" means—
  (a) the use of funds, or the making available of funds, for the purposes of terrorism, or
  (b) the acquisition, possession, concealment, conversion or transfer of funds that are (directly or indirectly) to be used or made available for those purposes.

(2) "Money laundering" means an act which falls within section 340(11) of the Proceeds of Crime Act 2002 (c 29).

(3) "Nuclear weapon" includes a nuclear explosive device that is not intended for use as a weapon.

(4) "Radiological weapon" means a device designed to cause destruction, damage or injury by means of the radiation produced by the decay of radioactive material.

(5) "Chemical weapon" means a chemical weapon as defined by section 1(1) of the Chemical Weapons Act 1996 (c 6), other than one whose intended use is only for permitted purposes (as defined by section 1(3) of that Act).

(6) "Biological weapon" means anything within section 1(1)(a) or (b) of the Biological Weapons Act 1974 (c 6).

[1814]

NOTES
Commencement: 27 November 2008.

PART 2
PERSONS TO WHOM A DIRECTION MAY BE GIVEN

Persons to whom a direction may be given

3.—(1) A direction under this Schedule may be given to—
  (a) a particular person operating in the financial sector,
  (b) any description of persons operating in that sector, or
  (c) all persons operating in that sector.

(2) In this Schedule "relevant person", in relation to a direction, means any of the persons to whom the direction is given.

(3) A direction may make different provision in relation to different descriptions of relevant person.

Persons operating in the financial sector

4.—(1) Any reference in this Schedule to a person operating in the financial sector is to a credit or financial institution that—
  (a) is a United Kingdom person, or
  (b) is acting in the course of a business carried on by it in the United Kingdom.

(2) This is subject to the exceptions in paragraph 6.

Meaning of "credit institution" and "financial institution"

5.—(1) "Credit institution" means—
  (a) a credit institution as defined in Article 4(1)(a) of the banking consolidation directive, or
  (b) a branch (within the meaning of Article 4(3) of that directive) located in an EEA state of—
    (i) an institution within sub-paragraph (a), or
    (ii) an equivalent institution whose head office is located in a non-EEA state,
when it accepts deposits or other repayable funds from the public or grants credits for its own account (within the meaning of the banking consolidation directive).

(2) "Financial institution" means—
  (a) an undertaking, including a money service business, when it carries out one or more of the activities listed in points 2 to 12 and 14 of Annex 1 to the banking consolidation directive, other than—

     (i)   a credit institution;

     (ii)   an undertaking whose only listed activity is trading for own account in one or more of the products listed in point 7 of Annex 1 to the banking consolidation directive where the undertaking does not have a customer,

and for this purpose "customer" means a person who is not a member of the same group as the undertaking;

    (b)   an insurance company duly authorised in accordance with the life assurance consolidation directive, when it carries out activities covered by that directive;

    (c)   a person whose regular occupation or business is the provision to other persons of an investment service or the performance of an investment activity on a professional basis, when providing or performing investment services or activities (within the meaning of the markets in financial instruments directive), other than a person falling within Article 2 of that directive;

    (d)   a collective investment undertaking, when marketing or otherwise offering its units or shares;

    (e)   an insurance intermediary as defined in Article 2(5) of Directive 2002/92/EC of the European Parliament and of the Council of 9th December 2002 on insurance mediation (other than a tied insurance intermediary as mentioned in Article 2(7) of that Directive), when it acts in respect of contracts of long-term insurance within the meaning given by article 3(1) of, and Part II of Schedule 1 to, the Financial Services and Markets Act 2000 (Regulated Activities) Order 2001 (SI 2001/544);

    (f)   a branch located in an EEA state of—

       (i)   a person referred to in any of paragraphs (a) to (e), or

       (ii)   a person equivalent to a person within any of those paragraphs whose head office is located in a non-EEA state,

when carrying out any activity mentioned in that paragraph;

    (g)   an insurance company (as defined by section 1165(3) of the Companies Act 2006 (c 46));

    (h)   the National Savings Bank;

    (i)   the Director of Savings, when money is raised under the auspices of the Director under the National Loans Act 1968 (c 13).

Exceptions

6.—(1)   For the purposes of this Schedule the following are not regarded as persons operating in the financial sector when carrying out any of the following activities—

    (a)   a society registered under the Industrial and Provident Societies Act 1965 (c 12), when it—

       (i)   issues withdrawable share capital within the limit set by section 6 of that Act (maximum shareholding in society); or

       (ii)   accepts deposits from the public within the limit set by section 7(3) of that Act (carrying on of banking by societies);

    (b)   a society registered under the Industrial and Provident Societies Act (Northern Ireland) 1969 (c 24 (NI)), when it—

       (i)   issues withdrawable share capital within the limit set by section 6 of that Act (maximum shareholding in society); or

       (ii)   accepts deposits from the public within the limit set by section 7(3) of that Act (carrying on of banking by societies);

    (c)   a person within any of paragraphs 1 to 23 or 25 to 51 of the Schedule to the Financial Services and Markets Act 2000 (Exemption) Order 2001 (SI 2001/1201), when carrying out an activity in respect of which the person is exempt;

    (d)   a person who was an exempted person for the purposes of section 45 of the Financial Services Act 1986 (c 60) (miscellaneous exemptions) immediately before its repeal, when exercising the functions specified in that section.

    (2)   A person who falls within the definition of "credit institution" or "financial institution" solely as a result of engaging in financial activity on an occasional or very limited basis is not regarded for the purposes of this Schedule as operating in the financial sector.

    (3)   For the purposes of sub-paragraph (2) a person is regarded as engaging in a financial activity on an occasional or very limited basis if—

    (a)   the person's total annual turnover in respect of the financial activity does not exceed £64,000,

    (b)   the financial activity is limited in relation to any customer to no more than one transaction exceeding 1,000 euro (whether the transaction is carried out in a single operation or a series of operations which appear to be linked),

    (c)   the financial activity does not exceed 5% of the person's total annual turnover,

    (d)   the financial activity is ancillary and directly related to the person's main activity,

    (e)   the financial activity is not the transmission or remittance of money (or any representation of monetary value) by any means,

(f)   the person's main activity is not that of a credit or financial institution, and
(g)   the financial activity is provided only to customers of the person's main activity.

Interpretation of this Part

7.——   In this Part of this Schedule—

"the banking consolidation directive" means Directive 2006/48/EC of the European Parliament and of the Council of 14th June 2006 relating to the taking up and pursuit of the business of credit institutions;

"the life assurance consolidation directive" means Directive 2002/83/EC of the European Parliament and of the Council of 5th November 2002 concerning life assurance;

"the markets in financial instruments directive" means Directive 2004/39/EC of the European Parliament and of the Council of 12th April 2004 on markets in financial instruments.

Power to amend

8.—(1)   The Treasury may by order amend paragraphs 4 to 7.

(2)   Any such order is subject to affirmative resolution procedure.

[1815]

NOTES

Commencement: 27 November 2008.

PART 3
REQUIREMENTS THAT MAY BE IMPOSED BY A DIRECTION

Requirements that may be imposed by a direction

9.—(1)   A direction under this Schedule may impose requirements in relation to transactions or business relationships with—
(a)   a person carrying on business in the country;
(b)   the government of the country;
(c)   a person resident or incorporated in the country.

(2)   The direction may impose requirements in relation to—
(a)   a particular person within sub-paragraph (1),
(b)   any description of persons within that sub-paragraph, or
(c)   all persons within that sub-paragraph.

(3)   In this Schedule "designated person", in relation to a direction, means any of the persons in relation to whom the direction is given.

(4)   The kinds of requirement that may be imposed by a direction under this Schedule are specified in—

paragraph 10 (customer due diligence);
paragraph 11 (ongoing monitoring);
paragraph 12 (systematic reporting);
paragraph 13 (limiting or ceasing business).

(5)   A direction may make different provision—
(a)   in relation to different descriptions of designated person, and
(b)   in relation to different descriptions of transaction or business relationship.

(6)   The requirements imposed by a direction must be proportionate having regard to the advice mentioned in paragraph 1(2) or, as the case may be, the risk mentioned in paragraph 1(3) or (4) to the national interests of the United Kingdom.

Customer due diligence

10.—(1)   A direction may require a relevant person to undertake enhanced customer due diligence measures—
(a)   before entering into a transaction or business relationship with a designated person, and
(b)   during a business relationship with such a person.

(2)   The direction may do either or both of the following—
(a)   impose a general obligation to undertake enhanced customer due diligence measures;
(b)   require a relevant person to undertake specific measures identified or described in the direction.

(3)   "Customer due diligence measures" means measures to—
(a)   establish the identity of the designated person,
(b)   obtain information about—
(i)   the designated person and their business, and

     (ii)   the source of their funds, and

(c)   assess the risk of the designated person being involved in relevant activities.

(4) In sub-paragraph (3)(c) "relevant activities" means—
   (a)   terrorist financing;
   (b)   money laundering; or
   (c)   the development or production of nuclear, radiological, biological or chemical weapons or the facilitation of that development or production.

(5) A direction may not impose requirements of a kind mentioned in this paragraph on a person who is regarded as operating in the financial sector by virtue only of paragraph 5(2)(g) (certain insurance companies).

Ongoing monitoring

11.—(1) A direction may require a relevant person to undertake enhanced ongoing monitoring of any business relationship with a designated person.

(2) The direction may do either or both of the following—
   (a)   impose a general obligation to undertake enhanced ongoing monitoring;
   (b)   require a relevant person to undertake specific measures identified or described in the direction.

(3) "Ongoing monitoring" of a business relationship means—
   (a)   keeping up to date information and documents obtained for the purposes of customer due diligence measures, and
   (b)   scrutinising transactions undertaken during the course of the relationship (and, where appropriate, the source of funds for those transactions) to ascertain whether the transactions are consistent with the relevant person's knowledge of the designated person and their business.

(4) A direction may not impose requirements of a kind mentioned in this paragraph on a person who is regarded as operating in the financial sector by virtue only of paragraph 5(2)(g) (certain insurance companies).

Systematic reporting

12.—(1) A direction may require a relevant person to provide such information and documents as may be specified in the direction relating to transactions and business relationships with designated persons.

(2) A direction imposing such a requirement must specify how the direction is to be complied with, including—
   (a)   the person to whom the information and documents are to be provided, and
   (b)   the period within which, or intervals at which, information and documents are to be provided.

(3) The power conferred by this paragraph is not exercisable in relation to information or documents in respect of which a claim to legal professional privilege (in Scotland, to confidentiality of communications) could be maintained in legal proceedings.

(4) The exercise of the power conferred by this paragraph and the provision of information under it is not otherwise subject to any restriction on the disclosure of information, whether imposed by statute or otherwise.

Limiting or ceasing business

13.— A direction may require a relevant person not to enter into or continue to participate in—
   (a)   a specified transaction or business relationship with a designated person,
   (b)   a specified description of transactions or business relationships with a designated person, or
   (c)   any transaction or business relationship with a designated person.

[1816]

NOTES
Commencement: 27 November 2008.

PART 4
PROCEDURAL PROVISIONS AND LICENSING

General directions to be given by order

14.—(1) A direction given to—
   (a)   a description of persons operating in the financial sector, or

(b)   all persons operating in that sector,

must be contained in an order made by the Treasury.

(2)   If the order contains requirements of a kind mentioned in paragraph 13 (limiting or ceasing business)—

    (a)   it must be laid before Parliament after being made, and

    (b)   if not approved by a resolution of each House of Parliament before the end of 28 days beginning with the day on which it is made, it ceases to have effect at the end of that period.

In calculating the period of 28 days, no account is to be taken of any time during which Parliament is dissolved or prorogued or during which both Houses are adjourned for more than 4 days.

(3)   An order's ceasing to have effect in accordance with sub-paragraph (2) does not affect anything done under the order.

(4)   An order to which sub-paragraph (2) does not apply is subject to negative resolution procedure.

(5)   If apart from this sub-paragraph an order under this paragraph would be treated for the purposes of the standing orders of either House of Parliament as a hybrid instrument, it is to proceed in that House as if it were not such an instrument.

Specific directions: notification and duration of directions

15.—(1)   This paragraph applies in relation to a direction given to a particular person.

(2)   The Treasury must give notice of the direction to the person.

(3)   The direction (if not previously revoked and whether or not varied) ceases to have effect at the end of the period of one year beginning with the day on which the direction is given.

This is without prejudice to the giving of a further direction.

(4)   The Treasury may vary or revoke the direction at any time.

(5)   Where the direction is varied or ceases to have effect (whether on revocation or otherwise), the Treasury must give notice of that fact to the person.

General directions: publication and duration of directions

16.—(1)   This paragraph applies to an order containing directions under paragraph 14 (general directions given by order).

(2)   The Treasury must take such steps as they consider appropriate to publicise the making of the order.

(3)   An order—

    (a)   revoking the order, or

    (b)   varying the order so as to make its provisions less onerous,

is subject to negative resolution procedure.

(4)   The order (if not previously revoked and whether or not varied) ceases to have effect at the end of the period of one year beginning with the day on which it was made.

This is without prejudice to the making of a further order.

(5)   Where the order is varied or ceases to have effect (whether on revocation or otherwise), the Treasury must take such steps as they consider appropriate to publicise that fact.

Directions limiting or ceasing business: exemption by licence

17.—(1)   The following provisions apply where a direction contains requirements of a kind mentioned in paragraph 13 (limiting or ceasing business).

(2)   The Treasury may grant a licence to exempt acts specified in the licence from those requirements.

(3)   A licence may be—

    (a)   general or granted to a description of persons or to a particular person;

    (b)   subject to conditions;

    (c)   of indefinite duration or subject to an expiry date.

(4)   The Treasury may vary or revoke a licence at any time.

(5)   On the grant, variation or revocation of a licence, the Treasury must—

    (a)   in the case of a licence granted to a particular person, give notice of the grant, variation or revocation to that person;

(b)   in the case of a general licence or a licence granted to a description of persons, take such steps as the Treasury consider appropriate to publicise the grant, variation or revocation of the licence.

[1817]

NOTES
Commencement: 27 November 2008.

PART 5
ENFORCEMENT: INFORMATION POWERS

Enforcement authorities and officers

18.—(1) In this Schedule "enforcement authority" means—
  (a) the Financial Services Authority ("the FSA"),
  (b) the Commissioners for Her Majesty's Revenue and Customs ("HMRC"),
  (c) the Office of Fair Trading ("the OFT"), or
  (d) in relation to credit unions in Northern Ireland, the Department of Enterprise, Trade and Investment in Northern Ireland ("DETINI").

(2) In this Part of this Schedule "enforcement officer" means—
  (a) an officer of the FSA, including a member of the staff or an agent of the FSA,
  (b) an officer of Revenue and Customs,
  (c) an officer of the OFT,
  (d) an officer of DETINI acting for the purposes of its functions under this Schedule in relation to credit unions in Northern Ireland, or
  (e) a local enforcement officer.

(3) A "local enforcement officer" means—
  (a) in Great Britain, an officer of a local weights and measures authority;
  (b) in Northern Ireland, an officer of DETINI acting pursuant to arrangements made with the OFT for the purposes of this Schedule.

Power to require information or documents

19.—(1) An enforcement officer may by notice to a relevant person require the person—
  (a) to provide such information as may be specified in the notice, or
  (b) to produce such documents as may be so specified.

(2) An officer may exercise powers under this paragraph only if the information or documents sought to be obtained as a result are reasonably required in connection with the exercise by the enforcement authority for whom the officer acts of its functions under this Schedule.

(3) Where an officer requires information to be provided or documents produced under this paragraph—
  (a) the notice must set out the reasons why the officer requires the information to be provided or the documents produced, and
  (b) the information must be provided or the documents produced—
    (i) before the end of such reasonable period as may be specified in the notice; and
    (ii) at such place as may be so specified.

(4) In relation to a document in electronic form the power to require production of it includes a power to require the production of a copy of it in legible form or in a form from which it can readily be produced in visible and legible form.

(5) An enforcement officer may take copies of, or make extracts from, any document produced under this paragraph.

(6) The production of a document does not affect any lien which a person has on the document.

Entry, inspection without a warrant etc

20.—(1) Where an enforcement officer has reasonable cause to believe that any premises are being used by a relevant person in connection with the person's business activities, the officer may on producing evidence of authority at any reasonable time—
  (a) enter the premises;
  (b) inspect the premises;
  (c) observe the carrying on of business activities by the relevant person;
  (d) inspect any document found on the premises;
  (e) require any person on the premises to provide an explanation of any document or to state where it may be found.

(2) An enforcement officer may take copies of, or make extracts from, any document found under sub-paragraph (1).

PART II
OTHER ACTS

(3)   An officer may exercise powers under this paragraph only if the information or document sought to be obtained as a result is reasonably required in connection with the exercise by the enforcement authority for whom the officer acts of its functions under this Schedule.

(4)   In this paragraph "premises" means any premises other than premises used only as a dwelling.

Entry to premises under warrant

21.—(1)   A justice may issue a warrant under this paragraph if satisfied on information on oath given by an enforcement officer that there are reasonable grounds for believing that the first, second or third set of conditions is satisfied.

(2)   The first set of conditions is—
    (a)   that there is on the premises specified in the warrant a document in relation to which a requirement could be imposed under paragraph 19(1)(b), and
    (b)   that if such a requirement were to be imposed—
        (i)   it would not be complied with, or
        (ii)   the document to which it relates would be removed, tampered with or destroyed.

(3)   The second set of conditions is—
    (a)   that a person on whom a requirement has been imposed under paragraph 19(1)(b) has failed (wholly or in part) to comply with it, and
    (b)   that there is on the premises specified in the warrant a document that has been required to be produced.

(4)   The third set of conditions is—
    (a)   that an enforcement officer has been obstructed in the exercise of a power under paragraph 20, and
    (b)   that there is on the premises specified in the warrant a document that could be inspected under paragraph 20(1)(d).

(5)   A justice may issue a warrant under this paragraph if satisfied on information on oath given by an officer that there are reasonable grounds for suspecting that—
    (a)   an offence under this Schedule has been, is being or is about to be committed by a relevant person, and
    (b)   there is on the premises specified in the warrant a document relevant to whether that offence has been, or is being or is about to be committed.

(6)   A warrant issued under this paragraph shall authorise an enforcement officer—
    (a)   to enter the premises specified in the warrant;
    (b)   to search the premises and take possession of anything appearing to be a document specified in the warrant or to take, in relation to any such document, any other steps which may appear to be necessary for preserving it or preventing interference with it;
    (c)   to take copies of, or extracts from, any document specified in the warrant;
    (d)   to require any person on the premises to provide an explanation of any document appearing to be of the kind specified in the warrant or to state where it may be found;
    (e)   to use such force as may reasonably be necessary.

(7)   Where a warrant is issued by a justice under sub-paragraph (1) or (5) on the basis of information on oath given by an officer of the FSA, for "an enforcement officer" in sub-paragraph (6) substitute "a constable".

(8)   In sub-paragraphs (1), (5) and (7), "justice" means—
    (a)   in relation to England and Wales, a justice of the peace;
    (b)   in relation to Scotland, a justice within the meaning of section 307 of the Criminal Procedure (Scotland) Act 1995 (c 46) (interpretation);
    (c)   in relation to Northern Ireland, a lay magistrate.

(9)   In the application of this paragraph to Scotland, the references in sub-paragraphs (1), (5) and (7) to information on oath are to be read as references to evidence on oath.

Restrictions on powers

22.—(1)   This paragraph applies in relation to the powers conferred by—
    (a)   paragraph 19 (power to require information or documents),
    (b)   paragraph 20 (entry, inspection without warrant etc), or
    (c)   paragraph 21 (entry to premises under warrant).

(2)   Those powers are not exercisable in relation to information or documents in respect of which a claim to legal professional privilege (in Scotland, to confidentiality of communications) could be maintained in legal proceedings.

(3)   The exercise of those powers and the provision of information or production of documents under them is not otherwise subject to any restriction on the disclosure of information, whether imposed by statute or otherwise.

Failure to comply with information requirement

23.—(1)	If on an application made by—
  (a)	an enforcement authority, or
  (b)	a local weights and measures authority or DETINI pursuant to arrangements made with the OFT—
    (i)	by or on behalf of the authority; or
    (ii)	by DETINI,

it appears to the court that a person (the "information defaulter") has failed to do something that they were required to do under paragraph 19(1), the court may make an order under this paragraph.

(2)	An order under this paragraph may require the information defaulter—
  (a)	to do the thing that they failed to do within such period as may be specified in the order;
  (b)	otherwise to take such steps to remedy the consequences of the failure as may be so specified.

(3)	If the information defaulter is a body corporate, a partnership or an unincorporated body of persons that is not a partnership, the order may require any officer of the body corporate, partnership or body, who is (wholly or partly) responsible for the failure to meet such costs of the application as are specified in the order.

(4)	In this paragraph "the court" means—
  (a)	in England and Wales and Northern Ireland, the High Court or the county court;
  (b)	in Scotland, the Court of Session or the sheriff court.

Powers of local enforcement officers

24.—(1)	A local enforcement officer may only exercise powers under this Part of this Schedule pursuant to arrangements made with the OFT—
  (a)	by or on behalf of the relevant local weights and measures authority, or
  (b)	by DETINI.

(2)	Anything done or omitted to be done by, or in relation to, a local enforcement officer in the exercise or purported exercise of a power in this Part of this Schedule is treated for all purposes as if done or omitted to be done by, or in relation to, an officer of the OFT.

(3)	Sub-paragraph (2) does not apply for the purposes of criminal proceedings brought against the local enforcement officer, the relevant local weights and measures authority, DETINI or the OFT, in respect of anything done or omitted to be done by the officer.

(4)	A local enforcement officer must not disclose to any person other than the OFT and the relevant local weights and measures authority or, as the case may be, DETINI information obtained by the officer in the exercise of powers under this Part of this Schedule unless—
  (a)	the officer has the approval of the OFT to do so, or
  (b)	the officer is under a duty to make the disclosure.

(5)	In this paragraph "the relevant local weights and measures authority", in relation to a local enforcement officer, means the authority of which the officer is an officer.

[1818]

NOTES

Commencement: 27 November 2008.

PART 6
ENFORCEMENT: CIVIL PENALTIES

Power to impose civil penalties

25.—(1)	An enforcement authority may impose a penalty of such amount as it considers appropriate on a person who fails to comply with a requirement imposed—
  (a)	by a direction under this Schedule, or
  (b)	by a condition of a licence under paragraph 17.

For this purpose "appropriate" means effective, proportionate and dissuasive.

(2)	No such penalty is to be imposed if the authority is satisfied that the person took all reasonable steps and exercised all due diligence to ensure that the requirement would be complied with.

(3)	In deciding whether to impose a penalty for failure to comply with a requirement, an enforcement authority must consider whether the person followed any relevant guidance which was at the time—
  (a)	issued by a supervisory authority or any other appropriate body,
  (b)	approved by the Treasury, and

(c)   published in a manner approved by the Treasury as suitable in their opinion to bring the guidance to the attention of persons likely to be affected by it.

(4)   In sub-paragraph (3) "appropriate body" means a body which regulates or is representative of any trade, profession, business or employment carried on by the person.

(5)   A person on whom a penalty is imposed under this paragraph is not liable to be proceeded against for an offence under paragraph 30 in respect of the same failure.

Imposition of penalty by HMRC: procedure and reviews

26.—(1)   This paragraph applies where HMRC decide to impose a penalty under paragraph 25 on a person.

(2)   HMRC must give the person notice of—
   (a)   their decision to impose the penalty and its amount,
   (b)   the reasons for imposing the penalty,
   (c)   the right to a review under this paragraph, and
   (d)   the right to appeal under paragraph 28.

(3)   The person may by notice to HMRC require them to review their decision.

(4)   A notice requiring a review may not be given after the end of the period of 45 days beginning with the day on which HMRC first gave the person notice under sub-paragraph (2).

(5)   On a review under this paragraph, HMRC must either—
   (a)   confirm the decision, or
   (b)   withdraw or vary the decision and take such further steps (if any) in consequence of the withdrawal or variation as they consider appropriate.

(6)   Where HMRC do not, within the period of 45 days beginning with the day the notice under sub-paragraph (3) was given, give notice to the person of their determination of the review, they are to be taken to have confirmed their decision.

Imposition of penalty by other enforcement authority: procedure

27.—(1)   This paragraph applies if the FSA, the OFT or DETINI ("the authority") proposes to impose a penalty under paragraph 25 on a person.

(2)   The authority must give the person notice of—
   (a)   the proposal to impose the penalty and the proposed amount,
   (b)   the reasons for imposing the penalty, and
   (c)   the right to make representations to the authority within a specified period (which may not be less than 28 days).

(3)   The authority must then decide, within a reasonable period, whether to impose a penalty under paragraph 25 and must give the person notice—
   (a)   if it decides not to impose a penalty, of that decision;
   (b)   if it decides to impose a penalty, of the following matters—
      (i)   the decision to impose a penalty and the amount,
      (ii)   the reasons for the decision, and
      (iii)   the right to appeal under paragraph 28.

Appeal against imposition of civil penalty

28.—(1)   A person may appeal to the tribunal against—
   (a)   a decision of HMRC on a review under paragraph 26;
   (b)   a decision of the FSA or the OFT under paragraph 27.

(2)   A person may appeal to the High Court in Northern Ireland against a decision of DETINI under paragraph 27.

(3)   On the appeal the tribunal or court may—
   (a)   set aside the decision appealed against, and
   (b)   impose any penalty that could have been imposed by the body whose decision is appealed or remit the matter to that body.

(4)   An appeal against a decision of HMRC may not be made after the end of the period of 30 days beginning with—
   (a)   the date of the document notifying the person of the decision, or
   (b)   if paragraph 26(6) (deemed confirmation of decision) applies, the day after the end of the period mentioned there.

(5)   In this paragraph "the tribunal" means the First-tier Tribunal or, where so provided by or determined under Tribunal Procedure Rules, the Upper Tribunal.

(6)   The Treasury may by order provide that, until a time specified in the order, appeals under sub-paragraph (1) are to be made—
   (a)   in the case of a decision of HMRC, to a VAT and duties tribunal;

(b)   in the case of a decision of the FSA, to the Financial Services and Markets Tribunal;

(c)   in the case of a decision of the OFT, to the Consumer Credit Appeals Tribunal;

(rather than to the tribunal).

(7)   An order under sub-paragraph (6) may provide that any enactment applies (with or without modifications) in relation to an appeal to a tribunal mentioned in paragraph (a), (b) or (c) of that sub-paragraph.

(8)   Such an order is subject to negative resolution procedure.

Payment and recovery of civil penalties

29.—(1)   A penalty imposed under paragraph 25 is payable to the enforcement authority that imposed it.

(2)   Any such penalty is a debt due to the authority and is recoverable accordingly.

[1819]

NOTES

Commencement: 27 November 2008.

PART 7
ENFORCEMENT: OFFENCES

Offences: failure to comply with requirement imposed by direction

30.—(1)   A person who fails to comply with a requirement imposed by a direction under this Schedule commits an offence, subject to the following provisions.

(2)   No offence is committed if the person took all reasonable steps and exercised all due diligence to ensure that the requirement would be complied with.

(3)   In deciding whether a person has committed an offence under this paragraph the court must consider whether the person followed any relevant guidance that was at the time—

(a)   issued by a supervisory authority or any other appropriate body,

(b)   approved by the Treasury, and

(c)   published in a manner approved by the Treasury as suitable in their opinion to bring the guidance to the attention of persons likely to be affected by it.

(4)   In sub-paragraph (3) "appropriate body" means a body that regulates or is representative of any trade, profession, business or employment carried on by the alleged offender.

(5)   A person guilty of an offence under this paragraph is liable—

(a)   on summary conviction, to a fine not exceeding the statutory maximum;

(b)   on conviction on indictment, to imprisonment for a term not exceeding two years or a fine or both.

(6)   A person who is convicted of an offence under this paragraph is not liable to a penalty under paragraph 25 in respect of the same failure.

Offences in connection with licences

31.—(1)   A person commits an offence who for the purpose of obtaining a licence under paragraph 17—

(a)   provides information that is false in a material respect or a document that is not what it purports to be, and

(b)   knows that, or is reckless as to whether, the information is false or the document is not what it purports to be.

(2)   A person guilty of an offence under this paragraph is liable on conviction on indictment to imprisonment for a term not exceeding two years or a fine or both.

Extra-territorial application of offences

32.—(1)   An offence under this Schedule may be committed by a United Kingdom person by conduct wholly or partly outside the United Kingdom.

(2)   Nothing in this paragraph affects any criminal liability arising otherwise than under this paragraph.

Prosecution of offences

33.—(1)   Proceedings for an offence under this Schedule may be instituted in England and Wales only by—

(a)   the FSA;

(b)   the Director of Revenue and Customs Prosecutions;

    (c)   the OFT;
    (d)   a local weights and measures authority; or
    (e)   the Director of Public Prosecutions.

    (2)   Proceedings for an offence under this Schedule may be instituted in Northern Ireland only by—
    (a)   the FSA;
    (b)   HMRC;
    (c)   the OFT;
    (d)   DETINI; or
    (e)   the Director of Public Prosecutions for Northern Ireland.

    (3), (4)   (*Amend the Financial Services and Markets Act 2000, ss 168, 402 at* **[196]**, **[429]**.)

    (5)   HMRC may conduct a criminal investigation into any offence under this Schedule.

    (6)   In sub-paragraph (5) "criminal investigation" has the meaning given by section 35(5)(b) of the Commissioners for Revenue and Customs Act 2005 (c 11).

Jurisdiction to try offences

34.   Where an offence under this Schedule is committed outside the United Kingdom—
    (a)   proceedings for the offence may be taken at any place in the United Kingdom, and
    (b)   the offence may for all incidental purposes be treated as having been committed at any such place.

Time limit for summary proceedings

35.—(1)   An information relating to an offence under this Schedule that is triable by a magistrates' court in England and Wales may be so tried if it is laid—
    (a)   at any time within three years after the commission of the offence, and
    (b)   within twelve months after the date on which evidence sufficient in the opinion of the prosecutor to justify the proceedings comes to the knowledge of the prosecutor.

    (2)   Summary proceedings in Scotland for an offence under this Schedule—
    (a)   must not be commenced after the expiration of three years from the commission of the offence;
    (b)   subject to that, may be commenced at any time within twelve months after the date on which evidence sufficient in the Lord Advocate's opinion to justify the proceedings came to the knowledge of the Lord Advocate.

Section 136(3) of the Criminal Procedure (Scotland) Act 1995 (c 46) (date when proceedings deemed to be commenced) applies for the purposes of this sub-paragraph as for the purposes of that section.

    (3)   A magistrates' court in Northern Ireland has jurisdiction to hear and determine a complaint charging the commission of a summary offence under this Schedule provided that the complaint is made—
    (a)   within three years from the time when the offence was committed, and
    (b)   within twelve months from the date on which evidence sufficient in the opinion of the prosecutor to justify the proceedings comes to the knowledge of the prosecutor.

    (4)   For the purposes of this paragraph a certificate of the prosecutor (or, in Scotland, the Lord Advocate) as to the date on which such evidence as is referred to above came to their notice is conclusive evidence.

Liability of officers of bodies corporate etc

36.—(1)   If an offence under this Schedule committed by a body corporate is shown—
    (a)   to have been committed with the consent or the connivance of an officer of the body corporate, or
    (b)   to be attributable to any neglect on the part of any such officer,
the officer as well as the body corporate is guilty of an offence and liable to be proceeded against and punished accordingly.

    (2)   If an offence under this Schedule committed by a partnership is shown—
    (a)   to have been committed with the consent or the connivance of a partner, or
    (b)   to be attributable to any neglect on the part of a partner,
the partner as well as the partnership is guilty of an offence and liable to be proceeded against and punished accordingly.

    (3)   If an offence under this Schedule committed by an unincorporated association (other than a partnership) is shown—
    (a)   to have been committed with the consent or the connivance of an officer of the association, or
    (b)   to be attributable to any neglect on the part of any such officer,

the officer as well as the association is guilty of an offence and liable to be proceeded against and punished accordingly.

(4)   If the affairs of a body corporate are managed by its members, sub-paragraph (1) applies in relation to the acts and defaults of a member in connection with the member's functions of management as if the member were a director of the body.

(5)   In this paragraph—
"officer"—
      (a)   in relation to a body corporate, means a director, manager, secretary, chief executive, member of the committee of management, or a person purporting to act in such a capacity, and
      (b)   in relation to an unincorporated association, means any officer of the association or any member of its governing body, or a person purporting to act in such capacity;
"partner" includes a person purporting to act as a partner.

Proceedings against unincorporated bodies

37.—(1)   Proceedings for an offence under this Schedule alleged to have been committed by a partnership or an unincorporated association must be brought in the name of the partnership or association (and not in that of its members).

(2)   In proceedings for such an offence brought against a partnership or unincorporated association—
      (a)   section 33 of the Criminal Justice Act 1925 (c 86) (procedure on charge of offence against corporation) and Schedule 3 to the Magistrates' Courts Act 1980 (c 43) (corporations) apply as they do in relation to a body corporate;
      (b)   section 70 of the Criminal Procedure (Scotland) Act 1995 (c 46) (proceedings against bodies corporate) applies as it does in relation to a body corporate;
      (c)   section 18 of the Criminal Justice (Northern Ireland) Act 1945 (c 15 (NI)) (procedure on charge) and Schedule 4 to the Magistrates' Courts (Northern Ireland) Order 1981 (SI 1981/1675 (NI 26)) (corporations) apply as they do in relation to a body corporate.

(3)   Rules of court relating to the service of documents have effect in relation to proceedings for an offence under this Schedule as if the partnership or association were a body corporate.

(4)   A fine imposed on the partnership or association on its conviction of such an offence is to be paid out of the funds of the partnership or association.
[1820]

NOTES
Commencement: 27 November 2008.

PART 8
SUPPLEMENTARY AND GENERAL

Report to Parliament

38.—(1)   As soon as reasonably practicable after the end of each calendar year, the Treasury must—
      (a)   prepare a report about their exercise during that year of their functions under this Schedule, and
      (b)   lay a copy of the report before Parliament.

(2)   Sub-paragraph (1) does not apply in relation to a year if no direction under this Schedule is in force at any time in that year.

Supervision by supervisory authority

39.—(1)   A supervisory authority must take appropriate measures to monitor persons operating in the financial sector for whom it is the supervisory authority for the purpose of securing compliance by those persons with the requirements of any directions under this Schedule.

(2)   For the purposes of this Schedule—
      (a)   the FSA is the supervisory authority for—
          (i)   credit institutions that are authorised persons;
          (ii)   financial institutions (except money service businesses that are not authorised persons and consumer credit financial institutions);
      (b)   the OFT is the supervisory authority for consumer credit financial institutions;
      (c)   HMRC are the supervisory authority for money service businesses that are not authorised persons;
      (d)   DETINI is the supervisory authority for credit unions in Northern Ireland.

(3)   Where under sub-paragraph (2) there is more than one supervisory authority for a person, the authorities may agree that one of them will act as the supervisory authority for that person for the purposes of this Schedule.

(4)   Where an agreement has been made under sub-paragraph (3), the authority that has agreed to act as the supervisory authority must—

(a)   where directions under this Schedule have been given to specified persons operating in the financial sector, notify those persons;

(b)   where such directions have been given to all persons operating in the financial sector or to a description of such persons, publish the agreement in such way as it considers appropriate.

(5)   Where no agreement has been made under sub-paragraph (3), the supervisory authorities for a person must co-operate in the performance of their functions under this paragraph.

Assistance in preparing guidance

40.   The Treasury must provide such assistance as may reasonably be required by a supervisory authority or other body drawing up guidance that, when issued and published with the approval of the Treasury, would be relevant guidance for the purposes of paragraph 25(3) (civil penalties) and 30(3) (offences: failure to comply with requirement imposed by direction).

Functions of Financial Services Authority

41.—(1)   The functions of the FSA under this Schedule shall be treated for the purposes of Parts 1, 2 and 4 of Schedule 1 to the Financial Services and Markets Act 2000 (c 8) (general provisions relating to the Authority) as if they were functions conferred on the FSA under that Act.

(2)   Any penalty under paragraph 25 (civil penalties) received by the FSA is to be applied towards expenses incurred by it in connection with its functions under this Schedule or for any incidental purpose.

Notices

42.—(1)   A notice under this Schedule may be given to a person—

(a)   by posting it to the person's last known address, or

(b)   where the person is a body corporate, partnership or unincorporated association, by posting it to the registered or principal office of the body, partnership or association.

(2)   Where the Treasury are under a duty to give a notice to a person but do not have an address for them, they must make arrangements for the notice to be given to the person at the first available opportunity.

Crown application

43.—(1)   This Schedule binds the Crown, subject as follows.

(2)   No contravention by the Crown of a provision of this Schedule makes the Crown criminally liable.

(3)   The following courts may, on the application of a person appearing to the court to have an interest, declare unlawful any act or omission of the Crown that constitutes such a contravention—

(a)   the High Court in England and Wales;

(b)   the Court of Session;

(c)   the High Court in Northern Ireland.

(4)   Nothing in this paragraph affects Her Majesty in her private capacity.

This is to be construed as if section 38(3) of the Crown Proceedings Act 1947 (c 44) (meaning of Her Majesty in her private capacity) were contained in this Schedule.

Meaning of "United Kingdom person"

44.—(1)   In this Schedule "United Kingdom person" means a United Kingdom national or a body incorporated or constituted under the law of any part of the United Kingdom.

(2)   For this purpose a United Kingdom national is an individual who is—

(a)   a British citizen, a British overseas territories citizen, a British National (Overseas) or a British Overseas citizen;

(b)   a person who under the British Nationality Act 1981 (c 61) is a British subject; or

(c)   a British protected person within the meaning of that Act.

(3)   Her Majesty may by Order in Council extend the definition in sub-paragraph (1) so as to apply to bodies incorporated or constituted under the law of any of the Channel Islands, the Isle of Man or any British overseas territory.

Interpretation

45.—(1)   In this Schedule—

"authorised person" means a person who is authorised for the purposes of the Financial Services and Markets Act 2000 (c 8);

"business relationship" means a business, professional or commercial relationship between a relevant person and a customer, which is expected by the relevant person, at the time when contact is established, to have an element of duration;

"conduct" includes acts and omissions;

"consumer credit financial institution" means a financial institution that under section 21 of the Consumer Credit Act 1974 (c 39) requires a licence to carry on a consumer credit business, other than—

(a)   a person covered by a group licence issued by the Office of Fair Trading under section 22 of that Act,

(b)   a money service business, or

(c)   an authorised person;

"country" includes territory;

"document" means information recorded in any form;

"money service business" means an undertaking which by way of business operates a currency exchange office, transmits money (or any representations of monetary value) by any means or cashes cheques which are made payable to customers;

"notice" means a notice in writing.

(2)   In this Schedule any reference to an amount in one currency includes the equivalent amount in any other currency.

(3)   Unless otherwise defined, expressions used in this Schedule and in—

(a)   Directive 2005/60/EC of the European Parliament and of the Council of 26th October 2005 on the prevention of the use of the financial system for the purpose of money laundering and terrorist financing, or

(b)   Commission Directive 2006/70/EC of 1st August 2006 laying down implementing measures for that directive,

have the same meaning as in the relevant directive.

Index of defined expressions

46.   In this Schedule the following expressions are defined or otherwise explained by the provisions indicated—

authorised person	paragraph 45(1)
the banking consolidation directive (in Part 2 of this Schedule)	paragraph 7
biological weapon	paragraph 2(6)
business relationship	paragraph 45(1)
chemical weapon	paragraph 2(5)
conduct	paragraph 45(1)
consumer credit financial institution	paragraph 45(1)
country	paragraph 45(1)
credit institution	paragraph 5(1)
customer due diligence measures	paragraph 10(3)
designated person, in relation to a direction	paragraph 9(3)
DETINI	paragraph 18(1)(d)
document	paragraph 45(1)
enforcement authority	paragraph 18(1)
enforcement officer (in Part 5 of this Schedule)	paragraph 18(2)
financial institution	paragraph 5(2)
the FSA	paragraph 18(1)(a)
HMRC	paragraph 18(1)(b)

the life assurance consolidation directive (in Part 2 of this Schedule)	paragraph 7
local enforcement officer	paragraph 18(3)
the markets in financial instruments directive (in Part 2 of this Schedule)	paragraph 7
money laundering	paragraph 2(2)
money service business	paragraph 45(1)
notice	paragraph 45(1)
nuclear weapon	paragraph 2(3)
the OFT	paragraph 18(1)(c)
persons operating in the financial sector	paragraph 4
radiological weapon	paragraph 2(4)
relevant person, in relation to a direction	paragraph 3(2)
supervisory authority	paragraph 39(2)
terrorist financing	paragraph 2(1)
United Kingdom person	paragraph 44

[1821]

NOTES
Commencement: 27 November 2008.

BANKING ACT 2009

(2009 c 1)

NOTES
The Banking Act 2009 (Commencement No 1) Order 2009 (SI 2009/296) was published after Parts I to V of this Handbook had been sent for typesetting. The Order is included in the Appendix to this work at **[A1]**. The Order brought into force large parts of this Act and therefore supersedes the commencement information given in the notes to each section below. In addition, another six statutory instruments were made under various powers conferred by this Act and they are also included in the Appendix.

ARRANGEMENT OF SECTIONS

PART 1
SPECIAL RESOLUTION REGIME

Transfer of property

Compensation

Incidental functions

An Act to make provision about banking

[12 February 2009]

PART 1
SPECIAL RESOLUTION REGIME

Introduction

1   Overview

(1)   The purpose of the special resolution regime for banks is to address the situation where all or part of the business of a bank has encountered, or is likely to encounter, financial difficulties.

(2)   The special resolution regime consists of—
  (a)   the three stabilisation options,
  (b)   the bank insolvency procedure (provided by Part 2), and
  (c)   the bank administration procedure (provided by Part 3).

(3)   The three "stabilisation options" are—
  (a)   transfer to a private sector purchaser (section 11),
  (b)   transfer to a bridge bank (section 12), and
  (c)   transfer to temporary public ownership (section 13).

(4)   Each of the three stabilisation options is achieved through the exercise of one or more of the "stabilisation powers", which are—
  (a)   the share transfer powers (sections 15, 16, 26 to 31 and 85), and
  (b)   the property transfer powers (sections 33 and 42 to 46).

(5)   Each of the following has a role in the operation of the special resolution regime—
  (a)   the Bank of England,
  (b)   the Treasury, and
  (c)   the Financial Services Authority.

(6)   The Table describes the provisions of this Part.

Sections	Topic
Sections 1 to 3	Introduction
Sections 4 to 6	Objectives and code
Sections 7 to 10	Exercise of powers: general
Sections 11 to 13	The stabilisation options
Sections 14 to 32	Transfer of securities
Sections 33 to 48	Transfer of property
Sections 49 to 62	Compensation
Sections 63 to 75	Incidental functions

PART II
OTHER ACTS

Sections	Topic
Sections 76 to 81	Treasury
Sections 82 and 83	Holding companies
Sections 84 to 89	Building societies, &c

[1822]

NOTES
Commencement: to be appointed.

2 Interpretation: "bank"

(1)   In this Part "bank" means a UK institution which has permission under Part 4 of the Financial Services and Markets Act 2000 to carry on the regulated activity of accepting deposits (within the meaning of section 22 of that Act, taken with Schedule 2 and any order under section 22).

(2)   But "bank" does not include—
  (a)   a building society (within the meaning of section 119 of the Building Societies Act 1986),
  (b)   a credit union within the meaning of section 31 of the Credit Unions Act 1979, or
  (c)   any other class of institution excluded by an order made by the Treasury.

(3)   In subsection (1) "UK institution" means an institution which is incorporated in, or formed under the law of any part of, the United Kingdom.

(4)   Where a stabilisation power is exercised in respect of a bank, it does not cease to be a bank for the purposes of this Part if it later loses the permission referred to in subsection (1).

(5)   An order under subsection (2)(c)—
  (a)   shall be made by statutory instrument, and
  (b)   may not be made unless a draft has been laid before and approved by resolution of each House of Parliament.

(6)   Section 84 applies this Part to building societies with modifications.

(7)   Section 89 allows the application of this Part to credit unions.

[1823]

NOTES
Commencement: to be appointed.

3 Interpretation: other expressions

In this Part—
  "the FSA" means the Financial Services Authority, and
  "financial assistance" has the meaning given by section 257.

[1824]

NOTES
Commencement: to be appointed.

Objectives and code

4 Special resolution objectives

(1)   This section sets out the special resolution objectives.

(2)   The relevant authorities shall have regard to the special resolution objectives in using, or considering the use of—
  (a)   the stabilisation powers,
  (b)   the bank insolvency procedure, or
  (c)   the bank administration procedure.

(3)   For the purpose of this section the relevant authorities are—
  (a)   the Treasury,
  (b)   the FSA, and
  (c)   the Bank of England.

(4)   Objective 1 is to protect and enhance the stability of the financial systems of the United Kingdom.

(5)   Objective 2 is to protect and enhance public confidence in the stability of the banking systems of the United Kingdom.

(6)   Objective 3 is to protect depositors.

(7)   Objective 4 is to protect public funds.

(8)   Objective 5 is to avoid interfering with property rights in contravention of a Convention right (within the meaning of the Human Rights Act 1998).

(9)   In subsection (4), the reference to the stability of the financial systems of the United Kingdom includes, in particular, a reference to the continuity of banking services.

(10)   The order in which the objectives are listed in this section is not significant; they are to be balanced as appropriate in each case.

[1825]

NOTES
Commencement: to be appointed.

5   Code of practice

(1)   The Treasury shall issue a code of practice about the use of—
     (a)   the stabilisation powers,
     (b)   the bank insolvency procedure, and
     (c)   the bank administration procedure.

(2)   The code may, in particular, provide guidance on—
     (a)   how the special resolution objectives are to be understood and achieved,
     (b)   the choice between different options,
     (c)   the information to be provided in the course of a consultation under this Part,
     (d)   the giving of advice by one relevant authority to another about whether, when and how the stabilisation powers are to be used,
     (e)   how to determine whether Condition 2 in section 7 is met,
     (f)   how to determine whether the test for the use of stabilisation powers in section 8 is satisfied,
     (g)   sections 63 and 66, and
     (h)   compensation.

(3)   Sections 12 and 13 require the inclusion in the code of certain matters about bridge banks and temporary public ownership.

(4)   The relevant authorities shall have regard to the code.

(5)   For the purpose of this section the relevant authorities are—
     (a)   the Treasury,
     (b)   the FSA, and
     (c)   the Bank of England.

[1826]

NOTES
Commencement: to be appointed.

6   Code of practice: procedure

(1)   Before issuing the code of practice the Treasury must consult—
     (a)   the FSA,
     (b)   the Bank of England, and
     (c)   the scheme manager of the Financial Services Compensation Scheme (established under Part 15 of the Financial Services and Markets Act 2000).

(2)   As soon as is reasonably practicable after issuing the code of practice the Treasury shall lay a copy before Parliament.

(3)   The Treasury may revise and re-issue the code of practice.

(4)   Subsections (1) and (2) apply to re-issue as to the first issue.

[1827]

NOTES
Commencement: to be appointed.

Exercise of powers: general

7   General conditions

(1)   A stabilisation power may be exercised in respect of a bank only if the FSA is satisfied that the following conditions are met.

(2)   Condition 1 is that the bank is failing, or is likely to fail, to satisfy the threshold conditions (within the meaning of section 41(1) of the Financial Services and Markets Act 2000 (permission to carry on regulated activities)).

(3)   Condition 2 is that having regard to timing and other relevant circumstances it is not reasonably likely that (ignoring the stabilisation powers) action will be taken by or in respect of the bank that will enable the bank to satisfy the threshold conditions.

(4)   The FSA shall treat Conditions 1 and 2 as met if satisfied that they would be met but for financial assistance provided by—
(a)   the Treasury, or
(b)   the Bank of England (disregarding ordinary market assistance offered by the Bank on its usual terms).

(5)   Before determining whether or not Condition 2 is met the FSA must consult—
(a)   the Bank of England, and
(b)   the Treasury.

(6)   The special resolution objectives are not relevant to Conditions 1 and 2.

(7)   The conditions for applying for and making a bank insolvency order are set out in sections 96 and 97.

(8)   The conditions for applying for and making a bank administration order are set out in sections 143 and 144.

[1828]

NOTES
Commencement: to be appointed.

8   Specific conditions: private sector purchaser and bridge bank

(1)   The Bank of England may exercise a stabilisation power in respect of a bank in accordance with section 11(2) or 12(2) only if satisfied that Condition A is met.

(2)   Condition A is that the exercise of the power is necessary, having regard to the public interest in—
(a)   the stability of the financial systems of the United Kingdom,
(b)   the maintenance of public confidence in the stability of the banking systems of the United Kingdom, or
(c)   the protection of depositors.

(3)   Before determining whether Condition A is met, and if so how to react, the Bank of England must consult—
(a)   the FSA, and
(b)   the Treasury.

(4)   Where the Treasury notify the Bank of England that they have provided financial assistance in respect of a bank for the purpose of resolving or reducing a serious threat to the stability of the financial systems of the United Kingdom, the Bank may exercise a stabilisation power in respect of the bank in accordance with section 11(2) or 12(2) only if satisfied that Condition B is met (instead of Condition A).

(5)   Condition B is that—
(a)   the Treasury have recommended the Bank of England to exercise the stabilisation power on the grounds that it is necessary to protect the public interest, and
(b)   in the Bank's opinion, exercise of the stabilisation power is an appropriate way to provide that protection.

(6)   The conditions in this section are in addition to the conditions in section 7.

[1829]

NOTES
Commencement: to be appointed.

9   Specific conditions: temporary public ownership

(1)   The Treasury may exercise a stabilisation power in respect of a bank in accordance with section 13(2) only if satisfied that one of the following conditions is met.

(2)   Condition A is that the exercise of the power is necessary to resolve or reduce a serious threat to the stability of the financial systems of the United Kingdom.

(3)   Condition B is that exercise of the power is necessary to protect the public interest, where the Treasury have provided financial assistance in respect of the bank for the purpose of resolving or reducing a serious threat to the stability of the financial systems of the United Kingdom.

(4)   Before determining whether a condition is met the Treasury must consult—

(a)   the FSA, and

(b)   the Bank of England.

(5)   The conditions in this section are in addition to the conditions in section 7.

[1830]

NOTES
Commencement: to be appointed.

10   Banking Liaison Panel

(1)   The Treasury shall make arrangements for a panel to advise the Treasury about the effect of the special resolution regime on—

(a)   banks,

(b)   persons with whom banks do business, and

(c)   the financial markets.

(2)   In particular, the panel may advise the Treasury about—

(a)   the exercise of powers to make statutory instruments under or by virtue of this Part, Part 2 or Part 3 (excluding the stabilisation powers, compensation scheme orders, resolution fund orders, third party compensation orders and orders under section 75(2)(b) and (c)),

(b)   the code of practice under section 5, and

(c)   anything else referred to the panel by the Treasury.

(3)   The Treasury shall ensure that the panel includes—

(a)   a member appointed by the Treasury,

(b)   a member appointed by the Bank of England,

(c)   a member appointed by the FSA,

(d)   a member appointed by the scheme manager of the Financial Services Compensation Scheme,

(e)   one or more persons who in the Treasury's opinion represent the interests of banks,

(f)   one or more persons who in the Treasury's opinion have expertise in law relating to the financial systems of the United Kingdom, and

(g)   one or more persons who in the Treasury's opinion have expertise in insolvency law and practice.

[1831]

NOTES
Commencement: to be appointed.

The stabilisation options

11   Private sector purchaser

(1)   The first stabilisation option is to sell all or part of the business of the bank to a commercial purchaser.

(2)   For that purpose the Bank of England may make—

(a)   one or more share transfer instruments;

(b)   one or more property transfer instruments.

[1832]

NOTES
Commencement: to be appointed.

12   Bridge bank

(1)   The second stabilisation option is to transfer all or part of the business of the bank to a company which is wholly owned by the Bank of England (a "bridge bank").

(2)   For that purpose the Bank of England may make one or more property transfer instruments.

(3)   The code of practice under section 5 must include provision about the management and control of bridge banks including, in particular, provision about—

(a)   setting objectives,

(b)   the content of the articles of association,

(c)   the content of reports under section 80(1),

(d)   different arrangements for management and control at different stages, and

(e)   eventual disposal.

(4)   Where property, rights or liabilities are first transferred by property transfer instrument to a bridge bank and later transferred (whether or not by the exercise of a power under this Part) to another company which is wholly owned by the Bank of England, that other company is an "onward bridge bank".

(5)   An onward bridge bank—
    (a)   is a bridge bank for the purposes of—
        (i)   subsection (3),
        (ii)   section 77,
        (iii)   section 79, and
        (iv)   section 80(5), but
    (b)   is not a bridge bank for the purposes of—
        (i)   section 30(1),
        (ii)   section 43(1), or
        (iii)   section 80(1).

[1833]

NOTES
Commencement: to be appointed.

13   Temporary public ownership

(1)   The third stabilisation option is to take the bank into temporary public ownership.

(2)   For that purpose the Treasury may make one or more share transfer orders in which the transferee is—
    (a)   a nominee of the Treasury, or
    (b)   a company wholly owned by the Treasury.

(3)   The code of practice under section 5 must include provision about the management of banks taken into temporary public ownership under this section.

[1834]

NOTES
Commencement: to be appointed.

Transfer of securities

14   Interpretation: "securities"

(1)   In this Part "securities" includes anything falling within any of the following classes.

(2)   Class 1: shares and stock.

(3)   Class 2: debentures, including—
    (a)   debenture stock,
    (b)   loan stock,
    (c)   bonds,
    (d)   certificates of deposit, and
    (e)   any other instrument creating or acknowledging a debt.

(4)   Class 3: warrants or other instruments that entitle the holder to acquire anything in Class 1 or 2.

(5)   Class 4: rights which—
    (a)   are granted by a deposit-taker, and
    (b)   form part of the deposit-taker's own funds for the purposes of section 1 of Chapter 2 of Title V of Directive 2006/48/EC (on the taking up and pursuit of the business of credit institutions).

[1835]

NOTES
Commencement: to be appointed.

15   Share transfer instrument

(1)   A share transfer instrument is an instrument which—
    (a)   provides for securities issued by a specified bank to be transferred;
    (b)   makes other provision for the purposes of, or in connection with, the transfer of securities issued by a specified bank (whether or not the transfer has been or is to be effected by that instrument, by another share transfer instrument or otherwise).

(2)   A share transfer instrument may relate to—
    (a)   specified securities, or
    (b)   securities of a specified description.

[1836]

NOTES
Commencement: to be appointed.

16 Share transfer order

(1)   A share transfer order is an order which—
  (a)   provides for securities issued by a specified bank to be transferred;
  (b)   makes other provision for the purposes of, or in connection with, the transfer of securities issued by a specified bank (whether or not the transfer has been or is to be effected by that order, by another share transfer order or otherwise).

(2)   A share transfer order may relate to—
  (a)   specified securities, or
  (b)   securities of a specified description.

[1837]

NOTES
Commencement: to be appointed.

---

17 Effect

(1)   In this section "transfer" means a transfer provided for by a share transfer instrument or order.

(2)   A transfer takes effect by virtue of the instrument or order (and in accordance with its provisions as to timing or other ancillary matters).

(3)   A transfer takes effect despite any restriction arising by virtue of contract or legislation or in any other way.

(4)   In subsection (3) "restriction" includes—
  (a)   any restriction, inability or incapacity affecting what can and cannot be assigned or transferred (whether generally or by a particular person), and
  (b)   a requirement for consent (by any name).

(5)   A share transfer instrument or order may provide for a transfer to take effect free from any trust, liability or other encumbrance (and may include provision about their extinguishment).

(6)   A share transfer instrument or order may extinguish rights to acquire securities falling within Class 1 or 2 in section 14.

[1838]

NOTES
Commencement: to be appointed.

---

18 Continuity

(1)   A share transfer instrument or order may provide for a transferee to be treated for any purpose connected with the transfer as the same person as the transferor.

(2)   A share transfer instrument or order may provide for agreements made or other things done by or in relation to a transferor to be treated as made or done by or in relation to the transferee.

(3)   A share transfer instrument or order may provide for anything (including legal proceedings) that relates to anything transferred and is in the process of being done by or in relation to the transferor immediately before the transfer date, to be continued by or in relation to the transferee.

(4)   A share transfer instrument or order may modify references (express or implied) in an instrument or document to a transferor.

(5)   A share transfer instrument or order may require or permit—
  (a)   a transferor to provide a transferee with information and assistance;
  (b)   a transferee to provide a transferor with information and assistance.

[1839]

NOTES
Commencement: to be appointed.

---

19 Conversion and delisting

(1)   A share transfer instrument or order may provide for securities to be converted from one form or class to another.

(2)   A share transfer instrument or order may provide for the listing of securities, under section 74 of the Financial Services and Markets Act 2000, to be discontinued.

[1840]

NOTES
Commencement: to be appointed.

PART II
OTHER ACTS

20 Directors

(1)   A share transfer instrument may enable the Bank of England—
  (a)   to remove a director of a specified bank;
  (b)   to vary the service contract of a director of a specified bank;
  (c)   to terminate the service contract of a director of a specified bank;
  (d)   to appoint a director of a specified bank.

(2)   A share transfer order may enable the Treasury—
  (a)   to remove a director of a specified bank;
  (b)   to vary the service contract of a director of a specified bank;
  (c)   to terminate the service contract of a director of a specified bank;
  (d)   to appoint a director of a specified bank.

(3)   Appointments under subsection (1)(d) are to be on terms and conditions agreed with the Bank of England.

(4)   Appointments under subsection (2)(d) are to be on terms and conditions agreed with the Treasury.

[1841]

NOTES
Commencement: to be appointed.

21 Ancillary instruments: production, registration, &c

(1)   A share transfer instrument or order may permit or require the execution, issue or delivery of an instrument.

(2)   A share transfer instrument or order may provide for a transfer to have effect irrespective of—
  (a)   whether an instrument has been produced, delivered, transferred or otherwise dealt with;
  (b)   registration.

(3)   A share transfer instrument or order may provide for the effect of an instrument executed, issued or delivered in accordance with the instrument or order.

(4)   A share transfer instrument or order may modify or annul the effect of an instrument.

(5)   A share transfer instrument or order may—
  (a)   entitle a transferee to be registered in respect of transferred securities;
  (b)   require a person to effect registration.

[1842]

NOTES
Commencement: to be appointed.

22 Termination rights, &c

(1)   In this section "default event provision" means a Type 1 or Type 2 default event provision as defined in subsections (2) and (3).

(2)   A Type 1 default event provision is a provision of a contract or other agreement that has the effect that if a specified event occurs or situation arises—
  (a)   the agreement is terminated, modified or replaced,
  (b)   rights or duties under the agreement are terminated, modified or replaced,
  (c)   a right accrues to terminate, modify or replace the agreement,
  (d)   a right accrues to terminate, modify or replace rights or duties under the agreement,
  (e)   a sum becomes payable or ceases to be payable,
  (f)   delivery of anything becomes due or ceases to be due,
  (g)   a right to claim a payment or delivery accrues, changes or lapses,
  (h)   any other right accrues, changes or lapses, or
  (i)   an interest is created, changes or lapses.

(3)   A Type 2 default event provision is a provision of a contract or other agreement that has the effect that a provision of the contract or agreement—
  (a)   takes effect only if a specified event occurs or does not occur,
  (b)   takes effect only if a specified situation arises or does not arise,
  (c)   has effect only for so long as a specified event does not occur,
  (d)   has effect only while a specified situation lasts,
  (e)   applies differently if a specified event occurs,
  (f)   applies differently if a specified situation arises, or
  (g)   applies differently while a specified situation lasts.

(4)   For the purposes of subsections (2) and (3) it is the effect of a provision that matters, not how it is described (nor, for example, whether it is presented in a positive or a negative form).

(5)   A share transfer instrument or order may provide for subsection (6) or (7) to apply (but need not apply either).

(6)   If this subsection applies, the share transfer instrument or order is to be disregarded in determining whether a default event provision applies.

(7)   If this subsection applies, the share transfer instrument or order is to be disregarded in determining whether a default event provision applies except in so far as the instrument or order provides otherwise.

(8)   In subsections (6) and (7) a reference to the share transfer instrument or order is a reference to—
   (a)   the making of the instrument or order,
   (b)   anything that is done by the instrument or order or is to be, or may be, done under or by virtue of the instrument or order, and
   (c)   any action or decision taken or made under this or another enactment in so far as it resulted in, or was connected to, the making of the instrument or order.

(9)   Provision under subsection (5) may apply subsection (6) or (7)—
   (a)   generally or only for specified purposes, cases or circumstances;
   (b)   differently for different purposes, cases or circumstances.

(10)   A thing is not done by virtue of an instrument or order for the purposes of subsection (8)(b) merely by virtue of being done under a contract or other agreement rights or obligations under which have been transferred by the instrument or order.

[1843]

NOTES
Commencement: to be appointed.

23   Incidental provision

(1)   A share transfer instrument or order may include incidental, consequential or transitional provision.

(2)   In relying on subsection (1) a share transfer instrument or order—
   (a)   may make provision generally or only for specified purposes, cases or circumstances, and
   (b)   may make different provision for different purposes, cases or circumstances.

[1844]

NOTES
Commencement: to be appointed.

24   Procedure: instruments

(1)   As soon as is reasonably practicable after making a share transfer instrument in respect of a bank the Bank of England shall send a copy to—
   (a)   the bank,
   (b)   the Treasury,
   (c)   the FSA, and
   (d)   any other person specified in the code of practice under section 5.

(2)   As soon as is reasonably practicable after making a share transfer instrument the Bank of England shall publish a copy—
   (a)   on the Bank's internet website, and
   (b)   in two newspapers, chosen by the Bank of England to maximise the likelihood of the instrument coming to the attention of persons likely to be affected.

(3)   Where the Treasury receive a copy of a share transfer instrument under subsection (1) they shall lay a copy before Parliament.

[1845]

NOTES
Commencement: to be appointed.

25   Procedure: orders

(1)   A share transfer order—
   (a)   shall be made by statutory instrument, and
   (b)   shall be subject to annulment in pursuance of a resolution of either House of Parliament.

(2)   As soon as is reasonably practicable after making a share transfer order in respect of a bank the Treasury shall send a copy to—
   (a)   the bank,

(b)   the Bank of England,

(c)   the FSA, and

(d)   any other person specified in the code of practice under section 5.

(3)   As soon as is reasonably practicable after making a share transfer order the Treasury shall publish a copy—

(a)   on the Treasury's internet website, and

(b)   in two newspapers, chosen by the Treasury to maximise the likelihood of the instrument coming to the attention of persons likely to be affected.

[1846]

NOTES
Commencement: to be appointed.

26 Supplemental instruments

(1)   This section applies where the Bank of England has made a share transfer instrument in accordance with section 11(2) ("the original instrument").

(2)   The Bank of England may make one or more supplemental share transfer instruments.

(3)   A supplemental share transfer instrument is a share transfer instrument which—

(a)   provides for the transfer of securities which were issued by the bank before the original instrument and have not been transferred by the original instrument or another supplemental share transfer instrument;

(a)   makes provision of a kind that a share transfer instrument may make under section 15(1)(b) (whether or not in connection with a transfer under the original instrument).

(4)   Sections 7 and 8 do not apply to a supplemental share transfer instrument (but it is to be treated in the same way as any other share transfer instrument for all other purposes, including for the purposes of the application of a power under this Part).

(5)   Before making a supplemental share transfer instrument the Bank of England must consult—

(a)   the FSA, and

(b)   the Treasury.

(6)   The possibility of making a supplemental share transfer instrument in reliance on subsection (2) is without prejudice to the possibility of making of a new instrument in accordance with section 11(2) (and not in reliance on subsection (2) above).

[1847]

NOTES
Commencement: to be appointed.

27 Supplemental orders

(1)   This section applies where the Treasury have made a share transfer order, in respect of securities issued by a bank, in accordance with section 13(2) ("the original order").

(2)   The Treasury may make one or more supplemental share transfer orders.

(3)   A supplemental share transfer order is a share transfer order which—

(a)   provides for the transfer of securities which were issued by the bank before the original order and have not been transferred by the original order or another supplemental share transfer order;

(b)   makes provision of a kind that a share transfer order may make under section 16(1)(b), whether in connection with a transfer under the original order or in connection with a transfer under that or another supplemental order.

(4)   Sections 7 and 9 do not apply to a supplemental share transfer order (but it is to be treated in the same way as any other share transfer order for all other purposes, including for the purposes of the application of a power under this Part).

(5)   Before making a supplemental share transfer order the Treasury must consult—

(a)   the FSA, and

(b)   the Bank of England.

(6)   The possibility of making a supplemental share transfer order in reliance on subsection (2) is without prejudice to the possibility of making of a new order in accordance with section 13(2) (and not in reliance on subsection (2) above).

[1848]

NOTES
Commencement: to be appointed.

28 Onward transfer

(1)   This section applies where the Treasury have made a share transfer order, in respect of securities issued by a bank, in accordance with section 13(2) ("the original order").

(2)   The Treasury may make one or more onward share transfer orders.

(3)   An onward share transfer order is a share transfer order which—
  (a)   provides for the transfer of—
      (i)   securities which were issued by the bank before the original order and have been transferred by the original order or a supplemental share transfer order, or
      (ii)   securities which were issued by the bank after the original order;
  (b)   makes other provision for the purposes of, or in connection with, the transfer of securities issued by the bank (whether the transfer has been or is to be effected by that order, by another share transfer order or otherwise).

(4)   An onward share transfer order may not transfer securities to the transferor under the original order.

(5)   Sections 7 and 9 do not apply to an onward share transfer order (but it is to be treated in the same way as any other share transfer order for all other purposes, including for the purposes of the application of a power under this Part).

(6)   Before making an onward share transfer order the Treasury must consult—
  (a)   the FSA, and
  (b)   the Bank of England.

(7)   Section 27 applies where the Treasury have made an onward share transfer order.

[1849]

NOTES
Commencement: to be appointed.

29 Reverse share transfer

(1)   This section applies where the Treasury have made a share transfer order in accordance with section 13(2) ("the original order") providing for the transfer of securities issued by a bank to a person ("the original transferee").

(2)   The Treasury may make one or more reverse share transfer orders in respect of securities issued by the bank and held by the original transferee (whether or not they were transferred by the original order).

(3)   If the Treasury makes an onward share transfer order in respect of securities transferred by the original order, the Treasury may make one or more reverse share transfer orders in respect of securities—
  (a)   issued by the bank, and
  (b)   held by a transferee under the onward share transfer order of any of the following kinds—
      (i)   a company wholly owned by the Bank of England,
      (ii)   a company wholly owned by the Treasury, or
      (iii)   a nominee of the Treasury.

(4)   A reverse share transfer order is a share transfer order which—
  (a)   provides for transfer to the transferor under the original order (where subsection (2) applies);
  (b)   provides for transfer to the original transferee (where subsection (3) applies);
  (c)   makes other provision for the purposes of, or in connection with, the transfer of securities which are, could be or could have been transferred under paragraph (a) or (b).

(5)   Sections 7, 9 and 51 do not apply to a reverse share transfer order (but it is to be treated in the same way as any other share transfer order for all other purposes including for the purposes of the application of a power under this Part).

(6)   Before making a reverse share transfer order the Treasury must consult—
  (a)   the FSA, and
  (b)   the Bank of England.

(7)   Section 27 applies where the Treasury have made a reverse share transfer order.

[1850]

NOTES
Commencement: to be appointed.

PART II
OTHER ACTS

30 Bridge bank: share transfers

(1)   This section applies where the Bank of England has made a property transfer instrument in respect of a bridge bank in accordance with section 12(2) ("the original instrument").

(2)   The Bank of England may make one or more bridge bank share transfer instruments.

(3)   A bridge bank share transfer instrument is a share transfer instrument which—
 (a)   provides for securities issued by the bridge bank to be transferred;
 (b)   makes other provision for the purposes of, or in connection with, the transfer of securities issued by the bridge bank (whether the transfer has been or is to be effected by that instrument, by another share transfer instrument or otherwise).

(4)   Sections 7 and 8 do not apply to a bridge bank share transfer instrument (but it is to be treated in the same way as any other share transfer instrument for all other purposes, including for the purposes of the application of a power under this Part).

(5)   Before making a bridge bank share transfer instrument the Bank of England must consult—
 (a)   the FSA, and
 (b)   the Treasury.

(6)   Section 26 applies where the Bank of England has made a bridge bank share transfer instrument.

[1851]

NOTES
Commencement: to be appointed.

31 Bridge bank: reverse share transfer

(1)   This section applies where the Bank of England has made a bridge bank share transfer instrument in accordance with section 30(2) ("the original instrument") providing for the transfer of securities to—
 (a)   a company wholly owned by the Bank of England,
 (b)   a company wholly owned by the Treasury, or
 (c)   a nominee of the Treasury.

(2)   The Bank of England may make one or more bridge bank reverse share transfer instruments in respect of securities issued by the bridge bank and held by a person within subsection (1)(a) to (c).

(3)   A bridge bank reverse share transfer instrument is a share transfer instrument which—
 (a)   provides for transfer to the transferor under the original instrument;
 (b)   makes other provision for the purposes of, or in connection with, the transfer of securities which are, could be or could have been transferred under paragraph (a).

(4)   Sections 7, 8 and 51 do not apply to a bridge bank reverse share transfer instrument (but it is to be treated in the same way as any other share transfer instrument for all other purposes including for the purposes of the application of a power under this Part).

(5)   Before making a bridge bank reverse share transfer instrument the Bank of England must consult—
 (a)   the FSA, and
 (b)   the Treasury.

(6)   Section 26 applies where the Bank of England has made a bridge bank reverse share transfer instrument.

[1852]

NOTES
Commencement: to be appointed.

32 Interpretation: general

In this group of sections—
 "service contract" has the meaning given by section 227 of the Companies Act 2006, and
 "transfer date" means the date or time on or at which a share transfer instrument or order (or the relevant part of it) takes effect.

[1853]

NOTES
Commencement: to be appointed.

Transfer of property

33   Property transfer instrument

(1)   A property transfer instrument is an instrument which—

   (a)   provides for property, rights or liabilities of a specified bank to be transferred;

   (b)   makes other provision for the purposes of, or in connection with, the transfer of property, rights or liabilities of a specified bank (whether the transfer has been or is to be effected by that instrument, by another property transfer instrument or otherwise).

(2)   A property transfer instrument may relate to—

   (a)   all property, rights and liabilities of the specified bank,

   (b)   all its property, rights and liabilities subject to specified exceptions,

   (c)   specified property, rights or liabilities, or

   (d)   property, rights or liabilities of a specified description.

[1854]

NOTES

Commencement: to be appointed.

34   Effect

(1)   In this section "transfer" means a transfer provided for by a property transfer instrument.

(2)   A transfer takes effect by virtue of the instrument (and in accordance with its provisions as to timing or other ancillary matters).

(3)   A transfer takes effect despite any restriction arising by virtue of contract or legislation or in any other way.

(4)   In subsection (3) "restriction" includes—

   (a)   any restriction, inability or incapacity affecting what can and cannot be assigned or transferred (whether generally or by a particular person), and

   (b)   a requirement for consent (by any name).

(5)   A property transfer instrument may provide for a transfer to be conditional upon a specified event or situation—

   (a)   occurring or arising, or

   (b)   not occurring or arising.

(6)   A property transfer instrument may include provision dealing with the consequences of breach of a condition imposed under subsection (5); and the consequences may include—

   (a)   automatic vesting in the original transferor;

   (b)   an obligation to effect a transfer back to the original transferor, with specified consequences for failure to comply (which may include provision conferring a discretion on a court or tribunal);

   (c)   provision making a transfer or anything done in connection with a transfer void or voidable.

(7)   Where a property transfer instrument makes provision in respect of property held on trust (however arising) it may also make provision about—

   (a)   the terms on which the property is to be held after the instrument takes effect (which provision may remove or alter the terms of the trust), and

   (b)   how any powers, provisions and liabilities in respect of the property are to be exercisable or have effect after the instrument takes effect.

[1855]

NOTES

Commencement: to be appointed.

35   Transferable property

(1)   A property transfer instrument may transfer any property, rights or liabilities including, in particular—

   (a)   property, rights and liabilities acquired or arising between the making of the instrument and the transfer date,

   (b)   rights and liabilities arising on or after the transfer date in respect of matters occurring before that date,

   (c)   property outside the United Kingdom,

   (d)   rights and liabilities under the law of a country or territory outside the United Kingdom, and

   (e)   rights and liabilities under an enactment (including legislation of the European Union).

(2)   Section 32 applies for the interpretation of this section (with the necessary modification).

[1856]

36 Continuity

(1)   A property transfer instrument may provide—
  (a)   for a transfer to be, or to be treated as, a succession;
  (b)   for a transferee to be treated for any purpose connected with the transfer as the same person as the transferor.

(2)   A property transfer instrument may provide for agreements made or other things done by or in relation to a transferor to be treated as made or done by or in relation to the transferee.

(3)   A property transfer instrument may provide for anything (including legal proceedings) that relates to anything transferred and is in the process of being done by or in relation to the transferor immediately before the transfer date, to be continued by or in relation to the transferee.

(4)   A property transfer instrument which transfers or enables the transfer of a contract of employment may include provision about continuity of employment.

(5)   A property transfer instrument may modify references (express or implied) in an instrument or document to a transferor.

(6)   In so far as rights and liabilities in respect of anything transferred are enforceable after transfer, a property transfer instrument may provide for apportionment between transferor and transferee to a specified extent and in specified ways.

(7)   A property transfer instrument may enable the transferor and transferee by agreement to modify a provision of the instrument; but a modification—
  (a)   must achieve a result that could have been achieved by the instrument, and
  (b)   may not transfer (or arrange for the transfer of) property, rights or liabilities.

(8)   A property transfer instrument may require or permit—
  (a)   a transferor to provide a transferee with information and assistance;
  (b)   a transferee to provide a transferor with information and assistance.

(9)   Section 32 applies for the interpretation of this section (with the necessary modification).

[1857]

37 Licences

(1)   A licence in respect of anything transferred by property transfer instrument shall continue to have effect despite the transfer.

(2)   A property transfer instrument may disapply subsection (1) to a specified extent.

(3)   Where a licence imposes rights or obligations, a property transfer instrument may apportion responsibility for exercise or compliance between transferor and transferee.

(4)   In this section "licence" includes permission and approval and any other permissive document in respect of anything transferred.

[1858]

38 Termination rights, &c

(1)   In this section "default event provision" means a Type 1 or Type 2 default event provision as defined in subsections (2) and (3).

(2)   A Type 1 default event provision is a provision of a contract or other agreement that has the effect that if a specified event occurs or situation arises—
  (a)   the agreement is terminated, modified or replaced,
  (b)   rights or duties under the agreement are terminated, modified or replaced,
  (c)   a right accrues to terminate, modify or replace the agreement,
  (d)   a right accrues to terminate, modify or replace rights or duties under the agreement,
  (e)   a sum becomes payable or ceases to be payable,
  (f)   delivery of anything becomes due or ceases to be due,
  (g)   a right to claim a payment or delivery accrues, changes or lapses,
  (h)   any other right accrues, changes or lapses, or
  (i)   an interest is created, changes or lapses.

(3)   A Type 2 default event provision is a provision of a contract or other agreement that has the effect that a provision of the contract or agreement—
    (a)   takes effect only if a specified event occurs or does not occur,
    (b)   takes effect only if a specified situation arises or does not arise,
    (c)   has effect only for so long as a specified event does not occur,
    (d)   has effect only while a specified situation lasts,
    (e)   applies differently if a specified event occurs,
    (f)   applies differently if a specified situation arises, or
    (g)   applies differently while a specified situation lasts.

(4)   For the purposes of subsections (2) and (3) it is the effect of a provision that matters, not how it is described (nor, for example, whether it is presented in a positive or a negative form).

(5)   A property transfer instrument may provide for subsection (6) or (7) to apply (but need not apply either).

(6)   If this subsection applies, the property transfer instrument is to be disregarded in determining whether a default event provision applies.

(7)   If this subsection applies, the property transfer instrument is to be disregarded in determining whether a default event provision applies except in so far as the instrument provides otherwise.

(8)   In subsections (6) and (7) a reference to the property transfer instrument is a reference to—
    (a)   the making of the instrument,
    (b)   anything that is done by the instrument or is to be, or may be, done under or by virtue of the instrument, and
    (c)   any action or decision taken or made under this or another enactment in so far as it resulted in, or was connected to, the making of the instrument.

(9)   Provision under subsection (5) may apply subsection (6) or (7)—
    (a)   generally or only for specified purposes, cases or circumstances;
    (b)   differently for different purposes, cases or circumstances.

(10)   A thing is not done by virtue of an instrument for the purposes of subsection (8)(b) merely by virtue of being done under a contract or other agreement rights or obligations under which have been transferred by the instrument.

[1859]

NOTES
Commencement: to be appointed.

39 Foreign property

(1)   This section applies where a property transfer instrument transfers foreign property.

(2)   In subsection (1) "foreign property" means—
    (a)   property outside the United Kingdom, and
    (b)   rights and liabilities under foreign law.

(3)   The transferor and the transferee must each take any necessary steps to ensure that the transfer is effective as a matter of foreign law (if it is not wholly effective by virtue of the property transfer instrument).

(4)   Until the transfer is effective as a matter of foreign law, the transferor must—
    (a)   hold the property or right for the benefit of the transferee (together with any additional property or right accruing by virtue of the original property or right), or
    (b)   discharge the liability on behalf of the transferee.

(5)   The transferee must meet any expenses of the transferor in complying with this section.

(6)   An obligation imposed by this section is enforceable as if created by contract between the transferor and transferee.

(7)   The transferor must comply with any directions of the Bank of England in respect of the obligations under subsections (3) and (4); and—
    (a)   a direction may disapply subsections (3) and (4) to a specified extent, and
    (b)   obligations imposed by direction are enforceable as if created by contract between the transferor and the Bank of England.

(8)   In this section "foreign law" means the law of a country or territory outside the United Kingdom.

[1860]

NOTES
Commencement: to be appointed.

PART II
OTHER ACTS

40 Incidental provision

(1)   A property transfer instrument may include incidental, consequential or transitional provision.

(2)   In relying on subsection (1) an instrument—

(a)   may make provision generally or only for specified purposes, cases or circumstances, and

(b)   may make different provision for different purposes, cases or circumstances.

[1861]

NOTES

Commencement: to be appointed.

41 Procedure

(1)   As soon as is reasonably practicable after making a property transfer instrument in respect of a bank the Bank of England shall send a copy to—

(a)   the bank,
(b)   the Treasury,
(c)   the FSA, and
(d)   any other person specified in the code of practice under section 5.

(2)   As soon as is reasonably practicable after making a property transfer instrument the Bank of England shall publish a copy—

(a)   on the Bank's internet website, and
(b)   in two newspapers, chosen by the Bank of England to maximise the likelihood of the instrument coming to the attention of persons likely to be affected.

(3)   Where the Treasury receive a copy of a property transfer instrument under subsection (1) they shall lay a copy before Parliament.

[1862]

NOTES

Commencement: to be appointed.

42 Supplemental instruments

(1)   This section applies where the Bank of England has made a property transfer instrument in accordance with section 11(2) or 12(2) ("the original instrument").

(2)   The Bank of England may make one or more supplemental property transfer instruments.

(3)   A supplemental property transfer instrument is a property transfer instrument which—

(a)   provides for property, rights or liabilities to be transferred from the transferor under the original instrument (whether accruing or arising before or after the original instrument);

(b)   makes other provision of a kind that an original property transfer instrument may make under section 33(1)(b) (whether in connection with a transfer under the original instrument or in connection with a transfer under that or another supplemental instrument).

(4)   Sections 7 and 8 do not apply to a supplemental property transfer instrument (but it is to be treated in the same way as any other property transfer instrument for all other purposes, including for the purposes of the application of a power under this Part).

(5)   Before making a supplemental property transfer instrument the Bank of England must consult—

(a)   the FSA, and
(b)   the Treasury.

(6)   The possibility of making a supplemental property transfer instrument in reliance on subsection (2) is without prejudice to the possibility of making of a new instrument in accordance with section 11(2) or 12(2) (and not in reliance on subsection (2) above).

[1863]

NOTES

Commencement: to be appointed.

43 Onward transfer

(1)   This section applies where the Bank of England has made a property transfer instrument in respect of a bridge bank in accordance with section 12(2) ("the original instrument").

(2)   The Bank of England may make one or more onward property transfer instruments.

(3)   An onward property transfer instrument is a property transfer instrument which—

(a) provides for property, rights or liabilities of the bridge bank to be transferred (whether accruing or arising before or after the original instrument);

(b) makes other provision for the purposes of, or in connection with, the transfer of property, rights or liabilities of the bridge bank (whether the transfer has been or is to be effected by that instrument, by another property transfer instrument or otherwise).

(4) An onward property transfer instrument may relate to property, rights or liabilities of the bridge bank whether or not they were transferred under the original instrument.

(5) An onward property transfer instrument may not transfer property, rights or liabilities to the transferor under the original instrument.

(6) Sections 7, 8 and 52 do not apply to an onward property transfer instrument (but for other purposes it is to be treated in the same way as any other property transfer instrument, including for the purposes of the application of a power under this Part).

(7) Before making an onward property transfer instrument the Bank of England must consult—
(a) the FSA, and
(b) the Treasury.

(8) Section 42 applies where the Bank of England has made an onward property transfer instrument.

[1864]

NOTES
Commencement: to be appointed.

44 Reverse property transfer

(1) This section applies where the Bank of England has made a property transfer instrument in accordance with section 12(2) ("the original instrument") providing for the transfer of property, rights or liabilities to a bridge bank.

(2) The Bank of England may make one or more reverse property transfer instruments in respect of property, rights or liabilities of the bridge bank.

(3) If the Bank of England makes an onward property transfer instrument under section 43 the Bank may make one or more reverse property transfer instruments in respect of property, rights or liabilities of a transferee of any of the following kinds under the onward property transfer instrument—
(a) a company wholly owned by the Bank of England,
(b) a company wholly owned by the Treasury, or
(c) a company wholly owned by a nominee of the Treasury.

(4) A reverse property transfer instrument is a property transfer instrument which—
(a) provides for transfer to the transferor under the original instrument (where subsection (2) applies);
(b) provides for transfer to the bridge bank (where subsection (3) applies);
(c) makes other provision for the purposes of, or in connection with, the transfer of property, rights or liabilities that are, could be or could have been transferred under paragraph (a) or (b) (whether the transfer has been or is to be effected by that instrument or otherwise).

(5) Sections 7, 8 and 52 do not apply to a reverse property transfer instrument (but it is to be treated in the same way as any other property transfer instrument for all other purposes including for the purposes of the application of a power under this Part).

(6) Before making a reverse property transfer instrument the Bank of England must consult—
(a) the FSA, and
(b) the Treasury.

(7) Section 42 applies where the Bank of England has made a reverse property transfer instrument.

[1865]

NOTES
Commencement: to be appointed.

45 Temporary public ownership: property transfer

(1) This section applies where the Treasury have made a share transfer order, in respect of securities issued by a bank, in accordance with section 13(2) ("the original order").

(2) The Treasury may make one or more property transfer orders.

(3) A property transfer order is an order which—
(a) provides for property, rights or liabilities of the bank to be transferred (whether accruing or arising before or after the original order);

   (b)   makes other provision for the purposes of, or in connection with, the transfer of property, rights or liabilities of the bank (whether the transfer has been or is to be effected by the order or otherwise).

(4)   Sections 7, 8 and 9 do not apply to a property transfer order.

(5)   A property transfer order is to be treated—
   (a)   in the same way as a share transfer order for the procedural purposes of section 25, but
   (b)   as a property transfer instrument for all other purposes (including for the purposes of the application of powers under this Part).

(6)   In the application of section 39 by virtue of subsection (5)(b) above, the power to give directions under section 39(7) vests in the Treasury (instead of the Bank of England).

(7)   Section 42 applies where the Treasury has made a property transfer order.

(8)   Before making a property transfer order the Treasury must consult—
   (a)   the FSA, and
   (b)   the Bank of England.

[1866]

NOTES
Commencement: to be appointed.

46 Temporary public ownership: reverse property transfer

(1)   This section applies where the Treasury have made a property transfer order in accordance with section 45(2) ("the original order") providing for the transfer of property, rights or liabilities to a company wholly owned by—
   (a)   the Bank of England,
   (b)   the Treasury, or
   (c)   a nominee of the Treasury.

(2)   The Treasury may make one or more reverse property transfer orders in respect of property, rights or liabilities of the transferee under the original order.

(3)   A reverse property transfer order is a property transfer order which—
   (a)   provides for transfer to the transferor under the original order;
   (b)   makes other provision for the purposes of, or in connection with, the transfer of property, rights or liabilities which are, could be or could have been transferred.

(4)   Sections 7, 8 and 9 do not apply to a reverse property transfer order.

(5)   A reverse property transfer order is to be treated—
   (a)   in the same way as a share transfer order for the procedural purposes of section 25, but
   (b)   as a property transfer instrument for all other purposes (including for the purposes of the application of a power under this Part).

(6)   In the application of section 39 by virtue of subsection (5)(b) above, the power to give directions under section 39(7) vests in the Treasury (instead of the Bank of England).

(7)   Before making a reverse property transfer order the Treasury must consult—
   (a)   the FSA, and
   (b)   the Bank of England.

(8)   Section 42 applies where the Treasury have made a reverse property transfer order.

[1867]

NOTES
Commencement: to be appointed.

47 Restriction of partial transfers

(1)   In this Part "partial property transfer" means a property transfer instrument which provides for the transfer of some, but not all, of the property, rights and liabilities of a bank.

(2)   The Treasury may by order—
   (a)   restrict the making of partial property transfers;
   (b)   impose conditions on the making of partial property transfers;
   (c)   require partial property transfers to include specified provision or provision to a specified effect;
   (d)   provide for a partial property transfer to be void or voidable, or for other consequences (including automatic transfer of other property, rights or liabilities) to arise, if or in so far as the partial property transfer is made or purported to be made in contravention of a provision of the order (or of another order under this section).

(3)   Provision under subsection (2) may, in particular, refer to particular classes of deposit.

(4)   An order may apply to transfers generally or only to transfers—

    (a)   of a specified kind, or

    (b)   made or applying in specified circumstances.

(5)   An order—

    (a)   shall be made by statutory instrument, and

    (b)   may not be made unless a draft has been laid before and approved by resolution of each House of Parliament.

[1868]

NOTES

Commencement: to be appointed.

48　Power to protect certain interests

(1)   In this section—

    (a)   "security interests" means arrangements under which one person acquires, by way of security, an actual or contingent interest in the property of another,

    (b)   "title transfer collateral arrangements" are arrangements under which Person 1 transfers assets to Person 2 on terms providing for Person 2 to transfer assets if specified obligations are discharged,

    (c)   "set-off" arrangements are arrangements under which two or more debts, claims or obligations can be set off against each other,

    (d)   "netting arrangements" are arrangements under which a number of claims or obligations can be converted into a net claim or obligation and include, in particular, "close-out" netting arrangements, under which actual or theoretical debts are calculated during the course of a contract for the purpose of enabling them to be set off against each other or to be converted into a net debt, and

    (e)   "protected arrangements" means security interests, title transfer collateral arrangements, set-off arrangements and netting arrangements.

(2)   The Treasury may by order—

    (a)   restrict the making of partial property transfers in cases that involve, or where they might affect, protected arrangements;

    (b)   impose conditions on the making of partial property transfers in cases that involve, or where they might affect, protected arrangements;

    (c)   require partial property transfers to include specified provision, or provision to a specified effect, in respect of or for purposes connected with protected arrangements;

    (d)   provide for a partial property transfer to be void or voidable, or for other consequences (including automatic transfer of other property, rights or liabilities) to arise, if or in so far as the partial property transfer is made or purported to be made in contravention of a provision of the order (or of another order under this section).

(3)   An order may apply to protected arrangements generally or only to arrangements—

    (a)   of a specified kind, or

    (b)   made or applying in specified circumstances.

(4)   An order may include provision for determining which arrangements are to be, or not to be, treated as protected arrangements; in particular, an order may provide for arrangements to be classified not according to their description by the parties but according to one or more indications of how they are treated, or are intended to be treated, in commercial practice.

(5)   In this section "arrangements" includes arrangements which—

    (a)   are formed wholly or partly by one or more contracts or trusts;

    (b)   arise under or are wholly or partly governed by the law of a country or territory outside the United Kingdom;

    (c)   wholly or partly arise automatically as a matter of law;

    (d)   involve any number of parties;

    (e)   operate partly by reference to other arrangements between other parties.

(6)   An order—

    (a)   shall be made by statutory instrument, and

    (b)   may not be made unless a draft has been laid before and approved by resolution of each House of Parliament.

[1869]

NOTES

Commencement: to be appointed.

PART II
OTHER ACTS

Compensation

49 Orders

(1)   This Part provides three methods of protecting the financial interests of transferors and others in connection with share transfer instruments and orders and property transfer instruments.

(2)   A "compensation scheme order" is an order—
  (a)   establishing a scheme for determining whether transferors should be paid compensation, or providing for transferors to be paid compensation, and
  (b)   establishing a scheme for paying any compensation.

(3)   A "resolution fund order" is an order establishing a scheme under which transferors become entitled to the proceeds of the disposal of things transferred—
  (a)   in specified circumstances, and
  (b)   to a specified extent.

(4)   A "third party compensation order" is provision made in accordance with section 59 for compensation to be paid to persons other than transferors.

[1870]

NOTES
Commencement: to be appointed.

50 Sale to private sector purchaser

(1)   This section applies if the Bank of England makes a share transfer instrument or a property transfer instrument in accordance with section 11(2).

(2)   The Treasury shall make a compensation scheme order.

(3)   An order made by virtue of subsection (2) may include a third party compensation order.

(4)   In the case of a partial property transfer, an order made by virtue of subsection (2) must include a third party compensation order.

[1871]

NOTES
Commencement: to be appointed.

51 Transfer to temporary public ownership

(1)   This section applies if the Treasury make a share transfer order in accordance with section 13(2).

(2)   The Treasury shall make either—
  (a)   a compensation scheme order, or
  (b)   a resolution fund order.

(3)   A resolution fund order made by virtue of subsection (2)(b) may include—
  (a)   a compensation scheme order;
  (b)   a third party compensation order (which may, in particular, make provision, in respect of specified classes of creditor, for rights in addition to any rights they may have by virtue of the resolution fund order).

(4)   A compensation scheme order made by virtue of subsection (2) may include a third party compensation order.

[1872]

NOTES
Commencement: to be appointed.

52 Transfer to bridge bank

(1)   This section applies if the Bank of England makes a property transfer instrument in accordance with section 12(2).

(2)   The Treasury shall make a resolution fund order.

(3)   An order made by virtue of subsection (2) may include—
  (a)   a compensation scheme order;
  (b)   a third party compensation order (which may, in particular, make provision, in respect of specified classes of creditor, for rights in addition to any rights they may have by virtue of the resolution fund order).

(4)   In the case of a partial property transfer, the resolution fund order must include a third party compensation order.

[1873]

NOTES
Commencement: to be appointed.

53 Onward and reverse transfers

(1)   This section applies where—
   (a)   the Treasury make an onward share transfer order under section 28,
   (b)   the Treasury makes a reverse share transfer order under section 29,
   (c)   the Bank of England makes a bridge bank share transfer instrument under section 30,
   (d)   the Bank of England makes a bridge bank reverse share transfer instrument under section 31,
   (e)   the Bank of England makes an onward property transfer instrument under section 43,
   (f)   the Bank of England makes a reverse property transfer instrument under section 44,
   (g)   the Treasury make a property transfer order under section 45, or
   (h)   the Treasury make a reverse property transfer order under section 46.

(2)   The Treasury may make—
   (a)   a compensation scheme order;
   (b)   a third party compensation order.

[1874]

NOTES
Commencement: to be appointed.

54 Independent valuer

(1)   A compensation scheme order may provide for the amount of any compensation payable to be determined by a person appointed in accordance with the order (the "independent valuer"); and subsections (2) to (5) apply to an order which includes provision for an independent valuer.

(2)   An order must provide for the independent valuer to be appointed by a person appointed by the Treasury ("the appointing person").

(3)   An order may either—
   (a)   require the Treasury to make arrangements to identify a number of possible independent valuers, one of whom is to be selected by the appointing person, or
   (b)   require the appointing person to make arrangements to select the independent valuer, having regard to any criteria specified in the order.

(4)   The independent valuer may be removed only—
   (a)   on the grounds of incapacity or serious misconduct, and
   (b)   by a person specified by the Treasury in accordance with the compensation scheme order.

(5)   An order must include provision for resignation and replacement of the independent valuer (and subsections (2) and (3) apply to replacement as to the first appointment).

[1875]

NOTES
Commencement: to be appointed.

55 Independent valuer: supplemental

(1)   An independent valuer may do anything necessary or desirable for the purposes of or in connection with the performance of the functions of the office.

(2)   The Treasury may by order confer specific functions on independent valuers; in particular, the order may—
   (a)   enable an independent valuer to apply to a court or tribunal for an order requiring the provision of information or the giving of oral or written evidence;
   (b)   enable or require independent valuers to publish, disclose or withhold information.

(3)   Provision under subsection (2) may—
   (a)   confer a discretion on independent valuers;
   (b)   confer jurisdiction on a court or tribunal;
   (c)   make provision about oaths, expenses and other procedural matters relating to the giving of evidence or the provision of information;
   (d)   create a criminal offence;
   (e)   make other provision about enforcement.

(4)   An independent valuer may appoint staff.

(5)   The Treasury may by order make provision about the procedure to be followed by independent valuers.

PART II
OTHER ACTS

(6)   The Treasury shall by order make provision for—
    (a)   reconsideration of a decision of an independent valuer, and
    (b)   appeal to a court or tribunal against a decision of an independent valuer.

(7)   Independent valuers (and their staff) are neither servants nor agents of the Crown (and, in particular, are not civil servants).

(8)   Records of an independent valuer are public records for the purposes of the Public Records Act 1958.

(9)   An order under this section—
    (a)   shall be made by statutory instrument, and
    (b)   shall be subject to annulment in pursuance of a resolution of either House of Parliament.

[1876]

NOTES
Commencement: to be appointed.

56 Independent valuer: money

(1)   The Treasury may by order provide for the payment by the Treasury of remuneration and allowances to—
    (a)   independent valuers,
    (b)   staff of independent valuers,
    (c)   appointing persons, and
    (d)   monitors.

(2)   An order—
    (a)   must provide for the appointment by the Treasury of a person to monitor the operation of the arrangements for remuneration and allowances for independent valuers;
    (b)   may require, or enable a compensation scheme order or third party compensation order to require, the monitor's approval before specified things may be done in the course of those arrangements;
    (c)   may include provision about records and accounts;
    (d)   may make provision about numbers of staff and the terms and conditions of their appointment (which may include provision requiring the approval of the Treasury or the monitor).

(3)   In subsection (1) a reference to the payment of allowances to a person includes a reference to the payment to or in respect of the person of sums by way of or in respect of pension.

(4)   Independent valuers (and their staff) are not liable for damages in respect of anything done in good faith for the purposes of or in connection with the functions of the office (subject to section 8 of the Human Rights Act 1998).

(5)   An order under this section—
    (a)   shall be made by statutory instrument, and
    (b)   shall be subject to annulment in pursuance of a resolution of either House of Parliament.

[1877]

NOTES
Commencement: to be appointed.

57 Valuation principles

(1)   A compensation scheme order may specify principles ("valuation principles") to be applied in determining the amount of compensation.

(2)   Valuation principles may, in particular, require an independent valuer—
    (a)   to apply, or not to apply, specified methods of valuation;
    (b)   to assess values or average values at specified dates or over specified periods;
    (c)   to take specified matters into account in a specified manner;
    (d)   not to take specified matters into account.

(3)   In determining an amount of compensation (whether or not in accordance with valuation principles) an independent valuer must disregard actual or potential financial assistance provided by the Bank of England or the Treasury (disregarding ordinary market assistance offered by the Bank on its usual terms).

(4)   Valuation principles may require or permit an independent valuer to make assumptions; such as, for example, that the bank—
    (a)   has had a permission under Part 4 of the Financial Services and Markets Act 2000 (regulated activities) varied or cancelled,
    (b)   is unable to continue as a going concern,
    (c)   is in administration, or

    (d)   is being wound up.

(5)   There is nothing to prevent the application of the valuation principles in an order from resulting in no compensation being payable to a transferor.

[1878]

NOTES
Commencement: to be appointed.

58 Resolution fund

(1)   A resolution fund order must include provision for determining—
    (a)   who will be entitled to a share of the proceeds on disposal of things transferred,
    (b)   the way in which the proceeds will be calculated, and
    (c)   the way in which shares will be calculated.

(2)   Provision under subsection (1)(b) may, in particular, provide for proceeds to be calculated net of—
    (a)   amounts required for the repayment of loans from public funds or for other payments in respect of public financial assistance;
    (b)   some or all of the administrative or other expenses incurred in connection with the provisions of this Part.

(3)   A resolution fund order may include provision for—
    (a)   an independent valuer to make a determination under the order (in which case sections 54(2) to (5), 55 and 56 shall apply);
    (b)   valuation principles to be applied in making a determination (in which case section 57(2) shall apply).

(4)   A resolution fund order may confer a discretionary function on—
    (a)   a Minister of the Crown,
    (b)   the Treasury,
    (c)   the Bank of England, or
    (d)   any other specified person.

(5)   A resolution fund order may include provision for the determination of disputes about the application of its provisions (whether by conferring jurisdiction on a court or tribunal or otherwise).

(6)   A resolution fund order may require the Bank of England in managing a bridge bank to aim to maximise the proceeds available for distribution in accordance with the order; and an order which includes a requirement must—
    (a)   specify its extent, and
    (b)   include provision about how the Bank is to comply with it.

(7)   A resolution fund order may require the Treasury to ensure that a bank in temporary public ownership in accordance with section 13(2) is managed with the aim of maximising the proceeds available for distribution in accordance with the order; and an order which includes a requirement must—
    (a)   specify its extent, and
    (b)   include provision about how the Treasury is to comply with it.

(8)   A requirement under subsection (6) or (7) is to be complied with only in so far as is compatible with—
    (a)   pursuit of the special resolution objectives, and
    (b)   compliance with the code of practice under section 5.

[1879]

NOTES
Commencement: to be appointed.

59 Third party compensation: discretionary provision

(1)   A power or duty in this Part to make a third party compensation order is a power or duty to make provision establishing a scheme for paying compensation to persons other than a transferor.

(2)   A third party compensation order may—
    (a)   form part of a compensation scheme order or resolution fund order, or
    (b)   be a separate order.

(3)   A third party compensation order may include provision for—
    (a)   an independent valuer (in which case sections 54 to 56 shall apply);
    (b)   valuation principles (in which case section 57(2) to (5) shall apply).

[1880]

PART II
OTHER ACTS

60 Third party compensation: mandatory provision

(1)   The Treasury may make regulations about third party compensation arrangements in the case of partial property transfers.

(2)   In making regulations the Treasury shall, in particular, have regard to the desirability of ensuring that if a residual bank enters insolvency after transfer, pre-transfer creditors do not receive less favourable treatment than they would have received had it entered insolvency immediately before transfer.

(3)   In subsection (2)—
- (a)   "residual bank" means a bank that is a transferor under a property transfer instrument,
- (b)   "pre-transfer creditor" means a person who—
  - (i)   is a creditor of a residual bank immediately before a property transfer instrument takes effect, and
  - (ii)   satisfies conditions specified by the regulations, and
- (c)   the reference to insolvency includes a reference to (i) liquidation, (ii) bank insolvency, (iii) administration, (iv) bank administration, (v) receivership, (vi) a composition with creditors, and (vii) a scheme of arrangement.

(4)   The regulations may—
- (a)   require a compensation scheme order or a resolution fund order to include a third party compensation order;
- (b)   require a third party compensation order to include provision of a specified kind or to specified effect;
- (c)   make provision which is to be treated as forming part of a third party compensation order (whether (i) generally, (ii) only if applied, (iii) unless disapplied, or (iv) subject to express modification).

(5)   Regulations may provide for whether compensation is to be paid, and if so what amount is to be paid, to be determined by reference to any factors or combination of factors; in particular, the regulations may provide for entitlement—
- (a)   to depend in part upon the amounts which are or may be payable under a resolution fund order;
- (b)   to be contingent upon the occurrence or non-occurrence of specified events;
- (c)   to be determined wholly or partly by an independent valuer (within the meaning of sections 54 to 56) appointed in accordance with a compensation scheme order or resolution fund order.

(6)   Regulations may make provision about payment including, in particular, provision for payments—
- (a)   on account subject to terms and conditions;
- (b)   by instalment.

(7)   Regulations—
- (a)   shall be made by statutory instrument, and
- (b)   may not be made unless a draft has been laid before and approved by resolution of each House of Parliament.

                                                                                        [1881]

61 Sources of compensation

(1)   This section applies to—
- (a)   compensation scheme orders,
- (b)   resolution fund orders,
- (c)   third party compensation orders, and
- (d)   regulations under section 60.

(2)   An order or regulations may provide for compensation or other payments to be made by—
- (a)   the Treasury,
- (b)   the Financial Services Compensation Scheme, subject to section 214B of the Financial Services and Markets Act 2000 (contribution to costs of special resolution regime – inserted by section 171 below), or
- (c)   any other specified person.

                                                                                        [1882]

NOTES
Commencement: to be appointed.

62 Procedure

(1)   This section applies to—
  (a)   compensation scheme orders,
  (b)   resolution fund orders, and
  (c)   third party compensation orders.

(2)   An order—
  (a)   shall be made by statutory instrument, and
  (b)   may not be made unless a draft has been laid before and approved by resolution of each House of Parliament.

[1883]

NOTES
Commencement: to be appointed.

Incidental functions

63   General continuity obligation: property transfers

(1)   In this section and section 64—
  (a)   "residual bank" means a bank all or part of whose business has been transferred in accordance with section 11(2)(b) or 12(2),
  (b)   "group company" means anything which is, or was immediately before the transfer, a group undertaking in relation to a residual bank,
  (c)   "group undertaking" has the meaning given by section 1161(5) of the Companies Act 2006 (interpretation),
  (d)   "the transferred business" means the part of the bank's business that has been transferred, and
  (e)   "transferee" means a commercial purchaser or bridge bank to whom all or part of the transferred business has been transferred.

(2)   The residual bank and each group company must provide such services and facilities as are required to enable a transferee to operate the transferred business, or part of it, effectively.

(3)   The duty under subsection (2) (the "continuity obligation") may be enforced as if created by contract between the residual bank or group company and the transferee.

(4)   The duty to provide services and facilities in pursuance of the continuity obligation is subject to a right to receive reasonable consideration.

(5)   The continuity obligation is not limited to the provision of services or facilities directly to a transferee.

(6)   The Bank of England may, with the consent of the Treasury, by notice to the residual bank or a group company state that in the Bank's opinion—
  (a)   specified activities are required to be undertaken in accordance with the continuity obligation;
  (b)   activities are required be undertaken in accordance with the continuity obligation on specified terms.

(7)   A notice under subsection (6) shall be determinative of the nature and extent of the continuity obligation as from the time when the notice is given.

[1884]

NOTES
Commencement: to be appointed.

64   Special continuity obligations: property transfers

(1)   Expressions in this section have the same meaning as in section 63.

(2)   The Bank of England may—
  (a)   cancel a contract or other arrangement between the residual bank and a group company (whether or not rights or obligations under it have been transferred to a transferee);
  (b)   modify the terms of a contract or other arrangement between the residual bank and a group company (whether or not rights or obligations under it have been transferred to a transferee);
  (c)   add or substitute a transferee as a party to a contract or other arrangement between the residual bank and a group company;

(d)   confer and impose rights and obligations on a group company and a transferee, which shall have effect as if created by contract between them;
(e)   confer and impose rights and obligations on the residual bank and a transferee which shall have effect as if created by contract between them.

(3)   In modifying or setting terms under subsection (2) the Bank of England shall aim, so far as is reasonably practicable, to preserve or include—
(a)   provision for reasonable consideration, and
(b)   any other provision that would be expected in arrangements concluded between parties dealing at arm's length.

(4)   The power under subsection (2)—
(a)   may be exercised only in so far as the Bank of England thinks it necessary to ensure the provision of such services and facilities as are required to enable the transferee to operate the transferred business, or part of it, effectively,
(b)   may be exercised only with the consent of the Treasury, and
(c)   must be exercised by way of provision in a property transfer instrument (or supplemental instrument).

[1885]

NOTES
Commencement: to be appointed.

65   Continuity obligations: onward property transfers

(1)   In this section—
(a)   "onward transfer" means a transfer of property, rights or liabilities (whether or not under a power in this Part) from—
(i)   a person who is a transferee under a property transfer instrument under section 12(2) (an "original transferee"), or
(ii)   a bank, securities issued by which were earlier transferred by a share transfer order under section 13(2), and
(b)   the person to whom the onward transfer is made is referred to as an "onward transferee".

(2)   The continuity authority may—
(a)   provide for an obligation under section 63 to apply in respect of an onward transferee;
(b)   extend section 64 so as to permit action to be taken under section 64(2) for the purpose of enabling an onward transferee to operate transferred business, or part of it, effectively.

(3)   "The continuity authority" means—
(a)   the Bank of England, where subsection (1)(a)(i) applies, and
(b)   the Treasury, where subsection (1)(a)(ii) applies.

(4)   Subsection (2) may be relied on to impose obligations on—
(a)   an original transferee (where the original transfer was a property transfer),
(b)   a residual bank within the meaning of section 63 (where the original transfer was a property transfer),
(c)   the bank (where the original transfer was a share transfer),
(d)   anything which is or was a group undertaking (within the meaning of section 1161(5) of the Companies Act 2006) of anything within paragraphs (a) to (c), or
(e)   any combination.

(5)   Subsection (2) may be used to impose obligations—
(a)   in addition to obligations under or by virtue of section 63 or 64, or
(b)   replacing obligations under or by virtue of either of those sections to a specified extent.

(6)   A power under subsection (2) is exercisable by giving a notice to each person—
(a)   on whom a continuity obligation is to be imposed under the power, or
(b)   who is expected to benefit from a continuity obligation under the power.

(7)   Sections 63(3) to (7) and 64(3) and (4) apply to an obligation as applied under subsection (2)—
(a)   construing "transferred business" as the business transferred by means of the onward transfer, and
(b)   with any other necessary modification.

(8)   The Bank of England may act under or by virtue of subsection (2) only with the consent of the Treasury.

[1886]

NOTES
Commencement: to be appointed.

66 General continuity obligation: share transfers

(1)   In this section and section 67—

    (a)   "transferred bank" means a bank all or part of the ownership of which has been transferred in accordance with section 11(2)(a) or 13(2),

    (b)   "former group company" means anything which was a group undertaking in relation to the transferred bank immediately before the transfer (whether or not it is also a group undertaking in relation to the transferred bank immediately after the transfer),

    (c)   "group undertaking" has the meaning given by section 1161(5) of the Companies Act 2006 (interpretation), and

    (d)   "the continuity authority" means—

        (i)   the Bank of England, where ownership was transferred in accordance with section 11(2)(a), and

        (ii)   the Treasury, where ownership was transferred in accordance with section 13(2).

(2)   Each former group company must provide such services and facilities as are required to enable the transferred bank to operate effectively.

(3)   The duty under subsection (2) (the "continuity obligation") may be enforced as if created by contract between the transferred bank and the former group company.

(4)   The duty to provide services and facilities in pursuance of the continuity obligation is subject to a right to receive reasonable consideration.

(5)   The continuity obligation is not limited to the provision of services or facilities directly to the transferred bank.

(6)   The continuity authority may by notice to a former group company state that in the authority's opinion—

    (a)   specified activities are required to be undertaken in accordance with the continuity obligation;

    (b)   activities are required be undertaken in accordance with the continuity obligation on specified terms.

(7)   A notice under subsection (6) shall be determinative of the nature and extent of the continuity obligation as from the time when the notice is given.

(8)   The Bank of England may act under or by virtue of subsection (6) only with the consent of the Treasury.

[1887]

NOTES

Commencement: to be appointed.

---

67 Special continuity obligations: share transfers

(1)   Expressions in this section have the same meaning as in section 66.

(2)   The continuity authority may—

    (a)   cancel a contract or other arrangement between the transferred bank and a former group company;

    (b)   modify the terms of a contract or other arrangement between the transferred bank and a former group company;

    (c)   confer and impose rights and obligations on a former group company and the transferred bank, which shall have effect as if created by contract between them.

(3)   In modifying or setting terms under subsection (2) the continuity authority shall aim, so far as is reasonably practicable, to preserve or include—

    (a)   provision for reasonable consideration, and

    (b)   any other provision that would be expected in arrangements concluded between parties dealing at arm's length.

(4)   The power under subsection (2)—

    (a)   may be exercised only in so far as the continuity authority thinks it necessary to ensure the provision of such services and facilities as are required to enable the transferred bank to operate effectively,

    (b)   may be exercised by the Bank of England only with the consent of the Treasury, and

    (c)   must be exercised by way of provision in a share transfer instrument or order (or supplemental instrument or order).

[1888]

NOTES

Commencement: to be appointed.

68 Continuity obligations: onward share transfers

(1)   In this section "onward transfer" means a transfer (whether or not under a power in this Part) of securities issued by a bank where—
   (a)   securities issued by the bank were earlier transferred by share transfer order under section 13(2), or
   (b)   the bank was the transferee under a property transfer instrument under section 12(2).

(2)   The continuity authority may—
   (a)   provide for an obligation under section 66 to apply in respect of the bank after the onward transfer;
   (b)   extend section 67 so as to permit action to be taken under section 67(2) to enable the bank to operate effectively after the onward transfer.

(3)   In this section "continuity authority" has the same meaning as in sections 66 and 67.

(4)   Subsection (2) may be relied on to impose obligations on—
   (a)   the bank,
   (b)   anything which is or was a group undertaking (within the meaning of section 1161(5) of the Companies Act 2006) of the bank,
   (c)   anything which is or was a group undertaking of the residual bank (in a case to which subsection (1)(b) applies), or
   (d)   any combination.

(5)   Subsection (2) may be used to impose obligations—
   (a)   in addition to obligations under or by virtue of section 66 or 67, or
   (b)   replacing obligations under or by virtue of either of those sections to a specified extent.

(6)   A power under subsection (2) is exercisable by giving a notice to each person—
   (a)   on whom a continuity obligation is to be imposed under the power, or
   (b)   who is expected to benefit from a continuity obligation under the power.

(7)   Sections 66(3) to (7) and 67(3) and (4) apply to an obligation as applied under subsection (2) with any necessary modification.

(8)   The Bank of England may act under or by virtue of subsection (2) only with the consent of the Treasury.

[1889]

NOTES
   Commencement: to be appointed.

69 Continuity obligations: consideration and terms

(1)   The Treasury may by order specify matters which are to be or not to be considered in determining—
   (a)   what amounts to reasonable consideration for the purpose of sections 63 to 68;
   (b)   what provisions to include in accordance with section 64(3)(b) or 67(3)(b).

(2)   An order—
   (a)   shall be made by statutory instrument, and
   (b)   shall be subject to annulment in pursuance of a resolution of either House of Parliament.

(3)   A continuity authority may give guarantees or indemnities in respect of consideration for services or facilities provided or to be provided in pursuance of a continuity obligation.

(4)   In this section "continuity authority"—
   (a)   in relation to sections 63 and 64, means the Bank of England, and
   (b)   in relation to sections 65 to 68, has the same meaning as in those sections.

[1890]

NOTES
   Commencement: to be appointed.

70 Continuity obligations: termination

(1)   The continuity authority may by notice terminate an obligation arising under section 63 or 66.

(2)   The power under subsection (1) is exercisable by giving a notice to each person—
   (a)   on whom the obligation is imposed, or
   (b)   who has benefited or might have expected to benefit from the obligation.

(3)   In this section "continuity authority"—
   (a)   in relation to section 63, means the Bank of England, and
   (b)   in relation to section 66, has the same meaning as in that section.

(4)   A reference in subsection (1) to obligations under a section includes a reference to obligations under that section as applied under section 65 or 68.

[1891]

NOTES
Commencement: to be appointed.

71   Pensions

(1)   This section applies to—
    (a)   share transfer orders,
    (b)   share transfer instruments, and
    (c)   property transfer instruments.

(2)   An order or instrument may make provision—
    (a)   about the consequences of a transfer for a pension scheme;
    (b)   about property, rights and liabilities of any pension scheme of the bank.

(3)   In particular, an order or instrument may—
    (a)   modify any rights and liabilities;
    (b)   apportion rights and liabilities;
    (c)   transfer property of, or accrued rights in, one pension scheme to another (with or without consent).

(4)   Provision by virtue of this section may (but need not) amend the terms of a pension scheme.

(5)   A share or property transfer instrument may make provision in reliance on this section only with the consent of the Treasury.

(6)   In this section—
    (a)   "pension scheme" includes any arrangement for the payment of pensions, allowances and gratuities, and
    (b)   a reference to a pension scheme of a bank is a reference to a scheme in respect of which the bank, or a group company of the bank, is or was an employer.

(7)   In subsection (6)(b) the reference to a group company of the bank is a reference to anything that is or was a group undertaking in relation to the bank within the meaning given by section 1161(5) of the Companies Act 2006.

[1892]

NOTES
Commencement: to be appointed.

72   Enforcement

(1)   The Treasury may by regulations make provision for the enforcement of obligations imposed by or under—
    (a)   a share transfer order,
    (b)   a share transfer instrument, or
    (c)   a property transfer instrument.

(2)   Regulations—
    (a)   may confer jurisdiction on a court or tribunal;
    (b)   may not impose a penalty or create a criminal offence;
    (c)   may make provision which has effect in respect of an order or instrument only if applied by the order or instrument.

(3)   Regulations—
    (a)   shall be made by statutory instrument, and
    (b)   shall be subject to annulment in pursuance of a resolution of either House of Parliament.

[1893]

NOTES
Commencement: to be appointed.

73   Disputes

(1)   This section applies to—
    (a)   share transfer orders,
    (b)   share transfer instruments, and
    (c)   property transfer instruments.

(2)   An order or instrument may include provision for disputes to be determined in a specified manner.

(3)   Provision by virtue of subsection (2) may, in particular—

(a)   confer jurisdiction on a court or tribunal;
(b)   confer discretion on a specified person.

[1894]

NOTES
Commencement: to be appointed.

74 Tax

(1)   The Treasury may by regulations make provision about the fiscal consequences of the exercise of a stabilisation power.

(2)   Regulations may relate to—
(a)   capital gains tax;
(b)   corporation tax;
(c)   income tax;
(d)   inheritance tax;
(e)   stamp duty;
(f)   stamp duty land tax;
(g)   stamp duty reserve tax.

(3)   Regulations may apply to—
(a)   anything done in connection with an instrument or order;
(b)   things transferred or otherwise affected by virtue of an instrument or order;
(c)   a transferor or transferee under an instrument or order;
(d)   persons otherwise affected by an instrument or order.

(4)   Regulations may—
(a)   modify or disapply an enactment;
(b)   provide for an action to have or not have specified consequences;
(c)   provide for specified classes of property (including securities), rights or liabilities to be treated, or not treated, in a specified way;
(d)   withdraw or restrict a relief;
(e)   extend, restrict or otherwise modify a charge to tax;
(f)   provide for matters to be determined by the Treasury in accordance with provision made by or in accordance with the regulations.

(5)   Regulations may make provision for the fiscal consequences of the exercise of a stabilisation power in respect of things done—
(a)   during the period of three months before the date on which the stabilisation power is exercised, or
(b)   on or after that date.

(6)   In relation to the exercise of a supplemental or onward instrument or order under section 26, 27, 28, 30, 42, 43 or 45, in subsection (5)(a) above "the stabilisation power" is a reference to the first stabilisation power in connection with which the supplemental or onward instrument or order is made.

(7)   The Treasury may by order amend subsection (2) so as to—
(a)   add an entry, or
(b)   remove an entry.

(8)   Regulations or an order under this section—
(a)   shall be made by statutory instrument, and
(b)   may not be made unless a draft has been laid before and approved by resolution of the House of Commons.

[1895]

NOTES
Commencement: to be appointed.

75 Power to change law

(1)   The Treasury may by order amend the law for the purpose of enabling the powers under this Part to be used effectively, having regard to the special resolution objectives.

(2)   An order may be made—
(a)   for the general purpose of the exercise of powers under this Part,
(b)   to facilitate a particular proposed or possible use of a power, or
(c)   in connection with a particular exercise of a power.

(3)   An order under subsection (2)(c) may make provision which has retrospective effect in so far as the Treasury consider it necessary or desirable for giving effect to the particular exercise of a

power under this Act in connection with which the order is made (but in relying on this subsection the Treasury shall have regard to the fact that it is in the public interest to avoid retrospective legislation).

(4)   In subsection (1) "amend the law" means—
   (a)   disapply or modify the effect of a provision of an enactment (other than a provision made by or under this Act),
   (b)   disapply or modify the effect of a rule of law not set out in legislation, or
   (c)   amend any provision of an instrument or order made in the exercise of a stabilisation power.

(5)   Provision under this section may relate to this Part as it applies—
   (a)   to banks,
   (b)   to building societies,
   (c)   to credit unions (by virtue of section 89), or
   (d)   to any combination.

(6)   Specific powers under this Part are without prejudice to the generality of this section.

(7)   An order—
   (a)   shall be made by statutory instrument, and
   (b)   may not be made unless a draft has been laid before and approved by resolution of each House of Parliament.

(8)   But if the Treasury think it necessary to make an order without complying with subsection (7)(b)—
   (a)   the order may be made,
   (b)   the order shall lapse unless approved by resolution of each House of Parliament during the period of 28 days (ignoring periods of dissolution, prorogation or adjournment of either House for more than 4 days) beginning with the day on which the order is made,
   (c)   the lapse of an order under paragraph (b) does not invalidate anything done under or in reliance on the order before the lapse and at a time when neither House has declined to approve the order, and
   (d)   the lapse of an order under paragraph (b) does not prevent the making of a new order (in new terms).

[1896]

PART II
OTHER ACTS

NOTES
Commencement: to be appointed.

Treasury

76   International obligation notice: general

(1)   The Bank of England may not exercise a stabilisation power in respect of a bank if the Treasury notify the Bank that the exercise would be likely to contravene an international obligation of the United Kingdom.

(2)   A notice under subsection (1)—
   (a)   must be in writing, and
   (b)   may be withdrawn (generally, partially or conditionally).

(3)   If the Treasury give a notice under subsection (1) the Bank of England must consider other exercises of the stabilisation powers with a view to—
   (a)   pursuing the special resolution objectives, and
   (b)   avoiding the objections on which the Treasury's notice was based.

(4)   The Treasury may by notice to the Bank of England disapply subsection (3) in respect of a bank; and a notice may be revoked by further notice.

[1897]

NOTES
Commencement: to be appointed.

77   International obligation notice: bridge bank

(1)   This section applies where the Bank of England has transferred all or part of a bank's business to a bridge bank.

(2)   The Bank of England must comply with any notice of the Treasury requiring the Bank, for the purpose of ensuring compliance by the United Kingdom with its international obligations—
   (a)   to take specified action under this Part in respect of the bridge bank, or
   (b)   not to take specified action under this Part in respect of the bridge bank.

(3)   A notice under subsection (1)—
   (a)   must be in writing, and

(b)   may be withdrawn (generally, partially or conditionally).

(4)   A notice may include requirements about timing.

[1898]

NOTES
Commencement: to be appointed.

78 Public funds: general

(1)   The Bank of England may not exercise a stabilisation power in respect of a bank without the Treasury's consent if the exercise would be likely to have implications for public funds.

(2)   In subsection (1)—
   (a)   "public funds" means the Consolidated Fund and any other account or source of money which cannot be drawn or spent other than by, or with the authority of, the Treasury, and
   (b)   action has implications for public funds if it would or might involve or lead to a need for the application of public funds.

(3)   The Treasury may by order specify considerations which are to be, or not to be, taken into account in determining whether action has implications for public funds for the purpose of subsection (1).

(4)   If the Treasury refuse consent under subsection (1), the Bank of England must consider other exercises of the stabilisation powers with a view to—
   (a)   pursuing the special resolution objectives, and
   (b)   avoiding the objections on which the Treasury's refusal was based.

(5)   The Treasury may by notice to the Bank of England disapply subsection (4) in respect of a bank; and a notice may be revoked by further notice.

(6)   An order under subsection (3)—
   (a)   shall be made by statutory instrument, and
   (b)   shall be subject to annulment in pursuance of a resolution of the House of Commons.

[1899]

NOTES
Commencement: to be appointed.

79 Public funds: bridge bank

(1)   This section applies where the Bank of England has transferred all or part of a bank's business to a bridge bank.

(2)   The Bank of England may not take action in respect of the bridge bank without the Treasury's consent if the action would be likely to have implications for public funds.

(3)   Section 78(2) and (3) have effect for the purposes of this section.

[1900]

NOTES
Commencement: to be appointed.

80 Bridge bank: report

(1)   Where the Bank of England transfers all or part of a bank's business to a bridge bank, the Bank must report to the Chancellor of the Exchequer about the activities of the bridge bank.

(2)   The first report must be made as soon as is reasonably practicable after the end of one year beginning with the date of the first transfer to the bridge bank.

(3)   A report must be made as soon as is reasonably practicable after the end of each subsequent year.

(4)   The Chancellor of the Exchequer must lay a copy of each report under subsection (2) or (3) before Parliament.

(5)   The Bank must comply with any request of the Treasury for a report dealing with specified matters in relation to a bridge bank.

(6)   A request under subsection (5) may include provision about—
   (a)   the content of the report;
   (b)   timing.

[1900A]

NOTES
Commencement: to be appointed.

81 Temporary public ownership: report

(1)   Where the Treasury make one or more share transfer orders under section 13(2) in respect of a bank, the Treasury must lay before Parliament a report about the activities of the bank.

(2)   The first report must be made as soon as is reasonably practicable after the end of one year beginning with the date of the first share transfer order.

(3)   A report must be made as soon as is reasonably practicable after the end of each subsequent year.

(4)   The obligation to produce reports continues to apply in respect of each year until the first during which no securities issued by the bank are owned by—
   (a)   a company wholly owned by the Treasury, or
   (b)   a nominee of the Treasury.

                                                                                     [1900B]

NOTES
Commencement: to be appointed.

Holding companies

82 Temporary public ownership

(1)   The Treasury may take a parent undertaking of a bank (the "holding company") into temporary public ownership, in accordance with section 13(2), if the following conditions are met.

(2)   Condition 1 is that the FSA are satisfied that the general conditions for the exercise of a stabilisation power set out in section 7 are met in respect of the bank.

(3)   Condition 2 is that the Treasury are satisfied that it is necessary to take action in respect of the holding company for the purpose specified in Condition A or B of section 9.

(4)   Condition 3 is that the holding company is an undertaking incorporated in, or formed under the law of any part of, the United Kingdom.

(5)   Before determining whether Condition 2 is met the Treasury must consult—
   (a)   the FSA, and
   (b)   the Bank of England.

(6)   Expressions used in this section have the same meaning as in the Companies Act 2006.

                                                                                     [1900C]

NOTES
Commencement: to be appointed.

83 Supplemental

(1)   In the following provisions references to banks include references to holding companies—
   (a)   section 10(1),
   (b)   section 13(3),
   (c)   section 16(1), and
   (d)   section 75(5)(a).

(2)   Where the Treasury take a bank's holding company into temporary public ownership in reliance on section 82—
   (a)   section 20(2) applies to (i) directors of the holding company, (ii) directors of the bank, and (iii) directors of a bank in the same group,
   (b)   section 25(2) applies as if references to a bank were references to a holding company,
   (c)   sections 27 to 29 apply as if references to a bank were references to a holding company,
   (d)   a share transfer may be made in respect of securities which were issued by the bank or by another bank which is or was in the same group; and a transfer—
      (i)   shall be made by onward share transfer order under section 28 or by reverse share transfer order under section 29 (in addition to any that may be made under those sections as applied by paragraph (c) above),
      (ii)   may be made under section 28 only in respect of securities held by (or for the benefit of) the holding company or a subsidiary undertaking of the holding company,
      (iii)   is not subject to section 28(4),
      (iv)   may be made under section 29 only in respect of securities held by a person of a kind listed in section 29(3)(b), and
      (v)   is not (otherwise) subject to section 29(3),
   (e)   section 45 applies as if—
      (i)   the reference to a bank in subsection (1) were a reference to a holding company, and

      (ii)   a reference to the bank in subsection (3) were a reference to the holding company, the bank and any other bank which is or was in the same group,

(f)   sections 65 to 68 apply, with—

      (i)   references to the bank or the transferred bank taken as references to the bank, the holding company and any other bank which is or was in the same group, and

      (ii) references to securities of the bank taken as including references to securities of the holding company (so that, in particular, sections 65(1)(a)(ii) and 68(1)(a) include references to the earlier transfer of securities issued by the holding company),

(g)   other provisions of this Act about share transfer orders apply with any necessary modifications,

(h)   section 214B of the Financial Services and Markets Act 2000 applies (contribution to costs of special resolution regime – inserted by section 171 below), and

(i)   the reference in section 214B(1)(b) to the bank, and later references in the section, are treated as including references to any other bank which is also a subsidiary undertaking of the holding company (but not to the holding company itself).

(3)   A reference in this Act or another enactment to a share transfer order in respect of securities issued by a bank includes (so far as the context permits) a reference to a share transfer order in respect of securities issued by a holding company.

(4)   In so far as sections 47 and 60 apply in relation to orders treated as property transfer instruments by virtue of section 45(5)(b) or 46(5)(b) (including those sections as applied by virtue of subsection (2) above) the reference in section 47(1) to the property of a bank includes a reference to the property of a holding company and of any other bank which is or was in the same group.

(5)   Expressions used in this section have the same meaning as in the Companies Act 2006.

(6)   A reference to two banks being in the same group is a reference to their being group undertakings in respect of each other.

[1900D]

NOTES

Commencement: to be appointed.

Building societies, &c

84 Application of Part 1: general

This Part shall apply to building societies (within the meaning of section 119 of the Building Societies Act 1986) as it applies to banks, subject to the provisions of the Table.

Section	Topic	Modification or note
11	Private sector purchaser	A share transfer instrument may not be made.
13	Temporary public ownership	The procedure provided by section 85 has effect in place of share transfer orders.
14 to 32	Transfer of securities	The procedure provided by section 85 has effect in place of share transfer orders; and— (a) sections 28 and 30 do not apply, and (b) section 27 applies following an order under section 85 as following a share transfer order.
33	Property transfer instrument: nature	A property transfer instrument in respect of a building society may— (a) cancel shares in the building society; (b) confer rights and impose liabilities in place of cancelled shares (whether by way of actual or deemed shares in a transferee building society or by way of other rights and liabilities in relation to a transferee bank).
33 and 36	Property transfer instrument: continuity	A property transfer instrument in respect of a bank which provides for transfer to a building society may confer rights and impose liabilities by way of actual or deemed shares in the building society.

Section	Topic	Modification or note
34	Property transfer instrument: effect	A property transfer instrument may, in particular, have effect without causing sections 93 to 102D of the Building Societies Act 1986 (mergers and transfers) to apply.
42	Supplemental property transfer instrument	A supplemental property transfer instrument in respect of a building society may— (a) cancel shares in the building society; (b) confer rights and impose liabilities in place of cancelled shares (whether by way of actual or deemed shares in a transferee building society or by way of other rights and liabilities in relation to a transferee bank).
45	Temporary public ownership: property transfer	(a) Section 45 applies following an order under section 85 as following a share transfer order. (b) A property transfer order in respect of a building society may cancel shares in the building society.
49 to 62	Compensation	(a) A reference to a share transfer order includes a reference to an order under section 85. (b) A resolution fund order may not be made under section 51(2)(b). (c) If and in so far as an order under section 85 provides for the issue of new deferred shares, section 51(2) shall not apply.
63 to 75	Incidental functions	A reference to a share transfer order includes a reference to an order under section 85.

[1900E]

PART II
OTHER ACTS

NOTES

Commencement: to be appointed.

85 Temporary public ownership

(1)   For the purpose of exercising the third stabilisation option in respect of a building society the Treasury may make one or more orders for the purposes of—
  (a)   arranging for deferred shares of a building society to be publicly owned,
  (b)   cancelling private membership rights in the building society,
  (c)   allowing the building society to continue in business while in public ownership, and
  (d)   eventually either winding up or dissolving the building society.

(2)   For the purpose specified in subsection (1)(a) an order may—
  (a)   arrange for the transfer of existing deferred shares;
  (b)   provide for new deferred shares.

(3)   For the purpose of arranging for the transfer of existing deferred shares an order may—
  (a)   provide for deferred shares to be transferred;
  (b)   make other provision for the purposes of, or in connection with, the transfer of deferred shares (whether or not the transfer has been or is to be effected by the order, by another order under this section or otherwise);
  (c)   relate to all or any specified class or description of deferred shares issued by the building society.

(4)   For the purpose of providing for new deferred shares an order may—
  (a)   issue or allow the Treasury to issue new deferred shares on behalf of the building society;
  (b)   specify or allow the Treasury to specify the terms and effect of new deferred shares;
  (c)   specify or allow the Treasury to specify the recipient of new deferred shares.

(5)   For the purpose specified in subsection (1)(b) an order may—
  (a)   cancel or permit the cancellation of shares (whether or not deferred) in the building society;
  (b)   confer rights and impose liabilities, or allow them to be conferred and imposed, in place of cancelled shares;

(c)   prevent the issue or acquisition of shares in or other rights in respect of the building society otherwise than in accordance with the order.

(6)   For the purpose specified in subsection (1)(c) an order may make any provision which the Treasury think desirable to facilitate the business of the building society after the making of provision in accordance with subsections (3) to (5).

(7)   An order in respect of a building society may—
  (a)   make provision expressly or impliedly disapplying or modifying the memorandum or rules of the building society;
  (b)   disapply or modify an enactment about, or in its application to, building societies.

(8)   The following sections apply to orders under this section as to share transfer orders: sections 17, 18, 20, 21, 22, 23, 25, 71, 72 and 73.

[1900F]

NOTES
Commencement: to be appointed.

86   Distribution of assets on dissolution or winding up

(1)   The Treasury may by order make provision about the distribution of surplus assets of a building society which—
  (a)   is the subject of a property transfer instrument or order, and
  (b)   is later wound up or dissolved by consent.

(2)   An order under section 85 may include provision about the distribution of surplus assets of the building society if it is later wound up or dissolved by consent.

(3)   "Surplus" means remaining after the satisfaction of liabilities to creditors and shareholders.

(4)   An order under or by virtue of this section—
  (a)   may include any provision of a kind that may be made by order under section 90B of the Building Societies Act 1986 (power to alter priorities on dissolution or winding up),
  (b)   may be made whether or not the power under that section has been exercised, and
  (c)   shall be treated for all procedural purposes in the same way as an order under that section.

[1900G]

NOTES
Commencement: to be appointed.

87   Interpretation

(1)   Expressions used in this group of sections and in the Building Societies Act 1986 have the same meaning in this group of sections as in that Act.

(2)   An order under section 119(1) of that Act defining "deferred shares"—
  (a)   may make special provision for the meaning of that expression in the application of this group of sections, and
  (b)   shall otherwise apply to this group of sections as to that Act.

[1900H]

NOTES
Commencement: to be appointed.

88   Consequential provision

(1)   The Treasury may by order make provision, in addition to the provisions of this group of sections, in consequence of the application of this Part to building societies.

(2)   An order may, in particular, amend or modify the effect of an enactment (including a fiscal enactment) passed before the commencement of this Part.

(3)   An order—
  (a)   shall be made by statutory instrument, and
  (b)   may not be made unless a draft has been laid before and approved by resolution of each House of Parliament.

[1900I]

NOTES
Commencement: to be appointed.

89   Credit unions

(1)   The Treasury may by order provide for the application of this Part to credit unions (within the meaning of section 31 of the Credit Unions Act 1979) subject to modifications set out in the order.

(2)   An order may disapply, modify or apply (with or without modifications) any enactment which relates, or in so far as it relates, to credit unions.

(3)   An order—
  (a)   shall be made by statutory instrument, and
  (b)   may not be made unless a draft has been laid before and approved by resolution of each House of Parliament.

(4)   Provision made under or by virtue of this Part may make special provision in relation to the application of this Part to credit unions.

(5)   In the application of this section to Northern Ireland the reference to section 31 of the Credit Unions Act 1979 is to be treated as a reference to Article 2 of the Credit Unions (Northern Ireland) Order 1985.

[1900J]

NOTES
Commencement: to be appointed.

PART 2
BANK INSOLVENCY

Introduction

90   Overview

(1)   This Part provides for a procedure to be known as bank insolvency.

(2)   The main features of bank insolvency are that—
  (a)   a bank enters the process by court order,
  (b)   the order appoints a bank liquidator,
  (c)   the bank liquidator aims to arrange for the bank's eligible depositors to have their accounts transferred or to receive their compensation from the FSCS,
  (d)   the bank liquidator then winds up the bank, and
  (e)   for those purposes, the bank liquidator has powers and duties of liquidators, as applied and modified by the provisions of this Part.

(3)   The Table describes the provisions of this Part.

Sections	*Topic*
Sections 90 to 93	Introduction
Sections 94 to 98	Bank insolvency order
Sections 99 to 105	Process of bank liquidation
Sections 106 to 112	Tenure of bank liquidator
Sections 113 to 116	Termination of process, &c
Sections 117 to 122	Other processes
Sections 123 to 135	Miscellaneous

[1900K]

NOTES
Commencement: to be appointed.

91   Interpretation: "bank"

(1)   In this Part "bank" means a UK institution which has permission under Part 4 of the Financial Services and Markets Act 2000 to carry on the regulated activity of accepting deposits (within the meaning of section 22 of that Act, taken with Schedule 2 and any order under section 22).

(2)   But "bank" does not include—
  (a)   a building society within the meaning of section 119 of the Building Societies Act 1986,
  (b)   a credit union within the meaning of section 31 of the Credit Unions Act 1979, or
  (c)   any other class of institution excluded by an order made by the Treasury.

PART II
OTHER ACTS

(3)   In subsection (1) "UK institution" means an institution which is incorporated in, or formed under the law of any part of, the United Kingdom.

(4)   An order under subsection (2)(c)—
  (a)   shall be made by statutory instrument, and
  (b)   may not be made unless a draft has been laid before and approved by resolution of each House of Parliament.

(5)   Section 130 makes provision for the application of this Part to building societies.

(6)   Section 131 makes provision for the application of this Part to credit unions.

[1900L]

NOTES
Commencement: to be appointed.

92 Interpretation: "the court"

In this Part "the court" means—
  (a)   in England and Wales, the High Court,
  (b)   in Scotland, the Court of Session, and
  (c)   in Northern Ireland, the High Court.

[1900M]

NOTES
Commencement: to be appointed.

93 Interpretation: other expressions

(1)   In this Part "the FSA" means the Financial Services Authority.

(2)   In this Part a reference to "the FSCS" is a reference to—
  (a)   the Financial Services Compensation Scheme (established under Part 15 of the Financial Services and Markets Act 2000), or
  (b)   where appropriate, the scheme manager of that Scheme.

(3)   In this Part "eligible depositors" means depositors who are eligible for compensation under the FSCS.

(4)   For the purposes of a reference in this Part to inability to pay debts—
  (a)   a bank that is in default on an obligation to pay a sum due and payable under an agreement, is to be treated as unable to pay its debts, and
  (b)   section 123 of the Insolvency Act 1986 (inability to pay debts) also applies; and
for the purposes of paragraph (a) "agreement" means an agreement the making or performance of which constitutes or is part of a regulated activity carried on by the bank.

(5)   Expressions used in this Part and in the Insolvency Act 1986 have the same meaning as in that Act.

(6)   Expressions used in this Part and in the Companies Act 2006 have the same meaning as in that Act.

(7)   A reference in this Part to action includes a reference to inaction.

(8)   The expression "fair" is used in this Part as a shorter modern equivalent of the expression "just and equitable" (and is not therefore intended to exclude the application of any judicial or other practice relating to the construction and application of that expression).

[1900N]

NOTES
Commencement: to be appointed.

Bank insolvency order

94 The order

(1)   A bank insolvency order is an order appointing a person as the bank liquidator of a bank.

(2)   A person is eligible for appointment as a bank liquidator if qualified to act as an insolvency practitioner.

(3)   An appointment may be made only if the person has consented to act.

(4)   A bank insolvency order takes effect in accordance with section 98; and—
  (a)   the process of a bank insolvency order having effect may be described as "bank insolvency" in relation to the bank, and
  (b)   while the order has effect the bank may be described as being "in bank insolvency".

[1900O]

NOTES
Commencement: to be appointed.

95　Application

(1)　An application for a bank insolvency order may be made to the court by—
  (a)　the Bank of England,
  (b)　the FSA, or
  (c)　the Secretary of State.

(2)　An application must nominate a person to be appointed as the bank liquidator.

(3)　The bank must be given notice of an application, in accordance with rules under section 411 of the Insolvency Act 1986 (as applied by section 125 below).

[1900P]

NOTES
Commencement: to be appointed.

96　Grounds for applying

(1)　In this section—
  (a)　Ground A is that a bank is unable, or likely to become unable, to pay its debts,
  (b)　Ground B is that the winding up of a bank would be in the public interest, and
  (c)　Ground C is that the winding up of a bank would be fair.

(2)　The Bank of England may apply for a bank insolvency order only if—
  (a)　the FSA has informed the Bank of England that the FSA is satisfied that Conditions 1 and 2 in section 7 are met, and
  (b)　the Bank of England is satisfied—
    (i)　that the bank has eligible depositors, and
    (ii)　that Ground A or C applies.

(3)　The FSA may apply for a bank insolvency order only if—
  (a)　the Bank of England consents, and
  (b)　the FSA is satisfied—
    (i)　that Conditions 1 and 2 in section 7 are met,
    (ii)　that the bank has eligible depositors, and
    (iii)　that Ground A or C applies.

(4)　The Secretary of State may apply for a bank insolvency order only if satisfied—
  (a)　that the bank has eligible depositors, and
  (b)　that Ground B applies.

(5)　The sources of information on the basis of which the Secretary of State may be satisfied of the matters specified in subsection (4) include those listed in section 124A(1) of the Insolvency Act 1986 (petition for winding up on grounds of public interest).

[1900Q]

NOTES
Commencement: to be appointed.

97　Grounds for making

(1)　The court may make a bank insolvency order on the application of the Bank of England or the FSA if satisfied—
  (a)　that the bank has eligible depositors, and
  (b)　that Ground A or C of section 96 applies.

(2)　The court may make a bank insolvency order on the application of the Secretary of State if satisfied—
  (a)　that the bank has eligible depositors, and
  (b)　that Grounds B and C of section 96 apply.

(3)　On an application for a bank insolvency order the court may—
  (a)　grant the application in accordance with subsection (1) or (2),
  (b)　adjourn the application (generally or to a specified date), or
  (c)　dismiss the application.

[1900R]

NOTES
Commencement: to be appointed.

98 Commencement

(1)   A bank insolvency order shall be treated as having taken effect in accordance with this section.

(2)   In the case where—
   (a)   notice has been given to the FSA under section 120 of an application for an administration order or a petition for a winding up order, and
   (b)   the FSA or the Bank of England applies for a bank insolvency order in the period of 2 weeks specified in Condition 3 in that section,

the bank insolvency order is treated as having taken effect when the application or petition was made or presented.

(3)   In any other case, the bank insolvency order is treated as having taken effect when the application for the order was made.

(4)   Unless the court directs otherwise on proof of fraud or mistake, proceedings taken in the bank insolvency, during the period for which it is treated as having had effect, are treated as having been taken validly.

[1900S]

NOTES
Commencement: to be appointed.

Process of bank liquidation

99 Objectives

(1)   A bank liquidator has two objectives.

(2)   Objective 1 is to work with the FSCS so as to ensure that as soon as is reasonably practicable each eligible depositor—
   (a)   has the relevant account transferred to another financial institution, or
   (b)   receives payment from (or on behalf of) the FSCS.

(3)   Objective 2 is to wind up the affairs of the bank so as to achieve the best result for the bank's creditors as a whole.

(4)   Objective 1 takes precedence over Objective 2 (but the bank liquidator is obliged to begin working towards both objectives immediately upon appointment).

[1900T]

NOTES
Commencement: to be appointed.

100 Liquidation committee

(1)   Following a bank insolvency order a liquidation committee must be established, for the purpose of ensuring that the bank liquidator properly exercises the functions under this Part.

(2)   The liquidation committee shall consist initially of 3 individuals, one nominated by each of—
   (a)   the Bank of England,
   (b)   the FSA, and
   (c)   the FSCS.

(3)   The bank liquidator must report to the liquidation committee about any matter—
   (a)   on request, or
   (b)   which the bank liquidator thinks is likely to be of interest to the liquidation committee.

(4)   In particular, the bank liquidator—
   (a)   must keep the liquidation committee informed of progress towards Objective 1 in section 99, and
   (b)   must notify the liquidation committee when in the bank liquidator's opinion Objective 1 in section 99 has been achieved entirely or so far as is reasonably practicable.

(5)   As soon as is reasonably practicable after receiving notice under subsection (4)(b) the liquidation committee must either—
   (a)   resolve that Objective 1 in section 99 has been achieved entirely or so far as is reasonably practicable (a "full payment resolution"), or
   (b)   apply to the court under section 168(5) of the Insolvency Act 1986 (as applied by section 103 below).

(6)   Where a liquidation committee passes a full payment resolution—
   (a)   the bank liquidator must summon a meeting of creditors,
   (b)   the meeting may elect 2 or 4 individuals as new members of the liquidation committee,
   (c)   those individuals replace the members nominated by the Bank of England and the FSA,

(d) the FSCS may resign from the liquidation committee (in which case 3 or 5 new members may be elected under paragraph (b)), and

(e) if no individuals are elected under paragraph (b), or the resulting committee would have fewer than 3 members or an even number of members, the liquidation committee ceases to exist at the end of the meeting.

(7) Subject to provisions of this section, rules under section 411 of the Insolvency Act 1986 (as amended by section 125 below) may make provision about—

(a) the establishment of liquidation committees,

(b) the membership of liquidation committees,

(c) the functions of liquidation committees, and

(d) the proceedings of liquidation committees.

[1900U]

NOTES

Commencement: to be appointed.

---

101 Liquidation committee: supplemental

(1) A meeting of the liquidation committee may be summoned—

(a) by any of the members, or

(b) by the bank liquidator.

(2) While the liquidation committee consists of the initial members (or their nominated replacements) a meeting is quorate only if all the members are present.

(3) A person aggrieved by any action of the liquidation committee before it has passed a full payment resolution may apply to the court, which may make any order (including an order for the repayment of money).

(4) The court may (whether on an application under subsection (3), on the application of a bank liquidator or otherwise) make an order that the liquidation committee is to be treated as having passed a full payment resolution.

(5) If a liquidation committee fails to comply with section 100(5) the bank liquidator must apply to the court—

(a) for an order under subsection (4) above, or

(b) for directions under or by virtue of section 168(3) or 169(2) of the Insolvency Act 1986 as applied by section 103 below.

(6) A nominating body under section 100(2) may replace its nominee at any time.

(7) After the removal of the nominated members under section 100(6)(c) the FSA and the Bank of England—

(a) may attend meetings of the liquidation committee,

(b) are entitled to copies of documents relating to the liquidation committee's business,

(c) may make representations to the liquidation committee, and

(d) may participate in legal proceedings relating to the bank insolvency.

(8) Where a liquidation committee ceases to exist by virtue of section 100(6)(e)—

(a) it may be re-formed by a creditors' meeting summoned by the bank liquidator for the purpose, and

(b) the bank liquidator must summon a meeting for the purpose if requested to do so by one-tenth in value of the bank's creditors.

(9) Where a liquidation committee ceases to exist by virtue of section 100(6)(e) and has not been re-formed under subsection (8) above or under section 141(2) or 142(2) of the Insolvency Act 1986 (as applied by section 103 below)—

(a) ignore a reference in this Part to the liquidation committee,

(b) for section 113(2) to (4) substitute requirements for the bank liquidator, before making a proposal—

(i) to produce a final report,

(ii) to send copies in accordance with section 113(2)(b),

(iii) to make it available in accordance with section 113(2)(c), and

(iv) to be satisfied as specified in section 113(4)(b),

(c) ignore Condition 2 in section 114, and

(d) for section 115(1) to (5) substitute a power for the bank liquidator to apply to the Secretary of State or Accountant of Court for release and requirements that before making an application the bank liquidator must—

(i) produce a final report,

(ii) send copies in accordance with section 115(2)(b),

(iii) make it available in accordance with section 115(2)(c), and

(iv)   notify the court and the registrar of companies of the intention to vacate office and to apply for release.

[1900V]

NOTES
Commencement: to be appointed.

102   Objective 1: (a) or (b)?

(1)   As soon as is reasonably practicable, a liquidation committee must recommend the bank liquidator to pursue—

(a)   Objective 1(a) in section 99,

(b)   Objective 1(b) in section 99, or

(c)   Objective 1(a) for one specified class of case and Objective 1(b) for another.

(2)   In making a recommendation the liquidation committee must consider—

(a)   the desirability of achieving Objective 1 as quickly as possible, and

(b)   Objective 2 in section 99.

(3)   If the liquidation committee thinks that the bank liquidator is failing to comply with their recommendation, they must apply to the court for directions under section 168(5) of the Insolvency Act 1986 (as applied by section 103 below).

(4)   Where the liquidation committee has not made a recommendation the bank liquidator may apply to the court under section 101(3); and the court may, in particular, make a direction in lieu of a recommendation if the liquidation committee fail to make one within a period set by the court.

[1900W]

NOTES
Commencement: to be appointed.

103   General powers, duties and effect

(1)   A bank liquidator may do anything necessary or expedient for the pursuit of the Objectives in section 99.

(2)   The following provisions of this section provide for—

(a)   general powers and duties of bank liquidators (by application of provisions about liquidators), and

(b)   the general process and effects of bank insolvency (by application of provisions about winding up).

(3)   The provisions set out in the Table apply in relation to bank insolvency as in relation to winding up, with—

(a)   the modifications set out in subsection (4),

(b)   any other modification specified in the Table, and

(c)   any other necessary modification.

(4)   The modifications are that—

(a)   a reference to the liquidator is a reference to the bank liquidator,

(b)   a reference to winding up is a reference to bank insolvency,

(c)   a reference to winding up by the court is a reference to the imposition of bank insolvency by order of the court,

(d)   a reference to being wound up under Part IV or V of the Insolvency Act 1986 is a reference to being made the subject of a bank insolvency order,

(e)   a reference to the commencement of winding up is a reference to the commencement of bank insolvency,

(f)   a reference to going into liquidation is a reference to entering bank insolvency,

(g)   a reference to a winding-up order is a reference to a bank insolvency order, and

(h)   a reference to a company is a reference to the bank.

(5)   Powers conferred by this Act, by the Insolvency Act 1986 (as applied) and the Companies Acts are in addition to, and not in restriction of, any existing powers of instituting proceedings against a contributory or debtor of a bank, or the estate of any contributory or debtor, for the recovery of any call or other sum.

(6)   A reference in an enactment or other document to anything done under a provision applied by this Part includes a reference to the provision as applied.

TABLE OF APPLIED PROVISIONS		
Provision of Insolvency Act 1986	*Subject*	*Modification or comment*
Section 127	Avoidance of property dispositions	Ignore section 127(2).
Section 128	Avoidance of attachment, &c	
Section 130	Consequences of winding-up order	Ignore section 130(4).
Section 131	Company's statement of affairs	(a) Treat references to the official receiver as references to the bank liquidator. (b) A creditor or contributory of the bank is entitled to receive a copy of a statement under section 131 on request to the bank liquidator.
Section 135	Provisional appointment	(a) Treat the reference to the presentation of a winding-up petition as a reference to the making of an application for a bank insolvency order. (b) Subsection (2) applies in relation to England and Wales and Scotland (and subsection (3) does not apply). (c) Ignore the reference to the official receiver. (d) Only a person who is qualified to act as an insolvency practitioner and who consents to act may be appointed. (e) A provisional bank liquidator may not pay dividends to creditors. (f) The appointment of a provisional bank liquidator lapses on the appointment of a bank liquidator.
Section 141	Liquidation Committee (England and Wales)	The application of section 141 is subject to— (a) sections 100, 101 and 109 of this Act, (b) rules under section 411 (as applied by section 125 of this Act) which may, in particular, adapt section 141 to reflect (i) the fact that the bank liquidator is appointed by the court and (ii) the possibility of calling creditors' meetings under other provisions, and (c) the omission of references to the official receiver.
Section 142	Liquidation Committee (Scotland)	The application of section 142 is subject to— (a) sections 100, 101 and 109 of this Act, (b) rules under section 411 (as applied by section 125 of this Act) which may, in particular, adapt section 142 to reflect (i) the fact that the bank liquidator is appointed by the court and (ii) the possibility of calling creditors' meetings under other provisions, and (c) the omission of references to the official receiver.
Section 143	General functions of liquidator	(a) Section 143(1) is subject to Objective 1 in section 99 above. (b) Ignore section 143(2).

PART II
OTHER ACTS

TABLE OF APPLIED PROVISIONS		
Provision of Insolvency Act 1986	*Subject*	*Modification or comment*
Section 144	Custody of property	
Section 145	Vesting of property	
Section 146	*Duty to summon final meeting*	*Section 146 is not applied—but section 115 below makes similar provision.*
Section 147	Power to stay or sist proceedings	An application may be made only by— (a) the bank liquidator, (b) the FSA, (c) the Bank of England, (d) the FSCS, or (e) a creditor or contributory (but only if the liquidation committee has passed a full payment resolution).
Section 148	List of contributories and application of assets	*By virtue of the Insolvency Rules the functions under this section are largely delegated to the liquidator—rules by virtue of section 125 may achieve a similar delegation to the bank liquidator.*
Section 149	Debts due from contributories	
Section 150	Power to make calls	
Section 152	Order on contributory: evidence	
Section 153	Exclusion of creditors	
Section 154	Adjustment of rights of contributories	
Section 155	Inspection of books by creditors	In making or considering whether to make an order under section 155 the court shall have regard to Objective 1 in section 99 above.
Section 156	Payment of expenses of winding up	
Section 157	Attendance at company meetings (Scotland)	
Section 158	Power to arrest absconding contributory	
Section 159	*Powers to be cumulative*	*Section 159 is not applied—but subsection (5) above makes similar provision.*
Section 160	Delegation of powers to liquidator (England and Wales)	
Section 161	Orders for calls on contributories (Scotland)	
Section 162	Appeals from orders (Scotland)	An appeal may be brought only if the liquidation committee has passed a full payment resolution.

	TABLE OF APPLIED PROVISIONS	
Provision of Insolvency Act 1986	*Subject*	*Modification or comment*
Section 167 and Schedule 4	General powers of liquidator	(a) An application to the court may not be made under section 167(3) unless the liquidation committee has passed a full payment resolution (although a creditor or contributory may apply to the court with respect to any action (or inaction) of the liquidation committee, under section 101(3) above). (b) In exercising or considering whether to exercise a power under Schedule 4 the bank liquidator shall have regard to Objective 1 in section 99. (c) A reference to the liquidation committee is to the liquidation committee established by section 100. (d) The power in paragraph 4 of Schedule 4 includes the power to submit matters to arbitration. *Some additional general powers are conferred by section 104 below.*
Section 168	Supplementary powers of liquidator	(a) A direction or request under section 168(2) has no effect unless the liquidation committee has passed a full payment resolution. (b) Section 168(5) also applies in the case of the imposition of bank insolvency by order of the Court of Session. (c) An application to the court may not be made under section 168(5) unless the liquidation committee has passed a full payment resolution (except as provided in section 100 or 102 above).
Section 169	Supplementary powers (Scotland)	(a) Ignore section 169(1). (b) Powers of the bank liquidator by virtue of section 169(2) are subject to Objective 1 in section 99 above.
Section 170	Liquidator's duty to make returns	The liquidation committee is added to the list of persons able to apply under section 170(2).
Section 172	Removal of liquidator	*Section 172 is not applied to a bank liquidator— but section 108 makes similar provision.* Section 172(1), (2) and (5) are applied to a provisional bank liquidator.
Section 174	*Release of liquidator*	*Section 174 is not applied—but section 115 makes similar provision.*
Section 175	Preferential debts	
Section 176	Preferential charge on goods restrained	
Section 176ZA	Expenses of winding up	
Section 176A	Share of assets for unsecured creditors	
Section 177	Appointment of special manager	
Section 178	Power to disclaim onerous property	

TABLE OF APPLIED PROVISIONS

Provision of Insolvency Act 1986	Subject	Modification or comment
Section 179	Disclaimer of leaseholds	
Section 180	Land subject to rentcharge	
Section 181	Disclaimer: powers of court	
Section 182	Leaseholds	
Section 183	Effect of execution or attachment (England and Wales)	
Section 184	Execution of writs (England and Wales)	
Section 185	Effect of diligence (Scotland)	In the application of section 37(1) of the Bankruptcy (Scotland) Act 1985 the reference to an order of the court awarding winding up is a reference to the making of the bank insolvency order.
Section 186	Rescission of contracts by court	
Section 187	Transfer of assets to employees	
Section 188	Publicity	
Section 189	Interest on debts	
Section 190	Exemption from stamp duty	
Section 191	Company's books as evidence	
Section 192	Information about pending liquidations	
Section 193	Unclaimed dividends (Scotland)	
Section 194	Resolutions passed at adjourned meetings	
Section 195	Meetings to ascertain wishes of creditors or contributories	The power to have regard to the wishes of creditors and contributories is subject to Objective 1 in section 99.
Section 196	Judicial notice of court documents	
Section 197	Commission for receiving evidence	
Section 198	Court order for examination of persons (Scotland)	
Section 199	Costs of application for leave to proceed (Scotland)	
Section 200	Affidavits	
Section 206	Fraud in anticipation of winding up	

TABLE OF APPLIED PROVISIONS

Provision of Insolvency Act 1986	Subject	Modification or comment
Section 207	Transactions in fraud of creditors	
Section 208	Misconduct in course of winding up	
Section 209	Falsification of company's books	
Section 210	Material omissions	
Section 211	False representations to creditors	
Section 212	Summary remedy against directors, &c	
Section 213	Fraudulent trading	
Section 214	Wrongful trading	
Section 215	Sections 213 & 214: procedure	
Section 216	Restriction on re-use of company names	
Section 217	Personal liability for debts	
Section 218	Prosecution of officers and members of company	(a) Ignore subsections (4) and (6). (b) In subsection (3), treat the second reference to the official receiver as a reference to the Secretary of State. (c) In subsection (5) treat the reference to subsection (4) as a reference to subsection (3).
Section 219	Obligations under section 218	
Section 231	Appointment of 2 or more persons	
Section 232	Validity of acts	
Section 233	Utilities	
Section 234	Getting in company's property	
Section 235	Co-operation with liquidator	Ignore references to the official receiver
Section 236	Inquiry into company's dealings	Ignore references to the official receiver
Section 237	Section 236: enforcement by court	
Section 238	Transactions at undervalue (England and Wales)	Anything done by the bank in connection with the exercise of a stabilisation power under Part 1 of this Act is not a transaction at an undervalue for the purposes of section 238.
Section 239	Preferences (England and Wales)	Action taken by the bank in connection with the exercise of a stabilisation power under Part 1 of this Act does not amount to giving a preference for the purpose of section 239.

PART II
OTHER ACTS

TABLE OF APPLIED PROVISIONS

Provision of Insolvency Act 1986	Subject	Modification or comment
Section 240	Sections 238 & 239: relevant time	
Section 241	Orders under sections 238 & 239	Having notice of the relevant proceedings means having notice of— (a) an application by the Bank of England, the FSA or the Secretary of State for a bank insolvency order, or (b) notice under section 120 below.
Section 242	Gratuitous alienations (Scotland)	Anything done by the bank in connection with the exercise of a stabilisation power under Part 1 of this Act is not a gratuitous alienation for the purpose of section 242 or any other rule of law.
Section 243	Unfair preferences (Scotland)	Action taken by the bank in connection with the exercise of a stabilisation power under Part 1 of this Act does not amount to an unfair preference for the purpose of section 243 or any other rule of law.
Section 244	Extortionate credit transactions	
Section 245	Avoidance of floating charges	
Section 246	Unenforceability of liens	
Sections 386 & 387, and Schedule 6 (and Schedule 4 to the Pension Schemes Act 1993)	Preferential debts	
Section 389	Offence of acting without being qualified	Treat references to acting as an insolvency practitioner as references to acting as a bank liquidator.
Section 390	Persons not qualified to act	Treat references to acting as an insolvency practitioner as references to acting as a bank liquidator.
Section 391	Recognised professional bodies	An order under section 391 has effect in relation to any provision applied for the purposes of bank insolvency.
Sections 423–425	Transactions defrauding creditors	Anything done by the bank in connection with the exercise of a stabilisation power under Part 1 of this Act is not a transaction at an undervalue for the purposes of section 423.
Sections 430 to 432 and Schedule 10	Offences	
Section 433	Statements: admissibility	For section 433(1)(a) and (b) substitute a reference to a statement prepared for the purposes of a provision of this Part.

104 Additional general powers

(1)   A bank liquidator has the following powers.

(2)   Power to effect and maintain insurances in respect of the business and property of the bank.

(3)   Power to do all such things (including the carrying out of works) as may be necessary for the realisation of the property of the bank.

(4)   Power to make any payment which is necessary or incidental to the performance of the bank liquidator's functions.

[1900Y]

105 Status of bank liquidator

A bank liquidator is an officer of the court.

[1900Z]

Tenure of bank liquidator

106 Term of appointment

A bank liquidator appointed by bank insolvency order remains in office until vacating office—
- (a)   by resigning under section 107,
- (b)   on removal under section 108 or 109,
- (c)   on disqualification under section 110,
- (d)   on the appointment of a replacement in accordance with section 112,
- (e)   in accordance with sections 113 to 115, or
- (f)   on death.

[1901]

107 Resignation

(1)   A bank liquidator may resign by notice to the court.

(2)   Rules under section 411 of the Insolvency Act 1986 (as applied by section 125 below) may restrict a bank liquidator's power to resign.

(3)   Resignation shall take effect in accordance with those rules (which shall include provision about release).

[1901A]

108 Removal by court

(1)   A bank liquidator may be removed by order of the court on the application of—
- (a)   the liquidation committee,
- (b)   the FSA, or
- (c)   the Bank of England.

(2)   Before making an application the FSA must consult the Bank of England.

(3)   Before making an application the Bank of England must consult the FSA.

(4)   A bank liquidator removed by order has release with effect from a time determined by—
- (a)   the Secretary of State, or
- (b)   in the case of a bank liquidator in Scotland, the Accountant of Court.

[1901B]

PART II
OTHER ACTS

109 Removal by creditors

(1)   A bank liquidator may be removed by resolution of a meeting of creditors held pursuant to section 195 of the Insolvency Act 1986 (as applied by section 103 above) provided that the following conditions are met.

(2)   Condition 1 is that the liquidation committee has passed a full payment resolution.

(3)   Condition 2 is that the notice given to creditors of the meeting includes notice of intention to move a resolution removing the bank liquidator.

(4)   Condition 3 is that the Bank of England and the FSA—
   (a)   receive notice of the meeting, and
   (b)   are given an opportunity to make representations to it.

(5)   A bank liquidator who is removed under this section has release with effect—
   (a)   from the time when the court is informed of the removal, or
   (b)   if the meeting removing the bank liquidator resolves to disapply paragraph (a), from a time determined by—
      (i)   the Secretary of State, or
      (ii)   in the case of a bank liquidator in Scotland, the Accountant of Court.

[1901C]

NOTES
Commencement: to be appointed.

110 Disqualification

(1)   If a bank liquidator ceases to be qualified to act as an insolvency practitioner, the appointment lapses.

(2)   A bank liquidator whose appointment lapses under subsection (1) has release with effect from a time determined by—
   (a)   the Secretary of State, or
   (b)   in the case of a bank liquidator in Scotland, the Accountant of Court.

[1901D]

NOTES
Commencement: to be appointed.

111 Release

A bank liquidator who is released is discharged from all liability in respect of acts or omissions in the bank insolvency and otherwise in relation to conduct as bank liquidator (but without prejudice to the effect of section 212 of the Insolvency Act 1986 as applied by section 103 above).

[1901E]

NOTES
Commencement: to be appointed.

112 Replacement

(1)   Where a bank liquidator vacates office the Bank of England must as soon as is reasonably practicable appoint a replacement bank liquidator.

(2)   But where a bank liquidator is removed by resolution of a meeting of creditors under section 109—
   (a)   a replacement may be appointed by resolution of the meeting, and
   (b)   failing that, subsection (1) above applies.

[1901F]

NOTES
Commencement: to be appointed.

Termination of process, &c

113 Company voluntary arrangement

(1)   A bank liquidator may make a proposal in accordance with section 1 of the Insolvency Act 1986 (company voluntary arrangement).

(2)   Before making a proposal the bank liquidator—
   (a)   shall present a final report on the bank liquidation to the liquidation committee,
   (b)   shall send a copy of the report to—
      (i)   the FSA,
      (ii)   the FSCS,

   (iii) the Bank of England,
   (iv) the Treasury, and
   (v) the registrar of companies, and
 (c) shall make the report available to members, creditors and contributories on request.

(3) A proposal may be made only with the consent of the liquidation committee.

(4) The liquidation committee may consent only if—
 (a) it has passed a full payment resolution, and
 (b) the bank liquidator is satisfied, as a result of arrangements made with the FSCS, that any depositor still eligible for compensation under the scheme will be dealt with in accordance with section 99(2)(a) or (b).

(5) The bank liquidator must be the nominee (see section 1(2) of the 1986 Act).

(6) Part 1 of the 1986 Act shall apply to a proposal made by a bank liquidator, with the following modifications.

(7) In section 3 (summoning of meetings) subsection (2) (and not (1)) applies.

(8) The action that may be taken by the court under section 5(3) (effect of approval) includes suspension of the bank insolvency order.

(9) On the termination of a company voluntary arrangement the bank liquidator may apply to the court to lift the suspension of the bank insolvency order.

                          [1901G]

NOTES
Commencement: to be appointed.

114 Administration

(1) A bank liquidator who thinks that administration would achieve a better result for the bank's creditors as a whole than bank insolvency may apply to the court for an administration order (under paragraph 38 of Schedule B1 to the Insolvency Act 1986).

(2) An application may be made only if the following conditions are satisfied.

(3) Condition 1 is that the liquidation committee has passed a full payment resolution.

(4) Condition 2 is that the liquidation committee has resolved that moving to administration might enable the rescue of the bank as a going concern.

(5) Condition 3 is that the bank liquidator is satisfied, as a result of arrangements made with the FSCS, that any depositors still eligible for compensation under the scheme will receive their payments or have their accounts transferred during administration.

                          [1901H]

NOTES
Commencement: to be appointed.

115 Dissolution

(1) A bank liquidator who thinks that the winding up of the bank is for practical purposes complete shall summon a final meeting of the liquidation committee.

(2) The bank liquidator—
 (a) shall present a final report on the bank insolvency to the meeting,
 (b) shall send a copy of the report to—
   (i) the FSA,
   (ii) the FSCS,
   (iii) the Bank of England,
   (iv) the Treasury, and
   (v) the registrar of companies, and
 (c) shall make the report available to members, creditors and contributories on request.

(3) At the meeting the liquidation committee shall—
 (a) consider the report, and
 (b) decide whether to release the bank liquidator.

(4) If the liquidation committee decides to release the bank liquidator, the bank liquidator—
 (a) shall notify the court and the registrar of companies, and
 (b) vacates office, and has release, when the court is notified.

(5) If the liquidation committee decides not to release the bank liquidator, the bank liquidator may apply to the Secretary of State for release; if the application is granted, the bank liquidator—
 (a) vacates office when the application is granted, and
 (b) has release from a time determined by the Secretary of State.

(6)   In the case of a bank liquidator in Scotland, a reference in subsection (5) to the Secretary of State is a reference to the Accountant of Court.

(7)   On receipt of a notice under subsection (4)(a) the registrar of companies shall register it.

(8)   At the end of the period of 3 months beginning with the day of the registration of the notice, the bank is dissolved (subject to deferral under section 116).

[1901I]

NOTES
Commencement: to be appointed.

116 Dissolution: supplemental

(1)   The Secretary of State may by direction defer the date of dissolution under section 115, on the application of a person who appears to the Secretary of State to be interested.

(2)   An appeal to the court lies from any decision of the Secretary of State on an application for a direction under subsection (1).

(3)   Subsection (1) does not apply where the bank insolvency order was made by the court in Scotland; but the court may by direction defer the date of dissolution on an application by a person appearing to the court to have an interest.

(4)   A person who obtains deferral under subsection (1) or (3) shall, within 7 days after the giving of the deferral direction, deliver a copy of the direction to the registrar of companies for registration.

(5)   A person who without reasonable excuse fails to comply with subsection (4) is liable to a fine and, for continued contravention, to a daily default fine, in each case of the same amount as for a contravention of section 205(6) of the Insolvency Act 1986 (dissolution).

(6)   The bank liquidator may give the notice summoning the final meeting under section 115 above at the same time as giving notice of any final distribution of the bank's property; but, if summoned for an earlier date the meeting shall be adjourned (and, if necessary, further adjourned) until a date on which the bank liquidator is able to report to the meeting that the winding up of the bank is for practical purposes complete.

(7)   A bank liquidator must retain sufficient sums to cover the expenses of the final meeting under section 115 above.

[1901J]

NOTES
Commencement: to be appointed.

Other processes

117 Bank insolvency as alternative order

(1)   On a petition for a winding up order or an application for an administration order in respect of a bank the court may, instead, make a bank insolvency order.

(2)   A bank insolvency order may be made under subsection (1) only—
   (a)   on the application of the FSA made with the consent of the Bank of England, or
   (b)   on the application of the Bank of England.

[1901K]

NOTES
Commencement: to be appointed.

118 Voluntary winding-up

A resolution for voluntary winding up of a bank under section 84 of the Insolvency Act 1986 shall have no effect without the prior approval of the court.

[1901L]

NOTES
Commencement: to be appointed.

119 Exclusion of other procedures

(1)   The following paragraphs of Schedule B1 to the Insolvency Act 1986 (administration) apply to a bank insolvency order as to an administration order.

(2)   Those paragraphs are—
   (a)   paragraph 40 (dismissal of pending winding-up petition), and
   (b)   paragraph 42 (moratorium on insolvency proceedings).

(3)   For that purpose—
  (a)   a reference to an administration order is a reference to a bank insolvency order,
  (b)   a reference to a company being in administration is a reference to a bank being in bank insolvency, and
  (c)   a reference to an administrator is a reference to a bank liquidator.

[1901M]

NOTES
  Commencement: to be appointed.

120   Notice to FSA of preliminary steps

(1)   An application for an administration order in respect of a bank may not be determined unless the conditions below are satisfied.

(2)   A petition for a winding up order in respect of a bank may not be determined unless the conditions below are satisfied.

(3)   A resolution for voluntary winding up of a bank may not be made unless the conditions below are satisfied.

(4)   An administrator of a bank may not be appointed unless the conditions below are satisfied.

(5)   Condition 1 is that the FSA has been notified—
  (a)   by the applicant for an administration order, that the application has been made,
  (b)   by the petitioner for a winding up order, that the petition has been presented,
  (c)   by the bank, that a resolution for voluntary winding up may be made, or
  (d)   by the person proposing to appoint an administrator, of the proposed appointment.

(6)   Condition 2 is that a copy of the notice complying with Condition 1 has been filed with the court (and made available for public inspection by the court).

(7)   Condition 3 is that—
  (a)   the period of 2 weeks, beginning with the day on which the notice is received, has ended, or
  (b)   both—
    (i)   the FSA has informed the person who gave the notice that it does not intend to apply for a bank insolvency order, and
    (ii)   the Bank of England has informed the person who gave the notice that it does not intend to apply for a bank insolvency order or to exercise a stabilisation power under Part 1.

(8)   Condition 4 is that no application for a bank insolvency order is pending.

(9)   Arranging for the giving of notice in order to satisfy Condition 1 can be a step with a view to minimising the potential loss to a bank's creditors for the purpose of section 214 of the Insolvency Act 1986 (wrongful trading).

(10)   Where the FSA receives notice under Condition 1—
  (a)   the FSA shall inform the Bank of England,
  (b)   the FSA shall inform the person who gave the notice, within the period in Condition 3(a), whether it intends to apply for a bank insolvency order, and
  (c)   if the Bank of England decides to apply for a bank insolvency order or to exercise a stabilisation power under Part 1, the Bank shall inform the person who gave the notice, within the period in Condition 3(a).

[1901N]

NOTES
  Commencement: to be appointed.

121   Disqualification of directors

(1)   In this section "the Disqualification Act" means the Company Directors Disqualification Act 1986.

(2)   In the Disqualification Act—
  (a)   a reference to liquidation includes a reference to bank insolvency,
  (b)   a reference to winding up includes a reference to making or being subject to a bank insolvency order,
  (c)   a reference to becoming insolvent includes a reference to becoming subject to a bank insolvency order, and
  (d)   a reference to a liquidator includes a reference to a bank liquidator.

PART II
OTHER ACTS

(3)   For the purposes of the application of section 7(3) of the Disqualification Act (disqualification order or undertaking) to a bank which is subject to a bank insolvency order, the responsible office-holder is the bank liquidator.

(4)   (*Inserts the Company Directors Disqualification Act 1986, s 21A.*)

[1901O]

NOTES
Commencement: to be appointed.

122   Application of insolvency law

(1)   The Secretary of State and the Treasury may by order made jointly—
  (a)   provide for an enactment about insolvency to apply to bank insolvency (with or without specified modifications);
  (b)   amend, or modify the application of, an enactment about insolvency in consequence of this Part.

(2)   An order under subsection (1)—
  (a)   shall be made by statutory instrument, and
  (b)   may not be made unless a draft has been laid before and approved by resolution of each House of Parliament.

[1901P]

NOTES
Commencement: to be appointed.

Miscellaneous

123   Role of FSCS

(1)   For the purpose of co-operating in the pursuit of Objective 1 in section 99 the FSCS—
  (a)   may make or arrange for payments to or in respect of eligible depositors of the bank, and
  (b)   may make money available to facilitate the transfer of accounts of eligible depositors of the bank.

(2)   The FSCS may include provision about expenditure under this section; and, in particular—
  (a)   money may be raised through the imposition of a levy under Part 15 of the Financial Services and Markets Act in respect of expenditure or possible expenditure under this section, and
  (b)   sums raised in connection with the scheme (whether or not under paragraph (a)) may be expended under this section.

(3)   (*Amends the Financial Services and Markets Act 2000, s 220 at* [248].)

(4)   The FSCS is entitled to participate in proceedings for or in respect of a bank insolvency order.

(5)   A bank liquidator must—
  (a)   comply with a request of the FSCS for the provision of information, and
  (b)   provide the FSCS with any other information which the bank liquidator thinks might be useful for the purpose of co-operating in the pursuit of Objective 1.

(6)   A bank liquidator may enter into an agreement under section 221A of the Financial Services and Markets Act 2000 (Compensation Scheme: delegation of functions) for the bank liquidator to exercise functions of the scheme manager for the purpose of facilitating the pursuit of Objective 1.

(7)   Where a bank insolvency order is made in respect of a bank, the fact that it later ceases to be an authorised person does not prevent the operation of the compensation scheme in respect of it; and for that purpose the bank is a relevant person within the meaning of section 213(9) of the Financial Services and Markets Act 2000 despite the lapse of authorisation.

[1901Q]

NOTES
Commencement: to be appointed.

124   Transfer of accounts

(1)   This section applies where a bank liquidator arranges, in pursuit of Objective 1 in section 99, for the transfer of eligible depositors' accounts from the bank to another financial institution.

(2)   The arrangements may disapply, or provide that they shall have effect despite, any restriction arising by virtue of contract or legislation or in any other way.

(3)   In subsection (2) "restriction" includes—

(a)　　any restriction, inability or incapacity affecting what can and cannot be assigned or transferred (whether generally or by a particular person), and

(b)　　a requirement for consent (by any name).

(4)　　In making the arrangements mentioned in subsection (1) the bank liquidator must ensure that eligible depositors will be able to remove money from transferred accounts as soon as is reasonably practicable after transfer.

[1901R]

NOTES

Commencement: to be appointed.

125, 126　　*(S 125 (Rules) amends the Insolvency Act 1986, s 411 (at **[1135]**) and Sch 8, and further provides that s 413(2) of the 1986 Act (duty to consult Insolvency Rules Committee) shall not apply to the first set of rules made in reliance on the amendments made to s 411 by this section; s 126 (Fees) amends s 414 of the 1986 Act.)*

127　Insolvency Services Account

A bank liquidator who obtains money by realising assets in the course of the bank insolvency must pay it into the Insolvency Services Account (kept by the Secretary of State).

[1901S]

NOTES

Commencement: to be appointed.

128　　*(S 128 (Evidence) amends the Insolvency Act 1986, s 433.)*

129　Co-operation between courts

(1)　　Provisions of or by virtue of this Part are "insolvency law" for the purposes of section 426 of the Insolvency Act 1986 (co-operation between courts).

(2)　　*(Amends the Insolvency Act 1986, s 426.)*

[1901T]

NOTES

Commencement: to be appointed.

130　Building societies

(1)　　The Treasury may by order provide for this Part to apply to building societies (within the meaning of section 119 of the Building Societies Act 1986) as it applies to banks, subject to modifications set out in the order.

(2)　　An order may—

(a)　　amend the Building Societies Act 1986 or any other enactment which relates, or in so far as it relates, to building societies;

(b)　　amend an enactment amended by this Part;

(c)　　replicate, with or without modifications, any provision of this Part;

(d)　　apply a provision made under or by virtue of this Part, with or without modifications, to this Part as it applies to building societies.

(3)　　An order—

(a)　　shall be made by statutory instrument, and

(b)　　may not be made unless a draft has been laid before and approved by resolution of each House of Parliament.

(4)　　Provision made under or by virtue of this Part may make special provision in relation to the application of this Part to building societies.

[1901U]

NOTES

Commencement: to be appointed.

131　Credit unions

(1)　　The Treasury may by order provide for this Part to apply to credit unions (within the meaning of section 31 of the Credit Unions Act 1979) as it applies to banks, subject to modifications set out in the order.

(2)　　An order may—

(a)　　amend the Credit Unions Act 1979, the Industrial and Providential Societies Act 1965 or any other enactment which relates, or in so far as it relates, to credit unions;

(b)　　amend an enactment amended by this Part;

(c)　　replicate, with or without modifications, any provision of this Part;

(d)   apply a provision made under or by virtue of this Part, with or without modifications, to this Part as it applies to credit unions.

(3)   An order—
(a)   shall be made by statutory instrument, and
(b)   may not be made unless a draft has been laid before and approved by resolution of each House of Parliament.

(4)   Provision made under or by virtue of this Part may make special provision in relation to the application of this Part to credit unions.

[1901V]

NOTES
Commencement: to be appointed.

132 Partnerships

(1)   The Lord Chancellor may, by order made with the concurrence of the Secretary of State and the Lord Chief Justice, modify provisions of this Part in their application to partnerships.

(2)   For procedural purposes an order under subsection (1) shall be treated in the same way as an order under section 420 of the Insolvency Act 1986 (partnerships).

(3)   This section does not apply in relation to partnerships constituted under the law of Scotland.

[1901W]

NOTES
Commencement: to be appointed.

133 Scottish partnerships

(1)   The Secretary of State may by order modify provisions of this Part in their application to partnerships constituted under the law of Scotland.

(2)   An order—
(a)   shall be made by statutory instrument, and
(b)   shall be subject to annulment in pursuance of a resolution of either House of Parliament.

[1901X]

NOTES
Commencement: to be appointed.

134 Northern Ireland

In the application of this Part to Northern Ireland—
(a)   a reference to an enactment is to be treated as a reference to the equivalent enactment having effect in relation to Northern Ireland,
(b)   where this Part amends an enactment an equivalent amendment (incorporating any necessary modification) is made to the equivalent enactment having effect in relation to Northern Ireland,
(c)   references to the Secretary of State, except in section 122, are to be treated as references to the Department of Enterprise, Trade and Investment,
(d)   a reference to the Insolvency Services Account is to be treated as a reference to the Insolvency Account,
(e)   a reference to section 31 of the Credit Unions Act 1979 is to be treated as a reference to Article 2 of the Credit Unions (Northern Ireland) Order 1985,
(f)   the Judgments Enforcement (Northern Ireland) Order 1981 has effect in place of sections 183 and 184 of the Insolvency Act 1986 (applied by section 103 above), and
(g)   the reference in section 132 to the Lord Chief Justice is a reference to the Lord Chief Justice in Northern Ireland.

[1901Y]

NOTES
Commencement: to be appointed.

135 Consequential provision

(1)   The Treasury may by order make provision in consequence of this Part.

(2)   An order may, in particular, amend or modify the effect of an enactment (including a fiscal enactment) passed before the commencement of this Part.

(3)   An order—
(a)   shall be made by statutory instrument, and

(b)   may not be made unless a draft has been laid before and approved by resolution of each House of Parliament.

[1901Z]

NOTES
Commencement: to be appointed.

PART 3
BANK ADMINISTRATION

Introduction

136   Overview

(1)   This Part provides for a procedure to be known as bank administration.

(2)   The main features of bank administration are that—
    (a)   it is used where part of the business of a bank is sold to a commercial purchaser in accordance with section 11 or transferred to a bridge bank in accordance with section 12 (and it can also be used in certain cases of multiple transfers under Part 1),
    (b)   the court appoints a bank administrator on the application of the Bank of England,
    (c)   the bank administrator is able and required to ensure that the non-sold or non-transferred part of the bank ("the residual bank") provides services or facilities required to enable the commercial purchaser ("the private sector purchaser") or the transferee ("the bridge bank") to operate effectively, and
    (d)   in other respects the process is the same as for normal administration under the Insolvency Act 1986, subject to specified modifications.

(3)   The Table describes the provisions of this Part.

Sections	Topic
Sections 136 to 140	Introduction
Sections 141 to 148	Process
Sections 149 to 152	Multiple transfers
Sections 153 and 154	Termination
Sections 155 to 168	Miscellaneous

[1902]

NOTES
Commencement: to be appointed.

137   Objectives

(1)   A bank administrator has two objectives—
    (a)   Objective 1: support for commercial purchaser or bridge bank (see section 138), and
    (b)   Objective 2: "normal" administration (see section 140).

(2)   Objective 1 takes priority over Objective 2 (but a bank administrator is obliged to begin working towards both objectives immediately upon appointment).

[1902A]

NOTES
Commencement: to be appointed.

138   Objective 1: supporting private sector purchaser or bridge bank

(1)   Objective 1 is to ensure the supply to the private sector purchaser or bridge bank of such services and facilities as are required to enable it, in the opinion of the Bank of England, to operate effectively.

(2)   For the purposes of Objective 1—
    (a)   the reference to services and facilities includes a reference to acting as transferor or transferee under a supplemental or reverse property transfer instrument, and
    (b)   the reference to "supply" includes a reference to supply by persons other than the residual bank.

(3)   In the case of bank administration following a private sector purchase the bank administrator must co-operate with any request of the Bank of England to enter into an agreement for the residual bank to provide services or facilities to the private sector purchaser; and—

(a)   in pursuing Objective 1 the bank administrator must have regard to the terms of that or any other agreement entered into between the residual bank and the private sector purchaser,

(b)   in particular, the bank administrator must avoid action that is likely to prejudice performance by the residual bank of its obligations in accordance with those terms,

(c)   if in doubt about the effect of those terms the bank administrator may apply to the court for directions under paragraph 63 of Schedule B1 to the Insolvency Act 1986 (applied by section 145 below), and

(d)   the private sector purchaser may refer to the court a dispute about any agreement with the residual bank, by applying for directions under paragraph 63 of Schedule B1.

(4)   In the case of bank administration following transfer to a bridge bank, the bank administrator must co-operate with any request of the Bank of England to enter into an agreement for the residual bank to provide services or facilities to the bridge bank; and—

(a)   the bank administrator must avoid action that is likely to prejudice performance by the residual bank of its obligations in accordance with an agreement,

(b)   the bank administrator must ensure that so far as is reasonably practicable an agreement entered into includes provision for consideration at market rate,

(c)   paragraph (b) does not prevent the bank administrator from entering into an agreement on any terms that the bank administrator thinks necessary in pursuit of Objective 1, and

(d)   this subsection does not apply after Objective 1 ceases.

(5)   Where a bank administrator requires the Bank of England's consent or approval to any action in accordance with this Part, the Bank may withhold consent or approval only on the grounds that the action might prejudice the achievement of Objective 1.

[1902B]

NOTES
Commencement: to be appointed.

139   Objective 1: duration

(1)   Objective 1 ceases if the Bank of England notifies the bank administrator that the residual bank is no longer required in connection with the private sector purchaser or bridge bank.

(2)   A bank administrator who thinks that Objective 1 is no longer required may apply to the court for directions under paragraph 63 of Schedule B1 to the Insolvency Act 1986 (applied by section 145 below); and the court may direct the Bank of England to consider whether to give notice under subsection (1) above.

(3)   If immediately upon the making of a bank administration order the Bank of England thinks that the residual bank is not required in connection with the private sector purchaser or bridge bank, the Bank of England may give a notice under subsection (1).

(4)   A notice under subsection (1) is referred to in this Part as an "Objective 1 Achievement Notice".

[1902C]

NOTES
Commencement: to be appointed.

140   Objective 2: "normal" administration

(1)   Objective 2 is to—

(a)   rescue the residual bank as a going concern ("Objective 2(a)"), or

(b)   achieve a better result for the residual bank's creditors as a whole than would be likely if the residual bank were wound up without first being in bank administration ("Objective 2(b)").

(2)   In pursuing Objective 2 a bank administrator must aim to achieve Objective 2(a) unless of the opinion either—

(a)   that it is not reasonably practicable to achieve it, or

(b)   that Objective 2(b) would achieve a better result for the residual bank's creditors as a whole.

(3)   In pursuing Objective 2(b) in bank administration following transfer to a bridge bank, the bank administrator may not realise any asset unless—

   (a)   the asset is on a list of realisable assets agreed between the bank administrator and the Bank of England, or

   (b)   the Bank of England has given an Objective 1 Achievement Notice.

[1902D]

NOTES
Commencement: to be appointed.

Process

141 Bank administration order

(1)   A bank administration order is an order appointing a person as the bank administrator of a bank.

(2)   A person is eligible for appointment as a bank administrator if qualified to act as an insolvency practitioner.

(3)   An appointment may be made only if the person has consented to act.

(4)   A bank administration order takes effect in accordance with its terms; and—

   (a)   the process of a bank administration order having effect may be described as "bank administration" in relation to the bank, and

   (b)   while the order has effect the bank may be described as being "in bank administration".

[1902E]

NOTES
Commencement: to be appointed.

142 Application

(1)   An application for a bank administration order may be made to the court by the Bank of England.

(2)   An application must nominate a person to be appointed as the bank administrator.

(3)   The bank must be given notice of an application, in accordance with rules under section 411 of the Insolvency Act 1986 (as applied by section 160 below).

[1902F]

NOTES
Commencement: to be appointed.

143 Grounds for applying

(1)   The Bank of England may apply for a bank administration order in respect of a bank if the following conditions are met.

(2)   Condition 1 is that the Bank of England has made or intends to make a property transfer instrument in respect of the bank in accordance with section 11(2) or 12(2).

(3)   Condition 2 is that the Bank of England is satisfied that the residual bank—

   (a)   is unable to pay its debts, or

   (b)   is likely to become unable to pay its debts as a result of the property transfer instrument which the Bank intends to make.

[1902G]

NOTES
Commencement: to be appointed.

144 Grounds for making

(1)   The court may make a bank administration order if satisfied that the conditions in section 143 were met.

(2)   On an application for a bank administration order the court may—

   (a)   grant the application,

   (b)   adjourn the application (generally or to a specified date), or

   (c)   dismiss the application.

[1902H]

NOTES
Commencement: to be appointed.

145 General powers, duties and effect

(1) A bank administrator may do anything necessary or expedient for the pursuit of the Objectives in section 137.

(2) The following provisions of this section provide for—
- (a) general powers and duties of bank administrators (by application of provisions about administrators), and
- (b) the general process and effects of bank administration (by application of provisions about administration).

(3) The provisions set out in the Tables apply in relation to bank administration as in relation to administration, with—
- (a) the modifications set out in subsection (4),
- (b) any other modification specified in the Tables, and
- (c) any other necessary modification.

(4) The modifications are that—
- (a) a reference to the administrator is a reference to the bank administrator,
- (b) a reference to administration is a reference to bank administration,
- (c) a reference to an administration order is a reference to a bank administration order,
- (d) a reference to a company is a reference to the bank,
- (e) a reference to the purpose of administration is a reference to the Objectives in section 137, and
- (f) in relation to provisions of the Insolvency Act 1986 other than Schedule B1, the modifications in section 103 above apply (but converting references into references to bank administration or administrators rather than to bank insolvency or liquidators).

(5) Powers conferred by this Act, by the Insolvency Act 1986 (as applied) and the Companies Acts are in addition to, and not in restriction of, any existing powers of instituting proceedings against a contributory or debtor of a bank, or the estate of any contributory or debtor, for the recovery of any call or other sum.

(6) A reference in an enactment or other document to anything done under a provision applied by this Part includes a reference to the provision as applied.

TABLE 1: APPLIED PROVISIONS: INSOLVENCY ACT 1986, SCHEDULE B1		
Provision of Sch B1	*Subject*	*Modification or comment*
Para 40(1)(a)	Dismissal of pending winding-up petition	
Para 41	Dismissal of administrative or other receiver	
Para 42	Moratorium on insolvency proceedings	Ignore sub-paras (4) and (5).
Para 43	Moratorium on other legal process	(a) In the case of bank administration following transfer to a bridge bank, unless the Bank of England has given an Objective 1 Achievement Notice consent of the bank administrator may not be given for the purposes of Para 43 without the approval of the Bank of England. (b) In the case of bank administration following transfer to a bridge bank, unless the Bank of England has given an Objective 1 Achievement Notice, in considering whether to give permission under sub-Para (6) to a winding-up the court must have regard to the Objectives in section 137. (c) In considering whether to give permission for the purposes of Para 43 the court must have regard to the Objectives in section 137.

TABLE 1: APPLIED PROVISIONS: INSOLVENCY ACT 1986, SCHEDULE B1

Provision of Sch B1	Subject	Modification or comment
Para 44(1)(a) and (5)	Interim moratorium	
Para 46	Announcement of appointment	Ignore sub-Para (6)(b) and (c).
Paras 47 & 48	Statement of affairs	
Para 49	Administrator's proposals	(a) Para 49 does not apply unless the Bank of England has given an Objective 1 Achievement Notice; for bank administrator's proposals before the Bank of England has given an Objective 1 Achievement Notice, see section 147. (b) Treat the reference in sub-Para (1) to the purpose of administration as a reference to Objective 2. (c) Before making proposals under sub-Para (1) in the case of bank administration following transfer to a bridge bank, the bank administrator must consult the Bank of England about the chances of a payment to the residual bank from a scheme established by resolution fund order under section 49(3). (d) Treat the reference in sub-Para (2)(b) to the Objective mentioned in Para 3(1)(a) or (b) as a reference to Objective 2(a). (e) Ignore sub-Para(3)(b). (f) Treat references in sub-Para (5) to the company's entering administration as references to satisfaction of the condition in Para (a) above.
Paras 50–58	Creditors' meeting	(a) Treat references in Para 51(2) to the company's entering administration as references to the giving of an Objective 1 Achievement Notice. (b) The bank administrator may comply with a request under Para 56(1)(a) only if satisfied that it will not prejudice pursuit of Objective 1 in section 137. (c) A creditors' meeting may not establish a creditors' committee in reliance on Para 57 until the Bank of England has given an Objective 1 Achievement Notice. (d) Until that time the Bank of England shall have the functions of the creditors' committee.
Para 59	General powers	A bank administrator may not rely on Para 59 (or subsection (1) above) for the purpose of recovering property transferred by property transfer instrument.
Para 60 and Schedule 1	General powers	(a) The exercise of powers under Schedule 1 is subject to section 137(2).

TABLE 1: APPLIED PROVISIONS: INSOLVENCY ACT 1986, SCHEDULE B1		
Provision of Sch B1	*Subject*	*Modification or comment*
		(b) In the case of bank administration following transfer to a bridge bank, until the Bank of England has given an Objective 1 Achievement Notice powers under the following paragraphs of Schedule 1 may be exercised only with the Bank of England's consent: 2, 3, 11, 14, 15, 16, 17, 18 and 21.
Para 61	Directors	
Para 62	Power to call meetings of creditors	
Para 63	Application to court for directions	(a) Before the Bank of England has given an Objective 1 Achievement Notice, the bank administrator may apply for directions if unsure whether a proposed action would prejudice the pursuit of Objective 1; and before making an application in reliance on this paragraph the bank administrator must give notice to the Bank of England, which shall be entitled to participate in the proceedings.
		(b) In making directions the court must have regard to the Objectives in section 137.
Para 64	Management powers.	
Para 65	Distribution to creditors	(a) In the case of bank administration following transfer to a bridge bank, until the Bank of England has given an Objective 1 Achievement Notice a bank administrator may make a distribution only with the Bank of England's consent.
		(b) Ignore sub Para (3).
Para 66	Payments	
Para 67	Taking custody of property	
Para 68	Management	Before the approval of proposals under Para 53 a bank administrator shall manage the bank's affairs, business and property in accordance with principles agreed between the bank administrator and the Bank of England.
Para 69	Agency	
Para 70	Floating charges	The bank administrator may take action only if satisfied that it will not prejudice pursuit of Objective 1 in section 137.
Para 71	Fixed charges	The court may make an order only if satisfied that it will not prejudice pursuit of Objective 1 in section 137.
Para 72	Hire-purchase property	In the case of administration following transfer to a bridge bank, until the Bank of England has given an Objective 1 Achievement Notice an application may be made only with the Bank of England's consent.

TABLE 1: APPLIED PROVISIONS: INSOLVENCY ACT 1986, SCHEDULE B1

Provision of Sch B1	Subject	Modification or comment
Para 73	Protection for secured and preferential creditors	(a) Treat a reference to proposals as including a reference to the principles specified in the modification of Para 68 set out above. (b) Para 73(1)(a) does not apply until the Bank of England has given an Objective 1 Achievement Notice.
Para 74	Challenge to administrator's conduct	(a) The Bank of England may make an application to the court, on any grounds, including grounds of insufficient pursuit of Objective 1 in section 137 (in addition to applications that may anyway be made under Para 74). (b) Until the Bank of England has given an Objective 1 Achievement Notice, an order may be made on the application of a creditor only if the court is satisfied that it would not prejudice pursuit of Objective 1 in section 137.
Para 75	Misfeasance	In addition to applications that may anyway be made under Para 75, an application may be made by the bank administrator or the Bank of England.
Para 80	Termination: successful rescue	*See section 153.*
Para 84	Termination: no more assets for distribution	*See section 154.*
Para 85	Discharge of administration order	
Para 86	Notice to Companies Registrar of end of administration	*See section 153.*
Para 87	Resignation	A bank administrator may resign only by notice in writing— (a) to the court, copied to the Bank of England, or (b) in the case of a bank administrator appointed by the creditors' committee under Para 90, to the creditors' committee.
Para 88	Removal	Until the Bank of England has given an Objective 1 Achievement Notice, an application for an order may be made only with the Bank of England's consent.
Para 89	Disqualification	The notice under sub-Para (2) must be given to the Bank of England.
Paras 90 & 91	Replacement	(a) Until an Objective 1 Notice has been given, the Bank of England, and nobody else, may make an application under Para 91(1). (b) After that, either the Bank of England or a creditors' committee may apply. (c) Ignore Para 91(1)(b) to (e) and (2).
Para 96	Substitution of floating charge-holder	Para 96 applies to a bank administrator, but—

TABLE 1: APPLIED PROVISIONS: INSOLVENCY ACT 1986, SCHEDULE B1		
Provision of Sch B1	*Subject*	*Modification or comment*
		(a) only after an Objective 1 Achievement Notice has been given, and (b) ignoring references to priority of charges.
Para 98	Discharge	Discharge takes effect— (a) where the person ceases to be bank administrator before an Objective 1 Achievement Notice has been given, at a time determined by the Bank of England, and (b) otherwise, at a time determined by resolution of the creditors' committee (for which purpose ignore sub-Para (3)).
Para 99	Vacation of office: charges and liabilities	In the application of sub-Para (3), payments may be made only— (a) in accordance with directions of the Bank of England, and (b) if the Bank is satisfied that they will not prejudice Objective 1 in section 137.
Paras 100–103	Joint administrators	Until an Objective 1 Achievement Notice has been given, an application under Para 103 may be made only by the Bank of England.
Para 104	Validity	
Para 106 (and section 430 and Schedule 10)	Fines	
Paras 107–109	Extension of time limits	(a) Until an Objective 1 Achievement Notice has been given, an application under Para 107 may be made only with the Bank of England's consent. (b) In considering an application under Para 107 the court must have regard to Objective 1 in section 137. (c) In Para 108(1) "consent" means consent of the Bank of England.
Para 110	*Amendment of provisions about time*	*An order under Para 110 may amend a provision of the Schedule as it applies by virtue of this section (whether or not in the same way as it amends the provision as it applies otherwise).*
Para 111	Interpretation	
Paras 112–116	Scotland	

TABLE 2: APPLIED PROVISIONS: OTHER PROVISIONS OF THE INSOLVENCY ACT 1986		
Section	*Subject*	*Modification or comment*
Section 135	Provisional appointment	(a) Treat the reference to the presentation of a winding-up petition as a reference to the making of an application for a bank administration order.

TABLE 2: APPLIED PROVISIONS: OTHER PROVISIONS OF THE INSOLVENCY ACT 1986

Section	Subject	Modification or comment
		(b) Subsection (2) applies in relation to England and Wales and Scotland (and subsection (3) does not apply).
		(c) Ignore the reference to the official receiver.
		(d) Only a person who is qualified to act as an insolvency practitioner and who consents to act may be appointed.
		(e) The court may only confer on a provisional bank administrator functions in connection with the pursuance of Objective 1; and section 138(2)(a) does not apply before a bank administration order is made.
		(f) A provisional bank administrator may not pursue Objective 2.
		(g) The appointment of a provisional bank administrator lapses on the appointment of a bank administrator.
		(h) Section 172(1), (2) and (5) apply to a provisional bank administrator.
Section 168(4) (and Para 13 of Schedule 4)	Discretion in managing and distributing assets	In the case of bank administration following transfer to a bridge bank, until the Bank of England has given an Objective 1 Achievement Notice distribution may be made only— (a) with the Bank of England's consent, or (b) out of assets which have been designated as realisable by agreement between the bank administrator and the Bank of England.
Section 176A	Unsecured creditors	In the case of bank administration following transfer to a bridge bank, until the Bank of England has given an Objective 1 Achievement Notice distribution may be made in reliance on s. 176A only— (a) with the Bank of England's consent, or (b) out of assets which have been designated as realisable by agreement between the bank administrator and the Bank of England.
Section 178	Disclaimer of onerous property	In the case of bank administration following transfer to a bridge bank, until the Bank of England has given an Objective 1 Achievement Notice notice of disclaimer may be given only with the Bank of England's consent.
Section 179	Disclaimer of leaseholds	
Section 180	Land subject to rentcharge	
Section 181	Disclaimer: powers of court	
Section 182	Leaseholds	

TABLE 2: APPLIED PROVISIONS: OTHER PROVISIONS OF THE INSOLVENCY ACT 1986		
Section	*Subject*	*Modification or comment*
Section 188	Publicity	
Section 213	Fraudulent trading	
Section 214	Wrongful trading	Ignore subsection (6).
Section 233	Utilities	
Section 234	Getting in company's property	
Section 235	Co-operation with liquidator	
Section 236	Inquiry into company's dealings	
Section 237	Section 236: enforcement by court	
Section 238	Transactions at undervalue (England and Wales)	
Section 239	Preferences (England and Wales)	
Section 240	Ss. 238 & 239: relevant time	
Section 241	Orders under ss. 238 & 239	(a) In considering making an order in reliance on section 241 the court must have regard to Objective 1 of section 137. (b) Ignore subsections (2A)(a) and (3) to (3C).
Section 242	Gratuitous alienations (Scotland)	
Section 243	Unfair preferences (Scotland)	In considering the grant of a decree under subsection (5) the court must have regard to Objective 1 of section 137.
Section 244	Extortionate credit transactions	
Section 245	Avoidance of floating charges	
Section 246	Unenforceability of liens	
Sections 386 & 387, and Schedule 6 (and Schedule 4 to the Pension Schemes Act 1993)	Preferential debts	
Section 389	Offence of acting without being qualified	Treat references to acting as an insolvency practitioner as references to acting as a bank administrator.
Section 390	Persons not qualified to act	Treat references to acting as an insolvency practitioner as references to acting as a bank administrator.
Section 391	Recognised professional bodies	An order under section 391 has effect in relation to any provision applied for the purposes of bank administration.
Sections 423–425	Transactions defrauding creditors	(a) In considering granting leave under section 424(1) the court must have regard to Objective 1 of section 137.

**TABLE 2: APPLIED PROVISIONS: OTHER PROVISIONS OF
THE INSOLVENCY ACT 1986**

Section	Subject	Modification or comment
		(b) In considering making an order in reliance on section 425 the court must have regard to Objective 1 of section 137.
Sections 430–432 & Schedule 10	Offences	
Section 433	Statements: admissibility	For section 433(1)(a) and (b) substitute a reference to a statement prepared for the purposes of a provision of this Part.

[1902I]

NOTES
Commencement: to be appointed.

146   Status of bank administrator

A bank administrator is an officer of the court.

[1902J]

NOTES
Commencement: to be appointed.

147   Administrator's proposals

(1)   This section applies before the giving of an Objective 1 Achievement Notice (at which point paragraph 49 of Schedule B1 to the Insolvency Act 1986 applies in accordance with section 145).

(2)   The bank administrator must as soon as is reasonably practicable after appointment make a statement setting out proposals for achieving the Objectives in section 137.

(3)   The statement must say whether the bank administrator proposes to pursue Objective 2(a) or 2(b) in section 140.

(4)   The statement must have been agreed with the Bank of England.

(5)   But a bank administrator who is unable to agree a statement with the Bank of England may apply to the court for directions under paragraph 63 of Schedule B1 to the Insolvency Act 1986 (as applied by section 145); and the court may make any order, including dispensing with the need for the Bank of England's agreement.

(6)   The bank administrator must send the statement to the FSA.

(7)   The bank administrator may revise the statement (and subsections (4) to (6) apply to a revised statement as to the original).

(8)   The statement shall be treated in the same way (subject to this section) as a statement under paragraph 49 of Schedule B1 to the Insolvency Act 1986.

[1902K]

NOTES
Commencement: to be appointed.

148   Sharing information

(1)   This section applies to bank administration following transfer to a bridge bank.

(2)   Within the period of 5 days beginning with the day on which the bank administrator is appointed, the Bank of England must give the bank administrator information about the financial positions of the residual bank and the bridge bank.

(3)   While the residual bank is in bank administration the bridge bank must give the bank administrator on request information about the financial position of the bridge bank that the bank administrator requires for the purposes of pursuing Objective 1 in section 137.

(4)   Until the Bank of England has given an Objective 1 Achievement Notice, the bank administrator must—
    (a)   give the Bank of England information on request,
    (b)   allow the Bank of England access to records on request,
    (c)   give the bridge bank information on request,
    (d)   allow the bridge bank access to records on request,

(e)   keep the Bank of England informed about, and allow the Bank to participate in, any discussions between the bank administrator and another person which relate to, or are likely to affect, pursuit of Objective 1 in section 137, and

(f)   keep the bridge bank informed about, and allow the bridge bank to participate in, any discussions between the bank administrator and another person which relate to, or are likely to affect, pursuit of Objective 1 in section 137.

(5)   The Treasury shall by regulations prescribe—

(a)   the classes of information that must be provided under subsections (2) to (4), and

(b)   the classes of record to which access must be allowed under subsection (4).

(6)   Regulations under subsection (5)—

(a)   shall be made by statutory instrument, and

(b)   shall be subject to annulment in pursuance of a resolution of either House of Parliament.

[1902L]

NOTES

Commencement: to be appointed.

Multiple transfers

149   General application of this Part

(1)   This section applies where more than one property transfer instrument is made in respect of a bank.

(2)   For that purpose "property transfer instrument" includes—

(a)   supplemental instruments under section 42,

(b)   onward property transfer instruments under section 43, and

(c)   property transfer orders under section 45.

(3)   This Part applies to the bank with any modifications specified by the Treasury in regulations.

(4)   The regulations—

(a)   shall be made by statutory instrument, and

(b)   may not be made unless a draft has been laid before and approved by resolution of each House of Parliament.

[1902M]

NOTES

Commencement: to be appointed.

150   Bridge bank to private purchaser

(1)   This section applies where the Bank of England gives a bank administrator—

(a)   an Objective 1 Achievement Notice in respect of a bridge bank, and

(b)   notice that Objective 1 is still required to be pursued in respect of a commercial purchaser who has acquired all or part of the business of the bridge bank.

(2)   An Objective 1 Achievement Notice accompanied by a notice under subsection (1)(b) is referred to in this Part as an Objective 1 Interim Achievement Notice.

(3)   Where an Objective 1 Interim Achievement Notice is given, Objective 1 continues to apply—

(a)   in accordance with section 138(3), and

(b)   with the commercial purchaser being treated as the "private sector purchaser".

(4)   An Objective 1 Interim Achievement Notice in respect of the bridge bank—

(a)   has effect as between the bank administrator and the bridge bank, but

(b)   has no other effect for the purposes of provisions of this Part which refer to the giving of an Objective 1 Achievement Notice.

(5)   When the Bank of England gives the bank administrator an Objective 1 Achievement Notice in respect of the commercial purchaser, section 139 and other provisions of this Part which refer to the giving of an Objective 1 Achievement Notice shall have effect.

[1902N]

NOTES

Commencement: to be appointed.

151   Property transfer from bridge bank

(1)   This section applies where the Bank of England—

(a) transfers all or part of the business of a bank ("the original bank") to a bridge bank ("the original bridge bank") by making a property transfer instrument in accordance with section 12(2), and

(b) later makes or proposes to make an onward property transfer instrument under section 43(2) from the bridge bank to a transferee ("the onward transferee").

(2) If the onward transferee is a company which is wholly owned by the Bank of England—

(a) the onward transferee is treated as a bridge bank for the purposes of this Part, and

(b) the original bridge bank is treated as a residual bank for the purposes of this Part.

(3) In any other case, the Bank of England may determine that the original bridge bank is to be treated as a residual bank for the purposes of this Part.

(4) Where the original bridge bank is put into bank administration in reliance on subsection (2)(b), Objective 1 shall apply in accordance with section 138(4) in relation to both—

(a) services provided by the original bank to the original bridge bank, and

(b) services provided by the original bridge bank to the onward transferee.

(5) Where the original bridge bank is put into bank administration in reliance on a determination under subsection (3), Objective 1 shall apply in accordance with—

(a) section 138(3) in relation to services provided by the original bridge bank to the onward transferee, and

(b) section 138(4) in relation to services provided by the original bank to the original bridge bank.

(6) But the Bank may determine—

(a) that subsection (5) does not apply, and

(b) that section 150 shall apply as if the Bank had given—

(i) an Objective 1 Interim Achievement Notice in respect of the original bridge bank, and

(ii) a notice under section 150(1)(b) in respect of the onward transferee.

[1902O]

NOTES

Commencement: to be appointed.

152 Property transfer from temporary public ownership

(1) This section applies where the Treasury—

(a) make a share transfer order, in respect of securities issued by a bank (or a bank's holding company), in accordance with section 13(2), and

(b) later make a property transfer order from the bank (or from another bank which is or was in the same group as the bank) under section 45(2).

(2) This Part applies to the transferor under the property transfer order as to the transferor under a property transfer instrument.

(3) For that purpose this Part applies with any modifications specified by the Treasury in regulations; and the regulations—

(a) shall be made by statutory instrument, and

(b) may not be made unless a draft has been laid before and approved by resolution of each House of Parliament.

[1902P]

NOTES

Commencement: to be appointed.

Termination

153 Successful rescue

(1) This section applies if—

(a) the Bank of England has given an Objective 1 Achievement Notice, and

(b) the bank administrator has pursued Objective 2(a) in section 140 and believes that it has been achieved.

(2) The bank administrator may give a notice under paragraph 80 of Schedule B1 to the Insolvency Act 1986 (notice bringing administrator's appointment to an end on achievement of objectives).

(3) A bank administrator who gives a notice in accordance with subsection (2) must send a copy to the FSA.

(4) Failure without reasonable excuse to comply with subsection (3) is an offence.

[1902Q]

154 Winding-up or voluntary arrangement

(1) This section applies if—
- (a) the Bank of England has given an Objective 1 Achievement Notice, and
- (b) the bank administrator pursues Objective 2(b) in section 140.

(2) The bank administrator may—
- (a) give a notice under paragraph 84 of Schedule B1 to the Insolvency Act 1986 (no more assets for distribution), or
- (b) make a proposal in accordance with section 1 of that Act (company voluntary arrangement).

(3) Part 1 of that Act shall apply to a proposal made by a bank administrator, with the following modifications.

(4) In section 3 (summoning of meetings) subsection (2) (and not (1)) applies.

(5) The action that may be taken by the court under section 5(3) (effect of approval) includes suspension of the bank administration order.

(6) On the termination of a company voluntary arrangement the bank administrator may apply to the court to lift the suspension of the bank administration order.

(7) The bank administrator may not act under subsection (2) above unless satisfied that the bank has received any funds it is likely to receive from any scheme under a resolution fund order under section 52.

[1902R]

Miscellaneous

155 Disqualification of directors

(1) In this section "the Disqualification Act" means the Company Directors Disqualification Act 1986.

(2) In the Disqualification Act—
- (a) a reference to liquidation includes a reference to bank administration,
- (b) a reference to winding up includes a reference to making or being subject to a bank administration order,
- (c) a reference to becoming insolvent includes a reference to becoming subject to a bank administration order, and
- (d) a reference to a liquidator includes a reference to a bank administrator.

(3) For the purposes of the application of section 7(3) of the Disqualification Act (disqualification order or undertaking) to a bank which is subject to a bank administration order, the responsible office-holder is the bank administrator.

(4) (*inserts the Company Directors Disqualification Act 1986, s 21B.*)

[1902S]

156 Application of other law

(1) The Secretary of State and the Treasury may by order made jointly—
- (a) provide for an enactment about insolvency or administration to apply to bank administration (with or without specified modifications);
- (b) amend, or modify the application of, an enactment about insolvency or administration in consequence of this Part.

(2) An order under subsection (1)—
- (a) shall be made by statutory instrument, and
- (b) may not be made unless a draft has been laid before and approved by resolution of each House of Parliament.

[1902T]

157 Other processes

(1) Before exercising an insolvency power in respect of a residual bank the FSA must give notice to the Bank of England, which may participate in any proceedings arising out of the exercise of the power.

(2) In subsection (1)—
- (a) "residual bank" means a bank all or part of whose business has been transferred to a commercial purchaser in accordance with section 11 or to a bridge bank in accordance with section 12, and
- (b) "insolvency power" means—
  - (i) section 359 of the Financial Services and Markets Act 2000 (application for administration order), and
  - (ii) section 367 of that Act (winding-up petition).

                                                   [1902U]

NOTES
Commencement: to be appointed.

158 Building societies

(1) The Treasury may by order provide for this Part to apply to building societies (within the meaning of section 119 of the Building Societies Act 1986) as it applies to banks, subject to modifications set out in the order.

(2) An order may—
- (a) amend the Building Societies Act 1986 or any other enactment which relates, or in so far as it relates, to building societies;
- (b) amend an enactment amended by this Part;
- (c) replicate, with or without modifications, a provision of this Part;
- (d) apply a provision made under or by virtue of this Part, with or without modifications, to this Part as it applies to building societies.

(3) An order—
- (a) shall be made by statutory instrument, and
- (b) may not be made unless a draft has been laid before and approved by resolution of each House of Parliament.

(4) Provision made under or by virtue of this Part may make special provision in relation to the application of this Part to building societies.

                                                   [1902V]

NOTES
Commencement: to be appointed.

159 Credit unions

(1) The Treasury may by order provide for this Part to apply to credit unions (within the meaning of section 31 of the Credit Unions Act 1979) as it applies to banks, subject to modifications set out in the order.

(2) An order may—
- (a) amend the Credit Union Act 1979, the Industrial and Providential Societies Act 1965 or any other enactment which relates, or in so far as it relates, to credit unions;
- (b) amend an enactment amended by this Part;
- (c) replicate, with or without modifications, a provision of this Part;
- (d) apply a provision made under or by virtue of this Part, with or without modifications, to this Part as it applies to credit unions.

(3) An order—
- (a) shall be made by statutory instrument, and
- (b) may not be made unless a draft has been laid before and approved by resolution of each House of Parliament.

(4) Provision made under or by virtue of this Part may make special provision in relation to the application of this Part to credit unions.

                                                   [1902W]

NOTES
Commencement: to be appointed.

160–162 *(S 160 (Rules) amends the Insolvency Act 1986, s 411 at* **[1135]**, *and further provides that s 413(2) of the 1986 Act (duty to consult Insolvency Rules Committee) shall not apply to the first set of rules made in reliance on the amendments made to s 411 by this section; s 161 (Fees) amends s 414 of the 1986 Act; s 162 (Evidence) amends s 433 of the 1986 Act.)*

PART II
OTHER ACTS

163 Partnerships

(1) The Lord Chancellor may, by order made with the concurrence of the Secretary of State and the Lord Chief Justice, modify provisions of this Part in their application to partnerships.

(2) For procedural purposes an order under subsection (1) shall be treated in the same way as an order under section 420 of the Insolvency Act 1986 (partnerships).

(3) This section does not apply in relation to partnerships constituted under the law of Scotland.

[1902X]

NOTES

Commencement: to be appointed.

164 Scottish partnerships

(1) The Secretary of State may by order modify provisions of this Part in their application to partnerships constituted under the law of Scotland.

(2) An order—
  (a) shall be made by statutory instrument, and
  (b) shall be subject to annulment in pursuance of a resolution of either House of Parliament.

[1902Y]

NOTES

Commencement: to be appointed.

165 Co-operation between courts

(1) Provisions of or by virtue of this Part are "insolvency law" for the purposes of section 426 of the Insolvency Act 1986 (co-operation between courts).

(2) *(Amends the Insolvency Act 1986, s 426.)*

[1902Z]

NOTES

Commencement: to be appointed.

166 Interpretation: general

(1) In this Part "the court" means—
  (a) in England and Wales, the High Court,
  (b) in Scotland, the Court of Session, and
  (c) in Northern Ireland, the High Court.

(2) In this Part "the FSA" means the Financial Services Authority.

(3) For the purposes of a reference in this Part to inability to pay debts—
  (a) a bank that is in default on an obligation to pay a sum due and payable under an agreement, is to be treated as unable to pay its debts, and
  (b) section 123 of the Insolvency Act 1986 (inability to pay debts) also applies; and

for the purposes of paragraph (a) "agreement" means an agreement the making or performance of which constitutes or is part of a regulated activity carried on by the bank.

(4) Expressions used in this Part and in the Insolvency Act 1986 have the same meaning as in that Act.

(5) Expressions used in this Part and in the Companies Act 2006 have the same meaning as in that Act.

(6) A reference in this Part to action includes a reference to inaction.

[1903]

NOTES

Commencement: to be appointed.

167 Northern Ireland

In the application of this Part to Northern Ireland—
  (a) a reference to an enactment is to be treated as a reference to the equivalent enactment having effect in relation to Northern Ireland,
  (b) where this Part amends an enactment an equivalent amendment (incorporating any necessary modification) is made to the equivalent enactment having effect in relation to Northern Ireland,
  (c) the reference in section 159 to section 31 of the Credit Unions Act 1979 is to be treated as a reference to Article 2 of the Credit Unions (Northern Ireland) Order 1985, and

    (d)   in section 163—
        (i)   the reference to the Secretary of State is to be treated as a reference to the Department for Enterprise, Trade and Investment, and
        (ii)   the reference to the Lord Chief Justice is a reference to the Lord Chief Justice in Northern Ireland.

[1903A]

NOTES
Commencement: to be appointed.

168 Consequential provision

(1)   The Treasury may by order make provision in consequence of this Part.

(2)   An order may, in particular, amend or modify the effect of an enactment (including a fiscal enactment) passed before the commencement of this Part.

(3)   An order—
    (a)   shall be made by statutory instrument, and
    (b)   may not be made unless a draft has been laid before and approved by resolution of each House of Parliament.

[1903B]

NOTES
Commencement: to be appointed.

PART 4
FINANCIAL SERVICES COMPENSATION SCHEME

169 Overview

This Part makes a number of amendments in connection with the Financial Services Compensation Scheme provided for by Part 15 of the Financial Services and Markets Act 2000.

[1903C]

NOTES
Commencement: to be appointed.

170–180   (*Ss 170–180 contain the following amendments to Part 15 of the Financial Services and Markets Act 2000 (Part 15 is at* **[240]** *et seq): s 170 (Contingency funding) inserts s 214A of the 2000 Act and amends ss 213, 218; s 171 (Special resolution regime) inserts s 214B of the 2000 Act and amends s 223; s 172 (Investing in National Loans Fund) inserts s 223A of the 2000 Act; s 173 (Borrowing from National Loans Fund) inserts s 223B of the 2000 Act; s 174 (Procedure for claims) inserts s 214(1A)–(1C) of the 2000 Act and amends s 417; s 175 (Rights in insolvency) amends s 215 of the 2000 Act; s 176 (Information) inserts s 218A of the 2000 Act and amends s 219; s 177 (Payments in error) inserts s 223C of the 2000 Act; s 178 (Regulations) amends s 429 of the 2000 Act; s 179 (Delegation of functions) inserts s 221A of the 2000 Act and amends s 222; s 180 inserts s 224A of the 2000 Act.*)

PART 5
INTER-BANK PAYMENT SYSTEMS

Introduction

181 Overview

This Part enables the Bank of England to oversee certain systems for payments between financial institutions.

[1903D]

NOTES
Commencement: to be appointed.

182 Interpretation: "inter-bank payment system"

(1)   In this Part "inter-bank payment system" means arrangements designed to facilitate or control the transfer of money between financial institutions who participate in the arrangements.

(2)   The fact that persons other than financial institutions can participate does not prevent arrangements from being an inter-bank payment system.

(3)   In subsection (1) "financial institutions" means—

(a)   banks, and

(b)   building societies.

(4)   In subsection (1) "money" includes credit.

(5)   A system is an inter-bank payment system for the purposes of this Part whether or not it operates wholly or partly in relation to persons or places outside the United Kingdom.

[1903E]

NOTES
Commencement: to be appointed.

183 Interpretation: other expressions

In this Part—

(a)   a reference to the "operator" of an inter-bank payment system is a reference to any person with responsibility under the system for managing or operating it,

(b)   a reference to the operation of a system includes a reference to its management,

(c)   "the UK financial system" has the meaning given to "the financial system" by section 3(2) of the Financial Services and Markets Act 2000 (market confidence),

(d)   a reference to the Bank of England's role as a monetary authority is to be construed in accordance with section 244(2)(c), and

(e)   "the FSA" means the Financial Services Authority.

[1903F]

NOTES
Commencement: to be appointed.

Recognised systems

184 Recognition order

(1)   The Treasury may by order ("recognition order") specify an inter-bank payment system as a recognised system for the purposes of this Part.

(2)   A recognition order must specify in as much detail as is reasonably practicable the arrangements which constitute the inter-bank payment system.

(3)   The Treasury may not specify an inter-bank system operated solely by the Bank of England.

[1903G]

NOTES
Commencement: to be appointed.

185 Recognition criteria

(1)   The Treasury may make a recognition order in respect of an inter-bank payment system only if satisfied that any deficiencies in the design of the system, or any disruption of its operation, would be likely—

(a)   to threaten the stability of, or confidence in, the UK financial system, or

(b)   to have serious consequences for business or other interests throughout the United Kingdom.

(2)   In considering whether to specify a system the Treasury must have regard to—

(a)   the number and value of the transactions that the system presently processes or is likely to process in the future,

(b)   the nature of the transactions that the system processes,

(c)   whether those transactions or their equivalent could be handled by other systems,

(d)   the relationship between the system and other systems, and

(e)   whether the system is used by the Bank of England in the course of its role as a monetary authority.

[1903H]

NOTES
Commencement: to be appointed.

186 Procedure

(1)   Before making a recognition order in respect of a payment system the Treasury must—

(a)   consult the Bank of England,

(b)   notify the operator of the system, and

(c)   consider any representations made.

(2)   The Treasury must also consult the FSA before making a recognition order in respect of a payment system the operator of which—

(a) is, or has applied to become, a recognised investment exchange within the meaning of section 285 of the Financial Services and Markets Act 2000,

(b) is, or has applied to become, a recognised clearing house within the meaning of that section, or

(c) has, or has applied for, permission under Part 4 of that Act (regulated activities).

(3) In considering whether to make a recognition order in respect of a payment system the Treasury may rely on information provided by the Bank of England or the FSA.

[1903I]

NOTES
Commencement: to be appointed.

187 De-recognition

(1) The Treasury may revoke a recognition order.

(2) The Treasury must revoke a recognition order if not satisfied that the criteria in section 185 are met in respect of the recognised inter-bank payment system.

(3) Before revoking a recognition order the Treasury must—
(a) consult the Bank of England,
(b) notify the operator of the recognised inter-bank payment system, and
(c) consider any representations made.

(4) The Treasury must also consult the FSA before revoking a recognition order in respect of a payment system the operator of which—
(a) is, or has applied to become, a recognised investment exchange within the meaning of section 285 of the Financial Services and Markets Act 2000,
(b) is, or has applied to become, a recognised clearing house within the meaning of that section, or
(c) has, or has applied for, permission under Part 4 of that Act (regulated activities).

(5) The Treasury must consider any request by the operator of a recognised inter-bank payment system for the revocation of its recognition order.

[1903J]

PART II
OTHER ACTS

NOTES
Commencement: to be appointed.

Regulation

188 Principles

(1) The Bank of England may publish principles to which operators of recognised inter-bank payment systems are to have regard in operating the systems.

(2) Before publishing principles the Bank must obtain the approval of the Treasury.

[1903K]

NOTES
Commencement: to be appointed.

189 Codes of practice

The Bank of England may publish codes of practice about the operation of recognised inter-bank payment systems.

[1903L]

NOTES
Commencement: to be appointed.

190 System rules

(1) The Bank of England may require the operator of a recognised inter-bank payment system—
(a) to establish rules for the operation of the system;
(b) to change the rules in a specified way or so as to achieve a specified purpose;
(c) to notify the Bank of any proposed change to the rules;
(d) not to change the rules without the approval of the Bank.

(2) A requirement under subsection (1)(c) or (d) may be general or specific.

[1903M]

191 Directions

(1)   The Bank of England may give directions to the operator of a recognised inter-bank payment system.

(2)   A direction may—
(a)   require or prohibit the taking of specified action in the operation of the system;
(b)   set standards to be met in the operation of the system.

(3)   Before giving a direction the Bank must notify the Treasury.

(4)   The Treasury may by order confer immunity from liability in damages in respect of action or inaction in accordance with a direction.

(5)   An immunity does not extend to action or inaction—
(a)   in bad faith, or
(b)   in contravention of section 6(1) of the Human Rights Act 1998.

(6)   An order—
(a)   shall be made by statutory instrument, and
(b)   shall be subject to annulment in pursuance of a resolution of either House of Parliament.

[1903N]

192 Role of FSA

(1)   In exercising powers under this Part the Bank of England shall have regard to any action that the FSA has taken or could take.

(2)   Before taking action under this Part in respect of a recognised inter-bank payment system the operator of which satisfies section 186(2), the Bank of England must consult the FSA.

(3)   If the FSA gives the Bank of England notice that the FSA is considering taking action in respect of the operator of a recognised inter-bank payment system who satisfies section 186(2), the Bank may not take action under this Part in respect of the operator unless—
(a)   the FSA consents, or
(b)   the notice is withdrawn.

[1903O]

Enforcement

193 Inspection

(1)   The Bank of England may appoint one or more persons to inspect the operation of a recognised inter-bank payment system.

(2)   The operator of a recognised inter-bank payment system must—
(a)   grant an inspector access, on request and at any reasonable time, to premises on or from which any part of the system is operated, and
(b)   otherwise co-operate with an inspector.

[1903P]

194 Inspection: warrant

(1)   A justice of the peace may on the application of an inspector issue a warrant entitling an inspector or a constable to enter premises if—
(a)   any part of the management or operation of a recognised inter-bank payment system is conducted on the premises (whether by an operator of the system or by someone providing services used by an operator), and
(b)   any of the following conditions is satisfied.

(2)   Condition 1 is that—
(a)   a requirement under section 204 in connection with the payment system has not been complied with, and

(b) there is reason to believe that information relevant to the requirement is on the premises.

(3) Condition 2 is that there is reason to suspect that if a requirement under section 204 were imposed in connection with the payment system in respect of information on the premises—
(a) the requirement would not be complied with, and
(b) the information would be destroyed or otherwise tampered with.

(4) Condition 3 is that an inspector—
(a) gave reasonable notice of a wish to enter the premises, and
(b) was refused entry.

(5) Condition 4 is that a person occupying or managing the premises has failed to co-operate with an inspector.

(6) A warrant—
(a) permits an inspector or a constable to enter the premises,
(b) permits an inspector or a constable to search the premises and copy or take possession of information or documents, and
(c) permits a constable to use reasonable force.

(7) Sections 15(5) to (8) and 16 of the Police and Criminal Evidence Act 1984 (warrants: procedure) apply to warrants under this section.

(8) In the application of this section to Scotland—
(a) the reference to a justice of the peace includes a reference to a sheriff, and
(b) ignore subsection (7).

(9) In the application of this section to Northern Ireland—
(a) the reference to a justice of the peace is a reference to a lay magistrate, and
(b) the reference to sections 15(5) to (8) and 16 of the Police and Criminal Evidence Act 1984 is a reference to the equivalent provisions of the Police and Criminal Evidence (Northern Ireland) Order 1989.

[1903Q]

NOTES
Commencement: to be appointed.

195 Independent report

(1) The Bank of England may require the operator of a recognised inter-bank payment system to appoint an expert to report on the operation of the system.

(2) The Bank may impose a requirement only if it thinks—
(a) the operator is not taking sufficient account of principles published by the Bank under section 188,
(b) the operator is failing to comply with a code of practice under section 189, or
(c) the report is likely for any other reason to assist the Bank in the performance of its functions under this Part.

(3) The Bank may impose requirements about—
(a) the nature of the expert to be appointed;
(b) the content of the report;
(c) treatment of the report (including disclosure and publication);
(d) timing.

[1903R]

NOTES
Commencement: to be appointed.

196 Compliance failure

In this Part "compliance failure" means a failure by the operator of a recognised inter-bank payment system to—
(a) comply with a code of practice under section 189,
(b) comply with a requirement under section 190,
(c) comply with a direction under section 191, or
(d) ensure compliance with a requirement under section 195.

[1903S]

NOTES
Commencement: to be appointed.

197 Publication

(1) The Bank of England may publish details of a compliance failure by the operator of a recognised inter-bank payment system.

(2) The Bank may publish details of a sanction imposed under sections 198 to 200.

[1903T]

NOTES
Commencement: to be appointed.

198 Penalty

(1) The Bank of England may require the operator of a recognised inter-bank payment system to pay a penalty in respect of a compliance failure.

(2) A penalty—
  (a) must be paid to the Bank of England, and
  (b) may be enforced by the Bank as a debt.

(3) The Bank must prepare a statement of the principles which it will apply in determining—
  (a) whether to impose a penalty, and
  (b) the amount of a penalty.

(4) The Bank must—
  (a) publish the statement on its internet website,
  (b) send a copy to the Treasury,
  (c) review the statement from time to time and revise it if necessary (and paragraphs (a) and (b) apply to a revision), and
  (d) in applying the statement to a compliance failure, apply the version in force when the failure occurred.

[1903U]

NOTES
Commencement: to be appointed.

199 Closure

(1) This section applies if the Bank of England thinks that a compliance failure—
  (a) threatens the stability of, or confidence in, the UK financial system, or
  (b) has serious consequences for business or other interests throughout the United Kingdom.

(2) The Bank may give the operator of the inter-bank payment system concerned an order to stop operating the system (a "closure order")—
  (a) for a specified period,
  (b) until further notice, or
  (c) permanently.

(3) A closure order may apply to—
  (a) all activities of the payment system, or
  (b) specified activities.

(4) An operator who fails to comply with a closure order commits an offence.

(5) A person guilty of an offence is liable—
  (a) on summary conviction, to a fine not exceeding the statutory maximum, or
  (b) on conviction on indictment, to a fine.

[1903V]

NOTES
Commencement: to be appointed.

200 Management disqualification

(1) The Bank of England may by order prohibit a specified person from being an operator of a recognised inter-bank payment system—
  (a) for a specified period,
  (b) until further notice, or
  (c) permanently.

(2) The Bank may by order prohibit a specified person from holding an office or position involving responsibility for taking decisions about the management of a recognised inter-bank payment system—
  (a) for a specified period,
  (b) until further notice, or
  (c) permanently.

(3)   A person who breaches a prohibition under subsection (1) or (2) commits an offence.

(4)   A person guilty of an offence is liable—
   (a)   on summary conviction, to a fine not exceeding the statutory maximum, or
   (b)   on conviction on indictment, to a fine.

[1903W]

NOTES
Commencement: to be appointed.

201   Warning

(1)   Before imposing a sanction on the operator of an inter-bank payment system or on another person the Bank of England must—
   (a)   give the operator or other person a notice (a "warning notice"),
   (b)   give the operator or other person at least 21 days to make representations,
   (c)   consider any representations made, and
   (d)   as soon as is reasonably practicable, give the operator or other person a notice stating whether or not the Bank intends to impose the sanction.

(2)   In subsection (1) "imposing a sanction" means—
   (a)   publishing details under section 197(1),
   (b)   requiring the payment of a penalty under section 198,
   (c)   giving a closure order under section 199, or
   (d)   making an order under section 200.

(3)   Despite subsection (1), if satisfied that it is necessary the Bank may without notice—
   (a)   give a closure order under section 199, or
   (b)   make an order under section 200.

[1903X]

NOTES
Commencement: to be appointed.

202   Appeal

(1)   Where the Bank of England notifies a person under section 201(1)(d) that the Bank intends to impose a sanction, the person may appeal to the Financial Services and Markets Tribunal.

(2)   Where the Bank of England imposes a sanction on a person without notice in reliance on section 201(3), the person may appeal to the Financial Services and Markets Tribunal.

(3)   Part 9 of the Financial Services and Markets Act 2000 applies to appeals under this section; and for that purpose—
   (a)   a reference to the FSA is to be taken as a reference to the Bank of England,
   (b)   for section 133(9) of that Act substitute the proposition that a sanction may not be imposed while an appeal could be brought or is pending.
   (c)   Part 9 is to be read with any other necessary modifications.

[1903Y]

NOTES
Commencement: to be appointed.

Miscellaneous

203   Fees

(1)   The Bank of England may require operators of recognised inter-bank payment systems to pay fees.

(2)   A requirement under subsection (1) must relate to a scale of fees approved by the Treasury by regulations.

(3)   Regulations under subsection (2)—
   (a)   shall be made by statutory instrument, and
   (b)   shall be subject to annulment in pursuance of a resolution of either House of Parliament.

(4)   A requirement under subsection (1) may be enforced by the Bank as a debt.

[1903Z]

NOTES
Commencement: to be appointed.

204   Information

(1)   The Bank of England may by notice in writing require a person to provide information—

PART II
OTHER ACTS

(a)   which the Bank thinks will help the Treasury in determining whether to make a recognition order, or

(b)   which the Bank otherwise requires in connection with its functions under this Part.

(2)   In particular, a notice may require the operator of a recognised inter-bank payment system to notify the Bank if events of a specified kind occur.

(3)   A notice may require information to be provided—
(a)   in a specified form or manner;
(b)   at a specified time;
(c)   in respect of a specified period.

(4)   The Bank may disclose information obtained by virtue of this section to—
(a)   the Treasury;
(b)   the FSA;
(c)   an authority in a country or territory outside the United Kingdom which exercises functions similar to those of the Treasury, the Bank of England or the FSA in relation to inter-bank payment systems;
(d)   the European Central Bank;
(e)   the Bank for International Settlements.

(5)   Subsection (4)—
(a)   overrides a contractual or other requirement to keep information in confidence, and
(b)   is without prejudice to any other power to disclose information.

(6)   The Treasury may by regulations permit the disclosure of information obtained by virtue of this section to a specified person.

(7)   The Bank may publish information obtained by virtue of this section.

(8)   The Treasury may make regulations about the manner and extent of publication under subsection (7).

(9)   Regulations under this section—
(a)   shall be made by statutory instrument, and
(b)   shall be subject to annulment in pursuance of a resolution of either House of Parliament.

(10)   It is an offence—
(a)   to fail without reasonable excuse to comply with a requirement under this section;
(b)   knowingly or recklessly to give false information in pursuance of this section.

(11)   A person guilty of an offence is liable—
(a)   on summary conviction, to a fine not exceeding the statutory maximum, or
(b)   on conviction on indictment, to a fine.

[1904]

NOTES
Commencement: to be appointed.

205 Pretending to be recognised

(1)   It is an offence for the operator of a non-recognised inter-bank payment system—
(a)   to assert that the system is recognised, or
(b)   to do anything which suggests that the system is recognised.

(2)   A person guilty of an offence is liable—
(a)   on summary conviction, to a fine not exceeding the statutory maximum, or
(b)   on conviction on indictment, to a fine.

[1904A]

NOTES
Commencement: to be appointed.

206 Saving for informal oversight

(1)   Nothing in this Part prevents the Bank of England from having dealings with the operators of payment systems to which this Part does not apply.

(2)   Nothing in this Part prevents the Bank from having dealings, other than through the provisions of this Part, with the operators of payment systems to which this Part does apply.

[1904B]

NOTES
Commencement: to be appointed.

207–227   (*Part 6 (Banknotes: Scotland and Northern Ireland) outside the scope of this work.*)

PART 7
MISCELLANEOUS

Treasury support for banks

228　Consolidated Fund

(1)　There shall be paid out of money provided by Parliament expenditure incurred—

    (a)　by the Treasury for any purpose in connection with Parts 1 to 3 of this Act,

    (b)　by the Treasury, or by the Secretary of State with the consent of the Treasury, in respect of, or in connection with giving, financial assistance to or in respect of a bank or other financial institution (other than in respect of loans made in accordance with section 229), or

    (c)　by the Treasury in respect of financial assistance to the Bank of England.

(2)　For the purpose of subsection (1)(b) expenditure is incurred in respect of financial assistance in respect of banks or other financial institutions if it is incurred in respect of an activity, transaction or arrangement, or class of activity, transaction or arrangement, which is expected to facilitate any part of the business of one or more banks or other financial institutions; and for that purpose it does not matter—

    (a)　whether or not that is the sole or principal expected effect of the activity, transaction or arrangement, or

    (b)　whether the sole or principal motive for the activity, transaction or arrangement is (i) its effect on banks or other financial institutions, (ii) its effect on the economy as a whole, (iii) its effect on a particular industry or sector of the economy, or (iv) its effect on actual or potential customers of banks or other financial institutions.

(3)　In this section "financial assistance" has the meaning given by section 257 (and an order under that section may restrict or expand the effect of subsection (2)).

(4)　This section has effect in relation to expenditure whether incurred—

    (a)　before or after Royal Assent, and

    (b)　in pursuance of obligations entered into before or after Royal Assent.

(5)　Expenditure which could be paid out of money provided by Parliament under subsection (1) shall be charged on and paid out of the Consolidated Fund if the Treasury are satisfied that the need for the expenditure is too urgent to permit arrangements to be made for the provision of money by Parliament.

(6)　Where money is paid in reliance on subsection (5) the Treasury shall as soon as is reasonably practicable lay a report before Parliament specifying the amount paid (but not the identity of the institution to or in respect of which it is paid).

(7)　If the Treasury think it necessary on public interest grounds, they may delay or dispense with a report under subsection (6).

[1904C]

NOTES

Commencement: to be appointed.

229　National Loans Fund

(1)　Where the Treasury propose to make a loan to or in respect of a bank or other financial institution, they may arrange for money to be paid out of the National Loans Fund.

(2)　The Treasury may make arrangements under subsection (1) only where they think it necessary to make the loan urgently in order to protect the stability of the financial systems of the United Kingdom.

(3)　The Treasury shall determine—

    (a)　the rate of interest on a loan, and

    (b)　other terms and conditions.

(4)　Sums received by the Treasury in respect of loans by virtue of this section shall be paid into the National Loans Fund.

(5)　Neither section 16 of the Banking (Special Provisions) Act 2008 (finance) nor any other enactment restricts the breadth of application of this section.

(6)　Where money is paid in reliance on subsection (1) the Treasury shall as soon as is reasonably practicable lay a report before Parliament specifying the amount paid (but not the identity of the institution to or in respect of which it is paid).

(7)　If the Treasury think it necessary on public interest grounds, they may delay or dispense with a report under subsection (6).

[1904D]

NOTES
Commencement: to be appointed.

230 "Financial institution"

(1)   The Treasury may by order provide that a specified institution, or an institution of a specified class, is or is not to be treated as a financial institution for the purposes of section 228 or 229.

(2)   An order—
   (a)   shall be made by statutory instrument, and
   (b)   shall be subject to annulment in pursuance of a resolution of either House of Parliament.
[1904E]

NOTES
Commencement: to be appointed.

231   Reports

(1)   The Treasury shall prepare reports about any arrangements entered into which involve or may require reliance on section 228(1).

(2)   A report must be prepared in respect of—
   (a)   the period beginning with 1st April 2009 and ending with 30th September 2009, and
   (b)   each successive period of 6 months;
but no report is required for a period in respect of which there is nothing to record.

(3)   The Treasury shall lay each report before the House of Commons as soon as is reasonably practicable.

(4)   A report must not—
   (a)   specify individual arrangements, or
   (b)   identify, or enable the identification of, individual beneficiaries.

(5)   The Treasury must aim to give as much information as possible in a report, subject to subsection (4) and other considerations of public interest.
[1904F]

NOTES
Commencement: to be appointed.

Investment banks

232   Definition

(1)   In this group of sections "investment bank" means an institution which satisfies the following conditions.

(2)   Condition 1 is that the institution has permission under Part 4 of the Financial Services and Markets Act 2000 to carry on the regulated activity of—
   (a)   safeguarding and administering investments,
   (b)   dealing in investments as principal, or
   (c)   dealing in investments as agent.

(3)   Condition 2 is that the institution holds client assets.

(4)   In this group of sections "client assets" means assets which an institution has undertaken to hold for a client (whether or not on trust and whether or not the undertaking has been complied with).

(5)   Condition 3 is that the institution is incorporated in, or formed under the law of any part of, the United Kingdom.

(6)   The Treasury may by order—
   (a)   provide that a specified class of institution, which has a permission under Part 4 of the Financial Services and Markets Act 2000 to carry on a regulated activity, is to be treated as an investment bank for the purpose of this group of sections;
   (b)   provide that a specified class of institution is not to be treated as an investment bank for the purpose of this group of sections;
   (c)   provide that assets of a specified kind, or held in specified circumstances, are to be or not to be treated as client assets for the purpose of this group of sections;
   (d)   amend a provision of this section in consequence of provision under paragraph (a), (b) or (c).

[1904G]

NOTES
Commencement: to be appointed.

233   Insolvency regulations

(1)   The Treasury may by regulations ("investment bank insolvency regulations")—
    (a)   modify the law of insolvency in its application to investment banks;
    (b)   establish a new procedure for investment banks where—
        (i)   they are unable, or are likely to become unable, to pay their debts (within the meaning of section 93(4)), or
        (ii)   their winding up would be fair (within the meaning of section 93(8)).

(2)   Investment bank insolvency regulations may, in particular—
    (a)   apply or replicate (with or without modifications) or make provision similar to provision made by or under the Insolvency Act 1986 or Part 2 or 3 of this Act;
    (b)   establish a new procedure either (i) to operate for investment banks in place of liquidation or administration (under the Insolvency Act 1986), or (ii) to operate alongside liquidation or administration in respect of a particular part of the business or affairs of investment banks.

(3)   In making investment bank insolvency regulations the Treasury shall have regard to the desirability of—
    (a)   identifying, protecting, and facilitating the return of, client assets,
    (b)   protecting creditors' rights,
    (c)   ensuring certainty for investment banks, creditors, clients, liquidators and administrators,
    (d)   minimising the disruption of business and markets, and
    (e)   maximising the efficiency and effectiveness of the financial services industry in the United Kingdom.

(4)   A reference to returning client assets includes a reference to—
    (a)   transferring assets to another institution, and
    (b)   returning or transferring assets equivalent to those which an institution undertook to hold for clients.

[1904H]

NOTES
Commencement: to be appointed.

234   Regulations: details

(1)   Investment bank insolvency regulations may provide for a procedure to be instituted—
    (a)   by a court, or
    (b)   by the action of one or more specified classes of person.

(2)   Investment bank insolvency regulations may—
    (a)   confer functions on persons appointed in accordance with the regulations (which may, in particular, (i) be similar to the functions of a liquidator or administrator under the Insolvency Act 1986, or (ii) involve acting as a trustee of client assets), and
    (b)   specify objectives to be pursued by a person appointed in accordance with the regulations.

(3)   Investment bank insolvency regulations may make the application of a provision depend—
    (a)   on whether an investment bank is, or is likely to become, unable to pay its debts,
    (b)   on whether the winding up of an investment bank would be fair, or
    (c)   partly on those and partly on other considerations.

(4)   Investment bank insolvency regulations may make provision about the relationship between a procedure established by the regulations and—
    (a)   liquidation or administration under the Insolvency Act 1986,
    (b)   bank insolvency or bank administration under Part 2 or 3 of this Act, and
    (c)   provision made by or under any other enactment in connection with insolvency.

(5)   Regulations by virtue of subsection (4) may, in particular—
    (a)   include provision for temporary or permanent moratoria;
    (b)   amend an enactment.

(6)   Investment bank insolvency regulations may include provision—
    (a)   establishing a mechanism for determining which assets are client assets (subject to section 232);
    (b)   establishing a mechanism for determining that assets are to be, or not to be, treated as client assets (subject to section 232);
    (c)   about the treatment of client assets;

PART II
OTHER ACTS

(d) about the treatment of unsettled transactions (and related collateral);

(e) for the transfer to another financial institution of assets or transactions;

(f) for the creation or enforcement of rights (including rights that take preference over creditors' rights) in respect of client assets or other assets;

(g) indemnifying a person who is exercising or purporting to exercise functions under or by virtue of the regulations;

(h) for recovery of assets transferred in error.

(7) Provision may be included under subsection (6)(f) only to the extent that the Treasury think it necessary having regard to the desirability of protecting both—

(a) client assets, and

(b) creditors' rights.

(8) Investment bank insolvency regulations may confer functions on—

(a) a court or tribunal,

(b) the Financial Services Authority,

(c) the Financial Services Compensation Scheme (established under Part 15 of the Financial Services and Markets Act 2000),

(d) the scheme manager of that Scheme, and

(e) any other specified person.

(9) Investment bank insolvency regulations may include provision about institutions that are or were group undertakings (within the meaning of section 1161(5) of the Companies Act 2006) of an investment bank.

(10) Investment bank insolvency regulations may replicate or apply, with or without modifications, a power to make procedural rules.

(11) Investment bank insolvency regulations may include provision for assigning or apportioning responsibility for the cost of the application of a procedure established or modified by the regulations.

[1904I]

NOTES

Commencement: to be appointed.

---

235 Regulations: procedure

(1) Investment bank insolvency regulations shall be made by statutory instrument.

(2) Investment bank insolvency regulations may not be made unless a draft has been laid before and approved by resolution of each House of Parliament.

(3) The Treasury must consult before laying draft investment bank insolvency regulations before Parliament.

(4) If the power to make investment bank insolvency regulations has not been exercised before the end of the period of 2 years beginning with the date on which this Act is passed, it lapses.

(5) An order under section 232(6)—

(a) shall be made by statutory instrument, and

(b) may not be made unless a draft has been laid before and approved by resolution of each House of Parliament.

[1904J]

NOTES

Commencement: to be appointed.

---

236 Review

(1) The Treasury shall arrange for a review of the effect of any investment bank insolvency regulations.

(2) The review must be completed during the period of 2 years beginning with the date on which the regulations come into force.

(3) The Treasury shall appoint one or more persons to conduct the review; and a person appointed must have expertise in connection with the law of insolvency or financial services.

(4) The review must consider, in particular—

(a) how far the regulations are achieving the objectives specified in section 233(3), and

(b) whether the regulations should continue to have effect.

(5) The review must result in a report to the Treasury.

(6) The Treasury shall lay a copy of the report before Parliament.

(7) If a review recommends further reviews—

(a)   the Treasury may arrange for the further reviews, and
(b)   subsections (3) to (6) (and this subsection) shall apply to them.

[1904K]

NOTES
    Commencement: to be appointed.

Banking (Special Provisions) Act 2008

237 Compensation: valuer

Without prejudice to the generality of section 12 of the Banking (Special Provisions) Act 2008 (consequential and supplementary provision), it is declared that the power under section 9 of that Act to make provision for the appointment of a valuer includes power to replicate, or to make provision of a kind that may be made under, section 55(1) to (3) of this Act.

[1904L]

NOTES
    Commencement: to be appointed.

Bank of England

NOTES
    Editorial note: although the following sections contain amendments only, the editor considers that some users may find it helpful to have all of the amending text set out in full.

238   UK financial stability

(1)   After section 2 of the Bank of England Act 1998 (functions of court of directors) insert—

> **"2A   Financial Stability Objective**
>
> (1)   An Objective of the Bank shall be to contribute to protecting and enhancing the stability of the financial systems of the United Kingdom (the "Financial Stability Objective").
>
> (2)   In pursuing the Financial Stability Objective the Bank shall aim to work with other relevant bodies (including the Treasury and the Financial Services Authority).
>
> (3)   The court of directors shall, consulting the Treasury, determine and review the Bank's strategy in relation to the Financial Stability Objective.
>
> **2B   Financial Stability Committee**
>
> (1)   There shall be a sub-committee of the court of directors of the Bank (the "Financial Stability Committee") consisting of—
>> (a)   the Governor of the Bank, who shall chair the Committee (when present),
>> (b)   the Deputy Governors of the Bank, and
>> (c)   4 directors of the Bank, appointed by the chair of the court of directors (designated under paragraph 13 of Schedule 1).
>
> (2)   The Committee shall have the following functions—
>> (a)   to make recommendations to the court of directors, which they shall consider, about the nature and implementation of the Bank's strategy in relation to the Financial Stability Objective,
>> (b)   to give advice about whether and how the Bank should act in respect of an institution, where the issue appears to the Committee to be relevant to the Financial Stability Objective,
>> (c)   in particular, to give advice about whether and how the Bank should use stabilisation powers under Part 1 of the Banking Act 2009 in particular cases,
>> (d)   to monitor the Bank's use of the stabilisation powers,
>> (e)   to monitor the Bank's exercise of its functions under Part 5 of the Banking Act 2009 (inter-bank payment systems), and
>> (f)   any other functions delegated to the Committee by the court of directors for the purpose of pursuing the Financial Stability Objective.
>
> (3)   The Treasury may appoint a person to represent the Treasury at meetings of the Committee; and the Treasury's representative—
>> (a)   may not vote in proceedings of the Committee,
>> (b)   shall in all other respects be a member of the Committee, and
>> (c)   may be replaced by the Treasury.
>
> (4)   The Committee may co-opt other non-voting members.
>
> (5)   The chair of the court of directors may replace members of the Committee appointed under subsection (1)(c).

2C Financial Stability Committee: supplemental

(1) The Committee shall determine its own procedure (including quorum).

(2) If a member of the Committee has any direct or indirect interest (including any reasonably likely future interest) in any dealing or business which falls to be considered by the Committee—

(a) he shall disclose his interest to the Committee when it considers the dealing or business, and

(b) he shall have no vote in proceedings of the Committee in relation to any question arising from its consideration of the dealing or business, unless the Committee has resolved that the interest does not give rise to a conflict of interest.

(3) The Committee may delegate a function under section 2B(2)(b) to (e) to two or more of its members, excluding—

(a) the Treasury representative, and

(b) co-opted non-voting members."

(2) At the end of section 2 of the Bank of England Act 1998 add—

"(5) Sections 2A and 11 set objectives for the Bank in relation to financial stability and monetary policy; and subsections (2) to (4) above are subject to those sections."

[1904M]

NOTES

Commencement: to be appointed.

239 Number of directors

(1) Section 1 of the Bank of England Act 1998 (court of directors) is amended as follows.

(2) In subsection (2) omit "16".

(3) After subsection (2) insert—

"(2A) The number of directors must not exceed 9."

(4) The directors immediately before the day on which this section comes into force shall vacate office on that day (without prejudice to re-appointment).

[1904N]

NOTES

Commencement: to be appointed.

240 Meetings

(1) Paragraph 12 of Schedule 1 to the Bank of England 1998 (court of directors: meetings) is amended as follows.

(2) In sub-paragraph (1) for "once a month" substitute "7 times in each calendar year".

(3) For sub-paragraph (2) substitute—

"(2) Either of the following may summon a meeting at any time on giving such notice as the circumstances appear to require—

(a) the Governor of the Bank (or in his absence a Deputy Governor), and

(b) the chair of the court."

[1904O]

NOTES

Commencement: to be appointed.

241 Chair of court

(1) For paragraph 13(3) of Schedule 1 to the Bank of England Act 1998 (court of directors: chairing meetings) substitute—

"(3) The Chancellor of the Exchequer may designate—

(a) a member of the court to chair its meetings ("the chair of the court"), and

(b) one or more members of the court as deputies to chair its meetings in the absence of the chair of the court."

(2) For section 3(4) of that Act (sub-committee: chair) substitute—

"(4) The chair of the court (designated under paragraph 13 of Schedule 1) shall chair meetings of the sub-committee (when present)."

[1904P]

NOTES
Commencement: to be appointed.

242 Quorum

(1)   The Bank of England Act 1998 is amended as follows.

(2)   In section 3 (functions delegated to sub-committee)—
  (a)   omit subsection (3),
  (b)   in subsection (7) for "(3)" substitute "(4)", and
  (c)   at the end of subsection (7) add "(including quorum)".

(3)   In paragraph 13 of Schedule 1 (court of directors: proceedings)—
  (a)   omit sub-paragraph (2),
  (b)   in sub-paragraph (6) for "(2)" substitute "(3)", and
  (c)   at the end of sub-paragraph (6) add "(including quorum)".

[1904Q]

NOTES
Commencement: to be appointed.

243 Tenure

(1)   At the end of paragraph 1 of Schedule 1 to the Bank of England Act 1998 (Governor and Deputies: appointment) add—

  "(3)   A person may not be appointed as Governor more than twice.

  (4)   A person may not be appointed as Deputy Governor more than twice."

(2)   At the end of paragraph 6 of that Schedule (re-appointment) insert "(subject to paragraph 1(3) and (4))".

(3)   After paragraphs 1 and 2 of Schedule 3 to that Act (Monetary Policy Committee: appointment) insert—

  "2A.   A person may not be appointed as a member of the Committee under section 13(2)(c) more than twice."

(4)   At the end of paragraph 6 of that Schedule (re-appointment) insert "(subject to paragraph 2A)".

[1904R]

NOTES
Commencement: to be appointed.

244 Immunity

(1)   The Bank of England has immunity in its capacity as a monetary authority.

(2)   In this section—
  (a)   a reference to the Bank of England is a reference to the Bank and anyone who acts or purports to act as a director, officer, servant or agent of the Bank,
  (b)   "immunity" means immunity from liability in damages in respect of action or inaction, and
  (c)   a reference to the Bank's capacity as a monetary authority includes a reference to functions exercised by the Bank for the purpose of or in connection with—
    (i)   acting as the central bank of the United Kingdom, or
    (ii)   protecting or enhancing the stability of the financial systems of the United Kingdom.

(3)   The immunity does not extend to action or inaction—
  (a)   in bad faith, or
  (b)   in contravention of section 6(1) of the Human Rights Act 1998.

[1904S]

NOTES
Commencement: to be appointed.

245   (*Repeals the Bank Charter Act 1844, s 6 (Bank to produce weekly account).*)

246 Information

(1)   The Bank of England may disclose information that it thinks relevant to the financial stability of—

(a)   individual financial institutions, or
(b)   one or more aspects of the financial systems of the United Kingdom.

(2)   Information about the business or other affairs of a specified or identifiable person may be disclosed under subsection (1) only to—
(a)   the Treasury;
(b)   the Financial Services Authority;
(c)   the scheme manager of the Financial Services Compensation Scheme (established under Part 15 of the Financial Services and Markets Act 2000);
(d)   an authority in a country or territory outside the United Kingdom which exercises functions similar to those of the Treasury, the Bank of England or the Financial Services Authority in relation to financial stability;
(e)   the European Central Bank.

(3)   This section—
(a)   overrides a contractual or other requirement to keep information in confidence, and
(b)   is without prejudice to any other power to disclose information.

[1904T]

NOTES
Commencement: to be appointed.

247 Bank of England Act 1946

Nothing in this Act affects the generality of section 4 of the Bank of England Act 1946 (directions and relations with other banks).

[1904U]

NOTES
Commencement: to be appointed.

Financial Services Authority

248   (*Amends the Financial Services and Markets Act 2000, s 45 at* **[45]**.)

249 Functions

(1)   A reference in an enactment to functions conferred on the Financial Services Authority by or under the Financial Services and Markets Act 2000 (or any part of it) includes a reference to functions conferred on the Authority by or under this Act.

(2)   A reference in an enactment to functions of the Financial Services Authority includes a reference to functions conferred by or under this Act (irrespective of whether the enactment was passed or made before or after the commencement of this Act).

(3)   The Treasury may by order disapply subsection (1) or (2) to a specified extent; and an order—
(a)   shall be made by statutory instrument, and
(b)   may not be made unless a draft has been laid before and approved by resolution of each House of Parliament.

(4)   (*Adds the Financial Services and Markets Act 2000, s 1(4) at* **[1]**.)

[1904V]

NOTES
Commencement: to be appointed.

250 Information

(1)   The Financial Services Authority shall collect information that it thinks is or may be relevant to the stability of—
(a)   individual financial institutions, or
(b)   one or more aspects of the financial systems of the United Kingdom.

(2)   The Authority may perform its function under subsection (1) by the exercise of the power in section 165 of the Financial Services and Markets Act 2000 (power to require information—as qualified by section 249 above) or in any other way.

[1904W]

NOTES
Commencement: to be appointed.

Central banks

251 Financial assistance to building societies

(1)   The Treasury may by order modify the Building Societies Act 1986 for the purpose of facilitating, or in connection with, the provision of financial assistance to building societies by—
  (a)   the Treasury,
  (b)   the Bank of England,
  (c)   another central bank of a Member State of the European Economic Area, or
  (d)   the European Central Bank.

(2)   An order may affect any provision of the Building Societies Act 1986 which appears to the Treasury otherwise capable of preventing, impeding or affecting the provision of financial assistance; including, in particular, provision—
  (a)   about the establishment, constitution or powers of building societies,
  (b)   restricting or otherwise dealing with raising funds or borrowing,
  (c)   restricting or otherwise dealing with what may be done by or in relation to building societies,
  (d)   about security, or
  (e)   about the application of insolvency law or other legislation relating to companies.

(3)   An order—
  (a)   may disapply or modify a provision;
  (b)   may (but need not) take the form of textual amendment.

(4)   Incidental provision of an order (included in reliance on section 259(1)(c)) may, in particular—
  (a)   impose conditions, limits or other restrictions on what may be done in reliance on a provision of the order;
  (b)   confer a discretion on the Treasury, the Bank of England or another person or class of person.

(5)   Incidental or consequential provision of an order (included in reliance on section 259(1)(c)) may disapply or modify an enactment, whether by textual amendment or otherwise.

(6)   An order—
  (a)   shall be made by statutory instrument, and
  (b)   may not be made unless a draft has been laid before and approved by resolution of each House of Parliament.

(7)   The Treasury may by order create exceptions to or otherwise modify the effect of section 9B of the Building Societies Act 1986 (restriction on creation of floating charges); and—
  (a)   the Treasury may make an order only if they think it is likely to help building societies to use, give effect to or take advantage of financial assistance of the kind specified in subsection (1),
  (b)   an order may have effect in relation to transactions between building societies and persons not listed in subsection (1),
  (c)   an order shall be made by statutory instrument, and
  (d)   an order may not be made unless a draft has been laid before and approved by resolution of each House of Parliament.

(8)   In this section, "financial assistance" has the meaning given by section 257.

[1904X]

NOTES
  Commencement: to be appointed.

252 Registration of charges

(1)   Part 25 of the Companies Act 2006 (registration of charges) does not apply to a charge if the person interested in it is—
  (a)   the Bank of England,
  (b)   the central bank of a country or territory outside the United Kingdom, or
  (c)   the European Central Bank.

(2)   The reference in subsection (1) to Part 25 of the Companies Act 2006 includes a reference to—
  (a)   Part 12 of the Companies Act 1985 (which has effect until the commencement of Part 25 of the 2006 Act),
  (b)   Part 13 of the Companies (Northern Ireland) Order 1986 (which has effect until the commencement of Part 25 of the 2006 Act), and
  (c)   any provision about registration of charges made under section 1052 of the Companies Act 2006 (overseas companies).

[1904Y]

NOTES
Commencement: to be appointed.

253, 254 (*S 253 amends the Bankruptcy and Diligence etc (Scotland) Act 2007; s 254 abolishes the "funds attached" rule in Scotland (both outside the scope of this work*).)

Financial collateral arrangements

255 Regulations

(1) The Treasury may make regulations about financial collateral arrangements.

(2) "Financial collateral arrangements" are arrangements under which financial collateral is used as security in respect of a loan or other liability; and for that purpose—
(a) collateral may be in cash, securities or any other form,
(b) use as security may involve transfer of the collateral or the creation or transfer of any kind of right, interest or charge (fixed or floating) in respect of it, and
(c) in particular, use as security can include use under arrangements of a kind described commercially as "title transfer financial collateral arrangements".

(3) The regulations—
(a) may make any provision that the Treasury think necessary or desirable for the purpose of, or in connection with, implementation of the Financial Collateral Arrangements Directive (2002/47/EC) (or any replacement), but
(b) are not restricted to provision required in connection with the Directive, and may make any provision that the Treasury think necessary or desirable for the purpose of enabling financial collateral arrangements, whether or not with an international element, to be commercially useful and effective.

(4) The regulations may, in particular—
(a) disapply or modify an enactment or rule of law about formalities or evidence,
(b) disapply or modify an enactment about insolvency, administration, receivership or any similar procedure,
(c) disapply or modify an enactment about property law,
(d) disapply or modify an enactment about companies or other commercial entities or groupings,
(e) provide for provisions of financial collateral arrangements to have effect despite a reorganisation, winding-up or other process affecting a party to the arrangements,
(f) make provision for the enforcement of financial collateral arrangements (which may include, in particular, provision—
  (i) about sale, appropriation and set-off,
  (ii) about the use of collateral while subject to the arrangements,
  (iii) about "close out netting arrangements", under which obligations under a number of contracts may be set off against each other in the event of default under a specified contract,
  (iv) permitting a person to foreclose or exercise another right under the arrangements with or without an order of a court,
  (v) permitting or requiring the disclosure of information, and
  (vi) for enforcement after the commencement of, and despite, reorganisation, winding-up or another process),
(g) make provision for the choice of law according to which, or under which, matters arising under financial collateral arrangements are to be determined, and
(h) apply to persons whether or not provisions of the Directive apply to them.

(5) The regulations may, in particular—
(a) do anything done or purported to be done by the Financial Collateral Arrangements (No 2) Regulations 2003,
(b) provide for those regulations, or a specified provision, to be treated as having had effect despite any lack of vires,
(c) provide for anything done under or in reliance on those regulations to be treated as having had effect despite any lack of vires, and
(d) make any provision which the Treasury think necessary or desirable to achieve or restore certainty and stability in connection with the matters to which those regulations relate.

[1904Z]

NOTES
Commencement: to be appointed.

256 Supplemental

(1) Regulations under section 255—

(a)   shall be made by statutory instrument, and

(b)   shall lapse unless approved by resolution of each House of Parliament during the period of 28 days (ignoring periods of dissolution, prorogation or adjournment of either House for more than 4 days) beginning with the day on which the regulations are made.

(2)   The lapse of regulations under subsection (1)(b)—

(a)   does not invalidate anything done under or in reliance on the regulations before the lapse and at a time when neither House has declined to approve the regulations, and

(b)   does not prevent the making of new regulations (in new terms).

[1905]

NOTES
Commencement: to be appointed.

PART 8
GENERAL

257   "Financial assistance"

(1)   In this Act "financial assistance" includes giving guarantees or indemnities and any other kind of financial assistance (actual or contingent).

(2)   The Treasury may by order provide that a specified activity or transaction, or class of activity or transaction, is to be or not to be treated as financial assistance for a specified purpose of this Act; and subsection (1) is subject to this subsection.

(3)   An order—

(a)   shall be made by statutory instrument, and

(b)   shall be subject to annulment in pursuance of a resolution of either House of Parliament.

[1905A]

NOTES
Commencement: to be appointed.

258   "Enactment"

In this Act "enactment" includes—

(a)   subordinate legislation,

(b)   an Act of the Scottish Parliament and an instrument under an Act of the Scottish Parliament, and

(c)   Northern Ireland legislation.

[1905B]

NOTES
Commencement: to be appointed.

259   Statutory instruments

(1)   A statutory instrument under this Act—

(a)   may make provision that applies generally or only for specified purposes, cases or circumstances,

(b)   may make different provision for different purposes, cases or circumstances, and

(c)   may include incidental, consequential or transitional provision.

(2)   No statutory instrument under this Act shall be treated as a hybrid instrument under Standing Orders of either House of Parliament.

(3)   The Table lists the powers to make statutory instruments under this Act and the arrangements for Parliamentary scrutiny in each case (which are subject to subsections (4) to (6)).

Section	Topic	Parliamentary scrutiny
PART 1—*Special resolution regime*		
2	Meaning of "bank"	Draft affirmative resolution
25	Share transfer orders	Negative resolution
47	Partial transfers	Draft affirmative resolution
48	Protection of interests	Draft affirmative resolution
55	Independent valuer	Negative resolution

PART II
OTHER ACTS

Section	Topic	Parliamentary scrutiny
PART 1—Special resolution regime		
56	Independent valuer: money	Negative resolution
60	Third party compensation	Draft affirmative resolution
62	Compensation orders	Draft affirmative resolution
69	Continuity obligations: consideration and terms	Negative resolution
72	Transfers: enforcement	Negative resolution
74	Tax	Draft affirmative resolution (Commons only)
75	Power to change law	Draft affirmative resolution (except for urgent cases)
78	Public funds	Negative resolution (Commons only)
85	Building societies: orders	Negative resolution
86	Building societies: assets	(As for orders under section 90B of the Building Societies Act 1986)
88	Building societies: consequential	Draft affirmative resolution
89	Credit unions	Draft affirmative resolution
PART 2—Bank insolvency		
91	Meaning of "bank"	Draft affirmative resolution
122	Application of insolvency law	Draft affirmative resolution
125	Rules	(Expansion of power in section 411 of the Insolvency Act 1986)
130	Building societies	Draft affirmative resolution
131	Credit unions	Draft affirmative resolution
132	Partnerships	(As for orders under section 420 of the Insolvency Act 1986)
133	Scottish partnerships	Negative resolution
135	Consequential provision	Draft affirmative resolution
PART 3—Bank administration		
148	Sharing information	Negative resolution
149	Multiple original transfers	Draft affirmative resolution
152	Transfer from temporary public ownership	Draft affirmative resolution
156	Application of other law	Draft affirmative resolution
158	Building societies	Draft affirmative resolution
159	Credit unions	Draft affirmative resolution
160	Rules	(Expansion of power in section 411 of the Insolvency Act 1986)
163	Partnerships	(As for orders under section 420 of the Insolvency Act 1986)
164	Scottish partnerships	Negative resolution
168	Consequential provision	Draft affirmative resolution
PART 4—Financial Services Compensation Scheme		
170	Contingency funding	Draft affirmative resolution
171	Special resolution regime	Draft affirmative resolution

Section	Topic	Parliamentary scrutiny
PART 4—*Financial Services Compensation Scheme*		
173	Borrowing from National Loans Fund	Negative resolution
PART 5—*Inter-bank payment systems*		
191	Bank of England directions: immunity	Negative resolution
203	Fees regulations	Negative resolution
204	Information	Negative resolution
PART 6—*Banknotes: Scotland and Northern Ireland*		
215	Banknote regulations	Draft affirmative resolution
PART 7—*Miscellaneous*		
230	Financial institution	Negative resolution
232	Investment banks: definition	Draft affirmative resolution
233	Investment banks: insolvency	Draft affirmative resolution
249	FSA—functions	Draft affirmative resolution
251	Central banks: assistance to building societies	Draft affirmative resolution
255	Financial collateral arrangements	Affirmative resolution
PART 8—*General*		
257	Financial assistance	Negative resolution
262	Repeal of Banking (Special Provisions) Act 2008	None
263	Commencement	None

(4) A power listed in subsection (5) may be exercised without a draft being laid before and approved by resolution of each House of Parliament if—

(a) the power is being exercised for the first time, and
(b) the person exercising it is satisfied that it is necessary to exercise it without laying a draft for approval.

(5) The powers are those in—
(a) section 2 (special resolution regime: meaning of "bank"),
(b) section 47 (special resolution regime: partial transfers),
(c) section 48 (special resolution regime: protection of interests),
(d) section 60 (special resolution regime: third party compensation),
(e) section 88 (special resolution regime: building societies: consequential),
(f) section 91 (bank insolvency: meaning of "bank"),
(g) section 122 (bank insolvency: application of insolvency law),
(h) section 130 (bank insolvency: building societies),
(i) section 135 (bank insolvency: consequential provision),
(j) section 149 (bank administration: multiple original transfers),
(k) section 152 (bank administration: transfer from temporary public ownership),
(l) section 156 (bank administration: application of other law),
(m) section 158 (bank administration: building societies),
(n) section 168 (bank administration: consequential provision), and
(o) section 171 (Financial Services Compensation Scheme: special resolution regime).

(6) Where an instrument is made in reliance on subsection (5)—
(a) it shall lapse unless approved by resolution of each House of Parliament during the period of 28 days (ignoring periods of dissolution, prorogation or adjournment of either House for more than 4 days) beginning with the day on which the instrument is made,
(b) the lapse of an instrument under paragraph (a) does not invalidate anything done under or in reliance on it before its lapse and at a time when neither House has declined to approve it, and
(c) the lapse of an instrument under paragraph (a) does not prevent the making of a new one (in new terms).

NOTES
Commencement: to be appointed.

260 Money

Expenditure of the Treasury under, by virtue of or in connection with a provision of this Act shall be paid out of money provided by Parliament.

[1905D]

NOTES
Commencement: to be appointed.

261 Index of defined terms

The Table sets out expressions defined in this Act for general purposes.

Expression	Section
Action	93 and 166
Bank (Part 1)	2
Bank (Part 2)	91
Bank administration	136
Bank administration order	141
Bank insolvency	90
Bank insolvency order	94
Bridge bank	12
Bridge bank reverse share transfer instrument	31
Bridge bank share transfer instrument	30
Compensation scheme order	49
The court (Part 2)	92
The court (Part 3)	166
Eligible depositors	93
Enactment	258
FSA	3, 93 & 166
FSCS	93
Fair	93
Financial assistance	257
Financial institution	230
Full payment resolution	100
Independent valuer	54
Inter-bank payment system	182
Liquidation committee	100
Objective 1 Achievement Notice	139
Onward bridge bank	12
Onward property transfer instrument	43
Onward share transfer order	28
Partial property transfer	47
Property transfer instrument	33
Property transfer order	45
Resolution fund order	49
Reverse property transfer instrument	44

Expression	Section
Reverse property transfer order	46
Reverse share transfer order	29
Securities	14
Share transfer instrument	15
Share transfer order	16
Special resolution regime	1
Special resolution objectives	4
Stabilisation options	1
Stabilisation powers	1
Supplemental property transfer instrument	42
Supplemental share transfer instrument or order	26 & 27
Third party compensation order	49 & 59
Unable to pay debts	93 & 166

[1905E]

NOTES
Commencement: to be appointed.

262 Repeal

(1) The Treasury may by order repeal the Banking (Special Provisions) Act 2008.

(2) An order—
    (a) may include savings, and
    (b) shall be made by statutory instrument.

(3) Subsection (2)(a) is without prejudice to the generality of, or the application to this section of, section 259.

[1905F]

NOTES
Commencement: to be appointed.

263 Commencement

(1) The preceding provisions of this Act shall come into force in accordance with provision made by the Treasury by order.

(2) Subsection (1) does not apply to section 254, which comes into force at the end of the period of 2 months beginning with the date of Royal Assent.

(3) An order under subsection (1)—
    (a) may make provision generally or only in relation to specific provisions or purposes,
    (b) may make different provision for different provisions or purposes,
    (c) may include incidental or transitional provision (including savings), and
    (d) shall be made by statutory instrument.

(4) Where the Treasury or another authority are required to consult or take other action before exercising a power or fulfilling a duty to make legislation or to do any other thing under, by virtue of or in connection with this Act, the Treasury or other authority may rely on consultation or other action carried out before the commencement of the relevant provision of this Act.

[1905G]

NOTES
Commencement: 12 February 2009.

264 Extent

(1) This Act extends to—
    (a) England and Wales,
    (b) Scotland, and
    (c) Northern Ireland.

(2) But—

PART II
OTHER ACTS

(a)   sections 253 and 254 extend to Scotland only, and
(b)   an amendment of an enactment has the same extent as the enactment (or the relevant part).

[1905H]

NOTES
Commencement: 12 February 2009.

265 Short title

This Act may be cited as the Banking Act 2009.

[1905I]–[2000]

NOTES
Commencement: 12 February 2009.

PART III
STATUTORY INSTRUMENTS

A.   FSMA 2000 COMMENCEMENT ORDERS

FINANCIAL SERVICES AND MARKETS ACT 2000 (COMMENCEMENT NO 1) ORDER 2001 (NOTE)

(SI 2001/516)

NOTES

Authority: Financial Services and Markets Act 2000, s 431(2).
See the Appendix of Commencement Dates at **[498]**.

[2001]

FINANCIAL SERVICES AND MARKETS ACT 2000 (COMMENCEMENT NO 2) ORDER 2001 (NOTE)

(SI 2001/1282)

NOTES

Authority: Financial Services and Markets Act 2000, s 431(2).
See the Appendix of Commencement Dates at **[498]**.

[2002]

FINANCIAL SERVICES AND MARKETS ACT 2000 (COMMENCEMENT NO 3) ORDER 2001 (NOTE)

(SI 2001/1820)

NOTES

Authority: Financial Services and Markets Act 2000, s 431(2).
See the Appendix of Commencement Dates at **[498]**.

[2003]

FINANCIAL SERVICES AND MARKETS ACT 2000 (COMMENCEMENT NO 4 AND TRANSITIONAL PROVISION) ORDER 2001

(SI 2001/2364)

NOTES

Made: 2 July 2001.
Authority: Financial Services and Markets Act 2000, ss 428(3), 431(2).
As of 1 February 2009, this Order had not been amended.

1   Citation

This Order may be cited as the Financial Services and Markets Act 2000 (Commencement No 4 and Transitional Provision) Order 2001.

[2004]

2   Appointed days

(1)   3rd July 2001 is the day appointed for the coming into force of—
    (a)   paragraph 6 of Schedule 20 to the Act (amendment of the Tribunals and Inquiries Act 1992); and
    (b)   section 432(1) of the Act, for the purpose of introducing Schedule 20 to that extent.

(2)   19th July 2001 is the day appointed for the coming into force of paragraphs 7 and 8 of Schedule 1 to the Act (arrangements for the investigation of complaints), for the purpose of enabling the Authority to make the complaints scheme and appoint the investigator.

[2005]

3 Transitional saving in relation to the Financial Services Tribunal

Notwithstanding paragraph 6 of Schedule 20 to the Act, Schedule 1 to the Tribunals and Inquiries Act 1992 (tribunals under supervision of the Council on Tribunals) is to be treated as if it still contained the existing entry relating to financial services and paragraph 18 (which refers to the Financial Services Tribunal established under section 96 of the Financial Services Act 1986), for as long as that Tribunal retains functions conferred by or under any enactment.

[2006]

FINANCIAL SERVICES AND MARKETS ACT 2000 (COMMENCEMENT NO 5) ORDER 2001 (NOTE)

(SI 2001/2632)

NOTES
Authority: Financial Services and Markets Act 2000, s 431(2).
See the Appendix of Commencement Dates at **[498]**.

[2007]

FINANCIAL SERVICES AND MARKETS ACT 2000 (COMMENCEMENT NO 6) ORDER 2001 (NOTE)

(SI 2001/3436)

NOTES
Authority: Financial Services and Markets Act 2000, s 431(2).
See the Appendix of Commencement Dates at **[498]**.

[2008]

FINANCIAL SERVICES AND MARKETS ACT 2000 (COMMENCEMENT NO 7) ORDER 2001 (NOTE)

(SI 2001/3538)

NOTES
Authority: Financial Services and Markets Act 2000, ss 428(3), 431(2).
See the Appendix of Commencement Dates at **[498]**.
Note that art 2(2) of this Order provides that: "Section 104 of the Act (control of business transfers) comes into force on the appointed day for the purposes of insurance business transfer schemes only". The application of this provision (which relates to the exclusivity of this regime as a means of transfers of business) to banking business transfer schemes has not been brought into force and is unlikely to be implemented.

[2009]

B.   FSMA 2000 STATUTORY INSTRUMENTS

FINANCIAL SERVICES AND MARKETS ACT 2000 (REGULATED ACTIVITIES) ORDER 2001

(SI 2001/544)

NOTES
Made: 26 February 2001.
Authority: Financial Services and Markets Act 2000, ss 22(1), (5), 426, 428(3), Sch 2, para 25.
Commencement: see art 2.
This Order is reproduced as amended by the following SIs:

2001	Financial Services and Markets Act 2000 (Regulated Activities) (Amendment) Order 2001, SI 2001/3544.
2002	Financial Services and Markets Act 2000 (Regulated Activities) (Amendment) Order 2002, SI 2002/682; Financial Services and Markets Act 2000 (Financial Promotion and Miscellaneous Amendments) Order 2002, SI 2002/1310; Financial Services and Markets Act 2000 (Regulated Activities) (Amendment) (No 2) Order 2002, SI 2002/1776; Financial Services and Markets Act 2000 (Commencement of Mortgage Regulation) (Amendment) Order 2002, SI 2002/1777.
2003	Financial Services and Markets Act 2000 (Regulated Activities) (Amendment) (No 1) Order 2003, SI 2003/1475; Financial Services and Markets Act 2000 (Regulated Activities) (Amendment) (No 2) Order 2003, SI 2003/1476; Financial Services and Markets Act 2000 (Regulated Activities) (Amendment) (No 3) Order 2003, SI 2003/2822.
2004	Financial Services and Markets Act 2000 (Regulated Activities) (Amendment) Order 2004, SI 2004/1610; Financial Services and Markets Act 2000 (Regulated Activities) (Amendment) (No 2) Order 2004, SI 2004/2737; Life Assurance Consolidation Directive (Consequential Amendments) Regulations 2004, SI 2004/3379.
2005	Financial Services and Markets Act 2000 (Regulated Activities) (Amendment) Order 2005, SI 2005/593; Financial Services and Markets Act 2000 (Regulated Activities) (Amendment) (No 2) Order 2005, SI 2005/1518; Civil Partnership Act 2004 (Amendments to Subordinate Legislation) Order 2005, SI 2005/2114.
2006	Financial Services and Markets Act 2000 (Regulated Activities) (Amendment) Order 2006, SI 2006/1969; Financial Services and Markets Act 2000 (Regulated Activities) (Amendment) (No 2) Order 2006, SI 2006/2383; Capital Requirements Regulations 2006, SI 2006/3221; Financial Services and Markets Act 2000 (Regulated Activities) (Amendment No 3) Order 2006, SI 2006/3384.
2007	Companies Act 2006 (Commencement No 2, Consequential Amendments, Transitional Provisions and Savings) Order 2007, SI 2007/1093; Financial Services and Markets Act 2000 (Regulated Activities) (Amendment) Order 2007, SI 2007/1339; Money Laundering Regulations 2007, SI 2007/2157; Financial Services and Markets Act 2000 (Reinsurance Directive) Order 2007, SI 2007/3254; Financial Services and Markets Act 2000 (Regulated Activities) (Amendment) (No 2) Order 2007, SI 2007/3510.
2008	Companies Act 2006 (Consequential Amendments etc) Order 2008, SI 2008/948.
2009	Payment Services Regulations 2009, SI 2009/209.

Transitional provisions (interim permissions and interim approvals): for transitional provisions relating to interim permissions and interim approvals in respect of regulated mortgage business, general insurance intermediaries, pension schemes, regulated home reversion plans, regulated home purchase plans, and, with effect from 30 June 2008, the provision of travel insurance, see the Financial Services and Markets Act 2000 (Transitional Provisions) (Mortgages) Order 2004, SI 2004/2615 at **[2735]**, the Financial Services and Markets Act 2000 (Transitional Provisions) (General Insurance Intermediaries) Order 2004, SI 2004/3351 at **[2750]**, the Financial Services and Markets Act 2000 (Regulated Activities) (Amendment) Order 2006, SI 2006/1969 at **[2853]**, the Financial Services and Markets Act 2000 (Regulated Activities) (Amendment) (No 2) Order 2006, SI 2006/2383 at **[2860]**, and the Financial Services and Markets Act 2000 (Regulated Activities) (Amendment) (No 2) Order 2007, SI 2007/3510 at **[2899]**.

ARRANGEMENT OF ARTICLES

PART I
GENERAL

PART III
STATUTORY INSTRUMENTS

PART II
SPECIFIED ACTIVITIES

CHAPTER I
General

CHAPTER II
ACCEPTING DEPOSITS

The activity

Exclusions

CHAPTER IIA
ELECTRONIC MONEY

The activity

Exclusions

Supplemental

CHAPTER III
INSURANCE

The activities

Exclusions

Supplemental

CHAPTER IV
DEALING IN INVESTMENTS AS PRINCIPAL

The activity

Exclusions

PART III
SPECIFIED INVESTMENTS

PART V
UNAUTHORISED PERSONS CARRYING ON INSURANCE MEDIATION ACTIVITIES

SCHEDULES:

PART I
GENERAL

1 Citation

This Order may be cited as the Financial Services and Markets Act 2000 (Regulated Activities)
Order 2001.

[2010]

2 Commencement

(1)   Except as provided by paragraph (2), this Order comes into force on the day on which
section 19 of the Act comes into force.

(2)   This Order comes into force—
   (a)   for the purposes of articles 59, 60 and 87 (funeral plan contracts) on 1st January 2002;
         and
   (b)   for the purposes of articles 61 to 63, 88, 90 and 91 (regulated mortgage contracts) [on
         such a day as the Treasury may specify].

[(3)   Any day specified under paragraph (2)(b) must be caused to be notified in the London,
Edinburgh and Belfast Gazettes published not later than one week before that day.]

[2011]

NOTES
Para (2): words in square brackets substituted by the Financial Services and Markets Act 2000 (Commencement of Mortgage Regulation) (Amendment) Order 2002, SI 2002/1777, art 2(1), (2), as from 30 August 2002.
Para (3): added by SI 2002/1777, art 2(1), (3), as from 30 August 2002.
On such a day as the Treasury may specify: 31 October 2004 (see the London Gazette, 14 July 2003).

3 Interpretation

(1) In this Order—
"the Act" means the Financial Services and Markets Act 2000;
"annuities on human life" does not include superannuation allowances and annuities payable out of any fund applicable solely to the relief and maintenance of persons engaged, or who have been engaged, in any particular profession, trade or employment, or of the dependants of such persons;
"buying" includes acquiring for valuable consideration;
"close relative" in relation to a person means—
  (a) his spouse [or civil partner];
  (b) his children and step children, his parents and step-parents, his brothers and sisters and his step-brothers and step-sisters; and
  (c) the spouse [or civil partner] of any person within sub-paragraph (b);
["the Commission Regulation" means Commission Regulation 1287/2006 of 10 August 2006;]
"contract of general insurance" means any contract falling within Part I of Schedule 1;
"contract of insurance" means any contract of insurance which is a contract of long-term insurance or a contract of general insurance, and includes—
  (a) fidelity bonds, performance bonds, administration bonds, bail bonds, customs bonds or similar contracts of guarantee, where these are—
    (i) effected or carried out by a person not carrying on a banking business;
    (ii) not effected merely incidentally to some other business carried on by the person effecting them; and
    (iii) effected in return for the payment of one or more premiums;
  (b) tontines;
  (c) capital redemption contracts or pension fund management contracts, where these are effected or carried out by a person who—
    (i) does not carry on a banking business; and
    (ii) otherwise carries on a regulated activity of the kind specified by article 10(1) or (2);
  (d) contracts to pay annuities on human life;
  (e) contracts of a kind referred to in article 1(2)(e) of the first life insurance directive (collective insurance etc); and
  (f) contracts of a kind referred to in article 1(3) of the first life insurance directive (social insurance);
but does not include a funeral plan contract (or a contract which would be a funeral plan contract but for the exclusion in article 60);
"contract of long-term insurance" means any contract falling within Part II of Schedule 1;
"contractually based investment" means—
  (a) rights under a qualifying contract of insurance;
  (b) any investment of the kind specified by any of articles 83, 84, 85 and 87; or
  (c) any investment of the kind specified by article 89 so far as relevant to an investment falling within (a) or (b);
["credit institution" means—
  (a) a credit institution authorised under the banking consolidation directive other than an institution to which Article 2.1 of the markets in financial instruments directive (the text of which is set out in Schedule 3) applies, or
  (b) an institution which would satisfy the requirements for authorisation as a credit institution under that directive (other than an institution to which Article 2.1 of the markets in financial instruments directive would apply) if it had its registered office (or if it does not have a registered office, its head office) in an EEA State;]
"deposit" has the meaning given by article 5;
["electronic money" means monetary value, as represented by a claim on the issuer, which is—
  (a) stored on an electronic device;
  (b) issued on receipt of funds; and
  (c) accepted as a means of payment by persons other than the issuer;]

["financial instrument" means any instrument listed in Section C of Annex I to the markets in financial instruments directive (the text of which is set out in Part 1 of Schedule 2) read with Chapter VI of the Commission Regulation (the text of which is set out in Part 2 of Schedule 2);]

"funeral plan contract" has the meaning given by article 59;

["home Member State", in relation to an investment firm, has the meaning given by Article 4.1.20 of the markets in financial instruments directive, and in relation to a credit institution, has the meaning given by Article 4.7 of the banking consolidation directive;]

["home purchase provider" has the meaning given by article 63F(3);

"home purchaser" has the meaning given by article 63F(3);]

"instrument" includes any record whether or not in the form of a document;

["investment firm" means a person whose regular occupation or business is the provision or performance of investment services and activities on a professional basis but does not include—

    (a)   a person to whom the markets in financial instruments directive does not apply by virtue of Article 2 of that directive (the text of which is set out in Schedule 3);

    (b)   a person whose home Member State is an EEA State other than the United Kingdom and to whom, by reason of the fact that the State has given effect to Article 3 of that directive, that directive does not apply by virtue of that Article;

    (c)   a person who does not have a home Member State and to whom (if he had his registered office in an EEA State, or, being a person other than a body corporate or a body corporate not having a registered office, if he had his head office in an EEA State) the markets in financial instruments directive would not apply by virtue of Article 2 of that directive;]

["investment services and activities" means—

    (a)   any service provided to third parties listed in Section A of Annex I to the markets in financial instruments directive (the text of which is set out in Part 3 of Schedule 2) read with Article 52 of Commission Directive 2006/73/EC of 10 August 2006 (the text of which is set out in Part 4 of Schedule 2), or

    (b)   any activity listed in Section A of Annex I to that directive,

relating to any financial instrument;]

"joint enterprise" means an enterprise into which two or more persons ("the participators") enter for commercial purposes related to a business or businesses (other than the business of engaging in a regulated activity) carried on by them; and, where a participator is a member of a group, each other member of the group is also to be regarded as a participator in the enterprise;

"local authority" means—

    (a)   in England and Wales, a local authority within the meaning of the Local Government Act 1972, the Greater London Authority, the Common Council of the City of London or the Council of the Isles of Scilly;

    (b)   in Scotland, a local authority within the meaning of the Local Government (Scotland) Act 1973;

    (c)   in Northern Ireland, a district council within the meaning of the Local Government Act (Northern Ireland) 1972;

["management company" has the meaning given by Article 1a.2 of the UCITS directive as amended by Directive 2001/107/EC;]

"managing agent" means a person who is permitted by the Council of Lloyd's in the conduct of his business as an underwriting agent to perform for a member of Lloyd's one or more of the following functions—

    (a)   underwriting contracts of insurance at Lloyd's;

    (b)   reinsuring such contracts in whole or in part;

    (c)   paying claims on such contracts;

["market operator" means a market operator within the meaning of Article 4.1.13 of the markets in financial instruments directive, or a person who would be a market operator if he had his registered office, or if he does not have a registered office his head office, in an EEA State, but does not include—

    (a)   a person to whom the markets in financial instruments directive does not apply by virtue of Article 2 of that directive (the text of which is set out in Schedule 3);

    (b)   a person who does not have a home Member State to whom (if he had his registered office, or if he does not have a registered office his head office, in an EEA State) the markets in financial instruments directive would not apply by virtue of Article 2 of that directive;]

["multilateral trading facility" means—

    (a)   a multilateral trading facility (within the meaning of Article 4.1.15 of the markets in financial instruments directive) operated by an investment firm, a credit institution or a market operator, or

    (b)   a facility which—

    (i) is operated by an investment firm, a credit institution or market operator which does not have a home Member State, and

    (ii) if its operator had a home Member State, would be a multilateral trading facility within the meaning of Article 4.1.15 of the markets in financial instruments directive;]

["occupational pension scheme" has the meaning given by section 1 of the Pension Schemes Act 1993 but with paragraph (b) of the definition omitted;]

"overseas person" means a person who—

  (a) carries on activities of the kind specified by any of articles 14, 21, 25, [25A,] [25B, 25C,] [25D,] 37[, 39A], 40, 45, 51, 52[, 53, 53A [, 53B, 53C, 61, 63B and 63F]] or, so far as relevant to any of those articles, article 64 (or activities of a kind which would be so specified but for the exclusion in article 72); but

  (b) does not carry on any such activities, or offer to do so, from a permanent place of business maintained by him in the United Kingdom;

"pension fund management contract" means a contract to manage the investments of pension funds (other than funds solely for the benefit of the officers or employees of the person effecting or carrying out the contract and their dependants or, in the case of a company, partly for the benefit of officers and employees and their dependants of its subsidiary or holding company or a subsidiary of its holding company); and for the purposes of this definition, "subsidiary" and "holding company" are to be construed in accordance with section 736 of the Companies Act 1985 or article 4 of the Companies (Northern Ireland) Order 1986;

["personal pension scheme" means a scheme or arrangement which is not an occupational pension scheme or a stakeholder pension scheme and which is comprised in one or more instruments or agreements, having or capable of having effect so as to provide benefits to or in respect of people—

  (a) on retirement,

  (b) on having reached a particular age, or

  (c) on termination of service in an employment;]

["plan provider" has the meaning given by paragraph (3) of article 63B, read with paragraphs (7) and (8) of that article;]

"property" includes currency of the United Kingdom or any other country or territory;

"qualifying contract of insurance" means a contract of long-term insurance which is not—

  (a) a reinsurance contract; nor

  (b) a contract in respect of which the following conditions are met—

    (i) the benefits under the contract are payable only on death or in respect of incapacity due to injury, sickness or infirmity;

    (ii) …

    (iii) the contract has no surrender value, or the consideration consists of a single premium and the surrender value does not exceed that premium; and

    (iv) the contract makes no provision for its conversion or extension in a manner which would result in it ceasing to comply with any of the above conditions;

["regulated home purchase plan" has the meaning given by article 63F(3);

"regulated home reversion plan" has the meaning given by article 63B(3);]

"regulated mortgage contract" has the meaning given by article 61(3);

["relevant investment" means—

  (a) rights under a qualifying contract of insurance;

  (b) rights under any other contract of insurance;

  (c) any investment of the kind specified by any of articles 83, 84, 85 and 87; or

  (d) any investment of the kind specified by article 89 so far as relevant to an investment falling within (a) or (c);]

["reversion seller" has the meaning given by article 63B(3);]

"security" means (except where the context otherwise requires) any investment of the kind specified by any of articles 76 to 82 or, so far as relevant to any such investment, article 89;

"selling", in relation to any investment, includes disposing of the investment for valuable consideration, and for these purposes "disposing" includes—

  (a) in the case of an investment consisting of rights under a contract—

    (i) surrendering, assigning or converting those rights; or

    (ii) assuming the corresponding liabilities under the contract;

  (b) in the case of an investment consisting of rights under other arrangements, assuming the corresponding liabilities under the arrangements; and

  (c) in the case of any other investment, issuing or creating the investment or granting the rights or interests of which it consists;

"stakeholder pension scheme" has the meaning given by section 1 of the Welfare Reform and Pensions Act 1999 [in relation to Great Britain and has the meaning given by article 3 of the Welfare Reform and Pensions (Northern Ireland) Order 1999 in relation to Northern Ireland];

"syndicate" means one or more persons, to whom a particular syndicate number has been assigned by or under the authority of the Council of Lloyd's, carrying out or effecting contracts of insurance written at Lloyd's;

"voting shares", in relation to a body corporate, means shares carrying voting rights attributable to share capital which are exercisable in all circumstances at any general meeting of that body corporate.

(2) For the purposes of this Order, a transaction is entered into through a person if he enters into it as agent or arranges, in a manner constituting the carrying on of an activity of the kind specified by article 25(1)[, 25A(1), 25B(1) or 25C(1)], for it to be entered into by another person as agent or principal.

(3) For the purposes of this Order, a contract of insurance is to be treated as falling within Part II of Schedule 1, notwithstanding the fact that it contains related and subsidiary provisions such that it might also be regarded as falling within Part I of that Schedule, if its principal object is that of a contract falling within Part II and it is effected or carried out by an authorised person who has permission to effect or carry out contracts falling within paragraph I of Part II of Schedule 1.

[2012]

NOTES

Para (1) is amended as follows:

Words in square brackets in the definition "close relative" inserted by the Civil Partnership Act 2004 (Amendments to Subordinate Legislation) Order 2005, SI 2005/2114, art 2(16), Sch 16, Pt 1, para 1(1), (2), as from 5 December 2005.

Definitions "the Commission Regulation", "credit institution", "financial instrument", "home Member State", "investment firm", "investment services and activities", "management company", "market operator", and "multilateral trading facility" inserted by the Financial Services and Markets Act 2000 (Regulated Activities) (Amendment No 3) Order 2006, SI 2006/3384, arts 2, 3(b), as from 1 April 2007 (for the purposes of enabling applications to be made for (i) a Pt IV permission, (ii) a variation of a Pt IV permission, and (iii) the Authority's approval under s 59 of the 2000 Act, in relation to an activity of the kind specified by art 25D of this Order, or in relation to an investment of the kind specified by arts 83, 84 or 85 of this Order), and as from 1 November 2007 (otherwise).

Definition "electronic money" inserted by the Financial Services and Markets Act 2000 (Regulated Activities) (Amendment) Order 2002, SI 2002/682, art 2, as from 27 April 2002 (subject to transitional provisions in relation to persons issuing electronic money immediately before that date contained in art 9 at **[2667]**).

Definitions "home purchase provider", "home purchaser", "plan provider", "regulated home purchase plan", "regulated home reversion plan", and "reversion seller" inserted by the Financial Services and Markets Act 2000 (Regulated Activities) (Amendment) (No 2) Order 2006, SI 2006/2383, arts 2, 3(1)(a), (c)–(e), as from 6 November 2006 (for the purposes of enabling applications to be made for (i) a Pt IV permission, or a variation of a Pt IV permission, in relation to activities of the kind specified by arts 25B, 25C, 53B, 53C, 63B or 63F or, so far as relevant to any such activity, art 64 of this Order; or (ii) the Authority's approval under FSMA 2000, s 59 in relation to any of those activities), and as from 6 April 2007 (otherwise) (for transitional provisions and effect see arts 36–40 of, and the Schedule to, the 2006 Order at **[2861]** et seq).

Definition "occupational pension scheme" substituted by the Financial Services and Markets Act 2000 (Regulated Activities) (Amendment) Order 2006, SI 2006/1969, art 2(1), (2)(a), as from 1 October 2006 (for the purposes of enabling applications to be made for Pt IV permission or for a variation of Pt IV permission in relation to the regulated activity specified by art 52(b) of this Order (as amended by SI 2006/1969) or in relation to an investment specified by art 82(2) of this Order (as so amended)), and as from 6 April 2007 (otherwise); for transitional provisions and effect see arts 3–7 of, and the Schedule to, the 2006 Order at **[2854]**.

In definition "overseas person" first figure in square brackets inserted, and words in the penultimate (outer) pair of square brackets substituted, by the Financial Services and Markets Act 2000 (Regulated Activities) (Amendment) (No 1) Order 2003, SI 2003/1475, art 3, as from 31 October 2004 (for transitional provisions see arts 26–29 at **[2700]** et seq); second figures in square brackets inserted, and words in final (inner) pair of square brackets substituted, by SI 2006/2383, arts 2, 3(1)(b), as from 6 November 2006 (for the purposes of enabling applications to be made for (i) a Pt IV permission, or a variation of a Pt IV permission, in relation to activities of the kind specified by arts 25B, 25C, 53B, 53C, 63B or 63F or, so far as relevant to any such activity, art 64 of this Order; or (ii) the Authority's approval under FSMA 2000, s 59 in relation to any of those activities), and as from 6 April 2007 (otherwise) (for transitional provisions and effect see arts 36–40 of, and the Schedule to, the 2006 Order at **[2861]** et seq); third figure in square brackets inserted by SI 2006/3384, arts 2, 3(a), as from 1 April 2007 (for the purposes of enabling applications to be made for (i) a Pt IV permission, (ii) a variation of a Pt IV permission, and (iii) the Authority's approval under s 59 of the 2000 Act, in relation to an activity of the kind specified by art 25D of this Order, or in relation to an investment of the kind specified by arts 83, 84 or 85 of this Order), and as from 1 November 2007 (otherwise); fourth figure in square brackets inserted by the Financial Services and Markets Act 2000 (Regulated Activities) (Amendment) (No 2) Order 2003, SI 2003/1476, art 3(1)(a), as from 31 October 2004 (in so far as relating to contracts of long-term care insurance), and as from 14 January 2005 (otherwise) (for transitional provisions see arts 22–27 of that Order at **[2706]** et seq).

Definition "personal pension scheme" inserted by SI 2006/1969, art 2(1), (2)(a), as from 1 October 2006 (for the purposes of enabling applications to be made for Pt IV permission or for a variation of Pt IV permission in relation to the regulated activity specified by art 52(b) of this Order (as amended by SI 2006/1969) or in relation to an investment specified by art 82(2) of this Order (as so amended)), and as from 6 April 2007 (otherwise); for transitional provisions and effect see arts 3–7 of, and the Schedule to, the 2006 Order at **[2854]** et seq.

In definition "qualifying contract of insurance" sub-para (b)(ii) revoked by the Financial Services and Markets Act 2000 (Regulated Activities) (Amendment) Order 2007, SI 2007/1339, arts 2, 3, as from 6 June 2007.

Definition "relevant investment" inserted by SI 2003/1476, art 3(1)(b), as from 31 October 2004 (in so far as relating to contracts of long-term care insurance), and as from 14 January 2005 (otherwise) (for transitional provisions see arts 22–27 of that Order at **[2706]** et seq).

Words in square brackets in definition "stakeholder pension scheme" added by SI 2005/593, art 2(1), (2)(b), as from 6 April 2005.

Para (2): words in square brackets inserted by SI 2006/2383, arts 2, 3(2), as from 6 November 2006 (for the purposes of enabling applications to be made for (i) a Pt IV permission, or a variation of a Pt IV permission, in relation to activities of the kind specified by arts 25B, 25C, 53B, 53C, 63B or 63F or, so far as relevant to any such activity, art 64 of this Order; or (ii) the Authority's approval under FSMA 2000, s 59 in relation to any of those activities), and as from 6 April 2007 (otherwise) (for transitional provisions and effect see arts 36–40 of, and the Schedule to, the 2006 Order at **[2861]** et seq).

Step-children, etc: as to the meaning of this and related expressions, see the Civil Partnership Act 2004, s 246 (as applied to this Order by the Civil Partnership Act 2004 (Relationships Arising Through Civil Partnership) Order 2005, SI 2005/3137, art 3, Schedule).

PART II
SPECIFIED ACTIVITIES

CHAPTER I
GENERAL

4   Specified activities: general

(1)   The following provisions of this Part specify kinds of activity for the purposes of section 22 of the Act (and accordingly any activity of one of those kinds, which is carried on by way of business, and relates to an investment of a kind specified by any provision of Part III and applicable to that activity, is a regulated activity for the purposes of the Act).

(2)   The kinds of activity specified by articles 51 and 52 are also specified for the purposes of section 22(1)(b) of the Act (and accordingly any activity of one of those kinds, when carried on by way of business, is a regulated activity when carried on in relation to property of any kind).

(3)   Subject to paragraph (4), each provision specifying a kind of activity is subject to the exclusions applicable to that provision (and accordingly any reference in this Order to an activity of the kind specified by a particular provision is to be read subject to any such exclusions).

[(4)   Where an investment firm or credit institution—
    (a)   provides or performs investment services and activities on a professional basis, and
    (b)   in doing so would be treated as carrying on an activity of a kind specified by a provision of this Part but for an exclusion in any of articles 15, 16, 19, 22, 23, 29, 38, 67, 68, 69, 70 and 72E,
that exclusion is to be disregarded and, accordingly, the investment firm or credit institution is to be treated as carrying on an activity of the kind specified by the provision in question.]

[(4A)   Where a person, other than a person specified by Article 1.2 of the insurance mediation directive (the text of which is set out in Part 1 of Schedule 4)—
    (a)   for remuneration, takes up or pursues insurance mediation or reinsurance mediation in relation to a risk or commitment located in an EEA State, and
    (b)   in doing so would be treated as carrying on an activity of a kind specified by a provision of this Part but for an exclusion in any of articles 30, 66 and 67,
that exclusion is to be disregarded (and accordingly that person is to be treated as carrying on an activity of the kind specified by the provision in question).]

(5)   In this article—

              .....

["insurance mediation" has the meaning given by Article 2.3 of the insurance mediation directive, the text of which is set out in Part II of Schedule 4;]

              .....

["reinsurance mediation" has the meaning given by Article 2.4 of the insurance mediation directive, the text of which is set out in Part III of Schedule 4.]

[2013]

NOTES

Para (4): substituted by the Financial Services and Markets Act 2000 (Regulated Activities) (Amendment No 3) Order 2006, SI 2006/3384, arts 2, 4(a), as from 1 April 2007 (for the purposes of enabling applications to be made for (i) a Pt IV permission, (ii) a variation of a Pt IV permission, and (iii) the Authority's approval under s 59 of the 2000 Act, in relation to an activity of the kind specified by art 25D of this Order, or in relation to an investment of the kind specified by arts 83, 84 or 85 of this Order), and as from 1 November 2007 (otherwise).

Para (4A): inserted by the Financial Services and Markets Act 2000 (Regulated Activities) (Amendment) (No 2) Order 2003, SI 2003/1476, art 3(2)(a), as from 31 October 2004 (in so far as relating to contracts of long-term care insurance), and as from 14 January 2005 (otherwise), for transitional provisions see arts 22–27 of that Order at **[2706]** et seq.

Para (5): definitions "insurance mediation" and "reinsurance mediation" inserted by SI 2003/1476, art 3(2)(b), as from 31 October 2004 (in so far as relating to contracts of long-term care insurance), and as from 14 January 2005 (otherwise), for transitional provisions see arts 22–27 of that Order at **[2706]** et seq; definitions "core investment service" and "investment firm" (omitted) revoked by SI 2006/3384, arts 2, 4(a), as from 1 April 2007 (for the purposes of enabling applications to be made for (i) a Pt IV permission, (ii) a variation of a Pt IV permission, and (iii) the Authority's approval under s 59 of the 2000 Act, in relation to an activity of the kind specified by art 25D of this Order, or in relation to an investment of the kind specified by arts 83, 84 or 85 of this Order), and as from 1 November 2007 (otherwise).

CHAPTER II
ACCEPTING DEPOSITS
The activity

5 Accepting deposits

(1)   Accepting deposits is a specified kind of activity if—
   (a)   money received by way of deposit is lent to others; or
   (b)   any other activity of the person accepting the deposit is financed wholly, or to a material extent, out of the capital of or interest on money received by way of deposit.

(2)   In paragraph (1), "deposit" means a sum of money, other than one excluded by any of [articles 6 to 9A], paid on terms—
   (a)   under which it will be repaid, with or without interest or premium, and either on demand or at a time or in circumstances agreed by or on behalf of the person making the payment and the person receiving it; and
   (b)   which are not referable to the provision of property (other than currency) or services or the giving of security.

(3)   For the purposes of paragraph (2), money is paid on terms which are referable to the provision of property or services or the giving of security if, and only if—
   (a)   it is paid by way of advance or part payment under a contract for the sale, hire or other provision of property or services, and is repayable only in the event that the property or services is or are not in fact sold, hired or otherwise provided;
   (b)   it is paid by way of security for the performance of a contract or by way of security in respect of loss which may result from the non-performance of a contract; or
   (c)   without prejudice to sub-paragraph (b), it is paid by way of security for the delivery up or return of any property, whether in a particular state of repair or otherwise.

[2014]

NOTES

Para (2): words in square brackets substituted by the Financial Services and Markets Act 2000 (Regulated Activities) (Amendment) Order 2002, SI 2002/682, art 3(1), as from 27 April 2002, subject to transitional provisions in relation to persons issuing electronic money immediately before that date contained in art 9 at **[2667]**.
   See the Financial Services and Markets Act 2000 (Carrying on Regulated Activities by Way of Business) Order 2001, SI 2001/1177, art 2 at **[2207]** in relation to deposit taking business.

Exclusions

6 Sums paid by certain persons

(1)   A sum is not a deposit for the purposes of article 5 if it is—
   (a)   paid by any of the following persons—
      (i) the Bank of England, the central bank of an EEA State other than the United Kingdom, or the European Central Bank;
      (ii) an authorised person who has permission to accept deposits, or to effect or carry out contracts of insurance;
      (iii) an EEA firm falling within paragraph 5(b), (c) or (d) of Schedule 3 to the Act (other than one falling within paragraph (ii) above);
      (iv) the National Savings Bank;
      (v) a municipal bank, that is to say a company which was, immediately before the coming into force of this article, exempt from the prohibition in section 3 of the Banking Act 1987 by virtue of section 4(1) of, and paragraph 4 of Schedule 2 to, that Act;
      (vi) Keesler Federal Credit Union;
      (vii) a body of persons certified as a school bank by the National Savings Bank or by an authorised person who has permission to accept deposits;
      (viii) a local authority;
      (xi) any body which by virtue of any enactment has power to issue a precept to a local authority in England and Wales or a requisition to a local authority in Scotland, or to the expenses of which, by virtue of any enactment, a local authority in the

United Kingdom is or can be required to contribute (and in this paragraph, "enactment" includes an enactment comprised in, or in an instrument made under, an Act of the Scottish Parliament);

   (x) the European Community, the European Atomic Energy Community or the European Coal and Steel Community;

   (xi) the European Investment Bank;

   (xii) the International Bank for Reconstruction and Development;

   (xiii) the International Finance Corporation;

   (xiv) the International Monetary Fund;

   (xv) the African Development Bank;

   (xvi) the Asian Development Bank;

   (xvii) the Caribbean Development Bank;

   (xviii) the Inter-American Development Bank;

   (xix) the European Bank for Reconstruction and Development;

[(xx) the Council of Europe Development Bank;]

  (b)   paid by a person other than one mentioned in sub-paragraph (a) in the course of carrying on a business consisting wholly or to a significant extent of lending money;

  (c)   paid by one company to another at a time when both are members of the same group or when the same individual is a majority shareholder controller of both of them; or

  (d)   paid by a person who, at the time when it is paid, is a close relative of the person receiving it or who is, or is a close relative of, a director or manager of that person or who is, or is a close relative of, a controller of that person.

(2)   For the purposes of paragraph (1)(c), an individual is a majority shareholder controller of a company if he is a controller of the company by virtue of paragraph (a), (c), (e) or (g) of section 422(2) of the Act, and if in his case the greatest percentage of those referred to in those paragraphs is 50 or more.

(3)   In the application of sub-paragraph (d) of paragraph (1) to a sum paid by a partnership, that sub-paragraph is to have effect as if, for the reference to the person paying the sum, there were substituted a reference to each of the partners.

                                                           [2015]

NOTES

Para (1): sub-para (a)(xx) substituted by the Financial Services and Markets Act 2000 (Financial Promotion and Miscellaneous Amendments) Order 2002, SI 2002/1310, art 4(1), as from 5 June 2002.

7 Sums received by solicitors etc

(1)   A sum is not a deposit for the purposes of article 5 if it is received by a practising solicitor acting in the course of his profession.

(2)   In paragraph (1), "practising solicitor" means—

  (a)   a solicitor who is qualified to act as such under section 1 of the Solicitors Act 1974, article 4 of the Solicitors (Northern Ireland) Order 1976 or section 4 of the Solicitors (Scotland) Act 1980;

  (b)   a recognised body;

  (c)   a registered foreign lawyer in the course of providing professional services as a member of a multi-national partnership;

  (d)   a registered European lawyer; or

  (e)   a partner of a registered European lawyer who is providing professional services in accordance with—

     (i)   rules made under section 31 of the Solicitors Act 1974;

     (ii)   regulations made under article 26 of the Solicitors (Northern Ireland) Order 1976; or

     (iii)   rules made under section 34 of the Solicitors (Scotland) Act 1980.

(3)   In this article—

  (a)   "a recognised body" means a body corporate recognised by—

     (i)   the Council of the Law Society under section 9 of the Administration of Justice Act 1985;

     (ii)   the Incorporated Law Society of Northern Ireland under article 26A of the Solicitors (Northern Ireland) Order 1976; or

     (iii)   the Council of the Law Society of Scotland under section 34 of the Solicitors (Scotland) Act 1980;

  (b)   "registered foreign lawyer" has the meaning given by section 89 of the Courts and Legal Services Act 1990 or, in Scotland, section 65 of the Solicitors (Scotland) Act 1980;

  (c)   "multi-national partnership" has the meaning given by section 89 of the Courts and Legal Services Act 1990 but, in Scotland, is a reference to a "multi-national practice" within the meaning of section 60A of the Solicitors (Scotland) Act 1980; and

  (d)   "registered European lawyer" has the meaning given by regulation 2(1) of the European

Communities (Lawyer's Practice) Regulations 2000 or regulation 2(1) of the European Communities (Lawyer's Practice) (Scotland) Regulation 2000.

[2016]

8 Sums received by persons authorised to deal etc

A sum is not a deposit for the purposes of article 5 if it is received by a person who is—
  (a) an authorised person with permission to carry on an activity of the kind specified by any of articles 14, 21, 25, 37, 51 and 52, or
  (b) an exempt person in relation to any such activity,

in the course of, or for the purpose of, [carrying on any such activity (or any activity which would be such an activity but for any exclusion made by this Part)] with or on behalf of the person by or on behalf of whom the sum is paid.

[2017]

NOTES
Words in square brackets substituted by the Financial Services and Markets Act 2000 (Regulated Activities) (Amendment) Order 2001, SI 2001/3544, arts 2, 3, as from 1 December 2001.

9 Sums received in consideration for the issue of debt securities

  (1) Subject to paragraph (2), a sum is not a deposit for the purposes of article 5 if it is received by a person as consideration for the issue by him of any investment of the kind specified by article 77 or 78.

  (2) The exclusion in paragraph (1) does not apply to the receipt by a person of a sum as consideration for the issue by him of commercial paper unless—
  (a) the commercial paper is issued to persons—
    (i) whose ordinary activities involve them in acquiring, holding, managing or disposing of investments (as principal or agent) for the purposes of their businesses; or
    (ii) who it is reasonable to expect will acquire, hold, manage or dispose of investments (as principal or agent) for the purposes of their businesses; and
  (b) the redemption value of the commercial paper is not less than £100,000 (or an amount of equivalent value denominated wholly or partly in a currency other than sterling), and no part of the commercial paper may be transferred unless the redemption value of that part is not less than £100,000 (or such an equivalent amount).

[(3) In paragraph (2), "commercial paper" means an investment of the kind specified by article 77 or 78 having a maturity of less than one year from the date of issue.]

[2018]

NOTES
Para (3): substituted by the Financial Services and Markets Act 2000 (Regulated Activities) (Amendment) Order 2002, SI 2002/682, art 12, as from 27 April 2002.

[9A Sums received in exchange for electronic money

A sum is not a deposit for the purposes of article 5 if it is immediately exchanged for electronic money.]

[2019]

NOTES
Inserted by the Financial Services and Markets Act 2000 (Regulated Activities) (Amendment) Order 2002, SI 2002/682, art 3(2), as from 27 April 2002, subject to transitional provisions in relation to persons issuing electronic money immediately before that date contained in art 9 at **[2667]**.

[9AA Information society services

Article 5 is subject to the exclusion in article 72A (information society services).]

[2020]

NOTES
Inserted by the Financial Services and Markets Act 2000 (Regulated Activities) (Amendment) (No 2) Order 2002, SI 2002/1776, art 3(1), (2), as from 21 August 2002.

[9AB Funds received for payment services

  (1) A sum is not a deposit for the purposes of article 5 if it is received by an authorised payment institution, an EEA authorised payment institution or a small payment institution from a payment service user with a view to the provision of payment services.

(2)   For the purposes of paragraph (1), "authorised payment institution", "EEA authorised payment institution", "small payment institution", "payment services" and "payment service user" have the meanings given in the Payment Services Regulations 2009.]

[2020A]

NOTES

Commencement: 1 November 2009.

Inserted by the Payment Services Regulations 2009, SI 2009/209, reg 126, Sch 6, Pt 2, para 4(a), as from 1 November 2009 (for the full commencement details of the 2009 Regulations, see reg 1 of those Regulations at **[4387]**).

[CHAPTER IIA
ELECTRONIC MONEY

The activity

9B   Issuing electronic money

Issuing electronic money is a specified kind of activity.]

[2021]

NOTES

Inserted, together with arts 9C–9K and the preceding heading, by the Financial Services and Markets Act 2000 (Regulated Activities) (Amendment) Order 2002, SI 2002/682, art 4, as from 27 April 2002, subject to transitional provisions in relation to persons issuing electronic money immediately before that date contained in art 9 at **[2667]**.

[Exclusions

9C   Persons certified as small issuers etc

(1)   There is excluded from article 9B the issuing of electronic money by a person to whom the Authority has given a certificate under this article (provided the certificate has not been revoked).

(2)   An application for a certificate may be made by—
(a)   a body corporate, or
(b)   a partnership,
(other than a credit institution as defined in [Article 4(1)(a)] of the banking consolidation directive) which has its head office in the United Kingdom.

(3)   The authority must, on the application of such a person ("A"), give A a certificate if it appears to the Authority that paragraph (4), (5) or (6) applies.

(4)   This paragraph applies if—
(a)   A does not issue electronic money except on terms that the electronic device on which the monetary value is stored is subject to a maximum storage amount of not more than 150 euro; and
(b)   A's total liabilities with respect to the issuing of electronic money do not (or will not) usually exceed 5 million euro and do not (or will not) ever exceed 6 million euro.

(5)   This paragraph applies if—
(a)   the condition in paragraph (4)(a) is met;
(b)   A's total liabilities with respect to the issuing of electronic money do not (or will not) exceed 10 million euro; and
(c)   electronic money issued by A is accepted as a means of payment only by—
(i)   subsidiaries of A which perform operational or other ancillary functions related to electronic money issued or distributed by A; or
(ii)   other members of the same group as A (other than subsidiaries of A).

(6)   This paragraph applies if—
(a)   the conditions in paragraphs (4)(a) and (5)(b) are met; and
(b)   electronic money issued by A is accepted as a means of payment, in the course of business, by not more than one hundred persons where—
(i)   those persons accept such electronic money only at locations within the same premises or limited local area; or
(ii)   those persons have a close financial or business relationship with A, such as a common marketing or distribution scheme.

(7)   For the purposes of paragraph (6)(b)(i), locations are to be treated as situated within the same premises or limited local area if they are situated within—
(a)   a shopping centre, airport, railway station, bus station, or campus of a university, polytechnic, college, school or similar educational establishment; or
(b)   an area which does not exceed four square kilometres;

but sub-paragraphs (a) and (b) are illustrative only and are not to be treated as limiting the scope of paragraph (6)(b)(i).

(8)   For the purposes of paragraph (6)(b)(ii), persons are not to be treated as having a close financial or business relationship with A merely because they participate in arrangements for the acceptance of electronic money issued by A.

(9)   In this article, references to amounts in euro include references to equivalent amounts in sterling.

(10)   A person to whom a certificate has been given under this article (and whose certificate has not been revoked) is referred to in this Chapter as a "certified person".]

[2022]

NOTES

Inserted as noted to art 9B at **[2021]**.

Para (2): words in square brackets substituted the Capital Requirements Regulations 2006, SI 2006/3221, reg 29(4), Sch 6, para 6(1), (2), as from 1 January 2007.

[9D   Applications for certificates

The following provisions of the Act apply to applications to the Authority for certificates under 9C (and the determination of such applications) as they apply to applications for Part IV permissions (and the determination of such applications)—

(a)   section 51(1)(b) and (3) to (6);

(b)   section 52, except subsections (6), (8) and (9)(a) and (b); and

(c)   section 55(1).]

[2023]

NOTES

Inserted as noted to art 9B at **[2021]**.

[9E   Revocation of certificate on Authority's own initiative

(1)   The Authority may revoke a certificate given to a person ("A") under article 9C if—

(a)   it appears to it that A does not meet the relevant conditions, or has failed to meet the relevant conditions at any time since the certificate was given; or

(b)   the person to whom the certificate was given has contravened any rule or requirement to which he is subject as a result of article 9G.

(2)   For the purposes of paragraph (1), A meets the relevant conditions at any time if, at that time, paragraph (4), (5) or (6) of article 9C applies.

(3)   Sections 54 and 55(2) of the Act apply to the revocation of a certificate under paragraph (1) as they apply to the cancellation of a Part IV permission on the Authority's own initiative, as if references in those sections to an authorised person were references to a certified person.]

[2024]

NOTES

Inserted as noted to art 9B at **[2021]**.

[9F   Revocation of certificate on request

(1)   A certified person ("B") may apply to the Authority for his certificate to be revoked, and the Authority must then revoke the certificate and give B written notice that it has done so.

(2)   An application under paragraph (1) must be made in such manner as the Authority may direct.

(3)   If—

(a)   B has made an application under Part IV of the Act for permission to carry on a regulated activity of the kind specified by article 9B (or for variation of an existing permission so as to add a regulated activity of that kind), and

(b)   on making an application for revocation of his certificate under paragraph (1), he requests that the revocation be conditional on the granting of his application under Part IV of the Act,

the revocation of B's certificate is to be conditional on the granting of his application under Part IV of the Act.]

[2025]

NOTES

Inserted as noted to art 9B at **[2021]**.

[9G   Obtaining information from certified persons etc

(1)   The Authority may make rules requiring certified persons to provide information to the Authority about their activities so far as relating to the issuing of electronic money, including the amount of their liabilities with respect to the issuing of electronic money.

(2)   Section 148 of the Act (modification or waiver of rules) applies in relation to rules made under paragraph (1) as if references in that section to an authorised person were references to a certified person.

(3)   Section 150 of the Act (actions for damages) applies in relation to a rule made under paragraph (1) as if the reference in subsection (1) of that section to an authorised person were a reference to a certified person.

(4)   The Authority may, by notice in writing given to a certified person, require him—
   (a)   to provide specified information or information of a specified description; or
   (b)   to produce specified documents or documents of a specified description.

(5)   Paragraph (4) applies only to information or documents reasonably required for the purposes of determining whether the certified person meets, or has met, the relevant conditions.

(6)   Subsections (2), (5) and (6) of section 165 of the Act (Authority's power to require information) apply to a requirement imposed under paragraph (4) as they apply to a requirement imposed under that section.

(7)   Section 166 of the Act (reports by skilled persons) has effect as if—
   (a)   the reference in subsection (1) of that section to section 165 included a reference to paragraph (4) above; and
   (b)   the reference in section 166(2)(a) of the Act to an authorised person included a reference to a certified person.

(8)   Subsection (4) of section 168 of the Act (appointment of persons to carry out investigations in particular cases) has effect as if it provided for subsection (5) of that section to apply if it appears to the Authority that there are circumstances suggesting that a certified person may not meet, or may not have met, the relevant conditions.

(9)   Sections 175 (information and documents: supplemental provisions), 176 (entry of premises under warrant) and 177 (offences) of the Act apply to a requirement imposed under paragraph (4) as they apply to a requirement imposed under section 165 of the Act (the reference in section 176(3)(a) to an authorised person being read as a reference to a certified person).

(10)   In this article—
   (a)   "specified", in paragraph (4), means specified in the notice mentioned in that paragraph;
   (b)   a certified person ("A") meets the relevant conditions at any time if, at that time, paragraph (4), (5) or (6) of article 9C applies.]

[2026]

NOTES
Inserted as noted to art 9B at **[2021]**.

[Supplemental

9H   Rules prohibiting the issue of electronic money at a discount

(1)   The Authority may make rules applying to authorised persons with permission to carry on an activity of the kind specified by article 9B, prohibiting the issue of electronic money having a monetary value greater than the funds received.

(2)   Section 148 of the Act (modification or waiver of rules) applies in relation to rules made under paragraph (1).]

[2027]

NOTES
Inserted as noted to art 9B at **[2021]**.

[9I   False claims to be a certified person

A person who is not a certified person is to be treated as guilty of an offence under section 24 of the Act (false claims to be authorised or exempt) if he—
   (a)   describes himself (in whatever terms) as a certified person;
   (b)   behaves, or otherwise holds himself out, in a manner which indicates (or which is reasonably likely to be understood as indicating) that he is a certified person.]

[2028]

NOTES
Inserted as noted to art 9B at **[2021]**.

[9J Exclusion of electronic money from the compensation scheme

The compensation scheme established under Part XV of the Act is not to provide for the compensation of persons in respect of claims made in connection with any activity of the kind specified by article 9B.]

[2029]

NOTES
Inserted as noted to art 9B at **[2021]**.

[9K Record of certified persons

The record maintained by the Authority under section 347 of the Act (public record of authorised persons etc) must include every certified person.]

[2030]

NOTES
Inserted as noted to art 9B at **[2021]**.

[9L Funds received for payment services

(1)   Any funds are not to be treated as electronic money for the purposes of this Order if they are received by an authorised payment institution, an EEA authorised payment institution or a small payment institution from a payment service user with a view to the provision of payment services.

(2)   For the purposes of paragraph (1), "authorised payment institution", "EEA authorised payment institution", "small payment institution", "payment services" and "payment service user" have the meanings given in the Payment Services Regulations 2009.]

[2030A]

NOTES
Commencement: 1 November 2009.
Inserted by the Payment Services Regulations 2009, SI 2009/209, reg 126, Sch 6, Pt 2, para 4(b), as from 1 November 2009 (for the full commencement details of the 2009 Regulations, see reg 1 of those Regulations at **[4387]**).

CHAPTER III
INSURANCE

The activities

10 Effecting and carrying out contracts of insurance

(1)   Effecting a contract of insurance as principal is a specified kind of activity.

(2)   Carrying out a contract of insurance as principal is a specified kind of activity.

[2031]

Exclusions

11 Community co-insurers

(1)   There is excluded from article 10(1) or (2) the effecting or carrying out of a contract of insurance by an EEA firm falling within paragraph 5(d) of Schedule 3 to the Act—
(a)   other than through a branch in the United Kingdom; and
(b)   pursuant to a Community co-insurance operation in which the firm is participating otherwise than as the leading insurer.

(2)   In paragraph (1), "Community co-insurance operation" and "leading insurer" have the same meaning as in the Council Directive of 30 May 1978 on the co-ordination of laws, regulations and administrative provisions relating to Community co-insurance (No 78/473/EEC).

[2032]

12 Breakdown insurance

(1)   There is excluded from article 10(1) or (2) the effecting or carrying out, by a person who does not otherwise carry on an activity of the kind specified by that article, of a contract of insurance which—
(a)   is a contract under which the benefits provided by that person ("the provider") are exclusively or primarily benefits in kind in the event of accident to or breakdown of a vehicle; and
(b)   contains the terms mentioned in paragraph (2).

(2)   Those terms are that—
(a)   the assistance takes either or both of the forms mentioned in paragraph (3)(a) and (b);

  (b)   the assistance is not available outside the United Kingdom and the Republic of Ireland except where it is provided without the payment of additional premium by a person in the country concerned with whom the provider has entered into a reciprocal agreement; and

  (c)   assistance provided in the case of an accident or breakdown occurring in the United Kingdom or the Republic of Ireland is, in most circumstances, provided by the provider's servants.

(3)   The forms of assistance are—

  (a)   repairs to the relevant vehicle at the place where the accident or breakdown has occurred; this assistance may also include the delivery of parts, fuel, oil, water or keys to the relevant vehicle;

  (b)   removal of the relevant vehicle to the nearest or most appropriate place at which repairs may be carried out, or to—

     (i)   the home, point of departure or original destination within the United Kingdom of the driver and passengers, provided the accident or breakdown occurred within the United Kingdom;

     (ii)   the home, point of departure or original destination within the Republic of Ireland of the driver and passengers, provided the accident or breakdown occurred within the Republic of Ireland or within Northern Ireland;

     (iii)   the home, point of departure or original destination within Northern Ireland of the driver and passengers, provided the accident or breakdown occurred within the Republic of Ireland;

and this form of assistance may include the conveyance of the driver or passengers of the relevant vehicle, with the vehicle, or (where the vehicle is to be conveyed only to the nearest or most appropriate place at which repairs may be carried out) separately, to the nearest location from which they may continue their journey by other means.

(4)   A contract does not fail to meet the condition in paragraph (1)(a) solely because the provider may reimburse the person entitled to the assistance for all or part of any sums paid by him in respect of assistance either because he failed to identify himself as a person entitled to the assistance or because he was unable to get in touch with the provider in order to claim the assistance.

(5)   In this article—

"the assistance" means the benefits to be provided under a contract of the kind mentioned in paragraph (1);

"breakdown" means an event—

  (a)   which causes the driver of the relevant vehicle to be unable to start a journey in the vehicle or involuntarily to bring the vehicle to a halt on a journey because of some malfunction of the vehicle or failure of it to function, and

  (b)   after which the journey cannot reasonably be commenced or continued in the relevant vehicle;

"the relevant vehicle" means the vehicle (including a trailer or caravan) in respect of which the assistance is required.

[2033]

[12A   Information society services

Article 10 is subject to the exclusion in article 72A (information society services), as qualified by paragraph (2) of that article.]

[2034]

NOTES

Inserted by the Financial Services and Markets Act 2000 (Regulated Activities) (Amendment) (No 2) Order 2002, SI 2002/1776, art 3(1), (3), as from 21 August 2002.

Supplemental

13   Application of sections 327 and 332 of the Act to insurance market activities

(1)   In sections 327(5) and (7) and 332(3)(b) of the Act (exemption from the general prohibition for members of the professions, and rules in relation to such persons), the references to "a regulated activity" and "regulated activities" do not include—

  (a)   any activity of the kind specified by article 10(1) or (2), where—

     (i)   P is a member of the Society; and

     (ii)   by virtue of section 316 of the Act (application of the Act to Lloyd's underwriting), the general prohibition does not apply to the carrying on by P of that activity; or

  (b)   any activity of the kind specified by article 10(2), where—

     (i)   P is a former underwriting member; and

     (ii)   the contract of insurance in question is one underwritten by P at Lloyd's.

(2) In paragraph (1)—
"member of the Society" has the same meaning as in Lloyd's Act 1982; and
"former underwriting member" has the meaning given by section 324(1) of the Act.

[2035]

CHAPTER IV
DEALING IN INVESTMENTS AS PRINCIPAL

The activity

14 Dealing in investments as principal

[(1)] Buying, selling, subscribing for or underwriting securities or contractually based investments (other than investments of the kind specified by article 87, or article 89 so far as relevant to that article) as principal is a specified kind of activity.

[(2) Paragraph (1) does not apply to a kind of activity to which article 25D applies.]

[2036]

NOTES
Para (1) numbered as such, and para (2) added, by the Financial Services and Markets Act 2000 (Regulated Activities) (Amendment No 3) Order 2006, SI 2006/3384, arts 2, 5, as from 1 April 2007 (for the purposes of enabling applications to be made for (i) a Pt IV permission, (ii) a variation of a Pt IV permission, and (iii) the Authority's approval under s 59 of the 2000 Act, in relation to an activity of the kind specified by art 25D of this Order, or in relation to an investment of the kind specified by arts 83, 84 or 85 of this Order), and as from 1 November 2007 (otherwise).
See the Financial Services and Markets Act 2000 (Carrying on Regulated Activities by Way of Business) Order 2001, SI 2001/1177, art 3 at **[2208]** in relation to investment business.

Exclusions

15 Absence of holding out etc

(1) Subject to paragraph (3), a person ("A") does not carry on an activity of the kind specified by article 14 by entering into a transaction which relates to a security or is the assignment (or, in Scotland, the assignation) of a qualifying contract of insurance (or an investment of the kind specified by article 89, so far as relevant to such a contract), unless—
   (a) A holds himself out as willing, as principal, to buy, sell or subscribe for investments of the kind to which the transaction relates at prices determined by him generally and continuously rather than in respect of each particular transaction;
   (b) A holds himself out as engaging in the business of buying investments of the kind to which the transaction relates, with a view to selling them;
   (c) A holds himself out as engaging in the business of underwriting investments of the kind to which the transaction relates; or
   (d) A regularly solicits members of the public with the purpose of inducing them, as principals or agents, to enter into transactions constituting activities of the kind specified by article 14, and the transaction is entered into as a result of his having solicited members of the public in that manner.

(2) In paragraph (1)(d), "members of the public" means any persons other than—
   (a) authorised persons or persons who are exempt persons in relation to activities of the kind specified by article 14;
   (b) members of the same group as A;
   (c) persons who are or who propose to become participators with A in a joint enterprise;
   (d) any person who is solicited by A with a view to the acquisition by A of 20 per cent or more of the voting shares in a body corporate;
   (e) if A (either alone or with members of the same group as himself) holds more than 20 per cent of the voting shares in a body corporate, any person who is solicited by A with a view to—
      (i) the acquisition by A of further shares in the body corporate; or
      (ii) the disposal by A of shares in the body corporate to the person solicited or to a member of the same group as the person solicited;
   (f) any person who—
      (i) is solicited by A with a view to the disposal by A of shares in a body corporate to the person solicited or to a member of the same group as that person; and
      (ii) either alone or with members of the same group holds 20 per cent or more of the voting shares in the body corporate;
   (g) any person whose head office is outside the United Kingdom, who is solicited by an approach made or directed to him at a place outside the United Kingdom and whose ordinary business involves him in carrying on activities of the kind specified by any of

articles 14, 21, 25, 37, 40, 45, 51, 52 and 53 or (so far as relevant to any of those articles) article 64, or would do so apart from any exclusion from any of those articles made by this Order.

(3)　This article does not apply where A enters into the transaction as bare trustee or, in Scotland, as nominee for another person and is acting on that other person's instructions (but the exclusion in article 66(1) applies if the conditions set out there are met).

[(4)　This article is subject to article 4(4).]

[2037]

NOTES

Para (4): added by the Financial Services and Markets Act 2000 (Regulated Activities) (Amendment No 3) Order 2006, SI 2006/3384, arts 2, 6, as from 1 April 2007 (for the purposes of enabling applications to be made for (i) a Pt IV permission, (ii) a variation of a Pt IV permission, and (iii) the Authority's approval under s 59 of the 2000 Act, in relation to an activity of the kind specified by art 25D of this Order, or in relation to an investment of the kind specified by arts 83, 84 or 85 of this Order), and as from 1 November 2007 (otherwise).

16　Dealing in contractually based investments

[(1)]　A person who is not an authorised person does not carry on an activity of the kind specified by article 14 by entering into a transaction relating to a contractually based investment—

　　(a)　with or through an authorised person, or an exempt person acting in the course of a business comprising a regulated activity in relation to which he is exempt; or

　　(b)　through an office outside the United Kingdom maintained by a party to the transaction, and with or through a person whose head office is situated outside the United Kingdom and whose ordinary business involves him in carrying on activities of the kind specified by any of articles 14, 21, 25, 37, 40, 45, 51, 52 and 53 or, so far as relevant to any of those articles, article 64 (or would do so apart from any exclusion from any of those articles made by this Order).

[(2)　This article is subject to article 4(4).]

[2038]

NOTES

Para (1) numbered as such, and para (2) added, by the Financial Services and Markets Act 2000 (Regulated Activities) (Amendment No 3) Order 2006, SI 2006/3384, arts 2, 7, as from 1 April 2007 (for the purposes of enabling applications to be made for (i) a Pt IV permission, (ii) a variation of a Pt IV permission, and (iii) the Authority's approval under s 59 of the 2000 Act, in relation to an activity of the kind specified by art 25D of this Order, or in relation to an investment of the kind specified by arts 83, 84 or 85 of this Order), and as from 1 November 2007 (otherwise).

17　Acceptance of instruments creating or acknowledging indebtedness

(1)　A person does not carry on an activity of the kind specified by article 14 by accepting an instrument creating or acknowledging indebtedness in respect of any loan, credit, guarantee or other similar financial accommodation or assurance which he has made, granted or provided.

(2)　The reference in paragraph (1) to a person accepting an instrument includes a reference to a person becoming a party to an instrument otherwise than as a debtor or a surety.

[2039]

NOTES

Modification: references in para (1) to securities, instruments or investments creating or acknowledging indebtedness (or creating or acknowledging a present or future indebtedness) includes a reference to uncertificated units of eligible debt securities; see the Uncertificated Securities (Amendment) (Eligible Debt Securities) Regulations 2003, SI 2003/1633, reg 15, Sch 2, para 8 (as from 24 June 2003).

Modification: references in para (2) to a person becoming party to an instrument includes a reference to a person assuming rights and obligations in respect of uncertificated units of an eligible debt security in accordance with its current terms of issue; see the Uncertificated Securities (Amendment) (Eligible Debt Securities) Regulations 2003, SI 2003/1633, reg 15, Sch 2, para 9 (as from 24 June 2003).

18　Issue by a company of its own shares etc

(1)　There is excluded from article 14 the issue by a company of its own shares or share warrants, and the issue by any person of his own debentures or debenture warrants.

(2)　In this article—

　　(a)　"company" means any body corporate other than an open-ended investment company;

　　(b)　"shares" and "debentures" include any investment of the kind specified by article 76 or 77;

　　(c)　"share warrants" and "debenture warrants" mean any investment of the kind specified by article 79 which relates to shares in the company concerned or, as the case may be, debentures issued by [the person concerned].

[2040]

[18A Dealing by a company in its own shares

(1)   A company does not carry on an activity of the kind specified by article 14 by purchasing its own shares where section 162A of the Companies Act 1985 (Treasury shares) applies to the shares purchased.

(2)   A company does not carry on an activity of the kind specified by article 14 by dealing in its own shares held as treasury shares, in accordance with section 162D of that Act (Treasury shares: disposal and cancellation).

(3)   In this article "shares held as treasury shares" has the same meaning as in that Act.]

[2041]

19 Risk management

(1)   A person ("B") does not carry on an activity of the kind specified by article 14 by entering as principal into a transaction with another person ("C") if—
   (a)   the transaction relates to investments of the kind specified by any of articles 83 to 85 (or article 89 so far as relevant to any of those articles);
   (b)   neither B nor C is an individual;
   (c)   the sole or main purpose for which B enters into the transaction (either by itself or in combination with other such transactions) is that of limiting the extent to which a relevant business will be affected by any identifiable risk arising otherwise than as a result of the carrying on of a regulated activity; and
   (d)   the relevant business consists mainly of activities other than—
      (i)   regulated activities; or
      (ii)   activities which would be regulated activities but for any exclusion made by this Part.

(2)   In paragraph (1), "relevant business" means a business carried on by—
   (a)   B;
   (b)   a member of the same group as B; or
   (c)   where B and another person are, or propose to become, participators in a joint enterprise, that other person.

[(3)   This article is subject to article 4(4).]

[2042]

20 Other exclusions

Article 14 is also subject to the exclusions in articles 66 (trustees etc), 68 (sale of goods and supply of services), 69 (groups and joint enterprises), 70 (sale of body corporate), 71 (employee share schemes)[, 72 (overseas persons) and 72A (information society services)].

[2043]

CHAPTER V
DEALING IN INVESTMENTS AS AGENT
The activity

21 Dealing in investments as agent

[(1)] Buying, selling, subscribing for or underwriting securities or [relevant investments] (other than investments of the kind specified by article 87, or article 89 so far as relevant to that article) as agent is a specified kind of activity.

[(2) Paragraph (1) does not apply to a kind of activity to which article 25D applies.]

[2044]

NOTES
Para (1) numbered as such, and para (2) added, by the Financial Services and Markets Act 2000 (Regulated Activities) (Amendment No 3) Order 2006, SI 2006/3384, arts 2, 9, as from 1 April 2007 (for the purposes of enabling applications to be made for (i) a Pt IV permission, (ii) a variation of a Pt IV permission, and (iii) the Authority's approval under s 59 of the 2000 Act, in relation to an activity of the kind specified by art 25D of this Order, or in relation to an investment of the kind specified by arts 83, 84 or 85 of this Order), and as from 1 November 2007 (otherwise).
Words in square brackets in para (1) substituted by the Financial Services and Markets Act 2000 (Regulated Activities) (Amendment) (No 2) Order 2003, SI 2003/1476, art 4(1), as from 31 October 2004 (in so far as relating to contracts of long-term care insurance), and as from 14 January 2005 (otherwise), for transitional provisions see arts 22–27 of that Order at **[2706]** et seq.
See the Financial Services and Markets Act 2000 (Carrying on Regulated Activities by Way of Business) Order 2001, SI 2001/1177, art 3 at **[2208]** in relation to investment business.

Exclusions

22 Deals with or through authorised persons

(1) A person who is not an authorised person does not carry on an activity of the kind specified by article 21 by entering into a transaction as agent for another person ("the client") with or through an authorised person if—
    (a) the transaction is entered into on advice given to the client by an authorised person; or
    (b) it is clear, in all the circumstances, that the client, in his capacity as an investor, is not seeking and has not sought advice from the agent as to the merits of the client's entering into the transaction (or, if the client has sought such advice, the agent has declined to give it but has recommended that the client seek such advice from an authorised person).

[(2) But the exclusion in paragraph (1) does not apply if—
    (a) the transaction relates to a contract of insurance; or
    (b) the agent receives from any person other than the client any pecuniary reward or other advantage, for which he does not account to the client, arising out of his entering into the transaction.]

[(3) This article is subject to article 4(4).]

[2045]

NOTES
Para (2): substituted by the Financial Services and Markets Act 2000 (Regulated Activities) (Amendment) (No 2) Order 2003, SI 2003/1476, art 4(2), as from 31 October 2004 (in so far as relating to contracts of long-term care insurance), and as from 14 January 2005 (otherwise), for transitional provisions see arts 22–27 of that Order at **[2706]**.
Para (3): added by the Financial Services and Markets Act 2000 (Regulated Activities) (Amendment No 3) Order 2006, SI 2006/3384, arts 2, 10, as from 1 April 2007 (for the purposes of enabling applications to be made for (i) a Pt IV permission, (ii) a variation of a Pt IV permission, and (iii) the Authority's approval under s 59 of the 2000 Act, in relation to an activity of the kind specified by art 25D of this Order, or in relation to an investment of the kind specified by arts 83, 84 or 85 of this Order), and as from 1 November 2007 (otherwise).

23 Risk management

(1) A person ("B") does not carry on an activity of the kind specified by article 21 by entering as agent for a relevant person into a transaction with another person ("C") if—
    (a) the transaction relates to investments of the kind specified by any of articles 83 to 85 (or article 89 so far as relevant to any of those articles);
    (b) neither B nor C is an individual;
    (c) the sole or main purpose for which B enters into the transaction (either by itself or in combination with other such transactions) is that of limiting the extent to which a relevant business will be affected by any identifiable risk arising otherwise than as a result of the carrying on of a regulated activity; and
    (d) the relevant business consists mainly of activities other than—
        (i) regulated activities; or

      (ii)   activities which would be regulated activities but for any exclusion made by this Part.

(2)   In paragraph (1), "relevant person" means—
    (a)   a member of the same group as B; or
    (b)   where B and another person are, or propose to become, participators in a joint enterprise, that other person;

and "relevant business" means a business carried on by a relevant person.

   [(3)   This article is subject to article 4(4).]

[2046]

NOTES

Para (3): added by the Financial Services and Markets Act 2000 (Regulated Activities) (Amendment No 3) Order 2006, SI 2006/3384, arts 2, 11, as from 1 April 2007 (for the purposes of enabling applications to be made for (i) a Pt IV permission, (ii) a variation of a Pt IV permission, and (iii) the Authority's approval under s 59 of the 2000 Act, in relation to an activity of the kind specified by art 25D of this Order, or in relation to an investment of the kind specified by arts 83, 84 or 85 of this Order), and as from 1 November 2007 (otherwise).

---

24 Other exclusions

Article 21 is also subject to the exclusions in articles 67 (profession or non-investment business), 68 (sale of goods and supply of services), 69 (groups and joint enterprises), 70 (sale of body corporate), 71 (employee share schemes)[, 72 (overseas persons)[, 72A (information society services), 72B (activities carried on by a provider of relevant goods or services) and 72D (large risks contracts where risk situated outside the EEA)]].

[2047]

NOTES

Words in first (outer) pair of square brackets substituted by the Financial Services and Markets Act 2000 (Regulated Activities) (Amendment) (No 2) Order 2002, SI 2002/1776, art 3(1), (5), as from 21 August 2002; words in second (inner) pair of square brackets substituted by the Financial Services and Markets Act 2000 (Regulated Activities) (Amendment) (No 2) Order 2003, SI 2003/1476, art 4(3), as from 31 October 2004 (in so far as relating to contracts of long-term care insurance), and as from 14 January 2005 (otherwise), for transitional provisions see arts 22–27 of that Order at **[2706]** et seq.

CHAPTER VI
ARRANGING DEALS IN INVESTMENTS
The activities

25 Arranging deals in investments

(1)   Making arrangements for another person (whether as principal or agent) to buy, sell, subscribe for or underwrite a particular investment which is—
    (a)   a security,
    (b)   a [relevant investment], or
    (c)   an investment of the kind specified by article 86, or article 89 so far as relevant to that article,

is a specified kind of activity.

(2)   Making arrangements with a view to a person who participates in the arrangements buying, selling, subscribing for or underwriting investments falling within paragraph (1)(a), (b) or (c) (whether as principal or agent) is also a specified kind of activity.

   [(3)   Paragraphs (1) and (2) do not apply to a kind of activity to which article 25D applies.]

[2048]

NOTES

Para (1): words in square brackets substituted by the Financial Services and Markets Act 2000 (Regulated Activities) (Amendment) (No 2) Order 2003, SI 2003/1476, art 5(1), as from 31 October 2004 (in so far as relating to contracts of long-term care insurance), and as from 14 January 2005 (otherwise), for transitional provisions see arts 22–27 of that Order at **[2706]** et seq.

Para (3): added by the Financial Services and Markets Act 2000 (Regulated Activities) (Amendment No 3) Order 2006, SI 2006/3384, arts 2, 12, as from 1 April 2007 (for the purposes of enabling applications to be made for (i) a Pt IV permission, (ii) a variation of a Pt IV permission, and (iii) the Authority's approval under s 59 of the 2000 Act, in relation to an activity of the kind specified by art 25D of this Order, or in relation to an investment of the kind specified by arts 83, 84 or 85 of this Order), and as from 1 November 2007 (otherwise).

See the Financial Services and Markets Act 2000 (Carrying on Regulated Activities by Way of Business) Order 2001, SI 2001/1177, art 3 at **[2208]** in relation to investment business, except in so far as that activity relates to investment of the kind specified by arts 86 or 89 of this order so far as relevant to that article.

[25A Arranging regulated mortgage contracts

(1)   Making arrangements—

(a)   for another person to enter into a regulated mortgage contract as borrower; or

(b)   for another person to vary the terms of a regulated mortgage contract entered into by him as borrower after the coming into force of article 61, in such a way as to vary his obligations under that contract,

is a specified kind of activity.

(2)   Making arrangements with a view to a person who participates in the arrangements entering into a regulated mortgage contract as borrower is also a specified kind of activity.

(3)   In this article "borrower" has the meaning given by article 61(3)(a)(i).]

[2049]

NOTES
Commencement: 31 October 2004.
Inserted by the Financial Services and Markets Act 2000 (Regulated Activities) (Amendment) (No 1) Order 2003, SI 2003/1475, art 4, as from 31 October 2004; for transitional provisions see arts 26–29 at **[2700]** et seq.
See the Financial Services and Markets Act 2000 (Carrying on Regulated Activities by Way of Business) Order 2001, SI 2001/1177, art 3A at **[2209]**.

[25B   Arranging regulated home reversion plans

(1)   Making arrangements—

(a)   for another person to enter into a regulated home reversion plan as reversion seller or as plan provider; or

(b)   for another person to vary the terms of a regulated home reversion plan, entered into on or after 6th April 2007 by him as reversion seller or as plan provider, in such a way as to vary his obligations under that plan,

is a specified kind of activity.

(2)   Making arrangements with a view to a person who participates in the arrangements entering into a regulated home reversion plan as reversion seller or as plan provider is also a specified kind of activity.]

[2049A]

NOTES
Commencement: 6 November 2006 (certain purposes); 6 April 2007 (otherwise) (see below).
Inserted, together with art 25C, by the Financial Services and Markets Act 2000 (Regulated Activities) (Amendment) (No 2) Order 2006, SI 2006/2383, arts 2, 4, as from 6 November 2006 (for the purposes of enabling applications to be made for (i) a Pt IV permission, or a variation of a Pt IV permission, in relation to activities of the kind specified by arts 25B, 25C, 53B, 53C, 63B or 63F or, so far as relevant to any such activity, art 64 of this Order; or (ii) the Authority's approval under FSMA 2000, s 59 in relation to any of those activities), and as from 6 April 2007 (otherwise) (for transitional provisions and effect see arts 36–40 of, and the Schedule to, the 2006 Order at **[2861]** et seq).
See the Financial Services and Markets Act 2000 (Carrying on Regulated Activities by Way of Business) Order 2001, SI 2001/1177, art 3B at **[2209A]**.

[25C   Arranging regulated home purchase plans

(1)   Making arrangements—

(a)   for another person to enter into a regulated home purchase plan as home purchaser; or

(b)   for another person to vary the terms of a regulated home purchase plan, entered into on or after 6th April 2007 by him as home purchaser, in such a way as to vary his obligations under that plan,

is a specified kind of activity.

(2)   Making arrangements with a view to a person who participates in the arrangements entering into a regulated home purchase plan as home purchaser is also a specified kind of activity.]

[2049B]

NOTES
Commencement: 6 November 2006 (certain purposes); 6 April 2007 (otherwise).
Inserted as noted to art 25B at **[2049A]**.
See the Financial Services and Markets Act 2000 (Carrying on Regulated Activities by Way of Business) Order 2001, SI 2001/1177, art 3C at **[2209B]**.

[25D   Operating a multilateral trading facility

(1)   The operation of a multilateral trading facility on which MiFID instruments are traded is a specified kind of activity.

(2)   In paragraph (1), "MiFID instrument" means any investment—

(a)   of the kind specified by article 76, 77, 78, 79, 80, 81, 83, 84 or 85; or

(b) of the kind specified by article 89 so far as relevant to an investment falling within sub-paragraph (a),

that is a financial instrument.]

[2049C]

NOTES
Commencement: 1 April 2007 (certain purposes); 1 November 2007 (otherwise) (see below).
Inserted by the Financial Services and Markets Act 2000 (Regulated Activities) (Amendment No 3) Order 2006, SI 2006/3384, arts 2, 13, as from 1 April 2007 (for the purposes of enabling applications to be made for (i) a Pt IV permission, (ii) a variation of a Pt IV permission, and (iii) the Authority's approval under s 59 of the 2000 Act, in relation to an activity of the kind specified by art 25D of this Order, or in relation to an investment of the kind specified by arts 83, 84 or 85 of this Order), and as from 1 November 2007 (otherwise).
See the Financial Services and Markets Act 2000 (Carrying on Regulated Activities by Way of Business) Order 2001, SI 2001/1177, art 3 at **[2206]** in relation to investment business.

Exclusions

26 Arrangements not causing a deal

There are excluded from [articles 25(1), 25A(1), 25B(1) and 25C(1)] arrangements which do not or would not bring about the transaction to which the arrangements relate.

[2050]

NOTES
Words in square brackets substituted by the Financial Services and Markets Act 2000 (Regulated Activities) (Amendment) (No 2) Order 2006, SI 2006/2383, arts 2, 5, as from 6 November 2006 (for the purposes of enabling applications to be made for (i) a Pt IV permission, or a variation of a Pt IV permission, in relation to activities of the kind specified by arts 25B, 25C, 53B, 53C, 63B or 63F or, so far as relevant to any such activity, art 64 of this Order; or (ii) the Authority's approval under FSMA 2000, s 59 in relation to any of those activities), and as from 6 April 2007 (otherwise) (for transitional provisions and effect see arts 36–40 of, and the Schedule to, the 2006 Order at **[2861]** et seq).

27 Enabling parties to communicate

A person does not carry on an activity of the kind specified by [article 25(2), 25A(2), 25B(2) or 25C(2)] merely by providing means by which one party to a transaction (or potential transaction) is able to communicate with other such parties.

[2051]

NOTES
Words in square brackets substituted by the Financial Services and Markets Act 2000 (Regulated Activities) (Amendment) (No 2) Order 2006, SI 2006/2383, arts 2, 6, as from 6 November 2006 (for the purposes of enabling applications to be made for (i) a Pt IV permission, or a variation of a Pt IV permission, in relation to activities of the kind specified by arts 25B, 25C, 53B, 53C, 63B or 63F or, so far as relevant to any such activity, art 64 of this Order; or (ii) the Authority's approval under FSMA 2000, s 59 in relation to any of those activities), and as from 6 April 2007 (otherwise) (for transitional provisions and effect see arts 36–40 of, and the Schedule to, the 2006 Order at **[2861]** et seq).

28 Arranging transactions to which the arranger is a party

(1) There are excluded from article 25(1) any arrangements for a transaction into which the person making the arrangements enters or is to enter as principal or as agent for some other person.

(2) There are excluded from article 25(2) any arrangements which a person makes with a view to transactions into which he enters or is to enter as principal or as agent for some other person.

[(3) But the exclusions in paragraphs (1) and (2) do not apply to arrangements made for or with a view to a transaction which relates to a contract of insurance, unless the person making the arrangements either—
(a) is the only policyholder; or
(b) as a result of the transaction, would become the only policyholder.]

[2052]

NOTES
Para (3): added by the Financial Services and Markets Act 2000 (Regulated Activities) (Amendment) (No 2) Order 2003, SI 2003/1476, art 5(2), as from 31 October 2004 (in so far as relating to contracts of long-term care insurance), and as from 14 January 2005 (otherwise), for transitional provisions see arts 22–27 of that Order at **[2706]** et seq.

[28A Arranging contracts [or plans] to which the arranger is a party

(1) There are excluded from [articles 25A(1), 25B(1) and 25C(1)] any arrangements—
(a) for a [contract or plan] into which the person making the arrangements enters or is to enter; or

(b)   for a variation of a [contract or plan] to which that person is (or is to become) a party.

(2)   There are excluded [articles 25A(2), 25B(2) and 25C(2)] any arrangements which a person makes with a view to contracts [or plans] into which he enters or is to enter.]

[2053]

NOTES

Commencement: 31 October 2004.

Inserted by the Financial Services and Markets Act 2000 (Regulated Activities) (Amendment) (No 1) Order 2003, SI 2003/1475, art 7, as from 31 October 2004; for transitional provisions see arts 26–29 at **[2700]** et seq.

Article heading: words in square brackets inserted by the Financial Services and Markets Act 2000 (Regulated Activities) (Amendment) (No 2) Order 2006, SI 2006/2383, arts 2, 7(1), as from 6 November 2006 (for the purposes of enabling applications to be made for (i) a Pt IV permission, or a variation of a Pt IV permission, in relation to activities of the kind specified by arts 25B, 25C, 53B, 53C, 63B or 63F or, so far as relevant to any such activity, art 64 of this Order; or (ii) the Authority's approval under FSMA 2000, s 59 in relation to any of those activities), and as from 6 April 2007 (otherwise) (for transitional provisions and effect see arts 36–40 of, and the Schedule to, the 2006 Order at **[2861]** et seq).

Para (1): words in square brackets substituted by SI 2006/2383, arts 2, 7(1)(a), as from 6 November 2006 (certain purposes), and as from 6 April 2007 (otherwise) (for purposes, transitional provisions, and effect, see the note "Article heading" above).

Para (2): words in first pair of square brackets substituted, and words in second pair of square brackets inserted, by SI 2006/2383, arts 2, 7(1)(b), as from 6 November 2006 (certain purposes), and as from 6 April 2007 (otherwise) (for purposes, transitional provisions, and effect, see the note "Article heading" above).

29 Arranging deals with or through authorised persons

(1)   There are excluded from [articles 25(1) and (2), 25A(1) and (2), 25B(1) and (2) and 25C(1) and (2)] arrangements made by a person ("A") who is not an authorised person for or with a view to a transaction which is or is to be entered into by a person ("the client") with or though an authorised person if—

(a)   the transaction is or is to be entered into on advice to the client by an authorised person; or

(b)   it is clear, in all the circumstances, that the client, in his capacity as an [investor, borrower, reversion seller, plan provider or (as the case may be) home purchaser], is not seeking and has not sought advice from A as to the merits of the client's entering into the transaction (or, if the client has sought such advice, A has declined to give it but has recommended that the client seek such advice from an authorised person).

[(2)   But the exclusion in paragraph (1) does not apply if—

(a)   the transaction relates, or would relate, to a contract of insurance; or

(b)   A receives from any person other than the client any pecuniary reward or other advantage, for which he does not account to the client, arising out of his making the arrangements.]

[(3)   This article is subject to article 4(4).]

[2054]

NOTES

Para (1): words in square brackets substituted by the Financial Services and Markets Act 2000 (Regulated Activities) (Amendment) (No 2) Order 2006, SI 2006/2383, arts 2, 8, as from 6 November 2006 (for the purposes of enabling applications to be made for (i) a Pt IV permission, or a variation of a Pt IV permission, in relation to activities of the kind specified by arts 25B, 25C, 53B, 53C, 63B or 63F or, so far as relevant to any such activity, art 64 of this Order; or (ii) the Authority's approval under FSMA 2000, s 59 in relation to any of those activities), and as from 6 April 2007 (otherwise) (for transitional provisions and effect see arts 36–40 of, and the Schedule to, the 2006 Order at **[2861]** et seq).

Para (2): substituted by the Financial Services and Markets Act 2000 (Regulated Activities) (Amendment) (No 2) Order 2003, SI 2003/1476, art 5(3), as from 31 October 2004 (in so far as relating to contracts of long-term care insurance), and as from 14 January 2005 (otherwise), for transitional provisions see arts 22–27 of that Order at **[2706]**.

Para (3): added by the Financial Services and Markets Act 2000 (Regulated Activities) (Amendment No 3) Order 2006, SI 2006/3384, arts 2, 14, as from 1 April 2007 (for the purposes of enabling applications to be made for (i) a Pt IV permission, (ii) a variation of a Pt IV permission, and (iii) the Authority's approval under s 59 of the 2000 Act, in relation to an activity of the kind specified by art 25D of this Order, or in relation to an investment of the kind specified by arts 83, 84 or 85 of this Order), and as from 1 November 2007 (otherwise).

[29A Arrangements made in the course of administration by authorised person

[(1)]   A person who is not an authorised person ("A") does not carry on an activity of the kind specified by article 25A(1)(b) as a result of—

(a)   anything done by an authorised person ("B") in relation to a regulated mortgage contract which B is administering pursuant to an arrangement of the kind mentioned in article 62(a); or

(b)   anything A does in connection with the administration of a regulated mortgage contract in circumstances falling within article 62(b).]

[(2)   A person who is not an authorised person ("A") does not carry on an activity of the kind specified by article 25B(1)(b) as a result of—

(a)   anything done by an authorised person ("B") in relation to a regulated home reversion plan which B is administering pursuant to an arrangement of the kind mentioned in article 63C(a); or

(b)   anything A does in connection with the administration of a regulated home reversion plan in circumstances falling within article 63C(b).

(3)   A person who is not an authorised person ("A") does not carry on an activity of the kind specified by article 25C(1)(b) as a result of—

(a)   anything done by an authorised person ("B") in relation to a regulated home purchase plan which B is administering pursuant to an arrangement of the kind mentioned in article 63G(a); or

(b)   anything A does in connection with the administration of a regulated home purchase plan in circumstances falling within article 63G(b).]

[2055]

NOTES

Commencement: 31 October 2004.

Inserted by the Financial Services and Markets Act 2000 (Regulated Activities) (Amendment) (No 1) Order 2003, SI 2003/1475, art 9, as from 31 October 2004; for transitional provisions see arts 26–29 at **[2700]** et seq.

Para (1) numbered as such, and paras (2), (3) added, by the Financial Services and Markets Act 2000 (Regulated Activities) (Amendment) (No 2) Order 2006, SI 2006/2383, arts 2, 9, as from 6 November 2006 (for the purposes of enabling applications to be made for (i) a Pt IV permission, or a variation of a Pt IV permission, in relation to activities of the kind specified by arts 25B, 25C, 53B, 53C, 63B or 63F or, so far as relevant to any such activity, art 64 of this Order; or (ii) the Authority's approval under FSMA 2000, s 59 in relation to any of those activities), and as from 6 April 2007 (otherwise) (for transitional provisions and effect see arts 36–40 of, and the Schedule to, the 2006 Order at **[2861]** et seq).

30   Arranging transactions in connection with lending on the security of insurance policies

(1)   There are excluded from article 25(1) and (2) arrangements made by a money-lender under which either—

[(a)   a relevant authorised person or a person acting on his behalf will introduce to the money-lender persons with whom the relevant authorised person has entered, or proposes to enter, into a relevant transaction, or will advise such persons to approach the money-lender, with a view to the money-lender lending money on the security of any contract effected pursuant to a relevant transaction;]

(b)   a relevant authorised person gives an assurance to the money-lender as to the amount which, on the security of any contract effected pursuant to a relevant transaction, will or may be received by the money-lender should the money-lender lend money to a person introduced to him pursuant to the arrangements.

(2)   In paragraph (1)—

"money-lender" means a person who is—

(a)   a money-lending company within the meaning of section 338 of the Companies Act 1985;

(b)   a body corporate incorporated under the law of, or of any part of, the United Kingdom relating to building societies; or

(c)   a person whose ordinary business includes the making of loans or the giving of guarantees in connection with loans;

"relevant authorised person" means an authorised person who has permission to effect [contracts of insurance] or to sell investments of the kind specified by article 89, so far as relevant to such contracts;

"relevant transaction" means the effecting of a [contract of insurance] or the sale of an investment of the kind specified by article 89, so far as relevant to such contracts.

[(3)   This article is subject to article 4(4A).]

[2056]

NOTES

Para (1): sub-para (a) substituted by the Financial Services and Markets Act 2000 (Regulated Activities) (Amendment) Order 2001, SI 2001/3544, arts 2, 5, as from 1 December 2001.

Para (2): words in square brackets in definitions "relevant authorised person" and "relevant transaction" substituted by the Financial Services and Markets Act 2000 (Regulated Activities) (Amendment) (No 2) Order 2003, SI 2003/1476, art 5(4), as from 31 October 2004 (in so far as relating to contracts of long-term care insurance), and as from 14 January 2005 (otherwise), for transitional provisions see arts 22–27 of that Order at **[2706]** et seq.

Para (3): added by the Financial Services and Markets Act 2000 (Regulated Activities) (Amendment No 3) Order 2006, SI 2006/3384, arts 2, 15, as from 1 April 2007 (for the purposes of enabling applications to be made for (i) a Pt IV permission, (ii) a variation of a Pt IV permission, and (iii) the Authority's approval under s 59 of the 2000 Act, in relation to an activity of the kind specified by art 25D of this Order, or in relation to an investment of the kind specified by arts 83, 84 or 85 of this Order), and as from 1 November 2007 (otherwise).

31   Arranging the acceptance of debentures in connection with loans

(1)   There are excluded from article 25(1) and (2) arrangements under which a person accepts or is to accept, whether as principal or agent, an instrument creating or acknowledging indebtedness in respect of any loan, credit, guarantee or other similar financial accommodation or assurance which is, or is to be, made, granted or provided by that person or his principal.

(2)   The reference in paragraph (1) to a person accepting an instrument includes a reference to a person becoming a party to an instrument otherwise than as a debtor or a surety.

[2057]

NOTES

Modification: references in para (1) to securities, instruments or investments creating or acknowledging indebtedness (or creating or acknowledging a present or future indebtedness) includes a reference to uncertificated units of eligible debt securities; see the Uncertificated Securities (Amendment) (Eligible Debt Securities) Regulations 2003, SI 2003/1633, reg 15, Sch 2, para 8 (as from 24 June 2003).

Modification: references in para (2) to a person becoming party to an instrument includes a reference to a person assuming rights and obligations in respect of uncertificated units of an eligible debt security in accordance with its current terms of issue; see the Uncertificated Securities (Amendment) (Eligible Debt Securities) Regulations 2003, SI 2003/1633, reg 15, Sch 2, para 9 (as from 24 June 2003).

32   Provision of finance

There are excluded from article 25(2) arrangements having as their sole purpose the provision of finance to enable a person to buy, sell, subscribe for or underwrite investments.

[2058]

33   Introducing

There are excluded from [articles 25(2), 25A(2), 25B(2) and 25C(2)] arrangements where—
(a)   they are arrangements under which persons ("clients") will be introduced to another person;
(b)   the person to whom introductions are to be made is—
    (i)   an authorised person;
    (ii)   an exempt person acting in the course of a business comprising a regulated activity in relation to which he is exempt; or
    (iii)   a person who is not unlawfully carrying on regulated activities in the United Kingdom and whose ordinary business involves him in engaging in an activity of the kind specified by any of articles 14, 21, 25, [25A,] [25B, 25C,] 37[, 39A], 40, 45, 51, [52, 53[, 53A, 53B and 53C]] (or, so far as relevant to any of those articles, article 64), or would do so apart from any exclusion from any of those articles made by this Order; ...
(c)   the introduction is made with a view to the provision of independent advice or the independent exercise of discretion in relation to investments generally or in relation to any class of investments to which the arrangements relate[; and
(d)   the arrangements are made with a view to a person entering into a transaction which does not relate to a contract of insurance].

[2059]

NOTES

Words in first pair of square brackets substituted by the Financial Services and Markets Act 2000 (Regulated Activities) (Amendment) (No 2) Order 2006, SI 2006/2383, arts 2, 10(a), as from 6 November 2006 (for the purposes of enabling applications to be made for (i) a Pt IV permission, or a variation of a Pt IV permission, in relation to activities of the kind specified by arts 25B, 25C, 53B, 53C, 63B or 63F or, so far as relevant to any such activity, art 64 of this Order; or (ii) the Authority's approval under FSMA 2000, s 59 in relation to any of those activities), and as from 6 April 2007 (otherwise) (for transitional provisions and effect see arts 36–40 of, and the Schedule to, the 2006 Order at **[2861]** et seq).

Figure in first pair of square brackets in para (b)(iii) inserted, and words in the penultimate (outer) pair of square brackets in that paragraph substituted, by the Financial Services and Markets Act 2000 (Regulated Activities) (Amendment) (No 1) Order 2003, SI 2003/1475, art 10, as from 31 October 2004, for transitional provisions see arts 26–29 at **[2700]** et seq.

Figures in second pair of square brackets in para (b)(iii) inserted, and words in final (inner) pair of square brackets substituted, by SI 2006/2383, arts 2, 10(b), as from 6 November 2006 (certain purposes), and as from 6 April 2007 (otherwise) (for purposes, transitional provisions, and effect, see the note above).

Figure in third pair of square brackets in para (b)(iii) inserted, word omitted from that paragraph revoked, and para (d) and the word immediately preceding it added, by the Financial Services and Markets Act 2000 (Regulated Activities) (Amendment) (No 2) Order 2003, SI 2003/1476, art 5(5), as from 31 October 2004 (in so far as relating to contracts of long-term care insurance), and as from 14 January 2005 (otherwise), for transitional provisions see arts 22–27 of that Order at **[2706]** et seq.

[33A Introducing to authorised persons etc

(1)   There are excluded from article 25A(2) arrangements where—
  (a)   they are arrangements under which a client is introduced to a person ("N") who is—
    (i)   an authorised person who has permission to carry on a regulated activity of the kind specified by any of articles 25A, 53A, and 61(1),
    (ii)   an appointed representative who may carry on a regulated activity of the kind specified by either of articles 25A and 53A without contravening the general prohibition, or
    (iii)   an overseas person who carries on activities specified by any of articles 25A, 53A and 61(1); and
  (b)   the conditions mentioned in paragraph (2) are satisfied.

[(1A)   There are excluded from article 25B(2) arrangements where—
  (a)   they are arrangements under which a client is introduced to a person ("N") who is—
    (i)   an authorised person who has permission to carry on a regulated activity of the kind specified by any of articles 25B, 53B and 63B(1),
    (ii)   an appointed representative who may carry on a regulated activity of the kind specified by either of articles 25B and 53B without contravening the general prohibition, or
    (iii)   an overseas person who carries on activities specified by any of articles 25B, 53B and 63B(1); and
  (b)   the conditions mentioned in paragraph (2) are satisfied.

(1B)   There are excluded from article 25C(2) arrangements where—
  (a)   they are arrangements under which a client is introduced to a person ("N") who is—
    (i)   an authorised person who has permission to carry on a regulated activity of the kind specified by any of articles 25C, 53C and 63F(1),
    (ii)   an appointed representative who may carry on a regulated activity of the kind specified by either of articles 25C and 53C without contravening the general prohibition, or
    (iii)   an overseas person who carries on activities specified by any of articles 25C, 53C and 63F(1); and
  (b)   the conditions mentioned in paragraph (2) are satisfied.]

(2)   Those conditions are—
  (a)   that the person making the introduction ("P") does not receive any money, other than money payable to P on his own account, paid by the client for or in connection with any transaction which the client enters into with or through N as a result of the introduction; and
  (b)   that before making the introduction P discloses to the client such of the information mentioned in paragraph (3) as applies to P.

(3)   That information is—
  (a)   that P is a member of the same group as N;
  (b)   details of any payment which P will receive from N, by way of fee or commission, for introducing the client to N;
  (c)   an indication of any other reward or advantage received or to be received by P that arises out of his introducing clients to N.

[(4)   In this article, "client" means—
  (a)   for the purposes of paragraph (1), a borrower within the meaning given by article 61(3)(a)(i), or a person who is or may be contemplating entering into a regulated mortgage contract as such a borrower;
  (b)   for the purposes of paragraph (1A), a reversion seller, a plan provider or a person who is or may be contemplating entering into a regulated home reversion plan as a reversion seller or as a plan provider;
  (c)   for the purposes of paragraph (1B), a home purchaser or a person who is or may be contemplating entering into a regulated home purchase plan as a home purchaser.]

                                                       [2060]

NOTES

Commencement: 31 October 2004.

Inserted by the Financial Services and Markets Act 2000 (Regulated Activities) (Amendment) (No 1) Order 2003, SI 2003/1475, art 11, as from 31 October 2004; for transitional provisions see arts 26–29 at **[2700]** et seq.

Paras (1A), (1B): inserted by the Financial Services and Markets Act 2000 (Regulated Activities) (Amendment) (No 2) Order 2006, SI 2006/2383, arts 2, 11(a), as from 6 November 2006 (for the purposes of enabling applications to be made for (i) a Pt IV permission, or a variation of a Pt IV permission, in relation to activities of the kind specified by arts 25B, 25C, 53B, 53C, 63B or 63F or, so far as relevant to any such activity, art 64 of this Order; or (ii) the Authority's approval under FSMA 2000, s 59 in relation to any of those activities), and as from 6 April 2007 (otherwise) (for transitional provisions and effect see arts 36–40 of, and the Schedule to, the 2006 Order at **[2861]** et seq).

Para (4): substituted by SI 2006/2383, arts 2, 11(b), as from 6 November 2006 (certain purposes), and as from 6 April 2007 (otherwise) (for purposes, transitional provisions, and effect, see the note above).

34   Arrangements for the issue of shares etc

(1)   There are excluded from article 25(1) and (2)—

    (a)   arrangements made by a company for the purposes of issuing its own shares or share warrants; and

    (b)   arrangements made by any person for the purposes of issuing his own debentures or debenture warrants;

and for the purposes of article 25(1) and (2), a company is not, by reason of issuing its own shares or share warrants, and a person is not, by reason of issuing his own debentures or debenture warrants, to be treated as selling them.

(2)   In paragraph (1), "company", "shares", "debentures", "share warrants" and "debenture warrants" have the meanings given by article 18(2).

[2061]

35   International securities self-regulating organisations

(1)   There are excluded from article 25(1) and (2) any arrangements made for the purposes of carrying out the functions of a body or association which is approved under this article as an international securities self-regulating organisation, whether the arrangements are made by the organisation itself or by a person acting on its behalf.

(2)   The Treasury may approve as an international securities self-regulating organisation any body corporate or unincorporated association with respect to which the conditions mentioned in paragraph (3) appear to them to be met if, having regard to such matters affecting international trade, overseas earnings and the balance of payments or otherwise as they consider relevant, it appears to them that to do so would be desirable and not result in any undue risk to investors.

(3)   The conditions are that—

    (a)   the body or association does not have its head office in the United Kingdom;

    (b)   the body or association is not eligible for recognition under section 287 or 288 of the Act (applications by investment exchanges and clearing houses) on the ground that (whether or not it has applied, and whether or not it would be eligible on other grounds) it is unable to satisfy the requirements of one or both of paragraphs (a) and (b) of section 292(3) of the Act (requirements for overseas investment exchanges and overseas clearing houses);

    (c)   the body or association is able and willing to co-operate with the Authority by the sharing of information and in other ways;

    (d)   adequate arrangements exist for co-operation between the Authority and those responsible for the supervision of the body or association in the country or territory in which its head office is situated;

    (e)   the body or association has a membership composed of persons falling within any of the following categories, that is to say, authorised persons, exempt persons, and persons whose head offices are outside the United Kingdom and whose ordinary business involves them in engaging in activities which are activities of a kind specified by this Order (or would be apart from any exclusion made by this Part); and

    (f)   the body or association facilitates and regulates the activity of its members in the conduct of international securities business.

(4)   In paragraph (3)(f), "international securities business" means the business of buying, selling, subscribing for or underwriting investments (or agreeing to do so), either as principal or agent, where—

    (a)   the investments are securities or [relevant investments] and are of a kind which, by their nature, and the manner in which the business is conducted, may be expected normally to be bought or dealt in by persons sufficiently expert to understand the risks involved; and

    (b)   either the transaction is international or each of the parties may be expected to be indifferent to the location of the other;

and, for the purposes of this definition, it is irrelevant that the investments may ultimately be bought otherwise than in the course of such business by persons not so expert.

(5)   Any approval under this article is to be given by notice in writing; and the Treasury may by a further notice in writing withdraw any such approval if for any reason it appears to them that it is not appropriate to it to continue in force.

[2062]

PART III
STATUTORY INSTRUMENTS

NOTES

Para (4): words in square brackets in sub-para (a) substituted by the Financial Services and Markets Act 2000 (Regulated Activities) (Amendment) (No 2) Order 2003, SI 2003/1476, art 5(6), as from 31 October 2004 (in so far as relating to contracts of long-term care insurance), and as from 14 January 2005 (otherwise), for transitional provisions see arts 22–27 of that Order at **[2706]** et seq.

36 Other exclusions

[(1)] Article 25 is also subject to the exclusions in articles 66 (trustees etc), 67 (profession or non-investment business), 68 (sale of goods and supply of services), 69 (groups and joint enterprises), 70 (sale of body corporate), 71 (employee share schemes)[, 72 (overseas persons)[, 72A (information society services), 72B (activities carried on by a provider of relevant goods or services), 72C (provision of information about contracts of insurance on an incidental basis) and 72D (large risks contracts where risk situated outside the EEA)]].

[(2) [Articles 25A, 25B and 25C are] also subject to the exclusions in articles 66 (trustees etc), 67 (profession or non-investment business), 72 (overseas persons) and 72A (information society services).]

[(3) Article 25D is also subject to the exclusion in article 72 (overseas persons).]

[2063]

NOTES

Para (1): numbered as such by the Financial Services and Markets Act 2000 (Regulated Activities) (Amendment) (No 1) Order 2003, SI 2003/1475, art 12(a), as from 31 October 2004 (for transitional provisions see arts 26–29 at **[2700]** et seq); words in first (outer) pair of square brackets substituted by the Financial Services and Markets Act 2000 (Regulated Activities) (Amendment) (No 2) Order 2002, SI 2002/1776, art 3(1), (6), as from 21 August 2002; words in second (inner) pair of square brackets substituted by the Financial Services and Markets Act 2000 (Regulated Activities) (Amendment) (No 2) Order 2003, SI 2003/1476, art 5(7), as from 31 October 2004 (in so far as relating to contracts of long-term care insurance), and as from 14 January 2005 (otherwise), for transitional provisions see arts 22–27 of that Order at **[2706]** et seq.

Para (2): added by SI 2003/1475, art 12(b), as from 31 October 2004, for transitional provisions see arts 26–29 at **[2700]** et seq; words in square brackets substituted by the Financial Services and Markets Act 2000 (Regulated Activities) (Amendment) (No 2) Order 2006, SI 2006/2383, arts 2, 12, as from 6 November 2006 (for the purposes of enabling applications to be made for (i) a Pt IV permission, or a variation of a Pt IV permission, in relation to activities of the kind specified by arts 25B, 25C, 53B, 53C, 63B or 63F or, so far as relevant to any such activity, art 64 of this Order; or (ii) the Authority's approval under FSMA 2000, s 59 in relation to any of those activities), and as from 6 April 2007 (otherwise) (for transitional provisions and effect see arts 36–40 of, and the Schedule to, the 2006 Order at **[2861]** et seq).

Para (3): added by the Financial Services and Markets Act 2000 (Regulated Activities) (Amendment No 3) Order 2006, SI 2006/3384, arts 2, 16, as from 1 April 2007 (for the purposes of enabling applications to be made for (i) a Pt IV permission, (ii) a variation of a Pt IV permission, and (iii) the Authority's approval under s 59 of the 2000 Act, in relation to an activity of the kind specified by art 25D of this Order, or in relation to an investment of the kind specified by arts 83, 84 or 85 of this Order), and as from 1 November 2007 (otherwise).

CHAPTER VII
MANAGING INVESTMENTS

The activity

37 Managing investments

Managing assets belonging to another person, in circumstances involving the exercise of discretion, is a specified kind of activity if—

(a) the assets consist of or include any investment which is a security or a contractually based investment; or

(b) the arrangements for their management are such that the assets may consist of or include such investments, and either the assets have at any time since 29th April 1988 done so, or the arrangements have at any time (whether before or after that date) been held out as arrangements under which the assets would do so.

[2064]

NOTES

See the Financial Services and Markets Act 2000 (Carrying on Regulated Activities by Way of Business) Order 2001, SI 2001/1177, art 3 at **[2208]** in relation to investment business, and art 4 at **[2210]** in respect of activities of managing investments where assets in question are held for the purposes of an occupational pension scheme.

Exclusions

38 Attorneys

[(1)] A person does not carry on an activity of the kind specified by article 37 if—

(a) he is a person appointed to manage the assets in question under a power of attorney; and

(b) all routine or day-to-day decisions, so far as relating to investments of a kind mentioned in article 37(a), are taken on behalf of that person by—

(i) an authorised person with permission to carry on activities of the kind specified by article 37; ...

      (ii)   a person who is an exempt person in relation to activities of that kind[; or

      (iii)   an overseas person.]

[(2)   This article is subject to article 4(4).]

[2065]

NOTES

Para (1) numbered as such, and para (2) added, by the Financial Services and Markets Act 2000 (Regulated Activities) (Amendment No 3) Order 2006, SI 2006/3384, arts 2, 17, as from 1 April 2007 (for the purposes of enabling applications to be made for (i) a Pt IV permission, (ii) a variation of a Pt IV permission, and (iii) the Authority's approval under s 59 of the 2000 Act, in relation to an activity of the kind specified by art 25D of this Order, or in relation to an investment of the kind specified by arts 83, 84 or 85 of this Order), and as from 1 November 2007 (otherwise). Note that the Queen's Printer's copy of SI 2006/3384 does not actually specify that the words "This article is subject to article 4(4)" should be numbered as paragraph (2) even though it does provide that the original text should be numbered as paragraph (1). It is assumed that this is an error.

Word omitted from para (1)(b)(i) revoked, and para (1)(b)(iii) and the word immediately preceding it added, by the Financial Services and Markets Act 2000 (Regulated Activities) (Amendment) Order 2001, SI 2001/3544, arts 2, 6, as from 1 December 2001.

39 Other exclusions

Article 37 is also subject to the exclusions in articles 66 (trustees etc), 68 (sale of goods and supply of services)[, 69 (groups and joint enterprises)[, 72A (information society services) and 72C (provision of information about contracts of insurance on an incidental basis)]].

[2066]

NOTES

Words in first (outer) pair of square brackets substituted by the Financial Services and Markets Act 2000 (Regulated Activities) (Amendment) (No 2) Order 2002, SI 2002/1776, art 3(1), (7), as from 21 August 2002; words in second (inner) pair of square brackets substituted by the Financial Services and Markets Act 2000 (Regulated Activities) (Amendment) (No 2) Order 2003, SI 2003/1476, art 6, as from 31 October 2004 (in so far as relating to contracts of long-term care insurance), and as from 14 January 2005 (otherwise), for transitional provisions see arts 22–27 of that Order at **[2706]** et seq.

[CHAPTER VIIA
ASSISTING IN THE ADMINISTRATION AND PERFORMANCE OF A
CONTRACT OF INSURANCE

The Activity

39A Assisting in the administration and performance of a contract of insurance

Assisting in the administration and performance of a contract of insurance is a specified kind of activity.]

[2067]

NOTES

Commencement: 31 October 2004 (in so far as relating to contracts of long-term care insurance); 14 January 2005 (otherwise).

Inserted, together with the preceding headings and arts 39B, 39C, by the Financial Services and Markets Act 2000 (Regulated Activities) (Amendment) (No 2) Order 2003, SI 2003/1476, art 7, as from 31 October 2004 (in so far as relating to contracts of long-term care insurance), and as from 14 January 2005 (otherwise); for transitional provisions see arts 22–27 of that Order at **[2706]** et seq.

[Exclusions

39B Claims management on behalf of an insurer etc

(1)   A person does not carry on an activity of the kind specified by article 39A if he acts in the course of carrying on the activity of—

    (a)   expert appraisal;

    (b)   loss adjusting on behalf of a relevant insurer; or

    (c)   managing claims on behalf of a relevant insurer,

and that activity is carried on in the course of carrying on any profession or business.

(2)   In this article—

    (a)   "relevant insurer" means—

      (i)   a person who has Part IV permission to carry on an activity of the kind specified by article 10;

      (ii)   a person to whom the general prohibition does not apply by virtue of section 316(1)(a) of the Act (members of the Society of Lloyd's);

      (iii) an EEA firm falling within paragraph 5(d) of Schedule 3 to the Act (insurance undertaking); or

      (iv) a relevant reinsurer;

(b) "relevant reinsurer" means a person whose main business consists of accepting risks ceded by—
  (i) a person falling within sub-paragraph (i), (ii) or (iii) of the definition of "relevant insurer"; …
  [(ii) an EEA firm falling within paragraph 5(da) of Schedule 3 to the Act (reinsurance undertaking); or
  (iii) a person established outside the United Kingdom and not falling within paragraph (ii) who carries on an activity of the kind specified by article 10 by way of business].]

[2068]

NOTES
Commencement: 31 October 2004 (in so far as relating to contracts of long-term care insurance); 14 January 2005 (otherwise).
Inserted as noted to art 39A at **[2067]**.
Para (2): word omitted from sub-para (b)(i) revoked, and sub-paras (b)(ii), (iii) substituted (for the original sub-para (b)(ii)) by the Financial Services and Markets Act 2000 (Reinsurance Directive) Order 2007, SI 2007/3254, reg 2, as from 10 December 2007.

[39C Other exclusions
Article 39A is also subject to the exclusions in articles 66 (trustees etc), 67 (profession or non-investment business), 72A (information society services), 72B (activities carried on by a provider of relevant goods or services), 72C (provision of information about contracts of insurance on an incidental basis) and 72D (large risks contracts where risk situated outside the EEA).]

[2069]

NOTES
Commencement: 31 October 2004 (in so far as relating to contracts of long-term care insurance); 14 January 2005 (otherwise).
Inserted as noted to art 39A at **[2067]**.

CHAPTER VIII
SAFEGUARDING AND ADMINISTERING INVESTMENTS
The activity

40 Safeguarding and administering investments
(1) The activity consisting of both—
  (a) the safeguarding of assets belonging to another, and
  (b) the administration of those assets,
or arranging for one or more other persons to carry on that activity, is a specified kind of activity if the condition in sub-paragraph (a) or (b) of paragraph (2) is met.
(2) The condition is that—
  (a) the assets consist of or include any investment which is a security or a contractually based investment; or
  (b) the arrangements for their safeguarding and administration are such that the assets may consist of or include such investments, and either the assets have at any time since 1st June 1997 done so, or the arrangements have at any time (whether before or after that date) been held out as ones under which such investments would be safeguarded and administered.
(3) For the purposes of this article—
  (a) it is immaterial that title to the assets safeguarded and administered is held in uncertificated form;
  (b) it is immaterial that the assets safeguarded and administered may be transferred to another person, subject to a commitment by the person safeguarding and administering them, or arranging for their safeguarding and administration, that they will be replaced by equivalent assets at some future date or when so requested by the person to whom they belong.

[2070]

NOTES
See the Financial Services and Markets Act 2000 (Carrying on Regulated Activities by Way of Business) Order 2001, SI 2001/1177, art 3 at **[2208]** in relation to investment business.

Exclusions

41   Acceptance of responsibility by third party

(1)   There are excluded from article 40 any activities which a person carries on pursuant to arrangements which—

(a)   are ones under which a qualifying custodian undertakes to the person to whom the assets belong a responsibility in respect of the assets which is no less onerous than the qualifying custodian would have if the qualifying custodian were safeguarding and administering the assets; and

(b)   are operated by the qualifying custodian in the course of carrying on in the United Kingdom an activity of the kind specified by article 40.

(2)   In paragraph (1), "qualifying custodian" means a person who is—

(a)   an authorised person who has permission to carry on an activity of the kind specified by article 40, or

(b)   an exempt person acting in the course of a business comprising a regulated activity in relation to which he is exempt.

[2071]

42   Introduction to qualifying custodians

(1)   There are excluded from article 40 any arrangements pursuant to which introductions are made by a person ("P") to a qualifying custodian with a view to the qualifying custodian providing in the United Kingdom a service comprising an activity of the kind specified by article 40, where the qualifying person (or other person who is to safeguard and administer the assets in question) is not connected with P.

(2)   For the purposes of paragraph (1)—

(a)   "qualifying custodian" has the meaning given by article 41(2); and

(b)   a person is connected with P if either he is a member of the same group as P, or P is remunerated by him.

[2072]

43   Activities not constituting administration

The following activities do not constitute the administration of assets for the purposes of article 40—

(a)   providing information as to the number of units or the value of any assets safeguarded;

(b)   converting currency;

(c)   receiving documents relating to an investment solely for the purpose of onward transmission to, from or at the direction of the person to whom the investment belongs.

[2073]

44   Other exclusions

Article 40 is also subject to the exclusions in articles 66 (trustees etc), 67 (profession or non-investment business), 68 (sale of goods and supply of services), 69 (groups and joint enterprises)[, 71 (employee share schemes)[, 72A (information society services) and 72C (provision of information about contracts of insurance on an incidental basis)]].

[2074]

NOTES

Words in first (outer) pair of square brackets substituted by the Financial Services and Markets Act 2000 (Regulated Activities) (Amendment) (No 2) Order 2002, SI 2002/1776, art 3(1), (8), as from 21 August 2002; words in second (inner) pair of square brackets substituted by the Financial Services and Markets Act 2000 (Regulated Activities) (Amendment) (No 2) Order 2003, SI 2003/1476, art 8, as from 31 October 2004 (in so far as relating to contracts of long-term care insurance), and as from 14 January 2005 (otherwise), for transitional provisions see arts 22–27 of that Order at **[2706]** et seq.

CHAPTER IX
SENDING DEMATERIALISED INSTRUCTIONS

The activities

45   Sending dematerialised instructions

(1)   Sending, on behalf of another person, dematerialised instructions relating to a security [or a contractually based investment] is a specified kind of activity, where those instructions are sent by means of a relevant system in respect of which an Operator is approved under the [2001] Regulations.

(2)   Causing dematerialised instructions relating to a security [or a contractually based investment] to be sent [on behalf of another person] by means of such a system is also a specified kind of activity where the person causing them to be sent is a system-participant.

(3)   In this Chapter—
  [(a)   "the 2001 Regulations" means the Uncertificated Securities Regulations 2001;]
  (b)   "dematerialised instruction", "Operator", "settlement bank" and "system-participant"
       have the meaning given by regulation 3 of the [2001] Regulations.

[2075]

NOTES
  Para (1): words in first pair of square brackets inserted, and date in second pair of square brackets substituted, by the Financial Services and Markets Act 2000 (Regulated Activities) (Amendment) Order 2002, SI 2002/682, art 13(1), as from 27 April 2002.
  Para (2): words in first pair of square brackets inserted by SI 2002/682, art 13(2), as from 27 April 2002; words in second pair of square brackets inserted by the Financial Services and Markets Act 2000 (Regulated Activities) (Amendment) Order 2001, SI 2001/3544, arts 2, 7, as from 1 December 2001.
  Para (3): words in square brackets substituted by SI 2002/682, art 13(3), as from 27 April 2002.
  See the Financial Services and Markets Act 2000 (Carrying on Regulated Activities by Way of Business) Order 2001, SI 2001/1177, art 3 at **[2208]** in relation to investment business.

Exclusions

46   Instructions on behalf of participating issuers

There is excluded from article 45 the act of sending, or causing to be sent, a dematerialised instruction where the person on whose behalf the instruction is sent or caused to be sent is a participating issuer within the meaning of the [2001] Regulations.

[2076]

NOTES
  Date in square brackets substituted by the Financial Services and Markets Act 2000 (Regulated Activities) (Amendment) Order 2002, SI 2002/682, art 13(4), as from 27 April 2002.

47   Instructions on behalf of settlement banks

There is excluded from article 45 the act of sending, or causing to be sent, a dematerialised instruction where the person on whose behalf the instruction is sent or caused to be sent is a settlement bank in its capacity as such.

[2077]

48   Instructions in connection with takeover offers

(1)   There is excluded from article 45 of the act of sending, or causing to be sent, a dematerialised instruction where the person on whose behalf the instruction is sent or caused to be sent is an offeror making a takeover offer.

(2)   In this article—
  (a)   "offeror" means, in the case of a takeover offer made by two or more persons jointly, the joint offers or any of them;
  (b)   "takeover offer" means—
    (i)   an offer to acquire shares (which in this sub-paragraph has the same meaning as in [section 974 of the Companies Act 2006]) in a body corporate incorporated in the United Kingdom which is a takeover offer within the meaning of [Chapter 3 of Part 28] of that Act (or would be such an offer if that Part of that Act applied in relation to any body corporate);
    (ii)   an offer to acquire all or substantially all the shares, or all the shares of a particular class, in a body corporate incorporated outside the United Kingdom; or
    (iii) an offer made to all the holders of shares, or shares of a particular class, in a body corporate to acquire a specified proportion of those shares;
  but in determining whether an offer falls within paragraph (ii) there are to be disregarded any shares which the offeror or any associate of his (within the meaning of [section 988 of the Companies Act 2006]) holds or has contracted to acquire; and in determining whether an offer falls within paragraph (iii) the offeror, any such associate and any person whose shares the offeror or any such associate has contracted to acquire is not to be regarded as a holder of shares.

[2078]

NOTES
  Para (2): words in square brackets in sub-para (b) substituted the Companies Act 2006 (Commencement No 2, Consequential Amendments, Transitional Provisions and Savings) Order 2007, SI 2007/1093, art 6(1), Sch 3, para 8, as from 6 April 2007, subject to transitional provisions in relation to a takeover offer where the date of the offer is before that date.

49   Instructions in the course of providing a network

There is excluded from article 45 the act of sending, or causing to be sent, a dematerialised instruction as a necessary part of providing a network, the purpose of which is to carry dematerialised instructions which are at all time properly authenticated (within the meaning of the [2001] Regulations).

[2079]

NOTES

Date in square brackets substituted by the Financial Services and Markets Act 2000 (Regulated Activities) (Amendment) Order 2002, SI 2002/682, art 13(4), as from 27 April 2002.

50   Other exclusions

Article 45 is also subject to the exclusions in articles 66 (trustees etc)[, 69 (groups and joint enterprises) and 72A (information society services)].

[2080]

NOTES

Words in square brackets substituted by the Financial Services and Markets Act 2000 (Regulated Activities) (Amendment) (No 2) Order 2002, SI 2002/1776, art 3(1), (9), as from 21 August 2002.

CHAPTER X
COLLECTIVE INVESTMENT SCHEMES

The activities

51   Establishing etc a collective investment scheme

(1)   The following are specified kinds of activity—
    (a)   establishing, operating or winding up a collective investment scheme;
    (b)   acting as trustee of an authorised unit trust scheme;
    (c)   acting as the depositary or sole director of an open-ended investment company.

(2)   In this article, "trustee", "authorised unit trust scheme" and "depositary" have the meaning given by section 237 of the Act.

[2081]

NOTES

See the Financial Services and Markets Act 2000 (Carrying on Regulated Activities by Way of Business) Order 2001, SI 2001/1177, art 3 at **[2208]** in relation to investment business.

[Exclusion

51A   Information society services

Article 51 is subject to the exclusion in article 72A (information society services).]

[2082]

NOTES

Inserted, together with the preceding heading by the Financial Services and Markets Act 2000 (Regulated Activities) (Amendment) (No 2) Order 2002, SI 2002/1776, art 3(1), (10), as from 21 August 2002.

CHAPTER XI
... PENSION SCHEMES

The activities

[52   Establishing etc a pension scheme

The following are specified kinds of activity—
    (a)   establishing, operating or winding up a stakeholder pension scheme;
    (b)   establishing, operating or winding up a personal pension scheme.]

[2083]

NOTES

Commencement: 1 October 2006 (certain purposes); 6 April 2007 (otherwise) (see below).

The word omitted from the Chapter heading preceding this article was revoked, and this article was substituted, by the Financial Services and Markets Act 2000 (Regulated Activities) (Amendment) Order 2006, SI 2006/1969, art 2(1), (3), (4), as from 1 October 2006 (for the purposes of enabling applications to be made for Pt IV permission or for a variation of Pt IV permission in relation to the regulated activity specified by art 52(b) of this Order (as so substituted)), and as from 6 April 2007 (otherwise); for transitional provisions and effect see arts 3–7 of, and the Schedule to, the 2006 Order at **[2854]** et seq.

See the Financial Services and Markets Act 2000 (Carrying on Regulated Activities by Way of Business) Order 2001, SI 2001/1177, art 3 at **[2208]** in relation to investment business.

[Exclusion

52A Information society services

Article 52 is subject to the exclusion in article 72A (information society services).]

[2084]

NOTES

Inserted, together with the preceding heading, by the Financial Services and Markets Act 2000 (Regulated Activities) (Amendment) (No 2) Order 2002, SI 2002/1776, art 3(1), (11), as from 21 August 2002.

[CHAPTER XIA
PROVIDING BASIC ADVICE ON STAKEHOLDER PRODUCTS

The Activity

52B Providing basic advice on stakeholder products

(1) Providing basic advice to a retail consumer on a stakeholder product is a specified kind of activity.

(2) For the purposes of paragraph (1), a person ("P") provides basic advice when—
- (a) he asks a retail consumer questions to enable him to assess whether a stakeholder product is appropriate for that consumer; and
- (b) relying on the information provided by the retail consumer P assesses that a stakeholder product is appropriate for the retail consumer and—
  - (i) describes that product to that consumer;
  - (ii) gives a recommendation of that product to that consumer; and
- (c) the retail consumer has indicated to P that he has understood the description and the recommendation in sub-paragraph (b).

(3) In this article—
"retail consumer" means any person who is advised by P on the merits of opening or buying a stakeholder product in the course of a business carried on by P and who does not receive the advice in the course of a business carried on by him;
"stakeholder product" means—
- (a) an account which qualifies as a stakeholder child trust fund within the meaning given by the Child Trust Funds Regulations 2004;
- [(b) rights under a stakeholder pension scheme;]
- (c) an investment of a kind specified in regulations made by the Treasury.]

[2085]

NOTES

Commencement: 6 April 2005.

Inserted, together with the preceding headings, by the Financial Services and Markets Act 2000 (Regulated Activities) (Amendment) (No 2) Order 2004, SI 2004/2737, arts, 2, 3, as from 6 April 2005. For transitional provisions, see the note below.

Para (3): in definition "stakeholder product", para (b) substituted by the Financial Services and Markets Act 2000 (Regulated Activities) (Amendment) Order 2005, SI 2005/593, art 2(3), as from 6 April 2005.

Transitional provisions: SI 2004/2737, art 4, provides as follows—

"4 Transitional provisions

(1) Part 4 of the Act shall apply in the case of persons who have permission at the date this Order comes into force to carry out the activity specified in article 53 of the principal Order and who wish to carry out the activity specified in article 52B of that Order as follows.

(2) Where P is a person to whom paragraph (1) applies—
- (a) the procedures established under sections 44 and 45 in respect of application for permission shall not apply in respect of permission to carry out the article 52B activity,
- (b) P shall be deemed to have such a permission if he has notified the Authority in writing of his wish to undertake the activity and the Authority has acknowledged receipt of P's notification in writing from the date of the acknowledgement.".

Regulations: the Financial Services and Markets 2000 (Stakeholder Products) Regulations 2004, SI 2004/2738 at **[2741]**.

CHAPTER XII
ADVISING ON INVESTMENTS

The activity

53 Advising on investments

Advising a person is a specified kind of activity if the advice is—
    (a)   given to the person in his capacity as an investor or potential investor, or in his capacity as agent for an investor or a potential investor; and
    (b)   advice on the merits of his doing any of the following (whether as principal or agent)—
        (i)   buying, selling, subscribing for or underwriting a particular investment which is a security or a [relevant investment], or
        (ii)   exercising any right conferred by such an investment to buy, sell, subscribe for or underwrite such an investment.

[2086]

NOTES

Words in square brackets substituted by the Financial Services and Markets Act 2000 (Regulated Activities) (Amendment) (No 2) Order 2003, SI 2003/1476, art 9(1), as from 31 October 2004 (in so far as relating to contracts of long-term care insurance), and as from 14 January 2005 (otherwise); for transitional provisions see arts 22–27 of that Order at **[2706]** et seq.

Transitional provisions: see the note to art 52B at **[2085]**.

See the Financial Services and Markets Act 2000 (Carrying on Regulated Activities by Way of Business) Order 2001, SI 2001/1177, art 3 at **[2208]** in relation to investment business.

[53A Advising on regulated mortgage contracts

    (1)   Advising a person is a specified kind of activity if the advice—
    (a)   is given to the person in his capacity as a borrower or potential borrower; and
    (b)   is advice on the merits of his doing any of the following—
        (i)   entering into a particular regulated mortgage contract, or
        (ii)   varying the terms of a regulated mortgage contract entered into by him after the coming into force of article 61 in such a way as to vary his obligations under that contract.
    (2)   In this article, "borrower" has the meaning given by article 61(3)(a)(i).]

[2087]

NOTES

Commencement: 31 October 2004.

Inserted by the Financial Services and Markets Act 2000 (Regulated Activities) (Amendment) (No 1) Order 2003, SI 2003/1475, art 13, as from 31 October 2004; for transitional provisions see arts 26–29 at **[2700]** et seq.

See the Financial Services and Markets Act 2000 (Carrying on Regulated Activities by Way of Business) Order 2001, SI 2001/1177, art 3A at **[2209]**.

[53B Advising on regulated home reversion plans

Advising a person is a specified kind of activity if the advice—
    (a)   is given to the person in his capacity as—
        (i)   a reversion seller or potential reversion seller, or
        (ii)   a plan provider or potential plan provider; and
    (b)   is advice on the merits of his doing either of the following—
        (i)   entering into a particular regulated home reversion plan, or
        (ii)   varying the terms of a regulated home reversion plan, entered into on or after 6th April 2007 by him, in such a way as to vary his obligations under that plan.]

[2087A]

NOTES

Commencement: 6 November 2006 (certain purposes); 6 April 2007 (otherwise) (see below).

Inserted, together with art 53C, by the Financial Services and Markets Act 2000 (Regulated Activities) (Amendment) (No 2) Order 2006, SI 2006/2383, arts 2, 13, as from 6 November 2006 (for the purposes of enabling applications to be made for (i) a Pt IV permission, or a variation of a Pt IV permission, in relation to activities of the kind specified by arts 25B, 25C, 53B, 53C, 63B or 63F or, so far as relevant to any such activity, art 64 of this Order; or (ii) the Authority's approval under FSMA 2000, s 59 in relation to any of those activities), and as from 6 April 2007 (otherwise) (for transitional provisions and effect see arts 36–40 of, and the Schedule to, the 2006 Order at **[2861]** et seq).

See the Financial Services and Markets Act 2000 (Carrying on Regulated Activities by Way of Business) Order 2001, SI 2001/1177, art 3B at **[2209A]**.

[53C Advising on regulated home purchase plans

Advising a person is a specified kind of activity if the advice—

(a)   is given to the person in his capacity as a home purchaser or potential home purchaser; and

(b)   is advice on the merits of his doing either of the following—
  (i)   entering into a particular regulated home purchase plan, or
  (ii)   varying the terms of a regulated home purchase plan, entered into on or after 6th April 2007 by him, in such a way as to vary his obligations under that plan.]

[2087B]

NOTES
Commencement: 6 November 2006 (certain purposes); 6 April 2007 (otherwise).
Inserted as noted to art 53B at **[2087A]**.
See the Financial Services and Markets Act 2000 (Carrying on Regulated Activities by Way of Business) Order 2001, SI 2001/1177, art 3C at **[2209B]**.

Exclusions

54   Advice given in newspapers etc

(1)   There is excluded from [articles 53, 53A, 53B and 53C] the giving of advice in writing or other legible form if the advice is contained in a newspaper, journal, magazine, or other periodical publication, or is given by way of a service comprising regularly updated news or information, if the principal purpose of the publication or service, taken as a whole and including any advertisements or other promotional material contained in it, is neither—

(a)   that of giving advice of a kind mentioned in article 53[, 53A, 53B or 53C, as the case may be]; nor

[(b)   that of leading or enabling persons—
  (i)   to buy, sell, subscribe for or underwrite securities or [relevant investments], or (as the case may be),
  (ii)   to enter as borrower into regulated mortgage contracts, or vary the terms of regulated mortgage contracts entered into by them as borrower;
  [(iii) to enter as reversion seller or plan provider into regulated home reversion plans, or vary the terms of regulated home reversion plans entered into by them as reversion seller or plan provider,
  (iv)   to enter as home purchaser into regulated home purchase plans, or vary the terms of regulated home purchase plans entered into by them as home purchaser].]

(2)   There is also excluded from [articles 53, 53A, 53B and 53C] the giving of advice in any service consisting of the broadcast or transmission of television or radio programmes, if the principal purpose of the service, taken as a whole and including any advertisements or other promotional material contained in it, is neither of those mentioned in paragraph (1)(a) and (b).

(3)   The Authority may, on the application of the proprietor of any such publication or service as is mentioned in paragraph (1) or (2), certify that it is of the nature described in that paragraph, and may revoke any such certificate if it considers that it is no longer justified.

(4)   A certificate given under paragraph (3) and not revoked is conclusive evidence of the matters certified.

[2088]

NOTES
Para (1) is amended as follows:
Words in first and second pairs of square brackets substituted by the Financial Services and Markets Act 2000 (Regulated Activities) (Amendment) (No 2) Order 2006, SI 2006/2383, arts 2, 14(a)(i), (ii), as from 6 November 2006 (for the purposes of enabling applications to be made for (i) a Pt IV permission, or a variation of a Pt IV permission, in relation to activities of the kind specified by arts 25B, 25C, 53B, 53C, 63B or 63F or, so far as relevant to any such activity, art 64 of this Order; or (ii) the Authority's approval under FSMA 2000, s 59 in relation to any of those activities), and as from 6 April 2007 (otherwise) (for transitional provisions and effect see arts 36–40 of, and the Schedule to, the 2006 Order at **[2861]** et seq).
Sub-para (b) substituted, by the Financial Services and Markets Act 2000 (Regulated Activities) (Amendment) (No 1) Order 2003, SI 2003/1475, art 14, as from 31 October 2004 (for transitional provisions see arts 26–29 at **[2700]** et seq).
Words in square brackets in sub-para (b)(i) substituted by the Financial Services and Markets Act 2000 (Regulated Activities) (Amendment) (No 2) Order 2003, SI 2003/1476, art 9(2), as from 31 October 2004 (in so far as relating to contracts of long-term care insurance), and as from 14 January 2005 (otherwise) (for transitional provisions see arts 22–27 of that Order at **[2706]** et seq).
Sub-paras (b)(iii), (iv) inserted by SI 2006/2383, arts 2, 14(a)(iii), as from 6 November 2006 (certain purposes), and as from 6 April 2007 (otherwise) (for purposes, transitional provisions, and effect, see the note above).
Para (2): words in square brackets substituted by SI 2006/2383, arts 2, 14(b), as from 6 November 2006 (certain purposes), and as from 6 April 2007 (otherwise) (for purposes, transitional provisions, and effect, see the note above).

[54A   Advice given in the course of administration by authorised person

[(1)]   A person who is not an authorised person ("A") does not carry on an activity of the kind specified by article 53A by reason of—

(a)   anything done by an authorised person ("B") in relation to a regulated mortgage contract which B is administering pursuant to arrangements of the kind mentioned in article 62(a); or

(b)   anything A does in connection with the administration of a regulated mortgage contract in circumstances falling within article 62(b).

[(2)   A person who is not an authorised person ("A") does not carry on an activity of the kind specified by article 53B by reason of—

(a)   anything done by an authorised person ("B") in relation to a regulated home reversion plan which B is administering pursuant to arrangements of the kind mentioned in article 63C(a); or

(b)   anything A does in connection with the administration of a regulated home reversion plan in circumstances falling within article 63C(b).

(3)   A person who is not an authorised person ("A") does not carry on an activity of the kind specified by article 53C by reason of—

(a)   anything done by an authorised person ("B") in relation to a regulated home purchase plan which B is administering pursuant to arrangements of the kind mentioned in article 63G(a); or

(b)   anything A does in connection with the administration of a regulated home purchase plan in circumstances falling within article 63G(b).]]

[2089]

NOTES

Commencement: 31 October 2004.

Inserted by the Financial Services and Markets Act 2000 (Regulated Activities) (Amendment) (No 1) Order 2003, SI 2003/1475, art 15, as from 31 October 2004; for transitional provisions see arts 26–29 at **[2700]** et seq.

Para (1) numbered as such, and paras (2), (3) added, by the Financial Services and Markets Act 2000 (Regulated Activities) (Amendment) (No 2) Order 2006, SI 2006/2383, arts 2, 15, as from 6 November 2006 (for the purposes of enabling applications to be made for (i) a Pt IV permission, or a variation of a Pt IV permission, in relation to activities of the kind specified by arts 25B, 25C, 53B, 53C, 63B or 63F or, so far as relevant to any such activity, art 64 of this Order; or (ii) the Authority's approval under FSMA 2000, s 59 in relation to any of those activities), and as from 6 April 2007 (otherwise) (for transitional provisions and effect see arts 36–40 of, and the Schedule to, the 2006 Order at **[2861]** et seq).

55   Other exclusions

[(1)]   Article 53 is also subject to the exclusions in articles 66 (trustees etc), 67, (profession or non-investment business), 68 (sale of goods and supply of services), 69 (groups and joint enterprises), 70 (sale of body corporate)[, 72 (overseas persons)[, 72A (information society services), 72B (activities carried on by a provider of relevant goods or services) and 72D (large risks contracts where risk situated outside the EEA)]].

[(2)   [Articles 53A, 53B and 53C are] also subject to the exclusions in articles 66 (trustees etc), 67 (profession or non-investment business) and 72A (information society services).]

[2090]

NOTES

Para (1): numbered as such by the Financial Services and Markets Act 2000 (Regulated Activities) (Amendment) (No 1) Order 2003, SI 2003/1475, art 16(a), as from 31 October 2004, for transitional provisions see arts 26–29 at **[2700]** et seq; words in first (outer) pair of square brackets substituted by the Financial Services and Markets Act 2000 (Regulated Activities) (Amendment) (No 2) Order 2002, SI 2002/1776, art 3(1), (12), as from 21 August 2002; words in second (inner) pair of square brackets substituted by the Financial Services and Markets Act 2000 (Regulated Activities) (Amendment) (No 2) Order 2003, SI 2003/1476, art 9(3), as from 31 October 2004 (in so far as relating to contracts of long-term care insurance), and as from 14 January 2005 (otherwise), for transitional provisions see arts 22–27 of that Order at **[2706]** et seq.

Para (2): added by SI 2003/1475, art 16(b), as from 31 October 2004 (for transitional provisions see arts 26–29 at **[2700]** et seq); words in square brackets substituted by the Financial Services and Markets Act 2000 (Regulated Activities) (Amendment) (No 2) Order 2006, SI 2006/2383, arts 2, 16, as from 6 November 2006 (for the purposes of enabling applications to be made for (i) a Pt IV permission, or a variation of a Pt IV permission, in relation to activities of the kind specified by arts 25B, 25C, 53B, 53C, 63B or 63F or, so far as relevant to any such activity, art 64 of this Order; or (ii) the Authority's approval under FSMA 2000, s 59 in relation to any of those activities), and as from 6 April 2007 (otherwise) (for transitional provisions and effect see arts 36–40 of, and the Schedule to, the 2006 Order at **[2861]** et seq).

CHAPTER XIII
LLOYD'S

The activities

56   Advice on syndicate participation at Lloyd's

Advising a person to become, or continue or cease to be, a member of a particular Lloyd's syndicate is a specified kind of activity.

[2091]

57   Managing the underwriting capacity of a Lloyd's syndicate

Managing the underwriting capacity of a Lloyd's syndicate as a managing agent at Lloyd's is a specified kind of activity.

[2092]

58   Arranging deals in contracts of insurance written at Lloyd's

The arranging, by the society incorporated by Lloyd's Act 1871 by the name of Lloyd's, of deals in contracts of insurance written at Lloyd's, is a specified kind of activity.

[2093]

[Exclusion

58A   Information society services

Articles 56 to 58 are subject to the exclusion in article 72A (information society services).]

[2094]

NOTES

Inserted, together with the preceding heading, by the Financial Services and Markets Act 2000 (Regulated Activities) (Amendment) (No 2) Order 2002, SI 2002/1776, art 3(1), (13), as from 21 August 2002.

CHAPTER XIV
FUNERAL PLAN CONTRACTS

The activity

59   Funeral plan contracts

(1)   Entering as provider into a funeral plan contract is a specified kind of activity.

(2)   A "funeral plan contract" is a contract (other than one excluded by article 60) under which—

    (a)   a person ("the customer") makes one or more payments to another person ("the provider"); and

    (b)   the provider undertakes to provide, or secure that another person provides, a funeral in the United Kingdom for the customer (or some other person who is living at the date when the contract is entered into) on his death;

unless, at the time of entering into the contract, the customer and the provider intend or expect the funeral to occur within one month.

[2095]

[Exclusions]

60   Plans covered by insurance or trust arrangements

(1)   There is excluded from article 59 any contract under which—

    (a)   the provider undertakes to secure that sums paid by the customer under the contract will be applied towards a contract of whole life insurance on the life of the customer (or other person for whom the funeral is to be provided), effected and carried out by an authorised person who has permission to effect and carry out such contracts of insurance, for the purpose of providing the funeral; or

    (b)   the provider undertakes to secure that sums paid by the customer under the contract will be held on trust for the purpose of providing the funeral, and that the following requirements are or will be met with respect to the trust—

        (i)   the trust must be established by a written instrument;

        (ii)   more than half of the trustees must be unconnected with the provider;

        (iii)   the trustees must appoint, or have appointed, an independent fund manager who is an authorised person who has permission to carry on an activity of the kind specified by article 37, and who is a person who is unconnected with the provider, to manage the assets of the trust;

        (iv)   annual accounts must be prepared, and audited by a person who is eligible for appointment as a [statutory auditor under Part 42 of the Companies Act 2006], with respect to the assets and liabilities of the trust; and

(v)   the assets and liabilities of the trust must, at least once every three years, be determined, calculated and verified by an actuary who is a Fellow of the Institute of Actuaries or of the Faculty of Actuaries.

(2)   For the purposes of paragraph (1)(b)(ii) and (iii), a person is unconnected with the provider if he is a person other than—

(a)   the provider;

(b)   a member of the same group as the provider;

(c)   a director, other officer or employee of the provider, or of any member of the same group as the provider;

(d)   a partner of the provider;

(e)   a close relative of a person falling within sub-paragraph (a), (c) or (d); or

(f)   an agent of any person falling within sub-paragraphs (a) to (e).

[2096]

NOTES

The heading preceding this article was substituted by the Financial Services and Markets Act 2000 (Regulated Activities) (Amendment) (No 2) Order 2002, SI 2002/1776, art 3(1), (14), as from 21 August 2002.

Para (1): words in square brackets substituted (for the original words "company auditor under section 25 of the Companies Act 1989") by the Companies Act 2006 (Consequential Amendments etc) Order 2008, SI 2008/948, art 3(1), Sch 1, Pt 1, para 1(tt), as from 6 April 2008 (for savings see art 6(4) of the 2008 Order which provides that where by virtue of any transitional provision, a provision of the Companies Act 2006 has effect only (a) on or after a specified date, or (b) in relation to matters occurring or arising on or after a specified date, any amendment substituting or inserting a reference to that provision has effect correspondingly).

[60A   Information society services

Article 59 is subject to the exclusion in article 72A (information society services).]

[2097]

NOTES

Inserted by the Financial Services and Markets Act 2000 (Regulated Activities) (Amendment) (No 2) Order 2002, SI 2002/1776, art 3(1), (15), as from 21 August 2002.

CHAPTER XV
REGULATED MORTGAGE CONTRACTS

The activities

61   Regulated mortgage contracts

(1)   Entering into a regulated mortgage contract as lender is a specified kind of activity.

(2)   Administering a regulated mortgage contract is also a specified kind of activity, where the contract was entered into [by way of business] after the coming into force of this article.

(3)   In this Chapter—

[(a)   a contract is a "regulated mortgage contract" if, at the time it is entered into, the following conditions are met—

(i)   the contract is one under which a person ("the lender") provides credit to an individual or to trustees ("the borrower");

(ii)   the contract provides for the obligation of the borrower to repay to be secured by a first legal mortgage on land (other than timeshare accommodation) in the United Kingdom;

(iii)   at least 40% of that land is used, or is intended to be used, as or in connection with a dwelling by the borrower or (in the case of credit provided to trustees) by an individual who is a beneficiary of the trust, or by a related person;

[but such a contract is not a regulated mortgage contract if it is a regulated home purchase plan;]]

(b)   "administering" a regulated mortgage contract means either or both of—

(i)   notifying the borrower of changes in interest rates or payments due under the contract, or of other matters of which the contract requires him to be notified; and

(ii)   taking any necessary steps for the purposes of collecting or recovering payments due under the contract from the borrower;

but a person is not to be treated as administering a regulated mortgage contract merely because he has, or exercises, a right to take action for the purposes of enforcing the contract (or to require that such action is or is not taken);

(c)   "credit" includes a cash loan, and any other form of financial accommodation.

(4)   For the purposes of [paragraph 3(a)]—

(a)   a "first legal mortgage" means a legal mortgage ranking in priority ahead of all other mortgages (if any) affecting the land in question, where "mortgage" includes charge and (in Scotland) a heritable security;

(b)   the area of any land which comprises a building or other structure containing two or more storeys is to be taken to be the aggregate of the floor areas of each of those storeys;

(c)   "related person", in relation to the borrower or (in the case of credit provided to trustees) a beneficiary of the trust, means—
  (i)   that person's spouse [or civil partner];
  (ii)   a person (whether or not of the opposite sex) whose relationship with that person has the characteristics of the relationship between husband and wife; or
  (iii)   that person's parent, brother, sister, child, grandparent or grandchild; and

(d)   "timeshare accommodation" has the meaning given by section 1 of the Timeshare Act 1992.

[2098]

NOTES
Commencement: 31 October 2004.
Para (2): words in square brackets inserted by the Financial Services and Markets Act 2000 (Regulated Activities) (Amendment) Order 2001, SI 2001/3544, arts 2, 8(a), as from 1 September 2002.
Para (3): sub-para (a) substituted by SI 2001/3544, arts 2, 8(b), as from 1 September 2002; words in square brackets inserted by the Financial Services and Markets Act 2000 (Regulated Activities) (Amendment) (No 2) Order 2006, SI 2006/2383, arts 2, 17, as from 6 November 2006 (for the purposes of enabling applications to be made for (i) a Pt IV permission, or a variation of a Pt IV permission, in relation to activities of the kind specified by arts 25B, 25C, 53B, 53C, 63B or 63F or, so far as relevant to any such activity, art 64 of this Order; or (ii) the Authority's approval under FSMA 2000, s 59 in relation to any of those activities), and as from 6 April 2007 (otherwise) (for transitional provisions and effect see arts 36–40 of, and the Schedule to, the 2006 Order at **[2861]** et seq).
Para (4): words in first pair of square brackets substituted by SI 2001/3544, arts 2, 8(c), as from 1 September 2002; words in second pair of square brackets inserted by the Civil Partnership Act 2004 (Amendments to Subordinate Legislation) Order 2005, SI 2005/2114, art 2(16), Sch 16, Pt 1, para 1(1), (3), as from 5 December 2005.

Exclusions

62   Arranging administration by authorised person

A person who is not an authorised person does not carry on an activity of the kind specified by article 61(2) in relation to a regulated mortgage contract where he—

(a)   arranges for another person, being an authorised person with permission to carry on an activity of that kind, to administer the contract; or

(b)   administers the contract himself during a period of not more than one month beginning with the day on which any such arrangement comes to an end.

[2099]

NOTES
Commencement: 31 October 2004.

63   Administration pursuant to agreement with authorised person

A person who is not an authorised person does not carry on an activity of the kind specified by article 61(2) in relation to a regulated mortgage contract where he administers the contract pursuant to an agreement with an authorised person who has permission to carry on an activity of that kind.

[2100]

NOTES
Commencement: 31 October 2004.

[63A   Other exclusions

Article 61 is also subject to the exclusions in articles 66 (trustees etc), 72 (overseas persons) and 72A (information society services).]

[2101]

NOTES
Commencement: 31 October 2004.
Inserted by the Financial Services and Markets Act 2000 (Regulated Activities) (Amendment) (No 2) Order 2002, SI 2002/1776, art 3(1), (16), as from 21 August 2002; substituted by the Financial Services and Markets Act 2000 (Regulated Activities) (Amendment) (No 1) Order 2003, SI 2003/1475, art 17, as from 31 October 2004 (for transitional provisions see arts 26–29 at **[2700]** et seq).

[CHAPTER 15A
REGULATED HOME REVERSION PLANS

The activities

63B   Entering into and administering regulated home reversion plans

(1)   Entering into a regulated home reversion plan as plan provider is a specified kind of activity.

(2)   Administering a regulated home reversion plan is also a specified kind of activity where the plan was entered into on or after 6th April 2007.

(3)   In this Chapter—
   (a)   a "regulated home reversion plan" is an arrangement comprised in one or more instruments or agreements, in relation to which the following conditions are met at the time it is entered into—
      (i)   the arrangement is one under which a person (the "plan provider") buys all or part of a qualifying interest in land (other than timeshare accommodation) in the United Kingdom from an individual or trustees (the "reversion seller");
      (ii)   the reversion seller (if he is an individual) or an individual who is a beneficiary of the trust (if the reversion seller is a trustee), or a related person, is entitled under the arrangement to occupy at least 40% of the land in question as or in connection with a dwelling, and intends to do so; and
      (iii)   the arrangement specifies one or more qualifying termination events, on the occurrence of which that entitlement will end;
   (b)   "administering" a regulated home reversion plan means any of—
      (i)   notifying the reversion seller of changes in payments due under the plan, or of other matters of which the plan requires him to be notified;
      (ii)   taking any necessary steps for the purposes of making payments to the reversion seller under the plan; and
      (iii)   taking any necessary steps for the purposes of collecting or recovering payments due under the plan from the reversion seller,
but a person is not to be treated as administering a regulated home reversion plan merely because he has, or exercises, a right to take action for the purposes of enforcing the plan (or to require that such action is or is not taken).

(4)   For the purposes of paragraph (3)—
   (a)   the reference to a "qualifying interest" in land—
      (i)   in relation to land in England or Wales, is to an estate in fee simple absolute or a term of years absolute, whether subsisting at law or in equity;
      (ii)   in relation to land in Scotland, is to the interest of an owner in land or the tenant's right over or interest in a property subject to a lease;
      (iii)   in relation to land in Northern Ireland, is to any freehold estate or any leasehold estate, whether subsisting at law or in equity;
   (b)   "timeshare accommodation" has the meaning given by section 1 of the Timeshare Act 1992;
   (c)   "related person" in relation to the reversion seller or, where the reversion seller is a trustee, a beneficiary of the trust, means—
      (i)   that person's spouse or civil partner;
      (ii)   a person (whether or not of the opposite sex) whose relationship with that person has the characteristics of the relationship between husband and wife; or
      (iii)   that person's parent, brother, sister, child, grandparent or grandchild; and
   (d)   "qualifying termination event", in relation to a person's entitlement to occupy land, means—
      (i)   the person becomes a resident of a care home;
      (ii)   the person dies;
      (iii)   the end of a specified period of at least twenty years beginning with the day on which the reversion seller entered into the arrangement.

(5)   For the purposes of paragraph (3)(a)(ii), the area of any land which comprises a building or other structure containing two or more storeys is to be taken to be the aggregate of the floor areas of each of those storeys.

(6)   For the purposes of the definition of "qualifying termination event" in paragraph (4), "care home"—
   (a)   in relation to England and Wales, has the meaning given by section 3 of the Care Standards Act 2000;
   (b)   in relation to Scotland, means accommodation provided by a "care home" within the meaning of section 2(3)of the Regulation of Care (Scotland) Act 2001;
   (c)   in relation to Northern Ireland, means—

(i) a residential care home within the meaning of article 10 of the Health and Personal Social Services (Quality, Improvement and Regulation) (Northern Ireland) Order 2003; or

(ii) a nursing home within the meaning of article 11 of that Order.

(7) In this Order—
  (a) references to entering into a regulated home reversion plan as plan provider include acquiring any obligations or rights (including his interest in land) of the plan provider, under such a plan; but
  (b) in relation to a person who acquires any such obligations or rights, an activity is a specified kind of activity for the purposes of articles 25B(1)(b) and 53B(b)(ii) and paragraph (2) only if the plan was entered into by the plan provider (rather than the obligations or rights acquired) on or after 6th April 2007.

(8) Accordingly, references in this Order to a plan provider, other than in paragraph (7), include a person who acquires any such obligations or rights.]

[2101A]

NOTES
Commencement: 6 November 2006 (certain purposes); 6 April 2007 (otherwise) (see below).
Chapters 15A, 15B (arts 63B–63I) inserted by the Financial Services and Markets Act 2000 (Regulated Activities) (Amendment) (No 2) Order 2006, SI 2006/2383, arts 2, 18, as from 6 November 2006 (for the purposes of enabling applications to be made for (i) a Pt IV permission, or a variation of a Pt IV permission, in relation to activities of the kind specified by arts 25B, 25C, 53B, 53C, 63B or 63F or, so far as relevant to any such activity, art 64 of this Order; or (ii) the Authority's approval under FSMA 2000, s 59 in relation to any of those activities), and as from 6 April 2007 (otherwise) (for transitional provisions and effect see arts 36–40 of, and the Schedule to, the 2006 Order at **[2861]** et seq).

[Exclusions

63C Arranging administration by authorised person

A person who is not an authorised person does not carry on an activity of the kind specified by article 63B(2) in relation to a regulated home reversion plan where he—
  (a) arranges for another person, being an authorised person with permission to carry on an activity of that kind, to administer the plan; or
  (b) administers the plan himself during a period of not more than one month beginning with the day on which any such arrangement comes to an end.]

[2101B]

NOTES
Commencement: 6 November 2006 (certain purposes); 6 April 2007 (otherwise).
Inserted as noted to art 63B at **[2101A]**.

[63D Administration pursuant to agreement with authorised person

A person who is not an authorised person does not carry on an activity of the kind specified by article 63B(2) in relation to a regulated home reversion plan where he administers the plan pursuant to an agreement with an authorised person who has permission to carry on an activity of that kind.]

[2101C]

NOTES
Commencement: 6 November 2006 (certain purposes); 6 April 2007 (otherwise).
Inserted as noted to art 63B at **[2101A]**.

[63E Other exclusions

Article 63B is also subject to the exclusions in articles 66 (trustees etc), 72 (overseas persons) and 72A (information society services).]

[2101D]

NOTES
Commencement: 6 November 2006 (certain purposes); 6 April 2007 (otherwise).
Inserted as noted to art 63B at **[2101A]**.

[CHAPTER 15B
REGULATED HOME PURCHASE PLANS

The activities

63F Entering into and administering regulated home purchase plans

(1) Entering into a regulated home purchase plan as home purchase provider is a specified kind of activity.

(2)   Administering a regulated home purchase plan is also a specified kind of activity where the plan was entered into by way of business on or after 6th April 2007.

(3)   In this Chapter—
    (a)   a "regulated home purchase plan" is an arrangement comprised in one or more instruments or agreements, in relation to which the following conditions are met at the time it is entered into—
        (i)   the arrangement is one under which a person (the "home purchase provider") buys a qualifying interest or an undivided share of a qualifying interest in land (other than timeshare accommodation) in the United Kingdom;
        (ii)   where an undivided share of a qualifying interest in land is bought, the interest is held on trust for the home purchase provider and the individual or trustees mentioned in paragraph (iii) as beneficial tenants in common;
        (iii)   the arrangement provides for the obligation of an individual or trustees (the "home purchaser") to buy the interest bought by the home purchase provider over the course of or at the end of a specified period; and
        (iv)   the home purchaser (if he is an individual) or an individual who is a beneficiary of the trust (if the home purchaser is a trustee), or a related person, is entitled under the arrangement to occupy at least 40% of the land in question as or in connection with a dwelling during that period, and intends to do so;
    (b)   "administering" a regulated home purchase plan means either or both of—
        (i)   notifying the home purchaser of changes in payments due under the plan, or of other matters of which the plan requires him to be notified; and
        (ii)   taking any necessary steps for the purposes of collecting or recovering payments due under the plan from the home purchaser;
but a person is not to be treated as administering a regulated home purchase plan merely because he has, or exercises, a right to take action for the purposes of enforcing the plan or to require that such action is or is not taken.

(4)   Article 63B(4)(a) to (c) applies for the purposes of paragraph (3)(a) with references to the "reversion seller" being read as references to the "home purchaser".

(5)   Article 63B(5) applies for the purposes of paragraph (3)(a)(iv) with the reference to "paragraph (3)(a)(ii)" being read as a reference to "paragraph (3)(a)(iv)".]

[2101E]

NOTES
Commencement: 6 November 2006 (certain purposes); 6 April 2007 (otherwise).
Inserted as noted to art 63B at **[2101A]**.

[Exclusions

63G   Arranging administration by authorised person

A person who is not an authorised person does not carry on an activity of the kind specified by article 63F(2) in relation to a regulated home purchase plan where he—
    (a)   arranges for another person, being an authorised person with permission to carry on an activity of that kind, to administer the plan; or
    (b)   administers the plan himself during a period of not more than one month beginning with the day on which any such arrangement comes to an end.]

[2101F]

NOTES
Commencement: 6 November 2006 (certain purposes); 6 April 2007 (otherwise).
Inserted as noted to art 63B at **[2101A]**.

[63H   Administration pursuant to agreement with authorised person

A person who is not an authorised person does not carry on an activity of the kind specified by article 63F(2) in relation to a regulated home purchase plan where he administers the plan pursuant to an agreement with an authorised person who has permission to carry on an activity of that kind.]

[2101G]

NOTES
Commencement: 6 November 2006 (certain purposes); 6 April 2007 (otherwise).
Inserted as noted to art 63B at **[2101A]**.

[63I   Other exclusions

Article 63F is also subject to the exclusions in articles 66 (trustees etc), 72 (overseas persons) and 72A (information society services).]

[2101H]

NOTES
Commencement: 6 November 2006 (certain purposes); 6 April 2007 (otherwise).
Inserted as noted to art 63B at **[2101A]**.

CHAPTER XVI
AGREEING TO CARRY ON ACTIVITIES

The activity

64   Agreeing to carry on specified kinds of activity

Agreeing to carry on an activity of the kind specified by any other provision of this Part (other than article 5, [9B,] 10, [25D,] 51 or 52) is a specified kind of activity.

[2102]

NOTES
First figure in square brackets inserted by the Financial Services and Markets Act 2000 (Regulated Activities) (Amendment) Order 2002, SI 2002/682, art 5, as from 27 April 2002, subject to transitional provisions in relation to persons issuing electronic money immediately before that date contained in art 9 at **[2667]**; second figure in square brackets inserted by the Financial Services and Markets Act 2000 (Regulated Activities) (Amendment No 3) Order 2006, SI 2006/3384, arts 2, 18, as from 1 April 2007 (for the purposes of enabling applications to be made for (i) a Pt IV permission, (ii) a variation of a Pt IV permission, and (iii) the Authority's approval under s 59 of the 2000 Act, in relation to an activity of the kind specified by art 25D of this Order, or in relation to an investment of the kind specified by arts 83, 84 or 85 of this Order), and as from 1 November 2007 (otherwise).
See also the Financial Services and Markets Act 2000 (Carrying on Regulated Activities by Way of Business) Order 2001, SI 2001/1177, arts 3, 3A, 3B, 3C at **[2208]**, **[2209]**, **[2209A]**, **[2209B]**.

[Exclusions

65   Overseas persons etc

Article 64 is subject to the exclusions in articles 72 (overseas persons) and 72A (information society services).]

[2103]

NOTES
Substituted, together with the preceding heading, by the Financial Services and Markets Act 2000 (Regulated Activities) (Amendment) (No 2) Order 2002, SI 2002/1776, art 3(1), (17), as from 21 August 2002.

CHAPTER XVII
EXCLUSIONS APPLYING TO SEVERAL SPECIFIED KINDS OF ACTIVITY

66   Trustees, nominees and personal representatives

(1)   A person ("X") does not carry on an activity of the kind specified by article 14 where he enters into a transaction as bare trustee or, in Scotland, as nominee for another person ("Y") and—
  (a)   X is acting on Y's instructions; and
  (b)   X does not hold himself out as providing a service of buying and selling securities or contractually based investments.

(2)   Subject to paragraph (7), there are excluded from [articles 25(1) and (2)[, 25A(1) and (2), 25B(1) and (2) and 25C(1) and (2)]] arrangements made by a person acting as trustee or personal representative for or with a view to a transaction which is or is to be entered into—
  (a)   by that person and a fellow trustee or personal representative (acting in their capacity as such); or
  (b)   by a beneficiary under the trust, will or intestacy.

(3)   Subject to paragraph (7), there is excluded from article 37 any activity carried on by a person acting as trustee or personal representative, unless—
  (a)   he holds himself out as providing a service comprising an activity of the kind specified by article 37; or
  (b)   the assets in question are held for the purposes of an occupational pension scheme, and, by virtue of article 4 of the Financial Services and Markets Act 2000 (Carrying on Regulated Activities by Way of Business) Order 2001, he is to be treated as carrying on that activity by way of business.

[(3A)   Subject to paragraph (7), there is excluded from article 39A any activity carried on by a person acting as trustee or personal representative, unless he holds himself out as providing a service comprising an activity of the kind specified by article 39A.]

(4)   Subject to paragraph (7), there is excluded from article 40 any activity carried on by a person acting as trustee or personal representative, unless he holds himself out as providing a service comprising an activity of the kind specified by article 40.

[(4A)   There is excluded from article 40 any activity carried on by a person acting as trustee which consists of arranging for one or more other persons to safeguard and administer trust assets where—

    (a)   that other person is a qualifying custodian; or

    (b)   that safeguarding and administration is also arranged by a qualifying custodian.

In this paragraph, "qualifying custodian" has the meaning given by article 41(2).]

(5)   A person does not, by sending or causing to be sent a dematerialised instruction (within the meaning of article 45), carry on an activity of the kind specified by that article if the instruction relates to an investment which that person holds as trustee or personal representative.

(6)   Subject to paragraph (7), there is excluded from [articles 53[, 53A, 53B and 53C]] the giving of advice by a person acting as trustee or personal representative where he gives the advice to—

    (a)   a fellow trustee or personal representative for the purposes of the trust or the estate; or

    (b)   a beneficiary under the trust, will or intestacy concerning his interest in the trust fund or estate.

[(6A)   Subject to paragraph (7), a person acting as trustee or personal representative does not carry on an activity of the kind specified by article 61(1) or (2) where the borrower under the regulated mortgage contract in question is a beneficiary under the trust, will or intestacy.]

[(6B)   Subject to paragraph (7), a person acting as trustee or personal representative does not carry on an activity of the kind specified by article 63B(1) or (2) where the reversion seller under the regulated home reversion plan in question is a beneficiary under the trust, will or intestacy.

(6C)   Subject to paragraph (7), a person acting as trustee or personal representative does not carry on an activity of the kind specified by article 63F(1) or (2) where the home purchaser under the regulated home purchase plan in question is a beneficiary under the trust, will or intestacy.]

(7)   Paragraphs (2), (3)[, (3A)], [(4), (6)[, (6A), (6B) and (6C)]] do not apply if the person carrying on the activity is remunerated for what he does in addition to any remuneration he receives as trustee or personal representative, and for these purposes a person is not to be regarded as receiving additional remuneration merely because his remuneration is calculated by reference to time spent.

[(8)   This article is subject to article 4(4A).]

[2104]

NOTES

Para (2): words in first (outer) pair of square brackets substituted by the Financial Services and Markets Act 2000 (Regulated Activities) (Amendment) (No 1) Order 2003, SI 2003/1475, art 18(a), as from 31 October 2004 (for transitional provisions see arts 26–29 at **[2700]** et seq); words in second (inner) pair of square brackets substituted by the Financial Services and Markets Act 2000 (Regulated Activities) (Amendment) (No 2) Order 2006, SI 2006/2383, arts 2, 19(a), as from 6 November 2006 (for the purposes of enabling applications to be made for (i) a Pt IV permission, or a variation of a Pt IV permission, in relation to activities of the kind specified by arts 25B, 25C, 53B, 53C, 63B or 63F or, so far as relevant to any such activity, art 64 of this Order; or (ii) the Authority's approval under FSMA 2000, s 59 in relation to any of those activities), and as from 6 April 2007 (otherwise) (for transitional provisions and effect see arts 36–40 of, and the Schedule to, the 2006 Order at **[2861]** et seq).

Para (3A): inserted by the Financial Services and Markets Act 2000 (Regulated Activities) (Amendment) (No 2) Order 2003, SI 2003/1476, art 10(1)(a), as from 31 October 2004 (in so far as relating to contracts of long-term care insurance), and as from 14 January 2005 (otherwise); for transitional provisions see arts 22–27 of that Order at **[2706]** et seq.

Para (4A): inserted by the Financial Services and Markets Act 2000 (Regulated Activities) (Amendment) Order 2005, SI 2005/593, art 2(4), as from 6 April 2005.

Para (6): words in first (outer) pair of square brackets substituted by SI 2003/1475, art 18(b), as from 31 October 2004 (for transitional provisions see arts 26–29 at **[2700]** et seq); words in second (inner) pair of square brackets substituted by SI 2006/2383, arts 2, 19(b), as from 6 November 2006 (certain purposes), and as from 6 April 2007 (otherwise) (for purposes, transitional provisions, and effect, see the para (2) note above).

Para (6A): inserted by SI 2003/1475, art 18(c), as from 31 October 2004; for transitional provisions see arts 26–29 at **[2700]** et seq.

Paras (6B), (6C): inserted by SI 2006/2383, arts 2, 19(c), as from 6 November 2006 (certain purposes), and as from 6 April 2007 (otherwise) (for purposes, transitional provisions, and effect, see the para (2) note above).

Para (7): figure in first pair of square brackets inserted by SI 2003/1476, art 10(1)(b), as from 31 October 2004 (in so far as relating to contracts of long-term care insurance), and as from 14 January 2005 (otherwise), for transitional provisions see arts 22–27 of that Order at **[2706]** et seq; words in second (outer) pair of square brackets substituted by SI 2003/1475, art 18(d), as from 31 October 2004, for transitional provisions see arts 26–29 at **[2700]** et seq; words in third (inner) pair of square brackets substituted by SI 2006/2383, arts 2, 19(d), as from 6 November 2006 (certain purposes), and as from 6 April 2007 (otherwise) (for purposes, transitional provisions, and effect, see the para (2) note above).

Para (8): added by the Financial Services and Markets Act 2000 (Regulated Activities) (Amendment No 3) Order 2006, SI 2006/3384, arts 2, 19, as from 1 April 2007 (for the purposes of enabling applications to be made for (i) a Pt IV permission, (ii) a variation of a Pt IV permission, and (iii) the Authority's approval under s 59 of the 2000 Act, in relation to an activity of the kind specified by art 25D of this Order, or in relation to an investment of the kind specified by arts 83, 84 or 85 of this Order), and as from 1 November 2007 (otherwise).

67 Activities carried on in the course of a profession or non-investment business

(1)   There is excluded from articles 21, 25(1) and (2)[, 25A], [25B, 25C,] [39A, 40], [53 [, 53A, 53B and 53C]] any activity which

    (a)   is carried on in the course of carrying on any profession or business which does not otherwise consist of [the carrying on of regulated activities in the United Kingdom]; and

    (b)   may reasonably be regarded as a necessary part of other services provided in the course of that profession or business.

(2)   But the exclusion in paragraph (1) does not apply if the activity in question is remunerated separately from the other services.

[(3)   This article is subject to article 4(4) and (4A).]

[2105]

NOTES

Para (1) is amended as follows:

Figure in first pair of square brackets inserted, and words in fourth (outer) pair of square brackets substituted, by the Financial Services and Markets Act 2000 (Regulated Activities) (Amendment) (No 1) Order 2003, SI 2003/1475, art 19, as from 31 October 2004, for transitional provisions see arts 26–29 at **[2700]** et seq.

Figures in second pair of square brackets inserted by the Financial Services and Markets Act 2000 (Regulated Activities) (Amendment) (No 2) Order 2006, SI 2006/2383, arts 2, 20(a), as from 6 November 2006 (for the purposes of enabling applications to be made for (i) a Pt IV permission, or a variation of a Pt IV permission, in relation to activities of the kind specified by arts 25B, 25C, 53B, 53C, 63B or 63F or, so far as relevant to any such activity, art 64 of this Order; or (ii) the Authority's approval under FSMA 2000, s 59 in relation to any of those activities), and as from 6 April 2007 (otherwise) (for transitional provisions and effect see arts 36–40 of, and the Schedule to, the 2006 Order at **[2861]** et seq).

Figures in third pair of square brackets substituted by the Financial Services and Markets Act 2000 (Regulated Activities) (Amendment) (No 2) Order 2003, SI 2003/1476, art 10(2), as from 31 October 2004 (in so far as relating to contracts of long-term care insurance), and as from 14 January 2005 (otherwise), for transitional provisions see arts 22–27 of that Order at **[2706]** et seq.

Words in fifth (inner) pair of square brackets substituted by SI 2006/2383, arts 2, 20(b), as from 6 November 2006 (certain purposes), and as from 6 April 2007 (otherwise) (for purposes, transitional provisions, and effect, see the note above).

Words in square brackets in sub-para (a) substituted by the Financial Services and Markets Act 2000 (Regulated Activities) (Amendment) Order 2001, SI 2001/3544, arts 2, 9, as from 1 December 2001.

Para (3): added by the Financial Services and Markets Act 2000 (Regulated Activities) (Amendment No 3) Order 2006, SI 2006/3384, arts 2, 20, as from 1 April 2007 (for the purposes of enabling applications to be made for (i) a Pt IV permission, (ii) a variation of a Pt IV permission, and (iii) the Authority's approval under s 59 of the 2000 Act, in relation to an activity of the kind specified by art 25D of this Order, or in relation to an investment of the kind specified by arts 83, 84 or 85 of this Order), and as from 1 November 2007 (otherwise).

68 Activities carried on in connection with the sale of goods or supply of services

(1)   Subject to paragraphs (9), (10) and (11), this article concerns certain activities carried on for the purposes of or in connection with the sale of goods or supply of services by a supplier to a customer, where—

"supplier" means a person whose main business is to sell goods or supply services and not to carry on any activities of the kind specified by any of articles 14, 21, 25, 37[, 39A], 40, 45, 51, 52 and 53 and, where the supplier is a member of a group, also means any other member of that group; and

"customer" means a person, other than an individual, to whom a supplier sells goods or supplies services, or agrees to do so, and, where the customer is a member of a group, also means any other member of that group;

and in this article "related sale or supply" means a sale of goods or supply of services to the customer otherwise than by the supplier, but for or in connection with the same purpose as the sale or supply mentioned above.

(2)   There is excluded from article 14 any transaction entered into by a supplier with a customer, if the transaction is entered into for the purposes of or in connection with the sale of goods or supply of services, or a related sale or supply.

(3)   There is excluded from article 21 any transaction entered into [by a supplier as agent for a customer], if the transaction is entered into for the purposes of or in connection with the sale of goods or supply of services, or a related sale or supply, and provided that—

    (a)   where the investment to which the transaction relates is a security, the supplier does not hold himself out (other than to the customer) as engaging in the business of buying securities of the kind to which the transaction relates with a view to selling them, and does not regularly solicit members of the public for the purpose of inducing them (as principals or agents) to buy, sell, subscribe for or underwrite securities;

    (b)   where the investment to which the transaction relates is a contractually based investment, the supplier enters into the transaction—

        (i)   with or through an authorised person, or an exempt person acting in the course of a business comprising a regulated activity in relation to which he is exempt; or

(ii)   through an office outside the United Kingdom maintained by a party to the transaction, and with or through a person whose head office is situated outside the United Kingdom and whose ordinary business involves him in carrying on activities of the kind specified by any of articles 14, 21, 25, 37, 40, 45, 51, 52 and 53 or, so far as relevant to any of those articles, article 64, or would do so apart from any exclusion from any of those articles made by this Order.

(4)   In paragraph (3)(a), "members of the public" has the meaning given by article 15(2), references to "A" being read as references to the supplier.

(5)   There are excluded from article 25(1) and (2) arrangements made by a supplier for, or with a view to, a transaction which is or is to be entered into by a customer for the purposes of or in connection with the sale of goods or supply of services, or a related sale or supply.

(6)   There is excluded from article 37 any activity carried on by a supplier where the assets in question—
   (a)   are those of a customer; and
   (b)   are managed for the purposes of or in connection with the sale of goods or supply of services, or a related sale or supply.

(7)   There is excluded from article 40 any activity carried on by a supplier where the assets in question are or are to be safeguarded and administered for the purposes of or in connection with the sale of goods or supply of services, or a related sale or supply.

(8)   There is excluded from article 53 the giving of advice by a supplier to a customer for the purposes of or in connection with the sale of goods or supply of services, or a related sale or supply, or to a person with whom the customer proposes to enter into a transaction for the purposes of or in connection with such a sale or supply or related sale or supply.

(9)   Paragraphs (2), (3) and (5) do not apply in the case of a transaction for the sale or purchase of a [contract of insurance], an investment of the kind specified by article 81, or an investment of the kind specified by article 89 so far as relevant to such a contract or such an investment.

(10)   Paragraph (6) does not apply where the assets managed consist of qualifying contracts of insurance, investments of the kind specified by article 81, or investments of the kind specified by article 89 so far as relevant to such contracts or such investments.

(11)   Paragraph (8) does not apply in the case of advice in relation to an investment which is a [contract of insurance], is of the kind specified by article 81, or is of the kind specified by article 89 so far as relevant to such a contract or such an investment.

[(12)   This article is subject to article 4(4).]

[2106]

NOTES

Para (1): figure in square brackets in definition "supplier" inserted by the Financial Services and Markets Act 2000 (Regulated Activities) (Amendment) (No 2) Order 2003, SI 2003/1476, art 10(3)(a), as from 31 October 2004 (in so far as relating to contracts of long-term care insurance), and as from 14 January 2005 (otherwise); for transitional provisions see arts 22–27 of that Order at **[2706]** et seq.

Para (3): words in square brackets substituted by the Financial Services and Markets Act 2000 (Regulated Activities) (Amendment) Order 2001, SI 2001/3544, arts 2, 10, as from 1 December 2001.

Paras (9), (11): words in square brackets substituted by SI 2003/1476, art 10(3)(b), (c), as from 31 October 2004 (in so far as relating to contracts of long-term care insurance), and as from 14 January 2005 (otherwise); for transitional provisions see arts 22–27 of that Order at **[2706]** et seq.

Para (12): added by the Financial Services and Markets Act 2000 (Regulated Activities) (Amendment No 3) Order 2006, SI 2006/3384, arts 2, 21, as from 1 April 2007 (for the purposes of enabling applications to be made for (i) a Pt IV permission, (ii) a variation of a Pt IV permission, and (iii) the Authority's approval under s 59 of the 2000 Act, in relation to an activity of the kind specified by art 25D of this Order, or in relation to an investment of the kind specified by arts 83, 84 or 85 of this Order), and as from 1 November 2007 (otherwise).

---

69   Groups and joint enterprises

(1)   There is excluded from article 14 any transaction into which a person enters as principal with another person if that other person is also acting as principal and—
   (a)   they are members of the same group; or
   (b)   they are, or propose to become, participators in a joint enterprise and the transaction is entered into for the purposes of or in connection with that enterprise.

(2)   There is excluded from article 21 any transaction into which a person enters as agent for another person if that other person is acting as principal, and the condition in paragraph (1)(a) or (b) is met, provided that—
   (a)   where the investment to which the transaction relates is a security, the agent does not hold himself out (other than to members of the same group or persons who are or propose to become participators with him in a joint enterprise) as engaging in the business of buying securities of the kind to which the transaction relates with a view to

selling them, and does not regularly solicit members of the public for the purpose of inducing them (as principals or agents) to buy, sell, subscribe for or underwrite securities;

    (b)   where the investment to which the transaction relates is a contractually based investment, the agent enters into the transaction—

        (i)   with or through an authorised person, or an exempt person acting in the course of a business comprising a regulated activity in relation to which he is exempt; or

        (ii) through an office outside the United Kingdom maintained by a party to the transaction, and with or through a person whose head office is situated outside the United Kingdom and whose ordinary business involves him in carrying on activities of the kind specified by any of articles 14, 21, 25, 37, 40, 45, 51, 52 and 53 or, so far as relevant to any of those articles, article 64, or would do so apart from any exclusion from any of those articles made by this Order.

(3)   In paragraph (2)(a), "members of the public" has the meaning given by article 15(2), references to "A" being read as references to the agent.

(4)   There are excluded from article 25(1) and (2) arrangements made by a person if—

    (a)   he is a member of a group and the arrangements in question are for, or with a view to, a transaction which is or is to be entered into, as principal, by another member of the same group; or

    (b)   he is or proposes to become a participator in a joint enterprise, and the arrangements in question are for, or with a view to, a transaction which is or is to be entered into, as principal, by another person who is or proposes to become a participator in that enterprise, for the purposes of or in connection with that enterprise.

(5)   There is excluded from article 37 any activity carried on by a person if—

    (a)   he is a member of a group and the assets in question belong to another member of the same group; or

    (b)   he is or proposes to become a participator in a joint enterprise with the person to whom the assets belong, and the assets are managed for the purposes of or in connection with that enterprise.

(6)   There is excluded from article 40 any activity carried on by a person if—

    (a)   he is a member of a group and the assets in question belong to another member of the same group; or

    (b)   he is or proposes to become a participator in a joint enterprise, and the assets in question—

        (i)   belong to another person who is or proposes to become a participator in that joint enterprise; and

        (ii) are or are to be safeguarded and administered for the purposes of or in connection with that enterprise.

(7)   A person who is a member of a group does not carry on an activity of the kind specified by article 45 where he sends a dematerialised instruction, or causes one to be sent, on behalf of another member of the same group, if the investment to which the instruction relates is one in respect of which a member of the same group is registered as holder in the appropriate register of securities, or will be so registered as a result of the instruction.

(8)   In paragraph (7), "dematerialised instruction" and "register of securities" have the meaning given by regulation 3 of the Uncertificated Securities Regulations [2001].

(9)   There is excluded from article 53 the giving of advice by a person if—

    (a)   he is a member of a group and gives the advice in question to another member of the same group; or

    (b)   he is, or proposes to become, a participator in a joint enterprise and the advice in question is given to another person who is, or proposes to become, a participator in that enterprise for the purposes of or in connection with that enterprise.

[(10) Paragraph (2) does not apply to a transaction for the sale or purchase of a contract of insurance.

(11) Paragraph (4) does not apply to arrangements for, or with a view to, a transaction for the sale or purchase of a contract of insurance.

(12) Paragraph (9) does not apply where the advice relates to a transaction for the sale or purchase of a contract of insurance.]

[(13) This article is subject to article 4(4).]

[2107]

NOTES
  Para (8): date in square brackets substituted by the Financial Services and Markets Act 2000 (Regulated Activities) (Amendment) Order 2002, SI 2002/682, art 13(4), as from 27 April 2002.

Paras (10)–(12): added by the Financial Services and Markets Act 2000 (Regulated Activities) (Amendment) (No 2) Order 2003, SI 2003/1476, art 10(4), as from 31 October 2004 (in so far as relating to contracts of long-term care insurance), and as from 14 January 2005 (otherwise); for transitional provisions see arts 22–27 of that Order at **[2706]** et seq.

Para (13): added by the Financial Services and Markets Act 2000 (Regulated Activities) (Amendment No 3) Order 2006, SI 2006/3384, arts 2, 22, as from 1 April 2007 (for the purposes of enabling applications to be made for (i) a Pt IV permission, (ii) a variation of a Pt IV permission, and (iii) the Authority's approval under s 59 of the 2000 Act, in relation to an activity of the kind specified by art 25D of this Order, or in relation to an investment of the kind specified by arts 83, 84 or 85 of this Order), and as from 1 November 2007 (otherwise).

70   Activities carried on in connection with the sale of a body corporate

(1)   A person does not carry on an activity of the kind specified by article 14 by entering as principal into a transaction if—

   (a)   the transaction is one to acquire or dispose of shares in a body corporate other than an open-ended investment company, or is entered into for the purposes of such an acquisition or disposal; and

   (b)   either—

      (i)   the conditions set out in paragraph (2) are met; or

      (ii)   those conditions are not met, but the object of the transaction may nevertheless reasonably be regarded as being the acquisition of day to day control of the affairs of the body corporate.

(2)   The conditions mentioned in paragraph (1)(b) are that—

   (a)   the shares consist of or include 50 per cent or more of the voting shares in the body corporate; or

   (b)   the shares, together with any already held by the person acquiring them, consist of or include at least that percentage of such shares; and

   (c)   in either case, the acquisition or disposal is between parties each of whom is a body corporate, a partnership, a single individual or a group of connected individuals.

(3)   In paragraph (2)(c), "a group of connected individuals" means—

   (a)   in relation to a party disposing of shares in a body corporate, a single group of persons each of whom is—

      (i)   a director or manager of the body corporate;

      (ii)   a close relative of any such director or manager;

      (iii)   a person acting as trustee for any person falling within paragraph (i) or (ii); and

   (b)   in relation to a party acquiring shares in a body corporate, a single group of persons each of whom is—

      (i)   a person who is or is to be a director or manager of the body corporate;

      (ii)   a close relative of any such person; or

      (iii)   a person acting as trustee for any person falling within paragraph (i) or (ii).

(4)   A person does not carry on an activity of the kind specified by article 21 by entering as agent into a transaction of the kind described in paragraph (1).

(5)   There are excluded from article 25(1) and (2) arrangements made for, or with a view to, a transaction of the kind described in paragraph (1).

(6)   There is excluded from article 53 the giving of advice in connection with a transaction (or proposed transaction) of the kind described in paragraph (1).

[(7)   Paragraphs (4), (5) and (6) do not apply in the case of a transaction for the sale or purchase of a contract of insurance.]

[(8)   This article is subject to article 4(4).]

[2108]

NOTES

Para (7): added by the Financial Services and Markets Act 2000 (Regulated Activities) (Amendment) (No 2) Order 2003, SI 2003/1476, art 10(5), as from 31 October 2004 (in so far as relating to contracts of long-term care insurance), and as from 14 January 2005 (otherwise); for transitional provisions see arts 22–27 of that Order at **[2706]** et seq.

Para (8): added by the Financial Services and Markets Act 2000 (Regulated Activities) (Amendment No 3) Order 2006, SI 2006/3384, arts 2, 23, as from 1 April 2007 (for the purposes of enabling applications to be made for (i) a Pt IV permission, (ii) a variation of a Pt IV permission, and (iii) the Authority's approval under s 59 of the 2000 Act, in relation to an activity of the kind specified by art 25D of this Order, or in relation to an investment of the kind specified by arts 83, 84 or 85 of this Order), and as from 1 November 2007 (otherwise).

71   Activities carried on in connection with employee share schemes

(1)   A person ("C"), a member of the same group as C or a relevant trustee does not carry on an activity of the kind specified by article 14 by entering as principal into a transaction the purpose of which is to enable or facilitate—

(a) transactions in shares in, or debentures issued by, C between, or for the benefit of, any of the persons mentioned in paragraph (2); or

(b) the holding of such shares or debentures by, or for the benefit of, such persons.

(2) The persons referred to in paragraph (1) are—

(a) the bona fide employees or former employees of C or of another member of the same group as C;

(b) the wives, husbands, widows, widowers, [civil partners, surviving civil partners,] or children or step-children under the age of eighteen of such employees or former employees.

(3) C, a member of the same group as C or a relevant trustee does not carry on an activity of the kind specified by article 21 by entering as agent into a transaction of the kind described in paragraph (1).

(4) There are excluded from article 25(1) or (2) arrangements made by C, a member of the same group as C or a relevant trustee if the arrangements in question are for, or with a view to, a transaction of the kind described in paragraph (1).

(5) There is excluded from article 40 any activity if the assets in question are, or are to be, safeguarded and administered by C, a member of the same group as C or a relevant trustee for the purpose of enabling or facilitating transactions of the kind described in paragraph (1).

(6) In this article—

(a) "shares" and "debentures" include—

(i) any investment of the kind specified by article 76 or 77;

(ii) any investment of the kind specified by article 79 or 80 so far as relevant to articles 76 and 77; and

(iii) any investment of the kind specified by article 89 so far as relevant to investments of the kind mentioned in paragraph (i) or (ii);

(b) "relevant trustee" means a person who, in pursuance of the arrangements made for the purpose mentioned in paragraph (1), holds, as trustee, shares in or debentures issued by C.

[2109]

NOTES

Para (2): words in square brackets in sub-para (b) inserted by the Civil Partnership Act 2004 (Amendments to Subordinate Legislation) Order 2005, SI 2005/2114, art 2(16), Sch 16, Pt 1, para 1(1), (4), as from 5 December 2005.

Step-children, etc: as to the meaning of this and related expressions, see the Civil Partnership Act 2004, s 246 (as applied to this Order by the Civil Partnership Act 2004 (Relationships Arising Through Civil Partnership) Order 2005, SI 2005/3137, art 3, Schedule).

72 Overseas persons

(1) An overseas person does not carry on an activity of the kind specified by article 14 [or 25D] by—

(a) entering into a transaction as principal with or though an authorised person, or an exempt person acting in the course of a business comprising a regulated activity in relation to which he is exempt; or

(b) entering into a transaction as principal with a person in the United Kingdom, if the transaction is the result of a legitimate approach.

(2) An overseas person does not carry on an activity of the kind specified by article 21 [or 25D] by—

(a) entering into a transaction as agent for any person with or through an authorised person or an exempt person acting in the course of a business comprising a regulated activity in relation to which he is exempt; or

(b) entering into a transaction with another party ("X") as agent for any person ("Y"), other than with or through an authorised person or such an exempt person, unless—

(i) either X or Y is in the United Kingdom; and

(ii) the transaction is the result of an approach (other than a legitimate approach) made by or on behalf of, or to, whichever of X or Y is in the United Kingdom.

(3) There are excluded from article 25(1) [or 25D] arrangements made by an overseas person with an authorised person, or an exempt person acting in the course of a business comprising a regulated activity in relation to which he is exempt.

(4) There are excluded from article 25(2) [or 25D] arrangements made by an overseas person with a view to transactions which are, as respects transactions in the United Kingdom, confined to—

(a) transactions entered into by authorised persons as principal or agent; and

(b) transactions entered into by exempt persons, as principal or agent, in the course of business comprising regulated activities in relation to which they are exempt.

(5)   There is excluded from article 53 the giving of advice by an overseas person as a result of a legitimate approach.

[(5A)   An overseas person does not carry on an activity of the kind specified by article 25A(1)(a), 25B(1)(a) or 25C(1)(a) if each person who may be contemplating entering into the relevant type of agreement in the relevant capacity is non-resident.

(5B)   There are excluded from articles 25A(1)(b), 25B(1)(b) and 25C(1)(b) arrangements made by an overseas person to vary the terms of a qualifying agreement.

(5C)   There are excluded from articles 25A(2), 25B(2) and 25C(2), arrangements made by an overseas person which are made solely with a view to non-resident persons who participate in those arrangements entering, in the relevant capacity, into the relevant type of agreement.

(5D)   An overseas person does not carry on an activity of the kind specified in article 61(1), 63B(1) or 63F(1) by entering into a qualifying agreement.

(5E)   An overseas person does not carry on an activity of the kind specified in article 61(2), 63B(2) or 63F(2) where he administers a qualifying agreement.

(5F)   In paragraphs (5A) to (5E)—
    (a)   "non-resident" means not normally resident in the United Kingdom;
    (b)   "qualifying agreement" means—
        (i)   in relation to articles 25A and 61, a regulated mortgage contract where the borrower (or each borrower) is non-resident when he enters into it;
        (ii)   in relation to articles 25B and 63B, a regulated home reversion plan where the reversion seller (or each reversion seller) is non-resident when he enters into it;
        (iii)   in relation to articles 25C and 63F, a regulated home purchase plan where the home purchaser (or each home purchaser) is non-resident when he enters into it;
    (c)   "the relevant capacity" means—
        (i)   in the case of a regulated mortgage contract, as borrower;
        (ii)   in the case of a regulated home reversion plan, as reversion seller or plan provider;
        (iii)   in the case of a regulated home purchase plan, as home purchaser;
    (d)   "the relevant type of agreement" means—
        (i)   in relation to article 25A, a regulated mortgage contract;
        (ii)   in relation to article 25B, a regulated home reversion plan;
        (iii)   in relation to article 25C, a regulated home purchase plan.]

(6)   There is excluded from article 64 any agreement made by an overseas person to carry on an activity of the kind specified by article 25(1) or (2), 37[, 39A], 40 or 45 if the agreement is the result of a legitimate approach.

(7)   In this article, "legitimate approach" means—
    (a)   an approach made to the overseas person which has not been solicited by him in any way, or has been solicited by him in a way which does not contravene section 21 of the Act; or
    (b)   an approach made by or on behalf of the overseas person in a way which does not contravene that section.

[(8)   Paragraphs (1) to (5) do not apply where the overseas person is an investment firm or credit institution—
    (a)   who is providing or performing investment services and activities on a professional basis; and
    (b)   whose home Member State is the United Kingdom.]

[2110]

NOTES

    Paras (1)–(4): figures in square brackets inserted by the Financial Services and Markets Act 2000 (Regulated Activities) (Amendment No 3) Order 2006, SI 2006/3384, arts 2, 24(a)–(d), as from 1 April 2007 (for the purposes of enabling applications to be made for (i) a Pt IV permission, (ii) a variation of a Pt IV permission, and (iii) the Authority's approval under s 59 of the 2000 Act, in relation to an activity of the kind specified by art 25D of this Order, or in relation to an investment of the kind specified by arts 83, 84 or 85 of this Order), and as from 1 November 2007 (otherwise).
    Paras (5A)–(5F): inserted by the Financial Services and Markets Act 2000 (Regulated Activities) (Amendment) (No 1) Order 2003, SI 2003/1475, art 20, as from 31 October 2004; and substituted by the Financial Services and Markets Act 2000 (Regulated Activities) (Amendment) (No 2) Order 2006, SI 2006/2383, arts 2, 21, as from 6 November 2006 (for the purposes of enabling applications to be made for (i) a Pt IV permission, or a variation of a Pt IV permission, in relation to activities of the kind specified by arts 25B, 25C, 53B, 53C, 63B or 63F or, so far as relevant to any such activity, art 64 of this Order; or (ii) the Authority's approval under FSMA 2000, s 59 in relation to any of those activities), and as from 6 April 2007 (otherwise) (for transitional provisions and effect see arts 36–40 of, and the Schedule to, the 2006 Order at **[2861]** et seq).
    Para (6): figure in square brackets inserted by the Financial Services and Markets Act 2000 (Regulated Activities) (Amendment) (No 2) Order 2003, SI 2003/1476, art 10(6), as from 31 October 2004 (in so far as relating to contracts of long-term care insurance), and as from 14 January 2005 (otherwise); for transitional provisions see arts 22–27 of that Order at **[2706]** et seq.

Para (8): added by SI 2006/3384, arts 2, 24(e), as from 1 April 2007 (for the purposes of enabling applications to be made for (i) a Pt IV permission, (ii) a variation of a Pt IV permission, and (iii) the Authority's approval under s 59 of the 2000 Act, in relation to an activity of the kind specified by art 25D of this Order, or in relation to an investment of the kind specified by arts 83, 84 or 85 of this Order), and as from 1 November 2007 (otherwise).

[72A Information society services

(1)   There is excluded from this Part any activity consisting of the provision of an information society service from an EEA State other than the United Kingdom.

(2)   The exclusion in paragraph (1) does not apply to the activity of effecting or carrying out a contract of insurance as principal, where—

(a)   the activity is carried on by an undertaking which has received official authorisation in accordance with [Article 4 of the life assurance consolidation directive] or the first non-life insurance directive, and

(b)   the insurance falls within the scope of any of the insurance directives.]

[2111]

NOTES
Inserted by the Financial Services and Markets Act 2000 (Regulated Activities) (Amendment) (No 2) Order 2002, SI 2002/1776, art 2, as from 21 August 2002.
Para (2): words in square brackets substituted by the Life Assurance Consolidation Directive (Consequential Amendments) Regulations 2004, SI 2004/3379, reg 17, as from 11 January 2005.

[72B Activities carried on by a provider of relevant goods or services

(1)   In this article—
"connected contract of insurance" means a contract of insurance which—

(a)   is not a contract of long-term insurance;

(b)   has a total duration (or would have a total duration were any right to renew conferred by the contract exercised) of five years or less;

(c)   has an annual premium (or, where the premium is paid otherwise than by way of annual premium, the equivalent of an annual premium) of 500 euro or less, or the equivalent amount in sterling or other currency;

(d)   covers the risk of—

(i)   breakdown, loss of, or damage to, non-motor goods supplied by the provider; or

[(ii)   damage to, or loss of, baggage and other risks linked to the travel booked with the provider ("travel risks") in circumstances where—

(aa)   the travel booked with the provider relates to attendance at an event organised or managed by that provider and the party seeking insurance is not an individual (acting in his private capacity) or a small business; or

(bb)   the travel booked with the provider is only the hire of an aircraft, vehicle or vessel which does not provide sleeping accommodation];

(e)   does not cover any liability risks (except, in the case of a contract which covers travel risks, where that cover is ancillary to the main cover provided by the contract);

(f)   is complementary to the non-motor goods being supplied or service being provided by the provider; and

(g)   is of such a nature that the only information that a person requires in order to carry on an activity of the kind specified by article 21, 25, 39A or 53 in relation to it is the cover provided by the contract;

"non-motor goods" means goods which are not mechanically propelled road vehicles;
"provider" means a person who supplies non-motor goods or provides services related to travel in the course of carrying on a profession or business which does not otherwise consist of the carrying on of regulated activities.
[For these purposes, the transfer of possession of an aircraft, vehicle or vessel under an agreement for hire which is not—

(a)   a hire-purchase agreement within the meaning of section 189(1) of the Consumer Credit Act 1974, or

(b)   any other agreement which contemplates that the property in those goods will also pass at some time in the future,

is the provision of a service related to travel, not a supply of goods];
["small business" means—

(a)   subject to paragraph (b) a sole trader, body corporate, partnership or an unincorporated association which had a turnover in the last financial year of less than £1,000,000;

(b)   where the business concerned is a member of a group within the meaning of section 262(1) of the Companies Act 1985 (and after the repeal of that section within the meaning of section 474(1) of the Companies Act 2006), reference to its turnover means the combined turnover of the group;

"turnover" means the amounts derived from the provision of goods and services falling within the business's ordinary activities, after deduction of trade discounts, value added tax and any other taxes based on the amounts so derived].

(2)   There is excluded from article 21 any transaction for the sale or purchase of a connected contract of insurance into which a provider enters as agent.

(3)   There are excluded from article 25(1) and (2) any arrangements made by a provider for, or with a view to, a transaction for the sale or purchase of a connected contract of insurance.

(4)   There is excluded from article 39A any activity carried on by a provider where the contract of insurance in question is a connected contract of insurance.

(5)   There is excluded from article 53 the giving of advice by a provider in relation to a transaction for the sale or purchase of a connected contract of insurance.

(6)   For the purposes of this article, a contract of insurance which covers travel risks is not to be treated as a contract of long-term insurance, notwithstanding the fact that it contains related and subsidiary provisions such that it might be regarded as a contract of long-term insurance, if the cover to which those provisions relate is ancillary to the main cover provided by the contract.]

[2112]

NOTES

Commencement: 31 October 2004 (in so far as relating to contracts of long-term care insurance); 14 January 2005 (otherwise).

Inserted, together with arts 72C, 72D, by the Financial Services and Markets Act 2000 (Regulated Activities) (Amendment) (No 2) Order 2003, SI 2003/1476, art 11, as from 31 October 2004 (in so far as relating to contracts of long-term care insurance), and as from 14 January 2005 (otherwise); for transitional provisions see arts 22–27 of that Order at **[2706]** et seq.

Para (1) is amended as follows:

In definition "connected contract of insurance" sub-para (d)(ii) substituted by the Financial Services and Markets Act 2000 (Regulated Activities) (Amendment) (No 2) Order 2007, SI 2007/3510, art 2(1), (2), as from 30 June 2008 (for the purposes of enabling applications to be made, pursuant to this amendment, for (i) a Pt IV permission, or a variation of a Pt IV permission, in relation to activities of the kind specified by arts 21, 25(1), 25(2), 39A, 53 or, so far as relevant to any such activity, art 64 of this Order, or (ii) the Authority's approval under s 59 of FSMA 2000 in relation to any of those activities), and as from 1 January 2009 (otherwise) (for transitional provisions see arts 3–9 of that Order at **[2900]** et seq).

Words in square brackets in definition "provider" inserted, and definitions "small business" and "turnover" added, by SI 2007/3510, art 2(1), (3), as from the same dates and for the same purposes as noted above (for transitional provisions see arts 3–9 of that Order at **[2900]** et seq).

[72C   Provision of information on an incidental basis

(1)   There is excluded from articles 25(1) and (2) the making of arrangements for, or with a view to, a transaction for the sale or purchase of a contract of insurance or an investment of the kind specified by article 89, so far as relevant to such a contract, where that activity meets the conditions specified in paragraph (4).

(2)   There is excluded from articles 37 and 40 any activity—

(a)   where the assets in question are rights under a contract of insurance or an investment of the kind specified by article 89, so far as relevant to such a contract; and

(b)   which meets the conditions specified in paragraph (4).

(3)   There is excluded from article 39A any activity which meets the conditions specified in paragraph (4).

(4)   The conditions specified in this paragraph are that the activity—

(a)   consists of the provision of information to the policyholder or potential policyholder;

(b)   is carried on by a person in the course of carrying on a profession or business which does not otherwise consist of the carrying on of regulated activities; and

(c)   may reasonably be regarded as being incidental to that profession or business.]

[2113]

NOTES

Commencement: 31 October 2004 (in so far as relating to contracts of long-term care insurance); 14 January 2005 (otherwise).

Inserted as noted to art 72B at **[2112]**.

[72D   Large risks contracts where risk situated outside the EEA

(1)   There is excluded from articles 21, 25(1) and (2), 39A and 53 any activity which is carried on in relation to a large risks contract of insurance, to the extent that the risk or commitment covered by the contract is not situated in an EEA State.

(2) In this article, a "large risks contract of insurance" is a contract of insurance the principal object of which is to cover—

(a) risks falling within paragraph 4 (railway rolling stock), 5 (aircraft), 6 (ships), 7 (goods in transit), 11 (aircraft liability) or 12 (liability of ships) of Part 1 of Schedule 1;

(b) risks falling within paragraph 14 (credit) or 15 (suretyship) of that Part provided that the risks relate to a business carried on by the policyholder; or

(c) risks falling within paragraph 3 (land vehicles), 8 (fire and natural forces), 9 (damage to property), 10 (motor vehicle liability), 13 (general liability) or 16 (miscellaneous financial loss) of that Part provided that the risks relate to a business carried on by the policyholder and that the condition specified in paragraph (3) is met in relation to that business.

(3) The condition specified in this paragraph is that at least two of the three following criteria were met in the most recent financial year for which information is available—

(a) the balance sheet total of the business (within the meaning of section 247(5) of the Companies Act 1985 or article 255(5) of the Companies (Northern Ireland) Order 1986) exceeded 6.2 million euro,

(b) the net turnover (within the meaning given to "turnover" by section 262(1) of that Act or article 270(1) of that Order) exceeded 12.8 million euro,

(c) the number of employees (within the meaning given by section 247(6) of that Act or article 255(6) of that Order) exceeded 250,

and for a financial year which is a company's financial year but not in fact a year, the net turnover of the policyholder shall be proportionately adjusted.

(4) For the purposes of paragraph (3), where the policyholder is a member of a group for which consolidated accounts (within the meaning of the Seventh Company Law Directive) are drawn up, the question whether the condition specified by that paragraph is met is to be determined by reference to those accounts.]

[2114]

NOTES

Commencement: 31 October 2004 (in so far as relating to contracts of long-term care insurance); 14 January 2005 (otherwise).

Inserted as noted to art 72B at **[2112]**.

[72E Business Angel-led Enterprise Capital Funds

(1) A body corporate of a type specified in paragraph (7) does not carry on the activity of the kind specified by article 21 by entering as agent into a transaction on behalf of the participants of a Business Angel-led Enterprise Capital Fund.

(2) There are excluded from article 25(1) and (2) arrangements, made by a body corporate of a type specified in paragraph (7), for or with a view to a transaction which is or is to be entered into by or on behalf of the participants in a Business Angel-led Enterprise Capital Fund.

(3) There is excluded from article 37 any activity, carried on by a body corporate of a type specified in paragraph (7), which consists in the managing of assets belonging to the participants in a Business Angel-led Enterprise Capital Fund.

(4) There is excluded from article 40 any activity, carried on by a body corporate of a type specified in paragraph (7), in respect of assets belonging to the participants in a Business Angel-led Enterprise Capital Fund.

(5) A body corporate of a type specified in paragraph (7) does not carry on the activity of the kind specified in article 51(1)(a) where it carries on the activity of establishing, operating or winding up a Business Angel-led Enterprise Capital Fund.

(6) A body corporate of a type specified in paragraph (7) does not carry on the activity of the kind specified in article 53 where it is advising the participants in a Business Angel-led Enterprise Capital Fund on investments to be made by or on behalf of the participants of that Business Angel-led Enterprise Capital Fund.

(7) The type of body corporate specified is a limited company—

(i) which operates a Business Angel-led Enterprise Capital Fund; and

(ii) the members of which are participants in the Business Angel-led Enterprise Capital Fund operated by that limited company and between them have invested at least 50 per cent of the total investment in that Business Angel-led Enterprise Capital Fund excluding any investment made by the Secretary of State.

(8) For the purposes of paragraph (7), "a limited company" means a body corporate with limited liability which is a company or firm formed in accordance with the law of an EEA State and having its registered office, central administration or principal place of business within the territory of an EEA State.

(9)   Nothing in this article has the effect of excluding a body corporate from the application of the Money Laundering Regulations [2007], in so far as those Regulations would have applied to it but for this article.

(10)   Nothing in this article has the effect of excluding a body corporate from the application of section 397 of the Act (misleading statements and practices), in so far as that section would have applied to it but for this article.]

[(11)   This article is subject to article 4(4).]

[2115]

NOTES

Commencement: 1 October 2005.

Inserted, together with art 72F, by the Financial Services and Markets Act 2000 (Regulated Activities) (Amendment) (No 2) Order 2005, SI 2005/1518, art 2(1), (3), as from 1 October 2005.

Para (9): date in square brackets substituted by the Money Laundering Regulations 2007, SI 2007/2157, reg 51, Sch 6, Pt 2, para 10, as from 15 December 2007.

Para (11): added by SI 2006/3384, arts 2, 25, as from 1 April 2007 (for the purposes of enabling applications to be made for (i) a Pt IV permission, (ii) a variation of a Pt IV permission, and (iii) the Authority's approval under s 59 of the 2000 Act, in relation to an activity of the kind specified by art 25D of this Order, or in relation to an investment of the kind specified by arts 83, 84 or 85 of this Order), and as from 1 November 2007 (otherwise).

[72F   Interpretation

(1)   For the purposes of this article and of article 72E—

"Business Angel-led Enterprise Capital Fund" means a collective investment scheme which—

    (a)   is established for the purpose of enabling participants to participate in or receive profits or income arising from the acquisition, holding, management or disposal of investments falling within one or more of—

        (i)   article 76, being shares in an unlisted company;

        (ii)   article 77, being instruments creating or acknowledging indebtedness in respect of an unlisted company; and

        (iii)   article 79, being warrants or other instruments entitling the holder to subscribe for shares in an unlisted company;

    (b)   has only the following as its participants—

        (i)   the Secretary of State;

        (ii)   a body corporate of a type specified in article 72E(7); and

        (iii)   one or more persons each of whom at the time they became a participant was—

            (aa)   a sophisticated investor;

            (bb)   a high net worth individual;

            (cc)   a high net worth company;

            (dd)   a high net worth unincorporated association;

            (ee)   a trustee of a high value trust; or

            (ff)   a self-certified sophisticated investor;

    (c)   is prevented, by the arrangements by which it is established, from—

        (i)   acquiring investments, other than those falling within paragraphs (i) to (iii) of sub-paragraph (a); and

        (ii)   acquiring investments falling within paragraphs (i) to (iii) of sub-paragraph (a) in an unlisted company, where the aggregated cost of those investments exceeds £2 million, unless that acquisition is necessary to prevent or reduce the dilution of an existing share-holding in that unlisted company;

"high net worth company" means a body corporate which—

    (a)   falls within article 49(2)(a) of the Financial Services and Markets Act 2000 (Financial Promotion) Order 2001 (high net worth companies, unincorporated associations etc); and

    (b)   has executed a document [(in a manner which binds the company)] in the following terms:

"This company is a high net worth company and falls within article 49(2)(a) of the Financial Services and Markets Act 2000 (Financial Promotion) Order 2001. We understand that any Business Angel-led Enterprise Capital Fund (within the meaning of article 72F of the Financial Services and Markets Act 2000 (Regulated Activities) Order 2001), in which this company participates, or any person who operates that Business Angel-led Enterprise Capital Fund, in which this company participates, will not be authorised under the Financial Services and Markets Act 2000 (and so will not have to satisfy the threshold conditions set out in Part I of Schedule 6 to that Act and will not be subject to Financial Services Authority rules such as those on holding client money). We understand that this means that redress through the Financial Services Authority, the Financial Ombudsman Scheme or the Financial Services Compensation Scheme will not be available. We also understand the risks associated in investing in a Business Angel-led Enterprise Capital Fund and are aware that it is open to us to seek advice from someone who is authorised under the Financial Services and Markets Act 2000 and who specialises in advising on this kind of investment."

"high net worth individual" means an individual who—

(a)   is a "certified high net worth individual" within the meaning of article 48(2) of the Financial Services and Markets Act 2000 (Financial Promotion) Order 2001 (certified high net worth individuals); and

(b)   has signed a statement in the following terms:

"I declare that I am a certified high net worth individual within the meaning of article 48(2) of the Financial Services and Markets Act 2000 (Financial Promotion) Order 2001 and that I understand that any Business Angel-led Enterprise Capital Fund (within the meaning of article 72F of the Financial Services and Markets Act 2000 (Regulated Activities) Order 2001), in which I participate, or any person who operates that Business Angel-led Enterprise Capital Fund, in which I participate, will not be authorised under the Financial Services and Markets Act 2000 (and so will not have to satisfy the threshold conditions set out in Part I of Schedule 6 to that Act and will not be subject to Financial Services Authority rules such as those on holding client money). I understand that this means that redress through the Financial Services Authority, the Financial Ombudsman Scheme or the Financial Services Compensation Scheme will not be available. I also understand the risks associated in investing in a Business Angel-led Enterprise Capital Fund and am aware that it is open to me to seek advice from someone who is authorised under the Financial Services and Markets Act 2000 and who specialises in advising on this kind of investment.";

"high net worth unincorporated association" means an unincorporated association—

(a)   which falls within article 49(2)(b) of the Financial Services and Markets Act 2000 (Financial Promotion) Order 2001; and

(b)   on behalf of which an officer of that association or a member of its governing body has signed a statement in the following terms:

"This unincorporated association is a high net worth unincorporated association and falls within article 49(2)(b) of the Financial Services and Markets Act 2000 (Financial Promotion) Order 2001. I understand that any Business Angel-led Enterprise Capital Fund (within the meaning of article 72F of the Financial Services and Markets Act 2000 (Regulated Activities) Order 2001), in which this association participates, or any person who operates that Business Angel-led Enterprise Capital Fund, in which this association participates, will not be authorised under the Financial Services and Markets Act 2000 (and so will not have to satisfy the threshold conditions set out in Part I of Schedule 6 to that Act and will not be subject to Financial Services Authority rules such as those on holding client money). I understand that this means that redress through the Financial Services Authority, the Financial Ombudsman Scheme or the Financial Services Compensation Scheme will not be available. I also understand the risks associated in investing in a Business Angel-led Enterprise Capital Fund and am aware that it is open to the association to seek advice from someone who is authorised under the Financial Services and Markets Act 2000 and who specialises in advising on this kind of investment.";

"high value trust" means a trust—

(a)   where the aggregate value of the cash and investments which form a part of the trust's assets (before deducting the amount of its liabilities) is £10 million or more;

(b)   on behalf of which a trustee has signed a statement in the following terms:

"This trust is a high value trust. I understand that any Business Angel-led Enterprise Capital Fund (within the meaning of article 72F of the Financial Services and Markets Act 2000 (Regulated Activities) Order 2001), in which this trust participates, or any person who operates that Business Angel-led Enterprise Capital Fund, in which this trust participates, will not be authorised under the Financial Services and Markets Act 2000 (and so will not have to satisfy the threshold conditions set out in Part I of Schedule 6 to that Act and will not be subject to Financial Services Authority rules such as those on holding client money). I understand that this means that redress through the Financial Services Authority, the Financial Ombudsman Scheme or the Financial Services Compensation Scheme will not be available. I also understand the risks associated in investing in a Business Angel-led Enterprise Capital Fund and am aware that it is open to the trust to seek advice from someone who is authorised under the Financial Services and Markets Act 2000 and who specialises in advising on this kind of investment.";

"self-certified sophisticated investor" means an individual who—

(a)   is a "self-certified sophisticated investor" within the meaning of article 50A of the Financial Services and Markets Act 2000 (Financial Promotion) Order 2001;

(b)   has signed a statement in the following terms:

"I declare that I am a self-certified sophisticated investor within the meaning of article 50A of the Financial Services and Markets Act 2000 (Financial Promotion) Order 2001 and that I understand that any Business Angel-led Enterprise Capital Fund (within the meaning of article 72F of the Financial Services and Markets Act 2000 (Regulated Activities) Order 2001), in which I participate, or any person who operates that Business Angel-led Enterprise Capital Fund, in which I participate, will not be authorised under the Financial Services and Markets Act 2000 (and so will not have to satisfy the threshold conditions set out in Part I of Schedule 6 to that Act and will not be subject to Financial Services Authority rules such as those on holding client money). I understand that this means that redress through the Financial Services Authority, the Financial Ombudsman Scheme or the Financial Services Compensation Scheme will not be available. I also understand the risks associated in investing in a Business Angel-led Enterprise Capital Fund and am aware that it is open to me to seek advice from someone who is authorised under the Financial Services and Markets Act 2000 and who specialises in advising on this kind of investment.";

"sophisticated investor" means an individual who—

(a)   is a "certified sophisticated investor" within the meaning of article 50(1) of the Financial Services and Markets Act 2000 (Financial Promotion) Order 2001; and

(b)   has signed a statement in the following terms:

"I declare that I am a certified sophisticated investor within the meaning of article 50(1) of the Financial Services and Markets Act 2000 (Financial Promotion) Order 2001 and that I understand that any Business Angel-led Enterprise Capital Fund (within the meaning of article 72F of the Financial Services and Markets Act 2000 (Regulated Activities) Order 2001), in which I participate, or any person who operates that Business Angel-led Enterprise Capital Fund, in which I participate, will not be authorised under the Financial Services and Markets Act 2000 (and so will not have to satisfy the threshold conditions set out in Part I of Schedule 6 to that Act and will not be subject to Financial Services Authority rules such as those on holding client money). I understand that this means that redress through the Financial Services Authority, the Financial Ombudsman Scheme or the Financial Services Compensation Scheme will not be available. I also understand the risks associated in investing in a Business Angel-led Enterprise Capital Fund and am aware that it is open to me to seek advice from someone who is authorised under the Financial Services and Markets Act 2000 and who specialises in advising on this kind of investment.";

"unlisted company" has the meaning given by article 3 of the Financial Services and Markets Act 2000 (Financial Promotion) Order 2001.

(2)   References in this Article and in Article 72E to a participant in a Business Angel-led Enterprise Capital Fund, doing things on behalf of such a participant and property belonging to such a participant are, respectively, references to that participant in that capacity, to doing things on behalf of that participant in that capacity or to the property of that participant held in that capacity.]

[2116]

NOTES

Commencement: 1 October 2005.

Inserted as noted to art 72E at **[2115]**.

Para (1): words in square brackets in definition "high net worth company" substituted by the Financial Services and Markets Act 2000 (Regulated Activities) (Amendment) (No 2) Order 2006, SI 2006/2383, arts 2, 22, as from 6 November 2006 (for the purposes of enabling applications to be made for (i) a Pt IV permission, or a variation of a Pt IV permission, in relation to activities of the kind specified by arts 25B, 25C, 53B, 53C, 63B or 63F or, so far as relevant to any such activity, art 64 of this Order; or (ii) the Authority's approval under FSMA 2000, s 59 in relation to any of those activities), and as from 6 April 2007 (otherwise) (for transitional provisions and effect see arts 36–40 of, and the Schedule to, the 2006 Order at **[2861]** et seq).

PART III

SPECIFIED INVESTMENTS

73 Investments: general

The following kinds of investment are specified for the purposes of section 22 of the Act.

[2117]

74 Deposits

A deposit.

[2118]

[74A Electronic money

Electronic money.]

[2119]

PART III
STATUTORY INSTRUMENTS

NOTES
Inserted by the Financial Services and Markets Act 2000 (Regulated Activities) (Amendment) Order 2002, SI 2002/682, art 6, as from 27 April 2002, subject to transitional provisions in relation to persons issuing electronic money immediately before that date contained in art 9 at **[2667]**.

75 Contracts of insurance

Rights under a contract of insurance.

[2120]

76 Shares etc

(1) Shares or stock in the share capital of—
    (a) any body corporate (wherever incorporated), and
    (b) any unincorporated body constituted under the law of a country or territory outside the United Kingdom.

(2) Paragraph (1) includes—
    (a) any shares of a class defined as deferred shares for the purposes of section 119 of the Building Societies Act 1986; and
    (b) any transferable shares in a body incorporated under the law of, or any part of, the United Kingdom relating to industrial and provident societies or credit unions, or in a body constituted under the law of another EEA State for purposes equivalent to those of such a body.

(3) But subject to paragraph (2) there are excluded from paragraph (1) shares or stock in the share capital of—
    (a) an open-ended investment company;
    (b) a building society incorporated under the law of, or any part of, the United Kingdom;
    (c) a body incorporated under the law of, or any part of, the United Kingdom relating to industrial and provident societies or credit unions;
    (d) any body constituted under the law of an EEA State for purposes equivalent to those of a body falling within sub-paragraph (b) or (c).

[2121]

77 Instruments creating or acknowledging indebtedness

(1) Subject to paragraph (2), such of the following as do not fall within article 78—
    (a) debentures;
    (b) debenture stock;
    (c) loan stock;
    (d) bonds;
    (e) certificates of deposit;
    (f) any other instrument creating or acknowledging indebtedness.

(2) If and to the extent that they would otherwise fall within paragraph (1), there are excluded from that paragraph—
    (a) an instrument acknowledging or creating indebtedness for, or for money borrowed to defray, the consideration payable under a contract for the supply of goods or services;
    (b) a cheque or other bill of exchange, a banker's draft or a letter of credit (but not a bill of exchange accepted by a banker);
    (c) a banknote, a statement showing a balance on a current, deposit or savings account, a lease or other disposition of property, or a heritable security; and
    (d) a contract of insurance.

(3) An instrument excluded from paragraph (1) of article 78 by paragraph (2)(b) of that article is not thereby to be taken to fall within paragraph (1) of this article.

[2122]

NOTES
Modification: references in para (1) to securities, instruments or investments creating or acknowledging indebtedness (or creating or acknowledging a present or future indebtedness) includes a reference to uncertificated units of eligible debt securities; see the Uncertificated Securities (Amendment) (Eligible Debt Securities) Regulations 2003, SI 2003/1633, reg 15, Sch 2, para 8 (as from 24 June 2003).
HM Treasury and the Financial Services Authority have issued a consultation paper, *Consultation on the legislative framework for the regulation of alternative finance investment bonds (sukuk) (December 2008)* which proposes the insertion of a new art 77A into this Order to make certain alternative finance investment bonds a specified investment for the purposes of the Act. The main effect of the Order (that is set out in draft) would be to regulate a form of Sharia compliant investment bond (known in the plural as 'sukuk' and in the singular as 'sakk') that is, in economic substance, similar to a debt security in an equivalent manner to conventional debt securities, where appropriate. Sukuk arrangements allow assets to be held for the benefit of investors in certificates issued by a company. The benefits may include the payment of a return that is economically equivalent to interest and redemption of the certificates out of the proceeds from the disposal of the assets.

78   Government and public securities

(1)   Subject to paragraph (2), loan stock, bonds and other instruments creating or acknowledging indebtedness, issued by or on behalf of any of the following—

    (a)   the government of the United Kingdom;
    (b)   the Scottish Administration;
    (c)   the Executive Committee of the Northern Ireland Assembly;
    (d)   the National Assembly for Wales;
    (e)   the government of any country or territory outside the United Kingdom;
    (f)   a local authority in the United Kingdom or elsewhere; or
    (g)   a body the members of which comprise—
        (i)   states including the United Kingdom or another EEA State; or
        (ii)   bodies whose members comprise states including the United Kingdom or another EEA State.

(2)   There are excluded from paragraph (1)—

    (a)   so far as applicable, the instruments mentioned in article 77(2)(a) to (d);
    (b)   any instrument creating or acknowledging indebtedness in respect of—
        (i)   money received by the Director of Savings as deposits or otherwise in connection with the business of the National Savings Bank;
        (ii)   money raised under the National Loans Act 1968 under the auspices of the Director of Savings or treated as so raised by virtue of section 11(3) of the National Debt Act 1972.

[2123]

NOTES
Modification: references in this article to securities, instruments or investments creating or acknowledging indebtedness (or creating or acknowledging a present or future indebtedness) includes a reference to uncertificated units of eligible debt securities; see the Uncertificated Securities (Amendment) (Eligible Debt Securities) Regulations 2003, SI 2003/1633, reg 15, Sch 2, para 8 (as from 24 June 2003).

79   Instruments giving entitlements to investments

(1)   Warrants and other instruments entitling the holder to subscribe for any investment of the kind specified by article 76, 77 or 78.

(2)   It is immaterial whether the investment to which the entitlement relates is in existence or identifiable.

(3)   An investment of the kind specified by this article is not to be regarded as falling within article 83, 84 or 85.

[2124]

80   Certificates representing certain securities

(1)   Subject to paragraph (2), certificates or other instruments which confer contractual or property rights (other than rights consisting of an investment of the kind specified by article 83)—

    (a)   in respect of any investment of the kind specified by any of articles 76 to 79, being an investment held by a person other than the person on whom the rights are conferred by the certificate or instrument; and
    (b)   the transfer of which may be effected without the consent of that person.

(2)   There is excluded from paragraph (1) any certificate or other instrument which confers rights in respect of two or more investments issued by different persons, or in respect of two or more different investments of the kind specified by article 78 and issued by the same person.

[2125]

81   Units in a collective investment scheme

Units in a collective investment scheme (within the meaning of Part XVII of the Act).

[2126]

[82   Rights under a pension scheme

(1)   Rights under a stakeholder pension scheme.

(2)   Rights under a personal pension scheme.]

[2127]

NOTES
Commencement: 1 October 2006 (certain purposes); 6 April 2007 (otherwise) (see below).
Substituted by the Financial Services and Markets Act 2000 (Regulated Activities) (Amendment) Order 2006, SI 2006/1969, art 2(1), (5), as from 1 October 2006 (for the purposes of enabling applications to be made for Pt IV permission or for a variation of Pt IV permission in relation to an investment specified by art 82(2) of this Order (as so substituted)), and as from 6 April 2007 (otherwise); for transitional provisions and effect see arts 3–7 of, and the Schedule to, the 2006 Order at **[2854]** et seq.

PART III
STATUTORY INSTRUMENTS

83 Options

[(1)]   Options to acquire or dispose of—
- (a)   a security or contractually based investment (other than one of a kind specified by this article);
- (b)   currency of the United Kingdom or any other country or territory;
- (c)   palladium, platinum, gold or silver; ...
- (d)   an option to acquire or dispose of an investment of the kind specified by this article by virtue of paragraph (a), (b) or (c);
- [(e)   subject to paragraph (4), an option to acquire or dispose of an option to which paragraph 5, 6, 7 or 10 of Section C of Annex I to the markets in financial instruments directive (the text of which is set out in Part I of Schedule 2) applies].

[(2)   Subject to paragraph (4), options—
- (a)   to which paragraph (1) does not apply;
- (b)   which relate to commodities;
- (c)   which may be settled physically; and
- (d)   either—
  - (i)   to which paragraph 5 or 6 of Section C of Annex I to the markets in financial instruments directive, the text of which is set out in Part 1 of Schedule 2, applies, or
  - (ii)   which in accordance with Article 38 of the Commission Regulation (the text of which is set out in Part 2 of Schedule 2) are to be considered as having the characteristics of other derivative financial instruments and not being for commercial purposes, and to which paragraph 7 of Section C of Annex I to the markets in financial instruments directive applies.

(3)   Subject to paragraph (4), options—
- (a)   to which paragraph (1) does not apply;
- (b)   which may be settled physically; and
- (c)   to which paragraph 10 of Section C of Annex I to the markets in financial instruments directive (read with the Commission Regulation) applies.

(4)   Paragraphs (1)(e), (2) and (3) only apply to options in relation to which—
- (a)   an investment firm or credit institution is providing or performing investment services and activities on a professional basis,
- (b)   a management company is providing, in accordance with Article 5(3) of the UCITS directive, the investment service specified in paragraph 4 or 5 of Section A, or the ancillary service specified in paragraph 1 of Section B, of Annex I to the markets in financial instruments directive, or
- (c)   a market operator is providing the investment service specified in paragraph 8 of Section A of Annex I to the markets in financial instruments directive.

(5)   Expressions used in paragraphs (1)(e), (2) and (3) and in the markets in financial instruments directive have the same meaning as in that directive.]

[2128]

NOTES

Para (1): numbered as such, word omitted from sub-para (c) revoked, and sub-para (e) inserted, by the Financial Services and Markets Act 2000 (Regulated Activities) (Amendment No 3) Order 2006, SI 2006/3384, arts 2, 26(a), (b), as from 1 April 2007 (for the purposes of enabling applications to be made for (i) a Pt IV permission, (ii) a variation of a Pt IV permission, and (iii) the Authority's approval under s 59 of the 2000 Act, in relation to an activity of the kind specified by art 25D of this Order, or in relation to an investment of the kind specified by arts 83, 84 or 85 of this Order), and as from 1 November 2007 (otherwise).

Paras (2)–(5): added by SI 2006/3384, arts 2, 26(c), as from the same dates and for the same purposes as noted above.

84 Futures

(1)   Subject to paragraph (2), rights under a contract for the sale of a commodity or property of any other description under which delivery is to be made at a future date and at a price agreed on when the contract is made.

[(1A)   Subject to paragraph (1D), futures—
- (a)   to which paragraph (1) does not apply;
- (b)   which relate to commodities;
- (c)   which may be settled physically; and
- (d)   to which paragraph 5 or 6 of Section C of Annex I to the markets in financial instruments directive applies.

(1B)   Subject to paragraph (1D), futures and forwards—
- (a)   to which paragraph (1) does not apply;
- (b)   which relate to commodities;
- (c)   which may be settled physically;

    (d)   which in accordance with Article 38 of the Commission Regulation (the text of which is set out in Part 2 of Schedule 2) are to be considered as having the characteristics of other derivative financial instruments and not being for commercial purposes; and

    (e)   to which paragraph 7 of Section C of Annex I to the markets in financial instruments directive applies.

(1C)   Subject to paragraph (1D), futures—

    (a)   to which paragraph (1) does not apply;

    (b)   which may be settled physically; and

    (c)   to which paragraph 10 of Section C of Annex I to the markets in financial instruments directive (read with the Commission Regulation) applies.

(1D)   Paragraph (1A), (1B) and (1C) only apply to futures or forwards in relation to which—

    (a)   an investment firm or credit institution is providing or performing investment services and activities on a professional basis,

    (b)   a management company is providing, in accordance with Article 5(3) of the UCITS directive, the investment service specified in paragraph 4 or 5 of Section A, or the ancillary service specified in paragraph 1 of Section B, of Annex I to the markets in financial instruments directive, or

    (c)   a market operator is providing the investment service specified in paragraph 8 of Section A of Annex I to the markets in financial instruments directive.

(1E)   Expressions used in paragraphs (1A) to (1C) and in the markets in financial instruments directive have the same meaning as in that directive.]

(2)   There are excluded from paragraph (1) rights under any contract which is made for commercial and not investment purposes.

(3)   A contract is to be regarded as made for investment purposes if it is made or traded on a recognised investment exchange, or is made otherwise than on a recognised investment exchange but is expressed to be as traded on such an exchange or on the same terms as those on which an equivalent contract would be made on such an exchange.

(4)   A contract not falling within paragraph (3) is to be regarded as made for commercial purposes if under the terms of the contract delivery is to be made within seven days, unless it can be shown that there existed an understanding that (notwithstanding the express terms of the contract) delivery would not be made within seven days.

(5)   The following are indications that a contract not falling within paragraph (3) or (4) is made for commercial purposes and the absence of them is an indication that it is made for investment purposes—

    (a)   one or more of the parties is a producer of the commodity or other property, or uses it in his business;

    (b)   the seller delivers or intends to deliver the property or the purchaser takes or intends to take delivery of it.

(6)   It is an indication that a contract is made for commercial purposes that the prices, the lot, the delivery date or other terms are determined by the parties for the purposes of the particular contract and not by reference (or not solely by reference) to regularly published prices, to standard lots or delivery dates or to standard terms.

(7)   The following are indications that a contract is made for investment purposes—

    (a)   it is expressed to be as traded on an investment exchange;

    (b)   performance of the contract is ensured by an investment exchange or a clearing house;

    (c)   there are arrangements for the payment or provision of margin.

(8)   For the purposes of paragraph (1), a price is to be taken to be agreed on when a contract is made—

    (a)   notwithstanding that it is left to be determined by reference to the price at which a contract is to be entered into on a market or exchange or could be entered into at a time and place specified in the contract; or

    (b)   in a case where the contract is expressed to be by reference to a standard lot and quality, notwithstanding that provision is made for a variation in the price to take account of any variation in quantity or quality on delivery.

[2129]

NOTES

Paras (1A)–(1E): inserted by the Financial Services and Markets Act 2000 (Regulated Activities) (Amendment No 3) Order 2006, SI 2006/3384, arts 2, 27, as from 1 April 2007 (for the purposes of enabling applications to be made for (i) a Pt IV permission, (ii) a variation of a Pt IV permission, and (iii) the Authority's approval under s 59 of the 2000 Act, in relation to an activity of the kind specified by art 25D of this Order, or in relation to an investment of the kind specified by arts 83, 84 or 85 of this Order), and as from 1 November 2007 (otherwise).

85 Contracts for differences etc

(1) Subject to paragraph (2), rights under—
  (a) a contract for differences; or
  (b) any other contract the purpose or pretended purpose of which is to secure a profit or avoid a loss by reference to fluctuations in—
     (i) the value or price of property of any description; or
     (ii) an index or other factor designated for that purpose in the contract.

(2) There are excluded from paragraph (1)—
  (a) rights under a contract if the parties intend that the profit is to be secured or the loss is to be avoided by one or more of the parties taking delivery of any property to which the contract relates;
  (b) rights under a contract under which money is received by way of deposit on terms that any interest or other return to be paid on the sum deposited will be calculated by reference to fluctuations in an index or other factor;
  (c) rights under any contract under which—
     (i) money is received by the Director of Savings as deposits or otherwise in connection with the business of the National Savings Bank; or
     (ii) money is raised under the National Loans Act 1968 under the auspices of the Director of Savings or treated as so raised by virtue of section 11(3) of the National Debt Act 1972;
  (d) rights under a qualifying contract of insurance.

[(3) Subject to paragraph (4), derivative instruments for the transfer of credit risk—
  (a) to which neither article 83 nor paragraph (1) applies; and
  (b) to which paragraph 8 of Section C of Annex I to the markets in financial instruments directive applies.

(4) Paragraph (3) only applies to derivatives in relation to which—
  (a) an investment firm or credit institution is providing or performing investment services and activities on a professional basis,
  (b) a management company is providing, in accordance with Article 5(3) of the UCITS directive, the investment service specified in paragraph 4 or 5 of Section A, or the ancillary service specified in paragraph 1 of Section B, of Annex I to the markets in financial instruments directive, or
  (c) a market operator is providing the investment service specified in paragraph 8 of Section A of Annex I to the markets in financial instruments directive.

(5) "Derivative instruments for the transfer of credit risk" has the same meaning as in the markets in financial instruments directive.]

[2130]

NOTES

Paras (3)–(5): added by the Financial Services and Markets Act 2000 (Regulated Activities) (Amendment No 3) Order 2006, SI 2006/3384, arts 2, 28, as from 1 April 2007 (for the purposes of enabling applications to be made for (i) a Pt IV permission, (ii) a variation of a Pt IV permission, and (iii) the Authority's approval under s 59 of the 2000 Act, in relation to an activity of the kind specified by art 25D of this Order, or in relation to an investment of the kind specified by arts 83, 84 or 85 of this Order), and as from 1 November 2007 (otherwise).

---

86 Lloyd's syndicate capacity and syndicate membership

(1) The underwriting capacity of a Lloyd's syndicate.

(2) A person's membership (or prospective membership) of a Lloyd's syndicate.

[2131]

87 Funeral plan contracts

Rights under a funeral plan contract.

[2132]

88 Regulated mortgage contracts

Rights under a regulated mortgage contract.

[2133]

NOTES

Commencement: 31 October 2004.

[88A Regulated home reversion plans

Rights under a regulated home reversion plan.]

[2133A]

NOTES
  Commencement: 6 November 2006 (certain purposes); 6 April 2007 (otherwise) (see below).
  Inserted, together with art 88B, by the Financial Services and Markets Act 2000 (Regulated Activities) (Amendment) (No 2) Order 2006, SI 2006/2383, arts 2, 23, as from 6 November 2006 (for the purposes of enabling applications to be made for (i) a Pt IV permission, or a variation of a Pt IV permission, in relation to activities of the kind specified by arts 25B, 25C, 53B, 53C, 63B or 63F or, so far as relevant to any such activity, art 64 of this Order; or (ii) the Authority's approval under FSMA 2000, s 59 in relation to any of those activities), and as from 6 April 2007 (otherwise) (for transitional provisions and effect see arts 36–40 of, and the Schedule to, the 2006 Order at **[2861]** et seq).

[88B   Regulated home purchase plans

Rights under a regulated home purchase plan.]

[2133B]

NOTES
  Commencement: 6 November 2006 (certain purposes); 6 April 2007 (otherwise).
  Inserted as noted to art 88A at **[2133A]**.

89   Rights to or interests in investments

  (1)   Subject to paragraphs (2) to (4), any right to or interest in anything which is specified by any other provision of this Part (other than [article 88, 88A or 88B]).

  (2)   Paragraph (1) does not include interests under the trusts of an occupational pension scheme.

  (3)   Paragraph (1) does not include—
   (a)   rights to or interests in a contract of insurance of the kind referred to in paragraph (1)(a) of article 60; or.
   (b)   interests under a trust of the kind referred to in paragraph (1)(b) of that article.

  (4)   Paragraph (1) does not include anything which is specified by any other provision of this Part.

[2134]

NOTES
  Para (1): words in square brackets substituted by the Financial Services and Markets Act 2000 (Regulated Activities) (Amendment) (No 2) Order 2006, SI 2006/2383, arts 2, 24, as from 6 November 2006 (for the purposes of enabling applications to be made for (i) a Pt IV permission, or a variation of a Pt IV permission, in relation to activities of the kind specified by arts 25B, 25C, 53B, 53C, 63B or 63F or, so far as relevant to any such activity, art 64 of this Order; or (ii) the Authority's approval under FSMA 2000, s 59 in relation to any of those activities), and as from 6 April 2007 (otherwise) (for transitional provisions and effect see arts 36–40 of, and the Schedule to, the 2006 Order at **[2861]** et seq).

90, 91   (*(Pt IV) Reg 90 amends the Consumer Credit Act 1974, ss 16, 43, 52, 53, 137, 151; reg 91 amended the Consumer Credit (Advertisements) Regulations 1989, SI 1989/1125 (revoked) and amends the Consumer Credit (Content of Quotations) and Consumer Credit (Advertisements) (Amendment) Regulations 1999, SI 1999/2725, reg 2.*)

[PART V
UNAUTHORISED PERSONS CARRYING ON INSURANCE MEDIATION ACTIVITIES

92   Interpretation
In this Part—
   "designated professional body" means a body which is for the time being designated by the Treasury under section 326 of the Act (designation of professional bodies);
   "insurance mediation activity" means any regulated activity of the kind specified by article 21, 25(1) or (2), 39A or 53, or, so far as relevant to any of those articles, article 64, which is carried on in relation to a contract of insurance;
   "the record" means the record maintained by the Authority under section 347 of the Act (public record of authorised persons etc);
   "recorded insurance intermediary" has the meaning given by article 93(4);
   "a relevant member", in relation to a designated professional body, means a member (within the meaning of section 325(2) of the Act) of the profession in relation to which that designated professional body is established, or a person who is controlled or managed by one or more such members.]

[2135]

NOTES
  Commencement: 31 October 2004 (in so far as relating to contracts of long-term care insurance); 14 January 2005 (otherwise).

Inserted, together with the preceding heading and arts 93–96, by the Financial Services and Markets Act 2000 (Regulated Activities) (Amendment) (No 2) Order 2003, SI 2003/1476, art 13, as from 31 October 2004 (in so far as relating to contracts of long-term care insurance), and as from 14 January 2005 (otherwise); for transitional provisions see arts 22–27 of that Order at **[2706]** et seq.

[93 Duty to maintain a record of persons carrying on insurance mediation activities

(1) Subject to articles 95 and 96, the Authority must include in the record every person who—
 (a) as a result of information obtained by virtue of its rules or by virtue of a direction given, or requirement imposed, under section 51(3) of the Act (procedure for applications under Part IV), appears to the Authority to fall within paragraph (2); or
 (b) as a result of information obtained by virtue of article 94, appears to the Authority to fall within paragraph (3).

(2) A person falls within this paragraph if he is, or has entered into a contract by virtue of which he will be, an appointed representative who carries on any insurance mediation activity.

(3) A person falls within this paragraph if—
 (a) he is a relevant member of a designated professional body who carries on, or is proposing to carry on, any insurance mediation activity; and
 (b) the general prohibition does not (or will not) apply to the carrying on of those activities by virtue of section 327 of the Act (exemption from the general prohibition).

(4) In this Part, "recorded insurance intermediary" means a person who is included in the record by virtue of paragraph (1).

(5) The record must include—
 (a) in the case of any recorded insurance intermediary, its address; and
 (b) in the case of a recorded insurance intermediary which is not an individual, the name of the individuals who are responsible for the management of the business carried on by the intermediary, so far as it relates to insurance mediation activities.]

[2136]

NOTES
Commencement: 31 October 2004 (in so far as relating to contracts of long-term care insurance); 14 January 2005 (otherwise).
Inserted as noted to art 92 at **[2135]**.

[94 Members of designated professional bodies

(1) A designated professional body must, by notice in writing, inform the Authority of—
 (a) the name,
 (b) the address, and
 (c) in the case of a relevant member which is not an individual, the name of the individuals who are responsible for the management of the business carried on by the member, so far as it relates to insurance mediation activities,
of any relevant member who falls within paragraph (2).

(2) A relevant member of a designated professional body falls within this paragraph if, in accordance with the rules of that body, he carries on, or proposes to carry on any insurance mediation activity but does not have, and does not propose to apply for, Part IV permission on the basis that the general prohibition does not (or will not) apply to the carrying on of that activity by virtue of section 327 of the Act.

(3) A designated professional body must also, by notice in writing, inform the Authority of any change in relation to the matters specified in sub-paragraphs (a) to (c) of paragraph (1).

(4) A designated professional body must inform the Authority when a relevant member to whom paragraph (2) applies ceases, for whatever reason, to carry on insurance mediation activities.

(5) The Authority may give directions to a designated professional body as to the manner in which the information referred to in paragraphs (1), (3) and (4) must be provided.]

[2137]

NOTES
Commencement: 31 October 2004 (in so far as relating to contracts of long-term care insurance); 14 January 2005 (otherwise).
Inserted as noted to art 92 at **[2135]**.

[95 Exclusion from record where not fit and proper to carry on insurance mediation activities

(1)   If it appears to the Authority that a person who falls within article 93(2) (appointed representatives) ("AR") is not a fit and proper person to carry on insurance mediation activities, it may decide not to include him in the record or, if that person is already included in the record, to remove him from the record.

(2)   Where the Authority proposes to make a determination under paragraph (1), it must give AR a warning notice.

(3)   If the Authority makes a determination under paragraph (1), it must give AR a decision notice.

(4)   If the Authority gives AR a decision notice under paragraph (3), AR may refer the matter to the Tribunal.

(5)   The Authority may, on the application of AR, revoke a determination under paragraph (1).

(6)   If the Authority decides to grant the application, it must give AR written notice of its decision.

(7)   If the Authority proposes to refuse the application, it must give AR a warning notice.

(8)   If the Authority decides to refuse the application, it must give AR a decision notice.

(9)   If the Authority gives AR a decision notice under paragraph (8), AR may refer the matter to the Tribunal.

(10)   Sections 393 and 394 of the Act (third party rights and access to Authority material) apply to a warning notice given in accordance with paragraph (2) or (7) and to a decision notice given in accordance with paragraph (3) or (8).]

[2138]

NOTES
Commencement: 31 October 2004 (in so far as relating to contracts of long-term care insurance); 14 January 2005 (otherwise).
Inserted as noted to art 92 at **[2135]**.

[96 Exclusion from the record where Authority has exercised its powers under Part XX of the Act

(1)   If a person who appears to the Authority to fall within article 93(3) (member of a designated professional body) falls within paragraph (2) or (3), the Authority must not include him in the record or, if that person is already included in the record, must remove him from the record.

(2)   A person falls within this paragraph if, by virtue of a direction given by the Authority under section 328(1) of the Act (directions in relation to the general prohibition), section 327(1) of the Act does not apply in relation to the carrying on by him of any insurance mediation activity.

(3)   A person falls within this paragraph if the Authority has made an order under section 329(2) of the Act (orders in relation to the general prohibition) disapplying section 327(1) of the Act in relation to the carrying on by him of any insurance mediation activity.]

[2139]

NOTES
Commencement: 31 October 2004 (in so far as relating to contracts of long-term care insurance); 14 January 2005 (otherwise).
Inserted as noted to art 92 at **[2135]**.

97   (*(Pt VI) added by the Financial Services and Markets Act 2000 (Regulated Activities) (Amendment) Order 2004, SI 2004/1610, art 3, as from 15 July 2004, and inserts the Financial Services and Markets Act 2000, s 49(2A) at* **[49]**.)

SCHEDULES

SCHEDULE 1
CONTRACTS OF INSURANCE
Article 3(1)

PART I
CONTRACTS OF GENERAL INSURANCE

1 Accident

Contracts of insurance providing fixed pecuniary benefits or benefits in the nature of indemnity (or a combination of both) against risks of the person insured or, in the case of a contract made by virtue

of section 140, 140A or 140B of the Local Government Act 1972 (or, in Scotland, section 86(1) of the Local Government (Scotland) Act 1973), a person for whose benefit the contract is made—
(a) sustaining injury as the result of an accident or of an accident of a specified class; or
(b) dying as a result of an accident or of an accident of a specified class; or
(c) becoming incapacitated in consequence of disease or of disease of a specified class,
including contracts relating to industrial injury and occupational disease but excluding contracts falling within paragraph 2 of Part I of, or paragraph IV of Part II of, this Schedule.

2 Sickness

Contracts of insurance providing fixed pecuniary benefits or benefits in the nature of indemnity (or a combination of both) against risks of loss to the persons insured attributable to sickness or infirmity but excluding contracts falling within paragraph IV of Part II of this Schedule.

3 Land vehicles

Contracts of insurance against loss of or damage to vehicles used on land, including motor vehicles but excluding railway rolling stock.

4 Railway rolling stock

Contract of insurance against loss of or damage to railway rolling stock.

5 Aircraft

Contracts of insurance upon aircraft or upon the machinery, tackle, furniture or equipment of aircraft.

6 Ships

Contracts of insurance upon vessels used on the sea or on inland water, or upon the machinery, tackle, furniture or equipment of such vessels.

7 Goods in transit

Contracts of insurance against loss of or damage to merchandise, baggage and all other goods in transit, irrespective of the form of transport.

8 Fire and natural forces

Contracts of insurance against loss of or damage to property (other than property to which paragraphs 3 to 7 relate) due to fire, explosion, storm, natural forces other than storm, nuclear energy or land subsidence.

9 Damage to property

Contracts of insurance against loss of or damage to property (other than property to which paragraphs 3 to 7 relate) due to hail or frost or any other event (such as theft) other than those mentioned in paragraph 8.

10 Motor vehicle liability

Contracts of insurance against damage arising out of or in connection with the use of motor vehicles on land, including third-party risks and carrier's liability.

11 Aircraft liability

Contracts of insurance against damage arising out of or in connection with the use of aircraft, including third-party risks and carrier's liability.

12 Liability of ships

Contracts of insurance against damage arising out of or in connection with the use of vessels on the sea or on inland water, including third party risks and carrier's liability.

13 General liability

Contracts of insurance against risks of the persons insured incurring liabilities to third parties, the risks in question not being risks to which paragraph 10, 11 or 12 relates.

14 Credit

Contracts of insurance against risks of loss to the persons insured arising from the insolvency of debtors of theirs or from the failure (otherwise than through insolvency) of debtors of theirs to pay their debts when due.

15 Suretyship

(1) Contracts of insurance against the risks of loss to the persons insured arising from their having to perform contracts of guarantee entered into by them.

(2) Fidelity bonds, performance bonds, administration bonds, bail bonds or customs bonds or similar contracts of guarantee, where these are—

(a)   effected or carried out by a person not carrying on a banking business;
(b)   not effected merely incidentally to some other business carried on by the person effecting them; and
(c)   effected in return for the payment of one or more premiums.

16 Miscellaneous financial loss

Contracts of insurance against any of the following risks, namely—
(a)   risks of loss to the persons insured attributable to interruptions of the carrying on of business carried on by them or to reduction of the scope of business so carried on;
(b)   risks of loss to the persons insured attributable to their incurring unforeseen expense (other than loss such as is covered by contracts falling within paragraph 18);
(c)   risks which do not fall within sub-paragraph (a) or (b) and which are not of a kind such that contracts of insurance against them fall within any other provision of this Schedule.

17 Legal expenses

Contracts of insurance against risks of loss to the persons insured attributable to their incurring legal expenses (including costs of litigation).

18 Assistance

Contracts of insurance providing either or both of the following benefits, namely—
(a)   assistance (whether in cash or in kind) for persons who get into difficulties while travelling, while away from home or while away from their permanent residence; or
(b)   assistance (whether in cash or in kind) for persons who get into difficulties otherwise than as mentioned in sub-paragraph (a).

[2140]

NOTES

Note: see also the FSA Perimeter Guidance Manual, PERG 6, for guidance on the identification of contracts of insurance.

PART II
CONTRACTS OF LONG-TERM INSURANCE

I Life and annuity

Contracts of insurance on human life or contracts to pay annuities on human life, but excluding (in each case) contracts within paragraph III.

II Marriage and birth

Contract of insurance to provide a sum on marriage [or the formation of a civil partnership] or on the birth of a child, being contracts expressed to be in effect for a period of more than one year.

III Linked long term

Contracts of insurance on human life or contracts to pay annuities on human life where the benefits are wholly or party to be determined by references to the value of, or the income from, property of any description (whether or not specified in the contracts) or by reference to fluctuations in, or in an index of, the value of property of any description (whether or not so specified).

IV Permanent health

Contracts of insurance providing specified benefits against risks of persons becoming incapacitated in consequence of sustaining injury as a result of an accident or of an accident of a specified class or of sickness or infirmity, being contracts that—
(a)   are expressed to be in effect for a period of not less than five years, or until the normal retirement age for the persons concerned, or without limit of time; and
(b)   either are not expressed to be terminable by the insurer, or are expressed to be so terminable only in special circumstances mentioned in the contract.

V Tontines

Tontines.

VI Capital redemption contracts

Capital redemption contracts, where effected or carried out by a person who does not carry on a banking business, and otherwise carries on a regulated activity of the kind specified by article 10(1) or (2).

VII Pension fund management
(a)   Pension fund management contracts, and
(b)   pension fund management contracts which are combined with contracts of insurance covering either conservation of capital or payment of a minimum interest,

where effected or carried out by a person who does not carry on a banking business, and otherwise carries on a regulated activity of the kind specified by article 10(1) or (2).

VIII Collective insurance etc

Contracts of a kind referred to in article 1(2)(e) of the first life insurance directive.

IX Social insurance

Contracts of a kind referred to in article 1(3) of the first life insurance directive.

[2141]

[SCHEDULE 2
SECTIONS A AND C OF ANNEX I TO THE MARKETS IN FINANCIAL INSTRUMENTS DIRECTIVE AND RELATED COMMUNITY SUBORDINATE LEGISLATION
Article 3(1)

PART 1
SECTION C OF ANNEX I TO THE MARKETS IN FINANCIAL INSTRUMENTS DIRECTIVE

Financial Instruments

1. Transferable securities;

2. Money-market instruments;

3. Units in collective investment undertakings;

4. Options, futures, swaps, forward rate agreements and any other derivative contracts relating to securities, currencies, interest rates or yields, or other derivatives instruments, financial indices or financial measures which may be settled physically or in cash;

5. Options, futures, swaps, forward rate agreements and any other derivative contracts relating to commodities that must be settled in cash or may be settled in cash at the option of one of the parties (otherwise than by reason of a default or other termination event);

6. Options, futures, swaps, and any other derivative contracts relating to commodities that can be physically settled provided that they are traded on a regulated market and/or an MTF;

7. Options, futures, swaps, forwards and any other derivative contracts relating to commodities, that can be physically settled not otherwise mentioned in C6 and not being for commercial purposes, which have the characteristics of other derivative financial instruments, having regard to whether, inter alia, they are cleared and settled through recognised clearing houses or are subject to regular margin calls;

8. Derivative instruments for the transfer of credit risk;

9. Financial contracts for differences;

10. Options, futures, swaps, forward rate agreements and any other derivative contracts relating to climatic variables, freight rates, emission allowances or inflation rates or other official economic statistics that must be settled in cash or may be settled in cash at the option of one of the parties (otherwise than by reason of a default or other termination event), as well as any other derivative contracts relating to assets, rights, obligations, indices and measures not otherwise mentioned in this Section, which have the characteristics of other derivative financial instruments, having regard to whether, inter alia, they are traded on a regulated market or an MTF, are cleared and settled through recognised clearing houses or are subject to regular margin calls.]

[2142]

[PART 2
CHAPTER VI OF THE COMMISSION REGULATION

DERIVATIVE FINANCIAL INSTRUMENTS

Article 38
Characteristics of other derivative financial instruments

1.   For the purposes of Section C(7) of Annex I to Directive 2004/39/EC, a contract which is not a spot contract within the meaning of paragraph 2 of this Article and which is not covered by paragraph 4 shall be considered as having the characteristics of other derivative financial instruments and not being for commercial purposes if it satisfies the following conditions:

   (a)   it meets one of the following sets of criteria:
      (i)   it is traded on a third country trading facility that performs a similar function to a regulated market or an MTF;
      (ii)   it is expressly stated to be traded on, or is subject to the rules of, a regulated market, an MTF or such a third country trading facility;
      (iii)   it is expressly stated to be equivalent to a contract traded on a regulated market, MTF or such a third country trading facility;
   (b)   it is cleared by a clearing house or other entity carrying out the same functions as a central counterparty, or there are arrangements for the payment or provision of margin in relation to the contract;
   (c)   it is standardised so that, in particular, the price, the lot, the delivery date or other terms are determined principally by reference to regularly published prices, standard lots or standard delivery dates.

2.   A spot contract for the purposes of paragraph 1 means a contract for the sale of a commodity, asset or right, under the terms of which delivery is scheduled to be made within the longer of the following periods:

   (a)   two trading days;
   (b)   the period generally accepted in the market for that commodity, asset or right as the standard delivery period.

However, a contract is not a spot contract if, irrespective of its explicit terms, there is an understanding between the parties to the contract that delivery of the underlying is to be postponed and not to be performed within the period mentioned in the first subparagraph.

3.   For the purposes of Section C(10) of Annex I to Directive 2004/39/EC, a derivative contract relating to an underlying referred to in that Section or in Article 39 shall be considered to have the characteristics of other derivative financial instruments if one of the following conditions is satisfied:

   (a)   that contract is settled in cash or may be settled in cash at the option of one or more of the parties, otherwise than by reason of a default or other termination event;
   (b)   that contract is traded on a regulated market or an MTF;
   (c)   the conditions laid down in paragraph 1 are satisfied in relation to that contract.

4.   A contract shall be considered to be for commercial purposes for the purposes of Section C(7) of Annex I to Directive 2004/39/EC, and as not having the characteristics of other derivative financial instruments for the purposes of Sections C(7) and (10) of that Annex, if it is entered into with or by an operator or administrator of an energy transmission grid, energy balancing mechanism or pipeline network, and it is necessary to keep in balance the supplies and uses of energy at a given time.

Article 39
Derivatives Within Section C(10) of Annex I to Directive 2004/39/EC

In addition to derivative contracts of a kind referred to in Section C(10) of Annex I to Directive 2004/39/EC, a derivative contract relating to any of the following shall fall within that Section if it meets the criteria set out in that Section and in Article 38(3):

   (a)   telecommunications bandwidth;
   (b)   commodity storage capacity;
   (c)   transmission or transportation capacity relating to commodities, whether cable, pipeline or other means;
   (d)   an allowance, credit, permit, right or similar asset which is directly linked to the supply, distribution or consumption of energy derived from renewable resources;
   (e)   a geological, environmental or other physical variable;
   (f)   any other asset or right of a fungible nature, other than a right to receive a service, that is capable of being transferred;
   (g)   an index or measure related to the price or value of, or volume of transactions in any asset, right, service or obligation.]

[2142A]

NOTES
Commencement: 1 April 2007 (certain purposes); 1 November 2007 (otherwise).
Substituted as noted to Part 1 at **[2142]**.
Note: Commission Regulation 1287/2006/EC is set out in full at **[5917]** et seq.

[PART 3
SECTION A OF ANNEX I TO THE MARKETS IN FINANCIAL INSTRUMENTS DIRECTIVE

INVESTMENT SERVICES AND ACTIVITIES

1.   Reception and transmission of orders in relation to one or more financial instruments.

2.   Execution of orders on behalf of clients.

3.   Dealing on own account.

4.   Portfolio management.

5.   Investment advice.

6.   Underwriting of financial instruments and/or placing of financial instruments on a firm commitment basis.

7.   Placing of financial instruments without a firm commitment basis.

8.   Operation of Multilateral Trading Facilities.]

[2142B]

NOTES
Commencement: 1 April 2007 (certain purposes); 1 November 2007 (otherwise).
Substituted as noted to Part 1 at **[2142]**.
Note: MiFID is set out in full at **[5522]** et seq.

[PART 4
ARTICLE 52 OF COMMISSION DIRECTIVE 2006/73/EC

Article 52
Investment Advice

For the purposes of the definition of "investment advice" in Article 4(1)(4) of Directive 2004/39/EC, a personal recommendation is a recommendation that is made to a person in his capacity as an investor or potential investor, or in his capacity as an agent for an investor or potential investor.

That recommendation must be presented as suitable for that person, or must be based on a consideration of the circumstances of that person, and must constitute a recommendation to take one of the following sets of steps:
   (a)   to buy, sell, subscribe for, exchange, redeem, hold or underwrite a particular financial instrument;
   (b)   to exercise or not to exercise any right conferred by a particular financial instrument to buy, sell, subscribe for, exchange, or redeem a financial instrument.

A recommendation is not a personal recommendation if it is issued exclusively through distribution channels or to the public.]

[2142C]

NOTES
Commencement: 1 April 2007 (certain purposes); 1 November 2007 (otherwise).
Substituted as noted to Part 1 at **[2142]**.
Note: Commission Directive 2006/73/EC is set out in full at **[5960]** et seq.

[SCHEDULE 3
ARTICLE 2 OF THE MARKETS IN FINANCIAL INSTRUMENTS DIRECTIVE

Article 2
Exemptions

1.   This Directive shall not apply to:
   (a)   insurance undertakings as defined in Article 1 of Directive 73/239/EEC or assurance undertakings as defined in Article 1 of Directive 2002/83/EC or undertakings carrying on the reinsurance and retrocession activities referred to in Directive 64/225/EEC;
   (b)   persons which provide investment services exclusively for their parent undertakings, for their subsidiaries or for other subsidiaries of their parent undertakings;
   (c)   persons providing an investment service where that service is provided in an incidental manner in the course of a professional activity and that activity is regulated by legal or regulatory provisions or a code of ethics governing the profession which do not exclude the provision of that service;

(d) persons who do not provide any investment services or activities other than dealing on own account unless they are market makers or deal on own account outside a regulated market or an MTF on an organised, frequent and systematic basis by providing a system accessible to third parties in order to engage in dealings with them;

(e) persons which provide investment services consisting exclusively in the administration of employee-participation schemes;

(f) persons which provide investment services which only involve both administration of employee-participation schemes and the provision of investment services exclusively for their parent undertakings, for their subsidiaries or for other subsidiaries of their parent undertakings;

(g) the members of the European System of Central Banks and other national bodies performing similar functions and other public bodies charged with or intervening in the management of the public debt;

(h) collective investment undertakings and pension funds whether coordinated at Community level or not and the depositaries and managers of such undertakings;

(i) persons dealing on own account in financial instruments, or providing investment services in commodity derivatives or derivative contracts included in Annex I, Section C10 to the clients of their main business, provided this is an ancillary activity to their main business, when considered on a group basis, and that main business is not the provision of investment services within the meaning of this Directive or banking services under Directive 2000/12/EC;

(j) persons providing investment advice in the course of providing another professional activity not covered by this Directive provided that the provision of such advice is not specifically remunerated;

(k) persons whose main business consists of dealing on own account in commodities and/or commodity derivatives. This exception shall not apply where the persons that deal on own account in commodities and/or commodity derivatives are part of a group the main business of which is the provision of other investment services within the meaning of this Directive or banking services under Directive 2000/12/EC;

(l) firms which provide investment services and/or perform investment activities consisting exclusively in dealing on own account on markets in financial futures or options or other derivatives and on cash markets for the sole purpose of hedging positions on derivatives markets or which deal for the accounts of other members of those markets or make prices for them and which are guaranteed by clearing members of the same markets, where responsibility for ensuring the performance of contracts entered into by such firms is assumed by clearing members of the same markets;

(m) associations set up by Danish and Finnish pensions funds with the sole aim of managing the assets of pension funds that are members of those associations;

(n) 'agenti di cambio' whose activities and functions are governed by Article 201 of Italian Legislative Decree No 58 of 24 February 1998.

2. The rights conferred by this Directive shall not extend to the provision of services as counterparty in transactions carried out by public bodies dealing with public debt or by members of the European System of Central Banks performing their tasks as provided for by the Treaty and the Statute of the European System of Central Banks and of the European Central Bank or performing equivalent functions under national provisions.

3. In order to take account of developments on financial markets, and to ensure the uniform application of this Directive, the Commission, acting in accordance with the procedure referred to in Article 64(2), may, in respect of exemptions (c), (i) and (k) define the criteria for determining when an activity is to be considered as ancillary to the main business on a group level as well as for determining when an activity is provided in an incidental manner.]

[2143]

NOTES

Commencement: 1 April 2007 (certain purposes); 1 November 2007 (otherwise) (see below).

Substituted by the Financial Services and Markets Act 2000 (Regulated Activities) (Amendment No 3) Order 2006, SI 2006/3384, arts 2, 30, as from 1 April 2007 (for the purposes of enabling applications to be made for (i) a Pt IV permission, (ii) a variation of a Pt IV permission, and (iii) the Authority's approval under s 59 of the 2000 Act, in relation to an activity of the kind specified by art 25D of this Order, or in relation to an investment of the kind specified by arts 83, 84 or 85 of this Order), and as from 1 November 2007 (otherwise).

Note: MiFID is set out in full at **[5522]** et seq.

[SCHEDULE 4
RELEVANT TEXT OF THE INSURANCE MEDIATION DIRECTIVE
Article 4

PART I
ARTICLE 1.2

This Directive shall not apply to persons providing mediation services for insurance contracts if all the following conditions are met:

    (a)   the insurance contract only requires knowledge of the insurance cover that is provided;

    (b)   the insurance contract is not a life assurance contract;

    (c)   the insurance contract does not cover any liability risks;

    (d)   the principal professional activity of the person is other than insurance mediation;

    (e)   the insurance is complementary to the product or service supplied by any provider, where such insurance covers:

        (i)   the risk of breakdown, loss of or damage to goods supplied by that provider; or

        (ii)   damage to or loss of baggage and other risks linked to the travel booked with that provider, even if the insurance covers life assurance or liability risks, provided that the cover is ancillary to the main cover for the risks linked to that travel;

    (f)   the amount of the annual premium does not exceed EUR 500 and the total duration of the insurance contract, including any renewals, does not exceed five years.]

[2144]

NOTES

Commencement: 31 October 2004 (in so far as relating to contracts of long-term care insurance); 14 January 2005 (otherwise).

Added by the Financial Services and Markets Act 2000 (Regulated Activities) (Amendment) (No 2) Order 2003, SI 2003/1476, art 12, as from 31 October 2004 (in so far as relating to contracts of long-term care insurance), and as from 14 January 2005 (otherwise); for transitional provisions see arts 22–27 of that Order at **[2706]** et seq.

Note: the Insurance Mediation Directive (European Parliament and Council Directive 2002/92/EC on insurance mediation) is set out in full at **[5412]** et seq.

[PART II
ARTICLE 2.3

"Insurance mediation" means the activities of introducing, proposing or carrying out other work preparatory to the conclusion of contracts of insurance, or of concluding such contracts, or of assisting in the administration and performance of such contracts, in particular in the event of a claim.

These activities when undertaken by an insurance undertaking or an employee of an insurance undertaking who is acting under the responsibility of the insurance undertaking shall not be considered as insurance mediation.

The provision of information on an incidental basis in the context of another professional activity provided that the purpose of that activity is not to assist the customer in concluding or performing an insurance contract, the management of claims of an insurance undertaking on a professional basis, and loss adjusting and expert appraisal of claims shall also not be considered as insurance mediation.]

[2145]

NOTES

Commencement: 31 October 2004 (in so far as relating to contracts of long-term care insurance); 14 January 2005 (otherwise).

Added as noted to Sch 4, Pt I at **[2144]**.

Note: the Insurance Mediation Directive (European Parliament and Council Directive 2002/92/EC on insurance mediation) is set out in full at **[5412]** et seq.

[PART III
ARTICLE 2.4

"Reinsurance mediation" means the activities of introducing, proposing or carrying out other work preparatory to the conclusion of contracts of reinsurance, or of concluding such contracts, or of assisting in the administration and performance of such contracts, in particular in the event of a claim.

These activities when undertaken by a reinsurance undertaking or an employee of a reinsurance undertaking who is acting under the responsibility of the reinsurance undertaking are not considered as reinsurance mediation.

The provision of information on an incidental basis in the context of another professional activity provided that the purpose of that activity is not to assist the customer in concluding or performing a reinsurance contract, the management of claims of a reinsurance undertaking on a professional basis, and loss adjusting and expert appraisal of claims shall also not be considered as reinsurance mediation.]

[2146]

NOTES
  Commencement: 31 October 2004 (in so far as relating to contracts of long-term care insurance); 14 January 2005 (otherwise).
  Added as noted to Sch 4, Pt I at **[2144]**.
  Note: the Insurance Mediation Directive (European Parliament and Council Directive 2002/92/EC on insurance mediation) is set out in full at **[5412]** et seq.

FINANCIAL SERVICES AND MARKETS ACT 2000 (RECOGNITION REQUIREMENTS FOR INVESTMENT EXCHANGES AND CLEARING HOUSES) REGULATIONS 2001

(SI 2001/995)

NOTES
  Made: 9 April 2001.
  Authority: Financial Services and Markets Act 2000, ss 286(1), 426, 427, 428(3).
  Commencement: see reg 2 at **[2148]**.
  These Regulations are reproduced as amended by: the Financial Services and Markets Act 2000 (Market Abuse) Regulations 2005, SI 2005/381; the Financial Services and Markets Act 2000 (Recognition Requirements for Investment Exchanges and Clearing Houses) (Amendment) Regulations 2006, SI 2006/3386.

ARRANGEMENT OF REGULATIONS

1   Citation

These Regulations may be cited as the Financial Services and Markets Act 2000 (Recognition Requirements for Investment Exchanges and Clearing Houses) Regulations 2001.

[2147]

2   Commencement

These Regulations come into force on the day on which sections 290(1) and 292(2) of the Act (which relate to the making of recognition orders) come into force.

[2148]

NOTES
  Note that ss 290(1) and 292(2) of the Act came into force on 3 September 2001 (for the purposes of recognition orders coming into force not sooner than 1 December 2001), and on 1 December 2001 (for all other purposes).

---

3   Interpretation

(1)   In these Regulations—
    "the Act" means the Financial Services and Markets Act 2000;

["branch" in relation to an investment firm has the meaning given in Article 4.1.26 of the markets in financial instruments directive and in relation to a credit institution has the meaning given in Article 4.3 of the banking consolidation directive;]

["central counterparty", "clearing" and "settlement" have the same meaning as in the markets in financial instruments directive;]

["the Commission Regulation" means Commission Regulation 1287/2006 of 10 August 2006;]

"the Companies Act" means the Companies Act 1989;

["competent authority", in relation to an investment firm or credit institution, means the competent authority in relation to that firm or institution for the purposes of the markets in financial instruments directive;]

["credit institution" means—

    (a)   a credit institution authorised under the banking consolidation directive, or

    (b)   an institution which would satisfy the requirements for authorisation as a credit institution under that directive if it had its registered office (or if it does not have a registered office, its head office) in an EEA State;]

"defaulter" and "default" are to be construed in accordance with section 188(2) of the Companies Act, and references to action taken under the default rules of an exchange or clearing house are to be construed in accordance with section 188(4) of that Act;

["disorderly trading conditions" has the same meaning as in the markets in financial instruments directive;]

"exempt activities", in relation to a recognised body, means the regulated activities in respect of which the body is exempt from the general prohibition as a result of section 285(2) or (3) of the Act;

"facilities", in relation to a recognised body, means the facilities and services it provides in the course of carrying on exempt activities, and references to the use of the facilities of an exchange is to be construed in accordance with paragraph (2);

"financial crime" is to be construed in accordance with section 6(3) and (4) of the Act;

["financial instrument" has the meaning given in Article 4.1.17 of the markets in financial instruments directive;]

"the Financial Services Act" means the Financial Services Act 1986;

"investments" means investments of a kind specified for the purposes of section 22 of the Act;

"market contract" has the meaning given in section 286(4) of the Act (with reference, in the case of a recognised investment exchange, to section 155(2) of the Companies Act or article 80(2) of the Northern Ireland Order, or in the case of a recognised clearing house, to section 155(3) of the Companies Act or article 80(3) of the Northern Ireland Order) and references to a party to a market contract are to be construed in accordance with section 187 of the Companies Act;

["multilateral trading facility" has the meaning given in Article 4.1.15 of the markets in financial instruments directive;]

"the Northern Ireland Order" means the Companies (No 2) (Northern Ireland) Order 1990; and

["regulated market" has the meaning given in Article 4.1.14 of the markets in financial instruments directive;]

"regulatory functions", in relation to a recognised body, has the meaning given in section 291(3) of the Act.

["transferable securities" has the meaning given in Article 4.1.18 of the markets in financial instruments directive;]

["UK firm" means an investment firm or credit institution which has a Part IV permission to carry on one or more regulated activities.]

(2)   In these Regulations, references to dealings on an exchange, or transactions effected on an exchange, are references to dealings or transactions which are effected by means of the exchange's facilities or which are governed by the rules of the exchange, and references to the use of the facilities of an exchange include use which consists of any such dealings or entering into any such transactions.

(3)   In these Regulations, except in regulation 6, references to the performance of the functions of a recognised body are references to the carrying on by it of exempt activities together with the performance of its regulatory functions.

[2149]

NOTES

Para (1): definitions in square brackets inserted by the Financial Services and Markets Act 2000 (Recognition Requirements for Investment Exchanges and Clearing Houses) (Amendment) Regulations 2006, SI 2006/3386, regs 2, 3, as from 1 November 2007.

4 Recognition requirements for investment exchanges

Parts I and II of the Schedule set out recognition requirements applying to bodies in respect of which a recognition order has been made under section 290(1)(a) of the Act, or which have applied for such an order under section 287 of the Act.

[2150]

5 Recognition requirements for clearing houses

Parts III and IV of the Schedule set out recognition requirements applying to bodies in respect of which a recognition order has been made under section 290(1)(b) of the Act, or which have applied for such an order under section 288 of the Act.

[2151]

6 Method of satisfying recognition requirements

(1)   In considering whether a recognised body or applicant satisfies recognition requirements applying to it under these Regulations, the Authority may take into account all relevant circumstances including the constitution of the person concerned and its regulatory provisions and practices within the meaning of section 302(1) of the Act.

(2)   Without prejudice to the generality of paragraph (1), a recognised body or applicant may satisfy recognition requirements applying to it under these Regulations by making arrangements for functions to be performed on its behalf by any other person.

(3)   Where a recognised body or applicant makes arrangements of the kind mentioned in paragraph (2), the arrangements do not affect the responsibility imposed by the Act on the recognised body or applicant to satisfy recognition requirements applying to it under these Regulations, but it is in addition a recognition requirement applying to the recognised body or applicant that the person who performs (or is to perform) the functions is a fit and proper person who is able and willing to perform them.

[2152]

7 Dealings and transactions not involving investments

Nothing in these Regulations is to be construed as requiring a recognised investment exchange to limit dealings on the exchange to dealings in investments, or as requiring a recognised investment exchange or recognised clearing house to limit the provision of its clearing services to clearing services in respect of transactions in investments.

[2153]

8 Exchanges and clearing houses which do not enter into market contracts

Nothing in Parts II or IV of the Schedule is to be taken as requiring a recognised investment exchange or recognised clearing house which does not enter into such contracts as are mentioned in section 155(2)(b) or (3) of the Companies Act to have default rules, or to make any arrangements, relating to such contracts.

[2154]

9 Effect of recognition under the Financial Services Act 1986

(1)   In this regulation, "commencement" means the beginning of the day on which subsections (2) and (3) of section 285 of the Act (exemption from the general prohibition for recognised investment exchanges and clearing houses) come into force.

(2)   Subject to paragraph (3), an order under section 37(3) of the Financial Services Act which was in force immediately before commencement has effect after commencement as if it were a recognition order made under section 290(1)(a) of the Act following an application under section 287 of the Act, declaring the body or association to which it relates to be a recognised investment exchange.

(3)   But if the order was made by virtue of section 40(2) of the Financial Services Act (recognition requirements for overseas investment exchanges and clearing houses), it has effect as if it were a recognition order made under section 292(2)(a) of the Act.

(4)   Subject to paragraph (5), an order under section 39(3) of the Financial Services Act which was in force immediately before commencement has effect after commencement as if it were a recognition order made under section 290(1)(b) of the Act following an application under section 288 of the Act, declaring the body or association to which it relates to be a recognised clearing house.

(5)   But if the order was made by virtue of section 40(2) of the Financial Services Act (recognition requirements for overseas investment exchanges and clearing houses), it has effect as if it were a recognition order made under section 292(2)(b) of the Act.

(6)   Where a recognition order has effect by virtue of this regulation, the Authority may not give a notice under section 298(1)(a) of the Act, giving notice of its intention to give a direction under section 296 or to make a revocation order under section 297(2) in relation to the recognised body concerned, earlier than one month after commencement.

PART III
STATUTORY INSTRUMENTS

(7)   Paragraph (6) is without prejudice to section 298(7) of the Act (which permits the Authority to give a direction under section 296 of the Act without following the procedure set out in section 298, if the Authority considers it essential to do so), or to the continued effect of any notice which has effect as a notice given under section 298(1)(a) of the Act by virtue of regulation 10(4) below.

[2155]

10   Revocation of recognition: action taken before commencement

(1)   In this regulation—
  (a)   "commencement" has the same meaning as in regulation 9 above, and
  (b)   "relevant person" means—
    (i)   in relation to action taken in respect of a body or association of the kind described in section 40(1) of the Financial Services Act (overseas investment exchanges and clearing houses), the Treasury, or
    (ii)   in any other case, the Authority.

(2)   This regulation applies to action taken by a relevant person before commencement pursuant to section 37(7) or 39(7) of the Financial Services Act (which relate to revocation of recognition orders under that Act), or pursuant to subsections (2) to (9) of section 11 of that Act as they had effect by virtue of section 37(7) or 39(7).

(3)   Paragraphs (4) to (8) apply where a relevant person has given notice to a body or association under section 11(3) of the Financial Services Act of its intention to revoke a recognition order made under that Act in relation to that body or association, but has not notified the body or association of its determination whether to proceed to revoke that recognition order.

(4)   The notice has effect after commencement as if it were a notice given by the Authority under section 298(1)(a) of the Act, giving notice of the Authority's intention to revoke the recognition order which is treated as having effect in relation to the body or association by virtue of regulation 9 above.

(5)   If before commencement the relevant person has complied with—
  (a)   the requirement in subsection (3) of section 11 of the Financial Services Act to bring the notice to the attention of members of the body or association in question, or
  (b)   the requirement in that subsection to publish the notice to other persons likely to be affected,
the Authority is to be treated as having complied with the equivalent requirement in section 298(1)(b) or (as the case may be) (c) of the Act, in relation to the notice under section 298(1)(a) which has effect by virtue of paragraph (4).

(6)   Nothing in paragraph (4) or in the Act is to be treated as changing the length or affecting the continuity of the period within which, in accordance with the notice as originally given, representations might be made by any person to the relevant person pursuant to section 11(5) of the Financial Services Act, but any such representations are to be considered by the Authority as if they were representations made to it pursuant to section 298(3) of the Act.

(7)   For the purposes of the Authority's consideration whether to proceed to exercise the power to make a revocation order under subsection (2) of section 297 of the Act (but without prejudice to any exercise by the Authority of that power where it has given a new notice under section 298(1)(a) after commencement), that subsection is to be read as if the reference in paragraph (a) to recognition requirements were a reference to recognition requirements other than new recognition requirements, and as if the reference in paragraph (b) to obligations were a reference to obligations other than new obligations.

(8)   A recognition requirement or obligation is to be treated as a new recognition requirement or obligation if its effect is not substantially the same as the effect of a requirement or obligation of the kind mentioned (or having effect as if mentioned) in section 37(7) (in the case of an investment exchange) or 39(7) (in the case of a clearing house) of the Financial Services Act (as those provisions had effect immediately before commencement).

(9)   Paragraph (10) applies where a relevant person has made an order ("the revoking order") under section 37(7) or 39(7) of the Financial Services Act, revoking a recognition order made in relation to a body or association under that Act, but either—
  (a)   the revoking order has not taken effect in accordance with section 11(2) of the Financial Services Act, or
  (b)   the revoking order has taken effect but contains transitional provisions pursuant to section 11(7) of the Financial Services Act which continued to have effect immediately before commencement.

(10)   The revoking order has effect after commencement as if it were a revocation order made by the Authority under section 297 of the Act, revoking (with effect from the date specified in the revoking order) the recognition order which is treated as having effect in relation to the body or

association by virtue of regulation 9 above, and as if any such transitional provisions were included in the revocation order by virtue of section 297(5) of the Act.

[2156]

SCHEDULE

Regulations 4 and 5

PART I

RECOGNITION REQUIREMENTS FOR INVESTMENT EXCHANGES

Financial resources

1.—(1)   The exchange must have financial resources sufficient for the proper performance of its functions as a recognised investment exchange.

(2)   In considering whether this requirement is satisfied, the Authority [must] (without prejudice to the generality of regulation 6(1)) take into account all the circumstances, including the exchange's connection with any person, and any activity carried on by the exchange, whether or not it is an exempt activity.

Suitability

2.—(1)   The exchange must be a fit and proper person to perform the functions of a recognised investment exchange.

(2)   In considering whether this requirement is satisfied, the Authority may (without prejudice to the generality of regulation 6(1)) take into account all the circumstances, including the exchange's connection with any person.

[(3)   The persons who effectively direct the business and operations of the exchange must be of sufficiently good repute and sufficiently experienced to ensure the sound and prudent management and operation of the financial markets operated by it.

(4)   The persons who are in a position to exercise significant influence over the management of the exchange, whether directly or indirectly, must be suitable.]

Systems and controls

3.—(1)   The exchange must ensure that the systems and controls used in the performance of its functions are adequate, and appropriate for the scale and nature of its business.

(2)   Sub-paragraph (1) applies in particular to systems and controls concerning—
   (a)   the transmission of information;
   (b)   the assessment[, mitigation] and management of risks to the performance of the exchange's functions;
   (c)   the effecting and monitoring of transactions on the exchange;
   [(ca) the technical operation of the exchange, including contingency arrangements for disruption to its facilities;]
   (d)   the operation of the arrangements mentioned in paragraph 4(2)(d) below; and
   (e)   (where relevant) the safeguarding and administration of assets belonging to users of the exchange's facilities.

Safeguards for investors

4.—(1)   The exchange must ensure that business conducted by means of its facilities is conducted in an orderly manner and so as to afford proper protection to investors.

(2)   Without prejudice to the generality of sub-paragraph (1), the exchange must ensure that—
   (a)   access to the exchange's facilities is subject to criteria designed to protect the orderly functioning of the market and the interests of investors [and is in accordance with paragraph 7B];
   [(aa) it has transparent and non-discretionary rules and procedures—
      (i)   to provide for fair and orderly trading, and
      (ii) to establish objective criteria for the efficient execution of orders;]
   (b)   ...
   (c)   appropriate arrangements are made for relevant information to be made available (whether by the exchange or, where appropriate, by issuers of the investments) to persons engaged in dealing in investments on the exchange;
   (d)   satisfactory arrangements[, which comply with paragraph 7D,] are made for securing the timely discharge (whether by performance, compromise or otherwise) of the rights and liabilities of the parties to transactions effected on the exchange (being rights and liabilities in relation to those transactions);
   (e)   satisfactory arrangements are made for recording transactions effected on the exchange, and transactions (whether or not effected on the exchange) which are cleared or to be cleared by means of its facilities;

[(ea) appropriate arrangements are made to—
      (i)   identify conflicts between the interests of the exchange, its owners and operators and the interests of the persons who make use of its facilities or the interests of the financial markets operated by it, and
      (ii) manage such conflicts so as to avoid adverse consequences for the operation of the financial markets operated by the exchange and for the persons who make use of its facilities;]

(f)   appropriate measures [(including the monitoring of transactions effected on the exchange)] are adopted to reduce the extent to which the exchange's facilities can be used for a purpose connected with market abuse or financial crime, and to facilitate their detection and monitor their incidence; and

(g)   where the exchange's facilities include making provision for the safeguarding and administration of assets belonging to users of those facilities, satisfactory arrangements are made for that purpose.

(3) In sub-paragraph (2)(c), "relevant information" means information which is relevant in determining the current value of the investments.

[Provision of pre-trade information about share trading

4A.—(1) The exchange must make arrangements for—
(a)   current bid and offer prices for shares, and
(b)   the depth of trading interest in shares at the prices which are advertised through its systems,

to be made available to the public on reasonable commercial terms and on a continuous basis during normal trading hours, subject to the requirements contained in Chapter IV of the Commission Regulation.

(2) If an exchange decides to give investment firms and credit institutions required to publish their quotes in shares—
(a)   in accordance with Article 27 of the markets in financial instruments directive, or
(b)   by the Authority,

access to the arrangements referred to in sub-paragraph (1), it must do so on reasonable commercial terms and on a non-discriminatory basis.

(3) The Authority may waive the requirements of sub-paragraph (1) in the circumstances specified—
(a)   in the case of shares to be traded on a multilateral trading facility operated by the exchange, in Article 29.2 of the markets in financial instruments directive and Chapter IV of the Commission Regulation; or
(b)   in the case of shares to be traded on a regulated market operated by the exchange, in Article 44.2 of that directive and Chapter IV of the Commission Regulation.

(4) In this paragraph, "shares" means shares admitted to trading on a regulated market.

Provision of post-trade information about share trading

4B.—(1) The exchange must make arrangements for the price, volume and time of transactions executed in shares to be made available to the public as soon as possible after the time of the transaction on reasonable commercial terms, subject to the requirements contained in Chapter IV of the Commission Regulation.

(2) If an exchange decides to give investment firms and credit institutions required to make public details of their transactions in shares—
(a)   in accordance with Article 28 of the markets in financial instruments directive, or
(b)   by the Authority,

access to the arrangements referred to in sub-paragraph (1), it must do so on reasonable commercial terms and on a non-discriminatory basis.

(3) The Authority may permit exchanges to defer the publication required by sub-paragraph (1) in the circumstances specified, and subject to the requirements contained—
(a)   in the case of shares traded on a multilateral trading facility operated by an exchange, in Article 30.2 of the markets in financial instruments directive and Chapter IV of the Commission Regulation; or
(b)   in the case of shares traded on a regulated market operated by an exchange, in Article 45.2 of that directive and Chapter IV of the Commission Regulation.

(4) If the Authority permits exchanges to defer the publication required by sub-paragraph (1), those exchanges must ensure that the existence of and the terms of the permission are disclosed to users and members of their facilities and to investors.

(5) In this paragraph, "shares" means shares admitted to trading on a regulated market.]

Disclosure by issuers of securities

5.   ...

Promotion and maintenance of standards

6.—(1)   The exchange must be able and willing to promote and maintain high standards of integrity and fair dealing in the carrying on of regulated activities by persons in the course of using the facilities provided by the exchange.

(2)   The exchange must be able and willing to cooperate, by the sharing of information or otherwise, with the Authority, with any other authority, body or person having responsibility in the United Kingdom for the supervision or regulation of any regulated activity or other financial service, or with an overseas regulator within the meaning of section 195 of the Act.

Rules and consultation

7.—(1)   The exchange must ensure that appropriate procedures are adopted for it to make rules, for keeping its rules under review and for amending them.

(2)   The procedures must include procedures for consulting users of the exchange's facilities in appropriate cases.

(3)   The exchange must consult users of its facilities on any arrangements it proposes to make for dealing with penalty income in accordance with paragraph 8(3) below (or on any changes which it proposes to make to those arrangements).

[Admission of financial instruments to trading

7A.—(1)   The exchange must make clear and transparent rules concerning the admission of financial instruments to trading on any financial market operated by it.

(2)   The rules must ensure that all financial instruments admitted to trading on a regulated market operated by the exchange are capable of being traded in a fair, orderly and efficient manner (in accordance with Chapter V of the Commission Regulation, where applicable).

(3)   The rules must ensure that—
   (a)   all transferable securities admitted to trading on a regulated market operated by the exchange are freely negotiable (in accordance with Chapter V of the Commission Regulation, where applicable); and
   (b)   all contracts for derivatives admitted to trading on a regulated market operated by the exchange are designed so as to allow for their orderly pricing as well as for the existence of effective settlement conditions.

(4)   The exchange must maintain arrangements to provide sufficient publicly available information (or satisfy itself that sufficient information is publicly available) to enable the users of a multilateral trading facility operated by it to form investment judgments, taking into account both the nature of the users and the types of instrument traded.

(5)   The exchange must maintain effective arrangements to verify that issuers of transferable securities admitted to trading on a regulated market operated by it comply with the disclosure obligations.

(6)   The exchange must maintain arrangements to assist users of a regulated market operated by it to obtain access to information made public under the disclosure obligations.

(7)   The exchange must maintain arrangements regularly to review whether the financial instruments admitted to trading on a regulated market operated by it comply with the admission requirements for those instruments.

(8)   The rules must provide that where an exchange, without obtaining the consent of the issuer, admits to trading on a regulated market operated by it a transferable security which has been admitted to trading on another regulated market, the exchange—
   (a)   must inform the issuer of that security as soon as is reasonably practicable, and
   (b)   may not require the issuer of that security to demonstrate compliance with the disclosure obligations.

(9)   The rules must provide that where an exchange, without obtaining the consent of the issuer, admits to trading on a multilateral trading facility operated by it a transferable security which has been admitted to trading on a regulated market, it may not require the issuer of that security to demonstrate compliance with the disclosure obligations.

(10)   In this paragraph—
   "derivatives" has the same meaning as in the markets in financial instruments directive;
   "the disclosure obligations" are the initial, ongoing and ad hoc disclosure requirements contained in the relevant articles and given effect—
      (a)   in the UK by Part 6 of the Act and Part 6 rules (within the meaning of section 73A of the Act); or

(b)   in another EEA State by legislation transposing the relevant articles in that State.
"issuer" has the same meaning as in the markets in financial instruments directive;
"the relevant articles" means—

(a)   Article 6.1 to 6.4 of Directive 2003/6/EC of the European Parliament and of the
Council of 28 January 2003 on insider dealing and market manipulation,

(b)   Articles 3, 5, 7, 8, 10, 14 and 16 of Directive 2003/71/EC of the European
Parliament and of the Council of 4 November 2003 on the prospectuses to be
published when securities are offered to the public or admitted to trading,

(c)   Articles 4 to 6, 14, 16 to 19 and 30 of Directive 2004/109/EC of the European
Parliament and of the Council of 15 December 2004 relating to the harmonisation
of transparency requirements in relation to information about issuers whose
securities are admitted to trading on a regulated market, and

(d)   Community legislation made under the provisions mentioned in paragraphs (a)
to (c).

(11)   This paragraph is without prejudice to the generality of paragraph 4.

Access to the exchange's facilities

7B.—(1)   The exchange must make transparent and non-discriminatory rules, based on objective
criteria, governing access to, or membership of, its facilities.

(2)   In particular those rules must specify the obligations for users or members of its facilities
arising from—

(a)   the constitution and administration of the exchange;

(b)   rules relating to transactions on the market;

(c)   its professional standards for staff of any investment firm or credit institution having
access to or membership of a financial market operated by the exchange;

(d)   conditions established under sub-paragraph (3)(c) for access to or membership of a
financial market operated by the exchange by persons other than investment firms or
credit institutions; and

(e)   the rules and procedures for clearing and settlement of transactions concluded on a
financial market operated by the exchange.

(3)   Rules of the exchange about access to, or membership of, a financial market operated by it
must permit the exchange to give access to or admit to membership (as the case may be) only—

(a)   an investment firm,

(b)   a credit institution, or

(c)   a person who—

(i)   is fit and proper,

(ii)   has a sufficient level of trading ability and competence,

(iii)   where applicable, has adequate organisational arrangements, and

(iv)   has sufficient resources for the role he is to perform, taking account of the
exchange's arrangements under paragraph 4(2)(d).

(4)   Rules under this paragraph must enable—

(a)   an investment firm authorised under Article 5 of the markets in financial instruments
directive, or

(b)   a credit institution authorised under the banking consolidation directive,

by the competent authority of another EEA State (including a branch established in the United
Kingdom of such a firm or institution) to have direct or remote access to, or membership of, any
financial market operated by the exchange on the same terms as a UK firm.

(5)   The exchange must make arrangements regularly to provide the Authority with a list of the
users or members of its facilities.

(6)   This paragraph is without prejudice to the generality of paragraph 4.

Access to central counterparty, clearing and settlement facilities

7C.—(1)   This paragraph applies to an exchange which provides central counterparty, clearing or
settlement facilities.

(2)   The exchange must make transparent and non-discriminatory rules, based on objective
criteria, governing access to those facilities.

(3)   The rules under sub-paragraph (2) must enable an investment firm or a credit institution
authorised by the competent authority of another EEA State (including a branch established in the
United Kingdom of such a firm or institution) to have access to those facilities on the same terms as
a UK firm for the purposes of finalising or arranging the finalisation of transactions in financial
instruments.

(4)   The exchange may refuse access to those facilities on legitimate commercial grounds.

Choice of settlement facilities

7D.—(1)   The rules of the exchange must permit a user or member of a regulated market operated by it to use whatever settlement facility he chooses for a transaction.

(2)   Sub-paragraph (1) only applies where—
  (a)   such links and arrangements exist between the chosen settlement facility and any other settlement facility as are necessary to ensure the efficient and economic settlement of the transaction; and
  (b)   the exchange is satisfied that the smooth and orderly functioning of the financial markets will be maintained.

Suspension and removal of financial instruments from trading

7E.   The rules of the exchange must provide that the exchange must not exercise its power to suspend or remove from trading on a regulated market operated by it any financial instrument which no longer complies with its rules, where such step would be likely to cause significant damage to the interests of investors or the orderly functioning of the financial markets.]

Discipline

8.—[(1)   The exchange must have—
  (a)   effective arrangements (which include the monitoring of transactions effected on the exchange) for monitoring and enforcing compliance with its rules, including rules in relation to the provision of clearing services in respect of transactions other than transactions effected on the exchange;
  (b)   effective arrangements for monitoring and enforcing compliance with the arrangements made by it as mentioned in paragraph 4(2)(d); and
  (c)   effective arrangements for monitoring transactions effected on the exchange in order to identify disorderly trading conditions.]

(2)   Arrangements made pursuant to sub-paragraph (1) must include procedures for—
  (a)   investigating complaints made to the exchange about the conduct of persons in the course of using the exchange's facilities; and
  (b)   the fair, independent and impartial resolution of appeals against decisions of the exchange.

(3)   Where arrangements made pursuant to sub-paragraph (1) include provision for requiring the payment of financial penalties, they must include arrangements for ensuring that any amount so paid is applied only in one or more of the following ways—
  (a)   towards meeting expenses incurred by the exchange in the course of the investigation of the breach in respect of which the penalty is paid, or in the course of any appeal against the decision of the exchange in relation to that breach;
  (b)   for the benefit of users of the exchange's facilities;
  (c)   for charitable purposes.

Complaints

9.—(1)   The exchange must have effective arrangements for the investigation and resolution of complaints arising in connection with the performance of, or failure to perform, any of its regulatory functions.

(2)   But sub-paragraph (1) does not extend to—
  (a)   complaints about the content of rules made by the exchange, or
  (b)   complaints about a decision against which the complainant has the right to appeal under procedures of the kind mentioned in paragraph 8(2)(b) above.

(3)   The arrangements must include arrangements for a complaint to be fairly and impartially investigated by a person independent of the exchange, and for him to report on the result of his investigation to the exchange and to the complainant.

(4)   The arrangements must confer on the person mentioned in sub-paragraph (3) the power to recommend, if he thinks it appropriate, that the exchange—
  (a)   makes a compensatory payment to the complainant,
  (b)   remedies the matter complained of,
or takes both of those steps.

(5)   Sub-paragraph (3) is not to be taken as preventing the exchange from making arrangements for the initial investigation of a complaint to be conducted by the exchange.

[Operation of a multilateral trading facility

9A.—(1)   An exchange operating a multilateral trading facility must also operate a regulated market.

(2)   An exchange operating a multilateral trading facility must comply with those requirements of—
  (a)   Chapter I of Title II of the markets in financial instruments directive, and
  (b)   Commission Directive 2006/73/EC of 10 August 2006,
which are applicable to a market operator (within the meaning of the directive) operating such a facility.

(3)   The requirements of this paragraph do not apply for the purposes of section 292(3)(a) of the Act (requirements for overseas investment exchanges and overseas clearing houses).]

[2157]

NOTES
  Para 1: word in square brackets in sub-para (2) substituted by the Financial Services and Markets Act 2000 (Recognition Requirements for Investment Exchanges and Clearing Houses) (Amendment) Regulations 2006, SI 2006/3386, regs 2, 4, as from 1 November 2007.
  Para 2: sub-paras (3), (4) added by SI 2006/3386, regs 2, 5, as from 1 November 2007.
  Para 3: sub-para (2)(ca) and the word in square brackets in sub-para (2)(b) inserted by SI 2006/3386, regs 2, 6, as from 1 November 2007.
  Para 4: sub-paras (2)(aa), (ea) and the words in square brackets in sub-paras (2)(a), (d), (f) inserted, and sub-para (2)(b) revoked, by SI 2006/3386, regs 2, 7, as from 1 November 2007.
  Paras 4A, 4B, 7A–7E, 9A: inserted by SI 2006/3386, regs 2, 8, 9, 11, as from 1 November 2007.
  Para 5: revoked by the Financial Services and Markets Act 2000 (Market Abuse) Regulations 2005, SI 2005/381, reg 11, as from 1 July 2005.
  Para 8: sub-para (1) substituted by SI 2006/3386, regs 2, 10, as from 1 November 2007.

PART II
RECOGNITION REQUIREMENTS FOR INVESTMENT EXCHANGES: DEFAULT RULES IN RESPECT OF MARKET CONTRACTS

Default rules in respect of market contracts

10.—(1)   The exchange must have default rules which, in the event of a member of the exchange being or appearing to be unable to meet his obligations in respect of one or more market contracts, enable action to be taken in respect of unsettled market contracts to which he is a party.

(2)   The rules may authorise the taking of the same or similar action in relation to a member who appears to be likely to become unable to meet his obligations in respect of one or more market contracts.

(3)   The rules must enable action to be taken in respect of all unsettled market contracts, other than those entered into ... for the purposes of or in connection with the provision of clearing services for the exchange.

Content of rules

11.—(1)   This paragraph applies as regards contracts falling within section 155(2)(a) of the Companies Act.

(2)   The rules mentioned in paragraph 10 must provide—
  (a)   for all rights and liabilities between those party as principal to unsettled market contracts to which the defaulter is party as principal to be discharged and for there to be paid by one party to the other such sum of money (if any) as may be determined in accordance with the rules;
  (b)   for the sums so payable in respect of different contracts between the same parties to be aggregated or set off so as to produce a net sum; and
  (c)   for the certification by or on behalf of the exchange of the net sum payable or, as the case may be, of the fact that no sum is payable.

(3)   The reference in sub-paragraph (2) to rights and liabilities between those party as principal to unsettled market contracts does not include rights and liabilities—
  (a)   in respect of margin; or
  (b)   arising out of a failure to perform a market contract.

(4)   The rules may make the same or similar provision, in relation to non-members designated in accordance with the procedures mentioned in sub-paragraph (5), as in relation to members of the exchange.

(5)   If such provision is made as is mentioned in sub-paragraph (4), the exchange must have adequate procedures—
  (a)   for designating the persons, or descriptions of person, in respect of whom action may be taken;
  (b)   for keeping under review the question which persons or descriptions of person should be or remain so designated; and
  (c)   for withdrawing such designation.

(6)   The procedures must be designed to secure that—

(a)   a person is not, or does not remain, designated if failure by him to meet his obligations in respect of one or more market contracts would be unlikely adversely to affect the operation of the market; and

(b)   a description of persons is not, or does not remain, designated if failure by a person of that description to meet his obligations in respect of one or more market contracts would be unlikely adversely to affect the operation of the market.

(7)   The exchange must have adequate arrangements—

(a)   for bringing a designation or withdrawal of designation to the attention of the person or description of persons concerned; and

(b)   where a description of persons is designated, or the designation of a description of persons is withdrawn, for ascertaining which persons fall within that description.

12.—(1)   This paragraph applies as regards contracts falling within section 155(2)(b) of the Companies Act.

(2)   The rules mentioned in paragraph 10 must provide—

(a)   for all rights and liabilities of the defaulter under or in respect of unsettled market contracts to be discharged and for there to be paid by or to the defaulter such sum of money (if any) as may be determined in accordance with the rules;

(b)   for the sums so payable by or to the defaulter in respect of different contracts to be aggregated or set off so as to produce a net sum;

(c)   for that sum—

(i)   if payable by the defaulter to the exchange, to be set off against any property provided by or on behalf of the defaulter as cover for margin (or the proceeds of realisation of such property) so as to produce a further net sum;

(ii)   if payable by the exchange to the defaulter, to be aggregated with any property provided by or on behalf of the defaulter as cover for margin (or the proceeds of realisation of such property); and

(d)   for the certification by or on behalf of the exchange of the sum finally payable or, as the case may be, of the fact that no sum is payable.

(3)   The reference in sub-paragraph (2) to the rights and liabilities of a defaulter under or in respect of an unsettled market contract includes (without prejudice to the generality of that provision) rights and liabilities arising in consequence of action taken under provisions of the rules authorising—

(a)   the effecting by the exchange of corresponding contracts in relation to unsettled market contracts to which the defaulter is party;

(b)   the transfer of the defaulter's position under an unsettled market contract to another member of the exchange;

(c)   the exercise by the exchange of any option granted by an unsettled market contract.

(4)   A "corresponding contract" means a contract on the same terms (except as to price or premium) as the market contract but under which the person who is the buyer under the market contract agrees to sell and the person who is the seller under the market contract agrees to buy.

(5)   Sub-paragraph (4) applies with any necessary modifications in relation to a market contract which is not an agreement to sell.

(6)   The reference in sub-paragraph (2) to the rights and liabilities of a defaulter under or in respect of an unsettled market contract does not include, where he acts as agent, rights or liabilities of his arising out of the relationship of principal and agent.

Notification to other parties affected

13.   The exchange must have adequate arrangements for ensuring that—

(a)   in the case of unsettled market contracts with a defaulter acting as principal, parties to the contract are notified as soon as reasonably practicable of the default and of any decision taken under the rules in relation to contracts to which they are a party; and

(b)   in the case of unsettled market contracts with a defaulter acting as agent, parties to the contract and the defaulter's principals are notified as soon as reasonably practicable of the default and of the identity of the other parties to the contract.

Cooperation with other authorities

14.   The exchange must be able and willing to cooperate, by the sharing of information and otherwise, with the Secretary of State, any relevant office-holder within the meaning of section 189 of the Companies Act, and any other authority or body having responsibility for any matter arising out of, or connected with, the default of a member of the exchange or any non-member designated in accordance with the procedures mentioned in paragraph 11(5) above.

PART III
STATUTORY INSTRUMENTS

Margin

15.—(1)   Where the exchange provides clearing services, the rules of the exchange must provide that in the event of a default, margin provided by the defaulter for his own account is not to be applied to meet a shortfall on a client account.

(2)   This paragraph is without prejudice to the requirements of any rules relating to clients' money made by the Authority under sections 138 and 139 of the Act.

[2158]

NOTES

Para 10: words omitted from sub-para (3) revoked by the Financial Services and Markets Act 2000 (Recognition Requirements for Investment Exchanges and Clearing Houses) (Amendment) Regulations 2006, SI 2006/3386, regs 2, 12, as from 1 November 2007.

PART III
RECOGNITION REQUIREMENTS FOR CLEARING HOUSES

Financial resources

16.—(1)   The clearing house must have financial resources sufficient for the proper performance of its functions as a recognised clearing house.

(2)   In considering whether this requirement is satisfied, the Authority may (without prejudice to the generality of regulation 6(1)) take into account all the circumstances, including the clearing house's connection with any person, and any activity carried on by the clearing house, whether or not it is an exempt activity.

Suitability

17.—(1)   The clearing house must be a fit and proper person to perform the functions of a recognised clearing house.

(2)   In considering whether this requirement is satisfied, the Authority may (without prejudice to the generality of regulation 6(1)) take into account all the circumstances, including the clearing house's connection with any person.

Systems and controls

18.—(1)   The clearing house must ensure that the systems and controls used in the performance of its functions are adequate, and appropriate for the scale and nature of its business.

(2)   This requirement applies in particular to systems and controls concerning—
- (a)   the transmission of information;
- (b)   the assessment and management of risks to the performance of the clearing house's functions;
- (c)   the operation of the matters mentioned in paragraph 19(2)(b) below; and
- (d)   (where relevant) the safeguarding and administration of assets belonging to users of the clearing house's facilities.

Safeguards for investors

19.—(1)   The clearing house must ensure that its facilities are such as to afford proper protection to investors.

(2)   Without prejudice to the generality of sub-paragraph (1), the clearing house must ensure that—
- (a)   access to the clearing house's facilities is subject to criteria designed to protect the orderly functioning of those facilities and the interests of investors;
- (b)   its clearing services involve satisfactory arrangements for securing the timely discharge (whether by performance, compromise or otherwise) of the rights and liabilities of the parties to transactions in respect of which it provides such services (being rights and liabilities in relation to those transactions);
- (c)   satisfactory arrangements are made for recording transactions which are cleared or to be cleared by means of its facilities;
- (d)   appropriate measures are adopted to reduce the extent to which the clearing house's facilities can be used for a purpose connected with market abuse or financial crime, and to facilitate their detection and monitor their incidence; and
- (e)   where the clearing house's facilities include making provision for the safeguarding and administration of assets belonging to users of those facilities, satisfactory arrangements are made for that purpose.

Promotion and maintenance of standards

20.—(1) The clearing house must be able and willing to promote and maintain high standards of integrity and fair dealing in the carrying on of regulated activities by persons in the course of using the facilities provided by the clearing house.

(2) The clearing house must be able and willing to cooperate, by the sharing of information or otherwise, with the Authority, with any other authority, body or person having responsibility in the United Kingdom for the supervision or regulation of any regulated activity or other financial service, or with an overseas regulator within the meaning of section 195 of the Act.

Rules

21.—(1) The clearing house must ensure that appropriate procedures are adopted for it to make rules, for keeping its rules under review and for amending them.

(2) The procedures must include procedures for consulting users of the clearing house's facilities in appropriate cases.

(3) The clearing house must consult users of its facilities on any arrangements it proposes to make for dealing with penalty income in accordance with paragraph 22(3) below (or on any changes which it proposes to make to those arrangements).

[Access to central counterparty, clearing and settlement facilities

21A.—(1) The clearing house must make transparent and non-discriminatory rules, based on objective criteria, governing access to central counterparty, clearing or settlement facilities provided by it.

(2) The rules under sub-paragraph (1) must enable an investment firm or a credit institution authorised by the competent authority of another EEA State (including a branch established in the United Kingdom of such a firm or institution) to have access to those facilities on the same terms as a UK firm for the purposes of finalising or arranging the finalisation of transactions in financial instruments.

(3) The clearing house may refuse access to those facilities on legitimate commercial grounds.]

Discipline

22.—(1) The clearing house must have effective arrangements for monitoring and enforcing compliance with its rules.

(2) The arrangements must include procedures for—
    (a) investigating complaints made to the clearing house about the conduct of persons in the course of using the clearing house's facilities; and
    (b) the fair, independent and impartial resolution of appeals against decisions of the clearing house.

(3) Where the arrangements include provision for requiring the payment of financial penalties, they must include arrangements for ensuring that any amount so paid is applied only in one or more of the following ways—
    (a) towards meeting expenses incurred by the clearing house in the course of the investigation of the breach in respect of which the penalty is paid, or in the course of any appeal against the decision of the clearing house in relation to that breach;
    (b) for the benefit of users of the clearing house's facilities;
    (c) for charitable purposes.

Complaints

23.—(1) The clearing house must have effective arrangements for the investigation and resolution of complaints arising in connection with the performance of, or failure to perform, any of its regulatory functions.

(2) But sub-paragraph (1) does not extend to—
    (a) complaints about the content of rules made by the clearing house, or
    (b) complaints about a decision against which the complainant has the right to appeal under procedures of the kind mentioned in paragraph 22(2)(b) above.

(3) The arrangements must include arrangements for a complaint to be fairly and impartially investigated by a person independent of the clearing house, and for him to report on the result of his investigation to the clearing house and to the complainant.

(4) The arrangements must confer on the person mentioned in sub-paragraph (3) the power to recommend, if he thinks it appropriate, that the clearing house—
    (a) makes a compensatory payment to the complainant,
    (b) remedies the matter complained of,
or takes both of those steps.

PART III
STATUTORY INSTRUMENTS

(5)   Sub-paragraph (3) is not to be taken as preventing the clearing house from making arrangements for the initial investigation of a complaint to be conducted by the clearing house.

[2159]

NOTES

Para 21A: inserted by the Financial Services and Markets Act 2000 (Recognition Requirements for Investment Exchanges and Clearing Houses) (Amendment) Regulations 2006, SI 2006/3386, regs 2, 13, as from 1 November 2007.

PART IV
RECOGNITION REQUIREMENTS APPLYING TO CLEARING HOUSES: DEFAULT RULES IN RESPECT OF MARKET CONTRACTS

Default rules in respect of market contracts

24.—(1)   The clearing house must have default rules which, in the event of a member of the clearing house being or appearing to be unable to meet his obligations in respect of one or more market contracts, enable action to be taken to close out his position in relation to all unsettled market contracts to which he is a party.

(2)   The rules may authorise the taking of the same or similar action where a member appears to be likely to become unable to meet his obligations in respect of one or more market contracts.

Content of rules

25.—(1)   The rules must provide—
  (a)   for all rights and liabilities of the defaulter under or in respect of unsettled market contracts to be discharged and for there to be paid by or to the defaulter such sum of money (if any) as may be determined in accordance with the rules;
  (b)   for the sums so payable by or to the defaulter in respect of different contracts to be aggregated or set off so as to produce a net sum;
  (c)   for that sum—
     (i)   if payable by the defaulter to the clearing house, to be set off against any property provided by or on behalf of the defaulter as cover for margin (or the proceeds of realisation of such property) so as to produce a further net sum;
     (ii)   if payable by the clearing house to the defaulter, to be aggregated with any property provided by or on behalf of the defaulter as cover for margin (or the proceeds of realisation of such property); and
  (d)   for the certification by or on behalf of the clearing house of the sum finally payable or, as the case may be, of the fact that no sum is payable.

(2)   The reference in sub-paragraph (1) to the rights and liabilities of a defaulter under or in respect of an unsettled market contract includes (without prejudice to the generality of that provision) rights and liabilities arising in consequence of action taken under provisions of the rules authorising—
  (a)   the effecting by the clearing house of corresponding contracts in relation to unsettled market contracts to which the defaulter is party;
  (b)   the transfer of the defaulter's position under an unsettled market contract to another member of the clearing house;
  (c)   the exercise by the clearing house of any option granted by an unsettled market contract.

(3)   A "corresponding contract" means a contract on the same terms (except as to price or premium) as the market contract but under which the person who is the buyer under the market contract agrees to sell and the person who is the seller under the market contract agrees to buy.

(4)   Sub-paragraph (3) applies with any necessary modifications in relation to a market contract which is not an agreement to sell.

(5)   The reference in sub-paragraph (1) to the rights and liabilities of a defaulter under or in respect of an unsettled market contract does not include, where he acts as agent, rights or liabilities of his arising out of the relationship of principal and agent.

Notification to other parties affected

26.   The clearing house must have adequate arrangements for ensuring that parties to unsettled market contracts with a defaulter are notified as soon as reasonably practicable of the default and of any decision taken under the rules in relation to contracts to which they are a party.

Cooperation with other authorities

27.   The clearing house must be able and willing to cooperate, by the sharing of information and otherwise, with the Secretary of State, any relevant office-holder within the meaning of section 189 of the Companies Act, and any other authority or body having responsibility for any matter arising out of or connected with the default of a member of the clearing house.

Margin

28.—(1) The rules of the clearing house must provide that in the event of a default, margin provided by the defaulter for his own account is not to be applied to meet a shortfall on a client account.

(2) This paragraph is without prejudice to the requirements of any rules relating to clients' money made by the Authority under sections 138 and 139 of the Act.

[2160]

FINANCIAL SERVICES AND MARKETS ACT 2000 (PRESCRIBED MARKETS AND QUALIFYING INVESTMENTS) ORDER 2001

(SI 2001/996)

NOTES
Made: 15 March 2001.
Authority: this Order was originally made under the Financial Services and Markets Act 2000, s 118(3). However, following the amendment of Part VIII by the Financial Services and Markets Act 2000 (Market Abuse) Regulations 2005, SI 2005/381, it now has effect as if made under s 130A(1).
Commencement: 1 December 2001.
This Order is reproduced as amended by: the Financial Services and Markets Act 2000 (Prescribed Markets and Qualifying Investments) (Amendment) Order 2001, SI 2001/3681; the Financial Services and Markets Act 2000 (Market Abuse) Regulations 2005, SI 2005/381; the Financial Services and Markets Act 2000 (Markets in Financial Instruments) Regulations 2007, SI 2007/126; the Definition of Financial Instrument Order 2008 SI 2008/3053.

1   Citation

This Order may be cited as the Financial Services and Markets Act 2000 (Prescribed Markets and Qualifying Investments) Order 2001.

[2161]

2   Commencement

This Order comes into force on the day on which section 123 of the Act (power to impose penalties in cases of market abuse) comes into force.

[2162]

3   Interpretation

In this Order—
    "the Act" means the Financial Services and Markets Act 2000; and
    ["regulated market" has the meaning given in [Article 4.1.14 of the markets in financial instruments directive];]
    "UK recognised investment exchange" means a body corporate or unincorporated association in respect of which there is in effect a recognition order made under section 290(1)(a) of the Act (recognition orders in respect of investment exchanges other than overseas investment exchanges).

[2163]

NOTES
Definition "regulated market" inserted by the Financial Services and Markets Act 2000 (Market Abuse) Regulations 2005, SI 2005/381, reg 10(1), as from 1 July 2005; words in square brackets in that definition substituted by the Financial Services and Markets Act 2000 (Markets in Financial Instruments) Regulations 2007, SI 2007/126, reg 3(6), Sch 6, Pt 2, para 15, as from 1 November 2007 (for the full commencement details of SI 2007/126, see reg 1 of those Regulations at **[4051]**).

[4   Prescribed Markets

(1) There are prescribed, as markets to which subsections (2), (3), (5), (6) and (7) of section 118 apply—
    (a)   all markets which are established under the rules of a UK recognised investment exchange,
    (b)   the market known as OFEX,
    (c)   all other markets which are regulated markets.

(2) There are prescribed, as markets to which subsections (4) and (8) of section 118 apply—
    (a)   all markets which are established under the rules of a UK recognised investment exchange;
    (b)   the market known as OFEX.]

[2164]

NOTES
Commencement: 1 July 2005.
Articles 4, 5 substituted for original arts 4, 4A, 5, by the Financial Services and Markets Act 2000 (Market Abuse) Regulations 2005, SI 2005/381, reg 10(2), as from 1 July 2005. Art 4A was previously inserted by the Financial Services and Markets Act 2000 (Prescribed Markets and Qualifying Investments) (Amendment) Order 2001, SI 2001/3681, art 2, as from 5 December 2001.

4A (*See the note to art 4 at* **[2164]**.)

[5 Qualifying Investments
There are prescribed, as qualifying investments in relation to the markets prescribed by article 4, all financial instruments within the meaning given in Article 1(3) of Directive 2003/6/EC of the European Parliament and the Council of 28 January 2003 on insider dealing and market manipulation (market abuse) [as modified by Article 69 of Directive 2004/39/EC on markets in financial instruments].]

[2165]

NOTES
Commencement: 1 July 2005.
Substituted as noted to art 4 at **[2164]**.
Words in square brackets inserted by the Definition of Financial Instrument Order 2008 SI 2008/3053, art 4, as from 31 January 2009.

FINANCIAL SERVICES AND MARKETS ACT 2000 (PROMOTION OF COLLECTIVE INVESTMENT SCHEMES) (EXEMPTIONS) ORDER 2001

(SI 2001/1060)

NOTES
Made: 19 March 2001.
Authority: Financial Services and Markets Act 2000, s 238(6), (7).
Commencement: 1 December 2001.
This Order is reproduced as amended by: the Financial Services and Markets Act 2000 (Financial Promotion) (Amendment) Order 2001, SI 2001/2633; the Financial Services and Markets Act 2000 (Financial Promotion and Miscellaneous Amendments) Order 2002, SI 2002/1310; the Financial Services and Markets Act 2000 (Financial Promotion) (Amendment) (Electronic Commerce Directive) Order 2002, SI 2002/2157; the Financial Services and Markets Act 2000 (Promotion of Collective Investment Schemes etc) (Exemptions) (Amendment) Order 2003, SI 2003/2067; the Financial Services and Markets Act 2000 (Financial Promotion and Promotion of Collective Investment Schemes) (Miscellaneous Amendments) Order 2005, SI 2005/270; the Financial Services and Markets Act 2000 (Promotion of Collective Investment Schemes) (Exemptions) (Amendment) Order 2005, SI 2005/1532; the Civil Partnership Act 2004 (Amendments to Subordinate Legislation) Order 2005, SI 2005/2114.

ARRANGEMENT OF ARTICLES

PART I
GENERAL AND INTERPRETATION

PART II
TERRITORIAL SCOPE

PART III
OTHER EXEMPTIONS

PART I
GENERAL AND INTERPRETATION

1   Citation and commencement

(1)   This Order may be cited as the Financial Services and Markets Act 2000 (Promotion of Collective Investment Schemes) (Exemptions) Order 2001.

(2)   This Order comes into force on the day on which section 19 of the Act comes into force.
[2166]

2   Interpretation: general

(1)   In this Order—
    "the Act" means the Financial Services and Markets Act 2000;
    "authorised unit trust scheme" has the meaning given by section 237 of the Act;
    "close relative", in relation to a person means—
        (a)   his spouse [or civil partner];
        (b)   his children and step-children, his parents and step-parents, his brothers and sisters and his step-brothers and step-sisters; and
        (c)   the spouse [or civil partner] of any person within sub-paragraph (b);
    "overseas scheme" means an unregulated scheme which is operated and managed in a country or territory outside the United Kingdom;
    "publication" means—
        (a)   a newspaper, journal, magazine or other periodical publication;
        (b)   a web site [or similar system for the electronic display of information];
        (c)   any programme forming part of a service consisting of the broadcast or transmission of television or radio programmes; and
        (d)   any teletext service, that is to say a service consisting of television transmissions consisting of a succession of visual displays (with or without accompanying sound) capable of being selected and held for separate viewing or other use;
    "qualifying contract of insurance" has the meaning given in the Regulated Activities Order;
    "the Regulated Activities Order" means the Financial Services and Markets Act 2000 (Regulated Activities) Order 2001;
    "relevant scheme activities" means—
        (i)   the activity specified by article 51 of the Regulated Activities Order; or
        (ii)   any activity specified by article 14, 21, 25, 37 or 53 of that Order when carried on in relation to units;
    "solicited real time communication" has the meaning given by article 5;
    "units" has the meaning given by section 237(2) of the Act;

"unregulated scheme" means a collective investment scheme which is not an authorised unit trust scheme nor a scheme constituted by an authorised open-ended investment company nor a recognised scheme for the purposes of Part XVII of the Act;

"unsolicited real time communication" has the meaning given by article 5.

(2) In this Order, any reference to the "scheme promotion restriction" means the restriction imposed by section 238(1) of the Act.

[2167]

NOTES

Para (1): words in square brackets in definition "close relative" inserted by the Civil Partnership Act 2004 (Amendments to Subordinate Legislation) Order 2005, SI 2005/2114, art 2(16), Sch 16, Pt 1, para 2, as from 5 December 2005; words in square brackets in definition "publication" inserted by the Financial Services and Markets Act 2000 (Financial Promotion and Miscellaneous Amendments) Order 2002, SI 2002/1310, art 3(1), (2), as from 5 June 2002.

Step-children, etc: as to the meaning of this and related expressions, see the Civil Partnership Act 2004, s 246 (as applied to this Order by the Civil Partnership Act 2004 (Relationships Arising Through Civil Partnership) Order 2005, SI 2005/3137, art 3, Schedule).

---

3 Interpretation: communications

In this Order—

(a) any reference to a communication is a reference to the communication, by an authorised person in the course of business, of an invitation or inducement to participate in an unregulated scheme;

(b) any reference to a communication being made to another person is a reference to a communication being addressed, whether verbally or in legible form, to a particular person or persons (for example where it is contained in a telephone call or letter);

(c) any reference to a communication being directed at persons is a reference to a communication being addressed to persons generally (for example where it is contained in a television broadcast or web site);

(d) "communicate" includes causing a communication to be made;

(e) a "recipient" of a communication is a person to whom the communication is made or, in the case of a non-real time communication which is directed at persons generally, any person who reads or hears the communication;

[(f) "electronic commerce communication" means a communication, the making of which constitutes the provision of an information society service;

(g) "incoming electronic commerce communication" means an electronic commerce communication made from an establishment in an EEA State other than the United Kingdom;

(h) "outgoing electronic commerce communication" means an electronic commerce communication made from an establishment in the United Kingdom to a person in an EEA State other than the United Kingdom].

[2168]

NOTES

Paras (f)–(h) added by the Financial Services and Markets Act 2000 (Financial Promotion) (Amendment) (Electronic Commerce Directive) Order 2002, SI 2002/2157, arts 7, 8(1), as from 21 August 2002.

---

4 Interpretation: real time communications

(1) In this Order, references to a real time communication are references to any communication made in the course of a personal visit, telephone conversation or other interactive dialogue.

(2) A non-real time communication is a communication not falling within paragraph (1).

(3) For the purposes of this Order, non-real time communications include communications made by letter or e-mail or contained in a publication.

(4) For the purposes of this Order, the factors in paragraph (5) are to be treated as indications that a communication is a non-real time communication.

(5) The factors are that—

(a) the communication is made to or directed at more than one recipient in identical terms (save for details of the recipient's identity);

(b) the communication is made or directed by way of a system which in the normal course constitutes or creates a record of the communication which is available to the recipient to refer to at a later time;

(c) the communication is made or directed by way of a system which in the normal course does not enable or require the recipient to respond immediately to it.

[2169]

5   Interpretation: solicited and unsolicited real time communications

(1)   A real time communication is solicited where it is made in the course of a personal visit, telephone call or other interactive dialogue if that call, visit or dialogue—
- (a)   was initiated by the recipient of the communication; or
- (b)   takes place in response to an express request from the recipient of the communication.

(2)   A real time communication is unsolicited where it is made otherwise than as described in paragraph (1).

(3)   For the purposes of paragraph (1)—
- (a)   a person is not to be treated as expressly requesting a call, visit or dialogue—
  - (i)   because he omits to indicate that he does not wish to receive any or any further visits or calls or to engage in any or any further dialogue;
  - (ii)   because he agrees to standard terms that state that such visits, calls or dialogue will take place, unless he has signified clearly that, in addition to agreeing to the terms, he is willing for them to take place;
- (b)   a communication is solicited only if it is clear from all the circumstances when the call, visit or dialogue is initiated or requested that during the course of the visit, call or dialogue communications will be made concerning the kind of activities or investments to which the communications in fact made relate;
- (c)   it is immaterial whether the express request is made before or after this Order comes into force.

(4)   Where a real time communication is solicited by a recipient ("R"), it is treated as having also been solicited by any other person to whom it is made at the same time as it is made to R if that other recipient is—
- (a)   a close relative of R; or
- (b)   expected to participate in the unregulated scheme jointly with R.

[2170]

[5A   Interpretation: outgoing electronic commerce communications

(1)   For the purposes of the application of those articles to outgoing electronic commerce communications—
- (a)   any reference in article 21(4)(d) or 23(1)(a) or (3)(d) to an authorised person includes a reference to a person who is entitled, under the law of an EEA State other than the United Kingdom, to carry on regulated activities in that State;
- (b)   any reference in article 21 or 22 to an amount in pounds sterling includes a reference to an equivalent amount in another currency.

(2)   For the purposes of the application of article 22 to outgoing electronic commerce communications, any reference in section 737 or 264(2) of the Companies Act 1985 (or the equivalent provision in the Companies (Northern Ireland) Order 1986) to a company includes a reference to a company registered under the law of an EEA State other than the United Kingdom.]

[2171]

NOTES

Inserted by the Financial Services and Markets Act 2000 (Financial Promotion) (Amendment) (Electronic Commerce Directive) Order 2002, SI 2002/2157, arts 7, 8(2), as from 21 August 2002.

---

6   Degree of prominence to be given to required indications

Where a communication must, if it is to fall within any provision of this Order, be accompanied by an indication of any matter, the indication must be presented to the recipient—
- (a)   in a way that can be easily understood; and
- (b)   in such manner as, depending on the means by which the communication is made or directed, is best calculated to bring the matter in question to the attention of the recipient and to allow him to consider it.

[2172]

7   Combination of different exemptions

Nothing in this Order is to be construed as preventing a person from relying on more than one exemption in respect of the same communication.

[2173]

PART II
TERRITORIAL SCOPE

8   Communications to overseas recipients

(1)   Subject to [paragraphs (2) and (7)], the scheme promotion restriction does not apply to any communication—

(a)   which is made (whether from inside or outside the United Kingdom) to a person who receives the communication outside the United Kingdom; or

(b)   which is directed (whether from inside or outside the United Kingdom) only at persons outside the United Kingdom.

(2)   Paragraph (1) does not apply to an unsolicited real time communication unless—

(a)   it is made from a place outside the United Kingdom; and

(b)   it relates to an overseas scheme.

(3)   For the purposes of paragraph (1)(b)—

(a)   if the conditions set out in paragraph (4)(a), (b), (c) and (d) are met, a communication directed from a place inside the United Kingdom is to be regarded as directed only at persons outside the United Kingdom;

(b)   if the conditions set out in paragraph (4)(c) and (d) are met, a communication directed from a place outside the United Kingdom is to be regarded as directed only at persons outside the United Kingdom;

(c)   in any other case where one or more of the conditions in paragraph (4)(a) to (e) are met, that fact shall be taken into account in determining whether the communication is to be regarded as directed only at persons outside the United Kingdom (but a communication may still be regarded as directed only at persons outside the United Kingdom even if none of the conditions in paragraph (4) is met).

(4)   The conditions are that—

(a)   the communication is accompanied by an indication that it is directed only at persons outside the United Kingdom;

(b)   the communication is accompanied by an indication that it must not be acted upon by persons in the United Kingdom;

(c)   the communication is not referred to in, or directly accessible from, any other communication which is made to a person or directed at persons in the United Kingdom by or on behalf of the same person;

(d)   there are in place proper systems and procedures to prevent recipients in the United Kingdom (other than those to whom the communication might otherwise lawfully have been made or directed) acquiring from the person directing the communication, a close relative of his or a company in the same group, units in the scheme to which the communication relates;

(e)   the communication is included in—

(i)   a web site, newspaper, journal, magazine or periodical publication which is principally accessed in or intended for a market outside the United Kingdom;

(ii)   a radio or television broadcast or teletext service transmitted principally for reception outside the United Kingdom.

(5)   For the purposes of paragraph (1)(b), a communication may be treated as directed only at persons outside the United Kingdom even if—

(a)   it is also directed, for the purposes of article 14(1)(b), at investment professionals falling within article 14(5) (but disregarding paragraph (6) of that article for this purpose);

(b)   it is also directed, for the purposes of article 22(1)(b), at high net worth persons to whom article 22 applies (but disregarding paragraph (2)(e) of that article for this purpose).

(6)   Where a communication falls within paragraph (5)—

(a)   the condition in paragraph (4)(a) is to be construed as requiring an indication that the communication is directed only at persons outside the United Kingdom or persons having professional experience in matters relating to investments or high net worth persons (as the case may be);

(b)   the condition in paragraph (4)(b) is to be construed as requiring an indication that the communication must not be acted upon by persons in the United Kingdom or by persons who do not have professional experience in matters relating to investments or who are not high net worth persons (as the case may be).

[(7)   Paragraph (1) does not apply to an outgoing electronic commerce communication.]

[2174]

NOTES

Para (1): words in square brackets substituted by the Financial Services and Markets Act 2000 (Financial Promotion) (Amendment) (Electronic Commerce Directive) Order 2002, SI 2002/2157, arts 7, 9(a), as from 21 August 2002.

Para (7): added by SI 2002/2157, arts 7, 9(b), as from 21 August 2002.

9   Solicited real time communications from overseas

The scheme promotion restriction does not apply to any solicited real time communication which is made from outside the United Kingdom and which relates to units in an overseas scheme.

[2175]

10   Communications from overseas to previously overseas customers

(1)   The scheme promotion restriction does not apply to a non-real time or unsolicited real time communication which—

(a)   is made from outside the United Kingdom by an authorised person to a previously overseas customer of his; and

(b)   relates to units in an overseas scheme.

(2)   In this article—

"previously overseas customer" means a person with whom the authorised person has done business within the period of twelve months ending with the day on which the communication was made ("the earlier business") and where—

(a)   at the time that the earlier business was done, the customer was neither resident in the United Kingdom nor had a place of business there; or

(b)   at the time the earlier business was done, the authorised person had on a former occasion done business with the customer, being business of the same description as the business to which the communication relates, and on that former occasion the customer was neither resident in the United Kingdom nor had a place of business there.

(3)   For the purposes of this article, an authorised person has done business with a customer if, in the course of his overseas business, he has—

(a)   effected a transaction, or arranged for a transaction to be effected, with the customer in respect of units in an overseas scheme; or

(b)   given, outside the United Kingdom, any advice on the merits of the customer buying or selling units in an overseas scheme.

[2176]

[10A   Incoming electronic commerce communications

(1)   The scheme promotion restriction does not apply to an incoming electronic commerce communication.

(2)   Paragraph (1) does not apply to—

(a)   a communication which constitutes an advertisement by the operator of a UCITS Directive scheme of units in that scheme; or

(b)   an unsolicited communication made by electronic mail.

(3)   In this article, "UCITS Directive scheme" means an undertaking for collective investment in transferable securities which is subject to [the UCITS directive], and has been authorised in accordance with Article 4 of that Directive.

(4)   For the purposes of this article, a communication by electronic mail is to be regarded as unsolicited, unless it is made in response to an express request from the recipient of the communication.]

[2177]

NOTES

Inserted by the Financial Services and Markets Act 2000 (Financial Promotion) (Amendment) (Electronic Commerce Directive) Order 2002, SI 2002/2157, arts 7, 10, as from 21 August 2002.

Para (3): words in square brackets substituted by the Financial Services and Markets Act 2000 (Promotion of Collective Investment Schemes etc) (Exemptions) (Amendment) Order 2003, SI 2003/2067, art 2(1), (2), as from 13 February 2004.

PART III
OTHER EXEMPTIONS

11   Follow up non-real time communications and solicited real time communications

(1)   Where an authorised person makes or directs a communication ("the first communication") which is exempt from the scheme promotion restriction because, in compliance with the requirements of another provision of this Order, it is accompanied by certain indications or contains certain information, then the scheme promotion restriction does not apply to any subsequent communication which complies with the requirements of paragraph (2).

(2)   The requirements of this paragraph are that the subsequent communication—

(a)   is a non-real time communication or a solicited real time communication;

(b)   is made by the same person who made the first communication;

(c)   is made to a recipient of the first communication;

(d)   relates to the same unregulated scheme as the first communication; and

(e)   is made within 12 months of the recipient receiving the first communication.

(3)   A communication made or directed before this Order comes into force is to be treated as a first communication falling within paragraph (1) if it would have fallen within that paragraph had it been made or directed after this Order comes into force.

[2178]

12   Introductions

(1)   If the requirements of paragraph (2) are met, the scheme promotion restriction does not apply to any real time communication which is made with a view to or for the purposes of introducing the recipient to—

(a)   an authorised person who carries on one or more relevant scheme activities in relation to units in unregulated schemes; or

(b)   a person who is exempt, as a result of an exemption order made under section 38(1) of the Act, in relation to one or more relevant scheme activities.

(2)   The requirements of this paragraph are that—

(a)   the maker of the communication ("A") is not a close relative of, nor a member of the same group as, the person to whom the introduction is, or is to be, made;

(b)   A does not carry on business in relevant scheme activities in relation to units in unregulated schemes;

(c)   A does not receive from any person other than the recipient any pecuniary reward or other advantage arising out of his making the introduction; and

(d)   it is clear in all the circumstances that the recipient, in his capacity as an investor, is not seeking and has not sought advice from A as to the merits of participating in an unregulated scheme (or, if the client has sought such advice, A has declined to give it, but has recommended that the recipient seek such advice from an authorised person specialising in that kind of investment).

[2179]

13   Generic promotions

The scheme promotion restriction does not apply to any communication which—

(a)   does not relate to units of a particular unregulated scheme identified (directly or indirectly) in the communication; and

(b)   does not identify (directly or indirectly) any person who operates a collective investment scheme or sells units.

[2180]

14   Investment professionals

(1)   The scheme promotion restriction does not apply to any communication which—

(a)   is made only to recipients whom the person making the communication believes on reasonable grounds to be investment professionals; or

(b)   may reasonably be regarded as directed only at such recipients.

(2)   For the purposes of paragraph (1)(b), if all the conditions set out in paragraph (4)(a) to (c) are met in relation to the communication, it is to be regarded as directed only at investment professionals.

(3)   In any other case in which one or more of the conditions set out in paragraph (4)(a) to (c) are met, that fact shall be taken into account in determining whether the communication is directed only at investment professionals (but a communication may still be regarded as so directed even if none of the conditions in paragraph (4) is met).

(4)   The conditions are that—

(a)   the communication is accompanied by an indication that it is directed at persons having professional experience of participating in unregulated schemes and that the units to which the communication relates are available only to such persons;

(b)   the communication is accompanied by an indication that persons who do not have professional experience in participating in unregulated schemes should not rely on it;

(c)   there are in place proper systems and procedures to prevent recipients other than investment professionals from acquiring from the person directing the communication, a close relative of his or a company in the same group, units in the scheme to which the communication relates.

(5)   "Investment professionals" means—

(a)   an authorised person;

(b)   a person who is exempt, as a result of an exemption order made under section 38(1) of the Act, in relation to one or more relevant scheme activities;

(c)   any other person—

(i)   whose ordinary activities involve him in participating in unregulated schemes for the purposes of a business carried on by him; or

(ii)   who it is reasonable to expect will so participate for the purposes of a business carried on by him;

(d)   a government, local authority (whether in the United Kingdom or elsewhere) or an international organisation;

(e)   a person ("A") who is a director, officer or employee of a person ("B") falling within any of sub-paragraphs (a) to (d), when the communication is made to A in that capacity and where A's responsibilities when acting in that capacity involve him in B's participation in unregulated schemes.

(6)   For the purposes of paragraph (1), a communication is to be treated as made only to or directed only at investment professionals even if it also made to or directed at other persons to whom it may lawfully be communicated.

(7)   In this article—

"government" means the government of the United Kingdom, the Scottish Administration, the Executive Committee of the Northern Ireland Assembly, the National Assembly for Wales and any government of any country or territory outside the United Kingdom;

"international organisation" means any body the members of which comprise—

(a)   states including the United Kingdom or another EEA State; or

(b)   bodies whose members comprise states including the United Kingdom or another EEA State.

[2181]

15   One off non-real time communications and solicited real time communications

(1)   The scheme promotion restriction does not apply to a one off communication which is either a non-real time communication or a solicited real time communication.

(2)   If both the conditions set out in paragraph (3) are met in relation to a communication it is to be regarded as a one off communication. In any other case in which either of those conditions is met, that fact is to be taken into account in determining whether the communication is a one off communication (but a communication may still be regarded as a one off communication even if neither of the conditions in paragraph (3) is met).

(3)   The conditions are that—

(a)   the communication is made only to one recipient or only to one group of recipients in the expectation that they would engage in any investment activity jointly;

(b)   the communication is not part of an organised marketing campaign.

[2182]

[15A   One off unsolicited real time communications

(1)   The scheme promotion restriction does not apply to an unsolicited real time communication if the conditions in paragraph (2) are met.

(2)   The conditions in this paragraph are that—

(a)   the communication is a one off communication;

(b)   the communicator believes on reasonable grounds that the recipient understands the risks associated with engaging in the investment activity to which the communication relates;

(c)   at the time the communication is made, the communicator believes on reasonable grounds that the recipient would expect to be contacted by him in relation to the investment activity to which the communication relates.

(3)   Paragraphs (2) and (3) of article 15 apply in determining whether a communication is a one off communication for the purposes of this article as they apply for the purposes of article 15.]

[2183]

NOTES

Inserted by the Financial Services and Markets Act 2000 (Financial Promotion) (Amendment) Order 2001, SI 2001/2633, art 3, as from 1 December 2001.

16   Communications required or authorised by enactments

The scheme promotion restriction does not apply to any communication which is required or authorised to be communicated by or under any enactment other than the Act.

[2184]

17   Persons in the business of placing promotional material

The scheme promotion restriction does not apply to any communication which is made to a person whose business it is to place, or arrange for the placing of, promotional material provided that it is communicated so that he can place or arrange for placing it.

[2185]

18   Existing participants in an unregulated scheme

The scheme promotion restriction does not apply to any communication which is—

    (a)   a non-real time communication or a solicited real time communication;

    (b)   communicated by the operator of an unregulated scheme; and

    (c)   communicated to persons whom the person making the communication believes on reasonable grounds to be persons who are entitled to units in that scheme.

[2186]

19 Group companies

The scheme promotion restriction does not apply to any communication made by one body corporate in a group to another body corporate in the same group.

[2187]

20 Persons in the business of disseminating information

(1)   The scheme promotion restriction does not apply to any communication which is made only to recipients whom the person making the communication believes on reasonable grounds to be persons to whom paragraph (2) applies.

(2)   This paragraph applies to—

    (a)   a person who receives the communication in the course of a business which involves the dissemination through a publication of information concerning investments;

    (b)   a person whilst acting in the capacity of director, officer or employee of a person falling within sub-paragraph (a) being a person whose responsibilities when acting in that capacity involve him in the business referred to in that sub-paragraph;

    (c)   any person to whom the communication may otherwise lawfully be made.

[2188]

[21 Certified high net worth individuals

(1)   If the requirements of paragraphs (4) and (7) are met, the scheme promotion restriction does not apply to any communication which—

    (a)   is a non-real time communication or a solicited real time communication;

    (b)   is made to an individual whom the person making the communication believes on reasonable grounds to be a certified high net worth individual;

    (c)   relates only to units falling within paragraph (8); and

    (d)   does not invite or induce the recipient to enter into an agreement under the terms of which he can incur a liability or obligation to pay or contribute more than he commits by way of investment.

(2)   "Certified high net worth individual" means an individual who has signed, within the period of twelve months ending with the day on which the communication is made, a statement complying with Part I of the Schedule.

(3)   The validity of a statement signed for the purposes of paragraph (2) is not affected by a defect in the form or wording of the statement, provided that the defect does not alter the statement's meaning and that the words shown in bold type in Part I of the Schedule are so shown in the statement.

(4)   The requirements of this paragraph are that either the communication is accompanied by the giving of a warning in accordance with paragraphs (5) and (6) or, where because of the nature of the communication this is not reasonably practicable,—

    (a)   a warning in accordance with paragraph (5) is given to the recipient orally at the beginning of the communication together with an indication that he will receive the warning in legible form and that, before receipt of that warning, he should consider carefully any decision to participate in a collective investment scheme to which the communication relates; and

    (b)   a warning in accordance with paragraphs (5) and (6) (d) to (h) is sent to the recipient of the communication within two business days of the day on which the communication is made.

(5)   The warning must be in the following terms—

"Reliance on this promotion for the purpose of buying the units to which the promotion relates may expose an individual to a significant risk of losing all of the property or other assets invested.".

But, where a warning is sent pursuant to paragraph (4)(b), for the words "this promotion" in both places where they occur there must be substituted wording which clearly identifies the promotion which is the subject of the warning.

(6)   The warning must—

    (a)   be given at the beginning of the communication;

    (b)   precede any other written or pictorial matter;

    (c)   be in a font size consistent with the text forming the remainder of the communication;

    (d)   be indelible;

    (e)   be legible;

(f)   be printed in black, bold type;
(g)   be surrounded by a black border which does not interfere with the text of the warning; and
(h)   not be hidden, obscured or interrupted by any other written or pictorial matter.

(7)   The requirements of this paragraph are that the communication is accompanied by an indication—
(a)   that it is exempt from the restriction on the promotion of unregulated schemes (in section 238 of the Act) on the grounds that the communication is made to a certified high net worth individual;
(b)   of the requirements that must be met for an individual to qualify as a certified high net worth individual;
(c)   that any individual who is in any doubt about the units to which the communication relates should consult an authorised person specialising in advising in participation in unregulated schemes.

(8)   A unit falls within this paragraph if it is in an unregulated scheme which invests wholly or predominantly in the shares in or debentures of one or more unlisted companies.

(9)   "Business day" means any day except a Saturday, a Sunday, Christmas Day, Good Friday or a day which is a bank holiday under the Banking and Financial Dealings Act 1971 in any part of the United Kingdom.

(10)   "Unlisted company" has the meaning given in the Financial Services and Markets Act 2000 (Financial Promotion) Order 2001.]

[2189]

NOTES
Commencement: 3 March 2005.
Substituted by the Financial Services and Markets Act 2000 (Financial Promotion and Promotion of Collective Investment Schemes) (Miscellaneous Amendments) Order 2005, SI 2005/270, art 3, Sch 2, para 1, as from 3 March 2005, subject to transitional provisions as noted below.
Transitional provisions: the Financial Services and Markets Act 2000 (Financial Promotion and Promotion of Collective Investment Schemes) (Miscellaneous Amendments) Order 2005, SI 2005/270, art 5 provides as follows—

"5   Transitional provision: CIS Exemptions Order
(1)   Paragraph (2) applies where, immediately before the coming into force of this Order, an individual is a certified high net worth individual within the meaning of article 21 of the CIS Exemptions Order.
(2)   That individual must, for so long as he holds a current certificate of high net worth, be treated as a certified high net worth individual for the purpose of article 21 of the CIS Exemptions Order as substituted by this Order.
(3)   For the purposes of this article, a certificate of high net worth—
(a)   means a certificate of high net worth which, immediately before the coming into force of this Order, satisfies the criteria in article 21(3)(a), (c) and (d) of the CIS Exemptions Order; and
(b)   is current if it is signed and dated—
(i)   within the period of twelve months ending with the day on which the communication (referred to in article 21 of the CIS Exemptions Order) is made; and
(ii)   prior to this Order coming into force.".

This article as it had effect prior to the coming into force of SI 2005/270 read as follows—

"21   Certified high net worth individuals
(1)   If the requirements of paragraphs (4) and (5) are met, the scheme promotion restriction does not apply to any communication which—
(a)   is a non-real time communication or a solicited real time communication;
(b)   is made to a certified high net-worth individual;
(c)   relates only to units falling within paragraph (6);
(d)   does not invite or induce the recipient to enter into an agreement under the terms of which he can incur a liability or obligation to pay or contribute more than he commits by way of investment.
(2)   "Certified high net-worth individual" means any individual—
(a)   who has a current certificate of high net worth; and
(b)   who has signed, within the period of twelve months ending with the day on which the communication is made, a statement in the following terms—

"I make this statement so that I am able to receive promotions of units in unregulated collective investment schemes where such promotions are exempt from the restriction in section 238 of the Financial Services and Markets Act 2000. The exemption relates to certified high net worth individuals and I declare that I qualify as such. I accept that the schemes to which the promotions will relate are not authorised or recognised for the purposes of that Act. I am aware that it is open to me to seek advice from an authorised person who specialises in advising on this kind of investment".

(3)   For the purposes of paragraph (2)(a) a certificate of high net worth—
(a)   must be in writing or other legible form;
(b)   is current if it is signed and dated within the period of twelve months ending with the day on which the communication is made;

(c)   must state that in the opinion of the person signing the certificate, the person to whom the certificate relates either—
   (i)   had, during the financial year immediately preceding the date on which the certificate is signed, an annual income of not less than £100,000; or
   (ii) held, throughout the financial year immediately preceding the date on which the certificate is signed, net assets to the value of not less than £250,000;
(d)   must be signed by the recipient's accountant or by the recipient's employer.

(4)   The requirements of this paragraph are that the communication is accompanied by an indication—
(a)   that it is exempt from the restriction on the promotion of unregulated schemes (in section 238 of the Financial Services and Markets Act 2000) on the grounds that the communication is made to a certified high net worth individual;
(b)   of the requirements that must be met for a person to qualify as a certified high net worth individual;
(c)   that buying the units to which the communication relates may expose the individual to a significant risk of losing all of the property invested;
(d)   that any person who is in any doubt about the units to which the communication relates should consult an authorised person specialising in advising on participation in unregulated schemes.

(5)   In determining an individual's "net assets", no account is to be taken of—
(a)   the property which is his primary residence or of any loan secured on that residence;
(b)   any rights of his under a qualifying contract of insurance; or
(c)   any benefits (in the form of pensions or otherwise) which are payable on the termination of his service or on his death or retirement and to which he is (or his dependents are), or may be, entitled.

(6)   A unit falls within this paragraph if it is in an unregulated scheme—
(a)   which is not operated by the person who has signed the certificate of high net worth referred to in paragraph (2)(a); and
(b)   which invests wholly or predominantly in the shares in or debentures of an unlisted company.

(7)   "Unlisted company" has the meaning given in the Financial Services and Markets Act 2000 (Financial Promotion) Order 2001.".

22 High net worth companies, unincorporated associations etc

(1)   The scheme promotion restriction does not apply to any communication which—
(a)   is made only to recipients whom the person making the communication believes on reasonable grounds to be persons to whom paragraph (2) applies; or
(b)   may reasonably be regarded as directed only at persons to whom paragraph (2) applies.

(2)   This paragraph applies to—
[(a)   any body corporate which has, or which is a member of the same group as an undertaking which has, a called-up share capital or net assets of not less than—
   (i)   if the body corporate has more than 20 members or is a subsidiary undertaking of an undertaking which has more than 20 members, £500,000;
   (ii) otherwise, £5 million;]
(b)   any unincorporated association or partnership which has net assets of not less than £5 million;
(c)   the trustee of a high value trust;
(d)   any person ("A") whilst acting in the capacity of director, officer or employee of a person ("B") falling within any of sub-paragraphs (a) to (c), where A's responsibilities, when acting in that capacity, involve him in B's participation in unregulated schemes;
(e)   any person to whom the communication might otherwise lawfully be made.

(3)   For the purposes of paragraph (1)(b)—
(a)   if all the conditions set out in paragraph (4)(a) to (c) are met in relation to the communication, it is to be regarded as directed at persons to whom paragraph (2) applies;
(b)   in any other case in which one or more of those conditions are met, that fact is to be taken into account in determining whether the communication is directed at persons to whom paragraph (2) applies (but a communication may still be regarded as so directed even if none of the conditions in paragraph (4) is met).

(4)   The conditions are that—
(a)   the communication includes an indication of the description of persons to whom it is directed and an indication of the fact that the units to which it relates are available only to such persons;
(b)   the communication includes an indication that persons of any other description should not rely upon it;
(c)   there are in place proper systems and procedures to prevent recipients other than persons to whom paragraph (2) applies from acquiring from the person directing the communication, a close relative of his or a company in the same group, units in the scheme to which the communication relates.

(5)   In this article—
"called-up share capital" has the meaning given in the Companies Act 1985 or in the Companies (Northern Ireland) Order 1986;

"high value trust" means a trust where the aggregate value of the cash and investments which form part of the trust's assets (before deducing the amount of its liabilities)—

    (a)   is £10 million or more; or

    (b)   has been £10 million or more at any time during the year immediately preceding the date on which communication in question was first made or directed;

"net assets" has the meaning given in section 264 of the Companies Act 1985 or the equivalent provision of the Companies (Northern Ireland) Order 1986.

[2190]

NOTES

Para (2): sub-para (a) substituted by the Financial Services and Markets Act 2000 (Financial Promotion and Miscellaneous Amendments) Order 2002, SI 2002/1310, art 3(1), (3), as from 5 June 2002.

23 Sophisticated investors

(1)   "Certified sophisticated investor" means a person—

    (a)   who has a current certificate in writing or other legible form signed by an authorised person to the effect that he is sufficiently knowledgeable to understand the risks associated with participating in unregulated schemes; and

    (b)   who has signed, within the period of twelve months ending with the day on which the communication is made, a statement in the following terms—

"I make this statement so that I can receive promotions which are exempt from the restriction on promotion of unregulated schemes in the Financial Services and Markets Act 2000. The exemption relates to certified sophisticated investors and I declare that I qualify as such. I accept that the schemes to which the promotions will relate are not authorised or recognised for the purposes of that Act. I am aware that it is open to me to seek advice from an authorised person who specialises in advising on this kind of investment".

[(1A)   The validity of a statement signed in accordance with paragraph (1)(b) is not affected by a defect in the wording of the statement, provided that the defect does not alter the statement's meaning.]

(2)   If the requirements of paragraph (3) are met, the scheme promotion restriction does not apply to any communication which—

    (a)   is made to a certified sophisticated investor; and

    (b)   does not invite or induce the recipient to participate in an unregulated scheme operated by the person who has signed the certificate referred to in paragraph (1)(a) or to acquire units from that person.

(3)   The requirements of this paragraph are that the communication is accompanied by an indication—

    (a)   that it is exempt from the scheme promotion restriction (in section 238 of the Financial Services and Markets Act 2000) on the communication of invitations or inducements to participate in unregulated schemes on the ground that it is made to a certified sophisticated investor;

    (b)   of the requirements that must be met for a person to qualify as a certified sophisticated investor;

    (c)   that buying the units to which the communication relates may expose the individual to a significant risk of losing all of the property invested;

    (d)   that any individual who is in any doubt about the investment to which the invitation or inducement relates should consult an authorised person specialising in advising on investments of the kind in question.

(4)   For the purposes of paragraph (1)(a), a certificate is current if it is signed and dated not more than three years before the date on which the communication is made.

[2191]

NOTES

Para (1A): inserted by the Financial Services and Markets Act 2000 (Financial Promotion and Promotion of Collective Investment Schemes) (Miscellaneous Amendments) Order 2005, SI 2005/270, art 3, Sch 2, para 2, as from 3 March 2005.

[23A Self-certified sophisticated investors

(1)   "Self-certified sophisticated investor" means an individual who has signed, within the period of twelve months ending with the day on which the communication is made, a statement complying with Part II of the Schedule.

(2)   The validity of a statement signed for the purposes of paragraph (1) is not affected by a defect in the form or wording of the statement, provided that the defect does not alter the statement's meaning and that the words shown in bold type in Part II of the Schedule are so shown in the statement.

(3)   If the requirements of paragraphs (4) and (7) are met, the scheme promotion restriction does not apply to any communication which—

  (a)   is made to an individual whom the person making the communication believes on reasonable grounds to be a self-certified sophisticated investor;

  (b)   relates only to units falling within paragraph (8); and

  (c)   does not invite or induce the recipient to enter into an agreement under the terms of which he can incur a liability or obligation to pay or contribute more than he commits by way of investment.

(4)   The requirements of this paragraph are—

  (a)   ...

  (b)   ... that either the communication is accompanied by the giving of a warning in accordance with paragraphs (5) and (6) or, where because of the nature of the communication this is not reasonably practicable,—

  (i)   a warning in accordance with paragraph (5) is given to the recipient orally at the beginning of the communication together with an indication that he will receive the warning in legible form and that, before receipt of that warning, he should consider carefully any decision to participate in a collective investment scheme to which the communication relates; and

  (ii)   a warning in accordance with paragraphs (5) and (6) (d) to (h) is sent to the recipient of the communication within two business days of the day on which the communication is made.

(5)   The warning must be in the following terms—

"Reliance on this promotion for the purpose of buying [the] units to which the promotion relates may expose an individual to a significant risk of losing all of the property or other assets invested.".

But, where a warning is sent pursuant to paragraph (4)(b), for the words "this promotion" in both places where they occur there must be substituted wording which clearly identifies the promotion which is the subject of the warning.

(6)   The warning must—

  (a)   be given at the beginning of the communication;

  (b)   precede any other written or pictorial matter;

  (c)   be in a font size consistent with the text forming the remainder of the communication;

  (d)   be indelible;

  (e)   be legible;

  (f)   be printed in black, bold type;

  (g)   be surrounded by a black border which does not interfere with the text of the warning; and

  (h)   not be hidden, obscured or interrupted by any other written or pictorial matter.

(7)   The requirements of this paragraph are that the communication is accompanied by an indication—

  (a)   that it is exempt from the scheme promotion restriction (in section 238 of the Act) on the communication of invitations or inducements to participate in unregulated schemes on the ground that it is made to a self-certified sophisticated investor;

  (b)   of the requirements that must be met for an individual to qualify as a self-certified sophisticated investor;

  (c)   that any individual who is in any doubt about the investment to which the invitation or inducement relates should consult an authorised person specialising in advising on investments of the kind in question.

(8)   A unit falls within this paragraph if it is in an unregulated scheme which invests wholly or predominantly in the shares in or debentures of one or more an unlisted companies.

(9)   "Business day" means any day except a Saturday, a Sunday, Christmas Day, Good Friday or a day which is a bank holiday under the Banking and Financial Dealings Act 1971 in any part of the United Kingdom.

(10)   "Unlisted company" has the meaning given in the Financial Services and Markets Act 2000 (Financial Promotion) Order 2001.]

[2192]

NOTES

Commencement: 3 March 2005.

Inserted by the Financial Services and Markets Act 2000 (Financial Promotion and Promotion of Collective Investment Schemes) (Miscellaneous Amendments) Order 2005, SI 2005/270, art 3, Sch 2, para 3, as from 3 March 2005.

Para (4): words omitted revoked by the Financial Services and Markets Act 2000 (Promotion of Collective Investment Schemes) (Exemptions) (Amendment) Order 2005, SI 2005/1532, art 2(1), (2)(a), (b), as from 1 July 2005.

Para (5): word in square brackets substituted by SI 2005/1532, art 2(1), (2)(c), as from 1 July 2005.

24 Associations of high net worth or sophisticated investors

The scheme promotion restriction does not apply to any non-real time communication or solicited real time communication which—

(a) is made to an association[, or to a member of an association,] the membership of which the person making the communication believes on reasonable grounds comprises wholly or predominantly persons who are—
  (i) certified high net worth individuals within the meaning of article 21;
  (ii) high net worth persons falling within article 22(2)(a) to (d);
  (iii) certified sophisticated investors within the meaning of article 23 [or 23A]; and

(b) does not invite or induce the recipient to enter into an agreement under the terms of which he can incur a liability or obligation to pay or contribute more than he commits by way of investment.

[2193]

NOTES

Words in square brackets inserted by the Financial Services and Markets Act 2000 (Promotion of Collective Investment Schemes) (Exemptions) (Amendment) Order 2005, SI 2005/1532, art 2(1), (3), as from 1 July 2005.

25 Settlors, trustees and personal representatives

The scheme promotion restriction does not apply to any communication which is made—

(a) by an authorised person when acting as a settlor or grantor of a trust, a trustee or a personal representative;

(b) to a trustee of the trust, a fellow trustee or a fellow personal representative (as the case may be),

if the communication is made for the purposes of the trust or estate.

[2194]

26 Beneficiaries of trust, will or intestacy

The scheme promotion restriction does not apply to any communication which is made—

(a) by an authorised person when acting as a settlor of a trust, trustee or personal representative to a beneficiary under the trust, will or intestacy; or

(b) by an authorised person who is a beneficiary under a trust, will or intestacy to another beneficiary under the same trust, will or intestacy,

if the communication relates to the management or distribution of that trust fund or estate.

[2195]

27 Remedy following report by Parliamentary Commissioner for Administration

The scheme promotion restriction does not apply to any communication made or directed by a person for the purpose of enabling any injustice, stated by the Parliamentary Commissioner for Administration in a report under section 10 of the Parliamentary Commissioner Act 1967 to have occurred, to be remedied with respect to the recipient.

[2196]

28 Persons placing promotional material in particular publications

The scheme promotion restriction does not apply to any communication received by a person who receives the publication in which the communication is contained because he has himself placed an advertisement in that publication.

[2197]

[29 Open-ended investment companies authorised in Northern Ireland

(1) The scheme promotion restriction does not apply in relation to a scheme constituted by an authorised Northern Ireland open-ended investment company.

(2) In this article—

(a) "authorised Northern Ireland open-ended investment company" means a body incorporated by virtue of regulations made under section 1 of the Open-Ended Investment Companies Act (Northern Ireland) 2002 in respect of which an authorisation order is in force; and

(b) "authorisation order" means an order made under (or having effect as made under) any provision of those regulations which is made by virtue of section 1(2)(1) of that Act (provision corresponding to Chapter 3 of Part 17 of the Act).]

[2198]

NOTES
  Added by the Financial Services and Markets Act 2000 (Promotion of Collective Investment Schemes etc) (Exemptions) (Amendment) Order 2003, SI 2003/2067, art 2(1), (3), as from 5 September 2003.

[30 EEA management companies
The scheme promotion restriction does not apply to any communication which is made by an EEA firm which—
  (a) falls within paragraph 5(f) of Schedule 3 to the Act (management companies of UCITS), and
  (b) qualifies for authorisation by virtue of paragraph 12 of that Schedule,
unless the Authority has given (and not withdrawn) a notice to that firm under paragraph 15A(2) of that Schedule (notice indicating that the way in which the firm intends to invite persons in the United Kingdom to become participants in any collective investment scheme which that firm manages does not comply with the law in force in the United Kingdom).]

[2199]

NOTES
  Commencement: 13 February 2004.
  Added by the Financial Services and Markets Act 2000 (Promotion of Collective Investment Schemes etc) (Exemptions) (Amendment) Order 2003, SI 2003/2067, art 2(1), (4), as from 13 February 2004.

[SCHEDULE
STATEMENTS FOR CERTIFIED HIGH NET WORTH INDIVIDUALS AND
SELF-CERTIFIED SOPHISTICATED INVESTORS
Articles 21 and 23A

PART I
STATEMENT FOR CERTIFIED HIGH NET WORTH INDIVIDUALS
1. The statement to be signed for the purposes of article 21(2) (definition of high net worth individual) must be in the following form and contain the following content—

"STATEMENT FOR CERTIFIED HIGH NET WORTH INDIVIDUAL
I declare that I am a certified high net worth individual for the purposes of the Financial Services and Markets Act 2000 (Promotion of Collective Investment Schemes) (Exemptions) Order 2001.
I understand that this means—
  (a) I can receive promotions, made by a person who is authorised by the Financial Services Authority, which relate to units in unregulated collective investment schemes that invest wholly or predominantly in unlisted companies;
  (b) the schemes to which the promotions will relate are not authorised or recognised for the purposes of the Financial Services and Markets Act 2000.
I am a certified high net worth individual because **at least one of the following applies**—
  (a) I had, during the financial year immediately preceding the date below, an annual income to the value of £100,000 or more;
  (b) I held, throughout the financial year immediately preceding the date below, net assets to the value of £250,000 or more. Net assets for these purposes do not include—
      (i) the property which is my primary residence or any loan secured on that residence;
      (ii) any rights of mine under a qualifying contract of insurance within the meaning of the Financial Services and Markets Act 2000 (Regulated Activities) Order 2001; or
      (iii) any benefits (in the form of pensions or otherwise) which are payable on the termination of my service or on my death or retirement and to which I am (or my dependants are), or may be, entitled.

I accept that I can lose my property and other assets from making investment decisions based on financial promotions.

I am aware that it is open to me to seek advice from someone who specialises in advising on unregulated collective investment schemes.
Signature...
Date ...."]

[2200]

NOTES

Commencement: 3 March 2005.

Added by the Financial Services and Markets Act 2000 (Financial Promotion and Promotion of Collective Investment Schemes) (Miscellaneous Amendments) Order 2005, SI 2005/270, art 3, Sch 2, para 4, as from 3 March 2005.

[PART II
STATEMENT FOR SELF-CERTIFIED SOPHISTICATED INVESTORS

2. The statement to be signed for the purposes of article 23A(1) (definition of self-certified sophisticated investor) must be in the following form and contain the following content—

"STATEMENT FOR SELF-CERTIFIED SOPHISTICATED INVESTOR

I declare that I am a self-certified sophisticated investor for the purposes of the Financial Services and Markets Act 2000 (Promotion of Collective Investment Schemes) (Exemptions) Order 2001.

I understand that this means—

   (a)   I can receive promotions, made by a person who is authorised by the Financial Services Authority, which relate to units in unregulated collective investment schemes that invest wholly or predominantly in unlisted companies;

   (b)   the schemes to which the promotions will relate are not authorised or recognised for the purposes of the Financial Services and Markets Act 2000.

I am a self-certified sophisticated investor because **at least one of the following applies**—

   (a)   I am a member of a network or syndicate of business angels and have been so for at least the last six months prior to the date below;

   (b)   I have made more than one investment in an unlisted company in the two years prior to the date below;

   (c)   I am working, or have worked in the two years prior to the date below, in a professional capacity in the private equity sector, or in the provision of finance for small and medium enterprises;

   (d)   I am currently, or have been in the two years prior to the date below, a director of a company with an annual turnover of at least £1 million.

I accept that I can lose my property and other assets from making investment decisions based on financial promotions.

I am aware that it is open to me to seek advice from someone who specialises in advising on unregulated collective investment schemes.

Signature...

Date ...."]

                                                                               [2201]

NOTES

Commencement: 3 March 2005.

Added as noted to Pt I at **[2200]**.

FINANCIAL SERVICES AND MARKETS ACT 2000 (COLLECTIVE INVESTMENT SCHEMES) ORDER 2001

(SI 2001/1062)

NOTES

Made: 19 March 2001.

Authority: Financial Services and Markets Act 2000, s 235(5).

Commencement: 1 December 2001.

This Order is reproduced as amended by: the Financial Services and Markets Act 2000 (Miscellaneous Provisions) Order 2001, SI 2001/3650; the Financial Services and Markets Act 2000 (Collective Investment Schemes) (Amendment) Order 2005, SI 2005/57; the Civil Partnership Act 2004 (Amendments to Subordinate Legislation) Order 2005, SI 2005/2114; the Financial Services and Markets Act 2000 (Regulated Activities) (Amendment) Order 2006, SI 2006/1969; the Financial Services and Markets Act 2000 (Regulated Activities) (Amendment No 3) Order 2006, SI 2006/3384; the Financial Services and Markets Act 2000 (Collective Investment Schemes) (Amendment) Order 2007, SI 2007/800; the Financial Services and Markets Act 2000 (Collective Investment Schemes) (Amendment) Order 2008, SI 2008/1641.

1 Citation and commencement

This Order may be cited as the Financial Services and Markets Act 2000 (Collective Investment Schemes) Order 2001 and comes into force on the day on which section 19 of the Act comes into force.

[2202]

2 Interpretation

In this Order—

"the Act" means the Financial Services and Markets Act 2000;

"the 1988 Act" means the Income and Corporation Taxes Act 1988;

"authorised unit trust scheme" has the meaning given by section 237(3) of the Act;

"contract of insurance" and "contract of long term insurance" have the meaning given by article 3(1) of the Regulated Activities Order;

"feeder fund" means an authorised unit trust scheme the sole object of which is investment in units of a single authorised unit trust scheme or shares in a single open-ended investment company;

"franchise arrangements" means arrangements under which a person earns profits or income by exploiting a right conferred by the arrangements to use a trade mark or design or other intellectual property or the good-will attached to it;

"funeral plan contract" has the meaning given by article 59 of the Regulated Activities Order;

"individual pension account" has the meaning given by regulation 4 of the Personal Pension Schemes (Restriction on Discretion to Approve) (Permitted Investments) Regulations 2001;

.....

["occupational pension scheme" has the meaning given by section 1 of the Pension Schemes Act 1993 but with paragraph (b) of the definition omitted;]

"the operator" has the meaning given by section 237(2) of the Act;

["personal pension scheme" means a scheme or arrangement which is not an occupational pension scheme and which is comprised in one or more instruments or agreements, having or capable of having effect so as to provide benefits to or in respect of people—

    (a)   on retirement,

    (b)   on having reached a particular age, or

    (c)   on termination of service in an employment;]

"personal pension unit trust" means a personal pension scheme which is an authorised unit trust scheme of a kind mentioned in Part I of Schedule 1 to the Personal Pension Schemes (Appropriate Schemes) Regulations 1997;

"recognised scheme" has the meaning given by section 237(3) of the Act;

"the Regulated Activities Order" means the Financial Services and Markets Act 2000 (Regulated Activities) Order 2001;

"timeshare rights" has the meaning given by section 1 of the Timeshare Act 1992.

[2203]

NOTES

Original (joint) definition "occupational pension scheme" and "personal pension scheme" (omitted) revoked, and new (separate) definitions "occupational pension scheme" and "personal pension scheme" inserted, by the Financial Services and Markets Act 2000 (Regulated Activities) (Amendment) Order 2006, SI 2006/1969, art 8, as from 6 April 2007.

---

3 Arrangements not amounting to a collective investment scheme

Arrangements of the kind specified by the Schedule to this Order do not amount to a collective investment scheme.

[2204]

SCHEDULE
ARRANGEMENTS NOT AMOUNTING TO A COLLECTIVE INVESTMENT SCHEME
Article 3

1 Individual investment management arrangements

Arrangements do not amount to a collective investment scheme if—

    (a)   the property to which the arrangements relate (other than cash awaiting investment) consists of investments of one or more of the following kinds:

        (i)   an investment of the kind specified by any of articles 76 to 80 of the Regulated Activities Order;

        (ii)   an investment of the kind specified by article 81 of that Order (units in a collective investment scheme) so far as relating to authorised unit trust schemes, recognised schemes or shares in an open-ended investment company; or

        (iii)   a contract of long term insurance;

    (b)   each participant is entitled to a part of that property and to withdraw that part at any time; and

(c)   the arrangements do not have the characteristics mentioned in section 235(3)(a) of the Act and have those mentioned in section 235(3)(b) only because the parts of the property to which different participants are entitled are not bought and sold separately except where a person becomes or ceases to be a participant.

2   Enterprise initiative schemes

(1)   Arrangements do not amount to a collective investment scheme if—
  (a)   the property to which the arrangements relate (other than cash awaiting investment) consists of shares;
  (b)   the arrangements constitute a complying fund;
  (c)   each participant is entitled to a part of the property to which the arrangements relate and—
    (i)   to the extent that the property to which he is entitled comprises relevant shares of a class which are admitted to official listing in an EEA State or to dealings on a recognised investment exchange, he is entitled to withdraw it at any time after the end of the period of five years beginning with the date on which the shares in question were issued;
    (ii)   to the extent that the property to which he is entitled comprises other relevant shares, he is entitled to withdraw it at any time after the end of the period of seven years beginning with the date on which the shares in question were issued;
    (iii)   to the extent that the property to which he is entitled comprises shares other than relevant shares, he is entitled to withdraw it at any time after the end of the period of six months beginning with the date on which the shares in question ceased to be relevant shares; and
    (iv)   to the extent that the property comprises cash which the operator has agreed (conditionally or unconditionally) to apply in subscribing for shares, he is entitled to withdraw it at any time; and
  (d)   the arrangements would meet the conditions described in paragraph 1(c) were it not for the fact that the operator is entitled to exercise all or any of the rights conferred by shares included in the property to which the arrangements relate.

(2)   In sub-paragraph (1)—
  (a)   "shares" means investments of the kind specified by article 76 of the Regulated Activities Order (shares etc) and shares are to be regarded as relevant shares if and so long as they are shares in respect of which neither—
    (i)   a claim for relief made in accordance with section 306 of the 1988 Act has been disallowed; nor
    (ii)   an assessment has been made pursuant to section 307 of the 1988 Act withdrawing or refusing relief by reason of the body corporate in which the shares are held having ceased to be a body corporate which is a qualifying company for the purposes of that Act;
  (b)   "complying fund" means arrangements which provide that—
    (i)   the operator will, so far as is practicable, make investments each of which, subject to each participant's individual circumstances, qualify for relief by virtue of Chapter III of Part VII of the 1988 Act; and
    (ii)   the minimum contribution to the arrangements which each participant must make is not less than £2000.

3   Pure deposit based schemes

Arrangements do not amount to a collective investment scheme if the whole amount of each participant's contribution is a deposit which is accepted by an authorised person with permission to carry on an activity of the kind specified by article 5 of the Regulated Activities Order (accepting deposits) or a person who is an exempt person in relation to such an activity.

4   Schemes not operated by way of business

Arrangements do not amount to a collective investment scheme if they are operated otherwise than by way of business.

5   Debt issues

(1)   Arrangements do not amount to a collective investment scheme if they are arrangements under which the rights or interests of participants are, except as provided in sub-paragraph (2), represented by investments of one, and only one, of the following descriptions:
  (a)   investments of the kind specified by article 77 of the Regulated Activities Order (instruments creating or acknowledging indebtedness) which are—
    (i)   issued by a single body corporate other than an open-ended investment company; or
    (ii)   issued by a single issuer who is not a body corporate and which are guaranteed by the government of the United Kingdom, the Scottish Administration, the

Executive Committee of the Northern Ireland Assembly, the National Assembly for Wales or the government of any country or territory outside the United Kingdom;

and which are not convertible into or exchangeable for investments of any other description;

(b)   investments falling within sub-paragraph (a)(i) or (ii) ("the former investments") which are convertible into or exchangeable for investments of the kind specified by article 76 of the Regulated Activities Order ("the latter investments") provided that the latter investments are issued by the same person who issued the former investments or are issued by a single other issuer;

(c)   investments of the kind specified by article 78 of the Regulated Activities Order (government and public securities) which are issued by a single issuer; or

(d)   investments of the kind specified by article 79 of the Regulated Activities Order (instruments giving entitlement to investments) which are issued otherwise than by an open-ended investment company and which confer rights in respect of investments, issued by the same issuer, of the kind specified by article 76 of that Order or within any of paragraphs (a) to (c).

(2)   Arrangements which would otherwise not amount to a collective investment scheme by virtue of the provisions of sub-paragraph (1) are not to be regarded as amounting to such a scheme by reason only that one or more of the participants ("the counterparty") is a person—

(a)   whose ordinary business involves him in carrying on activities of the kind specified by any of articles 14 (dealing in investments as principal), 21 (dealing in investments as agent), 25 (arranging deals in investments), [25D (operating a multilateral trading facility),] 37 (managing investments), 40 (safeguarding and administering investments), 45 (sending dematerialised instructions), 51 (establishing etc a collective investment scheme), 52 (establishing etc a stakeholder pension scheme) and 53 (advising on investments) or, so far as relevant to any of those articles, article 64 of the Regulated Activities Order (agreeing to carry on specified kinds of activities), or would do so apart from any exclusion from any of those articles made by that Order; and

(b)   whose rights or interests in the arrangements are or include rights or interests under a swap arrangement.

(3)   In sub-paragraph (2), "swap arrangement" means an arrangement the purpose of which is to facilitate the making of payments to participants whether in a particular amount or currency or at a particular time or rate of interest or all or any combination of those things, being an arrangement under which the counterparty—

(a)   is entitled to receive amounts, whether representing principal or interest, payable in respect of any property subject to the arrangements or sums determined by reference to such amounts; and

(b)   makes payments, whether or not of the same amount or in the same currency as the amounts or sums referred to in paragraph (a), which are calculated in accordance with an agreed formula by reference to those amounts or sums.

6 Common accounts

Arrangements do not amount to a collective investment scheme if—

(a)   they are arrangements under which the rights or interests of participants are rights to or interests in money held in a common account; and

(b)   that money is held in the account on the understanding that an amount representing the contribution of each participant is to be applied—

(i)   in making payments to him;

(ii)   in satisfaction of sums owed by him; or

(iii)   in the acquisition of property for him or the provision of services to him.

[7 Certain funds relating to leasehold property

Arrangements do not amount to a collective investment scheme if the rights or interests of the participants are rights or interests—

(a)   in a fund which is a trust fund within the meaning of section 42(1) of the Landlord and Tenant Act 1987 or which would be such a trust fund if the landlord were not an exempt landlord within the meaning of section 58(1) of that Act; or

(b)   in money held in a designated account by the scheme administrator under a tenancy deposit scheme within the meaning of section 212(2) of the Housing Act 2004.]

8 Certain employee share schemes

(1)   Arrangements do not amount to a collective investment scheme if they are operated by a person ("A"), a member of the same group as A or a relevant trustee for the purpose of enabling or facilitating—

(a)   transactions in shares in, or debentures issued by, A between, or for the benefit of, any of the persons mentioned in sub-paragraph (2); or

(b)   the holding of such shares or debentures by, or for the benefit of, any such persons.

(2)   The persons referred to in sub-paragraph (1) are—
  (a)   the bona fide employees or former employees of A or of another member of the same group; or
  (b)   the wives, husbands, widows, widowers, [civil partners, surviving civil partners,] or children or step-children under the age of eighteen of such employees or former employees.

(3)   For the purposes of this paragraph—
  (a)   "shares" and "debentures" have the meaning given by article 71(6)(a) of the Regulated Activities Order:
  (b)   "relevant trustee" means a person who, in pursuance of the arrangements, holds shares in or debentures issued by A.

[9 Schemes entered into for commercial purposes wholly or mainly related to existing business

(1)   Arrangements first entered into before 15th July 2008 do not amount to a collective investment scheme if—
  (a)   by virtue of paragraph 9 of the Schedule to the Financial Services and Markets Act 2000 (Collective Investment Schemes) Order 2001 as it had effect immediately before 15th July 2008 they did not then do so provided that all participants are permitted participants; or
  (b)   in the case of arrangements which amounted to a collective investment scheme immediately before 15th July 2008—
    (i)   all participants are permitted participants; and
    (ii)   at any time each person which is at that time a participant [agrees in writing in respect of the remaining life of the arrangements] that the arrangements do not amount to a collective investment scheme.

(2)   Arrangements first entered into on or after 15th July 2008 do not amount to a collective investment scheme if all participants are permitted participants.

(3)   The exclusion in sub-paragraph (2) shall not apply to arrangements falling within that sub-paragraph if [at any time each person which is at that time a permitted participant agrees in writing in respect of the life of the arrangements that the arrangements amount to a collective investment scheme].

(4)   If at any time a person which is not a permitted participant participates in arrangements then for as long as that person is a participant but not a permitted participant the exclusion in sub-paragraph (1) or, as the case may be, sub-paragraph (2) shall not apply to the arrangements.

(5)   For the purposes of this paragraph—
  "permitted participant" means a participant which—
  (a)   at the time of entering into the arrangements carries on a business which is not a specified business (the "first business") but which may be in addition to any specified business carried on by that participant at that time and—
    (i)   does not carry on that first business solely by virtue of being—
      (a)   a participant in the arrangements; or
      (b)   a member, partner or trust beneficiary of a body corporate, unincorporated association, partnership or trust which is itself a participant in the arrangements; and
    (ii)   enters into the arrangements for commercial purposes wholly or mainly related to the first business; or
  (b)   is a body corporate, unincorporated association[,] partnership, or trustee of a trust (unless that trustee is an individual) which—
    (i)   does not carry on a specified business; and
    (ii)   only has as its members, partners or trust beneficiaries persons which themselves qualify, or would qualify if they participated in the arrangements, as participants of the kind mentioned in paragraph (a) of this paragraph; and
  "specified business" means the business of engaging in any regulated activity of the kind specified by any of articles 14, 21, 25, 25D, 37, 40, 45, 51 to 53 or, so far as relevant to any of those articles, article 64 of the Regulated Activities Order.

(6)   For the purposes of this paragraph, neither the entry into arrangements by any person as a further participant nor the exit from arrangements by any participant shall in itself constitute the creation of new arrangements.

[(7)   An agreement made in respect of any arrangements in accordance with the provisions of sub-paragraph (1)(b)(ii) or sub-paragraph (3) is not affected by—
  (a)   the entry into such arrangements by any person as a further participant;
  (b)   the exit from such arrangements of any participant;

(c)   any later agreement in writing or otherwise under which, contrary to the earlier
        agreement, such arrangements do or, as the case may be, do not amount to a collective
        investment scheme.]]

10 Group schemes

Arrangements do not amount to a collective investment scheme if each of the participants is a body
corporate in the same group as the operator.

11 Franchise arrangements

Franchise arrangements do not amount to a collective investment scheme.

12 Trading schemes

Arrangements do not amount to a collective investment scheme if—
   (a)   the purpose of the arrangements is that participants should receive, by way of reward,
          payments or other benefits in respect of the introduction by any person of other persons
          who become participants;
   (b)   the arrangements are such that the payments or other benefits referred to in paragraph (a)
          are to be wholly or mainly funded out of the contributions of other participants; and
   (c)   the only reason why the arrangements have either or both of the characteristics
          mentioned in section 235(3) of the Act is because, pending their being used to fund those
          payments or other benefits, contributions of participants are managed as a whole by or
          on behalf of the operator of the scheme.

13 Timeshare schemes

Arrangements do not amount to a collective investment scheme if the rights or interests of the
participants are timeshare rights.

14 Other schemes relating to use or enjoyment of property

Arrangements do not amount to a collective investment scheme if—
   (a)   the predominant purpose of the arrangements is to enable the participants to share in the
          use or enjoyment of property or to make its use or enjoyment available gratuitously to
          others; and
   (b)   the property to which the arrangements relate does not consist of the currency of any
          country or territory and does not consist of or include any investment of the kind
          specified by Part III of the Regulated Activities Order or which would be of such a kind
          apart from any exclusion made by that Part of the Order.

15 Schemes involving the issue of certificates representing investments

Arrangements do not amount to a collective investment scheme if the rights or interests of the
participants are investments of the kind specified by article 80 of the Regulated Activities Order
(certificates representing certain securities).

16 Clearing services

Arrangements do not amount to a collective investment scheme if their purpose is the provision of
clearing services and they are operated by an authorised person, a recognised clearing house or a
recognised investment exchange.

17 Contracts of insurance

A contract of insurance does not amount to a collective investment scheme.

[18 Funeral plan contracts

Arrangements do not amount to a collective investment scheme if they consist of, or are made
pursuant to—
   (a)   a funeral plan contract; or
   (b)   a contract which would be a funeral plan contract but for—
          (i)   the proviso to article 59(2) of the Regulated Activities Order, or
          (ii)   the exclusion in article 60 of that Order.]

19 Individual pension accounts

An individual pension account does not amount to a collective investment scheme.

20 Occupational and personal pension schemes

   (1)   An occupational pension scheme does not amount to a collective investment scheme.

   (2)   A personal pension scheme does not amount to a collective investment scheme.

   (3)   Sub-paragraph (2) does not extend to a personal pension unit trust which is constituted as a
feeder fund or comprises feeder funds.

[21 Bodies corporate etc

(1) Subject to sub-paragraph (2), no body incorporated under the law of, or any part of, the United Kingdom relating to building societies or industrial and provident societies or registered under any such law relating to friendly societies, and no other body corporate other than an open-ended investment company, amounts to a collective investment scheme.

(2) Sub-paragraph (1) does not apply to any body incorporated as a limited liability partnership.]

[2205]

NOTES

Para 5: words in square brackets in sub-para (2)(a) inserted by the Financial Services and Markets Act 2000 (Regulated Activities) (Amendment No 3) Order 2006, SI 2006/3384, art 36(1), (2), as from 1 November 2007 (for the full commencement details of SI 2006/3384, see the Note for that Order at **[2866A]**).

Para 7: substituted by the Financial Services and Markets Act 2000 (Collective Investment Schemes) (Amendment) Order 2007, SI 2007/800, art 2, as from 6 April 2007.

Para 8: words in square brackets in sub-para (2)(b) inserted by the Civil Partnership Act 2004 (Amendments to Subordinate Legislation) Order 2005, SI 2005/2114, art 2(16), Sch 16, Pt 1, para 3, as from 5 December 2005.

Para 9: substituted by the Financial Services and Markets Act 2000 (Collective Investment Schemes) (Amendment) Order 2008, SI 2008/1641, art 2, as from 15 July 2008 (as amended by the Financial Services and Markets Act 2000 (Collective Investment Schemes) (Amendment) (No 2) Order 2008, SI 2008/1813, art 2, as from 14 July 2008).

Paras 18, 21: substituted by SI 2001/3650, art 2(1), (3), (4), as from 1 December 2001.

Step-children, etc: as to the meaning of this and related expressions, see the Civil Partnership Act 2004, s 246 (as applied to this Order by the Civil Partnership Act 2004 (Relationships Arising Through Civil Partnership) Order 2005, SI 2005/3137, art 3, Schedule).

FINANCIAL SERVICES AND MARKETS ACT 2000 (CARRYING ON REGULATED ACTIVITIES BY WAY OF BUSINESS) ORDER 2001

(SI 2001/1177)

NOTES

Made: 26 March 2001.

Authority: Financial Services and Markets Act 2000, ss 419, 428(3).

Commencement: 19 December 2001.

This Order is reproduced as amended by: the Financial Services and Markets Act 2000 (Regulated Activities) (Amendment) (No 1) Order 2003, SI 2003/1475; the Financial Services and Markets Act 2000 (Regulated Activities) (Amendment) (No 2) Order 2003, SI 2003/1476; the Financial Services and Markets Act 2000 (Carrying on Regulated Activities by Way of Business) (Amendment) Order 2005, SI 2005/922; the Financial Services and Markets Act 2000 (Regulated Activities) (Amendment) Order 2006, SI 2006/1969; the Financial Services and Markets Act 2000 (Regulated Activities) (Amendment) (No 2) Order 2006, SI 2006/2383; the Financial Services and Markets Act 2000 (Regulated Activities) (Amendment No 3) Order 2006, SI 2006/3384.

ARRANGEMENT OF ARTICLES

1 Citation, commencement and interpretation

(1) This Order may be cited as the Financial Services and Markets Act 2000 (Carrying on Regulated Activities by Way of Business) Order 2001, and comes into force on the day on which section 19 of the Financial Services and Markets Act 2000 comes into force.

(2) In this Order—

(a) the "Regulated Activities Order" means the Financial Services and Markets Act 2000 (Regulated Activities) Order 2001;

(b) ["contract of insurance",] "contractually based investment", "deposit", "overseas person" and "security" have the same meaning as in that Order;

(c) "shares" and "debentures" mean any investment of the kind specified by article 76 or 77 of that Order;

    (d)   "units in a collective investment scheme" means any investment of the kind specified by article 81 of that Order;

    (e)   "warrants" means any investment of the kind specified by article 79 of that Order.

[2206]

NOTES

Para (2): words in square brackets in sub-para (b) inserted by the Financial Services and Markets Act 2000 (Regulated Activities) (Amendment) (No 2) Order 2003, SI 2003/1476, art 18(1), (2), as from 31 October 2004 (in so far as relating to contracts of long-term care insurance), and as from 14 January 2005 (otherwise); for transitional provisions see arts 22–27 of that Order at **[2706]** et seq.

2 Deposit taking business

(1)   A person who carries on an activity of the kind specified by article 5 of the Regulated Activities Order (accepting deposits) is not to be regarded as doing so by way of business if—

    (a)   he does not hold himself out as accepting deposits on a day to day basis; and

    (b)   any deposits which he accepts are accepted only on particular occasions, whether or not involving the issue of any securities.

(2)   In determining for the purposes of paragraph (1)(b) whether deposits are accepted only on particular occasions, regard is to be had to the frequency of those occasions and to any characteristics distinguishing them from each other.

[2207]

3 Investment business

(1)   A person is not to be regarded as carrying on by way of business an activity to which [paragraph (2) applies], unless he carries on the business of engaging in one or more such activities.

(2)   [This paragraph] applies to an activity of the kind specified by any of the following provisions of the Regulated Activities Order, namely—

    (a)   article 14 (dealing in investments as principal);

    (b)   article 21 (dealing in investments as agent);

    (c)   article 25 (arranging deals in investments), except in so far as that activity relates to an investment of the kind specified by article 86 of that Order (Lloyd's syndicate capacity and syndicate membership), or article 89 of that Order (rights and interests) so far as relevant to that article;

    [(ca)   article 25D (operating a multilateral trading facility);]

    (d)   article 37 (managing investments);

    (e)   article 40 (safeguarding and administering investments);

    (f)   article 45 (sending dematerialised instructions);

    (g)   article 51 (establishing etc a collective investment scheme);

    (h)   article 52 (establishing etc a … pension scheme);

    (i)   article 53 (advising on investments); and

    [(j)   article 64 (agreeing) so far as relevant to any of the articles mentioned in sub-paragraphs (a) to (i),

but does not apply to any insurance mediation activity].

(3)   [Paragraph (1)] is without prejudice to article 4 of this Order.

[(4)   A person is not to be regarded as carrying on by way of business any insurance mediation activity unless he takes up or pursues that activity for remuneration.

(5)   In this article, "insurance mediation activity" means any activity of the kind specified by article 21, 25(1) or (2), 39A or 53 of the Regulated Activities Order, or, so far as relevant to any of those articles, article 64 of that Order, which is carried on in relation to a contract of insurance.]

[2208]

NOTES

Paras (1), (3): words in square brackets substituted by the Financial Services and Markets Act 2000 (Regulated Activities) (Amendment) (No 2) Order 2003, SI 2003/1476, art 18(1), (3)(a), (c), as from 31 October 2004 (in so far as relating to contracts of long-term care insurance), and as from 14 January 2005 (otherwise); for transitional provisions see arts 22–27 of that Order at **[2706]** et seq.

Para (2): words in first pair of square brackets substituted, and sub-para (j) (and the following words) substituted, by SI 2003/1476, art 18(1), (3)(b), as from 31 October 2004 (in so far as relating to contracts of long-term care insurance), and as from 14 January 2005 (otherwise), for transitional provisions see arts 22–27 of that Order at **[2706]** et seq; sub-para (ca) inserted by the Financial Services and Markets Act 2000 (Regulated Activities) (Amendment No 3) Order 2006, SI 2006/3384, art 37, as from 1 November 2007 (for the full commencement details of SI 2006/3384, see the Note for that Order at **[2866A]**); word omitted from sub-para (h) revoked by the Financial Services and Markets Act 2000 (Regulated Activities) (Amendment) Order 2006, SI 2006/1969, art 9(1), (2), as from 6 April 2007.

Paras (4), (5): added by SI 2003/1476, art 18(1), (3)(d), as from 31 October 2004 (in so far as relating to contracts of long-term care insurance), and as from 14 January 2005 (otherwise); for transitional provisions see arts 22–27 of that Order at **[2706]** et seq.

[3A   Arranging and advising on regulated mortgage contracts

A person is not to be regarded as carrying on by way of business an activity of the kind specified by—

(a)   article 25A of the Regulated Activities Order (arranging regulated mortgage contracts);

(b)   article 53A of that Order (advising on regulated mortgage contracts); or

(c)   article 64 of that Order (agreeing), so far as relevant to any of the articles mentioned in sub-paragraphs (a) and (b),

unless he carries on the business of engaging in that activity.]

[2209]

NOTES

Commencement: 31 October 2004.

Inserted by the Financial Services and Markets Act 2000 (Regulated Activities) (Amendment) (No 1) Order 2003, SI 2003/1475, art 25, as from 31 October 2004; for transitional provisions see arts 26–29 at **[2700]** et seq.

[3B   Arranging and advising on regulated home reversion plans

A person is not to be regarded as carrying on by way of business an activity specified by—

(a)   article 25B of the Regulated Activities Order (arranging regulated home reversion plans);

(b)   article 53B of that Order (advising on regulated home reversion plans); or

(c)   article 64 of that Order (agreeing), so far as relevant to either of the articles mentioned in sub-paragraphs (a) and (b),

unless he carries on the business of engaging in that activity.]

[2209A]

NOTES

Commencement: 6 April 2007.

Inserted, together with art 3C, by the Financial Services and Markets Act 2000 (Regulated Activities) (Amendment) (No 2) Order 2006, SI 2006/2383, art 29, as from 6 April 2007 (for the full commencement details of SI 2006/2383 and for transitional provisions and effect, see arts 1, 36–40 of, and the Schedule to, the 2006 Order at **[2860]** et seq).

[3C   Arranging and advising on regulated home purchase plans

A person is not to be regarded as carrying on by way of business an activity specified by—

(a)   article 25C of the Regulated Activities Order (arranging regulated home purchase plans);

(b)   article 53C of that Order (advising on regulated home purchase plans); or

(c)   article 64 of that Order (agreeing), so far as relevant to either of the articles mentioned in sub-paragraphs (a) and (b),

unless he carries on the business of engaging in that activity.]

[2209B]

NOTES

Commencement: 6 April 2007.

Inserted as noted to art 3B at **[2209A]**.

4   Managing investments: occupational pension schemes

(1)   A person who carries on an activity of the kind specified by article 37 of the Regulated Activities Order (managing investments), where the assets in question are held for the purposes of an occupational pension scheme, is to be regarded as carrying on that activity by way of business, except where—

(a)   he is a person to whom paragraph (2) applies; or

(b)   all ... day to day decisions in the carrying on of that activity (other than decisions falling within paragraph (6)), so far as relating to relevant assets, are taken on his behalf by—

(i)   an authorised person who has permission to carry on activities of the kind specified by article 37 of the Regulated Activities Order;

(ii)   a person who is an exempt person in relation to activities of that kind; or

(iii)   an overseas person.

(2)   This paragraph applies to—

(a)   any trustee of a relevant scheme who is a beneficiary or potential beneficiary under the scheme; and

(b)   any other trustee of a relevant scheme who takes no ... day to day decisions relating to the management of any relevant assets.

(3)   In this article—

["occupational pension scheme" has the meaning given by section 1 of the Pension Schemes Act 1993 but with paragraph (b) of the definition omitted;]

"relevant assets" means assets of the scheme in question which are securities or contractually based investments;

"relevant scheme" means any occupational pension scheme of a kind falling within paragraph (4) or (5).

(4)   A scheme falls within this paragraph if—
- (a)   it is constituted under an irrevocable trust:
- (b)   it has no more than twelve relevant members;
- (c)   all relevant members, other than any relevant member who is unfit to act, or is incapable of acting, as trustees of the scheme, are trustees of it; and
- (d)   all ... day to day decisions relating to the management of the assets of the scheme which are relevant assets are required to be taken by all, or a majority of, relevant members who are trustees of the scheme or by a person of a kind falling within paragraph (1)(b)(i) or (ii) acting alone or jointly with all, or a majority of, such relevant members;

and for these purposes a person is a relevant member of a scheme if he is an employee or former employee by or in respect of whom contributions to the scheme are being or have been made and to or in respect of whom benefits are or may become payable under the scheme.

(5)   A scheme falls within this paragraph if—
- (a)   it has no more than fifty members;
- (b)   the contributions made by or in respect of each member of the scheme are used in the acquisition of a contract of insurance on the life of that member or in the acquisition of a contract to pay an annuity on that life;
- (c)   the only decision of a kind described in paragraph (1)(b) which may be taken in relation to the scheme is the selection of such contracts; and
- (d)   each member is given the opportunity to select the contract which the contributions made by or in respect of him will be used to acquire.

(6)   A decision falls within this paragraph if—
- [(a)   it is a decision by the trustees of an occupational pension scheme to buy, sell or subscribe for—
  - (i)   units in a collective investment scheme;
  - (ii)   shares or debentures (or warrants relating to such shares or debentures) issued by a body corporate having as its purpose the investment of its funds with the aim of spreading investment risk and giving its members the benefit of the results of the management of those funds by or on behalf of that body; or
  - (iii)   rights under (or rights to or interests in) any contract of insurance;]
  ...
- [(b)   the decision is taken after advice has been obtained and considered from a person who falls within any of the cases in paragraph (7);]
- (c), (d) ...

[(7)   The cases are where the person is—
- (a)   an authorised person who has permission to carry on activities of the kind specified by article 53 of the Regulated Activities Order in relation to the decision in question;
- (b)   an exempt person in relation to such activities;
- (c)   exempt from the general prohibition by virtue of section 327 of the Financial Services and Markets Act 2000; or
- (d)   an overseas person.]

[2210]

NOTES

Paras (1), (2), (4): words omitted revoked by the Financial Services and Markets Act 2000 (Carrying on Regulated Activities by Way of Business) (Amendment) Order 2005, SI 2005/922, art 2(1), (2), as from 6 April 2005.

Para (3): definition "occupational pension scheme" substituted by the Financial Services and Markets Act 2000 (Regulated Activities) (Amendment) Order 2006, SI 2006/1969, art 9(1), (3), as from 6 April 2007.

Para (6): sub-paras (a), (b) substituted, the omitted words following sub-para (a) revoked, and sub-paras (c), (d) revoked, by SI 2005/922, art 2(1), (4)–(7), as from 6 April 2005.

Para (7): substituted by SI 2005/922, art 2(1), (8), as from 6 April 2005.

FINANCIAL SERVICES AND MARKETS ACT 2000 (EXEMPTION) ORDER 2001

(SI 2001/1201)

NOTES

Made: 26 March 2001.

Authority: Financial Services and Markets Act 2000, ss 38, 428(3).

Commencement: 1 December 2001.

This Order is reproduced as amended by: the Tourist Boards (Scotland) Act 2006; the Financial Services and Markets Act 2000 (Exemption) (Amendment) Order 2001, SI 2001/3623; the Financial Services and Markets Act 2000 (Financial Promotion and Miscellaneous Amendments) Order 2002, SI 2002/1310; the Financial Services and Markets Act 2000 (Exemption) (Amendment) Order 2003, SI 2003/47; the Financial Services and Markets Act 2000 (Exemption) (Amendment) (No 2) Order 2003, SI 2003/1675; the Financial Services and Markets Act 2000 (Exemption) (Amendment) Order 2005, SI 2005/592; the Civil Partnership Act 2004 (Amendments to Subordinate Legislation) Order 2005, SI 2005/2114; the Wales Tourist Board (Transfer of Functions to the National Assembly for Wales and Abolition) Order 2005, SI 2005/3225; the Charities and Trustee Investment (Scotland) Act 2005 (Consequential Provisions and Modifications) Order 2006, SI 2006/242; the Financial Services and Markets Act 2000 (Regulated Activities) (Amendment) Order 2006, SI 2006/1969; the Financial Services and Markets Act 2000 (Regulated Activities) (Amendment) (No 2) Order 2006, SI 2006/2383; the Financial Services and Markets Act 2000 (Exemption) (Amendment) Order 2007, SI 2007/125; the Tourist Boards (Scotland) Act 2006 (Consequential Modifications) Order 2007, SI 2007/1103; the Financial Services and Markets Act 2000 (Exemption) (Amendment No 2) Order 2007, SI 2007/1821; the Financial Services and Markets Act 2000 (Exemption) (Amendment) Order 2008, SI 2008/682; the Housing and Regeneration Act 2008 (Consequential Provisions) (No 2) Order 2008, SI 2008/2831; the Financial Services and Markets Act 2000 (Exemption) (Amendment) Order 2009, SI 2009/118; the Financial Services and Markets Act 2000 (Exemption) (Amendment) Order 2009, SI 2009/264.

ARRANGEMENT OF ARTICLES

1   Citation and commencement

This Order may be cited as the Financial Services and Markets Act 2000 (Exemption) Order 2001 and comes into force on the day on which section 19 of the Act comes into force.

[2211]

2   Interpretation

In this Order—
    "the Act" means the Financial Services and Markets Act 2000;
    "charity"—
       (a)   in relation to Scotland, means a [body entered in the Scottish Charity Register]; and
       (b)   otherwise, has the meaning given by section 96(1) of the Charities Act 1993 or by section 35 of the Charities Act (Northern Ireland) 1964;
    ["credit institution" has the meaning given by the Regulated Activities Order;]
    "deposit" has the meaning given by the Regulated Activities Order;
    "industrial and provident society" has the meaning given by section 417(1) of the Act but does not include a credit union within the meaning of the Credit Unions Act 1979 or the Credit Unions (Northern Ireland) Order 1985;
    ["investment firm" has the meaning given by the Regulated Activities Order;]
    "local authority" means—
       (a)   in England and Wales, a local authority within the meaning of the Local Government Act 1972, the Greater London Authority, the Common Council of the City of London or the Council of the Isles of Scilly;
       (b)   in Scotland, a local authority within the meaning of the Local Government (Scotland) Act 1973; and
       (c)   in Northern Ireland, a district council within the meaning of the Local Government Act (Northern Ireland) 1972;
    ["non-qualifying contract of insurance" means a contract of insurance (within the meaning of the Regulated Activities Order) which is not a qualifying contract of insurance (within the meaning of that Order);]
    "the Regulated Activities Order" means the Financial Services and Markets Act 2000 (Regulated Activities) Order 2001.

[2212]

3 Persons exempt in respect of any regulated activity other than insurance business

Each of the persons listed in Part I of the Schedule is exempt from the general prohibition in respect of any regulated activity other than an activity of the kind specified by article 10 of the Regulated Activities Order (effecting and carrying out contracts of insurance).

[2213]

4 Persons exempt in respect of accepting deposits

Subject to the limitations, if any, expressed in relation to him, each of the persons listed in Part II of the Schedule is exempt from the general prohibition in respect of any regulated activity of the kind specified by article 5 of the Regulated Activities Order (accepting deposits).

[2214]

5 Persons exempt in respect of particular regulated activities

(1) Subject to the limitation, if any, expressed in relation to him, each of the persons listed in Part III of the Schedule is exempt from the general prohibition in respect of any regulated activity of the kind specified by any of the following provisions of the Regulated Activities Order, or article 64 of that Order (agreeing to carry on specified kinds of activity) so far as relevant to any such activity—

   (a)   article 14 (dealing in investments as principal);
   (b)   article 21 (dealing in investments as agent);
   (c)   article 25 (arranging deals in investments);
 [(ca) article 25D (operating a multilateral trading facility);]
   (d)   article 37 (managing investments);
 [(da) article 39A (assisting in the administration and performance of a contract of insurance);]
   (e)   article 40 (safeguarding and administering investments);
   (f)   article 45 (sending dematerialised instructions);
   (g)   article 51 (establishing etc a collective investment scheme);
   (h)   article 52 (establishing etc a ... pension scheme);
   (i)   article 53 (advising on investments).

(2) Subject to the limitation, if any, expressed in relation to him, each of the persons listed in Part IV of the Schedule is exempt from the general prohibition in respect of any regulated activity of the kind referred to in relation to him, or an activity of the kind specified by article 64 of the Regulated Activities Order so far as relevant to any such activity.

[2215]

6 Transitional exemption for credit unions

A credit union, within the meaning of the Credit Unions Act 1979 ... , is exempt from the general prohibition in respect of any regulated activity of the kind specified by article 5 of the Regulated Activities Order, but only until 1st July 2002.

[2216]

— Article 4 sets out procedural provisions that relate to the requirement to reapply for permission.
— Article 5 provides that restrictions imposed under the Credit Unions Act 1979, s 19 have effect from commencement as if they were requirements imposed under s 43 of the 2000 Act. Article 5 also makes transitional provisions in relation to the lending powers of credit unions.
— Article 6 makes transitional provisions for people working for credit unions who will, after commencement, be subject to the regime for approved persons in Part V of the 2000 Act. Such persons are taken to have been approved by the Authority for the purposes of s 59 of that Act.
— Article 7 enables credit unions from 8 April 2002 ("applications day"), to apply for a variation of a requirement to which they will, by virtue of art 5, be subject from commencement. Applications may also be made for approval of persons who will, after commencement, be subject to the to the regime established under Part V of the 2000 Act (approved persons). The Authority may also initiate action under s 45 of the 2000 Act (exercise of own initiative powers) or s 56 (prohibition orders) from applications day. Nothing done under the 2000 Act by virtue of art 7 takes effect before commencement.
— Article 8 enables the Authority, from applications day, to exercise its powers under s 165 of the 2000 Act (information gathering) in relation to those credit unions which it has reasonable grounds to believe will be authorised persons at commencement.
— Article 9 makes certain transitional provisions in relation to St Paul's Mutual Aid Society. By virtue of art 20(4) of the Financial Services and Markets Act 2000 (Transitional Provisions) (Authorised Persons etc) Order 2001 (SI 2001/2636), the Society was exempt from the general prohibition imposed by s 19 of the 2000 Act until 1 July 2002.

SCHEDULE

Articles 3–5

PART I
PERSONS EXEMPT IN RESPECT OF ANY REGULATED ACTIVITY OTHER THAN INSURANCE BUSINESS

1. The Bank of England.
2. The central bank of an EEA State other than the United Kingdom.
3. The European Central Bank.
4. The European Community.
5. The European Atomic Energy Community.
6. The European Coal and Steel Community.
7. The European Investment Bank.
8. The International Bank for Reconstruction and Development.
9. The International Finance Corporation.
10. The International Monetary Fund.
11. The African Development Bank.
12. The Asian Development Bank.
13. The Caribbean Development Bank.
14. The Inter-American Development Bank.
15. The European Bank for Reconstruction and Development.
[15A. Bank for International Settlements.]
[15B. Bank of England Asset Purchase Facility Fund Limited.]

[2217]

NOTES
Para 15A: added by the Financial Services and Markets Act 2000 (Exemption) (Amendment) Order 2003, SI 2003/47, art 2, as from 1 March 2003.
Para 15B: added by the Financial Services and Markets Act 2000 (Exemption) (Amendment) Order 2009, SI 2009/118, art 2, as from 2 February 2009.

PART II
PERSONS EXEMPT IN RESPECT OF ACCEPTING DEPOSITS

16. A municipal bank, that is to say a company which was, immediately before the coming into force of this Order, exempted from the prohibition in section 3 of the Banking Act 1987 by virtue of section 4(1) of, and paragraph 4 of Schedule 2 to, that Act.

17.—(1) Keesler Federal Credit Union, in so far as it accepts deposits from members, or dependants of members, of a visiting force of the United States of America, or from members, or dependants of members, of a civilian component of such a force.

(2) In sub-paragraph (1), "member", "dependent" and "visiting force" have the meanings given by section 12 of the Visiting Forces Act 1952 and "member of a civilian component" has the meaning given by section 10 of that Act.

18.   A body of persons certified as a school bank by the National Savings Bank or by an authorised person who has permission to accept deposits.

19.   A local authority.

20.—(1)   Any body which by virtue of any enactment has power to issue a precept to a local authority in England or Wales or a requisition to a local authority in Scotland, or to the expenses of which, by virtue of any enactment, a local authority in the United Kingdom is or can be required to contribute.

   (2)   In sub-paragraph (1), "enactment" includes an enactment comprised in, or in an instrument made under, an Act of the Scottish Parliament.

[21.   The Council of Europe Development Bank.]

22.   A charity, in so far as it accepts deposits—
   (a)   from another charity; or
   (b)   in respect of which no interest or premium is payable.

23.   The National Children's Charities Fund in so far as—
   (a)   it accepts deposits in respect of which no interest or premium is payable; and
   (b)   the total value of the deposits made by any one person does not exceed £10,000.

24.   An industrial and provident society, in so far as it accepts deposits in the form of withdrawable share capital.

[24A.   A credit union, within the meaning of the Credit Unions (Northern Ireland) Order 1985.]

25.—(1)   The Student Loans Company Limited, in so far as it accepts deposits from the Secretary of State or the Scottish Ministers in connection with, or for the purposes of, enabling eligible students to receive loans.

   (2)   In sub-paragraph (1), "eligible student" means—
   (a)   any person who is an eligible student pursuant to regulations made under Part II of the Teaching and Higher Education Act 1998;
   (b)   any person to whom, or in respect of whom, loans may be paid under section 73(f) of the Education (Scotland) Act 1980;
   (c)   any person who is an eligible student pursuant to regulations made under article 3 of the Education (Student Support) (Northern Ireland) Order 1998; or
   (d)   any person who is in receipt of or who is eligible to receive a loan of the kind mentioned in article 3(1) of the Teaching and Higher Education Act 1998 (Commencement No 2 and Transitional Provisions) Order 1998 or article 3(1) of the Education (Student Support) (Northern Ireland) Order 1998 (Commencement and Transitional Provisions) Order (Northern Ireland) 1998.

[2218]

NOTES

   Para 21: substituted by the Financial Services and Markets Act 2000 (Financial Promotion and Miscellaneous Amendments) Order 2002, SI 2002/1310, art 4(2), as from 5 June 2002.
   Para 24A: inserted by the Financial Services and Markets Act 2000 (Exemption) (Amendment) Order 2001, SI 2001/3623, arts 2, 4, as from 1 December 2001.

PART III
PERSONS EXEMPT IN RESPECT OF ANY REGULATED ACTIVITY
MENTIONED IN ARTICLE 5(1)

26.   The National Debt Commissioners.

[27.   Partnerships UK.]

28.   The International Development Association.

29.   The English Tourist Board.

30.   …

[31.   VisitScotland].

32.   The Northern Ireland Tourist Board.

33.   Scottish Enterprise.

[33A.   Invest Northern Ireland.]

34.   The Multilateral Investment Guarantee Agency.

[34A.   The Board of the Pension Protection Fund.]

[34B.   Capital for Enterprise Limited, in so far as in carrying on any regulated activity it provides services only to the Crown.]

35.   A person acting as an official receiver within the meaning of section 399 of the Insolvency Act 1986 or article 2 of the Insolvency (Northern Ireland) Order 1989.

36.   ...

37.—[(1)   An Operator, in so far as he carries on—

    (a)   any regulated activity for the purposes of the performance of his functions as an Operator under the Uncertificated Securities Regulations 1995; or

    (b)   any other regulated activity for the purposes of operating a computer-based system and procedures which—

        (i)   enable title to investments to be evidenced and transferred without a written instrument; or

        (ii)   facilitate matters supplementary or incidental to those specified in sub-paragraph (i),

other than a regulated activity in respect of which a recognised clearing house is exempt from the general prohibition by virtue of section 285(3) of the Act.]

    (2)   In sub-paragraph (1), "Operator" means a person approved as such by the Treasury under the Uncertificated Securities Regulations 1995.

38.   A person acting as a judicial factor.

39.   A person acting as an insolvency practitioner within the meaning of section 388 of the Insolvency Act 1986 [or article 3 of the Insolvency (Northern Ireland) Order 1989].

[2219]

NOTES

   Para 27: substituted by the Financial Services and Markets Act 2000 (Exemption) (Amendment) (No 2) Order 2003, SI 2003/1675, art 2(1), (4)(a), as from 13 July 2003.

   Para 30: revoked by the Wales Tourist Board (Transfer of Functions to the National Assembly for Wales and Abolition) Order 2005, SI 2005/3225, art 6(2), Sch 2, Pt 2, para 4, as from 1 April 2006.

   Para 31: substituted by the Tourist Boards (Scotland) Act 2006, s 4, Sch 2, Pt 2, para 10, as from 1 April 2007 (in relation to Scotland), and by the Tourist Boards (Scotland) Act 2006 (Consequential Modifications) Order 2007, SI 2007/1103, art 2, Schedule, Pt 2, para 6, as from 29 March 2007 (in relation to England and Wales).

   Para 33A: inserted by the Financial Services and Markets Act 2000 (Exemption) (Amendment No 2) Order 2007, SI 2007/1821, art 2(1), (2), as from 20 July 2007.

   Para 34A: inserted by the Financial Services and Markets Act 2000 (Exemption) (Amendment) Order 2005, SI 2005/592, art 2(1), as from 6 April 2005.

   Para 34B: inserted by the Financial Services and Markets Act 2000 (Exemption) (Amendment) Order 2008, SI 2008/682, art 2, as from 1 April 2008.

   Para 36: revoked by the Financial Services and Markets Act 2000 (Exemption) (Amendment) Order 2007, SI 2007/125, art 5, as from 1 November 2007.

   Para 37: sub-para (1) substituted by the Financial Services and Markets Act 2000 (Exemption) (Amendment) Order 2001, SI 2001/3623, arts 2, 5, as from 1 December 2001.

   Para 39: words in square brackets added by SI 2001/3623, arts 2, 6, as from 1 December 2001.

PART IV
PERSONS EXEMPT IN RESPECT OF PARTICULAR REGULATED ACTIVITIES

Enterprise schemes

40.—(1)   Any body corporate which has as its principal object (or one of its principal objects)—

    (a)   the promotion or encouragement of industrial or commercial activity or enterprise in the United Kingdom or in any particular area of it; or

    (b)   the dissemination of information concerning persons engaged in such activity or enterprise or requiring capital to become so engaged;

is exempt from the general prohibition in respect of any regulated activity of the kind specified by article 25 of the Regulated Activities Order (arranging deals in investments) so long as it does not carry on that activity for, or with the prospect of, direct or indirect pecuniary gain.

    (2)   For the purposes of this paragraph, such sums as may reasonably be regarded as necessary to meet the costs of carrying on the activity mentioned in sub-paragraph (1) do not constitute a pecuniary gain.

   [(3)   This paragraph does not apply where an investment firm or credit institution—

    (a)   provides or performs investment services and activities on a professional basis, and

    (b)   in doing so, but for the operation of [sub-paragraph (1)], it would be treated as carrying on an activity of a kind specified by Part 2 of the Regulated Activities Order [in breach of the general prohibition].]

Employee share schemes in electricity industry shares

41.—(1)   Each of the persons to whom this paragraph applies is exempt from the general prohibition in respect of any regulated activity of the kind specified by article 14, 21 or 25 of the Regulated Activities Order (dealing in investments as principal or agent or arranging deals in investments) which he carries on for the purpose of—

    (a)   enabling or facilitating transactions in electricity industry shares or debentures between or for the benefit of any qualifying person; or

    (b)   the holding of electricity industry shares or debentures by or for the benefit of any qualifying person.

(2)   This paragraph applies to—
    (a)   The National Grid Holding plc;
    (b)   Electricity Association Limited;
    (c)   any body corporate in the same group as the person mentioned in sub-paragraph (a) or (b);
    (d)   any company listed in Schedule 1 to the Electricity Act 1989 (Nominated Companies) (England and Wales) Order 1990; and
    (e)   a person holding shares in or debentures of a body corporate as trustee in pursuance of arrangements made for either of the purposes mentioned in sub-paragraph (1) by the Secretary of State, by any of the bodies mentioned in sub-paragraphs (a) to (c) or by an electricity successor company or by some or all of them.

(3)   In this paragraph—
    (a)   "electricity industry shares or debentures" means—
        (i)   any investment of the kind specified by article 76 or 77 of the Regulated Activities Order (shares or instruments creating or acknowledging indebtedness) in or of an electricity successor company;
        (ii)   any investment of the kind specified by article 79 or 80 of that Order (instruments giving entitlement to investments and certificates representing certain securities), so far as relevant to the investments mentioned in sub-paragraph (i); and
        (iii)   any investment of the kind specified by article 89 of that Order (rights to or interests in investments) so far as relevant to the investments mentioned in sub-paragraphs (i) and (ii);
    (b)   "qualifying person" means—
        (i)   the bona fide employees or former employees of The National Grid Holding plc, Electricity Association Limited or any other body corporate in the same group as either of them; and
        (ii)   the wives, husbands, widows, widowers[, civil partners, surviving civil partners,] or children (including, in Northern Ireland, adopted children) or step-children under the age of eighteen of such employees or former employees;
    (c)   references to an electricity successor company include any body corporate that is in the same group and "electricity successor company" means a body corporate which is a successor company for the purposes of Part II of the Electricity Act 1989;
    (d)   "former employees" of a person ("the employer") include any person who has never been employed by the employer so long as he occupied a position in relation to some other person of such a kind that it may reasonably be assumed that he would have been a former employee of the employer had the reorganisation of the electricity industry under Part II of the Electricity Act 1989 been affected before he ceased to occupy the relevant position.

Gas industry

42.—(1)   Transco plc is exempt from the general prohibition in respect of any regulated activity of the kind specified by article 14, 21[, 25 or 25D] of the Regulated Activities Order (dealing in investments as principal or agent[, arranging deals in investments or operating a multilateral trading facility]) which it carries on—
    (a)   in its capacity as a gas transporter under the Transco Licence; and
    (b)   for the purposes of enabling or facilitating gas shippers to buy or sell an investment of the kind specified by article 84 or 85 of the Regulated Activities Order (futures or contracts for differences etc).

(2)   ENMO Ltd is exempt from the general prohibition in respect of any regulated activity of the kind specified by article 14, 21[, 25 or 25D] of the Regulated Activities Order (dealing in investments as principal or agent[, arranging deals in investments or operating a multilateral trading facility]) which it carries on—
    (a)   in its capacity as the operator of the balancing market; and
    (b)   for the purpose of enabling or facilitating Transco plc and relevant gas shippers, for the purpose of participating in the balancing market, to buy or sell investments of the kind specified by article 84 or 85 of that Order (futures or contracts for differences etc).

(3)   Transco plc and relevant gas shippers are exempt from the general prohibition in respect of any regulated activity of the kind specified by article 14 or 21 of the Regulated Activities Order (dealing in investments as principal or agent) in so far as that activity relates to an investment of the kind specified by article 84 or 85 of that Order (futures or contracts for differences etc) and is carried on for the purpose of participating in the balancing market.

(4)   In this paragraph—

(a)   "the balancing market" means the market to regulate the delivery and off-take of gas in Transco plc's pipeline system for the purpose of balancing the volume of gas in that system;

(b)   "gas shipper" has the same meaning as in Part I of the Gas Act 1986;

(c)   "relevant gas shippers" means gas shippers who have entered into a subscription agreement with ENMO Ltd for the purpose of participating in the balancing market;

(d)   "Transco Licence" means the licence treated as granted to Transco plc as a gas transporter under section 7 of the Gas Act 1986;

(e)   the reference to enabling or facilitating includes acting pursuant to rules governing the operation of the balancing market which apply in the event of one of the participants appearing to be unable, or likely to become unable, to meet his obligations in respect of one or more contracts entered into through the balancing market.

Trade unions and employers' associations

43.—(1)   A trade union or employers' association is exempt from the general prohibition in respect of any regulated activity of the kind specified by article 10 of the Regulated Activities Order (effecting and carrying out contracts of insurance) which it carries on in order to provide provident benefits or strike benefits for its members.

(2)   In sub-paragraph (1), "trade union" and "employers' association" have the meanings given by section 1 and section 122(1) of the Trade Union and Labour Relations (Consolidation) Act 1992 or, in Northern Ireland, the meanings given by article 3(1) and article 4(1) of the Industrial Relations (Northern Ireland) Order 1992.

Charities

44.—(1)   A charity is exempt from the general prohibition in respect of any regulated activity of the kind specified by article 51 of the Regulated Activities Order (establishing etc a collective investment scheme) which it carries on in relation to a fund established under—

(a)   section 22A of the Charities Act 1960;

(b)   section 25 of the Charities Act 1993; or

(c)   section 25 of the Charities Act (Northern Ireland) 1964.

(2)   A charity is exempt from the general prohibition in respect of any regulated activity of the kind specified by article 51 of the Regulated Activities Order (establishing etc a collective investment scheme) which it carries on in relation to a pooling scheme fund established under—

(a)   section 22 of the Charities Act 1960; or

(b)   section 24 of the Charities Act 1993.

(3)   In sub-paragraph (2), "pooling scheme fund" means a fund established by a common investment scheme the trusts of which provide that property is not to be transferred to the fund except by or on behalf of a charity, the charity trustees (within the meaning of section 97(1) of the Charities Act 1993) of which are the trustees appointed to manage the fund.

Schemes established under the Trustee Investments Act 1961

45.   A person acting in his capacity as manager or operator of a fund established under section 11 of the Trustee Investments Act 1961 is exempt from the general prohibition in respect of any regulated activity of the kind specified by article 51 of the Regulated Activities Order (establishing etc a collective investment scheme) which he carries on in relation to that fund.

Former members of Lloyd's

46.   Any person who ceased to be an underwriting member (within the meaning of Lloyd's Act 1982) of Lloyd's before 24th December 1996 is exempt from the general prohibition in respect of any regulated activity of the kind specified by article 10(2) of the Regulated Activities Order (carrying out contracts of insurance) which relates to contracts of insurance that he has underwritten at Lloyd's.

Local authorities

[47.   A local authority is exempt from the general prohibition in respect of any regulated activity of the kind specified by—

(a)   article 21, 25(1) or (2), 39A or 53 of the Regulated Activities Order (dealing in investments as agent, arranging deals in investments, assisting in the administration and performance of a contract of insurance or advising on investments) which relates to a non-qualifying contract of insurance; ...

(b)   article 25A, 53A or 61 of that Order (arranging, advising on, entering into or administering a regulated mortgage contract);

[(c)   article 25B, 53B or 63B of that Order (arranging, advising on, entering into or administering a regulated home reversion plan); or

    (d)   article 25C, 53C or 63F of that Order (arranging, advising on, entering into or administering a regulated home purchase plan)].]

Social housing

[48.—(1)   A relevant housing body is exempt from the general prohibition in respect of any regulated activity of the kind specified by—

    (a)   article 21, 25(1) or (2), 39A or 53 of the Regulated Activities Order (dealing in investments as agent, arranging deals in investments, assisting in the administration and performance of a contract of insurance or advising on investments) which relates to a non-qualifying contract of insurance; ...

    (b)   article 25A, 53A or 61 of that Order (arranging, advising on, entering into or administering a regulated mortgage contract);

    [(c)   article 25B, 53B or 63B of that Order (arranging, advising on, entering into or administering a regulated home reversion plan); or

    (d)   article 25C, 53C or 63F of that Order (arranging, advising on, entering into or administering a regulated home purchase plan)].

  (2)   In this paragraph, "relevant housing body" means any of the following—

    (a)   a registered social landlord within the meaning of Part I of the Housing Act 1996;

    (b)   a registered social landlord within the meaning of the Housing (Scotland) Act 2001;

    (c)   [The Regulator of Social Housing];

    [(ca) the Homes and Communities Agency;]

    (d)   Scottish Homes;

    (e)   the body established under article 9 of the Housing (Northern Ireland) Order 1981 known as the Northern Ireland Housing Executive;

    [(f)   Communities Scotland]].

[Electricity industry

49.—(1)   NGC is exempt from the general prohibition in respect of any regulated activity of the kind specified by article 14, 21, 25[, 25D] or 53 of the Regulated Activities Order (dealing in investments as principal or agent, arranging deals in investments[, operating a multilateral trading facility] or advising on investments) which it carries on in the course of—

    (a)   its participation in the Balancing and Settlement Arrangements as operator of the electricity transmission system in [Great Britain] under the Transmission Licence; or

    (b)   the acquisition by it of Balancing Services in accordance with the Electricity Act 1989 and the Transmission Licence.

  (2)   ELEXON Clear Limited is exempt from the general prohibition in respect of any regulated activity of the kind specified by article 14, 21[, 25 or 25D] of that Order which it carries on in the course of its participation in the Balancing and Settlement Arrangements as clearer for the purposes of (among other things) receiving from and paying to BSC Parties trading and reconciliation charges arising under the Balancing and Settlement Arrangements.

  (3)   Each BSC Party is exempt from the general prohibition in respect of any regulated activity of the kind specified by article 14, 21, 25[, 25D] or 53 of that Order which it carries on in the course of—

    (a)   its participation in the Balancing and Settlement Arrangements; or

    (b)   the provision by it (or, in the case of an activity of the kind specified by article 21 of that Order, its principal) of Balancing Services to NGC.

  (4)   ELEXON Limited is exempt from the general prohibition in respect of any regulated activity of the kind specified by article 25 [or 25D] of that Order which it carries on in the course of its participation in the Balancing and Settlement Arrangements as administrator

  (5)   Each BSC Agent and each Volume Notification Agent is exempt from the general prohibition in respect of any regulated activity of the kind specified by article 25 [or 25D] of that Order which it carries on in that capacity.

  (6)   ...

  (7)   In this paragraph—

"Ancillary Services" means services which generators and suppliers of electricity and those making transfers of electricity across an Interconnector are required (as a condition of their connection to the transmission system in [Great Britain]), or have agreed, to make available to NGC for the purpose of securing the stability of the electricity transmission or any distribution system in [Great Britain] or any system linked to it by an Interconnector;

"Balancing and Settlement Arrangements" means—

    (a)   the Balancing Mechanism; and

    (b)   arrangements—

        (i)   for the determination and allocation to BSC Parties of the quantities of electricity that have been delivered to and taken off the electricity transmission system and any distribution system in [Great Britain]; and

(ii) which set, and provide for the determination and financial settlement of, BSC Parties' obligations arising by reference to the quantities referred to in sub-paragraph (i), including the difference between such quantities (after taking account of accepted bids and offers in the Balancing Mechanism) and the quantities of electricity contracted for sale and purchase between BSC Parties;

"Balancing Mechanism" means the arrangements pursuant to which BSC Parties may make, and NGC may accept, offers or bids to increase or decrease the quantities of electricity to be delivered to or taken off the electricity transmission system or any distribution system in [Great Britain] at any time or during any period so as to assist NGC in operating and balancing the electricity transmission system, and arrangements for the settlement of financial obligations arising from the acceptance of such offers and bids;

"Balancing Services" means—

(a)   offers and bids made in the Balancing Mechanism;

(b)   Ancillary Services; and

(c)   other services available to NGC which assist it in operating the electricity transmission system in accordance with the Electricity Act 1989 and the Transmission Licence;

"BSC Agents" means the persons for the time being engaged by or on behalf of ELEXON Limited for the purpose of providing services to all BSC Parties, NGC, ELEXON Limited and ELEXON Clear Limited in connection with the operation of the Balancing and Settlement Arrangements;

["BSC Framework Agreement" means the agreement of that title in the form approved by the Secretary of State for the purpose of conditions of the Transmission Licence and which is dated 14 August 2000; and "conditions" for the purposes of this definition means conditions determined by the Secretary of State under powers granted by section 137(1) of the Energy Act 2004. and incorporated into existing electricity transmission licences by a scheme made by the Secretary of State pursuant to section 138 of, and Schedule 17 to, that Act;]

"BSC Parties" means those persons (other than NGC, ELEXON Limited and ELEXON Clear Limited) who have signed or acceded to (in accordance with the terms of the BSC Framework Agreement), and not withdrawn from, the BSC Framework Agreement;

"Interconnector" means the electric lines and electrical plant [and meters] used [solely] for the transfer of electricity to or from the electricity transmission system ... in [Great Britain] into or out of [Great Britain];

"NGC" means ... National Grid Company plc;

.....

"the Transmission Licence" means the licence to [participate in the transmission of] electricity in [Great Britain] granted[, or treated as granted,] to NGC under section 6(1)(b) of the Electricity Act 1989; and

"Volume Notification Agents" means the persons for the time being appointed and authorised under and in accordance with the Balancing and Settlement Arrangements on behalf of BSC Parties to notify to the BSC Agent designated for that purpose pursuant to the Balancing and Settlement Arrangements quantities of electricity contracted for the sale and purchase between those BSC Parties to be taken into account for the purposes of the Balancing and Settlement Arrangements.]

[Freight Forwarders and Storage Firms

50.—(1)   A freight forwarder or storage firm is exempt from the general prohibition in respect of any regulated activity of the kind specified by article 21, 25, 39A or 53 of the Regulated Activities Order (dealing in investments as agent, arranging deals in investments, assisting in the administration and performance of a contract of insurance or advising on investments) in the circumstances referred to in paragraph 2.

(2)   The circumstances are—

(a)   where a freight forwarder ("F")—

(i)   holds a policy of insurance which insures F in respect of loss of or damage to goods which F transports or of which F arranges the transportation, and

(ii)   makes available to a customer rights under that policy to enable the customer to claim directly against the insurer in respect of loss or damage to those goods; or

(b)   where a storage firm ("S")—

(i)   holds a policy of insurance which insures S in respect of loss of or damage to goods which S stores or for which S arranges storage, and

(ii)   makes available to a customer rights under that policy to enable the customer to claim directly against the insurer in respect of loss or damage to those goods.

(3)   In this paragraph—

(a) "freight forwarder" means a person whose principal business is arranging or carrying out the transportation of goods;

(b) "storage firm" means a person whose principal business is storing goods or arranging storage for goods;

(c) "customer" means a person *who is not an individual* who uses the service of a freight forwarder or storage firm.

Policyholder Advocates

51.—(1) A person acting as a policyholder advocate is exempt from the general prohibition in respect of any regulated activity of the kind specified by article 25 or 53 of the Regulated Activities Order (arranging deals in investments or advising on investments) in so far as he carries on these activities in connection with, or for the purposes of, his role as policyholder advocate.

(2) In sub-paragraph (1), "policyholder advocate" means a person who is—

(a) appointed by an insurer ("I") to represent the interests of policyholders in negotiations with I about I's proposals to redefine the rights and interests in any surplus assets arising in I's with-profits fund; and

(b) approved or nominated by the Authority to carry out that role.

(3) In sub-paragraph (2), "with-profits fund" means a long-term insurance fund in which policyholders are eligible to participate in surplus assets of the fund.]

[2220]

NOTES

Para 40: sub-para (3) added by the Financial Services and Markets Act 2000 (Exemption) (Amendment) Order 2007, SI 2007/125, art 6(a), as from 1 November 2007; words in first pair of square brackets substituted, and words in second pair of square brackets added, by the Financial Services and Markets Act 2000 (Exemption) (Amendment No 2) Order 2007, SI 2007/1821, art 2(1), (3), as from 1 November 2007.

Para 41: words in square brackets in sub-para (3)(b)(ii) inserted by the Civil Partnership Act 2004 (Amendments to Subordinate Legislation) Order 2005, SI 2005/2114, art 2(16), Sch 16, Pt 1, para 4, as from 5 December 2005.

Para 42: words in square brackets substituted by SI 2007/125, art 6(b), as from 1 November 2007.

Para 47: substituted by the Financial Services and Markets Act 2000 (Exemption) (Amendment) (No 2) Order 2003, SI 2003/1675, art 2(1), (4)(b), as from 31 October 2004 (in so far as providing for an exemption in relation to any mortgage activity), and as from 14 January 2005 (otherwise); word omitted from sub-para (a) revoked, and sub-paras (c), (d) inserted, by the Financial Services and Markets Act 2000 (Regulated Activities) (Amendment) (No 2) Order 2006, SI 2006/2383, art 30(a), as from 6 April 2007 (for the full commencement details of SI 2006/2383 and for transitional provisions and effect, see arts 1, 36–40 of, and the Schedule to, the 2006 Order at **[2860]** et seq).

Para 48: substituted by SI 2003/1675, art 2(1), (4)(c), as from 31 October 2004 (in so far as providing for an exemption in relation to any mortgage activity), and as from 14 January 2005 (otherwise); word omitted from sub-para (1)(a) revoked, and sub-paras (1)(c), (d) inserted, by SI 2006/2383, art 30(b), as from 6 April 2007 (for the full commencement details of SI 2006/2383 and for transitional provisions and effect, see arts 1, 36–40 of, and the Schedule to, the 2006 Order at **[2860]** et seq); words in square brackets in sub-para (2)(c) substituted, and sub-para (2)(ca) inserted, by the Housing and Regeneration Act 2008 (Consequential Provisions) (No 2) Order 2008, SI 2008/2831, arts 3, 4, Sch 1, para 11, Sch 2, para 4, as from 1 December 2008; sub-para (2)(f) added by the Financial Services and Markets Act 2000 (Exemption) (Amendment) Order 2005, SI 2005/592, art 2(2), as from 6 April 2005.

Para 49: added by the Financial Services and Markets Act 2000 (Exemption) (Amendment) Order 2001, SI 2001/3623, arts 2, 8, as from 1 December 2001, and is amended as follows:

Words ", operating a multilateral trading facility" in square brackets in sub-para (1) inserted, figure ", 25D" in square brackets in sub-paras (1), (3) inserted, and words in square brackets in sub-pars (4), (5) inserted, by SI 2007/125, art 6(c)(i), (iii)–(v), as from 1 November 2007.

Words in square brackets in sub-para (2) substituted by SI 2007/125, art 6(c)(ii), as from 1 November 2007.

Other words in square brackets substituted or inserted, and words omitted revoked, by the Financial Services and Markets Act 2000 (Exemption) (Amendment) Order 2005, SI 2005/592, art 3, as from 1 April 2005.

Para 50: added, together with para 51, by SI 2007/1821, art 2(1), (4), as from 20 July 2007; the words in italics in the definition "customer" are revoked by the Financial Services and Markets Act 2000 (Exemption) (Amendment) Order 2009, SI 2009/264, art 2, as from 6 April 2009.

Para 51: added as noted above.

Transfer of functions: by the Housing (Scotland) Act 2001, s 84, the functions of Scottish Homes are transferred to the Scottish Ministers.

Step-children, etc: as to the meaning of this and related expressions, see the Civil Partnership Act 2004, s 246 (as applied to this Order by the Civil Partnership Act 2004 (Relationships Arising Through Civil Partnership) Order 2005, SI 2005/3137, art 3, Schedule).

FINANCIAL SERVICES AND MARKETS ACT 2000 (APPOINTED REPRESENTATIVES) REGULATIONS 2001

(SI 2001/1217)

NOTES
Made: 28 March 2001.
Authority: Financial Services and Markets Act 2000, ss 39(1), 417(1).
Commencement: 1 December 2001.
These Regulations are reproduced as amended by: the Financial Services and Markets Act 2000 (Appointed Representatives) (Amendment) Regulations 2001, SI 2001/2508; the Financial Services and Markets Act 2000 (Regulated Activities) (Amendment) (No 1) Order 2003, SI 2003/1475; the Financial Services and Markets Act 2000 (Regulated Activities) (Amendment) (No 2) Order 2003, SI 2003/1476; the Financial Services and Markets Act 2000 (Appointed Representatives) (Amendment) Regulations 2004, SI 2004/453; the Financial Services and Markets Act 2000 (Regulated Activities) (Amendment) (No 2) Order 2004, SI 2004/2737; the Financial Services and Markets Act 2000 (Regulated Activities) (Amendment) (No 2) Order 2006, SI 2006/2383; the Financial Services and Markets Act 2000 (Appointed Representatives) (Amendment) Regulations 2006, SI 2006/3414; the Financial Services and Markets Act 2000 (Markets in Financial Instruments) (Amendment) Regulations 2007, SI 2007/763.

1   Citation, commencement and interpretation

(1)   These Regulations may be cited as the Financial Services and Markets Act 2000 (Appointed Representatives) Regulations 2001, and come into force on the day on which section 19 of the Act comes into force.

(2)   In these Regulations—
"buy", "sell", "security"[, "contract of insurance", "[qualifying contract of insurance]" and "relevant investment"] have the same meaning as in the Regulated Activities Order;
["contract of long-term care insurance" means a contract of insurance in respect of which the following conditions are met—
    (a)   the purpose (or one of the purposes) of the policy is to protect the policyholder against the risk of becoming unable to live independently without assistance in consequence of a deterioration of mental or physical health, injury, sickness or other infirmity;
    (b)   benefits under the contract are payable in respect of—
        (i)   services,
        (ii)   accommodation, or
        (iii)   goods,
which are (or which is) necessary or desirable due to a deterioration of mental or physical health, injury, sickness or other infirmity;
    (c)   the contract is expressed to be in effect until the death of the policyholder (except that the contract may give the policyholder the option to surrender the policy); and
    (d)   the benefits under the contract are capable of being paid throughout the life of the policyholder;]
["EEA credit institution" means a credit institution authorised under the banking consolidation directive which has its relevant office in an EEA State other than the United Kingdom;
"EEA investment firm" means an investment firm as defined in section 424A of the Act which has its relevant office in an EEA State other than the United Kingdom;]
["home purchaser" has the same meaning as in article 63F(3) of the Regulated Activities Order;]
"other counterparties" means persons other than the principal;
["plan provider" has the meaning given by paragraph (3) of article 63B of the Regulated Activities Order, read with paragraphs (7) and (8) of that article;]
"the principal", in relation to a contract, means the party who is an authorised person, and "the representative" means the other party;
"the Regulated Activities Order" means the Financial Services and Markets Act 2000 (Regulated Activities) Order 2001;
["regulated home purchase plan" has the same meaning as in article 63F(3) of the Regulated Activities Order;
"regulated home reversion plan" has the same meaning as in article 63B(3) of the Regulated Activities Order;]
["regulated mortgage contract", and "borrower" in relation to such a contract, have the same meaning as in article 61(3) of the Regulated Activities Order;]
["reversion seller" has the same meaning as in article 63B(3) of the Regulated Activities Order].

NOTES

Para (2) is amended as follows:

In the first group of definitions (ie, the ones beginning with "buy"), words in first (outer) pair of square brackets substituted by the Financial Services and Markets Act 2000 (Regulated Activities) (Amendment) (No 2) Order 2003, SI 2003/1476, art 14(1), (2), as from 31 October 2004 (in so far as relating to contracts of long-term care insurance), and as from 14 January 2005 (otherwise), for transitional provisions see arts 22–27 of that Order at **[2706]** et seq; words in second (inner) pair of square brackets substituted by the Financial Services and Markets Act 2000 (Appointed Representatives) (Amendment) Regulations 2004, SI 2004/453, reg 2(1), (2), as from 25 April 2004.

Definition "contract of long-term care insurance" inserted by SI 2004/453, reg 2(1), (3), as from 31 October 2004.

Definitions "EEA credit institution" and "EEA investment firm" inserted by the Financial Services and Markets Act 2000 (Appointed Representatives) (Amendment) Regulations 2006, SI 2006/3414, regs 2, 3, as from 1 November 2007.

Definitions "home purchaser", "plan provider", "regulated home purchase plan", "regulated home reversion plan", and "reversion seller" inserted by the Financial Services and Markets Act 2000 (Regulated Activities) (Amendment) (No 2) Order 2006, SI 2006/2383, art 31(1), (2), as from 6 April 2007 (for the full commencement details of SI 2006/2383 and for transitional provisions and effect, see arts 1, 36–40 of, and the Schedule to, the 2006 Order at **[2860]** et seq).

Definition "regulated mortgage contract" inserted by the Financial Services and Markets Act 2000 (Regulated Activities) (Amendment) (No 1) Order 2003, SI 2003/1475, art 23(1), (2), as from 31 October 2004; for transitional provisions see arts 26–29 of that Order at **[2700]** et seq.

2 Descriptions of business for which appointed representatives are exempt

[(1)] [Subject to paragraph (2),] any business which comprises—

[(aa) an activity of the kind specified by article 21 of the Regulated Activities Order (dealing in investments as agent), where the transaction relates to [a contract of insurance which is not a qualifying contract of insurance or a contract of long-term care insurance];]

(a) an activity of the kind specified by article 25 of [that Order] (arranging deals in investments), where the arrangements are for or with a view to transactions relating to securities or [relevant investments];

[(ab) an activity of the kind specified by article 25A of that Order (arranging regulated mortgage contracts);]

[(aba) an activity of the kind specified by article 25B of that Order (arranging regulated home reversion plans);

(abb) an activity of the kind specified by article 25C of that Order (arranging regulated home purchase plans);]

[(ac) an activity of the kind specified by article 39A of that Order (assisting in the administration and performance of a contract of insurance) ... ;]

(b) an activity of the kind specified by article 40 of that Order (safeguarding and administering investments), where the activity consists of arranging for one or more other persons to safeguard and administer assets;

[(ba) an activity of the kind specified by article 52B of that Order (providing basic advice on stakeholder products);]

(c) an activity of the kind specified by article 53 of that Order (advising on investments); ...

[(ca) an activity of the kind specified by article 53A of that Order (advising on regulated mortgage contracts); ...]

[(cb) an activity of the kind specified by article 53B of that Order (advising on regulated home reversion plans);

(cc) an activity of the kind specified by article 53C of that Order (advising on regulated home purchase plans); or]

(d) an activity of the kind specified by article 64 of that Order (agreeing to carry on activities), so far as relevant to an activity falling within [sub-paragraph (aa), (a), (ab), (ac), [(aba), (abb), (b), (c), (ca), (cb) or (cc)]];

is prescribed for the purposes of subsection (1)(a)(i) of section 39 of the Act (exemption of appointed representatives).

[(1A) In its application to a contract with a principal who is an EEA investment firm or an EEA credit institution, the list in paragraph (1) shall be treated as including in addition—

(a) the activity of placing financial instruments,

(b) the activity of providing advice to clients or potential clients in relation to the placing of financial instruments.

(1B) In paragraph (1A), "clients" and "financial instruments" have the meanings given in, respectively, paragraphs 1.10 and 1.17 of Article 4 of the markets in financial instruments directive.]

[(2), (3) ...]

[2222]

NOTES

Para (1) is amended as follows:

Numbered as such, and words in first pair of square brackets inserted, by the Financial Services and Markets Act 2000 (Appointed Representatives) (Amendment) Regulations 2001, SI 2001/2508, reg 2(a), (b), as from 1 December 2001.

Sub-paras (aa), (ac) inserted, and words in square brackets in sub-para (a) substituted, by the Financial Services and Markets Act 2000 (Regulated Activities) (Amendment) (No 2) Order 2003, SI 2003/1476, art 14(1), (3)(a)–(c), as from 31 October 2004 (in so far as relating to contracts of long-term care insurance), and as from 14 January 2005 (otherwise); for transitional provisions see arts 22–27 of that Order at **[2706]** et seq.

Words in square brackets in sub-para (aa) substituted by the Financial Services and Markets Act 2000 (Appointed Representatives) (Amendment) Regulations 2004, SI 2004/453, reg 3(1), (2), as from 25 April 2004.

Sub-paras (ab), (ca) inserted, and word omitted from sub-para (c) revoked, by the Financial Services and Markets Act 2000 (Regulated Activities) (Amendment) (No 1) Order 2003, SI 2003/1475, art 23(1), (3)(a)–(c), as from 31 October 2004; for transitional provisions see arts 26–29 of that Order at **[2700]** et seq.

Sub-paras (aba), (abb), (cb), (cc) inserted, word omitted from sub-para (ca) revoked, and words in second (inner) pair of square brackets in sub-para (d) substituted, by the Financial Services and Markets Act 2000 (Regulated Activities) (Amendment) (No 2) Order 2006, SI 2006/2383, art 31(1), (3), as from 6 April 2007 (for the full commencement details of SI 2006/2383 and for transitional provisions and effect, see arts 1, 36–40 of, and the Schedule to, the 2006 Order at **[2860]** et seq).

Words omitted from sub-para (ac) revoked by SI 2004/453, reg 3(1), (3), as from 25 April 2004.

Sub-para (ba) inserted by the Financial Services and Markets Act 2000 (Regulated Activities) (Amendment) (No 2) Order 2004, SI 2004/2737, art 5(1), (2), as from 6 April 2005.

Words in first (outer) pair of square brackets in sub-para (d) substituted by a combination of SI 2003/1475, art 23(1), (3)(d), as from 31 October 2004 (for transitional provisions see arts 26–29 of that Order at **[2700]** et seq) and SI 2003/1476, art 14(1), (3)(d), as from 31 October 2004 (in so far as relating to contracts of long-term care insurance), and as from 14 January 2005 (otherwise) (for transitional provisions see arts 22–27 of that Order at **[2706]** et seq).

Paras (1A), (1B): inserted by the Financial Services and Markets Act 2000 (Appointed Representatives) (Amendment) Regulations 2006, SI 2006/3414, regs 2, 4(a), as from 1 November 2007.

Paras (2), (3): added by SI 2001/2508, reg 2(c), as from 1 December 2001; revoked by SI 2006/3414, regs 2, 4(b), as from 1 November 2007.

3 Requirements applying to contracts between authorised persons and appointed representatives

(1) [Except where paragraph (1A) applies to a contract between a principal and a representative, it is a prescribed requirement for the purposes of section 39(1)(a)(ii) of the Act that such a contract] must (unless it prohibits the representative from representing other counterparties) contain a provision enabling the principal to—

(a)   impose such a prohibition; or

(b)   impose restrictions as to the other counterparties which the representative may represent, or as to the types of investment in relation to which the representative may represent other counterparties.

[(1A)   This paragraph applies to a contract where the principal is an EEA investment firm or an EEA credit institution.]

(2)   For the purposes of paragraph (1) a representative is to be treated as representing other counterparties where he—

[(aa)   he enters into investment transactions as agent (in circumstances constituting the carrying on of an activity of the kind specified by article 21 of the Regulated Activities Order) for other counterparties;]

(a)   makes arrangements (in circumstances constituting the carrying on of an activity of the kind specified by article 25 of [that Order]) for persons to enter (or with a view to persons entering) into investment transactions with other counterparties;

[(ab)   he assists in the administration and performance of a contract of insurance (in circumstances constituting the carrying on of an activity of the kind specified by article 39A of that Order) for other counterparties;]

(b)   arranges (in circumstances constituting the carrying on of an activity of the kind specified by article 40 of that Order) for other counterparties to safeguard and administer assets; or

(c)   gives advice (in circumstances constituting the carrying on of an activity of the kind specified by article 53 of that Order) on the merits of entering into investment transactions with other counterparties;

where an "investment transaction" means a transaction to buy, sell, subscribe for or underwrite an investment which is a security or a [relevant investment].

[(3)   A representative is also to be treated as representing other counterparties for the purposes of paragraph (1) where he—

(a)   makes arrangements (in circumstances constituting the carrying on of an activity of the kind specified by article 25A of that Order)—

(i)   for persons to enter (or with a view to persons entering) as borrowers into regulated mortgage contracts with other counterparties, or

      (ii)   for a person to vary a regulated mortgage contract entered into by a person as borrower after the coming into force of article 61 of that Order with other counterparties; or

  (b)   gives advice (in circumstances constituting the carrying on of an activity of the kind specified by article 53A of that Order) on the merits of—

      (i)   persons entering as borrowers into regulated mortgage contracts with other counterparties, or

      (ii)   persons varying regulated mortgage contracts entered into by them as borrower after the coming into force of article 61 of that Order with other counterparties.]

[(3A)   A representative is also to be treated as representing other counterparties for the purposes of paragraph (1) where he—

  (a)   makes arrangements (in circumstances constituting the carrying on of an activity of the kind specified by article 25B of that Order)—

      (i)   for a person to enter (or with a view to a person entering) as reversion seller or plan provider into a regulated home reversion plan with other counterparties, or

      (ii)   for a person to vary a regulated home reversion plan entered into on or after 6th April 2007 by him as reversion seller or plan provider with other counterparties; or

  (b)   gives advice (in circumstances constituting the carrying on of an activity of the kind specified by article 53B of that Order) on the merits of—

      (i)   a person entering as reversion seller or plan provider into a regulated home reversion plan with other counterparties, or

      (ii)   a person varying a regulated home reversion plan entered into on or after 6th April 2007 by him as reversion seller or plan provider with other counterparties.

(3B)   A representative is also to be treated as representing other counterparties for the purposes of paragraph (1) where he—

  (a)   makes arrangements (in circumstances constituting the carrying on of an activity of the kind specified by article 25C of that Order)—

      (i)   for a person to enter (or with a view to a person entering) as home purchaser into a regulated home purchase plan with other counterparties, or

      (ii)   for a person to vary a regulated home purchase plan entered into on or after 6th April 2007 by a person as home purchaser with other counterparties; or

  (b)   gives advice (in circumstances constituting the carrying on of an activity of the kind specified by article 53C of that Order) on the merits of—

      (i)   a person entering as home purchaser into a regulated home purchase plan with other counterparties, or

      (ii)   a person varying a regulated home purchase plan entered into on or after 6th April 2007 by him as home purchaser with other counterparties.]

[(4)   Where the contract between the principal and the representative permits or requires the representative to carry on business which includes an activity—

  (a)   of the kind specified by article 21, 25, 39A or 53 of the Regulated Activities Order or an activity of the kind specified by article 64 of that Order, so far as relevant to any of those articles, and

  (b)   which relates to a contract of insurance,

paragraph (5) applies.

(5)   Where this paragraph applies, it is also a prescribed requirement for the purposes of subsection (1)(a)(ii) of section 39 of the Act that the contract between the principal and the representative contain a provision providing that the representative is not permitted or required to carry on business, so far as it comprises an activity of the kind specified by paragraph (4), unless he is included in the record maintained by the Authority under section 347 of the Act by virtue of article 93 of the Regulated Activities Order (recorded insurance intermediaries).]

[(6)   In the case of a representative to whom subsection (1A) of section 39 of the Act applies, it is a prescribed requirement for the purposes of subsection (1)(a)(ii) of that section, except where paragraph (1A) applies, that the contract between the principal and the representative must contain a provision that the representative is only permitted to provide the services and carry on the activities referred to in Article 4.1.25 of the markets in financial instruments directive while he is entered on the applicable register.]

[2223]

NOTES

    Para (1): words in square brackets substituted by the Financial Services and Markets Act 2000 (Appointed Representatives) (Amendment) Regulations 2006, SI 2006/3414, regs 2, 5(a), as from 1 November 2007.

    Paras (1A), (6): inserted and added respectively by SI 2006/3414, regs 2, 5(b), (c), as from 1 November 2007.

    Para (2): sub-paras (aa), (ab) inserted, words in square brackets in sub-para (a) and the final words in square brackets substituted, by the Financial Services and Markets Act 2000 (Regulated Activities) (Amendment)

(No 2) Order 2003, SI 2003/1476, art 14(1), (4)(a), as from 31 October 2004 (in so far as relating to contracts of long-term care insurance), and as from 14 January 2005 (otherwise); for transitional provisions see arts 22–27 of that Order at [2706] et seq.

Para (3): added by the Financial Services and Markets Act 2000 (Regulated Activities) (Amendment) (No 1) Order 2003, SI 2003/1475, art 23(1), (4), as from 31 October 2004; for transitional provisions see arts 26–29 at [2700] et seq.

Paras (3A), (3B): inserted by the Financial Services and Markets Act 2000 (Regulated Activities) (Amendment) (No 2) Order 2006, SI 2006/2383, art 31(1), (4), as from 6 April 2007 (for the full commencement details of SI 2006/2383 and for transitional provisions and effect, see arts 1, 36–40 of, and the Schedule to, the 2006 Order at [2860] et seq).

Paras (4), (5): added by SI 2003/1476, art 14(1), (4)(b), as from 31 October 2004 (in so far as relating to contracts of long-term care insurance), and as from 14 January 2005 (otherwise); for transitional provisions see arts 22–27 of that Order at [2706] et seq.

[4   Transitional provision in relation to contracts

Regulation 3(6) does not apply in relation to a contract made on or before 31st October 2007.]

[2223A]

NOTES
Commencement: 1 November 2007.
Added by the Financial Services and Markets Act 2000 (Markets in Financial Instruments) (Amendment) Regulations 2007, SI 2007/763, reg 7, as from 1 November 2007.

FINANCIAL SERVICES AND MARKETS ACT 2000 (DESIGNATED PROFESSIONAL BODIES) ORDER 2001

(SI 2001/1226)

NOTES
Made: 27 March 2001.
Authority: Financial Services and Markets Act 2000, s 326.
Commencement: 28 March 2001.
This Order is reproduced as amended by: the Financial Services and Markets Act 2000 (Designated Professional Bodies) (Amendment) Order 2004, SI 2004/3352; the Financial Services and Markets Act 2000 (Designated Professional Bodies) (Amendment) Order 2006, SI 2006/58.

1   Citation, commencement and interpretation

(1)   This Order may be cited as the Financial Services and Markets Act 2000 (Designated Professional Bodies) Order 2001.

(2)   This Order comes into force on the day after the day on which it is made.

(3)   In this Order, "the Act" means the Financial Services and Markets Act 2000.

[2224]

2   Designated professional bodies

The following bodies are designated under section 326(1) of the Act for the purposes of Part XX of the Act—

(a)   the Law Society;
(b)   the Law Society of Scotland;
(c)   the Law Society of Northern Ireland;
(d)   the Institute of Chartered Accountants in England and Wales;
(e)   the Institute of Chartered Accountants of Scotland;
(f)   the Institute of Chartered Accountants in Ireland;
(g)   the Association of Chartered Certified Accountants;
(h)   the Institute of Actuaries;
[(i)   the Council for Licensed Conveyancers];
[(j)   the Royal Institution of Chartered Surveyors].

[2225]

NOTES
Para (i) added by the Financial Services and Markets Act 2000 (Designated Professional Bodies) (Amendment) Order 2004, SI 2004/3352, art 2, as from 14 January 2005; para (j) added by the Financial Services and Markets Act 2000 (Designated Professional Bodies) (Amendment) Order 2006, SI 2006/58, art 2, as from 10 February 2006.

FINANCIAL SERVICES AND MARKETS ACT 2000 (PROFESSIONS) (NON-EXEMPT ACTIVITIES) ORDER 2001

(SI 2001/1227)

NOTES

Made: 27 March 2001.

Authority: Financial Services and Markets Act 2000, ss 327(6), 428(3).

Commencement: see art 1.

This Order is reproduced as amended by: the Financial Services and Markets Act 2000 (Miscellaneous Provisions) Order 2001, SI 2001/3650; the Financial Services and Markets Act 2000 (Regulated Activities) (Amendment) Order 2002, SI 2002/682; the Financial Services and Markets Act 2000 (Commencement of Mortgage Regulation) (Amendment) Order 2002, SI 2002/1777; the Financial Services and Markets Act 2000 (Regulated Activities) (Amendment) (No 1) Order 2003, SI 2003/1475; the Financial Services and Markets Act 2000 (Regulated Activities) (Amendment) (No 2) Order 2003, SI 2003/1476; the Financial Services and Markets Act 2000 (Regulated Activities) (Amendment) (No 2) Order 2004, SI 2004/2737; the Financial Services and Markets Act 2000 (Regulated Activities) (Amendment) Order 2006, SI 2006/1969; the Financial Services and Markets Act 2000 (Regulated Activities) (Amendment) (No 2) Order 2006, SI 2006/2383.

1 Citation and commencement

(1) This Order may be cited as the Financial Services and Markets Act 2000 (Professions) (Non-Exempt Activities) Order 2001.

(2) Subject to paragraph (3), this Order comes into force on the day on which section 19 of the Act comes into force.

(3) This Order comes into force—

    (a) for the purposes of article 4(g), on 1st January 2002; and

    (b) for the purposes of [article 6A], [on such a day as the Treasury may specify].

[(4) Any day specified under paragraph (3)(b) must be caused to be notified in the London, Edinburgh and Belfast Gazettes published not later than one week before that day.]

[2226]

NOTES

Para (3): words in first pair of square brackets substituted by the Financial Services and Markets Act 2000 (Miscellaneous Provisions) Order 2001, SI 2001/3650, art 3(a), as from 31 October 2004; words in second pair of square brackets substituted by the Financial Services and Markets Act 2000 (Commencement of Mortgage Regulation) (Amendment) Order 2002, SI 2002/1777, art 3(1), (2), as from 30 August 2002.

Para (4): added by SI 2002/1777, art 3(1), (3), as from 30 August 2002.

2 Interpretation

(1) In this Order—

"the Act" means the Financial Services and Markets Act 2000;

["contract of insurance" has the meaning given by article 3(1) of the Regulated Activities Order;]

"contractually based investment" has the meaning given by article 3(1) of the Regulated Activities Order;

["home purchase provider" has the meaning given by article 63F(3) of the Regulated Activities Order;

"home purchaser" has the meaning given by article 63F(3) of the Regulated Activities Order;]

"occupational pension scheme" and "personal pension scheme" have the meaning given by section 1 of the Pension Schemes Act 1993;

["plan provider" has the meaning given by paragraph (3) of article 63B of the Regulated Activities Order, read with paragraphs (7) and (8) of that article;]

["record of insurance intermediaries" means the record maintained by the Authority under section 347 of the Act (the public record) by virtue of article 93 of the Regulated Activities Order (recorded insurance intermediaries);]

"the Regulated Activities Order" means the Financial Services and Markets Act 2000 (Regulated Activities) Order 2001;

["regulated home purchase plan" has the meaning given by article 63F(3) of the Regulated Activities Order;

"regulated home reversion plan" has the meaning given by article 63B(3) of the Regulated Activities Order;

"regulated mortgage contract" has the meaning given by article 61 of the Regulated Activities Order;]

["relevant investment" has the meaning given by article 3(1) of the Regulated Activities Order;]

["reversion seller" has the meaning given by article 63B(3) of the Regulated Activities Order;]

"security" has the meaning given by article 3(1) of the Regulated Activities Order;

"syndicate" has the meaning given by article 3(1) of the Regulated Activities Order.

(2) For the purposes of this Order, a person is a member of a personal pension scheme if he is a person to or in respect of whom benefits are or may become payable under the scheme.

[2227]

NOTES

Para (1): definitions "contract of insurance" and "record of insurance intermediaries" inserted, and definition "relevant investment" substituted, by the Financial Services and Markets Act 2000 (Regulated Activities) (Amendment) (No 2) Order 2003, SI 2003/1476, art 16(1), (2), as from 31 October 2004 (in so far as relating to contracts of long-term care insurance), and as from 14 January 2005 (otherwise), for transitional provisions see arts 22–27 of that Order at **[2706]** et seq; definitions "home purchase provider", "home purchaser", "plan provider", "regulated home purchase plan", "regulated home reversion plan", "regulated mortgage contract", and "reversion seller" inserted by the Financial Services and Markets Act 2000 (Regulated Activities) (Amendment) (No 2) Order 2006, SI 2006/2383, art 32(1), (2), as from 6 April 2007 (for the full commencement details of SI 2006/2383 and for transitional provisions and effect, see arts 1, 36–40 of, and the Schedule to, the 2006 Order at **[2860]** et seq).

---

3   Activities to which exemption from the general prohibition does not apply

The activities in articles 4 to 8 are specified for the purposes of section 327(6) of the Act.

[2228]

4   An activity of the kind specified by any of the following provisions of the Regulated Activities Order—

(a)   article 5 (accepting deposits);
[(aa)   article 9B (issuing electronic money);]
(b)   article 10 (effecting and carrying out contracts of insurance);
(c)   article 14 (dealing in investments as principal);
(d)   article 51 (establishing etc a collective investment scheme);
(e)   article 52 (establishing etc a ... pension scheme);
[(ea)   article 52B (providing basic advice on stakeholder products);]
(f)   article 57 (managing the underwriting capacity of a Lloyd's syndicate);
(g)   article 59 (funeral plan contracts);
(h)   ...

[2229]

NOTES

Para (aa) inserted by the Financial Services and Markets Act 2000 (Regulated Activities) (Amendment) Order 2002, SI 2002/682, art 7(1), as from 27 April 2002;

Word omitted from para (e) revoked by the Financial Services and Markets Act 2000 (Regulated Activities) (Amendment) Order 2006, SI 2006/1969, art 11, as from 6 April 2007.

Para (ea) inserted by the Financial Services and Markets Act 2000 (Regulated Activities) (Amendment) (No 2) Order 2004, SI 2004/2737, art, 5(3), (4), as from 6 April 2005.

Para (h) revoked by the Financial Services and Markets Act 2000 (Miscellaneous Provisions) Order 2001, SI 2001/3650, art 3(b), as 31 October 2004.

[**4A**   An activity of the kind specified by article 21 or 25 of the Regulated Activities Order (dealing in investments as agent or arranging deals in investments) in so far as it—

(a)   relates to a transaction for the sale or purchase of rights under a contract of insurance; and

(b)   is carried on by a person who is not included in the record of insurance intermediaries.]

[2230]

NOTES

Commencement: 31 October 2004 (in so far as relating to contracts of long-term care insurance); 14 January 2005 (otherwise).

Inserted by the Financial Services and Markets Act 2000 (Regulated Activities) (Amendment) (No 2) Order 2003, SI 2003/1476, art 16(1), (3), as from 31 October 2004 (in so far as relating to contracts of long-term care insurance), and as from 14 January 2005 (otherwise); for transitional provisions see arts 22–27 of that Order at **[2706]** et seq.

5—(1)   An activity of the kind specified by article 37 of the Regulated Activities Order (managing investments) in so far as it consists of buying or subscribing for a [security or contractually based investment].

(2)   Paragraph (1) does not apply—

(a)   if all routine or day to day decisions, so far as relating to that activity, are taken by an authorised person with permission to carry on that activity or by a person who is an exempt person in relation to such an activity; or

(b)   to an activity undertaken in accordance with the advice of an authorised person with permission to give advice in relation to such an activity or a person who is an exempt person in relation to the giving of such advice.

[2231]

NOTES

Para (1): words in square brackets substituted by the Financial Services and Markets Act 2000 (Regulated Activities) (Amendment) (No 2) Order 2003, SI 2003/1476, art 16(1), (4), as from 31 October 2004 (in so far as relating to contracts of long-term care insurance), and as from 14 January 2005 (otherwise); for transitional provisions see arts 22–27 of that Order at [2706] et seq.

[5A An activity of the kind specified by article 39A of the Regulated Activities Order (assisting in the administration and performance of a contract of insurance) if it is carried on by a person who is not included in the record of insurance intermediaries.]

[2232]

NOTES

Commencement: 31 October 2004 (in so far as relating to contracts of long-term care insurance); 14 January 2005 (otherwise).
Inserted by the Financial Services and Markets Act 2000 (Regulated Activities) (Amendment) (No 2) Order 2003, SI 2003/1476, art 16(1), (5), as from 31 October 2004 (in so far as relating to contracts of long-term care insurance), and as from 14 January 2005 (otherwise); for transitional provisions see arts 22–27 of that Order at [2706] et seq.

6—(1) An activity of the kind specified by article 53 of the Regulated Activities Order (advising on investments) where the advice in question falls within [paragraph (2), (3) or (5)].

(2) Subject to paragraph (4), advice falls within this paragraph in so far as—
   (a) it is given to an individual (or his agent) other than where the individual acts—
      (i) in connection with the carrying on of a business of any kind by himself or by an undertaking of which he is, or would become as a result of the transaction to which the advice relates, a controller; or
      (ii) in his capacity as a trustee of an occupational pension scheme;
   (b) it consists of a recommendation to buy or subscribe for a particular [security or contractually based investment]; and
   (c) the transaction to which the advice relates would be made—
      (i) with a person acting in the course of carrying on the business of buying, selling, subscribing for or underwriting the [security or contractually based investment], whether as principal or agent;
      (ii) on an investment exchange or any other market to which that investment is admitted for dealing; or
      (iii) in response to an invitation to subscribe for [such an investment] which is, or is to be, admitted for dealing on an investment exchange or any other market.

(3) Subject to paragraph (4), advice falls within this paragraph in so far as it consists of a recommendation to a member of a personal pension scheme (or his agent) to dispose of any rights or interests which the member has in or under the scheme.

(4) Advice does not fall within paragraph (2) or (3) if it endorses a corresponding recommendation given to the individual (or, as the case may be, the member) by an authorised person with permission to give advice in relation to the proposed transaction or a person who is an exempt person in relation to the giving of such advice.

[(5) Advice falls within this paragraph in so far as—
   (a) it relates to a transaction for the sale or purchase of rights under a contract of insurance; and
   (b) it is given by a person who is not included in the record of insurance intermediaries.]

[2233]

NOTES

Paras (1), (2): words in square brackets substituted by the Financial Services and Markets Act 2000 (Regulated Activities) (Amendment) (No 2) Order 2003, SI 2003/1476, art 16(1), (6)(a), (b), as from 31 October 2004 (in so far as relating to contracts of long-term care insurance), and as from 14 January 2005 (otherwise); for transitional provisions see arts 22–27 of that Order at [2706] et seq.
Para (5): added by SI 2003/1476, art 16(1), (6)(c), as from 31 October 2004 (in so far as relating to contracts of long-term care insurance), and as from 14 January 2005 (otherwise); for transitional provisions see arts 22–27 of that Order at [2706] et seq.

[6A—(1) An activity of the kind specified by article 53A of the Regulated Activities Order (advising on regulated mortgage contracts) where the advice in question falls within paragraph (2).

(2) Subject to paragraph (3), advice falls within this paragraph in so far as—

(a)   it consists of a recommendation, given to an individual, to enter as borrower into a regulated mortgage contract with a particular person; and

(b)   in entering into a regulated mortgage contract that person would be carrying on an activity of the kind specified by article 61(1) of the Regulated Activities Order (regulated mortgage contracts).

(3)   Advice does not fall within paragraph (2) if it endorses a corresponding recommendation given to the individual by an authorised person with permission to carry on an activity of the kind specified by article 53A of the Regulated Activities Order or a person who is an exempt person in relation to an activity of that kind.]

[2234]

NOTES
Commencement: 31 October 2004.
Inserted by the Financial Services and Markets Act 2000 (Regulated Activities) (Amendment) (No 1) Order 2003, SI 2003/1475, art 24(1), (3), as from 31 October 2004; for transitional provisions see arts 26–29 at **[2700]** et seq.

[[6B]—(1)   An activity of the kind specified by article 61(1) or (2) of the Regulated Activities Order (regulated mortgage contracts).

(2)   Paragraph (1) does not apply to an activity carried on by a person in his capacity as a trustee or personal representative where the borrower under the regulated mortgage contract in question is a beneficiary under the trust, will or intestacy.]

[2235]

NOTES
Commencement: 31 October 2004.
Inserted (as art 6A) by the Financial Services and Markets Act 2000 (Miscellaneous Provisions) Order 2001, SI 2001/3650, art 3(c), as from 31 October 2004; renumbered as art 6B by the Financial Services and Markets Act 2000 (Regulated Activities) (Amendment) (No 1) Order 2003, SI 2003/1475, art 24(1), (2), as from 31 October 2004 (for transitional provisions see arts 26–29 at **[2700]** et seq).

[6C—(1)   An activity of the kind specified by article 53B of the Regulated Activities Order (advising on regulated home reversion plans) where the advice in question falls within paragraph (2).

(2)   Subject to paragraph (3), advice falls within this paragraph in so far as—
(a)   it consists of a recommendation, given to an individual to enter as reversion seller or plan provider into a regulated home reversion plan with a particular person; and
(b)   in entering into a regulated home reversion plan that person would be carrying on an activity of the kind specified by article 63B(1) of the Regulated Activities Order (regulated home reversion plans).

(3)   Advice does not fall within paragraph (2) if it endorses a corresponding recommendation given to the individual by an authorised person with permission to carry on an activity of the kind specified by article 53B of the Regulated Activities Order or a person who is an exempt person in relation to an activity of that kind.]

[2235A]

NOTES
Commencement: 6 April 2007.
Inserted, together with arts 6D–6F, by the Financial Services and Markets Act 2000 (Regulated Activities) (Amendment) (No 2) Order 2006, SI 2006/2383, art 32(1), (3), as from 6 April 2007 (for the full commencement details of SI 2006/2383 and for transitional provisions and effect, see arts 1, 36–40 of, and the Schedule to, the 2006 Order at **[2860]** et seq).

[6D—(1)   An activity of the kind specified by article 63B(1) or (2) of the Regulated Activities Order (regulated home reversion plans).

(2)   Paragraph (1) does not apply to an activity carried on by a person in his capacity as a trustee or personal representative where the reversion seller under the regulated home reversion plan in question is a beneficiary under the trust, will or intestacy.]

[2235B]

NOTES
Commencement: 6 April 2007.
Inserted as noted to art 6C at **[2235A]**.

[6E—(1)   An activity of the kind specified by article 53C of the Regulated Activities Order (advising on regulated home purchase plans) where the advice in question falls within paragraph (2).

(2)   Subject to paragraph (3), advice falls within this paragraph in so far as—
  (a)   it consists of a recommendation, given to an individual to enter as home purchaser into a regulated home purchase plan with a particular person; and
  (b)   in entering into a regulated home purchase plan that person would be carrying on an activity of the kind specified by article 63F(1) of the Regulated Activities Order (regulated home purchase plans).

(3)   Advice does not fall within paragraph (2) if it endorses a corresponding recommendation given to the individual by an authorised person with permission to carry on an activity of the kind specified by article 53C of the Regulated Activities Order or a person who is an exempt person in relation to an activity of that kind.]

[2235C]

NOTES
  Commencement: 6 April 2007.
  Inserted as noted to art 6C at **[2235A]**.

[6F—(1)   An activity of the kind specified by article 63F(1) or (2) of the Regulated Activities Order (regulated home purchase plans).

(2)   Paragraph (1) does not apply to an activity carried on by a person in his capacity as a trustee or personal representative where the home purchaser under the regulated home purchase plan in question is a beneficiary under the trust, will or intestacy.]

[2235D]

NOTES
  Commencement: 6 April 2007.
  Inserted as noted to art 6C at **[2235A]**.

7—(1)   Advising a person to become a member of a particular Lloyd's syndicate.

(2)   Paragraph (1) does not apply to advice which endorses that of an authorised person with permission to give such advice or a person who is an exempt person in relation to the giving of such advice.

[2236]

8   Agreeing to carry on any of the activities mentioned in articles 4 to 7 other than the activities mentioned in article 4(a), [(aa),] (b), (d) and (e).

[2237]

NOTES
  Reference "(aa)," in square brackets inserted by the Financial Services and Markets Act 2000 (Regulated Activities) (Amendment) Order 2002, SI 2002/682, art 7(2), as from 27 April 2002, subject to transitional provisions in relation to persons issuing electronic money immediately before that date contained in art 9 at **[2666]**.

OPEN-ENDED INVESTMENT COMPANIES REGULATIONS 2001

(SI 2001/1228)

NOTES
  Made: 27 March 2001.
  Authority: Financial Services and Markets Act 2000, ss 262, 428(3).
  Commencement: see art 1(2).
  These Regulations are reproduced as amended by: the Uncertificated Securities Regulations 2001, SI 2001/3755; the Collective Investment Schemes (Miscellaneous Amendments) Regulations 2003, SI 2003/2066; the Open-Ended Investment Companies (Amendment) Regulations 2005, SI 2005/923; the Civil Partnership Act 2004 (Amendments to Subordinate Legislation) Order 2005, SI 2005/2114; the Regulatory Reform (Financial Services and Markets Act 2000) Order 2007, SI 2007/1973; the Companies Act 2006 (Consequential Amendments etc) Order 2008, SI 2008/948.

ARRANGEMENT OF REGULATIONS

PART I
GENERAL

PART II
FORMATION, SUPERVISION AND CONTROL

General

Authorisation

Names

Alterations

Ending of authorisation

Powers of intervention

Investigations

Winding up

PART III
CORPORATE CODE

Organs

PART III
STATUTORY INSTRUMENTS

PART I
GENERAL

1 Citation, commencement and extent

(1) These Regulations may be cited as the Open-Ended Investment Companies Regulations 2001.

(2) These Regulations come into force—

    (a)   for the purpose of regulation 6, on the day on which sections 247 and 248 of the Act come into force for the purpose of making rules;

    (b)   for the purposes of regulations 7, 12, 13, 18(1) and (3), 74, 77 and 80 to 82, so far as relating to the making of applications for authorisation orders to be made on or after the day mentioned in sub-paragraph (c), on the day on which section 40 of the Act comes into force;

    (c)   for all remaining purposes, on the day on which section 19 of the Act comes into force.

(3) Subject to regulation 20(2)(b), these Regulations have effect in relation to any open-ended investment company which has its head office situated in Great Britain.

[2238]

2 Interpretation

(1) In these Regulations, except where the context otherwise requires—

"the Act" means the Financial Services and Markets Act 2000;

"the 1985 Act" means the Companies Act 1985;

"the 1986 Act" means the Insolvency Act 1986;

"annual general meeting" has the meaning given in regulation 37(1);

"annual report" has the meaning given in regulation 66(1)(a);

"the appropriate registrar" means—

    (a)   the registrar of companies for England and Wales if the company's instrument of incorporation states that its head office is to be situated in England and Wales, or that it is to be situated in Wales;

    (b)   the registrar of companies for Scotland if the company's instrument of incorporation states that its head office is to be situated in Scotland;

"authorisation order" means an order made by the Authority under regulation 14;

"bearer shares" has the meaning given in regulation 48;

"court", in relation to any proceedings under these Regulations involving an open-ended investment company the head office of which is situated—

    (a)   in England and Wales, means the High Court; and

    (b)   in Scotland, means the Court of Session;

"depositary", in relation to an open-ended investment company, has the meaning given in regulation 5(1);

"the designated person" means the person designated in the company's instrument of incorporation for the purposes of paragraph 4 of Schedule 4 to these Regulations;

"FSA rules" means any rules made by the Authority under regulation 6(1);

"larger denomination share" has the meaning given in regulation 45(5);

"officer", in relation to an open-ended investment company, includes a director or any secretary or manager;

"open-ended investment company" means an body incorporated by virtue of regulation 3(1) or a body treated as if it had been so incorporated by virtue of regulation 85(3)(a);

"prospectus" has the meaning given in regulation 6(2);

"relevant provision" means any requirement imposed by or under the Act;

"register of shareholders" means the register kept under paragraph 1(1) of Schedule 3 to these Regulations;

"scheme property", in relation to an open-ended investment company, means the property subject to the collective investment scheme constituted by the company;

"share certificate" has the meaning given in regulation 46(1);

"smaller denomination share" has the meaning given in regulation 45(5);

"transfer documents" has the meaning given in paragraph 5(3) of Schedule 4 to these Regulations;

"the Tribunal" means the Financial Services and Markets Tribunal;

"umbrella company" means an open-ended investment company whose instrument of incorporation provides for such pooling as is mentioned in section 235(3)(a) of the Act (collective investment schemes) in relation to separate parts of the scheme property and whose shareholders are entitled to exchange rights in one part for rights in another; and

.....

(2) In these Regulations any reference to a shareholder of an open-ended investment company is a reference to—

  (a) the person who holds the share certificate, or other documentary evidence of title relating to that share mentioned in regulation 48; and

  (b) the person whose name is entered on the company's register of shareholders in relation to any share other than a bearer share.

(3) In these Regulations, unless the contrary intention appears, expressions which are also used in [the Companies Acts (as defined in section 2 of the Companies Act 2006)] have the same meaning as in [those Acts].

[2239]

NOTES

Para (1): definitions "certificated form", "participating issuer", "participating security", "uncertificated form" and "uncertificated unit of a security" (omitted) revoked by the Uncertificated Securities Regulations 2001, SI 2001/3755, reg 51, Sch 7, Pt 2, para 24(a), as from 26 November 2001; definition "the UCITS directive" (omitted) revoked by the Collective Investment Schemes (Miscellaneous Amendments) Regulations 2003, SI 2003/2066, reg 13(7)(a), as from 13 February 2004.

Para (3): words in square brackets substituted by the Companies Act 2006 (Consequential Amendments etc) Order 2008, SI 2008/948, art 3(1), Sch 1, Pt 2, para 220, as from 6 April 2008.

PART II
FORMATION, SUPERVISION AND CONTROL

General

3 Open-ended investment company

(1) If the Authority makes an authorisation order then, immediately upon the coming into effect of the order, the body to which the authorisation order relates is to be incorporated as an open-ended investment company (notwithstanding that, at the point of its incorporation by virtue of this paragraph, the body will not have any shareholders or property).

(2) The name of an open-ended investment company is the name mentioned in the authorisation order made in respect of the company or, if it changes its name in accordance with these Regulations and FSA rules, its new name.

[2240]

4 Registration by the Authority

(1) Upon making an authorisation order under regulation 14, the Authority must forthwith register—

  (a) the instrument of incorporation of the company;

  (b) a statement of the address of the company's head office;

  (c) a statement, with respect to each person named in the application for authorisation as director of the company, of the particulars set out in regulation 13; and

  (d) a statement of the corporate name and registered or principal office of the person named in the application for authorisation as the depositary of the company.

(2) In this regulation any reference to the instrument of incorporation of a company is a reference to the instrument of incorporation supplied for the purposes of regulation 14(1)(c).

[2241]

5 Safekeeping of scheme property by depositary

(1) Subject to paragraph (2), all the scheme property of an open-ended investment company must be entrusted for safekeeping to a person appointed for the purpose ("a depositary").

(2) Nothing in paragraph (1)—

  (a) applies to any scheme property designated for the purposes of this regulation by FSA rules;

  (b) prevents a depositary from—

    (i) entrusting to a third party all or some of the assets in its safekeeping; or

    (ii) in a case falling within sub-paragraph (i), authorising the third party to entrust all or some of those assets to other specified persons.

(3) Schedule 1 to these Regulations makes provision with respect to depositaries of open-ended investment companies.

[2242]

6 FSA rules

(1)   The Authority's powers to make rules under section 247 (trust scheme rules) and section 248 (scheme particulars rules) of the Act in relation to authorised unit trust schemes are, subject to the provisions of these Regulations, exercisable in relation to open-ended investment companies—
    (a)   for like purposes; and
    (b)   subject to the same conditions.

(2)   In these Regulations any document which a person is required to submit and publish by virtue of rules made by the Authority under paragraph (1) for like purposes to those in section 248 of the Act is referred to as a prospectus.

[2243]

7 Modification or waiver of FSA rules

(1)   The Authority may, on the application or with the consent of any person to whom any FSA rules apply, direct that all or any of the FSA rules—
    (a)   are not to apply to him as respects a particular open-ended investment company; or
    (b)   are to apply to him as respects such a company with such modifications as may be specified in the direction.

(2)   The Authority may, on the application or with the consent of an open-ended investment company and its depositary acting jointly, direct that all or any of the FSA rules—
    (a)   are not to apply to the company; or
    (b)   are to apply to the company with such modifications as may be specified in the direction.

(3)   Section 148(3) to (9) and (11) of the Act (modification or waiver of rules) have effect in relation to a direction under paragraph (1) as they have effect in relation to a direction under section 148(2) of the Act but with the following modifications—
    (a)   …
    (b)   any reference to the [person] is to be read as a reference to the person mentioned in paragraph (1); and
    (c)   subsection (7)(b) is to be read, in relation to a shareholder, as if the word "commercial" were omitted.

(4)   Section 148(3) to (9) and (11) of the Act have effect in relation to a direction under paragraph (2) as they have effect in relation to a direction under section 148(2) of the Act but with the following modifications—
    (a)   subsection (4)(a) is to be read as if the words "by the … person" were omitted;
    (b)   subsections (7)(b), (8) and (11) are to be read as if the reference to the … person were a reference to each of the company and its depositary;
    (c)   subsection (7)(b) is to be read, in relation to a shareholder, as if the word "commercial" were omitted; and
    (d)   subsection (9) is to be read as if the reference to the … person were a reference to the company and its depositary acting jointly.

[2244]

NOTES
Para (3): sub-para (a) revoked, and word in square brackets in sub-para (b) substituted, by the Regulatory Reform (Financial Services and Markets Act 2000) Order 2007, SI 2007/1973, arts 2, 12(a), (b), as from 12 July 2007.
Para (4): words omitted revoked by SI 2007/1973, arts 2, 12(c), as from 12 July 2007.

8 Notices: general

Subject to the provisions of these Regulations—
    (a)   section 387 of the Act (warning notices) applies to a warning notice given under any provision of these Regulations in the same way as it applies to a warning notice given under any provision of the Act;
    (b)   section 388 of the Act (decision notices) applies to a decision notice given under any provision of these Regulations in the same way as it applies to a decision notice given under any provision of the Act;
    (c)   section 389 of the Act (notices of discontinuance) applies to the discontinuance of the action proposed in a warning notice or the action to which a decision notice relates given under any provision of these Regulations in the same way as it applies to a warning notice or decision notice given under any provision of the Act;
    (d)   section 390 of the Act (final notices) applies to a decision notice given under any provision of these Regulations in the same way as it applies to a decision notice given under any provision of the Act.

[2245]

9 Publication

Section 391 of the Act (publication) applies to the notices mentioned in regulation 8 in the same way as it applies to any such notice given under any provision of the Act.

[2246]

10 The Authority's procedures

Section 395 of the Act (the Authority's procedures) applies to the procedure relating to the Authority's functions in relation to supervisory notices, warning notices and decision notices given under any provision of these Regulations.

[2247]

11 The Tribunal

Section 133 of the Act (proceedings: general provision) applies to any reference to the Tribunal under these Regulations as it applies to any reference to the Tribunal under the Act.

[2248]

Authorisation

12 Applications for authorisation

(1) Any application for an authorisation order in respect of a proposed open-ended investment company—

(a) must be made in such manner as the Authority may direct;

(b) must state with respect to each person proposed in the application as a director of the company the particulars set out in regulation 13;

(c) must state the corporate name and registered or principal office of the person proposed in the application as depositary of the company; and

(d) must contain or be accompanied by such other information as the Authority may reasonably require for the purpose of determining the application.

(2) At any time after receiving an application and before determining it the Authority may require the applicant to furnish additional information.

(3) Different directions may be given and different requirements imposed in relation to different applications.

(4) Any information to be furnished to the Authority under this regulation must be in such form or verified in such manner as it may specify.

(5) A person commits an offence if—

(a) for the purposes of or in connection with any application under this regulation; or

(b) in purported compliance with any requirement imposed on him by or under this regulation;

he furnishes information which he knows to be false or misleading in a material particular or recklessly furnishes information which is false or misleading in a material particular.

(6) A person guilty of an offence under paragraph (5) is liable—

(a) on conviction on indictment, to imprisonment for a term not exceeding two years or to a fine or to both;

(b) on summary conviction, to imprisonment for a term not exceeding three months or to a fine not exceeding the statutory maximum or to both.

[2249]

13 Particulars of directors

(1) Subject to paragraph (2), an application for an authorisation order must contain the following particulars with respect to each person proposed as a director of the company—

(a) in the case of an individual, his present name, any former name, his usual residential address, his nationality, his business occupation (if any), particulars of any other directorships held by him or which have been held by him and his date of birth;

(b) in the case of a body corporate of Scottish firm, its corporate or firm name and the address of its registered or principal office.

(2) The application need not contain particulars of a directorship—

(a) which has not been held by a director at any time during the 5 years preceding the date on which the application is delivered to the Authority;

(b) which is held by a director in a body corporate which is dormant and, if he also held that directorship for any period during those 5 years, which was dormant for the whole of that period; or

(c) which was held by a director for any period during those 5 years in a body corporate which was dormant for the whole of that period.

(3) For the purposes of paragraph (2), a body corporate is dormant during a period in which no significant transaction occurs; and it ceases to be dormant on the occurrence of such a transaction.

(4)   In paragraph (1)(a)—
   (a)   name means a person's Christian name (or other forename) and surname, except that in the case of a peer, or an individual usually known by a title, the title may be stated instead of his Christian name (or other forename) and surname or in addition to either or both of them;
   (b)   the reference to a former name does not include—
      (i)   in the case of a peer, or an individual normally known by a British title, the name by which he was known previous to the adoption of or succession to the title;
      (ii)   in the case of any person, a former name which was changed or disused before he attained the age of 18 years or which has been changed or disused for 20 years or more; or
      (iii) in the case of a married woman, the name by which she was known previous to the marriage; and
   (c)   the reference to directorships is a reference to directorships in any body corporate whether or not incorporated in Great Britain.

(5)   In paragraph (3) the reference to a significant transaction is, in relation to a company within the meaning of section 735(1) of the 1985 Act, a reference to a significant accounting transaction within the meaning of [section 1169(2) of the Companies Act 2006, other than a transaction to which subsection (3) of that section applies].

[2250]

NOTES
   Para (5): words in square brackets substituted by the Companies Act 2006 (Consequential Amendments etc) Order 2008, SI 2008/948, art 3(1), Sch 1, Pt 2, para 221, as from 6 April 2008.

---

14   Authorisation

(1)   Where an application is duly made under regulation 12, the Authority may make an authorisation order in respect of an open-ended investment company if—
   (a)   it is satisfied that the company will, on the coming into effect of the authorisation order, comply with the requirements in regulation 15;
   (b)   it is satisfied that the company will, at that time, comply with the requirements of FSA rules;
   (c)   it has been provided with a copy of the proposed company's instrument of incorporation and a certificate signed by a solicitor to the effect that the instrument of incorporation complies with Schedule 2 to these Regulations and with such of the requirements of FSA rules as relate to the contents of that instrument of incorporation; and
   (d)   it has received a notification under regulation 18(3) from the appropriate registrar.

(2)   If the Authority makes an order under paragraph (1), it must give written notice of the order to the applicant.

(3)   In determining whether the requirement referred to in regulation 15(5) is satisfied in respect of any proposed director of a company, the Authority may take into account—
   (a)   any matter relating to any person who is or will be employed by or associated with the proposed director, for the purposes of the business of the company;
   (b)   if the proposed director is a body corporate, any matter relating to any director or controller of the body, to any other body corporate in the same group or to any director or controller of any such other body corporate;
   (c)   if the proposed director is a partnership, any matter relating to any of the partners; and
   (d)   if the proposed director is an unincorporated association, any matter relating to any member of the governing body of the association or any officer or controller of the association.

(4)   An application must be determined by the Authority before the end of the period of six months beginning with the date on which it receives a completed application.

(5)   The Authority may determine an incomplete application if it considers it appropriate to do so and, if it does so, it must determine the application within the period of twelve months beginning with the date on which it first receives the application.

(6)   The applicant may withdraw his application, by giving the Authority written notice, at any time before the Authority determines it.

(7)   An authorisation order must specify the date on which it is to come into effect.

(8)   Schedule 2 to these Regulations makes provision with respect to the contents, alteration and binding nature of the instrument of incorporation of an open-ended investment company.

[2251]

15   Requirements for authorisation

(1)   The requirements referred to in regulation 14(1)(a) are as follows.

(2)   The company and its instrument of incorporation must comply with the requirements of these regulations and FSA rules.

(3)   The head office of the company must be situated in England and Wales, Wales or Scotland.

(4)   The company must have at least one director.

(5)   The directors of the company must be fit and proper persons to act as such.

(6)   If the company has only one director, that director must be a body corporate which is an authorised person and which has permission under ... the Act to act as sole director of an open-ended investment company.

(7)   If the company has two or more directors, the combination of their experience and expertise must be such as is appropriate for the purposes of carrying on the business of the company.

(8)   The person appointed as the depositary of the company—
   (a)   must be a body corporate incorporated in the United Kingdom or another EEA State;
   (b)   must have a place of business in the United Kingdom;
   (c)   must have its affairs administered in the country in which it is incorporated;
   (d)   must be an authorised person;
   (e)   must have permission under Part IV of the Act to act as the depositary of an open-ended investment company; and
   (f)   must be independent of the company and of the persons appointed as directors of the company.

(9)   The name of the company must not be undesirable or misleading.

(10)   The aims of the company must be reasonably capable of being achieved.

(11)   The company must meet one or both of the following requirements—
   (a)   shareholders are entitled to have their shares redeemed or repurchased upon request at a price related to the net value of the scheme property and determined in accordance with the company's instrument of incorporation and FSA rules; or
   (b)   shareholders are entitled to sell their shares on an investment exchange at a price not significantly different from that mentioned in sub-paragraph (a).

[2252]

NOTES
Para (6): words omitted revoked by the Collective Investment Schemes (Miscellaneous Amendments) Regulations 2003, SI 2003/2066, reg 8, as from 13 February 2004.

16 Representations against refusal of authorisation

(1)   If the Authority proposes to refuse an application made under regulation 12, it must give the applicant a warning notice.

(2)   If the Authority decides to refuse the application—
   (a)   it must give the applicant a decision notice; and
   (b)   the applicant may refer the matter to the Tribunal.

[2253]

17 Certificates

(1)   If an open-ended investment company which complies with the conditions necessary to enable it to enjoy the rights conferred by [the UCITS directive] so requests, the Authority may issue a certificate to the effect that the company complies with those conditions.

(2)   Such a certificate may be issued on the making of an authorisation order in respect of the company or at any subsequent time.

[2254]

NOTES
Para (1): words in square brackets substituted by the Collective Investment Schemes (Miscellaneous Amendments) Regulations 2003, SI 2003/2066, reg 13(7)(b), as from 13 February 2004.

Names

18 Registrar's approval of names

(1)   Where, in respect of a proposed open-ended investment company, it appears to the Authority that the requirements of regulation 14(1)(a) to (c) are or will be met, the Authority must notify the appropriate registrar of the name by which it is proposed that the company should be incorporated.

(2)   Every open-ended investment company must obtain the Authority's approval to any proposed change in the name by which the company is incorporated and the Authority must notify the appropriate registrar of the proposed name.

(3)   If it appears to the appropriate registrar that the provisions of regulation 19(1) are not contravened in relation to the proposed name, he must notify the Authority to that effect.

[2255]

19   Prohibition on certain names

(1)   No open-ended investment company is to have a name that—
   (a)   includes any of the following words or expressions, that is to say—
      (i)   limited, unlimited or public limited company, or their Welsh equivalents ("cyfyngedig", "anghyfyngedig" and "cwmni cyfyngedig cyhoeddus" respectively); or
      (ii)   European Economic Interest Grouping or any equivalent set out in Schedule 3 to the European Economic Interest Grouping Regulations 1989;
   (b)   includes an abbreviation of any of the words or expressions referred to in sub-paragraph (a); or
   (c)   is the same as any other name appearing in the registrar's index of company names.

(2)   In determining for the purposes of paragraph (1)(c) whether one name is the same as another, there are to be disregarded—
   (a)   the definite article, where it is the first word of the name;
   (b)   the following word and expressions where they appear at the end of the name—
      "company" or its Welsh equivalent ("cwmni");
      "and company" or its Welsh equivalent ("a'r cwmni");
      "company limited" or its Welsh equivalent ("cwmni cyfyngedig");
      "limited" or its Welsh equivalent ("cyfyngedig");
      "unlimited" or its Welsh equivalent ("anghyfyngedig");
      "public limited company" or its Welsh equivalent ("cwmni cyfyngedig cyhoeddus");
      "European Economic Interest Grouping" or any equivalent set out in Schedule 3 to the European Economic Interest Grouping Regulations 1989;
      "investment company with variable capital" or its Welsh equivalent ("cwmni buddsoddi â chyfalaf newidiol");
      "open-ended investment company" or its Welsh equivalent ("cwmni buddsoddiant penagored");
   (c)   abbreviations of any of those words or expressions where they appear at the end of the name; and
   (d)   type and case of letters, accents, spaces between letters and punctuation marks;
and "and" and "&" are to be taken as the same.

[2256]

20   Registrar's index of company names

(1)   Upon making an authorisation order in respect of an open-ended investment company or upon approving any change in the name of such a company, the Authority must notify the appropriate registrar of the name by which the company is incorporated or, as the case may be, of the company's new name.

(2)   Section 714 of the 1985 Act (registrar's index of company and corporate names) has effect as if the bodies listed in subsection (1) of that section included—
   (a)   open-ended investment companies in respect of which an authorisation order has come into effect; and
   (b)   collective investment schemes which are open-ended investment companies and which have a head office situated in Northern Ireland.

[2257]

Alterations

21   The Authority's approval for certain changes in respect of a company

(1)   An open-ended investment company must give written notice to the Authority of—
   (a)   any proposed alteration to the company's instrument of incorporation;
   (b)   any proposed alteration to the company's prospectus which, if made, would be significant;
   (c)   any proposed reconstruction or amalgamation involving the company;
   (d)   any proposal to wind up the affairs of the company otherwise than by the court;
   (e)   any proposal to replace a director of the company, to appoint any additional director or to decrease the number of directors in post; and
   (f)   any proposal to replace the depositary of the company.

(2)   Any notice given under paragraph (1)(a) must be accompanied by a certificate signed by a solicitor to the effect that the change in question will not affect the compliance of the instrument of incorporation with Schedule 2 to these Regulations and with such of the requirements of FSA rules as relate to the contents of that instrument.

(3)   Effect must not be given to any proposal falling within paragraph (1) unless—
   (a)   the Authority, by written notice, has given its approval to the proposal; or
   (b)   one month, beginning with the date on which notice of the proposal was given, has expired without the company or the depositary having received from the Authority a warning notice under regulation 22 in respect of the proposal.

(4)   No change falling within paragraph (1)(e) may be made if any of the requirements set out in regulation 15(4) to (7) and (8)(f) would not be satisfied if the change were made and no change falling within paragraph (1)(f) may be made if any of the requirements in regulation 15(8) would not be satisfied if the change were made.

[2258]

22   Procedure when refusing approval of proposed changes

(1)   If the Authority proposes to refuse approval of a proposal to replace the depositary, or any director, of an open-ended investment company, it must give a warning notice to the company.

(2)   If the Authority proposes to refuse approval of any other proposal falling within regulation 21, it must give separate warning notices to the company and its depositary.

(3)   To be valid the warning notice must be received by that person before the end of one month beginning with the date on which notice of the proposal was given.

(4)   If, having given a warning notice to a person, the Authority decides to refuse approval—
   (a)   it must give him a decision notice; and
   (b)   he may refer the matter to the Tribunal.

(5)   If, having given a warning notice to a person, the Authority decides to approve the proposal, it must give him a [written] notice.

[2259]

NOTES
Para (5): word in square brackets substituted by the Open-Ended Investment Companies (Amendment) Regulations 2005, SI 2005/923, reg 2(1), (2), as from 6 April 2005.

Ending of authorisation

23   Ending of authorisation

(1)   The Authority may revoke an authorisation order if it appears to it that—
   (a)   any requirement for the making of the order is no longer satisfied;
   (b)   the company, any of its directors or its depositary—
      (i)   has contravened any relevant provision; or
      (ii)   has, in purported compliance with any such provision, knowingly or recklessly given the Authority information which is false or misleading in a material particular;
   (c)   no regulated activity has been carried on in relation to the company for the previous twelve months; or
   (d)   it is desirable to revoke the authorisation order in order to protect the interests of shareholders or potential shareholders in the company.

(2)   For the purposes of paragraph (1)(d), the Authority may take into account any matter relating to—
   (a)   the company or its depositary;
   (b)   any director or controller of the depositary;
   (c)   any person employed by or associated, for the purposes of the business of the company, with the company or its depositary;
   (d)   any director of the company;
   (e)   any person exercising influence over any director of the company or its depositary;
   (f)   any body corporate in the same group as any director of the company or its depositary;
   (g)   any director of any such body corporate;
   (h)   any person exercising influence over any such body corporate;
   (i)   any person who would be such a person as is mentioned in regulation 14(3)(a) to (d) were it to apply to a director as it applies to a proposed director.

(3)   Before revoking any authorisation order that has come into effect, the Authority must ensure that such steps as are necessary and appropriate to secure the winding up of the company (whether by the court or otherwise) have been taken.

[2260]

24   Procedure

(1)   If the Authority proposes to make an order revoking an authorisation order ("a revoking order"), it must give separate warning notices to the company and its depositary.

(2)　If, having given warning notices, the Authority decides to make a revoking order it must without delay give the company and its depositary a decision notice and either of them may refer the matter to the Tribunal.

(3)　Sections 393 and 394 of the Act apply to a warning notice or a decision notice given in accordance with this regulation.

[2261]

Powers of intervention

25　Directions

(1)　The Authority may give a direction under this regulation if it appears to the Authority that—
　(a)　one or more requirements for the making of an authorisation order are no longer satisfied;
　(b)　the company, any of its directors or its depositary—
　　(i)　has contravened or is likely to contravene any relevant provision; or
　　(ii)　has, in purported compliance with any such provision, knowingly or recklessly given the Authority information which is false or misleading in a material particular; or
　(c)　it is desirable to give a direction in order to protect the interests of shareholders or potential shareholders in the company.

(2)　A direction under this regulation may—
　(a)　require the company to cease the issue or redemption, or both the issue and redemption, of shares or any class of shares in the company;
　(b)　in the case of a director of the company who is the designated person, require that director to cease transfers to or from, or both to and from, his own holding of shares, or of any class of shares, in the company;
　(c)　in the case of an umbrella company, require that investments made in respect of one or more parts of the scheme property which are pooled separately be realised and, following the discharge of such liabilities of the company as are attributable to the relevant part or parts of the scheme property, that the resulting funds be distributed to shareholders in accordance with FSA rules;
　(d)　require any director of the company to present a petition to the court to wind up the company; or
　(e)　require that the affairs of the company be wound up otherwise than by the court.

(3)　Subject to paragraph (4), if the authorisation order is revoked, the revocation does not affect the operation of any direction under this regulation which is then in force; and a direction under this regulation may be given in relation to a company in the case of which an authorisation order has been revoked if a direction under this regulation was already in force at the time of revocation.

(4)　Where a winding-up order has been made by the court, no direction under this regulation is to have effect in relation to the company concerned.

(5)　For the purposes of paragraph (1)(c), the Authority may take into account any matter relating to any of the persons mentioned in regulation 23(2).

(6)　If a person contravenes a direction under this regulation, section 150 (actions for damages) applies to the contravention as it applies to a contravention mentioned in that section.

(7)　The Authority may, on its own initiative or on the application of the company or its depositary, revoke or vary a direction given under this regulation if it appears to the Authority—
　(a)　in the case of revocation, that it is no longer necessary for the direction to take effect or continue in force;
　(b)　in the case of variation, that the direction should take effect or continue in force in a different form.

[2262]

26　Applications to the court

(1)　This regulation applies if the Authority could give a direction under regulation 25 in relation to an open-ended investment company.

(2)　The Authority may apply to the court for an order removing the depositary or any director of the company and replacing any such person with a person or persons nominated by the Authority.

(3)　The Authority may nominate a person for the purposes of paragraph (2) only if it is satisfied that, if the order were made, the requirements of paragraphs (4) to (7) or, as the case may be, of paragraph (8) of regulation 15 would be met.

(4)　If it appears to the Authority that there is no person whom it may nominate for the purposes of paragraph (2), it may apply to the court for an order removing the director in question or the depositary (or both) and appointing an authorised person to wind up the company.

(5)　On an application under this regulation the court may make such order as it thinks fit.

(6) The court may, on the application of the Authority, rescind any such order as is mentioned in paragraph (4) and substitute such an order as is mentioned in paragraph (2).

(7) The Authority must—
  (a) give written notice of the making of an application under this section to—
      (i) the company;
      (ii) its depositary; and
      (iii) where the application seeks the removal of any director of the company, that director; and
  (b) take such steps as it considers appropriate for bringing the making of the application to the attention of the shareholders of the company.

[2263]

27 Procedure on giving directions under regulation 25 and varying them on Authority's own initiative

(1) A direction takes effect—
  (a) immediately, if the notice given under paragraph (3) states that that is the case;
  (b) on such date as may be specified in the notice; or
  (c) if no date is specified in the notice, when the matter to which it relates is no longer open to review.

(2) A direction may be expressed to take effect immediately (or on a specified date) only if the Authority, having regard to the ground on which it is exercising its power under regulation 25, considers that it is necessary for the direction to take effect immediately (or on that date).

(3) If the Authority proposes to give a direction under regulation 25, or gives such a direction with immediate effect, it must give separate written notices to the company and its depositary.

(4) The notice must—
  (a) give details of the direction;
  (b) inform the person to whom it is given of when the direction takes effect;
  (c) state the Authority's reasons for giving the direction and for its determination as to when the direction takes effect;
  (d) inform the person to whom it is given that he may make representations to the Authority within such period as may be specified in it (whether or not he has referred the matter to the Tribunal); and
  (e) inform him of his right to refer the matter to the Tribunal.

(5) If the direction imposes a requirement under regulation 25(2)(a) or (b), the notice must state that the requirement has effect until—
  (a) a specified date; or
  (b) a further direction.

(6) If the direction imposes a requirement under regulation 25(2)(d) or (e), the petition must be presented (or, as the case may be, the company must be wound up)—
  (a) by a date specified in the notice; or
  (b) if no date is specified, as soon as possible.

(7) The Authority may extend the period allowed under the notice for making representations.

(8) If, having considered any representations made by a person to whom the notice was given, the Authority decides—
  (a) to give the direction in the way proposed, or
  (b) if it has been given, not to revoke the direction,
it must give separate written notices to the company and its depositary.

(9) If, having considered any representations made by a person to whom the notice was given, the Authority decides—
  (a) not to give the direction in the way proposed,
  (b) to give the direction in a way other than that proposed, or
  (c) to revoke a direction which has effect,
it must give separate written notices to the company and its depositary.

(10) A notice given under paragraph (8) must inform the person to whom it is given of his right to refer the matter to the Tribunal.

(11) A notice under paragraph (9)(b) must comply with paragraph (4).

(12) If a notice informs a person of his right to refer a matter to the Tribunal, it must give an indication of the procedure on such a reference.

(13) This regulation applies to the variation of a direction on the Authority's own initiative as it applies to the giving of a direction.

(14) For the purposes of paragraph (1)(c), whether a matter is open to review is to be determined in accordance with section 391(8) of the Act.

(15)   Section 395 of the Act (the Authority's procedures) has effect as if subsection (13) included a reference to a notice given in accordance with paragraph (3), (8) or (9)(b).

[2264]

28   Procedure: refusal to revoke or vary direction

(1)   If on an application under regulation 25(7) for a direction to be revoked or varied the Authority proposes—

(a)   to vary the direction otherwise than in accordance with the application, or

(b)   to refuse to revoke or vary the direction,

it must give the applicant a warning notice.

(2)   If the Authority decides to refuse to revoke or vary the direction—

(a)   it must give the applicant a decision notice; and

(b)   the applicant may refer the matter to the Tribunal.

[2265]

29   Procedure: revocation of direction and grant of request for variation

(1)   If the Authority decides on its own initiative to revoke a direction under regulation 25 it must give separate written notices of its decision to the company and its depositary.

(2)   If on an application made under regulation 25(7) for a direction to be revoked or varied, the Authority decides to revoke or vary it in accordance with the application, it must give the applicant written notice of its decision.

(3)   A notice under this regulation must specify the date on which the decision takes effect.

(4)   The Authority may publish such information about the revocation or variation, in such way, as it considers appropriate.

[2266]

Investigations

30   Power to investigate

(1)   The Authority or the Secretary of State may appoint one or more competent persons to investigate and report on the affairs of, or of any director or depositary of, an open-ended investment company if it appears to either of them that it is in the interests of shareholders or potential shareholders of the company to do so or that the matter is of public concern.

(2)   A person appointed under paragraph (1) to investigate the affairs of, or of any director or depositary of, a company may also, if he thinks it necessary for the purposes of that investigation, investigate the affairs of (or of the directors, depositary, trustee or operator of)—

(a)   an open-ended investment company the directors of which include any of the directors of the company whose affairs are being investigated by virtue of that paragraph;

(b)   an open-ended investment company the directors of which include any of the directors of the depositary whose affairs are being investigated by virtue of that paragraph;

(c)   an open-ended investment company the depositary of which is—

(i)   the same as the depositary of the company whose affairs are being investigated by virtue of that paragraph; or

(ii)   the depositary whose affairs are being investigated by virtue of that paragraph;

(d)   an open-ended investment company the directors of which include—

(i)   the director whose affairs are being investigated by virtue of that paragraph; or

(ii)   any director of a body corporate which is the director whose affairs are being investigated by virtue of that paragraph;

(e)   a collective investment scheme the manager, depositary or operator of which is a director of the company whose affairs are being investigated by virtue of that paragraph;

(f)   a collective investment scheme the trustee of which is—

(i)   the same as the depositary of the company whose affairs are being investigated by virtue of that paragraph; or

(ii)   the depositary whose affairs are being investigated by virtue of that paragraph; or

(g)   a collective investment scheme the manager, depositary or operator of which is—

(i)   the director whose affairs are being investigated by virtue of that paragraph; or

(ii)   a director of a body corporate which is the director whose affairs are being investigated by virtue of that paragraph.

(3)   If the person ("A") appointed to conduct an investigation under this regulation considers that a person ("B") is or may be able to give information which is relevant to the investigation, A may require B—

(a)   to produce to A any documents in B's possession or under his control which appear to A to be relevant to that investigation;

(b)   to attend before A; and

(c)   otherwise to give A all such assistance in connection with the investigation which B is reasonably able to give;

and it is B's duty to comply with that requirement.

(4)   Subsection (5) to (9) of section 170 of the Act (investigations: general) apply if—
   (a)   the Authority appoints a person under this regulation to conduct an investigation on its behalf; or
   (b)   the Secretary of State appoints a person under this regulation to conduct an investigation on his behalf;
as they apply in the cases mentioned in subsection (1) of that section.

(5)   Section 174 of the Act (admissibility of statements made to investigators) applies to a statement made by a person in compliance with a requirement imposed on him under this regulation as it applies to a statement mentioned in that section.

(6)   Subsections (2) to (4) and (6) of section 175 (information and documents: supplemental provisions) and section 177 of the Act (offences) have effect as if this regulation were contained in Part XI of the Act (information gathering and investigations).

(7)   Subsections (1) to (9) of section 176 of the Act (entry of premises under warrant) apply in relation to a person appointed under paragraph (1) as if—
   (a)   references to an investigator were references to a person so appointed;
   (b)   references to an information requirement were references to a requirement imposed under this regulation by a person so appointed;
   (c)   the premises mentioned in section 176(3)(a) were the premises of a person whose affairs are the subject of an investigation under this regulation or of an appointed representative of such a person.

(8)   No person may be required under this regulation to disclose information or produce a document in respect of which he owes an obligation of confidence by virtue of carrying on a banking business unless—
   (a)   the imposition of the requirement is authorised by the Authority or the Secretary of State (as the case may be) or the person to whom the obligation of confidence is owed; or
   (b)   the person to whom it is owed is—
      (i)   a director or depositary of any open-ended investment company which is under investigation; or
      (ii)   any other person whose own affairs are under investigation.

[2267]

Winding up

31   Winding up by the court

(1)   Where an open-ended investment company is wound up as an unregistered company under Part V of the 1986 Act, the provisions of that Act apply for the purposes of the winding up with the following modifications.

(2)   A petition for the winding up of an open-ended investment company may be presented by the depositary of the company as well as by any person authorised under section 124 (application for winding up) or section 124A of the 1986 Act (petition for winding up on grounds of public interest), as those sections apply by virtue of Part V of that Act, to present a petition for the winding up of the company.

(3)   Where a petition for the winding up of an open ended investment company is presented by a person other than the Authority—
   (a)   that person must serve a copy of the petition on the Authority; and
   (b)   the Authority is entitled to be heard on the petition.

(4)   If, before the presentation of a petition for the winding up by the court of an open-ended investment company as an unregistered company under Part V of the 1986 Act, the affairs of the company are being wound up otherwise than by the court—
   (a)   section 129(2) of the 1986 Act (commencement of winding up by the court) is not to apply; and
   (b)   any winding up of the company by the court is to be deemed to have commenced—
      (i)   at the time at which the Authority gave its approval to a proposal mentioned in paragraph (1)(d) of regulation 21; or
      (ii)   in a case falling within paragraph (3)(b) of that regulation, on the day following the end of the one-month period mentioned in that paragraph.

[2268]

32   Dissolution on winding up by the court

(1)   Section 172(8) of the 1986 Act (final meeting of creditors and vacation of office by liquidator), as that section applies by virtue of Part V of that Act (winding up of unregistered companies) has effect, in relation to open-ended investment companies, as if the reference to the registrar of companies was a reference to the Authority.

(2) Where, in respect of an open-ended investment company, the Authority receives—

   (a)   a notice given for the purposes of section 172(8) of the 1986 Act (as aforesaid); or

   (b)   a notice from the official receiver that the winding up, by the court, of the company is complete;

the Authority must, on receipt of the notice, forthwith register it and, subject to the provisions of this regulation, at the end of the period of three months beginning with the day of the registration of the notice, the company is to be dissolved.

(3) The Secretary of State may, on the application of the official receiver or any other person who appears to the Secretary of State to be interested, give a direction deferring the date at which the dissolution of the company is to take effect for such period as the Secretary of State thinks fit.

(4) An appeal to the court lies from any decision of the Secretary of State on an application for a direction under paragraph (3).

(5) Paragraph (3) does not apply to a case where the winding-up order was made by the court in Scotland, but in such a case the court may, on an application by any person appearing to the court to have an interest, order that the date at which the dissolution of the company is to take effect be deferred for such period as the court thinks fit.

(6) It is the duty of the person—

   (a)   on whose application a direction is given under paragraph (3);

   (b)   in whose favour an appeal with respect to an application for such a direction is determined; or

   (c)   on whose application an order is made under paragraph (5);

not later than seven days after the giving of the direction, the determination of the appeal or the making of the order, to deliver to the Authority for registration a copy of the direction or determination or, in respect of an order, a certified copy of the interlocutor.

(7) If a person without reasonable excuse fails to deliver a copy as required by paragraph (6), he is guilty of an offence.

(8) A person guilty of an offence under paragraph (7) is liable, on summary conviction—

   (a)   to a fine not exceeding level 1 on the standard scale; and

   (b)   on a second or subsequent conviction instead of the penalty set out in sub-paragraph (a), to a fine of £100 for each day on which the contravention is continued.

[2269]

33 Dissolution in other circumstances

(1) Where the affairs of an open-ended investment company have been wound up otherwise than by the court, the Authority must, as soon as is reasonably practicable after the winding up is complete, register that fact and, subject to the provisions of this regulation, at the end of the period of three months beginning with the day of the registration, the company is to be dissolved.

(2) The court may, on the application of the Authority or the company, make an order deferring the date at which the dissolution of the company is to take effect for such period as the court thinks fit.

(3) It is the duty of the company, on whose application an order of the court under paragraph (2) is made, to deliver to the Authority, not later than seven days after the making of the order, a copy of the order for registration.

(4) Where any company, the head office of which is situated in England and Wales, or Wales, is dissolved by virtue of paragraph (1), any sum of money (including unclaimed distributions) standing to the account of the company at the date of the dissolution must on such date as is determined in accordance with FSA rules, be paid into court.

(5) Where any company, the head office of which is situated in Scotland, is dissolved by virtue of paragraph (1), any sum of money (including unclaimed dividends and unapplied or undistributable balances) standing to the account of the company at the date of the dissolution must—

   (a)   on such date as is determined in accordance with FSA rules, be lodged in an appropriate bank or institution as defined in section 73(1) of the Bankruptcy (Scotland) Act 1985 (interpretation) in the name of the Accountant of the Court; and

   (b)   thereafter be treated as if it were a sum of money lodged in such an account by virtue of section 193 of the 1986 Act (unclaimed dividends (Scotland)), as that section applies by virtue of Part V of that Act.

[2270]

PART III
CORPORATE CODE

Organs

34 Directors

(1)   On the coming into effect of an authorisation order in respect of an open-ended investment company, the persons proposed in the application under regulation 12 as directors of the company are deemed to be appointed as its first directors.

[(2)   Subject to regulations 21 and 26, any subsequent appointment as a director of a company must be made by the company in general meeting, save that the directors of the company may appoint a person to act as director to fill any vacancy until such time as the next annual general meeting of the company takes place or, if the company does not hold annual general meetings, the directors of the company may appoint a person to act as director.]

(3)   Any act of a director is valid notwithstanding—
   (a)   any defect that may thereafter be discovered in his appointment or qualifications; or
   (b)   that it is afterwards discovered that his appointment had terminated by virtue of any provision contained in FSA rules which required a director to retire upon attaining a specified age.

(4)   The business of a company must be managed—
   (a)   where a company has only one director, by that director; or
   (b)   where a company has more than one director, by the directors but subject to any provision contained in FSA rules as to the allocation between the directors of responsibilities for the management of the company (including any provision there may be as to the allocation of such responsibility to one or more directors to the exclusion of others).

(5)   Subject to the provisions of these Regulations, FSA rules and the company's instrument of incorporation, the directors of a company may exercise all the powers of the company.

[2271]

NOTES
Para (2): substituted by the Open-Ended Investment Companies (Amendment) Regulations 2005, SI 2005/923, reg 2(1), (3), as from 6 April 2005.

[34A   Removal of certain directors by ordinary resolution

(1)   The directors of an open-ended investment company must, on a members' requisition, forthwith proceed duly to convene an extraordinary general meeting of the company and this applies notwithstanding anything in the company's instrument of incorporation.

(2)   A members' requisition is a requisition—
   (a)   by members of the company holding at the date of the deposit of the requisition not less than one-tenth of such of the paid-up capital of the company as at that date carries the right of voting at general meetings of the company; and
   (b)   which states as the object of the meeting the removal of one or more directors appointed in accordance with regulation 34(2) and which must be signed by the requisitionists and deposited at the registered office of the company.

(3)   A company may by ordinary resolution at an extraordinary general meeting convened in accordance with paragraph (1) remove any director or directors appointed in accordance with regulation 34(2).

(4)   This regulation is not to be treated as depriving a person removed under it of compensation or damages payable to him in respect of the termination of his appointment as director or as derogating from any power to remove a director which exists apart from this regulation.]

[2272]

NOTES
Commencement: 6 April 2005.
Inserted by the Open-Ended Investment Companies (Amendment) Regulations 2005, SI 2005/923, reg 2(1), (4), as from 6 April 2005.

35 Directors to have regard to interests of employees

(1)   The matters to which a director of an open-ended investment company must have regard in the performance of his functions include the interests of the company's employees in general, as well as the interests of its shareholders.

(2) The duty imposed by this regulation on a director is owed by him to the company (and the company alone) and is enforceable in the same way as any other fiduciary duty owed to a company by its directors.

[2273]

36 Inspection of directors' service contracts

(1) Every open-ended investment company must keep at an appropriate place—
- (a) in the case of each director whose contract of service with the company is in writing, a copy of that contract; and
- (b) in the case of each director whose contract of service with the company is not in writing, a written memorandum setting out its terms.

(2) All copies and memoranda kept by a company in accordance with paragraph (1) must be kept at the same place.

(3) The following are appropriate places for the purposes of paragraph (1)—
- (a) the company's head office;
- (b) the place where the company's register of shareholders is kept; and
- (c) where the designated person is a director of the company and is a body corporate, the registered or principal office of that person.

(4) Every copy and memorandum required by paragraph (1) to be kept must be open to the inspection of any shareholder of the company.

(5) If such an inspection is refused, the court may by order compel an immediate inspection of the copy or memorandum concerned.

[(6) Every copy and memorandum required to be kept by paragraph (1) must be made available, for inspection, by the company at the company's annual general meeting or, if the company does not hold annual general meetings, sent to any shareholder at his request within ten days of the company's receipt of such request.]

(7) Paragraph (1) applies to a variation of a director's contract of service as it applies to the contract.

[2274]

NOTES
Para (6): substituted the Open-Ended Investment Companies (Amendment) Regulations 2005, SI 2005/923, reg 2(1), (5), as from 6 April 2005.

37 General meetings

(1) Subject to paragraph (2) [and regulation 37A], every open-ended investment company [incorporated before 6 April 2005] must in each year hold a general meeting ("annual general meeting") in addition to any other meetings, whether general or otherwise, it may hold in that year.

(2) If a company holds its first annual general meeting within 18 months of the date on which the authorisation order made by the Authority in respect of the company comes into effect, paragraph (1) does not require the company to hold any other meeting as its annual general meeting in the year of its incorporation or in the following year.

(3) Subject to paragraph (2) [and regulation 37A], not more than 15 months may elapse between the date of one annual general meeting of a company and the date of the next.

[2275]

NOTES
Paras (1), (3): words in square brackets inserted by the Open-Ended Investment Companies (Amendment) Regulations 2005, SI 2005/923, reg 2(1), (6), as from 6 April 2005.

[37A Election to dispense with annual general meetings

(1) The directors of an open-ended investment company may elect to dispense with the holding of an annual general meeting by giving sixty days' written notice to all the company's shareholders.

(2) An election has effect for the year in which it is made and subsequent years, but does not affect any liability already incurred by reason of default in holding an annual general meeting.]

[2276]

NOTES
Commencement: 6 April 2005.
Inserted by the Open-Ended Investment Companies (Amendment) Regulations 2005, SI 2005/923, reg 2(1), (7), as from 6 April 2005.

38 Capacity of company

(1) The validity of an act done by an open-ended investment company cannot be called into question on the ground of lack of capacity by reason of anything in these Regulations, FSA rules or the company's instrument of incorporation.

(2) Nothing in paragraph (1) affects the duty of the directors to observe any limitation on their powers.

[2277]

39 Power of directors and general meeting to bind the company

(1) In favour of a person dealing in good faith, the following powers, that is to say—
   (a) the power of the directors of an open-ended investment company (whether or not acting as a board) to bind the company, or authorise others to do so; and
   (b) the power of such a company in general meeting to bind the company, or authorise others to do so;
are deemed to be free of any limitation under the company's constitution.

(2) For the purposes of this regulation—
   (a) a person deals with a company if he is party to any transaction or other act to which the company is a party;
   (b) subject to paragraph (4), a person is not to be regarded as acting in bad faith by reason only of his knowing that, under the company's constitution, an act is beyond any of the powers referred to in paragraph (1)(a) or (b); and
   (c) subject to paragraph (4), a person is presumed to have acted in good faith unless the contrary is proved.

(3) The reference in paragraph (1) to any limitation under the company's constitution on the powers therein set out includes any limitation deriving from these Regulations, from FSA rules or from a resolution of the company in general meeting or of a meeting of any class of shareholders.

(4) Sub-paragraphs (b) and (c) of paragraph (2) do not apply where—
   (a) by virtue of a limitation deriving from these Regulations or from FSA rules, an act is beyond any of the powers referred to in paragraph (1)(a) or (b); and
   (b) the person in question—
      (i) has actual knowledge of that fact; or
      (ii) has deliberately failed to make enquiries in circumstances in which a reasonable and honest person would have done so.

(5) Paragraph (1) does not affect any liability incurred by the directors or any other person by reason of the directors exceeding their powers.

[2278]

40 No duty to enquire as to capacity etc

Subject to regulation 39(4)(b)(ii), a party to a transaction with an open-ended investment company is not bound to enquire—
   (a) as to whether the transaction is permitted by these Regulations, FSA rules or the company's instrument of incorporation; or
   (b) as to any limitation on the powers referred to in regulation 39(1)(a) or (b).

[2279]

41 Exclusion or deemed notice

A person is not to be taken to have notice of any matter merely because of its being disclosed in any document made available by an open-ended investment company for inspection; but this does not affect the question whether a person is affected by notice of any matter by reason of a failure to make such enquiries as ought reasonably to be made.

[2280]

42 Restraint and ratification by shareholders

(1) A shareholder of an open-ended investment company may bring proceedings to restrain the doing of an act which but for regulation 38(1) would be beyond the company's capacity.

(2) Paragraph (1) of regulation 39 does not affect any right of a shareholder of an open-ended investment company to bring proceedings to restrain the doing of an act which is beyond any of the powers referred to in that paragraph.

(3) No proceedings may be brought under paragraph (1) in respect of an act to be done in fulfilment of a legal obligation arising from a previous act of the company; and paragraph (2) does not have the effect of enabling proceedings to be brought in respect of any such act.

(4) Any action by the directors of a company—
   (a) which, but for regulation 38(1), would be beyond the company's capacity; or

(b)   which is within the company's capacity but beyond the powers referred to in regulation 39(1)(a);

may only be ratified by a resolution of the company in general meeting.

(5)   A resolution ratifying such action does not affect any liability incurred by the directors or any other person, relief from any such liability requiring agreement by a separate resolution of the company in general meeting.

(6)   Nothing in this regulation affects any power or right conferred by or arising under section 150 (actions for damages) or section 380, 382 or 384 of the Act (injunctions and restitution orders).

[2281]

43   Events affecting company status

(1)   Where either of the conditions mentioned in paragraph (2) is satisfied, an open-ended investment company is not entitled to rely against other persons on the happening of any of the following events—

(a)   any alteration of the company's instrument of incorporation;

(b)   any change among the directors of the company;

(c)   as regards service of any document on the company, any change in the situation of the head office of the company; or

(d)   the making of a winding-up order in respect of the company or, in circumstances in which the affairs of a company are to be wound up otherwise than by the court, the commencement of the winding up.

(2)   The conditions referred to in paragraph (1) are that—

(a)   the event in question had not been officially notified at the material time and is not shown by the company to have been known at that time by the other person concerned; and

(b)   if the material time fell on or before the 15th day after the date of official notification (or where the 15th day was a non-business day, on or before the next day that was a business day), it is shown that the other person concerned was unavoidably prevented from knowing of the event at that time.

(3)   In this regulation "official notification" means the notification in the Gazette (by virtue of regulation 78) of any document containing the information referred to in paragraph (1) above, and "officially notified" is to be construed accordingly.

[2282]

44   Invalidity of certain transactions involving directors

(1)   This regulation applies where—

(a)   an open-ended investment company enters into a transaction to which the parties include a director of the company or any person who is an associate of such a director; and

(b)   in connection with the transaction, the directors of the company (whether or not acting as a board) exceed any limitation on their powers under the company's constitution.

(2)   The transaction is voidable at the instance of the company.

(3)   Whether or not the transaction is avoided, any such party to the transaction as is mentioned in paragraph (1)(a), and any director of the company who authorised the transaction, is liable—

(a)   to account to the company for any gain which he has made directly or indirectly by the transaction; and

(b)   to indemnify the company for any loss or damage resulting from the transaction.

(4)   Nothing in paragraphs (1) to (3) is to be construed as excluding the operation of any other enactment or rule of law by virtue of which the transaction may be called into question or any liability to the company may arise.

(5)   The transaction ceases to be voidable if—

(a)   restitution of any money or other asset which was the subject-matter of the transaction is no longer possible;

(b)   the company is indemnified for any loss or damage resulting from the transaction;

(c)   rights which are acquired, bona fide for value and without actual notice of the directors concerned having exceeded their powers, by a person who is not a party to the transaction would be affected by the avoidance; or

(d)   the transaction is ratified by resolution of the company in general meeting.

(6)   A person other than a director of the company is not liable under paragraph (3) if he shows that at the time the transaction was entered into he did not know that the directors concerned were exceeding their powers.

(7)   This regulation does not affect the operation of regulation 39 in relation to any party to the transaction not within paragraph (1)(a); but where a transaction is voidable by virtue of this regulation and valid by virtue of that regulation in favour of such a person, the court may, on the

application of that person or of the company, make such order affirming, severing or setting aside the transaction, on such terms as appear to the court to be just.

(8)   For the purposes of this regulation—
    (a)   "associate", in relation to any person who is a director of the company, means that person's spouse, [civil partner,] child or stepchild (if under 18), employee, partner or any body corporate of which that person is a director; and if that person is a body corporate, any subsidiary undertaking or director of that body corporate (including any director or employee of such subsidiary undertaking);
    (b)   "transaction" includes any act; and
    (c)   the reference in paragraph (1)(b) to any limitation on directors' powers under the company's constitution includes any limitation deriving from these Regulations, from FSA rules or from a resolution of the company in general meeting or of a meeting of any class of shareholders.

[2283]

NOTES
Para (8): words in square brackets in sub-para (a) inserted by the Civil Partnership Act 2004 (Amendments to Subordinate Legislation) Order 2005, SI 2005/2114, art 2(16), Sch 16, Pt 1, para 5, as from 5 December 2005.
Stepchild, etc: as to the meaning of this and related expressions, see the Civil Partnership Act 2004, s 246 (as applied to these Regulations by the Civil Partnership Act 2004 (Relationships Arising Through Civil Partnership) Order 2005, SI 2005/3137, art 3, Schedule).

Shares

45   Shares

(1)   An open-ended investment company may issue more than one class of shares.

(2)   A shareholder may not have any interest in the scheme property of the company.

(3)   The rights which attach to each share of any given class are—
    (a)   the right, in accordance with the instrument of incorporation, to participate in or receive profits or income arising from the acquisition, holding, management or disposal of the scheme property;
    (b)   the right, in accordance with the instrument of incorporation, to vote at any general meeting of the company or at any relevant class meeting; and
    (c)   such other rights as may be provided for, in relation to shares of that class, in the instrument of incorporation of the company.

(4)   In respect of any class of shares, the rights referred to in paragraph (3) may, if the company's instrument of incorporation so provides, be expressed in two denominations; and in the case of any such class, one (the "smaller") denomination is to be such proportion of the other (the "larger") denomination as is fixed by the instrument of incorporation.

(5)   In respect of any class of shares within paragraph (4), any share to which are attached rights expressed in the smaller denomination is to be known as a smaller denomination share; and any share to which are attached rights expressed in the larger denomination is to be known as a larger denomination share.

(6)   In respect of any class of shares, the rights which attach to each share of that class are—
    (a)   except in respect of a class of shares within paragraph (4), equal to the rights that attach to each other share of that class; and
    (b)   in respect of a class of shares within that paragraph, equal to the rights that attach to each other share of that class of the same denomination.

(7)   In respect of any class of shares within paragraph (4), the rights that attach to any smaller denomination share of that class are to be a proportion of the rights that attach to any larger denomination share of that class and that proportion is to be the same as the proportion referred to in paragraph (4).

[2284]

46   Share certificates

(1)   Subject to regulations 47 and 48, an open-ended investment company must prepare documentary evidence of title to its shares ("share certificates") as follows—
    (a)   in respect of any new shares issued by it;
    (b)   where a shareholder has transferred part only of his holding back to the company, in respect of the remainder of that holding;
    (c)   where a shareholder has transferred part only of his holding to the designated person, in respect of the remainder of that holding;
    (d)   where a company has registered a transfer of shares made to a person other than the company or a person designated as mentioned in sub-paragraph (c)—
        (i)   in respect of the shares transferred to the transferee; and

    (ii)   in respect of any shares retained by the transferor which were evidenced by any certificate sent to the company for the purposes of registering the transfer;

  (e)   in respect of any holding of bearer shares for which a certificate evidencing title has already been issued but where the certificate has been surrendered to the company for the purpose of being replaced by two or more certificates which between them evidence title to the shares comprising that holding; and

  (f)   in respect of any shares for which a certificate has already been issued but where it appears to the company that the certificate needs to be replaced as a result of having been lost, stolen or destroyed or having become damaged or worn out.

(2)   A company must exercise due diligence and take all reasonable steps to ensure that certificates prepared in accordance with paragraph (1)(a) to (e) are ready for delivery as soon as reasonably practicable.

(3)   Certificates need be prepared in the circumstances referred to in paragraph (1)(e) and (f) only if the company has received—

  (a)   a request for a new certificate;

  (b)   the old certificate (if there is one);

  (c)   such indemnity as the company may require; and

  (d)   such reasonable sum as the company may require in respect of the expenses incurred by it in complying with the request.

(4)   Each share certificate must state—

  (a)   the number of shares the title to which is evidenced by the certificate;

  (b)   where the company has more than one class of shares, the class of shares title to which is evidenced by the certificate; and

  (c)   except in the case of bearer shares, the name of the holder.

(5)   Where, in respect of any class of shares, the rights that attach to shares of that class are expressed in two denominations, the reference in paragraph (4)(a) (as it applies to shares of that class) to the number of shares is a reference to the total of—

$N + n/p$

(6)   In paragraph (5)—

  (a) N is the relevant number of the larger denomination shares of the class in question;

  (b) n is the relevant number of the smaller denomination shares of that class; and

  (c) p is the number of smaller denomination shares of that class that are equivalent to one larger denomination share of that class.

(7)   Nothing in these Regulations is to be taken as preventing the total arrived at under paragraph (5) being expressed on the certificate as a single entry representing the result derived from the formula set out in that paragraph.

(8)   In England and Wales, a share certificate specifying any shares held by any person which is—

  (a)   under the common seal of the company; or

  (b)   authenticated in accordance with regulation 59;

is prima facie evidence of that person's title to the shares.

(9)   In Scotland, a share certificate specifying any shares held by any person which is—

  (a)   under the common seal of the company; or

  (b)   subscribed by the company in accordance with the Requirements of Writing (Scotland) Act 1995;

is, unless the contrary is shown, sufficient evidence of that person's title to the shares.

[2285]

47   Exceptions from regulation 46

(1)   …

(2)   Nothing in regulation 46 requires a company to prepare share certificates in the following cases.

(3)   Case 1 is any case where the company's instrument of incorporation states that share certificates will not be issued and contains provision as to other procedures for evidencing a person's entitlement to shares.

(4)   Case 2 is any case where a shareholder has indicated to the company in writing that he does not wish to receive a certificate.

(5)   Case 3 is any case where shares are issued or transferred to the designated person.

(6)   Case 4 is any case where shares are issued or transferred to a nominee of a recognised investment exchange who is designated for the purposes of this paragraph in the rules of the investment exchange in question.

[2286]

NOTES

Para (1): revoked by the Uncertificated Securities Regulations 2001, SI 2001/3755, reg 52(4), as from 26 November 2001.

48 Bearer shares

An open-ended investment company may, if its instrument of incorporation so provides, issue shares ("bearer shares") evidenced by a share certificate, or by any other documentary evidence of title for which provision is made in its instrument of incorporation, which indicates—

(a) that the holder of the document is entitled to the shares specified in it; and

(b) that no entry will be made on the register of shareholders identifying the holder of those shares.

[2287]

49 Register of shareholders

Schedule 3 to these Regulations makes provision with respect to the register of shareholders of an open-ended investment company.

[2288]

50 Power to close register

(1) Subject to paragraph (2), an open-ended investment company may, on giving notice by advertisement in a national newspaper circulating in all the countries in which shares in the company are sold, close the register of shareholders for any time or times not exceeding, in the whole, 30 days in each year.

[(2) Paragraph (1) has effect subject to any requirements contained in FSA rules].

[2289]

NOTES

Para (2): substituted by the Uncertificated Securities Regulations 2001, SI 2001/3755, reg 51, Sch 7, Pt 2, para 24(b), as from 26 November 2001.

51 Power of court to rectify register

(1) An application to the court may be made under this regulation if—

(a) the name of any person is, without sufficient cause, entered in or omitted from the register of shareholders of an open-ended investment company;

(b) default is made as to the details contained in any entry on the register in respect of a person's holding of shares in the company; or

(c) default is made or unnecessary delay takes place in amending the register so as to reflect the fact of any person having ceased to be a shareholder.

(2) An application under this regulation may be made by the person aggrieved, by any shareholder of the company or by the company itself.

(3) The court may refuse the application or may order rectification of the register of shareholders and payment by the company of any damages sustained by any party aggrieved.

(4) On such an application the court may decide any question necessary or expedient to be decided for rectification of the register of shareholders including, in particular, any question relating to the right of a person who is a party to the application to have his name entered in or omitted from the register (whether the question arises as between shareholders and alleged shareholders or as between shareholders or alleged shareholders on the one hand and the company on the other hand).

[2290]

52 Share transfers

Schedule 4 to these Regulations makes provision for the transfer of registered and bearer shares in an open-ended investment company.

[2291]

Operation

53 Power incidental to carrying on business

An open-ended investment company has power to do all such things as are incidental or conducive to the carrying on of its business.

[2292]

54 Name to appear in correspondence etc

(1) Every open-ended investment company must have its name mentioned in legible characters in all letters of the company and in all other documents issued by the company in the course of business.

(2)   If an officer of a company or a person on the company's behalf signs or authorises to be signed on behalf of the company any cheque or order for money or goods in which the company's name is not mentioned as required by paragraph (1) he is personally liable to the holder of the cheque or order for money or goods for the amount of it (unless it is duly paid by the company).

[2293]

55 Particulars to appear in correspondence etc

(1)   Every open-ended investment company must have the following particulars mentioned in legible characters in all letters of the company and in all other documents issued by the company in the course of business—
  (a)   the company's place of registration;
  (b)   the number with which it is registered;
  (c)   the address of its head office; and
  (d)   the fact that it is an investment company with variable capital.

(2)   Where, in accordance with regulation 72, the Authority makes any change of existing registered numbers in respect of any open-ended investment company then, for a period of three years beginning with the date on which the notification of the change is sent to the company by the Authority, the requirement of paragraph (1)(b) is, notwithstanding regulation 72(4), satisfied by the use of either the old number or the new.

[2294]

56 Contracts: England and Wales

Under the law of England and Wales a contract may be made—
  (a)   by an open-ended investment company by writing under its common seal; or
  (b)   on behalf of such a company, by any person acting under its authority (whether expressed or implied);

and any formalities required by law in the case of a contract made by an individual also apply, unless a contrary intention appears, to a contract made by or on behalf of such a company.

[2295]

57 Execution of documents: England and Wales

(1)   Under the law of England and Wales the following provisions have effect with respect to the execution of documents by an open-ended investment company.

(2)   A document is executed by a company by the affixing of its common seal.

(3)   A company need not have a common seal, however, and the following provisions of this regulation apply whether it does or not.

(4)   A document that is signed by at least one director and expressed (in whatever form of words) to be executed by the company has the same effect as if executed under the common seal of the company.

(5)   A document executed by a company which makes it clear on its face that it is intended by the person or persons making it to be a deed has effect, upon delivery, as a deed; and it is to be presumed, unless a contrary intention is proved, to be delivered upon its being executed.

(6)   In favour of a purchaser, a document is deemed to have been duly executed by a company if it purports to be signed by at least one director or, in the case of a director which is a body corporate, it purports to be executed by that director; and, where it makes it clear on its face that it is intended by the person or persons making it to be a deed, it is deemed to have been delivered upon its being executed.

(7)   In paragraph (6), "purchaser" means a purchaser in good faith for valuable consideration and includes a lessee, mortgagee or other person who for valuable consideration acquires an interest in property.

[2296]

58 Execution of deeds overseas: England and Wales

(1)   Under the law of England and Wales an open-ended investment company may, by writing under its common seal, empower any person, either generally or in respect of any specified matters, as its attorney, to execute deeds on its behalf in any place elsewhere than in the United Kingdom.

(2)   A deed executed by such an attorney on behalf of the company has the same effect as if it were executed under the company's common seal.

[2297]

59 Authentication of documents: England and Wales

A document or proceeding requiring authentication by an open-ended investment company is sufficiently authenticated for the purposes of the law of England and Wales—
  (a)   by the signature of a director or other authorised officer of the company; or

PART III
STATUTORY INSTRUMENTS

(b)   in the case of a director which is a body corporate, if it is executed by that director.

[2298]

60 Official seal for share certificates

(1)   An open-ended investment company which has a common seal may have, for use for sealing shares issued by the company and for sealing documents creating or evidencing shares so issued, an official seal which is a facsimile of its common seal with the addition on its face of the word "securities".

(2)   The official seal when duly affixed to a document has the same effect as the company's common seal.

(3)   Nothing in this regulation affects the right of an open-ended investment company whose head office is in Scotland to subscribe such shares and documents in accordance with the Requirements of Writing (Scotland) Act 1995.

[2299]

61 Personal liability for contracts and deeds

(1)   A contract, which purports to be made by or on behalf of an open-ended investment company at a time before the coming into effect of an authorisation order in relation to that company, has effect (subject to any agreement to the contrary) as a contract made with the person purporting to act for the company or as agent for it, and he is accordingly personally liable under the contract.

(2)   Paragraph (1) applies—
    (a)   to the making of a deed under the law of England and Wales; and
    (b)   to the undertaking of an obligation under the law of Scotland;
as it applies to the making of a contract.

(3)   If a company enters into a transaction at any time after the authorisation order made in respect of the company has been revoked and the company fails to comply with its obligations in respect of that transaction within 21 days of being called upon to do so, the person who authorised the transaction is liable, and where the transaction was authorised by two or more persons they are jointly and severally liable, to indemnify the other party to the transaction in respect of any loss or damage suffered by him by reason of the company's failure to comply with those obligations.

[2300]

62 Exemptions from liability to be void

(1)   This regulation applies to any provision, whether contained in the instrument of incorporation of an open-ended investment company or in any contract with the company or otherwise—
    (a)   which exempts any officer of the company or any person (whether or not an officer of the company) employed by the company as auditor from, or indemnifies him against, any liability which by virtue of any rule of law would otherwise attach to him in respect of any negligence, default, breach of duty or breach of trust of which he may be guilty in relation to the company; or
    (b)   which exempts the depositary of the company from, or indemnifies him against, any liability for any failure to exercise due care and diligence in the discharge of his functions in respect of the company.

(2)   Except as provided by the following paragraph, any such provision is void.

(3)   This regulation does not prevent a company—
    (a)   from purchasing and maintaining for any such officer, auditor or depositary insurance against any such liability; or
    (b)   from indemnifying any such officer, auditor or depositary against any liability incurred by him—
        (i)   in defending any proceedings (whether civil or criminal) in which judgment is given in his favour or he is acquitted; or
        (ii)   in connection with any application under regulation 63 in which relief is granted to him by the court.

[2301]

63 Power of court to grant relief in certain cases

(1)   This regulation applies to—
    (a)   any proceedings for negligence, default, breach of duty or breach of trust against an officer of an open-ended investment company or a person (whether or not an officer of the company) employed by the company as auditor; or
    (b)   any proceedings against the depository of such a company for failure to exercise due care and diligence in the discharge of his functions in respect of the company.

(2)   If, in any proceedings to which this regulation applies, it appears to the court hearing the case—

(a)   that the officer, auditor or depositary is or may be liable in respect of the cause of action in question;

(b)   that, nevertheless, he has acted honestly and reasonably; and

(c)   that having regard to all the circumstances of the case (including those connected with his appointment) he ought fairly to be excused from the liability sought to be enforced against him;

the court may relieve him, either wholly or partly, from his liability on such terms as it may think fit.

(3)   If any such officer, auditor or depositary has reason to apprehend that any claim will or might be made against him in proceedings to which this regulation applies, he may apply to the court for relief.

(4)   The court, on an application under paragraph (3), has the same power to relieve the applicant as under this regulation it would have had if it had been a court before which the relevant proceedings against the applicant had been brought.

(5)   Where a case to which paragraph (2) applies is being tried by a judge with a jury, the judge, after hearing the evidence, may, if he is satisfied that the defendant or defender ought in pursuance of that paragraph to be relieved either in whole or in part from the liability sought to be enforced against him, withdraw the case in whole or in part from the jury and forthwith direct judgment to be entered for the defendant or defender on such terms as to costs or otherwise as the judge may think proper.

[2302]

64   Punishment for fraudulent trading

(1)   If any business of an open-ended investment company is carried on with intent to defraud creditors of the company or creditors of any other person, or for any fraudulent purpose, every person who was knowingly a party to the carrying on of the business in that manner is guilty of an offence and liable—

(a)   on conviction on indictment, to imprisonment not exceeding a term of two years or to a fine or to both;

(b)   on summary conviction, to imprisonment not exceeding a term of three months or to a fine not exceeding the statutory maximum or to both.

(2)   This regulation applies whether or not the company has been, or is in the course of being, wound up (whether by the court or otherwise).

[2303]

65   Power to provide for employees on cessation or transfer of business

(1)   The powers of an open-ended investment company include power to make the following provision for the benefit of persons employed or formerly employed by the company, that is to say, provision in connection with the cessation or the transfer to any person of the whole or part of the undertaking of the company.

(2)   The power conferred by paragraph (1) is exercisable notwithstanding that its exercise is not in the best interests of the company.

(3)   The power which a company may exercise by virtue of paragraph (1) may only be exercised by the company—

(a)   in a case not falling within sub-paragraph (b) or (c), if sanctioned by a resolution of the company in general meeting;

(b)   if so authorised by the instrument of incorporation—

(i)   in the case of a company that has only one director, by a resolution of that director; and

(ii)   in any other case, by such resolution of directors as is required by FSA rules; or

(c)   if the instrument of incorporation requires the exercise of the power to be sanctioned by a resolution of the company in general meeting for which more than a simple majority of the shareholders voting is necessary, by a resolution of that majority;

and in any case after compliance with any other requirements of the instrument of incorporation applicable to the exercise of the power.

[2304]

Reports

66   Reports: preparation

(1)   The directors of an open-ended investment company must—

(a)   prepare a report ("annual report") for each annual accounting period of the company; and

(b) subject to paragraph (2), prepare a report ("half-yearly report") for each half-yearly accounting period of the company.

(2) Where a company's first annual accounting period is a period of less than 12 months, a half-yearly report need not be prepared for any part of that period.

(3) The directors of a company must lay copies of the annual report before the company in general meeting.

(4) Nothing in this regulation or in regulation 67 prejudices the generality of regulation 6(1).

(5) In this regulation any reference to annual and half-yearly accounting periods of a company is a reference to those periods as determined in relation to that company in accordance with FSA rules.

[2305]

67 Reports: accounts

(1) The annual report of an open-ended investment company must, in respect of the annual accounting period to which it relates, contain accounts of the company.

(2) The company's auditors must make a report to the company's shareholders in respect of the accounts of the company contained in its annual report.

(3) A copy of the auditor's report must form part of the company's annual report.

[2306]

68 Reports: voluntary revision

(1) If it appears to the directors of an open-ended investment company that any annual report of the company did not comply with the requirements of these Regulations or FSA rules, they may prepare a revised annual report.

(2) Where copies of the previous report have been laid before the company in general meeting or delivered to the Authority, the revisions must be confined to—
(a) the correction of anything in the previous report which did not comply with the requirements of these Regulations or FSA rules; and
(b) the making of any necessary consequential alterations.

[2307]

69 Auditors

Schedule 5 to these Regulations makes provision with respect to the auditors of open-ended investment companies.

[2308]

Mergers and divisions

70 Mergers and divisions

Schedule 6 to these Regulations makes provision with respect to mergers and divisions involving open-ended investment companies.

[2309]

PART IV
THE AUTHORITY'S REGISTRATION FUNCTIONS

71 Register of open-ended investment companies

(1) The Authority must maintain a register of open-ended investment companies.

(2) The Authority may keep the register in any form it thinks fit provided that it is possible to inspect the information contained on it and to obtain a copy of that information (or any part of it) for inspection.

[2310]

72 Companies' registered numbers

(1) The Authority must allocate to every open-ended investment company a number, which is to be known as the company's registered number.

(2) Companies' registered numbers must be in such form, consisting of one or more sequences of figures or letters, as the Authority may from time to time determine.

(3) The Authority may, upon adopting a new form of registered number, make such changes of existing registered numbers (including numbers allocated by the appropriate registrar) as appear to it to be necessary.

(4) A change in a company's registered number has effect from the date on which the company is notified by the Authority of the change.

[2311]

73   Delivery of documents to the Authority

Any document which is required by these Regulations to be delivered to the Authority to be recorded on the register maintained pursuant to regulation 71 must be delivered in such form as the Authority may from time to time specify.

[2312]

74   Keeping of company records by the Authority

(1)   The information contained in a document delivered to the Authority under any provision of these Regulations may be recorded and kept by it in any form it thinks fit, provided that it is possible to inspect the information and produce a copy of it in legible form.

(2)   The originals of documents delivered to the Authority under any provision of these Regulations in legible form must be kept by it for ten years after which they may be destroyed.

(3)   Where a company has been dissolved, the Authority may, at any time after the expiration of two years from the date of the dissolution, direct that any records in its custody relating to the company may be removed to the Public Record Office; and records in respect of which such a direction is given must be disposed of in accordance with the enactments relating to that Office and the rules made under them.

(4)   Paragraph (3) does not extend to Scotland.

[2313]

75   Inspection etc of records kept by the Authority

(1)   Any person may inspect any records kept by the Authority for the purposes of this Part of these Regulations and may require—
     (a)   a copy, in such form as the Authority considers appropriate, of any information contained in those records; or
     (b)   a certified copy of, or extract from, any such record.

(2)   The right of inspection extends to the originals of documents delivered to the Authority in legible form only where the record kept by the Authority of the contents of the document is illegible or unavailable.

(3)   A copy of or extract from a record kept by the Authority under these Regulations, on which is endorsed a certificate signed by a member of the Authority's staff authorised by it for that purpose certifying that it is an accurate record of the contents of any document delivered to the Authority under these Regulations, is in all legal proceedings admissible in evidence as of equal validity with the original document and as evidence of any fact stated therein of which direct oral evidence would be admissible.

(4)   No process for compelling the production of a document kept by the Authority under these Regulations is to issue from any court except with the leave of the court; and any such process must bear on it a statement that it is issued with the leave of the court.

[2314]

76   Provision by the Authority of documents in non-legible form

Any requirement of these Regulations as to the supply by the Authority of a document may, if the Authority thinks fit, be satisfied by the communication by the Authority of the information in any non-legible form it thinks appropriate.

[2315]

77   Documents relating to Welsh open-ended investment companies

(1)   This regulation applies to any document which is delivered to the Authority under these Regulations and relates to an open-ended investment company (whether already registered or to be registered) whose instrument of incorporation states that its head office is to be situated in Wales.

(2)   A document to which this regulation applies may be in Welsh but must be accompanied by a certified translation into English.

(3)   The requirement for a translation imposed by paragraph (2) does not apply—
     (a)   to documents of such description as may be specified in FSA rules; or
     (b)   to documents in a form prescribed in Welsh (or partly in Welsh and partly in English) by virtue of section 26 of the Welsh Language Act 1993 (powers to prescribe Welsh forms).

(4)   An open-ended investment company whose instrument of incorporation states that its head office is to be situated in Wales may deliver to the Authority a certified translation into Welsh of any document in English which relates to the company and which is or has been delivered to the Authority.

(5)   In this regulation "certified translation" means a translation which is certified in the manner specified in FSA rules to be a correct translation.

[2316]

78   (*Revoked by the Open-Ended Investment Companies (Amendment) Regulations 2005, SI 2005/923, reg 2(1), (7), as from 6 April 2005.*)

79   Exclusion of deemed notice

A person is not to be taken to have deemed notice of any matter merely because of its being disclosed in any document kept by the Authority (and thus available for inspection) under any provision of these Regulations.

[2317]

PART V
MISCELLANEOUS

80   Contraventions

Any of the following persons, that is to say—

    (a)   a person who contravenes any provision of these Regulations; and

    (b)   an open-ended investment company (including any director or depositary of such a company) which contravenes any provision of FSA rules,

is to be treated as having contravened rules made under section 138 of the Act (general rule-making power).

[2318]

81   Offences by bodies corporate etc

Section 400 of the Act (offences by bodies corporate etc) applies to an offence under these Regulations as it applies to an offence under the Act.

[2319]

82   Jurisdiction and procedure in respect of offences

Section 403 of the Act (jurisdiction and procedure in respect of offences) applies to offences under these Regulations as it applies to offences under the Act.

[2320]

83   Evidence of grant of probate etc

The production to a company of any document which is by law sufficient evidence of probate of the will, or letters of administration of the estate, or confirmation as executor, of a deceased person having been granted to some person must be accepted by the company as sufficient evidence of the grant.

[2321]

84   Minor and consequential amendments

The provisions mentioned in Schedule 7 to these Regulations (being minor amendments and amendments consequential on the provisions of these Regulations) have effect subject to the amendments specified in that Schedule.

[2322]

85   Revocation etc

    (1)   ...

    (2)   Anything done under or in accordance with the 1996 Regulations has effect as if done under or in accordance with these Regulations.

    (3)   Without prejudice to the generality of paragraph (2)—

    (a)   a body incorporated by virtue of regulation 3(1) of the 1996 Regulations is to be treated as if it had been incorporated by virtue of regulation 3(1) of these Regulations;

    (b)   where an application under regulation 7 of the 1996 Regulations had not been determined by the Authority at the time when this regulation comes into force, it is to be treated as if it were an application made under regulation 12 of these Regulations;

    (c)   the Authority's registration functions under Part IV of these Regulations apply to any documents or records delivered to the appropriate registrar pursuant to regulation 4 of, and Schedule 1 to, the 1996 Regulations.

[2323]

NOTES

Para (1): revokes the Open-Ended Investment Companies (Investment Companies with Variable Capital) Regulations 1996, SI 1996/2827.

SCHEDULES

SCHEDULE 1
DEPOSITARIES

Regulation 5

Appointment

1.   On the coming into effect of an authorisation order in respect of an open-ended investment company, the person named in the application under regulation 12 as depositary of the company is deemed to be appointed as its first depositary.

2.   Subject to regulations 21 and 26, any subsequent appointment of the depositary of a company must be made by the directors of the company.

Retirement

3.   The depositary of a company may not retire voluntarily except upon the appointment of a new depositary.

Rights

4.   The depositary of a company is entitled—
   (a)   to receive all such notices of, and other communications relating to, any general meeting of the company as a shareholder of the company is entitled to receive;
   (b)   to attend any general meeting of the company;
   (c)   to be heard at any general meeting which it attends on any part of the business of the meeting which concerns it as depositary;
   (d)   to convene a general meeting of the company when it sees fit;
   (e)   to require from the company's officers such information and explanations as it thinks necessary for the performance of its functions as depositary; and
   (f)   to have access, except in so far as they concern its appointment or removal, to any reports, statements or other papers which are to be considered at any meeting held by the directors of the company (when acting in their capacity as such), at any general meeting of the company or at any meeting of holders of shares of any particular class.

Statement by depositary ceasing to hold office

5.—(1)   Where the depositary of a company ceases, for any reason other than by virtue of a court order made under regulation 26, to hold office, it may deposit at the head office of the company a statement of any circumstances connected with its ceasing to hold office which it considers should be brought to the attention of the shareholders or creditors of the company or, if it considers that there are no such circumstances, a statement that there are none.

(2)   If the statement is of circumstances which the depositary considers should be brought to the attention of the shareholders or creditors of the company, the company must, not later than 14 days after the deposit of the statement, either—
   (a)   send a copy of the statement to each of the shareholders whose name appears on the register of shareholders (other than the designated person) and take such steps as FSA rules may require for the purpose of bringing the fact that the statement has been made to the attention of the holders of any bearer shares; or
   (b)   apply to the court;
and, where an application is made under sub-paragraph (b), the company must notify the depositary.

(3)   Unless the depositary receives notice of an application to the court before the end of the period of 21 days beginning with the day on which it deposited the statement, it must, not later than seven days after the end of that period, send a copy of the statement to the Authority.

(4)   If the court is satisfied that the depositary is using the statement to secure needless publicity for defamatory matter—
   (a)   it must direct that copies of the statement need not be sent out and that the steps required by FSA rules need not be taken; and
   (b)   it may further order the company's costs on the application to be paid in whole or in part by the depositary notwithstanding that the depositary is not a party to the application;
and the company must, not later than 14 days after the court's decision, take such steps in relation to a statement setting out the effect of the order as are required by sub-paragraph (2)(a) in relation to the statement deposited under sub-paragraph (1).

(5)   If the court is not so satisfied, the company must, not later than 14 days after the court's decision, take the steps required by sub-paragraph (2)(a) and notify the depositary of the court's decision.

(6)   The depositary must, not later than seven days after receiving such a notice, send a copy of the statement to the Authority.

(7)   Where a notice of appeal is filed not later than 14 days after the court's decision, any reference to that decision in sub-paragraphs (4) and (5) is to be construed as a reference to the final determination or withdrawal of that appeal (as the case may be).

6.—(1)   This paragraph applies where copies of a statement have been sent to shareholders under paragraph 5.

(2)   The depositary who made the statement has, notwithstanding that it has ceased to hold office, the rights conferred by paragraph 4(a) to (c) in relation to the general meeting of the company next following the date on which the copies were sent out.

(3)   The reference in paragraph 4(c) to business concerning the depositary as depositary is to be construed in relation to a depositary who has ceased to hold office as a reference to business concerning it as former depositary.

[2324]

SCHEDULE 2
INSTRUMENT OF INCORPORATION

Regulation 14

1.   The instrument of incorporation of an open-ended investment company must—
    (a)   contain the statements set out in paragraph 2; and
    (b)   contain provision made in accordance with paragraphs 3 and 4.

2.   The statements referred to in paragraph 1(a) are—
    (a)   the head office of the company is situated in England and Wales, Wales or Scotland (as the case may be);
    (b)   the company is an open-ended investment company with variable share capital;
    (c)   the shareholders are not liable for the debts of the company;
    (d)   the scheme property is entrusted to a depositary for safekeeping (subject to any exceptions permitted by FSA rules); and
    (e)   charges or expenses of the company may be taken out of the scheme property.

3.—(1)   The instrument of incorporation must contain provision as to the following matters—
    (a)   the object of the company;
    (b)   any matter relating to the procedure for the appointment, retirement and removal of any director of the company for which provision is not made in these Regulations or FSA rules; and
    (c)   the currency in which the accounts of the company are to be prepared.

(2)   The provision referred to in sub-paragraph (1)(a) as to the object of an open-ended investment company must state clearly the kind of property in which the company is to invest and must state that the object of the company is to invest in property of that kind with the aim of spreading investment risk and giving its shareholders the benefit of the results of the management of that property.

4.—(1)   The instrument of incorporation must also contain provision as to the following matters—
    (a)   the name of the company;
    (b)   the category, as specified in FSA rules, to which the company belongs;
    (c)   the maximum and minimum sizes of the company's capital;
    (d)   in the case of an umbrella company, the investment objectives applicable to each part of the scheme property that is pooled separately;
    (e)   the classes of shares that the company may issue indicating, in the case of an umbrella company, which class or classes of shares may be issued in respect of each part of the scheme property that is pooled separately;
    (f)   the rights attaching to shares of each class (including any provision for the expression in two denominations of such rights);
    (g)   if the company is to be able to issue bearer shares, a statement to that effect together with details of any limitations on the classes of the company's shares which are to include bearer shares;
    (h)   in the case of a company which is a participating issuer, a statement to that effect together with an indication of any class of shares in the company which is a class of participating securities;
    (i)   if the company is to dispense with the requirements of regulation 46, the details of any substituted procedures for evidencing title to the company's shares; and
    (j)   the form, custody and use of the company's common seal (if any).

(2)   For the purposes of sub-paragraph (1)(c), the size at any time of a company's capital is to be taken to be the value at that time, as determined in accordance with FSA rules, of the scheme property of the company less the liabilities of the company.

5.—(1)   Once an authorisation order has been made in respect of a company, no amendment may be made to the statements contained in the company's instrument of incorporation which are required by paragraph 2.

(2) Subject to sub-paragraph (1) and to any restriction imposed by FSA rules, a company may amend any provision which is contained in its instrument of incorporation.

(3) No amendment to a provision which is contained in a company's instrument of incorporation by virtue of paragraph 3 may be made unless it has been approved by the shareholders of the company in general meeting.

6.—(1) The provisions of a company's instrument of incorporation are binding on the officers and depositary of the company and on each of its shareholders; and all such persons (but no others) are to be taken to have notice of the provisions of the instrument.

(2) A person is not debarred from obtaining damages or other compensation from a company by reason only of his holding or having held shares in the company.

[2325]

SCHEDULE 3
REGISTER OF SHAREHOLDERS

Regulation 49

General

1.—(1) Subject to sub-paragraph (2), every open-ended investment company must keep a register of persons who hold shares in the company.

(2) Except to the extent that the aggregate numbers of shares mentioned in paragraphs 5(1)(b) and 7 include bearer shares, nothing in this Schedule requires any entry to be made in the register in respect of bearer shares.

2.—(1) ... , the register of shareholders is prima facie evidence of any matters which are by these Regulations directed or authorised to be contained in it.

(2) ...

3.—(1) In the case of companies registered in England and Wales, no notice of any trust, express, implied or constructive, is to be entered on the company's register or be receivable by the company.

(2) A company must exercise all due diligence and take all reasonable steps to ensure that the information contained in the register is at all times complete and up to date.

Contents

5.—(1) The register of shareholders must contain an entry consisting of—
    (a) the name of the designated person;
    (b) a statement of the aggregate number of all shares in the company held by that person; ...
    (c) ...

(2) In sub-paragraph (1), for the purposes of sub-paragraph (b), the designated person is to be taken as holding all shares in the company which are in issue and in respect of which no other person's name is entered on the register.

(3) The statements referred to in sub-paragraph (1)(b) and (c) must be up-dated at least once a day.

6.—(1) This paragraph does not apply to any issue or transfer of shares to the designated person.

(2) Where a company issues a share to any person and the name of that person is not already entered on the register, the company must enter his name on the register.

(3) In respect of any person whose name is entered on the register in accordance with sub-paragraph (2) or paragraph 6 of Schedule 4 to these Regulations, the register must contain an entry consisting of—
    (a) the address of the shareholder;
    (b) the date on which the shareholder's name was entered on the register;
    (c) a statement of the aggregate number of shares held by the shareholder, distinguishing each share by its number (if it has one) and, where the company has more than one class of shares, by its class; ...
    (d) ...

7. The register of shareholders must contain a monthly statement of the aggregate number of all the bearer shares in issue except for any bearer shares in issue which, at the time when the statement is made, are held by the designated person.

8.—(1) This paragraph applies where the aggregate number of shares referred to in paragraphs 5 to 7 includes any shares to which attach rights expressed in two denominations.

(2) In respect of each class of shares to which are attached rights expressed in two denominations, the number of shares of that class held by any person referred to in paragraph 5 or 6, or the number of bearer shares of that class referred to in paragraph 7, is to be taken to be the total of—

$N + n/p$

(3)　In sub-paragraph (2)—
  (a)　N is the relevant number of larger denomination shares of that class;
  (b)　n is the relevant number of smaller denomination shares of that class; and
  (c)　p is the number of smaller denomination shares of that class that are equivalent to one larger denomination share of that class,

(4)　Nothing in these Regulations is to be taken as preventing the total arrived at under sub-paragraph (2) being expressed on the register as a single entry representing the result derived from the formula set out in that sub-paragraph.

Location

9.　The register of shareholders of a company must be kept at its head office, except that—
  (a)　if the work of making it up is done at another office of the company, it may be kept there; and
  (b)　if the company arranges with some other person for the making up of the register to be undertaken on its behalf by that other person, it may be kept at the office of the other person at which the work is being done.

Index

10.—(1)　Every company must keep an index of the names of the holders of its registered shares.

(2)　The index must contain, in respect of each shareholder, a sufficient indication to enable the account of that shareholder in the register to be readily found.

(3)　The index must be at all times kept at the same place as the register of shareholders.

(4)　Not later than 14 days after the date on which any alteration is made to the register of shareholders, the company must make any necessary alteration in the index.

Inspection

11.—(1)　Subject to regulation 50 and to FSA rules, the register of shareholders and the index of names must be open to the inspection of any shareholder (including any holder of bearer shares) without charge.

(2)　Any shareholder may require a copy of the entries on the register relating to him and the company must cause any copy so required by a person to be sent to him free of charge.

(3)　If an inspection required under this paragraph is refused, or if a copy so required is not sent, the court may by order compel an immediate inspection of the register and index, or direct that the copy required be sent to the person requiring it.

Agent's default

12.—(1)　Sub-paragraphs (2) and (4) apply where, in accordance with paragraph 9(b), the register of shareholders is kept at the office of some person other than the company and by reason of any default of his the company fails to comply with any of the requirements of paragraph 10 or 11.

(2)　In a case to which this sub-paragraph applies, the person at whose office the register of shareholders is kept is guilty of an offence if he knowingly or recklessly authorises or permits the default in question.

(3)　A person guilty of an offence under sub-paragraph (2) is liable in respect of each default on summary conviction to a fine not exceeding level 1 on the standard scale.

(4)　The power of the court under paragraph 11(3) extends to the making of orders directed to the person at whose office the register of shareholders is kept and to any officer or employee of his.

[2326]

NOTES

Para 2: words omitted from sub-para (1) and the whole of sub-para (2) revoked by the Uncertificated Securities Regulations 2001, SI 2001/3755, regs 51, 52(4), Sch 7, Pt 2, para 24(c), as from 26 November 2001.

Para 5: sub-para (1)(c) and the word immediately preceding it revoked by SI 2001/3755, reg 52(4), as from 26 November 2001.

Para 6: sub-para (3)(d) and the word immediately preceding it revoked by SI 2001/3755, reg 52(4), as from 26 November 2001.

SCHEDULE 4
SHARE TRANSFERS

Regulation 52

General

1.   The instrument of incorporation of a company may contain provision as to share transfers in respect of any matter for which provision is not made in these Regulations or FSA rules.

2.   Where any shares are transferred to the company, the company must cancel those shares.

3.   ....

Transfer of registered shares

4.—(1)   Where a transfer of shares is made by the person (if any) who is designated in the company's instrument of incorporation for the purposes of this paragraph, the company may not register the transfer unless such evidence as the company may require to prove that the transfer has taken place has been delivered to the company.

(2)   Where for any reason a person ceases to be designated for the purposes of this paragraph—

    (a)   any shares held by that person which are not disposed of on or before his ceasing to be so designated are to be deemed to be the subject of a new transfer to him which takes effect immediately after he ceases to be so designated; and

    (b)   the company must make such adjustments to the register as are necessary to reflect his change of circumstances.

5.—(1)   Except in the case of any transfer of shares referred to in paragraph 4, the company may not register any transfer unless the transfer documents relating to that transfer have been delivered to the company.

(2)   No share certificate has to be delivered by virtue of sub-paragraph (1) in any case where shares are transferred by a nominee of a recognised investment exchange who is designated for the purposes of regulation 47(6) in the rules of the investment exchange in question.

(3)   In these Regulations "transfer documents", in relation to any transfer of registered shares, means—

    (a)   a stock transfer within the meaning of the Stock Transfer Act 1963 which complies with the requirements of that Act as to the execution and contents of a stock transfer or such other instrument of transfer as is authorised by, and completed and executed in accordance with any requirements in, the company's instrument of incorporation;

    (b)   except in a case falling within paragraph (3) or (4) of regulation 47, a share certificate relating to the shares in question;

    (c)   in a case falling within paragraph (3) of regulation 47, such other evidence of title to those shares as is required by the instrument of incorporation of the company; and

    (d)   such other evidence (if any) as the company may require to prove the right of the transferor to transfer the shares in question.

6.   In the case of any transfer of shares which meets the requirements of paragraph 4 or 5, the company must—

    (a)   register the transfer; and

    (b)   where the name of the transferee is not already entered on the register, enter that name on the register.

7.—(1)   A company may, before the end of the period of 21 days commencing with the date of receipt of the transfer documents relating to any transfer of shares, refuse to register the transfer if—

    (a)   there exists a minimum requirement as to the number or value of shares that must be held by any shareholder of the company and the transfer would result in either the transferor or transferee holding less than the required minimum; or

    (b)   the transfer would result in a contravention of any provision of the company's instrument of incorporation or would produce a result inconsistent with any provision of the company's prospectus.

(2)   A company must give the transferee written notice of any refusal to register a transfer of shares.

(3)   Nothing in these Regulations requires a company to register a transfer or give notice to any person of a refusal to register a transfer where registering the transfer or giving the notice would result in a contravention of any provision of law (including any law that is for the time being in force in a country or territory outside the United Kingdom).

8.—(1)   Where, in respect of any transfer of shares, the company certifies that it has received the transfer documents referred to in paragraph 5(3)(b) or (c) (as the case may be), that certification is to be taken as a representation by the company to any person acting on the faith of the certification that there has been produced to the company such evidence as on its face shows a prima facie title to the shares in the transferor named in the instrument of transfer.

PART III

STATUTORY INSTRUMENTS

(2)   For the purposes of sub-paragraph (1), a certification is made by a company if the instrument of transfer—

(a)   bears the words "certificate lodged" (or words to the like effect); and

(b)   is signed by a person acting under authority (whether express or implied) given by the company to issue and sign such certifications.

(3)   A certification under sub-paragraph (1) is not to be taken as a representation that the transferor has any title to the shares in question.

(4)   Where a person acts on the faith of a false certification by a company which is made negligently or fraudulently, the company is liable to pay to that person any damages sustained by him.

Transfer of bearer shares

9.   A transfer of title to any bearer share in a company is effected by the transfer from one person to another of the instrument mentioned in regulation 48 which relates to that share.

10.   Where the holder of bearer shares proposes to transfer to another person a number of shares which is less than the number specified in the instrument relating to those shares, he may only do so if he surrenders the instrument to the company and obtains a new instrument specifying the number of shares to be transferred.

Miscellaneous

11.   Nothing in the preceding provisions of this Schedule prejudices any power of the company to register as shareholder any person to whom the right to any shares in the company has been transmitted by operation of law.

12.   A transfer of registered shares that are held by a deceased person at the time of his death which is made by his personal representative is as valid as if the personal representative had been the holder of the shares at the time of the execution of the instrument of transfer.

13.   On the death of any one of the joint holders of any shares, the survivor is to be the only person recognised by the company as having any title to or any interest in those shares.

[2327]

NOTES

Para 3: revoked by the Uncertificated Securities Regulations 2001, SI 2001/3755, reg 52(4), as from 26 November 2001.

SCHEDULE 5
AUDITORS

Regulation 69

Eligibility

1.   No person is eligible for appointment as auditor of an open-ended investment company unless he is [eligible for appointment as a statutory auditor under Part 42 of the Companies Act 2006].

2.—(1)   A person is ineligible for appointment as auditor of an open-ended investment company if he is—

(a)   an officer or employee of the company; or

(b)   a partner or employee of such a person, or a partnership of which such a person is a partner.

(2)   For the purposes of sub-paragraph (1), an auditor of a company is not to be regarded as an officer or employee of the company.

[(3)   A person is also ineligible for appointment if there exists between that person, or any associate of that person, and the company a connection of any such description as may be specified by regulations made by the Secretary of State under section 1214(4) of the Companies Act 2006.

(4)   In sub-paragraph (3) "associate" has the same meaning as in Part 42 of that Act (see section 1260 of that Act).

(5)   The power of the Secretary of State to make regulations under section 1214(4) of that Act for the purposes of subsection (1) of that section in relation to statutory auditors is exercisable, subject to the same conditions, for the purposes of sub-paragraph (3) above in relation to auditors of open-ended investment companies.]

3.—(1)   No person is to act as auditor of a company if he is ineligible for appointment to the office.

(2)   If during his term of office an auditor of a company becomes ineligible for appointment to the office, he must thereupon vacate office and give notice in writing to the company concerned that he has vacated it by reason of ineligibility.

(3)   A person who acts as auditor of a company in contravention of sub-paragraph (1) or fails to give notice of vacating his office as required by sub-paragraph (2) is guilty of an offence and liable—

    (a)   on conviction on indictment, to a fine;

    (b)   on summary conviction, to a fine not exceeding the statutory maximum.

(4)   In the case of continued contravention he is liable on a second or subsequent summary conviction (instead of the fine mentioned in sub-paragraph (3)(b)) to a fine not exceeding £100 in respect of each day on which the contravention is continued.

(5)   In proceedings against a person for an offence under this paragraph it is a defence for him to show that he did not know and had no reason to believe that he was, or had become, ineligible for appointment.

Appointment

4.—(1)   Every company must appoint an auditor or auditors in accordance with this paragraph.

(2)   [Subject to sub-paragraphs (6) and (7), a company] must, at each general meeting at which the company's annual report is laid, appoint an auditor or auditors to hold office from the conclusion of that meeting until the conclusion of the next general meeting at which an annual report is laid.

(3)   [Subject to sub-paragraph (6), the first] auditors of a company may be appointed by the directors of the company at any time before the first general meeting of the company at which an annual report is laid; and auditors so appointed are to hold office until the conclusion of that meeting.

(4)   Where no appointment is made under sub-paragraph (3), the first auditors of any company may be appointed by the company in general meeting.

(5)   No rules made under section 340 of the Act (appointment of auditors) apply in relation to open-ended investment companies.

[(6)   On the date on which the holding of an annual general meeting is dispensed with in accordance with regulation 37A, any auditor or auditors appointed in accordance with sub-paragraph (2) or (3) ceases to hold office and the directors must forthwith re-appoint the auditor or auditors or appoint a new auditor or auditors.]

[(7)   The directors of any company which does not hold annual general meetings must appoint the auditor or auditors.]

5.   If, in any case, no auditors are appointed as required in paragraph 4, the Authority may appoint a person to fill the vacancy.

6.—(1)   The directors of a company, or the company in general meeting, may fill a casual vacancy in the office of auditor.

(2)   While such a vacancy continues, any surviving or continuing auditor or auditors may continue to act.

7.—(1)   Sub-paragraphs (2) to (5) apply to the appointment, as auditor of a company, of a partnership constituted under the law of England and Wales or Northern Ireland, or under the law of any country or territory in which a partnership is not a legal person; and sub-paragraphs (3) to (5) apply to the appointment as such an auditor of a partnership constituted under the law of Scotland, or under the law of any country or territory in which an partnership is a legal person.

(2)   The appointment is, unless the contrary intention appears, an appointment of the partnership as such and not of the partners.

(3)   Where the partnership ceases, the appointment is to be treated as extending to—

    (a)   any partnership which succeeds to the practice of that partnership and is eligible for the appointment; and

    (b)   any person who succeeds to that practice having previously carried it on in partnership and is eligible for the appointment.

(4)   For this purpose a partnership is to be regarded as succeeding to the practice of another partnership only if the members of the successor partnership are substantially the same as those of the former partnership; and a partnership or other person is to be regarded as succeeding to the practice of a partnership only if it or he succeeds to the whole or substantially the whole of the business of the former partnership.

(5)   Where the partnership ceases and no person succeeds to the appointment under sub-paragraph (3), the appointment may with the consent of the company be treated as extending to a partnership or other person eligible for the appointment who succeeds to the business of the former partnership or to such part of it as is agreed by the company to be treated as comprising the appointment.

Rights

8.—(1)   The auditors of a company have a right of access at all times to the company's books, accounts and vouchers and are entitled to require from the company's officers such information and explanations as they think necessary for the performance of their duties as auditors.

(2)   An officer of a company commits an offence if he knowingly or recklessly makes to the company's auditors a statement (whether written or oral) which—
   (a)   conveys or purports to convey any information or explanations which the auditors require, or are entitled to require, as auditors of the company; and
   (b)   is misleading, false or deceptive in a material particular.

(3)   A person guilty of an offence under sub-paragraph (2) is liable—
   (a)   on conviction on indictment, to imprisonment not exceeding a term of two years or to a fine or to both;
   (b)   on summary conviction, to imprisonment not exceeding a term of three months or to a fine not exceeding the statutory maximum or to both.

9.—(1)   The auditors of a company are entitled—
   (a)   to receive all such notices of, and other communications relating to, any general meeting of the company as a shareholder of the company is entitled to receive;
   (b)   to attend any general meeting of the company; and
   (c)   to be heard at any general meeting which they attend on any part of the business of the meeting which concerns them as auditors.

(2)   The right to attend and be heard at a meeting is exercisable in the case of a body corporate or partnership by an individual authorised by it in writing to act as its representative at the meeting.

Remuneration

10.—(1)   The remuneration of auditors of a company who are appointed by the company in general meeting must be fixed by the company in general meeting or in such manner as the company in general meeting may decide.

(2)   The remuneration of auditors who are appointed by the directors or the Authority must, as the case may be, be fixed by the directors or the Authority (and be payable by the company even where it is fixed by the Authority).

11.—(1)   Subject to sub-paragraph (2), the power of the Secretary of State to make regulations under [section 494 of the Companies Act 2006] (remuneration of auditors or their associates for non-audit work) in relation to company auditors is to be exercisable in relation to auditors of open-ended investment companies—
   (a)   for like purposes; and
   (b)   subject to the same conditions.

(2)   For the purposes of the exercise of the power to make regulations under [section 494 of the Companies Act 2006], as extended by sub-paragraph (1), the reference in [section 494(4)] to a note to a company's accounts is to be taken to be a reference to the annual report of an open-ended investment company.

Removal

12.—(1)   A company may by resolution remove an auditor from office notwithstanding anything in any agreement between it and him.

(2)   Where a resolution removing an auditor is passed at a general meeting of a company, the company must, not later than 14 days after the holding of the meeting, notify the Authority of the passing of the resolution.

(3)   Nothing in this paragraph is to be taken as depriving a person removed under it of compensation or damages payable to him in respect of the termination of his appointment as auditor or of any appointment terminating with that as auditor.

Rights on removal or non-reappointment

13.—(1)   A resolution at a general meeting of a company—
   (a)   removing an auditor before the expiration of his period of office; or
   (b)   appointing as auditor a person other than the retiring auditor;
is not effective unless notice of the intention to move it has been given to the open-ended investment company at least 28 days before the meeting at which it is moved.

(2)   On receipt of notice of such an intended resolution, the company must forthwith send a copy to the person proposed to be removed or, as the case may be, to the person proposed to be appointed and to the retiring auditor.

(3)   The auditor proposed to be removed or, as the case may be, the retiring auditor may make with respect to the intended resolution representations in writing to the company (not exceeding a reasonable length) and request their notification to the shareholders of the company.

(4)   The company must (unless the representations are received by the company too late for it to do so)—

(a)   in any notice of the resolution given to the shareholders of the company, state the fact of the representations having been made;

(b)   send a copy of the representations to each of the shareholders whose name appears on the register of shareholders (other than the designated person) and to whom notice of the meeting is or has been sent;

(c)   take such steps as FSA rules may require for the purpose of bringing the fact that the representations have been made to the attention of the holders of any bearer shares; and

(d)   at the request of any holder of bearer shares, provide a copy of the representations.

(5)   If a copy of any such representations is not sent out as required because they were received too late or because of the company's default or if, for either of those reasons, any steps required by sub-paragraph (4)(c) or (d) are not taken, the auditor may (without prejudice to his right to be heard orally) require that the representations be read out at the meeting.

(6)   Copies of the representations need not be sent out, the steps required by sub-paragraph (4)(c) or (d) need not be taken and the representations need not be read out at the meeting if, on the application of the company or any other person claiming to be aggrieved, the court is satisfied that the rights conferred by this paragraph are being abused to secure needless publicity for defamatory matter; and the court may order the costs of the company on such an application to be paid in whole or in part by the auditor, notwithstanding that he is not a party to the application.

14.—(1)   An auditor who has been removed from office has, notwithstanding his removal, the rights conferred by paragraph 9 in relation to any general meeting of the company at which his term of office would otherwise have expired or at which it is proposed to fill the vacancy caused by his removal.

(2)   The reference in paragraph 9 to business concerning the auditors as auditors is to be construed in relation to an auditor who has been removed from office as a reference to business concerning him as former auditor.

Resignation

15.—(1)   An auditor of a company may resign his office by depositing a notice in writing to that effect at the company's head office.

(2)   Such a notice is not effective unless it is accompanied by the statement required by paragraph 18.

(3)   An effective notice of resignation operates to bring the auditor's term of office to an end as of the date on which the notice is deposited or on such later date as may be specified in it.

(4)   The company must, not later than 14 days after the deposit of a notice of resignation, send a copy of the notice to the Authority.

16.—(1)   This paragraph applies where a notice of resignation of an auditor is accompanied by a statement of circumstances which he considers ought to be brought to the attention of the shareholders or creditors of the company.

(2)   An auditor may deposit with the notice a signed requisition that a general meeting of the company be convened forthwith for the purpose of receiving and considering such explanation of the circumstances connected with his resignation as he may wish to place before the meeting.

(3)   The company must, not later than 21 days after the date of the deposit of a requisition under this paragraph, proceed to convene a meeting for a day not later than 28 days after the date on which the notice convening the meeting is given.

(4)   The auditor may request the company to circulate a statement in writing (not exceeding a reasonable length) of the circumstances connected with his resignation to each of the shareholders of the company whose name appears on the register of shareholders (other than the designated person)—

(a)   before the meeting convened on his requisition; or

(b)   before any general meeting at which his term of office would otherwise have expired or at which it is proposed to fill the vacancy caused by his resignation;

and to take such steps as FSA rules may require for the purpose of bringing the fact that the statement has been made to the attention of the holders of any bearer shares.

(5)   The company must (unless the statement is received by it too late for it to do so)—

(a)   in any notice or advertisement of the meeting given or made to shareholders of the company, state the fact of the statement having been made;

(b)   send a copy of the statement to every shareholder of the company to whom notice of the meeting is or has been sent; and

(c)   at the request of any holder of bearer shares, provide a copy of the statement.

(6)   If a copy of the statement is not sent out or provided as required because it was received too late or because of the company's default the auditor may (without prejudice to his right to be heard orally) require that the statement be read out at the meeting.

(7)   Copies of a statement need not be sent out or provided and the statement need not be read out at the meeting if, on the application of the company or any other person claiming to be aggrieved, the court is satisfied that the rights conferred by this paragraph are being abused to secure needless publicity for defamatory matter; and the court may order the costs of the company on such an application to be paid in whole or in part by the auditor, notwithstanding that he is not a party to the application.

17.—(1)   An auditor who has resigned has, notwithstanding his removal, the rights conferred by paragraph 9 in relation to any such general meeting of the company as is mentioned in paragraph 16(4)(a) or (b).

(2)   The reference in paragraph 9 to business concerning the auditors as auditors is to be construed in relation to an auditor who has resigned as a reference to business concerning him as former auditor.

Statement by auditor ceasing to hold office

18.—(1)   Where an auditor ceases for any reason to hold office, he must deposit at the head office of the company a statement of any circumstances connected with his ceasing to hold office which he considers should be brought to the attention of the shareholders or creditors of the company or, if he considers that there are no such circumstances, a statement that there are none.

(2)   The statement must be deposited—
(a)   in the case of resignation, along with the notice of resignation;
(b)   in the case of failure to seek re-appointment, not less than 14 days before the end of the time allowed for next appointing auditors; and
(c)   in any other case, not later than the end of the period of 14 days beginning with the date on which he ceases to hold office.

(3)   If the statement is of circumstances which the auditor considers should be brought to the attention of the shareholders or creditors of the company, the company must, not later than 14 days after the deposit of the statement, either—
(a)   send a copy of the statement to each of the shareholders whose name appears on the register of shareholders (other than the designated person) and take such steps as FSA rules may require for the purpose of bringing the fact that the statement has been made to the attention of the holders of any bearer shares; or
(b)   apply to the court;
and, where an application is made under sub-paragraph (b), the company must notify the auditor.

(4)   Unless the auditor receives notice of an application to the court before the end of the period of 21 days beginning with the day on which he deposited the statement, he must, not later than seven days after the end of that period, send a copy of the statement to the Authority.

(5)   If the court is satisfied that the auditor is using the statement to secure needless publicity for defamatory matter—
(a)   it must direct that copies of the statement need not be sent out and that the steps required by FSA rules need not be taken; and
(b)   it may further order the company's costs on the application to be paid in whole or in part by the auditor notwithstanding that he is not a party to the application;
and the company must, not later than 14 days after the court's decision, take such steps in relation to a statement setting out the effect of the order as are required by sub-paragraph (3)(a) in relation to the statement deposited under sub-paragraph (1).

(6)   If the court is not so satisfied, the company must, not later than 14 days after the court's decision, send to each of the shareholders a copy of the auditor's statement and notify the auditor of the court's decision.

(7)   The auditor must, not later than 7 days after receiving such a notice, send a copy of the statement to the Authority.

(8)   Where notice of appeal is filed not later than 14 days after the court's decision, any reference to that decision in sub-paragraphs (5) and (6) is to be construed as a reference to the final determination or withdrawal of that appeal, as the case may be.

19.—(1)   If a person ceasing to hold office as auditor fails to comply with paragraph 18 he is guilty of an offence and liable—
(a)   on conviction on indictment, to a fine;
(b)   on summary conviction, to a fine not exceeding the statutory maximum.

(2)   In proceedings for an offence under sub-paragraph (1), it is a defence for the person charged to show that he took all reasonable steps and exercised all due diligence to avoid the commission of the offence.

20.   Section 249(1) of the Act (disqualification of auditor for breach of trust scheme rules) applies to a failure by an auditor to comply with a duty imposed on him by FSA rules as it applies to a breach of trust scheme rules.

[2328]

NOTES

Para 1: words in square brackets substituted (for the original words "also eligible under section 25 of the Companies Act 1989 for appointment as a company auditor") by the Companies Act 2006 (Consequential Amendments etc) Order 2008, SI 2008/948, art 3(1), Sch 1, Pt 1, para 28(1), (2), as from 6 April 2008 (for savings see art 6(4) of the 2008 Order which provides that where by virtue of any transitional provision, a provision of the Companies Act 2006 has effect only (a) on or after a specified date, or (b) in relation to matters occurring or arising on or after a specified date, any amendment substituting or inserting a reference to that provision has effect correspondingly).

Para 2: sub-paras (3)–(5) substituted, for original sub-para (3), by SI 2008/948, art 3(1), Sch 1, Pt 1, para 28(1), (3), as from 6 April 2008 (subject to savings as noted in the para 1 note above). The original sub-paragraph read as follows—

"(3)   The power of the Secretary of State to make regulations under section 27 of the Companies Act 1989 (ineligibility on ground of lack of independence) in relation to the appointment of company auditors is to be exercisable in relation to the appointment of auditors of open-ended investment companies—
     (a)   for like purposes; and
     (b)   subject to the same conditions.".

Para 4: words in square brackets in sub-paras (2), (3) substituted, and paras (6), (7) added, by the Open-Ended Investment Companies (Amendment) Regulations 2005, SI 2005/923, reg 2(1), (9), as from 6 April 2005.

Para 11: words in square brackets in sub-para (1), and words in first pair of square brackets in sub-para (2) substituted (for the original words "section 390B of the 1985 Act"), and words in second pair of square brackets in sub-para (2) substituted (for the original words "section 390B(3)"), by SI 2008/948, art 3(1), Sch 1, Pt 2, para 222, as from 6 April 2008 (subject to savings as noted in the para 1 note above).

SCHEDULE 6
MERGERS AND DIVISIONS

Regulation 70

1.   This Schedule applies to any reconstruction or amalgamation involving an open-ended investment company which takes the form of a scheme described in paragraph 4.

2.   An open-ended investment company may apply to the court under [section 896 or 899 of the Companies Act 2006] (power of company to compromise with creditors and members) [in respect of] a scheme falling within any of sub-paragraphs (a) to (c) of paragraph 4(1) where—
     (a)   the scheme in question involves a compromise or arrangement with its shareholders or creditors or any class of its shareholders or creditors; and
     (b)   the consideration for the transfer or each of the transfers envisaged by the scheme is to be—
          (i)   shares in the transferee company receivable by shareholders of the transferor company; or
          (ii)   where there is more than one transferor company and any one or more of them is a public company, shares in the transferee company receivable by shareholders or members of the transferor companies (as the case may be);
in each case with or without any cash payment to shareholders.

3.   A public company may apply to the court under [section 896 or 899 of the Companies Act 2006] [in respect of] a scheme falling within sub-paragraph (b) or (c) of paragraph 4(1) where—
     (a)   the scheme in question involves a compromise or arrangement with its members or creditors or any class of its members or creditors; and
     (b)   the consideration for the transfer or each of the transfers envisaged by the scheme is to be—
          (i)   shares in the transferee company receivable by members of the transferor company; or
          (ii)   where there is more than one transferor company and any one or more of them is an open-ended investment company, shares in the transferee company receivable by shareholders or members of the transferor companies (as the case may be),
in each case with or without any cash payment to shareholders.

4.—(1)   The schemes falling within this paragraph are—
     (a)   any scheme under which the undertaking, property and liabilities of an open-ended investment company are to be transferred to another such company, other than one formed for the purpose of, or in connection with the scheme;
     (b)   any scheme under which the undertaking, property and liabilities of two or more bodies corporate, each of which is either—

        (i)   an open-ended investment company; or
        (ii)   a public company,
are to be transferred to an open-ended investment company formed for the purpose of, or in connection with, the scheme;

   (c)   any scheme under which the undertaking, property and liabilities of an open-ended investment company or a public company are to be divided among and transferred to two or more open-ended investment companies whether or not formed for the purpose of, or in connection with, the scheme.

(2)   Nothing in this Schedule is to be taken as enabling the court to sanction a scheme under which the whole or any part of the undertaking, property or liabilities of an open-ended investment company may be transferred to any person other than another such company.

[5.   An application made by virtue of paragraph 2 or 3 shall be treated as one to which Part 27 of the Companies Act 2006 applies (mergers and divisions of public companies), and the provisions of that Part and Part 26 of that Act have effect accordingly, subject to paragraph 6.]

6.—(1)   [The provisions of the Companies Act 2006] referred to in paragraph 5 have effect with such modifications as are necessary or appropriate for the purposes of this Schedule.

(2)   In particular, any reference in those provisions to [a merger by absorption, a merger by formation of a new company or a division] is to be taken to be a reference to a scheme falling within sub-paragraph (a), (b) or (c) of paragraph 4(1).

(3)   Without prejudice to the generality of sub-paragraph (1), the following references in those provisions have effect as follows, unless the context otherwise requires—

   (a)   any reference to a scheme is to be taken to be a reference to a scheme falling within any of sub-paragraphs (a) to (c) of paragraph 4(1);

   (b)   any reference to a company is to be taken to be a reference to an open-ended investment company;

   (c)   any reference to members is to be taken to be a reference to shareholders of an open-ended investment company;

   (d)   any reference to the registered office of a company is to be taken to be a reference to the head office of an open-ended investment company;

   (e)   any reference to the memorandum and articles of a company is to be taken to be a reference to the instrument of incorporation of an open-ended investment company;

   (f)   any reference to a report under section 103 of the 1985 Act (non-cash consideration to be valued before allotment) is to be taken to be a reference to any report with respect to the valuation of any non-cash consideration given for shares in an open-ended investment company which may be required by FSA rules;

   (g)   any reference to annual accounts is to be taken to be a reference to the accounts contained in the annual report of an open-ended investment company;

   (h)   ...

   (i)   any reference to the requirements of [the Companies Act 2006] as to balance sheets forming part of a company's annual accounts is to be taken to be a reference to any requirements arising by virtue of FSA rules as to balance sheets drawn up for the purposes of the accounts contained in the annual report of an open-ended investment company;

   (j)   any reference to paid up capital is to be taken to be a reference to the share capital of an open-ended investment company.

                                                            [2329]

NOTES

Paras 2, 3: words in square brackets substituted by the Companies Act 2006 (Consequential Amendments etc) Order 2008, SI 2008/948, art 3(1), Sch 1, Pt 2, para 223(1)–(3), as from 6 April 2008.

Para 5: substituted by SI 2008/948, art 3(1), Sch 1, Pt 2, para 223(1), (4), as from 6 April 2008.

Para 6: words in square brackets substituted, and words omitted revoked by SI 2008/948, art 3(1), Sch 1, Pt 2, para 223(1), (5), as from 6 April 2008.

(*Sch 7 (Minor and Consequential Amendments) amends the Trustee Investments Act 1961, Sch 1, Pt III (repealed subject to savings), the Stock Transfer Act 1963, s 1, the Companies Act 1985, ss 26, 199, 209, 220, 718, and amended s 716 of that Act (repealed), the Company Directors Disqualification Act 1986, Sch 1, the Pension Schemes Act 1993, s 38, the Limited Liability Partnerships Act 2000, Schedule, and amended the Uncertificated Securities Regulations 1995, SI 1995/3272, regs 3, 19 (revoked).*)

FINANCIAL SERVICES AND MARKETS ACT 2000 (DISSOLUTION OF THE INSURANCE BROKERS REGISTRATION COUNCIL) (CONSEQUENTIAL PROVISIONS) ORDER 2001 (NOTE)

(SI 2001/1283)

NOTES
Made: 30 March 2001.
Authority: Financial Services and Markets Act 2000, ss 416(4), 428(3).
Commencement: 30 April 2001.
This Order makes provision consequential on the provisions of the Financial Services and Markets Act 2000, s 416 which repeal the Insurance Brokers (Registration) Act 1977 and dissolve the Insurance Brokers Registration Council. The relevant provisions of the Act were brought into force on 30 April 2001 by the Financial Services and Markets Act 2000 (Commencement No 2) Order 2001 (SI 2001/1282). The Grants Fund, comprising funds raised by levying practising insurance brokers and enrolled bodies, is transferred to the manager of the Investor Compensation Scheme established under section 54 of the Financial Services Act 1986. All other property, liabilities and rights to which the Council was entitled or subject immediately before 30 April 2001 transfer to the Treasury on that date. This Order also makes provision in respect of liabilities which the Council would have incurred if the Council had not been dissolved, legal proceedings to which the Council was, before 30 April 2001, a party and contracts, agreements and other instruments which relate to the property, rights and liabilities which, by virtue of this Order, become property, rights and liabilities of the Treasury. This Order also makes consequential amendments to other legislation which relates to the Council or which refers to the Insurance Brokers (Registration) Act 1977. The Order also permits the Treasury to disclose information which they acquire by virtue of this Order where the disclosure could have been made by the Council, but for its dissolution and the provisions of the Order.

[2330]

FINANCIAL SERVICES AND MARKETS ACT 2000 (SERVICE OF NOTICES) REGULATIONS 2001

(SI 2001/1420)

NOTES
Made: 10 April 2001.
Authority: Financial Services and Markets Act 2000, ss 414, 428(3).
Commencement: 18 June 2001.
These Regulations are reproduced as amended by: the Enterprise Act 2002; the Financial Services and Markets Act 2000 (Service of Notices) (Amendment) Regulations 2005, SI 2005/274.
Application of these Regulations to payment service providers: see the Payment Services Regulations 2009, SI 2009/209 at **[4387]**. In particular, see Sch 5, Pt 2 to those Regulations ("Application and Modification of Secondary Legislation").

1 Citation, commencement and interpretation

(1) These Regulations may be cited as the Financial Services and Markets Act 2000 (Service of Notices) Regulations 2001, and come into force on the day on which section 1 of the Act comes into force.

(2) In these Regulations—
"the Act" means the Financial Services and Markets Act 2000;
"appropriate person" means—
    (a)   an individual to whom a relevant document may be given, in accordance with regulation 3(1), in order to give that document to a person who is not an individual, or

    (b)   in the case of a relevant document given to an appointed representative, his principal;

"business day" means any day except Saturday, Sunday or a bank holiday, where "bank holiday" includes Christmas Day and Good Friday;

"document" means a notice, direction or document (as defined in section 417 of the Act) of any kind;

"host state regulator" has the meaning given in paragraph 11 of Schedule 3 to the Act;

"an investigating authority" means the Authority or the Secretary of State, as the case may be;

"investigator" means a person appointed by an investigating authority under section 97(2), 167, 168(3) or (5), 169(1)(b) or 284 of the Act, or under regulations made under section 262 of the Act, to carry out an investigation;

"nominee", in relation to any person to whom a document is to be given ("A"), means a person ("B") who is authorised for the time being to receive relevant documents on behalf of A, to whom relevant documents may be given—

    (a)   if A has notified the Authority in writing that B is so authorised, by any relevant authority, or

    (b)   if A has notified a relevant authority in writing that B is so authorised, by that relevant authority;

"ombudsman" has the meaning given in paragraph 1 of Schedule 17 to the Act;

"relevant authority" means—

    (a)   the Authority,

    (b)   the Secretary of State,

    (c)   the [Office of Fair Trading],

    (d)   an investigator,

    (e)   the scheme manager,

    (f)   the scheme operator, or

    (g)   an ombudsman;

"a relevant document" means—

    (a)   a document in relation to which a provision of or made under the Act (other than a provision of or made under Part IX or Part XXIV of the Act) requires a document of that kind to be given, or

    (b)   where a provision of or made under the Act (other than a provision of or made under Part IX or Part XXIV) authorises the imposition of a requirement, a document by which such a requirement is imposed.

(3)   For the purposes of these Regulations, the scheme operator and ombudsmen are treated as the same relevant authority (with the effect, in particular, that a document given to one is to be treated as also given to the other).

(4)   In these Regulations references to a requirement to give any document apply however the requirement is expressed (and so, in particular, include any requirement for a document to be served or sent).

(5)   For the purposes of these Regulations, writing includes any means of electronic communication which may be processed to produce a legible text.

(6)   These Regulations have effect subject to any contrary provision made by a relevant authority under the Act with respect to the service of documents.

            [2331]

NOTES

Para (2): words in square brackets in definition "relevant authority" substituted by virtue of the Enterprise Act 2002, s 2(1), as from 1 April 2003.

2 Methods of service

(1)   This regulation has effect in relation to any relevant document given by a relevant authority to any person ("the recipient") other than a relevant authority.

(2)   Any such document must be given by one of the following methods—

    (a)   by delivering it to the recipient, the recipient's nominee or the appropriate person;

    (b)   by leaving it at the proper address of the recipient, the recipient's nominee or the appropriate person, determined in accordance with regulation 4;

    (c)   by posting it to that address; or

    (d)   by transmitting it by fax or other means of electronic communication to the recipient, the recipient's nominee or the appropriate person, in accordance with regulation 5.

(3)   For the purposes of this regulation, "posting" a relevant document means sending that document pre-paid by a postal service which seeks to deliver documents by post within the United Kingdom no later than the next working day in all or the majority of cases, and to deliver by post outside the United Kingdom within such a period as is reasonable in all the circumstances.

            [2332]

3 Appropriate person to be served

(1)   A relevant document which is required to be given by a relevant authority to a person (other than a relevant authority) who is not an individual may—

(a)   where that person is a body corporate (other than a limited liability partnership), be given to the secretary or the clerk of that body, or to any person holding a senior position in that body;

(b)   where that person is a limited liability partnership, be given to any designated member, within the meaning given in section 8 of the Limited Liability Partnerships Act 2000;

(c)   where that person is a partnership (other than a limited liability partnership), be given to any partner;

(d)   where that person is an unincorporated association other than a partnership, be given to any member of the governing body of the association.

(2)   A relevant document which is required to be given to an appointed representative may be given to his principal.

(3)   For the purposes of this regulation, persons holding a senior position in a body corporate include—

(a)   a director, the treasurer, secretary or chief executive, and

(b)   a manager or other officer of that body who, in either case, has responsibility for the matter to which the relevant document relates.

[2333]

4 Proper address for service

(1)   The proper address—

(a)   in the case of any person who is required by any provision of or made under the Act to provide to the Authority an address of a place in the United Kingdom for the service of documents, is the address so provided, and

(b)   in the case of a person to whom no such requirement applies and subject to paragraph (3), is any current address provided by that person as an address for service of relevant documents.

(2)   In the case of any person who has not provided an address as mentioned in paragraph (1), the proper address is the last known address of that person (whether of his residence, or of a place where he carries on business or is employed), or any address under such of the following provisions as may be applicable—

(a)   in the case of a body corporate (other than a limited liability partnership), its secretary or its clerk, the address of its registered or principal office in the United Kingdom;

(b)   in the case of a limited liability partnership or any of its designated members, the address of its registered or principal office in the United Kingdom;

(c)   in the case of a partnership (other than a limited liability partnership) or any of its partners, the address of its principal office in the United Kingdom;

(d)   in the case of an unincorporated association other than a partnership, or its governing body, the address of its principal office in the United Kingdom;

(e)   in the case of a member of a designated professional body, if the member does not have a place of business in the United Kingdom, the address of that body.

(3)   Where the address mentioned in paragraph (1)(b) is situated in a country or territory other than the United Kingdom, a relevant authority may give a relevant document by leaving it at, or posting it to, any applicable address of a place in the United Kingdom falling within paragraph (2).

[2334]

5 Service by electronic means of communication

(1)   A relevant authority may give a relevant document by fax only if the person to whom it is to be given has indicated in writing to that authority (and has not withdrawn the indication)—

(a)   that he is willing to receive relevant documents by fax, and

(b)   the fax number to which such documents should be sent.

(2)   If a relevant authority gives a relevant document by fax it must, by the end of the business day following the day on which it did so, send a copy of that document to the person to whom the document is to be given by any method specified in regulation 2 other than fax.

(3)   A relevant authority may give a relevant document by any other electronic means of communication only if the person to whom it is to be given—

(a)   has indicated in writing to that authority (and has not withdrawn the indication) that he is willing to receive relevant documents by those means, and

(b)   has provided, in writing to that authority for this purpose, an e-mail address, or other electronic identification such as an ISDN or other telephonic link number.

(4)   A fax number, e-mail address or other electronic identification provided to the Authority for the purpose of accepting the service of relevant documents is sufficient indication, for any relevant authority, for the purposes of paragraph (1) or (3).

[2335]

6 Deemed service

(1)   Subject to regulation 11, a relevant document which is given by a relevant authority to any person in accordance with these Regulations is to be treated as having been received on the day shown in the table below.

Method of giving	Deemed day of receipt
Leaving the document at the proper address	The business day after the day on which it is left at the proper address
Post to an address in the United Kingdom	The second business day after posting
Post to an address in any EEA State (other than the United Kingdom)	The fifth business day after posting
Fax	The business day after the day on which the document is transmitted
Other electronic means of communication	The business day after the day on which the document is transmitted

(2)   Where a relevant document is given by fax, that document is to be treated as having been received on the deemed day of receipt of the fax, determined in accordance with paragraph (1), regardless of whether a relevant authority has sent a copy of that document in accordance with paragraph (2) of regulation 5.

[(3)   Where—

(a)   a notice given under section 53(4) (exercise of own-initiative power: procedure) of the Act states that a variation of an authorised person's Part IV permission takes effect immediately,

(b)   a notice given under section 78(2) (discontinuance or suspension: procedure) of the Act states that a discontinuance or suspension of the listing of any securities takes effect immediately, or

(c)   a notice given under section 259(3) (procedure on giving directions under section 257 and varying them on Authority's own initiative) of the Act, or under regulation 27 (procedure on giving directions under regulation 25 and varying them on Authority's own initiative) of the Open-Ended Investment Companies Regulations 2001 states that a direction to which it relates takes effect immediately,

that notice is to be treated as having been received at the time it is in fact received if that is earlier than the day on which paragraph (1) would otherwise require it to be treated as having been received.]

[2336]

NOTES

Para (3): added by the Financial Services and Markets Act 2000 (Service of Notices) (Amendment) Regulations 2005, SI 2005/274, reg 2, as from 6 April 2005.

7 Service on a relevant authority

(1)   Subject to paragraphs (2) and (3) and regulations 8 and 10, a relevant document which is to be given to a relevant authority may be given by any method of serving or transmitting documents.

(2)   Where a relevant document is given by delivering it to the relevant authority, it must be delivered—

(a)   to the employee or other individual with responsibility for the matter to which the document relates, if the identity of that individual is known, or

(b)   in any other case, to the published address of that authority.

(3)   Where a relevant document is given to a relevant authority by leaving it at, or posting it to, the address of a relevant authority, it must be left at or posted to the published address of that authority.

(4)   For the purposes of this regulation, "posting" a document means sending it by a pre-paid postal service.

[2337]

8   Electronic service on a relevant authority

(1)   Where a relevant document which is to be given to a relevant authority is given by fax or other electronic means it must be sent to a fax number, e-mail address or other electronic identification—

(a)   which has been notified to the sender by the relevant authority as the appropriate number, address or other electronic identification for the purpose of receiving relevant documents of the kind in question, or

(b)   in all other cases, which has been published by the relevant authority for the purpose of receiving relevant documents.

(2)   Where any provision of or made under the Act requires a person to give a relevant document to the Authority before the end of a specified period, that person may give that document by fax only if by the end of the business day following the day on which he did so, he sends a copy of that document to the Authority by any method other than fax.

[2338]

9   Day of service on a relevant authority

(1)   No relevant document which is to be given to a relevant authority is to be treated as given until it is received by that authority in legible form, and for the purposes of any provision of or made under the Act which requires a relevant authority to take any action within a specified period beginning with the day on which a document was received by that authority, that day is the day on which the document is actually received in legible form.

(2)   For the purposes of paragraph (1), where a relevant document is given by fax and a copy sent in accordance with paragraph (2) of regulation 8, that document is to be treated as given to the Authority on either the day on which the fax is actually received by the Authority or the day on which the copy is actually received by the Authority, whichever day is the earlier.

[2339]

10   Compliance with a requirement to serve a document on the Authority by a specified day

(1)   For the purposes of any provision of or made under the Act which requires a person to give a document to the Authority before the end of a specified period, that person is to be regarded as having complied with that requirement (irrespective of the day on which the document is in fact received by the Authority if it is sent by post, fax or other electronic means) if he sends the document to the Authority in accordance with any applicable directions before the end of the specified period or, where no such directions apply, if he—

(a)   delivers the document to an employee of the Authority with responsibility for the matter to which the document relates before the end of the specified period;

(b)   leaves the document at the Authority's address before the end of the specified period, and obtains a time stamped receipt;

(c)   posts the document to the Authority's address before the final day of the specified period;

(d)   sends the document to the Authority by fax before the end of the specified period, provided that he has also sent or subsequently sends a copy of that document in accordance with paragraph (2) of regulation 8; or

(e)   sends the document to the Authority by other electronic means of communication before the end of the specified period, and obtains electronic confirmation of receipt.

(2)   For the purposes of this regulation—

(a)   "posts" means—

(i)   where the person who is required to give a document is located in the United Kingdom, sending that document pre-paid by a postal service which seeks to deliver documents by post within the United Kingdom no later than the next working day in all or the majority of cases, and

(ii)   where the person who is required to give a document is located outside the United Kingdom, sending that document pre-paid by a postal service which seeks to deliver documents by post in the fastest time which is reasonable in the circumstances;

(b)   "applicable direction" means any direction given by the Authority under the Act which specifies the manner in which the relevant document in question is to be given.

[2340]

11   Day of service on a host state regulator

No relevant document is to be treated as given by a relevant authority to a host state regulator until it is received by that regulator.

[2341]

PART III
STATUTORY INSTRUMENTS

FINANCIAL SERVICES AND MARKETS ACT 2000
(COMPENSATION SCHEME: ELECTING PARTICIPANTS)
REGULATIONS 2001

(SI 2001/1783)

NOTES
Made: 9 May 2001.
Authority: Financial Services and Markets Act 2000, ss 213(10), 214(5), 224(4), 417(1), 428(3).
Commencement: 18 June 2001.
These Regulations are reproduced as amended by: the Financial Services and Markets Act 2000
(Regulated Activities) (Amendment) (No 2) Order 2003, SI 2003/1476; the Collective Investment Schemes
(Miscellaneous Amendments) Regulations 2003, SI 2003/2066; the Capital Requirements Regulations 2006,
SI 2006/3221.
Modified in relation to Gibraltar by the Financial Services and Markets Act 2000 (Gibraltar) Order 2001,
SI 2001/3084 at **[2495]** et seq.

1 Citation, commencement and interpretation

(1)   These Regulations may be cited as the Financial Services and Markets Act 2000
(Compensation Scheme: Electing Participants) Regulations 2001 and come into force on 18th June
2001.

(2)   In these Regulations—
"branch"—

(a)   in relation to an investment firm, has the meaning given by Article 1.5 of the
investor-compensation schemes directive;

(b)   in relation to a credit institution, has the meaning given by Article 1.5 of the
deposit-guarantee schemes directive;

[(c)   in relation to a relevant management company, has the meaning given by
Article 1.5 of the investor-compensation schemes directive (as applied by
Article 5f.2 of the UCITS directive);]

"credit institution" has the meaning given by [Article 4(1)] of the banking consolidation
directive;

"deposit-guarantee schemes directive" means Council and European Parliament Directive
94/19/EC on deposit-guarantee schemes;

"depositor" has the same meaning as in the deposit-guarantee schemes directive;

"Financial Services Compensation Scheme" means the compensation scheme established
pursuant to Part XV of the Act;

"home State deposit-guarantee scheme" means—

(a)   in relation to a credit institution which is exempted by the EEA State in which
that institution has its head office from the obligation to belong to a deposit-
guarantee scheme by virtue of belonging to a system which protects the credit
institution as mentioned in Article 3 of the deposit-guarantee schemes directive,
that system; and

(b)   in all other cases, the deposit-guarantee scheme officially recognised by that EEA
State for the purposes of Article 3.1 of the deposit-guarantee schemes directive;

"home State investor-compensation scheme" means—

(a)   in relation to a credit institution which is exempted by the EEA State in which
that institution has its head office from the obligation to belong to an investor-
compensation scheme by virtue of Article 2.1 of the investor-compensation
schemes directive (participation in a system that protects the credit institution),
that system; and

(b)   in all other cases, the investor-compensation scheme officially recognised by that
EEA State for the purposes of Article 2.1 of the investor-compensation schemes
directive;

["insurance intermediary" means an insurance intermediary (within the meaning of
Article 2(5) of the insurance mediation directive) or a reinsurance intermediary (within the
meaning of Article 2(6) of that Directive);]

"investment firm" has the meaning given by Article 1.1 of the investor-compensation schemes
directive;

"investor" has the meaning given by Article 1.4 of the investor-compensation schemes
directive;

"investor-compensation schemes directive" means the Council and European Parliament
Directive 97/9/EC on investor-compensation schemes;

["relevant management company" means an EEA firm falling within paragraph 5(f) of
Schedule 3 to the Act which—

(a)   is authorised by its home state regulator to provide services of the kind specified by Article 5.3(a) of the UCITS directive (management of portfolios of investments); and

(b)   is providing those services in the United Kingdom].

[2342]

NOTES

Para (2): in definition "branch" sub-para (c) inserted, and definition "relevant management company" added, by the Collective Investment Schemes (Miscellaneous Amendments) Regulations 2003, SI 2003/2066, reg 7(a), as from 13 February 2004; words in square brackets in definition "credit institution" substituted by the Capital Requirements Regulations 2006, SI 2006/3221, reg 29(4), Sch 6, para 7, as from 1 January 2007; definition "insurance intermediary" inserted by the Financial Services and Markets Act 2000 (Regulated Activities) (Amendment) (No 2) Order 2003, SI 2003/1476, art 15(1), (2), as from 31 October 2004 (in so far as relating to contracts of long-term care insurance), and as from 14 January 2005 (otherwise) (for transitional provisions see arts 22–27 of that Order at **[2706]** et seq).

2 Persons not to be regarded as relevant persons

For the purposes of section 213(10) of the Act (certain persons not to be regarded as relevant persons unless they elect to participate), the following categories are prescribed—

(a)   any investment firm; ...

(b)   any credit institution[; ...

(c)   any insurance intermediary][; and

(d)   any relevant management company.]

[2343]

NOTES

Word omitted from para (a) revoked, and para (c) and the word immediately preceding it inserted, by the Financial Services and Markets Act 2000 (Regulated Activities) (Amendment) (No 2) Order 2003, SI 2003/1476, art 15(1), (3), as from 31 October 2004 (in so far as relating to contracts of long-term care insurance), and as from 14 January 2005 (otherwise) (for transitional provisions see arts 22–27 of that Order at **[2706]** et seq); word omitted from para (b) revoked, and para (d) and the word immediately preceding it inserted, by the Collective Investment Schemes (Miscellaneous Amendments) Regulations 2003, SI 2003/2066, reg 7(b), as from 13 February 2004.

3 Persons who may elect to participate

(1)   For the purposes of section 214(5) of the Act (persons who may elect to participate), the following categories are prescribed—

(a)   any investment firm [or relevant management company] which has established a branch in the United Kingdom in exercise of an EEA right and is a member of a home State investor-compensation scheme which meets the condition in paragraph (2); ...

(b)   any credit institution which has established a branch in the United Kingdom in exercise of an EEA right and is a member of a home State deposit-guarantee scheme which meets the condition in paragraph (3)[; and

(c)   any insurance intermediary which is not an investment firm or a credit institution].

(2)   The condition mentioned in paragraph (1)(a) is that the scope or level (including percentage) of the protection afforded to investors by the Financial Services Compensation Scheme exceeds that afforded by the home State investor-compensation scheme.

(3)   The condition mentioned in paragraph (1)(b) is that the scope or level (including percentage) of the protection afforded to depositors by the Financial Services Compensation Scheme exceeds that afforded by the home State deposit-guarantee scheme.

[2344]

NOTES

Para (1): words in square brackets in sub-para (a) inserted by the Collective Investment Schemes (Miscellaneous Amendments) Regulations 2003, SI 2003/2066, reg 7(c), as from 13 February 2004; word omitted from sub-para (a) revoked, and sub-para (c) and the word immediately preceding it inserted, by the Financial Services and Markets Act 2000 (Regulated Activities) (Amendment) (No 2) Order 2003, SI 2003/1476, art 15(1), (4), as from 31 October 2004 (in so far as relating to contracts of long-term care insurance), and as from 14 January 2005 (otherwise) (for transitional provisions see arts 22–27 of that Order at **[2706]** et seq).

4 Persons in respect of whom inspection under section 224 does not apply

For the purposes of section 224(4) of the Act (power to inspect documents held by Official Receiver), the following categories are prescribed—

(a)   any investment firm; ...

(b)   any credit institution[; ...

(c)   any insurance intermediary][; and

(d)   any relevant management company.]

[2345]

NOTES
Word omitted from para (a) revoked, and para (c) and the word immediately preceding it inserted, by the Financial Services and Markets Act 2000 (Regulated Activities) (Amendment) (No 2) Order 2003, SI 2003/1476, art 15(1), (5), as from 31 October 2004 (in so far as relating to contracts of long-term care insurance), and as from 14 January 2005 (otherwise) (for transitional provisions see arts 22–27 of that Order at [2706] et seq); word omitted from para (b) revoked, and para (d) and the word immediately preceding it inserted, by the Collective Investment Schemes (Miscellaneous Amendments) Regulations 2003, SI 2003/2066, reg 7(d), as from 13 February 2004.

FINANCIAL SERVICES AND MARKETS ACT 2000 (DISCLOSURE OF INFORMATION BY PRESCRIBED PERSONS) REGULATIONS 2001

(SI 2001/1857)

NOTES
Made: 10 May 2001.
Authority: Financial Services and Markets Act 2000, ss 353(1), 417(1).
Commencement: 18 June 2001.
These Regulations are reproduced as amended by: the Financial Services and Markets Act 2000 (Disclosure of Information by Prescribed Persons) (Amendment) Regulations 2005, SI 2005/272.

1 Citation and commencement

These Regulations may be cited as the Financial Services and Markets Act 2000 (Disclosure of Information by Prescribed Persons) Regulations 2001 and come into force on 18th June 2001.

[2346]

2 Interpretation

In these Regulations—
   "the Act" means the Financial Services and Markets Act 2000;
   "Schedule person" means a person referred to in the Schedule;
   "scheme person" means the scheme manager, the scheme operator, or a member of the panel
      of ombudsmen appointed by the scheme operator pursuant to paragraph 4 of Schedule 17 to
      the Act.

[2347]

3 Permitted disclosure

   (1)   Subject to paragraph (2), Schedule persons and scheme persons are permitted to disclose information to which this regulation applies—
   (a)   for the purpose of enabling or assisting them to discharge their functions under the Act, or any rules or regulations made thereunder; or
   (b)   to the Authority, for the purpose of enabling or assisting the Authority to discharge any of its public functions.

   (2)   Schedule persons are permitted to disclose information in accordance with paragraph (1)(b) only if—
   (a)   the disclosure is made in good faith; and
   (b)   the person disclosing the information reasonably believes that the information is relevant to the discharge of a public function by the Authority.

   (3)   This regulation applies to the following kinds of information—
   (a)   information received by Schedule persons or scheme persons for the purposes of, or in the discharge of, any functions conferred on them by or under the Act;
   (b)   other information received by Schedule persons if the information is, or would have been relevant to the performance of those functions; or
   (c)   the opinions of Schedule persons or scheme persons in relation to information falling within sub-paragraph (a) or (b).

   (4)   This regulation does not apply to confidential information within the meaning of section 348(2) of the Act.

[2348]

SCHEDULE

Regulation 2

A Schedule person is a person who is performing or has performed any of the following functions—

   (a)   the verification of information in a manner required by the Authority pursuant to section 165(6)(a) of the Act;

   (b)   the authentication of a document in a manner required by the Authority pursuant to section 165(6)(b) of the Act;

   (c)   the making of a report under section 166 of the Act;

[(ca) the conduct of an investigation under section 113(2) of the Act;]

   (d)   the conduct of an investigation under section 167, 168(3) or (5) or 169(1)(b) of the Act;

   (e)   the conduct of an investigation under section 284 of the Act;

[(ea) the conduct of an investigation under section 376(10) of the Act;]

   (f)   the conduct of an investigation pursuant to regulations made under section 262 of the Act.

[2349]

NOTES

Paras (ca), (ea) inserted by the Financial Services and Markets Act 2000 (Disclosure of Information by Prescribed Persons) (Amendment) Regulations 2005, SI 2005/272, reg 2, as from 6 April 2005.

FINANCIAL SERVICES AND MARKETS ACT 2000 (DISCLOSURE OF CONFIDENTIAL INFORMATION) REGULATIONS 2001

(SI 2001/2188)

NOTES

Made: 15 June 2001.

Authority: Financial Services and Markets Act 2000, ss 349(1)(b), (2), (3), 417(1), 426, 427, 428(3).

Commencement: 18 June 2001.

Transitional provisions: see the Financial Services and Markets Act 2000 (Consequential and Transitional Provisions) (Miscellaneous) (No 2) Order 2001, SI 2001/2659, art 7, which makes transitional modifications of the 2001 Regulations in relation to exemptions from restrictions on disclosure.

These Regulations are reproduced as amended by: the Enterprise Act 2002; the Financial Services and Markets Act 2000 (Disclosure of Confidential Information) (Amendment) Regulations 2001, SI 2001/3437; the Financial Services and Markets Act 2000 (Disclosure of Confidential Information) (Amendment) (No 2) Regulations 2001, SI 2001/3624; the Electronic Commerce Directive (Financial Services and Markets) Regulations 2002, SI 2002/1775; the Financial Services and Markets Act 2000 (Disclosure of Confidential Information) (Amendment) Regulations 2003, SI 2003/693; the Financial Services and Markets Act 2000 (Disclosure of Confidential Information) (Amendment) Regulations 2003, SI 2003/1092 (revoked); the Insurance Mediation Directive (Miscellaneous Amendments) Regulations 2003, SI 2003/1473; the Collective Investment Schemes (Miscellaneous Amendments) Regulations 2003, SI 2003/2066; the Financial Services and Markets Act 2000 (Disclosure of Confidential Information) (Amendment) (No 2) Regulations 2003, SI 2003/2174; the Financial Services and Markets Act 2000 (Disclosure of Confidential Information) (Amendment) (No 3) Regulations 2003, SI 2003/2817; the Financial Conglomerates and Other Financial Groups Regulations 2004, SI 2004/1862; the Life Assurance Consolidation Directive (Consequential Amendments) Regulations 2004, SI 2004/3379; the Financial Services and Markets Act 2000 (Disclosure of Confidential Information) (Amendment) Regulations 2005, SI 2005/3071; the Capital Requirements Regulations 2006, SI 2006/3221; the Financial Services and Markets Act 2000 (Disclosure of Confidential Information) (Amendment) Regulations 2006, SI 2006/3413; the Financial Services and Markets Act 2000 (Reinsurance Directive) Regulations 2007, SI 2007/3255.

Application of these Regulations to payment service providers: see the Payment Services Regulations 2009, SI 2009/209 at [4387]. In particular, see Sch 5, Pt 2 to those Regulations ("Application and Modification of Secondary Legislation").

ARRANGEMENT OF REGULATIONS

PART I
PRELIMINARY

PART II
DISCLOSURE OF CONFIDENTIAL INFORMATION GENERALLY

PART III
DISCLOSURE OF SINGLE MARKET DIRECTIVE INFORMATION

PART IV
DISCLOSURE OF CONFIDENTIAL INFORMATION NOT SUBJECT TO DIRECTIVE RESTRICTIONS

PART V
TRANSITIONAL PROVISIONS

SCHEDULES:

PART I
PRELIMINARY

1 Citation and Commencement

These Regulations may be cited as the Financial Services and Markets Act 2000 (Disclosure of Confidential Information) Regulations 2001 and come into force on 18th June 2001.

[2350]

2 Interpretation

In these Regulations—
    "the Act" means the Financial Services and Markets Act 2000;
    "Authority worker" means—
        (a)   a person who is or has been employed by the Authority; or
        (b)   an auditor or expert instructed by the Authority;
    ["conglomerates directive" means Directive 2002/87/EC of the European Parliament and of the Council of 16th December 2002 on the supplementary supervision of credit institutions, insurance undertakings and investment firms in a financial conglomerate and amending Council Directives 73/239/EEC, 79/267/EEC, 92/49/EEC, 92/96/EEC, 93/6/EEC, 93/22/EEC, and Directives 98/78/EC and 2000/12/EC of the European Parliament and of the Council;]
    "criminal investigation" means an investigation of any crime, including an investigation of any alleged or suspected crime and an investigation of whether a crime has been committed;
    "dependent territory" means the Channel Islands, the Isle of Man and any territory outside the British Islands for whose external relations the United Kingdom is responsible;
    "dependent territory regulatory authority" means an overseas regulatory authority which exercises its functions in, and in relation to, a dependent territory;
    "directive restrictions" means the restrictions imposed on the disclosure of information by [articles 54 and 58 of the markets in financial instruments directive], [Section 2 of Chapter 1 of Title V of the banking consolidation directive], [Articles 16 and 17 of Directive 2002/83/EC of the European Parliament and of the Council of 5th November 2002 concerning life assurance as amended by the conglomerates directive], article 16 of the third non-life insurance directive, [articles 24 to 30 of the reinsurance directive,] article 50 of the UCITS directive [… and article 9 of the insurance mediation directive];
    "disciplinary proceedings authority" means a person responsible for initiating prescribed disciplinary proceedings or determining the outcome of such proceedings;
    "EEA competent authority" means a competent authority of an EEA state other than the United Kingdom for the purposes of any of the single market directives, … … ;

"EEA regulatory authority" means an EEA competent authority or an overseas regulatory authority which exercises its functions in, and in relation to, an EEA State other than the United Kingdom;

"former regulated activities" means activities carried on before the coming into force of section 19 of the Act and which constitute—

    (a)   investment business within the meaning of the Financial Services Act 1986;

    (b)   deposit-taking business within the meaning of the Banking Act 1987;

    (c)   insurance business within the meaning of the Insurance Companies Act 1982; or

    (d)   insurance business within the meaning of the Friendly Societies Act 1992;

"former regulated person" means a person who, at any time before the coming into force of section 19 of the Act, was—

    (a)   authorised under section 3 or 4 of the Insurance Companies Act 1982;

    (b)   an authorised person within the meaning of the Financial Services Act 1986, or an appointed representative within the meaning of section 44 (appointed representatives) of that Act;

    (c)   an authorised institution within the meaning of the Banking Act 1987;

    (d)   a European institution within the meaning of the Banking Coordination (Second Council Directive) Regulations 1992;

    (e)   a European investment firm within the meaning of the Investment Services Regulations 1995;

    (f)   an EC company within the meaning of the Insurance Companies Act 1982 able to carry on direct insurance business through a branch in the United Kingdom, or provide insurance in the United Kingdom by virtue of paragraph 1 or 8 of Schedule 2F to that Act;

    (g)   a friendly society authorised or treated as authorised for the purposes of Part IV of the Friendly Societies Act 1992, or permitted by virtue of section 31(2) or (3) of that Act to carry on activities without authorisation under that Part; or

    (h)   a building society authorised or treated as authorised for the purposes of the Building Societies Act 1986;

.....

["markets in financial instruments directive information" means confidential information received by the Authority in the course of discharging its functions as an EEA competent authority under the markets in financial instruments directive;]

"non-EEA regulatory authority" means an overseas regulatory authority other than an EEA regulatory authority or a dependent territory regulatory authority;

"overseas regulatory authority" means—

    (a)   an authority in a country or territory outside the United Kingdom which exercises any function of a kind mentioned in section 195(4) of the Act; or

    (b)   an overseas investment exchange or overseas clearing house;

"prescribed disciplinary proceedings" means the disciplinary proceedings prescribed in Schedule 3;

"Secretary of State worker" means—

    (a)   a person who is or has been employed by the Secretary of State; or

    (b)   an auditor or expert instructed by the Secretary of State;

"single market directive information" means confidential information received by the Authority in the course of discharging its functions as the competent authority under any of the single market directives [(except for the markets in financial instruments directive)] [or the conglomerates directive];

[["the third non-life insurance directive"] has the meaning given to it by paragraph 3 of Schedule 3 to the Act;]

.....
.....

[2351]

NOTES

Definition "conglomerates directive", and words in second pair of square brackets in definition "single market directive information", inserted by the Financial Conglomerates and Other Financial Groups Regulations 2004, SI 2004/1862, reg 11, as from 10 August 2004.

In definition "directive restrictions" words in first pair of square brackets substituted by the Financial Services and Markets Act 2000 (Disclosure of Confidential Information) (Amendment) Regulations 2006, SI 2006/3413, regs 2, 3(a)(i), as from 1 November 2007; words in second pair of square brackets substituted by the Capital Requirements Regulations 2006, SI 2006/3221, reg 29(4), Sch 6, para 8(1), (2), as from 1 January 2007; words in third pair of square brackets substituted by the Life Assurance Consolidation Directive (Consequential Amendments) Regulations 2004, SI 2004/3379, reg 19(1), (2)(a), as from 11 January 2005; words in fourth pair of square brackets inserted by the Financial Services and Markets Act 2000 (Reinsurance Directive) Regulations 2007, SI 2007/3255, reg 3(1), (2), as from 10 December 2007; words in final pair of square brackets substituted by the Insurance Mediation Directive (Miscellaneous Amendments) Regulations 2003, SI 2003/1473, reg 10, as from 14 January 2005; words omitted revoked by SI 2006/3413, regs 2, 3(a)(ii), as from 20 January 2007.

First words omitted from definition "EEA competent authority", and definitions "the UCITS directive" and "UCITS directive information" (omitted), revoked by the Collective Investment Schemes (Miscellaneous Amendments) Regulations 2003, SI 2003/2066, reg 12(a), as from 13 February 2004.

Second words omitted from definition "EEA competent authority" revoked by the Financial Services and Markets Act 2000 (Disclosure of Confidential Information) (Amendment) Regulations 2006, SI 2006/3413, regs 2, 3(b), as from 20 January 2007.

Definition "listing particulars directive" (omitted) revoked by SI 2006/3413, regs 2, 3(c), as from 20 January 2007.

Definition "markets in financial instruments directive information", and words in first pair of square brackets in definition "single market directive information", inserted by SI 2006/3413, regs 2, 3(d), (e), as from 1 November 2007.

The final definition in square brackets was originally inserted (as the definitions "the third life insurance directive" and "the third non-life insurance directive") by the Financial Services and Markets Act 2000 (Disclosure of Confidential Information) (Amendment) Regulations 2003, SI 2003/693, reg 3(a), as from 3 April 2003; words in square brackets subsequently substituted by SI 2004/3379, reg 19(1), (2)(b), as from 11 January 2005.

PART II
DISCLOSURE OF CONFIDENTIAL INFORMATION GENERALLY

3 Disclosure by and to the Authority, the Secretary of State and the Treasury etc

(1)   A disclosure of confidential information is permitted when it is made to any person—

    (a)   by the Authority or an Authority worker for the purpose of enabling or assisting the person making the disclosure to discharge any public functions of the Authority or (if different) of the Authority worker;

    (b)   by the Secretary of State or a Secretary of State worker for the purpose of enabling or assisting the person making the disclosure to discharge any public functions of the Secretary of State or (if different) of the Secretary of State worker;

    (c)   by the Treasury for the purpose of enabling or assisting the Treasury to discharge any of their public functions.

(2)   A disclosure of confidential information is permitted when it is made by any primary recipient, or person obtaining the information directly or indirectly from a primary recipient, to the Authority, the Secretary of State or the Treasury for the purpose of enabling or assisting the Authority, the Secretary of State or the Treasury (as the case may be) to discharge any of its, his or their public functions.

(3)   Paragraphs (1) and (2) do not permit disclosure in contravention of any of the directive restrictions.

[2352]

4 Disclosure for the purposes of criminal proceedings and investigations

A primary recipient of confidential information, or a person obtaining such information directly or indirectly from a primary recipient, is permitted to disclose such information to any person—

    (a)   for the purposes of any criminal investigation whatever which is being or may be carried out, whether in the United Kingdom or elsewhere;

    (b)   for the purposes of any criminal proceedings whatever which have been or may be initiated, whether in the United Kingdom or elsewhere; or

    [(ba) for the purposes of any proceedings under Part 2, 3 or 4 of the Proceeds of Crime Act 2002 which have been, or may be initiated;]

    (c)   for the purpose of initiating or bringing to an end any such investigation or proceedings, or of facilitating a determination of whether it or they should be initiated or brought to an end.

[2353]

NOTES

Para (ba) inserted by the Financial Services and Markets Act 2000 (Disclosure of Confidential Information) (Amendment) (No 2) Regulations 2003, SI 2003/2174, regs 2, 4(a), as from 23 August 2003 (see further the note below).

Note that an identical para (ba) was originally inserted by the Financial Services and Markets Act 2000 (Disclosure of Confidential Information) (Amendment) Regulations 2003, SI 2003/1092, as from 2 May 2003. However, those Regulations were revoked by SI 2003/2174, as from 23 August 2003 due to a number of drafting errors contained in those Regulations. The para (ba) as inserted by SI 2003/1092 did not contain any such drafting error so, in effect, has been in operation since 2 May 2003.

---

5 Disclosure for the purposes of certain other proceedings

(1)   Subject to paragraphs (4) and (5), a primary recipient of confidential information, or a person obtaining such information directly or indirectly from a primary recipient, is permitted to disclose such information to—

   (a)   a person mentioned in paragraph (3) for the purpose of initiating proceedings to which this regulation applies, or of facilitating a determination of whether they should be initiated; or

   (b)   any person for the purposes of proceedings to which this regulation applies and which have been initiated, or for the purpose of bringing to an end such proceedings, or of facilitating a determination of whether they should be brought to an end.

(2)   A person mentioned in paragraph (3) (or a person who is employed by the Authority or the Secretary of State) is permitted to disclose confidential information to any person for a purpose mentioned in paragraph (1)(a).

(3)   The persons referred to in paragraphs (1)(a) and (2) are—

   (a)   the Authority;

   (b)   the Secretary of State; and

   (c)   the Department of Enterprise, Trade and Investment in Northern Ireland.

(4)   This regulation does not permit the disclosure of information with a view to the institution of, or in connection with, proceedings of the kind referred to in paragraph (6)(e) to the extent that—

   (a)   the information relates to an authorised person, former authorised person or former regulated person ("A");

   (b)   the information also relates to another person ("B") who, to the knowledge of the primary recipient (or person obtaining confidential information directly or indirectly from him), is or has been involved in an attempt to rescue A, or A's business, from insolvency or impending insolvency; and

   (c)   B is not a director, controller or manager of A.

(5)   This regulation does not permit disclosure in contravention of any of the directive restrictions.

(6)   The proceedings to which this regulation applies are—

   (a)   civil proceedings arising under or by virtue of the Act, an enactment referred to in section 338 of the Act, the Banking Act 1979, the Friendly Societies Act 1974, the Insurance Companies Act 1982, the Financial Services Act 1986, the Building Societies Act 1986, the Banking Act 1987, the Friendly Societies Act 1992 or the Investment Services Regulations 1995;

   (b)   proceedings before the Tribunal;

   (c)   any other civil proceedings to which the Authority is, or is proposed to be, a party;

   (d)   proceedings under section 7 or 8 of the Company Directors Disqualification Act 1986 or article 10 or 11 of the Companies (Northern Ireland) Order 1989 in respect of a director or former director of an authorised person, former authorised person or former regulated person; or

   (e)   proceedings under Parts I to VI or IX to X of the Insolvency Act 1986, the Bankruptcy (Scotland) Act 1985 or Parts II to VII or IX or X of the Insolvency (Northern Ireland) Order 1989 in respect of an authorised person, former authorised person or former regulated person.

[2354]

6 Disclosure in pursuance of a Community obligation

A primary recipient of confidential information, or a person receiving such information directly or indirectly from a primary recipient, is permitted to disclose such information in pursuance of a Community obligation.

[2355]

7 Restrictions on use of confidential information

Where confidential information is disclosed under these Regulations to a person other than the Authority, the Secretary of State, the Treasury or the Bank of England, and the disclosure is made subject to any conditions as to the use to which the information may be put, the person to whom the information has been disclosed may not use the information in breach of any such condition, without the consent of the person who disclosed it to him.

[2356]

PART III

DISCLOSURE OF SINGLE MARKET DIRECTIVE INFORMATION ...

[8 Application of this Part

This Part applies to—

   (a)   single market directive information; and

   (b)   markets in financial instruments directive information, where that information has been received from—

       (i)   an overseas regulatory authority under a cooperation agreement referred to in article 63 of the markets in financial instruments directive; or

(ii)   an EEA competent authority under article 58.1 of the markets in financial instruments directive.]

[2357]

NOTES
Commencement: 1 November 2007.
Words omitted from the heading preceding this regulation revoked by the Collective Investment Schemes (Miscellaneous Amendments) Regulations 2003, SI 2003/2066, reg 12(b), (c), as from 13 February 2004.
Substituted by the Financial Services and Markets Act 2000 (Disclosure of Confidential Information) (Amendment) Regulations 2006, SI 2006/3413, regs 2, 4, as from 1 November 2007.

9   Disclosure by the Authority or Authority workers to certain other persons

(1)   Subject to paragraphs (2)[, (3) and (3A)], the Authority or an Authority worker is permitted to disclose information to which this Part applies to a person specified in the first column in Schedule 1 for the purpose of enabling or assisting that person to discharge any of the functions listed beside him in the second column in that Schedule.

(2)   Paragraph (1) does not permit disclosure to a person specified in the first column in Part 3 of Schedule 1 unless the disclosure is provided for by a cooperation agreement of the kind referred to in—

[(a)   article 63 of the markets in financial instruments directive;]
(b)   [article 46] of the banking consolidation directive;
(c)   [article 16.3 of the life assurance consolidation directive];
(d)   article 16.3 of the third non-life insurance directive, ...
(e)   article 50.4 of the UCITS directive[, or
(f)   article 26 of the reinsurance directive].

[(2A)   The references in paragraph (2) to the provisions mentioned in sub-paragraphs (a), ... (d) and (e) are to those provisions as replaced by Directive 2000/64/EC of the European Parliament and of the Council of 7 November 2000.]

(3)   Paragraph (1) does not permit disclosure to a person specified in the first column in Part 4 of Schedule 1—
(a)   of information obtained from an EEA competent authority, unless that authority has given its express consent to the disclosure; or
(b)   of information obtained in the course of an on-the-spot verification of the kind referred to in—
    (i)   ...
    (ii)   [article 43] of the banking consolidation directive,
    (iii)   [article 11 of the life assurance consolidation directive], ...
    (iv)   article 14 of the first non-life insurance directive[, or
    (v)   article 16 of the reinsurance directive],
unless the EEA competent authority of the state in which the on-the-spot verification was carried out has given its express consent to the disclosure.

[(3A)   Paragraph (1) does not permit disclosure of markets in financial instruments information to a person specified in the first column of Schedule 1 other than a person listed in paragraph (3B) where that information—
(a)   was obtained from an EEA competent authority under article 58.1 of the markets in financial instruments directive ("the directive") or an overseas regulatory authority under a cooperation agreement referred to in article 63 of the directive, and
(b)   that authority indicated at the time of communication that such information must not be disclosed,
unless that authority has given its express consent to the disclosure.

(3B)   The persons are—
(a)   the Bank of England,
(b)   the European Central Bank,
(c)   the central bank of any country or territory outside the United Kingdom, or
(d)   a body (other than a central bank) in a country or territory outside the United Kingdom having—
    (i)   functions as a monetary authority; or
    (ii)   responsibility for overseeing payment systems.]

[2358]

NOTES
Para (1): words in square brackets substituted by the Financial Services and Markets Act 2000 (Disclosure of Confidential Information) (Amendment) Regulations 2006, SI 2006/3413, regs 2, 5(a), as from 1 November 2007.
Para (2): sub-para (a) substituted by SI 2006/3413, regs 2, 5(b), as from 1 November 2007; words in square brackets in sub-para (b) substituted by the Capital Requirements Regulations 2006, SI 2006/3221, reg 29(4),

Sch 6, para 8(1), (3), as from 1 January 2007; words in square brackets in sub-para (c) substituted by the Life Assurance Consolidation Directive (Consequential Amendments) Regulations 2004, SI 2004/3379, reg 19(1), (3)(a), as from 11 January 2005 (with regard to this amendment see further the notes below); word omitted from sub-para (d) revoked, and sub-para (e) (and the word immediately preceding it) inserted, by the Financial Services and Markets Act 2000 (Reinsurance Directive) Regulations 2007, SI 2007/3255, reg 3(1), (3), as from 10 December 2007.

Para (2A): inserted by the Financial Services and Markets Act 2000 (Disclosure of Confidential Information) (Amendment) Regulations 2003, SI 2003/693, reg 3(b), as from 3 April 2003; word omitted revoked by SI 2004/3379, reg 19(1), (3)(b), as from 11 January 2005.

Para (3): sub-para (b)(i) revoked by SI 2006/3413, regs 2, 5(c), as from 1 November 2007; words in square brackets in sub-para (b)(ii) substituted by SI 2006/3221, reg 29(4), Sch 6, para 8(1), (3), (4), as from 1 January 2007; words in square brackets in sub-para (b)(iii) substituted by SI 2004/3379, reg 19(1), (3)(a), (c), as from 11 January 2005; word omitted from sub-para (b)(iii) revoked and sub-para (b)(v) (and the word immediately preceding it) inserted, by SI 2007/3255, reg 3(1), (4), as from 10 December 2007.

Paras (3A), (3B): added by SI 2006/3413, regs 2, 5(d), as from 1 November 2007.

Note: with regard to the amendment made by SI 2004/3379, reg 19(1), (3)(a) to para (2) above, reg 19(3) actually provides as follows—

"(3)   In regulation 9 (disclosure by the authority or authority of workers to certain other persons)—
   (a)   in paragraph 2(c), for "article 15.3 of the third life assurance directive" substitute "article 16.3 of the life assurance consolidation directive";".

The original words in para (2)(c) above were "article 15.3 of the third life *insurance* directive". However, the amendment has been incorporated as it is believed that this was merely a drafting error in the 2004 Regulations.

10   Disclosure by Schedule 1 person

A person specified in the first column in Schedule 1 is permitted to disclose information to which this Part applies for the purpose of enabling or assisting him to discharge any of the functions listed beside him in that Schedule.

[2359]

PART IV
DISCLOSURE OF CONFIDENTIAL INFORMATION NOT SUBJECT TO DIRECTIVE RESTRICTIONS

11   Application of this Part

This Part applies to confidential information other than—
   (a)   single market directive information;
   (b), (c) ...
   [(d)   markets in financial instruments directive information, where that information has been received from—
      (i)   an overseas regulatory authority under a cooperation agreement referred to in article 63 of the markets in financial instruments directive; or
      (ii)   an EEA competent under article 58.1 of the markets in financial instruments directive,
   unless that authority has given its express consent for disclosure that is covered by this Part].

[2360]

NOTES
   Para (b) revoked by the Collective Investment Schemes (Miscellaneous Amendments) Regulations 2003, SI 2003/2066, reg 12(d), as from 13 February 2004; para (c) revoked, and para (d) added, by the Financial Services and Markets Act 2000 (Disclosure of Confidential Information) (Amendment) Regulations 2006, SI 2006/3413, regs 2, 6, as from 1 April 2007 (in so far as relating to the revocation of para (c)), and as from 1 November 2007 (in so far as relating to the addition of para (d)).

12   Disclosure by and to a Schedule 1 or 2 person or disciplinary proceedings authority

(1)   A primary recipient of information to which this Part applies, or a person obtaining such information directly or indirectly from a primary recipient, is permitted to disclose such information to—
   (a)   a person specified in the first column in Schedule 1 or 2 for the purpose of enabling or assisting that person to discharge any function listed beside him in the second column in Schedule 1 or 2; or
   (b)   a disciplinary proceedings authority for the purposes of any prescribed disciplinary proceedings which have been or may be initiated, or for the purpose of initiating or bringing to an end any such proceedings, or of facilitating a determination of whether they should be initiated or brought to an end.

(2)   A person specified in the first column in Schedule 1 or 2 is permitted to disclose information to which this Part applies to any person for the purpose of enabling or assisting the person making the disclosure to discharge any function listed beside him in the second column in Schedule 1 or 2.

(3)   A disciplinary proceedings authority is permitted to disclose information to which this Part applies to any person for any of the purposes mentioned in paragraph (1)(b).

[2361]

[12A   The National Lottery Commission may disclose information to which this Part applies to the National Audit Office for the purpose of enabling or assisting the Comptroller and Auditor General to carry out an examination under Part II of the National Audit Act 1983 in relation to the Commission.]

[2362]

NOTES
Inserted by the Financial Services and Markets Act 2000 (Disclosure of Confidential Information) (Amendment) (No 2) Regulations 2001, SI 2001/3624, reg 2(1), (4), as from 1 December 2001.

[12B   Electronic commerce
The Authority may disclose information to which this Part applies for the purpose of publishing that information in accordance with regulation 10(8) of the Electronic Commerce Directive (Financial Services and Markets) Regulations 2002.]

[2363]

NOTES
Inserted by the Electronic Commerce Directive (Financial Services and Markets) Regulations 2002, SI 2002/1775, reg 16, as from 21 August 2002.

[12C   A primary recipient of information to which this Part applies, or a person obtaining such information directly or indirectly from a primary recipient is permitted to disclose such information to any person for the purposes of any proceedings under the Proceeds of Crime Act 2002 which have been or may be initiated.]

[2364]

NOTES
Inserted by the Financial Services and Markets Act 2000 (Disclosure of Confidential Information) (Amendment) (No 2) Regulations 2003, SI 2003/2174, regs 2, 4(c), as from 23 August 2003 (see further the note below).
Note: this Regulation was originally inserted as regulation 12B by the Financial Services and Markets Act 2000 (Disclosure of Confidential Information) (Amendment) Regulations 2003, SI 2003/1092, as from 2 May 2003. However, those Regulations were revoked by SI 2003/2174, as from 23 August 2003 due to a number of drafting errors contained in those Regulations (including the fact that this regulation should have been numbered as 12C as a regulation 12B had previously been inserted).

PART V
TRANSITIONAL PROVISIONS

13   Interpretation

In this Part—
"pre-commencement information" means information which is subject to restrictions (with or without qualifications or exceptions) on disclosure by virtue of a pre-commencement provision;
"pre-commencement provision" means—
(a)   any provision in—
(i)   Schedule 2B to the Insurance Companies Act 1982;
(ii)   Part VIII of the Financial Services Act 1986;
(iii)   Part V of the Banking Act 1987; or
(iv)   SRO rules;
which imposes restrictions on the disclosure of information, or creates exceptions or qualifications to such restrictions; or
(b)   regulation 48 of the Investment Services Regulations 1995;
"recognised self-regulating organisation" means a body which immediately before the coming into force of section 348 of the Act was a recognised self-regulating organisation within the meaning of section 8(1) of the Financial Services Act 1986, or a recognised self-regulating organisation for friendly societies within the meaning of Schedule 11 to that Act;
"SRO rules" means the rules of a recognised self-regulating organisation;
"transitional information" means information which immediately before the coming into force of section 19 of the Act was subject to restrictions on disclosure by virtue of a pre-commencement provision.

[2365]

14   Disclosure of pre-commencement information

(1)   Before the coming into force of section 19 of the Act, each pre-commencement provision is to be treated as permitting the disclosure of pre-commencement information—

    (a)   in accordance with regulation 3(1) as if it were confidential information;

    (b)   to the Authority, the Secretary of State or the Treasury for the purpose referred to in regulation 3(2);

    (c)   to any person for the purposes referred to in regulation 4; and

    (d)   to—

        (i)   a person mentioned in regulation 5(3) for the purpose referred to in regulation 5(1)(a); or

        (ii)   any person for the purposes referred to in regulation 5(1)(b),

but only if the proceedings in question are of the kind referred to in regulation 5(6)(a), (b) or (c).

(2)   Paragraph (1) is not to be taken as—

    (a)   precluding disclosure of pre-commencement information where that is otherwise permitted under the pre-commencement provision in question; or

    (b)   permitting disclosure in contravention of any of the directive restrictions.

[2366]

15   Disclosure of transitional information

(1)   After the coming into force of section 19 of the Act, sections 348, 349 and 352 of the Act apply in relation to transitional information in the same way as they apply in relation to confidential information within the meaning of section 348(2) of the Act.

(2)   Paragraph (1) does not apply to transitional information which—

    (a)   has been made available to the public by virtue of being disclosed in any circumstances in which, or for any purposes for which, disclosure is not precluded by section 348 of the Act or a pre-commencement provision; or

    (b)   satisfies the criterion set out in section 348(4)(b) of the Act.

(3)   For the purposes of sections 348 and 349 of the Act as they apply by virtue of paragraph (1)—

    (a)   a person who holds transitional information is to be treated as a primary recipient of the information if he—

        (i)   obtained it as mentioned in paragraph 1(2) or 5(1)(a) of Schedule 2B to the Insurance Companies Act 1982;

        (ii)   was a primary recipient of the information for the purposes of section 179 of the Financial Services Act 1986;

      [(iia)   obtained or received it as mentioned in subsection (5) of that section;]

        (iii)   received it as mentioned in section 82(1)(a) of the Banking Act 1987; or

        (iv)   received it as mentioned in regulation 48(1) of the Investment Services Regulations 1995;

    (b)   any other person who holds transitional information is to be treated as having obtained the information directly or indirectly from a primary recipient.

(4)   Transitional information which is subject to directive restrictions imposed by the single market directives ... is to be treated for the purposes of these Regulations as single market directive information ...

(5)   Part IV of these Regulations does not apply to transitional information which is subject to directive restrictions imposed by [article 107.3] of the listing particulars directive.

[2367]

16   Disclosure by recognised self-regulating organisations

If a recognised self-regulating organisation discloses any information to the Authority for the purpose of enabling or assisting the Authority to discharge functions corresponding to functions of the organisation, the disclosure is not to be taken as a contravention of any duty to which the organisation is subject.

[2368]

[17   Investment services directive information: transitional provision

In these Regulations confidential information received by the Authority in the course of discharging its functions as an EEA competent authority under Council Directive 93/22/EEC of 10th May 1993 on investment services in the securities field shall be deemed to have been received by the Authority in the course of discharging its functions as an EEA competent authority under the markets in financial instruments directive.]

[2368A]

NOTES
Commencement: 1 November 2007
Inserted by the Financial Services and Markets Act 2000 (Disclosure of Confidential Information) (Amendment) Regulations 2006, SI 2006/3413, regs 2, 7, as from 1 November 2007.

SCHEDULES

SCHEDULE 1
DISCLOSURE OF CONFIDENTIAL INFORMATION WHETHER OR NOT SUBJECT TO DIRECTIVE RESTRICTIONS

Regulations 9, 10 and 12

PART 1

Person	Functions
The Bank of England, the European Central Bank or the central bank of any country or territory outside the United Kingdom	(a) Its functions as a monetary authority
	(b) Its functions in relation to overseeing payment systems
A body (other than a central bank) in a country or territory outside the United Kingdom having (a) functions as a monetary authority or (b) responsibility for overseeing payment systems	Its functions as such
A recognised investment exchange (other than an overseas investment exchange)	Its functions as such
The body known as the Panel on Takeovers and Mergers	All of its functions
The Society of Lloyd's	Its regulatory functions
The [Office of Fair Trading]	(a) [Its] functions under the Act
	(b) [Its] functions under any other enactment in so far as they relate to the supervision of:
	(i) former authorised persons or persons who have carried on former regulated activities; or
	(ii) persons carrying on, or who have carried on, regulated activities[; or
	(iii) financial organisations within the meaning of article 30.5 of the banking consolidation directive]
The Competition Commission	(a) Its functions under the Act
	(b) Its functions under any other enactment in so far as they relate to the supervision of:
	(i) former authorised persons or persons who have carried on former regulated activities; or
	(ii) persons carrying on, or who have carried on, regulated activities[; or

Person	Functions
	(iii) financial organisations within the meaning of article 30.5 of the banking consolidation directive]
An official receiver appointed under section 399 of the Insolvency Act 1986, or an official receiver for Northern Ireland appointed under article 355 of the Insolvency (Northern Ireland) Order 1989	His functions under enactments relating to insolvency, in so far as they relate to—
	(i) former authorised persons or persons who have carried on former regulated activities; or
	(ii) persons carrying on, or who have carried on, regulated activities
The scheme manager	Its functions under Part XV of the Act
A body responsible, in an EEA State other than the United Kingdom, for administering a deposit-guarantee scheme recognised in accordance with directive 94/19/EC, or an investor-compensation scheme recognised in accordance with Directive 97/9/EC	Its functions as such
A designated professional body within the meaning of Part XX of the Act	Its functions as such
A body which was, immediately before the coming into force of section 19 of the Act, a recognised professional body within the meaning of the Financial Services Act 1986	Its functions as such under that Act or under the Act
A person appointed to make a report under section 166 of the Act	His functions as such
A person appointed to conduct an investigation under section 167 or section 168(3) or (5) of the Act	His functions as such
An auditor exercising functions conferred by or under the Act	Those functions
An auditor of an authorised person appointed under or as a result of an enactment (other than the Act)	His functions as such
An actuary exercising functions conferred by or under the Act	Those functions
A person appointed as an inspector under section 49 of the Industrial and Provident Societies Act 1965	His functions as such
A person appointed as an inspector under section 18 of the Credit Unions Act 1979	His functions as such
A person appointed to make a report under section 52(5)(d) of the Building Societies Act 1986	His functions as such
A person appointed as an investigator under section 55 of the Building Societies Act 1986 or as an inspector under section 56 of that Act	His functions as such
A person appointed to make a report under section 62(3)(d) of the Friendly Societies Act 1992	His functions as such
A person appointed as an investigator under section 65 of the Friendly Societies Act 1992 or as an inspector under section 66 of that Act	His functions as such

Person	Functions
A recognised supervisory body within the meaning of Part II of the Companies Act 1989 or Part III of the Companies (Northern Ireland) Order 1990	(a) Its functions as such a body under that Part
	(b) Its functions in relation to disciplinary proceedings against auditors
A qualifying body as defined by section 32 of the Companies Act 1989	Its functions as such
The Institute of Actuaries or the Faculty of Actuaries	[Their supervisory functions in relation to the exercise by an actuary of his professional duties, including the conduct of disciplinary proceedings and determining whether to institute or terminate such proceedings]
A recognised professional body within the meaning of section 391 of the Insolvency Act 1986 or article 350 of the Insolvency (Northern Ireland) Order 1989	(a) Its functions as such a body under that Act or that Order
	(b) Its functions in relation to disciplinary proceedings against insolvency practitioners
The Department of Enterprise, Trade and Investment in Northern Ireland	(a) Its functions under Part V of the Companies (No 2) (Northern Ireland) Order 1990 (financial markets and insolvency)
	(b) Its functions under Part XII of the Insolvency (Northern Ireland) Order 1989
	(c) Its functions under any other enactment in so far as they relate to the supervision of:
	(i) former authorised persons or persons who have carried on former regulated activities; or
	(ii) persons carrying on, or who have carried on, regulated activities
[The Pensions Regulator]	[Its functions as such] in so far as they relate to the supervision of:
	(i) former authorised persons or persons who have carried on former regulated activities; or
	(ii) persons carrying on, or who have carried on, regulated activities
The Charity Commissioners for England and Wales	Their functions under any enactment in so far as they relate to the supervision of:
	(i) former authorised persons or persons who have carried on former regulated activities; or
	(ii) persons carrying on, or who have carried on, regulated activities
The investigator appointed by the Authority in accordance with paragraph 7 of Schedule 1 to the Act	His functions as such
[A person appointed by the Treasury to hold an inquiry into matters relating to financial services (including an inquiry under section 15 of the Act), or an officer or member of staff of such an inquiry	His functions in carrying out the inquiry and reporting to the Treasury]

Person	Functions
[An investment exchange which has its head office in an EEA State other than the United Kingdom, and which is recognised as an investment exchange under the law of that state	Its functions as a supervisor of financial markets]
[A person upon whom functions are conferred by or under Part 2, 3 or 4 of the Proceeds of Crime Act 2002	Those functions]
[A person authorised by the Secretary of State for the purposes of section 245B(1)(b) of the Companies Act 1985	His functions as such]
[Any body carrying on activities concerned with any of the matters set out in section 16(2) of the Companies (Audit, Investigations and Community Enterprise) Act 2004	Its functions as such]
[Any body carrying on activities concerned with any of the matters set out in section 14 of the Companies (Audit, Investigations and Community Enterprise) Act 2004	Its functions as such]
[The Financial Reporting Council and its operating bodies	Their supervisory functions in relation to the exercise by an actuary of his professional duties, the conduct of disciplinary proceedings and determining whether to institute or terminate such proceedings]

[2369]

NOTES

In entry relating to the Office of Fair Trading words "Office of Fair Trading" and "Its" in square brackets substituted by virtue of the Enterprise Act 2002, s 2(1), as from 1 April 2003; sub-para (b)(iii) (and the word immediately preceding it) inserted by the Financial Services and Markets Act 2000 (Disclosure of Confidential Information) (Amendment) Regulations 2006, SI 2006/3413, regs 2, 8(1)(a), as from 20 January 2007.

In entry relating to the Competition Commission sub-para (b)(iii) (and the word immediately preceding it) inserted by SI 2006/3413, regs 2, 8(1)(b), as from 20 January 2007.

In entry relating to the Institute of Actuaries or the Faculty of Actuaries words in square brackets substituted by the Financial Services and Markets Act 2000 (Disclosure of Confidential Information) (Amendment) (No 3) Regulations 2003, SI 2003/2817, reg 2(a), as from 26 November 2003.

In entry relating to "The Pensions Regulator" (formerly "The Occupational Pensions Regulatory Authority") words in square brackets substituted by Financial Services and Markets Act 2000 (Disclosure of Confidential Information) (Amendment) Regulations 2005, SI 2005/3071, reg 2(1), (2), as from 25 November 2005.

First entry in square brackets added by the Financial Services and Markets Act 2000 (Disclosure of Confidential Information) (Amendment) Regulations 2001, SI 2001/3437, reg 2, as from 8 November 2001.

Second entry in square brackets added by the Financial Services and Markets Act 2000 (Disclosure of Confidential Information) (Amendment) (No 2) Regulations 2001, SI 2001/3624, reg 2(1), (6), as from 1 December 2001.

Third entry in square brackets inserted by the Financial Services and Markets Act 2000 (Disclosure of Confidential Information) (Amendment) (No 2) Regulations 2003, SI 2003/2174, regs 2, 4(b), as from 23 August 2003. Note that an identical entry was originally inserted by the Financial Services and Markets Act 2000 (Disclosure of Confidential Information) (Amendment) Regulations 2003, SI 2003/1092, as from 2 May 2003. However, those Regulations were revoked by SI 2003/2174, as from 23 August 2003 due to a number of drafting errors contained in those Regulations. The entry as inserted by SI 2003/1092 did not contain any such drafting error so, in effect, has been in operation since 2 May 2003.

Fourth entry in square brackets inserted by SI 2003/2817, reg 2(b), as from 26 November 2003.

Final three entries in square brackets added by SI 2006/3413, regs 2, 8(2), as from 20 January 2007.

Charity Commissioners: as to the abolition of the office of Charity Commissioner for England and Wales, the establishment of the Charity Commission for England and Wales, and the transfer of the functions, rights, liabilities, etc from the Charity Commissioners to the Charity Commission, see the Charities Act 2006, s 6.

PART 2

Person	Functions
An EEA regulatory authority	(a) Its functions as an EEA competent authority
	(b) Its functions corresponding to any of the functions specified in the second column of Part 1 of this Schedule

[2370]

PART 3

Person	Functions
A dependent territory regulatory authority	Its functions as such
A non-EEA regulatory authority	Its functions as such

[2371]

PART 4

Person	Functions
An inspector appointed under Part XIV of the Companies Act 1985	His functions as such
A person authorised to exercise powers under section 447 of the Companies Act 1985	His functions as such
A person authorised under section 84 of the Companies Act 1989 to exercise on behalf of the Secretary of State powers conferred by section 83 of that Act	His functions as such
The Department of Enterprise, Trade and Investment in Northern Ireland	(a) Its functions under Part XV of the Companies (Northern Ireland) Order 1986 (investigation of companies and their affairs; requisition of documents)
	(b) Its functions under Part III of the Companies (Northern Ireland) Order 1990 (eligibility for appointment as company auditor)
	(c) Its functions under the Companies (Northern Ireland) Order 1989 (disqualification of company directors)
An inspector appointed under Part XV of the Companies (Northern Ireland) Order 1986	His functions under that Part
A person appointed to exercise powers under article 440 of the Companies (Northern Ireland) Order 1986	His functions as such
A recognised clearing house (other than an overseas clearing house)	Its functions as a clearing house in so far as they are exercisable in relation to defaults or potential defaults by market participants
A person included on the list maintained by the Authority for the purposes of section 301 of the Act	His functions under settlement arrangements to which regulations made under that section relate

Person	Functions
A person approved under the Uncertificated Securities Regulations 1995 as an operator of a relevant system (within the meaning of those Regulations)	His functions as such in so far as they are exercisable in relation to defaults or potential defaults by market participants
[A clearing house or other similar body which has its head office in an EEA State other than the United Kingdom, and which is recognised under the law of that state as a provider of clearing or settlement services	Its functions in relation to defaults or potential defaults by market participants]

[2372]

NOTES

Entry in square brackets added by the Financial Services and Markets Act 2000 (Disclosure of Confidential Information) (Amendment) (No 2) Regulations 2001, SI 2001/3624, reg 2(1), (7), as from 1 December 2001.

SCHEDULE 2
DISCLOSURE OF CONFIDENTIAL INFORMATION NOT SUBJECT TO
DIRECTIVE RESTRICTION
Regulation 12

Person	Functions
The Bank of England	All its public functions (so far as not mentioned in Schedule 1)
The International Monetary Fund	All its functions
The [Office of Fair Trading]	[Its] functions under any enactment (so far as not mentioned in Schedule 1)
The Competition Commission	Its functions under any enactment (so far as not mentioned in Schedule 1)
The Gas and Electricity Markets Authority	Its functions under any enactment
A local weights and measures authority in Great Britain	Its functions as such under any enactment
An EEA regulatory authority	Its functions as such (so far as not mentioned in Schedule 1)
The Department of Enterprise, Trade and Investment in Northern Ireland	(a) Its functions under Part V of the Companies (No 2) (Northern Ireland) Order 1990 (Financial Markets and Insolvency)
	(b) Its functions under Part XII of the Insolvency (Northern Ireland) Order 1989
	(c) Its functions under any other enactment (so far as not mentioned in Schedule 1)
	(d) Its functions as a weights and measures authority for Northern Ireland
A recognised clearing house (other than an overseas clearing house)	Its functions as such (so far as not mentioned in Schedule 1)
A person approved under the Uncertificated Securities Regulations 1995 as an operator of a relevant system (within the meaning of those regulations)	His functions as such (so far as not mentioned in Schedule 1)
The scheme operator	Its functions as such

Person	Functions
The Chief Ombudsman appointed in accordance with paragraph 5 of Schedule 17 to the Act, and any other member of the panel of ombudsmen appointed in accordance with paragraph 4 of that Schedule	Their functions as such
An inspector appointed under section 284 of the Act	His functions as such
A person appointed in accordance with regulations made under section 262(1) of the Act to carry out an investigation in relation to an open-ended investment company	His functions as such
[The Pensions Regulator]	[Its functions as such] (so far as not mentioned in Schedule 1 to these Regulations)
The Charity Commissioners for England and Wales	Their functions under any enactment (so far as not mentioned in Schedule 1)
The Commissioners of Customs and Excise	Their functions under any enactment
The Postal Services Commission	Its functions under the Postal Services Act 2000
The Pensions Ombudsman	His functions under the Pension Schemes Act 1993 and the Pensions Act 1995
[The National Lottery Commission	All its public functions]
[A person upon whom functions are conferred by or under Part 2, 3 or 4 of the Proceeds of Crime Act 2002	Those functions]
[The Gambling Commission	Its functions as such]

[2373]

NOTES

In entry relating to "The Pensions Regulator" (formerly "The Occupational Pensions Regulatory Authority") words in square brackets substituted by Financial Services and Markets Act 2000 (Disclosure of Confidential Information) (Amendment) Regulations 2005, SI 2005/3071, reg 2(1), (3), as from 25 November 2005.

In entry relating to the Office of Fair Trading words in square brackets substituted by virtue of the Enterprise Act 2002, s 2(1), as from 1 April 2003.

First entry in square brackets added by the Financial Services and Markets Act 2000 (Disclosure of Confidential Information) (Amendment) (No 2) Regulations 2001, SI 2001/3624, reg 2(1), (8), as from 1 December 2001.

Second entry in square brackets inserted by the Financial Services and Markets Act 2000 (Disclosure of Confidential Information) (Amendment) (No 2) Regulations 2003, SI 2003/2174, regs 2, 4(d), as from 23 August 2003. Note that an identical entry was originally inserted by the Financial Services and Markets Act 2000 (Disclosure of Confidential Information) (Amendment) Regulations 2003, SI 2003/1092, as from 2 May 2003. However, those Regulations were revoked by SI 2003/2174, as from 23 August 2003 due to a number of drafting errors contained in those Regulations. The entry as inserted by SI 2003/1092 did not contain any such drafting error so, in effect, has been in operation since 2 May 2003.

Final entry in square brackets added by the Financial Services and Markets Act 2000 (Disclosure of Confidential Information) (Amendment) Regulations 2006, SI 2006/3413, regs 2, 9, as from 20 January 2007.

Commissioners of Customs and Excise: a reference to the Commissioners of Customs and Excise is now to be taken as a reference to the Commissioners for Her Majesty's Revenue and Customs; see the Commissioners for Revenue and Customs Act 2005, s 50(1), (7).

Charity Commissioners: see the note to Sch 1, Pt 1 at **[2369]**.

SCHEDULE 3
PRESCRIBED DISCIPLINARY PROCEEDINGS

Regulation 2

The following disciplinary proceedings are prescribed for the purposes of section 349(5)(d) of the Act—

   (a) disciplinary proceedings relating to the exercise by a barrister, solicitor, auditor, accountant, valuer or actuary of his professional duties;

   (b) disciplinary proceedings relating to the discharge of his duties by an officer or servant of—

       (i) the Crown;

>   (ii)   the Authority;
>   (iii)   the body known as the Panel on Takeovers and Mergers;
>   (iv)   the Charity Commissioners for England and Wales;
>   (v)   the [Office of Fair Trading];
>   (vi)   the Competition Commission;
>   (vii)   the Insolvency Practitioners Tribunal in relation to its functions under the Insolvency Act 1986;
>   (viii)   the Occupational Pensions Board in relation to its functions under the Social Security Act 1973 and the Social Security Acts 1975 to 1986;
>   (ix)   the organs of the Society of Lloyd's being organs constituted by or under Lloyd's Act 1982 in relation to their functions under Lloyd's Acts 1871–1982 and the byelaws made thereunder of the Society of Lloyd's;
>   (x)   the National Lottery Commission in relation to their functions under the National Lottery etc Act 1993.

[2374]

NOTES
  Words in square brackets substituted by virtue of the Enterprise Act 2002, s 2(1), as from 1 April 2003.
  Charity Commissioners: see the note to Sch 1, Pt 1 at **[2369]**.

FINANCIAL SERVICES AND MARKETS ACT 2000 (RIGHTS OF ACTION) REGULATIONS 2001

(SI 2001/2256)

NOTES
  Made: 20 June 2001.
  Authority: Financial Services and Markets Act 2000, ss 20(3), 71(2), (3), 150(3), (5), 202(2), 417(1), 428(3).
  Commencement: 1 December 2001.
  These Regulations are reproduced as amended by: the Electronic Commerce Directive (Financial Services and Markets) Regulations 2002, SI 2002/1775; the Financial Services and Markets Act 2000 (Fourth Motor Insurance Directive) Regulations 2002, SI 2002/2706.

ARRANGEMENT OF REGULATIONS

1 Citation and commencement

These Regulations may be cited as the Financial Services and Markets Act 2000 (Rights of Action) Regulations 2001 and come into force on the day on which section 19 of the Act comes into force.

[2375]

2 Interpretation

In these Regulations—
  "the Act" means the Financial Services and Markets Act 2000;
  "government" means—
>   (a)   the government of the United Kingdom;
>   (b)   the Scottish Administration;
>   (c)   the Executive Committee of the Northern Ireland Assembly;
>   (d)   the National Assembly for Wales; or
>   (e)   the government of any country or territory outside the United Kingdom;
  "international organisation" means any international organisation the members of which include the United Kingdom or any other state;
  "local authority", in relation to the United Kingdom, means—
>   (a)   in England and Wales, a local authority within the meaning of the Local Government Act 1972, the Greater London Authority, the Common Council of the City of London or the Council of the Isles of Scilly;
>   (b)   in Scotland, a local authority within the meaning of the Local Government (Scotland) Act 1973; and

(c)   in Northern Ireland, a district council within the meaning of the Local
Government Act (Northern Ireland) 1972;

"Part IV financial resources requirement" means a requirement imposed on an authorised
person by the Authority under Part IV of the Act to have or maintain financial resources;

"Part XIII financial resources requirement" means a requirement imposed on an incoming firm
(within the meaning of section 193(1) of the Act) by the Authority under Part XIII of the
Act to have or maintain financial resources;

"the Regulated Activities Order" means the Financial Services and Markets Act 2000
(Regulated Activities) Order 2001.

[2376]

3 Private person

(1)   In these Regulations, "private person" means—
  (a)   any individual, unless he suffers the loss in question in the course of carrying on—
    (i)   any regulated activity; or
    (ii)   any activity which would be a regulated activity apart from any exclusion made
by [article 72 (overseas persons) or 72A (information society services) of the
Regulated Activities Order]; and
  (b)   any person who is not an individual, unless he suffers the loss in question in the course
of carrying on business of any kind;

but does not include a government, a local authority (in the United Kingdom or elsewhere) or an
international organisation.

(2)   For the purposes of paragraph (1)(a), an individual who suffers loss in the course of
effecting or carrying out contracts of insurance (within the meaning of article 10 of the Regulated
Activities Order) written at Lloyd's is not to be taken to suffer loss in the course of carrying on a
regulated activity.

[2377]

NOTES

Para (1): words in square brackets in sub-para (a)(ii) substituted by the Electronic Commerce Directive
(Financial Services and Markets) Regulations 2002, SI 2002/1775, reg 18, as from 21 August 2002.

4 Authorised person acting otherwise than in accordance with permission

(1)   A case where the conditions specified by paragraph (2) are satisfied is prescribed for the
purposes of section 20(3) of the Act (and so in such a case the contravention of a requirement
imposed by the Authority under the Act is actionable at the suit of a person who suffers loss as a
result of that contravention).

(2)   The conditions specified by this paragraph are that—
  (a)   the action would be brought at the suit of—
    (i)   a private person; or
    (ii)   a person acting in a fiduciary or representative capacity on behalf of a private
person and any remedy would be exclusively for the benefit of that private person
and could not be effected through an action brought otherwise than at the suit of
the fiduciary or representative; and
  (b)   the contravention is not of a Part IV financial resources requirement.

[2378]

5 Prohibition orders and performance of a controlled function

(1)   The definition of "private person" in regulation 3 is prescribed for the purposes of
section 71(3) of the Act (and so the contravention of section 56(6) or 59(1) or (2) of the Act is
actionable at the suit of a person who falls within that definition and who suffers loss as a result of
that contravention).

(2)   A case where the condition specified by paragraph (3) is satisfied is prescribed for the
purposes of section 71(2) of the Act (and so in such a case the contravention of section 56(6)
or 59(1) or (2) of the Act is actionable at the suit of a person who is not a private person).

(3)   The condition specified by this paragraph is that the action would be brought at the suit of
a person (who is not a private person) acting in a fiduciary or representative capacity on behalf of a
private person and any remedy would be exclusively for the benefit of that private person and could
not be effected through an action brought otherwise than at the suit of the fiduciary or
representative.

[2379]

6   Authority rules

(1)   The definition of "private person" in regulation 3 is prescribed for the purposes of section 150(5) of the Act (and so the contravention by an authorised person of a rule is actionable at the suit of a person who falls within that definition and who suffers loss as a result of that contravention).

(2)   A case where any of the conditions specified by paragraph (3) is satisfied is prescribed for the purposes of section 150(3) of the Act (and so in such a case the contravention of a rule is actionable at the suit of a person who is not a private person).

(3)   The conditions specified by this paragraph are that—
  (a)   the rule that has been contravened prohibits an authorised person from seeking to make provision excluding or restricting any duty or liability;
  (b)   the rule that has been contravened is directed at ensuring that transactions in any security or contractually based investment (within the meaning of the Regulated Activities Order) are not effected with the benefit of unpublished information that, if made public, would be likely to affect the price of that security or investment;
  (c)   the action would be brought at the suit of a person (who is not a private person) acting in a fiduciary or representative capacity on behalf of a private person and any remedy would be exclusively for the benefit of that private person and could not be effected through an action brought otherwise than at the suit of the fiduciary or representative;
  [(d)   the rule that has been contravened requires a relevant authorised person to respond to a claim for compensation within a specified time limit, or to pay interest in specified circumstances in respect of any such claim.]

  [(4)   In this regulation—
  (a)   "relevant authorised person" means an authorised person with a Part IV permission—
      (i)   to effect or to carry out relevant contracts of insurance; or
      (ii)   to manage the underwriting capacity of a Lloyd's syndicate as a managing agent, the members of which effect or carry out relevant contracts of insurance underwritten at Lloyd's;
  where a "relevant contract of insurance" means a contract of insurance against damage arising out of or in connection with the use of motor vehicles on land (other than carrier's liability);
  (b)   "rule" has the meaning given by section 150(4) of the Act; and
  (c)   "specified" means specified in rules.]

[2380]

NOTES
Para (3): sub-para (d) added by the Financial Services and Markets Act 2000 (Fourth Motor Insurance Directive) Regulations 2002, SI 2002/2706, reg 3(a), as from 20 November 2002.
Para (4): added by SI 2002/2706, reg 3(b), as from 20 November 2002.

7   Incoming firms

(1)   A case where the conditions specified by paragraph (2) are satisfied is prescribed for the purposes of section 202(2) of the Act (and so in such a case the contravention of a requirement imposed by the Authority under Part XIII of the Act is actionable at the suit of a person who suffers loss as a result of that contravention).

(2)   The conditions specified by this paragraph are that—
  (a)   the action would be brought at the suit of—
      (i)   a private person; or
      (ii)   a person acting in a fiduciary or representative capacity on behalf of a private person and any remedy would be exclusively for the benefit of that private person and could not be effected through an action brought otherwise than at the suit of the fiduciary or representative; and
  (b)   the contravention is not of a Part XIII financial resources requirement.

[2381]

FINANCIAL SERVICES AND MARKETS ACT 2000 (MEANING OF "POLICY" AND "POLICYHOLDER") ORDER 2001

(SI 2001/2361)

NOTES
Made: 2 July 2001.
Authority: Financial Services and Markets Act 2000, ss 424(2), 428(3).
Commencement: 1 December 2001.
As of 1 February 2009, this Order had not been amended.

1   Citation, commencement and interpretation

(1)   This Order may be cited as the Financial Services and Markets Act 2000 (Meaning of "Policy" and "Policyholder") Order 2001 and comes into force on the day on which section 19 of the Act comes into force.

(2)   In this Order, "contract of insurance" has the meaning given by article 3 of the Financial Services and Markets Act 2000 (Regulated Activities) Order 2001.

[2382]

2   Meaning of "policy"

For the purposes of section 424(2) of the Act, "policy" means, as the context requires,

(a)   a contract of insurance, including one under which an existing liability has already accrued, or

(b)   any instrument evidencing such a contract.

[2383]

3   Meaning of "policyholder"

For the purposes of section 424(2) of the Act, "policyholder" means the person who for the time being is the legal holder of the policy, and includes any person to whom, under the policy, a sum is due, a periodic payment is payable or any other benefit is to be provided or to whom such a sum, payment or benefit is contingently due, payable or to be provided.

[2384]

FINANCIAL SERVICES AND MARKETS ACT 2000 (COLLECTIVE INVESTMENT SCHEMES CONSTITUTED IN OTHER EEA STATES) REGULATIONS 2001

(SI 2001/2383)

NOTES

Made: 4 July 2001.
Authority: Financial Services and Markets Act 2000, ss 264, 417(1).
Commencement: 1 December 2001.
These Regulations are reproduced as amended by: the Collective Investment Schemes (Miscellaneous Amendments) Regulations 2003, SI 2003/2066.

1   These Regulations may be cited as the Financial Services and Markets Act 2000 (Collective Investment Schemes Constituted in Other EEA States) Regulations 2001 and come into force on the day on which section 19 of the Act comes into force.

[2385]

2   In these Regulations—
"the Act" means the Financial Services and Markets Act 2000;
.....

[2386]

NOTES

Definition "the UCITS Directive" (omitted) revoked by the Collective Investment Schemes (Miscellaneous Amendments) Regulations 2003, SI 2003/2066, reg 11(a), as from 13 February 2004.

3   The requirements prescribed for the purposes of section 264 of the Act are that a collective investment scheme is one which, in accordance with [the UCITS directive], is an undertaking for collective investment in transferable securities subject to [that directive] ("the undertaking").

[2387]

NOTES

Words in square brackets substituted by the Collective Investment Schemes (Miscellaneous Amendments) Regulations 2003, SI 2003/2066, reg 11(b), as from 13 February 2004.

4   The notice to be given to the Authority under section 264(1) of the Act must contain or be accompanied by—
(a)   the undertaking's fund rules or instrument of incorporation;

[(b) its full and simplified prospectus (within the meaning of Section VI of the UCITS directive); and]

(c) where appropriate, its latest annual report and any subsequent half-yearly report.

[2388]

NOTES
Para (b): substituted by the Collective Investment Schemes (Miscellaneous Amendments) Regulations 2003, SI 2003/2066, reg 11(c), as from 13 February 2004.

FINANCIAL SERVICES AND MARKETS TRIBUNAL RULES 2001

(SI 2001/2476)

NOTES
Made: 9 July 2001.
Authority: Financial Services and Markets Act 2000, ss 132(3), 137(6), Sch 13, para 9.
Commencement: see r 1.
Transitional provisions: these Rules are modified by the Financial Services and Markets Act 2000 (Transitional Provisions) (Partly Completed Procedures) Order 2001, SI 2001/3592, arts 63, 80, 95, Schedule. Part VI of that Order deals with partly completed procedures of the recognised self-regulating organisations established under the Financial Services Act 1986 which ceased to exist after the commencement of FSMA 2000. Modifications are made to these Rules as they apply to proceedings before the Interim Tribunal established under that Order and the Financial Services Authority.
As to the application of these Rules to certain appeals to the Financial Services and Markets Tribunal made under the Money Laundering Regulations 2007, SI 2007/2157, see reg 44 of, and Sch 5, Pt 2, para 3 to, those Regulations at **[2877BR]**, **[2877CF]**.
Banking (Special Provisions) Act 2008: various Orders made under the Banking (Special Provisions) Act 2008 apply and modify certain provisions of these Rules in relation to the banks that are the subject of the Orders; see:
● the Northern Rock plc Compensation Scheme Order 2008, SI 2008/718 at **[4149]**;
● the Bradford & Bingley plc Compensation Scheme Order 2008, SI 2008/3249 at **[4376]**.
As of 1 February 2009, these Rules had not been amended.

ARRANGEMENT OF RULES

PART I
INTRODUCTION

PART II
PRELIMINARY MATTERS

PART III
HEARINGS

PART IV
APPEALS FROM THE TRIBUNAL

PART V
GENERAL

PART I
INTRODUCTION

1   Citation and commencement

These Rules may be cited as the Financial Services and Markets Tribunal Rules 2001 and shall come into force on the day on which section 132(2) of the Act comes into force.

[2389]

2   Interpretation

(1)   In these Rules, unless the context requires otherwise—
"the Act" means the Financial Services and Markets Act 2000;
"applicant" means a person who refers a case to the Tribunal and, if there is more than one such person, "applicant" means each such person;
"the Authority" means the Financial Services Authority;
"Authority notice" means the decision notice, supervisory notice or other notice relating to the referred action that was given to the applicant by the Authority;
"Chairman" means the person from time to time acting as chairman of the Tribunal in respect of a reference;
"direction" includes any direction, summons or order given or made by the Tribunal;
"documents" includes information recorded in any form and, in relation to information recorded otherwise than in legible form, references to its production include references to producing a copy of the information in legible form;
"file" means send to the Tribunal;
"further material" means documents which—
(a)   were considered by the Authority in reaching or maintaining the decision to give an Authority notice; or
(b)   were obtained by the Authority in connection with the matter to which that notice relates (whether they were obtained before or after giving the notice) but which were not considered by it in reaching or maintaining that decision,
but does not include documents on which the Authority relies in support of the referred action;
"party" means the applicant or the Authority (or, if there is more than one applicant, any of the applicants or the Authority) and "other party" shall be construed accordingly;
"protected item" has the meaning in section 413;
"reference" means a reference to the Tribunal under or by virtue of the Act or any other enactment (including an enactment comprised in subordinate legislation within the meaning of the Interpretation Act 1978);
"reference notice" means a notice filed under rule 4(1);
"referred action" means the act (or proposed act) on the part of the Authority that gave rise to the reference;
"register" means the register of references and decisions kept in connection with the Tribunal's functions and which is open to the inspection of any person without charge at all reasonable hours;
"reply" means a reply filed by the applicant under rule 6(1);
"representations" means written representations or (with the consent of the Tribunal, or at its request) oral representations;
"response document" means:
(a)   in relation to the Authority, its statement of case;
(b)   in relation to the applicant, his reply;
"the Secretary" means the person from time to time appointed as secretary to the Tribunal, being a member of staff appointed under paragraph 6(1) of Schedule 13;
"statement of case" means a statement filed by the Authority under rule 5(1);

"supplementary statement" means a statement that is supplementary to a response document and filed in accordance with a direction given under rule 10(1)(f); and

"the Tribunal" means the Financial Services and Markets Tribunal.

(2)   Unless the context requires otherwise—

   (a)   a reference in these Rules to a rule by number alone means the rule so numbered in these Rules;

   (b)   a reference in these Rules to a section or Schedule by number alone means the section or Schedule so numbered in the Act;

   (c)   words and expressions defined in the Act have the same meaning in these Rules; and

   (d)   anything permitted or required by these Rules to be done by a party may be done by any representative of that party.

[2390]

3   Application of these Rules

These Rules apply to all references to the Tribunal.

[2391]

PART II
PRELIMINARY MATTERS

4   Reference notice

(1)   A reference shall be made by way of a written notice ("the reference notice") signed by or on behalf of the applicant and filed by the applicant.

(2)   In any case not covered by section 133(1)(a) (which provides that a reference must be made before the end of the period of 28 days beginning with the date on which a decision notice or supervisory notice is given), the period specified for the purposes of section 133(1)(b) (such other period as may be specified for making a reference) shall be the period of 28 days beginning with the date on which the Authority notice is given.

(3)   The reference notice shall state—

   (a)   the name and address of the applicant;

   (b)   the name and address of the applicant's representative (if any);

   (c)   if no representative is named under sub-paragraph (b), the applicant's address for service in the United Kingdom (if different from the address notified under sub-paragraph (a));

   (d)   that the notice is a reference notice; and

   (e)   the issues concerning the Authority notice that the applicant wishes the Tribunal to consider.

(4)   In sub-paragraph (3)(a), "address", where the applicant is a corporation, means the address of the applicant's registered or principal office.

(5)   The applicant shall file with the reference notice a copy of any Authority notice to which the reference relates.

(6)   The applicant may include with the reference notice an application for directions, such as a direction extending any time limit for making a reference, a direction under rule 10(1)(e) (suspension of Authority's action) or a direction under rule 10(1)(p) (that the register shall include no particulars about the reference).

(7)   At the same time as he files the reference notice, the applicant shall send a copy of that notice (and of any application for directions in accordance with paragraph (6)) to the Authority.

(8)   In all cases where an application for directions is made under paragraph (6) the Secretary shall refer the application for directions to the Tribunal for determination and he shall take no further action in relation to the reference notice until the application for directions has been determined.

(9)   Subject to paragraph (8) and to any directions given by the Tribunal, upon receiving a reference notice the Secretary shall—

   (a)   enter particulars of the reference in the register; and

   (b)   inform the parties in writing of—

      (i)   the fact that the reference has been received;

      (ii)   the date when the Tribunal received the notice; and

      (iii) the Tribunal's decision on any application made for directions (and include a copy of any direction given),

and the Secretary when sending the parties this information shall specify the date on which he is sending it.

[2392]

5 Authority's statement of case

(1)   The Authority shall file a written statement ("a statement of case") in support of the referred action so that it is received by the Tribunal no later than 28 days after the day on which the Authority received the information sent by the Secretary in accordance with rule 4(9)(b).

(2)   The statement of case shall—
   (a)   specify the statutory provisions providing for the referred action;
   (b)   specify the reasons for the referred action;
   (c)   set out all the matters and facts upon which the Authority relies to support the referred action; and
   (d)   specify the date on which the statement of case is filed.

(3)   The statement of case shall be accompanied by a list of—
   (a)   the documents on which the Authority relies in support of the referred action; and
   (b)   the further material which in the opinion of the Authority might undermine the decision to take that action.

(4)   At the same time as it files the statement of case, the Authority shall send to the applicant a copy of the statement of case and of the list referred to in paragraph (3).

[2393]

6 Applicant's reply

(1)   The applicant shall file a written reply so that it is received by the Tribunal no later than 28 days after—
   (a)   the date on which the applicant received a copy of the statement of case; or
   (b)   if the Authority amends its statement of case, the date on which the applicant received a copy of the amended statement of case.

(2)   The reply shall—
   (a)   state the grounds on which the applicant relies in the reference;
   (b)   identify all matters contained in the statement of case which are disputed by the applicant;
   (c)   state the applicant's reasons for disputing them; and
   (d)   specify the date on which it is filed.

(3)   The reply shall be accompanied by a list of all the documents on which the applicant relies in support of his case.

(4)   At the same time as he files the reply, the applicant shall send to the Authority a copy of the reply and of the list referred to in paragraph (3).

[2394]

7 Secondary disclosure by the Authority

(1)   Following the filing of the applicant's reply, if there is any further material which might be reasonably expected to assist the applicant's case as disclosed by the applicant's reply and which is not mentioned in the list provided in accordance with rule 5(3), the Authority shall file a list of such further material.

(2)   Any list required to be filed by paragraph (1) shall be filed so that it is received no later than 14 days after the day on which the Authority received the applicant's reply.

(3)   At the same time as it files any list required by paragraph (1) the Authority shall send a copy to the applicant.

[2395]

8 Exceptions to disclosure

(1)   A list provided in accordance with rule 5(3) or 7(1) need not include any document that relates to a case involving a person other than the applicant which was taken into account by the Authority in the applicant's case only for the purposes of comparison with other cases.

(2)   A list provided in accordance with rule 5(3), 6(3) or 7(1) need not include any document that is material the disclosure of which for the purposes of or in connection with any legal proceedings is prohibited by section 17 of the Regulation of Investigatory Powers Act 2000.

(3)   A list provided in accordance with rule 5(3), 6(3) or 7(1) need not include any document in respect of which an application has been or is being made under paragraph (4).

(4)   A party may apply to the Tribunal (without giving notice to the other party) for a direction authorising that party not to include in the list required by rule 5(3), 6(3) or 7(1) a document on the ground that disclosure of the document—
   (a)   would not be in the public interest; or
   (b)   would not be fair, having regard to—
     (i)   the likely significance of the document to the applicant in relation to the matter referred to the Tribunal; and

      (ii)   the potential prejudice to the commercial interests of a person other than the applicant which would be caused by disclosure of the document.

(5)   For the purpose of deciding an application by a party under paragraph (4), the Tribunal may—

    (a)   require that the document be produced to the Tribunal together with a statement of the reasons why its inclusion in the list would—

        (i)   in the case of an application under paragraph (4)(a), not be in the public interest; or

        (ii)   in the case of an application under paragraph (4)(b), not be fair; and

    (b)   invite the other party to make representations.

(6)   If the Tribunal refuses an application under paragraph (4) for a direction authorising a party not to include a document in a list, it shall direct that party—

    (a)   to revise the list so as to include the document; and

    (b)   to file a copy of that list as revised and send a copy to the other party.

(7)   A party who has filed a list under rule 5(3), 6(3) or 7(1) shall, upon the request of the other party, provide that other party with a copy of any document specified in the list or make any such document available to that party for inspection or copying.

(8)   Paragraph (7) does not apply to any document that is a protected item.

[2396]

9 Directions

(1)   The Tribunal may at any time give directions to enable the parties to prepare for the hearing of the reference, to assist the Tribunal to determine the issues and generally to ensure the just, expeditious and economical determination of the reference.

(2)   The Tribunal may give directions on the application of any party or of all the parties or of its own initiative and, where it gives a direction of its own initiative, it may (but need not) give prior notice to the parties of its intention to do so.

(3)   Any application for directions shall include the reasons for making that application.

(4)   Except where it is made during the pre-hearing review or during the hearing of the reference, an application for directions shall be filed and, unless the application is accompanied by the written consent of all the parties or an application without notice is permitted by these Rules, the party making the application shall at the same time send a copy to the other party.

(5)   If any party objects to the directions applied for, the Tribunal shall consider the objection and, if it considers it necessary for the determination of the application, shall give the parties an opportunity to make representations.

(6)   Directions may be given orally or in writing and, unless the Tribunal decides otherwise in any particular case, notice of any written direction (or refusal to give a direction) shall be given to the parties.

(7)   Directions containing a requirement may specify a time limit for complying with the requirement and shall include a statement of the possible consequences of a party's failure to comply with the requirement.

(8)   A person to whom a direction is given under these Rules may apply to the Tribunal showing good cause why it should be varied or set aside, but the Tribunal shall not grant such an application without first notifying any person who applied for the direction and giving that party an opportunity to make representations.

(9)   The following paragraphs of this rule shall apply if the Chairman directs that it is appropriate to hold a pre-hearing review.

(10)   The Secretary shall give the parties not less than 14 days' notice of the time and place of the pre-hearing review.

(11)   At the pre-hearing review, which shall be held before the Chairman—

    (a)   the Chairman shall give all directions appearing necessary or desirable for securing the just, expeditious and economical conduct of the reference; and

    (b)   the Chairman shall endeavour to secure that the parties make all admissions and agreements as they ought reasonably to have made in relation to the proceedings.

(12)   In this rule, "pre-hearing review" means a review of the reference that may be held at any time before the hearing of the reference.

[2397]

10 Particular types of direction

(1)   Directions given by the Tribunal may—

    (a)   fix the time and place of the hearing of the reference and alter any time and place so fixed;

   (b)   provide for an oral hearing, upon such notice as the Tribunal may determine, in connection with any matter arising under the reference;

   (c)   adjourn any oral hearing;

   (d)   extend any time limit for making a reference under the Act or these Rules, or vary (whether by extending or shortening) any other time limit for anything to be done under these Rules;

   (e)   suspend the effect of an Authority notice (or prevent it taking effect) until the reference has been finally disposed of, or until any appeal against the Tribunal's determination of the reference has been finally disposed of, or both;

   (f)   permit or require any party to provide further information or supplementary statements or to amend a response document or a supplementary statement;

   (g)   require any party to file any document—

      (i)   that is in the custody or under the control of that party;

      (ii) that the Tribunal considers is or may be relevant to the determination of the reference; and

      (iii) that has neither been exempted from disclosure by direction given pursuant to rule 8(4) nor been made available pursuant to rule 8(7),

and may also require that any such document directed for filing as above shall be copied to the other party or else be made available to that other party for inspection and copying;

   (h)   require any party to provide a statement of relevant issues and facts, identifying those which are, and are not, agreed by the other party;

   (j)   require any party to file documents for any hearing under these Rules or to agree with the other party the documents to be filed;

   (k)   require any party to file—

      (i)   a list of the witnesses whom the party wishes to call to give evidence at the hearing of the reference; and

      (ii) statements of the evidence which those witnesses intend to give, if called;

   (l)   make provision as to any expert witnesses to be called including the number of such witnesses and the evidence to be given by them;

   (m) provide for the appointment of any expert under paragraph 7(4) of Schedule 13 and for that expert to send the parties copies of any report that he produces;

   (n)   provide for the manner in which any evidence may be given;

   (o)   provide for the use of languages in addition to English, including provision—

      (i)   as to the venue of any hearing under these Rules so as to ensure the availability of simultaneous translation facilities; and

      (ii) for the translation of any document;

   (p)   require that the register shall include no particulars about the reference; and

   (q)   where two or more reference notices have been filed—

      (i)   in respect of the same matter;

      (ii) in respect of separate interests in the same subject in dispute; or

      (iii) which involve the same issues,

provide that the references or any particular issue or matter raised in the references be consolidated or heard together.

(2)   In the case of an application for a direction under paragraph (1)(d) extending any time limit, the Tribunal may direct that the time limit be extended (whether or not it has already expired) if it is satisfied that to do so would be in the interests of justice but, in the case of an application for a direction extending any time limit for making a reference, the Tribunal shall not determine the application without—

   (a)   considering whether the Authority notice was such as to notify the applicant properly and effectively of the referred action; and

   (b)   considering whether the existence of the right to make the reference and the time limit had been notified to the applicant, whether in the Authority notice or otherwise.

(3)   A time limit extended under paragraph (2) may from time to time be further extended by directions of the Tribunal (whether or not that or any subsequent such time limit has already expired) made upon an application under paragraph (1)(d), but no such direction shall be given unless the Tribunal is satisfied that the further extension would be in the interests of justice.

(4)   Where a party files a response document or list later than any time limit imposed by or extended under these Rules but without applying for a direction under paragraph (1)(d) extending the time limit, that party shall be treated as applying for such a direction but no such direction shall be given unless the Tribunal is satisfied that such an extension would be in the interests of justice.

(5)   If a response document or list is not filed in accordance with the time limit imposed by (or extended under) these Rules, the Tribunal may of its own initiative direct that the document or list be filed by a specified date.

(6)   Where an application for a direction is made under paragraph (1)(e), the Tribunal may give such a direction only if it is satisfied that to do so would not prejudice—

    (a)   the interests of any persons (whether consumers, investors or otherwise) intended to be protected by the Authority notice; or

    (b)   the smooth operation or integrity of any market intended to be protected by that notice.

  (7) If the Tribunal gives a direction under paragraph (1)(f) to permit or require a party to provide a supplementary statement or to amend a response document or supplementary statement, the direction may require that party to file any such statement or amendment and send a copy to the other party.

  (8) The Tribunal shall not give a direction under paragraph (1)(g) or (1)(j) in relation to the disclosure of any document to the extent that the Tribunal is satisfied that—

    (a)   it is a protected item or would be included in an exemption provided by rule 8(1) or (2); or

    (b)   it should not be disclosed on one of the grounds specified in rule 8(4),

and, for the purpose of determining whether such a direction should be given in respect of any such document, the Tribunal may—

        (i)   require that the document be produced to the Tribunal;

       (ii)   hear the application in the absence of any party; and

      (iii)   invite any party to make representations.

  (9) In the case of an application for a direction under paragraph (1)(p) that the register should include no particulars about the reference, the Tribunal may give such a direction if it is satisfied that this is necessary, having regard to—

    (a)   the interests of morals, public order, national security or the protection of the private lives of the parties; or

    (b)   any unfairness to the applicant or prejudice to the interests of consumers that might result from the register including particulars about the reference.

[2398]

11 Filing of subsequent notices in relation to the referred action

Where, after the filing of a reference notice, the Authority gives the applicant any notice under the Act in relation to the referred action, the Authority shall without delay file a copy of that notice.

[2399]

12 Summoning of witnesses

  (1) The Tribunal may by summons require any person to—

    (a)   attend, at such time and place as is specified in the summons, to give evidence as a witness;

    (b)   file, within the time specified in the summons, any document in his custody or under his control which the Tribunal considers it necessary to examine; or

    (c)   both attend and file in accordance with sub-paragraphs (a) and (b) above.

  (2) No person may be required under this rule to file a document to the extent that the Tribunal is satisfied that—

    (a)   it is a protected item or would be included in an exemption provided by rule 8(1) or (2); or

    (b)   it should not be disclosed on one of the grounds specified in rule 8(4),

and, for the purpose of satisfying itself in respect of any such document, the Tribunal may—

        (i)   require that the document be produced to the Tribunal;

       (ii)   conduct any hearing in the absence of any party; and

      (iii)   invite any party to make representations.

  (3) A witness summons shall be sent so as to be received by the person to whom it is addressed not less than seven days before the time specified in the summons.

  (4) Every summons under paragraph (1) shall contain a statement warning of the effect of paragraph 11(3) to (5) of Schedule 13 (penalty for refusal or failure to attend or give evidence).

  (5) No person shall be required, in obedience to a summons under paragraph (1), to travel more than 16 kilometres from his place of residence unless the necessary expenses of his attendance are paid or tendered to him in advance, and when the summons is issued at the request of a party, those expenses shall be paid by that party.

  (6) The Tribunal may, upon the application of the person to whom the witness summons is addressed, direct that the witness summons be set aside or varied.

[2400]

13 Preliminary hearing

  (1) The Tribunal may direct that any question of fact or law which appears to be in issue in relation to the reference be determined at a preliminary hearing.

  (2) If, in the opinion of the Tribunal, the determination of that question substantially disposes of the reference, the Tribunal may treat the preliminary hearing as the hearing of the reference and may make such order by way of disposing of the reference as it thinks fit.

PART III
STATUTORY INSTRUMENTS

(3) If the parties so agree in writing, the Tribunal may determine the question without an oral hearing, but, in any such case, the Tribunal may not at the same time dispose of the reference unless the parties have agreed in writing that it may do so.

[2401]

14 Withdrawal of reference and unopposed references

(1) The applicant may withdraw the reference—
  (a) at any time before the hearing of the reference, without permission, by filing a notice to that effect; or
  (b) at the hearing of the reference, with the Tribunal's permission,
and the Tribunal may determine any reference that is so withdrawn.

(2) The Authority may state that it does not oppose the reference or that it is withdrawing its opposition to it—
  (a) at any time before the hearing of the reference, without permission, by filing a notice to that effect; or
  (b) at the hearing of the reference, with the Tribunal's permission.

(3) In any case where—
  (a) the Authority makes a statement within paragraph (2)(a);
  (b) the Authority does not file a statement of case within the time limit imposed by rule 5(1) (or any such time limit as extended under rule 10(1)(d)); or
  (c) the applicant does not file a reply within any time limit imposed by rule 6(1) (or any such time limit as extended under rule 10(1)(d)),
the Tribunal may (subject to its power to give a direction pursuant to rule 10(5)) determine the reference without an oral hearing in accordance with rule 16, but it shall not dismiss a reference without notifying the applicant that it is minded to do so and giving him an opportunity to make representations.

(4) When determining proceedings pursuant to paragraph (1) or (3), the Tribunal may make a costs order under rule 21.

[2402]

15 References by third parties

(1) In the case of any reference made by an applicant under section 393 (third party rights) these Rules apply subject to the modifications set out in this rule.

(2) The following definitions apply in place of the definitions of "Authority notice" and "referred action" given in rule 2(1)—
  (a) if the reference was made under section 393(9) (reference to the Tribunal by a third party to whom a decision notice was copied), "Authority notice" means the decision notice which was copied to the applicant by the Authority;
  (b) if the reference was made under section 393(11) (reference to the Tribunal by a third party who alleges that he was not given a copy of a decision notice), "Authority notice" means the decision notice which the applicant alleges was not copied to him; and
  (c) in either case, "referred action" means the action set out in the Authority notice.

(3) If the reference was made under section 393(11), rule 4(5) (requirement on applicant to file a copy of the Authority notice) does not apply.

(4) The duties of the Authority to set out information under rule 5(2) (statement of case) or to list material under rule 5(3) or 7(1) (lists of documents and further material) apply only to information, documents or material which relate to the matters referred to the Tribunal in accordance with section 393(9) or (as the case may be) section 393(11).

[2403]

PART III
HEARINGS

16 Determination without oral hearing

(1) The Tribunal may determine a reference, or any particular issue, without an oral hearing if—
  (a) the parties agree in writing;
  (b) the issue concerns an application for directions; or
  (c) rule 14(3) applies.

(2) Where a reference or an issue is determined in accordance with this rule, the Tribunal shall consider whether there are circumstances making it undesirable to make a public pronouncement of the whole or part of its decision and may in consequence take any steps, including any one or more of the steps specified in paragraph (3), but any such step shall be taken with a view to ensuring the minimum restriction on public pronouncement that is consistent with the need for the restriction.

(3)   The steps referred to in paragraph (2) are—
- (a)   anonymising the decision;
- (b)   editing the text of the decision;
- (c)   declining to publish the whole or part of the decision.

(4)   Before reaching a decision under paragraph (2), the Tribunal shall invite the parties to make representations on the matter.

[2404]

17   Hearings in public

(1)   In this rule, "hearing" means any hearing under these Rules but does not include any determination under rule 16(1) or the hearing of any application made to the Tribunal without notice to the other party.

(2)   Subject to the following paragraphs of this rule, all hearings shall be in public.

(3)   The Tribunal may direct that all or part of a hearing shall be in private—
- (a)   upon the application of all the parties; or
- (b)   upon the application of any party, if the Tribunal is satisfied that a hearing in private is necessary, having regard to—
  - (i)   the interests of morals, public order, national security or the protection of the private lives of the parties; or
  - (ii)   any unfairness to the applicant or prejudice to the interests of consumers that might result from a hearing in public,

if, in either case, the Tribunal is satisfied that a hearing in private would not prejudice the interests of justice.

(4)   Before determining an application under paragraph (3)(b), the Tribunal shall give the other party an opportunity to make representations.

(5)   Before giving a direction under paragraph (3) that the entire hearing should be in private, the Tribunal shall consider whether only part of the hearing should be heard in private.

(6)   The following persons shall be entitled to attend any hearing of the Tribunal whether or not it is in private—
- (a)   the parties and their representatives;
- (b)   the President or any member of the panel of chairmen or of the lay panel notwithstanding that they are not members of the Tribunal for the purpose of the reference to which the hearing relates;
- (c)   the Secretary and any member of the Tribunal's staff appointed under paragraph 6 of Schedule 13; and
- (d)   a member of the Council on Tribunals or the Scottish Committee of that Council.

(7)   The Tribunal may permit any other person to attend a hearing which is held in private.

(8)   The persons mentioned in paragraph (6)(b) and (d) shall be entitled to attend the deliberations of the Tribunal but shall take no part in those deliberations.

(9)   The Tribunal may exclude from the whole or part of a hearing any person whose conduct, in the opinion of the Tribunal, has disrupted or is likely to disrupt the hearing.

(10)   Subject to any direction under paragraph (11), the Secretary shall provide for the public inspection at the Tribunal's offices of a daily list of all hearings which are to be held together with information about the time and place fixed for the hearings.

(11)   Where all or part of a hearing is held or is to be held in private, the Tribunal may direct that information about the whole or part of the proceedings before the Tribunal (including information that might help to identify any person) shall not be made public, and such a direction may provide for the information (if any) that is to be entered in the register or removed from it.

[2405]

18   Representation at hearings

(1)   Subject to paragraph (2), the parties may appear at the hearing (with assistance from any person if desired), and may be represented by any person, whether or not that person is legally qualified.

(2)   If in any particular case the Tribunal is satisfied that there are good and sufficient reasons for doing so, it may refuse to permit a person to assist or represent a party at the hearing.

(3)   In this rule, "hearing" means any hearing under these Rules.

[2406]

19   Procedure at hearings

(1)   Subject to the Act and these Rules, the Tribunal shall conduct all hearings under these Rules in such manner as it considers most suitable to the clarification of the issues before it and generally to the just, expeditious and economical determination of the proceedings.

(2)   Subject to any directions by the Tribunal, the parties shall be entitled—
   (a)   to give evidence (and, with the consent of the Tribunal, to bring expert evidence);
   (b)   to call witnesses;
   (c)   to question any witnesses; and
   (d)   to address the Tribunal on the evidence, and generally on the subject matter of the reference.

(3)   Evidence may be admitted by the Tribunal whether or not it would be admissible in a court of law and whether or not it was available to the Authority when taking the referred action.

(4)   If a party fails to attend or be represented at any hearing of which it has been duly notified, the Tribunal may, if it is satisfied that there is no good and sufficient reason for the absence—
   (a)   in the case of the hearing of the reference, hear and determine the reference in the party's absence; or
   (b)   in the case of any other hearing, give any direction, determine any issue or adjourn the hearing.

[2407]

20   Decisions of Tribunal

(1)   Subject to paragraph (2) and to rule 16(2), the Tribunal shall make arrangements for the public pronouncement of its decisions, whether by giving its decisions orally in open court or by publishing its decisions in writing.

(2)   Where the whole or any part of any hearing under these Rules was in private, the Tribunal shall consider whether, having regard to—
   (a)   the reason for the hearing or any part of it being in private; and
   (b)   the outcome of the hearing,
it would be undesirable to make a public pronouncement of the whole or part of its decision and may in consequence take any steps, including one or more of the steps specified in paragraph (3), but any such step shall be taken with a view to ensuring the minimum restriction on public pronouncement that is consistent with the need for the restriction.

(3)   The steps referred to in paragraph (2) are—
   (b)   anonymising the decision;
   (b)   editing the text of the decision;
   (c)   declining to publish the whole or part of the decision.

(4)   Before reaching a decision under paragraph (2), the Tribunal shall invite the parties to make representations on the matter.

(5)   The Secretary shall as soon as may be practicable enter every decision (and the reasons for the decision) in the register, but this is subject to any steps taken under paragraph (2) or under rule 16(2) and to any direction given under rule 17(11).

(6)   Every notification of a decision determining a reference which is sent to the parties shall be accompanied by a notification of any provision of the Act relating to appeals from the Tribunal and of the time within which and the place at which such appeal or application for permission to appeal may be made.

[2408]

21   Costs

(1)   In this rule, "costs order" means an order under paragraph 13 of Schedule 13 (power of Tribunal to order payment of costs) that a party pay the whole or part of the costs or expenses incurred by another party, and "the paying party" and "the receiving party" mean, respectively, the parties against whom and in whose favour the Tribunal makes, or (as the case may be) considers making a costs order.

(2)   The Tribunal shall not make a costs order without first giving the paying party an opportunity to make representations against the making of the order.

(3)   Where the Tribunal makes a cost order it may order—
   (a)   that an amount fixed by the Tribunal shall be paid to the receiving party by way of costs or (as the case may be) expenses; or
   (b)   that the costs shall be assessed or (as the case may be) expenses shall be taxed on such basis as it shall specify—
      (i)   in England and Wales, by a costs official;
      (ii)   in Scotland, by the Auditor of the Court of Session;
      (iii) in Northern Ireland, by the Taxing Master of the Supreme Court of Northern Ireland.

[2409]

NOTES
Supreme Court of Northern Ireland: the Supreme Court of Judicature of Northern Ireland is renamed the Court of Judicature of Northern Irelands; see the Constitutional Reform Act 2005, s 59(2) (as from a day to be appointed).

22 Review of Tribunal's decision

(1)   If, on the application of a party or of its own initiative, the Tribunal is satisfied that—

   (a)   its decision determining a reference was wrongly made as a result of an error on the part of the Tribunal staff; or

   (b)   new evidence has become available since the conclusion of the hearing to which that decision relates, the existence of which could not have been reasonably known of or foreseen,

the Tribunal may review and, by certificate signed by the Chairman, set aside the relevant decision.

(2)   An application for the purposes of paragraph (1) may either be made immediately following the decision at the hearing of the reference or shall be filed (stating the grounds in full) not later than 14 days after the date on which notification of the decision was sent to the parties.

(3)   Where the Tribunal proposes to review its decision of its own initiative, it shall notify the parties of that proposal not later than 14 days after the date on which the decision was sent to the parties.

(4)   The parties shall have an opportunity to make representations on any application or proposal for review under this rule and the review shall be determined either by the same members of the Tribunal who decided the case or by a differently constituted Tribunal appointed by the President.

(5)   If, having reviewed the decision, the decision is set aside, the Tribunal shall substitute such decision as it thinks fit or order a re-hearing before either the same or a differently constituted Tribunal.

(6)   The certificate of the Chairman as to the setting aside of the Tribunal's decision under this rule shall be sent to the Secretary who shall immediately make such correction as may be necessary in the register and shall send a copy of the entry so corrected to each party.

[2410]

PART IV
APPEALS FROM THE TRIBUNAL

23 Application for permission to appeal

(1)   In this Part, "appeal" means appeal (or an appeal) under section 137(1) to the Court of Appeal or the Court of Session from a decision of the Tribunal disposing of a reference, and "appellant" means a party applying for permission to appeal.

(2)   An application to the Tribunal for permission to appeal may be made—

   (a)   orally at the hearing after the decision is announced by the Tribunal; or

   (b)   by way of written application filed not later than 14 days after the decision is sent to the party making the application.

(3)   When an application is made under paragraph (2)(b), it shall be signed by the appellant and shall—

   (a)   state the name and address of the appellant and any representative of the appellant;

   (b)   identify the decision of the Tribunal to which the application relates; and

   (c)   state the grounds on which the appellant intends to rely in the appeal.

(4)   An application under this rule may include an application for a direction under rule 10(1)(e) (suspension of Authority's action).

[2411]

24 Decision as to permission to appeal

(1)   An application to the Tribunal for permission to appeal may be decided by the Chairman, on consideration of the application.

(2)   Unless the decision is made immediately following an oral application or the Chairman considers that special circumstances render a hearing desirable, the application for permission to appeal shall be decided without an oral hearing.

(3)   The decision of the Tribunal on an application for permission to appeal, together with the reasons for its decision, shall be recorded in writing.

(4)   Unless the decision is given immediately following an oral application, the Secretary shall notify the appellant and each of the other parties of the decision and the reasons for the decision.

(5)   Where the Tribunal refuses the application, it shall issue a direction that the appellant, if he wishes to seek permission from the Court of Appeal or the Court of Session to appeal, must do so within 14 days of the Tribunal's refusal.

[2412]

25 Reference remitted for rehearing

(1)   The following paragraphs of this rule apply where the Court of Appeal or the Court of Session remits a reference to the Tribunal under section 137(3)(a) for rehearing and determination ("rehearing").

(2)   These Rules, so far as relevant, shall apply to the rehearing as they did to the original hearing of the reference.

(3)   The Tribunal shall, within 28 days of the remittal, give directions in relation to the rehearing.

[2413]

PART V
GENERAL

26 Miscellaneous powers of Tribunal

(1)   Any functions of the Secretary may be performed by an Assistant Secretary to the Tribunal or by some other member of the Tribunal staff authorised for the purpose by the Secretary.

(2)   Subject to the provisions of the Act and these Rules, the Tribunal may regulate its own procedure.

(3)   Without limiting any other powers conferred on it by the Act or by these Rules, the Tribunal may, if it thinks fit—
  (a)   order any response document, supplementary statement or written representation to be struck out at any stage of the proceedings on the ground that it is scandalous, frivolous or vexatious; or
  (b)   order any reference to be struck out for want of prosecution.

(4)   Before making any order under paragraph (3), the Tribunal shall give notice to the party against whom it is proposed that the order should be made, giving it an opportunity to make representations against the making of the order.

[2414]

27 Failure to comply

(1)   Where a party has, without reasonable excuse, failed to comply—
  (a)   with a direction given under these Rules; or
  (b)   with a provision of these Rules,
  the Tribunal may take any one or more of the following steps in respect of that party—
    (i)   make a costs order under rule 21 against that party;
    (ii)   where that party is the applicant, dismiss the whole or part of the reference (or, if there is more than one applicant, that applicant's reference);
    (iii)   where that party is the Authority, strike out the whole or part of the statement of case and, where appropriate, direct that the Authority be debarred from contesting the reference altogether.

(2)   The Tribunal shall not take any of these steps in respect of a party unless it has given that party notice giving it an opportunity to make representations against the taking of any such steps.

[2415]

28 Irregularities

(1)   Any irregularity resulting from failure to comply with any provision of these Rules or of any direction of the Tribunal before the Tribunal has reached its decision shall not of itself render the proceedings void.

(2)   Where any such irregularity comes to the attention of the Tribunal, the Tribunal may, and shall if it considers that any person may have been prejudiced by the irregularity, give such directions as it thinks just to cure or waive the irregularity.

(3)   Clerical mistakes in any document recording a direction or decision of the Chairman or the Tribunal, or errors arising in such a document from an accidental slip or omission, may be corrected by a certificate signed by the Chairman.

[2416]

29 Power of Chairman to exercise powers of Tribunal

Any matter (other than the determination of a reference or the setting aside of a decision on a reference) required or authorised by these Rules to be done by the Tribunal may be done by the Chairman.

[2417]

30 Proof of documents

(1) Any document purporting to a document duly executed or issued by the Chairman or the Secretary on behalf of the Tribunal shall, unless proved to the contrary, be deemed to be a document so executed or issued.

(2) A document purporting to be certified by the Secretary to be a true copy of any entry of a decision in the register shall, unless proved to the contrary, be sufficient evidence of the entry and of the matters referred to in it.

[2418]

31 Sending notices

(1) This rule applies to any notice sent under these Rules, and in this rule—
"send" to a person includes deliver or give to, or serve on, that person;
"notice" includes any notice or other thing required or authorised by these Rules to be sent or delivered to, or served on, any person; and
"recipient" means a person to or on whom any notice is required or authorised to be sent for the purposes of these Rules.

(2) A notice may be sent—
   (a)   by a postal service which seeks to deliver documents or other things by post no later than the next working day in all or in the majority of cases;
   (b)   by fax or other means of electronic communication; or
   (c)   by personal delivery.

(3) A notice shall be sent—
   (a)   in the case of a notice directed to the Tribunal, to the Tribunal's office;
   (b)   in the case of a notice directed to the applicant—
      (i)   to his representative; or
      (ii)   (in any case where there is no representative) to the applicant,
at the appropriate address notified to the Tribunal in accordance with rule 4(3);
   (c)   in the case of a notice directed to the Authority, to the Authority's head office; or
   (d)   otherwise, to the recipient's registered office or last known address.

(4) Subject to paragraphs (5) and (6), a notice that is sent shall be deemed, unless the contrary is proved, to have been received—
   (a)   where it was sent by post, on the second day after it was sent; and
   (b)   in any other case, on the day it was sent.

(5) Where a notice is sent by post to the Tribunal, it shall be deemed to have been received on the day it was actually received by the Tribunal.

(6) No notice shall be deemed to have been received if it is not received in legible form (or, in the case of a document received in electronic form, if the recipient is not readily able to elicit the information in legible form).

(7) Where the time prescribed by these Rules for doing any act expires on a Saturday, Sunday, Christmas Day, Good Friday or bank holiday, the act shall be in time if done on the next following working day.

(8) Paragraph (9) applies where—
   (a)   a recipient cannot be found;
   (b)   a recipient has died and has no known personal representative;
   (c)   a recipient has no address for service in the United Kingdom; or
   (d)   for any other reason service on a recipient cannot be readily effected.

(9) Where this paragraph applies the Chairman may dispense with service on the recipient or may make an order for alternative service on such other person or in such other form (whether by advertisement in a newspaper or otherwise) as the Chairman may think fit.

(10) In this rule, "bank holiday" means a day that is specified in, or appointed under, the Banking and Financial Dealings Act 1971.

[2419]

FINANCIAL SERVICES AND MARKETS ACT 2000 (VARIATION OF THRESHOLD CONDITIONS) ORDER 2001 (NOTE)

(SI 2001/2507)

NOTES
Made: 12 July 2001.
Authority: Financial Services and Markets Act 2000, s 428(3), Sch 6, paras 8, 9.
Commencement: 3 September 2001.
This Order is amended as noted below.
This Order varies the threshold conditions in Sch 6 to the Financial Services and Markets Act 2000 which authorised persons and applicants for authorisation under that Act must satisfy. Article 2 varies the condition set out in para 1(1) of Sch 6 with the effect that limited liability partnerships are not eligible to obtain permission to effect or carry out contracts of insurance. Article 3(1) sets out additional threshold conditions which must be satisfied by insurers having their head office outside the European Economic Area. Conversely, article 3(3) (as substituted by the Financial Services and Markets Act 2000 (Variation of Threshold Conditions) (Amendment) Order 2005, SI 2005/680, art 2(1), (2), as from 6 April 2005) provides that the conditions set out in paras 4, 5 of Sch 6 (relating to adequacy of resources, and fitness and properness) do not apply to Swiss general insurance companies (as defined in Article 1(2)). Note that prior to the amendment by SI 2005/680 paras 3–5 were disapplied. The 2005 Order also adds the following art 4 to this Order—

"4   Swiss general insurance companies

(1)   A Swiss general insurance company must, for the purposes of section 41 and Schedule 6, satisfy the following additional conditions—

(a)   the value of the assets of the business carried on by it in the United Kingdom must not fall below the amount of the liabilities of that business, that value and amount being determined in such manner as may be specified;

(b)   such assets must be maintained in such places as may be specified and must be of such a nature as may be specified as being appropriate in relation to the currency in which the liabilities of the company are or may be required to be met; and

(c)   when applying to the Authority for permission to carry on a regulated activity it must submit to the Authority a statement from the supervisory authorities in Switzerland—

   (i)   stating the classes of insurance business which the company is authorised to carry on in Switzerland,

   (ii)   specifying the risks covered there,

   (iii)   declaring that the company is constituted in Switzerland in a form permitted by Annex 3 of the Agreement signed on 10th October 1989 between the European Economic Community and the Swiss Confederation on direct insurance other than life assurance,

   (iv)   confirming that the company limits its business activities to insurance and to operations directly arising therefrom to the exclusion of all other commercial business, and

   (v)   declaring that the company has the required solvency margin or minimum guarantee fund.

(2)   In this article, "specified" means specified in rules.".

[2420]

FINANCIAL SERVICES AND MARKETS ACT 2000 (CONSULTATION WITH COMPETENT AUTHORITIES) REGULATIONS 2001

(SI 2001/2509)

NOTES
Made: 12 July 2001.
Authority: Financial Services and Markets Act 2000, ss 183(2), 188(2), 417(1), 428(3).
Commencement: 1 December 2001.
These Regulations are reproduced as amended by: the Collective Investment Schemes (Miscellaneous Amendments) Regulations 2003, SI 2003/2066; the Financial Conglomerates and Other Financial Groups Regulations 2004, SI 2004/1862; the Capital Requirements Regulations 2006, SI 2006/3221; the Financial Services and Markets Act 2000 (Regulated Activities) (Amendment No 3) Order 2006, SI 2006/3384; the Financial Services and Markets Act 2000 (Markets in Financial Instruments) Regulations 2007, SI 2007/126; the Financial Services and Markets Act 2000 (Reinsurance Directive) Regulations 2007, SI 2007/3255.

1   These Regulations may be cited as the Financial Services and Markets Act 2000 (Consultation with Competent Authorities) Regulations 2001 and come into force on the day on which section 19 of the Act comes into force.

[2421]

2   In these Regulations—

"the Act" means the Financial Services and Markets Act 2000;

["capital adequacy directive" means Council Directive 2006/49/EC of the European Parliament and of the Council of 14 June 2006 relating to the capital adequacy of investment firms and credit institutions;]

["EEA consolidated supervisor" means the competent authority responsible, under Articles 71 or 72 of the banking consolidation directive or under Articles 71 or 72 of the banking consolidation directive as applied by Articles 2(2) and 37(1) of the capital adequacy directive, for the exercise of supervision of—

    (a)   an EEA parent credit institution;

    (b)   an EEA parent investment firm; or

    (c)   credit institutions or investment firms controlled by an EEA parent financial holding company where the parent is authorised in a different EEA State to at least one of the subsidiary undertakings;]

"EEA credit institution" means an EEA firm falling within paragraph 5(b) of Schedule 3 to the Act;

["EEA insurance undertaking" means an EEA firm falling within paragraph 5(d) of Schedule 3 to the Act;]

"EEA investment firm" means an EEA firm falling within paragraph 5(a) of Schedule 3 to the Act;

["EEA management company" means an EEA firm falling within paragraph 5(f) of Schedule 3 to the Act;]

["EEA parent credit institution" means a parent credit institution in an EEA State which is not a subsidiary undertaking of another credit institution or investment firm authorised in any EEA State, or of a financial holding company set up in any EEA State;]

["EEA parent investment firm" means a parent investment firm in an EEA State which is not a subsidiary undertaking of another credit institution or investment firm authorised in any EEA State or of a financial holding company set up in any EEA State;]

["EEA parent financial holding company" means a parent financial holding company in an EEA State which is not a subsidiary undertaking of a credit institution or investment firm authorised in any EEA State or of another financial holding company set up in any EEA State;]

["EEA reinsurance undertaking" means an EEA firm falling within paragraph 5(da) of Schedule 3 to the Act;]

["financial holding company" has the meaning given by Article 4(19) of the banking consolidation directive;]

     .....

"the Regulated Activities Order" means the Financial Services and Markets Act 2000 (Regulated Activities) Order 2001;

["relevant competent authority" means a competent authority which is not the EEA consolidated supervisor and which has authorised a subsidiary undertaking of an EEA parent credit institution, a subsidiary undertaking of an EEA parent investment firm or a subsidiary undertaking of an EEA parent financial holding company.]

"UK authorised person" has the meaning given by section 178(4) of the Act.

                                                               [2422]

NOTES

Definitions "capital adequacy directive", "EEA consolidated supervisor", "EEA parent credit institution", "EEA parent investment firm", "EEA parent financial holding company", "financial holding company", and "relevant competent authority" inserted by the Capital Requirements Regulations 2006, SI 2006/3221, regs 18, 19, as from 1 January 2007.

Definition "EEA insurance undertaking" inserted by the Financial Conglomerates and Other Financial Groups Regulations 2004, SI 2004/1862, reg 13(1), (2), as from 10 August 2004.

Definition "EEA management company" inserted by the Collective Investment Schemes (Miscellaneous Amendments) Regulations 2003, SI 2003/2066, reg 6(a), as from 13 February 2004.

Definition "EEA reinsurance undertaking" inserted by the Financial Services and Markets Act 2000 (Reinsurance Directive) Regulations 2007, SI 2007/3255, reg 4(1), (2), as from 10 December 2007.

Definition "investment firm" (omitted) revoked by the Financial Services and Markets Act 2000 (Regulated Activities) (Amendment No 3) Order 2006, SI 2006/3384, art 38, as from 1 November 2007 (for the full commencement details of SI 2006/3384, see the Note for that Order at **[2866A]**).

---

3   Where [paragraph (1), (2), (3) or (4)] of regulation 5 applies, the requirement specified by regulation 6 is prescribed for the purposes of section 183(2) of the Act (and so must be complied with by the Authority before determining whether to approve of the change of control or to give a warning notice under section 183(3) or 185(3) of the Act).

                                                              [2423]

NOTES
Words in square brackets substituted by the Financial Conglomerates and Other Financial Groups Regulations 2004, SI 2004/1862, reg 13(1), (3), as from 10 August 2004.

4 Where—
 (a) [paragraph (1), (2), (3) or (4)] of regulation 5 applies; and
 (b) the Authority proposes to give a notice of objection under 187(1) of the Act;

the requirement specified by regulation 6 is prescribed for the purposes of section 188(2) of the Act (and so must be complied with by the Authority before it gives a warning notice under section 188(1) of the Act).

[2424]

NOTES
Words in square brackets substituted by the Financial Conglomerates and Other Financial Groups Regulations 2004, SI 2004/1862, reg 13(1), (4), as from 10 August 2004.

5—(1) This paragraph applies where—
 (a) a person ("the acquirer") proposes to acquire or has acquired control, an additional kind of control or an increase in a relevant kind of control over a UK authorised person in circumstances falling within section 178(1) or (2) of the Act;
 (b) that UK authorised person is an investment firm;
 [(c) the acquirer is any of the following—
  (i) an EEA investment firm;
  (ii) an EEA credit institution;
  (iii) an EEA insurance undertaking; or
  (iv) the parent undertaking of an EEA firm of a kind specified by paragraph (i), (ii) or (iii);] and
 (d) as a result of the acquisition or proposed acquisition, the acquirer is or would become a parent undertaking of the UK authorised person.

 (2) This paragraph applies where—
 (a) a person ("the acquirer") proposes to acquire or has acquired control, an additional kind of control or an increase in a relevant kind of control over a UK authorised person in circumstances falling within section 178(1) or (2) of the Act;
 (b) that UK authorised person has permission to accept deposits (within the meaning of the Regulated Activities Order);
 [(c) the acquirer is any of the following—
  (i) an EEA investment firm;
  (ii) an EEA credit institution;
  (iii) an EEA insurance undertaking; or
  (iv) the parent undertaking of an EEA firm of a kind specified by paragraph (i), (ii) or (iii);] and
 (d) as a result of the acquisition or proposed acquisition, the acquirer is or would become a parent undertaking of the UK authorised person.

 [(3) This paragraph applies where—
 (a) a person ("the acquirer") proposes to acquire or has acquired control, an additional kind of control or an increase in a relevant kind of control over a UK authorised person in circumstances falling within section 178(1) or (2) of the Act;
 (b) that UK authorised person has permission to operate a collective investment scheme;
 [(c) the acquirer is any of the following—
  (i) an EEA investment firm;
  (ii) an EEA credit institution;
  (iii) an EEA insurance undertaking;
  (iv) an EEA management company; or
  (v) the parent undertaking of an EEA firm of a kind specified by paragraph (i), (ii), (iii) or (iv);] and
 (d) as a result of the acquisition or proposed acquisition, the acquirer is or would become a parent undertaking of the UK authorised person.]

 [(4) This paragraph applies where—
 (a) a person ("the acquirer") proposes to acquire or has acquired control, an additional kind of control or an increase in a relevant kind of control over a UK authorised person in circumstances falling within section 178(1) or (2) of the Act;
 (b) that UK authorised person has permission to effect or carry on contracts of insurance (within the meaning of the Regulated Activities Order);
 (c) the acquirer is any of the following—

(i)   an EEA investment firm;
(ii)   an EEA credit institution;
(iii)   an EEA insurance undertaking; ...
[(iiia) an EEA reinsurance undertaking; or]
(iv)   the parent undertaking of an EEA firm of a kind specified by paragraph (i), (ii)[, (iii) or (iiia)]; and
(d)   as a result of the acquisition or proposed acquisition, the acquirer is or would become a parent undertaking of the UK authorised person.]

[2425]

NOTES
Para (1): sub-para (c) substituted by the Financial Conglomerates and Other Financial Groups Regulations 2004, SI 2004/1862, reg 13(1), (5)(a), as from 10 August 2004.
Para (2): sub-para (c) substituted by SI 2004/1862, reg 13(1), (5)(b), as from 10 August 2004.
Para (3): added by the Collective Investment Schemes (Miscellaneous Amendments) Regulations 2003, SI 2003/2066, reg 6(d), as from 13 February 2004; sub-para (c) substituted by SI 2004/1862, reg 13(1), (5)(c), as from 10 August 2004.
Para (4): added by SI 2004/1862, reg 13(1), (5)(d), as from 10 August 2004; word omitted from sub-para (c)(iii) revoked, sub-para (c)(iiia) inserted, and words in square brackets in sub-para (c)(iv) substituted, by the Financial Services and Markets Act 2000 (Reinsurance Directive) Regulations 2007, SI 2007/3255, reg 4(1), (4), as from 10 December 2007.

[6   The requirement specified by this regulation is that the Authority must, as the case may be, consult the home state regulator of any EEA firm that is mentioned in paragraph (1)(c), (2)(c), (3)(c) or (4)(c) of regulation 5.]

[2426]

NOTES
Commencement: 10 August 2004.
Substituted by the Financial Conglomerates and Other Financial Groups Regulations 2004, SI 2004/1862, reg 13(1), (6), as from 10 August 2004.

[7—(1)   Where paragraph (3) applies, the requirement specified by paragraph (5) is prescribed for the purposes of section 183(2) of the Act and so must be complied with by the Authority before it determines whether to approve the change of control or give a warning notice under section 183(3) or 185(3) of the Act.

(2)   Where paragraph (4) applies, the requirement specified by paragraph (5) is prescribed for the purposes of section 188(2) of the Act and so must be complied with by the Authority before it gives a warning notice under section 188(1) of the Act.

(3)   This paragraph applies where—
(a)   a person ("the acquirer") proposes to acquire or has acquired control, an additional kind of control or an increase in a relevant kind of control over a UK authorised person in circumstances falling within section 178(1) or (2) of the Act;
(b)   that UK authorised person has an EEA right to carry on an activity in an EEA State other than the United Kingdom which derives from any of—
(i)   the insurance directives;
(ii)   the banking consolidation directive;
(iii)   the [markets in financial instruments directive]; or
(iv)   the UCITS directive; and
(c)   that UK authorised person is a member of a financial conglomerate (within the meaning of article 2(14) of Directive 2002/87/EC of the European Parliament and of the Council of 16 December 2002 on the supplementary supervision of credit institutions, insurance undertakings and investment firms in a financial conglomerate and amending Council Directives 73/239/EEC, 79/267/EEC, 92/49/EEC, 93/6/EEC, 93/22/EEC and Directives 98/78/EC and 2000/12/EC of the European Parliament and of the Council).

(4)   This paragraph applies where—
(a)   a circumstance has arisen in respect of which the Authority may give a decision notice to a UK authorised person under section 187 of the Act;
(b)   that UK authorised person has an EEA right to carry on activity in an EEA State other than the United Kingdom which derives from any of—
(i)   the insurance directives;
(ii)   the banking consolidation directive;
(iii)   the [markets in financial instruments directive]; or
(iv)   the UCITS directive;
(c)   that UK authorised person is a member of a financial conglomerate (within the meaning of article 2(14) of Directive 2002/87/EC of the European Parliament and of the Council of 16 December 2002 on the supplementary supervision of credit institutions, insurance

undertakings and investment firms in a financial conglomerate and amending Council Directives 73/239/EEC, 79/267/EEC, 92/49/EEC, 93/6/EEC, 93/22/EEC and Directives 98/78/EC and 2000/12/EC of the European Parliament and of the Council).

(5) The requirement specified by this paragraph is that the Authority must, where it considers that the action it proposes to take—

    (a)   constitutes a major sanction or an exceptional measure; and

    (b)   is of importance for the supervisory tasks of the home state regulator of any EEA firm that is a member of a financial conglomerate and is—

        (i)   an EEA investment firm;

        (ii)   an EEA credit institution; or

        (iii)   an EEA insurance undertaking,

consult that home state regulator.

(6) But paragraph (5) does not apply where the Authority—

    (a)   considers that there is an urgent need to act;

    (b)   considers that such consultation may jeopardise the effectiveness of any action to be taken by it; or

    (c)   has already consulted that home state regulator regarding that matter.

(7) Where paragraph (5) does not apply by virtue of paragraph (6)(a) or (b), the Authority must inform the home state regulator in question as soon as is reasonably practicable.]

[2427]

NOTES

Commencement: 10 August 2004.

Added by the Financial Conglomerates and Other Financial Groups Regulations 2004, SI 2004/1862, reg 13(1), (7), as from 10 August 2004.

Paras (3), (4): words in square brackets in sub-para (b)(iii) substituted by the Financial Services and Markets Act 2000 (Markets in Financial Instruments) Regulations 2007, SI 2007/126, reg 3(6), Sch 6, Pt 2, para 16, as from 1 November 2007 (for the full commencement details of SI 2007/126, see reg 1 of those Regulations at **[4051]**).

[8—(1) Where paragraph (3) applies, the requirement specified by paragraph (5) is prescribed for the purposes of section 183(2) of the Act and so must be complied with by the Authority before it determines whether to approve the change of control or give a warning notice under section 183(3) or 185(3) of the Act.

(2) Where paragraph (4) applies, the requirement specified by paragraph (5) is prescribed for the purposes of section 188(2) of the Act and so must be complied with by the Authority before it gives a warning notice under section 188(1) of the Act.

(3) This paragraph applies where—

    (a)   a person ("the acquirer") proposes to acquire or has acquired control or an additional kind of control over a UK authorised person in circumstances falling within section 178(1) or (2) of the Act;

    (b)   that UK authorised person is, or is controlled by, an EEA parent credit institution or an EEA parent investment firm or is controlled by an EEA parent financial holding company which is subject to supervision on a consolidated basis in accordance with the banking consolidation directive or with the banking consolidation directive as applied by Articles 2(2) and 37(1) of the capital adequacy directive.

(4) This paragraph applies where—

    (a)   a circumstance has arisen in respect of which the Authority may give a decision notice to a UK authorised person under section 187 of the Act;

    (b)   that UK authorised person is, or is controlled by, an EEA parent credit institution or an EEA parent investment firm or is controlled by an EEA parent financial holding company which is subject to supervision on a consolidated basis in accordance with the banking consolidation directive or with the banking consolidation directive as applied by Articles 2(2) and 37(1) of the capital adequacy directive.

(5) The requirement specified by this paragraph is that the Authority must consult—

    (a)   the EEA consolidated supervisor where it considers that the action it proposes to take constitutes a major sanction or an exceptional measure; and

    (b)   a relevant competent authority where it considers that the action it proposes to take constitutes a major sanction or an exceptional measure which is of importance for the supervisory tasks of that relevant competent authority.

(6) Paragraphs (1) and (2) of this regulation do not apply where the Authority considers that—

    (a)   there is an urgent need to act; or

    (b)   such consultation may jeopardise the effectiveness of the actions referred to in paragraph (5), but in such a case the Authority must, without delay, inform the EEA consolidated supervisor and the relevant competent authorities referred to in paragraph (5)(b) of the action that it has taken.]

[2427A]

NOTES
Commencement: 1 January 2007.
Added by the Capital Requirements Regulations 2006, SI 2006/3221, regs 18, 20, as from 1 January 2007.

FINANCIAL SERVICES AND MARKETS ACT 2000 (GAMING CONTRACTS) ORDER 2001

(SI 2001/2510)

NOTES
Made: 12 July 2001.
Authority: Financial Services and Markets Act 2000, s 412(2), (6).
Commencement: 1 December 2001.
As of 1 February 2009, this Order had not been amended.

1 This Order may be cited as the Financial Services and Markets Act 2000 (Gaming Contracts) Order 2001 and comes into force on the day on which section 19 of the Act comes into force.

[2428]

2—(1) Any activity of the kind—
  (a) specified by article 14 or 21 of the Financial Services and Markets Act 2000 (Regulated Activities) Order 2001 ("the Regulated Activities Order") (dealing in investments as principal or agent);
  (b) specified by article 64 of that Order (agreeing to carry on specified kinds of activity), so far as relevant to either of those articles; or
  (c) which would be so specified apart from any exclusion from any of those articles made by that Order;
is specified for the purposes of paragraph (b) of subsection (2) of section 412 of the Act (contracts not to be void or unenforceable because of the law relating to gaming).

  (2) The class of investment consisting of securities and contractually based investments (within the meaning of the Regulated Activities Order) is specified for the purposes of paragraph (c) of subsection (2) of that section.

[2429]

FINANCIAL SERVICES AND MARKETS ACT 2000 (EEA PASSPORT RIGHTS) REGULATIONS 2001

(SI 2001/2511)

NOTES
Made: 12 July 2001.
Authority: Financial Services and Markets Act 2000, ss 417(1), 426–428, Sch 3, paras 13(1)(b)(iii), 14(1)(b), 17(a), (b), (c), 18, 22.
Commencement: see reg 1(1).
These Regulations are reproduced as amended by: the Electronic Money (Miscellaneous Amendments) Regulations 2002, SI 2002/765; the Insurance Mediation Directive (Miscellaneous Amendments) Regulations 2003, SI 2003/1473; the Collective Investment Schemes (Miscellaneous Amendments) Regulations 2003, SI 2003/2066; the Financial Conglomerates and Other Financial Groups Regulations 2004, SI 2004/1862; the Capital Requirements Regulations 2006, SI 2006/3221; the Financial Services and Markets Act 2000 (EEA Passport Rights) (Amendment) Regulations 2006, SI 2006/3385; the Financial Services and Markets Act 2000 (Markets in Financial Instruments) (Amendment) Regulations 2007, SI 2007/763; the Reinsurance Directive Regulations 2007, SI 2007/3253.

ARRANGEMENT OF REGULATIONS

PART I
GENERAL

PART II
EXERCISE OF PASSPORT RIGHTS BY EEA FIRMS

Contents of consent notice and regulator's notice

Changes relating to EEA firms

Cancellation of qualification for authorisation

Applications for approval under section 60 by EEA firms

PART III
EXERCISE OF PASSPORT RIGHTS BY UK FIRMS

Changes relating to UK firms

UK firms: scope of outward passport

PART IV
TRANSITIONAL PROVISIONS

PART I
GENERAL

1 Citation, commencement and interpretation

(1)   These Regulations may be cited as the Financial Services and Markets Act 2000 (EEA Passport Rights) Regulations 2001, and come into force on the day on which section 19 of the Act comes into force.

(2)   In these Regulations—
   "the 2BCD Regulations" means the Banking Coordination (Second Council Directive) Regulations 1992;
   "the Act" means the Financial Services and Markets Act 2000;
   "authorised agent" means, in relation to an EEA firm or UK firm, an agent or employee of the firm who has authority to bind the firm in its relations with third parties, and to represent the

firm in its relations with the Authority or the host state regulator (as the case may be) and with the courts in the United Kingdom or the EEA State concerned (as the case may be);

"claims representative", in relation to a UK firm and an EEA State, means a person who has been designated as the firm's representative in that EEA State, and has authority—

(a) to act on behalf of the firm and to represent, or to instruct others to represent, the firm in relation to any matters giving rise to claims made against policies issued by the firm, to the extent that they cover motor vehicles risks situated in the EEA State;

(b) to pay sums in settlement of such claims (but not to settle such claims); and

(c) to accept service on behalf of the firm of proceedings in respect of such claims;

"commencement" means the beginning of the day on which section 19 of the Act comes into force;

"contract of insurance", "contract of general insurance" and "contract of long-term insurance" have the same meaning as in the Regulated Activities Order;

"credit institution" means an EEA firm falling within paragraph 5(b) of Schedule 3;

["electronic money institution" means an electronic money institution as defined in Article 1 of directive 2000/46/EC of the European Parliament and of the Council of 18th September 2000 on the taking up, pursuit of and prudential supervision of the business of electronic money institutions;]

"EEA activities" means—

(a) in relation to an EEA firm, activities which the firm is seeking to carry on in the United Kingdom in exercise of an EEA right;

(b) in relation to a UK firm, activities which the firm is seeking to carry on in another EEA State in exercise of an EEA right;

"financial institution" means an EEA firm falling within paragraph 5(c) of Schedule 3;

"the Friendly Societies Act" means the Friendly Societies Act 1992;

"health insurance risks", in relation to an EEA State, means risks of a kind mentioned in paragraph 2 of Schedule 1 to the Regulated Activities Order (sickness), where—

(a) contracts of insurance covering those risks serve as a partial or complete alternative to the health cover provided by the statutory social security system in that EEA State; and

(b) the law of that EEA State requires such contracts to be operated on a technical basis similar to life assurance in accordance with all the conditions listed in the first sub-paragraph of Article 54(2) of the third non-life insurance directive;

"the Insurance Companies Act" means the Insurance Companies Act 1982;

"insurance firm" means an EEA firm falling within paragraph 5(d) of Schedule 3;

["insurance intermediary" means an EEA firm falling within paragraph 5(e) of Schedule 3;]

"investment firm" means an EEA firm falling within paragraph 5(a) of Schedule 3;

"the ISD Regulations" means the Investment Services Regulations 1995;

["management company" means an EEA firm falling within paragraph 5(f) of Schedule 3;]

"national bureau", in relation to an EEA State, means a professional organisation—

(a) which has been constituted in that EEA State in accordance with Recommendation No 5 adopted on 25th January 1949 by the Road Transport Sub-committee of the Inland Transport Committee of the United Nations Economic Commission for Europe; and

(b) which groups together undertakings which in that EEA State are authorised to conduct the business of motor vehicle liability insurance;

"national guarantee fund", in relation to an EEA State, means a body—

(a) which has been set up or authorised in that EEA State in accordance with Article 1(4) of Council Directive 84/5/EEC on the approximation of laws of the Member States relating to insurance against civil liability in respect of the use of motor vehicles; and

(b) which provides compensation for damage to property or personal injuries caused by unidentified vehicles or vehicles for which the insurance obligation provided for in Article 1(1) of that Directive has not been satisfied;

"the Regulated Activities Order" means the Financial Services and Markets Act 2000 (Regulated Activities) Order 2001;

"relevant motor vehicle risks" means risks of damage arising out of or in connection with the use of motor vehicles on land, including third party risks (but excluding carrier's liability);

"requisite details", in relation to a branch, means—

(a) particulars of the programme of operations carried on, or to be carried on, from the branch, including a description of the particular EEA activities to be carried on, and of the structural organisation of the branch;

(b) the address in the EEA State in which the branch is, or is to be, established from which information about the business may be obtained; and

(c) the names of the managers of the business;

"Schedule 3" means Schedule 3 to the Act;

["tied agent" has the meaning given in Article 4.1.25 of the markets in financial instruments directive;

"UK investment firm" means a UK firm—

    (a)   which is an investment firm [(within the meaning of section 424A of the Act)],

    (b)   whose EEA right derives from the markets in financial instruments directive].

[2430]

NOTES

Para (2) is amended as follows:

Definition "electronic money institution" inserted by the Electronic Money (Miscellaneous Amendments) Regulations 2002, SI 2002/765, reg 10(1), (2), as from 27 April 2002.

Definition "insurance intermediary" inserted by the Insurance Mediation Directive (Miscellaneous Amendments) Regulations 2003, SI 2003/1473, reg 8(1), (2), as from 14 January 2005.

Definition "management company" inserted by the Collective Investment Schemes (Miscellaneous Amendments) Regulations 2003, SI 2003/2066, reg 2(3), as from 13 February 2004.

Definitions "tied agent" and "UK investment firm" inserted by the Financial Services and Markets Act 2000 (EEA Passport Rights) (Amendment) Regulations 2006, SI 2006/3385, regs 2, 3, as from 1 November 2007.

Words in square brackets in definition "UK investment firm" inserted by the Financial Services and Markets Act 2000 (Markets in Financial Instruments) (Amendment) Regulations 2007, SI 2007/763, reg 8, as from 1 November 2007.

Modified in relation to Gibraltar by the Financial Services and Markets Act 2000 (Gibraltar) Order 2001, SI 2001/3084 at **[2495]** et seq.

PART II
EXERCISE OF PASSPORT RIGHTS BY EEA FIRMS

Contents of consent notice and regulator's notice

2 Establishment of a branch: contents of consent notice

(1)   The following information is prescribed for the purposes of paragraph 13(1)(b)(iii) of Schedule 3 (and is therefore to be included in a consent notice given to the Authority by a firm's home state regulator pursuant to paragraph 13(1)(a) of Schedule 3).

(2)   In the case of an investment firm, the prescribed information is—

    (a)   a statement that the firm is an investment firm;

    (b)   the requisite details of the branch; ...

    [(c)   details of the accredited compensation scheme of which the firm is a member in accordance with Directive 97/9/EC of the European Parliament and of the Council of 3rd March 1997 on investor-compensation schemes; and

    (d)   a statement of whether the firm intends to use a tied agent established in the United Kingdom.]

    [(2A)   In the case of a management company, the prescribed information is—

    (a)   a statement that the firm is a management company;

    (b)   the requisite details of the branch; and

    (c)   details of any compensation scheme which is intended to protect the branch's investors.]

(3)   In the case of a credit institution, the prescribed information is—

    (a)   a statement that the firm is a credit institution;

    (b)   the requisite details of the branch;

    (c)   the amount of the firm's own funds (as defined in Section 1 of Chapter 2 of Title V to the banking consolidation directive); and

    (d)   [except where the firm is an electronic money institution,] [the sum of the capital requirements under Article 75 of the banking consolidation directive].

(4)   In the case of a financial institution, the prescribed information is—

    (a)   a statement that—

        (i)   the firm is a financial institution;

        (ii)   the firm is a subsidiary undertaking of a credit institution [(other than an electronic money institution)] which is authorised in the EEA State in question and which holds at least 90 per cent of the voting rights in the firm (and for the purpose of this paragraph any two or more credit institutions which are authorised in that EEA State and hold voting rights in the firm are to be treated as a single credit institution, and as being "parent undertakings" of the firm);

        (iii)   the firm carries on in that EEA State the EEA activities in question;

        (iv)   the memorandum and articles of association, or other constituent instrument, of the firm permit it to carry on those activities;

        (v)   the consolidated supervision of the firm's parent undertaking or, if more than one, any one of them effectively includes supervision of the firm;

        (vi)   the firm's parent undertaking has guaranteed or, if more than one, they have jointly and severally guaranteed, the firm's obligations, with the consent of the home state regulator;

(vii) the firm's business is being conducted in a prudent manner;
(b) the requisite details of the branch;
(c) the amount of the firm's own funds (as defined in Section 1 of Chapter 2 of Title V to the banking consolidation directive); and
[(d) the sum of the capital requirements under Article 75 of the banking consolidation directive of the firm's parent undertaking.]

(5) In the case of an insurance firm, the prescribed information is—
(a) a scheme of operations prepared in accordance with such requirements as may be imposed by the firm's home state regulator, setting out (amongst other things) the types of business to be carried on and the structural organisation of the branch;
(b) the name of the firm's authorised agent;
(c) the address in the United Kingdom from which information about the business may be obtained, and a statement that this is the address for service on the firm's authorised agent;
(d) in the case of a firm which intends to cover relevant motor vehicle risks, a declaration by the firm that it has become a member of the Motor Insurers' Bureau (being a company limited by guarantee and incorporated under the Companies Act 1929 on the 14th June 1946); and
(e) a statement by the firm's home state regulator attesting that the firm has the minimum margin of solvency calculated in accordance with such of the following as are appropriate—
(i) Articles 16 and 17 of the first non-life insurance directive [(as last amended by Directive 2002/87/EC of the European Parliament and of the Council)], and
(ii) Articles 18, 19 and 20 of the first life insurance directive.

[2431]

NOTES

Para (2): word omitted from sub-para (b) revoked, and sub-paras (c), (d) substituted (for the original sub-para (c)), by the Financial Services and Markets Act 2000 (EEA Passport Rights) (Amendment) Regulations 2006, SI 2006/3385, regs 2, 4, as from 1 April 2007.

Para (2A): inserted by the Collective Investment Schemes (Miscellaneous Amendments) Regulations 2003, SI 2003/2066, reg 3(2)(a), as from 13 February 2004.

Para (3): words in first pair of square brackets in sub-para (d) inserted by the Electronic Money (Miscellaneous Amendments) Regulations 2002, SI 2002/765, reg 10(1), (2), as from 27 April 2002; words in second pair of square brackets in sub-para (d) substituted by the Capital Requirements Regulations 2006, SI 2006/3221, reg 29(4), Sch 6, para 9(1), (2), as from 1 January 2007.

Para (4): words in square brackets in sub-para (a) inserted by SI 2002/765, reg 10(1), (2), as from 27 April 2002; sub-para (d) substituted by SI 2006/3221, reg 29(4), Sch 6, para 9(1), (3), as from 1 January 2007.

Para (5): words in square brackets in sub-para (e)(i) inserted by the Financial Conglomerates and Other Financial Groups Regulations 2004, SI 2004/1862, reg 14(4), as from 10 August 2004.

3 Provision of services: contents of regulator's notice

(1) The following information is prescribed for the purposes of paragraph 14(1)(b) of Schedule 3 (and is therefore to be included in a regulator's notice given to the Authority by a firm's home state regulator pursuant to that paragraph).

(2) [Subject to paragraph (2ZA), in] the case of an investment firm, the prescribed information is—
(a) a statement that the firm is an investment firm; ...
(b) particulars of the programme of operations to be carried on in the United Kingdom, including a description of the particular EEA activities to be carried on[; and
(c) a statement of whether the firm intends to use a tied agent to provide services in the United Kingdom].

[(2ZA) In the case of an investment firm exercising the right under Article 31.5 of the markets in financial instruments directive, the prescribed information is—
(a) a statement that the firm is an investment firm; and
(b) a statement that the firm intends to exercise that right in the United Kingdom.]

[(2A) In the case of a management company, the prescribed information is—
(a) a statement that the firm is a management company;
(b) particulars of the programme of operations to be carried on in the United Kingdom including a description of the particular EEA activities to be carried on; and
(c) details of any compensation scheme which is intended to protect investors.]

(3) In the case of an insurance firm, the prescribed information is—
(a) a statement of the classes of business which the firm is authorised to carry on in accordance with Article 6 of the first non-life insurance directive or Article 6 of the first life insurance directive;
(b) the name and address of the firm;

    (c)   the nature of the risks or commitments which the firm proposes to cover in the United Kingdom;

    (d)   in the case of a firm which intends to cover relevant motor vehicle risks—

        (i)   the name and address of the claims representative; and

        (ii)   a declaration by the firm that it has become a member of the Motor Insurers' Bureau; and

    (e)   a statement by the firm's home state regulator attesting that the firm has the minimum margin of solvency calculated in accordance with such of the following as are appropriate—

        (i)   Articles 16 and 17 of the first non-life insurance directive [(as last amended by Directive 2002/87/EC of the European Parliament and of the Council)], and

        (ii)   Articles 18, 19 and 20 of the first life insurance directive.

[(4)   In the case of an insurance intermediary, the prescribed information is that the firm intends to carry on insurance mediation or reinsurance mediation (in each case, within the meaning of the insurance mediation directive) by providing services in the United Kingdom.]

[2432]

NOTES

Para (2): words in first pair of square brackets substituted, word omitted revoked, and sub-para (c) (and the word immediately preceding it) added, by the Financial Services and Markets Act 2000 (EEA Passport Rights) (Amendment) Regulations 2006, SI 2006/3385, regs 2, 5(a), as from 1 April 2007.

Para (2ZA): inserted by SI 2006/3385, regs 2, 5(b), as from 1 April 2007.

Para (2A): inserted by the Collective Investment Schemes (Miscellaneous Amendments) Regulations 2003, SI 2003/2066, reg 3(2)(b), as from 13 February 2004.

Para (3): words in square brackets in sub-para (e) inserted by Financial Conglomerates and Other Financial Groups Regulations 2004, SI 2004/1862, reg 14 (4), as from 10 August 2004.

Para (4): added by the Insurance Mediation Directive (Miscellaneous Amendments) Regulations 2003, SI 2003/1473, reg 8(1), (3), as from 14 January 2005.

Changes relating to EEA firms

4 [Management] [companies], credit institutions and financial institutions: changes to branch details

(1)   [A] [management company], credit institution or financial institution which has established a branch in the United Kingdom in exercise of an EEA right must not make a change in the requisite details of the branch, unless the relevant requirements have been complied with.

(2)   Where the relevant requirements have been complied with, the firm's permission is to be treated as varied accordingly.

(3)   For the purposes of this regulation, the "relevant requirements" are those of paragraph (4) or (if the change is occasioned by circumstances beyond the firm's control) paragraph (5).

(4)   The requirements of this paragraph are that—

    (a)   the firm has given a notice to the Authority and to its home state regulator stating the details of the proposed change;

    (b)   the Authority has received from the home state regulator a notice stating those details; and

    (c)   either the Authority has informed the firm that it may make the change, or the period of one month beginning with the day on which the firm gave the Authority the notice mentioned in sub-paragraph (a) has elapsed.

(5)   The requirements of this paragraph are that the firm has as soon as practicable (whether before or after the change) given a notice to the Authority and to its home state regulator, stating details of the change.

(6)   The Authority must, as soon as practicable after receiving a notice from [a] [management company], credit institution or financial institution under this regulation, inform the firm of any consequential changes in the applicable provisions (within the meaning of paragraph 13 of Schedule 3).

[2433]

NOTES

Regulation heading: word in first pair of square brackets substituted (for the original words "Investment firms, management") by the Financial Services and Markets Act 2000 (EEA Passport Rights) (Amendment) Regulations 2006, SI 2006/3385, regs 2, 6(a), as from 1 November 2007 (for transitional provisions see the note below); word in second pair of square brackets inserted by the Collective Investment Schemes (Miscellaneous Amendments) Regulations 2003, SI 2003/2066, reg 3(2)(c), as from 13 February 2004.

Para (1): word in first pair of square brackets substituted (for the original words "An investment firm") by SI 2006/3385, regs 2, 6(b), as from 1 November 2007 (for transitional provisions see the note below); words in second pair of square brackets inserted by SI 2003/2066, reg 3(2)(c), as from 13 February 2004.

Para (6): word in first pair of square brackets substituted (for the original words "an investment firm") by SI 2006/3385, regs 2, 6(b), as from 1 November 2007 (for transitional provisions see the note below); words in second pair of square brackets inserted by SI 2003/2066, reg 3(2)(c), as from 13 February 2004.

Transitional provisions: the Financial Services and Markets Act 2000 (EEA Passport Rights) (Amendment) Regulations 2006, SI 2006/3385, reg 15 (at **[2866C]**) provides as follows—

"15   Transitional and saving provisions

(1)   Where an investment firm has given notice to the Authority and to its home state regulator pursuant to regulation 4(4)(a) of the principal Regulations (of a change in the requisite details of its branch) on or before 31st October 2007, regulation 4 continues to apply in relation to that change as if it had not been amended by these Regulations, and regulation 4A of the principal Regulations (inserted by these Regulations) does not apply in relation to that change.

(2)   Where an investment firm has given notice to the Authority and to its home state regulator pursuant to regulation 5(3)(a) of the principal Regulations or before 31st October 2007 (in relation to a change in the matters referred to in regulation 3(2)(b) of those Regulations), regulation 5 continues to apply in relation to that change as if it had not been amended by these Regulations, and regulation 5A of the principal Regulations (inserted by these Regulations) does not apply in relation to that change.

(3)   Where on or before 31st October 2007—
    (a)   a UK investment firm has given notice to the Authority and to its host state regulator pursuant to regulation 11(2)(a) of the principal Regulations (of a change in the requisite details of the branch) on or before 31st October 2007, but
    (b)   the Authority has not performed its function under regulation 11(4) of those Regulations,
the Authority must inform the host state regulator of the change pursuant to regulation 11A(3) of the principal Regulations (inserted by these Regulations) instead of performing its function under regulation 11(4).

(4)   Where the Authority has performed its function under regulation 11(4) of the principal Regulations (in relation to a change in the requisite details of a branch by a UK investment firm) on or before 31st October 2007, regulation 11 of the principal Regulations continues to apply in relation to that change as if it had not been amended by these Regulations, and regulation 11A of the principal Regulations (inserted by these Regulations) does not apply in relation to that change.

(5)   Where a UK investment firm has given notice to the Authority and to its host state regulator pursuant to regulation 12(2)(a) of the principal Regulations (in relation to a change in its programme of operations or EEA activities) on or before 31st October 2007—
    (a)   regulation 12A of the principal Regulations (inserted by these Regulations) does not apply in relation to that change;
    (b)   the firm must not make the change to which the notice relates until the period of one month beginning with the day on which it gave the notice pursuant to regulation 12(2)(a) of the principal Regulations has elapsed; and
    (c)   the Authority must, as soon as reasonably practicable after receiving the notice, inform the host state regulator of the proposed change.

(6)   In this regulation, "UK investment firm" means a UK firm (within the meaning of Schedule 3)—
    (a)   which is an investment firm (within the meaning of the investment services directive); and
    (b)   whose EEA right derives from that directive.".

Transitional provisions: see also the Financial Services and Markets Act 2000 (Markets in Financial Instruments) Regulations 2007, SI 2007/126, reg 6A at **[4056A]** (transitional provisions: EEA investment firms exercising passport rights under the investment services directive).

[4A   Investment firms: changes to branch details

(1)   An investment firm which has established a branch in the United Kingdom in exercise of an EEA right must not—
    (a)   make a change in the requisite details of the branch,
    (b)   use, for the first time, any tied agent established in the United Kingdom, or
    (c)   cease to use tied agents established in the United Kingdom,
unless the requirements of paragraph (3) have been complied with.

(2)   Where those requirements have been complied with, the firm's permission is to be treated as varied accordingly.

(3)   The requirements are that—
    (a)   the firm has given a notice to its home state regulator stating the details of the proposed change, and
    (b)   the period of one month beginning with the day on which the firm gave the notice has elapsed.

(4)   Paragraph (1) does not apply to a change occasioned by circumstances beyond the firm's control.]

[2433A]

NOTES

Commencement: 1 April 2007 (certain purposes); 1 November 2007 (otherwise) (see below).

Inserted by the Financial Services and Markets Act 2000 (EEA Passport Rights) (Amendment) Regulations 2006, SI 2006/3385, regs 2, 7, as from 1 April 2007 (certain purposes), and as from 1 November 2007 (otherwise) (see below). For transitional provisions, see the note to reg 4 at **[2433]**.

Commencement of this regulation: the commencement of the Financial Services and Markets Act 2000 (EEA Passport Rights) (Amendment) Regulations 2006, SI 2006/3385 (which inserts this regulation) is provided for by reg 1(2), (3) of the 2006 Regulations (at **[2866B]**); those paragraphs read as follows—

"(2)   These Regulations come into force on 1st April 2007 for the purposes of—
    (a)   regulations 4 and 5;
    (b)   enabling the Authority to treat a notice referred to in regulation 4A(3)(a) or 5A(3)(a) of the principal Regulations (inserted by these Regulations) given on or after that date as effective for the purpose of regulation 4A(3) or 5A(3) (as the case may be);
    (c)   enabling the Authority, on receipt on or after that date of notice under regulation 11A(2)(a) or 12A(2)(a) of the principal Regulations (inserted by these Regulations), to inform the host state regulator of the proposed change in accordance with regulation 11A(3) or 12A(3) (as the case may be); and
    (d)   enabling the Authority to give notice under regulation 11A(3) or 12A(3) of the principal Regulations (inserted by these Regulations),

and for all other purposes on 1st November 2007.

(3)   Nothing in paragraph (2) gives an investment firm or a UK investment firm an EEA right to carry on, before 1st November 2007, an activity—
    (a)   which is an ancillary service listed in Section B of Annex I to the markets in financial instruments directive but which is not a non-core service listed in Section C of the Annex to the investment services directive;
    (b)   in relation to an investment which is a financial instrument listed in Section C of Annex I to the markets in financial instruments directive but which is not an instrument listed in Section B of the Annex to the investment services directive; or
    (c)   referred to in paragraph 5 of Section A of Annex I to the markets in financial instruments directive unless the firm has an EEA right to carry on one or more core services listed in Section A of the Annex to the investment services directive.".

5 [Management] [companies]: changes to services

(1)   ...

[(1A)   A management company which is providing services in the United Kingdom in the exercise of an EEA right must not make a change in any of the matters referred to in regulation 3(2A)(b), unless the relevant requirements have been complied with.]

(2)   Where the relevant requirements have been complied with, the firm's permission is to be treated as varied accordingly.

(3)   For the purposes of this regulation, the "relevant requirements" are that—
    (a)   the firm has given a notice to the Authority and to its home state regulator stating the details of the proposed change; or
    (b)   if the change is occasioned by circumstances beyond the firm's control, it has as soon as practicable (whether before or after the change) given to the Authority and to its home state regulator a notice stating the details of the change.

(4)   The Authority must, as soon as practicable after receiving a notice from an investment firm [or a management company] under this regulation, inform the firm of any consequential changes in the applicable provisions (within the meaning of paragraph 14 of Schedule 3).

[2434]

NOTES

Regulation heading: word in first pair of square brackets substituted (for the original words "Investment firms, management") by the Financial Services and Markets Act 2000 (EEA Passport Rights) (Amendment) Regulations 2006, SI 2006/3385, regs 2, 8(a), as from 1 November 2007 (for transitional provisions, see the note to reg 4 at **[2433]**); word in second pair of square brackets inserted by the Collective Investment Schemes (Miscellaneous Amendments) Regulations 2003, SI 2003/2066, reg 3(2)(d)(i), as from 13 February 2004.

Para (1): revoked by SI 2006/3385, regs 2, 8(b), as from 1 November 2007 (for transitional provisions, see the note to reg 4 at **[2433]**). The original paragraph read as follows—

"(1)   An investment firm which is providing services in the United Kingdom in exercise of an EEA right must not make a change in any of the matters referred to in regulation 3(2)(b), unless the relevant requirements have been complied with.".

Para (1A): inserted by SI 2003/2066, reg 3(2)(d)(ii), as from 13 February 2004.
Para (4): words in square brackets inserted by SI 2003/2066, reg 3(2)(d)(iii), as from 13 February 2004.
Transitional provisions: see also the Financial Services and Markets Act 2000 (Markets in Financial Instruments) Regulations 2007, SI 2007/126, reg 6A at **[4056A]** (transitional provisions: EEA investment firms exercising passport rights under the investment services directive).

[5A Investment firms: changes to services

(1)   An investment firm which is providing services in the United Kingdom in exercise of an EEA right must not—
    (a)   make a change in any of the matters referred to in regulation 3(2)(b),
    (b)   use, for the first time, any tied agent to provide services in the United Kingdom, or
    (c)   cease to use tied agents to provide services in the United Kingdom,

unless the requirements of paragraph (3) have been complied with.

(2)   Where those requirements have been complied with, the firm's permission is to be treated as varied accordingly.

(3)   The requirements are that—
  (a)   the firm has given a notice to its home state regulator stating the details of the proposed change, and
  (b)   the period of one month beginning with the day on which the firm gave the notice has elapsed.

(4)   Paragraph (1) does not apply to a change occasioned by circumstances beyond the firm's control.]

[2434A]

NOTES
   Commencement: 1 April 2007 (certain purposes); 1 November 2007 (otherwise) (see below).
   Inserted by the Financial Services and Markets Act 2000 (EEA Passport Rights) (Amendment) Regulations 2006, SI 2006/3385, regs 2, 9, as from 1 April 2007 (certain purposes), and as from 1 November 2007 (otherwise). For more information as to the commencement of this regulation, see the final note to reg 4A at **[2433A]**, and for transitional provisions, see the note to reg 4 at **[2433]**.

6   Insurance firms: changes to branch details

(1)   An insurance firm which has established a branch in the United Kingdom in exercise of an EEA right must not make a change in any of the details referred to in regulation 2(5)(a) to (c) with respect to the branch, unless the relevant requirements have been complied with.

(2)   Where the relevant requirements have been complied with, the firm's permission is to be treated as varied accordingly.

(3)   For the purposes of this regulation, the relevant requirements are those of paragraph (4) or (if the change is occasioned by circumstances beyond the firm's control) paragraph (5).

(4)   The requirements of this paragraph are that—
  (a)   the firm has given a notice to the Authority and to its home state regulator stating the details of the proposed change;
  (b)   the Authority has received from the home state regulator a notice stating that it has approved the proposed change;
  (c)   the period of one month beginning with the day on which the firm gave the Authority the notice mentioned in sub-paragraph (a) has elapsed; and
  (d)   either—
     (i)   a further period of one month has elapsed; or
     (ii)   the Authority has informed the home state regulator of any consequential changes in the applicable provisions (within the meaning of paragraph 13 of Schedule 3).

(5)   The requirements of this paragraph are that the firm has as soon as practicable (whether before or after the change) given a notice to the Authority and to its home state regulator, stating the details of the change.

(6)   The Authority must, as soon as practicable—
  (a)   acknowledge receipt of the documents sent under paragraph (4) or (5); and
  (b)   in the case of a notice under paragraph (5), inform the firm's home state regulator of any consequential changes in the applicable provisions (within the meaning of paragraph 13 of Schedule 3).

[2435]

7   Insurance firms: changes to services

(1)   An insurance firm which is providing services in the United Kingdom in exercise of an EEA right must not make a change in any of the matters referred to in regulation 3(3)(b), (c) or (d), unless the relevant requirements have been complied with.

(2)   Where the relevant requirements have been complied with, the firm's permission is to be treated as varied accordingly.

(3)   For the purposes of this regulation, the "relevant requirements" are those of paragraph (4) or (if the change is occasioned by circumstances beyond the firm's control) paragraph (5).

(4)   The requirements of this paragraph are that—
  (a)   the firm has given a notice to its home state regulator stating the details of the proposed change; and
  (b)   the home state regulator has passed to the Authority the information contained in that notice.

(5)   The requirements of this paragraph are that the firm has as soon as practicable (whether before or after the change) given to its home state regulator a notice stating the details of the change.

[2436]

Cancellation of qualification for authorisation

8   EEA firms ceasing to carry on regulated activities in the United Kingdom

Where an EEA firm which is qualified for authorisation under Schedule 3—
  (a)   has ceased, or is to cease to carry on regulated activities in the United Kingdom, and
  (b)   gives notice of that fact to the Authority,
the notice is to be treated as a request for cancellation of the firm's qualification for authorisation under Schedule 3 (and hence as a request under section 34(2) of the Act).

[2437]

9   Financial institutions giving up right to authorisation

  (1)   The Authority may, on an application by a financial institution which is qualified for authorisation under Schedule 3, direct that the firm's qualification for authorisation under Schedule 3 is cancelled from such date as may be specified in the direction.

  (2)   The Authority must not give such a direction unless—
  (a)   the firm has given notice to its home state regulator; and
  (b)   the Authority has agreed with the home state regulator that the direction should be given.

  (3)   The date specified in such a direction—
  (a)   must not be earlier than the date requested in the application; but
  (b)   subject to that, is to be such date as may be agreed between the Authority and the firm's home state regulator.

  (4)   The Authority must, as soon as practicable, send a copy of the direction to the firm and to the firm's home state regulator.

  (5)   A firm in respect of which such a direction has been given may (notwithstanding subsection (3) of section 40 of the Act) apply for permission under that section, to take effect not earlier than the date referred to in paragraph (1).

[2438]

Applications for approval under section 60 by EEA firms

10   Applications for approval under section 60 by EEA firms

In section 60 of the Act (applications for approval for persons to perform controlled functions), "the authorised person concerned" includes—
  [(a)]   an EEA firm with respect to which the Authority has received a consent notice [or regulator's notice] under paragraph 13 of Schedule 3 or a regulator's notice under paragraph 14 of that Schedule, and which will be the authorised person concerned if it qualifies for authorisation under that Schedule[; and
  (b)   an EEA firm which falls within paragraph 5(da) of Schedule 3 which establishes a branch in the United Kingdom].

[2439]

NOTES
  Para (a) designated as such, and para (b) (and the word immediately preceding it) inserted, by the Reinsurance Directive Regulations 2007, SI 2007/3253, reg 2(2), Sch 2, para 1, (a), as from 10 December 2007.
  Words in square brackets in para (a) inserted by the Insurance Mediation Directive (Miscellaneous Amendments) Regulations 2003, SI 2003/1473, reg 8(1), (4), as from 14 January 2005.

PART III
EXERCISE OF PASSPORT RIGHTS BY UK FIRMS
Changes relating to UK firms

11   UK ... [management companies], credit institutions and financial institutions: changes to branch details

  (1)   A UK firm which has exercised an EEA right, deriving from ... [the UCITS directive] or the banking consolidation directive, to establish a branch must not make a change in the requisite details of the branch unless the requirements of paragraph (2) or (if the change is occasioned by circumstances beyond the firm's control) paragraph (3) have been complied with.

  (2)   The requirements of this paragraph are that—
  (a)   the firm has given a notice to the Authority and to the host state regulator stating the details of the proposed change;
  (b)   the Authority has given the host state regulator a notice under paragraph (5)(a); and
  (c)   either the host state regulator has informed the firm that it may make the change, or the period of one month beginning with the day on which the firm gave the host state regulator the notice mentioned in sub-paragraph (a) has elapsed.

(3)   The requirements of this paragraph are that the firm has as soon as practicable (whether before or after the change) given a notice to the Authority and to the host state regulator, stating the details of the change.

(4)   the Authority must, within the period of one month beginning with the day on which it received the notice referred to in paragraph (2)(a), either consent to the change or refuse to consent to the change.

(5)   If the Authority consents to the change, it must—
    (a)   give a notice to the host state regulator informing it of the details of the proposed change; and
    (b)   inform the firm that if has given that notice, stating the date on which it did so.

(6)   If the Authority refuses to consent to the change—
    (a)   the firm may refer the matter to the Tribunal; and
    (b)   the Authority must give notice to the firm of the refusal, stating the reasons for it, and giving an indication of the firm's right to refer the matter to the Tribunal, and the procedure on such a reference.

(7)   The Authority may not refuse to consent to the change unless, having regard to the change and to the EEA activities which the firm is seeking to carry on, it doubts the adequacy of the administrative structure or the financial situation of the firm; and in reaching a determination as to the adequacy of the administrative structure, the Authority may have regard to the adequacy of management, systems and controls and the presence of relevant skills needed for the EEA activities to be carried on.

[2440]

NOTES
    Regulation heading: words omitted revoked by the Financial Services and Markets Act 2000 (EEA Passport Rights) (Amendment) Regulations 2006, SI 2006/3385, regs 2, 10, as from 1 November 2007 (for transitional provisions, see the note to reg 4 at **[2433]**) (the original words were "Investment firms,"); words in square brackets inserted by the Collective Investment Schemes (Miscellaneous Amendments) Regulations 2003, SI 2003/2066, reg 4(2)(a), as from 13 February 2004.
    Para (1): words omitted revoked by SI 2006/3385, regs 2, 10, as from 1 November 2007 (for transitional provisions, see the note to reg 4 at **[2433]**) (the original words were "the investment services directive,"); words in square brackets inserted by SI 2003/2066, reg 4(2)(a), as from 13 February 2004.
    Transitional provisions: see also the Financial Services and Markets Act 2000 (Markets in Financial Instruments) Regulations 2007, SI 2007/126, reg 7 at **[4057]** (transitional provisions: UK investment firms exercising passport rights under the investment services directive), and reg 7A at **[4057A]** (transitional provision: investment research and financial analysis).

[11A   UK investment firms: changes to branch details

(1)   A UK investment firm which has exercised an EEA right deriving from the markets in financial instruments directive to establish a branch must not—
    (a)   make a change in the requisite details of the branch,
    (b)   use, for the first time, any tied agent established in the EEA State in which the branch is established, or
    (c)   cease to use tied agents established in the EEA State in which the branch is established,
unless the requirements of paragraph (2) have been complied with.

(2)   The requirements are that—
    (a)   the firm has given a notice to the Authority stating the details of the proposed change, and
    (b)   the period of one month beginning with the day on which the firm gave the notice has elapsed.

(3)   The Authority must, as soon as reasonably practicable after receiving a notice under paragraph (2), inform the host state regulator of the proposed change.

(4)   Paragraph (1) does not apply to a change occasioned by circumstances beyond the firm's control.]

[2440A]

NOTES
    Commencement: 1 April 2007 (certain purposes); 1 November 2007 (otherwise) (see below).
    Inserted by the Financial Services and Markets Act 2000 (EEA Passport Rights) (Amendment) Regulations 2006, SI 2006/3385, regs 2, 11, as from 1 April 2007 (certain purposes), and as from 1 November 2007 (otherwise). For more information as to the commencement of this regulation, see the final note to reg 4A at **[2433A]**, and for transitional provisions, see the note to reg 4 at **[2433]**.

12 UK … [management companies]: changes to services

(1)   A UK firm which is providing services in exercise of an EEA right, deriving from … [the UCITS directive], must not make a change in the programme of operations, or the EEA activities, to be carried on in exercise of that right, unless the relevant requirements have been complied with.

(2)   For the purposes of this regulation, the "relevant requirements" are that—
   (a)   the firm has given a notice to the Authority and to the host state regulator stating the details of the proposed change; or
   (b)   if the change is occasioned by circumstances beyond the firm's control, it has as soon as practicable (whether before or after the change) given a notice to the Authority and to the host state regulator, stating the details of the change.

[2441]

NOTES

Regulation heading: words omitted revoked by the Financial Services and Markets Act 2000 (EEA Passport Rights) (Amendment) Regulations 2006, SI 2006/3385, regs 2, 12, as from 1 November 2007 (for transitional provisions, see the note to reg 4 at **[2433]**) (the original words were "investment firms and"); words in square brackets inserted by the Collective Investment Schemes (Miscellaneous Amendments) Regulations 2003, SI 2003/2066, reg 4(2)(b), as from 13 February 2004.

Para (1): words omitted revoked by SI 2006/3385, regs 2, 12, as from 1 November 2007 (for transitional provisions, see the note to reg 4 at **[2433]**) (the original words were "the investment services directive or"); words in square brackets inserted by SI 2003/2066, reg 4(2)(b), as from 13 February 2004.

Transitional provisions: see also the Financial Services and Markets Act 2000 (Markets in Financial Instruments) Regulations 2007, SI 2007/126, reg 7 at **[4057]** (transitional provisions: UK investment firms exercising passport rights under the investment services directive), and reg 7A at **[4057A]** (transitional provision: investment research and financial analysis).

[12A UK investment firms: changes to services

(1)   A UK investment firm which is providing services in a particular EEA State in exercise of an EEA right deriving from the markets in financial instruments directive must not—
   (a)   make a change in the programme of operations, or the EEA activities, to be carried on in exercise of that right,
   (b)   use, for the first time, any tied agent to provide services in the territory of that State, or
   (c)   cease to use tied agents to provide services in the territory of that State,
unless the requirements of paragraph (2) have been complied with.

(2)   The requirements are that—
   (a)   the firm has given a notice to the Authority stating the details of the proposed change, and
   (b)   the period of one month beginning with the day on which the firm gave the notice has elapsed.

(3)   The Authority must, as soon as reasonably practicable after receiving a notice under paragraph (2), inform the host state regulator of the proposed change.

(4)   Paragraph (1) does not apply to a change occasioned by circumstances beyond the firm's control.]

[2441A]

NOTES

Commencement: 1 April 2007 (certain purposes); 1 November 2007 (otherwise) (see below).

Inserted by the Financial Services and Markets Act 2000 (EEA Passport Rights) (Amendment) Regulations 2006, SI 2006/3385, regs 2, 13, as from 1 April 2007 (certain purposes), and as from 1 November 2007 (otherwise). For more information as to the commencement of this regulation, see the final note to reg 4A at **[2433A]**, and for transitional provisions, see the note to reg 4 at **[2433]**.

13 UK insurance firms: changes to relevant EEA details of branches

(1)   A UK firm which has exercised an EEA right, deriving from any of the insurance directives, to establish a branch must not make a change in the relevant EEA details (as defined in regulation 14), unless the requirements of paragraph (2) or (if the change is occasioned by circumstances beyond the firm's control) paragraph (3) have been complied with.

(2)   The requirements of this paragraph are that—
   (a)   the firm has given a notice to the Authority and to the host state regulator stating the details of the proposed change;
   (b)   the Authority has given the host state regulator a notice under paragraph (5)(a);
   (c)   the period of one month beginning with the day on which the firm gave the Authority the notice mentioned in sub-paragraph (a) has elapsed; and
   (d)   either—
      (i)   a further period of one month has elapsed; or
      (ii)   the Authority has informed the firm of any consequential changes in the

applicable provisions (within the meaning of paragraph 19 of Schedule 3) of which the Authority has been notified by the host state regulator.

(3)   The requirements of this paragraph are that the firm has as soon as practicable (whether before or after the change) given a notice to the Authority and to the host state regulator, stating the details of the change.

(4)   The Authority must, within one month of receiving the notice referred to in paragraph (2)(a), either consent to the change or refuse to consent to the change.

(5)   If the Authority consents to the change, it must—

    (a)   give a notice to the host state regulator informing it of the details of the proposed change; and

    (b)   inform the firm that it has given that notice, stating the date on which it did so.

(6)   If the Authority refuses to consent to the change—

    (a)   the firm may refer the matter to the Tribunal; and

    (b)   the Authority must give notice to the firm of the refusal, stating the reasons for it, and giving an indication of the firm's right to refer the matter to the Tribunal, and the procedure on such a reference.

(7)   The Authority may not refuse to consent to the change unless, having regard to the change, the Authority has reason—

    (a)   to doubt the adequacy of the firm's administrative structure or financial situation, or

    (b)   to question the reputation, qualifications or experience of the directors or managers of the firm or the authorised agent,

in relation to the business conducted, or to be conducted, through the branch.

[2442]

14   Relevant EEA details for the purposes of regulation 13

(1)   For the purposes of regulation 13, the relevant EEA details, with respect to a branch, are—

    (a)   the address of the branch;

    (b)   the name of the UK firm's authorised agent and, in the case of a member of Lloyd's, confirmation that the authorised agent has power to accept service of proceedings on behalf of Lloyd's;

    (c)   the classes or parts of classes of business carried on, or to be carried on, and the nature of the risks or commitments covered, or to be covered, in the EEA State concerned;

    (d)   details of the structural organisation of the branch;

    (e)   the guiding principles as to reinsurance of business carried on, or to be carried on, in the EEA State concerned, including the firm's maximum retention per risk or event after all reinsurance ceded;

    (f)   estimates of—

       (i)   the costs of installing administrative services and the organisation for securing business in the EEA State concerned;

       (ii)   the resources available to cover those costs; and

       (iii)   if contracts of a kind falling within paragraph 18 of Schedule 1 to the Regulated Activities Order (assistance) are, or are to be, effected or carried out, the resources available for providing assistance;

    (g)   for each of the first three years following the establishment of the branch—

       (i)   estimates of the firm's margin of solvency and the margin of solvency required, and the method of calculation;

       (ii)   if the firm carries on, or intends to carry on, business comprising the effecting or carrying out of contracts of long-term insurance, the details mentioned in paragraph (2) as respects the business carried on, or to be carried on, in the EEA State concerned; and

       (iii)   if the firm carries on, or intends to carry on, business comprising the effecting or carrying out of contracts of general insurance, the details mentioned in paragraph (3) as respects the business carried on, or to be carried on, in the EEA State concerned;

    (h)   if the insurer covers, or intends to cover, relevant motor vehicle risks, details of the firm's membership of the national bureau and the national guarantee fund in the EEA State concerned; and

    (i)   if the firm covers, or intends to cover, health insurance risks, the technical bases used, or to be used, for calculating premiums in respect of such risks.

(2)   The details referred to in paragraph (1)(g)(ii) are—

    (a)   the following information, on both optimistic and pessimistic bases, for each type of contract or treaty—

       (i)   the number of contracts or treaties expected to be issued;

       (ii)   the total premium income, both gross and net of reinsurance ceded; and

       (iii)   the total sums assured or the total amounts payable each year by way of annuity;

(b)   detailed estimates, on both optimistic and pessimistic bases, of income and expenditure in respect of direct business, reinsurance acceptances and reinsurance cessions; and

(c)   estimates relating to the financial resources intended to cover underwriting liabilities.

(3)   The details referred to in paragraph (1)(g)(iii) are—

(a)   estimates relating to expenses of management (other than costs of installation), and in particular those relating to current expenses and commissions;

(b)   estimates relating to premiums or contributions (both gross and net of all reinsurance ceded) and to claims (after all reinsurance recoveries); and

(c)   estimates relating to the financial resources to cover underwriting liabilities.

[2443]

15 UK insurance firms: changes to relevant UK details of branches

(1)   A UK firm which has exercised an EEA right, deriving from any of the insurance directives, to establish a branch must not make a change falling within paragraph (2) with respect to the branch, unless—

(a)   the firm has given a notice to the Authority stating the details of the proposed change at least one month before the change is effected; or

(b)   if the change is occasioned by circumstances beyond the firm's control, the firm has as soon as practicable (whether before or after the change) given a notice to the Authority stating the details of the change.

(2)   A change falls within this paragraph if it is a change in any of the information which the UK firm was required to provide to the Authority by or under paragraph 19(2) of Schedule 3, other than a change in the relevant EEA details referred to in regulation 13.

[2444]

16 UK insurance firms: changes to services

(1)   A UK firm which is providing services in exercise of an EEA right, deriving from any of the insurance directives, must not make a change in the relevant details (as defined in regulation 17), unless the relevant requirements have been complied with.

(2)   For the purposes of this regulation, the "relevant requirements" are those of paragraph (3) or (if the change is occasioned by circumstances beyond the firm's control) paragraph (4).

(3)   The requirements of this paragraph are that—

(a)   the firm has given a notice to the Authority stating the details of the proposed change; and

(b)   the Authority has given the host state regulator a notice under paragraph (6)(a).

(4)   The requirements of this paragraph are that the firm has as soon as practicable (whether before or after the change) given a notice to the Authority stating the details of the change.

(5)   The Authority must, within one month of receiving a notice under paragraph (3)(a), either consent to the change or refuse to consent to the change.

(6)   If the Authority consents to the change, it must—

(a)   give a notice to the host state regulator informing it of the details of the proposed change; and

(b)   inform the firm that it has given that notice, stating the date on which it did so.

(7)   If the Authority refuses to consent to the change—

(a)   the firm may refer the matter to the Tribunal; and

(b)   the Authority must give notice to the firm of the refusal, stating the reasons for it, and giving an indication of the firm's right to refer the matter to the Tribunal, and the procedure on such a reference.

[2445]

17 Relevant details for the purposes of regulation 16

The relevant details for the purposes of regulation 16 are—

(a)   the EEA State in which the EEA activities are carried on, or are to be carried on;

(b)   the nature of the risks or commitments covered, or to be covered, in the EEA State concerned;

(c)   if the firm covers, or intends to cover, relevant motor vehicle risks—

    (i)   the name and address of the claims representative; and

    (ii)   details of the firm's membership of the national bureau and the national guarantee fund in the EEA State concerned; and

(d)   if the insurer covers, or intends to cover, health insurance risks, the technical bases used, or to be used, for calculating premiums in respect of such risks.

[2446]

18   Offences relating to failure to notify changes

(1)   If a UK firm which is not an authorised person contravenes the prohibition imposed by regulation 11(1), [11A(1),] 12(1), [12A(1),] 13(1), 15(1), or 16(1) it is guilty of an offence, punishable—

    (a)   on summary conviction, by a fine not exceeding the statutory maximum; or

    (b)   on conviction on indictment, by a fine.

(2)   In proceedings for an offence under paragraph (1), it is a defence for the firm to show that it took all reasonable precautions and exercised all due diligence to avoid committing the offence.

[2447]

NOTES

Para (1): figures in square brackets inserted by the Financial Services and Markets Act 2000 (EEA Passport Rights) (Amendment) Regulations 2006, SI 2006/3385, regs 2, 14, as from 1 November 2007.

UK firms: scope of outward passport

19   UK firms: scope of outward passport

  [(1)]   Where—

    (a)   the activities identified in a notice of intention under paragraph 19 or 20 of Schedule 3 include (in accordance with paragraph 19(3) or 20(2) of that Schedule) any activity which is not a regulated activity, and

    (b)   that activity is one which the UK firm in question is able to carry on in the EEA State in question without contravening any provision of the law of the United Kingdom (or any part of the United Kingdom),

the UK firm is to be treated, for the purposes of the exercise of its EEA right, as being authorised to carry on that activity.

  [(2)   Where—

    (a)   the activities of a UK firm which pursues the activity of reinsurance (within the meaning of Article 2.1(a) of the reinsurance directive) includes any activity which is not a regulated activity, and

    (b)   that activity is one which the UK firm in question is able to carry on in the EEA State in question without contravening any provision of the law of the United Kingdom (or any part of the United Kingdom),

the UK firm is to be treated, for the purpose of the exercise of its EEA right, as being authorised to carry on that activity.]

[2448]

NOTES

Para (1) numbered as such, and para (2) added, by the Reinsurance Directive Regulations 2007, SI 2007/3253, reg 2(2), Sch 2, para (b), as from 10 December 2007.

PART IV

TRANSITIONAL PROVISIONS

20   Changes relating to EEA firms: procedures partly completed at commencement

(1)   If before commencement—

    (a)   an EEA firm which was a European institution within the meaning of the 2BCD Regulations gave a notice under paragraph 4(1)(a) of Schedule 2 to those Regulations (changes to details of branch), and

    (b)   not all the other requirements set out in paragraph 4(1) of that Schedule were satisfied,

the notice is to be treated as given under regulation 4(4)(a), and the other requirements set out in regulation 4(4) treated as satisfied to the extent to which the corresponding requirements in paragraph 4(1) of that Schedule had been satisfied.

(2)   If before commencement—

    (a)   an EEA firm which was a European investment firm within the meaning of the ISD Regulations gave a notice under paragraph 5(1)(a) of Schedule 3 to those Regulations (changes to details of branch), and

    (b)   not all the other requirements set out in paragraph 5(1) of that Schedule were satisfied,

the notice is to be treated as given under regulation 4(4)(a), and the other requirements set out in regulation 4(4) treated as satisfied to the extent to which the corresponding requirements in paragraph 5(1) of that Schedule had been satisfied.

(3)   In a case falling within paragraph (1) or (2), regulation 4(6) applies unless the Authority had, before commencement, complied with the duty in regulation 8(3) of the 2BCD Regulations or regulation 8(4) of the ISD Regulations.

(4)   If before commencement—

(a)   an EEA firm which was an EC company within the meaning of the Insurance Companies Act gave a notice under paragraph 2(2)(a) of Schedule 2F to that Act (changes to details of branch), and

(b)   not all the other requirements set out in paragraph 2(2) of that Schedule were satisfied,

the notice is to be treated as given under regulation 6(4)(a), and the other requirements set out in regulation 6(4) treated as satisfied to the extent to which the corresponding requirements in paragraph 2(2) of that Schedule had been satisfied.

(5)   In a case falling within paragraph (4), regulation 6(6) applies except to the extent that the duty in paragraph 2(4) of Schedule 2F to the Insurance Companies Act had been complied with before commencement.

(6)   If before commencement—

(a)   an EEA firm which was an EC company within the meaning of the Insurance Companies Act gave a notice under paragraph 9(2)(a) of Schedule 2F to that Act (changes relating to the provision of services), and

(b)   the requirement in paragraph 9(2)(b) of that Schedule was not satisfied,

the notice is to be treated as given under regulation 7(4)(a).

[2449]

21 Changes relating to UK firms: procedures partly completed at commencement

(1)   If before commencement a UK firm gave notice under paragraph 5(1)(a) of Schedule 6 to the 2BCD Regulations or paragraph 6(1)(a) of Schedule 6 to the ISD Regulations (changes to details of branch)—

(a)   the notice is to be treated as given under regulation 11(2)(a), and

(b)   any notice given under paragraph 5(1)(b) of Schedule 6 to the 2BCD Regulations or paragraph 6(1)(b) of Schedule 6 to the ISD Regulations is to be treated as given under regulation 11(2)(b),

unless paragraph (2) applies.

(2)   This paragraph applies if, before commencement, either—

(a)   all the requirements set out in paragraph 5(1) of Schedule 6 to the 2BCD Regulations or paragraph 6(1) of Schedule 6 to the ISD Regulations had been satisfied, or

(b)   in response to the notice a notice of refusal was given to the firm under paragraph 6(5)(b) of Schedule 6 to the 2BCD Regulations or paragraph 7(5)(b) of Schedule 6 to the ISD Regulations, and the refusal was not at commencement capable of being reversed on an appeal, reference to a tribunal or a review as mentioned in paragraph 7(5) of Schedule 6 to the ISD Regulations.

(3)   If before commencement a UK firm gave notice under paragraph 2(2)(a) of Schedule 2G to the Insurance Companies Act or Schedule 13B to the Friendly Societies Act (changes to details of branch)—

(a)   the notice is to be treated as given to the Authority under regulation 13(2)(a), and

(b)   the other requirements set out in regulation 13(2) are to be treated as satisfied to the extent to which the corresponding requirements in paragraph 2(2) of Schedule 2G to the Insurance Companies Act or of Schedule 13B to the Friendly Societies Act had been satisfied,

unless paragraph (4) applies.

(4)   This paragraph applies if, before commencement, either—

(a)   all the requirements set out in paragraph 2(2) of Schedule 2G to the Insurance Companies Act or of Schedule 13B to the Friendly Societies Act had been satisfied, or

(b)   in response to the notice a notice of refusal was given to the firm under paragraph 2(5)(b) of that Schedule.

(5)   If before commencement a UK firm gave notice under paragraph 6(2)(a) of Schedule 2G to the Insurance Companies Act or of Schedule 13B to the Friendly Societies Act (changes relating to the provision of services)—

(a)   the notice is to be treated as given to the Authority under regulation 16(3)(a) and

(b)   if a notice was sent under paragraph 6(2)(b) of Schedule 2G to the Insurance Companies Act or of Schedule 13B to the Friendly Societies Act, that notice is to be treated as given under regulation 16(3)(b),

unless, before commencement, the firm had been notified under paragraph 6(5)(a) or (b) of Schedule 2G to the Insurance Companies Act or of Schedule 13B to the Friendly Societies Act of the decision taken in response to the notice.

[2450]

FINANCIAL SERVICES AND MARKETS ACT 2000 (COMMUNICATIONS BY AUDITORS) REGULATIONS 2001

(SI 2001/2587)

NOTES
Made: 17 July 2001.
Authority: Financial Services and Markets Act 2000, ss 342(5), 343(5), 428(3).
Commencement: 1 December 2001.

As of 1 February 2009, these Regulations had not been amended.

1 Citation, commencement and interpretation

(1) These Regulations may be cited as the Financial Services and Markets Act 2000 (Communications by Auditors) Regulations 2001 and come into force on the day on which section 19 of the Act (the general prohibition) comes into force.

(2) In these Regulations—
"the Act" means the Financial Services and Markets Act 2000;
"the person concerned" means—
    (a)   in relation to an auditor of an authorised person, that authorised person;
    (b)   in relation to an auditor of a person who has close links (within the meaning of section 343 of the Act) with an authorised person, that authorised person;
"relevant requirement" means—
    (a)   a requirement which is imposed by or under any provision of the Act other than Part VI (listing) and which relates to authorisation under the Act (whether by way of permission under Part IV of the Act or otherwise) or to the carrying on of any regulated activity; or
    (b)   a requirement which is imposed by or under any other Act and whose contravention constitutes an offence which the Authority has power to prosecute under the Act.

[2451]

2 Circumstances in which an auditor is to communicate

(1) An auditor to whom section 342 or 343 of the Act applies must communicate to the Authority information on, or his opinion on, matters mentioned in section 342(3)(a) or 343(3)(a) of the Act (matters of which he has, or had, become aware in his capacity as auditor of an authorised person or as auditor of a person who has close links with an authorised person) in the following circumstances.

(2) The circumstances are that—
    (a)   the auditor reasonably believes that, as regards the person concerned—
        (i)   there is or has been, or may be or may have been, a contravention of any relevant requirement that applies to the person concerned; and
        (ii)   that contravention may be of material significance to the Authority in determining whether to exercise, in relation to the person concerned, any functions conferred on the Authority by or under any provision of the Act other than Part VI;
    (b)   the auditor reasonably believes that the information on, or his opinion on, those matters may be of material significance to the Authority in determining whether the person concerned satisfies and will continue to satisfy the threshold conditions;
    (c)   the auditor reasonably believes that the person concerned is not, may not be or may cease to be a going concern;
    (d)   the auditor is precluded from stating in his report that the annual accounts or, where they are required to be made by any of the following provisions, other financial reports of the person concerned—
        (i)   have been properly prepared in accordance with the Companies Act 1985 or, where applicable, give a true and fair view of the matters referred to in section 235(2) of that Act;
        (ii)   have been prepared so as to conform with the requirements of Part VIII of the Building Societies Act 1986 and the regulations made under it or, where applicable, give a true and fair view of the matters referred to in subsection (4) or (7) of section 78 of that Act;
        (iii)   have been prepared so as to conform with the Friendly Societies Act 1992 and the regulations made under it or, where applicable, give a true and fair view of the matters referred to in section 73(5) of that Act;
        (iv)   have been prepared so as to conform with the requirements of the Friendly and Industrial and Provident Societies Act 1968 or, where applicable, give a true and fair view of the matters referred to in section 9(2) and (3) of that Act; or

(v)   have been prepared so as to conform with the requirements of rules made under the Act where the auditor is, by rules made under section 340 of the Act, required to make such a statement;

as the case may be; or

(e)   where applicable, the auditor is required to state in his report in relation to the person concerned any of the facts referred to in subsection (2), (3) or (4A) of section 237 of the Companies Act 1985.

[2452]

FINANCIAL SERVICES AND MARKETS ACT 2000 (MUTUAL SOCIETIES) ORDER 2001

(SI 2001/2617)

NOTES

Made: 18 July 2001.

Authority: Financial Services and Markets Act 2000, ss 334(1), (2), 335(1), (2), (3), (4), 336(1), (2), 337, 338(1), (2), 339(1), (2), 426, 427, 428(3).

Commencement: 17 August 2001 (in so far as relating to arts 4(3), 8, Sch 2); 1 December 2001 (otherwise).

As of 1 February 2009, the provisions of this Order reproduced here had not been amended.

ARRANGEMENT OF ARTICLES

PART I
GENERAL

PART II
TRANSFERRED FUNCTIONS

PART III
DISSOLUTIONS

PART IV
AMENDMENTS, REPEALS ETC

SCHEDULES:

PART I
GENERAL

1 Citation

This Order may be cited as the Financial Services and Markets Act 2000 (Mutual Societies) Order 2001.

[2453]

2   Commencement

This Order comes into force—

(a)   for the purposes of article 8, and for the purposes of article 4(3) and Schedule 2, on 17th August 2001, and

(b)   for all other purposes, on the day on which section 19 of the 2000 Act (the general prohibition) comes into force.

[2454]

3   Interpretation

(1)   In this Order—

"the 2000 Act" means the Financial Services and Markets Act 2000,

"assistant registrar" means an assistant registrar of friendly societies for the central registration area,

"the assistant registrar for Scotland" means the assistant registrar of friendly societies for Scotland,

"the Board" means the Building Societies Investor Protection Board,

"building society" has the same meaning as in the Building Societies Act 1986,

"the central office" means the central office of the registry of friendly societies,

"the central registration area" means the area defined by section 4(1)(a) of the Friendly Societies Act 1974 (as it had effect immediately before its repeal by the 2000 Act),

"the Chief Registrar" means the Chief Registrar of friendly societies,

"commencement" means the beginning of the day on which section 19 of the 2000 Act comes into force,

"enactment" includes an enactment contained in subordinate legislation within the meaning of the Interpretation Act 1978, and

"the last period" means the period beginning with 1st April 2001 and ending at commencement.

(2)   In this Order, "transferred function" means any function transferred by article 4 and, in relation to any transferred function, "transferor" means the person from whom the function is transferred and "transferee" means the person to whom it is transferred.

(3)   In this Order, unless the context otherwise requires, any reference to an article by number alone is a reference to the article so numbered in this Order.

[2455]

PART II
TRANSFERRED FUNCTIONS

4   Transfer of functions

(1)   The functions—

(a)   of the Chief Registrar, the assistant registrar for Scotland, the assistant registrars and the central office listed in Part I of Schedule 1 to this Order,

(b)   of the Friendly Societies Commission listed in Part II of Schedule 1 to this Order, and

(c)   of the Building Societies Commission listed in Part III of Schedule 1 to this Order,

are transferred to the Treasury.

(2)   All other functions which, immediately before commencement were functions—

(a)   of the Chief Registrar, the assistant registrar for Scotland, the assistant registrars or the central office,

(b)   of the Friendly Societies Commission, or

(c)   of the Building Societies Commission,

are transferred to the Authority, subject to any repeal or amendment made by any provision of this Order or by any other provision of or made under the 2000 Act.

(3)   Schedule 2 makes provision about the application of the 2000 Act in relation to functions transferred (or to be transferred) to the Authority by paragraph (2) above.

(4)   For the purposes of the Transfer of Undertakings (Protection of Employment) Regulations 1981, paragraph (2) above is to be regarded as giving rise to the transfer of an undertaking by virtue of each of sub-paragraphs (a), (b) and (c) of that paragraph, whether or not it would otherwise be so regarded.

[2456]

5   Consequential and transitional provisions in relation to transferred functions

(1)   The transfer of any function by virtue of article 4 does not affect the validity of anything done before commencement—

(a)   by the transferor in the exercise of the transferred function, or

(b)   by any other person in relation to the exercise by the transferor of the transferred function, and any such thing is to have effect for all purposes as if done by (or, as the case may be, in relation to the exercise of the function by) the transferee.

(2) Paragraph (1) also has effect in relation to anything which is in the process of being done at commencement, and any such thing may be carried on and completed by (or, as the case may be, in relation to the exercise of the function by) the transferee.

(3) If, at commencement, a transferor is a party to any legal proceedings in relation to its exercise of any transferred function, the transferee is substituted for the transferor in those proceedings.

(4) If, at commencement, a transferor holds any monies which have been deposited with the transferor as security for any costs in relation to its exercise of any transferred function, the monies are transferred to the transferee at commencement to be held for the same purpose and on the same terms.

(5) This article has effect subject to any transitional provision or saving contained in Schedule 5 to this Order or in any other provision made under the 2000 Act.

[2457]

6 Requirements to provide documents etc

(1) Paragraph (2) applies where, by virtue of any provision of or made under any enactment, a person ("A") other than a transferor was before commencement required or entitled—

   (a)   to provide any account, application, list, notice, plan, report, return, or any other document or material (including a copy of any document or material),

   (b)   to give any explanation or provide any other information, or

   (c)   to notify, report on, or make representations or a statement on, any matter,

to any transferor, or to any other person ("B") on behalf of any transferor, in connection with the exercise by the transferor of any function which is transferred by article 4(2) to the Authority, but had not provided that document or material, given that explanation or information, or notified, reported on or made representations on that matter, before commencement.

(2) After commencement A is required or (as the case may be) entitled to provide that document or material, to give that explanation or information, or to notify, report on, or make representations on, that matter, to the Authority (or, as the case may be, to B on behalf of the Authority), but otherwise in the same form and containing the same particulars as would have been required before commencement.

(3) Paragraph (1) has effect no matter how the requirement or entitlement is expressed.

(4) Where the requirement or entitlement mentioned in paragraph (1) was subject to any provision requiring A to comply with the requirement or exercise the entitlement within a specified time (however expressed), that provision continues to apply in relation to the requirement imposed or entitlement given by paragraph (2), and the time period is to be treated as continuing to run without interruption.

(5) Where any person does anything after commencement in compliance with paragraph (2) in relation to which, if that thing had been done before commencement, a fee would have been payable to the transferor, he is required to pay that fee to the Authority, and the fee (insofar as it is not so paid) may be recovered by the Authority as a debt due to it.

(6) This article is without prejudice to the generality of article 5(1) and (2).

(7) This article has effect subject to any transitional provision or saving contained in Schedule 5 to this Order or in any other provision made under the 2000 Act.

[2458]

7 Consequential modification of non-statutory provisions

(1) Where a relevant provision is predicated on the continuing exercise of any transferred function by the transferor, any reference in the provision to the transferor has effect, in relation to any time after commencement, as a reference to the transferee.

(2) Paragraph (3) applies where—

   (a)   a relevant provision contains a requirement for consent to be given by the Building Societies Commission before the repayment by a building society of any sum owed by it, and

   (b)   the requirement was included in the relevant provision so as to comply with the terms of—

      (i)   an order made under section 45(5) of the Building Societies Act 1986 as that section had effect before the coming into force of section 21 of the Building Societies Act 1997,

      (ii)   an order made under section 119(1) of the Building Societies Act 1986, or

      (iii)   guidance issued by the Building Societies Commission pursuant to section 45AA of that Act.

(3)   Unless the context otherwise requires, the requirement has effect, in relation to any time after commencement, as a requirement for consent to be given by the Authority.

(4)   Paragraph (5) applies where a relevant provision prohibits the payment or crediting of interest on any sum owed by a building society if the board of directors of the society is of the opinion that—

(a)   there has been a failure on the part of the society to satisfy a criterion of prudent management, set out in section 45(3) of the Building Societies Act 1986 as it had effect at any time before commencement, relating to the maintenance of adequate reserves and other capital resources, or

(b)   there would be such a failure if the interest was paid or credited.

(5)   Unless the context otherwise requires, any reference in that provision to that criterion has effect, in relation to any time after commencement, as a reference to the condition set out in paragraph 4(1) of Schedule 6 to the 2000 Act (adequate resources).

(6)   "Relevant provision" means a provision which—

(a)   is contained in the rules of a building society, friendly society or industrial and provident society, or in any other contract, deed or document other than an enactment, and

(b)   has effect before, as well as after, commencement,

but for the purposes only of paragraph (1) above also includes a provision in any document which is provided to the Authority after commencement pursuant to article 6(2).

[2459]

8   Anticipatory exercise of powers

(1)   This article applies where by virtue of any amendment made by Schedule 3 to this Order—

(a)   the Authority will, with effect from commencement, have power to make rules, or have power to give directions as to the form of or particulars to be included in any document or as to the manner in which any application is to be made, or

(b)   the Treasury will, with effect from commencement, have power to make any rules, order or regulations.

(2)   Where this article applies, the Authority or the Treasury (as the case may be) may exercise the power referred to in paragraph (1) before commencement for the purposes of bringing the rules, directions, order or regulations into effect at commencement.

(3)   In exercising any power before commencement by virtue of paragraph (2), the Authority or the Treasury (as the case may be) are to be treated as being subject to the same requirements or conditions, as to the procedure to be followed in exercising the power or otherwise, as would apply in relation to the exercise of that power if this Order were fully in force.

[2460]

PART III
DISSOLUTIONS

9   The Building Societies Commission

(1)   As soon as practicable after commencement, the Building Societies Commission must lay before the Treasury and before Parliament a report on the discharge of its functions during the last period.

(2)   Before the end of the period of seven months beginning at commencement, the Building Societies Commission must send to the Treasury and to the Comptroller and Auditor General a statement of accounts in respect of the last period.

(3)   The Comptroller and Auditor General must examine, certify and report on the statement of accounts received by him from the Building Societies Commission under paragraph (2), and lay a copy of the statement and of his report before Parliament.

(4)   The Building Societies Commission is to cease to exist on the day after the first day on which paragraphs (1) and (3) have both been complied with.

(5)   Immediately before the Building Societies Commission ceases to exist by virtue of paragraph (4), all assets, rights and liabilities which at that time are held or enjoyed by the Commission, or to which at that time it is subject, are transferred to the Treasury, except as provided in paragraphs (7) and (9).

(6)   Paragraph (7) applies in relation to income received by the Building Societies Commission under section 2 of the Building Societies Act 1986, in respect of the last period or in relation to applications submitted to it during the last period ("relevant income").

(7)   Insofar as relevant income is not applied before commencement in accordance with section 2 of the Building Societies Act 1986 towards expenses of the Commission, it is to be paid to the Authority.

(8)   Paragraph (9) applies where, before commencement—

(a) any fee or charge, or any sum in respect of costs or expenses, was payable to the Building Societies Commission, but

(b) that fee, charge or sum, or any part of it, was not so paid ("the unpaid sum").

(9) Notwithstanding any amendment, repeal or revocation made by this Order or by any other provision of or made under the 2000 Act, the unpaid sum is payable after commencement to the Authority in substitution for the Commission and (insofar as it is not so paid) may be recovered by the Authority as a debt due to it.

(10) The Authority must, so far as practicable, ensure that—

(a) relevant income paid to it in accordance with paragraph (7), and

(b) any sum paid to it or recovered by it in accordance with paragraph (9),

is used only in connection with any functions of the Authority in relation to building societies or, to the extent that it is not so used, is applied for the benefit of building societies.

[2461]

10 The Friendly Societies Commission

(1) As soon as practicable after commencement, the Friendly Societies Commission must lay before the Treasury and before Parliament a report on the discharge of its functions during the last period.

(2) Before the end of the period of seven months beginning at commencement, the Friendly Societies Commission must send to the Treasury and to the Comptroller and Auditor General a statement of accounts in respect of the last period.

(3) The Comptroller and Auditor General must examine, certify and report on the statement of accounts received by him from the Friendly Societies Commission under paragraph (2), and lay a copy of the statement and of his report before Parliament.

(4) The Friendly Societies Commission is to cease to exist on the day after the first day on which paragraphs (1) and (3) have both been complied with.

(5) Immediately before the Friendly Societies Commission ceases to exist by virtue of paragraph (4), all assets, rights and liabilities which at that time are held or enjoyed by the Commission, or to which at that time it is subject, are transferred to the Treasury, except as provided in paragraphs (7) and (9).

(6) Paragraph (7) applies in relation to income received by the Friendly Societies Commission under section 2 of the Friendly Societies Act 1992, in respect of the last period or in relation to applications submitted to it during the last period ("relevant income").

(7) Insofar as relevant income is not applied before commencement in accordance with section 2 of the Friendly Societies Act 1992 towards expenses of the Commission, it is to be paid to the Authority.

(8) Paragraph (9) applies where, before commencement—

(a) any fee or charge, or any sum in respect of costs or expenses, was payable to the Friendly Societies Commission, but

(b) that fee, charge or sum, or any part of it, was not so paid ("the unpaid sum").

(9) Notwithstanding any amendment, repeal or revocation made by this Order or by any other provision of or made under the 2000 Act, the unpaid sum is payable after commencement to the Authority in substitution for the Commission and (insofar as it is not so paid) may be recovered by the Authority as a debt due to it.

(10) The Authority must, so far as practicable, ensure that—

(a) relevant income paid to it in accordance with paragraph (7), and

(b) any sum paid to it or recovered by it in accordance with paragraph (9),

is used only in connection with any functions of the Authority in relation to friendly societies or, to the extent that it is not so used, is applied for the benefit of friendly societies.

[2462]

11 The Building Societies Investor Protection Board

(1) As soon as practicable after commencement, the Board must prepare—

(a) a report on the discharge of its functions during the last period, and

(b) a statement of accounts showing the state of affairs and income and expenditure of the Board in respect of the last period.

(2) The statement of accounts must be audited by auditors appointed by the Board and the auditors must report to the Board stating whether in their opinion the provisions of paragraph 6(2) of Schedule 5 to the Building Societies Act 1986 (as it had effect immediately before its repeal by this Order) were complied with in respect of the last period.

(3) As soon as practicable after paragraphs (1) and (2) above have been complied with, the Board must publish, in such manner as it thinks appropriate, the report prepared in accordance with paragraph (1)(a) and the statement of accounts prepared in accordance with paragraph (1)(b).

(4)   The Board is to cease to exist on the day after paragraph (3) is complied with.

[2463]

12   The Chief Registrar, assistant registrar for Scotland, and assistant registrars

(1)   As soon as practicable after the Building Societies Commission and the Friendly Societies Commission have ceased to exist by virtue of articles 9 and 10, the Chief Registrar must lay before Parliament a report of his proceedings and those of the assistant registrar for Scotland and the assistant registrars, of the principal matters transacted by him and them, and of the valuations returned to him or them, in relation to the period beginning with 1st October 2001 and ending at commencement.

(2)   The report which the Chief Registrar is required to make by virtue of paragraph (1) may be combined with the report which he is required to make pursuant to section 6(1) of the Friendly Societies Act 1974 in respect of the year ending 30th September 2001.

(3)   The office of Chief Registrar, the office of assistant registrar for Scotland, and the offices of assistant registrar are to cease to exist on the day after paragraph (1) is complied with.

(4)   Immediately before the offices mentioned in paragraph (3) cease to exist by virtue of that paragraph, all assets, rights and liabilities which at that time attach to those offices (including records maintained or held by, and any other assets, rights and liabilities of, the central office) are transferred to the Treasury.

[2464]

PART IV
AMENDMENTS, REPEALS ETC

13   Amendments, repeals, transitional provisions and savings

(1)   The enactments specified in Schedule 3 to this Order have effect with the amendments made by that Schedule.

(2)   The enactments specified in Schedule 4 to this Order are repealed to the extent specified in that Schedule.

(3)   The amendments and repeals made by Schedules 3 and 4 are subject to the transitional provisions and savings contained in Schedule 5 to this Order and to any other transitional provisions or savings made under the 2000 Act.

[2465]

SCHEDULES

SCHEDULE 1
FUNCTIONS TRANSFERRED TO THE TREASURY
Article 4(1)

PART I
FUNCTIONS OF THE CHIEF REGISTRAR, ASSISTANT REGISTRAR FOR SCOTLAND,
ASSISTANT REGISTRARS AND THE CENTRAL OFFICE

Act	Provision	Function
The Superannuation and other Trust Funds (Validation) Act 1927 c 41.	Section 8	Making regulations prescribing the qualifications required to be held by an actuary for the purposes of the Act.
The Friendly and Industrial and Provident Societies Act 1968 c 55.	Section 4(8)	Making regulations substituting any sum or number, and prescribing receipts and payments to be taken into account, for the purposes of section 4(2) of the Act (exemption from obligation to appoint auditor).
	Section 10(1)	Making regulations prescribing maximum rates for remuneration of auditors and reporting accountants.
	Section 13(3)	Making regulations prescribing accounts to be comprised and particulars to be contained in group accounts.

Act	Provision	Function
The Friendly Societies Act 1974 c 46.	Section 31(5)	Making regulations substituting any sum, number or percentage, and prescribing receipts and payments to be taken into account, for the purposes of section 31(2) or (3) of the Act (exemption from obligation to appoint auditor).
	Section 40(1)	Making regulations under section 10 of the Friendly and Industrial and Provident Societies Act 1968 prescribing maximum rates for remuneration of auditors and reporting accountants.
	Section 42(1)	Making regulations specifying class of society or branch for whom application of section 41(1) of the Act is modified (valuation report required every 3 years rather than every 5 years).
	Section 42(2)	Making regulations specifying class of society or branch for whom application of section 41(1) of the Act is modified (valuation report required every 3 years rather than every 5 years in respect of specified class of business).
	Section 47(1)	Prescribing other UK Government securities for the purchase of which, on behalf of its members, a society or branch registered under the Act (and also an industrial and provident society, by virtue of section 11 of the Industrial and Provident Societies Act 1965) may set up a fund.
	Section 86(2)	Making regulations specifying requirements to be complied with in procedure for proxy voting.
The Industrial and Provident Societies Act 1975 c 41.	Section 2	Making an order substituting sum in section 6(1) of the Industrial and Provident Societies Act 1965 (maximum shareholding of a member of an industrial and provident society) and making related provision.
The Industrial and Provident Societies Act 1978 c 34.	Section 2	Making an order substituting sums in section 7(3) of the Industrial and Provident Societies Act 1965 (limits on taking deposits at one time or from one depositor) and making related provision.
The Credit Unions Act 1979 c 34.	Section 5(4)	Making an order substituting sum in section 5(3) of the Act (maximum shareholding of a member of a credit union).
	Section 9(4) and (5)	Making an order substituting amount in section 9(1) of the Act (limit on taking deposits from someone too young to be a member of a credit union) and making related provision.
	Section 11(7)	Making an order specifying maximum period within which loan by credit union must be repaid (section 11(4) of the Act) and maximum rate of interest charged (section 11(5) of the Act).
	Section 13(1)	Making an order authorising manner in which surplus funds of credit union may be invested.
	Section 14(4)	Making an order specifying maximum rate of dividend payable on shares of credit union.
	Section 15(3) and (4)	Making regulations prescribing matters mentioned in section 15(2)(a) and (b) of the Act (which relate to requirement to insure against fraud or dishonesty).
The Building Societies Act 1986 c 53.	Schedule 2A paragraph 3(1)	Making rules prescribing form of receipt for discharge of mortgage under paragraph 1 of the Schedule.

Act	Provision	Function
The Social Security Contributions and Benefits Act 1992 c 4.	Schedule 1 paragraph 11(2)	Making regulations prescribing procedure for making amendments to rules of a registered friendly society in compliance with regulations under paragraph 11(1) of the Schedule (sickness payments).

[2466]

PART II
FUNCTIONS OF THE FRIENDLY SOCIETIES COMMISSION

Act	Provision	Function
The Friendly Societies Act 1974 c 46.	Section 65A(8)	Making regulations under section 11(7) of the Friendly Societies Act 1992 (manner of carrying on group insurance business etc) applying to registered friendly societies.
The Friendly Societies Act 1992 c 40.	Section 5(4)	Making an order varying Schedule 2 (activities of an incorporated friendly society).
	Section 11(7)	Making regulations specifying manner in which group insurance business may be carried on by incorporated friendly societies.
	Section 69(4) and (5)	Making regulations exempting incorporated friendly societies from preparing group accounts.
	Section 70(6)	Making regulations about contents and form of annual accounts.
	Section 71(1)(b)	Making regulations prescribing information to be contained in annual report.
	Section 71(2)(a)	Making regulations prescribing information to be contained in annual report of an incorporated friendly society which has subsidiaries or jointly controls other bodies.
	Section 91(8)	Making regulations providing for regulation of conversion of friendly societies into companies.
	Section 93(14)	Making an order prescribing the day on which the transitional period ends (period within which societies must comply with the Act).
	Section 99(3)	Making an order substituting sum in section 99(1) (maximum benefit payable on death under the age of 10).
	Section 112(4)	Making regulations in connection with records which are kept otherwise than in legible form.
	Schedule 3 paragraph 13(4)	Making an order prescribing maximum fee chargeable by incorporated friendly society for providing copies of its statutory documents.
	Schedule 5 paragraph 2(5)	Making an order substituting a sum in paragraph 2(3) or (4) of the Schedule (loan fund).
	Schedule 5 paragraph 3(1)	Prescribing other UK Government securities for the purchase of which, on behalf of its members, an incorporated friendly society may set up a fund.
	Schedule 11 paragraph 16(1)	Making an order prescribing series of monetary amounts ("prescribed bands") for the purposes of Part II of Schedule 11 (dealings with members of committee of management).

Act	Provision	Function
	Schedule 12 paragraph 5(2)	Making regulations prescribing when rules of societies may exclude or limit voting rights of members according to amount of subscriptions.
	Schedule 12 paragraph 7(6)	Making regulations prescribing requirements for procedure to be adopted for proxy voting.
	Schedule 14 paragraph 5(3)	Making regulations specifying descriptions of connections which make auditors ineligible for appointment.
	Schedule 14 paragraph 7(4)	Making regulations substituting sum, number or percentage, and prescribing receipts and payments which must be taken into account, for the purposes of paragraph 7(1) and (3) of the Schedule (exemption from requirement for auditor to be a member of a recognised supervisory body).
	Schedule 14 paragraph 17(1)	Making regulations to secure the disclosure of the amount of remuneration of auditors and their associates.
	Schedule 15 paragraph 3(1)(a)	Making regulations to prescribe matters to be dealt with in a statement to members (statements relating to conversion of society into a company).

[2467]

PART III
FUNCTIONS OF THE BUILDING SOCIETIES COMMISSION

Act	Provision	Function
The Building Societies Act 1986 c 53.	Section 6(7) and (8)	Making an order modifying or applying section 6(2) and (3) (lending limit) in relation to assets of subsidiary or associated undertakings, and making related provision.
	Section 6A(2)(b) and (5)	Making an order prescribing description and circumstances of creation of equitable interest (for the purposes of determining when a loan is to be treated as secured on land), and making related provision.
	Section 6A(4) and (5)	Making an order providing for provisions of the Act to have effect in relation to loans secured on land outside the EEA with appropriate modifications, and making related provision.
	Section 7(7) and (8)	Making an order modifying or applying section 7(2) and (3) (funding limit) in relation to liabilities of subsidiary or associated undertakings, and making related provision.
	Section 8(12)	Making an order varying subsections (2), (9) and (10) of the section (provision about raising funds and borrowing), and making related provision.
	Section 9A(12)	Making an order substituting an amount or percentage in subsections (2), (3) or (6), or varying subsection (4)(b), of the section (restrictions on certain transactions).
	Section 42B(8)	Making regulations specifying matters of which particulars must be contained in statements under paragraphs 3 and 9 of Schedule 8A.

Act	Provision	Function
	Section 60(9) and (16)	Making an order substituting maximum amount which rules of a society may require as shareholding of director, and making related provision.
	Section 61(4) and (5)	Making an order substituting amount, number or percentage in subsections (1) to (3), or varying subsection (3A), of the section (rules as to election of directors), and making related provision.
	Section 64(3)	Making an order substituting any of the amounts in subsection (2) (requisite cash value of assets for the purposes of transactions with directors or persons connected with them).
	Section 65(8)	Making an order to substitute sums in the section (loans to directors or persons connected with them).
	Section 68(9)	Making an order substituting amounts in subsections (7) and (8) (exceptions from obligations imposed by the section in relation to transactions with directors or persons connected with them).
	Section 69(5)	Making an order designating relevant services for the purpose of the section (disclosure and record of income of related businesses), and making related provision.
	Section 69(12)	Making an order substituting a sum in the subsection in relation to volume of business.
	Section 72(7) and (8)	Making regulations as to documents to be comprised in annual accounts, and matters to be included in such documents, including modification of Part VIII of the Act, and making related provision.
	Section 73(6) to (8)	Making regulations as to contents and form of annual accounts of a building society.
	Section 74(3) and (4)	Making regulations prescribing contents and form of annual business statement.
	Section 75(1)(b)	Making regulations prescribing information to be contained in the directors' annual report.
	Section 76(3)	Making regulations with respect to the form and content of summary financial statement.
	Section 92A(10)	Making an order substituting percentages in subsections (4) and (5) of the section (acquisition or establishment of new business), and making related provision.
	Section 92A(11)	Making an order varying subsections (5) and (9) of the section, and making related provision.
	Section 96(2)	Making regulations authorising payments of compensation to directors or other officers on amalgamation or transfer of engagements.
	Section 96(5)	Making regulations authorising distribution of funds to members on amalgamation or transfer of engagements.
	Section 99(3)	Making regulations authorising payment of compensation to directors or other officers on transfers of business under section 97.
	Section 102(1) and (2)	Making regulations regulating transfers of business under section 97.
	Section 102D(11)	Making regulations prescribing time periods for notices under section 102B(4).

Act	Provision	Function
	Section 114(4)	Making regulations about records kept otherwise than in legible form.
	Section 119(1)	Making an order defining class of shares which are "deferred shares" for the purpose of the Act.
	Schedule 2 paragraphs 10A(3) and 10C(6)	Making regulations specifying words or expressions the use of which in a business name requires the Authority's approval (and specifying bodies whose comments must be sought), and making related provision.
	Schedule 2 paragraphs 10B(5) and 10C(6)	Making regulations as to form and display of notice under paragraph 10B(3) and (4) of the Schedule (notice of registered name and address of society), and making related provision.
	Schedule 2 paragraph 12(4)	Making an order prescribing amount in paragraph 12(1)(b) of the Schedule (maximum amount which may be charged by a building society for providing copies of its statutory documents).
	Schedule 2 paragraph 20A(13)	Making an order substituting number or sum in paragraph 20A(2) or (7) of the Schedule (members' requisitions of special meetings), and making related provision.
	Schedule 2 paragraph 32(4) and (6)	Making an order varying definitions of "requisite number" or "qualified member" in paragraph 31(2) or descriptions of provisions rendered void by paragraph 31(3) of the Schedule, and making related provision.
	Schedule 2 paragraph 36(1) and (3)	Making an order specifying prescribed amount for the purposes of Part III of the Schedule, and making related provision.
	Schedule 10 paragraph 9(1) and (2)	Making an order prescribing series of numbers or monetary amounts ("prescribed bands") for the purposes of Part II of the Schedule.
	Schedule 11 paragraph 5(1)(b)	Making an order designating bodies of accountants the members of whom are qualified for appointment as auditor of a building society.
	Schedule 15A paragraph 25	Making regulations prescribing the form of receivership accounts for the purposes of section 38 of the Insolvency Act 1986.
	Schedule 15A paragraph 47	Making regulations prescribing the form of receivership accounts for the purposes of article 48 of the Insolvency (Northern Ireland) Order 1989.
	Schedule 17 paragraph 5(1)	Specifying particulars to be given in transfer statement.
	Schedule 17 paragraph 5(2)	Specifying information to be contained in transfer summary.

[2468]

SCHEDULE 2
APPLICATION OF FINANCIAL SERVICES AND MARKETS ACT 2000 TO TRANSFERRED FUNCTIONS

Article 4(3)

Interpretation

1. In this Schedule—
  (a) "mutuals expenditure" means expenditure of the Authority incurred—
    (i) in carrying out relevant functions, or for any purpose incidental to the carrying out of relevant functions, or
    (ii) in repaying the principal of, or paying any interest on, any money which it has

           borrowed and which has been used for the purpose of meeting expenses incurred in relation to its assumption of relevant functions,

  (b)   "the mutuals legislation" means the Friendly Societies Act 1974, the Building Societies Act 1986, the Friendly Societies Act 1992, and the enactments relating to industrial and provident societies and credit unions referred to in section 338(1),

  (c)   "relevant functions" means functions transferred to the Authority by virtue of article 4(2) (and includes, in relation to any time before commencement, such functions as they are to be transferred with effect from commencement), and

  (d)   any reference to a section or Schedule is a reference to that section or Schedule in the 2000 Act.

General

2.   For the purposes of section 1(3) and Schedule 1 (which make general provision in relation to the Authority and its functions), relevant functions are to be treated as functions conferred on the Authority under a provision of the 2000 Act.

3.   If the Authority maintains arrangements designed to enable it to determine whether persons are complying with requirements imposed on them by or under the mutuals legislation, paragraph 6(2) of Schedule 1 (which permits functions to be performed by a body or person other than the Authority) applies to those arrangements as it applies to arrangements of the kind mentioned in paragraph 6(1) of that Schedule, but does not affect the Authority's responsibility for relevant functions or for any other matter under the mutuals legislation.

4.   The Authority's determination of the general policy and principles by reference to which it performs relevant functions is not to be treated as a general function of the Authority by virtue of subsection (4)(d) of section 2 (functions of the Authority to which the Authority's general duties apply).

5.   Section 8 (which requires the Authority to make arrangements for consulting consumers and practitioners on its general policies and practices) does not apply in relation to the Authority's general policies and practices with respect to the exercise of relevant functions.

6.   In the application of section 12 (which makes provision for reviews of the economy, efficiency and effectiveness with which the Authority has used its resources in discharging its functions) to relevant functions, section 12(3) is to be read as if, for the words from "pursuing" to the end there were substituted "exercising its functions".

7.   For the purposes of section 159(1) (interpretation of Chapter III of Part X), relevant functions are not to be treated as functions under the 2000 Act.

8.   For the purposes of section 415 (jurisdiction in civil proceedings), relevant functions are to be treated as functions of the Authority under the 2000 Act.

Rules relating to fees

9.   Paragraphs 10 and 11 apply where the Authority—

  (a)   makes (or proposes to make) rules under paragraph 17(1) of Schedule 1 which require the payment to the Authority of fees which relate in whole or in part to mutuals expenditure, or

  (b)   designates any provisions in accordance with article 4 of the Financial Services and Markets Act 2000 (Transitional Provisions and Savings) (Rules) Order 2001 with a view to their having effect after commencement as such rules.

10.   In the application of paragraph 17(1) of Schedule 1 to the rules, the reference to fees and charges provided for by any other provision of the 2000 Act includes a reference to fees and charges provided for by any provision of the mutuals legislation.

11.   To the extent that the fees relate to mutuals expenditure—

  (a)   the making of the rules is not to be treated as a general function of the Authority by virtue of subsection (4)(a) of section 2 (functions of the Authority to which the Authority's general duties apply),

  (b)   section 155(2)(c) (requirement to include in consultation a statement that rules are compatible with general duties) (or, in any case covered by paragraph 9(b) above, article 4(2)(f) of the Order referred to in that paragraph) does not apply in relation to the rules, and

  (c)   the rules are not to be treated as regulating provisions for the purposes of section 159(1) (interpretation of Chapter III of Part X).

Guidance

12.   For the purposes of sections 157(3) and 158(5) (guidance to regulated persons generally), guidance given to building societies, friendly societies and industrial and provident societies

generally or to a class of such societies is to be treated as if given to regulated persons generally or to a class of regulated persons, whether or not those societies would otherwise be "regulated persons" within the meaning of those sections.

13. Paragraph 14 applies where guidance is given by the Authority under section 157 on the operation of a rule of the kind mentioned in paragraph 9 above (whether made as mentioned in sub-paragraph (a) of that paragraph, or designated as mentioned in sub-paragraph (b) of that paragraph).

14. To the extent that the fees required to be paid by the rule relate to mutuals expenditure—
    (a)   the giving of the guidance is not to be treated as a general function of the Authority by virtue of subsection (4)(c) of section 2 (functions of the Authority to which the Authority's general duties apply),
    (b)   section 155(2)(c) (requirement to include in consultation a statement that rules are compatible with general duties) does not apply in relation to the guidance, and
    (c)   the guidance is not to be treated as a regulating provision for the purposes of section 159(1) (interpretation of Chapter III of Part X).

15. Paragraphs 16 and 17 apply where general guidance is given by the Authority under section 157 with respect to any matter relating to relevant functions, or with respect to any provision of or made under the mutuals legislation, unless paragraph 14 above applies.

16. The giving of the guidance is not to be treated as a general function of the Authority by virtue of subsection (4)(c) of section 2 (functions of the Authority to which the Authority's general duties apply).

17. The guidance is not to be treated as a regulating provision for the purposes of section 159(1) (interpretation of Chapter III of Part X).

[2469]

(Sch 3 contains consequential amendments; Sch 4 contains repeals; Sch 5 contains transitional provisions and savings.)

FINANCIAL SERVICES AND MARKETS ACT 2000 (INSOLVENCY) (DEFINITION OF "INSURER") ORDER 2001

(SI 2001/2634)

NOTES
Made: 20 July 2001.
Authority: Financial Services and Markets Act 2000, ss 355(2), 428(3).
Commencement: 1 December 2001.
This Order is reproduced as amended by: the Financial Services and Markets Act 2000 (Administration Orders Relating to Insurers) Order 2002, SI 2002/1242.

1—(1) This Order may be cited as the Financial Services and Markets Act 2000 (Insolvency) (Definition of "Insurer") Order 2001 and comes into force on the day on which section 19 of the Act comes into force.

(2) In this Order, the "Regulated Activities Order" means the Financial Services and Markets Act 2000 (Regulated Activities) Order 2001.

[2470]

2 In Part XXIV of the Act (insolvency), ... "insurer" means any person who is carrying on a regulated activity of the kind specified by article 10(1) or (2) of the Regulated Activities Order (effecting and carrying out contracts of insurance) but who is not—
    (a)   exempt from the general prohibition in respect of that regulated activity;
    (b)   a friendly society; or
    (c)   a person who effects or carries out contracts of insurance all of which fall within paragraphs 14 to 18 of Part I of Schedule 1 to the Regulated Activities Order in the course of, or for the purposes of, a banking business.

[2471]

NOTES
Words omitted revoked by the Financial Services and Markets Act 2000 (Administration Orders Relating to Insurers) Order 2002, SI 2002/1242, art 2, as from 31 May 2002.

FINANCIAL SERVICES AND MARKETS ACT 2000 (LAW APPLICABLE TO CONTRACTS OF INSURANCE) REGULATIONS 2001

(SI 2001/2635)

NOTES
Made: 19 July 2001.
Authority: Financial Services and Markets Act 2000, ss 417(1), 424(3), 428(3).
Commencement: 1 December 2001.
These Regulations are reproduced as amended by: the Financial Services and Markets Act 2000 (Law Applicable to Contracts of Insurance) (Amendment) Regulations 2001, SI 2001/3542; the Financial Services and Markets Act 2000 (Motor Insurance) Regulations 2007, SI 2007/2403.

ARRANGEMENT OF REGULATIONS

PART I
GENERAL

PART II
CONTRACTS OF GENERAL INSURANCE

PART III
CONTRACTS OF LONG-TERM INSURANCE

PART I
GENERAL

1   Citation and commencement

These Regulations may be cited as the Financial Services and Markets Act 2000 (Law Applicable to Contracts of Insurance) Regulations 2001 and come into force on the day on which section 19 of the Act comes into force.

[2472]

2   Interpretation

(1)   In these Regulations—
"the Act" means the Financial Services and Markets Act 2000;
"the 1990 Act" means the Contracts (Applicable Law) Act 1990;
"applicable law", in relation to a contract of insurance, means the law that is applicable to that contract;
"contract of general insurance" and "contract of long-term insurance" have the meanings given by the Regulated Activities Order;
"EEA State of the commitment" means, in relation to a contract of long-term insurance entered into on a date—
    (a)   if the policyholder is an individual, the EEA State in which he resides on that date; or
    (b)   otherwise, the EEA State in which the establishment of the policyholder to which the contract relates is situated on that date;
"establishment", in relation to a person ("A"), means—
    (a)   A's head office;
    (b)   any of A's agencies;
    (c)   any of A's branches; or
    (d)   any permanent presence of A in an EEA State, which need not take the form of a branch or agency and which may consist of an office managed by A's staff or by a person who is independent of A but has permanent authority to act for A as if he were an agency;

"large risk" has the meaning given by Article 5(d) of the first non-life insurance directive and includes risks specified by paragraph (iii) of that definition insured by professional associations, joint ventures or temporary groups;

"mandatory rules" means the rules from which the law allows no derogation by way of contract;

"the Regulated Activities Order" means the Financial Services and Markets Act 2000 (Regulated Activities) Order 2001.

(2) References to the EEA State where the risk covered by a contract of insurance is situated are to—

    (a)   if the contract relates to buildings or to buildings and their contents (in so far as the contents are covered by the same contract of insurance), the EEA State in which the property is situated;

    (b)   if the contract relates to vehicles of any type, the EEA State of registration;

    (c)   if the contract covers travel or holidays risks and has a duration of four months or less, the EEA State in which the policyholder entered into the contract;

    (d)   in any other case—

        (i)   if the policyholder is an individual, the EEA State in which he resides on the date the contract is entered into;

        (ii)   otherwise, the EEA State in which the establishment of the policyholder to which the contract relates is situated on that date.

[(2A) If the contract of insurance relates to a vehicle dispatched from one EEA State to another, in respect of the period of 30 days beginning with the day on which the purchaser accepts delivery a reference to the EEA State in which a risk is situated is a reference to the State of destination (and not, as provided by paragraph (2)(b), to the State of registration).]

(3) References to the country in which a person resides are to—

    (a)   if he is an individual, the country in which he has his habitual residence;

    (b)   in any other case, the country in which he has his central administration.

(4) Where an EEA State (including the United Kingdom) includes several territorial units, each of which has its own laws concerning contractual obligations, each unit is to be considered as a separate state for the purposes of identifying the applicable law under these Regulations.

[2473]

NOTES

Para (2A): inserted by the Financial Services and Markets Act 2000 (Motor Insurance) Regulations 2007, SI 2007/2403, reg 3, as from 5 September 2007.

3 Scope of these Regulations

(1) These Regulations do not apply to contracts of reinsurance.

(2) These Regulations apply to contracts of insurance which are entered into by friendly societies as follows—

    (a)   Part II applies to a contract of insurance entered into by a friendly society to which section 37(3) of the Friendly Societies Act 1992 applies;

    (b)   Part III applies to a contract of insurance entered into by a friendly society to which section 37(2) of that Act applies; and

    (c)   Part II applies to any other contract of insurance entered into by a friendly society which covers a risk situated in an EEA State with the following modifications—

        (i)   paragraph (1) of regulation 4 does not apply;

        (ii)   regulation 4 applies only where the policyholder is an individual; ...

        [(iii)   regulation 7(1) applies as if for the words "the 1990 Act is to be treated as applying", there were substituted "a court in any part of the United Kingdom must apply the general rules of private international law of that part of the United Kingdom concerning contractual obligations"; and

        (iv)   regulation 7(2) and (3) apply as if for the words "the 1990 Act is to be treated as applying" in each case, there were substituted the words "the general rules of private international law of that part of the United Kingdom concerning contractual obligations apply".]

[2474]

NOTES

Para (2): word omitted from sub-para (c)(ii) revoked, and sub-paras (c)(iii), (iv) substituted for original sub-para (c)(iii), by the Financial Services and Markets Act 2000 (Law Applicable to Contracts of Insurance) (Amendment) Regulations 2001, SI 2001/3542, reg 2, as from 1 December 2001.

PART II
CONTRACTS OF GENERAL INSURANCE

4 Applicable law

(1) This Part applies to a contract of general insurance which covers risks situated in an EEA State.

(2) If the policyholder resides in the EEA State in which the risk is situated, the applicable law is the law of that EEA State unless, if such a choice is permitted under the law of that EEA State, the parties to the contract choose the law of another country.

(3) If the policyholder does not reside in the EEA State in which the risk is situated, the parties to the contract may choose as the applicable law either—

     (a)   the law of the EEA State in which the risk is situated; or

     (b)   the law of the country in which the policyholder resides.

(4) If the policyholder carries on a business (including a trade or profession) and the contract covers two or more risks relating to that business which are situated in different EEA States, the freedom of the parties to choose the applicable law conferred by this regulation extends to the law of any of those EEA States and of the country in which the policyholder resides.

(5) If any of the EEA States referred to in paragraph (3) or (4) grant greater freedom of choice of the applicable law, the parties to the contract may take advantage of that freedom.

(6) Notwithstanding paragraphs (2) to (4), if the risks covered by the contract are limited to events occurring in one EEA State other than the EEA State in which the risk is situated, the parties may choose the law of the former EEA State as the applicable law.

(7) Notwithstanding paragraphs (2) to (4), if the risk covered by the contract is a large risk the parties may choose any law as the applicable law.

(8) Where the foregoing provisions of this regulation allow the parties to the contract to choose the applicable law and if no choice has been made, or no choice has been made which satisfies the requirement set out in regulation 6(1), the applicable law is the law of the country, from amongst those considered in the relevant paragraph ("the relevant countries"), which is most closely connected with the contract; however, where a severable part of the contract has a closer connection with another relevant country, the law applicable to that part is, by way of exception, the law of that relevant country.

(9) For the purposes of paragraph (8), the contract is rebuttably presumed to be most closely connected with the EEA State in which the risk is situated.

           [2475]

5 Mandatory rules

(1) Nothing in regulation 4 restricts the application of the mandatory rules of any part of the United Kingdom, irrespective of the applicable law of the contract.

(2) If the parties to the contract choose the applicable law under regulation 4 and if all the other elements relevant to the situation at the time when the parties make their choice are connected with one EEA State only, the application of the mandatory rules of that EEA State is not prejudiced.

           [2476]

6 Choice of law

(1) Any choice made by the parties under regulation 4 must be expressed or demonstrated with reasonable certainty by the terms of the contract or the circumstances of the case.

(2) Where the parties to the contract may choose the applicable law under regulation 4, and where the risk to which the contract relates is covered by Community co-insurance (within the meaning of Council Directive 78/473/EEC on the coordination of laws, regulations and administrative provisions relating to Community co-insurance)), co-insurers other than the leading insurer (within the meaning of that Directive) are not to be treated as parties to the contract.

           [2477]

7 The 1990 Act

(1) Subject to the preceding provisions of this Part, the 1990 Act is to be treated as applying to the contract for the purposes of determining the applicable law.

(2) In determining whether the mandatory rules of another EEA State should be applied in accordance with regulation 5(2) where the parties have chosen the law of a part of the United Kingdom as the applicable law, the 1990 Act is to be treated as applying to the contract.

(3) In determining what freedom of choice the parties have under the law of a part of the United Kingdom, the 1990 Act is to be treated as applying to the contract.

           [2478]

PART III
STATUTORY INSTRUMENTS

PART III
CONTRACTS OF LONG-TERM INSURANCE

8 Applicable law

(1) This Part applies to a contract of long-term insurance if—
   (a)   where the policyholder is an individual, he resides in an EEA State;
   (b)   otherwise, the establishment of the policyholder to which the contract relates is situated in an EEA State.

(2) The applicable law is the law of the EEA State of the commitment unless, if such a choice is permitted under the law of that EEA State, the parties choose the law of another country.

(3) If the policyholder is an individual and resides in one EEA State but is a national or citizen of another, the parties to the contract may choose the law of the EEA State of which he is a national or citizen as the applicable law.

[2479]

9 Mandatory rules

Nothing in regulation 8 affects the application of the mandatory rules of any part of the United Kingdom, irrespective of the applicable law of the contract.

[2480]

10 The 1990 Act

(1) Subject to the preceding provisions of this Part, the 1990 Act is to be treated as applying to the contract for the purposes of determining the applicable law.

(2) In determining what freedom of choice the parties have under the law of a part of the United Kingdom, the 1990 Act is to be treated as applying to the contract.

[2481]

FINANCIAL SERVICES AND MARKETS ACT 2000 (CONTROLLERS) (EXEMPTION) ORDER 2001

(SI 2001/2638)

NOTES
Made: 19 July 2001.
Authority: Financial Services and Markets Act 2000, ss 192(a), 428(3).
Commencement: 1 December 2001.

As of 1 February 2009, this Order had not been amended.

1 Citation and commencement

This Order may be cited as the Financial Services and Markets Act 2000 (Controllers) (Exemption) Order 2001 and comes into force on the day on which section 19 of the Act comes into force.

[2482]

2 Friendly societies

(1) In any case where a person ("the acquirer")—
   (a)   proposes to take, in relation to a relevant friendly society, such a step as is mentioned in section 178(1) of the Act, or
   (b)   acquires control, an additional kind of control or an increase in a relevant kind of control (in each case, within the meaning of Part XII of the Act) over a relevant friendly society without himself taking any such step,

the acquirer is exempt from any obligation imposed by section 178 of the Act to notify the Authority of his proposal or acquisition.

(2) In any case where a controller of a relevant friendly society—
   (a)   proposes to take, in relation to that relevant friendly society, such a step as is mentioned in section 190(1) of the Act, or
   (b)   ceases to have or reduces a relevant kind of control (within the meaning of Part XII of the Act) over that relevant friendly society without himself taking any such step,

the controller is exempt from any obligation imposed by section 190 of the Act to notify the Authority.

(3) In this article, "relevant friendly society" means any UK authorised person (within the meaning of Part XII of the Act) who is a friendly society to which neither subsection (2) nor (3) of section 37 of the Friendly Societies Act 1992 applies.

[2483]

FINANCIAL SERVICES AND MARKETS ACT 2000 (OWN-INITIATIVE POWER) (OVERSEAS REGULATORS) REGULATIONS 2001

(SI 2001/2639)

NOTES
Made: 19 July 2001.
Authority: Financial Services and Markets Act 2000, ss 47(1), (3), 417(1), 428(3).
Commencement: see reg 1.
As of 1 February 2009, these Regulations had not been amended.

1 Citation and commencement

These Regulations may be cited as the Financial Services and Markets Act 2000 Own-initiative Power) (Overseas Regulators) Regulations 2001 and come into force on the day on which section 19 of the Act comes into force.

[2484]

2 Overseas regulators

(1)   The kind of regulator to which paragraph (2) applies is prescribed for the purposes of section 47(1)(b) of the Act.

(2)   This paragraph applies to a regulator who exercises—
   (a)   a function corresponding to any function of the Authority under the Act;
   (b)   a function corresponding to any function exercised by the competent authority under Part VI of the Act (official listing);
   (c)   a function corresponding to any function exercised by the Secretary of State under the Companies Act 1985; or
   (d)   a function in connection with—
      (i)   the investigation of conduct of the kind prohibited by Part V of the Criminal Justice Act 1993 (insider dealing); or
      (ii)   the enforcement of rules (whether or not having the force of law) relating to such conduct.

[2485]

3 Duty to consider Community obligation

(1)   The kinds of regulator to which paragraph (2) applies are prescribed for the purposes of section 47(3)(b) of the Act.

(2)   This paragraph applies to—
   (a)   any host state regulator (within the meaning of Schedule 3 to the Act); and
   (b)   the supervisory authority in Switzerland (within the meaning of the Agreement between the European Economic Community and the Swiss Confederation on direct insurance other than life assurance, signed at Luxembourg on 10th October 1989 ("the Agreement")).

(3)   The following kinds of provisions are prescribed for the purposes of section 47(3)(c) of the Act—
   (a)   in the case of a regulator to whom paragraph (2)(a) applies—
      (i)   any provision of Community legislation; and
      (ii)   any rule of law in force in an EEA State for purposes connected with the implementation of any such provision;
   (b)   in the case of a regulator to whom paragraph (2)(b) applies—
      (i)   any provision of the Agreement; and
      (ii)   any rule of law in force in Switzerland for purposes connected with the implementation of any such provision.

[2486]

FINANCIAL SERVICES AND MARKETS ACT 2000 (OFFICIAL LISTING OF SECURITIES) REGULATIONS 2001

(SI 2001/2956)

NOTES
Made: 22 August 2001.

Authority: Financial Services and Markets Act 2000, ss 75(3), 79(3), 103(1), 417(1), 428(3), Sch 10, para 9, Sch 11, paras 16(3), (4), 20(2).

Commencement: 1 December 2001.

These Regulations are reproduced as amended by: the Financial Services and Markets Act 2000 (Official Listing of Securities) (Amendment) Regulations 2001, SI 2001/3439; the Prospectus Regulations 2005, SI 2005/1433.

ARRANGEMENT OF REGULATIONS

PART 1
GENERAL

PART 2
MISCELLANEOUS MATTERS PRESCRIBED FOR THE PURPOSES OF PART VI OF THE ACT

PART 3
PERSONS RESPONSIBLE FOR LISTING PARTICULARS, PROSPECTUSES
AND NON-LISTING PROSPECTUSES

PART 1
GENERAL

1 Citation and commencement

These Regulations may be cited as the Financial Services and Markets Act 2000 (Official Listing of Securities) Regulations 2001 and come into force on the day on which section 74(1) comes into force.

[2487]

2 Interpretation

(1)   In these Regulations—
"the Act" means the Financial Services and Markets Act 2000;
"competent authority" is to be construed in accordance with section 72;
"the Financial Promotion Order" means the Financial Services and Markets Act 2000 (Financial Promotion) Order 2001;
"issuer" has the same meaning as is given, for the purposes of section 103(1), in regulation 4 below;
"non-listing prospectus" has the meaning given in section 87(2); and
"the Regulated Activities Order" means the Financial Services and Markets Act 2000 (Regulated Activities) Order 2001.

(2)   Any reference in these Regulations to a section or Schedule is, unless otherwise stated or unless the context otherwise requires, a reference to that section of or Schedule to the Act.

[2488]

PART 2
MISCELLANEOUS MATTERS PRESCRIBED FOR THE PURPOSES OF
PART VI OF THE ACT

3 Bodies whose securities may not be listed

For the purposes of section 75(3) (which provides that no application for listing may be entertained in respect of securities issued by a body of a prescribed kind) there are prescribed the following kinds of body—
(a)   [where the securities are securities within the meaning of the Regulated Activities Order,] a private company within the meaning of section 1(3) of the Companies Act 1985 or article 12(3) of the Companies (Northern Ireland) Order 1986;
(b)   an old public company within the meaning of section 1 of the Companies Consolidation (Consequential Provisions) Act 1985 or article 3 of the Companies Consolidation (Consequential Provisions) (Northern Ireland) Order 1986.

[2489]

NOTES
Words in square brackets in para (a) inserted by the Financial Services and Markets Act 2000 (Official Listing of Securities) (Amendment) Regulations 2001, SI 2001/3439, reg 2, as from 1 December 2001.

4   Meaning of "issuer"

(1)   For the purposes of section 103(1), "issuer" has the meaning given in this regulation.

(2)   In relation to certificates or other instruments falling within article 80 of the Regulated Activities Order (certificates representing certain securities), "issuer" means—
  (a)   …
  (b)   for all other purposes, the person who issued or is to issue the securities to which the certificates or instruments relate.

(3)   In relation to any other securities, "issuer" means the person by whom the securities have been or are to be issued.

[2490]

NOTES
Para (2): sub-para (a) revoked by the Prospectus Regulations 2005, SI 2005/1433, reg 2(3), Sch 3, para 3, as from 1 July 2005.

5   (*Reg 5 provided that for the purposes of the Financial Services and Markets Act 2000, Sch 10, para 9 "approved exchange" means a recognised investment exchange approved by the Treasury for the purposes of the Public Offers of Securities Regulations 1995 (either generally or in relation to dealings in securities). Sch 9 to the 2000 Act applied various provisions of Part VI of that Act in relation to a non-listing prospectus, subject to the modifications specified in that Schedule. Sch 9, para 5 provided that Sch 10 would have effect in such circumstances with the addition of a new paragraph 9. Sch 10, para 9 therefore effectively ceased to exist on the repeal of Sch 9 by the Prospectus Regulations 2005, SI 2005/1433, reg 2(1), Sch 1, para 16, as from 1 July 2005 and, therefore, this regulation is spent.*)

PART 3
PERSONS RESPONSIBLE FOR LISTING PARTICULARS, PROSPECTUSES AND NON-LISTING PROSPECTUSES

6   Responsibility for listing particulars

(1)   Subject to the following provisions of this Part, for the purposes of Part VI of the Act the persons responsible for listing particulars (including supplementary listing particulars) are—
  (a)   the issuer of the securities to which the particulars relate;
  (b)   where the issuer is a body corporate, each person who is a director of that body at the time when the particulars are submitted to the competent authority;
  (c)   where the issuer is a body corporate, each person who has authorised himself to be named, and is named, in the particulars as a director or as having agreed to become a director of that body either immediately or at a future time;
  (d)   each person who accepts, and is stated in the particulars as accepting, responsibility for the particulars;
  (e)   each person not falling within any of the foregoing sub-paragraphs who has authorised the contents of the particulars.

(2)   A person is not to be treated as responsible for any particulars by virtue of paragraph (1)(b) above if they are published without his knowledge or consent and on becoming aware of their publication he forthwith gives reasonable public notice that they were published without his knowledge or consent.

(3)   When accepting responsibility for particulars under paragraph (1)(d) above or authorising their contents under paragraph (1)(e) above, a person may state that he does so only in relation to certain specified parts of the particulars, or only in certain specified respects, and in such a case he is responsible under paragraph (1)(d) or (e) above—
  (a)   only to the extent specified; and
  (b)   only if the material in question is included in (or substantially in) the form and context to which he has agreed.

(4)   Nothing in this regulation is to be construed as making a person responsible for any particulars by reason of giving advice as to their contents in a professional capacity.

(5)   Where by virtue of this regulation the issuer of any shares pays or is liable to pay compensation under section 90 for loss suffered in respect of shares for which a person has

subscribed no account is to be taken of that liability or payment in determining any question as to the amount paid on subscription for those shares or as to the amount paid up or deemed to be paid up on them.

[2491]

7 Securities issued in connection with takeovers and mergers

(1)   This regulation applies where—
  (a)   listing particulars relate to securities which are to be issued in connection with—
    (i)   an offer by the issuer (or by a wholly-owned subsidiary of the issuer) for securities issued by another person ("A");
    (ii)   an agreement for the acquisition by the issuer (or by a wholly-owned subsidiary of the issuer) of securities issued by another person ("A"); or
    (iii)   any arrangement whereby the whole of the undertaking of another person ("A") is to become the undertaking of the issuer (or of a wholly-owned subsidiary of the issuer, or of a body corporate which will become such a subsidiary by virtue of the arrangement); and
  (b)   each of the specified persons is responsible by virtue of regulation 6(1)(d) above for any part ("the relevant part") of the particulars relating to A or to the securities or undertaking to which the offer, agreement or arrangement relates.

(2)   In paragraph (1)(b) above the "specified persons" are—
  (a)   A; and
  (b)   where A is a body corporate—
    (i)   each person who is a director of A at the time when the particulars are submitted to the competent authority; and
    (ii)   each other person who has authorised himself to be named, and is named, in the particulars as a director of A.

(3)   Where this regulation applies, no person is to be treated as responsible for the relevant part of the particulars under regulation 6(1)(a), (b) or (c) above but without prejudice to his being responsible under regulation 6(1)(d).

(4)   In this regulation—
  (a)   "listing particulars" includes supplementary listing particulars; and
  (b)   "wholly-owned subsidiary" is to be construed in accordance with section 736 of the Companies Act 1985 (and, in relation to an issuer which is not a body corporate, means a body corporate which would be a wholly-owned subsidiary of the issuer within the meaning of that section if the issuer were a body corporate).

[2492]

8 Successor companies under legislation relating to electricity

(1)   Where—
  (a)   the same document contains listing particulars relating to the securities of—
    (i)   two or more successor companies within the meaning of Part II of the Electricity Act 1989, or
    (ii)   two or more successor companies within the meaning of Part III of the Electricity (Northern Ireland) Order 1992; and
  (b)   the responsibility of any person for any information included in the document ("the relevant information") is stated in the document to be confined to its inclusion as part of the particulars relating to the securities of any one of those companies,

that person is not to be treated as responsible, by virtue of regulation 6 above, for the relevant information in so far as it is stated in the document to form part of the particulars relating to the securities of any other of those companies.

(2)   "Listing particulars" includes supplementary listing particulars.

[2493]

9 Specialist securities

(1)   This regulation applies where listing particulars relate to securities of a kind specified by listing rules for the purposes of section 82(1)(c), other than securities which are to be issued in the circumstances mentioned in regulation 7(1)(a) above.

(2)   No person is to be treated as responsible for the particulars under regulation 6(1)(a), (b) or (c) above but without prejudice to his being responsible under regulation 6(1)(d).

(3)   "Listing particulars" includes supplementary listing particulars.

[2494]

10–12   (*Revoked by the Prospectus Regulations 2005, SI 2005/1433, reg 2(3), Sch 3, para 3, as from 1 July 2005.*)

FINANCIAL SERVICES AND MARKETS ACT 2000 (GIBRALTAR) ORDER 2001

(SI 2001/3084)

NOTES
Made: 11 September 2001.
Authority: Financial Services and Markets Act 2000, ss 409(1), 428(3).
Commencement: 5 October 2001 (for the purpose of making rules): 1 December 2001 (otherwise).
This Order is reproduced as amended by: the Financial Services and Markets Act 2000 (Gibraltar) (Amendment) Order 2005, SI 2005/1; the Financial Services and Markets Act 2000 (Gibraltar) (Amendment) Order 2006, SI 2006/1805; the Capital Requirements Regulations 2006, SI 2006/3221; the Markets in Financial Instruments Directive (Consequential Amendments) Regulations 2007, SI 2007/2932; the Financial Services and Markets Act 2000 (Reinsurance Directive) Order 2007, SI 2007/3254.

1 Citation, commencement and interpretation

(1) This Order may be cited as the Financial Services and Markets Act 2000 (Gibraltar) Order 2001 and comes into force—

    (a)   for the purpose of making rules, on 5th October 2001;

    (b)   otherwise, on the day on which section 19 of the Act comes into force.

(2) In this Order—

    "the Act" means the Financial Services and Markets Act 2000;

    "Gibraltar-based firm" means a firm which has its head office in Gibraltar;

    "the Passport Rights Regulations" means the Financial Services and Markets Act 2000 (EEA Passport Rights) Regulations 2001;

    "Schedule 3" means Schedule 3 to the Act.

[2495]

2 Exercise of deemed passport rights by Gibraltar-based firms

(1) Schedule 3 applies in relation to a Gibraltar-based firm as follows.

[(1A) A Gibraltar-based firm falling within paragraph 5(a) of Schedule 3 is to be treated as having an entitlement, corresponding to its EEA right deriving from the [markets in financial instruments directive], to establish a branch or provide services in the United Kingdom.]

(2) A Gibraltar-based firm falling within paragraph 5(b) or (c) of Schedule 3 is to be treated as having an entitlement, corresponding to its EEA right deriving from the banking consolidation directive … , to establish a branch or provide services in the United Kingdom.

(3) A Gibraltar-based firm falling within paragraph 5(d) of Schedule 3 is to be treated as having an entitlement, corresponding to its EEA right deriving from any of the insurance directives, to establish a branch or provide services in the United Kingdom.

[(3A) A Gibraltar-based firm falling within paragraph 5(e) of Schedule 3 is to be treated as having an entitlement, corresponding to its EEA right deriving from the insurance mediation directive, to establish a branch or provide services in the United Kingdom.]

[(3B) A Gibraltar-based firm falling within paragraph 5(da) of Schedule 3 is to be treated as having an entitlement, corresponding to its EEA right deriving from the reinsurance directive, to establish a branch or provide services in the United Kingdom.]

(4) For the purposes of paragraphs [(1A),] [(2), (3)[, (3A) and (3B)]], references in paragraph [[5(a), (b)], (d)[, (da)] and (e)] of Schedule 3 to the home state regulator are to be treated as references to the competent authority (within the meaning of the relevant single market directive) in Gibraltar in relation to the Gibraltar-based firm concerned.

(5) In relation to such a Gibraltar-based firm as is mentioned in paragraph [(1A),] [(2), (3)[, (3A) or (3B)]], references in Schedule 3, the Passport Rights Regulations [(other than in relation to a Gibraltar-based firm falling within paragraph 5(da) of Schedule 3)] and the Financial Services and Markets Act 2000 (Compensation Scheme: Electing Participants) Regulations 2001 to—

    (a)   "an EEA State" are to be treated as references to Gibraltar;

    (b)   "an EEA right" are to be treated as references to the entitlement mentioned in paragraph [(1A),] [(2), (3)[, (3A) or (3B)]];

    (c)   rights deriving from a single market directive are to be treated as references to that entitlement, so far as corresponding to those rights; and

    (d)   "EEA activities" are to be treated as references to the activities which the firm is seeking to carry on in exercise of that entitlement.

(6) Paragraph 16 of Schedule 3 does not apply to Gibraltar-based firms.

(7) For the avoidance of doubt, a Gibraltar-based firm which is exercising, or has exercised, the entitlement mentioned in paragraph [(1A),] [(2), (3)[, (3A) or (3B)]] is to be taken to be an

"incoming firm" for the purposes of Part XIII of the Act (incoming firms: intervention by the Authority); but section 199(7) of the Act has effect, in relation to such a Gibraltar-based firm, as if the words "and the Commission" were omitted.

[2496]

NOTES

Para (1A): inserted by the Financial Services and Markets Act 2000 (Gibraltar) (Amendment) Order 2006, SI 2006/1805, art 2(1), (2), as from 31 July 2006; words in square brackets substituted by the Markets in Financial Instruments Directive (Consequential Amendments) Regulations 2007, SI 2007/2932, reg 6, as from 1 November 2007.

Para (2): words omitted revoked by SI 2006/1805, art 2(1), (3), as from 31 July 2006.

Para (3A): inserted by the Financial Services and Markets Act 2000 (Gibraltar) (Amendment) Order 2005, SI 2005/1, art 2(1), (2), as from 14 January 2005.

Para (3B): inserted by the Financial Services and Markets Act 2000 (Reinsurance Directive) Order 2007, SI 2007/3254, reg 3(1), (2)(a), as from 10 December 2007.

Para (4) is amended as follows:

Figure in first pair of square brackets inserted by SI 2006/1805, art 2(1), (4)(a), as from 31 July 2006.

Words in second (outer) pair of square brackets substituted by SI 2005/1, art 2(1), (3), as from 14 January 2005.

Words in third (inner) pair of square brackets substituted by SI 2007/3254, reg 3(1), (2)(b), as from 10 December 2007.

Words in fourth (outer) pair of square brackets substituted by SI 2005/1, art 2(1), (3)(b), as from 14 January 2005.

Figure "5(a), (b)" in fifth (inner) pair of square brackets substituted by SI 2006/1805, art 2(1), (4)(b), as from 31 July 2006.

Reference ", (da)" in sixth (inner) pair of square brackets inserted by SI 2007/3254, art 3(1), (2)(b), as from 10 December 2007.

Para (5) is amended as follows:

Reference to "(1A)" in square brackets in both places it occurs inserted by SI 2006/1805, art 2(1), (5), as from 31 July 2006.

Words in second (outer) pair of square brackets substituted by SI 2005/1, art 2(1), (4), as from 14 January 2005.

Words ", (3A) or (3B)" in square brackets in both places they occur substituted by SI 2007/3254, art 3(1), (2)(c)(ii), as from 10 December 2007.

Words "(other than in relation to a Gibraltar-based firm falling within paragraph 5(da) of Schedule 3)" in square brackets inserted by SI 2007/3254, art 3(1), (2)(c)(i), as from 10 December 2007.

Words in second (outer) pair of square brackets in sub-para (b) substituted by SI 2005/1, art 2(1), (4), as from 14 January 2005.

Para (7): figure in first pair of square brackets inserted by SI 2006/1805, art 2(1), (5), as from 31 July 2006; words in second (outer) pair of square brackets substituted by SI 2005/1, art 2(1), (4), as from 14 January 2005; words in third (inner) pair of square brackets substituted by SI 2007/3254, art 3(1), (2)(d), as from 10 December 2007.

3 EEA firms satisfying conditions under Gibraltar law

(1) A relevant EEA firm which—

    (a) has satisfied Gibraltar establishment conditions (whether before or after commencement), and

    (b) has (whether before or after commencement) established a branch in the United Kingdom for the purpose of carrying on any relevant activity,

is to be treated as having satisfied the establishment conditions within the meaning of Part II of Schedule 3, and accordingly qualifies for authorisation under paragraph 12(1) of that Schedule.

(2) A relevant EEA firm which—

    (a) has satisfied Gibraltar service conditions (whether before or after commencement), and

    (b) is carrying on any relevant activity by providing services in the United Kingdom,

is to be treated as having satisfied the service conditions within the meaning of Part II of Schedule 3, and accordingly qualifies for authorisation under paragraph 12(2) of that Schedule.

(3) Where a relevant EEA firm has (whether before or after commencement) established a branch, or is providing services, in Gibraltar (but not in the United Kingdom) in exercise of an EEA right, regulations 4 to 7 of the Passport Rights Regulations apply to changes affecting that firm (so far as those changes relate to the establishment of a branch, or the provision of services, in the United Kingdom) as they apply to changes affecting a firm which has established a branch, or is providing services, in the United Kingdom in exercise of an EEA right.

(4) In relation to a firm falling within paragraph (1) or (2)—

    (a) the references in paragraph 15 of Schedule 3 to a "permitted activity" are references to a relevant activity; and

    (b) the reference in paragraph 15(2) of Schedule 3 to the consent notice, regulator's notice or notice of intention is a reference to whichever of the corresponding notices mentioned in paragraph (5)(d) is applicable.

(5) In this article—

(a) "commencement" means the beginning of the day on which section 19 of the Act comes into force;

(b) "Gibraltar establishment conditions" means conditions under the law of Gibraltar corresponding to those in paragraph 13(1) of Schedule 3; and

(c) "Gibraltar service conditions" means conditions under the law of Gibraltar corresponding to those in paragraph 14(1) of Schedule 3;

(d) "relevant activity" means an activity specified in the notice corresponding to—
  (i) the consent notice (within the meaning of paragraph 13 of Schedule 3), or
  (ii) the regulator's notice or the notice of intention (within the meaning of paragraph 14 of Schedule 3),

as the case may be, which was given to the relevant authority in Gibraltar pursuant to the Gibraltar establishment conditions or the Gibraltar service conditions;

(e) "relevant EEA firm" means an EEA firm[, other than a firm falling within paragraph 5(da) of Schedule 3,] other than a Gibraltar-based firm.

[2497]

NOTES
Para (5): words in square brackets in sub-para (e) inserted by the Financial Services and Markets Act 2000 (Reinsurance Directive) Order 2007, SI 2007/3254, reg 3(1), (3), as from 10 December 2007.

4   Exercise by UK firms of deemed passport rights in Gibraltar

(1)   Schedule 3 applies in relation to the establishment by a UK firm of a branch in Gibraltar, or the provision by a UK firm of services in Gibraltar, as follows.

(2)   A UK firm is to be treated as having an entitlement, corresponding to its EEA right, to establish a branch or provide services in Gibraltar.

(3)   In relation to a UK firm, references in Schedule 3, the Passport Rights Regulations and article 77 of the Financial Services and Markets Act 2000 (Transitional Provisions) (Authorised Persons etc) Order 2001 to—

(a) "an EEA State" are to be treated as including references to Gibraltar;

(b) "an EEA right" are to be treated as including references to the entitlement mentioned in paragraph (2);

(c) rights deriving from a single market directive are to be treated as including references to that entitlement, so far as corresponding to those rights; and

(d) "EEA activities" are to be treated as including references to the activities which the firm is seeking to carry on in exercise of that entitlement.

(4)   In paragraph 24(1)(b) of Schedule 3, the reference to the right conferred by [Article 24] of the banking consolidation directive includes a reference to the entitlement mentioned in paragraph (2), so far as corresponding to that right.

[2498]

NOTES
Para (4): words in square brackets substituted by the Capital Requirements Regulations 2006, SI 2006/3221, reg 29(4), Sch 6, para 10, as from 1 January 2007.

FINANCIAL SERVICES AND MARKETS ACT 2000 (CONTROLLERS) (EXEMPTION) (NO 2) ORDER 2001

(SI 2001/3338)

NOTES
Made: 4 October 2001.
Authority: Financial Services and Markets Act 2000, ss 192(a), 428(3).
Commencement: 1 December 2001.

As of 1 February 2009, this Order had not been amended.

1   Citation, commencement and interpretation

(1)   This Order may be cited as the Financial Services and Markets Act 2000 (Controllers) (Exemption) (No 2) Order 2001 and comes into force on the day on which section 19 of the Act comes into force.

(2)   In this Order—
"the Act" means the Financial Services and Markets Act 2000;
"associate" has the meaning given by section 422(4) of the Act;

"authorised building society" means a building society (within the meaning of the Building Societies Act 1986) which is a UK authorised person for the purposes of Part XII of the Act;

"capital", in relation to an authorised building society, consists of the following—

(a) any shares of a class defined as deferred shares for the purposes of section 119 of the Building Societies Act 1986 which have been issued by that society; and

(b) the general reserves of that society.

[2499]

2 Acquiring and increasing control over an authorised building society

(1) In any case where a person ("the acquirer")—

(a) proposes to take a step which would result in his—

(i) acquiring control over an authorised building society in the case mentioned in paragraph (a) of subsection (2) of section 179 of the Act (holding of 10% or more of the shares), or

(ii) acquiring an additional kind of control over such a society of the kind mentioned in paragraph (a) of subsection (4) of that section (holding of shares), or

(b) without himself taking any such step, has acquired such control or such an additional kind of control over such a society,

the acquirer is exempt from any obligation imposed by section 178 of the Act to notify the Authority of his proposal or his acquisition unless paragraph (2) applies.

(2) This paragraph applies if the proposed step would result in the acquirer holding, or the acquirer holds, a holding of 10% or more of the capital of that authorised building society.

(3) In paragraph (2), "acquirer" means—

(a) the acquirer;

(b) any of the acquirer's associates; or

(c) the acquirer and any of his associates.

(4) In any case where a controller of an authorised building society—

(a) proposes to take a step which would result in his acquiring an increase of his control over that society in the circumstances mentioned in paragraph (a) of subsection (1) of section 180 of the Act (increase in percentage of shares), or

(b) without himself taking any such step, has acquired increased control over that society in those circumstances,

the controller is exempt from any obligation imposed by section 178 of the Act to notify the Authority of his proposal or his acquisition unless paragraph (5) applies.

(5) This paragraph applies if the proposed step would result in the controller increasing, or the controller has increased, his holding of the capital of that authorised building society by any of the steps mentioned in section 180(2) of the Act.

(6) In paragraph (5), "controller" means—

(a) the controller;

(b) any of the controller's associates; or

(c) the controller and any of his associates.

[2500]

3 Reducing control over an authorised building society

(1) In any case where a controller of an authorised building society—

(a) proposes to take a step which would result in his ceasing to have control of the kind mentioned in paragraph (a) of subsection (4) of section 179 of the Act (holding of shares) over that society, or

(b) without himself taking any such step, has ceased to have such control,

the controller is exempt from any obligation imposed by section 190 of the Act to notify the Authority of his proposal or that cessation unless paragraph (2) applies.

(2) This paragraph applies if the proposed step would result in the controller ceasing, or the controller has ceased, to hold 10% or more of the capital of that authorised building society.

(3) In any case where a controller of an authorised building society—

(a) proposes to take a step which would result in his reducing his control over that society in the circumstances mentioned in paragraph (a) of subsection (1) of section 181 of the Act (decrease in percentage of shares), or

(b) without himself taking any such step, has reduced his control in those circumstances,

the controller is exempt from any obligation imposed by section 190 of the Act to notify the Authority of his proposal or that reduction unless paragraph (4) applies.

(4) This paragraph applies if the proposed step would result in the controller reducing, or the controller has reduced, his holding of the capital of that authorised building society by any of the steps mentioned in section 181(2) of the Act.

(5) In paragraphs (2) and (4), "controller" means—

(a)   the controller;
(b)   any of the controller's associates; or
(c)   the controller and any of his associates.

[2501]

FINANCIAL SERVICES AND MARKETS ACT 2000 (INTERIM PERMISSIONS) ORDER 2001

(SI 2001/3374)

NOTES
Made: 10 October 2001.
Authority: Financial Services and Markets Act 2000, ss 426–428.
Commencement: 31 October 2001.
As of 1 February 2009, this Order had not been amended.

ARRANGEMENT OF ARTICLES

1   Citation and commencement

This Order may be cited as the Financial Services and Markets Act 2000 (Interim Permissions) Order 2001 and comes into force on the twenty first day after it is laid before Parliament.

[2502]

2   Definitions

(1)   In this Order—
"the Act" means the Financial Services and Markets Act 2000;
"commencement" means the beginning of the day on which section 19 comes into force;
"an interim permission" means a Part IV permission conferred by article 6 or 7(2);
"the relevant date" means—
    (a)   commencement, in respect of—
        (i)   newly regulated activities which are regulated activities immediately after commencement; and
        (ii)   overseas regulated activity;
    (b)   1 January 2002 in respect of newly regulated activities which are not regulated activities before that date.

(2)   In this Order—
"the Banking Act" means the Banking Act 1987;
"the Building Societies Act" means the Building Societies Act 1986;
"the Financial Services Act" means the Financial Services Act 1986;
"the Friendly Societies Act" means the Friendly Societies Act 1992;
"the Insurance Companies Act" means the Insurance Companies Act 1982;
"the 2BCD Regulations" means the Banking Coordination (Second Council Directive) Regulations 1992;
"the ISD Regulations" means the Investment Services Regulations 1995;
"the 3ID Regulations" means the Insurance Companies (Third Insurance Directives) Regulations 1994;
"the Authorised Persons Order" means the Financial Services and Markets Act 2000 (Transitional Provisions) (Authorised Persons etc) Order 2001;
"the Regulated Activities Order" means the Financial Services and Markets Act 2000 (Regulated Activities) Order 2001.

(3)   Any reference in this Order to a section or Part is, unless the context otherwise requires, a reference to that section or Part of the Act.

[2503]

3   Relevant Applicant

(1)   This Order applies to a person who—
- (a)   has, on or before 31 October 2001, made an application to the Authority—
    - (i)   under section 40 for permission to carry on a newly regulated activity; or
    - (ii)   under section 44 to add a newly regulated activity to his Part IV permission; and
- (b)   was at 3 September 2001 carrying on by way of business the newly regulated activity to which the application mentioned in sub-paragraph (a) relates.

(2)   This Order also applies to a person who—
- (a)   has on or before 31 October 2001 made an application to the Authority—
    - (i)   under section 40 for permission to carry on an overseas regulated activity; or
    - (ii)   under section 44 for variation to add an overseas regulated activity to his Part IV permission; and
- (b)   was at 3 September 2001 carrying on by way of business that overseas regulated activity in a country or territory outside the United Kingdom.

(3)   In this Order, a person to whom this Order applies in accordance with this article is referred to as a "Relevant Applicant".

[2504]

4   Newly regulated activity

(1)   In this Order a "newly regulated activity" is an activity—
- (a)   which the Relevant Applicant was able to carry on in the United Kingdom before commencement without contravening a regulatory enactment;
- (b)   for which the Relevant Applicant needs permission under the Act if he continues to carry on that activity after the relevant date without contravening either the general prohibition or section 20; and
- (c)   which the Relevant Applicant does not have a Part IV permission to carry on by virtue of the Authorised Persons Order.

(2)   The reference in paragraph (1) to an activity which the Relevant Applicant was able to carry on without contravening a regulatory enactment does not include an activity in respect of which he was—
- (a)   an exempt person under Chapter IV of Part I of the Financial Services Act;
- (b)   exempt by virtue of Schedule 2 to the Banking Act.

(3)   A "regulatory enactment" means—
- (a)   section 3 of the Banking Act;
- (b)   section 3 of the Financial Services Act;
- (c)   section 2(1) of the Insurance Companies Act;
- (d)   section 31(1) of the Friendly Societies Act;
- (e)   section 9(1) of the Building Societies Act.

[2505]

5   Overseas regulated activity

In this Order an "overseas regulated activity" is a regulated activity which the Relevant Applicant—
- (a)   is regarded as carrying on in the United Kingdom after the relevant date only by virtue of section 418; and
- (b)   which the Relevant Applicant was carrying on at 3 September 2001 without contravening—
    - (i)   regulation 20 of the ISD Regulations;
    - (ii)   regulation 22 of the 2BCD Regulations;
    - (iii)   paragraph 1 or 5 of Schedule 2G to the Insurance Companies Act;
    - (iv)   paragraph 1 or 5 of Schedule 13B to the Friendly Societies Act.

[2506]

6   Interim permission

(1)   Subject to article 10, if—
- (a)   the Relevant Applicant notifies the Authority before 31 October 2001 that he wishes to have a Part IV permission by virtue of this article; and
- (b)   his application has not been withdrawn or decided before the relevant date,

he is to be treated as having, at the relevant date, a Part IV permission to carry on any newly regulated activity or overseas regulated activity covered by his application.

(2)   For the purposes of paragraph (1)(b), an application has been decided if—
- (a)   the Authority has given permission to the Relevant Applicant to carry on the activity

without exercising its powers under section 42(7)(a) or (b) or section 43(1) and the grant of permission under section 42(2) takes effect from the relevant date;

    (b)   in a case where the Relevant Applicant refers the determination of his application to the Tribunal under section 55 then if the reference has been determined in respect of that activity;

    (c)   the Authority has refused permission, or given permission but exercised its power under section 42(7)(a) or (b) or section 43(1) in respect of the carrying on of the activity and the time for referring the matter to the Tribunal has expired before the relevant date without the Relevant Applicant making such a reference.

[2507]

7 Subsidiary of person with paragraph 23 permission

(1)   This article applies where—

    (a)   a person ("S") is a subsidiary undertaking of another person ("PP");

    (b)   PP is a person in respect of whom a paragraph 23 permission was in effect immediately before commencement;

    (c)   S has, on or before 31 October 2001, made an application to the Authority under section 40 or 44 for permission under Part IV to carry on regulated activities which relate to the paragraph 23 permitted business carried on by PP;

    (d)   PP was, at the date when S made the application referred to in sub-paragraph (c), carrying on paragraph 23 permitted business;

    (e)   PP has not made an application to the Authority under section 40 or 44 for permission under Part IV to carry on regulated activities which correspond to his paragraph 23 permitted business;

    (f)   S notifies the Authority on or before 31 October 2001 that he wishes to have a Part IV permission by virtue of this article.

(2)   In a case where this article applies—

    (a)   S is to be treated as a Relevant Applicant for the purposes of this Order; and

    (b)   S is to be treated as having, at commencement, a Part IV permission to carry on the paragraph 23 permitted business covered by his application.

(3)   For the purposes of this article—

    (a)   a "paragraph 23 permission" is a permission granted to a person under paragraph 23 of Schedule 1 to the Financial Services Act;

    (b)   "paragraph 23 permitted business" is business which PP was able to carry on before commencement without contravening section 3 of the Financial Services Act by reason of his paragraph 23 permission.

[2508]

8 Duration of interim permission

(1)   A Relevant Applicant who has an interim permission to carry on a particular regulated activity may not after commencement withdraw his application for permission to carry on that activity, unless the Authority consents to his withdrawing it.

(2)   Subject to paragraph (4) and without prejudice to the exercise by the Authority of its powers under Part IV, a Relevant Applicant's interim permission to carry on a particular activity lapses on whichever is the earliest of the following dates—

    (a)   in a case where the Relevant Applicant withdraws his application for permission to carry on that activity, then when the application is withdrawn;

    (b)   in a case where the Authority gives permission to carry on the activity and does not exercise its power under section 42(7)(a) or (b) or section 43(1), then from the date when the permission given under section 42(2) takes effect;

    (c)   in a case where the Relevant Applicant refers the determination of his application to the Tribunal under section 55, then when the reference is determined in respect of that activity;

    (d)   in a case where—

        (i)   the Authority refuses permission or gives permission but exercises its power under section 42(7)(a) or (b) or section 43(1) in respect of the carrying on of the activity; and

        (ii)   the Relevant Applicant does not refer the matter to the Tribunal,

    then on the date when the right to refer the matter to the Tribunal expires.

(3)   For the purposes of paragraph (1)(c), an application is decided when it has been determined and there is no possibility (or no further possibility) of the determination being reversed or varied on a reference to a tribunal or an appeal.

(4)   Where—

    (a)   the Authority has exercised its powers under section 53 in respect of the activities covered by a Relevant Applicant's interim permission; and

(b) the operation of paragraph (2) would result in there being no regulated activities for which the Relevant Applicant has a Part IV permission,

the interim permission does not lapse but remains in force (as varied by the Authority under section 53) until it is cancelled by the Authority; and the Authority must cancel the interim permission once it is satisfied that it is no longer necessary to keep the interim permission in force.

[2509]

9 Approved persons performing controlled functions for Relevant Applicant

(1) Where a person ("E") has transitional approval to perform a controlled function in relation to the carrying on by a Relevant Applicant of a regulated activity for which that Relevant Applicant has interim permission, that transitional approval lapses on whichever is the earliest of the following dates—

(a) the date when the Relevant Applicant's interim permission lapses in accordance with article 8;

(b) if E has applied for approval under section 59 to perform that function and that application is granted, then the date when that application is granted;

(c) if E has applied for approval under section 59 to perform that function and the application is refused, then the date when either—

(i) any reference of that refusal under section 62(4) is determined by the Tribunal; or

(ii) the right to refer the refusal to the Tribunal expires without such a reference having been made.

(2) For the purposes of paragraph (1), E has transitional approval to perform a controlled function if he is to be taken, by virtue of the Authorised Persons Order, to have been approved by the Authority for the performance of that function.

[2510]

10 Effect of overriding prohibition

(1) Articles 6 and 8 do not apply to a Relevant Applicant who is subject, immediately before the relevant date, to an overriding prohibition.

(2) For the purposes of this article, a Relevant Applicant is subject to an "overriding prohibition" if—

(a) his authorisation has been suspended under section 28 or section 33 of the Financial Services Act;

(b) he is prohibited under section 65 of the Financial Services Act from entering into transactions which constitute investment business (within the meaning of that Act);

(c) immediately before commencement he was a member of a recognised self-regulating organisation for the purposes of section 7 of the Financial Services Act but was subject to a direction imposed by that organisation preventing him from carrying on investment business (within the meaning of that Act);

(d) he was prevented by a restriction under section 12 or a direction under section 19 of the Banking Act from accepting deposits;

(e) he had ceased to be authorised by virtue of a direction under section 11 or section 12A of the Insurance Companies Act to effect contracts of insurance (within the meaning of those sections);

(f) he was subject to a direction under section 40(1)(a) of the Friendly Societies Act withdrawing his authorisation to effect contracts of insurance (within the meaning of that section);

(g) he had been forbidden under section 51(1) of the Friendly Societies Act to accept any new members;

(h) he was subject to a condition imposed under section 42 of the Building Societies Act preventing him from issuing shares, accepting deposits or making advances or other loans;

(i) he was prohibited under regulation 9 or 15 of the 2BCD Regulations from accepting deposits in the United Kingdom or from carrying on home-regulated investment business in the United Kingdom (within the meaning of those Regulations);

(j) he was restricted under regulation 10 of the 2BCD Regulations from carrying on in the United Kingdom any home regulated activity (within the meaning of that regulation);

(k) he was prohibited under regulation 9 of the ISD Regulations from providing in the United Kingdom any listed services (within the meaning of that regulation).

(3) Articles 6 and 8 do not apply to a Relevant Applicant who is subject, immediately before the relevant date, to a requirement which—

(a) is imposed (or is treated, by virtue of the Authorised Persons Order, as having been imposed) on him under section 43; and

(b) prohibits him from carrying on the newly regulated activity or overseas regulated activity to which his application relates.

[2511]

11 Transitional provision

(1)   The following transitional provisions apply until the relevant date.

(2)   In sections 45, 46, 47, 48, 50, 52, 53, 54 and 55 (variation of Part IV permissions etc) sections 56 and 60 (performance of regulated activities) and section 148 (modification or waiver of rules)—

    (a)   the references to an authorised person are to be read as references to a Relevant Applicant; and

    (b)   references to Part IV permissions are to be read as references to interim permissions even though not yet in force.

[2512]

12 Application of rules etc to Relevant Applicants with interim permission

(1)   The Authority may direct that any relevant provision which would otherwise apply to Relevant Applicants by virtue of their interim permission is not to apply, or is to apply to them as modified in the way specified in the direction.

(2)   Where the Authority makes a rule or gives guidance which applies only to persons who are Relevant Applicants with an interim permission (or only to a class of such persons), section 155 does not apply to that rule or guidance.

(3)   For the purposes of paragraph (1) a relevant provision is any provision made as a result of the exercise by the Authority of its legislative functions within the meaning of paragraph 1 of Schedule 1 to the Act.

[2513]

13 Application of the Act etc

The Schedule to this Order makes provision about the application of the Act and of certain provisions made under the Act in relation to a Relevant Applicant with an interim permission.

[2514]

SCHEDULE
APPLICATION OF THE ACT TO RELEVANT APPLICANTS
WITH INTERIM PERMISSION

Article 13

1.   Paragraphs 2 and 3 apply to every Relevant Applicant with an interim permission.

2.   For the purposes of section 20, the Relevant Applicant's interim permission is treated as having been given to him by the Authority under Part IV.

3.   A Relevant Applicant's interim permission is to be disregarded for the purposes of sections 38(2), 40(2) and 42 to 44.

4.   Paragraphs 5 to 13 apply to a Relevant Applicant who falls within section 31(1) only by virtue of having an interim permission.

5.   A Relevant Applicant is to be treated after commencement as an authorised person for the purposes of the Act (and of any provision made under the Act), unless otherwise expressly provided for by this Schedule.

6.   For the purposes of section 21(1) and 25(2)(a) a Relevant Applicant is not to be treated as an authorised person for the purposes of communicating or approving the content of a communication except where the communication invites or induces a person to enter into (or offer to enter into) an agreement the making or performance of which constitutes a controlled activity which corresponds to a regulated activity which is covered by his interim permission.

7.   A Relevant Applicant may still be an appointed representative within the meaning of section 39(2) (and hence may be treated as exempt from the general prohibition as a result of section 39(1) for the purposes of section 42(3)(a)).

8.   A Relevant Applicant is not to be treated as an authorised person for the purposes of Chapter II of Part XVII of the Act.

9.   A Relevant Applicant is not to be treated as an authorised person for the purposes of subsections (8) and (9) of section 272.

10.   For the purposes of article 22 of the Regulated Activities Order, a Relevant Applicant who does not have an interim permission to carry on an activity of the kind specified by article 21 of that Order—

    (a)   is to be treated as an authorised person for the purpose of considering whether he is able to benefit from the exclusion (so that he is not "a person who is not an authorised person" for the purposes of the article); but

    (b)   is not to be treated as an authorised person for the other purposes of the article (so that a person does not benefit from the exclusion by entering into a transaction with or through the Relevant Applicant or because a Relevant Applicant has given advice to the client).

11. For the purposes of article 29 of the Regulated Activities Order, a Relevant Applicant who does not have an interim permission to carry on an activity of the kind specified by article 25 of that Order—

    (a)   is to be treated as an authorised person for the purpose of considering whether he is able to benefit from the exclusion (so that he is not "a person who is not an authorised person" for the purposes of the article); but

    (b)   is not to be treated as an authorised person for the other purposes of the article (so that a person does not benefit from the exclusion in relation to arrangements made for or with a view to a transaction which is or is to be entered into with or through a Relevant Applicant or because a Relevant Applicant has given advice to the client).

12. For the purposes of article 72(1)(a), (2)(a), (3), or (4)(a) of the Regulated Activities Order, a Relevant Applicant is not to be treated as an authorised person (so that an overseas person does not benefit from the exclusion in relation to transactions entered into with or through the Relevant Applicant).

[2515]

BANKRUPTCY (FINANCIAL SERVICES AND MARKETS ACT 2000) (SCOTLAND) RULES 2001 (NOTE)

(SI 2001/3591)

NOTES

Made: 5 November 2001.

Authority: Financial Services and Markets Act 2000, ss 372(4)(c), (9)(b), 428(3).

Commencement: 1 December 2001.

These Rules relate to demands by the Financial Services Authority (under section 372(4)(a) of FSMA 2000) to an individual to establish to the Authority's satisfaction that that individual has a reasonable prospect of being able to pay a regulated activity debt when it falls due. Rule 3 makes provision for the form of a demand. Rule 4 relates to service of a demand. Rules 5 and 6 relate to the setting aside of a demand. The Rules apply to Scotland only.

As of 1 February 2009, these Rules had not been amended.

[2516]

FINANCIAL SERVICES AND MARKETS ACT 2000 (CONTROL OF BUSINESS TRANSFERS) (REQUIREMENTS ON APPLICANTS) REGULATIONS 2001

(SI 2001/3625)

NOTES

Made: 7 November 2001.

Authority: Financial Services and Markets Act 2000, ss 108, 417(1), 428(3), Sch 12, para 6(2).

Commencement: 1 December 2001.

These Regulations are reproduced as amended by: the Life Assurance Consolidation Directive (Consequential Amendments) Regulations 2004, SI 2004/3379; the Financial Services and Markets Act 2000 (Reinsurance Directive) Regulations 2007, SI 2007/3255; the Financial Services and Markets Act 2000 (Control of Business Transfers) (Requirements on Applicants) (Amendment) Regulations 2008, SI 2008/1467.

1 Citation, commencement and interpretation

(1) These Regulations may be cited as the Financial Services and Markets Act 2000 (Control of Business Transfers) (Requirements on Applicants) Regulations 2001 and come into force on 1st December 2001.

(2) In these Regulations—

"the Act" means the Financial Services and Markets Act 2000;

"the parties" means the authorised person concerned and the transferee (within the meaning of section 105(2) or, as the case may be, section 106(2) of the Act);

"the report" means the scheme report mentioned in section 109(1) of the Act;

"State of the commitment" has the meaning given by paragraph 6(1) of Schedule 12 to the Act;

"State in which the risk is situated" has the meaning given by paragraph 6(3) of Schedule 12 to the Act;

"a summary of the report" means a summary of the report sufficient to indicate the opinion of the person making the report of the likely effects of the insurance business transfer scheme on the policyholders of the parties.

[2517]

2 Meaning of "commitment"

There is prescribed for the purposes of paragraph 6(2) of Schedule 12 to the Act any contract of insurance of a kind referred to in [Article 2 of the life assurance consolidation directive].

[2518]

NOTES
   Words in square brackets substituted by the Life Assurance Consolidation Directive (Consequential Amendments) Regulations 2004, SI 2004/3379, reg 20, as from 11 January 2005.

3 Transfer of an insurance business

   (1)   An applicant under section 107 of the Act for an order sanctioning an insurance business transfer scheme ("the scheme") must comply with the following requirements.

   (2)   A notice stating that the application has been made must be—
   (a)   published—
      (i)   in the London, Edinburgh and Belfast Gazettes;
      (ii)   in two national newspapers in the United Kingdom; ...
      (iii)   where, as regards any policy [(other than a policy which evidences a contract of reinsurance)] included in the proposed transfer, an EEA State other than the United Kingdom is the State of the commitment or the State in which the risk is situated, in two national newspapers in that EEA State; and
      [(iv)   where, as regards any policy included in the proposed transfer which evidences a contract of reinsurance, an EEA State other than the United Kingdom is the State in which the establishment of the policyholder to which the policy relates is situated at the date when the contract was entered into, in one business newspaper which is published or circulated in that EEA State; ...]
   (b)   sent to every policyholder of the parties[; and
   (c)   sent—
      (i)   to every reinsurer of the authorised person concerned (within the meaning of section 105(2) of the Act) any of whose contracts of reinsurance (in whole or part) are to be transferred by the scheme; or
      (ii)   in a case where such a contract has been placed with or through a person authorised to act on behalf of the reinsurer, then to that person; or
      (iii)   in a case where such a contract has been placed with more than one reinsurer, then to the person or persons authorised to act on behalf of those reinsurers or groups of reinsurers].

   (3)   The notices mentioned in paragraph (2) must—
   (a)   be approved by the Authority prior to publication (or, as the case may be, being sent); and
   (b)   contain the address from which the documents mentioned in paragraph (4) may be obtained.

   (4)   A copy of the report and a statement setting out the terms of the scheme and containing a summary of the report must be given free of charge to any person who requests them.

   (5)   A copy of the application, the report and the statement mentioned in paragraph (4) must be given free of charge to the Authority.

   (6)   In the case of any such scheme as is mentioned in section 105(5) of the Act, copies of the documents listed in paragraph 6(1) of Schedule 15B to the Companies Act 1985 or in paragraph 6(1) of Schedule 15B to the Companies (Northern Ireland) Order 1986 (application of provisions about compromises and arrangements to mergers and divisions of public companies) must be given to the Authority by the beginning of the period referred to in paragraph 3(e) of that Schedule.

[2519]

NOTES
   Para (2): word omitted from sub-para (a)(ii) revoked, words in square brackets in sub-para (a)(iii) inserted, and sub-para (a)(iv) inserted, by the Financial Services and Markets Act 2000 (Reinsurance Directive) Regulations 2007, SI 2007/3255, reg 2(1), (2), as from 10 December 2007; word omitted from sub-para (a)(iv) revoked, and sub-para (c) (and the word immediately preceding it) added, by the Financial Services and Markets Act 2000 (Control of Business Transfers) (Requirements on Applicants) (Amendment) Regulations 2008, SI 2008/1467, reg 2(a), (b), as from 30 June 2008.

4—(1)   Subject to paragraph (2) [or (3)], the court may not determine an application under section 107 for an order sanctioning an insurance business transfer scheme—

(a)   where the applicant has failed to comply with the requirements in regulation 3(2), (3) or (6); and

(b)   until a period of not less than twenty-one days has elapsed since the Authority was given the documents mentioned in regulation 3(5).

(2)   The requirements in regulation 3(2)(a)(ii)[, (iii) and (iv)][, (b) and (c)] may be waived by the court in such circumstances and subject to such conditions as the court considers appropriate.

[(3)   The requirement in regulation 3(2)(a)(iv) must be waived where an applicant demonstrates that he has notified all policyholders of contracts of reinsurance.]

[2520]

NOTES
Para (1): words in square brackets inserted by the Financial Services and Markets Act 2000 (Reinsurance Directive) Regulations 2007, SI 2007/3255, reg 2(1), (3), as from 10 December 2007.
Para (2): words in first pair of square brackets substituted by SI 2007/3255, reg 2(1), (4), as from 10 December 2007; words in second pair of square brackets substituted by the Financial Services and Markets Act 2000 (Control of Business Transfers) (Requirements on Applicants) (Amendment) Regulations 2008, SI 2008/1467, reg 2(c), as from 30 June 2008.
Para (3): added by SI 2007/3255, reg 2(1), (5), as from 10 December 2007.

5   Transfer of a banking business

(1)   An applicant under section 107 of the Act for an order sanctioning a banking business transfer scheme ("the scheme") must comply with the following requirements.

(2)   A notice stating that the application has been made must be published—
(a)   in the London, Edinburgh and Belfast Gazettes; and
(b)   in two national newspapers in the United Kingdom.

(3)   The notice mentioned in paragraph (2) must—
(a)   be approved by the Authority prior to its publication; and
(b)   contain the address from which the statement mentioned in paragraph (4) may be obtained.

(4)   A statement setting out the terms of the scheme must be given free of charge to any person who requests it.

(5)   Copies of the application and the statement mentioned in paragraph (4) must be given free of charge to the Authority.

[2521]

6—(1)   Subject to paragraph (2), the court may not determine an application under section 107 for an order sanctioning a banking business transfer scheme—
(a)   where the applicant has failed to comply with the requirements in regulation 5(2) or (3); and
(b)   until a period of not less than twenty-one days has elapsed since the Authority was given the documents mentioned in regulation 5(5).

(2)   The requirement in regulation 5(2)(b) may be waived by the court in such circumstances and subject to such conditions as the court considers appropriate.

[2522]

FINANCIAL SERVICES AND MARKETS ACT 2000 (CONTROL OF TRANSFERS OF BUSINESS DONE AT LLOYD'S) ORDER 2001

(SI 2001/3626)

NOTES
Made: 7 November 2001.
Authority: Financial Services and Markets Act 2000, ss 323, 428(3).
Commencement: 1 December 2001.
This Order is reproduced as amended by: the Financial Services and Markets Act 2000 (Control of Transfers of Business Done at Lloyd's) (Amendment) Order 2008, SI 2008/1725.

1   Citation and commencement

This Order may be cited as the Financial Services and Markets Act 2000 (Control of Transfers of Business Done at Lloyd's) Order 2001 and comes into force on 1st December 2001.

[2523]

2   Interpretation

In this Order—
   "the Act" means the Financial Services and Markets Act 2000;
   "the Council" and "the Society" have the same meaning as in Lloyd's Act 1982;
   .....

[2524]

NOTES
   Definition "former underwriting member" (omitted) revoked by the Financial Services and Markets Act 2000 (Control of Transfers of Business Done at Lloyd's) (Amendment) Order 2008, SI 2008/1725, art 2(1), (2), as from 23 July 2008.

3   The following provisions, that is to say—
   (a)   sections 104 and [107 to 114A] of the Act;
   (b)   any regulations made under section 108 of the Act; and
   (c)   Part I of Schedule 12 to the Act;

apply in relation to schemes for the transfer of the whole or any part of the business carried on by one or more [underwriting members of the Society or by one or more persons who have ceased to be such a member (whether before, on or after 24th December 1996)] ("the members concerned") in the same way as they apply in relation to insurance business transfer schemes, but only if the conditions specified by article 4 are satisfied.

[2525]

NOTES
   Words in square brackets substituted by the Financial Services and Markets Act 2000 (Control of Transfers of Business Done at Lloyd's) (Amendment) Order 2008, SI 2008/1725, art 2(1), (3), as from 23 July 2008.

4   The conditions referred to in article 3 are—
   (a)   that the scheme results in the business transferred being carried on from an establishment of the transferee in an EEA State;
   [(b)   that the Council of Lloyd's has—
       (i)   by resolution authorised one person to act, or
       (ii)   certified that one person has authority to act,
   in connection with the transfer for the members concerned, as transferor;
   (c)   that a copy of the resolution or the certificate has been give to the Authority.]

[2526]

NOTES
   Paras (b), (c) substituted by the Financial Services and Markets Act 2000 (Control of Transfers of Business Done at Lloyd's) (Amendment) Order 2008, SI 2008/1725, art 2(1), (4), as from 23 July 2008.

5—(1)   The provisions which apply by virtue of paragraph (a) and (b) of article 3 do so as if—
   (a)   any reference to the authorised person concerned were a reference to the members concerned; and
   (b)   anything done in connection with the transfer by the person authorised[, or the person certified to have authority,] in accordance with [paragraph (b) of article 4] had been done by the members concerned for whom he acted.

   (2)   In the application of Part I of Schedule 12 to the Act to the members concerned, the conditions in sub-paragraphs (2)(a), (3)(a) and (4)(a) of paragraph 1 of that Schedule are treated as satisfied.

   [(3)   A transfer scheme carried out by virtue of this Order may transfer to an establishment of the transferee business written on different syndicates and in different years of account of syndicates.]

[2527]

NOTES
   Para (1): words in first pair of square brackets inserted, and words in second pair of square brackets substituted, by the Financial Services and Markets Act 2000 (Control of Transfers of Business Done at Lloyd's) (Amendment) Order 2008, SI 2008/1725, art 2(1), (5), as from 23 July 2008.
   Para (3): added by SI 2008/1725, art 2(1), (6), as from 23 July 2008.

FINANCIAL SERVICES AND MARKETS TRIBUNAL (LEGAL ASSISTANCE) REGULATIONS 2001

(SI 2001/3632)

NOTES
Made: 8 November 2001.
Authority: Financial Services and Markets Act 2000, ss 134, 135, 428(1), (3).
Commencement: 30 November 2001.

As of 1 February 2009, these Regulations had not been amended.

ARRANGEMENT OF REGULATIONS

PART I
GENERAL

PART II
ELIGIBILITY, ASSESSMENT AND CONTRIBUTIONS

PART III
ASSIGNMENT OF REPRESENTATIVE

PART IV
WITHDRAWAL OF LEGAL ASSISTANCE

PART V
CONSTITUTION

PART I
GENERAL

1   Citation and commencement

These Regulations may be cited as the Financial Services and Markets Tribunal (Legal Assistance) Regulations 2001 and shall come into force on 30th November 2001.

[2528]

2   Interpretation

In these Regulations—
    "the Act" means the Financial Services and Markets Act 2000;
    "advocate" means—
        (a)   a barrister, or a solicitor who has obtained a higher courts advocacy qualification in accordance with regulations and rules of conduct of the Law Society; or

    (b)   in relation to Scotland, a member of the Faculty of Advocates or a solicitor who holds rights of audience under section 25A of the Solicitors (Scotland) Act 1980;

"assisted person" means a person in receipt of legal assistance;

"the Authority" means the Financial Services Authority;

"decision notice" means a decision notice given by the Authority under section 127(1) of the Act;

"disposable income" and "disposable capital" mean, respectively, income and capital, calculated in accordance with regulations 16 to 34;

"legal assistance" means legal assistance in connection with proceedings which are before the Tribunal pursuant to a reference under section 127(4) of the Act and with regard to which a determination of the Tribunal disposing of the reference has not yet been made, and include advice, assistance and representation for the purpose of those proceedings;

"partner" except in the expression "partner in a business" means a person with whom the applicant lives as a couple, and includes a person with whom the applicant is not currently living but from whom he is not living separate and apart;

"representative" means a solicitor or an advocate; and

"the Tribunal" means the Financial Services and Markets Tribunal established under section 132 of the Act, and, for the purposes of these Regulations, includes—

    (a)   any member of the panel of chairmen of the Tribunal established under paragraph 3 of Schedule 13 to the Act acting alone; and

    (b)   any person acting on behalf of the Tribunal in accordance with regulation 43.

[2529]

3 Scope

(1)   The Lord Chancellor shall fund such legal assistance as the Tribunal directs regarding a relevant reference.

(2)   For the purposes of this regulation, a relevant reference is a reference which the Tribunal is to determine in relation to any individual who—

    (a)   has received a decision notice from the Authority;

    (b)   has referred the matter to the Tribunal under section 127(4) of the Act; and

    (c)   fulfils the criteria set out in regulation 8.

[2530]

4 Applications for legal assistance

(1)   Any application shall be made in writing to the Tribunal.

(2)   The application shall state—

    (a)   the name and address of the applicant;

    (b)   the name and address of the applicant's solicitor;

    (c)   the Tribunal reference number allocated to the case, if known;

    (d)   the reasons why the applicant considers it to be in the interests of justice for legal assistance to be granted; and

    (e)   details of the financial resources of the applicant and of any other person whose resources are to be treated as his resources under these Regulations.

[2531]

5 Provision of information

(1)   The Tribunal may direct the applicant to provide any information it requires in order to decide whether to grant his application.

(2)   The applicant shall provide the Tribunal with any information it requires under paragraph (1).

[2532]

6 Legal assistance order

(1)   Where an application for legal assistance is granted, the Tribunal shall—

    (a)   issue a legal assistance order; and

    (b)   send a copy of the order to—

        (i)   the applicant;

        (ii)   the applicant's solicitor; and

        (iii)   the Authority.

(2)   The legal assistance order shall include details of any contribution payable.

[2533]

7 Refusal of legal assistance

(1)   Where an application for legal assistance is refused, the Tribunal shall send written reasons for the refusal to the applicant.

(2)   An applicant whose application for legal assistance has been refused may make a renewed application in writing to the Tribunal.

(3)   Any renewed application to the Tribunal under paragraph (2) shall specify any new or additional factors which the applicant wishes the Tribunal to take into account.

[2534]

PART II
ELIGIBILITY, ASSESSMENT AND CONTRIBUTIONS

8 Eligibility

The Tribunal shall grant legal assistance to an individual if it is satisfied that—
- (a)   it is in the interests of justice to do so; and
- (b)   his financial resources are such that he requires assistance in meeting the legal costs he would, but for these Regulations, be likely to incur in relation to the proceedings before the Tribunal.

[2535]

9 Interests of justice test

In deciding whether it is in the interests of justice for legal assistance to be granted, the Tribunal shall take all relevant factors into account, including—
- (a)   whether the individual would, if any matter arising in the proceedings before the Tribunal is decided against him, be likely to lose his livelihood or suffer serious damage to his reputation;
- (b)   whether the determination of any matter arising in the proceedings may involve consideration of a substantial question of law;
- (c)   whether the individual may be unable to understand the proceedings or to state his own case;
- (d)   whether the proceedings may involve the tracing, interviewing or expert cross-examination of witnesses on behalf of the individual; and
- (e)   whether it is in the interests of another person that the individual be represented.

[2536]

10 Financial eligibility

(1)   Where a doubt arises as to whether the financial resources of an individual are such that he requires legal assistance, the doubt shall be resolved in his favour.

(2)   The Tribunal shall determine the financial eligibility of the applicant and any contribution payable in accordance with these Regulations.

(3)   The Tribunal may appoint an expert to prepare a report with regard to the financial resources of the applicant.

[2537]

11 Resources of other persons

(1)   In calculating the disposable income and disposable capital of the applicant, the resources of his partner shall be treated as his resources.

(2)   Where it appears to the Tribunal that—
- (a)   another person is, has been or is likely to be substantially maintaining the applicant; or
- (b)   any of the resources of another person have been or are likely to be made available to the applicant

the Tribunal may treat all or any part of the resources of that other person as the resources of the applicant.

(3)   In this regulation and regulation 12 "person" includes a company, partnership, body of trustees and any body of persons, whether corporate or not corporate.

[2538]

12 Deprivation or conversion of resources

If it appears to the Tribunal that the applicant has, with intent to reduce the amount of his disposable income or disposable capital, whether for the purpose of making himself eligible to receive legal assistance, reducing his liability to pay a contribution, or otherwise—
- (a)   directly or indirectly deprived himself of any resources;
- (b)   transferred any resources to another person; or
- (c)   converted any part of his resources into resources which under these Regulations are to be wholly or partly disregarded

the resources which he has so deprived himself of, transferred or converted shall be treated as part of his resources or as not so converted as the case may be.

[2539]

13 Duty to report change in financial circumstances

The assisted person shall immediately inform the Tribunal of any change in his financial circumstances (or those of any other person whose resources are to be treated as his resources under these Regulations) of which he is, or should reasonably be aware, which has occurred since any assessment of his resources, and which might affect the terms on which he was assessed as eligible to receive legal assistance.

[2540]

14   Amendment of assessment due to error or receipt of new information

Where—

(a)   it appears to the Tribunal that there has been an error in the assessment of a person's resources or contribution, or in any calculation or estimate upon which such assessment was based; or

(b)   new information which is relevant to the assessment has come to light

the Tribunal may make an amended assessment, and may take such steps equitable to give effect to it in relation to any period during which legal assistance has already been provided.

[2541]

15   Further assessments

(1)   Where it appears that the circumstances of the assisted person may have altered so that—

(a)   his disposable income has increased by an amount greater than £750 or decreased by an amount greater than £300; or

(b)   his disposable capital has increased by an amount greater than £750

the Tribunal shall, subject to paragraph (6), make a further assessment of the assisted person's resources and any contribution which he is required to pay under regulation 35, in accordance with these Regulations.

(2)   Where a further assessment is made, the period of calculation for the purposes of disposable income shall be the period of 12 months following the date of the change of circumstances or such other period of 12 months as the Tribunal considers appropriate.

(3)   Where a further assessment is made, the amount or value of every resource of a capital nature acquired since the date of the original application shall be ascertained as at the date of receipt of that resource.

(4)   Any capital contribution which becomes payable as a result of a further assessment shall be payable in respect of the cost of the legal assistance, including costs already incurred.

(5)   Where legal assistance is withdrawn as a result of a further assessment of capital, the Tribunal may require a contribution to be paid in respect of costs already incurred.

(6)   The Tribunal may decide not to make a further assessment under paragraph (1) if it considers such a further assessment inappropriate, having regard in particular to the period during which legal assistance is likely to continue to be provided to the assisted person.

[2542]

16   Calculation of income

(1)   The income of the individual from any source shall be taken to be the income which he may reasonable expect to receive (in cash or in kind) during the period of calculation.

(2)   For the purpose of this regulation and regulation 32, the period of calculation shall be the 12 months starting on the date of the application for legal assistance or such other 12 month period as the Tribunal considers appropriate.

[2543]

17—(1)   The income from a trade, business or gainful occupation other than an occupation at a wage or salary shall be deemed to be whichever of the following the Tribunal considers more appropriate and practicable—

(a)   the profits which have accrued or will accrue to the individual in respect of the period of calculation; or

(b)   the drawings of the individual.

(2)   In calculating the profits under paragraph (1)(a)—

(a)   the Tribunal may have regard to the profits of the last accounting period of such trade, business or gainful occupation for which accounts have been prepared; and

(b)   there shall be deducted all sums necessarily expended to earn those profits, but no deduction shall be made in respect of the living expenses of the individual or any member of his family or household, except in so far as that person is wholly or mainly employed in that trade or business and such living expenses form part of his remuneration.

[2544]

18—(1)   For the purposes of this regulation, "national insurance contributions" means contributions under Part I of the Social Security Contributions and Benefits Act 1992.

(2)   In calculating the disposable income of the individual, any income tax and national insurance contributions paid or payable on that income in respect of the period of calculation shall be deducted.

[2545]

19—(1)   For the purposes of this regulation, "the Schedule" means Schedule 2 to the Income Support (General) Regulations 1987.

(2)   Subject to paragraph (3), in calculating the disposable income of the individual there shall be a deduction at or equivalent to the following rates (as they applied at the beginning of the period of calculation)—

(a)   in respect of the maintenance of his partner, the difference between the income support allowance for a couple both aged not less than 18 (which is specified in column 2 of paragraph 1(3)(d) of the Schedule), and the allowance for a single person aged not less than 25 (which is specified in column 2 of paragraph 1(1)(e) of the Schedule); and

(b)   in respect of the maintenance of any dependant child or dependant relative of his, where such persons are members of his household—

(i)   in the case of a dependant child or a dependant relative aged 15 or under at the beginning of the period of calculation, the amount specified at (a) in column 2 in paragraph 2(1) of the Schedule; and

(ii)   in the case of a dependant child or a dependant relative aged 16 or over at the beginning of the period of calculation, the amount specified at (b) in column 2 in paragraph 2(1) of the Schedule.

(3)   The Tribunal may reduce any rate provided by virtue of paragraph (2)(b) by taking into account the income and other resources of the dependant child or dependant relative to such extent as appears to the Tribunal to be equitable.

(4)   In ascertaining whether a child is a dependant child or whether a person is a dependant relative for the purpose of this regulation, regard shall be had to their income and other resources.

[2546]

20   Where the individual is making and, throughout such period as the Tribunal considers adequate, has regularly made payments for the maintenance of—

(a)   a former partner;

(b)   a child; or

(c)   a relative

who is not a member of his household, in calculating the disposable income of the individual a reasonable amount shall be deducted in respect of such payments.

[2547]

21   In calculating the disposable income of the individual from any source, the Tribunal shall disregard such amount (if any) as it considers reasonable, having regard to the nature of the income or to any other circumstances.

[2548]

22   In calculating the disposable income of the individual, any sums (net of council tax benefit) payable by him in respect of the council tax to which he is liable by virtue of section 6 of the Local Government Finance Act 1992 shall be deducted.

[2549]

23   Where the income of the individual consists, wholly or partly, of a wage or salary from employment, in calculating his disposable income there shall be deducted—

(a)   the reasonable expenses of travelling to and from his place of employment;

(b)   the amount of any payments reasonably made for membership of a trade union or professional organisation;

(c)   where it would be reasonable to do so, an amount to provide for the care of any dependant child living with the individual during the time that he is absent from home by reason of his employment; and

(d)   the amount of any contribution paid, whether under a legal obligation or not, to an occupational pension scheme or a personal pension scheme within the meaning of section 1 of the Pension Schemes Act 1993.

[2550]

24—(1)   Paragraphs (2) to (5) apply only if the individual is a householder.

(2)   In calculating the disposable income of the individual, the net rent payable by him in respect of his main or only dwelling, or such part of it as is reasonable in the circumstances, shall be deducted.

(3)   Where the individual lives in more than one dwelling, the Tribunal shall decide which is the main dwelling.

(4)   For the purpose of this regulation, "net rent" includes—

   (a)   any annual rent payable;

   (b)   any annual instalment (whether of interest or capital) in respect of a mortgage debt or heritable security up to a maximum of an amount bearing the same proportion to the amount of the annual instalment as £100,000 bears to the debt secured; and

   (c)   a sum in respect of yearly outgoings borne by the householder including, in particular, any water and sewerage charges, and a reasonable allowance towards any necessary expenditure on repairs and insurance.

(5)   In calculating the amount of net rent payable, there shall be deducted—

   (a)   any housing benefit paid under the Social Security Contributions and Benefits Act 1992;

   (b)   any proceeds of sub-letting any part of the premises; and

   (c)   an amount reasonably attributable to any person other than the individual, his partner or any dependant, who is accommodated in the premises otherwise than as a sub-tenant.

(6)   If the individual is not a householder, a reasonable amount in respect of the cost of his living accommodation shall be deducted.

[2551]

25 Calculation of capital

Subject to the provisions of these Regulations, in calculating the disposable capital of the individual, the amount or value of every resource of a capital nature belonging to him on the date on which the application for legal assistance is made shall be included.

[2552]

26   In so far as any resource of a capital nature does not consist of money, its value shall be taken to be—

   (a)   the amount which that resource would realise if sold; or

   (b)   the value assessed in such other manner as appears to the Tribunal to be equitable.

[2553]

27   Where money is due to the individual, whether it is payable immediately or otherwise and whether payment is secured or not, its value shall be taken to be its present value.

[2554]

28   The value to the individual of any life insurance or endowment policy shall be taken to be the amount which he could readily borrow on the security of that policy.

[2555]

29   Other than in circumstances which are exceptional having regard in particular to the quantity or value of the items concerned, nothing shall be included in the disposable capital of the individual in respect of—

   (a)   the household furniture and effects of the main or only dwelling house occupied by him;

   (b)   articles of personal clothing; and

   (c)   the tools and equipment of his trade, unless they form part of the plant or equipment of a business to which the provisions of regulation 30 apply.

[2556]

30—(1)   Where the individual is the sole owner of or partner in a business, the value of the business to him shall be taken to be the greater of—

   (a)   such sum, or his share of such sum, as could be withdrawn from the assets of his business without substantially impairing its profits or normal development; and

   (b)   such sum as the individual could borrow on the security of his interest in the business without substantially injuring its commercial credit.

(2)   Where the individual stands in relation to a company in a position analogous to that of a sole owner or partner in a business, the Tribunal may, instead of ascertaining the value of his stocks, shares, bonds or debentures in that company, treat him as if he were a sole owner or partner in a business and calculate the amount of his capital in respect of that resource in accordance with paragraph (1).

(3)   Where the individual owns solely, jointly or in common with other persons, any interest on the termination of a prior estate, whether

   (a)   legal or equitable;

   (b)   vested or contingent;

   (c)   in reversion or remainder; and

   (d)   whether in real or personal property or in a trust or other fund the value of such interest shall be calculated in such manner as is both equitable and practicable.

(4)   In Scotland, the value of any interest, whether vested or contingent, of the individual in the fee of any heritable or moveable property forming the whole or part of any trust or other estate, shall be calculated in such manner as is both equitable and practicable.

[2557]

31—(1)   In calculating the disposable capital of the individual, the value of any interest in land shall be taken to be the amount for which that interest could be sold less the amount of any mortgage debt or heritable security, subject to the following—
> (a)   in calculating the value of his interests, the total amount to be deducted in respect of all mortgage debts or heritable securities shall not exceed £100,000;
> (b)   in making the deductions in sub-paragraph (a), any mortgage debt or heritable security in respect of the main or only dwelling shall be deducted last; and
> (c)   the first £100,000 of the value of his interest (if any) in the main or only dwelling in which he resides, after the application of sub-paragraphs (a) and (b), shall be disregarded.

(2)   Where the individual resides in more than one dwelling, the Tribunal shall decide which is the main dwelling.

[2558]

32   Where under any statute, bond, covenant, guarantee or other instrument the individual is under a contingent liability to pay any sum or is liable to pay a sum not yet ascertained, the Tribunal shall disregard such amount as is reasonably likely to become payable within the period of calculation in regulation 16(2).

[2559]

33   In calculating the disposable capital of the individual, the Tribunal may disregard any capital resource where—
> (a)   the individual is restrained from dealing with that resource by order of a court;
> (b)   he has requested the court which made the order to release part or all of that resource for use in connection with the proceedings before the Tribunal; and
> (c)   that request has been refused.

[2560]

34   In calculating the disposable capital of the individual, the Tribunal may disregard such amount of capital (if any) as it considers reasonable, having regard to the nature of the capital or to any other circumstances.

[2561]

35 Contributions
> (1)   The assisted person shall make the following contributions—
>> (a)   where his annual disposable income exceeds £3,110, monthly contributions of one thirty-sixth of the excess; and
>> (b)   where his disposable capital exceeds £3,000, a contribution of the whole of the amount of the excess.

(2)   All contributions shall be payable in such manner as the Tribunal directs.

(3)   All contributions payable under paragraph (1)(a) shall be payable monthly throughout the period the legal assistance order is in force.

(4)   All contributions payable under paragraph (1)(b) shall be payable upon assessment, or at such other time as the Tribunal directs.

(5)   Where the contribution made by the assisted person exceeds the cost to the Tribunal of the legal assistance provided to him, the excess shall be refunded to the assisted person.

[2562]

36—(1)   Where, on determining a reference, the Tribunal directs the Authority to—
> (a)   take no action against the assisted person;
> (b)   impose a penalty on the assisted person of a lesser amount than that stated in the decision notice; or
> (c)   instead of imposing a penalty on the assisted person, publish a statement to the effect that he has engaged in market abuse

the Tribunal may, at the hearing of the reference, order the refund of some or all of any contribution made by the assisted person.

(2)   In making a decision under paragraph (1), the Tribunal shall have regard to all the circumstances of the case, including the conduct of the parties.

[2563]

PART III
ASSIGNMENT OF REPRESENTATIVE

37—(1)   A legal assistance order may provide for legal assistance to be provided by a solicitor alone, or by a solicitor and one or more advocates.

(2)   The Tribunal, in deciding what legal assistance to grant under paragraph (1), shall take all relevant factors into account, including—
- (a)   whether the case appears to involve substantial, novel or complex issues of law or fact;
- (b)   whether the case is exceptional compared with the generality of such cases; and
- (c)   the number and level of advocates instructed on behalf of the Authority.

[2564]

38   Where the Authority has issued a decision notice against more than one assisted person in the same case, the Tribunal may, unless it considers it not to be in the interests of justice to do so, assign the same solicitor and, if any, advocate, to each of those individuals.

[2565]

39   Amendment of legal assistance order

(1)   An application may be made to the Tribunal to amend a legal assistance order, and any such application shall state the grounds on which it is made.

(2)   The Tribunal may grant or refuse any application made under paragraph (1).

(3)   The Tribunal may, before granting legal assistance for more than one advocate, require written advice from any advocate already assigned to the assisted person on the question of what legal assistance is required in the proceedings.

[2566]

40—(1)   Where an application for legal assistance has been granted, an application may be made to the Tribunal to select a representative in place of a representative previously assigned and any such application shall state the grounds on which it is made.

(2)   The Tribunal may grant or refuse any application made under paragraph (1).

[2567]

PART IV
WITHDRAWAL OF LEGAL ASSISTANCE

41—(1)   The Tribunal may withdraw legal assistance where—
- (a)   the assisted person has requested that it do so;
- (b)   there has been a change of circumstances in relation to any of the factors which the Tribunal took into account in deciding that legal assistance should be granted;
- (c)   the assisted person has failed to provide any relevant information or evidence;
- (d)   the assisted person has made a false statement regarding his financial resources;
- (e)   the assisted person has failed to pay all or part of any contribution required by the Tribunal; or
- (f)   it appears to the Tribunal to be in the interests of justice to do so.

(2)   Before the Tribunal withdraws legal assistance, it shall take into account any representations which are made within a reasonable time by or on behalf of the assisted person.

(3)   Where legal assistance is withdrawn, the Tribunal shall provide written notification of the withdrawal and of the reason for it to the assisted person and his solicitor, who shall inform any assigned advocate.

(4)   On any subsequent application by the assisted person for legal assistance in respect of the same proceedings, he shall declare the withdrawal of legal assistance and the reason for it.

[2568]

42   Duty to report abuse

Notwithstanding the relationship between or rights of a representative and client or any privilege arising out of any such relationship, where the representative for an assisted person knows or suspects that that person—
- (a)   has intentionally failed to comply with any provision of these Regulations concerning the information to be provided by him; or

(b)   in providing such information has knowingly made a false statement or false
        representation

the representative shall immediately report the circumstances to the Tribunal.

[2569]

PART V
CONSTITUTION

43   Any act required or authorised by these Regulations to be done by the Tribunal may be done by
a member of the panel of chairmen of the Tribunal acting alone or by a person authorised by the
Tribunal to carry out that act.

[2570]

FINANCIAL SERVICES AND MARKETS TRIBUNAL (LEGAL ASSISTANCE SCHEME—COSTS) REGULATIONS 2001

(SI 2001/3633)

NOTES
Made: 8 November 2001.
Authority: Financial Services and Markets Act 2000, ss 134, 135, 428(1), (3).
Commencement: 30 November 2001.

As of 1 February 2009, these Regulations had not been amended.

ARRANGEMENT OF REGULATIONS

1   Citation, commencement and extent

(1)   These Regulations may be cited as the Financial Services and Markets Tribunal (Legal
Assistance Scheme—Costs) Regulations 2001 and shall come into force on 30th November 2001.

(2)   These Regulations apply to the whole of the United Kingdom, except that—
        (a)   regulations 20, 21 and 23(5) do not apply in relation to a Tribunal reference in Scotland;
                and
        (b)   regulation 22 only applies in relation to a Tribunal reference in Scotland.

[2571]

2 Interpretation

In these Regulations—

"the Act" means the Financial Services and Markets Act 2000;

"advocate" means—

(a)   a barrister, or a solicitor who has obtained a higher courts advocacy qualification in accordance with regulations and rules of conduct of the Law Society; or

(b)   in relation to Scotland, a member of the Faculty of Advocates or a solicitor who holds rights of audience under section 25A of the Solicitors (Scotland) Act 1980;

"appropriate officer" means a costs officer of the Supreme Court Costs Office;

"assisted person" means a person in receipt of legal assistance;

"the Authority" means the Financial Services Authority;

"costs", in relation to Scotland, means expenses;

"legal assistance" means legal assistance in connection with proceedings which are before the Tribunal pursuant to a reference under section 127(4) of the Act and with regard to which a determination of the Tribunal disposing of the reference has not yet been made, and includes advice, assistance and representation for the purpose of those proceedings;

"legal assistance order" means a document granting a right to legal assistance in respect of proceedings before the Tribunal;

"the main hearing" means the hearing at which a decision of the Tribunal disposing of the reference is made;

"representative" means a solicitor or an advocate;

"the Tribunal" means the Financial Services and Markets Tribunal established under section 132 of the Act, and includes any person authorised by it to act on its behalf in that regard.

[2572]

3 Determination of costs

(1)   Costs in respect of work done under a legal assistance order shall be determined by the appropriate officer in accordance with these Regulations.

(2)   In determining costs, the appropriate officer shall, subject to the provisions of these Regulations—

(a)   take into account all the relevant circumstances of the case including the nature, importance, complexity or difficulty of the work and the time involved; and

(b)   allow a reasonable amount in respect of all work actually and reasonably done.

[2573]

4 Authorisation of expenditure

(1)   Where it appears to the solicitor necessary for the proper conduct of proceedings before the Tribunal for costs to be incurred under the legal assistance order by taking any of the following steps—

(a)   obtaining a written report or opinion of one or more experts;

(b)   employing a person to provide a written report or opinion (otherwise than as an expert); or

(c)   performing an act which is either unusual in its nature or involves unusually large expenditure

he may apply to the Tribunal for prior authority to do so.

(2)   Where the Tribunal authorises the taking of any step specified in paragraph (1), it shall also authorise the maximum to be paid in respect of that step.

[2574]

5 Authorisation of travelling and accommodation expenses

A representative assigned to an assisted person in any proceedings before the Tribunal may apply to the Tribunal for prior authority for the incurring of travelling and accommodation expenses in order to attend at any hearing in those proceedings.

[2575]

6 Interim payment of disbursements

(1)   A solicitor may submit a claim to the appropriate officer for payment of a disbursement for which he has incurred liability in proceedings before the Tribunal in accordance with the provisions of this regulation.

(2)   A claim for payment may be made where—

(a)   a solicitor has obtained prior authority to incur expenditure of £100 or more under regulation 4 or 5; and

(b)   he has incurred such a liability.

(3)   Without prejudice to regulation 14(2), a claim under paragraph (1) shall not exceed the maximum fee authorised under the prior authority.

(4)   A claim for payment under paragraph (1) may be made at any time before the solicitor submits a claim for costs under regulation 12(2).

(5)   A claim under paragraph (1) shall be submitted to the appropriate officer in such form and manner as he may direct and shall be accompanied by the authority to incur expenditure and any invoices or other documents in support of the claim.

(6)   The appropriate officer shall allow the disbursement subject to the limit in paragraph (3) if it appears to have been reasonably incurred in accordance with the prior authority.

(7)   Where the appropriate officer allows the disbursement, he shall notify the solicitor and, where the disbursement includes the fees or charges of any person, that person, of the amount payable, and shall authorise payment to the solicitor accordingly.

(8)   Regulations 19 to 22 (redetermination etc) shall not apply to a payment under this regulation.

[2576]

7   Interim disbursements and final determination of costs

(1)   On a final determination of costs, regulations 12(2) and (3)(e) and 14 shall apply notwithstanding that a payment has been made under regulation 6.

(2)   Where the amount found to be due under regulation 14 in respect of a disbursement is less than the amount paid under regulation 6 ("the interim disbursement"), the appropriate officer shall deduct the difference from the sum otherwise payable to the solicitor on the determination of costs, and where the amount due under regulation 14 exceeds the interim disbursement, the appropriate officer shall add the difference to the amount otherwise payable to the solicitor.

[2577]

8   Staged payments in long cases

(1)   A representative may submit a claim to the appropriate officer for a staged payment of his fees in relation to proceedings before the Tribunal.

(2)   Where a claim is submitted in accordance with the provisions of this regulation, a staged payment shall be allowed where the appropriate officer is satisfied—
(a)   that the claim relates to fees for a period of preparation of 100 hours or more, for which the representative will, subject to final determination of the costs payable, be entitled to be paid in accordance with these Regulations; and
(b)   that the period from the date of the legal assistance order to the conclusion of the proceedings before the Tribunal will be likely to exceed 12 months, having regard, amongst other matters, to the number of individuals against whom a decision notice has been issued in the same case, and the weight and complexity of the case.

(3)   In this regulation, "preparation" means work done before the main hearing, including—
(a)   reading the papers in the case;
(b)   attendance at conferences;
(c)   contact with the Authority;
(d)   providing written or oral advice;
(e)   researching the law;
(f)   preparation for the examination of witnesses and of oral submissions for the main hearing;
(g)   preparation of written submissions, notices or other documents for use at the main hearing;
(h)   attendance at any hearing before the main hearing; and
(i)   all preparation within the meaning of regulation 13(1)(a) not falling within the preceding sub-paragraphs.

(4)   The amount to be allowed for preparation falling within paragraph (3)(a) to (h) shall be computed by reference to the number of hours of preparation which it appears to the appropriate officer, without prejudice to the final determination of the costs payable, has been reasonably done, multiplied by the relevant hourly rate, namely—
(a)   in the case of an advocate who is a Queen's Counsel, the hourly rate for subsidiary fees for Queen's Counsel prescribed in Table 2 in Schedule 2;
(b)   in the case of any other advocate, the hourly rate for subsidiary fees for junior counsel prescribed in Table 1 in Schedule 2.

(5)   The amount to be allowed for preparation falling within paragraph (3)(i) shall be computed by reference to the number of hours of preparation which it appears to the appropriate officer, without prejudice to the final determination of the costs payable, has been reasonably done, multiplied by the relevant hourly rate prescribed in Schedule 1, applicable to the class of work and the grade of fee-earner.

(6)   A claim shall be submitted in such form and manner as the appropriate officer may direct, including such case plan as he may require for the purposes of paragraph (2)(a).

(7)   A representative may claim further staged payments in accordance with this regulation in respect of further periods of preparation exceeding 100 hours which were not included in an earlier claim.

(8)   Regulations 19 to 22 (redetermination etc) shall not apply to a payment under this regulation.

[2578]

9   Interim payments for attendance at hearing and refreshers

(1)   A representative may submit a claim to the appropriate officer for an interim payment in respect of attendance at the Tribunal or refreshers where the main hearing lasts for a qualifying period.

(2)   Where a claim is submitted in accordance with the provisions of this regulation, an interim payment shall, without prejudice to the final determination of the costs payable, be allowed—
- (a)   to a solicitor where he or a fee-earner representing him has attended at the hearing on each day of the qualifying period;
- (b)   to an advocate where he has undertaken advocacy on the first day of the main hearing or carried out preparation or advocacy on any other day.

(3)   The qualifying period for the purposes of this regulation shall be 20 days (which need not be continuous), and a day shall qualify as part of that period if the hearing begins at any time on that day.

(4)   The amount payable in respect of each day which qualifies as part of the qualifying period shall be—
- (a)   in the case of a solicitor—
  - (i)   where the hearing begins before and ends after the luncheon adjournment, five times the hourly rate for a trainee or fee-earner of equivalent experience attending court where more than one representative is assigned as prescribed in Schedule 1;
  - (ii)   where the hearing begins and ends before the luncheon adjournment, or begins after the luncheon adjournment, two and a half times the hourly rate referred to in (i) above;
- (b)   in the case of an advocate who is a Queen's Counsel, the maximum amount of the full day refresher fee for Queen's Counsel prescribed in Table 2 in Schedule 2;
- (c)   in the case of an advocate retained solely for the purpose of making a note of any hearing, one-half of the maximum amount of the full day refresher fee for junior counsel prescribed in Table 1 in Schedule 2;
- (d)   in the case of any other advocate, the maximum amount of the full day refresher fee for junior counsel prescribed in Table 1 in Schedule 2.

(5)   A claim for an interim payment may be made in respect of a qualifying period and shall be submitted in such form and manner as the appropriate officer may direct.

(6)   Further interim payments under this regulation may be claimed if the hearing lasts for further qualifying periods.

(7)   A representative who has obtained prior approval under regulation 5 for the incurring of travelling or accommodation expenses may, at the same time as he submits a claim for an interim payment under this regulation, submit a claim for an interim payment of all such expenses incurred to date (less any expenses previously recovered by him by way of interim payment under this regulation).

(8)   A claim under paragraph (7) shall be submitted in such form and manner as the appropriate officer may direct, and shall be supported by such evidence of the expense claimed as he may require.

(9)   Regulations 19 to 22 (redetermination etc) shall not apply to a payment under this regulation.

[2579]

10   Hardship payments

(1)   The appropriate officer may allow a hardship payment to a representative in the circumstances set out in paragraph (2), subject to the provisions of this regulation.

(2)   Those circumstances are that the representative—
- (a)   represents the assisted person in proceedings before the Tribunal;
- (b)   applies for such payment, in such form and manner as the appropriate officer may direct, not less than six months after he was first instructed in those proceedings;
- (c)   is not, at the date of the application, entitled to any payment under regulation 8 (staged payments) or 9 (interim payments);
- (d)   is unlikely to receive final payment in respect of the proceedings, as determined under regulation 13 or 16, within the three months following the application for the hardship payment; and

    (e)   satisfies the appropriate officer that, by reason of the circumstance in sub-paragraph (d), he is likely to suffer financial hardship.

(3)   Every application for a hardship payment shall be accompanied by such information and documents as the appropriate officer may require as evidence of—

    (a)   the work done by the representative in relation to the proceedings up to the date of the application; and

    (b)   the likelihood of financial hardship.

(4)   The amount of any hardship payment shall be in the discretion of the appropriate officer, but shall not exceed such sum as would be reasonable remuneration for the work done by the representative in the proceedings up to the date of the application.

(5)   No hardship payment shall be made if it appears to the appropriate officer that the sum which would be reasonable remuneration for the representative, or the sum required to relieve his financial hardship, is less than £5,000 (excluding any VAT).

(6)   Any hardship payment shall be set off against the remuneration finally payable to the representative under regulation 13 or 16.

[2580]

11 Computation of final claim

(1)   At the conclusion of a case in which one or more payments have been made to a representative under regulation 8, 9 or 10 he shall submit a claim under regulation 12 or 15 for the determination of his overall remuneration, whether or not such a claim will result in any payment additional to those already made.

(2)   In the determination of the amount payable to a representative under regulation 13 or 16, the appropriate officer shall deduct the amount of any advance payment made under regulation 8, 9 or 10 in respect of the same case from the amount that would otherwise be payable; and, if the amount of the advance payment is greater than the amount that would otherwise be payable, the appropriate officer shall be entitled to recover the amount of the difference, either by way of repayment by the representative or by way of deduction from any other amount that may be due to him.

[2581]

12 Claims for costs by solicitors

(1)   Subject to regulation 23, no claim by a solicitor for costs in respect of work done under a legal assistance order shall be considered unless he submits it within three months of the conclusion of the proceedings to which it relates.

(2)   A claim for costs shall be submitted to the appropriate officer in such form and manner as he may direct and shall be accompanied by the legal assistance order and any receipts or other documents in support of any disbursement claimed.

(3)   A claim shall—

    (a)   summarise the items of work in respect of which fees are claimed according to the classes of work specified in regulation 13(1);

    (b)   state, where appropriate, the dates on which the items of work were done, the time taken, the sums claimed and whether the work was done for more than one individual;

    (c)   specify, where appropriate, the fee-earner who undertook each of the items of work claimed;

    (d)   give particulars of any work done in relation to a rehearing; and

    (e)   specify any disbursements claimed, the circumstances in which they were incurred and the amounts claimed in respect of them.

(4)   Where the solicitor claims that paragraph 3 of Schedule 1 (enhanced rates) should be applied in relation to an item of work, he shall give full particulars in support of his claim.

(5)   The solicitor shall supply such further particulars, information and documents as the appropriate officer may require.

[2582]

13 Determination of solicitors' fees

(1)   The appropriate officer may allow work done by fee-earners in the following classes—

    (a)   preparation, including taking instructions, advising, interviewing witnesses, ascertaining the Authority's case, preparing and perusing documents, dealing with letters and telephone calls which are not routine, preparing for advocacy, instructing an advocate and expert witnesses, conferences and consultations;

    (b)   advocacy;

    (c)   attending at court where an advocate is assigned, including conferences with the advocate at court;

    (d)   travelling and waiting; and

    (e)   dealing with routine letters written and routine telephone calls.

(2) The appropriate officer shall consider the claim, any further particulars, information or documents submitted by the solicitor under regulation 12 and any other relevant information and shall allow—

    (a)   such work as appears to him to have been reasonably done under the legal assistance order by a fee-earner, classifying such work according to the classes specified in paragraph (1) as he considers appropriate; and

    (b)   such time in each class of work allowed by him (other than routine letters written and routine telephone calls) as he considers reasonable.

(3) In respect of all cases where the solicitor acts as advocate before the Tribunal, the appropriate officer shall proceed in accordance with the provisions of regulation 16 as if the fee-earner who did the work had been an advocate.

(4) In respect of all other classes of work, the provisions of this regulation shall apply.

(5) Subject to paragraph (2), (3), (4) and (6), the appropriate officer shall allow fees for work allowed by him under this regulation in accordance with Schedule 1.

(6) The fees allowed in accordance with Schedule 1 shall be those appropriate to such of the following grades of fee-earner as the appropriate officer considers reasonable—

    (a)   senior solicitor;

    (b)   solicitor, legal executive or fee-earner of equivalent experience;

    (c)   trainee or fee-earner of equivalent experience.

[2583]

14   Determination of solicitors' disbursements

(1) Subject to the provisions of this regulation, the appropriate officer shall allow such disbursements claimed under regulation 12 as appear to him to have been reasonably incurred.

(2) No question as to the propriety of any step, or as to the amount of the payment within the maximum authorised, with regard to which prior authority has been given under regulation 4 or 5, shall be raised on any determination of costs unless the representative knew or should reasonably have known that the purpose for which it was given had become unnecessary.

(3) Payment may be allowed on a determination of costs in respect of any step with regard to which prior authority may be given, notwithstanding that no such authority was given or that the maximum authorised was exceeded.

[2584]

15   Claims for fees by an advocate

(1) Subject to regulation 23, no claim by an advocate for fees in respect of work done under a legal assistance order shall be considered unless he submits it within three months of the conclusion of the proceedings to which it relates.

(2) A claim for fees shall be submitted to the appropriate officer in such form and manner as he may direct.

(3) A claim shall—

    (a)   summarise the items of work in respect of which fees are claimed according to the classes of fee specified in regulation 16(2);

    (b)   state, where appropriate, the dates on which the items of work were done, the time taken, the sums claimed and whether the work was done for more than one individual; and

    (c)   give particulars of any work done in relation to a rehearing.

(4) Where an advocate claims that the provision for enhanced rates in regulation 16(3) should be applied in relation to an item of work, he shall give full particulars in support of his claim.

(5) The advocate shall supply such further particulars, information and documents as the appropriate officer may require.

[2585]

16   Determination of advocates' fees

(1) The appropriate officer shall consider the claim, any further particulars and information submitted by an advocate under regulation 15 and any other relevant information and shall allow such work as appears to him to have been reasonably done.

(2) The appropriate officer may allow any of the following classes of fee to an advocate in respect of work allowed by him under this regulation—

    (a)   a basic fee for preparation including preparation for any hearing before the main hearing and, where appropriate, the first day of the main hearing including, where they took place on that day, short conferences, consultations, applications and appearances, and any other preparation;

    (b)   a refresher fee for any day or part of a day during which a hearing continued, including, where they took place on that day, short conferences, consultations, applications and appearances, and any other preparation;

(c)   subsidiary fees for—
     (i)   attendance at conferences and consultations not covered by (a) or (b) above;
     (ii)   written advices or other written work; and
     (iii)   attendance at hearings before the main hearing, applications and appearances not covered by (a) or (b) above.

(3)   The appropriate officer shall allow such fees in respect of such work as he considers reasonable in such amounts as he may determine in accordance with Schedule 2, provided that where it appears to the appropriate officer, taking into account all the relevant circumstances of the case, that owing to the exceptional circumstances of the case the amount payable by way of fees in accordance with Schedule 2 would not provide reasonable remuneration for some or all of the work he has allowed, he may allow such amounts as appear to him to be reasonable remuneration for the relevant work.

[2586]

17   Payment of costs

(1)   Having determined the costs payable to a representative in accordance with these Regulations, the appropriate officer shall notify the representative of the costs payable and authorise payment accordingly.

(2)   Where the costs payable under paragraph (1) are varied as a result of any redetermination or appeal made or brought pursuant to these Regulations—
    (a)   where the costs are increased, the appropriate officer shall authorise payment of the increase;
    (b)   where the costs are decreased, the representative shall repay the amount of such decrease; and
    (c)   where the payment of any costs of the representative is ordered under regulation 20(14) or 21(8), the appropriate officer shall authorise payment.

[2587]

18   Recovery of overpayments

(1)   This regulation applies where a representative is entitled to be paid a certain sum ("the amount due") by virtue of the provisions of these Regulations and, for whatever reason, he is paid an amount greater than that sum.

(2)   Where the circumstances in paragraph (1) arise, the appropriate officer may—
    (a)   require immediate repayment of the amount in excess of the amount due ("the excess amount") and the representative shall on demand repay the excess amount to the appropriate officer; or
    (b)   deduct the excess amount from any other sum which is or becomes payable to the representative by virtue of the provisions of these Regulations.

(3)   The appropriate officer may proceed under paragraph (2)(b) without first proceeding under paragraph (2)(a).

(4)   Paragraph (2) shall apply notwithstanding that the representative to whom the excess amount was paid is exercising, or may exercise, a right under regulations 19 to 22.

[2588]

19   Redetermination of costs by appropriate officer

(1)   Where a representative is dissatisfied with the costs determined in accordance with the provisions of these Regulations by the appropriate officer, he may apply to the appropriate officer to redetermine those costs.

(2)   Subject to regulation 23, the application shall be made within 21 days of the receipt of notification of the costs payable under regulation 17.

(3)   The application shall be made by giving notice to the appropriate officer in such form as he may direct specifying the matters in respect of which the application is made and the grounds of objection.

(4)   The notice of application shall be accompanied by the particulars, information and documents supplied under regulation 12 or 15, as appropriate.

(5)   The notice of application shall state whether the applicant wishes to appear or to be represented and, if the applicant so wishes, the appropriate officer shall notify the applicant of the time at which he is prepared to hear him or his representative.

(6)   The applicant shall supply such further particulars, information and documents as the appropriate officer may require.

(7)   The appropriate officer shall redetermine the costs, whether by way of increase or decrease in the amount previously determined, in the light of the objections made by the applicant or on his behalf, and shall notify the applicant of his decision.

(8)   The applicant may request the appropriate officer to give reasons in writing for his decision and the appropriate officer shall comply with any such request.

(9)   Subject to regulation 23, any request under paragraph (8) shall be made within 21 days of the receipt of notification of the decision.

[2589]

20   Appeals to a Costs Judge

(1)   Where the appropriate officer has given his reasons for his decisions under regulation 19, a representative who is dissatisfied with that decision may appeal to a Costs Judge.

(2)   Subject to regulation 23, an appeal shall be brought within 21 days of the receipt of the appropriate officer's reasons, by giving notice of appeal in writing to the Senior Costs Judge.

(3)   The appellant shall send a copy of any notice given under paragraph (2) to the appropriate officer.

(4)   The notice of appeal shall—
  (a)   be in such form as the Senior Costs Judge may direct;
  (b)   specify separately each item appealed against, showing (where appropriate) the amount claimed for the item, the amount determined and the grounds of the objection to the determination; and
  (c)   state whether the appellant wishes to appear or to be represented or whether he will accept a decision given in his absence.

(5)   The notice of appeal shall be accompanied by—
  (a)   a copy of the written representations given under regulation 19(3);
  (b)   the appropriate officer's reasons for his decision given under regulation 19(8); and
  (c)   the particulars, information and documents supplied to the appropriate officer under regulation 19.

(6)   The Senior Costs Judge may, and if so directed by the Lord Chancellor either generally or in a particular case shall, send to the Lord Chancellor a copy of the notice of appeal together with copies of such other documents as the Lord Chancellor may require.

(7)   The Lord Chancellor may arrange for written or oral representations to be made on his behalf and, if he intends to do so, he shall inform the Senior Costs Judge and the appellant.

(8)   Any written representations made on behalf of the Lord Chancellor under paragraph (7) shall be sent to the Senior Costs Judge and the appellant and, in the case of oral representations, the Senior Costs Judge and the appellant shall be informed of the grounds on which such representations will be made.

(9)   The appellant shall be permitted a reasonable opportunity to make representations in reply.

(10)   The Costs Judge shall inform the appellant (or his representative) and the Lord Chancellor, where representations have been or are to be made on his behalf, of the date of any hearing and, subject to the provisions of this regulation, may give directions as to the conduct of the appeal.

(11)   The Costs Judge may consult the Tribunal or the appropriate officer and may require the appellant to provide any further information which he requires for the purpose of the appeal and, unless the Costs Judge otherwise directs, no further evidence shall be received on the hearing of the appeal and no ground of objection shall be valid which was not raised under regulation 19.

(12)   The Costs Judge shall have the same powers as the appropriate officer under these Regulations and, in the exercise of such powers, may alter the redetermination of the appropriate officer in respect of any sum allowed, whether by increase or decrease as he thinks fit.

(13)   The Costs Judge shall inform the appellant, the Lord Chancellor and the appropriate officer of his decision and the reasons for it in writing.

(14)   Except where he confirms or decreases the sums redetermined under regulation 19, the Costs Judge may allow the appellant a sum in respect of part or all of any reasonable costs (including any fee payable in respect of an appeal) incurred by him in connection with the appeal.

[2590]

21   Appeals to the High Court

(1)   A representative who is dissatisfied with the decision of the Costs Judge on an appeal under regulation 20 may apply to a Costs Judge to certify a point of principle of general importance.

(2)   Subject to regulation 23, an application under paragraph (1) shall be made within 21 days of notification of the Costs Judge's decision under regulation 20(13).

(3)   Where a Costs Judge certifies a point of principle of general importance, the representative may appeal to the High Court against the decision of the Costs Judge on an appeal under regulation 20, and the Lord Chancellor shall be a respondent to such an appeal.

(4)   Subject to regulation 23, an appeal under paragraph (3) shall be brought within 21 days of receipt of the Costs Judge's certificate under paragraph (1).

(5)   Where the Lord Chancellor is dissatisfied with the decision of the Costs Judge on an appeal under regulation 20, he may, if no appeal has been made by the representative under paragraph (3) appeal to the High Court against that decision, and the representative shall be a respondent to the appeal.

(6)   Subject to regulation 23, an appeal under paragraph (5) shall be brought within 21 days of receipt of notification of the Costs Judge's decision under regulation 20(13).

(7)   An appeal under paragraph (3) or (5) shall—
  (a)   be brought in the Queen's Bench Division of the High Court;
  (b)   follow the procedure set out in Part 8 of the Civil Procedure Rules 1998; and
  (c)   be heard and determined by a single judge, whose decision shall be final.

(8)   The judge shall have the same powers as the appropriate officer and the Costs Judge under these Regulations and may reverse, affirm or amend the decision appealed against or make such other order as he thinks fit.

[2591]

22   Reference to the Auditor in Scottish cases

(1)   Where the appropriate officer has given his reasons for his decisions under regulation 19, a representative who is dissatisfied with that decision may refer the matter for taxation by the auditor.

(2)   The auditor shall give reasonable notice of the diet of taxation to the representative and the appropriate officer, and shall issue a report of the taxation.

(3)   The appropriate officer and any other party to a reference to the auditor under paragraph (1) may make written representations to the Court of Session in relation to the auditor's report within 14 days of the issue of that report, and may be heard thereon, and rule 42.4 of the Act of Sederunt (Rules of the Court of Session 1994) 1994 shall apply to the determination of any such representations.

(4)   In this regulation, "auditor" means the Auditor of the Court of Session.

[2592]

23   Time limits

(1)   Subject to paragraph (2), the time limit within which any act is required or authorised to be done may, for good reason, be extended—
  (a)   In the case of acts required or authorised to be done under regulations 20 to 22, by a Costs Judge, the High Court or the Court of Session, as the case may be; and
  (b)   in the case of acts required or authorised to be done by a representative under any other regulation, by the appropriate officer.

(2)   Where a representative without good reason has failed (or, if an extension were not granted, would fail) to comply with a time limit, the appropriate officer, a Costs Judge, the High Court, or the Court of Session, as the case may be—
  (a)   may, in exceptional circumstances, extend the time limit; and
  (b)   shall consider whether it is reasonable in the circumstances to reduce the costs.

(3)   Costs shall not be reduced under paragraph (2)(b) unless the representative has been allowed a reasonable opportunity to show cause orally or in writing why they should not be reduced.

(4)   A representative may appeal to a Costs Judge, or, in Scotland, to the Court of Session, against a decision made under this regulation by an appropriate officer.

(5)   An appeal against a decision made under this regulation shall be brought within 21 days of receipt of the decision by giving notice in writing to the Senior Costs Judge specifying the grounds of appeal.

[2593]

SCHEDULES

SCHEDULE 1
SOLICITORS' FEES

Fees Determined Under Regulation 13

1.   Subject to paragraph 2, the appropriate officer shall allow fees for work allowed by him under regulation 13 at the following prescribed rates—

Class of work	Grade of fee-earner	Rate
Preparation	Senior solicitor	£55.75 per hour

Class of work	Grade of fee-earner	Rate
	Solicitor, legal executive or fee-earner of equivalent experience	£47.25 per hour
	Trainee or fee-earner of equivalent experience	£34.00 per hour
Attendance at the Tribunal where more than one representative assigned	Senior solicitor	£42.25 per hour
	Solicitor, legal executive or fee-earner of equivalent experience	£34.00 per hour
	Trainee or fee-earner of equivalent experience	£20.50 per hour
Travelling and waiting	Senior solicitor, solicitor, legal executive or fee-earner of equivalent experience	£24.75 per hour
	Trainee or fee-earner of equivalent experience	£12.50 per hour
Routine letters written and routine telephone calls		£3.60 per item

2.   In respect of any item of work, the appropriate officer may allow fees at less than the relevant prescribed rate specified in paragraph 1 where it appears to him reasonable to do so having regard to the competence and despatch with which the work was done.

3.—(1)   Upon a determination in respect of any case the appropriate officer may allow fees at more than the relevant prescribed rate specified in paragraph 1, subject to the provisions of this paragraph, where it appears to him, taking into account all the relevant circumstances of the case, that—

(a)   the work was done with exceptional competence, skill or expertise;
(b)   the work was done with exceptional despatch; or
(c)   the case involved exceptional circumstances or complexity.

(2)   Where the appropriate officer considers that any item or class of work should be allowed at more than the prescribed rate, he shall apply to that item or class of work a percentage enhancement in accordance with the following provisions of this paragraph.

(3)   In determining the percentage by which fees should be enhanced above the prescribed rate the appropriate officer should have regard to—
(a)   the degree of responsibility accepted by the solicitor and his staff;
(b)   the care, speed and economy with which the case was prepared; and
(c)   the novelty, weight and complexity of the case.

(4)   The percentage above the relevant prescribed rate by which fees for work may be enhanced shall not exceed 200 per cent.

[2594]

SCHEDULE 2
ADVOCATES' FEES

1.   The appropriate officer shall allow such fee in respect of an item of work allowed under regulation 16(3), not exceeding the maximum amount specified in respect of that item of work, as appears to him to provide reasonable remuneration.

2.   Where an hourly rate is specified in a Table in this Schedule in respect of an item of work allowed under regulation 16(3), the appropriate officer shall determine any fee for such work in accordance with that hourly rate, provided that the fee determined shall not be less than the minimum amount specified.

3.   Where a refresher fee is claimed in respect of less than a full day, the appropriate officer shall allow such fee as appears to him reasonable having regard to the fee which would be allowable for a full day.

<table>
<tbody>
<tr><td colspan="5" align="center">*Table 1:*
Junior Counsel/Solicitor Advocate</td></tr>
</tbody>
</table>

Basic fee	Full day refresher	Subsidiary fees		
		Attendance at consultations and conferences	Written work	Attendance at hearings before the main hearing
Maximum amount: £545.50	Maximum amount: £178.75	£33.50 per hour Minimum amount: £16.75	Maximum amount: £58.25	Maximum amount: £110

Table 2:
Queen's Counsel

Basic fee	Full day refresher	Subsidiary fees		
		Attendance at consultations and conferences	Written work	Attendance at hearings before the main hearing
Maximum amount: £5,400.00	Maximum amount: £330.50	£62.50 per hour Minimum amount: £32.00	Maximum amount: £119.50	Maximum amount: £257.50

[2595]

INSURERS (WINDING UP) RULES 2001

(SI 2001/3635)

NOTES
Made: 9 November 2001.
Authority: Insolvency Act 1986, s 411; Financial Services and Markets Act 2000, s 379.
Commencement: 1 December 2001.
These Rules are reproduced as amended by: the Insurers (Reorganisation and Winding Up)
Regulations 2003, SI 2003/1102; the Insurers (Reorganisation and Winding Up) Regulations 2004, SI 2004/353.

ARRANGEMENT OF RULES

1   Citation, commencement and revocation

(1)   These Rules may be cited as the Insurers (Winding Up) Rules 2001 and come into force on 1st December 2001.

(2)   The Insurance Companies (Winding Up) Rules 1985 are revoked.

[2596]

2   Interpretation

(1)   In these Rules, unless the context otherwise requires—
   "the 1923 Act" means the Industrial Assurance Act 1923;
   "the 1985 Act" means the Companies Act 1985;
   "the 1986 Act" means the Insolvency Act 1986;
   "the 2000 Act" means the Financial Services and Markets Act 2000;
   "the Authority" means the Financial Services Authority;
   "company" means an insurer which is being wound up;
   "contract of general insurance" and "contract of long-term insurance" have the meaning given
      by article 3(1) of the Financial Services and Markets Act 2000 (Regulated Activities)
      Order 2001;
   "excess of the long-term business assets" means the amount, if any, by which the value of the
      assets representing the fund or funds maintained by the company in respect of its long-term
      business as at the liquidation date exceeds the value as at that date of the liabilities of the
      company attributable to that business;
   "excess of the other business assets" means the amount, if any, by which the value of the assets
      of the company which do not represent the fund or funds maintained by the company in
      respect of its long-term business as at the liquidation date exceeds the value as at that date
      of the liabilities of the company (other than liabilities in respect of share capital) which are
      not attributable to that business;
   "Financial Services Compensation Scheme" means the scheme established under section 213
      of the 2000 Act;
   "general business" means the business of effecting or carrying out a contract of general
      insurance;
   "the general regulations" means the Insolvency Regulations 1994;
   "the Industrial Assurance Acts" means the 1923 Act and the Industrial Assurance and Friendly
      Societies Act 1948;
   "insurer" has the meaning given by article 2 of the Financial Services and Markets Act 2000
      (Insolvency) (Definition of "Insurer") Order 2001;
   "linked liability" means any liability under a policy the effecting of which constitutes the
      carrying on of long-term business the amount of which is determined by reference to—
         (a)   the value of property of any description (whether or not specified in the policy),
         (b)   fluctuations in the value of such property,
         (c)   income from any such property, or
         (d)   fluctuations in an index of the value of such property;
   "linked policy" means a policy which provides for linked liabilities and a policy which when
      made provided for linked liabilities is deemed to be a linked policy even if the policy holder
      has elected to convert his rights under the policy so that at the liquidation date there are no
      longer linked liabilities under the policy;
   "liquidation date" means the date of the winding-up order or the date on which a resolution for
      the winding up of the company is passed by the members of the company (or the
      policyholders in the case of a mutual insurance company) and, if both a winding-up order
      and winding-up resolution have been made, the earlier date;
   "long-term business" means the business of effecting or carrying out any contract of long-term
      insurance;

"non-linked policy" means a policy which is not a linked policy;

"other business", in relation to a company carrying on long-term business, means such of the business of the company as is not long-term business;

"the principal rules" means the Insolvency Rules 1986;

"stop order", in relation to a company, means an order of the court, made under section 376(2) of the 2000 Act, ordering the liquidator to stop carrying on the long-term business of the company;

"unit" in relation to a policy means any unit (whether or not described as a unit in the policy) by reference to the numbers and value of which the amount of the liabilities under the policy at any time is measured.

(2)   Unless the context otherwise requires, words or expressions contained in these Rules bear the same meaning as in the principal rules, the general regulations, the 1986 Act, the 2000 Act or any statutory modification thereof respectively.

[2597]

3 Application

(1)   These Rules apply to proceedings for the winding up of an insurer which commence on or after the date on which these Rules come into force.

(2)   These Rules supplement the principal rules and the general regulations which continue to apply to the proceedings in the winding up of an insurer under the 1986 Act as they apply to proceedings in the winding up of any company under that Act; but in the event of a conflict between these Rules and the principal rules or the general regulations these Rules prevail.

[2598]

4 Appointment of liquidator

Where the court is considering whether to appoint a liquidator under—

(a)   section 139(4) of the 1986 Act (appointment of liquidator where conflict between creditors and contributories), or

(b)   section 140 of the 1986 Act (appointment of liquidator following administration or voluntary arrangement),

the manager of the Financial Services Compensation Scheme may appear and make representations to the court as to the person to be appointed.

[2599]

[5 Maintenance of separate financial records for long-term and other business in winding up

(1)   This rule applies in the case of a company carrying on long-term business in whose case no stop order has been made.

(2)   The liquidator shall prepare and keep separate financial records in respect of the long-term business and the other business of the company.

(3)   Paragraphs (4) and (5) apply in the case of a company to which this rule applies which also carries on permitted general business ('a hybrid insurer').

(4)   Where, before the liquidation date, a hybrid insurer has, or should properly have, apportioned the assets and liabilities attributable to its permitted general business to its long term business for the purposes of any accounts, those assets and liabilities must be apportioned to its long term business for the purposes of complying with paragraph (2) of this rule.

(5)   Where, before the liquidation date, a hybrid insurer has, or should properly have, apportioned the assets and liabilities attributable to its permitted general business other than to its long term business for the purposes of any accounts, those assets and liabilities must be apportioned to its other business for the purposes of complying with paragraph (2) of this rule.

(6)   Regulation 10 of the general regulations (financial records) applies only in relation to the company's other business.

(7)   In relation to the long-term business, the liquidator shall, with a view to the long-term business of the company being transferred to another insurer, maintain such accounting, valuation and other records as will enable such other insurer upon the transfer being effected to comply with the requirements of any rules made by the Authority under Part X of the 2000 Act relating to accounts and statements of insurers.

(8)   In paragraphs (4) and (5)—

(a)   "accounts" means any accounts or statements maintained by the company in compliance with a requirement under the Companies Act 1985 or any rules made by the Authority under Part X of the 2000 Act;

(b)   "permitted general business" means the business of effecting or carrying out a contract of general insurance where the risk insured against relates to either accident or sickness.]

[2600]

NOTES

Substituted by the Insurers (Reorganisation and Winding Up) Regulations 2003, SI 2003/1102, regs 52, 53(1), as from 20 April 2003.

6   Valuation of general business policies

Except in relation to amounts which have fallen due for payment before the liquidation date and liabilities referred to in paragraph 2(1)(b) of Schedule 1, the holder of a general business policy shall be admitted as a creditor in relation to his policy without proof for an amount equal to the value of the policy and for this purpose the value of a policy shall be determined in accordance with Schedule 1.

[2601]

7   Valuation of long-term policies

(1)   This rule applies in relation to a company's long-term business where no stop order has been made.

(2)   In relation to a claim under a policy which has fallen due for payment before the liquidation date, a policy holder shall be admitted as a creditor without proof for such amount as appears from the records of the company to be due in respect of that claim.

(3)   In all other respects a policy holder shall be admitted as a creditor in relation to his policy without proof for an amount equal to the value of the policy and for this purpose the value of a policy of any class shall be determined in the manner applicable to policies of that class provided by Schedules 2, 3 and 4.

(4)   This rule applies in relation to a person entitled to apply for a free paid-up policy under section 24 of the 1923 Act (provisions as to forfeited policies) and to whom no such policy has been issued before the liquidation date (whether or not it was applied for) as if such a policy had been issued immediately before the liquidation date—

    (a)   for the minimum amount determined in accordance with section 24(2) of the 1923 Act, or

    (b)   if the liquidator is satisfied that it was the practice of the company during the five years immediately before the liquidation date to issue policies under that section in excess of the minimum amounts so determined, for the amount determined in accordance with that practice.

[2602]

8—(1)   This rule applies in relation to a company's long-term business where a stop order has been made.

(2)   In relation to a claim under a policy which has fallen due for payment on or after the liquidation date and before the date of the stop order, a policy holder shall be admitted as a creditor without proof for such amount as appears from the records of the company and of the liquidator to be due in respect of that claim.

(3)   In all other respects a policy holder shall be admitted as a creditor in relation to his policy without proof for an amount equal to the value of the policy and for this purpose the value of a policy of any class shall be determined in the manner applicable to policies of that class provided by Schedule 5.

(4)   Paragraph (4) of rule 7 applies for the purposes of this rule as if references to the liquidation date (other than that in sub-paragraph (b) of that paragraph) were references to the date of the stop order.

[2603]

9   Attribution of liabilities to company's long-term business

(1)   This rule applies in the case of a company carrying on long-term business if at the liquidation date there are liabilities of the company in respect of which it is not clear from the accounting and other records of the company whether they are or are not attributable to the company's long-term business.

(2)   The liquidator shall, in such manner and according to such accounting principles as he shall determine, identify the liabilities referred to in paragraph (1) as attributable or not attributable to a company's long-term business and those liabilities shall for the purposes of the winding-up be deemed as at the liquidation date to be attributable or not as the case may be.

(3)   For the purposes of paragraph (2) the liquidator may—

    (a)   determine that some liabilities are attributable to the company's long-term business and that others are not (the first method); or

    (b)   determine that a part of a liability shall be attributable to the company's long-term business and that the remainder of the liability is not (the second method), and he may use the first method for some of the liabilities and the second method for the remainder of them.

(4)　Notwithstanding anything in the preceding paragraphs of this rule, the court may order that the determination of which (if any) of the liabilities referred to in paragraph (1) are attributable to the company's long-term business and which (if any) are not shall be made in such manner and by such methods as the court may direct or the court may itself make the determination.

[2604]

10　Attribution of assets to company's long-term business

(1)　This rule applies in the case of a company carrying on long-term business if at the liquidation date there are assets of the company in respect of which—

(a)　it is not clear from the accounting and other records of the company whether they do or do not represent the fund or funds maintained by the company in respect of its long-term business, and

(b)　it cannot be inferred from the source of the income out of which those assets were provided whether they do or do not represent those funds.

(2)　Subject to paragraph (6) the liquidator shall determine which (if any) of the assets referred to in paragraph (1) are attributable to those funds and which (if any) are not and those assets shall, for the purposes of the winding up, be deemed as at the liquidation date to represent those funds or not in accordance with the liquidator's determination.

(3)　For the purposes of paragraph (2) the liquidator may—

(a)　determine that some of those assets shall be attributable to those funds and that others of them shall not (the first method); or

(b)　determine that a part of the value of one of those assets shall be attributable to those funds and that the remainder of that value shall not (the second method),

and he may use the first method for some of those assets and the second method for others of them.

(4)

(a)　In making the attribution the liquidator's objective shall in the first instance be so far as possible to reduce any deficit that may exist, at the liquidation date and before any attribution is made, either in the company's long-term business or in its other business.

(b)　If there is a deficit in both the company's long-term business and its other business the attribution shall be in the ratio that the amount of the one deficit bears to the amount of the other until the deficits are eliminated.

(c)　Thereafter the attribution shall be in the ratio which the aggregate amount of the liabilities attributable to the company's long-term business bears to the aggregate amount of the liabilities not so attributable.

(5)　For the purposes of paragraph (4) the value of a liability of the company shall, if it falls to be valued under rule 6 or 7, have the same value as it has under that rule but otherwise it shall have such value as would have been included in relation to it in a balance sheet of the company prepared in accordance with the 1985 Act as at the liquidation date; and, for the purpose of determining the ratio referred to in paragraph (4) but not for the purpose of determining the amount of any deficit therein referred to, the net balance of shareholders' funds shall be included in the liabilities not attributable to the company's long-term business.

(6)　Notwithstanding anything in the preceding paragraphs of this rule, the court may order that the determination of which (if any) of the assets referred to in paragraph (1) are attributable to the fund or funds maintained by the company in respect of its long-term business and which (if any) are not shall be made in such manner and by such methods as the court may direct or the court may itself make the determination.

[2605]

11　Excess of long-term business assets

(1)　Where the company is one carrying on long-term business [and in whose case no stop order has been made], for the purpose of determining the amount, if any, of the excess of the long-term business assets, there shall be included amongst the liabilities of the company attributable to its long-term business an amount determined by the liquidator in respect of liabilities and expenses likely to be incurred in connection with the transfer of the company's long-term business as a going concern to another insurance company being liabilities not included in the valuation of the long-term policies made in pursuance of rule 7.

(2)　Where the liquidator is carrying on the long-term business of an insurer with a view to that business being transferred as a going concern to a person or persons ("transferee") who may lawfully carry out those contracts (or substitute policies being issued by another insurer), the liquidator may, in addition to any amounts paid by the Financial Services Compensation Scheme for the benefit of the transferee to secure such a transfer or to procure substitute policies being issued, pay to the transferee or other insurer all or part of such funds or assets as are attributable to the long-term business being transferred or substituted.

[2606]

NOTES

Para (1): words in square brackets inserted by the Insurers (Reorganisation and Winding Up) Regulations 2003, SI 2003/1102, regs 52, 54, as from 20 April 2003.

12 Actuarial advice

(1) Before doing any of the following, that is to say—
- (a) determining the value of a policy in accordance with Schedules 1 to 5 (other than paragraph 3 of Schedule 1);
- (b) identifying long-term liabilities and assets in accordance with rules 9 and 10;
- (c) determining the amount (if any) of the excess of the long-term business assets in accordance with rule 11;
- (d) determining the terms on which he will accept payment of overdue premiums under rule 21(1) or the amount and nature of any compensation under rule 21(2);

the liquidator shall obtain and consider advice thereon (including an estimate of any value or amount required to be determined) from an actuary.

(2) Before seeking, for the purpose of valuing a policy, the direction of the court as to the assumption of a particular rate of interest or the employment of any rates of mortality or disability, the liquidator shall obtain and consider advice thereon from an actuary.

[2607]

13 Utilisation of excess of assets

(1) Except at the direction of the court, no distribution may be made out of and no transfer to another insurer may be made of—
- (a) any part of the excess of the long-term business assets which has been transferred to the other business; or
- (b) any part of the excess of the other business assets, which has been transferred to the long-term business.

(2) Before giving a direction under paragraph (1) the court may require the liquidator to advertise the proposal to make a distribution or a transfer in such manner as the court shall direct.

[2608]

14 In the case of a company carrying on long-term business in whose case no stop order has been made, regulation 5 of the general regulations (payments into the Insolvency Services Account) applies only in relation to the company's other business.

[2609]

15 Custody of assets

(1) The Secretary of State may, in the case of a company carrying on long-term business in whose case no stop order has been made, require that the whole or a specified proportion of the assets representing the fund or funds maintained by the company in respect of its long-term business shall be held by a person approved by him for the purpose as trustee for the company.

(2) No assets held by a person as trustee for a company in compliance with a requirement imposed under this rule shall, so long as the requirement is in force, be released except with the consent of the Secretary of State but they may be transposed by the trustee into other assets by any transaction or series of transactions on the written instructions of the liquidator.

(3) The liquidator may not grant any mortgage or charge of assets which are held by a person as trustee for the company in compliance with a requirement imposed under this rule except with the consent of the Secretary of State.

[2610]

16 Maintenance of accounting, valuation and other records

(1) In the case of a company carrying on long-term business in whose case no stop order has been made, regulation 10 of the general regulations (financial records) applies only in relation to the company's other business.

(2) The liquidator of such company shall, with a view to the long-term business of the company being transferred to another insurer, maintain such accounting, valuation and other records as will enable such other insurer upon the transfer being effected to comply with the requirements of any rules made by the Authority under Part X of the 2000 Act relating to accounts and statements of insurers.

[2611]

17 Additional powers in relation to long-term business

(1) In the case of a company carrying on long-term business in whose case no stop order has been made, regulation 9 of the general regulations (investment or otherwise handling of funds in winding up of companies and payment of interest) applies only in relation to the company's other business.

(2) The liquidator of a company carrying on long-term business shall, so long as no stop order has been made, have power to do all such things as may be necessary to the performance of his duties under section 376(2) of the 2000 Act (continuation of contracts of long-term insurance where insurer in liquidation) but the Secretary of State may require him—

    (a)   not to make investments of a specified class or description,

    (b)   to realise, before the expiration of a specified period, the whole or a specified proportion of investments of a specified class or description held by the liquidator.

[2612]

18 Accounts and audit

(1) In the case of a company carrying on long-term business in whose case no stop order has been made, regulation 12 of the general regulations (liquidator carrying on business) applies only in relation to the company's other business.

(2) The liquidator of such a company shall supply the Secretary of State, at such times or intervals as he may specify, with such accounts as he may specify and audited in such manner as he may require and with such information about specified matters and verified in such specified manner as he may require.

(3) The liquidator of such a company shall, if required to do so by the Secretary of State, instruct at actuary to investigate the financial condition of the company's long-term business and to report thereon in such manner as the Secretary of State may specify.

[2613]

19 Security by the liquidator and special manager

In the case of a company carrying on long-term business in whose case no stop order has been made, rule 4.207 of the principal rules (security) applies separately to the company's long-term business and to its other business.

[2614]

20 Proof of debts

(1) This rule applies in the case of a company carrying on long-term business [in whose case no stop order has been made].

(2) The liquidator may in relation to the company's long-term business and to its other business fix different days on or before which the creditors of the company who are required to prove their debts or claims are to prove their debts or claims and he may fix one of those days without at the same time fixing the other.

(3) In submitting a proof of any debt a creditor may claim the whole or any part of such debt as attributable to the company's long-term business or to its other business or he may make no such attribution.

(4) When he admits any debt, in whole or in part, the liquidator shall state in writing how much of what he admits is attributable to the company's long-term business and how much to the company's other business.

[2615]

NOTES

Para (1): words in square brackets added by the Insurers (Reorganisation and Winding Up) Regulations 2003, SI 2003/1102, regs 52, 55, as from 20 April 2003.

---

21 Failure to pay premiums

(1) The liquidator may in the course of carrying on the company's long-term business and on such terms as he thinks fit accept payment of a premium even though the payment is tendered after the date on which under the terms of the policy it was finally due to be paid.

(2) The liquidator may in the course of carrying on the company's long-term business, and having regard to the general practice of insurers, compensate a policy holder whose policy has lapsed in consequence of a failure to pay any premium by issuing a free paid-up policy for reduced benefits or otherwise as the liquidator thinks fit.

[2616]

22 Notice of valuation of policy

(1) Before paying a dividend respect of claims other than under contracts of long-term insurance, the liquidator shall give notice of the value of each general business policy, as determined

by him in accordance with rule 6, to the persons appearing from the records of the company or otherwise to be entitled to an interest in that policy and he shall do so in such manner as the court may direct.

(2)　Before paying a dividend in respect of claims under contracts of long-term insurance and where a stop order has not been made in relation to the company, the liquidator shall give notice to the persons appearing from the records of the company or otherwise to be entitled to a payment under or to an interest in a long-term policy of the amount of that payment or the value of that policy as determined by him in accordance with rule 7(2) or (3), as the case may be.

(3)　If a stop order is made in relation to the company, the liquidator shall give notice to all the persons appearing from the records of the company or otherwise to be entitled to a payment under or to an interest in a long-term policy of the amount of that payment or the value of that policy as determined by him in accordance with rule 8(2) or (3), as the case may be, and he shall give that notice in such manner as the court may direct.

(4)　Any person to whom notice is so given shall be bound by the value so determined unless and until the court otherwise orders.

(5)　Paragraphs (2) and (3) of this rule have effect as though references therein to persons appearing to be entitled to an interest in a long-term policy and to the value of that policy included, respectively, references to persons appearing to be entitled to apply for a free paid-up policy under section 24 of the 1923 Act and to the value of that entitlement under rule 7 (in the case of paragraph (2) of this rule) or under rule 8 (in the case of paragraph (3) of this rule).

(6)　Where the liquidator summons a meeting of creditors in respect of liabilities of the company [attributable to either or both] its long-term business or other business, he may adopt any valuation carried out in accordance with rules 6, 7 or 8 as the case may be or, if no such valuation has been carried out by the time of the meeting, he may conduct the meeting using such estimates of the value of policies as he thinks fit.

[2617]

NOTES

　Para (6): words in square brackets substituted by the Insurers (Reorganisation and Winding Up) Regulations 2003, SI 2003/1102, regs 52, 56, as from 20 April 2003.

23　Dividends to creditors

(1)　This rule applies in the case of a company carrying on long-term business.

(2)　Part II of the principal rules applies separately in relation to the two separate companies assumed for the purposes of rule 5 above.

(3)　The court may, at any time before the making of a stop order, permit a dividend to be declared and paid on such terms as thinks fit in respect only of debts which fell due to payment before the liquidation date or, in the case of claims under long-term policies, which have fallen due for payment on or after the liquidation date.

[2618]

24　Meetings of creditors

　[(1)　In the case of a company carrying on long-term business in whose case no stop order has been made, the creditors entitled to participate in creditors' meetings may be—
- (a)　in relation to the long-term business assets of the company, only those who are creditors in respect of liabilities attributable to the long-term business of the company; and
- (b)　in relation to the other business assets of the company, only those who are creditors in respect of liabilities attributable to the other business of the company.

(1A)　In a case where separate general meetings of the creditors are summoned by the liquidator pursuant to—
- (a)　paragraph (1) above; or
- (b)　[regulation 29 of the Insurers (Reorganisation and Winding Up) Regulations 2004] (composite insurers: general meetings of creditors),

chapter 8 of Part 4 and Part 8 of the principal rules apply to each such separate meeting.]

(2)　In relation to any such separate meeting—
- (a)　rule 4.61(3) of the principal rules (expenses of summoning meetings) has effect as if the reference therein to assets were a reference to the assets available under the above-mentioned Regulations for meeting the liabilities of the company owed to the creditors summoned to the meeting, and
- (b)　rule 4.63 of the principal rules (resolutions) applies as if the reference therein to value in relation to a creditor who is not, by virtue of rule 6, 7 or 8 above, required to prove his debt, were a reference to the value most recently notified to him under rule 22 above or, if the court has determined a different value in accordance with rule 22(4), as if it were a reference to that different value.

[(3)   In paragraph (1)—
"long-term business assets" means the assets representing the fund or funds maintained by the company in respect of its long-term business;
"other business assets" means any assets of the company which are not long-term business assets.]

[2619]

NOTES
Para (1): substituted, together with para (1A) for original para (1), by the Insurers (Reorganisation and Winding Up) Regulations 2003, SI 2003/1102, regs 52, 57(1), (2), as from 20 April 2003.
Para (1A): substituted as noted above; words in square brackets in sub-para (b) substituted by the Insurers (Reorganisation and Winding Up) Regulations 2004, SI 2004/353, reg 51(1), (2), as from 18 February 2004 (as amended by the Insurers (Reorganisation and Winding Up) (Amendment) Regulations 2004, SI 2004/546, reg 2(6), as from 3 March 2004 (note that this amendment corrected a drafting error in SI 2004/353)).
Para (3): added by SI 2003/1102, regs 52, 57(1), (3), as from 20 April 2003.

25   Remuneration of liquidator carrying on long-term business

(1)   So long as no stop order has been made in relation to a company carrying on long-term business, the liquidator is entitled to receive remuneration for his services as such in relation to the carrying on of that business provided for in this rule.

(2)   The remuneration shall be fixed by the liquidation committee by reference to the time properly given by the liquidator and his staff in attending to matters arising in the winding up.

(3)   If there is no liquidation committee or the committee does not make the requisite determination, the liquidator's remuneration may be fixed (in accordance with paragraph (2)) by a resolution of a meeting of creditors.

(4)   If not fixed as above, the liquidator's remuneration shall be in accordance with the scale laid down for the Official Receiver by the general regulations.

(5)   If the liquidator's remuneration has been fixed by the liquidation committee, and the liquidator considers the amount to be insufficient, he may request that it be increased by resolution of the creditors.

[2620]

26   Apportionment of costs payable out of the assets

(1)   [Where no stop order has been made in relation to a company, rule 4.218] of the principal rules (general rule as to priority) applies separately to the assets of the company's long-term business and to the assets of the company's other business.

(2)   But where any fee, expense, cost, charge, disbursement or remuneration does not relate exclusively to the assets of the company's long-term business or to the assets of the company's other business, the liquidator shall apportion it amongst those assets in such manner as he shall determine.

[2621]

NOTES
Para (1): words in square brackets substituted by the Insurers (Reorganisation and Winding Up) Regulations 2003, SI 2003/1102, regs 52, 58(1), as from 20 April 2003.

27   Notice of stop order

(1)   When a stop order has been made in relation to the company, the court shall, on the same day send to the Official Receiver a notice informing him that the stop order has been made.

(2)   The notice shall be in Form No 1 set out in Schedule 6 with such variation as circumstances may require.

(3)   Three copies of the stop order sealed with the seal of the court shall forthwith be sent by the court to the Official Receiver.

(4)   The Official Receiver shall cause a sealed copy of the order to be served upon the liquidator by prepaid letter or upon such other person or persons, or in such other manner as the court may direct, and shall forward a copy of the order to the registrar of companies.

(5)   The liquidator shall forthwith on receipt of a sealed copy of the order—
   (a)   cause notice of the order in Form 2 set out in Schedule 6 to be gazetted, and
   (b)   advertise the making of the order in the newspaper in which the liquidation date was advertised, by notice in Form No 3 set out in Schedule 6.

[2622]

SCHEDULES

SCHEDULE 1
RULES FOR VALUING GENERAL BUSINESS POLICIES
Rule 6

1.—(1)   This paragraph applies in relation to periodic payments under a general business policy which fall due for payment after the liquidation date where the event giving rise to the liability to make the payments occurred before the liquidation date.

(2)   The value to be attributed to such periodic payments shall be determined on such actuarial principles and assumptions in regard to all relevant factors as the court shall direct.

2.—(1)   This paragraph applies in relation to liabilities under a general business policy which arise from events which occurred before the liquidation date but which have not—

    (a)   fallen due for payment before the liquidation date; or

    (b)   been notified to the company before the liquidation date.

(2)   The value to be attributed to such liabilities shall be determined on such actuarial principles and assumptions in regard to all relevant factors as the court shall direct.

3.—(1)   This paragraph applies in relation to liabilities under a general business policy not dealt with by paragraphs 1 or 2.

(2)   The value to be attributed to those liabilities shall—

    (a)   if the terms of the policy provide for a repayment of premium upon the early termination of the policy or the policy is expressed to run from one definite date to another or the policy may be terminated by any of the parties with effect from a definite date, be the greater of the following two amounts—

        (i)   the amount (if any) which under the terms of the policy would have been repayable on early termination of the policy had the policy terminated on the liquidation date, and

        (ii)   where the policy is expressed to run from one definite date to another or may be terminated by any of the parties with effect from a definite date, such proportion of the last premium paid as is proportionate to the unexpired portion of the period in respect of which that premium was paid; and

    (b)   in any other case, be a just estimate of that value.

[2623]

SCHEDULE 2
RULES FOR VALUING NON-LINKED LIFE POLICIES, NON-LINKED DEFERRED ANNUITY POLICIES, NON-LINKED ANNUITIES IN PAYMENT, UNITISED NON-LINKED POLICIES AND CAPITAL REDEMPTION POLICIES
Rule 7

1 General

In valuing a policy—

    (a)   where it is necessary to calculate the present value of future payments by or to the company, interest shall be assumed at such fair and reasonable rate or rates as the court may direct;

    (b)   where relevant, the rates of mortality and the rates of disability to be employed shall be such rates as the court considers appropriate after taking into account—

        (i)   relevant published tables of rates of mortality and rates of disability, and

        (ii)   the rates of mortality and the rates of disability experienced in connection with similar policies issued by the company;

    (c)   there shall be determined—

        (i)   the present value of the ordinary benefits,

        (ii)   the present value of additional benefits;

        (iii)   the present value of options, and

        (iv)   if further premiums fall to be paid under the policy on or after the liquidation date, the present value of the premiums;

and for the purposes of this Schedule if the ordinary benefits only take into account premiums paid to date, the present value of future premiums shall be taken as nil.

2 Present value of the ordinary benefits

(1)   Ordinary benefits are the benefits which will become payable to the policy holder on or after the liquidation date without his having to exercise any option under the policy (including any bonus or addition to the sum assured or the amount of annuity declared before the liquidation date) and for this purpose "option" includes a right to surrender the policy.

(2)   Subject to sub-paragraph (3), the present value of the ordinary benefits shall be the value at the liquidation date of the reversion in the ordinary benefits according to the contingency upon which those benefits are payable calculated on the basis of the rates of interest, mortality and disability referred to in paragraph 1.

(3)   For accumulating with profits policies—
  (a)   where the benefits are not expressed in the form of units in a with-profits fund, the value of the ordinary benefits is the amount that would have been payable, excluding any discretionary additions, if the policyholder had been able to exercise a right to terminate the policy at the liquidation date; and
  (b)   where the benefits are expressed in the form of units in a with-profits fund, the value of the ordinary benefits is the number of units held by the policy holder at the liquidation date valued at the unit price in force at that time or, if that price is not calculated on a daily basis, such price as the court may determine having regard to the last published unit price and any change in the value of assets attributable to the fund since the date of the last published unit price.

(4)   Where—
  (a)   sub-paragraph (3) applies, and
  (b)   paragraph 3(1) of Schedule 3 applies to the calculation of the unit price (or as the case may be) the fund value,
the value shall be adjusted on the basis set out in paragraph 3(3) to (5) of Schedule 3.

(5)   Where sub-paragraph (3) applies, the value may be further adjusted by reference to the value of the assets underlying the unit price (or as the case may be) the value of the fund, if the liquidator considers such an adjustment to be necessary.

3   Present value of additional benefits

(1)   Where under the terms of the policy or on the basis of the company's established practice the policy holder has a right to receive or an expectation of receiving benefits additional to the minimum benefits guaranteed under those terms, the court shall determine rates of interest, bonus (whether reversionary, terminal or any other type of bonus used by the company), mortality and disability to provide for the present value (if any) of that right or expectation.

(2)   In determining what (if any) value to attribute to any such expectations the court shall have regard to the premium payable in relation to the minimum guaranteed benefits and the amount (if any) an insurer is required to provide in respect of those expectations in any rules made by the Authority under Part X of the 2000 Act.

4   Present value of options

The amount of the present value of options shall be the amount which, in the opinion of the liquidator, is necessary to be provided at the liquidation date (in addition to the amount of the present value of the ordinary benefits) to cover the additional liabilities likely to arise upon the exercise on or after that date by the policy holder of any option conferred upon him by the terms of the policy or, in the case of an industrial assurance policy, by the Industrial Assurance Acts other than an option whereby the policy holder can secure a guaranteed cash payment within the period of 12 months beginning with that date.

5   Present value of premiums

The present value of the premiums shall be the value at the liquidation date of the premiums which fall due to be paid by the policy holder after the liquidation date calculated on the basis of the rates of interest, mortality and disability referred to in paragraph 1.

6   Value of the policy

(1)   Subject to sub-paragraph (2)—
  (a)   if no further premiums fall due to be paid under the policy on or after the liquidation date, the value of the policy shall be the aggregate of—
    (i)   the present value of the ordinary benefits;
    (ii)   the present value of options; and
    (iii) the present value of additional benefits;
  (b)   if further premiums fall due to be so paid and the aggregate value referred to in sub-paragraph (a) exceeds the present value of the premiums, the value of the policy shall be the amount of that excess; and
  (c)   if further premiums fall due to be so paid and that aggregate does not exceed the present value of the premiums, the policy shall have no value.

(2)   Where the policy holder has a right conferred upon him by the terms of the policy or by the Industrial Assurance Acts whereby the policy holder can secure a guaranteed cash payment within the period of 12 months beginning with the liquidation date, the liquidator shall determine the amount which in his opinion it is necessary to provide at that date to cover the liabilities which will

(2)   Where this paragraph applies the value of the policy shall be the greater of the following two amounts—

(a)   the value the policy would have had at the date of the stop order had the policy been a non-linked policy, that is to say, had the linked liabilities provided by the policy not been so provided but the policy had otherwise been on the same terms, and

(b)   the value the policy would have had at the date of the stop order had the policy not included any guarantees of payments on maturity or surrender worth a minimum amount calculable in money terms.

[2627]

SCHEDULE 6
FORMS

Rule 27

FORM NO 1

Notification to Official Receiver of order made under section 376(2) of the Financial Services and Markets Act 2000

(Title)

To the Official Receiver of the Court

(Address)

Order made this day by the Honourable Mr Justice .... (or, *as the case may be*) that the liquidator or (insert name of company) shall not carry on the long-term business of the company.

[2628]

FORM NO 2

Notice for London Gazette

Notice of order made under section 376(2) of the Financial Services and Markets Act 2000 for cessation of long-term business

Name of Company .... Address of Registered Office

Court .... Number of Matter .... Date of Order

Date of liquidation date

[2629]

FORM NO 3

Notice for Newspaper

Notice of order made under section 376(2) of the Financial Services and Markets Act 2000 for cessation of long-term business

Name of Company

Date of Liquidation date

Date of Order

[Liquidator]

[2630]

FINANCIAL SERVICES AND MARKETS ACT 2000 (MISLEADING STATEMENTS AND PRACTICES) ORDER 2001

(SI 2001/3645)

NOTES

Made: 9 November 2001.

Authority: Financial Services and Markets Act 2000, s 397(9), (10), (14).

Commencement: see art 1(2).

This Order is reproduced as amended by: the Financial Services and Markets Act 2000 (Commencement of Mortgage Regulation) (Amendment) Order 2002, SI 2002/1777; the Financial Services and Markets Act 2000 (Misleading Statements and Practices) (Amendment) Order 2003, SI 2003/1474; the Financial Services and Markets Act 2000 (Regulated Activities) (Amendment) (No 2) Order 2003, SI 2003/1476.

1   Citation and commencement

(1)   This order may be cited as the Financial Services and Markets Act 2000 (Misleading Statements and Practices) Order 2001.

(2) This Order comes into force—
    (a)   for the purposes of articles 3(b) and 4(b), on 1st January 2002;
    (b)   for the purposes of articles 3(c) and 4(c), [on such a day as the Treasury may specify];
    (c)   for all other purposes, on 1st December 2001.

[(3)   Any day specified under paragraph (2)(b) must be caused to be notified in the London, Edinburgh and Belfast Gazettes published not later than one week before that day.]

[2631]

NOTES
Para (2): words in square brackets substituted by the Financial Services and Markets Act 2000 (Commencement of Mortgage Regulation) (Amendment) Order 2002, SI 2002/1777, art 6(1), (2), as from 30 August 2002.
Para (3): added by SI 2002/1777, art 6(1), (3), as from 30 August 2002.

2 Interpretation

In this Order—
    "the Act" means the Financial Services and Markets Act 2000;
    ["contract of insurance" has the meaning given by article 3(1) of the Regulated Activities Order;]
    "controlled activity" means an activity which falls within Part I of Schedule 1 to the Financial Promotion Order other than an activity which falls within—
        (a)   [paragraph 9, 10, 10A or 10B] of that Schedule, or
        (b)   paragraph 11 so far as relating to [paragraph 9, 10, 10A or 10B];
    "controlled investment" means an investment which falls within Part II of Schedule 1 to the Financial Promotion Order other than an investment which falls within paragraph 25 or 26 of that Schedule;
    "the Financial Promotion Order" means the Financial Services and Markets Act 2000 (Financial Promotion) Order 2001;
    ["Regulated Activities Order" means the Financial Services and Markets Act 2000 (Regulated Activities) Order 2001].

[2632]

NOTES
Para (1): definitions "contract of insurance" and "Regulated Activities Order" inserted by the Financial Services and Markets Act 2000 (Regulated Activities) (Amendment) (No 2) Order 2003, SI 2003/1476, art 17(1), (2), as from 31 October 2004 (in so far as relating to contracts of long-term care insurance), and as from 14 January 2005 (otherwise) (for transitional provisions see arts 22–27 of that Order at **[2706]** et seq); in definition "controlled activity" words in square brackets substituted by the Financial Services and Markets Act 2000 (Misleading Statements and Practices) (Amendment) Order 2003, SI 2003/1474, art 2(1), (2), as from 31 October 2004.

3 Specified kinds of activity

The following kinds of activity are specified for the purposes of section 397(9)(a) of the Act—
    (a)   a controlled activity;
    (b)   an activity which falls within paragraph 9 (providing funeral plan contracts) of Schedule 1 to the Financial Promotion Order, or agreeing to carry on such an activity;
    (c)   an activity which falls within paragraph 10 (providing qualifying credit) of that Schedule, or agreeing to carry on such an activity;
    [(ca)   an activity which falls within paragraph 10A (arranging qualifying credit) or 10B (advising on qualifying credit) of that Schedule, or agreeing to carry on any such activity;]
    (d)   an activity of the kind specified by article 45 (sending dematerialised instructions), 51 (establishing etc a collective investment scheme), 52 (establishing etc a stakeholder pension scheme) or 57 (managing the underwriting capacity of a Lloyd's syndicate) of [the Regulated Activities Order];
    [(e)   (so far as not already specified by paragraph (a)), an activity of the kind specified by—
        (i)   article 14 of the Regulated Activities Order (dealing in investments as principal),
        (ii)   article 21 of that Order (dealing in investments as agent),
        (iii)   article 25(1) or (2) of that Order (arranging deals in investments),
        (iv)   article 39A of that Order (assisting in the administration and performance of a contract of insurance),
        (v)   article 53 of that Order (advising on investments), or
        (vi)   so far as relevant to any of those articles, article 64 of that Order (agreeing),
    so far as it relates to a contract of insurance].

[2633]

PART III
DISCLOSURE OF INFORMATION OBTAINED UNDER COMPANIES LEGISLATION

5 Information to which this Part applies

(1)   This Part applies to information disclosed after commencement to the Bank—
  (a)   under subsection (1) of section 449 of the Companies Act 1985, or
  (b)   under paragraph (1) of Article 442 of the Companies (Northern Ireland) Order 1986,

in its capacity as a competent authority under section 449(3) of that Act or Article 442(3) of that Order (as the case may be) ("companies information").

(2)   Subject to paragraphs (3) and (4), companies information may be disclosed in accordance with section 349 of the Act and the Disclosure Regulations as if—
  (a)   it were confidential information within the meaning of section 348(2) of the Act; and
  (b)   the Bank were a primary recipient of the information.

(3)   The Bank may disclose companies information in accordance with Part IV of the Disclosure Regulations only with—
  (a)   in the case of information disclosed as mentioned in paragraph (1)(a), the consent of the Secretary of State, or
  (b)   in the case of information disclosed as mentioned in paragraph (1)(b), the consent of the Department of Enterprise, Trade and Investment in Northern Ireland.

(4)   A person other than the Bank must not disclose such information under paragraph (2) except with the consent of—
  (a)   in the case of information disclosed as mentioned in paragraph (1)(a), the consent of the Secretary of State, or
  (b)   in the case of information disclosed as mentioned in paragraph (1)(b), the consent of the Department of Enterprise, Trade and Investment in Northern Ireland.

[2639]

PART IV
TRANSITIONAL PROVISIONS

6 Information supplied before commencement by an overseas regulatory authority

(1)   This article applies to information which fell within section 86(1) of the Banking Act 1987 and immediately before commencement was subject to restrictions on disclosure by virtue of section 82 of that Act, as those sections had effect by virtue of paragraph 57 of Schedule 5 to the 1998 Act ("transitional overseas regulatory information").

(2)   Subject to paragraphs (3) and (4), regulation 15 of the Disclosure Regulations (disclosure of transitional information) has effect in relation to transitional overseas regulatory information which the Bank holds after commencement as if the persons to be treated as a primary recipient by virtue of paragraph (3)(a) of that regulation included the Bank in relation to such information.

(3)   Transitional overseas regulatory information which fell within section 86(1)(a) of the Banking Act 1987 and was supplied by an EEA regulatory authority is to be treated for the purposes of the Disclosure Regulations as single market directive information (within the meaning of those Regulations).

(4)   Transitional overseas regulatory information which fell within section 86(1)(b) of the Banking Act 1987 is to be treated for the purposes of the Disclosure Regulations as single market directive information which is obtained in the course of an on-the-spot verification of the kind referred to in [Article 43] of the banking consolidation directive.

(5)   For the purposes of this article, references in Part III of the Disclosure Regulations (disclosure of single market directive information) to the Authority are to be treated as including the Bank.

[2640]

NOTES
  Para (4): words in square brackets substituted by the Capital Requirements Regulations 2006, SI 2006/3221, reg 29(4), Sch 6, para 11, as from 1 January 2007.

7 Companies information supplied before commencement

(1)   This article applies to information ("transitional companies information")—
  (a)   disclosed before commencement to the Bank under section 449(1) of the Companies Act 1985, or under Article 442(1) of the Companies (Northern Ireland) Order 1986, in its capacity as a competent authority under section 449(3) of that Act or Article 442(3) of that Order (as the case may be); and
  (b)   which immediately before commencement was subject to any of the powers of disclosure conferred by subsection (2) or (3) of section 87 of the Banking Act 1987, as that section had effect by virtue of paragraph 59 of Schedule 5 to the 1998 Act.

(2) Subject to paragraphs (3) and (4), transitional companies information may be disclosed in accordance with section 349 of the Act and the Disclosure Regulations as if—

    (a) it were confidential information within the meaning of section 348(2) of the Act; and

    (b) the Bank were a primary recipient of the information.

(3) The Bank may disclose transitional companies information in accordance with Part IV of the Disclosure Regulations only with the consent of—

    (a) in the case of information of the kind mentioned in paragraph (1)(a), the Secretary of State, or

    (b) in the case of information of the kind mentioned in paragraph (1)(b), the Department of Enterprise, Trade and Investment in Northern Ireland.

(4) A person other than the Bank must not disclose such information under paragraph (2) except with the consent of—

    (a) in the case of information disclosed as mentioned in paragraph (1)(a), the Secretary of State, or

    (b) in the case of information disclosed as mentioned in paragraph (1)(b), the Department of Enterprise, Trade and Investment in Northern Ireland.

[2641]

8 Information supplied before commencement by the Building Societies Commission

(1) This article applies to information ("transitional building societies information")—

    (a) disclosed before commencement by the Building Societies Commission to the Bank for the purpose of enabling or assisting the Bank to discharge its relevant functions; and

    (b) which immediately before commencement was subject to the powers of disclosure conferred by section 87(3A) of the Banking Act 1987, as that section had effect by virtue of paragraph 59 of Schedule 5 to the 1998 Act.

(2) Transitional building societies information may be disclosed in accordance with section 349 of the Act and the Disclosure Regulations as if—

    (a) it were confidential information within the meaning of section 348(2) of the Act; and

    (b) the Bank were a primary recipient of the information.

[2642]

FINANCIAL SERVICES AND MARKETS ACT 2000 (MISCELLANEOUS PROVISIONS) ORDER 2001

(SI 2001/3650)

NOTES

Made: 9 November 2001.

Authority: Financial Services and Markets Act 2000, ss 21(5), (9), (10), 235(5), 327(6), 426–428, Sch 2, para 25.

Commencement: see art 1 at **[2643]**.

This Order is reproduced as amended by: the Financial Services and Markets Act 2000 (Scope of Permission Notices) Order 2001, SI 2001/3771; the Financial Services and Markets Act 2000 (Commencement of Mortgage Regulation) (Amendment) Order 2002, SI 2002/1777; the Financial Services and Markets Act 2000 (Financial Promotion) Order 2005, SI 2005/1529.

ARRANGEMENT OF ARTICLES

PART I
GENERAL

PART III
MISCELLANEOUS PROVISIONS

PART I
GENERAL

1   Citation and commencement

[(1)]   This Order may be cited as the Financial Services and Markets Act 2000 (Miscellaneous Provisions) Order 2001 and comes into force—

(a)   save as provided for in paragraph (b), on 1st December 2001;

(b)   for the purposes of article 3, [on such a day as the Treasury may specify].

[(2)   Any day specified under paragraph (1)(b) must be caused to be notified in the London, Edinburgh and Belfast Gazettes published not later than one week before that day.]

[2643]

NOTES

Para (1): numbered as such, and words in square brackets in sub-para (b) substituted, by the Financial Services and Markets Act 2000 (Commencement of Mortgage Regulation) (Amendment) Order 2002, SI 2002/1777, art 7(1)–(3), as from 30 August 2002.

Para (2): added by SI 2002/1777, art 7(1), (4), as from 30 August 2002.

2–12   *(Pt II (arts 2–12) contains amendments only. Art 2 amends the Financial Services and Markets Act 2000 (Collective Investment Schemes) Order 2001, SI 2001/1062, Schedule at* **[2205]***; art 3 amends the Financial Services and Markets Act 2000 (Professions) (Non-Exempt Activities) Order 2001, SI 2001/1227, arts 1, 4 at* **[2226]***,* **[2229]** *and inserts art 6B at* **[2235]** *(note that this was originally inserted as art 6A but has subsequently been renumbered); arts 4, 5 revoked by the Financial Services and Markets Act 2000 (Financial Promotion) Order 2005, SI 2005/1529, art 74, Sch 6, as from 1 July 2005; arts 6–10 amend the Financial Services and Markets Act 2000 (Transitional Provisions) (Authorised Persons etc) Order 2001, SI 2001/2636; arts 11, 12 amend the Financial Services and Markets Act 2000 (Transitional Provisions) (Controllers) Order 2001, SI 2001/2637.)*

PART III
MISCELLANEOUS PROVISIONS

13   Interpretation

(1)   In this Part—

"the 2BCD Regulations" means the Banking Coordination (Second Council Directive) Regulations 1992;

"the Act" means the Financial Services and Markets Act 2000;

"the Authorised Persons Order" means the Financial Services and Markets Act 2000 (Transitional Provisions) (Authorised Persons etc) Order 2001;

"the Banking Act" means the Banking Act 1987;

"the Building Societies Act" means the Building Societies Act 1986;

"commencement" means the beginning of 1 December 2001;

"the Financial Services Act" means the Financial Services Act 1986;

"the Friendly Societies Act" means the Friendly Societies Act 1992;

"the Insurance Companies Act" means the Insurance Companies Act 1982;

"the ISD Regulations" means the Investment Services Regulations 1995.

(2)   In this Part, any reference to a section or Schedule is, unless the context otherwise requires, a reference to that section of or Schedule to the Act.

[2644]

14   Winding up of persons previously authorised under the Financial Services Act etc

(1)   This article applies in the case of a body of a kind mentioned in section 367(1) (winding-up petitions) which was, immediately before commencement, an authorised person or appointed representative (in each case within the meaning of the Financial Services Act) to whom section 72(1) of that Act applied.

(2)   In such a case, subsection (5) of section 367 has effect as if it provided for "agreement" to include (in addition to such an agreement as is mentioned in that subsection) any investment agreement, within the meaning of the Financial Services Act.

[2645]

15   Winding up of persons previously authorised under the Banking Act

(1)   This article applies in the case of a body of a kind mentioned in section 367(1) which was, immediately before commencement, an authorised institution within the meaning of the Banking Act.

(2)   Such a body is to be treated for the purpose of section 367(3)(a) as unable to pay its debts if it is in default on an obligation to pay a sum due and payable in respect of a deposit.

(3)   In paragraph (2), "deposit" has the meaning given by section 5 of the Banking Act except that it includes any sum which would otherwise be excluded from that meaning by paragraph (a), (b) or (e) of subsection (3) of that section.

(4)   This article does not affect the application of section 367(4) and (5).

[2646]

16   The Rehabilitation of Offenders Act 1974

(1)   Notwithstanding—
  (a)   any repeal of section 189 of, or Part I of Schedule 14 to, the Financial Services Act;
  (b)   any repeal of section 95(2) of the Banking Act;
  (c)   any amendment or revocation of article 5(2) of, or paragraph 8 of Schedule 3 to, the Rehabilitation of Offenders Act 1974 (Exceptions) Order 1975 which comes into force on or after commencement,

those provisions continue to have effect in relation to any proceedings which are specified in those provisions, whether or not those proceedings have been initiated before commencement, as if they had not been repealed, amended or revoked (as the case may be).

(2)   In paragraph (1), "proceedings" means proceedings before a judicial authority within the meaning of section 4(6) of the Rehabilitation of Offenders Act 1974.

[2647]

17   Disqualification of members of the Financial Services Tribunal

Notwithstanding—
  (a)   paragraphs 1(a), 2(a) and 7(3)(a) of Schedule 20 (which omit provisions in the House of Commons Disqualifications Act 1975, the Northern Ireland Assembly Disqualification Act 1975 and the Judicial Pensions and Retirement Act 1993 relating to the Financial Services Tribunal), and
  (b)   the corresponding repeals in Schedule 22,

the provisions so omitted continue to have effect for so long as the Financial Services Tribunal continues to have functions conferred by or under any enactment.

[2648]

18   Duty of auditors to communicate matters to the Authority

(1)   Notwithstanding any repeal of the enactments specified by paragraph (2), those enactments, and any rules, regulations or orders made under those enactments in force immediately before commencement, continue to have effect in relation to any matter of which an auditor becomes aware in his capacity as an auditor that relates to things done (or not done) before commencement, subject to the modifications in paragraph (4) and, where relevant, paragraph (3).

(2)   The enactments specified by this paragraph are—
  (a)   section 109 of the Financial Services Act (communication by auditor with Authority), to the extent that it relates to the obligation to communicate a matter;
  (b)   section 47 of the Banking Act (communication by auditor with the Authority), to the extent that it relates to the obligation to communicate a matter;
  (c)   section 21A of the Insurance Companies Act (communication by auditor), to the extent that it relates to the obligation to communicate a matter;
  (d)   section 82(8) to (11) of the Building Societies Act (auditors' duties to Commission), to the extent that it relates to the obligation to furnish information; and
  (e)   section 79(8) to (11) of the Friendly Societies Act (auditors' duties to Commission), to the extent that it relates to the obligation to furnish information.

(3)   For each reference to the Secretary of State, the Treasury, the Building Societies Commission or the Friendly Societies Commission, there is substituted a reference to the Authority (and so any communication made pursuant to those enactments must be made to the Authority).

(4)   Where an enactment specified by paragraph (2) refers to an auditor of a person ("A") who has a particular status, that enactment applies after commencement as if that reference was to A having that status immediately before commencement.

[2649]

19   Reports under the Financial Services Act and the Banking Act

(1)   The first report of the Authority made under paragraph 10(1) of Schedule 1 must include the last Financial Services Act report and the last Banking Act report.

(2)   The "last Financial Services Act report" is the report, in respect of the year during which commencement occurs, which the Authority would be required by section 117(1) of the Financial Services Act to make, but for the repeal of that section.

(3)   The "last Banking Act report" is a report on the Authority's activities under the Banking Act during the financial year (within the meaning of section 1(3) of that Act) during which commencement occurs.

[2650]

20   Report under the Insurance Companies Act

(1)   Notwithstanding any repeal of section 98 of the Insurance Companies Act (annual report by the Treasury), the Treasury must, when they lay the first copy of the Authority's annual report in accordance with paragraph 10(3) of Schedule 1, lay before Parliament a general report of matters within the Insurance Companies Act that covers the relevant period.

(2)   In paragraph (1), the relevant period is the period from (but not including) the last day of the period to which the last report under section 98 of the Insurance Companies Act related to commencement.

[2651]

21   Transfer of property, rights and liabilities

(1)   The Authority must make a scheme under this article for the transfer to it of such of the property, rights and liabilities of each transferor body as appear to the Authority appropriate to be so transferred as a consequence of the Act coming into force.

(2)   Provided that the transferor body notifies the Authority of its agreement to the Scheme, the property, rights and liabilities of the transferor body to which a scheme under this article relates, shall on the date specified by the scheme (or, if different dates are specified in the scheme in relation to different property, rights or liabilities, on the relevant date specified by the scheme), by virtue of this article and without further assurance, be transferred to and vested in the Authority in accordance with the provisions of the scheme.

(3)   The property, rights and liabilities capable of being transferred in accordance with a scheme under this article may include property, rights and liabilities that would not otherwise be capable of being transferred or assigned by the transferor body.

(4)   A scheme made under this article may make such supplemental, consequential and transitional provision for the purposes of, or in connection with, any transfer of property, rights or liabilities for which the scheme provides or in connection with such other provisions contained in the scheme as the Authority considers appropriate.

(5)   Each of the following is a "transferor body" for the purposes of this article—
    (a)   the Personal Investment Authority Limited;
    (b)   the Investment Management Regulatory Organisation Limited;
    (c)   the Securities and Futures Authority Limited.

[2652]

22   Transfer of liabilities

(1)   Notwithstanding any term of any scheme made under article 21 any liability incurred by a transferor body as a result of an act or omission occurring before commencement is to be treated on and after commencement as a liability of the Authority.

(2)   The reference to liabilities in paragraph (1) and in article 21 does not include any liability transferred as a result of article 17 of the Financial Services and Markets Act 2000 (Transitional Provisions) (Ombudsman Scheme and Complaints Scheme) Order 2001.

[2653]

23   Legal proceedings

(1)   If, at commencement, a transferor body is a party to any legal proceedings the Authority is substituted for the transferor body in those proceedings.

(2)   Where legal proceedings for an injunction commenced under a provision of the Financial Services Act or the Banking Act are concluded on or after commencement, the court may, instead of granting an injunction restraining a contravention of the kind mentioned in that provision, grant an

PART III
STATUTORY INSTRUMENTS

injunction restraining (or in Scotland, an interdict prohibiting) such conduct as the court considers appropriate, having regard to any provision made by or under the Act.

(3) For the purposes of this article, "transferor body" has the same meaning as in article 21.

[2654]

24 Exemption from liability in damages

(1) Notwithstanding their repeal, the provisions mentioned in paragraph (2) continue to have effect—

    (a)   in relation to things done or omitted to be done before commencement, and

    (b)   in relation to anything done on or after commencement for the purposes of or in connection with any proceedings arising from anything done or omitted to be done before commencement.

(2) The provisions mentioned in this paragraph are—

    (a)   section 1(4) of the Banking Act (immunity in relation to things done or omitted in discharge of functions);

    (b)   section 43(5) of the Financial Services Act (listed money market institutions);

    (c)   section 187 of the Financial Services Act (exemption from liability for damages) (including as extended in relation to the Authority by regulation 56(1) of the ISD Regulations and in relation to the recognised self-regulating organisations by regulation 30 of the ISD Regulations);

    (d)   section 171(6A) of the Companies Act 1989 (certain money market institutions).

(3) Notwithstanding the revocation of the Financial Markets and Insolvency (Money Market) Regulations 1995, regulation 29 of those Regulations continues to have effect to the extent provided for by paragraph 20(5) of Schedule 1 to the Bank of England Act 1998 (Consequential Amendments to Subordinate Legislation) Order 1998.

(4) The reference in paragraph (2)(a) to section 1(4) of the Banking Act is a reference to that provision—

    (a)   as amended by paragraph 2 of Schedule 5 to the Bank of England Act 1998;

    (b)   as continued in effect without those amendments by paragraph 1 of Schedule 8 to that Act (but as if the references in paragraphs (1) above to "commencement" were to 1st June 1998); and

    (c)   as extended by paragraph 2 of Schedule 8 to the 2BCD Regulations.

(5) The Authority may rely on section 187(1) of the Financial Services Act in relation to any liability transferred to it by virtue of paragraph (1) of article 22 or of article 21 to the same extent as the transferor body from which the liability was transferred could have relied on it before commencement in relation to that liability.

(6) For the avoidance of doubt, the Authority's functions for the purposes of paragraph 19 of Schedule 1 (exemption from liability in damages) include any functions exercisable by the Authority after commencement as a result of any saving made by or under the Act from the effect of any repeal or revocation so made.

[2655]

25 Fees for the exercise of certain Authority functions

(1) For the purposes of paragraph 17 of Schedule 1 (fees) the following are to be treated as functions of the Authority under the Act—

    (a)   the Authority's functions under—

        (i)   the Financial Services Act (other than Part IV of that Act);

        (ii)   the Banking Act;

        (iii)   the 2BCD Regulations;

        (iv)   the ISD Regulations,

with respect to which the Authority incurs expenditure after commencement;

    (b)   any function exercisable by the Authority after commencement as a result of any saving made by or under the Act from the effect of any repeal or revocation so made.

(2) For the purposes of paragraph 17 of Schedule 1, expenditure incurred in meeting a liability transferred to the Authority by virtue of paragraph (1) of article 22 or of article 21 is to be treated as having been incurred in connection with the discharge by the Authority of functions under the Act.

(3) For the purposes of section 99(2), expenditure incurred in meeting a liability arising from the exercise by the Authority of its functions as the competent authority under Part IV of the Financial Services Act is to be treated as having been incurred in carrying out its functions as competent authority under Part VI of the Act.

[2656]

26 Fees under the Insurance Companies Act

(1) Any relevant authorised person who has not paid the final Insurance Companies Act fee must, by or on his final day, pay to the Authority his relevant pre-commencement fee.

(2)   By 26th April 2002—

   (a)   the Authority must inform the Treasury of the amount which it has received pursuant to paragraph (1) ("X"); and

   (b)   the Treasury must inform the Authority of the amount which they received before commencement as fees under the 2001 Fees Order ("Y").

(3)   On or before 31st December 2002—

   (a)   if two-thirds of X exceeds one third of Y, the Authority must pay the difference to the Treasury;

   (b)   if one third of Y exceeds two thirds of X, the Treasury must pay the difference to the Authority.

(4)   Any sum received by the Treasury under paragraph (3) must be paid into the Consolidated Fund.

(5)   In this article—

"the 2001 Fees Order" means the Insurance (Fees) Order 2001;

"final day", in relation to any person, means the day by which that person would have been required to deposit documents with the Treasury under section 22(1) of the Insurance Companies Act, but for the repeal of that Act;

"relevant authorised person" means an authorised person who was, immediately before commencement, authorised under section 3 or 4 of the Insurance Companies Act but was not an EC company (as defined by that Act);

"relevant pre-commencement fee", in relation to any person, means the amount which, had he deposited documents under section 22(1) of the Insurance Companies Act immediately before commencement, he would have been obliged to pay to the Treasury as a fee under the 2001 Fees Order.

(6)   For the purposes of this article, a person has paid the final Insurance Companies Act fee if he has, before commencement, paid to the Treasury a fee under the 2001 Fees Order.

(7)   This article applies notwithstanding any repeal of section 94A of the Insurance Companies Act or any revocation of the 2001 Fees Order.

[2657]

27   Fees in respect of the existing deficit

(1)   Before 30th April 2002 the Treasury must inform the Authority of an amount ("the relevant amount"), which must not exceed the existing deficit, for the purposes of this article.

(2)   The Authority must make rules providing for the payment to it in the transitional period by authorised persons who have Part IV permission to effect and carry out contracts of insurance of such fees as it considers will enable it to repay the relevant amount to the Treasury.

(3)   In making rules under paragraphs (2) for the first year of the transitional period, the Authority must have regard to the object of securing (so far as practicable) that the amount of fees payable in that year is equal to one half of the relevant amount.

(4)   On each of 31st July 2003 and 31st July 2004, the Authority must pay to the Treasury the sums that it has received by virtue of rules made under paragraph (2) in the relevant period which expires immediately before that date.

(5)   Any sums received by the Treasury pursuant to this article must be paid into the Consolidated Fund.

(6)   Nothing in this article affects the Authority's power to make rules under paragraph 17 of Schedule 1 (fees).

(7)   In this article—

"the existing deficit" means the cost incurred by the Treasury in exercising functions which were, when they were exercised, relevant functions for the purposes of subsection (6) of section 94A of the Insurance Companies Act, less the amount that the Treasury received before commencement as fees by virtue of orders made under that section and any amount that the Treasury receive (or are to receive) by virtue of article 26(3);

"the relevant period" is the period running from 1st July in one year to 30th June in the next year;

"transitional period" means the period from 1st July 2002 to 30th June 2004.

[2658]

28   The Contracting Out Order

(1)   The Contracting Out (Functions in Relation to Insurance) Order 1998 is revoked.

(2)   Notwithstanding paragraph (1), any contract made between the Treasury and the Authority that relates to the exercise of functions listed in the Schedule to that Order which is subsisting immediately before commencement, continues to have effect on and after commencement, to the extent that it relates to matters ancillary to the exercise of those functions including—

   (a)   payment; and

PART III
STATUTORY INSTRUMENTS

(b)   retention and inspection of documents.

(3)   Any obligation of the Authority under such a contract which continues to have effect after commencement is to be treated as a function conferred on the Authority by or under a provision of the Act for the purposes of Schedule 1.

(4)   The Authority must comply in a reasonable time with any direction that the Treasury give to it that relates to the conduct of relevant litigation or the handling of any proposal to initiate such litigation.

(5)   In paragraph (4), "relevant litigation" means any litigation that arises from or relates to the exercise of the functions listed in the Schedule to that Order by the Authority, whether or not the Authority is or the Treasury are a party.

[2659]

29 Correction of scope of permission notices as a result of this Order

(1)   This article applies where—
  (a)   the Authority has sent before commencement a scope of permission notice under article 55 of the Authorised Persons Order to a person who has a permission conferred on him at commencement as a result of article 6, 7, 8 or 9;
  (b)   that person has before commencement notified the Authority in accordance with article 56(1)(a) of that Order that he agrees with the matters stated in the notice;
  (c)   the Authority has, before commencement, sent to the person a notice ("revision notice") revising the scope of permission notice so that it includes the permission conferred on the person as a result of article 6, 7, 8 or 9 (as the case may be).

[(2)   Where this article applies if the person does not, on or before 4 January 2002, notify the Authority that he objects to the revision notice, then article 57(1) of the Authorised Persons Order applies as if—
  (a)   the reference to the scope of permission notice in that article were to the scope of permission notice as revised by the revision notice; and
  (b)   the person had agreed to that notice as so revised.

(3)   If the person notifies the Authority on or before 4 January 2002 that he objects to the revision notice, then article 57(1) of the Authorised Persons Order applies as if the revision notice had not been sent.]

[2660]

NOTES
Paras (2), (3): substituted by the Financial Services and Markets Act 2000 (Scope of Permission Notices) Order 2001, SI 2001/3771, art 5(1), (2), as from 1 December 2001.

30 Correction of scope of permission notices for PIA firms

(1)   This article applies where—
  (a)   the Authority has sent, before commencement, a scope of permission notice under article 55 of the Authorised Persons Order to a person who, at the time the notice was sent, was a member of the Personal Investment Authority Limited;
  (b)   that person has before commencement notified the Authority in accordance with article 56(1)(a) of that Order that he agrees with the matters stated in the notice;
  (c)   the scope of permission notice thereby agreed purported to provide for the person to have a permission to agree to carry on all regulated activities so far as carried on in respect of an investment of the kind specified by article 76 of the Regulated Activities Order (shares etc) and in relation to an "intermediate customer";
  (d)   the Authority has, before commencement, sent to the firm a notice ("a revision notice") revising the scope of permission notice so that it states that the person has permission to agree to carry on any regulated activity which the scope of permission notice states that he has a Part IV permission to carry on (in so far as agreeing to carry on that activity itself constitutes, by virtue of article 64 of the Regulated Activities Order, a regulated activity).

[(2)   Where this article applies if the person does not, on or before 4 January 2002, notify the Authority that he objects to the revision notice, then article 57(1) of the Authorised Persons Order applies as if—
  (a)   the reference to the scope of permission notice in that article were to the scope of permission notice as revised by the revision notice; and
  (b)   the person had agreed to that notice as so revised.

(3)   If the person notifies the Authority on or before 4 January 2002 that he objects to the revision notice, then article 57(1) of the Authorised Persons Order applies as if the revision notice had not been sent.]

(4)   For the purpose of this article "the Regulated Activities Order" means the Financial Services and Markets Act 2000 (Regulated Activities) Order 2001.

[2661]

NOTES
Paras (2), (3): substituted by the Financial Services and Markets Act 2000 (Scope of Permission Notices) Order 2001, SI 2001/3771, art 5(1), (3), as from 1 December 2001.

FINANCIAL SERVICES AND MARKETS ACT 2000 (SCOPE OF PERMISSION NOTICES) ORDER 2001

(SI 2001/3771)

NOTES
Made: 26 November 2001.
Authority: Financial Services and Markets Act 2000, ss 426–428.
Commencement: 1 December 2001.

As of 1 February 2009, this Order had not been amended.

1   Citation, commencement and interpretation

(1)   This Order may be cited as the Financial Services and Markets Act 2000 (Scope of Permission Notices) Order 2001 and comes into force on 1st December 2001.

(2)   In this Order—
"the Act" means the Financial Services and Markets Act 2000;
"the Authorised Persons Order" means the Financial Services and Markets Act 2000 (Transitional Provisions) (Authorised Persons etc) Order 2001;
"commencement" means the beginning of 1st December 2001;
"the Regulated Activities Order" means the Financial Services and Markets Act 2000 (Regulated Activities) Order 2001.

[2662]

2   Revision of scope of permission notices

(1)   This article applies where—
(a)   the Authority has given, before commencement, a scope of permission notice under article 55 of the Authorised Persons Order;
(b)   that notice falls within one of the cases specified in article 3;
(c)   the recipient of the notice has, before commencement, notified the Authority in accordance with article 56(1)(a) of the Authorised Persons Order that he agrees with the matters stated in the notice;
(d)   the Authority has, before commencement, given that recipient a notice ("the revision notice") revising the scope of permission notice in a permitted manner.

(2)   If the recipient of the scope of permission notice does not, on or before 4 January 2002, notify the Authority that he objects to the revision notice, then article 57(1) of the Authorised Persons Order applies as if—
(a)   the reference to the scope of permission notice in that article were to the scope of permission notice as revised by the revision notice; and
(b)   the person has agreed to that notice as so revised.

(3)   If the recipient of the scope of permission notice notifies the Authority on or before 4 January 2002 that he objects to the revision notice, then article 57(1) of the Authorised Persons Order applies as if the revision notice had not been sent.

[2663]

3   Cases in which scope of permission notices may be revised

The cases specified in this article are as follows—

Case 1

Where—
(a)   the recipient of the scope of permission notice was, at the time the notice was sent, an authorised person within the meaning of the Financial Services Act 1986;
(b)   that person is to be treated, by virtue of Part II of the Authorised Persons Order, as having a Part IV permission to carry on a regulated activity of the kind specified by

**PART III
STATUTORY INSTRUMENTS**

article 14 of the Regulated Activities Order (dealing in investments as principal) in so far as the activity consists of his entering into a transaction relating to contractually based investments;

(c)   the person is not subject, by virtue of Part III of the Authorised Persons Order, to a requirement imposed under section 43 of the Act preventing him from carrying on the regulated activity in paragraph (b); and

(d)   the scope of permission notice did not specify that the person had a Part IV permission to carry on the regulated activity in paragraph (b).

Case 2

Where—

(a)   the recipient of the scope of permission notice was, at the time the notice was sent, a member of the Personal Investment Authority Limited;

(b)   the scope of permission notice specified that he had a Part IV permission to carry on a regulated activity of the kind specified by article 53 of the Regulated Activities Order (advising on investments) in relation to a particular specified kind of investment ("investment A");

(c)   the person is to be treated, by virtue of Part II of the Authorised Persons Order, as having a Part IV permission to carry on that regulated activity also in relation to rights to or interests in (within the meaning of activity 89 of the Regulated Activities Order) investment A;

(d)   the person is not subject, by virtue of Part III of the Authorised Persons Order, to a requirement imposed under section 43 of the Act preventing him from carrying on that regulated activity in relation to rights to or interests in investment A; and

(e)   the scope of permission notice did not specify that he had a Part IV permission to carry on that regulated activity in relation to rights to or interests in investment A.

Case 3

Where—

(a)   the scope of permission notice specified that the recipient of the notice has a Part IV permission to carry on a regulated activity in relation to a particular specified kind of investment ("investment B"); and

(b)   the scope of permission notice purported also to specify that he had permission to carry on that regulated activity in relation to rights to and interests in investments generally rather than only in relation to rights to or interests in investment B.

Case 4

Where—

(a)   the recipient of the scope of permission notice was, at the time the notice was sent, a member of either the Investment Management Regulatory Organisation Limited or the Personal Investment Authority Limited;

(b)   the scope of permission notice specified that he had a Part IV permission to carry on a regulated activity of the kind specified by article 40 of the Regulated Activities Order (safeguarding and administering investments);

(c)   the scope of permission notice also specified that he was subject to a requirement under section 43 of the Act that he should not hold or control client money; and

(d)   the person is not subject, by virtue of Part III of the Authorised Persons Order, to that requirement.

Case 5

Where—

(a)   the recipient of the scope of permission notice was, at the time the notice was sent, a member of either the Investment Management Regulatory Organisation Limited or the Personal Investment Authority Limited;

(b)   the scope of permission notice specified that he had a Part IV permission to carry on a regulated activity of the kind specified by either article 51 of the Regulated Activities Order (establishing etc a collective investment scheme) or article 52 of that Order (establishing etc a stakeholder pension scheme);

(c)   the scope of permission notice purported to limit that permission to carrying on the activity in relation to a specified kind of investment; and

(d)   the Part IV permission that the person is to be treated as having by virtue of Parts II and III of the Authorised Persons Order is not subject to that limitation.

Case 6

Where—
(a)   the recipient of the scope of permission notice was, at the time the notice was sent, a member of the Investment Management Regulatory Organisation Limited;
(b)   the scope of permission notice specified that he had a Part IV permission to carry on a regulated activity of the kind specified by article 21 of the Regulated Activities Order (dealing in investments as agent) for the purpose of stock lending activities;
(c)   the scope of permission notice purported further to limit his permission so that he could not carry on that activity in relation to investments of the kind specified by article 78 of the Regulated Activities Order (government and public securities); and
(d)   the Part IV permission that the person is to be treated as having by virtue of Parts II and III of the Authorised Persons Order is not subject to that limitation.

[2664]

4   Permitted revisions

For the purposes of article 2(1)(d), a revision notice revises the scope of permission notice in a permitted manner if—
(a)   in Case 1 in article 3, it results in the scope of permission notice specifying that the recipient has a Part IV permission to carry on the regulated activities described in paragraph (b) of that Case;
(b)   in Case 2 in article 3, it results in the scope of permission notice specifying that the recipient has a Part IV permission to carry on the regulated activity described in paragraph (c) of that Case;
(c)   in Case 3 in article 3, it results in the scope of permission notice specifying that his Part IV permission to carry on a particular regulated activity in relation to rights to or interests in investments is limited to rights to or interests in investment B (as defined in that Case);
(d)   in Case 4 in article 3, it results either in the lifting of the requirement that the recipient should not control client money or in the lifting of the requirement that he should not hold or control client money;
(e)   in Case 5 in article 3, it results in the removal of the limitation described in paragraph (c) of that Case;
(f)   in Case 6 in article 3, it results in the removal of the limitation described in paragraph (c) of that Case;
(g)   in any Case in article 3, it results in the scope of permission notice specifying that the recipient has a Part IV permission to carry on a regulated activity of the kind specified by article 64 of the Regulated Activities Order (agreeing to carry on specified kinds of activity) to the extent appropriate having regard to paragraphs (a) to (f) above.

[2665]

5   (*Substitutes the Financial Services and Markets Act 2000* (*Miscellaneous Provisions*) *Order 2001, SI 2001/3650, arts 29(2), (3), 30(2), (3) at* **[2660]**, **[2661]**.)

FINANCIAL SERVICES AND MARKETS ACT 2000 (REGULATED ACTIVITIES) (AMENDMENT) ORDER 2002

(SI 2002/682)

NOTES
Made: 14 March 2002.
Authority: Financial Services and Markets Act 2000, ss 22(1), (5), 428(3), Sch 2, para 25.
Commencement: 11 April 2002 (for certain purposes); 27 April 2002 (otherwise).
This Order is reproduced as amended by: the Capital Requirements Regulations 2006, SI 2006/3221.

PART I
PRELIMINARY

1   Citation, commencement and interpretation

(1)   This Order may be cited as the Financial Services and Markets Act 2000 (Regulated Activities) (Amendment) Order 2002.

(2)   This Order comes into force—
(a)   on 11th April 2002, for the purpose of making rules under articles 9G and 9H of the principal Order (as inserted by article 4 of this Order);
(b)   on 27th April 2002, for all other purposes.

(3)   In this Order—
    (a)   "the Act" means the Financial Services and Markets Act 2000;
    (b)   "the principal Order" means the Financial Services and Markets Act 2000 (Regulated Activities) Order 2001.

        [2666]

PART II
ELECTRONIC MONEY

2–6   (*Amend the Financial Services and Markets Act 2000 (Regulated Activities) Order 2001, SI 2001/544, arts 3, 5, 64 at* **[2012]**, **[2014]**, **[2102]**, *insert arts 9A–9K, 74A at* **[2019]**–**[2030]**, **[2119]**.)

Supplemental and transitional provisions

7, 8   (*Amend the Financial Services and Markets Act 2000 (Professions) (Non-Exempt Activities) Order 2001, SI 2001/1227, arts 4, 8 at* **[2229]**, **[2237]**, *and the Financial Services and Markets Act 2000, Sch 6 at* **[472]**.)

9   Transitional provisions for persons issuing electronic money at commencement

(1)   Where, immediately before commencement, a credit institution with Part IV permission to accept deposits was carrying on by way of business in the United Kingdom the activity of issuing electronic money, the institution's permission is to be treated as including, for a period of six months beginning at commencement, permission to carry on an activity of the kind specified by article 9B of the principal Order.

(2)   Where, immediately before commencement—
    (a)   an EEA firm of the kind mentioned in paragraph 5(b) or (c) of Schedule 3 to the Act qualified for authorisation under that Schedule, and
    (b)   the activities which were treated as permitted activities for the purposes of paragraph 13 or 14 of that Schedule as it applied to that firm included the issuing of electronic money,
the firm's permission under paragraph 15 of that Schedule is to be treated, at commencement, as including permission to carry on that activity.

(3)   Where an existing issuer having his head office in the United Kingdom is, after commencement, granted a Part IV permission to carry on an activity of the kind specified by article 9B (and hence becomes a UK firm, within the meaning of Schedule 3 to the Act, in relation to that activity)—
    (a)   if, immediately before commencement, the existing issuer was carrying on the activity of issuing electronic money from a branch established in another EEA State, the conditions in paragraph 19(2) to (5) of that Schedule are to be treated as satisfied with respect to that branch;
    (b)   if, immediately before commencement, the existing issuer was carrying on the activity of issuing electronic money by providing services in another EEA State, the conditions in paragraph 20(1) of that Schedule are to be treated as satisfied with respect to the provision of those services in that EEA State.

(4)   An existing issuer having his head office in an EEA State other than the United Kingdom who, after commencement, becomes authorised (within the meaning of [Article 4(2)] of the banking consolidation directive) by his home state regulator (and hence becomes an EEA firm)—
    (a)   is to be treated as having complied with the establishment conditions (within the meaning of paragraph 13 of Schedule 3 to the Act) where, immediately before commencement, he was carrying on the activity of issuing electronic money from a branch established in the United Kingdom;
    (b)   is to be treated as having complied with the service conditions (within the meaning of paragraph 14 of that Schedule) where, immediately before commencement, he was carrying on the activity of issuing electronic money by providing services in the United Kingdom.

(5)   Where paragraph (4)(a) or (b) applies, the existing issuer is to be treated as having permission to carry on the activity mentioned in that paragraph through its United Kingdom branch or (as the case may be) by providing services in the United Kingdom.

(6)   There is excluded from article 9B of the principal Order any activity carried on by an existing issuer before 27th October 2002, unless he has been granted a Part IV permission to carry on that activity, or has permission to carry on that activity as a result of paragraph (5).

(7)   There is also excluded from article 9B of the principal Order any activity carried on by an existing issuer after the beginning of 27th October 2002, provided—
    (a)   he has made an application before 27th June 2002 under section 40 of the Act for permission to carry on that activity, and has not withdrawn it; and

   (b)   the application has not been finally determined.

(8)   For the purposes of paragraph (7), an application is to be treated as finally determined—

   (a)   in a case where the Authority gives permission to carry on the activity and does not exercise its power under section 42(7)(a) or (b) or section 43(1) of the Act, on the date on which the permission takes effect;

   (b)   in a case where the Authority refuses permission, or gives permission but exercises its power under section 42(7)(a) or (b) or section 43 of the Act, at the time when the matter ceases to be open to review (within the meaning of section 391(8) of the Act).

(9)   In this article—

   (a)   "commencement" means the beginning of 27th April 2002;

   (b)   "credit institution" means a credit institution as defined in [Article 4(1)(a)] of the banking consolidation directive;

   (c)   an "existing issuer" means a body corporate or partnership (other than one falling within paragraph (1) or (2)) which, immediately before commencement—

      (i)   has its head office in the United Kingdom, and is carrying on by way of business in the United Kingdom the activity of issuing electronic money; or

      (ii)   has its head office in an EEA State other than the United Kingdom, and is carrying on such an activity by way of business in the United Kingdom without contravening the law of that other EEA State;

   (d)   in paragraph (1) and in sub-paragraph (c) of this paragraph, the references to carrying on an activity in the United Kingdom are to be construed without reference to section 418 of the Act (carrying on regulated activities in the United Kingdom).

[2667]

NOTES

Paras (4), (9): words in square brackets substituted by the Capital Requirements Regulations 2006, SI 2006/3221, reg 29(4), Sch 6, para 13, as from 1 January 2007.

10 Anticipatory consultation on rules

If—

   (a)   before 11th April 2002 any steps were taken in relation to a draft of rules which the Authority proposes to make under article 9G(1) or 9H of the principal Order (as inserted by article 4 of this Order), and

   (b)   those steps, had they been taken after that day, would to any extent have satisfied the requirements of section 155 of the Act,

those requirements are to that extent to be taken to have been satisfied.

[2668]

11–13 ((*Pt III*) *amend the Financial Services and Markets Act 2000 (Regulated Activities) Order 2001, SI 2001/544, arts 4, 9, 45, 46, 49 and 69 at* **[2013]**, **[2018]**, **[2075]**, **[2076]**, **[2079]**, **[2107]**.)

FINANCIAL SERVICES AND MARKETS ACT 2000 (ADMINISTRATION ORDERS RELATING TO INSURERS) ORDER 2002

(SI 2002/1242)

NOTES

Made: 2 May 2002.

Authority: Financial Services and Markets Act 2000, ss 355(2), 360, 426, 428(3).

Commencement: 31 May 2002.

This Order is reproduced as amended by: the Financial Services and Markets Act 2000 (Administration Orders Relating to Insurers) (Amendment) Order 2003, SI 2003/2134; the Insurers (Reorganisation and Winding Up) Regulations 2004, SI 2004/353.

1 Citation, commencement and interpretation

(1)   This Order may be cited as the Financial Services and Markets Act 2000 (Administration Orders Relating to Insurers) Order 2002 and comes into force on 31st May 2002.

(2)   In this Order—

"the 1986 Act" means the Insolvency Act 1986;

["initial creditors' meeting" has the meaning given by paragraph 51(1) of Schedule B1;
"Schedule B1" means Schedule B1 to the 1986 Act.]

[2669]

NOTES
Para (2): definitions "initial creditors' meeting" and "Schedule B1" substituted for original definition
"section 23 meeting" by the Financial Services and Markets Act 2000 (Administration Orders Relating to
Insurers) (Amendment) Order 2003, SI 2003/2134, arts 2, 3, as from 15 September 2003, except in relation to
any case where a petition for an administration order has been presented to the court before that date.

2 (*Amends the Financial Services and Markets Act 2000 (Insolvency) (Definition of "Insurer")
Order 2001, SI 2001/2634, art 2 at* **[2471]**.)

3 Modification of Part II of the 1986 Act in relation to insurers

Part II of the 1986 Act (administration orders)[, other than paragraph 14 of Schedule B1 (power of
holder of floating charge to appoint administrator) and paragraph 22 of Schedule B1 (power of
company or directors to appoint administrator),] applies in relation to insurers with the
modifications specified in the Schedule to this Order, and accordingly [paragraph 9(2) of
Schedule B1] does not preclude the making of an administration order in relation to an insurer.

[2670]

NOTES
Words in first pair of square brackets inserted by the Insurers (Reorganisation and Winding Up)
Regulations 2004, SI 2004/353, reg 52, as from 18 February 2004; words in second pair of square brackets
substituted by the Financial Services and Markets Act 2000 (Administration Orders Relating to Insurers)
(Amendment) Order 2003, SI 2003/2134, arts 2, 4, as from 15 September 2003, except in relation to any case
where a petition for an administration order has been presented to the court before that date.

4 Modification of the Insolvency Rules 1986 in relation to insurers

The Insolvency Rules 1986, so far as they give effect to Part II of the 1986 Act, have effect in
relation to insurers with the modification that in [Rule 2.12] of those Rules (the hearing) there is
inserted after sub-paragraph (a) the following sub-paragraph—
    "(aa) the Financial Services Authority;".

[2671]

NOTES
Words in square brackets substituted by the Financial Services and Markets Act 2000 (Administration Orders
Relating to Insurers) (Amendment) Order 2003, SI 2003/2134, arts 2, 5, as from 15 September 2003, except in
relation to any case where a petition for an administration order has been presented to the court before that date.

[5 Mutual credit and set-off

Where an insurer, in relation to which an administration order has been made, subsequently goes
into liquidation, sums due from the insurer to another party are not to be included in the account of
mutual dealings rendered under rule 4.90 of the Insolvency Rules 1986 (mutual credit and set-off) if,
at the time they became due—
    (a)   an administration application had been made under paragraph 12 of Schedule B1 in
           relation to the insurer;
    (b)   in the case of an appointment of an administrator under paragraph 14 of Schedule B1, a
           notice of appointment had been filed with the court under paragraph 18 of that Schedule
           in relation to the insurer; or
    (c)   in the case of an appointment of an administrator under paragraph 22 of Schedule B1, a
           notice of intention to appoint had been filed with the court under paragraph 27 of that
           Schedule in relation to the insurer.]

[2672]

NOTES
Substituted by the Financial Services and Markets Act 2000 (Administration Orders Relating to Insurers)
(Amendment) Order 2003, SI 2003/2134, arts 2, 6, as from 15 September 2003, except in relation to any case
where a petition for an administration order has been presented to the court before that date.

SCHEDULE
MODIFICATIONS OF PART II OF THE INSOLVENCY ACT 1986
IN RELATION TO INSURERS
Article 3

[1. In paragraph 49(4) of Schedule B1 (administrator's proposals), at the end of paragraph (c)
add—

"and
> (d)   to the Financial Services Authority".

2.   In paragraph 53(2) of Schedule B1 (business and result of initial creditors' meeting), at the end of paragraph (c), add—
> "and
> (d)   the Financial Services Authority".

3.   In paragraph 54(2)(b) of Schedule B1 (revision of administrator's proposals), after "creditor" insert "and to the Financial Services Authority".

4.   In paragraph 76(1) of Schedule B1 (automatic end of administration), for "one year" substitute "30 months".

5.   In paragraph 76(2)(b) of Schedule B1 (extension of administrator's term of office by consent) for "six" substitute "twelve".

6.   In paragraph 79(1) of Schedule B1 (court ending administration on application of administrator), after the first reference to "company" insert "or the Financial Services Authority".

7.   In paragraph 91(1) of Schedule B1 (supplying vacancy in office of administrator), at the end of paragraph (e) add—
> "or
> (f)   the Financial Services Authority".]

[8].—(1)   The powers of the administrator referred to in Schedule 1 to the 1986 Act (powers of administrator or administrative receiver) include the power to make—
> (a)   any payments due to a creditor; or
> (b)   any payments on account of any sum which may become due to a creditor.

(2)   Any payments to a creditor made pursuant to sub-paragraph (1) must not exceed, in aggregate, the amount which the administrator reasonably considers that the creditor would be entitled to receive on a distribution of the insurer's assets in a winding up.

(3)   The powers conferred by sub-paragraph (1) may be exercised until [an initial creditors' meeting] but may only be exercised thereafter—
> (a)   if the following conditions are met—
>> (i)   the administrator has laid before [that meeting] or any subsequent creditors' meeting ("the relevant meeting") a statement containing the information mentioned in sub-paragraph (4); and
>> (ii)   the powers are exercised with the consent of a majority in number representing three-fourths in value of the creditors present and voting either in person or by proxy at the relevant meeting; or
> (b)   with the consent of the court.

(4)   The information referred to in sub-paragraph (3)(a) is an estimate of the aggregate amount of—
> (a)   the insurer's assets and liabilities (whether actual, contingent or prospective); and
> (b)   all payments which the administrator proposes to make to creditors pursuant to sub-paragraph (1);
including any assumptions which the administrator has made in calculating that estimate.

[2673]

NOTES

Paras 1–7 substituted for original paras 1–5, para 8 renumbered as such, and words in square brackets in para 8(3) substituted, by the Financial Services and Markets Act 2000 (Administration Orders Relating to Insurers) (Amendment) Order 2003, SI 2003/2134, arts 2, 7, as from 15 September 2003, except in relation to any case where a petition for an administration order has been presented to the court before that date.

ELECTRONIC COMMERCE DIRECTIVE (FINANCIAL SERVICES AND MARKETS) REGULATIONS 2002

(SI 2002/1775)

NOTES

Made: 12 July 2002.

Authority: European Communities Act 1972, s 2(2); Financial Services and Markets Act 2000, ss 349(1), 414, 428(3).

Commencement: 18 July 2002 (for the purpose of enabling the Authority to make rules); 21 August 2002 (otherwise).

These Regulations are reproduced as amended by: the Electronic Commerce Directive (Financial Services and Markets) (Amendment) Regulations 2002, SI 2002/2015; the Electronic Commerce Directive (Financial Services and Markets) (Amendment) Regulations 2004, SI 2004/3378; the Financial Services (EEA State) Regulations 2007, SI 2007/108.

ARRANGEMENT OF REGULATIONS

PART 1
GENERAL

PART 2
MODIFICATION OF FUNCTIONS OF THE FINANCIAL SERVICES AUTHORITY

PART 3
ARTICLE 3.4 OF THE ELECTRONIC COMMERCE DIRECTIVE

PART 4
ENFORCEMENT

PART 6
MISCELLANEOUS AND CONSEQUENTIAL PROVISIONS

PART 1
GENERAL

1 Citation and commencement

These Regulations may be cited as the Electronic Commerce Directive (Financial Services and Markets) Regulations 2002, and come into force—

    (a)   for the purpose of enabling the Authority to make rules, on 18th July 2002;

    (b)   otherwise, on 21st August 2002.

[2674]

2 Interpretation

    (1)   In these Regulations—

"the 2000 Act" means the Financial Services and Markets Act 2000;

"authorised incoming provider" means an incoming provider who is an authorised person within the meaning of the 2000 Act;

"the Authority" means the Financial Services Authority;

"commercial communication" means a communication, in any form, designed to promote, directly or indirectly, the goods, services or image of any person pursuing a commercial activity or exercising a regulated profession, other than a communication—

    (a)   consisting only of information allowing direct access to the activity of that person, including a geographic address, domain name or electronic mail address; or

    (b)   relating to the goods, services or image of that person provided that the communication has been prepared independently of the person making it (and for this purpose, a communication prepared without financial consideration is to be taken to have been prepared independently unless the contrary is shown);

"the Commission" means the Commission of the European Communities;

"consumer" means any individual who is acting for purposes other than those of his trade, business or profession;

"country of origin" in relation to an incoming electronic commerce activity means the EEA State in which is situated the establishment from which the information society service in question is provided;

"criminal conduct" means conduct which constitutes an offence in any part of the United Kingdom, or would constitute an offence in any part of the United Kingdom if it occurred there;

"direction" means a direction made, or proposed to be made, by the Authority under regulation 6;

"EEA regulator" means an authority in an EEA State other than the United Kingdom which exercises any function of a kind mentioned in section 195(4) of the 2000 Act;

["EEA State" has the meaning given by Schedule 1 to the Interpretation Act 1978;]

"electronic commerce directive" means Directive 2000/31/EC of the European Parliament and of the Council of 8 June 2000 on certain legal aspects of information society services, in particular electronic commerce, in the Internal Market (Directive on electronic commerce);

"financial instrument" includes an investment of a kind specified by any of articles 76 to 85 of the Regulated Activities Order;

"incoming electronic commerce activity" means an activity—

    (a)   which consists of the provision of an information society service from an establishment in an EEA State other than the United Kingdom to a person or persons in the United Kingdom, and

    (b)   which would, but for article 72A of the Regulated Activities Order (and irrespective of the effect of article 72 of that Order), be a regulated activity within the meaning of the 2000 Act;

"incoming provider" means a person carrying on an incoming electronic commerce activity;

"information society service" means an information society service within the meaning of Article 2(a) of the electronic commerce directive;

"investment" means an investment of a kind specified by any provision of Part III of the Regulated Activities Order;

"Regulated Activities Order" means the Financial Services and Markets Act 2000 (Regulated Activities) Order 2001;

"regulated profession" means any profession within the meaning of—

    (a)   Article 1(d) of Directive 89/48/EEC of the Council of the European Communities of 21 December 1988 on a general system for the recognition of higher-education diplomas awarded on completion of professional education and training of at least three years' duration, or

    (b)   Article 1(f) of Directive 92/51/EEC of the Council of the European Communities of 18 June 1992 on a second general system for the recognition of professional education and training to supplement Directive 89/48/EEC;

"relevant EEA regulator", in relation to a direction, means the EEA regulator in the country of origin of the incoming electronic commerce activity to which the direction does, or would if made, relate, and which is responsible in that country for the regulation of that activity;

"rule" means a rule made by the Authority under the 2000 Act;

"Tribunal" means the Financial Services and Markets Tribunal referred to in section 132 of the 2000 Act;

"UCITS Directive" means Directive 85/611/EEC of the Council of the European Communities of 20 December 1985 on the co-ordination of laws, regulations and administrative provisions relating to undertakings for collective investment in transferable securities;

"UCITS Directive scheme" means an undertaking for collective investment in transferable securities which is subject to the UCITS Directive, and has been authorised in accordance with Article 4 of that Directive;

"unauthorised incoming provider" means an incoming provider who is not an authorised person within the meaning of the 2000 Act.

(2)   A reference in these Regulations to a requirement imposed by the Authority under these Regulations is a reference to—

    (a)   a requirement (including a requirement that a person no longer carry on an incoming electronic commerce activity) imposed by a direction; or

    (b)   a requirement imposed by a rule applicable to incoming providers in accordance with regulation 3(4).

(3)   For the purposes of these Regulations—

    (a)   an establishment, in connection with an information society service, is the place at which the provider of the service (being a national of an EEA State or a company or firm as mentioned in Article 48 of the treaty establishing the European Community) effectively pursues an economic activity for an indefinite period;

    (b)   the presence or use in a particular place of equipment or other technical means of providing an information society service does not, of itself, constitute that place as an establishment of the kind mentioned in sub-paragraph (a);

    (c)   where it cannot be determined from which of a number of establishments a given information society service is provided, that service is to be regarded as provided from the establishment where the provider has the centre of his activities relating to the service;

(d)   a communication by electronic mail is to be regarded as unsolicited, unless it is made in response to an express request from the recipient of the communication.

[2675]

NOTES
Para (1): definition "EEA State" substituted by the Financial Services (EEA State) Regulations 2007, SI 2007/108, reg 6, as from 13 February 2007.

PART 2

MODIFICATION OF FUNCTIONS OF THE FINANCIAL SERVICES AUTHORITY

3 Consumer contract requirements: modification of rule-making power

(1)   The power to make rules conferred by section 138 of the 2000 Act is to be taken to include a power to make rules applying to unauthorised incoming providers.

(2)   In consequence of paragraph (1)—

(a)   any reference in sections 138(4), (5) and (7) to (9), 148, 150 and 156 of the 2000 Act to an authorised person includes a reference to an unauthorised incoming provider;

(b)   any reference in those sections to a regulated activity includes a reference to an incoming electronic commerce activity.

(3)   For the purpose of the exercise by the Authority of the power conferred by section 138 of the 2000 Act to make rules applying to incoming providers with respect to the carrying on by them of incoming electronic commerce activities, subsections (7) and (9) of that section have effect as if the reference to "person" where first occurring were a reference to an individual acting for purposes other than those of his trade, business or profession.

(4)   Rules made by the Authority under section 138 of the 2000 Act do not apply to incoming providers with respect to the carrying on by them of incoming electronic commerce activities unless they—

(a)   impose consumer contract requirements;

(b)   apply with respect to communications that constitute an advertisement by the operator of a UCITS Directive scheme of units in that scheme; or

(c)   relate to the permissibility of unsolicited commercial communications by electronic mail.

[(4A)   Notwithstanding paragraph (4)(a), rules made by the Authority under section 138 of the 2000 Act which impose consumer contract requirements do not apply to an incoming provider with respect to the carrying on by him of an incoming electronic commerce activity which consists of the provision of an information society service from an establishment in an EEA State other than the United Kingdom, if the provisions by which that State has transposed the Financial Services Distance Marketing Directive, or the obligations in the domestic law of that State corresponding to those provided for in that Directive, as the case may be, apply to that activity.]

(5)   A consumer contract rule may provide that conduct engaged in by a person to whom the rule applies, and which is in conformity with a provision corresponding to the rule made by a body or authority in an EEA State other than the United Kingdom, is to be treated as conduct in conformity with the rule.

(6)   "Consumer contract requirement" means a requirement—

(a)   that information of a kind referred to in regulation 4 be provided to a consumer before he enters into a contract for the provision of one or more information society services, or

(b)   as to the manner in which such information is to be provided.

[(6A)   "The Financial Services Distance Marketing Directive" means Directive 2002/65/EC of the European Parliament and the Council of 23 September 2002 concerning the distance marketing of consumer financial services and amending Council Directive 90/619/EEC and Directives 97/7/EC and 98/27/EC.]

(7)   "Consumer contract rule" means a rule made by the Authority under section 138 of the 2000 Act which imposes a consumer contract requirement on incoming providers.

[2676]

NOTES
Paras (4A), (6A): inserted by the Electronic Commerce Directive (Financial Services and Markets) (Amendment) Regulations 2004, SI 2004/3378, reg 2, as from 11 January 2005.

4 Consumer contract requirements: information

The information which may be the subject of a consumer contract requirement is—

(a) the identity and description of the main business of the other party to the proposed contract ("the supplier"), the geographic address at which the supplier is established, and any other geographic address relevant to the consumer's relations with the supplier;

(b) if the supplier has a representative established in the consumer's country of residence with whom the consumer is to have dealings, the identity and geographic address of the representative, and any other geographic address relevant to the consumer's relations with the representative;

(c) if the consumer is to have dealings with any professional person in connection with the contract, the identity of that person, a statement of the capacity in which he is to act, and the geographic address relevant to the consumer's relations with him;

(d) if the supplier is registered on any public register in connection with the carrying on of his business (or such of his business as is relevant to the contract), the name of that register, and any registration number or other means of identifying the relevant entry on the register;

(e) if the carrying on of the supplier's business (or such of it as is relevant to the contract) is subject to a requirement that he be authorised by a person or body in order to carry it on, the name and geographic address of that person or body;

(f) a description of the main features of the service or services to which the contract relates;

(g) either—

  (aa) the total price to be paid by the consumer under the contract, including all related fees, charges and expenses, and all taxes paid by or through the supplier (in so far as these are reflected in the total price); or

  (bb) if the total price cannot be given, the basis for the calculation of the total price, in a form enabling the consumer to verify the total price when calculated by the supplier;

(h) where the service to be provided under the contract relates to one or more financial instruments—

  (aa) if the instruments are subject to special risks relating to their specific features or operations to be executed in relation to them, notice of the existence of those risks,

  (bb) if the price of the instruments is subject to fluctuation depending on market conditions outside the supplier's control, notice of that fact, and

  (cc) notice that movements in the price of the instruments in the past are not necessarily an indicator of future performance;

(i) notice of the possibility that taxes or other costs may exist which are not imposed or paid by or through the supplier;

(j) the arrangements for payment under, and the performance of, the contract;

(k) any specific additional cost imposed by the supplier on the consumer in relation to the consumer's use of the means for concluding the contract or communicating with the supplier;

(l) the existence or absence of any legal right of the consumer to withdraw from the contract after it has been entered into, the conditions attached to the exercise of any such right, and the consequences for the consumer of not exercising it;

(m) where the contract relates to services to be performed on an indefinite or recurrent basis, the minimum duration of the contract;

(n) any rights of the consumer or the supplier to terminate the contract in accordance with one of its express terms, any contractual penalties which may apply in that event, and the procedure to be followed by the consumer in that event (including the address to which any notification of withdrawal from the contract should be sent);

(o) the state or states whose laws are taken by the supplier as a basis for the establishment of relations with the consumer before the contract is concluded;

(p) any express term in the contract relating to the law governing it, or to the jurisdiction of courts;

(q) the language or languages in which the supplier—

  (aa) proposes to offer the terms of, and information concerning, the contract, and

  (bb) undertakes (with the agreement of the consumer) to communicate with the consumer during the existence of the contract;

(r) whether any mechanism other than redress through a court (including guarantee funds and compensation schemes and arrangements) is available to the consumer in relation to matters arising in connection with the contract, and if so, the procedure to be followed by the consumer in order to gain access to it;

(s) any limitations, of which the supplier could reasonably be taken to be aware, of the period for which any information referred to in paragraphs (a) to (r) will be valid.

[2677]

5 Application of certain rules

Rules made by the Authority under section 140 or 141 of the 2000 Act do not apply to incoming providers to the extent that they specify an activity which is an incoming electronic commerce activity.

[2678]

PART 3
ARTICLE 3.4 OF THE ELECTRONIC COMMERCE DIRECTIVE

6 Direction by Authority

(1)   If the policy conditions and the procedural conditions are met, the Authority may direct that an incoming provider may no longer carry on a specified incoming electronic commerce activity, or may only carry it on subject to specified requirements.

(2)   A direction—
  (a)   must be in writing;
  (b)   has effect from—
    (i)   a specified date (which may be the date on which it is made); or
    (ii)   if no date is specified, the date on which the direction is no longer open to review;
  (c)   must include a statement to the effect that the person to whom it applies may refer the matter to the Tribunal;
  (d)   may have effect for a specified period, until the occurrence of a specified event, until specified conditions are met, or for an indefinite period.

(3)   The requirements referred to in paragraph (1) may include the requirement that the person to whom the direction applies must comply with one or more rules (with such modifications (if any) as may be specified) with respect to the carrying on by him of an incoming electronic commerce activity.

(4)   If a requirement of a kind mentioned in subsection (3) of section 48 of the 2000 Act is specified in a direction, the requirement has the same effect in relation to the person to whom the direction applies as it would have if it had been imposed on that person by the Authority acting under section 45 of that Act.

(5)   Contravention of a specified requirement does not make a person guilty of an offence, or make any transaction void or unenforceable.

(6)   Contravention of a specified requirement by an incoming provider is actionable at the suit of a person who suffers loss as a result of the contravention, subject to—
  (a)   the defences and other incidents applying to actions for breach of statutory duty; and
  (b)   the conditions mentioned in regulation 7(2) of the Financial Services and Markets Act 2000 (Rights of Action) Regulations 2001 ("the Rights of Action Regulations").

(7)   For the purposes of paragraph (6)(b), the reference in regulation 7(2)(b) of the Rights of Action Regulations to a Part XIII financial resources requirement is to be taken to include a reference to a specified requirement to have or maintain financial resources.

(8)   For the purposes of this regulation, a direction is no longer open to review if any of the conditions in section 391(8) (a) to (d) of the 2000 Act are satisfied.

(9)   In this regulation, "specified" in relation to a direction means specified in the direction.

[2679]

7 Policy conditions

The policy conditions are that—
  (a)   the Authority considers—
    (i)   the making of the direction to be necessary for—
      (aa)   the prevention, investigation, detection or prosecution of criminal conduct;
      (bb)   the protection of consumers; or
      (cc)   other reasons of public policy relevant to the regulatory objectives set out in Part I of the 2000 Act; and
    (ii)   that the carrying on of the incoming electronic commerce activity by the person to whom the direction is to apply prejudices, or presents a serious and grave risk of prejudice to, any of the objectives referred to in sub-paragraph (i); and
  (b)   the direction appears to the Authority to be a proportionate means of achieving, or addressing the prejudice or risk of prejudice to, any of those objectives.

[2680]

8 Procedural conditions

The procedural conditions are that—
  (a)   the Authority has requested the relevant EEA regulator to take measures to remedy the situation giving rise to the request;

(b)   the relevant EEA regulator—
  (i)   has not, within what appears to the Authority to be a reasonable time, taken such measures; or
  (ii)   has taken such measures, but the measures appear to the Authority to be inadequate in the circumstances;
(c)   the Authority has notified the Commission and the relevant EEA regulator of its intention to make the direction; and
(d)   the Authority has notified the person to whom the direction is to apply of its proposal to make the direction, and afforded that person the opportunity to make representations to the Authority in such manner, and within such period, as the Authority may determine.

[2681]

9   Urgent cases

(1)   If the case appears to the Authority to be one of urgency, it may make a direction regardless of whether the procedural conditions are met.

(2)   If the Authority makes a direction in reliance on paragraph (1), it must notify the Commission and the relevant EEA regulator as soon as possible that the direction has been made, and provide each of those bodies with a statement of its reasons for considering the case to be one of urgency.

[2682]

10   Directions made under regulation 6

(1)   Subject to the following provisions of this regulation, the Authority may vary or revoke a direction by notice in writing to the person to whom the direction applies.

(2)   The Authority may vary or revoke a direction under this regulation on its own initiative, or on the application of the person to whom the direction applies.

(3)   If the Authority decides to refuse an application for the variation or revocation of a direction made under this regulation, it must notify the applicant in writing of its decision.

(4)   The Authority must not vary a direction on its own initiative under this regulation unless it has afforded the person to whom the direction applies the opportunity to make representations to the Authority in such manner, and within such period, as the Authority may determine.

(5)   Paragraph (4) does not apply if the case appears to the Authority to be one of urgency.

(6)   A decision by the Authority to vary a direction has effect from—
  (a)   a date referred to in the notice given under paragraph (1) (which must not be earlier than the date on which the decision was made); or
  (b)   if no such date is referred to, the date on which the decision was made.

(7)   If the case is one to which regulation 11(b) or (c) applies, a notice under paragraph (1) or (3) must include a statement to the effect that the person to whom the direction applies may refer the matter to the Tribunal.

(8)   If the Authority makes a direction it may publish, in such manner as it considers appropriate, such information about the matter to which the direction relates as it considers appropriate in furtherance of any of the objectives referred to in regulation 7(a)(i).

(9)   The Authority may not publish information under paragraph (8) if publication of it would, in the Authority's opinion, be unfair to the person to whom the direction applies or prejudicial to the interests of consumers.

[2683]

11   Referral to the Tribunal

If the Authority—
  (a)   makes a direction;
  (b)   varies a direction on its own initiative; or
  (c)   decides to refuse an application for the variation or revocation of a direction,
the person to whom the direction applies may refer the matter to the Tribunal.

[2684]

PART 4
ENFORCEMENT

12   Application of certain provisions of the 2000 Act

(1)   For the purposes of sections 205 to 209 and 384 of the 2000 Act, a requirement imposed by the Authority under these Regulations upon an authorised incoming provider is to be treated as imposed on him by or under that Act.

(2)   For the purposes of sections 380, 382 and 398 of, and paragraph 6 of Schedule 1 to, the 2000 Act, a requirement imposed by the Authority under these Regulations upon an incoming provider is to be treated as imposed on him by or under that Act.

(3)   Any reference in sections 165 to 168 and 176 of the 2000 Act to an authorised person includes a reference to an unauthorised incoming provider.

(4)   Any reference in sections 132 and 133 of the 2000 Act to that Act includes a reference to these Regulations.

(5)   The reference in section 168(4)(c) of the 2000 Act to a rule made by the Authority includes a reference to a requirement imposed by the Authority under these Regulations.

[2685]

13   *((Pt 5) amends the Financial Services and Markets Act 2000, ss 417, 418 at* **[443]**, **[444]**.)

PART 6
MISCELLANEOUS AND CONSEQUENTIAL PROVISIONS

14 Disclosure of information

In any enactment that requires or permits the disclosure of information to or by the Authority, a reference (however expressed) to powers or functions conferred on the Authority by or under the 2000 Act includes, for the purposes of such disclosure, a reference to the Authority's functions under these Regulations.

[2686]

15 Notices

The Financial Services and Markets Act 2000 (Service of Notices) Regulations 2001 apply for the purposes of these Regulations as if any reference in those Regulations to "the Act" included a reference to these Regulations.

[2687]

16   *(Inserts the Financial Services and Markets Act 2000 (Disclosure of Confidential Information) Regulations 2001, SI 2001/2188, reg 12B, at* **[2363]**.)

17 Functions of the Authority

For the purposes of the 2000 Act, a function conferred on the Authority by these Regulations is to be taken to be a function conferred on the Authority by or under that Act.

[2688]

18   *(Amends the Financial Services and Markets Act 2000 (Rights of Action) Regulations 2001, SI 2001/2256, reg 3 at* **[2377]**.)

[19 Exclusion of general regulations

(1)   Regulation 4(1) of the general regulations does not affect any legal requirement imposed by or under the 2000 Act or these Regulations.

(2)   Regulation 4(2) and (3) of the general regulations do not apply to the Authority or any enforcement authority in respect of its responsibility in relation to a requirement of the kind mentioned in paragraph (1).

(3)   A rule that corresponds to a relevant regulation applies instead of that regulation.

(4)   The reference in regulation 22(a) of the general regulations to regulation 6(1)(c) of those regulations is to be taken to include a reference to a provision in a rule that corresponds to regulation 6(1)(c) (and so applies in its stead by virtue of paragraph (3)).

(5)   In this regulation—
   "enforcement authority" has the same meaning as in the general regulations;
   "general regulations" means the Electronic Commerce (EC Directive) Regulations 2002;
   "relevant regulation" means regulation 6 to 9, 11 or 15 of the general regulations.]

[2689]

NOTES
Added by the Electronic Commerce Directive (Financial Services and Markets) (Amendment) Regulations 2002, SI 2002/2015, reg 2, as from 21 August 2002.

FINANCIAL SERVICES AND MARKETS ACT 2000 (FOURTH MOTOR INSURANCE DIRECTIVE) REGULATIONS 2002

(SI 2002/2706)

NOTES
Made: 28 October 2002.
Authority: European Communities Act 1972, s 2(2); Financial Services and Markets Act 2000, ss 150(3), 417(1).
Commencement: 20 November 2002.

As of 1 February 2009, these Regulations had not been amended.

1 Citation and commencement

These Regulations may be cited as the Financial Services and Markets Act 2000 (Fourth Motor Insurance Directive) Regulations 2002 and come into force on 20th November 2002.

[2690]

2 Power of the Authority to make rules under section 138 of the Financial Services and Markets Act 2000

(1) Rules made by the Authority under section 138 of the Financial Services and Markets Act 2000 ("the 2000 Act") (general rule-making power) may require a relevant authorised person to pay interest in specified circumstances in respect of claims made for compensation.

(2) In paragraph (1)—
    (a)   "relevant authorised person" means an authorised person with a Part IV permission (within the meaning of the 2000 Act)—
         (i)   to effect or carry out relevant contracts of insurance; or
         (ii)   to manage the underwriting capacity of a Lloyd's syndicate as a managing agent, the members of which effect or carry out relevant contracts of insurance underwritten at Lloyd's;
    where a "relevant contract of insurance" means a contract of insurance against damage arising out of or in connection with the use of motor vehicles on land (other than carrier's liability);
    (b)   "specified" means specified in the rules.

(3) Rules made pursuant to paragraph (1) may not come into force before 19th January 2003.

[2691]

3   (*Amends the Financial Services and Markets Act 2000 (Rights of Action) Regulations 2001, SI 2001/2256, reg 6 at* **[2380]**.)

FINANCIAL SERVICES AND MARKETS ACT 2000 (COLLECTIVE INVESTMENT SCHEMES) (DESIGNATED COUNTRIES AND TERRITORIES) ORDER 2003

(SI 2003/1181)

NOTES
Made: 29 April 2003.
Authority: Financial Services and Markets Act 2000, ss 270, 426, 428(3).
Commencement: 21 May 2003.

As of 1 February 2009, this Order had not been amended.

1 Citation and commencement

This Order may be cited as the Financial Services and Markets Act 2000 (Collective Investment Schemes) (Designated Countries and Territories) Order 2003 and comes into force on 21st May 2003.

[2692]

2 Designation of territories

Guernsey, Jersey and the Isle of Man are designated for the purposes of section 270 of the Act (collective investment schemes authorised in designated countries or territories).

[2693]

3 Specification of classes of collective investment schemes

(1)   The following classes of collective investment scheme are specified for the purposes of subsection (1)(b) of section 270 of the Act—

(a)   where the scheme is managed in, and authorised under the law of, Guernsey, any authorised scheme (within the meaning of the Collective Investment Schemes (Class A) Rules 2002, as amended by the Collective Investment Schemes (Class A) Rules 2002 (Amendment) Rules 2003) which is not—
   (i)   a feeder-fund; or
   (ii)   a protected cell scheme;

(b)   where the scheme is managed in, and authorised under the law of, Jersey, any scheme which is a recognised fund within the meaning of the Collective Investment Funds (Recognised Funds) (Rules) (Jersey) Order 2003 and which is not a feeder-fund; and

(c)   where the scheme is managed in, and authorised under the law of, the Isle of Man, any scheme which is an authorised scheme within the meaning of the Financial Supervision Act 1988 (an Act of Tynwald) (as last amended by the Corporate Service Providers Act 2000) and which is not a feeder-fund.

(2)   For the purposes of this article—

(a)   "feeder-fund" means a collective investment scheme which has as its purpose the investment of its funds in securities (within the meaning of article 3 of the Financial Services and Markets Act 2000 (Regulated Activities) Order 2001) issued by one other collective investment scheme; and

(b)   "protected cell scheme" means a collective investment scheme which, under the law of Guernsey, has been incorporated as, or converted into, a protected cell company under the Protected Cell Companies Ordinance 1997 (as last amended by the Protected Cell Companies (Amendment) Ordinance 1998).

[2694]

4 Revocation of transitional provisions

Article 67(1) of the Financial Services and Markets Act 2000 (Transitional Provisions) (Authorised Persons etc) Order 2001, in so far as it relates to any order under section 87(1) of the Financial Services Act 1986 which designated Guernsey, Jersey or the Isle of Man for the purposes of that section, is revoked.

[2695]

FINANCIAL SERVICES AND MARKETS ACT 2000 (COMMUNICATIONS BY ACTUARIES) REGULATIONS 2003

(SI 2003/1294)

NOTES
Made: 12 May 2003.
Authority: Financial Services and Markets Act 2000, ss 342(5), 343(5), 428(3).
Commencement: 1 September 2003.

As of 1 February 2009, these Regulations had not been amended.

---

1   Citation, commencement and interpretation

(1)   These Regulations may be cited as the Financial Services and Markets Act 2000 (Communications by Actuaries) Regulations 2003 and come into force on 1st September 2003.

(2)   In these Regulations—
   "the Act" means the Financial Services and Markets Act 2000;
   "contract of long-term insurance" has the same meaning as in the Financial Services and Markets Act 2000 (Regulated Activities) Order 2001;
   "relevant requirement" means—

(a)   a requirement which is imposed by or under any provision of the Act other than Part VI (official listing); or

(b)   a requirement which is imposed by or under any other Act and whose contravention constitutes an offence which the Authority has power to prosecute under the Act.

[2696]

2   Circumstances in which an actuary is to communicate

(1)   This regulation applies to any person who is, or has been, an actuary acting for an authorised person ("A") and who is or was—

(a)   appointed under or as a result of rules made by the Authority under section 340 of the Act; or

(b)   appointed under or as a result of any other statutory provision and subject to duties imposed by such rules.

(2)   An actuary to whom this regulation applies must communicate to the Authority information on, or his opinion on, matters mentioned in section 342(3)(a) of the Act (matters of which he has, or had, become aware in his capacity as actuary acting for an authorised person) in the circumstances specified in paragraph (4).

(3)   An actuary—

(a)   to whom this regulation applies, and

(b)   who is or has been an actuary acting for a person who has close links with A (within the meaning of section 343(8) of the Act),

must communicate to the Authority information on, or his opinion on, matters mentioned in section 343(3)(a) of the Act (information on a matter concerning A of which he has, or had, become aware in his capacity as actuary acting for the person who has close links with A) in the circumstances specified in paragraph (4).

(4)   The circumstances are that the actuary reasonably believes that—

(a)   as regards A—

(i)   there is or has been, or may be or may have been, a contravention of any relevant requirement that applies to A; and

(ii)   that contravention may be of material significance to the Authority in determining whether to exercise, in relation to A, any functions conferred on the Authority by or under any provision of the Act other than Part VI;

(b)   the information on, or his opinion on, those matters may be of material significance to the Authority in determining whether A satisfies and will continue to satisfy the threshold conditions;

(c)   where applicable, there is a significant risk that assets representing a fund or funds maintained by A in respect of contracts of long-term insurance effected or carried out by him are or may be, or may become, insufficient to meet his liabilities attributable to such contracts; or

(d)   where applicable, there is a significant risk that A—

(i)   did not,

(ii)   does not or is unable to, or

(iii)   will not, may not or may become unable to,

take into account in a reasonable and proportionate manner the interests of the policyholders of contracts of long-term insurance effected or carried out by him.

(5)   In determining whether there is a significant risk of the kind specified by paragraph (4)(d), the actuary may take into account—

(a)   the manner in which A exercises his discretion in relation to the operation of the fund or funds maintained by A in respect of contracts of long-term insurance effected or carried out by him, including the distribution and use of surplus assets;

(b)   the methodology used to determine bonuses;

(c)   the manner in which A takes into account the interests of different classes of policyholder;

(d)   the application of fixed or discretionary charges or benefits payable under such contracts;

(e)   representations made by A to policyholders or potential policyholders; and

(f)   any obligation (however phrased) imposed on A under the Act to treat policyholders fairly.

[2697]

FINANCIAL SERVICES AND MARKETS ACT 2000 (REGULATED ACTIVITIES) (AMENDMENT) (NO 1) ORDER 2003

(SI 2003/1475)

NOTES
Made: 5 June 2003.
Authority: Financial Services and Markets Act 2000, ss 22(1), (5), 426, 427, 428(3), Sch 2, para 25.
Commencement: 1 January 2004 (arts 26–29); 31 October 2004 (otherwise).
As of 1 February 2009, this Order had not been amended.

PART III
STATUTORY INSTRUMENTS

PART 1
GENERAL

1   Citation and commencement

(1)   This Order may be cited as the Financial Services and Markets Act 2000 (Regulated Activities) (Amendment) (No 1) Order 2003.

(2)   Articles 26 to 29 come into force on 1st January 2004.

(3)   Otherwise, this Order comes into force on 31st October 2004.

[2698]

NOTES

Commencement: 31 October 2004.

2   Interpretation

In this Order, "the Regulated Activities Order" means the Financial Services and Markets Act 2000 (Regulated Activities) Order 2001.

[2699]

NOTES

Commencement: 31 October 2004.

3–25   *(Arts 3–20 (Pt 2) amend the Financial Services and Markets Act 2000 (Regulated Activities) Order 2001, SI 2001/544 at* **[2010]** *et seq; arts 21, 22 (Pt 3) amend the Consumer Credit Act 1974; arts 23–25 (Pt 4) amend the Financial Services and Markets Act 2000 (Carrying on Regulated Activities by Way of Business) Order 2001, SI 2001/1177 at* **[2206]** *et seq, the Financial Services and Markets Act 2000 (Appointed Representatives) Regulations 2001, SI 2001/1217 at* **[2221]** *et seq, and the Financial Services and Markets Act 2000 (Professions) (Non-Exempt Activities) Order 2001, SI 2001/1227 at* **[2226]** *et seq.)*

PART 5
TRANSITIONAL PROVISIONS

26   Interpretation

In this Part—
 "the Act" means the Financial Services and Markets Act 2000;
 "commencement" means the beginning of 31st October 2004;
 "mortgage mediation activity" means any regulated activity of the kind specified by article 25A or 53A of the Regulated Activities Order (arranging or advising on regulated mortgage contracts), or article 64 of that Order, so far as relevant to any such activity.

[2700]

27   Applications for Part IV permission

(1)   This article applies to any completed application for Part IV permission which is made before 30th April 2004 by a person who is not an authorised person, to the extent that the application relates to any mortgage mediation activity ("an early Part IV application").

(2)   Section 52(1) of the Act (applications to be determined by the Authority within six months) does not apply to early Part IV applications.

(3)   If the Authority has not determined an early Part IV application before the end of the period of six months beginning on the date on which it received the completed application, it must inform the applicant of the progress being made on the application (unless it has already done so).

(4)   In any event, the Authority must determine all early Part IV applications before commencement.

[2701]

28 Applications for approval

(1)   This article applies to any application made before 31st July 2004 under section 59 of the Act (approval of the performance of controlled functions) by a person who is not an authorised person for the Authority's approval of the performance by a person of any controlled function (within the meaning of section 59(3) of the Act), to the extent that that function relates to the carrying on of any mortgage mediation activity ("an early Part V application").

(2)   Section 61(3) of the Act (applications to be determined by the Authority within three months) does not apply to early Part V applications.

(3)   If the Authority has not determined an early Part V application before the end of the period of six months beginning on the date on which it received the application, it must inform the applicant of the progress being made on the application (unless it has already done so).

(4)   In any event, the Authority must determine all early Part V applications before commencement.

[2702]

29 Modifications and waivers

(1)   Before commencement, section 148 of the Act (modification or waiver of rules) has effect as if the references to "authorised person" (except in subsection (9)) included a reference to a person who has Part IV permission to carry on any mortgage mediation activity, albeit that that permission is not in force.

(2)   To the extent that it relates to any mortgage mediation activity, any direction given by the Authority under section 148(2) of the Act as modified by paragraph (1) may not come into force before commencement.

[2703]

FINANCIAL SERVICES AND MARKETS ACT 2000 (REGULATED ACTIVITIES) (AMENDMENT) (NO 2) ORDER 2003

(SI 2003/1476)

NOTES
Made: 5 June 2003.
Authority: Financial Services and Markets Act 2000, ss 22(1), (5), 192(a), 426, 427, 428(3), Sch 2, para 25.
Commencement: 1 January 2004 (arts 22–27); 31 October 2004 (arts 1–21 in so far as they relate to contracts of long-term care insurance); 14 January 2005 (otherwise).
This Order is reproduced as amended by: the Financial Services and Markets Act 2000 (Regulated Activities) (Amendment) Order 2004, SI 2004/1610.

ARRANGEMENT OF ARTICLES

PART 1
GENERAL

PART 5
MISCELLANEOUS

PART 6
TRANSITIONAL PROVISIONS

PART 1
GENERAL

1 Citation, commencement and interpretation

(1) This Order may be cited as the Financial Services and Markets Act 2000 (Regulated Activities) (Amendment) (No 2) Order 2003.

(2) Articles 22 to 27 of this Order come into force on 1st January 2004.

(3) The other provisions of this Order come into force—
   (a) in so far as they relate to contracts of long-term care insurance, on 31st October 2004;
   (b) for all other purposes, on 14th January 2005.

(4) In this Order—
   "the Act" means the Financial Services and Markets Act 2000;
   "contract of long-term care insurance" means a contract of insurance (within the meaning of the principal Order) in respect of which the following conditions are met—
   (a) the purpose (or one of the purposes) of the policy is to protect the policyholder against the risk of becoming unable to live independently without assistance in consequence of a deterioration of mental or physical health, injury, sickness or other infirmity;
   (b) benefits under the contract are payable in respect of—
      (i) services,
      (ii) accommodation, or
      (iii) goods,
   which are (or which is) necessary or desirable due to a deterioration of mental or physical health, injury, sickness or other infirmity;
   (c) the contract is expressed to be in effect until the death of the policyholder (except that the contract may give the policyholder the option to surrender the policy); and
   (d) the benefits under the contract are capable of being paid throughout the life of the policyholder;
   "the principal Order" means the Financial Services and Markets Act 2000 (Regulated Activities) Order 2001.

[2704]

NOTES

Commencement: 31 October 2004 (in so far as relating to contracts of long-term care insurance); 14 January 2005 (otherwise).

2–18 *(Arts 2–13 (Pts 2, 3) amend the Financial Services and Markets Act 2000 (Regulated Activities) Order 2001, SI 2001/544 at* **[2010]** *et seq; arts 14–18 (Pt 4) amend the Financial Services and Markets Act 2000 (Carrying on Regulated Activities by Way of Business) Order 2001, SI 2001/1177 at* **[2206]** *et seq, the Financial Services and Markets Act 2000 (Appointed Representatives) Regulations 2001, SI 2001/1217 at* **[2221]** *et seq, the Financial Services and Markets Act 2000 (Professions) (Non-Exempt Activities) Order 2001, SI 2001/1227 at* **[2226]** *et seq, the Financial Services and Markets Act 2000 (Compensation Scheme: Electing Participants) Regulations 2001, SI 2001/1783 at* **[2342]** *et seq, and the Financial Services and Markets Act 2000 (Misleading Statements and Practices) Order 2001, SI 2001/3645 at* **[2631]** *et seq.)*

PART 5
MISCELLANEOUS

19, 20 *(Art 19 amends the Financial Services and Markets Act 2000, Sch 6, Pt I, para 2, at* **[472]**; *art 20(1), (2) amend s 49(2) of that Act at* **[49]**; *art 20(3) revoked by the Financial Services and Markets Act 2000 (Regulated Activities) (Amendment) Order 2004, SI 2004/1610, art 2, as from 15 July 2004.)*

21 Controllers of insurance intermediaries

(1) In any case where a person ("the acquirer")—
   (a) proposes to take, in relation to a UK insurance intermediary ("A"), such a step as is mentioned in section 178(1) of the Act (obligation to notify the Authority of control over authorised persons), or
   (b) acquires control, an additional kind of control or an increase in a relevant kind of control over a UK insurance intermediary without himself taking any such step,
the acquirer is exempt from any obligation imposed by section 178 of the Act to notify the Authority of his proposal or acquisition unless paragraph (2) applies.

(2) This paragraph applies—

   (a)   where the acquirer falls within paragraph (1)(a), if the acquirer does not currently, but would if he took the proposed step, fall within any of the cases in paragraph (3); or

   (b)   where the acquirer falls within paragraph (1)(b), if the acquirer did not immediately before acquiring control, but as a result of that acquisition does, fall within any of those cases.

(3)   The cases are where the acquirer—

   (a)   holds 20% or more of the shares in A;

   (b)   is able to exercise significant influence over the management of A by virtue of his shareholding in A;

   (c)   holds 20% or more of the shares in a parent undertaking ("P") of A;

   (d)   is able to exercise significant influence over the management of P by virtue of his shareholding in P;

   (e)   is entitled to exercise, or control the exercise of, 20% or more of the voting power in A;

   (f)   is able to exercise significant influence over the management of A by virtue of his voting power in A;

   (g)   is entitled to exercise, or control the exercise of, 20% or more of the voting power in P; or

   (h)   is able to exercise a significant influence over the management of P by virtue of his voting power in P.

(4)   In paragraph (3), "the acquirer" means—

   (a)   the acquirer;

   (b)   any of the acquirer's associates; or

   (c)   the acquirer and any of his associates.

(5)   In any case where a controller of A—

   (a)   proposes to take, in relation to A, such a step as is mentioned in section 190(1) of the Act (obligation to notify the Authority of a reduction in control over an authorised person), or

   (b)   ceases to have, or reduces a relevant kind of, control over A without himself taking any such step,

the controller is exempt from any obligation imposed by subsection (1) or (2) of section 190 of the Act to notify the Authority unless paragraph (6) applies.

(6)   This paragraph applies if—

   (a)   the percentage of shares held by the controller in A decreases (or would decrease) from 20% or more to less than 20%;

   (b)   the percentage of shares held by the controller in a parent undertaking ("P") of A decreases (or would decrease) from 20% or more to less than 20%;

   (c)   the percentage of voting power which the controller is entitled to exercise, or control the exercise of, in A decreases (or would decrease) from 20% or more to less than 20%; or

   (d)   the percentage of voting power which the controller is entitled to exercise, or control the exercise of, in P decreases (or would decrease) from 20% or more to less than 20%.

(7)   In paragraph (6), "the controller" means—

   (a)   the controller;

   (b)   any of the controller's associates; or

   (c)   the controller and any of his associates.

(8)   References in this article to acquiring control, or an additional kind of control, increasing control and reducing control are to be read with Part XII of the Act.

(9)   In this article—

"associate", "shares" and "voting power" have the same meaning as in section 422 of the Act;

"UK insurance intermediary" means any UK authorised person (within the meaning of section 178(4) of the Act) who has Part IV permission to carry on any regulated activity of the kind specified by article 21, 25(1) or (2), 39A or 53 of the principal Order, or, so far as relevant to any of those articles, article 64 of that Order, which is carried on in relation to a contract of insurance, but who does not have Part IV permission to carry on any other regulated activity.

[2705]

NOTES

Commencement: 31 October 2004 (in so far as relating to contracts of long-term care insurance); 14 January 2005 (otherwise).

PART 6
TRANSITIONAL PROVISIONS

22 Interpretation

In this Part—

"commencement" means the beginning of 14th January 2005;

"general insurance mediation activity" means any regulated activity of the kind specified by article 21, 25(1) or (2), 39A or 53 of the principal Order, or, so far as relevant to any of those articles, article 64 of that Order, which is carried on in relation to a contract of insurance which is not—

    (a)   a qualifying contract of insurance; or

    (b)   a contract of long-term care insurance;

"long-term care insurance mediation activity" means any regulated activity of the kind specified by article 21, 25(1) or (2), 39A or 53 of the principal Order, or, so far as relevant to any of those articles, article 64 of that Order, which is carried on in relation to a contract of insurance which is a contract of long-term care insurance.

[2706]

23 Applications for Part IV permission—general insurance mediation

(1)   This article applies to any completed application for Part IV permission which is made before 14th July 2004 by a person who is not an authorised person, to the extent that the application relates to any general insurance mediation activity ("an early Part IV application").

(2)   Section 52(1) of the Act (applications to be determined by the Authority within six months) does not apply to early Part IV applications.

(3)   If the Authority has not determined an early Part IV application before the end of the period of six months beginning on the date on which it received the completed application, it must inform the applicant of the progress being made on the application (unless it has already done so).

(4)   In any event, the Authority must determine all early Part IV applications before 14th January 2005.

[2707]

24 Application for approval—general insurance mediation

(1)   This article applies to any application made before 14th October 2004 under section 59 of the Act (approval of the performance of controlled functions) by a person who is not an authorised person for the Authority's approval of the performance by a person of any controlled function (within the meaning of section 59(3) of the Act), to the extent that that function relates to the carrying on of any general insurance mediation activity ("an early Part V application").

(2)   Section 61(3) of the Act (applications to be determined by the Authority within three months) does not apply to early Part V applications.

(3)   If the Authority has not determined an early Part V application before the end of the period of six months beginning on the date on which it received the application, it must inform the applicant of the progress being made on the application (unless it has already done so).

(4)   In any event, the Authority must determine all early Part V applications before 14th January 2005.

[2708]

25 Applications for Part IV permission—long-term care insurance mediation

(1)   This article applies to any completed application for Part IV permission which is made before 30th April 2004 by a person who is not an authorised person, to the extent that the application relates to any long-term care insurance mediation activity ("an early Part IV long-term care application").

(2)   Section 52(1) of the Act (applications to be determined by the Authority within six months) does not apply to early Part IV long-term care applications.

(3)   If the Authority has not determined an early Part IV long-term care application before the end of the period of six months beginning on the date on which it received the completed application, it must inform the applicant of the progress being made on the application (unless it has already done so).

(4)   In any event, the Authority must determine all early Part IV long-term care applications before 31st October 2004.

[2709]

26 Application for approval—long-term care insurance mediation

(1)   This article applies to any application made before 31st July 2004 under section 59 of the Act (approval of the performance of controlled functions) by a person who is not an authorised person for the Authority's approval of the performance by a person of any controlled function

(within the meaning of section 59(3) of the Act), to the extent that that function relates to the carrying on of any long-term care insurance mediation activity ("an early Part V long-term care application").

(2)   Section 61(3) of the Act (applications to be determined by the Authority within three months) does not apply to early Part V long-term care applications.

(3)   If the Authority has not determined an early Part V long-term care application before the end of the period of six months beginning on the date on which it received the application, it must inform the applicant of the progress being made on the application (unless it has already done so).

(4)   In any event, the Authority must determine all early Part V long-term care applications before 31st October 2004.

[2710]

27   Modifications and waivers

(1)   Before commencement, section 148 of the Act (modification or waiver of rules) has effect as if the references to "authorised person" (except in subsection (9)) included a reference to a person who has Part IV permission to carry on any general insurance mediation activity or any long-term care insurance mediation activity, albeit that that permission is not in force.

(2)   To the extent that it relates to any general insurance mediation activity, any direction given by the Authority under section 148(2) of the Act as modified by paragraph (1) may not come into force before commencement.

(3)   To the extent that it relates to any long-term care insurance mediation activity, any such direction may not come into force before 31st October 2004.

[2711]

FINANCIAL SERVICES AND MARKETS ACT 2000 (TRANSITIONAL PROVISIONS) (COMPLAINTS RELATING TO GENERAL INSURANCE AND MORTGAGES) ORDER 2004

(SI 2004/454)

NOTES
Made: 25 February 2004.
Authority: Financial Services and Markets Act 2000, ss 426–428.
Commencement: 31 October 2004 (in so far as it relates to a complaint relating to an activity to which, immediately before that date, the MCAS Scheme applied); 14 January 2005 (otherwise).
This Order is reproduced as amended by: the Financial Services and Markets Act 2000 (Transitional Provisions) (Complaints Relating to General Insurance and Mortgages) (Amendment) Order 2004, SI 2004/1609.

ARRANGEMENT OF ARTICLES

1   Citation, commencement and interpretation

(1)   This Order may be cited as the Financial Services and Markets Act 2000 (Transitional Provisions) (Complaints Relating to General Insurance and Mortgages) Order 2004.

(2)   This Order comes into force—
  (a)   in so far as it relates to a complaint relating to an activity to which, immediately before 31st October 2004, the MCAS Scheme applied, on 31st October 2004;
  (b)   for all other purposes, on 14th January 2005.

(3)   In this Order—
  "the Act" means the Financial Services and Markets Act 2000;
  "former scheme" means the GISC Facility or, as the case may be, the MCAS Scheme;

"GISC Facility" means the Dispute Resolution Facility established by the General Insurance Standards Council;

"MCAS Scheme" means the Mortgage Code Arbitration Scheme;

"new scheme" means the ombudsman scheme provided for by Part 16 of the Act [(the ombudsman scheme)];

"relevant commencement date" means—

(a)   in relation to a complaint which relates to an activity to which, immediately before 14th January 2005, the GISC Facility applied, ... 14th January 2005;

(b)   in relation to a complaint which relates to an activity to which, immediately before 31st October 2004, the MCAS Scheme applied, ... 31st October 2004.

[2712]

NOTES

Commencement: 31 October 2004 (in so far as it relates to a complaint relating to an activity to which, immediately before that date, the MCAS Scheme applied); 14 January 2005 (otherwise).

Para (3): words in square brackets in definition "new scheme" substituted, and words omitted from definition "relevant commencement date" revoked, by the Financial Services and Markets Act 2000 (Transitional Provisions) (Complaints Relating to General Insurance and Mortgages) (Amendment) Order 2004, SI 2004/1609, reg 2, as from 15 July 2004.

2   Complaints made after commencement about acts or omissions before commencement

(1)   Subject to the provisions of this Order, the compulsory jurisdiction resulting from section 226 of the Act applies to a complaint referred to the new scheme [on or] after the relevant commencement date which relates to an act or omission occurring before that date if the conditions mentioned in paragraph (2) are satisfied (notwithstanding that the conditions in subsection (2)(b) and (c) of that section are not met).

(2)   The conditions are that—

(a)   the act or omission is that of a person ("R") who, at the time of that act or omission, was subject to a former scheme;

(b)   R was an authorised person on or after the relevant commencement date;

(c)   the act or omission occurred in the carrying on by R of an activity to which that former scheme applied; and

(d)   the complainant is eligible and wishes to have the complaint dealt with under the new scheme.

(3)   For the purposes of paragraph (2)(d), where the complainant is not eligible in accordance with the rules made under section 226(6) and (7) of the Act (power to specify in rules the classes of persons who are eligible complainants), an ombudsman may nonetheless, if he considers it appropriate, treat the complainant as eligible if he would have been entitled to refer an equivalent complaint to the former scheme in question immediately before the relevant commencement date.

(4)   Where the former scheme in question is the GISC Facility, a complainant is not to be treated as eligible for the purposes of paragraph (2)(d) unless—

(a)   he is an individual; and

(b)   he is acting otherwise than solely for the purposes of his business.

(5)   Where the former scheme in question is the MCAS Scheme, a complainant is not to be treated as eligible for the purposes of paragraph (2)(d) if—

(a)   the complaint does not relate to a breach of the Mortgage Code;

(b)   the complaint concerns physical injury, illness, nervous shock or their consequences; or

(c)   the complainant is claiming a sum of money that exceeds £100,000.

(6)   A complaint falling within paragraph (1) is referred to in this Order as a "relevant transitional complaint".

[2713]

NOTES

Commencement: 31 October 2004 (in so far as it relates to a complaint relating to an activity to which, immediately before that date, the MCAS Scheme applied); 14 January 2005 (otherwise).

Para (1): words in square brackets inserted by the Financial Services and Markets Act 2000 (Transitional Provisions) (Complaints Relating to General Insurance and Mortgages) (Amendment) Order 2004, SI 2004/1609, reg 3, as from 15 July 2004.

3   Procedure applying to relevant transitional complaints

In paragraph 13 of Schedule 17 to the Act (Authority's procedural rules)—

(a)   the references to a complaint are to be taken to include a relevant transitional complaint; and

(b)   the references to the ombudsman scheme are, in relation to a relevant transitional complaint, to be taken to mean the new scheme as it applies to such complaints by virtue of this Order; and

(c)   in sub-paragraph (4), the reference to complaints which may be referred to the scheme is to be taken to include any complaint which may be referred to the scheme as a relevant transitional complaint.

[2714]

NOTES

Commencement: 31 October 2004 (in so far as it relates to a complaint relating to an activity to which, immediately before that date, the MCAS Scheme applied); 14 January 2005 (otherwise).

4   Scheme rules applying to relevant transitional complaints

(1)   In paragraph 14 of Schedule 17 to the Act (the scheme operator's rules)—

(a)   references to "complaints" are to be taken to include relevant transitional complaints;

(b)   sub-paragraph (2)(a) (matters which are to be taken into account in making determinations) does not apply to a relevant transitional complaint.

(2)   In deciding whether a relevant transitional complaint is to be dismissed without consideration of its merits as mentioned in paragraph 14(2)(b) of that Schedule, an ombudsman must take into account whether an equivalent complaint would have been so dismissed under the former scheme in question, as it had effect immediately before the relevant commencement date; and any scheme rules made under paragraph 14(2)(b) and (3) of that Schedule (rejection of a complaint without consideration of its merits) are to be construed accordingly.

[2715]

NOTES

Commencement: 31 October 2004 (in so far as it relates to a complaint relating to an activity to which, immediately before that date, the MCAS Scheme applied); 14 January 2005 (otherwise).

5   Determination of relevant transitional complaints

(1)   Sections 228 to 232 of the Act apply in relation to a relevant transitional complaint as they apply in relation to a complaint of the kind mentioned in section 226(1) of the Act (compulsory jurisdiction), subject to paragraph (2).

(2)   In determining, in relation to a relevant transitional complaint—

(a)   what is fair and reasonable in all the circumstances of the case, for the purposes of section 228(2) of the Act, and

(b)   what amount (if any) constitutes fair compensation for the purposes of section 229(2)(a) of the Act,

an ombudsman is to take into account what determination might have been expected to be made under the former scheme in question, and what amount (if any) might have been expected to be awarded or recommended by way of compensation under that scheme, in relation to an equivalent complaint dealt with under the former scheme immediately before the relevant commencement date.

[2716]

NOTES

Commencement: 31 October 2004 (in so far as it relates to a complaint relating to an activity to which, immediately before that date, the MCAS Scheme applied); 14 January 2005 (otherwise).

6   Funding and fees

(1)   In section 234(1) of the Act (industry funding), the reference to the operation of the new scheme in relation to the compulsory jurisdiction is to be taken to include the operation of the scheme in relation to relevant transitional complaints.

(2)   In paragraph 15 of Schedule 17 to the Act (fees), the references to a complaint are to be taken to include a relevant transitional complaint.

(3)   Any fee which, by reason of paragraph (2), is owed to the scheme operator by a respondent who is not an authorised person, may be recovered as a debt due to the scheme operator.

[2717]

NOTES

Commencement: 31 October 2004 (in so far as it relates to a complaint relating to an activity to which, immediately before that date, the MCAS Scheme applied); 14 January 2005 (otherwise).

PART III
STATUTORY INSTRUMENTS

7 Exemption from liability in damages

In paragraph 10(1) of Schedule 17 to the Act (exemption from liability in damages), the reference to functions under the Act in relation to the compulsory jurisdiction is to be taken to include functions exercisable by virtue of this Order.

[2718]

NOTES

Commencement: 31 October 2004 (in so far as it relates to a complaint relating to an activity to which, immediately before that date, the MCAS Scheme applied); 14 January 2005 (otherwise).

8 Privilege

In paragraph 11 of Schedule 17 to the Act (privilege), the reference to a complaint which is subject to the compulsory jurisdiction is to be taken to include a relevant transitional complaint.

[2719]

NOTES

Commencement: 31 October 2004 (in so far as it relates to a complaint relating to an activity to which, immediately before that date, the MCAS Scheme applied); 14 January 2005 (otherwise).

9 Record-keeping and reporting requirements relating to relevant transitional complaints

The Authority may make rules applying to authorised persons with respect to the keeping of records and the making of reports in relation to relevant transitional complaints.

[2720]

NOTES

Commencement: 31 October 2004 (in so far as it relates to a complaint relating to an activity to which, immediately before that date, the MCAS Scheme applied); 14 January 2005 (otherwise).

10 (*Revoked by the Financial Services and Markets Act 2000 (Transitional Provisions) (Complaints Relating to General Insurance and Mortgages) (Amendment) Order 2004, SI 2004/1609, reg 3, as from 15 July 2004.*)

11 Information

(1) Any information held by any person responsible for the operation of a former scheme ("the former holder") in connection with the operation of a former scheme may be disclosed by that person to the scheme operator or to an ombudsman ("the new holder").

(2) Any such disclosure is not to be treated as contravening any restriction on disclosure of the information (imposed by statute or otherwise) to which the former holder is subject.

(3) When information has been disclosed in accordance with this article, the new holder is to be treated as subject to any such restriction on disclosure as would have applied to the former holder (subject to any exceptions which would have so applied).

(4) But paragraph (3) does not prevent the application of section 31(4A) of the Data Protection Act 1998 to information which has been disclosed in accordance with this article.

(5) Sections 231 and 232 apply in relation to relevant transitional complaints as they apply in relation to complaints relating to acts or omissions occurring [on or after the relevant commencement date].

[2721]

NOTES

Commencement: 31 October 2004 (in so far as it relates to a complaint relating to an activity to which, immediately before that date, the MCAS Scheme applied); 14 January 2005 (otherwise).
Para (5): words in square brackets substituted by the Financial Services and Markets Act 2000 (Transitional Provisions) (Complaints Relating to General Insurance and Mortgages) (Amendment) Order 2004, SI 2004/1609, reg 5, as from 15 July 2004.

[12 Application of rules etc in relation to relevant matters

(1) If the Authority proposes to make any rules or give guidance in relation to relevant matters, sections 155 and 157(3) of the Act do not apply to the proposed rules or guidance.

(2) When the scheme operator proposes to make any scheme rules in relation to relevant matters, sub-paragraphs (4) to (6) of paragraph 14 of Schedule 17 to the Act do not apply to the proposed rules.

(3) In this article, "relevant matters" means—
(a) the effect of this Order;

(b)   the application of rules or guidance made or to be made before the relevant commencement date relating to relevant transitional complaints.]

[2722]

NOTES
Commencement: 15 July 2004.
Added by the Financial Services and Markets Act 2000 (Transitional Provisions) (Complaints Relating to General Insurance and Mortgages) (Amendment) Order 2004, SI 2004/1609, reg 6, as from 15 July 2004.

FINANCIAL CONGLOMERATES AND OTHER FINANCIAL GROUPS REGULATIONS 2004

(SI 2004/1862)

NOTES
Made: 19 July 2004.
Authority: European Communities Act 1972, s 2(2); Financial Services and Markets Act 2000, ss 183(2), 188(2), 417(1), 428(3).
Commencement: 10 August 2004.
These Regulations are reproduced as amended by: the Capital Requirements Regulations 2006, SI 2006/3221; the Financial Services and Markets Act 2000 (Markets in Financial Instruments) Regulations 2007, SI 2007/126.

ARRANGEMENT OF REGULATIONS

PART 1
INTRODUCTION

PART 1
INTRODUCTION

1   Citation, commencement and interpretation

(1)   These Regulations may be cited as the Financial Conglomerates and Other Financial Groups Regulations 2004 and come into force on 10th August 2004.

(2)   In these Regulations—
"the Act" means the Financial Services and Markets Act 2000;

["the European Banking Committee" means the Committee established pursuant to a Commission Decision of 5 November 2003 establishing the European Banking Committee (No 2004/10/EC);]

"the capital adequacy directive" means [Directive 2006/49/EC of the European Parliament and of the Council of 14 June 2006] on the capital adequacy of investment firms and credit institutions;

"competent authority", except in the term "third-country competent authority" as defined in regulation 7(1), means any national authority of an EEA State which is empowered by law or regulation to supervise regulated entities, whether on an individual or group-wide basis;

"the conglomerates directive" means Directive 2002/87/EC of the European Parliament and of the Council of 16th December 2002 on the supplementary supervision of credit institutions, insurance undertakings and investment firms in a financial conglomerate and amending Council Directives 73/239/EEC, 79/267/EEC, 92/49/EEC, 92/96/EEC, 93/6/EEC, 93/22/EEC, and Directives 98/78/EC and 2000/12/EC of the European Parliament and of the Council;

"co-ordinator" means the competent authority which has been appointed, for the purposes of Article 10 of the conglomerates directive, as the competent authority which is responsible for the co-ordination and exercise of supplementary supervision of a financial conglomerate;

"directive requirement" means any procedural requirement (including a requirement to consult or obtain consent) imposed on a competent authority by—

(a)　the conglomerates directive; or

(b)　[Article 143] of the banking consolidation directive (as it is applied by that directive or by [Article 2 and 37(1)] of the capital adequacy directive);

"financial conglomerate", except in the term "third-country financial conglomerate" as defined in regulation 7(1), has the meaning given by Article 2(14) of the conglomerates directive;

"the Financial Conglomerates Committee" means the Committee established pursuant to Article 21 of the conglomerates directive;

"relevant competent authorities" means those competent authorities, within the meaning of Article 2(17) of the conglomerates directive, which are, or which have been appointed as, relevant competent authorities in relation to a financial conglomerate;

"regulated entity" means—

(a)　a credit institution (within the meaning of the second sub-paragraph of [Article 4(1)] of the banking consolidation directive);

(b)　an insurance undertaking (within the meaning of Article 4 of Directive 2002/83/EC of the European Parliament and of the Council of 5th November 2002 concerning life assurance, Article 6 of the first non-life insurance directive or Article 1(b) of Directive 98/78/EC of the European Parliament and of the Council of 27th October 1998 on the supplementary supervision of insurance undertakings in an insurance group);

(c)　a management company (within the meaning of Article 1a(2) of the UCITS directive) or an undertaking which is outside the EEA but which would require authorisation in accordance with Article 5 of the UCITS directive if it had its registered office in the EEA; or

(d)　an investment firm (within the meaning of [Article 4.1.1 of the markets in financial instruments directive], [including the undertakings referred to in Article 3(1)(b)] of the capital adequacy directive); and

"supplementary supervision" means the supervision of a regulated entity to the extent and in the manner prescribed by the conglomerates directive.

(3)　Save as is otherwise provided, any expression used in these Regulations which is defined for the purposes of the Act has the meaning given by the Act.

[2723]

NOTES

Commencement: 10 August 2004.

Para (2): definition "the European Banking Committee" substituted (for original definition "the Banking Advisory Committee"), and words in square brackets in the definitions "the capital adequacy directive" and "directive requirement" substituted, by the Capital Requirements Regulations 2006, SI 2006/3221, reg 29(3), Sch 5, para 1(1), (2)(a)–(c), as from 1 January 2007; words in first and third pairs of square brackets in definition "regulated entity" substituted by SI 2006/3221, reg 29(3), Sch 5, para 1(1), (2)(d), as from 1 January 2007; words in second pair of square brackets in that definition substituted by the Financial Services and Markets Act 2000 (Markets in Financial Instruments) Regulations 2007, SI 2007/126, reg 3(6), Sch 6, Pt 2, para 19(1), (2), as from 1 November 2007 (for the full commencement details of SI 2007/126, see reg 1 of those Regulations at **[4051]**).

PART 2

EXERCISE OF SUPPLEMENTARY SUPERVISION OF REGULATED ENTITIES IN A FINANCIAL CONGLOMERATE

2 Notification of identification as a financial conglomerate and choice of co-ordinator

(1)   Where the Authority has become the co-ordinator for a financial conglomerate, it must notify—

    (a)   the relevant member of that financial conglomerate;

    (b)   any competent authority which has given EEA authorisation to a regulated entity which is a member of that financial conglomerate;

    (c)   the competent authorities of the EEA State in which the parent undertaking of that financial conglomerate has its head office, unless that parent undertaking is a regulated entity; and

    (d)   the Commission,

that the group has been identified as a financial conglomerate for the purposes of Article 4 of the conglomerates directive and that the Authority is the co-ordinator for that financial conglomerate.

(2)   Paragraph (3) applies if—

    (a)   the Authority is a relevant competent authority in relation to a financial conglomerate, and

    (b)   the Authority, in conjunction with the other relevant competent authorities, proposes to waive the criteria specified in Article 10(2) of the conglomerates directive (selection of the co-ordinator) and appoint a different competent authority as co-ordinator.

(3)   Before the Authority, in conjunction with the other relevant competent authorities, waives the criteria specified in Article 10(2) of the conglomerates directive and appoints a different competent authority as co-ordinator, the Authority must, where there is a directive requirement to do so, give the financial conglomerate an opportunity to make representations.

(4)   In this regulation, "the relevant member" of a financial conglomerate is—

    (a)   the parent undertaking at the head of the financial conglomerate; or

    (b)   where there is no parent undertaking at the head of the financial conglomerate, the regulated entity which—

        (i)   is in the most important financial sector (within the meaning given by Article 3(2) of the conglomerates directive); and

        (ii)   has the largest balance-sheet total in that sector.

[2724]

NOTES

Commencement: 10 August 2004.

---

3 Exercise of functions under Part IV of the Act for the purposes of carrying on supplementary supervision

(1)   This regulation applies if the Authority is considering varying the Part IV permission of any person ("A") where—

    (a)   A is a member of a financial conglomerate; and

    (b)   the Authority is acting in the course of carrying on supplementary supervision for the purposes of any provision (other than Article 11, 12, 16, 17 or 18(3)) of the conglomerates directive.

(2)   Section 49(2) of the Act (obligation to consult home state regulators of connected persons) does not apply.

(3)   Before varying the Part IV permission of A, the Authority must, where there is a directive requirement to do so—

    (a)   consult the relevant competent authorities in relation to the financial conglomerate of which A is a member;

    (b)   obtain the consent of those competent authorities; and

    (c)   consult the financial conglomerate of which A is a member.

[2725]

NOTES

Commencement: 10 August 2004.

---

4 Exercise of functions under section 148 of the Act for the purposes of carrying on supplementary supervision

(1)   Paragraph (2) applies if the Authority is considering exercising any of the powers conferred on it by section 148 of the Act (modification or waiver of rules) in the course of carrying on supplementary supervision of a financial conglomerate for the purposes of any provision (other than Article 11, 12, 16, 17 or 18(3)) of the conglomerates directive.

(2)   Before the Authority exercises such a power in relation to an authorised person who is a member of a financial conglomerate, the Authority must, where there is a directive requirement to do so—

    (a)   consult the relevant competent authorities in relation to the financial conglomerate of which that person is a member;

    (b)   obtain the consent of those competent authorities; and

    (c)   consult the financial conglomerate of which that person is a member.

[2726]

NOTES
    Commencement: 10 August 2004.

5   Consultation in the case of major sanctions or exceptional measures

(1)   Before the Authority—

    (a)   varies the Part IV permission of a member of a financial conglomerate ("D");

    (b)   publishes a statement under section 205 of the Act (public censure) that it considers that D has contravened a requirement imposed on him by or under the Act;

    (c)   imposes a penalty on D in respect of such a contravention under section 206 of the Act (financial penalties); or

    (d)   exercises any of its powers (other than its powers under section 381, 383 or 384(2)) under Part XXV of the Act (injunctions and restitution) in relation to D,

it must, if it considers that the action constitutes a major sanction or an exceptional measure and is of importance for the supervisory tasks of the competent authority of any regulated entity which is a member of the same financial conglomerate as D, consult that competent authority.

(2)   But paragraph (1) does not apply—

    (a)   where the Authority considers that there is an urgent need to act;

    (b)   where the Authority considers that such consultation may jeopardise the effectiveness of the action mentioned in paragraph (1); or

    (c)   where regulation 3, 8(3) or (4), 9 or 10 applies.

(3)   Where paragraph (1) does not apply by virtue of paragraph (2)(a) or (b), the Authority must, as soon as is reasonably practicable, inform the competent authority referred to in paragraph (1) of the action that it has taken.

[2727]

NOTES
    Commencement: 10 August 2004.

6   Authority functions and service of notifications

(1)   Any function carried out by the Authority (whether in the capacity of a co-ordinator, a relevant competent authority or otherwise) for the purposes of the conglomerates directive (including a function conferred by these Regulations) is to be treated as a function conferred on the Authority by a provision of the Act.

(2)   The Financial Services and Markets Act 2000 (Service of Notices) Regulations 2001 apply to any notifications given under regulation 2(1)(a) as they apply to any notice, direction or document of any kind given under the Act.

[2728]

NOTES
    Commencement: 10 August 2004.

PART 3
SUPPLEMENTARY SUPERVISION OF THIRD-COUNTRY FINANCIAL CONGLOMERATES AND THIRD-COUNTRY GROUPS

7   Supervision of third-country financial conglomerates and third-country groups—interpretation

(1)   For the purposes of this Part—

    "asset management company" means—

        (a)   any EEA firm falling within paragraph 5(f) of Schedule 3 to the Act; or

        (b)   any UK firm whose EEA right derives from the UCITS directive;

    "credit institution" means—

        (a)   any EEA firm falling within paragraph 5(b) of Schedule 3 to the Act; or

        (b)   any UK firm whose EEA right derives from the banking consolidation directive;

    "investment firm" means—

        (a)   any EEA firm falling within paragraph 5(a) of Schedule 3 to the Act; or

  (b) any UK firm whose EEA right derives from the [markets in financial instruments directive];

"third-country competent authority" means the authority of a country or territory which is not an EEA State which is empowered by law or regulation to supervise (whether on an individual or group-wide basis) regulated entities;

"third-country financial conglomerate" means a group—

  (a) which, subject to Article 3 of the conglomerates directive, meets the conditions in Article 2(14) of that directive, and

  (b) in which the parent undertaking has its head office outside the EEA;

"third-country group" means a group of which the parent undertaking has its head office outside the EEA.

(2) For the purposes of this Part a regulated entity is in a third-country group if the parent undertaking of the group in which it is a member has its head office outside the EEA.

[2729]

NOTES

Commencement: 10 August 2004.

Para (1): words in square brackets in para (b) of the definition "investment firm" substituted by the Financial Services and Markets Act 2000 (Markets in Financial Instruments) Regulations 2007, SI 2007/126, reg 3(6), Sch 6, Pt 2, para 19(1), (3), as from 1 November 2007 (for the full commencement details of SI 2007/126, see reg 1 of those Regulations at **[4051]**).

---

8 Supervision of third-country financial conglomerates

(1) Where the Authority is, for the purposes of Article 18(1) of the conglomerates directive (parent undertakings outside the Community), verifying whether the regulated entities in a third-country financial conglomerate are subject to supervision, by a third-country competent authority, which is equivalent to that provided for by the provisions of the conglomerates directive, it must, where there is a directive requirement to do so, before completing this verification—

  (a) consult the other relevant competent authorities in relation to that third-county financial conglomerate;

  (b) consult the Financial Conglomerates Committee for the purposes of obtaining any applicable guidance prepared by that Committee in accordance with Article 21(5) of the conglomerates directive (guidance on whether third-country competent authorities are likely to achieve objectives of supplementary supervision); and

  (c) take into account any such guidance.

(2) Paragraphs (3) and (4) apply if the Authority, for the purposes of Article 18(3) of the conglomerates directive (application of other methods for the purposes of ensuring appropriate supplementary supervision of the regulated entities in a third-country financial conglomerate), exercises its powers to—

  (a) vary the Part IV permission of a regulated entity in a third-country financial conglomerate;

  (b) disapply from, or apply in a modified form to, such a regulated entity the rules specified in subsection (1) of section 148 of the Act (modification or waiver of rules) in accordance with that section;

  (c) impose conditions under section 185 of the Act (conditions attached to approval of change of control) on a person who is, or proposes to be, a controller of such a regulated entity; or

  (d) give a notice under section 186 or 187 of the Act (notice of objection to acquisition of, or existing, control) to a person who is, or proposes to be, a controller of such a regulated entity.

(3) Where there is a directive requirement to do so, the Authority must before taking the action specified in paragraph (2)—

  (a) where the Authority is the co-ordinator, consult the relevant competent authorities in relation to that third-country financial conglomerate; or

  (b) where the Authority is not the co-ordinator, obtain the consent of the co-ordinator for that third-country financial conglomerate to take that action.

(4) If the Authority decides to take that action, it must, where there is a directive requirement to do so, notify—

  (a) the competent authority of each regulated entity in that third-country financial conglomerate, and

  (b) the Commission,

that it has done so.

[2730]

PART III
STATUTORY INSTRUMENTS

NOTES

Commencement: 10 August 2004.

---

9   Supervision of third-country banking groups

(1)   Where the Authority is, for the purposes of [Article 143] of the banking consolidation directive (third-country parent undertakings), verifying whether a credit institution in a third-country group is subject to supervision by a third-country competent authority which is equivalent to that governed by the principles laid down in [Articles 71, 72 and 73(1) and (3)] of that directive (supervision on a consolidated basis of credit institutions), it must, where there is a directive requirement to do so, before completing this verification—

    (a)   consult any competent authority which supervises a credit institution in that third-country group;

    (b)   consult [the European Banking Committee] for the purposes of obtaining any applicable guidance prepared by that Committee in accordance with [the first sub-paragraph of Article 143(2)] of that directive; and

    (c)   take into account any such guidance.

(2)   Paragraphs (3) and (4) apply if the Authority exercises, for the purposes of [Article 143(3)] of the banking consolidation directive, its powers to—

    (a)   vary the Part IV permission of a credit institution in a third-country group;

    (b)   disapply from, or apply in modified form to, such a credit institution, the rules specified in subsection (1) of section 148 of the Act in accordance with that section;

    (c)   impose conditions under section 185 of the Act on a person who is, or proposes to be, a controller of such a credit institution; or

    (d)   give a notice under section 186 or 187 of the Act to a person who is, or proposes to be, a controller of such a credit institution.

(3)   Where there is a directive requirement to do so, the Authority must before exercising its powers to take the action specified in paragraph (2)—

    (a)   where the Authority would be responsible for supervising that third-country group for the purposes of [Articles 125 or 126] of the banking consolidation directive (competent authorities responsible for exercising supervision on a consolidated basis) if alternative techniques were not applied, consult the competent authorities which are involved in the supervision of any of the credit institutions in that third-country group; and

    (b)   where the Authority would not be so responsible, obtain the consent of the competent authority which would be responsible for supervising that third-country group for the purposes of [Articles 125 or 126] of the banking consolidation directive if alternative techniques were not applied.

(4)   If the Authority decides to take that action, it must, where there is a directive requirement to do so, notify—

    (a)   any competent authority which supervises a credit institution in that third-country group; and

    (b)   the Commission,

that it has done so.

(5)   Where the Authority has, for the purposes of Article 30 of the conglomerates directive (asset management companies), included an asset management company in the scope of supervision of a credit institution in a third-country group, each reference in this regulation to a "credit institution" is to be treated as including a reference to that asset management company.

                                                         [2731]

NOTES

Commencement: 10 August 2004.

Paras (1)–(3): words in square brackets substituted by the Capital Requirements Regulations 2006, SI 2006/3221, reg 29(3), Sch 5, para 1(1), (3), as from 1 January 2007.

10   Supervision of third-country groups subject to the capital adequacy directive

(1)   Paragraph (2) applies if—

    [(a)   the Authority is, for the purposes of Article 143 of the banking consolidation directive, as applied by Articles 2(1) and 37(1) of the capital adequacy directive (supervision) verifying whether a credit institution or an investment firm in a third-country group is subject to supervision by a third-country competent authority which is equivalent to that governed by the principles laid down in Articles 2(1) and 37(1) of the capital adequacy directive; or]

    (b)   the Authority is, for the purposes of [Article 143] of the banking consolidation directive, as applied by [Articles 2(2) and 37(1)] of the capital adequacy directive (groups containing investment firms but no credit institutions), verifying whether an investment firm in a third-country group is subject to supervision, by a third-country competent authority, which is equivalent to that governed by the principles laid down in [Articles 2(2) and 37(1)] of the capital adequacy directive.

(2)   The Authority must, where there is a directive requirement to do so, before completing the verification referred to in paragraph (1)—

    (a)   consult any competent authority which supervises an investment firm or a credit institution (if any) in that third-country group;

    (b)   consult [the European Banking Committee] for the purposes of obtaining any applicable guidance prepared by that Committee in accordance with [Article 143(2)] of that directive; and

    (c)   take into account any such guidance.

(3)   Paragraphs (4) and (5) apply if the Authority exercises, for the purposes of [Article 143(3)] of the banking consolidation directive as applied by [Articles 2 and 37(1)] of the capital adequacy directive, its powers to—

    (a)   vary the Part IV permission of an investment firm or credit institution in a third-country group;

    (b)   disapply from or apply in modified form to, such an investment firm or credit institution the rules specified in subsection (1) of section 148 of the Act in accordance with that section;

    (c)   impose conditions under section 185 of the Act on a person who is, or proposes to be, a controller of such an investment firm or credit institution; or

    (d)   give a notice under section 186 or 187 of the Act to a person who is, or proposes to be, a controller of such an investment firm or credit institution.

(4)   Where there is a directive requirement to do so, the Authority must, before exercising its powers to take the action specified in paragraph (3)—

    (a)   where the Authority would be responsible for supervision of that third-country group for the purposes of [Articles 125 or 126] of the banking consolidation directive, as applied by [Articles 2 and 37(1)] of the capital adequacy directive, if alternative techniques were not applied, consult the competent authorities which are involved in the supervision of any of the investment firms or credit institutions (if any) in that third-country group; and

    (b)   where the Authority would not be so responsible, obtain the consent of the competent authority which would be responsible for supervision of that third-country group for the purposes of [Articles 125 or 126] of the banking consolidation directive, as applied by [Articles 2 and 37(1)] of the capital adequacy directive, if alternative techniques were not applied.

(5)   If the Authority decides to take that action, it must, where there is a directive requirement to do so, notify—

    (a)   any competent authority which supervises an investment firm or a credit institution (if any) in that third-country group; and

    (b)   the Commission,

that it has done so.

(6)   If the Authority has, for the purposes of Article 30 of the conglomerates directive, included an asset management company in the scope of supervision of—

    (a)   credit institutions and investment firms in a third-country group; or

    (b)   investment firms in a third-country group,

each reference in this regulation to an "investment firm" is to be treated as including a reference to that asset management company.

[2732]

NOTES

Commencement: 10 August 2004.

Paras (1)–(4): words in square brackets substituted by the Capital Requirements Regulations 2006, SI 2006/3221, reg 29(3), Sch 5, para 1(1), (4), as from 1 January 2007.

PART 4
PROVISIONS RELATING TO INFORMATION

11   (*Amends the Financial Services and Markets Act 2000 (Disclosure of Confidential Information) Regulations 2001, SI 2001/2188, reg 2 at* **[2351]**.)

12   Obtaining information—avoidance of duplication of reporting

(1)   Paragraph (2) applies if the Authority is the co-ordinator in relation to any financial conglomerate.

(2)   If the Authority requires any disclosed information in connection with its functions as the co-ordinator, it must so far as possible obtain that information by requesting the competent authority which holds that information to disclose it to the Authority.

(3)   In this regulation, "disclosed information" means information which a regulated entity in a financial conglomerate has disclosed to its competent authority.

[2733]

NOTES
Commencement: 10 August 2004.

PART 5
MISCELLANEOUS

13, 14   (*Reg 13 amends the Financial Services and Markets Act 2000 (Consultation with Competent Authorities) Regulations 2001, SI 2001/2509, regs 2–5 at* **[2422]**–**[2425]**, *substitutes reg 6 at* **[2426]**, *and adds reg 7 at* **[2427]**; *reg 14 amends the Building Societies Act 1986, s 119, the Bank of England Act 1998, s 17, the Cash Ratio Deposits (Eligible Liabilities) Order 1998, SI 1998/1130, art 2 at* **[3528]**, *and the Financial Services and Markets Act 2000 (EEA Passport Rights) Regulations 2001, SI 2001/2511, regs 2, 3 at* **[2431]**, **[2432]**.)

15   Extension of power to vary Part IV permissions

(1)   Subject to paragraph (2), the Authority may exercise its own-initiative power (within the meaning of section 45 of the Act (variation etc on the Authority's own initiative)) in relation to an authorised person, if it appears to it that it is desirable to do so for the purpose of—

(a)   carrying out supplementary supervision in accordance with the conglomerates directive;

(b)   acting in accordance with any of [Articles 133, 134, 136, 138, 141, 142 or 143] of the banking consolidation directive (as they are applied by that directive or by [Article 2(1) or (2) and 37(1)] of the capital adequacy directive); or

(c)   acting in accordance with Article 8(2) or Annex I.1.B of Directive 98/78/EC of the European Parliament and of the Council of 27 October 1998 on the supplementary supervision of insurance undertakings in an insurance group.

(2)   The Authority may exercise its own-initiative power, for the purposes set out in paragraph (1), to vary a Part IV permission in any of the ways mentioned in section 44(1) of the Act (variation etc at request of authorised person); and this extends to including any provision in the permission as varied that could be included if a fresh permission were given in response to an application under section 40 of the Act (application for permission).

(3)   The duty imposed by subsection (2) of section 41 of the Act (the threshold conditions) does not prevent the Authority from exercising its own-initiative power for the purposes set out in paragraph (1).

[2734]

NOTES
Commencement: 10 August 2004.
Para (1): words in square brackets in sub-para (b) substituted by the Capital Requirements Regulations 2006, SI 2006/3221, reg 29(3), Sch 5, para 1(1), (5), as from 1 January 2007.

FINANCIAL SERVICES AND MARKETS ACT 2000 (TRANSITIONAL PROVISIONS) (MORTGAGES) ORDER 2004 (NOTE)

(SI 2004/2615)

NOTES
Made: 7 October 2004.
Authority: Financial Services and Markets Act 2000, ss 426–428.
Commencement: 29 October 2004 (for the purposes of art 4 (Application of the Authority's rules etc to persons with interim permission or interim approval)); 31 October 2004 (otherwise).
Article 2 of this Order conferred an interim permission on certain applicants who had applied to the FSA for permission under Pt IV of FSMA 2000 to carry on certain mortgage mediation activities (viz arranging or advising on regulated mortgage contracts) and whose application was pending on the date (31 October 2004) when those activities became regulated activities within the meaning of s 22 of FSMA 2000 (by reason of the Financial Services and Markets Act 2000 (Regulated Activities) (Amendment) (No 1) Order 2003, SI 2003/1475). Article 3 conferred interim approval, in similar terms to those in art 2, on people who were working for a person who benefited from an interim permission and who needed approval under Pt V of the Act. Article 4 allowed the FSA to modify, inter alia, its rules in their application to persons with interim permission or interim approval, and art 5 (and the Schedule) provided for the application of provisions in, or made under, the Act to persons with interim permission or interim approval. Interim permission or interim approval continued until the firm's application was determined and permission granted, or until the applicant withdrew their

application, or until the Financial Services Tribunal confirmed the FSA's decision to refuse the application for permission. In any event, interim permission and interim approval ended on 31 October 2005 for regulated mortgage firms and, after this date, no firms have interim permission to carry on these activities. This Order effectively became spent on that date.

[2735]–[2740]

FINANCIAL SERVICES AND MARKETS ACT 2000 (STAKEHOLDER PRODUCTS) REGULATIONS 2004

(SI 2004/2738)

NOTES
Made: 16 November 2004.
Authority: Financial Services and Markets Act 2000, s 428; Financial Services and Markets Act 2000 (Regulated Activities) Order, SI 2001/544, art 52B(3).
Commencement: 6 April 2005.
These Regulations are reproduced as amended by: the Financial Services and Markets Act 2000 (Stakeholder Products) (Amendment) Regulations 2005, SI 2005/594.

ARRANGEMENT OF REGULATIONS

1 Citation and commencement

These Regulations may be cited as the Financial Services and Markets 2000 (Stakeholder Products) Regulations 2004 and come into force on 6th April 2005.

[2741]

NOTES
Commencement: 6 April 2005.
Note: this regulation is reproduced as it appears in the Queen's Printer's copy, ie, without the word "Act" preceding "2000".

2 Interpretation

(1) In these Regulations—
"the 2000 Act" means the Financial Services and Markets Act 2000;
"account-holder" means the holder of a deposit account;
"Bank of England base rate" means the rate announced from time to time by the Monetary Policy Committee of the Bank of England as the official dealing rate, being the rate at which the Bank of England is willing to enter into transactions for providing short-term liquidity in the money markets;
"the Conduct of Business Rules" means the Conduct of Business Rules made by the Financial Services Authority under section 153 of the 2000 Act;
"relevant contract of insurance" means a contract of insurance—
    (a)   which, or any part of which, is one or more of the following kinds—
        (i)   life and annuity,
        (ii)   linked long-term, and
    (b)   which is carried out by an insurer who has permission, as the case may be, under—
        (i)   Part 4 of the 2000 Act, or
        (ii)   paragraph 15 of Schedule 3 to the 2000 Act,
    to effect or carry out contracts of insurance of that kind, and
    (c)   is not a with-profits policy and does not include rights in a with-profits fund;
"deposit account" means a deposit account with a deposit-taker and includes a share account with a building society within the meaning of the Building Societies Act 1986;
"deposit-taker" means—
    (a)   a person who has permission under Part 4 of the 2000 Act to accept deposits, or

(b)   an EEA firm of the kind mentioned in paragraph 5(b) of Schedule 3 to the 2000 Act which has permission under paragraph 15 of that Schedule (as a result of qualifying for authorisation under paragraph 12 of that Schedule) to accept deposits;

"dilution levy" has the meaning given by the handbook made by the Financial Services Authority under section 153 of the 2000 Act;

"insurer" means—

    (a)   a person who has permission under Part 4 of the 2000 Act to effect or carry out contracts of insurance, or

    (b)   an EEA firm of the kind mentioned in paragraph 5(d) of Schedule 3 to that Act, which has permission under paragraph 15 of that Schedule (as a result of qualifying for authorisation under paragraph 12 of that Schedule) to effect or carry out contracts of insurance;

"investor" means a member of a collective investment scheme which complies with regulation 5 or an underlying fund which complies with regulation 6 as the case may be;

"investment property" means the scheme property of a collective investment scheme which complies with regulation 5 or an underlying fund which complies with regulation 6 as the case may be;

"investment scheme" means a collective investment scheme which complies with regulation 5 or a linked long-term contract which complies with regulation 6 as the case may be;

"land and buildings" means interests in any land or buildings which satisfy the conditions in rule 5A.8.5R of the Collective Investment Schemes Sourcebook made by the Financial Services Authority under section 153 of the 2000 Act;

"linked long-term contract" means a contract of long-term insurance as specified in paragraph 3 of Part 2 of Schedule 1 to the principal Order;

"manager" means the manager of a relevant collective investment scheme or the insurer of a relevant linked long-term contract as the case may be;

"the principal Order" means the Financial Services and Markets Act 2000 (Regulated Activities) Order 2001;

"relevant collective investment scheme" means an authorised unit trust scheme, an authorised open-ended investment company or a recognised scheme, as the case may be, as defined in section 237(3) of the 2000 Act;

"relevant investments" means—

    (a)   shares issued by a company wherever incorporated and officially listed on a recognised stock exchange;

    (b)   units in a relevant collective investment scheme where a substantial proportion of the scheme property is invested, directly or indirectly, in shares, as defined in paragraph (a) or land and buildings; and

    (c)   rights under a contract of insurance where a substantial proportion of the assets of the funds held in respect of that contract are invested, directly or indirectly, in shares as set out in sub-paragraph (a) or land and buildings;

"relevant linked long-term contract" means a linked long-term contract which meets the conditions and characteristics specified in regulation 6(1);

"units" means the rights or interests (however described) of the members of a relevant collective investment scheme.

(2)   The definitions of "deposit-taker" and "insurer" in paragraph (1) must be read with—

    (a)   section 22 of the 2000 Act,

    (b)   any relevant order under that section, and

    (c)   Schedule 2 to that Act.

[2742]

NOTES
Commencement: 6 April 2005.

3 Meaning of stakeholder product

These Regulations specify kinds of investment for the purposes of sub-paragraph (c) of the definition of "stakeholder product" in article 52B(3) of the principal Order and accordingly an investment of one of these kinds is a stakeholder product for the purposes of article 52B of that Order.

[2743]

NOTES
Commencement: 6 April 2005.

4 Certain deposit accounts

A deposit account ("the account") is a stakeholder product if the following conditions are fulfilled—

(a)   the minimum amount which an account-holder may deposit on a single occasion is £10, except where the deposit-taker permits a smaller payment;

(b)   the deposit-taker permits [payment to the account by any of the following means, at the option of the account-holder]—

     (i)   cash;

     (ii)   cheque;

     (iii)   ...

     (iv)   standing order;

     (v)   direct credit (other than standing order),

excluding payments by credit card or debit card or any combination including a payment by credit card or debit card;

(c)   interest accrues on the account on a daily basis at a rate that is not less than the Bank of England base rate minus 1 per cent per annum ("the interest rate");

(d)   when the Bank of England base rate increases, the interest rate must be raised within one month of the date of that increase;

(e)   on the instructions of the account holder, any cash and interest held in the account is transferred or paid to the account holder within a period which may not exceed seven days ("withdrawal instructions"); and

(f)   there is no limitation on the frequency with which an account holder may issue withdrawal instructions.

[2744]

NOTES

Commencement: 6 April 2005.

Words in square brackets in para (b) substituted, and para (b)(iii) revoked, by the Financial Services and Markets Act 2000 (Stakeholder Products) (Amendment) Regulations 2005, SI 2005/594, reg 2(1), (2), as from 6 April 2005.

5 Units in certain collective investment schemes

Units in a relevant collective investment scheme are a stakeholder product where that scheme has the characteristics, and complies with the conditions, set out in regulation 7.

[2745]

NOTES

Commencement: 6 April 2005.

6 Rights under certain linked long-term contracts

(1)   Rights under a linked long-term contract are a stakeholder product where the insurer ensures that the fund held in respect of that contract ("the underlying fund")—

(a)   has the characteristics and complies with the conditions set out in regulation 7; and

(b)   where the investment returns are smoothed, complies with the conditions set out in regulation 8.

(2)   For the purposes of this regulation and regulations 8 and 9, investment returns are smoothed when the insurer offers the product on the basis that the amount in respect of the investment returns earned from time to time by the underlying funds to be attributed under the contract to the policyholder will be managed and attributed with a view to reducing the volatility of such returns over given periods, and "smoothing", "smoothed" and "unsmoothed" are to be construed accordingly.

[2746]

NOTES

Commencement: 6 April 2005.

7 Characteristics and conditions applicable to certain stakeholder products

(1)   The characteristics in relation to an investment scheme are—

(a)   no more than 60 per cent in value of the investment property, calculated in accordance with paragraph (3), consists of relevant investments;

(b)   the investment property should be selected and managed having regard to the need to achieve a balance between—

     (i)   the opportunity for the investor to benefit from growth in the value of investments generally; and

     (ii)   control of the risk of loss of value in the investment; and

(c)   the manager has regard to—

     (i)   the need for diversification of the investment property, in so far as appropriate to the circumstances of the investment scheme; and

     (ii)   the suitability for the purposes of the scheme of any investment option proposed.

(2)   The conditions with which the investment scheme must comply are—

(a)   the minimum amount which an investor may contribute to the investment scheme on a single occasion is £20, except where the manager permits a smaller amount;

(b)   the manager must permit [payment to the investment scheme by any of the following means, at the option of the investor]—

    (i)   cheque;
    (ii)   direct debit;
    (iii)   standing order;
    (iv)   direct credit (other than standing order),

and excluding payments by cash, credit card or debit card or any combination including a payment by cash, credit card or debit card;

(c)   the value of an investor's rights in the investment scheme and the value of the investment property may be reduced in the circumstances and to the extent set out in regulation 9; and

(d)   where the stakeholder product consists of—

    (i)   units in a relevant collective investment scheme, it must be a requirement of that scheme that the purchase and sale price of those units shall, at any given time, not differ from each other and that price must be made available to the public on a daily basis;

    (ii)   rights under a relevant linked long-term contract which are expressed as shares in funds, it must be a requirement of that contract that the purchase and sale price of those shares shall, at any given time, not differ from each other and that price must be made available to the public on a daily basis.

(3)   For the purposes of the calculation set out in paragraph (1)(a), the following provisions apply—

(a)   where any of the investment property is invested in units in a relevant collective investment scheme, only such of the assets of that scheme as are invested, directly or indirectly, in relevant investments shall be taken into account; and

(b)   the calculation shall be taken as an average over a period of 3 months.

(4)   When calculating the average over a period of 3 months for the purposes of paragraph (3)(b) ("the average"), where the manager has specified under paragraph (5) that the calculation is to be carried out weekly or monthly—

(a)   where the average is to be calculated weekly, it is to be carried out on such day of the week ("the specified day") as has been so specified by the manager (except that, where that day is not a working day, the average is to be calculated on the next working day), and the average on each subsequent day prior to the next specified day is to be taken to be the average on the previous specified day; and

(b)   where the average is to be calculated monthly, it is to be so calculated on such day in each month ("the specified day") as has been so specified by the manager (except that, where that date is not a working day, the average is to be calculated on the next working day), and the average on each subsequent day prior to the next specified date is to be taken to be the average on the previous specified date.

(5)   For the purposes of paragraph (4)—

(a)   the frequency, which must be daily, weekly or monthly, with which the average is to be calculated; and

(b)   where the average is to be calculated using weekly or monthly figures, that day of the week or, as the case may be, the date in the month on which it is to take place,

must be specified in writing by the manager; and the specification may not be amended during the period of 12 months after the date on which it is made.

(6)   Where, following the calculation under paragraph (4), the average value of the investment property comprises more than 60 per cent of relevant investments, the manager must take steps to bring that average value within the limit prescribed in regulation 7(1)(a) as soon as reasonably practicable and in any event within 3 months.

[2747]

NOTES

Commencement: 6 April 2005.

Para (2): words in square brackets in sub-para (b) substituted by the Financial Services and Markets Act 2000 (Stakeholder Products) (Amendment) Regulations 2005, SI 2005/594, reg 2(1), (3), as from 6 April 2005.

8   Additional conditions applicable to smoothed linked long-term contracts

The conditions under this paragraph are—

(a)   the manager must make available, to each investor who is also a policyholder or to anyone else requesting it, the information necessary to enable a person making such a request properly to understand the essential elements of the insurer's commitment under the terms of the policy;

(b)   the manager must make available, to each investor and anyone else requesting it, information on its policy on and charges for smoothing;

(c)   no payment may be made or property attributed from the underlying fund to any person other than an investor, except for permitted reductions in the investor's rights and investment property in accordance with regulation 9;

(d)   the manager must manage the underlying fund with the aim of attributing to each investor on the maturity or surrender of his rights under the linked long-term contract a value that falls within a target range which is notified to each investor before he enters into the linked long-term contract;

(e)   except as provided for in paragraph (f), there is no guarantee of the value of an investor's rights under the linked long-term contract;

(f)   the manager may guarantee that, on the death of an investor, the value of an investor's rights under the linked long-term contract are no more than 101 per cent of the total of the value of the units allocated to that contract.

[2748]

NOTES
Commencement: 6 April 2005.

9 Permitted reductions in investor's rights and investment property

(1)   The value of an investor's rights in an investment scheme may be reduced in the circumstances, and to the extent, set out in paragraphs (3) to (5).

(2)   The value of the investment property may be reduced in the circumstances, and to the extent, set out in paragraph (9).

(3)   To the extent that an investor's rights in an investment scheme are represented by a fund allocated to him to the exclusion of other investors, the value of those rights may be reduced by the making of deductions from that fund no greater than, at the choice of the manager—

(a)   the relevant percentage of its value for each day on which it is held; or

(b)   the proportion attributable to the investor's fund of the relevant percentage of the value of the investment property for each day on which the investor's fund is held for the purposes of the scheme.

(4)   To the extent that an investor's rights in an investment scheme are represented by a share of funds held for the purposes of the scheme, the amount of that share not being determined by reference to a discretion exercisable by any person, the value of those rights may be reduced by the making of deductions from that share no greater than, at the choice of the manager—

(a)   the relevant percentage of its value for each day on which it is held; or

(b)   the proportion attributable to the investor's share of the relevant percentage of the value of the investment property for each day on which the investor's share is held for the purposes of the scheme.

(5)   To the extent that an investor's rights are represented by rights under a linked long-term contract to which regulations 6(1)(b) and 8 apply, the value of those rights may be reduced by the making of deductions from those rights no greater than, at the choice of the manager—

(a)   the relevant percentage of the value of the investor's rights under the contract; or

(b)   the proportion attributable to the investor's rights of the relevant percentage of the value of the underlying fund for each day on which the investor has rights under the contract.

(6)   When calculating the value of the rights of an investor for the purposes of paragraphs (3) to (5) above, where the manager has specified under paragraph (7) that such rights are to be valued weekly or monthly—

(a)   where such rights are to be valued weekly, they are to be valued on such day of the week ("the specified day") as has been so specified by the manager (except that, where that day is not a working day, the rights are to be valued on the next working day), and the value of the rights on each subsequent day prior to the next specified day is to be taken to be the value of the rights on the previous specified day; and

(b)   where the rights are to be valued monthly, they are to be valued on such date in each month ("the specified date") as has been so specified by the manager (except that, where that date is not a working day, the rights are to be valued on the next working day), and the value of the rights on each subsequent day prior to the next specified date is to be taken to be the value of the rights on the previous specified date.

(7)   For the purposes of paragraph (6)—

(a)   the frequency, which must be daily, weekly or monthly, with which rights are to be valued; and

(b)   where valuation is to take place weekly or monthly, the day of the week or, as the case may be, the date in the month on which it is to take place,

must be specified in writing by the manager; and the specification may not be amended during the period of 12 months after the date on which it is made.

(8)   For the purposes of paragraphs (3) to (5), "the relevant percentage" means—
   (a)   during the period of 10 years beginning with the day on which the first contribution is made by the investor to the investment scheme or linked long-term contract (as the case may be), 3/730 per cent;
   (b)   otherwise 1/365 per cent.

(9)   The value of the investment property may be reduced—
   (a)   where any stamp duty, stamp duty reserve tax, value added tax or other charge (including any dilution levy) are incurred by the manager directly or indirectly in or consequent upon the sale or purchase of investments held for the purposes of the investment scheme, by the amount of those charges;
   (b)   where any amount of tax is paid or anticipated to be payable in respect of income received or capital gains realised by the manager in respect of investments held for the purposes of the investment scheme, by the amount so deducted or anticipated;
   (c)   where any charges or expenses are incurred by the manager directly or indirectly in maintaining or repairing any land or building in which the investment property is invested or in connection with the collection of rent, service charge or other sum due under the terms of a lease from occupiers of any land or building in which the investment property is invested, by the amount of those charges or expenses;
   (d)   where any charges or expenses are incurred by the manager directly or indirectly in complying with an order of the court or any similar requirements imposed by law, by the amount of those charges or expenses;
   (e)   to the extent that the manager incurs any expenses in complying with a requirement—
      (i)   to arrange for the investor to receive a copy of the annual report and accounts issued to investors by any company, unit trust, open-ended investment company or other entity in which the investment scheme is invested directly or indirectly ("the relevant entities"), or
      (ii)   to arrange for the investor to attend, vote or receive any other information issued to investors by the relevant entities,
   by the amount of such of those expenses; and
   (f)   in respect of a linked long-term contract referred to in regulation 6 which is subject to smoothing, by the amount of the charges or expenses incurred by the manager in providing funds to smooth investment returns but only when the provision of such funds is in accordance with the manager's stated policy on smoothing.

(10)   Where the value of the investment property is reduced by reference to an amount of charges or expenses referred to in paragraph (9), then, for the purposes of calculating any reduction in the investor's rights under paragraphs (3), (4) or (5), the value of those rights is to be calculated after the deductions of any such amount.

(11)   Where an investment scheme is brought to an end by a manager and the investor takes up a transfer facility to another investment scheme, the relevant percentage for the purposes of paragraphs (3) to (5) shall be the same as that which would have been applied under or in respect of the original investment scheme as if the original investment scheme were continuing, notwithstanding any rules of the new investment scheme.

[2749]

NOTES
Commencement: 6 April 2005.

FINANCIAL SERVICES AND MARKETS ACT 2000 (TRANSITIONAL PROVISIONS) (GENERAL INSURANCE INTERMEDIARIES) ORDER 2004 (NOTE)

(SI 2004/3351)

NOTES
Made: 16 December 2004.
Authority: Financial Services and Markets Act 2000, ss 426–428.
Commencement: 10 January 2005 (for the purposes of art 4 (Application of the Authority's rules etc to persons with interim permission or interim approval)); 14 January 2005 (otherwise).
Article 2 of this Order conferred an interim permission on certain applicants who had applied to the FSA for permission under Pt IV of FSMA 2000 to carry on certain general insurance mediation activities and whose application was pending on the date (14 January 2005) when those activities became regulated activities within the meaning of s 22 of FSMA 2000 (by reason of the Financial Services and Markets Act 2000 (Regulated Activities) (Amendment) (No 2) Order 2003, SI 2003/1476). Article 3 conferred interim approval, in similar terms to those in art 2, on people who were working for a person who benefited from an interim permission and who needed approval under Pt V of the Act. Article 4 allowed the FSA to modify, inter alia, its rules in their

application to persons with interim permission or interim approval, and art 5 (and the Schedule) provided for the application of provisions in, or made under, the Act to persons with interim permission or interim approval. Article 6 disapplied, in relation to persons with an interim permission and their appointed representatives, the Authority's duty to have in place compensation arrangements under the financial services compensation scheme. Interim permission or interim approval continued until the firm's application was determined and permission granted, or until the applicant withdrew their application, or until the Financial Services Tribunal confirmed the FSA's decision to refuse the application for permission. In any event, interim permission and interim approval ended on 14 January 2006 for insurance mediation activities and, after this date, no firms have interim permission to carry on these activities. This Order effectively became spent on that date.

[2750]–[2756]

FINANCIAL SERVICES AND MARKETS ACT 2000 (FINANCIAL PROMOTION) ORDER 2005

(SI 2005/1529)

NOTES
Made: 8 June 2005.
Authority: Financial Services and Markets Act 2000, ss 21(5), (6), (9), (10), 428(3), Sch 2, para 25.
Commencement: 1 July 2005.
Note: this Order revokes and re-enacts, with certain amendments, the Financial Services and Markets Act 2000 (Financial Promotion) Order 2001, SI 2001/1335 (as amended).
This Order is reproduced as amended by: the Financial Services and Markets Act 2000 (Financial Promotion) (Amendment) Order 2005, SI 2005/3392; the Financial Services and Markets Act 2000 (Regulated Activities) (Amendment) Order 2006, SI 2006/1969; the Financial Services and Markets Act 2000 (Regulated Activities) (Amendment) (No 2) Order 2006, SI 2006/2383; the Financial Services and Markets Act 2000 (Regulated Activities) (Amendment No 3) Order 2006, SI 2006/3384; the Financial Services and Markets Act 2000 (Financial Promotion) (Amendment) Order 2007, SI 2007/1083; the Companies Act 2006 (Commencement No 2, Consequential Amendments, Transitional Provisions and Savings) Order 2007, SI 2007/1093; the Financial Services and Markets Act 2000 (Financial Promotion) (Amendment No 2) Order 2007, SI 2007/2615.

ARRANGEMENT OF ARTICLES

PART I
CITATION, COMMENCEMENT AND INTERPRETATION

PART II
CONTROLLED ACTIVITIES AND CONTROLLED INVESTMENTS

PART III
EXEMPTIONS: INTERPRETATION AND APPLICATION

PART IV
EXEMPT COMMUNICATIONS: ALL CONTROLLED ACTIVITIES

SCHEDULES:

PART I
CITATION, COMMENCEMENT AND INTERPRETATION

1   Citation and commencement

This Order may be cited as the Financial Services and Markets Act 2000 (Financial Promotion) Order 2005 and comes into force on 1st July 2005.

[2757]

NOTES

Commencement: 1 July 2005.

2   Interpretation: general

(1)   In this Order, except where the context otherwise requires—

"the 1985 Act" means the Companies Act 1985;

"the 1986 Order" means the Companies (Northern Ireland) Order 1986;

"the Act" means the Financial Services and Markets Act 2000;

"close relative" in relation to a person means—

(a)   his spouse [or civil partner];

(b)   his children and step-children, his parents and step-parents, his brothers and sisters and his step-brothers and step-sisters; and

(c)   the spouse [or civil partner] of any person within sub-paragraph (b);

"controlled activity" has the meaning given by article 4 and Schedule 1;

"controlled investment" has the meaning given by article 4 and Schedule 1;

"deposit" means a sum of money which is a deposit for the purposes of article 5 of the Regulated Activities Order;

"equity share capital" has the meaning given in the 1985 Act or in the 1986 Order;

"financial promotion restriction" has the meaning given by article 5;

"government" means the government of the United Kingdom, the Scottish Administration, the Executive Committee of the Northern Ireland Assembly, the National Assembly for Wales and any government of any country or territory outside the United Kingdom;

"instrument" includes any record whether or not in the form of a document;

"international organisation" means any body the members of which comprise—

(a)   states including the United Kingdom or another EEA State; or

(b)   bodies whose members comprise states including the United Kingdom or another EEA State;

"overseas communicator" has the meaning given by article 30;

"previously overseas customer" has the meaning given by article 31;

"publication" means—

(a)   a newspaper, journal, magazine or other periodical publication;

(b)   a web site or similar system for the electronic display of information;

(c)   any programme forming part of a service consisting of the broadcast or transmission of television or radio programmes;

(d)   any teletext service, that—is to say a service consisting of television transmissions consisting of a succession of visual displays (with or without accompanying sound) capable of being selected and held for separate viewing or other use;

"qualifying contract of insurance" has the meaning given in the Regulated Activities Order;

"qualifying credit" has the meaning given by paragraph 10 of Schedule 1;

"the Regulated Activities Order" means the Financial Services and Markets Act 2000 (Regulated Activities) Order 2001;

"relevant insurance activity" has the meaning given by article 21;

"relevant investment activities" has the meaning given by article 30;

"solicited real time communication" has the meaning given by article 8;

"units", in a collective investment scheme, has the meaning given by Part XVII of the Act;

"unsolicited real time communication" has the meaning given by article 8.

(2) References to a person engaging in investment activity are to be construed in accordance with subsection (8) of section 21 of the Act; and for these purposes, "controlled activity" and "controlled investment" in that subsection have the meaning given in this Order.

[2758]

NOTES

Commencement: 1 July 2005.

Para (1): in definition "close relative" words in square brackets inserted by the Financial Services and Markets Act 2000 (Financial Promotion) (Amendment) Order 2005, SI 2005/3392, art 2(1), (2), as from 21 December 2005.

Step-children, etc: as to the meaning of this and related expressions, see the Civil Partnership Act 2004, s 246 (as applied to this Order by the Civil Partnership Act 2004 (Relationships Arising Through Civil Partnership) Order 2005, SI 2005/3137, art 3, Schedule).

3 Interpretation: unlisted companies

(1) In this Order, an "unlisted company" means a body corporate the shares in which are not—

(a) listed or quoted on an investment exchange whether in the United Kingdom or elsewhere;

(b) shares in respect of which information is, with the agreement or approval of any officer of the company, published for the purpose of facilitating deals in the shares indicating prices at which persons have dealt or are willing to deal in them other than persons who, at the time the information is published, are existing members of a relevant class; or

(c) subject to a marketing arrangement which accords to the company the facilities referred to in section 163(2)(b) of the 1985 Act or article 173(2)(b) of the 1986 Order.

(2) For the purpose of paragraph (1)(b), a person is to be regarded as a member of a relevant class if he was, at the relevant time—

(a) an existing member or debenture holder of the company;

(b) an existing employee of the company;

(c) a close relative of such a member or employee; or

(d) a trustee (acting in his capacity as such) of a trust, the principal beneficiary of which is a person within any of sub-paragraphs (a), (b) and (c).

(3) In this Order references to shares in and debentures of an unlisted company are references to—

(a) in the case of a body corporate which is a company within the meaning of the 1985 Act, shares and debentures within the meaning of that Act;

(b) in the case of a body corporate which is a company within the meaning of the 1986 Order, shares and debentures within the meaning of that Order;

(c) in the case of any other body corporate, investments falling within paragraph 14 or 15 of Schedule 1 to this Order.

[2759]

NOTES

Commencement: 1 July 2005.

PART II
CONTROLLED ACTIVITIES AND CONTROLLED INVESTMENTS

4 Definition of controlled activities and controlled investments

(1) For the purposes of section 21(9) of the Act, a controlled activity is an activity which falls within any of paragraphs 1 to 11 of Schedule 1.

(2) For the purposes of section 21(10) of the Act, a controlled investment is an investment which falls within any of paragraphs 12 to 27 of Schedule 1.

[2760]

NOTES

Commencement: 1 July 2005.

PART III
EXEMPTIONS: INTERPRETATION AND APPLICATION

5   Interpretation: financial promotion restriction

In this Order, any reference to the financial promotion restriction is a reference to the restriction in section 21(1) of the Act.

[2761]

NOTES
Commencement: 1 July 2005.

6   Interpretation: communications

In this Order—

(a)   any reference to a communication is a reference to the communication, in the course of business, of an invitation or inducement to engage in investment activity;

(b)   any reference to a communication being made to another person is a reference to a communication being addressed, whether orally or in legible form, to a particular person or persons (for example where it is contained in a telephone call or letter);

(c)   any reference to a communication being directed at persons is a reference to a communication being addressed to persons generally (for example where it is contained in a television broadcast or web site);

(d)   "communicate" includes causing a communication to be made or directed;

(e)   a "recipient" of a communication is the person to whom the communication is made or, in the case of a non-real time communication which is directed at persons generally, any person who reads or hears the communication;

(f)   "electronic commerce communication" means a communication, the making of which constitutes the provision of an information society service;

(g)   "incoming electronic commerce communication" means an electronic commerce communication made from an establishment in an EEA State other than the United Kingdom;

(h)   "outgoing electronic commerce communication" means an electronic commerce communication made from an establishment in the United Kingdom to a person in an EEA State other than the United Kingdom.

[2762]

NOTES
Commencement: 1 July 2005.

7   Interpretation: real time communications

(1)   In this Order, references to a real time communication are references to any communication made in the course of a personal visit, telephone conversation or other interactive dialogue.

(2)   A non-real time communication is a communication not falling within paragraph (1).

(3)   For the purposes of this Order, non-real time communications include communications made by letter or e-mail or contained in a publication.

(4)   For the purposes of this Order, the factors in paragraph (5) are to be treated as indications that a communication is a non-real time communication.

(5)   The factors are that—

(a)   the communication is made to or directed at more than one recipient in identical terms (save for details of the recipient's identity);

(b)   the communication is made or directed by way of a system which in the normal course constitutes or creates a record of the communication which is available to the recipient to refer to at a later time;

(c)   the communication is made or directed by way of a system which in the normal course does not enable or require the recipient to respond immediately to it.

[2763]

NOTES
Commencement: 1 July 2005.

8   Interpretation: solicited and unsolicited real time communications

(1)   A real time communication is solicited where it is made in the course of a personal visit, telephone call or other interactive dialogue if that call, visit or dialogue—

(a)   was initiated by the recipient of the communication; or

(b)   takes place in response to an express request from the recipient of the communication.

(2)   A real time communication is unsolicited where it is made otherwise than as described in paragraph (1).

(3)   For the purposes of paragraph (1)—
    (a)   a person is not to be treated as expressly requesting a call, visit or dialogue—
        (i)   because he omits to indicate that he does not wish to receive any or any further visits or calls or to engage in any or any further dialogue;
        (ii)   because he agrees to standard terms that state that such visits, calls or dialogue will take place, unless he has signified clearly that, in addition to agreeing to the terms, he is willing for them to take place;
    (b)   a communication is solicited only if it is clear from all the circumstances when the call, visit or dialogue is initiated or requested that during the course of the visit, call or dialogue communications will be made concerning the kind of controlled activities or investments to which the communications in fact made relate;
    (c)   it is immaterial whether the express request was made before or after this article comes into force.

(4)   Where a real time communication is solicited by a recipient ("R"), it is treated as having also been solicited by any other person to whom it is made at the same time as it is made to R if that other recipient is—
    (a)   a close relative of R; or
    (b)   expected to engage in any investment activity jointly with R.

[2764]

NOTES
Commencement: 1 July 2005.

8A   Interpretation: outgoing electronic commerce communications

(1)   For the purposes of the application of those articles to outgoing electronic commerce communications—
    (a)   any reference in article 48(7)(c), 50(1)(a) or (3)(e) or 52(3)(c) to an authorised person includes a reference to a person who is entitled, under the law of an EEA State other than the United Kingdom, to carry on regulated activities in that State;
    (b)   any reference in article 68(1) or 71 to rules or legislation includes a reference to provisions corresponding to those rules or legislation in the law of an EEA State other than the United Kingdom;
    (c)   any reference in article 49 to an amount in pounds sterling includes a reference to an equivalent amount in another currency.

(2)   For the purposes of the application of article 49 to outgoing electronic commerce communications, any reference in section 264(2) or 737 of the 1985 Act (or the equivalent provisions in the 1986 Order) to a body corporate or company includes a reference to a body corporate or company registered under the law of an EEA State other than the United Kingdom.

(3)   For the purposes of the application of article 3 in respect of outgoing electronic commerce communications—
    (a)   any reference in section 163(2)(b) of the 1985 Act (or the equivalent provision in the 1986 Order) to a company includes a reference to a company registered under the law of an EEA State other than the United Kingdom;
    (b)   any reference in that section to an investment exchange includes a reference to an investment exchange which is recognised as an investment exchange under the law of an EEA State other than the United Kingdom.

[2765]

NOTES
Commencement: 1 July 2005.

9   Degree of prominence to be given to required indications

Where a communication must, if it is to fall within any provision of this Order, be accompanied by an indication of any matter, the indication must be presented to the recipient—
    (a)   in a way that can be easily understood; and
    (b)   in such manner as, depending on the means by which the communication is made or directed, is best calculated to bring the matter in question to the attention of the recipient and to allow him to consider it.

[2766]

NOTES
Commencement: 1 July 2005.

10 Application to qualifying contracts of insurance

(1)   Nothing in this Order exempts from the application of the financial promotion restriction a communication which invites or induces a person to enter into a qualifying contract of insurance with a person who is not—

(a)   an authorised person;

(b)   an exempt person who is exempt in relation to effecting or carrying out contracts of insurance of the class to which the communication relates;

(c)   a company which has its head office in an EEA State other than the United Kingdom and which is entitled under the law of that State to carry on there insurance business of the class to which the communication relates;

(d)   a company which has a branch or agency in an EEA State other than the United Kingdom and is entitled under the law of that State to carry on there insurance business of the class to which the communication relates;

(e)   a company authorised to carry on insurance business of the class to which the communication relates in any country or territory which is listed in Schedule 2.

(2)   In this article, references to a class of insurance are references to the class of insurance contract described in Schedule 1 to the Regulated Activities Order into which the effecting or carrying out of the contract to which the communication relates would fall.

[2767]

NOTES

Commencement: 1 July 2005.

11 Combination of different exemptions

(1)   In respect of a communication relating to—

(a)   a controlled activity falling within paragraph 2 of Schedule 1 carried on in relation to a qualifying contract of insurance; or

(b)   a controlled activity falling within any of paragraphs 3 to 11 of Schedule 1,

a person may rely on the application of one or more of the exemptions in Parts IV and VI.

(2)   In respect of a communication relating to—

(a)   an activity falling within paragraph 1 of Schedule 1; or

(b)   a relevant insurance activity,

a person may rely on one or more of the exemptions in Parts IV and V; and, where a communication relates to any such activity and also to an activity mentioned in paragraph (1)(a) or (b), a person may rely on one or more of the exemptions in Parts IV and V in respect of the former activity and on one or more of the exemptions in Parts V and VI in respect of the latter activity.

[2768]

NOTES

Commencement: 1 July 2005.

PART IV
EXEMPT COMMUNICATIONS: ALL CONTROLLED ACTIVITIES

12 Communications to overseas recipients

(1)   Subject to paragraphs (2) and (7), the financial promotion restriction does not apply to any communication—

(a)   which is made (whether from inside or outside the United Kingdom) to a person who receives the communication outside the United Kingdom; or

(b)   which is directed (whether from inside or outside the United Kingdom) only at persons outside the United Kingdom.

(2)   Paragraph (1) does not apply to an unsolicited real time communication unless—

(a)   it is made from a place outside the United Kingdom; and

(b)   it is made for the purposes of a business which is carried on outside the United Kingdom and which is not carried on in the United Kingdom.

(3)   For the purposes of paragraph (1)(b)—

(a)   if the conditions set out in paragraph (4)(a), (b), (c) and (d) are met, a communication directed from a place inside the United Kingdom is to be regarded as directed only at persons outside the United Kingdom;

(b)   if the conditions set out in paragraph (4)(c) and (d) are met, a communication directed from a place outside the United Kingdom is to be regarded as directed only at persons outside the United Kingdom;

(c)   in any other case where one or more of the conditions in paragraph (4)(a) to (e) are met, that fact is to be taken into account in determining whether or not a communication is to be regarded as directed only at persons outside the United Kingdom (but a communication may still be regarded as directed only at persons outside the United Kingdom even if none of the conditions in paragraph (4) is met).

(4) The conditions are that—
  (a) the communication is accompanied by an indication that it is directed only at persons outside the United Kingdom;
  (b) the communication is accompanied by an indication that it must not be acted upon by persons in the United Kingdom;
  (c) the communication is not referred to in, or directly accessible from, any other communication made to a person or directed at persons in the United Kingdom by the person directing the communication;
  (d) there are in place proper systems and procedures to prevent recipients in the United Kingdom (other than those to whom the communication might otherwise lawfully have been made by the person directing it or a member of the same group) engaging in the investment activity to which the communication relates with the person directing the communication, a close relative of his or a member of the same group;
  (e) the communication is included in—
    (i) a web site, newspaper, journal, magazine or periodical publication which is principally accessed in or intended for a market outside the United Kingdom;
    (ii) a radio or television broadcast or teletext service transmitted principally for reception outside the United Kingdom.

(5) For the purpose of paragraph (1)(b), a communication may be treated as directed only at persons outside the United Kingdom even if—
  (a) it is also directed, for the purposes of article 19(1)(b), at investment professionals falling within article 19(5) (but disregarding paragraph (6) of that article for this purpose);
  (b) it is also directed, for the purposes of article 49(1)(b), at high net worth persons to whom article 49 applies (but disregarding paragraph (2)(e) of that article for this purpose) and it relates to a controlled activity to which article 49 applies;
  (c) it is a communication to which article 31 applies.

(6) Where a communication falls within paragraph (5)(a) or (b)—
  (a) the condition in paragraph (4)(a) is to be construed as requiring an indication that the communication is directed only at persons outside the United Kingdom or persons having professional experience in matters relating to investments or high net worth persons (as the case may be);
  (b) the condition in paragraph (4)(b) is to be construed as requiring an indication that the communication must not be acted upon by persons in the United Kingdom except by persons who have professional experience in matters relating to investments or who are not high net worth persons (as the case may be);
  (c) the condition in paragraph (4)(c) will not apply where the other communication referred to in that paragraph is made to a person or directed at a person in the United Kingdom to whom paragraph (5) applies.

(7) Paragraph (1) does not apply to an outgoing electronic commerce communication.

[2769]

NOTES
Commencement: 1 July 2005.

13 Communications from customers and potential customers

(1) The financial promotion restriction does not apply to any communication made by or on behalf of a person ("customer") to one other person ("supplier")—
  (a) in order to obtain information about a controlled investment available from or a controlled service provided by the supplier; or
  (b) in order that the customer can acquire a controlled investment from that supplier or be supplied with a controlled service by that supplier.

(2) For the purposes of paragraph (1), a controlled service is a service the provision of which constitutes engaging in a controlled activity by the supplier.

[2770]

NOTES
Commencement: 1 July 2005.

14 Follow up non-real time communications and solicited real time communications

(1) Where a person makes or directs a communication ("the first communication") which is exempt from the financial promotion restriction because, in compliance with the requirements of another provision of this Order, it is accompanied by certain indications or contains certain

information, then the financial promotion restriction does not apply to any subsequent communication which complies with the requirements of paragraph (2).

(2) The requirements of this paragraph are that the subsequent communication—
  (a) is a non-real time communication or a solicited real time communication;
  (b) is made by, or on behalf of, the same person who made the first communication;
  (c) is made to a recipient of the first communication;
  (d) relates to the same controlled activity and the same controlled investment as the first communication; and
  (e) is made within 12 months of the recipient receiving the first communication.

(3) The provisions of this article only apply in the case of a person who makes or directs a communication on behalf of another where the first communication is made by that other person.

(4) Where a person makes or directs a communication on behalf of another person in reliance on the exemption contained in this article the person on whose behalf the communication was made or directed remains responsible for the content of that communication.

(5) A communication made or directed before this article comes into force is to be treated as a first communication falling within paragraph (1) if it would have fallen within that paragraph had it been made or directed after this article comes into force.

[2771]

NOTES
Commencement: 1 July 2005.

15 Introductions

(1) If the requirements of paragraph (2) are met, the financial promotion restriction does not apply to any communication which is made with a view to or for the purposes of introducing the recipient to—
  (a) an authorised person who carries on the controlled activity to which the communication relates; or
  (b) an exempt person where the communication relates to a controlled activity which is also a regulated activity in relation to which he is an exempt person.

(2) The requirements of this paragraph are that—
  (a) the maker of the communication ("A") is not a close relative of, nor a member of the same group as, the person to whom the introduction is, or is to be, made;
  (b) A does not receive from any person other than the recipient any pecuniary reward or other advantage arising out of his making the introduction; and
  (c) it is clear in all the circumstances that the recipient, in his capacity as an investor, is not seeking and has not sought advice from A as to the merits of the recipient engaging in investment activity (or, if the client has sought such advice, A has declined to give it, but has recommended that the recipient seek such advice from an authorised person).

[2772]

NOTES
Commencement: 1 July 2005.

16 Exempt persons

(1) The financial promotion restriction does not apply to any communication which—
  (a) is a non-real time communication or a solicited real time communication;
  (b) is made or directed by an exempt person; and
  (c) is for the purposes of that exempt person's business of carrying on a controlled activity which is also a regulated activity in relation to which he is an exempt person.

(2) The financial promotion restriction does not apply to any unsolicited real time communication made by a person ("AR") who is an appointed representative (within the meaning of section 39(2) of the Act) where—
  (a) the communication is made by AR in carrying on the business—
    (i) for which his principal ("P") has accepted responsibility for the purposes of section 39 of the Act; and
    (ii) in relation to which AR is exempt from the general prohibition by virtue of that section; and
  (b) the communication is one which, if it were made by P, would comply with any rules made by the Authority under section 145 of the Act (financial promotion rules) which are relevant to a communication of that kind.

[2773]

NOTES
Commencement: 1 July 2005.

17 Generic promotions

The financial promotion restriction does not apply to any communication which—
- (a) does not identify (directly or indirectly) a person who provides the controlled investment to which the communication relates; and
- (b) does not identify (directly or indirectly) any person as a person who carries on a controlled activity in relation to that investment.

[2774]

NOTES
Commencement: 1 July 2005.

17A Communications caused to be made or directed by unauthorised persons

(1) If a condition in paragraph (2) is met, the financial promotion restriction does not apply to a communication caused to be made or directed by an unauthorised person which is made or directed by an authorised person.

(2) The conditions in this paragraph are that—
- (a) the authorised person prepared the content of the communication; or
- (b) it is a real-time communication.

[2775]

NOTES
Commencement: 1 July 2005.

18 Mere conduits

(1) Subject to paragraph (4), the financial promotion restriction does not apply to any communication which is made or directed by a person who acts as a mere conduit for it.

(2) A person acts as a mere conduit for a communication if—
- (a) he communicates it in the course of an activity carried on by him, the principal purpose of which is transmitting or receiving material provided to him by others;
- (b) the content of the communication is wholly devised by another person; and
- (c) the nature of the service provided by him in relation to the communication is such that he does not select, modify or otherwise exercise control over its content prior to its transmission or receipt.

(3) For the purposes of paragraph (2)(c) a person does not select, modify or otherwise exercise control over the content of a communication merely by removing or having the power to remove material—
- (a) which is, or is alleged to be, illegal, defamatory or in breach of copyright;
- (b) in response to a request to a body which is empowered by or under any enactment to make such a request; or
- (c) when otherwise required to do so by law.

(4) Nothing in paragraph (1) prevents the application of the financial promotion restriction in so far as it relates to the person who has caused the communication to be made or directed.

(5) This article does not apply to an electronic commerce communication.

[2776]

NOTES
Commencement: 1 July 2005.

18A Electronic commerce communications: mere conduits, caching and hosting

The financial promotion restriction does not apply to an electronic commerce communication in circumstances where—
- (a) the making of the communication constitutes the provision of an information society service of a kind falling within paragraph 1 of Article 12, 13 or 14 of the electronic commerce directive ("mere conduit", "caching" and "hosting"); and
- (b) the conditions mentioned in the paragraph in question, to the extent that they are applicable at the time of, or prior to, the making of the communication, are or have been met at that time.

[2777]

NOTES
Commencement: 1 July 2005.

19 Investment professionals

(1)   The financial promotion restriction does not apply to any communication which—
- (a)   is made only to recipients whom the person making the communication believes on reasonable grounds to be investment professionals; or
- (b)   may reasonably be regarded as directed only at such recipients.

(2)   For the purposes of paragraph (1)(b), if all the conditions set out in paragraph (4)(a) to (c) are met in relation to the communication, it is to be regarded as directed only at investment professionals.

(3)   In any other case in which one or more of the conditions set out in paragraph (4)(a) to (c) are met, that fact is to be taken into account in determining whether the communication is directed only at investment professionals (but a communication may still be regarded as so directed even if none of the conditions in paragraph (4) is met).

(4)   The conditions are that—
- (a)   the communication is accompanied by an indication that it is directed at persons having professional experience in matters relating to investments and that any investment or investment activity to which it relates is available only to such persons or will be engaged in only with such persons;
- (b)   the communication is accompanied by an indication that persons who do not have professional experience in matters relating to investments should not rely on it;
- (c)   there are in place proper systems and procedures to prevent recipients other than investment professionals engaging in the investment activity to which the communication relates with the person directing the communication, a close relative of his or a member of the same group.

(5)   "Investment professionals" means—
- (a)   an authorised person;
- (b)   an exempt person where the communication relates to a controlled activity which is a regulated activity in relation to which the person is exempt;
- (c)   any other person—
    - (i)   whose ordinary activities involve him in carrying on the controlled activity to which the communication relates for the purpose of a business carried on by him; or
    - (ii)   who it is reasonable to expect will carry on such activity for the purposes of a business carried on by him;
- (d)   a government, local authority (whether in the United Kingdom or elsewhere) or an international organisation;
- (e)   a person ("A") who is a director, officer or employee of a person ("B") falling within any of sub-paragraphs (a) to (d) where the communication is made to A in that capacity and where A's responsibilities when acting in that capacity involve him in the carrying on by B of controlled activities.

(6)   For the purposes of paragraph (1), a communication may be treated as made only to or directed only at investment professionals even if it is also made to or directed at other persons to whom it may lawfully be communicated.

[2778]

NOTES
Commencement: 1 July 2005.

20 Communications by journalists

(1)   Subject to paragraph (2), the financial promotion restriction does not apply to any non-real time communication if—
- (a)   the content of the communication is devised by a person acting in the capacity of a journalist;
- (b)   the communication is contained in a qualifying publication; and
- (c)   in the case of a communication requiring disclosure, one of the conditions in paragraph (2) is met.

(2)   The conditions in this paragraph are that—
- (a)   the communication is accompanied by an indication explaining the nature of the author's financial interest or that of a member of his family (as the case may be);
- (b)   the authors are subject to proper systems and procedures which prevent the publication of communications requiring disclosure without the explanation referred to in sub-paragraph (a); or

PART III
STATUTORY INSTRUMENTS

    (c)   the qualifying publication in which the communication appears falls within the remit of—

        (i)   the Code of Practice issued by the Press Complaints Commission;

        (ii)   the OFCOM Broadcasting Code; or

        (iii) the Producers' Guidelines issued by the British Broadcasting Corporation.

(3)   For the purposes of this article, a communication requires disclosure if—

    (a)   an author of the communication or a member of his family is likely to obtain a financial benefit or avoid a financial loss if people act in accordance with the invitation or inducement contained in the communication;

    (b)   the communication relates to a controlled investment of a kind falling within paragraph (4); and

    (c)   the communication identifies directly a person who issues or provides the controlled investment to which the communication relates.

(4)   A controlled investment falls within this paragraph if it is—

    (a)   an investment falling within paragraph 14 of Schedule 1 (shares or stock in share capital);

    (b)   an investment falling within paragraph 21 of that Schedule (options) to acquire or dispose of an investment falling within sub-paragraph (a);

    (c)   an investment falling within paragraph 22 of that Schedule (futures) being rights under a contract for the sale of an investment falling within sub-paragraph (a); or

    (d)   an investment falling within paragraph 23 of that Schedule (contracts for differences etc) being rights under a contract relating to, or to fluctuations in, the value or price of an investment falling within sub-paragraph (a).

(5)   For the purposes of this article—

    (a)   the authors of the communication are the person who devises the content of the communication and the person who is responsible for deciding to include the communication in the qualifying publication;

    (b)   a "qualifying publication" is a publication or service of the kind mentioned in paragraph (1) or (2) of article 54 of the Regulated Activities Order and which is of the nature described in that article, and for the purposes of this article, a certificate given under paragraph (3) of article 54 of that Order and not revoked is conclusive evidence of the matters certified;

    (c)   the members of a person's family are his spouse [or civil partner] and any children of his under the age of 18 years.

                                                                     [2779]

NOTES

Commencement: 1 July 2005.

Para (5): words in square brackets in sub-para (c) inserted by the Financial Services and Markets Act 2000 (Financial Promotion) (Amendment) Order 2005, SI 2005/3392, art 2(1), (3), as from 21 December 2005.

20A Promotion broadcast by company director etc

(1)   The financial promotion restriction does not apply to a communication which is communicated as part of a qualifying service by a person ("D") who is a director or employee of an undertaking ("U") where—

    (a)   the communication invites or induces the recipient to acquire—

        (i)   a controlled investment of the kind falling within article 20(4) which is issued by U (or by an undertaking in the same group as U); or

        (ii)   a controlled investment issued or provided by an authorised person in the same group as U;

    (b)   the communication—

        (i)   comprises words which are spoken by D and not broadcast, transmitted or displayed in writing; or

        (ii)   is displayed in writing only because it forms part of an interactive dialogue to which D is a party and in the course of which D is expected to respond immediately to questions put by a recipient of the communication;

    (c)   the communication is not part of an organised marketing campaign; and

    (d)   the communication is accompanied by an indication that D is a director or employee (as the case may be) of U.

(2)   For the purposes of this article, a "qualifying service" is a service—

    (a)   which is broadcast or transmitted in the form of television or radio programmes; or

    (b)   displayed on a web site (or similar system for the electronic display of information) comprising regularly updated news and information,

provided that the principal purpose of the service, taken as a whole and including any advertisements and other promotional material contained in it, is neither of the purposes described in article 54(1)(a) or (b) of the Regulated Activities Order.

(3)   For the purposes of paragraph (2), a certificate given under article 54(3) of the Regulated Activities Order and not revoked is conclusive evidence of the matters certified.

[2780]

NOTES
Commencement: 1 July 2005.

20B   Incoming electronic commerce communications

(1)   The financial promotion restriction does not apply to an incoming electronic commerce communication.

(2)   Paragraph (1) does not apply to—
  (a)   a communication which constitutes an advertisement by the operator of a UCITS directive scheme of units in that scheme;
  (b)   a communication consisting of an invitation or inducement to enter into a contract of insurance, where—
       (i)   the communication is made by an undertaking which has received official authorisation in accordance with Article 4 of the life assurance consolidation directive or the first non-life insurance directive, and
       (ii)   the insurance falls within the scope of any of the insurance directives; or
  (c)   an unsolicited communication made by electronic mail.

(3)   In this article, "UCITS directive scheme" means an undertaking for collective investment in transferable securities which is subject to Directive 85/611/EEC of the Council of the European Communities of 20 December 1985 on the co-ordination of laws, regulations and administrative provisions relating to undertakings for collective investment in transferable securities, and has been authorised in accordance with Article 4 of that Directive.

(4)   For the purposes of this article, a communication by electronic mail is to be regarded as unsolicited, unless it is made in response to an express request from the recipient of the communication.

[2781]

NOTES
Commencement: 1 July 2005.

PART V
EXEMPT COMMUNICATIONS: DEPOSITS AND INSURANCE

21   Interpretation: relevant insurance activity

In this Part, a "relevant insurance activity" means a controlled activity falling within paragraph 2 of Schedule 1 carried on in relation to an investment falling within paragraph 13 of that Schedule where that investment is not a qualifying contract of insurance.

[2782]

NOTES
Commencement: 1 July 2005.

22   Deposits: non-real time communications

(1)   If the requirements of paragraph (2) are met, the financial promotion restriction does not apply to any non-real time communication which relates to a controlled activity falling within paragraph 1 of Schedule 1.

(2)   The requirements of this paragraph are that the communication is accompanied by an indication—
  (a)   of the full name of the person with whom the investment which is the subject of the communication is to be made ("deposit-taker");
  (b)   of the country or territory in which a deposit-taker that is a body corporate is incorporated (described as such);
  (c)   if different, of the country or territory in which the deposit-taker's principal place of business is situated (described as such);
  (d)   whether or not the deposit-taker is regulated in respect of his deposit-taking business;
  (e)   if the deposit-taker is so regulated, of the name of the regulator in the deposit-taker's principal place of business, or if there is more than one such regulator, the prudential regulator;
  (f)   whether any transaction to which the communication relates would, if entered into by the recipient and the deposit-taker, fall within the jurisdiction of any dispute resolution scheme or deposit guarantee scheme and if so, identifying each such scheme;
  (g)   the necessary capital information.

PART III
STATUTORY INSTRUMENTS

(3)   In this article—

"full name", in relation to a person, means the name under which that person carries on business and, if different, that person's corporate name;

"liabilities" includes provisions where such provisions have not been deducted from the value of the assets;

"necessary capital information" means—

(a)   in relation to a deposit-taker which is a body corporate, either the amount of its paid up capital and reserves, described as such, or a statement that the amount of its paid up capital and reserves exceeds a particular amount (stating it);

(b)   in relation to a deposit-taker which is not a body corporate, either the amount of the total assets less liabilities (described as such) or a statement that the amount of its total assets exceeds a particular amount (stating it) and that its total liabilities do not exceed a particular amount (stating it).

[2783]

NOTES
Commencement: 1 July 2005.

23   Deposits: real time communications

The financial promotion restriction does not apply to any real time communication (whether solicited or unsolicited) which relates to an activity falling within paragraph 1 of Schedule 1.

[2784]

NOTES
Commencement: 1 July 2005.

24   Relevant insurance activity: non-real time communications

(1)   If the requirements of paragraph (2) are met, the financial promotion restriction does not apply to any non-real time communication which relates to a relevant insurance activity.

(2)   The requirements of this paragraph are that the communication is accompanied by an indication—

(a)   of the full name of the person with whom the investment which is the subject of the communication is to be made ("the insurer");

(b)   of the country or territory in which the insurer is incorporated (described as such);

(c)   if different, of the country or territory in which the insurer's principal place of business is situated (described as such);

(d)   whether or not the insurer is regulated in respect of its insurance business;

(e)   if the insurer is so regulated, of the name of the regulator of the insurer in its principal place of business or, if there is more than one such regulator, the name of the prudential regulator;

(f)   whether any transaction to which the communication relates would, if entered into by the recipient and the insurer, fall within the jurisdiction of any dispute resolution scheme or compensation scheme and if so, identifying each such scheme.

(3)   In this article "full name", in relation to a person, means the name under which that person carries on business and, if different, that person's corporate name.

[2785]

NOTES
Commencement: 1 July 2005.

25   Relevant insurance activity: non-real time communications: reinsurance and large risks

(1)   The financial promotion restriction does not apply to any non-real time communication which relates to a relevant insurance activity and concerns only—

(a)   a contract of reinsurance; or

(b)   a contract that covers large risks.

(2)   "Large risks" means—

(a)   risks falling within paragraph 4 (railway rolling stock), 5 (aircraft), 6 (ships), 7 (goods in transit), 11 (aircraft liability) or 12 (liability of ships) of Schedule 1 to the Regulated Activities Order;

(b)   risks falling within paragraph 14 (credit) or 15 (suretyship) of that Schedule provided that the risks relate to a business carried on by the recipient;

(c)   risks falling within paragraph 3 (land vehicles), 8 (fire and natural forces), 9 (damage to property), 10 (motor vehicle liability), 13 (general liability) or 16 (miscellaneous financial loss) of that Schedule provided that the risks relate to a business carried on by the recipient and that the condition specified in paragraph (3) is met in relation to that business.

(3)   The condition specified in this paragraph is that at least two of the three following criteria were exceeded in the most recent financial year for which information is available prior to the making of the communication—

(a)   the balance sheet total of the business (within the meaning of section 247(5) of the 1985 Act or article 255(5) of the 1986 Order) was 6.2 million euros;

(b)   the net turnover (within the meaning given to "turnover" by section 262(1) of the 1985 Act or article 270(1) of the 1986 Order) was 12.8 million euros;

(c)   the number of employees (within the meaning given by section 247(6) of the 1985 Act or article 255(6) of the 1986 Order) was 250;

and for a financial year which is a company's financial year but not in fact a year, the net turnover of the recipient shall be proportionately adjusted.

(4)   For the purposes of paragraph (3), where the recipient is a member of a group for which consolidated accounts (within the meaning of the Seventh Company Law Directive) are drawn up, the question whether the condition met in that paragraph is met is to be determined by reference to those accounts.

[2786]

NOTES
Commencement: 1 July 2005.

26   Relevant insurance activity: real time communication

The financial promotion restriction does not apply to any real time communication (whether solicited or unsolicited) which relates to a relevant insurance activity.

[2787]

NOTES
Commencement: 1 July 2005.

PART VI
EXEMPT COMMUNICATIONS: CERTAIN CONTROLLED ACTIVITIES

27   Application of exemptions in this Part

Except where otherwise stated, the exemptions in this Part apply to communications which relate to—

(a)   a controlled activity falling within paragraph 2 of Schedule 1 carried on in relation to a qualifying contract of insurance;

(b)   controlled activities falling within any of paragraphs 3 to 11 of Schedule 1.

[2788]

NOTES
Commencement: 1 July 2005.

28   One off non-real time communications and solicited real time communications

(1)   The financial promotion restriction does not apply to a one off communication which is either a non-real time communication or a solicited real time communication.

(2)   If all the conditions set out in paragraph (3) are met in relation to a communication it is to be regarded as a one off communication. In any other case in which one or more of those conditions are met, that fact is to be taken into account in determining whether the communication is a one off communication (but a communication may still be regarded as a one off communication even if none of the conditions in paragraph (3) is met).

(3)   The conditions are that—

(a)   the communication is made only to one recipient or only to one group of recipients in the expectation that they would engage in any investment activity jointly;

(b)   the identity of the product or service to which the communication relates has been determined having regard to the particular circumstances of the recipient;

(c)   the communication is not part of an organised marketing campaign.

[2789]

NOTES
Commencement: 1 July 2005.

28A One off unsolicited real time communications

(1) The financial promotion restriction does not apply to an unsolicited real time communication if the conditions in paragraph (2) are met.

(2) The conditions in this paragraph are that—
    (a) the communication is a one off communication;
    (b) the communicator believes on reasonable grounds that the recipient understands the risks associated with engaging in the investment activity to which the communication relates;
    (c) at the time that the communication is made, the communicator believes on reasonable grounds that the recipient would expect to be contacted by him in relation to the investment activity to which the communication relates.

(3) Paragraphs (2) and (3) of article 28 apply in determining whether a communication is a one off communication for the purposes of this article as they apply for the purposes of article 28.

[2790]

NOTES
Commencement: 1 July 2005.

28B Real time communications: introductions …

(1) If the requirements of paragraph (2) are met, the financial promotion restriction does not apply to any real time communication which—
    (a) relates to a controlled activity falling within [paragraph 10, 10A, 10B, 10C, 10D, 10E, 10F, 10G or 10H] of Schedule 1; and
    (b) is made for the purpose of, or with a view to, introducing the recipient to a person ("N") who is—
        (i) an authorised person who carries on the controlled activity to which the communication relates,
        (ii) an appointed representative, where the controlled activity to which the communication relates is also a regulated activity in respect of which he is exempt from the general prohibition, or
        (iii) an overseas person who carries on the controlled activity to which the communication relates.

(2) The requirements of this paragraph are that the maker of the communication ("M")—
    (a) does not receive any money, other than money payable to M on his own account, paid by the recipient for or in connection with any transaction which the recipient enters into with or through N as a result of the introduction; and
    (b) before making the introduction, discloses to the recipient such of the information mentioned in paragraph (3) as applies to M.

(3) That information is—
    (a) that M is a member of the same group as N;
    (b) details of any payment which M will receive from N, by way of fee or commission, for introducing the recipient to N;
    (c) an indication of any other reward or advantage received or to be received by M that arises out of his making introductions to N.

(4) In this article, "overseas person" means a person who carries on controlled activities which fall within paragraph 10, 10A or 10B of Schedule 1, but who does not carry on any such activity, or offer to do so, from a permanent place of business maintained by him in the United Kingdom.

[2791]

NOTES
Commencement: 1 July 2005.
Article heading: words omitted revoked by the Financial Services and Markets Act 2000 (Regulated Activities) (Amendment) (No 2) Order 2006, SI 2006/2383, art 35(1), (2), as from 6 April 2007 (for the full commencement details of SI 2006/2383 and for transitional provisions and effect, see arts 1, 36–40 of, and the Schedule to, the 2006 Order at **[2860]** et seq).
Para (1): words in square brackets substituted by SI 2006/2383, art 35(1), (3), as from 6 April 2007 (for the full commencement details of SI 2006/2383 and for transitional provisions and effect, see arts 1, 36–40 of, and the Schedule to, the 2006 Order at **[2860]** et seq).

29 Communications required or authorised by enactments

(1) Subject to paragraph (2), the financial promotion restriction does not apply to any communication which is required or authorised by or under any enactment other than the Act.

(2)   This article does not apply to a communication which relates to a controlled activity falling within paragraph 10, 10A or 10B of Schedule 1 or within paragraph 11 in so far as it relates to that activity.

[2792]

NOTES
Commencement: 1 July 2005.

30   Overseas communicators: solicited real time communications

(1)   The financial promotion restriction does not apply to any solicited real time communication which is made by an overseas communicator from outside the United Kingdom in the course of or for the purposes of his carrying on the business of engaging in relevant investment activities outside the United Kingdom.

(2)   In this article—
    "overseas communicator" means a person who carries on relevant investment activities outside the United Kingdom but who does not carry on any such activity from a permanent place of business maintained by him in the United Kingdom;
    "relevant investment activities" means controlled activities which fall within paragraphs 3 to 7 or 10 to 10B of Schedule 1 or, so far as relevant to any of those paragraphs, paragraph 11 of that Schedule.

[2793]

NOTES
Commencement: 1 July 2005.

31   Overseas communicators: non-real time communications to previously overseas customers

(1)   The financial promotion restriction does not apply to any non-real time communication which is communicated by an overseas communicator from outside the United Kingdom to a previously overseas customer of his.

(2)   In this article a "previously overseas customer" means a person with whom the overseas communicator has done business within the period of twelve months ending with the day on which the communication was received ("the earlier business") and where—
    (a)   at the time that the earlier business was done, the customer was neither resident in the United Kingdom nor had a place of business there; or
    (b)   at the time the earlier business was done, the overseas communicator had on a former occasion done business with the customer, being business of the same description as the business to which the communication relates, and on that former occasion the customer was neither resident in the United Kingdom nor had a place of business there.

(3)   For the purposes of this article, an overseas communicator has done business with a customer if, in the course of carrying on his relevant investment activities outside the United Kingdom, he has—
    (a)   effected a transaction, or arranged for a transaction to be effected, with the customer;
    (b)   provided, outside the United Kingdom, a service to the customer as described in paragraph 6 of Schedule 1 (whether or not that paragraph was in force at the time the business was done); or
    (c)   given, outside the United Kingdom, any advice to the customer as described in paragraph 7 of that Schedule (whether or not that paragraph was in force at the time the business was done).

[2794]

NOTES
Commencement: 1 July 2005.

32   Overseas communicators: unsolicited real time communications to previously overseas customers

(1)   If the requirements of paragraphs (2) and (3) are met, the financial promotion restriction does not apply to an unsolicited real time communication which is made by an overseas communicator from outside the United Kingdom to a previously overseas customer of his.

(2)   The requirements of this paragraph are that the terms on which previous transactions and services had been effected or provided by the overseas communicator to the previously overseas customer were such that the customer would reasonably expect, at the time that the unsolicited real time communication is made, to be contacted by the overseas communicator in relation to the investment activity to which the communication relates.

(3)   The requirements of this paragraph are that the previously overseas customer has been informed by the overseas communicator on an earlier occasion—

    (a)   that the protections conferred by or under the Act will not apply to any unsolicited real time communication which is made by the overseas communicator and which relates to that investment activity;

    (b)   that the protections conferred by or under the Act may not apply to any investment activity that may be engaged in as a result of the communication; and

    (c)   whether any transaction between them resulting from the communication would fall within the jurisdiction of any dispute resolution scheme or compensation scheme or, if there is no such scheme, of that fact.

[2795]

NOTES
Commencement: 1 July 2005.

33 Overseas   communicators: unsolicited   real   time   communications   to knowledgeable customers

(1)   If the requirements of paragraphs (2), (3) and (4) are met, the financial promotion restriction does not apply to an unsolicited real time communication which is made by an overseas communicator from outside the United Kingdom in the course of his carrying on relevant investment activities outside the United Kingdom.

(2)   The requirements of this paragraph are that the overseas communicator believes on reasonable grounds that the recipient is sufficiently knowledgeable to understand the risks associated with engaging in the investment activity to which the communication relates.

(3)   The requirements of this paragraph are that, in relation to any particular investment activity, the recipient has been informed by the overseas communicator on an earlier occasion—

    (a)   that the protections conferred by or under the Act will not apply to any unsolicited real time communication which is made by him and which relates to that activity;

    (b)   that the protections conferred by or under the Act may not apply to any investment activity that may be engaged in as a result of the communication; and

    (c)   whether any transaction between them resulting from the communication would fall within the jurisdiction of any dispute resolution scheme or compensation scheme or, if there is no such scheme, of that fact.

(4)   The requirements of this paragraph are that the recipient, after being given a proper opportunity to consider the information given to him in accordance with paragraph (3), has clearly signified that he understands the warnings referred to in paragraph (3)(a) and (b) and that he accepts that he will not benefit from the protections referred to.

[2796]

NOTES
Commencement: 1 July 2005.

34 Governments, central banks etc

The financial promotion restriction does not apply to any communication which—

    (a)   is a non-real time communication or a solicited real time communication;

    (b)   is communicated by and relates only to controlled investments issued, or to be issued, by—

        (i)   any government;

        (ii)   any local authority (in the United Kingdom or elsewhere);

        (iii)   any international organisation;

        (iv)   the Bank of England;

        (v)   the European Central Bank;

        (vi)   the central bank of any country or territory outside the United Kingdom.

[2797]

NOTES
Commencement: 1 July 2005.

35 Industrial and provident societies

The financial promotion restriction does not apply to any communication which—

    (a)   is a non-real time communication or a solicited real time communication;

    (b)   is communicated by an industrial and provident society; and

    (c)   relates only to an investment falling within paragraph 15 of Schedule 1 issued, or to be issued, by the society in question.

[2798]

NOTES
Commencement: 1 July 2005.

36 Nationals of EEA States other than United Kingdom

The financial promotion restriction does not apply to any communication which—
   (a)   is a non-real time communication or a solicited real time communication;
   (b)   is communicated by a national of an EEA State other than the United Kingdom in the course of any controlled activity lawfully carried on by him in that State; and
   (c)   conforms with any rules made by the Authority under section 145 of the Act (financial promotion rules) which are relevant to a communication of that kind.

[2799]

NOTES
Commencement: 1 July 2005.

37 Financial markets

(1)   The financial promotion restriction does not apply to any communication—
   (a)   which is a non-real time communication or a solicited real time communication;
   (b)   which is communicated by a relevant market; and
   (c)   to which paragraph (2) or (3) applies.

(2)   This paragraph applies to a communication if—
   (a)   it relates only to facilities provided by the market; and
   (b)   it does not identify (directly or indirectly)—
      (i)   any particular investment issued, or to be issued, by or available from an identified person as one that may be traded or dealt in on the market; or
      (ii)   any particular person as a person through whom transactions on the market may be effected.

(3)   This paragraph applies to a communication if—
   (a)   it relates only to a particular investment falling within paragraph 21, 22 or 23 of Schedule 1; and
   (b)   it identifies the investment as one that may be traded or dealt in on the market.

(4)   "Relevant market" means a market which—
   (a)   meets the criteria specified in Part I of Schedule 3; or
   (b)   is specified in, or is established under the rules of an exchange specified in, Part II, III or IV of that Schedule.

[2800]

NOTES
Commencement: 1 July 2005.

38 Persons in the business of placing promotional material

The financial promotion restriction does not apply to any communication which is made to a person whose business it is to place, or arrange for the placing of, promotional material provided that it is communicated so that he can place or arrange for placing it.

[2801]

NOTES
Commencement: 1 July 2005.

39 Joint enterprises

(1)   The financial promotion restriction does not apply to any communication which is made or directed by a participator in a joint enterprise to or at another participator in the same joint enterprise in connection with, or for the purposes of, that enterprise.

(2)   "Joint enterprise" means an enterprise into which two or more persons ("the participators") enter for commercial purposes related to a business or businesses (other than the business of engaging in a controlled activity) carried on by them; and, where a participator is a member of a group, each other member of the group is also to be regarded as a participator in the enterprise.

(3)   "Participator" includes potential participator.

[2802]

NOTES
Commencement: 1 July 2005.

40 Participants in certain recognised collective investment schemes

The financial promotion restriction does not apply to any non-real time communication or solicited real time communication which is made—

(a) by a person who is the operator of a scheme recognised under section 270 or 272 of the Act; and

(b) to persons in the United Kingdom who are participants in any such recognised scheme operated by the person making the communication,

and which relates only to such recognised schemes as are operated by that person or to units in such schemes.

[2803]

NOTES

Commencement: 1 July 2005.

41 Bearer instruments: promotions required or permitted by market rules

(1) The financial promotion restriction does not apply to any communication which—

(a) is a non-real time communication or a solicited real time communication;

(b) is communicated by a body corporate ("A") that is not an open-ended investment company;

(c) is made to or may reasonably be regarded as directed at persons entitled to bearer instruments issued by A, a parent undertaking of A or a subsidiary undertaking of A; and

(d) is required or permitted by the rules of a relevant market to be communicated to holders of instruments of a class which consists of or includes the bearer instruments in question.

(2) "Bearer instrument" means any of the following investments title to which is capable of being transferred by delivery—

(a) any investment falling within paragraph 14 or 15 of Schedule 1;

(b) any investment falling within paragraph 17 or 18 of that Schedule which confers rights in respect of an investment falling within paragraph 14 or 15.

(3) For the purposes of this article, a bearer instrument falling within paragraph 17 or 18 of Schedule 1 is treated as issued by the person ("P") who issued the investment in respect of which the bearer instrument confers rights if it is issued by—

(a) an undertaking in the same group as P; or

(b) a person acting on behalf of, or pursuant to arrangements made with, P.

(4) "Relevant market", in relation to instruments of any particular class, means any market on which instruments of that class can be traded or dealt in and which—

(a) meets the criteria specified in Part I of Schedule 3; or

(b) is specified in, or established under the rules of an exchange specified in, Part II or III of that Schedule.

[2804]

NOTES

Commencement: 1 July 2005.

42 Bearer instruments: promotions to existing holders

(1) The financial promotion restriction does not apply to any communication which—

(a) is a non-real time communication or a solicited real time communication;

(b) is communicated by a body corporate ("A") that is not an open-ended investment company;

(c) is made to or may reasonably be regarded as directed at persons entitled to bearer instruments issued by A, a parent undertaking of A or a subsidiary undertaking of A;

(d) relates only to instruments of a class which consists of or includes either the bearer instruments to which the communication relates or instruments in respect of which those bearer instruments confer rights; and

(e) is capable of being accepted or acted on only by persons who are entitled to instruments (whether or not bearer instruments) issued by A, a parent undertaking of A or a subsidiary undertaking of A.

(2) "Bearer instruments" has the meaning given by article 41.

(3) For the purposes of this article, an instrument falling within paragraph 17 or 18 of Schedule 1 is treated as issued by the person ("P") who issued the investment in respect of which the bearer instrument confers rights if it is issued by—

(a) an undertaking in the same group as P; or

(b) a person acting on behalf of, or pursuant to arrangements made with, P.

[2805]

NOTES
Commencement: 1 July 2005.

43   Members and creditors of certain bodies corporate

(1)   The financial promotion restriction does not apply to any non-real time communication or solicited real time communication which is communicated—

   (a)   by, or on behalf of, a body corporate ("A") that is not an open-ended investment company; and

   (b)   to persons whom the person making or directing the communication believes on reasonable grounds to be persons to whom paragraph (2) applies,

and which relates only to a relevant investment which is issued or to be issued by A, or by an undertaking ("U") in the same group as A that is not an open-ended investment company.

(2)   This paragraph applies to—

   (a)   a creditor or member of A or of U;

   (b)   a person who is entitled to a relevant investment which is issued, or to be issued, by A or by U;

   (c)   a person who is entitled, whether conditionally or unconditionally, to become a member of A or of U but who has not yet done so;

   (d)   a person who is entitled, whether conditionally or unconditionally, to have transferred to him title to a relevant investment which is issued by A or by U but has not yet acquired title to the investment.

(3)   "Relevant investment" means—

   (a)   an investment falling within paragraph 14 or 15 of Schedule 1;

   (b)   an investment falling within paragraph 17 or 18 of that Schedule so far as relating to any investments within sub-paragraph (a).

(4)   For the purposes of this article, an investment falling within paragraph 17 or 18 of Schedule 1 is treated as issued by the person ("P") who issued the investment in respect of which the instrument confers rights if it is issued by—

   (a)   an undertaking in the same group as P; or

   (b)   a person acting on behalf of, or pursuant to arrangements made with, P.

[2806]

NOTES
Commencement: 1 July 2005.

44   Members and creditors of open-ended investment companies

(1)   The financial promotion restriction does not apply to any communication which—

   (a)   is a non-real time communication or a solicited real time communication;

   (b)   is communicated by, or on behalf of, a body corporate ("A") that is an open-ended investment company;

   (c)   is communicated to persons whom the person making or directing the communication believes on reasonable grounds to be persons to whom paragraph (2) applies; and

   (d)   relates only to an investment falling within paragraph 15, 17 or 19 of Schedule 1 which is issued, or to be issued, by A.

(2)   This paragraph applies to—

   (a)   a creditor or member of A;

   (b)   a person who is entitled to an investment falling within paragraph 15, 17 or 19 of Schedule 1 which is issued, or to be issued, by A;

   (c)   a person who is entitled, whether conditionally or unconditionally, to become a member of A but who has not yet done so;

   (d)   a person who is entitled, whether conditionally or unconditionally, to have transferred to him title to an investment falling within paragraph 15, 17 or 19 of Schedule 1 which is issued by A but has not yet acquired title to the investment.

(3)   For the purposes of this article, an investment falling within paragraph 17 of Schedule 1 is treated as issued by the person ("P") who issued the investment in respect of which the instrument confers rights if it is issued by—

   (a)   an undertaking in the same group as P; or

   (b)   a person acting on behalf of, or pursuant to arrangements made with, P.

[2807]

NOTES
Commencement: 1 July 2005.

45 Group companies

The financial promotion restriction does not apply to any communication made by one body corporate in a group to another body corporate in the same group.

[2808]

NOTES
Commencement: 1 July 2005.

46 Qualifying credit to bodies corporate

The financial promotion restriction does not apply to any communication which relates to a controlled activity falling within paragraph 10, 10A or 10B of Schedule 1 (or within paragraph 11 so far as it relates to that activity) if the communication is—
  (a)   made to or directed at bodies corporate only; or
  (b)   accompanied by an indication that the qualifying credit to which it relates is only available to bodies corporate.

[2809]

NOTES
Commencement: 1 July 2005.

47 Persons in the business of disseminating information

(1)   The financial promotion restriction does not apply to any communication which is made only to recipients whom the person making the communication believes on reasonable grounds to be persons to whom paragraph (2) applies.

(2)   This paragraph applies to—
  (a)   a person who receives the communication in the course of a business which involves the dissemination through a publication of information concerning controlled activities;
  (b)   a person whilst acting in the capacity of director, officer or employee of a person falling within sub-paragraph (a) being a person whose responsibilities when acting in that capacity involve him in the business referred to in that sub-paragraph;
  (c)   any person to whom the communication may otherwise lawfully be made.

[2810]

NOTES
Commencement: 1 July 2005.

48 Certified high net worth individuals

(1)   If the requirements of paragraphs (4) and (7) are met, the financial promotion restriction does not apply to any communication which—
  (a)   is a non-real time communication or a solicited real time communication;
  (b)   is made to an individual whom the person making the communication believes on reasonable grounds to be a certified high net worth individual, and
  (c)   relates only to one or more investments falling within paragraph (8).

(2)   "Certified high net worth individual" means an individual who has signed, within the period of twelve months ending with the day on which the communication is made, a statement complying with Part I of Schedule 5.

(3)   The validity of a statement signed for the purposes of paragraph (2) is not affected by a defect in the form or wording of the statement, provided that the defect does not alter the statement's meaning and that the words shown in bold type in Part I of Schedule 5 are so shown in the statement.

(4)   The requirements of this paragraph are that either the communication is accompanied by the giving of a warning in accordance with paragraphs (5) and (6) or where, because of the nature of the communication, this is not reasonably practicable,—
  (a)   a warning in accordance with paragraph (5) is given to the recipient orally at the beginning of the communication together with an indication that he will receive the warning in legible form and that, before receipt of that warning, he should consider carefully any decision to engage in investment activity to which the communication relates; and
  (b)   a warning in accordance with paragraphs (5) and (6) (d) to (h) is sent to the recipient of the communication within two business days of the day on which the communication is made.

(5)   The warning must be in the following terms—

"The content of this promotion has not been approved by an authorised person within the meaning of the Financial Services and Markets Act 2000. Reliance on this promotion for the purpose of engaging in any investment activity may expose an individual to a significant risk of losing all of the property or other assets invested.".

But where a warning is sent pursuant to paragraph (4)(b), for the words "this promotion" in both places where they occur there must be substituted wording which clearly identifies the promotion which is the subject of the warning.

(6) The warning must—
- (a) be given at the beginning of the communication;
- (b) precede any other written or pictorial matter;
- (c) be in a font size consistent with the text forming the remainder of the communication;
- (d) be indelible;
- (e) be legible;
- (f) be printed in black, bold type;
- (g) be surrounded by a black border which does not interfere with the text of the warning; and
- (h) not be hidden, obscured or interrupted by any other written or pictorial matter.

(7) The requirements of this paragraph are that the communication is accompanied by an indication—
- (a) that it is exempt from the general restriction (in section 21 of the Act) on the communication of invitations or inducements to engage in investment activity on the ground that it is made to a certified high net worth individual;
- (b) of the requirements that must be met for an individual to qualify as a certified high net worth individual; and
- (c) that any individual who is in any doubt about the investment to which the communication relates should consult an authorised person specialising in advising on investments of the kind in question.

(8) An investment falls within this paragraph if—
- (a) it is an investment falling within paragraph 14 of Schedule 1 being stock or shares in an unlisted company;
- (b) it is an investment falling within paragraph 15 of Schedule 1 being an investment acknowledging the indebtedness of an unlisted company;
- (c) it is an investment falling within paragraph 17 or 18 of Schedule 1 conferring entitlement or rights with respect to investments falling within sub-paragraph (a) or (b);
- (d) it comprises units in a collective investment scheme being a scheme which invests wholly or predominantly in investments falling within sub-paragraph (a) or (b);
- (e) it is an investment falling within paragraph 21 of Schedule 1 being an option to acquire or dispose of an investment falling within sub-paragraph (a), (b) or (c);
- (f) it is an investment falling within paragraph 22 of Schedule 1 being rights under a contract for the sale of an investment falling within sub-paragraph (a), (b) or (c);
- (g) it is an investment falling within paragraph 23 of Schedule 1 being a contract relating to, or to fluctuations in value or price of, an investment falling within sub-paragraph (a), (b) or (c),

provided in each case that it is an investment under the terms of which the investor cannot incur a liability or obligation to pay or contribute more than he commits by way of investment.

(9) "Business day" means any day except a Saturday, a Sunday, Christmas Day, Good Friday or a day which is a bank holiday under the Banking and Financial Dealings Act 1971 in any part of the United Kingdom.

[2811]

NOTES

Commencement: 1 July 2005.

---

49 High net worth companies, unincorporated associations etc

(1) The financial promotion restriction does not apply to any communication which—
- (a) is made only to recipients whom the person making the communication believes on reasonable grounds to be persons to whom paragraph (2) applies; or
- (b) may reasonably be regarded as directed only at persons to whom paragraph (2) applies.

(2) This paragraph applies to—
- (a) any body corporate which has, or which is a member of the same group as an undertaking which has, a called-up share capital or net assets of not less than—
  - (i) if the body corporate has more than 20 members or is a subsidiary undertaking of an undertaking which has more than 20 members, £500,000;
  - (ii) otherwise, £5 million;
- (b) any unincorporated association or partnership which has net assets of not less than £5 million;
- (c) the trustee of a high value trust;

PART III
STATUTORY INSTRUMENTS

(d) any person ("A") whilst acting in the capacity of director, officer or employee of a person ("B") falling within any of sub-paragraphs (a) to (c) where A's responsibilities, when acting in that capacity, involve him in B's engaging in investment activity;

(e) any person to whom the communication may otherwise lawfully be made.

(3) For the purposes of paragraph (1)(b)—

(a) if all the conditions set out in paragraph (4)(a) to (c) are met, the communication is to be regarded as directed at persons to whom paragraph (2) applies;

(b) in any other case in which one or more of those conditions are met, that fact is to be taken into account in determining whether the communication is directed at persons to whom paragraph (2) applies (but a communication may still be regarded as so directed even if none of the conditions in paragraph (4) is met).

(4) The conditions are that—

(a) the communication includes an indication of the description of persons to whom it is directed and an indication of the fact that the controlled investment or controlled activity to which it relates is available only to such persons;

(b) the communication includes an indication that persons of any other description should not act upon it;

(c) there are in place proper systems and procedures to prevent recipients other than persons to whom paragraph (2) applies engaging in the investment activity to which the communication relates with the person directing the communication, a close relative of his or a member of the same group.

(5) "Called-up share capital" has the meaning given in the 1985 Act or in the 1986 Order.

(6) "High value trust" means a trust where the aggregate value of the cash and investments which form part of the trust's assets (before deducting the amount of its liabilities)—

(a) is £10 million or more; or

(b) has been £10 million or more at anytime during the year immediately preceding the date on which the communication in question was first made or directed.

(7) "Net assets" has the meaning given by section 264 of the 1985 Act or the equivalent provision of the 1986 Order.

[2812]

NOTES

Commencement: 1 July 2005.

50 Sophisticated investors

(1) "Certified sophisticated investor", in relation to any description of investment, means a person—

(a) who has a current certificate in writing or other legible form signed by an authorised person to the effect that he is sufficiently knowledgeable to understand the risks associated with that description of investment; and

(b) who has signed, within the period of twelve months ending with the day on which the communication is made, a statement in the following terms:

"I make this statement so that I am able to receive promotions which are exempt from the restrictions on financial promotion in the Financial Services and Markets Act 2000. The exemption relates to certified sophisticated investors and I declare that I qualify as such in relation to investments of the following kind [list them]. I accept that the contents of promotions and other material that I receive may not have been approved by an authorised person and that their content may not therefore be subject to controls which would apply if the promotion were made or approved by an authorised person. I am aware that it is open to me to seek advice from someone who specialises in advising on this kind of investment.".

(1A) The validity of a statement signed in accordance with paragraph (1)(b) is not affected by a defect in the wording of the statement, provided that the defect does not alter the statement's meaning.

(2) If the requirements of paragraph (3) are met, the financial promotion restriction does not apply to any communication which—

(a) is made to a certified sophisticated investor;

(b) does not invite or induce the recipient to engage in investment activity with the person who has signed the certificate referred to in paragraph (1)(a); and

(c) relates only to a description of investment in respect of which that investor is certified.

(3) The requirements of this paragraph are that the communication is accompanied by an indication—

(a) that it is exempt from the general restriction (in section 21 of the Act) on the communication of invitations or inducements to engage in investment activity on the ground that it is made to a certified sophisticated investor;

    (b)   of the requirements that must be met for a person to qualify as a certified sophisticated investor;

    (c)   that the content of the communication has not been approved by an authorised person and that such approval is, unless this exemption or any other exemption applies, required by section 21 of the Act;

    (d)   that reliance on the communication for the purpose of engaging in any investment activity may expose the individual to a significant risk of losing all of the property invested or of incurring additional liability;

    (e)   that any person who is in any doubt about the investment to which the communication relates should consult an authorised person specialising in advising on investments of the kind in question.

(4)   For the purposes of paragraph (1)(a), a certificate is current if it is signed and dated not more than three years before the date on which the communication is made.

[2813]

NOTES

Commencement: 1 July 2005.

50A   Self-certified sophisticated investors

(1)   "Self-certified sophisticated investor" means an individual who has signed within the period of twelve months ending with the day on which the communication is made, a statement complying with Part II of Schedule 5.

(2)   The validity of a statement signed for the purposes of paragraph (1) is not affected by a defect in the form or wording of the statement, provided that the defect does not alter the statement's meaning and that the words shown in bold type in Part II of Schedule 5 are so shown in the statement.

(3)   If the requirements of paragraphs (4) and (7) are met, the financial promotion restriction does not apply to any communication which—

    (a)   is made to an individual whom the person making the communication believes on reasonable grounds to be a self-certified sophisticated investor; and

    (b)   relates only to one or more investments falling within paragraph (8).

(4)   The requirements of this paragraph are that either the communication is accompanied by the giving of a warning in accordance with paragraphs (5) and (6) or where, because of the nature of the communication this is not reasonably practicable—

    (a)   a warning in accordance with paragraph (5) is given to the recipient orally at the beginning of the communication together with an indication that he will receive the warning in legible form and that, before receipt of that warning, he should consider carefully any decision to engage in investment activity to which the communication relates; and

    (b)   a warning in accordance with paragraphs (5) and (6) (d) to (h) is sent to the recipient of the communication within two business days of the day on which the communication is made.

(5)   The warning must be in the following terms—

"The content of this promotion has not been approved by an authorised person within the meaning of the Financial Services and Markets Act 2000. Reliance on this promotion for the purpose of engaging in any investment activity may expose an individual to a significant risk of losing all of the property or other assets invested.".

But where a warning is sent pursuant to paragraph (4)(b), for the words "this promotion" in both places where they occur there must be substituted wording which clearly identifies the promotion which is the subject of the warning.

(6)   The warning must—

    (a)   be given at the beginning of the communication;

    (b)   precede any other written or pictorial matter;

    (c)   be in a font size consistent with the text forming the remainder of the communication;

    (d)   be indelible;

    (e)   be legible;

    (f)   be printed in black, bold type;

    (g)   be surrounded by a black border which does not interfere with the text of the warning; and

    (h)   not be hidden, obscured or interrupted by any other written or pictorial matter.

(7)   The requirements of this paragraph are that the communication is accompanied by an indication—

    (a)   that it is exempt from the general restriction (in section 21 of the Act) on the

PART III
STATUTORY INSTRUMENTS

communication of invitations or inducements to engage in investment activity on the
ground that it is made to a self-certified sophisticated investor;

(b)   of the requirements that must be met for an individual to qualify as a self-certified
sophisticated investor;

(c)   that any individual who is in any doubt about the investment to which the
communication relates should consult an authorised person specialising in advising on
investments of the kind in question.

(8)   An investment falls within this paragraph if—

(a)   it is an investment falling within paragraph 14 of Schedule 1 being stock or shares in an
unlisted company;

(b)   it is an investment falling within paragraph 15 of Schedule 1 being an investment
acknowledging the indebtedness of an unlisted company;

(c)   it is an investment falling within paragraph 17 or 18 of Schedule 1 conferring
entitlement or rights with respect to investments falling within sub-paragraph (a) or (b);

(d)   it comprises units in a collective investment scheme being a scheme which invests
wholly or predominantly in investments falling within sub-paragraph (a) or (b);

(e)   it is an investment falling within paragraph 21 of Schedule 1 being an option to acquire
or dispose of an investment falling within sub-paragraph (a), (b) or (c);

(f)   it is an investment falling within paragraph 22 of Schedule 1 being rights under a
contract for the sale of an investment falling within sub-paragraph (a), (b) or (c);

(g)   it is an investment falling within paragraph 23 of Schedule 1 being a contract relating to,
or to fluctuations in value or price of, an investment falling within sub-paragraph (a), (b)
or (c),

provided in each case that it is an investment under the terms of which the investor cannot incur a
liability or obligation to pay or contribute more than he commits by way of investment.

(9)   "Business day" means any day except a Saturday, a Sunday, Christmas Day, Good Friday or
a day which is a bank holiday under the Banking and Financial Dealings Act 1971 in any part of the
United Kingdom.

[2814]

NOTES

Commencement: 1 July 2005.

51 Associations of high net worth or sophisticated investors

The financial promotion restriction does not apply to any non-real time communication or solicited
real time communication which—

(a)   is made to an association, or to a member of an association, the membership of which
the person making the communication believes on reasonable grounds comprises wholly
or predominantly persons who are—

    (i)   certified or self-certified high net worth individuals within the meaning of
article 48;

    (ii)   high net worth persons falling within article 49(2)(a) to (d);

    (iii)   certified or self-certified sophisticated investors within the meaning of article 50
or 50A; and

(b)   relates only to an investment under the terms of which a person cannot incur a liability
or obligation to pay or contribute more than he commits by way of investment.

[2815]

NOTES

Commencement: 1 July 2005.

52 Common interest group of a company

(1)   "Common interest group", in relation to a company, means an identified group of persons
who at the time the communication is made might reasonably be regarded as having an existing and
common interest with each other and that company in—

(a)   the affairs of the company; and

(b)   what is done with the proceeds arising from any investment to which the communication
relates.

(2)   If the requirements of paragraphs (3) and either (4) or (5) are met, the financial promotion
restriction does not apply to any communication which—

(a)   is a non-real time communication or a solicited real time communication;

(b)   is made only to persons who are members of a common interest group of a company, or
may reasonably be regarded as directed only at such persons; and

(c)   relates to investments falling within paragraph 14 or 15 of Schedule 1 which are issued,
or to be issued, by that company.

(3)   The requirements of this paragraph are that the communication is accompanied by an indication—

    (a)   that the directors of the company (or its promoters named in the communication) have taken all reasonable care to ensure that every statement of fact or opinion included in the communication is true and not misleading given the form and context in which it appears;

    (b)   that the directors of the company (or its promoters named in the communication) have not limited their liability with respect to the communication; and

    (c)   that any person who is in any doubt about the investment to which the communication relates should consult an authorised person specialising in advising on investments of the kind in question.

(4)   The requirements of this paragraph are that the communication is accompanied by an indication—

    (a)   that the directors of the company (or its promoters named in the communication) have taken all reasonable care to ensure that any person belonging to the common interest group (and his professional advisers) can have access, at all reasonable times, to all the information that he or they would reasonably require, and reasonably expect to find, for the purpose of making an informed assessment of the assets and liabilities, financial position, profits and losses and prospects of the company and of the rights attaching to the investments in question; and

    (b)   describing the means by which such information can be accessed.

(5)   The requirements of this paragraph are that the communication is accompanied by an indication that any person considering subscribing for the investments in question should regard any subscription as made primarily to assist the furtherance of the company's objectives (other than any purely financial objectives) and only secondarily, if at all, as an investment.

(6)   For the purposes of paragraph (2)(b)—

    (a)   if all the conditions set out in paragraph (7) are met, the communication is to be regarded as directed at persons who are members of the common interest group;

    (b)   in any other case in which one or more of those conditions are met, that fact shall be taken into account in determining whether the communication is directed at persons who are members of the common interest group (but a communication may still be regarded as directed only at such persons even if none of the conditions in paragraph (7) is met).

(7)   The conditions are that—

    (a)   the communication is accompanied by an indication that it is directed at persons who are members of the common interest group and that any investment or activity to which it relates is available only to such persons;

    (b)   the communication is accompanied by an indication that it must not be acted upon by persons who are not members of the common interest group;

    (c)   there are in place proper systems and procedures to prevent recipients other than members of the common interest group engaging in the investment activity to which the communication relates with the person directing the communication, a close relative of his or a member of the same group.

(8)   Persons are not to be regarded as having an interest of the kind described in paragraph (1) if the only reason why they would be so regarded is that—

    (a)   they will have such an interest if they become members or creditors of the company;

    (b)   they all carry on a particular trade or profession; or

    (c)   they are persons with whom the company has an existing business relationship, whether by being its clients, customers, contractors, suppliers or otherwise.

[2816]

NOTES

Commencement: 1 July 2005.

53 Settlors, trustees and personal representatives

The financial promotion restriction does not apply to any communication which is made between—

    (a)   a person when acting as a settlor or grantor of a trust, a trustee or a personal representative; and

    (b)   a trustee of the trust, a fellow trustee or a fellow personal representative (as the case may be),

if the communication is made for the purposes of the trust or estate.

[2817]

NOTES

Commencement: 1 July 2005.

54 Beneficiaries of trust, will or intestacy

The financial promotion restriction does not apply to any communication which is made—

    (a)   between a person when acting as a settlor or grantor of a trust, trustee or personal representative and a beneficiary under the trust, will or intestacy; or

    (b)   between a beneficiary under a trust, will or intestacy and another beneficiary under the same trust, will or intestacy,

if the communication relates to the management or distribution of that trust fund or estate.

[2818]

NOTES

Commencement: 1 July 2005.

55 Communications by members of professions

(1) The financial promotion restriction does not apply to a real time communication (whether solicited or unsolicited) which—

    (a)   is made by a person ("P") who carries on a regulated activity to which the general prohibition does not apply by virtue of section 327 of the Act; and

    (b)   is made to a recipient who has, prior to the communication being made, engaged P to provide professional services,

where the controlled activity to which the communication relates is an excluded activity which would be undertaken by P for the purposes of, and incidental to, the provision by him of professional services to or at the request of the recipient.

(2) "Professional services" has the meaning given in section 327 of the Act.

(3) An "excluded activity" is an activity to which the general prohibition would apply but for the application of—

    (a)   section 327 of the Act; or

    (b)   article 67 of the Regulated Activities Order.

[2819]

NOTES

Commencement: 1 July 2005.

55A Non-real time communication by members of professions

(1) The financial promotion restriction does not apply to a non-real time communication which is—

    (a)   made by a person ("P") who carries on Part XX activities; and

    (b)   limited to what is required or permitted by paragraphs (2) and (3).

(2) The communication must be in the following terms—

"This [firm/company] is not authorised under the Financial Services and Markets Act 2000 but we are able in certain circumstances to offer a limited range of investment services to clients because we are members of [relevant designated professional body]. We can provide these investment services if they are an incidental part of the professional services we have been engaged to provide."

(3) The communication may in addition set out the Part XX activities which P is able to offer to his clients, provided it is clear that these are the investment services to which the statement in paragraph (2) relates.

(4) The validity of a communication made in accordance with paragraph (2) is not affected by a defect in the wording of it provided that the defect does not alter the communication's meaning.

(5) "Part XX activities" means the regulated activities to which the general prohibition does not apply when they are carried on by P by virtue of section 327 of the Act.

[2820]

NOTES

Commencement: 1 July 2005.

56 Remedy following report by Parliamentary Commissioner for Administration

The financial promotion restriction does not apply to any communication made or directed by a person for the purpose of enabling any injustice, stated by the Parliamentary Commissioner for Administration in a report under section 10 of the Parliamentary Commissioner Act 1967 to have occurred, to be remedied with respect to the recipient.

[2821]

57   Persons placing promotional material in particular publications

The financial promotion restriction does not apply to any communication received by a person who receives the publication in which the communication is contained because he has himself placed an advertisement in that publication.

[2822]

NOTES
Commencement: 1 July 2005.

58   Acquisition of interest in premises run by management companies

(1)   "Management company" means a company established for the purpose of—
  (a)   managing the common parts or fabric of premises used for residential or business purposes; or
  (b)   supplying services to such premises.

(2)   The financial promotion restriction does not apply to any non-real time communication or solicited real time communication if it relates to an investment falling within paragraph 14 of Schedule 1 which—
  (a)   is issued, or to be issued, by a management company; and
  (b)   is to be acquired by any person in connection with the acquisition of an interest in the premises in question.

[2823]

NOTES
Commencement: 1 July 2005.

59   Annual accounts and directors' report

(1)   If the requirements in paragraphs (2) to (5) are met, the financial promotion restriction does not apply to any communication by a body corporate (other than an open-ended investment company) which—
  (a)   consists of, or is accompanied by, the whole or any part of the annual accounts of a body corporate (other than an open-ended investment company); or
  (b)   is accompanied by any report which is prepared and approved by the directors of such a body corporate under—
    (i)   sections 234 and 234A of the 1985 Act;
    (ii)   the corresponding Northern Ireland enactment; or
    (iii)   the law of an EEA State other than the United Kingdom which corresponds to the provisions mentioned in paragraph (i) or (ii).

(2)   The requirements of this paragraph are that the communication—
  (a)   does not contain any invitation to persons to underwrite, subscribe for, or otherwise acquire or dispose of, a controlled investment; and
  (b)   does not advise persons to engage in any of the activities within sub-paragraph (a).

(3)   The requirements of this paragraph are that the communication does not contain any invitation to persons to—
  (a)   effect any transaction with the body corporate (or with any named person) in the course of that body's (or person's) carrying on of any activity falling within any of paragraphs 3 to 11 of Schedule 1; or
  (b)   make use of any services provided by that body corporate (or by any named person) in the course of carrying on such activity.

(4)   The requirements of this paragraph are that the communication does not contain any inducement relating to an investment other than one issued, or to be issued, by the body corporate (or another body corporate in the same group) which falls within—
  (a)   paragraph 14 or 15 of Schedule 1; or
  (b)   paragraph 17 or 18 of that Schedule, so far as relating to any investments within sub-paragraph (a).

(5)   The requirements of this paragraph are that the communication does not contain any reference to—
  (a)   the price at which investments issued by the body corporate have in the past been bought or sold; or
  (b)   the yield on such investments,

unless it is also accompanied by an indication that past performance cannot be relied on as a guide to future performance.

(6)   For the purposes of paragraph (5)(b), a reference, in relation to an investment, to earnings, dividend or nominal rate of interest payable shall not be taken to be a reference to the yield on the investment.

(7)   "Annual accounts" means—

(a)   accounts produced by virtue of Part VII of the 1985 Act (or of that Part as applied by virtue of any other enactment);

(b)   accounts produced by virtue of the corresponding Northern Ireland enactment (or of that enactment as applied by virtue of any other enactment);

(c)   a summary financial statement prepared under section 251 of the 1985 Act;

(d)   accounts delivered to the registrar under Chapter II of Part XXIII of the 1985 Act;

(e)   accounts which are produced or published by virtue of the law of an EEA State other than the United Kingdom and which correspond to accounts within any of sub-paragraphs (a) to (d).

[2824]

NOTES

Commencement: 1 July 2005.

60   Participation in employee share schemes

(1)   The financial promotion restriction does not apply to any communication by a person ("C"), a member of the same group as C or a relevant trustee where the communication is for the purposes of an employee share scheme and relates to any of the following investments issued, or to be issued, by C—

(a)   investments falling within paragraph 14 or 15 of Schedule 1;

(b)   investments falling within paragraph 17 or 18 so far as relating to any investments within sub-paragraph (a); or

(c)   investments falling within paragraph 21 or 27 so far as relating to any investments within sub-paragraph (a) or (b).

(2)   "Employee share scheme", in relation to any investments issued by C, means arrangements made or to be made by C or by a person in the same group as C to enable or facilitate—

(a)   transactions in the investments specified in paragraphs (1)(a) or (b) between or for the benefit of—

(i)   the bona fide employees or former employees of C or of another member of the same group as C;

(ii)   the wives, husbands, widows, widowers[, civil partners, surviving civil partners] or children or step-children under the age of eighteen of such employees or former employees; or

(b)   the holding of those investments by, or for the benefit of, such persons.

(3)   "Relevant trustee" means a person who, in pursuance of an actual or proposed employee share scheme, holds as trustee or will hold as trustee investments issued by C

[2825]

NOTES

Commencement: 1 July 2005.

Para (2): words in square brackets in sub-para (a)(ii) inserted by the Financial Services and Markets Act 2000 (Financial Promotion) (Amendment) Order 2005, SI 2005/3392, art 2(1), (4), as from 21 December 2005.

Step-children, etc: as to the meaning of this and related expressions, see the Civil Partnership Act 2004, s 246 (as applied to this Order by the Civil Partnership Act 2004 (Relationships Arising Through Civil Partnership) Order 2005, SI 2005/3137, art 3, Schedule).

61   Sale of goods and supply of services

(1)   In this article—

"supplier" means a person whose main business is to sell goods or supply services and not to carry on controlled activities falling within any of paragraphs 3 to 7 of Schedule 1 and, where the supplier is a member of a group, also means any other member of that group;

"customer" means a person, other than an individual, to whom a supplier sells goods or supplies services, or agrees to do so, and, where the customer is a member of a group, also means any other member of that group;

"a related sale or supply" means a sale of goods or supply of services to the customer otherwise than by the supplier, but for or in connection with the same purpose as the sale or supply mentioned above.

(2)   The financial promotion restriction does not apply to any non-real time communication or any solicited real time communication made by a supplier to a customer of his for the purposes of, or in connection with, the sale of goods or supply of services or a related sale or supply.

(3)   But the exemption in paragraph (2) does not apply if the communication relates to—

(a)   a qualifying contract of insurance or units in a collective investment scheme; or

(b)   investments falling within paragraph 27 of Schedule 1 so far as relating to investments within paragraph (a).

[2826]

NOTES
Commencement: 1 July 2005.

62   Sale of body corporate

(1)   The financial promotion restriction does not apply to any communication by, or on behalf of, a body corporate, a partnership, a single individual or a group of connected individuals which relates to a transaction falling within paragraph (2).

(2)   A transaction falls within this paragraph if—
    (a)   it is one to acquire or dispose of shares in a body corporate other than an open-ended investment company, or is entered into for the purposes of such an acquisition or disposal; and
    (b)   either—
        (i)   the conditions set out in paragraph (3) are met; or
        (ii)   those conditions are not met, but the object of the transaction may nevertheless reasonably be regarded as being the acquisition of day to day control of the affairs of the body corporate.

(3)   The conditions mentioned in paragraph (2)(b) are that—
    (a)   the shares consist of or include 50 per cent or more of the voting shares in the body corporate; or
    (b)   the shares, together with any already held by the person acquiring them, consist of or include at least that percentage of such shares; and
    (c)   in either case, the acquisition or disposal is, or is to be, between parties each of whom is a body corporate, a partnership, a single individual or a group of connected individuals.

(4)   "A group of connected individuals" means—
    (a)   in relation to a party disposing of shares in a body corporate, a single group of persons each of whom is—
        (i)   a director or manager of the body corporate;
        (ii)   a close relative of any such director or manager; or
        (iii)   a person acting as trustee for, or nominee of, any person falling within paragraph (i) or (ii); and
    (b)   in relation to a party acquiring shares in a body corporate, a single group of persons each of whom is—
        (i)   a person who is or is to be a director or manager of the body corporate;
        (ii)   a close relative of any such person; or
        (iii)   a person acting as trustee for or nominee of any person falling within paragraph (i) or (ii).

(5)   "Voting shares" in relation to a body corporate, means shares carrying voting rights attributable to share capital which are exercisable in all circumstances at any general meeting of that body corporate.

[2827]

NOTES
Commencement: 1 July 2005.

63   Takeovers of relevant unlisted companies: interpretation

(1)   In this article and in articles 64, 65 and 66, a "relevant unlisted company", in relation to a takeover offer, means a company which is an unlisted company at the time that the offer is made and which has been an unlisted company throughout the period of ten years immediately preceding the date of the offer.

(2)   In this article and in articles 64, 65 and 66, references to a takeover offer for a relevant unlisted company are references to an offer which meets the requirements of Part I of Schedule 4 and which is an offer—
    (a)   for all the shares in, or all the shares comprised in the equity or non-equity share capital of, a relevant unlisted company (other than any shares already held by or on behalf of the person making the offer); or
    (b)   for all the debentures of such a company (other than debentures already held by or on behalf of the person making the offer).

(3)   Shares in or debentures of an unlisted company are to be regarded as being held by or on behalf of the person making the offer if the person who holds them, or on whose behalf they are held, has agreed that an offer should not be made in respect of them.

[2828]

64 Takeovers of relevant unlisted companies

(1) If the requirements of paragraphs (2) and (3) are met, the financial promotion restriction does not apply to any communication which is communicated in connection with a takeover offer for a relevant unlisted company.

(2) The requirements of this paragraph are that the communication is accompanied by the material listed in Part II of Schedule 4.

(3) The requirements of this paragraph are that the material listed in Part III of Schedule 4 is available at a place in the United Kingdom at all times during normal office hours for inspection free of charge.

[2829]

65 Takeovers of relevant unlisted companies: warrants etc

The financial promotion restriction does not apply to any communication which—
   (a) is communicated at the same time as, or after, a takeover offer for a relevant unlisted company is made; and
   (b) relates to investments falling within paragraph 17 or 18 of Schedule 1 so far as relating to the shares in or debentures of the unlisted company which are the subject of the offer.

[2830]

66 Takeovers of relevant unlisted companies: application forms

The financial promotion restriction does not apply to any communication made in connection with a takeover offer for a relevant unlisted company which is a form of application for—
   (a) shares in or debentures of the unlisted company; or
   (b) investments falling within paragraphs 17 or 18 of Schedule 1 so far as relating to the shares in or debentures of the company which are the subject of the offer.

[2831]

67 Promotions required or permitted by market rules

(1) The financial promotion restriction does not apply to any communication which—
   (a) is a non-real time communication or a solicited real time communication;
   (b) relates to an investment which falls within any of paragraphs 14 to 18 of Schedule 1 and which is permitted to be traded or dealt in on a relevant market; and
   (c) is required or permitted to be communicated by—
      (i) the rules of the relevant market;
      (ii) a body which regulates the market; or
      (iii) a body which regulates offers or issues of investments to be traded on such a market.

(2) "Relevant market" means a market which—
   (a) meets the criteria specified in Part I of Schedule 3; or
   (b) is specified in, or established under the rules of an exchange specified in, Part II or III of that Schedule.

[2832]

68 Promotions in connection with admission to certain EEA markets

(1) The financial promotion restriction does not apply to any communication—
   (a) which is a non-real time communication or a solicited real time communication;
   (b) which a relevant EEA market requires to be communicated before an investment can be admitted to trading on that market;

    (c)   which, if it were included in a prospectus issued in accordance with prospectus rules made under Part VI of the Act, would be required to be communicated by those rules; and

    (d)   which is not accompanied by any information other than information which is required or permitted to be published by the rules of that market.

(2)   In this article "relevant EEA market" means any market on which investments can be traded or dealt in and which—

    (a)   meets the criteria specified in Part I of Schedule 3; or

    (b)   is specified in, or established under the rules of an exchange specified in, Part II of that Schedule.

[2833]

NOTES

Commencement: 1 July 2005.

69   Promotions of securities already admitted to certain markets

(1)   In this article—

"relevant investment" means any investment falling within—

    (a)   paragraph 14 or 15 of Schedule 1; or

    (b)   paragraph 17 or 18 of that Schedule so far as relating to any investment mentioned in sub-paragraph (a);

"relevant market" means any sub-market on which investments can be traded and which—

    (a)   meets the criteria specified in Part I of Schedule 3; or

    (b)   is specified in, or established under, the rules of an exchange specified in, Part II or III of that Schedule.

(2)   If the requirements of paragraph (3) are met, the financial promotion restriction does not apply to any communication which—

    (a)   is a non-real time communication or a solicited real time communication;

    (b)   is communicated by a body corporate ("A"), other than an open-ended investment company; and

    (c)   relates only to relevant investments issued, or to be issued, by A or by another body corporate in the same group,

if relevant investments issued by A or by any such body corporate are permitted to be traded on a relevant market.

(3)   The requirements of this paragraph are that the communication—

    (a)   is not, and is not accompanied by, an invitation to engage in investment activity;

    (b)   is not, and is not accompanied by, an inducement relating to an investment other than one issued, or to be issued, by A (or another body corporate in the same group);

    (c)   is not, and is not accompanied by, an inducement relating to a relevant investment which refers to—

        (i)   the price at which relevant investments have been bought or sold in the past, or

        (ii)   the yield on such investments,

unless the inducement also contains an indication that past performance cannot be relied on as a guide to future performance.

(4)   For the purposes of this article, an investment falling within paragraph 17 or 18 of Schedule 1 is treated as issued by the person ("P") who issued the investment in respect of which the investment confers rights if it is issued by—

    (a)   an undertaking in the same group as P; or

    (b)   a person acting on behalf of, or pursuant to, arrangements made with P.

(5)   For the purposes of paragraph (3)(a), "engaging in investment activity" has the meaning given in section 21(8) of the Act; and for the purposes of paragraph (3)(c)(ii), a reference, in relation to an investment, to earnings, dividend or nominal rate of interest payable shall not be taken to be a reference to the yield on the investment.

[2834]

NOTES

Commencement: 1 July 2005.

70   Promotions included in listing particulars etc

(1)   The financial promotion restriction does not apply to any non-real time communication which is included in—

    (a)   listing particulars;

    (b)   supplementary listing particulars;

    [(c)   a prospectus or supplementary prospectus approved—

        (i)   by the competent authority in accordance with Part 6 of the Act; or

PART III
STATUTORY INSTRUMENTS

(ii)   by the competent authority of an EEA State other than the United Kingdom, provided the requirements of section 87H of the Act have been met,

or part of such a prospectus or supplementary prospectus; or]

(d)   any other document required or permitted to be published by listing rules or prospectus rules under Part VI of the Act (except an advertisement within the meaning of the prospectus directive).

[(1A)   The financial promotion restriction does not apply to any non-real time communication—

(a)   comprising the final terms of an offer or the final offer price or amount of securities which will be offered to the public; and

(b)   complying with Articles 5(4), 8(1) and 14(2) of the prospectus directive.]

(2)   In this article "listing particulars", "listing rules", "the prospectus directive" and "prospectus rules" have the meaning given by Part VI of the Act.

[2835]

NOTES

Commencement: 1 July 2005.

Para (1): sub-para (c) substituted by the Financial Services and Markets Act 2000 (Financial Promotion) (Amendment No 2) Order 2007, SI 2007/2615, art 2(1), (2), as from 1 October 2007.

Para (1A): inserted by SI 2007/2615, art 2(1), (3), as from 1 October 2007.

71   Material relating to prospectus for public offer of unlisted securities

(1)   The financial promotion restriction does not apply to any non-real time communication relating to a prospectus or supplementary prospectus where the only reason for considering it to be an invitation or inducement is that it does one or more of the following—

(a)   it states the name and address of the person by whom the transferable securities to which the prospectus or supplementary prospectus relates are to be offered;

(b)   it gives other details for contacting that person;

(c)   it states the nature and the nominal value of the transferable securities to which the prospectus or supplementary prospectus relates, the number offered and the price at which they are offered;

(d)   it states that a prospectus or supplementary prospectus is or will be available (and, if it is not yet available, when it is expected to be);

(e)   it gives instructions for obtaining a copy of the prospectus or supplementary prospectus.

(2)   In this article—

(a)   "transferable securities" has the same meaning as in section 102A(3) of the Act;

(b)   references to a prospectus or supplementary prospectus are references to a prospectus or supplementary prospectus which is published in accordance with prospectus rules made under Part VI of the Act.

[2836]

NOTES

Commencement: 1 July 2005.

72   Pension products offered by employers

(1)   If the requirements of paragraph (2) are met, the financial promotion restriction does not apply to any communication which is made by an employer to an employee in relation to a group personal pension scheme or a stakeholder pension scheme.

(2)   The requirements of this paragraph are that—

(a)   the employer will make a contribution to the group personal pension scheme or stakeholder pension scheme to which the communication relates in the event of the employee becoming a member of the scheme and the communication contains a statement informing the employee of this;

(b)   the employer has not received, and will not receive, any direct financial benefit from the scheme;

(c)   the employer notifies the employee in writing prior to the employee becoming a member of the scheme of the amount of the contribution that the employer will make to the scheme in respect of that employee; and

(d)   in the case of a non-real time communication, the communication contains, or is accompanied by, a statement informing the employee of his right to seek advice from an authorised person or an appointed representative.

(3)   For the purposes of paragraph (2)(b) "direct financial benefit" includes—

(a)   any commission paid to the employer by the provider of the scheme; and

(b)   any reduction in the amount of the premium payable by the employer in respect of any insurance policy issued to the employer by the provider of the scheme.

(4)   In this article—

"group personal pension scheme" means arrangements administered on a group basis under a personal pension scheme and which are available to employees of the same employer or of employers within a group;

["personal pension scheme" means a scheme or arrangement which is not an occupational pension scheme or a stakeholder pension scheme and which is comprised in one or more instruments or agreements, having or capable of having effect so as to provide benefits to or in respect of people—

    (a)   on retirement,

    (b)   on having reached a particular age, or

    (c)   on termination of service in an employment.]

"stakeholder pension scheme" has the meaning given by section 1 of the Welfare Reform and Pensions Act 1999.

[2837]

NOTES

Commencement: 1 July 2005.

Para (4): definition "personal pension scheme" substituted by the Financial Services and Markets Act 2000 (Regulated Activities) (Amendment) Order 2006, SI 2006/1969, art 12(1), (2), as from 6 April 2007.

73   Advice centres

(1)   If the requirements of paragraph (2) are met, the financial promotion restriction does not apply to any communication which is made by a person in the course of carrying out his duties as an adviser for, or employee of, an advice centre.

(2)   The requirements of this paragraph are that the communication relates to—

    (a)   qualifying credit;

    (b)   rights under, or rights to or interests in rights under, qualifying contracts of insurance; ...

    (c)   a child trust fund;

    [(d)   a regulated home reversion plan; or

    (e)   a regulated home purchase plan].

(3)   In this article—

"adequate professional indemnity insurance", in relation to an advice centre, means insurance providing cover that is adequate having regard to—

    (a)   the claims record of the centre;

    (b)   the financial resources of the centre; and

    (c)   the right of clients of the centre to be compensated for loss arising from the negligent provision of financial advice;

"advice centre" means a body which—

    (a)   gives advice which is free and in respect of which the centre does not receive any fee, commission or other reward;

    (b)   provides debt advice as its principal financial services activity; and

    (c)   in the case of a body which is not part of a local authority, holds adequate professional indemnity insurance or a guarantee providing comparable cover;

"child trust fund" has the meaning given by section 1(2) of the Child Trust Funds Act 2004;

"local authority" has the meaning given in article 2 of the Financial Services and Markets Act 2000 (Exemption) Order 2001.

[2838]

NOTES

Commencement: 1 July 2005.

Para (2): word omitted from sub-para (b) revoked, and sub-paras (d), (e) inserted, by the Financial Services and Markets Act 2000 (Regulated Activities) (Amendment) (No 2) Order 2006, SI 2006/2383, art 35(1), (4), as from 6 April 2007 (for the full commencement details of SI 2006/2383 and for transitional provisions and effect, see arts 1, 36–40 of, and the Schedule to, the 2006 Order at [2860] et seq).

74   Revocation

The Orders specified in the first column of Schedule 6 are revoked to the extent specified in the third column of that Schedule.

[2839]

NOTES

Commencement: 1 July 2005.

SCHEDULES

SCHEDULE 1
Article 4

PART I
CONTROLLED ACTIVITIES

1 Accepting deposits

Accepting deposits is a controlled activity if—
  (a)   money received by way of deposit is lent to others; or
  (b)   any other activity of the person accepting the deposit is financed wholly, or to a material extent, out of the capital of or interest on money received by way of deposit,
and the person accepting the deposit holds himself out as accepting deposits on a day to day basis.

2 Effecting or carrying out contracts of insurance

(1)   Effecting a contract of insurance as principal is a controlled activity.

(2)   Carrying out a contract of insurance as principal is a controlled activity.

(3)   There is excluded from sub-paragraph (1) or (2) the effecting or carrying out of a contract of insurance of the kind described in article 12 of the Regulated Activities Order by a person who does not otherwise carry on an activity falling within those sub-paragraphs.

3 Dealing in securities and contractually based investments

(1)   Buying, selling, subscribing for or underwriting securities or contractually based investments (other than investments of the kind specified by paragraph 25, or paragraph 27 so far as relevant to that paragraph) as principal or agent is a controlled activity.

(2)   A person does not carry on the activity in sub-paragraph (1) by accepting an instrument creating or acknowledging indebtedness in respect of any loan, credit, guarantee or other similar financial accommodation or assurance which he has made, granted or provided.

(3)   The reference in sub-paragraph (2) to a person accepting an instrument includes a reference to a person becoming a party to an instrument otherwise than as a debtor or a surety.

4 Arranging deals in investments

(1)   Making arrangements for another person (whether as principal or agent) to buy, sell, subscribe for or underwrite a particular investment which is—
  (a)   a security;
  (b)   a contractually based investment; or
  (c)   an investment of the kind specified by paragraph 24, or paragraph 27 so far as relevant to that paragraph,
is a controlled activity.

(2)   Making arrangements with a view to a person who participates in the arrangements buying, selling, subscribing for or underwriting investments falling within sub-paragraph (1)(a), (b) or (c) (whether as principal or agent) is a controlled activity.

(3)   A person does not carry on an activity falling within paragraph (2) merely by providing means by which one party to a transaction (or potential transaction) is able to communicate with other such parties.

[4A Operating a multilateral trading facility

Operating a multilateral trading facility on which MiFID instruments are traded is a controlled activity.]

5 Managing investments

Managing assets belonging to another person, in circumstances involving the exercise of discretion, is a controlled activity if—
  (a)   the assets consist of or include any investment which is a security or a contractually based investment; or
  (b)   the arrangements for their management are such that the assets may consist of or include such investments, and either the assets have at any time since 29th April 1988 done so, or the arrangements have at any time (whether before or after that date) been held out as arrangements under which the assets would do so.

6 Safeguarding and administering investments

(1)   The activity consisting of both—
  (a)   the safeguarding of assets belonging to another; and
  (b)   the administration of those assets,

or arranging for one or more other persons to carry on that activity, is a controlled activity if either the condition in paragraph (a) or (b) of sub-paragraph (2) is met.

(2)   The condition is that—
- (a)   the assets consist of or include any investment which is a security or a contractually based investment; or
- (b)   the arrangements for their safeguarding and administration are such that the assets may consist of or include investments of the kind mentioned in sub-paragraph (a) and either the assets have at any time since 1st June 1997 done so, or the arrangements have at any time (whether before or after that date) been held out as ones under which such investments would be safeguarded and administered.

(3)   For the purposes of this article—
- (a)   it is immaterial that title to the assets safeguarded and administered is held in uncertificated form;
- (b)   it is immaterial that the assets safeguarded and administered may be transferred to another person, subject to a commitment by the person safeguarding and administering them, or arranging for their safeguarding and administration, that they will be replaced by equivalent assets at some future date or when so requested by the person to whom they belong.

(4)   For the purposes of this article, the following activities do not constitute the administration of assets—
- (a)   providing information as to the number of units or the value of any assets safeguarded;
- (b)   converting currency;
- (c)   receiving documents relating to an investment solely for the purpose of onward transmission to, from or at the direction of the person to whom the investment belongs.

7   Advising on investments

Advising a person is a controlled activity if the advice is—
- (a)   given to the person in his capacity as an investor or potential investor, or in his capacity as agent for an investor or a potential investor; and
- (b)   advice on the merits of his doing any of the following (whether as principal or agent)—
  - (i)   buying, selling, subscribing for or underwriting a particular investment which is a security or a contractually based investment; or
  - (ii)   exercising any right conferred by such an investment to buy, sell, subscribe for or underwrite such an investment.

8   Advising on syndicate participation at Lloyd's

Advising a person to become, or continue or cease to be, a member of a particular Lloyd's syndicate is a controlled activity.

9   Providing funeral plan contracts

(1)   Entering as provider into a qualifying funeral plan contract is a controlled activity.

(2)   A "qualifying funeral plan contract" is a contract under which—
- (a)   a person ("the customer") makes one or more payments to another person ("the provider");
- (b)   the provider undertakes to provide, or to secure that another person provides, a funeral in the United Kingdom for the customer (or some other person who is living at the date when the contract is entered into) on his death; and
- (c)   the provider is a person who carries on the regulated activity specified in article 59 of the Regulated Activities Order.

10   Providing qualifying credit

(1)   Providing qualifying credit is a controlled activity.

(2)   "Qualifying credit" is a credit provided pursuant to an agreement under which—
- (a)   the lender is a person who carries on the regulated activity specified in article 61 of the Regulated Activities Order; and
- (b)   the obligation of the borrower to repay is secured (in whole or in part) on land.

(3)   "Credit" includes a cash loan and any other form of financial accommodation.

10A   Arranging qualifying credit etc

Making arrangements—
- (a)   for another person to enter as borrower into an agreement for the provision of qualifying credit; or

    (b)   for a borrower under a regulated mortgage contract, within the meaning of article 61(3) of the Regulated Activities Order, entered into after the coming into force of that article, to vary the terms of that contract in such a way as to vary his obligations under that contract,

is a controlled activity.

10B Advising on qualifying credit etc

(1)   Advising a person is a controlled activity if the advice is—
    (a)   given to the person in his capacity as a borrower or potential borrower; and
    (b)   advice on the merits of his doing any of the following—
        (i)   entering into an agreement for the provision of qualifying credit, or
        (ii)   varying the terms of a regulated mortgage contract entered into by him after the coming into force of article 61 of the Regulated Activities Order in such a way as to vary his obligations under that contract.

(2)   In this paragraph, "borrower" and "regulated mortgage contract" have the meaning given by article 61(3) of the Regulated Activities Order.

[10C Providing a regulated home reversion plan

Entering into a regulated home reversion plan as plan provider is a controlled activity.

10D Arranging a regulated home reversion plan

Making arrangements—
    (a)   for another person to enter as reversion seller or plan provider into a regulated home reversion plan; or
    (b)   for a reversion seller or a plan provider under a regulated home reversion plan, entered into on or after 6th April 2007 by him, to vary the terms of that plan in such a way as to vary his obligations under that plan,

is a controlled activity.

10E Advising on a regulated home reversion plan

Advising a person is a controlled activity if the advice is—
    (a)   given to the person in his capacity as reversion seller, potential reversion seller, plan provider or potential plan provider; and
    (b)   advice on the merits of his doing either of the following—
        (i)   entering into a regulated home reversion plan, or
        (ii)   varying the terms of a regulated home reversion plan, entered into on or after 6th April 2007 by him, in such a way as to vary his obligations under that plan.

10F Providing a regulated home purchase plan

Entering into a regulated home purchase plan as home purchase provider is a controlled activity.

10G Arranging a regulated home purchase plan

Making arrangements—
    (a)   for another person to enter as home purchaser into a regulated home purchase plan; or
    (b)   for a home purchaser under a regulated home purchase plan, entered into on or after 6th April 2007 by him, to vary the terms of that plan in such a way as to vary his obligations under that plan,

is a controlled activity.

10H Advising on a regulated home purchase plan

Advising a person is a controlled activity if the advice is—
    (a)   given to the person in his capacity as home purchaser or potential home purchaser; and
    (b)   advice on the merits of his doing either of the following—
        (i)   entering into a regulated home purchase plan, or
        (ii)   varying the terms of a regulated home purchase plan, entered into on or after 6th April 2007 by him, in such a way as to vary his obligations under that plan.]

11 Agreeing to carry on specified kinds of activity

Agreeing to carry on any controlled activity falling within any of paragraphs 3 to 10B [(other than paragraph 4A)] above is a controlled activity.

            [2840]

NOTES

Commencement: 1 July 2005.

Para 4A: inserted by the Financial Services and Markets Act 2000 (Regulated Activities) (Amendment No 3) Order 2006, SI 2006/3384, art 40(1), (2)(a), as from 1 November 2007 (for the full commencement details of SI 2006/3384, see the Note for that Order at **[2866A]**).

Paras 10C–10H: inserted by the Financial Services and Markets Act 2000 (Regulated Activities) (Amendment) (No 2) Order 2006, SI 2006/2383, art 35(1), (5), as from 6 April 2007 (for the full commencement details of SI 2006/2383 and for transitional provisions and effect, see arts 1, 36–40 of, and the Schedule to, the 2006 Order at **[2860]** et seq).

Para 11: words in square brackets inserted by SI 2006/3384, art 40(1), (2)(b), as from 1 November 2007 (for the full commencement details of SI 2006/3384, see the Note for that Order at **[2866A]**).

PART II
CONTROLLED INVESTMENTS

12.   A deposit.

13.   Rights under a contract of insurance.

14.—(1)   Shares or stock in the share capital of—
  (a)   any body corporate (wherever incorporated);
  (b)   any unincorporated body constituted under the law of a country or territory outside the United Kingdom.

  (2)   Sub-paragraph (1) includes—
  (a)   any shares of a class defined as deferred shares for the purposes of section 119 of the Building Societies Act 1986;
  (b)   any transferable shares in a body incorporated under the law of, or any part of, the United Kingdom relating to industrial and provident societies or credit unions or in a body constituted under the law of another EEA State for purposes equivalent to those of such a body.

  (3)   But subject to sub-paragraph (2) there are excluded from sub-paragraph (1) shares or stock in the share capital of—
  (a)   an open-ended investment company;
  (b)   a building society incorporated under the law of, or any part of, the United Kingdom;
  (c)   any body incorporated under the law of, or any part of, the United Kingdom relating to industrial and provident societies or credit unions;
  (d)   any body constituted under the law of an EEA State for purposes equivalent to those of a body falling within paragraph (b) or (c).

15   Instruments creating or acknowledging indebtedness

  (1)   Subject to sub-paragraph (2), such of the following as do not fall within paragraph 16—
  (a)   debentures;
  (b)   debenture stock;
  (c)   loan stock;
  (d)   bonds;
  (e)   certificates of deposit;
  (f)   any other instrument creating or acknowledging a present or future indebtedness.

  (2)   If and to the extent that they would otherwise fall within sub-paragraph (1), there are excluded from that sub-paragraph—
  (a)   any instrument acknowledging or creating indebtedness for, or for money borrowed to defray, the consideration payable under a contract for the supply of goods or services;
  (b)   a cheque or other bill of exchange, a banker's draft or a letter of credit (but not a bill of exchange accepted by a banker);
  (c)   a banknote, a statement showing a balance on a current, deposit or saving account, a lease or other disposition of property, a heritable security; and
  (d)   a contract of insurance.

  (3)   An instrument excluded from sub-paragraph (1) of paragraph 16 by paragraph 16(2)(b) is not thereby to be taken to fall within sub-paragraph (1) of this paragraph.

16   Government and public securities

  (1)   Subject to sub-paragraph (2), loan stock, bonds and other instruments—
  (a)   creating or acknowledging indebtedness; and
  (b)   issued by or on behalf of a government, local authority (whether in the United Kingdom or elsewhere) or international organisation.

  (2)   There are excluded from sub-paragraph (1)—
  (a)   so far as applicable, the instruments mentioned in paragraph 15(2)(a) to (d);
  (b)   any instrument creating or acknowledging indebtedness in respect of—
    (i)   money received by the Director of Savings as deposits or otherwise in connection with the business of the National Savings Bank;
    (ii)   money raised under the National Loans Act 1968 under the auspices of the Director of Savings or treated as so raised by virtue of section 11(3) of the National Debt Act 1972.

17 Instruments giving entitlements to investments

(1) Warrants and other instruments entitling the holder to subscribe for any investment falling within paragraph 14, 15 or 16.

(2) It is immaterial whether the investment to which the entitlement relates is in existence or identifiable.

(3) An investment falling within this paragraph shall not be regarded as falling within paragraph 21, 22 or 23.

18 Certificates representing certain securities

(1) Subject to sub-paragraph (2), certificates or other instruments which confer contractual or property rights (other than rights consisting of an investment of the kind specified by paragraph 21)—

    (a) in respect of any investment of the kind specified by any of paragraphs 14 to 17 being an investment held by a person other than the person on whom the rights are conferred by the certificate or instrument; and

    (b) the transfer of which may be effected without the consent of that person.

(2) There is excluded from sub-paragraph (1) any instrument which confers rights in respect of two or more investments issued by different persons, or in respect of two or more different investments of the kind specified by paragraph 16 and issued by the same person.

19 Units in a collective investment scheme

Units in a collective investment scheme.

[20 Rights under a pension scheme

(1) Rights under a stakeholder pension scheme.

(2) Rights under a personal pension scheme.

(3) "Stakeholder pension scheme" and "personal pension scheme" have the meanings given by article 72(4).]

21 Options

    [(1)] Options to acquire or dispose of—

    (a) a security or contractually based investment (other than one of a kind specified in this paragraph);

    (b) currency of the United Kingdom or of any other country or territory;

    (c) palladium, platinum, gold or silver; ...

    (d) an option to acquire or dispose of an investment falling within this paragraph by virtue of sub-paragraph (a), (b) or (c);

    [(e) subject to sub-paragraph (4), an option to acquire or dispose of an option to which paragraph 5, 6, 7 or 10 of Section C of Annex I to the markets in financial instruments directive applies].

    [(2) Subject to sub-paragraph (4), options—

    (a) to which sub-paragraph (1) does not apply;

    (b) which relate to commodities;

    (c) which may be settled physically; and

    (d) either—

        (i) to which paragraph 5 or 6 of Section C of Annex I to the markets in financial instruments directive applies, or

        (ii) which in accordance with Article 38 of the Commission Regulation are to be considered as having the characteristics of other derivative financial instruments and not being for commercial purposes, and to which paragraph 7 of Section C of Annex I to the markets in financial instruments directive applies.

(3) Subject to sub-paragraph (4), options—

    (a) to which sub-paragraph (1) does not apply;

    (b) which may be settled physically; and

    (c) to which paragraph 10 of Section C of Annex I to the markets in financial instruments directive (read with the Commission Regulation) applies.

(4) Sub-paragraphs (1)(e), (2) and (3) only apply to options in relation to which—

    (a) an investment firm or credit institution is providing or performing investment services and activities on a professional basis,

    (b) a management company is providing, in accordance with Article 5(3) of the UCITS directive, the investment service specified in paragraph 4 or 5 of Section A, or the ancillary service specified in paragraph 1 of Section B, of Annex I to the markets in financial instruments directive, or

    (c) a market operator is providing the investment service specified in paragraph 8 of Section A of Annex I to the markets in financial instruments directive.

(5)   Expressions used in sub-paragraphs (1)(e), (2) and (3) and in the markets in financial instruments directive have the same meaning as in that directive.]

22 Futures

(1)   Subject to sub-paragraph (2), rights under a contract for the sale of a commodity or property of any other description under which delivery is to be made at a future date and at a price agreed on when the contract is made.

[(1A)   Subject to sub-paragraph (1D), futures—
   (a)   to which sub-paragraph (1) does not apply;
   (b)   which relate to commodities;
   (c)   which may be settled physically; and
   (d)   to which paragraph 5 or 6 of Section C of Annex I to the markets in financial instruments directive applies.

(1B)   Subject to sub-paragraph (1D), futures and forwards—
   (a)   to which sub-paragraph (1) does not apply;
   (b)   which relate to commodities;
   (c)   which may be settled physically;
   (d)   which in accordance with Article 38 of the Commission Regulation are to be considered as having the characteristics of other derivative financial instruments and not being for commercial purposes; and
   (e)   to which paragraph 7 of Section C of Annex I to the markets in financial instruments directive applies.

(1C)   Subject to sub-paragraph (1D), futures—
   (a)   to which sub-paragraph (1) does not apply;
   (b)   which may be settled physically; and
   (c)   to which paragraph 10 of Section C of Annex I to the markets in financial instruments directive (read with the Commission Regulation) applies.

(1D)   Sub-paragraphs (1A), (1B) and (1C) only apply to futures or forwards in relation to which—
   (a)   an investment firm or credit institution is providing or performing investment services and activities on a professional basis,
   (b)   a management company is providing, in accordance with Article 5(3) of the UCITS directive, the investment service specified in paragraph 4 or 5 of Section A, or the ancillary service specified in paragraph 1 of Section B, of Annex I to the markets in financial instruments directive, or
   (c)   a market operator is providing the investment service specified in paragraph 8 of Section A of Annex I to the markets in financial instruments directive.

(1E)   Expressions used in sub-paragraphs (1A) to (1C) and in the markets in financial instruments directive have the same meaning as in that directive.]

(2)   There are excluded from sub-paragraph (1) rights under any contract which is made for commercial and not investment purposes.

(3)   For the purposes of sub-paragraph (2), in considering whether a contract is to be regarded as made for investment purposes or for commercial purposes, the indicators set out in article 84 of the Regulated Activities Order shall be applied in the same way as they are applied for the purposes of that article.

23 Contracts for differences etc

(1)   Subject to sub-paragraph (2), rights under—
   (a)   a contract for differences; or
   (b)   any other contract the purpose or pretended purpose of which is to secure a profit or avoid a loss by reference to fluctuations in—
      (i)   the value or price of property of any description;
      (ii)   an index or other factor designated for that purpose in the contract.

(2)   There are excluded from sub-paragraph (1)—
   (a)   rights under a contract if the parties intend that the profit is to be secured or the loss is to be avoided by one or more of the parties taking delivery of any property to which the contract relates;
   (b)   rights under a contract under which money is received by way of deposit on terms that any interest or other return to be paid on the sum deposited will be calculated by reference to fluctuations in an index or other factor;
   (c)   rights under any contract under which—
      (i)   money is received by the Director of Savings as deposits or otherwise in connection with the business of the National Savings Bank; or

        (ii)   money is raised under the National Loans Act 1968 under the auspices of the Director of Savings or treated as so raised by virtue of section 11(3) of the National Debt Act 1972;

   (d)   rights under a qualifying contract of insurance.

[(3)   Subject to sub-paragraph (4), derivative instruments for the transfer of credit risk—

   (a)   to which neither paragraph 21 nor sub-paragraph (1) applies; and

   (b)   to which paragraph 8 of Section C of Annex I to the markets in financial instruments directive applies.

(4)   Sub-paragraph (3) only applies to derivatives in relation to which—

   (a)   an investment firm or credit institution is providing or performing investment services and activities on a professional basis,

   (b)   a management company is providing, in accordance with Article 5(3) of the UCITS directive, the investment service specified in paragraph 4 or 5 of Section A, or the ancillary service specified in paragraph 1 of Section B, of Annex I to the markets in financial instruments directive, or

   (c)   a market operator is providing the investment service specified in paragraph 8 of Section A of Annex I to the markets in financial instruments directive.

(5)   "Derivative instruments for the transfer of credit risk" has the same meaning as in the markets in financial instruments directive.]

24 Lloyd's syndicate capacity and syndicate membership

(1)   The underwriting capacity of a Lloyd's syndicate.

(2)   A person's membership (or prospective membership) of a Lloyd's syndicate.

25 Funeral plan contracts

Rights under a qualifying funeral plan contract.

26 Agreements for qualifying credit

Rights under an agreement for qualifying credit.

[26A Regulated home reversion plans

Rights under a regulated home reversion plan.

26B Regulated home purchase plans

Rights under a regulated home purchase plan.]

27 Rights to or interests in investments

(1)   Subject to sub-paragraphs (2) and (3), any right to or interest in anything which is specified by any other provision of this Part of this Schedule (other than [paragraph 26, 26A or 26B]).

(2)   Sub-paragraph (1) does not apply to interests under the trusts of an occupational pension scheme.

(2A)   Sub-paragraph (1) does not apply to any right or interest acquired as a result of entering into a funeral plan contract (and for this purpose a "funeral plan contract" is a contract of a kind described in paragraph 9(2)(a) and (b)).

(3)   Sub-paragraph (1) does not apply to anything which falls within any other provision of this Part of this Schedule.

28 Interpretation

In this Schedule—

   "buying" includes acquiring for valuable consideration;

   ["Commission Regulation" means Commission Regulation 1287/2006 of 10 August 2006;]

   "contract of insurance" has the meaning given in the Regulated Activities Order;

   "contractually based investment" means—

   (a)   rights under a qualifying contract of insurance;

   (b)   any investment of the kind specified by any of paragraphs 21, 22, 23 and 25;

   (c)   any investment of the kind specified by paragraph 27 so far as relevant to an investment falling within (a) or (b);

   ["credit institution" has the meaning given in the Regulated Activities Order;]

   ["home purchase provider" and "home purchaser" have the meanings given in article 63F(3) of the Regulated Activities Order;]

   ["investment firm" has the meaning given in the Regulated Activities Order;]

   ["investment services and activities" has the meaning given in the Regulated Activities Order;]

   ["management company" has the meaning given in the Regulated Activities Order;]

   ["market operator" has the meaning given in the Regulated Activities Order;]

   ["MiFID instrument" has the meaning given in article 25D(2) of the Regulated Activities Order;]

["multilateral trading facility" has the meaning given in the Regulated Activities Order;]

["occupational pension scheme" has the meaning given by section 1 of the Pension Schemes Act 1993 but with paragraph (b) of the definition omitted;]

["plan provider" has the meaning given by paragraph (3) of article 63B of the Regulated Activities Order, read with paragraphs (7) and (8) of that article;]

"property" includes currency of the United Kingdom or any other country or territory;

"qualifying funeral plan contract" has the meaning given by paragraph 9;

["regulated home purchase plan" has the meaning given in article 63F(3) of the Regulated Activities Order;

"regulated home reversion plan" and "reversion seller" have the meanings given in article 63B(3) of the Regulated Activities Order;]

"security" means a controlled investment falling within any of paragraphs 14 to 20 or, so far as relevant to any such investment, paragraph 27;

"selling", in relation to any investment, includes disposing of the investment for valuable consideration, and for these purposes "disposing" includes—

    (a)   in the case of an investment consisting of rights under a contract—

        (i)   surrendering, assigning or converting those rights; or

        (ii)   assuming the corresponding liabilities under the contract;

    (b)   in the case of an investment consisting of rights under other arrangements, assuming the corresponding liabilities under the arrangements; and

    (c)   in the case of any other investment, issuing or creating the investment or granting the rights or interests of which it consists;

"syndicate" has the meaning given in the Regulated Activities Order.

[2841]

NOTES

Commencement: 1 July 2005.

Para 20: substituted by the Financial Services and Markets Act 2000 (Regulated Activities) (Amendment) Order 2006, SI 2006/1969, art 12(1), (3), as from 6 April 2007.

Para 21: sub-para (1) numbered as such, word omitted from sub-para (1)(c) revoked, and sub-paras (1)(e), (2)–(5) inserted, by the Financial Services and Markets Act 2000 (Regulated Activities) (Amendment No 3) Order 2006, SI 2006/3384, art 40(1), (3), as from 1 November 2007 (for the full commencement details of SI 2006/3384, see the Note for that Order at **[2866A]**).

Para 22: sub-paras (1A)–(1E) inserted by SI 2006/3384, art 40(1), (4), as from 1 November 2007 (for the full commencement details of SI 2006/3384, see the Note for that Order at **[2866A]**).

Para 23: sub-paras (3)–(5) added by SI 2006/3384, art 40(1), (5), as from 1 November 2007 (for the full commencement details of SI 2006/3384, see the Note for that Order at **[2866A]**).

Paras 26A, 26B: inserted by the Financial Services and Markets Act 2000 (Regulated Activities) (Amendment) (No 2) Order 2006, SI 2006/2383, art 35(1), (6)(a), as from 6 April 2007 (for the full commencement details of SI 2006/2383 and for transitional provisions and effect, see arts 1, 36–40 of, and the Schedule to, the 2006 Order at **[2860]** et seq).

Para 27: words in square brackets substituted by SI 2006/2383, art 35(1), (6)(b), as from 6 April 2007 (for the full commencement details of SI 2006/2383 and for transitional provisions and effect, see arts 1, 36–40 of, and the Schedule to, the 2006 Order at **[2860]** et seq).

Para 28 is amended as follows:

Definitions "Commission Regulation", "credit institution", "investment firm", "investment services and activities", "management company", "market operator", "MiFID instrument", and "multilateral trading facility" inserted by SI 2006/3384, art 40(1), (6), as from 1 November 2007 (for the full commencement details of SI 2006/3384, see the Note for that Order at **[2866A]**).

Definitions "home purchase provider", "home purchaser", "plan provider", "regulated home purchase plan", "regulated home reversion plan", and "reversion seller" inserted by SI 2006/2383, art 35(1), (6)(c), as from 6 April 2007 (for the full commencement details of SI 2006/2383 and for transitional provisions and effect, see arts 1, 36–40 of, and the Schedule to, the 2006 Order at **[2860]** et seq).

Definition "occupational pension scheme" substituted by SI 2006/1969, art 12(1), (4), as from 6 April 2007.

SCHEDULE 2
COUNTRIES AND TERRITORIES

Article 10

1.   The Bailiwick of Guernsey.

2.   The Isle of Man.

3.   The Commonwealth of Pennsylvania.

4.   The State of Iowa.

5.   The Bailiwick of Jersey.

[2842]

NOTES

Commencement: 1 July 2005.

SCHEDULE 3
MARKETS AND EXCHANGES
Articles 37, 41, 67, 68 and 69

PART I
CRITERIA FOR RELEVANT EEA MARKETS

The criteria are—
  (a)   the head office of the market must be situated in an EEA State; and
  (b)   the market must be subject to requirements in the EEA State in which its head office is
         situated as to—
         (i)   the manner in which it operates;
         (ii)   the means by which access may be had to the facilities it provides;
         (iii) the conditions to be satisfied before an investment may be traded or dealt in by
                means of its facilities;
         (iv)   the reporting and publication of transactions effected by means of its facilities.
                                                                              [2843]

NOTES
  Commencement: 1 July 2005.

[PART II
CERTAIN INVESTMENT EXCHANGES OPERATING RELEVANT EEA MARKETS

Aktietorget I Norden (Sweden).

Amsterdam Options Exchange (Netherlands).

Athens Stock Exchange (Greece).

Athens Derivative Exchange (Greece).

Barcelona Stock Exchange (Spain).

Bavarian Stock Exchange (Germany).

Belgian Secondary Market for Treasury Certificates (Belgium).

Berlin-Bremen Stock Exchange (Germany).

Bilbao Stock Exchange (Spain).

Böag Borsen AG (Germany).

Bratislava Stock Exchange (Slovakia).

Bucharest Stock Exchange (Romania).

Budapest Stock Exchange (Hungary).

Bulgaria Stock Exchange (Bulgaria).

Copenhagen Stock Exchange (Denmark).

Cyprus Stock Exchange (Cyprus).

Danish Authorised Market Place (Denmark).

Dusseldorf Stock Market (Germany).

EDX (UK).

Eurex Deutschland (Germany).

Euronext Amsterdam (Netherlands).

Euronext Brussels (Belgium).

Euronext Lisbon (Portugal).

Euronext Paris (France).

Frankfurt Stock Exchange (Germany).

Helsinki Stock Exchange and Securities and Derivatives Exchange (Finland).

Irish Stock Exchange (Ireland).

Italian and Foreign Government Bonds Market (Italy).

Italian Stock Exchange (Italy).

Ljubliana Stock Exchange (Slovenia).

London International Financial Futures and Options Exchange (UK).

London Stock Exchange (UK).

Luxembourg Stock Exchange (Luxembourg).

Madrid Stock Exchange (Spain)

Malta Stock Exchange (Malta).

Market for Public Debt (Spain).

MEFF Renta Variable Futures Options Exchange (Spain).

MEFF Renta Fija Equity Futures Exchange (Spain).

MTS Italy (Italy).

MTS Poland (Poland).

MTS Portugal (Portugal).

National Stock Exchange of Lithuania (Lithuania).

Nordic Growth Market (Sweden).

PLUS (UK).

Prague Stock Exchange (Czech Republic).

Riga Stock Exchange (Latvia).

ShareMark (UK).

Stockholm Stock Exchange (Sweden).

Stuttgart Stock Exchange (Germany).

Tallinn Stock Exchange (Estonia).

Valencia Stock Exchange (Spain).

Vienna Stock Exchange (Austria).

Virt-x (UK).

Warsaw Stock Exchange (Poland).]

[2844]

NOTES

Commencement: 20 April 2007.

Substituted by the Financial Services and Markets Act 2000 (Financial Promotion) (Amendment) Order 2007, SI 2007/1083, art 2, as from 20 April 2007.

PART III
CERTAIN NON-EEA INVESTMENT EXCHANGES OPERATING RELEVANT MARKETS

America Stock Exchange.

Australian Stock Exchange.

Basler Effektenbourse.

Boston Stock Exchange.

Bourse de Geneve.

Buenos Aires Stock Exchange.

Canadian Venture Exchange.

Chicago Board Options Exchange.

Chicago Stock Exchange.

Effektenborsenverein Zurich.

Fukuoka Stock Exchange.

Hiroshima Stock Exchange.

Iceland Stock Exchange.

Johannesburg Stock Exchange.

Korean Stock Exchange.

Kuala Lumpur Stock Exchange.

Kyoto Stock Exchange.

Midwest Stock Exchange.

Montreal Stock Exchange.

Nagoya Stock Exchange.

NASDAQ.

National Stock Exchange.

New York Stock Exchange.

New Zealand Stock Exchange Limited.

Niigita Stock Exchange.

Osaka Stock Exchange.

Oslo Stock Exchange.

Pacific Stock Exchange.

Philadelphia Stock Exchange.

Sapporo Stock Exchange.

Singapore Stock Exchange.

Stock Exchange of Hong Kong Limited.

Stock Exchange of Thailand.

Tokyo Stock Exchange.

Toronto Stock Exchange.

[2845]

NOTES
Commencement: 1 July 2005.

PART IV
OTHER RELEVANT MARKETS

American Commodity Exchange.

Australian Financial Futures Market.

Chicago Board of Trade.

Chicago Mercantile Exchange.

Chicago Rice and Cotton Exchange.

Commodity Exchange Inc.

Eurex US.

Eurex Zurich.

International Securities Market Association.

International Petroleum Exchange.

Kansas City Board of Trade.

London Metal Exchange.

Minneapolis Grain Exchange.

New York Board of Trade.

New York Futures Exchange.

New York Mercantile Exchange.

New Zealand Futures Exchange.

Pacific Commodity Exchange.

Philadelphia Board of Trade.

Singapore International Monetary Exchange.

Sydney Futures Exchange.

Toronto Futures Exchange.

[2846]

NOTES
Commencement: 1 July 2005.

SCHEDULE 4
TAKEOVERS OF RELEVANT UNLISTED COMPANIES
Articles 63 and 64

PART I
REQUIREMENTS RELATING TO THE OFFER

1.   The terms of the offer must be recommended by all the directors of the company other than any director who is—

    (a)   the person by whom, or on whose behalf, an offer is made ("offeror"); or

(b)   a director of the offeror.

2.—(1)   This paragraph applies to an offer for debentures or for non-equity share capital.

(2)   Where, at the date of the offer, shares carrying 50 per cent or less of the voting rights attributable to the equity share capital are held by or on behalf of the offeror, the offer must include or be accompanied by an offer made by the offeror for the rest of the shares comprised in the equity share capital.

3.—(1)   This paragraph applies to an offer for shares comprised in the equity share capital.

(2)   Where, at the date of the offer, shares which carry 50 per cent or less of the categories of voting rights described in sub-paragraph (3) are held by or on behalf of the offeror, it must be a condition of the offer that sufficient shares will be acquired or agreed to be acquired by the offeror pursuant to or during the offer so as to result in shares carrying more than 50 per cent of one or both categories of relevant voting rights being held by him or on his behalf.

(3)   The categories of voting rights mentioned in sub-paragraph (2) are—
(a)   voting rights exercisable in general meetings of the company;
(b)   voting rights attributable to the equity share capital.

4.—(1)   Subject to sub-paragraph (2), the offer must be open for acceptance by every recipient for the period of at least 21 days beginning with the day after the day on which the invitation or inducement in question was first communicated to recipients of the offer.

(2)   Sub-paragraph (1) does not apply if the offer is totally withdrawn and all persons are released from any obligation incurred under it.

5.   The acquisition of the shares or debentures to which the offer relates must not be conditional upon the recipients approving, or consenting, to any payment or other benefit being made or given to any director or former director of the company in connection with, or as compensation or consideration for—
(a)   his ceasing to be a director;
(b)   his ceasing to hold any office held in conjunction with any directorship; or
(c)   in the case of a former director, his ceasing to hold any office which he held in conjunction with his former directorship and which he continued to hold after ceasing to be a director.

6.   The consideration for the shares or debentures must be—
(a)   cash; or
(b)   in the case of an offeror which is a body corporate other than an open-ended investment company, either cash or shares in, or debentures of, the body corporate or any combination of such cash, shares or debentures.

[2847]

NOTES

Commencement: 1 July 2005.

PART II
ACCOMPANYING MATERIAL

7.   An indication of the identity of the offeror and, if the offer is being made on behalf of another person, the identity of that person.

8.   An indication of the fact that the terms of the offer are recommended by all directors of the company other than (if that is the case) any director who is the offeror or a director of the offeror.

9.   An indication to the effect that any person who is in any doubt about the invitation or inducement should consult a person authorised under the Act.

10.   An indication that, except insofar as the offer may be totally withdrawn and all persons released from any obligation incurred under it, the offer is open for acceptance by every recipient for the period of at least 21 days beginning with the day after the day on which the invitation or inducement in question was first communicated to recipients of the offer.

11.   An indication of the date on which the invitation or inducement was first communicated to the recipients of the offer.

12.   An indication that the acquisition of the shares or debentures to which the offer relates is not conditional upon the recipients approving, or consenting, to any payment or other benefit being made or given to any director or former director of the company in connection with, or as compensation or consideration for—
(a)   his ceasing to be a director;
(b)   his ceasing to hold any office held in conjunction with any directorship; or
(c)   in the case of a former director, his ceasing to hold any office which he held in conjunction with his former directorship and which he continued to hold after ceasing to be a director.

13. An indication of the place where additional material listed in Part III may be inspected.

14. The audited accounts of the company in respect of the latest accounting reference period for which the period for laying and delivering accounts under the 1985 Act or the 1986 Order has passed or, if accounts in respect of a later accounting reference period have been delivered under the relevant legislation, as shown in those accounts and not the earlier accounts.

15. Advice to the directors of the company on the financial implications of the offer which is given by a competent person who is independent of and who has no substantial financial interest in the company or the offeror, being advice which gives the opinion of that person in relation to the offer.

16. An indication by the directors of the company, acting as a board, of the following matters—
    (a) whether or not there has been any material change in the financial position or prospects of the company since the end of the latest accounting reference period in respect of which audited accounts have been delivered to the relevant registrar of companies under the relevant legislation;
    (b) if there has been any such change, the particulars of it;
    (c) any interests, in percentage terms, which any of them have in the shares in or debentures of the company and which are required to be entered in the register kept by the company under section 325 of the 1985 Act or article 333 of the 1986 Order;
    (d) any interests, in percentage terms, which any of them have in the shares in or debentures of any offeror which is a body corporate and which, if the director were a director of the offeror, would—
        (i) in the case of a company within the meaning of the 1985 Act or the 1986 Order, be required to be entered in the register kept by the offeror under section 325 of the 1985 Act or article 333 of the 1986 Order; and
        (ii) in any other case, be required to be so entered if the offeror were such a company.

17. An indication of any material interest which any director has in any contract entered into by the offeror and in any contract entered into by any member of any group of which the offeror is a member.

18. An indication as to whether or not each director intends to accept the offer in respect of his own beneficial holdings in the company.

19. In the case of an offeror which is a body corporate and the shares in or debentures of which are to be the consideration or any part of the consideration for the offer, an indication by the directors of the offeror that the information concerning the offeror and those shares or debentures contained in the document is correct.

20. If the offeror is making the offer on behalf of another person—
    (a) an indication by the offeror as to whether or not he has taken any steps to ascertain whether that person will be in a position to implement the offer;
    (b) if he has taken any such steps, an indication by him as to what those steps are; and
    (c) the offeror's opinion as to whether that person will be in a position to implement the offer.

21. An indication that each of the following—
    (a) each of the directors of the company;
    (b) the offeror; and
    (c) if the offeror is a body corporate, each of the directors of the offeror;

is responsible for the information required by Part I and this Part of this Schedule insofar as it relates to themselves or their respective bodies corporate and that, to the best of their knowledge and belief (having taken all reasonable care to ensure that such is the case) the information is in accordance with the facts and that no material fact has been omitted.

22. The particulars of—
    (a) all shares in or debentures of the company; and
    (b) all investments falling within paragraph 17, 19 or 21 of Schedule 1 so far as relating to shares in or debentures of the company;

which are held by or on behalf of the offeror or each offeror, if there is more than one, or if none are so held an appropriate negative statement.

23. An indication as to whether or not the offer is conditional upon acceptance in respect of a minimum number of shares or debentures being received and, if the offer is so conditional, what the minimum number is.

24. Where the offer is conditional upon acceptances, an indication of the date which is the latest date on which it can become unconditional.

25. If the offer is, or has become, unconditional an indication of the fact that it will remain open until further notice and that at least 14 days' notice will be given before it is closed.

26. An indication as to whether or not, if circumstances arise in which an offeror is able compulsorily to acquire shares of any dissenting minority under [Chapter 3 of Part 28 of the Companies Act 2006 (c 46)], that offeror intends to so acquire those shares.

27. If shares or debentures are to be acquired for cash, an indication of the period within which the payment will be made.

28.—(1) Subject to sub-paragraph (2), if the consideration or any part of the consideration for the shares or debentures to be acquired is shares in or debentures of an offeror—

(a) an indication of the nature and particulars of the offeror's business, its financial and trading prospects and its place of incorporation;

(b) the following information, in respect of any offeror which is a body corporate and in respect of the company, for the period of five years immediately preceding the date on which the invitation or inducement in question was first communicated to recipients of the offer—

(i) turnover,

(ii) profit on ordinary activities before and after tax,

(iii) extraordinary items,

(iv) profits and loss, and

(v) the rate per cent of any dividends paid, adjusted as appropriate to take account of relevant changes over the period and the total amount absorbed thereby.

(2) In the case of a body corporate—

(a) which was incorporated during the period of five years immediately preceding the date on which the invitation or inducement in question was first communicated to recipients of the offer; or

(b) which has, at any time during that period, been exempt from the provisions of Part VII of the 1985 Act relating to the audit of accounts by virtue of section 249A or 249AA of that Act or been exempt from the provisions of Part VIII of the 1986 Order relating to the audit of accounts by virtue of article 257A or 257AA of that Order;

the information described in sub-paragraph (1) with respect to that body corporate need be included only in relation to the period since its incorporation or since it last ceased to be exempt from those provisions of Part VII of the 1985 Act or Part VIII of the 1986 Order as the case may be.

29. Particulars of the first dividend in which any such shares or debentures will participate and of the rights attaching to them (including in the case of debentures, rights as to interest) and of any restrictions on their transfer.

30. An indication of the effect of the acceptance on the capital and income position of the holder of the shares in or debentures of the company.

31. Particulars of all material contracts (not being contracts which were entered into in the ordinary course of business) which were entered into by each of the company and the offeror during the period of two years immediately preceding the date on which the invitation or inducement in question was first communicated to recipients of the offer.

32. Particulars of the terms on which shares in or debentures of the company acquired in pursuance of the offer will be transferred and any restrictions on their transfer.

33. An indication as to whether or not it is proposed, in connection with the offer, that any payment or other benefit be made or given to any director or former director of the company in connection with, or as compensation or consideration for—

(a) his ceasing to be a director;

(b) his ceasing to hold any office held in conjunction with any directorship; or

(c) in the case of a former director, his ceasing to hold any office which he held in conjunction with his former directorship and which he continued to hold after ceasing to be a director;

and, if such payments or benefits are proposed, details of each one.

34. An indication as to whether or not there exists any agreement or arrangement between—

(a) the offeror or any person with whom the offeror has an agreement of the kind described in section 204 of the 1985 Act or article 216 of the 1986 Order; and

(b) any director or shareholder of the company or any person who has been such a director or shareholder;

at any time during the period of twelve months immediately preceding the date on which the invitation or inducement in question was first communicated to recipients of the offer, being an agreement or arrangement which is connected with or dependent on the offer and, if there is any such agreement or arrangement, particulars of it.

35. An indication whether or not the offeror has reason to believe that there has been any material change in the financial position or prospects of the company since the end of the accounting reference period to which the accounts referred to in paragraph 14 relate, and if the offeror has reason to believe that there has been such a change, the particulars of it.

36.   An indication as to whether or not there is any agreement or arrangement whereby any shares or debentures acquired by the offeror in pursuance of the offer will or may be transferred to any other person, together with the names of the parties to any such agreement or arrangement and particulars of all shares and debentures in the company held by such persons.

37.   Particulars of any dealings—
    (a)   in the shares in or debentures of the company; and
    (b)   if the offeror is a body corporate, in the shares in or debentures of the offeror;
which took place during the period of twelve months immediately preceding the date on which the invitation or inducement in question was first communicated to recipients of the offer and which were entered into by every person who was a director of either the company or the offeror during that period; and, if there have been no such dealings, an indication to that effect.

38.   In a case in which the offeror is a body corporate which is required to deliver accounts under the 1985 Act or the 1986 Order, particulars of the assets and liabilities as shown in its audited accounts in respect of the latest accounting reference period for which the period for laying and delivering accounts under the relevant legislation has passed or, if accounts in respect of a later accounting reference period have been delivered under the relevant legislation, as shown in those accounts and not the earlier accounts.

39.   Where valuations of assets are given in connection with the offer, the basis on which the valuation was made and the names and addresses of the persons who valued them and particulars of any relevant qualifications.

40.   If any profit forecast is given in connection with the offer, an indication of the assumptions on which the forecast is based.

[2848]

NOTES
Commencement: 1 July 2005.
Para 26: words in square brackets substituted by the Companies Act 2006 (Commencement No 2, Consequential Amendments, Transitional Provisions and Savings) Order 2007, SI 2007/1093, art 6(1), Sch 3, para 10, as from 6 April 2007.

PART III
ADDITIONAL MATERIAL AVAILABLE FOR INSPECTION
41.   The memorandum and articles of association of the company.

42.   If the offeror is a body corporate, the memorandum and articles of association of the offeror or, if there is no such memorandum and articles, any instrument constituting or defining the constitution of the offeror and, in either case, if the relevant document is not written in English, a certified translation in English.

43.   In the case of a company that does not fall within paragraph 45—
    (a)   the audited accounts of the company in respect of the last two accounting reference periods for which the laying and delivering of accounts under the 1985 Act or the 1986 Order has passed; and
    (b)   if accounts have been delivered to the relevant registrar of companies, in respect of a later accounting reference period, a copy of those accounts.

44.   In the case of an offeror which is required to deliver accounts to the registrar of companies and which does not fall within paragraph 45—
    (a)   the audited accounts of the offeror in respect of the last two accounting reference periods for which the laying and delivering of accounts under the 1985 Act or the 1986 Order has passed; and
    (b)   if accounts have been delivered to the relevant registrar of companies in respect of a later accounting reference period, a copy of those accounts.

45.   In the case of a company or an offeror—
    (a)   which was incorporated during the period of three years immediately preceding the date on which the invitation or inducement in question was first communicated to recipients of the offer; or
    (b)   which has, at any time during that period, been exempt from the provisions of Part VII of the 1985 Act relating to the audit of accounts by virtue of section 249A or 249AA of that Act or been exempt from the provisions of Part VIII of the 1986 Order relating to the audit of accounts by virtue of article 257A or 257AA of that Order;
the information described in whichever is relevant of paragraph 43 or 44 with respect to that body corporate need be included only in relation to the period since its incorporation or since it last ceased to be exempt from those provisions of Part VII of the 1985 Act or Part VIII of the 1986 Order, as the case may be.

46.   All existing contracts of service entered into for a period of more than one year between the company and any of its directors and, if the offeror is a body corporate, between the offeror and any of its directors.

47.   Any report, letter, valuation or other document any part of which is exhibited or referred to in the information required to be made available by Part II and this Part of this Schedule.

48.   If the offer document contains any statement purporting to have been made by an expert, that expert's written consent to the inclusion of that statement.

49.   All material contracts (if any) of the company and of the offeror (not, in either case, being contracts which were entered into in the ordinary course of business) which were entered into during the period of two years immediately preceding the date on which the invitation or inducement in question was first communicated to recipients of the offer.

[2849]

NOTES
  Commencement: 1 July 2005.

SCHEDULE 5
STATEMENTS FOR CERTIFIED HIGH NET WORTH INDIVIDUALS AND SELF-CERTIFIED SOPHISTICATED INVESTORS
Articles 48 and 50A

PART I
STATEMENT FOR CERTIFIED HIGH NET WORTH INDIVIDUALS

1.   The statement to be signed for the purposes of article 48(2) (definition of high net worth individual) must be in the following form and contain the following content—

"STATEMENT FOR CERTIFIED HIGH NET WORTH INDIVIDUAL

I declare that I am a certified high net worth individual for the purposes of the Financial Services and Markets Act 2000 (Financial Promotion) Order 2005.

I understand that this means:
  (a)   I can receive financial promotions that may not have been approved by a person authorised by the Financial Services Authority;
  (b)   the content of such financial promotions may not conform to rules issued by the Financial Services Authority;
  (c)   by signing this statement I may lose significant rights;
  (d)   I may have no right to complain to either of the following—
        (i)   the Financial Services Authority; or
        (ii)   the Financial Ombudsman Scheme;
  (e)   I may have no right to seek compensation from the Financial Services Compensation Scheme.

I am a certified high net worth individual because **at least one of the following applies—**
  (a)   I had, during the financial year immediately preceding the date below, an annual income to the value of £100,000 or more;
  (b)   I held, throughout the financial year immediately preceding the date below, net assets to the value of £250,000 or more. Net assets for these purposes do not include—
        (i)   the property which is my primary residence or any loan secured on that residence;
        (ii)   any rights of mine under a qualifying contract of insurance within the meaning of the Financial Services and Markets Act 2000 (Regulated Activities) Order 2001; or
        (iii) any benefits (in the form of pensions or otherwise) which are payable on the termination of my service or on my death or retirement and to which I am (or my dependants are), or may be, entitled.

I accept that I can lose my property and other assets from making investment decisions based on financial promotions.

I am aware that it is open to me to seek advice from someone who specialises in advising on investments.

Signature...

Date...",

[2850]

NOTES
  Commencement: 1 July 2005.

PART III
STATUTORY INSTRUMENTS

PART II
STATEMENT FOR SELF-CERTIFIED SOPHISTICATED INVESTORS

2.   The statement to be signed for the purposes of article 50A(1) (definition of self-certified sophisticated investor) must be in the following form and contain the following content—

"STATEMENT FOR SELF-CERTIFIED SOPHISTICATED INVESTOR

I declare that I am a self-certified sophisticated investor for the purposes of the Financial Services and Markets Act (Financial Promotion) Order 2005.

I understand that this means:

(a)   I can receive financial promotions that may not have been approved by a person authorised by the Financial Services Authority;

(b)   the content of such financial promotions may not conform to rules issued by the Financial Services Authority;

(c)   **by signing this statement I may lose significant rights;**

(d)   I may have no right to complain to either of the following—
  (i)   the Financial Services Authority; or
  (ii)   the Financial Ombudsman Scheme;

(e)   I may have no right to seek compensation from the Financial Services Compensation Scheme.

I am a self-certified sophisticated investor because **at least one of the following applies—**

(a)   I am a member of a network or syndicate of business angels and have been so for at least the last six months prior to the date below;

(b)   I have made more than one investment in an unlisted company in the two years prior to the date below;

(c)   I am working, or have worked in the two years prior to the date below, in a professional capacity in the private equity sector, or in the provision of finance for small and medium enterprises;

(d)   I am currently, or have been in the two years prior to the date below, a director of a company with an annual turnover of at least £1 million.

I accept that I can lose my property and other assets from making investment decisions based on financial promotions.

I am aware that it is open to me to seek advice from someone who specialises in advising on investments.

Signature..

Date.. ".

[2851]

NOTES
  Commencement: 1 July 2005.

SCHEDULE 6
REVOCATION
Article 74

Order	Reference	Extent of revocation
The Financial Services and Markets Act 2000 (Financial Promotion) Order 2001	SI 2001/1335	The whole Order
The Financial Services and Markets Act 2000 (Financial Promotion) (Amendment) Order 2001	SI 2001/2633	The whole Order
The Financial Services and Markets Act 2000 (Miscellaneous Provisions) Order 2001	SI 2001/3650	Article 4 and 5
The Financial Services and Markets Act 2000 (Financial Promotion) (Amendment No 2) Order 2001	SI 2001/3800	The whole Order
The Financial Services and Markets Act 2000 (Financial Promotion and Miscellaneous Amendments) Order 2002	SI 2002/1310	Article 2

Order	Reference	Extent of revocation
The Financial Services and Markets Act 2000 (Commencement of Mortgage Regulation) (Amendment) Order 2002	SI 2002/1777	Article 4
The Financial Services and Markets Act 2000 (Financial Promotion) (Amendment) (Electronic Communications Directive) Order 2002	SI 2002/2157	The whole Order
The Financial Services and Markets Act 2000 (Financial Promotion) (Amendment) Order 2003	SI 2003/1676	The whole Order
The Financial Services and Markets Act 2000 (Financial Promotion and Promotion of Collective Investment Schemes) (Miscellaneous Amendments) Order 2005	SI 2005/270	Article 2 and Schedule 1

[2852]

NOTES
Commencement: 1 July 2005.

FINANCIAL SERVICES AND MARKETS ACT 2000 (REGULATED ACTIVITIES) (AMENDMENT) ORDER 2006

(SI 2006/1969)

NOTES
Made: 28 June 2006.
Authority: Financial Services and Markets Act 2000, ss 22(1), (5), 426, 427, 428(3), Sch 2, para 25.
Commencement: 1 October 2006 (arts 1, 2, 4, for the purposes of enabling applications to be made for Part IV permission or for a variation of Part IV permission in relation to the regulated activity specified by art 52(b) of the Regulated Activities Order 2001 as amended by this Order or in relation to an investment specified by art 82(2) of the 2001 Order as amended by this Order); 6 April 2007 (otherwise).

As of 1 February 2009, this Order had not been amended.

ARRANGEMENT OF ARTICLES

1   Citation, commencement and interpretation

(1)   This Order may be cited as the Financial Services and Markets Act 2000 (Regulated Activities) (Amendment) Order 2006.

(2)   Articles 1, 2 and 4 of this Order come in to force—
   (a)   for the purposes of enabling applications to be made for Part IV permission or for a variation of Part IV permission in relation to the regulated activity specified by article 52(b) of the Principal Order as amended by this Order or in relation to an investment specified by article 82(2) of the Principal Order as amended by this Order on 1st October 2006;
   (b)   and for all other purposes on 6th April 2007.

(3)   All other articles of this Order come into force on 6th April 2007.

(4)   In this Order—
   "the Principal Order" means the Financial Services and Markets Act 2000 (Regulated Activities) Order 2001;

"the Act" means the Financial Services and Markets Act 2000;
"commencement" means 6th April 2007.

[2853]

NOTES
Commencement: 1 October 2006 (for certain purposes); 6 April 2007 (otherwise) (see para (2) above).

2 (*Amends the Financial Services and Markets Act 2000 (Regulated Activities) Order 2001, SI 2001/544, art 3 at* **[2012]**, *substitutes arts 52, 82 at* **[2083]**, **[2127]**, *and amends the Chapter heading preceding art 52.*)

3 Transitional provisions

(1) Paragraph (2) applies to a person ("A") who immediately before commencement had Part IV permission to carry on an activity of the kind specified by article 52 of the Principal Order.

(2) On commencement A is to be treated as also having Part IV permission to carry on the activity of establishing, operating or winding up a personal pension scheme.

(3) Paragraph (4) applies to a person ("B") who immediately before commencement had Part IV permission to carry on an activity of the kind specified by article—

(a)   14 (dealing in investments as principal),

(b)   21 (dealing in investments as agent),

(c)   25 (arranging deals in investments),

(d)   37 (managing investments),

(e)   40 (safeguarding and administering investments),

(f)   45 (sending dematerialised instructions),

(g)   53 (advising on investments), or

(h)   in so far as relevant to any activity specified in this paragraph or by article 52 of the Principal Order, 64 (agreeing to carry on specified kinds of activity),

of the Principal Order in relation to rights under a stakeholder pension scheme ("a relevant permission").

(4) On commencement B is to be treated as also having Part IV permission to carry on, in relation to rights under a personal pension scheme, any of the activities of a kind mentioned in paragraph (3) for which he had a relevant permission immediately before commencement.

(5) No person shall be treated as having his Part IV permission extended in accordance with this article if on or before 23rd March 2007 he gave written notice to the Authority that he did not wish to have his permission extended.

[2854]

NOTES
Commencement: 6 April 2007.

4 Interim permission

(1) This article applies where—

(a)   a person has submitted an application for Part IV permission or a variation of Part IV permission ("the applicant"), to the extent that the application relates to—

    (i)   a regulated activity specified by article 52(b) of the Principal Order (as amended by this Order),

    (ii)   an investment specified by article 82(2) of the Principal Order (as amended by this Order);

(b)   on or before 1st October 2006, the applicant had been carrying on an activity that following commencement will be—

    (i)   a regulated activity of establishing, operating or winding up a personal pension scheme; or

    (ii)   an activity of a kind specified by article—

        (aa)   14 (dealing in investments as principal),

        (bb)   21 (dealing in investments as agent),

        (cc)   25 (arranging deals in investments),

        (dd)   37 (managing investments),

        (ee)   40 (safeguarding and administering investments),

        (ff)   45 (sending dematerialised instructions),

        (gg)   53 (advising on investments), or

        (hh)   in so far as relevant to any activity specified in this sub-paragraph, 64 (agreeing to carry on specified kinds of activity),

    of the Principal Order in relation to rights under a personal pension scheme;

(c)   the Authority received the application on or before 23rd March 2007; and

(d)   the application had not been finally decided before commencement.

(2)   The applicant is to be treated as having at commencement the permission to which the application relates.

(3)   A permission which an applicant is to be treated as having is referred to in this Order as an "interim permission".

(4)   Without prejudice to the exercise by the Authority of its powers under Part 4 of the Act an interim permission lapses when the application has been finally decided.

(5)   In this article "finally decided" means—
  (a)   subject to paragraph (6), when the application is withdrawn;
  (b)   when the Authority grants permission under section 42 of the Act (giving permission) to carry on the activity in question;
  (c)   where the Authority has refused an application and the matter is not referred to the Tribunal, when the time for referring the matter to the Tribunal has expired;
  (d)   where the Authority has refused an application and the matter is referred to the Tribunal when—
    (i)   if the reference is determined by the Tribunal (including a determination following remission back to the Tribunal for rehearing in accordance with subsection (3)(a) of section 137 of the Act (appeal on a point of law)), the time for bringing an appeal has expired, or
    (ii)   on an appeal from a determination by the Tribunal on a point of law, the Court itself determines the application in accordance with section 137 of the Act.

(6)   An applicant who is treated as having interim permission may not withdraw the application without first obtaining the consent of the Authority.

(7)   Where—
  (a)   the Authority exercises its power under section 45 (variation etc on the Authority's own initiative) in relation to an authorised person who holds an interim permission; and
  (b)   as a result of the variation there are no longer any regulated activities for which the authorised person has permission,

the Authority must, once it is satisfied that it is no longer necessary to keep the interim permission in force, cancel it.

[2855]

NOTES

Commencement: 1 October 2006 (for certain purposes); 6 April 2007 (otherwise) (see art 1(2)).

---

5   Interim approval

(1)   This article applies where—
  (a)   an applicant (within the meaning of article 4(1)) has submitted, before commencement, an application to the Authority under section 60 of the Act (applications for approval); and
  (b)   the application has not been finally decided.

(2)   The person in respect of whom the application is made is to be treated as having at commencement the Authority's approval for the purposes of section 59 of the Act (approval for particular arrangements) in relation to the functions to which the application relates.

(3)   An approval which an applicant is to be treated as having is referred to in this Order as an "interim approval".

(4)   Without prejudice to the exercise by the Authority of its powers under Part 4 of the Act an interim approval lapses when the application has been finally decided.

(5)   In this article, "finally decided" means—
  (a)   when the application is withdrawn;
  (b)   when the Authority grants the application for approval under section 62 of the Act (applications for approval: procedure and right to refer to Tribunal);
  (c)   where the Authority has refused an application and the matter is not referred to the Tribunal, when the time for referring the matter to the Tribunal has expired;
  (d)   where the Authority has refused an application and the matter is referred to the Tribunal, when—
    (i)   if the reference is determined by the Tribunal (including a determination following remission back to the Tribunal for rehearing in accordance with subsection (3)(a) of section 137 of the Act), the time for bringing an appeal has expired, or
    (ii)   on an appeal from a determination by the Tribunal on a point of law, the Court itself determines the application in accordance with section 137 of the Act.

[2856]

NOTES
   Commencement: 6 April 2007.

6 Application of the Authority's rules etc to persons with interim permission or interim approval

(1)   The Authority may direct in writing that any relevant provision which would otherwise apply to a person by virtue of his interim permission or interim approval is not to apply, or is to apply to him as modified in the way specified in the direction.

(2)   Where the Authority makes a rule, gives guidance or issues a statement or code which applies only to persons with an interim permission or an interim approval (or only to a class of such persons), sections 65 (statements and codes: procedure) and 155 (consultation) and subsection (3) of section 157 (guidance) of the Act do not apply to that rule, guidance, statement or code.

(3)   For the purposes of paragraph (1), a "relevant provision" is any provision made as a result of the exercise by the Authority of any of its legislative functions mentioned in paragraph 1(2) of Schedule 1 to the Act (the Financial Services Authority).

[2857]

NOTES
   Commencement: 6 April 2007.

7 Application of the Act etc

The Schedule modifies the application of the Act and the Principal Order in relation to persons with an interim permission or an interim approval.

[2858]

NOTES
   Commencement: 6 April 2007.

8–12   (*Art 8 amends the Financial Services and Markets Act 2000 (Collective Investment Schemes) Order 2001, SI 2001/1062, art 2 at* [2203]*; art 9 amends the Financial Services and Markets Act 2000 (Carrying on Regulated Activities by Way of Business) Order 2001, SI 2001/1177, arts 3, 4 at* [2208]*,* [2209]*; art 10 amends the Financial Services and Markets Act 2000 (Exemption) Order 2001, SI 2001/1201, art 5 at* [2215]*; art 11 amends the Financial Services and Markets Act 2000 (Professions) (Non-Exempt Activities) Order 2001, SI 2001/1227, art 4 at* [2229]*; art 12 amends the Financial Services and Markets Act 2000 (Financial Promotion) Order 2005, SI 2005/1529, art 72, Sch 1, Pt II at* [2837]*,* [2841]*.*)

SCHEDULE
APPLICATION OF THE ACT AND THE PRINCIPAL ORDER TO PERSONS WITH AN
INTERIM PERMISSION OR AN INTERIM APPROVAL

Article 7

1.   Paragraphs 2 and 3 apply to every person with interim permission.

2.   For the purposes of section 20 (authorised persons acting without permission), a person's interim permission is treated as having been given to him under Part 4 of the Act.

3.   A person's interim permission is to be disregarded for the purposes of—
   (a)   subsection (2) of section 38 (exemption orders),
   (b)   subsection (2) of section 40 (application for permission),
   (c)   subject to paragraph 7, section 42 (giving permission),
   (d)   section 43 (imposition of requirements), and
   (e)   subsections (1), (4) and (5) of section 44 (variation etc at request of authorised person).

4.   Paragraphs 5(1), 6 to 9, 11, 12 and 13 apply to a person who falls within subsection (1) of section 31 (authorised persons) only by virtue of having an interim permission.

5.—(1)   A person with interim permission is to be treated after commencement as an authorised person for the purposes of the Act (and any provision made under the Act), unless otherwise expressly provided for by this Schedule.

(2)   A person with an interim approval is to be treated after commencement as an approved person for the purposes of the Act (and any provision made under the Act), unless otherwise expressly provided for by this Schedule.

6.   For the purposes of subsection (1) of section 21 (restrictions on financial promotion) a person with an interim permission is not to be treated as an authorised person for the purposes of communicating or approving the content of a communication except where the communication

invites or induces a person to enter into (or offer to enter into) an agreement the making or the performance of which constitutes a controlled activity which corresponds to a regulated activity which is covered by his interim permission.

7.   A person with an interim permission may still be an appointed representative within the meaning of subsection (2) of section 39 (exemption of appointed representatives) (and hence may be treated as exempt from the general prohibition as a result of section 39(1) for the purposes of subsection (3)(a) of section 42 (giving permission)).

8.   Subsection (3)(a) of section 213 (the compensation scheme) does not apply to a person who is a relevant person (within the meaning of that section) only by virtue of his having interim permission.

9.   Subsection (1)(a) of section 347 (the record of authorised persons etc) is disapplied in relation to persons with interim permission.

10.   Section 347(1)(h) is disapplied in relation to persons with interim approval.

11.   In article 22 of the Principal Order (deals with or through authorised persons), with the exception of the first reference, the references to an "authorised person" do not include a person with interim permission.

12.   In article 29 of the Principal Order (arranging deals with or through authorised persons), with the exception of the first reference, the references to an "authorised person" do not include a person with interim permission.

13.   For the purposes of paragraphs (1)(a), (2)(a), (3) and (4)(a) of article 72 of the Principal Order (overseas persons), a person with an interim permission is not to be treated as an authorised person.

[2859]

NOTES
    Commencement: 6 April 2007.

FINANCIAL SERVICES AND MARKETS ACT 2000 (REGULATED ACTIVITIES) (AMENDMENT) (NO 2) ORDER 2006

(SI 2006/2383)

NOTES
    Made: 12 September 2006.
    Authority: Financial Services and Markets Act 2000, ss 22(1), (5), 426, 427, 428(3), Sch 2, para 25.
    Commencement: 6 November 2006 (for the purposes of enabling applications to be made for (i) a Pt IV permission, or a variation of a Pt IV permission, in relation to activities of the kind specified by arts 25B, 25C, 53B, 53C, 63B or 63F or, so far as relevant to any such activity, art 64 of the Regulated Activities Order 2001, or (ii) the Authority's approval under FSMA 2000, s 59 in relation to any of those activities); 6 April 2007 (otherwise).

    As of 1 February 2009, this Order had not been amended.

ARRANGEMENT OF ARTICLES

PART 1
GENERAL

PART 5
TRANSITIONAL PROVISIONS

PART 1
GENERAL

1 Citation and commencement

(1)   This Order may be cited as the Financial Services and Markets Act 2000 (Regulated Activities) (Amendment) (No 2) Order 2006.

(2)   This Order comes into force—

   (a)   for the purposes of enabling applications to be made for—

      (i)   a Part IV permission, or a variation of a Part IV permission, in relation to activities of the kind specified by article 25B, 25C, 53B, 53C, 63B or 63F or, so far as relevant to any such activity, article 64 of the Financial Services and Markets Act 2000 (Regulated Activities) Order 2001; or

      (ii)   the Authority's approval under section 59 of the Financial Services and Markets Act 2000 in relation to any of those activities,

   on 6th November 2006; and

   (b)   for all other purposes, on 6th April 2007.

[2860]

NOTES

Commencement: 6 November 2006 (certain purposes); 6 April 2007 (otherwise) (see para (2) above).

2–24   *(Arts 2–24 (Pt 2) amend the Financial Services and Markets Act 2000 (Regulated Activities) Order 2001, SI 2001/544, arts 3, 26, 27, 28A, 29, 29A, 33, 33A, 36, 54, 54A, 55, 61, 66, 67, 72, 72F, 89, and insert arts 25B, 25C, 53B, 53C, 63B–63I, 88A, 88B (see the 2001 Order at* **[2010]** *et seq); arts 25–28 (Pt 3) amend the Consumer Credit Act 1974 (outside the scope of this work), the Companies Act 1985, s 262 (repealed), the Law of Property (Miscellaneous Provisions) Act 1989, s 2 at* **[1150]**, *and the Financial Services and Markets Act 2000, s 49 at* **[49]**; *arts 29–35 (Pt 4) add the Financial Services and Markets Act 2000 (Carrying on Regulated Activities by Way of Business) Order 2001, SI 2001/1177, arts 3B, 3C at* **[2209A]**, **[2209B]**, *amend the Financial Services and Markets Act 2000 (Exemption) Order 2001, SI 2001/1201, Schedule, Pt IV at* **[2220]**, *the Financial Services and Markets Act 2000 (Appointed Representatives) Regulations 2001, SI 2001/1217, regs 1–3 at* **[2221]**–**[2223]**, *the Financial Services and Markets Act 2000 (Professions) (Non-Exempt Activities) Order 2001, SI 2001/1227, art 2 at* **[2227]**, *and insert arts 6C–6F of that Order at* **[2235A]**–**[2235D]**, *amend the Financial Services and Markets Act 2000 (Financial Promotion) Order 2005, SI 2005/1529, arts 28B, 73, Sch 1, Pts I, II at* **[2791]**, **[2838]**, **[2840]**, **[2841]**, *the Consumer Credit (Advertisement) Regulations 2004, SI 2004/1484 (outside the scope of this work), and amended the Money Laundering Regulations 2003, SI 2003/3075 (revoked).)*

PART 5
TRANSITIONAL PROVISIONS

36 Interpretation

In this Part—

   "the Act" means the Financial Services and Markets Act 2000;

   "commencement" means the beginning of 6th April 2007;

   "the Regulated Activities Order" means the Financial Services and Markets Act 2000 (Regulated Activities) Order 2001.

[2861]

NOTES

Commencement: 6 November 2006 (certain purposes); 6 April 2007 (otherwise) (see art 1).

37 Interim permission

(1)   This article applies where—

   (a)   a person ("the applicant") has submitted to the Authority an application for Part IV permission or a variation of a Part IV permission, to the extent that the application relates to an activity of the kind specified by any of the following articles of the Regulated Activities Order (as amended by this Order)—

      (i)   article 25B (arranging regulated home reversion plans);

      (ii)   article 25C (arranging regulated home purchase plans);

      (iii)   article 53B (advising on regulated home reversion plans);

      (iv)   article 53C (advising on regulated home purchase plans);

      (v)   article 63B (entering into and administering regulated home reversion plans);

      (vi)   article 63F (entering into and administering regulated home purchase plans); or

      (vii)   article 64 (agreeing to carry on specified kinds of activity), so far as relevant to any of the above activities;

(b)   the applicant had carried on such activity before 6th November 2006;
(c)   the Authority received the application on or before 23rd March 2007; and
(d)   the application has not been finally decided before commencement.

(2)   The applicant is to be treated as having on commencement the permission to which the application relates.

(3)   A permission which an applicant is to be treated as having is referred to in this Part as an "interim permission".

(4)   Without prejudice to the exercise by the Authority of its powers under Part 4 of the Act, an interim permission lapses—
(a)   where the application relates to an activity of the kind specified by article 63B or 63F of the Regulated Activities Order or article 64 of that Order, so far as relevant to any such activity, when the application has been finally decided;
(b)   where the application relates to an activity of the kind specified by article 25B, 25C, 53B or 53C of the Regulated Activities Order or article 64 of that Order, so far as relevant to any such activity—
(i)   when the application has been finally decided; or
(ii)   at the beginning of 6th April 2008,
whichever is the earlier.

(5)   In this article, "finally decided" means—
(a)   subject to paragraph (6), when the application is withdrawn;
(b)   when the Authority grants permission under section 42 of the Act (giving permission) to carry on the activity in question;
(c)   when the Authority varies a permission under section 44 of the Act (variation etc at request of authorised person) to add the activity in question;
(d)   where the Authority has refused an application and the matter is not referred to the Tribunal, when the time for referring the matter to the Tribunal has expired;
(e)   where the Authority has refused an application and the matter is referred to the Tribunal, when—
(i)   if the reference is determined by the Tribunal (including a determination following remission back to the Tribunal for rehearing in accordance with section 137(3)(a) of the Act (appeal on a point of law)), the time for bringing an appeal has expired; or
(ii)   on an appeal from a determination by the Tribunal on a point of law, the Court itself determines the application in accordance with section 137 of the Act.

(6)   An applicant who is treated as having an interim permission may not withdraw the application without first obtaining the consent of the Authority.

(7)   Where—
(a)   the Authority exercises its powers under section 45 (variation etc on the Authority's own initiative) in relation to an authorised person who holds an interim permission; and
(b)   as a result of the variation there are no longer any regulated activities for which the authorised person has permission,
the Authority must, once it is satisfied that it is no longer necessary to keep the interim permission in force, cancel it.

[2862]

NOTES

Commencement: 6 November 2006 (certain purposes); 6 April 2007 (otherwise) (see art 1).

---

38   Interim approval

(1)   This article applies where—
(a)   the applicant (within the meaning of article 37(1)(a)) has submitted to the Authority an application made under section 60 of the Act (applications for approval); and
(b)   the application has not been finally decided before commencement.

(2)   The person in respect of whom the application is made is to be treated as having on commencement the approval of the Authority for the purposes of section 59 of the Act (approval for particular arrangements) in relation to the functions to which the application relates.

(3)   An approval which a person is to be treated as having is referred to in this Part as an "interim approval".

(4)   Without prejudice to the exercise by the Authority of its powers under Part 5 of the Act, an interim approval lapses—
(a)   where the application relates to an activity of the kind specified by article 63B or 63F of the Regulated Activities Order or article 64 of that Order, so far as relevant to any such activity, when the application has been finally decided;

    (b)   where the application relates to an activity of the kind specified by article 25B, 25C, 53B or 53C of the Regulated Activities Order or article 64 of that Order, so far as relevant to any such activity—

        (i)   when the application has been finally decided; or

       (ii)   at the beginning of 6th April 2008,

whichever is the earlier.

    (5)   In this article, "finally decided" means—

    (a)   when the application is withdrawn;

    (b)   when the Authority grants the application for approval under section 62 of the Act (applications for approval: procedure and right to refer to Tribunal);

    (c)   where the Authority has refused an application and the matter is not referred to the Tribunal, when the time for referring the matter to the Tribunal has expired;

    (d)   where the Authority has refused an application and the matter is referred to the Tribunal, when—

        (i)   if the reference is determined by the Tribunal (including a determination following remission back to the Tribunal for rehearing in accordance with section 137(3)(a) of the Act), the time for bringing an appeal has expired; or

       (ii)   on an appeal from a determination by the Tribunal on a point of law, the Court itself determines the application in accordance with section 137 of the Act.

[2863]

NOTES

Commencement: 6 November 2006 (certain purposes); 6 April 2007 (otherwise) (see art 1).

39 Application of the Authority's rules etc to persons with an interim permission or an interim approval

    (1)   The Authority may direct in writing that any relevant provision which would otherwise apply to a person by virtue of his interim permission or interim approval is not to apply or is to apply to him as modified in the way specified in the direction.

    (2)   Where the Authority makes a rule, gives guidance or issues a statement or code which applies only to persons with an interim permission or an interim approval (or only to a class of such persons), sections 65 (statements and codes: procedure), 155 (consultation) and 157(3) (guidance) of the Act do not apply to that rule, guidance, statement or code.

    (3)   For the purposes of paragraph (1) a "relevant provision" is any provision made as a result of the exercise by the Authority of any of its legislative functions mentioned in paragraph 1(2) of Schedule 1 to the Act (the Financial Services Authority).

[2864]

NOTES

Commencement: 6 November 2006 (certain purposes); 6 April 2007 (otherwise) (see art 1).

40 Application of the Act etc

The Schedule modifies the application of the Act and the Regulated Activities Order in relation to persons with an interim permission or an interim approval.

[2865]

NOTES

Commencement: 6 November 2006 (certain purposes); 6 April 2007 (otherwise) (see art 1).

SCHEDULE
APPLICATION OF THE ACT AND THE REGULATED ACTIVITIES ORDER TO PERSONS WITH AN INTERIM PERMISSION OR AN INTERIM APPROVAL

Article 40

1.   Paragraphs 2 and 3 apply to every person with an interim permission.

2.   For the purposes of section 20 (authorised persons acting without permission), a person's interim permission is treated as having been given to him under Part 4 of the Act.

3.   A person's interim permission is to be disregarded for the purposes of—

    (a)   section 38(2) (exemption orders);

    (b)   section 40(2) (application for permission);

    (c)   subject to paragraph 7, section 42 (giving permission);

    (d)   section 43 (imposition of requirements); and

    (e)   section 44(1), (4) and (5) (variation etc at request of authorised person).

4.   Paragraphs 5(1) and 6 to 10 apply to a person who falls within section 31(1) (authorised persons) by virtue only of having an interim permission.

5.—(1)   A person with an interim permission is to be treated on or after commencement as an authorised person for the purposes of the Act (and any provision made under the Act), unless otherwise expressly provided for by this Schedule.

(2)   A person with an interim approval is to be treated on or after commencement as an approved person for the purposes of the Act (and any provision made under the Act).

6.   For the purposes of section 21(2) (restrictions on financial promotion), a person with an interim permission is not to be treated as an authorised person for the purposes of communicating or approving the content of a communication except where the communication invites or induces a person to enter into (or offer to enter into) an agreement the making or performance of which constitutes a controlled activity which corresponds to a regulated activity which is covered by his interim permission.

7.   A person with an interim permission may still be an appointed representative within the meaning of section 39(2) (exemption of appointed representatives) (and hence may be treated as exempt from the general prohibition as a result of section 39(1) for the purposes of section 42(3)(a) (giving permission)).

8.   Subsection (3)(a) of section 213 (the compensation scheme) does not apply to—
   (a)   a person who is a relevant person, within the meaning of that section, by virtue only of having an interim permission; or
   (b)   an appointed representative of such person.

9.   In article 29 of the Regulated Activities Order (arranging deals with or through authorised persons), with the exception of the first reference, the references to an "authorised person" do not include a person with an interim permission.

10.   In sub-paragraph (a) of both paragraphs (2) and (3) of article 29A of the Regulated Activities Order (arrangements made in the course of administration by authorised person), the references to an "authorised person" do not include a person with an interim permission.

[2866]

NOTES
   Commencement: 6 November 2006 (certain purposes); 6 April 2007 (otherwise) (see art 1).

FINANCIAL SERVICES AND MARKETS ACT 2000 (REGULATED ACTIVITIES) (AMENDMENT NO 3) ORDER 2006 (NOTE)

(SI 2006/3384)

NOTES
   This Order was made on 18 December 2006 under FSMA 2000, ss 22(1), (5), 428(3), Sch 2, para 25. It amends the Financial Services and Markets Act 2000 (Regulated Activities) Order 2001, SI 2001/544 at **[2010]** et seq. It also contains consequential amendments to the Companies Act 1989 at **[1153]** et seq, the Terrorism Act 2000 at **[1247]** et seq, the Financial Services and Markets Act 2000 (Collective Investment Schemes) Order 2001, SI 2001/1062 at **[2202]** et seq, the Financial Services and Markets Act 2000 (Carrying on Regulated Activities by Way of Business) Order 2001, SI 2001/1177 at **[2206]** et seq, the Financial Services and Markets Act 2000 (Consultation with Competent Authorities) Regulations 2001, SI 2001/2509 at **[2421]** et seq, the Money Laundering Regulations 2003, SI 2003/3075 (revoked), the Financial Services and Markets Act 2000 (Financial Promotion) Order 2005, SI 2005/1529 at **[2757]** et seq, and various other enactments that are outside the scope of this work. In so far as relevant to this work, these amendments have been incorporated at the appropriate place. Article 1 of this Order provides that this Order comes into force (a) on 1 April 2007 for the purposes of enabling applications to be made for (i) a Part IV permission, (ii) a variation of a Part IV permission, (iii) the Authority's approval under FSMA 2000, s 59, in relation to an activity of the kind specified by art 25D of the Regulated Activities Order, or in relation to an investment of the kind specified by arts 83, 84 or 85 of that Order; and (b) for all other purposes, on 1 November 2007. This Order does not contain any transitional provisions or savings.

[2866A]

FINANCIAL SERVICES AND MARKETS ACT 2000 (EEA PASSPORT RIGHTS) (AMENDMENT) REGULATIONS 2006

(SI 2006/3385)

NOTES
   Made: 18 December 2006.
   Authority: Financial Services and Markets Act 2000, s 428(3), Sch 3, paras 13(1)(b)(iii), 14(1)(b), 17(b), 22.

PART III
STATUTORY INSTRUMENTS

Commencement: 1 April 2007 (certain purposes); 1 November 2007 (otherwise).

As of 1 February 2009, these Regulations had not been amended.

1 Citation, commencement and interpretation

(1)   These Regulations may be cited as the Financial Services and Markets Act 2000 (EEA Passport Rights) (Amendment) Regulations 2006.

(2)   These Regulations come into force on 1st April 2007 for the purposes of—
(a)   regulations 4 and 5;
(b)   enabling the Authority to treat a notice referred to in regulation 4A(3)(a) or 5A(3)(a) of the principal Regulations (inserted by these Regulations) given on or after that date as effective for the purpose of regulation 4A(3) or 5A(3) (as the case may be);
(c)   enabling the Authority, on receipt on or after that date of notice under regulation 11A(2)(a) or 12A(2)(a) of the principal Regulations (inserted by these Regulations), to inform the host state regulator of the proposed change in accordance with regulation 11A(3) or 12A(3) (as the case may be); and
(d)   enabling the Authority to give notice under regulation 11A(3) or 12A(3) of the principal Regulations (inserted by these Regulations),
and for all other purposes on 1st November 2007.

(3)   Nothing in paragraph (2) gives an investment firm or a UK investment firm an EEA right to carry on, before 1st November 2007, an activity—
(a)   which is an ancillary service listed in Section B of Annex I to the markets in financial instruments directive but which is not a non-core service listed in Section C of the Annex to the investment services directive;
(b)   in relation to an investment which is a financial instrument listed in Section C of Annex I to the markets in financial instruments directive but which is not an instrument listed in Section B of the Annex to the investment services directive; or
(c)   referred to in paragraph 5 of Section A of Annex I to the markets in financial instruments directive unless the firm has an EEA right to carry on one or more core services listed in Section A of the Annex to the investment services directive.

(4)   In these Regulations, "the principal Regulations" means the Financial Services and Markets Act 2000 (EEA Passport Rights) Regulations 2001 and "the investment services directive" means Council Directive 93/22/EEC of 10 May 1993 on investment services in the securities field.

[2866B]

NOTES
Commencement: 1 April 2007 (certain purposes); 1 November 2007 (otherwise) (see above).

2–14   (*Amend the Financial Services and Markets Act 2000 (EEA Passport Rights) Regulations 2001, SI 2001/2511 at* **[2430]** *et seq.*)

15 Transitional and saving provisions

(1)   Where an investment firm has given notice to the Authority and to its home state regulator pursuant to regulation 4(4)(a) of the principal Regulations (of a change in the requisite details of its branch) on or before 31st October 2007, regulation 4 continues to apply in relation to that change as if it had not been amended by these Regulations, and regulation 4A of the principal Regulations (inserted by these Regulations) does not apply in relation to that change.

(2)   Where an investment firm has given notice to the Authority and to its home state regulator pursuant to regulation 5(3)(a) of the principal Regulations or before 31st October 2007 (in relation to a change in the matters referred to in regulation 3(2)(b) of those Regulations), regulation 5 continues to apply in relation to that change as if it had not been amended by these Regulations, and regulation 5A of the principal Regulations (inserted by these Regulations) does not apply in relation to that change.

(3)   Where on or before 31st October 2007—
(a)   a UK investment firm has given notice to the Authority and to its host state regulator pursuant to regulation 11(2)(a) of the principal Regulations (of a change in the requisite details of the branch) on or before 31st October 2007, but
(b)   the Authority has not performed its function under regulation 11(4) of those Regulations,
the Authority must inform the host state regulator of the change pursuant to regulation 11A(3) of the principal Regulations (inserted by these Regulations) instead of performing its function under regulation 11(4).

(4)   Where the Authority has performed its function under regulation 11(4) of the principal Regulations (in relation to a change in the requisite details of a branch by a UK investment firm) on or before 31st October 2007, regulation 11 of the principal Regulations continues to apply in

relation to that change as if it had not been amended by these Regulations, and regulation 11A of the principal Regulations (inserted by these Regulations) does not apply in relation to that change.

(5)   Where a UK investment firm has given notice to the Authority and to its host state regulator pursuant to regulation 12(2)(a) of the principal Regulations (in relation to a change in its programme of operations or EEA activities) on or before 31st October 2007—

(a)   regulation 12A of the principal Regulations (inserted by these Regulations) does not apply in relation to that change;

(b)   the firm must not make the change to which the notice relates until the period of one month beginning with the day on which it gave the notice pursuant to regulation 12(2)(a) of the principal Regulations has elapsed; and

(c)   the Authority must, as soon as reasonably practicable after receiving the notice, inform the host state regulator of the proposed change.

(6)   In this regulation, "UK investment firm" means a UK firm (within the meaning of Schedule 3)—

(a)   which is an investment firm (within the meaning of the investment services directive); and

(b)   whose EEA right derives from that directive.

[2866C]

NOTES
Commencement: 1 April 2007 (certain purposes); 1 November 2007 (otherwise) (see reg 1).

FINANCIAL SERVICES AND MARKETS ACT 2000 (OMBUDSMAN SCHEME) (CONSUMER CREDIT JURISDICTION) ORDER 2007

(SI 2007/383)

NOTES
Made: 7 February 2007.
Authority: Financial Services and Markets Act 2000, s 226A(2)(e).
Commencement: 8 March 2007 (certain purposes); 1 October 2008 (otherwise).

As of 1 February 2009, this Order had not been amended.

1 Citation and commencement

This Order may be cited as the Financial Services and Markets Act 2000 (Ombudsman Scheme) (Consumer Credit Jurisdiction) Order 2007 and shall come into force—

(a)   for the purposes of article 2(a) to (f) and (i) on 8th March 2007; and

(b)   for all other purposes on the day sections 24 and 25 of the Consumer Credit Act 2006 come fully into force.

[2867]

NOTES
Commencement: 8 March 2007.
Note: the Consumer Credit Act 2006, ss 24, 25 came into force for all purposes on 1 October 2008 (see the Consumer Credit Act 2006 (Commencement No 3) Order 2007, SI 2007/3300).

2 Types of Business

The Secretary of State specifies the following types of business for the purposes of section 226A(2)(e) of the Financial Services and Markets Act 2000—

(a)   a consumer credit business;

(b)   a consumer hire business;

(c)   a business so far as it comprises or relates to credit brokerage;

(d)   a business so far as it comprises or relates to debt-adjusting;

(e)   a business so far as it comprises or relates to debt-counselling;

(f)   a business so far as it comprises or relates to debt-collecting;

(g)   a business so far as it comprises or relates to debt administration;

(h)   a business so far as it comprises or relates to the provision of credit information services;

(i)   a business so far as it comprises or relates to the operation of a credit reference agency.

[2868]

NOTES
Commencement: 8 March 2007 (paras (a)–(f), (i)); 1 October 2008 (paras (g), (h)).

FINANCIAL SERVICES AND MARKETS ACT 2000 (MARKETS IN FINANCIAL INSTRUMENTS) (AMENDMENT) REGULATIONS 2007

(SI 2007/763)

NOTES
Made: 8 March 2007.
Authority: Financial Services and Markets Act 2000, ss 39(1), 349(1)–(3), 417(1), 428(3), Sch 3, para 22; European Communities Act 1972, s 2(2).
Commencement: 1 April 2007 (certain purposes); 1 November 2007 (otherwise).
As of 1 February 2009, these Regulations had not been amended.
Note: although the provisions of these Regulations only amend other statutory instruments, the editor considers that some users may find it helpful to have all of the amending provisions set out in one place, particularly those provisions in relation to the MiFID Article 3 exemption.

ARRANGEMENT OF REGULATIONS

1 Citation, commencement and interpretation

(1)   These Regulations may be cited as the Financial Services and Markets Act 2000 (Markets in Financial Instruments) (Amendment) Regulations 2007.

(2)   These Regulations come into force—
  (a)   on 1st April 2007—
    (i)   for the purposes of enabling notices to be given in accordance with regulation 9A(3)(b) of the principal regulations (inserted by regulation 3) and enabling the Authority to give directions in accordance with that regulation as to the form of such notices,
    (ii)   for the purposes of enabling notice to be given under regulation 9B(2), 9C(2) or 9D(2) of the principal regulations (inserted by regulation 4),
    (iii)   for the purposes of regulation 9; and
  (b)   for all other purposes, on 1st November 2007.

(3)   In these Regulations, "the principal regulations" means the Financial Services and Markets Act 2000 (Markets in Financial Instruments) Regulations 2007.

[2869]

NOTES
Commencement: 1 April 2007 (certain purposes); 1 November 2007 (otherwise) (see reg 1).

2 Exempt investment firms

(1)   In regulation 2 of the principal regulations (interpretation) after the definition of "Part IV permission" insert—
    ""regulated activity" has the meaning given in section 22 of the Act;".

(2)   In Part 2 of the principal regulations (Part IV permission: investment firms)—
  (a)   immediately before regulation 4, insert the heading—

"General   restriction on giving Part IV permission";
  (b)   after regulation 4 insert—

"4A   Applications to be an exempt investment firm

  (1)   A person may apply in accordance with section 40 of the Act for a Part IV permission to carry on regulated activities as an exempt investment firm.

  (2)   An authorised person may become entitled to carry on regulated activities as an exempt investment firm only by applying for a variation of his Part IV permission in accordance with section 44 of the Act.

  (3)   For the purposes of this regulation, and regulations 4B and 4C, "exempt investment firm" means an authorised person who—
    (a)   is an investment firm within the meaning given in Article 4.1.1 of the markets in financial instruments directive, and

(b)   has a Part IV permission,

but to whom Title II of the markets in financial instruments directive does not apply.

(4)   A person may only apply for a Part IV permission as mentioned in paragraph (1), and an authorised person may only apply for a variation of his Part IV permission as mentioned in paragraph (2), if the person or authorised person has his relevant office in the United Kingdom.

(5)   In paragraph (4) "relevant office" means—
(a)   in relation to a body corporate, its registered office or, if it has no registered office, its head office, and
(b)   in relation to a person or authorised person other than a body corporate, the person's head office.

4B   Limitation on exempt investment firms

An exempt investment firm has no entitlement—
(a)   to establish a branch by making use of the procedures in paragraph 19 of Schedule 3, or
(b)   to provide any service by making use of the procedures in paragraph 20 of Schedule 3,

in a case where the entitlement of the firm to do so would, but for this regulation, derive from the markets in financial instruments directive.

4C   Requirements to be applied to exempt investment firms

(1)   If the Authority—
(a)   gives to a person who has applied as mentioned in regulation 4A(1) a Part IV permission to carry on regulated activities as an exempt investment firm, or
(b)   varies the Part IV permission of an authorised person who has applied as mentioned in regulation 4A(2) for a variation to permit him to carry on regulated activities as an exempt investment firm,

the requirements specified in paragraph (3) ("the specified requirements") shall be treated as being included in the permission by the Authority under section 43 of the Act.

(2)   Notwithstanding paragraph (1)—
(a)   the inclusion of the specified requirements in the Part IV permission does not—
(i)   amount, for the purpose of section 52(6) of the Act, to a proposal to exercise the power of the Authority under section 43(1) of the Act,
(ii)   amount, for the purpose of section 52(9) of the Act, to a decision to exercise the power of the Authority under section 43(1) of the Act, or
(iii)   entitle the person to refer a matter under section 55(1) of the Act;
(b)   the specified requirements shall not expire until the person ceases to be an exempt investment firm and, accordingly, section 43(5) shall not be treated as requiring the Authority to specify a period at the end of which they expire; and
(c)   no application under section 44 of the Act to vary the permission by cancelling or varying any of the specified requirements may be made by the person unless he informs the Authority when making the application that he wishes to cease to be an exempt investment firm.

(3)   The requirements are that the person—
(a)   does not hold clients' funds or securities and does not, for that reason, at any time, place himself in debt with his clients;
(b)   does not provide any investment service other than—
(i)   the reception and transmission of orders in transferable securities and units in collective investment undertakings, and
(ii)   the provision of investment advice in relation to the financial instruments mentioned in paragraph (i);
(c)   in the course of providing the investment services mentioned in sub-paragraph (b), transmits orders only to—
(i)   investment firms authorised in accordance with the markets in financial instruments directive,
(ii)   credit institutions authorised in accordance with the banking consolidation directive,
(iii)   branches of investment firms or of credit institutions which are authorised in a third country and which are subject to and comply with prudential rules considered by the Authority to be at least as stringent as those laid down in the markets in financial instruments directive, the banking consolidation directive or Directive 2006/49/EC of the European Parliament and of the Council of 14 June 2006 on the capital adequacy of investment firms and credit institutions,

       (iv)   collective investment undertakings authorised under the law of a Member State to market units to the public and to the managers of such undertakings,

       (v)   investment companies with fixed capital, as defined in Article 15(4) of Second Council Directive 77/91/EEC of 13 December 1976 on the coordination of safeguards required of public companies in respect of their formation and the maintenance and alteration of their capital, the securities of which are listed or dealt in on a regulated market in a Member State.

(4)   In paragraph (3)—

   (a)   terms and expressions defined in Article 4 of the markets in financial instruments directive and used in the paragraph have the meanings given in that Article;

   (b)   "the banking consolidation directive" means Directive 2006/48/EC of the European Parliament and of the Council of 14 June 2006 relating to the taking up and pursuit of the business of credit institutions;

   (c)   other terms and expressions used both in the paragraph and in Article 3 of or Annex 1 to the markets in financial instruments directive have the same meanings in the paragraph as in that Article or Annex; and

   (d)   "Member State", in sub-paragraph (c)(iv), includes an EEA State that is not a Member State.".

(3)   In regulation 10 of the principal regulations (interpretation of Part 3) omit the definitions of "regulated activity" and "Schedule 3".

                                                         [2870]

NOTES
Commencement: 1 November 2007.

3 Transitional provision in relation to exempt investment firms

In Part 3 of the principal regulations (transitional and saving provisions), after regulation 9, insert—

"9A Transitional provision: exempt investment firms

(1)   Except where paragraph (3) applies, an authorised person who immediately before 1st November 2007—

   (a)   is an investment firm within the meaning given in Article 4.1.1 of the markets in financial instruments directive,

   (b)   has his relevant office in the United Kingdom, and

   (c)   fulfils all the requirements set out in regulation 4C(3),

becomes an exempt investment firm with effect from that day as if he had applied as mentioned in regulation 4A(2) for a variation of his Part IV permission to permit him to carry on regulated activities as an exempt investment firm and the Authority had so varied the permission on that day.

(2)   In paragraph (1) "relevant office" has the meaning given in regulation 4A(5).

(3)   This paragraph applies—

   (a)   to an authorised person having a Part IV permission that, immediately before 1st November 2007—

       (i)   includes no requirement having the effect of prohibiting the person from holding clients' funds, or

       (ii)   permits the person, in connection with the carrying on of regulated activities comprising any investment services and activities (excluding activities to which, by virtue of Article 2, the markets in financial instruments directive does not apply), to carry on the activity consisting of both the safeguarding of assets belonging to another and the administration of those assets; and

   (b)   to an authorised person who, before 1st November 2007, gives the Authority notice, in such form as the Authority may direct, that he does not wish to become an exempt investment firm.

(4)   In paragraph (3)—

   (a)   "clients' funds", in sub-paragraph (a)(i), has the same meaning as in Article 3 of the markets in financial instruments directive, and

   (b)   sub-paragraph (a)(ii) is to be construed in accordance with section 22 of the Act, any relevant order made under that section and Schedule 2 to the Act.

(5)   The variation of a person's Part IV permission effected by paragraph (1) does not amount to the grant of an application for variation of a Part IV permission for the purpose of section 52(4) of the Act or to the determination of an application under Part IV for the purpose of section 55(1) of the Act.".

[2871]

NOTES
Commencement: 1 April 2007 (certain purposes); 1 November 2007 (otherwise) (see reg 1).

4   Transitional provision in relation to Part IV permissions

In Part 3 of the principal regulations, after regulation 9A (inserted by regulation 3), insert—

"9B   Transitional provision: operators of alternative trading systems

(1)   Any person who immediately before 1st November 2007—
- (a)   had a Part IV permission to carry on an activity of the kind specified by article 14, 21 or 25 of the principal Order in relation to an investment of a particular kind; and
- (b)   operated an alternative trading system (within the meaning of the Alternative Trading Systems Instrument 2003 (2003/45) made by the Authority under the Act on 19th June 2003),

is, subject to regulation 9C, from 1st November 2007 to be treated as having a Part IV permission to carry on the kind of activity specified by article 25D of the principal Order (inserted by the 2006 Order) in relation to an investment of the same kind which is a financial instrument.

(2)   Where the person concerned gave written notice to the Authority on or before 1st October 2007 to that effect, paragraph (1) shall not apply to him.

9C   Transitional provision for investment firms and credit institutions in relation to options, futures and contracts for differences

(1)   Any person who immediately before 1st November 2007—
- (a)   was an investment firm or a credit institution (in each case within the meaning of the principal Order as amended by the 2006 Order); and
- (b)   had a Part IV permission to carry on an activity of the kind specified by article 14, 21, 25, 37 or 53 of the principal Order in relation to an investment specified in the first column in the table in Schedule 8,

is from 1st November 2007 also to be treated as having a Part IV permission to carry on that kind of activity in relation to an investment specified in the second column of the table opposite that investment (in so far as he does not already have such permission).

(2)   Where the person concerned gave written notice to the Authority on or before 1st October 2007 to that effect, paragraph (1) shall not apply to him.

9D   Transitional provision for management companies in relation to options, futures and contracts for differences

(1)   Any person who immediately before 1st November 2007—
- (a)   was a management company (within the meaning of the principal Order as amended by the 2006 Order);
- (b)   was providing, in accordance with Article 5.3 of Council Directive 85/611/EEC of 20 December 1985 on the coordination of laws, regulations and administrative provisions relating to undertakings for collective investment in transferable securities, the investment service specified in paragraph 4 or 5 of Section A, or the ancillary service specified in paragraph 1 of Section B, of Annex I to the markets in financial instruments directive; and
- (c)   had a Part IV permission to carry on an activity of the kind specified by article 14, 21, 25, 37, 40 or 53 of the principal Order in relation to an investment specified in the first column in the table in Schedule 8,

is from 1st November 2007 also to be treated as having a Part IV permission to carry on that kind of activity in relation to an investment specified in the second column of the table opposite that investment (in so far as he does not already have such permission).

(2)   Where the person concerned gave written notice to the Authority on or before 1st October 2007 to that effect, paragraph (1) shall not apply to him.".

[2872]

NOTES
Commencement: 1 April 2007 (certain purposes); 1 November 2007 (otherwise) (see reg 1).

PART III
STATUTORY INSTRUMENTS

5 In regulation 10 of the principal regulations, before the definition of "ancillary service" insert—
    ""the principal Order" means the Financial Services and Markets Act 2000 (Regulated
        Activities) Order 2001;
        "the 2006 Order" means the Financial Services and Markets Act 2000 (Regulated
        Activities) (Amendment No 3) Order 2006;".

[2873]

NOTES
Commencement: 1 November 2007.

6
After Schedule 7 to the principal regulations, insert—

"SCHEDULE 8
TRANSITIONAL PROVISION FOR PART IV PERMISSIONS
Table
Regulations 9C and 9D

Investment in relation to which the person has Part IV permission immediately before 1st November 2007	Additional investments to which the person's Part IV permission is extended from 1st November 2007
Option (excluding commodity options and options on a commodity future) within the meaning of the General Provisions and Glossary Instrument 2001 (2001/7) made by the Authority under the Act on 21st June 2001("the 2001 Instrument") as amended by the Handbook Administration (No 3) Instrument 2006 (2006/21) made by the Authority under the Act on 22nd June 2006 and the CRD (Consequential Amendments) Instrument 2006 (2006/53) made by the Authority under the Act on 23rd November 2006	Those options within the meaning of the 2001 Instrument as last amended by the Glossary (MIFID) Instrument 2007 (2007/1) made by the Authority under the Act on 25th January 2007 ("the 2007 Instrument") which are options falling within paragraph 10 of Section C of Annex I to the markets in financial instruments directive ("Section C")
Commodity option within the meaning of the 2001 Instrument[1]	Those commodity options within the meaning of the 2001 Instrument as last amended by the 2007 Instrument which are options falling within paragraphs 4, 5, 6 and 7 of Section C
Option on a commodity future within the meaning of the 2001 Instrument	Those options on a commodity future within the meaning of the 2001 Instrument as last amended by the 2007 Instrument which are options falling within paragraphs 4, 5, 6 and 7 of Section C
Future (excluding commodity futures and rolling spot forex contracts[2]) within the meaning of the 2001 Instrument	Those futures[3] (excluding commodity futures and rolling spot forex contracts) which are futures falling within paragraph 10 of Section C
Commodity future within the meaning of the 2001 Instrument	Those commodity futures within the meaning of the 2001 Instrument as last amended by the 2007 Instrument which are futures falling within paragraphs 5, 6 and 7 of Section C
Contract for differences (excluding spread bets[4] and rolling spot forex contracts) within the meaning of the 2001 Instrument	Those contracts for differences (excluding spread bets and rolling spot forex contracts) within the meaning of the 2001 Instrument as last amended by the 2007 Instrument which are derivative instruments for the transfer of credit risk falling within paragraph 8 of Section C.

---

[1] "Commodity" is amended by the CRD (Consequential Amendments) Instrument 2006 and the Handbook Administration (No 4) Instrument 2006 (2006/64) made by the Authority under the Act on 21st December 2006.

[2] "Rolling spot forex contract" is defined in the 2001 Instrument.

(3) The definition of "future" in the 2001 Instrument is from 1st November 2007 affected by the amendment made to article 84 of the Financial Services and Markets Act 2000 (Regulated Activities) Order 2001 (SI 2001/544) by article 27 of the Financial Services and Markets Act 2000 (Regulated Activities) (Amendment No 3) Order 2006 (SI 2006/3384).

(4) "Spread bet" is defined in the 2001 Instrument.".

[2874]

NOTES
Commencement: 1 November 2007.

7 Amendment of the Appointed Representatives Regulations

In the Financial Services and Markets Act 2000 (Appointed Representatives) Regulations 2001, after regulation 3 insert—

"4 Transitional provision in relation to contracts

Regulation 3(6) does not apply in relation to a contract made on or before 31st October 2007.".

[2875]

NOTES
Commencement: 1 November 2007.

8 Amendment of the EEA Passport Rights Regulations

In regulation 1(2) of the Financial Services and Markets Act 2000 (EEA Passport Rights) Regulations 2001, in paragraph (a) of the definition of "UK investment firm", after "investment firm" insert "(within the meaning of section 424A of the Act)".

[2876]

NOTES
Commencement: 1 November 2007.

9 Amendment of the Disclosure of Confidential Information Amendment Regulations

In regulation 1(2) of the Financial Services and Markets Act 2000 (Disclosure of Confidential Information) (Amendment) Regulations 2006—
(a) at the end of sub-paragraph (a) omit "and";
(b) after sub-paragraph (a) insert—
"(aa) for the purposes of regulation 6(a) on 1st April 2007; and".

[2877]

NOTES
Commencement: 1 April 2007.

MONEY LAUNDERING REGULATIONS 2007

(SI 2007/2157)

NOTES
Made: 24 July 2007.
Authority: European Communities Act 1972, s 2(2); Financial Services and Markets Act 2000, ss 168(4)(b), 402(1)(b), 417(1), 428(3).
Commencement: 15 December 2007.
These Regulations are reproduced as amended by: the Money Laundering (Amendment) Regulations 2007, SI 2007/3299; the Payment Services Regulations 2009, SI 2009/209.

ARRANGEMENT OF REGULATIONS

PART 1
GENERAL

PART 2
CUSTOMER DUE DILIGENCE

PART 3
RECORD-KEEPING, PROCEDURES AND TRAINING

PART 4
SUPERVISION AND REGISTRATION

Interpretation

Supervision

Registration of high value dealers, money service businesses and trust or company service providers

Requirement to inform the authority

Registration of Annex I financial institutions, estate agents etc

Financial provisions

PART 5
ENFORCEMENT

Powers of designated authorities

Civil penalties, review and appeals

PART 1
GENERAL

1 Citation, commencement etc

(1) These Regulations may be cited as the Money Laundering Regulations 2007 and come into force on 15th December 2007.

(2) These Regulations are prescribed for the purposes of sections 168(4)(b) (appointment of persons to carry out investigations in particular cases) and 402(1)(b) (power of the Authority to institute proceedings for certain other offences) of the 2000 Act.

(3) The Money Laundering Regulations 2003 are revoked.

[2877AA]

NOTES
Commencement: 15 December 2007.

2 Interpretation

(1) In these Regulations—
  "the 2000 Act" means the Financial Services and Markets Act 2000;
  "Annex I financial institution" has the meaning given by regulation 22(1);
  "auditor", except in regulation 17(2)(c) and (d), has the meaning given by regulation 3(4) and (5);
  "authorised person" means a person who is authorised for the purposes of the 2000 Act;
  "the Authority" means the Financial Services Authority;
  "the banking consolidation directive" means Directive 2006/48/EC of the European Parliament and of the Council of 14th June 2006 relating to the taking up and pursuit of the business of credit institutions;
  "beneficial owner" has the meaning given by regulation 6;
  ["bill payment service provider" means an undertaking which provides a payment service enabling the payment of utility and other household bills;]
  "business relationship" means a business, professional or commercial relationship between a relevant person and a customer, which is expected by the relevant person, at the time when contact is established, to have an element of duration;
  "cash" means notes, coins or travellers' cheques in any currency;
  "casino" has the meaning given by regulation 3(13);
  "the Commissioners" means the Commissioners for Her Majesty's Revenue and Customs;
  "consumer credit financial institution" has the meaning given by regulation 22(1);
  "credit institution" has the meaning given by regulation 3(2);
  "customer due diligence measures" has the meaning given by regulation 5;
  "DETI" means the Department of Enterprise, Trade and Investment in Northern Ireland;

"the electronic money directive" means Directive 2000/46/EC of the European Parliament and of the Council of 18th September 2000 on the taking up, pursuit and prudential supervision of the business of electronic money institutions;

"estate agent" has the meaning given by regulation 3(11);

"external accountant" has the meaning given by regulation 3(7);

"financial institution" has the meaning given by regulation 3(3);

"firm" means any entity, whether or not a legal person, that is not an individual and includes a body corporate and a partnership or other unincorporated association;

"high value dealer" has the meaning given by regulation 3(12);

"the implementing measures directive" means Commission Directive 2006/70/EC of 1st August 2006 laying down implementing measures for the money laundering directive;

"independent legal professional" has the meaning given by regulation 3(9);

"insolvency practitioner", except in regulation 17(2)(c) and (d), has the meaning given by regulation 3(6);

"the life assurance consolidation directive" means Directive 2002/83/EC of the European Parliament and of the Council of 5th November 2002 concerning life assurance;

"local weights and measures authority" has the meaning given by section 69 of the Weights and Measures Act 1985 (local weights and measures authorities);

"the markets in financial instruments directive" means Directive 2004/39/EC of the European Parliament and of the Council of 12th April 2004 on markets in financial instruments;

"money laundering" means an act which falls within section 340(11) of the Proceeds of Crime Act 2002;

"the money laundering directive" means Directive 2005/60/EC of the European Parliament and of the Council of 26th October 2005 on the prevention of the use of the financial system for the purpose of money laundering and terrorist financing;

"money service business" means an undertaking which by way of business operates a currency exchange office, transmits money (or any representations of monetary value) by any means or cashes cheques which are made payable to customers;

"nominated officer" means a person who is nominated to receive disclosures under Part 7 of the Proceeds of Crime Act 2002 (money laundering) or Part 3 of the Terrorism Act 2000 (terrorist property);

"non-EEA state" means a state that is not an EEA state;

"notice" means a notice in writing;

"occasional transaction" means a transaction (carried out other than as part of a business relationship) amounting to 15,000 euro or more, whether the transaction is carried out in a single operation or several operations which appear to be linked;

"the OFT" means the Office of Fair Trading;

"ongoing monitoring" has the meaning given by regulation 8(2);

["payment services" has the meaning given by regulation 2(1) of the Payment Services Regulations 2009;]

"regulated market"—

    (a)   within the EEA, has the meaning given by point 14 of Article 4(1) of the markets in financial instruments directive; and

    (b)   outside the EEA, means a regulated financial market which subjects companies whose securities are admitted to trading to disclosure obligations which are contained in international standards and are equivalent to the specified disclosure obligations;

"relevant person" means a person to whom, in accordance with regulations 3 and 4, these Regulations apply;

"the specified disclosure obligations" means disclosure requirements consistent with—

    (a)   Article 6(1) to (4) of Directive 2003/6/EC of the European Parliament and of the Council of 28th January 2003 on insider dealing and market manipulation;

    (b)   Articles 3, 5, 7, 8, 10, 14 and 16 of Directive 2003/71/EC of the European Parliament and of the Council of 4th November 2003 on the prospectuses to be published when securities are offered to the public or admitted to trading;

    (c)   Articles 4 to 6, 14, 16 to 19 and 30 of Directive 2004/109/EC of the European Parliament and of the Council of 15th December 2004 relating to the harmonisation of transparency requirements in relation to information about issuers whose securities are admitted to trading on a regulated market; or

    (d)   Community legislation made under the provisions mentioned in sub-paragraphs (a) to (c);

"supervisory authority" in relation to any relevant person means the supervisory authority specified for such a person by regulation 23;

"tax adviser" (except in regulation 11(3)) has the meaning given by regulation 3(8);

["telecommunication, digital and IT payment service provider" means an undertaking which provides payment services falling within paragraph 1(g) of Schedule 1 to the Payment Services Regulations 2009;]

"terrorist financing" means an offence under—

(a) section 15 (fund-raising), 16 (use and possession), 17 (funding arrangements), 18 (money laundering) or 63 (terrorist finance: jurisdiction) of the Terrorism Act 2000;

(b) paragraph 7(2) or (3) of Schedule 3 to the Anti-Terrorism, Crime and Security Act 2001 (freezing orders);

(c) article 7, 8 or 10 of the Terrorism (United Nations Measures) Order 2006; or

(d) article 7, 8 or 10 of the Al-Qaida and Taliban (United Nations Measures) Order 2006;

"trust or company service provider" has the meaning given by regulation 3(10).

(2) In these Regulations, references to amounts in euro include references to equivalent amounts in another currency.

(3) Unless otherwise defined, expressions used in these Regulations and the money laundering directive have the same meaning as in the money laundering directive and expressions used in these Regulations and in the implementing measures directive have the same meaning as in the implementing measures directive.

[2877AB]

NOTES

Commencement: 15 December 2007.

Para (1): definitions "bill payment service provider", "payment services", and "telecommunication, digital and IT payment service provider" inserted by the Payment Services Regulations 2009, SI 2009/209, reg 126, Sch 6, Pt 2, para 6(a), as from 1 November 2009 (for the full commencement details of the 2009 Regulations, see reg 1 of those Regulations at **[4387]**).

3 Application of the Regulations

(1) Subject to regulation 4, these Regulations apply to the following persons acting in the course of business carried on by them in the United Kingdom ("relevant persons")—

(a) credit institutions;

(b) financial institutions;

(c) auditors, insolvency practitioners, external accountants and tax advisers;

(d) independent legal professionals;

(e) trust or company service providers;

(f) estate agents;

(g) high value dealers;

(h) casinos.

(2) "Credit institution" means—

(a) a credit institution as defined in Article 4(1)(a) of the banking consolidation directive; or

(b) a branch (within the meaning of Article 4(3) of that directive) located in an EEA state of an institution falling within sub-paragraph (a) (or an equivalent institution whose head office is located in a non-EEA state) wherever its head office is located,

when it accepts deposits or other repayable funds from the public or grants credits for its own account (within the meaning of the banking consolidation directive).

(3) "Financial institution" means—

(a) an undertaking, including a money service business, when it carries out one or more of the activities listed in points 2 to 12 and 14 of Annex 1 to the banking consolidation directive (the relevant text of which is set out in Schedule 1 to these Regulations), other than—

(i) a credit institution;

(ii) an undertaking whose only listed activity is trading for own account in one or more of the products listed in point 7 of Annex 1 to the banking consolidation directive where the undertaking does not have a customer,

and, for this purpose, "customer" means a third party which is not a member of the same group as the undertaking;

(b) an insurance company duly authorised in accordance with the life assurance consolidation directive, when it carries out activities covered by that directive;

(c) a person whose regular occupation or business is the provision to other persons of an investment service or the performance of an investment activity on a professional basis, when providing or performing investment services or activities (within the meaning of the markets in financial instruments directive), other than a person falling within Article 2 of that directive;

(d) a collective investment undertaking, when marketing or otherwise offering its units or shares;

(e) an insurance intermediary as defined in Article 2(5) of Directive 2002/92/EC of the European Parliament and of the Council of 9th December 2002 on insurance mediation, with the exception of a tied insurance intermediary as mentioned in Article 2(7) of that

Directive, when it acts in respect of contracts of long-term insurance within the meaning given by article 3(1) of, and Part II of Schedule 1 to, the Financial Services and Markets Act 2000 (Regulated Activities) Order 2001;

(f)   a branch located in an EEA state of a person referred to in sub-paragraphs (a) to (e) (or an equivalent person whose head office is located in a non-EEA state), wherever its head office is located, when carrying out any activity mentioned in sub-paragraphs (a) to (e);

(g)   the National Savings Bank;

(h)   the Director of Savings, when money is raised under the auspices of the Director under the National Loans Act 1968.

(4)   "Auditor" means any firm or individual who is a statutory auditor within the meaning of Part 42 of the Companies Act 2006 (statutory auditors), when carrying out statutory audit work within the meaning of section 1210 of that Act.

(5)   Before the entry into force of Part 42 of the Companies Act 2006 the reference in paragraph (4) to—

(a)   a person who is a statutory auditor shall be treated as a reference to a person who is eligible for appointment as a company auditor under section 25 of the Companies Act 1989 (eligibility for appointment) or article 28 of the Companies (Northern Ireland) Order 1990; and

(b)   the carrying out of statutory audit work shall be treated as a reference to the provision of audit services.

(6)   "Insolvency practitioner" means any person who acts as an insolvency practitioner within the meaning of section 388 of the Insolvency Act 1986 (meaning of "act as insolvency practitioner") or article 3 of the Insolvency (Northern Ireland) Order 1989.

(7)   "External accountant" means a firm or sole practitioner who by way of business provides accountancy services to other persons, when providing such services.

(8)   "Tax adviser" means a firm or sole practitioner who by way of business provides advice about the tax affairs of other persons, when providing such services.

(9)   "Independent legal professional" means a firm or sole practitioner who by way of business provides legal or notarial services to other persons, when participating in financial or real property transactions concerning—

(a)   the buying and selling of real property or business entities;

(b)   the managing of client money, securities or other assets;

(c)   the opening or management of bank, savings or securities accounts;

(d)   the organisation of contributions necessary for the creation, operation or management of companies; or

(e)   the creation, operation or management of trusts, companies or similar structures,

and, for this purpose, a person participates in a transaction by assisting in the planning or execution of the transaction or otherwise acting for or on behalf of a client in the transaction.

(10)   "Trust or company service provider" means a firm or sole practitioner who by way of business provides any of the following services to other persons—

(a)   forming companies or other legal persons;

(b)   acting, or arranging for another person to act—

(i)   as a director or secretary of a company;

(ii)   as a partner of a partnership; or

(iii)   in a similar position in relation to other legal persons;

(c)   providing a registered office, business address, correspondence or administrative address or other related services for a company, partnership or any other legal person or arrangement;

(d)   acting, or arranging for another person to act, as—

(i)   a trustee of an express trust or similar legal arrangement; or

(ii)   a nominee shareholder for a person other than a company whose securities are listed on a regulated market,

when providing such services.

(11)   "Estate agent" means—

(a)   a firm; or

(b)   sole practitioner,

who, or whose employees, carry out estate agency work (within the meaning given by section 1 of the Estate Agents Act 1979 (estate agency work)), when in the course of carrying out such work.

(12)   "High value dealer" means a firm or sole trader who by way of business trades in goods (including an auctioneer dealing in goods), when he receives, in respect of any transaction, a payment or payments in cash of at least 15,000 euros in total, whether the transaction is executed in a single operation or in several operations which appear to be linked.

(13) "Casino" means the holder of a casino operating licence and, for this purpose, a "casino operating licence" has the meaning given by section 65(2) of the Gambling Act 2005 (nature of licence).

(14) In the application of this regulation to Scotland, for "real property" in paragraph (9) substitute "heritable property".

[2877AC]

NOTES
Commencement: 15 December 2007.

4 Exclusions

(1) These Regulations do not apply to the following persons when carrying out any of the following activities—

(a) a society registered under the Industrial and Provident Societies Act 1965, when it—
  (i) issues withdrawable share capital within the limit set by section 6 of that Act (maximum shareholding in society); or
  (ii) accepts deposits from the public within the limit set by section 7(3) of that Act (carrying on of banking by societies);

(b) a society registered under the Industrial and Provident Societies Act (Northern Ireland) 1969, when it—
  (i) issues withdrawable share capital within the limit set by section 6 of that Act (maximum shareholding in society); or
  (ii) accepts deposits from the public within the limit set by section 7(3) of that Act (carrying on of banking by societies);

(c) a person who is (or falls within a class of persons) specified in any of paragraphs 2 to 23, 25 to 38 or 40 to 49 of the Schedule to the Financial Services and Markets Act 2000 (Exemption) Order 2001, when carrying out any activity in respect of which he is exempt;

(d) a person who was an exempted person for the purposes of section 45 of the Financial Services Act 1986 (miscellaneous exemptions) immediately before its repeal, when exercising the functions specified in that section;

(e) a person whose main activity is that of a high value dealer, when he engages in financial activity on an occasional or very limited basis as set out in paragraph 1 of Schedule 2 to these Regulations; or

(f) a person, when he prepares a home information pack or a document or information for inclusion in a home information pack.

(2) These Regulations do not apply to a person who falls within regulation 3 solely as a result of his engaging in financial activity on an occasional or very limited basis as set out in paragraph 1 of Schedule 2 to these Regulations.

(3) Parts 2 to 5 of these Regulations do not apply to—
(a) the Auditor General for Scotland;
(b) the Auditor General for Wales;
(c) the Bank of England;
(d) the Comptroller and Auditor General;
(e) the Comptroller and Auditor General for Northern Ireland;
(f) the Official Solicitor to the Supreme Court, when acting as trustee in his official capacity;
(g) the Treasury Solicitor.

(4) In paragraph (1)(f), "home information pack" has the same meaning as in Part 5 of the Housing Act 2004 (home information packs).

[2877AD]

NOTES
Commencement: 15 December 2007.

PART 2
CUSTOMER DUE DILIGENCE

5 Meaning of customer due diligence measures

"Customer due diligence measures" means—
(a) identifying the customer and verifying the customer's identity on the basis of documents, data or information obtained from a reliable and independent source;
(b) identifying, where there is a beneficial owner who is not the customer, the beneficial owner and taking adequate measures, on a risk-sensitive basis, to verify his identity so that the relevant person is satisfied that he knows who the beneficial owner is, including,

in the case of a legal person, trust or similar legal arrangement, measures to understand the ownership and control structure of the person, trust or arrangement; and
   (c)   obtaining information on the purpose and intended nature of the business relationship.

[2877AE]

NOTES
Commencement: 15 December 2007.

6 Meaning of beneficial owner

(1)   In the case of a body corporate, "beneficial owner" means any individual who—
   (a)   as respects any body other than a company whose securities are listed on a regulated market, ultimately owns or controls (whether through direct or indirect ownership or control, including through bearer share holdings) more than 25% of the shares or voting rights in the body; or
   (b)   as respects any body corporate, otherwise exercises control over the management of the body.

(2)   In the case of a partnership (other than a limited liability partnership), "beneficial owner" means any individual who—
   (a)   ultimately is entitled to or controls (whether the entitlement or control is direct or indirect) more than a 25% share of the capital or profits of the partnership or more than 25% of the voting rights in the partnership; or
   (b)   otherwise exercises control over the management of the partnership.

(3)   In the case of a trust, "beneficial owner" means—
   (a)   any individual who is entitled to a specified interest in at least 25% of the capital of the trust property;
   (b)   as respects any trust other than one which is set up or operates entirely for the benefit of individuals falling within sub-paragraph (a), the class of persons in whose main interest the trust is set up or operates;
   (c)   any individual who has control over the trust.

(4)   In paragraph (3)—
"specified interest" means a vested interest which is—
   (a)   in possession or in remainder or reversion (or, in Scotland, in fee); and
   (b)   defeasible or indefeasible;
"control" means a power (whether exercisable alone, jointly with another person or with the consent of another person) under the trust instrument or by law to—
   (a)   dispose of, advance, lend, invest, pay or apply trust property;
   (b)   vary the trust;
   (c)   add or remove a person as a beneficiary or to or from a class of beneficiaries;
   (d)   appoint or remove trustees;
   (e)   direct, withhold consent to or veto the exercise of a power such as is mentioned in sub-paragraph (a), (b), (c) or (d).

(5)   For the purposes of paragraph (3)—
   (a)   where an individual is the beneficial owner of a body corporate which is entitled to a specified interest in the capital of the trust property or which has control over the trust, the individual is to be regarded as entitled to the interest or having control over the trust; and
   (b)   an individual does not have control solely as a result of—
      (i)   his consent being required in accordance with section 32(1)(c) of the Trustee Act 1925 (power of advancement);
      (ii)   any discretion delegated to him under section 34 of the Pensions Act 1995 (power of investment and delegation);
      (iii)   the power to give a direction conferred on him by section 19(2) of the Trusts of Land and Appointment of Trustees Act 1996 (appointment and retirement of trustee at instance of beneficiaries); or
      (iv)   the power exercisable collectively at common law to vary or extinguish a trust where the beneficiaries under the trust are of full age and capacity and (taken together) absolutely entitled to the property subject to the trust (or, in Scotland, have a full and unqualified right to the fee).

(6)   In the case of a legal entity or legal arrangement which does not fall within paragraph (1), (2) or (3), "beneficial owner" means—
   (a)   where the individuals who benefit from the entity or arrangement have been determined, any individual who benefits from at least 25% of the property of the entity or arrangement;

    (b)   where the individuals who benefit from the entity or arrangement have yet to be determined, the class of persons in whose main interest the entity or arrangement is set up or operates;

    (c)   any individual who exercises control over at least 25% of the property of the entity or arrangement.

(7)   For the purposes of paragraph (6), where an individual is the beneficial owner of a body corporate which benefits from or exercises control over the property of the entity or arrangement, the individual is to be regarded as benefiting from or exercising control over the property of the entity or arrangement.

(8)   In the case of an estate of a deceased person in the course of administration, "beneficial owner" means—

    (a)   in England and Wales and Northern Ireland, the executor, original or by representation, or administrator for the time being of a deceased person;

    (b)   in Scotland, the executor for the purposes of the Executors (Scotland) Act 1900.

(9)   In any other case, "beneficial owner" means the individual who ultimately owns or controls the customer or on whose behalf a transaction is being conducted.

(10)   In this regulation—

    "arrangement", "entity" and "trust" means an arrangement, entity or trust which administers and distributes funds;

    "limited liability partnership" has the meaning given by the Limited Liability Partnerships Act 2000.

[2877AF]

NOTES

Commencement: 15 December 2007.

7 Application of customer due diligence measures

(1)   Subject to regulations 9, 10, 12, 13, 14, 16(4) and 17, a relevant person must apply customer due diligence measures when he—

    (a)   establishes a business relationship;

    (b)   carries out an occasional transaction;

    (c)   suspects money laundering or terrorist financing;

    (d)   doubts the veracity or adequacy of documents, data or information previously obtained for the purposes of identification or verification.

(2)   Subject to regulation 16(4), a relevant person must also apply customer due diligence measures at other appropriate times to existing customers on a risk-sensitive basis.

(3)   A relevant person must—

    (a)   determine the extent of customer due diligence measures on a risk-sensitive basis depending on the type of customer, business relationship, product or transaction; and

    (b)   be able to demonstrate to his supervisory authority that the extent of the measures is appropriate in view of the risks of money laundering and terrorist financing.

(4)   Where—

    (a)   a relevant person is required to apply customer due diligence measures in the case of a trust, legal entity (other than a body corporate) or a legal arrangement (other than a trust); and

    (b)   the class of persons in whose main interest the trust, entity or arrangement is set up or operates is identified as a beneficial owner,

the relevant person is not required to identify all the members of the class.

(5)   Paragraph (3)(b) does not apply to the National Savings Bank or the Director of Savings.

[2877AG]

NOTES

Commencement: 15 December 2007.

8 Ongoing monitoring

(1)   A relevant person must conduct ongoing monitoring of a business relationship.

(2)   "Ongoing monitoring" of a business relationship means—

    (a)   scrutiny of transactions undertaken throughout the course of the relationship (including, where necessary, the source of funds) to ensure that the transactions are consistent with the relevant person's knowledge of the customer, his business and risk profile; and

    (b)   keeping the documents, data or information obtained for the purpose of applying customer due diligence measures up-to-date.

PART III
STATUTORY INSTRUMENTS

(3)   Regulation 7(3) applies to the duty to conduct ongoing monitoring under paragraph (1) as it applies to customer due diligence measures.

[2877AH]

NOTES
Commencement: 15 December 2007.

9 Timing of verification

(1)   This regulation applies in respect of the duty under regulation 7(1)(a) and (b) to apply the customer due diligence measures referred to in regulation 5(a) and (b).

(2)   Subject to paragraphs (3) to (5) and regulation 10, a relevant person must verify the identity of the customer (and any beneficial owner) before the establishment of a business relationship or the carrying out of an occasional transaction.

(3)   Such verification may be completed during the establishment of a business relationship if—
  (a)   this is necessary not to interrupt the normal conduct of business; and
  (b)   there is little risk of money laundering or terrorist financing occurring,
provided that the verification is completed as soon as practicable after contact is first established.

(4)   The verification of the identity of the beneficiary under a life insurance policy may take place after the business relationship has been established provided that it takes place at or before the time of payout or at or before the time the beneficiary exercises a right vested under the policy.

(5)   The verification of the identity of a bank account holder may take place after the bank account has been opened provided that there are adequate safeguards in place to ensure that—
  (a)   the account is not closed; and
  (b)   transactions are not carried out by or on behalf of the account holder (including any payment from the account to the account holder),
before verification has been completed.

[2877AI]

NOTES
Commencement: 15 December 2007.

10 Casinos

(1)   A casino must establish and verify the identity of—
  (a)   all customers to whom the casino makes facilities for gaming available—
    (i)   before entry to any premises where such facilities are provided; or
    (ii)   where the facilities are for remote gaming, before access is given to such facilities; or
  (b)   if the specified conditions are met, all customers who, in the course of any period of 24 hours—
    (i)   purchase from, or exchange with, the casino chips with a total value of 2,000 euro or more;
    (ii)   pay the casino 2,000 [euro] or more for the use of gaming machines; or
    (iii) pay to, or stake with, the casino 2,000 euro or more in connection with facilities for remote gaming.

(2)   The specified conditions are—
  (a)   the casino verifies the identity of each customer before or immediately after such purchase, exchange, payment or stake takes place, and
  (b)   the Gambling Commission is satisfied that the casino has appropriate procedures in place to monitor and record—
    (i)   the total value of chips purchased from or exchanged with the casino;
    (ii)   the total money paid for the use of gaming machines; or
    (iii) the total money paid or staked in connection with facilities for remote gaming,
  by each customer.

(3)   In this regulation—
  "gaming", "gaming machine", "remote operating licence" and "stake" have the meanings given by, respectively, sections 6(1) (gaming & game of chance), 235 (gaming machine), 67 (remote gambling) and 353(1) (interpretation) of the Gambling Act 2005;
  "premises" means premises subject to—
    (a)   a casino premises licence within the meaning of section 150(1)(a) of the Gambling Act 2005 (nature of licence); or

    (b)   a converted casino premises licence within the meaning of paragraph 65 of Part 7 of Schedule 4 to the Gambling Act 2005 (Commencement No 6 and Transitional Provisions) Order 2006;

"remote gaming" means gaming provided pursuant to a remote operating licence.

[2877AJ]

NOTES

Commencement: 15 December 2007.

Para (1): word in square brackets in sub-para (b)(ii) inserted by the Money Laundering (Amendment) Regulations 2007, SI 2007/3299, reg 2(a), as from 15 December 2007.

11 Requirement to cease transactions etc

(1)   Where, in relation to any customer, a relevant person is unable to apply customer due diligence measures in accordance with the provisions of this Part, he—

    (a)   must not carry out a transaction with or for the customer through a bank account;

    (b)   must not establish a business relationship or carry out an occasional transaction with the customer;

    (c)   must terminate any existing business relationship with the customer;

    (d)   must consider whether he is required to make a disclosure by Part 7 of the Proceeds of Crime Act 2002 or Part 3 of the Terrorism Act 2000.

(2)   Paragraph (1) does not apply where a lawyer or other professional adviser is in the course of ascertaining the legal position for his client or performing his task of defending or representing that client in, or concerning, legal proceedings, including advice on the institution or avoidance of proceedings.

(3)   In paragraph (2), "other professional adviser" means an auditor, accountant or tax adviser who is a member of a professional body which is established for any such persons and which makes provision for—

    (a)   testing the competence of those seeking admission to membership of such a body as a condition for such admission; and

    (b)   imposing and maintaining professional and ethical standards for its members, as well as imposing sanctions for non-compliance with those standards.

[2877AK]

NOTES

Commencement: 15 December 2007.

12 Exception for trustees of debt issues

(1)   A relevant person—

    (a)   who is appointed by the issuer of instruments or securities specified in paragraph (2) as trustee of an issue of such instruments or securities; or

    (b)   whose customer is a trustee of an issue of such instruments or securities,

is not required to apply the customer due diligence measure referred to in regulation 5(b) in respect of the holders of such instruments or securities.

(2)   The specified instruments and securities are—

    (a)   instruments which fall within article 77 of the Financial Services and Markets Act 2000 (Regulated Activities) Order 2001; and

    (b)   securities which fall within article 78 of that Order.

[2877AL]

NOTES

Commencement: 15 December 2007.

13 Simplified due diligence

(1)   A relevant person is not required to apply customer due diligence measures in the circumstances mentioned in regulation 7(1)(a), (b) or (d) where he has reasonable grounds for believing that the customer, transaction or product related to such transaction, falls within any of the following paragraphs.

(2)   The customer is—

    (a)   a credit or financial institution which is subject to the requirements of the money laundering directive; or

    (b)   a credit or financial institution (or equivalent institution) which—

        (i)   is situated in a non-EEA state which imposes requirements equivalent to those laid down in the money laundering directive; and

        (ii)   is supervised for compliance with those requirements.

(3) The customer is a company whose securities are listed on a regulated market subject to specified disclosure obligations.

(4) The customer is an independent legal professional and the product is an account into which monies are pooled, provided that—
    (a) where the pooled account is held in a non-EEA state—
        (i) that state imposes requirements to combat money laundering and terrorist financing which are consistent with international standards; and
        (ii) the independent legal professional is supervised in that state for compliance with those requirements; and
    (b) information on the identity of the persons on whose behalf monies are held in the pooled account is available, on request, to the institution which acts as a depository institution for the account.

(5) The customer is a public authority in the United Kingdom.

(6) The customer is a public authority which fulfils all the conditions set out in paragraph 2 of Schedule 2 to these Regulations.

(7) The product is—
    (a) a life insurance contract where the annual premium is no more than 1,000 euro or where a single premium of no more than 2,500 euro is paid;
    (b) an insurance contract for the purposes of a pension scheme where the contract contains no surrender clause and cannot be used as collateral;
    (c) a pension, superannuation or similar scheme which provides retirement benefits to employees, where contributions are made by an employer or by way of deduction from an employee's wages and the scheme rules do not permit the assignment of a member's interest under the scheme (other than an assignment permitted by section 44 of the Welfare Reform and Pensions Act 1999 (disapplication of restrictions on alienation) or section 91(5)(a) of the Pensions Act 1995 (inalienability of occupational pension)); or
    (d) electronic money, within the meaning of Article 1(3)(b) of the electronic money directive, where—
        (i) if the device cannot be recharged, the maximum amount stored in the device is no more than 150 euro; or
        (ii) if the device can be recharged, a limit of 2,500 euro is imposed on the total amount transacted in a calendar year, except when an amount of 1,000 euro or more is redeemed in the same calendar year by the bearer (within the meaning of Article 3 of the electronic money directive).

(8) The product and any transaction related to such product fulfils all the conditions set out in paragraph 3 of Schedule 2 to these Regulations.

(9) The product is a child trust fund within the meaning given by section 1(2) of the Child Trust Funds Act 2004.

[2877AM]

NOTES
Commencement: 15 December 2007.

---

14 Enhanced customer due diligence and ongoing monitoring

(1) A relevant person must apply on a risk-sensitive basis enhanced customer due diligence measures and enhanced ongoing monitoring—
    (a) in accordance with paragraphs (2) to (4);
    (b) in any other situation which by its nature can present a higher risk of money laundering or terrorist financing.

(2) Where the customer has not been physically present for identification purposes, a relevant person must take specific and adequate measures to compensate for the higher risk, for example, by applying one or more of the following measures—
    (a) ensuring that the customer's identity is established by additional documents, data or information;
    (b) supplementary measures to verify or certify the documents supplied, or requiring confirmatory certification by a credit or financial institution which is subject to the money laundering directive;
    (c) ensuring that the first payment is carried out through an account opened in the customer's name with a credit institution.

(3) A credit institution ("the correspondent") which has or proposes to have a correspondent banking relationship with a respondent institution ("the respondent") from a non-EEA state must—
    (a) gather sufficient information about the respondent to understand fully the nature of its business;

(b)   determine from publicly-available information the reputation of the respondent and the quality of its supervision;

(c)   assess the respondent's anti-money laundering and anti-terrorist financing controls;

(d)   obtain approval from senior management before establishing a new correspondent banking relationship;

(e)   document the respective responsibilities of the respondent and correspondent; and

(f)   be satisfied that, in respect of those of the respondent's customers who have direct access to accounts of the correspondent, the respondent—

    (i)   has verified the identity of, and conducts ongoing monitoring in respect of, such customers; and

    (ii)   is able to provide to the correspondent, upon request, the documents, data or information obtained when applying customer due diligence measures and ongoing monitoring.

(4)   A relevant person who proposes to have a business relationship or carry out an occasional transaction with a politically exposed person must—

(a)   have approval from senior management for establishing the business relationship with that person;

(b)   take adequate measures to establish the source of wealth and source of funds which are involved in the proposed business relationship or occasional transaction; and

(c)   where the business relationship is entered into, conduct enhanced ongoing monitoring of the relationship.

(5)   In paragraph (4), "a politically exposed person" means a person who is—

(a)   an individual who is or has, at any time in the preceding year, been entrusted with a prominent public function by—

    (i)   a state other than the United Kingdom;

    (ii)   a Community institution; or

    (iii)   an international body,

including a person who falls in any of the categories listed in paragraph 4(1)(a) of Schedule 2;

(b)   an immediate family member of a person referred to in sub-paragraph (a), including a person who falls in any of the categories listed in paragraph 4(1)(c) of Schedule 2; or

(c)   a known close associate of a person referred to in sub-paragraph (a), including a person who falls in either of the categories listed in paragraph 4(1)(d) of Schedule 2.

(6)   For the purpose of deciding whether a person is a known close associate of a person referred to in paragraph (5)(a), a relevant person need only have regard to information which is in his possession or is publicly known.

[2877AN]

NOTES

Commencement: 15 December 2007.

15   Branches and subsidiaries

(1)   A credit or financial institution must require its branches and subsidiary undertakings which are located in a non-EEA state to apply, to the extent permitted by the law of that state, measures at least equivalent to those set out in these Regulations with regard to customer due diligence measures, ongoing monitoring and record-keeping.

(2)   Where the law of a non-EEA state does not permit the application of such equivalent measures by the branch or subsidiary undertaking located in that state, the credit or financial institution must—

(a)   inform its supervisory authority accordingly; and

(b)   take additional measures to handle effectively the risk of money laundering and terrorist financing.

(3)   In this regulation "subsidiary undertaking"—

(a)   except in relation to an incorporated friendly society, has the meaning given by section 1162 of the Companies Act 2006 (parent and subsidiary undertakings) and, in relation to a body corporate in or formed under the law of an EEA state other than the United Kingdom, includes an undertaking which is a subsidiary undertaking within the meaning of any rule of law in force in that state for purposes connected with implementation of the European Council Seventh Company Law Directive 83/349/EEC of 13th June 1983 on consolidated accounts;

(b)   in relation to an incorporated friendly society, means a body corporate of which the society has control within the meaning of section 13(9)(a) or (aa) of the Friendly Societies Act 1992 (control of subsidiaries and other bodies corporate).

(4)   Before the entry into force of section 1162 of the Companies Act 2006 the reference to that section in paragraph (3)(a) shall be treated as a reference to section 258 of the Companies Act 1985 (parent and subsidiary undertakings).

[2877AO]

NOTES
Commencement: 15 December 2007.

16   Shell banks, anonymous accounts etc

(1)   A credit institution must not enter into, or continue, a correspondent banking relationship with a shell bank.

(2)   A credit institution must take appropriate measures to ensure that it does not enter into, or continue, a corresponding banking relationship with a bank which is known to permit its accounts to be used by a shell bank.

(3)   A credit or financial institution carrying on business in the United Kingdom must not set up an anonymous account or an anonymous passbook for any new or existing customer.

(4)   As soon as reasonably practicable on or after 15th December 2007 all credit and financial institutions carrying on business in the United Kingdom must apply customer due diligence measures to, and conduct ongoing monitoring of, all anonymous accounts and passbooks in existence on that date and in any event before such accounts or passbooks are used.

(5)   A "shell bank" means a credit institution, or an institution engaged in equivalent activities, incorporated in a jurisdiction in which it has no physical presence involving meaningful decision-making and management, and which is not part of a financial conglomerate or third-country financial conglomerate.

(6)   In this regulation, "financial conglomerate" and "third-country financial conglomerate" have the meanings given by regulations 1(2) and 7(1) respectively of the Financial Conglomerates and Other Financial Groups Regulations 2004.

[2877AP]

NOTES
Commencement: 15 December 2007.

17   Reliance

(1)   A relevant person may rely on a person who falls within paragraph (2) (or who the relevant person has reasonable grounds to believe falls within paragraph (2)) to apply any customer due diligence measures provided that—
   (a)   the other person consents to being relied on; and
   (b)   notwithstanding the relevant person's reliance on the other person, the relevant person remains liable for any failure to apply such measures.

(2)   The persons are—
   (a)   a credit or financial institution which is an authorised person;
   (b)   a relevant person who is—
      (i)   an auditor, insolvency practitioner, external accountant, tax adviser or independent legal professional; and
      (ii)   supervised for the purposes of these Regulations by one of the bodies listed in Part 1 of Schedule 3;
   (c)   a person who carries on business in another EEA state who is—
      (i)   a credit or financial institution, auditor, insolvency practitioner, external accountant, tax adviser or independent legal professional;
      (ii)   subject to mandatory professional registration recognised by law; and
      (iii) supervised for compliance with the requirements laid down in the money laundering directive in accordance with section 2 of Chapter V of that directive; or
   (d)   a person who carries on business in a non-EEA state who is—
      (i)   a credit or financial institution (or equivalent institution), auditor, insolvency practitioner, external accountant, tax adviser or independent legal professional;
      (ii)   subject to mandatory professional registration recognised by law;
      (iii) subject to requirements equivalent to those laid down in the money laundering directive; and
      (iv)   supervised for compliance with those requirements in a manner equivalent to section 2 of Chapter V of the money laundering directive.

(3)   In paragraph (2)(c)(i) and (d)(i), "auditor" and "insolvency practitioner" includes a person situated in another EEA state or a non-EEA state who provides services equivalent to the services provided by an auditor or insolvency practitioner.

(4) Nothing in this regulation prevents a relevant person applying customer due diligence measures by means of an outsourcing service provider or agent provided that the relevant person remains liable for any failure to apply such measures.

(5) *In this regulation, "financial institution" excludes money service businesses.*

[2877AQ]

NOTES
Commencement: 15 December 2007.
Para (5): substituted by the Payment Services Regulations 2009, SI 2009/209, reg 126, Sch 6, Pt 2, para 6(b), as from 1 November 2009 as follows (for the full commencement details of the 2009 Regulations, see reg 1 of those Regulations at **[4387]**)—

"(5) In this regulation, "financial institution" excludes—
  (a) any money service business;
  (b) any authorised payment institution, EEA authorised payment institution or small payment institution (within the meaning of the Payment Services Regulations 2009) which provides payment services mainly falling within paragraph 1(f) of Schedule 1 to those Regulations.".

18 Directions where Financial Action Task Force applies counter-measures

The Treasury may direct any relevant person—
  (a) not to enter into a business relationship;
  (b) not to carry out an occasional transaction; or
  (c) not to proceed any further with a business relationship or occasional transaction,

with a person who is situated or incorporated in a non-EEA state to which the Financial Action Task Force has decided to apply counter-measures.

[2877AR]

NOTES
Commencement: 15 December 2007.

PART 3
RECORD-KEEPING, PROCEDURES AND TRAINING

19 Record-keeping

(1) Subject to paragraph (4), a relevant person must keep the records specified in paragraph (2) for at least the period specified in paragraph (3).

(2) The records are—
  (a) a copy of, or the references to, the evidence of the customer's identity obtained pursuant to regulation 7, 8, 10, 14 or 16(4);
  (b) the supporting records (consisting of the original documents or copies) in respect of a business relationship or occasional transaction which is the subject of customer due diligence measures or ongoing monitoring.

(3) The period is five years beginning on—
  (a) in the case of the records specified in paragraph (2)(a), the date on which—
    (i) the occasional transaction is completed; or
    (ii) the business relationship ends; or
  (b) in the case of the records specified in paragraph (2)(b)—
    (i) where the records relate to a particular transaction, the date on which the transaction is completed;
    (ii) for all other records, the date on which the business relationship ends.

(4) A relevant person who is relied on by another person must keep the records specified in paragraph (2)(a) for five years beginning on the date on which he is relied on for the purposes of regulation 7, 10, 14 or 16(4) in relation to any business relationship or occasional transaction.

(5) A person referred to in regulation 17(2)(a) or (b) who is relied on by a relevant person must, if requested by the person relying on him within the period referred to in paragraph (4)—
  (a) as soon as reasonably practicable make available to the person who is relying on him any information about the customer (and any beneficial owner) which he obtained when applying customer due diligence measures; and
  (b) as soon as reasonably practicable forward to the person who is relying on him copies of any identification and verification data and other relevant documents on the identity of the customer (and any beneficial owner) which he obtained when applying those measures.

(6) A relevant person who relies on a person referred to in regulation 17(2)(c) or (d) (a "third party") to apply customer due diligence measures must take steps to ensure that the third party will, if requested by the relevant person within the period referred to in paragraph (4)—

(a)   as soon as reasonably practicable make available to him any information about the customer (and any beneficial owner) which the third party obtained when applying customer due diligence measures; and

(b)   as soon as reasonably practicable forward to him copies of any identification and verification data and other relevant documents on the identity of the customer (and any beneficial owner) which the third party obtained when applying those measures.

(7)   Paragraphs (5) and (6) do not apply where a relevant person applies customer due diligence measures by means of an outsourcing service provider or agent.

(8)   For the purposes of this regulation, a person relies on another person where he does so in accordance with regulation 17(1).

[2877AS]

NOTES
Commencement: 15 December 2007.

20 Policies and procedures

(1)   A relevant person must establish and maintain appropriate and risk-sensitive policies and procedures relating to—
(a)   customer due diligence measures and ongoing monitoring;
(b)   reporting;
(c)   record-keeping;
(d)   internal control;
(e)   risk assessment and management;
(f)   the monitoring and management of compliance with, and the internal communication of, such policies and procedures,
in order to prevent activities related to money laundering and terrorist financing.

(2)   The policies and procedures referred to in paragraph (1) include policies and procedures—
(a)   which provide for the identification and scrutiny of—
  (i)   complex or unusually large transactions;
  (ii)   unusual patterns of transactions which have no apparent economic or visible lawful purpose; and
  (iii) any other activity which the relevant person regards as particularly likely by its nature to be related to money laundering or terrorist financing;
(b)   which specify the taking of additional measures, where appropriate, to prevent the use for money laundering or terrorist financing of products and transactions which might favour anonymity;
(c)   to determine whether a customer is a politically exposed person;
(d)   under which—
  (i)   an individual in the relevant person's organisation is a nominated officer under Part 7 of the Proceeds of Crime Act 2002 and Part 3 of the Terrorism Act 2000;
  (ii)   anyone in the organisation to whom information or other matter comes in the course of the business as a result of which he knows or suspects or has reasonable grounds for knowing or suspecting that a person is engaged in money laundering or terrorist financing is required to comply with Part 7 of the Proceeds of Crime Act 2002 or, as the case may be, Part 3 of the Terrorism Act 2000; and
  (iii) where a disclosure is made to the nominated officer, he must consider it in the light of any relevant information which is available to the relevant person and determine whether it gives rise to knowledge or suspicion or reasonable grounds for knowledge or suspicion that a person is engaged in money laundering or terrorist financing.

(3)   Paragraph (2)(d) does not apply where the relevant person is an individual who neither employs nor acts in association with any other person.

(4)   A credit or financial institution must establish and maintain systems which enable it to respond fully and rapidly to enquiries from financial investigators accredited under section 3 of the Proceeds of Crime Act 2002 (accreditation and training), persons acting on behalf of the Scottish Ministers in their capacity as an enforcement authority under that Act, officers of Revenue and Customs or constables as to—
(a)   whether it maintains, or has maintained during the previous five years, a business relationship with any person; and
(b)   the nature of that relationship.

(5)   A credit or financial institution must communicate where relevant the policies and procedures which it establishes and maintains in accordance with this regulation to its branches and subsidiary undertakings which are located outside the United Kingdom.

(6)   In this regulation—

"politically exposed person" has the same meaning as in regulation 14(4);
"subsidiary undertaking" has the same meaning as in regulation 15.

[2877AT]

NOTES
Commencement: 15 December 2007.

21 Training

A relevant person must take appropriate measures so that all relevant employees of his are—
   (a)   made aware of the law relating to money laundering and terrorist financing; and
   (b)   regularly given training in how to recognise and deal with transactions and other activities which may be related to money laundering or terrorist financing.

[2877AU]

NOTES
Commencement: 15 December 2007.

PART 4
SUPERVISION AND REGISTRATION
Interpretation

22 Interpretation

(1) In this Part—
"Annex I financial institution" means any undertaking which falls within regulation 3(3)(a) other than—
   (a)   a consumer credit financial institution;
   (b)   a money service business; *or*
   (c)   an authorised person;
   [(d)   a bill payment service provider; or
   (e)   a telecommunication, digital and IT payment service provider;]
"consumer credit financial institution" means any undertaking which falls within regulation 3(3)(a) and which requires, under section 21 of the Consumer Credit Act 1974 (businesses needing a licence), a licence to carry on a consumer credit business, other than—
   (a)   a person covered by a group licence issued by the OFT under section 22 of that Act (standard and group licences);
   (b)   a money service business; *or*
   (c)   an authorised person;
   [(d)   a bill payment service provider; or
   (e)   a telecommunication, digital and IT payment service provider].

(2) In paragraph (1), "consumer credit business" has the meaning given by section 189(1) of the Consumer Credit Act 1974 (definitions) and, on the entry into force of section 23(a) of the Consumer Credit Act 2006 (definitions of "consumer credit business" and "consumer hire business"), has the meaning given by section 189(1) of the Consumer Credit Act 1974 as amended by section 23(a) of the Consumer Credit Act 2006.

[2877AV]

NOTES
Commencement: 15 December 2007.
Para (1): in both of the definitions "Annex I financial institution" and "consumer credit financial institution" the word "or" at the end of sub-para (b) is revoked, and sub-para (d), (e) are added, by the Payment Services Regulations 2009, SI 2009/209, reg 126, Sch 6, Pt 2, para 6(c), as from 1 November 2009 (for the full commencement details of the 2009 Regulations, see reg 1 of those Regulations at **[4387]**).
Note: the Consumer Credit Act 2006, s 23 entered into force on 6 April 2008.

Supervision

23 Supervisory authorities

(1) Subject to paragraph (2), the following bodies are supervisory authorities—
   (a)   the Authority is the supervisory authority for—
      (i)   credit and financial institutions which are authorised persons;
      (ii)   trust or company service providers which are authorised persons;
      (iii)   Annex I financial institutions;
   (b)   the OFT is the supervisory authority for—
      (i)   consumer credit financial institutions;
      (ii)   estate agents;

PART III
STATUTORY INSTRUMENTS

(c)   each of the professional bodies listed in Schedule 3 is the supervisory authority for relevant persons who are regulated by it;

(d)   the Commissioners are the supervisory authority for—

    (i)   high value dealers;

    (ii)   money service businesses which are not supervised by the Authority;

    (iii)   trust or company service providers which are not supervised by the Authority or one of the bodies listed in Schedule 3;

    (iv)   auditors, external accountants and tax advisers who are not supervised by one of the bodies listed in Schedule 3;

    [(v)   bill payment service providers which are not supervised by the Authority;

    (vi)   telecommunication, digital and IT payment service providers which are not supervised by the Authority].

(e)   the Gambling Commission is the supervisory authority for casinos;

(f)   DETI is the supervisory authority for—

    (i)   credit unions in Northern Ireland;

    (ii)   insolvency practitioners authorised by it under article 351 of the Insolvency (Northern Ireland) Order 1989;

(g)   the Secretary of State is the supervisory authority for insolvency practitioners authorised by him under section 393 of the Insolvency Act 1986 (grant, refusal and withdrawal of authorisation).

(2)   Where under paragraph (1) there is more than one supervisory authority for a relevant person, the supervisory authorities may agree that one of them will act as the supervisory authority for that person.

(3)   Where an agreement has been made under paragraph (2), the authority which has agreed to act as the supervisory authority must notify the relevant person or publish the agreement in such manner as it considers appropriate.

(4)   Where no agreement has been made under paragraph (2), the supervisory authorities for a relevant person must cooperate in the performance of their functions under these Regulations.

[2877AW]

NOTES

Commencement: 15 December 2007.

Para (1): sub-paras (d)(v), (vi) inserted by the Payment Services Regulations 2009, SI 2009/209, reg 126, Sch 6, Pt 2, para 6(d), as from 1 November 2009 (for the full commencement details of the 2009 Regulations, see reg 1 of those Regulations at **[4387]**).

24 Duties of supervisory authorities

(1)   A supervisory authority must effectively monitor the relevant persons for whom it is the supervisory authority and take necessary measures for the purpose of securing compliance by such persons with the requirements of these Regulations.

(2)   A supervisory authority which, in the course of carrying out any of its functions under these Regulations, knows or suspects that a person is or has engaged in money laundering or terrorist financing must promptly inform the Serious Organised Crime Agency.

(3)   A disclosure made under paragraph (2) is not to be taken to breach any restriction, however imposed, on the disclosure of information.

(4)   The functions of the Authority under these Regulations shall be treated for the purposes of Parts 1, 2 and 4 of Schedule 1 to the 2000 Act (the Financial Services Authority) as functions conferred on the Authority under that Act.

[2877AX]

NOTES

Commencement: 15 December 2007.

Registration of high value dealers, money service businesses and trust or company service providers

25 Duty to maintain registers

(1)   The Commissioners must maintain registers of—

    (a)   high value dealers;

    (b)   money service businesses for which they are the supervisory authority; *and*

    (c)   trust or company service providers for which they are the supervisory authority;

    [(d)   bill payment service providers for which they are the supervisory authority; and

    (e)   telecommunication, digital and IT payment service providers for which they are the supervisory authority].

(2)   The Commissioners may keep the registers in any form they think fit.

(3)   The Commissioners may publish or make available for public inspection all or part of a register maintained under this regulation.

[2877AY]

NOTES
Commencement: 15 December 2007.
Para (1): the word "and" at the end of sub-para (b) is revoked, and sub-paras (d), (e) are added, by the Payment Services Regulations 2009, SI 2009/209, reg 126, Sch 6, Pt 2, para 6(e), as from 1 November 2009 (for the full commencement details of the 2009 Regulations, see reg 1 of those Regulations at **[4387]**).

26   Requirement to be registered

(1)   A person in respect of whom the Commissioners are required to maintain a register under regulation 25 must not act as a—
    (a)   high value dealer;
    (b)   money service business; *or*
    (c)   trust or company service provider,
    [(d)   bill payment service provider; or
    (e)   telecommunication, digital and IT payment service provider,]
unless he is included in the register.

(2)   Paragraph (1) and regulation 29 are subject to the transitional provisions set out in regulation 50.

[2877AZ]

NOTES
Commencement: 15 December 2007.
Para (1): the word "or" at the end of sub-para (b) is revoked, and sub-paras (d), (e) are added, by the Payment Services Regulations 2009, SI 2009/209, reg 126, Sch 6, Pt 2, para 6(f), as from 1 November 2009 (for the full commencement details of the 2009 Regulations, see reg 1 of those Regulations at **[4387]**).

27   Applications for registration in a register maintained under regulation 25

(1)   An applicant for registration in a register maintained under regulation 25 must make an application in such manner and provide such information as the Commissioners may specify.

(2)   The information which the Commissioners may specify includes—
    (a)   the applicant's name and (if different) the name of the business;
    (b)   the nature of the business;
    (c)   the name of the nominated officer (if any);
    (d)   in relation to a money service business or trust or company service provider—
        (i)   the name of any person who effectively directs or will direct the business and any beneficial owner of the business; and
        (ii)   information needed by the Commissioners to decide whether they must refuse the application pursuant to regulation 28.

(3)   At any time after receiving an application and before determining it, the Commissioners may require the applicant to provide, within 21 days beginning with the date of being requested to do so, such further information as they reasonably consider necessary to enable them to determine the application.

(4)   If at any time after the applicant has provided the Commissioners with any information under paragraph (1) or (3)—
    (a)   there is a material change affecting any matter contained in that information; or
    (b)   it becomes apparent to that person that the information contains a significant inaccuracy,
he must provide the Commissioners with details of the change or, as the case may be, a correction of the inaccuracy within 30 days beginning with the date of the occurrence of the change (or the discovery of the inaccuracy) or within such later time as may be agreed with the Commissioners.

(5)   The obligation in paragraph (4) applies also to material changes or significant inaccuracies affecting any matter contained in any supplementary information provided pursuant to that paragraph.

(6)   Any information to be provided to the Commissioners under this regulation must be in such form or verified in such manner as they may specify.

[2877BA]

NOTES
Commencement: 15 December 2007.

28   Fit and proper test

(1)   The Commissioners must refuse to register an applicant as a money service business or trust or company service provider if they are satisfied that—

PART III
STATUTORY INSTRUMENTS

(a)   the applicant;

(b)   a person who effectively directs, or will effectively direct, the business or service provider;

(c)   a beneficial owner of the business or service provider; or

(d)   the nominated officer of the business or service provider,

is not a fit and proper person.

(2)   For the purposes of paragraph (1), a person is not a fit and proper person if he—

  (a)   has been convicted of—

     (i)   an offence under the Terrorism Act 2000;

    (ii)   an offence under paragraph 7(2) or (3) of Schedule 3 to the Anti-Terrorism, Crime and Security Act 2001 (offences);

    (iii)   an offence under the Terrorism Act 2006;

    (iv)   an offence under Part 7 (money laundering) of, or listed in Schedule 2 (lifestyle offences: England and Wales), 4 (lifestyle offences: Scotland) or 5 (lifestyle offences: Northern Ireland) to, the Proceeds of Crime Act 2002;

    (v)   an offence under the Fraud Act 2006 or, in Scotland, the common law offence of fraud;

    (vi)   an offence under section 72(1), (3) or (8) of the Value Added Tax Act 1994 (offences); or

    (vii)   the common law offence of cheating the public revenue;

  (b)   has been adjudged bankrupt or sequestration of his estate has been awarded and (in either case) he has not been discharged;

  (c)   is subject to a disqualification order under the Company Directors Disqualification Act 1986;

  (d)   is or has been subject to a confiscation order under the Proceeds of Crime Act 2002;

  (e)   has consistently failed to comply with the requirements of these Regulations, the Money Laundering Regulations 2003 or the Money Laundering Regulations 2001;

  (f)   has consistently failed to comply with the requirements of regulation 2006/1781/EC of the European Parliament and of the Council of 15th November 2006 on information on the payer accompanying the transfer of funds;

  (g)   has effectively directed a business which falls within sub-paragraph (e) or (f);

  (h)   is otherwise not a fit and proper person with regard to the risk of money laundering or terrorist financing.

(3)   For the purposes of this regulation, a conviction for an offence listed in paragraph (2)(a) is to be disregarded if it is spent for the purposes of the Rehabilitation of Offenders Act 1974.

[2877BB]

NOTES
Commencement: 15 December 2007.

29 Determination of applications under regulation 27

(1)   Subject to regulation 28, the Commissioners may refuse to register an applicant for registration in a register maintained under regulation 25 only if—

  (a)   any requirement of, or imposed under, regulation 27 has not been complied with;

  (b)   it appears to the Commissioners that any information provided pursuant to regulation 27 is false or misleading in a material particular; or

  (c)   the applicant has failed to pay a charge imposed by them under regulation 35(1).

(2)   The Commissioners must within 45 days beginning either with the date on which they receive the application or, where applicable, with the date on which they receive any further information required under regulation 27(3), give the applicant notice of—

  (a)   their decision to register the applicant; or

  (b)   the following matters—

     (i)   their decision not to register the applicant;

    (ii)   the reasons for their decision;

    (iii)   the right to require a review under regulation 43; and

    (iv)   the right to appeal under regulation 44(1)(a).

(3)   The Commissioners must, as soon as practicable after deciding to register a person, include him in the relevant register.

[2877BC]

NOTES
Commencement: 15 December 2007.

30 Cancellation of registration in a register maintained under regulation 25

(1)   The Commissioners must cancel the registration of a money service business or trust or company service provider in a register maintained under regulation 25(1) if, at any time after registration, they are satisfied that he or any person mentioned in regulation 28(1)(b), (c) or (d) is not a fit and proper person within the meaning of regulation 28(2).

(2)   The Commissioners may cancel a person's registration in a register maintained by them under regulation 25 if, at any time after registration, it appears to them that they would have had grounds to refuse registration under regulation 29(1).

(3)   Where the Commissioners decide to cancel a person's registration they must give him notice of—

 (a)   their decision and, subject to paragraph (4), the date from which the cancellation takes effect;

 (b)   the reasons for their decision;

 (c)   the right to require a review under regulation 43; and

 (d)   the right to appeal under regulation 44(1)(a).

(4)   If the Commissioners—

 (a)   consider that the interests of the public require the cancellation of a person's registration to have immediate effect; and

 (b)   include a statement to that effect and the reasons for it in the notice given under paragraph (3),

the cancellation takes effect when the notice is given to the person.

[2877BD]

NOTES
Commencement: 15 December 2007.

Requirement to inform the authority

31 Requirement on authorised person to inform the Authority

(1)   An authorised person whose supervisory authority is the Authority must, before acting as a money service business or a trust or company service provider or within 28 days of so doing, inform the Authority that he intends, or has begun, to act as such.

(2)   Paragraph (1) does not apply to an authorised person who—

 (a)   immediately before 15th December 2007 was acting as a money service business or a trust or company service provider and continues to act as such after that date; and

 (b)   before 15th January 2008 informs the Authority that he is or was acting as such.

(3)   Where an authorised person whose supervisory authority is the Authority ceases to act as a money service business or a trust or company service provider, he must immediately inform the Authority.

(4)   Any requirement imposed by this regulation is to be treated as if it were a requirement imposed by or under the 2000 Act.

(5)   Any information to be provided to the Authority under this regulation must be in such form or verified in such manner as it may specify.

[2877BE]

NOTES
Commencement: 15 December 2007.

Registration of Annex I financial institutions, estate agents etc

32 Power to maintain registers

(1)   The supervisory authorities mentioned in paragraph (2), (3) or (4) may, in order to fulfil their duties under regulation 24, maintain a register under this regulation.

(2)   The Authority may maintain a register of Annex I financial institutions.

(3)   The OFT may maintain registers of—

 (a)   consumer credit financial institutions; and

 (b)   estate agents.

(4)   The Commissioners may maintain registers of—

 (a)   auditors;

 (b)   external accountants; and

 (c)   tax advisers,

who are not supervised by the Secretary of State, DETI or any of the professional bodies listed in Schedule 3.

(5)   Where a supervisory authority decides to maintain a register under this regulation, it must take reasonable steps to bring its decision to the attention of those relevant persons in respect of whom the register is to be established.

(6)   A supervisory authority may keep a register under this regulation in any form it thinks fit.

(7)   A supervisory authority may publish or make available to public inspection all or part of a register maintained by it under this regulation.

[2877BF]

NOTES
Commencement: 15 December 2007.

33 Requirement to be registered

Where a supervisory authority decides to maintain a register under regulation 32 in respect of any description of relevant persons and establishes a register for that purpose, a relevant person of that description may not carry on the business or profession in question for a period of more than six months beginning on the date on which the supervisory authority establishes the register unless he is included in the register.

[2877BG]

NOTES
Commencement: 15 December 2007.

34 Applications for and cancellation of registration in a register maintained under regulation 32

(1)   Regulations 27, 29 (with the omission of the words "Subject to regulation 28" in regulation 29(1)) and 30(2), (3) and (4) apply to registration in a register maintained by the Commissioners under regulation 32 as they apply to registration in a register maintained under regulation 25.

(2)   Regulation 27 applies to registration in a register maintained by the Authority or the OFT under regulation 32 as it applies to registration in a register maintained under regulation 25 and, for this purpose, references to the Commissioners are to be treated as references to the Authority or the OFT, as the case may be.

(3)   The Authority and the OFT may refuse to register an applicant for registration in a register maintained under regulation 32 only if—
  (a)   any requirement of, or imposed under, regulation 27 has not been complied with;
  (b)   it appears to the Authority or the OFT, as the case may be, that any information provided pursuant to regulation 27 is false or misleading in a material particular; or
  (c)   the applicant has failed to pay a charge imposed by the Authority or the OFT, as the case may be, under regulation 35(1).

(4)   The Authority or the OFT, as the case may be, must, within 45 days beginning either with the date on which it receives an application or, where applicable, with the date on which it receives any further information required under regulation 27(3), give the applicant notice of—
  (a)   its decision to register the applicant; or
  (b)   the following matters—
     (i)   that it is minded not to register the applicant;
     (ii)   the reasons for being minded not to register him; and
     (iii)   the right to make representations to it within a specified period (which may not be less than 28 days).

(5)   The Authority or the OFT, as the case may be, must then decide, within a reasonable period, whether to register the applicant and it must give the applicant notice of—
  (a)   its decision to register the applicant; or
  (b)   the following matters—
     (i)   its decision not to register the applicant;
     (ii)   the reasons for its decision; and
     (iii)   the right to appeal under regulation 44(1)(b).

(6)   The Authority or the OFT, as the case may be, must, as soon as reasonably practicable after deciding to register a person, include him in the relevant register.

(7)   The Authority or the OFT may cancel a person's registration in a register maintained by them under regulation 32 if, at any time after registration, it appears to them that they would have had grounds to refuse registration under paragraph (3).

(8)   Where the Authority or the OFT proposes to cancel a person's registration, it must give him notice of—
  (a)   its proposal to cancel his registration;
  (b)   the reasons for the proposed cancellation; and

(c)   the right to make representations to it within a specified period (which may not be less than 28 days).

(9)   The Authority or the OFT, as the case may be, must then decide, within a reasonable period, whether to cancel the person's registration and it must give him notice of—

    (a)   its decision not to cancel his registration; or

    (b)   the following matters—

        (i)   its decision to cancel his registration and, subject to paragraph (10), the date from which cancellation takes effect;

       (ii)   the reasons for its decision; and

     (iii)   the right to appeal under regulation 44(1)(b).

(10)   If the Authority or the OFT, as the case may be—

    (a)   considers that the interests of the public require the cancellation of a person's registration to have immediate effect; and

    (b)   includes a statement to that effect and the reasons for it in the notice given under paragraph (9)(b),

the cancellation takes effect when the notice is given to the person.

(11)   In paragraphs (3) and (4), references to regulation 27 are to be treated as references to that paragraph as applied by paragraph (2) of this regulation.

[2877BH]

NOTES
Commencement: 15 December 2007.

Financial provisions

35   Costs of supervision

(1)   The Authority, the OFT and the Commissioners may impose charges—

    (a)   on applicants for registration;

    (b)   on relevant persons supervised by them.

(2)   Charges levied under paragraph (1) must not exceed such amount as the Authority, the OFT or the Commissioners (as the case may be) consider will enable them to meet any expenses reasonably incurred by them in carrying out their functions under these Regulations or for any incidental purpose.

(3)   Without prejudice to the generality of paragraph (2), a charge may be levied in respect of each of the premises at which a person carries on (or proposes to carry on) business.

(4)   The Authority must apply amounts paid to it by way of penalties imposed under regulation 42 towards expenses incurred in carrying out its functions under these Regulations or for any incidental purpose.

(5)   In paragraph (2), "expenses" in relation to the OFT includes expenses incurred by a local weights and measures authority or DETI pursuant to arrangements made for the purposes of these Regulations with the OFT—

    (a)   by or on behalf of the authority; or

    (b)   by DETI.

[2877BI]

NOTES
Commencement: 15 December 2007.

PART 5
ENFORCEMENT

Powers of designated authorities

36   Interpretation

In this Part—

   "designated authority" means—

      (a)   the Authority;

      (b)   the Commissioners;

      (c)   the OFT; and

      (d)   in relation to credit unions in Northern Ireland, DETI;

   "officer", except in regulations 40(3), 41 and 47 means—

      (a)   an officer of the Authority, including a member of the Authority's staff or an agent of the Authority;

      (b)   an officer of Revenue and Customs;

      (c)   an officer of the OFT;

(d)   a relevant officer; or

(e)   an officer of DETI acting for the purposes of its functions under these Regulations in relation to credit unions in Northern Ireland;

"recorded information" includes information recorded in any form and any document of any nature;

"relevant officer" means—

(a)   in Great Britain, an officer of a local weights and measures authority;

(b)   in Northern Ireland, an officer of DETI acting pursuant to arrangements made with the OFT for the purposes of these Regulations.

[2877BJ]

NOTES

Commencement: 15 December 2007.

37 Power to require information from, and attendance of, relevant and connected persons

(1)   An officer may, by notice to a relevant person or to a person connected with a relevant person, require the relevant person or the connected person, as the case may be—

(a)   to provide such information as may be specified in the notice;

(b)   to produce such recorded information as may be so specified; or

(c)   to attend before an officer at a time and place specified in the notice and answer questions.

(2)   For the purposes of paragraph (1), a person is connected with a relevant person if he is, or has at any time been, in relation to the relevant person, a person listed in Schedule 4 to these Regulations.

(3)   An officer may exercise powers under this regulation only if the information sought to be obtained as a result is reasonably required in connection with the exercise by the designated authority for whom he acts of its functions under these Regulations.

(4)   Where an officer requires information to be provided or produced pursuant to paragraph (1)(a) or (b)—

(a)   the notice must set out the reasons why the officer requires the information to be provided or produced; and

(b)   such information must be provided or produced—

(i)   before the end of such reasonable period as may be specified in the notice; and

(ii)   at such place as may be so specified.

(5)   In relation to information recorded otherwise than in legible form, the power to require production of it includes a power to require the production of a copy of it in legible form or in a form from which it can readily be produced in visible and legible form.

(6)   The production of a document does not affect any lien which a person has on the document.

(7)   A person may not be required under this regulation to provide or produce information or to answer questions which he would be entitled to refuse to provide, produce or answer on grounds of legal professional privilege in proceedings in the High Court, except that a lawyer may be required to provide the name and address of his client.

(8)   Subject to paragraphs (9) and (10), a statement made by a person in compliance with a requirement imposed on him under paragraph (1)(c) is admissible in evidence in any proceedings, so long as it also complies with any requirements governing the admissibility of evidence in the circumstances in question.

(9)   In criminal proceedings in which a person is charged with an offence to which this paragraph applies—

(a)   no evidence relating to the statement may be adduced; and

(b)   no question relating to it may be asked,

by or on behalf of the prosecution unless evidence relating to it is adduced, or a question relating to it is asked, in the proceedings by or on behalf of that person.

(10)   Paragraph (9) applies to any offence other than one under—

(a)   section 5 of the Perjury Act 1911 (false statements without oath);

(b)   section 44(2) of the Criminal Law (Consolidation) (Scotland) Act 1995 (false statements and declarations); or

(c)   Article 10 of the Perjury (Northern Ireland) Order 1979 (false unsworn statements).

(11)   In the application of this regulation to Scotland, the reference in paragraph (7) to—

(a)   proceedings in the High Court is to be read as a reference to legal proceedings generally; and

(b)   an entitlement on grounds of legal professional privilege is to be read as a reference to an entitlement on the grounds of confidentiality of communications[—

(i)   between a professional legal adviser and his client; or

     (ii)   made in connection with or in contemplation of legal proceedings and for the purposes of those proceedings].

[2877BK]

NOTES
Commencement: 15 December 2007.
Para (11): words in square brackets added by the Money Laundering (Amendment) Regulations 2007, SI 2007/3299, reg 2(b), as from 15 December 2007.

38 Entry, inspection without a warrant etc

(1)   Where an officer has reasonable cause to believe that any premises are being used by a relevant person in connection with his business or professional activities, he may on producing evidence of his authority at any reasonable time—

    (a)   enter the premises;
    (b)   inspect the premises;
    (c)   observe the carrying on of business or professional activities by the relevant person;
    (d)   inspect any recorded information found on the premises;
    (e)   require any person on the premises to provide an explanation of any recorded information or to state where it may be found;
    (f)   in the case of a money service business or a high value dealer, inspect any cash found on the premises.

(2)   An officer may take copies of, or make extracts from, any recorded information found under paragraph (1).

(3)   Paragraphs (1)(d) and (e) and (2) do not apply to recorded information which the relevant person would be entitled to refuse to disclose on grounds of legal professional privilege in proceedings in the High Court, except that a lawyer may be required to provide the name and address of his client and, for this purpose, regulation 37(11) applies to this paragraph as it applies to regulation 37(7).

(4)   An officer may exercise powers under this regulation only if the information sought to be obtained as a result is reasonably required in connection with the exercise by the designated authority for whom he acts of its functions under these Regulations.

(5)   In this regulation, "premises" means any premises other than premises used only as a dwelling.

[2877BL]

NOTES
Commencement: 15 December 2007.

39 Entry to premises under warrant

(1)   A justice may issue a warrant under this paragraph if satisfied on information on oath given by an officer that there are reasonable grounds for believing that the first, second or third set of conditions is satisfied.

(2)   The first set of conditions is—
    (a)   that there is on the premises specified in the warrant recorded information in relation to which a requirement could be imposed under regulation 37(1)(b); and
    (b)   that if such a requirement were to be imposed—
       (i)   it would not be complied with; or
      (ii)   the recorded information to which it relates would be removed, tampered with or destroyed.

(3)   The second set of conditions is—
    (a)   that a person on whom a requirement has been imposed under regulation 37(1)(b) has failed (wholly or in part) to comply with it; and
    (b)   that there is on the premises specified in the warrant recorded information which has been required to be produced.

(4)   The third set of conditions is—
    (a)   that an officer has been obstructed in the exercise of a power under regulation 38; and
    (b)   that there is on the premises specified in the warrant recorded information or cash which could be inspected under regulation 38(1)(d) or (f).

(5)   A justice may issue a warrant under this paragraph if satisfied on information on oath given by an officer that there are reasonable grounds for suspecting that—
    (a)   an offence under these Regulations has been, is being or is about to be committed by a relevant person; and
    (b)   there is on the premises specified in the warrant recorded information relevant to whether that offence has been, or is being or is about to be committed.

(6)   A warrant issued under this regulation shall authorise an officer—
  (a)   to enter the premises specified in the warrant;
  (b)   to search the premises and take possession of any recorded information or anything appearing to be recorded information specified in the warrant or to take, in relation to any such recorded information, any other steps which may appear to be necessary for preserving it or preventing interference with it;
  (c)   to take copies of, or extracts from, any recorded information specified in the warrant;
  (d)   to require any person on the premises to provide an explanation of any recorded information appearing to be of the kind specified in the warrant or to state where it may be found;
  (e)   to use such force as may reasonably be necessary.

(7)   Where a warrant is issued by a justice under paragraph (1) or (5) on the basis of information [on oath] given by an officer of the Authority, for "an officer" in paragraph (6) substitute "a constable".

(8)   In paragraphs (1), (5) and (7), "justice" means—
  (a)   in relation to England and Wales, a justice of the peace;
  (b)   in relation to Scotland, a justice within the meaning of section 307 of the Criminal Procedure (Scotland) Act 1995 (interpretation);
  (c)   in relation to Northern Ireland, a lay magistrate.

(9)   In the application of this regulation to Scotland, the references in paragraphs [(1), (5) and (7)] to information on oath are to be read as references to evidence on oath.

[2877BM]

NOTES
Commencement: 15 December 2007.
Para (7): words in square brackets inserted by the Money Laundering (Amendment) Regulations 2007, SI 2007/3299, reg 2(c)(i), as from 15 December 2007.
Para (9): words in square brackets substituted by SI 2007/3299, reg 2(c)(ii), as from 15 December 2007.

40   Failure to comply with information requirement

(1)   If, on an application made by—
  (a)   a designated authority; or
  (b)   a local weights and measures authority or DETI pursuant to arrangements made with the OFT—
      (i)   by or on behalf of the authority; or
      (ii)   by DETI,
it appears to the court that a person (the "information defaulter") has failed to do something that he was required to do under regulation 37(1), the court may make an order under this regulation.

(2)   An order under this regulation may require the information defaulter—
  (a)   to do the thing that he failed to do within such period as may be specified in the order;
  (b)   otherwise to take such steps to remedy the consequences of the failure as may be so specified.

(3)   If the information defaulter is a body corporate, a partnership or an unincorporated body of persons which is not a partnership, the order may require any officer of the body corporate, partnership or body, who is (wholly or partly) responsible for the failure to meet such costs of the application as are specified in the order.

(4)   In this regulation, "court" means—
  (a)   in England and Wales and Northern Ireland, the High Court or the county court;
  (b)   in Scotland, the Court of Session or the sheriff [court].

[2877BN]

NOTES
Commencement: 15 December 2007.
Para (4): word in square brackets in sub-para (b) inserted by the Money Laundering (Amendment) Regulations 2007, SI 2007/3299, reg 2(d), as from 15 December 2007.

41   Powers of relevant officers

(1)   A relevant officer may only exercise powers under regulations 37 to 39 pursuant to arrangements made with the OFT—
  (a)   by or on behalf of the local weights and measures authority of which he is an officer ("his authority"); or
  (b)   by DETI.

(2)   Anything done or omitted to be done by, or in relation to, a relevant officer in the exercise or purported exercise of a power in this Part shall be treated for all purposes as having been done or omitted to be done by, or in relation to, an officer of the OFT.

(3) Paragraph (2) does not apply for the purposes of any criminal proceedings brought against the relevant officer, his authority, DETI or the OFT, in respect of anything done or omitted to be done by the officer.

(4) A relevant officer shall not disclose to any person other than the OFT and his authority or, as the case may be, DETI information obtained by him in the exercise of such powers unless—
(a) he has the approval of the OFT to do so; or
(b) he is under a duty to make the disclosure.

[2877BO]

NOTES
Commencement: 15 December 2007.

Civil penalties, review and appeals

42 Power to impose civil penalties

(1) A designated authority may impose a penalty of such amount as it considers appropriate on a relevant person who fails to comply with any requirement in regulation 7(1), (2) or (3), 8(1) or (3), 9(2), 10(1), 11(1), 14(1), 15(1) or (2), 16(1), (2), (3) or (4), 19(1), (4), (5) or (6), 20(1), (4) or (5), 21, 26, 27(4) or 33 or a direction made under regulation 18 and, for this purpose, "appropriate" means effective, proportionate and dissuasive.

(2) The designated authority must not impose a penalty on a person under paragraph (1) where there are reasonable grounds for it to be satisfied that the person took all reasonable steps and exercised all due diligence to ensure that the requirement would be complied with.

(3) In deciding whether a person has failed to comply with a requirement of these Regulations, the designated authority must consider whether he followed any relevant guidance which was at the time—
(a) issued by a supervisory authority or any other appropriate body;
(b) approved by the Treasury; and
(c) published in a manner approved by the Treasury as suitable in their opinion to bring the guidance to the attention of persons likely to be affected by it.

(4) In paragraph (3), an "appropriate body" means any body which regulates or is representative of any trade, profession, business or employment carried on by the [person].

(5) Where the Commissioners decide to impose a penalty under this regulation, they must give the person notice of—
(a) their decision to impose the penalty and its amount;
(b) the reasons for imposing the penalty;
(c) the right to a review under regulation 43; and
(d) the right to appeal under regulation 44(1)(a).

(6) Where the Authority, the OFT or DETI proposes to impose a penalty under this regulation, it must give the person notice of—
(a) its proposal to impose the penalty and the proposed amount;
(b) the reasons for imposing the penalty; and
(c) the right to make representations to it within a specified period (which may not be less than 28 days).

(7) The Authority, the OFT or DETI, as the case may be, must then decide, within a reasonable period, whether to impose a penalty under this regulation and it must give the person notice of—
(a) its decision not to impose a penalty; or
(b) the following matters—
(i) its decision to impose a penalty and the amount;
(ii) the reasons for its decision; and
(iii) the right to appeal under regulation 44(1)(b).

(8) A penalty imposed under this regulation is payable to the designated authority which imposes it.

[2877BP]

NOTES
Commencement: 15 December 2007.
Para (4): word in square brackets substituted by the Money Laundering (Amendment) Regulations 2007, SI 2007/3299, reg 2(e), as from 15 December 2007.

43 Review procedure

(1) This regulation applies to decisions of the Commissioners made under—
(a) regulation 29, to refuse to register an applicant;
(b) regulation 30, to cancel the registration of a registered person; and
(c) regulation 42, to impose a penalty.

(2)   Any person who is the subject of a decision to which this regulation applies may by notice to the Commissioners require them to review that decision.

(3)   The Commissioners need not review any decision unless the notice requiring the review is given within 45 days beginning with the date on which they first gave notice of the decision to the person requiring the review.

(4)   Where the Commissioners are required under this regulation to review any decision they must either—
(a)   confirm the decision; or
(b)   withdraw or vary the decision and take such further steps (if any) in consequence of the withdrawal or variation as they consider appropriate.

(5)   Where the Commissioners do not, within 45 days beginning with the date on which the review was required by a person, give notice to that person of their determination of the review, they are to be taken for the purposes of these Regulations to have confirmed the decision.

[2877BQ]

NOTES
   Commencement: 15 December 2007.

44   Appeals

(1)   A person may appeal from a decision by—
(a)   the Commissioners on a review under regulation 43; and
(b)   the Authority, the OFT or DETI under regulation 34 or 42.

(2)   An appeal from a decision by—
(a)   the Commissioners is to a VAT and duties tribunal;
(b)   the Authority is to the Financial Services and Markets Tribunal;
(c)   the OFT is to the Consumer Credit Appeals Tribunal; and
(d)   DETI is to the High Court.

(3)   The provisions of Part 5 of the Value Added Tax Act 1994 (appeals), subject to the modifications set out in paragraph 1 of Schedule 5, apply in respect of appeals to a VAT and duties tribunal made under this regulation as they apply in respect of appeals made to such a tribunal under section 83 (appeals) of that Act.

(4)   The provisions of Part 9 of the 2000 Act (hearings and appeals), subject to the modifications set out in paragraph 2 of Schedule 5, apply in respect of appeals to the Financial Services and Markets Tribunal made under this regulation as they apply in respect of references made to that Tribunal under that Act.

(5)   Sections 40A (the Consumer Credit Appeals Tribunal), 41 (appeals to the Secretary of State under Part 3) and 41A (appeals from the Consumer Credit Appeals Tribunal) of the Consumer Credit Act 1974 apply in respect of appeals to the Consumer Credit Appeal Tribunal made under this regulation as they apply in respect of appeals made to that Tribunal under section 41 of that Act.

(6)   A VAT and duties tribunal hearing an appeal under paragraph (2) has the power to—
(a)   quash or vary any decision of the supervisory authority, including the power to reduce any penalty to such amount (including nil) as they think proper; and
(b)   substitute their own decision for any decision quashed on appeal.

(7)   Notwithstanding paragraph (2)(c), until the coming into force of section 55 of the Consumer Credit Act 2006 (the Consumer Credit Appeals Tribunal), an appeal from a decision by the OFT is to the Financial Services and Markets Tribunal and, for these purposes, the coming into force of that section shall not affect—
(a)   the hearing and determination by the Financial Service and Markets Tribunal of an appeal commenced before the coming into force of that section ("the original appeal"); or
(b)   any appeal against the decision of the Financial Services and Markets Tribunal with respect to the original appeal.

(8)   The modifications in Schedule 5 have effect for the purposes of appeals made under this regulation.

[2877BR]

NOTES
   Commencement: 15 December 2007.
   Note: the Consumer Credit Act 2006, s 55 (which inserts the Consumer Credit Act 1974, s 40A) comes into force for certain purposes on 1 December 2007 and 6 April 2008 (see the Consumer Credit Act 2006 (Commencement No 3) Order 2007, SI 2007/3300).

Criminal offences

45   Offences

(1)   A person who fails to comply with any requirement in regulation 7(1), (2) or (3), 8(1) or (3), 9(2), 10(1), 11(1)(a), (b) or (c), 14(1), 15(1) or (2), 16(1), (2), (3) or (4), 19(1), (4), (5) or (6), 20(1), (4) or (5), 21, 26, 27(4) or 33, or a direction made under regulation 18, is guilty of an offence and liable—

    (a)   on summary conviction, to a fine not exceeding the statutory maximum;

    (b)   on conviction on indictment, to imprisonment for a term not exceeding two years, to a fine or to both.

(2)   In deciding whether a person has committed an offence under paragraph (1), the court must consider whether he followed any relevant guidance which was at the time—

    (a)   issued by a supervisory authority or any other appropriate body;

    (b)   approved by the Treasury; and

    (c)   published in a manner approved by the Treasury as suitable in their opinion to bring the guidance to the attention of persons likely to be affected by it.

(3)   In paragraph (2), an "appropriate body" means any body which regulates or is representative of any trade, profession, business or employment carried on by the alleged offender.

(4)   A person is not guilty of an offence under this regulation if he took all reasonable steps and exercised all due diligence to avoid committing the offence.

(5)   Where a person is convicted of an offence under this regulation, he shall not also be liable to a penalty under regulation 42.

[2877BS]

NOTES
Commencement: 15 December 2007.

46   Prosecution of offences

(1)   Proceedings for an offence under regulation 45 may be instituted by—

    (a)   the Director of Revenue and Customs Prosecutions or by order of the Commissioners;

    (b)   the OFT;

    (c)   a local weights and measures authority;

    (d)   DETI;

    (e)   the Director of Public Prosecutions; or

    (f)   the Director of Public Prosecutions for Northern Ireland.

(2)   Proceedings for an offence under regulation 45 may be instituted only against a relevant person or, where such a person is a body corporate, a partnership or an unincorporated association, against any person who is liable to be proceeded against under regulation 47.

(3)   Where proceedings under paragraph (1) are instituted by order of the Commissioners, the proceedings must be brought in the name of an officer of Revenue and Customs.

(4)   Where a local weights and measures authority in England or Wales proposes to institute proceedings for an offence under regulation 45 it must give the OFT notice of the intended proceedings, together with a summary of the facts on which the charges are to be founded.

(5)   A local weights and measures authority must also notify the OFT of the outcome of the proceedings after they are finally determined.

(6)   A local weights and measures authority must, whenever the OFT requires, report in such form and with such particulars as the OFT requires on the exercise of its functions under these Regulations.

(7)   Where the Commissioners investigate, or propose to investigate, any matter with a view to determining—

    (a)   whether there are grounds for believing that an offence under regulation 45 has been committed by any person; or

    (b)   whether such a person should be prosecuted for such an offence,

that matter is to be treated as an assigned matter within the meaning of section 1(1) of the Customs and Excise Management Act 1979.

(8)   Paragraphs (1) and (3) to (6) do not extend to Scotland.

[(9)   In its application to the Commissioners acting in Scotland, paragraph (7)(b) shall be read as referring to the Commissioners determining whether to refer the matter to the Crown Office and Procurator Fiscal Service with a view to the Procurator Fiscal determining whether a person should be prosecuted for such an offence.]

[2877BT]

NOTES
Commencement: 15 December 2007.
Para (9): added by the Money Laundering (Amendment) Regulations 2007, SI 2007/3299, reg 2(f), as from 15 December 2007.

47 Offences by bodies corporate etc

(1) If an offence under regulation 45 committed by a body corporate is shown—

    (a) to have been committed with the consent or the connivance of an officer of the body corporate; or

    (b) to be attributable to any neglect on his part,

the officer as well as the body corporate is guilty of an offence and liable to be proceeded against and punished accordingly.

(2) If an offence under regulation 45 committed by a partnership is shown—

    (a) to have been committed with the consent or the connivance of a partner; or

    (b) to be attributable to any neglect on his part,

the partner as well as the partnership is guilty of an offence and liable to be proceeded against and punished accordingly.

(3) If an offence under regulation 45 committed by an unincorporated association (other than a partnership) is shown—

    (a) to have been committed with the consent or the connivance of an officer of the association; or

    (b) to be attributable to any neglect on his part,

that officer as well as the association is guilty of an offence and liable to be proceeded against and punished accordingly.

(4) If the affairs of a body corporate are managed by its members, paragraph (1) applies in relation to the acts and defaults of a member in connection with his functions of management as if he were a director of the body.

(5) Proceedings for an offence alleged to have been committed by a partnership or an unincorporated association must be brought in the name of the partnership or association (and not in that of its members).

(6) A fine imposed on the partnership or association on its conviction of an offence is to be paid out of the funds of the partnership or association.

(7) Rules of court relating to the service of documents are to have effect as if the partnership or association were a body corporate.

(8) In proceedings for an offence brought against the partnership or association—

    (a) section 33 of the Criminal Justice Act 1925 (procedure on charge of offence against corporation) and Schedule 3 to the Magistrates' Courts Act 1980 (corporations) apply as they do in relation to a body corporate;

    (b) section 70 (proceedings against bodies corporate) of the Criminal Procedure (Scotland) Act 1995 applies as it does in relation to a body corporate;

    (c) section 18 of the Criminal Justice (Northern Ireland) Act 1945 (procedure on charge) and Schedule 4 to the Magistrates' Courts (Northern Ireland) Order 1981 (corporations) apply as they do in relation to a body corporate.

(9) In this regulation—

  "officer"—

    (a) in relation to a body corporate, means a director, manager, secretary, chief executive, member of the committee of management, or a person purporting to act in such a capacity; and

    (b) in relation to an unincorporated association, means any officer of the association or any member of its governing body, or a person purporting to act in such capacity; and

  "partner" includes a person purporting to act as a partner.

[2877BU]

NOTES
Commencement: 15 December 2007.

PART 6
MISCELLANEOUS

48 Recovery of charges and penalties through the court

Any charge or penalty imposed on a person by a supervisory authority under regulation 35(1) or 42(1) is a debt due from that person to the authority, and is recoverable accordingly.

[2877BV]

NOTES
Commencement: 15 December 2007.

49 Obligations on public authorities

(1)   The following bodies and persons must, if they know or suspect or have reasonable grounds for knowing or suspecting that a person is or has engaged in money laundering or terrorist financing, as soon as reasonably practicable inform the Serious Organised Crime Agency—

(a)   the Auditor General for Scotland;
(b)   the Auditor General for Wales;
(c)   the Authority;
(d)   the Bank of England;
(e)   the Comptroller and Auditor General;
(f)   the Comptroller and Auditor General for Northern Ireland;
(g)   the Gambling Commission;
(h)   the OFT;
(i)   the Official Solicitor to the Supreme Court;
(j)   the Pensions Regulator;
(k)   the Public Trustee;
(l)   the Secretary of State, in the exercise of his functions under enactments relating to companies and insolvency;
(m)   the Treasury, in the exercise of their functions under the 2000 Act;
(n)   the Treasury Solicitor;
(o)   a designated professional body for the purposes of Part 20 of the 2000 Act (provision of financial services by members of the professions);
(p)   a person or inspector appointed under section 65 (investigations on behalf of Authority) or 66 (inspections and special meetings) of the Friendly Societies Act 1992;
(q)   an inspector appointed under section 49 of the Industrial and Provident Societies Act 1965 (appointment of inspectors) or section 18 of the Credit Unions Act 1979 (power to appoint inspector);
(r)   an inspector appointed under section 431 (investigation of a company on its own application), 432 (other company investigations), 442 (power to investigate company ownership) or 446 (investigation of share dealing) of the Companies Act 1985 or under Article 424, 425, 435 or 439 of the Companies (Northern Ireland) Order 1986;
(s)   a person or inspector appointed under section 55 (investigations on behalf of Authority) or 56 (inspections and special meetings) of the Building Societies Act 1986;
(t)   a person appointed under section 167 (appointment of persons to carry out investigations), 168(3) or (5) (appointment of persons to carry out investigations in particular cases), 169(1)(b) (investigations to support overseas regulator) or 284 (power to investigate affairs of a scheme) of the 2000 Act, or under regulations made under section 262(2)(k) (open-ended investment companies) of that Act, to conduct an investigation; and
(u)   a person authorised to require the production of documents under section 447 of the Companies Act 1985 (Secretary of State's power to require production of documents), Article 440 of the Companies (Northern Ireland) Order 1986 or section 84 of the Companies Act 1989 (exercise of powers by officer).

(2)   A disclosure made under paragraph (1) is not to be taken to breach any restriction on the disclosure of information however imposed.

[2877BW]

NOTES
Commencement: 15 December 2007.

[49A   Disclosure by the Commissioners

(1)   The Commissioners may disclose to the Authority information held in connection with their functions under these Regulations if the disclosure is made for the purpose of enabling or assisting the Authority to discharge any of its functions under the Payment Services Regulations 2009.

(2)   Information disclosed to the Authority under subsection (1) may not be disclosed by the Authority or any person who receives the information directly or indirectly from the Authority except—

    (a)   to, or in accordance with authority given by, the Commissioners;

    (b)   with a view to the institution of, or otherwise for the purposes of, any criminal proceedings;

    (c)   with a view to the institution of any other proceedings by the Authority, for the purposes of any such proceedings instituted by the Authority, or for the purposes of any reference to the Tribunal under the Payment Services Regulations 2009; or

    (d)   in the form of a summary or collection of information so framed as not to enable information relating to any particular person to be ascertained from it.

(3)   Any person who discloses information in contravention of subsection (2) is guilty of an offence and liable—

    (a)   on summary conviction, to imprisonment for a term not exceeding three months, to a fine not exceeding the statutory maximum, or to both;

    (b)   on conviction on indictment, to imprisonment for a term not exceeding two years to a fine, or to both.

(4)   It is a defence for a person charged with an offence under this regulation of disclosing information to prove that they reasonably believed

    (a)   that the disclosure was lawful; or

    (b)   that the information had already and lawfully been made available to the public.]

[2877BWA]

NOTES

Commencement: 2 March 2009.

Inserted by the Payment Services Regulations 2009, SI 2009/209, reg 126, Sch 6, Pt 2, para 6(g), as from 2 March 2009 (for the full commencement details of the 2009 Regulations, see reg 1 of those Regulations at **[4387]**).

50   Transitional provisions: requirement to be registered

(1)   Regulation 26 does not apply to an existing money service business, an existing trust or company service provider *or an existing high value dealer* until—

    (a)   where it has applied in accordance with regulation 27 before the specified date for registration in a register maintained under regulation 25(1) (a "new register")—

        (i)   the date it is included in a new register following the determination of its application by the Commissioners; or

        (ii)   where the Commissioners give it notice under regulation 29(2)(b) of their decision not to register it, the date on which the Commissioners state that the decision takes effect or, where a statement is included in accordance with paragraph (3)(b), the time at which the Commissioners give it such notice;

    (b)   in any other case, the specified date.

(2)   The specified date is—

    (a)   in the case of an existing money service business, 1st February 2008;

    (b)   in the case of an existing trust or company service provider, 1st April 2008;

    (c)   in the case of an existing high value dealer, the first anniversary which falls on or after 1st January 2008 of the date of its registration in a register maintained under regulation 10 of the Money Laundering Regulations 2003;

    [(d)   in the case of an existing bill payment service provider or an existing telecommunication, digital and IT payment service provider, 1st March 2010].

(3)   In the case of an application for registration in a new register made before the specified date by an existing money service business, an existing trust or company service provider *or an existing high value dealer*, the Commissioners must include in a notice given to it under regulation 29(2)(b)—

    (a)   the date on which their decision is to take effect; or

    (b)   if the Commissioners consider that the interests of the public require their decision to have immediate effect, a statement to that effect and the reasons for it.

(4)   In the case of an application for registration in a new register made before the specified date by an existing money services business or an existing trust or company service provider, the Commissioners must give it a notice under regulation 29(2) by—

    (a)   in the case of an existing money service business, 1st June 2008;

    (b)   in the case of an existing trust or company service provider, 1st July 2008; or

    (c)   where applicable, 45 days beginning with the date on which they receive any further information required under regulation 27(3).

(5)   In this regulation—

"existing bill payment service provider" and "existing telecommunication, digital and IT payment service provider" mean a bill payment service provider or a telecommunication, digital and IT payment service provider carrying on business in the United Kingdom immediately before 1st November 2009;"

"existing money service business" and an "existing high value dealer" mean a money service business or a high value dealer which, immediately before 15th December 2007, was included in a register maintained under regulation 10 of the Money Laundering Regulations 2003;

"existing trust or company service provider" means a trust or company service provider carrying on business in the United Kingdom immediately before 15th December 2007.

[2877BX]

NOTES

Commencement: 15 December 2007.

Paras (1), (3): for the words in italics there are substituted the words ", an existing high value dealer, an existing bill payment service provider or an existing telecommunication, digital and IT payment service provider" by the Payment Services Regulations 2009, SI 2009/209, reg 126, Sch 6, Pt 2, para 6(h)(i), (iii), as from 1 November 2009 (for the full commencement details of the 2009 Regulations, see reg 1 of those Regulations at **[4387]**).

Para (2): sub-para (d) added by SI 2009/209, reg 126, Sch 6, Pt 2, para 6(h)(ii), as from 1 November 2009 (for the full commencement details of the 2009 Regulations, see reg 1 of those Regulations at **[4387]**).

Para (5): definitions "existing bill payment service provider" and "existing telecommunication, digital and IT payment service provider" inserted by SI 2009/209, reg 126, Sch 6, Pt 2, para 6(h)(iv), as from 1 November 2009 (for the full commencement details of the 2009 Regulations, see reg 1 of those Regulations at **[4387]**).

51   Minor and consequential amendments

Schedule 6, which contains minor and consequential amendments to primary and secondary legislation, has effect.

[2877BY]

NOTES

Commencement: 15 December 2007.

SCHEDULES

SCHEDULE 1
ACTIVITIES LISTED IN POINTS 2 TO 12 AND 14 OF ANNEX I TO THE BANKING CONSOLIDATION DIRECTIVE

Regulation 3(3)(a)

2.   Lending including, inter alia: consumer credit, mortgage credit, factoring, with or without recourse, financing of commercial transactions (including forfeiting).

3.   Financial leasing.

4.   *Money transmission services.*

5.   *Issuing and administering means of payment (e g credit cards, travellers' cheques and bankers' drafts).*

6.   Guarantees and commitments.

7.   Trading for own account or for account of customers in:
    (a)   money market instruments (cheques, bills, certificates of deposit, etc);
    (b)   foreign exchange;
    (c)   financial futures and options;
    (d)   exchange and interest-rate instruments; or
    (e)   transferable securities.

8.   Participation in securities issues and the provision of services related to such issues.

9.   Advice to undertakings on capital structure, industrial strategy and related questions and advice as well as services relating to mergers and the purchase of undertakings.

10.   Money broking.

11.   Portfolio management and advice.

12.   Safekeeping and administration of securities.

14.   Safe custody services.

[2877BZ]

NOTES

Commencement: 15 December 2007.

Paras 4, 5: substituted by the Payment Services Regulations 2009, SI 2009/209, reg 126, Sch 6, Pt 2, para 6(i), as from 1 November 2009, as follows (for the full commencement details of the 2009 Regulations, see reg 1 of those Regulations at **[4387]**)—

"4.   Payment services as defined in Article 4(3) of Directive 2007/64/EC of the European Parliament and of the Council of 13 November 2007 on payment services in the internal market.

5.   Issuing and administering other means of payment (including travellers' cheques and bankers' drafts) insofar as this activity is not covered by point 4.".

Note: the Banking Consolidation Directive, ie, Directive of the European Parliament and of the Council (2006/48/EC) relating to the taking up and pursuit of the business of credit institutions (recast) is set out in full at **[5784]**.

SCHEDULE 2
FINANCIAL ACTIVITY, SIMPLIFIED DUE DILIGENCE AND POLITICALLY EXPOSED PERSONS

Regulations 4(1)(e) and (2),
13(6) and (8) and 14(5)

Financial activity on an occasional or very limited basis

1.   For the purposes of regulation 4(1)(e) and (2), a person is to be considered as engaging in financial activity on an occasional or very limited basis if all the following conditions are fulfilled—
   (a)   the person's total annual turnover in respect of the financial activity does not exceed £64,000;
   (b)   the financial activity is limited in relation to any customer to no more than one transaction exceeding 1,000 euro, whether the transaction is carried out in a single operation, or a series of operations which appear to be linked;
   (c)   the financial activity does not exceed 5% of the person's total annual turnover;
   (d)   the financial activity is ancillary and directly related to the person's main activity;
   (e)   the financial activity is not the transmission or remittance of money (or any representation of monetary value) by any means;
   (f)   the person's main activity is not that of a person falling within regulation 3(1)(a) to (f) or (h);
   (g)   the financial activity is provided only to customers of the person's main activity and is not offered to the public.

Simplified due diligence

2.   For the purposes of regulation 13(6), the conditions are—
   (a)   the authority has been entrusted with public functions pursuant to the Treaty on the European Union, the Treaties on the European Communities or Community secondary legislation;
   (b)   the authority's identity is publicly available, transparent and certain;
   (c)   the activities of the authority and its accounting practices are transparent;
   (d)   either the authority is accountable to a Community institution or to the authorities of an EEA state, or otherwise appropriate check and balance procedures exist ensuring control of the authority's activity.

3.   For the purposes of regulation 13(8), the conditions are—
   (a)   the product has a written contractual base;
   (b)   any related transaction is carried out through an account of the customer with a credit institution which is subject to the money laundering directive or with a credit institution situated in a non-EEA state which imposes requirements equivalent to those laid down in that directive;
   (c)   the product or related transaction is not anonymous and its nature is such that it allows for the timely application of customer due diligence measures where there is a suspicion of money laundering or terrorist financing;
   (d)   the product is within the following maximum threshold—
       (i)   in the case of insurance policies or savings products of a similar nature, the annual premium is no more than 1,000 euro or there is a single premium of no more than 2,500 euro;
       (ii)   in the case of products which are related to the financing of physical assets where the legal and beneficial title of the assets is not transferred to the customer until the termination of the contractual relationship (whether the transaction is carried out in a single operation or in several operations which appear to be linked), the annual payments do not exceed 15,000 euro;
       (iii) in all other cases, the maximum threshold is 15,000 euro;
   (e)   the benefits of the product or related transaction cannot be realised for the benefit of third parties, except in the case of death, disablement, survival to a predetermined advanced age, or similar events;

   (f)   in the case of products or related transactions allowing for the investment of funds in financial assets or claims, including insurance or other kinds of contingent claims—

      (i)   the benefits of the product or related transaction are only realisable in the long term;

     (ii)   the product or related transaction cannot be used as collateral; and

   (iii)   during the contractual relationship, no accelerated payments are made, surrender clauses used or early termination takes place.

Politically exposed persons

4.—(1)   For the purposes of regulation 14(5)—

   (a)   individuals who are or have been entrusted with prominent public functions include the following—

      (i)   heads of state, heads of government, ministers and deputy or assistant ministers;

     (ii)   members of parliaments;

   (iii)   members of supreme courts, of constitutional courts or of other high-level judicial bodies whose decisions are not generally subject to further appeal, other than in exceptional circumstances;

   (iv)   members of courts of auditors or of the boards of central banks;

   (v)   ambassadors, chargés d'affaires and high-ranking officers in the armed forces; and

   (vi)   members of the administrative, management or supervisory bodies of state-owned enterprises;

   (b)   the categories set out in paragraphs (i) to (vi) of sub-paragraph (a) do not include middle-ranking or more junior officials;

   (c)   immediate family members include the following—

      (i)   a spouse;

     (ii)   a partner;

   (iii)   children and their spouses or partners; and

   (iv)   parents;

   (d)   persons known to be close associates include the following—

      (i)   any individual who is known to have joint beneficial ownership of a legal entity or legal arrangement, or any other close business relations, with a person referred to in regulation 14(5)(a); and

     (ii)   any individual who has sole beneficial ownership of a legal entity or legal arrangement which is known to have been set up for the benefit of a person referred to in regulation 14(5)(a).

   (2)   In paragraph (1)(c), "partner" means a person who is considered by his national law as equivalent to a spouse.

[2877CA]

NOTES
   Commencement: 15 December 2007.

SCHEDULE 3
PROFESSIONAL BODIES

Regulations 17(2)(b), 23(1)(c) and 32(4)

PART 1

1.   Association of Chartered Certified Accountants

2.   Council for Licensed Conveyancers

3.   Faculty of Advocates

4.   General Council of the Bar

5.   General Council of the Bar of Northern Ireland

6.   Institute of Chartered Accountants in England and Wales

7.   Institute of Chartered Accountants in Ireland

8.   Institute of Chartered Accountants of Scotland

9.   Law Society

10.   Law Society of Scotland

11.   Law Society of Northern Ireland

[2877CB]

NOTES
   Commencement: 15 December 2007.

PART 2

12.   Association of Accounting Technicians

13.   Association of International Accountants

14.   Association of Taxation Technicians

15.   Chartered Institute of Management Accountants

16.   Chartered Institute of Public Finance and Accountancy

17.   Chartered Institute of Taxation

18.   Faculty Office of the Archbishop of Canterbury

19.   Insolvency Practitioners Association

20.   Institute of Certified Bookkeepers

21.   Institute of Financial Accountants

[22.   International Association of Book-keepers]

[2877CC]

NOTES
  Commencement: 15 December 2007.
  Para 22: added by the Money Laundering (Amendment) Regulations 2007, SI 2007/3299, reg 2(g), as from
15 December 2007.

SCHEDULE 4
CONNECTED PERSONS

Regulation 37(2)

Corporate bodies

1.   If the relevant person is a body corporate ("BC"), a person who is or has been—
  (a)   an officer or manager of BC or of a parent undertaking of BC;
  (b)   an employee of BC;
  (c)   an agent of BC or of a parent undertaking of BC

Partnerships

2.   If the relevant person is a partnership, a person who is or has been a member, manager,
employee or agent of the partnership.

Unincorporated associations

3.   If the relevant person is an unincorporated association of persons which is not a partnership, a
person who is or has been an officer, manager, employee or agent of the association.

Individuals

4.   If the relevant person is an individual, a person who is or has been an employee or agent of that
individual.

[2877CD]

NOTES
  Commencement: 15 December 2007.

SCHEDULE 5
MODIFICATIONS IN RELATION TO APPEALS

Regulation 44(8)

PART 1
PRIMARY LEGISLATION

1   The Value Added Tax Act 1994 (c 23)

Part 5 of the Value Added Tax Act 1994 (appeals) is modified as follows—
  (a)   omit section 84; and
  (b)   in paragraphs (1)(a), (2)(a) and (3)(a) of section 87, omit ", or is recoverable as, VAT".

2   The Financial Services and Markets Act 2000 (c 8)

Part 9 of the 2000 Act (hearings and appeals) is modified as follows—
  (a)   in the application of section 133 and Schedule 13 to any appeal commenced before the
coming into force of section 55 of the Consumer Credit Act 2006, for all the references
to "the Authority", substitute "the Authority or the OFT (as the case may be)";

(b)   in section 133(1)(a) for "decision notice or supervisory notice in question" substitute "notice under regulation 34(5) or (9) or 42(7) of the Money Laundering Regulations 2007";

(c)   in section 133 omit subsections (6), (7), (8) and (12); and

(d)   in section 133(9) for "decision notice" in both places where it occurs substitute "notice under regulation 34(5) or (9) or 42(7) of the Money Laundering Regulations 2007".

[2877CE]

NOTES
Commencement: 15 December 2007.
Note: the Consumer Credit Act 2006, s 55 (which inserts the Consumer Credit Act 1974, s 40A) comes into force for certain purposes on 1 December 2007 and 6 April 2008 (see the Consumer Credit Act 2006 (Commencement No 3) Order 2007, SI 2007/3300).

PART 2
SECONDARY LEGISLATION

3   The Financial Services and Markets Tribunal Rules 2001
In the application of the Financial Services and Markets Tribunal Rules 2001 to any appeal commenced before the coming into force of section 55 of the Consumer Credit Act 2006, for all the references to "the Authority" substitute "the Authority or the OFT (as the case may be)".

[2877CF]

NOTES
Commencement: 15 December 2007.
Note: the Consumer Credit Act 2006, s 55 (which inserts the Consumer Credit Act 1974, s 40A) comes into force for certain purposes on 1 December 2007 and 6 April 2008 (see the Consumer Credit Act 2006 (Commencement No 3) Order 2007, SI 2007/3300).

(Sch 6, Pt 1 amends the Criminal Justice and Police Act 2001, Sch 1, Pt 1 at **[1309]** *and contains various other amendments to the Value Added Tax Act 1994 and the Northern Ireland Act 1998 (outside the scope of this work); Sch 6 Pt 2 amends the Financial Services and Markets Act 2000 (Regulated Activities) Order 2001, SI 2001/544, art 72E at* **[2115]**, *the Proceeds of Crime Act 2002 (Failure to Disclose Money Laundering: Specified Training) Order 2003, SI 2003/171 art 2 at* **[3703]**, *and contains various other amendments to the Independent Qualified Conveyancers (Scotland) Regulations 1997, the Executry Practitioners (Scotland) Regulations 1997, the Cross-Border Credit Transfers Regulations 1999, the Terrorism Act 2000 (Crown Servants and Regulators) Regulations 2001, the Representation of the People (England and Wales) Regulations 2001, the Representation of the People (Scotland) Regulations 2001, the Public Contracts (Scotland) Regulations 2006, the Utilities Contracts (Scotland) Regulations 2006, the Public Contracts Regulations 2006, and the Utilities Contracts Regulations 2006 (outside the scope of this work).)*

TRANSFER OF FUNDS (INFORMATION ON THE PAYER) REGULATIONS 2007

(SI 2007/3298)

NOTES
Made: 22 November 2007.
Authority: Financial Services and Markets Act 2000, ss 168(4)(b), 402(1)(b), 417(1), 428(3); European Communities Act 1972, s 2(2).
Commencement: 15 December 2007.

As of 1 February 2009, these Regulations had not been amended.

ARRANGEMENT OF REGULATIONS

PART 1
GENERAL

PART 1
GENERAL

1   Citation, commencement etc

(1)   These Regulations may be cited as the Transfer of Funds (Information on the Payer) Regulations 2007 and come into force on 15th December 2007.

(2)   These Regulations are prescribed for the purposes of sections 168(4)(b) (appointment of persons to carry out investigations in particular cases) and 402(1)(b) (power of the Authority to institute proceedings for certain other offences) of the 2000 Act.

[2878]

NOTES
Commencement: 15 December 2007.

2   Interpretation

(1)   In these Regulations—
"the 2000 Act" means the Financial Services and Markets Act 2000;
"authorised person" means a person who is authorised for the purposes of the 2000 Act;
"the Authority" means the Financial Services Authority;
"the Commissioners" means the Commissioners for Her Majesty's Revenue and Customs;
"money laundering" means an act which falls within section 340(11) of the Proceeds of Crime Act 2002;
"notice" means a notice in writing;
"the payments regulation" means Regulation 1781/2006/EC of the European Parliament and of the Council of 15th November 2006 on information on the payer accompanying transfers of funds;
"supervisory authority" in relation to any payment service provider means the supervisory authority specified for such a payment service provider by regulation 3;
"terrorist financing" means an offence under—
    (a)   section 15 (fund-raising), 16 (use and possession), 17 (funding arrangements), 18 (money laundering) or 63 (terrorist finance: jurisdiction) of the Terrorism Act 2000;
    (b)   paragraph 7(2) or (3) of Schedule 3 to the Anti-Terrorism, Crime and Security Act 2001 (freezing orders);

      (c)   article 7, 8 or 10 of the Terrorism (United Nations Measures) Order 2006; or

      (d)   article 7, 8 or 10 of the Al-Qaida and Taliban (United Nations Measures) Order 2006;

(2)   Unless otherwise defined, expressions used in these Regulations and the payments regulation have the same meaning as in the payments regulation.

(3)   References in these Regulations to numbered Articles are references to Articles of the payments regulation.

[2879]

NOTES

Commencement: 15 December 2007.

PART 2
SUPERVISION

3 Supervisory authorities

(1)   The Authority is the supervisory authority for payment service providers who are authorised persons.

(2)   The Commissioners are the supervisory authority for payment service providers who are not authorised persons.

[2880]

NOTES

Commencement: 15 December 2007.

4 Duties of supervisory authorities

(1)   A supervisory authority must effectively monitor the payment service providers for whom it is the supervisory authority and take necessary measures for the purpose of securing compliance by such payment service providers with the requirements of the payments regulation.

(2)   A supervisory authority which, in the course of carrying out any of its functions under these Regulations, knows or suspects that a payment service provider is or has engaged in money laundering or terrorist financing must promptly inform the Serious Organised Crime Agency.

(3)   A disclosure made under paragraph (2) is not to be taken to breach any restriction, however imposed, on the disclosure of information.

(4)   The functions of the Authority under these Regulations shall be treated for the purposes of Parts 1, 2 and 4 of Schedule 1 to the 2000 Act (the Financial Services Authority) as functions conferred on the Authority under that Act.

[2881]

NOTES

Commencement: 15 December 2007.

5 Costs of supervision

(1)   The Authority and the Commissioners may impose charges on payment service providers supervised by them.

(2)   Charges levied under paragraph (1) must not exceed such amount as the Authority or the Commissioners (as the case may be) consider will enable them to meet any expenses reasonably incurred by them in carrying out their functions under these Regulations or for any incidental purpose.

(3)   Without prejudice to the generality of paragraph (2), a charge may be levied in respect of each of the premises at which a payment service provider carries on (or proposes to carry on) business.

(4)   The Authority must apply amounts paid to it by way of penalties imposed under regulation 11 towards expenses incurred in carrying out its functions under these Regulations or for any incidental purpose.

[2882]

NOTES

Commencement: 15 December 2007.

PART 3
ENFORCEMENT

Powers of Supervisory Authorities

6 Interpretation

In this Part—
"officer", except in regulations 10(3) and 16, means—
(a) an officer of the Authority, including a member of the Authority's staff or an agent of the Authority; or
(b) an officer of Revenue and Customs;
"recorded information" includes information recorded in any form and any document of any nature.

[2883]

NOTES
Commencement: 15 December 2007.

7 Power to require information from, and attendance of, relevant and connected persons

(1) An officer may, by notice to a payment service provider or to a person connected with a payment service provider, require the payment service provider or the connected person, as the case may be—
(a) to provide such information as may be specified in the notice;
(b) to produce such recorded information as may be so specified; or
(c) to attend before an officer at a time and place specified in the notice and answer questions.

(2) For the purposes of paragraph (1), a person is connected with a payment service provider if he is, or has at any time been, in relation to the payment service provider, a person listed in Schedule 1 to these Regulations.

(3) An officer may exercise powers under this regulation only if the information sought to be obtained as a result is reasonably required in connection with the exercise by the supervisory authority for which he acts of its functions under these Regulations.

(4) Where an officer requires information to be provided or produced pursuant to paragraph (1)(a) or (b)—
(a) the notice must set out the reasons why the officer requires the information to be provided or produced; and
(b) such information must be provided or produced—
    (i) before the end of such reasonable period as may be specified in the notice; and
    (ii) at such place as may be so specified.

(5) In relation to information recorded otherwise than in legible form, the power to require production of it includes a power to require the production of a copy of it in legible form or in a form from which it can readily be produced in visible and legible form.

(6) The production of a document does not affect any lien which a person has on the document.

(7) A person may not be required under this regulation to provide or produce information or to answer questions which that person would be entitled to refuse to provide, produce or answer on grounds of legal professional privilege in proceedings in the High Court, except that a lawyer may be required to provide the name and address of his client.

(8) Subject to paragraphs (9) and (10), a statement made by a person in compliance with a requirement imposed on that person under paragraph (1)(c) is admissible in evidence in any proceedings, so long as it also complies with any requirements governing the admissibility of evidence in the circumstances in question.

(9) In criminal proceedings in which a person is charged with an offence to which this paragraph applies—
(a) no evidence relating to the statement may be adduced; and
(b) no question relating to it may be asked,
by or on behalf of the prosecution unless evidence relating to it is adduced, or a question relating to it is asked, in the proceedings by or on behalf of that person.

(10) Paragraph (9) applies to any offence other than one under—
(a) section 5 of the Perjury Act 1911 (false statements without oath);
(b) section 44(2) of the Criminal Law (Consolidation) (Scotland) Act 1995 (false statements and declarations); or
(c) Article 10 of the Perjury (Northern Ireland) Order 1979 (false unsworn statements).

(11) In the application of this regulation to Scotland, the reference in paragraph (7) to—

  (a)   proceedings in the High Court is to be read as a reference to proceedings in the Court of Session; and

  (b)   an entitlement on grounds of legal professional privilege is to be read as a reference to an entitlement on the grounds of confidentiality of communications—

       (i)   between a professional legal adviser and his client; or

       (ii)   made in connection with or in contemplation of legal proceedings and for the purposes of those proceedings.

[2884]

NOTES

Commencement: 15 December 2007.

8   Entry, inspection without a warrant etc

(1)   Where an officer has reasonable cause to believe that any premises are being used by a payment service provider in connection with the payment service provider's business or professional activities, he may on producing evidence of his authority at any reasonable time—

  (a)   enter the premises;

  (b)   inspect the premises;

  (c)   observe the carrying on of business or professional activities by the payment service provider;

  (d)   inspect any recorded information found on the premises;

  (e)   require any person on the premises to provide an explanation of any recorded information or to state where it may be found;

  (f)   inspect any cash found on the premises.

(2)   An officer may take copies of, or make extracts from, any recorded information found under paragraph (1).

(3)   Paragraphs (1)(d) and (e) and (2) do not apply to recorded information which the payment service provider would be entitled to refuse to disclose on grounds of legal professional privilege in proceedings in the High Court, except that a lawyer may be required to provide the name and address of his client and, for this purpose, regulation 7(11) applies to this paragraph as it applies to regulation 7(7).

(4)   An officer may exercise powers under this regulation only if the information sought to be obtained as a result is reasonably required in connection with the exercise by the supervisory authority for which he acts of its functions under these Regulations.

(5)   In this regulation, "premises" means any premises other than premises used only as a dwelling.

[2885]

NOTES

Commencement: 15 December 2007.

9   Entry to premises under warrant

(1)   A justice may issue a warrant under this paragraph if satisfied on information on oath given by an officer that there are reasonable grounds for believing that the first, second or third set of conditions is satisfied.

(2)   The first set of conditions is—

  (a)   that there is on the premises specified in the warrant recorded information in relation to which a requirement could be imposed under regulation 7(1)(b); and

  (b)   that if such a requirement were to be imposed—

       (i)   it would not be complied with; or

       (ii)   the recorded information to which it relates would be removed, tampered with or destroyed.

(3)   The second set of conditions is—

  (a)   that a person on whom a requirement has been imposed under regulation 7(1)(b) has failed (wholly or in part) to comply with it; and

  (b)   that there is on the premises specified in the warrant recorded information which has been required to be produced.

(4)   The third set of conditions is—

  (a)   that an officer has been obstructed in the exercise of a power under regulation 8; and

  (b)   that there is on the premises specified in the warrant recorded information or cash which could be inspected under regulation 8(1)(d) or (f).

(5)   A justice may issue a warrant under this paragraph if satisfied on information on oath given by an officer that there are reasonable grounds for suspecting that—

(a) an offence under these Regulations has been, is being or is about to be committed by a payment service provider; and

(b) there is on the premises specified in the warrant recorded information relevant to whether that offence has been, or is being or is about to be committed.

(6) A warrant issued under this regulation shall authorise an officer—

(a) to enter the premises specified in the warrant;

(b) to search the premises and take possession of any recorded information or anything appearing to be recorded information specified in the warrant or to take, in relation to any such recorded information, any other steps which may appear to be necessary for preserving it or preventing interference with it;

(c) to take copies of, or extracts from, any recorded information specified in the warrant;

(d) to require any person on the premises to provide an explanation of any recorded information appearing to be of the kind specified in the warrant or to state where it may be found;

(e) to use such force as may reasonably be necessary.

(7) Where a warrant is issued by a justice under paragraph (1) or (5) on the basis of information on oath given by an officer of the Authority, for "an officer" in paragraph (6) substitute "a constable".

(8) In paragraphs (1), (5) and (7), "justice" means—

(a) in relation to England and Wales, a justice of the peace;

(b) in relation to Scotland, a justice within the meaning of section 307 of the Criminal Procedure (Scotland) Act 1995 (interpretation);

(c) in relation to Northern Ireland, a lay magistrate.

(9) In the application of this regulation to Scotland, the references in paragraphs (1), (5) and (7) to information on oath are to be read as references to evidence on oath.

[2886]

NOTES

Commencement: 15 December 2007.

---

10 Failure to comply with information requirement

(1) If, on an application made by a supervisory authority it appears to the court that a person (the "information defaulter") has failed to do something that he was required to do under regulation 7(1), the court may make an order under this regulation.

(2) An order under this regulation may require the information defaulter—

(a) to do the thing that he failed to do within such period as may be specified in the order;

(b) otherwise to take such steps to remedy the consequences of the failure as may be so specified.

(3) If the information defaulter is a body corporate, a partnership or an unincorporated body of persons which is not a partnership, the order may require any officer of the body corporate, partnership or body, who is (wholly or partly) responsible for the failure to meet such costs of the application as are specified in the order.

(4) In this regulation, "court" means—

(a) in England and Wales and Northern Ireland, the High Court or the county court;

(b) in Scotland, the Court of Session or the sheriff court.

[2887]

NOTES

Commencement: 15 December 2007.

Civil Penalties, Review and Appeals

11 Power to impose civil penalties

(1) A supervisory authority may impose a penalty of such amount as it considers appropriate on a payment service provider in respect of any transfer of funds to which the payments regulation applies—

(a) in the case of the payment service provider of the payer, if he fails to comply with any requirement in—

(i) Article 5(1) read with Article 6(1) (information accompanying transfers of funds within the EEA);

(ii) Article 5(2) read with Article 5(3) or (4) (whichever is relevant) (verification of information);

(iii) Article 5(5) (record keeping);

(iv) Article 6(2) (information to be provided following request);

      (v)   Article 7(1) read with Article 7(2) (information accompanying transfers of funds from the EEA to outside the EEA);

    (b)   in the case of the payment service provider of the payee, if he fails to comply with any requirement in Article 8 (detection of missing information), 9(1) (transfers of funds with missing or incomplete information), 9(2) sub-paragraph 2 (reporting) or 11 (record keeping);

    (c)   in the case of the intermediary payment service provider, if he fails to comply with any requirement in Article 12 (keeping information on the payer with the transfer) or 13(3), (4) or (5) (use of a payment system with technical limitations);

and, for this purpose, "appropriate" means effective, proportionate and dissuasive.

(2)   The supervisory authority must not impose a penalty on a person under paragraph (1) where there are reasonable grounds for it to be satisfied that the person took all reasonable steps and exercised all due diligence to ensure that the requirement would be complied with.

(3)   In deciding whether a person has failed to comply with any requirement of the payments regulation, the supervisory authority must consider whether the person followed any relevant guidance which was at the time—

    (a)   issued by a supervisory authority or any other appropriate body;

    (b)   approved by the Treasury; and

    (c)   published in a manner approved by the Treasury as suitable in their opinion to bring the guidance to the attention of persons likely to be affected by it.

(4)   In paragraph (3), an "appropriate body" means any body which regulates or is representative of any trade, profession, business or employment carried on by the payment service provider.

(5)   Where the Commissioners decide to impose a penalty under this regulation, they must give the payment service provider notice of—

    (a)   their decision to impose the penalty and its amount;

    (b)   the reasons for imposing the penalty;

    (c)   the right to a review under regulation 12; and

    (d)   the right to appeal under regulation 13(1)(b).

(6)   Where the Authority proposes to impose a penalty under this regulation, it must give the payment service provider notice of—

    (a)   its proposal to impose the penalty and the proposed amount;

    (b)   the reasons for imposing the penalty; and

    (c)   the right to make representations to it within a specified period (which may not be less than 28 days).

(7)   The Authority must then decide, within a reasonable period, whether to impose a penalty under this regulation and it must give the payment service provider notice of—

    (a)   its decision not to impose a penalty; or

    (b)   the following matters—

        (i)   its decision to impose a penalty and the amount;

        (ii)   the reasons for its decision; and

        (iii)   the right to appeal under regulation 13(1)(a).

(8)   A penalty imposed under this regulation is payable to the supervisory authority which imposes it.

                                                                               [2888]

NOTES

Commencement: 15 December 2007.

---

12 Review procedure

(1)   Any payment service provider who is the subject of a decision by the Commissioners to impose a penalty under regulation 11 may by notice to the Commissioners require them to review that decision.

(2)   The Commissioners need not review any decision unless the notice requiring the review is given within 45 days beginning with the date on which they first gave notice of the decision to the payment service provider requiring the review.

(3)   Where the Commissioners are required under this regulation to review any decision they must either—

    (a)   confirm the decision; or

    (b)   withdraw or vary the decision and take such further steps (if any) in consequence of the withdrawal or variation as they consider appropriate.

(4) Where the Commissioners do not, within 45 days beginning with the date on which the review was required by a payment service provider, give notice to that person of their determination of the review, they are to be taken for the purposes of these Regulations to have confirmed the decision.

[2889]

NOTES
Commencement: 15 December 2007.

13 Appeals

(1) A payment service provider may appeal from a decision by—
  (a) the Authority under regulation 11(7); and
  (b) the Commissioners on a review under regulation 12.

(2) An appeal from a decision by—
  (a) the Authority is to the Financial Services and Markets Tribunal; and
  (b) the Commissioners is to a VAT and duties tribunal.

(3) The provisions of Part 9 of the 2000 Act (hearings and appeals), subject to the modifications set out in paragraph 1 of Schedule 2, apply in respect of appeals to the Financial Services and Markets Tribunal made under this regulation as they apply in respect of references made to that Tribunal under that Act.

(4) The provisions of Part 5 of the Value Added Tax Act 1994 (appeals), subject to the modifications set out in paragraph 2 of Schedule 2, apply in respect of appeals to a VAT and duties tribunal made under this regulation as they apply in respect of appeals made to such a tribunal under section 83 (appeals) of that Act.

(5) A VAT and duties tribunal hearing an appeal under paragraph (2) has the power to—
  (a) quash or vary any decision of the supervisory authority, including the power to reduce any penalty to such amount (including nil) as they think proper; and
  (b) substitute their own decision for any decision quashed on appeal.

[2890]

NOTES
Commencement: 15 December 2007.

Criminal Offences

14 Offences

(1) A payment service provider is guilty of an offence in respect of any transfer of funds to which the payments regulation applies—
  (a) in the case of the payment service provider of the payer, if he fails to comply with any requirement in—
     (i) Article 5(1) read with Article 6(1) (information accompanying transfers of funds within the EEA);
     (ii) Article 5(2) read with Article 5(3) or (4) (whichever is relevant) (verification of information);
     (iii) Article 5(5) (record keeping);
     (iv) Article 6(2) (information to be provided following request);
     (v) Article 7(1) read with Article 7(2) (information accompanying transfers of funds from the EEA to outside the EEA);
  (b) in the case of the payment service provider of the payee, if he fails to comply with any requirement in Article 8 (detection of missing information), 9(1) or the third paragraph of Article 9 (transfers of funds with missing or incomplete information) or Article 11 (record keeping);
  (c) in the case of the intermediary payment service provider, if he fails to comply with any requirement in Article 12 (keeping information on the payer with the transfer) or 13(3), (4) or (5) (use of a payment system with technical limitations).

(2) A payment service provider who is guilty of an offence under paragraph (1) is liable—
  (a) on summary conviction, to a fine not exceeding the statutory maximum;
  (b) on conviction on indictment, to imprisonment for a term not exceeding two years, to a fine or to both.

(3) In deciding whether a person has committed an offence under paragraph (1), the court must consider whether the person followed any relevant guidance which was at the time—
  (a) issued by a supervisory authority or any other appropriate body;
  (b) approved by the Treasury; and
  (c) published in a manner approved by the Treasury as suitable in their opinion to bring the guidance to the attention of persons likely to be affected by it.

(4) In paragraph (3), an "appropriate body" means any body which regulates or is representative of any trade, profession, business or employment carried on by the alleged offender.

(5) A person is not guilty of an offence under this regulation if he took all reasonable steps and exercised all due diligence to avoid committing the offence.

(6) Where a person is convicted of an offence under this regulation, he shall not also be liable to a penalty under regulation 11.

[2891]

NOTES
Commencement: 15 December 2007.

15 Prosecution of offences

(1) Proceedings for an offence under regulation 14 may be instituted by—
   (a)   the Director of Revenue and Customs Prosecutions or by order of the Commissioners;
   (b)   the Director of Public Prosecutions; or
   (c)   the Director of Public Prosecutions for Northern Ireland.

(2) Proceedings for an offence under regulation 14 may be instituted only against a payment service provider or, where the payment service provider is a body corporate, a partnership or an unincorporated association, against any person who is liable to be proceeded against under regulation 16.

(3) Where proceedings under paragraph (1) are instituted by order of the Commissioners, the proceedings must be brought in the name of an officer of Revenue and Customs.

(4) Where the Commissioners investigate, or propose to investigate, any matter with a view to determining—
   (a)   whether there are grounds for believing that an offence under regulation 14 has been committed by any person; or
   (b)   whether a person should be prosecuted for such an offence,
that matter is to be treated as an assigned matter within the meaning of section 1(1) of the Customs and Excise Management Act 1979.

(5) Paragraphs (1) and (3) do not extend to Scotland and, in its application to the Commissioners acting in Scotland, paragraph (4)(b) shall be read as referring to the Commissioners determining whether to refer the matter to the Crown Office and Procurator Fiscal Service with a view to the Procurator Fiscal determining whether a person should be prosecuted for such an offence.

[2892]

NOTES
Commencement: 15 December 2007.

16 Offences by bodies corporate etc

(1) If an offence under regulation 14 committed by a body corporate is shown—
   (a)   to have been committed with the consent or the connivance of an officer of the body corporate; or
   (b)   to be attributable to any neglect on his part,
the officer as well as the body corporate is guilty of an offence and liable to be proceeded against and punished accordingly.

(2) If an offence under regulation 14 committed by a partnership is shown—
   (a)   to have been committed with the consent or the connivance of a partner; or
   (b)   to be attributable to any neglect on his part,
the partner as well as the partnership is guilty of an offence and liable to be proceeded against and punished accordingly.

(3) If an offence under regulation 14 committed by an unincorporated association (other than a partnership) is shown—
   (a)   to have been committed with the consent or the connivance of an officer of the association; or
   (b)   to be attributable to any neglect on his part,
the officer as well as the association is guilty of an offence and liable to be proceeded against and punished accordingly.

(4) If the affairs of a body corporate are managed by its members, paragraph (1) applies in relation to the acts and defaults of a member in connection with his functions of management as if he were a director of the body.

(5)   Proceedings for an offence alleged to have been committed by a partnership or an unincorporated association must be brought in the name of the partnership or association (and not in that of its members).

(6)   A fine imposed on the partnership or association on its conviction of an offence is to be paid out of the funds of the partnership or association.

(7)   Rules of court relating to the service of documents are to have effect as if the partnership or association were a body corporate.

(8)   In proceedings for an offence brought against the partnership or association—
  (a)   section 33 of the Criminal Justice Act 1925 (procedure on charge of offence against corporation) and Schedule 3 to the Magistrates' Courts Act 1980 (corporations) apply as they do in relation to a body corporate;
  (b)   section 70 of the Criminal Procedure (Scotland) Act 1995 (proceedings against bodies corporate) applies as it does in relation to a body corporate;
  (c)   section 18 of the Criminal Justice (Northern Ireland) Act 1945 (procedure on charge) and Schedule 4 to the Magistrates' Courts (Northern Ireland) Order 1981 (corporations) apply as they do in relation to a body corporate.

(9)   In this regulation—
  "officer"—
  (a)   in relation to a body corporate, means a director, manager, secretary, chief executive, member of the committee of management, or a person purporting to act in such a capacity; and
  (b)   in relation to an unincorporated association, means any officer of the association or any member of its governing body, or a person purporting to act in such capacity; and
  "partner" includes a person purporting to act as a partner.

[2893]

NOTES
  Commencement: 15 December 2007.

PART 4
MISCELLANEOUS

17 Recovery of charges and penalties through the court

Any charge or penalty imposed on a payment service provider by a supervisory authority under regulation 5(1) or 11(1) is a debt due from that person to the authority, and is recoverable accordingly.

[2894]

NOTES
  Commencement: 15 December 2007.

18 Transfers between the United Kingdom and the Channel Islands and the Isle of Man

In determining whether a person has failed to comply with any requirement in the payments regulation, any transfer of funds between the United Kingdom and—
  (a)   the Channel Islands; or
  (b)   the Isle of Man,
shall be treated as a transfer of funds within the United Kingdom.

[2895]

NOTES
  Commencement: 15 December 2007.

19 Consequential amendments

Schedule 3, which contains consequential amendments, has effect.

[2896]

NOTES
  Commencement: 15 December 2007.

SCHEDULES

SCHEDULE 1
CONNECTED PERSONS
Regulation 7(2)

Corporate Bodies
1.   If the payment service provider is a body corporate ("BC"), a person who is or has been—
    (a)   an officer or manager of BC or of a parent undertaking of BC;
    (b)   an employee of BC;
    (c)   an agent of BC or of a parent undertaking of BC

Partnerships
2.   If the payment service provider is a partnership, a person who is or has been a member, manager, employee or agent of the partnership.

Unincorporated Associations
3.   If the payment service provider is an unincorporated association of persons which is not a partnership, a person who is or has been an officer, manager, employee or agent of the association.

Individuals
4.   If the payment service provider is an individual, a person who is or has been an employee or agent of that individual.

[2897]

NOTES
Commencement: 15 December 2007.

SCHEDULE 2
MODIFICATIONS IN RELATION TO APPEALS
Regulation 13(3) and (4)

1   The Financial Services and Markets Act 2000

Section 133 of the 2000 Act (hearings and appeals) is modified as follows—
    (a)   in paragraph (a) of subsection (1), for "decision notice or supervisory notice in question" substitute "notice under regulation 11(7) of the Transfer of Funds (Information on the Payer) Regulations 2007";
    (b)   omit subsections (6), (7), (8) and (12); and
    (c)   in subsection (9)—
        (i)   for "decision notice" where it first occurs substitute "notice under regulation 11(7) of the Transfer of Funds (Information on the Payer) Regulations 2007";
        (ii) in paragraph (a), omit "decision".

2   The Value Added Tax Act 1994

Part 5 of the Value Added Tax Act 1994 (appeals) is modified as follows—
    (a)   omit section 84; and
    (b)   in section 87, in paragraph (a) of each of subsections (1), (2) and (3), omit ", or is recoverable as, VAT".

[2898]

NOTES
Commencement: 15 December 2007.

(Sch 3 (Consequential Amendments) amends the Northern Ireland Act 1998, Sch 3 (outside the scope of this work), the Criminal Justice and Police Act 2001, s 68 (outside the scope of this work) and Sch 1, Pt 1 to the 2001 Act at **[1309]**.*)*

PART III
STATUTORY INSTRUMENTS

FINANCIAL SERVICES AND MARKETS ACT 2000 (REGULATED ACTIVITIES) (AMENDMENT) (NO 2) ORDER 2007

(SI 2007/3510)

NOTES

Made: 13 December 2007.
Authority: Financial Services and Markets Act 2000, ss 22(1), (5), 426(1), 427, 428(3), Sch 2, para 25.
Commencement: 30 June 2008 (certain purposes); 1 January 2009 (otherwise).

As of 1 February 2009, this Order had not been amended.

PART 1
GENERAL

1 Citation and commencement

(1) This Order may be cited as the Financial Services and Markets Act 2000 (Regulated Activities) (Amendment) (No 2) Order 2007.

(2) This Order comes into force—
  (a) for the purposes of enabling applications to be made, pursuant to the amendments made to article 72B of the Financial Services and Markets Act 2000 (Regulated Activities) Order 2001 by article 2 of this Order, for—
    (i) a Part IV permission, or a variation of a Part IV permission, in relation to activities of the kind specified by article 21, 25(1), 25(2), 39A, 53 or, so far as relevant to any such activity, article 64 of the Financial Services and Markets Act 2000 (Regulated Activities) Order 2001; or
    (ii) the Authority's approval under section 59 of the Financial Services and Markets Act 2000 in relation to any of those activities, on 30th June 2008;
  (b) for all other purposes, on 1st January 2009.

[2899]

NOTES

Commencement: 30 June 2008 (certain purposes); 1 January 2009 (otherwise) (see above).

2 *(Art 2 (Pt 2) amends the Financial Services and Markets Act 2000 (Regulated Activities) Order 2001, SI 2001/544, art 72B at* **[2112]***.)*

PART 3
TRANSITIONAL PROVISIONS

3 Interpretation

In this Part—
  "the Act" means the Financial Services and Markets Act 2000;
  "commencement" means the beginning of 1st January 2009;
  "the Regulated Activities Order" means the Financial Services and Markets Act 2000 (Regulated Activities) Order 2001.

[2900]

NOTES

Commencement: 30 June 2008 (certain purposes); 1 January 2009 (otherwise) (see art 1).

4 Interim permission

(1) This article applies where—
  (a) a person who is a provider within the meaning of article 72B of the Regulated Activities Order ("the applicant") has submitted to the Authority an application for Part IV permission or a variation of a Part IV permission to the extent that the application—
    (i) relates to an activity of the kind specified in any of the following articles of the Regulated Activities Order—
      (aa) article 21 (dealing in investments as agent);
      (bb) article 25(1) and (2) (arranging deals in investments);
      (cc) article 39A (assisting in the administration and performance of a contract of insurance);
      (dd) article 53 (advising on investments); or
      (ee) article 64 (agreeing to carry on specified kinds of activity) in so far as it relates to any of the activities mentioned in (aa) to (dd); and

    (ii)   is made pursuant to the amendments made to article 72B of the Regulated Activities Order by article 2 of this Order;

  (b)   the Authority received the application on or before 15th November 2008; and

  (c)   the application has not been finally decided before commencement.

(2)   The applicant is to be treated as having on commencement the permission to which the application relates.

(3)   A permission which an applicant is to be treated as having is referred to in this Part as an "interim permission".

(4)   Without prejudice to the exercise by the Authority of its powers under Part 4 of the Act, an interim permission lapses—

  (a)   when the application has been finally decided; or

  (b)   at the end of 31st December 2009,

whichever is the earlier.

(5)   In this article "finally decided" means—

  (a)   when the application is withdrawn;

  (b)   when the Authority grants permission under section 42 of the Act (giving permission) to carry on the activity in question;

  (c)   when the Authority varies a permission under section 44 of the Act (variation etc at request of authorised person) to add the activity in question;

  (d)   where the Authority has refused an application and the matter is not referred to the Tribunal, when the time for referring the matter to the Tribunal has expired;

  (e)   where the Authority has refused an application and the matter is referred to the Tribunal, when—

    (i)   if the reference is determined by the Tribunal (including a determination following remission back to the Tribunal for rehearing in accordance with section 137(3)(a) of the Act (appeal on a point of law)), the time for bringing an appeal has expired; or

    (ii)   on an appeal from a determination by the Tribunal on a point of law, the Court itself determines the application in accordance with section 137 of the Act.

(6)   An applicant who is treated as having an interim permission may not withdraw the application without first obtaining the consent of the Authority.

(7)   Where—

  (a)   the Authority exercises its powers under section 45 (variation etc on the Authority's own initiative) in relation to an authorised person who holds an interim permission; and

  (b)   as a result of the variation there are no longer any regulated activities for which the authorised person has permission,

the Authority must, once it is satisfied that it is no longer necessary to keep the interim permission in force, cancel it.

[2901]

NOTES

Commencement: 30 June 2008 (certain purposes); 1 January 2009 (otherwise) (see art 1).

---

5 Interim approval

(1)   This article applies where—

  (a)   the applicant (within the meaning of article 4(1)(a)) has submitted to the Authority an application made under section 60 of the Act (applications for approval) pursuant to the amendments made to article 72B of the Regulated Activities Order by article 2 of this Order; and

  (b)   the application has not been finally decided before commencement.

(2)   The person in respect of whom the application is made is to be treated as having on commencement the approval of the Authority for the purposes of section 59 of the Act (approval for particular arrangements) in relation to the functions to which the application relates.

(3)   An approval which a person is to be treated as having is referred to in this Part as an "interim approval".

(4)   Without prejudice to the exercise by the Authority of its powers under Part 5 of the Act, an interim approval lapses—

  (a)   when the application has been finally decided; or

  (b)   at the end of 31st December 2009,

whichever is the earlier.

(5)   In this article, "finally decided" means—

  (a)   when the application is withdrawn;

(b)   when the Authority grants the application for approval under section 62 of the Act (applications for approval: procedure and right to refer to the Tribunal);

(c)   where the Authority has refused an application and the matter is not referred to the Tribunal, when the time for referring the matter to the Tribunal has expired;

(d)   where the Authority has refused an application and the matter is referred to the Tribunal, when—

    (i)   if the reference is determined by the Tribunal (including a determination following remission back to the Tribunal for rehearing in accordance with section 137(3)(a) of the Act), the time for bringing an appeal has expired; or

    (ii)   on an appeal from a determination by the Tribunal on a point of law, the Court itself determines the application in accordance with section 137 of the Act.

[2902]

NOTES

Commencement: 30 June 2008 (certain purposes); 1 January 2009 (otherwise) (see art 1).

6 Application of the Authority's rules etc to persons with an interim permission or an interim approval

(1)   The Authority may direct in writing that any relevant provision which would otherwise apply to a person by virtue of his interim permission or interim approval is not to apply or is to apply to him as modified in the way specified in the direction.

(2)   Where the Authority makes a rule, gives guidance or issues a statement or code which applies only to persons with an interim permission or an interim approval (or only to a class of such persons), sections 65 (statements and codes: procedure), 155 (consultation) and 157(3) (guidance) of the Act do not apply to that rule, guidance, statement or code.

(3)   For the purposes of paragraph (1) a "relevant provision" is any provision made as a result of the exercise by the Authority of any of its legislative functions mentioned in paragraph 1(2) of Schedule 1 to the Act (the Financial Services Authority).

[2903]

NOTES

Commencement: 30 June 2008 (certain purposes); 1 January 2009 (otherwise) (see art 1).

7 Application of the Act to persons with an interim permission or an interim approval

(1)   This article applies to every person with interim permission.

(2)   For the purpose of section 20 (authorised persons acting without permission), a person's interim permission is treated as having been given to him under Part 4 of the Act.

(3)   A person's interim permission is to be disregarded for the purposes of—

(a)   section 38(2) (exemption orders);

(b)   section 40(2) (application for permission);

(c)   subject to article 8(4), section 42 (giving permission);

(d)   section 43 (imposition of requirements); and

(e)   section 44(1), (4) and (5) (variation etc at request of authorised person).

[2904]

NOTES

Commencement: 30 June 2008 (certain purposes); 1 January 2009 (otherwise) (see art 1).

8—(1)   This article applies to a person who falls within section 31(1) (authorised persons) by virtue only of having an interim permission.

(2)   A person with an interim permission is to be treated on or after commencement as an authorised person for the purposes of the Act (and any provision made under the Act), unless otherwise expressly provided for by this Part.

(3)   For the purposes of section 21(2) (restrictions on financial promotion), a person with an interim permission is not to be treated as an authorised person for the purposes of communicating or approving the content of a communication except where the communication invites or induces a person to enter into (or offer to enter into) an agreement the making or performance of which constitutes a controlled activity which corresponds to a regulated activity which is covered by his interim permission.

(4)   A person with an interim permission may still be an appointed representative within the meaning of section 39(2) (exemption of appointed representatives) (and hence may be treated as exempt from the general prohibition as a result of section 39(1) for the purposes of section 42(3)(a) (giving permission)).

(5)   Subsection (3)(a) of section 213 (the compensation scheme) does not apply to—

(a)   a person who is a relevant person, within the meaning of that section, by virtue only of having an interim permission; or

(b)   an appointed representative of such person.

[2905]

NOTES

Commencement: 30 June 2008 (certain purposes); 1 January 2009 (otherwise) (see art 1).

9   A person with an interim approval is to be treated on or after commencement as an approved person for the purposes of the Act (and any provision made under the Act).

[2906]–[3499]

NOTES

Commencement: 30 June 2008 (certain purposes); 1 January 2009 (otherwise) (see art 1).

Appendix 2

STATUTORY INSTRUMENTS MADE UNDER THE FINANCIAL SERVICES AND MARKETS ACT 2000

NOTES

This table lists all statutory instruments made under the Financial Services and Markets Act 2000 that are of general UK application. Statutory instruments applying to Northern Ireland only are not listed. Statutory instruments which are no longer in force are printed in italics.

2009 Statutory Instruments

SI 2009/264: Financial Services and Markets Act 2000 (Exemption) (Amendment) Order 2009
Authority: FSMA 2000, s 38. This Order (which has an identical name to the Order listed below) also amends the Financial Services and Markets Act 2000 (Exemption) Order 2001, SI 2001/1201. It extends the exemption in para 50 of the Schedule to the 2001 Order applying in relation to freight forwarders and storage firms, so that such firms may extend rights under their insurance policies to both their commercial and to their retail customers without becoming subject to regulation under the Act (see **[2220]**).

SI 2009/118: Financial Services and Markets Act 2000 (Exemption) (Amendment) Order 2009
Authority: FSMA 2000, ss 38, 428(3). This Order amends the Financial Services and Markets Act 2000 (Exemption) Order 2001, SI 2001/1201. It adds the Bank of England Asset Purchase Facility Fund Limited to the list of persons in Part 1 of the Schedule who are exempt in respect of any regulated activity other than insurance business (see **[2217]**).

2008 Statutory Instruments

SI 2008/2673: Financial Services and Markets Act 2000 (Consequential Amendments) (Taxes) Order 2008
Authority: FSMA 2000, ss 426, 428. This Order amends the Income and Corporation Taxes Act 1988, s 444BA. It substitutes a reference to the Insurance Prudential Sourcebook for the existing reference to the Integrated Prudential Sourcebook.

SI 2008/1813: Financial Services and Markets Act 2000 (Collective Investment Schemes) (Amendment) (No 2) Order 2008
Authority: FSMA 2000, ss 235(5), 428(3). This Order amends the Financial Services and Markets Act 2000 (Collective Investment Schemes) (Amendment) Order 2008, SI 2008/1641 which itself amended the Schedule to the Financial Services and Markets Act 2000 (Collective Investment Schemes) Order 2001, SI 2001/1062 (see below). It corrects errors in SI 2008/1641 and comes into force on the day before that Order comes into force.

SI 2008/1725: Financial Services and Markets Act 2000 (Control of Transfers of Business Done at Lloyd's) (Amendment) Order 2008
Authority: FSMA 2000, ss 323, 428(3). This Order amends the Financial Services and Markets Act 2000 (Control of Transfers of Business Done at Lloyd's) Order 2001, SI 2001/3626 (at **[2523]**). The 2001 Order applies Part VII of the Financial Services and Markets Act 2000 to the Lloyd's market (control of business transfers). This Order amends the 2001 Order so that the provisions of Part VII, that were applied by that Order to members and to some former members of Lloyd's, apply to all insurance business whenever written in the Lloyd's market.

SI 2008/1641: Financial Services and Markets Act 2000 (Collective Investment Schemes) (Amendment) Order 2008
Authority: FSMA 2000, ss 235(5), 428(3). This Order amends the Schedule to the Financial Services and Markets Act 2000 (Collective Investment Schemes) Order 2001 (SI 2001/1062) which sets out arrangements which are not to be regarded as a collective investment scheme for the purposes of the Financial Services and Markets Act 2000. It substitutes a new paragraph 9 in that Schedule (see **[2202]** et seq).

2008 Statutory Instruments

SI 2008/1468: Financial Services and Markets Act 2000 (Amendments to Part 7) Regulations 2008

Authority: FSMA 2000, ss 117(b), 428(3). These Regulations amend Part VII of the 2000 Act (see [127] et seq). New s 112(2A)–(2C) make clear that the power of the court to make an order under s 112 is to be taken as always having included the power to transfer, for example, contracts which include provisions prohibiting their transfer or contracts in relation to which there is a query as to their transferability in the absence of consent of a counterparty or contracts where there is a contravention, liability or interference with a right or interest which arises as a result of the transfer. A new s 112A also makes clear that the specified entitlements arising as a result of something done or likely to be done by or under Pt VII of the Act will only be enforceable after the order under s 112(1) has been made and only in so far as the court makes provision to that effect in that order.

SI 2008/1467: Financial Services and Markets Act 2000 (Control of Business Transfers) (Requirements on Applicants) (Amendment) Regulations 2008

Authority: FSMA 2000, ss 108, 428(3). These Regulations amend the Financial Services and Markets Act 2000 (Control of Business Transfers) (Requirements on Applicants) Regulations 2001, SI 2001/3625 (see [2517] et seq). The effect of the amendments is to oblige a person applying to court for an order sanctioning an insurance business transfer under s 107 of the 2000 Act to give notice of the application to a reinsurer (or a person acting on its behalf) any of whose contracts of reinsurance are proposed to be transferred as part of the insurance business transfer scheme.

SI 2008/733: Financial Services and Markets Act 2000 (Consequential Amendments) Order 2008

Authority: FSMA 2000, s 426. This Order amends the Consumer Credit Act 1974, s 82(2A). Section 82 deals with the variation of agreements and sub-s (2) makes provision for the treatment of agreements which have been varied for the purposes of the 1974 Act. Sub-s (2A) provides that sub-s (2) does not apply in certain circumstances. The circumstances are where the modifying agreement is an agreement secured by land mortgage or an agreement which is (or forms part of) a regulated home purchase plan, and where entering into the agreement as lender or home purchase provider is a regulated activity for the purposes of FSMA 2000. These types of agreements are exempt under s 16(6C) of the 1974 Act. The amendment to s 82(2A) provides that sub-s (2) also does not apply where the earlier agreement which is being modified is exempt from the application of the 1974 Act under s 16(6C).

SI 2008/682: Financial Services and Markets Act 2000 (Exemption) (Amendment) Order 2008

Authority: FSMA 2000, ss 38, 428(3). This Order amends the Schedule to the Financial Services and Markets Act 2000 (Exemption) Order 2001 (SI 2001/1201) which provides for certain persons to be exempt from the general prohibition imposed by FSMA 2000, s 19 on carrying on a regulated activity in the UK unless authorised under the 2000 Act (see [2211] et seq). This Order adds Capital for Enterprise Limited to the Schedule of the 2001 Order. This provides that Capital for Enterprise Limited is exempt in relation to the regulated activities listed at art 5(1) of the 2001 Order carried on by it provided that in doing so it provides services only to the Crown.

2007 Statutory Instruments

SI 2007/3510: Financial Services and Markets Act 2000 (Regulated Activities) (Amendment) (No 2) Order 2007

Authority: FSMA 2000, ss 22(1), (5), 426(1), 427, 428(3), Sch 2, para 25. At [2899]. This Order amends art 72B(1)(d)(ii) of the Regulated Activities Order to limit the exemption from regulation in respect of the activities specified in arts 21, 25(1) and (2), 39A, 53 and 64 of that Order for travel insurance to circumstances where a contract of insurance is linked to (a) travel to an event organised by the travel provider where the person seeking insurance is not an individual or a business with a group annual turnover of less than £1,000,000; or (b) the hire of a vehicle.

2007 Statutory Instruments

SI 2007/3298: Transfer of Funds (Information on the Payer) Regulations 2007
Authority: FSMA 2000, ss 168(4)(b), 402(1)(b), 417(1), 428(3). At **[2878]**. These Regulations make provision for the enforcement of the obligations set out in Regulation 1781/2006/EC of the European Parliament and of the Council on information on the payer accompanying transfers of funds. The 2006 Regulation imposes obligations on payment services providers when they make or receive a transfer of funds. Part 2 makes provision for the supervision of payment service providers (individuals or businesses whose business includes services for the electronic transfer of funds on behalf of a payer). Part 3 provides enforcement powers for the supervisors. These include powers to obtain information from payment service providers etc, to enter and inspect premises, and to apply to court when a provider has failed to comply with a requirement to produce information to a supervisor. Provision is also made for civil penalties and criminal offences. Part 4 contains provision for the recovery of penalties and charges through the court, and provides that transfers of funds between the UK and any of the Crown Dependencies are to be treated as transfers within the UK.

SI 2007/3255: Financial Services and Markets Act 2000 (Reinsurance Directive) Regulations 2007
Authority: FSMA 2000, ss 108, 183(2), 188(2), 349(1)(b), (2), (3), 417(1), 428(3). These Regulations implement, in part, Directive 2005/68/EC of the European Parliament and of the Council of 16 November 2005 on reinsurance ("the Reinsurance Directive"). They amend the Financial Services and Markets Act 2000 (Control of Business Transfers) (Requirements on Applicants) Regulations 2001, SI 2001/3625 (at **[2517]** et seq), the Financial Services and Markets Act 2000 (Disclosure of Confidential Information) Regulations 2001, SI 2001/2188 (at **[2350]** et seq), and the Financial Services and Markets Act 2000 (Consultation with Competent Authorities) Regulations 2001, SI 2001/2509 (at **[2421]** et seq).

SI 2007/3254: Financial Services and Markets Act 2000 (Reinsurance Directive) Order 2007
Authority: FSMA 2000, ss 22(1), (5), 409(1)(a), (5), 428(3), Sch 2, para 25. This Order implements, in part, Directive 2005/68/EC of the European Parliament and of the Council of 16 November 2005 on reinsurance ("the Reinsurance Directive"). It amends the Regulated Activities Order (at **[2010]** et seq) and the Financial Services and Markets Act 2000 (Gibraltar) Order 2001, SI 2001/3084 (at **[2495]** et seq).

SI 2007/2615: Financial Services and Markets Act 2000 (Financial Promotion) (Amendment No 2) Order 2007
Authority: FSMA 2000, ss 21(5), (6), 428(3). This Order amends the Financial Services and Markets Act 2000 (Financial Promotion) Order 2005, SI 2005/1529 at **[2757]** et seq. The amendment made by this Order extends the exemptions from the restriction on financial promotions to prospectuses (and their constituent parts) which have been approved by another Member State and which approval has been notified to the competent authority in the UK in accordance with s 87H of FSMA 2000. It also extends the exemption to communications made in accordance with the Prospectus Directive comprising the final terms of the offer or the final offer price or amount of securities to be offered to the public.

SI 2007/2403: Financial Services and Markets Act 2000 (Motor Insurance) Regulations 2007
Authority: FSMA 2000, ss 117, 417(1), 424(3), 428(3). These Regulations amend FSMA 2000 and the Financial Services and Markets Act 2000 (Law Applicable to Contracts of Insurance) Regulations 2001, SI 2001/2635 to change the meaning of "EEA State in which a risk is situated" in certain circumstances in the context of vehicle insurance. They implement, in part, Article 4a(1) of Council Directive 1990/232/EEC on the approximation of the laws of the Member States relating to insurance against civil liability in respect of the use of motor vehicles (the "Third Motor Insurance Directive") which was inserted into the Directive by Article 4(4) of Directive 2005/14/EC of the European Parliament and of the Council.

SI 2007/2157: Money Laundering Regulations 2007
Authority: FSMA 2000, ss 168(4)(b), 402(1)(b), 417(1), 428(3); European Communities Act 1972, s 2(2). At **[2877AA]**. These Regulations revoke and replace the Money Laundering Regulations 2003, 2003/3075 (at **[3787]**) as from 15 December 2007.

SI 2007/1821: Financial Services and Markets Act 2000 (Exemption) (Amendment No 2) Order 2007
Authority: FSMA 2000, ss 38, 428(3). This Order amends the Financial Services and Markets Act 2000 (Exemption) Order 2001, SI 2001/1201 (at **[2211]**)

SI 2007/1339: Financial Services and Markets Act 2000 (Regulated Activities) (Amendment) Order 2007
Authority: FSMA 2000, ss 22(1), (5), 428(3), Sch 2, para 25. This Order amends the definition of "qualifying contracts of insurance" in art 2 of the RAO (at **[2012]**)

2007 Statutory Instruments

SI 2007/1083: Financial Services and Markets Act 2000 (Financial Promotion) (Amendment) Order 2007
Authority: FSMA 2000, s 21(5), (6). This Order substitutes the Financial Services and Markets Act 2000 (Financial Promotion) Order 2005, SI 2005/1529, Sch 3, Pt II at **[2844]** (certain investment exchanges operating relevant EEA markets)

SI 2007/800: Financial Services and Markets Act 2000 (Collective Investment Schemes) (Amendment) Order 2007
Authority: FSMA 2000, s 235(5). This Order amends the Schedule to the Financial Services Markets Act 2000 (Collective Investment Schemes) Order 2001, SI 2001/1062 (at **[2205]**) which sets out arrangements which are not to be regarded as collective investment schemes for the purposes of FSMA 2000. Paragraph 7 of that Schedule excludes certain funds relating to leasehold property. The amendment made by this Order extends this exclusion to arrangements where the participants have rights or interests in money held under a tenancy deposit scheme as provided for by Chapter 4 of Part 6 of the Housing Act 2004

SI 2007/763: Financial Services and Markets Act 2000 (Markets in Financial Instruments) (Amendment) Regulations 2007
Authority: FSMA 2000, ss 39(1), 349(1)–(3), 417(1), 428(3), Sch 3, para 22; European Communities Act 1972, s 2(2). At **[2869]**. These Regulations amend the Financial Services and Markets Act 2000 (Markets in Financial Instruments) Regulations 2007, SI 2007/126 (at **[4051]** et seq), the Financial Services and Markets Act 2000 (EEA Passport Rights) Regulations 2001, SI 2001/2511, reg 1 (at **[2430]**), and add the Financial Services and Markets Act 2000 (Appointed Representatives) Regulations 2001, SI 2001/1217, reg 4 (at **[2223A]**). They also make a consequential amendment to the Financial Services and Markets Act 2000 (Disclosure of Confidential Information) (Amendment) Regulations 2006, SI 2006/3413 (relating to the commencement of those Regulations). The Regulations implement, in part, Directive 2004/39/EC of the European Parliament and of the Council of 21 April 2004 on markets in financial instruments (MiFID)

SI 2007/383: Financial Services and Markets Act 2000 (Ombudsman Scheme) (Consumer Credit Jurisdiction) Order 2007
Authority: FSMA 2000, s 226A(2)(e). At **[2867]**. Section 226A of the 2000 Act was inserted by the Consumer Credit Act 2006. It provides that a complaint, relating to an act or omission of a licensee under a standard licence or a person authorised to carry on an activity by virtue of s 34A of the Consumer Credit Act 1974, qualifies to be dealt with under the financial ombudsman scheme if certain conditions are satisfied. One of the conditions is that at the time the act or omission occurs it has to have occurred in the course of a business of a type specified in an order made by the Secretary of State. This Order specifies the types of business for the purposes of section 226A(2)(e)

SI 2007/125: Financial Services and Markets Act 2000 (Exemption) (Amendment) Order 2007
Authority: FSMA 2000, ss 38, 428(3). This Order, which amends the Financial Services and Markets Act 2000 (Exemption) Order 2001, SI 2001/1201 at **[2211]**, implements, in part, Directive 2004/39/EC of the European Parliament and of the Council of 21 April 2004 on markets in financial instruments (MiFID)

2006 Statutory Instruments

SI 2006/3414: Financial Services and Markets Act 2000 (Appointed Representatives) (Amendment) Regulations 2006
Authority: FSMA 2000, ss 39(1), 417(1), 428(3). These Regulations, which amend the Financial Services and Markets Act 2000 (Appointed Representatives) Regulations 2001, SI 2001/1217 at **[2221]**, implement, in part, Directive 2004/39/EC of the European Parliament and of the Council of 21 April 2004 on markets in financial instruments (MiFID)

SI 2006/3413: Financial Services and Markets Act 2000 (Disclosure of Confidential Information) (Amendment) Regulations 2006
Authority: FSMA 2000, ss 349(1), (2), (3), 417(1), 428(3). These Regulations, which amend the Financial Services and Markets Act 2000 (Disclosure of Confidential Information) Regulations 2001, SI 2001/2188 at **[2350]**, implement, in part, Directive 2004/39/EC of the European Parliament and of the Council of 21 April 2004 on markets in financial instruments (MiFID)

2006 Statutory Instruments

SI 2006/3386: Financial Services and Markets Act 2000 (Recognition Requirements for Investment Exchanges and Clearing Houses) (Amendment) Regulations 2006
Authority: FSMA 2000, ss 286(1), (4A), (4B), (4C), (4D), 292(3)(a), 428(3). These Regulations amend the Financial Services and Markets Act 2000 (Recognition Requirements for Investment Exchanges and Clearing Houses) Regulations 2001, SI 2001/995 at [2147]. These Regulations implement, in part, Directive 2004/39/EC of the European Parliament and of the Council of 21 April 2004 on markets in financial instruments (MiFID)

SI 2006/3385: Financial Services and Markets Act 2000 (EEA Passport Rights) (Amendment) Regulations 2006
Authority: FSMA 2000, ss 428(3), Sch 3, paras 13(1)(b)(iii), 14(1)(b), 17(b), 22. At [2866B]. These Regulations implement, in part, Directive 2004/39/EC of the European Parliament and of the Council on markets in financial instruments (MiFID). They amend the Financial Services and Markets Act 2000 (EEA Passport Rights) Regulations 2001, SI 2001/2511 at [2430]

SI 2006/3384: Financial Services and Markets Act 2000 (Regulated Activities) (Amendment No 3) Order 2006
Authority: FSMA 2000, ss 22(1), (5), 428(3), Sch 2, para 25. This Order implements, in part, Directive 2004/39/EC of the European Parliament and of the Council on markets in financial instruments (MiFID). Part 2 of the Order amends the Financial Services and Markets Act 2000 (Regulated Activities) Order 2001, SI 2001/544. Parts 3 and 4 contain consequential amendments to other Acts and statutory instruments (including the Companies Act 1989, the Terrorism Act 2000, the Financial Services and Markets Act 2000 (Collective Investment Schemes) Order 2001, SI 2001/1062, the Financial Services and Markets Act 2000 (Carrying on Regulated Activities by Way of Business) Order 2001, SI 2001/1177, the Financial Services and Markets Act 2000 (Consultation with Competent Authorities) Regulations 2001, SI 2001/2509, the Money Laundering Regulations 2003, SI 2003/3075, and the Financial Services and Markets Act 2000 (Financial Promotion) Order 2005, SI 2005/1529)

SI 2006/3273: Lloyd's Sourcebook (Finance Act 1993 and Finance Act 1994) (Amendment) Order 2006
Authority: FSMA 2000, ss 417(1), 426(1). This Order substitutes references in the Finance Act 1993 and the Finance Act 1994 to the Lloyd's Sourcebook with references to the Insurance Prudential Sourcebook in consequence of the application of the latter Sourcebook to the operation of the market at Lloyd's. It revokes the Lloyd's Sourcebook (Amendment of the Finance Act 1993 and the Finance Act 1994) Order 2005, SI 2005/1538

SI 2006/2383: Financial Services and Markets Act 2000 (Regulated Activities) (Amendment) (No 2) Order 2006
Authority: FSMA 2000, ss 22(1), (5), 426, 427, 428(3), Sch 2, para 25. At [2860]. This Order amends the Regulated Activities Order at [2010]. The effect of the Order is that the activities of entering into, administering, arranging and advising on regulated home reversion plans and regulated home purchase plans become regulated activities for the purposes of FSMA 2000. It also makes consequential amendments to primary legislation including CA 1985 and FSMA 2000 and various SIs made under FSMA 2000 (see [2860] et seq)

SI 2006/1969: the Financial Services and Markets Act 2000 (Regulated Activities) (Amendment) Order 2006
Authority: FSMA 2000, ss 22(1), (5), 426, 427, 428(3), Sch 2, para 25. At [2853]. This Order amends the Regulated Activities Order at [2010]. The effect of the Order is that establishing, operating or winding up a personal pension scheme becomes a regulated activity for the purposes of FSMA 2000. It also makes consequential amendments to other SIs made under FSMA 2000 (see [2853] et seq)

SI 2006/1805: the Financial Services and Markets Act 2000 (Gibraltar) (Amendment) Order 2006
Authority: FSMA 2000, s 409(1). Amends the Financial Services and Markets Act 2000 (Gibraltar) Order 2001, SI 2001/3084 at [2495]

SI 2006/58: the Financial Services and Markets Act 2000 (Designated Professional Bodies) (Amendment) Order 2006
Authority: FSMA 2000, s 326. Amends the Financial Services and Markets Act 2000 (Designated Professional Bodies) Order 2001, SI 2001/1226 at [2224]

2005 Statutory Instruments
SI 2005/3392: Financial Services and Markets Act 2000 (Financial Promotion) (Amendment) Order 2005 Authority: FSMA 2000, ss 21(5), (6), 428(3). Amends the Financial Services and Markets Act 2000 (Financial Promotion) Order 2005, SI 2005/1529 at **[2757]**
SI 2005/3071: Financial Services and Markets Act 2000 (Disclosure of Confidential Information) (Amendment) Regulations 2005 Authority: FSMA 2000, ss 349(1)(b), (2), (3), 417(1). Amends the Financial Services and Markets Act 2000 (Disclosure of Confidential Information) Regulations 2001, SI 2001/2188 at **[2350]**
SI 2005/2967: Financial Services and Markets Act 2000 (Consequential Amendments) Order 2005 Authority: FSMA 2000, ss 426, 428(3). Amends the Consumer Credit Act 1974
SI 2005/1538: Lloyd's Sourcebook (Amendment of the Finance Act 1993 and the Finance Act 1994) Order 2005 Authority: FSMA 2000, ss 417(1), 426(1). Revoked by the Lloyd's Sourcebook (Finance Act 1993 and Finance Act 1994) (Amendment) Order 2006, SI 2006/3273
SI 2005/1532: Financial Services and Markets Act 2000 (Promotion of Collective Investment Schemes) (Exemptions) (Amendment) Order 2005 Authority: FSMA 2000, ss 238(6), (7), 428(3). Amends the Financial Services and Markets Act 2000 (Promotion of Collective Investment Schemes) (Exemptions) Order 2001, SI 2001/1060 at **[2166]**
SI 2005/1529: Financial Services and Markets Act 2000 (Financial Promotion) Order 2005 Authority: FSMA 2000, ss 21(5), (6), (9), (10), 428(3), Sch 2, para 25. At **[2757]**
SI 2005/1518: Financial Services and Markets Act 2000 (Regulated Activities) (Amendment) (No 2) Order 2005 Authority: FSMA 2000, ss 22(1), (5), 428(3), Sch 2, para 25. Amends the Financial Services and Markets Act 2000 (Regulated Activities) Order 2001, SI 2001/544 at **[2010]**
SI 2005/923: Open-Ended Investment Companies (Amendment) Regulations 2005 Authority: FSMA 2000, s 262. Amend the Open-Ended Investment Companies Regulations 2001, SI 2001/1228 at **[2238]**
SI 2005/922: Financial Services and Markets Act 2000 (Carrying on Regulated Activities by Way of Business) (Amendment) Order 2005 Authority: FSMA 2000, ss 419, 428(3). Amends the Financial Services and Markets Act 2000 (Carrying on Regulated Activities by way of Business) Order 2001, SI 2001/1177 at **[2206]**
SI 2005/680: Financial Services and Markets Act 2000 (Variation of Threshold Conditions) (Amendment) Order 2005 Authority: FSMA 2000, s 428(3), Sch 6, paras 8, 9. Amends the Financial Services and Markets Act 2000 (Variation of Threshold Conditions) Order 2001, SI 2001/2507. See the note relating to the 2001 Order at **[2420]**
SI 2005/594: Financial Services and Markets Act 2000 (Stakeholder Products) (Amendment) Regulations 2005 Authority: FSMA 2000, s 428 and SI 2001/544, art 52B(3). Amend the Financial Services and Markets Act 2000 (Stakeholder Products) Regulations 2004, SI 2004/2738 at **[2741]**
SI 2005/593: Financial Services and Markets Act 2000 (Regulated Activities) (Amendment) Order 2005 Authority: FSMA 2000, s 22(1), (5), 428(3), Sch 2, para 25. Amends the Financial Services and Markets Act 2000 (Regulated Activities) Order 2001, SI 2001/544 at **[2010]**
SI 2005/592: Financial Services and Markets Act 2000 (Exemption) (Amendment) Order 2005 Authority: FSMA 2000, ss 38, 428(3). Amends the Financial Services and Markets Act 2000 (Exemption) Order 2001, SI 2001/1201 at **[2211]**
SI 2005/274: Financial Services and Markets Act 2000 (Service of Notices) (Amendment) Regulations 2005 Authority: FSMA 2000, s 414. Amend the Financial Services and Markets Act 2000 (Service of Notices) Regulations 2001, SI 2001/1420 at **[2331]**
SI 2005/272: Financial Services and Markets Act 2000 (Disclosure of Information by Prescribed Persons) (Amendment) Regulations 2005 Authority: FSMA 2000, ss 353(1), 417(1). Amend the Financial Services and Markets Act 2000 (Disclosure of Information by Prescribed Persons) Regulations 2001, SI 2001/1857 at **[2346]**

PART III
STATUTORY INSTRUMENTS

2005 Statutory Instruments

SI 2005/270: Financial Services and Markets Act 2000 (Financial Promotion and Promotion of Collective Investment Schemes) (Miscellaneous Amendments) Order 2005
Authority: FSMA 2000, ss 21(5), (6), 238(6), (7), 428(3). Amends the Financial Services and Markets Act 2000 (Promotion of Collective Investment Schemes) (Exemptions) Order 2001, SI 2001/1060 at **[2166]**, and the Financial Services and Markets Act 2000 (Financial Promotion) Order 2001, SI 2001/1335

SI 2005/57: Financial Services and Markets Act 2000 (Collective Investment Schemes) (Amendment) Order 2005
Authority: FSMA 2000, s 235(5). Amends the Financial Services and Markets Act 2000 (Collective Investment Schemes) Order 2001, SI 2001/1062 at **[2202]**

SI 2005/1: Financial Services and Markets Act 2000 (Gibraltar) (Amendment) Order 2005
Authority: FSMA 2000, s 409(1). Amends the Financial Services and Markets Act 2000 (Gibraltar) Order 2001, SI 2001/3084 at **[2495]**

2004 Statutory Instruments

SI 2004/3352: Financial Services and Markets Act 2000 (Designated Professional Bodies) (Amendment) Order 2004
Authority: FSMA 2000, s 326. Amends the Financial Services and Markets Act 2000 (Designated Professional Bodies) Order 2001, SI 2001/1226 at **[2224]**

SI 2004/3351: Financial Services and Markets Act 2000 (Transitional Provisions) (General Insurance Intermediaries) Order 2004
Authority: FSMA 2000, ss 426–428. This Order is spent; see the note at **[2750]**

SI 2004/2738: Financial Services and Markets Act 2000 (Stakeholder Products) Regulations 2004
Authority: FSMA 2000, s 428 and SI 2001/544, art 52B(3). At **[2741]**

SI 2004/2737: Financial Services and Markets Act 2000 (Regulated Activities) (Amendment) (No 2) Order 2004
Authority: FSMA 2000, ss 22(1), (5), 428(3), Sch 2, para 25. Amends the Financial Services and Markets Act 2000 (Regulated Activities) Order 2001, SI 2001/544 at **[2010]**

SI 2004/2615: Financial Services and Markets Act 2000 (Transitional Provisions) (Mortgages) Order 2004
Authority: FSMA 2000, ss 426–428. This Order is spent; see the note at **[2735]**

SI 2004/1862: Financial Conglomerates and Other Financial Groups Regulations 2004
Authority: European Communities Act 1972, s 2(2); FSMA 2000, ss 183(2), 188(2), 417(1), 428(3). At **[2723]**. These Regulations implement, in part, European Parliament and Council Directive 2002/87/EC on the supplementary supervision of credit institutions, insurance undertakings and investment firms in a financial conglomerate and amending Council Directives 73/239/EEC, 79/267/EEC, 92/49/EEC, 92/96/EEC, 93/6/EEC, 93/22/EEC, and Directives 98/78/EC and 2000/12/EC of the European Parliament and of the Council ("the conglomerates directive")

SI 2004/1610: Financial Services and Markets Act 2000 (Regulated Activities) (Amendment) Order 2004
Authority: FSMA 2000, ss 22(1), (5), 428(3), Sch 2, para 25. Amends the Financial Services and Markets Act 2000 (Regulated Activities) Order 2001, SI 2001/544 at **[2010]**, and the Financial Services and Markets Act 2000 (Regulated Activities) (Amendment) (No 2) Order 2003, SI 2003/1476 at **[2704]**

SI 2004/1609: Financial Services and Markets Act 2000 (Transitional Provisions) (Complaints Relating to General Insurance and Mortgages) (Amendment) Order 2004
Authority: FSMA 2000, ss 426–428. Amends the Financial Services and Markets Act 2000 (Transitional Provisions) (Complaints Relating to General Insurance and Mortgages) Order 2004, SI 2004/454 at **[2712]**

SI 2004/952: Financial Services and Markets Act 2000 (Transitional Provisions, Repeals and Savings) (Financial Services Compensation Scheme) (Amendment) Order
Authority: FSMA 2000, ss 360, 426–428. Amends the Financial Services and Markets Act 2000 (Transitional Provisions, Repeals and Savings) (Financial Services Compensation Scheme) Order 2001, SI 2001/2967

2004 Statutory Instruments

SI 2004/454: Financial Services and Markets Act 2000 (Transitional Provisions) (Complaints Relating to General Insurance and Mortgages) Order 2004
Authority: FSMA 2000, ss 426–428. At **[2712]**

SI 2004/453: Financial Services and Markets Act 2000 (Appointed Representatives) (Amendment) Regulations 2004
Authority: FSMA 2000, ss 39(1), 417(1), 428(3). Amend the Financial Services and Markets Act 2000 (Appointed Representatives) Regulations 2001, SI 2001/1217 at **[2221]**

SI 2004/355: Financial Services and Markets Act 2000 (Consequential Amendments) Order 2004
Authority: FSMA 2000, s 426. Amends the Companies Act 1985 at **[1031]**, the Building Societies Act 1986, the Finance Act 1994, the Pensions Act 1995, the Public Offers of Securities Regulations 1995, SI 1995/1537, and the Financial Services and Markets Act 2000 (Consequential Amendments) Order 2002, SI 2002/1555. Also contains various amendments to Northern Ireland legislation

2003 Statutory Instruments

SI 2003/3075: Money Laundering Regulations 2003
Authority: European Communities Act 1972, s 2(2); FSMA 2000, ss 168(4)(b), 402(1)(b), 417(1), 428(3). At **[3787]**. These Regulations implement European Parliament and Council Directive 2001/97/EC amending Council Directive 91/308/EEC on prevention of the use of the financial system for the purpose of money laundering. These Regulations are revoked and replaced by the Money Laundering Regulations 2007, SI 2007/2157, as from 15 December 2007 (at **[2877AA]**)

SI 2003/2822: Financial Services and Markets Act 2000 (Regulated Activities) (Amendment) (No 3) Order 2003
Authority: FSMA 2000, ss 22(1), (5), 428(3), Sch 2, para 25. Amends the Financial Services and Markets Act 2000 (Regulated Activities) Order 2001, SI 2001/544 at **[2010]**

SI 2003/2817: Financial Services and Markets Act 2000 (Disclosure of Confidential Information) (Amendment) (No 3) Regulations 2003
Authority: FSMA 2000, ss 349(1)(b), (2), 417(1). Amend the Financial Services and Markets Act 2000 (Disclosure of Confidential Information) Regulations 2001, SI 2001/2188 at **[2350]**

SI 2003/2174: Financial Services and Markets Act 2000 (Disclosure of Confidential Information) (Amendment) (No 2) Regulations 2003
Authority: FSMA 2000, ss 349(1)(b), (2), 417(1). Amend the Financial Services and Markets Act 2000 (Disclosure of Confidential Information) Regulations 2001, SI 2001/2188 at **[2350]**

SI 2003/2134: Financial Services and Markets Act 2000 (Administration Orders Relating to Insurers) (Amendment) Order 2003
Authority: FSMA 2000, ss 360, 426–428. Amends the Financial Services and Markets Act 2000 (Administration Orders Relating to Insurers) Order 2002, SI 2002/1242 at **[2669]**, and the Financial Services and Markets Act 2000 (Transitional Provisions, Repeals and Savings) (Financial Services Compensation Scheme) Order 2001, SI 2001/2967

SI 2003/2067: Financial Services and Markets Act 2000 (Promotion of Collective Investment Schemes etc) (Exemptions) (Amendment) Order 2003
Authority: FSMA 2000, ss 21(5), 238(6), (7), 428(3). Amends the Financial Services and Markets Act 2000 (Promotion of Collective Investment Schemes) (Exemptions) Order 2001, SI 2001/1060 at **[2166]**, and the Financial Services and Markets Act 2000 (Financial Promotion) Order 2001, SI 2001/1335. This Order implements, in part, (i) European Parliament and Council Directive 2001/107/EC amending Council Directive 85/611/EEC on the coordination of laws, regulations and administrative provisions relating to undertakings for collective investment in transferable securities (UCITS) with a view to regulating management companies and simplified prospectuses, and (ii) European Parliament and Council Directive 2001/108/EC amending Council Directive 85/611/EEC on the coordination of laws, regulations and administrative provisions relating to undertakings for collective investment in transferable securities (UCITS) with regard to investments of UCITS

PART III
STATUTORY INSTRUMENTS

2003 Statutory Instruments

SI 2003/2066: Collective Investment Schemes (Miscellaneous Amendments) Regulations 2003
Authority: European Communities Act 1972, s 2(2); FSMA 2000, ss 183(2), 188(2), 213(10), 214(5), 224(4), 264(3), 349(1)(b), (2), (3), 417(1), 428(3), Sch 3, paras 13(1)(b)(iii), 14(1)(b), 17(b), 22. These Regulations amend the Financial Services and Markets Act 2000 at [1], the Financial Services and Markets Act 2000 (EEA Passport Rights) Regulations 2001, SI 2001/2511 at [2430], the Financial Services and Markets Act 2000 (Consultation with Competent Authorities) Regulations 2001, SI 2001/2509 at [2421], the Financial Services and Markets Act 2000 (Compensation Scheme: Electing Participants) Regulations 2001, SI 2001/1783 at [2342], the Financial Services and Markets Act 2000 (Collective Investment Schemes Constituted in Other EEA States) Regulations 2001, SI 2001/2383 at [2385], the Financial Services and Markets Act 2000 (Disclosure of Confidential Information) Regulations 2001, SI 2001/2188 at [2350], and the Open-Ended Investment Companies Regulations 2001, SI 2001/1228 at [2238]. The Regulations also contains minor and consequential amendments to CA 1985 and other statutory instruments that are outside the scope of this work. These Regulations implement, in part, (i) European Parliament and Council Directive 2001/107/EC amending Council Directive 85/611/EEC on the coordination of laws, regulations and administrative provisions relating to undertakings for collective investment in transferable securities (UCITS) with a view to regulating management companies and simplified prospectuses, and (ii) European Parliament and Council Directive 2001/108/EC amending Council Directive 85/611/EEC on the coordination of laws, regulations and administrative provisions relating to undertakings for collective investment in transferable securities (UCITS) with regard to investments of UCITS

SI 2003/1676: *Financial Services and Markets Act 2000 (Financial Promotion) (Amendment) Order 2003*
Authority: FSMA 2000, ss 21(5), (9), (10), 428(3). Revoked by the Financial Services and Markets Act 2000 (Financial Promotion) Order 2005, SI 2005/1529

SI 2003/1675: Financial Services and Markets Act 2000 (Exemption) (Amendment) (No 2) Order 2003
Authority: FSMA 2000, ss 38, 428(3). Amends the Financial Services and Markets Act 2000 (Exemption) Order 2001, SI 2001/1201 at [2211]

SI 2003/1476: Financial Services and Markets Act 2000 (Regulated Activities) (Amendment) (No 2) Order 2003
Authority: FSMA 2000, ss 22(1), (5), 192(a), 426, 427, 428(3). At [2704]. This Order implements, in part, European Parliament and Council Directive 2002/92/EC on insurance mediation

SI 2003/1475: Financial Services and Markets Act 2000 (Regulated Activities) (Amendment) (No 1) Order 2003
Authority: FSMA 2000, ss 22(1), (5), 426, 427, 428(3). At [2698]

SI 2003/1474: Financial Services and Markets Act 2000 (Misleading Statements and Practices) (Amendment) Order 2003
Authority: FSMA 2000, s 397(9), (14). Amends the Financial Services and Markets Act 2000 (Misleading Statements and Practices) Order 2001, SI 2001/3645 at [2631]

SI 2003/1473: Insurance Mediation Directive (Miscellaneous Amendments) Regulations 2003
Authority: European Communities Act 1972, s 2(2); FSMA 2000, ss 349(1)(b), (2), (3), 417(1), 428(3), Sch 3 paras 14(1)(b), 17(a). Amend the Financial Services and Markets Act 2000 at [1], the Financial Services and Markets Act 2000 (EEA Passport Rights) Regulations 2001, SI 2001/2511 at [2430], and the Financial Services and Markets Act 2000 (Disclosure of Confidential Information) Regulations 2001, SI 2001/2188 at [2350]. These Regulations implement, in part, European Parliament and Council Directive 2002/92/EC on insurance mediation

SI 2003/1294: Financial Services and Markets Act 2000 (Communications by Actuaries) Regulations 2003
Authority: FSMA 2000, ss 342(5), 343(5), 428(3). At [2696]

SI 2003/1181: Financial Services and Markets Act 2000 (Collective Investment Schemes) (Designated Countries and Territories) Order 2003
Authority: FSMA 2000, ss 270, 426, 428(3). At [2692]

SI 2003/1092: *Financial Services and Markets Act 2000 (Disclosure of Confidential Information) (Amendment) Regulations 2003*
Authority: FSMA 2000, ss 349(1)(b), (2), 417(1). Revoked by the Financial Services and Markets Act 2000 (Disclosure of Confidential Information) (Amendment) (No 2) Regulations 2003, SI 2003/2174

2003 Statutory Instruments

SI 2003/693: Financial Services and Markets Act 2000 (Disclosure of Confidential Information) (Amendment) Regulations 2003
Authority: FSMA 2000, ss 349(1)(b), (2), 417(1), 428(3). Amend the Financial Services and Markets Act 2000 (Disclosure of Confidential Information) Regulations 2001, SI 2001/2188 at **[2350]**. These Regulations implement, in part, European Parliament and Council Directive 2000/64/EC amending Council Directives 85/611/EEC, 92/49/EEC, 92/96/EEC and 93/22/EEC as regards exchange of information with third countries

SI 2003/47: Financial Services and Markets Act 2000 (Exemption) (Amendment) Order 2003
Authority: FSMA 2000, ss 38, 428(3). Amends the Financial Services and Markets Act 2000 (Exemption) Order 2001, SI 2001/1201 at **[2211]**

2002 Statutory Instruments

SI 2002/2707: Financial Services and Markets Act 2000 (Variation of Threshold Conditions) Order 2002
Authority: FSMA 2000, s 428(3), Sch 6, para 9. Amends the Financial Services and Markets Act 2000 at **[1]**. This Order implements, in part, European Parliament and Council Directive 2000/26/EC on the approximation of the laws of the Member States relating to insurance against civil liability in respect of the use of motor vehicles and amending Council Directives 73/239/EEC and 88/357/EEC (Fourth motor insurance Directive)

SI 2002/2706: Financial Services and Markets Act 2000 (Fourth Motor Insurance Directive) Regulations 2002
Authority: European Communities Act 1972, s 2(2); FSMA 2000, ss 150(3), 417(1). At **[2690]**. These Regulations implement, in part, European Parliament and Council Directive 2000/26/EC on the approximation of the laws of the Member States relating to insurance against civil liability in respect of the use of motor vehicles and amending Council Directives 73/239/EEC and 88/357/EEC (Fourth motor insurance Directive)

SI 2002/2157: Financial Services and Markets Act 2000 (Financial Promotion) (Amendment) (Electronic Commerce Directive) Order 2002
Authority: FSMA 2000, ss 21(5), (6), 238(6),(7), 428(3). Revoked by the Financial Services and Markets Act 2000 (Financial Promotion) Order 2005, SI 2005/1529

SI 2002/1777: Financial Services and Markets Act 2000 (Commencement of Mortgage Regulation) (Amendment) Order 2002
Authority: FSMA 2000, ss 21(5), (9), (10), 22(1), (5), 327(6), 397(9), (10), (14), 428(3), Sch 2, para 25. Amends the Financial Services and Markets Act 2000 (Regulated Activities) Order 2001, SI 2001/544 at **[2010]**, the Financial Services and Markets Act 2000 (Professions) (Non-exempt Activities) Order 2001, SI 2001/1227 at **[2226]**, the Financial Services and Markets Act 2000 (Financial Promotion) Order 2001, SI 2001/1335, the Financial Services and Markets Act 2000 (Regulated Activities) (Amendment) Order 2001, SI 2001/3544, the Financial Services and Markets Act 2000 (Misleading Statements and Practices) Order 2001, SI 2001/3645 at **[2631]**, and the Financial Services and Markets Act 2000 (Miscellaneous Provisions) Order 2001, SI 2001/3650 at **[3643]**

SI 2002/1776: Financial Services and Markets Act 2000 (Regulated Activities) (Amendment) (No 2) Order 2002
Authority: FSMA 2000, ss 22(1), (5), 428(3). Amends the Financial Services and Markets Act 2000 (Regulated Activities) Order 2001, SI 2001/544 at **[2010]**. This Order implements, in part, European Parliament and Council Directive 2000/31/EC on certain legal aspects of information society services, in particular electronic commerce, in the internal market ("Directive on electronic commerce")

SI 2002/1775: Electronic Commerce Directive (Financial Services and Markets) Regulations 2002
Authority: European Communities Act 1972, s 2(2); FSMA 2000, ss 349(1), 414, 428(3). At **[2674]**. These Regulations implement, in part, European Parliament and Council Directive 2000/31/EC on certain legal aspects of information society services, in particular electronic commerce, in the internal market ("Directive on electronic commerce")

PART III
STATUTORY INSTRUMENTS

2002 Statutory Instruments

SI 2002/1555: Financial Services and Markets Act 2000 (Consequential Amendments) Order 2002
Authority: FSMA 2000, ss 416(4), 426, 427. This Order is supplementary to the Financial Services and Markets Act 2000 (Consequential Amendments and Repeals) Order 2001, SI 2001/3649. It corrects or adjusts amendments made by SI 2001/3649, and makes additional amendments which are consequential upon the repeal of the legislation which established the regulatory regimes which have been replaced by FSMA 2000. It amends a large amount of legislation, the majority of which is not reproduced in this Handbook.

SI 2002/1501: Financial Services and Markets Act 2000 (Consequential Amendments and Transitional Provisions) (Credit Unions) Order 2002
Authority: FSMA 2000, ss 426–428. Amends the Credit Unions Act 1979, the Trustee Savings Banks Act 1985, the Financial Services and Markets Act 2000 (Permission and Applications) (Credit Unions etc) Order 2002, SI 2002/704, and revokes various statutory instruments made under the 1979 Act

SI 2002/1409: Financial Services and Markets Act 2000 (Consequential Amendments) (Taxes) Order 2002
Authority: FSMA 2000, s 426. Amends the Income and Corporation Taxes Act 1988, the Finance Act 1989, the Insurance Companies (Taxation of Reinsurance Business) Regulations 1995, SI 1995/1730, the Insurance Companies (Reserves) (Tax) Regulations 1996, SI 1996/2991, the Friendly Societies (Modification of the Corporation Tax Acts) Regulations 1997, SI 1997/473, and the Individual Savings Account Regulations 1998, SI 1998/1870

SI 2002/1310: Financial Services and Markets Act 2000 (Financial Promotion and Miscellaneous Amendments) Order 2002
Authority: FSMA 2000, ss 21(5), (6), 22(1), (5), 38, 238(6), (7), 428(3), Sch 2, para 25. Amends the Financial Services and Markets Act 2000 (Financial Promotion) Order 2001, SI 2001/1335, the Financial Services and Markets Act 2000 (Promotion of Collective Investment Schemes) (Exemptions) Order 2001, SI 2001/1060 at **[2166]**, and the Financial Services and Markets Act 2000 (Regulated Activities) Order 2001, SI 2001/544 at **[2010]**.

SI 2002/1242: Financial Services and Markets Act 2000 (Administration Orders Relating to Insurers) Order 2002
Authority: FSMA 2000, ss 355(2), 360, 426, 428(3). At **[2669]**

SI 2002/765: Electronic Money (Miscellaneous Amendments) Regulations 2002
Authority: European Communities Act 1972, s 2(2); FSMA 2000, ss 417, 428(3), Sch 3, para 13(1)(b)(iii). Amend the Companies Act 1985 at **[1031]**, the Financial Services and Markets Act 2000 at **[1]**, the Public Offers of Securities Regulations 1995, SI 1995/1537, the Cross-Border Credit Transfers Regulations 1999, SI 1999/1876, the Financial Markets and Insolvency (Settlement Finality) Regulations 1999, SI 1999/2979, the Competition Act 1998 (Small Agreements and Conduct of Minor Significance) Regulations 2000, SI 2000/262, the Competition Act 1998 (Determination of Turnover for Penalties) Order 2000, SI 2000/309, the Financial Services and Markets Act 2000 (EEA Passport Rights) Regulations 2001, SI 2001/2511 at **[2430]**, and the Companies (Northern Ireland) Order 1986. These Regulations implement, in part, European Parliament and Council Directive 2000/46/EC on the taking up, pursuit of and prudential supervision of the business of electronic money institutions, and European Parliament and Council Directive 2000/28/EC amending Directive 2000/12/EC relating to the taking up and pursuit of the business of credit institutions

SI 2002/704: Financial Services and Markets Act 2000 (Permission and Applications) (Credit Unions etc) Order 2002
Authority: FSMA 2000, ss 426–428. This Order sets out the transitional provisions relating to the expiry (on 2 July 2002) of the transitional exemption of credit unions from the general prohibition imposed by FSMA 2000, s 19; see the Financial Services and Markets Act 2000 (Exemption) Order 2001, SI 2001/1201, art 6

SI 2002/682: Financial Services and Markets Act 2000 (Regulated Activities) (Amendment) Order 2002
Authority: FSMA 2000, ss 22(1), (5), 428(3), Sch 2, para 25. At **[2666]**. This Order implements, in part, European Parliament and Council Directive 2000/46/EC on the taking up, pursuit of and prudential supervision of the business of electronic money institutions, and European Parliament and Council Directive 2000/28/EC amending Directive 2000/12/EC relating to the taking up and pursuit of the business of credit institutions

2001 Statutory Instruments

SI 2001/4040: Insurers (Winding Up) (Scotland) Rules 2001
Authority: IA 1986, s 411; FSMA 2000, s 379. These Rules supplement the Insolvency (Scotland) Rules 1986, SI 1986/1915 in relation to the winding up of insurers in Scotland. They revoke and replace, with modifications, the Insurance Companies (Winding Up) (Scotland) Rules 1986, SI 1986/1918

SI 2001/3801: Financial Services and Markets Act 2000 (Consequential Amendments) (No 2) Order 2001
Authority: FSMA 2000, ss 426, 427. Amends the Terrorism (United Nations Measures) Order 2001, SI 2001/3365 and the Terrorism (United Nations Measures) (Overseas Territories) Order 2001, SI 2001/3366

SI 2001/3800: Financial Services and Markets Act 2000 (Financial Promotion) (Amendment No 2) Order 2001
Authority: FSMA 2000, s 21(5). Revoked by the Financial Services and Markets Act 2000 (Financial Promotion) Order 2005, SI 2005/1529

SI 2001/3771: Financial Services and Markets Act 2000 (Scope of Permission Notices) Order 2001
Authority: FSMA 2000, ss 426–428. At **[2662]**

SI 2001/3681: Financial Services and Markets Act 2000 (Prescribed Markets and Qualifying Investments) (Amendment) Order 2001
Authority: FSMA 2000, s 118(3). This Order amended the Financial Services and Markets Act 2000 (Prescribed Markets and Qualifying Investments) Order 2001, SI 2001/996 by inserting a new art 4A. That article was effectively revoked as from 1 July 2005 and this Order became spent on that date

SI 2001/3650: Financial Services and Markets Act 2000 (Miscellaneous Provisions) Order 2001
Authority: FSMA 2000, ss 21(5), (9), (10), 235(5), 327(6), 426–428, Sch 2, para 25. At **[2643]**

SI 2001/3649: Financial Services and Markets Act 2000 (Consequential Amendments and Repeals) Order 2001
Authority: FSMA 2000, ss 426, 427. This Order (which is made up of 610 articles) sets out the amendments to primary and secondary legislation consequential on the coming into force of FSMA 2000. The large majority of the amendments are consequential on the principal repeals and revocations made by art 3 (ie, the Policyholders Protection Act 1975, the Insurance Companies Act 1982, the Financial Services Act 1986, the Banking Act 1987, the Insurance Companies (Reserves) Act 1995, the Policyholders Protection Act 1997, the Banking Coordination (Second Council Directive) Regulations 1992, SI 1992/3218, the Insurance Companies (Third Insurance Directives) Regulations 1994, SI 1994/1696, and the Investment Services Regulations 1995, SI 1995/3275). References in other legislation to the enactments repealed and revoked, or to expressions used in those enactments, are amended so that they refer to the appropriate provision or expression in FSMA 2000

SI 2001/3648: Financial Services and Markets Act 2000 (Confidential Information) (Bank of England) (Consequential Provisions) Order 2001
Authority: FSMA 2000, ss 426, 427. At **[2635]**

SI 2001/3647: Financial Services and Markets Act 2000 (Consequential Amendments and Savings) (Industrial Assurance) Order 2001
Authority: FSMA 2000, ss 339(1)–(3), 416(4), 426, 427. This Order makes transitional savings and consequential amendments pursuant to the repeal, by FSMA 2000, s 416, of the Industrial Assurance Act 1923, the Industrial Assurance and Friendly Societies Act 1948, and the revocation of the Industrial Assurance (Northern Ireland) Order 1978. It amends a large amount of legislation that is outside the scope of this Handbook

SI 2001/3646: Financial Services and Markets Act 2000 (Transitional Provisions and Savings) (Information Requirements and Investigations) Order 2001
Authority: FSMA 2000, ss 426, 427, 428(3). This Order makes transitional provisions for requirements to provide information under the Banking Act 1987, the Financial Services Act 1986, and the Insurance Companies Act 1982 and requirements made by recognised self-regulating organisations that are outstanding on 1 December 2001 ("commencement"). The Order also makes transitional provisions for requirements to supply a report by a skilled person that are pending at commencement which were made under the Banking Act 1987 or Insurance Companies Act 1982. The Order also makes transitional provisions for investigators appointed under the Insurance Companies Act 1982, the Banking Act 1987 and the Financial Services Act 1986 where the investigations are in progress at commencement

PART III
STATUTORY INSTRUMENTS

2001 Statutory Instruments

SI 2001/3645: Financial Services and Markets Act 2000 (Misleading Statements and Practices) Order 2001
Authority: FSMA 2000, s 397(9), (10), (14). At **[2631]**.

SI 2001/3640: Financial Services and Markets Act 2000 (Savings, Modifications and Consequential Provisions) (Rehabilitation of Offenders) (Scotland) Order 2001
Authority: FSMA 2000, ss 426, 427, 428(3). This Order makes amendments, savings and modifications (in relation to Scotland only) that relate to the Rehabilitation of Offenders Act 1974. These provisions are necessary following the repeal of the Insurance Companies Act 1982, the Financial Services Act 1986, and the Banking Act 1987. It also makes consequential amendments to the Rehabilitation of Offenders Act 1974 (Exceptions) Order 1975, SI 1975/1023 at **[3505]**

SI 2001/3639: Financial Services and Markets Act 2000 (Transitional Provisions and Savings) (Business Transfers) Order 2001
Authority: FSMA 2000, ss 426–428. This Order makes savings and transitional provisions for applications under the Insurance Companies Act 1982, Sch 2C for approval of a transfer of the whole or part of the long term business carried on by an insurance company, or approval of the transfer of rights and obligations under contracts of general insurance (including transfers of business to or from members of Lloyd's). In relation to any application that has been made, but not determined, before 1 December 2001, the relevant provisions of Sch 2C are saved, subject to modifications

SI 2001/3635: Insurers (Winding Up) Rules 2001
Authority: IA 1986, s 411; FSMA 2000, s 379. At **[2596]**

SI 2001/3633: Financial Services and Markets Tribunal (Legal Assistance Scheme—Costs) Regulations 2001
Authority: FSMA 2000, ss 134, 135, 428(1), (3). At **[2571]**

SI 2001/3632: Financial Services and Markets Tribunal (Legal Assistance) Regulations 2001
Authority: FSMA 2000, ss 134, 135, 428(1), (3). At **[2528]**

SI 2001/3629: Financial Services and Markets Act 2000 (Consequential Amendments) (Taxes) Order 2001
Authority: FSMA 2000, ss 426–428. This Order makes consequential amendments to primary and secondary legislation relating to matters under the care and management of the Commissioners of Inland Revenue (now the Commissioners for Her Majesty's Revenue and Customs). The matters involved include income tax, corporation tax, capital gains tax, national insurance contributions, inheritance tax, stamp duty and stamp duty reserve tax. It amends a large amount of legislation that is outside the scope of this Handbook

SI 2001/3626: Financial Services and Markets Act 2000 (Control of Transfers of Business Done at Lloyd's) Order 2001
Authority: FSMA 2000, ss 323, 428(3). At **[2523]**

SI 2001/3625: Financial Services and Markets Act 2000 (Control of Business Transfers) (Requirements on Applicants) Regulations 2001
Authority: FSMA 2000, ss 108, 417(1), 428(3), Sch 12, para 6(2). At **[2517]**

SI 2001/3624: Financial Services and Markets Act 2000 (Disclosure of Confidential Information) (Amendment) (No 2) Regulations 2001
Authority: FSMA 2000, ss 349(1)(b), (2), 417(1), 426, 427, 428(3). Amend the Financial Services and Markets Act 2000 (Disclosure of Confidential Information) Regulations 2001, SI 2001/2188 at **[2350]**. These Regulations implement, in part, European Parliament and Council Directive 2001/34/EC on the admission of securities to official stock exchange listing and on information to be published on those securities

SI 2001/3623: Financial Services and Markets Act 2000 (Exemption) (Amendment) Order 2001
Authority: FSMA 2000, ss 38, 428(3). Amends the Financial Services and Markets Act 2000 (Exemption) Order 2001, SI 2001/1201 at **[2211]**

2001 Statutory Instruments

SI 2001/3592: Financial Services and Markets Act 2000 (Transitional Provisions) (Partly Completed Procedures) Order 2001
Authority: FSMA 2000, ss 426–428. This Order makes transitional provision for procedures which are partly completed on the day on which the main provisions of FSMA 2000 come into force (1 December 2001). Part I of the Order provides for commencement and interpretation. Part II sets out how applications which have been made under the repealed legislation are to be treated after commencement, and deals with situations where the FSA has started proceedings on its own initiative to withdraw, suspend or restrict authorisation under that legislation. Part III deals with similar matters relating to friendly societies and building societies. Part IV concerns pending authorisations of unit trust schemes and recognition of collective investment schemes. Part V provides for the transition of other partly completed procedures, namely those in relation to (i) applications by people who will need to be approved persons for the purposes of Part V of FSMA 2000; (ii) the making of public statements of misconduct under FSA 1986, s 60; (iii) persons who are subject to proceedings for disqualification under FSA 1986. Part VI provides for the partly completed procedures of the recognised self-regulating organisations established under FSA 1986. Part VII contains supplemental provisions regarding the content of notices served before commencement which are to be carried forward as a notice under an equivalent provision in FSMA 2000. Part VIII deals with the position where an EEA firm is part way through exercising its EEA right to establish a branch or provide services in the UK, and where a UK firm is part way through exercising its EEA right to "passport" into another member State. Part IX of the Order contains transitional provisions relating to appeals which are pending at commencement

SI 2001/3591: Bankruptcy (Financial Services and Markets Act 2000) (Scotland) Rules 2001
Authority: FSMA 2000, ss 372(4)(c), (9)(b), 428(3). See the note at **[2516]**

SI 2001/3582: Financial Services and Markets Act 2000 (Dissolution of the Board of Banking Supervision) (Transitional Provisions) Order 2001
Authority: FSMA 2000, ss 426, 427, 428(3). This Order makes transitional provisions in connection with the final report of the Board of Banking Supervision (which is dissolved by FSMA 2000, s 416(3)(d))

SI 2001/3544: Financial Services and Markets Act 2000 (Regulated Activities) (Amendment) Order 2001
Authority: FSMA 2000, ss 22(1), (5), 428(3), Sch 2, para 25. Amends the Financial Services and Markets Act 2000 (Regulated Activities) Order 2001, SI 2001/544 at **[2010]**

SI 2001/3542: Financial Services and Markets Act 2000 (Law Applicable to Contracts of Insurance) (Amendment) Regulations 2001
Authority: FSMA 2000, ss 424(3), 417(1), 428(3). Amend the Financial Services and Markets Act 2000 (Law Applicable to Contracts of Insurance) Regulations 2001, SI 2001/2635 at **[2472]**

SI 2001/3538: Financial Services and Markets Act 2000 (Commencement No 7) Order 2001
Authority: FSMA 2000, ss 431(2), 428(3). For details relating to the commencement of FSMA 2000, see the Appendix of commencement dates at **[498]**

SI 2001/3439: Financial Services and Markets Act 2000 (Official Listing of Securities) (Amendment) Regulations 2001
Authority: FSMA 2000, ss 75(3), 417(1), 428(3). Amend the Financial Services and Markets Act 2000 (Official Listing of Securities) Regulations 2001, SI 2001/2956 at **[2487]**

SI 2001/3437: Financial Services and Markets Act 2000 (Disclosure of Confidential Information) (Amendment) Regulations 2001
Authority: FSMA 2000, ss 349(1)(b), (2), (3), 417(1). Amend the Financial Services and Markets Act 2000 (Disclosure of Confidential Information) Regulations 2001, SI 2001/2188 at **[2350]**

SI 2001/3436: Financial Services and Markets Act 2000 (Commencement No 6) Order 2001
Authority: FSMA 2000, s 431(2). For details relating to the commencement of FSMA 2000, see the Appendix of commencement dates at **[498]**

SI 2001/3374: Financial Services and Markets Act 2000 (Interim Permissions) Order 2001
Authority: FSMA 2000, ss 426–428. At **[2502]**

SI 2001/3338: Financial Services and Markets Act 2000 (Controllers) (Exemption) (No 2) Order 2001
Authority: FSMA 2000, ss 192(a), 428(3). At **[2499]**

2001 Statutory Instruments

SI 2001/3084: Financial Services and Markets Act 2000 (Gibraltar) Order 2001
Authority: FSMA 2000, ss 409(1), 428(3). At **[2495]**. This Order implements, in part, European Parliament and Council Directive 2000/12/EC relating to the taking up and pursuit of the business of credit institutions, and "the insurance directives" (ie, 73/239/EEC, 88/357/EEC, 92/49/EEC, 79/267/EEC, 90/619/EEC, and 92/96/EEC)

SI 2001/3083: Financial Services and Markets Act 2000 (Transitional Provisions and Savings) (Civil Remedies, Discipline, Criminal Offences etc) (No 2) Order 2001
Authority: FSMA 2000, ss 426, 427, 428(3). This Order revokes and re-enacts with certain modifications the Financial Services and Markets Act 2000 (Transitional Provisions and Savings) (Civil Remedies, Discipline, Criminal Offences etc) Order 2001, SI 2001/2657. It relates to the civil, prosecutorial and disciplinary powers of the FSA in relation to conduct that took place before the commencement of FSMA 2000, s 19 (the general prohibition). It also makes consequential amendments to the Financial Services and Markets Act 2000 (Consequential and Transitional Provisions) (Miscellaneous) (No 2) Order 2001, SI 2001/2659

SI 2001/2968: Financial Services and Markets Act 2000 (Treatment of Assets of Insurers on Winding Up) Regulations 2001
Authority: FSMA 2000, ss 378, 428(3). Revoked by the Insurers (Reorganisation and Winding Up) Regulations 2003, SI 2003/1102

SI 2001/2967: Financial Services and Markets Act 2000 (Transitional Provisions, Repeals and Savings) (Financial Services Compensation Scheme) Order 2001
Authority: FSMA 2000, ss 339(3), 416(4), 426–428. This Order makes transitional provisions in connection with the Financial Services Compensation Scheme which supersedes eight former compensation schemes; ie, the Policyholders Protection Scheme, the Deposit Protection Scheme, the Building Societies Investor Protection Scheme, the Investor Compensation Scheme, the section 43 Compensation Scheme, the Friendly Societies Protection Scheme, the Personal Investment Authority indemnity scheme, and the arrangements described in the ABI/ICS agreement ("the ABI scheme"). It implements, in part, European Parliament and Council Directive 94/19/EC on deposit-guarantee schemes, and European Parliament and Council Directive 97/9/EC on investor-compensation schemes

SI 2001/2966: Financial Services and Markets Act 2000 (Consequential Amendments) (Pre-Commencement Modifications) Order 2001
Authority: FSMA 2000, ss 426, 427. The modifications made by this Order are consequential on a number of provisions of FSMA 2000 which were brought into force by the Financial Services and Markets Act 2000 (Commencement No 5) Order 2001, SI 2001/2632. These include provisions relating to the making of applications and the granting of permissions to come into force on the day on which s 19 of the Act comes into force, the doing of other preparatory acts by the FSA in advance of that day, and certain provisions relating to the Financial Services and Markets Tribunal. The modifications made by this Order ceased to have effect when s 19 came into force.

SI 2001/2958: Financial Services and Markets Act 2000 (Offers of Securities) Order 2001
Authority: FSMA 2000, s 87(4), Sch 11, paras 8(2), 15, 17, 21, 22, 23, 25. Revoked by the Prospectus Regulations 2005, SI 2005/1433

SI 2001/2957: Financial Services and Markets Act 2000 (Official Listing of Securities) (Transitional Provisions) Order 2001
Authority: FSMA 2000, ss 426, 427, 428(3). This Order makes transitional provisions in connection with the official listing of securities following the repeal of FSA 1986, Pt IV and its replacement with the new regime in Pt VI of FSMA 2000. It provides, inter alia, for the continued effect of listing rules after commencement, and deals with the contravention of those rules before commencement and appeals in relation to decisions taken before commencement. These Regulations implement, in part, Council Directive 79/279/EEC coordinating the conditions for the admission of securities to official stock exchange listing, Council Directive 80/390/EEC coordinating the requirements for the drawing up, scrutiny and distribution of the listing particulars to be published for the admission of securities to official stock exchange listing (and the amending Directives 82/148/EEC, 87/345/EEC, 90/211/EEC and 94/18/EC), and Council Directive 82/121/EEC on information to be published on a regular basis by companies the shares of which have been admitted to official stock-exchange listing

2001 Statutory Instruments
SI 2001/2956: Financial Services and Markets Act 2000 (Official Listing of Securities) Regulations 2001 Authority: FSMA 2000, ss 75(3), 79(3), 103(1), 417(1), 428(3), Sch 10, para 9, Sch 11, paras 16(3), 16(4), 20(2). At **[2487]**. This Order implements, in part, Council Directive 79/279/EEC coordinating the conditions for the admission of securities to official stock exchange listing, Council Directive 80/390/EEC coordinating the requirements for the drawing up, scrutiny and distribution of the listing particulars to be published for the admission of securities to official stock exchange listing (and the amending Directives 82/148/EEC, 87/345/EEC, 90/211/EEC and 94/18/EC), and Council Directive 82/121/EEC on information to be published on a regular basis by companies the shares of which have been admitted to official stock-exchange listing
SI 2001/2659: Financial Services and Markets Act 2000 (Consequential and Transitional Provisions) (Miscellaneous) (No 2) Order 2001 Authority: FSMA 2000, ss 426, 427, 428(3). This Order makes consequential and transitional provisions for the purposes of a number of provisions of FSMA 2000 which were brought into force by the Financial Services and Markets Act 2000 (Commencement No 5) Order 2001, SI 2001/2632. Those provisions include the making of applications under the Act for permission or authorisation coming into force on the day on which s 19 of the Act comes into force, and in connection with Part XI of the Act (information gathering and investigations)
SI 2001/2657: Financial Services and Markets Act 2000 (Transitional Provisions and Savings) (Civil Remedies, Discipline, Criminal Offences etc) Order 2001 Authority: FSMA 2000, ss 426, 427, 428(3). Revoked before coming into force by the Financial Services and Markets Act 2000 (Transitional Provisions and Savings) (Civil Remedies, Discipline, Criminal Offences etc) (No 2) Order 2001, SI 2001/3083
SI 2001/2639: Financial Services and Markets Act 2000 (Own-initiative Power) (Overseas Regulators) Regulations 2001 Authority: FSMA 2000, ss 47(1), (3), 417(1), 428(3). At **[2484]**. These Regulations implement, in part, Council Directive 92/49/EEC on the coordination of laws, regulations and administrative provisions relating to direct insurance other than life assurance and amending Directives 73/239/EEC and 88/357/EEC (third non-life insurance Directive), Council Directive 92/96/EEC on the coordination of laws, regulations and administrative provisions relating to direct life assurance and amending Directives 79/267/EEC and 90/619/EEC (third life assurance Directive), Council Directive 91/371/EEC on the implementation of the Agreement between the European Economic Community and the Swiss Confederation concerning direct insurance other than life assurance, Council Directive 93/22/EEC on investment services in the securities field, and European Parliament and Council Directive 2000/12/EC relating to the taking up and pursuit of the business of credit institutions
SI 2001/2638: Financial Services and Markets Act 2000 (Controllers) (Exemption) Order 2001 Authority: FSMA 2000, ss 192(a), 428(3). At **[2482]**
SI 2001/2637: Financial Services and Markets Act 2000 (Transitional Provisions) (Controllers) Order 2001 Authority: FSMA 2000, ss 426–428. This Order makes transitional provision for people who are subject to a regime requiring them to notify a significant shareholding in an authorised person and who will fall within Part XII of FSMA 2000. It deals both with the status after commencement of people who have been approved as shareholder controllers under existing regimes and with partly completed procedures.
SI 2001/2636: Financial Services and Markets Act 2000 (Transitional Provisions) (Authorised Persons etc) Order 2001 Authority: FSMA 2000, ss 426–428. This Order sets out the transitional arrangements for ensuring that people who have been authorised to carry on particular business under the various regulatory regimes replaced by FSMA 2000 are treated as authorised persons with the appropriate permission for the purposes of that Act. The regulatory regimes covered by this Order are the Financial Services Act 1986, the Banking Act 1987, the Insurance Companies Act 1982, the Friendly Societies Act 1992, the Building Societies Act 1986, the Banking Coordination (Second Council Directive) Regulations 1992, SI 1992/3218, and the Investment Services Regulations 1995, SI 1995/3275
SI 2001/2635: Financial Services and Markets Act 2000 (Law Applicable to Contracts of Insurance) Regulations 2001 Authority: FSMA 2000, ss 424(3), 417(1), 428(3). At **[2472]**. These Regulations implement, in part, Council Directive 78/473/EEC on the coordination of laws, regulations and administrative provisions relating to Community co-insurance

2001 Statutory Instruments

SI 2001/2634: Financial Services and Markets Act 2000 (Insolvency) (Definition of "Insurer") Order 2001
Authority: FSMA 2000, ss 355(2), 428(3). At **[2470]**

SI 2001/2633: Financial Services and Markets Act 2000 (Financial Promotion) (Amendment) Order 2001
Authority: FSMA 2000, ss 21(5), 238(6). Revoked by the Financial Services and Markets Act 2000 (Financial Promotion) Order 2005, SI 2005/1529

SI 2001/2632: Financial Services and Markets Act 2000 (Commencement No 5) Order 2001
Authority: FSMA 2000, s 431(2). For details relating to the commencement of FSMA 2000, see the Appendix of commencement dates at **[498]**

SI 2001/2617: Financial Services and Markets Act 2000 (Mutual Societies) Order 2001
Authority: FSMA 2000, ss 334(1), (2), 335(1)–(4), 336(1), (2), 337, 338(1), (2), 339(1), (2), 426, 427, 428(3). At **[2453]**

SI 2001/2587: Financial Services and Markets Act 2000 (Communications by Auditors) Regulations 2001
Authority: FSMA 2000, ss 342(5), 343(5), 428(3). At **[2451]**. These Regulations implement, in part, European Parliament and Council Directive 95/26/EC amending Directives 77/780/EEC and 89/646/EEC in the field of credit institutions, Directives 73/239/EEC and 92/49/EEC in the field of non- life insurance, Directives 79/267/EEC and 92/96/EEC in the field of life assurance, Directive 93/22/EEC in the field of investment firms and Directive 85/611/EEC in the field of undertakings for collective investment in transferable securities (UCITS), with a view to reinforcing prudential supervision

SI 2001/2512: Financial Services and Markets Act 2000 (Transitional Provisions) (Reviews of Pensions Business) Order 2001
Authority: FSMA 2000, ss 426–428. This Order makes transitional provisions with respect to the reviews of pension selling being conducted under the Financial Services Act 1986. The reviews concern (a) the selling of personal pension schemes between 29 April 1988 and 30 June 1994, and (b) the selling of free standing additional voluntary contribution schemes between 29 April 1988 and 15 August 1999

SI 2001/2511: Financial Services and Markets Act 2000 (EEA Passport Rights) Regulations 2001
Authority: FSMA 2000, ss 417(1), 426–428, Sch 3, paras 13(1)(b)(iii), 14(1)(b), 17(a)–(c), 18, 22. At **[2430]**

SI 2001/2510: Financial Services and Markets Act 2000 (Gaming Contracts) Order 2001
Authority: FSMA 2000, s 412(2), (6). At **[2428]**

SI 2001/2509: Financial Services and Markets Act 2000 (Consultation with Competent Authorities) Regulations 2001
Authority: FSMA 2000, ss 183(2), 188(2), 417(1), 428(3). At **[2421]**. These Regulations implement, in part, Council Directive 93/22/EEC on investment services in the securities field, and European Parliament and Council Directive 2000/12/EC relating to the taking up and pursuit of the business of credit institutions.

SI 2001/2508: Financial Services and Markets Act 2000 (Appointed Representatives) (Amendment) Regulations 2001
Authority: FSMA 2000, ss 39(1), 417(1). Amend the Financial Services and Markets Act 2000 (Appointed Representatives) Regulations 2001, SI 2001/1217 at **[2221]**

SI 2001/2507: Financial Services and Markets Act 2000 (Variation of Threshold Conditions) Order 2001
Authority: FSMA 2000, s 428(3), Sch 6, paras 8, 9. See the note at **[2420]**

SI 2001/2476: Financial Services and Markets Tribunal Rules 2001
Authority: FSMA 2000, ss 132(3), 137(6), Sch 13, para 9. At **[2389]**

SI 2001/2383: Financial Services and Markets Act 2000 (Collective Investment Schemes constituted in other EEA States) Regulations 2001
Authority: FSMA 2000, ss 264, 417(1). At **[2385]**. These Regulations implement, in part, Council Directive 85/611/EEC on the coordination of laws, regulations and administrative provisions relating to undertakings for collective investment in transferable securities (UCITS)

2001 Statutory Instruments
SI 2001/2364: Financial Services and Markets Act 2000 (Commencement No 4 and Transitional Provision) Order 2001 Authority: FSMA 2000, ss 431(2), 428(3). At **[2004]**. For details relating to the commencement of FSMA 2000, see the Appendix of commencement dates at **[498]**
SI 2001/2361: Financial Services and Markets Act 2000 (Meaning of "Policy" and "Policyholder") Order 2001 Authority: FSMA 2000, ss 424(2), 428(3). At **[2382]**
SI 2001/2326: Financial Services and Markets Act 2000 (Transitional Provisions) (Ombudsman Scheme and Complaints Scheme) Order 2001 Authority: FSMA 2000, ss 426–428. Articles 2–17 of this Order make transitional provision in relation to Part XVI of FSMA 2000, which provides for the establishment of an ombudsman scheme. The Order provides for certain complaints relating to acts or omissions occurring before the commencement of Part XVI, which fell (or would have fallen) within the scope of one of the "former schemes" (listed in art 1(2)), to be dealt with under the new scheme. The remainder of the Order makes transitional provisions concerned with complaints relating to certain matters occurring before the coming into force of FSMA 2000, s 19
SI 2001/2256: Financial Services and Markets Act 2000 (Rights of Action) Regulations 2001 Authority: FSMA 2000, ss 20(3), 71(2), (3), 150(3), (5), 202(2), 417(1), 428(3). At **[2375]**
SI 2001/2255: Financial Services and Markets Act 2000 (Transitional Provisions) (Designated Date for The Securities and Futures Authority) Order 2001 Authority: FSMA 2000, s 428(3), Sch 21, para 1. Schedule 21 to FSMA 2000 makes transitional provisions in relation to the provisions of the Financial Services Act 1986 which relate to the recognition and subsequent supervision of recognised self-regulating organisations, pending the repeal of the 1986 Act. Schedule 21 came into force on the passing of FSMA 2000 but applies in part from a date designated by the Treasury. This Order designates 13 July 2001 as the designated date for the Securities and Futures Authority Limited
SI 2001/2188: Financial Services and Markets Act 2000 (Disclosure of Confidential Information) Regulations 2001 Authority: FSMA 2000, ss 349(1)(b), (2), (3), 417(1), 426, 427, 428(3). At **[2350]**
SI 2001/1858: Financial Services and Markets Act 2000 (Competition Information) (Specification of Enactment etc) Order 2001 Authority: FSMA 2000, s 428(3), Sch 19. Lapsed on the repeal of FSMA 2000, Sch 19 by the Enterprise Act 2002, ss 247(k), 278(2), Sch 26
SI 2001/1857: Financial Services and Markets Act 2000 (Disclosure of Information by Prescribed Persons) Regulations 2001 Authority: FSMA 2000, ss 353(1), 417(1). At **[2346]**
SI 2001/1821: Financial Services and Markets Act 2000 (Consequential and Transitional Provisions) (Miscellaneous) Order 2001 Authority: FSMA 2000, ss 426–428. This Order makes consequential and transitional provisions in consequence of the Financial Services and Markets Act 2000 (Commencement No 3) Order, SI 2001/1820 which brought into force the provisions of FSMA 2000 relating to the constitution and rule making powers of the FSA and the scheme operator of the Ombudsman scheme
SI 2001/1820: Financial Services and Markets Act 2000 (Commencement No 3) Order 2001 Authority: FSMA 2000, s 431(2). For details relating to the commencement of FSMA 2000, see the Appendix of commencement dates at **[498]**
SI 2001/1819: Financial Services and Markets Act 2000 (Regulations Relating to Money Laundering) Regulations 2001 Authority: FSMA 2000, ss 168(4)(b), 402(1)(b), 417(1). Revoked by the Money Laundering Regulations 2003, SI 2003/3075
SI 2001/1783: Financial Services and Markets Act 2000 (Compensation Scheme: Electing Participants) Regulations 2001 Authority: FSMA 2000, ss 213(10), 214(5), 224(4), 417(1), 428(3). At **[2342]**. These Regulations implement, in part, European Parliament and Council Directive 94/19/EC on deposit-guarantee schemes, and European Parliament and Council Directive 97/9/EC on investor-compensation schemes

2001 Statutory Instruments

SI 2001/1534: Financial Services and Markets Act 2000 (Transitional Provisions and Savings) (Rules) Order 2001
Authority: FSMA 2000, ss 426–428. This Order makes transitional provision in relation to the rule making powers conferred on the FSA under FSMA 2000. Part I contains the commencement and interpretation provisions. Part II concerns the power of the FSA to designate existing rules and legislative provisions which will be repealed or will lapse at commencement so that they continue in effect after commencement as if they were rules made by the FSA. This is an alternative to the FSA making new rules under its FSMA 2000 powers. Part III of the Order contains transitional provisions in relation to consultation which the FSA has carried out in anticipation of the powers to be conferred on it by FSMA 2000. Where such consultations about rules, codes, statements of policy, etc, to be made under the Act was carried out before FSMA 2000 received Royal Assent, the procedure adopted may not have been fully compliant with the requirements laid down in the Act

SI 2001/1420: Financial Services and Markets Act 2000 (Service of Notices) Regulations 2001
Authority: FSMA 2000, ss 414, 428(3). At **[2331]**

SI 2001/1335: Financial Services and Markets Act 2000 (Financial Promotion) Order 2001
Authority: FSMA 2000, ss 22(1), (5), 428(3), Sch 2, para 25. Revoked by the Financial Services and Markets Act 2000 (Financial Promotion) Order 2005, SI 2005/1529

SI 2001/1283: Financial Services and Markets Act 2000 (Dissolution of the Insurance Brokers Registration Council) (Consequential Provisions) Order 2001
Authority: FSMA 2000, ss 416(4), 428(3). See the note at **[2330]**

SI 2001/1282: Financial Services and Markets Act 2000 (Commencement No 2) Order 2001
Authority: FSMA 2000, s 431(2). For details relating to the commencement of FSMA 2000, see the Appendix of commencement dates at **[498]**

SI 2001/1228: Open-Ended Investment Companies Regulations 2001
Authority: FSMA 2000, ss 262, 428(3). At **[2238]**

SI 2001/1227: Financial Services and Markets Act 2000 (Professions) (Non-Exempt Activities) Order 2001
Authority: FSMA 2000, ss 327(6), 428(3). At **[2226]**

SI 2001/1226: Financial Services and Markets Act 2000 (Designated Professional Bodies) Order 2001
Authority: FSMA 2000, s 326. At **[2224]**

SI 2001/1217: Financial Services and Markets Act 2000 (Appointed Representatives) Regulations 2001
Authority: FSMA 2000, ss 39(1), 417(1). At **[2221]**

SI 2001/1201: Financial Services and Markets Act 2000 (Exemption) Order 2001
Authority: FSMA 2000, ss 38, 428(3). At **[2211]**

SI 2001/1177: Financial Services and Markets Act 2000 (Carrying on Regulated Activities by Way of Business) Order 2001
Authority: FSMA 2000, ss 419, 428(3). At **[2206]**

SI 2001/1062: Financial Services and Markets Act 2000 (Collective Investment Schemes) Order 2001
Authority: FSMA 2000, s 235(5). At **[2202]**

SI 2001/1060: Financial Services and Markets Act 2000 (Promotion of Collective Investment Schemes) (Exemptions) Order 2001
Authority: FSMA 2000, s 238(6), (7). At **[2166]**

SI 2001/996: Financial Services and Markets Act 2000 (Prescribed Markets and Qualifying Investments) Order 2001
Authority: originally made under FSMA 2000, s 118(3). However, following the amendment of Pt VIII of that Act by the Financial Services and Markets Act 2000 (Market Abuse) Regulations 2005, SI 2005/381, it now has effect as if made under s 130A(1). At **[2161]**

SI 2001/995: Financial Services and Markets Act 2000 (Recognition Requirements for Investment Exchanges and Clearing Houses) Regulations 2001
Authority: FSMA 2000, ss 286(1), 426, 427, 428(3). At **[2147]**

SI 2001/544: Financial Services and Markets Act 2000 (Regulated Activities) Order 2001
Authority: FSMA 2000, ss 22(1), (5), 426, 428(3), Sch 2, para 25. At **[2010]**. This Order implements, in part, Council Directive 93/22/EEC on investment services in the securities field

---

2001 Statutory Instruments

SI 2001/516: Financial Services and Markets Act 2000 (Commencement No 1) Order 2001
Authority: FSMA 2000, s 431(2). For details relating to the commencement of FSMA 2000, see the Appendix of commencement dates at **[498]**

2000 Statutory Instruments

SI 2000/1734: Financial Services and Markets (Transitional Provisions) (Designated Date for Certain Self-Regulating Organisations) Order 2000
Authority: FSMA 2000, s 428, Sch 21, paras 1, 2. Schedule 21 to FSMA 2000 makes transitional provisions in relation to the provisions of the Financial Services Act 1986 which relate to the recognition and subsequent supervision of recognised self-regulating organisations, pending the repeal of the 1986 Act. Schedule 21 came into force on the passing of FSMA 2000 but applies in part from a date designated by the Treasury. This Order designates 25 July 2000 as the designated date for the Personal Investment Authority Limited and for the Investment Management Regulatory Organisation Limited

[3500]

C. OTHER STATUTORY INSTRUMENTS

STOCK TRANSFER (RECOGNISED STOCK EXCHANGES) ORDER 1973

(SI 1973/536)

NOTES
Made: 26 March 1973.
Authority: Stock Transfer Act 1963, s 4.
Commencement: 26 March 1973.

As of 1 February 2009, this Order had not been amended.

1   This Order may be cited as the Stock Transfer (Recognised Stock Exchanges) Order 1973.

[3501]

2   The Interpretation Act 1889 shall apply for the interpretation of this Order as it applies for the interpretation of an Act of Parliament.

[3502]

NOTES
Interpretation Act 1889: repealed; see now the Interpretation Act 1978.

3   The Stock Exchange shall be a recognised stock exchange for the purposes of the Stock Transfer Act 1963.

[3503]

4   The Stock Transfer (Recognition of Stock Exchanges) Order 1966 is hereby revoked.

[3504]

REHABILITATION OF OFFENDERS ACT 1974 (EXCEPTIONS) ORDER 1975

(SI 1975/1023)

NOTES
Made: 24 June 1975.
Authority: Rehabilitation of Offenders Act 1974, ss 4(4), 7(4).
Commencement: 1 July 1975.
This Order is reproduced as amended by: the Criminal Justice Act 1988; the Osteopaths Act 1993; the Chiropractors Act 1994; the Rehabilitation of Offenders Act 1974 (Exceptions) (Amendment) Order 1986, SI 1986/1249; the Rehabilitation of Offenders Act 1974 (Exceptions) (Amendment No 2) Order 1986, SI 1986/2268; the Postal Services Act 2000 (Consequential Modifications No 1) Order 2001, SI 2001/1149; the Rehabilitation of Offenders Act 1974 (Exceptions) (Amendment) Order 2001, SI 2001/1192; the Rehabilitation of Offenders Act 1974 (Exceptions) (Amendment) (No 2) Order 2001, SI 2001/3816; the Rehabilitation of Offenders Act 1974 (Exceptions) (Amendment) Order 2002, SI 2002/441; the Rehabilitation of Offenders Act 1974 (Exclusions and Exceptions) (Scotland) Order 2003, SSI 2003/231; the Rehabilitation of Offenders Act 1974 (Exceptions) (Amendment) (England and Wales) Order 2003, SI 2003/965; the Health Professions Order 2001 (Consequential Amendments) Order 2003, SI 2003/1590; the Courts Act 2003 (Consequential Provisions) (No 2) Order 2005, SI 2005/617; the Opticians Act 1989 (Amendment) Order 2005, SI 2005/848; the Manufacture and Storage of Explosives Regulations 2005, SI 2005/1082; the Dentists Act 1984 (Amendment) Order 2005, SI 2005/2011; the Serious Organised Crime and Police Act 2005 (Consequential and Supplementary Amendments to Secondary Legislation) Order 2006, SI 2006/594; the Rehabilitation of Offenders Act 1974 (Exceptions) (Amendment) (England and Wales) Order 2006, SI 2006/2143; the Rehabilitation of Offenders Act 1974 (Exceptions) (Amendment No 2) (England and Wales) Order 2006, SI 2006/3290; the Pharmacists and Pharmacy Technicians Order 2007, SI 2007/289; the Rehabilitation of Offenders Act 1974 (Exceptions) (Amendment) (England and Wales) Order 2007, SI 2007/2149; the Secretaries of State for Children, Schools and Families, for Innovation, Universities and Skills and for Business, Enterprise and Regulatory Reform Order 2007, SI 2007/3224; the Tribunals, Courts and Enforcement Act 2007 (Transitional and Consequential Provisions) Order 2008, SI 2008/2683; the Rehabilitation of Offenders Act 1974 (Exceptions) (Amendment) (England and Wales) Order 2008, SI 2008/3259. See also the note below.
Note: this Order is revoked in relation to Scotland by the Rehabilitation of Offenders Act 1974 (Exclusions and Exceptions) (Scotland) Order 2003, SSI 2003/231, art 6(a), as from 29 March 2003. The 2003 Scottish Order consolidates this Order and the amending SI 1986/1249 and SI 1986/2268 which exclude and make exceptions to the provisions of the Rehabilitation of Offenders Act 1974, s 4 (effect of rehabilitation). It excludes

further proceedings and types of work from certain provisions within that section and updates the terms used to reflect recent Scottish legislation, including the Regulation of Care (Scotland) Act 2001 and the Protection of Children (Scotland) Act 2003. Amendments made to this Order before 29 March 2003 which applied to Scotland only have now been omitted from the Order as reproduced here.

1   This Order may be cited as the Rehabilitation of Offenders Act 1974 (Exceptions) Order 1975 and shall come into operation on 1st July 1975.

[3505]

NOTES
Revoked in relation to Scotland as noted at the beginning of this Order.

2—[(1)   In this Order, except where the context otherwise requires—
["the 2000 Act" means the Financial Services and Markets Act 2000;]
"the Act" means the Rehabilitation of Offenders Act 1974;
["administration of justice offence" means—
    (a)   the offence of perverting the course of justice,
    (b)   any offence under section 51 of the Criminal Justice and Public Order Act 1994 (intimidation etc of witnesses, jurors and others),
    (c)   an offence under section 1, 2, 6 or 7 of the Perjury Act 1911 (perjury),
or any offence committed under the law of any part of the United Kingdom (other than England or Wales) or of any other country where the conduct which constitutes the offence would, if it all took place in England or Wales, constitute one or more of the offences specified by paragraph (a) to (c);]
["adoption agency" has the meaning given to it by section 1 of the Adoption Act 1976;]
["associate", in relation to a person ("A"), means someone who is a controller, director or manager of A or, where A is a partnership, any partner of A;]

.....

["child minding" means—
    [(a)   child minding within the meaning of section 79A of the Children Act 1989; and
    (b)   early years childminding within the meaning of section 96(4) of the Childcare Act 2006, or later years childminding within the meaning of section 96(8) of that Act;]]
["collective investment scheme" has the meaning given by section 235 of the 2000 Act;]
["the competent authority for listing" means the competent authority for the purposes of Part VI of the 2000 Act (listing);]
["contracting authority" means a contracting authority within the meaning of Article 1(9) of Directive 2004/18/EC;]
["contracting entity" means a contracting entity within the meaning of Article 2(2) of Directive 2004/17/EC;]
["controller" has the meaning given by section 422 of the 2000 Act;]
["Council" has the meaning given to it by section 54 of the Care Standards Act 2000;]
["Council of Lloyd's" means the council constituted by section 3 of Lloyd's Act 1982;]
["day care" means—
    [(a)   day care for which registration is required by section 79D(5) of the Children Act 1989; and
    (b)   early years provision within the meaning of section 96(2) of the Childcare Act 2006 (other than early years childminding), or later years provision within the meaning of section 96(6) of that Act (other than later years childminding), for which registration is required, or permitted, under Part 3 of that Act;]]
["day care premises" means any premises on which day care is provided, but does not include any part of the premises where children are not looked after;]
["Directive 2004/17/EC" means Directive 2004/17/EC of the European Parliament and of the Council of 31 March 2004;]
["Directive 2004/18/EC" means Directive 2004/18/EC of the European Parliament and of the Council of 31 March 2004;]
["director" has the meaning given by section 417 of the 2000 Act;]
["key worker", in relation to any body ("A"), means any individual who is likely, in the course of the duties of his office or employment—
    (a)   where A is the Authority, to play a significant role in the decision making process of the Authority in relation to the exercise of the Authority's public functions (within the meaning of section 349(5) of the 2000 Act) under any provision of the 2000 Act other than Part VI, or to support directly such a person;
    (b)   where A is the competent authority for listing, to play a significant role in the

PART III
STATUTORY INSTRUMENTS

decision making process of the competent authority for listing in relation to the exercise of its functions under Part VI of the 2000 Act, or to support directly such a person;]

["manager" has the meaning given by section 423 of the 2000 Act;]

["open-ended investment company" has the meaning given by section 236 of the 2000 Act]

[Part IV permission" has the meaning given by section 40(4) of the 2000 Act;]

["relevant collective investment scheme" means a collective investment scheme which is recognised under section 264 (schemes constituted in other EEA States), 270 (schemes authorised in designated countries or territories) or 272 (individually recognised overseas schemes) of the 2000 Act;]

.....

["taxi driver licence" means a licence granted under—

   [(i)   section 46 of the Town Police Clauses Act 1847;]

   (ii)   section 8 of the Metropolitan Public Carriage Act 1869;

   (iii)   section 9 of the Plymouth City Council Act 1975;

   (iv)   section 51 of the Local Government (Miscellaneous Provisions) Act 1976; or

   (v)   section 13 of the Private Hire Vehicles (London) Act 1998;]

["trustee", in relation to a unit trust scheme, has the meaning given by section 237 of the 2000 Act;]

["UK recognised clearing house" means a clearing house in relation to which a recognition order under section 290 of the 2000 Act, otherwise than by virtue of section 292(2) of that Act (overseas clearing houses), is in force;]

["UK recognised investment exchange" means an investment exchange in relation to which a recognition order under section 290 of the 2000 Act, otherwise than by virtue of section 292(2) of that Act (overseas investment exchanges), is in force;]

["work" includes—

   (a)   work of any kind, whether paid or unpaid, and whether under a contract of service or apprenticeship, under a contract for services, or otherwise than under a contract; and

   (b)   an office established by or by virtue of an enactment;]

["work with children" means work of the kind described in paragraph 14 of [Part 2 of] Schedule 1 to this Order;]

...

(2)   Where, by virtue of this Order, the operation of any of the provisions of the Act is excluded in relation to spent convictions the exclusion shall be taken to extend to spent convictions for offences of every description ...].

(3)   Part IV of Schedule 1 to this Order shall have effect for the interpretation of expressions used in that Schedule.

(4)   In this Order a reference to any enactment shall be construed as a reference to that enactment as amended, extended or applied by or under any other enactment.

[(4A)   In this Order any reference to a conviction shall where relevant include a reference to a caution, and any reference to spent convictions shall be construed accordingly.]

(5)   The Interpretation Act 1889 shall apply to the interpretation of this Order as it applies to the interpretation of an Act of Parliament.

[3506]

NOTES

Revoked in relation to Scotland as noted at the beginning of this Order.

Para (1) is amended as follows:

Substituted, together with para (2), by the Rehabilitation of Offenders Act 1974 (Exceptions) (Amendment No 2) Order 1986, SI 1986/2268, art 2(1), Schedule, para 1, as from 1 January 1987.

Definitions "the 2000 Act", "administration of justice offence", "associate", "collective investment scheme", "the competent authority for listing", "controller", "Council of Lloyd's", "director", "key worker", "manager", "open-ended investment company", "relevant collective investment scheme", "trustee", "UK recognised clearing house", and "UK recognised investment exchange" inserted by the Rehabilitation of Offenders Act 1974 (Exceptions) (Amendment) (No 2) Order 2001, SI 2001/3816, arts 2, 3(1), as from 30 November 2001.

Definitions "adoption agency", "child minding", "day care", "day care premises", "work", and "work with children" inserted by the Rehabilitation of Offenders Act 1974 (Exceptions) (Amendment) Order 2001, SI 2001/1192, arts 2, 3, as from 31 March 2001. Paras (a), (b) of definitions "child minding" and "day care" subsequently substituted, and words in square brackets in definition "work with children" inserted, by the Rehabilitation of Offenders Act 1974 (Exceptions) (Amendment) (England and Wales) Order 2008, SI 2008/3259, arts 2, 3(1), as from 18 December 2008.

Definition "the Building Societies Commission" (omitted) revoked by SI 2001/3816, arts 2, 3(3), as from 30 November 2001.

Definitions "contracting authority", "contracting entity", "Directive 2004/17/EC", and "Directive 2004/18/EC" inserted by the Rehabilitation of Offenders Act 1974 (Exceptions) (Amendment) (England and Wales) Order 2006, SI 2006/2143, arts 2, 3(b), as from 26 July 2006.

Definition "Council" inserted by the Rehabilitation of Offenders Act 1974 (Exceptions) (Amendment) (England and Wales) Order 2003, SI 2003/965, arts 2, 3(a), as from 1 April 2003.

Definition "Part IV permission" inserted by SI 2001/3816, arts 2, 3(1), as from 30 November 2001.

Definition "relevant offence" (omitted) revoked by the Rehabilitation of Offenders Act 1974 (Exceptions) (Amendment) (England and Wales) Order 2007, SI 2007/2149, arts 2, 3(1), as from 22 July 2007.

Definition "taxi driver licence" inserted by SI 2003/965, arts 2, 3(a), as from 1 April 2003; para (i) substituted by SI 2006/2143, arts 2, 3(a), as from 26 July 2006.

Final words omitted revoked by SI 2001/3816, arts 2, 3(3), as from 30 November 2001.

Para (2): substituted as noted above; words omitted revoked by SI 2007/2149, arts 2, 3(2), as from 22 July 2007.

Para (4A): inserted by SI 2008/3259, arts 2, 3(2), as from 18 December 2008.

Adoption Act 1976, s 1: repealed by the Adoption and Children Act 2002, s 139(3), Sch 5. As to the meaning of "adoption agency", see now s 2(1) of the 2002 Act.

Interpretation Act 1889: repealed and replaced by the Interpretation Act 1978.

---

3   [Neither section 4(2) of, nor paragraph 3(3) of Schedule 2 to,] the Act shall apply in relation to—

(a)   any question asked by or on behalf of any person, in the course of the duties of his office or employment, in order to assess the suitability—

   (i)   of the person to whom the question relates for admission to any of the professions specified in Part I of Schedule 1 to this Order; or

  [(ii)   of the person to whom the question relates for any office or employment specified in Part II of the said Schedule 1 or for any other work specified in paragraph [13, 14, 20, 21, 35, 36, 37, 40 or 43] of Part II of the said Schedule 1; or]

  (iii)   of the person to whom the question relates or of any other person to pursue any occupation specified in Part III of the said Schedule 1 or to pursue it subject to a particular condition or restriction; or

  (iv)   of the person to whom the question relates or of any other person to hold a licence, certificate or permit of a kind specified in Schedule 2 to this Order or to hold it subject to a particular condition or restriction,

where the person questioned is informed at the time the question is asked that, by virtue of this Order, spent convictions are to be disclosed;

[(aa)   any question asked by or on behalf of any person, in the course of the duties of his work, in order to assess the suitability of a person to work with children, where—

  (i)   the question relates to the person whose suitability is being assessed;

  (ii)   the person whose suitability is being assessed lives on the premises where his work with children would normally take place and the question relates to a person living in the same household as him;

  (iii)   the person whose suitability is being assessed lives on the premises where his work with children would normally take place and the question relates to a person who regularly works on those premises at a time when the work with children usually takes place; or

  (iv)   the work for which the person's suitability is being assessed is child minding which would normally take place on premises other than premises where that person lives and the question relates to a person who lives on those other premises or to a person who regularly works on them at a time when the child minding takes place,

and where the person to whom the question relates is informed at the time the question is asked that, by virtue of this Order, spent convictions are to be disclosed;]

[(ab)   ...]

(b)   any question asked by or on behalf of any person, in the course of his duties as a person employed in the service of the Crown, the United Kingdom Atomic Energy Authority, [or] ... [the Financial Services Authority] in order to assess, for the purpose of safeguarding national security, the suitability of the person to whom the question relates or of any other person for any office or employment where the person questioned is informed at the time the question is asked that, by virtue of this Order, spent convictions are to be disclosed for the purpose of safeguarding national security;

[(bb)   any question asked by or on behalf of

  (i)   the Civil Aviation Authority,

  (ii)   any other person authorised to provide air traffic services under section 4 or section 5 of the Transport Act 2000 (in any case where such person is a company, an "authorised company"),

  (iii)   any company which is a subsidiary (within the meaning given by section 736(1) of the Companies Act 1985) of an authorised company, or

  (iv)   any company of which an authorised company is a subsidiary,

where, in the case of sub-paragraphs (iii) and (iv) of this paragraph the question is put in relation to the provision of air traffic services, and in all cases, where the question is put in order to assess, for the purpose of safeguarding national security, the suitability of the person to whom the question relates or of any other person for any office or employment where the person questioned is informed at the time the question is asked that, by virtue of this Order, spent convictions are to be disclosed for the purpose of safeguarding national security;]

   [(e)   any question asked by or on behalf of any person in the course of his duties as a person employed by an adoption agency for the purpose of assessing the suitability of any person to adopt children in general or a child in particular where—
      (i)   the question relates to the person whose suitability is being assessed; or
      (ii)   the question relates to a person over the age of 18 living in the same household as the person whose suitability is being assessed,

and where the person to whom the question relates is informed at the time the question is asked that, by virtue of this Order, spent convictions are to be disclosed;

   (f)   any question asked by or on behalf of any person, in the course of the duties of his work, in order to assess the suitability of a person to provide day care where—
      (i)   the question relates to the person whose suitability is being assessed; or
      (ii)   the question relates to a person who lives on the premises which are or are proposed to be day care premises,

and where the person to whom the question relates is informed at the time the question is asked that, by virtue of this Order, spent convictions are to be disclosed];

   [(g)   any question asked by, or on behalf of, the person listed in the second column of any entry in the table below to the extent that it relates to a conviction … (or any circumstances ancillary to … a conviction) of any individual, but only if—
      (i)   the person questioned is informed at the time the question is asked that, by virtue of this Order, spent convictions … are to be disclosed; and
      (ii)   the question is asked in order to assess the suitability of the individual to whom the question relates to have the status specified in the first column of that entry.

Status			*Questioner*
1		A person with Part IV permission.	The Financial Services Authority.
2	(a)	An approved person (within the meaning of Part V of the 2000 Act (performance of regulated activities)).	The Financial Services Authority or the authorised person (within the meaning of section 31(2) of the 2000 Act) or the applicant for Part IV permission who made the application for the Authority's approval under section 59 of the 2000 Act in relation to the person mentioned in sub-paragraph (a) of the first column.
	(b)	An associate of the person (whether or not an individual) mentioned in sub-paragraph (a).	
3	(a)	The manager or trustee of an authorised unit trust scheme, within the meaning of section 237 of the 2000 Act.	The Financial Services Authority or the unit trust scheme mentioned in the first column.
	(b)	An associate of the person (whether or not an individual) mentioned in sub-paragraph (a).	
4	(a)	A director of an open-ended investment company.	The Financial Services Authority or the open-ended investment company mentioned in the first column.
	(b)	An associate of the person (whether or not an individual) mentioned in sub-paragraph (a).	
5		An associate of the operator or trustee of a relevant collective investment scheme.	The Financial Services Authority or the collective investment scheme mentioned in the first column.
6		An associate of a UK recognised investment exchange or UK recognised clearing house.	The Financial Services Authority or the investment exchange or clearing house mentioned in the first column.

Status			*Questioner*		
7		A controller of a person with Part IV permission.			The Financial Services Authority or the person with Part IV permission mentioned in the first column.
8	(a)	A person who carries on a regulated activity (within the meaning of section 22 of the 2000 Act) but to whom the general prohibition does not apply by virtue of section 327 of the 2000 Act (exemption from the general prohibition for members of a designated professional body).	(a)		The Financial Services Authority.
	(b)	An associate of the person (whether or not an individual) mentioned in sub-paragraph (a).	(b)		In the case of a person mentioned in sub-paragraph (b) of the first column, the person mentioned in sub-paragraph (a) of that column.
9		A key worker of the Financial Services Authority.			The Financial Services Authority.
10		An ombudsman (within the meaning of Schedule 17 to the 2000 Act) of the Financial Ombudsman Service.			The scheme operator (within the meaning of section 225 of the 2000 Act) of the Financial Ombudsman Service.
11		An associate of the issuer of securities which have been admitted to the official list maintained by the competent authority for listing under section 74 of the 2000 Act.			The competent authority for listing.
12		A sponsor (within the meaning of section 88(2) of the 2000 Act).			The competent authority for listing.
13		A key worker of the competent authority for listing.			The competent authority for listing.
14		An associate of a person who has Part IV permission and who is admitted to Lloyd's as an underwriting agent (within the meaning of section 2 of Lloyd's Act 1982).	(a)		The Council of Lloyd's.
			(b)		The person with Part IV permission specified in the first column (or a person applying for such permission).
15		An associate of the Council of Lloyd's.			The Council of Lloyd's.
16	(a)	Any member of a UK recognised investment exchange or UK recognised clearing house.	(a)		The UK recognised investment exchange or UK recognised clearing house specified in the first column.
	(b)	Any associate of the person (whether or not an individual) mentioned in sub-paragraph (a).	(b)		In the case of a person mentioned in sub-paragraph (b) of the first column, the person mentioned in sub-paragraph (a) of that column];

[(h) any question asked by or on behalf of the National Lottery Commission for the purpose of determining whether to grant or revoke a licence under Part I of the National Lottery etc Act 1993 where the question relates to an individual—

    (i) who manages the business or any part of the business carried on under the licence (or who is likely to do so if the licence is granted), or

    (ii) for whose benefit that business is carried on (or is likely to be carried on if the licence is granted),

and where the person to whom the question relates is informed at the time that the question is asked that, by virtue of this Order, spent convictions are to be disclosed];

[(i) any question asked by or on behalf of the Council for the purpose of determining whether or not to grant an application for registration under Part IV of the Care Standards Act 2000, where the person questioned is informed at the time the question is asked that, by virtue of this Order, spent convictions are to be disclosed];

[(j) any question asked by or on behalf of a contracting authority or contracting entity in

relation to a conviction within the meaning of Article 45(1) of Directive 2004/18/EC which is a spent conviction (or any circumstances ancillary to such a conviction) for the purpose of determining whether or not to treat a person as ineligible:
  (i)   for the purposes of regulation 23 of the Public Contracts Regulations 2006 or regulation 23 of the Utilities Contracts Regulations 2006; or
  (ii) to participate in a design contest for the purposes of regulation 33 of the Public Contracts Regulations 2006 or regulation 34 of the Utilities Contracts Regulations 2006,
where the person questioned is informed at the time the question is asked that, by virtue of this Order, convictions within the meaning of Article 45(1) of Directive 2004/18/EC which are spent convictions are to be disclosed;
  (k)   any question asked, by or on behalf of the Football Association[, Football League] or Football Association Premier League in order to assess the suitability of the person to whom the question relates or of any other person to be approved as able to undertake, in the course of acting as a steward at a sports ground at which football matches are played or as a supervisor or manager of such a person, licensable conduct within the meaning of the Private Security Industry Act 2001 without a licence issued under that Act, in accordance with ... section 4 of that Act];
  [(l) any question asked by the Secretary of State for the purpose of considering the suitability of an individual to have access to information released under sections 113A and 113B of the Police Act 1997].

[3507]

NOTES
Revoked in relation to Scotland as noted at the beginning of this Order.
Words in first pair of square brackets substituted by the Rehabilitation of Offenders Act 1974 (Exceptions) (Amendment) (England and Wales) Order 2008, SI 2008/3259, arts 2, 4, as from 18 December 2008.
Para (a): sub-para (ii) substituted by the Rehabilitation of Offenders Act 1974 (Exceptions) (Amendment) Order 2001, SI 2001/1192, arts 2, 4(1), as from 31 March 2001; words in square brackets in sub-para (ii) substituted by the Rehabilitation of Offenders Act 1974 (Exceptions) (Amendment) (England and Wales) Order 2007, SI 2007/2149, arts 2, 4(1), as from 22 July 2007.
Para (aa): inserted by the Rehabilitation of Offenders Act 1974 (Exceptions) (Amendment) Order 1986, SI 1986/1249, art 2, Schedule, as from 18 July 1986; substituted by SI 2001/1192, arts 2, 4(2), as from 31 March 2001.
Para (ab): inserted by the Rehabilitation of Offenders Act 1974 (Exceptions) (Amendment No 2) Order 1986, SI 1986/2268, art 2(1), Schedule, para 2, as from 1 January 1987; revoked by the Rehabilitation of Offenders Act 1974 (Exceptions) (Amendment) (No 2) Order 2001, SI 2001/3816, arts 2, 4(1), (2), as from 30 November 2001.
Para (b): word in first pair of square brackets inserted by the Postal Services Act 2000 (Consequential Modifications No 1) Order 2001, SI 2001/1149, art 3(1), Sch 1, para 41, as from 26 March 2001; words omitted revoked by a combination of SI 2002/441, arts 2, 3(2), as from 1 March 2002 and SI 2001/1149, art 3(2), Sch 2, as from 26 March 2001; words in second pair of square brackets inserted by SI 2001/3816, arts 2, 4(1), (3), as from 30 November 2001.
Para (bb): inserted by SI 2002/441, arts 2, 3(3), as from a day to be appointed (ie, the day on which the Police Act 1997, s 133(d) comes into force in England and Wales).
Paras (e), (f): added by SI 2001/1192, arts 2, 4(3), as from 31 March 2001. Note that SI 2001/1192 purports to insert these paragraphs after para (d) but it is believed that this is a drafting error as this article doesn't contain a para (d).
Para (g): added by SI 2001/3816, arts 2, 4(1), (4), as from 30 November 2001; words omitted revoked by SI 2007/2149, arts 2, 4(2), (3), as from 22 July 2007.
Para (h): added by SI 2002/441, arts 2, 3(4), as from 1 March 2002.
Para (i): added by SI 2003/965, arts 2, 5, as from 1 April 2003.
Para (j): added, together with para (k), by the Rehabilitation of Offenders Act 1974 (Exceptions) (Amendment) (England and Wales) Order 2006, SI 2006/2143, arts 2, 4, as from 26 July 2006.
Para (k): added as noted above; words in square brackets inserted, and words omitted revoked, by the Rehabilitation of Offenders Act 1974 (Exceptions) (Amendment No 2) (England and Wales) Order 2006, SI 2006/3290, art 2, as from 7 December 2006.
Para (l): added by SI 2007/2149, arts 2, 4(4), as from 22 July 2007.

4 [Neither paragraph (b) of section 4(3) of, nor paragraph 3(5) of Schedule 2 to, the Act shall apply] in relation to—
  (a)   the dismissal or exclusion of any person from any profession specified in Part I of Schedule 1 to this Order;
  [(b) any office, employment or occupation specified in Part II or Part III of the said Schedule 1 or any other work specified in paragraph [13, 14, 20, 21, 35, 36, 37, 40 or 43] of Part II of the said Schedule 1;]
  (c)   any action taken for the purpose of safeguarding national security;
  [(d) any decision by the Financial Services Authority—
        (i)   to refuse an application for Part IV permission under the 2000 Act,
        (ii) to vary or to cancel such permission (or to refuse to vary or cancel such permission) or to impose a requirement under section 43 of that Act or,

(iii) to make, or to refuse to vary or revoke, an order under section 56 of that Act (prohibition orders),

(iv) to refuse an application for the Authority's approval under section 59 of that Act or to withdraw such approval,

(v) to refuse to make, or to revoke, an order declaring a unit trust scheme to be an authorised unit trust scheme under section 243 of the 2000 Act or to refuse to give its approval under section 251 of the 2000 Act to a proposal to replace the manager or trustee of such a scheme,

(vi) to give a direction under section 257 of the 2000 Act (authorised unit trust schemes), or to vary (or to refuse to vary or revoke) such a direction,

(vii) to refuse to make, or to revoke, an authorisation order under regulation 14 of the Open-Ended Investment Companies Regulations 2001 or to refuse to give its approval under regulation 21 of those Regulations to a proposal to replace a director or to appoint an additional director of an open-ended investment company,

(viii) to give a direction to an open-ended investment company under regulation 25 of those Regulations or to vary (or refuse to vary or revoke) such a direction,

(ix) to refuse to give its approval to a collective investment scheme being recognised under section 270 of the 2000 Act or to direct that such a scheme cease to be recognised by virtue of that section or to refuse to make, or to revoke, an order declaring a collective investment scheme to be a recognised scheme under section 272 of that Act,

(x) to refuse to make, or to revoke, a recognition order under section 290 of the 2000 Act, otherwise than by virtue of section 292(2) of that Act, or to give a direction to a UK recognised investment exchange or UK recognised clearing house under section 296 of the 2000 Act,

(xi) to make, or to refuse to vary or to revoke, an order under section 329 (orders in respect of members of a designated professional body in relation to the general prohibition), or

(xii) to dismiss, fail to promote or exclude a person from being a key worker of the Authority,

by reason of, or partly by reason of, a spent conviction of an individual ..., or of any circumstances ancillary to such a conviction or of a failure (whether or not by that individual) to disclose such a conviction or any such circumstances;

(e) any decision by the scheme operator (within the meaning of section 225 of the 2000 Act) of the Financial Ombudsman Service to dismiss, or not to appoint, an individual as, an ombudsman (within the meaning of Schedule 17 to the 2000 Act) of the Financial Ombudsman Service by reason of, or partly by reason of, his spent conviction ..., or of any circumstances ancillary to such a conviction or of a failure (whether or not by that individual) to disclose such a conviction or any such circumstances;

(f) any decision of the competent authority for listing—

(i) to refuse an application for listing under Part VI of the 2000 Act or to discontinue or suspend the listing of any securities under section 77 of that Act,

(ii) to refuse to grant a person's application for approval as a sponsor under section 88 of the 2000 Act or to cancel such approval, or

(iii) to dismiss, fail to promote or exclude a person from being a key worker of the competent authority for listing,

by reason of, or partly by reason of, a spent conviction of an individual ..., or of any circumstances ancillary to such a conviction or of a failure (whether or not by that individual) to disclose such a conviction or any such circumstances;

(g) any decision of anyone who is specified in any of sub-paragraphs 2 to 4 or 5 to 7 of the second column of the table in article 3(g), other than the Authority, to dismiss an individual who has, or to fail to promote or exclude an individual who is seeking to obtain, the status specified in the corresponding entry in the first column of that table (but not, where applicable, the status of being an associate of another person), by reason of, or partly by reason of, a spent conviction of that individual or of his associate ..., or of any circumstances ancillary to such a conviction or of a failure (whether or not by that individual) to disclose such a conviction or any such circumstances;

(h) any decision of anyone who is specified in sub-paragraph 8(a), 14(a) or 16(a) of the second column of the table in article 3(g) to dismiss an individual who has, or to fail to promote or exclude an individual who is seeking to obtain, the status specified in the corresponding entry in sub-paragraph (b) of the first column of that table (associate), by reason of, or partly by reason of, a spent conviction of that individual ..., or of any circumstances ancillary to such a conviction or of a failure (whether or not by that individual) to disclose such a conviction or any such circumstances;

(i) any decision of the Council of Lloyd's—

(i) to refuse to admit any person as, or to exclude, an underwriting agent (within the meaning of section 2 of Lloyd's Act 1982), where that person has, or who has applied for, Part IV permission, or

(ii) to dismiss, or to exclude a person from being, an associate of the Council of Lloyd's,

by reason of, or partly by reason of, a spent conviction of an individual ..., or of any circumstances ancillary to such a conviction or of a failure (whether or not by that individual) to disclose such a conviction or any such circumstances;

(j) any decision of a UK recognised investment exchange or UK recognised clearing house to refuse to admit any person as, or to exclude, a member by reason of, or partly by reason of, a spent conviction of an individual ..., or of any circumstances ancillary to such a conviction or of a failure (whether or not by that individual) to disclose such a conviction or any such circumstances;]

[(k) any decision by the Council to refuse to grant an application for registration under Part IV of the Care Standards Act 2000 or to suspend, remove or refuse to restore a person's registration under that Part;

(l) any decision to refuse to grant a taxi driver licence, to grant such a licence subject to conditions or to suspend, revoke or refuse to renew such a licence;

(m) any decision by the Security Industry Authority to refuse to grant a licence under section 8 of the Private Security Industry Act 2001, to grant such a licence subject to conditions, to modify such a licence (including any of the conditions of that licence) or to revoke such a licence;]

[(n) any decision by the Football Association[, Football League] or Football Association Premier League to refuse to approve a person as able to undertake, in the course of acting as a steward at a sports ground at which football matches are played or as a supervisor or manager of such a person, licensable conduct within the meaning of the Private Security Industry Act 2001 without a licence issued under that Act, in accordance with ... section 4 of that Act].

[3508]

NOTES
Revoked in relation to Scotland as noted at the beginning of this Order.
Words in first pair of square brackets substituted by the Rehabilitation of Offenders Act 1974 (Exceptions) (Amendment) (England and Wales) Order 2008, SI 2008/3259, arts 2, 5, as from 18 December 2008.
Para (b): substituted by the Rehabilitation of Offenders Act 1974 (Exceptions) (Amendment) Order 2001, SI 2001/1192, arts 2, 5, as from 31 March 2001; words in square brackets substituted by the Rehabilitation of Offenders Act 1974 (Exceptions) (Amendment) (England and Wales) Order 2007, SI 2007/2149, arts 2, 5(2), as from 22 July 2007.
Para (d): inserted by the Rehabilitation of Offenders Act 1974 (Exceptions) (Amendment No 2) Order 1986, SI 1986/2268, art 2(1), Schedule, para 3, as from 1 January 1987, and substituted (by new paras (d)–(j)) by the Rehabilitation of Offenders Act 1974 (Exceptions) (Amendment) (No 2) Order 2001, SI 2001/3816, arts 2, 5, as from 30 November 2001; words omitted revoked by SI 2007/2149, arts 2, 5(1), as from 22 July 2007.
Paras (e)–(j): substituted as noted above; words omitted revoked by SI 2007/2149, arts 2, 5(1), as from 22 July 2007.
Paras (k)–(m): added by SI 2003/965, arts 2, 7, as from 1 April 2003.
Para (n): added by the Rehabilitation of Offenders Act 1974 (Exceptions) (Amendment) (England and Wales) Order 2006, SI 2006/2143, arts 2, 5, as from 26 July 2006; words in square brackets inserted, and words omitted revoked, by the Rehabilitation of Offenders Act 1974 (Exceptions) (Amendment No 2) (England and Wales) Order 2006, SI 2006/3290, art 2, as from 7 December 2006.

[**5**—(1) [Neither section 4(1) of, nor paragraph 3(1) of Schedule 2 to, the Act shall]—

(a) apply in relation to any proceedings specified in Schedule 3 to this Order;

(b) apply in relation to any proceedings specified in paragraph (2) below to the extent that there falls to be determined therein any issue relating to a person's spent conviction ... or to circumstances ancillary thereto;

(c) prevent, in any proceedings specified in paragraph (2) below, the admission or requirement of any evidence relating to a person's spent conviction ... or to circumstances ancillary thereto.

[(2) The proceedings referred to in paragraph (1) above are any proceedings with respect to a decision or proposed decision of the kind specified in article 4(d) to [(n)].]]

[3509]

NOTES
Revoked in relation to Scotland as noted at the beginning of this Order.
Substituted by the Rehabilitation of Offenders Act 1974 (Exceptions) (Amendment No 2) Order 1986, SI 1986/2268, art 2(1), Schedule, para 4, as from 1 January 1987.
Para (1): words in square brackets substituted by the Rehabilitation of Offenders Act 1974 (Exceptions) (Amendment) (England and Wales) Order 2008, SI 2008/3259, arts 2, 6(1), as from 18 December 2008; words omitted revoked by the Rehabilitation of Offenders Act 1974 (Exceptions) (Amendment) (England and Wales) Order 2007, SI 2007/2149, arts 2, 6, as from 22 July 2007.

Para (2): substituted by the Rehabilitation of Offenders Act 1974 (Exceptions) (Amendment) (No 2) Order 2001, SI 2001/3816, arts 2, 6, as from 30 November 2001; reference to "(n)" in square brackets substituted by SI 2008/3259, arts 2, 6(2), as from 18 December 2008.

SCHEDULES

SCHEDULE 1
[EXCEPTED PROFESSIONS, OFFICES, EMPLOYMENTS, WORK AND OCCUPATIONS]
Article 2(3), 3, 4

PART I
PROFESSIONS

1. Medical practitioner.

2. Barrister (in England and Wales), advocate (in Scotland), solicitor.

3. Chartered accountant, certified accountant.

4. Dentist, dental hygienist, [dental therapist].

5. Veterinary surgeon.

6. Nurse, midwife.

7. [optometrist], dispensing optician.

[8. Registered pharmacist.

8A. Registered pharmacy technician.]

9. Registered teacher (in Scotland).

10. Any profession to which the [Health Professions Order 2001] applies and which is undertaken following registration under that Act.

[11. Registered osteopath.]

[12. Registered chiropractor.]

[13. Chartered psychologist.

14. Actuary.

15. Registered foreign lawyer.

16. Legal executive.

17. Receiver appointed by the Court of Protection.]

[18. Home inspector.]

[3510]

NOTES
Revoked in relation to Scotland as noted at the beginning of this Order.
Schedule heading: substituted by the Rehabilitation of Offenders Act 1974 (Exceptions) (Amendment) Order 2001, SI 2001/1192, arts 2, 6(1), as from 31 March 2001.
Para 4: words in square brackets substituted by the Dentists Act 1984 (Amendment) Order 2005, SI 2005/2011, art 49, Sch 6, Pt II, para 7, as from 31 July 2006.
Para 7: words in square brackets substituted by the Opticians Act 1989 (Amendment) Order 2005, SI 2005/848, art 28, Sch 1, Pt 3, para 14, as from 30 June 2005.
Para 8: the original para 8 (pharmaceutical chemist) was substituted by new paras 8, 8A, by the Pharmacists and Pharmacy Technicians Order 2007, SI 2007/289, art 67, Sch 1, Pt 2, para 12(a), as from 30 March 2007 (in so far as relating to the new para 8), and as from a day to be appointed (in so far as relating to para 8A).
Para 8A: see the para 8 note above.
Para 10: words in square brackets substituted by the Health Professions Order 2001 (Consequential Amendments) Order 2003, SI 2003/1590, art 3, Schedule, Pt 2, para 26, as from 9 July 2003.
Para 11: added by the Osteopaths Act 1993, s 39(2), as from 1 April 1998.
Para 12: added by the Chiropractors Act 1994, s 40(2), as from 15 June 1999.
Paras 13–17: added by the Rehabilitation of Offenders Act 1974 (Exceptions) (Amendment) Order 2002, SI 2002/441, arts 2, 5(1), as from 1 March 2002.
Para 18: added by the Rehabilitation of Offenders Act 1974 (Exceptions) (Amendment) (England and Wales) Order 2006, SI 2006/2143, arts 2, 6, as from 26 July 2006.
Solicitor: the reference to a solicitor should now be read as including a reference to a registered European lawyer, see the European Communities (Lawyer's Practice) Regulations 2000, SI 2000/1119, reg 37(3), Sch 4, para 19.

PART II
[OFFICES, EMPLOYMENTS AND WORK]

1. Judicial appointments.

[2. The Director of Public Prosecutions and any office or employment in the Crown Prosecution Service.]

3. ...

[4. [Designated officers for magistrates' courts, for justices of the peace or for local justice areas], justices' clerks [and assistants to justices' clerks].]

5. Clerks (including depute and assistant clerks) and officers of the High Court of Justiciary, the Court of Session and the district court, sheriff clerks (including sheriff clerks depute) and their clerks and assistants.

6. Constables, persons appointed as police cadets to undergo training with a view to becoming constables and persons employed for the purposes of, or to assist the constables of, a police force established under any enactment; naval, military and air force police.

7. Any employment which is concerned with the administration of, or is otherwise normally carried out wholly or partly within the precincts of, a prison, remand centre, [removal centre, short-term holding facility,] [young offender institution] or young offenders institution, and members of boards of visitors appointed under section 6 of the Prison Act 1952 or of visiting committees appointed under section 7 of the Prisons (Scotland) Act 1952.

8. Traffic wardens appointed under section 81 of the Road Traffic Regulation Act 1967 or section 9 of the Police (Scotland) Act 1967.

9. Probation officers appointed under Schedule 3 to the Powers of Criminal Courts Act 1973.

10, 11. ...

[12. Any office or employment which is concerned with:
    (a)   the provision of care services to vulnerable adults; or
    (b)   the representation of, or advocacy services for, vulnerable adults by a service that has been approved by the Secretary of State or created under any enactment;
and which is of such a kind as to enable a person, in the course of his normal duties, to have access to vulnerable adults in receipt of such services.]

[13. Any employment or other work which is concerned with the provision of health services and which is of such a kind as to enable the holder of that employment or the person engaged in that work to have access to persons in receipt of such services in the course of his normal duties.]

[14. Any work which is—
    (a)   work in a regulated position; or
    (b)   work in a further education institution where the normal duties of that work involve regular contact with persons aged under 18.]

[15. Any employment in the Royal Society for the Prevention of Cruelty to Animals where the person employed or working, as part of his duties, may carry out the [humane] killing of animals.

16. Any office or employment in the Serious Fraud Office.

17. Any office or employment in the [Serious Organised Crime Agency].

[18. The Commissioners for Her Majesty's Revenue and Customs and any office or employment in their service.

18A. The Director and any office or employment in the Revenue and Customs Prosecutions Office.]

19. Any employment which is concerned with the monitoring, for the purposes of child protection, of communications by means of the internet.]

[20. Any employment or other work which is normally carried out in premises approved under section 9 of the Criminal Justice and Court Services Act 2000.

21. Any employment or other work which is normally carried out in a hospital used only for the provision of high security psychiatric services.]

[22. An individual designated under section 2 of the Traffic Management Act 2004.

23. Judges' clerks, secretaries and legal secretaries within the meaning of section 98 of the Supreme Court Act 1981.

24. Court officers and court contractors, who in the course of their work, have face to face contact with judges of the Supreme Court, or access to such judges' lodgings.

25. Persons who in the course of their work have regular access to personal information relating to an identified or identifiable member of the judiciary.

26. Court officers and court contractors, who, in the course of their work, attend either the Royal Courts of Justice or the Central Criminal Court.

27.   Court security officers, and tribunal security officers.

28.   Court contractors, who, in the course of their work, have unsupervised access to court-houses, offices and other accommodation used in relation to the courts.

29.   Contractors, sub-contractors, and any person acting under the authority of such a contractor or sub-contractor, who, in the course of their work, have unsupervised access to tribunal buildings, offices and other accommodation used in relation to tribunals.

30.   The following persons—
  (a)   Court officers who execute county court warrants;
  (b)   High Court enforcement officers;
  (c)   sheriffs and under-sheriffs;
  (d)   tipstaffs;
  (e)   any other persons who execute High Court writs or warrants who act under the authority of a person listed at (a) to (d);
  (f)   persons who execute writs of sequestration;
  (g)   civilian enforcement officers as defined in section 125A of the Magistrates' Courts Act 1980;
  (h)   persons who are authorised to execute warrants under section 125B(1) of the Magistrates' Courts Act 1980 , and any other person, (other than a constable), who is authorised to execute a warrant under section 125(2) of the 1980 Act;
  (i)   persons who execute clamping orders, as defined in paragraph 38(2) of Schedule 5 to the Courts Act 2003.

31.   The Official Solicitor and his deputy.

32.   Persons appointed to the office of Public Trustee or deputy Public Trustee, and officers of the Public Trustee.

33.   Court officers and court contractors who exercise functions in connection with the administration and management of funds in court including the deposit, payment, delivery and transfer in, into and out of any court of funds in court and regulating the evidence of such deposit, payment, delivery or transfer and court officers and court contractors, who receive payments in pursuance of a conviction or order of a magistrates' court.]

[34.   People working in [the Department for Children, Schools and Families], the Office for Standards in Education, Children's Services and Skills or in the Government Offices for the English Regions with access to sensitive or personal information about children or vulnerable adults.

35.   Any office, employment or other work which is concerned with the establishment or operation of a database under section 12 of the Children Act 2004, and which is of such a kind as to enable the holder of that office or employment, or the person engaged in that work, to have access to information included in the database.

36.   Any office, employment or other work which is of such a kind that the person is or may be permitted or required to be given access to a database under section 12 of the Children Act 2004.

37.   Any work which is normally concerned with the provision of any form of information, advice or guidance wholly or mainly to children which relates to their physical, emotional or educational well-being and is provided by means of telephone or other form of electronic communication including the internet and mobile telephone text messaging.

38.   The chairman, other members, and members of staff (including any person seconded to serve as a member of staff) of the Independent Barring Board.

39.   Staff working within the Public Guardianship Office, (to be known as the Office of the Public Guardian from October 2007), with access to data relating to children and vulnerable adults.

40.   The Commissioner for Older People in Wales, and his deputy, and any person appointed by the Commissioner to assist him in the discharge of his functions or authorised to discharge his functions on his behalf.

41.   The Commissioners for the Gambling Commission and any office or employment in their service.

42.   Individuals seeking authorisation from the Secretary of State for the Home Department to become authorised search officers.

43.   Any employment or other work where the normal duties
  (a)   involve caring for, training, supervising, or being solely in charge of, persons aged under 18 serving in the naval, military or air forces of the Crown; or
  (b)   include supervising or managing a person employed or working in a capacity referred to in paragraph (a).]

[3511]

PART III
STATUTORY INSTRUMENTS

NOTES
  Revoked in relation to Scotland as noted at the beginning of this Order.
  Schedule heading: see note to Pt I at **[3510]**.

Part heading: substituted by the Rehabilitation of Offenders Act 1974 (Exceptions) (Amendment) Order 2001, SI 2001/1192, arts 2, 6(21), as from 31 March 2001.

Para 2: substituted by the Rehabilitation of Offenders Act 1974 (Exceptions) (Amendment) Order 2002, SI 2002/441, arts 2, 5(2)(a), (b), as from 1 March 2002.

Para 3: revoked by the Rehabilitation of Offenders Act 1974 (Exceptions) (Amendment) (England and Wales) Order 2006, SI 2006/2143, arts 2, 7(a), as from 26 July 2006.

Para 4: substituted by SI 2001/1192, arts 2, 6(3), as from 31 March 2001; words in first pair of square brackets substituted by the Courts Act 2003 (Consequential Provisions) (No 2) Order 2005, SI 2005/617, art 2, Schedule, para 55, as from 1 April 2005; words in second pair of square brackets substituted by SI 2006/2143, arts 2, 7(b)(i), as from 26 July 2006.

Para 7: words in first pair of square brackets inserted by SI 2006/2143, arts 2, 7(b)(ii), as from 26 July 2006; words in second pair of square brackets substituted by virtue of the Criminal Justice Act 1988, s 123(6), Sch 8, paras 1, 3, as from 1 October 1988.

Paras 10, 11: revoked by the Rehabilitation of Offenders Act 1974 (Exceptions) (Amendment) Order 1986, SI 1986/1249, art 2, Schedule, as from 18 July 1986.

Para 12: substituted by SI 2006/2143, arts 2, 7(c), as from 26 July 2006.

Para 13: substituted by SI 2001/1192, arts 2, 6(4), as from 31 March 2001.

Para 14: substituted, for original paras 14, 15, by SI 1986/1249, art 2, Schedule, as from 18 July 1986; further substituted by SI 2001/1192, arts 2, 6(5), as from 31 March 2001.

Para 15: added (together with paras 16, 17, 18, 19) by SI 2002/441, arts 2, 5(2)(c), as from 1 March 2002; word in square brackets inserted by SI 2006/2143, arts 2, 7(b)(iii), as from 26 July 2006.

Paras 16, 19: added as noted above.

Para 17: added as noted above; words in square brackets substituted by the Serious Organised Crime and Police Act 2005 (Consequential and Supplementary Amendments to Secondary Legislation) Order 2006, SI 2006/594, art 2, Schedule, para 2, as from 1 April 2006.

Paras 18, 18A: para 18 originally added as noted above; subsequently substituted by new paras 18, 18A by SI 2006/2143, arts 2, 7(d), as from 26 July 2006.

Paras 20, 21: added by the Rehabilitation of Offenders Act 1974 (Exceptions) (Amendment) (England and Wales) Order 2003, SI 2003/965, arts 2, 8, as from 1 April 2003.

Paras 22–33: added by SI 2006/2143, arts 2, 7(e), as from 26 July 2006.

Paras 34–43: added by the Rehabilitation of Offenders Act 1974 (Exceptions) (Amendment) (England and Wales) Order 2007, SI 2007/2149, arts 2, 7, as from 22 July 2007; words in square brackets in para 34 substituted by the Secretaries of State for Children, Schools and Families, for Innovation, Universities and Skills and for Business, Enterprise and Regulatory Reform Order 2007, SI 2007/3224, art 15, Schedule, Pt 2, para 11, as from 12 December 2007.

Road Traffic Regulation Act 1967, s 81: repealed by the Road Traffic Regulation Act 1984 and replaced by s 95 of that Act.

Powers of Criminal Courts Act 1973, Sch 3: repealed by the Probation Service Act 1993, and replaced by s 4 thereof; s 4 was in turn repealed by the Criminal Justice and Court Services Act 2000, s 75, Sch 8. As to the National Probation Service for England and Wales, see now Chapter I of Pt I of the 2000 Act.

PART III
REGULATED OCCUPATIONS

1. Firearms dealer.

2. Any occupation in respect of which an application to the Gaming Board for Great Britain for a licence, certificate or registration is required by or under any enactment.

3. ...

4. *Dealer in securities.*

5. *Manager or trustee under a unit trust scheme.*

6. Any occupation which is concerned with—
    (a) the management of a place in respect of which the approval of the Secretary of State is required by section 1 of the Abortion Act 1967; or
    (b) in England and Wales, carrying on a nursing home in respect of which registration is required by section 187 of the Public Health Act 1936 or section 14 of the Mental Health Act 1959; or
    (c) in Scotland, carrying on a nursing home in respect of which registration is required under section 1 of the Nursing Homes Registration (Scotland) Act 1938 or a private hospital in respect of which registration is required under section 15 of the Mental Health (Scotland) Act 1960.

7. Any occupation which is concerned with carrying on an establishment in respect of which registration is required by section 37 of the National Assistance Act 1948 or section 61 of the Social Work (Scotland) Act 1968.

8. Any occupation in respect of which the holder, as occupier of premises on which explosives are kept, is required [pursuant to regulations 4 and 7 of the Control of Explosives Regulations 1991 to obtain from the chief officer of police a valid explosives certificate certifying him to be a fit person to acquire or acquire and keep explosives].

[9. ...]

[10. Approved legal services body manager.]

NOTES

Revoked in relation to Scotland as noted at the beginning of this Order.

Schedule heading: see the note to Pt I at **[3510]**.

Para 3: revoked by the Rehabilitation of Offenders Act 1974 (Exceptions) (Amendment) (No 2) Order 2001, SI 2001/3816, arts 2, 7(a), as from 30 November 2001.

Paras 4, 5: revoked by the Rehabilitation of Offenders Act 1974 (Exceptions) (Amendment No 2) Order 1986, SI 1986/2268, art 2(2)(a), as from the date on which the Financial Services Act 1986, s 189, Sch 14 are brought into force for the purposes of this revocation. Note, however, that the 1986 Act was repealed by the Financial Services and Markets Act 2000 (Consequential Amendments and Repeals) Order 2001, SI 2001/3649, art 3(1)(c), as from 1 December 2001, without ever having been brought into force for these purposes. Therefore, these revocations cannot, under the present drafting of SI 1986/2268, ever be brought into force.

Para 8: words in square brackets substituted by the Manufacture and Storage of Explosives Regulations 2005, SI 2005/1082, reg 28(1), Sch 5, Pt 2, para 27(1), (2), as from 26 April 2005.

Para 9: added by the Rehabilitation of Offenders Act 1974 (Exceptions) (Amendment) Order 2002, SI 2002/441, arts 2, 5(3)(a), as from 1 March 2002; revoked by the Rehabilitation of Offenders Act 1974 (Exceptions) (Amendment) (England and Wales) Order 2003, SI 2003/965, arts 2, 9, as from 1 April 2003.

Para 10: added by the Rehabilitation of Offenders Act 1974 (Exceptions) (Amendment) (England and Wales) Order 2008, SI 2008/3259, arts 2, 7(1), as from 18 December 2008.

Gaming Board for Great Britain: functions, etc, transferred to the Gambling Commission by the Gambling Act 2005, s 21, Sch 5.

Public Health Act 1936, s 187, Mental Health Act 1959, s 14, National Assistance Act 1948, s 37: all of these provisions are repealed; as to the registration, etc, of care homes, see now the Care Standards Act 2000.

PART IV
INTERPRETATION

In this Schedule—

["actuary" means a member of the Institute of Actuaries or a member or student of the Faculty of Actuaries;

["approved legal services body manager" means a person who must be approved by the Law Society under section 9A(2)(e) of the Administration of Justice Act 1985;]

["assistants to justices' clerks" has the meaning given by section 27(5) of the Courts Act 2003;]

["authorised search officer" means a person authorised to carry out searches in accordance with sections 40 and 41 of the Immigration, Asylum and Nationality Act 2006;]

"care services" means

    (i)   accommodation and nursing or personal care in a care home (where "care home" has the same meaning as in the Care Standards Act 2000);

    (ii)   personal care or nursing or support for a person to live independently in his own home;

    (iii)   social care services; or

    (iv)   any services provided in an establishment catering for a person with learning difficulties;]

"certified accountant" means a member of the Association of Certified Accountants;

"chartered accountant" means a member of the Institute of Chartered Accountants in England and Wales or of the Institute of Chartered Accountants of Scotland;

["chartered psychologist" means a psychologist included in the British Psychological Society's Register of Chartered Psychologists;]

["child" means a person under the age of eighteen (and "children" is to be construed accordingly);]

["court contractor" means a person who has entered into a contract with the Lord Chancellor under section 2(4) of the Courts Act 2003, such a person's sub-contractor, and persons acting under the authority of such a contractor or sub-contractor for the purpose of discharging the Lord Chancellor's general duty in relation to the courts;]

["court officer" means a person appointed by the Lord Chancellor under section 2(1) of the Courts Act 2003;]

["court security officers" has the meaning given by section 51 of the Courts Act 2003;]

"dealer in securities" means a person dealing in securities within the meaning of section 26(1) of the Prevention of Fraud (Investments) Act 1958;

"firearms dealer" has the meaning assigned to that expression by section 57(4) of the Firearms Act 1968;

["funds in court" has the meaning given by section 47 of the Administration of Justice Act 1982;]

"further education" has the meaning assigned to that expression by section 41 of the Education Act 1944 or, in Scotland, section 4 of the Education (Scotland) Act 1962;

["further education institution" has the meaning given to it by paragraph 3 of the Education (Restriction of Employment) Regulations 2000;]

"health services" means services provided under the National Health Service Acts 1946 to 1973 or the National Health Service (Scotland) Acts 1947 to 1973 and similar services provided otherwise than under the National Health Service;

["high security psychiatric services" has the meaning given by section 4 of the National Health Service Act 1977;]

["home inspector" means a person who is a member of a certification scheme approved by the Secretary of State in accordance with section 164(3) of the Housing Act 2004;]

.....

["judges of the Supreme Court" means the Lord Chief Justice, the Master of the Rolls, the President of the Queen's Bench Division, the President of the Family Division, the Chancellor of the High Court, the Lords Justices of Appeal and the puisne judges of the High Court;]

"judicial appointment" means an appointment to any office by virtue of which the holder has power (whether alone or with others) under any enactment or rule of law to determine any question affecting the rights, privileges, obligations or liabilities of any person;

["legal executive" means a fellow of the Institute of Legal Executives;]

["members of the judiciary" means persons appointed to any office by virtue of which the holder has power (whether alone or with others) under any enactment or rule of law to determine any question affecting the rights, privileges, obligations or liabilities of any person;]

["personal information" means any information which is of a personal or confidential nature and is not in the public domain and it includes information in any form but excludes anything disclosed for the purposes of proceedings in a particular cause or matter;]

"proprietor" and "independent school" have the meanings assigned to those expressions by section 114(1) of the Education Act 1944 or, in Scotland, section 145 of the Education (Scotland) Act 1962;

["registered chiropractor" has the meaning given by section 43 of the Chiropractors Act 1994.]

["registered foreign lawyer" has the meaning given by section 89 of the Courts and Legal Services Act 1990;]

["registered osteopath" has the meaning given by section 41 of the Osteopaths Act 1993.]

["registered pharmacist" means a person who is registered in the register maintained under article 10(1) of the Pharmacists and Pharmacy Technicians Order 2007;

"registered pharmacy technician" means a person who is registered in the register maintained under article 21(1) of the Pharmacists and Pharmacy Technicians Order 2007;]

"registered teacher" means a teacher registered under the Teaching Council (Scotland) Act 1965 and includes a provisionally registered teacher;

["regulated position" means a position which is a regulated position for the purposes of Part II of the Criminal Justice and Court Services Act 2000;]

["removal centre" and "short-term holding facility" have the meaning given by section 147 of the Immigration and Asylum Act 1999;]

"school" has the meaning assigned to that expression by section 114(1) of the Education Act 1944 or, in Scotland, section 145 of the Education (Scotland) Act 1962;

.....

[.....]

"teacher" includes a warden of a community centre, leader of a youth club or similar institution, youth worker and, in Scotland, youth and community worker;

["tribunal security officers" means persons who, in the course of their work, guard tribunal buildings, offices and other accommodation used in relation to tribunals against unauthorised access or occupation, against outbreaks of disorder or against damage;]

["tribunals" means any person exercising the judicial power of the State, that is not a court listed in section 1(1) of the Courts Act 2003;]

"unit trust scheme" has the meaning assigned to that expression by section 26(1) of the Prevention of Fraud (Investments) Act 1958 and, in relation thereto, "manager" and "trustee" shall be construed in accordance with section 26(3) of that Act

["vulnerable adult" means a person aged 18 or over who has a condition of the following type:
    (i)   a substantial learning or physical disability;
    (ii)   a physical or mental illness or mental disorder, chronic or otherwise, including an addiction to alcohol or drugs; or
    (iii)   a significant reduction in physical or mental capacity].

[3513]

NOTES

Revoked in relation to Scotland as noted at the beginning of this Order.

Schedule heading: see the note to Pt I at [3510].

Definitions "actuary", "care services", "chartered psychologist", "legal executive", "registered foreign lawyer", and "vulnerable adult" inserted by the Rehabilitation of Offenders Act 1974 (Exceptions) (Amendment) Order 2002, SI 2002/441, arts 2, 5(4), as from 1 March 2002.

Definition "approved legal services body manager" inserted by the Rehabilitation of Offenders Act 1974 (Exceptions) (Amendment) (England and Wales) Order 2008, SI 2008/3259, arts 2, 7(2), as from 18 December 2008.

Definitions "assistants to justices' clerks", "court contractor", "court officer", "court security officers", "funds in court", "home inspector", "judges of the Supreme Court", "members of the judiciary", "personal information", "removal centre", "short-term holding facility", "tribunal security officers", and "tribunals" inserted by the Rehabilitation of Offenders Act 1974 (Exceptions) (Amendment) (England and Wales) Order 2006, SI 2006/2143, arts 2, 8, as from 26 July 2006.

Definitions "authorised search officer" and "child" inserted by the Rehabilitation of Offenders Act 1974 (Exceptions) (Amendment) (England and Wales) Order 2007, SI 2007/2149, arts 2, 8, as from 22 July 2007.

Definitions "dealer in securities" and "unit trust scheme" revoked by the Rehabilitation of Offenders Act 1974 (Exceptions) (Amendment No 2) Order 1986, SI 1986/2268, art 2(2)(a), as from the date on which the Financial Services Act 1986, s 189, Sch 14 are brought into force for the purposes of this revocation. Note, however, that the 1986 Act was repealed by the Financial Services and Markets Act 2000 (Consequential Amendments and Repeals) Order 2001, SI 2001/3649, art 3(1)(c), as from 1 December 2001, without ever having been brought into force for these purposes. Therefore, these revocations cannot, under the present drafting of SI 1986/2268, ever be brought into force.

Definitions "further education institution" and "regulated position" inserted by the Rehabilitation of Offenders Act 1974 (Exceptions) (Amendment) Order 2001, SI 2001/1192, arts 2, 6(6)(a), (b), as from 31 March 2001.

Definition "high security psychiatric services" inserted by the Rehabilitation of Offenders Act 1974 (Exceptions) (Amendment) (England and Wales) Order 2003, SI 2003/965, arts 2, 10(a), as from 1 April 2003.

Definition "insurance company" (omitted) revoked by the Rehabilitation of Offenders Act 1974 (Exceptions) (Amendment) (No 2) Order 2001, SI 2001/3816, arts 2, 7(b), as from 30 November 2001.

Definition "registered chiropractor" inserted by the Chiropractors Act 1994, s 40(4), as from 15 June 1999.

Definition "registered osteopath" inserted by the Osteopaths Act 1993, s 39(4), as from 1 April 1998.

Definitions "registered pharmacist" and "registered pharmacy technician" inserted by the Pharmacists and Pharmacy Technicians Order 2007, SI 2007/289, art 67, Sch 1, Pt 2, para 12(b), as from 30 March 2007 (in so far as relating to "registered pharmacist"), and as from a day to be appointed (in so far as relating to "registered pharmacy technician").

Definition "social services" (omitted) revoked by SI 2002/441, arts 2, 5(4)(e), as from 1 March 2002.

Definition "taxi driver" (omitted) originally inserted by SI 2002/441, arts 2, 5(4), as from 1 March 2002, and revoked by SI 2003/965, arts 2, 10(b), as from 1 April 2003.

Prevention of Fraud (Investments) Act 1958: repealed by the Financial Services Act 1986, s 212, Sch 17 (now itself repealed).

Education Act 1944, ss 41, 114(1): repealed by the Education Act 1996, s 582(2), Sch 38, Pt I.

National Health Service Acts 1946 to 1973: repealed and consolidated in the National Health Service Act 1977. The 1977 Act has either been repealed, or is prospectively repealed, by the National Health Service (Consequential Provisions) Act 2006. See now, generally, the National Health Service Act 2006 and the National Health Service (Wales) Act 2006.

Education (Restriction of Employment) Regulations 2000: revoked by the Education (Prohibition from Teaching or Working with Children) Regulations 2003, SI 2003/1184.

SCHEDULE 2
EXCEPTED LICENCES, CERTIFICATES AND PERMITS
Article 3

1. Firearm certificates and shot gun certificates issued under the Firearms Act 1968, and permits issued under section 7(1), 9(2) or 13(1)(c) of that Act.

2. Licences issued under section 25 of the Children and Young Persons Act 1933 (which relates to persons under the age of 18 going abroad for the purpose of performing or being exhibited for profit).

[3. Explosives certificates issued by a chief officer of police pursuant to regulations 4 and 7 of the Control of Explosives Regulations 1991 as to the fitness of a person to acquire or acquire and keep explosives.]

[4. Taxi driver licences.

5. Licences granted under section 8 of the Private Security Industry Act 2001.]

[3514]

NOTES
Revoked in relation to Scotland as noted at the beginning of this Order.
Para 3: substituted by the Manufacture and Storage of Explosives Regulations 2005, SI 2005/1082, reg 28(1), Sch 5, Pt 2, para 27(1), (3), as from 26 April 2005.
Paras 4, 5: added by the Rehabilitation of Offenders Act 1974 (Exceptions) (Amendment) (England and Wales) Order 2003, SI 2003/965, arts 2, 11, as from 1 April 2003.

SCHEDULE 3
EXCEPTED PROCEEDINGS
Article 5

1. Proceedings in respect of a person's admission to, or disciplinary proceedings against a member of, any profession specified in Part I of Schedule 1 to this Order.

2. Proceedings before the Court of Appeal of the High Court in the exercise of their disciplinary jurisdiction in respect of solicitors.

3. Disciplinary proceedings against a constable.

4. Proceedings before the Gaming Board for Great Britain.

[5. Proceedings under the Mental Health Act 1983 before any tribunal.]

6. Proceedings under the Firearms Act 1968 in respect of—
   (a) the registration of a person as a firearms dealer, the removal of person's name from a register of firearms dealers or the imposition, variation or revocation of conditions of any such registration; or
   (b) the grant, renewal, variation or revocation of a firearm certificate; or
   (c) the grant, renewal or revocation of a shot gun certificate; or
   (d) the grant of a permit under section 7(1), 9(2) or 13(1)(c) of that Act.

7. Proceedings in respect of the grant, renewal or variation of a licence under section 25 of the Children and Young Persons Act 1933 (which relates to persons under the age of 18 going abroad for the purpose of performing or being exhibited for profit).

8. …

[9. Proceedings in respect of a direction given under section 142 of the Education Act 2002 or of any prohibition or restriction on a person's employment or work which has effect as if it were contained in such a direction.]

10. *Proceedings under the Prevention of Fraud (Investments) Act 1958 in respect of an application for, or revocation of,—*
   (a) *a licence to deal in securities; or*
   (b) *an order by the Secretary of State declaring a person to be an exempted dealer for the purposes of that Act; or*
   (c) *an order by the Secretary of State declaring a unit trust scheme to be an authorised unit trust scheme for the purposes of that Act,*

(including proceedings under section 6 of that Act before the tribunal of inquiry constituted under that section in respect of a licence to deal in securities).

11. Proceedings in respect of an application for, or cancellation of,—
   (a) the Secretary of State's approval of a place under section 1 of the Abortion Act 1967; or
   (b) in England and Wales, registration in respect of a nursing home under section 187 of the Public Health Act 1936 or section 14 of the Mental Health Act 1959; or
   (c) in Scotland, registration in respect of a nursing home under section 1 of the Nursing Homes Registration (Scotland) Act 1938 or of a private hospital under section 15 of the Mental Health (Scotland) Act 1960.

12. Proceedings in respect of an application for, or cancellation of, registration under section 37 of the National Assistance Act 1948 or section 61 of the Social Work (Scotland) Act 1968 in respect of any such establishment as is mentioned in those sections.

13. Proceedings on an application to the [chief officer of police for an explosives certificate pursuant to regulations 4 and 7 of the Control of Explosives Regulations 1991 as to the fitness of the applicant to acquire or acquire and keep explosives].

14. Proceedings by way of appeal against, or review of, any decision taken, by virtue of any of the provisions of this Order, on consideration of a spent conviction.

15. Proceedings held for the receipt of evidence affecting the determination of any question arising in any proceedings specified in this Schedule.

[16. Proceedings relating to a taxi driver licence.]

[17. Proceedings—
   (a) before the National Lottery Commission in respect of the grant or revocation of a licence under Part I of the National Lottery etc Act 1993; or
   (b) by way of appeal to the Secretary of State against the revocation of any such licence by the National Lottery Commission.]

[18. Proceedings relating to registration under Part IV of the Care Standards Act 2000.

19. Proceedings under section 11 of the Private Security Industry Act 2001.]

[20. Proceedings before the Parole Board.

21. Proceedings under section 7D of the Criminal Injuries Compensation Act 1995.

22. The following proceedings under the Proceeds of Crime Act 2002—
   (a) proceedings under Chapter 2 of Part 5;
   (b) proceedings pursuant to a notice under section 317(2);
   (c) proceedings pursuant to an application under Part 8 in connection with a civil recovery investigation (within the meaning of section 341).

23. Proceedings brought before the Football Association[, Football League] or Football Association Premier League against a decision taken by the body before which the proceedings are brought to refuse to approve a person as able to undertake, in the course of acting as a steward at a sports ground at which football matches are played or as a supervisor or manager of such a person, licensable conduct within the meaning of the Private Security Industry Act 2001 without a licence issued under that Act, in accordance with … section 4 of that Act.]

[3515]

NOTES

Revoked in relation to Scotland as noted at the beginning of this Order.

Para 5: substituted by the Tribunals, Courts and Enforcement Act 2007 (Transitional and Consequential Provisions) Order 2008, SI 2008/2683, art 6(1), Sch 1, para 6, as from 3 November 2008.

Para 8: revoked by the Rehabilitation of Offenders Act 1974 (Exceptions) (Amendment) (No 2) Order 2001, SI 2001/3816, arts 2, 7(c), as from 30 November 2001.

Para 9: substituted by the Rehabilitation of Offenders Act 1974 (Exceptions) (Amendment) (England and Wales) Order 2006, SI 2006/2143, arts 2, 9(a), as from 26 July 2006.

Para 10: revoked by the Rehabilitation of Offenders Act 1974 (Exceptions) (Amendment No 2) Order 1986, SI 1986/2268, art 2(2)(b), as from the date on which the Financial Services Act 1986, s 189, Sch 14 are brought into force for the purposes of this revocation. Note, however, that the 1986 Act was repealed by the Financial Services and Markets Act 2000 (Consequential Amendments and Repeals) Order 2001, SI 2001/3649, art 3(1)(c), as from 1 December 2001, without ever having been brought into force for these purposes. Therefore, these revocations cannot, under the present drafting of SI 1986/2268, ever be brought into force.

Para 13: words in square brackets substituted by the Manufacture and Storage of Explosives Regulations 2005, SI 2005/1082, reg 28(1), Sch 5, Pt 2, para 27(1), (4), as from 26 April 2005.

Para 16: added by the Rehabilitation of Offenders Act 1974 (Exceptions) (Amendment) Order 2002, SI 2002/441, arts 2, 6(1), as from 1 March 2002; substituted by the Rehabilitation of Offenders Act 1974 (Exceptions) (Amendment) (England and Wales) Order 2003, SI 2003/965, arts 2, 12, as from 1 April 2003.

Para 17: added by SI 2002/441, arts 2, 6(2), as from a day to be appointed (ie, the day on which the Police Act 1997, s 133(d) comes into force in England and Wales).

Paras 18, 19: added by SI 2003/965, arts 2, 13, as from 1 April 2003.

Paras 20–22: added, together with para 23, by SI 2006/2143, arts 2, 9(b), as from 26 July 2006.

Para 23: added as noted above; words in square brackets inserted, and words omitted revoked, by the Rehabilitation of Offenders Act 1974 (Exceptions) (Amendment No 2) (England and Wales) Order 2006, SI 2006/3290, art 2, as from 7 December 2006.

Gaming Board for Great Britain: functions, etc, transferred to the Gambling Commission by the Gambling Act 2005, s 21, Sch 5.

Mental Health Act 1959: largely repealed; see now the Mental Health Act 1983, Pt V.

Education Act 1944, s 72: repealed by the Education Act 1996, s 582(2), Sch 38, Pt I.

Prevention of Fraud (Investments) Act 1958: repealed by the Financial Services Act 1986, s 212, Sch 17 (now itself repealed).

Public Health Act 1936, s 187, Mental Health Act 1959, s 14, National Assistance Act 1948, s 37: all of these provisions are repealed; as to the registration, etc, of care homes, see now the Care Standards Act 2000.

FINANCIAL MARKETS AND INSOLVENCY REGULATIONS 1991

(SI 1991/880)

NOTES

Made: 27 March 1991.

Authority: CA 1989, ss 155(4), (5), 158(4), (5), 160(5), 173(4), (5), 174(2)–(4), 185, 186, 187(3).

Commencement: 25 April 1991.

These Regulations are reproduced as amended by: the Financial Markets and Insolvency (Amendment) Regulations 1992, SI 1992/716; the Financial Markets and Insolvency (CGO Service) Regulations 1999, SI 1999/1209; the Financial Services and Markets Act 2000 (Consequential Amendments and Repeals) Order 2001, SI 2001/3649; the Enterprise Act 2002 (Insolvency) Order 2003, SI 2003/2096.

ARRANGEMENT OF REGULATIONS

PART I
GENERAL

PART I
GENERAL

1 Citation and commencement

These Regulations may be cited as the Financial Markets and Insolvency Regulations 1991 and shall come into force on 25th April 1991.

[3515A]

2 Interpretation: general

(1) In these Regulations "the Act" means the Companies Act 1989.

(2) A reference in any of these Regulations to a numbered regulation shall be construed as a reference to the regulation bearing that number in these Regulations.

(3) A reference in any of these Regulations to a numbered paragraph shall, unless the reference is to a paragraph of a specified regulation, be construed as a reference to the paragraph bearing that number in the regulation in which the reference is made.

[3515B]

3–6 ((*Pts II–IV) amend the Companies Act 1989, ss 155, 159, 160, 162 at* **[1154]**, **[1157]**, **[1158]**, **[1160]**.)

PART V
MARKET CHARGES

7 Interpretation of Part V

In this Part of these Regulations, unless the context otherwise requires—
  "the Bank" means the Bank of England;
  "business day" has the same meaning as in section 167(3) of the Act;
      .....
  "CGO" means the Central Gilts Office of the Bank;
  "CGO Service" means the computer-based system established by the Bank and The Stock
    Exchange to facilitate the transfer of specified securities;
  "CGO Service charge" means a charge of the kind described in section 173(1)(c) of the Act;
  "CGO Service member" means a person who is entitled by contract with [CRESTCo Limited
    (which is now responsible for operating the CGO Service)] to use the CGO Service;
  "former CGO Service member" means a person whose entitlement ... to use the CGO Service
    has been terminated or suspended;
  "market charge" means a charge which is a market charge for the purposes of Part VII of
    the Act;
  "settlement bank" means a person who has agreed under a contract with [CRESTCo Limited
    (which is now responsible for operating the CGO Service)] to make payments of the kind
    mentioned in section 173(1)(c) of the Act;
  "specified securities" has the meaning given in section 173(3) of the Act;
  "Talisman" means The Stock Exchange settlement system known as Talisman;
  "Talisman charge" means a charge granted in favour of The Stock Exchange over property
    credited to an account within Talisman maintained in the name of the chargor in respect of
    certain property beneficially owned by the chargor; and
  "transfer" when used in relation to specified securities has the meaning given in section 173(3)
    of the Act.

[3515C]

NOTES
Definition "CGO" (omitted) revoked, words in square brackets in definitions "CGO Service member" and "settlement bank" substituted, and words omitted from definition "former CGO Service member" revoked, by the Financial Markets and Insolvency (CGO Service) Regulations 1999, SI 1999/1209, reg 3(1), as from 24 May 1999.

8   Charges on land or any interest in land not to be treated as market charges

(1)   No charge, whether fixed or floating, shall be treated as a market charge to the extent that it is a charge on land or any interest in land.

(2)   For the purposes of paragraph (1), a charge on a debenture forming part of an issue or series shall not be treated as a charge on land or any interest in land by reason of the fact that the debenture is secured by a charge on land or any interest in land.

[3515D]

9   (*Amends the Companies Act 1989, s 173 at* **[1169]**.)

10   Extent to which charge granted in favour of recognised investment exchange to be treated as market charge

(1)   A charge granted in favour of a recognised investment exchange other than The Stock Exchange shall be treated as a market charge only to the extent that—
  (a)   it is a charge over property provided as margin in respect of market contracts entered into by the exchange for the purposes of or in connection with the provision of clearing services;
  (b)   in the case of a recognised UK investment exchange, it secures the obligation to pay to the exchange the net sum referred to in paragraph 9(2)(a) of Schedule 21 of the Act as it applies by virtue of paragraph 1(4) of that Schedule; and
  (c)   in the case of a recognised overseas investment exchange, it secures the obligation to reimburse the cost (other than fees and other incidental expenses) incurred by the exchange in settling unsettled market contracts in respect of which the charged property is provided as margin.

(2)   A charge granted in favour of The Stock Exchange shall be treated as a market charge only to the extent that—
  (a)   it is a charge of the kind described in paragraph (1); or
  (b)   it is a Talisman charge and secures an obligation of either or both of the kinds mentioned in paragraph (3).

(3)   The obligations mentioned in this paragraph are—
  (a)   the obligation of the chargor to reimburse The Stock Exchange for payments (including stamp duty and taxes but excluding Stock Exchange fees and incidental expenses arising from the operation by The Stock Exchange of settlement arrangements) made by The Stock Exchange in settling, through Talisman, market contracts entered into by the chargor; and
  (b)   the obligation of the chargor to reimburse The Stock Exchange the amount of any payment it has made pursuant to a short term certificate.

(4)   In paragraph (3), "short term certificate" means an instrument issued by The Stock Exchange undertaking to procure the transfer of property of a value and description specified in the instrument to or to the order of the person to whom the instrument is issued or his endorsee or to a person acting on behalf of either of them and also undertaking to make appropriate payments in cash, in the event that the obligation to procure the transfer of property cannot be discharged in whole or in part.

[3515E]

11   Extent to which charge granted in favour of recognised clearing house to be treated as market charge

A charge granted in favour of a recognised clearing house shall be treated as a market charge only to the extent that—
  (a)   it is a charge over property provided as margin in respect of market contracts entered into by the clearing house;
  (b)   in the case of a recognised UK clearing house, it secures the obligation to pay to the clearing house the net sum referred to in paragraph 9(2)(a) of Schedule 21 to the Act; and
  (c)   in the case of a recognised overseas clearing house, it secures the obligation to reimburse the cost (other than fees or other incidental expenses) incurred by the clearing house in settling unsettled market contracts in respect of which the charged property is provided as margin.

[3515F]

12 Circumstances in which CGO Service charge to be treated as market charge

A CGO Service charge shall be treated as a market charge only if—
(a)   it is granted to a settlement bank by a person for the purpose of securing debts or liabilities of the kind mentioned in section 173(1)(c) of the Act incurred by that person through his use of the CGO Service as a CGO Service member; and
(b)   it contains provisions which refer expressly to the [CGO Service].

[3515G]

NOTES
Words in square brackets substituted by the Financial Markets and Insolvency (CGO Service) Regulations 1999, SI 1999/1209, reg 3(2), as from 24 May 1999.

13   Extent to which CGO Service charge to be treated as market charge

A CGO Service charge shall be treated as a market charge only to the extent that—
(a)   it is a charge over any one or more of the following—
   (i)   specified securities held within the CGO Service to the account of a CGO Service member or a former CGO Service member;
   (ii)   specified securities which were held as mentioned in sub-paragraph (i) above immediately prior to their being removed from the CGO Service consequent upon the person in question becoming a former CGO Service member;
   (iii)   sums receivable by a CGO Service member or former CGO Service member representing interest accrued on specified securities held within the CGO Service to his account or which were so held immediately prior to their being removed from the CGO Service consequent upon his becoming a former CGO Service member;
   (iv)   sums receivable by a CGO Service member or former CGO Service member in respect of the redemption or conversion of specified securities which were held within the CGO Service to his account at the time that the relevant securities were redeemed or converted or which were so held immediately prior to their being removed from the CGO Service consequent upon his becoming a former CGO Service member; and
   (v)   sums receivable by a CGO Service member or former CGO Service member in respect of the transfer by him of specified securities through the medium of the CGO Service; and
(b)   it secures the obligation of a CGO Service member or former CGO Service member to reimburse a settlement bank for the amount due from him to the settlement bank as a result of the settlement bank having discharged or become obliged to discharge payment obligations in respect of transfers or allotments of specified securities made to him through the medium of the CGO Service.

[3515H]

14   [Limitation on disapplication of moratorium on certain legal processes under Schedule B1 to the Insolvency Act 1986 (administration) in relation to CGO Service charges]

(1)   In this regulation "qualifying period" means the period beginning with the fifth business day before the day on which [an application] for the making of an administration order in relation to the relevant CGO Service member or former CGO Service member is presented and ending with the second business day after the day on which an administration order is made in relation to the relevant CGO Service member or former CGO Service member pursuant to the petition.

[(1A)   A reference in paragraph (1) to an application for an administration order shall be treated as including a reference to—
(a)   appointing an administrator under paragraph 14 or 22 of Schedule B1 to the Insolvency Act 1986, or
(b)   filing with the court a notice of intention to appoint an administrator under either of those paragraphs,
and a reference to "an administration order" shall include the appointment of an administrator under paragraph 14 or 22 of Schedule B1 to the Insolvency Act 1986.]

(2)   [The disapplication of paragraph 43(2) of Schedule B1 to the Insolvency Act 1986 (including that provisions as applied by paragraph 44 of that Schedule)] by section 175(1)(a) of the Act shall be limited in respect of a CGO Service charge so that it has effect only to the extent necessary to enable there to be realised, whether through the sale of specified securities or otherwise, a sum equal to whichever is less of the following—
(a)   the total amount of payment obligations discharged by the settlement bank in respect of transfers and allotments of specified securities made during the qualifying period to the relevant CGO Service member or former CGO Service member through the medium of the CGO Service less the total amount of payment obligations discharged to the

settlement bank in respect of transfers of specified securities made during the qualifying period by the relevant CGO Service member or former CGO Service member through the medium of the CGO Service; and

(b) the amount (if any) described in regulation 13(b) due to the settlement bank from the relevant CGO Service member or former CGO Service member.

[3515I]

NOTES

Regulation heading: substituted by the Enterprise Act 2002 (Insolvency) Order 2003, SI 2003/2096, arts 5, 6, Schedule, Pt 2, paras 47, 48(a), as from 15 September 2003, except in relation to any case where a petition for an administration order was presented before that date.

Paras (1), (2): words in square brackets substituted by SI 2003/2096, arts 5, 6, Schedule, Pt 2, paras 47, 48(b), (d), as from 15 September 2003, except in relation to any case where a petition for an administration order was presented before that date. Note, it is assumed that the words "the petition" at the end of para (1) should have been similarly substituted, but the Queen's Printer's copy of SI 2003/2096 made no such provision.

Para (1A): inserted by SI 2003/2096, arts 5, 6, Schedule, Pt 2, paras 47, 48(c), as from 15 September 2003, except in relation to any case where a petition for an administration order was presented before that date.

15 Ability of administrator or receiver to recover assets in case of property subject to CGO Service charge or Talisman charge

(1) [The disapplication—
(a) by section 175(1)(b) of the Act, of paragraphs 70, 71 and 72 of Schedule B1 to the Insolvency Act 1986, and
(b) by section 175(3) of the Act, of sections 43 and 61 of the 1986 Act,

shall cease to have effect] in respect of a charge which is either a CGO Service charge or a Talisman charge after the end of the second business day after the day on which an administration order is made or, as the case may be, an administrative receiver or a receiver is appointed, in relation to the grantor of the charge, in relation to property subject to it which—

(a) in the case of a CGO Service charge, is not, on the basis of a valuation in accordance with paragraph (2), required for the realisation of whichever is the less of the sum referred to in regulation 14(2)(a) and the amount referred to in regulation 14(2)(b) due to the settlement bank at the close of business on the second business day referred to above; and
(b) in the case of a Talisman charge is not, on the basis of a valuation in accordance with paragraph (2), required to enable The Stock Exchange to reimburse itself for any payment it has made of the kind referred to in regulation 10(3).

[(1A) A reference in paragraph (1) to "an administration order" shall include the appointment of an administrator under paragraph 14 or 22 of Schedule B1 to the Insolvency Act 1986.]

(2) For the purposes of paragraph (1) the value of property shall, except in a case falling within paragraph (3), be such as may be agreed between whichever is relevant of the administrator, administrative receiver or receiver on the one hand and the settlement bank or The Stock Exchange on the other.

(3) For the purposes of paragraph (1), the value of any investment for which a price for the second business day referred to above is quoted in the Daily Official List of The Stock Exchange shall—

(a) in a case in which two prices are so quoted, be an amount equal to the average of those two prices, adjusted where appropriate to take account of any accrued interest; and
(b) in a case in which one price is so quoted, be an amount equal to that price, adjusted where appropriate to take account of any accrued interest.

[3515J]

NOTES

Para (1): words in square brackets substituted by the Enterprise Act 2002 (Insolvency) Order 2003, SI 2003/2096, arts 5, 6, Schedule, Pt 2, paras 47, 49(a), as from 15 September 2003, except in relation to any case where a petition for an administration order was presented before that date.

Para (1A): inserted by SI 2003/2096, arts 5, 6, Schedule, Pt 2, paras 47, 49(b), as from 15 September 2003, except in relation to any case where a petition for an administration order was presented before that date.

PART VI

CONSTRUCTION OF REFERENCES TO PARTIES TO MARKET CONTRACTS

16 Circumstances in which member or designated non-member dealing as principal to be treated as acting in different capacities

(1) In this regulation "relevant transaction" means—
(a) a market contract effected as principal by a member or designated non-member of a recognised investment exchange or a member of a recognised clearing house being a market contract—

[(i)   which is a relevant investment; and]

(ii)   in relation to which money received by the member or designated non-member is client money for the purposes of [the Financial Services (Client Money) Regulations 1991] or would be client money for the purposes of those regulations were it not money which, in accordance with those regulations, may be regarded as immediately due and payable to the member or designated non-member for his own account; and

(b)   a market contract which would be regarded as a relevant transaction by virtue of sub-paragraph (a) above were it not for the fact that no money is received by the member or designated non-member in relation to the contract

(2)   For the purposes of subsection (1) of section 187 of the Act (construction of references to parties to market contracts) a member or designated non-member of a recognised investment exchange or a member of a recognised clearing house shall be treated as effecting relevant transactions in a different capacity from other market contracts he has effected as principal.

[(3)   In paragraph (1)(a)(i) "relevant investment" means an investment of one of the following kinds—

(a)   options;
(b)   futures;
(c)   contracts for differences;
(d)   rights to or interests in an investment of a kind mentioned in sub-paragraphs (a) to (c).

(4)   Paragraph (3) must be read with—
(a)   section 22 of the Financial Services and Markets Act 2000;
(b)   any relevant order under that section; and
(c)   Schedule 2 to that Act.]

[3515K]

NOTES

Para (1): sub-para (a)(i) substituted by the Financial Services and Markets Act 2000 (Consequential Amendments and Repeals) Order 2001, SI 2001/3649, art 415(1), (2), as from 1 December 2001; words in square brackets in sub-para (a)(ii) substituted by the Financial Markets and Insolvency (Amendment) Regulations 1992, SI 1992/716, as from 1 May 1992.

Paras (3), (4): added by SI 2001/3649, art 415(1), (3), as from 1 December 2001.

17   ((*Pt VII*) *Amends the Companies Act 1989, Sch 21.*)

PART VIII
LEGAL PROCEEDINGS

18   (*Amends the Companies Act 1989, s 175 at* **[1171]**.)

19   Court having jurisdiction in respect of proceedings under Part VII of Act

(1)   For the purposes of sections 161, 163, 164, 175(5) and 182 of the Act (various legal proceedings under Part VII of Act) "the court" shall be the court which has last heard an application in the proceedings under the Insolvency Act 1986 or the Bankruptcy (Scotland) Act 1985 in which the relevant office-holder is acting or, as the case may be, any court having jurisdiction to hear applications in those proceedings.

(2)   For the purposes of subsection (2) [and (2A)] of section 175 of the Act (administration orders etc), "the court" shall be the court which has made the administration order or, as the case may be, to which the [application] for an administration order has been presented [or the notice of intention to appoint has been filed].

(3)   The rules regulating the practice and procedure of the court in relation to applications to the court in England and Wales under sections 161, 163, 164, 175 and 182 of the Act shall be the rules applying in relation to applications to that court under the Insolvency Act 1986.

[3515L]

NOTES

Para (2): words in first and third pairs of square brackets inserted, and word in second pair of square brackets substituted, by the Enterprise Act 2002 (Insolvency) Order 2003, SI 2003/2096, arts 5, 6, Schedule, Pt 2, paras 47, 50, as from 15 September 2003, except in relation to any case where a petition for an administration order was presented before that date.

INSIDER DEALING (SECURITIES AND REGULATED MARKETS) ORDER 1994

(SI 1994/187)

NOTES
Made: 1 February 1994.
Authority: Criminal Justice Act 1993, ss 54(1), 60(1), 62(1), 64(3).
Commencement: 1 March 1994.
This Order is reproduced as amended by: the Insider Dealing (Securities and Regulated Markets) (Amendment) Order 1996, SI 1996/1561; the Insider Dealing (Securities and Regulated Markets) (Amendment) Order 2000, SI 2000/1923; the Insider Dealing (Securities and Regulated Markets) (Amendment) Order 2002, SI 2002/1874.

ARRANGEMENT OF ARTICLES

1 Title, commencement and interpretation

This Order may be cited as the Insider Dealing (Securities and Regulated Markets) Order 1994 and shall come into force on the twenty eighth day after the day on which it is made.

[3516]

2

In this Order a "State within the European Economic Area" means a State which is a member of the European Communities and the Republics of Austria, Finland and Iceland, the Kingdoms of Norway and Sweden and the Principality of Liechtenstein.

[3517]

3 Securities

Articles 4 to 8 set out conditions for the purposes of section 54(1) of the Criminal Justice Act 1993 (securities to which Part V of the Act of 1993 applies).

[3518]

4

The following condition applies in relation to any security which falls within any paragraph of Schedule 2 to the Act of 1993, that is, that it is officially listed in a State within the European Economic Area or that it is admitted to dealing on, or has its price quoted on or under the rules of, a regulated market.

[3519]

5

The following alternative condition applies in relation to a warrant, that is, that the right under it is a right to subscribe for any share or debt security of the same class as a share or debt security which satisfies the condition in article 4.

[3520]

6

The following alternative condition applies in relation to a depositary receipt, that is, that the rights under it are in respect of any share or debt security which satisfies the condition in article 4.

[3521]

7

The following alternative conditions apply in relation to an option or a future, that is, that the option or rights under the future are in respect of—

    (a)   any share or debt security which satisfies the condition in article 4, or

    (b)   any depositary receipt which satisfies the condition in article 4 or article 6.

[3522]

8

The following alternative condition applies in relation to a contract for differences, that is, that the purpose or pretended purpose of the contract is to secure a profit or avoid a loss by reference to fluctuations in—

    (a)   the price of any shares or debt securities which satisfy the condition in article 4, or

    (b)   an index of the price of such shares or debt securities.

[3523]

9 Regulated markets

The following markets are regulated markets for the purposes of Part V of the Act of 1993—

[(a)] any market which is established under the rules of an investment exchange specified in the Schedule to this Order
[(b) the market known as OFEX ...]

[3524]

NOTES
Para (a) designated as such, and para (b) added, by the Insider Dealing (Securities and Regulated Markets) (Amendment) Order 2000, SI 2000/1923, art 2(1), (2), as from 20 July 2000; words omitted from para (b) revoked by the Insider Dealing (Securities and Regulated Markets) (Amendment) Order 2002, SI 2002/1874, art 2(1), (2) as from 19 July 2002.

10 United Kingdom regulated markets

The regulated markets which are regulated in the United Kingdom for the purposes of Part V of the Act of 1993 are any market which is established under the rules of—
[(a) the London Stock Exchange Limited;]
(b) LIFFE Administration & Management; ...
(c) OMLX, the London Securities and Derivatives Exchange Limited [...
(d) [virt-x Exchange Limited].]
[(e) [the exchange known as COREDEALMTS];
together with the market known as OFEX ...]

[3525]

NOTES
Para (a) substituted, word omitted from para (b) revoked, and para (d) and the word immediately preceding it added, by the Insider Dealing (Securities and Regulated Markets) (Amendment) Order 1996, SI 1996/1561, art 3, as from 1 July 1996; word omitted from para (c) revoked, and para (e) added, by the Insider Dealing (Securities and Regulated Markets) (Amendment) Order 2000, SI 2000/1923, art 2(1), (3), as from 20 July 2000; words in square brackets in paras (d), (e) substituted, and final words omitted revoked, by the Insider Dealing (Securities and Regulated Markets) (Amendment) Order 2002, SI 2002/1874, art 2(1), (3) as from 19 July 2002.
Note that on 3 March 2008 virt-x Exchange Limited changed its name to SWX Europe Limited.

SCHEDULE
REGULATED MARKETS
Article 9
Any market which is established under the rules of one of the following investment exchanges:

Amsterdam Stock Exchange.

Antwerp Stock Exchange.

Athens Stock Exchange.

Barcelona Stock Exchange.

Bavarian Stock Exchange.

Berlin Stock Exchange.

Bilbao Stock Exchange.

Bologna Stock Exchange.

...

Bremen Stock Exchange.

Brussels Stock Exchange.

Copenhagen Stock Exchange.

[The exchange known as COREDEALMTS.]

Dusseldorf Stock Exchange.

[The exchange known as EASDAQ.]

Florence Stock Exchange.

Frankfurt Stock Exchange.

Genoa Stock Exchange.

...

Hamburg Stock Exchange.

Hanover Stock Exchange.

Helsinki Stock Exchange.

[Iceland Stock Exchange.

The Irish Stock Exchange Limited.]

...

...

Lisbon Stock Exchange.

LIFFE Administration & Management.

[The London Stock Exchange Limited.]

Luxembourg Stock Exchange.

Lyon Stock Exchange.

Madrid Stock Exchange.

...

Milan Stock Exchange.

...

...

Naples Stock Exchange.

The exchange known as NASDAQ.

[The exchange known as the Nouveau Marché.]

OMLX, the London Securities and Derivatives Exchange Limited.

Oporto Stock Exchange.

Oslo Stock Exchange.

Palermo Stock Exchange.

Paris Stock Exchange.

Rome Stock Exchange.

...

Stockholm Stock Exchange.

Stuttgart Stock Exchange.

[The exchange known as SWX Swiss Exchange.]

[...]

Trieste Stock Exchange.

Turin Stock Exchange.

Valencia Stock Exchange.

Venice Stock Exchange.

Vienna Stock Exchange.

[virt-x Exchange Limited.]

[3525A]

NOTES

First to seventh entries omitted revoked, entries "Iceland Stock Exchange" and "The Irish Stock Exchange Limited" substituted, and entries "The London Stock Exchange Limited" and "The exchange known as the Nouveau Marché" inserted, by the Insider Dealing (Securities and Regulated Markets) (Amendment) Order 1996, SI 1996/1561, art 4, as from 1 July 1996; entry "The exchange known as COREDEALMTS" inserted by the Insider Dealing (Securities and Regulated Markets) (Amendment) Order 2000, SI 2000/1923, art 2(1), (4)(a), as from 20 July 2000, and substituted by the Insider Dealing (Securities and Regulated Markets) (Amendment) Order 2002, SI 2002/1874, art 2(1), (4)(a) as from 19 July 2002; entry "The exchange known as EASDAQ" inserted, and eighth entry omitted revoked, by SI 2000/1923, art 2(1), (4)(b), (c), as from 20 July 2000; entries "The exchange known as SWX Swiss Exchange" and "virt-x Exchange Limited" inserted by SI 2002/1874, art 2(1), (4)(b), (d) as from 19 July 2002; final entry omitted originally inserted by SI 1996/1561, art 4, as from 1 July 1996, and revoked by SI 2002/1874, art 2(1), (4)(c) as from 19 July 2002.

Note that on 3 March 2008 virt-x Exchange Limited changed its name to SWX Europe Limited.

PART III
STATUTORY INSTRUMENTS

TRADED SECURITIES (DISCLOSURE) REGULATIONS 1994 (NOTE)

(SI 1994/188)

NOTES
Revoked by the Financial Services and Markets Act 2000 (Market Abuse) Regulations 2005, SI 2005/381, reg 9, as from 1 July 2005.

[3525B]

PUBLIC OFFERS OF SECURITIES REGULATIONS 1995 (NOTE)

(SI 1995/1537)

NOTES
Revoked by the Prospectus Regulations 2005, SI 2005/1433, reg 2(3), Sch 3, para 2, as from 1 July 2005.

[3526]

FINANCIAL MARKETS AND INSOLVENCY REGULATIONS 1996

(SI 1996/1469)

NOTES
Made: 5 June 1996.
Authority: CA 1989, ss 185, 186.
Commencement: 15 July 1996.
These Regulations are reproduced as amended by: the Uncertificated Securities Regulations 2001, SI 2001/3755; the Enterprise Act 2002 (Insolvency) Order 2003, SI 2003/2096; the Enterprise Act 2002 (Insolvency) Order 2004, SI 2004/2312.

ARRANGEMENT OF REGULATIONS

PART I
GENERAL

PART I
GENERAL

1   Citation and commencement

These Regulations may be cited as the Financial Markets and Insolvency Regulations 1996 and shall come into force on 15th July 1996.

[3526A]

2   Interpretation

(1)   In these Regulations—
"the Act" means the Companies Act 1989;

"business day" means any day which is not a Saturday or Sunday, Christmas Day, Good Friday or a bank holiday in any part of the United Kingdom under the Banking and Financial Dealings Act 1971;

"issue", in relation to an uncertificated unit of a security, means to confer on a person title to a new unit;

"register of securities"—
    (a)   in relation to shares, means a register of members; and
    (b)   in relation to units of a security other than shares, means [a register, whether maintained by virtue of the Uncertificated Securities Regulations 2001 or otherwise], of persons holding the units;

        .....

"relevant nominee" means a system-member who is a subsidiary undertaking of the Operator designated by him as such in accordance with such rules and practices as are mentioned in [paragraph 25(f) of Schedule 1 to the Uncertificated Securities Regulations 2001];

"settlement bank" means a person who has contracted with an Operator to make payments in connection with transfers, by means of a relevant system, of title to uncertificated units of a security and of interests of system-beneficiaries in relation to such units;

"system-beneficiary" means a person on whose behalf a system-member or former system-member holds or held uncertificated units of a security;

"system-charge" means a charge of a kind to which regulation 3(2) applies;

"system-member" means a person who is permitted by an Operator to transfer by means of a relevant system title to uncertificated units of a security held by him; and "former system-member" means a person whose participation in the relevant system is terminated or suspended;

"transfer", in relation to title to uncertificated units of a security, means [the registration of a transfer of title to those units in the relevant Operator register of securities;] and in relation to an interest of a system-beneficiary in relation to uncertificated units of a security, means the transfer of the interest to another system-beneficiary by means of a relevant system; and

other expressions used in these Regulations which are also used in [the Uncertificated Securities Regulations 2001] have the same meanings as in those Regulations.

(2)   For the purposes of these Regulations, a person holds a unit of a security if—
    (a)   in the case of an uncertificated unit, he is entered on a register of securities in relation to the unit in accordance with [regulation 20, 21 or 22 of the Uncertificated Securities Regulations 2001]; and
    (b)   in the case of a certificated unit, he has title to the unit.

(3)   A reference in any of these Regulations to a numbered regulation shall be construed as a reference to the regulation bearing that number in these Regulations.

(4)   A reference in any of these Regulations to a numbered paragraph shall, unless the reference is to a paragraph of a specified regulation, be construed as a reference to the paragraph bearing that number in the regulation in which the reference is made.

[3526B]

NOTES

Para (1): words in square brackets substituted, and definition "the 1995 Regulations" (omitted) revoked, by the Uncertificated Securities Regulations 2001, SI 2001/3755, reg 51, Sch 7, Pt 2, para 20(a), as from 26 November 2001.

Para (2): words in square brackets substituted by SI 2001/3755, reg 51, Sch 7, Pt 2, para 20(b), as from 26 November 2001.

PART II
SYSTEM-CHARGES

3 Application of Part VII of the Act in relation to system-charges

(1)   Subject to the provisions of these Regulations, Part VII of the Act shall apply in relation to—
    (a)   a charge to which paragraph (2) applies ("a system-charge") and any action taken to enforce such a charge; and
    (b)   any property subject to a system-charge,
in the same way as it applies in relation to a market charge, any action taken to enforce a market charge and any property subject to a market charge.

(2)   This paragraph applies in relation to a charge granted in favour of a settlement bank for the purpose of securing debts or liabilities arising in connection with any of the following—
    (a)   a transfer of uncertificated units of a security to a system-member by means of a relevant system whether the system-member is acting for himself or on behalf of a system-beneficiary;

(b)   a transfer, by one system-beneficiary to another and by means of a relevant system, of his interests in relation to uncertificated units of a security held by a relevant nominee where the relevant nominee will continue to hold the units;

(c)   an agreement to make a transfer of the kind specified in paragraph (a);

(d)   an agreement to make a transfer of the kind specified in paragraph (b); and

(e)   an issue of uncertificated units of a security to a system-member by means of a relevant system whether the system-member is acting for himself or on behalf of a system-beneficiary.

(3) In its application, by virtue of these Regulations, in relation to a system-charge, section 173(2) of the Act shall have effect as if the references to "purposes specified" and "specified purposes" were references to any one or more of the purposes specified in paragraph (2).

[3526C]

4   Circumstances in which Part VII applies in relation to system-charge

(1) Part VII of the Act shall apply in relation to a system-charge granted by a system-member and in relation to property subject to such a charge only if—

(a)   it is granted to a settlement bank by a system-member for the purpose of securing debts or liabilities arising in connection with any of the transactions specified in regulation 3(2), being debts or liabilities incurred by that system-member or by a system-beneficiary on whose behalf he holds uncertificated units of a security; and

(b)   it contains provisions which refer expressly to the relevant system in relation to which the grantor is a system-member.

(2) Part VII of the Act shall apply in relation to a system-charge granted by a system-beneficiary and in relation to property subject to such a charge only if—

(a)   it is granted to a settlement bank by a system-beneficiary for the purpose of securing debts or liabilities arising in connection with any of the transactions specified in regulation 3(2), incurred by that system-beneficiary or by a system-member who holds uncertificated units of a security on his behalf; and

(b)   it contains provisions which refer expressly to the relevant system in relation to which the system-member who holds the uncertificated units of a security in relation to which the system-beneficiary has the interest is a system-member.

[3526D]

5   Extent to which Part VII applies to a system-charge

Part VII of the Act shall apply in relation to a system-charge only to the extent that—

(a)   it is a charge over any one or more of the following—

    (i)   uncertificated units of a security held by a system-member or a former system-member;

    (ii)   interests of a kind specified in [regulation 31(2)(b) or 31(4)(b) of the Uncertificated Securities Regulations 2001] in uncertificated units of a security in favour of a system member or a former system-member;

    (iii)   interests of a system-beneficiary in relation to uncertificated units of a security;

    (iv)   units of a security which are no longer in uncertificated form because the person holding the units has become a former system-member;

    (v)   sums or other benefits receivable by a system-member or former system-member by reason of his holding uncertificated units of a security, or units which are no longer in uncertificated form because the person holding the units has become a former system-member;

    (vi)   sums or other benefits receivable by a system-beneficiary by reason of his having an interest in relation to uncertificated units of a security or in relation to units which are no longer in uncertificated form because the person holding the units has become a former system-member;

    (vii)   sums or other benefits receivable by a system-member or former system-member by way of repayment, bonus, preference, redemption, conversion or accruing or offered in respect of uncertificated units of a security, or units which are no longer in uncertificated form because the person holding the units has become a former system-member;

    (viii)   sums or other benefits receivable by a system-beneficiary by way of repayment, bonus, preference, redemption, conversion or accruing or offered in respect of uncertificated units of a security in relation to which he has an interest or in respect of units in relation to which the system-beneficiary has an interest and which are no longer in uncertificated form because the person holding the units has become a former system-member;

    (ix)   sums or other benefits receivable by a system-member or former system-member in respect of the transfer of uncertificated units of a security by or to him by means of a relevant system;

      (x)   sums or other benefits receivable by a system-member or former system-member in respect of an agreement to transfer uncertificated units of a security by or to him by means of a relevant system;

      (xi) sums or other benefits receivable by a system-beneficiary in respect of the transfer of the interest of a system-beneficiary in relation to uncertificated units of a security by or to him by means of a relevant system or in respect of the transfer of uncertificated units of a security by or to a system-member acting on his behalf by means of a relevant system;

      (xii) sums or other benefits receivable by a system-beneficiary in respect of an agreement to transfer the interest of a system-beneficiary in relation to uncertificated units of a security by or to him by means of a relevant system, or in respect of an agreement to transfer uncertificated units of a security by or to a system-member acting on his behalf by means of a relevant system; and

  (b) it secures—

      (i)   the obligation of a system-member or former system-member to reimburse a settlement bank, being an obligation which arises in connection with any of the transactions specified in regulation 3(2) and whether the obligation was incurred by the system-member when acting for himself or when acting on behalf of a system-beneficiary; or

      (ii) the obligation of a system-beneficiary to reimburse a settlement bank, being an obligation which arises in connection with any of the transactions specified in regulation 3(2) and whether the obligation was incurred by the system-beneficiary when acting for himself or by reason of a system-member acting on his behalf.

[3526E]

NOTES

  Words in square brackets in sub-para (a)(ii) substituted by the Uncertificated Securities Regulations 2001, SI 2001/3755, reg 51, Sch 7, Pt 2, para 20(c), as from 26 November 2001.

---

6 [Limitation on disapplication of moratorium on certain legal processes under Schedule B1 to the Insolvency Act 1986 (administration) in relation to system-charges]

  (1) This regulation applies where an administration order is made in relation to a system-member or former system-member.

  [(1A) A reference in paragraph (1) to "an administration order" shall include the appointment of an administrator under paragraph 14 or 22 of Schedule B1 to the Insolvency Act 1986].

  (2) [The disapplication of paragraph 43(2) of Schedule B1 to the Insolvency Act 1986 (including that provision as applied by paragraph 44 of that Schedule)] by section 175(1)(a) of the Act shall have effect, in relation to a system-charge granted by a system-member or former system-member, only to the extent necessary to enable there to be realised, whether through the sale of uncertificated units of a security or otherwise, the lesser of the two sums specified in paragraphs (3) and (4).

  (3) The first sum of the two sums referred to in paragraph (2) is the net sum of—

  (a) all payment obligations discharged by the settlement bank in connection with—

      (i)   transfers of uncertificated units of a security by means of a relevant system made during the qualifying period to or by the relevant system-member or former system-member, whether acting for himself or on behalf of a system-beneficiary;

      (ii) agreements made during the qualifying period to transfer uncertificated units of a security by means of a relevant system to or from the relevant system-member or former system-member, whether acting for himself or on behalf of a system-beneficiary; and

      (iii) issues of uncertificated units of a security by means of a relevant system made during the qualifying period to the relevant system-member or former system-member, whether acting for himself or on behalf of a system-beneficiary; less

  (b) all payment obligations discharged to the settlement bank in connection with transactions of any kind described in paragraph (3)(a)(i) and (ii).

  (4) The second of the two sums referred to in paragraph (2) is the sum (if any) due to the settlement bank from the relevant system-member or former system-member by reason of an obligation of the kind described in regulation 5(b)(i).

  (5) In this regulation and regulation 7, "qualifying period" means the period—

  (a) beginning with the fifth business day before the day on which [an application] for the making of the administration order was presented; and

  (b) ending with the second business day after the day on which the administration order is made.

  [(5A) A reference in paragraph (5) to an application for an administration order shall be treated as including a reference to—

PART III
STATUTORY INSTRUMENTS

(a) appointing an administrator under [paragraph 14] or 22 of Schedule B1 to the Insolvency Act 1986, or

(b) filing with the court a notice of intention to appoint an administrator under either of those paragraphs,

and a reference to "an administration order" shall include the appointment of an administrator under paragraph 14 or 22 of Schedule B1 to the Insolvency Act 1986.]

[3526F]

NOTES

Regulation heading: substituted by the Enterprise Act 2002 (Insolvency) Order 2003, SI 2003/2096, arts 5, 6, Schedule, Pt 2, paras 61, 62(a), as from 15 September 2003, except in relation to any case where a petition for an administration order was presented before that date.

Para (1A): inserted by SI 2003/2096, arts 5, 6, Schedule, Pt 2, paras 61, 62(b), as from 15 September 2003, except in relation to any case where a petition for an administration order was presented before that date.

Paras (2), (5): words in square brackets substituted by SI 2003/2096, arts 5, 6, Schedule, Pt 2, paras 61, 62(c), (d), as from 15 September 2003, except in relation to any case where a petition for an administration order was presented before that date.

Para (5A): added by SI 2003/2096, arts 5, 6, Schedule, Pt 2, paras 61, 62(e), as from 15 September 2003, except in relation to any case where a petition for an administration order was presented before that date; words in square brackets substituted by the Enterprise Act 2002 (Insolvency) Order 2004, SI 2004/2312, art 3, as from 15 October 2004.

7 [Limitation on disapplication of moratorium on certain legal processes under Schedule B1 to the Insolvency Act 1986 (administration) in relation to system-charges granted by a system-beneficiary]

(1) This regulation applies where an administration order is made in relation to a system-beneficiary.

[(1A) A reference in paragraph (1) to "an administration order" shall include the appointment of an administrator under paragraph 14 or 22 of Schedule B1 to the Insolvency Act 1986].

(2) [The disapplication of paragraph 43(2) of Schedule B1 to the Insolvency Act 1986 (including that provision as applied by paragraph 44 of that Schedule)] by section 175(1)(a) of the Act shall have effect, in relation to a system-charge granted by a system-beneficiary, only to the extent necessary to enable there to be realised, whether through the sale of interests of a system-beneficiary in relation to uncertificated units of a security or otherwise, the lesser of the two sums specified in paragraphs (3) and (4).

(3) The first of the two sums referred to in paragraph (2) is the net sum of—

(a) all payment obligations discharged by the settlement bank in connection with—

    (i) transfers, to or by the relevant system-beneficiary by means of a relevant system made during the qualifying period, of interests of the system-beneficiary in relation to uncertificated units of a security held by a relevant nominee, where the relevant nominee has continued to hold the units;

    (ii) agreements made during the qualifying period to transfer, to or from the relevant system-beneficiary by means of a relevant system, interests of the system-beneficiary in relation to uncertificated units of a security held by a relevant nominee, where the relevant nominee will continue to hold the units;

    (iii) transfers, during the qualifying period and by means of a relevant system, of uncertificated units of a security, being transfers made to or by a system-member acting on behalf of the relevant system-beneficiary;

    (iv) agreements made during the qualifying period to transfer uncertificated units of a security by means of a relevant system to or from a system-member acting on behalf of the relevant system-beneficiary; and

    (v) issues of uncertificated units of a security made during the qualifying period and by means of a relevant system, being issues to a system-member acting on behalf of the relevant system-beneficiary; less

(b) all payment obligations discharged to the settlement bank in connection with transactions of any kind described in paragraph (3)(a)(i) to (iv).

(4) The second of the two sums referred to in paragraph (2) is the sum (if any) due to the settlement bank from the relevant system-beneficiary by reason of an obligation of the kind described in regulation 5(b)(ii).

[3526G]

NOTES

Regulation heading: substituted by the Enterprise Act 2002 (Insolvency) Order 2003, SI 2003/2096, arts 5, 6, Schedule, Pt 2, paras 61, 63(a), as from 15 September 2003, except in relation to any case where a petition for an administration order was presented before that date.

Para (1A): inserted by SI 2003/2096, arts 5, 6, Schedule, Pt 2, paras 61, 63(b), as from 15 September 2003, except in relation to any case where a petition for an administration order was presented before that date.

Para (2): words in square brackets substituted by SI 2003/2096, arts 5, 6, Schedule, Pt 2, paras 61, 63(c), as from 15 September 2003, except in relation to any case where a petition for an administration order was presented before that date.

8 Ability of administrator or receiver to recover assets in case of property subject to system-charge

(1) This regulation applies where an administration order is made or an administrator or an administrative receiver or a receiver is appointed, in relation to a system-member, former system-member or system-beneficiary.

[(1A) A reference in paragraph (1) to "an administration order" shall include the appointment of an administrator under paragraph 14 or 22 of Schedule B1 to the Insolvency Act 1986.]

(2) [The disapplication—
   (a)   by section 175(1)(b) of the Act, of paragraphs 70, 71 and 72 of Schedule B1 to the Insolvency Act 1986, and
   (b)   by section 175(3) of the Act, of sections 43 and 61 of the 1986 Act,
shall cease to have effect] after the end of the relevant day in respect of any property which is subject to a system-charge granted by the system-member, former system-member or system-beneficiary if on the basis of a valuation in accordance with paragraph (3), the charge is not required for the realisation of the sum specified in paragraph (4) or (5).

(3) For the purposes of paragraph (2), the value of property shall, except in a case falling within paragraph (6), be such as may be agreed between the administrator, administrative receiver or receiver on the one hand and the settlement bank on the other.

(4) Where the system-charge has been granted by a system-member or former system-member, the sum referred to in paragraph (2) is whichever is the lesser of—
   (a)   the sum referred to in regulation 6(3);
   (b)   the sum referred to in regulation 6(4) due to the settlement bank at the close of business on the relevant day.

(5) Where the system-charge has been granted by a system-beneficiary, the sum referred to in paragraph (2) is whichever is the lesser of—
   (a)   the sum referred to in regulation 7(3);
   (b)   the sum referred to in regulation 7(4) due to the settlement bank at the close of business on the relevant day.

(6) For the purposes of paragraph (2), the value of any property for which a price for the relevant day is quoted in the Daily Official List of The London Stock Exchange Limited shall—
   (a)   in a case in which two prices are so quoted, be an amount equal to the average of those two prices, adjusted where appropriate to take account of any accrued dividend or interest; and
   (b)   in a case in which one price is so quoted, be an amount equal to that price, adjusted where appropriate to take account of any accrued dividend or interest.

(7) In this regulation "the relevant day" means the second business day after the day on which the [company enters administration], or the administrative receiver or receiver is appointed.

[3526H]

NOTES
   Para (1A): inserted by the Enterprise Act 2002 (Insolvency) Order 2003, SI 2003/2096, arts 5, 6, Schedule, Pt 2, paras 61, 64(a), as from 15 September 2003, except in relation to any case where a petition for an administration order was presented before that date.
   Paras (2), (7): words in square brackets substituted by SI 2003/2096, arts 5, 6, Schedule, Pt 2, paras 61, 64(b), (c), as from 15 September 2003, except in relation to any case where a petition for an administration order was presented before that date.

9   ((Pt III) spent; amended the Companies Act 1989, s 156 (repealed).)

CASH RATIO DEPOSITS (ELIGIBLE LIABILITIES) ORDER 1998

(SI 1998/1130)

NOTES
   Made: 24 April 1998.
   Authority: Bank of England Act 1998, Sch 2, para 2(2).
   Commencement: 1 June 1998.
   This Order is reproduced as amended by: the Cash Ratio Deposits (Eligible Liabilities) (Amendment) Order 2005, SI 2005/3203; the Capital Requirements Regulations 2006, SI 2006/3221.

1 Citation and commencement

This Order may be cited as the Cash Ratio Deposits (Eligible Liabilities) Order 1998 and shall come into force on 1st June 1998.

[3527]

2 Interpretation

(1)   In this Order—

"the Act" means the Bank of England Act 1998;

"credit items in the course of transmission", in relation to an eligible institution, means standing orders and other credit transfers debited to customers' accounts, and payment orders including cheques and bankers' payments, in respect of which the eligible institution is required to make a payment and has not yet made it;

"debit items in the course of collection", in relation to an eligible institution, means payment orders including cheques (other than cheques passed to United Kingdom offices of other eligible institutions for collection) and bankers' payments in respect of which the eligible institution is entitled to receive a payment and has not yet received it;

"ecu" means—

(a)   the European currency unit as defined in Article 1 of Council Regulation No 3320/94/EC; or

(b)   any other unit of account which is defined by reference to the European currency unit as so defined;

"eligible institution" means an eligible institution for the purposes of Schedule 2 to the Act;

"finance lease" means a lease granted on terms which have the effect of transferring to the lessee all or substantially all of the risk and rewards of ownership of the asset or assets subject to the lease;

"fixed assets", in relation to an eligible institution, means assets which are intended for use on a continuing basis in the institution's activities;

"group" has the meaning given by section 262 of the Companies Act 1985;

"items in suspense" means all credit balances in the books of an eligible institution not in customers' names, but relating to funds held on behalf of customers or others, including, without prejudice to the generality of the foregoing—

(a)   accounts holding funds awaiting transfer to customers (other than accounts relating to interest accruing and interest suspense accounts);

(b)   returnable application monies for issues of securities;

(c)   funds of any customer awaiting investment which have been transferred to an account not in the name of the customer;

(d)   funds transferred from the account of any customer to an account not in the name of the customer to meet acceptances, confirmed credits and similar obligations;

(e)   funds placed on account to meet travellers' cheques issued by the eligible institution but not yet presented;

(f)   valuation fees awaiting transfer to a person who has made a report on the value of land; and

(g)   accounts holding funds which the eligible institution has received as collecting agent on behalf of a charity;

but excluding balances awaiting settlement of securities transactions held in an account not in the name of the customer;

"net sterling liabilities to non-resident offices", in relation to an eligible institution, means the amount (if any) by which the institution's total sterling liabilities to non-resident offices exceed its total sterling claims on non-resident offices;

"non-resident banking subsidiary", in relation to an eligible institution or a non-resident parent, means a body corporate incorporated in a country or territory outside the United Kingdom, or a partnership or other unincorporated association formed under the law of such a country or territory, whose sole or main business is banking and (in the case of an undertaking with a share capital) all of whose voting share capital is, or (in the case of any other undertaking) all of whose shares are, beneficially owned by that eligible institution or, as the case may be, that non-resident parent;

"non-resident offices", in relation to an eligible institution, means the offices outside the United Kingdom of—
    (a)   that institution;
    (b)   any non-resident banking subsidiary of that institution; and
    (c)   if that institution has a non-resident parent, that non-resident parent and its non-resident banking subsidiaries (if any);

"non-resident parent", in relation to an eligible institution, means a body corporate incorporated in a country or territory outside the United Kingdom, or a partnership or other unincorporated association formed under the law of such a country or territory, which beneficially owns (in the case of an undertaking with a share capital) all of the voting share capital of, or (in the case of any other undertaking) all of the shares in, that institution;

"over two year deposits", in relation to an eligible institution, means deposits made with the institution on terms to the effect that repayment cannot be required before the end of the period of two years beginning with the day on which the deposit is made (other than in exceptional circumstances outside the control of the depositor specified at the time the deposit is made), and which have been reported as such deposits by the institution to the Bank;

"retransfer agreement" means—
    (a)   a sale and repurchase agreement;
    (b)   an agreement under which one party sells securities or other assets to another, and by a related transaction undertakes to purchase the same or equivalent securities or assets from that other party on a specified date, or at call, at a specified price; or
    (c)   an agreement under which one party otherwise transfers securities or other assets to another in return for a cash payment, and as part of the same transaction undertakes to make a cash payment to that other party upon the transfer to it by that other party of the same or equivalent securities or assets on a specified date, or at call;

"sale and repurchase agreement" means an agreement under which one party sells securities or other assets to another, and as part of the same transaction undertakes to purchase the same or equivalent securities or assets from that other party on a specified date, or at call, at a specified price;

"the Schedule" means the Schedule to this Order;

"securities" means shares, stock, debentures, debenture stock, loan stock, bonds, and other securities of any description;

"sterling deposit liabilities to non-resident offices", in relation to an eligible institution, means sterling liabilities of the United Kingdom offices of that institution to its non-resident offices which fall within paragraph 1 or paragraph 3 of the Schedule, and which have been reported as such liabilities by the institution to the Bank;

"stored value card" means a card (which includes any token, coupon, stamp, form, booklet or other document or thing) issued by an eligible institution under an agreement which provides that the institution will or, as the case may be, a third party may, upon production of the card, supply to the holder of the card goods or services (which includes the payment of cash) of a value not exceeding the amount of any payment or payments previously made to the institution by the holder of the card (or the balance thereof remaining after previous transactions);

"total sterling claims on non-resident offices", in relation to an eligible institution, means the total sterling claims of the United Kingdom offices of that institution on its non-resident offices, which have been reported as such claims by the institution to the Bank;

"total sterling liabilities to non-resident offices", in relation to an eligible institution, means the total sterling liabilities of the United Kingdom offices of that institution to its non-resident offices, which have been reported as such liabilities by the institution to the Bank;

"undertaking" has the meaning given by section 259 of the Companies Act 1985;

"voting share capital", in relation to an undertaking, means issued shares carrying rights to vote in all or substantially all circumstances at general meetings of the undertaking; and, in determining for the purposes of this Order whether any shares carry rights to vote as aforesaid, any temporary suspension of voting rights attaching to those shares shall be ignored.

(2)   In paragraph (1), in the definitions of "non-resident banking subsidiary" and "non-resident parent" references to shares shall be construed in accordance with section 259 of the Companies Act 1985.

(3)   In this Order, references to deposits made with an eligible institution include, in relation to an eligible institution which is a building society within the meaning of the Building Societies Act 1986 or an institution which is incorporated in or formed under the law of the Republic of Ireland and whose characteristics correspond as nearly as may be to those of such a building society, shares in the institution other than shares which are own funds within the meaning given by

[Directive 2006/48/EC of the European Parliament and of the Council of 14 June 2006 relating to the taking up and pursuit of the business of credit institutions].

(4)   In this Order, references to liabilities in respect of sterling deposits made with United Kingdom offices of an eligible institution include sterling liabilities of the institution in respect of—

(a)   finance leases entered into by United Kingdom offices of the institution;

(b)   accounts of such offices with United Kingdom offices of other eligible institutions which are overdrawn; and

(c)   stored value cards issued by such offices;

but exclude such liabilities in respect of—

(d)   deposits made by non-resident offices of the institution with United Kingdom offices of the institution solely for the purpose of enabling the eligible institution to purchase fixed assets; and

(e)   deposits made solely for the purpose of funding the depositor's participation in a loan made, or to be made, to a third party.

(5)   In this Order, references to certificates of deposit include negotiable or transferable deposits made on terms in all respects identical to those applying to deposits in respect of which a certificate of deposit could have been issued but where no such certificate has been issued, but exclude any certificates of deposit issued by an eligible institution which are then held by that institution.

(6)   In this Order, references to currencies other than sterling include ecus.

(7)   Any transaction which is treated in the books and records of an eligible institution as having been entered into by, or with, an office of that institution in a particular country or territory shall be so treated for the purposes of determining that institution's eligible liabilities and, in particular, but without prejudice to the generality of the foregoing—

(a)   any transaction which is treated in the books and records of that institution as giving rise to a liability on the part of a United Kingdom office of that institution to a non-resident office of that institution shall be treated as giving rise to such a liability, and, in particular, where such liability relates to a deposit that deposit shall be treated as made with that United Kingdom office; and

(b)   any transaction which is treated in the books and records of that institution as giving rise to a claim on a non-resident office of that institution by a United Kingdom office of that institution shall be treated as giving rise to such a claim.

(8)   Any transaction which is treated in the books and records of an eligible institution as having been entered into by, or with, a United Kingdom office of another eligible institution shall be so treated for the purposes of determining the first-mentioned institution's eligible liabilities.

[3528]

NOTES

Para (3): words in square brackets substituted by the Capital Requirements Regulations 2006, SI 2006/3221, reg 29(4), Sch 6, para 1, as from 1 January 2007.

Eligible debt securities: as to the application of this article to eligible debt securities, see the Uncertificated Securities (Amendment) (Eligible Debt Securities) Regulations 2003, SI 2003/1633, reg 15, Sch 2, para 5 (as from 24 June 2003).

3 Eligible liabilities

For the purposes of paragraph 2 of Schedule 2 to the Act, the eligible liabilities of an eligible institution means the aggregate of the amounts referred to in paragraphs 1 to 7 of the Schedule, less the aggregate of the amounts referred to in [paragraphs 9 to 13] of the Schedule.

[3529]

NOTES

Words in square brackets substituted by the Cash Ratio Deposits (Eligible Liabilities) (Amendment) Order 2005, SI 2005/3203, art 2(1), (2), as from 1 March 2006.

4 Liabilities in respect of sterling deposits

(1)   In calculating the amount of an eligible institution's liabilities in respect of sterling deposits made with United Kingdom offices of the institution—

(a)   except in a case where sub-paragraph (b) applies, the total credit balances on the relevant accounts of any customer with those offices shall be reduced by the total debit balances on those accounts;

(b)   where the institution provides banking facilities to different undertakings within the same group, and compliance with any limit on the amount of those facilities is determined by reference to net amounts, the total credit balances on the relevant accounts of such undertakings with those offices shall be reduced by the total debit balances on those accounts; and

(c)   any interest which has accrued but has not yet been credited to an account shall be ignored.

(2)   For the purposes of paragraph (1), an account with an eligible institution is a relevant account if the following conditions are satisfied—

   (a)   the account is denominated in sterling;

   (b)   where the account is held in the name of an individual, that individual is resident in the United Kingdom;

   (c)   where the account is held in the name of an undertaking, the account is an account of a United Kingdom office of that undertaking;

   (d)   the account and all other accounts which the institution treats as netted with that account are managed and controlled on a net basis; and

   (e)   the institution has received a written opinion or, as the case may be, written opinions from its legal advisers that a legally enforceable right of set-off exists in respect of the account and all other accounts which the institution treats as netted with that account under the law of each jurisdiction whose law could affect the enforceability of such a right (including upon default, liquidation or bankruptcy or any analogous event under the law of such jurisdiction).

[3530]

5   Liabilities and claims in respect of retransfer agreements

(1)   In calculating the amount of an eligible institution's liability to make a payment for the purchase of, or otherwise in return for the transfer to it of, securities or other assets under a retransfer agreement, the amount of the institution's liability to make such a payment shall be reduced by the amount of any deposit paid by the institution under that agreement.

(2)   In calculating the amount of an eligible institution's claim to receive a payment for the sale of, or otherwise in return for the transfer by it of, securities or other assets under a retransfer agreement, the amount of the institution's claim shall be reduced by the amount of any deposit paid to the institution under that agreement.

(3)   In calculating the amount payable by or to an eligible institution under a retransfer agreement involving the purchase of securities or other assets, no account shall be taken of any amount by which the purchase price under the agreement exceeds the sale price of the securities or other assets originally sold under the agreement (but ignoring in the case of both purchase price and sale price any amount payable in respect of any income which has accrued on the securities or other assets purchased or sold).

[3531]

6   Holdings of securities

(1)   For the purposes of this Order, securities held by United Kingdom offices of an eligible institution shall include any security which the institution is required to purchase, or accept a transfer of, under a retransfer agreement entered into by any such office, and exclude any security which the institution is required to sell or transfer under such an agreement.

(2)   In paragraph (1), where the retransfer agreement in question provides for the purchase or transfer of equivalent securities, references to any security are to the amount of any security, being a security of a type which may be sold or transferred under that agreement, which the eligible institution is required to purchase, or accept a transfer of, or (as the case may be) sell or transfer, under the agreement.

[3532]

7   Avoidance of double-counting

(1)   If any liability of an eligible institution would fall within more than one of the descriptions of liability set out in paragraphs 1 to 7 of the Schedule, that liability shall be counted as a liability only once when aggregating the amounts referred to in those paragraphs for the purposes of article 3.

(2)   If any item relating to an eligible institution would fall within more than one of the descriptions set out in [paragraphs 9 to 13] of the Schedule, that item shall be counted only once when aggregating the amounts referred to in those paragraphs for the purposes of article 3.

[3533]

NOTES

Para (2): words in square brackets substituted by the Cash Ratio Deposits (Eligible Liabilities) (Amendment) Order 2005, SI 2005/3203, art 2(1), (2), as from 1 March 2006.

PART III
STATUTORY INSTRUMENTS

SCHEDULE
ELIGIBLE LIABILITIES

Article 3

1.   The amount of the eligible institution's liabilities in respect of sterling deposits (other than those evidenced by an instrument falling within paragraph 2 below) made with United Kingdom offices of the eligible institution, except for over two year deposits [and except for deposits made by the Bank].

2.   The amount of the eligible institution's liabilities in respect of certificates of deposit, commercial paper, bonds, notes and other similar instruments denominated in each case in sterling and issued by United Kingdom offices of the eligible institution on terms requiring repayment not later than five years from the date of issue.

3.   The amount of the eligible institution's liabilities to make payments in sterling for the purchase of, or otherwise in return for the transfer to it of, securities or other assets under retransfer agreements entered into by United Kingdom offices of the eligible institution, other than any such agreements entered into with the Bank.

4.   The amount of all sterling items in suspense held by United Kingdom offices of the eligible institution.

5.   60% of the amount of sterling credit items in the course of transmission by United Kingdom offices of the eligible institution to the Bank, any other United Kingdom office of the eligible institution or a United Kingdom office of any other eligible institution.

6.   ...

7.   The amount (if any) by which the total liabilities of the United Kingdom offices of the eligible institution denominated in currencies other than sterling, as reported to the Bank, exceed the total assets of those offices denominated in such currencies, as so reported.

LESS

8.   ...

9.—(a)   The amount of any sterling deposits made by United Kingdom offices of the eligible institution with, and sterling loans made by such offices to, United Kingdom offices of other eligible institutions (including certificates of deposit and commercial paper which are—
  (i)   denominated in sterling;
  (ii)   held by United Kingdom offices of the eligible institution; and
  (iii)   issued by United Kingdom offices of other eligible institutions;
but excluding any instrument which falls within paragraph 11 below).

  (b)   Sterling amounts payable to United Kingdom offices of the eligible institution by United Kingdom offices of any other eligible institution under the terms of any finance lease.

  (c)   The amount of sterling cheques passed by United Kingdom offices of the eligible institution to United Kingdom offices of other eligible institutions for collection.

10.   The amount of the eligible institution's claims to receive payments in sterling for the sale of, or otherwise in return for the transfer by it of, securities or other assets under retransfer agreements entered into by United Kingdom offices of the eligible institution with United Kingdom offices of other eligible institutions.

11.   The value of the preference shares, bonds, notes and other similar debt instruments (other than certificates of deposit and commercial paper but including subordinated loan capital not represented by the issue of securities) denominated in sterling and issued by a United Kingdom office of any other eligible institution on terms requiring redemption or repayment not later than five years from the date of issue which are held by United Kingdom offices of the eligible institution for its own account.

12.   60% of the amount of sterling debit items in the course of collection by United Kingdom offices of the eligible institution from the Bank, any other United Kingdom office of the eligible institution or a United Kingdom office of any other eligible institution.

13.   The amount (if any) by which the eligible institution's sterling deposit liabilities to non-resident offices exceed the institution's net sterling liabilities to non-resident offices.

[3534]

NOTES

 Para 1: words in square brackets added by the Cash Ratio Deposits (Eligible Liabilities) (Amendment) Order 2005, SI 2005/3203, art 2(1), (3)(a), as from 1 March 2006.

 Paras 6, 8: revoked by SI 2005/3203, art 2(1), (3)(b), as from 1 March 2006.

 Eligible debt securities: as to the application of this article in relation to eligible debt securities, see the Uncertificated Securities (Amendment) (Eligible Debt Securities) Regulations 2003, SI 2003/1633, reg 15, Sch 2, para 5 (as from 24 June 2003).

PUBLIC INTEREST DISCLOSURE (PRESCRIBED PERSONS) ORDER 1999 (NOTE)

(SI 1999/1549)

NOTES
Made: 5 June 1999.
Authority: Employment Rights Act 1996, s 43F.
Commencement: 2 July 1999.
This Order prescribes persons for the purposes of s 43F of the Employment Rights Act 1996, to whom protected disclosures may be made and matters for which they are prescribed. The broad effect of the Order, taken with section 43F, is that a worker potentially protected by the provisions of the 1996 Act will be protected by the 1996 Act if he makes a qualifying disclosure in good faith to a person prescribed in the Order, reasonably believing that the failure disclosed falls within the matters in respect of which that person is prescribed and that the information disclosed, and any allegation contained in it, are substantially true.

[3535]

UNFAIR TERMS IN CONSUMER CONTRACTS REGULATIONS 1999

(SI 1999/2083)

NOTES
Made: 22 July 1999.
Authority: European Communities Act 1972, s 2(2).
Commencement: 1 October 1999.
These Regulations are reproduced as amended by: the Enterprise Act 2002; the Railways and Transport Safety Act 2003; the Unfair Terms in Consumer Contracts (Amendment) Regulations 2001, SI 2001/1186; the Financial Services and Markets Act 2000 (Consequential Amendments and Repeals) Order 2001, SI 2001/3649; the Communications Act 2003 (Consequential Amendments No 2) Order 2003, SI 2003/3182; the Financial Services (Distance Marketing) Regulations 2004, SI 2004/2095; the Unfair Terms in Consumer Contracts (Amendment) and Water Act 2003 (Transitional Provision) Regulations 2006, SI 2006/523.

ARRANGEMENT OF REGULATIONS

1 Citation and commencement

These Regulations may be cited as the Unfair Terms in Consumer Contracts Regulations 1999 and shall come into force on 1st October 1999.

[3536]

2   (*Revokes the Unfair Terms in Consumer Contracts Regulations 1994, SI 1994/3159.*)

3 Interpretation

(1)   In these Regulations—
    "the Community" means the European Community;

"consumer" means any natural person who, in contracts covered by these Regulations, is acting for purposes which are outside his trade, business or profession;

"court" in relation to England and Wales and Northern Ireland means a county court or the High Court, and in relation to Scotland, the Sheriff or the Court of Session;

["OFT" means the Office of Fair Trading];

"EEA Agreement" means the Agreement on the European Economic Area signed at Oporto on 2nd May 1992 as adjusted by the protocol signed at Brussels on 17th March 1993;

"Member State" means a State which is a contracting party to the EEA Agreement;

"notified" means notified in writing;

"qualifying body" means a person specified in Schedule 1;

"seller or supplier" means any natural or legal person who, in contracts covered by these Regulations, is acting for purposes relating to his trade, business or profession, whether publicly owned or privately owned;

"unfair terms" means the contractual terms referred to in regulation 5.

[(1A)   The references—
(a)   in regulation 4(1) to a seller or a supplier, and
(b)   in regulation 8(1) to a seller or supplier,

include references to a distance supplier and to an intermediary.

(1B)   In paragraph (1A) and regulation 5(6)—
"distance supplier" means—
(a)   a supplier under a distance contract within the meaning of the Financial Services (Distance Marketing) Regulations 2004, or
(b)   a supplier of unsolicited financial services within regulation 15 of those Regulations; and

"intermediary" has the same meaning as in those Regulations.]

(2)   In the application of these Regulations to Scotland for references to an "injunction" or an "interim injunction" there shall be substituted references to an "interdict" or "interim interdict" respectively.

[3537]

NOTES
Para (1): Definition "OFT" substituted by virtue of the Enterprise Act 2002, s 2(1), as from 1 April 2003.
Paras (1A), (1B): inserted by the Financial Services (Distance Marketing) Regulations 2004, SI 2004/2095, reg 24(1), (2), as from 31 October 2004.

4   Terms to which these Regulations apply

(1)   These Regulations apply in relation to unfair terms in contracts concluded between a seller or a supplier and a consumer.

(2)   These Regulations do not apply to contractual terms which reflect—
(a)   mandatory statutory or regulatory provisions (including such provisions under the law of any Member State or in Community legislation having effect in the United Kingdom without further enactment);
(b)   the provisions or principles of international conventions to which the Member States or the Community are party.

[3538]

5   Unfair Terms

(1)   A contractual term which has not been individually negotiated shall be regarded as unfair if, contrary to the requirement of good faith, it causes a significant imbalance in the parties' rights and obligations arising under the contract, to the detriment of the consumer.

(2)   A term shall always be regarded as not having been individually negotiated where it has been drafted in advance and the consumer has therefore not been able to influence the substance of the term.

(3)   Notwithstanding that a specific term or certain aspects of it in a contract has been individually negotiated, these Regulations shall apply to the rest of a contract if an overall assessment of it indicates that it is a pre-formulated standard contract.

(4)   It shall be for any seller or supplier who claims that a term was individually negotiated to show that it was.

(5)   Schedule 2 to these Regulations contains an indicative and non-exhaustive list of the terms which may be regarded as unfair.

[(6)   Any contractual term providing that a consumer bears the burden of proof in respect of showing whether a distance supplier or an intermediary complied with any or all of the obligations placed upon him resulting from the Directive and any rule or enactment implementing it shall always be regarded as unfair.

(7) In paragraph (6)—

"the Directive" means Directive 2002/65/EC of the European Parliament and of the Council of 23 September 2002 concerning the distance marketing of consumer financial services and amending Council Directive 90/619/EEC and Directives 97/7/EC and 98/27/EC; and

"rule" means a rule made by the Financial Services Authority under the Financial Services and Markets Act 2000 or by a designated professional body within the meaning of section 326(2) of that Act.]

[3539]

NOTES

Paras (6), (7): added by the Financial Services (Distance Marketing) Regulations 2004, SI 2004/2095, reg 24(1), (2), as from 31 October 2004.

6 Assessment of unfair terms

(1) Without prejudice to regulation 12, the unfairness of a contractual term shall be assessed, taking into account the nature of the goods or services for which the contract was concluded and by referring, at the time of conclusion of the contract, to all the circumstances attending the conclusion of the contract and to all the other terms of the contract or of another contract on which it is dependent.

(2) In so far as it is in plain intelligible language, the assessment of fairness of a term shall not relate—

(a) to the definition of the main subject matter of the contract, or

(b) to the adequacy of the price or remuneration, as against the goods or services supplied in exchange.

[3540]

7 Written contracts

(1) A seller or supplier shall ensure that any written term of a contract is expressed in plain, intelligible language.

(2) If there is doubt about the meaning of a written term, the interpretation which is most favourable to the consumer shall prevail but this rule shall not apply in proceedings brought under regulation 12.

[3541]

8 Effect of unfair term

(1) An unfair term in a contract concluded with a consumer by a seller or supplier shall not be binding on the consumer.

(2) The contract shall continue to bind the parties if it is capable of continuing in existence without the unfair term.

[3542]

9 Choice of law clauses

These Regulations shall apply notwithstanding any contract term which applies or purports to apply the law of a non-Member State, if the contract has a close connection with the territory of the Member States.

[3543]

10 Complaints—consideration by [OFT]

(1) It shall be the duty of the [OFT] to consider any complaint made to [it] that any contract term drawn up for general use is unfair, unless—

(a) the complaint appears to the [OFT] to be frivolous or vexatious; or

(b) a qualifying body has notified the [OFT] that it agrees to consider the complaint.

(2) The [OFT] shall give reasons for [its] decision to apply or not to apply, as the case may be, for an injunction under regulation 12 in relation to any complaint which these Regulations require [it] to consider.

(3) In deciding whether or not to apply for an injunction in respect of a term which the [OFT] considers to be unfair, [it] may, if [it] considers it appropriate to do so, have regard to any undertakings given to [it] by or on behalf of any person as to the continued use of such a term in contracts concluded with consumers.

[3544]

NOTES

Words in square brackets substituted by virtue of the Enterprise Act 2002, s 2(1), as from 1 April 2003.

PART III
STATUTORY INSTRUMENTS

11 Complaints—consideration by qualifying bodies

(1) If a qualifying body specified in Part One of Schedule 1 notifies the [OFT] that it agrees to consider a complaint that any contract term drawn up for general use is unfair, it shall be under a duty to consider that complaint.

(2) Regulation 10(2) and (3) shall apply to a qualifying body which is under a duty to consider a complaint as they apply to the [OFT].

[3545]

NOTES

Words in square brackets substituted by virtue of the Enterprise Act 2002, s 2(1), as from 1 April 2003.

12 Injunctions to prevent continued use of unfair terms

(1) The [OFT] or, subject to paragraph (2), any qualifying body may apply for an injunction (including an interim injunction) against any person appearing to the [OFT] or that body to be using, or recommending use of, an unfair term drawn up for general use in contracts concluded with consumers.

(2) A qualifying body may apply for an injunction only where—
- (a) it has notified the [OFT] of its intention to apply at least fourteen days before the date on which the application is made, beginning with the date on which the notification was given; or
- (b) the [OFT] consents to the application being made within a shorter period.

(3) The court on an application under this regulation may grant an injunction on such terms as it thinks fit.

(4) An injunction may relate not only to use of a particular contract term drawn up for general use but to any similar term, or a term having like effect, used or recommended for use by any person.

[3546]

NOTES

Words in square brackets substituted by virtue of the Enterprise Act 2002, s 2(1), as from 1 April 2003.

13 Powers of the [OFT] and qualifying bodies to obtain documents and information

(1) The [OFT] may exercise the power conferred by this regulation for the purpose of—
- (a) facilitating [its] consideration of a complaint that a contract term drawn up for general use is unfair; or
- (b) ascertaining whether a person has complied with an undertaking or court order as to the continued use, or recommendation for use, of a term in contracts concluded with consumers.

(2) A qualifying body specified in Part One of Schedule 1 may exercise the power conferred by this regulation for the purpose of—
- (a) facilitating its consideration of a complaint that a contract term drawn up for general use is unfair; or
- (b) ascertaining whether a person has complied with—
  - (i) an undertaking given to it or to the court following an application by that body, or
  - (ii) a court order made on an application by that body,
  as to the continued use, or recommendation for use, of a term in contracts concluded with consumers.

(3) The [OFT] may require any person to supply to [it], and a qualifying body specified in Part One of Schedule 1 may require any person to supply to it—
- (a) a copy of any document which that person has used or recommended for use, at the time the notice referred to in paragraph (4) below is given, as a pre-formulated standard contract in dealings with consumers;
- (b) information about the use, or recommendation for use, by that person of that document or any other such document in dealings with consumers.

(4) The power conferred by this regulation is to be exercised by a notice in writing which may—
- (a) specify the way in which and the time within which it is to be complied with; and
- (b) be varied or revoked by a subsequent notice.

(5) Nothing in this regulation compels a person to supply any document or information which he would be entitled to refuse to produce or give in civil proceedings before the court.

(6) If a person makes default in complying with a notice under this regulation, the court may, on the application of the [OFT] or of the qualifying body, make such order as the court thinks fit for requiring the default to be made good, and any such order may provide that all the costs or expenses

of and incidental to the application shall be borne by the person in default or by any officers of a company or other association who are responsible for its default.

[3547]

NOTES
Words in square brackets substituted by virtue of the Enterprise Act 2002, s 2(1), as from 1 April 2003.

14 Notification of undertakings and orders to [OFT]

A qualifying body shall notify the [OFT]—
    (a)   of any undertaking given to it by or on behalf of any person as to the continued use of a term which that body considers to be unfair in contracts concluded with consumers;
    (b)   of the outcome of any application made by it under regulation 12, and of the terms of any undertaking given to, or order made by, the court;
    (c)   of the outcome of any application made by it to enforce a previous order of the court.

[3548]

NOTES
Words in square brackets substituted by virtue of the Enterprise Act 2002, s 2(1), as from 1 April 2003.

15 Publication, information and advice

(1) The [OFT] shall arrange for the publication in such form and manner as [it] considers appropriate, of—
    (a)   details of any undertaking or order notified to [it] under regulation 14;
    (b)   details of any undertaking given to [it] by or on behalf of any person as to the continued use of a term which the [OFT] considers to be unfair in contracts concluded with consumers;
    (c)   details of any application made by [it] under regulation 12, and of the terms of any undertaking given to, or order made by, the court;
    (d)   details of any application made by the [OFT] to enforce a previous order of the court.

(2) The [OFT] shall inform any person on request whether a particular term to which these Regulations apply has been—
    (a)   the subject of an undertaking given to the [OFT] or notified to [it] by a qualifying body; or
    (b)   the subject of an order of the court made upon application by [it] or notified to [it] by a qualifying body;

and shall give that person details of the undertaking or a copy of the order, as the case may be, together with a copy of any amendments which the person giving the undertaking has agreed to make to the term in question.

(3) The [OFT] may arrange for the dissemination in such form and manner as [it] considers appropriate of such information and advice concerning the operation of these Regulations as may appear to [it] to be expedient to give to the public and to all persons likely to be affected by these Regulations.

[3549]

NOTES
Words in square brackets substituted by virtue of the Enterprise Act 2002, s 2(1), as from 1 April 2003.

[16 The functions of the Financial Services Authority

The functions of the Financial Services Authority under these Regulations shall be treated as functions of the Financial Services Authority under the [Financial Services and Markets Act 2000].]

[3550]

NOTES
Added by the Unfair Terms in Consumer Contracts (Amendment) Regulations 2001, SI 2001/1186, reg 2(a), as from 1 May 2001.
Words in square brackets substituted by the Financial Services and Markets Act 2000 (Consequential Amendments and Repeals) Order 2001, SI 2001/3649, art 583, as from 1 December 2001.

SCHEDULES

SCHEDULE 1
QUALIFYING BODIES

Regulation 3

PART 1

[1.   The Information Commissioner.

2. The Gas and Electricity Markets Authority.
3. The Director General of Electricity Supply for Northern Ireland.
4. The Director General of Gas for Northern Ireland.
5. [The Office of Communications].
6. [The Water Services Regulation Authority.]
7. [The Office of Rail Regulation.]
8. Every weights and measures authority in Great Britain.
9. The Department of Enterprise, Trade and Investment in Northern Ireland.
10. The Financial Services Authority.]

[3551]

NOTES
   Substituted by the Unfair Terms in Consumer Contracts (Amendment) Regulations 2001, SI 2001/1186, reg 2(b), as from 1 May 2001.
   Para 5: words in square brackets substituted by the Communications Act 2003 (Consequential Amendments No 2) Order 2003, SI 2003/3182, art 2, as from 29 December 2003.
   Para 6: words in square brackets substituted by the Unfair Terms in Consumer Contracts (Amendment) and Water Act 2003 (Transitional Provision) Regulations 2006, SI 2006/523, art 2, as from 1 April 2006.
   Para 7: words in square brackets substituted by virtue of the Railways and Transport Safety Act 2003, s 16(4), (5), Sch 3, para 4, as from 5 July 2004.

PART 2

11. Consumers' Association

[3552]

SCHEDULE 2
INDICATIVE AND NON-EXHAUSTIVE LIST OF TERMS WHICH MAY BE REGARDED
AS UNFAIR
Regulation 5(5)

1. Terms which have the object or effect of—
    (a) excluding or limiting the legal liability of a seller or supplier in the event of the death of a consumer or personal injury to the latter resulting from an act or omission of that seller or supplier;
    (b) inappropriately excluding or limiting the legal rights of the consumer vis-à-vis the seller or supplier or another party in the event of total or partial non-performance or inadequate performance by the seller or supplier of any of the contractual obligations, including the option of offsetting a debt owed to the seller or supplier against any claim which the consumer may have against him;
    (c) making an agreement binding on the consumer whereas provision of services by the seller or supplier is subject to a condition whose realisation depends on his own will alone;
    (d) permitting the seller or supplier to retain sums paid by the consumer where the latter decides not to conclude or perform the contract, without providing for the consumer to receive compensation of an equivalent amount from the seller or supplier where the latter is the party cancelling the contract;
    (e) requiring any consumer who fails to fulfil his obligation to pay a disproportionately high sum in compensation;
    (f) authorising the seller or supplier to dissolve the contract on a discretionary basis where the same facility is not granted to the consumer, or permitting the seller or supplier to retain the sums paid for services not yet supplied by him where it is the seller or supplier himself who dissolves the contract;
    (g) enabling the seller or supplier to terminate a contract of indeterminate duration without reasonable notice except where there are serious grounds for doing so;
    (h) automatically extending a contract of fixed duration where the consumer does not indicate otherwise, when the deadline fixed for the consumer to express his desire not to extend the contract is unreasonably early;
    (i) irrevocably binding the consumer to terms with which he had no real opportunity of becoming acquainted before the conclusion of the contract;
    (j) enabling the seller or supplier to alter the terms of the contract unilaterally without a valid reason which is specified in the contract;
    (k) enabling the seller or supplier to alter unilaterally without a valid reason any characteristics of the product or service to be provided;
    (l) providing for the price of goods to be determined at the time of delivery or allowing a seller of goods or supplier of services to increase their price without in both cases giving

the consumer the corresponding right to cancel the contract if the final price is too high in relation to the price agreed when the contract was concluded;

(m)   giving the seller or supplier the right to determine whether the goods or services supplied are in conformity with the contract, or giving him the exclusive right to interpret any term of the contract;

(n)   limiting the seller's or supplier's obligation to respect commitments undertaken by his agents or making his commitments subject to compliance with a particular formality;

(o)   obliging the consumer to fulfil all his obligations where the seller or supplier does not perform his;

(p)   giving the seller or supplier the possibility of transferring his rights and obligations under the contract, where this may serve to reduce the guarantees for the consumer, without the latter's agreement;

(q)   excluding or hindering the consumer's right to take legal action or exercise any other legal remedy, particularly by requiring the consumer to take disputes exclusively to arbitration not covered by legal provisions, unduly restricting the evidence available to him or imposing on him a burden of proof which, according to the applicable law, should lie with another party to the contract.

2.   Scope of paragraphs 1(g), (j) and (l)

(a)   Paragraph 1(g) is without hindrance to terms by which a supplier of financial services reserves the right to terminate unilaterally a contract of indeterminate duration without notice where there is a valid reason, provided that the supplier is required to inform the other contracting party or parties thereof immediately.

(b)   Paragraph 1(j) is without hindrance to terms under which a supplier of financial services reserves the right to alter the rate of interest payable by the consumer or due to the latter, or the amount of other charges for financial services without notice where there is a valid reason, provided that the supplier is required to inform the other contracting party or parties thereof at the earliest opportunity and that the latter are free to dissolve the contract immediately.

Paragraph 1(j) is also without hindrance to terms under which a seller or supplier reserves the right to alter unilaterally the conditions of a contract of indeterminate duration, provided that he is required to inform the consumer with reasonable notice and that the consumer is free to dissolve the contract.

(c)   Paragraphs 1(g), (j) and (l) do not apply to:

—   transactions in transferable securities, financial instruments and other products or services where the price is linked to fluctuations in a stock exchange quotation or index or a financial market rate that the seller or supplier does not control;

—   contracts for the purchase or sale of foreign currency, traveller's cheques or international money orders denominated in foreign currency.

(d)   Paragraph 1(1) is without hindrance to price indexation clauses, where lawful, provided that the method by which prices vary is explicitly described.

[3553]

FINANCIAL MARKETS AND INSOLVENCY (SETTLEMENT FINALITY) REGULATIONS 1999

(SI 1999/2979)

NOTES

Made: 2 November 1999.

Authority: European Communities Act 1972, s 2(2).

Commencement: 11 December 1999.

These Regulations are reproduced as amended by: the Civil Jurisdiction and Judgments Order 2001, SI 2001/3929; the Financial Services and Markets Act 2000 (Consequential Amendments) Order 2002, SI 2002/1555; the Enterprise Act 2002 (Insolvency) Order 2003, SI 2003/2096; the Financial Markets and Insolvency (Settlement Finality) (Amendment) Regulations 2006, SI 2006/50; the Capital Requirements Regulations 2006, SI 2006/3221; the Financial Services (EEA State) Regulations 2007, SI 2007/108; the Financial Services and Markets Act 2000 (Markets in Financial Instruments) Regulations 2007, SI 2007/126; the Financial Markets and Insolvency (Settlement Finality) (Amendment) Regulations 2007, SI 2007/832; the Civil Jurisdiction and Judgments Regulations 2007, SI 2007/1655.

ARRANGEMENT OF REGULATIONS

PART I
GENERAL

PART II
DESIGNATED SYSTEMS

PART III
TRANSFER ORDERS EFFECTED THROUGH A DESIGNATED SYSTEM AND
COLLATERAL SECURITY

Collateral security charges

General

PART I
GENERAL

1 Citation, commencement and extent

(1)   These Regulations may be cited as the Financial Markets and Insolvency (Settlement Finality) Regulations 1999 and shall come into force on 11th December 1999.

(2)   ...

[3553A]

NOTES

Para (2): revoked by the Financial Markets and Insolvency (Settlement Finality) (Amendment) Regulations 2006, SI 2006/50, reg 2(1), (2), as from 2 February 2006. Note that para (2) previously provided that these Regulations do not extend to Northern Ireland.

2 Interpretation

(1)   In these Regulations—
    ["the 2000 Act" means the Financial Services and Markets Act 2000;]
    "central bank" means a central bank of an EEA State or the European Central Bank;
    "central counterparty" means a body corporate or unincorporated association interposed between the institutions in a designated system and which acts as the exclusive counterparty of those institutions with regard to transfer orders;
    "charge" means any form of security, including a mortgage and, in Scotland, a heritable security;

"clearing house" means a body corporate or unincorporated association which is responsible for the calculation of the net positions of institutions and any central counterparty or settlement agent in a designated system;

"collateral security" means any realisable assets provided under a charge or a repurchase or similar agreement, or otherwise (including money provided under a charge)—

(a)   for the purpose of securing rights and obligations potentially arising in connection with a designated system ("collateral security in connection with participation in a designated system"); or

(b)   to a central bank for the purpose of securing rights and obligations in connection with its operations in carrying out its functions as a central bank ("collateral security in connection with the functions of a central bank");

"collateral security charge" means, where collateral security consists of realisable assets (including money) provided under a charge, that charge;

["credit institution" means a credit institution as defined in Article 4(1)(a) of Directive 2006/48/EC of the European Parliament and of the Council of 14 June 2006 relating to the taking up and pursuit of the business of credit institutions, including the bodies set out in the list in Article 2;]

"creditors' voluntary winding-up resolution" means a resolution for voluntary winding up (within the meaning of the Insolvency Act 1986 [or the Insolvency (Northern Ireland) Order 1989]) where the winding up is a creditors' winding up (within the meaning of that Act [or that Order]);

"default arrangements" means the arrangements put in place by a designated system to limit systemic and other types of risk which arise in the event of a participant appearing to be unable, or likely to become unable, to meet its obligations in respect of a transfer order, including, for example, any default rules within the meaning of Part VII [or Part V] or any other arrangements for—

(a)   netting,

(b)   the closing out of open positions, or

(c)   the application or transfer of collateral security;

"defaulter" means a person in respect of whom action has been taken by a designated system under its default arrangements;

"designated system" means a system which is declared by a designation order for the time being in force to be a designated system for the purposes of these Regulations;

"designating authority" means—

(a)   in the case of a system—

(i)   which is, or the operator of which is, a recognised investment exchange or a recognised clearing house for the purposes of [the 2000 Act],

(ii)   which is, or the operator of which is, a listed person within the meaning of the Financial Markets and Insolvency (Money Market) Regulations 1995, or

(iii)   through which securities transfer orders are effected (whether or not payment transfer orders are also effected through that system),

the Financial Services Authority;

(b)   in any other case, the Bank of England;

"designation order" has the meaning given by regulation 4;

["EEA State" has the meaning given by Schedule 1 to the Interpretation Act 1978;]

"guidance", in relation to a designated system, means guidance issued or any recommendation made by it which is intended to have continuing effect and is issued in writing or other legible form to all or any class of its participants or users or persons seeking to participate in the system or to use its facilities and which would, if it were a rule, come within the definition of a rule;

"indirect participant" means a credit institution for which payment transfer orders are capable of being effected through a designated system pursuant to its contractual relationship with an institution;

"institution" means—

(a)   a credit institution;

(b)   an investment firm as defined in [Article 4.1.1 of Directive 2004/39/EC of the European Parliament and of the Council of 21 April 2004 on markets in financial instruments, other than a person to whom Article 2 applies];

(c)   a public authority or publicly guaranteed undertaking;

(d)   any undertaking whose head office is outside the European Community and whose functions correspond to those of a credit institution or investment firm as defined in (a) and (b) above; or

(e)   any undertaking which is treated by the designating authority as an institution in accordance with regulation 8(1),

which participates in a designated system and which is responsible for discharging the financial obligations arising from transfer orders which are effected through the system;

"netting" means the conversion into one net claim or obligation of different claims or obligations between participants resulting from the issue and receipt of transfer orders between them, whether on a bilateral or multilateral basis and whether through the interposition of a clearing house, central counterparty or settlement agent or otherwise;

["Part V" means Part V of the Companies (No 2) (Northern Ireland) Order 1990;]

"Part VII" means Part VII of the Companies Act 1989;

"participant" means—
  (a)   an institution,
  (b)   a body corporate or unincorporated association which carries out any combination of the functions of a central counterparty, a settlement agent or a clearing house, with respect to a system, or
  (c)   an indirect participant which is treated as a participant, or is a member of a class of indirect participants which are treated as participants, in accordance with regulation 9;

"protected trust deed" and "trust deed" shall be construed in accordance with section 73(1) of the Bankruptcy (Scotland) Act 1985 (interpretation);

"relevant office-holder" means—
  (a)   the official receiver;
  (b)   any person acting in relation to a company as its liquidator, provisional liquidator, or administrator;
  (c)   any person acting in relation to an individual (or, in Scotland, any debtor within the meaning of the Bankruptcy (Scotland) Act 1985) as his trustee in bankruptcy or interim receiver of his property or as permanent or interim trustee in the sequestration of his estate or as his trustee under a protected trust deed; or
  (d)   any person acting as administrator of an insolvent estate of a deceased person;

and in sub-paragraph (b), "company" means any company, society, association, partnership or other body which may be wound up under the Insolvency Act 1986 [or the Insolvency (Northern Ireland) Order 1989];

"rules", in relation to a designated system, means rules or conditions governing the system with respect to the matters dealt with in these Regulations;

"securities" means (except for the purposes of the definition of "charge") any instruments referred to in section [C of Annex I to Directive 2004/39/EC of the European Parliament and of the Council of 21 April 2004 on markets in financial instruments];

"settlement account" means an account at a central bank, a settlement agent or a central counterparty used to hold funds or securities (or both) and to settle transactions between participants in a designated system;

"settlement agent" means a body corporate or unincorporated association providing settlement accounts to the institutions and any central counterparty in a designated system for the settlement of transfer orders within the system and, as the case may be, for extending credit to such institutions and any such central counterparty for settlement purposes;

"the Settlement Finality Directive" means Directive 98/26/EC of the European Parliament and of the Council of 19th May 1998 on settlement finality in payment and securities settlement systems;

"transfer order" means—
  (a)   an instruction by a participant to place at the disposal of a recipient an amount of money by means of a book entry on the accounts of a credit institution, a central bank or a settlement agent, or an instruction which results in the assumption or discharge of a payment obligation as defined by the rules of a designated system ("a payment transfer order"); or
  (b)   an instruction by a participant to transfer the title to, or interest in, securities by means of a book entry on a register, or otherwise ("a securities transfer order");

"winding up" means—
  (a)   winding up by the court, or
  (b)   creditors' voluntary winding up,

within the meaning of the Insolvency Act 1986 [or the Insolvency (Northern Ireland) Order 1989] (but does not include members' voluntary winding up within the meaning of that Act [or that Order]).

(2)   In these Regulations—
  (a)   references to the law of insolvency include references to every provision made by or under the Insolvency Act 1986[, the Insolvency (Northern Ireland) Order 1989] or the Bankruptcy (Scotland) Act 1985; and in relation to a building society references to insolvency law or to any provision of the Insolvency Act 1986 [or the Insolvency (Northern Ireland) Order 1989] are to that law or provision as modified by the Building Societies Act 1986;
  (b)   in relation to Scotland, references to—
      (i)   sequestration include references to the administration by a judicial factor of the insolvent estate of a deceased person,

(ii)   an interim or permanent trustee include references to a judicial factor on the insolvent estate of a deceased person, and

(iii)   "set off" include compensation.

(3)   Subject to paragraph (1), expressions used in these Regulations which are also used in the Settlement Finality Directive have the same meaning in these Regulations as they have in the Settlement Finality Directive.

(4)   References in these Regulations to things done, or required to be done, by or in relation to a designated system shall, in the case of a designated system which is neither a body corporate nor an unincorporated association, be treated as references to things done, or required to be done, by or in relation to the operator of that system.

[3553B]

NOTES

Para (1) is amended as follows:

Definition "the 2000 Act" substituted (for original definition "the 1986 Act"), and words in square brackets in definition "designating authority" substituted, by the Financial Services and Markets Act 2000 (Consequential Amendments) Order 2002, SI 2002/1555, art 39(1), (2), as from 3 July 2002.

Definition "credit institution" substituted by the Capital Requirements Regulations 2006, SI 2006/3221, reg 29(4), Sch 6, para 3, as from 1 January 2007.

Words in square brackets in definitions "creditors' voluntary winding up resolution", "default arrangements", "relevant office-holder", and "winding up" inserted, and definition "Part V" inserted, by the Financial Markets and Insolvency (Settlement Finality) (Amendment) Regulations 2006, SI 2006/50, reg 2(1), (3), as from 2 February 2006.

Definition "EEA State" substituted by the Financial Services (EEA State) Regulations 2007, SI 2007/108, reg 5, as from 13 February 2007.

Words in square brackets in the definitions "institution" and "securities" substituted by the Financial Services and Markets Act 2000 (Markets in Financial Instruments) Regulations 2007, SI 2007/126, reg 3(6), Sch 6, Pt 2, para 14, as from 1 November 2007 (for the full commencement details of SI 2007/126, see reg 1 of those Regulations at **[4051]**).

Para (2): words in square brackets inserted by SI 2006/50, reg 2(1), (4), as from 2 February 2006.

PART II
DESIGNATED SYSTEMS

3   Application for designation

(1)   Any body corporate or unincorporated association may apply to the designating authority for an order declaring it, or any system of which it is the operator, to be a designated system for the purposes of these Regulations.

(2)   Any such application—

(a)   shall be made in such manner as the designating authority may direct; and

(b)   shall be accompanied by such information as the designating authority may reasonably require for the purpose of determining the application.

(3)   At any time after receiving an application and before determining it, the designating authority may require the applicant to furnish additional information.

(4)   The directions and requirements given or imposed under paragraphs (2) and (3) may differ as between different applications.

(5)   Any information to be furnished to the designating authority under this regulation shall be in such form or verified in such manner as it may specify.

(6)   Every application shall be accompanied by copies of the rules of the system to which the application relates and any guidance relating to that system.

[3553C]

4   Grant and refusal of designation

(1)   Where—

(a)   an application has been duly made under regulation 3;

(b)   the applicant has paid any fee charged by virtue of regulation 5(1); and

(c)   the designating authority is satisfied that the requirements of the Schedule are satisfied with respect to the system to which the application relates;

the designating authority may make an order (a "designation order") declaring the system to be a designated system for the purposes of these Regulations.

(2)   In determining whether to make a designation order, the designating authority shall have regard to systemic risks.

(3)   Where an application has been made to the Financial Services Authority under regulation 3 in relation to a system through which both securities transfer orders and payment transfer orders are effected, the Authority shall consult the Bank of England before deciding whether to make a designation order.

PART III
STATUTORY INSTRUMENTS

(4)　A designation order shall state the date on which it takes effect.

(5)　Where the designating authority refuses an application for a designation order it shall give the applicant a written notice to that effect stating the reasons for the refusal.

[3553D]

5　Fees

(1)　The designating authority may charge a fee to an applicant for a designation order.

(2)　The designating authority may charge a designated system a periodical fee.

(3)　Fees chargeable by the designating authority under this regulation shall not exceed an amount which reasonably represents the amount of costs incurred or likely to be incurred—
- (a)　in the case of a fee charged to an applicant for a designation order, in determining whether the designation order should be made; and
- (b)　in the case of a periodical fee, in satisfying itself that the designated system continues to meet the requirements of the Schedule and is complying with any obligations to which it is subject by virtue of these Regulations.

[3553E]

6　Certain bodies deemed to satisfy requirements for designation

(1)　Subject to paragraph (2), an investment exchange or clearing house declared by an order for the time being in force to be a recognised investment exchange or recognised clearing house for the purposes of [the 2000 Act], whether that order was made before or is made after the coming into force of these Regulations, shall be deemed to satisfy the requirements in paragraphs 2 and 3 of the Schedule.

(2)　Paragraph (1) does not apply to overseas investment exchanges or overseas clearing houses within the meaning of the 1986 Act.

[3553F]

NOTES

Para (1): words in square brackets substituted by the Financial Services and Markets Act 2000 (Consequential Amendments) Order 2002, SI 2002/1555, art 39(1), (3), as from 3 July 2002.

7　Revocation of designation

(1)　A designation order may be revoked by a further order made by the designating authority if at any time it appears to the designating authority—
- (a)　that any requirement of the Schedule is not satisfied in the case of the system to which the designation order relates; or
- (b)　that the system has failed to comply with any obligation to which it is subject by virtue of these Regulations.

(2)　[Subsections (1) to (7) of section 298 of the 2000 Act] shall apply in relation to the revocation of a designation order under paragraph (1) as they apply in relation to the revocation of a recognition order under [section 297(2) of that Act]; and in those subsections as they so apply—
- [(a)　any reference to a recognised body shall be taken to be a reference to a designated system;
- (b)　any reference to members of a recognised body shall be taken to be a reference to participants in a designated system;
- (c)　references to the Authority shall, in cases where the Bank of England is the designating authority, be taken to be a reference to the Bank of England; and
- (d)　subsection (4)(a) shall have effect as if for "two months" there were substituted "three months".]

[(3)　An order revoking a designation order—
- (a)　shall state the date on which it takes effect, being no earlier than three months after the day on which the revocation order is made; and
- (b)　may contain such transitional provisions as the designating authority thinks necessary or expedient.

(4)　A designation order may be revoked at the request or with the consent of the designated system, and any such revocation shall not be subject to the restriction imposed by paragraph (3)(a), or to the requirements imposed by subsections (1) to (6) of section 298 of the 2000 Act.]

[3553G]

NOTES

Para (2): words in square brackets substituted by the Financial Services and Markets Act 2000 (Consequential Amendments) Order 2002, SI 2002/1555, art 39(1), (4), as from 3 July 2002. With regard to the words in the second pair of square brackets, note that art 39(4)(b) of the 2002 Order actually provides—

"for "*under* subsection (1) of that section" substitute "section 297(2) of that Act"";

It is believed that this is an error and that the word "under" should not be removed from para (2).
Paras (3), (4): added by SI 2002/1555, art 39(1), (5), as from 3 July 2002.

8 Undertakings treated as institutions

(1)   A designating authority may treat as an institution any undertaking which participates in a designated system and which is responsible for discharging financial obligations arising from transfer orders effected through that system, provided that—

    (a)   the designating authority considers such treatment to be required on grounds of systemic risk, and

    (b)   the designated system is one in which at least three institutions (other than any undertaking treated as an institution by virtue of this paragraph) participate and through which securities transfer orders are effected.

(2)   Where a designating authority decides to treat an undertaking as an institution in accordance with paragraph (1), it shall give written notice of that decision to the designated system in which the undertaking is to be treated as a participant.

[3553H]

9 Indirect participants treated as participants

(1)   A designating authority may treat—

    (a)   an indirect participant as a participant in a designated system, or

    (b)   a class of indirect participants as participants in a designated system,

where it considers this to be required on grounds of systemic risk, and shall give written notice of any decision to that effect to the designated system.

[3553I]

10 Provision of information by designated systems

(1)   A designated system shall, on being declared to be a designated system, provide to the designating authority in writing a list of its participants and shall give written notice to the designating authority of any amendment to the list within seven days of such amendment.

(2)   The designating authority may, in writing, require a designated system to furnish to it such other information relating to that designated system as it reasonably requires for the exercise of its functions under these Regulations, within such time, in such form, at such intervals and verified in such manner as the designating authority may specify.

(3)   When a designated system amends, revokes or adds to its rules or its guidance, it shall within fourteen days give written notice to the designating authority of the amendment, revocation or addition.

(4)   A designated system shall give the designating authority at least fourteen days' written notice of any proposal to amend, revoke or add to its default arrangements.

(5)   Nothing in this regulation shall require a designated system to give any notice or furnish any information to the Financial Services Authority which it has given or furnished to the Authority pursuant to any requirement imposed by or under [section 293 of the 2000 Act] (notification requirements) or any other enactment.

[3553J]

NOTES
Para (5): words in square brackets substituted by the Financial Services and Markets Act 2000 (Consequential Amendments) Order 2002, SI 2002/1555, art 39(1), (6), as from 3 July 2002.

11 Exemption from liability in damages

(1)   Neither the designating authority nor any person who is, or is acting as, a member, officer or member of staff of the designating authority shall be liable in damages for anything done or omitted in the discharge, or purported discharge, of the designating authority's functions under these Regulations.

(2)   Paragraph (1) does not apply—

    (a)   if the act or omission is shown to have been in bad faith; or

    (b)   so as to prevent an award of damages made in respect of an act or omission on the ground that the act or omission was unlawful as a result of section 6(1) of the Human Rights Act 1998 (acts of public authorities).

[3553K]

12 Publication of information and advice

A designating authority may publish information or give advice, or arrange for the publication of information or the giving of advice, in such form and manner as it considers appropriate with respect to any matter dealt with in these Regulations.

[3553L]

PART III
STATUTORY INSTRUMENTS

PART III
TRANSFER ORDERS EFFECTED THROUGH A DESIGNATED SYSTEM AND COLLATERAL SECURITY

13 Modifications of the law of insolvency

(1)   The general law of insolvency has effect in relation to—
  (a)   transfer orders effected through a designated system and action taken under the rules of a designated system with respect to such orders; and
  (b)   collateral security,

subject to the provisions of this Part.

(2)   Those provisions apply in relation to—
  (a)   insolvency proceedings in respect of a participant in a designated system; and
  (b)   insolvency proceedings in respect of a provider of collateral security in connection with the functions of a central bank, in so far as the proceedings affect the rights of the central bank to the collateral security;

but not in relation to any other insolvency proceedings, notwithstanding that rights or liabilities arising from transfer orders or collateral security fall to be dealt with in the proceedings.

(3)   Subject to regulation 21, nothing in this Part shall have the effect of disapplying Part VII [or Part V].

[3553M]

NOTES

Para (3): words in square brackets added by the Financial Markets and Insolvency (Settlement Finality) (Amendment) Regulations 2006, SI 2006/50, reg 2(1), (5), as from 2 February 2006.

14 Proceedings of designated system take precedence over insolvency proceedings

(1)   None of the following shall be regarded as to any extent invalid at law on the ground of inconsistency with the law relating to the distribution of the assets of a person on bankruptcy, winding up, sequestration or under a protected trust deed, or in the administration of an insolvent estate—
  (a)   a transfer order;
  (b)   the default arrangements of a designated system;
  (c)   the rules of a designated system as to the settlement of transfer orders not dealt with under its default arrangements;
  (d)   a contract for the purpose of realising collateral security in connection with participation in a designated system otherwise than pursuant to its default arrangements; or
  (e)   a contract for the purpose of realising collateral security in connection with the functions of a central bank.

(2)   The powers of a relevant office-holder in his capacity as such, and the powers of the court under the Insolvency Act 1986[, the Insolvency (Northern Ireland) Order 1989] or the Bankruptcy (Scotland) Act 1985, shall not be exercised in such a way as to prevent or interfere with—
  (a)   the settlement in accordance with the rules of a designated system of a transfer order not dealt with under its default arrangements;
  (b)   any action taken under its default arrangements;
  (c)   any action taken to realise collateral security in connection with participation in a designated system otherwise than pursuant to its default arrangements; or
  (d)   any action taken to realise collateral security in connection with the functions of a central bank.

This does not prevent the court from afterwards making any such order or decree as is mentioned in regulation 17(1) or (2).

(3)   Nothing in the following provisions of this Part shall be construed as affecting the generality of the above provisions.

(4)   A debt or other liability arising out of a transfer order which is the subject of action taken under default arrangements may not be proved in a winding up or bankruptcy, or in Scotland claimed in a winding up, sequestration or under a protected trust deed, until the completion of the action taken under default arrangements.

A debt or other liability which by virtue of this paragraph may not be proved or claimed shall not be taken into account for the purposes of any set-off until the completion of the action taken under default arrangements.

(5)   Paragraph (1) has the effect that the following provisions (which relate to preferential debts and the payment of expenses etc) apply subject to paragraph (6), namely—
  (a)   in the case of collateral security provided by a company (within the meaning of section 735 of the Companies Act 1985 [or Article 3 of the Companies (Northern Ireland) Order 1986])—

        (i)   section 175 of the Insolvency Act 1986 [or Article 149 of the Insolvency (Northern Ireland) Order 1989], and

        (ii)   where the company is [in administration], [section 40 (or, in Scotland, section 59 and 60(1)(e)) of the Insolvency Act 1986, paragraph 99(3) of Schedule B1 to that Act] [or paragraph 100(3) of Schedule B1 to, and Article 50 of, the Insolvency (Northern Ireland) Order 1989], and section 196 of the Companies Act 1985 [or Article 205 of the Companies (Northern Ireland) Order 1986]; and

   (b)   in the case of collateral security provided by an individual, section 328(1) and (2) of the Insolvency Act 1986[or, in Northern Ireland, Article 300(1) and (2) of the Insolvency (Northern Ireland) Order 1989] or, in Scotland, in the case of collateral security provided by an individual or a partnership, section 51 of the Bankruptcy (Scotland) Act 1985 and any like provision or rule of law affecting a protected trust deed.

  (6)   The claim of a participant or central bank to collateral security shall be paid in priority to—

   (a)   the expenses of the winding up mentioned in sections 115 and 156 of the Insolvency Act 1986 [or Articles 100 and 134 of the Insolvency (Northern Ireland) Order 1989], the expenses of the bankruptcy within the meaning of that Act [or that Order] or, as the case may be, the remuneration and expenses of the administrator mentioned in [paragraph 99(3) of Schedule B1 to that Act] [or in paragraph 100(3) to Schedule B1 to that Order], and

   (b)   the preferential debts of the company or the individual (as the case may be) within the meaning given by section 386 of that Act [or Article 346 of that Order],

unless the terms on which the collateral security was provided expressly provide that such expenses, remuneration or preferential debts are to have priority.

  (7)   As respects Scotland—

   (a)   the reference in paragraph (6)(a) to the expenses of bankruptcy shall be taken to be a reference to the matters mentioned in paragraphs (a) to (d) of section 51(1) of the Bankruptcy (Scotland) Act 1985, or any like provision or rule of law affecting a protected trust deed; and

   (b)   the reference in paragraph (6)(b) to the preferential debts of the individual shall be taken to be a reference to the preferred debts of the debtor within the meaning of the Bankruptcy (Scotland) Act 1985, or any like definition applying with respect to a protected trust deed by virtue of any provision or rule of law affecting it.

[3553N]

NOTES

Para (2): words in square brackets inserted by the Financial Markets and Insolvency (Settlement Finality) (Amendment) Regulations 2006, SI 2006/50, reg 2(1), (6)(a), as from 2 February 2006.

Para (5): words in first, second, sixth and seventh pairs of square brackets inserted by SI 2006/50, reg 2(1), (6)(b), (c), (e), as from 2 February 2006; words in fifth pair of square brackets originally inserted by SI 2006/50, reg 2(1), (6)(d), as from 2 February 2006, and substituted by the Financial Markets and Insolvency (Settlement Finality) (Amendment) Regulations 2007, SI 2007/832, reg 2(1), (2), as from 6 April 2007; other words in square brackets substituted by the Enterprise Act 2002 (Insolvency) Order 2003, SI 2003/2096, arts 5, 6, Schedule, Pt 2, paras 74, 75, as from 15 September 2003, except in relation to any case where a petition for an administration order was presented before that date.

Para (6): words in first, second, and fifth pairs of square brackets inserted by SI 2006/50, reg 2(1), (6)(f), (g), as from 2 February 2006; words in fourth pair of square brackets originally inserted by SI 2006/50, reg 2(1), (6)(f), as from 2 February 2006, and substituted by SI 2007/832, reg 2(1), (3), as from 6 April 2007; other words in square brackets substituted by SI 2003/2096, arts 5, 6, Schedule, Pt 2, paras 74, 75, as from 15 September 2003, except in relation to any case where a petition for an administration order was presented before that date.

---

15 Net sum payable on completion of action taken under default arrangements

  (1)   The following provisions apply with respect to any sum which is owed on completion of action taken under default arrangements by or to a defaulter but do not apply to any sum which (or to the extent that it) arises from a transfer order which is also a market contract within the meaning of Part VII [or Part V], in which case sections 162 and 163 of the Companies Act 1989 [or Articles 85 and 86 of the Companies (No 2) (Northern Ireland) Order 1990] apply subject to the modification made by regulation 21.

  (2)   If, in England and Wales [or Northern Ireland], a bankruptcy or winding-up order has been made or a creditors' voluntary winding-up resolution has been passed, the debt—

   (a)   is provable in the bankruptcy or winding up or, as the case may be, is payable to the relevant office-holder; and

   (b)   shall be taken into account, where appropriate, under section 323 of the Insolvency Act 1986 [or Article 296 of the Insolvency (Northern Ireland) Order 1989] (mutual dealings and set-off) or the corresponding provision applicable in the case of winding up;

in the same way as a debt due before the commencement of bankruptcy, the date on which the body corporate goes into liquidation (within the meaning of section 247 of the Insolvency Act 1986 [or Article 6 of the Insolvency (Northern Ireland) Order 1989]) or, in the case of a partnership, the date of the winding-up order.

(3)　If, in Scotland, an award of sequestration or a winding-up order has been made, or a creditors' voluntary winding-up resolution has been passed, or a trust deed has been granted and it has become a protected trust deed, the debt—

    (a)　may be claimed in the sequestration or winding up or under the protected trust deed or, as the case may be, is payable to the relevant office-holder; and

    (b)　shall be taken into account for the purposes of any rule of law relating to set-off applicable in sequestration, winding up or in respect of a protected trust deed;

in the same way as a debt due before the date of sequestration (within the meaning of section 73(1) of the Bankruptcy (Scotland) Act 1985) or the commencement of the winding up (within the meaning of section 129 of the Insolvency Act 1986) or the grant of the trust deed.

[3553O]

NOTES

Paras (1), (2): words in square brackets inserted by the Financial Markets and Insolvency (Settlement Finality) (Amendment) Regulations 2006, SI 2006/50, reg 2(1), (7), as from 2 February 2006.

16　Disclaimer of property, rescission of contracts, &c

(1)　Sections 178, 186, 315 and 345 of the Insolvency Act 1986 [or Articles 152, 157, 288 and 318 of the Insolvency (Northern Ireland) Order 1989] (power to disclaim onerous property and court's power to order rescission of contracts, &c) do not apply in relation to—

    (a)　a transfer order; or

    (b)　a contract for the purpose of realising collateral security.

In the application of this paragraph in Scotland, the reference to sections 178, 315 and 345 shall be construed as a reference to any rule of law having the like effect as those sections.

(2)　In Scotland, a permanent trustee on the sequestrated estate of a defaulter or a liquidator or a trustee under a protected trust deed granted by a defaulter is bound by any transfer order given by that defaulter and by any such contract as is mentioned in paragraph (1)(b) notwithstanding section 42 of the Bankruptcy (Scotland) Act 1985 or any rule of law having the like effect applying in liquidations or any like provision or rule of law affecting the protected trust deed.

(3)　Sections 127 and 284 of the Insolvency Act 1986 [or Articles 107 and 257 of the Insolvency (Northern Ireland) Order 1989] (avoidance of property dispositions effected after commencement of winding up or presentation of bankruptcy petition), section 32(8) of the Bankruptcy (Scotland) Act 1985 (effect of dealing with debtor relating to estate vested in permanent trustee) and any like provision or rule of law affecting a protected trust deed, do not apply to—

    (a)　a transfer order, or any disposition of property in pursuance of such an order;

    (b)　the provision of collateral security;

    (c)　a contract for the purpose of realising collateral security or any disposition of property in pursuance of such a contract; or

    (d)　any disposition of property in accordance with the rules of a designated system as to the application of collateral security.

[3553P]

NOTES

Paras (1), (3): words in square brackets inserted by the Financial Markets and Insolvency (Settlement Finality) (Amendment) Regulations 2006, SI 2006/50, reg 2(1), (8), as from 2 February 2006.

17　Adjustment of prior transactions

(1)　No order shall be made in relation to a transaction to which this regulation applies under—

    (a)　section 238 or 339 of the Insolvency Act 1986 [or Article 202 or 312 of the Insolvency (Northern Ireland) Order 1989] (transactions at an undervalue);

    (b)　section 239 or 340 of that Act [or Article 203 or 313 of that Order] (preferences); or

    (c)　section 423 of that Act [or Article 367 of that Order] (transactions defrauding creditors).

(2)　As respects Scotland, no decree shall be granted in relation to any such transaction—

    (a)　under section 34 or 36 of the Bankruptcy (Scotland) Act 1985 or section 242 or 243 of the Insolvency Act 1986 (gratuitous alienations and unfair preferences); or

    (b)　at common law on grounds of gratuitous alienations or fraudulent preferences.

(3)　This regulation applies to—

    (a)　a transfer order, or any disposition of property in pursuance of such an order;

    (b)　the provision of collateral security;

    (c)　a contract for the purpose of realising collateral security or any disposition of property in pursuance of such a contract; or

(d)   any disposition of property in accordance with the rules of a designated system as to the application of collateral security.

[3553Q]

NOTES
Para (1): words in square brackets inserted by the Financial Markets and Insolvency (Settlement Finality) (Amendment) Regulations 2006, SI 2006/50, reg 2(1), (9), as from 2 February 2006.

Collateral security charges

18   Modifications of the law of insolvency

The general law of insolvency has effect in relation to a collateral security charge and the action taken to enforce such a charge, subject to the provisions of regulation 19.

[3553R]

19   Administration orders, &c

(1)   The following provisions of [Schedule B1 to] the Insolvency Act 1986 (which relate to administration orders and administrators) do not apply in relation to a collateral security charge—
[(a)   paragraph 43(2) including that provision as applied by paragraph 44; and
(b)   paragraphs 70, 71 and 72 of that Schedule,]
and [paragraph 41(2) of that Schedule] (receiver to vacate office when so required by administrator) does not apply to a receiver appointed under such a charge.

[(1A)   The following provisions of [Schedule B1 to] the Insolvency (Northern Ireland) Order 1989 (which relate to administration orders and administrators) do not apply in relation to a collateral security charge—
[(a)   paragraph 44(2), including that provision as applied by paragraph 45 (restrictions on enforcement of security where company in administration or where administration application has been made); and
(b)   paragraphs 71, 72 and 73 (charged and hire purchase property);]
and [paragraph 42(2)] (receiver to vacate office when so required by administrator) does not apply to a receiver appointed under such a charge.]

(2)   However, where a collateral security charge falls to be enforced after an administration order has been made or a petition for an administration order has been presented, and there exists another charge over some or all of the same property ranking in priority to or *pari passu* with the collateral security charge, on the application of any person interested, the court may order that there shall be taken after enforcement of the collateral security charge such steps as the court may direct for the purpose of ensuring that the chargee under the other charge is not prejudiced by the enforcement of the collateral security charge.

[(2A)   A reference in paragraph (2) to "an administration order" shall include the appointment of an administrator under paragraph 14 or 22 of Schedule B1 to the Insolvency Act 1986 [or under paragraph 15 or 23 of Schedule B1 to the Insolvency (Northern Ireland) Order 1989].]

(3)   Sections 127 and 284 of the Insolvency Act 1986 [or Articles 107 and 257 of the Insolvency (Northern Ireland) Order 1989] (avoidance of property dispositions effected after commencement of winding up or presentation of bankruptcy petition), section 32(8) of the Bankruptcy (Scotland) Act 1985 (effect of dealing with debtor relating to estate vested in permanent trustee) and any like provision or rule of law affecting a protected trust deed, do not apply to a disposition of property as a result of which the property becomes subject to a collateral security charge or any transactions pursuant to which that disposition is made.

[3553S]

NOTES
Para (1): words in first pair of square brackets inserted, words in third pair of square brackets substituted, and sub-paras (a), (b) substituted, by the Enterprise Act 2002 (Insolvency) Order 2003, SI 2003/2096, arts 5, 6, Schedule, Pt 2, paras 74, 76(a), as from 15 September 2003, except in relation to any case where a petition for an administration order was presented before that date.
Para (1A): inserted by the Financial Markets and Insolvency (Settlement Finality) (Amendment) Regulations 2006, SI 2006/50, reg 2(1), (10)(a), as from 2 February 2006; words in square brackets substituted by the Financial Markets and Insolvency (Settlement Finality) (Amendment) Regulations 2007, SI 2007/832, reg 2(1), (4), as from 6 April 2007.
Para (2A): inserted by SI 2003/2096, arts 5, 6, Schedule, Pt 2, paras 74, 76(b), as from 15 September 2003, except in relation to any case where a petition for an administration order was presented before that date; words in square brackets inserted by SI 2007/832, reg 2(1), (5), as from 6 April 2007.
Para (3): words in square brackets inserted by SI 2006/50, reg 2(1), (10)(b), as from 2 February 2006.

General

20 Transfer order entered into designated system following insolvency

(1)   This Part does not apply in relation to any transfer order given by a participant which is entered into a designated system after—

    (a)   a court has made an order of a type referred to in regulation 22 in respect of that participant, or

    (b)   that participant has passed a creditors' voluntary winding-up resolution, or

    (c)   a trust deed granted by that participant has become a protected trust deed,

unless the conditions mentioned in paragraph (2) are satisfied.

(2)   The conditions referred to in paragraph (1) are that—

    (a)   the transfer order is carried out on the same day that the event specified in paragraph (1)(a), (b) or (c) occurs, and

    (b)   the settlement agent, the central counterparty or the clearing house can show that it did not have notice of that event at the time of settlement of the transfer order.

(3)   For the purposes of paragraph (2)(b), the relevant settlement agent, central counterparty or clearing house shall be taken to have notice of an event specified in paragraph (1)(a), (b) or (c) if it deliberately failed to make enquiries as to that matter in circumstances in which a reasonable and honest person would have done so.

[3553T]

21 Disapplication of certain provisions of Part VII [and Part V]

(1)   The provisions of the Companies Act 1989 [or the Companies (No 2) (Northern Ireland) Order 1990] mentioned in paragraph (2) do not apply in relation to—

    (a)   a market contract which is also a transfer order effected through a designated system; or

    (b)   a market charge which is also a collateral security charge.

(2)   The provisions referred to in paragraph (1) are as follows—

    (a)   section 163(4) to (6) [and Article 86(3) to (5)] (net sum payable on completion of default proceedings);

    (b)   section 164(4) to (6) [and Article 87(3) to (5)] (disclaimer of property, rescission of contracts, &c); and

    (c)   section 175(5) and (6) [and Article 97(5) and (6)] (administration orders, &c).

[3553U]

NOTES

Words in square brackets inserted by the Financial Markets and Insolvency (Settlement Finality) (Amendment) Regulations 2006, SI 2006/50, reg 2(1), (11), as from 2 February 2006.

22 Notification of insolvency order or passing of resolution for creditors' voluntary winding up

(1)   Upon the making of an order for bankruptcy, sequestration, administration or winding up in respect of a participant in a designated system, the court shall forthwith notify both the system and the designating authority that such an order has been made.

(2)   Following receipt of—

    (a)   such notification from the court, or

    (b)   notification from a participant of the passing of a creditors' voluntary winding-up resolution or of a trust deed becoming a protected trust deed, pursuant to paragraph 5(4) of the Schedule,

the designating authority shall forthwith inform the Treasury of the notification.

[3553V]

23 Applicable law relating to securities held as collateral security

Where—

    (a)   securities (including rights in securities) are provided as collateral security to a participant or a central bank (including any nominee, agent or third party acting on behalf of the participant or the central bank), and

    (b)   a register, account or centralised deposit system located in an EEA State legally records the entitlement of that person to the collateral security,

the rights of that person as a holder of collateral security in relation to those securities shall be governed by the law of the EEA State or, where appropriate, the law of the part of the EEA State, where the register, account, or centralised deposit system is located.

[3553W]

24 Applicable law where insolvency proceedings are brought

Where insolvency proceedings are brought in any jurisdiction against a person who participates, or has participated, in a system designated for the purposes of the Settlement Finality Directive, any question relating to the rights and obligations arising from, or in connection with, that participation and falling to be determined by a court in England and Wales[, the High Court in Northern Ireland] or in Scotland shall (subject to regulation 23) be determined in accordance with the law governing that system.

[3553X]

NOTES
Words in square brackets inserted by the Financial Markets and Insolvency (Settlement Finality) (Amendment) Regulations 2006, SI 2006/50, reg 2(1), (12), as from 2 February 2006.

25   Insolvency proceedings in other jurisdictions

(1)   The references to insolvency law in section 426 of the Insolvency Act 1986 (co-operation between courts exercising jurisdiction in relation to insolvency) include, in relation to a part of the United Kingdom, this Part and, in relation to a relevant country or territory within the meaning of that section, so much of the law of that country or territory as corresponds to this Part.

(2)   A court shall not, in pursuance of that section or any other enactment or rule of law, recognise or give effect to—
- (a)   any order of a court exercising jurisdiction in relation to insolvency law in a country or territory outside the United Kingdom, or
- (b)   any act of a person appointed in such a country or territory to discharge any functions under insolvency law,

in so far as the making of the order or the doing of the act would be prohibited in the case of a court in England and Wales or Scotland[, the High Court in Northern Ireland] or a relevant office-holder by this Part.

(3)   Paragraph (2) does not affect the recognition or enforcement of a judgment required to be recognised or enforced under or by virtue of the Civil Jurisdiction and Judgments Act 1982 [or Council Regulation (EC) No 44/2001 of 22nd December 2000 on jurisdiction and the recognition and enforcement of judgments in civil and commercial matters][, as amended from time to time and as applied by the Agreement made on 19th October 2005 between the European Community and the Kingdom of Denmark on jurisdiction and the recognition and enforcement of judgments in civil and commercial matters].

[3553Y]

NOTES
Para (2): words in square brackets inserted by the Financial Markets and Insolvency (Settlement Finality) (Amendment) Regulations 2006, SI 2006/50, reg 2(1), (13), as from 2 February 2006.
Para (3): words in first pair of square brackets added by the Civil Jurisdiction and Judgments Order 2001, SI 2001/3929, art 5, Sch 3, para 27, as from 1 March 2002; words in second pair of square brackets added by the Civil Jurisdiction and Judgments Regulations 2007, SI 2007/1655, reg 5, Schedule, Pt 2, para 32, as from 1 July 2007.

26   Systems designated in other EEA States ... and Gibraltar

(1)   Where an equivalent overseas order or equivalent overseas security is subject to the insolvency law of England and Wales or Scotland [or Northern Ireland], this Part shall apply—
- (a)   in relation to the equivalent overseas order as it applies in relation to a transfer order; and
- (b)   in relation to the equivalent overseas security as it applies in relation to collateral security in connection with a designated system.

(2)   In paragraph (1)—
- (a)   "equivalent overseas order" means an order having the like effect as a transfer order which is effected through a system designated for the purposes of the Settlement Finality Directive in another EEA State ... or Gibraltar; and
- (b)   "equivalent overseas security" means any realisable assets provided under a charge or a repurchase or similar agreement, or otherwise (including money provided under a charge) for the purpose of securing rights and obligations potentially arising in connection with such a system.

[3553Z]

NOTES
Words omitted revoked, and words in square brackets inserted, by the Financial Markets and Insolvency (Settlement Finality) (Amendment) Regulations 2006, SI 2006/50, reg 2(1), (14), as from 2 February 2006.

SCHEDULE
REQUIREMENTS FOR DESIGNATION OF SYSTEM
Regulation 4(1)

1 Establishment, participation and governing law

(1) The head office of at least one of the participants in the system must be in [the United Kingdom] and the law of England and Wales[, Northern Ireland] or Scotland must be the governing law of the system.

(2) There must be not less than three institutions participating in the system, unless otherwise determined by the designating authority in any case where—
  (a) there are two institutions participating in a system; and
  (b) the designating authority considers that designation is required on the grounds of systemic risk.

(3) The system must be a system through which transfer orders are effected.

(4) Where orders relating to financial instruments other than securities are effected through the system—
  (a) the system must primarily be a system through which securities transfer orders are effected; and
  (b) the designating authority must consider that designation is required on grounds of systemic risk.

2 Arrangements and resources

The system must have adequate arrangements and resources for the effective monitoring and enforcement of compliance with its rules or, as respects monitoring, arrangements providing for that function to be performed on its behalf (and without affecting its responsibility) by another body or person who is able and willing to perform it.

3 Financial resources

The system must have financial resources sufficient for the proper performance of its functions as a system.

4 Co-operation with other authorities

The system must be able and willing to co-operate, by the sharing of information and otherwise, with—
  (a) the Financial Services Authority,
  (b) the Bank of England,
  (c) any relevant office-holder, and
  (d) any authority, body or person having responsibility for any matter arising out of, or connected with, the default of a participant.

5 Specific provision in the rules

(1) The rules of the system must—
  (a) specify the point at which a transfer order takes effect as having been entered into the system,
  (b) specify the point after which a transfer order may not be revoked by a participant or any other party, and
  (c) prohibit the revocation by a participant or any other party of a transfer order from the point specified in accordance with paragraph (b).

(2) The rules of the system must require each institution which participates in the system to provide upon payment of a reasonable charge the information mentioned in sub-paragraph (3) to any person who requests it, save where the request is frivolous or vexatious. The rules must require the information to be provided within fourteen days of the request being made.

(3) The information referred to in sub-paragraph (2) is as follows—
  (a) details of the systems which are designated for the purposes of the Settlement Finality Directive in which the institution participates, and
  (b) information about the main rules governing the functioning of those systems.

(4) The rules of the system must require each participant upon—
  (a) the passing of a creditors' voluntary winding up resolution, or
  (b) a trust deed granted by him becoming a protected trust deed,
to notify forthwith both the system and the designating authority that such a resolution has been passed, or, as the case may be, that such a trust deed has become a protected trust deed.

6 Default arrangements

The system must have default arrangements which are appropriate for that system in all the circumstances.

[3553ZA]

NOTES
Para 1: words in first pair of square brackets substituted, and words in second pair of square brackets inserted, by the Financial Markets and Insolvency (Settlement Finality) (Amendment) Regulations 2006, SI 2006/50, reg 2(1), (15), as from 2 February 2006.

LIMITED LIABILITY PARTNERSHIPS (FORMS) REGULATIONS 2001 (NOTE)

(SI 2001/927)

NOTES
Made: 9 March 2001.
Authority: CA 1985, ss 190, 225, 244, 363, 391, 395, 397, 398, 400, 401, 403, 405, 410, 413, 416, 417, 419, 466, 652A, 652D.
Note that ss 190, 225, 244 were repealed by the Companies Act 2006 as from 6 April 2008 though they are specifically saved in relation to their application to LLPs. Section 466 is repealed by the Bankruptcy and Diligence etc (Scotland) Act 2007, s 46(1), as from a day to be appointed. The remaining sections listed above are all repealed by the 2006 Act as from 1 October 2009.
Commencement: 6 April 2001.
These Regulations set out the forms (listed in the first table below) to be used for the purposes of the specified provisions of CA 1985 by limited liability partnerships, with such variations as the circumstances require. The Regulations also provide that the particulars or information contained in the forms listed in the second table below are the particulars or information prescribed for the purposes of the specified provisions of the 1985 Act.
As of 1 February 2009, these Regulations had not been amended.
In these Regulations, references to a section or to a numbered section are to a section of CA 1985 as applied to limited liability partnerships by the Limited Liability Partnerships Regulations 2001, SI 2001/1090, regs 3, 4.

		Limited Liability Partnerships (Forms) Regulations 2001
Form No	*Section*	*Description*
LLP190	190	Location of register of debenture holders of a Limited Liability Partnership
LLP225	225	Change of accounting reference date of a Limited Liability Partnership
LLP244	244	Notice of extension of accounts delivery period of a Limited Liability Partnership
LLP363[1]	363	Annual return of a Limited Liability Partnership
LLP391	391	Notice of removal of auditor from a Limited Liability Partnership
LLP395	395	Particulars of a charge in respect of a Limited Liability Partnership
LLP397	397	Particulars for the registration of a charge to secure a series of debentures in respect of a Limited Liability Partnership
LLP397a	397	Particulars of an issue of secured debentures in a series in respect of a Limited Liability Partnership
LLP398	398	Limited Liability Partnership: Certificate of registration in Scotland or Northern Ireland of a charge comprising property situated there
LLP400	400	Particulars of a mortgage or charge on a property that has been acquired by a Limited Liability Partnership
LLP401	401	Register of charges, memoranda of satisfaction and appointments and cessations of receivers
LLP403a	403	Limited Liability Partnership: Declaration of satisfaction in full or part of mortgage or charge

Limited Liability Partnerships (Forms) Regulations 2001

Form No	Section	Description
LLP403b	403	Declaration that part of the property or undertaking charged (a) has been released from the charge; (b) no longer forms part of the limited liability partnership's property or undertaking
LLP405(1)	405	Notice of appointment of receiver or manager in respect of a Limited Liability Partnership
LLP405(2)	405	Notice of ceasing to act as receiver or manager in respect of a Limited Liability Partnership
LLP410(Scot)	410	Particulars of a charge created by a Limited Liability Partnership registered in Scotland
LLP413(Scot)	413	Particulars for the registration of a charge to secure a series of debentures in respect of a Limited Liability Partnership
LLP413a(Scot)	413	Particulars of an issue of debentures out of a series of secured debentures in respect of a Limited Liability Partnership
LLP416(Scot)	416	Particulars of a charge subject to which property has been acquired by a Limited Liability Partnership registered in Scotland
LLP417(Scot)	417	Register of charges, memoranda of satisfaction and appointments and cessations of receivers
LLP419a(Scot)	419	Limited Liability Partnership: Memorandum of satisfaction in full or part of a registered charge
LLP419b(Scot)	419	Limited Liability Partnership: Memorandum of fact that a part of a property charged (a) has been released from the charge; (b) no longer forms part of the LLP's property
LLP466(Scot)	466	Particulars of an instrument of alteration to a floating charge created by a Limited Liability Partnership registered in Scotland
LLP652a	652A	Application for striking off a Limited Liability Partnership
LLP652c	652D	Withdrawal of application for voluntary strike off a Limited Liability Partnership

Prescribed particulars or information

Form	Section
LLP395	395
LLP397	397
LLP397a	397
LLP400	400
LLP401	401
LLP410 (Scot)	410
LLP413	413
LLP413a	413
LLP416	416
LLP417	417
LLP466	466
LLP652a	652A

NOTES

1   The Limited Liability Partnerships (Forms) Regulations 2002, SI 2002/690 which come into force on 2 April 2002 prescribe a new Form LLP363. The new form is prescribed as an alternative which may be used in any circumstances but which must be used where a member of a limited liability partnership is the beneficiary of a confidentiality order made under CA 1985, s 723B, as applied to limited liability partnerships (see SI 2002/690, *post*).

Wales: the Limited Liability Partnerships (Welsh Language Forms) Regulations 2001, SI 2001/2917 (made under CA 1985, ss 225, 363, 652A, 652D, and in force on 17 September 2001) prescribe forms that correspond to those prescribed by SI 2001/927 and are in Welsh as well as English. See also the Limited Liability Partnerships (Welsh Language Forms) Regulations 2003, SI 2003/61 (details of which are given in the note to SI 2002/690, *post*).

[3553ZB]

LIMITED LIABILITY PARTNERSHIPS REGULATIONS 2001

(SI 2001/1090)

NOTES
Made: 19 March 2001.
Authority: Limited Liability Partnerships Act 2000, ss 14–17.
Commencement: 6 April 2001.
These Regulations are reproduced as amended by: the Financial Services and Markets Act 2000 (Consequential Amendments) Order 2004, SI 2004/355; the Limited Liability Partnerships (Amendment) Regulations 2005, SI 2005/1989; the Civil Partnership Act 2004 (Amendments to Subordinate Legislation) Order 2005, SI 2005/2114; the Companies Act 1985 (Operating and Financial Review) (Repeal) Regulations 2005, SI 2005/3442; the Companies Act 1985 (Small Companies' Accounts and Audit) Regulations 2006, SI 2006/2782; the Limited Liability Partnerships (Amendment) Regulations 2007, SI 2007/2073; the Markets in Financial Instruments Directive (Consequential Amendments) Regulations 2007, SI 2007/2932; the Companies (Late Filing Penalties) and Limited Liability Partnerships (Filing Periods and Late Filing Penalties) Regulations 2008, SI 2008/497; the Limited Liability Partnerships (Accounts and Audit) (Application of Companies Act 2006) Regulations 2008, SI 2008/1911.
Savings for the Companies Act 1985 as applied by these Regulations: nothing in any of the following Orders affects any provision of the Companies Act 1985 as applied by these Regulations; ie, the Companies Act 2006 (Commencement No 1, Transitional Provisions and Savings) Order 2006 (SI 2006/3428), the Companies Act 2006 (Commencement No 2, Consequential Amendments, Transitional Provisions and Savings) Order 2007 (SI 2007/1093), the Companies Act 2006 (Commencement No 3, Consequential Amendments, Transitional Provisions and Savings) Order 2007 (SI 2007/2194), the Companies Act 2006 (Commencement No 5, Transitional Provisions and Savings) Order 2007 (SI 2007/3495), the Companies Act 2006 (Commencement No 6, Saving and Commencement Nos 3 and 5 (Amendment)) Order 2008 (SI 2008/674), the Companies Act 2006 (Commencement No 7, Transitional Provisions and Savings) Order 2008 (SI 2008/1886), and the Companies Act 2006 (Consequential Amendments etc) Order 2008 (SI 2008/948); see art 8 of the fist commencement Order, art 11 of the second commencement Order, art 12 of the third commencement Order, art 12 of the fifth commencement Order, art 6 of the sixth commencement Order, art 7 of the seventh commencement Order, and art 11 of SI 2008/948.
Prospective revocation: as to the prospective revocation of art 4 of these Regulations and specified entries in Sch 2 (as from 1 October 2009), see the Draft Limited Liability Partnerships (Application of Companies Act 2006) Regulations 2009 on the BERR website at: www.berr.gov.uk

ARRANGEMENT OF REGULATIONS

PART I
CITATION, COMMENCEMENT AND INTERPRETATION

PART II
ACCOUNTS AND AUDIT

PART III
COMPANIES ACT 1985 AND COMPANY DIRECTORS
DISQUALIFICATION ACT 1986

PART III
STATUTORY INSTRUMENTS

PART I
CITATION, COMMENCEMENT AND INTERPRETATION

1   Citation and commencement

These Regulations may be cited as the Limited Liability Partnerships Regulations 2001 and shall
come into force on 6th April 2001.

[3554]

2   Interpretation

In these Regulations—
   "the 1985 Act" means the Companies Act 1985;
   "the 1986 Act" means the Insolvency Act 1986;
   "the 2000 Act" means the Financial Services and Markets Act 2000;
   "devolved", in relation to the provisions of the 1986 Act, means the provisions of the 1986 Act
       which are listed in Schedule 4 and, in their application to Scotland, concern wholly or
       partly, matters which are set out in Section C 2 of Schedule 5 to the Scotland Act 1998 as
       being exceptions to the reservations made in that Act in the field of insolvency;
   "limited liability partnership agreement", in relation to a limited liability partnership, means
       any agreement express or implied between the members of the limited liability partnership
       or between the limited liability partnership and the members of the limited liability
       partnership which determines the mutual rights and duties of the members, and their rights
       and duties in relation to the limited liability partnership;
   "the principal Act" means the Limited Liability Partnerships Act 2000; and
   "shadow member", in relation to limited liability partnerships, means a person in accordance
       with whose directions or instructions the members of the limited liability partnership are
       accustomed to act (but so that a person is not deemed a shadow member by reason only that
       the members of the limited partnership act on advice given by him in a professional
       capacity).

[3555]

PART II
ACCOUNTS AND AUDIT

3 Application of the accounts and audit provisions of the 1985 Act to limited liability partnerships

(1) Subject to paragraph (2), the provisions of Part VII of the 1985 Act (*Accounts and Audit*) shall apply to limited liability partnerships.

(2) The enactments referred to in paragraph (1) shall apply to limited liability partnerships, except where the context otherwise requires, with the following modifications—

(a) references to a company shall include references to a limited liability partnership;

(b) references to a director or to an officer of a company shall include references to a member of a limited liability partnership;

(c) references to other provisions of the 1985 Act and to provisions of the Insolvency Act 1986 shall include references to those provisions as they apply to limited liability partnerships in accordance with Parts III and IV of these Regulations;

(d) the modifications set out in Schedule 1 to these Regulations; and

(e) such further modifications as the context requires for the purpose of giving effect to those provisions as applied by this Part of these Regulations.

[3556]

NOTES

Revoked by the Limited Liability Partnerships (Accounts and Audit) (Application of Companies Act 2006) Regulations 2008, SI 2008/1911, reg 58(1)(a), as from 1 October 2008, except in relation to accounts for, and otherwise as regards, financial years beginning before that date (see reg 58(3) at **[4226]**).

PART III
COMPANIES ACT 1985 AND COMPANY DIRECTORS
DISQUALIFICATION ACT 1986

4 Application of the remainder of the provisions of the 1985 Act and of the provisions of the Company Directors Disqualification Act 1986 to limited liability partnerships

(1) The provisions of the 1985 Act specified in the first column of Part I of Schedule 2 to these Regulations shall apply to limited liability partnerships, except where the context otherwise requires, with the following modifications—

(a) references to a company shall include references to a limited liability partnership;

(b) references to the Companies Acts shall include references to the principal Act and regulations made thereunder;

(c) references to the Insolvency Act 1986 shall include references to that Act as it applies to limited liability partnerships by virtue of Part IV of these Regulations;

(d) references in a provision of the 1985 Act to other provisions of that Act shall include references to those other provisions as they apply to limited liability partnerships by virtue of these Regulations;

(e) references to the memorandum of association of a company shall include references to the incorporation document of a limited liability partnership;

(f) references to a shadow director shall include references to a shadow member;

(g) references to a director of a company or to an officer of a company shall include references to a member of a limited liability partnership;

(h) the modifications, if any, specified in the second column of Part I of Schedule 2 opposite the provision specified in the first column; and

(i) such further modifications as the context requires for the purpose of giving effect to that legislation as applied by these Regulations.

(2) The provisions of the Company Director Disqualification Act 1986 shall apply to limited liability partnerships, except where the context otherwise requires, with the following modifications—

(a) references to a company shall include references to a limited liability partnership;

(b) references to the Companies Acts shall include references to the principal Act and regulations made thereunder and references to the companies legislation shall include references to the principal Act, regulations made thereunder and to any enactment applied by regulations to limited liability partnerships;

(d) references to the Insolvency Act 1986 shall include references to that Act as it applies to limited liability partnerships by virtue of Part IV of these Regulations;

(e) references to the memorandum of association of a company shall include references to the incorporation document of a limited liability partnership;

(f) references to a shadow director shall include references to a shadow member;

(g) references to a director of a company or to an officer of a company shall include references to a member of a limited liability partnership;

(h)   the modifications, if any, specified in the second column of Part II of Schedule 2 opposite the provision specified in the first column; and

(i)   such further modifications as the context requires for the purpose of giving effect to that legislation as applied by these Regulations.

[3557]

PART IV
WINDING UP AND INSOLVENCY

5   Application of the 1986 Act to limited liability partnerships

(1)   Subject to paragraphs (2) and (3), the following provisions of the 1986 Act, shall apply to limited liability partnerships—

(a)   Parts I, II, III, IV, VI and VII of the First Group of Parts (company insolvency; companies winding up),

(b)   the Third Group of Parts (miscellaneous matters bearing on both company and individual insolvency; general interpretation; final provisions).

(2)   The provisions of the 1986 Act referred to in paragraph (1) shall apply to limited liability partnerships, except where the context otherwise requires, with the following modifications—

(a)   references to a company shall include references to a limited liability partnership;

(b)   references to a director or to an officer of a company shall include references to a member of a limited liability partnership;

(c)   references to a shadow director shall include references to a shadow member;

(d)   references to the 1985 Act, the Company Directors Disqualification Act 1986, the Companies Act 1989 or to any provisions of those Acts or to any provisions of the 1986 Act shall include references to those Acts or provisions as they apply to limited liability partnerships by virtue of the principal Act;

(e)   references to the memorandum of association of a company and to the articles of association of a company shall include references to the limited liability partnership agreement of a limited liability partnership;

(f)   the modifications set out in Schedule 3 to these Regulations; and

(g)   such further modifications as the context requires for the purpose of giving effect to that legislation as applied by these Regulations.

(3)   In the application of this regulation to Scotland, the provisions of the 1986 Act referred to in paragraph (1) shall not include the provisions listed in Schedule 4 to the extent specified in that Schedule.

[3558]

PART V
FINANCIAL SERVICES AND MARKETS

6   Application of provisions contained in Parts XV and XXIV of the 2000 Act to limited liability partnerships

(1)   Subject to paragraph (2), sections 215(3),(4) and (6), 356, 359(1) to (4), 361 to 365, 367, 370 and 371 of the 2000 Act shall apply to limited liability partnerships.

(2)   The provisions of the 2000 Act referred to in paragraph (1) shall apply to limited liability partnerships, except where the context otherwise requires, with the following modifications—

(a)   references to a company shall include references to a limited liability partnership;

(b)   references to body shall include references to a limited liability partnership; and

(c)   references to the 1985 Act, the 1986 Act or to any of the provisions of those Acts shall include references to those Acts or provisions as they apply to limited liability partnerships by virtue of the principal Act.

[3559]

PART VI
DEFAULT PROVISION

7   Default provision for limited liability partnerships

The mutual rights and duties of the members and the mutual rights and duties of the limited liability partnership and the members shall be determined, subject to the provisions of the general law and to the terms of any limited liability partnership agreement, by the following rules:

(1)   All the members of a limited liability partnership are entitled to share equally in the capital and profits of the limited liability partnership.

(2)   The limited liability partnership must indemnify each member in respect of payments made and personal liabilities incurred by him—

(a)   in the ordinary and proper conduct of the business of the limited liability partnership; or

(b)   in or about anything necessarily done for the preservation of the business or property of the limited liability partnership.

(3)   Every member may take part in the management of the limited liability partnership.

(4)   No member shall be entitled to remuneration for acting in the business or management of the limited liability partnership.

(5)   No person may be introduced as a member or voluntarily assign an interest in a limited liability partnership without the consent of all existing members.

(6)   Any difference arising as to ordinary matters connected with the business of the limited liability partnership may be decided by a majority of the members, but no change may be made in the nature of the business of the limited liability partnership without the consent of all the members.

(7)   The books and records of the limited liability partnership are to be made available for inspection at the registered office of the limited liability partnership or at such other place as the members think fit and every member of the limited liability partnership may when he thinks fit have access to and inspect and copy any of them.

(8)   Each member shall render true accounts and full information of all things affecting the limited liability partnership to any member or his legal representatives.

(9)   If a member, without the consent of the limited liability partnership, carries on any business of the same nature as and competing with the limited liability partnership, he must account for and pay over to the limited liability partnership all profits made by him in that business.

(10)   Every member must account to the limited liability partnership for any benefit derived by him without the consent of the limited liability partnership from any transaction concerning the limited liability partnership, or from any use by him of the property of the limited liability partnership, name or business connection.

[3560]

8 Expulsion

No majority of the members can expel any member unless a power to do so has been conferred by express agreement between the members.

[3561]

PART VII
MISCELLANEOUS

9 General and consequential amendments

(1)   Subject to paragraph (2), the enactments mentioned in Schedule 5 shall have effect subject to the amendments specified in that Schedule.

(2)   In the application of this regulation to Scotland—

(a)   paragraph 15 of Schedule 5 which amends section 110 of the 1986 Act shall not extend to Scotland; and

(b)   paragraph 22 of Schedule 5 which applies to limited liability partnerships the culpable officer provisions in existing primary legislation shall not extend to Scotland insofar as it relates to matters which have not been reserved by Schedule 5 to the Scotland Act 1998.

[3562]

10 Application of subordinate legislation

(1)   The subordinate legislation specified in Schedule 6 shall apply as from time to time in force to limited liability partnerships and—

(a)   in the case of the subordinate legislation listed in Part I of that Schedule with such modifications as the context requires for the purpose of giving effect to the provisions of the Companies Act 1985 which are applied by these Regulations;

(b)   in the case of the subordinate legislation listed in Part II of that Schedule with such modifications as the context requires for the purpose of giving effect to the provisions of the Insolvency Act 1986 which are applied by these Regulations; and

(c)   in the case of the subordinate legislation listed in Part III of that Schedule with such modifications as the context requires for the purpose of giving effect to the provisions of the Business Names Act 1985 and the Company Directors Disqualification Act 1986 which are applied by these Regulations.

(2)   In the case of any conflict between any provision of the subordinate legislation applied by paragraph (1) and any provision of these Regulations, the latter shall prevail.

[3563]

SCHEDULES

SCHEDULE 1
MODIFICATIONS TO PROVISIONS OF PART VII OF THE 1985 ACT APPLIED BY THESE REGULATIONS
Regulation 3

Provision of Part VII	*Modification*
Section 222 (*Where and for how long accounting records to be kept*)	
subsection (5)	In paragraph (*a*), omit the words "*in the case of a private company*," and the word "*and*".
	Omit paragraph (*b*).
Section 224 (*accounting reference periods and accounting reference date*)	
subsections (2) and (3)	*Omit subsections* (2) *and* (3).
subsection (3A)	*Omit the words* "*incorporated on or after 1st April 1996*".
Section 225 (*alteration of accounting reference date*)	
subsection (5)	For the words "*laying and delivering accounts and reports*" substitute "*delivering the accounts and the auditors' report*".
[Section 226 (*duty to prepare individual accounts*).	*Omit subsection* (3).
Section 227 (*duty to prepare group accounts*)	*Omit subsection* (4).]
Section 228 (*exemption for parent companies included in accounts of larger group*)	*Omit subsection* (4).
[Section 228A (*exemption for parent companies included in non-EEA group accounts*)	*Omit subsection* (4).]
Section 231 (*disclosure required in notes to accounts: related undertakings*)	
subsection (3)	*Omit the words from* "*This subsection*" *to the end*.
Section 232 (*disclosure in notes to accounts: emoluments etc of directors and others*)	*Omit section 232, save that Schedule 6 shall apply for the purpose of paragraph 56A of Schedule 4, as inserted by this Schedule.*
Section 233 (*approval and signing of accounts*)	
subsection (1)	For subsection (1) substitute—
	"(1) *A limited liability partnership's annual accounts shall be approved by the members, and shall be signed on behalf of all the members by a designated member.*".
subsection (3)	Omit the words from "*laid before*" to "*otherwise*", and for the words "*the board*" substitute "*the members of the limited liability partnership*".
subsection (4)	For the words "*the board by a director of the company*" substitute "*the members by a designated member*".
subsection (6)	In paragraph (*a*), omit the words "*laid before the company, or otherwise*".

Provision of Part VII	Modification
[Sections 234 to 234ZZB (duty to prepare directors' report)	Omit sections 234 to 234ZZB.
Section 234ZA (statement as to disclosure of information to auditors)	Omit section 234ZA.
Section 234A (approval and signing of directors' report)	Omit section 234A.
…	…
Sections 234B (duty to prepare directors' remuneration report) and 234C (approval and signing of directors' remuneration report)	Omit sections 234B and 234C]
Section 235 (auditors' report)	
subsection (1)	For subsection (1) substitute—
	"(1) The limited liability partnership's annual accounts shall be submitted to its auditors, who shall make a report on them to the members of the limited liability partnership.".
[subsections (3) to (5)]	Omit [subsections (3) to (5)].
Section 236 (signature of auditors' report)	
subsection (2)	For subsection (2) substitute—
	"(2) Every copy of the auditors' report which is circulated, published or issued shall state the names of the auditors.".
subsection (4)	In paragraph (a) omit the words "laid before the company, or otherwise".
Section 237 (duties of auditors)	
subsection (4)	Omit subsection (4).
Section 238 (persons entitled to receive copies of accounts and report)	
subsection (1)	For subsection (1) substitute—
	"(1) A copy of the limited liability partnership's annual accounts, together with a copy of the auditors' report on those accounts, shall be sent to every member of the limited liability partnership and to every holder of the limited liability partnership's debentures, within one month of their being signed in accordance with section 233(1) and in any event not later than 10 months after the end of the relevant accounting reference period."
[subsection (1A)	Omit subsection (1A)(b) to (d).]
subsection (2)	(a) In paragraph (a), omit the words from "who is" to "meetings and", and (b) in paragraph (b) and (c), omit the words "shares or" in both places where they occur.
subsections (3) and (4)	Omit subsections (3) and (4).
subsection (4A)	Omit the words ", of the directors' report".
subsections (4C) to (4E)	Omit subsections (4C) to (4E).
Section 239 (right to demand copies of accounts and report)	
[subsection (1)	(a) Omit paragraphs (b), … and (c), and
	(b) in paragraph (d), omit the words from "and that directors' report" to the end.]

Provision of Part VII	Modification
subsection (2B)	*Omit subsection (2B).*
Section 240 (requirements in connection with publication of accounts)	
subsection (1)	*(a) Omit the words from "or, as the case may be," to the end.*
subsection (3)	*(a) In paragraph (c) omit the words from "and, if no such report has been made", to "any financial year",*
	[(b) omit paragraph (e), and]
	(c) omit the words "or any report made for the purposes of section 249A(2)".
Section 241 (accounts and report to be laid before general meeting)	*Omit section 241.*
[Section 241A (members' approval of directors' remuneration report)	*Omit section 241A.]*
Section 242 (accounts and report to be delivered to registrar)	
[subsection (1)	*(a) For the words "The directors of a company" substitute "The designated members of a limited liability partnership",*
	(b) omit paragraphs (b), … and (c),
	(c) in paragraph (d), omit from "and that directors' report" to the end, and
	(d) for "the directors must annex" substitute "the designated members must annex".]
subsection (2)	*(a) For the words "laying and delivering accounts and reports", substitute "delivering the accounts and the auditors' report", and*
	(b) for the word "director" substitute the words "designated member".
subsection (3)	*For the words "the directors" in each place where they occur substitute the words "the designated members".*
subsection (4)	*For the words "laying and delivering accounts and reports", substitute "delivering the accounts and the auditors' report".*
Section 242A (civil penalty for failure to deliver accounts)	
subsection (1)	*(a) For the words "laying and delivering accounts and reports" substitute "delivering the accounts and the auditors' report", and*
	(b) for the words "the directors" substitute "the designated members".
subsection (2)	*(a) For the words "laying and delivering accounts and reports" substitute "delivering the accounts and the auditors' report",*
	(b) omit the words ", and whether the company is a public or private company,",
	(c) omit the heading "Public company" and all entries under it, and
	(d) for the heading "Private company" substitute "Amount of penalty".
[subsection (2A)	*Omit subsection (2A)]*

Provision of Part VII	Modification
Section 242B (delivery and publications of accounts in euros)	
subsection (2)	For the words "the directors of a company" substitute "the designated members of a limited liability partnership".
...	...
Section 244 (period allowed for delivering accounts and report)	
subsection (1)	For subsection (1), substitute the following—
	"(1) The period allowed for delivering the accounts and the auditors' report is [9 months] after the end of the relevant accounting reference period.
	This is subject to the following provisions of this section."
subsection (2)	[In paragraph (a), for the words "10 months or 7 months, as the case may be" substitute "9 months".]
...	...
subsection (4)	For the words "laying and delivering accounts" substitute "delivering the accounts and the auditors' report".
[Section 245 (voluntary revision of accounts)	
subsection (1)	For subsection (1) substitute—
	"(1) If it appears to the members of a limited liability partnership that any annual accounts did not comply with the requirements of this Act, they may prepare revised accounts.".
subsection (2)	[(a) Omit the words "or report" in both places where they occur, and]
	(b) omit the words "laid before the company in general meeting or".
subsection (3)	Omit the words from "or a revised summary financial statement" to the end.
subsection (4)	[(a) In paragraph (a), omit the words ", statement or report",
	(b) in paragraph (b), omit the words "or reporting accountant" and the words ", statement or report", and
	(c) in paragraph (c)—
	(i) for "where the previous accounts or report" substitute "where the previous accounts",]
	(ii) omit sub-paragraph (ii), and
	(iii) omit the words from ", or where a summary financial statement" to the end.]
[Section 245A (Secretary of State's notice in respect of annual accounts)	
subsection (1)	(a) For paragraphs (a) and (b) substitute—
	"a copy of a limited liability partnership's annual accounts has been delivered to the registrar,", and
	[(b) omit the words "or report".]

Provision of Part VII	Modification
subsection (2)	*[Omit the words "or report" and the words "or a revised report".]*
subsection (3)	*[Omit the words "or report" in both places where they occur.]*
subsection (4)	*[Omit the words "and revised directors' reports" and the words "or reports" in both places where they occur.]]*
[Section 245B (application in respect of defective accounts, reports and reviews)	
subsection (1)	*[Omit the words ", or a directors' report does not comply," and the words "or a revised report".]*
subsection (3)	Omit paragraph (b).
subsection (3A)	Omit subsection (3A).
subsection (4)	*[Omit the words "or report" in each place where they occur and the words "or a revised report".]*
subsection (5)	*[Omit the words "or report" in both places where they occur.]*
subsection (7)	*[Omit the words "and revised directors' reports" and the words "or reports" in both places where they occur.]]*
[Section 245C (other persons authorised to apply to court)	
subsection (1)	*[Omit the words "and directors' reports" in both places where they occur.]]*
Section 246 (special provisions for small companies)	
subsection (3)	Omit paragraph (a), and paragraph (b)(ii), (iii) and (iv).
subsection (4)	Omit subsection (4).
subsection (5)	(a) For the words "the directors of the company" substitute "the designated members of the limited liability partnership", and (b) omit paragraph (b).
subsection (6)	Omit paragraphs (b) and (c).
subsection (8)	Omit paragraph (b) and the words ", in the report" and ", 234A".
Section 246A (special provisions for medium-sized companies)	
[subsection (2A)	Omit subsection (2A).]
subsection (3)	(a) For the words "The company" substitute "The designated members", and (b) for paragraph (a), substitute the following— "(a) which includes a profit and loss account in which the following items listed in the profit and loss account formats set out in Part I of Schedule 4 are combined as one item under the heading "gross profit or loss"— Items 1 to 3 and 6 in Format 1 Items 1 to 5 in Format 2.".
Section 247 (qualification of company as small or medium sized)	

Provision of Part VII	Modification
subsection (5)	In paragraph (a), for the words "items A to D" substitute "items B to D".
[Section 247A (cases in which special provisions do not apply)	
[subsection (1B)	Omit paragraphs (a) and (c), and the words "an authorised insurance company, a banking company," in paragraph (b).
Subsection (1C)	Omit paragraphs (a) and (c).
	In paragraph (b), after "it" insert "is a person (other than a banking limited liability partnership) who".]]
Section 247B (special auditors' report)	
subsection (1)	(a) In paragraph (a), for the words "the directors of a company" substitute "the designated members of a limited liability partnership", and
	(b) in paragraph (b) omit the words "or (2)".
Section 249A (exemptions from audit)	
subsection (2)	Omit subsection (2).
subsection (3A)	Omit subsection (3A).
subsection (4)	Omit subsection (4).
subsection (6)	Omit the words "or gross income".
subsection (6A)	Omit the words "or (2)".
subsection (7)	Omit the words from ", and 'gross income'" to the end.
Section 249AA (dormant companies)	
subsection (1)	For the words section 249B(2) to (5) substitute "section 249B (4) and (5)".
subsection (2)	[In paragraph (a), omit "(1B)(a) or (1C)(a)"].
[subsection (3)	For subsection (3) substitute the following—
	"(3) Subsection (1) does not apply if at any time in the financial year in question the limited liability partnership was an e-money issuer, [a MiFID investment firm] or a UCITS management company."]
subsection (5)	In paragraph (b), omit the words "(6) or".
subsection (6)	Omit subsection (6).
subsection (7)	In paragraph (a), for the words "section 28 (change of name)" substitute "paragraph 5 of the Schedule to the Limited Liability Partnerships Act 2000".
	Omit paragraph (b).
Section 249B (cases where audit exemption not available)	
subsection (1)	[(a) omit the words "or (2)" and paragraphs (a) and (bb), and
	[in paragraph (b), omit the words "an authorised insurance company, a banking company,".].]

Provision of Part VII	*Modification*
subsection (1C)	For paragraph (b), substitute "that the group's aggregate turnover in that year (calculated in accordance with section 249) is not more than £1 million net (or £1.2 million gross),".
subsections (2) and (3)	Omit subsections (2) and (3).
subsection (4)	(a) Omit the words "or (2)" in both places where they occur, and (b) omit paragraph (b).
Sections 249C (the report required for the purposes of section 249A(2)) and 249D (the reporting accountant)	Omit sections 249C and 249D.
Section 249E (effect of exemption from audit)	
subsection (1)	(a) In paragraph (b) omit the words from "or laid" to the end, and
	(b) omit paragraph (c).
subsection (2)	Omit subsection (2).
Section 251 (provision of summary financial statement by listed public companies)	Omit section 251.
Sections 252 and 253 (private company election to dispense with laying of accounts and reports)	Omit section 252 and 253.
Section 254 (exemption for unlimited companies from requirement to deliver accounts and reports)	Omit section 254.
Section 255 (special provisions for banking and insurance companies)	Omit section 255.
Section 255A (special provisions for banking and insurance groups)	Omit section 255A.
Section 255B (modification of disclosure requirements in relation to banking company or group)	Omit section 255B.
Section 255D (power to apply provisions to banking partnerships)	Omit section 255D.
[...	...]
Section 257 (power of Secretary of State to alter accounting requirements)	Omit section 257.
Section 260 (participating interests)	
subsection (6)	For the words from ", Schedule 8A," to "Schedule 9A" substitute the words "and Schedule 8A".
Section 262 (minor definitions)	
subsection (1)	(a) Omit the definitions of "annual report", ["credit institution" and "quoted company"], and
	(b) insert the following [definitions] at the appropriate place—
	[""banking limited liability partnership" means a limited liability partnership which has permission under Part 4 of the Financial Services and Markets Act 2000 to accept deposits (but does not include such a partnership which has permission to accept deposits only for the purpose of carrying on another regulated activity in accordance with that permission);"]

Provision of Part VII	Modification
	""limited liability partnership" means a limited liability partnership formed and registered under the Limited Liability Partnerships Act 2000;".
subsection (2)	Omit subsection (2).
[subsection (3)	Insert the following subsection after subsection (3)—
	"(3A) The definition of banking limited liability partnership in subsection (1) must be read with—
	(a) section 22 of the Financial Services and Markets Act 2000,
	(b) any relevant order under that section, and
	(c) Schedule 2 to that Act.".]
Section 262A (index of defined expressions)	In the index of defined expressions—
	(a) the entries relating to "annual report" "credit institution" ["quoted company"] and "reporting accountant", and all entries relating to sections 255 and 255A and to Schedules 9 and 9A, shall be omitted, and
	(b) the following [entries] shall be inserted at the appropriate place—
	[""banking limited liability partnership" section 262"]
	""limited liability partnership" section 262".
Schedule 4 (form and content of company accounts)	
Paragraph 1	In sub-paragraph (1)(b), for the words "any one of" substitute "either of".
Paragraph 3	In sub-paragraph (2)(b), omit the words "shares or".
	…
Balance Sheet Format 1	Omit the following items and the notes on the balance sheet formats which relate to them—
	(a) item A (called up share capital not paid),
	(b) item B.III.7 (own shares),
	(c) item C.II.5 (called up share capital not paid), and
	(d) item C.III.2 (own shares).
	For item K (capital and reserves) substitute—
	"K. Loans and other debts due to members (12)
	L. Members' other interests
	I Members' capital
	II Revaluation reserve
	III Other reserves."
Balance Sheet Format 2	Omit the following items and the notes on the balance sheet format which relate to them—
	(a) Assets item A (called up share capital not paid),
	(b) Assets item B.III.7 (own shares),
	(c) Assets item C.II.5 (called up share capital not paid), and

PART III
STATUTORY INSTRUMENTS

Provision of Part VII	*Modification*
	(*d*) *Assets item C.III.2 (own shares).*
	For Liabilities item A (capital and reserves) substitute—
	"A. Loans and other debts due to members (12)
	AA. Members' other interests
	I Members' capital
	II Revaluation reserve
	III Other reserves."
Notes on the balance sheet formats	
Note (12)	*Substitute the following as Note (12)—*
	"(12) Loans and other debts due to members (Format 1, item K and Format 2, item A)
	The following amounts shall be shown separately under this item—
	(*a*) *the aggregate amount of money advanced to the limited liability partnership by the members by way of loan,*
	(*b*) *the aggregate amount of money owed to members by the limited liability partnership in respect of profits,*
	(*c*) *any other amounts.*"
Profit and Loss Account Formats	*In Format 1, for item 20 (profit or loss for the financial year) substitute* "20. Profit or loss for the financial year before members' remuneration and profit shares"
	In Format 2, for item 22 (profit or loss for the financial year) substitute "22. Profit or loss for the financial year before members' remuneration and profit shares"
	Omit Profit and Loss Account Formats 3 and 4 and the notes on the profit and loss account formats which relate to them.
Notes on the profit and loss account Formats	
Note (15) (income from other fixed asset investments: other interest receivable and similar income)	*At the end of Note (15) insert the words* "Interest receivable from members shall not be included under this item."
Note (16) (interest payable and similar charges)	*At the end of Note (16) insert* "Interest payable to members shall not be included under this item."
Accounting principles and rules	
Paragraph 12	*In sub-paragraph (b) omit the words* "on behalf of the board of directors".
Paragraph 34	*Omit sub-paragraph (3), (3A) and (3B).*
Notes to the accounts	
[*Paragraph 35A*	*Omit paragraphs (b), (c) and (d).*]
Paragraph 37	*For the words* "38 to 51" *substitute the words* "41 to 51(1)".
Insertion of new paragraph after paragraph 37	*Insert the following new paragraph after paragraph 37—*
	"Loans and other debts due to members
	37A. The following information shall be given—

Provision of Part VII	Modification
	(a) the aggregate amounts of loans and other debts due to members as at the date of the beginning of the financial year,
	(b) the aggregate amounts contributed by members during the financial year,
	(c) the aggregate amounts transferred to or from the profit and loss account during that year,
	(d) the aggregate amounts withdrawn by members or applied on behalf of members during that year,
	(e) the aggregate amount of loans and other debts due to members as at the balance sheet date, and
	(f) the aggregate amount of loans and other debts due to members that fall due after one year.".
Paragraphs 38 to 40	*Omit paragraphs 38 to 40.*
Paragraphs 49 and 51(2)	*Omit paragraphs 49 and 51(2).*
Paragraph 56	*Insert the following paragraph after paragraph 56—*
	"Particulars of members
	56A(1) Particulars shall be given of the average number of members of the limited liability partnership in the financial year, which number shall be determined by dividing the relevant annual number by the number of months in the financial year.
	(2) The relevant annual number shall be determined by ascertaining for each month in the financial year the number of members of the limited liability partnership for all or part of that month, and adding together all the monthly numbers.
	(3) Where the amount of the profit of the limited liability partnership for the financial year before members' remuneration and profit shares exceeds £200,000, there shall be disclosed the amount of profit (including remuneration) which is attributable to the member with the largest entitlement to profit (including remuneration).
	For the purpose of determining the amount to be disclosed, "remuneration" includes any emoluments specified in paragraph 1(1)(a), (c) or (d) of Schedule 6 to this Act which are paid by or receivable from—
	(i) the limited liability partnership; and
	(ii) the limited liability partnership's subsidiary undertakings; and
	(iii) any other person.".
Paragraph 58	*Omit sub-paragraph (3)(c).*
Special provisions where the company is an investment company	
Paragraphs 71 to 73	*Omit paragraphs 71 to 73.*

Provision of Part VII	Modification
Schedule 4A (*form and content of group accounts*)	
Paragraph 1	*Omit sub-paragraph (3).*
Paragraph 10	*Omit sub-paragraph (1)(a) to (c).*
	Omit sub-paragraph (2).
Paragraph 11	*For sub-paragraph (1), substitute—*
	"(1) Where a limited liability partnership adopts the merger method of accounting, it must comply with this paragraph, and with generally accepted accounting principles or practice."
	Omit sub-paragraphs (5) to (7).
Paragraph 17	*(a) In sub-paragraph (2)(a), for the words "item K" substitute "item L",*
	(b) in sub-paragraph (2)(b), for the words "item A" substitute "item AA", and
	(c) In sub-paragraphs (3) and (4), omit paragraphs (c) and (d).
Paragraph 21	*In sub-paragraph (3), omit paragraphs (c) and (d).*
Schedule 5 (*disclosure of information: related undertakings*)	
Paragraph 6	*Omit paragraph 6.*
Paragraph 9A	*Omit paragraph 9A.*
Paragraph 20	*Omit paragraph 20.*
Paragraph 28A	*Omit paragraph 28A.*
Schedule 8 (*form and content of accounts prepared by small companies*)	
Paragraph 1	*In sub-paragraph (1)(b), for the words "any one of" substitute "either of".*
Paragraph 3	*In sub-paragraph (2)(b), omit the words "shares or".*
	...
Balance Sheet Format 1	*Omit item A (called up share capital not paid) and note (1) on the balance sheet format.*
	For item K (capital and reserves) substitute—
	"K. Loans and other debts due to members (9)
	L. Members' other interests
	I Members' capital
	II Revaluation reserve
	III Other reserves".
Balance Sheet Format 2	*Omit Assets item A (called up share capital not paid) and note (1) on the balance sheet format.*
	For Liabilities item A (capital and reserves) substitute—
	"A. Loans and other debts due to members (9)
	AA. Members' other interests
	I Members' capital
	II Revaluation reserve
	III Other reserves".

Provision of Part VII	Modification
Notes on the balance sheet formats	
Note (4) (Others: Other investments)	*Omit Note (4).*
Note (9)	*Substitute the following as Note (9)—*
	"(9) Loans and other debts due to members
	(Format 1, item K and Format 2, item A)
	The following amounts shall be shown separately under this item—
	(a) the aggregate amount of money advanced to the limited liability partnership by the members by way of loan,
	(b) the aggregate amount of money owed to members by the limited liability partnership in respect of profits,
	(c) any other amounts.".
Profit and Loss Account Formats	*In Format 1, for item 20 (profit or loss for the financial year) substitute "20. Profit or loss for the financial year before members' remuneration and profit shares"*
	In Format 2, for item 22 (profit or loss for the financial year) substitute "22. Profit or loss for the financial year before members' remuneration and profit shares"
	Omit Profit and Loss Account Formats 3 and 4 and the notes on the profit and loss account formats which relate to them.
Notes on the profit and loss account formats	
Note (12) (income from other fixed asset investments: other interest receivable and similar income)	*At the end of Note (12) insert the words "Interest receivable from members shall not be included under this item."*
Note (13) (interest payable and similar charges)	*At the end of Note (13) insert "Interest payable to members shall not be included under this item.".*
Accounting principles and rules	
Paragraph 12	*In sub-paragraph (b), omit the words "on behalf of the board of directors".*
Paragraph 34	*Omit sub-paragraphs (3), (4) and (5).*
Notes to the accounts	
[Paragraph 35A	*Omit paragraphs (b), (c) and (d).]*
Paragraph 37	*For the words "Paragraphs 38 to 47" substitute "Paragraphs 40 to 47".*
Insertion of new paragraph after paragraph 37	*Insert the following new paragraph after paragraph 37—*
	"Loans and other debts due to members
	37A. The following information shall be given—
	(a) the aggregate amount of loans and other debts due to members as at the date of the beginning of the financial year,
	(b) the aggregate amounts contributed by members during the financial year,
	(c) the aggregate amounts transferred to or from the profit and loss account during that year,

Provision of Part VII	Modification
	(d) the aggregate amounts withdrawn by members or applied on behalf of members during that year,
	(e) the aggregate amount of loans and other debts due to members as at the balance sheet date, and
	(f) the aggregate amount of loans and other debts due to members that fall due after one year.".
Paragraphs 38 and 39	*Omit paragraphs 38 and 39.*
Paragraph 45	*Omit paragraph 45.*
Paragraph 51	*Omit sub-paragraph (3)(c).*
Schedule 8A *(form and content of abbreviated accounts of small companies delivered to registrar)*	
Balance Sheet Format 1	*Omit item A (called up share capital not paid). For item K (capital and reserves) substitute—*
	"K. Loans and other debts due to members
	L. Members' other interests
	I Members' capital
	II Revaluation reserve
	III Other reserves".
Balance Sheet Format 2	*Omit Assets item A (called up share capital not paid).*
	For Liabilities item A (capital and reserves) substitute—
	"A. Loans and other debts due to members
	AA. Members' other interests
	I Members' capital
	II Revaluation reserve
	III Other reserves".
Notes to the accounts	
Paragraphs 5 and 6	*Omit paragraphs 5 and 6.*
Paragraph 9	*Omit sub-paragraph (3)(c).*

[3564]

NOTES

Revoked by the Limited Liability Partnerships (Accounts and Audit) (Application of Companies Act 2006) Regulations 2008, SI 2008/1911, reg 58(1)(a), as from 1 October 2008, except in relation to accounts for, and otherwise as regards, financial years beginning before that date (see reg 58(3) at **[4226]**).

Entries relating to ss 226, 227 inserted by the Limited Liability Partnerships (Amendment) Regulations 2005, SI 2005/1989, reg 2, Sch 1, paras 1, 2, as from 1 October 2005, in relation to financial years which begin on or after 1 January 2005 and which end on or after 1 October 2005.

Entry relating to s 228A inserted by SI 2005/1989, reg 2, Sch 1, paras 1, 3, as from 1 October 2005, in relation to financial years which begin on or after 1 January 2005 and which end on or after 1 October 2005.

Entries relating to ss 234–234ZZB, 234ZA, 234A, 234AA, 234AB, 234B, 234C substituted (for original entries relating to ss 234, 234A) by SI 2005/1989, reg 2, Sch 1, paras 1, 4, as from 1 October 2005, in relation to financial years which begin on or after 1 January 2005 and which end on or after 1 October 2005.

Entries relating to ss 234AA, 234AB revoked by the Companies Act 1985 (Operating and Financial Review) (Repeal) Regulations 2005, SI 2005/3442, reg 2(2)(b), Sch 2, para 3(1), (2), as from 12 January 2006.

In entry relating to s 235 words in square brackets substituted by SI 2005/1989, reg 2, Sch 1, paras 1, 5, as from 1 October 2005, in relation to financial years which begin on or after 1 January 2005 and which end on or after 1 October 2005.

Entry relating to s 238(1A) inserted by SI 2005/1989, reg 2, Sch 1, paras 1, 6, as from 1 October 2005, in relation to financial years which begin on or after 1 January 2005 and which end on or after 1 October 2005.

Entry relating to s 239(1) substituted by SI 2005/1989, reg 2, Sch 1, paras 1, 7, as from 1 October 2005, in relation to financial years which begin on or after 1 January 2005 and which end on or after 1 October 2005.

Word omitted from entry relating to s 239(1) revoked by SI 2005/3442, reg 2(2)(b), Sch 2, para 3(1), (3), as from 12 January 2006.

In entry relating to s 240(3), para (b) substituted by SI 2005/1989, reg 2, Sch 1, paras 1, 8, as from 1 October 2005, in relation to financial years which begin on or after 1 January 2005 and which end on or after 1 October 2005.

Entry relating to s 241A inserted by SI 2005/1989, reg 2, Sch 1, paras 1, 9, as from 1 October 2005, in relation to financial years which begin on or after 1 January 2005 and which end on or after 1 October 2005.

Entry relating to 242(1) substituted by SI 2005/1989, reg 2, Sch 1, paras 1, 10, as from 1 October 2005, in relation to financial years which begin on or after 1 January 2005 and which end on or after 1 October 2005.

Word omitted from entry relating to s 242(1) revoked by SI 2005/3442, reg 2(2)(b), Sch 2, para 3(1), (3), as from 12 January 2006.

Words in square brackets in entry relating to s 242A inserted by the Companies (Late Filing Penalties) and Limited Liability Partnerships (Filing Periods and Late Filing Penalties) Regulations 2008, SI 2008/497, reg 6, Schedule, Pt 2, para 1, as from 6 April 2008, in relation to accounts and auditors' reports for financial years beginning on or after that date.

Entry relating to s 243 revoked by SI 2005/1989, reg 2, Sch 1, paras 1, 11, as from 1 October 2005, in relation to financial years which begin on or after 1 January 2005 and which end on or after 1 October 2005.

In the entry relating to s 244(1) words in square brackets substituted (for the original words "10 months") by SI 2008/497, reg 6, Schedule, Pt 2, para 2, as from 6 April 2008, in relation to accounts and auditors' reports for financial years beginning on or after that date.

In the entry relating to s 244(2) words in square brackets substituted (for the original words "In paragraph (a), omit the words "or 7 months, as the case may be,"") by SI 2008/497, reg 6, Schedule, Pt 2, para 3, as from 6 April 2008, in relation to accounts and auditors' reports for financial years beginning on or after that date.

Entry relating to s 244(3) revoked by SI 2005/1989, reg 2, Sch 1, paras 1, 12, as from 1 October 2005, in relation to financial years which begin on or after 1 January 2005 and which end on or after 1 October 2005.

Entry relating to s 245 substituted by SI 2005/1989, reg 2, Sch 1, paras 1, 13, as from 1 October 2005, in relation to financial years which begin on or after 1 January 2005 and which end on or after 1 October 2005.

Words in square brackets in entry relating to s 245 substituted by SI 2005/3442, reg 2(2)(b), Sch 2, para 3(1), (4), as from 12 January 2006.

Entries relating to ss 245A, 245B substituted by SI 2005/1989, reg 2, Sch 1, paras 1, 14, 15, as from 1 October 2005, in relation to financial years which begin on or after 1 January 2005 and which end on or after 1 October 2005.

Words in square brackets in entries relating to ss 245A, 245B substituted by SI 2005/3442, reg 2(2)(b), Sch 2, para 3(1), (5), (6), as from 12 January 2006.

Entry relating to s 245C inserted by SI 2005/1989, reg 2, Sch 1, paras 1, 16, as from 1 October 2005, in relation to financial years which begin on or after 1 January 2005 and which end on or after 1 October 2005.

Words in square brackets in entry relating to s 245C(1) substituted by SI 2005/3442, reg 2(2)(b), Sch 2, para 3(1), (5), (7), as from 12 January 2006.

Entry relating to s 246A(2A) inserted by SI 2005/1989, reg 2, Sch 1, paras 1, 17, as from 1 October 2005, in relation to financial years which begin on or after 1 January 2005 and which end on or after 1 October 2005.

Entry relating to s 247A substituted by SI 2005/1989, reg 2, Sch 1, paras 1, 18, as from 1 October 2005, in relation to financial years which begin on or after 1 January 2005 and which end on or after 1 October 2005; words in square brackets substituted by the Companies Act 1985 (Small Companies' Accounts and Audit) Regulations 2006, SI 2006/2782, reg 7(1), (2), as from 8 November 2006, in relation to annual accounts and reports in respect of financial years ending on or after 31 December 2006.

In entry relating to s 249AA words in square brackets in entry relating to subsection (2) substituted, and whole of entry relating to subsection (3) substituted, by SI 2006/2782, reg 6(1), (3), as from 8 November 2006, in relation to annual accounts and reports in respect of financial years ending on or after 31 December 2006; words in square brackets in the entry relating to subsection (3) substituted (for the original words "an ISD investment firm") by the Markets in Financial Instruments Directive (Consequential Amendments) Regulations 2007, SI 2007/2932, reg 5, in relation to financial years ending on or after 1 November 2007 (for transitional provisions see the note below).

In entry relating to s 249B words in first (outer) pair of square brackets substituted by SI 2004/355, art 8(1), (4), as from 4 March 2004; words in second (inner) pair of square brackets substituted by SI 2006/2782, reg 6(1), (4), as from 8 November 2006, in relation to annual accounts and reports in respect of financial years ending on or after 31 December 2006.

Entry relating to s 256A inserted by SI 2005/1989, reg 2, Sch 1, paras 1, 19, as from 1 October 2005, in relation to financial years which begin on or after 1 January 2005 and which end on or after 1 October 2005; revoked by SI 2005/3442, reg 2(2)(b), Sch 2, para 3(1), (2), as from 12 January 2006.

In entry relating to s 262 words ""credit institution" and "quoted company"" in square brackets substituted by SI 2005/1989, reg 2, Sch 1, paras 1, 20, as from 1 October 2005, in relation to financial years which begin on or after 1 January 2005 and which end on or after 1 October 2005; other words in square brackets substituted or inserted by SI 2004/355, art 8(1), (5), as from 4 March 2004.

In entry relating to s 262A(1) words ""quoted company"" in square brackets inserted by SI 2005/1989, reg 2, Sch 1, paras 1, 21, as from 1 October 2005, in relation to financial years which begin on or after 1 January 2005 and which end on or after 1 October 2005; other words in square brackets substituted or inserted by SI 2004/355, art 8(1), (6), as from 4 March 2004.

In entry relating to Sch 4, para 3 words omitted revoked by SI 2005/1989, reg 2, Sch 1, paras 1, 22, as from 1 October 2005, in relation to financial years which begin on or after 1 January 2005 and which end on or after 1 October 2005.

Entry relating to Sch 4, para 35A inserted by SI 2005/1989, reg 2, Sch 1, paras 1, 23, as from 1 October 2005, in relation to financial years which begin on or after 1 January 2005 and which end on or after 1 October 2005.

In entry relating to Sch 8, para 3 words omitted revoked by SI 2005/1989, reg 2, Sch 1, paras 1, 24, as from 1 October 2005, in relation to financial years which begin on or after 1 January 2005 and which end on or after 1 October 2005.

Entry relating to Sch 8, para 35A inserted by SI 2005/1989, reg 2, Sch 1, paras 1, 25, as from 1 October 2005, in relation to financial years which begin on or after 1 January 2005 and which end on or after 1 October 2005.

Transitional provisions: the Markets in Financial Instruments Directive (Consequential Amendments) Regulations 2007, SI 2007/2932, reg 8 provides as follows—

"8 Transitional provision: accounting and audit requirements

(1) This regulation has effect for a financial year ("the transitional financial year") beginning before, but ending on or after, 1st November 2007.

(2) In the enactments amended by regulations 2, 4, 5 and 7 the references to a "MiFID investment firm" do not include a person who satisfies conditions A and B.

(3) Condition A is satisfied if, at any time that is within the transitional financial year and is before 1st November 2007, the person would have been a MiFID investment firm if Directive 2004/39/EC of the European Parliament and of the Council of 21 April 2004 on markets in financial instruments had had effect at that time.

(4) In paragraph (3), "MiFID investment firm" has the same meaning as in section 262 of the Companies Act 1985 (as it has effect on 1st November 2007, disregarding this regulation).

(5) Condition B is satisfied if the person—
  (a) was not, at any time that is within the transitional financial year and is before 1st November 2007, an ISD investment firm within the meaning of section 262 of the Companies Act 1985 (as it had effect at that time), and
  (b) would not, at any time that is within the transitional financial year and is on or after 1st November 2007, have been such a firm if that section and Council Directive 93/22/EC of 10 May 1993 on investment services in the securities field had had effect at that time as they had effect immediately before 1st November 2007.".

SCHEDULE 2

PART I
MODIFICATIONS TO PROVISIONS OF THE 1985 ACT APPLIED TO LIMITED LIABILITY PARTNERSHIPS

Regulation 4

Provisions	Modification
Formalities of Carrying on Business	
24 (minimum membership for carrying on business)	In the first paragraph omit the words ", other than a private company limited by shares or by guarantee,".
36 (company contracts England and Wales)	
36A (execution of documents England and Wales)	In subsection (4) for "a director and the secretary of a company, or by two directors of a company," substitute "two members of a limited liability partnership".
	In subsection (6) for "a director and the secretary of a company, or by two directors of the company" substitute "two members of a limited liability partnership".
36C (pre-incorporation contracts, deeds and obligations)	
37 (bills of exchange and promissory notes)	
38 (execution of deeds abroad)	
39 (power of company to have official seal for use abroad)	In subsection (1), omit the words "whose objects require or comprise the transaction of business in foreign countries may, if authorised by its articles" and before the word "have" insert the word "may".
41 (authentication of documents)	For "director, secretary or other authorised officer" substitute "member".
42 (events affecting a company's status)	
subsection (1)	In subsection (1), for "other persons" substitute "persons other than members of the limited liability partnership".
subsection (1)(b)	In subsection (1)(b) omit the words "or articles".

Provisions	Modification
subsection (1)(c)	Omit subsection (1)(c).

Miscellaneous provisions about shares and debentures

183 (transfer and registration)

subsection (1)	Subsection (1), omit the words "shares in or".
	For the words "company's articles" substitute "limited liability partnership agreement.".
subsection (2)	Subsection (2), omit the words "shareholder or" together with the words "shares in or".
subsection (3)	Omit subsection (3).
subsection (4)	Omit subsection (4).
subsection (5)	Omit the words "shares or".

184 (certification of transfers)

subsection (1)	Subsection (1), omit the words "shares in or" together with the words "shares or".

185 (duty of company as to issue of certificates)

subsection (1)	Subsection (1), omit the words "shares," in each of the four places that it occurs.
subsection (3)	Omit subsection (3).
subsection (4)	Omit the words "shares or" together with the words "shares,".

Debentures

190 (register of debenture holders)

191 (right to inspect register)

subsection (1)	In subsection (1), paragraph (a), for the words "or any holder of shares in the company" substitute "or any member of the limited liability partnership".
subsection (2)	In subsection (2), delete "or holder of shares".
subsection (6)	In subsection (6), delete the words "in the articles or".

192 (liability of trustees of debentures)

193 (perpetual debentures)

194 (power to re-issue redeemed debentures)

subsection (1)(a)	In subsection (1)(a), omit the words "in the articles or".
subsection (1)(b)	In subsection (1)(b), for "passing a resolution" substitute "making a determination".

195 (contract to subscribe for debentures)

196 (payment of debts out of assets subject to floating charge (England and Wales))

Officers and registered office

287 (registered office)   For section 287 there shall be substituted—

Provisions	Modification
	"(1) The change of registered office takes effect upon the notice of change of registered office (delivered to the registrar in accordance with paragraph 10 of the Schedule to the Limited Liability Partnerships Act 2000), being registered by the registrar, but until the end of the period of 14 days beginning with the date on which it is registered a person may validly serve any document on the limited liability partnership at its previous registered office.
	(2) Where a limited liability partnership unavoidably ceases to perform at its registered office any duty to keep at its registered office any register, index or other document or to mention the address of its registered office in any document in circumstances in which it was not practicable to give prior notice to the registrar of a change in the situation of the registered office, but—
	(a) resumes performance of that duty at other premises as soon as practicable, and
	(b) gives notice accordingly to the registrar of a change in the situation of its registered office within 14 days of doing so it shall not be treated as having failed to comply with that duty".
288 (register of directors and secretaries)	For section 288 there shall be substituted—
	"Where a person becomes a member or designated member of a limited liability partnership the notice to be delivered to the registrar under section 9(1)(a) of the Limited Liability Partnerships Act 2000 shall contain the following particulars with respect to that person—
	(1) name, which
	(a) in the case of an individual means his forename and surname (or, in the case of a peer or other person usually known by a title, his title instead of or in addition to either or both his forename and surname), and
	(b) if a corporation or a Scottish firm, its corporate or firm name; and
	(2) address, which—
	(a) in the case of an individual means his usual residential address; and
	(b) if a corporation or a Scottish firm, its registered or principal office; and
	(3) in the case of an individual, the date of his birth."

Company Identification

348 (company name to appear outside place of business)	
349 (company's name to appear in its correspondence)	
350 (company seal)	

Provisions	Modification
351 (particulars in correspondence etc)	In subsection (1) for paragraph (c) substitute the words "in the case of a limited liability partnership, whose name ends with the abbreviation "llp", "LLP", "pac" or "PAC", the fact that it is a limited liability partnership or a partneriaeth atebolrwydd cyfyngedig."
	Also in subsection (1) delete paragraph (d) and delete subsection (2).

Annual Return

Provisions	Modification
363 (duty to deliver annual returns)	Section 363 of the 1985 Act shall apply to a limited liability partnership being modified so as to read as follows—
	"(1) Every limited liability partnership shall deliver to the registrar successive annual returns each of which is made up to a date not later than the date which is from time to time the "return date" of the limited liability partnership, that is—
	(a) the anniversary of the incorporation of the limited liability partnership, or
	(b) if the last return delivered by the limited liability partnership in accordance with this section was made up to a different date, the anniversary of that date.
	(2) Each return shall—
	(a) be in a form approved by the registrar,
	(b) contain the information required by section 364, and
	(c) be signed by a designated member of the limited liability partnership.
	(3) If a limited liability partnership fails to deliver an annual return in accordance with this section before the end of the period of 28 days after the return date, the limited liability partnership is guilty of an offence and liable on summary conviction to a fine not exceeding level 5 on the standard scale. The contravention continues until such time as an annual return made up to that return date and complying with the requirements of subsection (2) (except as to date of delivery) is delivered by the limited liability partnership to the registrar.
	(4) Where a limited liability partnership is guilty of an offence under subsection (3) every designated member of the limited liability partnership is similarly liable unless he shows that he took all reasonable steps to avoid the commission of or the continuance of the offence."
364 (contents of annual return: general)	For section 364 substitute the following—
	"Every annual return shall state the date to which it is made up and shall contain the following information—
	(a) the address of the registered office of the limited liability partnership,

Provisions	Modification
	(b) the names and usual residential addresses of the members of the limited liability partnership and, if some only of them are designated members, which of them are designated members, and
	(c) if any register of debenture holders (or a duplicate of any such register or a part of it) is not kept at the registered office of the limited liability partnership, the address of the place where it is kept."

Auditors

Provisions	Modification
384 *(duty to appoint auditors)*	
subsection (2)	*In subsection (2), for the words from "(appointment at general meeting at which accounts are laid)" to the end substitute the words "(appointment of auditors)".*
subsection (3)	*In subsection (3), omit the words from "or 385A(2)" to the end.*
subsection (4)	*For subsection (4) substitute the following subsection—*
	"(4) A person is eligible for appointment by a limited liability partnership as auditor only if, were the limited liability partnership a company, he would be eligible under Part II of the Companies Act 1989 for appointment as a "company auditor"."
subsection (5)	*Insert a new subsection (5)—*
	"(5) Part II of the Companies Act 1989 shall apply in respect of auditors of limited liability partnerships as if the limited liability partnerships were companies formed and registered under this Act, and references in Part II to an officer of a company shall include reference to a member of a limited liability partnership."
385 *(appointment at general meeting at which accounts laid)*	
title to the section	*In the title to the section for the existing wording substitute "Appointment of auditors".*
subsection (1)	*Omit subsection (1).*
subsection (2)	*For subsection (2) substitute—*
	"(2) The designated members of a limited liability partnership shall appoint the auditors for the first financial year in respect of which auditors are appointed before the end of that financial year and thereafter before the expiration of not more than two months following the approval of the accounts for the preceding financial year in accordance with section 233.".
subsection (3)	*For subsection (3) substitute—*
	"(3) The auditor of a limited liability partnership shall hold office until not later than the expiration of two months following the approval in accordance with section 233 of the accounts for the financial year in respect of which the auditor was appointed."

Provisions	Modification
subsection (4)	*For subsection (4) substitute—*
	"(4) If the designated members fail to exercise their powers under subsection (2), the powers may be exercised by the members of the limited liability partnership in a meeting convened for the purpose".
387 *(appointment by Secretary of State in default of appointment by company)*	
subsection (1)	*In subsection (1), omit the words "re-appointed or deemed to be re-appointed".*
subsection (2)	*In subsection (2), for the word "officer" substitute the words "designated member".*
388 *(filling of casual vacancies)*	
subsection (1)	*In subsection (1), for "directors, or the company in general meeting," substitute "designated members".*
subsection (3)	*Omit subsection (3).*
subsection (4)	*Omit subsection (4).*
388A *(certain companies exempt from obligation to appoint auditors)*	
subsection (3)	*For subsection (3) substitute—*
	"(3) The designated members may appoint auditors and the auditors so appointed shall hold office until the expiration of two months following the approval in accordance with section 233 of the accounts for the financial year in respect of which the auditor was appointed."
subsection (4)	*Omit subsection (4).*
subsection (5)	*For subsection (5) substitute—*
	"(5) If the designated members fail to exercise their powers under subsection (3), the powers may be exercised by the members of the limited liability partnership in a meeting convened for the purpose."
389A *(rights to information)*	
390 *(right to attend company meetings)*	
subsection (1)	*In paragraph (a), (b) and (c) of subsection (1) omit the word "general" in each place where it occurs.*
	At the end of paragraph (a) add the words "and where any part of the business of the meeting concerns them as auditors."
	At the end of paragraph (b) add the words "where any part of the business of the meeting concerns them as auditors."
subsection (1A)	*Omit subsection (1A).*
subsection (2)	*Omit subsection (2).*
390A *(remuneration of auditors)*	
subsection (1)	*For subsection (1) substitute—*

Provisions	Modification
	"The remuneration of auditors appointed by the limited liability partnership shall be fixed by the designated members or in such manner as the members of the limited liability partnership may determine".
subsection (2)	*In subsection (2), omit the words "directors or the", in both places where they occur, and omit the words "as the case may be".*
390B (remuneration of auditors or their associates for non-audit work)	
391 (removal of auditors)	
subsection (1)	*In subsection (1), for the words "A company may by ordinary resolution" substitute "The designated members of a limited liability partnership may" and for the words "between it and" substitute "with".*
subsection (2)	*(a) In subsection (2), for the words "a resolution removing an auditor is passed at a general meeting of a company, the company" substitute the words "the designated members of the limited liability partnership have made a determination to remove an auditor, the designated members".*
	(b) For the words "every officer of it who is in default" substitute "every designated member of it who is in default".
subsection (4)	*In subsection (4), omit the word "general".*
391A (rights of auditors who are removed or not re-appointed)	
subsection (1)	*For subsection (1) substitute—*
	"The designated members shall give seven days' prior written notice to
	(a) any auditor whom it is proposed to remove before the expiration of his term of office; or
	(b) a retiring auditor where it is proposed to appoint as auditor a person other than the retiring auditor."
subsection (2)	*Omit subsection (2).*
subsection (3)	*In subsection (3), for the words "intended resolution" substitute the word "proposal" and omit the words "of the company".*
subsection (4)	*Omit the words "(unless the representations are received by it too late for it to do so)".*
	Omit subsection (4)(a).
	In subsection (4)(b), for the words "of the company to whom notice in writing of the meeting is or has been sent." Substitute "within twenty one days of receipt.".
subsection (5)	*For subsection (5) substitute—*

Provisions	Modification
	"If a copy of the representations is not sent out as required by subsection (4), then unless subsection (6) applies, the limited liability partnership and any designated member in default commits an offence. A person guilty of an offence under this section is liable on summary conviction to a fine not exceeding level 3 on the standard scale."
subsection (6)	*In subsection (6), the words "and the representations need not be read at the meeting" shall be omitted.*
392 (*resignation of auditors*)	
subsection (3)	*In the second paragraph of subsection (3) for "and every officer of it who is in default" substitute "and every designated member of it who is in default".*
392A (*rights of resigning auditors*)	
subsection (2)	*In subsection (2), for "directors" substitute "designated members" and for "an extraordinary general meeting of the company" substitute "a meeting of the members of the limited liability partnership".*
subsection (3)	*In subsection (3), omit ", or" from paragraph (a) and omit paragraph (b).*
subsection (5)	*In subsection (5), for "directors" substitute "designated members" and for "director" substitute "designated member".*
subsection (8)	*In subsection (8), omit the word "general" and the phrase "(a) or (b)".*
394 (*statement by person ceasing to hold office as auditor*)	
394A (*offences of failing to comply with section 394*)	

Registration of charges

The following references are to sections of the 1985 Act which were replaced by section 92 of the Companies Act 1989. They will apply to limited liability partnerships until the said section 92 is commenced.

395 (certain charges void if not registered)	
396 (charges which have to be registered)	In subsection (1) delete paragraphs (b) and (g).
397 (formalities of registration (debentures))	In subsection (1), paragraph (b) for the word "resolutions" substitute "determinations of the limited liability partnership".
398 (verification of charge on property outside United Kingdom)	
399 (company's duty to register charges it creates)	
400 (charges existing on property acquired)	
401 (register of charges to be kept by registrar of companies)	
402 (endorsement of certificate on debentures)	
403 (entries of satisfaction and release)	In subsection (1A), after "of the company" insert "or designated member, administrator or administrative receiver of the limited liability partnership".

Provisions	Modification
404 (rectification of register of charges)	In subsection (1), omit the words "or shareholders".
405 (registration of enforcement of security)	
406 (companies to keep copies of instruments creating charges)	
407 (company's register of charges)	In subsection (1), for "limited company" substitute "company (including limited liability partnership)".
408 (right to inspect instruments which create charges etc)	In subsection (1) delete "in general meeting".
410 (charges void unless registered)	In subsection (4) delete paragraph (b) and sub-paragraph (ii) of paragraph (c). In subsection (5) for "an incorporated company" substitute "a limited liability partnership".
411 (charges on property outside the United Kingdom)	
412 (negotiable instrument to secure book debts)	
413 (charges associated with debentures)	In subsection (2)(b), for the word "resolutions" substitute "determinations of the limited liability partnership".
414 (charge by way of ex facie absolute disposition, etc)	
415 (company's duty to register charges created by it)	
416 (duty to register charges existing on property acquired)	
417 (register of charges to be kept by registrar of companies)	
418 (certificate of registration to be issued)	
419 (entries of satisfaction and relief)	In subsection (1A), after the words "of the company" insert "or a designated member, liquidator, receiver or administrative receiver of the limited liability partnership".
420 (rectification of the register)	Omit the words "or shareholders".
421 (copies of instruments creating charges to be kept by the company)	
422 (company's register of charges)	
423 (right to inspect copies of instruments, and the company's register)	In subsection (1) delete "in general meeting".

Arrangements and Reconstructions

425 (power of company to compromise with creditors and members)	
subsection (3)	Omit the words "and a copy of every such order shall be annexed to every copy of the company's memorandum issued after the order has been made or, in the case of a company not having a memorandum, of every copy so issued of the instrument constituting the company or defining its constitution." For the semi-colon after the word "registration" substitute a full stop.
subsection (6)	Omit subsection (6).

Provisions	Modification
426 (information as to compromise to be circulated)	
subsection (2)	Omit the words "as directors or".
427 (provisions for facilitating company reconstruction or amalgamation)	
subsection (3)	In paragraph (b) for the words "policies or other like interests" substitute "policies, other like interests or, in the case of a limited liability partnership, property or interests in the limited liability partnership".
subsection (6)	For the words ""company" includes only accompany as defined in section 735(1)" substitute ""company" includes only a company as defined in section 735(1) or a limited liability partnership".

Investigation of companies and their affairs: Requisition of documents

Provisions	Modification
431 (investigation of a company on its own application or that of its members)	For subsection (2) substitute the following— "(2) The appointment may be made on the application of the limited liability partnership or on the application of not less than one-fifth in number of those who appear from notifications made to the registrar of companies to be currently members of the limited liability partnership."
432 (other company investigations)	
subsection (4)	For the words "but to whom shares in the company have been transferred or transmitted by operation of law" substitute "but to whom a member's share in the limited liability partnership has been transferred or transmitted by operation of law."
433 (inspectors' powers during investigation)	
434 (production of documents and evidence to inspectors)	
436 (obstruction of inspectors treated as contempt of court)	
437 (inspectors' reports)	
438 (power to bring civil proceedings on company's behalf)	
439 (expenses of investigating a company's affairs)	
subsection (5)	Omit paragraph (b) together with the word "or" at the end of paragraph (a).
441 (inspectors' report to be evidence)	
447 (Secretary of State's power to require production of documents)	
[447A (information provided: evidence)]	
448 (entry and search of premises)	
[448A (protection in relation to certain disclosures: information provided to Secretary of State)]	
449 (provision for security of information obtained)	

Provisions	Modification
450 (punishment for destroying, mutilating etc company documents)	[Omit subsection (1A).]
451 (punishment for furnishing false information)	
451A (disclosure of information by Secretary of State or inspector)	In subsection (1), for the words "sections 434 to 446" substitute "sections 434 to 441".
	Omit subsection (5).
452 (privileged information)	In subsection (1), for the words "sections 431 to 446" substitute "sections 431 to 441".
	In subsection (1A), for the words "sections 434, 443 or 446" substitute "section 434".
[453A (power to enter and remain on premises)	In subsection (7), for the words "section 431, 432 or 442" substitute "section 431 or 432.
453B (power to enter and remain on premises: procedural)	
453C (failure to comply with certain requirements)]	

Fraudulent Trading

458 (punishment for fraudulent trading)	

Protection of company's members against unfair prejudice

459 (order on application of company member)	At the beginning of subsection (1), insert the words "Subject to subsection (1A),". After subsection (1) insert as subsection (1A)—
	"The members of a limited liability partnership may by unanimous agreement exclude the right contained in subsection 459(1) for such period as shall be agreed. The agreement referred to in this subsection shall be recorded in writing."
	Omit subsections (2) and (3).
460 (order on application of Secretary of State)	…
	Omit subsection (2).
461 (provisions as to orders and petitions under this Part)	In subsection (2)(d) for the words "the shares of any members of the company by other members or by the company itself and, in the case of a purchase by the company itself, the reduction of the company's capital accordingly" substitute the words "the shares of any members in the limited liability partnership by other members or by the limited liability partnership itself.".
	In subsection (3) for the words "memorandum or articles" substitute the words "limited liability partnership agreement".
	For the existing words of subsection (4) substitute the words "Any alteration in the limited liability partnership agreement made by virtue of an order under this Part is of the same effect as if duly agreed by the members of the limited liability partnership and the provisions of this Act apply to the limited liability partnership agreement as so altered accordingly.".
	Omit subsection (5).

Provisions	Modification

Floating charges and Receivers (Scotland)

Provisions	Modification
464 (ranking of floating charges)	In subsection (1), for the words "section 462" substitute "the law of Scotland".
466 (alteration of floating charges)	Omit subsections (1), (2), (3) and (6).
486 (interpretation for Part XVIII generally)	For the current definition of "company" substitute ""company" means a limited liability partnership;" Omit the definition of "Register of Sasines".
487 (extent of Part XVIII)	

Matters arising subsequent to winding up

Provisions	Modification
651 (power of court to declare dissolution of company void)	
652 (registrar may strike defunct company off the register)	In subsection (6) paragraph (a) omit the word "director".
652A (registrar may strike private company off the register on application)	In this section the references to "a private company" shall include a reference to "a limited liability partnership".
subsection (1)	In subsection (1) the following shall be substituted for the existing wording— "On application by two or more designated members of a limited liability partnership, the registrar of companies may strike the limited liability partnership's name off the register". Omit subsection 2(a) and in subsection 2(b) after the word "be" insert the word "made". In subsection (6), omit the word "director".
652B (duties in connection with making an application under section 652A)	In paragraph (a) of subsection (5) for "no meetings are" substitute "no meeting is". In paragraph (b) of subsection (5) for "meetings summoned under that section fail" substitute "the meeting summoned under that section fails". In paragraph (c) of subsection (5) for "meetings" substitute "a meeting". In paragraph (d) of subsection (5) for "at previous meetings" substitute "at a previous meeting".
652C (directors' duties following application under section 652A)	In subsection (2), for the words "is a director of the company" substitute "is a designated member of the limited liability partnership". In subsection (2) omit paragraph (d). In subsection (5) for the words "is a director of the company" substitute "is a designated member of the limited liability partnership". In subsection (6), omit paragraph (d).
652D (sections 652B and 652C: supplementary provisions)	
652E (sections 652B and 652C: enforcement)	
652F (other offences connected with section 652A)	
653 (objection to striking off by person aggrieved)	

Provisions	Modification
654 (property of dissolved company to be bona vacantia)	
655 (effect on section 654 of company's revival after dissolution)	
656 (crown disclaimer of property vesting as bona vacantia)	
657 (effect of crown disclaimer under section 656)	
658 (liability for rentcharge on company's land after dissolution)	

Oversea Limited Liability Partnerships

Provisions	Modification
693 (obligation to state name and other particulars)	For the wording of subsection (1) there shall be substituted the following words— "Every oversea limited liability partnership shall— (a) in every prospectus inviting subscriptions for its debentures in Great Britain, state the country in which the limited liability partnership is incorporated, (b) conspicuously exhibit on every place where it carries on business in Great Britain the name of the limited liability partnership and the country in which it is incorporated, (c) cause the name of the limited liability partnership and the country in which it is incorporated to be stated in legible characters in all bill heads, letter paper, and in all notices and other official publications and communications of the limited liability partnership." For subsection (2) there shall be substituted the following words "For the purposes of this section "oversea limited liability partnership" means a body incorporated or otherwise established outside Great Britain whose name under its law of incorporation or establishment includes the words "limited liability partnership."". Subsections (3) and (4) shall be omitted.

The Registrar of Companies: His functions and offices

Provisions	Modification
704 (registration offices)	
705 (companies' registered numbers)	Omit subsection (5).
706 (delivery to the registrar of documents in legible form)	In subsection (2)(a), omit the words from "and, if the document is delivered" to the end of that paragraph.
707A (the keeping of company records by the registrar)	Omit subsection (4).
707B (delivery to the registrar using electronic communications)	In subsection (3), omit the "or" at the end of paragraph (a) and omit paragraph (b).
708 (fees payable to the registrar)	
709 (inspection of records kept by the registrar)	
710 (certificate of incorporation)	
710A (provision and authentication by registrar of documents in non-legible form)	

Provisions	Modification
710B (documents relating to Welsh companies)	In subsection (7), omit the words "272(5) and 273(7) and paragraph 7(3) of Part II of Schedule 9".
711 (public notice by registrar of receipt and issue of certain documents)	In subsection (1) delete "or articles" in paragraph (b) and delete paragraphs (d) to (j), (l), (m) and (s) to (z).
713 (enforcement of company's duty to make returns)	In subsection (1), in the penultimate line for "any officer" substitute "any designated member".
	In subsections (2) and (3) for "officers" substitute "designated members".
714 (registrar's index of company and corporate names)	
715A (interpretation)	

Miscellaneous and supplementary provisions

721 (production and inspection of books where offence suspected)	In subsection (2)(b), for the words "the secretary of the company or such other" substitute "such".
722 (form of company registers, etc)	
723 (use of computers for company records)	Omit subsection (2).
723A (obligations of company as to inspections of registers, & etc)	
725 (service of documents)	In subsection (2), for the words "other head officer" substitute "a designated member".
726 (costs and expenses in actions by certain limited companies)	References to a "limited company" shall include references to a "limited liability partnership".
727 (power of court to grant relief in certain cases)	In subsection (1) delete the words "an officer of a company or" and "officer or".
	In subsection (2), delete the words "officer or".
728 (enforcement of High Court orders)	
729 (annual report by Secretary of State)	
730 (punishment of offences)	
731 (summary proceedings)	
732 (prosecution by public authorities)	Delete the references to sections 210, 324, 329 and 455.
	Omit subsection (2) paragraphs (a) and (c). In subsection (2)(b), for the words "either one of those two persons" substitute "either the Secretary of State, the Director of Public Prosecutions".
	Omit subsection (3).
733 (offences by bodies corporate)	
subsection (1)	In subsection (1), delete the references to section 210 and 216(3).
subsection (2)	In subsection (2), omit the word "secretary".
subsection (3)	Omit subsection (3).
734 (criminal proceedings against unincorporated bodies)	

Interpretation

735A (relationship of this Act to the Insolvency Act)	In subsection (1), delete all the references to provisions of the 1985 Act other than the references to sections 425(6)(a), 460(2) and 728.

PART III
STATUTORY INSTRUMENTS

Provisions	Modification
736 ("subsidiary", "holding company", and "wholly-owned subsidiary")	
subsection (1)	For subsection (1) there shall be substituted the following words—
	"(1) Subject to subsection (1A), a company is a subsidiary of a limited liability partnership, its "holding company", if that limited liability partnership—
	(a) holds a majority of the voting rights in it, or
	(b) is a member of it and has the right to appoint or remove a majority of its board of directors, or
	(c) is a member of it and controls alone, pursuant to an agreement with other shareholders or members, a majority of the voting rights in it,
	or if it is a subsidiary of a company or limited liability partnership which is itself a subsidiary of that other company."
subsection (1A)	Insert as subsection (1A)—
	"(1A) A limited liability partnership is a subsidiary of a company or a subsidiary of another limited liability partnership, (such company or limited liability partnership being referred to in this section as its "holding company") if that company or limited liability partnership—
	(a) holds a majority of the voting rights in it;
	(b) is a member of it and has the right to appoint or remove a majority of other members; or
	(c) is a member of it and controls, alone or pursuant to an agreement with other members, a majority of voting rights in it,
	or if it is a subsidiary of a company or limited liability partnership which is itself a subsidiary of that holding company".
subsection (2)	For subsection (2) substitute "A company or a limited liability partnership is a "wholly-owned subsidiary" of another company or limited liability partnership if it has no members except that other and that other's wholly-owned subsidiaries or persons acting on behalf of that other or its wholly owned subsidiaries."
736A (provisions supplementing section 736)	After subsection (1) insert a new subsection (1A) in the following form—
	"(1A) In section 736(1A)(a) and (c) the references to the voting rights in a limited liability partnership are to the rights conferred on members in respect of their interest in the limited liability partnership to vote on those matters which are to be decided upon by a vote of the members of the limited liability partnership."
	After subsection (2) insert the new subsection (2A) in the following form—

Provisions	Modification
	"(2A) In section 736(1A)(b) the reference to the right to appoint or remove a majority of the members of the limited liability partnership is to the right to appoint or remove members holding a majority of the voting rights referred to in subsection (1A) and for this purpose—
	(a) a person shall be treated as having the right to appoint a member if
	(i) a person's appointment as member results directly from his appointment as a director or member of the holding company, or
	(ii) the member of the limited liability partnership is the company or limited liability partnership which is the holding company; and
	(b) a right to appoint or remove which is exercisable only with the consent or concurrence of another person shall be left out of account."
	In subsection (7) after the words "Rights attached to shares" insert the words "or to a member's interest in a limited liability partnership".
	In subsection (8) after the words "held by a company", in both places where they occur, insert "or a limited liability partnership".
	In subsection (9) after the words "in the interest of company" insert "or a limited liability partnership" and after the words "that company" in both places where they occur insert "or limited liability partnership".
	In subsection (10) after the words "a company" insert the words "or a limited liability partnership" and after the words "by the company" insert the words "or the limited liability partnership".
	In subsection (12) for the existing words substitute "In this section "company" includes a body corporate other than a limited liability partnership."
739 ("non-cash asset")	
740 ("body corporate" and "corporation")	
741 ("director" and "shadow director")	Omit subsection (3).
742 (*expressions used in connection with accounts*)	
743A (meaning of "office copy" in Scotland)	
744 (expressions used generally in this Act)	Delete the definitions of expressions not used in provisions which apply to limited liability partnerships and insert the following definitions—
	""limited liability partnership" has the meaning given it in section 1(2) of the Limited Liability Partnerships Act 2000".
	""shadow member" has the same meaning as it has in the Limited Liability Partnerships Regulations 2001".

PART III
STATUTORY INSTRUMENTS

Provisions	Modification
744A (index of defined expressions)	Delete the references to expressions not used in provisions which apply to limited liability partnerships including, in particular, the following expressions—
	Allotment (and related expressions)
	Section 738
	Annual general meeting
	Section 366
	Authorised minimum
	Section 118
	Called up share capital
	Section 737(1)
	Capital redemption reserve
	Section 170(1)
	Elective resolution
	Section 379A
	Employees' share scheme
	Section 743
	Existing company
	Section 735(1)
	Extraordinary general meeting
	Section 368
	Extraordinary resolution
	Section 378(1)
	The former Companies Acts
	Section 735(1)
	The Joint Stock Companies Acts
	Section 735(3)
	Overseas branch register
	Section 362
	Paid up (and related expressions)
	Section 738
	Registered office (of a company)
	Section 287
	Resolution for reducing share capital
	Section 135(3)
	Share premium account
	Section 130(1)
	Share warrant
	Section 188
	Special notice (in relation to a resolution)
	Section 379
	Special resolution
	Section 378(2)
	Uncalled share capital
	Section 737(2)

Provisions	Modification
	Undistributable reserves
	Section 264(3)
	Unlimited company
	Section 1(2)
	Unregistered company
	Section 718
[SCHEDULE 15C (SECURITY OF INFORMATION OBTAINED: SPECIFIED PERSONS)	
SCHEDULE 15D (SECURITY OF INFORMATION OBTAINED: SPECIFIED DISCLOSURES)]	
SCHEDULE 24 (PUNISHMENT OF OFFENCES UNDER THIS ACT)	Delete the references to those sections which are not applied to limited liability partnerships including, in particular, the following sections—
	Section 6(3) company failing to deliver to the registrar notice or other document, following alteration of its objects;
	Section 18(3) company failing to register change in memorandum or articles;
	Section 19(2) company failing to send to one of its members a copy of the memorandum or articles, when so required by the member;
	Section 20(2) where company's memorandum altered, company issuing copy of the memorandum without the alteration;
	Section 28(5) company failing to change name on direction of Secretary of State;
	Section 31(5) company altering its memorandum or articles, so ceasing to be exempt from having "limited" after its name;
	Section 31(6) company failing to change name, on Secretary of State's direction, so as to have "limited" (or Welsh equivalent) at the end;
	Section 32(4) company failing to comply with the Secretary of State's direction to change its name, on grounds that the name is misleading;
	Section 33 trading under misleading name (use of "public limited company" or Welsh equivalent when not so entitled); purporting to be a private company;
	Section 34 trading or carrying on business with improper use of "limited" or "cyfyngedig";
	Section 54(10) public company failing to give notice, or copy of court order, to registrar, concerning application to reregister as private company;
	Section 80(9) directors exercising company's power of allotment without the authority required by section 80(1);
	Section 81(2) private company offering shares to the public, or allotting shares with a view to their being so offered;

PART III
STATUTORY INSTRUMENTS

Provisions	Modification
	Section 82(5) allotting shares or debentures before third day after issue of prospectus;
	Section 86(6) company failing to keep money in separate bank account, where received in pursuance of prospectus stating that stock exchange listing is to be applied for;
	Section 87(4) offeror of shares for sale failing to keep proceeds in separate bank account;
	Section 88(5) officer of company failing to deliver return of allotments, etc to the registrar;
	Section 95(6) knowingly or recklessly authorising or permitting misleading, false or deceptive material in statement by directors under section 95(5);
	Section 97(4) company failing to deliver to registrar the prescribed form disclosing amount or rate of share commission;
	Section 110(2) making misleading, false or deceptive statement in connection with valuation under section 103 or 104;
	Section 111(3) officer of company failing to deliver copy of asset valuation report to registrar;
	Section 111(4) company failing to deliver to registrar copy of resolution under Section 104(4), with respect to transfer of an asset as consideration for allotment;
	Section 114 contravention of any of the provisions of sections 99 to 104, 106;
	Section 117(7) company doing business or exercising borrowing powers contrary to section 117;
	Section 122(2) company failing to give notice to registrar of reorganisation of share capital;
	Section 123(4) company failing to give notice to registrar of increase of share capital;
	Section 127(5) company failing to forward to registrar copy of court order, when application made to cancel resolution varying shareholders' rights;
	Section 128(5) company failing to send to registrar statement or notice required by section 128 (particulars of shares carrying special rights);
	Section 129(4) company failing to deliver to registrar statement or notice required by section 129 (registration of newly created class rights);
	Section 141 officer of company concealing name of creditor entitled to object to reduction of capital, or wilfully misrepresenting the nature or amount of debt or claim, etc;
	Section 142(2) director authorising or permitting non-compliance with section 142 (requirement to convene company meeting to consider serious loss of capital);

Provisions	Modification
	Section 143(2) company acquiring its own shares in breach of section 143;
	Section 149(2) company failing to cancel its own shares acquired by itself, as required by section 146(2); or failing to apply for reregistration as private company as so required in the case there mentioned;
	Section 151(3) company giving financial assistance towards acquisition of its own shares;
	Section 156(6) company failing to register statutory declaration under section 155;
	Section 156(7) director making statutory declaration under section 155, without having reasonable grounds for opinion expressed in it;
	Section 169(6) default by company's officer in delivering to registrar the return required by section 169 (disclosure by company of purchase of its own shares);
	Section 169(7) company failing to keep copy of contract, etc, at registered office; refusal of inspection to person demanding it;
	Section 173(6) director making statutory declaration under section 173 without having reasonable grounds for the opinion expressed in the declaration;
	Section 175(7) refusal of inspection of statutory declaration and auditor's report under section 173, etc;
	Section 176(4) company failing to give notice to registrar of application to court under section 176, or to register court order;
	Section 183(6) company failing to send notice of refusal to register a transfer of shares or debentures;
	Section 185(5) company default in compliance with section 185(1) (certificates to be made ready following allotment or transfer of shares, etc);
	Section 189(1) offences of fraud and forgery in connection with share warrants in Scotland;
	Section 189(2) unauthorised making of, or using or possessing apparatus for making share warrants in Scotland;
	Section 210(3) failure to discharge obligation of disclosure under Part VI; other forms of non-compliance with that Part;
	Section 211(10) company failing to keep register of interests disclosed under Part IV; other contraventions of section 211;
	Section 214(5) company failing to exercise powers under section 212, when so required by the members;
	Section 215(8) company default in compliance with section 215 (company report of investigation of shareholdings on members' requisition);

PART III
STATUTORY INSTRUMENTS

Provisions	Modification
	Section 216(3) failure to comply with company notice under section 212;
	Making false statement in response etc;
	Section 217(7) company failing to notify a person that he has been named as a shareholder; on removal of name from register, failing to alter associated index;
	Section 218(3) improper removal of entry from register of interests disclosed;
	company failing to restore entry improperly removed;
	Section 219(3) refusal of inspection of register or report under Part VI; failure to send copy when required;
	Section 232(4) default by director or officer of a company in giving notice of matters relating to himself for purposes of Schedule 6 Part I;
	Section 234(5) non-compliance with Part VII as to directors' report and its content;
	directors individually liable;
	Section 234A(4) laying, circulating or delivering directors' report without required signature;
	Section 241(2) failure to lay accounts and reports before the company in general meeting before the end of the period allowed for doing this;
	Section 251(6) failure to comply with requirements in relation to summary financial statements;
	Section 288(4) default in complying with section 288 (keeping register of directors and secretaries, refusal of inspection);
	Section 291(5) acting as director of a company without having the requisite share qualification;
	Section 294(3) director failing to give notice of his attaining retirement age;
	acting as director under appointment invalid due to his attaining it;
	Section 305(3) company default in complying with section 305 (directors' name to appear on company correspondence, etc);
	Section 306(4) failure to state that liability of proposed director or manager is unlimited; failure to give notice of that fact to person accepting office;
	Section 314(3) director failing to comply with section 314;
	Section 317(7) director failing to disclose interest in contract;
	Section 318(8) company in default in complying with section 318(1) or (5);

Provisions	Modification
	Section 322B(4) terms of unwritten contract between sole member of a private company limited by shares or by guarantee and the company not set out in a written memorandum or recorded in minutes of a directors' meeting;
	Section 323(2) director dealing in options to buy or sell company's listed shares or debentures;
	Section 324(7) director failing to notify interest in company's shares; making false statement in purported notification;
	Section 326(2), (3), (4) and (5) various defaults in connection with company register of directors' interests;
	Section 328(6) director failing to notify company that members of his family etc have or have exercised options to buy shares or debentures; making false statement in purported notification;
	Section 329(3) company failing to notify investment exchange of acquisition of its securities by a director;
	Section 342(1) director or relevant company authorising or permitting company to enter into transaction or arrangement, knowing or suspecting it to contravene section 330;
	Section 342(2) relevant company entering into transaction or arrangement for a director in contravention of section 330;
	Section 342(3) procuring a relevant company to enter into transaction or arrangement known to be contrary to section 330;
	Section 343(8) company failing to maintain register of transactions etc made with and for directors and not disclosed in company accounts; failing to make register available at registered office or at company meeting;
	Section 352(5) company default in complying with section 352 (requirement to keep register of members and their particulars);
	Section 352A(3) company default in complying with section 352A (statement that company has only one member);
	Section 353(4) company failing to send notice to registrar as to place where register of members is kept;
	Section 354(4) company failing to keep index of members;
	Section 356(5) refusal of inspection of members' register; failure to send copy on requisition;
	Section 364(4) company without share capital failing to complete and register annual return in due time;
	Section 366(4) company default in holding annual general meeting;
	Section 367(3) company default in complying with Secretary of State's direction to hold a company meeting;

PART III
STATUTORY INSTRUMENTS

Provisions	Modification
	Section 367(5) company failing to register resolution that meeting held under section 367 is to be its annual general meeting;
	Section 372(4) failure to give notice, to member entitled to vote at company meeting, that he may do so by proxy;
	Section 372(6) officer of company authorising or permitting issue of irregular invitations to appoint proxies;
	Section 376(7) officer of company in default as to circulation of members' resolutions for company meeting;
	Section 380(5) company failing to comply with section 380 (copies of certain resolutions etc to be sent to registrar of companies);
	Section 380(6) company failing to include copy of resolution to which section 380 applies in articles; failing to forward copy to member on request;
	Section 381B(2) director or secretary of company failing to notify auditors of proposed written resolution;
	Section 382(5) company failing to keep minutes of proceedings at company and board meetings, etc;
	Section 382B(2) failure of sole member to provide the company with a written record of a decision;
	Section 383(4) refusal of inspection of minutes of general meeting; failure to send copy of minutes on member's request;
	Section 389(10) person acting as a company auditor knowing himself to be disqualified: failing to give notice vacating office when he becomes disqualified;
	Section 429(6) offeror failing to send copy of notice or making statutory declaration knowing it to be false etc;
	Section 430A(6) offeror failing to give rights to minority shareholder;
	Section 444(3) failing to give Secretary of State, when required to do so, information about interests in shares etc; giving false information;
	Section 455(1) exercising a right to dispose of, or vote in respect of, shares which are subject to restrictions under Part XV; failing to give notice in respect of shares so subject; entering into agreement void under section 454(2), (3);
	Section 455(2) issuing shares in contravention of restrictions under Part XV;
	Section 461(5) failure to register office copy of court order under Part XVII altering, or giving leave to alter, company's memorandum;
	Section 697(1) oversea company failing to comply with any of sections 691 to 693 or 696;

Provisions	Modification
	Section 697(2) oversea company contravening section 694(6) (carrying on business under its corporate name after Secretary of State's direction);
	Section 697(3) oversea company failing to comply with section 695A or Schedule 21A;
	Section 703(1) oversea company failing to comply with requirements as to accounts and reports;
	Section 703D(5) oversea company failing to deliver particulars of charge to registrar;
	Section 703R(1) company failing to register winding up or commencement of insolvency proceedings etc;
	Section 703R(2) liquidator failing to register appointment, termination of winding up or striking off of company;
	Section 720(4) insurance company etc failing to send twice yearly statement in form of Schedule 23;
	Schedule 14, Pt II, paragraph 1(3) company failing to give notice of location of overseas branch register, etc;
	Schedule 14, Pt II, paragraph 4(2) company failing to transmit to its registered office in Great Britain copies of entries in overseas branch register or to keep duplicate of overseas branch register;
	Schedule 21C, Pt I, paragraph 7 credit or financial institution failing to deliver accounting documents;
	Schedule 21C, Pt II, paragraph 15 credit or financial institution failing to deliver accounts and reports;
	Schedule 21D, Pt I, paragraph 5 company failing to deliver accounting documents;
	Schedule 21D, Pt I, Paragraph 13 company failing to deliver accounts and reports.

[3565]

NOTES

Entries relating to ss 384, 385, 387, 388, 388A, 389A, 390, 390A, 390B, 391, 391A, 392, 392A, 394, 394A and 742 revoked by the Limited Liability Partnerships (Accounts and Audit) (Application of Companies Act 2006) Regulations 2008, SI 2008/1911, reg 58(1)(b), as from 1 October 2008 (for transitional provision and effect see reg 58(3)–(11) at **[4226]**).

Entries relating to ss 447A, 448A, 453A–453C, Schs 15C, 15D inserted by the Limited Liability Partnerships (Amendment) Regulations 2007, SI 2007/2073, regs 2, 3, as from 1 October 2007.

Words in square brackets in entry relating to s 450 substituted, and words omitted from entry relating to s 460 revoked, by the Financial Services and Markets Act 2000 (Consequential Amendments) Order 2004, SI 2004/355, art 9, as from 4 March 2004.

PART III
STATUTORY INSTRUMENTS

PART II
MODIFICATIONS TO THE COMPANY DIRECTORS DISQUALIFICATION ACT 1986

Part II of Schedule I	After paragraph 8 insert—
	"8A The extent of the member's and shadow members' responsibility for events leading to a member or shadow member, whether himself or some other member or shadow member, being declared by the court to be liable to make a contribution to the assets of the limited liability partnership under section 214A of the Insolvency Act 1986."

[3566]

SCHEDULE 3
MODIFICATIONS TO THE 1986 ACT

Regulation 5

Provisions	Modifications
Section 1 (those who may propose an arrangement)	
subsection (1)	For "The directors of a company" substitute "A limited liability partnership" and delete "to the company and".
subsection (3)	At the end add "but where a proposal is so made it must also be made to the limited liability partnership".
[Section 1A (moratorium)	
subsection (1)	For "the directors of an eligible company intend" substitute "an eligible limited liability partnership intends".
	For "they" substitute "it".]

The following modifications to sections 2 to 7 apply where a proposal under section 1 has been made by the limited liability partnership.

Section 2 (procedure where the nominee is not the liquidator or administrator)	
[subsection (1)	[For "the directors do" substitute "the limited liability partnership does".
subsection (2)	In paragraph [(aa)] for "meetings of the company and of it creditors" substitute "a meeting of the creditors of the limited liability partnership";
	In paragraph (b) for the first "meetings" substitute "a meeting" and for the second "meetings" substitute "meeting".
subsection (3)	For "the person intending to make the proposal" substitute "the designated members of the limited liability partnership".
subsection (4)	[In paragraph (a)] for "the person intending to make the proposal" substitute "the designated members of the limited liability partnership". [In paragraph (b) for "that person" substitute "those designated members".]

Provisions	Modifications
Section 3 (summoning of meetings)	
subsection (1)	For "such meetings as are mentioned in section 2(2)" substitute "a meeting of creditors" and for "those meetings" substitute "that meeting".
subsection (2)	Delete subsection (2).
Section 4 (decisions of meetings)	
subsection (1)	For "meetings" substitute "meeting".
subsection (5)	For "each of the meetings" substitute "the meeting".
new subsection (5A)	Insert a new subsection (5A) as follows—
	"(5A) If modifications to the proposal are proposed at the meeting the chairman of the meeting shall, before the conclusion of the meeting, ascertain from the limited liability partnership whether or not it accepts the proposed modifications; and if at that conclusion the limited liability partnership has failed to respond to a proposed modification it shall be presumed not to have agreed to it."
subsection (6)	For "either" substitute "the"; after "the result of the meeting", in the first place where it occurs, insert "(including, where modifications to the proposal were proposed at the meeting, the response to those proposed modifications made by the limited liability partnership)"; and at the end add "and to the limited liability partnership".
[Section 4A (approval of arrangement)	
subsection (2)	Omit "—(a)".
	For "both meetings" substitute "the meeting".
	Omit the words from ", or" to "that section".
subsection (3)	Omit.
subsection (4)	Omit.
subsection (5)	Omit.
subsection (6)	Omit.]
Section 5 (effect of approval)	
…	…
subsection (4)	For "each of the reports" substitute "the report".
Section 6 (challenge of decisions)	
subsection (1)	For … "either of the meetings" substitute "the meeting".
subsection (2)	For "either of the meetings" substitute "the meeting" and after paragraph [(aa)] add a new paragraph [(ab) as follows—
	"(ab)] any member of the limited liability partnership; and".
	Omit the word "and" at the end of paragraph (b) and omit paragraph (c).

PART III
STATUTORY INSTRUMENTS

Provisions	Modifications
subsection (3)	For "each of the reports" substitute "the report".
subsection (4)	For subsection (4) substitute the following—
	"(4) Where on such an application the court is satisfied as to either of the grounds mentioned in subsection (1), it may do one or both of the following, namely—
	(a) revoke or suspend [any decision approving the voluntary arrangement which has effect under section 4A];
	(b) give a direction to any person for the summoning of a further meeting to consider any revised proposal the limited liability partnership may make or, in a case falling within subsection (1)(b), a further meeting to consider the original proposal.".
subsection (5)	For … "meetings" substitute "a meeting", for … and for "person who made the original proposal" substitute "limited liability partnership".
[Section 6A (false representations, etc)	
subsection (1)	Omit "members or".]
Section 7 (implementation of proposal)	
…	…
[subsection (2)	In paragraph (a) omit "one or both of" and for "meetings" substitute "meeting".]

The following modifications to sections 2 and 3 apply where a proposal under section 1 has been made, where [the limited liability partnership is in administration], by the administrator or, where the limited liability partnership is being wound up, by the liquidator.

Provisions	Modifications
Section 2 (procedure where the nominee is not the liquidator or administrator)	
subsection (2)	In paragraph (a) for "meetings of the company" substitute "meetings of the members of the limited liability partnership".
Section 3 (summoning of meetings)	
subsection (2)	For "meetings of the company" substitute "a meeting of the members of the limited liability partnership".
…	…
…	…
…	…
…	…
…	…
…	…
Section 73 (alternative modes of winding up)	
subsection (1)	Delete ", within the meaning given to that expression by section 735 of the Companies Act,".
Section 74 (liability as contributories of present and past members)	For section 74 there shall be substituted the following—

Provisions	Modifications
	"74. When a limited liability partnership is wound up every present and past member of the limited liability partnership who has agreed with the other members or with the limited liability partnership that he will, in circumstances which have arisen, be liable to contribute to the assets of the limited liability partnership in the event that the limited liability partnership goes into liquidation is liable, to the extent that he has so agreed, to contribute to its assets to any amount sufficient for payment of its debts and liabilities, and the expenses of the winding up, and for the adjustment of the rights of the contributories among themselves.
	However, a past member shall only be liable if the obligation arising from such agreement survived his ceasing to be a member of the limited liability partnership."
Section 75 to 78	Delete sections 75 to 78.
Section 79 (meaning of "contributory")	
subsection (1)	In subsection (1) for "every person" substitute "(a) every present member of the limited liability partnership and (b) every past member of the limited liability partnership".
subsection (2)	After "section 214 (wrongful trading)" insert "or 214A (adjustment of withdrawals)".
subsection (3)	Delete subsection (3).
Section 83 (companies registered under Companies Act, Part XXII, Chapter II)	Delete section 83.
Section 84 (circumstances in which company may be wound up voluntarily)	
subsection (1)	For subsection (1) substitute the following—
	"(1) A limited liability partnership may be wound up voluntarily when it determines that it is to be wound up voluntarily."
subsection (2)	Omit subsection (2).
[subsection (2A)	For "company passes a resolution for voluntary winding up" substitute "limited liability partnership determines that it is to be wound up voluntarily" and for "resolution" where it appears for the second time substitute "determination".
subsection (2B)	For "resolution for voluntary winding up may be passed only" substitute "determination to wind up voluntarily may only be made" and in sub-paragraph (b), for "passing of the resolution" substitute "making of the determination".]
subsection (3)	For subsection (3) substitute the following—

Provisions	Modifications
	"(3) Within 15 days after a limited liability partnership has determined that it be wound up there shall be forwarded to the registrar of companies either a printed copy or else a copy in some other form approved by the registrar of the determination."
subsection [(5)]	After subsection [(4)] insert a new subsection [(5)]—
	"[(5)] If a limited liability partnership fails to comply with this regulation the limited liability partnership and every designated member of it who is in default is liable on summary conviction to a fine not exceeding level 3 on the standard scale."
Section 85 (notice of resolution to wind up)	
subsection (1)	For subsection (1) substitute the following—
	"(1) When a limited liability partnership has determined that it shall be wound up voluntarily, it shall within 14 days after the making of the determination give notice of the determination by advertisement in the Gazette."
Section 86 (commencement of winding up)	Substitute the following new section—
	"86. A voluntary winding up is deemed to commence at the time when the limited liability partnership determines that it be wound up voluntarily.".
Section 87 (effect on business and status of company)	
subsection (2)	In subsection (2), for "articles" substitute "limited liability partnership agreement".
Section 88 (avoidance of share transfers, etc after winding-up resolution)	
	For "shares" substitute "the interest of any member in the property of the limited liability partnership".
Section 89 (statutory declaration of solvency)	
	For "director(s)" wherever it appears in section 89 substitute "designated member(s)";
subsection (2)	For paragraph (a) substitute the following—
	"(a) it is made within the 5 weeks immediately preceding the date when the limited liability partnership determined that it be wound up voluntarily or on that date but before the making of the determination, and".
subsection (3)	For "the resolution for winding up is passed" substitute "the limited liability partnership determined that it be wound up voluntarily".
subsection (5)	For "in pursuance of a resolution passed" substitute "voluntarily".

Provisions	Modifications
Section 90 (distinction between "members" and "creditors" voluntary winding up)	
	For "directors'" substitute "designated members'".
Section 91 (appointment of liquidator)	
subsection (1)	Delete "in general meeting".
subsection (2)	For the existing wording substitute—
	"(2) On the appointment of a liquidator the powers of the members of the limited liability partnership shall cease except to the extent that a meeting of the members of the limited liability partnership summoned for the purpose or the liquidator sanctions their continuance."
	After subsection (2) insert—
	"(3) Subsections (3) and (4) of section 92 shall apply for the purposes of this section as they apply for the purposes of that section."
Section 92 (power to fill vacancy in office of liquidator)	
subsection (1)	For "the company in general meeting" substitute "a meeting of the members of the limited liability partnership summoned for the purpose".
subsection (2)	For "a general meeting" substitute "a meeting of the members of the limited liability partnership".
subsection (3)	In subsection (3), for "articles" substitute "limited liability partnership agreement".
new subsection (4)	Add a new subsection (4) as follows—
	"(4) The quorum required for a meeting of the members of the limited liability partnership shall be any quorum required by the limited liability partnership agreement for meetings of the members of the limited liability partnership and if no requirement for a quorum has been agreed upon the quorum shall be 2 members."
Section 93 (general company meeting at each year's end)	
subsection (1)	For "a general meeting of the company" substitute "a meeting of the members of the limited liability partnership".
new subsection (4)	Add a new subsection (4) as follows—
	"(4) subsections (3) and (4) of section 92 shall apply for the purposes of this section as they apply for the purposes of that section."
Section 94 (final meeting prior to dissolution)	
subsection (1)	For "a general meeting of the company" substitute "a meeting of the members of the limited liability partnership".
new subsection (5A)	Add a new subsection (5A) as follows

PART III
STATUTORY INSTRUMENTS

Provisions	Modifications
	"(5A) Subsections (3) and (4) of section 92 shall apply for the purposes of this section as they apply for the purposes of that section."
subsection (6)	For "a general meeting of the company" substitute "a meeting of the members of the limited liability partnership".
Section 95 (effect of company's insolvency)	
subsection (1)	For "directors'" substitute "designated members'".
subsection (7)	For subsection (7) substitute the following—
	"(7) In this section "the relevant period" means the period of 6 months immediately preceding the date on which the limited liability partnership determined that it be wound up voluntarily."
Section 96 (conversion to creditors' voluntary winding up)	
paragraph (a)	For "directors'" substitute "designated members'".
paragraph (b)	Substitute a new paragraph (b) as follows—
	"(b) the creditors' meeting was the meeting mentioned in section 98 in the next Chapter;".
Section 98 (meeting of creditors)	
subsection (1)	For paragraph (a) substitute the following—
	"(a) cause a meeting of its creditors to be summoned for a day not later than the 14th day after the day on which the limited liability partnership determines that it be wound up voluntarily;".
subsection (5)	For "were sent the notices summoning the company meeting at which it was resolved that the company be wound up voluntarily" substitute "the limited liability partnership determined that it be wound up voluntarily".
Section 99 (directors to lay statement of affairs before creditors)	
subsection (1)	For "the directors of the company" substitute "the designated members" and for "the director so appointed" substitute "the designated member so appointed".
subsection (2)	For "directors" substitute "designated members".
subsection (3)	For "directors" substitute "designated members" and for "director" substitute "designated member".
Section 100 (appointment of liquidator)	
subsection (1)	For "The creditors and the company at their respective meetings mentioned in section 98" substitute "The creditors at their meeting mentioned in section 98 and the limited liability partnership".
subsection (3)	Delete "director,".

Provisions	Modifications
Section 101 (appointment of liquidation committee)	
subsection (2)	For subsection (2) substitute the following—
	"(2) If such a committee is appointed, the limited liability partnership may, when it determines that it be wound up voluntarily or at any time thereafter, appoint such number of persons as they think fit to act as members of the committee, not exceeding 5."
Section 105 (meetings of company and creditors at each year's end)	
subsection (1)	For "a general meeting of the company" substitute "a meeting of the members of the limited liability partnership".
new subsection (5)	Add a new subsection (5) as follows—
	"(5) Subsections (3) and (4) of section 92 shall apply for the purposes of this section as they apply for the purposes of that section."
Section 106 (final meeting prior to dissolution)	
subsection (1)	For "a general meeting of the company" substitute "a meeting of the members of the limited liability partnership".
new subsection (5A)	After subsection (5) insert a new subsection (5A) as follows—
	"(5A) Subsections (3) and (4) of section 92 shall apply for the purposes of this section as they apply for the purposes of that section."
subsection (6)	For "a general meeting of the company" substitute "a meeting of the members of the limited liability partnership".
Section 110 (acceptance of shares, etc, as consideration for sale of company property)	
	For the existing section substitute the following—
	"(1) This section applies, in the case of a limited liability partnership proposed to be, or being, wound up voluntarily, where the whole or part of the limited liability partnership's business or property is proposed to be transferred or sold to another company whether or not it is a company within the meaning of the Companies Act ("the transferee company") or to a limited liability partnership ("the transferee limited liability partnership").

Provisions	Modifications
	(2) With the requisite sanction, the liquidator of the limited liability partnership being, or proposed to be, wound up ("the transferor limited liability partnership") may receive, in compensation or part compensation for the transfer or sale, shares, policies or other like interests in the transferee company or the transferee limited liability partnership for distribution among the members of the transferor limited liability partnership.
	(3) The sanction required under subsection (2) is—
	(a) in the case of a members' voluntary winding up, that of a determination of the limited liability partnership at a meeting of the members of the limited liability partnership conferring either a general authority on the liquidator or an authority in respect of any particular arrangement, (subsections (3) and (4) of section 92 to apply for this purpose as they apply for the purposes of that section), and
	(b) in the case of a creditor's voluntary winding up, that of either court or the liquidation committee.
	(4) Alternatively to subsection (2), the liquidator may (with the sanction) enter into any other arrangement whereby the members of the transferor limited liability partnership may, in lieu of receiving cash, shares, policies or other like interests (or in addition thereto), participate in the profits, or receive any other benefit from the transferee company or the transferee limited liability partnership.
	(5) A sale or arrangement in pursuance of this section is binding on members of the transferor limited liability partnership.
	(6) A determination by the limited liability partnership is not invalid for the purposes of this section by reason that it is made before or concurrently with a determination by the limited liability partnership that it be wound up voluntarily or for appointing liquidators; but, if an order is made within a year for winding up the limited liability partnership by the court, the determination by the limited liability partnership is not valid unless sanctioned by the court."
Section 111 (dissent from arrangement under section 110)	
subsections (1)–(3)	For subsections (1)–(3) substitute the following—
	"(1) This section applies in the case of a voluntary winding up where, for the purposes of section 110(2) or (4), a determination of the limited liability partnership has provided the sanction requisite for the liquidator under that section.

Provisions	Modifications
	(2) If a member of the transferor limited liability partnership who did not vote in favour of providing the sanction required for the liquidator under section 110 expresses his dissent from it in writing addressed to the liquidator and left at the registered office of the limited liability partnership within 7 days after the date on which that sanction was given, he may require the liquidator either to abstain from carrying the arrangement so sanctioned into effect or to purchase his interest at a price to be determined by agreement or arbitration under this section.
	(3) If the liquidator elects to purchase the member's interest, the purchase money must be paid before the limited liability partnership is dissolved and be raised by the liquidator in such manner as may be determined by the limited liability partnership."
subsection (4)	Omit subsection (4).
Section 117 (high court and county court jurisdiction)	
subsection (2)	Delete "Where the amount of a company's share capital paid up or credited as paid up does not exceed £120,000, then (subject to this section)".
subsection (3)	Delete subsection (3).
Section 120 (court of session and sheriff court jurisdiction)	
subsection (3)	Delete "Where the amount of a company's share capital paid up or credited as paid up does not exceed £120,000,".
subsection (5)	Delete subsection (5).
Section 122 (circumstances in which company may be wound up by the court)	
subsection (1)	For subsection (1) substitute the following—
	"(1) A limited liability partnership may be wound up by the court if—
	(a) the limited liability partnership has determined that the limited liability partnership be wound up by the court,
	(b) the limited liability partnership does not commence its business within a year from its incorporation or suspends its business for a whole year,
	(c) the number of members is reduced below two,
	(d) the limited liability partnership is unable to pay its debts …
	[(da) at the time at which a moratorium for the limited liability partnership under section 1A comes to an end, no voluntary arrangement approved under Part I has effect in relation to the limited liability partnership,]

PART III
STATUTORY INSTRUMENTS

Provisions	Modifications
	(e) the court is of the opinion that it is just and equitable that the limited liability partnership should be wound up."
Section 124 (application for winding up)	
subsections (2), (3) and (4)(a)	Delete these subsections.
[subsection (3A)	For "122(1)(fa)" substitute "122(1)(da)".]
Section 124A (petition for winding-up on grounds of public interest)	
subsection (1)	[Omit paragraphs (b) and (bb).]
Section 126 (power to stay or restrain proceedings against company)	
subsection (2)	Delete subsection (2).
Section 127 (avoidance of property dispositions, etc)	
[subsection (1)]	For "any transfer of shares" substitute "any transfer by a member of the limited liability partnership of his interest in the property of the limited liability partnership".
Section 129 (commencement of winding up by the court)	
subsection (1)	For "a resolution has been passed by the company" substitute "a determination has been made" and for "at the time of the passing of the resolution" substitute "at the time of that determination".
Section 130 (consequences of winding-up order)	
subsection (3)	Delete subsection (3).
Section 148 (settlement of list of contributories and application of assets)	
subsection (1)	Delete ", with power to rectify the register of members in all cases where rectification is required in pursuance of the Companies Act or this Act,".
Section 149 (debts due from contributory to company)	
subsection (1)	Delete "the Companies Act or".
subsection (2)	Delete subsection (2).
subsection (3)	Delete ", whether limited or unlimited,".
Section 160 (delegation of powers to liquidator (England and Wales))	
subsection (1)	In subsection (1)(b) delete "and the rectifying of the register of members".
subsection (2)	For subsection (2) substitute the following—
	"(2) But the liquidator shall not make any call without the special leave of the court or the sanction of the liquidation committee."
Section 165 (voluntary winding up)	
subsection (2)	In paragraph (a) for "an extraordinary resolution of the company" substitute "a determination by a meeting of the members of the limited liability partnership".
subsection (4)	For paragraph (c) substitute the following—

Provisions	Modifications
	"(c) summon meetings of the members of the limited liability partnership for the purpose of obtaining their sanction or for any other purpose he may think fit."
new subsection (4A)	Insert a new subsection (4A) as follows—
	"(4A) Subsections (3) and (4) of section 92 shall apply for the purposes of this section as they apply for the purposes of that section."
Section 166 (creditors' voluntary winding up)	
subsection (5)	In paragraph (b) for "directors" substitute "designated members".
Section 171 (removal, etc (voluntary winding up))	
subsection (2)	For paragraph (a) substitute the following—
	"(a) in the case of a members' voluntary winding up, by a meeting of the members of the limited liability partnership summoned specially for that purpose, or".
subsection (6)	In paragraph (a) for "final meeting of the company" substitute "final meeting of the members of the limited liability partnership" and in paragraph (b) for "final meetings of the company" substitute "final meetings of the members of the limited liability partnership".
new subsection (7)	Insert a new subsection (7) as follows—
	"(7) Subsections (3) and (4) of section 92 are to apply for the purposes of this section as they apply for the purposes of that section."
Section 173 (release (voluntary winding up))	
subsection (2)	In paragraph (a) for "a general meeting of the company" substitute "a meeting of the members of the limited liability partnership".
Section 183 (effect of execution or attachment (England and Wales))	
subsection (2)	Delete paragraph (a).
Section 184 (duties of sheriff (England and Wales))	
subsection (1)	For "a resolution for voluntary winding up has been passed" substitute "the limited liability partnership has determined that it be wound up voluntarily".
subsection (4)	Delete "or of a meeting having been called at which there is to be proposed a resolution for voluntary winding up," and "or a resolution is passed (as the case may be)".
Section 187 (power to make over assets to employees)	
	Delete section 187.
Section 194 (resolutions passed at adjourned meetings)	
	After "contributories" insert "or of the members of a limited liability partnership".

Provisions	Modifications
Section 195 (meetings to ascertain wishes of creditors or contributories)	
subsection (3)	Delete "the Companies Act or".
Section 206 (fraud, etc in anticipation of winding up)	
subsection (1)	For "passes a resolution for voluntary winding up" substitute "makes a determination that it be wound up voluntarily".
Section 207 (transactions in fraud of creditors)	
subsection (1)	For "passes a resolution for voluntary winding up" substitute "makes a determination that it be wound up voluntarily".
Section 210 (material omissions from statement relating to company's affairs)	
subsection (2)	For "passed a resolution for voluntary winding up" substitute "made a determination that it be wound up voluntarily".
Section 214 (wrongful trading)	
subsection (2)	Delete from "but the court shall not" to the end of the subsection.
After section 214	Insert the following new section 214A—

"**214A Adjustment of withdrawals**

(1) This section has effect in relation to a person who is or has been a member of a limited liability partnership where, in the course of the winding up of that limited liability partnership, it appears that subsection (2) of this section applies in relation to that person.

(2) This subsection applies in relation to a person if—

(a) within the period of two years ending with the commencement of the winding up, he was a member of the limited liability partnership who withdrew property of the limited liability partnership, whether in the form of a share of profits, salary, repayment of or payment of interest on a loan to the limited liability partnership or any other withdrawal of property, and

(b) it is proved by the liquidator to the satisfaction of the court that at the time of the withdrawal he knew or had reasonable ground for believing that the limited liability partnership—

(i) was at the time of the withdrawal unable to pay its debts within the meaning of section 123, or

Provisions	Modifications
	(ii) would become so unable to pay its debts after the assets of the limited liability partnership had been depleted by that withdrawal taken together with all other withdrawals (if any) made by any members contemporaneously with that withdrawal or in contemplation when that withdrawal was made.
	(3) Where this section has effect in relation to any person the court, on the application of the liquidator, may declare that that person is to be liable to make such contribution (if any) to the limited liability partnership's assets as the court thinks proper.
	(4) The court shall not make a declaration in relation to any person the amount of which exceeds the aggregate of the amounts or values of all the withdrawals referred to in subsection (2) made by that person within the period of two years referred to in that subsection.
	(5) The court shall not make a declaration under this section with respect to any person unless that person knew or ought to have concluded that after each withdrawal referred to in subsection (2) there was no reasonable prospect that the limited liability partnership would avoid going into insolvent liquidation.
	(6) For the purposes of subsection (5) the facts which a member ought to know or ascertain and the conclusions which he ought to reach are those which would be known, ascertained, or reached by a reasonably diligent person having both:
	(a) the general knowledge, skill and experience that may reasonably be expected of a person carrying out the same functions as are carried out by that member in relation to the limited liability partnership, and
	(b) the general knowledge, skill and experience that that member has.
	(7) For the purposes of this section a limited liability partnership goes into insolvent liquidation if it goes into liquidation at a time when its assets are insufficient for the payment of its debts and other liabilities and the expenses of the winding up.
	(8) In this section "member" includes a shadow member.
	(9) This section is without prejudice to section 214."
Section 215 (proceedings under ss 213, 214)	
subsection (1)	Omit the word "or" between the words "213" and "214" and insert after "214" "or 214A".

PART III
STATUTORY INSTRUMENTS

Provisions	Modifications
subsection (2)	For "either section" substitute "any of those sections".
subsection (4)	For "either section" substitute "any of those sections".
subsection (5)	For "Sections 213 and 214" substitute "Sections 213, 214 or 214A".
Section 218 (prosecution of delinquent officers and members of company)	
subsection (1)	For "officer, or any member, of the company" substitute "member of the limited liability partnership".
subsections (3), (4) and (6)	For "officer of the company, or any member of it," substitute "officer or member of the limited liability partnership".
...	...
Section 247 ("insolvency" and "go into liquidation")	
subsection (2)	For "passes a resolution for voluntary winding up" substitute "makes a determination that it be wound up voluntarily" and for "passing such a resolution" substitute "making such a determination".
[subsection (3)	For "resolution for voluntary winding up" substitute "determination to wind up voluntarily".]
Section 249 ("connected with a company")	For the existing words substitute— "For the purposes of any provision in this Group of Parts, a person is connected with a company (including a limited liability partnership) if— (a) he is a director or shadow director of a company or an associate of such a director or shadow director (including a member or a shadow member of a limited liability partnership or an associate of such a member or shadow member); or (b) he is an associate of the company or of the limited liability partnership."
Section 250 ("member" of a company)	Delete section 250.
Section 251 (expressions used generally)	Delete the word "and" appearing after the definition of "the rules" and insert the word "and" after the definition of "shadow director". After the definition of "shadow director" insert the following—

Provisions	Modifications
	""shadow member", in relation to a limited liability partnership, means a person in accordance with whose directions or instructions the members of the limited liability partnership are accustomed to act (but so that a person is not deemed a shadow member by reason only that the members of the limited liability partnership act on advice given by him in a professional capacity);".
Section 386 (categories of preferential debts)	
subsection (1)	In subsection (1), omit the words "or an individual".
subsection (2)	In subsection (2), omit the words "or the individual".
Section 387 ("the relevant date")	
subsection (3)	[In paragraph (ab) for "passed a resolution for voluntary winding up" substitute "made a determination that it be wound up voluntarily".]
	In paragraph (c) for "passing of the resolution for the winding up of the company" substitute "making of the determination by the limited liability partnership that it be wound up voluntarily".
subsection (5)	Omit subsection (5).
subsection (6)	Omit subsection (6).
Section 388 (meaning of "act as insolvency practitioner")	
subsection (2)	Omit subsection (2).
subsection (3)	Omit subsection (3).
subsection (4)	Delete ""company" means a company within the meaning given by section 735(1) of the Companies Act or a company which may be wound up under Part V of this Act (unregistered companies);" and delete ""interim trustee" and "permanent trustee" mean the same as the Bankruptcy (Scotland) Act 1985".
Section 389 (acting without qualification an offence)	
subsection (1)	Omit the words "or an individual".
[Section 389A (authorisation of nominees and supervisors)	
subsection (1)	Omit "or Part VIII".]
Section 402 (official petitioner)	Delete section 402.
Section 412 (individual insolvency rules (England and Wales))	Delete section 412.
Section 415 (Fees orders (individual insolvency proceedings in England and Wales))	Delete section 415.
Section 416 (monetary limits (companies winding up))	

Provisions	Modifications
subsection (1)	In subsection (1), omit the words "section 117(2) (amount of company's share capital determining whether county court has jurisdiction to wind it up);" and the words "section 120(3) (the equivalent as respects sheriff court jurisdiction in Scotland);".
subsection (3)	In subsection (3), omit the words "117(2), 120(3) or".
Section 418 (monetary limits (bankruptcy))	Delete section 418.
Section 420 (insolvent partnerships)	Delete section 420.
Section 421 (insolvent estates of deceased persons)	Delete section 421.
Section 422 (recognised banks, etc)	Delete section 422.
[Section 426A (disqualification from Parliament (England and Wales))	Omit.
Section 426B (devolution)	Omit.
Section 426C (irrelevance of privilege)	Omit.]
Section 427 (parliamentary disqualification)	Delete section 427.
Section 429 (disabilities on revocation or administration order against an individual)	Delete section 429.
Section 432 (offences by bodies corporate) subsection (2)	Delete "secretary or".
Section 435 (meaning of "associate") new subsection (3A)	Insert a new subsection (3A) as follows— "(3A) A member of a limited liability partnership is an associate of that limited liability partnership and of every other member of that limited liability partnership and of the husband or wife [or civil partner] or relative of every other member of that limited liability partnership.".
subsection (11)	For subsection (11) there shall be substituted— "(11) In this section "company" includes any body corporate (whether incorporated in Great Britain or elsewhere); and references to directors and other officers of a company and to voting power at any general meeting of a company have effect with any necessary modifications.".
Section 436 (expressions used generally)	The following expressions and definitions shall be added to the section— ""designated member" has the same meaning as it has in the Limited Liability Partnerships Act 2000;

Provisions	Modifications
	"limited liability partnership" means a limited liability partnership formed and registered under the Limited Liability Partnerships Act 2000;
	"limited liability partnership agreement", in relation to a limited liability partnership, means any agreement, express or implied, made between the members of the limited liability partnership or between the limited liability partnership and the members of the limited liability partnership which determines the mutual rights and duties of the members, and their rights and duties in relation to the limited liability partnership.".
Section 437 (transitional provisions, and savings)	Delete section 437.
Section 440 (extent (Scotland))	
subsection (2)	In subsection (2), omit paragraph (b).
Section 441 (extent (Northern Ireland))	
	Delete section 441.
Section 442 (extent (other territories))	
	Delete section 442.
[Schedule A1	
Paragraph 6	
sub-paragraph (1)	For "directors of a company wish" substitute "limited liability partnership wishes".
	For "they" substitute "the designated members of the limited liability partnership".
sub-paragraph (2)	For "directors" substitute "the designated members of the limited liability partnership".
	In sub-paragraph (c), for "meetings of the company and" substitute "a meeting of".
Paragraph 7	
sub-paragraph (1)	For "directors of a company" substitute "designated members of the limited liability partnership".
	In sub-paragraph (e)(iii), for "meetings of the company and" substitute "a meeting of".
Paragraph 8	
sub-paragraph (2)	For "meetings" substitute "meeting".
	For "are" substitute "is".
	Omit the words in parenthesis.
sub-paragraph (3)	For "either of those meetings" substitute "the meeting".
	For "those meetings were" substitute "that meeting was".
	Omit the words in parenthesis.
sub-paragraph (4)	For "either" substitute "the".
sub-paragraph (6)(c)	For "one or both of the meetings" substitute "the meeting".

PART III
STATUTORY INSTRUMENTS

Provisions	Modifications
Paragraph 9	
sub-paragraph (1)	For "directors" substitute "designated members of the limited liability partnership".
sub-paragraph (2)	For "directors" substitute "designated members of the limited liability partnership".
Paragraph 12	
sub-paragraph (1)(b)	Omit.
sub-paragraph (1)(c)	For "resolution may be passed" substitute "determination that it may be wound up may be made".
sub-paragraph (2)	For "transfer of shares" substitute "any transfer by a member of the limited liability partnership of his interest in the property of the limited liability partnership".
Paragraph 20	
sub-paragraph (8)	For "directors" substitute "designated members of the limited liability partnership".
sub-paragraph (9)	For "directors" substitute "designated members of the limited liability partnership".
Paragraph 24	
sub-paragraph (2)	For "directors" substitute "designated members of the limited liability partnership".
Paragraph 25	
sub-paragraph (2)(c)	For "directors" substitute "designated members of the limited liability partnership".
Paragraph 26	
sub-paragraph (1)	Omit ", director".
Paragraph 29	
sub-paragraph (1)	For "meetings of the company and its creditors" substitute "a meeting of the creditors of the limited liability partnership".
Paragraph 30	
sub-paragraph (1)	For "meetings" substitute "meeting".
new sub-paragraph (2A)	Insert new sub-paragraph (2A) as follows—
	"(2A) If modifications to the proposal are proposed at the meeting the chairman of the meeting shall, before the conclusion of the meeting, ascertain from the limited liability partnership whether or not it accepts the proposed modifications; and if at that conclusion the limited liability partnership has failed to respond to a proposed modification it shall be presumed not to have agreed to it.".
sub-paragraph (3)	For "either" substitute "the".

Provisions	Modifications
	After "the result of the meeting" in the first place where it occurs insert "(including, where modifications to the proposal were proposed at the meeting, the response to those proposed modifications made by the limited liability partnership)".
	At the end add "and to the limited liability partnership".
Paragraph 31	
sub-paragraph (1)	For "meetings" substitute "meeting".
sub-paragraph (7)	For "directors of the company" substitute "designated members of the limited liability partnership".
	For "meetings (or either of them)" substitute "meeting".
	For "directors" substitute "limited liability partnership".
	For "those meetings" substitute "that meeting".
Paragraph 32	
sub-paragraph (2)	For sub-paragraphs (a) and (b) substitute "with the day on which the meeting summoned under paragraph 29 is first held.".
Paragraph 36	
sub-paragraph (2)	For sub-paragraph (2) substitute—
	"(2) The decision has effect if, in accordance with the rules, it has been taken by the creditors' meeting summoned under paragraph 29.".
sub-paragraph (3)	Omit.
sub-paragraph (4)	Omit.
sub-paragraph (5)	Omit.
Paragraph 37	
sub-paragraph (5)	For "each of the reports of the meetings" substitute "the report of the meeting".
Paragraph 38	
sub-paragraph (1)(a)	For "one or both of the meetings" substitute "the meeting".
sub-paragraph (1)(b)	For "either of those meetings" substitute "the meeting".
sub-paragraph (2)(a)	For "either of the meetings" substitute "the meeting".
	After sub-paragraph (2)(a) insert new (aa) as follows—
	"(aa) any member of the limited liability partnership;".
sub-paragraph (2)(b)	Omit "creditors'".
sub-paragraph (3)(a)	For "each of the reports" substitute "the report".
sub-paragraph (3)(b)	Omit "creditors'".
sub-paragraph (4)(a)(ii)	Omit "in question".

PART III
STATUTORY INSTRUMENTS

Provisions	Modifications
sub-paragraph (4)(b)(i)	For "further meetings" substitute "a further meeting" and for "directors" substitute "limited liability partnership".
sub-paragraph (4)(b)(ii)	Omit "company or (as the case may be) creditors'".
sub-paragraph (5)	For "directors do" substitute "limited liability partnerships does".
Paragraph 39	
sub-paragraph (1)	For "one or both of the meetings" substitute "the meeting".
Schedule B1	
Paragraph 2	
sub-paragraph (c)	For "company or its directors" substitute "limited liability partnership".
Paragraph 8	
sub-paragraph (1)(a)	For "resolution for voluntary winding up" substitute "determination to wind up voluntarily".
Paragraph 9	Omit.
Paragraph 12	
sub-paragraph (1)(b)	Omit.
Paragraph 22	For sub-paragraph (1) substitute—
	"(1) A limited liability partnership may appoint an administrator.".
	Omit sub-paragraph (2).
Paragraph 23	
sub-paragraph (1)(b)	Omit "or its directors".
Paragraph 42	
sub-paragraph (2)	For "resolution may be passed for the winding up of" substitute "determination to wind up voluntarily may be made by".
Paragraph 61	For paragraph 61 substitute—"
	"61. The administrator has power to prevent any person from taking part in the management of the business of the limited liability partnership and to appoint any person to be a manager of that business.".
Paragraph 62	At the end add the following—
	"Subsections (3) and (4) of section 92 shall apply for the purposes of this paragraph as they apply for the purposes of that section.".
Paragraph 83	
sub-paragraph (6)(b)	For "resolution for voluntary winding up" substitute "determination to wind up voluntarily".
sub-paragraph (8)(b)	For "passing of the resolution for voluntary winding up" substitute "determination to wind up voluntarily".
sub-paragraph (8)(e)	For "passing of the resolution for voluntary winding up" substitute "determination to wind up voluntarily".

Provisions	Modifications
Paragraph 87	
sub-paragraph (2)(b)	Insert at the end "or".
sub-paragraph (2)(c)	Omit ", or".
sub-paragraph (2)(d)	Omit the words from "(d)" to "company".
Paragraph 89	
sub-paragraph (2)(b)	Insert at the end "or".
sub-paragraph (2)(c)	Omit ", or".
sub-paragraph (2)(d)	Omit the words from "(d)" to "company".
Paragraph 91	
sub-paragraph (1)(c)	Omit.
Paragraph 94	Omit.
Paragraph 95	For "to 94" substitute "and 93".
Paragraph 97	
sub-paragraph (1)(a)	Omit "or directors".
Paragraph 103	
sub-paragraph (5)	Omit.
Paragraph 105	Omit.]
Schedule 1	
Paragraph 19	For paragraph 19 substitute the following—
	"19. Power to enforce any rights the limited liability partnership has against the members under the terms of the limited liability partnership agreement."
Schedule 10	
[Section 6A(1)	In the entry relating to section 6A omit "members' or".]
Section 85(2)	In the entry relating to section 85(2) for "resolution for voluntary winding up" substitute "making of determination for voluntary winding up".
Section 89(4)	In the entry relating to section 89(4) for "Director" substitute "Designated member".
Section 93(3)	In the entry relating to section 93(3) for "general meeting of the company" substitute "meeting of members of the limited liability partnership".
Section 99(3)	In the entries relating to section 99(3) for "director" and "directors" where they appear substitute "designated member" or "designated members" as appropriate.
Section 105(3)	In the entry relating to section 105(3) for "company general meeting" substitute "meeting of the members of the limited liability partnership".
Section 106(6)	In the entry relating to section 106(6) for "final meeting of the company" substitute "final meeting of the members of the limited liability partnership".
Sections 353(1) to 362	Delete the entries relating to sections 353(1) to 362 inclusive.
Section 429(5)	Delete the entry relating to section 429(5).

Provisions	Modifications
[Schedule A1, paragraph 9(2)	For "Directors" substitute "Designated Members".
Schedule A1, paragraph 20(9)	For "Directors" substitute "Designated Members".
Schedule B1, paragraph 27(4)	Omit "or directors".
Schedule B1, paragraph 29(7)	Omit "or directors".
Schedule B1, paragraph 32	Omit "or directors".]

[3567]

NOTES

Entries relating to ss 1A, 4A, 6A, 389A, 426A–426C inserted by the Limited Liability Partnerships (Amendment) Regulations 2005, SI 2005/1989, reg 3, Sch 2, paras 1, 2, 3(b), (e), 12, 13, as from 1 October 2005, except in relation to a case where a petition for an administration order has been presented before that date.

In the entry relating to s 2, words in first, third and fourth pairs of square brackets inserted, and "(aa)" substituted, by SI 2005/1989, reg 3, Sch 2, paras 1, 3(a), as from 1 October 2005, except in relation to a case where a petition for an administration order has been presented before that date.

Entry relating to s 5(1) revoked by SI 2005/1989, reg 3, Sch 2, paras 1, 3(c), as from 1 October 2005, except in relation to a case where a petition for an administration order has been presented before that date.

Words omitted from entry relating to s 6 revoked, and words in square brackets substituted, by SI 2005/1989, reg 3, Sch 2, paras 1, 3(d), as from 1 October 2005, except in relation to a case where a petition for an administration order has been presented before that date.

Entry relating to s 7(1) revoked, and entry relating to s 7(2) inserted, by SI 2005/1989, reg 3, Sch 2, paras 1, 3(f), as from 1 October 2005, except in relation to a case where a petition for an administration order has been presented before that date.

In the paragraph following the entry for s 7 words in square brackets substituted by SI 2005/1989, reg 3, Sch 2, paras 1, 3(g), as from 1 October 2005, except in relation to a case where a petition for an administration order has been presented before that date.

Entries relating to ss 8, 9, 10, 11, 13, 14 revoked by SI 2005/1989, reg 3, Sch 2, paras 1, 4, as from 1 October 2005, except in relation to a case where a petition for an administration order has been presented before that date.

Entries relating to s 84(2A), (2B) inserted, and in the entry relating to s 84(5) figures in square brackets substituted, by SI 2005/1989, reg 3, Sch 2, paras 1, 5, as from 1 October 2005, except in relation to a case where a petition for an administration order has been presented before that date.

Words in square brackets in entries relating to ss 122, 124, 127, 247, 387 inserted by SI 2005/1989, reg 3, Sch 2, paras 1, 6–8, 10, 11, as from 1 October 2005, except in relation to a case where a petition for an administration order has been presented before that date.

In entry relating to s 124A, words in square brackets substituted by the Financial Services and Markets Act 2000 (Consequential Amendments) Order 2004, SI 2004/355, art 10(1), (3), as from 4 March 2004.

Entry relating to s 233 revoked by SI 2005/1989, reg 3, Sch 2, paras 1, 9, as from 1 October 2005, except in relation to a case where a petition for an administration order has been presented before that date.

In entry relating to s 435, words in square brackets inserted by the Civil Partnership Act 2004 (Amendments to Subordinate Legislation) Order 2005, SI 2005/2114, art 2(18), Sch 18, Pt 1, para 3, as from 5 December 2005.

Entries relating to Sch A1 and Sch B1 inserted by SI 2005/1989, reg 3, Sch 2, paras 1, 14, as from 1 October 2005, except in relation to a case where a petition for an administration order has been presented before that date.

Words in square brackets in entry relating to Sch 10 inserted by SI 2005/1989, reg 3, Sch 2, paras 1, 15, as from 1 October 2005, except in relation to a case where a petition for an administration order has been presented before that date.

SCHEDULE 4

Regulation 5(3)

The provisions listed in this Schedule are not applied to Scotland to the extent specified below—
   Sections 50 to 52;
   Section 53(1) and (2), to the extent that those subsections do not relate to the requirement for a copy of the instrument and notice being forwarded to the registrar of companies;
   Section 53(4) (6) and (7);
   Section 54(1), (2), (3) (to the extent that that subsection does not relate to the requirement for a copy of the interlocutor to be sent to the registrar of companies), and subsections (5), (6) and (7);
   Sections 55 to 58;
   Section 60, other than subsection (1);
   Section 61, including subsections (6) and (7) to the extent that those subsections do not relate to anything to be done or which may be done to or by the registrar of companies;
   Section 62, including subsection (5) to the extent that that subsection does not relate to anything to be done or which may be done to or by the registrar of companies;
   Sections 63 to 66;
   Section 67, including subsections (1) and (8) to the extent that those subsections do not relate to anything to be done or which may be done to the registrar of companies;

Section 68;

Section 69, including subsections (1) and (2) to the extent that those subsections do not relate to anything to be done or which may be done by the registrar of companies;

Sections 70 and 71;

Subsection 84(3), to the extent that it does not concern the copy of the resolution being forwarded to the registrar of companies within 15 days;

Sections 91 to 93;

Section 94, including subsections (3) and (4) to the extent that those subsections do not relate to the liquidator being required to send to the registrar of companies a copy of the account and a return of the final meeting;

Section 95;

Section 97;

Sections 100 to 102;

Sections 104 to 105;

Section 106, including subsections (3), (4) and (5) to the extent that those subsections do not relate to the liquidator being required to send to the registrar of companies a copy of the account of winding up and a return of the final meeting/quorum;

Sections 109 to 111;

Section 112, including subsection (3) to the extent that that subsection does not relate to the liquidator being required to send to the registrar a copy of the order made by the court;

Sections 113 to 115;

Sections 126 to 128;

Section 130(1) to the extent that that subsection does not relate to a copy of the order being forwarded by the court to the registrar;

Section 131;

Sections 133 to 135;

Sections 138 to 140;

Sections 142 to 146;

Section 147, including subsection (3) to the extent that that subsection does not relate to a copy of the order being forwarded by the company to the registrar;

Section 162 to the extent that that section concerns the matters set out in Section C.2 of Schedule 5 to the Scotland Act 1998 as being exceptions to the insolvency reservation;

Sections 163 to 167;

Section 169;

Section 170, including subsection (2) to the extent that that subsection does not relate to an application being made by the registrar to make good the default;

Section 171;

Section 172, including subsection (8) to the extent that that subsection does not relate to the liquidator being required to give notice to the registrar;

Sections 173 and 174;

Section 177;

Sections 185 to 189;

Sections 191 to 194;

Section 196 to the extent that that section applies to the specified devolved functions of Part IV of the Insolvency Act 1986;

Section 199;

Section 200 to the extent that it applies to the specified devolved functions of Part IV of the First Group of Parts of the 1986 Act;

Sections 206 to 215;

Section 218 subsections (1), (2), (4) and (6);

Section 231 to 232 to the extent that the sections apply to administrative receivers, liquidators and provisional liquidators;

Section 233, to the extent that that section applies in the case of the appointment of an administrative receiver, of a voluntary arrangement taking effect, of a company going into liquidation or where a provisional liquidator is appointed;

Section 234 to the extent that that section applies to situations other than those where an administration order applies;

Section 235 to the extent that that section applies to situations other than those where an administration order applies;

Sections 236 to 237 to the extent that those sections apply to situations other than administration orders and winding up;

Sections 242 to 243;

Section 244 to the extent that that section applies in circumstances other than a company which is subject to an administration order;

Section 245;

Section 251, to the extent that that section contains definitions which apply only to devolved matters;

Section 416(1) and (4), to the extent that those subsections apply to section 206(1)(a) and (b) in connection with the offence provision relating to the winding up of a limited liability partnership;

Schedule 2;

Schedule 3;

Schedule 4;

Schedule 8, to the extent that that Schedule does not apply to voluntary arrangements or administrations within the meaning of Parts I and II of the 1986 Act.

In addition, Schedule 10, which concerns punishment of offences under the Insolvency Act 1986, lists various sections of the Insolvency Act 1986 which create an offence. The following sections, which are listed in Schedule 10, are devolved in their application to Scotland:

Section 51(4);

Section 51(5);

Sections 53(2) to 62(5) to the extent that those subsections relate to matters other than delivery to the registrar of companies;

Section 64(2);

Section 65(4);

Section 66(6);

Section 67(8) to the extent that that subsection relates to matters other than delivery to the registrar of companies;

Section 93(3);

Section 94(4) to the extent that that subsection relates to matters other than delivery to the registrar of companies;

Section 94(6);

Section 95(8);

Section 105(3);

Section 106(4) to the extent that that subsection relates to matters other than delivery to the registrar of companies;

Section 106(6);

Section 109(2);

Section 114(4);

Section 131(7);

Section 164;

Section 166(7);

Section 188(2);

Section 192(2);

Sections 206 to 211; and

Section 235(5) to the extent that it relates to matters other than administration orders.

[3568]

SCHEDULE 5
GENERAL AND CONSEQUENTIAL AMENDMENTS IN OTHER LEGISLATION
Regulation 9

1–21.   (*Amend the Financial Services and Markets Act 2000, ss 177(2), 221(2) and 232(2) at* **[205]**, **[249]**, **[260]***; and contain miscellaneous amendments to the Bills of Sale Act (1878) Amendment Act 1882, the Third Parties (Rights Against Insurers) Act 1930, the Corporate Bodies' Contracts Act 1960, the Criminal Justice Act 1967, the Solicitors Act 1974, the Sex Discrimination Act 1975, the Race Relations Act 1976, the Betting and Gaming Duties Act 1981, the Companies Act 1985, the Business Names Act 1985, the Administration of Justice Act 1985, the Insolvency Act 1986, the Building Societies Act 1986, the Courts and Legal Services Act 1990, the Employment Rights Act 1996, and the Contracts (Rights of Third Parties) Act 1999.*)

Culpable officer provisions

22.—(1)   A culpable officer provision applies in the case of a limited liability partnership as if the reference in the provision to a director (or a person purporting to act as a director) were a reference to a member (or a person purporting to act as a member) of the limited liability partnership.

(2)   A culpable officer provision is a provision in any Act or subordinate legislation (within the meaning of the Interpretation Act 1978) to the effect that where—

(a)   a body corporate is guilty of a particular offence, and

(b)   the offence is proved to have been committed with the consent or connivance of, or to be attributable to the neglect on the part of, (among others) a director of the body corporate,

he (as well as the body corporate) is guilty of the offence.

[3569]

SCHEDULE 6
APPLICATION OF SUBORDINATE LEGISLATION

Regulation 10

PART I
REGULATIONS MADE UNDER THE 1985 ACT

1. *The Companies (Revision of Defective Accounts and Report) Regulations 1990*
2. The Companies (Defective Accounts) (Authorised Person) Order 1991
3. *The Accounting Standards (Prescribed Body) Regulations 1990*
4. The Companies (Inspection and Copying of Registers, Indices and Documents) Regulations 1991
5. The Companies (Registers and other Records) Regulations 1985
6. *Companies Act 1985 (Disclosure of Remuneration for Non-Audit Work) Regulations 1991.*
7. The Companies Act 1985 (Power to Enter and Remain on Premises: Procedural) Regulations 2005.]   **[357*]**

NOTES

Paras 1–3, 6.
Act 2006) Regulanked by the Limited Liability Partnerships (Accounts and Audit) (Application of Companies for, and otherwise as 2008, SI 2008/1911, reg 58(1)(c), as from 1 October 2008, except in relation to accounts financial years beginning before that date (see reg 58(3) at **[4226]**).

Para 7: added by the Ltd, ed Liability Partnerships (Amendment) Regulations 2007, SI 2007/2073, reg 4, as from 1 October 2007.

Companies (Revision of Dete ve Accounts and Report) Regulations 1990, SI 1990/2570: revoked and replaced by the Companies (Revisio of Defective Accounts and Reports) Regulations 2008, SI 2008/373, as from 6 April 2008, except in relation to mpanies' financial years beginning before that date.

Companies (Defective Accounts) (Author ed Person) Order 1991, SI 1991/13: revoked and replaced by the Companies (Defective Accounts) (Authorised Person) Order 2005, SI 2005/699. The 2005 Regulations were subsequently revoked by the Companies (Defective Accounts and Directors' Reports) (Authorised Person) and Supervision of Accounts and Reports (Prescribed Body) Order 2008, SI 2008/623, as from 6 April 2008 (subject to transitional provisions).

Accounting Standards (Prescribed Body) Regulations 1990, SI 1990/1667: revoked and replaced by the Accounting Standards (Prescribed Body) Regulations 2005, SI 2005/697. The 2005 Regulations were subsequently revoked and replaced by the Accounting Standards (Prescribed Body) Regulations 2008, SI 2008/651, as from 6 April 2008 (subject to transitional provisions).

Companies (Inspection and Copying of Registers, Indices and Documents) Regulations 1991, SI 1991/1998: revoked by the Companies (Company Records) Regulations 2008, SI 2008/3006, reg 2, as from 1 October 2009, subject to savings in relation to any request made before that date to be provided with a copy of a company record.

Companies Act 1985 (Disclosure of Remuneration for Non-Audit Work) Regulations 1991, SI 1991/2128: these Regulations are disapplied in relation to the accounts of a company for any financial year beginning on or after 1 October 2005; see the Companies (Disclosure of Auditor Remuneration) Regulations 2005, SI 2005/2417. The 2005 Regulations were subsequently revoked by the Companies (Disclosure of Auditor Remuneration and Liability Limitation Agreements) Regulations 2008, SI 2008/469, as from 6 April 2008, except in relation to the accounts of a company for any financial year beginning before that date.

PART II
REGULATIONS MADE UNDER THE 1986 ACT

1. Insolvency Practitioners Regulations 1990
2. The Insolvency Practitioners (Recognised Professional Bodies) Order 1986
3. The Insolvency Rules 1986 and the Insolvency (Scotland) Rules 1986 (except in so far as they relate to the exceptions to the reserved matters specified in section C 2 of Part II of Schedule 5 to the Scotland Act 1998)
4. The Insolvency Fees Order 1986
5. The Co-operation of Insolvency Courts (Designation of Relevant Countries and Territories) Order 1986
6. The Co-operation of Insolvency Courts (Designation of Relevant Countries and Territories) Order 1996
7. The Co-operation of Insolvency Courts (Designation of Relevant Country) Order 1998
8. Insolvency Proceedings (Monetary Limits) Order 1986
9. Insolvency Practitioners Tribunal (Conduct of Investigations) Rules 1986
10. Insolvency Regulations 1994
11. Insolvency (Amendment) Regulations 2000.   **[3571]**

NOTES

Insolvency Practitioners Regulations 1990, SI 1990/439: revoked and replaced by the Insolvency Practitioners Regulations 2005, SI 2005/524.

Insolvency Fees Order 1986, SI 1986/2030: revoked and replaced by the Insolvency Proceedings (Fees) Order 2004, SI 2004/593.

Co-operation of Insolvency Courts (Designation of Relevant Countries and Territories) Order 1996: it is assumed that this refers to the Co-operation of Insolvency Courts (Designation of Relevant Countries) Order 1996, SI 1996/253.

PART III
REGULATIONS MADE UNDER OTHER LEGISLATION

1. Company and Business Names Regulations 1981
2. The Companies (Disqualification Orders) Regulations 1986
3. The Insolvent Companies (Disqualification of Unfit Directors) Proceedings Rules 1987
4. The Contracting Out (Functions of the Official Receiver) Order 1995
5. The Uncertificated Securities Regulations 1995
6. The Insolvent Companies (Reports on Conduct of Directors) Rules 1996
7. The Insolvent Companies (Reports on Conduct of Directors) (Scotland) Rules 1996.

[3572]

NOTES

Companies (Disqualification Orders) Regulations 1986, SI 1986/2067: revoked and replaced by the Companies (Disqualification Orders) Regulations 2001, SI 2001/967.

Uncertificated Securities Regulations 1995, SI 1995/3272: revoked and replaced by the Uncertificated Securities Regulations 2001, SI 2001/3755.

LIMITED LIABILITY PARTNERSHIPS (SCOTLAND)
REGULATIONS 2001

(SSI 2001/128)

NOTES

Made: 28 March 2001.
Authority: Limited Liability Partnerships Act 2000, ss 14(1), (2), 15, 16, 17(1), (3).
Commencement: 6 April 2001.
As of 1 February 2009, these Regulations had not been amended.

ARRANGEMENT OF REGULATIONS

PART I
CITATION, COMMENCEMENT, EXTENT AND INTERPRETATION

PART II
COMPANIES ACT 1985

PART III
WINDING UP AND INSOLVENCY

PART IV
MISCELLANEOUS

SCHEDULES

PART I
CITATION, COMMENCEMENT EXTENT AND INTERPRETATION

1 Citation, commencement and extent

(1) These Regulations may be cited as the Limited Liability Partnerships (Scotland) Regulations 2001 and shall come into force on 6th April 2001.

(2) These Regulations extend to Scotland only.

[3572A]

2 Interpretation

In these Regulations—

"the 1985 Act" means the Companies Act 1985;

"the 1986 Act" means the Insolvency Act 1986;

"limited liability partnership agreement", in relation to a limited liability partnership, means any agreement, express or implied, made between the members of the limited liability partnership or between the limited liability partnership and the members of the limited liability partnership which determines the mutual rights and duties of the members, and their rights and duties in relation to the limited liability partnership;

"the principal Act" means the Limited Liability Partnerships Act 2000; and

"shadow member", in relation to a limited liability partnership, means a person in accordance with whose directions or instructions the members of the limited liability partnership are accustomed to act (but so that a person is not deemed a shadow member by reason only that the members of the limited liability partnership act on advice given by that person in a professional capacity).

[3572B]

PART II
COMPANIES ACT

3 Application of the 1985 Act to limited liability partnerships

The provisions of the 1985 Act specified in the first column of Schedule 1 to these Regulations shall apply to limited liability partnerships, with the following modifications—

(a) references to a company shall include references to a limited liability partnership;

(b) references to the Companies Acts shall include references to the principal Act and any regulations made thereunder;

(c) references to the 1986 Act shall include references to that Act as it applies to limited liability partnerships by virtue of Part III of these Regulations;

(d) references in a provision of the 1985 Act to other provisions of that Act shall include references to those other provisions as they apply to limited liability partnerships by virtue of these Regulations; and

(e) the modifications, if any, specified in the second column of Schedule 1 of the provision specified opposite them in the first column.

[3572C]

PART III
WINDING UP AND INSOLVENCY

4 Application of the 1986 Act to limited liability partnerships

(1) Subject to paragraph (2), the provisions of the 1986 Act listed in Schedule 2 shall apply in relation to limited liability partnerships as they apply in relation to companies.

(2) The provisions of the 1986 Act referred to in paragraph (1) shall so apply, with the following modifications—

(a) references to a company shall include references to a limited liability partnership;

(b) references to a director or to an officer of a company shall include references to a member of a limited liability partnership;

(c) references to a shadow director shall include references to a shadow member;

(d) references to the 1985 Act, the Company Directors Disqualification Act 1986, the Companies Act 1989 or to any provisions of those Acts or to any provisions of the 1986 Act shall include references to those Acts or provisions as they apply to limited liability partnerships by virtue of the principal Act or these Regulations; and

(e) the modifications set out in Schedule 3 to these Regulations.

[3572D]

PART IV
MISCELLANEOUS

5 General and consequential amendments

The enactments referred to in Schedule 4 shall have effect subject to the amendments specified in that Schedule.

[3572E]

6 Application of subordinate legislation

(1)   The Insolvency (Scotland) Rules 1986 shall apply to limited liability partnerships with such modifications as the context requires for the purpose of giving effect to the provisions of the Insolvency Act 1986 which are applied by these Regulations.

(2)   In the case of any conflict between any provision of the subordinate legislation applied by paragraph (1) and any provision of these Regulations, the latter shall prevail.

[3572F]

SCHEDULES

SCHEDULE 1
MODIFICATIONS TO PROVISIONS OF THE 1985 ACT
Regulation 3

Formalities of Carrying on Business

36B (execution of documents by companies)

Floating charges and Receivers (Scotland)

462 (power of incorporated company to create floating charge)	In subsection (1), for the words "an incorporated company (whether a company within the meaning of this Act or not)," substitute "a limited liability partnership", and the words "(including uncalled capital)" are omitted.
463 (effect of floating charge on winding up)	
466 (alteration of floating charges) Subsections (1), (2), (3) and (6)	
486 (interpretation for Part XVIII generally)	For the definition of "company" substitute ""company" means a limited liability partnership;"
487 (extent of Part XVIII)	

[3572G]

SCHEDULE 2
PROVISIONS OF THE 1986 ACT
Regulation 4(1)

The relevant provisions of the 1986 Act are as follows:

Sections 50 to 52;

Section 53(1) and (2), to the extent that those subsections do not relate to the requirement for a copy of the instrument and notice being delivered to the registrar of companies;

Section 53(4), (6) and (7);

Section 54(1), (2), (3) (to the extent that that subsection does not relate to the requirement for a copy of the interlocutor to be delivered to the registrar of companies), and subsections (5), (6) and (7);

Sections 55 to 58;

Section 60, other than subsection (1);

Section 61, including subsections (6) and (7) to the extent that those subsections do not relate to anything to be done or which may be sent to the registrar of companies;

Section 62, including subsection (5) to the extent that that subsection does not relate to anything to be done or which may be sent to the registrar of companies;

Sections 63 to 66;

Section 67, including subsections (1) and (8) to the extent that those subsections do not relate to anything to be sent to the registrar of companies;

Section 68;

Section 69, including subsections (1) and (2) to the extent that those subsections do not relate to anything to be done or which may be done by the registrar of companies;

Sections 70 and 71;

Subsection 84(3) to the extent that it does not concern the copy of the resolution being forwarded to the registrar of companies within 15 days;

Sections 91 to 93;

Section 94, including subsections (3) and (4) to the extent that those subsections do not relate to the liquidator being required to send to the registrar of companies a copy of the account and a return of the final meeting;

Section 95;

Section 97;

Sections 100 to 102;

Sections 104 to 105;

Section 106, including subsections (3), (4) and (5) to the extent that those subsections do not relate to the liquidator being required to send to the registrar of companies a copy of the account of winding up and a return of the final meeting/quorum;

Sections 109 to 111;

Section 112, including subsection (3) to the extent that that subsection does not relate to the liquidator being required to send to the registrar of companies a copy of the order made by the court;

Sections 113 to 115;

Sections 126 to 128;

Section 130(1) to the extent that that subsection does not relate to a copy of the order being forwarded by the court to the registrar of companies;

Section 131;

Sections 133 to 135;

Sections 138 to 140;

Sections 142 to 146;

Section 147, including subsection (3) to the extent that that subsection does not relate to a copy of the order being forwarded by the company to the registrar of companies;

Section 162 to the extent that the section concerns the matters set out in Section C 2 of Schedule 5 to the Scotland Act 1998 as being exceptions to the reservation of insolvency;

Sections 163 to 167;

Section 169;

Section 170, including subsection (2) to the extent that that subsection does not relate to an application being made by the registrar to make good the default;

Section 171;

Section 172, including subsection (8) to the extent that that subsection does not relate to the liquidator being required to give notice to the registrar of companies;

Sections 173 and 174;

Section 177;

Sections 185 to 189;

Sections 191 to 194;

Section 196;

Section 199;

Section 200;

Sections 206 to 215;

Section 218 subsections (1), (2),(4) and (6);

Sections 231 to 232 to the extent that the sections apply to administrative receivers, liquidators and provisional liquidators;

Section 233 to the extent that that section applies in the case of the appointment of an administrative receiver, of a voluntary arrangement taking effect, of a company going into liquidation or where a provisional liquidator is appointed;

Section 234 to the extent that that section applies to situations other than those where an administration order applies;

Section 235 to the extent that that section applies to situations other than those where an administration order applies;

Sections 236 to 237 to the extent that those sections apply to situations other than administration orders and winding up;

Sections 242 to 243;

Section 244 to the extent that that section applies in circumstances other than a company which is subject to an administration order;

Section 245;

Section 251;

Section 416(1) and (4) to the extent that those subsections apply to section 206(1)(a) and (b) in connection with the offence provision relating to the winding up of a limited liability partnership;

Section 430;

Section 436;

Schedule 2;

Schedule 3;

Schedule 4;

Schedule 8 to the extent that that Schedule does not apply to voluntary arrangements or administrations within the meaning of Parts I and II of the 1986 Act;

Schedule 10 to the extent that it refers to any of the sections referred to above.

[3572H]

SCHEDULE 3
MODIFICATIONS TO PROVISIONS OF THE 1986 ACT

Regulation 4(2)

Provisions	Modifications
Section 84 (circumstances in which company may be wound up voluntarily)	
Subsection (3)	For subsection (3) substitute the following—
	"(3) Within 15 days after a limited liability partnership has determined that it be wound up there shall be forwarded to the registrar of companies either a printed copy or a copy in some other form approved by the registrar of the determination."
	After subsection (3) insert a new subsection—
Subsection (4)	"(4) If a limited liability partnership fails to comply with this regulation the limited liability partnership and every designated member of it who is in default is liable on summary conviction to a fine not exceeding level 3 on the standard scale."
Section 91 (appointment of liquidator)	
Subsection (1)	Delete "in general meeting".
Subsection (2)	For subsection (2) substitute the following—
	"(2) On the appointment of a liquidator the powers of the members of the limited liability partnership shall cease except to the extent that a meeting of the members of the limited liability partnership summoned for the purpose or the liquidator sanctions their continuance."
	After subsection (2) insert—
	"(3) Subsections (3) and (4) of section 92 shall apply for the purposes of this section as they apply for the purposes of that section."
Section 92 (power to fill vacancy in office of liquidator)	

Provisions	Modifications
Subsection (1)	For "the company in general meeting" substitute "a meeting of the members of the limited liability partnership summoned for the purpose".
Subsection (2)	For "a general meeting" substitute "a meeting of the members of the limited liability partnership".
Subsection (3)	In subsection (3), for "articles" substitute "limited liability partnership agreement".
new subsection (4)	Add a new subsection (4) as follows—
	"(4) The quorum required for a meeting of the members of the limited liability partnership shall be any quorum required by the limited liability partnership agreement for meetings of the members of the limited liability partnership and if no requirement for a quorum has been agreed upon the quorum shall be 2 members."
Section 93 (general company meeting at each year's end)	
subsection (1)	For "a general meeting of the company" substitute "a meeting of the members of the limited liability partnership".
new subsection (4)	Add a new subsection (4) as follows—
	"(4) Subsections (3) and (4) of section 92 shall apply for the purposes of this section as they apply for the purposes of that section."
Section 94 (final meeting prior to dissolution)	
subsection (1)	For "a general meeting of the company" substitute "a meeting of the members of the limited liability partnership".
new subsection (5A)	Add a new subsection (5A) as follows—
	"(5A) Subsections (3) and (4) of section 92 shall apply for the purposes of this section as they apply for the purposes of that section."
subsection (6)	For "a general meeting of the company" substitute "a meeting of the members of the limited liability partnership".
Section 95 (effect of company's insolvency)	
subsection (1)	For "directors'" substitute "designated members'".
subsection (7)	For subsection (7) substitute the following—
	"(7) In this section 'the relevant period' means the period of 6 months immediately preceding the date on which the limited liability partnership determined that it be wound up voluntarily."
Section 100 (appointment of liquidator)	
subsection (1)	For "The creditors and the company at their respective meetings mentioned in section 98" substitute "The creditors at their meeting mentioned in section 98 and the limited liability partnership".
subsection (3)	Delete "director,".
Section 101(appointment of liquidation committee)	
subsection (2)	For subsection (2) substitute the following—
	"(2) If such a committee is appointed, the limited liability partnership may, when it determines that it be wound up voluntarily or at any time thereafter, appoint such number of persons as they think fit to act as members of the committee, not exceeding 5."
Section 105 (meetings of company and creditors at each year's end)	
subsection (1)	For "a general meeting of the company" substitute "a meeting of the members of the limited liability partnership".

Provisions	Modifications
new subsection (5)	Add a new subsection (5) as follows—
	"(5) Subsections (3) and (4) of section 92 shall apply for the purposes of this section as they apply for the purposes of that section."

Section 106 (final meeting prior to dissolution)

subsection (1)	For "a general meeting of the company" substitute "a meeting of the members of the limited liability partnership".
new subsection (5A)	After subsection (5) insert a new subsection (5A) as follows—
	"(5A) Subsections (3) and (4) of section 92 shall apply for the purposes of this section as they apply for the purposes of that section."
subsection (6)	For "a general meeting of the company" substitute "a meeting of the members of the limited liability partnership".

Sections 110 (acceptance of shares, etc, as consideration for sale of company property)

For the existing section substitute the following:

"(1) This section applies, in the case of a limited liability partnership proposed to be, or being, wound up voluntarily, where the whole or part of the limited liability partnership's business or property is proposed to be transferred or sold to another company whether or not it is a company within the meaning of the Companies Act ("the transferee company") or to a limited liability partnership ("the transferee limited liability partnership").

(2) With the requisite sanction, the liquidator of the limited liability partnership being, or proposed to be, wound up ("the transferor limited liability partnership") may receive, in compensation or part compensation for the transfer or sale, shares, policies or other like interests in the transferee company or the transferee limited liability partnership for distribution among the members of the transferor limited liability partnership.

(3) The sanction required under subsection (2) is—

(a) in the case of a members' voluntary winding up, that of a determination of the limited liability partnership at a meeting of the members of the limited liability partnership conferring either a general authority on the liquidator or an authority in respect of any particular arrangement, (subsections (3) and (4) of section 92 to apply for this purpose as they apply for the purposes of that section), and

(b) in the case of a creditor's voluntary winding up, that of either court or the liquidation committee.

(4) Alternatively to subsection (2), the liquidator may (with the sanction) enter into any other arrangement whereby the members of the transferor limited liability partnership may, in lieu of receiving cash, shares, policies or other like interests (or in addition thereto), participate in the profits, or receive any other benefit from the transferee company or the transferee limited liability partnership.

(5) A sale or arrangement in pursuance of this section is binding on members of the transferor limited liability partnership.

Provisions	Modifications
	(i) was at the time of the withdrawal unable to pay its debts within the meaning of section 123 of the Act, or
	(ii) would become so unable to pay its debts after the assets of the limited liability partnership had been depleted by that withdrawal taken together with all other withdrawals (if any) made by any members contemporaneously with that withdrawal or in contemplation when that withdrawal was made.
	(3) Where this section has effect in relation to any person the court, on the application of the liquidator, may declare that that person is to be liable to make such contribution (if any) to the limited liability partnership's assets as the court thinks proper.
	(4) The court shall not make a declaration in relation to any person the amount of which exceeds the aggregate of the amounts or values of all the withdrawals referred to in subsection (2) made by that person within the period of 2 years referred to in that subsection.
	(5) The court shall not make a declaration under this section with respect to any person unless that person knew or ought to have concluded that after each withdrawal referred to in subsection (2) there was no reasonable prospect that the limited liability partnership would avoid going into insolvent liquidation.
	(6) For the purposes of subsection (5) the facts which a member ought to know or ascertain, the conclusions which he ought to reach and the steps which he ought to have taken are those which would be known or ascertained, or reached or taken, by a reasonably diligent person having both:
	(a) the general knowledge, skill and experience that may reasonably be expected of a person carrying out the same functions as are carried out by that member in relation to the limited liability partnership, and
	(b) the general knowledge, skill and experience that that member has.
	(7) For the purposes of this section a limited liability partnership goes into insolvent liquidation if it goes into liquidation at a time when its assets are insufficient for the payment of its debts and other liabilities and the expenses of the winding up.
	(8) In this section "member" includes a shadow member.
	(9) This section is without prejudice to section 214."
Section 215 (proceedings under ss 213, 214)	
subsection (1)	Omit the word "or" between the words "213" and "214" and insert after "214" "or 214A".
subsection (2)	For "either section" substitute "any of those sections".
subsection (4)	For "either section" substitute "any of those sections".
subsection (5)	For "Sections 213 and 214" substitute "Sections 213, 214 or 214A".
Section 218 (prosecution of delinquent officers and members of company)	
subsection (1)	For "officer, or any member, of the company" substitute "member of the limited liability partnership"

PART III
STATUTORY INSTRUMENTS

2 Interpretation

In these Rules—

"the Act" means the Financial Services and Markets Act 2000;

"the Authority" means the Financial Services Authority;

"debt" means the sum referred to in section 372(4)(a) of the Act;

"demand" means a demand made under section 372(4)(a) of the Act;

"individual" has the meaning given by section 372(7) of the Act;

"person" excludes a body of persons corporate or unincorporate; .

"the 1986 Rules" means the Insolvency Rules 1986.

[3574]

3 Modification of the 1986 Rules

The 1986 Rules apply in relation to a demand with the following modifications.

[3575]

4 Rule 6.1

(1) Rule 6.1 (form and content of statutory demand) is disapplied.

(2) A demand must be dated and signed by a member of the Authority's staff authorised by it for that purpose.

(3) A demand must specify that it is made under section 372(4)(a) of the Act.

(4) A demand must state the amount of the debt, to whom it is owed and the consideration for it or, if there is no consideration, the way in which it arises; but if the person to whom the debt is owed holds any security in respect of the debt of which the Authority is aware—

(a) the demand must specify the nature of the security and the value which the Authority puts upon it as at the date of the demand; and

(b) the amount of which payment is claimed by the demand must be the full amount of the debt less the amount specified as the value of the security.

(5) A demand must state the grounds on which it is alleged that the individual appears to have no reasonable prospect of paying the debt.

[3576]

5 Rule 6.2

(1) Rule 6.2 (information to be given in statutory demand) is disapplied—

(2) The demand must include an explanation to the individual of the following matters—

(a) the purpose of the demand and the fact that, if the individual does not comply with the demand, bankruptcy proceedings may be commenced against him;

(b) the time within which the demand must be complied with, if that consequence is to be avoided;

(c) the methods of compliance which are open to the individual; and

(d) the individual's right to apply to the court for the demand to be set aside.

(3) The demand must specify the name and address (and telephone number, if any) of one or more persons with whom the individual may, if he wishes, enter into communication with a view to establishing to the Authority's satisfaction that there is a reasonable prospect that the debt will be paid when it falls due or (as the case may be) that the debt will be scoured or compounded.

[3577]

6 Rules 6.3, 6.5, 6.11 and 6.25

(1) Rules 6.3 (requirements as to service), 6.5 (hearing of application to set aside), 6.11, (proof of service of statutory demand) and 6.25 (decision on the hearing) apply as if—

(a) references to the debtor were references to an individual;

(b) references (other than in rule 6.5(2) and (4)(c)) to the creditor were references to the Authority; and

(c) references to the creditor in rule 6.5(2) and (4)(c) were references to the person to whom the debt is owed.

(2) Rule 6.5(2) applies as if the reference to the creditor also included a reference to the Authority.

(3) Rule 6.5(5) is disapplied and there is substituted the following—

"Where the person to whom the debt is owed holds some security in respect of his debt, and rule 4(4) of the Bankruptcy (Financial Services and Markets Act 2000) Rules 2001 is complied with in respect of it but the court is satisfied that the security is undervalued in the demand, the Authority may be required to amend the demand accordingly (but without prejudice to its right to present a bankruptcy by reference to the original demand)."

[3578]

7 Rule 6.4

Rule 6.4 (application to set aside statutory demand) applies as if—
- (a) references to the debtor were references to an individual;
- (b) the words in paragraph (2), "the creditor issuing the statutory demand is a Minister of the Crown or a Government Department, and" were omitted; and
- (c) the reference to the creditor in paragraph (2)(b) was a reference to the Authority.

[3579]

8 Rule 6.9

Rule 6.9 (court in which petition to be presented) applies as if, for paragraph (1)(a), there were substituted—

     "(a) if in any demand on which the petition is based the Authority has indicated the intention to present a bankruptcy petition to that Court,".

[3580]

UNCERTIFICATED SECURITIES REGULATIONS 2001

(SI 2001/3755)

NOTES

Made: 23 November 2001.

Authority: Companies Act 1989, s 207. Note that s 207 was repealed by the Companies Act 2006, s 1295, Sch 16, as from 6 April 2008. By virtue of s 1297 of that Act at **[1729FM]** (continuity of law) these Regulations now have effect as if made under ss 783, 784(3), 785 and 788 of the 2006 Act.

Commencement: 26 November 2001.

These Regulations are reproduced as amended by: the Enterprise Act 2002; the Enterprise Act 2002 (Consequential and Supplemental Provisions) Order 2003, SI 2003/1398; the Uncertificated Securities (Amendment) (Eligible Debt Securities) Regulations 2003, SI 2003/1633; the Enterprise Act 2002 and Media Mergers (Consequential Amendments) Order 2003, SI 2003/3180; the Government Stock (Consequential and Transitional Provision) (No 2) Order 2004, SI 2004/1662; the Local Authorities (Capital Finance) (Further Consequential and Saving Provisions) Order 2004, SI 2004/2044; the Capital Requirements Regulations 2006, SI 2006/3221; the Uncertificated Securities (Amendment) Regulations 2007, SI 2007/124; the Companies Act 2006 (Commencement No 2, Consequential Amendments, Transitional Provisions and Savings) Order 2007, SI 2007/1093; the Companies Act 2006 (Commencement No 3, Consequential Amendments, Transitional Provisions and Savings) Order 2007, SI 2007/2194.

ARRANGEMENT OF REGULATIONS

PART 1
CITATION, COMMENCEMENT AND INTERPRETATION

PART 2
THE OPERATOR

Approval and compliance

Supervision

Miscellaneous

PART 3
PARTICIPATING SECURITIES

Participation by issuers

PART 1
CITATION, COMMENCEMENT, AND INTERPRETATION

1 Citation and commencement

These Regulations may be cited as the Uncertificated Securities Regulations 2001 and shall come into force on 26th November 2001.

[3581]

2 Purposes and basic definition

(1)   These Regulations enable title to units of a security to be evidenced otherwise than by a certificate and transferred otherwise than by a written instrument, and make provision for certain supplementary and incidental matters; and in these Regulations "relevant system" means a computer-based system, and procedures, which enable title to units of a security to be evidenced and transferred without a written instrument, and which facilitate supplementary and incidental matters.

(2)   Where a title to a unit of a security is evidenced otherwise than by a certificate by virtue of these Regulations, the transfer of title to such a unit of a security shall be subject to these Regulations.

[3582]

3 Interpretation

(1)   In these Regulations—
["the 1877 Act" means the Treasury Bills Act 1877;
"the 1950 Act" means the Exchequer and Financial Provisions Act (Northern Ireland) 1950;]
"the 1985 Act" means the Companies Act 1985;
"the 1986 Act" means the Financial Services Act 1986;
[.....]
"the 2000 Act" means the Financial Services and Markets Act 2000;
"the 1986 Order" means the Companies (Northern Ireland) Order 1986;
.....
["the 1968 Regulations" means the Treasury Bills Regulations 1968;]
"the 1974 Regulations" means the Local Authority (Stocks and Bonds) Regulations 1974; ...
[.....]
"the 1995 Regulations" means the Uncertificated Securities Regulations 1995;
["the 2003 Regulations" means the Uncertificated Securities (Amendment) (Eligible Debt Securities) Regulations 2003;]
["the 2004 Regulations" means the Government Stock Regulations 2004;]
"the Authority" means the Financial Services Authority referred to in section 1 of the 2000 Act;
"certificate" means any certificate, instrument or other document of, or evidencing, title to units of a security;
"company" means a company within the meaning of section 735(1) of the 1985 Act;
"dematerialised instruction" means an instruction sent or received by means of a relevant system;
[.....]
"designated agency" has the meaning given by regulation 11(1);
["eligible debt security" means—
(a)   a security that satisfies the following conditions—
(i)   the security is constituted by an order, promise, engagement or acknowledgement to pay on demand, or at a determinable future time, a sum in money to, or to the order of, the holder of one or more units of the security; and
(ii)   the current terms of issue of the security provide that its units may only be held in uncertificated form and title to them may only be transferred by means of a relevant system;
(b)   an eligible Northern Ireland Treasury Bill; or
(c)   an eligible Treasury bill;
"eligible Northern Ireland Treasury Bill" means a security—
(a)   constituted by a Northern Ireland Treasury Bill issued in accordance with the 1950 Act as modified by Part 2 of Schedule 1 to the 2003 Regulations; and
(b)   whose current terms of issue provide that its units may only be held in uncertificated form and title to them may only be transferred by means of a relevant system;
"eligible Treasury bill" means a security—
(a)   constituted by a Treasury bill issued in accordance with the 1877 Act and the 1968 Regulations as modified by Part 1 of Schedule 1 to the 2003 Regulations; and

(b) whose current terms of issue provide that its units may only be held in uncertificated form and title to them may only be transferred by means of a relevant system;]

"enactment" includes an enactment comprised in any subordinate legislation within the meaning of the Interpretation Act 1978, and an enactment comprised in, or in an instrument made under, an Act of the Scottish Parliament;

["general local authority security" means a local authority security that is not an eligible debt security;

"general public sector security" means a public sector security that is not an eligible debt security;

"general UK Government security" means a UK Government security that is not an eligible debt security;]

"generate", in relation to an Operator-instruction, means to initiate the procedures by which the Operator-instruction comes to be sent;

"guidance", in relation to an Operator, means guidance issued by him which is intended to have continuing effect and is issued in writing or other legible form, which if it were a rule, would come within the definition of a rule;

"instruction" includes any instruction, election, acceptance or any other message of any kind;

"interest in a security" means any legal or equitable interest or right in relation to a security, including—

(a) an absolute or contingent right to acquire a security created, allotted or issued or to be created, allotted or issued; and

(b) the interests or rights of a person for whom a security is held on trust or by a custodian or depositary;

"issue", in relation to a new unit of a security, means to confer title to a new unit on a person;

"issuer-instruction" means a properly authenticated dematerialised instruction attributable to a participating issuer;

"issuer register of members" has the meaning given by regulation 20(1)(a);

"issuer register of securities"—

(a) in relation to shares, means an issuer register of members; and

[(b) in relation to units of securities other than—

(i) shares,

(ii) securities in respect of which regulation 22(3) applies, or

(iii) wholly dematerialised securities,

means a register of persons holding the units, maintained by or on behalf of the issuer or, in the case of general public sector securities, by or on behalf of the person specified in regulation 21(3);]

["local authority"—

(a) in relation to a security referred to in paragraph (a)(i) of the definition of "local authority security", has the same meaning as in the 1974 Regulations;

[(b) in relation to a security referred to in paragraph (b) of the definition of "local authority security", has the same meaning as in section 23 of the Local Government Act 2003 ("local authority");]]

["local authority security" means a security which is either—

(a) a security other than an eligible debt security which, when held in certificated form is—

(i) transferable in accordance with regulation 7(1) of the 1974 Regulations and title to which must be registered in accordance with regulation 5 of those Regulations; or

(ii) ...

(b) an eligible debt security issued by a local authority;]

"officer", in relation to an Operator or a participating issuer, includes—

(a) where the Operator or the participating issuer is a company, such persons as are mentioned in section 744 of the 1985 Act;

(b) where the Operator or the participating issuer is a partnership, a partner; or in the event that no partner is situated in the United Kingdom, a person in the United Kingdom who is acting on behalf of a partner; and

(c) where the Operator or the participating issuer is neither a company nor a partnership, any member of its governing body; or in the event that no member of its governing body is situated in the United Kingdom, a person in the United Kingdom who is acting on behalf of any member of its governing body;

"Operator" means a person approved by the Treasury under these Regulations as Operator of a relevant system (and in Schedule 1 includes a person who has applied to the Treasury under regulation 4 for their approval of him as an Operator);

"Operator-instruction" means a properly authenticated dematerialised instruction attributable to an Operator;

"Operator register of corporate securities" has the meaning given by regulation 22(2)(a)(i);

["Operator register of eligible debt securities" has the meaning given by regulation 22(3A)(a);
"Operator register of general public sector securities" has the meaning given by regulation 21(1)(a);]

"Operator register of members" has the meaning given by regulation 20(1)(b);

"Operator register of securities"—

    (a)   in relation to shares, means an Operator register of members;

    (b)   in relation to units of a security other than shares, means an Operator register of corporate securities, an Operator register of [general public sector securities, an Operator register of eligible debt securities or, as the case may be, a register maintained by an Operator in accordance with regulation 22(3)(a)];

"Operator's conversion rules" means the rules made and practices instituted by the Operator in order to comply with paragraph 18 of Schedule 1;

"Operator-system" means those facilities and procedures which are part of the relevant system, which are maintained and operated by or for an Operator, by which he generates Operator-instructions and receives dematerialised instructions from system-participants and by which persons change the form in which units of a participating security are held;

"participating issuer" means (subject to paragraph (3)) a person who has issued a security which is a participating security;

"participating security" means a security title to units of which is permitted by an Operator to be transferred by means of a relevant system;

"public sector securities" means UK Government securities and local authority securities;

["record of uncertificated general public sector securities" has the meaning given by regulation 21(2)(a);]

"record of securities" means any of a record of uncertificated corporate securities, a record of uncertificated shares and a record of uncertificated [general public sector securities];

"record of uncertificated corporate securities" has the meaning given by regulation 22(2)(b)(ii);

"record of uncertificated shares" has the meaning given by regulation 20(6)(a);

"register of members" means either or both of an issuer register of members and an Operator register of members;

"register of securities" means either or both of an issuer register of securities and an Operator register of securities;

"relevant system" has the meaning given by regulation 2(1); and "relevant system" includes an Operator-system;

"rules", in relation to an Operator, means rules made or conditions imposed by him with respect to the provision of the relevant system;

"securities" means shares, stock, debentures, debenture stock, loan stock, bonds, units of a collective investment scheme within the meaning of section 235 of the 2000 Act, rights under a depositary receipt within the meaning of paragraph 4 of Schedule 2 to the Criminal Justice Act 1993, and other securities of any description, and interests in a security;

"settlement", [except in paragraph 28 of Schedule 1,] in relation to a transfer of uncertificated units of a security between two system-members by means of a relevant system, means the delivery of those units to the transferee and, where appropriate, the creation of any associated obligation to make payments, in accordance with the rules and practices of the Operator; and "settle" shall be construed accordingly;

"settlement bank", in relation to a relevant system, means a person who has contracted to make payments in connection with transfers of title to uncertificated units of a security by means of that system;

"share" means share (or stock) in the share capital of a company;

"system-member", in relation to a relevant system, means a person who is permitted by an Operator to transfer by means of that system title to uncertificated units of a security held by him, and shall include, where relevant, two or more persons who are jointly so permitted;

"system-member instruction" means a properly authenticated dematerialised instruction attributable to a system-member;

"system-participant", in relation to a relevant system, means a person who is permitted by an Operator to send and receive properly authenticated dematerialised instructions; and "sponsoring system-participant" means a system-participant who is permitted by an Operator to send properly authenticated dematerialised instructions attributable to another person and to receive properly authenticated dematerialised instructions on another person's behalf;

"system-user", in relation to a relevant system, means a person who as regards that system is a participating issuer, a system-member, system-participant or settlement bank;

"UK Government security" means a security issued by Her Majesty's Government in the United Kingdom or by a Northern Ireland department;

"uncertificated", in relation to a unit of a security, means (subject to Regulation 42(11)(a)) that title to the unit is recorded on the relevant Operator register of securities, and may, by virtue of these Regulations, be transferred by means of a relevant system; and "certificated", in relation to a unit of a security, means that the unit is not an uncertificated unit;

"unit", in relation to a security, means the smallest possible transferable unit of the security (for example a single share);

"wholly dematerialised security" means—

(a) a strip, in relation to any stock or bond, within the meaning of section 47(1B) of the Finance Act 1942; or

(b) a participating security whose terms of issue (or, in the case of shares, where its terms of issue or the articles of association of the company in question) provide that its units may only be held in uncertificated form and title to them may only be transferred by means of a relevant system;

and other expressions have the meanings given to them by the 1985 Act.

(2) For the purposes of these Regulations—

(a) a dematerialised instruction is properly authenticated if it complies with the specifications referred to in paragraph 5(3) of Schedule 1; or if it was given, and not withdrawn, before these Regulations came into force and was properly authenticated within the meaning of regulation 3(2)(a) of the 1995 Regulations;

(b) a dematerialised instruction is attributable to a person if it is expressed to have been sent by that person, or if it is expressed to have been sent on behalf of that person, in accordance with the rules and specifications referred to in paragraph 5(4) of Schedule 1; and a dematerialised instruction may be attributable to more than one person.

(3) In respect of a participating security which is a [general] public sector security, references in these Regulations to the participating issuer shall, other than in Regulation 41, be taken to be references—

(a) in the case of a local authority security—

(i) to the relevant local authority; or

(ii) if the local authority has appointed another person to act as registrar for the purpose of the 1974 Regulations in respect of that security, to the person so appointed […

(iii) …]; and

(b) in the case of any other [general] public sector security, to [the Registrar of Government Stock].

[(4) In respect of a security which is an eligible debt security, references in these regulations to the issuer or the participating issuer of that security (or units of that security) shall be taken to be references to—

(a) a person ("P") who undertakes as principal to perform the payment obligation constituted by the security in accordance with its current terms of issue; and

(b) any other person who undertakes as principal to perform that obligation in accordance with those terms in the event that P fails to do so.

(5) For the purposes of paragraph (4)(b), a person who undertakes to perform an obligation under a contract of guarantee or other contract of suretyship is not to be regarded as undertaking to perform it as principal.

(6) For the purposes of paragraph (a) of the definition of "eligible debt security" in paragraph (1), a sum of money—

(a) is to be regarded as payable at a determinable future time if it is payable—

(i) at a future time fixed by or in accordance with the current terms of issue of the security; or

(ii) at the expiry of a fixed period after the occurrence of a specified event which is certain to happen, though the time of happening may be uncertain; and

(b) is not to be regarded as payable at a determinable future time if it is payable on a contingency.]

[3583]

NOTES

Para (1) is amended as follows:

Definitions "the 1877 Act", "the 1950 Act", "the 1968 Regulations", "the 2003 Regulations", "eligible debt security", "eligible Northern Ireland Treasury Bill", "eligible Treasury bill", "general local authority security", "general public sector security", "general UK Government security", "local authority", "Operator register of eligible debt securities" and "Operator register of general public sector securities" inserted, words omitted from definition "the 1974 Regulations", and the definition "Operator register of public sector securities" (omitted) revoked, words in square brackets in definitions "issuer register of securities", "Operator register of securities" and "record of securities" substituted, and definition "record of uncertificated general public sector securities" substituted (for original definition "record of uncertificated public sector securities"), by the Uncertificated Securities (Amendment) (Eligible Debt Securities) Regulations 2003, SI 2003/1633, reg 3, as from 24 June 2003.

Definitions "the 1989 Act", "the 1990 Regulations" and "dematerialised loan instrument" (omitted) originally inserted by SI 2003/1633, reg 3, as from 24 June 2003, and revoked by the Local Authorities (Capital Finance) (Further Consequential and Saving Provisions) Order 2004, SI 2004/2044, art 6(1)(a), as from 1 October 2004.

Definition "the 1965 Regulations" (omitted) revoked, and definition "the 2004 Regulations" inserted, by the Government Stock (Consequential and Transitional Provision) (No 2) Order 2004, SI 2004/1662, art 2, Schedule, Pt 3, para 29(1), (2)(a), as from 1 July 2004.

In definition "local authority" para (b) substituted by SI 2004/2044, art 6(1)(b), as from 1 October 2004.

Definition "local authority security" substituted by SI 2003/1633, reg 3, as from 24 June 2003; para (a)(ii) revoked by SI 2004/2044, art 6(1)(c), as from 1 October 2004.

Words in square brackets in definition "settlement" inserted by the Uncertificated Securities (Amendment) Regulations 2007, SI 2007/124, reg 2, as from 1 November 2007.

Para (3): the word "general" in square brackets in both places it occurs inserted by SI 2003/1633, reg 4(1)(a), as from 24 June 2003; sub-para (a)(iii) and the word immediately preceding it originally inserted by SI 2003/1633, reg 4(1)(b), as from 24 June 2003, and revoked by SI 2004/2044, art 6(1)(d), as from 1 October 2004; words in final pair of square brackets substituted by SI 2004/1662, art 2, Schedule, Pt 3, para 29(1), (2)(b), as from 1 July 2004.

Paras (4)–(6): added by SI 2003/1633, reg 4(2), as from 24 June 2003.

Note: in the original Queen's Printer's copy of these Regulations there were two definitions of "record of securities" in para (1) above. It is believed that the second one (ie, the one that followed the definition "register of members") should be the definition "*register* of securities". The above text has been changed accordingly, but no correction slip has been issued to confirm this.

Financial Services Act 1986: repealed by the Financial Services and Markets Act 2000 (Consequential Amendments and Repeals) Order 2001, SI 2001/3649, art 3(1)(c), as from 1 December 2001.

Uncertificated Securities Regulations 1995, SI 1995/3272: revoked by these Regulations.

PART 2
THE OPERATOR

Approval and Compliance

4   Applications for approval

(1)   Any person may apply to the Treasury for their approval of him as Operator of a relevant system.

(2)   The application shall be made in such manner as the Treasury may direct and shall be accompanied by—

    (a)   a copy of the rules and any guidance to be issued by the applicant; and

    (b)   such other information as the Treasury may reasonably require for the purpose of determining the application.

(3)   At any time after receiving an application and before determining it, the Treasury may require the applicant to provide such further information as they reasonably consider necessary to enable them to determine the application.

(4)   Information which the Treasury require under this regulation shall, if they so require, be provided in such form, or verified in such manner, as they may direct.

(5)   Different directions may be given, or requirements imposed, by the Treasury with respect to different applications.

[3584]

5   Grant and refusal of approval

(1)   If, on an application made under regulation 4, it appears to the Treasury that the requirements of Schedule 1 (which imposes requirements which must appear to the Treasury to be satisfied with respect to an Operator, his rules and practices and the relevant system) are satisfied with respect to the application, they may—

    (a)   subject to the payment of any fee charged by virtue of regulation 6(1); and

    (b)   subject to the provisions of Schedule 2,

approve the applicant as Operator of a relevant system.

(2)   In considering an application, the Treasury may have regard to any information which they consider is relevant to the application.

(3)   An approval under this regulation shall be by instrument in writing and shall state the date on which it is to take effect.

(4)   Schedule 3 shall have effect in relation to a decision to refuse an application made under regulation 4 as if references to an Operator were to the applicant.

(5)   Provided that it had not been withdrawn before these Regulations came into force, an approval granted to a person under regulation 5 of the 1995 Regulations shall be treated as having been granted under this regulation.

[3585]

6 Fees charged by the Treasury

(1) The Treasury may charge a fee to a person seeking approval as Operator of a relevant system.

(2) The Treasury may charge an Operator a periodical fee.

(3) Any fee chargeable by the Treasury under this regulation shall not exceed an amount which reasonably represents the amount of costs incurred—

    (a)   in the case of a fee charged to a person seeking approval, in determining whether to grant approval; and

    (b)   in the case of a periodical fee, in satisfying themselves that the Operator, his rules and practices and the relevant system continue to meet the requirements of Schedule 1 and that the Operator is complying with any obligations imposed on him by or under these Regulations.

(4) For the purposes of paragraph (3), the costs incurred by the Treasury shall be determined on the basis that they include such proportion of the following matters as are properly attributable to the performance of the relevant function—

    (a)   expenditure on staff, equipment, premises, facilities, research and development;

    (b)   the allocation, over a period of years, whether before or after the coming into force of these Regulations, of any initial expenditure incurred wholly and exclusively to perform the function or to prepare for its performance;

    (c)   any notional interest incurred on any capital expended on or in connection with the performance of the function or in preparing for its performance and, in a case in which any function is exercisable by the designated agency, any actual interest payable on any sums borrowed which have been so expended; and

    (d)   any other matter which, in accordance with generally accepted accounting principles, may properly be taken account of in ascertaining the costs properly attributable to the performance of the function.

(5) For the purposes of paragraph (4)(c)—

    (a)   "notional interest" means any interest which that person might reasonably have been expected to have been liable to pay had the sums expended been borrowed at arm's length; and

    (b)   "actual interest" means the actual interest paid on sums borrowed in a transaction at arm's length and, where a sum has been borrowed otherwise than in such a transaction, means whichever is the lesser of the interest actually paid and the interest that might reasonably have been expected to be paid had the transaction been at arm's length.

(6) Any fee received by the Treasury under this regulation shall be paid into the Consolidated Fund.

(7) Any fee received by the designated agency under this regulation may be retained by it.

[3586]

Supervision

7 Withdrawal of approval

(1) The Treasury may withdraw an Operator's approval at the request, or with the consent, of the Operator.

(2) If it appears to the Treasury that—

    (a)   any requirement of Schedule 1 is not satisfied in relation to an Operator; or

    (b)   an Operator is failing or has failed to comply with any obligation imposed on him by or under these Regulations,

they may withdraw approval from that Operator by written instrument even though the Operator does not wish his approval to be withdrawn.

(3) Schedule 3 shall have effect as regards the procedure to be followed before withdrawing an Operator's approval under paragraph (2).

(4) An instrument withdrawing an Operator's approval shall state the date on which it is to take effect.

(5) In the case of an instrument withdrawing an Operator's approval under paragraph (2), the date stated shall not be earlier than the end of the period of three months beginning with the day on which the instrument is executed.

(6) An instrument withdrawing an Operator's approval may contain such transitional provisions as the Treasury think necessary or expedient.

[3587]

8 Compliance orders and directions

(1) This regulation applies if it appears to the Treasury that—

(a)   any requirement of Schedule 1 is not satisfied, or is likely not to be satisfied, in relation to an Operator; or

(b)   an Operator has failed to comply with any obligation imposed on him by or under these Regulations.

(2)   The Treasury may—

(a)   make an application to the court; or

(b)   subject to paragraph (4), direct the Operator to take specified steps for the purpose of securing—

    (i)   that the relevant requirement of Schedule 1 is satisfied in relation to the Operator; or

    (ii)   the Operator's compliance with any obligation of the kind in question.

(3)   If on any application by the Treasury under paragraph (2)(a) the court is satisfied that the relevant requirement of Schedule 1 is not satisfied or is likely not to be satisfied, or, as the case may be, that the Operator has failed to comply with the obligation in question, it may order the Operator to take such steps as the court directs for securing that the requirement is satisfied or that the obligation is complied with.

(4)   Schedule 3 shall have effect as regards the procedure to be followed before giving a direction under paragraph (2)(b).

(5)   A direction under paragraph (2)(b) is enforceable, on the application of the Treasury, by an injunction or, in Scotland, by an order for specific performance under section 45 of the Court of Session Act 1988.

(6)   The jurisdiction conferred by paragraph (3) shall be exercisable by the High Court and the Court of Session.

(7)   The fact that a rule made or condition imposed by an Operator has been altered in response to a direction given by the Treasury under paragraph (2)(b) or an order of the court under paragraph (3) does not prevent it from being subsequently altered or revoked by the Operator.

[3588]

9 Injunctions and restitution orders

(1)   If on the application of the Treasury the court is satisfied—

(a)   that there is a reasonable likelihood that any person will contravene a relevant rule; or

(b)   that any person has contravened a relevant rule, and that there is a reasonable likelihood that the contravention will continue or be repeated,

the court may make an order restraining (or in Scotland an interdict prohibiting) the contravention.

(2)   If on the application of the Treasury the court is satisfied—

(a)   that any person has contravened a relevant rule; and

(b)   that there are steps which could be taken for remedying the contravention,

the court may make an order requiring that person and any other person who appears to the court to have been knowingly concerned in the contravention to take such steps as the court may direct to remedy it.

(3)   No application shall be made by the Treasury under paragraph (1) or (2) in respect of a relevant rule unless it appears to them that the Operator of the relevant system is unable or unwilling to take appropriate steps to restrain the contravention or to require the person concerned to take such steps as are mentioned in paragraph (2)(b).

(4)   If on the application of the Treasury the court is satisfied that any person may have—

(a)   contravened a relevant rule; or

(b)   been knowingly concerned in the contravention of a relevant rule,

the court may make an order restraining (or in Scotland an interdict prohibiting) him from disposing of, or otherwise dealing with, any assets of his which it is satisfied he is reasonably likely to dispose of or otherwise deal with.

(5)   The court may, on the application of the Treasury, make an order under paragraph (6) if it is satisfied that a person has contravened a relevant rule, or been knowingly concerned in the contravention of such a rule, and—

(a)   that profits have accrued to him as a result of the contravention; or

(b)   that one or more persons have suffered loss or been otherwise adversely affected as a result of the contravention.

(6)   The court may order the person concerned to pay to the Treasury such sum as appears to the court to be just having regard—

(a)   in a case within subparagraph (a) of paragraph (5), to the profits appearing to the court to have accrued;

(b)   in a case within subparagraph (b) of that paragraph, to the extent of the loss or other adverse effect; or

    (c)   in a case within both of those subparagraphs, to the profits appearing to the court to have accrued and to the extent of the loss or other adverse effect.

(7)   Subsections (3) to (5) and (8) of section 382 of the 2000 Act shall apply in relation to an application of the Treasury under paragraph (5) as they have effect in relation to an application of the Authority under subsection (1) of that section; and in those subsections as they so apply—

    (a)   the references to subsections (1) and (2) shall be taken to be references to paragraphs (5) and (6) respectively;

    (b)   the references to paragraphs (a) and (b) of subsection (1) shall be taken to be references to subparagraphs (a) and (b) respectively of paragraph (5).

(8)   The jurisdiction conferred by this Regulation shall be exercisable by the High Court and the Court of Session.

(9)   Nothing in this regulation affects the right of any person other than the Treasury to bring proceedings in respect of matters to which this regulation applies.

(10)   In this regulation, "relevant rule" means any provision of the rules of an Operator to which the person in question is subject and which regulate the carrying on by that person of business of any of the following kinds—

    (a)   dealing in investments as principal;

    (b)   dealing in investments as agent;

    (c)   arranging deals in investments;

    (d)   managing investments;

    (e)   safeguarding and administering investments;

    (f)   sending dematerialised instructions;

    (g)   establishing etc a collective investment scheme;

    (h)   advising on investments; or

    (i)   agreeing to carry on any of the activities mentioned in paragraphs (a) to (h).

(11)   In paragraph (2), references to remedying a contravention include references to mitigating its effect.

(12)   Paragraph (10) shall be read with—

    (a)   section 22 of the 2000 Act;

    (b)   any relevant order under that section; and

    (c)   Schedule 2 to that Act.

          [3589]

10 Provision of information by Operators

(1)   The Treasury may, in writing, require an Operator to give them such information as they may specify.

(2)   The Treasury may also, in writing, require an Operator to give them, at such times or in respect of such periods as they may specify, such information relating to that Operator as they may specify.

(3)   Any information required to be given under this regulation shall be only such as the Treasury may reasonably require for the exercise of their functions under these Regulations.

(4)   The Treasury may require information to be given by a specified time, in a specified form and to be verified in a specified manner.

(5)   If an Operator—

    (a)   alters or revokes any of his rules or guidance; or

    (b)   makes new rules or issues new guidance,

he shall give written notice to the Treasury without delay.

          [3590]

11 Delegation of Treasury functions

(1)   Subject to paragraphs (2) and (5), the Treasury may by instrument in writing delegate all or any of the functions conferred by this Part of these Regulations to the Authority; and references in these Regulations to the "designated agency" are references to the Authority so far as such functions are so delegated.

(2)   The functions conferred on the Treasury by regulation 12 may not be delegated.

(3)   The designated agency shall send to the Treasury a copy of any guidance issued by virtue of these Regulations and any requirements imposed by it on an Operator by virtue of regulation 10, and give them written notice of any amendment or revocation of, or addition to, any such guidance or requirements.

(4)   The designated agency shall—

    (a)   send to the Treasury a copy of any guidance issued by it which is intended to have continuing effect and is issued in writing or other legible form; and

(b)   give them written notice of any amendment or revocation of, or addition to, guidance issued by it,

but notice need not be given of the revocation of guidance other than is mentioned in subparagraph (a) or of any amendment or addition which does not result in or consist of such guidance as is there mentioned.

(5)   The Treasury shall not delegate any function to the Authority unless they are satisfied that—

(a)   any guidance issued by it in the exercise of its functions under these Regulations;

(b)   any requirements imposed by it on an Operator by virtue of regulation 10;

(c)   any guidance proposed to be issued by it in the exercise of its functions under these Regulations; and

(d)   any requirements it proposes to impose on an Operator by virtue of regulation 10,

do not have, and are not intended or likely to have, to any significant extent the effect of restricting, distorting or preventing competition, or if they have or are intended or likely to have that effect to any significant extent, that the effect is not greater than is necessary for the protection of investors.

(6)   The powers conferred by paragraph (7) shall be exercisable by the Treasury if at any time it appears to them that—

(a)   any guidance issued by the designated agency in the exercise of its functions under these Regulations;

(b)   any requirements imposed by the designated agency on an Operator by virtue of regulation 10; or

(c)   any practices of the designated agency followed in the exercise of its functions under these Regulations,

have, or are intended or likely to have, to any significant extent the effect of restricting, distorting or preventing competition and that the effect is greater than is necessary for the protection of investors.

(7)   The powers exercisable under this paragraph are—

(a)   to resume all or any of the functions delegated to the designated agency by the written instrument referred to in paragraph (1); or

(b)   to direct the designated agency to take specified steps for the purpose of securing that the guidance, requirements or practices in question do not have the effect mentioned in paragraph (6).

(8)   The Treasury may by written instrument—

(a)   at the request or with the consent of the designated agency; or

(b)   if at any time it appears to them that the designated agency is unable or unwilling to discharge all or any of the functions delegated to it,

resume all or any of the functions delegated to the designated agency under paragraph (1).

(9)   Neither the designated agency nor any person who is, or is acting as, a member, officer or member of staff of the designated agency shall be liable in damages for anything done or omitted in the discharge or purported discharge of functions delegated under paragraph (1) unless the act or omission is shown to have been in bad faith.

(10)   In this regulation—

(a)   any reference to guidance issued to an Operator by the designated agency is a reference to any guidance issued or any recommendation made by the designated agency in writing, or other legible form, which is intended to have continuing effect, and is issued or made to an Operator; and

(b)   references to the practices of the designated agency are references to the practices of the designated agency in its capacity as such.

(11)   If under paragraph (1) the Treasury delegate to the designated agency the Treasury's function of making applications to the court under regulation 9(5), the reference to the Treasury in regulation 9(6) shall, unless the Treasury otherwise provide in the instrument by which that function is delegated, be taken as a reference to the designated agency.

[3591]

12   International obligations

(1)   If it appears to the Treasury that any action proposed to be taken by an Operator or the designated agency would be incompatible with Community obligations or any other international obligations of the United Kingdom they may direct the Operator or the designated agency, as the case may be, not to take that action.

(2)   If it appears to the Treasury that any action which an Operator or the designated agency has power to take is required for the purpose of implementing any such obligations, they may direct the Operator or the designated agency, as the case may be, to take that action.

(3)   A direction under this regulation—

(a)   may include such supplemental or incidental requirements as the Treasury consider necessary or expedient; and

(b) is enforceable, on an application made by the Treasury, by injunction or, in Scotland, by an order for specific performance under section 45 of the Court of Session Act 1988.

[3592]

13 Prevention of restrictive practices

Schedule 2 (prevention of restrictive practices) shall have effect.

[3593]

PART 3
PARTICIPATING SECURITIES

Participation by Issuers

14 Participation in respect of shares

Where—
    (a) an Operator permits title to shares of a class in relation to which regulation 15 applies, or in relation to which a directors' resolution passed in accordance with regulation 16 is effective, to be transferred by means of a relevant system; and
    (b) the company in question permits the holding of shares of that class in uncertificated form and the transfer of title to any such shares by means of a relevant system,

title to shares of that class which are recorded on an Operator register of members may be transferred by means of that relevant system.

[3594]

15 This regulation applies to a class of shares if the company's articles of association are in all respects consistent with—
    (a) the holding of shares of that class in uncertificated form;
    (b) the transfer of title to shares of that class by means of a relevant system; and
    (c) these Regulations.

[3595]

16—(1) This regulation applies to a class of shares if a company's articles of association in any respect are inconsistent with—
    (a) the holding of shares of that class in uncertificated form;
    (b) the transfer of title to shares of that class by means of a relevant system; or
    (c) any provision of these Regulations.

(2) A company may resolve, subject to paragraph (6)(a), by resolution of its directors (in this Part referred to as a "director's resolution") that title to shares of a class issued or to be issued by it may be transferred by means of a relevant system.

(3) Upon a directors' resolution becoming effective in accordance with its terms, and for as long as it is in force, the articles of association in relation to the class of shares which were the subject of the directors' resolution shall not apply to any uncertificated shares of that class to the extent that they are inconsistent with—
    (a) the holding of shares of that class in uncertificated form;
    (b) the transfer of title to shares of that class by means of a relevant system; or
    (c) any provision of these Regulations.

(4) Unless a company has given notice to every member of the company in accordance with its articles of association of its intention to pass a directors' resolution before the passing of such a resolution, it shall give such notice within 60 days of the passing of the resolution.

(5) Notice given by the company before the coming into force of these Regulations of its intention to pass a directors' resolution which, if it had been given after the coming into force of these Regulations would have satisfied the requirements of paragraph (4), shall be taken to satisfy the requirements of that paragraph.

(6) In respect of a class of shares, the members of a company may by ordinary resolution—
    (a) if a directors' resolution has not been passed, resolve that the directors of the company shall not pass a directors' resolution;
    (b) if a directors' resolution has been passed but not yet come into effect in accordance with its terms, resolve that it shall not come into effect;
    (c) if a directors' resolution has been passed and is effective in accordance with its terms but the class of shares has not yet been permitted by the Operator to be a participating security, resolve that the directors' resolution shall cease to have effect; or
    (d) if a directors' resolution has been passed and is effective in accordance with its terms and the class of shares has been permitted by the Operator to be a participating security, resolve that the directors shall take the necessary steps to ensure that title to shares of the

class that was the subject of the directors' resolution shall cease to be transferable by means of a relevant system and that the directors' resolution shall cease to have effect, and the directors shall be bound by the terms of any such ordinary resolution.

[(7) In the event of default in complying with paragraph (4), an offence is committed by every officer of the issuer who is in default.

(7A) A person guilty of such an offence is liable—
(a) on conviction on indictment, to a fine;
(b) on summary conviction, to a fine not exceeding the statutory maximum.]

(8) A company shall not permit the holding of shares in such a class as is referred to in paragraph (1) in uncertificated form, or the transfer of title to shares in such a class by means of a relevant system, unless in relation to that class of shares a directors' resolution is effective.

[(8A) Chapter 3 of Part 3 of the Companies Act 2006 (resolutions affecting a company's constitution) applies to—
(a) a directors' resolution passed by virtue of paragraph (2), or
(b) a resolution of a company passed by virtue of paragraph (6) preventing or reversing such a resolution.]

(9) This regulation shall not be taken to exclude the right of the members of a company to amend the articles of association of the company, in accordance with the articles, to allow the holding of any class of its shares in uncertificated form and the transfer of title to shares in such a class by means of a relevant system.

[3596]

NOTES
Paras (7), (7A): substituted, for original para (7), by the Companies Act 2006 (Commencement No 3, Consequential Amendments, Transitional Provisions and Savings) Order 2007, SI 2007/2194, art 10(1), Sch 4, Pt 3, para 97(1), (2), as from 1 October 2007.
Para (8A): inserted by SI 2007/2194, art 10(1), Sch 4, Pt 3, para 97(1), (3), as from 1 October 2007.

17—(1) A class of shares in relation to which, immediately before the coming into force of these Regulations—
(a) regulation 15 of the 1995 Regulations applied; or
(b) a directors' resolution passed in accordance with regulation 16 of the 1995 Regulations was effective,
shall be taken to be a class of shares in relation to which regulation 15 of these Regulations applies or, as the case may be, a directors' resolution passed in accordance with regulation 16 is effective.

(2) On the coming into force of these Regulations a company's articles of association in relation to any such class of shares, and the terms of issue of any such class of shares, shall cease to apply to the extent that they are inconsistent with any provision of these Regulations.

[3597]

18 Interpretation of regulations 15, 16 and 17
For the purposes of regulations 15, 16 and 17 any shares with respect to which share warrants to bearer are issued under section 188 of the 1985 Act shall be regarded as forming a separate class of shares.

[3598]

19 Participation in respect of securities other than shares
(1) Subject to paragraph (2), where—
(a) an Operator permits title to a security other than a share to be transferred by means of a relevant system; and
(b) the issuer permits the holding of units of that security in uncertificated form and the transfer of title to units of that security by means of a relevant system,
title to units of that security which are recorded on an Operator register of securities may be transferred by means of that relevant system.

(2) In relation to any security other than a share, if the law under which it is constituted is not the law of England and Wales, Northern Ireland or Scotland, or if the current terms of its issue are in any respect inconsistent with—
(a) the holding of title to units of that security in uncertificated form;
(b) the transfer of title to units of that security by means of a relevant system; or
(c) subject to paragraph (3), these Regulations,
[an issuer of that security] shall not permit the holding of units of that security in uncertificated form, or the transfer of title to units of that security by means of a relevant system.

52 Revocations

(1) The following provisions of the 1965 Regulations are hereby revoked, namely—

regulation 4(3) and (4);

regulations 4A and 4B;

regulation 6(5);

regulation 17(7);

regulation 18(5);

regulation 19(2);

regulation 20(2); and

Schedule 1.

(2) The following provisions of the 1974 Regulations are hereby revoked, namely—

regulation 6(6);

regulation 6A;

regulation 7(1)(b), (4) and (5);

regulation 8(2) and (3);

regulation 9(4);

regulation 10(3);

regulation 16(4);

regulation 21(3); and

Schedule 2.

(3) The 1995 Regulations are hereby revoked.

(4) The following provisions of the Open-Ended Investment Companies Regulations 2001 are hereby revoked, namely—

regulation 47(1);

in Schedule 3—

paragraph 2(2),

paragraph 5(1)(c) and the word "and" immediately before it, and

paragraph 6(3)(d) and the word "and" immediately before it;

paragraph 3 of Schedule 4; and

paragraph 12 of Schedule 7.

[3632]

SCHEDULES

SCHEDULE 1

REQUIREMENTS FOR APPROVAL OF A PERSON AS OPERATOR

Regulation 5(1)

Arrangements and resources

1. An Operator must have adequate arrangements and resources for the effective monitoring and enforcement of compliance with his rules or, as respects monitoring, arrangements providing for that function to be performed on his behalf (and without affecting his responsibility) by another body or person who is able and willing to perform it.

Financial resources

2. An Operator must have financial resources sufficient for the proper performance of his functions as an Operator.

Promotion and maintenance of standards

3. An Operator must be able and willing to promote and maintain high standards of integrity and fair dealing in the operation of the relevant system and to cooperate, by the sharing of information or otherwise, with the Treasury and any other authority, body or person having responsibility for the supervision or regulation of investment business or other financial services.

Operation of the relevant system

4.—(1) Except in the circumstances referred to in subparagraph (2), where an Operator causes or permits a part of the relevant system which is not the Operator-system to be operated by another person (other than as his agent) the Operator—

(a) shall monitor compliance by the person and that part with the requirements of this Schedule; and

(b) shall have arrangements to ensure that the person provides him with such information and such assistance as he may require in order to meet his obligations under these Regulations.

(2) Where a part of the relevant system which is not the Operator-system comprises procedures which enable dematerialised instructions to be authenticated in accordance with paragraph 5(3)(b),

the Operator shall have arrangements to ensure that he is provided with such information and such assistance as he may require in order to keep under review his agreement to the specifications by which those dematerialised instructions may be authenticated.

System security

5.—(1)   A relevant system must be so constructed and operate in such a way that it satisfies the requirements of subparagraphs (2) to (6).

(2)   The relevant system must minimise the possibility of unauthorised access to, or modification of, any program or data held in any computer forming part of the Operator-system.

(3)   Each dematerialised instruction must be authenticated—
    (a)   in accordance with the specifications of the Operator, and those specifications shall provide that each dematerialised instruction—
        (i)   is identifiable as being from the computers of the Operator or of a particular system-participant; and
        (ii)   is designed to minimise fraud and forgery; or
    (b)   if it is sent to the Operator by, or by the Operator to, a depositary, a clearing house or an exchange, in accordance with specifications of that depositary, clearing house or exchange to which the Operator has agreed and which provide that each dematerialised instruction—
        (i)   is identifiable as being from the computers of the Operator or of the depositary, clearing house or exchange which sent it; and
        (ii)   is designed to minimise fraud and forgery.

(4)   Each dematerialised instruction must, in accordance with any relevant rules of the Operator and with the specifications of the Operator or the specifications referred to in subparagraph (3)(b) (as the case may be), express by whom it has been sent and, where relevant, on whose behalf it has been sent.

(5)   Each dematerialised instruction must, in accordance with any relevant rules of the Operator and with the specifications of the Operator or the specifications referred to in subparagraph (3)(b) (as the case may be), indicate—
    (a)   where it is sent to a system-participant or the Operator, that it is addressed to that system-participant or the Operator;
    (b)   where it is sent to a person who is using the facilities of a sponsoring system-participant to receive dematerialised instructions, that it is addressed to that person and the sponsoring system-participant; and
    (c)   where it is sent to the Operator in order for him to send an Operator-instruction to a system-participant, that it is addressed to the Operator, to the system-participant and, if the system-participant is acting as a sponsoring system-participant, to the relevant person on whose behalf the sponsoring system-participant receives dematerialised instructions; and

(6)   The relevant system must minimise the possibility for a system-participant to send a dematerialised instruction on behalf of a person from whom he has no authority.

(7)   For the purposes of this paragraph—
    "clearing house" means a body or association—
    (a)   which is a recognised clearing house within section 285(1)(b) of the 2000 Act;
    (b)   which is authorised under that Act to provide clearing services in the United Kingdom; or
    (c)   which provides services outside the United Kingdom which are similar in nature to those provided by any such body or association, and which is regulated or supervised in the provision of those services by a regulatory body or agency of government;
    "depositary" means a body or association carrying on business outside the United Kingdom with whom an Operator has made arrangements—
    (a)   to enable system-members to hold (whether directly or indirectly) and transfer title to securities (other than participating securities) by means of facilities provided by that body or association; or
    (b)   to enable that body or association to permit persons to whom it provides services in the course of its business to hold (whether directly or indirectly) and transfer title to participating securities by means of the Operator's relevant system; and
    "exchange" means a body or association—
    (a)   which is a recognised investment exchange within section 285(1)(a) of the 2000 Act;
    (b)   which is authorised under that Act to provide a facility for the matching and execution of transactions in securities in the United Kingdom; or
    (c)   which provides services outside the United Kingdom which are similar in nature

Rules and Practices

25. An Operator's rules and practices—
   (a) must bind system-members and participating issuers—
      (i) so as to ensure the efficient processing of transfers of title to uncertificated units of a security in response to Operator-instructions; and
      (ii) as to the action to be taken where transfer of title in response to a system-member instruction or an Operator-instruction cannot be effected;
   (b) must make provision as to the manner in which a system-member or the relevant participating issuer may change the form in which that system-member holds units of a participating security (other than a wholly dematerialised security);
   (c) must make provision for a participating issuer to cease to participate in respect of a participating security so as—
      (i) to minimise so far as practicable any disruption to system-members in respect of their ability to transfer the relevant security; and
      (ii) to provide the participating issuer with any relevant information held by the Operator relating to the uncertificated units of the relevant security held by system-members;
   (d) must make provision for the orderly termination of participation by system-members and system-participants whose participation is disruptive to other system-members or system-participants or to participating issuers;
   (e) must make provision—
      (i) as to which of the Operator's records are to constitute an Operator register of securities in relation to a participating security, or a participating security of a particular kind; and
      (ii) as to the times at which, and the manner in which, a participating issuer may inspect an Operator register of securities [(other than an Operator register of eligible debt securities)] in accordance with paragraph 12;
   (f) if they make provision for the designation of a subsidiary undertaking as a relevant nominee, must require that the relevant nominee maintain adequate records of—
      (i) the names of the persons who have an interest in the securities it holds; and
      (ii) the nature and extent of their interests; and
   (g) must make provision for the authentication by the Operator of any written notification given under regulation 25(3) or 32(2)(c).

26. An Operator's rules and practices must require—
   (a) that each system-participant is able to send and receive properly authenticated dematerialised instructions;
   (b) that each system-member has arrangements—
      (i) for properly authenticated dematerialised instructions attributable to him to be sent;
      (ii) for properly authenticated dematerialised instructions to be received by or for him; and
      (iii) with a settlement bank for payments to be made, where appropriate, for units of a security transferred by means of the relevant system; and
   (c) that each participating issuer is able to respond with sufficient speed to Operator-instructions.

27. An Operator must have rules which require system-users and former system-users to provide him with such information in their possession as he may require in order to meet his obligations under these Regulations.

[Access to central counterparty, clearing and settlement facilities

28.—(1) The Operator must make transparent and non-discriminatory rules, based on objective criteria, governing access to his settlement facilities.

(2) The rules under sub-paragraph (1) must enable an investment firm or a credit institution authorised by the competent authority of another EEA State (including a branch established in the United Kingdom of such a firm or institution) to have access to those facilities on the same terms as a UK firm for the purposes of finalising or arranging the finalisation of transactions in financial instruments.

(3) The Operator may refuse access to those facilities on legitimate commercial grounds.

(4) In this paragraph—
"banking consolidation directive" means Directive 2006/48/EC of the European Parliament and of the Council of 14th June 2006 relating to the taking up and pursuit of the business of credit institutions;
"branch" in relation to an investment firm has the meaning given in Article 4.1.26 of the markets in financial instruments directive and in relation to a credit institution has the meaning given in Article 4.3 of the banking consolidation directive;

"competent authority", in relation to an investment firm or credit institution, means the competent authority in relation to that firm or institution for the purposes of the markets in financial instruments directive;

"credit institution" means—

(a) a credit institution authorised under the banking consolidation directive, or

(b) an institution which would satisfy the requirements for authorisation as a credit institution under that directive if it had its registered office (or if it does not have a registered office, its head office) in an EEA State;

"EEA State" has the meaning given by paragraph 8 of Schedule 3 to the 2000 Act;

"financial instrument" has the meaning given by Article 4.1.17 of the markets in financial instruments directive;

"investment firm" has the meaning given by section 424A of the 2000 Act;

"markets in financial instruments directive" means Directive 2004/39/EC of the European Parliament and of the Council of 21st April 2004 on markets in financial instruments;

"regulated activity" has the meaning given by section 22 of the 2000 Act;

"settlement" has the same meaning as in the markets in financial instruments directive;

"UK firm" means an investment firm or credit institution which has a permission given by the Authority under Part 4 of the 2000 Act (or having effect as if so given) to carry on one or more regulated activities.]

[3633]

NOTES

Paras 12, 25: words in square brackets inserted by the Uncertificated Securities (Amendment) (Eligible Debt Securities) Regulations 2003, SI 2003/1633, reg 12, as from 24 June 2003.

Para 28: added by the Uncertificated Securities (Amendment) Regulations 2007, SI 2007/124, reg 3, as from 1 November 2007.

SCHEDULE 2
PREVENTION OF RESTRICTIVE PRACTICES

Regulation 13

Examination of rules and practices

1.—(1) The Treasury shall not approve a person as Operator of a relevant system unless they are satisfied that the rules and any guidance of which copies are furnished with the application for approval—

(a) do not have, and are not intended or likely to have, to any significant extent the effect of restricting, distorting or preventing competition; or

(b) if they have or are intended to have that effect to any significant extent, that the effect is not greater than is necessary for the protection of investors, or for compliance with [Directive 2006/48/EC of the European Parliament and of the Council of 14 June 2006 relating to the taking up and pursuit of the business of credit institutions].

(2) Subject to subparagraph (5), the powers conferred by subparagraph (3) shall be exercisable by the Treasury if at any time it appears to them that—

(a) any rules made or guidance issued by an Operator;

(b) any practices of an Operator in his capacity as such; or

(c) any practices of a system-user,

have, or are intended or likely to have, to a significant extent the effect of restricting, distorting or preventing competition and that the effect is greater than is necessary for the protection of investors or for compliance with Directive 2000/12/EC of the European Parliament and of the Council.

(3) the powers exercisable under this paragraph are—

(a) to withdraw approval from the Operator;

(b) to direct the Operator to take specified steps for the purpose of securing that the rules, guidance or practices in question do not have the effect mentioned in subparagraph (2); or

(c) to make alterations in the rules of the Operator for that purpose.

(4) The practices referred to in subparagraph (2)(c) are practices in relation to business in respect of which system-users are subject to the rules of the Operator and which are required or contemplated by his rules or guidance or otherwise attributable to his conduct in his capacity as Operator.

(5) The provisions of Schedule 3 shall apply as regards the procedure to be followed before—

(a) refusing to approve a person as Operator of a relevant system pursuant to subparagraph (1); or

(b) exercising any of the powers conferred by subparagraph (3).

PART III
STATUTORY INSTRUMENTS

Modification of paragraph 1 where delegation order is made

2.—(1)   This paragraph applies instead of paragraph 1 where the function of approving a person as Operator has been delegated to the designated agency by virtue of regulation 11.

(2)   The designated agency—
   (a)   shall send to the Treasury a copy of the rules and any guidance copies of which accompany the application for approval together with any other information supplied with or in connection with the application; and
   (b)   shall not grant the approval without the leave of the Treasury,

and the Treasury shall not give leave in any case in which they would (apart from the delegation of functions to the designated agency) have been precluded by paragraph 1(1) from granting approval.

(3)   The designated agency shall send to the Treasury a copy of any notice received by it from an Operator under regulation 10(5).

(4)   If at any time it appears to the Treasury that there are circumstances such that (apart from the delegation of functions to the designated agency) they would have been able to exercise any of the powers conferred by paragraph 1(3) they may, notwithstanding the delegation of functions to the designated agency but subject to paragraph 1(5)—
   (a)   themselves exercise the power conferred by paragraph 1(3)(a); or
   (b)   direct the designated agency to exercise the power conferred by paragraph 1(3)(b) or (c) in such manner as they may specify.

(5)   The provisions of Schedule 3 shall apply as regards the procedure to be followed before the Treasury exercise their power to refuse leave under subparagraph (2), or their power to give a direction under subparagraph (4), in respect of an Operator.

Reports by the [Office of Fair Trading]

3.—(1)   The Treasury shall before deciding—
   (a)   whether to refuse to approve a person as Operator of a relevant system pursuant to paragraph 1(1); or
   (b)   Whether to refuse for the granting of an approval pursuant to paragraph 2(2),

send to the [Office of Fair Trading (in this Schedule referred to as "the OFT")] a copy of the rules and of any guidance which the Treasury are required to consider in making that decision together with such other information as the Treasury consider will assist in discharging [its] functions under subparagraph (2).

(2)   The [OFT] shall report to the Treasury whether, in [its] opinion, the rules and guidance copies of which are sent to [it] under subparagraph (1) have, or are intended or likely to have, to any significant extent the effect of restricting, distorting or preventing competition and, if so, what that effect is likely to be; and in making any decision as is mentioned in subparagraph (1) the Treasury shall have regard to the [OFT's] report.

(3)   The Treasury shall send to the [OFT] copies of any notice received by them under regulation 10(5) or paragraph 2(3) together with such other information as the Treasury consider will assist the [OFT] in discharging [its] functions under subparagraphs (4) and (5).

(4)   The [OFT] shall keep under review—
   (a)   the rules, guidance and practices mentioned in paragraph 1(2); and
   (b)   the matters specified in the notices of which copies are sent to [it] under subparagraph (3),

and if at any time [it] is of the opinion that any such rules or guidance taken together with any such matters, have, or are intended or likely to have, to any significant extent the effect mentioned in subparagraph (2), [it] shall report [its] opinion to the Treasury stating what in [its] opinion that effect is or is likely to be.

(5)   The [OFT] may report to the Treasury [its] opinion that any such matter as is mentioned in subparagraph (4)(b) does not in [its] opinion have, and is not intended or likely to have, to any significant extent the effect mentioned in subparagraph (2).

(6)   The [OFT] may from time to time consider whether any such practices as are mentioned in paragraph 1(2) have, or are intended or likely to have, to any significant extent the effect mentioned in subparagraph (2) and, if so, what that effect is or is likely to be; and if [it] is of that opinion [it] shall make a report to the Treasury stating [its] opinion and what the effect is or is likely to be.

(7)   The Treasury shall not exercise their powers under paragraph 1(3) or 2(4) except after receiving a report from the [OFT] under subparagraph (4) or (6).

(8)   The [OFT] may, if [it] thinks fit, publish any report made by [it] under this paragraph but shall exclude from a published report, so far as practicable, any matter which relates to the affairs of a particular person (other than the person seeking approval as an Operator) the publication of which would or might in [its] opinion seriously and prejudicially affect the interests of that person.

Investigations by the [Office of Fair Trading]

4.—(1) For the purpose of investigating any matter with a view to his consideration under paragraph 3 the [OFT] may by a notice in writing—

    (a)   require any person to produce, at any time and place specified in the notice, to the [OFT] or to any person appointed by [it] for the purpose, any documents which are specified or described in the notice and which are documents in his custody or under his control and relating to any matter relevant to the investigation; or

    (b)   require any person carrying on business to furnish to the [OFT] such information as may be specified or described in the notice, and specify the time within which, and the manner and form in which, any such information is to be furnished.

    (2)   A person shall not under this paragraph be required to produce any document or disclose any information which he would be entitled to refuse to produce or disclose on grounds of legal professional privilege in proceedings in the High Court or on grounds of confidentiality as between client and professional legal adviser proceedings in the Court of Session.

    (3)   ...

[Enforcement

4A.—(1) The court may, on an application by the OFT, enquire into whether any person ("the defaulter") has refused or otherwise failed, without reasonable excuse, to comply with a notice under paragraph 4(1).

    (2)   An application under sub-paragraph (1) shall include details of the possible failure which the OFT considers has occurred.

    (3)   In enquiring into a case under sub-paragraph (1), the court shall hear any witness who may be produced against or on behalf of the defaulter and any statement which may be offered in defence.

    (4)   Sub-paragraphs (5) and (6) apply where the court is satisfied, after hearing any witnesses and statements as mentioned in sub-paragraph (3), that the defaulter has refused or otherwise failed, without reasonable excuse, to comply with a notice under paragraph 4(1).

    (5)   The court may punish the defaulter as it would have been able to punish him had he been guilty of contempt of court.

    (6)   Where the defaulter is a body corporate or is a partnership constituted under the law of Scotland, the court may punish any director, officer or (as the case may be) partner of the defaulter as it would have been able to punish that director, officer or partner had he been guilty of contempt of court.

    (7)   In this paragraph "the court"—

    (a)   in relation to England and Wales or Northern Ireland, means the High Court, and

    (b)   in relation to Scotland, means the Court of Session.

4B.—(1) A person commits an offence if he intentionally alters, suppresses or destroys a document which he has been required to produce by a notice under paragraph 4(1).

    (2)   A person who commits an offence under sub-paragraph (1) shall be liable—

    (a)   on summary conviction, to a fine not exceeding the statutory maximum;

    (b)   on conviction on indictment, to imprisonment for a term not exceeding two years or to a fine or to both.]

...

5.   ...

Exemptions from the Competition Act 1998

6.—(1) The Chapter I prohibition does not apply to—

    (a)   an agreement for the constitution of an Operator; or

    (b)   an agreement for the constitution of a person who has applied for approval as an Operator in accordance with these Regulations and whose application has not yet been determined,

to the extent to which the agreement relates to rules made or guidance issued by the Operator.

    (2)   The Chapter I prohibition does not apply to a decision made by an Operator to the extent to which the decision relates to any of the rules made or guidance issued by that Operator or to the Operator's specified practices.

    (3)   The Chapter I prohibition does not apply to the specified practices of—

    (a)   an Operator; or

    (b)   a person who is subject to the rules of an Operator.

PART III
STATUTORY INSTRUMENTS

(4)   The Chapter I prohibition does not apply to any agreement the parties to which consist of or include—

(a)   an Operator; or

(b)   a person who is subject to the rules of an Operator,

to the extent to which the agreement consists of provisions the inclusion of which is required or contemplated by these Regulations or by any rules made or guidance issued by the Operator or by the Operator's specified practices.

(5)   In this paragraph—

"the Chapter I prohibition" means the prohibition imposed by section 2(1) of the Competition Act 1998; and

"specified practices" means—

(a)   any practices of an Operator in its capacity as such; or

(b)   any practices of persons who are members of, or otherwise subject to rules made by, an Operator and which are practices—

(i)   in relation to business in respect of which the persons in question are subject to the rules of the Operator where those practices are required or contemplated by the rules of the Operator or by guidance issued by the Operator; or

(ii)   otherwise attributable to the conduct of the Operator as such;

and expressions used in this paragraph which are also used in Part I of the Competition Act 1998 are to be interpreted in same way as for the purposes of that Part of that Act.

Supplementary provisions

7.—(1)   Any direction given under this Schedule shall, on the application of the person by whom it was given, be enforceable by injunction or, in Scotland, by an order for specific performance under section 45 of the Court of Session Act 1988.

(2)   The fact that any rules made by an Operator have been altered by or pursuant to a direction given by the Treasury under this Schedule shall not preclude their subsequent alteration or revocation by the Operator.

(3)   In determining under this Schedule whether any guidance has, or is likely to have, any particular effect the Treasury and the [OFT] may assume that the persons to whom it is addressed will act in conformity with it.

[3634]

NOTES

Para 1: words in square brackets substituted by the Capital Requirements Regulations 2006, SI 2006/3221, reg 29(4), Sch 6, para 12, as from 1 January 2007.

Para 3: all words in square brackets (with the exception of the penultimate word in square brackets in sub-para (8)) substituted by the Enterprise Act 2002 (Consequential and Supplemental Provisions) Order 2003, SI 2003/1398, art 2, Schedule, para 43(1), (2)(a), as from 20 June 2003; the penultimate word in square brackets in sub-para (8) substituted by the Enterprise Act 2002 and Media Mergers (Consequential Amendments) Order 2003, SI 2003/3180, art 2, Schedule, para 9, as from 29 December 2003.

Para 4: words in square brackets substituted, and sub-para (3) revoked, by SI 2003/1398, art 2, Schedule, para 43(1), (2)(b), as from 20 June 2003.

Paras 4A, 4B: inserted by SI 2003/1398, art 2, Schedule, para 43(1), (2)(c), as from 20 June 2003.

Para 5: revoked by SI 2003/1398, art 2, Schedule, para 43(1), (2)(d), as from 20 June 2003.

Para 7: word in square brackets substituted by virtue of the Enterprise Act 2002, s 2, as from 1 April 2003.

SCHEDULE 3
PROCEDURE FOR REFUSAL OR WITHDRAWAL OR APPROVAL AS AN OPERATOR, OR FOR GIVING DIRECTIONS, ETC

Regulations 5(4), 7(3) and 8(4)

1.   Before—

(a)   refusing an application for approval as an Operator made under regulation 4 (whether or not pursuant to paragraph 1(1) of Schedule 2);

(b)   withdrawing an Operator's approval under regulation 7(2);

(c)   giving a direction under regulation 8;

(d)   exercising any power conferred by paragraph 1(3) of Schedule 2;

(e)   exercising the power to refuse leave under paragraph 2(2) of Schedule 2; or

(f)   giving a direction under paragraph 2(4) of Schedule 2, the Treasury shall—

(i)   give written notice of their intention to do so to the Operator;

(ii)   take such steps as they consider reasonably practicable to bring the notice to the attention of system-users; and

(iii)   publish the notice in such manner as they think appropriate for bringing it to the attention of other persons who are, in their opinion, likely to be affected.

2.   A notice under paragraph 1 shall—

    (a)   state why the Treasury intend to refuse the application, withdraw the approval, give the
            direction, or exercise the power in question; and
    (b)   draw attention to the right to make representations conferred by paragraph 3.

3.   Before the end of the period for making representations—
    (a)   the Operator,
    (b)   any system-user, and
    (c)   any other person who is likely to be affected by the proposed withdrawal or direction,
            may make representations to the Treasury.

4.   The period for making representations is—
    (a)   two months beginning—
          (i)   with the date on which the notice under paragraph 1 is served on the Operator; or
          (ii)   if later, with the date on which that notice is published; or
    (b)   such longer period as the Treasury may allow in the particular case.

5.   In deciding whether to refuse the application, withdraw the approval, give the direction, or
exercise the power in question, the Treasury shall have regard to any representations made in
accordance with paragraph 3.

6.   When the Treasury have decided whether to refuse the application, withdraw the approval, give
the direction, or exercise the power in question they shall, if they have decided to refuse the
application, withdraw the Operator's approval under regulation 7(2), give a direction under
regulation 8 or exercise a power conferred by paragraph 1(3) of Schedule 2—
    (a)   give the Operator written notice of their decision; and
    (b)   take such steps as they consider reasonably practicable for bringing their decision to the
            attention of system-users and of any other persons who are, in the Treasury's opinion,
            likely to be affected.

7.   If the Treasury consider it essential to do so, they may withdraw an Operator's approval under
regulation 7(2) or give a direction under regulation 8—
    (a)   without following the procedure set out in this Schedule; or
    (b)   if the Treasury have begun to follow that procedure, regardless of whether the period for
            making representations has expired.

8.   If the Treasury have, in relation to a particular matter, followed the procedure set out in
paragraphs 1 to 5, they need not follow it again if, in relation to that matter, they decide to take
action other than that specified in their notice under paragraph 1.

[3635]

SCHEDULE 4
KEEPING OF REGISTERS AND RECORDS OF PARTICIPATING SECURITIES
Regulation 23(4)

Interpretation

1.   In this Schedule—
    "uncertificated shares" means shares title to which may be transferred by means of a relevant
    system; and
    "certificated shares" means shares which are not uncertificated shares; and "uncertificated
    stock" means stock title to which may be transferred by means of a relevant system; and
    "certificated stock" means stock which is not uncertificated stock.

Registers of members

2.—(1)   Every participating issuer which is a company shall enter in its issuer register of
members—
    (a)   the names and addresses of the members;
    (b)   the date on which each person was registered as a member; and
    (c)   the date at which any person ceased to be a member.

  (2)   With the names and addresses of the members there shall be entered a statement—
    (a)   of the certificated shares held by each member, distinguishing each share by its number
            (so long as the share has a number) and, where the company has more than one class of
            issued shares, by its class; and
    (b)   of the amount paid or agreed to be considered as paid on the certificated shares of each
            member.

  (3)   Where the company has converted any of its shares into stock and given notice of the
conversion to the registrar of companies, the issuer register of members shall show the amount and
class of the certificated stock held by each member, instead of the amount of shares and the
particulars relating to shares specified in subparagraph (2).

  (4)   Subject to subparagraph (5), section 352 of the 1985 Act shall not apply to a company
which is a participating issuer, other than as respects any overseas branch register.

PART III
STATUTORY INSTRUMENTS

(a) the names and address of the persons holding units of the relevant participating security in uncertificated form; and

(b) how many units of that security each such person holds in that form.

[(2) The following provisions of the 2004 Regulations shall not apply in respect of units of general UK Government securities held in uncertificated form—

regulations 7 to 9;

regulations 12 to 14;

regulations 16 to 24;

regulation 28; and

regulations 30 to 31.]

(3) The following provisions of the 1974 Regulations shall not apply in respect of units of [general] local authority securities held in uncertificated form—

regulations 5 and 6;

regulations 8 to 14;

regulation 16; and

regulation 21.

Records of uncertificated [general] public sector securities

13.—(1) The participating issuer shall enter in a record of uncertificated [general] public sector securities the same particulars, so far as is practicable, as are required by paragraph 12(1) to be entered in the relevant Operator register of [general] public sector securities.

(2) In respect of every participating security which is a [general] UK Government security, the record of uncertificated [general] public sector securities shall be kept [by the Registrar of Government Stock].

(3) The participating issuer shall, unless it is impracticable to do so by virtue of circumstances beyond his control, ensure that the record of uncertificated [general] public sector securities is regularly reconciled with the Operator register of [general] public sector securities.

(4) Provided that he has complied with subparagraph (3), a participating issuer shall not be liable in respect of any act or thing done or omitted to be done by him or on his behalf in reliance upon the assumption that the particulars entered in any record of uncertificated [general] public sector securities which he is required to keep by these Regulations accord with particulars entered in the Operator register of [general] public sector securities to which the record relates.

(5) The provisions of the Bankers' Books Evidence Act 1879 shall apply for the purpose of proving any entry in the record of uncertificated [general] public sector securities as if the participating issuer were a bank and a banker within the meaning of that Act, and as if such entry in the record, or, where the information recorded therein is not in readable form and is later transcribed into readable form, the transcribed version of such entry, were an entry in a banker's book.

Registers of corporate securities

14.—(1) Where an Operator of a relevant system is required to maintain an Operator register of corporate securities, that register shall comprise the following particulars which the Operator shall enter on it, namely—

(a) the names and addresses of the persons holding units of the relevant participating security in uncertificated form; and

(b) how many units of that security each such person holds in that form.

(2) Sections 190 and 191 of the 1985 Act shall not apply to any part of an Operator register of corporate securities.

Records of uncertificated corporate securities

15.—(1) A participating issuer shall enter in a record of uncertificated corporate securities the same particulars, so far as is practicable, as are required by paragraph 14(1) to be entered in the relevant Operator register of corporate securities.

(2) A participating issuer to which this paragraph applies shall, unless it is impracticable to do so by virtue of circumstances beyond its control, ensure that the record of uncertificated corporate securities is regularly reconciled with the Operator register of corporate securities.

(3) Provided that it has complied with subparagraph (2), a participating issuer shall not be liable in respect of any act or thing done or omitted to be done by it or on its behalf in reliance upon the assumption that the particulars entered in any record of uncertificated corporate securities which the participating issuer is required to keep by these Regulations accord with particulars entered in any Operator register of corporate securities relating to it.

(4) In the case of a participating issuer which is a company, the record of uncertificated corporate securities shall be kept at the same place as the part of any register of debenture holders maintained by the company would be required to be kept.

(5) Section 191(1), (2), (4) and (5) of the 1985 Act shall apply in relation to a record of uncertificated corporate securities maintained by a participating issuer which is a company, so far as that record relates to debentures, as it applies or would apply to any register of debenture holders maintained by the company; and references to the 1985 Act in the Companies (Inspection and Copying of Registers, Indices and Documents) Regulations 1991 shall be construed accordingly.

(6) Any provision of an enactment or instrument which requires a register of persons holding securities (other than shares or public sector securities) to be open to inspection shall also apply to the record of uncertificated corporate securities relating to any units of those securities which are participating securities.

Miscellaneous

16.—(1) Every register which an Operator is required to maintain by virtue of these Regulations shall be kept in the United Kingdom.

(2) Provided that it is kept in the United Kingdom, any such register [(other than an Operator register of eligible debt securities)] which relates to securities issued by a company shall be deemed to be kept—

    (a) in the case of a company registered in England and Wales, in England and Wales; or

    (b) in the case of a company registered in Scotland, in Scotland.

17.—(1) An entry in a register of securities or in a record of securities relating to a person who no longer holds the securities which are the subject of the entry may be removed from the register or the record (as the case may be) after the expiration of 20 years beginning with the day on which the person ceased to hold any of those securities.

(2) Subparagraph (1) does not apply in respect of an entry in a register of members.

18. Sections 722 and 723(1) and (2) of the 1985 Act shall apply—

    (a) to any register, record or index required to be kept by any person in accordance with these Regulations as they apply to any register, record or index required by the Companies Acts to be kept by a company; and

    (b) to an Operator and its officers as they apply to a company and its officers.

19.—(1) Such sanctions as apply to a company and its officers in the event of a default in complying with section 352 of the 1985 Act shall apply to an Operator and his officers in the event of a default in complying with paragraph 4, 12 or 14.

(2) Such sanctions as apply to the registrar, within the meaning of the 1974 Regulations, in the event of a default in complying with regulation 5 of those Regulations shall apply to a participating issuer and his officers in the event of a default in complying with paragraph 13 in respect of a local authority security [falling within paragraph (a)(i) of the definition of "local authority security" in regulation 3(1)].

[(2A) ...]

(3) Such sanctions as apply in the event of a default in complying with the requirement to maintain a register imposed by the relevant enactment or instrument referred to in Regulation 22(1) shall apply to—

    (a) a participating issuer other than a company; and

    (b) a participating issuer which is a company, in relation to so much of the record of uncertificated corporate securities as does not relate to debentures,

and his officers in the event of a default in complying with paragraph 15.

(4) Subparagraphs (2) and (3) shall not apply to any of the following or its officers—

    (a) the Crown;

    (b) any person acting on behalf of the Crown;

    [(c) the Bank of England;

    (d) the Registrar of Government Stock;

    (e) any previous Registrar of Government Stock; or

    (f) in respect of a security which immediately before it became a participating security was transferable by exempt transfer within the meaning of the Stock Transfer Act 1982, a participating issuer].

20. An officer of a participating issuer shall be in default in complying with, or in contravention of paragraph 2, 5, 6, 7, 13 or 15, or section 722(2) of the 1985 Act as applied by paragraph 18, if, and only if, he knowingly and wilfully authorised or permitted the default or contravention.

21. An officer of an Operator shall be in default in complying with, or in contravention of, the provisions referred to in paragraph 19(1) of this Schedule, or of section 722(2) of the 1985 Act as applied by paragraph 18, if, and only if, he knowingly and wilfully authorised or permitted the default or contravention.

[3636]–[3638]

Provision of Part VII	Modification
	In subsection (7)(a), for "company of which he becomes a director, secretary or permanent representative" substitute "limited liability partnership of which he becomes a member or a designated member".
	In subsection (8), for "A company is an affected company" substitute "A limited liability partnership is an affected limited liability partnership".
Section 723D (construction of sections 723B and 723C)	In subsection (1), for "'relevant company'" substitute "'relevant limited liability partnership'".
	In subsection (1)(a) for "a company formed and registered under this Act or an existing company" substitute "a limited liability partnership formed and registered under the Limited Liability Partnerships Act 2000"; and delete the words "or (b) an oversea company".
	Omit subsection (2).
	In subsection (4), omit "'director' and 'secretary', in relation to an oversea company, have the same meanings as in Chapter 1 of Part 23 of this Act;".
	In subsection (7), for "company" in the first place where it occurs substitute "limited liability partnership" and for "company or a company to which section 690A applies" substitute "limited liability partnership".
Section 723F (Regulations under sections 723B to 723E)	Omit the words "In section 288 (register of directors and secretaries), after subsection (6) there shall be inserted—
	"(7) Subsections (3) and (5) are subject to section 723B."

[3638E]

NOTES
  See also the note to reg 3 at **[3638D]**.

LIMITED LIABILITY PARTNERSHIPS (PARTICULARS OF USUAL RESIDENTIAL ADDRESS) (CONFIDENTIALITY ORDERS) REGULATIONS 2002

(SI 2002/915)

NOTES
Made: 31 March 2002.
Authority: Companies Act 1985, ss 723B–723F.
Commencement: 2 April 2002.
These Regulations are reproduced as amended by: the Enterprise Act 2002.
Prospective revocation: as to the prospective revocation of these Regulations (as from 1 October 2009), see the Draft Limited Liability Partnerships (Application of Companies Act 2006) Regulations 2009 on the BERR website at: www.berr.gov.uk

ARRANGEMENT OF REGULATIONS

1   Citation, commencement and interpretation

(1)   These Regulations may be cited as the Limited Liability Partnerships (Particulars of Usual Residential Address) (Confidentiality Orders) Regulations 2002.

(2)   These Regulations shall come into force on 2nd April 2002.

(3)   In these Regulations—
"the 1985 Act" means the Companies Act 1985 as applied to limited liability partnerships by the Limited Liability Partnerships Regulations 2001 and by the Limited Liability Partnerships (No 2) Regulations 2002;
"the 2000 Act" means the Limited Liability Partnerships Act 2000;
"beneficiary of an order" means an individual in relation to whom a confidentiality order is in force;
"Companies (Particulars of Usual Residential Address) Regulations" means the Companies (Particulars of Usual Residential Address) (Confidentiality Orders) Regulations 2002;
"competent authority" means any authority specified in Schedule 1 to these Regulations;
"police force" means a police force within the meaning of section 101(1) of the Police Act 1996 or section 50 of the Police (Scotland) Act 1967;
"member" includes "designated member";
"principal Regulations" means the Limited Liability Partnerships Regulations 2001;
"service address" means the address specified pursuant to regulation 2(2)(b) in an application made under section 723B(1) of the 1985 Act or, if another address has been substituted under regulation 7, the address most recently substituted under that regulation; and
"working day" means any day other than a Saturday, a Sunday, Christmas Day, Good Friday or a day which is a bank holiday in any part of England or Wales under or by virtue of the Banking and Financial Dealings Act 1971.

(4)   In these Regulations unless the contrary intention appears, expressions which are also used in the 2000 Act or in the principal Regulations shall have the same meanings as in that Act or in those Regulations.

[3638F]

PART I

2   Applications for confidentiality orders under section 723B of the 1985 Act

(1)   An application for a confidentiality order shall be made to the Secretary of State.

(2)   An application for a confidentiality order shall—
(a)   be in such form and contain such information and be accompanied by such evidence as the Secretary of State may from time to time direct;
(b)   specify each limited liability partnership of which the applicant is or proposes to become a member and shall specify an address complying with regulation 9.

(3)   The Secretary of State may from time to time direct different information or evidence be provided for different cases or categories of application.

(4)   The Secretary of State may require any information or evidence delivered by an applicant to be verified in such manner as she may direct.

(4) Where a confidentiality order is made in relation to an application in respect of which no fee has been paid pursuant to paragraph (8) of regulation 2 that order shall remain in force for a period equal to the period for which the confidentiality order referred to in paragraph (8) of regulation 2, made under the Companies (Particulars of Usual Residential Address) Regulations, is to remain in force.

[3638O]

11 Revocation of a confidentiality order

(1) The Secretary of State may revoke a confidentiality order at any time if she is satisfied that—

(a) the beneficiary of the order, or any other person, in purported compliance with any provision of these Regulations, has furnished the Secretary of State with false, misleading or inaccurate information; or

(b) the registrar has not received, within the period of 28 days beginning with the date on which the beneficiary of the order was sent notice under regulation 4 of the Secretary of State's decision, in relation to each limited liability partnership of which that beneficiary is a member, the information in respect of the service address required to be delivered to the registrar under section 9 of the 2000 Act, by virtue of the making of the order; or

(c) the registrar has not received, within the period of 28 days from—

(i) any change or alteration among, or to, the members by virtue of the appointment of a beneficiary of an order; or

(ii) any change in the particulars of the usual residential address or the service address of the beneficiary of an order, in relation to each limited liability partnership of which that beneficiary is a member,

the information required to be delivered to the registrar under section 9 of the 2000 Act or sections 288 or 288A of the 1985 Act, of any such change or alteration, whether that change or alteration occurred before or after the making of the confidentiality order; or

(d) any statement delivered to the registrar under sections 2 and 3 of the 2000 Act naming as a member an individual in respect of whom a confidentiality order under the 1985 Act has been made did not contain the service address of the beneficiary or was not accompanied by a statement under the 2000 Act containing the usual residential address of the beneficiary; or

(e) any address purporting to be the service address of a beneficiary of an order which has been notified to the registrar under any provision of the 1985 Act or of the 2000 Act which does not comply with all the requirements of regulation 9.

(2) Where a beneficiary is also the beneficiary of a confidentiality order made under the Companies (Particulars of Usual Residential Address) Regulations which is revoked, any confidentiality order made in respect of that beneficiary as a member of a limited liability partnership is also revoked.

(3) If the Secretary of State proposes to revoke an order under this regulation, other than one revoked under paragraph (2), she shall send the beneficiary of the order notice.

(4) The notice must—

(a) state the grounds on which it is proposed to revoke the order;

(b) inform the beneficiary that he may, within a period of 21 days beginning with the date of the notice, deliver representations to the Secretary of State; and

(c) state that if representations are not received by the Secretary of State within that period, the order will be revoked at the expiry of that period.

(5) If the beneficiary delivers representations as to why the order should not be revoked within the period specified in paragraph (4), the Secretary of State shall have regard to the representations in determining whether to revoke the order, and shall send the beneficiary notice of her decision, and such notice shall be sent within five working days of the decision being made.

(6) Any communication by the Secretary of State in respect of the revocation or proposed revocation of a confidentiality order shall be sent to the beneficiary at his usual residential address.

[3638P]

12 Notification of cessation of a confidentiality order

On a confidentiality order ceasing to have effect, for whatever reason, the beneficiary of that order shall notify every relevant limited liability partnership within the meaning of section 723D(1)(a) of the 1985 Act of which he is a member, of that order ceasing to have effect within five days of its so ceasing to have effect.

[3638Q]

PART IV

13   Access to confidential records

(1)   Subject to paragraph (2), a competent authority is entitled to inspect, and take copies of, confidential records.

(2)   The circumstances in which a competent authority may inspect, and take copies of, confidential records are that the registrar has made a determination, in respect of that competent authority, as to the manner in which that competent authority and its officers, servants and representatives may inspect, and take copies of, confidential records.

(3)   The registrar may from time to time vary or revoke any determination with the consent of the competent authority in respect of whom it has been made.

[3638R]

14   Disclosure of relevant information

(1)   Subject to regulation 13 the disclosure of relevant information by any person is prohibited in the following circumstances—

(a)   where the information disclosed was delivered to the registrar, after the making of a confidentiality order in relation to the beneficiary of an order to whom the information relates, in the course the performance of the duties of the registrar under the 1985 Act or the 2000 Act in respect of that information and the information was obtained by the person disclosing it from the registrar;

(b)   where the information disclosed was provided to a limited liability partnership, of which the beneficiary of the order to which the information relates was a member, after the making of that order, for the purpose of enabling the limited liability partnership to comply with the requirements of the 2000 Act and of the 1985 Act, as the case may be, and the information was obtained by the person disclosing it from the limited liability partnership.

(2)   Paragraph (1) does not prohibit the disclosure of relevant information by a competent authority which is made for the purpose of facilitating the carrying out of a public function and "public function" includes—

(a)   any function conferred by or in accordance with any provision contained in any enactment or subordinate legislation;

(b)   any function conferred by or in accordance with any provision contained in the Community Treaties or any Community instrument;

(c)   any similar function conferred on persons by or under provisions having effect as part of the law of a country or territory outside the United Kingdom;

(d)   any function exercisable in relation to the investigation of any criminal offence or for the purposes of any criminal proceedings,

and disclosure for the purpose of facilitating the carrying out of a public function includes disclosure in relation to, and for the purpose of, any proceedings whether civil, criminal or disciplinary in which the competent authority engages while carrying out its public functions.

(3)   Paragraph (1) does not prohibit the disclosure of relevant information where the disclosure—

(a)   facilitates the creation and maintenance of confidential records of a limited liability partnership, and the provision of facilities for the inspection and copying of confidential records; or

(b)   is by the registrar, or any person performing functions on his behalf, of any relevant information obtained in the circumstances described in sub-paragraph (1)(a), included in any document delivered to the registrar under any provision of the 1985 Act or of the 2000 Act where that document is prescribed or approved by the registrar in respect of the delivery to the registrar of any information which is not relevant information and that document is made available for inspection and copying as if that were required by section 709(1) of the 1985 Act; or

(c)   is by any person of any relevant information obtain by that person from any document as is referred to in sub-paragraph (b).

(4)   Paragraph (1) does not prohibit the disclosure by any person of relevant information obtained in the course of the performance of their duties or functions, where that disclosure occurred notwithstanding the exercise by that person of the due care and diligence in maintaining the confidentiality, required by the 1985 Act and these Regulations, of that information, that could reasonably by expected of a person performing those duties and functions.

(5)   In this regulation—
"enactment" includes—

(a)   an Act of the Scottish Parliament;

(b)   Northern Ireland legislation;

PART III
STATUTORY INSTRUMENTS

"subordinate legislation" has the meaning given in the Interpretation Act 1978 and also includes an instrument made under an Act of the Scottish Parliament or under Northern Ireland legislation.

[3638S]

PART V

15 Form and delivery of notices etc

(1) Any notice—
   (a)   by the Secretary of State under regulation 4, 11(3) or 11(5); or
   (b)   to the Secretary of State under regulation 2(9);

and any representations made to the Secretary of State under regulation 11 shall be legible form.

(2) Where any notice is required to be sent by the Secretary of State to the usual residential address of any person, that notice is validly sent if sent to the address of that person, shown in the records of the registrar available for inspection or copying under section 709 of the 1985 Act or the confidential records as the case may be when the notice is sent.

[3638T]

16 Amendments of enactments

The enactments mentioned in Schedule 2 to these Regulations shall have effect with the amendments specified being amendments supplemental to, and consequential upon, the making of these Regulations.

[3638U]

17 Offence and penalties

(1) Any person who, in an application under 723B of the 1985 Act, makes a statement which he knows to be false in a material particular, or recklessly makes a statement which is false in a material particular, shall be guilty of an offence.

(2) Any person who discloses information in contravention of regulation 14 shall be guilty of an offence.

(3) A person guilty of an offence under paragraph (1) or (2) shall be liable—
   (a)   on conviction on indictment, to imprisonment for a term not exceeding two years or to a fine or to both; and
   (b)   on summary conviction, to imprisonment not exceeding six months, or to a fine not exceeding the statutory maximum or to both.

[3638V]

SCHEDULES

SCHEDULE 1
COMPETENT AUTHORITIES

Regulation 1

the Secretary of State;

the registrar and the registrar of companies for Northern Ireland;

an inspector appointed under Part XIV of the Companies Act 1985 or regulation 30 of the Open-Ended Investment Companies Regulations 2001;

any person authorised to exercise powers under section 447 of the Companies Act 1985 or section 84 of the Companies Act 1989;

any person exercising functions conferred by Part VI of the Financial Services and Markets Act 2000 or the competent authority under that Part;

a person appointed to make a report under section 166 of the Financial Services and Markets Act 2000;

a person appointed to conduct an investigation under section 167 or 168(3) or (5) of the Financial Services and Markets Act 2000;

an inspector appointed under section 284 of the Financial Services and Markets Act 2000;

the Department of Enterprise, Trade and Investment in Northern Ireland;

the Scottish Executive;

the Scotland Office;

the National Assembly for Wales;

the Wales Office (Office of the Secretary of State for Wales);

the Treasury;

the Commissioners of HM Customs and Excise;

the Commissioners of Inland Revenue;

the Bank of England;

the Director of Public Prosecutions and the Director of Public Prosecutions in Northern Ireland;

the Serious Fraud Office;

the Secret Intelligence Service;

the Security Service;

the Financial Services Authority;

the Competition Commission;

the Occupational Pensions Regulatory Authority;

the Panel on Takeovers and Mergers;

the Chief Registrar of Friendly Societies and the Registrar for Credit Unions and Industrial and Provident Societies for Northern Ireland;

the [Office of Fair Trading];

the Office of the Information Commissioner;

the Friendly Societies Commission;

a local weights and measures authority;

the Charity Commission;

an official receiver appointed under section 399 of the Insolvency Act 1986;

a person acting as an insolvency practitioner within the meaning of section 388 of the Insolvency Act 1986;

an inspector appointed under Part XV of the Companies (Northern Ireland) Order 1986 or Regulation 22 of the Open-Ended Investment Companies (Companies with Variable Capital) Regulations (Northern Ireland) 1997;

any person authorised to exercise powers under Article 440 of the Companies (Northern Ireland) Order 1986;

the Official Receiver for Northern Ireland;

a police force;

any procurator fiscal;

an overseas regulatory authority within the meaning of section 82 of the Companies Act 1989.

[3638W]

NOTES

Words in square brackets substituted by virtue of the Enterprise Act 2002, s 2(1), as from 1 April 2003.

Commissioners of Inland Revenue; Commissioners of Customs and Excise: references to the Commissioners of Inland Revenue and the Commissioners of Customs and Excise are now to be taken as a reference to the Commissioners for Her Majesty's Revenue and Customs; see the Commissioners for Revenue and Customs Act 2005, s 50(1), (7).

(Sch 2 inserts the Limited Liability Partnerships Act 2000, ss 2(2A), (2B), 9(3A), (3B), and CA 1985 s 288A.)

ELECTRONIC COMMERCE (EC DIRECTIVE) REGULATIONS 2002

(SI 2002/2013)

NOTES

Made: 30 July 2002.

Authority: European Communities Act 1972, s 2(2).

Commencement: 21 August 2002 (regs 1–15, 17–22); 23 October 2002 (reg 16).

These Regulations are reproduced as amended by: the Electronic Commerce (EC Directive) (Extension) Regulations 2004, SI 2004/1178.

ARRANGEMENT OF REGULATIONS

1   Citation and commencement

(1)   These Regulations may be cited as the Electronic Commerce (EC Directive) Regulations 2002 and except for regulation 16 shall come into force on 21st August 2002.

(2)   Regulation 16 shall come into force on 23rd October 2002.

[3639]

2   Interpretation

(1)   In these Regulations and in the Schedule—

"commercial communication" means a communication, in any form, designed to promote, directly or indirectly, the goods, services or image of any person pursuing a commercial, industrial or craft activity or exercising a regulated profession, other than a communication—

    (a)   consisting only of information allowing direct access to the activity of that person including a geographic address, a domain name or an electronic mail address; or

    (b)   relating to the goods, services or image of that person provided that the communication has been prepared independently of the person making it (and for this purpose, a communication prepared without financial consideration is to be taken to have been prepared independently unless the contrary is shown);

"the Commission" means the Commission of the European Communities;

"consumer" means any natural person who is acting for purposes other than those of his trade, business or profession;

"coordinated field" means requirements applicable to information society service providers or information society services, regardless of whether they are of a general nature or specifically designed for them, and covers requirements with which the service provider has to comply in respect of—

    (a)   the taking up of the activity of an information society service, such as requirements concerning qualifications, authorisation or notification, and

    (b)   the pursuit of the activity of an information society service, such as requirements concerning the behaviour of the service provider, requirements regarding the quality or content of the service including those applicable to advertising and contracts, or requirements concerning the liability of the service provider,

but does not cover requirements such as those applicable to goods as such, to the delivery of goods or to services not provided by electronic means;

"the Directive" means Directive 2000/31/EC of the European Parliament and of the Council of 8 June 2000 on certain legal aspects of information society services, in particular electronic commerce, in the Internal Market (Directive on electronic commerce);

"EEA Agreement" means the Agreement on the European Economic Area signed at Oporto on 2 May 1992 as adjusted by the Protocol signed at Brussels on 17 March 1993;

"enactment" includes an enactment comprised in Northern Ireland legislation and comprised in, or an instrument made under, an Act of the Scottish Parliament;

"enforcement action" means any form of enforcement action including, in particular—

    (a)   in relation to any legal requirement imposed by or under any enactment, any action taken with a view to or in connection with imposing any sanction (whether criminal or otherwise) for failure to observe or comply with it; and

    (b)   in relation to a permission or authorisation, anything done with a view to removing or restricting that permission or authorisation;

"enforcement authority" does not include courts but, subject to that, means any person who is authorised, whether by or under an enactment or otherwise, to take enforcement action;

"established service provider" means a service provider who is a national of a member State or a company or firm as mentioned in Article 48 of the Treaty and who effectively pursues an economic activity by virtue of which he is a service provider using a fixed establishment in a member State for an indefinite period, but the presence and use of the technical means and technologies required to provide the information society service do not, in themselves, constitute an establishment of the provider; in cases where it cannot be determined from which of a number of places of establishment a given service is provided, that service is to be regarded as provided from the place of establishment where the provider has the centre of his activities relating to that service; references to a service provider being established or to the establishment of a service provider shall be construed accordingly;

"information society services" (which is summarised in recital 17 of the Directive as covering "any service normally provided for remuneration, at a distance, by means of electronic equipment for the processing (including digital compression) and storage of data, and at the individual request of a recipient of a service") has the meaning set out in Article 2(a) of the Directive, (which refers to Article 1(2) of Directive 98/34/EC of the European Parliament and of the Council of 22 June 1998 laying down a procedure for the provision of information in the field of technical standards and regulations, as amended by Directive 98/48/EC of 20 July 1998);

"member State" includes a State which is a contracting party to the EEA Agreement;

"recipient of the service" means any person who, for professional ends or otherwise, uses an information society service, in particular for the purposes of seeking information or making it accessible;

"regulated profession" means any profession within the meaning of either Article 1(d) of Council Directive 89/48/EEC of 21 December 1988 on a general system for the recognition of higher-education diplomas awarded on completion of professional education and training of at least three years' duration or of Article 1(f) of Council Directive 92/51/EEC of 18 June 1992 on a second general system for the recognition of professional education and training to supplement Directive 89/48/EEC;

"service provider" means any person providing an information society service;

"the Treaty" means the treaty establishing the European Community.

(2)   In regulation 4 and 5, "requirement" means any legal requirement under the law of the United Kingdom, or any part of it, imposed by or under any enactment or otherwise.

(3)   Terms used in the Directive other than those in paragraph (1) above shall have the same meaning as in the Directive.

[3640]

3   Exclusions

(1)   Nothing in these Regulations shall apply in respect of—
   (a)   the field of taxation;
   (b)   questions relating to information society services covered by the Data Protection Directive and the Telecommunications Data Protection Directive and Directive 2002/58/EC of the European Parliament and of the Council of 12th July 2002 concerning the processing of personal data and the protection of privacy in the electronic communications sector (Directive on privacy and electronic communications);
   (c)   questions relating to agreements or practices governed by cartel law; and
   (d)   the following activities of information society services—
      (i)   the activities of a public notary or equivalent professions to the extent that they involve a direct and specific connection with the exercise of public authority,
      (ii)   the representation of a client and defence of his interests before the courts, and
      (iii)   betting, gaming or lotteries which involve wagering a stake with monetary value.

[(2)   These Regulations shall not apply in relation to any Act passed on or after the date these Regulations are made or in relation to the exercise of a power to legislate after that date.]

(3)   In this regulation—
"cartel law" means so much of the law relating to agreements between undertakings, decisions by associations of undertakings or concerted practices as relates to agreements to divide the market or fix prices;
"Data Protection Directive" means Directive 95/46/EC of the European Parliament and of the Council of 24 October 1995 on the protection of individuals with regard to the processing of personal data and on the free movement of such data; and
"Telecommunications Data Protection Directive" means Directive 97/66/EC of the European Parliament and of the Council of 15 December 1997 concerning the processing of personal data and the protection of privacy in the telecommunications sector.

[3641]

(b) whether or not the concluded contract will be filed by the service provider and whether it will be accessible;

(c) the technical means for identifying and correcting input errors prior to the placing of the order; and

(d) the languages offered for the conclusion of the contract.

(2) Unless parties who are not consumers have agreed otherwise, a service provider shall indicate which relevant codes of conduct he subscribes to and give information on how those codes can be consulted electronically.

(3) Where the service provider provides terms and conditions applicable to the contract to the recipient, the service provider shall make them available to him in a way that allows him to store and reproduce them.

(4) The requirements of paragraphs (1) and (2) above shall not apply to contracts concluded exclusively by exchange of electronic mail or by equivalent individual communications.

[3647]

10 Other information requirements

Regulations 6, 7, 8 and 9(1) have effect in addition to any other information requirements in legislation giving effect to Community law.

[3648]

11 Placing of the order

(1) Unless parties who are not consumers have agreed otherwise, where the recipient of the service places his order through technological means, a service provider shall—

(a) acknowledge receipt of the order to the recipient of the service without undue delay and by electronic means; and

(b) make available to the recipient of the service appropriate, effective and accessible technical means allowing him to identify and correct input errors prior to the placing of the order.

(2) For the purposes of paragraph (1)(a) above—

(a) the order and the acknowledgement of receipt will be deemed to be received when the parties to whom they are addressed are able to access them; and

(b) the acknowledgement of receipt may take the form of the provision of the service paid for where that service is an information society service.

(3) The requirements of paragraph (1) above shall not apply to contracts concluded exclusively by exchange of electronic mail or by equivalent individual communications.

[3649]

12 Meaning of the term "order"

Except in relation to regulation 9(1)(c) and regulation 11(1)(b) where "order" shall be the contractual offer, "order" may be but need not be the contractual offer for the purposes of regulations 9 and 11.

[3650]

13 Liability of the service provider

The duties imposed by regulations 6, 7, 8, 9(1) and 11(1)(a) shall be enforceable, at the suit of any recipient of a service, by an action against the service provider for damages for breach of statutory duty.

[3651]

14 Compliance with Regulation 9(3)

Where on request a service provider has failed to comply with the requirement in regulation 9(3), the recipient may seek an order from any court having jurisdiction in relation to the contract requiring that service provider to comply with that requirement.

[3652]

15 Right to rescind contract

Where a person—

(a) has entered into a contract to which these Regulations apply, and

(b) the service provider has not made available means of allowing him to identify and correct input errors in compliance with regulation 11(1)(b),

he shall be entitled to rescind the contract unless any court having jurisdiction in relation to the contract in question orders otherwise on the application of the service provider.

[3653]

16 (*Spent: amended the Stop Now Orders (EC Directive) Regulations 2001, SI 2001/1422 (revoked).*)

17 Mere conduit

(1)   Where an information society service is provided which consists of the transmission in a communication network of information provided by a recipient of the service or the provision of access to a communication network, the service provider (if he otherwise would) shall not be liable for damages or for any other pecuniary remedy or for any criminal sanction as a result of that transmission where the service provider—

    (a)   did not initiate the transmission;

    (b)   did not select the receiver of the transmission; and

    (c)   did not select or modify the information contained in the transmission.

(2)   The acts of transmission and of provision of access referred to in paragraph (1) include the automatic, intermediate and transient storage of the information transmitted where:

    (a)   this takes place for the sole purpose of carrying out the transmission in the communication network, and

    (b)   the information is not stored for any period longer than is reasonably necessary for the transmission.

[3654]

18 Caching

Where an information society service is provided which consists of the transmission in a communication network of information provided by a recipient of the service, the service provider (if he otherwise would) shall not be liable for damages or for any other pecuniary remedy or for any criminal sanction as a result of that transmission where—

    (a)   the information is the subject of automatic, intermediate and temporary storage where that storage is for the sole purpose of making more efficient onward transmission of the information to other recipients of the service upon their request, and

    (b)   the service provider—

        (i)   does not modify the information;

        (ii)   complies with conditions on access to the information;

        (iii)   complies with any rules regarding the updating of the information, specified in a manner widely recognised and used by industry;

        (iv)   does not interfere with the lawful use of technology, widely recognised and used by industry, to obtain data on the use of the information; and

        (v)   acts expeditiously to remove or to disable access to the information he has stored upon obtaining actual knowledge of the fact that the information at the initial source of the transmission has been removed from the network, or access to it has been disabled, or that a court or an administrative authority has ordered such removal or disablement.

[3655]

19 Hosting

Where an information society service is provided which consists of the storage of information provided by a recipient of the service, the service provider (if he otherwise would) shall not be liable for damages or for any other pecuniary remedy or for any criminal sanction as a result of that storage where—

    (a)   the service provider—

        (i)   does not have actual knowledge of unlawful activity or information and, where a claim for damages is made, is not aware of facts or circumstances from which it would have been apparent to the service provider that the activity or information was unlawful; or

        (ii)   upon obtaining such knowledge or awareness, acts expeditiously to remove or to disable access to the information, and

    (b)   the recipient of the service was not acting under the authority or the control of the service provider.

[3656]

20 Protection of rights

(1)   Nothing in regulations 17, 18 and 19 shall—

    (a)   prevent a person agreeing different contractual terms; or

    (b)   affect the rights of any party to apply to a court for relief to prevent or stop infringement of any rights.

(2)   Any power of an administrative authority to prevent or stop infringement of any rights shall continue to apply notwithstanding regulations 17, 18 and 19.

[3657]

PART III
STATUTORY INSTRUMENTS

    (j)   section 211(2) (discharge and variation of receivership orders—Northern Ireland);

    (k)   section 212(2) and (6) (discharge of management receiver—Northern Ireland);

    (l)   section 213(6) (appeal to Court of Appeal in respect of receivership matters—Northern Ireland);

    (m)   section 214(3) (appeal to House of Lords in respect of receivership matters—Northern Ireland),

but does not include an order made in proceedings for the enforcement, in Northern Ireland, of an order made under or for the purposes of the provisions listed above;

"a Northern Ireland restraint order" means an order made under or for the purposes of the following provisions of the Act—

    (a)   section 190(1) (restraint orders—Northern Ireland);

    (b)   section 190(7) (orders for the purpose of making restraint orders effective—Northern Ireland);

    (c)   section 191(5) (discharge and variation of restraint orders—Northern Ireland);

    (d)   section 192(3) (appeal to Court of Appeal in respect of restraint order—Northern Ireland);

    (e)   section 193(3) (appeal to House of Lords in respect of restraint order—Northern Ireland),

but does not include an order made in proceedings for the enforcement, in Northern Ireland, of an order made under or for the purposes of the provisions listed above;

"a Scottish administration order" means an order made under or for the purposes of the following provisions of the Act—

    (a)   section 125 (management administrators—Scotland);

    (b)   section 128 (enforcement administrators—Scotland);

    (c)   section 129(2) (management administrators: discharge—Scotland;

    (d)   section 130(4) (sums in administrator's hands—Scotland);

    (e)   section 135(2) (recall and variation of administration order—Scotland);

    (f)   section 136(6) (appeal in respect of administrators—Scotland);

    (g)   paragraph 5(4) of Schedule 3 (vesting of property in administrator—Scotland);

    (h)   paragraph 8(1) of Schedule 3 (supervision of administrators—Scotland),

but does not include an order made in proceedings for the enforcement, in Scotland, of an order made under or for the purposes of the provisions listed above;

"a Scottish restraint order" means an order made under or for the purposes of the following provisions of the Act—

    (a)   section 120(1) (restraint orders—Scotland);

    (b)   section 120(6) (orders for the purpose of making restraint orders effective—Scotland);

    (c)   section 121(7) (recall and variation of restraint orders—Scotland);

    (d)   section 122 (appeal in respect of restraint orders—Scotland),

but does not include an order made in proceedings for the enforcement, in Scotland, of an order made under or for the purposes of the provisions listed above.

[3664]

PART II
ENFORCEMENT OF SCOTTISH AND NORTHERN IRELAND ORDERS IN ENGLAND AND WALES

3 Restraint orders

(1)   Any Northern Ireland restraint order or Scottish restraint order has effect in England and Wales.

(2)   Proceedings for or with respect to the enforcement or contravention of a Northern Ireland restraint order or a Scottish restraint order may only be taken if the order is registered in accordance with article 6.

[3665]

4 Administrators and receivers

(1)   Any Northern Ireland receivership order or Scottish administration order has effect in England and Wales and the functions of—

    (a)   an administrator appointed in pursuance of Part 3 of the Act; and

    (b)   a receiver appointed in pursuance of Part 4 of the Act,

are exercisable in England and Wales.

(2)   Proceedings for or with respect to the enforcement or contravention of a Northern Ireland receivership order or a Scottish administration order may only be taken if the order is registered in accordance with article 6.

[3666]

5 Enforcement

(1) If any order is registered in accordance with article 6—

   (a) the Crown Court in England and Wales shall have, in relation to its enforcement, the same power;

   (b) proceedings for or with respect to its enforcement may be taken; and

   (c) proceedings for or with respect to any contravention of the order may be taken,

as if the Crown Court in England and Wales had made the order itself.

(2) Paragraph (1) shall have effect whether the contravention of the order occurs before or after the registration of the order.

[3667]

6 Registration

(1) Where an application for the registration of a Northern Ireland receivership order, a Northern Ireland restraint order, a Scottish administration order or a Scottish restraint order is made to the Crown Court in England and Wales, the Crown Court must direct that the order be registered in that court.

(2) Where the Crown Court has directed that an order be registered, it may make such order as it believes is appropriate for the purpose of—

   (a) ensuring that the order is effective; or

   (b) assisting an administrator appointed in pursuance of Part 3 of the Act or a receiver appointed in pursuance of Part 4 of the Act to exercise his functions.

[3668]

7 Supplementary

(1) Section 47 of the Act (which makes provision about land registration) applies in relation to restraint orders made under section 120(1) of the Act and section 190(1) of the Act as it applies in relation to restraint orders made under section 41(1) of the Act.

(2) A document purporting to be a copy of a Northern Ireland receivership order, a Northern Ireland restraint order, a Scottish administration order or a Scottish restraint order and certified as such by a proper officer of the court which made the order is admissible in evidence in the Crown Court in England and Wales without further proof.

[3669]

PART III
ENFORCEMENT OF ENGLISH, WELSH AND NORTHERN IRELAND ORDERS
IN SCOTLAND

8 Restraint orders

(1) Any English or Welsh restraint order or Northern Ireland restraint order has effect in Scotland.

(2) Proceedings for or with respect to the enforcement or contravention of an English or Welsh restraint order or a Northern Ireland restraint order may only be taken if the order is registered in accordance with article 11.

[3670]

9 Receivers

(1) Any English or Welsh receivership order or Northern Ireland receivership order has effect in Scotland and the functions of a receiver appointed in pursuance of Part 2 or Part 4 of the Act are exercisable in Scotland.

(2) Proceedings for or with respect to the enforcement or contravention of an English or Welsh receivership order or a Northern Ireland receivership order may only be taken if the order is registered in accordance with article 11.

[3671]

10 Enforcement

(1) If any order is registered in accordance with article 11—

   (a) the Court of Session shall have, in relation to its enforcement, the same power;

   (b) proceedings for or with respect to its enforcement may be taken; and

   (c) proceedings for or with respect to any contravention of the order may be taken,

as if the Court of Session had made the order itself.

(2) Paragraph (1) shall have effect whether the contravention of the order occurs before or after the registration of the order.

[3672]

2 Commencement of provisions

(1) The provisions of the Act listed in column 1 of the Schedule to this Order shall come into force on 24th February 2003, subject to the transitional provisions and savings contained in this Order.

(2) But where a particular purpose is specified in relation to any such provision in column 2 of that Schedule, the provision concerned shall come into force only for that purpose.

[3696]

3 Transitional provisions and savings for the principal money laundering offences

The new principal money laundering offences shall not have effect where the conduct constituting an offence under those provisions began before 24th February 2003 [and ended on or after that date] and the old principal money laundering offences shall continue to have effect in such circumstances.

[3697]

NOTES

Words in square brackets substituted by the Proceeds of Crime Act 2002 (Commencement No 5, Transitional Provisions, Savings and Amendment) Order 2003, SI 2003/333, art 14, as from 20 February 2003.

4 Transitional provisions and savings for the failure to disclose offences

The new failure to disclose offences shall not have effect where the information or other matter on which knowledge or suspicion that another person is engaged in money laundering is based, or which gives reasonable grounds for such knowledge or suspicion, came to a person before 24th February 2003 and the old failure to disclose offences shall continue to have effect in such circumstances.

[3698]

5 Transitional provisions and savings for the offences of tipping-off and prejudicing an investigation

(1) Section 342 of the Act shall not have effect where the conduct constituting an offence under that section began before 24th February 2003 [and ended on or after that date] and the following provisions shall continue to have effect in such circumstances—

    (a) sections 93D(1) of the Criminal Justice Act 1988;

    (b) sections 53(1) and 58 of the Drug Trafficking Act 1994;

    (c) sections 36 and 40(1) of the Criminal Law (Consolidation) (Scotland) Act 1995; and

    (d) articles 48(1) and 53 of the Proceeds of Crime (Northern Ireland) Order 1996.

(2) Section 93D(2) and (3) of the Criminal Justice Act 1988 shall continue to have effect where the disclosure mentioned in section 93D(2)(a) or 93D(3)(a), as the case may be, of that Act was made before 24th February 2003.

(3) Section 53(2) and (3) of the Drug Trafficking Act 1994 shall continue to have effect where the disclosure mentioned in section 53(2)(a) or 53(3)(a), as the case may be, of that Act was made before 24th February 2003.

(4) Section 40(2) and (3) of the Criminal Law (Consolidation) (Scotland) Act 1995 shall continue to have effect where the disclosure mentioned in section 40(2)(a) or 40(3)(a), as the case may be, of that Act was made before 24th February 2003.

(5) Article 48(2) and (3) of the Proceeds of Crime (Northern Ireland) Order 1996 shall continue to have effect where the disclosure mentioned in article 48(2)(a) or 48(3)(a), as the case may be, of that Order was made before 24th February 2003.

[3699]

NOTES

Para (1): words in square brackets substituted by the Proceeds of Crime Act 2002 (Commencement No 5, Transitional Provisions, Savings and Amendment) Order 2003, SI 2003/333, art 14, as from 20 February 2003.

6 Savings in relation to prosecution by Customs and Excise, application of offences to Crown servants and investigations

The following provisions shall continue to have effect in respect of offences committed before 24th February 2003 and offences committed by virtue of articles 3 to 5 of this Order—

    (a) sections 93F to 93J of the Criminal Justice Act 1988;

    (b) sections 55 to 57 and 59 to 61 of the Drug Trafficking Act 1994;

    (c) sections 31 to 35 and 42 of the Criminal Law (Consolidation) (Scotland) Act 1995; and

    (d) articles 49 to 52, and 54 to 56 of and Schedule 2 to the Proceeds of Crime (Northern Ireland) Order 1996.

[3700]

NOTES

Customs and Excise: a reference to Customs and Excise is now to be taken as a reference to the Commissioners for Her Majesty's Revenue and Customs; see the Commissioners for Revenue and Customs Act 2005, s 50(1), (7).

7 Transitional provision in relation to the Extradition Act 1989

Notwithstanding paragraph 18 of Schedule 11 to the Act (which amends the Extradition Act 1989), section 22(4)(h) of, and paragraph 15 of Schedule 1 to, the Extradition Act 1989 shall have effect as if they continued to contain references to—

(a) an offence under section 49, 50 or 51 of the Drug Trafficking Act 1994;

(b) an offence under section 14 of the Criminal Justice (International Co-operation) Act 1990;

(c) an offence under section 37 or 38 of the Criminal Law (Consolidation) (Scotland) Act 1995; and

(d) an offence under article 45, 46 or 47 of the Proceeds of Crime (Northern Ireland) Order 1996,

where the conduct constituting such offences occurred before 24th February 2003 or constituted an offence by virtue of articles 3 to 5 of this Order.

[3701]

(The Schedule sets out the provisions of the Proceeds of Crime Act 2002 that come into force on 24 February 2003. The relevant provisions of 2002 Act are set out at **[1310]** *et seq and all commencement information is noted to those provisions.)*

PROCEEDS OF CRIME ACT 2002 (FAILURE TO DISCLOSE MONEY LAUNDERING: SPECIFIED TRAINING) ORDER 2003

(SI 2003/171)

NOTES

Made: 29 January 2003.
Authority: Proceeds of Crime Act 2002, s 330(7)(b).
Commencement: 24 February 2003.
This Order is reproduced as amended by: the Money Laundering Regulations 2007, SI 2007/2157.

1 This Order may be cited as the Proceeds of Crime Act 2002 (Failure to Disclose Money Laundering: Specified Training) Order 2003 and shall come into force on 24th February 2003.

[3702]

2 The training specified for the purposes of section 330 of the Proceeds of Crime Act 2002 is the training required to be provided under [regulation 21 of the Money Laundering Regulations 2007].

[3703]

NOTES

Words in square brackets substituted by the Money Laundering Regulations 2007, SI 2007/2157, reg 51, Sch 6, Pt 2, para 11, as from 15 December 2007.

PROCEEDS OF CRIME ACT 2002 (REFERENCES TO FINANCIAL INVESTIGATORS) ORDER 2003

(SI 2003/172)

NOTES

Made: 29 January 2003.
Authority: Proceeds of Crime Act 2002, ss 453, 459(2).
Commencement: 24 February 2003.
This Order is reproduced as amended by: the Proceeds of Crime Act 2002 (References to Financial Investigators) (Amendment) Order 2004, SI 2004/8; the Proceeds of Crime Act 2002 (References to Financial Investigators) (Amendment No 2) Order 2004, SI 2004/3339; the Proceeds of Crime Act 2002 (References to Financial Investigators) (Amendment) Order 2005, SI 2005/386; the Proceeds of Crime Act 2002 (References to Financial Investigators) (Amendment) Order 2006, SI 2006/57; the Special Health Authorities Abolition

PART III
STATUTORY INSTRUMENTS

Column 1	Column 2
	(m) the Royal Mail and is not below the grade of Business Personal Contract Holder Grade 9;
	(n) the Home Office and is not below the grade of Senior Executive Officer];
	or is an immigration officer who is not below the grade of immigration inspector.]
Section 191(2)(c) (application for restraint order under Part 4)	An accredited financial investigator who is—
	(a) a constable of the Police Service of Northern Ireland;
	(b) a member of staff of the Police Service of Northern Ireland;
	(c) a customs officer;
	(d) a member of staff of the Financial Services Authority;
	(e) a member of staff of the Inland Revenue;
	(f) a member of staff of the Medicines and Healthcare Products Regulatory Agency;
	(g) a member of staff of the Department for Social Development in Northern Ireland; ...
	(h) a member of staff of the Department of Health, Social Services and Public Safety in Northern Ireland;
	[(i) an immigration officer;
	(j) a member of staff of the Occupational Pensions Regulatory Authority;
	(k) a member of staff of the Department of the Environment in Northern Ireland;
	(l) a member of staff of the Department of Agriculture and Rural Development in Northern Ireland];
	[(m) a member of staff of SOCA;
	(n) a member of staff of the Royal Mail;
	(o) a member of staff of the Home Office].
Section 216(3)(c) (authorisation for application for restraint order under Part 4)	An accredited financial investigator who is a member of staff of—
	(a) the Financial Services Authority and is not below the grade designated by the Financial Services Authority as Head of Department;
	(b) the Inland Revenue and is not below the grade designated by the Commissioners of Inland Revenue as grade 6;
	(c) the Medicines and Healthcare Products Regulatory Agency and is not below the grade designated by the Secretary of State for Health as integrated pay band 3 (upper); ...
	(d) the Department for Social Development in Northern Ireland and is not below the grade designated by the Department of Finance and Personnel in Northern Ireland as Deputy Principal;
	[(e) the Occupational Pensions Regulatory Authority and is not below the grade of regulatory manager;
	(f) the Department of the Environment in Northern Ireland and is not below the grade of senior scientific officer;

Column 1	Column 2
	(g) the Department of Agriculture and Rural Development in Northern Ireland and is not below the grade of deputy principal;
	[(h) SOCA and is not below the grade of grade 2 Senior Manager;
	(i) the Royal Mail and is not below the grade of Business Personal Contract Holder Grade 9;
	(j) the Home Office and is not below the grade of Senior Executive Officer];
	or is an immigration officer who is not below the grade of immigration inspector];
Section 378(1)(b) (appropriate officers for the purposes of confiscation investigations)	In relation to England and Wales, an accredited financial investigator who is a member of staff of—
	(a) a police force in England and Wales;
	(b) the Serious Fraud Office;
	(c) the Financial Services Authority;
	(d) the Inland Revenue;
	(e) the Medicines and Healthcare Products Regulatory Agency;
	(f) the Department for Work and Pensions;
	(g) the Investigations Branch of the Department for Environment, Food and Rural Affairs;
	(h) the Rural Payments Agency; …
	(i) [the Department for Business, Enterprise and Regulatory Reform];
	[(j) the Environment Agency; …
	(k) [the Counter Fraud and Security Management Services division of the NHS Business Services Authority]];
	[(l) a local authority;
	(m) the Occupational Pensions Regulatory Authority;
	[(n) SOCA;
	(o) the Royal Mail;
	(p) the Home Office];
	or is an immigration officer.]
	In relation to Northern Ireland, an accredited financial investigator who is a member of staff of—
	(a) the Police Service of Northern Ireland;
	(b) the Serious Fraud Office;
	(c) the Financial Services Authority;
	(d) the Inland Revenue;
	(e) the Medicines and Healthcare Products Regulatory Agency;
	(f) the Department for Social Development in Northern Ireland; …
	(g) the Department of Health, Social Services and Public Safety in Northern Ireland;
	[(h) the Occupational Pensions Regulatory Authority;
	(i) the Department of the Environment in Northern Ireland;

Column 1	Column 2
	(j) the Department of Agriculture and Rural Development in Northern Ireland;
	[(k) SOCA;
	(l) the Royal Mail;
	(m) the Home Office];
	or is an immigration officer];
Section 378(2)(d) (senior appropriate officers for the purposes of confiscation investigations)	In relation to England and Wales, an accredited financial investigator who is a member of staff of—
	(a) the Serious Fraud Office and is not below the grade designated by the Director of the Serious Fraud Office as grade 6;
	(b) the Financial Services Authority and is not below the grade designated by the Financial Services Authority as Head of Department;
	(c) the Inland Revenue and is not below the grade designated by the Commissioners of Inland Revenue as grade 6;
	(d) the Medicines and Healthcare Products Regulatory Agency and is not below the grade designated by the Secretary of State for Health as integrated pay band 3 (upper);
	(e) the Department for Work and Pensions and is not below the grade designated by the Secretary of State for Work and Pensions as Senior Executive Officer;
	(f) the Investigation Branch of the Department for Environment, Food and Rural Affairs and is not below the grade designated by the Secretary of State for Environment, Food and Rural Affairs as Senior Investigation Officer;
	(g) the Rural Payments Agency and is not below the grade designated by the Chief Executive of the Agency as Senior Investigation Officer; ...
	(h) [the Department for Business, Enterprise and Regulatory Reform] and is a Deputy Chief Investigation Officer or Chief Investigation Officer not below the grade designated by [the Secretary of State for Business, Enterprise and Regulatory Reform] as range 9;
	[(i) the Environment Agency and is not below the grade designated by the Secretary of State for Environment, Food and Rural Affairs as Area Environment Manager—EA Grade 7; ...
	[(j) the Counter Fraud and Security Management Services division of the NHS Business Services Authority and is not below the grade of Agenda for Change pay band 8b]];
	[(k) a local authority and holds an appropriate office;
	(l) the Occupational Pensions Regulatory Authority and is not below the grade of regulatory manager;
	[(m) SOCA and is not below the grade of grade 2 Senior Manager;
	(n) the Royal Mail and is not below the grade of Business Personal Contract Holder Grade 9;
	(o) the Home Office and is not below the grade of Senior Executive Officer].

Column 1	Column 2
	or is an immigration officer who is not below the grade of immigration inspector].
	In relation to Northern Ireland, an accredited financial investigator who is a member of staff of—
	(a) the Serious Fraud Office and is not below the grade designated by the Director of the Serious Fraud Office as grade 6;
	(b) the Financial Services Authority and is not below the grade designated by the Financial Services Authority as Head of Department;
	(c) the Inland Revenue and is not below the grade designated by the Commissioners of Inland Revenue as grade 6;
	(d) the Medicines and Healthcare Products Regulatory Agency and is not below the grade designated by the Secretary of State for Health as integrated pay band 3 (upper); ...
	(e) the Department for Social Development in Northern Ireland and is not below the grade designated by the Department of Finance and Personnel in Northern Ireland as Deputy Principal;
	[(f) the Occupational Pensions Regulatory Authority and is not below the grade of regulatory manager;
	(g) the Department of the Environment in Northern Ireland and is not below the grade of senior scientific officer;
	(h) the Department of Agriculture and Rural Development in Northern Ireland and is not below the grade of deputy principal;
	[(i) SOCA and is not below the grade of grade 2 Senior Manager;
	(j) the Royal Mail and is not below the grade of Business Personal Contract Holder Grade 9;
	(k) the Home Office and is not below the grade of Senior Executive Officer];
	or is an immigration officer who is not below the grade of immigration inspector].
Section 378(4)(a) (appropriate officers for the purposes of money laundering investigations)	In relation to England and Wales, an accredited financial investigator who is a member of staff of—
	(a) a police force in England and Wales;
	(b) the Serious Fraud Office;
	(c) the Medicines and Healthcare Products Regulatory Agency;
	(d) the Department for Work and Pensions; ...
	(e) [the Department for Business, Enterprise and Regulatory Reform];
	[(f) the Inland Revenue].
	[(g) a local authority;
	(h) the Occupational Pensions Regulatory Authority;
	[(i) SOCA;
	(j) the Royal Mail;
	(k) the Home Office];

Column 1	Column 2
	or is an immigration officer].
	In relation to Northern Ireland, an accredited financial investigator who is a member of staff of—
	(a) the Police Service of Northern Ireland;
	(b) the Serious Fraud Office;
	(c) the Medicines and Healthcare Products Regulatory Agency; ...
	(d) the Department for Social Development in Northern Ireland;
	[(e) the Inland Revenue];
	[(f) the Occupational Pensions Regulatory Authority;
	(g) the Department of the Environment in Northern Ireland;
	(h) the Department of Agriculture and Rural Development in Northern Ireland;
	[(i) SOCA;
	(j) the Royal Mail;
	(k) the Home Office];
	or is an immigration officer].
Section 378(6)(c) (senior appropriate officers for the purposes of money laundering investigations)	In relation to England and Wales, an accredited financial investigator who is a member of staff of—
	(a) the Serious Fraud Office and is not below the grade designated by the Director of the Serious Fraud Office as grade 6;
	(b) the Medicines and Healthcare Products Regulatory Agency and is not below the grade designated by the Secretary of State for Health as integrated pay band 3 (upper);
	(c) the Department for Work and Pensions and is not below the grade designated by the Secretary of State for Work and Pensions as Senior Executive Officer; ...
	(d) [the Department for Business, Enterprise and Regulatory Reform] and is a Deputy Chief Investigation Officer or Chief Investigation Officer not below the grade designated by [the Secretary of State for Business, Enterprise and Regulatory Reform] as range 9;
	[(e) the Inland Revenue and is not below the grade designated by the Commissioners of Inland Revenue as Grade 6];
	[(f) a local authority and holds an appropriate office;
	(g) the Occupational Pensions Regulatory Authority and is not below the grade of regulatory manager;
	[(h) SOCA and is not below the grade of grade 2 Senior Manager;
	(i) the Royal Mail and is not below the grade of Business Personal Contract Holder Grade 9;
	(j) the Home Office and is not below the grade of Senior Executive Officer];
	or is an immigration officer who is not below the grade of immigration inspector].
	In relation to Northern Ireland, an accredited financial investigator who is a member of staff of—

Column 1	Column 2
	(a) the Serious Fraud Office and is not below the grade designated by the Director of the Serious Fraud Office as grade 6;
	(b) the Medicines and Healthcare Products Regulatory Agency and is not below the grade designated by the Secretary of State for Health as integrated pay band 3 (upper); …
	(c) the Department for Social Development in Northern Ireland who is not below the grade designated by the Department of Finance and Personnel in Northern Ireland as Deputy Principal;
	[(d) the Inland Revenue and is not below the grade designated by the Commissioners of Inland Revenue as Grade 6];
	[(e) the Occupational Pensions Regulatory Authority and is not below the grade of regulatory manager;
	(f) the Department of the Environment in Northern Ireland and is not below the grade of senior scientific officer;
	(g) the Department of Agriculture and Rural Development in Northern Ireland and is not below the grade of deputy principal;
	[(h) SOCA and is not below the grade of grade 2 Senior Manager;
	(i) the Royal Mail and is not below the grade of Business Personal Contract Holder Grade 9;
	(j) the Home Office and is not below the grade of Senior Executive Officer];
	or is an immigration officer who is not below the grade of immigration inspector].

[3707]

NOTES

All references to "the Secretary of State for Business, Enterprise and Regulatory Reform" and "the Department for Business, Enterprise and Regulatory Reform" substituted by the Secretaries of State for Children, Schools and Families, for Innovation, Universities and Skills and for Business, Enterprise and Regulatory Reform Order 2007, SI 2007/3224, art 15, Schedule, Pt 2, para 34, as from 12 December 2007.

In the entry relating to section 42(2)(c), paras (k), (l) added by the Proceeds of Crime Act 2002 (References to Financial Investigators) (Amendment) Order 2004, SI 2004/8, art 2, Schedule, paras 1, 2, as from 16 February 2004; paras (m)–(o) added by the Proceeds of Crime Act 2002 (References to Financial Investigators) (Amendment) Order 2005, SI 2005/386, arts 2, 4, as from 1 April 2005; word omitted from the end of paras (k) and (i) revoked, and paras (p)–(r) added, by the Proceeds of Crime Act 2002 (References to Financial Investigators) (Amendment) Order 2006, SI 2006/57, arts 2, 4, as from 1 March 2006; words in square brackets in para (l) substituted by the Special Health Authorities Abolition Order 2006, SI 2006/635, art 3, Sch 2, para 11(1), (2)(a), as from 1 April 2006.

In the entry relating to section 68(3)(c), paras (h), (i) added by SI 2004/8, art 2, Schedule, paras 1, 3, as from 16 February 2004; paras (j), (k) (and the words "or is an immigration officer who is not below the grade of immigration inspector") added by SI 2005/386, arts 2, 5, as from 1 April 2005; word omitted from the end of paras (f) and (h) revoked, and paras (l)–(m) added, by SI 2006/57, arts 2, 5, as from 1 March 2006; para (i) substituted by SI 2006/635, art 3, Sch 2, para 11(1), (3)(a), as from 1 April 2006.

In the entry relating to section 191(2)(c), paras (i)–(l) added by SI 2005/386, arts 2, 6, as from 1 April 2005; word omitted from the end of para (g) revoked, and paras (m)–(o) added, by SI 2006/57, arts 2, 6, as from 1 March 2006.

In the entry relating to section 216(3)(c), paras (e)–(g) (and the words "or is an immigration officer who is not below the grade of immigration inspector") added by SI 2005/386, arts 2, 7, as from 1 April 2005; word omitted from the end of para (c) revoked, and paras (h)–(j) added, by SI 2006/57, arts 2, 7, as from 1 March 2006.

In the entry relating to section 378(1)(b) (in relation to England and Wales), paras (j), (k) added by SI 2004/8, art 2, Schedule, paras 1, 4, as from 16 February 2004; words in square brackets in para (k) substituted by SI 2006/635, art 3, Sch 2, para 11(1), (2)(b), as from 1 April 2006; para (l), (m) (and the words "or is an immigration officer") added by SI 2005/386, arts 2, 8, as from 1 April 2005; word omitted from the end of paras (h) and (j) revoked, and paras (n)–(p) added, by SI 2006/57, arts 2, 8, as from 1 March 2006.

In the entry relating to section 378(1)(b) (in relation to Northern Ireland), paras (h)–(j) (and the words "or is an immigration officer") added by SI 2005/386, arts 2, 9, as from 1 April 2005; word omitted from the end of para (f) revoked, and paras (k)–(m) added, by SI 2006/57, arts 2, 9, as from 1 March 2006.

In the entry relating to section 378(2)(d) (in relation to England and Wales), paras (i), (j) added by SI 2004/8, art 2, Schedule, paras 1, 5, as from 16 February 2004; para (j) substituted by SI 2006/635, art 3, Sch 2,

PART III
STATUTORY INSTRUMENTS

(b) in subsection (2), for "Such a warrant", there is substituted "A search and seizure warrant issued under section 352 of the Proceeds of Crime Act 2002";

(c) in subsection (2), for "constable", there is substituted "appropriate person (within the meaning of Part 8 of the Proceeds of Crime Act 2002)";

(d) for "the constable", in each subsequent place where it occurs, there is substituted "the appropriate person";

(e) for "a constable", in each subsequent place where it occurs, there is substituted "an appropriate person";

(f) at the beginning of subsection (9), there is inserted "In the case of a warrant which is issued because the judge is satisfied that the requirement in section 352(6)(a) of the Proceeds of Crime Act 2002 is satisfied (production order made and not complied with),";

(g) in subsection (9)(a), for "articles or persons sought were", there is substituted "material sought was";

(h) in subsection (9)(b), for "articles were seized, other than articles which were", there is substituted "material was seized, other than material which was";

(i) for sub-paragraphs (i) and (ii) of subsection (10), there is substituted "to an officer of the court at which it was issued.";

(j) for paragraphs (a) and (b) of subsection (11), there is substituted "by an officer of the court at which it was issued.".

[3713]

4 Application of section 21 of the Police and Criminal Evidence Act 1984

(1) Section 21 of the Police and Criminal Evidence Act 1984 (access and copying) applies to powers of seizure under search and seizure warrants sought for the purposes of a confiscation investigation or a money laundering investigation, with the modifications in paragraph (2).

(2) The modifications are that—

(a) in subsection (1), for "A constable", there is substituted, "An appropriate person (within the meaning of Part 8 of the Proceeds of Crime Act 2002)";

(b) in subsection (1), for "in the exercise of a power conferred by any enactment, including an enactment contained in an Act passed after this Act,", there is substituted "under a search and seizure warrant issued under section 352 of the Proceeds of Crime Act 2002 for the purposes of a confiscation investigation or a money laundering investigation";

(c) in subsection (2), for "officer", there is substituted "appropriate person";

(d) in subsection (3), for "a constable" where first occurring, there is substituted, "an appropriate person";

(e) in subsection (3)(b), for "the police", there is substituted "the appropriate person or an appropriate officer (within the meaning of Part 8 of the Proceeds of Crime Act 2002)";

(f) in subsection (3)(b), the words "for the purpose of investigating an offence" are omitted;

(g) in subsection (3), before "officer in charge of the investigation", there is inserted "appropriate";

(h) in subsection (3), for "a constable" in the second place where it occurs, there is substituted "an appropriate officer";

(i) in subsection (4), before "officer in charge of the investigation", there is inserted "appropriate";

(j) in subsection (4)(a), for "a constable", there is substituted "an appropriate officer";

(k) in subsection (5), for "A constable", there is substituted "An appropriate person";

(l) in subsection (8), before "officer in charge of the investigation", there is inserted "appropriate";

(m) in subsection (8)(b), the words "other than the offence for the purposes of investigating which the thing was seized" are omitted;

(n) in subsection (8)(c), after "criminal proceedings", there is inserted "(including proceedings related to the making of a confiscation order)".

[3714]

5 Application of section 22 of the Police and Criminal Evidence Act 1984

(1) Section 22 of the Police and Criminal Evidence Act 1984 (retention) applies to powers of seizure under search and seizure warrants sought for the purposes of a confiscation investigation or a money laundering investigation, with the modifications in paragraph (2).

(2) The modifications are that—

(a) in subsection (1), for "a constable" where first occurring, there is substituted "an appropriate person (within the meaning of Part 8 of the Proceeds of Crime Act 2002)";

(b) in subsection (1), for "a constable" in the second place where it occurs, there is substituted "an appropriate person";

(c) in subsection (1), for "following a requirement made by virtue of section 19 or 20 above", there is substituted "under a search and seizure warrant issued under section 352 of the Proceeds of Crime Act 2002 for the purposes of a confiscation investigation or a money laundering investigation";

(d) in subsection (1), after "retained", there is inserted "by the appropriate person or an appropriate officer (within the meaning of Part 8 of the Proceeds of Crime Act 2002)";

(e) in subsection (2), for "criminal investigation", there is substituted "confiscation investigation or money laundering investigation";

(f) after subsection (2)(a)(i), the word "or" is omitted;

(g) after subsection (2)(a)(ii), the word "and" is omitted;

(h) after subsection (2)(a)(ii), there is inserted—

"(iii) for use as evidence in proceedings relating to the making of a confiscation order under the Drug Trafficking Offences Act 1986, Part VI of the Criminal Justice Act 1988, Part I of the Drug Trafficking Act 1994 or Part 2 of the Proceeds of Crime Act 2002; or

(iv) for forensic examination or for investigation in connection with a confiscation investigation or money laundering investigation; and";

(i) subsections (3), (5) and (6) are omitted.

[3715]

6 Application of article 17 of the Police and Criminal Evidence (Northern Ireland) Order 1989

(1) Article 17 of the Police and Criminal Evidence (Northern Ireland) Order 1989 (search warrants—safeguards) applies to search and seizure warrants sought for the purposes of a confiscation investigation or a money laundering investigation, with the modifications in paragraph (2).

(2) The modifications are that—

(a) for paragraph (1), there is substituted—

"(1) This article and article 18 have effect in relation to the issue to an appropriate officer (within the meaning of Part 8 of the Proceeds of Crime Act 2002) of a search and seizure warrant under section 352 of the Proceeds of Crime Act 2002 for the purposes of a confiscation investigation or a money laundering investigation and an entry on or search of premises under such a warrant is unlawful unless the warrant complies with this article and is executed in accordance with article 18.";

(b) in paragraph (2), for "a constable", there is substituted "an appropriate officer";

(c) in paragraph (2), sub-paragraph (b) is omitted;

(d) in paragraph (2), sub-paragraph (c) is omitted;

(e) in paragraph (3), the words "supported by a complaint in writing and" are omitted;

(f) in paragraph (4), for "constable", there is substituted "appropriate officer";

(g) in paragraph (4), the words "justice of the peace or" are omitted;

(h) in paragraph (6), for sub-paragraph (iii) of sub-paragraph (a), there is substituted—

"(iii) the statutory power under which it is issued and, unless the judge orders otherwise, an indication of the nature of the investigation in respect of which it is issued; and";

(i) in paragraph (6), at the beginning of sub-paragraph (b), there is inserted "in the case of a warrant which is issued because the judge is satisfied that the requirement in section 352(6)(a) of the Proceeds of Crime Act 2002 is satisfied (production order made and not complied with),";

(j) in paragraph (6)(b), for "articles or persons", there is substituted "material";

(k) in paragraph (8), the words "justice of the peace or" are omitted.

[3716]

7 Application of article 18 of the Police and Criminal Evidence (Northern Ireland) Order 1989

(1) Article 18 of the Police and Criminal Evidence (Northern Ireland) Order 1989 (execution of warrants) applies to search and seizure warrants sought for the purposes of a confiscation investigation or a money laundering investigation, with the modifications in paragraph (2).

(2) The modifications are that—

(a) paragraph (1) is omitted;

(b) in paragraph (2) for "Such a warrant", there is substituted "A search and seizure warrant issued under section 352 of the Proceeds of Crime Act 2002";

(c) in paragraph (2), for "constable", there is substituted "appropriate person (within the meaning of Part 8 of the Proceeds of Crime Act 2002)";

(d) for "the constable", in each subsequent place where it occurs, there is substituted "the appropriate person";

(e) for "a constable", in each subsequent place where it occurs, there is substituted "an appropriate person";

(f) at the beginning of paragraph (9), there is inserted "In the case of a warrant which is

(4)   Entry and search under a warrant must be at a reasonable hour unless it appears to the appropriate person executing it that the purpose of a search may be frustrated on an entry at a reasonable hour.

(5)   Where the occupier of premises which are to be entered and searched is present at the time when an appropriate person seeks to execute a warrant to enter and search them, the appropriate person—

(a)   shall identify himself to the occupier and, if not in uniform, shall produce to him documentary evidence that he is an appropriate person;

(b)   shall produce the warrant to him; and

(c)   shall supply him with a copy of it.

(6)   Where—

(a)   the occupier of such premises is not present at the time when an appropriate person seeks to execute such a warrant; but

(b)   some other person who appears to the appropriate person to be in charge of the premises is present, subsection (5) above shall have effect as if any reference to the occupier were a reference to that other person.

(7)   If there is no person present who appears to the appropriate person to be in charge of the premises, he shall leave a copy of the warrant in a prominent place on the premises.

(8)   A search under a warrant may only be a search to the extent required for the purpose for which the warrant was issued.

(9)   In the case of a warrant which is issued because the judge is satisfied that the requirement in section 352(6)(a) of the Proceeds of Crime Act 2002 is satisfied (production order made but not complied with), an appropriate person executing a warrant shall make an endorsement on it stating—

(a)   whether the material sought was found; and

(b)   whether any material was seized, other than material which was sought.

(10)   A warrant which—

(a)   has been executed; or

(b)   has not been executed within the time authorised for its execution,

shall be returned to an officer of the court at which it was issued.

(11)   A warrant which is returned under subsection (10) above shall be retained for 12 months from its return by an officer of the court at which it was issued.

(12)   If during the period for which a warrant is to be retained the occupier of the premises to which it relates asks to inspect it, he shall be allowed to do so.

21   Access and copying

(1)   An appropriate person (within the meaning of Part 8 of the Proceeds of Crime Act 2002) who seizes anything under a search and seizure warrant issued under section 352 of the Proceeds of Crime Act 2002 for the purposes of a confiscation investigation or a money laundering investigation shall, if so requested by a person showing himself—

(a)   to be the occupier of premises on which it was seized; or

(b)   to have had custody or control of it immediately before the seizure,

provide that person with a record of what he seized.

(2)   The appropriate person shall provide the record within a reasonable time from the making of the request for it.

(3)   Subject to subsection (8) below, if a request for permission to be granted access to anything which—

(a)   has been seized by an appropriate person; and

(b)   is retained by the appropriate person or an appropriate officer (within the meaning of Part 8 of the Proceeds of Crime Act 2002),

is made to the appropriate officer in charge of the investigation by a person who had custody or control of the thing immediately before it was so seized or by someone acting on behalf of such a person, the officer shall allow the person who made the request access to it under the supervision of an appropriate officer.

(4)   Subject to subsection (8) below, if a request for a photograph or copy of any such thing is made to the appropriate officer in charge of the investigation by a person who had custody or control of the thing immediately before it was so seized, or by someone acting on behalf of such a person, the officer shall—

(a)   allow the person who made the request access to it under the supervision of an appropriate officer for the purpose of photographing or copying it; or

(b)   photograph or copy it, or cause it to be photographed or copied.

(5)   An appropriate person may also photograph or copy, or have photographed or copied, anything which he has power to seize, without a request being made under subsection (4) above.

(6)   Where anything is photographed or copied under subsection (4)(b) above, the photograph or copy shall be supplied to the person who made the request.

(7)   The photograph or copy shall be so supplied within a reasonable time from the making of the request.

(8)   There is no duty under this section to grant access to, or to supply a photograph or copy of, anything if the appropriate officer in charge of the investigation for the purposes of which it was seized has reasonable grounds for believing that to do so would prejudice—
   (a)   that investigation;
   (b)   the investigation of an offence; or
   (c)   any criminal proceedings (including proceedings related to the making of a confiscation order) which may be brought as a result of—
      (i)   the investigation of which he is in charge; or
      (ii)   any such investigation as is mentioned in paragraph (b) above.

22   Retention

(1)   Subject to subsection (4) below, anything which has been seized by an appropriate person (within the meaning of Part 8 of the Proceeds of Crime Act 2002) or taken away by an appropriate person under a search and seizure warrant issued under section 352 of the Proceeds of Crime Act 2002 for the purposes of a confiscation investigation or a money laundering investigation may be retained by the appropriate person or an appropriate officer (within the meaning of Part 8 of the Proceeds of Crime Act 2002) so long as is necessary in all the circumstances.

(2)   Without prejudice to the generality of subsection (1) above—
   (a)   anything seized for the purposes of a confiscation investigation or money laundering investigation may be retained, except as provided by subsection (4) below,—
      (i)   for use as evidence at a trial for an offence;
      (ii)   for forensic examination or for investigation in connection with an offence;
      (iii)   for use as evidence in proceedings relating to the making of a confiscation order under the Drug Trafficking Offences Act 1986, Part VI of the Criminal Justice Act 1988, Part I of the Drug Trafficking Act 1994 or Part 2 of the Proceeds of Crime Act 2002; or
      (iv)   for forensic examination or for investigation in connection with a confiscation investigation or money laundering investigation; and
   (b)   anything may be retained in order to establish its lawful owner, where there are reasonable grounds for believing that it has been obtained in consequence of the commission of an offence.

(3)   …

(4)   Nothing may be retained for either of the purposes mentioned in subsection (2)(a) above if a photograph or copy would be sufficient for that purpose.

(5), (6)   …

[3721]

SCHEDULE 2
ARTICLES 17, 18, 23 AND 24 OF THE POLICE AND CRIMINAL EVIDENCE (NORTHERN IRELAND) ORDER 1989, AS MODIFIED
Article 10

17   Search warrants—safeguards

(1)   This article and article 18 have effect in relation to the issue to an appropriate officer (within the meaning of Part 8 of the Proceeds of Crime Act 2002) of a search and seizure warrant under section 352 of the Proceeds of Crime Act 2002 for the purposes of a confiscation investigation or a money laundering investigation and an entry on or search of premises under such a warrant is unlawful unless the warrant complies with this article and is executed in accordance with article 18.

(2)   Where an appropriate officer applies for any such warrant, it shall be his duty—
   (a)   to state—
      (i)   the ground on which he makes the application; and
      (ii)   the statutory provision under which the warrant would be issued;
   (b), (c) …

(3)   An application for such a warrant shall be substantiated on oath.

(4)   The appropriate officer shall answer any question that the judge hearing the application asks him.

(5)   A warrant shall authorise an entry on one occasion only.

(6)   A warrant—
   (a)   shall specify—
      (i)   the name of the person who applies for it;

      (ii)   the date on which it is issued;

      (iii) the statutory provision under which it is issued and, unless the judge orders otherwise, an indication of the nature of the investigation in respect of which it is issued; and

      (iv) the premises to be searched; and

  (b)   in the case of a warrant which issued because the judge is satisfied that the requirement in section 352(6)(a) of the Proceeds of Crime Act 2002 is satisfied (production order made and not complied with) shall identify, so far as is practicable, the material to be sought.

(7)   Two copies shall be made of a warrant.

(8)   The copies shall be clearly certified as copies by the judge who issues the warrant.

18 Execution of warrants

(1)   ...

(2)   A search and seizure warrant issued under section 352 of the Proceeds of Crime Act 2002 may authorise persons to accompany any appropriate person (within the meaning of Part 8 of the Proceeds of Crime Act 2002) who is executing it.

(3)   Entry and search under a warrant must be within one month from the date of its issue.

(4)   Entry and search under a warrant must be at a reasonable hour unless it appears to the appropriate person executing it that the purpose of a search may be frustrated on an entry at a reasonable hour.

(5)   Where the occupier of premises which are to be entered and searched is present at the time when an appropriate person seeks to execute a warrant to enter and search them, the appropriate person—

  (a)   shall identify himself to the occupier and, if not in uniform, shall produce to him documentary evidence that he is an appropriate person;

  (b)   shall produce the warrant to him; and

  (c)   shall supply him with a certified copy of it.

(6)   Where—

  (a)   the occupier of such premises is not present at the time when an appropriate person seeks to execute such a warrant; but

  (b)   some other person who appears to the appropriate person to be in charge of the premises is present,

paragraph (5) shall have effect as if any reference to the occupier were a reference to that other person.

(7)   If there is no person present who appears to the appropriate person to be in charge of the premises, he shall leave or affix a copy of the warrant in a prominent place on the premises.

(8)   A search under a warrant may only be a search to the extent required for the purpose for which the warrant was issued.

(9)   In the case of a warrant which is issued because the judge is satisfied that the requirement in section 352(6)(a) of the Proceeds of Crime Act 2002 is satisfied (production order made and not complied with), an appropriate person executing a warrant shall make an endorsement on it stating—

  (a)   whether the material sought was found; and

  (b)   whether any material was seized, other than material which was sought.

(10)   A warrant which—

  (a)   has been executed; or

  (b)   has not been executed within the time authorised for its execution,

shall be returned to the chief clerk for the county court division in which the property is situated.

(11)   A warrant which is returned under paragraph (10) shall be retained for 12 months from its return.

(12)   If during the period for which a warrant is to be retained the occupier of the premises to which it relates asks to inspect it, he shall be allowed to do so.

23 Access and copying

(1)   An appropriate person (within the meaning of Part 8 of the Proceeds of Crime Act 2002) who seizes anything under a search and seizure warrant issued under section 352 of the Proceeds of Crime Act 2002 for the purposes of a confiscation investigation or a money laundering investigation shall, if so requested by a person showing himself—

  (a)   to be the occupier of premises on which it was seized; or

  (b)   to have had custody or control of it immediately before the seizure,

provide that person with a record of what he seized.

(2)   The appropriate person shall provide the record within a reasonable time from the making of the request for it.

(3)   Subject to paragraph (8), if a request for permission to be granted access to anything which—

(a)   has been seized by an appropriate person; and

(b)   is retained by the appropriate person or an appropriate officer (within the meaning of Part 8 of the Proceeds of Crime Act 2002),

is made to the appropriate officer in charge of the investigation by a person who had custody or control of the thing immediately before it was so seized or by someone acting on behalf of such a person, the officer shall allow the person who made the request access to it under the supervision of an appropriate officer.

(4)   Subject to paragraph (8), if a request for a photograph or copy of any such thing is made to the appropriate officer in charge of the investigation by a person who had custody or control of the thing immediately before it was so seized, or by someone acting on behalf of such a person, the officer shall—

(a)   allow the person who made the request access to it under the supervision of an appropriate officer for the purpose of photographing or copying it; or

(b)   photograph or copy it, or cause it to be photographed or copied.

(5)   An appropriate person may also photograph or copy, or have photographed or copied, anything which he has power to seize, without a request being made under paragraph (4).

(6)   Where anything is photographed or copied under paragraph (4)(b), the photograph or copy shall be supplied to the person who made the request.

(7)   The photograph or copy shall be so supplied within a reasonable time from the making of the request.

(8)   There is no duty under this Article to grant access to, or to supply a photograph or copy of, anything if the appropriate officer in charge of the investigation for the purposes of which it was seized has reasonable grounds for believing that to do so would prejudice—

(a)   that investigation;

(b)   the investigation of an offence; or

(c)   any criminal proceedings (including proceedings related to the making of a confiscation order) which may be brought as a result of—

(i)   the investigation of which he is in charge; or

(ii)   any such investigation as is mentioned in sub-paragraph (b).

24   Retention

(1)   Subject to paragraph (4), anything which has been seized by an appropriate person (within the meaning of Part 8 of the Proceeds of Crime Act 2002) or taken away by an appropriate person under a search and seizure warrant issued under section 352 of the Proceeds of Crime Act 2002 for the purposes of a confiscation investigation or a money laundering investigation may be retained by the appropriate person or an appropriate officer (within the meaning of Part 8 of the Proceeds of Crime Act 2002) so long as is necessary in all the circumstances.

(2)   Without prejudice to the generality of paragraph (1)—

(a)   anything seized for the purposes of a confiscation investigation or money laundering investigation may be retained, except as provided by paragraph (4)—

(i)   for use as evidence at a trial for an offence;

(ii)   for forensic examination or for investigation in connection with an offence;

(iii)   for use as evidence in proceedings relating to the making of a confiscation order under the Criminal Justice (Confiscation) (Northern Ireland) Order 1990, the Proceeds of Crime (Northern Ireland) Order 1996 or Part 4 of the Proceeds of Crime Act 2002; or

(iv)   for forensic examination or for investigation in connection with a confiscation investigation or money laundering investigation; and

(b)   anything may be retained in order to establish its lawful owner, where there are reasonable grounds for believing that it has been obtained in consequence of the commission of an offence.

(3)   …

(4)   Nothing may be retained for either of the purposes mentioned in paragraph (2)(a) if a photograph or copy would be sufficient for that purpose.

(5), (6)   …

PART III
STATUTORY INSTRUMENTS

PROCEEDS OF CRIME ACT 2002 (INVESTIGATIONS IN ENGLAND, WALES AND NORTHERN IRELAND: CODE OF PRACTICE) ORDER 2003 (NOTE)

(SI 2003/334)

NOTES

This Order was made on 20 February 2003 under the powers conferred by the Proceeds of Crime Act 2002, 377(4) and came into force on 24 February 2003. It has been superseded by the Proceeds of Crime Act 2002 (Investigations in England, Wales and Northern Ireland: Code of Practice) Order 2008, SI 2008/946 at **[4156]**.

[3730]–[3731]

PROCEEDS OF CRIME ACT 2002 (DISCLOSURE OF INFORMATION) ORDER 2003 (NOTE)

(SI 2003/335)

NOTES

This Order was revoked by the Proceeds of Crime Act 2002 (Disclosure of Information) Order 2008, SI 2008/1909, art 4, as from 23 July 2008. The 2008 Order is at **[4164]**.

[3732]–[3739]

PROCEEDS OF CRIME ACT 2002 (INVESTIGATIONS IN DIFFERENT PARTS OF THE UNITED KINGDOM) ORDER 2003

(SI 2003/425)

NOTES

Made: 27 February 2003.
Authority: Proceeds of Crime Act 2002, ss 443(1)(d), (e), (3), (4), 459(2).
Commencement: 1 April 2003.
This Order is reproduced as amended by: the Proceeds of Crime Act 2002 (Investigations in different parts of the United Kingdom) (Amendment) Order 2008, SI 2008/298.

ARRANGEMENT OF ARTICLES

PART 1
INTRODUCTION

PART 2
ENFORCEMENT IN ENGLAND AND WALES OF SCOTTISH AND NORTHERN IRELAND ORDERS AND WARRANTS

PART 3
ENFORCEMENT IN NORTHERN IRELAND OF ENGLISH, WELSH AND SCOTTISH ORDERS AND WARRANTS

PART 4
ENFORCEMENT IN SCOTLAND OF ENGLISH, WELSH AND NORTHERN IRELAND
ORDERS AND WARRANTS

PART 5
SUPPLEMENTARY PROVISIONS RELATING TO CONFISCATION INVESTIGATIONS
AND MONEY LAUNDERING INVESTIGATIONS

PART 1
INTRODUCTION

1   Title and commencement

This Order may be cited as the Proceeds of Crime Act 2002 (Investigations in different parts of the United Kingdom) Order 2003 and shall come into force on 1st April 2003.

[3740]

2   Interpretation

In this Order—
  "the Act" means the Proceeds of Crime Act 2002;
  "an English or Welsh account monitoring order" means an order made in England and Wales under section 370(1) of the Act for the purposes of a confiscation investigation or a money laundering investigation;
  "an English or Welsh appropriate officer" means—
    (a)   in relation to a confiscation investigation—
      (i)   [a member of SOCA's staff];
      (ii)   an accredited financial investigator;
      (iii)   a constable of a police force in England and Wales; or
      (iv)   a customs officer;
    (b)   in relation to a money laundering investigation—
      (i)   an accredited financial investigator;
      (ii)   a constable of a police force in England and Wales; or
      (iii)   a customs officer;
  "an English or Welsh customer information order" means an order made in England and Wales under section 363(1) of the Act for the purposes of a confiscation investigation or a money laundering investigation;
  "an English or Welsh disclosure order" means an order made in England and Wales under section 357(1) of the Act for the purposes of a confiscation investigation;
  "an English or Welsh production order" means an order made in England and Wales under section 345(1) of the Act for the purposes of a confiscation investigation or a money laundering investigation;
  "an English or Welsh search and seizure warrant" means a warrant issued in England and Wales under section 352(1) of the Act for the purposes of a confiscation investigation or a money laundering investigation;
  "a Northern Ireland account monitoring order" means an order made in Northern Ireland under section 370(1) of the Act for the purposes of a confiscation investigation or a money laundering investigation;
  "a Northern Ireland appropriate officer" means—
    (a)   in relation to a confiscation investigation—
      (i)   [a member of SOCA's staff]*r*;

(ii)   an accredited financial investigator;

(iii)   a constable of the Police Service of Northern Ireland; or

(iv)   a customs officer;

(b)   in relation to a money laundering investigation—

(i)   an accredited financial investigator;

(ii)   a constable of the Police Service of Northern Ireland; or

(iii)   a customs officer;

"a Northern Ireland customer information order" means an order made in Northern Ireland under section 363(1) of the Act for the purposes of a confiscation investigation or a money laundering investigation;

"a Northern Ireland disclosure order" means an order made in Northern Ireland under section 357(1) of the Act for the purposes of a confiscation investigation;

"a Northern Ireland production order" means an order made in Northern Ireland under section 345(1) of the Act for the purposes of a confiscation investigation or a money laundering investigation;

"a Northern Ireland search and seizure warrant" means a warrant issued in Northern Ireland under section 352(1) of the Act for the purposes of a confiscation investigation or a money laundering investigation;

"the Police and Criminal Evidence Order" means the Proceeds of Crime Act 2002 (Application of Police and Criminal Evidence Act 1984 and Police and Criminal Evidence (Northern Ireland) Order 1989) Order 2003;

"a Scottish account monitoring order" means an order made under section 404(1) of the Act for the purposes of a confiscation investigation or a money laundering investigation;

"a Scottish customer information order" means an order made under section 397(1) of the Act for the purposes of a confiscation investigation or a money laundering investigation;

"a Scottish disclosure order" means an order made under section 391(1) of the Act for the purposes of a confiscation investigation;

"a Scottish production order" means an order made under section 380(1) of the Act for the purposes of a confiscation investigation or a money laundering investigation;

"a Scottish search warrant" means a warrant issued under section 387(1) of the Act for the purposes of a confiscation investigation or a money laundering investigation;

references to a constable of a police force in Scotland include references to a customs officer.

[3741]

NOTES

Words in square brackets in definitions "an English or Welsh appropriate officer" and "a Northern Ireland appropriate officer" substituted by the Proceeds of Crime Act 2002 (Investigations in different parts of the United Kingdom) (Amendment) Order 2008, SI 2008/298, art 2(1), (2), as from 1 April 2008.

PART 2

ENFORCEMENT IN ENGLAND AND WALES OF SCOTTISH AND NORTHERN IRELAND
ORDERS AND WARRANTS

3 Northern Ireland production orders

(1)   This article applies where—

(a)   a Northern Ireland production order requires a person in England and Wales in possession or control of material in England and Wales to produce the material or give access to the material; or

(b)   an order to grant entry to premises in England and Wales is made in respect of a Northern Ireland production order under section 347 of the Act.

(2)   Subject to paragraph (7), the production order or the order to grant entry, as the case may be, may be served—

(a)   by sending it by post, facsimile transmission or electronic mail to the person in possession of the material; or

(b)   by an English or Welsh appropriate officer or a Northern Ireland appropriate officer serving the order personally,

and any rules of court as to the service of documents (other than rules of court made by virtue of section 446 of the Act) or other requirements in law as to the service of documents do not apply.

(3)   Sections 345(4), 347(3), 348(5) and (7) and 349 of the Act have effect with the modifications in paragraph (4).

(4)   The modifications are that for "an appropriate officer" in each place where it occurs, there is substituted, "whichever of an English or Welsh appropriate officer, a Northern Ireland appropriate officer or an English or Welsh appropriate officer and a Northern Ireland appropriate officer acting together the order specifies".

(5)   The production order or the order to grant entry, as the case may be, has effect as if it were an order of the Crown Court in England and Wales.

(6)   Section 348(1) to (4) of the Act (further provisions) has effect as if the production order were an English or Welsh production order.

(7)   Section 350 of the Act (government departments) has effect as if the production order were an English or Welsh production order and, in particular—

(a)   if the order is not brought to the attention of the officer concerned within the period stated in the order (in pursuance of section 345(4) of the Act) the person on whom it is served must report the reasons for the failure to a judge entitled to exercise the jurisdiction of the Crown Court in England and Wales; and

(b)   the production order must be served as if the proceedings were civil proceedings started against the department in England and Wales.

[3742]

4   Scottish production orders

(1)   This article applies where—

(a)   a Scottish production order requires a person in England and Wales in possession or control of material in England and Wales to produce the material or give access to the material; or

(b)   an order to grant entry to premises in England and Wales is made in respect of a Scottish production order under section 382 of the Act.

(2)   Subject to paragraph (7), the production order or the order to grant entry, as the case may be, may be served—

(a)   by sending it by post, facsimile transmission or electronic mail to the person in possession of the material; or

(b)   by an English or Welsh appropriate officer or a constable of a police force in Scotland serving the order personally,

and the Summary Jurisdiction (Process) Act 1881, any rules of court as to the service of documents (other than rules of court made by virtue of section 446 of the Act) and any other requirement in law as to the service of documents do not apply.

(3)   Sections 380(5), 382(3), 383(3) and (5) and 384 of the Act have effect with the modifications in paragraph (4).

(4)   The modifications are that for "a proper person" in each place where it occurs, there is substituted "whichever of an English or Welsh appropriate officer, a constable of a police force in Scotland or an English or Welsh appropriate officer and a constable of a police force in Scotland acting together the order specifies".

(5)   The production order or the order to grant entry, as the case may be, has effect as if it were an order of the Crown Court in England and Wales.

(6)   Section 383(1) and (2) of the Act (further provisions) does not apply and section 348(1) to (4) of the Act (further provisions) has effect as if the production order were an English or Welsh production order.

(7)   Section 385 of the Act (government departments) does not apply and section 350 of the Act (government departments) has effect as if the production order were an English or Welsh production order and, in particular—

(a)   if the order is not brought to the attention of the officer concerned within the period stated in the order (in pursuance of section 380(5) of the Act) the person on whom it is served must report the reasons for the failure to a judge entitled to exercise the jurisdiction of the Crown Court in England and Wales; and

(b)   the production order must be served as if the proceedings were civil proceedings started against the department in England and Wales.

[3743]

5   Northern Ireland search and seizure warrants

(1)   This article applies where a Northern Ireland search and seizure warrant authorises entry into and search of premises in England and Wales.

(2)   Section 352(4) of the Act (definition of a search and seizure warrant) has effect with the modification that for "an appropriate person", there is substituted "one or more appropriate persons, as the warrant specifies".

(3)   Section 352(5) of the Act (definition of an appropriate person) has effect with the modifications in paragraph (4).

[(4)   The modifications are—

(a)   for paragraphs (a), (b) and (c), there are substituted—

"(a)   an officer of Revenue and Customs;

(b)   a constable of a police force in England and Wales;

PART III

STATUTORY INSTRUMENTS

    (c)   a constable of the Police Service of Northern Ireland; or

    (d)   an accredited financial investigator."; and

  (b)   in subsection (7), for "paragraph (a) or (c)" substitute "paragraph (d)".]

(5)   Section 354 of the Act (further provisions) applies as if the warrant were an English or Welsh search and seizure warrant.

(6)   Article 7 of the Police and Criminal Evidence Order (application of article 18 of the Police and Criminal Evidence (Northern Ireland) Order 1989) does not apply to the execution of the warrant in England and Wales.

(7)   Article 3 of the Police and Criminal Evidence Order (application of section 16 of the Police and Criminal Evidence Act 1984) has effect in relation to the execution of the warrant in England and Wales as it has effect in relation to the execution of an English or Welsh search and seizure warrant.

(8)   Article 22 of the Police and Criminal Evidence (Northern Ireland) Order 1989 (extension of powers to computerised information) does not apply to a power of seizure under the warrant exercised in England and Wales.

(9)   Section 20 of the Police and Criminal Evidence Act 1984 (extension of powers to computerised information) has effect in relation to a power of seizure under the warrant exercised in England and Wales as it has effect in relation to the exercise of a power of seizure conferred by an enactment to which that section applies and as if the reference to a constable included a constable of the Police Service of Northern Ireland or a customs officer exercising functions by virtue of paragraphs (2) to (4).

(10)   Articles 8 and 9 of the Police and Criminal Evidence Order (application of articles 23 and 24 of the Police and Criminal Evidence (Northern Ireland) Order 1989) have effect as if the warrant had been executed in Northern Ireland.

(11)   Articles 4 and 5 of the Police and Criminal Evidence Order (application of sections 21 and 22 of the Police and Criminal Evidence Act 1984) do not apply.

[3744]

NOTES

Para (4): substituted by the Proceeds of Crime Act 2002 (Investigations in different parts of the United Kingdom) (Amendment) Order 2008, SI 2008/298, art 2(1), (3), as from 6 April 2008.

6 Scottish search warrants

(1)   This article applies where a Scottish search warrant authorises entry into and search of premises in England and Wales.

(2)   Section 387(4) of the Act (definition of search warrant) has effect with the modification that for "a proper person", there is substituted "a constable of a police force in England and Wales, a constable of a police force in Scotland or both acting together, as the warrant specifies".

(3)   Section 389 of the Act (further provisions) does not apply and section 354 of the Act (further provisions) applies as if the warrant were an English or Welsh search and seizure warrant.

(4)   Article 3 of the Police and Criminal Evidence Order (application of section 16 of the Police and Criminal Evidence Act 1984) has effect in relation to the execution of the warrant in England and Wales as it has effect in relation to the execution of an English or Welsh search and seizure warrant.

(5)   Section 390(3) of the Act (which deals with computerised information in relation to Scottish search warrants) does not apply to the execution of the warrant in England and Wales.

(6)   Section 20 of the Police and Criminal Evidence Act 1984 (extension of powers to computerised information) has effect in relation to a power of seizure under the warrant exercised in England and Wales as it has effect in relation to the exercise of a power of seizure conferred by an enactment to which that section applies and as if the reference to a constable included a constable of a police force in Scotland exercising functions by virtue of paragraph (2).

(7)   Section 390(4) of the Act (which states that copies may be taken of material seized under a Scottish search warrant) has effect as if the warrant had been executed in Scotland.

(8)   Articles 4 and 5 of the Police and Criminal Evidence Order (application of sections 21 and 22 of the Police and Criminal Evidence Act 1984) do not apply.

(9)   The Summary Jurisdiction (Process) Act 1881 does not apply.

[3745]

7 Northern Ireland disclosure orders

(1)   Paragraphs (2) to (4) apply where [a Northern Ireland appropriate officer] gives a notice under a Northern Ireland disclosure order which requires a person in England and Wales to—

    (a)   answer questions in England and Wales; or

(b)   provide information or produce documents in England and Wales.

(2)   Proceedings for an offence under section 359 of the Act may be brought in England and Wales.

(3)   Section 360 of the Act (statements) applies in relation to criminal proceedings brought in England and Wales, as well as criminal proceedings brought in Northern Ireland.

(4)   Section 361 of the Act (further provisions) applies as if the order were an English or Welsh disclosure order.

(5)   Paragraph (6) applies where [a Northern Ireland appropriate officer] gives a notice under a Northern Ireland disclosure order which requires a person in England and Wales to—
(a)   answer questions in Northern Ireland; or
(b)   provide information or produce documents in Northern Ireland.

(6)   Proceedings for an offence under section 359 may be brought in England and Wales, as well as in Northern Ireland.

[3746]

NOTES
Paras (1), (5): words in square brackets substituted by the Proceeds of Crime Act 2002 (Investigations in different parts of the United Kingdom) (Amendment) Order 2008, SI 2008/298, art 2(1), (4), as from 1 April 2008.

8 Scottish disclosure orders

(1)   Paragraphs (2) to (5) apply where the Lord Advocate gives a notice under a Scottish disclosure order which requires a person in England and Wales to—
(a)   answer questions in England and Wales; or
(b)   provide information or produce documents in England and Wales.

(2)   Section 393 of the Act (offences) does not apply and section 359 of the Act (offences) applies as if the order were an English or Welsh disclosure order.

(3)   Section 394 of the Act (statements) applies in relation to criminal proceedings brought in England and Wales, as well as criminal proceedings brought in Scotland, with the modifications in paragraph (4).

(4)   The modifications are that in subsection (2)—
(a)   in paragraph (b), after "section 393(1) or (3)", there is inserted "or an offence under section 359(1) or (3)";
(b)   in paragraph (c), after "perjury", there is inserted "or an offence under section 5 of the Perjury Act 1911".

(5)   Section 395 of the Act (further provisions) does not apply and section 361 of the Act (further provisions) applies as if the order were an English or Welsh disclosure order, with the [modifications in paragraph (5A)].

[(5A)   The modifications are that—
(a)   in subsection (7), for "An appropriate officer" there is substituted "The Lord Advocate"; and
(b)   in subsection (9), for "an appropriate officer" there is substituted "the Lord Advocate".]

(6)   Paragraphs (7) and (8) apply where the Lord Advocate gives a notice under a Scottish disclosure order which requires a person in England and Wales to—
(a)   answer questions in Scotland; or
(b)   provide information or produce documents in Scotland.

(7)   Section 359 of the Act (offences) applies as if the order were an English or Welsh disclosure order, as well as section 393 of the Act (offences) and, for the avoidance of doubt, section 361 of the Act does not apply in determining whether the person has committed an offence under section 359(1) or (3) of the Act.

(8)   Section 394 of the Act (statements) does not prevent a statement made by the person in response to a requirement imposed by the notice from being used in evidence on a prosecution in England and Wales for an offence under section 359(1) or (3).

[3747]

NOTES
Para (5): words in square brackets substituted by the Proceeds of Crime Act 2002 (Investigations in different parts of the United Kingdom) (Amendment) Order 2008, SI 2008/298, art 2(1), (5)(a), as from 6 April 2008.
Para (5A): inserted by SI 2008/298, art 2(1), (5)(b), as from 6 April 2008.

9 Northern Ireland customer information orders

(1)   This article applies where a Northern Ireland appropriate officer gives a notice under a Northern Ireland customer information order which requires a financial institution in England and Wales to provide customer information.

(2)   Proceedings for an offence under section 366 of the Act may be brought in England and Wales, as well as in Northern Ireland.

(3)   Section 367 of the Act (statements) applies in relation to criminal proceedings brought in England and Wales, as well as criminal proceedings brought in Northern Ireland.

(4)   Section 368 of the Act (disclosure of information) applies as if the order were an English or Welsh customer information order.

[3748]

10 Scottish customer information orders

(1)   This article applies where the procurator fiscal gives a notice under a Scottish customer information order which requires a financial institution in England and Wales to provide customer information.

(2)   Section 366 of the Act (offences) applies as if the order were an English or Welsh customer information order, as well as section 400 of the Act (offences).

(3)   Section 401 of the Act (statements) applies in relation to criminal proceedings brought in England and Wales, as well as criminal proceedings brought in Scotland, with the modification that in paragraph (b) of subsection (2), after "section 400(1) or (3)", there is inserted "or an offence under section 366(1) or (3)".

(4)   Section 368 of the Act (disclosure of information) applies as if the order were an English or Welsh customer information order.

[3749]

11 Northern Ireland account monitoring orders

(1)   This article applies where a Northern Ireland account monitoring order is made in respect of a financial institution in England and Wales.

(2)   The account monitoring order may be served—
   (a)   by sending it by post, facsimile transmission or electronic mail to the person in possession of the material; or
   (b)   by an English or Welsh appropriate officer or a Northern Ireland appropriate officer serving the order personally,

and any rules of court (other than rules of court made by virtue of section 446 of the Act) as to the service of documents or other requirements in law as to the service of documents do not apply.

(3)   Section 370(6) of the Act (definition of account monitoring order) has effect with the modification that for "an appropriate officer", there is substituted, "whichever of an English or Welsh appropriate officer, a Northern Ireland appropriate officer or an English or Welsh appropriate officer and Northern Ireland appropriate officer acting together the order specifies".

(4)   The account monitoring order has effect as if it were an order of the Crown Court in England and Wales.

(5)   Section 372 of the Act (statements) applies to criminal proceedings brought in England and Wales, as well as criminal proceedings brought in Northern Ireland.

(6)   Section 374 of the Act (disclosure of information) has effect as if the order were an English or Welsh account monitoring order.

[3750]

12 Scottish account monitoring orders

(1)   This article applies where a Scottish account monitoring order is made in respect of a financial institution in England and Wales.

(2)   The account monitoring order may be served—
   (a)   by sending it by post, facsimile transmission or electronic mail to the person in possession of the material; or
   (b)   by an English or Welsh appropriate officer or a constable of a police force in Scotland serving the order personally,

and the Summary Jurisdiction (Process) Act 1881, any rules of court as to the service of documents (other than rules of court made by virtue of section 446 of the Act) and any other requirements in law as to the service of documents do not apply.

(3)   Section 404(7) of the Act (definition of account monitoring order) has effect with the modification that for "the proper person", there is substituted "whichever of an English or Welsh appropriate officer, a constable of a police force in Scotland or an English or Welsh appropriate officer and a constable of a police force in Scotland acting together the order specifies".

(4)   The account monitoring order has effect as if it were an order of the Crown Court in England and Wales.

(5)   Section 406 of the Act (statements) applies to criminal proceedings brought in England and Wales, as well as criminal proceedings brought in Scotland.

(6)   Section 374 of the Act (disclosure of information) has effect as if the order were an English or Welsh account monitoring order.

[3751]

PART 3
ENFORCEMENT IN NORTHERN IRELAND OF ENGLISH, WELSH AND SCOTTISH ORDERS AND WARRANTS

13   English or Welsh production orders

(1)   This article applies where—
  (a)   an English or Welsh production order requires a person in Northern Ireland in possession or control of material in Northern Ireland to produce the material or give access to the material; or
  (b)   an order to grant entry to premises in Northern Ireland is made in respect of an English or Welsh production order under section 347 of the Act.

(2)   Subject to paragraph (7), the production order or the order to grant entry, as the case may be, may be served—
  (a)   by sending it by post, facsimile transmission or electronic mail to the person in possession of the material; or
  (b)   by a Northern Ireland appropriate officer or an English or Welsh appropriate officer serving the order personally,
and any rules of court as to the service of documents (other than rules of court made by virtue of section 446 of the Act) or other requirements in law as to the service of documents do not apply.

(3)   Sections 345(4), 347(3), 348(5) and (7) and 349 of the Act have effect with the modifications in paragraph (4).

(4)   The modifications are that for "an appropriate officer" in each place where it occurs, there is substituted, "whichever of an English or Welsh appropriate officer, a Northern Ireland appropriate officer or an English or Welsh appropriate officer and a Northern Ireland appropriate officer acting together the order specifies".

(5)   The production order or the order to grant entry, as the case may be, has effect as if it were an order of the Crown Court in Northern Ireland.

(6)   Section 348(1) to (4) of the Act (further provisions) has effect as if the production order were a Northern Ireland production order.

(7)   Section 350 of the Act (government departments) has effect as if the production order were a Northern Ireland production order and, in particular—
  (a)   if the order is not brought to the attention of the officer concerned within the period stated in the order (in pursuance of section 345(4) of the Act) the person on whom it is served must report the reasons for the failure to a Crown Court judge in Northern Ireland; and
  (b)   the production order must be served as if the proceedings were civil proceedings started against the department in Northern Ireland.

[3752]

14   Scottish production orders

(1)   This article applies where—
  (a)   a Scottish production order requires a person in Northern Ireland in possession or control of material in Northern Ireland to produce the material or give access to the material; or
  (b)   an order to grant entry to premises in Northern Ireland is made in respect of a Scottish production order under section 382 of the Act.

(2)   Subject to paragraph (7), the production order or the order to grant entry, as the case may be, may be served—
  (a)   by sending it by post, facsimile transmission or electronic mail to the person in possession of the material; or
  (b)   by a Northern Ireland appropriate officer or a constable of a police force in Scotland serving the order personally,
and the Summary Jurisdiction (Process) Act 1881, any rules of court as to the service of documents (other than rules of court made by virtue of section 446 of the Act) and any other requirements in law as to the service of documents do not apply.

(3)   Sections 380(5), 382(3), 383(3) and (5) and 384 of the Act have effect with the modifications in paragraph (4).

(4)   The modifications are that for "a proper person" in each place where it occurs, there is substituted "whichever of a Northern Ireland appropriate officer, a constable of a police force in Scotland or a Northern Ireland appropriate officer and a constable of a police force in Scotland acting together the order specifies".

(5)   The production order or the order to grant entry, as the case may be, has effect as if it were an order of the Crown Court in Northern Ireland.

(6)   Section 383(1) and (2) of the Act (further provisions) does not apply and section 348(1) to (4) of the Act (further provisions) has effect as if the production order were a Northern Ireland production order.

(7)   Section 385 of the Act (government departments) does not apply and section 350 of the Act (government departments) has effect as if the production order were a Northern Ireland production order and, in particular—

(a)   if the order is not brought to the attention of the officer concerned within the period stated in the order (in pursuance of section 380(5) of the Act) the person on whom it is served must report the reasons for the failure to a Crown Court judge in Northern Ireland; and

(b)   the production order must be served as if the proceedings were civil proceedings started against the department in Northern Ireland.

[3753]

15   English or Welsh search and seizure warrants

(1)   This article applies where an English or Welsh search and seizure warrant authorises entry into and search of premises in Northern Ireland.

(2)   Section 352(4) of the Act (definition of search and seizure warrant) has effect with the modification that for "an appropriate person", there is substituted "one or more appropriate persons, as the warrant specifies".

(3)   Section 352(5) of the Act (definition of appropriate person) has effect with the modifications in paragraph (4).

[(4)   The modifications are that—

(a)   for paragraphs (a), (b) and (c), there are substituted—
   "(a)   an officer of Revenue and Customs;
   (b)   a constable of a police force in England and Wales;
   (c)   a constable of the Police Service of Northern Ireland; or
   (d)   an accredited financial investigator."; and

(b)   in subsection (7), for "paragraph (a) or (c)" substitute "paragraph (d)".]

(5)   Section 354 of the Act (further provisions) applies as if the warrant were a Northern Ireland search and seizure warrant.

(6)   Article 3 of the Police and Criminal Evidence Order (application of section 16 of the Police and Criminal Evidence Act 1984) does not apply to the execution of the warrant in Northern Ireland.

(7)   Article 7 of the Police and Criminal Evidence Order (application of article 18 of the Police and Criminal Evidence (Northern Ireland) Order 1989) has effect in relation to the execution of the warrant in Northern Ireland as it has effect in relation to the execution of a Northern Ireland search and seizure warrant.

(8)   Section 20 of the Police and Criminal Evidence Act 1984 (extension of powers to computerised information) does not apply to a power of seizure under the warrant exercised in Northern Ireland.

(9)   Article 22 of the Police and Criminal Evidence (Northern Ireland) Order 1989 (extension of powers to computerised information) has effect in relation to a power of seizure under the warrant exercised in Northern Ireland as it has effect in relation to the exercise of a power of seizure conferred by an enactment to which that article applies and as if the reference to a constable included a constable of a police force in England and Wales or customs officer exercising functions by virtue of paragraphs (2) to (4).

(10)   Articles 4 and 5 of the Police and Criminal Evidence Order (application of sections 21 and 22 of the Police and Criminal Evidence Act 1984) have effect as if the warrant had been executed in England and Wales.

(11)   Articles 8 and 9 of the Police and Criminal Evidence Order (application of articles 23 and 24 of the Police and Criminal Evidence (Northern Ireland) Order 1989) do not apply.

[3754]

NOTES
Para (4): substituted by the Proceeds of Crime Act 2002 (Investigations in different parts of the United Kingdom) (Amendment) Order 2008, SI 2008/298, art 2(1), (6), as from 6 April 2008.

16   Scottish search warrants

(1)   This article applies where a Scottish search warrant authorises entry into and search of premises in Northern Ireland.

(2)   Section 387(4) of the Act (definition of search warrant) has effect with the modification that for "a proper person", there is substituted "a constable of the Police Service of Northern Ireland, a constable of a police force in Scotland or both acting together, as the warrant specifies".

(3)   Section 389 of the Act (further provisions) does not apply and section 354 of the Act (further provisions) applies as if the warrant were a Northern Ireland search and seizure warrant.

(4)   Article 7 of the Police and Criminal Evidence Order (application of article 18 of the Police and Criminal Evidence (Northern Ireland) Order 1989) has effect in relation to the execution of the warrant in Northern Ireland as it has effect in relation to the execution of a Northern Ireland search and seizure warrant.

(5)   Section 390(3) of the Act (which deals with computerised information in relation to Scottish search warrants) does not apply to the execution of the warrant in Northern Ireland.

(6)   Article 22 of the Police and Criminal Evidence (Northern Ireland) Order 1989 (extension of powers to computerised information) has effect in relation to a power of seizure under the warrant exercised in Northern Ireland as it has effect in relation to the exercise of a power of seizure conferred by an enactment to which that article applies and as if the reference to a constable included a constable of a police force in Scotland exercising functions by virtue of paragraph (2).

(7)   Section 390(4) of the Act (which states that copies may be taken of material seized under a Scottish search warrant) has effect as if the warrant had been executed in Scotland.

(8)   Articles 8 and 9 of the Police and Criminal Evidence Order (application of articles 23 and 24 of the Police and Criminal Evidence (Northern Ireland) Order 1989) do not apply.

(9)   The Summary Jurisdiction (Process) Act 1881 does not apply.

[3755]

17   English or Welsh disclosure orders

(1)   Paragraphs (2) to (4) apply where [an English or Welsh appropriate officer] gives a notice under an English or Welsh disclosure order which requires a person in Northern Ireland to—
   (a)   answer questions in Northern Ireland; or
   (b)   provide information or produce documents in Northern Ireland.

(2)   Proceedings for an offence under section 359 of the Act may be brought in Northern Ireland.

(3)   Section 360 of the Act (statements) applies in relation to criminal proceedings brought in Northern Ireland, as well as criminal proceedings brought in England and Wales.

(4)   Section 361 of the Act (further provisions) applies as if the order were a Northern Ireland disclosure order.

(5)   Paragraph (6) applies where [an English or Welsh appropriate officer] gives a notice under an English or Welsh disclosure order which requires a person in Northern Ireland to—
   (a)   answer questions in England or Wales; or
   (b)   provide information or produce documents in England or Wales.

(6)   Proceedings for an offence under section 359 may be brought in Northern Ireland, as well as in England and Wales.

[3756]

NOTES
Paras (1), (5): words in square brackets substituted by the Proceeds of Crime Act 2002 (Investigations in different parts of the United Kingdom) (Amendment) Order 2008, SI 2008/298, art 2(1), (7), as from 1 April 2008.

18   Scottish disclosure orders

(1)   Paragraphs (2) to (5) apply where the Lord Advocate gives a notice under a Scottish disclosure order which requires a person in Northern Ireland to—
   (a)   answer questions in Northern Ireland; or
   (b)   provide information or produce documents in Northern Ireland.

(2)   Section 393 of the Act (offences) does not apply and section 359 of the Act (offences) applies as if the order were a Northern Ireland disclosure order.

(3)   Section 394 of the Act (statements) applies in relation to criminal proceedings brought in Northern Ireland, as well as criminal proceedings brought in Scotland, with the modifications in paragraph (4).

(4)   The modifications are that in subsection (2)—
  (a)   in paragraph (b), after "section 393(1) or (3)", there is inserted "or an offence under section 359(1) or (3)";
  (b)   in paragraph (c), after "perjury", there is inserted "or an offence under article 10 of the Perjury (Northern Ireland) Order 1979".

(5)   Section 395 of the Act (further provisions) does not apply and section 361 of the Act (further provisions) applies as if the order were a Northern Ireland disclosure order, with the [modifications in paragraph (5A)].

[(5A)   The modifications are that—
  (a)   in subsection (7), for "An appropriate officer" there is substituted "The Lord Advocate"; and
  (b)   in subsection (9), for "an appropriate officer" there is substituted "the Lord Advocate".]

(6)   Paragraphs (7) and (8) apply where the Lord Advocate gives a notice under a Scottish disclosure order which requires a person in Northern Ireland to—
  (a)   answer questions in Scotland; or
  (b)   provide information or produce documents in Scotland.

(7)   Section 359 of the Act (offences) applies as if the order were a Northern Ireland disclosure order, as well as section 393 of the Act (offences) and, for the avoidance of doubt, section 361 of the Act does not apply in determining whether the person has committed an offence under section 359(1) or (3) of the Act.

(8)   Section 394 of the Act (statements) does not prevent a statement made by the person in response to a requirement imposed by the notice from being used in evidence on a prosecution in Northern Ireland for an offence under section 359(1) or (3).

[3757]

NOTES
  Para (5): words in square brackets substituted by the Proceeds of Crime Act 2002 (Investigations in different parts of the United Kingdom) (Amendment) Order 2008, SI 2008/298, art 2(1), (8)(a), as from 6 April 2008.
  Para (5A): inserted by SI 2008/298, art 2(1), (8)(b), as from 6 April 2008.

19   English or Welsh customer information orders

(1)   This article applies where an English or Welsh appropriate officer gives a notice under an English or Welsh customer information order which requires a financial institution in Northern Ireland to provide customer information.

(2)   Proceedings for an offence under section 366 of the Act may be brought in Northern Ireland, as well as in England and Wales.

(3)   Section 367 of the Act (statements) applies in relation to criminal proceedings brought in Northern Ireland, as well as criminal proceedings brought in England and Wales.

(4)   Section 368 of the Act (disclosure of information) applies as if the order were a Northern Ireland customer information order.

[3758]

20   Scottish customer information orders

(1)   This article applies where the procurator fiscal gives a notice under a Scottish customer information order which requires a financial institution in Northern Ireland to provide customer information.

(2)   Section 366 of the Act (offences) applies as if the order were a Northern Ireland customer information order, as well as section 400 of the Act (offences).

(3)   Section 401 of the Act (statements) applies in relation to criminal proceedings brought in Northern Ireland, as well as criminal proceedings brought in Scotland, with the modification that in paragraph (b) of subsection (2), after "section 400(1) or (3)", there is inserted "or an offence under section 366(1) or (3)".

(4)   Section 368 of the Act (disclosure of information) applies as if the order were a Northern Ireland customer information order.

[3759]

21   English or Welsh account monitoring orders

(1)   This article applies where an English or Welsh account monitoring order is made in respect of a financial institution in Northern Ireland.

(2)   The account monitoring order may be served—

   (a)   by sending it by post, facsimile transmission or electronic mail to the person in possession of the material; or

   (b)   by a Northern Ireland appropriate officer or an English or Welsh appropriate officer serving the order personally,

and any rules of court as to the service of documents (other than rules of court made by virtue of section 446 of the Act) or other requirements in law as to the service of documents do not apply.

   (3)   Section 370(6) of the Act (definition of account monitoring order) has effect with the modification that for "an appropriate officer", there is substituted, "whichever of an English or Welsh appropriate officer, a Northern Ireland appropriate officer or an English or Welsh appropriate officer and a Northern Ireland appropriate officer acting together the order specifies".

   (4)   The account monitoring order has effect as if it were an order of the Crown Court in Northern Ireland.

   (5)   Section 372 of the Act (statements) applies to criminal proceedings brought in Northern Ireland, as well as criminal proceedings brought in England and Wales.

   (6)   Section 374 of the Act (disclosure of information) has effect as if the order were a Northern Ireland account monitoring order.

[3760]

22   Scottish account monitoring orders

   (1)   This article applies where a Scottish account monitoring order is made in respect of a financial institution in Northern Ireland.

   (2)   The account monitoring order may be served—

   (a)   by sending it by post, facsimile transmission or electronic mail to the person in possession of the material; or

   (b)   by a Northern Ireland appropriate officer or a constable of a police force in Scotland serving the order personally,

and the Summary Jurisdiction (Process) Act 1881, any rules of court as to the service of documents (other than rules of court made by virtue of section 446 of the Act) and any other requirement in law as to the service of documents do not apply.

   (3)   Section 404(7) of the Act (definition of account monitoring order) has effect with the modification that for "the proper person", there is substituted "whichever of a Northern Ireland appropriate officer, a constable of a police force in Scotland or a Northern Ireland appropriate officer and a constable of a police force in Scotland acting together the order specifies".

   (4)   The account monitoring order has effect as if it were an order of the Crown Court in Northern Ireland.

   (5)   Section 406 of the Act (statements) applies to criminal proceedings brought in Northern Ireland, as well as criminal proceedings brought in Scotland.

   (6)   Section 374 of the Act (disclosure of information) has effect as if the order were a Northern Ireland account monitoring order.

[3761]

PART 4
ENFORCEMENT IN SCOTLAND OF ENGLISH, WELSH AND NORTHERN IRELAND ORDERS AND WARRANTS

23   English or Welsh production orders

   (1)   This article applies where—

   (a)   an English or Welsh production order requires a person in Scotland in possession or control of material in Scotland to produce the material or give access to the material; or

   (b)   an order to grant entry to premises in Scotland is made in respect of an English or Welsh production order under section 347 of the Act.

   (2)   The production order or the order to grant entry, as the case may be, may be served—

   (a)   by sending it by post, facsimile transmission or electronic mail to the person in possession of the material; or

   (b)   by a constable of a police force in Scotland or an English or Welsh appropriate officer serving the order personally,

and any rules of court as to the service of documents (other than rules of court made by virtue of section 446 of the Act) or other requirements in law as to the service of documents do not apply.

   (3)   Sections 345(4), 347(3), 348(5) and (7) and 349 of the Act have effect with the modifications in paragraph (4).

(4)   The modifications are that for "an appropriate officer" in each place where it occurs, there is substituted, "whichever of an English or Welsh appropriate officer, a constable of a police force in Scotland or an English or Welsh appropriate officer and a constable of a police force in Scotland acting together the order specifies".

(5)   The sheriff has, in relation to the enforcement of the production order, the same powers as if he had made the order himself and proceedings for or with respect to any failure to comply with the order may be taken accordingly.

(6)   Section 348(1) to (4) of the Act (further provisions) does not apply and section 383(1) and (2) of the Act (further provisions) has effect as if the production order were a Scottish production order.

(7)   Section 350 of the Act (government departments) does not apply and section 385 of the Act (government departments) has effect as if the production order were a Scottish production order and, in particular, if the order is not brought to the attention of the officer concerned within the period stated in the order (in pursuance of section 345(4) of the Act) the person on whom it is served must report the reasons for the failure to the sheriff.

[3762]

24   Northern Ireland production orders

(1)   This article applies where—
  (a)   a Northern Ireland production order requires a person in Scotland in possession or control of material in Scotland to produce the material or give access to the material; or
  (b)   an order to grant entry to premises in Scotland is made in respect of a Northern Ireland production order under section 347 of the Act.

(2)   The production order or the order to grant entry, as the case may be, may be served—
  (a)   by sending it by post, facsimile transmission or electronic mail to the person in possession of the material; or
  (b)   by a constable of a police force in Scotland or a Northern Ireland appropriate officer serving the order personally,
and any rules of court as to the service of documents (other than rules of court made by virtue of section 446 of the Act) or other requirements in law as to the service of documents do not apply.

(3)   Sections 345(4), 347(3), 348(5) and (7) and 349 of the Act have effect with the modifications in paragraph (4).

(4)   The modifications are that for "an appropriate officer" in each place where it occurs, there is substituted, "whichever of a constable of a police force in Scotland, a Northern Ireland appropriate officer or a constable of a police force in Scotland and a Northern Ireland appropriate officer acting together the order specifies".

(5)   The sheriff has, in relation to the enforcement of the production order, the same powers as if he had made the order himself and proceedings for or with respect to any failure to comply with the order may be taken accordingly.

(6)   Section 348(1) to (4) of the Act (further provisions) does not apply and section 383(1) and (2) of the Act (further provisions) has effect as if the production order were a Scottish production order.

(7)   Section 350 of the Act (government departments) does not apply and section 385 of the Act (government departments) has effect as if the production order were a Scottish production order and, in particular, if the order is not brought to the attention of the officer concerned within the period stated in the order (in pursuance of section 345(4) of the Act) the person on whom it is served must report the reasons for the failure to the sheriff.

[3763]

25   English or Welsh search and seizure warrants

(1)   This article applies where an English or Welsh search and seizure warrant authorises entry into and search of premises in Scotland.

(2)   Section 352(4) of the Act (definition of search and seizure warrant) has effect with the modification that for "an appropriate person", there is substituted "one or more appropriate persons, as the warrant specifies".

(3)   Section 352(5) of the Act (definition of appropriate person) has effect with the modifications in paragraph (4).

(4)   The modifications are that for paragraphs (a) and (b), there are substituted—
      "(a)   a constable of a police force in England and Wales; or
      (b)   a constable of a police force in Scotland.".

(5)   Section 354 of the Act (further provisions) does not apply and section 389 of the Act (further provisions) applies as if the warrant were a Scottish search warrant.

(6)   Article 3 of the Police and Criminal Evidence Order (application of section 16 of the Police and Criminal Evidence Act 1984) does not apply to the execution of the warrant in Scotland.

(7)   Section 20 of the Police and Criminal Evidence Act 1984 (extension of powers to computerised information) does not apply to a power of seizure under the warrant exercised in Scotland.

(8)   Section 390(3) of the Act (which deals with computerised information in relation to Scottish search warrants) has effect in relation to the execution of the warrant in Scotland as it has effect in relation to the execution of a Scottish search warrant.

(9)   Articles 4 and 5 of the Police and Criminal Evidence Order (application of sections 21 and 22 of the Police and Criminal Evidence Act 1984) have effect as if the warrant had been executed in England and Wales.

(10)   Section 390(4) of the Act (which states that copies may be taken of material seized under a Scottish search warrant) does not apply.

[3764]

26   Northern Ireland search and seizure warrants

(1)   This article applies where a Northern Ireland search and seizure warrant authorises entry into and search of premises in Scotland.

(2)   Section 352(4) of the Act (definition of search and seizure warrant) has effect with the modification that for "an appropriate person", there is substituted "one or more appropriate persons, as the warrant specifies".

(3)   Section 352(5) of the Act (definition of appropriate person) has effect with the modifications in paragraph (4).

(4)   The modifications are that for paragraphs (a) and (b), there are substituted—
  "(a)   a constable of the Police Service of Northern Ireland; or
  (b)   a constable of a police force in Scotland.".

(5)   Section 354 of the Act (further provisions) does not apply and section 389 of the Act (further provisions) applies as if the warrant were a Scottish search warrant.

(6)   Article 7 of the Police and Criminal Evidence Order (application of article 18 of the Police and Criminal Evidence (Northern Ireland) Order 1989) does not apply to the execution of the warrant in Scotland.

(7)   Article 22 of the Police and Criminal Evidence (Northern Ireland) Order 1989 (extension of powers to computerised information) does not apply to a power of seizure under the warrant exercised in Scotland.

(8)   Section 390(3) of the Act (which deals with computerised information in relation to Scottish search warrants) has effect in relation to the execution of the warrant in Scotland as it has effect in relation to the execution of a Scottish search warrant.

(9)   Articles 8 and 9 of the Police and Criminal Evidence Order (application of articles 23 and 24 of the Police and Criminal Evidence (Northern Ireland) Order 1989) have effect as if the warrant had been executed in Northern Ireland.

(10)   Section 390(4) of the Act (which states that copies may be taken of material seized under a Scottish search warrant) does not apply.

[3765]

27   English or Welsh disclosure orders

(1)   Paragraphs (2) to (5) apply where [an English or Welsh appropriate officer] gives a notice under an English or Welsh disclosure order which requires a person in Scotland to—
  (a)   answer questions in Scotland; or
  (b)   provide information or produce documents in Scotland.

(2)   Section 359 of the Act (offences) does not apply and section 393 of the Act (offences) applies as if the order were a Scottish disclosure order.

(3)   Section 360 of the Act (statements) applies in relation to criminal proceedings brought in Scotland, as well as criminal proceedings brought in England and Wales, with the modifications in paragraph (4).

(4)   The modifications are that in subsection (2)—
  (a)   in paragraph (b), after "section 359(1) or (3)", there is inserted "or an offence under section 393(1) or (3)";
  (b)   in paragraph (c), after "prosecution for", there is inserted "perjury in the law of Scotland,".

(5) Section 361 of the Act (further provisions) does not apply and section 395 of the Act (further provisions) applies as if the order were a Scottish disclosure order, with the modification that for "the Lord Advocate", in each place where it occurs, there is substituted "[an English or Welsh appropriate officer]".

(6) Paragraphs (7) and (8) apply where [an English or Welsh appropriate officer] gives a notice under an English or Welsh disclosure order which requires a person in Scotland to—
  (a) answer questions in England and Wales; or
  (b) provide information or produce documents in England and Wales.

(7) Section 393 of the Act (offences) applies as if the order were a Scottish disclosure order, as well as section 359 of the Act (offences) and, for the avoidance of doubt, section 395 of the Act does not apply in determining whether the person has committed an offence under section 393(1) or (3) of the Act.

(8) Section 360 of the Act (statements) does not prevent a statement made by the person in response to a requirement imposed by the notice from being used in evidence on a prosecution in Scotland for an offence under section 393(1) or (3).

[3766]

NOTES

Paras (1), (5), (6): words in square brackets substituted by the Proceeds of Crime Act 2002 (Investigations in different parts of the United Kingdom) (Amendment) Order 2008, SI 2008/298, art 2(1), (9), as from 1 April 2008.

28 Northern Ireland disclosure orders

(1) Paragraphs (2) to (5) apply where [an English or Welsh appropriate officer] gives a notice under a Northern Ireland disclosure order which requires a person in Scotland to—
  (a) answer questions in Scotland; or
  (b) provide information or produce documents in Scotland.

(2) Section 359 of the Act (offences) does not apply and section 393 of the Act (offences) applies as if the order were a Scottish disclosure order.

(3) Section 360 of the Act (statements) applies in relation to criminal proceedings brought in Scotland, as well as criminal proceedings brought in Northern Ireland, with the modifications in paragraph (4).

(4) The modifications are that in subsection (2)—
  (a) in paragraph (b), after "section 359(1) or (3)", there is inserted "or an offence under section 393(1) or (3)";
  (b) in paragraph (c), after "prosecution for", there is inserted "perjury in the law of Scotland,".

(5) Section 361 of the Act (further provisions) does not apply and section 395 of the Act (further provisions) applies as if the order were a Scottish disclosure order, with the modification that for "the Lord Advocate", in each place where it occurs, there is substituted "[an English or Welsh appropriate officer]".

(6) Paragraphs (7) and (8) apply where [an English or Welsh appropriate officer] gives a notice under a Northern Ireland disclosure order which requires a person in Scotland to—
  (a) answer questions in Northern Ireland; or
  (b) provide information or produce documents in Northern Ireland.

(7) Section 393 of the Act (offences) applies as if the order were a Scottish disclosure order, as well as section 359 of the Act (offences) and, for the avoidance of doubt, section 395 of the Act does not apply in determining whether the person has committed an offence under section 393(1) or (3) of the Act.

(8) Section 360 of the Act (statements) does not prevent a statement made by the person in response to a requirement imposed by the notice from being used in evidence on a prosecution in Scotland for an offence under section 393(1) or (3).

[3767]

NOTES

Paras (1), (5), (6): words in square brackets substituted by the Proceeds of Crime Act 2002 (Investigations in different parts of the United Kingdom) (Amendment) Order 2008, SI 2008/298, art 2(1), (10), as from 1 April 2008.

29 English or Welsh customer information orders

(1) This article applies where an English or Welsh appropriate officer gives a notice under an English or Welsh customer information order which requires a financial institution in Scotland to provide customer information.

(2) Section 400 of the Act (offences) applies as if the order were a Scottish customer information order, as well as section 366 of the Act (offences).

(3) Section 367 of the Act (statements) applies in relation to criminal proceedings brought in Scotland, as well as criminal proceedings brought in England and Wales, with the modification that in paragraph (b) of subsection (2), after "section 366(1) or (3)", there is inserted "or an offence under section 400(1) or (3)".

(4) Section 402 of the Act (further provisions) applies as if the order were a Scottish customer information order.

[3768]

30 Northern Ireland customer information orders

(1) This article applies where a Northern Ireland appropriate officer gives a notice under a Northern Ireland customer information order which requires a financial institution in Scotland to provide customer information.

(2) Section 400 of the Act (offences) applies as if the order were a Scottish customer information order, as well as section 366 of the Act (offences).

(3) Section 367 of the Act (statements) applies in relation to criminal proceedings brought in Scotland, as well as criminal proceedings brought in Northern Ireland, with the modification that in paragraph (b) of subsection (2), after "section 366(1) or (3)", there is inserted "or an offence under section 400(1) or (3)".

(4) Section 402 of the Act (further provisions) applies as if the order were a Scottish customer information order.

[3769]

31 English or Welsh account monitoring orders

(1) This article applies where an English or Welsh account monitoring order is made in respect of a financial institution in Scotland.

(2) The account monitoring order may be served—
(a) by sending it by post, facsimile transmission or electronic mail to the person in possession of the material; or
(b) by an English or Welsh appropriate officer or a constable of a police force in Scotland serving the order personally,

and any rules of court as to the service of documents (other than rules of court made by virtue of section 446 of the Act) or other requirements in law as to the service of documents do not apply.

(3) Section 370(6) of the Act (definition of account monitoring order) has effect with the modification that for "an appropriate officer", there is substituted, "whichever of an English or Welsh appropriate officer, a constable of a police force in Scotland or an English or Welsh appropriate officer and a constable of a police force in Scotland acting together the order specifies".

(4) The sheriff has, in relation to the enforcement of the account monitoring order, the same powers as if he had made the order himself and proceedings for or with respect to any failure to comply with the order may be taken accordingly.

(5) Section 372 of the Act (statements) applies to criminal proceedings brought in Scotland, as well as criminal proceedings brought in England and Wales.

(6) Section 407 of the Act (further provisions) has effect as if the order were a Scottish account monitoring order.

[3770]

32 Northern Ireland account monitoring orders

(1) This article applies where a Northern Ireland account monitoring order is made in respect of a financial institution in Scotland.

(2) The account monitoring order may be served—
(a) by sending it by post, facsimile transmission or electronic mail to the person in possession of the material; or
(b) by a Northern Ireland appropriate officer or a constable of a police force in Scotland serving the order personally,

and any rules of court as to the service of documents (other than rules of court made by virtue of section 446 of the Act) or other requirements in law as to the service of documents do not apply.

(3) Section 370(6) of the Act (definition of account monitoring order) has effect with the modification that for "an appropriate officer", there is substituted, "whichever of a Northern Ireland appropriate officer, a constable of a police force in Scotland or a Northern Ireland appropriate officer and a constable of a police force in Scotland acting together the order specifies".

(4)   The sheriff has, in relation to the enforcement of the account monitoring order, the same powers as if he had made the order himself and proceedings for or with respect to any failure to comply with the order may be taken accordingly.

(5)   Section 372 of the Act (statements) applies to criminal proceedings brought in Scotland, as well as criminal proceedings brought in Northern Ireland.

(6)   Section 407 of the Act (further provisions) has effect as if the order were a Scottish account monitoring order.

[3771]

PART 5
SUPPLEMENTARY PROVISIONS RELATING TO CONFISCATION INVESTIGATIONS AND MONEY LAUNDERING INVESTIGATIONS

33   Applications for discharge and variation and Code of Practice

(1)   This article applies where an order made, or warrant issued, under Part 8 of the Act for the purposes of a confiscation investigation or a money laundering investigation in one part of the United Kingdom is enforced in another part of the United Kingdom, in accordance with the preceding provisions of this Order.

(2)   Any application for the discharge or variation of the order or warrant must be made in the part of the United Kingdom in which the order was made.

(3)   The Code of Practice for the time being in operation by virtue of an order made by the Secretary of State under section 377(4) of the Act applies to any act done in England and Wales or in Northern Ireland in respect of the order or warrant by—
    (a)   an English or Welsh appropriate officer;
    (b)   a Northern Ireland appropriate officer; or
    (c)   a constable of a police force in Scotland,
and the Code of Practice for the time being in operation by virtue of an order made by the Scottish Ministers under section 410(4) of the Act does not apply in such circumstances.

(4)   The Code of Practice for the time being in operation by virtue of an order made by the Scottish Ministers under section 410(4) of the Act applies to any act done in Scotland in respect of the order or warrant by—
    (a)   an English or Welsh appropriate officer;
    (b)   a Northern Ireland appropriate officer; or
    (c)   a constable of a police force in Scotland,
and the Code of Practice for the time being in operation by virtue of an order made by the Secretary of State under section 377(4) of the Act does not apply in such circumstances.

[3772]–[3786]

34   *((Pt 6) amends the Civil Jurisdiction and Judgments Act 1982, s 18.)*

MONEY LAUNDERING REGULATIONS 2003 (NOTE)

(SI 2003/3075)

NOTES
These Regulations were revoked and replaced by the Money Laundering Regulations 2007, SI 2007/2157, reg 1(3), as from 15 December 2007. The 2007 Regulations are at **[2877AA]** et seq.

[3787]–[3817]

FINANCIAL COLLATERAL ARRANGEMENTS (NO 2) REGULATIONS 2003

(SI 2003/3226)

NOTES
Made: 10 December 2003.
Authority: European Communities Act 1972, s 2(2).
Commencement: 11 December 2003 (reg 2); 26 December 2003 (otherwise).

As of 1 February 2009, these Regulations had not been amended.

PART 1
GENERAL

1   Citation and commencement

(1)   These Regulations may be cited as the Financial Collateral Arrangements (No 2) Regulations 2003.

(2)   Regulation 2 shall come into force on 11th December 2003 and all other Regulations thereof shall come into force on 26th December 2003.

[3818]

2   *(Revokes the Financial Collateral Arrangements Regulations 2003, SI 2003/3112.)*

3   Interpretation

In these Regulations—

"book entry securities collateral" means financial collateral subject to a financial collateral arrangement which consists of financial instruments, title to which is evidenced by entries in a register or account maintained by or on behalf of an intermediary;

"cash" means money in any currency, credited to an account, or a similar claim for repayment of money and includes money market deposits and sums due or payable to, or received between the parties in connection with the operation of a financial collateral arrangement or a close-out netting provision;

"close-out netting provision" means a term of a financial collateral arrangement, or of an arrangement of which a financial collateral arrangement forms part, or any legislative provision under which on the occurrence of an enforcement event, whether through the operation of netting or set-off or otherwise—

    (a)   the obligations of the parties are accelerated to become immediately due and expressed as an obligation to pay an amount representing the original obligation's estimated current value or replacement cost, or are terminated and replaced by an obligation to pay such an amount; or

    (b)   an account is taken of what is due from each party to the other in respect of such obligations and a net sum equal to the balance of the account is payable by the party from whom the larger amount is due to the other party;

"enforcement event" means an event of default, or any similar event as agreed between the parties, on the occurrence of which, under the terms of a financial collateral arrangement or by operation of law, the collateral-taker is entitled to realise or appropriate financial collateral or a close-out netting provision comes into effect;

"equivalent financial collateral" means—

    (a)   in relation to cash, a payment of the same amount and in the same currency;

    (b)   in relation to financial instruments, financial instruments of the same issuer or debtor, forming part of the same issue or class and of the same nominal amount, currency and description or, where the financial collateral arrangement provides for the transfer of other assets following the occurrence of any event relating to or affecting any financial instruments provided as financial collateral, those other assets;

and includes the original financial collateral provided under the arrangement;

"financial collateral arrangement" means a title transfer financial collateral arrangement or a security financial collateral arrangement, whether or not these are covered by a master agreement or general terms and conditions;

"financial collateral" means either cash or financial instruments;

"financial instruments" means—

    (a)   shares in companies and other securities equivalent to shares in companies;

    (b)   bonds and other forms of instruments giving rise to or acknowledging indebtedness if these are tradeable on the capital market; and

    (c)   any other securities which are normally dealt in and which give the right to acquire any such shares, bonds, instruments or other securities by subscription, purchase or exchange or which give rise to a cash settlement (excluding instruments of payment);

and includes units of a collective investment scheme within the meaning of the Financial Services and Markets Act 2000, eligible debt securities within the meaning of the Uncertificated Securities Regulations 2001, money market instruments, claims relating to or rights in or in respect of any of the financial instruments included in this definition and any rights, privileges or benefits attached to or arising from any such financial instruments;

"intermediary" means a person that maintains registers or accounts to which financial instruments may be credited or debited, for others or both for others and for its own account but does not include—

    (a)   a person who acts as a registrar or transfer agent for the issuer of financial instruments; or

    (b)   a person who maintains registers or accounts in the capacity of operator of a system for the holding and transfer of financial instruments on records of the issuer or other records which constitute the primary record of entitlement to financial instruments as against the issuer;

"non-natural person" means any corporate body, unincorporated firm, partnership or body with legal personality except an individual, including any such entity constituted under the law of a country or territory outside the United Kingdom or any such entity constituted under international law;

"relevant account" means, in relation to book entry securities collateral which is subject to a financial collateral arrangement, the register or account, which may be maintained by the collateral-taker, in which entries are made, by which that book entry securities collateral is transferred or designated so as to be in the possession or under the control of the collateral-taker or a person acting on its behalf;

"relevant financial obligations" means the obligations which are secured or otherwise covered by a financial collateral arrangement, and such obligations may consist of or include—

    (a)   present or future, actual or contingent or prospective obligations (including such obligations arising under a master agreement or similar arrangement);

    (b)   obligations owed to the collateral-taker by a person other than the collateral-provider;

    (c)   obligations of a specified class or kind arising from time to time;

"reorganisation measures" means—

(a) administration within the meaning of the Insolvency Act 1986 or the Insolvency (Northern Ireland) Order 1989;

(b) a company voluntary arrangement within the meaning of that Act or that Order;

(c) administration of a partnership within the meaning of that Act or that Order or, in the case of a Scottish partnership, the Bankruptcy (Scotland) Act 1985;

(d) a partnership voluntary arrangement within the meaning of the Insolvency Act 1986 or the Insolvency (Northern Ireland) Order 1989 or, in the case of a Scottish partnership, the Bankruptcy (Scotland) Act 1985; and

(e) the making of an interim order on an administration application;

"security financial collateral arrangement" means an agreement or arrangement, evidenced in writing, where—

(a) the purpose of the agreement or arrangement is to secure the relevant financial obligations owed to the collateral-taker;

(b) the collateral-provider creates or there arises a security interest in financial collateral to secure those obligations;

(c) the financial collateral is delivered, transferred, held, registered or otherwise designated so as to be in the possession or under the control of the collateral-taker or a person acting on its behalf; any right of the collateral-provider to substitute equivalent financial collateral or withdraw excess financial collateral shall not prevent the financial collateral being in the possession or under the control of the collateral-taker; and

(d) the collateral-provider and the collateral-taker are both non-natural persons;

"security interest" means any legal or equitable interest or any right in security, other than a title transfer financial collateral arrangement, created or otherwise arising by way of security including—

(a) a pledge;

(b) a mortgage;

(c) a fixed charge;

(d) a charge created as a floating charge where the financial collateral charged is delivered, transferred, held, registered or otherwise designated so as to be in the possession or under the control of the collateral-taker or a person acting on its behalf; any right of the collateral-provider to substitute equivalent financial collateral or withdraw excess financial collateral shall not prevent the financial collateral being in the possession or under the control of the collateral-taker; or

(e) a lien;

"title transfer financial collateral arrangement" means an agreement or arrangement, including a repurchase agreement, evidenced in writing, where—

(a) the purpose of the agreement or arrangement is to secure or otherwise cover the relevant financial obligations owed to the collateral-taker;

(b) the collateral-provider transfers legal and beneficial ownership in financial collateral to a collateral-taker on terms that when the relevant financial obligations are discharged the collateral-taker must transfer legal and beneficial ownership of equivalent financial collateral to the collateral-provider; and

(c) the collateral-provider and the collateral-taker are both non-natural persons;

"winding-up proceedings" means—

(a) winding up by the court; or

(b) voluntary winding up;

within the meaning of the Insolvency Act 1986 or the Insolvency (Northern Ireland) Order 1989 or, in the case of Scottish partnerships, the Bankruptcy (Scotland) Act 1985.

[3819]

PART 2

MODIFICATION OF LAW REQUIRING FORMALITIES

4 Certain legislation requiring formalities not to apply to financial collateral arrangements

(1) Section 4 of the Statute of Frauds 1677 (no action on a third party's promise unless in writing and signed) shall not apply (if it would otherwise do so) in relation to a financial collateral arrangement.

(2) Section 53(1)(c) of the Law of Property Act 1925 (disposition of equitable interest to be in writing and signed) shall not apply (if it would otherwise do so) in relation to a financial collateral arrangement.

(3) Section 136 of the Law of Property Act 1925 (legal assignments of things in action) shall not apply (if it would otherwise do so) in relation to a financial collateral arrangement, to the extent that the section requires an assignment to be signed by the assignor or a person authorised on its behalf, in order to be effectual in law.

(4)   Section 395 of the Companies Act 1985 (certain charges void if not registered) shall not apply (if it would otherwise do so) in relation to a security financial collateral arrangement or any charge created or otherwise arising under a security financial collateral arrangement.

(5)   Section 4 of the Industrial and Provident Societies Act 1967 (filing of information relating to charges) shall not apply (if it would otherwise do so) in relation to a security financial collateral arrangement or any charge created or otherwise arising under a security financial collateral arrangement.

[3820]

5 Certain legislation affecting Scottish companies not to apply to financial collateral arrangements

Section 410 of the Companies Act 1985 (certain charges void if not registered (Scotland)) shall not apply (if it would otherwise do so) in relation to a security financial collateral arrangement or any charge created or otherwise arising under a security financial collateral arrangement.

[3821]

6 No additional formalities required for creation of a right in security over book entry securities collateral in Scotland

(1)   Where under the law of Scotland an act is required as a condition for transferring, creating or enforcing a right in security over any book entry securities collateral, that requirement shall not apply (if it would otherwise do so).

(2)   For the purposes of paragraph (1) an "act"—
   (a)   is any act other than an entry on a register or account maintained by or on behalf of an intermediary which evidences title to the book entry securities collateral;
   (b)   includes the entering of the collateral-taker's name in a company's register of members.

[3822]

7 Certain legislation affecting Northern Ireland companies and requiring formalities not to apply to financial collateral arrangements

Article 402 of the Companies (Northern Ireland) Order 1986 (certain charges void if not registered) shall not apply (if it would otherwise do so) in relation to a security financial collateral arrangement or any charge created or otherwise arising under a security financial collateral arrangement.

[3823]

PART 3
MODIFICATION OF INSOLVENCY LAW

8 Certain legislation restricting enforcement of security not to apply to financial collateral arrangements

(1)   The following provisions of Schedule B1 to the Insolvency Act 1986 (administration) shall not apply to any security interest created or otherwise arising under a financial collateral arrangement—
   (a)   paragraph 43(2) (restriction on enforcement of security or repossession of goods) including that provision as applied by paragraph 44 (interim moratorium); and
   (b)   paragraphs 70 and 71 (power of administrator to deal with charged property).

(2)   Paragraph 41(2) of Schedule B1 to the Insolvency Act 1986 (receiver to vacate office when so required by administrator) shall not apply to a receiver appointed under a charge created or otherwise arising under a financial collateral arrangement.

(3)   The following provisions of the Insolvency Act 1986 (administration) shall not apply in relation to any security interest created or otherwise arising under a financial collateral arrangement—
   (a)   sections 10(1)(b) and 11(3)(c) (restriction on enforcement of security while petition for administration order pending or order in force); and
   (b)   section 15(1) and 15(2) (power of administrator to deal with charged property).

(4)   Section 11(2) of the Insolvency Act 1986 (receiver to vacate office when so required by administrator) shall not apply to a receiver appointed under a charge created or otherwise arising under a financial collateral arrangement.

(5)   Paragraph 20 and sub-paragraph 12(1)(g) of Schedule A1 to the Insolvency Act 1986 (Effect of moratorium on creditors) shall not apply (if it would otherwise do so) to any security interest created or otherwise arising under a financial collateral arrangement.

[3824]

9 Certain Northern Ireland legislation restricting enforcement of security not to apply to financial collateral arrangements

(1) The following provisions of the Insolvency (Northern Ireland) Order 1989 (administration) shall not apply to any security interest created or otherwise arising under a financial collateral arrangement—

(a) Article 23(1)(b) and Article 24(3)(c) (restriction on enforcement of security while petition for administration order pending or order in force); and

(b) Article 28(1) and (2) (power of administrator to deal with charged property).

(2) Article 24(2) of that Order (receiver to vacate office at request of administrator) shall not apply to a receiver appointed under a charge created or otherwise arising under a financial collateral arrangement.

[3825]

10 Certain insolvency legislation on avoidance of contracts and floating charges not to apply to financial collateral arrangements

(1) In relation to winding-up proceedings of a collateral-taker or collateral-provider, section 127 of the Insolvency Act 1986 (avoidance of property dispositions, etc) shall not apply (if it would otherwise do so)—

(a) to any property or security interest subject to a disposition or created or otherwise arising under a financial collateral arrangement; or

(b) to prevent a close-out netting provision taking effect in accordance with its terms.

(2) Section 88 of the Insolvency Act 1986 (avoidance of share transfers, etc after winding-up resolution) shall not apply (if it would otherwise do so) to any transfer of shares under a financial collateral arrangement.

(3) Section 176A of the Insolvency Act 1986 (share of assets for unsecured creditors) shall not apply (if it would otherwise do so) to any charge created or otherwise arising under a financial collateral arrangement.

(4) Section 178 of the Insolvency Act 1986 (power to disclaim onerous property) or, in Scotland, any rule of law having the same effect as that section, shall not apply where the collateral-provider or collateral-taker under the arrangement is being wound up, to any financial collateral arrangement.

(5) Section 245 of the Insolvency Act 1986 (avoidance of certain floating charges) shall not apply (if it would otherwise do so) to any charge created or otherwise arising under a security financial collateral arrangement.

(6) Section 196 of the Companies Act 1985 (payment of debts out of assets subject to a floating charge (England and Wales) shall not apply (if it would otherwise do so) to any charge created or otherwise arising under a financial collateral arrangement.

[3826]

11 Certain Northern Ireland insolvency legislation on avoidance of contracts and floating charges not to apply to financial collateral arrangements

(1) In relation to winding-up proceedings of a collateral-provider or collateral-taker, Article 107 of the Insolvency (Northern Ireland) Order 1989 (avoidance of property dispositions effected after commencement of winding up) shall not apply (if it would otherwise do so)—

(a) to any property or security interest subject to a disposition or created or otherwise arising under a financial collateral arrangement; or

(b) to prevent a close-out netting provision taking effect in accordance with its terms.

(2) Article 74 of that Order (avoidance of share transfers, etc after winding-up resolution) shall not apply (if it would otherwise do so) to any transfer of shares under a financial collateral arrangement.

(3) Article 152 of that Order (power to disclaim onerous property) shall not apply where the collateral-provider or collateral-taker under the arrangement is being wound-up, to any financial collateral arrangement.

(4) Article 207 of that Order (avoidance of certain floating charges) shall not apply (if it would otherwise do so) to any charge created or otherwise arising under a security financial collateral arrangement.

(5) Article 205 of the Companies (Northern Ireland) Order 1986 (payment of debts out of assets subject to a floating charge) shall not apply (if it would otherwise do so) to any charge created or otherwise arising under a financial collateral arrangement.

[3827]

12 Close-out netting provisions to take effect in accordance with their terms

(1)   A close-out netting provision shall, subject to paragraph (2), take effect in accordance with its terms notwithstanding that the collateral-provider or collateral-taker under the arrangement is subject to winding-up proceedings or reorganisation measures.

(2)   Paragraph (1) shall not apply if at the time that a party to a financial collateral arrangement entered into such an arrangement or that the relevant financial obligations came into existence—

(a)   that party was aware or should have been aware that winding up proceedings or re-organisation measures had commenced in relation to the other party;

(b)   that party had notice that a meeting of creditors of the other party had been summoned under section 98 of the Insolvency Act 1986, or Article 84 of the Companies (Northern Ireland) Order 1989 or that a petition for the winding-up of the other party was pending;

(c)   that party had notice that an application for an administration order was pending or that any person had given notice of an intention to appoint an administrator; or

(d)   that party had notice that an application for an administration order was pending or that any person had given notice of an intention to appoint an administrator and liquidation of the other party to the financial collateral arrangement was immediately preceded by an administration of that party.

(3)   For the purposes of paragraph (2)—

(a)   winding-up proceedings commence on the making of a winding-up order by the court; and

(b)   reorganisation measures commence on the appointment of an administrator, whether by a court or otherwise.

(4)   Rules 2.85 (4)(a) and (c) and 4.90 (3)(b) of the Insolvency Rules 1986 (mutual credit and set-off) shall not apply to a close-out netting provision unless sub-paragraph (2)(a) applies.

[3828]

13 Financial collateral arrangements to be enforceable where collateral-taker not aware of commencement of winding-up proceedings or reorganisation measures

(1)   Where any of the events specified in paragraph (2) occur on the day of, but after the moment of commencement of, winding-up proceedings or reorganisation measures those events, arrangements and obligations shall be legally enforceable and binding on third parties if the collateral-taker can show that he was not aware, nor should have been aware, of the commencement of such proceedings or measures.

(2)   The events referred to in paragraph (1) are—

(a)   a financial collateral arrangement coming into existence;

(b)   a relevant financial obligation secured by a financial collateral arrangement coming into existence; or

(c)   the delivery, transfer, holding, registering or other designation of financial collateral so as to be in the possession or under the control of the collateral-taker.

(3)   For the purposes of paragraph (1)—

(a)   the commencement of winding-up proceedings means the making of a winding-up order by the court; and

(b)   commencement of reorganisation measures means the appointment of an administrator, whether by a court or otherwise.

[3829]

14 Modification of the Insolvency Rules 1986 and the Insolvency Rules (Northern Ireland) 1991

Where the collateral-provider or the collateral-taker under a financial collateral arrangement goes into liquidation or administration and the arrangement or a close out netting provision provides for, or the mechanism provided under the arrangement permits, either—

(a)   the debt owed by the party in liquidation or administration under the arrangement, to be assessed or paid in a currency other than sterling; or

(b)   the debt to be converted into sterling at a rate other than the official exchange rate prevailing on the date when that party went into liquidation or administration;

then rule 4.91 (liquidation), or rule 2.86 (administration) of the Insolvency Rules 1986 (debt in foreign currency), or rule 4.097 of the Insolvency Rules (Northern Ireland) 1991 (liquidation, debt in foreign currency), as appropriate, shall not apply unless the arrangement provides for an unreasonable exchange rate or the collateral-taker uses the mechanism provided under the arrangement to impose an unreasonable exchange rate in which case the appropriate rule shall apply.

[3830]

15 Modification of the Insolvency (Scotland) Rules 1986

Where the collateral-provider or the collateral-taker under a financial collateral arrangement goes into liquidation or, in the case of a partnership, sequestration and the arrangement provides for, or the mechanism provided under the arrangement permits, either—

   (a)   the debt owed by the party in liquidation or sequestration under the arrangement, to be assessed or paid in a currency other than sterling; or

   (b)   the debt to be converted into sterling at a rate other than the official exchange rate prevailing on the date when that party went into liquidation or sequestration;

then rules 4.16 and 4.17 of the Insolvency (Scotland) Rules 1986 and section 49(3) of the Bankruptcy (Scotland) Act 1985 as applied by rule 4.16 (1)(c) of those rules (claims in foreign currency), as appropriate, shall not apply unless the arrangement provides for an unreasonable exchange rate or the collateral-taker uses the mechanism provided under the arrangement to impose an unreasonable exchange rate in which case the appropriate rule shall apply.

[3831]

PART 4
RIGHT OF USE AND APPROPRIATION

16   Right of use under a security financial collateral arrangement

(1)   If a security financial collateral arrangement provides for the collateral-taker to use and dispose of any financial collateral provided under the arrangement, as if it were the owner of it, the collateral-taker may do so in accordance with the terms of the arrangement.

(2)   If a collateral-taker exercises such a right of use, it is obliged to replace the original financial collateral by transferring equivalent financial collateral on or before the due date for the performance of the relevant financial obligations covered by the arrangement or, if the arrangement so provides, it may set off the value of the equivalent financial collateral against or apply it in discharge of the relevant financial obligations in accordance with the terms of the arrangement.

(3)   The equivalent financial collateral which is transferred in discharge of an obligation as described in paragraph (2), shall be subject to the same terms of the security financial collateral arrangement as the original financial collateral was subject to and shall be treated as having been provided under the security financial collateral arrangement at the same time as the original financial collateral was first provided.

(4)   If a collateral-taker has an outstanding obligation to replace the original financial collateral with equivalent financial collateral when an enforcement event occurs, that obligation may be the subject of a close-out netting provision.

[3832]

17   No requirement to apply to court to appropriate financial collateral under a security financial collateral arrangement

Where a legal or equitable mortgage is the security interest created or arising under a security financial collateral arrangement on terms that include a power for the collateral-taker to appropriate the collateral, the collateral-taker may exercise that power in accordance with the terms of the security financial collateral arrangement, without any order for foreclosure from the courts.

[3833]

18   Duty to value collateral and account for any difference in value on appropriation

(1)   Where a collateral-taker exercises a power contained in a security financial collateral arrangement to appropriate the financial collateral the collateral-taker must value the financial collateral in accordance with the terms of the arrangement and in any event in a commercially reasonable manner.

(2)   Where a collateral-taker exercises such a power and the value of the financial collateral appropriated differs from the amount of the relevant financial obligations, then as the case may be, either—

   (a)   the collateral-taker must account to the collateral-provider for the amount by which the value of the financial collateral exceeds the relevant financial obligations; or

   (b)   the collateral-provider will remain liable to the collateral-taker for any amount whereby the value of the financial collateral is less than the relevant financial obligations.

[3834]

PART 5
CONFLICT OF LAWS

19   Standard test regarding the applicable law to book entry securities financial collateral arrangements

(1)   This regulation applies to financial collateral arrangements where book entry securities collateral is used as collateral under the arrangement and are held through one or more intermediaries.

(2)   Any question relating to the matters specified in paragraph (4) of this regulation which arises in relation to book entry securities collateral which is provided under a financial collateral arrangement shall be governed by the domestic law of the country in which the relevant account is maintained.

(3)   For the purposes of paragraph (2) "domestic law" excludes any rule under which, in deciding the relevant question, reference should be made to the law of another country.

(4)   The matters referred to in paragraph (2) are—
  (a)   the legal nature and proprietary effects of book entry securities collateral;
  (b)   the requirements for perfecting a financial collateral arrangement relating to book entry securities collateral and the transfer or passing of control or possession of book entry securities collateral under such an arrangement;
  (c)   the requirements for rendering a financial collateral arrangement which relates to book entry securities collateral effective against third parties;
  (d)   whether a person's title to or interest in such book entry securities collateral is overridden by or subordinated to a competing title or interest; and
  (e)   the steps required for the realisation of book entry securities collateral following the occurrence of any enforcement event.

[3835]

INSURERS (REORGANISATION AND WINDING UP) REGULATIONS 2004

(SI 2004/353)

NOTES
Made: 12 February 2004.
Authority: European Communities Act 1972, s 2.
Commencement: 18 February 2004.
These Regulations are reproduced as amended by: the Insurers (Reorganisation and Winding Up) (Amendment) Regulations 2004, SI 2004/546; the Insurers (Reorganisation and Winding Up) (Lloyd's) Regulations 2005, SI 2005/1998; the Financial Services (EEA State) Regulations 2007, SI 2007/108; the Financial Services and Markets Act 2000 (Markets in Financial Instruments) Regulations 2007, SI 2007/126; the Insurers (Reorganisation and Winding Up) (Amendment) Regulations 2007, SI 2007/851.
Note: see the Insurers (Reorganisation and Winding Up) (Lloyd's) Regulations 2005, SI 2005/1998 (at **[3933]**) with regard to the application of these Regulations in relation to Lloyd's.

ARRANGEMENT OF REGULATIONS

PART I
GENERAL

PART II
INSOLVENCY MEASURES AND PROCEEDINGS: JURISDICTION
IN RELATION TO INSURERS

PART III
MODIFICATIONS OF THE LAW OF INSOLVENCY: NOTIFICATION AND PUBLICATION

PART I
GENERAL

1 Citation and Commencement

These Regulations may be cited as the Insurers (Reorganisation and Winding Up) Regulations 2004, and come into force on 18th February 2004.

[3836]

NOTES
Commencement: 18 February 2004.

2 Interpretation

(1) In these Regulations—
   "the 1985 Act" means the Companies Act 1985;
   "the 1986 Act" means the Insolvency Act 1986;
   "the 2000 Act" means the Financial Services and Markets Act 2000;
   "the 1989 Order" means the Insolvency (Northern Ireland) Order 1989;

"administrator" has the meaning given by paragraph 13 of Schedule B1[, or by paragraph 14 of Schedule B1 to the 1989 Order];

"Article 418 compromise or arrangement" means a compromise or arrangement sanctioned by the court in relation to a UK insurer under Article 418 of the Companies Order, but does not include a compromise or arrangement falling within Article 420 or Articles 420A of that Order (reconstruction and amalgamations);

"the Authority" means the Financial Services Authority;

"branch", in relation to an EEA or UK insurer has the meaning given by Article 1(b) of the life insurance directive or the third non-life insurance directive;

"claim" means a claim submitted by a creditor of a UK insurer in the course of—

    (a)   a winding up,

    (b)   an administration, or

    (c)   a voluntary arrangement,

with a view to recovering his debt in whole or in part, and includes a proof of debt, within the meaning of Rule 4.73(4) of the Insolvency Rules, Rule 4.079(4) of the Insolvency Rules (Northern Ireland) or in Scotland a claim made in accordance with rule 4.15 of the Insolvency (Scotland) Rules;

"the Companies Order" means the Companies (Northern Ireland) Order 1986;

"creditors' voluntary winding up" has the meaning given by section 90 of the 1986 Act or Article 76 of the 1989 Order;

"debt"—

    (a)   in England and Wales and Northern Ireland—

        (i)   in relation to a winding up or administration of a UK insurer, has the meaning given by Rule 13.12 of the Insolvency Rules or Article 5 of the 1989 Order, and

        (ii)   in a case where a voluntary arrangement has effect, in relation to a UK insurer, means a debt which would constitute a debt in relation to the winding up of that insurer, except that references in paragraph (1) of Rule 13.12 or paragraph (1) of Article 5 of the 1989 Order to the date on which the company goes into liquidation are to be read as references to the date on which the voluntary arrangement has effect;

    (b)   in Scotland—

        (i)   in relation to a winding up of a UK insurer, shall be interpreted in accordance with Schedule 1 to the Bankruptcy (Scotland) Act 1985 as applied by Chapter 5 of Part 4 of the Insolvency (Scotland) Rules, and

        (ii)   in a case where a voluntary arrangement has effect in relation to a UK insurer, means a debt which would constitute a debt in relation to the winding up of that insurer, except that references in Chapter 5 of Part 4 of the Insolvency (Scotland) Rules to the date of commencement of winding up are to be read as references to the date on which the voluntary arrangement has effect;

"directive reorganisation measure" means a reorganisation measure as defined in Article 2(c) of the reorganisation and winding-up directive which was adopted or imposed on or after 20th April 2003;

"directive winding up proceedings" means winding up proceedings as defined in Article 2(d) of the reorganisation and winding-up directive which were opened on or after 20th April 2003;

"EEA creditor" means a creditor of a UK insurer who—

    (a)   in the case of an individual, is ordinarily resident in an EEA State, and

    (b)   in the case of a body corporate or unincorporated association of persons, has its head office in an EEA State;

"EEA insurer" means an undertaking, other than a UK insurer, pursuing the activity of direct insurance (within the meaning of Article 1 of the first life insurance directive or the first non-life insurance directive) which has received authorisation under Article 6 from its home state regulator;

"EEA regulator" means a competent authority (within the meaning of Article 1(1) of the life insurance directive or Article 1(k) of the third non-life insurance directive, as the case may be) of an EEA State;

["EEA State" has the meaning given by Schedule 1 to the Interpretation Act 1978;]

"the first non-life insurance directive" means the Council Directive (73/239/EEC) of 24 July 1973 on the co-ordination of laws, regulations and administrative provisions relating to the taking up and pursuit of the business of direct insurance other than life assurance;

"home state regulator", in relation to an EEA insurer, means the relevant EEA regulator in the EEA State where its head office is located;

"the Insolvency Rules" means the Insolvency Rules 1986;

"the Insolvency Rules (Northern Ireland)" means the Insolvency Rules (Northern Ireland) 1991;

"the Insolvency (Scotland) Rules" means the Insolvency (Scotland) Rules 1986;

"insurance claim" means any claim in relation to an insurance debt;

"insurance creditor" means a person who has an insurance claim against a UK insurer (whether or not he has claims other than insurance claims against that insurer);

"insurance debt" means a debt to which a UK insurer is, or may become liable, pursuant to a contract of insurance, to a policyholder or to any person who has a direct right of action against that insurer, and includes any premium paid in connection with a contract of insurance (whether or not that contract was concluded) which the insurer is liable to refund;

"life insurance directive" means the Directive (2002/83/EC) of the European Parliament and of the Council concerning life assurance;

"officer", in relation to a company, has the meaning given by section 744 of the 1985 Act or Article 2 of the Companies Order;

"official language" means a language specified in Article 1 of Council Regulation No 1 of 15th April 1958 determining the languages to be used by the European Economic Community (Regulation 1/58/EEC) , most recently amended by paragraph (a) of Part XVIII of Annex I to the Act of Accession 1994 (194 N);

"policyholder" has the meaning given by the Financial Services and Markets Act 2000 (Meaning of "Policy" and "Policyholder") Order 2001;

"the reorganisation and winding-up directive" means the Directive (2001/17/EC) of the European Parliament and of the Council of 19 March 2001 on the reorganisation and winding-up of insurance undertakings;

"Schedule B1" means Schedule B1 to the 1986 Act as inserted by section 248 of the Enterprise Act 2002[, unless specified otherwise];

"section 425 compromise or arrangement" means a compromise or arrangement sanctioned by the court in relation to a UK insurer under section 425 of the 1985 Act, but does not include a compromise or arrangement falling within section 427 or section 427A of that Act (reconstructions or amalgamations);

"section 425 or Article 418 compromise or arrangement" means a section 425 compromise or arrangement or an Article 418 compromise or arrangement;

"supervisor" has the meaning given by section 7 of the 1986 Act or Article 20 of the 1989 Order;

"the third non-life insurance directive" means the Council Directive (92/49/EEC) of 18th June 1992 on the co-ordination of laws, etc, and amending directives 73/239/EEC and 88/357/EEC);

"UK insurer" means a person who has permission under Part IV of the 2000 Act to effect or carry out contracts of insurance, but does not include a person who, in accordance with that permission, carries on that activity exclusively in relation to reinsurance contracts;

"voluntary arrangement" means a voluntary arrangement which has effect in relation to a UK insurer in accordance with section 4A of the 1986 Act or Article 17A of the 1989 Order; and

"winding up" means—

    (a)   winding up by the court, or

    (b)   a creditors' voluntary winding up.

(2)   In paragraph (1)—

    (a)   for the purposes of the definition of "directive reorganisation measure", a reorganisation measure is adopted or imposed at the time when it is treated as adopted or imposed by the law of the relevant EEA State; and

    (b)   for the purposes of the definition of "directive winding up proceedings", winding up proceedings are opened at the time when they are treated as opened by the law of the relevant EEA State,

and in this paragraph "relevant EEA State" means the EEA State under the law of which the reorganisation is adopted or imposed, or the winding up proceedings are opened, as the case may be.

(3)   In these Regulations, references to the general law of insolvency of the United Kingdom include references to every provision made by or under the 1986 Act or the 1989 Order; and in relation to friendly societies or to industrial and provident societies references to the law of insolvency or to any provision of the 1986 Act or the 1989 Order are to that law as modified by the Friendly Societies Act 1992 or by the Industrial and Provident Societies Act 1965 or the Industrial and Provident Societies Act (Northern Ireland) 1969 (as the case may be).

(4)   References in these Regulations to a "contract of insurance" must be read with—

    (a)   section 22 of the 2000 Act;

    (b)   any relevant order made under that section; and

    (c)   Schedule 2 to that Act,

but for the purposes of these Regulations a contract of insurance does not include a reinsurance contract.

(5)   Functions imposed or falling on the Authority by or under these Regulations shall be deemed to be functions under the 2000 Act.

[3837]

NOTES
Commencement: 18 February 2004.
Para (1): words in square brackets in definitions "administrator" and "Schedule B1" inserted by the Insurers (Reorganisation and Winding Up) (Amendment) Regulations 2007, SI 2007/851, reg 2(1), (2), as from 6 April 2007; definition "EEA State" substituted by the Financial Services (EEA State) Regulations 2007, SI 2007/108, reg 8, as from 13 February 2007.

3 Scope

For the purposes of these Regulations, neither the Society of Lloyd's nor the persons specified in section 316(1) of the 2000 Act are UK insurers.

[3838]

NOTES
Commencement: 18 February 2004.

PART II
INSOLVENCY MEASURES AND PROCEEDINGS: JURISDICTION
IN RELATION TO INSURERS

4 Prohibition against winding up etc EEA insurers in the United Kingdom

(1)   On or after the relevant date a court in the United Kingdom may not, in relation to an EEA insurer or any branch of an EEA insurer—
    (a)   make a winding up order pursuant to section 221 of the 1986 Act or Article 185 of the 1989 Order;
    (b)   appoint a provisional liquidator;
    (c)   make an administration order.

(2)   Paragraph (1)(a) does not prevent—
    (a)   the court from making a winding up order after the relevant date in relation to an EEA insurer if—
        (i)   a provisional liquidator was appointed in relation to that insurer before the relevant date, and
        (ii)   that appointment continues in force until immediately before that winding up order is made;
    (b)   the winding up of an EEA insurer after the relevant date pursuant to a winding up order which was made, and has not been discharged, before that date.

(3)   Paragraph (1)(b) does not prevent a provisional liquidator of an EEA insurer appointed before the relevant date from acting in relation to that insurer after that date.

(4)   Paragraph (1)(c) does not prevent an administrator appointed before the relevant date from acting after that date in a case in which the administration order under which he or his predecessor was appointed remains in force after that date.

(5)   An administrator may not, in relation to an EEA insurer, be appointed under paragraphs 14 or 22 of Schedule B1 [or paragraph 15 or 23 of Schedule B1 to the 1989 Order].

(6)   A proposed voluntary arrangement shall not have effect in relation to an EEA insurer if a decision, under section 4 of the 1986 Act or Article 17 of the 1989 Order, with respect to the approval of that arrangement was made after the relevant date.

(7)   Section 377 of the 2000 Act (reducing the value of contracts instead of winding up) does not apply in relation to an EEA insurer.

[(8)   An order under section 254 of the Enterprise Act 2002 (application of insolvency law to a foreign company) or under Article 9 of the Insolvency (Northern Ireland) Order 2005 (application of insolvency law to company incorporated outside Northern Ireland) may not provide for any of the following provisions of the 1986 Act or of the 1989 Order to apply in relation to an EEA insurer—
    (a)   Part I of the 1986 Act or Part II of the 1989 Order (company voluntary arrangements);
    (b)   Part II of the 1986 Act or Part III of the 1989 Order (administration);
    (c)   Chapter VI of Part IV of the 1986 Act (winding up by the Court) or Chapter VI of Part V of the 1989 Order (winding up by the High Court).]

(9)   In this regulation and regulation 5, "relevant date" means 20th April 2003.

[3839]

NOTES
Commencement: 18 February 2004.

Para (5): words in square brackets inserted by the Insurers (Reorganisation and Winding Up) (Amendment) Regulations 2007, SI 2007/851, reg 2(1), (3), as from 6 April 2007.
Para (8): substituted by SI 2007/851, reg 2(1), (4), as from 6 April 2007.

5   Schemes of arrangement: EEA insurers

(1)   For the purposes of section 425(6)(a) of the 1985 Act or Article 418(5)(a) of the Companies Order, an EEA insurer or a branch of an EEA insurer is to be treated as a company liable to be wound up under the 1986 Act or the 1989 Order if it would be liable to be wound up under that Act or Order but for the prohibition in regulation 4(1)(a).

(2)   But a court may not make a relevant order under section 425(2) of the 1985 Act or Article 418(2) of the Companies Order in relation to an EEA insurer which is subject to a directive reorganisation measure or directive winding up proceedings, or a branch of an EEA insurer which is subject to such a measure or proceedings unless the conditions set out in paragraph (3) are satisfied.

(3)   Those conditions are—
  (a)   the person proposing the section 425 or Article 418 compromise or arrangement ("the proposal") has given—
    (i)   the administrator or liquidator, and
    (ii)   the relevant competent authority,
  reasonable notice of the details of that proposal; and
  (b)   no person notified in accordance with sub-paragraph (a) has objected to the proposal.

(4)   Nothing in this regulation invalidates a compromise or arrangement which was sanctioned by the court by an order made before the relevant date.

(5)   For the purposes of paragraph (2), a relevant order means an order sanctioning a section 425 or Article 418 compromise or arrangement which—
  (a)   is intended to enable the insurer, and the whole or any part of its undertaking, to survive as a going concern and which affects the rights of persons other than the insurer or its contributories; or
  (b)   includes among its purposes a realisation of some or all of the assets of the EEA insurer to which the order relates and the distribution of the proceeds to creditors, with a view to terminating the whole or any part of the business of that insurer.

(6)   For the purposes of this regulation—
  (a)   "administrator" means an administrator, as defined by Article 2(i) of the reorganisation and winding up directive, who is appointed in relation to the EEA insurer in relation to which the proposal is made;
  (b)   "liquidator" means a liquidator, as defined by Article 2(j) of the reorganisation and winding up directive, who is appointed in relation to the EEA insurer in relation to which the proposal is made;
  (c)   "competent authority" means the competent authority, as defined by Article 2(g) of the reorganisation and winding up directive, which is competent for the purposes of the directive reorganisation measure or directive winding up proceedings mentioned in paragraph (2).

[3840]

NOTES
Commencement: 18 February 2004.

6   Reorganisation measures and winding up proceedings in respect of EEA insurers effective in the United Kingdom

(1)   An EEA insolvency measure has effect in the United Kingdom in relation to—
  (a)   any branch of an EEA insurer,
  (b)   any property or other assets of that insurer,
  (c)   any debt or liability of that insurer
as if it were part of the general law of insolvency of the United Kingdom.

(2)   Subject to paragraph (4)—
  (a)   a competent officer who satisfies the condition mentioned in paragraph (3); or
  (b)   a qualifying agent appointed by a competent officer who satisfies the condition mentioned in paragraph (3),
may exercise in the United Kingdom, in relation to the EEA insurer which is subject to an EEA insolvency measure, any function which, pursuant to that measure, he is entitled to exercise in relation to that insurer in the relevant EEA State.

(3)   The condition mentioned in paragraph (2) is that the appointment of the competent officer is evidenced—
  (a)   by a certified copy of the order or decision by a judicial or administrative authority in the relevant EEA State by or under which the competent officer was appointed; or

(b)   by any other certificate issued by the judicial or administrative authority which has jurisdiction in relation to the EEA insolvency measure,

and accompanied by a certified translation of that order, decision or certificate (as the case may be).

(4)   In exercising functions of the kind mentioned in paragraph (2), the competent officer or qualifying agent—

    (a)   may not take any action which would constitute an unlawful use of force in the part of the United Kingdom in which he is exercising those functions;

    (b)   may not rule on any dispute arising from a matter falling within Part V of these Regulations which is justiciable by a court in the part of the United Kingdom in which he is exercising those functions; and

    (c)   notwithstanding the way in which functions may be exercised in the relevant EEA State, must act in accordance with relevant laws or rules as to procedure which have effect in the part of the United Kingdom in which he is exercising those functions.

(5)   For the purposes of paragraph (4)(c), "relevant laws or rules as to procedure" mean—

    (a)   requirements as to consultation with or notification of employees of an EEA insurer;

    (b)   law and procedures relevant to the realisation of assets;

    (c)   where the competent officer is bringing or defending legal proceedings in the name of, or on behalf of, an EEA insurer, the relevant rules of court.

(6)   In this regulation—

"competent officer" means a person appointed under or in connection with an EEA insolvency measure for the purpose of administering that measure;

"qualifying agent" means an agent validly appointed (whether in the United Kingdom or elsewhere) by a competent officer in accordance with the relevant law in the relevant EEA State;

"EEA insolvency measure" means, as the case may be, a directive reorganisation measure or directive winding up proceedings which has effect in relation to an EEA insurer by virtue of the law of the relevant EEA State;

"relevant EEA State", in relation to an EEA insurer, means the EEA State in which that insurer has been authorised in accordance with Article 4 of the life insurance directive or Article 6 of the first non-life insurance directive.

[3841]

NOTES

Commencement: 18 February 2004.

7   Confirmation by the court of a creditors' voluntary winding up

(1)   Rule 7.62 of the Insolvency Rules or Rule 7.56 of the Insolvency Rules (Northern Ireland) applies in relation to a UK insurer with the modification specified in paragraph (2) or (3).

(2)   In Rule 7.62 paragraph (1), after the words

"the Insurers (Reorganisation and Winding Up) Regulations 2003" insert the words "or the Insurers (Reorganisation and Winding Up) Regulations 2004".

In Rule 7.56 of the Insolvency Rules (Northern Ireland) paragraph (1), after the words "the Insurers (Reorganisation and Winding Up) Regulations 2003" insert the words "or the Insurers (Reorganisation and Winding Up) Regulations 2004".

[3842]

NOTES

Commencement: 18 February 2004.

PART III
MODIFICATIONS OF THE LAW OF INSOLVENCY: NOTIFICATION AND PUBLICATION

8   Modifications of the law of insolvency

The general law of insolvency has effect in relation to UK insurers subject to the provisions of this Part.

[3843]

NOTES

Commencement: 18 February 2004.

9   Notification of relevant decision to the Authority

(1)   Where on or after [3rd March 2004] the court makes a decision, order or appointment of any of the following kinds—

   (a)   an administration order under paragraph 13 of Schedule B1[, or paragraph 14 of Schedule B1 to the 1989 Order];

   (b)   a winding up order under section 125 of the 1986 Act or Article 105 of the 1989 Order;

   (c)   the appointment of a provisional liquidator under section 135(1) of the 1986 Act or Article 115(1) of the 1989 Order;

   (d)   an interim order under paragraph 13(1)(d) of Schedule B1 [or paragraph 14(1)(d) of Schedule B1 to the 1989 Order];

   (e)   a decision to reduce the value of one or more of the insurer's contracts, in accordance with section 377 of the 2000 Act,

it must immediately inform the Authority, or cause the Authority to be informed of the decision, order or appointment which has been made.

(2) Where a decision with respect to the approval of a voluntary arrangement has effect, and the arrangement which is the subject of that decision is a qualifying arrangement, the supervisor must forthwith inform the Authority of the arrangement.

(3) Where a liquidator is appointed as mentioned in section 100 of the 1986 Act, paragraph 83 of Schedule B1[, paragraph 84 of Schedule B1 to the 1989 Order] or Article 86 of the 1989 Order (appointment of liquidator in a creditors' voluntary winding up), the liquidator must inform the Authority forthwith of his appointment.

(4) Where in the case of a members' voluntary winding up, section 95 of the 1986 Act (effect of company's insolvency) or Article 81 of the 1989 Order applies, the liquidator must inform the Authority forthwith that he is of that opinion.

(6) Paragraphs (1), (2) and (3) do not apply in any case where the Authority was represented at all hearings in connection with the application in relation to which the decision, order or appointment is made.

(7) For the purposes of paragraph (2), a "qualifying arrangement" means a voluntary arrangement which—

   (a)   varies the rights of creditors as against the insurer and is intended to enable the insurer, and the whole or any part of its undertaking, to survive as a going concern; or

   (b)   includes a realisation of some or all of the assets of the insurer and distribution of the proceeds to creditors, with a view to terminating the whole or any part of the business of that insurer.

(8) An administrator, supervisor or liquidator who fails without reasonable excuse to comply with paragraph (2), (3), or (4) (as the case may be) commits an offence and is liable on summary conviction to a fine not exceeding level 3 on the standard scale.

[3844]

NOTES

   Commencement: 18 February 2004.

   Para (1): words in first pair of square brackets substituted by the Insurers (Reorganisation and Winding Up) (Amendment) Regulations 2004, SI 2004/546, reg 2(1), (2), as from 3 March 2004; words in square brackets in sub-paras (a), (d) inserted by the Insurers (Reorganisation and Winding Up) (Amendment) Regulations 2007, SI 2007/851, reg 2(1), (5), as from 6 April 2007.

   Para (3): words in square brackets inserted by SI 2007/851, reg 2(1), (6), as from 6 April 2007.

10 Notification of relevant decision to EEA regulators

(1) Where the Authority is informed of a decision, order or appointment in accordance with regulation 9, the Authority must as soon as is practicable inform the EEA regulators in every EEA State—

   (a)   that the decision, order or appointment has been made; and

   (b)   in general terms, of the possible effect of a decision, order or appointment of that kind on—

      (i)   the business of an insurer, and

      (ii)   the rights of policyholders under contracts of insurance effected and carried out by an insurer.

(2) Where the Authority has been represented at all hearings in connection with the application in relation to which the decision, order or appointment has been made, the Authority must inform the EEA regulators in every EEA State of the matters mentioned in paragraph (1) as soon as is practicable after that decision, order or appointment has been made.

[3845]

NOTES

   Commencement: 18 February 2004.

PART III — STATUTORY INSTRUMENTS

11 Publication of voluntary arrangement, administration order, winding up order or scheme of arrangement

(1)   This regulation applies where a qualifying decision has effect, or a qualifying order or qualifying appointment is made, in relation to a UK insurer on or after 20th April 2003.

(2)   For the purposes of this regulation—
   (a)   a qualifying decision means a decision with respect to the approval of a proposed voluntary arrangement, in accordance with section 4A of the 1986 Act or Article 17A of the 1989 Order;
   (b)   a qualifying order means—
      (i)   an administration order under paragraph 13 of Schedule B1 [or under paragraph 14 of Schedule B1 to the 1989 Order],
      (ii)   an order appointing a provisional liquidator in accordance with section 135 of the 1986 Act or Article 115 of the 1989 Order, or
      (iii)   a winding up order made by the court under Part IV of the 1986 Act or Part V of the 1989 Order.
   (c)   a qualifying appointment means the appointment of a liquidator as mentioned in section 100 of the 1986 Act or Article 86 of the 1989 Order (appointment of liquidator in a creditors' voluntary winding up).

(3)   Subject to paragraph (8), as soon as is reasonably practicable after a qualifying decision has effect, or a qualifying order or a qualifying appointment has been made, the relevant officer must publish, or cause to be published, in the Official Journal of the European Communities the information mentioned in paragraph (4) and (if applicable) paragraphs (5), (6) or (7).

(4)   That information is—
   (a)   a summary of the terms of the qualifying decision or qualifying appointment or the provisions of the qualifying order (as the case may be);
   (b)   the identity of the relevant officer; and
   (c)   the statutory provisions in accordance with which the qualifying decision has effect or the qualifying order or appointment has been made or takes effect.

(5)   In the case of a qualifying appointment falling within paragraph (2)(c), that information includes the court to which an application under section 112 of the 1986 Act (reference of questions to the court) or Article 98 of the 1989 Order (reference of questions to the High Court) may be made.

(6)   In the case of a qualifying decision, that information includes the court to which an application under section 6 of the 1986 Act or Article 19 of the 1989 Order (challenge of decisions) may be made.

(7)   Paragraph (3) does not apply where a qualifying decision or qualifying order falling within paragraph (2)(b)(i) affects the interests only of the members, or any class of members, or employees of the insurer (in their capacity as members or employees).

(8)   This regulation is without prejudice to any requirement to publish information imposed upon a relevant officer under any provision of the general law of insolvency.

(9)   A relevant officer who fails to comply with paragraph (3) of this regulation commits an offence and is liable on summary conviction to a fine not exceeding level 3 on the standard scale.

(10)   A qualifying decision, qualifying order or qualifying appointment is not invalid or ineffective if the relevant official fails to comply with paragraph (3) of this regulation.

(11)   In this regulation, "relevant officer" means—
   (a)   in the case of a voluntary arrangement, the supervisor;
   (b)   in the case of an administration order or the appointment of an administrator, the administrator;
   (c)   in the case of a creditors' voluntary winding up, the liquidator;
   (d)   in the case of winding up order, the liquidator;
   (e)   in the case of an order appointing a provisional liquidator, the provisional liquidator.

                                          [3846]

NOTES
Commencement: 18 February 2004.
Para (2): words in square brackets in sub-para (b)(i) inserted by the Insurers (Reorganisation and Winding Up) (Amendment) Regulations 2007, SI 2007/851, reg 2(1), (7), as from 6 April 2007.

12 Notification to creditors: winding up proceedings

(1)   When a relevant order or appointment is made, or a relevant decision is taken, in relation to a UK insurer on or after 20th April 2003, the appointed officer must as soon as is reasonably practicable—
   (a)   notify all known creditors of that insurer in writing of—
      (i)   the matters mentioned in paragraph (4), and

    (ii) the matters mentioned in paragraph (5); and
  (b) notify all known insurance creditors of that insurer in writing of the matters mentioned in paragraph 6,

in any case.

(2) The appointed officer may comply with the requirement in paragraph (1)(a)(i) and the requirement in paragraph (1)(a)(ii) by separate notifications.

(3) For the purposes of this regulation—
  (a) "relevant order" means—
    (i) an administration order made under section 8 of the 1986 Act before 15th September 2003, or made on or after that date under paragraph 13 of Schedule B1 in the prescribed circumstances [or under paragraph 14 of Schedule B1 to the 1989 Order in the prescribed circumstances],
    (ii) a winding up order under section 125 of the 1986 Act (powers of the court on hearing a petition) or Article 105 of the 1989 Order (powers of High Court on hearing of petition),
    (iii) the appointment of a liquidator in accordance with section 138 of the 1986 Act (appointment of a liquidator in Scotland), and
    (iv) an order appointing a provisional liquidator in accordance with section 135 of that Act or Article 115 of the 1989 Order;
  (b) "relevant appointment" means the appointment of a liquidator as mentioned in section 100 of the 1986 Act or Article 86 of the 1989 Order (appointment of liquidator in a creditors' voluntary winding up); and
  (c) "relevant decision" means a decision as a result of which a qualifying voluntary arrangement has effect.

(4) The matters which must be notified to all known creditors in accordance with paragraph (1)(a)(i) are as follows—
  (a) that a relevant order or appointment has been made, or a relevant decision taken, in relation to the UK insurer; and
  (b) the date from which that order, appointment or decision has effect.

(5) The matters which must be notified to all known creditors in accordance with paragraph (1)(a)(ii) are as follows—
  (a) if applicable, the date by which a creditor must submit his claim in writing;
  (b) the matters which must be stated in a creditor's claim;
  (c) details of any category of debt in relation to which a claim is not required;
  (d) the person to whom any such claim or any observations on a claim must be submitted; and
  (e) the consequences of any failure to submit a claim by any specified deadline.

(6) The matters which must be notified to all known insurance creditors, in accordance with paragraph (1)(b), are as follows—
  (a) the effect which the relevant order, appointment or decision will, or is likely, to have on the kind of contract of insurance under, or in connection with, which that creditor's insurance claim against the insurer is founded; and
  (b) the date from which any variation (resulting from the relevant order or relevant decision) to the risks covered by, or the sums recoverable under, that contract has effect.

(7) Subject to paragraph (8), where a creditor is notified in accordance with paragraph (1)(a)(ii), the notification must be headed with the words "Invitation to lodge a claim: time limits to be observed", and that heading must be given in—
  (a) the official language, or one of the official languages, of the EEA State in which that creditor is ordinarily resident; or
  (b) every official language.

(8) Where a creditor notified in accordance with paragraph (1) is—
  (a) an insurance creditor; and
  (b) ordinarily resident in an EEA State,
the notification must be given in the official language, or one of the official languages, of that EEA State.

(9) The obligation under paragraph (1)(a)(ii) may be discharged by sending a form of proof in accordance with Rule 4.74 of the Insolvency Rules, Rule 4.080 of the Insolvency Rules (Northern Ireland) or Rule 4.15(2) of the Insolvency (Scotland) Rules as applicable in cases where any of those rules applies, provided that the form of proof complies with paragraph (7) or (8) (whichever is applicable).

[(10) The prescribed circumstances are where the administrator includes in the statement required under Rule 2.3 of the Insolvency Rules or under Rule 2.003 of the Insolvency Rules

(Northern Ireland) a statement to the effect that the objective set out in paragraph 3(1)(a) of Schedule B1 or in paragraph 4(1)(a) of Schedule B1 to the 1989 Order is not reasonably likely to be achieved.]

(11)   Where, after the appointment of an administrator, the administrator concludes that it is not reasonably practicable to achieve the objective specified in paragraph 3(1)(a) of Schedule B1 [or in paragraph 4(1)(a) of Schedule B1 to the 1989 Order], he shall inform the court and the Authority in writing of that conclusion and upon so doing the order by which he was appointed shall be a relevant order for the purposes of this regulation and the obligation under paragraph (1) shall apply as from the date on which he so informs the court and the Authority.

(12)   An appointed officer commits an offence if he fails without reasonable excuse to comply with an applicable requirement under this regulation, and is liable on summary conviction to a fine not exceeding level 3 on the standard scale.

(13)   For the purposes of this regulation—
(a)   "appointed officer" means—
  (i)   in the case of a relevant order falling within paragraph (3)(a)(i) or a relevant appointment falling within paragraph (3)(b)(i), the administrator,
  (ii)   in the case of a relevant order falling within paragraph (3)(a)(ii) or (iii) or a relevant appointment falling within paragraph (3)(b)(ii), the liquidator,
  (iii)   in the case of a relevant order falling within paragraph (3)(a)(iv), the provisional liquidator, or
  (iv)   in the case of a relevant decision, the supervisor; and
(b)   a creditor is a "known" creditor if the appointed officer is aware, or should reasonably be aware of—
  (i)   his identity,
  (ii)   his claim or potential claim, and
  (iii)   a recent address where he is likely to receive a communication.

(14)   For the purposes of paragraph (3), and of regulations 13 and 14, a voluntary arrangement is a qualifying voluntary arrangement if its purposes include a realisation of some or all of the assets of the UK insurer to which the order relates and a distribution of the proceeds to creditors, with a view to terminating the whole or any part of the business of that insurer.

[3847]

NOTES
Commencement: 18 February 2004.
Paras (3), (11): words in square brackets inserted by the Insurers (Reorganisation and Winding Up) (Amendment) Regulations 2007, SI 2007/851, reg 2(1), (8), (10), as from 6 April 2007.
Para (10): substituted by SI 2007/851, reg 2(1), (9), as from 6 April 2007.

13   Submission of claims by EEA creditors

(1)   An EEA creditor who on or after 20th April 2003 submits a claim or observations relating to his claim in any relevant proceedings (irrespective of when those proceedings were commenced or had effect) may do so in his domestic language, provided that the requirements in paragraphs (3) and (4) are complied with.

(2)   For the purposes of this regulation, "relevant proceedings" means—
(a)   a winding up;
(b)   a qualifying voluntary arrangement;
(c)   administration.

(3)   Where an EEA creditor submits a claim in his domestic language, the document must be headed with the words "Lodgement of claim" (in English).

(4)   Where an EEA creditor submits observations on his claim (otherwise than in the document by which he submits his claim), the observations must be headed with the words "Submission of observations relating to claims" (in English).

(5)   Paragraph (3) does not apply where an EEA creditor submits his claim using—
(a)   in the case of a winding up, a form of proof supplied by the liquidator in accordance with Rule 4.74 of the Insolvency Rules, Rule 4.080 of the Insolvency Rules (Northern Ireland) or rule 4.15(2) of the Insolvency (Scotland) Rules as the case may be;
(b)   in the case of a qualifying voluntary arrangement, a form approved by the court for that purpose.

(6)   In this regulation—
(a)   "domestic language", in relation to an EEA creditor, means the official language, or one of the official languages, of the EEA State in which he is ordinarily resident or, if the creditor is not an individual, in which the creditor's head office is located; and
(b)   "qualifying voluntary arrangement" has the meaning given by regulation 12(12).

[3848]

NOTES
Commencement: 18 February 2004.

14   Reports to creditors

(1)   This regulation applies where, on or after 20th April 2003—

(a)   a liquidator is appointed in accordance with section 100 of the 1986 Act or Article 86 of the 1989 Order (creditors' voluntary winding up: appointment of liquidator) or, on or after 15th September 2003, paragraph 83 of Schedule B1 [or paragraph 84 of Schedule B1 to the 1989 Order] (moving from administration to creditors' voluntary liquidation);

(b)   a winding up order is made by the court;

(c)   a provisional liquidator is appointed; or

(d)   [an administrator is appointed under paragraph 13 of Schedule B1] [or under paragraph 14 of Schedule B1 to the 1989 Order].

(2)   The liquidator or provisional liquidator (as the case may be) must send to every known creditor a report once in every 12 months beginning with the date when his appointment has effect.

(3)   The requirement in paragraph (2) does not apply where a liquidator or provisional liquidator is required by order of the court to send a report to creditors at intervals which are more frequent than those required by this regulation.

(4)   This regulation is without prejudice to any requirement to send a report to creditors, imposed by the court on the liquidator or provisional liquidator, which is supplementary to the requirements of this regulation.

(5)   A liquidator or provisional liquidator commits an offence if he fails without reasonable excuse to comply with an applicable requirement under this regulation, and is liable on summary conviction to a fine not exceeding level 3 on the standard scale.

(6)   For the purposes of this regulation—

(a)   "known creditor" means—

(i)   a creditor who is known to the liquidator or provisional liquidator, and

(ii)   in a case falling within paragraph (1)(b) or (c), a creditor who is specified in the insurer's statement of affairs (within the meaning of section 131 of the 1986 Act or Article 111 of the 1989 Order); and

(b)   "report" means a written report setting out the position generally as regards the progress of the winding up or provisional liquidation (as the case may be).

[3849]

NOTES
Commencement: 18 February 2004.
Para (1): words in square brackets in sub-para (a) and words in second pair of square brackets in sub-para (d) inserted by the Insurers (Reorganisation and Winding Up) (Amendment) Regulations 2007, SI 2007/851, reg 2(1), (11), as from 6 April 2007; words in first pair of square brackets in sub-para (d) substituted by the Insurers (Reorganisation and Winding Up) (Amendment) Regulations 2004, SI 2004/546, reg 2(1), (3), as from 3 March 2004.

15   Service of notices and documents

(1)   This regulation applies to any notification, report or other document which is required to be sent to a creditor of a UK insurer by a provision of this Part ("a relevant notification").

(2)   A relevant notification may be sent to a creditor by either of the following methods—

(a)   posting it to the proper address of the creditor;

(b)   transmitting it electronically, in accordance with paragraph (4).

(3)   For the purposes of paragraph (2)(a), the proper address of a creditor is any current address provided by that creditor as an address for service of a relevant notification or, if no such address is provided—

(a)   the last known address of that creditor (whether his residence or a place where he carries on business);

(b)   in the case of a body corporate, the address of its registered or principal office; or

(c)   in the case of an unincorporated association, the address of its principal office.

(4)   A relevant notification may be transmitted electronically only if it is sent to—

(a)   an electronic address notified to the relevant officer by the creditor for this purpose; or

(b)   if no such address has been notified, an electronic address at which the relevant officer reasonably believes the creditor will receive the notification.

(5)   Any requirement in this part to send a relevant notification to a creditor shall also be treated as satisfied if—

(a)   the creditor has agreed with—

      (i)   the UK insurer which is liable under the creditor's claim, or

      (ii)   the relevant officer,

that information which is required to be sent to him (whether pursuant to a statutory or contractual obligation, or otherwise) may instead be accessed by him on a web site;

(b)   the agreement applies to the relevant notification in question;

(c)   the creditor is notified of—

      (i)   the publication of the relevant notification on a web site,

      (ii)   the address of that web site,

      (iii) the place on that web site where the relevant notification may be accessed, and how it may be accessed; and

(d)   the relevant notification is published on that web site throughout a period of at least one month beginning with the date on which the creditor is notified in accordance with sub-paragraph (c):

(6)   Where, in a case in which paragraph (5) is relied on for compliance with a requirement of regulation 12 or 14—

(a)   a relevant notification is published for a part, but not all, of the period mentioned in paragraph (5)(d); but

(b)   the failure to publish it throughout that period is wholly attributable to circumstances which it would not be reasonable to have expected the relevant officer to prevent or avoid,

no offence is committed under regulation 12(10) or regulation 14(5) (as the case may be) by reason of that failure.

(7)   In this regulation—

(a)   "electronic address" includes any number or address used for the purposes of receiving electronic communications;

(b)   "electronic communication" means an electronic communication within the meaning of the Electronic Communications Act 2000 the processing of which on receipt is intended to produce writing; and

(c)   "relevant officer" means (as the case may be) an administrator, liquidator, provisional liquidator or supervisor who is required to send a relevant notification to a creditor by a provision of this Part.

[3850]

NOTES

Commencement: 18 February 2004.

16 Disclosure of confidential information received from an EEA regulator

(1)   This regulation applies to information ("insolvency information") which—

(a)   relates to the business or affairs of any other person; and

(b)   is supplied to the Authority by an EEA regulator acting in accordance with Articles 5, 8 or 30 of the reorganisation and winding up directive.

(2)   Subject to paragraphs (3) and (4), sections 348, 349 and 352 of the 2000 Act apply in relation to insolvency information in the same way as they apply in relation to confidential information within the meaning of section 348(2) of the 2000 Act.

(3)   Insolvency information is not subject to the restrictions on disclosure imposed by section 348(1) of the 2000 Act (as it applies by virtue of paragraph (2)) if it satisfies any of the criteria set out in section 348(4) of the 2000 Act.

(4)   The Disclosure Regulations apply in relation to insolvency information as they apply in relation to single market directive information (within the meaning of those Regulations).

(5)   In this regulation, "the Disclosure Regulations" means the Financial Services and Markets Act 2000 (Disclosure of Confidential Information) Regulations 2001.

[3851]

NOTES

Commencement: 18 February 2004.

PART IV
PRIORITY OF PAYMENT OF INSURANCE CLAIMS IN WINDING UP ETC

17 Interpretation of this Part

(1)   For the purposes of this Part—

"composite insurer" means a UK insurer who is authorised to carry on both general business and long term business, in accordance with article 18(2) of the life insurance directive;

"floating charge" has the meaning given by section 251 of the 1986 Act or paragraph (1) of Article 5 of the 1989 Order;

"general business" means the business of effecting or carrying out a contract of general insurance;

"general business assets" means the assets of a composite insurer which are, or should properly be, apportioned to that insurer's general business, in accordance with the requirements of Article 18(3) of the life insurance directive (separate management of long term and general business of a composite insurer);

"general business liabilities" means the debts of a composite insurer which are attributable to the general business carried on by that insurer;

"general insurer" means a UK insurer who carries on exclusively general business;

"long term business" means the business of effecting or carrying out a contract of long term insurance;

"long term business assets" means the assets of a composite insurer which are, or should properly be, apportioned to that insurer's long term business, in accordance with the requirements of Article 18(3) of the first life insurance directive (separate management of long term and general business of a composite insurer);

"long term business liabilities" means the debts of a composite insurer which are attributable to the long term business carried on by that insurer;

"long term insurer" means a UK insurer who—

(a)　carries on long term business exclusively, or

(b)　carries on long term business and permitted general business;

"non-transferring composite insurer" means a composite insurer the long term business of which has not been, and is not to be, transferred as a going concern to a person who may lawfully carry out those contracts, in accordance with section 376(2) of the 2000 Act;

"other assets" means any assets of a composite insurer which are not long term business assets or general business assets;

"other business", in relation to a composite insurer, means such of the business (if any) of the insurer as is not long term business or general business;

"permitted general business" means the business of effecting or carrying out a contract of general insurance where the risk insured against relates to either accident or sickness;

"preferential debt" means a debt falling into any of categories 4 or 5 of the debts listed in Schedule 6 to the 1986 Act or Schedule 4 to the 1989 Order, that is—

(a)　contributions to occupational pension schemes, etc, and

(b)　remuneration etc of employees;

"society" means—

(a)　a friendly society incorporated under the Friendly Societies Act 1992,

(b)　a society which is a friendly society within the meaning of section 7(1)(a) of the Friendly Societies Act 1974, and registered within the meaning of that Act, or

(c)　an industrial and provident society registered or deemed to be registered under the Industrial and Provident Societies Act 1965 or the Industrial and Provident Societies Act (Northern Ireland) 1969.

(2)　In this Part, references to assets include a reference to proceeds where an asset has been realised, and any other sums representing assets.

(3)　References in paragraph (1) to a contract of long term or of general insurance must be read with—

(a)　section 22 of the 2000 Act;

(b)　any relevant order made under that section; and

(c)　Schedule 2 to that Act.

[3852]

NOTES

Commencement: 18 February 2004.

18　Application of regulations 19 to 27

(1)　Subject to paragraph (2), regulations 19 to 27 apply in the winding up of a UK insurer where—

(a)　in the case of a winding up by the court, the winding up order is made on or after 20th April 2003; or

(b)　in the case of a creditors' voluntary winding up, the liquidator is appointed, as mentioned in section 100 of the 1986 Act, paragraph 83 of Schedule B1[, paragraph 84 of Schedule B1 to the 1989 Order] or Article 86 of the 1989 Order, on or after 20th April 2003.

(2)　Where a relevant section 425 or Article 418 compromise or arrangement is in place,

(a)　no winding up proceedings may be opened without the permission of the court, and

(b)   the permission of the court is to be granted only if required by the exceptional circumstances of the case.

(3)   For the purposes of paragraph (2), winding up proceedings include proceedings for a winding up order or for a creditors' voluntary liquidation with confirmation by the court.

(4)   Regulations 20 to 27 do not apply to a winding up falling within paragraph (1) where, in relation to a UK insurer—
(a)   an administration order was made before 20th April 2003, and that order is not discharged until the commencement date; or
(b)   a provisional liquidator was appointed before 20th April 2003, and that appointment is not discharged until the commencement date.

(5)   For purposes of this regulation, "the commencement date" means the date when a UK insurer goes into liquidation within the meaning given by section 247(2) of the 1986 Act or Article 6(2) of the 1989 Order.

[3853]

NOTES
Commencement: 18 February 2004.
Para (1): words in square brackets in sub-para (b) inserted by the Insurers (Reorganisation and Winding Up) (Amendment) Regulations 2007, SI 2007/851, reg 2(1), (12), as from 6 April 2007.

19   Application of this Part: assets subject to a section 425 or Article 418 compromise or arrangement

(1)   For the purposes of this Part, the insolvent estate of a UK insurer shall not include any assets which at the commencement date are subject to a relevant section 425 or Article 418 compromise or arrangement.

(2)   In this regulation—
(a)   "assets" has the same meaning as "property" in section 436 of the 1986 Act or Article 2(2) of the 1989 Order;
(b)   "commencement date" has the meaning given in [regulation 18(5)];
(c)   "insolvent estate"—
(i)   in England, Wales and Northern Ireland has the meaning given by Rule 13.8 of the Insolvency Rules or Rule 0.2 of the Insolvency Rules (Northern Ireland), and
(ii)   in Scotland means the company's assets;
(d)   "relevant section 425 or Article 418 compromise or arrangement" means
(i)   a section 425 or Article 418 compromise or arrangement which was sanctioned by the court before 20th April 2003, or
(ii)   any subsequent section 425 or Article 418 compromise or arrangement sanctioned by the court to amend or replace a compromise or arrangement of a kind mentioned in paragraph (i).

[3854]

NOTES
Commencement: 18 February 2004.
Para (2): words in square brackets in sub-para (b) substituted by the Insurers (Reorganisation and Winding Up) (Lloyd's) Regulations 2005, SI 2005/1998, reg 49, as from 10 August 2005.

20   Preferential debts: disapplication of section 175 of the 1986 Act or Article 149 of the 1989 Order

Except to the extent that they are applied by regulation 27, section 175 of the 1986 Act or Article 149 of the 1989 Order (preferential debts (general provision)) does not apply in the case of a winding up of a UK insurer, and instead the provisions of regulations 21 to 26 have effect.

[3855]

NOTES
Commencement: 18 February 2004.

21   Preferential debts: long term insurers and general insurers

(1)   This regulation applies in the case of a winding up of—
(a)   a long term insurer;
(b)   a general insurer;
(c)   a composite insurer, where the long term business of that insurer has been or is to be transferred as a going concern to a person who may lawfully carry out the contracts in that long term business in accordance with section 376(2) of the 2000 Act.

(2)   Subject to paragraph (3), the debts of the insurer must be paid in the following order of priority—

(a)   preferential debts;
(b)   insurance debts;
(c)   all other debts.

(3)   Preferential debts rank equally among themselves [after the expenses of the winding up] and must be paid in full, unless the assets are insufficient to meet them, in which case they abate in equal proportions

(4)   Insurance debts rank equally among themselves and must be paid in full, unless the assets available after the payment of preferential debts are insufficient to meet them, in which case they abate in equal proportions.

(5)   Subject to paragraph (6), so far as the assets of the insurer available for the payment of unsecured creditors are insufficient to meet the preferential debts, those debts (and only those debts) have priority over the claims of holders of debentures secured by, or holders of, any floating charge created by the insurer, and must be paid accordingly out of any property comprised in or subject to that charge.

(6)   The order of priority specified in paragraph (2)(a) and (b) applies for the purposes of any payment made in accordance with paragraph (5).

(7)   Section 176A of the 1986 Act [and Article 150A of the 1989 Order] [have] effect with regard to an insurer so that insurance debts must be paid out of the prescribed part in priority to all other unsecured debts.

[3856]

NOTES
Commencement: 18 February 2004.
Para (3): words in square brackets inserted by the Insurers (Reorganisation and Winding Up) (Amendment) Regulations 2004, SI 2004/546, reg 2(1), (4), as from 3 March 2004.
Para (7): words in first pair of square brackets inserted, and word in second pair of square brackets substituted, by the Insurers (Reorganisation and Winding Up) (Amendment) Regulations 2007, SI 2007/851, reg 2(1), (13), as from 6 April 2007.

22   Composite insurers: preferential debts attributable to long term and general business

(1)   This regulation applies in the case of the winding up of a non-transferring composite insurer.

(2)   Subject to the payment of costs in accordance with regulation 30, the long term business assets and the general business assets must be applied separately in accordance with paragraphs (3) and (4).

(3)   Subject to paragraph (6), the long term business assets must be applied in discharge of the long term business preferential debts in the order of priority specified in regulation 23(1).

(4)   Subject to paragraph (8), the general business assets must be applied in discharge of the general business preferential debts in the order of priority specified in regulation 24(1).

(5)   Paragraph (6) applies where the value of the long term business assets exceeds the long term business preferential debts and the general business assets are insufficient to meet the general business preferential debts.

(6)   Those long term business assets which represent the excess must be applied in discharge of the outstanding general business preferential debts of the insurer, in accordance with the order of priority specified in regulation 24(1).

(7)   Paragraph (8) applies where the value of the general business assets exceeds the general business preferential debts, and the long term business assets are insufficient to meet the long term business preferential debts.

(8)   Those general business assets which represent the excess must be applied in discharge of the outstanding long term business preferential debts of the insurer, in accordance with the order of priority specified in regulation 23(1).

(9)   For the purposes of this regulation and regulations 23 and 24—
    "long term business preferential debts" means those debts mentioned in regulation 23(1) and, unless the court orders otherwise, any expenses of the winding up which are apportioned to the long term business assets in accordance with regulation 30;
    "general business preferential debts" means those debts mentioned in regulation 24(1) and, unless the court orders otherwise, any expenses of the winding up which are apportioned to the general business assets in accordance with regulation 30.

(10)   For the purposes of paragraphs (6) and (8)—
    "outstanding long term business preferential debts" means those long term business preferential debts, if any, which remain unpaid, either in whole or in part, after the application of the long term business assets, in accordance with paragraph (3);

PART III
STATUTORY INSTRUMENTS

"outstanding general business preferential debts" means those general business preferential debts, if any, which remain unpaid, either in whole or in part, after the application of the general business assets, in accordance with paragraph (3).

[3857]

NOTES
Commencement: 18 February 2004.

23 Preferential debts: long term business of a non-transferring composite insurer

(1)   For the purpose of compliance with the requirement in regulation 22(3), the long term business assets of a non-transferring composite insurer must be applied in discharge of the following debts and in the following order of priority—
   (a)   relevant preferential debts;
   (b)   long term insurance debts.

(2)   Relevant preferential debts rank equally among themselves, unless the long term business assets, any available general business assets and other assets (if any) applied in accordance with regulation 24 are insufficient to meet them, in which case they abate in equal proportions.

(3)   Long term insurance debts rank equally among themselves, unless the long term business assets available after the payment of relevant preferential debts and any available general business assets and other assets (if any) applied in accordance with regulation 25 are insufficient to meet them, in which case they abate in equal proportions.

(4)   So far as the long term business assets, and any available general business assets, which are available for the payment of unsecured creditors are insufficient to meet the relevant preferential debts, those debts (and only those debts) have priority over the claims of holders of debentures secured by, or holders of, any floating charge created by the insurer over any of its long term business assets, and must be paid accordingly out of any property comprised in or subject to that charge.

(5)   The order of priority specified in paragraph (1) applies for the purposes of any payment made in accordance with paragraph (4).

(6)   For the purposes of this regulation—
   "available general business assets" means those general business assets which must be applied in discharge of the insurer's outstanding long term business preferential debts, in accordance with regulation 22(8);
   "long term insurance debt" means an insurance debt which is attributable to the long term business of the insurer;
   "relevant preferential debt" means a preferential debt which is attributable to the long term business of the insurer.

[3858]

NOTES
Commencement: 18 February 2004.

24 Preferential debts: general business of a composite insurer

(1)   For the purpose of compliance with the requirement in regulation 22(4), the long term business assets of a non-transferring composite insurer must be applied in discharge of the following debts and in the following order of priority—
   (a)   relevant preferential debts;
   (b)   general insurance debts.

(2)   Relevant preferential debts rank equally among themselves, unless the general business assets, any available long term business assets, and other assets (if any) applied in accordance with regulation 25 are insufficient to meet them, in which case they abate in equal proportions.

(3)   General insurance debts rank equally among themselves, unless the general business assets available after the payment of relevant preferential debts, any available long term business assets, and other assets (if any) applied in accordance with regulation 26 are insufficient to meet them, in which case they abate in equal proportions.

(4)   So far as the other business assets and available long term assets of the insurer which are available for the payment of unsecured creditors are insufficient to meet relevant preferential debts, those debts (and only those debts) have priority over the claims of holders of debentures secured by, or holders of, any floating charge created by the insurer, and must be paid accordingly out of any property comprised in or subject to that charge.

(5)   The order of priority specified in paragraph (1) applies for the purposes of any payment made in accordance with paragraph (4).

(6)   For the purposes of this regulation—

"available long term business assets" means those long term business assets which must be applied in discharge of the insurer's outstanding general business preferential debts, in accordance with regulation 22(6);

"general insurance debt" means an insurance debt which is attributable to the general business of the insurer;

"relevant preferential debt" means a preferential debt which is attributable to the general business of the insurer.

[3859]

NOTES
Commencement: 18 February 2004.

25 Insufficiency of long term business assets and general business assets

(1)   This regulation applies in the case of the winding up of a non-transferring composite insurer where the long term business assets and the general business assets, applied in accordance with regulation 22, are insufficient to meet in full the preferential debts and insurance debts.

(2)   In a case in which this regulation applies, the other assets (if any) of the insurer must be applied in the following order of priority—
  (a)   outstanding preferential debts;
  (b)   unattributed preferential debts;
  (c)   outstanding insurance debts;
  (d)   all other debts.

(3)   So far as the long term business assets, and any available general business assets, which are available for the payment of unsecured creditors are insufficient to meet the outstanding preferential debts and the unattributed preferential debts, those debts (and only those debts) have priority over the claims of holders of debentures secured by, or holders of, any floating charge created by the insurer over any of its other assets, and must be paid accordingly out of any property comprised in or subject to that charge.

(4)   For the purposes of this regulation—
  "outstanding insurance debt" means any insurance debt, or any part of an insurance debt, which was not discharged by the application of the long term business assets and the general business assets in accordance with regulation 22;
  "outstanding preferential debt" means any preferential debt attributable either to the long term business or the general business of the insurer which was not discharged by the application of the long term business assets and the general business assets in accordance with regulation 23;
  "unattributed preferential debt" means a preferential debt which is not attributable to either the long term business or the general business of the insurer.

[3860]

NOTES
Commencement: 18 February 2004.

26 Composite insurers: excess of long term business assets and general business assets

(1)   This regulation applies in the case of the winding up of a non-transferring composite insurer where the value of the long term business assets and the general business assets, applied in accordance with regulation 22, exceeds the value of the sum of the long term business preferential debts and the general business preferential debts.

(2)   In a case to which this regulation applies, long term business assets or general business assets which have not been applied in discharge of long term business preferential debts or general business preferential debts must be applied in accordance with regulation 27.

(3)   In this regulation, "long term business preferential debts" and "general business preferential debts" have the same meaning as in regulation 22.

[3861]

NOTES
Commencement: 18 February 2004.

27 Composite insurers: application of other assets

(1)   This regulation applies in the case of the winding up of a non-transferring composite insurer where regulation 25 does not apply.

(2)   The other assets of the insurer, together with any outstanding business assets, must be paid in discharge of the following debts in accordance with section 175 of the 1986 Act or Article 149 of the 1989 Order—

(a) unattributed preferential debts;

(b) all other debts.

(3) In this regulation—

"unattributed preferential debt" has the same meaning as in regulation 25;

"outstanding business assets" means assets of the kind mentioned in regulation 26(2).

[3862]

NOTES

Commencement: 18 February 2004.

28 Composite insurers: proof of debts

(1) This regulation applies in the case of the winding up of a non-transferring composite insurer in compliance with the requirement in regulation 23(2).

(2) The liquidator may in relation to the insurer's long term business assets and its general business assets fix different days on or before which the creditors of the company who are required to prove their debts or claims are to prove their debts or claims, and he may fix one of those days without at the same time fixing the other.

(3) In submitting a proof of any debt a creditor may claim the whole or any part of such debt as is attributable to the company's long term business or to its general business, or he may make no such attribution.

(4) When he admits any debt, in whole or in part, the liquidator must state in writing how much of what he admits is attributable to the company's long term business, how much is attributable to the company's general business, and how much is attributable to its other business (if any).

(5) Paragraph (2) does not apply in Scotland.

[3863]

NOTES

Commencement: 18 February 2004.

29 Composite insurers: general meetings of creditors

(1) This regulation applies in the same circumstances as regulation 28.

(2) The creditors mentioned in section 168(2) of the 1986 Act, Article 143(2) of the 1989 Order or rule 4.13 of the Insolvency (Scotland) Rules (power of liquidator to summon general meetings of creditors) are to be—

(a) in relation to the long term business assets of that insurer, only those who are creditors in respect of long term business liabilities; and

(b) in relation to the general business assets of that insurer, only those who are creditors in respect of general business liabilities,

and, accordingly, any general meetings of creditors summoned for the purposes of that section, Article or rule are to be separate general meetings of creditors in respect of long term business liabilities and general business liabilities.

[3864]

NOTES

Commencement: 18 February 2004.

30 Composite insurers: apportionment of costs payable out of the assets

(1) In the case of the winding up of a non-transferring composite insurer, Rule 4.218 of the Insolvency Rules or Rule 4.228 of the Insolvency Rules (Northern Ireland) (general rules as to priority) or rule 4.67 (order of priority of expenses of liquidation) of the Insolvency (Scotland) Rules applies separately to long-term business assets and to the general business assets of that insurer.

(2) But where any fee, expense, cost, charge, or remuneration does not relate exclusively to the long-term business assets or to the general business assets of that insurer, the liquidator must apportion it amongst those assets in such manner as he shall determine.

[3865]

NOTES

Commencement: 18 February 2004.

31 Summary remedy against liquidators

Section 212 of the 1986 Act or Article 176 of the 1989 Order (summary remedy against delinquent directors, liquidators etc) applies in relation to a liquidator who is required to comply with regulations 21 to 27, as it applies in relation to a liquidator who is required to comply with section 175 of the 1986 Act or Article 149 of the 1989 Order.

[3866]

NOTES
  Commencement: 18 February 2004.

32   Priority of subrogated claims by the Financial Services Compensation Scheme

(1)   This regulation applies where an insurance creditor has assigned a relevant right to the scheme manager ("a relevant assignment").

(2)   For the purposes of regulations 21, 23 and 24, where the scheme manager proves for an insurance debt in the winding up of a UK insurer pursuant to a relevant assignment, that debt must be paid to the scheme manager in the same order of priority as any other insurance debt.

(3)   In this regulation—
    "relevant right" means any direct right of action against a UK insurer under a contract of insurance, including the right to prove for a debt under that contract in a winding up of that insurer;
    "scheme manager" has the meaning given by section 212(1) of the 2000 Act.

[3867]

NOTES
  Commencement: 18 February 2004.

33   Voluntary arrangements: treatment of insurance debts

(1)   The modifications made by paragraph (2) apply where a voluntary arrangement is proposed under section 1 of the 1986 Act or Article 14 of the 1989 Order in relation to a UK insurer, and that arrangement includes—
    (a)   a composition in satisfaction of any insurance debts; and
    (b)   a distribution to creditors of some or all of the assets of that insurer in the course of, or with a view to, terminating the whole or any part of the business of that insurer.

(2)   Section 4 of the 1986 Act (decisions of meetings) has effect as if—
    (a)   after subsection (4) there were inserted—

    "(4A)   A meeting so summoned and taking place on or after 20th April 2003 shall not approve any proposal or modification under which any insurance debt of the company is to be paid otherwise than in priority to such of its debts as are not insurance debts or preferential debts.

      (4B)   Paragraph (4A) does not apply where—
        (a)   a winding up order made before 20th April 2003 is in force; or
        (b)   a relevant insolvency appointment made before 20th April 2003 has effect,
    in relation to the company.";
    (b)   for subsection (7) there were substituted—

    "(7)   References in this section to preferential debts mean debts falling into any of categories 4 and 5 of the debts listed in Schedule 6 to this Act; and references to preferential creditors are to be construed accordingly."; and
    (c)   after subsection (7) as so substituted there were inserted—

    "(8)   For the purposes of this section—
      (a)   "insurance debt" has the meaning it has in the Insurers (Reorganisation and Winding up) Regulations 2004; and
      (b)   "relevant insolvency measure" means—
          (i)   the appointment of a provisional liquidator, or
          (ii)   the appointment of an administrator,
    where an effect of the appointment will be, or is intended to be, a realisation of some or all of the assets of the insurer and the distribution of the proceeds to creditors, with a view to terminating the whole or any part of the business of that insurer.".

(3)   Article 17 of the 1989 Order (decisions of meetings) has effect as if—
    (a)   after paragraph (4) there were inserted—

    "(4A)   A meeting so summoned and taking place on or after 20th April 2003 shall not approve any proposal or modification under which any insurance debt of the company is to be paid otherwise than in priority to such of its debts as are not insurance debts or preferential debts.

      (4B)   Paragraph (4A) does not apply where—
        (a)   a winding up order made before 20th April 2003 is in force; or

(b)   a relevant insolvency appointment made before 20th April 2003 has effect, in relation to the company.";
(b)   for paragraph (7) there were substituted—

"(7)   References in this Article to preferential debts mean debts falling into any of categories 4 and 5 of the debts listed in Schedule 4 to this Order, and references to preferential creditors are to be construed accordingly."; and
(c)   after paragraph (7) as so substituted there were inserted—

"(8)   For the purposes of this section—
(a)   "insurance debt" has the meaning it has in the Insurers (Reorganisation and Winding Up) Regulations 2004 and
(b)   "relevant insolvency measure" means—
    (i)   the appointment of a provisional liquidator, or
    (ii)   the appointment of an administrator,
where an effect of the appointment will be, or is intended to be, a realisation of some or all of the assets of the insurer and the distribution of the proceeds to creditors, with a view to terminating the whole or any part of the business of that insurer.".

[3868]

NOTES
Commencement: 18 February 2004.
Note that the Insurers (Reorganisation and Winding Up) (Amendment) Regulations 2004, SI 2004/546, reg 2(5) provides as follows; it is assumed that this is an error and the amendment has not been incorporated—
(5)   In the modifications to section 4 of the Insolvency Act 1986 in regulation 33(2) and in those to Article 17 of the Insolvency (Northern Ireland) Order 1989 in regulation 33(3), in the new subsection 4B(b) and paragraph 4B(b) (respectively), insert "2003" after "20th April".

PART V
REORGANISATION OR WINDING UP OF UK INSURERS:
RECOGNITION OF EEA RIGHTS

34   Application of this Part
(1)   This Part applies—
(a)   where a decision with respect to the approval of a proposed voluntary arrangement having a qualifying purpose is made under section 4A of the 1986 Act or Article 17A of the 1989 Order on or after 20th April 2003 in relation to a UK insurer;
(b)   where an administration order made under section 8 of the 1986 Act on or after 20th April 2003 or, on or after 15th September 2003, made under paragraph 13 of Schedule B1 [or under paragraph 14 of Schedule B1 to the 1989 Order] is in force in relation to a UK insurer;
(c)   where on or after 20th April 2003 the court reduces the value of one or more of the contracts of a UK insurer under section 377 of the 2000 Act or section 24(5) of the Friendly Societies Act 1992;
(d)   where a UK insurer is subject to a relevant winding up;
(e)   where a provisional liquidator is appointed in relation to a UK insurer on or after 20th April 2003.

(2)   For the purposes of paragraph (1)(a), a voluntary arrangement has a qualifying purpose if it—
(a)   varies the rights of the creditors as against the insurer and is intended to enable the insurer, and the whole or any part of its undertaking, to survive as a going concern; or
(b)   includes a realisation of some or all of the assets of the insurer to which it relates and the distribution of the proceeds to creditors, with a view to terminating the whole or any part of the business of that insurer.

(3)   For the purposes of paragraph (1)(d), a winding up is a relevant winding up if—
(a)   in the case of a winding up by the court, the winding up order is made on or after 20th April 2003; or
(b)   in the case of a creditors' voluntary winding up, the liquidator is appointed in accordance with section 100 of the 1986 Act, paragraph 83 of Schedule B1[, paragraph 84 of Schedule B1 to the 1989 Order] or Article 86 of the 1989 Order on or after 20th April 2003.

[3869]

NOTES
Commencement: 18 February 2004.
Paras (1), (3): words in square brackets in sub-para (b) inserted by the Insurers (Reorganisation and Winding Up) (Amendment) Regulations 2007, SI 2007/851, reg 2(1), (14), (15), as from 6 April 2007.

35 Application of this Part: assets subject to a section 425 or Article 418 compromise or arrangement

(1) For the purposes of this Part, the insolvent estate of a UK insurer shall not include any assets which at the commencement date are subject to a relevant section 425 or Article 418 compromise or arrangement.

(2) In this regulation—

(a) "assets" has the same meaning as "property" in section 436 of the 1986 Act or Article 2(2) of the 1989 Order;

(b) "commencement date" has the meaning given in regulation 18(4);

(c) "insolvent estate" in England and Wales and Northern Ireland has the meaning given by Rule 13.8 of the Insolvency Rules or Rule 0.2 of the Insolvency Rules (Northern Ireland) and in Scotland means the company's assets;

(d) "relevant section 425 or Article 418 compromise or arrangement" means—

(i) a section 425 or Article 418 compromise or arrangement which was sanctioned by the court before 20th April 2003, or

(ii) any subsequent section 425 or Article 418 compromise or arrangement sanctioned by the court to amend or replace a compromise or arrangement of the kind mentioned in paragraph (i).

[3870]

NOTES
Commencement: 18 February 2004.

36 Interpretation of this Part

(1) For the purposes of this Part—

(a) "affected insurer" means a UK insurer which is the subject of a relevant reorganisation or a relevant winding up;

(b) "relevant reorganisation or a relevant winding up" means any voluntary arrangement, administration order, winding up, or order referred to in regulation 34(1)(d) t o which this Part applies; and

(c) "relevant time" means the date of the opening of a relevant reorganisation or a relevant winding up.

(2) In this Part, references to the opening of a relevant reorganisation or a relevant winding up mean—

(a) in the case of winding up proceedings—

(i) in the case of a winding up by the court, the date on which the winding up order is made, or

(ii) in the case of a creditors' voluntary winding up, the date on which the liquidator is appointed in accordance with section 100 of the 1986 Act, paragraph 83 of Schedule B1 or Article 86 of the 1989 Order [or paragraph 84 of Schedule B1 to the 1989 Order];

(b) in the case of a voluntary arrangement, the date when a decision with respect to that voluntary arrangement has effect in accordance with section 4A(2) of the 1986 Act or Article 17A(2) of the 1989 Order;

(c) in a case where an administration order under paragraph 13 of Schedule B1 [or under paragraph 14 of Schedule B1 to the 1989 Order] is in force, the date of the making of that order;

(d) in a case where an administrator is appointed under paragraphs 14 or 22 of Schedule B1 [or under paragraph 15 or 23 of Schedule B1 to the 1989 Order,] the date on which that appointment takes effect;

(e) in a case where the court reduces the value of one or more of the contracts of a UK insurer under section 377 of the 2000 Act or section 24(5) of the Friendly Societies Act 1992, the date the court exercises that power; and

(f) in a case where a provisional liquidator has been appointed, the date of that appointment,

and references to the time of an opening must be construed accordingly.

[3871]

NOTES
Commencement: 18 February 2004.
Para (2): words in square brackets inserted by the Insurers (Reorganisation and Winding Up) (Amendment) Regulations 2007, SI 2007/851, reg 2(1), (16), as from 6 April 2007.

37 EEA rights: applicable law in the winding up of a UK insurer

(1) This regulation is subject to the provisions of regulations 38 to 47.

PART III
STATUTORY INSTRUMENTS

(2) In a relevant winding up, the matters mentioned in paragraph (3) in particular are to be determined in accordance with the general law of insolvency of the United Kingdom.

(3) Those matters are—
- (a) the assets which form part of the estate of the affected insurer;
- (b) the treatment of assets acquired by, or devolving on, the affected insurer after the opening of the relevant winding up;
- (c) the respective powers of the affected insurer and the liquidator or provisional liquidator;
- (d) the conditions under which set-off may be revoked;
- (e) the effects of the relevant winding up on current contracts to which the affected insurer is a party;
- (f) the effects of the relevant winding up on proceedings brought by creditors;
- (g) the claims which are to be lodged against the estate of the affected insurer;
- (h) the treatment of claims against the affected insurer arising after the opening of the relevant winding up;
- (i) the rules governing—
    - (i) the lodging, verification and admission of claims,
    - (ii) the distribution of proceeds from the realisation of assets,
    - (iii) the ranking of claims,
    - (iv) the rights of creditors who have obtained partial satisfaction after the opening of the relevant winding up by virtue of a right in rem or through set-off;
- (j) the conditions for and the effects of the closure of the relevant winding up, in particular by composition;
- (k) the rights of creditors after the closure of the relevant winding up;
- (l) who is to bear the cost and expenses incurred in the relevant winding up;
- (m) the rules relating to the voidness, voidability or unenforceability of legal acts detrimental to all the creditors.

(4) In this regulation, "relevant winding up" has the meaning given by regulation 34(3).

[3872]

NOTES
Commencement: 18 February 2004.

38 Employment contracts and relationships

(1) The effects of a relevant reorganisation or a relevant winding up on any EEA employment contract and any EEA employment relationship are to be determined in accordance with the law of the EEA State to which that contract or that relationship is subject.

(2) In this regulation, an employment contract is an EEA employment contract, and an employment relationship is an EEA employment relationship, if it is subject to the law of an EEA State.

[3873]

NOTES
Commencement: 18 February 2004.

39 Contracts in connection with immovable property

The effects of a relevant reorganisation or a relevant winding up on a contract conferring the right to make use of or acquire immovable property situated within the territory of an EEA State are to be determined in accordance with the law of that State.

[3874]

NOTES
Commencement: 18 February 2004.

40 Registrable rights

The effects of a relevant reorganisation or a relevant winding up on rights of the affected insurer with respect to—
- (a) immovable property,
- (b) a ship, or
- (c) an aircraft

which is subject to registration in a public register kept under the authority of an EEA State are to be determined in accordance with the law of that State.

[3875]

NOTES
Commencement: 18 February 2004.

41   Third parties' rights in rem

(1)   A relevant reorganisation or a relevant winding up shall not affect the rights in rem of creditors or third parties in respect of tangible or intangible, movable or immovable assets (including both specific assets and collections of indefinite assets as a whole which change from time to time) belonging to the affected insurer which are situated within the territory of an EEA State at the relevant time.

(2)   The rights in rem referred to in paragraph (1) shall in particular include—

    (a)   the right to dispose of the assets in question or have them disposed of and to obtain satisfaction from the proceeds of or the income from those assets, in particular by virtue of a lien or a mortgage;

    (b)   the exclusive right to have a claim met out of the assets in question, in particular a right guaranteed by a lien in respect of the claim or by assignment of the claim by way of guarantee;

    (c)   the right to demand the assets in question from, or to require restitution by, any person having possession or use of them contrary to the wishes of the party otherwise entitled to the assets;

    (d)   a right in rem to the beneficial use of assets.

(3)   A right, recorded in a public register and enforceable against third parties, under which a right in rem within the meaning of paragraph (1) may be obtained, is also to be treated as a right in rem for the purposes of this regulation.

(4)   Paragraph (1) does not preclude actions for voidness, voidability or unenforceability of legal acts detrimental to creditors under the general law of insolvency of the United Kingdom, as referred to in regulation 37(3)(m).

[3876]

NOTES
Commencement: 18 February 2004.

---

42   Reservation of title agreements etc

(1)   The opening of a relevant reorganisation or a relevant winding up in relation to an insurer purchasing an asset shall not affect the seller's rights based on a reservation of title where at the time of that opening the asset is situated within the territory of an EEA State.

(2)   The opening of a relevant reorganisation or a relevant winding up in relation to an insurer selling an asset, after delivery of the asset, shall not constitute grounds for rescinding or terminating the sale and shall not prevent the purchaser from acquiring title where at the time of that opening the asset sold is situated within the territory of an EEA State.

(3)   Paragraphs (1) and (2) do not preclude actions for voidness, voidability or unenforceability of legal acts detrimental to creditors under the general law of insolvency of the United Kingdom, as referred to in regulation 37(3)(m).

[3877]

NOTES
Commencement: 18 February 2004.

---

43   Creditors' rights to set off

(1)   A relevant reorganisation or a relevant winding up shall not affect the right of creditors to demand the set-off of their claims against the claims of the affected insurer, where such a set-off is permitted by the applicable EEA law.

(2)   In paragraph (1), "applicable EEA law" means the law of the EEA State which is applicable to the claim of the affected insurer.

(3)   Paragraph (1) does not preclude actions for voidness, voidability or unenforceability of legal acts detrimental to creditors under the general law of insolvency of the United Kingdom, as referred to in regulation 37(3)(m).

[3878]

NOTES
Commencement: 18 February 2004.

---

44   Regulated markets

(1)   Without prejudice to regulation 40, the effects of a relevant reorganisation measure or winding up on the rights and obligations of the parties to a regulated market operating in an EEA State must be determined in accordance with the law applicable to that market.

PART III
STATUTORY INSTRUMENTS

(2)   Paragraph (1) does not preclude actions for voidness, voidability or unenforceability of legal acts detrimental to creditors under the general law of insolvency of the United Kingdom, as referred to in regulation 37(3)(m).

(3)   For the purposes of this regulation, "regulated market" has the meaning given by [Article 4.1.14 of Directive 2004/39/EC of the European Parliament and of the Council of 21 April 2004 on markets in financial instruments].

[3879]

NOTES
Commencement: 18 February 2004.
Para (3): words in square brackets substituted by the Financial Services and Markets Act 2000 (Markets in Financial Instruments) Regulations 2007, SI 2007/126, reg 3(6), Sch 6, Pt 2, para 17, as from 1 November 2007 (for the full commencement details of SI 2007/126, see reg 1 of those Regulations at **[4051]**).

45   Detrimental acts pursuant to the law of an EEA State

(1)   In a relevant reorganisation or a relevant winding up, the rules relating to detrimental transactions shall not apply where a person who has benefited from a legal act detrimental to all the creditors provides proof that—

(a)   the said act is subject to the law of an EEA State; and

(b)   that law does not allow any means of challenging that act in the relevant case.

(2)   For the purposes of paragraph (1), "the rules relating to detrimental transactions" means any provisions of the general law of insolvency relating to the voidness, voidability or unenforceability of legal acts detrimental to all the creditors, as referred to in regulation 37(3)(m).

[3880]

NOTES
Commencement: 18 February 2004.

46   Protection of third party purchasers

(1)   This regulation applies where, by an act concluded after the opening of a relevant reorganisation or a relevant winding up, an affected insurer disposes for a consideration of—

(a)   an immovable asset situated within the territory of an EEA State;

(b)   a ship or an aircraft subject to registration in a public register kept under the authority of an EEA State; or

(c)   securities whose existence or transfer presupposes entry into a register or account laid down by the law of an EEA State or which are placed in a central deposit system governed by the law of an EEA State.

(2)   The validity of that act is to be determined in accordance with the law of the EEA State within whose territory the immovable asset is situated or under whose authority the register, account or system is kept, as the case may be.

[3881]

NOTES
Commencement: 18 February 2004.

47   Lawsuits pending

(1)   The effects of a relevant reorganisation or a relevant winding up on a relevant lawsuit pending in an EEA State shall be determined solely in accordance with the law of that EEA State.

(2)   In paragraph (1), "relevant lawsuit" means a lawsuit concerning an asset or right of which the affected insurer has been divested.

[3882]

NOTES
Commencement: 18 February 2004.

PART VI
THIRD COUNTRY INSURERS

48   Interpretation of this Part

(1)   In this Part—

(a)   "relevant measure", in relation to a third country insurer, means

(i)   a winding up;

(ii)   an administration order made under paragraph 13 of Schedule B1 [or under paragraph 14 of Schedule B1 to the 1989 Order]; or

      (iii)   a decision of the court to reduce the value of one or more of the insurer's contracts, in accordance with section 377 of the 2000 Act;

  (b)   "third country insurer" means a person—

      (i)   who has permission under the 2000 Act to effect or carry out contracts of insurance; and

      (ii)   whose head office is not in the United Kingdom or an EEA State.

(2)   In paragraph (1), the definition of "third country insurer" must be read with—

  (a)   section 22 of the 2000 Act;

  (b)   any relevant order made under that section; and

  (c)   Schedule 2 to that Act.

[3883]

NOTES
Commencement: 18 February 2004.
Para (1): words in square brackets in sub-para (a)(ii) inserted by the Insurers (Reorganisation and Winding Up) (Amendment) Regulations 2007, SI 2007/851, reg 2(1), (17), as from 6 April 2007.

49   Application of these Regulations to a third country insurer

Parts III, IV and V of these Regulations apply where a third country insurer is subject to a relevant measure, as if references in those Parts to a UK insurer included a reference to a third country insurer.

[3884]

NOTES
Commencement: 18 February 2004.

50   Disclosure of confidential information: third country insurers

(1)   This regulation applies to information ("insolvency practitioner information") which—

  (a)   relates to the business or other affairs of any person; and

  (b)   is information of a kind mentioned in paragraph (2).

(2)   Information falls within paragraph (1)(b) if it is supplied to—

  (a)   the Authority by an EEA regulator; or

  (b)   an insolvency practitioner by an EEA administrator or liquidator,

in accordance with or pursuant to Article 30 of the reorganisation and winding up directive.

(3)   Subject to paragraphs (4), (5) and (6), sections 348, 349 and 352 of the 2000 Act apply in relation to insolvency practitioner information in the same way as they apply in relation to confidential information within the meaning of section 348(2) of that Act.

(4)   For the purposes of this regulation, sections 348, 349 and 352 of the 2000 Act and the Disclosure Regulations have effect as if the primary recipients specified in subsection (5) of section 348 of the 2000 Act included an insolvency practitioner.

(5)   Insolvency practitioner information is not subject to the restrictions on disclosure imposed by section 348(1) of the 2000 Act (as it applies by virtue of paragraph (3)) if it satisfies any of the criteria set out in section 348(4) of the 2000 Act.

(6)   The Disclosure Regulations apply in relation to insolvency practitioner information as they apply in relation to single market directive information (within the meaning of those Regulations).

(7)   In this regulation—

"the Disclosure Regulations" means the Financial Services and Markets Act 2000 (Disclosure of Confidential Information) Regulations 2001;

"EEA administrator" and "EEA liquidator" mean respectively an administrator or liquidator within the meaning of the reorganisation and winding up directive;

"insolvency practitioner" means an insolvency practitioner, within the meaning of section 388 of the 1986 Act or Article 3 of the 1989 Order, who is appointed or acts in relation to a third country insurer.

[3885]

NOTES
Commencement: 18 February 2004.

PART III
STATUTORY INSTRUMENTS

PART VII
REVOCATION AND AMENDMENTS

51, 52   (*Reg 51 amends the Insurers (Winding Up) Rules 2001, SI 2001/3635, r 24 at* **[2619]**, *and the Insurers (Winding Up) (Scotland) Rules 2001, SI 2001/4040, r 24; reg 52 amends the Financial Services and Markets Act 2000 (Administration Orders Relating to Insurers) Order 2002, SI 2002/1242, reg 3 at* **[2670]**.)

53   Revocation and Transitional

   (1)   Except as provided in this regulation, the Insurers (Reorganisation and Winding Up) Regulations 2003 are revoked.

   (2)   Subject to (3), the provisions of Parts III and IV shall continue in force in respect of decisions orders or appointments referred to therein and made before the coming into force of these Regulations.

   (3)   Where an administrator has been appointed in respect of a UK insurer on or after 15th September 2003, he shall be treated as being so appointed on the date these regulations come into force.

[3886]–[3889]

NOTES
Commencement: 18 February 2004.

CREDIT INSTITUTIONS (REORGANISATION AND WINDING UP) REGULATIONS 2004

(SI 2004/1045)

NOTES
Made: 1 April 2004.
Authority: European Communities Act 1972, s 2.
Commencement: 5 May 2004.
These Regulations are reproduced as amended by: the Capital Requirements Regulations 2006, SI 2006/3221; the Financial Services (EEA State) Regulations 2007, SI 2007/108; the Financial Services and Markets Act 2000 (Markets in Financial Instruments) Regulations 2007, SI 2007/126; the Credit Institutions (Reorganisation and Winding Up) (Amendment) Regulations 2007, SI 2007/830.

ARRANGEMENT OF REGULATIONS

PART 1
GENERAL

PART 2
INSOLVENCY MEASURES AND PROCEEDINGS: JURISDICTION IN RELATION TO
CREDIT INSTITUTIONS

PART 3
MODIFICATIONS OF THE LAW OF INSOLVENCY: NOTIFICATION AND PUBLICATION

PART 4
REORGANISATION OR WINDING UP OF UK CREDIT INSTITUTIONS:
RECOGNITION OF EEA RIGHTS

PART 5
THIRD COUNTRY CREDIT INSTITUTIONS

PART 1
GENERAL

1 Citation and commencement

These Regulations may be cited as the Credit Institutions (Reorganisation and Winding up) Regulations 2004, and come into force on 5th May 2004.

[3889A]

NOTES

Commencement: 5 May 2004.

2 Interpretation

(1)   In these Regulations—
"the 1985 Act" means the Companies Act 1985;
"the 1986 Act" means the Insolvency Act 1986;
"the 2000 Act" means the Financial Services and Markets Act 2000;
"the 1989 Order" means the Insolvency (Northern Ireland) Order 1989;
"administrator" has the meaning given by paragraph 13 of Schedule B1 to the 1986 Act[, paragraph 14 of Schedule B1 to the 1989 Order,] section 8(2) of the 1986 Act [or Article 21(2) of the 1989 Order] as the case may be;
"Article 418 compromise or arrangement" means a compromise or arrangement sanctioned by the court in relation to a UK credit institution under Article 418 of the Companies Order, but does not include a compromise or arrangement falling within Article 420 or Article 420A of that Order (reconstructions or amalgamations);
"the Authority" means the Financial Services Authority;
["banking consolidation directive" means Directive 2006/48/EC of the European Parliament and of the Council of 14 June 2006 relating to the taking up and pursuit of the business of credit institutions;]
"branch", in relation to an EEA or UK credit institution has the meaning given by [Article 4(3)] of the banking consolidation directive;
"claim" means a claim submitted by a creditor of a UK credit institution in the course of—
    (a)   a winding up,
    (b)   an administration, or
    (c)   a voluntary arrangement,
with a view to recovering his debt in whole or in part, and includes a proof, within the meaning of rule 2.72 of the Insolvency Rules, or a proof of debt within the meaning of rule 4.73(4) of

PART III
STATUTORY INSTRUMENTS

the Insolvency Rules or Rule 4.079(4) of the Insolvency Rules (Northern Ireland), as the case may be, or in Scotland a claim made in accordance with rule 4.15 of the Insolvency (Scotland) Rules;

"the Companies Order" means the Companies (Northern Ireland) Order 1986;

"creditors' voluntary winding up" has the meaning given by section 90 of the 1986 Act or Article 76 of the 1989 Order as the case may be;

"debt"—

(a) in relation to a winding up or administration of a UK credit institution, has the meaning given by rule 13.12 of the Insolvency Rules or Article 5(1) of the 1989 Order except that where the credit institution is not a company, references in rule 13.12 or Article 5(1) to a company are to be read as references to the credit institution, and

(b) in a case where a voluntary arrangement has effect, in relation to a UK credit institution, means a debt which would constitute a debt in relation to the winding up of that credit institution, except that references in paragraph (1) of rule 13.12 or paragraph (1) of Article 5 of the 1989 Order to the date on which the company goes into liquidation are to be read as references to the date on which the voluntary arrangement has effect;

(c) in Scotland—

(i) in relation to the winding up of a UK credit institution, shall be interpreted in accordance with Schedule 1 of the Bankruptcy (Scotland) Act 1985 as applied by Chapter 5 of Part 4 of the Insolvency (Scotland) Rules; and

(ii) in a case where a voluntary arrangement has effect in relation to a UK credit institution, means a debt which would constitute a debt in relation to the winding up of that credit institution, except that references in Chapter 5 of Part 4 of the Insolvency (Scotland) Rules to the date of commencement of winding up are to be read as references to the date on which the voluntary arrangement has effect;

"directive reorganisation measure" means a reorganisation measure as defined in Article 2 of the reorganisation and winding up directive which was adopted or imposed on or after the 5th May 2004;

"directive winding-up proceedings" means winding-up proceedings as defined in Article 2 of the reorganisation and winding up directive which were opened on or after the 5th May 2004;

"Disclosure Regulations" means the Financial Services and Markets Act 2000 (Disclosure of Confidential Information) Regulations 2001;

"EEA credit institution" means an EEA undertaking, other than a UK credit institution, of the kind mentioned in [Article 4(1) and (3) and subject to the exclusion of the undertakings referred to in Article 2] of the banking consolidation directive;

"EEA creditor" means a creditor of a UK credit institution who—

(a) in the case of an individual, is ordinarily resident in an EEA State; and

(b) in the case of a body corporate or unincorporated association of persons, has its head office in an EEA State;

"EEA regulator" means a competent authority (within the meaning of [Article 4(4)] of the banking consolidation directive) of an EEA State;

["EEA State" has the meaning given by Schedule 1 to the Interpretation Act 1978;]

"home state regulator", in relation to an EEA credit institution, means the relevant EEA regulator in the EEA State where its head office is located;

"the Insolvency Rules" means the Insolvency Rules 1986;

"the Insolvency Rules (Northern Ireland)" means the Insolvency Rules (Northern Ireland) 1991;

"the Insolvency (Scotland) Rules" means the Insolvency (Scotland) Rules 1986;

"liquidator", except for the purposes of regulation 4, includes any person or body appointed by the administrative or judicial authorities whose task is to administer winding-up proceedings in respect of a UK credit institution which is not a body corporate;

"officer", in relation to a company, has the meaning given by section 744 of the 1985 Act or Article 2 of the Companies Order;

"official language" means a language specified in Article 1 of Council Regulation No 1 of 15 April 1958 determining the languages to be used by the European Economic Community (Regulation 1/58/EEC), most recently amended by paragraph (a) of Part XVIII of Annex I to the Act of Accession 1994 (194 N);

"the reorganisation and winding up directive" means the directive of the European Parliament and of the Council of 4 April 2001 on the reorganisation and winding up of credit institutions (2001/24/EC);

"section 425 compromise or arrangement" means a compromise or arrangement sanctioned by the court in relation to a UK credit institution under section 425 of the 1985 Act, but does not include a compromise or arrangement falling within section 427 or section 427A of that Act (reconstructions or amalgamations);

"supervisor" has the meaning given by section 7 of the 1986 Act or Article 20 of the 1989 Order as the case may be;

"UK credit institution" means an undertaking whose head office is in the United Kingdom with permission under Part 4 of the 2000 Act to accept deposits or to issue electronic money as the case may be but does not include—

    (a)   an undertaking which also has permission under Part 4 of the 2000 Act to effect or carry out contracts of insurance; or

    (b)   a credit union within the meaning of section 1 of the Credit Unions Act 1979;

"voluntary arrangement" means a voluntary arrangement which has effect in relation to a UK credit institution in accordance with section 4A of the 1986 Act or Article 17A of the 1989 Order as the case may be; and

"winding up" means—

    (a)   winding up by the court, or

    (b)   a creditors' voluntary winding up.

(2)   In paragraph (1)—

    (a)   for the purposes of the definition of "directive reorganisation measure", a reorganisation measure is adopted at the time when it is treated as adopted or imposed by the law of the relevant EEA State; and

    (b)   for the purposes of the definition of "directive winding-up proceedings", winding-up proceedings are opened at the time when they are treated as opened by the law of the relevant EEA State,

and in this paragraph "relevant EEA State" means the EEA State under the law of which the reorganisation is adopted or imposed, or the winding-up proceedings are opened, as the case may be.

(3)   In these Regulations, references to the law of insolvency of the United Kingdom include references to every provision made by or under the 1986 Act or the 1989 Order as the case may be; and in relation to partnerships, limited liability partnerships or building societies, references to the law of insolvency or to any provision of the 1986 Act or the 1989 Order are to that law as modified by the Insolvent Partnerships Order 1994, the Insolvent Partnerships Order (Northern Ireland) 1995, the Limited Liability Partnerships Regulations 2001[, the Limited Liability Partnerships Regulations (Northern Ireland) 2004] or the Building Societies Act 1986 (as the case may be).

(4)   References in these Regulations to "accepting deposits" and a "contract of insurance" must be read with—

    (a)   section 22 of the 2000 Act;

    (b)   any relevant order made under that section; and

    (c)   Schedule 2 to that Act.

(5)   For the purposes of the 2000 Act, functions imposed or falling on the Authority under these Regulations shall be deemed to be functions under the 2000 Act.

[3889B]

NOTES

Commencement: 5 May 2004.

Para (1) is amended as follows:

Words in first pair of square brackets in definition "administrator" substituted, and words in second pair of square brackets inserted, by the Credit Institutions (Reorganisation and Winding Up) (Amendment) Regulations 2007, SI 2007/830, reg 2(1), (2), as from 6 April 2007.

Definition "banking consolidation directive" substituted by the Capital Requirements Regulations 2006, SI 2006/3221, reg 29(4), Sch 6, para 17(1), (2)(a), as from 1 January 2007.

Words in square brackets in definitions "branch", "EEA credit institution", and "EEA regulator" substituted by SI 2006/3221, reg 29(4), Sch 6, para 17(1), (2)(b)–(d) as from 1 January 2007.

Definition "EEA State" substituted by the Financial Services (EEA State) Regulations 2007, SI 2007/108, reg 9, as from 13 February 2007.

Para (3): words in square brackets inserted by SI 2007/830, reg 2(1), (3), as from 6 April 2007.

PART 2

INSOLVENCY MEASURES AND PROCEEDINGS: JURISDICTION IN RELATION TO CREDIT INSTITUTIONS

3 Prohibition against winding up etc EEA credit institutions in the United Kingdom

(1)   On or after the relevant date a court in the United Kingdom may not, in relation to an EEA credit institution or any branch of an EEA credit institution—

    (a)   make a winding-up order pursuant to section 221 of the 1986 Act or Article 185 of the 1989 Order;

   (b)   appoint a provisional liquidator;

   (c)   make an administration order.

(2)   Paragraph (1)(a) does not prevent—

   (a)   the court from making a winding-up order on or after the relevant date in relation to an EEA credit institution if—

       (i)   a provisional liquidator was appointed in relation to that credit institution before the relevant date, and

       (ii)   that appointment continues in force until immediately before that winding-up order is made;

   (b)   the winding up of an EEA credit institution on or after the relevant date pursuant to a winding-up order which was made, and has not been discharged, before that date.

(3)   Paragraph (1)(b) does not prevent a provisional liquidator of an EEA credit institution appointed before the relevant date from acting in relation to that credit institution on or after that date.

(4)   Paragraph (1)(c) does not prevent an administrator appointed before the relevant date from acting on or after that date in a case in which the administration order under which he or his predecessor was appointed remains in force after that date.

(5)   On or after the relevant date, an administrator may not, in relation to an EEA credit institution, be appointed under paragraphs 14 or 22 of Schedule B1 [to] the 1986 Act [or paragraphs 15 or 23 of Schedule B1 to the 1989 Order].

(6)   A proposed voluntary arrangement shall not have effect in relation to an EEA credit institution if a decision under section 4 of the 1986 Act or Article 17 of the 1989 Order with respect to the approval of that arrangement was taken on or after the relevant date.

[(7)   An order under section 254 of the Enterprise Act 2002 (application of insolvency law to a foreign company) or under Article 9 of the Insolvency (Northern Ireland) Order 2005 (application of insolvency law to company incorporated outside Northern Ireland) may not provide for any of the following provisions of the 1986 Act or of the 1989 Order to apply in relation to an incorporated EEA credit institution—

   (a)   Part 1 of the 1986 Act or Part 2 of the 1989 Order (company voluntary arrangements);

   (b)   Part 2 of the 1986 Act or Part 3 of the 1989 Order (administration);

   (c)   Chapter 4 of Part 4 of the 1986 Act or chapter 4 of Part 5 of the 1989 Order (creditors' voluntary winding up);

   (d)   Chapter 6 of Part 4 of the 1986 Act (winding up by the Court).]

(8)   In this regulation and regulation 4, "relevant date" means the 5th May 2004.

[3889C]

NOTES

Commencement: 5 May 2004.

Para (5): word in first pair of square brackets substituted, and words in second pair of square brackets, inserted, by the Credit Institutions (Reorganisation and Winding Up) (Amendment) Regulations 2007, SI 2007/830, reg 2(1), (4), as from 6 April 2007.

Para (7): substituted by SI 2007/830, reg 2(1), (5), as from 6 April 2007.

---

4 Schemes of arrangement

(1)   For the purposes of section 425(6)(a) of the 1985 Act or Article 418(5)(a) of the Companies Order, an EEA credit institution or a branch of an EEA credit institution is to be treated as a company liable to be wound up under the 1986 Act or the 1989 Order if it would be liable to be wound up under that Act or Order but for the prohibition in regulation 3(1)(a).

(2)   But a court may not make a relevant order under section 425(2) of the 1985 Act or Article 418(2) of the Companies Order in relation to an EEA credit institution which is subject to a directive reorganisation measure or directive winding-up proceedings, or a branch of an EEA credit institution which is subject to such a measure or proceedings, unless the conditions set out in paragraph (3) are satisfied.

(3)   Those conditions are—

   (a)   the person proposing the section 425 or Article 418 compromise or arrangement ("the proposal") has given—

       (i)   the administrator or liquidator, and

       (ii)   the relevant administrative or judicial authority,

   reasonable notice of the details of that proposal; and

   (b)   no person notified in accordance with sub-paragraph (a) has objected to the proposal.

(4)   Nothing in this regulation invalidates a compromise or arrangement which was sanctioned by the court by an order made before the relevant date.

(5)   For the purposes of paragraph (2), a relevant order means an order sanctioning a section 425 or Article 418 compromise or arrangement which—

(a)   is intended to enable the credit institution, and the whole or any part of its undertaking, to survive as a going concern and which affects the rights of persons other than the credit institution or its contributories; or

(b)   includes among its purposes a realisation of some or all of the assets of the EEA credit institution to which the order relates and the distribution of the proceeds to creditors, with a view to terminating the whole or any part of the business of that credit institution.

(6)   For the purposes of this regulation—

(a)   "administrator" means an administrator, as defined by Article 2 of the reorganisation and winding up directive, who is appointed in relation to the EEA credit institution in relation to which the proposal is made;

(b)   "liquidator" means a liquidator, as defined by Article 2 of the reorganisation and winding up directive, who is appointed in relation to the EEA credit institution in relation to which the proposal is made;

(c)   "administrative or judicial authority" means the administrative or judicial authority, as defined by Article 2 of the reorganisation and winding up directive, which is competent for the purposes of the directive reorganisation measure or directive winding-up proceedings mentioned in paragraph (2).

[3889D]

NOTES

Commencement: 5 May 2004.

5   Reorganisation measures and winding-up proceedings in respect of EEA credit institutions effective in the United Kingdom

(1)   An EEA insolvency measure has effect in the United Kingdom in relation to—

(a)   any branch of an EEA credit institution,

(b)   any property or other assets of that credit institution,

(c)   any debt or liability of that credit institution,

as if it were part of the general law of insolvency of the United Kingdom.

(2)   Subject to paragraph (4)—

(a)   a competent officer who satisfies the condition mentioned in paragraph (3); or

(b)   a qualifying agent appointed by a competent officer who satisfies the condition mentioned in paragraph (3),

may exercise in the United Kingdom, in relation to the EEA credit institution which is subject to an EEA insolvency measure, any function which, pursuant to that measure, he is entitled to exercise in relation to that credit institution in the relevant EEA State.

(3)   The condition mentioned in paragraph (2) is that the appointment of the competent officer is evidenced—

(a)   by a certified copy of the order or decision by a judicial or administrative authority in the relevant EEA State by or under which the competent officer was appointed; or

(b)   by any other certificate issued by the judicial or administrative authority which has jurisdiction in relation to the EEA insolvency measure,

and accompanied by a certified translation of that order, decision or certificate (as the case may be).

(4)   In exercising the functions of the kind mentioned in paragraph (2), the competent officer or qualifying agent—

(a)   may not take any action which would constitute an unlawful use of force in the part of the United Kingdom in which he is exercising those functions;

(b)   may not rule on any dispute arising from a matter falling within Part 4 of these Regulations which is justiciable by a court in the part of the United Kingdom in which he is exercising those functions; and

(c)   notwithstanding the way in which functions may be exercised in the relevant EEA State, must act in accordance with relevant laws or rules as to procedure which have effect in the part of the United Kingdom in which he is exercising those functions.

(5)   For the purposes of paragraph (4)(c), "relevant laws or rules as to procedure" means—

(a)   requirements as to consultation with or notification of employees of an EEA credit institution;

(b)   law and procedures relevant to the realisation of assets;

(c)   where the competent officer is bringing or defending legal proceedings in the name of, or on behalf of an EEA credit institution, the relevant rules of court.

(6)   In this regulation—

"competent officer" means a person appointed under or in connection with an EEA insolvency measure for the purpose of administering that measure;

PART III
STATUTORY INSTRUMENTS

"qualifying agent" means an agent validly appointed (whether in the United Kingdom or elsewhere) by a competent officer in accordance with the relevant law in the relevant EEA State;

"EEA insolvency measure" means, as the case may be, a directive reorganisation measure or directive winding-up proceedings which have effect in relation to an EEA credit institution by virtue of the law of the relevant EEA State;

"relevant EEA State", in relation to an EEA credit institution, means the EEA State in which that credit institution has been authorised in accordance with [Article 6] of the banking consolidation directive.

[3889E]

NOTES
Commencement: 5 May 2004.
Para (6): words in square brackets in definition "relevant EEA State" substituted by the Capital Requirements Regulations 2006, SI 2006/3221, reg 29(4), Sch 6, para 17(1), (3), as from 1 January 2007.

6 Confirmation by the court of a creditors' voluntary winding up

(1) Rule 7.62 of the Insolvency Rules or Rule 7.56 of the Insolvency Rules (Northern Ireland) applies in relation to a UK credit institution with the modification specified in paragraph (2) or (3).

(2) For the purposes of this regulation, rule 7.62 has effect as if there were substituted for paragraph (1)—

"(1) Where a UK credit institution (within the meaning of the Credit Institutions (Reorganisation and Winding up) Regulations 2004) has passed a resolution for voluntary winding up, and no declaration under section 89 has been made, the liquidator may apply to court for an order confirming the creditors' voluntary winding up for the purposes of Articles 10 and 28 of directive 2001/24/EC of the European Parliament and of the Council of 4 April 2001 on the reorganisation and winding up of credit institutions.".

(3) For the purposes of this regulation, Rule 7.56 of the Insolvency Rules (Northern Ireland) has effect as if there were substituted for paragraph (1)—

"(1) Where a UK credit institution (within the meaning of the Credit Institutions (Reorganisation and Winding up) Regulations 2004) has passed a resolution for voluntary winding up, and no declaration under Article 75 has been made, the liquidator may apply to court for an order confirming the creditors' voluntary winding up for the purposes of Articles 10 and 28 of directive 2001/24/EC of the European Parliament and of the Council of 4 April 2001 on the reorganisation and winding up of credit institutions.".

[3889F]

NOTES
Commencement: 5 May 2004.

PART 3
MODIFICATIONS OF THE LAW OF INSOLVENCY: NOTIFICATION AND PUBLICATION

7 Modifications of the law of insolvency

The general law of insolvency has effect in relation to UK credit institutions subject to the provisions of this Part.

[3889G]

NOTES
Commencement: 5 May 2004.

8 Consultation of the Authority prior to a voluntary winding up

(1) Where, on or after 5th May 2004, a UK credit institution ("the institution") intends to pass a resolution to wind up the institution under paragraph (b) or (c) of section 84(1) of the 1986 Act or sub-paragraph (b) or (c) of Article 70(1) of the 1989 Order, the institution must give written notice of the resolution to the Authority before it passes the resolution.

(2) Where notice is given under paragraph (1), the resolution may be passed only after the end of the period of five business days beginning with the day on which the notice was given.

[3889H]

NOTES
Commencement: 5 May 2004.

9 Notification of relevant decision to the Authority

(1) Where on or after 5th May 2004 the court makes a decision, order or appointment of any of the following kinds—

   (a)   an administration order under paragraph 13 of Schedule B1 to the 1986 Act[, paragraph 14 of Schedule B1 to the 1989 Order,] section 8(1) of the 1986 Act [or Article 21(1) of the 1989 Order];

   (b)   a winding-up order under section 125 of the 1986 Act or Article 105 of the 1989 Order;

   (c)   the appointment of a provisional liquidator under section 135(1) of the 1986 Act or Article 115(1) of the 1989 Order;

   (d)   the appointment of an administrator in an interim order under paragraph 13(1)(d) of Schedule B1 to the 1986 Act[, paragraph 14(1)(d) of Schedule B1 to the 1989 Order, section 9(4) of the 1986 Act] or Article 22(4) of the 1989 Order,

it must immediately inform the Authority, or cause the Authority to be informed, of the order or appointment which has been made.

(2) Where a decision with respect to the approval of a voluntary arrangement has effect, and the arrangement which is the subject of that decision is a qualifying arrangement, the supervisor must forthwith inform the Authority of the arrangement which has been approved.

(3) Where a liquidator is appointed as mentioned in section 100 of the 1986 Act, paragraph 83 of Schedule B1 to the 1986 Act[, paragraph 84 of Schedule B1 to the 1989 Order] or Article 86 of the 1989 Order (appointment of liquidator in a creditors' voluntary winding up), the liquidator must inform the Authority forthwith of his appointment.

(4) Where in the case of a members' voluntary winding up, section 95 of the 1986 Act (effect of company's insolvency) or Article 81 of the 1989 Order applies, the liquidator must inform the Authority forthwith that he is of that opinion.

(5) Paragraphs (1), (2) and (3) do not apply in any case where the Authority was represented at all hearings in connection with the application in relation to which the order or appointment is made.

(6) For the purposes of paragraph (2), a "qualifying arrangement" means a voluntary arrangement which—

   (a)   varies the rights of creditors as against the credit institution and is intended to enable the credit institution, and the whole or any part of its undertaking, to survive as a going concern; or

   (b)   includes a realisation of some or all of the assets of the credit institution, with a view to terminating the whole or any part of the business of that credit institution.

(7) A supervisor, administrator or liquidator who fails without reasonable excuse to comply with paragraph (2), (3), or (4) (as the case may be) commits an offence and is liable on summary conviction to a fine not exceeding level 3 on the standard scale.

[3889I]

NOTES

Commencement: 5 May 2004.

Para (1): words in first pair of square brackets in sub-para (a) substituted, words in second pair of square brackets in that sub-paragraph inserted, and words in square brackets in sub-para (d) inserted, by the Credit Institutions (Reorganisation and Winding Up) (Amendment) Regulations 2007, SI 2007/830, reg 2(1), (6), as from 6 April 2007.

Para (3): words in square brackets inserted by SI 2007/830, reg 2(1), (7), as from 6 April 2007.

10 Notification to EEA regulators

(1) Where the Authority is informed of a decision, order or appointment in accordance with regulation 9, the Authority must as soon as is practicable inform the relevant person—

   (a)   that the decision, order or appointment has been made; and

   (b)   in general terms, of the possible effect of a decision, order or appointment of that kind on the business of a credit institution.

(2) Where the Authority has been represented at all hearings in connection with the application in relation to which the decision, order or appointment has been made, the Authority must inform the relevant person of the matters mentioned in paragraph (1) as soon as is practicable after that decision, order or appointment has been made.

(3) Where, on or after 5th May 2004, it appears to the Authority that a directive reorganisation measure should be adopted in relation to or imposed on an EEA credit institution which has a branch in the United Kingdom, it will inform the home state regulator as soon as is practicable.

(4) In this regulation, the "relevant person" means the EEA regulator of any EEA State in which the UK credit institution has a branch.

[3889J]

NOTES
Commencement: 5 May 2004.

11 Withdrawal of authorisation

(1) For the purposes of this regulation—
  (a) a qualifying decision means a decision with respect to the approval of a voluntary arrangement where the voluntary arrangement includes a realisation of some or all of the assets of the credit institution with a view to terminating the whole or any part of the business of that credit institution;
  (b) a qualifying order means—
    (i) a winding-up order under section 125 of the 1986 Act or Article 105 of the 1989 Order; or
    (ii) an administration order under paragraph 13 of Schedule B1 to the 1986 Act [or paragraph 14 of Schedule B1 to the 1989 Order] in the prescribed circumstances;
  (c) a qualifying appointment means—
    (i) the appointment of a provisional liquidator under section 135(1) of the 1986 Act or Article 115(1) of the 1989 Order; or
    (ii) the appointment of a liquidator as mentioned in section 100 of the 1986 Act, Article 86 of the 1989 Order (appointment of liquidator in a creditors' voluntary winding up) or paragraph 83 of Schedule B1 to the 1986 Act [or paragraph 84 of Schedule B1 to the 1989 Order] (moving from administration to creditors' voluntary liquidation).

(2) The prescribed circumstances are where, after the appointment of an administrator, the administrator concludes that it is not reasonably practicable to achieve the objective specified in paragraph 3(1)(a) of Schedule B1 to the 1986 Act [or paragraph 4(1)(a) of Schedule B1 to the 1989 Order].

(3) When the Authority is informed of a qualifying decision, qualifying order or qualifying appointment, the Authority will as soon as reasonably practicable exercise its power under section 45 of the 2000 Act to vary or to cancel the UK credit institution's permission under Part 4 of that Act to accept deposits or to issue electronic money as the case may be.

[3889K]

NOTES
Commencement: 5 May 2004.
Paras (1), (2): words in square brackets inserted by the Credit Institutions (Reorganisation and Winding Up) (Amendment) Regulations 2007, SI 2007/830, reg 2(1), (8), (9), as from 6 April 2007.

12 Publication of voluntary arrangement, administration order, winding-up order or scheme of arrangement

(1) This regulation applies where a qualifying decision is approved, or a qualifying order or qualifying appointment is made, in relation to a UK credit institution on or after 5th May 2004.

(2) For the purposes of this regulation—
  (a) a qualifying decision means a decision with respect to the approval of a proposed voluntary arrangement, in accordance with section 4A of the 1986 Act or Article 17A of the 1989 Order;
  (b) a qualifying order means—
    (i) an administration order under paragraph 13 of Schedule B1 to the 1986 Act[, paragraph 14 of Schedule B1 to the 1989 Order,] section 8(1) of the 1986 Act [or Article 21(1) of the 1989 Order],
    (ii) an order appointing a provisional liquidator in accordance with section 135 of that Act or Article 115 of that Order, or
    (iii) a winding-up order made by the court under Part 4 of that Act or Part V of the 1989 Order;
  (c) a qualifying appointment means the appointment of a liquidator as mentioned in section 100 of the 1986 Act or Article 86 of the 1989 Order (appointment of liquidator in a creditors' voluntary winding up).

(3) Subject to paragraph (7), as soon as is reasonably practicable after a qualifying decision has effect or a qualifying order or a qualifying appointment has been made, the relevant officer must publish, or cause to be published, in the Official Journal of the European Communities and in 2 national newspapers in each EEA State in which the UK credit institution has a branch the information mentioned in paragraph (4) and (if applicable) paragraphs (5) or (6).

(4) That information is—
  (a) a summary of the terms of the qualifying decision, qualifying appointment or the provisions of the qualifying order (as the case may be);

    (b)   the identity of the relevant officer;

    (c)   the statutory provisions in accordance with which the qualifying decision has effect or the qualifying order or appointment has been made or takes effect.

(5)   In the case of a qualifying appointment, that information includes the court to which an application under section 112 of the 1986 Act (reference of questions to the court) … or Article 98 of the 1989 Order (reference of questions to the High Court) may be made.

(6)   In the case of a qualifying decision, that information includes the court to which an application under section 6 of the 1986 Act or Article 19 of the 1989 Order (challenge of decisions) may be made.

(7)   Paragraph (3) does not apply where a qualifying decision or qualifying order falling within paragraph (2)(b)(i) affects the interests only of the members, or any class of members, or employees of the credit institution (in their capacity as members or employees).

(8)   This regulation is without prejudice to any requirement to publish information imposed upon a relevant officer under any provision of the general law of insolvency.

(9)   A relevant officer who fails to comply with paragraph (3) of this regulation commits an offence and is liable on summary conviction to a fine not exceeding level 3 on the standard scale.

(10)   A qualifying decision, qualifying order or qualifying appointment is not invalid or ineffective if the relevant official fails to comply with paragraph (3) of this regulation.

(11)   In this regulation, "relevant officer" means—

    (a)   in the case of a voluntary arrangement, the supervisor;

    (b)   in the case of an administration order, the administrator;

    (c)   in the case of a creditors' voluntary winding up, the liquidator;

    (d)   in the case of winding-up order, the liquidator; or

    (e)   in the case of an order appointing a provisional liquidator, the provisional liquidator.

(12)   The information to be published in accordance with paragraph (3) of this regulation shall be—

    (a)   in the case of the Official Journal of the European Communities, in the official language or languages of each EEA State in which the UK credit institution has a branch;

    (b)   in the case of the national newspapers of each EEA State in which the UK credit institution has a branch, in the official language or languages of that EEA State.

[3889L]

NOTES

Commencement: 5 May 2004.

Para (2): words in first pair of square brackets in sub-para (b)(i) substituted, and words in second pair of square brackets in that sub-paragraph inserted, by the Credit Institutions (Reorganisation and Winding Up) (Amendment) Regulations 2007, SI 2007/830, reg 2(1), (10), as from 6 April 2007.

Para (5): words omitted revoked by SI 2007/830, reg 2(1), (11), as from 6 April 2007.

---

13   Honouring of certain obligations

(1)   This regulation applies where, on or after 5th May 2004, a relevant obligation has been honoured for the benefit of a relevant credit institution by a relevant person.

(2)   Where a person has honoured a relevant obligation for the benefit of a relevant credit institution, he shall be deemed to have discharged that obligation if he was unaware of the winding up of that credit institution.

(3)   For the purposes of this regulation—

    (a)   a relevant obligation is an obligation which, after the commencement of the winding up of a relevant credit institution, should have been honoured for the benefit of the liquidator of that credit institution;

    (b)   a relevant credit institution is a UK credit institution which—

        (i)   is not a body corporate; and

        (ii)   is the subject of a winding up;

    (c)   a relevant person is a person who at the time the obligation is honoured—

        (i)   is in the territory of an EEA State; and

        (ii)   is unaware of the winding up of the relevant credit institution.

(4)   For the purposes of paragraph (3)(c)(ii) of this regulation—

    (a)   a relevant person shall be presumed, in the absence of evidence to the contrary, to have been unaware of the winding up of a relevant credit institution where the relevant obligation was honoured before date of the publication provided for in regulation 12 in relation to that winding up;

    (b)   a relevant person shall be presumed, in the absence of evidence to the contrary, to have been aware of the winding up of the relevant credit institution where the relevant

PART III
STATUTORY INSTRUMENTS

obligation was honoured on or after the date of the publication provided for in regulation 12 in relation to that winding up.

[3889M]

NOTES
Commencement: 5 May 2004.

14 Notification to creditors: winding-up proceedings

(1)   When a relevant order or appointment is made, or a relevant decision is taken, in relation to a UK credit institution on or after 5th May 2004, the appointed officer must, as soon as is reasonably practicable, notify in writing all known creditors of that credit institution—
    (a)   of the matters mentioned in paragraph (4); and
    (b)   of the matters mentioned in paragraph (5).

(2)   The appointed officer may comply with the requirement in paragraphs (1)(a) and the requirement in paragraph (1)(b) by separate notifications.

(3)   For the purposes of this regulation—
    (a)   "relevant order" means—
        (i)   an administration order under paragraph 13 of Schedule B1 to the 1986 Act [or paragraph 14 of Schedule B1 to the 1989 Order] in the prescribed circumstances or an administration order made for the purposes set out in section 8(3)(b) or (d) of the 1986 Act [or Article 21(3) (b) or (d) of the 1989 Order], as the case may be,
        (ii)   a winding-up order under section 125 of the 1986 Act (powers of the court on hearing a petition) or Article 105 of the 1989 Order (powers of High Court on hearing of petition),
        (iii)   the appointment of a liquidator in accordance with section 138 of the 1986 Act (appointment of a liquidator in Scotland), or
        (iv)   an order appointing a provisional liquidator in accordance with section 135 of that Act or Article 115 of the 1989 Order;
    (b)   a "relevant appointment" means the appointment of a liquidator as mentioned in section 100 of the 1986 Act or Article 86 of the 1989 Order (appointment of liquidator in a creditors' voluntary winding up); and
    (c)   a "relevant decision" means a decision as a result of which a qualifying voluntary arrangement has effect.

(4)   The matters which must be notified to all known creditors in accordance with paragraph (1)(a) are as follows—
    (a)   that a relevant order or appointment has been made, or a relevant decision taken, in relation to the UK credit institution; and
    (b)   the date from which that order, appointment or decision has effect.

(5)   The matters which must be notified to all known creditors in accordance with paragraph (1)(b) are as follows—
    (a)   if applicable, the date by which a creditor must submit his claim in writing;
    (b)   the matters which must be stated in a creditor's claim;
    (c)   details of any category of debt in relation to which a claim is not required;
    (d)   the person to whom any such claim or any observations on a claim must be submitted; and
    (e)   the consequences of any failure to submit a claim by any specified deadline.

(6)   Where a creditor is notified in accordance with paragraph (1)(b), the notification must be headed with the words "Invitation to lodge a claim. Time limits to be observed", and that heading must be given in every official language.

(7)   The obligation under paragraph (1)(b) may be discharged by sending a form of proof in accordance with rule 4.74 of the Insolvency Rules, Rule 4.080 of the Insolvency Rules (Northern Ireland) or Rule 4.15(2) of the (Insolvency) Scotland Rules as applicable in cases where any of those rules applies, provided that the form of proof complies with paragraph (6).

[(8)   The prescribed circumstances are where the administrator includes in the statement required under Rule 2.3 of the Insolvency Rules or under Rule 2.003 of the Insolvency Rules (Northern Ireland) a statement to the effect that the objective set out in paragraph 3(1)(a) of Schedule B1 to the 1986 Act or in paragraph 4(1)(a) of Schedule B1 to the 1989 Order is not reasonably likely to be achieved.]

(9)   Where, after the appointment of an administrator, the administrator concludes that it is not reasonably practicable to achieve the objective specified in paragraph 3(1)(a) of Schedule B1 to the 1986 Act [or paragraph 4(1)(a) of Schedule B1 to the 1989 Order], he shall inform the court and the Authority in writing of that conclusion and upon so doing the order by which he was appointed shall be a relevant order for the purposes of this regulation and the obligation under paragraph (1) shall apply as from the date on which he so informs the court and the Authority.

(10)   An appointed officer commits an offence if he fails without reasonable excuse to comply with a requirement under paragraph (1) of this regulation, and is liable on summary conviction to a fine not exceeding level 3 on the standard scale.

(11)   For the purposes of this regulation—
- (a)   "appointed officer" means—
  - (i)   in the case of a relevant order falling within paragraph (3)(a)(i), the administrator,
  - (ii)   in the case of a relevant order falling within paragraph (3)(a)(ii) or (iii) or a relevant appointment falling within paragraph (3)(b), the liquidator,
  - (iii)   in the case of a relevant order falling within paragraph (3)(a)(iv), the provisional liquidator, or
  - (iv)   in the case of a relevant decision, the supervisor; and
- (b)   a creditor is a "known" creditor if the appointed officer is aware of—
  - (i)   his identity,
  - (ii)   his claim or potential claim, and
  - (iii)   a recent address where he is likely to receive a communication.

(12)   For the purposes of paragraph (3), a voluntary arrangement is a qualifying voluntary arrangement if its purposes include a realisation of some or all of the assets of the UK credit institution to which the order relates with a view to terminating the whole or any part of the business of that credit institution.

[3889N]

NOTES
Commencement: 5 May 2004.
Paras (3), (9): words in square brackets inserted by the Credit Institutions (Reorganisation and Winding Up) (Amendment) Regulations 2007, SI 2007/830, reg 2(1), (12)(a), (c), as from 6 April 2007.
Para (8): substituted by SI 2007/830, reg 2(1), (12)(b), as from 6 April 2007.

15   Submission of claims by EEA creditors

(1)   An EEA creditor who, on or after 5th May 2004, submits a claim or observations relating to his claim in any relevant proceedings (irrespective of when those proceedings were commenced or had effect) may do so in his domestic language, provided that the requirements in paragraphs (3) and (4) are complied with.

(2)   For the purposes of this regulation, "relevant proceedings" means—
- (a)   a winding up;
- (b)   a qualifying voluntary arrangement; or
- (c)   administration.

(3)   Where an EEA creditor submits a claim in his domestic language, the document must be headed with the words "Lodgement of claim" (in English).

(4)   Where an EEA creditor submits observations on his claim (otherwise than in the document by which he submits his claim), the observations must be headed with the words "Submission of observations relating to claims" (in English).

(5)   Paragraph (3) does not apply where an EEA creditor submits his claim using—
- (a)   in the case of a winding up, a form of proof supplied by the liquidator in accordance with rule 4.74 of the Insolvency Rules, Rule 4.080 of the Insolvency Rules (Northern Ireland) or rule 4.15(2) of the Insolvency (Scotland) Rules;
- (b)   in the case of a qualifying voluntary arrangement, a form approved by the court for that purpose.

(6)   In this regulation—
- (a)   "domestic language", in relation to an EEA creditor, means the official language, or one of the official languages, of the EEA State in which he is ordinarily resident or, if the creditor is not an individual, in which the creditor's head office is located; and
- (b)   "qualifying voluntary arrangement" means a voluntary arrangement whose purposes include a realisation of some or all of the assets of the UK credit institution to which the order relates with a view to terminating the whole or any part of the business of that credit institution.

[3889O]

NOTES
Commencement: 5 May 2004.

16   Reports to creditors

(1)   This regulation applies where, on or after 5th May 2004—
- (a)   a liquidator is appointed in accordance with section 100 of the 1986 Act, Article 86 of [the 1989 Order] (creditors' voluntary winding up: appointment of liquidator) or

paragraph 83 of Schedule B1 to the 1986 Act [or paragraph 84 of Schedule B1 to the 1989 Order] (moving from administration to creditors' voluntary liquidation);

(b) a winding-up order is made by the court;

(c) a provisional liquidator is appointed; or

[(d) an administrator is appointed under paragraph 13 of Schedule B1 to the 1986 Act or paragraph 14 of Schedule B1 to the 1989 Order].

(2) The liquidator, provisional liquidator or administrator (as the case may be) must send a report to every known creditor once in every 12 months beginning with the date when his appointment has effect.

(3) The requirement in paragraph (2) does not apply where a liquidator, provisional liquidator or administrator is required by order of the court to send a report to creditors at intervals which are more frequent than those required by this regulation.

(4) This regulation is without prejudice to any requirement to send a report to creditors, imposed by the court on the liquidator, provisional liquidator or administrator, which is supplementary to the requirements of this regulation.

(5) A liquidator, provisional liquidator or administrator commits an offence if he fails without reasonable excuse to comply with an applicable requirement under this regulation, and is liable on summary conviction to a fine not exceeding level 3 on the standard scale.

(6) For the purposes of this regulation—

(a) "known creditor" means—

(i) a creditor who is known to the liquidator, provisional liquidator or administrator, and

(ii) in a case falling within paragraph (1)(b) or (c), a creditor who is specified in the credit institution's statement of affairs (within the meaning of section 131 of the 1986 Act or Article 111 of the 1989 Order);

(b) "report" means a written report setting out the position generally as regards the progress of the winding up, provisional liquidation or administration (as the case may be).

[3889P]

NOTES

Commencement: 5 May 2004.

Para (1): words in first pair of square brackets in sub-para (a) and the whole of sub-para (d) substituted, and words in second pair of square brackets in sub-para (a) inserted, by the Credit Institutions (Reorganisation and Winding Up) (Amendment) Regulations 2007, SI 2007/830, reg 2(1), (13), as from 6 April 2007.

17 Service of notices and documents

(1) This regulation applies to any notification, report or other document which is required to be sent to a creditor of a UK credit institution by a provision of this Part ("a relevant notification").

(2) A relevant notification may be sent to a creditor by one of the following methods—

(a) by posting it to the proper address of the creditor;

(b) by transmitting it electronically, in accordance with paragraph (4).

(3) For the purposes of paragraph (2)(a), the proper address of a creditor is any current address provided by that person as an address for service of a relevant notification and, if no such address is provided—

(a) the last known address of that creditor (whether his residence or a place where he carries on business);

(b) in the case of a body corporate, the address of its registered or principal office; or

(c) in the case of an unincorporated association, the address of its principal office.

(4) A relevant notification may be transmitted electronically only if it is sent to—

(a) an electronic address notified to the relevant officer by the creditor for this purpose; or

(b) if no such address has been notified, to an electronic address at which the relevant officer reasonably believes the creditor will receive the notification.

(5) Any requirement in this Part to send a relevant notification to a creditor shall also be treated as satisfied if the conditions set out in paragraph (6) are satisfied.

(6) The conditions of this paragraph are satisfied in the case of a relevant notification if—

(a) the creditor has agreed with—

(i) the UK credit institution which is liable under the creditor's claim, or

(ii) the relevant officer,

that information which is required to be sent to him (whether pursuant to a statutory or contractual obligation, or otherwise) may instead be accessed by him on a web site;

(b) the agreement applies to the relevant notification in question;

(c) the creditor is notified of—

(i) the publication of the relevant notification on a web site,

(ii) the address of that web site,

      (iii)   the place on that web site where the relevant notification may be accessed, and how it may be accessed; and

  (d)   the relevant notification is published on that web site throughout a period of at least one month beginning with the date on which the creditor is notified in accordance with sub-paragraph (c).

(7)   Where, in a case in which paragraph (5) is relied on for compliance with a requirement of regulation 14 or 16—

  (a)   a relevant notification is published for a part, but not all, of the period mentioned in paragraph (6)(d) but

  (b)   the failure to publish it throughout that period is wholly attributable to circumstances which it would not be reasonable to have expected the relevant officer to prevent or avoid,

no offence is committed under regulation 14(10) or regulation 16(5) (as the case may be) by reason of that failure.

(8)   In this regulation—

  (a)   "electronic address" includes any number or address used for the purposes of receiving electronic communications which are sent electronically;

  (b)   "electronic communication" means an electronic communication within the meaning of the Electronic Communications Act 2000 the processing of which on receipt is intended to produce writing; and

  (c)   "relevant officer" means (as the case may be) an administrator, liquidator, provisional liquidator or supervisor who is required to send a relevant notification to a creditor by a provision of this Part.

[3889Q]

NOTES
Commencement: 5 May 2004.

18   Disclosure of confidential information received from an EEA regulator

(1)   This regulation applies to information ("insolvency information") which—

  (a)   relates to the business or affairs of any other person; and

  (b)   is supplied to the Authority by an EEA regulator acting in accordance with Articles 4, 5, 9, or 11 of the reorganisation and winding up directive.

(2)   Subject to paragraphs (3) and (4), sections 348, 349 and 352 of the 2000 Act apply in relation to insolvency information as they apply in relation to confidential information within the meaning of section 348(2) of the 2000 Act.

(3)   Insolvency information is not subject to the restrictions on disclosure imposed by section 348(1) of the 2000 Act (as it applies by virtue of paragraph (2)) if it satisfies any of the criteria set out in section 348(4) of the 2000 Act.

(4)   The Disclosure Regulations apply in relation to insolvency information as they apply in relation to single market directive information (within the meaning of those Regulations).

[3889R]

NOTES
Commencement: 5 May 2004.

PART 4
REORGANISATION OR WINDING UP OF UK CREDIT INSTITUTIONS: RECOGNITION OF EEA RIGHTS

19   Application of this Part

(1)   This Part applies as follows—

  (a)   where a decision with respect to the approval of a proposed voluntary arrangement having a qualifying purpose is made under section 4A of the 1986 Act or Article 17A of the 1989 Order on or after 5th May 2004 in relation to a UK credit institution;

  (b)   where an administration order made under paragraph 13 of Schedule B1 to the 1986 Act[, paragraph 14 of Schedule B1 to the 1989 Order,] section 8(1) of the 1986 Act [or Article 21(1) of the 1989 Order] on or after 5th May 2004 is in force in relation to a UK credit institution;

  (c)   where a UK credit institution is subject to a relevant winding up; or

  (d)   where a provisional liquidator is appointed in relation to a UK credit institution on or after 5th May 2004.

(2)   For the purposes of paragraph (1)(a), a voluntary arrangement has a qualifying purpose if it—

(a)   varies the rights of the creditors as against the credit institution and is intended to enable the credit institution, and the whole or any part of its undertaking, to survive as a going concern; or

(b)   includes a realisation of some or all of the assets of the credit institution to which the compromise or arrangement relates, with a view to terminating the whole or any part of the business of that credit institution.

(3)   For the purposes of paragraph (1)(c), a winding up is a relevant winding up if—

(a)   in the case of a winding up by the court, the winding-up order is made on or after 5th May 2004; or

(b)   in the case of a creditors' voluntary winding up, the liquidator is appointed in accordance with section 100 of the 1986 Act, Article 86 of the 1989 Order or paragraph 83 of Schedule B1 to the 1986 Act [or paragraph 84 of Schedule B1 to the 1989 Order] on or after 5th May 2004.

[3889S]

NOTES

Commencement: 5 May 2004.

Para (1): words in first pair of square brackets in sub-para (b) substituted, and words in second pair of square brackets in that sub-paragraph inserted, by the Credit Institutions (Reorganisation and Winding Up) (Amendment) Regulations 2007, SI 2007/830, reg 2(1), (14), as from 6 April 2007.

Para (3): words in square brackets in sub-para (b) inserted by SI 2007/830, reg 2(1), (15), as from 6 April 2007.

20 Application of this Part: assets subject to a section 425 or Article 418 compromise or arrangement

(1)   For the purposes of this Part, the insolvent estate of a UK credit institution shall not include any assets which at the commencement date are subject to a relevant section 425 or Article 418 compromise or arrangement.

(2)   In this regulation—

(a)   "assets" has the same meaning as "property" in section 436 of the 1986 Act or Article 2(2) of the 1989 Order;

(b)   "commencement date" means the date when a UK credit institution goes into liquidation within the meaning given by section 247(2) of the 1986 Act or Article 6(2) of the 1989 Order;

(c)   "insolvent estate" has the meaning given by rule 13.8 of the Insolvency Rules or Rule 0.2 of the Insolvency Rules (Northern Ireland) and in Scotland means the company's assets;

(d)   "relevant section 425 or Article 418 compromise or arrangement" means—

(i)   a section 425 or Article 418 compromise or arrangement which was sanctioned by the court before 5th May 2004, or

(ii)   any subsequent section 425 or Article 418 compromise or arrangement sanctioned by the court to amend or replace a compromise or arrangement of a kind mentioned in paragraph (i).

[3889T]

NOTES

Commencement: 5 May 2004.

21 Interpretation of this Part

(1)   For the purposes of this Part—

(a)   "affected credit institution" means a UK credit institution which is the subject of a relevant reorganisation or winding up;

(b)   "relevant reorganisation" or "relevant winding up" means any voluntary arrangement, administration, winding up, or order referred to in regulation 19(1) to which this Part applies; and

(c)   "relevant time" means the date of the opening of a relevant reorganisation or a relevant winding up.

(2)   In this Part, references to the opening of a relevant reorganisation or a relevant winding up mean—

(a)   in the case of winding-up proceedings—

(i)   in the case of a winding up by the court, the date on which the winding-up order is made, or

(ii)   in the case of a creditors' voluntary winding up, the date on which the liquidator is appointed in accordance with section 100 of the 1986 Act, Article 86 of the 1989 Order or paragraph 83 of Schedule B1 to the 1986 Act [or paragraph 84 of Schedule B1 to the 1989 Order];

(b)   in the case of a voluntary arrangement, the date when a decision with respect to the approval of that voluntary arrangement has effect in accordance with section 4A(2) of the 1986 Act or Article 17A(2) of the 1989 Order;

(c)   in a case where an administration order under paragraph 13 of Schedule B1 to the 1986 Act[, paragraph 14 of Schedule B1 to the 1989 Order,] section 8(1) of the 1986 Act [or Article 21(1) of the 1989 Order] is in force, the date of the making of that order; and

(d)   in a case where a provisional liquidator has been appointed, the date of that appointment,

and references to the time of an opening must be construed accordingly.

[3889U]

NOTES
Commencement: 5 May 2004.
Para (2): words in square brackets in sub-para (a) and words in second pair of square brackets in sub-para (c) inserted, and words in first pair of square brackets in sub-para (c) substituted, by the Credit Institutions (Reorganisation and Winding Up) (Amendment) Regulations 2007, SI 2007/830, reg 2(1), (16), as from 6 April 2007.

22   EEA rights: applicable law in the winding up of a UK credit institution

(1)   This regulation is subject to the provisions of regulations 23 to 35.

(2)   In a relevant winding up, the matters mentioned in paragraph (3) are to be determined in accordance with the general law of insolvency of the United Kingdom.

(3)   Those matters are—
    (a)   the assets which form part of the estate of the affected credit institution;
    (b)   the treatment of assets acquired by the affected credit institution after the opening of the relevant winding up;
    (c)   the respective powers of the affected credit institution and the liquidator or provisional liquidator;
    (d)   the conditions under which set-off may be invoked;
    (e)   the effects of the relevant winding up on current contracts to which the affected credit institution is a party;
    (f)   the effects of the relevant winding up on proceedings brought by creditors;
    (g)   the claims which are to be lodged against the estate of the affected credit institution;
    (h)   the treatment of claims against the affected credit institution arising after the opening of the relevant winding up;
    (i)   the rules governing—
        (i)   the lodging, verification and admission of claims,
        (ii)   the distribution of proceeds from the realisation of assets,
        (iii)   the ranking of claims,
        (iv)   the rights of creditors who have obtained partial satisfaction after the opening of the relevant winding up by virtue of a right in rem or through set-off;
    (j)   the conditions for and the effects of the closure of the relevant winding up, in particular by composition;
    (k)   the rights of creditors after the closure of the relevant winding up;
    (l)   who is to bear the cost and expenses incurred in the relevant winding up;
    (m)   the rules relating to the voidness, voidability or unenforceability of legal acts detrimental to all the creditors.

[3889V]

NOTES
Commencement: 5 May 2004.

23   Employment contracts and relationships

(1)   The effects of a relevant reorganisation or a relevant winding up on EEA employment contracts and EEA employment relationships are to be determined in accordance with the law of the EEA State to which that contract or that relationship is subject.

(2)   In this regulation, an employment contract is an EEA employment contract, and an employment relationship is an EEA employment relationship if it is subject to the law of an EEA State.

[3889W]

NOTES
Commencement: 5 May 2004.

24 Contracts in connection with immovable property

(1)   The effects of a relevant reorganisation or a relevant winding up on a contract conferring the right to make use of or acquire immovable property situated within the territory of an EEA State shall be determined in accordance with the law of that State.

(2)   The law of the EEA State in whose territory the property is situated shall determine whether the property is movable or immovable.

[3889X]

NOTES

Commencement: 5 May 2004.

25 Registrable rights

The effects of a relevant reorganisation or a relevant winding up on rights of the affected UK credit institution with respect to—

(a)   immovable property,

(b)   a ship, or

(c)   an aircraft

which is subject to registration in a public register kept under the authority of an EEA State are to be determined in accordance with the law of that State.

[3889Y]

NOTES

Commencement: 5 May 2004.

26 Third parties' rights in rem

(1)   A relevant reorganisation or a relevant winding up shall not affect the rights in rem of creditors or third parties in respect of tangible or intangible, movable or immovable assets (including both specific assets and collections of indefinite assets as a whole which change from time to time) belonging to the affected credit institution which are situated within the territory of an EEA State at the relevant time.

(2)   The rights in rem referred to in paragraph (1) shall mean—

(a)   the right to dispose of assets or have them disposed of and to obtain satisfaction from the proceeds of or the income from those assets, in particular by virtue of a lien or a mortgage;

(b)   the exclusive right to have a claim met, in particular a right guaranteed by a lien in respect of the claim or by assignment of the claim by way of guarantee;

(c)   the right to demand the assets from, or to require restitution by, any person having possession or use of them contrary to the wishes of the party so entitled;

(d)   a right in rem to the beneficial use of assets.

(3)   A right, recorded in a public register and enforceable against third parties, under which a right in rem within the meaning of paragraph (1) may be obtained, is also to be treated as a right in rem for the purposes of this regulation.

(4)   Paragraph (1) does not preclude actions for voidness, voidability or unenforceability of legal acts detrimental to creditors under the general law of insolvency of the United Kingdom.

[3889Z]

NOTES

Commencement: 5 May 2004.

27 Reservation of title agreements etc

(1)   The adoption of a relevant reorganisation or opening of a relevant winding up in relation to a credit institution purchasing an asset shall not affect the seller's rights based on a reservation of title where at the time of that adoption or opening the asset is situated within the territory of an EEA State.

(2)   The adoption of a relevant reorganisation or opening of a relevant winding up in relation to a credit institution selling an asset, after delivery of the asset, shall not constitute grounds for rescinding or terminating the sale and shall not prevent the purchaser from acquiring title where at the time of that adoption or opening the asset sold is situated within the territory of an EEA State.

(3)   Paragraphs (1) and (2) do not preclude actions for voidness, voidability or unenforceability of legal acts detrimental to creditors under the general law of insolvency of the United Kingdom.

[3889ZA]

NOTES

Commencement: 5 May 2004.

28 Creditors' rights to set off

(1) A relevant reorganisation or a relevant winding up shall not affect the right of creditors to demand the set-off of their claims against the claims of the affected credit institution, where such a set-off is permitted by the law applicable to the affected credit institution's claim.

(2) Paragraph (1) does not preclude actions for voidness, voidability or unenforceability of legal acts detrimental to creditors under the general law of insolvency of the United Kingdom.

[3889ZB]

NOTES
Commencement: 5 May 2004.

29 Regulated markets

(1) Subject to regulation 33, the effects of a relevant reorganisation or winding up on transactions carried out in the context of a regulated market operating in an EEA State must be determined in accordance with the law applicable to those transactions.

(2) For the purposes of this regulation, "regulated market" has the meaning given by the [Article 4.1.14 of Directive 2004/39/EC of the European Parliament and of the Council of 21 April 2004 on markets in financial instruments].

[3889ZC]

NOTES
Commencement: 5 May 2004.
Para (2): words in square brackets substituted by the Financial Services and Markets Act 2000 (Markets in Financial Instruments) Regulations 2007, SI 2007/126, reg 3(6), Sch 6, Pt 2, para 18(1), (2), as from 1 November 2007 (for the full commencement details of SI 2007/126, see reg 1 of those Regulations at **[4051]**).

30 Detrimental acts pursuant to the law of an EEA State

(1) In a relevant reorganisation or a relevant winding up, the rules relating to detrimental transactions shall not apply where a person who has benefited from a legal act detrimental to all the creditors provides proof that—
    (a)   the said act is subject to the law of an EEA State; and
    (b)   that law does not allow any means of challenging that act in the relevant case.

(2) For the purposes of paragraph (1), "the rules relating to detrimental transactions" means any provision of the general law of insolvency relating to the voidness, voidability or unenforceability of legal acts detrimental to all the creditors.

[3889ZD]

NOTES
Commencement: 5 May 2004.

31 Protection of third party purchasers

(1) This regulation applies where, by an act concluded after the adoption of a relevant reorganisation or opening of a relevant winding up, an affected credit institution disposes for a consideration of—
    (a)   an immovable asset situated within the territory of an EEA State;
    (b)   a ship or an aircraft subject to registration in a public register kept under the authority of an EEA State;
    (c)   relevant instruments or rights in relevant instruments whose existence or transfer presupposes entry into a register or account laid down by the law of an EEA State or which are placed in a central deposit system governed by the law of an EEA State.

(2) The validity of that act is to be determined in accordance with the law of the EEA State within whose territory the immoveable asset is situated or under whose authority the register, account or system is kept, as the case may be.

(3) In this regulation, "relevant instruments" means the instruments referred to in [Section C of Annex I to Directive 2004/39/EC of the European Parliament and of the Council of 21 April 2004 on markets in financial instruments].

[3889ZE]

NOTES
Commencement: 5 May 2004.
Para (3): words in square brackets substituted by the Financial Services and Markets Act 2000 (Markets in Financial Instruments) Regulations 2007, SI 2007/126, reg 3(6), Sch 6, Pt 2, para 18(1), (3), as from 1 November 2007 (for the full commencement details of SI 2007/126, see reg 1 of those Regulations at **[4051]**).

PART III
STATUTORY INSTRUMENTS

32 Lawsuits pending

(1)   The effects of a relevant reorganisation or a relevant winding up on a relevant lawsuit pending in an EEA State shall be determined solely in accordance with the law of that EEA State.

(2)   In paragraph (1), "relevant lawsuit" means a lawsuit concerning an asset or right of which the affected credit institution has been divested.

[3889ZF]

NOTES
Commencement: 5 May 2004.

33 Lex rei sitae

(1)   The effects of a relevant reorganisation or a relevant winding up on the enforcement of a relevant proprietary right shall be determined by the law of the relevant EEA State.

(2)   In this regulation—
"relevant proprietary right" means proprietary rights in relevant instruments or other rights in relevant instruments the existence or transfer of which is recorded in a register, an account or a centralised deposit system held or located in an EEA state;
"relevant EEA State" means the Member State where the register, account or centralised deposit system in which the relevant proprietary right is recorded is held or located;
"relevant instrument" has the meaning given by regulation 31(3).

[3889ZG]

NOTES
Commencement: 5 May 2004.

34 Netting agreements

The effects of a relevant reorganisation or a relevant winding up on a netting agreement shall be determined in accordance with the law applicable to that agreement.

[3889ZH]

NOTES
Commencement: 5 May 2004.

35 Repurchase agreements

Subject to regulation 33, the effects of a relevant reorganisation or a relevant winding up on a repurchase agreement shall be determined in accordance with the law applicable to that agreement.

[3889ZI]

NOTES
Commencement: 5 May 2004.

PART 5
THIRD COUNTRY CREDIT INSTITUTIONS

36 Interpretation of this Part

(1)   In this Part—
(a)   "relevant measure", in relation to a third country credit institution, means—
(i)   a winding up;
(ii)   a provisional liquidation; or
(iii)   an administration order made under paragraph 13 of Schedule B1 to the 1986 Act[, paragraph 14 of Schedule B1 to the 1989 Order,] section 8(1) of the 1986 Act [or Article 21(1) of the 1989 Order] as the case may be.
(b)   "third country credit institution" means a person—
(i)   who has permission under the 2000 Act to accept deposits or to issue electronic money as the case may be; and
(ii)   whose head office is not in the United Kingdom or an EEA State.

(2)   In paragraph (1), the definition of "third country credit institution" must be read with—
(a)   section 22 of the 2000 Act;
(b)   any relevant order made under that section; and
(c)   Schedule 2 to that Act.

[3889ZJ]

NOTES
Commencement: 5 May 2004.

Para (1): words in first pair of square brackets in sub-para (a)(iii) substituted, and words in second pair of square brackets in that sub-paragraph inserted, by the Credit Institutions (Reorganisation and Winding Up) (Amendment) Regulations 2007, SI 2007/830, reg 2(1), (17), as from 6 April 2007.

37   Application of these Regulations to a third country credit institution

Regulations 9 and 10 apply where a third country credit institution is subject to a relevant measure, as if references in those regulations to a UK credit institution included a reference to a third country credit institution.

[3889ZK]

NOTES
Commencement: 5 May 2004.

38   Disclosure of confidential information: third country credit institution

(1)   This regulation applies to information ("insolvency practitioner information") which—
    (a)   relates to the business or other affairs of any person; and
    (b)   is information of a kind mentioned in paragraph (2).

(2)   Information falls within paragraph (1)(b) if it is supplied to—
    (a)   the Authority by an EEA regulator; or
    (b)   an insolvency practitioner by an EEA administrator or liquidator,
in accordance with or pursuant to Articles 8 or 19 of the reorganisation and winding up directive.

(3)   Subject to paragraphs (4), (5) and (6), sections 348, 349 and 352 of the 2000 Act apply in relation to insolvency practitioner information in the same way as they apply in relation to confidential information within the meaning of section 348(2) of that Act.

(4)   For the purposes of this regulation, sections 348, 349 and 352 of the 2000 Act and the Disclosure Regulations have effect as if the primary recipients specified in subsection (5) of section 348 of the 2000 Act included an insolvency practitioner.

(5)   Insolvency practitioner information is not subject to the restrictions on disclosure imposed by section 348(1) of the 2000 Act (as it applies by virtue of paragraph (2)) if it satisfies any of the criteria set out in section 348(4) of the 2000 Act.

(6)   The Disclosure Regulations apply in relation to insolvency practitioner information as they apply in relation to single market directive information (within the meaning of those Regulations).

(7)   In this regulation—
"EEA administrator" and "EEA liquidator" mean an administrator or liquidator of a third country credit institution as the case may be within the meaning of the reorganisation and winding up directive;
"insolvency practitioner" means an insolvency practitioner, within the meaning of section 388 of the 1986 Act or Article 3 of the 1989 Order, who is appointed or acts in relation to a third country credit institution.

[3889ZL]

NOTES
Commencement: 5 May 2004.

CASH RATIO DEPOSITS (VALUE BANDS AND RATIOS) ORDER 2004 (NOTE)

(SI 2004/1270)

NOTES
Revoked by the Cash Ratio Deposits (Value Bands and Ratios) Order 2008, SI 2008/1344, as from 2 June 2008. The 2008 Order is at **[4162]** et seq.

[3890]–[3891]

FINANCIAL SERVICES (DISTANCE MARKETING) REGULATIONS 2004

(SI 2004/2095)

NOTES
Made: 4 August 2004.
Authority: European Communities Act 1972, s 2(2).
Commencement: 31 October 2004.
These Regulations are reproduced as amended by: the Financial Services (EEA State) Regulations 2007, SI 2007/108; the Consumer Protection from Unfair Trading Regulations 2008, SI 2008/1277; the Payment Services Regulations 2009, SI 2009/209.

ARRANGEMENT OF REGULATIONS

1 Citation, commencement and extent

These Regulations may be cited as the Financial Services (Distance Marketing) Regulations 2004 and come into force on 31st October 2004.

[3892]

NOTES
Commencement: 31 October 2004.

2 Interpretation

(1)   In these Regulations—

"the 1974 Act" means the Consumer Credit Act 1974;

"the 2000 Act" means the Financial Services and Markets Act 2000;

"the Authority" means the Financial Services Authority;

"appointed representative" has the same meaning as in section 39(2) of the 2000 Act (exemption of appointed representatives);

"authorised person" has the same meaning as in section 31(2) of the 2000 Act (authorised persons);

"breach" means a contravention by a supplier of a prohibition in, or a failure by a supplier to comply with a requirement of, these Regulations;

"business" includes a trade or profession;

"consumer" means any individual who, in contracts to which these Regulations apply, is acting for purposes which are outside any business he may carry on;

"court" in relation to England and Wales and Northern Ireland means a county court or the High Court, and in relation to Scotland means the Sheriff Court or the Court of Session;

"credit" includes a cash loan and any other form of financial accommodation, and for this purpose "cash" includes money in any form;

"designated professional body" has the same meaning as in section 326(2) of the 2000 Act (designation of professional bodies);

"the Directive" means Directive 2002/65/EC of the European Parliament and of the Council of 23 September 2002 concerning the distance marketing of consumer financial services and amending Council Directive 90/619/EEC and Directives 97/7/EC and 98/27/EC;

"distance contract" means any contract concerning one or more financial services concluded between a supplier and a consumer under an organised distance sales or service-provision scheme run by the supplier or by an intermediary, who, for the purpose of that contract, makes exclusive use of one or more means of distance communication up to and including the time at which the contract is concluded;

"durable medium" means any instrument which enables a consumer to store information addressed personally to him in a way accessible for future reference for a period of time adequate for the purposes of the information and which allows the unchanged reproduction of the information stored;

"EEA supplier" means a supplier who is a national of an EEA State, or a company or firm (within the meaning of Article 48 of the Treaty establishing the European Community) formed in accordance with the law of an EEA State;

["EEA State" has the meaning given by Schedule 1 to the Interpretation Act 1978;]

"exempt regulated activity" has the same meaning as in section 325(2) of the 2000 Act;

"financial service" means any service of a banking, credit, insurance, personal pension, investment or payment nature;

"means of distance communication" means any means which, without the simultaneous physical presence of the supplier and the consumer, may be used for the marketing of a service between those parties;

"the OFT" means the Office of Fair Trading;

"regulated activity" has the same meaning as in section 22 of the 2000 Act (the classes of activity and categories of investment);

"Regulated Activities Order" means the Financial Services and Markets Act 2000 (Regulated Activities) Order 2001;

"rule" means a rule—
    (a)   made by the Authority under the 2000 Act, or
    (b)   made by a designated professional body, and approved by the Authority, under section 332 of the 2000 Act,

as the context requires;

"supplier" means any person who, acting in his commercial or professional capacity, is the contractual provider of services.

(2) In these Regulations, subject to paragraph (1), any expression used in these Regulations which is also used in the Directive has the same meaning as in the Directive.

[3893]

NOTES

Commencement: 31 October 2004.

Para (1): definition "EEA State" substituted by the Financial Services (EEA State) Regulations 2007, SI 2007/108, reg 10, as from 13 February 2007.

3 Scope of these Regulations

(1) Regulations 7 to 14 apply, subject to regulations 4 and 5, in relation to distance contracts made on or after 31st October 2004.

(2) Regulation 15 applies in relation to financial services supplied on or after 31st October 2004 under an organised distance sales or service-provision scheme run by the supplier or by an intermediary, who, for the purpose of that supply, makes exclusive use of one or more means of distance communication up to and including the time at which the financial services are supplied.

[3894]

NOTES

Commencement: 31 October 2004.

4—(1) Where an EEA State, other than the United Kingdom, has transposed the Directive or has obligations in its domestic law corresponding to those provided for in the Directive—
    (a)   regulations 7 to 14 do not apply in relation to any contract made between an EEA supplier contracting from an establishment in that EEA State and a consumer in the United Kingdom, and
    (b)   regulation 15 does not apply to any supply of financial services by an EEA supplier from an establishment in that EEA State to a consumer in the United Kingdom,

if the provisions by which that State has transposed the Directive, or the obligations in the domestic law of that State corresponding to those provided for in the Directive, as the case may be, apply to that contract or that supply.

 (2) Subject to paragraph (5) and regulation 6(3) and (4)—
  (a) regulations 7 to 11 do not apply in relation to any contract made by a supplier who is an authorised person, the making or performance of which constitutes or is part of a regulated activity carried on by him;
  (b) regulation 15 does not apply to any supply of financial services by a supplier who is an authorised person, where that supply constitutes or is part of a regulated activity carried on by him.

 (3) Subject to regulation 6(3) and (4)—
  (a) regulations 7 and 8 do not apply in relation to any contract made by a supplier who is an appointed representative, the making or performance of which constitutes or is part of a regulated activity (other than an exempt regulated activity) carried on by him;
  (b) regulation 15 does not apply to any supply of financial services by a supplier who is an appointed representative, where that supply constitutes or is part of a regulated activity (other than an exempt regulated activity) carried on by him.

 (4) Subject to regulation 6(3) and (4)—
  (a) regulations 7 and 8 do not apply in relation to any contract where—
   (i) the supplier is bound, or is controlled or managed by one or more persons who are bound, by rules of a designated professional body which are equivalent to those regulations, and
   (ii) the making or performance of that contract constitutes or is part of an exempt regulated activity carried on by the supplier;
  (b) regulation 15 does not apply to any supply of financial services where—
   (i) the supplier is bound, or is controlled or managed by one or more persons who are bound, by rules of a designated professional body which are equivalent to that regulation, and
   (ii) that supply constitutes or is part of an exempt regulated activity carried on by the supplier.

 (5) Paragraph (2) does not apply in relation to any contract or supply of financial services made by a supplier who is the operator, trustee or depositary of a scheme which is a recognised scheme by virtue of section 264 of the 2000 Act (schemes constituted in other EEA States), where the making or performance of the contract or the supply of the financial services constitutes or is part of a regulated activity for which he has permission in that capacity.

 (6) In paragraph (5)—
 "the operator", "trustee" and "depositary" each has the same meaning as in section 237(2) of the 2000 Act (other definitions); and
 "permission" has the same meaning as in section 266 of that Act (disapplication of rules).

                       [3895]

NOTES
Commencement: 31 October 2004.

5—(1) Where a consumer and a supplier enter an initial service agreement and—
 (a) successive operations of the same nature, or
 (b) a series of separate operations of the same nature,
are subsequently performed between them over time and within the framework of that agreement, then, if any of regulations 7 to 14 apply, they apply only to the initial service agreement.

 (2) Where a consumer and a supplier do not enter an initial service agreement and—
 (a) successive operations of the same nature, or
 (b) a series of separate operations of the same nature,
are performed between them over time, then, if regulations 7 and 8 apply, they apply only—
  (i) when the first operation is performed, and
  (ii) to any operation which is performed more than one year after the previous operation.

 (3) For the purposes of this regulation, "initial service agreement" includes, for example, an agreement for the provision of—
 (a) a bank account;
 (b) a credit card; or
 (c) portfolio management services.

 (4) For the purposes of this regulation, "operations" includes, for example—
 (a) deposits to or withdrawals from a bank account;
 (b) payments by a credit card;

(c)　　transactions carried out within the framework of an initial service agreement for portfolio management services; and

(d)　　subscriptions to new units of the same collective investment fund,

but does not include adding new elements to an existing initial service agreement, for example adding the possibility of using an electronic payment instrument together with an existing bank account.

[3896]

NOTES

Commencement: 31 October 2004.

6　Financial services marketed by an intermediary

(1)　This regulation applies where a financial service is marketed by an intermediary.

(2)　These Regulations have effect as if—

(a)　　each reference to a supplier in the definition of "breach" in regulation 2(1) were a reference to a supplier or an intermediary;

(b)　　the reference to the supplier in the definition of "means of distance communication" in regulation 2(1), each reference to the supplier in regulations 7, 8(1) and (2), 10 and 11(3)(b), and the first reference to the supplier in regulation 8(4), were a reference to the intermediary;

(c)　　the reference to the supplier in regulation 8(3) were a reference to the supplier or the intermediary;

(d)　　for regulation 11(2) there were substituted—

"(2)　Paragraph (1) does not apply to a distance contract if the intermediary has not complied with regulation 8(1) (and the supplier has not done what the intermediary was required to do by regulation 8(1)), unless—

(a)　　the circumstances fall within regulation 8(1)(b); and

(b)　　either—

(i)　　the intermediary has complied with regulation 7(1) and (2) or, if applicable, regulation 7(4)(b), and with regulation 7(5), or

(ii)　　the supplier has done what the intermediary was required to do by regulation 7(1) and (2) or, if applicable, regulation 7(4)(b), and by regulation 7(5).";

(e)　　the reference to a supplier in regulation 22(1) were a reference to an intermediary; and

(f)　　each reference to the supplier in paragraphs 2, 4, 5 and 19 of Schedule 1 were a reference to the supplier and the intermediary.

(3)　Notwithstanding paragraphs (2) to (4) of regulation 4, regulations 7 and 8 apply in relation to the intermediary unless—

(a)　　the intermediary is an authorised person and the marketing of the financial service constitutes or is part of a regulated activity carried on by him;

(b)　　the intermediary is an appointed representative and the marketing of the financial service constitutes or is part of a regulated activity (other than an exempt regulated activity) carried on by him; or

(c)　　the intermediary is not an authorised person, but—

(i)　　he is bound, or is controlled or managed by one or more persons who are bound, by rules of a designated professional body which are equivalent to regulations 7 and 8, and

(ii)　　the marketing of the financial service constitutes or is part of an exempt regulated activity carried on by him.

(4)　Notwithstanding paragraphs (2) to (4) of regulation 4, regulation 15 applies to the intermediary unless—

(a)　　the intermediary is an authorised person and is acting in the course of a regulated activity carried on by him;

(b)　　the intermediary is an appointed representative and is acting in the course of a regulated activity (other than an exempt regulated activity) carried on by him; or

(c)　　the intermediary is not an authorised person, but—

(i)　　he is bound, or is controlled or managed by one or more persons who are bound, by rules of a designated professional body which are equivalent to regulation 15, and

(ii)　　he is acting in the course an exempt regulated activity carried on by him.

[3897]

NOTES

Commencement: 31 October 2004.

7 Information required prior to the conclusion of the contract

(1)   Subject to *paragraph (4)*, in good time prior to the consumer being bound by any distance contract, the supplier shall provide to the consumer the information specified in Schedule 1.

[(1A)   Where a distance contract to which paragraph (1) applies is also a contract for payment services to which the Payment Services Regulations 2009 apply, the supplier is required to provide to the consumer only the information specified in paragraphs 8 to 13, 16, 17 and 21 of Schedule 1.]

(2)   The supplier shall provide the information specified in Schedule 1 in a clear and comprehensible manner appropriate to the means of distance communication used, with due regard in particular to the principles of good faith in commercial transactions and the principles governing the protection of those who are unable to give their consent such as minors.

(3)   Subject to paragraph (4), the supplier shall make clear his commercial purpose when providing the information specified in Schedule 1.

(4)   In the case of a voice telephone communication—
   (a)   the supplier shall make clear his identity and the commercial purpose of any call initiated by him at the beginning of any conversation with the consumer; and
   (b)   if the consumer explicitly consents, only the information specified in Schedule 2 need be given.

(5)   The supplier shall ensure that the information he provides to the consumer pursuant to this regulation, regarding the contractual obligations which would arise if the distance contract were concluded, accurately reflects the contractual obligations which would arise under the law presumed to be applicable to that contract.

[3898]

NOTES
Commencement: 31 October 2004.
Para (1): for the words in italics there are substituted the words "paragraphs (1A) and (4)" by the Payment Services Regulations 2009, SI 2009/209, reg 126, Sch 6, Pt 2, para 5(a)(i), as from 1 November 2009 (for the full commencement details of the 2009 Regulations, see reg 1 of those Regulations at [4387]).
Para (1A): inserted by SI 2009/209, reg 126, Sch 6, Pt 2, para 5(a)(ii), as from 1 November 2009 (for the full commencement details of the 2009 Regulations, see reg 1 of those Regulations at [4387]).

8 Written and additional information

(1)   [Subject to paragraph (1A),] the supplier under a distance contract shall communicate to the consumer on paper, or in another durable medium which is available and accessible to the consumer, all the contractual terms and conditions and the information specified in Schedule 1, either—
   (a)   in good time prior to the consumer being bound by that distance contract; or
   (b)   immediately after the conclusion of the contract, where the contract has been concluded at the consumer's request using a means of distance communication which does not enable provision in accordance with sub-paragraph (a) of the contractual terms and conditions and the information specified in Schedule 1.

[(1A)   Where a distance contract to which paragraph (1) applies is also a contract for payment services to which the Payment Services Regulations 2009 apply, the supplier is required to communicate to the consumer all the contractual terms and conditions and the information specified in paragraphs 8 to 13, 16, 17 and 21 of Schedule 1.]

(2)   The supplier shall communicate the contractual terms and conditions to the consumer on paper, if the consumer so requests at any time during their contractual relationship.

(3)   Paragraph (2) does not apply if the supplier has already communicated the contractual terms and conditions to the consumer on paper during that contractual relationship, and those terms and conditions have not changed since they were so communicated.

(4)   The supplier shall change the means of distance communication with the consumer if the consumer so requests at any time during his contractual relationship with the supplier, unless that is incompatible with the distance contract or the nature of the financial service provided to the consumer.

[3899]

NOTES
Commencement: 31 October 2004.
Para (1): words in square brackets inserted by the Payment Services Regulations 2009, SI 2009/209, reg 126, Sch 6, Pt 2, para 5(b)(i), as from 1 November 2009 (for the full commencement details of the 2009 Regulations, see reg 1 of those Regulations at [4387]).
Para (1A): inserted by SI 2009/209, reg 126, Sch 6, Pt 2, para 5(b)(ii), as from 1 November 2009 (for the full commencement details of the 2009 Regulations, see reg 1 of those Regulations at [4387]).

9   Right to cancel

(1)   Subject to regulation 11, if within the cancellation period set out in regulation 10 notice of cancellation is properly given by the consumer to the supplier, the notice of cancellation shall operate to cancel the distance contract.

(2)   Cancelling the contract has the effect of terminating the contract at the time at which the notice of cancellation is given.

(3)   For the purposes of these Regulations, a notice of cancellation is a notification given—
-   (a)   orally (where the supplier has informed the consumer that notice of cancellation may be given orally),
-   (b)   in writing, or
-   (c)   in another durable medium available and accessible to the supplier,

which, however expressed, indicates the intention of the consumer to cancel the contract by that notification.

(4)   Notice of cancellation given under this regulation by a consumer to a supplier is to be treated as having been properly given if the consumer—
-   (a)   gives it orally to the supplier (where the supplier has informed the consumer that notice of cancellation may be given orally);
-   (b)   leaves it at the address of the supplier last known to the consumer and addressed to the supplier by name (in which case it is to be taken to have been given on the day on which it was left);
-   (c)   sends it by post to the address of the supplier last known to the consumer and addressed to the supplier by name (in which case it is to be taken to have been given on the day on which it was posted);
-   (d)   sends it by facsimile to the business facsimile number of the supplier last known to the consumer (in which case it is to be taken to have been given on the day on which it was sent);
-   (e)   sends it by electronic mail to the business electronic mail address of the supplier last known to the consumer (in which case it is to be taken to have been given on the day on which it is sent); or
-   (f)   by other electronic means—
    -   (i)   sends it to an internet address or web-site which the supplier has notified the consumer may be used for the purpose, or
    -   (ii)   indicates it on such a web-site in accordance with instructions which are on the web-site or which the supplier has provided to the consumer,
    (in which case it is to be taken to have been given on the day on which it is sent to that address or web-site or indicated on that web-site).

(5)   The references in paragraph (4)(b) and (c) to the address of the supplier shall, in the case of a supplier which is a body corporate, be treated as including a reference to the address of the secretary or clerk of that body.

(6)   The references in paragraph (4)(b) and (c) to the address of the supplier shall, in the case of a supplier which is a partnership, be treated as including a reference to the address of a partner or a person having control or management of the partnership business.

(7)   In this regulation—
-   (a)   every reference to the supplier includes a reference to any other person previously notified by or on behalf of the supplier to the consumer as a person to whom notice of cancellation may be given;
-   (b)   the references to giving notice of cancellation orally include giving such notice by voice telephone communication, where the supplier has informed the consumer that notice of cancellation may be given in that way; and
-   (c)   "electronic mail" has the same meaning as in regulation 2(1) of the Privacy and Electronic Communications (EC Directive) Regulations 2003 (interpretation).

[3900]

NOTES

Commencement: 31 October 2004.

10   Cancellation period

(1)   For the purposes of regulation 9, the cancellation period begins on the day on which the distance contract is concluded ("conclusion day") and ends as provided for in paragraphs (2) to (5).

(2)   Where the supplier complies with regulation 8(1) on or before conclusion day, the cancellation period ends on the expiry of fourteen calendar days beginning with the day after conclusion day.

(3)   Where the supplier does not comply with regulation 8(1) on or before conclusion day, but subsequently communicates to the consumer on paper, or in another durable medium which is

available and accessible to the consumer, all the contractual terms and conditions and the information required under regulation 8(1), the cancellation period ends on the expiry of fourteen calendar days beginning with the day after the day on which the consumer receives the last of those terms and conditions and that information.

(4)   In the case of a distance contract relating to life insurance, for the references to conclusion day in paragraphs (2) and (3) there are substituted references to the day on which the consumer is informed that the distance contract has been concluded.

(5)   In the case of a distance contract relating to life insurance or a personal pension, for the references to fourteen calendar days in paragraphs (2) and (3) there are substituted references to thirty calendar days.

[3901]

NOTES
Commencement: 31 October 2004.

11   Exceptions to the right to cancel

(1)   Subject to paragraphs (2) and (3), regulation 9 does not confer on a consumer a right to cancel a distance contract which is—

   (a)   a contract for a financial service where the price of that service depends on fluctuations in the financial market outside the supplier's control, which may occur during the cancellation period, such as services related to—
      (i)   foreign exchange,
      (ii)   money market instruments,
      (iii)   transferable securities,
      (iv)   units in collective investment undertakings,
      (v)   financial-futures contracts, including equivalent cash-settled instruments,
      (vi)   forward interest-rate agreements,
      (vii)   interest-rate, currency and equity swaps,
      (viii)   options to acquire or dispose of any instruments referred to in sub-paragraphs (i) to (vii), including cash-settled instruments and options on currency and on interest rates;
   (b)   a contract whose performance has been fully completed by both parties at the consumer's express request before the consumer gives notice of cancellation;
   (c)   a contract which—
      (i)   is a connected contract of insurance within the meaning of article 72B(1) of the Regulated Activities Order (activities carried on by a provider of relevant goods or services),
      (ii)   covers travel risks within the meaning of article 72B(1)(d)(ii) of that Order, and
      (iii)   has a total duration of less than one month;
   (d)   a contract under which a supplier provides credit to a consumer and the consumer's obligation to repay is secured by a legal mortgage on land;
   (e)   a credit agreement cancelled under regulation 15(1) of the Consumer Protection (Distance Selling) Regulations 2000 (automatic cancellation of a related credit agreement);
   (f)   a credit agreement cancelled under section 6A of the Timeshare Act 1992 (automatic cancellation of timeshare credit agreement); or
   (g)   a restricted-use credit agreement (within the meaning of the 1974 Act) to finance the purchase of land or an existing building, or an agreement for a bridging loan in connection with the purchase of land or an existing building.

(2)   Paragraph (1) does not apply to a distance contract if the supplier has not complied with regulation 8(1), unless—

   (a)   the circumstances fall within regulation 8(1)(b); and
   (b)   the supplier has complied with regulation 7(1) and (2) or, if applicable, regulation 7(4)(b), and with regulation 7(5).

(3)   Where—

   (a)   the conditions in sub-paragraphs (a) and (b) of paragraph (2) are satisfied in relation to a distance contract falling within paragraph (1),
   (b)   the supplier has not complied with regulation 8(1), and
   (c)   the consumer has not, by the end of the sixth day after the day on which the distance contract is concluded, received all the contractual terms and conditions and the information required under regulation 8(1),

the consumer may cancel the contract under regulation 9 during the period beginning on the seventh day after the day on which the distance contract is concluded and ending when he receives the last of the contractual terms and conditions and the information required under regulation 8(1).

[3902]

NOTES
Commencement: 31 October 2004.

12   Automatic cancellation of an attached distance contract

(1)   For the purposes of this regulation, where there is a distance contract for the provision of a financial service by a supplier to a consumer ("the main contract") and there is a further distance contract ("the secondary contract") for the provision to that consumer of a further financial service by—

    (a)   the same supplier, or

    (b)   a third party, the further financial service being provided pursuant to an agreement between the third party and the supplier under the main contract,

then the secondary contract (referred to in these Regulations as an "attached contract") is attached to the main contract if any of the conditions in paragraph (2) are satisfied.

(2)   The conditions referred to in paragraph (1) are—

    (a)   the secondary contract is entered into in compliance with a term of the main contract;

    (b)   the main contract is, or is to be, financed by the secondary contract;

    (c)   the main contract is a debtor-creditor-supplier agreement within the meaning of the 1974 Act, and the secondary contract is, or is to be, financed by the main contract;

    (d)   the secondary contract is entered into by the consumer to induce the supplier to enter into the main contract;

    (e)   performance of the secondary contract requires performance of the main contract.

(3)   Where a main contract is cancelled by a notice of cancellation given under regulation 9—

    (a)   the cancellation of the main contract also operates to cancel, at the time at which the main contract is cancelled, any attached contract which is not a contract or agreement of a type listed in regulation 11(1); and

    (b)   the supplier under the main contract shall, if he is not the supplier under the attached contract, forthwith on receipt of the notice of cancellation inform the supplier under the attached contract.

(4)   Paragraph (3)(a) does not apply to an attached contract if, at or before the time at which the notice of cancellation in respect of the main contract is given, the consumer has given and not withdrawn a notice to the supplier under the main contract that cancellation of the main contract is not to operate to cancel that attached contract.

(5)   Where a main contract made by an authorised person, the making or performance of which constitutes or is part of a regulated activity carried on by him, is cancelled under rules made by the Authority corresponding to regulation 9—

    (a)   the cancellation of the main contract also operates to cancel, at the time at which the main contract is cancelled, any attached contract which is not a contract or agreement of a type listed in regulation 11(1); and

    (b)   the supplier under the main contract shall, if he is not the supplier under the attached contract, inform the supplier under the attached contract forthwith on receiving notification of the consumer's intention to cancel the main contract by that notification.

(6)   Paragraph (5)(a) does not apply to an attached contract if, at or before the time at which the consumer gives notification of his intention to cancel the main contract by that notification, the consumer has given and not withdrawn a notice to the supplier under the main contract that cancellation of the main contract is not to operate to cancel that attached contract.

[3903]

NOTES
Commencement: 31 October 2004.

13   Payment for services provided before cancellation

(1)   This regulation applies where a cancellation event occurs in relation to a distance contract.

(2)   In this regulation, "cancellation event" means the cancellation of a distance contract under regulation 9 or 12.

(3)   The supplier shall refund any sum paid by or on behalf of the consumer under or in relation to the contract to the person by whom it was paid, less any charge made in accordance with paragraph (6), as soon as possible and in any event within a period not exceeding 30 calendar days beginning with—

    (a)   the day on which the cancellation event occurred; or

    (b)   if the supplier proves that this is later—

        (i)   in the case of a contract cancelled under regulation 9, the day on which the supplier in fact received the notice of cancellation, or

        (ii)   in the case of an attached contract under which the supplier is not the supplier under the main contract, the day on which, pursuant to regulation 12(3)(b) or (5)(b), he was in fact informed by the supplier under the main contract of the cancellation of the main contract.

(4)   The reference in paragraph (3) to any sum paid on behalf of the consumer includes any sum paid by any other person ("the creditor"), who is not the supplier, under an agreement between the consumer and the creditor by which the creditor provides the consumer with credit of any amount.

(5)   Where any security has been provided in relation to the contract, the security (so far as it has been provided) shall, on cancellation under regulation 9 or 12, be treated as never having had effect; and any property lodged solely for the purposes of the security as so provided shall be returned forthwith by the person with whom it is lodged.

(6)   Subject to paragraphs (7), (8) and (9), the supplier may make a charge for any service actually provided by the supplier in accordance with the contract.

(7)   The charge shall not exceed an amount which is in proportion to the extent of the service provided to the consumer prior to the time at which the cancellation event occurred (including the service of arranging to provide the financial service) in comparison with the full coverage of the contract, and in any event shall not be such that it could be construed as a penalty.

(8)   The supplier may not make any charge unless he can prove on the balance of probabilities that the consumer was informed about the amount payable in accordance with—
(a)   regulation 7(1) and paragraph 13 of Schedule 1,
(b)   regulation 7(4) and paragraph 5 of Schedule 2, or
(c)   rules corresponding to those provisions,
as the case may be.

(9)   The supplier may not make any charge if, without the consumer's prior request, he commenced performance of the contract prior to the expiry of the relevant cancellation period.

(10)   In paragraph (9), the relevant cancellation period is the cancellation period which—
(a)   in the case of a main contract, is applicable to that contract, or
(b)   in the case of an attached contract, would be applicable to that contract if that contract were a main contract,
under regulation 10, or under rules corresponding to that regulation, as the case may be.

(11)   The consumer shall, as soon as possible and in any event within a period not exceeding 30 calendar days beginning with the day on which the cancellation event occurred—
(a)   refund any sum paid by or on behalf of the supplier under or in relation to that contract to the person by whom it was paid; and
(b)   either restore to the supplier any property of which he has acquired possession under that contract, or deliver or send that property to any person to whom, under regulation 9, a notice of cancellation could have been given in respect of that contract.

(12)   Breach of a duty imposed by paragraph (11) on a consumer is actionable as a breach of statutory duty.

[3904]

NOTES

Commencement: 31 October 2004.

14   Payment by card

(1)   Subject to paragraph (2), where—
(a)   a payment card has been issued to an individual who, when entering the contract for the provision of that card, was acting for purposes which were outside any business he may carry on ("the card-holder"), and
(b)   fraudulent use is made of that card to make a payment under or in connection with a distance contract to which these Regulations apply, by another person who is neither acting, nor to be treated as acting, as the card-holder's agent,
the card-holder may request cancellation of that payment, and is entitled to be recredited with the sum paid, or to have it returned, by the card issuer.

(2)   Where paragraph (1) applies and, in any proceedings, the card-holder alleges that any use made of the payment card was not authorised by him, it is for the card issuer to prove that the use was so authorised.

(3)   Paragraph (1) does not apply if the contract for the provision of the payment card is an agreement to which section 83(1) of the 1974 Act (liability for misuse of credit facilities) applies.

(4)   ...

(5)   For the purposes of this regulation—
"card issuer" means the owner of the card;

"payment card" includes a credit card, a charge card, a debit card and a store card.

[3905]

NOTES
Commencement: 31 October 2004.
Revoked by the Payment Services Regulations 2009, SI 2009/209, reg 126, Sch 6, Pt 2, para 5(c), as from 1 November 2009 (for the full commencement details of the 2009 Regulations, see reg 1 of those Regulations at **[4387]**).
Para (4): inserts the Consumer Credit Act 1974, s 84(3C).

15 Unsolicited services

(1)   A person ("the recipient") who receives unsolicited financial services for purposes other than those of his business from another person who supplies those services in the course of his business, shall not thereby become subject to any obligation (to make payment, or otherwise).

(2), (3)   …

(4)   In this regulation, "unsolicited" means, in relation to financial services supplied to any person, that they are supplied without any prior request made by or on behalf of that person.

(5)–(7)   …

(8)   This regulation is without prejudice to any right a supplier may have at any time, by contract or otherwise, to renew a distance contract with a consumer without any request made by or on behalf of that consumer prior to the renewal of that contract.

[3906]

NOTES
Commencement: 31 October 2004.
Paras (2), (3), (5)–(7): revoked by the Consumer Protection from Unfair Trading Regulations 2008, SI 2008/1277, reg 30(1), (3), Sch 2, Pt 2, para 110(1), (2), Sch 4, Pt 2, as from 26 May 2008.

16 Prevention of contracting-out

(1)   A term contained in any contract is void if, and to the extent that, it is inconsistent with the application of a provision of these Regulations to a distance contract or the application of regulation 15 to a supply of unsolicited financial services.

(2)   Where a provision of these Regulations specifies a duty or liability of the consumer in certain circumstances, a term contained in a contract is inconsistent with that provision if it purports to impose, directly or indirectly, an additional or greater duty or liability on him in those circumstances.

(3)   These Regulations apply notwithstanding any contract term which applies or purports to apply the law of a State which is not an EEA State if the contract or supply has a close connection with the territory of an EEA State.

[3907]

NOTES
Commencement: 31 October 2004.

17 Enforcement authorities

(1)   For the purposes of regulations 18 to 21—
    (a)   in relation to any alleged breach concerning a specified contract, the Authority is the enforcement authority;
    (b)   in relation to any alleged breach concerning a contract under which the supplier is a local authority, but which is not a specified contract, the OFT is the enforcement authority;
    (c)   in relation to any other alleged breach—
        (i)   the OFT, and
        (ii)   in Great Britain every local weights and measures authority, and in Northern Ireland the Department of Enterprise, Trade and Investment,
    is an enforcement authority.

(2)   For the purposes of paragraph (1) and regulation 22(6), each of the following is a specified contract—
    (a)   a contract the making or performance of which constitutes or is part of a regulated activity carried on by the supplier;
    (b)   a contract for the provision of a debit card;
    (c)   a contract relating to the issuing of electronic money by a supplier to whom the Authority has given a certificate under article 9C of the Regulated Activities Order (persons certified as small issuers etc);
    (d)   a contract the effecting or carrying out of which is excluded from article 10(1) or (2) of

the Regulated Activities Order (effecting and carrying out contracts of insurance) by article 12 of that order (breakdown insurance), where the supplier is a person who does not otherwise carry on an activity of the kind specified by article 10 of that order;

(e)   a contract under which a supplier provides credit to a consumer and the obligation of the consumer to repay is secured by a first legal mortgage on land;

(f)   a contract, made before 14th January 2005, for insurance mediation activity other than in respect of a contract of long-term care insurance.

(3)   For the purposes of the application of this regulation and regulations 18 to 22 in relation to breaches of, and offences under, regulation 15, "contract"—

(a)   wherever it appears in this regulation other than in the expression "contract of long-term care insurance", and

(b)   in regulation 22(6),

is to be taken to mean "supply of financial services".

(4)   For the purposes of this regulation—

"contract of long-term care insurance" has the same meaning as in the Financial Services and Markets Act 2000 (Regulated Activities) (Amendment) (No 2) Order 2003;

"insurance mediation activity" means any activity which is not a regulated activity at the time the contract is made but will be a regulated activity of the kind specified by article 21, 25(1) or (2), 39A or 53 of the Regulated Activities Order when the amendments to that order made by the Financial Services and Markets Act 2000 (Regulated Activities) (Amendment) (No 2) Order 2003 come into force;

"local authority" means—

(a)   in England and Wales, a local authority within the meaning of the Local Government Act 1972, the Greater London Authority, the Common Council of the City of London or the Council of the Isles of Scilly,

(b)   in Scotland, a council constituted under section 2 of the Local Government etc (Scotland) Act 1994, and

(c)   in Northern Ireland, a district council within the meaning of the Local Government Act (Northern Ireland) 1972.

[3908]

NOTES
Commencement: 31 October 2004.

18 Consideration of complaints

(1)   An enforcement authority shall consider any complaint made to it about a breach unless—

(a)   the complaint appears to that authority to be frivolous or vexatious; or

(b)   that authority is aware that another enforcement authority has notified the OFT that it agrees to consider the complaint.

(2)   If an enforcement authority notifies the OFT that it agrees to consider a complaint made to another enforcement authority, the first mentioned authority shall be under a duty to consider the complaint.

[3909]

NOTES
Commencement: 31 October 2004.

19 Injunctions to secure compliance with these Regulations

(1)   Subject to paragraph (2), an enforcement authority may apply for an injunction (including an interim injunction) against any person who appears to that authority to be responsible for a breach.

(2)   An enforcement authority, other than the OFT or the Authority, may apply for an injunction only where—

(a)   that authority has notified the OFT, at least fourteen days before the date on which the application is to be made, of its intention to apply; or

(b)   the OFT consents to the application being made within a shorter period.

(3)   On an application made under this regulation, the court may grant an injunction on such terms as it thinks fit to secure compliance with these Regulations.

(4)   An enforcement authority which has a duty under regulation 18 to consider a complaint shall give reasons for its decision to apply or not to apply, as the case may be, for an injunction.

(5)   In deciding whether or not to apply for an injunction in respect of a breach, an enforcement authority may, if it considers it appropriate to do so, have regard to any undertaking as to compliance with these Regulations given to it or to another enforcement authority by or on behalf of any person.

(6)   In the application of this regulation to Scotland, for references to an "injunction" or an "interim injunction" there are substituted references to an "interdict" or an "interim interdict" respectively.

[3910]

NOTES
Commencement: 31 October 2004.

20   Notification of undertakings and orders to the OFT

An enforcement authority, other than the OFT and the Authority, shall notify the OFT of—
   (a)   any undertaking given to it by or on behalf of any person who appears to it to be responsible for a breach;
   (b)   the outcome of any application made by it under regulation 19 and the terms of any undertaking given to, or order made by, the court; and
   (c)   the outcome of any application made by it to enforce a previous order of the court.

[3911]

NOTES
Commencement: 31 October 2004.

21   Publication, information and advice

(1)   The OFT shall arrange for the publication, in such form and manner as it considers appropriate, of details of any undertaking or order notified to it under regulation 20.

(2)   Each of the OFT and the Authority shall arrange for the publication in such form and manner as it considers appropriate of—
   (a)   details of any undertaking as to compliance with these Regulations given to it by or on behalf of any person;
   (b)   details of any application made by it under regulation 18, and of the terms of any undertaking given to, or order made by, the court; and
   (c)   details of any application made by it to enforce a previous order of the court.

(3)   Each of the OFT and the Authority may arrange for the dissemination, in such form and manner as it considers appropriate, of such information and advice concerning the operation of these Regulations as may appear to it to be expedient to give to the public and to all persons likely to be affected by these Regulations.

[3912]

NOTES
Commencement: 31 October 2004.

22   Offences

(1)   A supplier under a distance contract who fails to comply with regulation 7(3) or (4)(a) or regulation 8(2) or (4) is guilty of an offence and liable, on summary conviction, to a fine not exceeding level 3 on the standard scale.

(2)   If an offence under paragraph (1) ... committed by a body corporate is shown—
   (a)   to have been committed with the consent or connivance of any director, manager, secretary or other similar officer of the body corporate, or any person who was purporting to act in any such capacity, or
   (b)   to be attributable to any neglect on his part,
he as well as the body corporate is guilty of the offence and liable to be proceeded against and punished accordingly.

(3)   If the affairs of a body corporate are managed by its members, paragraph (2) applies in relation to the acts and defaults of a member in connection with his functions of management as if he were a director of the body.

(4)   If an offence under paragraph (1) ... committed by a partnership is shown—
   (a)   to have been committed with the consent or connivance of any partner, or any person who was purporting to act as a partner, or
   (b)   to be attributable to any neglect on his part,
he as well as the partnership is guilty of an offence and liable to be proceeded against and punished accordingly.

(5)   If an offence under paragraph (1) ... committed by an unincorporated association (other than a partnership) is shown—
   (a)   to have been committed with the consent or connivance of an officer of the association or a member of its governing body, or any person who was purporting to act in any such capacity, or

(b)   to be attributable to any neglect on his part,

he as well as the association is guilty of an offence and liable to be proceeded against and punished accordingly.

(6)   Except in Scotland—
    (a)   the Authority may institute proceedings for an offence under these Regulations which relates to a specified contract;
    (b)   the OFT, and—
        (i)   in Great Britain, every local weights and measures authority,
        (ii)   in Northern Ireland, the Department of Enterprise, Trade and Investment,

may institute proceedings for any other offence under these Regulations.

[3913]

NOTES
Commencement: 31 October 2004.
Paras (2), (4), (5): words omitted revoked by the Consumer Protection from Unfair Trading Regulations 2008, SI 2008/1277, reg 30(1), (3), Sch 2, Pt 2, para 110(1), (3), Sch 4, Pt 2, as from 26 May 2008.

23   Functions of the Authority

The functions conferred on the Authority by these Regulations shall be treated as if they were conferred by the 2000 Act.

[3914]

NOTES
Commencement: 31 October 2004.

24–28   (*Reg 24 amends the Unfair Terms in Consumer Contracts Regulations 1999, SI 1999/2083, regs 3, 5 at* **[3537]**, **[3539]***; regs 25–28 contain amendments to the Consumer Protection (Distance Selling) Regulations 2000, SI 2000/2334, the Enterprise Act 2002, the Enterprise Act 2002 (Part 8 Community Infringements Specified UK Laws) Order 2003, SI 2003/1374, and the Enterprise Act 2002 (Part 8 Notice to OFT of Intended Prosecution Specified Enactments, Revocation and Transitional Provision) Order 2003, SI 2003/1376 (outside the scope of this work).*)

29   Transitional provisions

(1)   In relation to any contract made before 31st May 2005 which is a consumer credit agreement within the meaning of the 1974 Act and a regulated agreement within the meaning of that Act—
    (a)   regulations 7, 8, 10 and 11 apply subject to the modifications in paragraphs (2) to (5); and
    (b)   references in these Regulations to regulations 7, 8, 10 and 11 or to provisions contained in them shall be construed accordingly.

(2)   In regulation 7—
    (a)   in paragraphs (1) to (3), before "Schedule 1" at each place where it occurs insert "paragraph 13 of"; and
    (b)   in paragraph (4)(b), before "Schedule 2" insert "paragraph 5 of".

(3)   In regulation 8(1), for "contractual terms and conditions and the information specified in" at each place where it occurs substitute "information specified in paragraph 13 of".

(4)   In regulation 10(3), omit—
    (a)   "the contractual terms and conditions and"; and
    (b)   "those terms and conditions and".

(5)   In regulation 11(3), omit "the contractual terms and conditions and" at each place where it occurs.

[3915]

NOTES
Commencement: 31 October 2004.

SCHEDULES

SCHEDULE 1
INFORMATION REQUIRED PRIOR TO THE CONCLUSION OF THE CONTRACT
Regulations 7(1) and 8(1)

1.   The identity and the main business of the supplier, the geographical address at which the supplier is established and any other geographical address relevant to the consumer's relations with the supplier.

2.   Where the supplier has a representative established in the consumer's State of residence, the identity of that representative and the geographical address relevant to the consumer's relations with him.

3.   Where the consumer's dealings are with any professional other than the supplier, the identity of that professional, the capacity in which he is acting with respect to the consumer, and the geographical address relevant to the consumer's relations with that professional.

4.   Where the supplier is registered in a trade or similar public register, the particulars of the register in which the supplier is entered and his registration number or an equivalent means of identification in that register.

5.   Where the supplier's activity is subject to an authorisation scheme, the particulars of the relevant supervisory authority.

6.   A description of the main characteristics of the financial service.

7.   The total price to be paid by the consumer to the supplier for the financial service, including all related fees, charges and expenses, and all taxes paid via the supplier or, where an exact price cannot be indicated, the basis for the calculation of the price enabling the consumer to verify it.

8.   Where relevant, notice indicating that: (i) the financial service is related to instruments involving special risks related to their specific features or the operations to be executed or whose price depends on fluctuations in the financial markets outside the supplier's control; and (ii) historical performances are no indicators for future performances.

9.   Notice of the possibility that other taxes or costs may exist that are not paid via the supplier or imposed by him.

10.   Any limitations of the period for which the information provided is valid.

11.   The arrangements for payment and for performance.

12.   Any specific additional cost for the consumer of using the means of distance communication, if such additional cost is charged.

13.   Whether or not there is a right of cancellation and, where there is a right of cancellation, its duration and the conditions for exercising it, including information on the amount which the consumer may be required to pay in accordance with regulation 13, as well as the consequences of not exercising that right.

14.   The minimum duration of the distance contract in the case of financial services to be performed indefinitely or recurrently.

15.   Information on any rights the parties may have to terminate the distance contract early or unilaterally by virtue of the terms of the contract, including any penalties imposed by the contract in such cases.

16.   Practical instructions for exercising the right to cancel in accordance with regulation 9 indicating, among other things, the address at which the notice of cancellation should be left or to which it should be sent by post, and any facsimile number or electronic mail address to which it should be sent.

17.   The EEA State or States whose laws are taken by the supplier as a basis for the establishment of relations with the consumer prior to the conclusion of the distance contract.

18.   Any contractual clause on the law applicable to the distance contract or on the competent court.

19.   In which language, or languages: (i) the contractual terms and conditions, and the prior information specified in this Schedule, are supplied; and (ii) the supplier, with the agreement of the consumer, undertakes to communicate during the duration of the distance contract.

20.   Whether or not there is an out-of-court complaint and redress mechanism for the consumer and, if so, the methods for having access to it.

21.   The existence of guarantee funds or other compensation arrangements, except to the extent that they are required by Directive 94/19/EC of the European Parliament and of the Council of 30 May 1994 on deposit guarantee schemes or Directive 97/9/EC of the European Parliament and of the Council of 3 March 1997 on investor compensation schemes.

[3916]

NOTES

Commencement: 31 October 2004.

SCHEDULE 2
INFORMATION REQUIRED IN THE CASE OF VOICE TELEPHONE COMMUNICATIONS

Regulation 7(4)(b)

1.   The identity of the person in contact with the consumer and his link with the supplier.

2.   A description of the main characteristics of the financial service.

3.   The total price to be paid by the consumer to the supplier for the financial service including all taxes paid via the supplier or, if an exact price cannot be indicated, the basis for the calculation of the price enabling the consumer to verify it.

4.   Notice of the possibility that other taxes or costs may exist that are not paid via the supplier or imposed by him.

5.   Whether or not there is a right to cancel and, where there is such a right, its duration and the conditions for exercising it, including information on the amount which the consumer may be required to pay in accordance with regulation 13, as well as the consequences of not exercising that right.

6.   That other information is available on request and the nature of that information.

[3917]

NOTES
    Commencement: 31 October 2004.

FINANCIAL SERVICES AND MARKETS ACT 2000 (MARKET ABUSE) REGULATIONS 2005 (NOTE)

(SI 2005/381)

NOTES
    Made: 23 February 2005.
    Authority: European Communities Act 1972, s 2(2).
    Commencement: 17 March 2005 (regs 2, 3 8, Sch 1, paras 2, 3, 6, 11); 1 July 2005 (otherwise).

As of 1 February 2009, these Regulations had not been amended.
    These Regulations implement, in part, European Parliament and Council Directive 2003/6/EC on insider dealing and market manipulation (at **[5430]**) and the following measures which were made under Article 17 of that Directive—

* Commission Regulation (EC) No 2273/2003 implementing Directive 2003/6/EC of the European Parliament and of the Council as regards exemptions for buy-back programmes and stabilisation of financial instruments (at **[5490]**);
* Commission Directive 2003/124/EC implementing Directive 2003/6 of the European Parliament and of the Council as regards the definition and public disclosure of inside information and the definition of market manipulation (at **[5502]**); and
* Commission Directive 2004/72/EC implementing Directive 2003/6 of the European Parliament and of the Council as regards accepted market practices, the definition of inside information in relation to derivatives on commodities, the drawing up of lists of insiders, the notification of managers' transactions and the notification of suspicious transactions (at **[5597]**).

Reg 1 of these Regulations provides for citation and commencement.
    Reg 2 provides for interpretation.
    Reg 3 amends the Criminal Justice Act 1993, Sch 1, para 5(1) at **[1233]**.
    Reg 4 introduces Sch 1 to these Regulations (amendments of FSMA 2000, Part VI).
    Reg 5 introduces Sch 2 to these Regulations (amendments of FSMA 2000, Part VIII).
    Reg 6 amends FSMA 2000, s 150(4) at **[178]**.
    Reg 7 amends FSMA 2000, s 395(13) at **[422]**.
    Reg 8 amends FSMA 2000, s 397(4), (5) at **[424]**.
    Reg 9 revokes the Traded Securities (Disclosure) Regulations 1994, SI 1994/188.
    Reg 10 amends the Financial Services and Markets Act 2000 (Prescribed Markets and Qualifying Investments) Order 2001, SI 2001/996 at **[2161]**.
    Reg 11 amends the Financial Services and Markets Act 2000 (Recognition Requirements for Investment Exchanges and Clearing Houses) Regulations 2001, SI 2001/995 at **[2147]**.
    Sch 1 amends FSMA 2000, Pt VI (Official listing) at **[72]** et seq.
    Sch 2 amends FSMA 2000, Pt VIII (Penalties for market abuse) at **[141]** et seq.

[3918]

INVESTMENT RECOMMENDATION (MEDIA) REGULATIONS 2005

(SI 2005/382)

NOTES
    Made: 23 February 2005.
    Authority: European Communities Act 1972, s 2(2).
    Commencement: 1 July 2005.

These Regulations are reproduced as amended by: the Financial Services (EEA State) Regulations 2007, SI 2007/108; the Financial Services and Markets Act 2000 (Markets in Financial Instruments) Regulations 2007, SI 2007/126.

ARRANGEMENT OF REGULATIONS

PART 1
CITATION, INTERPRETATION AND APPLICATION

PART 2
PRODUCTION OF INVESTMENT RECOMMENDATIONS

PART 3
DISSEMINATION OF INVESTMENT RECOMMENDATIONS PRODUCED BY THIRD PARTIES

PART 4
TERRITORIAL SCOPE AND ACTIONS FOR DAMAGES

PART 1
CITATION, INTERPRETATION AND APPLICATION

1   Citation and commencement

These Regulations may be cited as the Investment Recommendation (Media) Regulations 2005 and come into force on 1st July 2005.

[3919]

NOTES

Commencement: 1 July 2005.

2   Interpretation

In these Regulations—

["EEA State" has the meaning given by Schedule 1 to the Interpretation Act 1978;]

"financial instrument" means any of the instruments listed in Article 1(3) of Directive 2003/6/EC of the European Parliament and the Council of 28 January 2003 on insider dealing and market manipulation that are admitted to trading on a regulated market (as defined in article [4.1.14 of Directive 2004/39/EC of the European Parliament and of the Council of 21 April 2004 on markets in financial instruments]) in an EEA State or for which a request for admission to trading on such a market has been made;

"investment recommendation" means information that directly recommends the buying, selling, subscribing for or the underwriting of a financial instrument or the exercise of any right conferred by such instrument to buy, sell, subscribe for or underwrite it; and

"media" means—

(a)   a newspaper, journal, magazine or other periodical publication;

(b)   a service consisting of the broadcast or transmission of television or radio programmes; or

(c)   a service (including the internet) comprising regularly updated news or information;

but excluding any such publication or service the principal purpose of which (taken as a whole and including any advertisements or other promotional material contained in it) is a purpose mentioned in article 54(1)(a) or (b) of the Financial Services and Markets Act 2000 (Regulated Activities) Order 2001.

[3920]

NOTES

Commencement: 1 July 2005.

Definition "EEA State" substituted by the Financial Services (EEA State) Regulations 2007, SI 2007/108, reg 11, as from 13 February 2007.

Words in square brackets in the definition "financial instrument" substituted by the Financial Services and Markets Act 2000 (Markets in Financial Instruments) Regulations 2007, SI 2007/126, reg 3(6), Sch 6, Pt 2, para 20, as from 1 November 2007 (for the full commencement details of SI 2007/126, see reg 1 of those Regulations at **[4051]**).

3 Application of Regulations

(1)   These Regulations apply in respect of the production and the dissemination of an investment recommendation which the producer of that recommendation intends to be, or to become, publicly available in or through the media.

(2)   Subject to paragraphs (3) and (4), any person whose business or profession is in the media and who, in the conduct of that business, or in the exercise of that profession, either—

(a)   produces an investment recommendation, or

(b)   disseminates an investment recommendation produced by a third party,

must do so in accordance with Parts 2 and 3; and references to a "person producing an investment recommendation" and to a "person disseminating an investment recommendation produced by a third party" are references respectively to such persons.

(3)   These Regulations do not apply to—

(a)   a person (being an authorised person within section 31 of the Financial Services and Markets Act 2000) ("the Act") producing an investment recommendation where such production by him is regulated pursuant to section 22 of the Act; and

(b)   a person (being an authorised person within section 31 of the Act) disseminating an investment recommendation produced by a third party where such dissemination is regulated pursuant to section 22 of the Act.

(4)   Parts 2 and 3 do not apply to the production and dissemination of an investment recommendation where—

(a)   the media in or through which the recommendation appears is subject either to a self-regulatory code or to an appropriate system or procedure with respect to the presentation of investment recommendations and to the disclosure of financial interests and conflicts of interest, and

(b)   the publication, programme or regularly updated news or information service in or through which the recommendation appears includes a clear and prominent reference to the relevant code, system or procedure.

(5)   In paragraph (4)(a), a "self-regulatory code" means the Code of Practice issued by the Press Complaints Commission, the Producers' Guidelines issued by the British Broadcasting Corporation and any code published by the Office of Communications pursuant to section 324 of the Communications Act 2003.

[3921]

NOTES

Commencement: 1 July 2005.

PART 2
PRODUCTION OF INVESTMENT RECOMMENDATIONS

4 Disclosure of identity of producers

A person producing an investment recommendation must disclose clearly and prominently in that recommendation his identity, in particular, the name and job title of the individual who prepared it and the name of the legal person responsible for its production.

[3922]

NOTES

Commencement: 1 July 2005.

5 Fair presentation

Reasonable care must be taken by a person producing an investment recommendation to ensure that in that recommendation—

(a)   facts are clearly distinguished from interpretations, estimates, opinions and other types of non-factual information;

(b)   all the documents, figures, names and other records used are reliable and if there is any doubt as to their reliability that this is clearly indicated; and

(c)   all projections, forecasts and price targets are clearly labelled as such and that any material assumptions made in producing or using them are indicated.

[3923]

NOTES
Commencement: 1 July 2005.

6 Disclosure of interests etc

(1)   Subject to paragraph (6), a person producing an investment recommendation must disclose, in the recommendation itself, all relationships and circumstances that may reasonably be expected to impair the objectivity of that recommendation, in particular, where he has—

(a)   a significant financial interest in one or more of the financial instruments which are the subject of the investment recommendation, or

(b)   a significant conflict of interest with respect to an issuer of a financial instrument to which the investment recommendation (directly or indirectly) relates.

(2)   For the purposes of paragraph (1)(a), a "significant" financial interest includes—

(a)   in relation to a legal person, a holding exceeding 5% of the total issued share capital in the issuer of the shares in question, and

(b)   in relation to a natural person, a holding exceeding £3000 of the total issued share capital in the issuer of the shares in question.

(3)   Where the person producing the investment recommendation is a legal person—

(a)   the significant financial interests and the significant conflicts of interest that it must disclose under paragraph (1) include any such interests or interest that it (or any connected legal person) has that are—

(i)   accessible, or reasonably expected to be accessible, to the persons involved in the preparation of the recommendation, or

(ii)   that are known to persons who, although not involved in the preparation of the recommendation, had, or could reasonably be expected to have, access to the recommendation prior to its being disseminated to customers or to the public; and

(b)   the requirement of disclosure of significant financial interests and of significant conflicts of interest under paragraph (1) applies also to any person who (whether under a contract of employment or otherwise) works for the person producing the investment recommendation and who was directly involved in preparing that recommendation.

(4)   The reference in paragraph (3)(a) to a legal person being "connected" to the person ("A") producing the investment recommendation, means—

(a)   a parent undertaking of A;

(b)   a subsidiary undertaking of A;

(c)   a subsidiary undertaking of the parent undertaking of A;

(d)   a parent undertaking of a subsidiary undertaking of A; or

(e)   an undertaking in which A or an undertaking mentioned in sub-paragraph (a), (b), (c) or (d) has a participating interest.

(5)   In paragraph (4)—

"parent undertaking" in sub-paragraphs (a), (c) and (d) has the same meaning as in Part 7 of the Companies Act 1985 (or Part 8 of the Companies (Northern Ireland) Order 1986); and includes an individual who would be a parent undertaking for the purposes of those provisions if he were an undertaking (and "subsidiary undertaking" is to be read accordingly).

"subsidiary undertaking" in sub-paragraphs (b), (c) and (d) has the same meaning as in Part 7 of the Companies Act 1985 (or Part 8 of the Companies (Northern Ireland) Order 1986); and includes, in relation to a body incorporated in or formed under the law of any EEA State other than the United Kingdom, an undertaking which is a subsidiary undertaking within the meaning of any rule of law in that State for the purposes of the Seventh Company Law Directive (and "parent undertaking" is to be read accordingly); and

"participating interest" in sub-paragraph (e) has the same meaning as in Part 7 of the Companies Act 1985 (or Part 8 of the Companies (Northern Ireland) Order 1986); and includes an interest held by an individual which would be a participating interest for the purposes of these provisions if he were taken to be an undertaking.

(6)   A person producing an investment recommendation may, if he considers that the disclosure required under paragraph (1) would be disproportionate in relation to the length of that recommendation, comply with the requirements of that paragraph—

(a)   by including in the recommendation itself a clear and prominent reference to the place where the disclosure can be directly and easily accessed by the public (such as an appropriate internet site of his from which a direct internet link can be made to such disclosures), or

(b)   where he produces two or more recommendations which appear together, by including in one of the recommendations a single clear and prominent reference to the place where the disclosures required for all the recommendations can be directly and easily accessed by the public.

[3924]

NOTES
Commencement: 1 July 2005.

7 Non-written investment recommendations

(1) A person producing a non-written investment recommendation may comply with the requirements of regulations 4 to 6 to disclose information or indicate certain matters—

(a) by including in the recommendation itself a clear and prominent reference to the place where the information and matters that would otherwise have to be disclosed or indicated in it can be directly and easily accessed by the public (such as at an appropriate internet site to which a direct internet link can be made to those matters or to that information), or

(b) where he produces two or more recommendations which appear together, by including in one of the recommendations a single clear and prominent reference to the place where the information and matters required to be disclosed or indicated for all the recommendations can be directly and easily accessed by the public.

(2) A "non-written investment recommendation" is an investment recommendation that is—

(a) broadcast or transmitted in the form of a television or radio programme, or

(b) displayed on a web site (or similar system for the electronic display of information).

[3925]

NOTES
Commencement: 1 July 2005.

PART 3
DISSEMINATION OF INVESTMENT RECOMMENDATIONS PRODUCED BY THIRD PARTIES

8 Disclosure of identity of persons disseminating investment recommendations

If a person having no authority from the person who produced an investment recommendation to do so nevertheless on his own behalf disseminates that recommendation, he must indicate his own identity clearly and prominently in the recommendation or ensure that it is otherwise clearly and prominently indicated to the persons to whom that recommendation is being disseminated.

[3926]

NOTES
Commencement: 1 July 2005.

9 Dissemination of altered investment recommendations

(1) A person disseminating an investment recommendation produced by a third party who makes a change to the direction of the recommendation (such as the change of a recommendation to "buy" into one to "hold" or to "sell" (or vice versa)), must comply with regulations 4 to 6.

(2) A person disseminating an investment recommendation produced by a third party who does not make a change to the direction of the recommendation but who makes some other substantial alteration, must ensure that the details of that alteration are clearly indicated.

(3) Where the dissemination referred to in paragraph (2) is by a legal person (either itself or through a natural person) that legal person must have a formal written policy so that those receiving the information are directed to where they can have access to—

(a) the identity of the person who produced that recommendation,

(b) the investment recommendation itself, and

(c) any disclosures of the financial interests and conflicts of interest of the person who produced the recommendation which have been made pursuant to regulation 6(1) or in accordance with any rules made by the Financial Services Authority.

[3927]

NOTES
Commencement: 1 July 2005.

10 Dissemination of summaries of investment recommendations

Where an investment recommendation produced by a third party is summarised and the summary is then disseminated, the summary must—

(a)   be clear and not misleading,

(b)   mention the document in which the investment recommendation appears, and

(c)   indicate where any disclosures as to the financial interests and conflicts of interest of the person who produced the investment recommendation which have been disclosed pursuant to regulation 6(1) or in accordance with any rules made by the Financial Services Authority, can be directly and clearly accessed by the public.

[3928]

NOTES
Commencement: 1 July 2005.

11 News reporting on investment recommendations

Where no change is made to the essence of an investment recommendation produced by a third party or where a summary is made of an investment recommendation produced by a third party, the requirements respectively of regulations 9 and 10 need not be complied with as respects news reporting on that recommendation or summary in or through the media.

[3929]

NOTES
Commencement: 1 July 2005.

PART 4
TERRITORIAL SCOPE AND ACTIONS FOR DAMAGES

12 Territorial scope

These Regulations apply to any act or course of conduct of—

(a)   a person producing an investment recommendation, if his act is done, or his course of conduct is engaged in, in the United Kingdom, regardless of whether that recommendation is then disseminated in or from the United Kingdom or in or from another EEA State;

(b)   a person disseminating an investment recommendation produced by a third party, if his act is done, or his course of conduct is engaged in, in or from—

    (i)   his registered office (or if he does not have a registered office his head office), or

    (ii)   another establishment maintained by him,

in the United Kingdom, regardless of whether any person to whom that recommendation is disseminated is in the United Kingdom or in another EEA State.

[3930]

NOTES
Commencement: 1 July 2005.

13 Actions for damages

(1)   A contravention of a provision in Part 2 or 3 is actionable at the suit of a private person who suffers loss as a result of the contravention, subject to the defences and other incidents applying to actions for breach of statutory duty.

(2)   A "private person" is a person who is a private person within regulation 3(1) of the Financial Services and Markets Act 2000 (Rights of Action) Regulations 2001.

[3931]

NOTES
Commencement: 1 July 2005.

PROSPECTUS REGULATIONS 2005 (NOTE)

(SI 2005/1433)

NOTES
Made: 26 May 2005.
Authority: European Communities Act 1972, s 2(2).
Commencement: 1 July 2005.
As of 1 February 2009, these Regulations had not been amended.
These Regulations implement Directive 2003/71/EC of the European Parliament and of the Council of 4th November 2003 on the prospectus to be published when securities are offered to the public or admitted to trading on a regulated market ("the prospectus directive") at **[5452]**.

They substitute FSMA 2000, ss 84–87 with new ss 84–87, 87A–87R (at **[84]** et seq).

Section 84 sets out the matters that may be dealt with in prospectus rules which the FSA will make. These matters include the form and content of a prospectus, the period of validity of a prospectus and the ways in which a prospectus may be published.

Section 85 states the general rule that a person may not make an offer of securities to the public in the UK, or seek admission to trading on a regulated market in the UK, unless a prospectus approved by the FSA has been published. Prospectuses approved by the competent authorities of other EEA States are treated in the same way as those approved by the FSA provided the conditions in s 87H are complied with. Section 85 and Schedule 11A exempt certain securities from the s 85 requirement. Section 86 exempts certain offers from that requirement.

Section 87A states the criteria by which the FSA will approve a prospectus. Section 87B allows the FSA to authorise the omission of information which a prospectus would otherwise have to contain. Section 87C contains the time limits during which applications need to be processed by the FSA and allows the FSA to seek further information in relation to applications for approval of a prospectus. Section 87D contains the procedure to be followed when the FSA approves, proposes not to approve or decides not to approve a prospectus. Sections 87E and 87F allow applications for approval to be transferred between competent authorities within the EEA. Section 87G states when a supplementary prospectus must be produced.

Sections 87J to 87M deal with the powers of the FSA, including conditions precedent to approval (s 87J), the power to suspend or prohibit offers to the public (s 87K), the power to suspend or prohibit admission to trading on a regulated market (s 87L) and the power publicly to censure (s 87M).

These Regulations also replace Schedule 11 to the 2000 Act with a new Schedule 11A (Transferable Securities) at **[478]** et seq.

These Regulations also revoke the Public Offers of Securities Regulations 1995 (SI 1995/1537) and the Financial Services and Markets Act 2000 (Offers of Securities) Order 2001 (SI 2001/2958), and make minor and consequential amendments to CA 1989, the Companies (Audit, Investigations and Community Enterprise) Act 2004, and the Financial Services and Markets Act 2000 (Official Listing of Securities) Regulations 2001 (SI 2001/2956). All amendments have been incorporated at the appropriate place in this Handbook.

[3932]

INSURERS (REORGANISATION AND WINDING UP) (LLOYD'S) REGULATIONS 2005

(SI 2005/1998)

NOTES

Made: 19 July 2005.
Authority: European Communities Act 1972, s 2(2).
Commencement: 10 August 2005.
These Regulations are reproduced as amended by: the Insurers (Reorganisation and Winding Up) (Amendment) Regulations 2007, SI 2007/851.

ARRANGEMENT OF REGULATIONS

PART 1
GENERAL

PART 2
LLOYD'S MARKET REORGANISATION ORDER

PART 3
MODIFICATION OF LAW OF INSOLVENCY: NOTIFICATION AND PUBLICATION

PART 4
APPLICATION OF PARTS 4 AND 5 OF THE PRINCIPAL REGULATIONS

PART 1
GENERAL

1   Citation and commencement

These Regulations may be cited as the Insurers (Reorganisation and Winding Up) (Lloyd's)
Regulations 2005, and come into force on 10 August 2005.

[3933]

NOTES
   Commencement: 10 August 2005.

---

2   Interpretation

(1)   In these Regulations—
   "the Administration for Insurers Order" means the Financial Services and Markets Act 2000
      (Administration Orders Relating to Insurers) Order 2002 [and the "Administration for
      Insurers (Northern Ireland) Order" means the Financial Services and Markets Act 2000
      (Administration Relating to Insurers) (Northern Ireland) Order 2007];
   "affected market participant" means any member, former member, managing agent, members'
      agent, Lloyd's broker, approved run-off company or coverholder to whom the Lloyd's
      market reorganisation order applies;
   "approved run-off company" means a company with the permission of the Society to perform
      executive functions, insurance functions or administrative and processing functions on
      behalf of a managing agent;
   "the association of underwriters known as Lloyd's" has the meaning it has for the purposes of
      the First Council Directive of 24 July 1973 on the coordination of laws, regulations and
      administrative provisions relating to the taking and pursuit of the business of direct
      insurance other than life assurance (73/239/EEC) and Directive 2002/83/EC of the
      European Parliament and of the Council of 5 November 2002 concerning life assurance;
   "central funds" means the New Central Fund as provided for in the New Central Fund Byelaw
      (No 23 of 1996) and the Central Fund as provided for in the Central Fund Byelaw (No 4
      of 1986);

"company" means a company within the meaning of section 735 of the 1985 Act or Article 3 of the Companies Order or a company incorporated elsewhere than in Great Britain that is a member of Lloyd's;

"corporate member" means a company admitted to membership of Lloyd's as an underwriting member;

"coverholder" means a company or partnership authorised by a managing agent to enter into, in accordance with the terms of a binding authority, a contract or contracts of insurance to be underwritten by the members of a syndicate managed by that managing agent;

"former member" means a person who has ceased to be a member, whether by resignation or otherwise, in accordance with Lloyd's Act 1982 and any byelaw made under it or in accordance with the provisions of Lloyd's Acts 1871–1982 then in force at the time the person ceased to be a member;

"Gazette" means the London Gazette, the Edinburgh Gazette and the Belfast Gazette;

"individual member" means a member or former member who is an individual;

"insurance market activity" has the meaning given by section 316(3) of the 2000 Act;

"insurance market debt" means an insurance debt under or in connection with a contract of insurance written at Lloyd's;

"Lloyd's Acts 1871–1982" means Lloyd's Act 1871, Lloyd's Act 1911, Lloyd's Act 1951 and Lloyd's Act 1982;

"Lloyd's broker" has the meaning given by section 2(1) of Lloyd's Act 1982;

"managing agent" has the meaning given by article 3(1) of the Financial Services and Markets Act 2000 (Regulated Activities) Order 2001;

"member" means an underwriting member of the Society;

"members' agent" means a person who carries out the activity of advising a person to become, or continue or cease to be, a member of a particular Lloyd's syndicate;

"overseas business regulatory deposit" means a deposit provided or maintained in respect of the overseas insurance and reinsurance business carried on by members in accordance with binding legal or regulatory requirements from time to time in force in the country or territory in which the deposit is held;

"overseas insurance business" means insurance business and reinsurance business transacted by members in a country or territory that is not or is not part of an EEA State;

"the principal Regulations" means the Insurers (Reorganisation and Winding Up) Regulations 2004;

"relevant trust fund" means any funds held on trust under a trust deed entered into by the member in accordance with the requirements of the Authority and the Byelaws of the Society for the payment of an obligation arising in connection with insurance market activity carried on by the member or for the establishment of a Lloyd's deposit and includes funds held on further trusts declared by the Society or the trustee of such a trust deed in respect of any class of insurance market activity;

"the Room" has the meaning given by section 2(1) of Lloyd's Act 1982;

"the Society" means the Society incorporated by Lloyd's Act 1871;

"subsidiary of the Society" means a company that is a subsidiary of the Society within the meaning of section 736 of the 1985 Act or Article 4 of the Companies Order;

"syndicate" has the meaning given by article 3(1) of the Financial Services and Markets Act 2000 (Regulated Activities) Order 2001.

(2) Subject to paragraph (3), words and phrases used in these Regulations have the same meaning as in the principal Regulations except where otherwise specified or where the context requires otherwise.

(3) For the purposes of these Regulations, "UK insurer" is to be treated as including a member or a former member.

(4) These Regulations have effect notwithstanding the provisions of section 360 of the 2000 Act.

[3934]

NOTES

Commencement: 10 August 2005.

Para (1): words in square brackets in definition "the Administration for Insurers Order" inserted by the Insurers (Reorganisation and Winding Up) (Amendment) Regulations 2007, SI 2007/851, reg 3(1), (2), as from 6 April 2007.

PART 2

LLOYD'S MARKET REORGANISATION ORDER

3 Lloyd's market reorganisation order

(1) In these Regulations "Lloyd's market reorganisation order" means an order which—

(a) is made by the court in relation to the association of underwriters known as Lloyd's;

(b)   appoints a reorganisation controller; and
(c)   on the making of which there comes into force a moratorium on the commencement of—
    (i)   proceedings, or
    (ii)   other legal processes
set out in regulation 8 in respect of affected market participants, the Society and subsidiaries of the Society.

(2)   A Lloyd's market reorganisation order applies to—
(a)   every member, former member, managing agent, members' agent, Lloyd's broker and approved run-off company who has not been excluded from the order in accordance with regulation 7;
(b)   every coverholder who has been included in the order in accordance with regulation 7;
(c)   the Society; and
(d)   subsidiaries of the Society.

[3935]

NOTES
Commencement: 10 August 2005.

4   Condition for making order

(1)   The court may make a Lloyd's market reorganisation order if it is satisfied that—
(a)   any regulatory solvency requirement is not, or may not be, met; and
(b)   an order is likely to achieve one or both of the objectives in regulation 5.

(2)   In paragraph (1), "regulatory solvency requirement" means a requirement to maintain adequate financial resources in respect of insurance business at Lloyd's, imposed under the 2000 Act, whether on a member or former underwriting member, either singly or together with other members or former underwriting members, or on the Society and includes a requirement to maintain a margin of solvency.

(3)   In paragraph (2), "former underwriting member" has the meaning given by section 324(1) of the 2000 Act.

[3936]

NOTES
Commencement: 10 August 2005.

5   Objectives of a Lloyd's market reorganisation order

The objectives of a Lloyd's market reorganisation order are—
(a)   to preserve or restore the financial situation of, or market confidence in, the association of underwriters known as Lloyd's in order to facilitate the carrying on of insurance market activities by members at Lloyd's;
(b)   to assist in achieving an outcome that is in the interests of creditors of members, and insurance creditors in particular.

[3937]

NOTES
Commencement: 10 August 2005.

6   Application for a Lloyd's market reorganisation order

(1)   An application for a Lloyd's market reorganisation order may be made by the Authority or by the Society, or by both.

(2)   If the application is made by only one of those bodies it must inform the other body of its intention to make the application as soon as possible, and in any event before the application is lodged at the court.

(3)   The Authority and the Society are entitled to be heard at the hearing of the application, regardless of which body makes the application.

(4)   An application must clearly designate—
(a)   any member, former member, managing agent, members' agent, Lloyd's broker, or approved run-off company to whom the order should not apply; and
(b)   every coverholder to whom the order should apply.

(5)   The applicant must give notice of the application by—
(a)   ensuring the posting of a copy in the Room,
(b)   displaying a copy on its website, and
(c)   publishing a copy
    (i)   in the Gazette, and

    (ii)   in such newspaper or newspapers within the United Kingdom and elsewhere as the applicant considers appropriate to bring the application to the attention of those likely to be affected by it.

(6)   The notice must be given as soon as reasonably practicable after the making of the application, unless the court orders otherwise.

[3938]

NOTES
Commencement: 10 August 2005.

7 Powers of the court

(1)   On hearing an application for a Lloyd's market reorganisation order, the court may make—
    (a)   a Lloyd's market reorganisation order, and
    (b)   any other order in addition to a Lloyd's market reorganisation order which the court thinks appropriate for the attainment of either or both of the objectives in regulation 5.

(2)   A Lloyd's market reorganisation order comes into force—
    (a)   at the time appointed by the court; or
    (b)   if no time is so appointed, when the order is made

and remains in force until revoked by the court.

(3)   The court may on an application made by the Authority or the Society at the same time as an application under regulation 6 or the reorganisation controller, the Authority, the Society, a subsidiary of the Society or any affected market participant at any time while the Lloyd's market reorganisation order is in force, amend or vary a Lloyd's market reorganisation order so that it—
    (a)   does not apply to—
        (i)   particular assets, or
        (ii)   particular members, former members, member's agents, managing agents, Lloyd's brokers, approved run-off companies or subsidiaries of the Society,
    specified in the order; and
    (b)   does apply to any coverholder specified in the order.

(4)   The court—
    (a)   must appoint one or more persons to be the reorganisation controller;
    (b)   must specify the powers and duties of the reorganisation controller;
    (c)   may establish or approve the respective duties and functions of two or more persons appointed to be the reorganisation controller, including specifying that one of them shall have precedence; and
    (d)   may from time to time vary the powers of a reorganisation controller.

(5)   An application made under paragraph (3) other than at the time of the application under regulation 6 shall be served on the reorganisation controller and the Authority who shall each be entitled to attend and be heard at a hearing of such an application.

[3939]

NOTES
Commencement: 10 August 2005.

8 Moratorium

(1)   Except with the permission of the court, for the period during which a Lloyd's market reorganisation order is in force, no proceedings or other legal process may be commenced or continued against:
    (a)   an affected market participant;
    (b)   the Society; or
    (c)   a subsidiary of the Society to which the order applies.

(2)   In paragraph (1),
    (a)   "court" means in England and Wales the High Court, in Northern Ireland the High Court and in Scotland the Court of Session; and
    (b)   "proceedings" means proceedings of every description and includes:
        (i)   a petition under section 124 or 124A of the 1986 Act or Article 104 or 104A of the 1989 Order for the appointment of a liquidator or provisional liquidator;
        (ii)   an application under section 252 of the 1986 Act or Article 226 of the 1989 Order for an interim order;
        (iii)   a petition for a bankruptcy order under Part 9 of the 1986 Act or Part 9 of the 1989 Order; and
        (iv)   a petition for sequestration under section 5 or 6 of the Bankruptcy (Scotland) Act, but
    does not include prosecution for a criminal offence.

(3)   Except with the permission of the court, for the period during which a Lloyd's market reorganisation order is in force, no execution may be commenced or continued, no security may be enforced, and no distress may be levied, against (or against the assets of or in the possession of):

(a)   any person specified in paragraph (1);

(b)   a relevant trust fund (or the trustees of a relevant trust fund); and

(c)   an overseas business regulatory deposit.

(4)   Paragraph (3) does not prevent the enforcement of—

(a)   approved security granted to secure payment of approved debts of a member incurred in connection with an overseas regulatory deposit arrangement; or

(b)   security granted by a Lloyd's broker over assets not being assets constituting or representing assets received or held by the Lloyd's broker as intermediary in respect of any contract of insurance or reinsurance written at Lloyd's or any contract of reinsurance reinsuring a member of Lloyd's in respect of a contract or contracts of insurance or reinsurance written by that member at Lloyd's.

(5)   In the application of paragraph (3) to Scotland, references to execution being commenced or continued include references to diligence being carried out or continued, and references to distress being levied shall be omitted.

(6)   For the period during which a Lloyd's market reorganisation order is in force, no action or step may be taken in respect of any of the persons specified in paragraph (1) by any person who is or may be entitled—

(a)   under any provision in Schedule B1 [or in Schedule B1 to the 1989 Order] to appoint an administrator;

(b)   to appoint an administrative receiver or receiver;

(c)   under section 425 of the 1985 Act or Article 418 of the Companies Order to propose a compromise or arrangement,

unless he has complied with paragraph (7).

(7)   A person intending to take any such action or step shall give notice [in writing] to the reorganisation controller before doing so.

(8)   Where a person fails to comply with paragraph (7),

(a)   an appointment to which sub-paragraph (6)(a) or (b) applies shall be void, and

(b)   no application under section 425 or Article 418 may be entertained by the court,

except where the court, having heard the reorganisation controller, orders otherwise.

(9)   Every application pursuant to paragraph (1) or paragraph (3) must be served on the reorganisation controller.

(10)   For the period during which a Lloyd's market reorganisation order is in force, an affected market participant in Scotland may not grant a trust deed for his creditors without the consent of the reorganisation controller.

(11)   Where a person who is subject to a Lloyd's market reorganisation order is, at the date of the order, in administration or liquidation or has been adjudged bankrupt or is a person whose estate is being sequestrated or who has granted a trust deed for his creditors—

(a)   any application to the court for permission to take any action that would be subject to a moratorium arising in those earlier proceedings shall be served on the reorganisation controller and the reorganisation controller shall be entitled to be heard on the application; and

(b)   the court shall take into account the achievement of the objectives for which the Lloyd's market reorganisation order was made.

(12)   In this regulation—

(a)   "approved debt" means a debt approved by the Society at the time it is incurred;

(b)   "approved security" means security approved by the Society at the time it is granted over or in respect of assets comprised in the member's premiums trust funds or liable in the future to become comprised therein;

(c)   "overseas regulatory deposit arrangement" means an arrangement approved by the Society and notified to the Authority whose purpose is to facilitate funding of any overseas business regulatory deposit.

[3940]

NOTES

Commencement: 10 August 2005.

Paras (6), (7): words in square brackets inserted by the Insurers (Reorganisation and Winding Up) (Amendment) Regulations 2007, SI 2007/851, reg 3(1), (3), as from 6 April 2007.

---

9   Reorganisation controller

(1)   The reorganisation controller is an officer of the court.

(2)   A person may be appointed as reorganisation controller only if he is qualified to act as an insolvency practitioner under Part 13 of the 1986 Act [or under Part 12 of the 1989 Order] and the court considers that he has appropriate knowledge, expertise and experience.

(3)   On an application by the reorganisation controller, the court may appoint one or more additional reorganisation controllers to act jointly or severally with the first reorganisation controller on such terms as the court sees fit.

[3941]

NOTES
Commencement: 10 August 2005.
Para (2); words in square brackets inserted by the Insurers (Reorganisation and Winding Up) (Amendment) Regulations 2007, SI 2007/851, reg 3(1), (4), as from 6 April 2007.

10   Announcement of appointment of controller

(1)   This regulation applies when the court makes a Lloyd's market reorganisation order.

(2)   As soon as is practicable after the order has been made, the Authority must inform the EEA regulators in every EEA State—

(a)   that the order has been made; and
(b)   in general terms, of the possible effect of a Lloyd's market reorganisation order on—
    (i)   the effecting or carrying out of contracts of insurance at Lloyd's, and
    (ii)   the rights of policyholders under or in respect of contracts of insurance written at Lloyd's.

(3)   As soon as is reasonably practicable after a person becomes the reorganisation controller, he must—

(a)   procure that notice of his appointment is posted—
    (i)   in the Room,
    (ii)   on the Society's website, and
    (iii)   on the Authority's website; and
(b)   publish a notice of his appointment—
    (i)   once in the Gazette, and
    (ii)   once in such newspapers as he thinks most appropriate for securing so far as possible that the Lloyd's market reorganisation order comes to the notice of those who may be affected by it.

[3942]

NOTES
Commencement: 10 August 2005.

11   Market reorganisation plan

(1)   The reorganisation controller may require any affected market participant, and any Lloyd's broker, approved run-off company, coverholder, the Society, subsidiary of the Society or trustee of a relevant trust fund—

(a)   to provide him with any information he considers useful to him in the achievement of the objectives set out in regulation 5; and
(b)   to carry out such work as may be necessary to prepare or organise information as the reorganisation controller may consider useful to him in the achievement of those objectives.

(2)   As soon as is reasonably practicable and in any event by such date as the court may require, the reorganisation controller must prepare a plan ("the market reorganisation plan") for achieving the objectives of the Lloyd's market reorganisation order.

(3)   The reorganisation controller must send a copy of the market reorganisation plan to the Authority and to the Society.

(4)   Before the end of a period of one month beginning with the day on which it receives the market reorganisation plan, the Authority must notify the reorganisation controller and the Society in writing of its decision to—

(a)   approve the plan;
(b)   reject the plan; or
(c)   approve the plan provisionally, subject to modifications set out in the notification.

(5)   Where the Authority rejects the plan, the notification must—

(a)   give reasons for its decision; and
(b)   specify a date by which the reorganisation controller may submit a new market reorganisation plan.

(6)   Where the reorganisation controller submits a new market reorganisation plan, he must send a copy to the Authority and to the Society.

(7)   Before the end of a period of one month beginning with the day on which the Authority receives that plan, the Authority must—
- (a)   accept it;
- (b)   reject it; or
- (c)   accept it provisionally subject to modifications.

(8)   Before the end of a period of one month beginning with the day on which he receives the notification from the Authority of the modifications required by it, the reorganisation controller must—
- (a)   accept the plan as modified by the Authority; or
- (b)   reject the plan as so modified.

(9)   The reorganisation controller must—
- (a)   file with the court the market reorganisation plan that has been approved by him and the Authority, and
- (b)   send a copy of it to—
  - (i)   every member, former member, managing agent and member's agent who requests it, and
  - (ii)   every other person who requests it, on payment of a reasonable charge.

(10)   Paragraph (11) applies if—
- (a)   the Authority rejects the market reorganisation plan and the reorganisation controller decides not to submit a new market reorganisation plan;
- (b)   the Authority rejects the new market reorganisation plan submitted by the reorganisation controller; or
- (c)   the reorganisation controller rejects the modifications made by the Authority to a new market reorganisation plan.

(11)   As soon as is reasonably practicable after any such rejection, the reorganisation controller must apply to the court for directions.

(12)   The Authority or the reorganisation controller as the case may be may apply to the court for an extension of the period specified in paragraph (4), (7) or (8) by a period of not more than one month. The court may not grant more than one such extension in respect of each period.

(13)   Where any person is under an obligation to publish anything under this regulation, that obligation is subject to the provisions of sections 348 and 349 of the 2000 Act.

[3943]

NOTES
Commencement: 10 August 2005.

12   Remuneration of the reorganisation controller

(1)   The reorganisation controller shall be entitled to receive remuneration and to recover expenses properly incurred in connection with the performance of his functions under or in connection with a Lloyd's market reorganisation order.

(2)   Subject to paragraph (3), the remuneration so charged is payable by—
- (a)   members,
- (b)   former members,
- (c)   the Society, and
- (d)   managing agents.

(3)   The court must give directions as to the payment of the remuneration and expenses of the reorganisation controller and in particular may provide for—
- (a)   apportionment of the amounts so charged between the classes of persons set out in paragraph (2) and between groups of persons within those classes; and
- (b)   payment of such remuneration and expenses out of relevant trust funds.

(4)   Amounts of such remuneration and expenses paid by any of the persons described in paragraph (2) are to be treated as payments of the expenses of a liquidator, administrator, trustee in bankruptcy or in Scotland an interim or permanent trustee.

(5)   The reorganisation controller may pay the reasonable charges of those to whom he has addressed a request for assistance or information under regulation 11 or anyone else from whom he has requested assistance in the performance of his functions.

(6)   The provision of such information or assistance in good faith does not constitute a breach of
- (a)   any duty owed by any person involved in its preparation or delivery to any company or partnership of which he is an officer, member or employee,
- (b)   any duty owed by an agent to his principal, or
- (c)   any duty of confidence, subject to sections 348 and 349 of the 2000 Act.

[3944]

PART III
STATUTORY INSTRUMENTS

NOTES
Commencement: 10 August 2005.

13 Treatment of members

(1)   Paragraph (2) applies where, after the making of a Lloyd's market reorganisation order, any of the following occurs pursuant to the 1986 Act, the 1989 Order or the Bankruptcy (Scotland) Act—

(a)   a person seeks to exercise an entitlement to appoint an administrator,

(b)   an application is made to the court for the appointment of an administrator,

(c)   a petition for the winding up of a corporate member is presented to the court,

(d)   a petition for a bankruptcy order or sequestration is presented to the court,

in respect of a member.

(2)   These Regulations, the principal Regulations[, the Administration for Insurers Order and the Administration for Insurers (Northern Ireland) Order] shall apply to the member and—

(a)   for the purposes of the principal Regulations (notwithstanding regulation 3 of those Regulations), the member shall be treated as if it, he or she were a UK insurer; and

(b)   for the purposes of the Administration for Insurers Order [or the Administration for Insurers (Northern Ireland) Order], a member that is a company shall be treated as if it were an insurance company.

(3)   Paragraph (2) does not apply where the court so orders, on the application of the administrator, liquidator, provisional liquidator, receiver or trustee in bankruptcy, the Accountant in Bankruptcy or trustee under a trust deed for creditors or the person referred to in paragraph (1)(b) or (c) seeking the appointment or presenting the petition.

(4)   A person who exercises an entitlement, makes an application or submits a petition to which paragraph (1) applies shall—

(a)   if he intends to make an application under paragraph (3) make the application before doing any of those things; and

(b)   include in any statement to be made under Schedule B1 [or in Schedule B1 to the 1989 Order], or in any application or petition, a statement as to whether an order under paragraph (3) has been made in respect of the member concerned.

(5)   An application under paragraph (3) must be notified [in writing] to the reorganisation controller.

(6)   The court must take account of any representation made by the reorganisation controller in relation to the application.

(7)   The court may not make an order under paragraph (3) unless the court considers it likely that the insurance market debts of the member will be satisfied.

(8)   In this regulation and regulation 14, references to a member include references to a former member.

[3945]

NOTES
Commencement: 10 August 2005.
Para (2): words in first pair of square brackets substituted, and words in second pair of square brackets inserted, by the Insurers (Reorganisation and Winding Up) (Amendment) Regulations 2007, SI 2007/851, reg 3(1), (5)(a), (b), as from 6 April 2007.
Paras (4), (5): words in square brackets inserted SI 2007/851, reg 3(1), (5)(c), (d), as from 6 April 2007.

14 Revocation of an order under regulation 13

(1)   This regulation applies in the case of a member in respect of whom an order has been made under regulation 13(3).

(2)   If the Society does not meet any request for payment of a cash call made by or on behalf of such a member, it must so inform the reorganisation controller, the Authority and the court.

(3)   If it appears to the reorganisation controller that, in respect of any such member, the insurance market debts of the member are not likely to be satisfied, he must apply to the court for the revocation of that order.

(4)   If the court revokes an order made under regulation 13(3), the provisions of these Regulations, the principal Regulations and the Administration for Insurers Order [or the Administration for Insurers (Northern Ireland) Order] apply to the member and from the date of the revocation a relevant officer is to be treated as having been appointed by the court.

(5)   For the purposes of paragraph (4), a relevant officer means—

(a)   an administrator,

(b)   a liquidator,

   (c)   a receiver,
   (d)   a trustee in bankruptcy, or
   (e)   in Scotland, an interim or permanent trustee,
as the case may be.

(6)   For the purposes of this regulation, a "cash call" means a request or demand made by a managing agent to a member of a syndicate to make payments to the trustees of any relevant trust fund to be held for the purpose of discharging or providing for the liabilities incurred by that member as a member of the syndicate.

[3946]

NOTES
   Commencement: 10 August 2005.
   Para (4): words in square brackets inserted by the Insurers (Reorganisation and Winding Up) (Amendment) Regulations 2007, SI 2007/851, reg 3(1), (6), as from 6 April 2007.

15   Reorganisation controller's powers: voluntary arrangements in respect of a member

(1)   The directors of a corporate member or former corporate member may make a proposal for a voluntary arrangement under Part 1 of the 1986 Act (or Part 2 of the 1989 Order) in relation to the member only if the reorganisation controller consents to the terms of that arrangement.

(2)   Section 1A of that Act or Article 14A of that Order do not apply to a corporate member or former corporate member if—
   (a)   a Lloyd's market reorganisation order applies to it; and
   (b)   there is no order under regulation 13(3) in force in relation to it.

(3)   The reorganisation controller is entitled to be heard at any hearing of an application relating to the arrangement.

[3947]

NOTES
   Commencement: 10 August 2005.

16   Reorganisation controller's powers: individual voluntary arrangements in respect of a member

(1)   The reorganisation controller is entitled to be heard on an application under section 253 of the 1986 Act (or Article 227 of the 1989 Order) by an individual member or former member.

(2)   When considering such an application the court shall have regard to the objectives of the Lloyd's market reorganisation order.

(3)   Paragraphs (4) to (7) apply if an interim order is made on the application of such a person.

(4)   The reorganisation controller, or a person appointed by him for that purpose, may attend any meeting of creditors of the member or former member summoned under section 257 of the 1986 Act (or Article 231 of the 1989 Order) (summoning of creditors meeting).

(5)   Notice of the result of a meeting so summoned must be given [in writing] to the reorganisation controller by the chairman of the meeting.

(6)   The reorganisation controller may apply to the court under section 262 (challenge of meeting's decision) or 263 (implementation and supervision of approved voluntary arrangement) of the 1986 Act (or Article 236 or 237 or the 1989 Order).

(7)   If a person other than the reorganisation controller makes an application to the court under any provision mentioned in paragraph (6), the reorganisation controller is entitled to be heard at any hearing relating to the application.

[3948]

NOTES
   Commencement: 10 August 2005.
   Para (5): words in square brackets inserted by the Insurers (Reorganisation and Winding Up) (Amendment) Regulations 2007, SI 2007/851, reg 3(1), (7), as from 6 April 2007.

17   Reorganisation controller's powers: trust deeds for creditors in Scotland

(1)   This regulation applies to the granting at any time by a debtor who is a member or former member of a trust deed for creditors.

(2)   The debtor must inform the person who is or is proposed to be the trustee at or before the time that the trust deed is granted that he is a member or former member of Lloyd's.

(3)   As soon as practicable after the making of the Lloyd's market reorganisation order the trustee must send to the reorganisation controller—
   (a)   in every case, a copy of the trust deed;

PART III
STATUTORY INSTRUMENTS

(b)   where any other document or information is sent to every creditor known to the trustee in pursuance of paragraph 5(1)(c) of Schedule 5 to the Bankruptcy (Scotland) Act 1985, a copy of such document or information.

(4)   If the debtor or the trustee fails without reasonable excuse to comply with any obligation in paragraph (2) or (3) he shall be guilty of an offence and shall be liable on summary conviction to a fine not exceeding level 5 on the statutory scale or to imprisonment for a term not exceeding 3 months or both.

(5)   Paragraph 7 of that Schedule applies to the reorganisation controller as if he were a qualified creditor who has not been sent a copy of the notice as mentioned in paragraph 5(1)(c) of the Schedule.

(6)   The reorganisation controller must be given the same notice as the creditors of any meeting of creditors held in relation to the trust deed.

(7)   The reorganisation controller, or a person appointed by him for the purpose, is entitled to attend and participate in (but not to vote at) any such meeting of creditors as if the reorganisation controller were a creditor under the deed.

(8)   Expressions used in this regulation and in the Bankruptcy (Scotland) Act 1985 have the same meaning in this regulation as in that Act.

[3949]

NOTES

Commencement: 10 August 2005.

18 Powers of reorganisation controller: section 425 or Article 418 compromise or arrangement

(1)   The reorganisation controller may apply to the court for an order that a meeting or meetings be summoned under section 425(1) of the 1985 Act or Article 418(1) of the Companies Order (power of company to compromise with creditors and members) in connection with a compromise or arrangement in relation to a member or former member.

(2)   Where a member, its creditors or members make an application under section 425(1) or Article 418 the reorganisation controller is entitled to attend and be heard at any hearing.

(3)   Where a meeting is summoned under section 425(1) or Article 418(1), the reorganisation controller is entitled to attend the meeting so summoned and to participate in it (but not to vote at it).

[3950]

NOTES

Commencement: 10 August 2005.

19 Appointment of an administrator, receiver or interim trustee in relation to a member

(1)   Where a Lloyd's market reorganisation order is in force, the following appointments may be made in relation to a member or former member only where an order has been made under regulation 13(3) and has not been revoked and shall be notified to the reorganisation controller—

(a)   the appointment of an administrator under paragraph 14 of Schedule B1 [or under paragraph 15 of Schedule B1 to the 1989 Order];

(b)   the appointment of an administrator under paragraph 22 of Schedule B1 [or under paragraph 23 of Schedule B1 to the 1989 Order];

(c)   the appointment of an administrative receiver;

(d)   the appointment of an interim receiver; and

(e)   the appointment of an interim trustee, within the meaning of the Bankruptcy (Scotland) Act 1985.

(2)   The notification to the reorganisation controller under paragraph (1) must be in writing.

(3)   If the requirement to notify the reorganisation controller in paragraph (1) is not complied with the administrator, administrative receiver, interim receiver or interim trustee is guilty of an offence and is liable on conviction to a fine not exceeding level 3 on the standard scale.

[3951]

NOTES

Commencement: 10 August 2005.

Para (1): words in square brackets inserted by the Insurers (Reorganisation and Winding Up) (Amendment) Regulations 2007, SI 2007/851, reg 3(1), (8), as from 6 April 2007.

20 Reorganisation controller's powers: administration orders in respect of members

(1)   The reorganisation controller may make an administration application under paragraph 12 of Schedule B1 [or under paragraph 13 of Schedule B1 to the 1989 Order] in respect of a member or former member.

(2)   Paragraphs (3) to (5) apply if—
   (a)   a person other than the reorganisation controller makes an administration application under Schedule B1[, or under Schedule B1 to the 1989 Order,] in relation to a member or former member; and
   (b)   an order under regulation 13(3) is not in force in respect of that member.

(3)   The reorganisation controller is entitled to be heard—
   (a)   at the hearing of the administration application; and
   (b)   at any other hearing of the court in relation to the member under Schedule B1 [or under Schedule B1 to the 1989 Order].

(4)   Any notice or other document required to be sent to a creditor of the member must also be sent to the reorganisation controller.

(5)   The reorganisation controller, or a person appointed by him for the purpose, may—
   (a)   attend any meeting of creditors of the member summoned under any enactment;
   (b)   attend any meeting of a committee established under paragraph 57 of Schedule B1 [or under paragraph 58 of Schedule B1 to the 1989 Order]; and
   (c)   make representations as to any matter for decision at such a meeting.

(6)   If, during the course of the administration of a member, a compromise or arrangement is proposed between the member and its creditors, or any class of them, the reorganisation controller may apply to court under section 425 of the 1985 Act (or Article 418 of the Companies Order).

[3952]

NOTES
Commencement: 10 August 2005.
Paras (1), (2), (5): words in square brackets inserted by the Insurers (Reorganisation and Winding Up) (Amendment) Regulations 2007, SI 2007/851, reg 3(1), (9)(a), (b), (d), as from 6 April 2007.
Para (3): words in square brackets substituted by SI 2007/851, reg 3(1), (9)(c), as from 6 April 2007.

21   Reorganisation controller's powers: receivership in relation to members

(1)   This regulation applies if a receiver has been appointed in relation to a member or former member.

(2)   The reorganisation controller may be heard on an application made under section 35 or 63 of the 1986 Act (or Article 45 of the 1989 Order).

(3)   The reorganisation controller may make an application under section 41(1)(a) or 69(1)(a) of the 1986 Act (or Article 51(1)(a) of the 1989 Order).

(4)   A report under section 48(1) or 67(1) of the 1986 Act (or Article 58(1) of the 1989 Order) must be sent by the person making it to the reorganisation controller.

(5)   The reorganisation controller, or a person appointed by him for the purpose, may—
   (a)   attend any meeting of creditors of the member or former member summoned under any enactment;
   (b)   attend any meeting of a committee established under section 49 or 68 of the 1986 Act (or [Article 59] of the 1989 Order);
   (c)   attend any meeting of a committee of creditors of a member or former member in Scotland; and
   (d)   make representations as to any matter for decision at such a meeting.

(6)   Where an administration application is made in respect of a member by the reorganisation controller (and there is an administrative receiver, or in Scotland a receiver, of that member), paragraph 39 of Schedule B1 [or paragraph 40 of Schedule B1 to the 1989 Order] does not require the court to dismiss the application if it thinks that—
   (a)   the objectives of the Lloyd's market reorganisation order are more likely to be achieved by the appointment of an administrator than by the appointment or continued appointment of a receiver in respect of that member, and
   (b)   the interests of the person by or on behalf of whom the receiver was appointed will be adequately protected.

[3953]

NOTES
Commencement: 10 August 2005.
Para (5): words in square brackets substituted by the Insurers (Reorganisation and Winding Up) (Amendment) Regulations 2007, SI 2007/851, reg 3(1), (10)(a), as from 6 April 2007.
Para (6): words in square brackets inserted by SI 2007/851, reg 3(1), (10)(b), as from 6 April 2007.

22   Syndicate set-off

(1)   This regulation applies where—
   (a)   a member ("the debtor") is subject to a relevant insolvency proceeding; and
   (b)   no order under regulation 13(3) is in effect in relation to the debtor.

(2)   In the application of section 323 of the 1986 Act or Article 296 of the 1989 Order, Rule 2.85 and Rule 4.90 of the Insolvency Rules or [Rule 2.086 and] R4.096 of the Insolvency Rules (Northern Ireland) to the debtor, the following paragraphs apply in relation to each syndicate of which the debtor is a member, and for that purpose each reference to the debtor is to the debtor as a member of that syndicate only.

(3)   Subject to paragraphs (4) and (5), where there have been mutual credits, mutual debts or other mutual dealings between the debtor in the course of his business as a member of the syndicate ("syndicate A") and a creditor, an account shall be taken of what is due from the debtor to that creditor, and of what is due from that creditor to the debtor, such account to be taken in respect of business transacted by the debtor as a member of syndicate A only and the sums due from one party shall be set off against the sums due from the other.

(4)   Where the creditor is a member (whether or not a member of syndicate A) and there have been mutual credits, mutual debts or other mutual dealings between the debtor as a member of syndicate A and the creditor in the course of the creditor's business as a member of syndicate A or of another syndicate of which he is a member, paragraph (5) applies.

(5)   A separate account must be taken in relation to each syndicate of which the creditor is a member of what is due from the debtor to the creditor, and of what is due from the creditor to the debtor, in respect only of business transacted between the debtor as a member of syndicate A and the creditor as a member of the syndicate in question (and not in respect of business transacted by the creditor as a member of any other syndicate or otherwise), and the sums due from one party shall be set off against the sums due from the other.

(6)   In this regulation—
    (a)   references to a member include references to a former member; and
    (b)   "relevant insolvency proceedings" means proceedings in respect of an application or petition referred to in regulation 13(1).

[3954]

NOTES
Commencement: 10 August 2005.
Para (2): words in square brackets inserted by the Insurers (Reorganisation and Winding Up) (Amendment) Regulations 2007, SI 2007/851, reg 3(1), (11), as from 6 April 2007.

23 Voluntary winding up of members: consent of reorganisation controller

(1)   During any period in which a Lloyd's market reorganisation order is in force, a member or former member that is a company may not be wound up voluntarily without the consent of the reorganisation controller.

(2)   Before a member or former member passes a resolution for voluntary winding up it must give written notice to the reorganisation controller.

(3)   Where notice is given under paragraph (2), a resolution for voluntary winding up may be passed only—
    (a)   after the end of a period of five business days beginning with the day on which the notice was given, if the reorganisation controller has not refused his consent, or
    (b)   if the reorganisation controller has consented in writing to the passing of the resolution.

(4)   A copy of a resolution for the voluntary winding up of a member forwarded to the registrar of companies in accordance with section 380 of the 1985 Act (or Article 388 of the Companies Order) must be accompanied by a certificate issued by the reorganisation controller stating that he consents to the voluntary winding up of the member.

(5)   If paragraph (4) is complied with, the voluntary winding up is to be treated as having commenced at the time the resolution was passed.

(6)   If paragraph (4) is not complied with, the resolution has no effect.

[3955]

NOTES
Commencement: 10 August 2005.

24 Voluntary winding up of members: powers of reorganisation controller

(1)   This regulation applies in relation to a member or former member that is a company and which is being wound up voluntarily with the consent of the reorganisation controller.

(2)   The reorganisation controller may apply to the court under section 112 of the 1986 Act (reference of questions to court) (or Article 98 of the 1989 Order) in respect of the member.

(3)   The reorganisation controller is entitled to be heard at any hearing of the court in relation to the voluntary winding up of the member.

(4)   Any notice or other document required to be sent to a creditor of the member must also be sent to the reorganisation controller.

(5)   The reorganisation controller, or a person appointed by him for the purpose, is entitled—
  (a)   to attend any meeting of creditors of the member summoned under any enactment;
  (b)   to attend any meeting of a committee established under section 101 of the 1986 Act (or Article 87 of the 1989 Order); and
  (c)   to make representations as to any matter for decision at such a meeting.

(6)   If, during the course of the winding up of the member, a compromise or arrangement is proposed between the member and its creditors, or any class of them, the reorganisation controller may apply to court under section 425 of the 1985 Act (or Article 418 of the Companies Order).

[3956]

NOTES
Commencement: 10 August 2005.

25   Petition for winding up of a member by reorganisation controller

(1)   The reorganisation controller may present a petition to the court for the winding up of a member or former member that is a company.

(2)   The petition is to be treated as made under section 124 of the 1986 Act or Article 104 of the 1989 Order.

(3)   Section 122(1) of the 1986 Act, or [Article 102] of the 1989 Order must, in the case of an application made by the reorganisation controller be read as if they included the following grounds—
  (a)   the member is in default of an obligation to pay an insurance market debt which is due and payable; or
  (b)   the court considers that the member is or is likely to be unable to pay insurance market debts as they fall due; and
  (c)   in the case of either (a) or (b), the court thinks that the winding up of the member is necessary or desirable for achieving the objectives of the Lloyd's market reorganisation order.

[3957]

NOTES
Commencement: 10 August 2005.
Para (3): words in square brackets substituted by the Insurers (Reorganisation and Winding Up) (Amendment) Regulations 2007, SI 2007/851, reg 3(1), (12), as from 6 April 2007.

26   Winding up of a member: powers of reorganisation controller

(1)   This regulation applies if a person other than the reorganisation controller presents a petition for the winding up of a member or former member that is a company.

(2)   Any notice or other document required to be sent to a creditor of the member must also be sent to the reorganisation controller.

(3)   The reorganisation controller may be heard—
  (a)   at the hearing of the petition; and
  (b)   at any other hearing of the court in relation to the member under or by virtue of Part 4 or 5 of the 1986 Act (or Part 5 or 6 of the 1989 Order).

(4)   The reorganisation controller, or a person appointed by him for the purpose, may—
  (a)   attend any meeting of the creditors of the member;
  (b)   attend any meeting of a committee established for the purposes of Part 4 or 5 of the 1986 Act under section 101 of that Act or under section 141 or 142 of that Act;
  (c)   attend any meeting of a committee established for the purposes of Part 5 or 6 of the 1989 Order under Article 87 or Article 120 of that Order;
  (d)   make representations as to any matter for decision at such a meeting.

(5)   If, during the course of the winding up of a member, a compromise or arrangement is proposed between the member and its creditors, or any class of them, the reorganisation controller may apply to the court under section 425 of the 1985 Act (or Article 418 of the Companies Order).

[3958]

NOTES
Commencement: 10 August 2005.

27 Petition for bankruptcy of a member by reorganisation controller

(1) The reorganisation controller may present a petition to the court for a bankruptcy order to be made against an individual member or, in Scotland, for the sequestration of the estate of an individual.

(2) The application shall be treated as made under section 264 of the 1986 Act (or Article 238 of the 1989 Order) or in Scotland under section 5 or 6 of the Bankruptcy (Scotland) Act 1985.

(3) On such a petition, the court may make a bankruptcy order or in Scotland an award of sequestration if (and only if)—

    (a)   the member is in default of an obligation to pay an insurance market debt which is due and payable; and

    (b)   the court thinks that the making of a bankruptcy order or award of sequestration in respect of that member is necessary or desirable for achieving the objectives of the Lloyd's market reorganisation order.

[3959]

NOTES
Commencement: 10 August 2005.

28 Bankruptcy of a member: powers of reorganisation controller

(1) This regulation applies if a person other than the reorganisation controller presents a petition to the court—

    (a)   under section 264 of the 1986 Act (or Article 238 of the 1989 Order) for a bankruptcy order to be made against an individual member;

    (b)   under section 5 of the Bankruptcy (Scotland) Act 1985 for the sequestration of the estate of an individual member; or

    (c)   under section 6 of that Act for the sequestration of the estate belonging to or held for or jointly by the members of an entity mentioned in subsection (1) of that section.

(2) The reorganisation controller is entitled to be heard—

    (a)   at the hearing of the petition, and

    (b)   at any other hearing in relation to the individual member or entity under—

        (i)   Part 9 of the 1986 Act,

        (ii)   Part 9 of the 1989 Order; or

        (iii)   the Bankruptcy (Scotland) Act 1985.

(3) A copy of the report prepared under section 274 of the 1986 Act (or Article 248 of the 1989 Order) must also be sent to the reorganisation controller.

(4) The reorganisation controller, or a person appointed by him for the purpose, is entitled—

    (a)   to attend any meeting of the creditors of the individual member or entity;

    (b)   to attend any meeting of a committee established under section 301 of the 1986 Act (or Article 274 of the 1989 Order);

    (c)   to attend any meeting of commissioners held under paragraph 17 or 18 of Schedule 6 to the Bankruptcy (Scotland) Act; and

    (d)   to make representations as to any matter for decision at such a meeting.

(5) In this regulation—

    (a)   references to an individual member include references to a former member who is an individual;

    (b)   "entity" means an entity which is a member or a former member.

[3960]

NOTES
Commencement: 10 August 2005.

29 Petition for winding up of the Society by reorganisation controller

(1) The reorganisation controller may present a petition to the court for the winding up of the Society in the circumstances set out in section 221(5) (winding up of unregistered companies) of the 1986 Act.

(2) Section 221(1) of that Act shall apply in respect of a petition presented by the reorganisation controller.

[3961]

NOTES
Commencement: 10 August 2005.

30   Winding up of the Society: service of petition etc on reorganisation controller

(1)   This regulation applies if a person other than the reorganisation controller presents a petition for the winding up of the Society.

(2)   The petitioner must serve a copy of the petition on the reorganisation controller.

(3)   Any notice or other document required to be sent to a creditor of the Society must also be sent to the reorganisation controller.

(4)   The reorganisation controller is entitled to be heard—
(a)   at the hearing of the petition; and
(b)   at any other hearing of the court in relation to the Society under or by virtue of Part 5 of the 1986 Act (winding up of unregistered companies).

(5)   The reorganisation controller, or a person appointed by him for the purpose, is entitled—
(a)   to attend any meeting of the creditors of the Society;
(b)   to attend any meeting of a committee established for the purposes of Part 5 of the 1986 Act under section 101 of that Act (appointment of liquidation committee);
(c)   to make representations as to any matter for decision at such a meeting.

(6)   If, during the course of the winding up of the Society, a compromise or arrangement is proposed between the Society and its creditors, or any class of them, the reorganisation controller may apply to the court under section 425 of the 1985 Act.

[3962]

NOTES
Commencement: 10 August 2005.

31   Payments from central funds

(1)   Unless otherwise agreed in writing between the Society, the reorganisation controller and the Authority, before making a payment from central funds during the period of the Lloyd's market reorganisation order, the Society must give 5 working days [written] notice to the reorganisation controller.

(2)   Notice under paragraph (1) must specify—
(a)   the amount of the proposed payment;
(b)   the purpose for which it is proposed to be made;
(c)   the recipient of the proposed payment.

(3)   An agreement under paragraph (1) may in particular provide for payments—
(a)   to a specified person;
(b)   to a specified class of person;
(c)   for a specified purpose;
(d)   for a specified class of purposes,
to be made without the notice provided for in paragraph (1)

(4)   If before the end of the period of 5 working days from the date on which he receives the notice under paragraph (1) the reorganisation controller considers that the payment should not be made, he must within that period—
(a)   apply to the court for a determination that the payment not be made; and
(b)   give notice [in writing] of his application to the Society and the Authority on or before the making of the application,
and the Society must not make payment without the permission of the court.

(5)   The Society and the Authority may be heard at any hearing in connection with any such application.

(6)   Where the reorganisation controller makes an application under paragraph (4), the Society commits an offence if it makes a payment from central funds without the permission of the court.

(7)   If an offence under paragraph (6) is shown to have been committed with the consent or connivance of an officer of the Society, the officer as well as the Society is guilty of the offence.

(8)   A person guilty of an offence under this regulation is liable—
(a)   on summary conviction, to a fine not exceeding the statutory maximum;
(b)   on conviction on indictment, to a fine.

(9)   In this regulation "working day" means any day other than a Saturday, a Sunday, Christmas Day, Good Friday or a day which is a bank holiday under the Banking and Financial Dealings Act 1971 in any part of the United Kingdom.

(10)   In paragraph (7), "officer", in relation to the Society, means the Chairman of Lloyd's, a Deputy Chairman of Lloyd's, the Chairman of the Committee established by section 5 of Lloyd's Act 1982, a deputy Chairman of the Committee, or a member of the Council established by section 3 of that Act.

[3963]

NOTES
Commencement: 10 August 2005.
Paras (1), (4): words in square brackets inserted by the Insurers (Reorganisation and Winding Up) (Amendment) Regulations 2007, SI 2007/851, reg 3(1), (13), as from 6 April 2007.

PART 3
MODIFICATION OF LAW OF INSOLVENCY: NOTIFICATION AND PUBLICATION

32 Application of Parts 3 and 4

Parts 3 and 4 of these Regulations apply where a Lloyd's market reorganisation order is in force and in respect of a member or former member in relation to whom no order under regulation 13(3) is in force.

[3964]

NOTES
Commencement: 10 August 2005.

33 Notification of relevant decision to Authority

(1) Regulation 9 of the principal Regulations applies to a member or former member in the circumstances set out in paragraph (2) and has effect as if the modifications set out in paragraphs (3) and (4) were included in it as regards members or former members.

(2) The circumstances are where—
  (a) the member or former member is subject to a Lloyd's market reorganisation order which remains in force; and
  (b) no order has been made in respect of that member or former member under regulation 13(3) of these Regulations and has not been revoked.

(3) In paragraph (1) of regulation 9 of the principal Regulations, insert—
  (a) after sub-paragraph (b)—
    "(ba) a bankruptcy order under section 264 of the 1986 Act or under [Article 238] of the 1989 Order;
    (bb) an award of sequestration under the Bankruptcy (Scotland) Act 1985;";
  (b) after paragraph (c)—
    "(ca) the appointment of an interim trustee under section 286 or 287 of the 1986 Act or under Article 259 or 260 of the 1989 Order;
    (cb) the appointment of a trustee in bankruptcy under sections 295, 296 or 300 of that Act or under Articles 268, 269 or 273 of that Order;
    (cc) the appointment of an interim or permanent trustee under the Bankruptcy (Scotland) Act 1985;".

(4) In paragraph (2) of that regulation after "voluntary arrangement", insert "or individual voluntary arrangement" and after "supervisor" insert "or nominee (as the case may be)".

(5) In paragraph (7) of that regulation, in the definition of "qualifying arrangement",
  (a) after "voluntary arrangement" insert "or individual voluntary arrangement"; and
  (b) for "insurer", wherever appearing substitute "member or former member".

(6) In paragraph (8), after "supervisor" insert ", nominee, trustee in bankruptcy, trustee under a trust deed for creditors".

[3965]

NOTES
Commencement: 10 August 2005.
Para (3): words in square brackets substituted by the Insurers (Reorganisation and Winding Up) (Amendment) Regulations 2007, SI 2007/851, reg 3(1), (14), as from 6 April 2007.

34 Notification of relevant decision to EEA Regulators

Regulation 10 of the principal Regulations applies as if—
  (a) in paragraph (1)(b)(i) for "the business of an insurer" there were substituted "the insurance business of a member or former member"; and
  (b) in paragraph (1)(b)(ii) for "an insurer" there were substituted "a member or former member".

[3966]

NOTES
Commencement: 10 August 2005.

35 Application of certain publication requirements in the principal Regulations to members

(1) Regulation 11 of the principal Regulations (publication of voluntary arrangement, administration order, winding up order or scheme of arrangement) applies, with the following, where a qualifying decision has effect, or a qualifying order or appointment is made, in relation to a member or former member.

(2) References in regulation 11(2) to a "qualifying decision", a "qualifying order" and a "qualifying appointment" have the same meaning as in that regulation, subject to the modifications set out in paragraphs (3) and (5).

(3) Regulation 11(2)(a) has effect as if a qualifying decision included a decision with respect to the approval of a proposed individual voluntary arrangement in relation to a member in accordance with section 258 of the 1986 Act or Article 232 of the 1989 Order (decisions of creditors' meeting: individual voluntary arrangements) or in Scotland the grant of a trust deed (within the meaning of the Bankruptcy (Scotland) Act 1985).

(4) In the case of a qualifying decision of a kind mentioned in paragraph (3) above, regulation 11(4) has effect as if the information mentioned therein included the court to which an application under sections 262 (challenge of the meeting's decision) and 263(3) (implementation and supervision of approved voluntary arrangement) of the 1986 Act may be made or Articles 236 (challenge of the meeting's decision) and 237(3) (implementation and supervision of approved voluntary arrangement) of the 1989 Order, or in Scotland under paragraph 12 of Schedule 5 to the Bankruptcy (Scotland) Act 1985.

(5) Regulation 11(2)(b) has effect as if a qualifying order included in relation to a member or former member a bankruptcy order under Part 9 of the 1986 Act or Part 9 of the 1989 Order, or in Scotland, an award of sequestration under the Bankruptcy (Scotland) Act.

(6) In the case of a qualifying order of the kind mentioned in paragraph (5) above, regulation 11(4) has effect as if the information mentioned therein included the court to which an application may be made under section 303 or 375 of the 1986 Act or Article 276 of the 1989 Order, or in Scotland included the court having jurisdiction to sequestrate.

(7) Regulation 11(11) has effect as if the meaning of "relevant officer" included—
  (a) in the case of a voluntary arrangement under Part 9 of the 1986 Act or Part 9 of the 1989 Order, the nominee;
  (b) in the case of a bankruptcy order, the trustee in bankruptcy;
  (c) in Scotland,
    (i) the trustee acting under a trust deed;
    (ii) in the case of an award of sequestration, the interim or permanent trustee, as the case may be.

[3967]

NOTES

Commencement: 10 August 2005.

36 Notification to creditors: winding up proceedings relating to members

(1) Regulation 12 of the principal Regulations (notification to creditors: winding up proceedings) applies, with the following modifications, where a relevant order or appointment is made, or a relevant decision is taken, in relation to a member or former member.

(2) References in paragraph (3) of that regulation to a "relevant order", a "relevant appointment" and a "relevant decision" have the meaning they have in that regulation, subject to the modifications set out in paragraphs (3) and (7).

(3) Paragraph (3) of that regulation has effect, for the purposes of this regulation, as if—
  (a) a relevant order included a bankruptcy order made in relation to a member or former member under Part 9 of the 1986 Act or Part 9 of the 1989 Order or an award of sequestration under the Bankruptcy (Scotland) Act 1985; and
  (b) a relevant decision included a decision as a result of which a qualifying individual voluntary arrangement in relation to a member or former member has effect in accordance with section 258 of the 1986 Act or Article 232 of the 1989 Order (decisions of creditors' meeting: individual voluntary arrangements) or in Scotland the grant of a qualifying trust deed.

(4) Paragraph (4)(a) of that regulation has effect as if the reference to a UK insurer included a reference to a member or former member who is to be treated as a UK insurer for the purposes of the application of the principal Regulations.

(5) Paragraph (9) of that regulation has effect as if, in a case where a bankruptcy order is made in relation to a member or former member, it permitted the obligation under paragraph (1)(a)(ii) of that regulation to be discharged by sending a form of proof in accordance with rule 6.97 of the Insolvency Rules or Rule 6.095 of the Insolvency Rules (Northern Ireland) or submitting a claim in

accordance with section 48 of the Bankruptcy (Scotland) Act 1985, provided that the form of proof or submission of claim complies with paragraph (7) or (8) of that regulation (whichever is applicable).

(6) Paragraph (13)(a) of that regulation has effect as if the meaning of "appointed officer" included—

(a) in the case of a qualifying individual voluntary arrangement approved in relation to a member or former member, the nominee;

(b) in the case of a bankruptcy order in relation to an individual member or former member, the trustee in bankruptcy;

(c) in Scotland in the case of a sequestration, the interim or permanent trustee; and

(d) in Scotland in the case of a relevant decision, the trustee.

(7) For the purposes of paragraph (3) of that regulation, an individual voluntary arrangement approved in relation to an individual member or former member is a qualifying individual voluntary arrangement and a trust deed within section 5(4A) of the Bankruptcy (Scotland) Act 1985 is a qualifying trust deed if its purposes or objects, as the case may be, include a realisation of some or all of the assets of that member or former member and a distribution of the proceeds to creditors, with a view to terminating the whole or any part of the business of that member carried on or formerly carried on in connection with contracts of insurance written at Lloyd's.

[3968]

NOTES
Commencement: 10 August 2005.

37 Submission of claims by EEA creditor

(1) Regulation 13 of the principal Regulations (submission of claims by EEA creditors) applies, with the modifications set out in paragraphs (3) to (6) below, in the circumstances set out in paragraph (2) below, in the same way as it applies where an EEA creditor submits a claim or observations in the circumstances set out in paragraph (1) of that regulation.

(2) Those circumstances are where, after the date these Regulations come into force an EEA creditor submits a claim or observations relating to his claim in any relevant proceedings in respect of a member or former member (irrespective of when those proceedings were commenced or had effect).

(3) Paragraph (2) of that regulation has effect as if the "relevant proceedings" included—

(a) bankruptcy or sequestration; or

(b) a qualifying individual voluntary arrangement or in Scotland a qualifying trust deed for creditors.

(4) Paragraph (5) of that regulation has effect as if it also provided that paragraph (3) of that regulation does not apply where an EEA creditor submits his claim using—

(a) in a case of a bankruptcy or an award of sequestration of a member or former member, a form of proof in accordance with Rule 6.97 of Insolvency Rules or Rule 4.080 of the Insolvency Rules (Northern Ireland) or section 48 of the Bankruptcy (Scotland) Act 1985;

(b) in the case of a qualifying trust deed, the form prescribed by the trustee; and

(c) in the case of a qualifying individual voluntary arrangement, a form approved by the court for that purpose.

(5) For the purposes of that regulation (as applied in the circumstances set out in paragraph (2) above), an individual voluntary arrangement approved in relation to an individual member is a qualifying individual voluntary arrangement and a trust deed for creditors within section 5(4A) of the Bankruptcy (Scotland) Act 1985 is a qualifying trust deed for creditors if its purposes or objects as the case may be include a realisation of some or all of the assets of that member or former member and a distribution of the proceeds to creditors including insurance creditors, with a view to terminating the whole or any part of the business of that member carried on in connection with effecting or carrying out contracts of insurance written at Lloyd's.

[3969]

NOTES
Commencement: 10 August 2005.

38 Reports to creditors

(1) Regulation 14 of the principal Regulations (reports to creditors) applies with the modifications set out in paragraphs (2) to (4) where—

(a) a liquidator is appointed in respect of a member or former member in accordance with—

(i) section 100 of the 1986 Act or Article 86 of the 1989 Order (creditors' voluntary winding up: appointment of a liquidator), or

      (ii)   paragraph 83 of Schedule B1 [or paragraph 84 of Schedule B1 to the 1989 Order] (moving from administration to creditors' voluntary liquidation);

(b)   a winding up order is made by the court in respect of a member or former member;

(c)   a provisional liquidator is appointed in respect of a member or former member;

[(d)   an administrator (within the meaning given by paragraph 1(1) of Schedule B1 or paragraph 2(1) of Schedule B1 to the 1989 Order) of a member or former member includes in the statement required by Rule 2.3 of the Insolvency Rules or by Rule 2.003 of the Insolvency Rules (Northern Ireland) a statement to the effect that the objective set out in paragraph 3(1)(a) of Schedule B1 or paragraph 4(1)(a) of Schedule B1 to the 1989 Order is not reasonably likely to be achieved;]

(e)   a bankruptcy order or award of sequestration is made in respect of a member or former member.

(2)   Paragraphs (2) to (5) of that regulation have effect as if they each included a reference to—

(a)   an administrator who has made a statement to the effect that the objective set out in paragraph 3(1)(a) of Schedule B1 [or in paragraph 4(1)(a) of Schedule B1 to the 1989 Order] is not reasonably likely to be achieved;

(b)   the official receiver or a trustee in bankruptcy; and

(c)   in Scotland, an interim or permanent trustee.

(3)   Paragraph (6)(a) of that regulation has effect as if the meaning of "known creditor" included—

(a)   a creditor who is known to the administrator, the trustee in bankruptcy or the trustee, as the case may be;

(b)   in a case where a bankruptcy order is made in respect of a member or former member, a creditor who is specified in a report submitted under section 274 of the 1986 Act or [Article 248] of the 1989 Order or a statement of affairs submitted under section 288 or Article 261 in respect of the member or former member;

(c)   in a case where an administrator of a member has made a statement to the effect that the objective set out in paragraph 3(1)(a) of Schedule B1 [or in paragraph 4(1)(a) of Schedule B1 to the 1989 Order] is not reasonably likely to be achieved, a creditor who is specified in the statement of the member's affairs required by the administrator under paragraph 47(1) of [Schedule B1 or under paragraph 48(1) of Schedule B1 to the 1989 Order];

(d)   in a case where a sequestration has been awarded, a creditor who is specified in a statement of assets and liabilities under section 19 of the Bankruptcy (Scotland) Act 1985.

(4)   Paragraph (6)(b) of that regulation has effect as if "report" included a written report setting out the position generally as regards the progress of—

(a)   the bankruptcy or sequestration; or

(b)   the administration.

[3970]

NOTES

Commencement: 10 August 2005.

Para (1): words in square brackets in sub-para (a)(ii) inserted, and sub-para (d) substituted, by the Insurers (Reorganisation and Winding Up) (Amendment) Regulations 2007, SI 2007/851, reg 3(1), (15)(a), (b), as from 6 April 2007.

Para (2): words in square brackets in sub-para (a) inserted by SI 2007/851, reg 3(1), (15)(c), as from 6 April 2007.

Para (3): words in square brackets in sub-para (b) and words in second pair of square brackets in sub-para (c) substituted, and words in first pair of square brackets in sub-para (c) inserted, by SI 2007/851, reg 3(1), (15)(d), (e), as from 6 April 2007.

39 Service of notices and documents

(1)   Regulation 15 of the principal Regulations (service of notices and documents) applies, with the modifications set out in paragraphs (2) and (3) below, to any notification, report or other document which is required to be sent to a creditor of a member or former member by a provision of Part III of those Regulations as applied and modified by regulations 33 to 35 above.

(2)   Paragraph 15(5)(a)(i) of that regulation has effect as if the reference to the UK insurer which is liable under the creditor's claim included a reference to the member or former member who or which is liable under the creditor's claim.

(3)   Paragraph (7)(c) of that regulation has effect as if "relevant officer" included a trustee in bankruptcy, nominee, receiver or, in Scotland, an interim or permanent trustee under a trust deed within the meaning of section 5(4A) of the Bankruptcy (Scotland) Act who is required to send a notification to a creditor by a provision of Part III of the principal Regulations as applied and modified by regulations 33 to 37 above.

[3971]

NOTES
Commencement: 10 August 2005.

PART 4
APPLICATION OF PARTS 4 AND 5 OF THE PRINCIPAL REGULATIONS

40 Priority for insurance claims

(1) Part 4 of the principal Regulations applies with the modifications set out in paragraphs (2) to (11).

(2) References, in relation to a UK insurer, to a winding up by the court have effect as if they included a reference to the bankruptcy or sequestration of a member or former member.

(3) References to the making of a winding up order in relation to a UK insurer have effect as if they included a reference to the making of a bankruptcy order or, in Scotland, an award of sequestration in relation to an individual member or a member or former member that is a Scottish limited partnership.

(4) References to an administration order in relation to a UK insurer have effect as if they included a reference to an individual voluntary arrangement in relation to an individual member and a trust deed for creditors within the meaning of section 5(4A) of the Bankruptcy (Scotland) Act.

(5) Regulation 20 (preferential debts: disapplication of section 175 of the 1986 Act or Article 149 of the 1989 Order) has effect as if the references to section 175 of the 1986 Act and Article 149 of the 1989 Order included a reference to section 328 of that Act, Article 300 of that Order and section 51(1) (d) to (h) of the Bankruptcy (Scotland) Act 1985.

(6) Regulation 21(3) (preferential debts: long term insurers and general insurers) has effect as if after the words "rank equally among themselves" there were inserted the words "after the expenses of the bankruptcy or sequestration".

(7) Regulation 27 (composite insurers: application of other assets) has effect as if the reference to section 175 of the 1986 Act or Article 149 of the 1989 Order included a reference to section 328 of that Act, Article 300 of that Order and section 51(1) (e) to (h) of the Bankruptcy (Scotland) Act.

(8) Regulation 29 (composite insurers: general meetings of creditors) has effect as if after paragraph (2) there were inserted—

> "(3) If the general meeting of the bankrupt's creditors proposes to establish a creditors' committee pursuant to section 301(1) of the 1986 Act or Article 274(1) of the 1989 Order, it must establish separate committees of creditors in respect of long-term business liabilities and creditors in respect of general business liabilities.

> (4) The committee of creditors in respect of long-term business liabilities may exercise the functions of a creditors' committee under the 1986 Act or the 1989 Order in relation to long term business liabilities only.

> (5) The committee of creditors in respect of general business liabilities may exercise the functions of a creditors' committee under the 1986 Act or the 1989 Order in relation to general business liabilities only.

> (6) If, in terms of section 30(1) of the Bankruptcy (Scotland) Act 1985, at the statutory meeting or any subsequent meeting of creditors it is proposed to elect one or more commissioners (or new or additional commissioners) in the sequestration, it shall elect separate commissioners in respect of the long-term business liabilities and the general business liabilities.

> (7) Any commissioner elected in respect of the long-term business liabilities shall exercise his functions under the Bankruptcy (Scotland) Act 1985 in respect of the long-term business liabilities only.

> (8) Any commissioner elected in respect of the general business liabilities shall exercise his functions under the Bankruptcy (Scotland) Act 1985 in respect of the general business liabilities only.".

(9) Regulation 30 (composite insurers: apportionment of costs payable out of the assets) has effect as if in its application to members or former members who are individuals or Scottish limited partnerships—

(a) in England and Wales, the reference to Rule 4.218 of the Insolvency Rules (general rule as to priority) included a reference to Rule 6.224 of the Insolvency Rules (general rule as to priority (bankruptcy));

(b) in Northern Ireland, the reference to Rule 4.228 of the Insolvency Rules (Northern Ireland) (general rule as to priority) included a reference to Rule 6.222 of the Insolvency Rules (Northern Ireland) (general rule as to priority (bankruptcy)); and

(c)   in Scotland, the reference to Rule 4.67 of the Insolvency (Scotland) Rules includes reference to—

  (i)   any finally determined outlays or remuneration in a sequestration within the meaning of section 53 of the Bankruptcy (Scotland) Act 1985 and shall be calculated and applied separately in respect of the long-term business assets and the general business assets of that member; and

  (ii)   the remuneration and expenses of a trustee under a trust deed for creditors within the meaning of the Bankruptcy (Scotland) Act 1985,

and references to a liquidator include references to a trustee in bankruptcy, interim or permanent trustee, trustee under a trust deed for creditors, Accountant in Bankruptcy or Commissioners where appropriate.

(10)   Regulation 31 (summary remedies against liquidators) has effect as if—

(a)   the reference to section 212 of the 1986 Act or Article 176 of the 1989 Order included a reference to section 304 of that Act or Article 277 of that Order (liability of trustee);

(b)   the references to a liquidator included a reference to a trustee in bankruptcy in respect of a qualifying insolvent member; and

(c)   the reference to section 175 of the 1986 Act or Article 149 of the 1989 Order included a reference to section 328 of that Act or Article 300 of that Order.

(11)   Regulation 33 (voluntary arrangements: treatment of insurance debts) has effect as if after paragraph (3) there were inserted—

"(4)   The modifications made by paragraph (5) apply where an individual member proposes an individual voluntary arrangement in accordance with Part 8 of the 1986 Act or Part 8 of the 1989 Order, and that arrangement includes—

(a)   a composition in satisfaction of any insurance debts; and

(b)   a distribution to creditors of some or all of the assets of that member in the course of, or with a view to, terminating the whole or any part of the insurance business of that member carried on at Lloyd's.

(5)   Section 258 of the 1986 Act (decisions of creditors' meeting) has effect as if—

(a)   after subsection (5) there were inserted—

"(5A)   A meeting so summoned in relation to an individual member and taking place when a Lloyd's market reorganisation order is in force shall not approve any proposal or modification under which any insurance debt of that member is to be paid otherwise than in priority to such of his debts as are not insurance debts or preferential debts.";

(b)   after subsection (7) there were inserted—

"(8)   For the purposes of this section—

(a)   "insurance debt" has the meaning it has in the Insurers (Reorganisation and Winding Up) Regulations 2004;

(b)   "Lloyd's market reorganisation order" and "individual member" have the meaning they have in the Insurers (Reorganisation and Winding Up) (Lloyd's) Regulations 2005.".

(6)   Article 232 of the 1989 Order (Decisions of creditors' meeting) has effect as if—

(a)   after paragraph (6) there were inserted—

"(6A)   A meeting so summoned in relation to an individual member and taking place when a Lloyd's market reorganisation order is in force shall not approve any proposal or modification under which any insurance debt of that member is to be paid otherwise than in priority to such of his debts as are not insurance debts or preferential debts.";

(b)   after paragraph (9) there were inserted—

"(10)   For the purposes of this Article—

(a)   "insurance debt" has the meaning it has in the Insurers (Reorganisation and Winding Up) Regulations 2004;

(b)   "Lloyd's market reorganisation order" and "individual member" have the meaning they have in the Insurers (Reorganisation and Winding Up) (Lloyd's) Regulations 2005.".

(7)   In Scotland, where a member or former member grants a trust deed for creditors, Schedule 5 to the Bankruptcy (Scotland) Act 1985 shall be read as if after paragraph 4 there were included paragraphs 4A and 4B as follows—

"4A.   Whether or not provision is made in any trust deed, where such a trust deed includes a composition in satisfaction of any insurance debts of a member or former member and a distribution to creditors of some or all of the assets of that member or former member in the course of or with a view to meeting obligations of his insurance business carried on at Lloyd's, the trustee may not provide for any insurance debt to be paid otherwise than in priority to such of his debts as are not insurance debts or preferred debts within the meaning of section 51(2).

4B.   For the purposes of paragraph 4A,

(a) "insurance debt" has the meaning it has in the Insurance (Reorganisation and Winding Up) Regulations 2004; and

(b) "member " and "former member" have the meaning given in regulation 2(1) of the Insurers (Reorganisation and Winding Up) (Lloyd's) Regulations 2005.".".

(12) The power to apply to court in section 303 of the 1986 Act or Article 276 of the 1989 Order or section 63 of the Bankruptcy (Scotland) Act (general control of trustee by court) may be exercised by the reorganisation controller if it appears to him that any act, omission or decision of a trustee of the estate of a member contravenes the provisions of Part 4 of the principal Regulations (as applied by this regulation).

[3972]

NOTES

Commencement: 10 August 2005.

41 Treatment of liabilities arising in connection with a contract subject to reinsurance to close

(1) Where in respect of a member or former member who is subject to a Lloyd's market reorganisation order any of the events specified in paragraph (2)(a) have occurred, for the purposes of the application of Part 4 of the principal Regulations to that member (and only for those purposes), an obligation of that member under a reinsurance to close contract in respect of a debt due or treated as due under a contract of insurance written at Lloyd's is to be treated as an insurance debt.

(2) For the purposes of this regulation—
  (a) The events are—
    (i) in respect of a member which is a corporation the appointment of a liquidator, provisional liquidator or administrator;
    (ii) in respect of an individual member, the appointment of a receiver or trustee in bankruptcy; and
    (iii) in respect of a member in Scotland being either an individual or a Scottish limited partnership, the making of a sequestration order or the appointment of an interim or permanent trustee;
  (b) "reinsurance to close contract" means a contract under which, in accordance with the rules or practices of Lloyd's, underwriting members ("the reinsured members") who are members of a syndicate for a year of account ("the closed year") agree with underwriting members who constitute that or another syndicate for a later year of account ("the reinsuring members") that the reinsuring members will indemnify the reinsured members against all known and unknown liabilities of the reinsured members arising out of the insurance business underwritten through that syndicate and allocated to the closed year (including liabilities under any reinsurance to close contract underwritten by the reinsured members).

[3973]

NOTES

Commencement: 10 August 2005.

42 Assets of members

(1) This regulation applies where a member or former member is treated as a UK insurer in accordance with regulations 13 and 40 above.

(2) Subject to paragraphs (3) and (4), the undistributed assets of the member are to be treated as assets of the insurer for the purposes of the application of Part 4 of the principal Regulations in accordance with regulation 43 below.

(3) For the purposes of this regulation, the undistributed assets of the member so treated do not include any asset held in a relevant trust fund.

(4) But any asset released from a relevant trust fund and received by such a member is to be treated as an asset of the insurer for the purposes of the application of Part 4 of the principal Regulations.

[3974]

NOTES

Commencement: 10 August 2005.

43   Application of Part 4 of the principal Regulations: protection of settlements

(1)   This regulation applies where a member or former member is subject to an insolvency measure mentioned in paragraph (4) at the time that a Lloyd's market reorganisation order comes into force.

(2)   Nothing in these Regulations or Part 4 of the principal Regulations affects the validity of any payment or disposition made, or any settlement agreed, by the relevant officer before the date when the Lloyd's market reorganisation order came into force.

(3)   For the purposes of the application of Part 4 of the principal Regulations, the insolvent estate of the member or former member shall not include any assets which are subject to a relevant section 425 or Article 418 compromise or arrangement, a relevant individual voluntary arrangement, or a relevant trust deed for creditors.

(4)   In paragraph (2) "relevant officer" means—
(a)   where the insolvency measure is a voluntary arrangement, the nominee;
(b)   where the insolvency measure is administration, the administrator;
(c)   where the insolvency measure is the appointment of a provisional liquidator, the provisional liquidator;
(d)   where the insolvency measure is a winding up, the liquidator;
(e)   where the insolvency measure is an individual voluntary arrangement, the nominee or supervisor;
(f)   where the insolvency measure is bankruptcy, the trustee in bankruptcy;
(g)   where the insolvency measure is sequestration, the interim or permanent trustee; and
(h)   where the insolvency measure is a trust deed for creditors, the trustee.

(5)   For the purposes of paragraph (3)—
(a)   "assets" has the same meaning as "property" in section 436 of the 1986 Act or Article 2(2) of the 1989 Order;
(b)   "insolvent estate" in England and Wales and Northern Ireland has the meaning given by Rule 13.8 of the Insolvency Rules or Rule 0.2 of the Insolvency Rules (Northern Ireland), and in Scotland means the whole estate of the member;
(c)   "a relevant section 425 or Article 418 compromise or arrangement" means—
(i)   a section 425 or Article 418 compromise or arrangement which was sanctioned by the court before the date on which an application for a Lloyd's market reorganisation order was made, or
(ii)   any subsequent section 425 or Article 418 compromise or arrangement sanctioned by the court to amend or replace a compromise or arrangement of the kind mentioned in paragraph (i);
(d)   "a relevant individual voluntary arrangement" and "a relevant trust deed for creditors" mean an individual voluntary arrangement or trust deed for creditors which was sanctioned by the court or entered into before the date on which an application for a Lloyd's market reorganisation order was made.

[3975]

NOTES
Commencement: 10 August 2005.

44   Challenge by reorganisation controller to conduct of insolvency practitioner

(1)   The reorganisation controller may apply to the court claiming that a relevant officer is acting, has acted, or proposes to act in a way that fails to comply with a requirement of Part 4 of the principal Regulations.

(2)   The reorganisation controller must send a copy of an application under paragraph (1) to the relevant officer in respect of whom the application is made.

(3)   In the case of a relevant officer who is acting in respect of a member or former member subject to the jurisdiction of a Scottish court, the application must be made to the Court of Session.

(4)   The court may—
(a)   dismiss the application;
(b)   make an interim order;
(c)   make any other order it thinks appropriate.

(5)   In particular, an order under this regulation may—
(a)   regulate the relevant officer's exercise of his functions;
(b)   require that officer to do or not do a specified thing;
(c)   make consequential provision.

(6)   An order may not be made under this regulation if it would impede or prevent the implementation of—
(a)   a voluntary arrangement approved under Part 1 of the 1986 Act or Part 2 of the 1989 Order before the date when the Lloyd's market reorganisation order was made;

(b)   an individual voluntary arrangement approved under Part 8 of that Act or Part 8 of that Order before the date when the Lloyd's market reorganisation order was made; or

(c)   a section 425 or Article 418 compromise or arrangement which was sanctioned by the court before the date when the Lloyd's market reorganisation order was made.

(7)   In this regulation "relevant officer" means—

(a)   a liquidator,

(b)   a provisional liquidator,

(c)   an administrator

(d)   the official receiver or a trustee in bankruptcy, or

(e)   in Scotland, an interim or permanent trustee or a trustee for creditors,

who is appointed in relation to a member or former member.

[3976]

NOTES

Commencement: 10 August 2005.

45 Application of Part 5 of the principal Regulations

(1)   Part 5 of the principal Regulations (reorganisation or winding up of UK insurers: recognition of EEA rights) applies with the modifications set out in regulation 46 where, on or after the date that a Lloyd's market reorganisation order comes into force, a member or former member is or becomes subject to a reorganisation or insolvency measure.

(2)   For the purposes of this regulation a "reorganisation or insolvency measure" means—

(a)   a voluntary arrangement, having a qualifying purpose, approved in accordance with section 4A of the 1986 Act or Article 17A of the 1989 Order;

(b)   administration pursuant to an order under paragraph 13 of Schedule B1 [or under paragraph 14 of Schedule B1 to the 1989 Order];

(c)   the reduction by the court of the value of one or more relevant contracts of insurance under section 377 of the 2000 Act or section 24(5) of the Friendly Societies Act 1992;

(d)   winding up;

(e)   the appointment of a provisional liquidator in accordance with section 135 of the 1986 Act or Article 115 of the 1989 Order;

(f)   an individual voluntary arrangement, having a qualifying purpose, approved in accordance with section 258 of the 1986 Act or Article 232 of the 1989 Order;

(g)   in Scotland a qualifying trust deed for creditors within the meaning of section 5(4A) of the Bankruptcy (Scotland) Act 1985;

(h)   bankruptcy, in accordance with Part 9 of the 1986 Act or Part 9 of the 1989 Order; or

(i)   sequestration under the Bankruptcy (Scotland) Act 1985.

(3)   A measure imposed under the law of a State or country other than the United Kingdom is not a reorganisation or insolvency measure for the purposes of this regulation.

(4)   For the purposes of sub-paragraphs (a), (f) and (g) of paragraph (2), a voluntary arrangement or individual voluntary arrangement has a qualifying purpose and a trust deed is a qualifying trust deed if it—

(a)   varies the rights of creditors as against the member and is intended to enable the member to continue to carry on an insurance market activity at Lloyd's; or

(b)   includes a realisation of some or all of the assets of the member and the distribution of proceeds to creditors, with a view to terminating the whole or any part of that member's business at Lloyd's.

[3977]

NOTES

Commencement: 10 August 2005.

Para (2): words in square brackets in sub-para (b) inserted by the Insurers (Reorganisation and Winding Up) (Amendment) Regulations 2007, SI 2007/851, reg 3(1), (16), as from 6 April 2007.

46 Modification of provisions in Part 5 of the principal Regulations

(1)   The modifications mentioned in regulation 45(1) are as follows.

(2)   Regulation 35 is disapplied.

(3)   Regulation 36 (interpretation of Part 5) has effect as if—

(a)   in paragraph (1)—

(i)   the meaning of "affected insurer" included a member or former member who, on or after the date that a Lloyd's market reorganisation order comes into force, is or becomes subject to a reorganisation or insolvency measure within the meaning given by regulation 44(2)of these Regulations;

(ii)   the meaning of "relevant reorganisation or relevant winding up" included any reorganisation or insolvency measure, in respect of a member or former member, to which Part 5 of the principal Regulations applies by virtue of regulation 45(1) of these Regulations;

    (iii)   in the case of sequestration, the date of sequestration within the meaning of section 12 of the Bankruptcy (Scotland) Act 1985; and

  (b)   in paragraph (2) references to the opening of a relevant reorganisation or a relevant winding up meant (in addition to the meaning in the cases set out in that paragraph)—

    (i)   in the case of an individual voluntary arrangement, the date when a decision with respect to that arrangement has effect in accordance with section 258 of the 1986 Act or Article 232 of the 1989 Order;

    (ii)   in the case of bankruptcy, the date on which the bankruptcy order is made under Part 9 of the 1986 Act or Part 9 of the 1989 Order;

    (iii)   in the case of a trust deed for creditors under the Bankruptcy (Scotland) Act 1985 the date when the trust deed was granted.

(4)   Regulation 37 of the principal Regulations (EEA rights: applicable law in the winding up of a UK insurer) has effect as if—

  (a)   references to a relevant winding up included (in each case) a reference to a reorganisation or insolvency measure within the meaning given by sub-paragraphs (d), (g) (h) and (i) of regulation 45(2) of these Regulations (winding up and bankruptcy) in respect of a member or former member; and

  (b)   the reference in paragraph (3)(c) to the liquidator included a reference to the trustee in bankruptcy or in Scotland to the interim or permanent trustee.

(5)   Regulation 42 (reservation of title agreements etc) has effect as if the reference to an insurer in paragraphs (1) and (2) included a reference to a member or former member.

[3978]

NOTES
Commencement: 10 August 2005.

47 Application of Part 5 of the principal Regulations: protection of dispositions etc made before a Lloyd's market reorganisation order comes into force

(1)   This regulation applies where—

  (a)   a member or former member is subject to a reorganisation or insolvency measure on the date when a Lloyd's market reorganisation order comes into force; and

  (b)   Part 5 of the principal Regulations applies in relation to that reorganisation or insolvency measure by virtue of regulation 45 above.

(2)   Nothing in Part 5 of the principal Regulations affects the validity of any payment or disposition made, or any settlement agreed, by the relevant officer before the date when the Lloyd's market reorganisation order came into force.

(3)   For the purposes of the application of Part 5 of the principal Regulations, the insolvent estate of the member does not include any assets which are subject to a relevant section 425 or Article 418 compromise or arrangement, a relevant individual voluntary arrangement, or a relevant trust deed for creditors.

(4)   In paragraph (2) "relevant officer" means—

  (a)   where the member is subject to a voluntary arrangement in accordance with section 4A of the 1986 Act or Article 17A of the 1989 Order, the supervisor;

  (b)   where the member is in administration in accordance with Schedule B1 [or with Schedule B1 to the 1989 Order], the administrator;

  (c)   where a provisional liquidator has been appointed in relation to a member in accordance with section 135 of the 1986 Act or Article 115 of the 1989 Order, the provisional liquidator;

  (d)   where the member is being wound up under Part 4 of the 1986 Act or Part 5 of the 1989 Order, the liquidator;

  (e)   where the member has made a voluntary arrangement in accordance with Part 8 of the 1986 Act or Part 8 of the 1989 Order, the nominee;

  (f)   where the member is bankrupt within the meaning of Part 9 of the 1986 Act or Part 9 of the 1989 Order, the official receiver or trustee in bankruptcy;

  (g)   where the member is being sequestrated, the interim or permanent trustee; and

  (h)   where a trust deed for creditors has been granted, the trustee.

(5)   For the purposes of paragraph (3)—

  (a)   "assets" has the same meaning as "property" in section 436 of the 1986 Act or Article 2(2) of the 1989 Order, except in relation to relevant trust deeds;

  (b)   "insolvent estate" in England and Wales and Northern Ireland has the meaning given by Rule 13.8 of the Insolvency Rules or Rule 0.2 of the Insolvency Rules (Northern Ireland), and in Scotland means the assets of the member;

    (c)   "relevant section 425 or Article 418 compromise or arrangement" means—

        (i)   a section 425 or Article 418 compromise or arrangement which was sanctioned by the court before the date when the Lloyd's market reorganisation order came into force, or

        (ii)   any subsequent section 425 or Article 418 compromise or arrangement sanctioned by the court to amend or replace a compromise or arrangement of the kind mentioned in paragraph (i);

    (d)   "relevant individual voluntary arrangement" means—

        (i)   an individual voluntary arrangement approved under Part 8 of the 1986 Act [or Part 8 of the 1989 Order] before the date when a Lloyd's market reorganisation order came in to force, and

        (ii)   any subsequent individual voluntary arrangement sanctioned by the court to amend or replace an arrangement of the kind mentioned in paragraph (i); and

    (e)   "relevant trust deed" means a trust deed granted by a member or former member before the date when the Lloyd's market reorganisation order entered into force.

[3979]

NOTES

Commencement: 10 August 2005.

Paras (4), (5): words in square brackets inserted by the Insurers (Reorganisation and Winding Up) (Amendment) Regulations 2007, SI 2007/851, reg 3(1), (17), as from 6 April 2007.

48 Non-EEA countries

In respect of a member or former member who is established in a country outside the EEA, the court or the Authority may, subject to sections 348 and 349 of the 2000 Act, make such disclosures as each considers appropriate to a court or to a regulator with a role equivalent to that of the Authority for the purpose of facilitating the work of the reorganisation controller.

[3980]

NOTES

Commencement: 10 August 2005.

49   (*Amends the Insurers (Reorganisation and Winding Up) Regulations 2004, SI 2004/353, reg 19 at* **[3854]**.)

PROCEEDS OF CRIME ACT 2002 (EXTERNAL REQUESTS AND ORDERS) ORDER 2005

(SI 2005/3181)

NOTES

Made: 15 November 2005.

Authority: Proceeds of Crime Act 2002, ss 444, 459(2).

Commencement: 1 January 2006.

This Order is reproduced as amended by: the Serious Organised Crime and Police Act 2005 (Consequential and Supplementary Amendments to Secondary Legislation) Order 2006, SI 2006/594; the Proceeds of Crime Act 2002 (External Requests and Orders) (Amendment) Order 2008, SI 2008/302.

ARRANGEMENT OF ARTICLES

PART 1
GENERAL PROVISIONS

PART 2
GIVING EFFECT IN ENGLAND AND WALES TO EXTERNAL REQUESTS IN CONNECTION WITH CRIMINAL INVESTIGATIONS OR PROCEEDINGS AND TO EXTERNAL ORDERS ARISING FROM SUCH PROCEEDINGS

CHAPTER 1
EXTERNAL REQUESTS

PART 3
GIVING EFFECT IN SCOTLAND TO EXTERNAL REQUESTS IN CONNECTION WITH CRIMINAL
INVESTIGATIONS OR PROCEEDINGS AND TO EXTERNAL ORDERS ARISING FROM
SUCH PROCEEDINGS

CHAPTER 1
EXTERNAL REQUESTS

CHAPTER 3
GENERAL

PART 1
GENERAL PROVISIONS

1 Title and commencement

This Order may be cited as the Proceeds of Crime Act 2002 (External Requests and Orders) Order 2005 and shall come into force on 1st January 2006.

[3980AA]

NOTES

Commencement: 1 January 2006.

2 Interpretation

In this Order—

"the Act" means the Proceeds of Crime Act 2002;
.....

"country" includes territory;

"external order" has the meaning set out in section 447(2) of the Act;

"external request" has the meaning set out in section 447(1) of the Act;

"a relevant officer of Revenue and Customs" means such an officer exercising functions by virtue of section 6 of the Commissioners for Revenue and Customs Act 2005.

[3980AB]

NOTES

Commencement: 1 January 2006.

Definition "the Agency" (omitted) revoked by the Proceeds of Crime Act 2002 (External Requests and Orders) (Amendment) Order 2008, SI 2008/302, art 2(1), (2), as from 1 April 2008.

3 Insolvency practitioners

(1) Paragraphs (2) and (3) apply if a person acting as an insolvency practitioner seizes or disposes of any property in relation to which his functions are not exercisable because—

    (a)   it is for the time being subject to a restraint order made under article 8, 58 or 95; or

    (b)   it is for the time being subject to a property freezing order made under article 147, an interim receiving order made under article 151, a prohibitory property order made under article 161 or an interim administration order made under article 167,

and at the time of the seizure or disposal he believes on reasonable grounds that he is entitled (whether in pursuance of an order of a court or otherwise) to seize or dispose of the property.

(2) He is not liable to any person in respect of any loss or damage resulting from the seizure or disposal, except so far as the loss or damage is caused by his negligence.

(3) He has a lien on the property or the proceeds of its sale—

    (a)   for such of his expenses as were incurred in connection with the liquidation, bankruptcy, sequestration or other proceedings in relation to which he purported to make the seizure or disposal, and

    (b)   for so much of his remuneration as may reasonably be assigned to his acting in connection with those proceedings.

(4)   Paragraph (2) does not prejudice the generality of any provision of the 1985 Act, the 1986 Act, the 1989 Order or any Act or Order which confers a protection from liability on him.

(5)   Paragraph (7) applies if—
   (a)   property is subject to a restraint order made under article 8, 58 or 95,
   (b)   a person acting as an insolvency practitioner incurs expenses in respect of property subject to the restraint order, and
   (c)   he does not know (and has no reasonable grounds to believe) that the property is subject to the restraint order.

(6)   Paragraph (7) also applies if—
   (a)   property is subject to a restraint order made under article 8, 58 or 95,
   (b)   a person acting as an insolvency practitioner incurs expenses which are not ones in respect of property subject to the restraint order, and
   (c)   the expenses are ones which (but for the effect of the restraint order) might have been met by taking possession of and realising property subject to it.

(7)   Whether or not he has seized or disposed of any property, he is entitled to payment of the expenses under—
   (a)   article 33(2) [or 34(3)] if the restraint order was made under article 7,
   (b)   article 77(2) or 78(3) if the restraint order was made under article 58,
   (c)   article 119(2) [or 120(3)] if the restraint order was made under article 95.

(8)   Paragraph (10) applies if—
   (a)   property is subject to a property freezing order made under article 147, an interim receiving order made under article 151, a prohibitory property order made under article 161 or an interim administration order made under article 167,
   (b)   a person acting as an insolvency practitioner incurs expenses in respect of property subject to the order, and
   (c)   he does not know (and has no reasonable grounds to believe) that the property is subject to the order.

(9)   Paragraph (10) also applies if—
   (a)   property is subject to a property freezing order made under article 147, an interim receiving order made under article 151, a prohibitory property order made under article 161 or an interim administration order made under article 167,
   (b)   a person acting as an insolvency practitioner incurs expenses which are not ones in respect of property subject to the order, and
   (c)   the expenses are ones which (but for the effect of the order) might have been met by taking possession of and realising property subject to it.

(10)   Whether or not he has seized or disposed of any property, he is entitled to payment of the expenses under article 191.

[3980AC]

NOTES

Commencement: 1 January 2006.

Para (7): words in square brackets substituted by the Proceeds of Crime Act 2002 (External Requests and Orders) (Amendment) Order 2008, SI 2008/302, art 2(1), (3), as from 1 April 2008.

---

4   Insolvency practitioners: interpretation

(1)   This article applies for the purposes of article 3.

(2)   A person acts as an insolvency practitioner if he so acts within the meaning given by section 388 of the 1986 Act or Article 3 of the 1989 Order; but this is subject to paragraphs (3) to (5).

(3)   The expression "person acting as an insolvency practitioner" includes the official receiver acting as receiver or manager of the property concerned.

(4)   In applying section 388 of the 1986 Act under paragraph (2) above—
   (a)   the reference in section 388(2)(a) to a permanent or interim trustee in sequestration must be taken to include a reference to a trustee in sequestration;
   (b)   section 388(5) (which includes provision that nothing in the section applies to anything done by the official receiver or the Accountant in Bankruptcy) must be ignored.

(5)   In applying Article 3 of the 1989 Order under paragraph (2) above, paragraph (5) (which includes provision that nothing in the Article applies to anything done by the official receiver) must be ignored.

(6)   The following sub-paragraphs apply to references to Acts or Orders—
   (a)   the 1913 Act is the Bankruptcy (Scotland) Act 1913;
   (b)   the 1914 Act is the Bankruptcy Act 1914;
   (c)   the 1985 Act is the Bankruptcy (Scotland) Act 1985;
   (d)   the 1986 Act is the Insolvency Act 1986;

(e)   the 1989 Order is the Insolvency (Northern Ireland) Order 1989.

(7)   An award of sequestration is made on the date of sequestration within the meaning of section 12(4) of the 1985 Act.

[3980AD]

NOTES
Commencement: 1 January 2006.

5   Orders and regulations

(1)   References in this article to subordinate legislation are to—
(a)   any order under this Order (other than one falling to be made by a court);
(b)   any regulations under this Order.

(2)   Subordinate legislation—
(a)   may make different provision for different purposes;
(b)   may include supplementary, incidental, saving or transitional provisions.

(3)   Any power to make subordinate legislation is exercisable by statutory instrument and, subject to paragraph (4), is subject to annulment in pursuance of a resolution of either House of Parliament.

(4)   A statutory instrument containing regulations made under paragraph 6(2) of Schedule 1 is subject to annulment in pursuance of a resolution of the Scottish Parliament.

[3980AE]

NOTES
Commencement: 1 January 2006.

PART 2
GIVING EFFECT IN ENGLAND AND WALES TO EXTERNAL REQUESTS IN CONNECTION WITH CRIMINAL INVESTIGATIONS OR PROCEEDINGS AND TO EXTERNAL ORDERS ARISING FROM SUCH PROCEEDINGS

CHAPTER 1
EXTERNAL REQUESTS

6   Action on receipt of external request in connection with criminal investigations or proceedings

(1)   Except where paragraph (2) applies, the Secretary of State may refer an external request in connection with criminal investigations or proceedings in the country from which the request was made and concerning relevant property in England or Wales to—
(a)   ...
(b)   the Director of Public Prosecutions;
(c)   the Director of Revenue and Customs Prosecutions,
to process it.

(2)   This paragraph applies where it appears to the Secretary of State that the request—
(a)   is made in connection with criminal investigations or proceedings which relate to an offence involving serious or complex fraud, and
(b)   concerns relevant property in England or Wales.

(3)   Where paragraph (2) applies, the Secretary of State may refer the request to the Director of the Serious Fraud Office to process it.

(4)   In this Chapter "the relevant Director" means the Director to whom an external request is referred under paragraph (1) or (3).

(5)   The relevant Director may ask the overseas authority which made the request for such further information as may be necessary to determine whether the request is likely to satisfy either of the conditions in article 7.

(6)   A request under paragraph (5) may include a request for statements which may be used as evidence.

(7)   Where a request concerns relevant property which is in Scotland or Northern Ireland as well as England or Wales, so much of the request as concerns such property shall be dealt with under Part 3 or 4, respectively.

[3980AF]

NOTES
Commencement: 1 January 2006.

PART III
STATUTORY INSTRUMENTS

Para (1): sub-para (a) revoked by the Proceeds of Crime Act 2002 (External Requests and Orders) (Amendment) Order 2008, SI 2008/302, art 2(1), (4), as from 1 April 2008.

7   Conditions for Crown Court to give effect to external request

(1)   The Crown Court may exercise the powers conferred by article 8 if either of the following conditions is satisfied.

(2)   The first condition is that—
  (a)   relevant property in England and Wales is identified in the external request;
  (b)   a criminal investigation has been started in the country from which the external request was made with regard to an offence, and
  (c)   there is reasonable cause to believe that the alleged offender named in the request has benefited from his criminal conduct.

(3)   The second condition is that—
  (a)   relevant property in England and Wales is identified in the external request;
  (b)   proceedings for an offence have been started in the country from which the external request was made and not concluded, and
  (c)   there is reasonable cause to believe that the defendant named in the request has benefited from his criminal conduct.

(4)   In determining whether the conditions are satisfied and whether the request is an external request within the meaning of the Act, the Court must have regard to the definitions in subsections (1), (4) to (8) and (11) of section 447 of the Act.

(5)   If the first condition is satisfied, references in this Chapter to the defendant are to the alleged offender.

[3980AG]

NOTES
Commencement: 1 January 2006.

8   Restraint orders

(1)   If either condition set out in article 7 is satisfied, the Crown Court may make an order ("a restraint order") prohibiting any specified person from dealing with relevant property which is identified in the external request and specified in the order.

(2)   A restraint order may be made subject to exceptions, and an exception may in particular—
  (a)   make provision for reasonable living expenses and reasonable legal expenses in connection with the proceedings seeking a restraint order or the registration of an external order;
  (b)   make provision for the purpose of enabling any person to carry on any trade, business, profession or occupation;
  (c)   be made subject to conditions.

(3)   Paragraph (4) applies if—
  (a)   a court makes a restraint order, and
  (b)   the applicant for the order applies to the court to proceed under paragraph (4) (whether as part of the application for the restraint order or at any time afterwards).

(4)   The court may make such order as it believes is appropriate for the purpose of ensuring that the restraint order is effective.

(5)   A restraint order does not affect property for the time being subject to a charge under any of these provisions—
  (a)   section 9 of the Drug Trafficking Offences Act 1986;
  (b)   section 78 of the Criminal Justice Act 1988;
  (c)   Article 14 of the Criminal Justice (Confiscation) (Northern Ireland) Order 1990;
  (d)   section 27 of the Drug Trafficking Act 1994;
  (e)   Article 32 of the Proceeds of Crime (Northern Ireland) Order 1996.

(6)   Dealing with property includes removing it from England and Wales.

[3980AH]

NOTES
Commencement: 1 January 2006.

9   Application, discharge and variation of restraint orders

(1)   A restraint order—
  (a)   may be made only on an application by the relevant Director;
  (b)   may be made on an ex parte application to a judge in chambers.

(2)   An application to discharge or vary a restraint order or an order under article 8(4) may be made to the Crown Court by—
  (a)   the relevant Director;
  (b)   any person affected by the order.

(3)   Paragraphs (4) to (7) apply to an application under paragraph (2).

(4)   The court—
  (a)   may discharge the order;
  (b)   may vary the order.

(5)   If the condition in article 7 which was satisfied was that proceedings were started, the court must discharge the order if, at the conclusion of the proceedings, no external order has been made.

(6)   If the condition in article 7 which was satisfied was that proceedings were started, the court must discharge the order if within a reasonable time an external order has not been registered under Chapter 2 of this Part.

(7)   If the condition in article 7 which was satisfied was that an investigation was started, the court must discharge the order if within a reasonable time proceedings for the offence are not started.

[3980AI]

NOTES
Commencement: 1 January 2006.

10   Appeal to Court of Appeal about restraint orders

(1)   If on an application for a restraint order the Crown Court decides not to make one, the relevant Director may appeal to the Court of Appeal against the decision.

(2)   If an application is made under article 9(2) in relation to a restraint order or an order under article 8(4), the following persons may appeal to the Court of Appeal in respect of the Crown Court's decision on the application—
  (a)   the relevant Director;
  (b)   any person affected by the order.

(3)   On an appeal under paragraph (1) or (2) the Court of Appeal may—
  (a)   confirm the decision, or
  (b)   make such order as it believes is appropriate.

[3980AJ]

NOTES
Commencement: 1 January 2006.

11   Appeal to House of Lords about restraint orders

(1)   An appeal lies to the House of Lords from a decision of the Court of Appeal on an appeal under article 10.

(2)   An appeal under this article lies at the instance of any person who was a party to the proceedings before the Court of Appeal.

(3)   On an appeal under this article the House of Lords may—
  (a)   confirm the decision of the Court of Appeal, or
  (b)   make such order as it believes is appropriate.

[3980AK]

NOTES
Commencement: 1 January 2006.

12   Seizure in pursuance of restraint order

(1)   If a restraint order is in force a constable or a relevant officer of Revenue and Customs may seize any property which is specified in it to prevent its removal from England and Wales.

(2)   Property seized under paragraph (1) must be dealt with in accordance with the directions of the court which made the order.

[3980AL]

NOTES
Commencement: 1 January 2006.

13   Hearsay evidence in restraint proceedings

(1)   Evidence must not be excluded in restraint proceedings on the ground that it is hearsay (of whatever degree).

(2)   Sections 2 to 4 of the Civil Evidence Act 1995 apply in relation to restraint proceedings as those sections apply in relation to civil proceedings.

(3)   Restraint proceedings are proceedings—
  (a)   for a restraint order;
  (b)   for the discharge or variation of a restraint order;
  (c)   on an appeal under article 10 or 11.

(4)   Hearsay is a statement which is made otherwise than by a person while giving oral evidence in the proceedings and which is rendered as evidence of the matters stated.

(5)   Nothing in this article affects the admissibility of evidence which is admissible apart from this article.

[3980AM]

NOTES
Commencement: 1 January 2006.

14   Supplementary (restraint orders)

(1)   The registration Acts—
  (a)   apply in relation to restraint orders as they apply in relation to orders which affect land and are made by the court for the purpose of enforcing judgments or recognisances;
  (b)   apply in relation to applications for restraint orders as they apply in relation to other pending land actions.

(2)   The registration Acts are—
  (a)   the Land Charges Act 1972;
  (b)   the Land Registration Act 2002.

(3)   But no notice may be entered in the register of title under the Land Registration Act 2002 in respect of a restraint order.

[3980AN]

NOTES
Commencement: 1 January 2006.

15   Appointment of management receivers

(1)   Paragraph (2) applies if—
  (a)   the Crown Court makes a restraint order, and
  (b)   the relevant Director applies to the court to proceed under paragraph (2) (whether as part of the application for the restraint order or at any time afterwards).

(2)   The Crown Court may by order appoint a receiver in respect of any property which is specified in the restraint order.

[3980AO]

NOTES
Commencement: 1 January 2006.

16   Powers of management receivers

(1)   If the court appoints a receiver under article 15 it may act under this article on the application of the relevant Director.

(2)   The court may by order confer on the receiver the following powers in relation to any property which is specified in the restraint order—
  (a)   power to take possession of the property;
  (b)   power to manage or otherwise deal with the property;
  (c)   power to start, carry on or defend any legal proceedings in respect of the property;
  (d)   power to realise so much of the property as is necessary to meet the receiver's remuneration and expenses.

(3)   The court may by order confer on the receiver power to enter any premises in England and Wales and to do any of the following—
  (a)   search for or inspect anything authorised by the court;
  (b)   make or obtain a copy, photograph or other record of anything so authorised;
  (c)   remove anything which the receiver is required or authorised to take possession of in pursuance of an order of the court.

(4)   The court may by order authorise the receiver to do any of the following for the purpose of the exercise of his functions—
  (a)   hold property;
  (b)   enter into contracts;

   (c)   sue and be sued;

   (d)   employ agents;

   (e)   execute powers of attorney, deeds or other instruments;

   (f)   take any other steps the court thinks appropriate.

(5)   The court may order any person who has possession of property which is specified in the restraint order to give possession of it to the receiver.

(6)   The court—

   (a)   may order a person holding an interest in property which is specified in the restraint order to make to the receiver such payment as the court specifies in respect of a beneficial interest held by the defendant or the recipient of a tainted gift;

   (b)   may (on the payment being made) by order transfer, grant or extinguish any interest in the property.

(7)   Paragraphs (2), (5) and (6) do not apply to property for the time being subject to a charge under any of these provisions—

   (a)   section 9 of the Drug Trafficking Offences Act 1986;

   (b)   section 78 of the Criminal Justice Act 1988;

   (c)   Article 14 of the Criminal Justice (Confiscation) (Northern Ireland) Order 1990;

   (d)   section 27 of the Drug Trafficking Act 1994;

   (e)   Article 32 of the Proceeds of Crime (Northern Ireland) Order 1996.

(8)   The court must not—

   (a)   confer the power mentioned in paragraph (2)(b) or (d) in respect of property, or

   (b)   exercise the power conferred on it by paragraph (6) in respect of property,

unless it gives persons holding interests in the property a reasonable opportunity to make representations to it.

[(8A)   Paragraph (8), so far as relating to the power mentioned in paragraph (2)(b), does not apply to property which—

   (a)   is perishable; or

   (b)   ought to be disposed of before its value diminishes.]

(9)   The court may order that a power conferred by an order under this article is subject to such conditions and exceptions as it specifies.

(10)   Managing or otherwise dealing with property includes—

   (a)   selling the property or any part of it or interest in it;

   (b)   carrying on or arranging for another person to carry on any trade or business the assets of which are or are part of the property;

   (c)   incurring capital expenditure in respect of the property.

[3980AP]

NOTES

Commencement: 1 January 2006.

Para (8A): inserted by the Proceeds of Crime Act 2002 (External Requests and Orders) (Amendment) Order 2008, SI 2008/302, art 2(1), (5), as from 1 April 2008.

17   Restrictions relating to restraint orders

(1)   Paragraphs (2) to (4) apply if a court makes a restraint order.

(2)   No distress may be levied against any property which is specified in the order except with the leave of the Crown Court and subject to any terms the Crown Court may impose.

(3)   If the order applies to a tenancy of any premises, no landlord or other person to whom rent is payable may exercise a right within paragraph (4) except with the leave of the Crown Court and subject to any terms the Crown Court may impose.

(4)   A right is within this paragraph if it is a right of forfeiture by peaceable re-entry in relation to the premises in respect of any failure by the tenant to comply with any term or condition of the tenancy.

(5)   If a court in which proceedings are pending in respect of any property is satisfied that a restraint order has been applied for or made in respect of the property, the court may either stay the proceedings or allow them to continue on any terms it thinks fit.

(6)   Before exercising any power conferred by paragraph (5), the court must give an opportunity to be heard to—

   (a)   the relevant Director, and

   (b)   any receiver appointed in respect of the property under article 15 [or 27].

[3980AQ]

NOTES

Commencement: 1 January 2006.

Para (6): words in square brackets substituted by the Proceeds of Crime Act 2002 (External Requests and Orders) (Amendment) Order 2008, SI 2008/302, art 2(1), (6), as from 1 April 2008.

CHAPTER 2
EXTERNAL ORDERS

18   Action on receipt of external order in connection with criminal convictions

(1)   Except where paragraph (2) applies, the Secretary of State may refer an external order arising from a criminal conviction in the country from which the order was sent and concerning relevant property in England or Wales to—

    (a)   ...

    (b)   the Director of Public Prosecutions;

    (c)   the Director of Revenue and Customs Prosecutions,

to process it.

(2)   This paragraph applies where it appears to the Secretary of State that—

    (a)   the property or sum of money specified in the order was found, or was believed, to have been obtained as a result of, or in connection with, criminal conduct involving serious or complex fraud, and

    (b)   the order concerns relevant property in England or Wales.

(3)   Where paragraph (2) applies, the Secretary of State may refer the order to the Director of the Serious Fraud Office to process it.

(4)   In this Chapter "the relevant Director" means the Director to whom an external order is referred under paragraph (1) or (3).

(5)   Where an order concerns relevant property which is in Scotland or Northern Ireland as well as England or Wales, so much of the request as concerns such property shall be dealt with under Part 3 or 4, respectively.

[3980AR]

NOTES

Commencement: 1 January 2006.

Para (1): sub-para (a) revoked by the Proceeds of Crime Act 2002 (External Requests and Orders) (Amendment) Order 2008, SI 2008/302, art 2(1), (7), as from 1 April 2008.

19   Authentication by the overseas court

(1)   Paragraph (2) applies where an overseas court has authenticated its involvement in—

    (a)   any judgment,

    (b)   any order,

    (c)   any other document concerned with such a judgment or order or proceedings relating to it.

(2)   Where this paragraph applies, any statement in the judgment, order or document is admissible in evidence in proceedings under this Chapter.

[3980AS]

NOTES

Commencement: 1 January 2006.

20   Applications to give effect to external orders

(1)   An application may be made by the relevant Director to the Crown Court to give effect to an external order.

(2)   No application to give effect to such an order may be made otherwise than under paragraph (1).

(3)   An application under paragraph (1)—

    (a)   shall include a request to appoint the relevant Director as the enforcement authority for the order;

    (b)   may be made on an ex parte application to a judge in chambers.

[3980AT]

NOTES

Commencement: 1 January 2006.

21   Conditions for Crown Court to give effect to external orders

(1)   The Crown Court must decide to give effect to an external order by registering it where all of the following conditions are satisfied.

(2) The first condition is that the external order was made consequent on the conviction of the person named in the order and no appeal is outstanding in respect of that conviction.

(3) The second condition is that the external order is in force and no appeal is outstanding in respect of it.

(4) The third condition is that giving effect to the external order would not be incompatible with any of the Convention rights (within the meaning of the Human Rights Act 1998) of any person affected by it.

(5) The fourth condition applies only in respect of an external order which authorises the confiscation of property other than money that is specified in the order.

(6) That condition is that the specified property must not be subject to a charge under any of the following provisions—
   (a) section 9 of the Drug Trafficking Offences Act 1986;
   (b) section 78 of the Criminal Justice Act 1988;
   (c) Article 14 of the Criminal Justice (Confiscation) (Northern Ireland) Order 1990;
   (d) section 27 of the Drug Trafficking Act 1994;
   (e) Article 32 of the Proceeds of Crime (Northern Ireland) Order 1996.

(7) In determining whether the order is an external order within the meaning of the Act, the Court must have regard to the definitions in subsections (2), (4), (5), (6), (8) and (10) of section 447 of the Act.

(8) In paragraph (3) "appeal" includes—
   (a) any proceedings by way of discharging or setting aside the order; and
   (b) an application for a new trial or stay of execution.

[3980AU]

NOTES
Commencement: 1 January 2006.

22 Registration of external orders

(1) Where the Crown Court decides to give effect to an external order, it must—
   (a) register the order in that court;
   (b) provide for notice of the registration to be given to any person affected by it; and
   (c) appoint the relevant Director as the enforcement authority for the order.

(2) Only an external order registered by the Crown Court may be implemented under this Chapter.

(3) The Crown Court may cancel the registration of the external order, or vary the property to which it applies, on an application by the relevant Director or any person affected by it if, or to the extent that, the court is of the opinion that any of the conditions in article 21 is not satisfied.

(4) The Crown Court must cancel the registration of the external order, on an application by the relevant Director or any person affected by it, if it appears to the court that the order has been satisfied—
   (a) in the case of an order for the recovery of a sum of money specified in it, by payment of the amount due under it, or
   (b) in the case of an order for the recovery of specified property, by the surrender of the property, or
   (c) by any other means.

(5) Where the registration of an external order is cancelled or varied under paragraph (3) or (4), the Crown Court must provide for notice of this to be given to the relevant Director and any person affected by it.

[3980AV]

NOTES
Commencement: 1 January 2006.

23 Appeal to Court of Appeal about external orders

(1) If on an application for the Crown Court to give effect to an external order by registering it, the court decides not to do so, the relevant Director may appeal to the Court of Appeal against the decision.

(2) If an application is made under article 22(3) or (4) in relation to the registration of an external order, the following persons may appeal to the Court of Appeal in respect of the Crown Court's decision on the application—
   (a) the relevant Director;
   (b) any person affected by the registration.

(3) On an appeal under paragraph (1) or (2) the Court of Appeal may—

(a) confirm or set aside the decision to register; or

(b) direct the Crown Court to register the external order (or so much of it as relates to property other than to which article 21(6) applies).

[3980AW]

NOTES
Commencement: 1 January 2006.

24 Appeal to House of Lords about external orders

(1) An appeal lies to the House of Lords from a decision of the Court of Appeal on an appeal under article 23.

(2) An appeal under this article lies at the instance of any person who was a party to the proceedings before the Court of Appeal.

(3) On an appeal under this article the House of Lords may—

(a) confirm or set aside the decision of the Court of Appeal, or

(b) direct the Crown Court to register the external order (or so much of it as relates to property other than property to which article 21(6) applies).

[3980AX]

NOTES
Commencement: 1 January 2006.

25 Sums in currency other than sterling

(1) This article applies where the external order which is registered under article 22 specifies a sum of money.

(2) If the sum of money which is specified is expressed in a currency other than sterling, the sum of money to be recovered is to be taken to be the sterling equivalent calculated in accordance with the rate of exchange prevailing at the end of the working day immediately preceding the day when the Crown Court registered the external order under article 22.

(3) The sterling equivalent must be calculated by the relevant Director.

(4) The notice referred to in article 22(1)(b) and (5) must set out the amount in sterling which is to be paid.

(5) In this article "working day" means any day other than—

(a) a Saturday or Sunday;

(b) Christmas Day;

(c) Good Friday;

(d) any day that is a bank holiday in England and Wales under the Banking and Financial Dealings Act 1971.

[3980AY]

NOTES
Commencement: 1 January 2006.

26 Time for payment

(1) This article applies where the external order is for the recovery of a specified sum of money.

(2) Subject to paragraphs (3) to (6), the amount ordered to be paid under—

(a) an external order that has been registered under article 22, or

(b) where article 25(2) applies, the notice under article 22(1)(b),

must be paid on the date on which the notice under article 22(1)(b) is delivered to the person affected by it.

(3) Where there is an appeal under article 23 or 24 and a sum falls to be paid when the appeal has been determined or withdrawn, the duty to pay is delayed until the day on which the appeal is determined or withdrawn.

(4) If the person affected by an external order which has been registered shows that he needs time to pay the amount ordered to be paid, the Crown Court which registered the order may make an order allowing payment to be made in a specified period.

(5) The specified period—

(a) must start with the day on which the notice under article 22(1)(b) was delivered to the person affected by the order or the day referred to in paragraph (3), as the case may be, and

(b) must not exceed six months.

(6)   If within the specified period the person affected by an external order applies to the Crown Court which registered the order for the period to be extended and the court believes that there are exceptional circumstances, it may make an order extending the period.

(7)   The extended period—
   (a)   must start with the day on which the notice under article 22(1)(b) was delivered to the person affected by it or the day referred to in paragraph (3), as the case may be, and
   (b)   must not exceed 12 months.

(8)   An order under paragraph (6)—
   (a)   may be made after the end of the specified period, but
   (b)   must not be made after the end of the extended period.

(9)   The court must not make an order under paragraph (4) or (6) unless it gives the relevant Director an opportunity to make representations.

[3980AZ]

NOTES
Commencement: 1 January 2006.

27   Appointment of enforcement receivers

(1)   This article applies if—
   (a)   an external order is registered,
   (b)   it is not satisfied, and
   (c)   in the case of an external order for the recovery of a specified sum of money, any period specified by order under article 26 has expired.

(2)   On the application of the relevant Director ... the Crown Court may by order appoint a receiver in respect of—
   (a)   where the external order is for the recovery of a specified sum of money, realisable property;
   (b)   where the external order is for the recovery of specified property, that property.

[3980BA]

NOTES
Commencement: 1 January 2006.
Para (2): words omitted revoked by the Proceeds of Crime Act 2002 (External Requests and Orders) (Amendment) Order 2008, SI 2008/302, art 2(1), (8), as from 1 April 2008.

28   Powers of enforcement receivers in respect of monetary external orders

(1)   If the court appoints a receiver under article 27, it may act under this article on the application of the relevant Director ... where the external order is for the recovery of a specified sum of money.

(2)   The court may by order confer on the receiver the following powers in relation to any realisable property—
   (a)   power to take possession of the property;
   (b)   power to manage or otherwise deal with the property;
   (c)   power to realise the property, in such manner as the court may specify;
   (d)   power to start, carry on or defend any legal proceedings in respect of the property.

(3)   The court may by order confer on the receiver power to enter any premises in England and Wales and to do any of the following—
   (a)   search for or inspect anything authorised by the court;
   (b)   make or obtain a copy, photograph or other record, of anything so authorised;
   (c)   remove anything which the receiver is required or authorised to take possession of in pursuance of an order of the court.

(4)   The court may by order authorise the receiver to do any of the following for the purposes of the exercise of his functions—
   (a)   hold property;
   (b)   enter into contracts;
   (c)   sue and be sued;
   (d)   employ agents;
   (e)   execute powers of attorney, deeds or other instruments;
   (f)   take any other steps the court thinks appropriate.

(5)   The court may order any person who has possession of realisable property to give possession of it to the receiver.

(6)   The court—

(a) may order a person holding an interest in realisable property to make to the receiver such payment as the court specifies in respect of a beneficial interest held by the defendant or the recipient of a tainted gift;

(b) may (on payment being made) by order transfer, grant or extinguish any interest in the property.

(7) Paragraphs (2), (5) and (6) do not apply to property for the time being subject to a charge under any of these provisions—

(a) section 9 of the Drug Trafficking Offences Act 1986;

(b) section 78 of the Criminal Justice Act 1988;

(c) Article 14 of the Criminal Justice (Confiscation) (Northern Ireland) Order 1990;

(d) section 27 of the Drug Trafficking Act 1994;

(e) Article 32 of the Proceeds of Crime (Northern Ireland) Order 1996.

(8) The court must not—

(a) confer the power mentioned in paragraph (2)(b) or (c) in respect of property, or

(b) exercise the power conferred on it by paragraph (6) in respect of property,

unless it gives persons holding interests in the property a reasonable opportunity to make representations to it.

[(8A) Paragraph (8), so far as relating to the power mentioned in paragraph (2)(b), does not apply to property which—

(a) is perishable; or

(b) ought to be disposed of before its value diminishes.]

(9) The court may order that a power conferred by an order under this article is subject to such conditions and exceptions as it specifies.

(10) Managing or otherwise dealing with property includes—

(a) selling the property or any part of it or interest in it;

(b) carrying on or arranging for another person to carry on any trade or business the assets of which are or are part of the property;

(c) incurring capital expenditure in respect of the property.

[3980BB]

NOTES

Commencement: 1 January 2006.

Para (1): words omitted revoked by the Proceeds of Crime Act 2002 (External Requests and Orders) (Amendment) Order 2008, SI 2008/302, art 2(1), (8), as from 1 April 2008.

Para (8A): inserted by SI 2008/302, art 2(1), (9), as from 1 April 2008.

---

29 Powers of enforcement receivers in respect of external orders for the recovery of specified property

(1) If the court appoints a receiver under article 27, it may act under this article on the application of the relevant Director ... where the external order is for the recovery of property specified in the order ("the specified property").

(2) The court may by order confer on the receiver the following powers in relation to the specified property—

(a) power to take possession of the property;

(b) power to manage or otherwise deal with the property;

(c) power to realise the property, in such manner as the court may specify;

(d) power to start, carry on or defend any legal proceedings in respect of the property.

(3) The court may by order confer on the receiver power to enter any premises in England and Wales and to do any of the following—

(a) search for or inspect anything authorised by the court;

(b) make or obtain a copy, photograph or other record of anything so authorised;

(c) remove anything which the receiver is required or authorised to take possession of in pursuance of an order of the court.

(4) The court may by order authorise the receiver to do any of the following for the purposes of the exercise of his functions—

(a) hold property;

(b) enter into contracts;

(c) sue and be sued;

(d) employ agents;

(e) execute powers of attorney, deeds or other instruments;

(f) take any other steps the court thinks appropriate.

(5) The court may order any person who has possession of the specified property to give possession of it to the receiver.

(6) The court—

   (a)   may order a person holding an interest in the specified property to make to the receiver such payment as the court specifies in respect of a beneficial interest held by the defendant or the recipient of a tainted gift;

   (b)   may (on the payment being made) by order transfer, grant or extinguish any interest in the property.

(7)   The court must not—

   (a)   confer the power mentioned in paragraph (2)(b) or (c) in respect of property, or

   (b)   exercise the power conferred on it by paragraph (6) in respect of property,

unless it gives persons holding interests in the property a reasonable opportunity to make representations to it.

[(7A)   Paragraph (7), so far as relating to the power mentioned in paragraph (2)(b), does not apply to property which—

   (a)   is perishable; or

   (b)   ought to be disposed of before its value diminishes.]

(8)   The court may order that a power conferred by an order under this article is subject to such conditions and exceptions as it specifies.

(9)   Managing or otherwise dealing with property includes—

   (a)   selling the property or any part of it or interest in it;

   (b)   carrying on or arranging for another person to carry on any trade or business the assets of which are or are part of the property;

   (c)   incurring capital expenditure in respect of the property.

[3980BC]–[3980BF]

NOTES

Commencement: 1 January 2006.

Para (1): words omitted revoked by the Proceeds of Crime Act 2002 (External Requests and Orders) (Amendment) Order 2008, SI 2008/302, art 2(1), (10)(a), as from 1 April 2008.

Para (7A): inserted by SI 2008/302, art 2(1), (10)(b), as from 1 April 2008.

30–32   *(Revoked by the Proceeds of Crime Act 2002 (External Requests and Orders) (Amendment) Order 2008, SI 2008/302, art 2(1), (11), as from 1 April 2008.)*

33   Application of sums by enforcement receivers

(1)   This article applies to sums which are in the hands of a receiver appointed under article 27 if they are—

   (a)   the proceeds of the realisation of property under article 28 or 29;

   (b)   where article 28 applies, sums (other than those mentioned in sub-paragraph (a)) in which the defendant holds an interest.

(2)   The sums must be applied as follows—

   (a)   first, they must be applied in payment of such expenses incurred by a person acting as an insolvency practitioner as are payable under this paragraph by virtue of article 3;

   (b)   second, they must be applied in making any payments directed by the Crown Court;

   (c)   third, they must be applied on the defendant's behalf towards satisfaction of the external order.

(3)   If the amount payable under the external order has been fully paid and any sums remain in the receiver's hands he must distribute them—

   (a)   among such persons who held (or hold) interests in the property concerned as the Crown Court directs; and

   (b)   in such proportions as it directs.

(4)   Before making a direction under paragraph (3) the court must give persons who held (or hold) interests in the property concerned a reasonable opportunity to make representations to it.

(5)   For the purposes of paragraphs (3) and (4) the property concerned is—

   (a)   the property represented by the proceeds mentioned in paragraph (1)(a);

   (b)   the sums mentioned in paragraph (1)(b).

(6)   The receiver applies sums as mentioned in paragraph (2)(c) by paying them to the relevant Director on account of the amount payable under the order.

[3980BG]

NOTES

Commencement: 1 January 2006.

34   Sums received by relevant Director

(1)   This article applies if a relevant Director receives sums on account of the amount payable under a registered external order or the value of the property specified in the order.

(2)   The relevant Director's receipt of the sums reduces the amount payable under the order, but he must apply the sums received as follows.

(3)   First he must apply them in payment of such expenses incurred by a person acting as an insolvency practitioner as—
(a)   are payable under this paragraph by virtue of article 3, but
(b)   are not already paid under article 33(2)(a).

(4)   He must next apply them—
(a)   first, in payment of the remuneration and expenses of a receiver appointed under article 15 to the extent that they have not been met by virtue of the exercise by that receiver of a power conferred under article 16(2)(d);
(b)   second, in payment of the remuneration and expenses of the receiver appointed under article 27.

(5)   Any sums which remain after the relevant Director has made any payments required by the preceding provisions of this article must be paid into the Consolidated Fund.

(6)   Paragraph (4) does not apply if the receiver is a member of the staff of the Crown Prosecution Service, the Serious Fraud Office or the Revenue and Customs Prosecution Office; and it is immaterial whether he is a permanent or temporary member or he is on secondment from elsewhere.

[3980BH]–[3980BJ]

NOTES
Commencement: 1 January 2006.

35, 36   *(Revoked by the Proceeds of Crime Act 2002 (External Requests and Orders) (Amendment) Order 2008, SI 2008/302, art 2(1), (12), as from 1 April 2008.)*

37   Satisfaction of external order

(1)   A registered external order is satisfied when no amount is due under it.

(2)   Where such an order authorises the recovery of property specified in it, no further amount is due under the order when all of the specified property has been sold.

[3980BK]

NOTES
Commencement: 1 January 2006.

38   Restrictions relating to enforcement receivers

(1)   Paragraphs (2) to (4) apply if a court makes an order under article 27 appointing a receiver in respect of any realisable property or specified property.

(2)   No distress may be levied against the property except with the leave of the Crown Court and subject to any terms the Crown Court may impose.

(3)   If the receiver is appointed in respect of a tenancy of any premises, no landlord or other person to whom rent is payable may exercise a right within paragraph (4) except with the leave of the Crown Court and subject to any terms the Crown Court may impose.

(4)   A right is within this paragraph if it is a right of forfeiture by peaceable re-entry in relation to the premises in respect of any failure by the tenant to comply with any term or condition of the tenancy.

(5)   If a court in which proceedings are pending in respect of any property is satisfied that an order under article 27 appointing a receiver in respect of the property has been applied for or made, the court may either stay the proceedings or allow them to continue on any terms it thinks fit.

(6)   Before exercising any power conferred by paragraph (5), the court must give an opportunity to be heard to—
(a)   the relevant Director … , and
(b)   the receiver (if the order under article 27 has been made).

[3980BL]–[3980BM]

NOTES
Commencement: 1 January 2006.
Para (6): words omitted revoked by the Proceeds of Crime Act 2002 (External Requests and Orders) (Amendment) Order 2008, SI 2008/302, art 2(1), (13), as from 1 April 2008.

39   *(Revoked by the Proceeds of Crime Act 2002 (External Requests and Orders) (Amendment) Order 2008, SI 2008/302, art 2(1), (14), as from 1 April 2008.)*

CHAPTER 3
RECEIVERS AND PROCEDURE

40 Protection of receiver appointed under articles 15, 27 and 30

If a receiver appointed under article 15 [or 27]—

    (a)   takes action in relation to property which is not realisable property or, as the case may be, the specified property,

    (b)   would be entitled to take the action if it were realisable property or, as the case may be, the specified property, and

    (c)   believes on reasonable grounds that he is entitled to take the action,

he is not liable to any person in respect of any loss or damage resulting from the action, except so far as the loss or damage is caused by his negligence.

[3980BN]

NOTES

Commencement: 1 January 2006.
Words in square brackets substituted by the Proceeds of Crime Act 2002 (External Requests and Orders) (Amendment) Order 2008, SI 2008/302, art 2(1), (15), as from 1 April 2008.

41 Further applications by receivers

(1)   This article applies to a receiver appointed under article 15 [or 27].

(2)   The receiver may apply to the Crown Court for an order giving directions as to the exercise of his powers.

(3)   The following persons may apply to the Crown Court—

    (a)   any person affected by action taken by the receiver;

    (b)   any person who may be affected by action the receiver proposes to take.

(4)   On an application under this article the court may make such order as it believes is appropriate.

[3980BO]

NOTES

Commencement: 1 January 2006.
Para (1): words in square brackets substituted by the Proceeds of Crime Act 2002 (External Requests and Orders) (Amendment) Order 2008, SI 2008/302, art 2(1), (15), as from 1 April 2008.

42 Discharge and variation of receiver orders

(1)   The following persons may apply to the Crown Court to vary or discharge an order made under article 15, 16 or 27 [to 29]—

    (a)   the receiver;

    (b)   the relevant Director;

    (c)   any person affected by the order.

(2)   On an application under this article the court—

    (a)   may discharge the order;

    (b)   may vary the order.

(3)   But in the case of an order under article 15 or 16—

    (a)   if the condition in article 7 which was satisfied was that proceedings were started, the court must discharge the order if at the conclusion of the proceedings no external order has been made;

    (b)   if the condition which was satisfied was that proceedings were started, the court must discharge the order if within a reasonable time an external order has not been registered under Chapter 2 of this Part;

    (c)   if the condition which was satisfied was that an investigation was started, the court must discharge the order if within a reasonable time proceedings for the offence are not started.

[3980BP]

NOTES

Commencement: 1 January 2006.
Para (1): words in square brackets substituted by the Proceeds of Crime Act 2002 (External Requests and Orders) (Amendment) Order 2008, SI 2008/302, art 2(1), (16), as from 1 April 2008.

43 Management receivers: discharge

(1)   This article applies if—

    (a)   a receiver stands appointed under article 15 in respect of property which is identified in the restraint order (the management receiver), and

(b)   the court appoints a receiver under article 27 ...

(2)   The court must order the management receiver to transfer to the other receiver all property held by the management receiver by virtue of the powers conferred on him by article 16.

(3)   ...

(4)   Paragraph (2) does not apply to property which the management receiver holds by virtue of the exercise by him of his power under article 16(2)(d).

(5)   If the management receiver complies with an order under paragraph (2) he is discharged—
(a)   from his appointment under article 15;
(b)   from any obligation under this Order arising from his appointment.

(6)   If this article applies the court may make such a consequential or incidental order as it believes is appropriate.

[3980BQ]

NOTES
Commencement: 1 January 2006.
Para (1): words omitted revoked by the Proceeds of Crime Act 2002 (External Requests and Orders) (Amendment) Order 2008, SI 2008/302, art 2(1), (17)(a), as from 1 April 2008.
Para (3): revoked by SI 2008/302, art 2(1), (17)(b), as from 1 April 2008.

44 Appeal to Court of Appeal about receivers

(1)   If on an application for an order under any of articles 15, 16 [or 27 to 29] the court decides not to make one, the person who applied for the order may appeal to the Court of Appeal against the decision.

(2)   If the court makes an order under any of articles 15, 16 [or 27 to 29], the following persons may appeal to the Court of Appeal in respect of the court's decision—
(a)   the person who applied for the order;
(b)   any person affected by the order.

(3)   If on an application for an order under article 41 the court decides not to make one, the person who applied for the order may appeal to the Court of Appeal against the decision.

(4)   If the court makes an order under article 41 the following persons may appeal to the Court of Appeal in respect of the court's decision—
(a)   the person who applied for the order;
(b)   any person affected by the order;
(c)   the receiver.

(5)   The following persons may appeal to the Court of Appeal against a decision of the court on an application under article 42—
(a)   the person who applied for the order in respect of which the application was made ... ;
(b)   any person affected by the court's decision;
(c)   the receiver.

(6)   On an appeal under this article the Court of Appeal may—
(a)   confirm the decision, or
(b)   make such order as it believes is appropriate.

[3980BR]

NOTES
Commencement: 1 January 2006.
Paras (1), (2): words in square brackets substituted by the Proceeds of Crime Act 2002 (External Requests and Orders) (Amendment) Order 2008, SI 2008/302, art 2(1), (18)(a), as from 1 April 2008.
Para (5): words omitted by SI 2008/302, art 2(1), (18)(b), as from 1 April 2008.

45 Appeal to the House of Lords about receivers

(1)   An appeal lies to the House of Lords from a decision of the Court of Appeal on an appeal under article 44.

(2)   An appeal under this article lies at the instance of any person who was a party to the proceedings before the Court of Appeal.

(3)   On an appeal under this article the House of Lords may—
(a)   confirm the decision of the Court Appeal, or
(b)   make such order as it believes is appropriate.

[3980BS]

NOTES
Commencement: 1 January 2006.

46 Powers of court and receiver

(1) This article applies to—
  (a) the powers conferred on a court by this Part;
  (b) the powers of a receiver appointed under article 15 [or 27].

(2) The powers—
  (a) must be exercised with a view to the value for the time being of realisable property or specified property being made available (by the property's realisation) for satisfying an external order that has been or may be made against the defendant;
  (b) must be exercised, in a case where an external order has not been made, with a view to securing that there is no diminution in the value of the property identified in the external request;
  (c) must be exercised without taking account of any obligation of a defendant or a recipient of a tainted gift if the obligation conflicts with the object of satisfying any external order against the defendant that has been or may be registered under article 22;
  (d) may be exercised in respect of a debt owed by the Crown.

(3) Paragraph (2) has effect subject to the following rules—
  (a) the powers must be exercised with a view to allowing a person other than the defendant or a recipient of a tainted gift to retain or recover the value of any interest held by him;
  (b) in the case of realisable property or specified property held by a recipient of a tainted gift, the powers must be exercised with a view to realising no more than the value for the time being of the gift;
  (c) in a case where an external order has not been made against the defendant, property must not be sold if the court so orders under paragraph (4).

(4) If on an application by the defendant or the recipient of a tainted gift, the court decides that property cannot be replaced it may order that it must not be sold.

(5) An order under paragraph (4) may be revoked or varied.

[3980BT]

NOTES
  Commencement: 1 January 2006.
  Para (1): words in square brackets substituted by the Proceeds of Crime Act 2002 (External Requests and Orders) (Amendment) Order 2008, SI 2008/302, art 2(1), (19), as from 1 April 2008.

47 Procedure on appeal to Court of Appeal under Part 2

(1) An appeal to the Court of Appeal under this Part lies only with the leave of that Court.

(2) Subject to rules of court made under section 53(1) of the Supreme Court Act 1981 (distribution of business between civil and criminal divisions) the criminal division of the Court of Appeal is the division—
  (a) to which an appeal to that Court under this Part is to lie, and
  (b) which is to exercise that Court's jurisdiction under this Part.

(3) In relation to appeals to the Court of Appeal under this Part, the Secretary of State may make an order containing provision corresponding to any provision in the Criminal Appeal Act 1968, subject to any specified modifications.

(4) Subject to any rules of court, the costs of and incidental to all proceedings on an appeal to the criminal division of the Court of Appeal under article 10, 23 or 44 are in the discretion of the court.

(5) The court shall have full power to determine by whom and to what extent the costs are to be paid.

(6) In any proceedings mentioned in paragraph (4), the court may—
  (a) disallow, or
  (b) (as the case may be) order the legal or other representative concerned to meet,
the whole of any wasted costs or such part of them as may be determined in accordance with rules of court.

(7) In paragraph (6) "wasted costs" means any costs incurred by a party—
  (a) as a result of any improper, unreasonable or negligent act or omission on the part of any legal or other representative or any employee of such a representative, or
  (b) which, in the light of any such act or omission occurring after they were incurred, the court considers it unreasonable to expect that party to pay.

(8) "Legal or other representative", in relation to a party to proceedings, means any person exercising a right of audience or right to conduct litigation on his behalf.

[3980BU]

PART III
STATUTORY INSTRUMENTS

NOTES
Commencement: 1 January 2006.

48 Procedure on appeal to House of Lords under Part 2

(1)   Section 33(3) of the Criminal Appeal Act 1968 (limitation on appeal from criminal division of the Court of Appeal) does not prevent an appeal to the House of Lords under this Part.

(2)   In relation to appeals to the House of Lords under this Part, the Secretary of State may make an order containing provision corresponding to any provision in the Criminal Appeal Act 1968, subject to any specified modifications.

[3980BV]

NOTES
Commencement: 1 January 2006.

CHAPTER 4
INTERPRETATION

49 Property

(1)   In this Part, "realisable property" means in a case where the external order specifies a sum of money, any free property held by the defendant or by the recipient of a tainted gift.

(2)   "Free property" has the same meaning as in section 82 of the Act (free property).

(3)   The rules in paragraphs (a) and (c) to (g) of section 84(2) of the Act (property: general provisions) apply in relation to property under this Order (in addition to section 447(4) to (6) of the Act (interpretation)) as they apply in relation to property under Part 2 of the Act.

[3980BW]

NOTES
Commencement: 1 January 2006.

50 Tainted gifts

(1)   In this Part, a gift is tainted if it was made by the defendant at any time after—
   (a)   the date on which the offence to which the external order or external request relates was committed, or
   (b)   if his criminal conduct consists of two or more such offences and they were committed on different dates, the date of the earliest.

(2)   For the purposes of paragraph (1), an offence which is a continuing offence is committed on the first occasion when it is committed.

(3)   A gift may be a tainted gift whether it was made before or after the coming into force of this Order.

[3980BX]

NOTES
Commencement: 1 January 2006.

51 Gifts and their recipients

(1)   In this Part, a defendant is to be treated as making a gift if he transfers property to another person for a consideration whose value is significantly less than the value of the property at the time of the transfer.

(2)   If paragraph (1) applies, the property given is to be treated as such share in the property transferred as is represented by the fraction—
   (a)   whose numerator is the difference between the two values mentioned in paragraph (1), and
   (b)   whose denominator is the value of the property at the time of the transfer.

(3)   In this Part references to a recipient of a tainted gift are to a person to whom the defendant has made the gift.

[3980BY]

NOTES
Commencement: 1 January 2006.

52 Value: the basic rule

(1)   Subject to article 53, this article applies where it is necessary under this Part to decide the value at any time of property then held by a person.

(2)   Its value is the market value of the property at that time.

(3)   But if at that time another person holds an interest in the property its value, in relation to the person mentioned in paragraph (1), is the market value of his interest at that time, ignoring any charging order under a provision listed in paragraph (4).

(4)   Those provisions are—
   (a)   section 9 of the Drug Trafficking Offences Act 1986;
   (b)   section 78 of the Criminal Justice Act 1988;
   (c)   Article 14 of the Criminal Justice (Confiscation) (Northern Ireland) Order 1990;
   (d)   section 27 of the Drug Trafficking Act 1994;
   (e)   Article 32 of the Proceeds of Crime (Northern Ireland) Order 1996.

[3980BZ]

NOTES
Commencement: 1 January 2006.

53   Value of tainted gifts

(1)   The value at any time (the material time) of a tainted gift is the greater of the following—
   (a)   the value (at time of the gift) of the property given, adjusted to take account of later changes in the value of money;
   (b)   the value (at the material time) of the property found under paragraph (2).

(2)   The property found under this paragraph is as follows—
   (a)   if the recipient holds the property given, the property found under this paragraph is that property;
   (b)   if the recipient holds no part of the property given, the property found under this paragraph is any property which directly or indirectly represents it in his hands;
   (c)   if the recipient holds part of the property given, the property found under this paragraph is that part and any property which directly or indirectly represents the other part in his hands.

(3)   The references in paragraph (1)(a) and (b) to the value are to the value found in accordance with article 52.

[3980CA]

NOTES
Commencement: 1 January 2006.

54   Meaning of "defendant"

In this Part "defendant"—
   (a)   in relation to a restraint order means—
      (i)   in a case in which the first condition in article 7 is satisfied, the alleged offender;
      (ii)   in a case in which the second condition in article 7 is satisfied, the person against whom proceedings for an offence have been started in a country outside the United Kingdom (whether or not he has been convicted);
   (b)   in relation to an external order, the person convicted of criminal conduct.

[3980CB]

NOTES
Commencement: 1 January 2006.

55   Other interpretation

In this Part—
   "relevant Director" has the meaning—
      (a)   in the context of an external request, set out in article 6(4);
      (b)   in the context of an external order, set out in article 18(4);
   "relevant property" means property which satisfies the test in section 447(7) of the Act;
   "specified property" means property specified in an external order (other than an order that specifies a sum of money).

[3980CC]

NOTES
Commencement: 1 January 2006.

PART 3
GIVING EFFECT IN SCOTLAND TO EXTERNAL REQUESTS IN CONNECTION WITH CRIMINAL INVESTIGATIONS OR PROCEEDINGS AND TO EXTERNAL ORDERS ARISING FROM SUCH PROCEEDINGS

CHAPTER 1
EXTERNAL REQUESTS

56 Action on receipt of external request in connection with criminal investigations or proceedings

(1) The Lord Advocate may make an application under article 59 where—
  (a) he receives an external request in relation to relevant property in Scotland; and
  (b) he considers that the request is likely to satisfy either of the conditions in article 57.

(2) The Lord Advocate may ask the overseas authority which made the request for such further information as may be necessary to determine whether the request is likely to satisfy either of the conditions in article 57.

(3) Where a request concerns relevant property which is in England and Wales or Northern Ireland as well as Scotland, so much of the request as concerns such property shall be dealt with under Part 2 or 4 respectively.

[3980CD]

NOTES
Commencement: 1 January 2006.

57 Conditions for court to give effect to external request

(1) The court may exercise the powers conferred by article 58 if either of the following conditions is satisfied.

(2) The first condition is that—
  (a) relevant property within Scotland is identified in the external request;
  (b) a criminal investigation has been instituted in the country from which the external request was made with regard to an offence; and
  (c) there is reasonable cause to believe that the alleged offender named in the request has benefited from his criminal conduct.

(3) The second condition is that—
  (a) relevant property within Scotland is identified in the external request;
  (b) proceedings for an offence have been instituted in the country from which the external request was made and not concluded, and
  (c) there is reasonable cause to believe that the accused named in the request has benefited from his criminal conduct.

(4) In determining whether the conditions are satisfied and whether the request is an external request within the meaning of the Act, the court must have regard to the definitions in subsections (1), (4) to (8) and (11) of section 447 of the Act.

(5) If the first condition is satisfied references in this Chapter to the accused are to the alleged offender.

[3980CE]

NOTES
Commencement: 1 January 2006.

58 Restraint orders

(1) If either condition set out in article 57 is satisfied, the court may make an order ("a restraint order") interdicting any specified person from dealing with relevant property which is identified in the external request and specified in the order.

(2) A restraint order may be made subject to exceptions, and an exception may in particular–
  (a) make provision for reasonable living expenses and reasonable legal expenses in connection with the proceedings seeking a restraint order or the registration of an external order;
  (b) make provision for the purpose of enabling any person to carry on any trade, business, profession or occupation;
  (c) be made subject to conditions.

(3) But an exception to a restraint order must not make provision for any legal expenses which—
  (a) relate to the criminal conduct mentioned in article 57(2), if the first condition is satisfied, or article 57(3), if the second condition is satisfied; and

(b) are incurred by a person against whom proceedings for the offence have been instituted or by a recipient of a tainted gift.

(4) The court may make such order as it believes is appropriate for the purpose of ensuring that the restraint order is effective.

(5) A restraint order does not affect property for the time being subject to a charge under—
   (a) section 9 of the Drug Trafficking Offences Act 1986;
   (b) section 78 of the Criminal Justice Act 1988;
   (c) Article 14 of the Criminal Justice (Confiscation) (Northern Ireland) Order 1990;
   (d) section 27 of the Drug Trafficking Act 1994;
   (e) Article 32 of the Proceeds of Crime (Northern Ireland) Order 1996.

(6) Dealing with property includes removing the property from Scotland.

[3980CF]

NOTES
Commencement: 1 January 2006.

59 Application, recall and variation

(1) A restraint order may be made on an ex parte application by the Lord Advocate, which may be heard in chambers.

(2) The Lord Advocate must intimate an order to every person affected by it.

(3) Paragraph (2) does not affect the time when the order becomes effective.

(4) The Lord Advocate and any person affected by the order may apply to the court to recall the order or to vary it and paragraphs (5) to (7) apply in such a case.

(5) If an application under paragraph (4) in relation to an order has been made but not determined, realisable property to which the order applies must not be realised.

(6) The court may—
   (a) recall the order;
   (b) vary the order.

(7) If the condition in article 57 which was satisfied was that proceedings were instituted, the court must recall the order if, at the conclusion of the proceedings, no external order has been made.

(8) If the condition in article 57 which was satisfied was that proceedings were instituted, the court must recall the order if within a reasonable time an external order has not been registered under Chapter 2 of this Part.

(9) If the condition in article 57 which was satisfied was that an investigation was instituted, the court must recall the order if within a reasonable time proceedings for the offence are not instituted.

[3980CG]

NOTES
Commencement: 1 January 2006.

60 Appeals

(1) If on an application for a restraint order the court decides not to make one, the Lord Advocate may reclaim against the decision.

(2) The Lord Advocate and any person affected by the order may reclaim against the decision of the court on an application under article 59(4).

[3980CH]

NOTES
Commencement: 1 January 2006.

61 Inhibition of property affected by order

(1) On the application of the Lord Advocate, the court may, in relation to the property mentioned in paragraph (2), grant warrant for inhibition against any person specified in a restraint order.

(2) That property is the heritable realisable property to which the restraint order applies (whether generally or such of it as is specified in the application).

(3) The warrant for inhibition—
   (a) has effect as if granted on the dependence of an action for debt by the Lord Advocate against the person and may be executed, recalled, loosed or restricted accordingly, and
   (b) has the effect of letters of inhibition and must forthwith be registered by the Lord Advocate in the Register of Inhibitions and Adjudications.

(4)   Section 155 of the Titles to Land Consolidation (Scotland) Act 1868 (effective date of inhibition) applies in relation to an inhibition for which warrant is granted under paragraph (1) as it applies to an inhibition by separate letters or contained in a summons.

(5)   The execution of an inhibition under this article in respect of property does not prejudice the exercise of an administrator's powers under or for the purposes of this Part in respect of that property.

(6)   An inhibition executed under this article ceases to have effect when, or in so far as, the restraint order ceases to apply in respect of the property in relation to which the warrant for inhibition was granted.

(7)   If an inhibition ceases to have effect to any extent by virtue of paragraph (6) the Lord Advocate must—

    (a)   apply for the recall or, as the case may be, the restriction of the inhibition, and

    (b)   ensure that the recall or restriction is reflected in the Register of Inhibitions and Adjudications.

[3980CI]

NOTES
Commencement: 1 January 2006.

62   Arrestment of property affected by order

(1)   On the application of the Lord Advocate the court may, in relation to moveable realisable property to which a restraint order applies (whether generally or such of it as is specified in the application), grant warrant for arrestment.

(2)   Such a warrant for arrestment may be granted only if the property would be arrestable if the person entitled to it were a debtor.

(3)   A warrant under paragraph (1) has effect as if granted on the dependence of an action for debt at the instance of the Lord Advocate against the person and may be executed, recalled, loosed or restricted accordingly.

(4)   The execution of an arrestment under this article in respect of property does not prejudice the exercise of an administrator's powers under or for the purposes of this Part in respect of that property.

(5)   An arrestment executed under this article ceases to have effect when, or in so far as, the restraint order ceases to apply in respect of the property in relation to which the warrant for arrestment was granted.

(6)   If an arrestment ceases to have effect to any extent by virtue of paragraph (5) the Lord Advocate must apply to the court for an order recalling, or as the case may be, restricting the arrestment.

[3980CJ]

NOTES
Commencement: 1 January 2006.

63   Management administrators

(1)   If the court makes a restraint order it may at any time, on the application of the Lord Advocate—

    (a)   appoint an administrator to take possession of any realisable property to which the order applies and (in accordance with the court's directions) to manage or otherwise deal with the property;

    (b)   order a person who has possession of property in respect of which an administrator is appointed to give him possession of it.

(2)   An appointment of an administrator may be made subject to conditions or exceptions.

(3)   Where the court makes an order under paragraph (1)(b), the clerk of court must notify the accused and any person subject to the order of the making of the order.

(4)   Any dealing of the accused or any such person in relation to property to which the order applies is of no effect in a question with the administrator unless the accused or, as the case may be, that person had no knowledge of the administrator's appointment.

(5)   The court—

    (a)   may order a person holding an interest in realisable property to which the restraint order applies to make to the administrator such payment as the court specifies in respect of a beneficial interest held by the accused or the recipient of a tainted gift;

    (b)   may (on the payment being made) by order transfer, grant or extinguish any interest in the property.

(6)　The court must not—
 (a) confer the power mentioned in paragraph (1) to manage or otherwise deal with the property, or
 (b) exercise the power conferred on it by paragraph (5),
unless it gives persons holding interests in the property a reasonable opportunity to make representations to it.

(7)　The court may order that a power conferred by an order under this article is subject to such conditions and exceptions as it specifies.

(8)　Managing or otherwise dealing with property includes—
 (a) selling the property or any part of it or interest in it;
 (b) carrying on or arranging for another person to carry on any trade or business the assets of which are or are part of the property;
 (c) incurring capital expenditure in respect of the property.

(9)　Paragraphs (1)(b) and (5) do not apply to property for the time being subject to a charge under—
 (a) section 9 of the Drug Trafficking Offences Act 1986;
 (b) section 78 of the Criminal Justice Act 1988;
 (c) Article 14 of the Criminal Justice (Confiscation) (Northern Ireland) Order 1990;
 (d) section 27 of the Drug Trafficking Act 1994;
 (e) Article 32 of the Proceeds of Crime (Northern Ireland) Order 1996.

[3980CK]

NOTES
Commencement: 1 January 2006.

64　Seizure in pursuance of restraint order

(1)　If a restraint order is in force a constable or a relevant officer of Revenue and Customs may seize any realisable property to which it applies to prevent its removal from Scotland.

(2)　Property seized under paragraph (1) must be dealt with in accordance with the directions of the court which made the order.

[3980CL]

NOTES
Commencement: 1 January 2006.

65　Restraint orders: restrictions on proceedings and remedies

(1)　While a restraint order has effect, the court may sist any action, execution or any legal process in respect of the property to which the order applies.

(2)　If the court in which proceedings are pending in respect of any property is satisfied that a restraint order has been applied for or made in respect of the property, the court may either sist the proceedings or allow them to continue on any terms it thinks fit.

(3)　Before exercising any power conferred by paragraph (2), the court must give an opportunity to be heard to—
 (a) the Lord Advocate, and
 (b) any administrator appointed in respect of the property under article 63.

[3980CM]

NOTES
Commencement: 1 January 2006.

CHAPTER 2
EXTERNAL ORDERS

66　Application to give effect to external orders

(1)　Where the Lord Advocate receives an external order arising from a criminal conviction and concerning relevant property in Scotland, he may make an ex parte application to the court to give effect to the order.

(2)　No application to give effect to such an order may be made otherwise than under paragraph (1).

(3)　An application under paragraph (1) may be heard in chambers.

(4)   Where an order concerns relevant property which is in England and Wales or Northern Ireland as well as Scotland, so much of the request as concerns such property shall be dealt with under Part 2 or 4 respectively.

[3980CN]

NOTES
Commencement: 1 January 2006.

67 Authentication by an overseas court

(1)   Paragraph (2) applies where an overseas court has authenticated its involvement in—
- (a)   any judgement;
- (b)   any order;
- (c)   any other document concerned with such a judgement or order or proceedings relating to it.

(2)   Where this paragraph applies, any statement in the judgement, order or document is admissible in evidence in proceedings under this Chapter.

[3980CO]

NOTES
Commencement: 1 January 2006.

68 Conditions for the court to give effect to external orders

(1)   The court must decide to give effect to an external order by registering it where all of the following conditions are satisfied.

(2)   The first condition is that the external order was made consequent on the conviction of the person named in the order and no appeal is outstanding in respect of that conviction.

(3)   The second condition is that the order is in force and no appeal is outstanding in respect of it.

(4)   The third condition is that giving effect to the order would not be incompatible with any of the Convention rights (within the meaning of the Human Rights Act 1998) of any person affected by it.

(5)   The fourth condition applies only in respect of an external order which authorises the confiscation of property other than money that is specified in the order.

(6)   That condition is that the specified property must not be subject to a charge under—
- (a)   section 9 of the Drug Trafficking Offences Act 1986;
- (b)   section 78 of the Criminal Justice Act 1988;
- (c)   Article 14 of the Criminal Justice (Confiscation) (Northern Ireland) Order 1990;
- (d)   section 27 of the Drug Trafficking Act 1994; or
- (e)   Article 32 of the Proceeds of Crime (Northern Ireland) Order 1996.

(7)   In determining whether the order is an external order within the meaning of the Act the court must have regard to the definitions in subsections (2), (4), (5), (6), (8) and (10) of section 447 of the Act.

(8)   In paragraph (3) "appeal" includes—
- (a)   any proceedings by way of discharging or setting aside the order; and
- (b)   an application for a new trial or suspension or delay in execution of any penalty or sentence.

[3980CP]

NOTES
Commencement: 1 January 2006.

69 Registration of external orders

(1)   Where the court decides to give effect to an external order, it must—
- (a)   register the order;
- (b)   provide for notice of the registration to be given to any person affected by it; and
- (c)   appoint a sheriff clerk for the purposes of the receipt of payment under articles 72(2) and 77(6).

(2)   Only an external order registered by the court may be implemented under this Chapter.

(3)   The court may cancel the registration of the external order, or vary the property to which it applies, on an application by the Lord Advocate or any person affected by it if, or to the extent that, the court is of the opinion that any of the conditions in article 68 is not satisfied.

(4)   Notice of an application under paragraph (3) must be given—

(a)   in the case of an application by the Lord Advocate, to any person affected by the registration of the external order; and

(b)   in any other case, to the Lord Advocate and any other person affected by the registration of the external order.

(5)   The court shall not cancel the registration of the external order or vary the property to which it applies under paragraph (3) unless it gives the Lord Advocate and any person affected by it the opportunity to make representations to it.

(6)   The court must cancel the registration of the external order on an application by the Lord Advocate or any person affected by it, if it appears to the court that the order has been satisfied—

(a)   in the case of an order for the recovery of a sum of money specified in it, by payment of the amount due under it, or

(b)   in the case of an order for the recovery of specified property, by the surrender of the property, or

(c)   by any other means.

(7)   Where the registration of an external order is cancelled or varied under paragraph (3) or (6), the court must provide for notice of this to be given to the Lord Advocate and any person affected by it.

[3980CQ]

NOTES

Commencement: 1 January 2006.

70   Appeal about external orders

(1)   If on an application for the court to give effect to an external order by registering it, the court decides not to do so, the Lord Advocate may reclaim against the decision.

(2)   If an application is made under article 69(3) or (6) in relation to the registration of an external order, the following persons may reclaim against the court's decision on the application—

(a)   the Lord Advocate;

(b)   any person affected by the registration.

(3)   On a reclaiming motion under paragraph (1) or (2) the court may—

(a)   confirm or set aside the decision to register; or

(b)   direct the court to register the external order (or so much of it as relates to property other than that to which article 68(6) applies).

[3980CR]

NOTES

Commencement: 1 January 2006.

71   Sums in currency other than sterling

(1)   This article applies where the external order which is registered under article 69 specifies a sum of money.

(2)   If the sum of money which is specified is expressed in a currency other than sterling, the sum of money to be recovered is to be taken to be the sterling equivalent calculated in accordance with the rate of exchange prevailing at the end of the working day immediately preceding the day when the court registered the external order under article 69.

(3)   The sterling equivalent must be calculated by the Lord Advocate.

(4)   The notice referred to in article 69(1)(b) and (7) must set out the amount in sterling which is to be paid.

(5)   In this article "working day" means any day other than—

(a)   a Saturday or Sunday;

(b)   Christmas Day; or

(c)   Good Friday;

(d)   any day that is a bank holiday in Scotland under the Banking and Financial Dealings Act 1971.

[3980CS]

NOTES

Commencement: 1 January 2006.

72   Time for payment

(1)   This article applies where the external order is for the recovery of a specified sum of money.

(2)   Subject to paragraphs (3) to (6), the amount ordered to be paid under—

    (a)   an external order that has been registered under article 69; or

    (b)   where article 71 applies, the notice under article 69(1)(b),

must be paid to the appropriate clerk of court on the date on which the notice under article 69(1)(b) is delivered to the person affected by it.

(3)   Where there is a reclaiming motion under article 70 the duty to pay is delayed until the day on which the reclaiming motion is determined or withdrawn.

(4)   If the person affected by an external order which has been registered shows that he needs time to pay the amount ordered to be paid, the court may make an order allowing payment to be made within a specified period.

(5)   The specified period—

    (a)   must start with the day on which the notice under article 69(1)(b) was delivered to the person affected by the order or the day referred to in paragraph (3) as the case may be; and

    (b)   must not exceed six months.

(6)   If within the specified period the person affected by an external order applies to the court for the period to be extended and the court believes that there are exceptional circumstances, it may make an order extending the period.

(7)   The extended period—

    (a)   must start with the day on which the notice under article 69(1)(b) was delivered to the person affected by it; and

    (b)   must not exceed 12 months.

(8)   An order under paragraph (6)—

    (a)   may be made after the end of the specified period; but

    (b)   must not be made after the end of the extended period.

(9)   The court must not make an order under paragraph (4) or (6) unless it gives the Lord Advocate an opportunity to make representations.

(10)   The appropriate clerk of court is the sheriff clerk appointed under article 69(1).

[3980CT]

NOTES

Commencement: 1 January 2006.

73 Appointment of enforcement administrators

(1)   This article applies if—

    (a)   an external order is registered;

    (b)   it is not satisfied; and

    (c)   in the case of an external order for the recovery of a specified sum of money, any period specified by order under article 72 has expired.

(2)   On the application of the Lord Advocate the court may appoint an administrator in respect of—

    (a)   where the external order is for the recovery of a specified sum of money, realisable property;

    (b)   where the external order is for the recovery of specified property, that property.

[3980CU]

NOTES

Commencement: 1 January 2006.

74 Powers of enforcement administrators in respect of monetary external orders

(1)   If the court appoints an administrator under article 73, it may act under this article on the application of the Lord Advocate where the external order is for the recovery of a specified sum of money.

(2)   The court may confer on the administrator the following powers in relation to any realisable property—

    (a)   power to take possession of the property;

    (b)   power to manage or otherwise deal with the property;

    (c)   power to realise the property in such manner as the court may specify.

(3)   The court may order any person who has possession of realisable property to give possession of it to the administrator.

(4)   The clerk of court must notify the offender and any person subject to an order under paragraph (3) of the making of that order.

(5)   Any dealing of the offender or any such persons in relation to property to which the order applies is of no effect in a question with the administrator unless the offender or, as the case may be, that person had no knowledge of the administrator's appointment.

(6)   The court—
   (a)   may order a person holding an interest in realisable property to make to the administrator such payment as the court specifies in respect of a beneficial interest held by the offender or the recipient of a tainted gift;
   (b)   may (on payment being made) by order transfer, grant or extinguish any interest in the property.

(7)   The court must not—
   (a)   confer the power mentioned in paragraph (2)(b) or (c) in respect of the property, or
   (b)   exercise the power conferred on it by paragraph (6) in respect of the property,

unless it gives persons holding interests in the property a reasonable opportunity to make representations to it.

(8)   Managing or otherwise dealing with property includes—
   (a)   selling the property or any part of it or interest in it;
   (b)   carrying on or arranging for another person to carry on any trade or business the assets of which are part of the property;
   (c)   incurring capital expenditure in respect of the property.

(9)   The court may order that a power conferred by an order under this article is subject to such conditions and exceptions as it specifies.

(10)   Paragraph (2) does not apply to property for the time being subject to a charge under—
   (a)   section 9 of the Drug Trafficking Offences Act 1986;
   (b)   section 78 of the Criminal Justice Act 1988;
   (c)   Article 14 of the Criminal Justice (Confiscation) (Northern Ireland) Order 1990;
   (d)   section 27 of the Drug Trafficking Act 1994;
   (e)   Article 32 of the Proceeds of Crime (Northern Ireland) Order 1996.

[3980CV]

NOTES
Commencement: 1 January 2006.

75   Powers of enforcement administrators in respect of external orders for the recovery of specified property

(1)   If the court appoints an administrator under article 73, it may act under this article on the application of the Lord Advocate where the external order is for the recovery of property specified in the order ("the specified property").

(2)   The court may confer on the administrator the following powers in relation to the specified property—
   (a)   power to take possession of the property;
   (b)   power to manage or otherwise deal with the property;
   (c)   power to realise the property in such manner as the court may specify.

(3)   The court may order any person who has possession of the specified property to give possession of it to the administrator.

(4)   The clerk of court must notify the offender and any person subject to an order under paragraph (3) of the making of that order.

(5)   Any dealing of the offender or any such person in relation to property to which the order applies is of no effect in a question with the administrator unless the person had no knowledge of the administrator's appointment.

(6)   The court—
   (a)   may order a person holding an interest in the specified property to make to the administrator such payment as the court specifies in respect of a beneficial interest held by the offender or the recipient of a tainted gift;
   (b)   may (on the payment being made) by order transfer, grant or extinguish any interest in the property.

(7)   The court must not—
   (a)   confer the power mentioned in paragraph (2)(b) or (c) in respect of the property; or
   (b)   exercise the power conferred on it by paragraph (6) in respect of property,

unless it gives persons holding interests in the property a reasonable opportunity to make representations about it.

(8)   The court may order that a power conferred by an order under this article is subject to such conditions and exceptions as it specifies.

PART III
STATUTORY INSTRUMENTS

(9)   Managing or otherwise dealing with property includes—
  (a)   selling the property or any part of it or interest in it;
  (b)   carrying on or arranging for another person to carry on any trade or business the assets of which are or are part of the property;
  (c)   incurring capital expenditure in respect of the property.

[3980CW]

NOTES
Commencement: 1 January 2006.

76   Disposal of family home

(1)   This article applies where the court confers power on the administrator under article 74(2) in respect of the offender's family home.

(2)   Where this article applies, then, before the administrator disposes of any right or interest in the offender's family home he shall—
  (a)   obtain the relevant consent; or
  (b)   where he is unable to do so, apply to the court for authority to carry out the disposal.

(3)   On an application being made to it under paragraph (2)(b), the court, after having regard to all the circumstances of the case including—
  (a)   the needs and financial resources of the spouse of the offender;
  (b)   the needs and financial resources of any child of the family;
  (c)   the length of the period during which the family home has been used as a residence by any of the persons referred to in sub-paragraph (a) or (b),
may refuse to grant the application or may postpone the granting of the application for such period (not exceeding 12 months) as it may consider reasonable in the circumstances or may grant the application subject to such conditions as it may prescribe.

(4)   Paragraph (3) shall apply—
  (a)   to an action for division and sale of the family home of the person concerned; or
  (b)   to an action for the purpose of obtaining vacant possession of that home,
brought by an administrator as it applies to an application under paragraph (2)(b) and, for the purposes of this paragraph, any reference in paragraph (3) to the granting of the application shall be construed as a reference to the granting of decree in the action.

(5)   In this article—
  "family home", in relation to any offender means any property in which the offender has or had (whether alone or in common with any other person) a right or interest, being property which is occupied as a residence by the offender and his or her spouse or by the offender's spouse or former spouse (in any case with or without a child of the family) or by the offender with a child of the family;
  "child of the family" includes any child or grandchild of either the offender or his or her spouse or former spouse, and any person who has been treated by either the offender or his or her spouse or former spouse, whatever the age of such a child, grandchild or person may be; and
  "relevant consent" means in relation to the disposal of any right or interest in a family home—
    (a)   in a case where the family home is occupied by the spouse or former spouse of the offender, the consent of the spouse or, as the case may be, of the former spouse, whether or not the family home is also occupied by the offender;
    (b)   where sub-paragraph (a) does not apply, in a case where the family home is occupied by the offender with a child of the family, the consent of the offender.

[3980CX]

NOTES
Commencement: 1 January 2006.

77   Application of sums by enforcement administrator

(1)   This article applies to sums which are in the hands of an administrator appointed under article 73 if they are—
  (a)   the proceeds of the realisation of property under article 74 or 75;
  (b)   where article 74 applies, sums (other than those mentioned in sub-paragraph (a)) in which the offender holds an interest.

(2)   The sums must be applied as follows—
  (a)   first, they must be applied in payment of such expenses incurred by a person acting as an insolvency practitioner as are payable under this paragraph by virtue of article 3;
  (b)   second, they must be applied in making any payments as directed by the court;
  (c)   third, they must be applied on the offender's behalf towards satisfaction of the external order.

(3)   If the amount payable under the external order has been fully paid and any sums remain in the administrator's hands he must distribute them—

(a)   among such persons who held (or hold) interests in the property concerned as the court directs; and

(b)   in such proportions as it directs.

(4)   Before making a direction under paragraph (3) the court must give persons who held (or hold) interests in the property concerned a reasonable opportunity to make representations to it.

(5)   For the purposes mentioned in paragraphs (3) and (4) the property concerned is—

(a)   the property represented by the proceeds mentioned in paragraph (1)(a);

(b)   the sums mentioned in paragraph (1)(b).

(6)   The administrator applies sums as mentioned in paragraph (2)(c) by paying them to the appropriate clerk of court on account of the amount payable under the order.

(7)   The appropriate clerk of court is the sheriff clerk appointed article 69(1).

[3980CY]

NOTES

Commencement: 1 January 2006.

78   Sums received by clerk of court

(1)   This section applies if a clerk of court receives sums on account of the amount payable under a registered external order or the value of the property specified in the order.

(2)   The clerk of court's receipt of the sums reduces the amount payable under the order, but he must apply the sums received as follows.

(3)   First he must apply them in payment of such expenses incurred by a person acting as an insolvency practitioner as—

(a)   are payable under this paragraph by virtue of article 3; but

(b)   are not already paid under article 77(2)(a).

(4)   If the Lord Advocate has reimbursed the administrator in respect of remuneration or expenses under article 80 the clerk of court must next apply the sums in reimbursing the Lord Advocate.

(5)   If the clerk of court received the sums under article 77 he must next apply them in payment of the administrator's remuneration and expenses.

(6)   If any amount remains after the clerk of court makes any payments required by the preceding paragraphs of this article, the amount must be disposed of in accordance with section 211(5) of the Criminal Procedure (Scotland) Act 1995 as if it were a fine imposed in the High Court.

[3980CZ]

NOTES

Commencement: 1 January 2006.

79   Satisfaction of external order

(1)   A registered external order is satisfied when no amount is due under it.

(2)   Where such an order authorises the recovery of property specified in it, no amount is due under the order when all of the specified property has been sold.

[3980DA]

NOTES

Commencement: 1 January 2006.

CHAPTER 3
ADMINISTRATORS AND PROCEDURE

80   Protection of administrator appointed under article 63 or 73

(1)   If an administrator appointed under article 63 or 73—

(a)   takes action in relation to property which is not realisable property, or as the case may be, the specified property;

(b)   would be entitled to take the action if it were realisable property or, as the case may be, the specified property; and

(c)   believes on reasonable grounds that he is entitled to take action,

he is not liable to any person in respect of any loss or damage resulting from the action, except so far as the loss or damage is caused by his negligence.

(2)   Paragraph (3) applies if an administrator incurs expenses in the exercise of his functions at a time when—
  (a)   an external order has not been registered; and
  (b)   an external order has been registered but the administrator has recovered no money.

(3)   As soon as practicable after they have been incurred the expenses must be reimbursed by the Lord Advocate.

(4)   Paragraph (5) applies if—
  (a)   an amount is due in respect of the administrator's remuneration and expenses; but
  (b)   nothing (or not enough) is available to be applied in payment of them under article 78(4).

(5)   The remuneration and expenses must be paid (to the extent of the shortfall) by the Lord Advocate.

[3980DB]

NOTES
Commencement: 1 January 2006.

81   Protection of persons affected

(1)   This paragraph applies where an administrator is appointed under article 63 or 73.

(2)   The following persons may apply to the court—
  (a)   any person affected by action taken by the administrator;
  (b)   any person who may be affected by action the administrator proposes to take.

(3)   On an application under this article the court may make such order as it thinks appropriate.

[3980DC]

NOTES
Commencement: 1 January 2006.

82   Recall and variation of order

(1)   The Lord Advocate, an administrator and any other person affected by an order made under article 63 or articles 73 to 75 may apply to the court to vary or recall the order.

(2)   On an application under this article the court—
  (a)   may vary the order;
  (b)   may recall the order.

(3)   But in the case of an order under article 63—
  (a)   if the condition in article 57 which was satisfied was that proceedings were instituted, the court must recall the order if at the conclusion of the proceedings no external order (within the meaning of section 447(2) of the Act) has now been made;
  (b)   if the condition which was satisfied was that an investigation was instituted the court must recall the order if within a reasonable period proceedings for the offence are not instituted.

[3980DD]

NOTES
Commencement: 1 January 2006.

83   Management administrators: discharge

(1)   This article applies if—
  (a)   an administrator stands appointed under article 63 in respect of property which is identified in the restraint order (the management administrator); and
  (b)   the court appoints an administrator under article 73.

(2)   The Court must order the management administrator to transfer to the other administrator all property held by the management administrator by virtue of the powers conferred on him by article 63.

(3)   If the management administrator complies with an order under paragraph (2) he is discharged—
  (a)   from his appointment under article 63;
  (b)   from any obligation under this Order arising from his appointment.

[3980DE]

NOTES
Commencement: 1 January 2006.

84 Appeals

(1) If on an application for an order under article 63 or articles 73 to 75 the court decides not to make one, the Lord Advocate may reclaim in respect of the decision.

(2) If the court makes an order under article 63 or articles 73 to 75 the following persons may reclaim in respect of the court's decision—
(a) the Lord Advocate;
(b) any person affected by the Order.

(3) If on an application for an order under article 81 the court decides not to make one, the person who applied for the order may reclaim in respect of the decision.

(4) If the court makes an order under article 81, the following persons may reclaim in respect of the court's decision—
(a) the person who applied for the order in respect of which the application was made;
(b) any person affected by the court's decision;
(c) the administrator.

(5) The following persons may reclaim in respect of a decision of the court on an application under article 82—
(a) the person who applied for the order in respect of which the application was made;
(b) any person affected by the court's decision;
(c) the administrator.

(6) On a reclaiming motion under this article the court may—
(a) confirm the decision;
(b) make such order as it believes is appropriate.

[3980DF]

NOTES
Commencement: 1 January 2006.

85 Administrators: further provision

Schedule 1 which makes further provision about administrators appointed under articles 63 and 73 has effect.

[3980DG]

NOTES
Commencement: 1 January 2006.

86 Administrators: restrictions on proceedings and remedies

(1) Where an administrator is appointed under article 73, the court may sist any action, execution or other legal process in respect of the property to which the order appointing the administrator relates.

(2) If a court (whether the Court of Session or any other court) in which proceedings are pending, in respect of any property is satisfied that an application has been made for the appointment of an administrator or that an administrator has been appointed in relation to that property, the court may either sist the proceedings or allow them to continue on any terms it thinks fit.

(3) Before exercising any power conferred by paragraph (2) the court must give an opportunity to be heard to—
(a) the Lord Advocate;
(b) if appointed, the administrator.

[3980DH]

NOTES
Commencement: 1 January 2006.

CHAPTER 4
INTERPRETATION

87 Property

(1) In this Part, "realisable property" means in a case where an external order specifies a sum of money, any free property held by the accused or offender, as the case may be, or the recipient of a tainted gift.

(2) The rules in paragraphs (a) and (c) to (g) of section 150(2) of the Act (property: general provisions) apply in relation to property under this Order (in addition to section 447(4) to (6)) of the Act (interpretation) as they apply in relation to property under Part 3 of the Act.

[3980DI]

PART III
STATUTORY INSTRUMENTS

NOTES
Commencement: 1 January 2006.

88   Tainted gifts and their recipients

(1)   In this Part, a gift is tainted if it was made by the accused or offender, as the case may be, at any time after—

    (a)   the date on which the offence to which the external order or external request relates was committed, or

    (b)   if his criminal conduct consists of two or more such offences and they were committed on different dates, the date of the earliest.

(2)   For the purposes of paragraph (1), an offence which is a continuing offence is committed on the first occasion when it is committed.

(3)   A gift may be a tainted gift whether it was made before or after the coming into force of this Order.

(4)   In this Part, an accused or offender, as the case may be, is to be treated as making a gift if he transfers property to another person for a consideration whose value is significantly less than the value of the property at the time of the transfer.

(5)   If paragraph (4) applies, the property given is to be treated as such share in the property transferred as is represented by the fraction—

    (a)   whose numerator is the difference between the two values mentioned in paragraph (4), and

    (b)   whose denominator is the value of the property at the time of the transfer.

(6)   In this Part, references to a recipient of a tainted gift are to a person to whom the accused or offender, as the case may be, has (whether directly or indirectly) made the gift.

[3980DJ]

NOTES
Commencement: 1 January 2006.

89   Value: the basic rule

(1)   Subject to article 90, this article applies where it is necessary under this Part to decide the value at any time of property then held by that person.

(2)   Its value is the market value of the property at that time.

(3)   But if at that time another person holds an interest in the property its value, in relation to the person mentioned in paragraph (1) is the market value of his interest at that time ignoring any charging order under a provision listed in paragraph (4).

(4)   Those provisions are—

    (a)   section 9 of the Drug Trafficking Offences Act 1986;

    (b)   section 78 of the Criminal Justice Act 1988;

    (c)   Article 14 of the Criminal Justice (Confiscation) (Northern Ireland) Order 1990;

    (d)   Section 27 of the Drug Trafficking Act 1994;

    (e)   Article 32 of the Proceeds of Crime (Northern Ireland) Order 1996.

[3980DK]

NOTES
Commencement: 1 January 2006.

90   Value of tainted gifts

(1)   The value at any time (the material time) of a tainted gift is the greater of the following—

    (a)   the value (at the time of the gift) of the property gives, adjusted to take account of later changes in the value of money;

    (b)   the value (at the material time) of the property found under paragraph (2).

(2)   The property found under this paragraph is as follows—

    (a)   if the recipient holds the property given, that property;

    (b)   if the recipient holds no part of the property given, any property which directly or indirectly represents it in his hands;

    (c)   if the recipient holds part of the property given, that part and any property which directly or indirectly represents the other part in his hands.

(3)   The references in paragraph (1)(a) and (b) to the value are to the value found in accordance with article 89.

[3980DL]

NOTES
Commencement: 1 January 2006.

91   Meaning of "accused" and "offender"

(1)   In this Part—
"accused", in relation to a restraint order means—
    (a)   in a case in which the first condition in article 57 is satisfied, the alleged offender;
    (b)   in a case in which the second condition in article 57 is satisfied, the person against whom proceedings for an offence have been instituted in a country outside the United Kingdom (whether or not he has been convicted);
"offender", in relation to an external order means the person convicted of criminal conduct.

[3980DM]

NOTES
Commencement: 1 January 2006.

92   Other interpretation

(1)   In this Part—
"court" means the Court of Session;
"relevant property" means property which satisfies the test set out in section 447(7) of the Act;
"specified property" means that property specified in the external request (other than a request that specifies a sum of money).

[3980DN]

NOTES
Commencement: 1 January 2006.

PART 4
GIVING EFFECT IN NORTHERN IRELAND TO EXTERNAL REQUESTS IN CONNECTION WITH CRIMINAL INVESTIGATIONS OR PROCEEDINGS AND TO EXTERNAL ORDERS ARISING FROM SUCH PROCEEDINGS

CHAPTER 1
EXTERNAL REQUESTS

93 Action on receipt of external request in connection with criminal investigations or proceedings

(1)   Except where paragraph (2) applies, the Secretary of State may refer an external request in connection with criminal investigations or proceedings in the country from which the request was made and concerning relevant property in Northern Ireland to—
    (a)   ...
    (b)   the Director of Public Prosecutions for Northern Ireland;
to process it.

(2)   This paragraph applies where it appears to the Secretary of State that the request—
    (a)   is made in connection with criminal investigations or proceedings which relate to an offence involving serious or complex fraud, and
    (b)   concerns relevant property in Northern Ireland.

(3)   Where paragraph (2) applies, the Secretary of State may refer the request to the Director of the Serious Fraud Office to process it.

(4)   In this Chapter "the relevant Director" means the Director to whom an external request is referred under paragraph (1) or (3).

(5)   The relevant Director may ask the overseas authority which made the request for such further information as may be necessary to determine whether the request is likely to satisfy either of the conditions in article 94.

(6)   A request under paragraph (5) may include a request for statements which may be used as evidence.

(7)   Where a request concerns relevant property which is in England, Wales or Scotland as well as Northern Ireland, so much of the request as concerns such property shall be dealt with under Part 2 or 3 respectively.

[3980DO]

NOTES
Commencement: 1 January 2006.

Para (1): sub-para (a) revoked by the Proceeds of Crime Act 2002 (External Requests and Orders) (Amendment) Order 2008, SI 2008/302, art 2(1), (20), as from 1 April 2008.

94 Conditions for High Court to give effect to external request

(1)   The High Court may exercise the powers conferred by article 95 if either of the following conditions is satisfied.

(2)   The first condition is that—
  (a)   relevant property in Northern Ireland is identified in the external request;
  (b)   a criminal investigation has been started in the country from which the external request was made with regard to an offence, and
  (c)   there is reasonable cause to believe that the alleged offender named in the request has benefited from his criminal conduct.

(3)   The second condition is that—
  (a)   relevant property in Northern Ireland is identified in the external request;
  (b)   proceedings for an offence have been started in the country from which the external request was made and not concluded, and
  (c)   there is reasonable cause to believe that the defendant named in the request has benefited from his criminal conduct.

(4)   In determining whether the conditions are satisfied and whether the request is an external request within the meaning of the Act, the court must have regard to the definitions in subsections (1), (4) to (8) and (11) of section 447 of the Act.

(5)   If the first condition is satisfied, references in this Chapter to the defendant are to the alleged offender.

[3980DP]

NOTES
Commencement: 1 January 2006.

95 Restraint orders

(1)   If either condition set out in article 94 is satisfied, the High Court may make an order ("a restraint order") prohibiting any specified person from dealing with relevant property which is identified in the external request and specified in the order.

(2)   A restraint order may be made subject to exceptions, and an exception may in particular—
  (a)   make provision for reasonable living expenses and reasonable legal expenses in connection with the proceedings seeking a restraint order or the registration of an external order;
  (b)   make provision for the purpose of enabling any person to carry on any trade, business, profession or occupation;
  (c)   be made subject to conditions.

(3)   Paragraph (4) applies if—
  (a)   a court makes a restraint order, and
  (b)   the applicant for the order applies to the court to proceed under paragraph (4) (whether as part of the application for the restraint order or at any time afterwards).

(4)   The court may make such order as it believes is appropriate for the purpose of ensuring that the restraint order is effective.

(5)   A restraint order does not affect property for the time being subject to a charge under any of these provisions—
  (a)   section 9 of the Drug Trafficking Offences Act 1986;
  (b)   section 78 of the Criminal Justice Act 1988;
  (c)   Article 14 of the Criminal Justice (Confiscation) (Northern Ireland) Order 1990;
  (d)   section 27 of the Drug Trafficking Act 1994;
  (e)   Article 32 of the Proceeds of Crime (Northern Ireland) Order 1996.

(6)   Dealing with property includes removing it from Northern Ireland.

[3980DQ]

NOTES
Commencement: 1 January 2006.

96 Application, discharge and variation of restraint orders

(1)   A restraint order—
  (a)   may be made only on an application by the relevant Director;
  (b)   may be made on an ex parte application to a judge in chambers.

(2)   An application to discharge or vary a restraint order or an order under article 95(4) may be made to the High Court by—
   (a)   the relevant Director;
   (b)   any person affected by the order.

(3)   Paragraphs (4) to (7) apply to an application under paragraph (2).

(4)   The court—
   (a)   may discharge the order;
   (b)   may vary the order.

(5)   If the condition in article 94 which was satisfied was that proceedings were started, the court must discharge the order if, at the conclusion of the proceedings, no external order has been made.

(6)   If the condition in article 94 which was satisfied was that proceedings were started, the court must discharge the order if within a reasonable time an external order has not been registered under Chapter 2 of this Part.

(7)   If the condition in article 94 which was satisfied was that an investigation was started, the court must discharge the order if within a reasonable time proceedings for the offence are not started.

[3980DR]

NOTES
Commencement: 1 January 2006.

97   Appeal to Court of Appeal about restraint orders

(1)   If on an application for a restraint order the High Court decides not to make one, the relevant Director may appeal to the Court of Appeal against the decision.

(2)   If an application is made under article 96(2) in relation to a restraint order or an order under article 95(4), the following persons may appeal to the Court of Appeal in respect of the High Court's decision on the application—
   (a)   the relevant Director;
   (b)   any person affected by the order.

(3)   On an appeal under paragraph (1) or (2) the Court of Appeal may—
   (a)   confirm the decision, or
   (b)   make such order as it believes is appropriate.

[3980DS]

NOTES
Commencement: 1 January 2006.

98   Appeal to House of Lords about restraint orders

(1)   An appeal lies to the House of Lords from a decision of the Court of Appeal on an appeal under article 97.

(2)   An appeal under this article lies at the instance of any person who was a party to the proceedings before the Court of Appeal.

(3)   On an appeal under this article the House of Lords may—
   (a)   confirm the decision of the Court of Appeal, or
   (b)   make such order as it believes is appropriate.

[3980DT]

NOTES
Commencement: 1 January 2006.

99   Seizure in pursuance of restraint order

(1)   If a restraint order is in force a constable may seize any property which is specified in it to prevent its removal from Northern Ireland.

(2)   Property seized under paragraph (1) must be dealt with in accordance with the directions of the court which made the order.

[3980DU]

NOTES
Commencement: 1 January 2006.

PART III
STATUTORY INSTRUMENTS

100 Supplementary (restraint orders)

(1)   The person applying for a restraint order must be treated for the purposes of section 66 of the Land Registration Act (Northern Ireland) 1970 (cautions) as a person interested in relation to any registered land to which—

(a)   the application relates, or

(b)   a restraint order made in pursuance of the application relates.

(2)   Upon being served with a copy of a restraint order, the Registrar shall, in respect of any registered land to which a restraint order or an application for a restraint order relates, make an entry inhibiting any dealing with the land without the consent of the High Court.

(3)   Subsections (2) and (4) of section 67 of the Land Registration Act (Northern Ireland) 1970 (inhibitions) shall apply to an entry made under subsection (2) as they apply to an entry made on the application of any person interested in the registered land under subsection (1) of that section.

(4)   Where a restraint order has been protected by an entry registered under the Land Registration Act (Northern Ireland) 1970 or the Registration of Deeds Acts, an order discharging the restraint order may require that the entry be vacated.

(5)   In this article—

"Registrar" and "entry" have the same meanings as in the Land Registration Act (Northern Ireland) 1970; and

"Registration Deeds Acts" has the meaning given by section 46(2) of the Interpretation Act (Northern Ireland) 1954.

[3980DV]

NOTES
Commencement: 1 January 2006.

101 Appointment of management receivers

(1)   Paragraph (2) applies if—

(a)   the High Court makes a restraint order, and

(b)   the relevant Director applies to the court to proceed under paragraph (2) (whether as part of the application for the restraint order or at any time afterwards).

(2)   The High Court may by order appoint a receiver in respect of any property which is specified in the restraint order.

[3980DW]

NOTES
Commencement: 1 January 2006.

102 Powers of management receivers

(1)   If the court appoints a receiver under article 101 it may act under this article on the application of the relevant Director.

(2)   The court may by order confer on the receiver the following powers in relation to any property which is specified in the restraint order—

(a)   power to take possession of the property;

(b)   power to manage or otherwise deal with the property;

(c)   power to start, carry on or defend any legal proceedings in respect of the property;

(d)   power to realise so much of the property as is necessary to meet the receiver's remuneration and expenses.

(3)   The court may by order confer on the receiver power to enter any premises in Northern Ireland and to do any of the following—

(a)   search for or inspect anything authorised by the court;

(b)   make or obtain a copy, photograph or other record of anything so authorised;

(c)   remove anything which the receiver is required or authorised to take possession of in pursuance of an order of the court.

(4)   The court may by order authorise the receiver to do any of the following for the purpose of the exercise of his functions—

(a)   hold property;

(b)   enter into contracts;

(c)   sue and be sued;

(d)   employ agents;

(e)   execute powers of attorney, deeds or other instruments;

(f)   take any other steps the court thinks appropriate.

(5)   The court may order any person who has possession of property which is specified in the restraint order to give possession of it to the receiver.

(6) The court—

    (a) may order a person holding an interest in property which is specified in the restraint order to make to the receiver such payment as the court specifies in respect of a beneficial interest held by the defendant or the recipient of a tainted gift;

    (b) may (on the payment being made)by order transfer, grant or extinguish any interest in the property.

(7) Paragraphs (2), (5) and (6) do not apply to property for the time being subject to a charge under any of these provisions—

    (a) section 9 of the Drug Trafficking Offences Act 1986;

    (b) section 78 of the Criminal Justice Act 1988;

    (c) Article 14 of the Criminal Justice (Confiscation) (Northern Ireland) Order 1990;

    (d) section 27 of the Drug Trafficking Act 1994;

    (e) Article 32 of the Proceeds of Crime (Northern Ireland) Order 1996.

(8) The court must not—

    (a) confer the power mentioned in paragraph (2)(b) or (d) in respect of property, or

    (b) exercise the power conferred on it by paragraph (6) in respect of property,

unless it gives persons holding interests in the property a reasonable opportunity to make representations to it.

[(8A) Paragraph (8), so far as relating to the power mentioned in paragraph (2)(b), does not apply to property which—

    (a) is perishable; or

    (b) ought to be disposed of before its value diminishes.]

(9) The court may order that a power conferred by an order under this article is subject to such conditions and exceptions as it specifies.

(10) Managing or otherwise dealing with property includes—

    (a) selling the property or any part of it or interest in it;

    (b) carrying on or arranging for another person to carry on any trade or business the assets of which are or are part of the property;

    (c) incurring capital expenditure in respect of the property.

[3980DX]

NOTES

Commencement: 1 January 2006.

Para (8A): inserted by the Proceeds of Crime Act 2002 (External Requests and Orders) (Amendment) Order 2008, SI 2008/302, art 2(1), (21), as from 1 April 2008.

103 Restrictions relating to restraint orders

(1) Paragraphs (2) and (3) apply if a court makes a restraint order.

(2) If the order applies to a tenancy of any premises, no landlord or other person to whom rent is payable may exercise a right within paragraph (3) except with the leave of the High Court and subject to any terms the High Court may impose.

(3) A right is within this paragraph if it is a right of forfeiture by peaceable re-entry in relation to the premises in respect of any failure by the tenant to comply with any term or condition of the tenancy.

(4) If a court in which proceedings are pending in respect of any property is satisfied that a restraint order has been applied for or made in respect of the property, the court may either stay the proceedings or allow them to continue on any terms it thinks fit.

(5) Before exercising any power conferred by paragraph (4), the court must give an opportunity to be heard to—

    (a) the relevant Director, and

    (b) any receiver appointed in respect of the property under article 101 [or 113].

[3980DY]

NOTES

Commencement: 1 January 2006.

Para (5): words in square brackets substituted by the Proceeds of Crime Act 2002 (External Requests and Orders) (Amendment) Order 2008, SI 2008/302, art 2(1), (22), as from 1 April 2008.

PART III
STATUTORY INSTRUMENTS

CHAPTER 2
EXTERNAL ORDERS

104 Action on receipt of external order in connection with criminal convictions

(1) Except where paragraph (2) applies, the Secretary of State may refer an external order arising from a criminal conviction in the country from which the order was sent and concerning relevant property in Northern Ireland to—

(a) ...

(b) the Director of Public Prosecutions for Northern Ireland;

to process it.

(2) This paragraph applies where it appears to the Secretary of State that—

(a) the property or sum of money specified in the order was found, or was believed, to have been obtained as a result of, or in connection with, criminal conduct involving serious or complex fraud, and

(b) the order concerns relevant property in Northern Ireland.

(3) Where paragraph (2) applies, the Secretary of State may refer the order to the Director of the Serious Fraud Office to process it.

(4) In this Chapter "the relevant Director" means the Director to whom an external order is referred under paragraph (1) or (3).

(5) Where an order concerns relevant property which is in England, Wales or Scotland as well as Northern Ireland, so much of the request as concerns such property shall be dealt with under Part 2 or 3, respectively.

[3980DZ]

NOTES

Commencement: 1 January 2006.

Para (1): sub-para (a) revoked by the Proceeds of Crime Act 2002 (External Requests and Orders) (Amendment) Order 2008, SI 2008/302, art 2(1), (23), as from 1 April 2008.

105 Authentication by the overseas court

(1) Paragraph (2) applies where an overseas court has authenticated its involvement in—

(a) any judgment,

(b) any order,

(c) any other document concerned with such a judgment or order or proceedings relating to it.

(2) Where this paragraph applies, any statement in the judgment, order or document is admissible in evidence in proceedings under this Chapter.

[3980EA]

NOTES

Commencement: 1 January 2006.

106 Applications to give effect to external orders

(1) An application may be made by the relevant Director to the Crown Court to give effect to an external order.

(2) No application to give effect to such an order may be made otherwise than under paragraph (1).

(3) An application under paragraph (1)—

(a) shall include a request to appoint the relevant Director as the enforcement authority for the order;

(b) may be made on an ex parte application to a judge in chambers.

[3980EB]

NOTES

Commencement: 1 January 2006.

107 Conditions for Crown Court to give effect to external orders

(1) The Crown Court must decide to give effect to an external order by registering it where all of the following conditions are satisfied.

(2) The first condition is that the external order was made consequent on the conviction of the person named in the order and no appeal is outstanding in respect of that conviction.

(3) The second condition is that the external order is in force and no appeal is outstanding in respect of it.

(4)   The third condition is that giving effect to the external order would not be incompatible with any of the Convention rights (within the meaning of the Human Rights Act 1998) of any person affected by it.

(5)   The fourth condition applies only in respect of an external order which authorises the confiscation of property other than money that is specified in the order.

(6)   That condition is that the specified property must not be subject to a charge under any of the following provisions—
  (a)   section 9 of the Drug Trafficking Offences Act 1986;
  (b)   section 78 of the Criminal Justice Act 1988;
  (c)   Article 14 of the Criminal Justice (Confiscation) (Northern Ireland) Order 1990;
  (d)   section 27 of the Drug Trafficking Act 1994;
  (e)   Article 32 of the Proceeds of Crime (Northern Ireland) Order 1996.

(7)   In determining whether the order is an external order within the meaning of the Act, the Court must have regard to the definitions in subsections (2), (4), (5), (6), (8) and (10) of section 447 of the Act.

(8)   In paragraph (3) "appeal" includes—
  (a)   any proceedings by way of discharging or setting aside the order; and
  (b)   an application for a new trial or stay of execution.

                                                                                [3980EC]

NOTES
Commencement: 1 January 2006.

108   Registration of external orders

(1)   Where the Crown Court decides to give effect to an external order, it must—
  (a)   register the order in that court;
  (b)   provide for notice of the registration to be given to any person affected by it; and
  (c)   appoint the relevant Director as the enforcement authority for the order.

(2)   Only an external order registered by the Crown Court may be implemented under this Chapter.

(3)   The Crown Court may cancel the registration of the external order, or vary the property to which it applies, on an application by the relevant Director or any person affected by it if, or to the extent that, the court is of the opinion that any of the conditions in article 107 is not satisfied.

(4)   The Crown Court must cancel the registration of the external order, on an application by the relevant Director or any person affected by it, if it appears to the court that the order has been satisfied—
  (a)   in the case of an order for the recovery of a sum of money specified in it, by payment of the amount due under it, or
  (b)   in the case of an order for the recovery of specified property, by the surrender of the property, or
  (c)   by any other means.

(5)   Where the registration of an external order is cancelled or varied under paragraph (3) or (4), the Crown Court must provide for notice of this to be given to the relevant Director and any person affected by it.

                                                                                [3980ED]

NOTES
Commencement: 1 January 2006.

109   Appeal to Court of Appeal about external orders

(1)   If on an application for the Crown Court to give effect to an external order by registering it, the court decides not to do so, the relevant Director may appeal to the Court of Appeal against the decision.

(2)   If an application is made under article 108(3) in relation to the registration of an external order, the following persons may appeal to the Court of Appeal in respect of the Crown Court's decision on the application—
  (a)   the relevant Director;
  (b)   any person affected by the registration.

(3)   On an appeal under paragraph (1) or (2) the Court of Appeal may—
  (a)   confirm the decision or set aside the decision to register; or
  (b)   direct the Crown Court to register the external order (or so much of it as relates to property other than that to which article 107(6) applies).

                                                                                [3980EE]

NOTES
Commencement: 1 January 2006.

110 Appeal to House of Lords about external orders

(1) An appeal lies to the House of Lords from a decision of the Court of Appeal on an appeal under article 109.

(2) An appeal under this article lies at the instance of any person who was a party to the proceedings before the Court of Appeal.

(3) On an appeal under this article the House of Lords may—
(a) confirm or set aside the decision of the Court of Appeal, or
(b) direct the Crown Court to register the external order (or so much of it as relates to property other than that to which article 107(6) applies).

[3980EF]

NOTES
Commencement: 1 January 2006.

111 Sums in currency other than sterling

(1) This article applies where the external order which is registered under article 108 specifies a sum of money.

(2) If the sum of money which is specified is expressed in a currency other than sterling, the sum of money to be recovered is to be taken to be the sterling equivalent calculated in accordance with the rate of exchange prevailing at the end of the working day immediately preceding the day when the Crown Court registered the external order under article 108.

(3) The sterling equivalent must be calculated by the relevant Director.

(4) The notice referred to in article 108(1)(b) and (5) must set out the amount in sterling which is to be paid.

(5) In this article "working day" means any day other than—
(a) a Saturday or Sunday;
(b) Christmas Day;
(c) Good Friday;
(d) any day that is a bank holiday in Northern Ireland under the Banking and Financial Dealings Act 1971.

[3980EG]

NOTES
Commencement: 1 January 2006.

112 Time for payment

(1) This article applies where the external order is for the recovery of a specified sum of money.

(2) Subject to paragraphs (3) to (6), the amount ordered to be paid under—
(a) an external order that has been registered under article 108, or
(b) where article 111(2) applies, the notice under article 108(1)(b),
must be paid on the date on which the notice under article 108(1)(b) is delivered to the person affected by it.

(3) Where there is an appeal under article 109 or 110 and a sum falls to be paid when the appeal has been determined or withdrawn, the duty to pay is delayed until the day on which the appeal is determined or withdrawn.

(4) If the person affected by an external order which has been registered shows that he needs time to pay the amount ordered to be paid, the Crown Court which registered the order may make an order allowing payment to be made in a specified period.

(5) The specified period—
(a) must start with the day on which the notice under 108(1)(b) was delivered to the person affected by the order or the day referred to in paragraph (3), as the case may be, and
(b) must not exceed six months.

(6) If within the specified period the person affected by an external order applies to the Crown Court which registered the order for the period to be extended and the court believes that there are exceptional circumstances, it may make an order extending the period.

(7) The extended period—
(a) must start with the day on which the notice under article 108(1)(b) was delivered to the person affected by it or the day referred to in paragraph (3), as the case may be, and

(b)   must not exceed 12 months.

(8)   An order under paragraph (6)—
    (a)   may be made after the end of the specified period, but
    (b)   must not be made after the end of the extended period.

(9)   The court must not make an order under paragraph (4) or (6) unless it gives the relevant Director an opportunity to make representations.

[3980EH]

NOTES
Commencement: 1 January 2006.

113   Appointment of enforcement receivers

(1)   This article applies if—
    (a)   an external order is registered,
    (b)   it is not satisfied, and
    (c)   in the case of an external order for the recovery of a specified sum of money, any period specified by order under article 112 has expired.

(2)   On the application of the relevant Director ... the Crown Court may by order appoint a receiver in respect of—
    (a)   where the external order is for the recovery of a specified sum of money, realisable property;
    (b)   where the external order is for the recovery of specified property, that property.

[3980EI]

NOTES
Commencement: 1 January 2006.
Para (2): words omitted revoked by the Proceeds of Crime Act 2002 (External Requests and Orders) (Amendment) Order 2008, SI 2008/302, art 2(1), (24), as from 1 April 2008.

114   Powers of enforcement receivers in respect of monetary external orders

(1)   If the court appoints a receiver under article 113, it may act under this article on the application of the relevant Director ... where the external order is for the recovery of a specified sum of money.

(2)   The court may by order confer on the receiver the following powers in relation to any realisable property—
    (a)   power to take possession of the property;
    (b)   power to manage or otherwise deal with the property;
    (c)   power to realise the property, in such manner as the court may specify;
    (d)   power to start, carry on or defend any legal proceedings in respect of the property.

(3)   The court may by order confer on the receiver power to enter any premises in Northern Ireland and to do any of the following—
    (a)   search for or inspect anything authorised by the court;
    (b)   make or obtain a copy, photograph or other record, of anything so authorised;
    (c)   remove anything which the receiver is required or authorised to take possession of in pursuance of an order of the court.

(4)   The court may by order authorise the receiver to do any of the following for the purposes of the exercise of his functions—
    (a)   hold property;
    (b)   enter into contracts;
    (c)   sue and be sued;
    (d)   employ agents;
    (e)   execute powers of attorney, deeds or other instruments;
    (f)   take any other steps the court thinks appropriate.

(5)   The court may order any person who has possession of realisable property to give possession of it to the receiver.

(6)   The court—
    (a)   may order a person holding an interest in realisable property to make to the receiver such payment as the court specifies in respect of a beneficial interest held by the defendant or the recipient of a tainted gift;
    (b)   may (on payment being made) by order transfer, grant or extinguish any interest in the property.

(7)   Paragraphs (2), (5) and (6) do not apply to property for the time being subject to a charge under any of these provisions—
    (a)   section 9 of the Drug Trafficking Offences Act 1986;

    (b)   section 78 of the Criminal Justice Act 1988;

    (c)   Article 14 of the Criminal Justice (Confiscation) (Northern Ireland) Order 1990;

    (d)   section 27 of the Drug Trafficking Act 1994;

    (e)   Article 32 of the Proceeds of Crime (Northern Ireland) Order 1996.

  (8)   The court must not—

    (a)   confer the power mentioned in paragraph (2)(b) or (c) in respect of property, or

    (b)   exercise the power conferred on it by paragraph (6) in respect of property,

unless it gives persons holding interests in the property a reasonable opportunity to make representations to it.

[(8A)   Paragraph (8), so far as relating to the power mentioned in paragraph (2)(b), does not apply to property which—

    (a)   is perishable; or

    (b)   ought to be disposed of before its value diminishes.]

  (9)   The court may order that a power conferred by an order under this article is subject to such conditions and exceptions as it specifies.

  (10)   Managing or otherwise dealing with property includes—

    (a)   selling the property or any part of it or interest in it;

    (b)   carrying on or arranging for another person to carry on any trade or business the assets of which are or are part of the property;

    (c)   incurring capital expenditure in respect of the property.

[3980EJ]

NOTES

Commencement: 1 January 2006.

Para (1): words omitted revoked by the Proceeds of Crime Act 2002 (External Requests and Orders) (Amendment) Order 2008, SI 2008/302, art 2(1), (24), as from 1 April 2008.

Para (8A): inserted by SI 2008/302, art 2(1), (25), as from 1 April 2008.

115 Powers of enforcement receivers in respect of external orders for the recovery of specified property

  (1)   If the court appoints a receiver under article 113, it may act under this article on the application of the relevant Director … where the external order is for the recovery of property specified in the order ("the specified property").

  (2)   The court may by order confer on the receiver the following powers in relation to the specified property—

    (a)   power to take possession of the property;

    (b)   power to manage or otherwise deal with the property;

    (c)   power to realise the property, in such manner as the court may specify;

    (d)   power to start, carry on or defend any legal proceedings in respect of the property.

  (3)   The court may by order confer on the receiver power to enter any premises in Northern Ireland and to do any of the following—

    (a)   search for or inspect anything authorised by the court;

    (b)   make or obtain a copy, photograph or other record of anything so authorised;

    (c)   remove anything which the receiver is required or authorised to take possession of in pursuance of an order of the court.

  (4)   The court may by order authorise the receiver to do any of the following for the purposes of the exercise of his functions—

    (a)   hold property;

    (b)   enter into contracts;

    (c)   sue and be sued;

    (d)   employ agents;

    (e)   execute powers of attorney, deeds or other instruments;

    (f)   take any other steps the court thinks appropriate.

  (5)   The court may order any person who has possession of the specified property to give possession of it to the receiver.

  (6)   The court—

    (a)   may order a person holding an interest in the specified property to make to the receiver such payment as the court specifies in respect of a beneficial interest held by the defendant or the recipient of a tainted gift;

    (b)   may (on the payment being made) by order transfer, grant or extinguish any interest in the property.

  (7)   The court must not—

    (a)   confer the power mentioned in paragraph (2)(b) or (c) in respect of property, or

    (b)   exercise the power conferred on it by paragraph (6) in respect of property, unless it gives persons holding interests in the property a reasonable opportunity to make representations to it.

[(7A)   Paragraph (7), so far as relating to the power mentioned in paragraph (2)(b), does not apply to property which—
(a)   is perishable; or
(b)   ought to be disposed of before its value diminishes.]

(8)   The court may order that a power conferred by an order under this article is subject to such conditions and exceptions as it specifies.

(9)   Managing or otherwise dealing with property includes—
(a)   selling the property or any part of it or interest in it;
(b)   carrying on or arranging for another person to carry on any trade or business the assets of which are or are part of the property;
(c)   incurring capital expenditure in respect of the property.

[3980EK]–[3980EN]

NOTES
Commencement: 1 January 2006.
Para (1): words omitted revoked by the Proceeds of Crime Act 2002 (External Requests and Orders) (Amendment) Order 2008, SI 2008/302, art 2(1), (26)(a), as from 1 April 2008.
Para (7A): inserted by SI 2008/302, art 2(1), (26)(b), as from 1 April 2008.

116–118   *(Revoked by the Proceeds of Crime Act 2002 (External Requests and Orders) (Amendment) Order 2008, SI 2008/302, art 2(1), (27), as from 1 April 2008.)*

119   Application of sums by enforcement receivers

(1)   This article applies to sums which are in the hands of a receiver appointed under article 113 if they are—
(a)   the proceeds of the realisation of property under article 114 or 115;
(b)   where article 114 applies, sums (other than those mentioned in sub-paragraph (a)) in which the defendant holds an interest.

(2)   The sums must be applied as follows—
(a)   first, they must be applied in payment of such expenses incurred by a person acting as an insolvency practitioner as are payable under this paragraph by virtue of article 3;
(b)   second, they must be applied in making any payments directed by the Crown Court;
(c)   third, they must be applied on the defendant's behalf towards satisfaction of the external order.

(3)   If the amount payable under the external order has been fully paid and any sums remain in the receiver's hands he must distribute them—
(a)   among such persons who held (or hold) interests in the property concerned as the Crown Court directs; and
(b)   in such proportions as it directs.

(4)   Before making a direction under paragraph (3) the court must give persons who held (or hold) interests in the property concerned a reasonable opportunity to make representations to it.

(5)   For the purposes of paragraphs (3) and (4) the property concerned is—
(a)   the property represented by the proceeds mentioned in paragraph (1)(a);
(b)   the sums mentioned in paragraph (1)(b).

(6)   The receiver applies sums as mentioned in paragraph (2)(c) by paying them to the appropriate chief clerk on account of the amount payable under the order.

(7)   The appropriate chief clerk is the chief clerk of the court at the place where the external order was registered.

[3980EO]

NOTES
Commencement: 1 January 2006.

120   Sums received by appropriate chief clerk

(1)   This article applies if the appropriate chief clerk receives sums on account of the amount payable under a registered external order or the value of the property specified in the order.

(2)   The appropriate chief clerk's receipt of the sums reduces the amount payable under the order, but he must apply the sums received as follows.

(3)   First he must apply them in payment of such expenses incurred by a person acting as an insolvency practitioner as—
(a)   are payable under this paragraph by virtue of article 3, but

(b)   are not already paid under article 119(2)(a).

(4)   He must next apply them—

(a)   first, in payment of the remuneration and expenses of a receiver appointed under article 101 to the extent that they have not been met by virtue of the exercise by that receiver of a power conferred under article 102(2)(d);

(b)   second, in payment of the remuneration and expenses of the receiver appointed under article 113.

(5)   If any amount remains after the appropriate chief clerk makes any payments required by the preceding provisions of this article, the amount must be treated for the purposes of section 20 of the Administration of Justice Act (Northern Ireland) 1954 (application of fines) as if it were a fine.

(6)   Paragraph (4) does not apply if the receiver is a member of the staff of the Public Prosecution Service for Northern Ireland, or the Serious Fraud Office; and it is immaterial whether he is a permanent or temporary member or he is on secondment from elsewhere.

[3980EP]–[3980ER]

NOTES
Commencement: 1 January 2006.

121, 122   *(Revoked by the Proceeds of Crime Act 2002 (External Requests and Orders) (Amendment) Order 2008, SI 2008/302, art 2(1), (28), as from 1 April 2008.)*

123   Satisfaction of external order

(1)   A registered external order is satisfied when no amount is due under it.

(2)   Where such an order authorises the recovery of property specified in it, no further amount is due under the order when all of the specified property has been sold.

[3980ES]

NOTES
Commencement: 1 January 2006.

124   Restrictions relating to enforcement receivers

(1)   Paragraphs (2) and (3) apply if a court makes an order under article 113 appointing a receiver in respect of any realisable property or specified property.

(2)   If the receiver is appointed in respect of a tenancy of any premises, no landlord or other person to whom rent is payable may exercise a right within paragraph (3) except with the leave of the Crown Court and subject to any terms the Crown Court may impose.

(3)   A right is within this paragraph if it is a right of forfeiture by peaceable re-entry in relation to the premises in respect of any failure by the tenant to comply with any term or condition of the tenancy.

(4)   If a court in which proceedings are pending in respect of any property is satisfied that an order under article 113 appointing a receiver in respect of the property has been applied for or made, the court may either stay the proceedings or allow them to continue on any terms it thinks fit.

(5)   Before exercising any power conferred by paragraph (4), the court must give an opportunity to be heard to—

(a)   the relevant Director … , and

(b)   the receiver (if the order under article 113 has been made).

[3980ET]–[3980EU]

NOTES
Commencement: 1 January 2006.
Para (5): words omitted revoked by the Proceeds of Crime Act 2002 (External Requests and Orders) (Amendment) Order 2008, SI 2008/302, art 2(1), (29), as from 1 April 2008.

125   *(Revoked by the Proceeds of Crime Act 2002 (External Requests and Orders) (Amendment) Order 2008, SI 2008/302, art 2(1), (30), as from 1 April 2008.)*

CHAPTER 3
RECEIVERS AND PROCEDURE

126   Protection of receiver appointed under articles 101, 113 and 116

(1)   If a receiver appointed under article 101 [or 113]—

(a)   takes action in relation to property which is not realisable property or, as the case may be, the specified property,

(b)   would be entitled to take the action if it were realisable property or, as the case may be, the specified property, and

(c)   believes on reasonable grounds that he is entitled to take the action,

he is not liable to any person in respect of any loss or damage resulting from the action, except so far as the loss or damage is caused by his negligence.

[3980EV]

NOTES

Commencement: 1 January 2006.

Para (1): words in square brackets substituted by the Proceeds of Crime Act 2002 (External Requests and Orders) (Amendment) Order 2008, SI 2008/302, art 2(1), (31), as from 1 April 2008.

127   Further applications by receivers

(1)   This article applies to a receiver appointed under article 101 [or 113].

(2)   The receiver may apply to—
(a)   the High Court if he is appointed under article 101;
(b)   the Crown Court if he is appointed under article 113 …

for an order giving directions as to the exercise of his powers.

(3)   The following persons may apply to the High Court if the receiver is appointed under article 101 or to the Crown Court if the receiver is appointed under article 113 … —
(a)   any person affected by action taken by the receiver;
(b)   any person who may be affected by action the receiver proposes to take.

(4)   On an application under this article the court may make such order as it believes is appropriate.

[3980EW]

NOTES

Commencement: 1 January 2006.

Para (1): words in square brackets substituted by the Proceeds of Crime Act 2002 (External Requests and Orders) (Amendment) Order 2008, SI 2008/302, art 2(1), (31), as from 1 April 2008.

Paras (2), (3): words omitted revoked by SI 2008/302, art 2(1), (32), as from 1 April 2008.

128   Discharge and variation of receiver orders

(1)   The following persons may apply to the High Court to vary or discharge an order made under article 101 or 102 or to the Crown Court to vary or discharge an order made under any of articles 113 [to 115]—
(a)   the receiver;
(b)   the relevant Director;
(c)   any person affected by the order.

(2)   On an application under this article the court—
(a)   may discharge the order;
(b)   may vary the order.

(3)   But in the case of an order under article 101 or 102—
(a)   if the condition in article 94 which was satisfied was that proceedings were started, the court must discharge the order if at the conclusion of the proceedings no external order has been made;
(b)   if the condition which was satisfied was that proceedings were started, the court must discharge the order if within a reasonable time an external order has not been registered under Chapter 2 of this Part;
(c)   if the condition which was satisfied was that an investigation was started, the court must discharge the order if within a reasonable time proceedings for the offence are not started.

[3980EX]

NOTES

Commencement: 1 January 2006.

Para (1): words in square brackets substituted by the Proceeds of Crime Act 2002 (External Requests and Orders) (Amendment) Order 2008, SI 2008/302, art 2(1), (33), as from 1 April 2008.

129   Management receivers: discharge

(1)   This article applies if—
(a)   a receiver stands appointed under article 101 in respect of property which is identified in the restraint order (the management receiver), and
(b)   the court appoints a receiver under article 113 …

(2) The court must order the management receiver to transfer to the other receiver all property held by the management receiver by virtue of the powers conferred on him by article 102.

(3) …

(4) Paragraph (2)does not apply to property which the management receiver holds by virtue of the exercise by him of his power under article 102(2)(d).

(5) If the management receiver complies with an order under paragraph (2) he is discharged—
  (a) from his appointment under article 101;
  (b) from any obligation under this Order arising from his appointment.

(6) If this article applies the court may make such a consequential or incidental order as it believes is appropriate.

[3980EY]

NOTES
Commencement: 1 January 2006.
Para (1): words omitted revoked by the Proceeds of Crime Act 2002 (External Requests and Orders) (Amendment) Order 2008, SI 2008/302, art 2(1), (34)(a), as from 1 April 2008.
Para (3): revoked by SI 2008/302, art 2(1), (34)(b), as from 1 April 2008.

130 Appeal to Court of Appeal about receivers

(1) If on an application for an order under any of articles 101, 102 [or 113 to 115], the court decides not to make one, the person who applies for the order may appeal to the Court of Appeal against the decision.

(2) If the court makes an order under any of articles 101, 102 [or 113 to 115], the following persons may appeal to the Court of Appeal in respect of the court's decision—
  (a) the person who applied for the order;
  (b) any person affected by the order.

(3) If on an application for an order under article 127 the court decides not to make one, the person who applied for the order may appeal to the Court of Appeal against the decision.

(4) If the court makes an order under article 127 the following persons may appeal to the Court of Appeal in respect of the court's decision—
  (a) the person who applied for the order;
  (b) any person affected by the order;
  (c) the receiver.

(5) The following persons may appeal to the Court of Appeal against a decision of the court on an application under article 128—
  (a) the person who applied for the order in respect of which the application was made … ;
  (b) any person affected by the court's decision;
  (c) the receiver.

(6) On an appeal under this article the Court of Appeal may—
  (a) confirm the decision, or
  (b) make such order as it believes is appropriate.

[3980EZ]

NOTES
Commencement: 1 January 2006.
Paras (1), (2): words in square brackets substituted by the Proceeds of Crime Act 2002 (External Requests and Orders) (Amendment) Order 2008, SI 2008/302, art 2(1), (35)(a), as from 1 April 2008.
Para (5): words omitted revoked by SI 2008/302, art 2(1), (35)(b), as from 1 April 2008.

131 Appeal to the House of Lords about receivers

(1) An appeal lies to the House of Lords from a decision of the Court of Appeal on an appeal under article 130.

(2) An appeal under this article lies at the instance of any person who was a party to the proceedings before the Court of Appeal.

(3) On an appeal under this article the House of Lords may—
  (a) confirm the decision of the Court Appeal, or
  (b) make such order as it believes is appropriate.

[3980FA]

NOTES
Commencement: 1 January 2006.

132 Powers of court and receiver

(1) This article applies to—

    (a)   the powers conferred on a court by this Part;

    (b)   the powers of a receiver appointed under article 101 [or 113].

  (2)   The powers—

    (a)   must be exercised with a view to the value for the time being of realisable property or specified property being made available (by the property's realisation)for satisfying an external order that has been or may be made against the defendant;

    (b)   must be exercised, in a case where an external order has not been made, with a view to securing that there is no diminution in the value of the property identified in the external request;

    (c)   must be exercised without taking account of any obligation of a defendant or a recipient of a tainted gift if the obligation conflicts with the object of satisfying any external order against the defendant that has been or may be registered under article 108;

    (d)   may be exercised in respect of a debt owed by the Crown.

  (3)   Paragraph (2) has effect subject to the following rules—

    (a)   the powers must be exercised with a view to allowing a person other than the defendant or a recipient of a tainted gift to retain or recover the value of any interest held by him;

    (b)   in the case of realisable property or specified property held by a recipient of a tainted gift, the powers must be exercised with a view to realising no more than the value for the time being of the gift;

    (c)   in a case where an external order has not been made against the defendant, property must not be sold if the court so orders under paragraph (4).

  (4)   If on an application by the defendant or the recipient of a tainted gift, the court decides that property cannot be replaced it may order that it must not be sold.

  (5)   An order under paragraph (4) may be revoked or varied.

                                                                      [3980FB]

NOTES

Commencement: 1 January 2006.

Para (1): words in square brackets substituted by the Proceeds of Crime Act 2002 (External Requests and Orders) (Amendment) Order 2008, SI 2008/302, art 2(1), (36), as from 1 April 2008.

133 Procedure on appeal to Court of Appeal under Part 4

  (1)   An appeal to the Court of Appeal under this Part lies only with the leave of that Court.

  (2)   In relation to appeals to the Court of Appeal under this Part, the Secretary of State may make an order containing provision corresponding to any provision in the Criminal Appeal (Northern Ireland) Act 1980, subject to any specified modifications.

  (3)   Subject to any rules of court, the costs of and incidental to all proceedings on an appeal to the Court of Appeal under article 97, 109 or 130 are in the discretion of the court.

  (4)   The court shall have full power to determine by whom and to what extent the costs are to be paid.

  (5)   In any proceedings mentioned in paragraph (3), the court may—

    (a)   disallow, or

    (b)   (as the case may be) order the legal or other representative concerned to meet,

the whole of any wasted costs or such part of them as may be determined in accordance with rules of court.

  (6)   In paragraph (5) "wasted costs" means any costs incurred by a party—

    (a)   as a result of any improper, unreasonable or negligent act or omission on the part of any legal or other representative or any employee of such a representative, or

    (b)   which, in the light of any such act or omission occurring after they were incurred, the court considers it unreasonable to expect that party to pay.

  (7)   Legal or other representative", in relation to a party to proceedings, means any person exercising a right of audience or right to conduct litigation on his behalf.

                                                                     [3980FC]

NOTES

Commencement: 1 January 2006.

134 Procedure on appeal to House of Lords under Part 4

  (1)   In relation to appeals to the House of Lords under this Part, the Secretary of State may make an order containing provision corresponding to any provision in the Criminal Appeal (Northern Ireland) Act 1980, subject to any specified modifications.

                                                                       [3980FD]

NOTES
Commencement: 1 January 2006.

CHAPTER 4
INTERPRETATION

135 Property

(1) In this Part, "realisable property" means in a case where the external order specifies a sum of money, any free property held by the defendant or by the recipient of a tainted gift.

(2) "Free property" has the same meaning as in section 230 of the Act (free property).

(3) The rules in paragraphs (a) and (c) to (g) of section 232(2) of the Act (property: general provisions) apply in relation to property under this Order (in addition to section 447(4) to (6) of the Act (interpretation)) as they apply in relation to property under Part 4 of the Act.

[3980FE]

NOTES
Commencement: 1 January 2006.

136 Tainted gifts

(1) In this Part, a gift is tainted if it was made by the defendant at any time after—
  (a) the date on which the offence to which the external order or external request relates was committed, or
  (b) if his criminal conduct consists of two or more such offences and they were committed on different dates, the date of the earliest.

(2) For the purposes of paragraph (1), an offence which is a continuing offence is committed on the first occasion when it is committed.

(3) A gift may be a tainted gift whether it was made before or after the coming into force of this Order.

[3980FF]

NOTES
Commencement: 1 January 2006.

137 Gifts and their recipients

(1) In this Part, a defendant is to be treated as making a gift if he transfers property to another person for a consideration whose value is significantly less than the value of the property at the time of the transfer.

(2) If paragraph (1) applies, the property given is to be treated as such share in the property transferred as is represented by the fraction—
  (a) whose numerator is the difference between the two values mentioned in paragraph (1), and
  (b) whose denominator is the value of the property at the time of the transfer.

(3) In this Part references to a recipient of a tainted gift are to a person to whom the defendant has made the gift.

[3980FG]

NOTES
Commencement: 1 January 2006.

138 Value: the basic rule

(1) Subject to article 139, this article applies where it is necessary under this Part to decide the value at any time of property then held by a person.

(2) Its value is the market value of the property at that time.

(3) But if at that time another person holds an interest in the property its value, in relation to the person mentioned in paragraph (1), is the market value of his interest at that time, ignoring any charging order under a provision listed in paragraph (4).

(4) Those provisions are—
  (a) section 9 of the Drug Trafficking Offences Act 1986;
  (b) section 78 of the Criminal Justice Act 1988;
  (c) Article 14 of the Criminal Justice (Confiscation) (Northern Ireland) Order 1990;
  (d) section 27 of the Drug Trafficking Act 1994;

(e)   Article 32 of the Proceeds of Crime (Northern Ireland) Order 1996.

[3980FH]

NOTES
Commencement: 1 January 2006.

139   Value of tainted gifts

(1)   The value at any time (the material time) of a tainted gift is the greater of the following—
     (a)   the value (at time of the gift) of the property given, adjusted to take account of later changes in the value of money;
     (b)   the value (at the material time) of the property found under paragraph (2).

(2)   The property found under this paragraph is as follows—
     (a)   if the recipient holds the property given, the property found under this paragraph is that property;
     (b)   if the recipient holds no part of the property given, the property found under this paragraph is any property which directly or indirectly represents it in his hands;
     (c)   if the recipient holds part of the property given, the property found under this paragraph is that part and any property which directly or indirectly represents the other part in his hands.

(3)   The references in paragraph (1)(a) and (b) to the value are to the value found in accordance with article 138.

[3980FI]

NOTES
Commencement: 1 January 2006.

140   Meaning of "defendant"

In this Part "defendant"—
     (a)   in relation to a restraint order means—
         (i)   in a case in which the first condition in article 94 is satisfied, the alleged offender;
         (ii)   in a case in which the second condition in article 94 is satisfied, the person against whom proceedings for an offence have been started in a country outside the United Kingdom (whether or not he has been convicted);
     (b)   in relation to an external order, the person convicted of criminal conduct.

[3980FJ]

NOTES
Commencement: 1 January 2006.

141   Other interpretation

In this Part–
     "relevant Director" has the meaning—
         (a)   in the context of an external request, set out in article 93(4);
         (b)   in the context of an external order, set out in article 104(4);
     "relevant property" means property which satisfies the test in section 447(7) of the Act;
     "specified property" means property specified in an external order (other than an order that specifies a sum of money).

[3980FK]

NOTES
Commencement: 1 January 2006.

PART 5
GIVING EFFECT IN THE UNITED KINGDOM TO EXTERNAL ORDERS BY MEANS OF
CIVIL RECOVERY

CHAPTER 1
INTRODUCTION

142   Action to give effect to an order

(1)   The Secretary of State may forward an external order to the enforcement authority.

(2)   This Part has effect for the purpose of enabling the enforcement authority to realise recoverable property (within the meaning of article 202) in civil proceedings before the High Court or Court of Session for the purpose of giving effect to an external order.

(3)   The powers conferred by this Part are exercisable in relation to any property whether or not proceedings have been brought in the country from which the external order was sent for criminal conduct (within the meaning of section 447(8) of the Act) in connection with the property.

[3980FL]

NOTES
Commencement: 1 January 2006.

CHAPTER 2
CIVIL RECOVERY IN THE HIGH COURT OR COURT OF SESSION
Proceedings for recovery orders

143   Proceedings for recovery orders in England and Wales or Northern Ireland

(1)   Proceedings for a recovery order pursuant to the registration of an external order may be taken by the enforcement authority in the High Court against any person who the authority thinks holds recoverable property.

(2)   The enforcement authority must serve the claim form—
  (a)   on the respondent, and
  (b)   unless the court dispenses with service, on any other person who the authority thinks holds any associated property which the authority wishes to be subject to a recovery order,
wherever domiciled, resident or present.

(3)   In the case of an external order which is for the recovery of property other than a sum of money which is specified in the external order ("the specified property"), that property must also be specified in the claim form.

(4)   Paragraph (5) applies in the case of an external order which is for the recovery of a specified sum of money.

(5)   If any property which the enforcement authority wishes to be subject to a recovery order is not specified in the claim form, it must be described in the form in general terms and the form must state whether it is alleged to be recoverable property or associated property.

(6)   The references above to the claim form include the particulars of claim, where they are served subsequently.

[3980FM]

NOTES
Commencement: 1 January 2006.

144   Proceedings for recovery orders in Scotland

(1)   Proceedings for a recovery order pursuant to the registration of an external order may be taken by the enforcement authority in the Court of Session against any person who the authority thinks holds recoverable property.

(2)   The enforcement authority must serve the application—
  (a)   on the respondent, and
  (b)   unless the court dispenses with service, on any other person who the authority thinks holds any associated property which the authority wishes to be subject to a recovery order,
wherever domiciled, resident or present.

(3)   In the case of an external order which is for the recovery of property other than a sum of money which is specified in the external order ("the specified property"), the property must also be specified in the application.

(4)   Paragraph (5) applies in the case of an external order which is for the recovery of a specified sum of money.

(5)   If any property which the enforcement authority wishes to be subject to a recovery order is not specified in the application it must be described in the application in general terms; and the application must state whether it is alleged to be recoverable property or associated property.

[3980FN]

NOTES
Commencement: 1 January 2006.

145   Sums in a currency other than sterling

(1)   This article applies where the external order in respect of which proceedings for a recovery order are taken specifies a sum of money.

(2)   If the sum of money which is specified in an external order is expressed in a currency other than sterling, the sum of money to be recovered is to be taken to be the sterling equivalent calculated in accordance with the rate of exchange prevailing at the end of day on which the external order was made.

(3)   This amount must be specified—
(a)   in England and Wales or Northern Ireland, in the claim form or the particulars of claim where they are served subsequently, or
(b)   in Scotland, in the application.

[3980FO]

NOTES
Commencement: 1 January 2006.

146   "Associated property"

(1)   "Associated property" means property of any of the following descriptions (including property held by the respondent) which is not itself the recoverable property—
(a)   any interest in the recoverable property,
(b)   any other interest in the property in which the recoverable property subsists,
(c)   if the recoverable property is a tenancy in common, the tenancy of the other tenant,
(d)   if (in Scotland) the recoverable property is owned in common, the interest of the other owner,
(e)   if the recoverable property is part of a larger property, but not a separate part, the remainder of that property.

(2)   References to property being associated with recoverable property are to be read accordingly.

(3)   No property is to be treated as associated with recoverable property consisting of rights under a pension scheme (within the meaning of articles 184 to 186).

[3980FP]

NOTES
Commencement: 1 January 2006.

Property freezing orders (England and Wales and Northern Ireland)

147   Application for property freezing order

(1)   Where the enforcement authority may take proceedings for a recovery order pursuant to the registration of an external order in the High Court, the authority may apply to the court for a property freezing order (whether before or after starting the proceedings).

(2)   A property freezing order is an order that—
(a)   specifies or describes the property to which it applies, and
(b)   subject to any exclusions (see article 149(1)(b) and (2)), prohibits any person to whose property the order applies from in any way dealing with property.

(3)   An application for a property freezing order may be made without notice if the circumstances are such that notice of the application would prejudice any right of the enforcement authority to obtain a recovery order in respect of any property.

(4)   The court may make a property freezing order on an application if it is satisfied that the condition in paragraph (5) is met and, where applicable, that the condition in paragraph (6) is met.

(5)   The first condition is that there is a good arguable case—
(a)   that the property to which the application for the order relates is or includes recoverable property, and
(b)   that, if any of it is not recoverable property, it is associated property.

(6)   The second condition is that, if—
(a)   the property to which the application for the order relates includes property alleged to be associated property, and
(b)   the enforcement authority has not established the identity of the person who holds it, the authority has taken all reasonable steps to do so.

[3980FQ]

NOTES
Commencement: 1 January 2006.

148   Variation and setting aside of property freezing order

(1)   The court may at any time vary or set aside a property freezing order.

(2) If the court makes an interim receiving order that applies to all of the property to which a property freezing order applies, it must set aside the property freezing order.

(3) If the court makes an interim receiving order that applies to some but not all of the property to which a property freezing order applies, it must vary the property freezing order so as to exclude any property to which the interim receiving order applies.

(4) If the court decides that any property to which a property freezing order applies is neither recoverable property nor associated property, it must vary the order so as to exclude the property.

(5) Before exercising the power to vary or set aside a property freezing order, the court must (as well as giving the parties to the proceedings an opportunity to be heard)give such an opportunity to any person who may be affected by its decision.

(6) Paragraph (5) does not apply where the court is acting as required by paragraph (2) or (3).

[3980FR]

NOTES
Commencement: 1 January 2006.

149 Property freezing orders: exclusions

(1) The power to vary a property freezing order includes (in particular) power to make exclusions as follows—
  (a) power to exclude property from the order, and
  (b) power, otherwise than by excluding property from the order, to make exclusions from the prohibition on dealing with the property to which the order applies.

(2) Exclusions from the prohibition on dealing with the property to which the order applies (other than exclusions of property from the order) may also be made when the order is made.

(3) An exclusion may, in particular, make provision for the purpose of enabling any person—
  (a) to meet his reasonable living expenses. or
  (b) to carry on any trade, business, profession or occupation.

(4) An exclusion may be made subject to conditions.

(5) Where the court exercises the power to make an exclusion for the purpose of enabling a person to meet legal expenses that he has incurred, or may incur, in respect of proceedings under this Part, it must ensure that the exclusion—
  (a) is limited to reasonable legal expenses that the person has reasonably incurred or that he reasonably incurs,
  (b) specifies the total amount that may be released for legal expenses in pursuance of the exclusion, and
  (c) is made subject to the required conditions (see article 198) in addition to any conditions imposed under paragraph (4).

(6) The court, in deciding whether to make an exclusion for the purpose of enabling a person to meet legal expenses of his in respect of proceedings under this Part—
  (a) must have regard (in particular) to the desirability of the person being represented in any proceedings under this Part in which he is a participant, and
  (b) must, where the person is the respondent, disregard the possibility that legal representation of the person in any such proceedings might, were an exclusion not made, be funded by the Legal Services Commission or the Northern Ireland Legal Services Commission.

(7) If excluded property is not specified in the order it must be described in the order in general terms.

(8) The power to make exclusions must, subject to paragraph (6), be exercised with a view to ensuring, so far as practicable, that the satisfaction of any right of the enforcement authority to recover the property which satisfies the tests in article 202(1) and (2) is not unduly prejudiced.

(9) Paragraph (8) does not apply where the court is acting as required by article 148(3) or (4).

[3980FS]

NOTES
Commencement: 1 January 2006.

150 Property freezing orders: restrictions on proceedings and remedies

(1) While a property freezing order has effect—
  (a) the court may stay any action, execution or other legal process in respect of the property to which the order applies, and
  (b) no distress may be levied against the property to which the order applies except with the leave of the court and subject to any terms the court may impose.

(2)   If a court (whether the High Court or any other court) in which proceedings are pending in respect of any property is satisfied that a property freezing order has been applied for or made in respect of the property, it may either stay the proceedings or allow them to continue on any terms it thinks fit.

(3)   If a property freezing order applies to a tenancy of any premises, no landlord or other person to whom rent is payable may exercise the right of forfeiture by peaceable re-entry in relation to the premises in respect of any failure by the tenant to comply with any term or condition of the tenancy, except with the leave of the court and subject to any terms the court may impose.

(4)   Before exercising any power conferred by this article, the court must (as well as giving the parties to any of the proceedings concerned an opportunity to be heard) give such an opportunity to any person who may be affected by the court's decision.

                                                                                                          [3980FT]

NOTES
  Commencement: 1 January 2006.

[150A   Receivers in connection with property freezing orders

(1)   Paragraph (2) applies if—
  (a)   the High Court makes a property freezing order on an application by an enforcement authority, and
  (b)   the authority applies to the court to proceed under paragraph (2) (whether as part of the application for the property freezing order or at any time afterwards).

(2)   The High Court may by order appoint a receiver in respect of any property to which the property freezing order applies.

(3)   An application for an order under this article may be made without notice if the circumstances are such that notice of the application would prejudice any right of the enforcement authority to obtain a recovery order in respect of any property.

(4)   In its application for an order under this article, the enforcement authority must nominate a suitably qualified person for appointment as a receiver.

(5)   Such a person may be a member of staff of the enforcement authority.

(6)   The enforcement authority may apply a sum received by it under article 191(2) in making payment of the remuneration and expenses of a receiver appointed under this article.

(7)   Paragraph (6) does not apply in relation to the remuneration of the receiver if he is a member of the staff of the enforcement authority (but it does apply in relation to such remuneration if the receiver is a person providing services under arrangements made by the enforcement authority).]

                                                                                                          [3980FTA]

NOTES
  Commencement: 6 April 2008.
  Inserted by the Proceeds of Crime Act 2002 (External Requests and Orders) (Amendment) Order 2008, SI 2008/302, art 3(1), as from 6 April 2008.

[150B   Powers of receivers appointed under article 150A

(1)   If the High Court appoints a receiver under article 150A on an application by an enforcement authority, the court may act under this article on the application of the authority.

(2)   The court may by order authorise or require the receiver—
  (a)   to exercise any of the powers mentioned in paragraph 5 of Schedule 2 (management powers) in relation to any property in respect of which the receiver is appointed,
  (b)   to take any other steps the court thinks appropriate in connection with the management of any such property (including securing the detention, custody or preservation of the property in order to manage it).

(3)   The court may by order require any person in respect of whose property the receiver is appointed—
  (a)   to bring the property to a place (in England and Wales, or as the case may be, Northern Ireland) specified by the receiver or to place it in the custody of the receiver (if, in either case, he is able to do so),
  (b)   to do anything he is reasonably required to do by the receiver for the preservation of the property.

(4)   The court may by order require any person in respect of whose property the receiver is appointed to bring any documents relating to the property which are in his possession or control to a place (in England and Wales or, as the case may be, Northern Ireland) specified by the receiver or to place them in the custody of the receiver.

(5)   In paragraph (4), "document" means anything in which information of any description is recorded.

(6)   Any prohibition on dealing with property imposed by a property freezing order does not prevent a person from complying with any requirements imposed by virtue of this article.

(7)   If—
  (a)   the receiver deals with any property which is not property in respect of which he is appointed under article 150A, and
  (b)   at the time he deals with the property he believes on reasonable grounds that he is entitled to do so by virtue of his appointment,

the receiver is not liable to any person in respect of any loss or damage resulting from his dealing with the property except so far as the loss or damage is caused by his negligence.]

[3980FTB]

NOTES
Commencement: 6 April 2008.
Inserted by the Proceeds of Crime Act 2002 (External Requests and Orders) (Amendment) Order 2008, SI 2008/302, art 3(1), as from 6 April 2008.

[150C   Supervision of article 150A receiver and variations

(1)   Any of the following persons may at any time apply to the High Court for directions as to the exercise of the functions of a receiver appointed under article 150A—
  (a)   the receiver,
  (b)   any party to the proceedings for the appointment of the receiver or the property freezing order concerned,
  (c)   any person affected by any action taken by the receiver,
  (d)   any person who may be affected by any action proposed to be taken by the receiver.

(2)   Before giving any directions under paragraph (1), the court must give an opportunity to be heard to—
  (a)   the receiver,
  (b)   the parties to the proceedings for the appointment of the receiver and for the property freezing order concerned,
  (c)   any person who may be interested in the application under paragraph (1).

(3)   The court may at any time vary or set aside the appointment of a receiver under article 150A, any order under article 150B or any directions under this article.

(4)   Before exercising any power under paragraph (3), the court must give an opportunity to be heard to—
  (a)   the receiver,
  (b)   the parties to the proceedings for the appointment of the receiver, for the order under article 150B or, as the case may be, for the directions under this article,
  (c)   the parties to the proceedings for the property freezing order concerned,
  (d)   any person who may be affected by the court's decision.]

[3980FTC]

NOTES
Commencement: 6 April 2008.
Inserted by the Proceeds of Crime Act 2002 (External Requests and Orders) (Amendment) Order 2008, SI 2008/302, art 3(1), as from 6 April 2008.

Interim receiving orders (England and Wales and Northern Ireland)

151   Application for interim receiving order

(1)   Where the enforcement authority may take proceedings for a recovery order pursuant to the registration of an external order in the High Court, the authority may apply to the court for an interim receiving order (whether before or after starting the proceedings).

(2)   An interim receiving order is an order for—
  (a)   the detention, custody or preservation of property, and
  (b)   the appointment of an interim receiver.

(3)   An application for an interim receiving order may be made without notice if the circumstances are such that notice of the application would prejudice any right of the enforcement authority to obtain a recovery order in respect of any property.

(4)   The court may make an interim receiving order on the application if it is satisfied that the conditions in paragraphs (5) and, where applicable, (6) are met.

(5)   The first condition is that there is a good arguable case—
  (a)   that the property to which the application for the order relates is or includes recoverable property, and

(b)   that, if any of it is not recoverable property, it is associated property.

(6)   The second condition is that, if—
(a)   the property to which the application for the order relates includes property alleged to be associated property, and
(b)   the enforcement authority has not established the identity of the person who holds it,
the authority has taken all reasonable steps to do so.

(7)   In its application for an interim receiving order, the enforcement authority must nominate a suitably qualified person for appointment as interim receiver, but the nominee may not be a member of the staff of the [enforcement authority].

(8)   The extent of the power to make an interim receiving order is not limited by articles 152 to 160.

[3980FU]

NOTES
Commencement: 1 January 2006.
Para (7): words in square brackets substituted by the Proceeds of Crime Act 2002 (External Requests and Orders) (Amendment) Order 2008, SI 2008/302, art 2(1), (37), as from 1 April 2008.

152   Functions of interim receiver

(1)   An interim receiving order may authorise or require the interim receiver—
(a)   to exercise any of the powers mentioned in Schedule 2,
(b)   to take any other steps the court thinks appropriate,
for the purpose of securing the detention, custody or preservation of the property to which the order applies or of taking any steps under paragraph (2).

(2)   An interim receiving order—
(a)   must require the interim receiver to take any steps which the court thinks necessary to establish whether or not the property to which the order applies is recoverable property or associated property, and
(b)   may require him to take any steps which the court thinks necessary to establish whether or not any other property is recoverable property (which satisfies the tests in article 202(1) and (2) or 203) and, if it is, who holds it.

(3)   If—
(a)   the interim receiver deals with any property which is not property to which the order applies, and
(b)   at the time he deals with the property he believes on reasonable grounds that he is entitled to do so in pursuance of the order,
the interim receiver is not liable to any person in respect of any loss or damage resulting from his dealing with the property except so far as the loss or damage is caused by negligence.

[3980FV]

NOTES
Commencement: 1 January 2006.

Property freezing orders and interim receiving orders: registration

153   Registration of property freezing orders and interim receiving orders

(1)   The registration Acts—
(a)   apply in relation to property freezing orders, and in relation to interim receiving orders as they apply in relation to orders which affect land and are made by the court for the purpose of enforcing judgments or recognisances,
(b)   apply in relation to applications for property freezing orders and in relation to applications for interim receiving orders as they apply in relation to other pending land actions.

(2)   The registration Acts are—
(a)   the Land Charges Act 1972, and
(b)   the Land Registration Act 2002.

(3)   But no notice may be entered in the register of title under the Land Registration Act 2002 in respect of a property freezing order or an interim receiving order.

[3980FW]

NOTES
Commencement: 1 January 2006.

154 Registration (Northern Ireland) of such orders

(1)   A person applying for a property freezing order or an interim receiving order must be treated for the purposes of section 66 of the Land Registration Act (Northern Ireland) 1970 (cautions) as a person interested in relation to any registered land to which—

(a)   the application relates, or

(b)   a property freezing order or an interim receiving order made in pursuance of the application relates.

(2)   Upon being served with a copy of a property freezing order, the Registrar must, in respect of any registered land to which a property freezing order or an application for a property freezing order relates, make an entry inhibiting any dealing with the land without the consent of the High Court.

(3)   Upon being served with a copy of an interim receiving order, the Registrar must, in respect of any registered land to which an interim receiving order or an application for an interim receiving order relates, make an entry inhibiting any dealing with the land without the consent of the High Court.

(4)   Subsections (2)and (4) of section 67 of the Land Registration Act (Northern Ireland) 1970 (inhibitions) apply to an entry made under paragraph (2) or (3) as they apply to an entry made on the application of any person interested in the registered land under subsection (1) of that section.

(5)   Where a property freezing order or an interim receiving order has been protected by an entry registered under the Land Registration Act (Northern Ireland) 1970 or the Registration of Deeds Acts, an order setting aside the property freezing order or interim receiving order may require that entry to be vacated.

(6)   In this article—

"Registrar" and "entry" have the same meanings as in the Land Registration Act (Northern Ireland) 1970; and

"Registration of Deeds Acts" has the meaning given by section 46(2) of the Interpretation Act (Northern Ireland) 1954.

[3980FX]

NOTES

Commencement: 1 January 2006.

Interim receiving orders: further provisions

155 Interim receiving orders: duties of respondent etc

(1)   An interim receiving order may require any person to whose property the order applies—

(a)   to bring the property to a place (in England and Wales or, as the case may be, Northern Ireland) specified by the interim receiver or place it in the custody of the interim receiver (if, in either case, he is able to do so),

(b)   to do anything he is reasonably required to do by the interim receiver for the preservation of the property.

(2)   An interim receiving order may require any person to whose property the order applies to bring any documents relating to the property which are in his possession or control to a place (in England and Wales, or, as the case may be, Northern Ireland) specified by the interim receiver or to place them in the custody of the interim receiver.

"Document" means anything in which information of any description is recorded.

[3980FY]

NOTES

Commencement: 1 January 2006.

156 Supervision of interim receiver and variation of order

(1)   The interim receiver, any party to the proceedings and any person affected by any action taken by the interim receiver, or who may be affected by any action proposed to be taken by him, may at any time apply to the court for directions as to the exercise of the interim receiver's functions.

(2)   Before giving any directions under paragraph (1), the court must (as well as giving the parties to the proceedings an opportunity to be heard) give such an opportunity to the interim receiver and to any person who may be interested in the application.

(3)   The court may at any time vary or set aside an interim receiving order.

(4)   Before exercising any power to vary or set aside an interim receiving order, the court must (as well as giving the parties to the proceedings an opportunity to be heard) give such an opportunity to the interim receiver and to any person who may be affected by the court's decision.

[3980FZ]

NOTES
Commencement: 1 January 2006.

157   Interim receiving orders: restrictions on dealing etc with property

(1)   An interim receiving order must, subject to any exclusions made in accordance with this article, prohibit any person to whose property the order applies from dealing with the property.

(2)   Exclusions may be made when the interim receiving order is made or on an application to vary the order.

(3)   An exclusion may, in particular, make provision for the purpose of enabling any person—
     (a)   to meet his reasonable living expenses, or
     (b)   to carry on any trade, business, profession or occupation,
     (c)   and may be made subject to conditions.

(4)   Where the court exercises the power to make an exclusion for the purpose of enabling a person to meet legal expenses that he has incurred, or may incur, in respect of proceedings under this Part, it must ensure that the exclusion—
     (a)   is limited to reasonable legal expenses that the person has reasonably incurred or that he reasonably incurs,
     (b)   specifies the total amount that may be released for legal expenses in pursuance of the exclusion, and
     (c)   is made subject to the required conditions (see article 198) in addition to any conditions imposed under paragraph (3).

(5)   The court, in deciding whether to make an exclusion for the purposes of enabling a person to meet legal expenses of his in respect of proceedings under this Part—
     (a)   must have regard (in particular) to the desirability of the person being represented in any proceedings under this Part in which he is a participant, and
     (b)   must, where the person is the respondent, disregard the possibility that legal representation of the person in any such proceedings might, were an exclusion not made, be funded by the Legal Services Commission or the Northern Ireland Legal Services Commission.

(6)   If the excluded property is not specified in the order it must be described in the order in general terms.

(7)   The power to make exclusions must, subject to paragraph (5), be exercised with a view to ensuring so far as practicable, that the satisfaction of any right of the enforcement authority to recover the property obtained through conduct which satisfies the test in article 202(2) is not unduly prejudiced.

[3980GA]

NOTES
Commencement: 1 January 2006.

158   Interim receiving orders: restriction on proceedings and remedies

(1)   While an interim receiving order has effect—
     (a)   the court may stay any action, execution or other legal process in respect of the property to which the order applies,
     (b)   no distress may be levied against the property to which the order applies except with the leave of the court and subject to any terms the court may impose.

(2)   If a court (whether the High Court or any other court) in which proceedings are pending in respect of any property is satisfied that an interim receiving order has been applied for or made in respect of the property, the court may either stay the proceedings or allow them to continue on any terms it thinks fit.

(3)   If the interim receiving order applies to a tenancy of any premises, no landlord or other person to whom rent is payable may exercise any right of forfeiture by peaceable re-entry in relation to the premises in respect of any failure by the tenant to comply with any term or condition of the tenancy, except with the leave of the court and subject to any terms the court may impose.

(4)   Before exercising any power conferred by this article, the court must (as well as giving the parties to any of the proceedings in question an opportunity to be heard) give such an opportunity to the interim receiver (if appointed) and any person who may be affected by the court's decision.

[3980GB]

NOTES
Commencement: 1 January 2006.

159 Exclusion of property which is not recoverable etc under interim receiving order

(1)   If the court decides that any property to which an interim receiving order applies is neither recoverable property nor associated property, it must vary the order so as to exclude it.

(2)   The court may vary an interim receiving order so as to exclude from the property to which the order applies any property which is alleged to be associated property if the court thinks that the satisfaction of any right of the enforcement authority to recover the property which satisfies the tests in article 202(1) and (2) will not be prejudiced.

(3)   The court may exclude any property within paragraph (2) on any terms or conditions, applying while the interim receiving order has effect, which the court thinks necessary or expedient.

[3980GC]

NOTES
Commencement: 1 January 2006.

160 Reporting under interim receiving order

(1)   An interim receiving order must require the interim receiver to inform the enforcement authority and the court as soon as reasonably practicable if he thinks that—
   (a)   any property to which the order applies by virtue of a claim that it is recoverable property is not recoverable property,
   (b)   any property to which the order applies by virtue of a claim that it is associated property is not associated property,
   (c)   any property to which the order does not apply is recoverable property (which satisfies the tests in article 202(1) and (2)) or associated property, or
   (d)   any property to which the order applies is held by a person who is different from the person it is claimed holds it,
or if he thinks that there has been any other material change of circumstances.

(2)   An interim receiving order must require the interim receiver—
   (a)   to report his findings to the court,
   (b)   to serve copies of his report on the enforcement authority and on any person who holds any property to which the order applies or who may otherwise be affected by the report.

[3980GD]

NOTES
Commencement: 1 January 2006.

Prohibitory property orders (Scotland)

161 Application for prohibitory property order

(1)   Where the enforcement authority may take proceedings for a recovery order pursuant to the registration of an external order in the Court of Session, the authority may apply to the court for a prohibitory property order (whether before or after starting the proceedings).

(2)   A prohibitory property order is an order that—
   (a)   specifies or describes the property to which it applies, and
   (b)   subject to any exclusions (see article 163(1)(b) and (2)), prohibits any person to whose property the order applies from in any way dealing with the property.

(3)   An application for a prohibitory property order may be made without notice if the circumstances are such that notice of the application would prejudice any right of the enforcement authority to obtain a recovery order in respect of any property.

(4)   The court may make a prohibitory property order on an application if it is satisfied that the condition in paragraph (5) is met and, where applicable, that the condition in paragraph (6) is met.

(5)   The first condition is that there is a good arguable case—
   (a)   that the property to which the application for the order relates is or includes recoverable property, and
   (b)   that, if any of it is not recoverable property, it is associated property.

(6)   The second condition is that, if—
   (a)   the property to which the application for the order relates includes property alleged to be associated property, and
   (b)   the enforcement authority has not established the identity of the person who holds it,
the authority has taken all reasonable steps to so.

[3980GE]

NOTES
Commencement: 1 January 2006.

162 Variation and recall of prohibitory property order

(1) The court may at any time vary or recall a prohibitory property order.

(2) If the court makes an interim administration order that applies to all of the property to which a prohibitory property order applies, it must recall the prohibitory property order.

(3) If the court makes an interim administration order that applies to some but not all of the property to which a prohibitory property order applies, it must vary the prohibitory property order so as to exclude any property to which the interim administration order applies.

(4) If the court decides that any property to which a prohibitory property order applies is neither recoverable property nor associated property, it must vary the order so as to exclude the property.

(5) Before exercising power under this Chapter to vary or recall a prohibitory property order, the court must (as well as giving the parties to the proceedings an opportunity to be heard) give such an opportunity to any person who may be affected by its decision.

(6) Paragraph (5) does not apply where the court is acting as required by paragraph (2) or (3).

[3980GF]

NOTES

Commencement: 1 January 2006.

163 Prohibitory property orders: exclusions

(1) The power to vary a prohibitory property order includes (in particular) power to make exclusion as follows—

    (a) power to exclude property from the order, and

    (b) power, otherwise than by excluding property from the order, to make exclusions from the prohibition on dealing with the property to which the order applies.

(2) Exclusions from the prohibition on dealing with the property to which the order applies (other than exclusions of property from the order) may also be made when the order is made.

(3) An exclusion may, in particular, make provision for the purpose of enabling any person—

    (a) to meet his reasonable living expenses, or

    (b) to carry on any trade, business, profession or occupation.

(4) An exclusion may be made subject to conditions.

(5) An exclusion may not be made for the purpose of enabling any person to meet any legal expenses in respect of proceedings under this Part.

(6) If excluded property is not specified in the order it must be described in the order in general terms.

(7) The power to make exclusions must be exercised with a view to ensuring, so far as practicable, that the satisfaction of any right of the enforcement authority to recover the property which satisfies the tests in article 202(1) and (2) is not unduly prejudiced.

(8) Paragraph (7) does not apply where the court is acting as required by article 162(3) or (4).

[3980GG]

NOTES

Commencement: 1 January 2006.

164 Prohibitory property orders: restriction on proceedings and remedies

(1) While a prohibitory property order has effect the court may sist any action, execution or other legal process in respect of the property to which the order applies.

(2) If a court (whether the Court of Session or any other court) in which proceedings are pending in respect of any property is satisfied that a prohibitory property order has been applied for or made in respect of the property, it may either sist the proceedings or allow them to continue on any terms it thinks fit.

(3) Before exercising any power conferred by this article, the court must (as well as giving the parties to any of the proceedings concerned an opportunity to be heard) give such an opportunity to any person who may be affected by the court's decision.

[3980GH]

NOTES

Commencement: 1 January 2006.

165 Arrestment of property affected by prohibitory property order

(1) On the application of the enforcement authority the Court of Session may, in relation to moveable recoverable property to which a prohibitory property order applies (whether generally or to such of it as is specified in the application), grant warrant for arrestment.

(2) An application under paragraph (1) may be made at the same time as the application for the prohibitory property order or at any time thereafter.

(3) Such a warrant for arrestment may be granted only if the property would be arrestable if the person entitled to it were a debtor.

(4) A warrant under paragraph (1) has effect as if granted on the dependence of an action for debt at the instance of the enforcement authority against the person and may be executed, recalled, loosed or restricted accordingly.

(5) An arrestment executed under this article ceases to have effect when, or in so far as, the prohibitory property order ceases to apply in respect of the property to which the warrant for arrestment was granted.

(6) If an arrestment ceases to have effect to any extent by virtue of paragraph (5) the enforcement authority must apply to the Court of Session for an order recalling or, as the case may be, restricting the arrestment.

[3980GI]

NOTES
Commencement: 1 January 2006.

166 Inhibition of property affected by prohibitory property order

(1) On the application of the enforcement authority, the Court of Session may, in relation to the property mentioned in paragraph (2), grant warrant for inhibition against any person specified in a prohibitory property order.

(2) That property is heritable property situated in Scotland to which the prohibitory property order applies (whether generally or to such of it as is specified in the application).

(3) The warrant for inhibition—
   (a)   has effect as if granted on the dependence of an action for debt by the enforcement authority against the person and may be executed, recalled, loosed or restricted accordingly, and
   (b)   has the effect of letters of inhibition and must forthwith be registered by the enforcement authority in the register of inhibition and adjudications.

(4) Section 155 of the Titles to Land Consolidation (Scotland) Act 1868 (effective date of inhibition) applies in relation to an inhibition for which warrant is granted under paragraph (1) as it applies to an inhibition by separate letters or contained in a summons.

(5) An inhibition executed under this article ceases to have effect when, or in so far as, the prohibitory property order ceases to apply in respect of the property in relation to which the warrant for inhibition was granted.

(6) If an inhibition ceases to have effect to any extent by virtue of paragraph (5) the enforcement authority must—
   (a)   apply for the recall or, as the case may be, the restriction of the inhibition, and
   (b)   ensure that the recall or restriction is reflected in the register of inhibitions and adjudications.

[3980GJ]

NOTES
Commencement: 1 January 2006.

Interim administration orders (Scotland)

167 Application for interim administration order

(1) Where the enforcement authority may take proceedings for a recovery order pursuant to the registration of an external order in the Court of Session, the authority may apply to the court for an interim administration order (whether before or after starting the proceedings).

(2) An interim administration order is an order for—
   (a)   the detention, custody or preservation of property, and
   (b)   the appointment of an interim administrator.

(3) An application for an interim administration order may be made without notice if the circumstances are such that notice of the application would prejudice any right of the enforcement authority to obtain a recovery order in respect of any property.

(4)   The court may make an interim administration order on the application if it is satisfied that the conditions in paragraphs (5) and, where applicable, (6) are met.

(5)   The first condition is that there is a probabilis causa litigandi—

    (a)   that the property to which the application for the order relates is or includes recoverable property, and

    (b)   that , if any of it is not recoverable property, it is associated property.

(6)   The second condition is that, if—

    (a)   the property to which the application for the order relates includes property alleged to be associated property, and

    (b)   the enforcement authority has not established the identity of the person who holds it,

the authority has taken all reasonable steps to do so.

(7)   In its application for an interim administration order, the enforcement authority must nominate a suitably qualified person for appointment as interim administrator, but the nominee may not be a member of the staff of the Scottish Administration.

(8)   The extent of the power to make an interim administration order is not limited by articles 168 to 175.

[3980GK]

NOTES

Commencement: 1 January 2006.

168   Functions of interim administrator

(1)   An interim administrator order may authorise or require the interim administrator—

    (a)   to exercise any of the powers mentioned in Schedule 2,

    (b)   to take any other steps the court thinks appropriate,

for the purpose of securing the detention, custody or preservation of the property to which the order applies or of taking any steps under paragraph (2).

(2)   An interim administration order must require the interim administrator to take any steps which the court thinks necessary to establish—

    (a)   whether or not the property to which the order applies is recoverable property or associated property,

    (b)   whether or not any other property is recoverable property (which satisfies the tests in article 202(1) and (2) or 203), and, if it is, who holds it.

(3)   If—

    (a)   the interim administrator deals with any property which is not property to which the order applies, and

    (b)   at the time he deals with the property he believes on reasonable grounds that he is entitled to do so in pursuance of the order,

the interim administrator is not liable to any person in respect of any loss or damage resulting from his dealing with the property except so far as the loss or damage is caused by his negligence.

[3980GL]

NOTES

Commencement: 1 January 2006.

169   Inhibition of property affected by order

(1)   On the application of the enforcement authority, the Court of Session may, in relation to the property mentioned in paragraph (2), grant warrant for inhibition against any person specified in an interim administration order.

(2)   That property is heritable property situated in Scotland to which the interim administration order applies (whether generally or such of it as is specified in the application).

(3)   The warrant for inhibition—

    (a)   has effect as if granted on the dependence of an action for debt by the enforcement authority against the person and may be executed, recalled, loosed or restricted accordingly, and

    (b)   has the effect of letters of inhibition and must forthwith be registered by the enforcement authority in the register of inhibitions and adjudications.

(4)   Section 155 of the Titles to Land Consolidation (Scotland)Act 1868 (effective date of inhibition) applies in relation to an inhibition for which warrant is granted under paragraph (1) as it applies to an inhibition by separate letters or contained in a summons.

(5)   The execution of an inhibition under this article in respect of property does not prejudice the exercise of an interim administrator's powers under or for the purposes of this Part in respect of that property.

PART III
STATUTORY INSTRUMENTS

(6)   An inhibition under this article ceases to have effect when, or in so far as, the interim administration order ceases to apply in respect of the property in relation to which the warrant for inhibition was granted.

(7)   If an inhibition ceases to have effect to any extent by virtue of paragraph (6) the enforcement authority must—

(a)   apply for the recall or, as the case may be, the restriction of the inhibition, and

(b)   ensure that the recall or restriction is reflected in the register of inhibitions and adjudications.

[3980GM]

NOTES
Commencement: 1 January 2006.

170   Interim administration orders: duties of respondent etc

(1)   An interim administration order may require any person to whose property the order applies—

(a)   to bring the property to a place (in Scotland)specified by the interim administrator or place it in the custody of the interim administrator (if, in either case, he is able to do so),

(b)   to do anything he is reasonably required to do by the interim administrator for the preservation of the property.

(2)   An interim administration order may require any person to whose property the order applies to bring any documents relating to the property which are in his possession or control to a place (in Scotland) specified by the interim administrator or to place them in the custody of the interim administrator.

"Document" means anything in which information of any description is recorded.

[3980GN]

NOTES
Commencement: 1 January 2006.

171   Supervision of interim administrator and variation of order

(1)   The interim administrator, any party to the proceedings and any person affected by an action taken by the interim administrator, or who may be affected by any action proposed to be taken by him, may at any time apply to the court for directions as to the exercise of the interim administrator's functions.

(2)   Before giving any directions under paragraph (1), the court must (as well as giving the parties to the proceedings an opportunity to be heard) give such an opportunity to the interim administrator and to any person who may be interested in the application.

(3)   The court may at any time vary or recall an interim administration order.

(4)   Before exercising any power to vary or set aside an interim administration order, the court must (as well as giving the parties to the proceedings an opportunity to be heard) give such an opportunity to the interim administrator and to any person who may be affected by the court's decision.

[3980GO]

NOTES
Commencement: 1 January 2006.

172   Interim administration orders: restrictions on dealing etc with property

(1)   An interim administration order must, subject to any exclusions made in accordance with this article, prohibit any person to whose property the order applies from dealing with the property.

(2)   Exclusions may be made when the interim administration order is made or on an application to vary the order.

(3)   An exclusion may, in particular, make provision for the purpose of enabling any person—

(a)   to meet his reasonable living expenses, or

(b)   to carry on any trade, business, profession or occupation,

and may be made subject to conditions.

(4)   But an exclusion may not be made for the purpose of enabling any person to meet any legal expenses in respect of proceedings under this Part.

(5)   If the excluded property is not specified in the order it must be described in the order in general terms.

(6)   The power to make exclusions must be exercised with a view to ensuring, so far as practicable, that the satisfaction of any right of the enforcement authority to recover the property obtained through conduct which satisfies the test in article 202(2) is not unduly prejudiced.

[3980GP]

NOTES
Commencement: 1 January 2006.

173   Interim administration orders: restrictions on proceedings and remedies

(1)   While an interim administration order has effect, the court may sist any action, execution or other legal process in respect of the property to which the order applies.

(2)   If a court (whether the Court of Session or any other court) in which proceedings are pending in respect of any property is satisfied that an interim administration order has been applied for or made in respect of the property, the court may either sist the proceedings or allow them to continue on any terms it thinks fit.

(3)   Before exercising any power conferred by this article, the court must (as well as giving the parties to any of the proceedings in question an opportunity to be heard) give such an opportunity to the interim administrator (if appointed) and any person who may be affected by the court's decision.

[3980GQ]

NOTES
Commencement: 1 January 2006.

174   Exclusion of property which is not recoverable etc under interim administration order

(1)   If the court decides that any property to which an interim administration order applies is neither recoverable property nor associated property, it must vary the order so as to exclude it.

(2)   The court may vary an interim administration order so as to exclude from the property to which the order applies any property which is alleged to be associated property if the court thinks that the satisfaction of any right of the enforcement authority to recover the property which satisfies the tests in article 202(1) and (2) will not be prejudiced.

(3)   The court may exclude any property within paragraph (2) on any terms or conditions, applying while the interim administration order has effect, which the court thinks necessary or expedient.

[3980GR]

NOTES
Commencement: 1 January 2006.

175   Reporting under interim administration order

(1)   An interim administration order must require the interim administrator to inform the enforcement authority and the court as soon as reasonably practicable if he thinks that—
  (a)   any property to which the order applies by virtue of a claim that it is recoverable property is not recoverable property,
  (b)   any property to which the order applies by virtue of a claim that it is associated property is not associated property,
  (c)   any property to which the order does not apply is recoverable property (which satisfies the tests in article 202(1) and (2)) or associated property, or
  (d)   any property to which the order applies is held by a person who is different from the person it is claimed holds it,
or if he thinks that there has been any other material change of circumstances.

(2)   An interim administration order must require the interim administrator—
  (a)   to report his findings to the court,
  (b)   to serve copies of his report on the enforcement authority and on any person who holds any property to which the order applies or who may otherwise be affected by the report.

[3980GS]

NOTES
Commencement: 1 January 2006.

176   Arrestment of property affected by interim administration order

(1)   On the application of the enforcement authority or the interim administrator the Court of Session may, in relation to moveable recoverable property to which an interim administration order applies (whether generally or such of it as is specified in the application), grant warrant for arrestment.

(2)   An application by the enforcement authority under paragraph (1) may be made at the same time as the application for the interim administration order or at any time thereafter.

(3)   Such a warrant for arrestment may be granted only if the property would be arrestable if the person entitled to it were a debtor.

(4)   A warrant under paragraph (1) has effect as if granted on the dependence of an action for debt at the instance of the enforcement authority or, as the case may be, the interim administrator against the person and may be executed, recalled, loosed or restricted accordingly.

(5)   The execution of an arrestment under this article in respect of property does not prejudice the exercise of an interim administrator's powers under or for the purposes of this Part in respect of that property.

(6)   An arrestment executed under this article ceases to have effect when, or in so far as, the interim administration order ceases to apply in respect of the property in relation to which the warrant for arrestment was granted.

(7)   If an arrestment ceases to have effect to any extent by virtue of paragraph (6) the enforcement authority or, as the case may be, the interim administrator must apply to the Court of Session for an order recalling or, as the case may be, restrict the arrestment.

[3980GT]

NOTES
Commencement: 1 January 2006.

Vesting and realisation of recoverable property

177   Recovery orders

(1)   The court must decide to give effect to an external order which falls within the meaning of section 447(2) of the Act by registering it and making a recovery order if it determines that any property or sum of money which is specified in it is recoverable property.

(2)   In making such a determination the court must have regard to—
    (a)   the definitions in subsections (2), (4), (5), (6), (8) and (10) of section 447 of the Act, and
    (b)   articles 202 to 207.

(3)   The recovery order must vest the recoverable property in the trustee for civil recovery.

(4)   But the court may not make in a recovery order—
    (a)   any provision in respect of any recoverable property if each of the conditions in paragraph (5) or (as the case may be) (6) is met and it would not be just and equitable to do so, or
    (b)   any provision which is incompatible with any of the Convention rights (within the meaning of the Human Rights Act 1998).

(5)   In relation to a court in England and Wales or Northern Ireland, the conditions referred to in paragraph (4)(a) are that—
    (a)   the respondent obtained the recoverable property in good faith,
    (b)   he took steps after obtaining the property which he would not have taken if he had not obtained it or he took steps before obtaining the property which he would not have taken if he had not believed he was going to obtain it,
    (c)   when he took the steps, he had no notice that the property was recoverable,
    (d)   if a recovery order were made in respect of the property, it would, by reason of the steps, be detrimental to him.

(6)   In relation to a court in Scotland, the conditions referred to in paragraph (4)(a) are that—
    (a)   the respondent obtained the recoverable property in good faith,
    (b)   he took steps after obtaining the property which he would not have taken if he had not obtained it or he took steps before obtaining the property which he would not have taken if he had not believed he was going to obtain it,
    (c)   when he took steps, he had no reasonable grounds for believing that the property was recoverable,
    (d)   if a recovery order were made in respect of the property, it would, by reason of the steps, be detrimental to him.

(7)   In deciding whether it would be just and equitable to make the provision in the recovery order where the conditions in paragraph (5) or (as the case may be) (6) are met, the court must have regard to—
    (a)   the degree of detriment that would be suffered by the respondent if the provision were made,
    (b)   the enforcement authority's interest in receiving the realised proceeds of the recoverable property.

(8)   A recovery order may sever any property.

(9)   A recovery order may impose conditions as to the manner in which the trustee for civil recovery may deal with any property vested by the order for the purpose of realising it.

(10)   A recovery order made by a court in England and Wales or Northern Ireland may provide for payment under article 191 of reasonable legal expenses that a person has reasonably incurred, or may reasonably incur, in respect of—

(a)   the proceedings under this Part in which the order is made, or

(b)   any related proceedings under this Part.

(11)   If regulations under article 199 apply to an item of expenditure, a sum in respect of the item is not payable under article 199 in pursuance of provision under paragraph (10) unless—

(a)   the enforcement authority agrees to its payment, or

(b)   the court has assessed the amount allowed by the regulations in respect of that item and the sum is paid in respect of the assessed amount.

(12)   This article is subject to articles 181 to 189.

[3980GU]

NOTES

Commencement: 1 January 2006.

178   Functions of the trustee for civil recovery

(1)   The trustee for civil recovery is a person appointed by the court to give effect to a recovery order.

(2)   The enforcement authority must nominate a suitably qualified person for appointment as the trustee.

(3)   The functions of the trustee are—

(a)   to secure the detention, custody or preservation of any property vested in him by the recovery order,

(b)   in the case of property other than money, to realise the value of the property for the benefit of the enforcement authority, and

(c)   to perform any other functions conferred on him by virtue of this Chapter.

(4)   In performing his functions, the trustee acts on behalf of the enforcement authority and must comply with any directions given by the authority.

(5)   The trustee is to realise the value of property vested in him by the recovery order, so far as practicable, in the manner best calculated to maximise the amount payable to the enforcement authority.

(6)   The trustee has the powers mentioned in Schedule 3.

(7)   References in this article to a recovery order include an order under article E46 and references to property vested in the trustee by a recovery order include property vested in him in pursuance of an order under article 187.

[3980GV]

NOTES

Commencement: 1 January 2006.

179   Recording of recovery order (Scotland)

(1)   The clerk of the court must immediately after the making of a recovery order which relates to heritable property situated in Scotland send a certified copy of it to the keeper of the register of inhibitions and adjudications for recording in that register.

(2)   Recording under paragraph (1) is to have the effect as from the date of the recovery order, of an inhibition at the instance of the trustee for civil recovery against the person in whom the heritable property was vest prior to that date.

[3980GW]

NOTES

Commencement: 1 January 2006.

180   Rights of pre-emption etc

(1)   A recovery order is to have effect in relation to any property despite any provision (of whatever nature) which would otherwise prevent, penalise or restrict the vesting of the property.

(2)   A right of pre-emption, right of irritancy, right of return or other similar right does not operate or become exercisable as a result of the vesting of any property under a recovery order.

A right of return means any right under a provision for the return or reversion of property in specified circumstances.

(3)   Where property is vested under a recovery order, any such right is to have effect as if the person in whom the property is vested were the same person in law as the person who held the property and as if no transfer of the property had taken place.

(4)   References to rights in paragraphs (2) and (3) do not include any rights in respect of which the recovery order was made.

(5)   This article applies in relation to the creation of interests, or the doing of anything else, by a recovery order as it applies in relation to the vesting of property.

[3980GX]

NOTES
Commencement: 1 January 2006.

181   Associated and joint property

(1)   Articles 182 and 183 apply if the court makes a recovery order in respect of any recoverable property in a case within paragraph (2) or (3).

(2)   A case is within this paragraph if—
- (a)   the property to which the proceedings relate includes property which is associated with the recoverable property and is specified or described in the claim form or (in Scotland) application, and
- (b)   if the associated property is not the respondent's property, the claim form or application has been served on the person whose property it is or the court has dispensed with service.

(3)   A case is within this paragraph if—
- (a)   the recoverable property belongs to joint tenants, and
- (b)   one of the tenants is an excepted joint owner.

(4)   An excepted joint owner is a person who obtained the property in circumstances in which it would not be recoverable as against him; and references to the excepted joint owner's share of the recoverable property are to so much of the recoverable property as would have been his if the joint tenancy had been severed.

(5)   Paragraphs (3) and (4) do not extend to Scotland.

[3980GY]

NOTES
Commencement: 1 January 2006.

182   Agreements about associated and joint property

(1)   Where—
- (a)   this article applies, and
- (b)   the enforcement authority (on the one hand) and the person who holds the associated property or who is the excepted joint owner (on the other) agree,

the recovery order may, instead of vesting the recoverable property in the trustee for civil recovery, require the person who holds the associated property or who is the excepted joint owner to make a payment to the trustee.

(2)   A recovery order which makes any requirement under paragraph (1) may, so far as required for giving effect to the agreement, include provision for vesting, creating, or extinguishing any interest in property.

(3)   The amount of the payment is to be the amount which the enforcement authority and that person agree represents—
- (a)   in a case within article 181(2), the value of the recoverable property,
- (b)   in a case within article 181(3), the value of the recoverable property less the value of the excepted joint owner's share.

(4)   But if—
- (a)   a property freezing order, an interim receiving order, a prohibitory property order or an interim administration order applied at any time to the associated property or joint tenancy, and
- (b)   the enforcement authority agrees that the person has suffered loss as a result of the order mentioned in sub-paragraph (a),

the amount of the payment may be reduced by any amount the enforcement authority and that person agree is reasonable, having regard to that loss and to any other relevant circumstances.

(5)   If there is more than one such item of associated property or excepted joint owner, the total amount to be paid to the trustee, and the part of that amount which is to be provided by each person who holds any such associated property or who is an excepted joint owner, is to be agreed between both (or all) of them and the enforcement authority.

(6)   A recovery order which makes any requirement under paragraph (1) must make provision for any recoverable property to cease to be recoverable.

[3980GZ]

NOTES
Commencement: 1 January 2006.

183   Associated and joint property: default of agreement

(1)   Where this article applies, the court may make the following provision if—
   (a)   there is no agreement under article 182, and
   (b)   the court thinks it just and equitable to do so.

(2)   The recovery order may provide—
   (a)   for the associated property to vest in the trustee for civil recovery or (as the case may be) for the excepted joint owner's interest to be extinguished, or
   (b)   in the case of an excepted joint owner, for the severance of his interest.

(3)   A recovery order making any provision by virtue of paragraph (2)(a) may provide—
   (a)   for the trustee to pay an amount to the person who holds the associated property or who is an excepted joint owner, or
   (b)   for the creation of interests in favour of that person, or the imposition of liabilities or conditions, in relation to the property vested in the trustee,
or for both.

(4)   In making any provision in a recovery order by virtue of paragraph (2) or (3), the court must have regard to—
   (a)   the rights of any person who holds the associated property or who is an excepted joint owner and the value to him of that property or, as the case may be, of his share (including any value which cannot be assessed in terms of money),
   (b)   the enforcement authority's interest in receiving the realised proceeds of the recoverable property.

(5)   If—
   (a)   a property freezing order, an interim receiving order, a prohibitory property order or an interim administration order applied at any time to the associated property or joint tenancy, and
   (b)   the court is satisfied that the person who holds the associated property or who is an excepted joint owner has suffered loss as a result of the order mentioned in sub-paragraph (a),
a recovery order making any provision by virtue of paragraph (2) or (3) may require the enforcement authority to pay compensation to that person.

(6)   The amount of compensation to be paid under paragraph (5) is the amount the court thinks reasonable, having regard to the person's loss and to any other relevant circumstances.

[(7)   In subsection (5) the reference to the enforcement authority is, in the case of an enforcement authority in relation to England and Wales or Northern Ireland, a reference to the enforcement authority which obtained the property freezing order or interim receiving order concerned.]

[3980HA]

NOTES
Commencement: 1 January 2006.
Para (7): added by the Proceeds of Crime Act 2002 (External Requests and Orders) (Amendment) Order 2008, SI 2008/302, art 2(1), (38), as from 1 April 2008.

184   Payments in respect of rights under pension schemes

(1)   This article applies to recoverable property consisting of rights under a pension scheme.

(2)   A recovery order in respect of the property must, instead of vesting the property in the trustee for civil recovery, require the trustees or managers of the pension scheme—
   (a)   to pay to the trustee for civil recovery within the period determined in accordance with paragraph 5 of Schedule 4 ("the prescribed period") the amount determined by the trustees or managers to be equal to the value of the rights, and
   (b)   to give effect to any other provision made by virtue of this article and the two following articles in respect of the scheme.
This paragraph is subject to articles 187 to 189.

(3)   A recovery order made by virtue of paragraph (2) overrides the provisions of the pension scheme to the extent that they conflict with the provisions of the order.

(4) A recovery order made by virtue of paragraph (2) may provide for the recovery by the trustees or managers of the scheme (whether by deduction from any amount which they are required to pay to the trustee for civil recovery or otherwise) of costs incurred by them in—
  (a) complying with the recovery order, or
  (b) providing information, before the order was made, to the enforcement authority, [receiver appointed under article 150A,] interim receiver or interim administrator.

(5) None of the following provisions applies to a court making a recovery order by virtue of paragraph (2)—
  (a) any provision of section 159 of the Pension Schemes Act 1993, section 155 of the Pension Schemes (Northern Ireland) Act 1993, section 91 of the Pensions Act 1995 or Article 89 of the Pensions (Northern Ireland) Order 1995 (which prevent assignment and the making of orders that restrain a person from receiving anything which he is prevented from assigning),
  (b) any provision of any enactment (whenever passed or made) corresponding to any of the provisions mentioned in sub-paragraph (a),
  (c) any provision of the pension scheme in question corresponding to any to those provisions.

[3980HB]

185 Consequential adjustment of liabilities under pension schemes

(1) A recovery order made by virtue of article 184(2) must require the trustees or managers of the pension scheme to make such reduction in the liabilities of the scheme as they think necessary in consequence of the payment made in pursuance of that paragraph.

(2) Accordingly, the order must require the trustees or managers to provide for the liabilities of the pension scheme in respect of the respondent's recoverable property to which article 184 applies to cease.

(3) So far as the trustees or managers are required by the recovery order to provide for the liabilities of the pension scheme in respect of the respondent's recoverable property to which article 184 applies to cease, their powers include (in particular) power to reduce the amount of—
  (a) any benefit or future benefit to which the respondent may be entitled under the scheme,
  (b) any future benefit to which any other person may be entitled under the scheme in respect of that property.

[3980HC]

186 Pension schemes: supplementary

(1) Schedule 4 has effect for the purposes of the exercise by trustees or managers of their powers under articles 184 and 185, including provision about the calculation and verification of the value at any time of rights and liabilities.

(2) A pension scheme means an occupational pension scheme or a personal pension scheme; and those expressions have the same meaning as in the Pension Schemes Act 1993 or, in relation to Northern Ireland, the Pension Schemes (Northern Ireland) Act 1993.

(3) In relation to an occupational pension scheme or a personal pension scheme, the trustees or managers means—
  (a) in the case of a scheme established under a trust, the trustees,
  (b) in any other case, the managers.

(4) References to a pension scheme include—
  (a) a retirement annuity contract (within the meaning of Part 3 of the Welfare Reform and Pensions Act 1999 or, in relation to Northern Ireland, Part 4 of the Welfare Reform and Pensions (Northern Ireland) Order 1999),
  (b) an annuity or insurance policy purchased, or transferred, for the purpose of giving effect to rights under an occupational pension scheme or a personal scheme,
  (c) an annuity purchased, or entered into, for the purpose of discharging any liability in respect of a pension credit under section 29(1)(b) of the Welfare Reform and Pensions Act 1999 or, in relation to Northern Ireland, Article 26(1)(b) of the Welfare Reform and Pensions (Northern Ireland) Order 1999.

(5) References to the trustees or managers—

(a)   in relation to a retirement annuity contract or other annuity, are to the provider of the annuity,

(b)   in relation to an insurance policy, are to the insurer.

(6)   Paragraphs (2) to (5) have effect for the purposes of this group of articles (that is, articles 184, 185 and this article).

[3980HD]

_____

NOTES
Commencement: 1 January 2006.

_____

187   Consent orders

(1)   The court may make an order staying (in Scotland, sisting) any proceedings for a recovery order on terms agreed by the parties for the disposal of the proceedings if each person to whose property the proceedings, or the agreement, relates is a party both to the proceedings and the agreement.

(2)   An order under paragraph (1) may, as well as staying (or sisting) the proceedings on terms—

(a)   make provision for any property which may be recoverable property to cease to be recoverable,

(b)   make any further provision which the court thinks appropriate.

(3)   Article 191 applies to property vested in the trustee for civil recovery, or money paid to him, in pursuance of the agreement as it applies to property vested in him by a recovery order or money paid under article 182.

[3980HE]

_____

NOTES
Commencement: 1 January 2006.

_____

188   Consent orders: pensions

(1)   This article applies where recoverable property to which proceedings under this Chapter relate includes rights under a pension scheme.

(2)   An order made under article 187—

(a)   may not stay (in Scotland, sist) the proceedings on terms that the rights are vested in any other person, but

(b)   may include provision imposing the following requirement, if the trustees or managers of the scheme are parties to the agreement by virtue of which the order is made.

(3)   The requirement is that the trustees or managers of the pension scheme—

(a)   make a payment in accordance with the agreement, and

(b)   give effect to any other provision made by virtue of this article in respect of the scheme.

(4)   The trustees or managers of the pension scheme have power to enter into an agreement in respect of the proceedings on any terms on which an order made under article 187 may stay (in Scotland, sist) the proceedings.

(5)   The following provisions apply in respect of an order under article 187, so far as it includes the requirement mentioned in paragraph (3).

(6)   The order overrides the provisions of the pension scheme to the extent that they conflict with the requirement.

(7)   The order may provide for the recovery by the trustees or managers of the scheme (whether by deduction from any amount which they are required to pay in pursuance of the agreement or otherwise) of costs incurred by them in—

(a)   complying with the order, or

(b)   providing information, before the order was made, to the enforcement authority, [receiver appointed under article 150A,] interim receiver or interim administrator.

(8)   Articles 184(5) and 185 (read with article 186) apply as if the requirement were included in an order made by virtue of article 184(2).

(9)   Paragraphs (4) to (7) of article 186 have effect for the purposes of this article.

[3980HF]

_____

NOTES
Commencement: 1 January 2006.
Para (7): words in square brackets inserted by the Proceeds of Crime Act 2002 (External Requests and Orders) (Amendment) Order 2008, SI 2008/302, art 3(2), as from 6 April 2008.

_____

189 Limit on recovery

(1)   This article applies if the enforcement authority seeks a recovery order—
  (a)   in respect of both property which is or represents property which satisfies the tests in article 202(1) or (2) and related property, or
  (b)   in respect of property which is or represents property which satisfies those tests where such an order, or an order under article 187, has previously been made in respect of related property.

(2)   For the purposes of this article—
  (a)   the original property means the property specified in the external order or a sum of money so specified,
  (b)   the original property, and any items of property which represent the original property, are to be treated as related to each other.

(3)   The court is not to make a recovery order if it thinks that the enforcement authority's right to recover the original property has been satisfied by a previous recovery order or order under article 187.

(4)   Subject to paragraph (3), the court may act under paragraph (5) if it thinks that—
  (a)   a recovery order may be made in respect of two or more related items of recoverable property, but
  (b)   the making of a recovery order in respect of both or all of them is not required in order to satisfy the enforcement authority's right to recover the original property.

(5)   The court may in order to satisfy that right to the extent required make a recovery order in respect of—
  (a)   only some of the related items of property, or
  (b)   only a part of any of the related items of property,
or both.

(6)   Where the court may make a recovery order in respect of any property, this article does not prevent the recovery of any profits which have accrued in respect of the property.

(7)   If—
  (a)   an order is made under section 298 of the Act for the forfeiture of recoverable property, and
  (b)   the enforcement authority subsequently seeks a recovery order in respect of related property,
the order under section 298 is to be treated, for the purposes of this article as if it were a recovery order obtained by the enforcement authority in respect of the forfeited property.

(8)   If—
  (a)   in pursuance of a judgment in civil proceedings (whether in the United Kingdom or elsewhere), the claimant has obtained property from the defendant ("the judgment property"),
  (b)   the claim was based on the defendant's having obtained the judgment property or related property through unlawful conduct within the meaning of section 242 of the Act, and
  (c)   the enforcement authority subsequently seeks a recovery order in respect of property which is related to the judgment property,
the judgment is to be treated for the purposes of this article as if it were a recovery order obtained by the enforcement authority in respect of the judgment property.

In relation to Scotland, "claimant" and "defendant" are to be read as "pursuer" and "defender".

(9)   If—
  (a)   property has been taken into account in deciding the amount of a person's benefit from criminal conduct for the purpose of making a confiscation order, and
  (b)   the enforcement authority subsequently seeks a recovery order in respect of related property,
the confiscation order is to be treated for the purposes of this article as it were a recovery order obtained by the enforcement authority in respect of the property referred to in sub-paragraph (a).

(10)   In paragraph (9), a confiscation order means—
  (a)   an order under section 6, 92 or 156 of the Act or an external order registered under Parts 2, 3 or 4 of this Order,
  (b)   an order under a corresponding provision of an enactment mentioned in section 8(7)(a) to (g) of the Act,
and, in relation to an order mentioned in sub-paragraph (b), the reference to the amount of a person's benefit from criminal conduct is to be read as a reference to the corresponding amount under the enactment in question.

[3980HG]

NOTES
Commencement: 1 January 2006.

190   Article 189: supplementary

(1)   Paragraphs (2) and (3) give examples of the satisfaction of the enforcement authority's right to recover the original property.

(2)   If—
   (a)   there is a disposal, other than a part disposal, of the original property, and
   (b)   other property (the representative property) is obtained in its place,

the enforcement authority's right to recover the original property is satisfied by the making of a recovery order in respect of either the original property or the representative property.

(3)   If—
   (a)   there is a part disposal of the original property, and
   (b)   other property (the representative property) is obtained in place of the property disposed of,

the enforcement authority's right to recover the original property is satisfied by the making of a recovery order in respect of the remainder of the original property together with either the representative property or the property disposed of.

(4)   In this article—
   (a)   a part disposal means a disposal to which article 211(1) applies,
   (b)   the original property has the same meaning as in article 189.

[3980HH]

NOTES
Commencement: 1 January 2006.

191   Applying realised proceeds

(1)   This article applies to—
   (a)   sums which represent the realised proceeds of property which was vested in the trustee for civil recovery by a recovery order or which he obtained in pursuance of a recovery order,
   (b)   sums vested in the trustee by a recovery order or obtained by him in pursuance of a recovery order.

(2)   The trustee is to make out of the sums—
   (a)   first, any payment required to be made by him by virtue of article 183,
   (b)   next, any payment of legal expenses which, after giving effect to article 177(11), are payable under this paragraph in pursuance of provision under article 177(10) contained in the recovery order,
   (c)   next, any payment of expenses incurred by a person acting as an insolvency practitioner which are payable under this paragraph by virtue of article 3(10),

and any sum which remains is to be paid to the enforcement authority.

(3)   The [enforcement authority (unless it is the Scottish Ministers)] may apply a sum received by [it] under paragraph (2) in making payment of the remuneration and expenses of—
   (a)   the trustee, or
   (b)   any interim receiver appointed in, or in anticipation of, the proceedings for the recovery order.

(4)   Paragraph (3)(a) does not apply in relation to the remuneration of the trustee if the trustee is a member of the staff of the [enforcement authority concerned].

[3980HI]

NOTES
Commencement: 1 January 2006.
Paras (3), (4): words in square brackets substituted by the Proceeds of Crime Act 2002 (External Requests and Orders) (Amendment) Order 2008, SI 2008/302, art 2(1), (39), as from 1 April 2008.

Exemptions etc

192   Victims of theft etc

(1)   In proceedings for a recovery order, a person who claims that any property alleged to be recoverable property, or any part of the property, belongs to him may apply for a declaration under this article.

(2)   If the applicant appears to the court to meet the following condition, the court may make a declaration to that effect.

(3) The condition is that—
  (a) the person was deprived of the property he claims, or of property which it represents, by unlawful conduct within the meaning of section 241 of the Act,
  (b) the property he was deprived of was not recoverable property immediately before he was deprived of it, and
  (c) the property he claims belongs to him.

(4) Property to which a declaration under this article applies is not recoverable property.

[3980HJ]

NOTES
  Commencement: 1 January 2006.

193 Other exemptions

(1) Proceedings for a recovery order may not be taken against the Financial Services Authority in respect of any recoverable property held by the authority.

(2) Proceedings for a recovery order may not be taken in respect of any property which is subject to any of the following charges—
  (a) a collateral security charge, within the meaning of the Financial Markets and Insolvency (Settlement Finality) Regulations 1999,
  (b) a market charge, within the meaning of Part 7 of the Companies Act 1989,
  (c) a money market charge, within the meaning of the Financial Markets and Insolvency (Money Market) Regulations 1995,
  (d) a system charge, within the meaning of the Financial Markets and Insolvency Regulations 1996 or the Financial Markets and Insolvency Regulations (Northern Ireland) 1996.

(3) Proceedings for a recovery order may not be taken against any person in respect of any recoverable property which he holds by reason of his acting or having acted, as an insolvency practitioner.

Acting as an insolvency practitioner has the same meaning as in article 4.

[3980HK]

NOTES
  Commencement: 1 January 2006.

Miscellaneous

194 Compensation

(1) If, in the case of any property to which a property freezing order, an interim receiving order, a prohibitory property order or an interim administration order has at any time applied, the court does not in the course of the proceedings, decide that the property is recoverable property or associated property, the person whose property it is may make an application to the court for compensation.

(2) Paragraph (1) does not apply if the court—
  (a) has made a declaration in respect of the property by virtue of article 192, or
  (b) makes an order under article 187.

(3) If the court has made a decision by reason of which no recovery order could be made in respect of the property, the application for compensation must be made within the period of three months beginning—
  (a) in relation to a decision of the High Court in England and Wales, with the date of the decision or, if any application is made for leave to appeal, with the date on which the application is withdrawn or refused or (if the application is granted) on which any proceedings on appeal are finally concluded,
  (b) in relation to a decision of the Court of Session or of the High Court in Northern Ireland, with the date of the decision or, if there an appeal against the decision, with the date on which any proceedings on appeal are finally concluded.

(4) If, in England and Wales or Northern Ireland, the proceedings in respect of the property have been discontinued, the application for compensation must be made within the period of three months beginning with the discontinuance.

(5) If the court is satisfied that the applicant has suffered loss as a result of the order mentioned in paragraph (1), it may require the enforcement authority to pay compensation to him.

(6) If, but for article 180(2), any right mentioned there would have operated in favour of, or become exercisable by, any person, he may make an application to the court for compensation.

(7) The application for compensation under paragraph (6) must be made within the period of three months beginning with the vesting referred to in article 180(2).

(8)   If the court is satisfied that, in consequence of the operation of article 180, the right in question cannot subsequently operate in favour of the applicant or (as the case may be) become exercisable by him, it may require the enforcement authority to pay compensation to him.

(9)   The amount of compensation to be paid under this article is the amount the court thinks reasonable, having regard to the loss suffered and any other relevant circumstances.

[(10)   In the case of an enforcement authority in relation to England and Wales or Northern Ireland—

    (a)   the reference in paragraph (5) to the enforcement authority is a reference to the enforcement authority which obtained the property freezing order or interim receiving order concerned, and

    (b)   the reference in paragraph (8) to the enforcement authority is a reference to the enforcement authority which obtained the recovery order concerned.]

[3980HL]

NOTES
Commencement: 1 January 2006.
Para (10): added by the Proceeds of Crime Act 2002 (External Requests and Orders) (Amendment) Order 2008, SI 2008/302, art 2(1), (40), as from 1 April 2008.

195   Payment of interim administrator or trustee (Scotland)

(1)   Any fees or expenses incurred by an interim administrator, or a trustee for civil recovery appointed by the Court of Session, in the exercise of his functions are to be reimbursed by the Scottish Ministers as soon as is practicable after they have been incurred.

(2)   The Scottish Ministers may apply a sum received by them under article 191(2) in making payment of such fees or expenses.

(3)   Paragraph (2) does not apply in relation to the fees of a trustee for civil recovery if the trustee is a member of their staff.

[3980HM]

NOTES
Commencement: 1 January 2006.

196   Effect on diligence of recovery order (Scotland)

(1)   An arrestment or poinding of any recoverable property executed on or after the appointment of the trustee for civil recovery is ineffectual in a question with the trustee.

(2)   Any recoverable property so arrested or poinded, or (if the property has been sold) the proceeds of sale, must be handed over to the trustee for civil recovery.

(3)   A poinding of the ground in respect of recoverable property on or after such an appointment is ineffectual in a question with the trustee for civil recovery except for the interest mentioned in paragraph (4).

(4)   That interest is—

    (a)   interest on the debt of a secured creditor for the current half yearly term, and

    (b)   arrears of interest on that debt for one year immediately before the commencement of that term.

(5)   On and after such appointment no other person may raise or insist in an adjudication against recoverable property or be confirmed as an executor-creditor on that property.

(6)   An inhibition on recoverable property shall cease to have effect in relation to any heritable property comprised in the recoverable property on such appointment.

(7)   The provision of this article apply in relation to—

    (a)   an action of mails and duties, and

    (b)   an action for sequestration of rent,

as they apply in relation to an arrestment or poinding.

[3980HN]

NOTES
Commencement: 1 January 2006.

197   Scope of powers (Scotland)

(1)   Orders under this Chapter may be made by the Court of Session in respect of a person wherever domiciled, resident or present.

(2)   But such an order in respect of a person's moveable property may not be made by the Court of Session where—

    (a)   the person is not domiciled, resident or present in Scotland, and

(b)   the property is not situated in Scotland,

unless the conduct which satisfies the test in article 202(2) took place in Scotland.

[3980HO]

NOTES

Commencement: 1 January 2006.

198 Legal expenses excluded from freezing: required conditions

(1)   The Lord Chancellor may by regulations specify the required conditions for the purposes of article 149(5) or 157(4).

(2)   A required condition may (in particular)—
- (a)   restrict who may receive sums released in pursuance of the exclusion (by, for example, requiring released sums to be paid to professional legal advisers), or
- (b)   be made for the purpose of controlling the amount of any sum released in pursuance of the exclusion in respect of an item of expenditure.

(3)   A required condition made for the purpose mentioned in paragraph (2)(b) may (for example)—
- (a)   provide for sums to be released only with the agreement of the enforcement authority;
- (b)   provide for a sum to be released in respect of an item of expenditure only if the court has assessed the amount allowed by regulations under article 199 in respect of that item and the sum is released for payment of the assessed amount;
- (c)   provide for a sum to be released in respect of an item of expenditure only if—
  - (i)   the enforcement authority agrees to its release, or
  - (ii)   the court has assessed the amount allowed by regulations under article 199 in respect of that item and the sum is released for payment of the assessed amount.

(4)   Before making regulations under this article, the Lord Chancellor must consult such persons as he considers appropriate.

[3980HP]

NOTES

Commencement: 1 January 2006.

Orders: the Proceeds of Crime Act 2002 (Legal Expenses in Civil Recovery Proceedings) (Amendment) Regulations 2008, SI 2008/523.

199 Legal expenses: regulations for purposes of article 177(11) or 198(3)

(1)   The Lord Chancellor may by regulations—
- (a)   make provision for the purposes of article 177(11);
- (b)   make provision for the purposes of required conditions that make provision of the kind mentioned in article 198(3)(b) or (c).

(2)   Regulations under this article may (in particular)—
- (a)   limit the amount of remuneration allowable to representatives for a unit of time worked;
- (b)   limit the total amount of remuneration allowable to representatives for work done in connection with proceedings or a step in proceedings;
- (c)   limit the amount allowable in respect of an item of expense incurred by a representative or incurred, otherwise than in respect of the remuneration of a representative, by a party to proceedings.

(3)   Before making regulations under this article, the Lord Chancellor must consult such persons as he considers appropriate.

[3980HQ]

NOTES

Commencement: 1 January 2006.

Orders: the Proceeds of Crime Act 2002 (Legal Expenses in Civil Recovery Proceedings) (Amendment) Regulations 2008, SI 2008/523.

200 Financial threshold

(1)   The enforcement authority may not start proceedings for a recovery order unless the authority reasonably believes that the aggregate value of the recoverable property which the authority wishes to be subject to a recovery order is not less than £10,000.

(2)   If the authority applies for a property freezing order, an interim receiving order, a prohibitory property order or an interim administration order before starting the proceedings, paragraph (1) applies to the application instead of to the start of the proceedings.

(3)   This article does not affect the continuation of proceedings for a recovery order which have been properly started or the making or continuing effect of a property freezing order, an interim receiving order, a prohibitory property order or an interim administration order which has been properly applied for.

[3980HR]

NOTES
Commencement: 1 January 2006.

201   (*Inserts the Limitation Act 1980, s 27B, the Prescription and Limitation (Scotland) Act 1973, s 19C, and the Limitation (Northern Ireland) Order 1989, art 72B.*)

CHAPTER 3
GENERAL

Recoverable property

202   Recoverable property: property or sum of money specified in the external order

(1)   Property or a sum of money is recoverable property if it is specified in an external order (within the meaning of section 447(2) of the Act).

(2)   Accordingly, the property (including money) must have been found to have been obtained as a result of or in connection with criminal conduct (within the meaning of section 447(8) of the Act) or must have been believed to have been so obtained.

(3)   But if property (including money) which is specified in the external order has been disposed of (since it was so obtained), it is recoverable property only if it is held by a person into whose hands it may be followed.

(4)   Recoverable property specified in an external order may be followed into the hands of a person obtaining it on a disposal by—
  (a)   the person who through the conduct obtained the property, or
  (b)   a person into whose hands it may (by virtue of this paragraph) be followed.

(5)   Where an external order specifies property other than a sum of money, only that property is recoverable property.

[3980HS]

NOTES
Commencement: 1 January 2006.

203   Tracing property, etc

(1)   This article applies only where an external order specifies a sum of money.

(2)   Where property which satisfies the tests in article 202(1) and (2) ("the original property") is or has been recoverable, property which represents the original property is also recoverable property.

(3)   If a person enters into a transaction by which—
  (a)   he disposes of recoverable property, whether the original property or property which (by virtue of this Chapter) represents the original property, and
  (b)   he obtains other property in place of it,
the other property represents the original property.

(4)   If a person disposes of recoverable property which represents the original property, the property may be followed into the hands of the person who obtains it (and it continues to represent the original property).

[3980HT]

NOTES
Commencement: 1 January 2006.

204   Mixing property

(1)   This article applies only where an external order specifies a sum of money.

(2)   Paragraph (3) applies if a person's recoverable property is mixed with other property (whether his property or another's).

(3)   The portion of the mixed property which is attributable to the recoverable property represents the property which satisfies the tests in article 202(1) and (2).

(4)   Recoverable property is mixed with other property if (for example) it is used—
  (a)   to increase funds held in a bank account,

(b) in part payment for the acquisition of an asset,
(c) for the restoration or improvement of land,
(d) by a person holding a leasehold interest in the property to acquire the freehold.

[3980HU]

NOTES
Commencement: 1 January 2006.

205 Recoverable property: general exceptions

(1) If—
(a) a person disposes of recoverable property, and
(b) the person who obtains it on the disposal does so in good faith, for value and without notice that it was recoverable property,

the property may not be followed into that person's hands and, accordingly, it ceases to be recoverable.

(2) If recoverable property is vested, forfeited or otherwise disposed of in pursuance of powers conferred by virtue of this Part, it ceases to be recoverable.

(3) If—
(a) in pursuance of a judgment in civil proceedings (whether in the United Kingdom or elsewhere), the defendant makes a payment to the claimant or the claimant otherwise obtains property from the defendant,
(b) the claimant's claim is based on any conduct by the defendant which satisfies the test in article 202(2), and
(c) apart from this paragraph, the sum received, or the property obtained, by the claimant would be recoverable property,

the property ceases to be recoverable.

In relation to Scotland, "claimant" and "defendant" are to be read as "pursuer" and "defender".

(4) If—
(a) a payment is made to a person in pursuance of a compensation order under Article 14 of the Criminal Justice (Northern Ireland) Order 1994, section 249 of the Criminal Procedure (Scotland) Act 1995 or section 130 of the Powers of Criminal Court (Sentencing) Act 2000, and
(b) apart from this paragraph, the sum received would be recoverable property,

the property ceases to be recoverable.

(5) If—
(a) a payment is made to a person in pursuance of a restitution order under section 27 of the Theft Act (Northern Ireland) 1969 or section 148(2) of the Powers of Criminal Courts (Sentencing) Act 2000 or a person otherwise obtains any property in pursuance of such an order, and
(b) apart from this paragraph, the sum received, or the property obtained, would be recoverable property,

the property ceases to be recoverable.

(6) If—
(a) in pursuance of an order made by the court under section 382(3) or 383(5) of the Financial Services and Markets Act 2000 (restitution orders), an amount is paid to or distributed among any persons in accordance with the court's directions, and
(b) apart from this paragraph, the sum received by them would be recoverable property,

the property ceases to be recoverable.

(7) If—
(a) in pursuance of a requirement of the Financial Services Authority under section 384(5) of the Financial Services and Markets Act 2000 (power of authority to pursue restitution), an amount is paid to or distributed among any persons and
(b) apart from this paragraph, the sum received by them would be recoverable property,

the property ceases to be recoverable.

(8) Property is not recoverable while a restraint order applies to it, that is—
(a) an order under section 41, 120 or 190 of the Act or article 8, 58 or 95 of this Order, or
(b) an order under any corresponding provision of an enactment mentioned in section 8(7)(a) to (g) of the Act.

(9) Property is not recoverable if it has been taken into account in deciding the amount of a person's benefit from criminal conduct for the purpose of making a confiscation order, that is—
(a) an order under section 6, 92 or 156 of the Act or an external order registered under Part 2, 3 or 4 of this Order, or

(b)   an order under a corresponding provision of an enactment mentioned in section 8(7)(a) to (g) of the Act,

and, in relation to an order mentioned in sub-paragraph (b), the reference to the amount of a person's benefit from criminal conduct is to be read as a reference to the corresponding amount under the enactment in question.

(10)   Where—
(a)   a person enters into a transaction to which article 203(3) applies, and
(b)   the disposal is one to which paragraph (1) or (2) applies,

this article does not affect the recoverability (by virtue of article 203(3)) of any property obtained on the transaction in place of the property disposed of.

[3980HV]

NOTES
Commencement: 1 January 2006.

206   Other exemptions

(1)   Property, which apart from this article, would be recoverable property and is—
(a)   forfeited in pursuance of powers conferred by the customs and excise Acts, as defined by section 1(1) of the Customs and Excise Management Act 1979, or
(b)   disposed of in pursuance of an enactment prescribed in Schedule 5,

is not recoverable or (as the case may be) associated property.

(2)   But where particular circumstances are prescribed in Schedule 5 in relation to an enactment, paragraph (1)(b) applies only in those circumstances.

[3980HW]

NOTES
Commencement: 1 January 2006.

207   Granting interests

(1)   If a person grants an interest in his recoverable property, the question whether the interest is also recoverable is to be determined in the same manner as it is on any other disposal of recoverable property.

(2)   Accordingly, on his granting an interest in the property ("the property in question")—
(a)   where the property in question is property which satisfies the tests in article 202(1) and (2), the interest is also to be treated as satisfying those tests,
(b)   where the property in question represents in his hands property which satisfies the tests in article 202(1) and (2), the interest is also to be treated as representing in his hands property which satisfies those tests.

[3980HX]

NOTES
Commencement: 1 January 2006.

Insolvency

208   Insolvency

(1)   Proceedings for a recovery order may not be taken or continued in respect of property to which paragraph (2) applies unless the appropriate court gives leave and the proceedings are taken or (as the case may be) continued in accordance with any terms imposed by that court.

(2)   This paragraph applies to recoverable property, or property associated with it, if—
(a)   it is an asset of a company being wound up in pursuance of a resolution for voluntary winding up,
(b)   it is an asset of a company and a voluntary arrangement under Part 1 of the 1986 Act or Part 2 of the 1989 Order, has effect in relation to the company,
(c)   an order under section 2 of the 1985 Act, section 286 of the 1986 Act or Article 259 of the 1989 Order (appointment of interim trustee or interim receiver) has effect in relation to the property,
(d)   it is an asset comprised in the estate of an individual who has been adjudged bankrupt or, in relation to Scotland, of a person whose estate has been sequestrated,
(e)   it is an asset of an individual and a voluntary arrangement under Part 8 of the 1986 Act, or Part 8 of the 1989 Order, has effect in relation to him, or
(f)   in relation to Scotland, it is property comprised in the estate of a person who has granted a trust deed within the meaning of the 1985 Act.

(3)   An application under this article, or under any provision of the 1986 Act or the 1989 Order, for leave to take proceedings for a recovery order may be made without notice to any person.

(4)   Paragraph (3) does not affect any requirement for notice of an application to given to any person acting as an insolvency practitioner or to the official receiver (whether or not acting as an insolvency practitioner).

(5)   References to the provisions of the 1986 Act in sections 420 and 421 of that Act, or to the provisions of the 1989 Order in Articles 364 or 365 of that Order, (insolvent partnerships and estates of deceased persons) include paragraphs (1) and (2) above.

(6)   In this article—
   (a)   the 1985 Act means the Bankruptcy (Scotland) Act 1985,
   (b)   the 1986 Act means the Insolvency Act 1986,
   (c)   the 1989 Order means the Insolvency (Northern Ireland) Order 1989,

and in paragraph (7) "the applicable enactment" means whichever enactment mentioned in sub-paragraphs (a) to (c) is relevant to the resolution, arrangement, order or trust deed mentioned in paragraph (2).

(7)   In this article—
   (a)   an asset means any property within the meaning of the applicable enactment or, where the 1985 Act is the applicable enactment, any property comprised in an estate to which the 1985 Act applies,
   (b)   the appropriate court means the court which, in relation to the resolution, arrangement, order or trust deed mentioned in paragraph (2), is the court for the purposes of the applicable enactment or, in relation to Northern Ireland, the High Court,
   (c)   acting as an insolvency practitioner has the same meaning as in article 4,
   (d)   other expressions used in this article and in the applicable enactment have the same meaning as in that enactment.

[3980HY]

NOTES
Commencement: 1 January 2006.

Delegation of enforcement functions

209   Performance of functions of Scottish Ministers by constables in Scotland

(1)   In Scotland, a constable engaged in temporary service with the Scottish Ministers in connection with their functions under this Part may perform functions, other than those specified in subsection (2), on behalf of the Scottish Ministers.

(2)   The specified functions are the functions conferred on the Scottish Ministers by—
   (a)   articles 144(1) and (2) and 167(1) and (7) (proceedings in the Court of Session),
   (b)   article 178(2) (trustee for civil recovery),
   (c)   articles 182(3) and (4) and 183(5) (agreements about associated and joint property),
   (d)   article 186(3) (pension schemes),
   (e)   article 193(1) (exemptions),
   (f)   article 194(5) and (8) (compensation),
   (g)   article 200(2) (financial threshold).

[3980HZ]–[3980IA]

NOTES
Commencement: 1 January 2006.

210   *(Revoked by the Proceeds of Crime Act 2002 (External Requests and Orders) (Amendment) Order 2008, SI 2008/302, art 2(1), (41), as from 1 April 2008.)*

Interpretation

211   Obtaining and disposing of property

(1)   References to a person disposing of his property include a reference—
   (a)   to his disposing of a part of it, or
   (b)   to his granting an interest in it,

(or to both), and references to the property disposed of are to any property obtained on the disposal.

(2)   A person who makes a payment to another is to be treated as making a disposal of his property to the other, whatever form the payment takes.

(3)   Where a person's property passes to another under a will or intestacy or by operation of law, it is to be treated as disposed of by him to the other.

(4)   A person is only to be treated as having obtained his property for value in a case where he gave unexecuted consideration if the consideration has become executed consideration.

[3980IB]

NOTES
Commencement: 1 January 2006.

212   Northern Ireland courts

(1)   In relation to the practice and procedure of courts in Northern Ireland, expressions used in this Part are to be read in accordance with rules of court.

[3980IC]

NOTES
Commencement: 1 January 2006.

213   General interpretation

(1)   In this Part—
"associated property" has the meaning given by article 146,
"constable", in relation to Northern Ireland, means a police officer within the meaning of the Police (Northern Ireland) Act 2000,
"the court" except in articles 158(2) and (3) and 173(2) and (3) means the High Court or (in relation to proceedings in Scotland) the Court of Session,
"dealing" with property includes disposing of it, taking possession of it or removing it from the United Kingdom,

.....

"enforcement authority"—
    [(a)   in relation to England and Wales, means SOCA, the Director of Public Prosecutions, the Director of Revenue and Customs Prosecutions or the Director of the Serious Fraud Office,]
    (b)   in relation to Scotland, means the Scottish Ministers,
    [(c)   in relation to Northern Ireland, means SOCA, the Director of the Serious Fraud Office or the Director of Public Prosecutions for Northern Ireland,]
"excepted joint owner" has the meaning given by article 181(4),
"interest", in relation to land—
    (a)   in the case of land in England and Wales or Northern Ireland, means any legal estate and any equitable interest or power,
    (b)   in the case of land in Scotland, means any estate, interest, servitude or other heritable right in or over land, including a heritable security,
"interest", in relation to property other than land, includes any right (including a right to possession of the property),
"interim administration order" has the meaning given by article 167(2),
"interim receiving order" has the meaning given by article 151(2),
"part", in relation to property, includes a portion,
"premises" has the same meaning as in the Police and Criminal Evidence Act 1984,
"prohibitory property order" has the meaning given in article 171(2),
"property freezing order" has the meaning given in article 147(2),
"recoverable property" is to be read in accordance with articles 202 to 207,
"recovery order" means an order made under article 177,
"respondent" means—
    (a)   where proceedings are brought by the enforcement authority, the person against whom the proceedings are brought,
    (b)   where no such proceedings have been brought but the enforcement authority has applied for a property freezing order, an interim receiving order, a prohibitory property order or an interim administration order, the person against whom he intends to bring such proceedings,
"share", in relation to an excepted joint owner, has the meaning given by article 181(4),
"specified property" means property other than a sum of money that is specified in an external order,
"value" means market value.

(2)   The following provisions apply for the purposes of this Part.

(3)   For the purpose of deciding whether or not property was recoverable at any time (including times before commencement), it is to be assumed that this Part was in force at that and any other relevant time.

(4)   Property is all property wherever situated and includes—
    (a)   money,
    (b)   all forms of property, real or personal, heritable or moveable,

(c)   things in action and other intangible or incorporeal property.

(5)   Any reference to a person's property (whether expressed as a reference to the property he holds or otherwise) is to be read as follows.

(6)   In relation to land, it is a reference to any interest which he holds in the land.

(7)   In relation to property other than land, it is a reference—
    (a)   to the property (if it belongs to him), or
    (b)   to any other interest which he holds in the property.

(8)   References to the satisfaction of the enforcement authority's right to recover any property which satisfies the tests in article 202(1) and (2) are to read in accordance with article 189.

[(8A)   In relation to an order in England and Wales or Northern Ireland which is a recovery order, a property freezing order, an interim receiving order or an order under article 187, references to the enforcement authority are, unless the context otherwise requires, references to the enforcement authority which is seeking, or (as the case may be) has obtained, the order.]

[3980ID]

NOTES

Commencement: 1 January 2006.
Para (1): definition "Director" (omitted) revoked, para (a) of definition "enforcement authority" substituted, and para (c) of that definition inserted, by the Proceeds of Crime Act 2002 (External Requests and Orders) (Amendment) Order 2008, SI 2008/302, art 2(1), (42)(a), (b), as from 1 April 2008.
Para (8A): added by the Proceeds of Crime Act 2002 (External Requests and Orders) (Amendment) Order 2008, SI 2008/302, art 2(1), (42)(c), as from 1 April 2008.

SCHEDULES

SCHEDULE 1
ADMINISTRATORS (SCOTLAND): FURTHER PROVISION

Article 85

General

1.   In this Schedule, unless otherwise expressly provided—
    (a)   references to an administrator are to an administrator appointed under article 63 or 73(2);
    (b)   references to realisable property are to the realisable property in respect of which the administrator is appointed; and
    (c)   references to specified property are to the specified property in respect of which the administrator is appointed.

Appointment etc

2.—(1)   If the office of administrator is vacant, for whatever reason, the court must appoint a new administrator.

(2)   Any property vested in the previous administrator by virtue of paragraph 5(4) vests in the new administrator.

(3)   Any order under article 63, 74(3) or 75(3) in relation to the previous administrator applies in relation to the new administrator when he gives written notice of his appointment to the person subject to the order.

(4)   The administration of property by an administrator must be treated as continuous despite any temporary vacancy in that office.

(5)   The appointment of an administrator is subject to such conditions as to caution as the accountant of court may impose.

(6)   The premium of any bond of caution or other security required by such conditions must be treated as part of the administrator's expenses in the exercise of his functions.

Functions

3.—(1)   An administrator—
    (a)   may, if appointed under article 63; and
    (b)   must, if appointed under article 73(2), as soon as practicable take possession of the realisable property or specified property, as the case may be, and of the documents mentioned in sub-paragraph (2).

(2)   Those documents are any document which—
    (a)   is in the possession or control of the person ("A") in whom the property is vested (or would be vested but for an order made under paragraph 5(4)); and
    (b)   relates to the property or to A's assets, business or financial affairs.

(3)   An administrator is entitled to have access to, and to copy, any document relating to the property or to A's assets, business or financial affairs ad not falling within sub-paragraph (2)(a).

(4)   An administrator may bring, defend or continue any legal proceedings relating to the property.

(5)   An administrator may borrow money so far as it is necessary to do so to safeguard the property and may for the purposes of such borrowing create a security over any part of the property.

(6)   An administrator may, if he considers that it would be beneficial for the management or realisation of the property—

    (a)   carry on any business of A;

    (b)   exercise any right of A as holder of securities in a company;

    (c)   grant a lease of the property or take on lease any other property;

    (d)   enter into any contract, or execute any deed, as regards the property or as regards A's business.

(7)   An administrator may, where any right, option or other power forms part of A's estate, make payments or incur liabilities with a view to—

    (a)   obtaining property which is the subject of; or

    (b)   maintaining,

the right, option or power.

(8)   An administrator may effect or maintain insurance policies as regards the property on A's business.

(9)   An administrator may, if appointed under article 73(2), complete any uncompleted title which A has to any heritable estate; but completion of title in A's name does not validate by accretion any unperfected right in favour of any person other than the administrator.

(10)   An administrator may sell, purchase or exchange property or discharge any security for an obligation due to A; but it is incompetent for the administrator or an associate of his (within the meaning of section 74 of the Bankruptcy (Scotland) Act 1985) to purchase any of A's property in pursuance of this sub-paragraph.

(11)   An administrator may claim, vote and draw dividends in the sequestration of the estate for bankruptcy or liquidation) of a debtor of A and may accede to a voluntary trust deed for creditors of such a debtor.

(12)   An administrator may discharge any of his functions through agents or employees, but is personally liable to meet the fees and expenses of any such agent or employee out of which remuneration as is payable to the administrator on a determination by the accountant of court.

(13)   An administrator may take such professional advice as he considers necessary in connection with the exercise of his functions.

(14)   An administrator may at any time apply to the court for directions as regards the exercise of his functions.

(15)   An administrator may exercise any power specifically conferred on him by the court, whether conferred on his appointment or subsequently.

(16)   An administrator may—

    (a)   enter any premises;

    (b)   search for or inspect anything authorised by the court;

    (c)   make or obtain a copy, photograph or other record of anything so authorised;

    (d)   remove anything which the administrator is required or administered to take possession of in pursuance of an order of the court.

(17)   An administrator may do anything incidental to the powers and duties listed in the previous provisions of this paragraph.

Consent of accountant of court

4.   An administrator proposing to exercise any power conferred by paragraph 3(4) to (7) must first obtain the consent of the accountant of court.

Dealings in good faith with administrator

5.—(1)   A person dealing with an administrator in good faith and for value is not concerned to enquire whether the administrator is acting within the powers mentioned in paragraph 3.

(2)   Sub-paragraph (1) does not apply where the administrator or an associate purchases property in contravention of paragraph 3(10).

(3)   The validity of any title is not challengeable by reason only of the administrator having acted out with the powers mentioned in paragraph 3.

(4) The exercise of a power mentioned in paragraph 3(4) to (11) must be in A's name except where and in so far as an order made by the court under this sub-paragraph vests the property in the administrator (or in a previous administrator).

(5) The court may make an order under sub-paragraph (4) on the application of the administrator or on its own motion.

Money received by administrator

6.—(1) All money received by an administrator in the exercise of his functions must be deposited by him, in the name (unless vested in the administrator by virtue of paragraph 5(4)) of the holder of the property realised, in an appropriate bank or institution.

(2) But the administrator may at any time retain in his hands a sum not exceeding £200 or such other sum as may be prescribed by the Scottish Ministers by regulations.

(3) In sub-paragraph (1), "appropriate bank or institution" means a bank or institution mentioned in section 3(1) of the Banking Act 1987 or for the time being specified in Schedule 2 to that Act.

Effect of appointment of administrator on diligence

7.—(1) An arrestment or poinding of realisable property or specified property, as the case may be, executed on or after the appointment of an administrator does not create a preference for the arrester or poinder.

(2) Any realisable property or specified property so arrested or poinded, or (if the property has been sold) the proceeds of sale, must be handed over to the administrator.

(3) A poinding of the ground in respect of realisable property or specified property on or after such appointment is ineffectual in a question with the administrator except for the interest mentioned in sub-paragraph (4).

(4) That interest is—
    (a) interest on the debt of a secured creditor for the current half-yearly term; and
    (b) arrears of interest on that debt for one year immediately before the commencement of that term.

(5) On and after such appointment no other person may raise or insist in an adjudication against realisable property or specified property or be confirmed as executor – creditor on that property.

(6) An inhibition on realisable property or specified property which takes effect on or after such appointment does not create a preference for the inhibitor in a question with the administrator.

(7) This paragraph is without prejudice to articles 61 and 62.

(8) In this paragraph, the reference to an administrator is to an administrator appointed under article 73(2).

Supervision

8.—(1) If the accountant of court reports to the court that an administrator has failed to perform any duty imposed on him, the court may, after giving the administrator an opportunity to be heard as regards the matter—
    (a) remove him from office;
    (b) censure him; or
    (c) make such order as it thinks fit.

(2) Section 6 of the Judicial Factors (Scotland) Act 1889 does not apply in relation to an administrator.

Accounts and remuneration

9.—(1) Not later than two weeks after the issuing of any determination by the accountant of court as to the remuneration and expenses payable to the administrator, the administrator or the Lord Advocate may appeal against it to the court.

(2) The amount of remuneration payable to the administrator must be determined on the basis of the value of the work reasonably undertaken by him, regard being had to the extent of the responsibilities involved.

(3) The accountant of court may authorise the administrator to pay without taxation an account in respect of legal services incurred by the administrator.

Discharge of administrator

10.—(1) After an administrator has lodged his final accounts under paragraph 9(1), he may apply to the accountant of court to be discharged from office.

(2)   A discharge, if granted, frees the administrator from all liability (other than liability arising from fraud) in respect of any act or omission of his in exercising his functions as administrator.

[3980IE]

NOTES
Commencement: 1 January 2006.

SCHEDULE 2
POWERS OF INTERIM RECEIVER OR ADMINISTRATOR
Articles 152 and 168

Seizure

1.   Power to seize property to which the order applies.

Information

2.—(1)   Power to obtain information or to require a person to answer any question.

(2)   A requirement imposed in the exercise of the power has effect in spite of any restriction on the disclosure of information (however imposed).

(3)   An answer given by a person in pursuance of such a requirement may not be used in evidence against him in criminal proceedings.

(4)   Sub-paragraph (3) does not apply—
   (a)   on a prosecution for an offence under section 5 of the Perjury Act 1911, section 44(2) of the Criminal Law (Consolidation) (Scotland) Act 1995 or Article 10 of the Perjury (Northern Ireland) Order 1979 (false statements), or
   (b)   on a prosecution for some other offence where, in giving evidence, he makes a statement inconsistent with it.

(5)   But an answer may not be used by virtue of sub-paragraph (4)(b) against a person unless—
   (a)   evidence relating to it is adduced, or
   (b)   a question relating to it is asked,
by him or on his behalf in the proceedings arising out of the prosecution.

Entry, search, etc

3.—(1)   Power to—
   (a)   enter any premises in the United Kingdom to which the interim receiving order applies, and
   (b)   take any of the following steps.

(2)   Those steps are—
   (a)   to carry out a search for or inspection of anything described in the order,
   (b)   to make or obtain a copy, photograph or other record of anything so described,
   (c)   to remove anything which he is required to take possession of in pursuance of the order or which may be required as evidence in the proceedings under Chapter 2 of Part 5.

(3)   The order may describe anything generally, whether by reference to a class or otherwise.

Supplementary

4.—(1)   An order making any provision under paragraph 2 or 3 must make provision in respect of legal professional privilege (in Scotland, legal privilege within the meaning of Chapter 3 of Part 8 of the Act).

(2)   An order making any provision under paragraph 3 may require any person—
   (a)   to give the interim receiver or administrator access to any premises which he may enter in pursuance of paragraph 3,
   (b)   to give the interim receiver or administrator any assistance he may require for taking the steps mentioned in that paragraph.

Management

5.—(1)   Power to manage any property to which the order applies.

(2)   Managing property includes—
   (a)   selling or otherwise disposing of assets comprised in the property which are perishable or which ought to be disposed of before their value diminishes,
   (b)   where the property comprises assets of a trade or business, carrying on, or arranging for another to carry on, the trade or business,
   (c)   incurring capital expenditure in respect of the property.

[3980IF]

NOTES
Commencement: 1 January 2006.

SCHEDULE 3
POWERS OF TRUSTEE FOR CIVIL RECOVERY
Article 178

Sale

1.   Power to sell the property or any part of it or interest in it.

Expenditure

2.   Power to incur expenditure for the purpose of—
    (a)   acquiring any part of the property, or any interest in it, which is not vested in him,
    (b)   discharging any liabilities, or extinguishing any rights, to which the property is subject.

Management

3.—(1)   Power to manage property.

    (2)   Managing property includes doing anything mentioned in paragraph 5(2) of Schedule 1.

Legal proceedings

4.   Power to start, carry on or defend any legal proceedings in respect of the property.

Compromise

5.   Power to make any compromise or other arrangement in connection with any claim relating to the property.

Supplementary

6.—(1)   For the purpose of, or in connection with, the exercise of any of his powers—
    (a)   power by his official name to do any of the things mentioned in sub-paragraph (2),
    (b)   power to do any other act which is necessary or expedient.

    (2)   Those things are—
    (a)   holding property,
    (b)   entering into contracts,
    (c)   suing and being sued,
    (d)   employing agents,
    (d)   executing a power of attorney, deed or other instrument.

[3980IG]

NOTES
Commencement: 1 January 2006.

SCHEDULE 4
RECOVERY FROM PENSION SCHEMES
Articles 184 and 186

Interpretation

1.   In this Schedule—
    "destination arrangement" means a pension arrangement under which some or all of the rights are derived, directly or indirectly, from a pension sharing transaction;
    "pension recovery order" means a recovery order made by virtue of article 184(2);
    "pension sharing transaction" means an order or provision falling within section 28(1) of the Welfare Reform and Pensions Act 1999 (activation of pension sharing) or article 25(1) of the Welfare Reform and Pensions (Northern Ireland) Order 1999 (activation of pension sharing);
    "relevant person" means the person whose rights under a pension scheme are the subject of a pension recovery order; and
    "valuation date" means a date within the period prescribed by paragraph 5 in respect of which the trustees or managers of the pension scheme decide to value the relevant person's pension rights in accordance with paragraph 2 or 3.

Calculation and verification of the value of rights under pension schemes

2.—(1)   This paragraph applies where the High Court or the Court of Session makes a pension recovery order, other than in respect of rights derived from a pension sharing transaction under a destination arrangement in a pension scheme.

(2)   The trustees or managers of the pension scheme in respect of which the pension recovery order has been made must calculate and verify the cash equivalent of the value at the valuation date of the rights which are the subject of the pension recovery order and must pay to the trustee for civil recovery a sum equal to that cash equivalent.

(3)   In relation to the calculation and verification by the trustees or managers of the cash equivalent referred to in sub-paragraph (2)—

   (a)   in the case of a pension scheme wholly or mainly administered in England and Wales, regulation 3 of the Pensions on Divorce etc (Provision of Information) Regulations 2000 (information about pensions and divorce: valuation of pension benefits), except paragraph (2) thereof, shall have effect as it has effect for the valuation of benefits in connection with the supply of information in connection with domestic and overseas divorce etc in England and Wales, with the modification that for "the date on which the request for valuation was received" in each place where it appears in that regulation, there shall be substituted "the valuation date for the purposes of Schedule 4 to the Proceeds of Crime Act 2002 (External Requests and Orders) Order 2005";

   (b)   in the case of a pension scheme wholly or mainly administered in Scotland, regulation 3 of the Divorce etc (Pensions) (Scotland) Regulations 2000 (valuation), except paragraph (11) thereof, shall have effect as it has effect for the valuation of benefits in connection with the supply of information in connection with divorce in Scotland, with the modification that for "the relevant date" in each place where it appears in that regulation, there shall be substituted "the valuation date for the purposes of Schedule 4 to the Proceeds of Crime Act 2002 (External Requests and Orders) Order 2005"; and

   (c)   in the case of a pension scheme wholly or mainly administered in Northern Ireland, regulation 3 of the Pensions on Divorce etc (Provision of Information) Regulations (Northern Ireland) 2000 (information about pensions on divorce: valuation of pension benefits), except paragraph (2) thereof, shall have effect as it has effect for the valuation of benefits in connection with the supply of information in connection with domestic and overseas divorce etc in Northern Ireland, with the modification that, for "the date on which the request for the valuation was received" in each place where it appears in that regulation, there shall be substituted "the valuation date for the purposes of Schedule 4 to the Proceeds of Crime Act 2002 (External Requests and Orders) Order 2005."

Calculation and verification of the value of rights under destination arrangements

3.—(1)   This paragraph applies where the High Court or the Court of Session makes a pension recovery order in respect of rights derived from a pension sharing transaction under a destination arrangement in a pension scheme.

(2)   The trustees or managers of the pension scheme in respect of which the pension recovery order has been made must calculate and verify the cash equivalent of the value at the valuation date of the rights which are the subject of the pension recovery order and must pay to the trustee for civil recovery a sum equal to that cash equivalent.

(3)   In relation to the calculation and verification by the trustees or managers of the cash equivalent referred to in sub-paragraph (2)—

   (a)   in the case of a pension arrangement in a scheme that is wholly or mainly administered in either England and Wales or Scotland, regulation 24 of the Pension Sharing (Pension Credit Benefit) Regulations 2000 (manner of calculation and verification of cash equivalents) shall have effect as it has effect for the calculation and verification of pension credit for the purposes of those Regulations; and

   (b)   in the case of a pension arrangement in a scheme that is wholly or mainly administered in Northern Ireland, regulation 24 of the Pension Sharing (Pension Credit and Benefit) Regulations (Northern Ireland) 2000 (manner of calculation and verification of cash equivalents) shall have effect as it has effect for the calculation and verification of pension credit for the purposes of those Regulations.

Approval of manner of calculation and verification of the value of rights

4.—(1)   This paragraph applies where the relevant person is also a trustee or manager of the pension scheme in respect of which the pension recovery order has been made.

(2)   When the trustees or managers of the pension scheme have, under paragraph 2 or 3, calculated and verified the value of the rights which are the subject of a pension recovery order, the manner in which the trustees or managers have calculated and verified the value of the rights must be approved by—

   (a)   a Fellow of the Institute of Actuaries; or

(b)   a Fellow of the Faculty of Actuaries.

(3)   Where the person referred to in sub-paragraph (2) is not able to approve the manner in which the trustees or managers have calculated and verified the value of the rights which are the subject of a pension recovery order, he must give notice in writing of that fact to the trustee for civil recovery and the trustees or managers of the scheme.

(4)   Where the trustees or managers of the scheme have been given notice under sub-paragraph (3), they must re-calculate and re-verify the value of the rights which are the subject of a pension recovery order for the purposes of paragraph 2 or 3.

Time for compliance with a pension recovery order

5.—(1)   In this paragraph, "the prescribed period" means the period prescribed for the purposes of article 184(2)(a).

(2)   Subject to sub-paragraphs (3) and (4), the prescribed period is the period of 60 days beginning on the day on which the pension recovery order is made.

(3)   Where an application for permission to appeal the pension recovery order is made within the period referred to in sub-paragraph (2), the prescribed period is the period of 60 days beginning on—

(a)   the day on which permission to appeal is finally refused;
(b)   the day on which the appeal is withdrawn; or
(c)   the day on which the appeal is dismissed,

as the case may be.

(3)   Where the person referred to in paragraph 4(2) gives notice, in accordance with paragraph 4(3) and within the period referred to in sub-paragraph (2), to the trustee for civil recovery and trustees or managers of the scheme that he is unable to approve the manner in which the trustees or managers have calculated the value of the rights which are the subject of the pension recovery order, the prescribed period is the period of 60 days beginning on the day on which such notice is given.

[3980IH]

NOTES

Commencement: 1 January 2006.

SCHEDULE 5
PRESCRIBED ENACTMENTS—PROPERTY WHICH IS NOT RECOVERABLE PROPERTY
Article 206

Section 31 of the Salmon Fisheries (Scotland) Act 1868 (forfeiture of articles found in possession of any offender).

Section 8 of the Diseases of Fish Act 1937 (penalties and legal proceedings).

Sections 19 and 20 of the Salmon and Freshwater Fisheries (Protection) (Scotland) Act 1951.

Section 138 of the Army Act 1955 (restitution or compensation for theft etc) (including where it has effect by virtue of paragraph 17 of Schedule 3 to the Armed Forces Act 1976), in circumstances other than where the disposal is of money which is paid as or towards compensation under section 138(5) of that Act or the disposal is the restitution of property given in exchange under section 138(6) of that Act.

Section 138 of the Air Force Act 1955 (restitution or compensation for theft etc) in circumstances other than where the disposal is of money is paid as or towards compensation under section 138(5) of that Act or the disposal is the restitution of property given in exchange under section 138(6) of that Act.

Section 76 of the Naval Discipline Act 1957 (restitution or compensation on conviction of larceny etc), in circumstances other than where the disposal is the restitution of property given in exchange under section 76(2)(a) of that Act or the disposal is of money which is paid as or towards compensation under section 76(2)(b) or (3) of that Act.

Section 3 of the Obscene Publications Act 1959 (powers of search and seizure).

Section 11(2) of the Sea Fish (Conservation) Act 1967 (penalties for offences).

Section 46(4) of the Courts-Martial (Appeals) Act 1968 (restitution of property), in circumstances where if the order had been made by the court-martial or Defence Council this Order would have provided that the property was not recoverable or (as the case may be) associated property.

Section 52 of the Firearms Act 1968 (forfeiture and disposal of firearms).

Section 27 of the Misuse of Drugs Act 1971 (forfeiture).

Sections 7 and 24 of the Forgery and Counterfeiting Act 1981 (powers of search, forfeiture etc).

Section 4(4) of the Inshore Fishing (Scotland) Act 1984.

Section 25 of the Public Order Act 1986 (power to order forfeiture).

Section 66 of the Criminal Justice and Public Order Act 1994 (power of court to forfeit sound equipment) in the circumstances where no order is made under section 66(5) by virtue of section 66(6) of that Act for the delivery of property to a person appearing to be the owner of the property.

Section 43 of the Drug Trafficking Act 1994 (forfeiture).

Section 22 of the Proceeds of Crime (Scotland) Act 1995 (forfeiture: district court).

Section 24 of the Proceeds of Crime (Scotland) Act 1995 (forfeiture of property subject to suspended forfeiture order), in the circumstances where no order is made under section 26 of that Act in relation to the property.

Paragraph 3 of the Schedule to the Noise Act 1996 (forfeiture), in the circumstances where no order is made under paragraph 4 of that Schedule for the delivery of the equipment to a person appearing to be the owner of the equipment.

Section 6 of the Knives Act 1997 (forfeiture of knives and publications), in the circumstances where no order is made under section 7 of that Act for the delivery of property to a person appearing to be the owner of the property.

Section 143 of the Powers of Criminal Courts (Sentencing) Act 2000 (powers to deprive offender of property used etc for purposes of crime), in the circumstances where no order is made under the Police (Property) Act 1897, as applied by section 144 of the Powers of Criminal Courts (Sentencing) Act 2000, for the delivery of the property to a person appearing to be the owner of the property.

Section 23 of the Terrorism Act 2000 (forfeiture).

Section 6 of the Royal Parks (Trading) Act 2000 (seizure, retention, disposal and forfeiture of property).

Paragraph 6 of Schedule 1 to the Anti-terrorism, Crime and Security Act 2001 (forfeiture).

Regulations 15 (disposal of vehicles) and 17 (disposal of contents) of the Goods Vehicles (Enforcement Powers) Regulations 2001, in the circumstances where the proceeds of sale have not been applied in meeting a claim to the proceeds of sale established under regulation 18(2) of those Regulations.

[3980II]

NOTES
  Commencement: 1 January 2006.

PROCEEDS OF CRIME ACT 2002 (MONEY LAUNDERING: EXCEPTIONS TO OVERSEAS CONDUCT DEFENCE) ORDER 2006

(SI 2006/1070)

NOTES
  Made: 5 April 2006.
  Authority: Proceeds of Crime Act 2002, ss 327(2A)(b)(ii), 328(3)(b)(ii), 329(2A)(b)(ii).
  Commencement: 15 May 2006.

As of 1 February 2009, this Order had not been amended.

1   This Order may be cited as the Proceeds of Crime Act 2002 (Money Laundering: Exceptions to Overseas Conduct Defence) Order 2006 and shall come into force on 15th May 2006.

[3981]

NOTES
  Commencement: 15 May 2006.

2—(1)   Relevant criminal conduct of a description falling within paragraph (2) is prescribed for the purposes of sections 327(2A)(b)(ii), 328(3)(b)(ii) and 329(2A)(b)(ii) of the Proceeds of Crime Act 2002 (exceptions to defence where overseas conduct is legal under local law).

   (2)   Such relevant criminal conduct is conduct which would constitute an offence punishable by imprisonment for a maximum term in excess of 12 months in any part of the United Kingdom if it occurred there other than—

   (a)   an offence under the Gaming Act 1968;

(b)   an offence under the Lotteries and Amusements Act 1976, or

(c)   an offence under section 23 or 25 of the Financial Services and Markets Act 2000.

[3982]

NOTES
Commencement: 15 May 2006.

TAKEOVERS DIRECTIVE (INTERIM IMPLEMENTATION) REGULATIONS 2006 (NOTE)

(SI 2006/1183)

NOTES
These Regulations were made on 25 April 2006 under the European Communities Act 1972, s 2(2) and came into force on 20 May 2006. They implemented the Takeovers Directive (ie, Directive 2004/25/EC of the European Parliament and of the Council of 21 April 2004 on Takeover Bids). The Directive had to be implemented in the UK by 20 May 2006 and, as the Companies Act 2006 had not completed Parliamentary passage by that date, this was achieved by means of these interim Regulations.

These Regulations were revoked by the Companies Act 2006 (Commencement No 2, Consequential Amendments, Transitional Provisions and Savings) Order 2007, SI 2007/1093, art 7, Sch 5, as from 6 April 2007, subject to savings in Sch 6, paras 2, 3 to that Order as follows—

"Savings for provisions relating to takeovers

2.   The revocation of the Interim Regulations by article 7 does not affect the operation of Part 5 of those Regulations (squeeze-out and sell-out) in relation to a takeover offer where the date of the offer is before 6th April 2007.

3.   The revocation of the Interim Regulations by article 7, and the coming into force of section 949 of the Companies Act 2006 (offence of disclosure in contravention of section 948), and in particular of section 949(2)(b), by virtue of article 2, does not affect the continued operation of regulation 8(2)(b) of the Interim Regulations in respect of offences committed prior to 6th April 2007.".

Part 28 of the Companies Act 2006 (Takeovers etc) was brought into force on the same date (see **[1676]** et seq).

[3983]–[4021]

CAPITAL REQUIREMENTS REGULATIONS 2006

(SI 2006/3221)

NOTES
Made: 4 December 2006.
Authority: European Communities Act 1972, s 2(2).
Commencement: 1 January 2007.

As of 1 February 2009, these Regulations had not been amended.

ARRANGEMENT OF REGULATIONS

PART 1
INTRODUCTION

PART 2
APPLICATIONS FOR PERMISSIONS

PART 3
EXERCISE OF SUPERVISION

PART 1
INTRODUCTION

1 Citation, commencement and interpretation

(1) These Regulations may be cited as the Capital Requirements Regulations 2006 and come into force on 1st January 2007.

(2) In these Regulations—
"the Act" means the Financial Services and Markets Act 2000;
"application" unless the context otherwise requires means an application—
    (a) for a permission;
    (b) to vary or revoke a permission; or
    (c) to vary or revoke the terms and conditions to which a permission is subject;
"banking consolidation directive" means Council Directive 2006/48/EC of the European Parliament and of the Council of 14 June 2006 relating to the taking up and pursuit of the business of credit institutions;
"capital adequacy directive" means Council Directive 2006/49/EC of the European Parliament and of the Council of 14 June 2006 relating to the capital adequacy of investment firms and credit institutions;
"decision" means a decision made by the EEA consolidated supervisor in relation to an application or a proposal;
"EEA consolidated supervisor" means the competent authority responsible, under the banking consolidation directive or under the banking consolidation directive as applied by Articles 2(2) and 37(1) of the capital adequacy directive, for the exercise of supervision on a consolidated basis of—
    (a) an EEA parent credit institution;
    (b) an EEA parent investment firm; or
    (c) credit institutions or investment firms controlled by an EEA parent financial holding company where the parent is authorised in a different EEA State to at least one of the subsidiaries;
"EEA parent credit institution" means a parent credit institution in an EEA State which is not a subsidiary of another credit institution or investment firm authorised in any EEA State, or of a financial holding company set up in any EEA State;
"EEA parent investment firm" means a parent investment firm in an EEA State which is not a subsidiary of another credit institution or investment firm authorised in any EEA State or of a financial holding company set up in any EEA State;
"EEA parent financial holding company" means a parent financial holding company in an EEA State which is not a subsidiary of another credit institution or investment firm authorised in any EEA State or of another financial holding company set up in any EEA State;
"joint decision" means a decision, made jointly by all relevant competent authorities and the EEA consolidated supervisor, in relation to an application or a proposal;

"national consolidated supervisor" means the competent authority responsible, under the banking consolidation directive or under the banking consolidation directive as applied by Articles 2(2) and 37(1) of the capital adequacy directive, for the exercise of supervision on a consolidated basis of—

   (a)   a parent credit institution in an EEA State;
   (b)   a parent investment firm in an EEA State; or
   (c)   credit institutions or investment firms controlled by a parent financial holding company in an EEA State;

"parent credit institution in an EEA State" means a credit institution which has a credit institution, an investment firm or a financial institution as a subsidiary or which holds a participation in such an institution, and which is not itself a subsidiary of another credit institution or investment firm authorised in the same EEA State, or of a financial holding company set up in the same EEA State;

"parent investment firm in an EEA State" means an investment firm which has a credit institution, an investment firm or a financial institution as a subsidiary or which holds a participation in such an institution, and which is not itself a subsidiary of another credit institution or investment firm authorised in the same EEA State or of a financial holding company set up in the same EEA State;

"parent financial holding company in an EEA State" means a financial holding company which is not itself a subsidiary of a credit institution or investment firm authorised in the same EEA State, or of another financial holding company set up in the same EEA State;

"permission" means a permission referred to in Article 84(1) or 87(9) of the banking consolidation directive, an approval referred to in Article 105 or Annex III, Part 6 of the banking consolidation directive or recognition referred to in Annex V of the capital adequacy directive;

"proposal" means a proposal made by the EEA consolidated supervisor to vary or revoke a permission or vary or revoke the terms or conditions to which it is subject;

"relevant competent authority" means a competent authority which is not the EEA consolidated supervisor and which has authorised a subsidiary of an EEA parent credit institution, a subsidiary of an EEA parent investment firm or a subsidiary of an EEA parent financial holding company.

   (3)   Save as provided by paragraph (2)—
   (a)   any expression used in these Regulations which is used in the banking consolidation directive or the capital adequacy directive shall have the meaning given by those directives; and
   (b)   any other expression used in these Regulations which is defined for the purposes of the Act has the meaning given by the Act.

[4022]

NOTES
Commencement: 1 January 2007.

PART 2
APPLICATIONS FOR PERMISSIONS

2 Application for permission

   (1)   This regulation applies where the Authority is the EEA consolidated supervisor.

   (2)   An application may be made to the Authority—
   (a)   by an EEA parent credit institution and its subsidiaries;
   (b)   by an EEA parent investment firm and its subsidiaries; or
   (c)   jointly by the subsidiaries of an EEA parent financial holding company.

   (3)   An application must be made in such manner as the Authority may direct.

[4023]

NOTES
Commencement: 1 January 2007.

3 Applications to the Authority as EEA consolidated supervisor

   (1)   This regulation applies where the Authority is the EEA consolidated supervisor and has received an application.

   (2)   The Authority must—
   (a)   forward the complete application to the relevant competent authorities without delay;
   (b)   work together, in full consultation with the relevant competent authorities, and do everything in its power to reach a joint decision within six months from the date on which it received the complete application; and

(c)   provide the applicants with a document containing the fully reasoned joint decision, if any.

(3)   If a joint decision is not made by the Authority and the relevant competent authorities within the period specified in paragraph (2)(b), the Authority must—

(a)   make its own decision on the application, taking account of the views and reservations of the relevant competent authorities expressed during that period; and

(b)   provide the applicant and the relevant competent authorities with a document containing the fully reasoned decision.

[4024]

NOTES
Commencement: 1 January 2007.

4 Applications forwarded to the Authority as a relevant competent authority

(1)   This regulation applies where the Authority is a relevant competent authority and has been forwarded a complete application by the EEA consolidated supervisor.

(2)   The Authority must work together, in full consultation with the EEA consolidated supervisor and the other relevant competent authorities, and do everything in its power to reach a joint decision within six months from the date on which the EEA consolidated supervisor received the complete application.

[4025]

NOTES
Commencement: 1 January 2007.

5 Proposals to vary or revoke a decision or joint decision

(1)   This regulation applies where the Authority is the EEA consolidated supervisor and intends to make a proposal.

(2)   The Authority must give written notice to those persons to whom the permission, which is the subject of the intended proposal, applies.

(3)   The notice must—

(a)   give details of the intended proposal; and

(b)   inform the persons to whom the permission applies that they may make representations to the Authority within such period as may be specified in the notice.

(4)   If after the period specified in the notice has expired the Authority makes the proposal, it must—

(a)   send the proposal and forward any representations received during that period to the relevant competent authorities;

(b)   work together, in full consultation with the relevant competent authorities, taking account of such representations and do everything in its power to reach a joint decision within six months from the date on which the proposal was made; and

(c)   provide the persons to whom the permission applies with a document containing the fully reasoned joint decision, if any.

(5)   If a joint decision is not made by the Authority and the relevant competent authorities within the period specified in paragraph (4)(b), the Authority must—

(a)   make its own decision on the proposal, taking account of the views and reservations of the relevant competent authorities expressed during that period and of any representations made by the persons to whom the permission applies;

(b)   provide the persons to whom the permission applies and the relevant competent authorities with a document containing the fully reasoned decision.

[4026]

NOTES
Commencement: 1 January 2007.

6   Where the Authority is a relevant competent authority and receives a proposal from the EEA consolidated supervisor, it must work together, in full consultation with the EEA consolidated supervisor and the other relevant competent authorities, and do everything in its power to reach a joint decision within six months from the date on which the proposal was made.

[4027]

NOTES
Commencement: 1 January 2007.

7 Recognition and application of a decision or joint decision

The Authority must recognise a decision or a joint decision as determinative and apply it in respect of any authorised person to whom the banking consolidation directive or the capital adequacy directive applies.

[4028]

NOTES
Commencement: 1 January 2007.

8 Exercise of functions under section 148 of the Act for the purpose of applying a decision or a joint decision

(1) The Authority may exercise the powers conferred by section 148 of the Act (modification or waiver of rules) if it appears desirable to do so for the purpose of applying a decision or a joint decision.

(2) In such a case the requirements contained in—
    (a) subsections (2) and (9)(b) of section 148 for the Authority's powers to be exercisable only on the application or with the consent of an authorised person; and
    (b) section 148(4),
shall not apply.

[4029]

NOTES
Commencement: 1 January 2007.

9—(1) Where the Authority proposes to exercise the powers conferred by section 148 of the Act in relation to an authorised person for the purpose of applying a decision or a joint decision, other than on the application or with the consent of that person, it must give him written notice and have regard to any representations received within such period as is specified in the notice.

(2) The notice must—
    (a) give details of any proposed direction or variation of a direction;
    (b) give details of any proposed conditions;
    (c) inform the person that, within such period as may be specified in the notice, he may make representations to the Authority;
    (d) inform the person when the proposed direction, variation or condition takes effect.

[4030]

NOTES
Commencement: 1 January 2007.

PART 3
EXERCISE OF SUPERVISION

10 The Authority's duties as an EEA consolidated supervisor

Regulations 11 and 12 apply where the Authority is the EEA consolidated supervisor.

[4031]

NOTES
Commencement: 1 January 2007.

11—(1) The Authority must take such steps, in going concern and emergency situations, as it considers appropriate—
    (a) to co-ordinate the gathering and dissemination of relevant or essential information; and
    (b) in co-operation with the relevant competent authorities, to plan and co-ordinate supervisory activities.

(2) The Authority must provide a relevant competent authority with all information which the Authority considers to be essential for the exercise of the relevant competent authority's supervisory tasks.

(3) For the purposes of this regulation, information shall be regarded as essential if it could materially influence the assessment of the financial soundness of a credit institution, financial institution or investment firm in another EEA State. In particular essential information shall include:
    (a) the group structure of all major credit institutions or investment firms in a group;
    (b) the relevant competent authorities of the credit institutions or investment firms in a group;

(c) procedures for the collection and verification of information from credit institutions or investment firms in a group;

(d) adverse developments in credit institutions or investment firms or in other entities of a group, which could seriously affect other credit institutions or investment firms of that group;

(e) major sanctions and exceptional measures taken by the EEA consolidated supervisor or any of the relevant competent authorities under the banking consolidation directive or under the banking consolidation directive as applied by Articles 2(2) and 37(1) of the capital adequacy directive.

[4032]

NOTES
Commencement: 1 January 2007.

12—(1) On request, the Authority must provide a relevant competent authority with all the information which the Authority considers to be relevant for the exercise of the relevant competent authority's supervisory tasks.

(2) In determining the extent of relevant information, the Authority must have regard to the importance of the subsidiary within the financial system of the EEA State in which it is authorised.

[4033]

NOTES
Commencement: 1 January 2007.

13 The Authority's duties as EEA consolidated supervisor or national consolidated supervisor

Regulations 14, 15 and 16 apply where the Authority is either the EEA consolidated supervisor or the national consolidated supervisor.

[4034]

NOTES
Commencement: 1 January 2007.

14—(1) Where an emergency situation arises within a banking group which potentially jeopardises the stability of the financial system in any EEA State where an entity of a group has been authorised, the Authority must notify as soon as practicable—

(a) the central bank and other bodies with a similar function in their capacity as monetary authorities; and

(b) the department of the central government administration responsible for legislation on the supervision of credit institutions, financial institutions, investment services and insurance companies;

of the EEA State in which the entity has been authorised.

(2) The Authority, in notifying any body under paragraph (1), may share any information which it is not prevented from disclosing.

[4035]

NOTES
Commencement: 1 January 2007.

15 The Authority must, so far as necessary to facilitate and establish effective supervision and wherever possible, have written co-ordination and co-operation agreements in place with other competent authorities.

[4036]

NOTES
Commencement: 1 January 2007.

16—(1) Where the Authority is considering, in relation to a credit institution, an investment firm or a financial institution, whether to take action against that person which it considers will impose a major sanction or exceptional measure it must, before making a decision, consult the EEA consolidated supervisor, and where its decision would be of importance to a competent authority's supervisory tasks, that authority.

(2) Paragraph (1) does not apply where the Authority considers that—

(a) there is an urgent need to act; or

(b) such consultation may jeopardise the effectiveness of the decision referred to in paragraph (1).

(3) Where paragraph (1) does not apply by virtue of paragraph (2), the Authority must, without delay, inform the EEA consolidated supervisor and the other competent authorities referred to in paragraph (1) of the action that it has taken.

(4) In this regulation, the Authority may impose a major sanction or exceptional measure by—

  (i) varying a Part IV permission;

  (ii) exercising any of the powers conferred on it by section 148 of the Act;

  (iii) publishing a statement under section 205 of the Act (public censure);

  (iv) imposing a penalty in respect of a contravention under section 206 of the Act (financial penalties);

  (v) exercising any of its powers (other than its powers under section 381, 383 or 384(2)) under Part XXV of the Act (injunctions and restitution).

[4037]

NOTES
Commencement: 1 January 2007.

17 Disclosed information

(1) Where the Authority is the EEA consolidated supervisor or a national consolidated supervisor and it needs information which has already been given to another competent authority, it must, wherever possible, obtain that information by requesting that the other competent authority which holds the information disclose it to the Authority.

(2) Where the Authority is the competent authority which has authorised a subsidiary of an EEA parent credit institution or a subsidiary of an EEA parent investment firm, and it needs information regarding the implementation of approaches and methodologies set out in the banking consolidation directive or the capital adequacy directive which may already be available to the EEA consolidated supervisor, it must, wherever possible, obtain that information by requesting that the EEA consolidated supervisor discloses the information to the Authority.

[4038]

NOTES
Commencement: 1 January 2007.

18–20 (*Amend the Financial Services and Markets Act 2000* (*Consultation with Competent Authorities*) *Regulations 2001, SI 2001/2509 at* **[2421]** *et seq.*)

PART 4
CREDIT INSTITUTIONS AND EXTERNAL CREDIT ASSESSMENT INSTITUTIONS

21 Interpretation

In this Part—

  "assessment methodology" means a methodology for assigning credit assessments;

  "ECAI" means an external credit assessment institution;

  "exposure risk-weighting purposes" means the purposes of determining the risk weight of an exposure in accordance with Article 80 of the banking consolidation directive;

  "securitisation risk-weighting purposes" means the purposes of determining the risk weight of a securitisation position in accordance with Article 96 of the banking consolidation directive.

[4039]

NOTES
Commencement: 1 January 2007.

22 Recognition for exposure risk-weighting purposes

(1) The Authority must recognise an ECAI as eligible for exposure risk-weighting purposes only if the Authority is satisfied, taking into account the requirements set out in Schedule 1, that—

  (a) the ECAI's assessment methodology complies with the requirements of objectivity, independence, ongoing review and transparency; and

  (b) the ECAI's credit assessments meet the requirements of credibility and transparency.

(2) The Authority may recognise an ECAI as eligible for exposure risk-weighting purposes without carrying out its own evaluation process if the ECAI has been recognised as eligible for those purposes by a competent authority of another EEA State.

(3)   Where the Authority recognises an ECAI as eligible for exposure risk-weighting purposes, it must determine, taking into account the requirements set out in Schedule 2, with which of the credit quality steps set out in Part 1 of Annex VI of the banking consolidation directive the relevant credit assessments of the ECAI are to be associated.

(4)   The Authority's determinations must be objective and consistent.

(5)   The Authority may recognise, without carrying out its own determination process, a determination of the kind mentioned in paragraph (3) which has been made by a competent authority of another EEA State.

[4040]

NOTES
Commencement: 1 January 2007.

23   Recognition for securitisation risk-weighting purposes

(1)   The Authority must recognise an ECAI as eligible for securitisation risk-weighting purposes only if the Authority is satisfied—
- (a)   taking into account the requirements set out in Schedule 1, that—
  - (i)   the ECAI's assessment methodology complies with the requirements of objectivity, independence, ongoing review and transparency; and
  - (ii)   the ECAI's credit assessments meet the requirements of credibility and transparency; and
- (b)   that the ECAI has a demonstrated ability in the area of securitisation.

(2)   A demonstrated ability in the area of securitisation may be evidenced by a strong market acceptance.

(3)   The Authority may recognise an ECAI as eligible for securitisation risk-weighting purposes without carrying out its own evaluation process if the ECAI has been recognised as eligible for those purposes by a competent authority of another Member State.

(4)   Where the Authority recognises an ECAI as eligible for securitisation risk-weighting purposes, it must determine with which of the credit quality steps set out in Part 4 of Annex IX of the banking consolidation directive the relevant credit assessments of the ECAI are to be associated.

(5)   The Authority's determinations must be objective and consistent.

(6)   The Authority must, when making its determination—
- (a)   differentiate between the relative degrees of risk expressed by each assessment; and
- (b)   consider—
  - (i)   quantitative factors (such as default rates and loss rates); and
  - (ii)   qualitative factors (such as the range of transactions assessed by the ECAI and the meaning of the credit assessment).

(7)   The Authority must seek to ensure that securitisation positions to which the same risk weight is applied on the basis of credit assessments of eligible ECAIs are subject to equivalent degrees of credit risk and, for this purpose the Authority may modify its determination as to the credit quality step with which a credit assessment is to be associated.

(8)   The Authority may recognise, without carrying out its own determination process, a determination of the kind mentioned in paragraph (4) which has been made by a competent authority of another EEA State.

[4041]

NOTES
Commencement: 1 January 2007.

24   Publishing recognition process and list of ECAIs

The Authority must make publicly available—
- (a)   an explanation of its recognition process, and
- (b)   a list of eligible ECAIs.

[4042]

NOTES
Commencement: 1 January 2007.

25   Revoking recognition

The Authority may revoke the recognition of an ECAI—
- (a)   where the ECAI is recognised in accordance with paragraph (1) of regulation 22 or, as the case may be, paragraph (1) of regulation 23, if the Authority considers that the requirements of the applicable paragraph are no longer met; and

PART III
STATUTORY INSTRUMENTS

(b) where an ECAI is recognised in accordance with paragraph (2) of regulation 22 or, as the case may be, paragraph (3) of regulation 23, if the condition in the applicable paragraph is no longer met.

[4043]

NOTES
Commencement: 1 January 2007.

PART 5
MISCELLANEOUS

26 Restriction on disclosure

(1) This regulation applies where—
    (a) a credit institution or investment firm does not meet a requirement of the banking consolidation directive, and
    (b) by adopting a relevant measure, the Authority requires the credit institution or investment firm to take the necessary action or steps at an early stage to address the situation.

(2) A measure is relevant if its adoption—
    (a) obliges the credit institution or investment firm to hold own funds in excess of the minimum level laid down in Article 75 of the banking consolidation directive;
    (b) reinforces the arrangements, processes, mechanisms and strategies implemented to comply with Articles 22 and 123 of the banking consolidation directive;
    (c) requires the credit institution or investment firm to apply a specific provisioning policy or treatment of assets in terms of own funds requirements;
    (d) restricts or limits the business, operations or network of the credit institution or investment firm; or
    (e) requires the reduction of the risk inherent in the credit institution's or investment firm's activities, products and systems.

(3) In such circumstances, sections 348, 349 and 352 of the Act apply to information about the adoption of the relevant measure—
    (a) in the same way as they apply in relation to confidential information within the meaning of section 348(2) of the Act (subject to paragraph (4) of that section), and
    (b) as if the Authority were a recipient of such information.

[4044]

NOTES
Commencement: 1 January 2007.

27 Functions of the Authority

Any function conferred by Part 2, 3 or 4 of these Regulations on the Authority (whether in the capacity of an EEA consolidated supervisor, a national consolidated supervisor, a relevant competent authority or otherwise) is to be treated as a function conferred on the Authority by a provision of the Act.

[4045]

NOTES
Commencement: 1 January 2007.

28 Service of notices

The Financial Services and Markets Act 2000 (Service of Notices) Regulations 2001 applies to any document given under regulation 3, 5 or 9 as they apply to any notice, direction or document of any kind under the Act.

[4046]

NOTES
Commencement: 1 January 2007.

29 Consequential amendments to primary and secondary legislation

(1) Schedule 3 (which amends the Act in consequence of the adoption of the banking consolidation directive) has effect.

(2) Schedule 4 (which amends other primary legislation in consequence of the adoption of the banking consolidation directive) has effect.

(3)   Schedule 5 (which amends the Financial Conglomerates and other Financial Groups Regulations 2004 in consequence of the adoption of the banking consolidation directive and the capital adequacy directive) has effect.

(4)   Schedule 6 (which amends other secondary legislation in consequence of the adoption of the banking consolidation directive and the capital adequacy directive) has effect.

[4047]

NOTES

Commencement: 1 January 2007.

SCHEDULES

SCHEDULE 1
RECOGNITION OF ECAIS

Regulations 22 and 23

PART 1
METHODOLOGY

Objectivity

1.   The Authority must verify that an ECAI's assessment methodology is rigorous, systematic, continuous and subject to validation based on historical experience.

Independence

2.   The Authority must verify that an ECAI's assessment methodology is free from external political influences or constraints, and from economic pressures that may influence a credit assessment.

3.   The Authority must assess the independence of an ECAI's assessment methodology according to factors such as the following—
     (a)   ownership and organisation structure of the ECAI;
     (b)   financial resources of the ECAI;
     (c)   staffing and expertise of the ECAI;
     (d)   corporate governance of the ECAI.

Ongoing review

4.   The Authority must verify that an ECAI's credit assessments—
     (a)   are subject to ongoing review, taking place after all significant events and at least annually; and
     (b)   are responsive to changes in the financial conditions.

5.   The Authority must verify that the assessment methodology for each market segment is established according to standards such as the following—
     (a)   that backtesting has been established for at least one year;
     (b)   that the Authority monitors the regularity of the review process by the ECAI;
     (c)   that the Authority is able to receive from the ECAI information as to the extent of the ECAI's contacts with the senior management of the entities which it rates.

6.   The Authority must take such steps as it considers necessary to ensure that it is promptly informed by an ECAI of any material changes in the methodology that the ECAI uses for assigning credit assessments.

Transparency and disclosure

7.   The Authority must take such steps as it considers necessary to ensure that the principles of the methodology employed by an ECAI for the formulation of its credit assessments are publicly available so as to enable all potential users to decide whether they are derived in a reasonable way.

[4048]

NOTES

Commencement: 1 January 2007.

PART 2
CREDIT ASSESSMENTS

Credibility and market acceptance

8.   The Authority must verify that the individual credit assessments of each ECAI are recognised in the market as credible and reliable by the users of such credit assessments.

9. The Authority must assess credibility according to factors such as the following—
    (a) market share of the ECAI;
    (b) revenues generated by the ECAI;
    (c) financial resources of the ECAI;
    (d) whether there is any pricing on the basis of the rating;
    (e) whether at least two credit institutions use the individual credit assessments of the ECAI for—
        (i) bond issuing, or
        (ii) assessing credit risks.

Transparency and Disclosure

10. The Authority must verify that individual credit assessments are—
    (a) accessible on equivalent terms to all credit institutions and investment firms having a legitimate interest in those individual credit assessments, and
    (b) available to non-domestic parties on equivalent terms as to domestic credit institutions and investment firms having a legitimate interest in those individual credit assessments.

[4049]

NOTES
Commencement: 1 January 2007.

SCHEDULE 2
MAPPING

Regulation 22

1.—(1) In order to differentiate between the relative degrees of risk expressed by each credit assessment, the Authority must consider quantitative factors such as the long-term default rate associated with all items assigned the same credit assessment.

(2) For recently established ECAIs and for those that have compiled only a short record of default data, the Authority must ask the ECAI what it believes to be the long-term default rate associated with all items assigned the same credit assessment.

2. In order to differentiate between the relative degrees of risk expressed by each credit assessment, the Authority must consider qualitative factors such as—
    (a) the pool of issuers that the ECAI covers;
    (b) the range of credit assessments that the ECAI assigns;
    (c) each credit assessment meaning;
    (d) the ECAI's definition of default.

3. The Authority must compare default rates experienced for each credit assessment of an ECAI and compare them with a benchmark built on the basis of default rates experienced by other ECAIs on a population of issuers which the Authority believes to present an equivalent level of credit risk.

4. Where the Authority believes that the default rates experienced for the credit assessment of an ECAI are materially and systematically higher than the benchmark, the Authority must assign a higher credit quality step in the credit quality assessment scale to the ECAI's credit assessment.

5. Where the Authority has increased the associated risk weight for a credit assessment of an ECAI, if the ECAI demonstrates that the default rates experienced for its credit assessment are no longer materially and systematically higher than the benchmark, the Authority may decide to restore the original credit quality step in the credit quality assessment scale for the ECAI's credit assessment.

[4050]

NOTES
Commencement: 1 January 2007.

(Sch 3 (Consequential Amendments to the Act) amends the Financial Services and Markets Act 2000, s 405, Sch 3, Pts I, III Sch 11A, Pt 2 at **[432]**, **[467]**, **[469]**, **[479]**; *Sch 4 (Consequential Amendments to other Primary Legislation) amends the Companies Act 1985, the Terrorism Act 2000 at* **[1247]** *et seq, the Proceeds of Crime Act 2002 at* **[1310]** *et seq, the Consumer Credit Act 1974, the Building Societies Act 1986, the Bank of England Act 1998, and the Criminal Justice Act 1993 (in so far as these amendments are still in force and relevant they have been taken in at the appropriate place); Sch 5 (Consequential Amendments to the Financial Conglomerates and other Financial Groups Regulations 2004) amends the Financial Conglomerates and Other Financial Groups Regulations 2004, SI 2004/1862 at* **[2723]** *et seq; Sch 6 (Consequential Amendments to Other Secondary Legislation) amends the Cash Ratio Deposits (Eligible Liabilities) Order 1998, SI 1998/1130 at* **[3527]** *et seq, the Financial Markets and Insolvency (Settlement Finality) Regulations 1999, SI 1999/2979 at* **[3553A]** *et seq, the Financial Services and Markets Act 2000 (Regulated Activities) Order 2001, SI 2001/544 at* **[2010]** *et seq, the Financial Services and Markets*

Act 2000 (Compensation Scheme: Electing Participants) Regulations 2001, SI 2001/1783 at **[2342]** *et seq, the Financial Services and Markets Act 2000 (Disclosure of Confidential Information) Regulations 2001, SI 2001/2188 at* **[2350]** *et seq, the Financial Services and Markets Act 2000 (EEA Passport Rights) Regulations 2001, SI 2001/2511 at* **[2430]** *et seq, the Financial Services and Markets Act 2000 (Gibraltar) Order 2001, SI 2001/3084 at* **[2495]** *et seq, the Financial Services and Markets Act 2000 (Confidential Information) (Bank of England) (Consequential Provisions) Order 2001, SI 2001/3648 at* **[2635]** *et seq, the Uncertificated Securities Regulations 2001, SI 2001/3755 at* **[3581]** *et seq, the Financial Services and Markets Act 2000 (Regulated Activities) (Amendment) Order 2002, SI 2002/682 at* **[2666]** *et seq, the Money Laundering Regulations 2003, SI 2003/3075 (revoked), and contains various other amendments that are outside the scope of this work.)*

FINANCIAL SERVICES AND MARKETS ACT 2000 (MARKETS IN FINANCIAL INSTRUMENTS) REGULATIONS 2007

(SI 2007/126)

NOTES
Made: 24 January 2007.
Authority: European Communities Act 1972, s 2(2).
Commencement: 1 April 2007 (certain purposes); 1 November 2007 (otherwise) (see reg 1(2)).
These Regulations are reproduced as amended by: the Financial Services and Markets Act 2000 (Markets in Financial Instruments) (Amendment) Regulations 2007, SI 2007/763; the Financial Services and Markets Act 2000 (Markets in Financial Instruments) (Amendment No 2) Regulations 2007, SI 2007/2160.

ARRANGEMENT OF REGULATIONS

PART 1
GENERAL

PART 2
PART IV PERMISSION: INVESTMENT FIRMS

PART 3
TRANSITIONAL AND SAVING PROVISIONS

SCHEDULES:

PART III
STATUTORY INSTRUMENTS

PART 1

GENERAL

1 Citation and commencement

(1)   These Regulations may be cited as the Financial Services and Markets Act 2000 (Markets in Financial Instruments) Regulations 2007.

(2)   These Regulations come into force on 1st April 2007 for the purposes of—

    (a)   enabling the Authority to receive a notice under subsection (1)(b) of section 312A of the Act (inserted by these Regulations) in preparation for the making of arrangements as mentioned in that section by an EEA market operator on or after 1st November 2007;

    (b)   enabling a recognised investment exchange to give notice under subsection (2) of section 312C of the Act (inserted by these Regulations), and enabling the Authority to send a copy of the notice to the host state regulator as required by subsection (3) of that section;

    (c)   enabling applications to be made for approval under section 412A of the Act (inserted by these Regulations);

    (d)   enabling the Authority to give a direction as to the manner in which an application under section 412A is to be made and as to the content of the application and information to accompany it, and enabling the Authority to require the applicant to provide further information in accordance with section 412A(3);

    (e)   enabling the Authority, on receipt on or after that date of a consent notice under paragraph 13(1)(a) of Schedule 3 in relation to a EEA firm exercising an EEA right deriving from the markets in financial instruments directive, to prepare for the firm's supervision in accordance with paragraph 13(2)(a) of that Schedule;

    (f)   enabling the Authority, on receipt of a regulator's notice under paragraph 14 of Schedule 3 or a notice referred to in paragraph 14(1)(ba) of that Schedule (inserted by these Regulations) in relation to a EEA firm exercising an EEA right deriving from the markets in financial instruments directive, to prepare for the firm's supervision in accordance with paragraph 14(2)(a) of that Schedule;

    (g)   enabling—

        (i)   a UK firm to give a notice of intention under paragraph 19 of Schedule 3 (as amended by these Regulations) in exercise of an EEA right deriving from the markets in financial instruments directive,

        (ii)   the Authority to give a consent notice referred to in paragraph 19(4) of that Schedule to the host state regulator or a notice referred to in paragraph 19(8), (11) or (12) of that Schedule in relation to the exercise of that EEA right, and

        (iii)   the firm to make a reference to the Tribunal in accordance with paragraph 19(12)(b) of that Schedule in relation to the exercise of that EEA right;

    (h)   enabling—

        (i)   a UK firm to give a notice of intention under paragraph 20 of Schedule 3 (as amended by these Regulations) in exercise of an EEA right deriving from the markets in financial instruments directive,

        (ii)   the Authority to send a copy of such a notice to the host state regulator under paragraph 20(3) of that Schedule and notify the UK firm under paragraph 20(4) of that Schedule that it has done so,

and for all other purposes on 1st November 2007.

(3)   For the purposes of paragraph (2)(e) to (h)—

"EEA right" has the meaning given in paragraph 7 of Schedule 3;

an "EEA right deriving from the markets in financial instruments directive" means an EEA right to carry on an activity—

    (a)   which is an investment service or activity listed in Section A of Annex I to the markets in financial instruments directive;

    (b)   which is an ancillary service listed in Section B of Annex I to the markets in financial instruments directive; or

    (c)   in relation to an investment which is a financial instrument listed in Section C of Annex I to the markets in financial instruments directive;

"Schedule 3" means Schedule 3 to the Act.

(4)   Nothing in paragraph (2)(e) to (h) gives an EEA firm or a UK firm an EEA right to carry on, before 1st November 2007, an activity—

    (a)   which is an ancillary service listed in Section B of Annex I to the markets in financial instruments directive but which is not a non-core service listed in Section C of the Annex to the investment services directive;

    (b)   in relation to an investment which is a financial instrument listed in Section C of Annex I to the markets in financial instruments directive but which is not an instrument listed in Section B of the Annex to the investment services directive; or

    (c)   referred to in paragraph 5 of Section A of Annex I to the markets in financial instruments directive unless the firm has an EEA right to carry on one or more core services listed in Section A of the Annex to the investment services directive.

[4051]

NOTES
    Commencement: 1 April 2007 (certain purposes); 1 November 2007 (otherwise) (see above).

2   Interpretation

In these Regulations—
    "the Act" means the Financial Services and Markets Act 2000;
    "authorised person" has the meaning given in section 31(2) of the Act;
    "the Authority" means the Financial Services Authority;
    "investment services directive" means Council Directive 93/22/EEC of 10 May 1993 on investment services in the securities field;
    "markets in financial instruments directive" means Directive 2004/39/EC of the European Parliament and of the Council of 21 April 2004 on markets in financial instruments;
    "Part IV permission" has the meaning given in section 40(4) of the Act;
    ["regulated activity" has the meaning given in section 22 of the Act;]
    "Schedule 3" means Schedule 3 to the Act;

[4052]

NOTES
    Commencement: 1 April 2007 (certain purposes); 1 November 2007 (otherwise) (see reg 1(2)).
    Definition "regulated activity" inserted by the Financial Services and Markets Act 2000 (Markets in Financial Instruments) (Amendment) Regulations 2007, SI 2007/763, reg 2(1), as from 1 November 2007.

3   Amendments of primary and secondary legislation

    (1)   Schedule 1, which contains amendments of Part 13 of the Act (incoming firms: intervention by authority), has effect.

    (2)   Schedule 2, which contains amendments of Part 18 of the Act (recognised investment exchanges and clearing houses), has effect.

    (3)   Schedule 3, which inserts Part 18A of the Act, has effect.

    (4)   Schedule 4, which contains amendments of Schedule 3 to the Act (EEA passport rights), has effect.

    (5)   Schedule 5, which contains other amendments of the Act, has effect.

    (6)   Schedule 6, which contains consequential amendments of other enactments, has effect.

[4053]

NOTES
    Commencement: 1 April 2007 (certain purposes); 1 November 2007 (otherwise) (see reg 1(2)).

PART 2
PART IV PERMISSION: INVESTMENT FIRMS

4   [General restriction on giving Part IV permission]

    (1)   The Authority must not give a Part IV permission to an applicant who is an investment firm unless it is satisfied that the applicant complies with—
        (a)   the provisions contained in or made under the Act implementing Chapter I of Title II of the markets in financial instruments directive; and
        (b)   any directly applicable Community regulation made under that Chapter.

    (2)   Paragraph (1) also applies if an authorised person becomes an investment firm by virtue of a variation of his Part IV permission.

    (3)   "Investment firm" has the meaning given in section 424A of the Act.

[4054]

NOTES
    Commencement: 1 April 2007 (certain purposes); 1 November 2007 (otherwise) (see reg 1(2)).
    Regulation heading: inserted by the Financial Services and Markets Act 2000 (Markets in Financial Instruments) (Amendment) Regulations 2007, SI 2007/763, reg 2(2)(a), as from 1 November 2007.

[4A   Applications to be an exempt investment firm

    (1)   A person may apply in accordance with section 40 of the Act for a Part IV permission to carry on regulated activities as an exempt investment firm.

(2)   An authorised person may become entitled to carry on regulated activities as an exempt investment firm only by applying for a variation of his Part IV permission in accordance with section 44 of the Act.

(3)   For the purposes of this regulation, and regulations 4B and 4C, "exempt investment firm" means an authorised person who—
  (a)   is an investment firm within the meaning given in Article 4.1.1 of the markets in financial instruments directive, and
  (b)   has a Part IV permission,
but to whom Title II of the markets in financial instruments directive does not apply.

(4)   A person may only apply for a Part IV permission as mentioned in paragraph (1), and an authorised person may only apply for a variation of his Part IV permission as mentioned in paragraph (2), if the person or authorised person has his relevant office in the United Kingdom.

(5)   In paragraph (4) "relevant office" means—
  (a)   in relation to a body corporate, its registered office or, if it has no registered office, its head office, and
  (b)   in relation to a person or authorised person other than a body corporate, the person's head office.]

[4054A]

NOTES
Commencement: 1 November 2007.
Inserted, together with regs 4B, 4C, by the Financial Services and Markets Act 2000 (Markets in Financial Instruments) (Amendment) Regulations 2007, SI 2007/763, reg 2(2)(b), as from 1 November 2007.

[4B   Limitation on exempt investment firms

An exempt investment firm has no entitlement—
  (a)   to establish a branch by making use of the procedures in paragraph 19 of Schedule 3, or
  (b)   to provide any service by making use of the procedures in paragraph 20 of Schedule 3,
in a case where the entitlement of the firm to do so would, but for this regulation, derive from the markets in financial instruments directive.]

[4054B]

NOTES
Commencement: 1 November 2007.
Inserted as noted to reg 4A at **[4054A]**.

[4C   Requirements to be applied to exempt investment firms

(1)   If the Authority—
  (a)   gives to a person who has applied as mentioned in regulation 4A(1) a Part IV permission to carry on regulated activities as an exempt investment firm, or
  (b)   varies the Part IV permission of an authorised person who has applied as mentioned in regulation 4A(2) for a variation to permit him to carry on regulated activities as an exempt investment firm,
the requirements specified in paragraph (3) ("the specified requirements") shall be treated as being included in the permission by the Authority under section 43 of the Act.

(2)   Notwithstanding paragraph (1)—
  (a)   the inclusion of the specified requirements in the Part IV permission does not—
    (i)   amount, for the purpose of section 52(6) of the Act, to a proposal to exercise the power of the Authority under section 43(1) of the Act,
    (ii)   amount, for the purpose of section 52(9) of the Act, to a decision to exercise the power of the Authority under section 43(1) of the Act, or
    (iii) entitle the person to refer a matter under section 55(1) of the Act;
  (b)   the specified requirements shall not expire until the person ceases to be an exempt investment firm and, accordingly, section 43(5) shall not be treated as requiring the Authority to specify a period at the end of which they expire; and
  (c)   no application under section 44 of the Act to vary the permission by cancelling or varying any of the specified requirements may be made by the person unless he informs the Authority when making the application that he wishes to cease to be an exempt investment firm.

(3)   The requirements are that the person—
  (a)   does not hold clients' funds or securities and does not, for that reason, at any time, place himself in debt with his clients;
  (b)   does not provide any investment service other than—
    (i)   the reception and transmission of orders in transferable securities and units in collective investment undertakings, and

     (ii)   the provision of investment advice in relation to the financial instruments mentioned in paragraph (i);

  (c)   in the course of providing the investment services mentioned in sub-paragraph (b), transmits orders only to—

     (i)   investment firms authorised in accordance with the markets in financial instruments directive,

     (ii)   credit institutions authorised in accordance with the banking consolidation directive,

     (iii)   branches of investment firms or of credit institutions which are authorised in a third country and which are subject to and comply with prudential rules considered by the Authority to be at least as stringent as those laid down in the markets in financial instruments directive, the banking consolidation directive or Directive 2006/49/EC of the European Parliament and of the Council of 14 June 2006 on the capital adequacy of investment firms and credit institutions,

     (iv)   collective investment undertakings authorised under the law of a Member State to market units to the public and to the managers of such undertakings,

     (v)   investment companies with fixed capital, as defined in Article 15(4) of Second Council Directive 77/91/EEC of 13 December 1976 on the coordination of safeguards required of public companies in respect of their formation and the maintenance and alteration of their capital, the securities of which are listed or dealt in on a regulated market in a Member State.

  (4)   In paragraph (3)—

  (a)   terms and expressions defined in Article 4 of the markets in financial instruments directive and used in the paragraph have the meanings given in that Article;

  (b)   "the banking consolidation directive" means Directive 2006/48/EC of the European Parliament and of the Council of 14 June 2006 relating to the taking up and pursuit of the business of credit institutions;

  (c)   other terms and expressions used both in the paragraph and in Article 3 of or Annex 1 to the markets in financial instruments directive have the same meanings in the paragraph as in that Article or Annex; and

  (d)   "Member State", in sub-paragraph (c)(iv), includes an EEA State that is not a Member State.]

[4054C]

NOTES

Commencement: 1 November 2007.
Inserted as noted to reg 4A at **[4054A]**.

PART 3
TRANSITIONAL AND SAVING PROVISIONS

5 Transitional and saving provisions: market operators

  (1)   Section 312A(2) of the Act applies to arrangements made on or before 31st October 2007, in the United Kingdom, by an EEA market operator to facilitate access to, or use of, a regulated market or multilateral trading facility operated by it as it applies to arrangements under section 312A(1).

  (2)   Section 312C(2) and (4) of the Act does not apply in relation to arrangements made by a recognised investment exchange on or before 31st October 2007 in the territory of another EEA State to facilitate access to, or use of, a regulated market or multilateral trading facility operated by it by persons established in that State.

[4055]

NOTES

Commencement: 1 April 2007 (certain purposes); 1 November 2007 (otherwise) (see reg 1(2)).

6 Transitional and saving provisions: EEA firms

  (1)   Where the Authority has received a consent notice of the sort referred to in paragraph 13(1)(a) of Schedule 3 from the home state regulator of an EEA investment firm on or before 31st October 2007, paragraph 13 of Schedule 3 applies as if it had not been amended by paragraph 8 of Schedule 4 to these Regulations.

  (2)   In this regulation, "EEA investment firm" means an EEA firm falling within paragraph 5(a) of Schedule 3 (before its amendment by these Regulations).

[4056]

PART III
STATUTORY INSTRUMENTS

NOTES

Commencement: 1 April 2007 (certain purposes); 1 November 2007 (otherwise) (see reg 1(2)).

[6A Transitional provisions: EEA investment firms exercising passport rights under the investment services directive

(1) Where on or before 31st October 2007 an EEA investment firm has exercised an EEA right deriving from the investment services directive to establish a branch or to provide services in the United Kingdom, and the Authority has received in respect of that firm—

   (a) a consent notice under paragraph 13(1)(a) of Schedule 3 or a regulator's notice under paragraph 14(1)(b) of Schedule 3 in relation to an investment service specified in the first column in table 1 in Schedule 7 to these Regulations, or

   (b) notice of change under regulation 4(4) or 5(3) of the EEA Passport Rights Regulations in relation to an investment service specified in the first column in table 1 in Schedule 7 to these Regulations,

that notice is on 1st November 2007 to be treated as having been given in relation to the investment service or activity specified in the second column of table 1 opposite that investment service.

(2) Where on or before 31st October 2007 an EEA investment firm has exercised an EEA right deriving from the investment services directive to establish a branch or to provide services in the United Kingdom, and the Authority has received in respect of that firm—

   (a) a consent notice under paragraph 13(1)(a) of Schedule 3 or a regulator's notice under paragraph 14(1)(b) of Schedule 3 in relation to a non-core service specified in the first column in table 2 in Schedule 7 to these Regulations, or

   (b) notice of change under regulation 4(4) or 5(3) of the EEA Passport Rights Regulations in relation to a non-core service specified in the first column in table 2 in Schedule 7 to these Regulations,

that notice is on 1st November 2007 to be treated as having been given in relation to the ancillary service specified in the second column of table 2 opposite that non-core service.

(3) Where on or before 31st October 2007 an EEA investment firm has exercised an EEA right deriving from the investment services directive to establish a branch or to provide services in the United Kingdom, and the Authority has received in respect of that firm—

   (a) a consent notice under paragraph 13(1)(a) of Schedule 3 or a regulator's notice under paragraph 14(1)(b) of Schedule 3 in relation to the non-core service specified in paragraph 6 of Section C of the Annex to the investment services directive (investment advice concerning one or more of the instruments listed in Section B), or

   (b) notice of change under regulation 4(4) or 5(3) of the EEA Passport Rights Regulations in relation to the non-core service specified in paragraph 6 of Section C of the Annex to the investment services directive,

that notice is on 1st November 2007 to be treated as having been given in relation to the investment service specified in paragraph 5 of Section A of Annex I to the markets in financial instruments directive (investment advice).

(4) Where on or before 31st October 2007 an EEA investment firm has exercised an EEA right deriving from the investment services directive to establish a branch or to provide services in the United Kingdom, and the Authority has received in respect of that firm—

   (a) a consent notice under paragraph 13(1)(a) of Schedule 3 or a regulator's notice under paragraph 14(1)(b) of Schedule 3 in relation to an instrument specified in the first column in table 3 in Schedule 7 to these Regulations, or

   (b) notice of change under regulation 4(4) or 5(3) of the EEA Passport Rights Regulations in relation to an instrument specified in the first column in table 3 in Schedule 7 to these Regulations,

that notice is on 1st November 2007 to be treated as having been given in relation to the financial instrument specified in the second column of table 3 opposite that instrument.

(5) If this regulation conflicts with any law of an EEA investment firm's home state, the law of the firm's home state shall prevail.

(6) In this regulation—

   "EEA investment firm" means an EEA firm falling within paragraph 5(a) of Schedule 3 (before its amendment by these Regulations);

   "EEA right" has the meaning given in paragraph 7 of Schedule 3;

   "home state" in relation to an EEA investment firm means the EEA State which is the firm's home Member State for the purposes of the markets in financial instruments directive.]

[4056A]

NOTES

Commencement: 1 November 2007.

Inserted by the Financial Services and Markets Act 2000 (Markets in Financial Instruments) (Amendment No 2) Regulations 2007, SI 2007/2160, reg 2(1), (3), as from 1 November 2007.

7 Transitional provisions: UK investment firms exercising passport rights under the investment services directive

(1)   Where—
- (a)   a UK investment firm on or before 31st October 2007 has given—
  - (i)   notice of intention under paragraph 19(2) or 20(1) of Schedule 3 in relation to an investment service specified in the first column in table 1 in Schedule 7 to these Regulations, or
  - (ii)   notice of change under regulation 11(3) or 12(2)(a) of the EEA Passport Rights Regulations in relation to an investment service specified in the first column in table 1 in Schedule 7 to these Regulations, or
- (b)   the Authority on or before 31st October 2007 has given—
  - (i)   a consent notice under paragraph 19(4) of Schedule 3 or a notice referred to in paragraph 20(3) of Schedule 3 in relation to an investment service specified in the first column in table 1 in Schedule 7 to these Regulations, or
  - (ii)   a notice referred to in regulation 11(5) of the EEA Passport Rights Regulations in relation to an investment service specified in the first column in table 1 in Schedule 7 to these Regulations,

it is on 1st November 2007 to be treated as having given that notice in relation to the investment service or activity specified in the second column of table 1 opposite that investment service.

(2)   Where—
- (a)   a UK investment firm on or before 31st October 2007 has given—
  - (i)   notice of intention under paragraph 19(2) or 20(1) of Schedule 3 in relation to a non-core service specified in the first column in table 2 in Schedule 7 to these Regulations, or
  - (ii)   notice of change under regulation 11(3) or 12(2)(a) of the EEA Passport Rights Regulations in relation to a non-core service specified in the first column in table 2 in Schedule 7 to these Regulations, or
- (b)   the Authority on or before 31st October 2007 has given—
  - (i)   a consent notice under paragraph 19(4) of Schedule 3 or a notice referred to in paragraph 20(3) of Schedule 3 in relation to a non-core service specified in the first column in table 2 in Schedule 7 to these Regulations, or
  - (ii)   a notice referred to in regulation 11(5) of the EEA Passport Rights Regulations in relation to a non-core service specified in the first column in table 2 in Schedule 7 to these Regulations,

it is on 1st November 2007 to be treated as having given that notice in relation to the ancillary service specified in the second column of table 2 opposite that non-core service.

(3)   Where—
- (a)   a UK investment firm on or before 31st October 2007 has given—
  - (i)   notice of intention under paragraph 19(2) or 20(1) of Schedule 3 in relation to the non-core service specified in paragraph 6 of Section C of the Annex to the investment services directive (investment advice concerning one or more of the instruments listed in Section B), or
  - (ii)   notice of change under regulation 11(3) or 12(2)(a) of the EEA Passport Rights Regulations in relation to the non-core service specified in paragraph 6 of Section C of the Annex to the investment services directive, or
- (b)   the Authority on or before 31st October 2007 has given—
  - (i)   a consent notice under paragraph 19(4) of Schedule 3 or a notice referred to in paragraph 20(3) of Schedule 3 in relation to the non-core service specified in paragraph 6 of Section C of the Annex to the investment services directive, or
  - (ii)   a notice referred to in regulation 11(5) of the EEA Passport Rights Regulations in relation to the non-core service specified in paragraph 6 of Section C of the Annex to the investment services directive,

it is on 1st November 2007 to be treated as having given that notice in relation to the investment service specified in paragraph 5 of Section A of Annex I to the markets in financial instruments directive (investment advice) …

(4)   Where—
- (a)   a UK investment firm on or before 31st October 2007 has given—
  - (i)   notice of intention under 19(2) or 20(1) of Schedule 3 in relation to an instrument specified in the first column in table 3 in Schedule 7 to these Regulations, or
  - (ii)   notice of change under regulation 11(3) or 12(2)(a) of the EEA Passport Rights Regulations in relation to an instrument specified in the first column in table 3 in Schedule 7 to these Regulations, or

(b)   the Authority on or before 31st October 2007 has given—
    (i)   a consent notice under paragraph 19(4) of Schedule 3 or a notice referred to in paragraph 20(3) of Schedule 3 in relation to an instrument specified in the first column in table 3 in Schedule 7 to these Regulations, or
    (ii)   a notice referred to in regulation 11(5) of the EEA Passport Rights Regulations in relation to an instrument specified in the first column in table 3 in Schedule 7 to these Regulations,

it is on 1st November 2007 to be treated as having given that notice in relation to the financial instrument specified in the second column of table 3 opposite that instrument.

(5)   Nothing in this regulation gives a UK investment firm the right to carry on a regulated activity (or an activity which, if it were regarded as carried on in the United Kingdom, would be a regulated activity) which it would require Part IV permission to carry on but for which it does not have Part IV permission.

[4057]

NOTES
Commencement: 1 April 2007 (certain purposes); 1 November 2007 (otherwise) (see reg 1(2)).
Para (3): words omitted revoked by the Financial Services and Markets Act 2000 (Markets in Financial Instruments) (Amendment No 2) Regulations 2007, SI 2007/2160, reg 2(1), (3), as from 1 November 2007.

[7A   Transitional provision: investment research and financial analysis

(1)   This regulation applies where a UK investment firm on or before 15th August 2007 has given—
(a)   notice of intention under paragraph 19(2) or 20(1) of Schedule 3, or
(b)   notice of change under regulation 11(3) or 12(2)(a) of the EEA Passport Rights Regulations,

in relation to the non-core service specified in paragraph 6 of Section C of the Annex to the investment services directive (investment advice concerning one or more of the instruments listed in Section B).

(2)   The Authority may during the period starting on 1st September 2007 and ending on 31st October 2007 give notice to the UK investment firm's host state regulator (within the meaning of paragraph 11 of Schedule 3) that from 1st November 2007 the firm will offer the ancillary service specified in paragraph 5 of Section B of Annex I to the markets in financial instruments directive (investment research and financial analysis).

(3)   Regulation 11 or 12 of the EEA Passport Rights Regulations does not apply where the Authority has given a notice in accordance with paragraph (2).

(4)   Where the UK investment firm concerned gave written notice to the Authority on or before 31st August 2007 to that effect, this regulation shall not apply to him.]

[4057A]

NOTES
Commencement: 15 August 2007.
Inserted by the Financial Services and Markets Act 2000 (Markets in Financial Instruments) (Amendment No 2) Regulations 2007, SI 2007/2160, reg 2(1), (4), as from 15 August 2007.

8   Additional saving provision: UK investment firms

Where the Authority has given a consent notice under paragraph 19(4) of Schedule 3 in relation to a UK investment firm on or before 31st October 2007, paragraph 19(6) of that Schedule applies as if it had not been amended by paragraph 10(c) of Schedule 4 to these Regulations, and paragraph 19(7B) (inserted by paragraph 10(d) of Schedule 4 to these Regulations) does not apply.

[4058]

NOTES
Commencement: 1 April 2007 (certain purposes); 1 November 2007 (otherwise) (see reg 1(2)).

9   Transitional provision: appointed representatives and tied agents

(1)   A person—
(a)   to whom section 39(1A) or 39A(1) of the Act (both inserted by these Regulations) applies,
(b)   whose name appeared in the record maintained by the Authority under section 347(1)(i) of the Act immediately before 1st November 2007,

is deemed, with effect from 1st November 2007, to be included in the record maintained by the Authority under section 347(1)(ha) of the Act (inserted by paragraph 12 of Schedule 5 to these Regulations).

(2)   Paragraph (1) does not prevent the Authority from removing an entry from the record in accordance with section 347(3).

[4059]

NOTES

Commencement: 1 April 2007 (certain purposes); 1 November 2007 (otherwise) (see reg 1(2)).

[9A   Transitional provision: exempt investment firms

(1)   Except where paragraph (3) applies, an authorised person who immediately before 1st November 2007—
  (a)   is an investment firm within the meaning given in Article 4.1.1 of the markets in financial instruments directive,
  (b)   has his relevant office in the United Kingdom, and
  (c)   fulfils all the requirements set out in regulation 4C(3),
becomes an exempt investment firm with effect from that day as if he had applied as mentioned in regulation 4A(2) for a variation of his Part IV permission to permit him to carry on regulated activities as an exempt investment firm and the Authority had so varied the permission on that day.

(2)   In paragraph (1) "relevant office" has the meaning given in regulation 4A(5).

(3)   This paragraph applies—
  (a)   to an authorised person having a Part IV permission that, immediately before 1st November 2007—
    (i)   includes no requirement having the effect of prohibiting the person from holding clients' funds, or
    (ii)   permits the person, in connection with the carrying on of regulated activities comprising any investment services and activities (excluding activities to which, by virtue of Article 2, the markets in financial instruments directive does not apply), to carry on the activity consisting of both the safeguarding of assets belonging to another and the administration of those assets; and
  (b)   to an authorised person who, before 1st November 2007, gives the Authority notice, in such form as the Authority may direct, that he does not wish to become an exempt investment firm.

(4)   In paragraph (3)—
  (a)   "clients' funds", in sub-paragraph (a)(i), has the same meaning as in Article 3 of the markets in financial instruments directive, and
  (b)   sub-paragraph (a)(ii) is to be construed in accordance with section 22 of the Act, any relevant order made under that section and Schedule 2 to the Act.

(5)   The variation of a person's Part IV permission effected by paragraph (1) does not amount to the grant of an application for variation of a Part IV permission for the purpose of section 52(4) of the Act or to the determination of an application under Part IV for the purpose of section 55(1) of the Act.]

[4059A]

NOTES

Commencement: 1 April 2007 (certain purposes); 1 November 2007 (otherwise) (see further the note below).
Inserted by the Financial Services and Markets Act 2000 (Markets in Financial Instruments) (Amendment) Regulations 2007, SI 2007/763, reg 3, as from 1 April 2007 (certain purposes), and as from 1 November 2007 (otherwise) (see further the note below).
Note: reg 1(2) of the Financial Services and Markets Act 2000 (Markets in Financial Instruments) (Amendment) Regulations 2007, SI 2007/763 provides as follows—
  "(2)   These Regulations come into force—
    (a)   on 1st April 2007—
      (i)   for the purposes of enabling notices to be given in accordance with regulation 9A(3)(b) of the principal regulations (inserted by regulation 3) and enabling the Authority to give directions in accordance with that regulation as to the form of such notices,
      (ii)   for the purposes of enabling notice to be given under regulation 9B(2), 9C(2) or 9D(2) of the principal regulations (inserted by regulation 4),
      (iii) for the purposes of regulation 9; and
    (b)   for all other purposes, on 1st November 2007.".

[9B   Transitional provision: operators of alternative trading systems

(1)   Any person who immediately before 1st November 2007—
  (a)   had a Part IV permission to carry on an activity of the kind specified by article 14, 21 or 25 of the principal Order in relation to an investment of a particular kind; and
  (b)   operated an alternative trading system (within the meaning of the Alternative Trading Systems Instrument 2003 (2003/45) made by the Authority under the Act on 19th June 2003),

is, subject to regulation 9C, from 1st November 2007 to be treated as having a Part IV permission to carry on the kind of activity specified by article 25D of the principal Order (inserted by the 2006 Order) in relation to an investment of the same kind which is a financial instrument.

(2)   Where the person concerned gave written notice to the Authority on or before 1st October 2007 to that effect, paragraph (1) shall not apply to him.]

[4059B]

NOTES
Commencement: 1 April 2007 (certain purposes); 1 November 2007 (otherwise) (see further the note to reg 9A).
Inserted, together with regs 9C, 9D, by the Financial Services and Markets Act 2000 (Markets in Financial Instruments) (Amendment) Regulations 2007, SI 2007/763, reg 4, as from 1 April 2007 (certain purposes), and as from 1 November 2007 (otherwise) (see further the note to reg 9A at **[4059A]**).

[9C   Transitional provision for investment firms and credit institutions in relation to options, futures and contracts for differences

(1)   Any person who immediately before 1st November 2007—
  (a)   was an investment firm or a credit institution (in each case within the meaning of the principal Order as amended by the 2006 Order); and
  (b)   had a Part IV permission to carry on an activity of the kind specified by article 14, 21, 25, 37 or 53 of the principal Order in relation to an investment specified in the first column in the table in Schedule 8,

is from 1st November 2007 also to be treated as having a Part IV permission to carry on that kind of activity in relation to an investment specified in the second column of the table opposite that investment (in so far as he does not already have such permission).

(2)   Where the person concerned gave written notice to the Authority on or before 1st October 2007 to that effect, paragraph (1) shall not apply to him.]

[4059C]

NOTES
Commencement: 1 April 2007 (certain purposes); 1 November 2007 (otherwise) (see further the note to reg 9A).
Inserted as noted to reg 9B at **[4059B]**.

[9D   Transitional provision for management companies in relation to options, futures and contracts for differences

(1)   Any person who immediately before 1st November 2007—
  (a)   was a management company (within the meaning of the principal Order as amended by the 2006 Order);
  (b)   was providing, in accordance with Article 5.3 of Council Directive 85/611/EEC of 20 December 1985 on the coordination of laws, regulations and administrative provisions relating to undertakings for collective investment in transferable securities, the investment service specified in paragraph 4 or 5 of Section A, or the ancillary service specified in paragraph 1 of Section B, of Annex I to the markets in financial instruments directive; and
  (c)   had a Part IV permission to carry on an activity of the kind specified by article 14, 21, 25, 37, 40 or 53 of the principal Order in relation to an investment specified in the first column in the table in Schedule 8,

is from 1st November 2007 also to be treated as having a Part IV permission to carry on that kind of activity in relation to an investment specified in the second column of the table opposite that investment (in so far as he does not already have such permission).

(2)   Where the person concerned gave written notice to the Authority on or before 1st October 2007 to that effect, paragraph (1) shall not apply to him.]

[4059D]

NOTES
Commencement: 1 April 2007 (certain purposes); 1 November 2007 (otherwise) (see further the note to reg 9A).
Inserted as noted to reg 9B at **[4059B]**.

[9E   Transitional provision in relation to client classification

(1)   Any person who immediately before 1st November 2007 had a Part IV permission containing a limitation or requirement—
  (a)   in relation to the carrying on of any regulated activity except an activity mentioned in paragraph (2); and

(b)   described by reference to a category of clients specified in the first column in the table in Schedule 9,

is from 1st November 2007 to be treated as having a Part IV permission to carry on that regulated activity subject to the same limitation or requirement described by reference to the category of clients specified in the second column of that table opposite.

(2)   The activities are—

(a)   an insurance mediation activity (within the meaning of paragraph 2(5) of Schedule 6 to the Act) carried on in relation to a contract of insurance (within the meaning of article 3(1) of the principal Order) which is not a life policy (within the meaning of the Glossary (Conduct of Business and Other Sourcebooks) Instrument 2007 (2007/32) made by the Authority under the Act on 24th May 2007); and

(b)   activities of the kind specified in any of the following provisions of the principal Order—

    (i)   article 25A (arranging regulated mortgage contracts),

    (ii)   article 25B (arranging regulated home reversion plans),

    (iii)   article 25C (arranging regulated home purchase plans),

    (iv)   article 53A (advising on regulated mortgage contracts),

    (v)   article 53B (advising on regulated home reversion plans),

    (vi)   article 53C (advising on regulated home purchase plans),

    (vii)   article 61 (entering into and administering regulated mortgage contracts),

    (viii)   article 63B (entering into and administering regulated home reversion plans), and

    (ix)   article 63F (entering into and administering regulated home purchase plans).

(3)   Where the person concerned gave written notice to the Authority on or before 1st October 2007 to that effect, paragraph (1) shall not apply to him.]

[4059E]

NOTES

Commencement: 15 August 2007 (for the purposes of enabling notice to be given in accordance with para (3) above); 1 November 2007 (otherwise).

Inserted by the Financial Services and Markets Act 2000 (Markets in Financial Instruments) (Amendment No 2) Regulations 2007, SI 2007/2160, reg 2(1), (5), as from 15 August 2007 (for the purposes of enabling notice to be given in accordance with para (3) above), and as from 1 November 2007 (otherwise).

10   Interpretation of Part 3

In this Part—

["the principal Order" means the Financial Services and Markets Act 2000 (Regulated Activities) Order 2001;

"the 2006 Order" means the Financial Services and Markets Act 2000 (Regulated Activities) (Amendment No 3) Order 2006;]

"ancillary service" has the meaning given in Article 4.1.3 of the markets in financial instruments directive;

"EEA Passport Rights Regulations" means the Financial Services and Markets Act 2000 (EEA Passport Rights) Regulations 2001;

"EEA State" has the meaning given in paragraph 8 of Schedule 3;

"EEA market operator" has the meaning given in section 312D of the Act (inserted by these Regulations);

"financial instrument" has the meaning given in Article 4.1.17 of the markets in financial instruments directive;

"home state regulator" the meaning given in paragraph 9 of Schedule 3;

"instrument" (except in the expression "financial instrument") means any of the instruments listed in Section B of the Annex to the investment services directive;

"investment service" (except in the expression "investment services and activities") has the meaning given in Article 1.1 of the investment services directive;

"investment services and activities" has the meaning given in Article 4.1.2 of the markets in financial instruments directive;

"multilateral trading facility" has the meaning given in Article 4.1.15 of the markets in financial instruments directive;

"non-core service" means any of the services listed in Section C of the Annex to the investment services directive;

"recognised investment exchange" has the meaning given in section 285 of the Act;

.....

"regulated market" has the meaning given in Article 4.1.14 of the markets in financial instruments directive;

.....

"UK investment firm" means a UK firm (within the meaning of paragraph 10 of Schedule 3)—

(a)   which is an investment firm (within the meaning of the investment services directive); and

(b)   whose EEA right derives from that directive.

[4060]

NOTES
Commencement: 1 April 2007 (certain purposes); 1 November 2007 (otherwise) (see reg 1(2)).
Definitions "the principal Order" and "the 2006 Order" inserted, and definitions "regulated activity" and "Schedule 3" (omitted) revoked, by the Financial Services and Markets Act 2000 (Markets in Financial Instruments) (Amendment) Regulations 2007, SI 2007/763, regs 2(3), 5, as from 1 November 2007.

SCHEDULES

(Sch 1 inserts the Financial Services and Markets Act 2000, ss 194A, 195A at **[222A]**, **[223A]**, *and amends s 199 of that Act at* **[227]**; *Sch 2 amends ss 286, 287, 290, 296–298, 302, 303, 306, 307, 313 of the 2000 Act, and inserts ss 292A, 293A, 301A–301G, 312A–312D (all in Part XVIII of the 2000 Act at* **[311]** *et seq); Sch 3 inserts Part XVIIIA of the 2000 Act (ss 313A–313D) at* **[339A]** *et seq; Sch 4 amends Sch 3 to the 2000 Act at* **[467]** *et seq; Sch 5 (Other Amendments of the Act) contains various other amendments to the 2000 Act; Sch 6 (Consequential Amendments of other Enactments) amends the Companies Act 1985, ss 23, 162, 162E, 226, 227, 228, 228A (which are either already repealed, or are repealed as from 1 October 2009), the Financial Markets and Insolvency (Settlement Finality) Regulations 1999, SI 1999/2979 at* **[3553A]** *et seq, the Financial Services and Markets Act 2000 (Prescribed Markets and Qualifying Investments) Order 2001, SI 2001/996 at* **[2161]** *et seq, the Financial Services and Markets Act 2000 (Consultation with Competent Authorities) Regulations 2001, SI 2001/2509 at* **[2421]** *et seq, the Insurers (Reorganisation and Winding Up) Regulations 2004, SI 2004/353 at* **[3836]** *et seq, the Credit Institutions (Reorganisation and Winding up) Regulations 2004, SI 2004/1045 at* **[3889A]** *et seq, the Financial Conglomerates and Other Financial Groups Regulations 2004, SI 2004/1862 at* **[2723]** *et seq, and the Investment Recommendation (Media) Regulations 2005, SI 2005/382 at* **[3919]** *et seq, and contains various other amendments that are outside the scope of this work.)*

SCHEDULE 7
EXERCISE OF PASSPORT RIGHTS UNDER THE INVESTMENT SERVICES DIRECTIVE
[Regulations 6A and 7]

Table 1

Investment service in Section A of the Annex to the investment services directive	*Corresponding investment service or activity in Section A of Annex I to the markets in financial instruments directive*
1(a) (reception and transmission, on behalf of investors, of orders in relation to one or more of the instruments listed in Section B)	1 (reception and transmission of orders in relation to one or more financial instruments)
1(b) (execution of such orders other than for own account)	2 (execution of orders on behalf of clients)
2 (dealing in any of the instruments listed in Section B for own account)	3 (dealing on own account)
3 (managing portfolios of investments in accordance with mandates given by investors on a [discretionary], client-by-client basis where such portfolios include one or more of the instruments listed in Section B)	4 (portfolio management)
4 (underwriting in respect of issues of any of the instruments listed in Section B and/or the placing of such issues)	6 (underwriting of financial instruments and/or placing of financial instruments on a firm commitment basis) and 7 (placing of financial instruments without a firm commitment basis)

Table 2

Non-core service in Section C of the Annex to the investment services directive	Corresponding ancillary service in Section B of Annex I to the markets in financial instruments directive
1 (safekeeping and administration in relation to one or more of the instruments listed in Section B)	1 (safekeeping and administration of financial instruments for the account of clients, including custodianship and related services such as cash/collateral management)
2 (safe custody services)	1
3 (granting credits or loans to an investor to allow him to carry out a transaction in one or more of the instruments listed in Section B, where the firm granting the credit or loan is involved in the transaction)	2 (granting credits or loans to an investor to allow him to carry out a transaction in one or more financial instruments, where the firm granting the credit or loan is involved in the transaction)
4 (advice to undertakings on capital structure, industrial strategy and related matters and advice and service relating to mergers and the purchase of undertakings)	3 (advice to undertakings on capital structure, industrial strategy and related matters and advice and services relating to mergers and the purchase of undertakings)
5 (services related to underwriting)	6 (services related to underwriting)
7 (foreign-exchange services where these are connected with the provision of investment services)	4 (foreign exchange services where these are connected to the provision of investment services)

Table 3

Instrument in Section B of the Annex to the investment services directive	Corresponding financial instrument in Section C of Annex I to the markets in financial instruments directive
1(a) (transferable securities)	1 (transferable securities)
1(b) (units in collective investment undertakings)	3 (units in collective investment undertakings)
2 (money-market instruments)	2 (money-market instruments)
3 (financial-futures contracts, including equivalent cash-settled instruments)	4 (options, futures, swaps, forward rate agreements and any other derivative contracts relating to securities, currencies, interest rates or yields, or other derivative instruments, financial indices or financial measures which may be settled physically or in cash)
4 (forward interest-rate agreements)	4
5 (interest-rate, currency and equity swaps)	4
6 (options to acquire or dispose of any instruments falling within this section of the Annex, including equivalent cash-settled instruments. This category includes in particular options on currency and on interest rates)	4

[4061]

PART III
STATUTORY INSTRUMENTS

[SCHEDULE 8
TRANSITIONAL PROVISION FOR PART IV PERMISSIONS
Regulations 9C and 9D

Table

Investment in relation to which the person has Part IV permission immediately before 1st November 2007	*Additional investments to which the person's Part IV permission is extended from 1st November 2007*
Option (excluding commodity options and options on a commodity future) within the meaning of the General Provisions and Glossary Instrument 2001 (2001/7) made by the Authority under the Act on 21st June 2001("the 2001 Instrument") as amended by the Handbook Administration (No 3) Instrument 2006 (2006/21) made by the Authority under the Act on 22nd June 2006 and the CRD (Consequential Amendments) Instrument 2006 (2006/53) made by the Authority under the Act on 23rd November 2006	Those options within the meaning of the 2001 Instrument as last amended by the Glossary (MIFID) Instrument 2007 (2007/1) made by the Authority under the Act on 25th January 2007 ("the 2007 Instrument") which are options falling within paragraph 10 of Section C of Annex I to the markets in financial instruments directive ("Section C")
Commodity option within the meaning of the 2001 Instrument[1]	Those commodity options within the meaning of the 2001 Instrument as last amended by the 2007 Instrument which are options falling within paragraphs 4, 5, 6 and 7 of Section C
Option on a commodity future within the meaning of the 2001 Instrument	Those options on a commodity future within the meaning of the 2001 Instrument as last amended by the 2007 Instrument which are options falling within paragraphs 4, 5, 6 and 7 of Section C
Future (excluding commodity futures and rolling spot forex contracts[2]) within the meaning of the 2001 Instrument	Those futures[3] (excluding commodity futures and rolling spot forex contracts) which are futures falling within paragraph 10 of Section C
Commodity future within the meaning of the 2001 Instrument	Those commodity futures within the meaning of the 2001 Instrument as last amended by the 2007 Instrument which are futures falling within paragraphs 5, 6 and 7 of Section C
Contract for differences (excluding spread bets[4] and rolling spot forex contracts) within the meaning of the 2001 Instrument	Those contracts for differences (excluding spread bets and rolling spot forex contracts) within the meaning of the 2001 Instrument as last amended by the 2007 Instrument which are derivative instruments for the transfer of credit risk falling within paragraph 8 of Section C".

[1] "Commodity" is amended by the CRD (Consequential Amendments) Instrument 2006 and the Handbook Administration (No 4) Instrument 2006 (2006/64) made by the Authority under the Act on 21st December 2006.

[2] "Rolling spot forex contract" is defined in the 2001 Instrument.

[3] The definition of "future" in the 2001 Instrument is from 1st November 2007 affected by the amendment made to article 84 of the Financial Services and Markets Act 2000 (Regulated Activities) Order 2001 (SI 2001/544) by article 27 of the Financial Services and Markets Act 2000 (Regulated Activities) (Amendment No 3) Order 2006 (SI 2006/3384).

[4] "Spread bet" is defined in the 2001 Instrument.]

[4062]

NOTES
Commencement: 1 November 2007.
Added by the Financial Services and Markets Act 2000 (Markets in Financial Instruments) (Amendment) Regulations 2007, SI 2007/763, reg 6, as from 1 November 2007.

[SCHEDULE 9
TRANSITIONAL PROVISION IN RELATION TO CLIENT CLASSIFICATION
Regulation 9E

Category of clients in limitation or requirement in Part IV permission immediately before 1st November 2007	Category of clients in limitation or requirement in Part IV permission from 1st November 2007
Private customers only	Retail clients only
Intermediate customers only	Professional clients only
Private and intermediate customers only	Retail and professional clients only
Intermediate customers and market counterparties only	Professional clients and eligible counterparties only]

[4062A]

NOTES
Commencement: 1 November 2007.
Added by the Financial Services and Markets Act 2000 (Markets in Financial Instruments) (Amendment No 2) Regulations 2007, SI 2007/2160, reg 2(1), (7), as from 1 November 2007.

COMPENSATION (EXEMPTIONS) ORDER 2007 (NOTE)

(SI 2007/209)

NOTES
This Order was made on 30 January 2007 under the powers conferred by the Compensation Act 2006, s 6. It came into force on 31 January 2007.

Part 2 of the Compensation Act 2006 regulates claims management services. A person who provides "regulated claims management services" must be authorised under the 2006 Act to do so, or be exempted, or have the benefit of a waiver of the obligation to be authorised.

Under s 4 of the 2006 Act, a regulated claims management service is one declared to be regulated by Order made by the Secretary of State. The Compensation (Regulated Claims Management Services) Order 2006 (SI 2006/3319) declares certain kinds of services to be regulated when provided in connection with certain kinds of claim. The services include advertising for claimants, referral of claimants to legal practitioners, advice in relation to claims and investigation of claims – including claims relating to financial products and services.

Article 5 of this Order exempts persons who are carrying out a regulated claims management service that is an activity that is regulated by the FSA, have been exempted under FSMA 2000 or have the benefit of an exclusion under FSMA 2000. The exemption does not extend to persons who refer uninsured losses to a legal practitioner or authorised person.

Article 4 exempts legal practitioners (barristers, solicitors, advocates, legal executives and foreign lawyers) who are already regulated by their respective professional bodies from the obligation to be authorised. Articles 6–12 exempt various other persons that (i) do not provide regulated claims management services for profit (eg, charities and independent trade unions), (ii) do not provide services to the public generally (eg, the Motor Insurers' Bureau), or (iii) provide the service of referrals only as an adjunct to an unrelated business.

Art 13 (as added by SI 2007/1090) confers further exemption in circumstances where (a) a claim has been made by a person ("the claimant") against another person ("the defendant"); and (b) the service is provided to the defendant in connection with (i) the making of a counterclaim against the claimant (on the same facts) or (ii) the making of a claim against a third party (incidental to, or consequent on, the claim referred to in (a) above).

[4062B]

CONTROL OF CASH (PENALTIES) REGULATIONS 2007

(SI 2007/1509)

NOTES
Made: 22 May 2007.
Authority: European Communities Act 1972, s 2(2).
Commencement: 15 June 2007.
As of 1 February 2009, this Order had not been amended.

1 Citation and commencement

These Regulations may be cited as the Control of Cash (Penalties) Regulations 2007 and come into force on 15th June 2007.

[4063]

NOTES

Commencement: 15 June 2007.

2 Interpretation

In these Regulations -

"Community Regulation" means European Parliament and Council Regulation (EC) No 1889/2005 on controls of cash entering or leaving the Community;

"The Commissioners" means the Commissioners for Her Majesty's Revenue and Customs.

[4064]

NOTES

Commencement: 15 June 2007.

3 Power to impose penalties

(1)   The Commissioners may impose a penalty of such amount as they consider appropriate, not exceeding £5,000, on a person failing to comply with article 3 of the Community Regulation (obligation to declare cash of a value of 10,000 euros or more).

(2)   Where the Commissioners decide to impose a penalty under this regulation, they must forthwith inform the person, in writing, of—

(a)   their decision to impose the penalty and its amount;

(b)   their reasons for imposing the penalty;

(c)   the review procedure; and

(d)   the right to appeal to a tribunal.

(3)   Where a person is liable to a penalty under this regulation, the Commissioners may reduce the penalty to such amount (including nil) as they think proper.

[4065]

NOTES

Commencement: 15 June 2007.

4 Review procedure

(1)   Any person who is the subject of a decision to impose a penalty under regulation 3 may by notice in writing to the Commissioners require them to review that decision.

(2)   The Commissioners need not review any decision unless the notice requiring the review is given before the end of the period of 45 days beginning with the date on which written notification of the decision was first given to the person requiring the review.

(3)   A person may give a notice under this regulation to require a decision to be reviewed for a second or subsequent time only if—

(a)   the grounds on which he requires the further review are that the Commissioners did not, on any previous review, have the opportunity to consider certain facts or other matters; and

(b)   he does not, on the further review, require the Commissioners to consider any facts or matters which were considered on a previous review except insofar as they are relevant to any issue to which the facts or matters not previously considered relate.

(4)   Where the Commissioners are required under this regulation to review any decision they must either

(a)   confirm the decision; or

(b)   withdraw or vary the decision and take such further steps (if any) in consequence of the withdrawal or variation as they consider appropriate.

(5) Where the Commissioners do not, within 45 days beginning with the date on which the review was required by a person, give notice to that person of their determination of the review, they are to be assumed for the purposes of these Regulations to have confirmed the decision.

[4066]

NOTES
Commencement: 15 June 2007.

5 Appeals to a VAT and duties tribunal

An appeal lies to a VAT and duties tribunal with respect to a decision of the Commissioners on a review under regulation 4.

[4067]

NOTES
Commencement: 15 June 2007.

6 On an appeal under regulation 5, the tribunal has the power to—
    (a)   quash or vary any decision of the Commissioners, including the power to reduce any penalty to such amount (including nil) as it thinks proper; and
    (b)   substitute its own decision for any decision quashed on appeal.

[4068]

NOTES
Commencement: 15 June 2007.

7 An appeal shall not be entertained unless—
    (a)   the amount which the Commissioners have imposed by way of a penalty under regulation 2 has been paid to them; or
    (b)   on being satisfied that the appellant would otherwise suffer hardship the Commissioners agree or the tribunal decides that the appeal should be entertained notwithstanding that the amount has not been paid.

[4069]

NOTES
Commencement: 15 June 2007.

8 Retention of cash detained

Where the Commissioners have imposed a penalty under regulation 3 they may deduct from any cash detained pursuant to article 4(2) of the Community Regulation the amount of the penalty, and upon expiry of the period for appealing, or where an appeal has been made upon determination of the appeal, the amount payable shall be forfeit to them.

[4070]

NOTES
Commencement: 15 June 2007.

ELECTRONIC COMMERCE DIRECTIVE (TERRORISM ACT 2006) REGULATIONS 2007

(SI 2007/1550)

NOTES
Made: 23 May 2007.
Authority: European Communities Act 1972, s 2(2).
Commencement: 21 June 2007.

As of 1 February 2009, this Order had not been amended.

ARRANGEMENT OF REGULATIONS

PART III
STATUTORY INSTRUMENTS

1   Citation and commencement

These Regulations may be cited as the Electronic Commerce Directive (Terrorism Act 2006) Regulations 2007 and shall come into force on 21st June 2007.

[4071]

NOTES

Commencement: 21 June 2007.

2   Interpretation

(1)   In these Regulations—

"the Act" means the Terrorism Act 2006;

"article" has the meaning given in section 20(2) of the Act;

"the Directive" means Directive 2000/31/EC of the European Parliament and of the Council of 8th June 2000 on certain legal aspects of information society services, in particular electronic commerce, in the Internal Market (Directive on electronic commerce);

"information society services"—

    (a)   has the meaning given in Article 2(a) of the Directive (which refers to Article 1(2) of Directive 98/34/EC of the European Parliament and of the Council of 22nd June 1998 laying down a procedure for the provision of information in the field of technical standards and regulations); and

    (b)   is summarised in recital 17 of the Directive as covering "any service normally provided for remuneration, at a distance, by means of electronic equipment for the processing (including digital compression) and storage of data, and at the individual request of a recipient of a service";

"recipient of the service" means any person who, for professional ends or otherwise, uses an information society service, in particular for the purposes of seeking information or making it accessible;

"record" has the meaning given in section 20(2) of the Act;

"relevant offence" is an offence under section 1 or 2 of the Act;

"service provider" means a person providing an information society service;

"statement" is to be construed in accordance with section 20(6) of the Act.

(2)   For the purposes of these Regulations—

    (a)   a service provider is established in a particular EEA state if he effectively pursues an economic activity using a fixed establishment in that EEA state for an indefinite period and he is a national of an EEA state or a company or firm as mentioned in Article 48 of the EEC Treaty;

    (b)   the presence or use in a particular place of equipment or other technical means of providing an information society service does not, of itself, constitute the establishment of a service provider;

    (c)   where it cannot be determined from which of a number of establishments a given information society service is provided, that service is to be regarded as provided from the establishment where the service provider has the centre of his activities relating to the service,

and references to a person being established in any place must be construed accordingly.

[4072]

NOTES

Commencement: 21 June 2007.

3   Internal market: UK service providers

(1)   If—

    (a)   in the course of providing information society services, a service provider established in the United Kingdom does anything in an EEA state other than the United Kingdom, and

    (b)   his action, if done in a part of the United Kingdom, would constitute a relevant offence,

he shall be guilty in that part of the United Kingdom of the offence.

(2)   If paragraph (1) applies—

    (a)   proceedings for the offence may be taken at any place in the United Kingdom; and

    (b)   the offence may for all incidental purposes be treated as having been committed at any such place.

(3)   Paragraph (1) does not apply to a case to which section 17 of the Act applies.

(4)   If a person commits a relevant offence only by virtue of paragraph (1) he is liable—
   (a)   on conviction on indictment, to imprisonment for a term not exceeding two years;
   (b)   on summary conviction, to imprisonment for a term not exceeding the appropriate period or to a fine not exceeding the appropriate amount.

(5)   The appropriate period is—
   (a)   in the case of a conviction in England and Wales if the offence is committed after the commencement of section 154(1) of the Criminal Justice Act 2003, 12 months;
   (b)   in any other case, three months.

(6)   The appropriate amount is—
   (a)   if calculated on a daily basis, £100 per day;
   (b)   if not calculated on a daily basis, level 5 on the standard scale.

[4073]

NOTES
Commencement: 21 June 2007.

4   Internal market: non-UK service providers

(1)   Proceedings for a relevant offence shall not be instituted against a non-UK service provider unless the derogation condition is satisfied.

(2)   A notice under section 3(3) of the Act shall not be given to a non-UK service provider unless the derogation and cooperation conditions are satisfied.

(3)   The derogation condition is that the step mentioned in paragraph (1) or (2) (as the case may be)—
   (a)   is necessary to pursue any of the public interest objectives;
   (b)   relates to an information society service that prejudices that objective or presents a serious and grave risk of prejudice to it; and
   (c)   is proportionate to that objective.

(4)   The public interest objectives are—
   (a)   public policy, in particular the prevention, investigation, detection and prosecution of a relevant offence;
   (b)   public security, including the safeguarding of national security and defence.

(5)   The cooperation condition is that—
   (a)   a constable has requested the EEA state in which the service provider is established to take appropriate measures and the EEA state has failed to do so; and
   (b)   a constable has notified the Commission and the EEA state that it is proposed to take the step mentioned in paragraph (2).

(6)   The requirement in paragraph (2) to satisfy the cooperation condition does not apply if—
   (a)   it appears to a constable that the step mentioned in paragraph (2) should be taken as a matter of urgency; and
   (b)   in the shortest possible time after that step is taken, a constable notifies the Commission and the EEA state in which the service provider is established that the step has been taken, indicating the reason for the urgency.

(7)   Appropriate measures are measures which appear to the constable to have equivalent effect under the law of the EEA state to the giving of a notice under section 3(3) of the Act.

(8)   In this regulation—
   (a)   "the Commission" means the Commission of the European Communities;
   (b)   "non-UK service provider" means a service provider who is established in an EEA state other than the United Kingdom.

[4074]

NOTES
Commencement: 21 June 2007.

5   Exception for mere conduits

(1)   A service provider is not capable of being guilty of a relevant offence in respect of anything done in the course of providing so much of an information society service as consists in—
   (a)   the provision of access to a communication network; or
   (b)   the transmission in a communication network of information provided by a recipient of the service,
if the transmission condition is satisfied.

(2)   The transmission condition is that the service provider does not—
   (a)   initiate the transmission;
   (b)   select the recipient of the transmission; or

(c) select or modify the information contained in the transmission.

(3) Paragraph (1)(b) does not apply if the information is information to which regulation 6 applies.

(4) For the purposes of this regulation, the provision of access to a communication network and the transmission of information in the network includes the automatic, intermediate and transient storage of information for the purpose of carrying out the transmission in the network.

(5) Paragraph (4) does not apply if the information is stored for longer than is reasonably necessary for the transmission.

[4075]

NOTES

Commencement: 21 June 2007.

6 Exception for caching

(1) This regulation applies to information which—
- (a) is provided by a recipient of the service; and
- (b) is the subject of automatic, intermediate and temporary storage which is solely for the purpose of making the onward transmission of the information to other recipients of the service at their request more efficient.

(2) A service provider is not capable of being guilty of a relevant offence in respect of anything done in the course of providing so much of an information society service as consists in the transmission in a communication network of information to which this regulation applies if—
- (a) the service provider does not modify the information;
- (b) he complies with any conditions attached to having access to the information; and
- (c) in a case to which paragraph (3) applies, the service provider expeditiously removes the information or disables access to it.

(3) This paragraph applies if the service provider obtains actual knowledge that—
- (a) the information at the initial source of the transmission has been removed from the network;
- (b) access to such information has been disabled; or
- (c) a court or administrative authority has ordered the removal from the network of, or the disablement of access to, such information.

[4076]

NOTES

Commencement: 21 June 2007.

7 Exception for hosting

(1) A service provider is not capable of being guilty of a relevant offence in respect of anything done in the course of providing so much of an information society service as consists in the storage of information provided by a recipient of the service if—
- (a) the service provider did not know when the information was provided that it was unlawfully terrorism-related; or
- (b) upon obtaining actual knowledge that the information was unlawfully terrorism-related, the service provider expeditiously removed the information or disabled access to it.

(2) For the purposes of paragraph (1), information is unlawfully terrorism-related if it is constituted by a statement, or contained in an article or record, which is unlawfully terrorism-related by virtue of section 3(7) of the Act.

(3) Paragraph (1) does not apply if the recipient of the service is acting under the authority or control of the service provider.

[4077]

NOTES

Commencement: 21 June 2007.

REGULATION OF INVESTIGATORY POWERS (INVESTIGATION OF PROTECTED ELECTRONIC INFORMATION: CODE OF PRACTICE) ORDER 2007

(SI 2007/2200)

NOTES
Made: 26 July 2007.
Authority: Regulation of Investigatory Powers Act 2000, s 71(5).
Commencement: 1 October 2007.
As of 1 February 2009, this Order had not been amended.

1 This Order may be cited as the Regulation of Investigatory Powers (Investigation of Protected Electronic Information: Code of Practice) Order 2007 and shall come into force on 1st October 2007.

[4078]

NOTES
Commencement: 1 October 2007.

2 The code of practice entitled "Investigation of Protected Electronic Information", laid before each House of Parliament in draft on 7th June 2007, relating to the investigation of protected electronic information under Part 3 of the Regulation of Investigatory Powers Act 2000, shall come into force on 1st October 2007.

[4079]

NOTES
Commencement: 1 October 2007.
The full text of the Code of Practice is available on the Home Office website at:
http://security.homeoffice.gov.uk/ripa/publication-search/ripa-cop/electronic-information?view=Binary

ADMINISTRATIVE JUSTICE AND TRIBUNALS COUNCIL (LISTED TRIBUNALS) ORDER 2007 (NOTE)

(SI 2007/2951)

NOTES
This Order was made on 9 October 2007 under the powers conferred by the Tribunals, Courts and Enforcement Act 2007, Sch 7, para 25(2). It came into force on 1 November 2007.
The 2007 Act establishes the Administrative Justice and Tribunals Council (AJTC) to replace the Council on Tribunals and provides for the AJTC to keep under review, consider and report on matters relating to the listed tribunals. On the coming into force of the 2007 Act the only listed tribunals were the two new tribunals provided for in the 2007 Act, being the First-tier Tribunal and the Upper Tribunal.
This Order designates as listed tribunals additional entities which the AJTC will keep under review, consider and report on. This includes the Financial Services and Markets Tribunal established under FSMA 2000, s 32 (except for its functions in respect of Northern Ireland).

[4079A]

REGULATED COVERED BONDS REGULATIONS 2008

(SI 2008/346)

NOTES
Made: 13 February 2008.
Authority: European Communities Act 1972, s 2(2).
Commencement: 6 March 2008.
These Regulations are reproduced as amended by: the Regulated Covered Bonds (Amendment) Regulations 2008, SI 2008/1714.

ARRANGEMENT OF REGULATIONS

PART 1
INTRODUCTION

PART 2
THE AUTHORITY

PART 3
REGISTRATION

PART 4
ISSUERS

PART 5
OWNERS

PART 6
PRIORITY OF PAYMENT

PART 7
ENFORCEMENT

PART 8
THE TRIBUNAL

PART 9
MISCELLANEOUS

PART 1
INTRODUCTION

1 Citation, commencement and interpretation

(1) These Regulations may be cited as the Regulated Covered Bonds Regulations 2008 and come into force on 6th March 2008.

(2) In these Regulations—
"the 1986 Act" means the Insolvency Act 1986;
"the 2006 Act" means the Companies Act 2006;
"the 1989 Order" means the Insolvency (Northern Ireland) Order 1989;
"the Act" means the Financial Services and Markets Act 2000;
"asset" means any property, right, entitlement or interest;
"asset pool" has the meaning given by regulation 3;
"the Authority" means the Financial Services Authority;
"banking consolidation directive" means Directive 2006/48/EC of the European Parliament and of the Council of 14 June 2006 relating to the taking up and pursuit of the business of credit institutions;
["building society" means a building society incorporated (or deemed to be incorporated) under the Building Societies Act 1986;]
"centre of main interests" has the same meaning as in Article 3(1) of Council Regulation (EC) No 1346/2000 of 29 May 2000 on insolvency proceedings;
"connected person" has the meaning given by regulation 5;
"covered bond" means a bond in relation to which the claims attaching to that bond are guaranteed to be paid by an owner from an asset pool it owns;
"eligible property" has the meaning given by regulation 2;
"hedging agreement" means an agreement entered into or asset held as protection against possible financial loss;
"issuer" means a person which issues a covered bond;
"owner" has the meaning given by regulation 4;
"programme" means issues, or series of issues, of covered bonds which have substantially similar terms and are subject to a framework contract or contracts;
["registered office" in relation to a building society means its principal office;]
"register of issuers" means the register maintained under regulation 7(1)(a);
"register of regulated covered bonds" means the register maintained under regulation 7(1)(b);
"regulated covered bond" means a covered bond or a programme of covered bonds, as the case may be, which is admitted to the register of regulated covered bonds;
"relevant asset pool" in relation to a regulated covered bond means the asset pool from which the claims attaching to that bond are guaranteed to be paid by the owner of that pool in the event of the failure of the issuer;
"relevant persons" has the meaning given by regulation 27(2);
"the Tribunal" means the Financial Services and Markets Tribunal established under section 132 of the Act (the Financial Services and Markets Tribunal).

(3) Unless otherwise defined, any expression used in these Regulations and in Article 22(4) of directive 85/611/EEC of the Council of 20 December 1985 relating to undertakings for collective investment in transferable securities has the same meaning as in that Article of that Directive.

[4080]

NOTES

Commencement: 6 March 2008.
Para (2): definition building society" inserted, and definition "registered office" substituted, by the Regulated Covered Bonds (Amendment) Regulations 2008, SI 2008/1714, reg 2(1), (2), as from 22 July 2008.

2 Eligible property

(1) In these Regulations "eligible property" means any interest in—
    (a) eligible assets specified in and compliant with the requirements contained in paragraph 68 of Annex VI of the banking consolidation directive, provided that—
        (i) exposures to a body qualifying for credit quality step 2 on the credit quality assessment scale set out in that Annex shall not be eligible property; and
        (ii) senior units, issued by French Fonds Communs de Creances or by equivalent

securitisation entities governed by the laws of the United Kingdom or an EEA state, securitising residential real estate or commercial real estate exposures may only be assessed as eligible assets if—

    (aa) the residential real estate or commercial real estate exposures secured were originated or acquired by the issuer or a connected person; and

    (bb) the senior units have a credit assessment by a nominated external credit assessment institution which is the most favourable category of credit assessment made by that external credit assessment institution;

(b) loans to a registered social landlord or, in Northern Ireland, to a registered housing association where the loans are secured—

    (i) over housing accommodation; or

    (ii) by rental income from housing accommodation;

(c) loans to a person ("A") which provides loans directly to a registered social landlord or, in Northern Ireland, to a registered housing association, where the loans to A are secured directly or indirectly—

    (i) over housing accommodation; or

    (ii) by rental income from housing accommodation;

(d) loans to a project company of a project which is a public-private partnership project where the loans are secured by payments made by a public body with step-in rights;

(e) loans to a person ("B") which provides loans directly to a project company of a project which is a public-private partnership project where the loans to B are secured directly or indirectly by payments made by a public body with step-in rights.

(2) Eligible property (and any relevant security) must be situated in an EEA state, Switzerland, the United States of America, Japan, Canada, Australia, New Zealand, the Channel Islands or the Isle of Man.

(3) In this regulation—

"the 1996 Act" means the Housing Act 1996;

"the 2001 Act" means the Housing (Scotland) Act 2001;

"housing accommodation"—

    (a) in England and Wales, has the meaning given by section 63 of the 1996 Act (minor modifications: Part 1);

    (b) in Scotland, has the meaning given by section 111 of the 2001 Act (interpretation); and

    (c) in Northern Ireland, has the meaning given by Article 2 of the Housing (Northern Ireland) Order 1981;

"project company" has the meaning given by paragraph 4H of Schedule A1 to the 1986 Act or, in Northern Ireland, paragraph 12 of Schedule A1 to the 1989 Order;

"public body" means a body which exercises public functions;

"public-private partnership project" has the meaning given by paragraph 4I of Schedule A1 to the 1986 Act or, in Northern Ireland, paragraph 13 of Schedule A1 to the 1989 Order;

"registered housing association" means a body registered as a housing association under Chapter II of Part II of the Housing (Northern Ireland) Order 1992;

"registered social landlord"—

    (a) in England and Wales, means a body registered as a social landlord under Part 1 of the 1996 Act; and

    (b) in Scotland, means a body registered as a social landlord under Part 3 of the 2001 Act;

"step-in rights" has the meaning given by paragraph 4J of Schedule A1 to the 1986 Act or, in Northern Ireland, paragraph 14 of Schedule A1 to the 1989 Order.

(4) Unless otherwise defined, any expression used in this regulation and the banking consolidation directive has the same meaning as in that directive.

[4081]

NOTES

Commencement: 6 March 2008.

3 Asset Pool

(1) Subject to paragraph (2), in these Regulations an "asset pool" comprises the following assets—

    (a) sums derived from the issue of regulated covered bonds and lent to the owner in accordance with regulation 16;

    (b) eligible property which is acquired by the owner using sums lent to it in accordance with regulation 22;

    (c) eligible property transferred to the asset pool by the issuer or a connected person to enable the issuer or owner, as the case may be, to comply with—

        (i) the requirements specified in regulation 17(2);

    (ii)   a direction of the Authority under regulation 30; or

    (iii)   an order of the court under regulation 33;

(d)   eligible property transferred to the asset pool by the issuer or a connected person for the purpose of over collateralisation;

(e)   contracts relating to the asset pool or to a regulated covered bond;

(f)   eligible property acquired by the owner using sums derived from any of the assets referred to in sub-paragraph (b), (c), (d) or (e);

(g)   sums derived from any of the assets referred to in sub-paragraph (b), (c), (d), (e) or (f); and

(h)   sums lent by persons (other than the issuer) to the owner to enable it to comply with the requirements specified in regulation 24(1)(a).

(2)   Any of the assets referred to in sub-paragraphs (a) to (f) and (h) of paragraph (1) may only form part of an asset pool at any time if they are recorded at that time, pursuant to arrangements made in accordance with regulation 17, 23 or 24, as being in that pool.

(3)   In paragraph (1), "over collateralisation" means the provision of additional assets that assist the payment from the relevant asset pool of claims attaching to a regulated covered bond in the event of the failure of the issuer.

[4082]

NOTES

    Commencement: 6 March 2008.

4 Owner

In these Regulations "owner" means a person which—

(a)   owns an asset pool; and

(b)   issues a guarantee to pay from that asset pool claims attaching to a regulated covered bond in the event of a failure of the issuer of that bond.

[4083]

NOTES

    Commencement: 6 March 2008.

5 Connected person

(1)   In these Regulations "connected person" in relation to an issuer means a person which—

    (a)   is—

        (i)   a parent undertaking of the issuer;

        (ii)   a subsidiary undertaking of the issuer; or

        (iii)   a subsidiary undertaking of a parent undertaking of the issuer;

    (b)   has its registered office in the United Kingdom; and

    (c)   either—

        (i)   has its centre of main interests in the United Kingdom; or

        (ii)   is authorised under Part 4 of the Act (permission to carry on regulated activities) to carry on the regulated activity referred to in article 5 (accepting deposits) of the Financial Services and Markets Act 2000 (Regulated Activities) Order 2001.

(2)   In paragraph (1) "parent undertaking" and "subsidiary undertaking" have the meanings given by section 1162 of the 2006 Act (parent and subsidiary undertakings).

[4084]

NOTES

    Commencement: 6 March 2008.

PART 2
THE AUTHORITY

6 Functions of the Authority

(1)   The Authority is to have the functions conferred on it by these Regulations.

(2)   The Authority's general functions are—

    (a)   its functions in relation to the giving of guidance under regulation 42; and

    (b)   its function of determining the general policy and principles by reference to which it performs particular functions under these Regulations.

(3)   In discharging its general functions the Authority must have regard to—

    (a)   the need to preserve investor confidence in, and the desirability of maintaining the good reputation of, the regulated covered bonds sector in the United Kingdom by the issuance of high quality regulated covered bonds;

(b)   the international character of financial services and markets and the desirability of maintaining the competitive position of the United Kingdom;

(c)   the need to use its resources in the most efficient and economic way;

(d)   the principle that a burden or restriction which is imposed on a person, or on the carrying on of an activity, should be proportionate to the benefits, considered in general terms, which are expected to result from the imposition of that burden or restriction;

(e)   the need to minimise the adverse effects on competition that may arise from anything done in the discharge of those functions;

(f)   the desirability of facilitating competition in relation to regulated covered bonds.

[4085]

NOTES
Commencement: 6 March 2008.

PART 3
REGISTRATION

7   Registers

(1)   The Authority must maintain—

(a)   a register of issuers; and

(b)   a register of regulated covered bonds.

(2)   The Authority must publish the registers in such manner and at such times as it may determine.

[4086]

NOTES
Commencement: 6 March 2008.

8   Applications for registration

A person who proposes to issue a covered bond or a programme of covered bonds may apply to the Authority, in such manner as the Authority may direct—

(a)   for admission to the register of issuers; or

(b)   for the covered bond or the programme of covered bonds to be admitted to the register of regulated covered bonds.

[4087]

NOTES
Commencement: 6 March 2008.

9   Applications for admission to the register of issuers

Subject to regulation 11, the Authority must grant an application under regulation 8(a) if it is satisfied that the applicant—

(a)   has its registered office in the United Kingdom;

(b)   is authorised under Part 4 of the Act (permission to carry on regulated activities) to carry on the regulated activity referred to in article 5 (accepting deposits) of the Financial Services and Markets Act 2000 (Regulated Activities) Order 2001;

(c)   will comply with the requirements imposed upon issuers by or under these Regulations; and

(d)   complies with any other requirements imposed by the Authority in relation to the application.

[4088]

NOTES
Commencement: 6 March 2008.

10   Applications for admission to the register of regulated covered bonds

(1)   The Authority may not entertain an application under regulation 8(b) in respect of a covered bond or programme of covered bonds unless it knows—

(a)   the identity of the owner of the relevant asset pool;

(b)   the assets intended to be included in that asset pool; and

(c)   the arrangements to be made under regulation 17.

(2)   The Authority may grant an application under regulation 8(b) if it is satisfied that—

(a)   the applicant is an issuer which is admitted to the register of issuers;

(b)   the applicant and the owner of the relevant asset pool will comply with the requirements imposed upon them by or under these Regulations; and

(c)   the applicant complies with any other requirements imposed by the Authority in relation to the application.

[4089]

11   Refusal of applications for registration

An application under regulation 8 may be refused if, for any reason relating to—
(a)   in the case of an application under regulation 8(a), the applicant; or
(b)   in the case of an application under regulation 8(b), the issuer, the owner of the relevant asset pool or the quality of that asset pool,
the Authority considers that granting it would be detrimental to the interests of investors in regulated covered bonds or to the maintenance of the good reputation of the regulated covered bond sector in the United Kingdom.

[4090]

12   Applications: supplementary

(1)   The applicant must provide any information which the Authority requires in connection with an application under regulation 8 in such form, and verified in such manner, as the Authority may direct.

(2)   At any time after receiving an application under regulation 8 and before determining it, the Authority may require the applicant to provide such further information as it reasonably considers necessary to enable it to determine the application.

(3)   Different directions may be given, or requirements imposed, by the Authority with respect to different applications or categories of application.

[4091]

13   Decision on the application

(1)   The Authority must notify the applicant of its decision on an application under regulation 8—
(a)   before the end of the period of six months beginning with the date on which the application is received; or
(b)   if within that period the Authority has required the applicant to provide further information in connection with the application, before the end of the period of six months beginning with the date on which that information is provided.

(2)   The applicant may withdraw its application by giving the Authority written notice at any time before the Authority determines it.

(3)   If the Authority decides to grant an application under regulation 8, it must give the applicant written notice of its decision.

(4)   If the Authority proposes to refuse an application under regulation 8, it must give the applicant a warning notice.

(5)   The Authority must, having considered any representations made in response to the warning notice—
(a)   if it decides to refuse the application under regulation 8, give the applicant a decision notice; or
(b)   if it grants the application, give the applicant written notice of its decision.

(6)   If the Authority decides to refuse an application under regulation 8, the applicant may refer the matter to the Tribunal.

[4092]

14   Admission to the registers

(1)   If the Authority decides to grant an application under regulation 8 it must, within seven days of the date on which it gave written notice under regulation 13(3) or (5)(b), admit—

(a) the applicant to the register of issuers; or

(b) the covered bond or the programme of covered bonds to the register of regulated covered bonds.

(2) The Authority may remove a regulated covered bond from the register of regulated covered bonds only after the expiry of the whole period of validity of that bond.

[4093]

NOTES

Commencement: 6 March 2008.

PART 4
ISSUERS

15 Acting without registration

(1) A person may not issue, or purport to issue, a regulated covered bond unless—

(a) it is admitted to the register of issuers; and

(b) the bond is admitted to the register of regulated covered bonds.

(2) A person which has been removed from the register of issuers may not make any further issue under a programme of covered bonds which has been admitted to the register of regulated covered bonds.

(3) Contravention of the prohibition in paragraph (1) or (2) by a person is a contravention of a requirement imposed on it by these Regulations, but does not—

(a) make any transaction void or unenforceable; or

(b) give rise to any right of action for breach of statutory duty.

[4094]

NOTES

Commencement: 6 March 2008.

16 Sums derived from the issue of regulated covered bonds

An issuer must lend sums derived from the issue of a regulated covered bond to the owner of the relevant asset pool.

[4095]

NOTES

Commencement: 6 March 2008.

17 General requirements

(1) An issuer of a regulated covered bond must enter into arrangements with the owner of the relevant asset pool for the maintenance and administration of that pool.

(2) The arrangements must provide for the following requirements—

(a) a record is kept of each asset in the asset pool;

(b) the asset pool is, during the whole period of validity of the regulated covered bond, capable of covering—

(i) claims attaching to the bond; and

(ii) sums required for the maintenance, administration and winding up of the asset pool;

(c) there is timely payment of claims attaching to the bond to the regulated covered bond holder; and

(d) the asset pool is of sufficient quality to give investors confidence that in the event of the failure of the issuer there will be a low risk of default in the timely payment by the owner of claims attaching to the bond.

(3) This regulation does not apply in the event of the insolvency of the issuer.

[4096]

NOTES

Commencement: 6 March 2008.

18 Notification requirements

(1) An issuer must give the Authority such information in respect of—

(a) any regulated covered bond it issues;

(b) any series of covered bonds issued or proposed to be issued under a regulated covered bond;

(c) the assets in the relevant asset pool;

(d)   the steps it has taken to comply with regulation 16 or 17;

as the Authority may direct.

(2)   The issuer of a regulated covered bond must inform the Authority if at any time any of the requirements specified in regulation 17(2) are not, or are not likely to be, satisfied in respect of the relevant asset pool.

(3)   The information required under paragraphs (1) and (2) must be given at such times, in such form and verified in such manner, as the Authority may direct.

[4097]

NOTES

Commencement: 6 March 2008.

19 Change of issuer

(1)   An issuer of a regulated covered bond may transfer the benefits and obligations accruing to or falling upon it under all contracts relating to the relevant asset pool to another person only if that person has been admitted to the register of issuers.

(2)   Where a transfer takes place in accordance with paragraph (1), that person shall be an issuer of that regulated covered bond for the purposes of these Regulations.

[4098]

NOTES

Commencement: 6 March 2008.

20 Material changes to the regulated covered bond

(1)   Where an issuer of a regulated covered bond proposes to make a material change to the contractual terms of the bond, it must give the Authority such—
    (a)   notice of the proposed change; and
    (b)   information in respect of the proposed change;
as the Authority may direct.

(2)   The information required under paragraph (1) must be given at such time, in such form and verified in such manner, as the Authority may direct.

(3)   If it appears to the Authority that the proposed change will not prevent the issuer and owner of the relevant asset pool from continuing to comply with the requirements imposed on them by or under these Regulations, it must give the issuer written notice of its decision to approve the change before the end of a period of 3 months beginning with the date on which the information required under paragraph (1) is provided.

(4)   If it appears to the Authority that the proposed change may prevent the issuer or the owner of the relevant asset pool from complying with the requirements imposed upon them by or under these Regulations, it may decide not to approve the change and give the issuer a decision notice.

(5)   If the Authority proposes to give a decision notice under paragraph (4), it must give the issuer a warning notice before the end of a period of 3 months beginning with the date on which the information required under paragraph (1) is provided.

(6)   The Authority must, having considered any representations made in response to the warning notice—
    (a)   if it decides to do so, give a decision notice under paragraph (4); or
    (b)   if it decides not to give a decision notice, give the issuer a notice of discontinuance and written notice of its decision to approve the change.

(7)   If the Authority gives a decision notice under paragraph (4), the issuer may refer the matter to the Tribunal.

(8)   The issuer may not make the proposed change before it has received a written notice from the Authority approving the change.

[4099]

NOTES

Commencement: 6 March 2008.

PART 5
OWNERS

21 Prohibition

(1)   A person may not be an owner unless it—
    (a)   is a company or limited liability partnership; and

(b)   has its registered office and centre of main interests in the United Kingdom.

(2)   Regulation 15(3) applies to a contravention of the prohibition in paragraph (1) as it applies to a contravention of the prohibition in regulation 15(1) or (2).

[(3)   In paragraph (1)—

"company" has the meaning given by section 735 of the Companies Act 1985 ("company" etc) and article 3 of the Companies (Northern Ireland) Order 1986 ("company" etc) until the coming into force of section 1 of the 2006 Act (companies) when it will have the meaning given by that section;

"limited liability partnership" has the meaning given—

    (a)   in relation to Great Britain, by section 1 of the Limited Liability Partnerships Act 2000 (limited liability partnerships); and

    (b)   in relation to Northern Ireland, by section 1 of the Limited Liability Partnerships Act (Northern Ireland) 2002 (limited liability partnerships) until the coming into force of section 1286 of the 2006 Act (extension of GB enactments relating to certain other forms of business organisation), when it will have the meaning given by section 1 of the Limited Liability Partnerships Act 2000.]

[4100]

NOTES

Commencement: 6 March 2008.

Para (3): substituted by the Regulated Covered Bonds (Amendment) Regulations 2008, SI 2008/1714, reg 2(1), (3), as from 22 July 2008.

[22   Sums derived from the issue of regulated covered bonds

The owner of the relevant asset pool must, so far as necessary for the purpose of complying with arrangements made pursuant to regulation 23 or 24(1)(a), use the sums lent to it by the issuer of a regulated covered bond to acquire eligible property.]

[4101]

NOTES

Commencement: 22 July 2008.

Substituted by the Regulated Covered Bonds (Amendment) Regulations 2008, SI 2008/1714, reg 2(1), (4), as from 22 July 2008.

Requirements relating to the asset pool

23—(1)   The owner of the relevant asset pool must enter into arrangements with the issuer of a regulated covered bond for the maintenance and administration of the asset pool.

(2)   The arrangements must provide for the requirements specified in regulation 17(2).

[4102]

NOTES

Commencement: 6 March 2008.

24—(1)   On the insolvency of the issuer of a regulated covered bond, the owner of the relevant asset pool must—

    (a)   make arrangements for the maintenance and administration of the asset pool which provide for the following requirements—

        (i)   a record is kept of each asset in the asset pool;

        (ii)   the asset pool is capable of covering—

            (aa)   claims attaching to the bond; and

            (bb)   sums required for the maintenance, administration and winding up of the asset pool;

        (iii)   there is timely payment of claims attaching to the bond to the regulated covered bond holder;

    (b)   give the Authority such information in respect of—

        (i)   the composition of the asset pool; and

        (ii)   the steps it has taken to comply with sub-paragraph (a);

as the Authority may direct; and

    (c)   inform the Authority if at any time any of the requirements set out in sub-paragraph (a)(ii) or (iii) are not, or are not likely to be, satisfied.

(2)   The information required under paragraph (1)(b) and (c) must be given at such times, in such form and verified in such manner, as the Authority may direct.

[4103]

25 Change of owner

(1)   Where a regulated covered bond has been issued and the owner of the relevant asset pool proposes to transfer ownership of the asset pool and the benefits and obligations accruing to or falling upon it under all contracts relating to the asset pool to another person, it must make arrangements to give the Authority such—

    (a)   notice of the proposed change of ownership; and

    (b)   information in respect of the proposed new owner;

as the Authority may direct.

(2)   The information required under paragraph (1) must be given at such time, in such form and verified in such manner, as the Authority may direct.

(3)   If it appears to the Authority that the proposed owner will comply with the requirements imposed by arrangements made pursuant to regulation 23 or, as the case may be, 24(1)(a) it must give the owner written notice of its decision to approve the change before the end of a period of 3 months beginning with the date on which the information required under paragraph (1) is provided.

(4)   If it appears to the Authority that the proposed owner will be unable to comply with any of those requirements it may decide not to approve the change and give the owner a decision notice.

(5)   If the Authority proposes to give a decision notice under paragraph (4), it must give the owner a warning notice before the end of a period of 3 months beginning with the date on which the information required under paragraph (1) is provided.

(6)   The Authority must, having considered any representations made in response to the warning notice—

    (a)   if it decides to do so, give a decision notice under paragraph (4); or

    (b)   if it decides not to give a decision notice, give the owner a notice of discontinuance and written notice of its decision to approve the change.

(7)   If the Authority gives a decision notice under paragraph (4), the owner may refer the matter to the Tribunal.

(8)   The owner may not transfer the asset pool to a proposed new owner before it has received a written notice from the Authority approving the change.

[4104]

26 Transfer of title

Where an issuer of a regulated covered bond or a connected person holds any interest in an asset in the relevant asset pool on behalf of the owner, a liquidator or administrator appointed to wind up that issuer or connected person must, as soon as reasonably practicable, transfer or assist in the transfer of that interest to the owner.

[4105]

PART 6
PRIORITY OF PAYMENT

27 Priority in a winding up

(1)   Subject to—

    (a)   section 115 of the 1986 Act (expenses of voluntary winding up) or, in Northern Ireland, article 100 of the 1989 Order (expenses of voluntary winding up); and

    (b)   the priority of the expenses of the winding up in a compulsory liquidation;

where an owner is wound up, the claims of relevant persons shall be paid from the relevant asset pool in priority to all other creditors.

(2)   "Relevant persons" are—

    (a)   regulated covered bond holders;

    (b)   persons providing services for the benefit of those bond holders;

    (c)   the counter-parties to hedging instruments which are incidental to the maintenance and administration of the asset pool or to the terms of the regulated covered bond; and

    (d)   persons (other than the issuer) providing a loan to the owner to enable it to satisfy the claims of the persons mentioned in sub-paragraph (a), (b) or (c).

(3)   The claims of the persons mentioned in paragraph (2)(b), (c) and (d) may rank equally with, but not in priority to, the claims of the persons mentioned in paragraph (2)(a).

[4106]

NOTES
Commencement: 6 March 2008.

28 Realisation of a charge

(1)   Subject to regulation 29, if—
    (a)   any asset comprised in the asset pool is charged as security for claims in priority to any charge over that asset granted to secure the claims of relevant persons; and
    (b)   the charge which has priority is realised at any time when the owner is not in the course of being wound up;
the proceeds of the realisation of that charge must, after payment of the expenses referred to in regulation 29 and any other expenses relating to that charge, be first applied to satisfy the claims of relevant persons at such time as those claims fall due for payment.

(2)   Subject to regulation 29, if—
    (a)   any asset comprised in the asset pool is charged as security for several claims;
    (b)   any agreement between the creditors of that charge gives priority to the claims of any person above the claims of the relevant persons; and
    (c)   that charge is realised at any time when the owner is not in the course of being wound up;
the proceeds of the realisation of that charge must, after payment of the expenses referred to in regulation 29 and any other expenses relating to that charge, be first applied to satisfy the claims of the relevant persons at such time as those claims fall due for payment.

[(3)   For the purposes of paragraphs (1) and (2) the claims of the persons mentioned in regulation 27(2)(b), (c) and (d) may rank equally with, but not in priority to, the claims of the persons mentioned in regulation 27(2)(a).]

[4107]

NOTES
Commencement: 6 March 2008.
Para (3): added by the Regulated Covered Bonds (Amendment) Regulations 2008, SI 2008/1714, reg 2(1), (5), as from 22 July 2008.

[29 Expenses

(1)   Disbursements made by a liquidator, provisional liquidator, administrator, administrative receiver, receiver or manager of the owner in respect of costs which—
    (a)   are incurred after the commencement of any winding up, administration, administrative receivership or receivership; and
    (b)   relate to any of the persons mentioned in paragraph (2);
shall be expenses of the winding up, administration, administrative receivership or receivership, as the case may be, and shall rank equally among themselves in priority to all other expenses.

(2)   The persons referred to in paragraph (1)(b) are—
    (a)   persons providing services for the benefit of regulated covered bond holders;
    (b)   the counter-parties to hedging instruments which are incidental to the maintenance and administration of the asset pool or to the terms of the regulated covered bonds; and
    (c)   persons (other than the issuer) providing a loan to the owner to enable it to meet the claims of regulated covered bond holders or pay costs which relate to persons falling within sub-paragraph (a) or (b).]

[4108]

NOTES
Commencement: 22 July 2008.
Substituted by the Regulated Covered Bonds (Amendment) Regulations 2008, SI 2008/1714, reg 2(1), (6), as from 22 July 2008.

PART 7
ENFORCEMENT

30 Authority's power to give directions

(1)   If it appears to the Authority that a person has failed, or is likely to fail, to comply with any requirement imposed on it by or under these Regulations, the Authority may direct that person to take specified steps for the purpose of securing its compliance with any such requirement.

(2)   If it appears to the Authority that an owner has failed, or is likely to fail, to comply with any requirement imposed on it by or under these Regulations, the Authority may direct the winding up of that person.

(3)   A direction under this regulation is enforceable, on the application of the Authority, by an injunction or, in Scotland, by an order for specific performance under section 45 of the Court of Session Act 1988(restoration of possession and specific performance).

[4109]

NOTES
Commencement: 6 March 2008.

31 Removal from the register

(1)   The Authority may remove an issuer from the register of issuers—
   (a)   at the issuer's request;
   (b)   with its consent; or
   (c)   if it appears to the Authority that the issuer is failing, or has failed, to comply with any requirement imposed on it by or under these Regulations.

(2)   But these Regulations (apart from regulation 15(2)) apply to a person which has been removed from the register of issuers as if it were still a person which is admitted to the register.

[4110]

NOTES
Commencement: 6 March 2008.

32 Directions and revocation: procedure

(1)   Before—
   (a)   giving a direction under regulation 30; or
   (b)   removing an issuer from the register of issuers under regulation 31(1)(c),
the Authority must give a warning notice to the person concerned.

(2)   If, having considered any representations, the Authority decides to—
   (a)   make the direction; or
   (b)   remove the issuer from the register of issuers,
the Authority must give that person a decision notice.

(3)   If the Authority decides not to—
   (a)   make a direction; or
   (b)   remove the issuer from the register of issuers,
it must give that person written notice of its decision.

(4)   If the Authority decides to—
   (a)   make a direction; or
   (b)   remove the issuer from the register of issuers,
the person concerned may refer the matter to the Tribunal.

[4111]

NOTES
Commencement: 6 March 2008.

33 Powers of the court

(1)   If, on the application of the Authority, the court is satisfied that—
   (a)   there is a reasonable likelihood that a person will contravene a requirement imposed on it by or under these Regulations; or
   (b)   a person has contravened any such requirement and there is a reasonable likelihood that the contravention will continue or be repeated,
the court may make an order restraining (or in Scotland an interdict prohibiting) the contravention.

(2)   If, on the application of the Authority, the court is satisfied that—
   (a)   a person has contravened a requirement imposed on it by or under these Regulations; and

(b)   there are steps which could be taken for remedying the contravention;

the court may make an order requiring that person, and any other person who appears to have been knowingly concerned in the contravention, to take such steps as the court may direct to remedy it.

(3)   The jurisdiction conferred by this regulation is exercisable by the High Court, the Court of Session and the Northern Ireland High Court.

(4)   In paragraph (2), references to remedying a contravention include references to mitigating its effect.

[4112]

NOTES

Commencement: 6 March 2008.

Financial penalties

34—(1)   The Authority may impose a penalty of such amount as it considers appropriate on a person which has contravened a requirement imposed on it by or under these Regulations.

(2)   A penalty imposed under this regulation is payable to the Authority.

(3)   The Authority may not take action against a person under this regulation after the end of the period of two years beginning with the first day on which it knew of the contravention unless proceedings against that person, in respect of the contravention, were begun before the end of that period.

(4)   For the purposes of paragraph (3)—
   (a)   the Authority is to be treated as knowing of a contravention if it has information from which the contravention can reasonably be inferred; and
   (b)   proceedings against a person in respect of a contravention are to be treated as begun when a warning notice is given to it under regulation 35.

[4113]

NOTES

Commencement: 6 March 2008.

35—(1)   Where the Authority proposes to impose a penalty under regulation 34, it must give the person concerned a warning notice.

(2)   The warning notice must state the amount of the proposed penalty and the Authority's reasons for imposing it.

(3)   If, having considered any representations made in response to the warning notice, the Authority decides to impose a penalty under regulation 34, it must without delay give the person concerned a decision notice.

(4)   The decision notice must state the amount of the penalty.

(5)   If the Authority decides to impose a penalty on a person under regulation 34, that person may refer the matter to the Tribunal.

[4114]

NOTES

Commencement: 6 March 2008.

36   Sections 210 (statements of policy) and 211 (statements of policy: procedure) of the Act are to apply in respect of the imposition of penalties under these Regulations and the amount of such penalties as they apply in respect of the imposition of penalties under Part 14 of the Act (disciplinary measures) and the amount of penalties under that Part of that Act.

[4115]

NOTES

Commencement: 6 March 2008.

37   Paragraph 16 (penalties) of Schedule 1 to the Act is to apply for the purposes of these Regulations as it applies for the purposes of the Act but with the following modifications—
   (a)   in sub-paragraph (1) for "this Act" substitute "the Regulated Covered Bonds Regulations 2008";

(b)   in sub-paragraph (2) for "authorised persons" substitute "issuers (within the meaning given by regulation 1(2) of the Regulated Covered Bond Regulations 2008)";
(c)   omit sub-paragraphs (3) and (13).

[4116]

NOTES
Commencement: 6 March 2008.

38   Offence of misleading the Authority

(1)   Subsections (1) and (3) of section 398 (misleading the Authority: residual cases) of the Act are to apply in respect of requirements imposed by or under these Regulations as they apply in respect of requirements imposed by or under the Act.

(2)   Section 400 (offences by bodies corporate etc) and subsections (2), (3), (5) and (6) of section 401 (proceedings for offences) of the Act are to apply for the purposes of paragraph (1) as they apply for the purposes of the Act.

[4117]

NOTES
Commencement: 6 March 2008.

PART 8
THE TRIBUNAL

39   Functions of the Tribunal

The Tribunal is to have the functions conferred on it by these Regulations.

[4118]

NOTES
Commencement: 6 March 2008.

40   Hearings and appeals

Part 9 of the Act (hearings and appeals) is to apply for the purposes of these Regulations as it applies for the purposes of the Act.

[4119]

NOTES
Commencement: 6 March 2008.

PART 9
MISCELLANEOUS

41   Notification of the Commission

The Authority must, in such manner and at such times as it may determine, notify the European Commission of—
(a)   issuers included in the register of issuers;
(b)   regulated covered bonds included in the register of regulated covered bonds; and
(c)   the status of the guarantees offered in respect of such bonds.

[4120]

NOTES
Commencement: 6 March 2008.

42   Guidance

(1)   The Authority may give guidance consisting of such information and advice as it considers appropriate—
(a)   with respect to the operation of these Regulations;
(b)   with respect to any matters relating to functions of the Authority under these Regulations;
(c)   with respect to any other matters about which it appears to the Authority to be desirable to give information or advice.

(2)   The Authority must give guidance consisting of information and advice about the quality of an asset pool for the purposes of the requirement specified in regulation 17(2)(d) and the manner in which it will assess the issuer's and owner's compliance with that requirement.

PART III
STATUTORY INSTRUMENTS

(3) Guidance given under paragraph (2) must include information and advice on the factors which the Authority will take into account, such as—

(a) fluctuations in the value of assets and the income from assets;

(b) fluctuations in the value of interest and exchange rates;

(c) geographical concentration and diversification of assets in the asset pool;

(d) the risk of loss if a person fails to perform its obligations, or fails to perform them in a timely manner; and

(e) counterparty credit risk, in particular, in relation to any interest rate, currency or other hedging instruments relating to the asset pool.

(4) Subject to paragraph (5), if the Authority proposes to give guidance under this regulation to issuers or owners generally, or to a class of issuer or owner, subsections (1), (2)(d) and (4) of section 155 of the Act (consultation) apply to the proposed guidance as they apply to proposed rules made under the Act, unless the Authority considers that the delay in complying with them would be prejudicial to the interests of regulated covered bond holders.

(5) Paragraph (4) shall not apply to the first guidance given pursuant to paragraph (2).

(6) The Authority may—

(a) publish its guidance;

(b) offer copies of its published guidance for sale at a reasonable price; and

(c) if it gives guidance in response to a request made by any person, make a reasonable charge for that guidance.

[4121]

NOTES

Commencement: 6 March 2008.

43 Disclosure of information

(1) Sections 348 (restrictions on disclosure of confidential information by Authority), 349 (exceptions from section 348) and 352 (offences) of the Act apply to confidential information disclosed under these Regulations as they apply to confidential information under the Act.

(2) In paragraph (1) "confidential information" has the meaning given by section 348 of the Act.

[4122]

NOTES

Commencement: 6 March 2008.

44 Warning notices and decision notices

Part 26 of the Act (notices) is to apply for the purposes of these Regulations as it applies for the purposes of the Act.

[4123]

NOTES

Commencement: 6 March 2008.

45 Authority's exemption from liability in damages

The functions of the Authority under these Regulations are to be treated for the purposes of paragraph 19 (exemption from liability in damages) of Part 4 of Schedule 1 to the Act as functions conferred on the Authority under that Act.

[4124]

NOTES

Commencement: 6 March 2008.

46 Modifications of primary and secondary legislation

The Schedule (which modifies primary and secondary legislation) has effect.

[4125]

NOTES

Commencement: 6 March 2008.

SCHEDULE
MODIFICATIONS TO PRIMARY AND SECONDARY LEGISLATION
Regulation 46

PART 1
PRIMARY LEGISLATION

Modification of the Companies Act 1985

1.   Section 196 (payment of debts out of assets subject to floating charge (England and Wales)) of the Companies Act 1985 shall not apply to an owner.

Modifications of the 1986 Act

2.—(1)   Sections 40 (payment of debts out of assets subject to floating charge) and 43 (power to dispose of charged property) of the 1986 Act shall not apply to an owner.

(2)   Section 107 of the 1986 Act (distribution of company's property) shall apply only after payment has been made of the claims of relevant persons.

(3)   Section 156 of the 1986 Act (payment of expenses of winding up) shall apply only after payment has been made of the expenses referred to in regulation 29.

(4)   Section 175 (preferential debts (general provision)) and 176A (share of assets for unsecured creditors) of the 1986 Act shall not apply to an owner.

(5)   Paragraphs 65(1) and 66 of Schedule B1 (distributions) to the 1986 Act shall apply only after payment has been made of the claims of relevant persons.

Modifications of the Act

3.   Section 165 (Authority's power to require information) of the Act is to apply for the purposes of these Regulations as it applies for the purposes of the Act but with the modification that for references to "an authorised person" there is substituted references to "a person to whom the Regulated Covered Bonds Regulations 2008 apply".

4.   Section 166 (reports by skilled persons) of the Act is to apply for the purposes of these Regulations as it applies for the purposes of the Act but with the modification that for the reference in subsection (2)(a) to "an authorised person" there is substituted a reference to "a person to whom the Regulated Covered Bond Regulations 2008 apply".

5.   Paragraph 17 (fees) of Part 3 of Schedule 1 to the Act is to apply for the purposes of these Regulations as it applies for the purposes of the Act, but with the following modifications—
    (a)   in sub-paragraph (1), omit paragraphs (b) and (c);
    (b)   for the reference in sub-paragraph (2) to "penalties imposed by it under this Act" there is substituted a reference to "penalties imposed by it under the Regulated Covered Bonds Regulations 2008"; and
    (c)   omit sub-paragraph (3).

Modification of the 2006 Act

6.   Where an owner is wound up, section 754 of the 2006 Act (priorities where debentures secured by floating charge) shall apply only after payment has been made of the claims of relevant persons.
[4126]

NOTES
Commencement: 6 March 2008.

PART 2
SECONDARY LEGISLATION

Modifications of the Insolvency Rules 1986

7.—(1)   Rule 4.181(1) of the Insolvency Rules 1986 (debts of insolvent company to rank equally) shall apply only after payment has been made of the claims of relevant persons.

(2)   Rules 2.67, 4.218 and 4.219 of the Insolvency Rules 1986 (priority of expenses) shall apply to an owner subject to the provisions of regulation 29.

Modification to the Insolvency (Scotland) Rules 1986

[8.   Rules 2.39B (expenses of the administration) and 4.67 (order of priority of expenses of liquidation) of the Insolvency (Scotland) Rules 1986 shall apply to an owner subject to the provisions of regulation 29.]

Modifications of the 1989 Order

9.—(1)   Article 50 (payment of debts out of assets subject to floating charge) [and article 53 (power to dispose of charged property)] of the 1989 Order shall not apply to an owner.

[(2)   Article 93 of and paragraphs 66(1) and 67 of Schedule B1 to the 1989 Order (distribution of company's property) shall apply only after payment has been made of the claims of relevant persons.

(3)   Article 134 of the 1989 Order (payment of expenses) shall apply only after payment has been made of the expenses referred to in regulation 29.

(4)   Articles 149 (preferential debts (general provision)) and 150A (share of assets for unsecured creditors) of the 1989 Order shall not apply to an owner.]

Modifications of the Insolvency Rules (Northern Ireland) 1991

10.—(1)   Rule 4.190(1) of the Insolvency Rules (Northern Ireland) 1991 (debts of insolvent company to rank equally) shall apply only after payment has been made of the claims of relevant persons.

(2)   Rules 2.068, 4.228 and 4.229 of the Insolvency Rules (Northern Ireland) 1991 (priority of expenses) shall apply to an owner subject to the provisions of regulation 29.

Modification of the Cross-Border Insolvency Regulations 2006

11.   The Cross-Border Insolvency Regulations 2006 shall not apply to an owner.

Modification of the Cross-Border Insolvency (Northern Ireland) Regulations 2007

12.   The Cross-Border Insolvency (Northern Ireland) Regulations 2007 shall not apply to an owner.

[4127]

NOTES

Commencement: 6 March 2008.
Para 8: substituted by the Regulated Covered Bonds (Amendment) Regulations 2008, SI 2008/1714, reg 2(1), (7)(a), as from 22 July 2008.
Para 9: words in square brackets in sub-para (1) substituted, and sub-paras (2)–(4) substituted for the original sub-para (2), by SI 2008/1714, reg 2(1), (7)(b), (c), as from 22 July 2008.

NORTHERN ROCK PLC TRANSFER ORDER 2008

(SI 2008/432)

NOTES

Made: 21 February 2008.
Authority: Banking (Special Provisions) Act 2008, ss 3, 4, 12, 13(2).
Commencement: 22 February 2008.

As of 1 February 2009, this Order had not been amended.

ARRANGEMENT OF ARTICLES

PART 1
GENERAL

PART 2
TRANSFER AND REGISTRATION OF SHARES AND EXTINGUISHMENT OF RIGHTS ETC

PART 3
MEETINGS, DIRECTORS AND PROCEEDINGS

PART 1
GENERAL

1 Citation, commencement and interpretation

(1) This Order may be cited as the Northern Rock plc Transfer Order 2008.

(2) This Order comes into force on 22nd February 2008.

(3) In this Order—
"the Act" means the Banking (Special Provisions) Act 2008;
"the 1985 Act" means the Companies Act 1985;
"the 2006 Act" means the Companies Act 2006;
"the Authority" means the Financial Services Authority;
"the effective time" means the beginning of 22nd February 2008;
"Northern Rock" means Northern Rock plc, company registered number 3273685;
"Northern Rock's registrar" means the person appointed by Northern Rock, as its agent, among other things to maintain its register of members;
"relevant undertaking" means Northern Rock or any of its group undertakings;
"shares in Northern Rock" means the ordinary shares, foundation shares and preference shares issued by Northern Rock;
"the transfer" means the transfer effected by article 2(1);
"the Treasury Solicitor" has the same meaning as in the Treasury Solicitor Act 1876 and whose address is One Kemble Street, London WC2B 4TS;
"the USRs" means the Uncertificated Securities Regulations 2001.

[4128]

NOTES
Commencement: 22 February 2008.

PART 2
TRANSFER AND REGISTRATION OF SHARES AND EXTINGUISHMENT OF RIGHTS ETC

2 Transfers

(1) By virtue of this Order, the shares in Northern Rock are transferred to the Treasury Solicitor as nominee of the Treasury.

(2) The transfer of shares effected under paragraph (1) shall vest title in the Treasury Solicitor—
(a) free from all trusts, liabilities and incumbrances; and
(b) together with all rights, benefits or privileges which attach or accrue to or arise from such shares on or after the effective time.

(3) The transfer under paragraph (1) takes place at the effective time.

[4129]

NOTES
Commencement: 22 February 2008.

3 Registration of shares and issue of certificates

(1) The Treasury Solicitor is entitled with effect from the effective time to be entered in the register of members of Northern Rock as holder of the shares transferred by virtue of this Order without the need for delivery of any instrument of transfer or other instrument or document and notwithstanding—

    (a) the absence of any required consent or concurrence to or with the transfer; and

    (b) any other restriction relating to the transfer.

(2) The Operator of a relevant system in which any shares transferred by virtue of this Order ("relevant shares") are held immediately prior to the effective time shall forthwith after the effective time—

    (a) withdraw his permission for title to the relevant shares to be transferred by means of the relevant system with effect from the effective time; and

    (b) inform all the system-members and Northern Rock's registrar of the date and time the relevant shares ceased to be securities participating in the system.

(3) Northern Rock shall procure that Northern Rock's registrar shall forthwith after the effective time—

    (a) take such action as the Operator of a relevant system may require to convert any relevant shares held in such system immediately prior to the effective time into certificated form;

    (b) register in Northern Rock's register of members (including its issuer register of members) the Treasury Solicitor as the holder of shares in Northern Rock.

(4) The Operator of a relevant system in which any relevant shares are held immediately prior to the effective time, Northern Rock and Northern Rock's registrar shall each—

    (a) provide each other with such information as shall be necessary to comply with this article; and

    (b) co-operate to ensure that the issuer register of members of Northern Rock reconciles with the Operator register of members of Northern Rock immediately prior to the effective time.

(5) From the effective time and until the Treasury Solicitor is entered in Northern Rock's register of members (including its issuer register of members)—

    (a) he is deemed for all purposes (including for the purposes of the 1985 Act and, when the relevant provisions of the 2006 Act come into force, the purposes of that Act and the USRs) to be—

        (i) the sole member of Northern Rock; and

        (ii) entered as holder on the Operator register of members of Northern Rock; and

    (b) no other person may exercise or purport to exercise in respect of Northern Rock any right deriving from any shares in Northern Rock.

(6) The Treasury Solicitor is entitled from the effective time to all the rights and advantages of a member of Northern Rock to the exclusion of all other persons, notwithstanding that he is not entered in either Northern Rock's register of members (including its issuer register of members) or the Operator register of members of Northern Rock.

(7) Section 185 of the 1985 Act (duty of company as to issue of certificates) applies to Northern Rock with the following modifications—

    (a) the transfer by virtue of this Order is deemed to be a transfer of the first-mentioned type referred to in subsection (2) which is lodged with Northern Rock at the effective time;

    (b) subsections (3) to (4D) do not apply.

(8) The corresponding provision of the 2006 Act to that referred to in paragraph (7) shall have effect, when it comes into force, subject to modification to similar effect as referred to in that paragraph.

(9) In paragraph (8), "corresponding provision" has the same meaning as in section 1297 of the 2006 Act (continuity of the law).

(10) In this article "certificated", "issuer register of members", "Operator", "Operator register of members", "relevant system" and "system-member" have the meanings given in the USRs.

[4130]

NOTES

Commencement: 22 February 2008.

4 Extinguishment of rights in relation to shares

(1) By virtue of this Order any right or other entitlement granted by—

    (a) a relevant undertaking; or

    (b) a person not within sub-paragraph (a), by reason of or in connection with—

        (i) any individual's office or employment with a relevant undertaking; or

        (ii) the services provided by any individual to a relevant undertaking, to receive shares in Northern Rock (whether by subscription, conversion or otherwise) is extinguished with effect from the effective time.

(2)　This article shall not apply to any right or entitlement to which article 5 applies.

[4131]

NOTES

Commencement: 22 February 2008.

5　Interest payments in relation to Tier 1 notes

(1)　This article applies if, while Northern Rock is wholly owned by the Treasury, Northern Rock would, but for this article, be obliged under the terms of any Tier 1 notes or arrangements relating to Tier 1 notes to issue ordinary shares in Northern Rock to satisfy entitlements to interest payments.

(2)　The Treasury may give notice to Northern Rock and the trustee for the holders of Tier 1 notes ("the trustee") that they—

　(a)　intend to settle interest payments in respect of any Tier 1 notes in cash pursuant to paragraph (3); or

　(b)　require Northern Rock to settle interest payments in respect of any Tier 1 notes by Northern Rock issuing further Tier 1 notes to the trustee pursuant to paragraph (4).

(3)　Upon the giving of the notice referred to in paragraph (2)(a), unless and until the Treasury specify otherwise—

　(a)　any obligation of Northern Rock to issue ordinary shares to the trustee is replaced by an obligation of Northern Rock to issue ordinary shares or, if so specified in the notice, further Tier 1 notes, to the Treasury Solicitor;

　(b)　on each date when, but for this article, Northern Rock would be required to satisfy an entitlement referred to in paragraph (1) the Treasury shall pay an amount equal to the interest payments to or to the order of the trustee; and

　(c)　Northern Rock shall have no further obligation in respect of the interest payments.

(4)　Upon the giving of the notice referred to in paragraph (2)(b), unless and until the Treasury specify otherwise—

　(a)　any obligation of Northern Rock to issue ordinary shares to the trustee shall be replaced by an obligation of Northern Rock to issue further Tier 1 notes to the trustee;

　(b)　Northern Rock shall issue that number of further Tier 1 notes which is necessary to cover the entitlement of the holders of relevant Tier 1 notes in respect of the interest payments; and

　(c)　Northern Rock shall have no further obligation in respect of the interest payments.

(5)　In this article—

"further Tier 1 notes" means further Tier 1 notes which are on the same terms as the Tier 1 notes, subject to any modifications specified in the notice given by the Treasury under paragraph (2)(b) which the Treasury may consider appropriate, whether to ensure the inclusion of such notes in Northern Rock's innovative tier one capital resources or otherwise;

"Tier 1 notes" means—

　　(a)　the £200,000,000 7.053 per cent callable perpetual core tier one notes of Northern Rock constituted by a trust deed dated 21st August 2002, and

　　(b)　the £300,000,000 8.399 per cent, step-up callable perpetual reserve capital instruments of Northern Rock constituted by a trust deed dated 21 September 2000 as supplemented by a supplemental trust deed dated 24th May 2001;

"innovative tier one capital resources" has the meaning given in the Glossary to the Authority's Handbook;

"Handbook" means the handbook containing provisions made by the Authority under Part 10 of FSMA 2000.

[4132]

NOTES

Commencement: 22 February 2008.

6　Conversion of foundation shares into ordinary shares etc

(1)　Immediately after the effective time, each foundation share issued by Northern Rock shall, by virtue of this Order, convert into and be redesignated as one ordinary share in Northern Rock notwithstanding any provision in the articles of association of Northern Rock and without the need for approval of any person.

(2)　Northern Rock's company secretary shall within one month after the effective time notify the registrar of companies of the alteration of the share capital of Northern Rock in accordance with section 122 of the 1985 Act (notice to registrar of alteration).

(3)   The conversion and redesignation of the foundation shares by virtue of this Order shall be treated as having been carried out by Northern Rock under and in accordance with article 8.6 of its articles of association (save that article 8.22 shall not apply) and the Deed of Covenant made on 30th September 1997 between Northern Rock and the Northern Rock Foundation shall terminate immediately after such conversion and redesignation.

[4133]

NOTES

Commencement: 22 February 2008.

7   Minimum membership for carrying on business

(1)   While Northern Rock is wholly owned by the Treasury, section 24 of the 1985 Act (minimum membership for carrying on business) shall not apply in relation to Northern Rock or any member of Northern Rock.

(2)   No petition shall be presented for the winding up of Northern Rock on the ground that the number of its members is less than the number required by law, nor shall any person be liable on that ground as a member of the company for the payment of any of its debts.

[4134]

NOTES

Commencement: 22 February 2008.

PART 3
MEETINGS, DIRECTORS AND PROCEEDINGS

8   Resolutions and meetings

(1)   Any meeting of members of Northern Rock held while Northern Rock is wholly owned by the Treasury shall, if the Treasury Solicitor is present in person or by proxy or authorises a corporate representative to attend, be deemed to be a duly constituted general meeting of the company notwithstanding that it may not have been properly called, or notice of it may not have been properly given, or any quorum required by Northern Rock's articles of association may not be present.

(2)   Notwithstanding any provision in the articles of association of Northern Rock, an appointment of a proxy for the Treasury Solicitor—

   (a)   may be in any written form (including in an electronic communication);
   (b)   need not be given with any period of notice;
   (c)   shall not require the approval of the board of Northern Rock;
   (d)   is deemed to be given in accordance with the articles of association.

(3)   A resolution of the company is effective notwithstanding that special notice (notice of intention to move it given to company at least 28 days before the meeting at which it is moved) of the resolution is required by any provision of the 1985 Act or 2006 Act but has not been given.

[4135]

NOTES

Commencement: 22 February 2008.

9   Removal of directors

(1)   While Northern Rock is wholly owned by the Treasury, the Treasury may in accordance with this article—

   (a)   remove any person as a director of a relevant undertaking;
   (b)   terminate a director's service contract with any relevant undertaking.

(2)   For the purposes of any contract or arrangement between a person and a relevant undertaking, action taken under paragraph (1) shall be treated as having been carried out by the relevant undertaking and, in the case of paragraph (1)(a), under and in accordance with its articles of association.

(3)   The Treasury may remove a person as a director of a relevant undertaking and may terminate his service contract by written notice to the relevant undertaking.

(4)   Any notice given in accordance with paragraph (3) shall take effect from the date specified in the notice.

(5)   A relevant undertaking which receives notice under paragraph (3) shall notify the person to whom the notice relates of that fact as soon as reasonably practicable.

(6)   A person—
   (a)   removed as director of a relevant undertaking, or

(b)   whose service contract with a relevant undertaking is terminated,

in accordance with this article shall not have any right or claim against the Treasury or any company wholly owned by the Treasury (other than a relevant undertaking) in consequence of the Treasury's actions under this article.

(7)   This article is not to be taken—
   (a)   as depriving any person removed under it of compensation or damages payable to him by a relevant undertaking in respect of—
      (i)   the termination of his appointment as director or of any appointment terminating with that as director; or
      (ii)   the termination of his service contract; or
   (b)   as derogating from any power to remove a director or to terminate a director's service contract that may exist apart from this article.

(8)   In this article and in article 10, "service contract" has the meaning given by section 227 of the 2006 Act (directors' service contracts).

[4136]

NOTES
Commencement: 22 February 2008.

10 Appointment of directors

(1)   While Northern Rock is wholly owned by the Treasury, the Treasury may appoint one or more directors of a relevant undertaking in accordance with this article and notwithstanding any restriction in the articles of association of the relevant undertaking.

(2)   The Treasury may appoint a director of a relevant undertaking by written notice to the relevant undertaking provided the appointee has agreed to act in such a capacity.

(3)   The appointment shall take effect from the date specified in the notice.

(4)   The Treasury may determine the terms (including remuneration) of the service contract of a person appointed as a director under this article in whatever written form they see fit.

(5)   Any appointment, contract or arrangement which is made or the terms of which are determined under this article is to be treated as made or entered into by the relevant undertaking in question.

(6)   This article is not to be taken as derogating from any power to appoint a director or determine the remuneration and other terms and conditions of a director's service contract that may exist apart from this article.

[4137]

NOTES
Commencement: 22 February 2008.

11 Proceedings against directors of Northern Rock

(1)   No director of a relevant undertaking shall be liable for any act or omission of the director, acting in such capacity, which occurs while Northern Rock is wholly owned by the Treasury and accordingly no proceedings may be brought (or in Scotland, raised) against any such director in respect of such matters.

(2)   The Treasury may in writing—
   (a)   waive the effect of paragraph (1), and
   (b)   give consent to bring (or in Scotland, raise) such proceedings against such directors.

(3)   Where paragraph (1) applies, section 232 of the 2006 Act (provisions protecting directors from liability) shall not apply to a relevant undertaking.

(4)   In this article—
   "proceedings" includes proceedings under Part 11 of the 2006 Act (derivative claims and proceedings by members);
   "director" means—
      (a)   a person who is appointed as a director while Northern Rock is wholly owned by the Treasury, whether or not he has ceased to be a director when proceedings in respect of that liability commenced;
      (b)   a person who was a director immediately before the effective time and whose continuing appointment as director while Northern Rock is wholly owned by the Treasury, the Treasury approves in writing, whether or not he has ceased to be a director at the time when proceedings in respect of that liability commenced; and
      (c)   an alternate director of a person falling within sub-paragraph (a) or (b).

[4138]

NOTES
Commencement: 22 February 2008.

12 Modification of rights in relevant instruments

(1) The consequences specified in paragraph (3) shall not arise in respect of any relevant instrument as a result of the transfer or any other thing done, or matter arising, by virtue of or in connection with this Order.

(2) Any circumstances which, but for paragraph (1), would give rise to the consequences specified in paragraph (3) shall not be taken to have arisen for the purposes of any relevant instrument.

(3) The consequences are—
    (a) the termination of the relevant instrument or any rights or obligations under it;
    (b) any right to terminate the relevant instrument or any right or obligation under it becoming exercisable;
    (c) any amount becoming due and payable or capable of being declared due and payable;
    (d) any other change in the amount or timing of any payment falling to be made or due to be received by any person;
    (e) any right to withhold, net or set off any payment becoming exercisable;
    (f) any event of default or breach of any right arising;
    (g) any right not to advance any amount becoming exercisable;
    (h) any obligation to provide or transfer any deposit or collateral; or
    (i) any other right or remedy (whether or not similar in kind to those referred to in paragraphs (a) to (h)) arising or becoming exercisable.

(4) Without prejudice to paragraph (3), any provision in a relevant instrument that, as a result of the transfer or any other thing done, or matter arising, by virtue of or in connection with this Order, provides for an obligation not to be created, suspends or extinguishes (in whole or in part) such an obligation or renders such an obligation subject to conditions, shall be of no effect.

(5) This article does not apply to any action taken by the Treasury under article 9.

(6) In this article—
"relevant instrument" has the meaning given in paragraph 4(3) of Schedule 1 to the Act and the specified connection referred to in paragraph 4(3)(c) of that Schedule is between Northern Rock and those undertakings whose assets and liabilities, profits and losses are consolidated in the consolidated accounts of Northern Rock.

[4139]

NOTES
Commencement: 22 February 2008.

PART 4
DE-LISTING, APPROVAL ETC

13 De-listing

(1) By virtue of this Order, the listing of any shares of Northern Rock is discontinued with effect from the effective time without the need for any notice to, or consent of, Northern Rock or any other person.

(2) In paragraph (1), "listing" has the meaning given in section 74 of FSMA 2000.

[4140]

NOTES
Commencement: 22 February 2008.

14 Approved persons

(1) While Northern Rock is wholly owned by the Treasury the requirements imposed on Northern Rock and any subsidiary undertaking by section 59 of FSMA 2000 (approval for particular arrangements) in relation to directors (including non-executive directors) and the chief executive officer shall be deemed to be satisfied in relation to Northern Rock and any subsidiary undertaking, provided that at all material times the Authority is satisfied that at least two individuals who effectively direct the business of Northern Rock are of sufficiently good repute and have sufficient experience to perform controlled functions in that respect.

(2) The Treasury may give written notice to the Authority that paragraph (1) is no longer to apply.

(3) At least one month prior to giving a notice under paragraph (2) the Treasury shall give written notice to Northern Rock or the relevant undertaking of its intention to give a notice to the Authority under paragraph (2).

(4) In paragraph (1)—
"controlled functions" has the meaning given in section 59(3) of FSMA 2000.

[4141]

NOTES
Commencement: 22 February 2008.

PART 5
AUTHORITY'S RULE-MAKING POWER

15 Modification to Authority's rule-making power

(1) Subsections (1) and (1A) of section 138 of FSMA 2000 (general rule-making power) have effect as if modified by inserting after "protecting the interests of consumers"—

"or for the purposes of, to facilitate or in consequence of a transfer under section 3 of the Banking (Special Provisions) Act 2008".

(2) Section 148(2) of FSMA 2000 (modification or waiver of rules) shall also apply—
(a) in the absence of an application by a person subject to rules made by the Authority; and
(b) without any requirement for the consent of such a person.

(3) Section 148(4) of FSMA 2000 shall not prevent the Authority from modifying or waiving rules in relation to a relevant undertaking under section 148 of that Act provided that the Authority is satisfied that the modification or waiver is necessary for the purposes of, to facilitate or in consequence of the transfer.

[4142]

NOTES
Commencement: 22 February 2008.

16 Modification to Authority's duty to consult on rule changes

(1) Section 155(7) of FSMA 2000 (consultation) has effect as if modified by adding at the end—

"or if it is making rules for the purposes of, or to facilitate or in consequence of, a transfer under section 3 of the Banking (Special Provisions) Act 2008."

(2) Section 157 of FSMA 2000 (guidance) has effect as if modified by adding after subsection (3)—

"(3A) Section 155(7) applies to proposed guidance with the modification made by article 16(1) of the Northern Rock Plc Transfer Order 2008.".

[4143]

NOTES
Commencement: 22 February 2008.

PART 6
MISCELLANEOUS

17 Shadow directorship

(1) While Northern Rock is wholly owned by the Treasury, for the purposes of the provisions listed in the Schedule to this Order, none of the persons listed in paragraph (3) shall be regarded as a shadow director or (unless otherwise appointed as a director) a person discharging managerial responsibilities of a relevant undertaking.

(2) For the purposes of the definition of "director" in section 417 of FSMA 2000 (definitions), none of the persons listed in paragraph (3) shall be regarded as a person in accordance with whose directions or instructions (not being advice given in a professional capacity) the directors of a relevant undertaking are accustomed to act while Northern Rock is wholly owned by the Treasury.

(3) The persons are—
(a) a Minister of the Crown;
(b) the Treasury;
(c) the Treasury Solicitor;
(d) the Bank of England;
(e) persons—
(i) employed by or under; or

(ii)   acting on behalf of,
any of the persons in paragraph (3).

[4144]

NOTES
   Commencement: 22 February 2008.

18   Northern Rock and freedom of information

(1)   This article applies while Northern Rock is wholly owned by the Treasury.

(2)   A relevant undertaking shall be deemed—
   (a)   not to be a publicly-owned company for the purposes of section 3(1)(b);
   (b)   not to hold information on behalf of the Treasury for the purposes of section 3(2)(b);
of the Freedom of Information Act 2000 (public authorities).

[4145]

NOTES
   Commencement: 22 February 2008.

19   Notification requirement

(1)   The Treasury must notify the Authority of the making of this Order.

(2)   A notification under paragraph (1)—
   (a)   may be given by such means as the Treasury consider appropriate;
   (b)   must be given to the Authority as soon as reasonably practicable after the effective time.

(3)   On receiving a notification under paragraph (1), the Authority must in turn notify any relevant EEA authority of the making of the Order.

(4)   A notification under paragraph (3)—
   (a)   may be given by such means as the Authority considers appropriate;
   (b)   must be given to the relevant EEA authority as soon as reasonably practicable after the Authority is notified under paragraph (1).

(5)   "Relevant EEA authority" means any regulatory authority in an EEA state that exercises functions in relation to any office or branch of the authorised deposit-taker in question in that state.

[4146]

NOTES
   Commencement: 22 February 2008.

20   Modification of provision on liability in relation to Operator's functions

(1)   Section 291 of FSMA 2000 (liability in relation to recognised body's regulatory functions) shall have effect as if the following modifications are made.

(2)   In subsection (1)—
   (a)   after "its officers and staff" add "and an Operator and its officers and staff";
   (b)   after "recognised body's" add "or the Operator's".

(3)   In subsection (3) at the end add—

"and the functions of the Operator so far as relating to, or matters arising out of, the obligations to which the Operator is subject under the Northern Rock plc Transfer Order 2008.

(4)   In this section, "Operator" has the meaning given in the Uncertificated Securities Regulations 2001".

[4147]

NOTES
   Commencement: 22 February 2008.

SCHEDULE
SHADOW DIRECTORSHIP

Article 17(1)

1.   The following provisions of the 1985 Act—
   (a)   section 288 (register of directors);
   (b)   section 305 (directors' names on correspondence, etc);
   (c)   section 317 (disclosure of interests in contracts);
   (d)   section 320 (substantial property transactions involving directors);
   (e)   section 323 (prohibition on dealing in share options);
   (f)   section 324 (disclosure of shareholdings);

    (g)   section 325 (register of directors' interests);
    (h)   section 330 (restriction on loans);
    (i)   section 733 (offences by bodies corporate).

2.   The following provisions of the 2006 Act—
    (a)   section 84 (criminal consequences of failure to make required disclosure);
    (b)   section 162 (register of directors);
    (c)   section 165 (register of directors' residential addresses);
    (d)   section 167 (duty to notify registrar of changes);
    (e)   sections 170 to 177 (general duties of directors);
    (f)   sections 182 to 186 (declaration of interest in existing transaction) as applied to shadow directors by section 187;
    (g)   sections 188 and 189 (directors' service contracts);
    (h)   sections 190 to 196 (substantial property transactions);
    (i)   sections 197 to 214 (loans etc to directors);
    (j)   sections 215 to 222 (payments for loss of office) as applied to shadow directors by section 223(2);
    (k)   sections 227 to 230 (directors' service contracts);
    (l)   section 231 (contracts with sole members who are directors);
    (m)   sections 260 to 269 (derivative claims in England and Wales and Northern Ireland);
    (n)   sections 854 to 859 (annual return).

3.   The following provisions of the Insolvency Act 1986—
    (a)   section 214 (wrongful trading);
    (b)   section 249 ("connected" with a company).

4.   The following provisions of FSMA 2000—
    (a)   section 96A (disclosure of information requirements);
    (b)   section 96B (disclosure rules: persons responsible for compliance).

[4148]

NOTES
   Commencement: 22 February 2008.

NORTHERN ROCK PLC COMPENSATION SCHEME ORDER 2008

(SI 2008/718)

NOTES
   Made: 12 March 2008.
   Authority: Banking (Special Provisions) Act 2008, ss 5, 9, 12, 13(2).
   Commencement: 13 March 2008.

   As of 1 February 2009, this Order had not been amended.

1—(1)   This Order may be cited as the Northern Rock plc Compensation Scheme Order 2008.

   (2)   This Order comes into force on the day after the day on which it is made.

[4149]

NOTES
   Commencement: 13 March 2008.

2   The Northern Rock plc Compensation Scheme set out in the Schedule to this Order shall have effect.

[4150]

NOTES
   Commencement: 13 March 2008.

SCHEDULE
THE NORTHERN ROCK PLC COMPENSATION SCHEME

Article 2

PART 1
GENERAL PROVISIONS

1 Citation

This Scheme may be cited as the Northern Rock plc Compensation Scheme.

2 Interpretation

In this Scheme—

"assessment notice" has the meaning given by paragraph 11;

"Northern Rock" means Northern Rock plc, company registered number 3273685;

"revised assessment notice" has the meaning given by paragraph 12;

"shares in Northern Rock" means the ordinary shares, foundation shares and preference shares issued by Northern Rock;

"the Act" means the Banking (Special Provisions) Act 2008;

"the Transfer Order" means the Northern Rock plc Transfer Order 2008;

"the transfer time" means the beginning of 22nd February 2008;

"the Tribunal" means the Financial Services and Markets Tribunal;

"valuer" means the independent valuer appointed by the Treasury in accordance with paragraph 7.

[4151]

NOTES

Commencement: 13 March 2008.

PART 2
DETERMINATION OF AMOUNT OF COMPENSATION

3 Transfer of Northern Rock shares

(1) The amount of any compensation payable by the Treasury to persons who held shares in Northern Rock immediately before they were transferred by the Transfer Order shall be determined in accordance with this paragraph.

(2) The amount of compensation payable to a person shall be an amount equal to the value immediately before the transfer time of all shares in Northern Rock held immediately before the transfer time by that person.

(3) For the purposes of this Scheme, the holders of shares in Northern Rock, and the class and number of shares held by them, shall be identified by reference to—

(a) the Operator register of members of Northern Rock; and

(b) the issuer register of members of Northern Rock,

following the reconciliation required by article 3(4) of the Transfer Order.

(4) In sub-paragraph (3) "issuer register of members" and "Operator register of members" have the meanings given in the Uncertificated Securities Regulations 2001.

4 Extinguishment of subscription rights

(1) The amount of any compensation payable by the Treasury to persons whose subscription rights were extinguished by virtue of article 4 of the Transfer Order shall be determined in accordance with this paragraph.

(2) The amount of compensation payable to a person shall be an amount equal to the value immediately before the transfer time of that person's subscription rights.

(3) In this paragraph "subscription rights" means any right or other entitlement granted by—

(a) a relevant undertaking; or

(b) a person not within paragraph (a) by reason of or in connection with—

(i) any individual's office or employment with a relevant undertaking; or

(ii) the services provided by any individual to a relevant undertaking,

to receive shares in Northern Rock (whether by subscription, conversion or otherwise).

(4) In sub-paragraph (3) "relevant undertaking" means Northern Rock or any of its group undertakings.

5 Modification of rights in relevant instruments

(1)   Subject to sub-paragraph (4), the amount of any compensation payable by the Treasury to persons whose rights were extinguished by virtue of the provision made in article 12 of the Transfer Order (referred to in this paragraph as "consequential rights") shall be determined in accordance with this paragraph.

(2)   The amount of compensation payable to a person shall be such compensation as may be just in respect of that person's consequential rights.

(3)   The determination of any compensation in respect of rights extinguished by virtue of article 12(1) or (2) of the Transfer Order shall take into account—
  (a)   any diminution in the value of property; or
  (b)   any increase in the burden of any liability,
which is attributable to the consequences specified in article 12(3) of the Transfer Order not arising.

(4)   Compensation is payable in respect of a person's consequential rights only if such compensation is required to be paid to comply with the Convention rights (within the meaning given by section 1 of the Human Rights Act 1998).

6 Valuation assumptions

In determining the amount of any compensation payable by the Treasury to any person in accordance with paragraphs 3 to 5, it must be assumed (in addition to the assumptions required to be made by section 5(4) of the Act (compensation etc for securities transferred etc)) that Northern Rock—
  (a)   is unable to continue as a going concern; and
  (b)   is in administration.

[4152]

NOTES
Commencement: 13 March 2008.

PART 3
INDEPENDENT VALUER

7 Appointment of independent valuer

(1)   The Treasury shall appoint an independent valuer for the purposes of this Scheme.

(2)   The valuer so appointed shall determine the amount of any compensation payable by the Treasury in accordance with Part 2 of this Scheme.

(3)   The valuer is to hold and vacate office in accordance with the terms of his appointment.

(4)   The Treasury may remove the valuer only on the ground of incapacity or serious misbehaviour.

(5)   Before making any appointment under sub-paragraph (1) the Treasury must consult the Institute of Chartered Accountants in England and Wales.

8 Remuneration

The valuer shall be—
  (a)   paid such remuneration; and
  (b)   reimbursed such expenses;
as the Treasury may determine.

9 Appointment of staff

(1)   The valuer may appoint such staff as he or she may determine.

(2)   The valuer shall determine the remuneration and other conditions of service of the persons appointed under this paragraph.

(3)   The valuer may pay such pensions, allowances or gratuities to or in respect of the persons appointed under this paragraph as he or she may determine.

(4)   The references in sub-paragraph (3) to pensions, allowances or gratuities to or in respect of the persons appointed under this paragraph include reference to pensions, allowances or gratuities by way of compensation in respect of any of those persons who suffer loss of employment.

(5)   Any determination under sub-paragraphs (2) to (4) shall require the approval of the Treasury.

[4153]

NOTES
Commencement: 13 March 2008.

PART 4
ASSESSMENT OF COMPENSATION BY VALUER

10 Procedure

(1)   The valuer may make such rules as to the procedure in relation to the assessment of any compensation (including the procedure for the reconsideration of any decisions relating to the assessment of compensation) as he or she considers appropriate.

(2)   Rules made under sub-paragraph (1) may make different provision for different cases or circumstances.

11 Assessment notice

(1)   Where the valuer has assessed the amount of any compensation payable by the Treasury—
(a)   to any person; or
(b)   in respect of a class or description of shares or rights,
he or she shall issue an assessment notice.

(2)   An assessment notice shall contain the following information—
(a)   the date on which the notice is issued;
(b)   the amount of any compensation determined by the valuer as being payable; and
(c)   the reasons for the valuer's decision.

(3)   The valuer shall send a copy of the assessment notice to the Treasury.

12 Reconsideration of assessment notice

(1)   If—
(a)   the Treasury; or
(b)   any person who is affected by the determination of the amount of any compensation which is contained in an assessment notice,
are dissatisfied with the assessment notice, the Treasury or any such person may require the valuer to reconsider his or her determination.

(2)   Where the valuer is required to reconsider his or her determination in accordance with sub-paragraph (1) he or she shall issue a revised assessment notice.

(3)   A revised assessment notice shall contain the following information—
(a)   the date on which the notice is issued;
(b)   either—
(i)   notification that the valuer has upheld the assessment notice; or
(ii)   notification that the valuer has varied the assessment notice;
(c)   the amount of any compensation determined by the valuer as being payable; and
(d)   the reasons for the valuer's decision.

(4)   The valuer shall send a copy of the revised assessment notice to the Treasury.

13 Right to refer to the Tribunal

If—
(a)   the Treasury; or
(b)   any person who is affected by the determination of the amount of any compensation which is contained in the revised assessment notice,
are dissatisfied with the revised assessment notice, the Treasury or any such person may refer the matter to the Tribunal.

14 Payment of compensation

(1)   The Treasury shall pay the amount of any compensation determined by the valuer to be payable—
(a)   to any person; or
(b)   in respect of a class or description of shares or rights.

(2)   The Treasury shall not be required to make a payment in accordance with sub-paragraph (1) until—
(a)   they have received a copy of the assessment notice or revised assessment notice, as the case may be; or
(b)   if there is a reference to the Tribunal, the matter has been finally disposed of.

(3)   The Treasury may apply any of the provisions of article 149.1 of the articles of association of Northern Rock, as in effect immediately prior to the making of this Order, in making any payment of compensation to the holders of shares in Northern Rock, as if such payment were payment of a dividend by Northern Rock.

[4154]

NOTES

Commencement: 13 March 2008.

PART 5
REFERENCES TO THE TRIBUNAL

15 Application of FSMA 2000

(1)   The provisions of—
  (a)   Part 9 (hearing and appeals) of, and Schedule 13 (the Financial Services and Markets Tribunal) to, FSMA 2000; and
  (b)   the Financial Services and Markets Tribunal Rules 2001;
shall apply in respect of any reference made under paragraph 13, subject to the modifications set out in this Part.

Modification of FSMA 2000

16.   Part 9 of, and Schedule 13 to, FSMA 2000 are modified as follows.

17.   In section 133 (proceedings: general provisions) and Schedule 13, for "the Authority" in each place it occurs substitute "the independent valuer appointed under paragraph 7 of the Schedule to the Northern Rock plc Compensation Scheme Order 2008".

18.   In section 133—
  (i)   in subsection (1)(a) for "the decision notice or supervisory notice in question", substitute " the revised assessment notice issued by the valuer under paragraph 12(2) of the Schedule to the Northern Rock plc Compensation Scheme Order 2008";
  (ii)   for subsection (4) substitute—

"(4)   Where the Tribunal is satisfied that the decision as to the amount of compensation shown in the revised assessment notice was not a reasonable decision the Tribunal must remit the matter to the valuer for reconsideration in accordance with such directions (if any) as they consider appropriate.";
  (iii)   omit subsections (5) to (9) and (12).

19.   Omit sections 134 to 136.

Modification of Financial Services and Markets Tribunal Rules 2001

20.   The Financial Services and Markets Tribunal Rules 2001 are modified as follows.

21.   In each place where it occurs (other than in rule 2)—
  (a)   for "Authority" substitute "respondent";
  (b)   for "Authority notice" substitute "revised assessment notice";
  (c)   for "statement of case" substitute "response document".

22.   In rule 2 (interpretation)—
  (a)   omit the definitions for "the Authority", "Authority notice", "further material", "protected item", "reply" and "statement of case";
  (b)   in the definition of "party", for "Authority", in both places where it occurs, substitute "respondent";
  (c)   in the definition of "referred action" for "the act (or proposed act) on the part of the Authority" substitute "the revised assessment notice";
  (d)   for the definition of "response document" substitute "means a statement filed by the respondent under rule 5(1);"; and
  (e)   in the appropriate place insert—
    ""respondent" means the independent valuer appointed under paragraph 7 of the Schedule to the Northern Rock plc Compensation Scheme Order 2008;";
    "revised assessment notice" means the revised assessment notice issued by the respondent under paragraph 12 of the Schedule to the Northern Rock plc Compensation Scheme Order 2008;".

23.   In rule 4(6) (reference notice) omit ", a direction under rule 10(1)(e) (suspension of Authority's action) or".

24.   In rule 5 (Authority's statement of case)—
  (a)   for paragraphs (1) and (2) substitute—

"(1)   The respondent shall file a written statement ("a response document") dealing with any issues arising out of the reference notice that the respondent wishes the Tribunal to consider so that it is received by the Tribunal no later than 28 days after the day on which the respondent received the information sent by the Secretary in accordance with rule 4(9)(b).

(2)   At the same time as it files the response document, the respondent shall send a copy to the applicant.";
  (b)   omit paragraphs (3) and (4).

25.   Omit rules 6 (applicant's reply), 7 (secondary disclosure by the Authority), 8 (exceptions to disclosure), 11 (filling of subsequent notices in relation to the referred action), 12(2) (summoning of witnesses), 14(3)(c) (withdrawal of reference and unopposed references), 15 (references by third parties) and 23(4) (application for permission to appeal).

26. In rule 10 (particular types of directions) omit paragraphs (1)(e), (2)(a), (6) and (8).

27. After rule 10 (particular types of directions) insert—

"10A(1) The President may, of his own motion or on application by a party, direct that a reference is heard as a lead case where—

    (a) one or more references under paragraph 13 of the Schedule to the Northern Rock plc Compensation Scheme Order 2008 have been made, but have not yet been determined by the Tribunal; and

    (b) it appears to the President that those references give rise to common or related issues of fact or law ("same issues proceedings").

(2) The President may—

    (a) give such further directions as he considers appropriate for determination of the lead case; and

    (b) direct that pending determination of the lead case all other same issues proceedings before the Tribunal shall be stayed.

(3) All parties in same issues proceedings must be allowed to make representations prior to the President making a direction under paragraph (1) or (2).

(4) Without prejudice generally to the parties' rights of appeal and to paragraphs (5) to (7), the Tribunal's determination of the same issues in the lead case shall be binding on the parties to each of the same issues proceedings unless the Tribunal or the President directs otherwise.

(5) Any party to any of the same issues proceedings may apply to the President for a direction that the determination of the same issues in the lead case does not apply to that party's case.

(6) An application under paragraph (5) must be made not later than 21 days after the date on which that party received notice of the determination of the same issues in the lead case.

(7) Within 28 days beginning with the date of determination of the same issues in the lead case the President may give further directions in relation to—

    (a) the lead case and each of the same issues proceedings stayed pending the determination of the same issues in the lead case;

    (b) the extent to which the determination of the same issues in the lead case is binding on any subsequent proceedings; and

    (c) any further directions required as a result of an application under paragraph (5), including a direction as to any further hearing required in relation to those proceedings.

(8) Where a direction has been given for any proceedings to be heard as a lead case and those proceedings are withdrawn or discontinued either before or during the hearing, the President may direct—

    (a) that one of the remaining same issues proceedings be substituted as the lead case; and

    (b) the extent to which any directions made prior to substitution shall be binding in relation to the substituted proceedings.

(9) The Secretary must send notice of the directions to be made under paragraphs (1) and (2), a copy of the directions made under paragraphs (1), (2), (4), (5), (7) and (8) and the determination of the same issues in the lead case to all the parties to the same issues proceedings.

10B If it appears to the President or the Chairman, whether on the application of a party or otherwise, that it is desirable that any person other than the respondent be made a party to any proceedings, he may direct that such person be joined as a party in the proceedings and may give such further directions for giving effect to, or in connection with, the direction as he thinks fit.".

28. In rule 19(3) (procedure at hearings) omit "when taking the referred action".

                                                                 [4155]

NOTES

Commencement: 13 March 2008.

PROCEEDS OF CRIME ACT 2002 (INVESTIGATIONS IN ENGLAND, WALES AND NORTHERN IRELAND: CODE OF PRACTICE) ORDER 2008

(SI 2008/946)

NOTES
Made: 31 March 2008.
Authority: Proceeds of Crime Act 2002, ss 377(4), (8), 459(2)(b).
Commencement: 1 April 2008.
As of 1 February 2009, this Order had not been amended.
The Code of Practice can be accessed on the Serious Organised Crime Agency's website at:
http://www.crimereduction.homeoffice.gov.uk/crimereduction026.htm

1   Citation and commencement

This Order may be cited as the Proceeds of Crime Act 2002 (Investigations in England, Wales and Northern Ireland: Code of Practice) Order 2008 and shall come into force on 1st April 2008.

[4156]

NOTES
Commencement: 1 April 2008.

2   Revised code of practice

Subject to article 3, the revised code of practice entitled "Code of Practice issued under section 377 of the Proceeds of Crime Act 2002" laid before Parliament on 18th February 2008 shall come into operation on 1st April 2008.

[4157]

NOTES
Commencement: 1 April 2008.

3   Exercise of functions at time of coming into operation

The revised code of practice referred to in article 2 shall apply to the exercise of any function under Chapter 2 of Part 8 of the Proceeds of Crime Act 2002 by a person who must comply with the revised code of practice under section 377(5) of that Act after midnight on 31st March 2008, notwithstanding that the person may have started to exercise the function before that time.

[4158]–[4161]

NOTES
Commencement: 1 April 2008.

CASH RATIO DEPOSITS (VALUE BANDS AND RATIOS) ORDER 2008

(SI 2008/1344)

NOTES
Made: 22 May 2008.
Authority: Bank of England Act 1998, Sch 2, para 5.
Commencement: 2 June 2008.
As of 1 February 2009, this Order had not been amended.

1   Citation and commencement

This Order may be cited as the Cash Ratio Deposits (Value Bands and Ratios) Order 2008 and comes into force on 2nd June 2008.

[4162]

NOTES
Commencement: 2 June 2008.

2 *(Revokes the Cash Ratio Deposits (Value Bands and Ratios) Order 2004, SI 2004/1270.)*

3 Value bands and ratios

For the purposes of paragraph 4 of Schedule 2 to the Bank of England Act 1998 (cash ratio deposits), the value bands and the ratios applicable to them, expressed as a percentage, are as follows:

Value band	Ratio
£0 – £500 million	0%
Over £500 million	0.11%

[4163]

NOTES
Commencement: 2 June 2008.

CANCELLATION OF CONTRACTS MADE IN A CONSUMER'S HOME OR PLACE OF WORK ETC REGULATIONS 2008

(SI 2008/1816)

NOTES
Made: 8 July 2008.
Authority: European Communities Act 1972, s 2(2); Consumers, Estate Agents and Redress Act 2007, s 59.
Commencement: 1 October 2008.
As of 1 February 2009, these Regulations had not been amended.

ARRANGEMENT OF REGULATIONS

1 Citation and commencement

These Regulations may be cited as the Cancellation of Contracts made in a Consumer's Home or Place of Work etc Regulations 2008 and shall come into force on 1st October 2008.

[4163A]

NOTES
Commencement: 1 October 2008.

2 Interpretation

(1) In these Regulations:

"the 1974 Act" means the Consumer Credit Act 1974;

"cancellable agreement" has the same meaning as in section 189(1) of the 1974 Act;

"cancellation notice" means a notice in writing given by the consumer which indicates that he wishes to cancel the contract;

"cancellation period" means the period of 7 days starting with the date of receipt by the consumer of a notice of the right to cancel;

"consumer" means a natural person who in making a contract to which these Regulations apply is acting for purposes which can be regarded as outside his trade or profession;

"consumer credit agreement" means an agreement between the consumer and any other person by which the other person provides the consumer with credit of any amount;

"credit" includes a cash loan and any other form of financial accommodation, and for this purpose "cash" includes money in any form;

"enforcement authority" means any person mentioned in regulation 21;

"fixed sum credit" has the same meaning as in section 10(1) of the 1974 Act;

"notice of the right to cancel" means a notice given in accordance with regulation 7;

"related credit agreement" means a consumer credit agreement under which fixed sum credit which fully or partly covers the price under a contract which may be cancelled under regulation 7 is granted—

    (i)   by the trader; or

    (ii) by another person, under an arrangement made between that person and the trader;

"solicited visit" has the meaning given in regulation 6(3);

"specified contract" has the meaning given in regulation 9; and

"trader" means a person who, in making a contract to which these Regulations apply, is acting in his commercial or professional capacity and anyone acting in the name or on behalf of a trader.

(2) Paragraph 8(2) of Schedule 3 has effect for the purposes of paragraphs 7 and 8(1).

[4163B]

NOTES
Commencement: 1 October 2008.

Consequential amendments, revocations and saving

3 (*Reg 3 introduces Sch 1 to these Regulations* (*Consequential Amendments*).)

4—(1) Schedule 2 (Revocations) shall have effect.

(2) The Consumer Protection (Cancellation of Contracts Concluded away from Business Premises) Regulations 1987 ("the 1987 Regulations") shall continue to have effect in relation to a contract to which they applied before their revocation by these Regulations.

(3) These Regulations shall not apply to a contract to which the 1987 Regulations applied before their revocation.

[4163C]

NOTES
Commencement: 1 October 2008.

Scope of application

5 These Regulations apply to a contract, including a consumer credit agreement, between a consumer and a trader which is for the supply of goods or services to the consumer by a trader and which is made—

    (a)   during a visit by the trader to the consumer's home or place of work, or to the home of another individual;

    (b)   during an excursion organised by the trader away from his business premises; or

    (c)   after an offer made by the consumer during such a visit or excursion.

[4163D]

PART III
STATUTORY INSTRUMENTS

NOTES

Commencement: 1 October 2008.

6—(1)   These Regulations do not apply to—

    (a)   any contracts listed in Schedule 3 (Excepted Contracts);

    (b)   a cancellable agreement;

    (c)   a consumer credit agreement which may be cancelled by the consumer in accordance with the terms of the agreement conferring upon him similar rights as if the agreement were a cancellable agreement; or

    (d)   a contract made during a solicited visit or a contract made after an offer made by a consumer during a solicited visit where the contract is—

        (i)   a regulated mortgage, home purchase plan or home reversion plan if the making or performance of such a contract constitutes a regulated activity for the purposes of the Financial Services and Markets Act 2000;

        (ii)   a consumer credit agreement secured on land which is—

            (aa)   regulated under the 1974 Act; or

            (bb)   to the extent that it is not regulated under the 1974 Act, exempt under that Act; or

        (iii)   any other consumer credit agreement regulated under the 1974 Act.

(2)   Where any agreement referred to in paragraph (1)(b), (c) or (d)(iii) is a related credit agreement the provisions of regulations 11 and 12 shall apply to the cancellation of that agreement.

(3)   A solicited visit means a visit by a trader, whether or not he is the trader who supplies the goods or services, to a consumer's home or place of work or to the home of another individual, which is made at the express request of the consumer but does not include—

    (a)   a visit by a trader which is made after he, or a person acting in his name or on his behalf—

        (i)   telephones the consumer (otherwise than at the consumer's express request) and indicates during the course of the telephone call (either expressly or by implication) that he, or the trader in whose name or on whose behalf he is acting, is willing to visit the consumer; or

        (ii)   visits the consumer (otherwise than at the consumer's express request) and indicates during the course of that visit (either expressly or by implication) that he, or the trader in whose name or on whose behalf he is acting, is willing to make a subsequent visit to the consumer; or

    (b)   a visit during which the contract which is made relates to goods and services other than those concerning which the consumer requested the visit of the trader, provided that when the visit was requested the consumer did not know, or could not reasonably have known, that the supply of such goods or services formed part of the trader's commercial or professional activities.

[4163E]

NOTES

Commencement: 1 October 2008.

7   Right to cancel a contract to which these Regulations apply

(1)   A consumer has the right to cancel a contract to which these Regulations apply within the cancellation period.

(2)   The trader must give the consumer a written notice of his right to cancel the contract and such notice must be given at the time the contract is made except in the case of a contract to which regulation 5(c) applies in which case the notice must be given at the time the offer is made by the consumer.

(3)   The notice must—

    (a)   be dated;

    (b)   indicate the right of the consumer to cancel the contract within the cancellation period;

    (c)   be easily legible;

    (d)   contain—

        (i)   the information set out in Part I of Schedule 4; and

        (ii)   a cancellation form in the form set out in Part II of that Schedule provided as a detachable slip and completed by or on behalf of the trader in accordance with the notes; and

    (e)   indicate if applicable—

        (i)   that the consumer may be required to pay for the goods or services supplied if the performance of the contract has begun with his written agreement before the end of the cancellation period;

      (ii)   that a related credit agreement will be automatically cancelled if the contract for goods or services is cancelled.

(4)   Where the contract is wholly or partly in writing the notice must be incorporated in the same document.

(5)   If incorporated in the contract or another document the notice of the right to cancel must—

   (a)   be set out in a separate box with the heading "Notice of the Right to Cancel"; and

   (b)   have as much prominence as any other information in the contract or document apart from the heading and the names of the parties to the contract and any information inserted in handwriting.

(6)   A contract to which these Regulations apply shall not be enforceable against the consumer unless the trader has given the consumer a notice of the right to cancel and the information required in accordance with this regulation.

[4163F]

NOTES

Commencement: 1 October 2008.

8   Exercise of the right to cancel a contract

(1)   If the consumer serves a cancellation notice within the cancellation period then the contract is cancelled.

(2)   A contract which is cancelled shall be treated as if it had never been entered into by the consumer except where these Regulations provide otherwise.

(3)   The cancellation notice must indicate the intention of the consumer to cancel the contract and does not need to follow the form of cancellation notice set out in Part II of Schedule 4.

(4)   The cancellation notice must be served on the trader or another person specified in the notice of the right to cancel as a person to whom the cancellation notice may be given.

(5)   A cancellation notice sent by post is taken to have been served at the time of posting, whether or not it is actually received.

(6)   Where a cancellation notice is sent by electronic mail it is taken to have been served on the day on which it is sent.

[4163G]

NOTES

Commencement: 1 October 2008.

9   Cancellation of specified contracts commenced before expiry of the right to cancel

(1)   Where the consumer enters into a specified contract and he wishes the performance of the contract to begin before the end of the cancellation period, he must request this in writing.

(2)   Where the consumer cancels a specified contract in accordance with regulation 8 he shall be under a duty to pay in accordance with the reasonable requirements of the cancelled contract for goods or services that were supplied before the cancellation.

(3)   If the consumer fails to provide the request in writing referred to in paragraph (1) then—

   (a)   the trader is not obliged to begin performance of the specified contract before the end of the cancellation period; and

   (b)   the consumer is not bound by the duty referred to in paragraph (2) if he cancels the contract in accordance with regulation 8.

(4)   For the purposes of this regulation and regulation 13, a "specified contact" means a contract for any of the following—

   (a)   the supply of newspapers, periodicals or magazines;

   (b)   advertising in any medium;

   (c)   the supply of goods the price of which is dependent on fluctuations in the financial markets which cannot be controlled by the trader;

   (d)   the supply of goods to meet an emergency;

   (e)   the supply of goods made to a customer's specifications or clearly personalised and any services in connection with the provision of such goods;

   (f)   the supply of perishable goods;

   (g)   the supply of goods which by their nature are consumed by use and which, before the cancellation, were so consumed;

   (h)   the supply of goods which, before the cancellation, had become incorporated in any land or thing not comprised in the cancelled contract;

   (i)   the supply of goods or services relating to a funeral; or

   (j)   the supply of services of any other kind.

[4163H]

NOTES
Commencement: 1 October 2008.

10 Recovery of money paid by consumer

(1)   On the cancellation of a contract under regulation 8 any sum paid by or on behalf of the consumer in respect of the contract shall become repayable except where these Regulations provide otherwise.

(2)   If the consumer or any person on his behalf is in possession of any goods under the terms of the cancelled contract then he shall have a lien on them for any sum repayable to him under paragraph (1).

(3)   Where any security has been provided in relation to the cancelled contract, the security shall be treated as never having had effect for that purpose and the trader must immediately return any property lodged with him solely as security for the purposes of the cancelled contract.

[4163I]

NOTES
Commencement: 1 October 2008.

11 Automatic cancellation of related credit agreement

(1)   A cancellation notice which cancels a contract for goods or services shall have the effect of cancelling any related credit agreement.

(2)   Subject to paragraphs (3) and (4), where a related credit agreement has been cancelled under paragraph (1)—

(a)   the trader must, if he is not the same person as the creditor under that agreement, immediately on receipt of the cancellation notice inform the creditor that the notice has been given;

(b)   any sum paid by or on behalf of the consumer in relation to the credit agreement must be reimbursed, except for any sum which would have to be paid under sub-paragraph (c);

(c)   the agreement shall continue in force so far as it relates to repayment of the credit and payment of interest in accordance with regulation 12, but shall otherwise cease to be enforceable; and

(d)   any security provided under the related credit agreement shall be treated as never having had effect for that purpose and the creditor must immediately return any property lodged with him solely as security for the purposes of the related credit agreement.

(3)   Where a related credit agreement is a cancellable agreement—

(a)   its cancellation under paragraph (1) shall take effect as if a notice of cancellation within the meaning of the 1974 Act had been served;

(b)   that Act shall apply in respect of the consequences of such cancellation;

(c)   paragraph (2)(b) to (d) and regulation 12 shall not apply in respect of its cancellation; and

(d)   regulations 13 and 14 shall not apply in respect of the cancellation of the related contract for goods or services.

(4)   Where a related credit agreement of a kind referred to in regulation 6(1)(c) is cancelled under paragraph (1)—

(a)   paragraph (2)(b) to (d) and regulation 12 shall not apply in respect of its cancellation; and

(b)   regulations 13 and 14 shall not apply in respect of the cancellation of the related contract for goods or services.

(5)   Where a related credit agreement of a kind referred to in regulation 6(1)(d)(iii) is cancelled under paragraph (1)—

(a)   the provisions of this regulation and regulation 12 shall apply in respect of its cancellation; and

(b)   the provisions of regulations 13 and 14 shall apply in respect of the cancellation of the related contract for goods or services.

(6)   For the purposes of this regulation and regulation 12 "creditor" is the person who grants credit under a related credit agreement.

[4163J]

NOTES
Commencement: 1 October 2008.

12 Repayment of credit and interest

(1)   Where—

(a) a contract under which credit is provided to the consumer is cancelled under regulation 8; or

(b) a related credit agreement (other than a cancellable agreement or an agreement of a kind referred to in regulation 6(1)(c)) is cancelled as a result of the cancellation of a contract for goods or services,

the contract or agreement shall continue in force so far as it relates to repayment of the credit and payment of interest.

(2) If, following the cancellation of a contract or related credit agreement to which paragraph (1) applies, the consumer repays the whole or a portion of the credit—

(a) before the expiry of one month following service of the cancellation notice; or

(b) in the case of a credit repayable by instalments, before the date on which the first instalment is due,

no interest shall be payable on the amount repaid.

(3) If the whole of a credit repayable by instalments is not repaid on or before the date specified in paragraph (2)(b), the consumer shall not be liable to repay any of the credit except on receipt of a request in writing signed by the trader stating the amounts of the remaining instalments (recalculated by the trader as nearly as may be in accordance with the contract and without extending the repayment period), but excluding any sum other than principal and interest.

(4) Repayment of a credit, or payment of interest, under a cancelled contract or related credit agreement shall be treated as duly made if it is made to any person on whom, under regulation 8(4), a cancellation notice could have been served.

(5) Where any security has been provided in relation to the contract or consumer credit agreement, the duty imposed on the consumer by this regulation shall not be enforceable before the trader or creditor has discharged any duty imposed on him by regulation 10(3) or 11(2)(d) respectively.

[4163K]

NOTES
Commencement: 1 October 2008.

13 Return of goods by consumer after cancellation

(1) A consumer who has acquired possession of any goods by virtue of the contract shall on the cancellation of that contract be under a duty, subject to any lien, to restore the goods to the trader and meanwhile to retain possession of the goods and take reasonable care of them.

(2) The consumer shall not be under a duty to restore goods supplied under a specified contract in circumstances where—

(a) he is required to pay, in accordance with the reasonable requirements of the cancelled contract, for the supply of such goods before cancellation; or

(b) the trader has begun performance of the contract before the end of the cancellation period without a prior request in writing by the consumer.

(3) The consumer shall not be under any duty to deliver the goods except at his own premises and following a request in writing signed by the trader and served on the consumer either before, or at the time when, the goods are collected from those premises.

(4) If the consumer—

(a) delivers the goods (whether at his own premises or elsewhere) to any person on whom, under regulation 8(4), a cancellation notice could have been served; or

(b) sends the goods at his own expense to such a person,

he shall be discharged from any duty to retain possession of the goods or restore them to the trader.

(5) Where the consumer delivers the goods as mentioned in paragraph (4)(a), his obligation to take care of the goods shall cease; and if he send the goods as mentioned in paragraph (4)(b), he shall be under a duty to take reasonable care to see that they are received by the trader and not damaged in transit, but in other respects his duty to take care of the goods shall cease.

(6) Where, at any time during the period of 21 days following the cancellation, the consumer receives such a request as is mentioned in paragraph (3) and unreasonably refuses or unreasonably fails to comply with it, his duty to retain possession and take reasonable care of the goods shall continue until he delivers or sends the goods as mentioned in paragraph (4); but if within that period he does not receive such a request his duty to take reasonable care of the goods shall cease at the end of that period.

(7) Where any security has been provided in relation to the cancelled contract, the duty imposed on the consumer to restore goods shall not be enforceable before the trader has discharged any duty imposed on him by regulation 10(3).

PART III
STATUTORY INSTRUMENTS

(8) Breach of a duty imposed on a consumer by this regulation is actionable as a breach of statutory duty.

[4163L]

NOTES
Commencement: 1 October 2008.

14 Goods given in part-exchange

(1) This regulation applies on the cancellation of a contract where the trader agreed to take goods in part-exchange (the "part-exchange goods") and those goods have been delivered to him.

(2) Unless, before the end of the period of ten days beginning with the date of cancellation, the part-exchange goods are returned to the consumer in a condition substantially as good as when they were delivered to the trader, the consumer shall be entitled to recover from the trader a sum equal to the part-exchange allowance.

(3) During the period of ten days beginning with the date of cancellation, the consumer, if he is in possession of goods to which the cancelled contract relates, shall have a lien on them for—
    (a) delivery of the part-exchange goods in a condition substantially as good as when they were delivered to the trader; or
    (b) a sum equal to the part-exchange allowance,

and if the lien continues to the end of that period it shall thereafter subsist only as a lien for a sum equal to the part-exchange allowance.

(4) In this regulation the part-exchange allowance means the sum agreed as such in the cancelled contract, or if no such sum was agreed, such sum as it would have been reasonable to allow in respect of the part-exchange goods if no notice of cancellation had been served.

[4163M]

NOTES
Commencement: 1 October 2008.

15 No contracting-out of contracts to which these Regulations apply

(1) A term contained in a contract is void if, and to the extent that, it is inconsistent with a provision for the protection of the consumer contained in these Regulations.

(2) Where a provision of these Regulations specifies the duty or liability of the consumer in certain circumstances, a term contained in a contract is inconsistent with that provision if it purports to impose, directly or indirectly, an additional or different duty or liability on the consumer in those circumstances.

[4163N]

NOTES
Commencement: 1 October 2008.

16 Service of documents

(1) A document to be served under these Regulations on a person may be so served—
    (a) by delivering it to him, or by leaving it at his proper address or by sending it to him at that address;
    (b) if the person is a body corporate, by serving it in accordance with sub-paragraph (a) on the secretary or clerk of that body;
    (c) if the person is a partnership, by serving it in accordance with sub-paragraph (a) on a partner or on a person having the control or management of the partnership business; and
    (d) if the person is an unincorporated body, by serving it in accordance with sub-paragraph (a) on a person having control or management of that body.

(2) For the purposes of paragraph (1), the proper address of any person on whom a document is to be served under these Regulations is his last known address except that—
    (a) in the case of service on a body corporate or its secretary or clerk, it is the address of the registered or principal office of the body corporate in the United Kingdom; and
    (b) in the case of service on a partnership or partner or person having the control or management of a partnership business, it is the partnership's principal place of business in the United Kingdom.

(3) A person's electronic mail address may also be his proper address for the purposes of paragraph (1).

[4163O]

NOTES
Commencement: 1 October 2008.

Enforcement

17   Offence relating to the failure to give notice of the right to cancel

(1)   A trader is guilty of an offence if he enters into a contract to which these Regulations apply but fails to give the consumer a notice of the right to cancel in accordance with regulation 7.

(2)   A person who is guilty of an offence under paragraph (1) shall be liable on summary conviction to a fine not exceeding level 5 on the standard scale.

[4163P]

NOTES
Commencement: 1 October 2008.

18   Defence of due diligence

(1)   In any proceedings against a person for an offence under regulation 17 it is a defence for that person to prove—
- (a)   that the commission of the offence was due to—
  - (i)   the act or default of another, or
  - (ii)   reliance on information given by another, and
- (b)   that he took all reasonable precautions and exercised all due diligence to avoid the commission of such an offence by himself or any person under his control.

(2)   A person shall not be entitled to rely on the defence provided by paragraph (1) without leave of the court unless—
- (a)   he has served on the prosecutor a notice in writing giving such information identifying or assisting in the identification of that other person as was in his possession; and
- (b)   the notice is served on the prosecutor not less than seven clear days before the hearing of the proceedings or, in Scotland, the diet of trial.

[4163Q]

NOTES
Commencement: 1 October 2008.

19   Liability of persons other than the principal offender

Where the commission by a person of an offence under regulation 17 is due to the act or default of another person, that other person is guilty of the offence and may be proceeded against and punished whether or not proceedings are taken against the first person.

[4163R]

NOTES
Commencement: 1 October 2008.

20   Offences committed by bodies of persons

(1)   Where an offence under regulation 17 committed by a body corporate is proved—
- (a)   to have been committed with the consent or connivance of an officer of the body corporate or
- (b)   to be attributable to any neglect on his part,

the officer, as well as the body corporate shall be guilty of the offence and liable to be proceeded against and punished accordingly.

(2)   In paragraph (1) a reference to an officer of a body corporate includes a reference to—
- (a)   a director, manager, secretary or other similar officer; and
- (b)   a person purporting to act as a director, manager, secretary or other similar officer.

(3)   Where an offence under regulation 17 committed in Scotland by a Scottish partnership is proved—
- (a)   to have been committed with the consent or connivance of a partner; or
- (b)   to be attributable to any neglect on his part,

that partner, as well as the partnership shall be guilty of the offence and liable to be proceeded against and punished accordingly.

(4)   In paragraph (3) a reference to a partner includes a person purporting to act as a partner.

[4163S]

PART III
STATUTORY INSTRUMENTS

NOTES
Commencement: 1 October 2008.

21 Duty to enforce

(1) Subject to paragraphs (2) and (3)—
  (a) it shall be the duty of every weights and measures authority in Great Britain to enforce regulation 17 within its area; and
  (b) it shall be the duty of the Department of Enterprise Trade and Investment in Northern Ireland to enforce regulation 17 within Northern Ireland.

(2) No proceedings for an offence under these Regulations may be instituted in England and Wales except by or on behalf of an enforcement authority.

(3) Nothing in paragraph (1) shall authorise any weights and measures authority to bring proceedings in Scotland for an offence.

[4163T]

NOTES
Commencement: 1 October 2008.

22 Powers of investigation

(1) If a duly authorised officer of an enforcement authority has reasonable grounds for suspecting that an offence has been committed under regulation 17, he may require a person carrying on or employed in a business to produce any document relating to the business, and take copies of it or any entry in it for the purposes of ascertaining whether such an offence has been committed.

(2) If the officer has reasonable grounds for believing that any documents may be required as evidence in proceedings for such an offence, he may seize and detain them and shall, if he does so, inform the person from whom they are seized.

(3) In this regulation "document" includes information recorded in any form.

(4) The reference in paragraph (1) to production of documents is, in the case of a document which contains information recorded otherwise than in a legible form, a reference to the production of a copy of the information in a legible form.

(5) An officer seeking to exercise a power under this regulation must do so only at a reasonable hour and on production (if required) of his identification and authority.

(6) Nothing in this regulation requires a person to produce, or authorises the taking from a person of, a document which the other person would be entitled to refuse to produce in proceedings in the High Court on the grounds of legal professional privilege or (in Scotland) in the Court of Session on the grounds of confidentiality of communications.

(7) In paragraph (6) "communications" means—
  (a) communications between a professional legal adviser and his client; or
  (b) communications made in connection with, or in contemplation of legal proceedings and for the purpose of those proceedings.

[4163U]

NOTES
Commencement: 1 October 2008.

Obstruction of authorised officers

23—(1) A person is guilty of an offence if he—
  (a) intentionally obstructs an officer of an enforcement authority acting in pursuance of his functions under these Regulations;
  (b) without reasonable cause fails to comply with any requirement properly made of him by such an officer under regulation 22; or
  (c) without reasonable cause fails to give such an officer any other assistance or information which he may reasonably require of him for the purpose of the performance of his functions under these Regulations.

(2) A person is guilty of an offence if, in giving any information which is required of him under paragraph (1)(c), he makes any statement which he knows to be false in a material particular.

(3) A person guilty of an offence under paragraph (1) or (2) shall be liable on summary conviction to a fine not exceeding level 3 on the standard scale.

[4163V]

Signed

Name and Address

Date

[4163Z]

NOTES
   Commencement: 1 October 2008.

PROCEEDS OF CRIME ACT 2002 (DISCLOSURE OF INFORMATION) ORDER 2008

(SI 2008/1909)

NOTES
   Made: 17 July 2008.
   Authority: Proceeds of Crime Act 2002, ss 436(6), 438(9).
   Commencement: 23 July 2008.

   As of 1 February 2009, this Order had not been amended.

1   Citation and commencement

This Order may be cited as the Proceeds of Crime Act 2002 (Disclosure of Information) Order 2008 and shall come into force on 23rd July 2008.

[4164]

NOTES
   Commencement: 23 July 2008.

2   Disclosure of information to certain Directors

For the purposes of section 436 of the Proceeds of Crime Act 2002, the persons listed in column 1 of the Schedule to this Order are designated as permitted persons in respect of the functions specified in relation to those persons in column 2 of the Schedule to this Order, being functions which the Secretary of State believes are of a public nature.

[4165]

NOTES
   Commencement: 23 July 2008.

3   Disclosure of information by certain Directors

The following functions are designated for the purposes of section 438 of the Proceeds of Crime Act 2002 being functions which the Secretary of State thinks are of a public nature—
   (a)   protecting public health;
   (b)   the functions of the Financial Services Authority under the Financial Services and Markets Act 2000.

[4166]

NOTES
   Commencement: 23 July 2008.

4   Revocation of the Proceeds of Crime Act 2002 (Disclosure of Information) Order 2003

The Proceeds of Crime Act 2002 (Disclosure of Information) Order 2003 is revoked.

[4167]

NOTES
   Commencement: 23 July 2008.

SCHEDULE

Article 2

Column 1	Column 2
The Secretary of State	Functions exercised for the purposes of—
	(a) the prevention, detection, investigation or prosecution of offences relating to a social security matter or a scheme or arrangement under section 2 of the Employment and Training Act 1973; or
	(b) checking the accuracy of any benefit, payment or advantage in a social security matter or a scheme or arrangement under section 2 of the Employment and Training Act 1973.
	Functions exercised for the purposes of prevention, detection, investigation or prosecution of offences relating to the use of motor vehicles, passenger vehicles or goods vehicles.
	Functions under—
	(a) the Employment Agencies Act 1973;
	(b) Part XIV of the Companies Act 1985;
	(c) Part III of the Companies Act 1989;
	(d) Part XI of the Financial Services and Markets Act 2000; and
	(e) the Export of Goods, Transfer of Technology and Provision of Technical Assistance (Control) Order 2003.
An officer authorised under section 9 of the Employment Agencies Act 1973	Functions under section 9 of the Employment Agencies Act 1973.
A person appointed or authorised to exercise powers under Part XIV of the Companies Act 1985	Functions under Part XIV of the Companies Act 1985.
A person appointed to conduct an investigation under Part XI of the Financial Services and Markets Act 2000	Functions under Part XI of the Financial Services and Markets Act 2000.
The Civil Aviation Authority	Functions under—
	(a) the Civil Aviation Act 1982;
	(b) Part IV and sections 69 and 73 of the Airports Act 1986; and
	(c) Part I of the Transport Act 2000.
The Gambling Commission	Functions under Part 2 of the Gambling Act 2005.
The Common Services Agency for the Scottish Health Service	Functions under article 3 of the National Health Service (Functions of the Common Services Agency) (Scotland) Order 1974 exercised for the purposes of preventing or detecting crime.
A financial investigator appointed under article 49 of the Proceeds of Crime (Northern Ireland) Order 1996	Functions under articles 50 and 51 of, and Schedule 2 to, the Proceeds of Crime (Northern Ireland) Order 1996.
The Department for Social Development in Northern Ireland	Functions exercised for the purposes of—

Column 1	Column 2
	(a) the prevention, detection, investigation or prosecution of offences relating to a social security matter; or
	(b) checking the accuracy of any benefit, payment or advantage in a social security matter.
The Department for Employment and Learning in Northern Ireland	Functions exercised for the purposes of—
	(a) the prevention, detection, investigation or prosecution of offences relating to a scheme or arrangement under section 1 of the Employment and Training Act (Northern Ireland) 1950; or
	(b) checking the accuracy of any benefit, payment or advantage in a scheme or arrangement under section 1 of the Employment and Training Act (Northern Ireland) 1950.
The Department of the Environment in Northern Ireland	Functions exercised for the purposes of the prevention, detection, investigation or prosecution of offences relating to the use of motor vehicles, passenger vehicles or goods vehicles.

[4168]

NOTES
  Commencement: 23 July 2008.

LIMITED LIABILITY PARTNERSHIPS (ACCOUNTS AND AUDIT) (APPLICATION OF COMPANIES ACT 2006) REGULATIONS 2008

(SI 2008/1911)

NOTES
  Made: 17 July 2008.
  Authority: Limited Liability Partnerships Act 2000, ss 15, 17; Companies Act 2006, ss 1210(1)(h), 1292(2).
  Commencement: 1 October 2008

  As of 1 February 2009, this Order had not been amended.

ARRANGEMENT OF REGULATIONS

PART 1
GENERAL INTRODUCTORY PROVISIONS

PART 2
LLPS QUALIFYING AS SMALL

PART 3
ACCOUNTING RECORDS

PART 1
GENERAL INTRODUCTORY PROVISIONS

1 Citation and commencement

These Regulations may be cited as the Limited Liability Partnerships (Accounts and Audit) (Application of Companies Act 2006) Regulations 2008 and come into force on 1st October 2008.

[4169]

NOTES

Commencement: 1 October 2008.

---

2 Application

(1)   Subject to paragraphs (2) to (11), these Regulations apply to accounts for financial years beginning on or after 1st October 2008.

(2)   Any question whether—

(a)   for the purposes of section 382, 383, 384(3) or 467(3) of the Companies Act 2006, as applied to limited liability partnerships by regulations 5 and 26, a limited liability partnership or group qualified as small in a financial year beginning before 1st October 2008, or

(b)   for the purposes of section 465 or 466 of that Act, as applied to limited liability partnerships by regulation 26, a limited liability partnership or group qualified as medium-sized in any such financial year,

is to be determined by reference to the corresponding provisions of the Companies Act 1985 or the Companies (Northern Ireland) Order 1986 as applied to limited liability partnerships by the Limited Liability Partnerships Regulations 2001 or the Limited Liability Partnerships Regulations (Northern Ireland) 2004.

(3)   Sections 485 to 488 of the Companies Act 2006, as applied to limited liability partnerships by regulation 36, apply in relation to appointments of auditors for financial years beginning on or after 1st October 2008.

(4)   Sections 492, 494 and 499 to 501 of the Companies Act 2006, as applied to limited liability partnerships by regulations 37, 38 and 40, apply to auditors appointed for financial years beginning on or after 1st October 2008.

(5)   Section 502 of the Companies Act 2006, as applied to limited liability partnerships by regulation 40, applies to auditors appointed on or after 1st October 2008.

(6)   Sections 495, 498 and 503 to 509 of the Companies Act 2006, as applied to limited liability partnerships by regulations 39 to 42, apply to auditors' reports on accounts for financial years beginning on or after 1st October 2008.

(7)   Sections 510 to 513 of the Companies Act 2006, as applied to limited liability partnerships by regulations 43 and 44, apply where notice of the proposed removal is given to the auditor on or after 1st October 2008.

(8)   Section 515 of the Companies Act 2006, as applied to limited liability partnerships by regulation 45, applies to appointments of auditors for financial years beginning on or after 1st October 2008.

(9)   Sections 516 to 518 of the Companies Act 2006, as applied to limited liability partnerships by regulation 45, apply to resignations occurring on or after 1st October 2008.

(10)   Sections 519 to 525 of the Companies Act 2006, as applied to limited liability partnerships by regulation 46, apply where the auditor ceases to hold office on or after 1st October 2008.

(11)   Section 526 of the Companies Act 2006, as applied to limited liability partnerships by regulation 46, applies where the vacancy occurs on or after 1st October 2008.

[4170]

NOTES

Commencement: 1 October 2008.

3 Interpretation

(1)   In these Regulations—

"1985 Act" means the Companies Act 1985,

"1986 Order" means the Companies (Northern Ireland) Order 1986, and

"LLP" means a limited liability partnership formed under the Limited Liability Partnerships Act 2000 or the Limited Liability Partnerships Act (Northern Ireland) 2002.

(2)   In these Regulations, unless the context otherwise requires—

(a)   any reference to a numbered Part, section or Schedule is to the Part, section or Schedule so numbered in the Companies Act 2006,

(b)   references in provisions applied to LLPs to other provisions of the Companies Act 2006 are to those provisions as applied to LLPs by these Regulations, and

(c)   references in provisions applied to LLPs to provisions of the Insolvency Act 1986 or the Insolvency (Northern Ireland) Order 1989 are to those provisions as applied to LLPs by the Limited Liability Partnerships Regulations 2001 or the Limited Liability Partnerships Regulations (Northern Ireland) 2004.

[4171]

NOTES

Commencement: 1 October 2008.

4 Scheme of Part 15 as applied to LLPs

Section 380 applies to LLPs, modified so that it reads as follows—

"380 Scheme of this Part

(1)   The requirements of this Part as to accounts and auditors' reports apply in relation to each financial year of an LLP.

(2)   In certain respects different provisions apply to different kinds of LLP.

(3)   The main distinctions for this purpose are between LLPs subject to the small LLPs regime (see section 381) and LLPs that are not subject to that regime.

(4)   In this Part, where provisions do not apply to all kinds of LLP, provisions applying to LLPs subject to the small LLPs regime appear before the provisions applying to other LLPs."

[4172]

NOTES

Commencement: 1 October 2008.

PART 2
LLPS QUALIFYING AS SMALL

5 LLPs subject to the small LLPs regime

Sections 381 to 384 apply to LLPs, modified so that they read as follows—

"381 LLPs subject to the small LLPs regime

The small LLPs regime applies to an LLP for a financial year in relation to which the LLP—

(a)   qualifies as small (see sections 382 and 383), and

(b)   is not excluded from the regime (see section 384).

382   LLPs qualifying as small: general

(1)   An LLP qualifies as small in relation to its first financial year if the qualifying conditions are met in that year.

(2)   An LLP qualifies as small in relation to a subsequent financial year—
  (a)   if the qualifying conditions are met in that year and the preceding financial year;
  (b)   if the qualifying conditions are met in that year and the LLP qualified as small in relation to the preceding financial year;
  (c)   if the qualifying conditions were met in the preceding financial year and the LLP qualified as small in relation to that year.

(3)   The qualifying conditions are met by an LLP in a year in which it satisfies two or more of the following requirements—

1. Turnover	Not more than £6.5 million
2. Balance sheet total	Not more than £3.26 million
3. Number of employees	Not more than 50

(4)   For a period that is an LLP's financial year but not in fact a year the maximum figures for turnover must be proportionately adjusted.

(5)   The balance sheet total means the aggregate of the amounts shown as assets in the LLP's balance sheet.

(6)   The number of employees means the average number of persons employed by the LLP in the year, determined as follows—

  (a)   find for each month in the financial year the number of persons employed under contracts of service by the LLP in that month (whether throughout the month or not),
  (b)   add together the monthly totals, and
  (c)   divide by the number of months in the financial year.

(7)   This section is subject to section 383 (LLPs qualifying as small: parent LLPs).

383   LLPs qualifying as small: parent LLPs

(1)   A parent LLP qualifies as a small LLP in relation to a financial year only if the group headed by it qualifies as a small group.

(2)   A group qualifies as small in relation to the parent LLP's first financial year if the qualifying conditions are met in that year.

(3)   A group qualifies as small in relation to a subsequent financial year of the parent LLP—
  (a)   if the qualifying conditions are met in that year and the preceding financial year;
  (b)   if the qualifying conditions are met in that year and the group qualified as small in relation to the preceding financial year;
  (c)   if the qualifying conditions were met in the preceding financial year and the group qualified as small in relation to that year.

(4)   The qualifying conditions are met by a group in a year in which it satisfies two or more of the following requirements—

1. Aggregate turnover	Not more than £6.5 million net (or £7.8 million gross)
2. Aggregate balance sheet total	Not more than £3.26 million net (or £3.9 million gross)
3. Aggregate number of employees	Not more than 50

(5)   The aggregate figures are ascertained by aggregating the relevant figures determined in accordance with section 382 for each member of the group.

(6)   In relation to the aggregate figures for turnover and balance sheet total—

  "net" means after any set-offs and other adjustments made to eliminate group transactions—
  (a)   in the case of non-IAS accounts in accordance with Part 1 of Schedule 4 to the Small Limited Liability Partnerships (Accounts) Regulations 2008 (SI 2008/1912) or Schedule 3 to the Large and Medium-sized Limited Liability Partnerships (Accounts) Regulations 2008 (SI 2008/1913),

(b) in the case of IAS accounts, in accordance with international accounting standards; and

"gross" means without those set-offs and other adjustments.

An LLP may satisfy any relevant requirement on the basis of either the net or the gross figure.

(7) The figures for each subsidiary undertaking shall be those included in its individual accounts for the relevant financial year, that is—

(a) if its financial year ends with that of the parent LLP, that financial year, and

(b) if not, its financial year ending last before the end of the financial year of the parent LLP.

If those figures cannot be obtained without disproportionate expense or undue delay, the latest available figures shall be taken.

384 LLPs excluded from the small LLPs regime

(1) The small LLPs regime does not apply to an LLP that is, or was at any time within the financial year to which the accounts relate—

(a) an LLP whose securities are admitted to trading on a regulated market in an EEA State,

(b) an LLP that—

(i) is an authorised insurance company, a banking LLP, an e-money issuer, a MiFID investment firm or a UCITS management company, or

(ii) carries on insurance market activity, or

(c) a member of an ineligible group.

(2) A group is ineligible if any of its members is—

(a) a public company,

(b) a body corporate (other than a company) whose shares are admitted to trading on a regulated market in an EEA State,

(c) a person (other than a small company or small LLP) who has permission under Part 4 of the Financial Services and Markets Act 2000 (c.8) to carry on a regulated activity,

(d) a small company or small LLP that is an authorised insurance company, a banking company or banking LLP, an e-money issuer, a MiFID investment firm or a UCITS management company, or

(e) a person who carries on insurance market activity.

(3) A company or LLP is a small company or small LLP for the purposes of subsection (2) if it qualified as small in relation to its last financial year ending on or before the end of the financial year to which the accounts relate."

[4173]

NOTES

Commencement: 1 October 2008.

PART 3
ACCOUNTING RECORDS

6 LLP's accounting records

Sections 386 to 389 apply to LLPs, modified so that they read as follows—

"386 Duty to keep accounting records

(1) Every LLP must keep adequate accounting records.

(2) Adequate accounting records means records that are sufficient—

(a) to show and explain the LLP's transactions,

(b) to disclose with reasonable accuracy, at any time, the financial position of the LLP at that time, and

(c) to enable the members of the LLP to ensure that any accounts required to be prepared comply with the requirements of this Act.

(3) Accounting records must, in particular, contain—

(a) entries from day to day of all sums of money received and expended by the LLP and the matters in respect of which the receipt and expenditure takes place, and

(b) a record of the assets and liabilities of the LLP.

(4) If the LLP's business involves dealing in goods, the accounting records must contain—

(a) statements of stock held by the LLP at the end of each financial year of the LLP,

(b)   all statements of stocktakings from which any statement of stock as is mentioned in paragraph (a) has been or is to be prepared, and

(c)   except in the case of goods sold by way of ordinary retail trade, statements of all goods sold and purchased, showing the goods and the buyers and sellers in sufficient detail to enable all these to be identified.

(5)   A parent LLP that has a subsidiary undertaking in relation to which the above requirements do not apply must take reasonable steps to secure that the undertaking keeps such accounting records as to enable the members of the parent LLP to ensure that any accounts required to be prepared under this Part comply with the requirements of this Act.

387   Duty to keep accounting records: offence

(1)   If an LLP fails to comply with any provision of section 386 (duty to keep accounting records), an offence is committed by every member of the LLP who is in default.

(2)   It is a defence for a person charged with such an offence to show that he acted honestly and that in the circumstances in which the LLP's business was carried on the default was excusable.

(3)   A person guilty of an offence under this section is liable—
(a)   on conviction on indictment, to imprisonment for a term not exceeding two years or a fine (or both);
(b)   on summary conviction—
(i)   in England and Wales, to imprisonment for a term not exceeding twelve months or to a fine not exceeding the statutory maximum (or both);
(ii)   in Scotland or Northern Ireland, to imprisonment for a term not exceeding six months, or to a fine not exceeding the statutory maximum (or both).

388   Where and for how long records to be kept

(1)   An LLP's accounting records—
(a)   must be kept at its registered office or such other place as the members think fit, and
(b)   must at all times be open to inspection by the members of the LLP.

(2)   If accounting records are kept at a place outside the United Kingdom, accounts and returns with respect to the business dealt with in the accounting records so kept must be sent to, and kept at, a place in the United Kingdom, and must at all times be open to such inspection.

(3)   The accounts and returns to be sent to the United Kingdom must be such as to—
(a)   disclose with reasonable accuracy the financial position of the business in question at intervals of not more than six months, and
(b)   enable the members of the LLP to ensure that the accounts required to be prepared under this Part comply with the requirements of this Act.

(4)   Accounting records that an LLP is required by section 386 to keep must be preserved by it for three years from the date on which they are made.

(5)   Subsection (4) is subject to any provision contained in rules made under section 411 of the Insolvency Act 1986 (c.45) (company insolvency rules) or Article 359 of the Insolvency (Northern Ireland) Order 1989 (SI 1989/2405 (NI 19)).

389   Where and for how long records to be kept: offences

(1)   If an LLP fails to comply with any provision of subsections (1) to (3) of section 388 (requirements as to keeping of accounting records), an offence is committed by every member of the LLP who is in default.

(2)   It is a defence for a person charged with such an offence to show that he acted honestly and that in the circumstances in which the LLP's business was carried on the default was excusable.

(3)   A member of an LLP commits an offence if he—
(a)   fails to take all reasonable steps for securing compliance by the LLP with subsection (4) of that section (period for which records to be preserved), or
(b)   intentionally causes any default by the LLP under that subsection.

(4)   A person guilty of an offence under this section is liable—
(a)   on conviction on indictment, to imprisonment for a term not exceeding two years or a fine (or both);
(b)   on summary conviction—
(i)   in England and Wales, to imprisonment for a term not exceeding twelve months or to a fine not exceeding the statutory maximum (or both);
(ii)   in Scotland or Northern Ireland, to imprisonment for a term not exceeding six months, or to a fine not exceeding the statutory maximum (or both)."

[4174]

NOTES
Commencement: 1 October 2008.

PART 4
FINANCIAL YEARS

7   An LLP's financial year

(1)   Sections 390 to 392 apply to LLPs, modified so that they read as follows—

"390   An LLP's financial year

(1)   An LLP's financial year is determined as follows.

(2)   Its first financial year—
  (a)   begins with the first day of its first accounting reference period, and
  (b)   ends with the last day of that period or such other date, not more than seven days before or after the end of that period, as the members of the LLP may determine.

(3)   Subsequent financial years—
  (a)   begin with the day immediately following the end of the LLP's previous financial year, and
  (b)   end with the last day of its next accounting reference period or such other date, not more than seven days before or after the end of that period, as the members of the LLP may determine.

(4)   In relation to an undertaking that is not an LLP, references in this Act to its financial year are to any period in respect of which a profit and loss account of the undertaking is required to be made up (by its constitution or by the law under which it is established), whether that period is a year or not.

(5)   The members of a parent LLP must secure that, except where in their opinion there are good reasons against it, the financial year of each of its subsidiary undertakings coincides with the LLP's own financial year.

391   Accounting reference periods and accounting reference date

(1)   An LLP's accounting reference periods are determined according to its accounting reference date in each calendar year.

(2)   The accounting reference date of an LLP is the last day of the month in which the anniversary of its incorporation falls.

(3)   An LLP's first accounting reference period is the period of more than six months, but not more than 18 months, beginning with the date of its incorporation and ending with its accounting reference date.

(4)   Its subsequent accounting reference periods are successive periods of twelve months beginning immediately after the end of the previous accounting reference period and ending with its accounting reference date.

(5)   This section has effect subject to the provisions of section 392 (alteration of accounting reference date).

392   Alteration of accounting reference date

(1)   An LLP may by notice given to the registrar specify a new accounting reference date having effect in relation to—
  (a)   the LLP's current accounting reference period and subsequent periods, or
  (b)   the LLP's previous accounting reference period and subsequent periods.

An LLP's "previous accounting reference period" means the one immediately preceding its current accounting reference period.

(2)   The notice must state whether the current or previous accounting reference period—
  (a)   is to be shortened, so as to come to an end on the first occasion on which the new accounting reference date falls or fell after the beginning of the period, or
  (b)   is to be extended, so as to come to an end on the second occasion on which that date falls or fell after the beginning of the period.

(3)   A notice extending an LLP's current or previous accounting reference period is not effective if given less than five years after the end of an earlier accounting reference period of the LLP that was extended under this section.

This does not apply—
  (a)   to a notice given by an LLP that is a subsidiary undertaking or parent undertaking of another EEA undertaking if the new accounting reference date coincides with

that of the other EEA undertaking or, where that undertaking is not a company or an LLP, with the last day of its financial year, or

(b)   where the LLP is in administration under Part 2 of the Insolvency Act 1986 (c.45) or Part 3 of the Insolvency (Northern Ireland) Order 1989 (SI 1989/2405 (NI 19)), or

(c)   where the Secretary of State directs that it should not apply, which he may do with respect to a notice that has been given or that may be given.

(4)   A notice under this section may not be given in respect of a previous accounting reference period if the period for filing the accounts and auditor's report for the financial year determined by reference to that accounting reference period has already expired.

(5)   An accounting reference period may not be extended so as to exceed 18 months and a notice under this section is ineffective if the current or previous accounting reference period as extended in accordance with the notice would exceed that limit.

This does not apply where the LLP is in administration under Part 2 of the Insolvency Act 1986 (c.45) or Part 3 of the Insolvency (Northern Ireland) Order 1989 (SI 1989/2405 (NI 19)).

(6)   In this section "EEA undertaking" means an undertaking established under the law of any part of the United Kingdom or the law of any other EEA State."

(2)   Until section 1068(1) comes fully into force, the notice referred to in section 392 (notice of alteration of accounting reference date) as applied to LLPs by paragraph (1) must be given in the form prescribed for the purposes of—

(a)   section 225(1) of the 1985 Act as applied to LLPs by regulation 3 of, and Schedule 1 to, the Limited Liability Partnerships Regulations 2001, or

(b)   Article 233(1) of the 1986 Order as applied to LLPs by regulation 3 of, and Schedule 1 to, the Limited Liability Partnerships Regulations (Northern Ireland) 2004.

[4175]

NOTES
Commencement: 1 October 2008.

PART 5
ANNUAL ACCOUNTS

8   Annual accounts to give true and fair view

Section 393 applies to LLPs, modified so that it reads as follows—

"393   Accounts to give true and fair view

(1)   The members of an LLP must not approve accounts for the purposes of this Chapter unless they are satisfied that they give a true and fair view of the assets, liabilities, financial position and profit or loss—

(a)   in the case of the LLP's individual accounts, of the LLP;

(b)   in the case of the LLP's group accounts, of the undertakings included in the consolidation as a whole, so far as concerns members of the LLP.

(2)   The auditor of an LLP in carrying out his functions under this Act in relation to the LLP's annual accounts must have regard to the members' duty under subsection (1)."

[4176]

NOTES
Commencement: 1 October 2008.

9   Individual accounts

Sections 394 to 397 apply to LLPs, modified so that they read as follows—

"394   Duty to prepare individual accounts

The members of every LLP must prepare accounts for the LLP for each of its financial years.

Those accounts are referred to as the LLP's "individual accounts".

395   Individual accounts: applicable accounting framework

(1)   An LLP's individual accounts may be prepared—

(a)   in accordance with section 396 ("non-IAS individual accounts"), or

(b)   in accordance with international accounting standards ("IAS individual accounts").

This is subject to the following provisions of this section and to section 407 (consistency of financial reporting within group).

PART III
STATUTORY INSTRUMENTS

(2)   After the first financial year in which the members of an LLP prepare IAS individual accounts ("the first IAS year"), all subsequent individual accounts of the LLP must be prepared in accordance with international accounting standards unless there is a relevant change of circumstance.

(3)   There is a relevant change of circumstance if, at any time during or after the first IAS year—

(a)   the LLP becomes a subsidiary undertaking of another undertaking that does not prepare IAS individual accounts,

(b)   the LLP ceases to be a subsidiary undertaking,

(c)   the LLP ceases to be an LLP with securities admitted to trading on a regulated market in an EEA State, or

(d)   a parent undertaking of the LLP ceases to be an undertaking with securities admitted to trading on a regulated market in an EEA State.

(4)   If, having changed to preparing non-IAS individual accounts following a relevant change of circumstance, the members again prepare IAS individual accounts for the LLP, subsections (2) and (3) apply again as if the first financial year for which such accounts are again prepared were the first IAS year.

396   Non-IAS individual accounts

(1)   Non-IAS individual accounts must comprise—

(a)   a balance sheet as at the last day of the financial year, and

(b)   a profit and loss account.

(2)   The accounts must—

(a)   in the case of the balance sheet, give a true and fair view of the state of affairs of the LLP as at the end of the financial year, and

(b)   in the case of the profit and loss account, give a true and fair view of the profit or loss of the LLP for the financial year.

(3)   The accounts must comply with the provisions of—

(a)   regulation 3 of the Small Limited Liability Partnerships (Accounts) Regulations 2008 (non-IAS individual accounts of LLP subject to the small LLPs regime) (SI 2008/1912), or

(b)   regulations 3 and 4 of the Large and Medium-sized Limited Liability Partnerships (Accounts) Regulations 2008 (non-IAS individual accounts of large and medium-sized LLPs) (SI 2008/1913),

as to the form and content of the balance sheet and profit and loss account, and additional information to be provided by way of notes to the accounts..

(4)   If compliance with the regulations specified in subsection (3), and any other provision made by or under this Act as to the matters to be included in an LLP's individual accounts or in notes to those accounts, would not be sufficient to give a true and fair view, the necessary additional information must be given in the accounts or in a note to them.

(5)   If in special circumstances compliance with any of those provisions is inconsistent with the requirement to give a true and fair view, the members must depart from that provision to the extent necessary to give a true and fair view.

Particulars of any such departure, the reasons for it and its effect must be given in a note to the accounts.

397   IAS individual accounts

Where the members of an LLP prepare IAS individual accounts, they must state in the notes to the accounts that the accounts have been prepared in accordance with international accounting standards."

[4177]

NOTES

Commencement: 1 October 2008.

10   Group accounts

Sections 398 to 408 apply to LLPs, modified so that they read as follows—

"398   Option to prepare group accounts

If at the end of a financial year an LLP subject to the small LLPs regime is a parent LLP the members, as well as preparing individual accounts for the year, may prepare group accounts for the year.

399   Duty to prepare group accounts

(1)   This section applies to LLPs that are not subject to the small LLPs regime.

(2) If at the end of a financial year the LLP is a parent LLP the members, as well as preparing individual accounts for the year, must prepare group accounts for the year unless the LLP is exempt from that requirement.

(3) There are exemptions under—
  (a) section 400 (LLP included in EEA accounts of larger group),
  (b) section 401 (LLP included in non-EEA accounts of larger group), and
  (c) section 402 (LLP none of whose subsidiary undertakings need be included in the consolidation).

(4) An LLP to which this section applies but which is exempt from the requirement to prepare group accounts, may do so.

400 Exemption for LLP included in EEA group accounts of larger group

(1) An LLP is exempt from the requirement to prepare group accounts if it is itself a subsidiary undertaking and its immediate parent undertaking is established under the law of an EEA State, in the following cases—
  (a) where the LLP is a wholly-owned subsidiary of that parent undertaking;
  (b) where that parent undertaking holds more than 50% of the shares in the LLP and notice requesting the preparation of group accounts has not been served on the LLP by members holding in aggregate—
    (i)   more than half of the remaining shares in the LLP, or
    (ii) 5% of the total shares in the LLP.

Such notice must be served not later than six months after the end of the financial year before that to which it relates.

(2) Exemption is conditional upon compliance with all of the following conditions—
  (a) the LLP must be included in consolidated accounts for a larger group drawn up to the same date, or to an earlier date in the same financial year, by a parent undertaking established under the law of an EEA State;
  (b) those accounts must be drawn up and audited, and that parent undertaking's annual report must be drawn up, according to that law—
    (i)   in accordance with the provisions of the Seventh Directive (83/349/EEC) (as modified, where relevant, by the provisions of the Bank Accounts Directive (86/635/EEC) or the Insurance Accounts Directive (91/674/EEC)), or
    (ii) in accordance with international accounting standards;
  (c) the LLP must disclose in its individual accounts that it is exempt from the obligation to prepare and deliver group accounts;
  (d) the LLP must state in its individual accounts the name of the parent undertaking that draws up the group accounts referred to above and—
    (i)   if it is incorporated outside the United Kingdom, the country in which it is incorporated, or
    (ii) if it is unincorporated, the address of its principal place of business;
  (e) the LLP must deliver to the registrar, within the period for filing its accounts and auditor's report for the financial year in question, copies of those group accounts, together with the auditor's report on them;
  (f) any requirement of Part 35 of this Act as to the delivery to the registrar of a certified translation into English must be met in relation to any document comprised in the accounts and reports delivered in accordance with paragraph (e).

(3) For the purposes of subsection (1)(b) shares held by a wholly-owned subsidiary of the parent undertaking, or held on behalf of the parent undertaking or a wholly-owned subsidiary, shall be attributed to the parent undertaking.

(4) The exemption does not apply to an LLP any of whose securities are admitted to trading on a regulated market in an EEA State.

(5) In subsection (4) "securities" includes—
  (a) debentures, including debenture stock, loan stock, bonds, certificates of deposit and other instruments creating or acknowledging indebtedness,
  (b) warrants or other instruments entitling the holder to subscribe for securities falling within paragraph (a), and
  (c) certificates or other instruments that confer—
    (i)   property rights in respect of a security falling within paragraph (a) or (b),
    (ii)   any right to acquire, dispose of, underwrite or convert a security, being a right to which the holder would be entitled if he held any such security to which the certificate or other instrument relates, or
    (iii) a contractual right (other than an option) to acquire any such security otherwise than by subscription.

PART III
STATUTORY INSTRUMENTS

401 Exemption for LLP included in non-EEA group accounts of larger group

(1)   An LLP is exempt from the requirement to prepare group accounts if it is itself a subsidiary undertaking and its parent undertaking is not established under the law of an EEA State, in the following cases—

    (a)   where the LLP is a wholly-owned subsidiary of that parent undertaking;

    (b)   where that parent undertaking holds more than 50% of the shares in the LLP and notice requesting the preparation of group accounts has not been served on the LLP by members holding in aggregate—

        (i)   more than half of the remaining shares in the LLP, or

        (ii)   5% of the total shares in the LLP.

Such notice must be served not later than six months after the end of the financial year before that to which it relates.

(2)   Exemption is conditional upon compliance with all of the following conditions—

    (a)   the LLP and all of its subsidiary undertakings must be included in consolidated accounts for a larger group drawn up to the same date, or to an earlier date in the same financial year, by a parent undertaking;

    (b)   those accounts must be drawn up—

        (i)   in accordance with the provisions of the Seventh Directive (83/349/EEC) (as modified, where relevant, by the provisions of the Bank Accounts Directive (86/635/EEC) or the Insurance Accounts Directive (91/674/EEC)), or

        (ii)   in a manner equivalent to consolidated accounts so drawn up;

    (c)   the group accounts must be audited by one or more persons authorised to audit accounts under the law under which the parent undertaking which draws them up is established;

    (d)   the LLP must disclose in its individual accounts that it is exempt from the obligation to prepare and deliver group accounts;

    (e)   the LLP must state in its individual accounts the name of the parent undertaking which draws up the group accounts referred to above and—

        (i)   if it is incorporated outside the United Kingdom, the country in which it is incorporated, or

        (ii)   if it is unincorporated, the address of its principal place of business;

    (f)   the LLP must deliver to the registrar, within the period for filing its accounts and auditor's report for the financial year in question, copies of the group accounts, together with the auditor's report on them;

    (g)   any requirement of Part 35 of this Act as to the delivery to the registrar of a certified translation into English must be met in relation to any document comprised in the accounts and reports delivered in accordance with paragraph (f).

(3)   For the purposes of subsection (1)(b) shares held by a wholly-owned subsidiary of the parent undertaking, or held on behalf of the parent undertaking or a wholly-owned subsidiary, shall be attributed to the parent undertaking.

(4)   The exemption does not apply to an LLP any of whose securities are admitted to trading on a regulated market in an EEA State.

(5)   In subsection (4) "securities" includes—

    (a)   debentures, including debenture stock, loan stock, bonds, certificates of deposit and other instruments creating or acknowledging indebtedness,

    (b)   warrants or other instruments entitling the holder to subscribe for securities falling within paragraph (a), and

    (c)   certificates or other instruments that confer—

        (i)   property rights in respect of a security falling within paragraph (a) or (b),

        (ii)   any right to acquire, dispose of, underwrite or convert a security, being a right to which the holder would be entitled if he held any such security to which the certificate or other instrument relates, or

        (iii)   a contractual right (other than an option) to acquire any such security otherwise than by subscription.

402 Exemption if no subsidiary undertakings need be included in the consolidation

A parent LLP is exempt from the requirement to prepare group accounts if under section 405 all of its subsidiary undertakings could be excluded from consolidation in non-IAS group accounts.

403 Group accounts: applicable accounting framework

(1)   The group accounts of a parent LLP may be prepared—

    (a)   in accordance with section 404 (" non-IAS group accounts"), or

    (b)   in accordance with international accounting standards ("IAS group accounts").

This is subject to the following provisions of this section.

(2)   After the first financial year in which the members of a parent LLP prepare IAS group accounts ("the first IAS year"), all subsequent group accounts of the LLP must be prepared in accordance with international accounting standards unless there is a relevant change of circumstance.

(3)   There is a relevant change of circumstance if, at any time during or after the first IAS year—

(a)   the LLP becomes a subsidiary undertaking of another undertaking that does not prepare IAS group accounts,

(b)   the LLP ceases to be an LLP with securities admitted to trading on a regulated market in an EEA State, or

(c)   a parent undertaking of the LLP ceases to be an undertaking with securities admitted to trading on a regulated market in an EEA State.

(4)   If, having changed to preparing non-IAS group accounts following a relevant change of circumstance, the members again prepare IAS group accounts for the LLP, subsections (2) and (3) apply again as if the first financial year for which such accounts are again prepared were the first IAS year.

404   Non-IAS group accounts

(1)   Non-IAS group accounts must comprise—

(a)   a consolidated balance sheet dealing with the state of affairs of the parent LLP and its subsidiary undertakings, and

(b)   a consolidated profit and loss account dealing with the profit or loss of the parent LLP and its subsidiary undertakings.

(2)   The accounts must give a true and fair view of the state of affairs as at the end of the financial year, and the profit or loss for the financial year, of the undertakings included in the consolidation as a whole, so far as concerns members of the LLP.

(3)   The accounts must comply with the provisions of—

(a)   regulation 6 of the Small Limited Liability Partnerships (Accounts) Regulations 2008 (non-IAS group accounts of small parent LLP opting to prepare group accounts) (SI 2008/1912), or

(b)   regulation 6 of the Large and Medium-sized Limited Liability Partnerships (Accounts) Regulations 2008 (non-IAS group accounts of large and medium-sized parent LLPs) (SI 2008/1913),

as to the form and content of the consolidated balance sheet and consolidated profit and loss account, and additional information to be provided by way of notes to the accounts.

(4)   If compliance with the regulations specified in subsection (3), and any other provision made by or under this Act as to the matters to be included in an LLP's group accounts or in notes to those accounts, would not be sufficient to give a true and fair view, the necessary additional information must be given in the accounts or in a note to them.

(5)   If in special circumstances compliance with any of those provisions is inconsistent with the requirement to give a true and fair view, the members must depart from that provision to the extent necessary to give a true and fair view.

Particulars of any such departure, the reasons for it and its effect must be given in a note to the accounts.

405   Non-IAS group accounts: subsidiary undertakings included in the consolidation

(1)   Where a parent LLP prepares non-IAS group accounts, all the subsidiary undertakings of the LLP must be included in the consolidation, subject to the following exceptions.

(2)   A subsidiary undertaking may be excluded from consolidation if its inclusion is not material for the purpose of giving a true and fair view (but two or more undertakings may be excluded only if they are not material taken together).

(3)   A subsidiary undertaking may be excluded from consolidation where—

(a)   severe long-term restrictions substantially hinder the exercise of the rights of the parent LLP over the assets or management of that undertaking, or

(b)   the information necessary for the preparation of group accounts cannot be obtained without disproportionate expense or undue delay, or

(c)   the interest of the parent LLP is held exclusively with a view to subsequent resale.

(4)   The reference in subsection (3)(a) to the rights of the parent LLP and the reference in subsection (3)(c) to the interest of the parent LLP are, respectively, to rights and interests held by or attributed to the LLP for the purposes of the definition of "parent undertaking" (see section 1162) in the absence of which it would not be the parent LLP.

406 IAS group accounts

Where the members of an LLP prepare IAS group accounts, they must state in the notes to those accounts that the accounts have been prepared in accordance with international accounting standards.

407 Consistency of financial reporting within group

(1) The members of a parent LLP must secure that the individual accounts of—
    (a) the parent LLP, and
    (b) each of its subsidiary undertakings,
are all prepared using the same financial reporting framework, except to the extent that in their opinion there are good reasons for not doing so.

(2) Subsection (1) does not apply if the members do not prepare group accounts for the parent LLP.

(3) Subsection (1) only applies to accounts of subsidiary undertakings that are required to be prepared under this Part.

(4) Subsection (1)(a) does not apply where the members of a parent LLP prepare IAS group accounts and IAS individual accounts.

408 Individual profit and loss account where group accounts prepared

(1) This section applies where—
    (a) an LLP prepares group accounts in accordance with this Act, and
    (b) the notes to the LLP's individual balance sheet show the LLP's profit or loss for the financial year determined in accordance with this Act

(2) The LLP's individual profit and loss account need not contain the information specified in section 411 (information about employee numbers and costs).

(3) The LLP's individual profit and loss account must be approved in accordance with section 414(1) (approval by members) but may be omitted from the LLP's annual accounts for the purposes of the other provisions of this Act.

(4) The exemption conferred by this section is conditional upon its being disclosed in the LLP's annual accounts that the exemption applies."

[4178]

NOTES
Commencement: 1 October 2008.

---

11 Information to be given in notes to accounts

Section 409 to 411 apply to LLPs, modified so that they read as follows—

"409 Information about related undertakings

(1) The notes to the LLP's annual accounts must contain the information about related undertakings required by—
    (a) regulations 4 and 7 of the Small Limited Liability Partnerships (Accounts) Regulations 2008 (information about related undertakings: non-IAS or IAS individual or group accounts) (SI 2008/1912), or
    (b) regulation 5 of the Large and Medium-sized Limited Liability Partnerships (Accounts) Regulations 2008 (information about related undertakings: non-IAS or IAS individual or group accounts) (SI 2008/1913).

(2) That information need not be disclosed with respect to an undertaking that—
    (a) is established under the law of a country outside the United Kingdom, or
    (b) carries on business outside the United Kingdom,
if the following conditions are met.

(4) The conditions are—
    (a) that in the opinion of the members of the LLP the disclosure would be seriously prejudicial to the business of—
        (i) that undertaking,
        (ii) the LLP,
        (iii) any of the LLP's subsidiary undertakings, or
        (iv) any other undertaking which is included in the consolidation;
    (b) that the Secretary of State agrees that the information need not be disclosed.

(5) Where advantage is taken of any such exemption, that fact must be stated in a note to the LLP's annual accounts.

410   Information about related undertakings: alternative compliance

(1)   This section applies where the members of an LLP are of the opinion that the number of undertakings in respect of which the LLP is required to disclose information under any provision of the regulations specified in section 409(1) (related undertakings) is such that compliance with that provision would result in information of excessive length being given in notes to the LLP's annual accounts.

(2)   The information need only be given in respect of—
    (a)   the undertakings whose results or financial position, in the opinion of the members, principally affected the figures shown in the LLP's annual accounts, and
    (b)   where the LLP prepares group accounts, undertakings excluded from consolidation under section 405(3) (undertakings excluded on grounds other than materiality).

(3)   If advantage is taken of subsection (2)—
    (a)   there must be included in the notes to the LLP's annual accounts a statement that the information is given only with respect to such undertakings as are mentioned in that subsection, and
    (b)   the full information (both that which is disclosed in the notes to the accounts and that which is not) must be annexed to the LLP's next annual return.

For this purpose the "next annual return" means that next delivered to the registrar after the accounts in question have been approved under section 414.

(4)   If an LLP fails to comply with subsection (3)(b), an offence is committed by—
    (a)   the LLP, and
    (b)   every member of the LLP who is in default.

(5)   A person guilty of an offence under subsection (4) is liable on summary conviction to a fine not exceeding level 3 on the standard scale and, for continued contravention, a daily default fine not exceeding one-tenth of level 3 on the standard scale.

410A   Information about off-balance sheet arrangements

(1)   In the case of an LLP that is not subject to the small LLPs regime, if in any financial year—
    (a)   the LLP is or has been party to arrangements that are not reflected in its balance sheet, and
    (b)   at the balance sheet date the risks or benefits arising form those arrangements are material,
the information required by this section must be given in notes to the LLP's annual accounts.

(2)   The information required is—
    (a)   the nature and business purpose of the arrangements, and
    (b)   the financial impact of the arrangements on the LLP.

(3)   The information need only be given to the extent necessary for enabling the financial position of the LLP to be assessed.

(4)   If the LLP qualifies as medium-sized in relation to the financial year (see sections 465 to 467) it need not comply with subsection (2)(b).

(5)   This section applies in relation to group accounts as if the undertakings included in the consolidation were a single LLP.

411   Information about employee numbers and costs

(1)   In the case of an LLP not subject to the small LLPs regime, the following information with respect to the employees of the LLP must be given in notes to the LLP's annual accounts—
    (a)   the average number of persons employed by the LLP in the financial year, and
    (b)   the average number of persons so employed within each category of persons employed by the LLP.

(2)   The categories by reference to which the number required to be disclosed by subsection (1)(b) is to be determined must be such as the members may select having regard to the manner in which the LLP's activities are organised.

(3)   The average number required by subsection (1)(a) or (b) is determined by dividing the relevant annual number by the number of months in the financial year.

(4)   The relevant annual number is determined by ascertaining for each month in the financial year—
    (a)   for the purposes of subsection (1)(a), the number of persons employed under contracts of service by the LLP in that month (whether throughout the month or not);
    (b)   for the purposes of subsection (1)(b), the number of persons in the category in question of persons so employed;

PART III
STATUTORY INSTRUMENTS

and adding together all the monthly numbers.

(5)   In respect of all persons employed by the LLP during the financial year who are taken into account in determining the relevant annual number for the purposes of subsection (1)(a) there must also be stated the aggregate amounts respectively of—

(a)   wages and salaries paid or payable in respect of that year to those persons;

(b)   social security costs incurred by the LLP on their behalf; and

(c)   other pension costs so incurred.

This does not apply in so far as those amounts, or any of them, are stated elsewhere in the LLP's accounts.

(6)   In subsection (5)—

"pension costs" includes any costs incurred by the LLP in respect of—

(a)   any pension scheme established for the purpose of providing pensions for persons currently or formerly employed by the LLP,

(b)   any sums set aside for the future payment of pensions directly by the LLP to current or former employees, and

(c)   any pensions paid directly to such persons without having first been set aside;

"social security costs" means any contributions by the LLP to any state social security or pension scheme, fund or arrangement.

(7)   This section applies in relation to group accounts as if the undertakings included in the consolidation were a single LLP."

[4179]

NOTES

Commencement: 1 October 2008.

12   Approval and signing of accounts

Section 414 applies to LLPs, modified so that it reads as follows—

"414   Approval and signing of accounts

(1)   An LLP's annual accounts must be approved by the members, and signed on behalf of all the members by a designated member.

(2)   The signature must be on the LLP's balance sheet.

(3)   If the accounts are prepared in accordance with the provisions applicable to LLPs subject to the small LLPs regime, the balance sheet must contain a statement to that effect in a prominent position above the signature.

(4)   If annual accounts are approved that do not comply with the requirements of this Act, every member of the LLP who—

(a)   knew that they did not comply, or was reckless as to whether they complied, and

(b)   failed to take reasonable steps to secure compliance with those requirements or, as the case may be, to prevent the accounts from being approved,

commits an offence.

(5)   A person guilty of an offence under this section is liable—

(a)   on conviction on indictment, to a fine;

(b)   on summary conviction, to a fine not exceeding the statutory maximum."

[4180]

NOTES

Commencement: 1 October 2008.

PART 6
PUBLICATION OF ACCOUNTS AND AUDITOR'S REPORT

13   Publication of accounts and auditor's report

Section 423 applies to LLPs, modified so that it reads as follows—

"423   Duty to circulate copies of annual accounts and auditor's report

(1)   Every LLP must send a copy of its annual accounts and auditor's report for each financial year to—

(a)   every member of the LLP, and

(b)   every holder of the LLP's debentures,

not later than the end of the period for filing accounts and the auditor's report on them, or, if earlier, the date on which it actually delivers its accounts and the auditor's report on those accounts to the registrar.

(2)   Copies need not be sent to a person for whom the LLP does not have a current address.

(3)   An LLP has a "current address" for a person if—
    (a)   an address has been notified to the LLP by the person as one at which documents may be sent to him, and
    (b)   the LLP has no reason to believe that documents sent to him at that address will not reach him.

(4)   Where copies are sent out over a period of days, references in this Act to the day on which copies are sent out shall be read as references to the last day of that period."

[4181]

NOTES
Commencement: 1 October 2008.

14   Default in sending out copies of accounts and auditor's report

Section 425 applies to LLPs, modified so that it reads as follows—

"425   Default in sending out copies of accounts and auditor's report: offences

(1)   If default is made in complying with section 423, an offence is committed by—
    (a)   the LLP, and
    (b)   every member of the LLP who is in default.

(2)   A person guilty of an offence under this section is liable—
    (a)   on conviction on indictment, to a fine;
    (b)   on summary conviction, to a fine not exceeding the statutory maximum."

[4182]

NOTES
Commencement: 1 October 2008.

15   Right of member or debenture holder to copies of accounts and auditor's report

Section 431 applies to LLPs, modified so that it reads as follows—

"431   Right of member or debenture holder to copies of accounts and auditor's report

(1)   A member of, or holder of debentures of, an LLP is entitled to be provided, on demand and without charge, with a copy of—
    (a)   the LLP's last annual accounts, and
    (b)   the auditor's report on those accounts.

(2)   The entitlement under this section is to a single copy of those documents, but that is in addition to any copy to which a person may be entitled under section 423.

(3)   If a demand made under this section is not complied with within seven days of receipt by the LLP, an offence is committed by—
    (a)   the LLP, and
    (b)   every member of the LLP who is in default.

(4)   A person guilty of an offence under this section is liable on summary conviction to a fine not exceeding level 3 on the standard scale and, for continued contravention, a daily default fine not exceeding one-tenth of level 3 on the standard scale."

[4183]

NOTES
Commencement: 1 October 2008.

16   Requirements in connection with publication of accounts and auditor's report

Sections 433 to 436 apply to LLPs, modified so that they read as follows—

"433   Name of signatory to be stated in published copies of accounts

(1)   Every copy of the LLP's balance sheet that is published by or on behalf of the LLP must state the name of the person who signed it on behalf of the members of the LLP.

(2)   If a copy is published without the required statement of the signatory's name, an offence is committed by—
    (a)   the LLP, and
    (b)   every member of the LLP who is in default.

(3)   A person guilty of an offence under this section is liable on summary conviction to a fine not exceeding level 3 on the standard scale.

434 Requirements in connection with publication of statutory accounts

(1) If an LLP publishes any of its statutory accounts, they must be accompanied by the auditor's report on those accounts (unless the LLP is exempt from audit and the members have taken advantage of that exemption).

(2) An LLP that prepares statutory group accounts for a financial year must not publish its statutory individual accounts for that year without also publishing with them its statutory group accounts.

(3) An LLP's "statutory accounts" are its accounts for a financial year as required to be delivered to the registrar under section 441.

(4) If an LLP contravenes any provision of this section, an offence is committed by—
    (a)   the LLP, and
    (b)   every member of the LLP who is in default.

(5) A person guilty of an offence under this section is liable on summary conviction to a fine not exceeding level 3 on the standard scale.

435 Requirements in connection with publication of non-statutory accounts

(1) If an LLP publishes non-statutory accounts, it must publish with them a statement indicating—
    (a)   that they are not the LLP's statutory accounts,
    (b)   whether statutory accounts dealing with any financial year with which the non-statutory accounts purport to deal have been delivered to the registrar, and
    (c)   whether an auditor's report has been made on the LLP's statutory accounts for any such financial year, and if so whether the report—
        (i)   was qualified or unqualified, or included a reference to any matters to which the auditor drew attention by way of emphasis without qualifying the report, or
        (ii)   contained a statement under section 498(2) (accounting records or returns inadequate or accounts not agreeing with records and returns), or section 498(3) (failure to obtain necessary information and explanations).

(2) The LLP must not publish with non-statutory accounts the auditor's report on the LLP's statutory accounts.

(3) References in this section to the publication by an LLP of "non-statutory accounts" are to the publication of—
    (a)   any balance sheet or profit and loss account relating to, or purporting to deal with, a financial year of the LLP, or
    (b)   an account in any form purporting to be a balance sheet or profit and loss account for a group headed by the LLP relating to, or purporting to deal with, a financial year of the LLP,
otherwise than as part of the LLP's statutory accounts.

(4) In subsection (3)(b) "a group headed by the LLP" means a group consisting of the LLP and any other undertaking (regardless of whether it is a subsidiary undertaking of the LLP) other than a parent undertaking of the LLP.

(5) If an LLP contravenes any provision of this section, an offence is committed by—
    (a)   the LLP, and
    (b)   every member of the LLP who is in default.

(6) A person guilty of an offence under this section is liable on summary conviction to a fine not exceeding level 3 on the standard scale.

436 Meaning of "publication" in relation to accounts and auditor's report

(1) This section has effect for the purposes of—
    •   section 433 (name of signatory to be stated in published copies of accounts),
    •   section 434 (requirements in connection with publication of statutory accounts), and
    •   section 435 (requirements in connection with publication of non-statutory accounts).

(2) For the purposes of those sections an LLP is regarded as publishing a document if it publishes, issues or circulates it or otherwise makes it available for public inspection in a manner calculated to invite members of the public generally, or any class of members of the public, to read it."

[4184]

NOTES
Commencement: 1 October 2008.

PART 7
FILING OF ACCOUNTS AND AUDITOR'S REPORT

17 Duty to file accounts and reports

(1) Sections 441 to 444 apply to LLPs, modified so that they read as follow—

"441 Duty to file accounts and auditor's report with the registrar

The designated members of an LLP must deliver to the registrar for each financial year the accounts and auditor's report required by—

- section 444 (filing obligations of LLPs subject to small LLPs regime),
- section 445 (filing obligations of medium-sized LLPs), or
- section 446 (filing obligations of large LLPs).

442 Period allowed for filing accounts

(1) This section specifies the period allowed for the designated members of an LLP to comply with their obligation under section 441 to deliver accounts and the auditor's report for a financial year to the registrar.

This is referred to in this Act as the "period for filing" those accounts and that report.

(2) The period is nine months after the end of the relevant accounting reference period.

This is subject to the following provisions of this section.

(3) If the relevant accounting reference period is the LLP's first and is a period of more than twelve months, the period is—

- (a) nine months from the first anniversary of the incorporation of the LLP, or
- (b) three months after the end of the accounting reference period,

whichever last expires.

(4) If the relevant accounting reference period is treated as shortened by virtue of a notice given by the LLP under section 392 (alteration of accounting reference date), the period is—

- (a) that applicable in accordance with the above provisions, or
- (b) three months from the date of the notice under that section,

whichever last expires.

(5) If for any special reason the Secretary of State thinks fit he may, on an application made before the expiry of the period otherwise allowed, by notice in writing to an LLP extend that period by such further period as may be specified in the notice.

(6) In this section "the relevant accounting reference period" means the accounting reference period by reference to which the financial year for the accounts in question was determined.

443 Calculation of period allowed

(1) This section applies for the purposes of calculating the period for filing an LLP's accounts and auditor's report which is expressed as a specified number of months from a specified date or after the end of a specified previous period.

(2) Subject to the following provisions, the period ends with the date in the appropriate month corresponding to the specified date or the last day of the specified previous period.

(3) If the specified date, or the last day of the specified previous period, is the last day of a month, the period ends with the last day of the appropriate month (whether or not that is the corresponding date).

(4) If—

- (a) the specified date, or the last day of the specified previous period, is not the last day of a month but is the 29th or 30th, and
- (b) the appropriate month is February,

the period ends with the last day of February.

(5) "The appropriate month" means the month that is the specified number of months after the month in which the specified date, or the end of the specified previous period, falls.

444 Filing obligations of LLPs subject to small LLPs regime

(1) The designated members of an LLP subject to the small LLPs regime—

- (a) must deliver to the registrar for each financial year a copy of a balance sheet drawn up as at the last day of that year, and
- (b) may also deliver to the registrar a copy of the LLP's profit and loss account for that year.

(2) The designated members must also deliver to the registrar a copy of the auditor's report on the accounts that they deliver.

This does not apply if the LLP is exempt from audit and the members have taken advantage of that exemption.

(3)   The copies of accounts and auditors' reports delivered to the registrar must be copies of the LLP's annual accounts and auditor's report, except that where the LLP prepares non-IAS accounts the designated members may deliver to the registrar a copy of a balance sheet drawn up in accordance with regulation 5 of the Small Limited Liability Partnerships (Accounts) Regulations 2008 (non-IAS individual accounts for delivery to registrar of companies) (SI 2008/1912).

These are referred to in this Part as "abbreviated accounts".

(4)   If abbreviated accounts are delivered to the registrar the obligation to deliver a copy of the auditor's report on the accounts is to deliver a copy of the special auditor's report required by section 449.

(5)   Where the designated members of an LLP subject to the small LLPs regime deliver to the registrar IAS accounts, or non-IAS accounts that are not abbreviated accounts, and in accordance with this section do not deliver to the registrar a copy of the LLP's profit and loss account, the copy of the balance sheet delivered to the registrar must contain in a prominent position a statement that the LLP's annual accounts have been delivered in accordance with the provisions applicable to LLPs subject to the small LLPs regime.

(6)   The copy of the balance sheet delivered to the registrar under this section must state the name of the person who signed it on behalf of the members.

(7)   The copy of the auditor's report delivered to the registrar under this section must—
   (a)   state the name of the auditor and (where the auditor is a firm) the name of the person who signed it as senior statutory auditor, or
   (b)   if the conditions in section 506 (circumstances in which names may be omitted) are met, state that a determination has been made and notified to the Secretary of State in accordance with that section."

(2)   Until section 1068 comes fully into force, for subsections (6) and (7) of section 444 as applied to LLPs by paragraph (1) substitute—

"(6)   The copy of the balance sheet delivered to the registrar under this section must—
   (a)   state the name of the person who signed it on behalf of the members under section 414, and
   (b)   be signed on behalf of the members by a designated member.

(7)   The copy of the auditor's report delivered to the registrar under this section must—
   (a)   state the name of the auditor and (where the auditor is a firm) the name of the person who signed it as senior statutory auditor, and
   (b)   be signed by the auditor or (where the auditor is a firm) in the name of the firm by a person authorised to sign on its behalf,

or, if the conditions in section 506 (circumstances in which names may be omitted) are met, state that a determination has been made and notified to the Secretary of State in accordance with that section."

[4185]

NOTES
Commencement: 1 October 2008.

18   Filing obligations of medium-sized LLPs

(1)   Section 445 applies to LLPs, modified so that it reads as follows—

"445   Filing obligations of medium-sized LLPs

(1)   The designated members of an LLP that qualifies as a medium-sized LLP in relation to a financial year (see sections 465 to 467) must deliver a copy of the LLP's annual accounts to the registrar.

(2)   They must also deliver to the registrar a copy of the auditor's report on those accounts.

(3)   Where the LLP prepares non-IAS accounts, the designated members may deliver to the registrar a copy of the LLP's annual accounts for the financial year—
   (a)   that includes a profit and loss account in which items are combined in accordance with regulation 4 of the Large and Medium-sized Limited Liability Partnerships (Accounts) Regulations 2008 (exemptions for non-IAS individual accounts of medium-sized LLPs) (SI 2008/1913), and
   (b)   that does not contain items whose omission is authorised by that regulation.

These are referred to in this Part as "abbreviated accounts".

(4)   If abbreviated accounts are delivered to the registrar the obligation to deliver a copy of the auditor's report on the accounts is to deliver a copy of the special auditor's report required by section 449.

(5)   The copy of the balance sheet delivered to the registrar under this section must state the name of the person who signed it on behalf of the members.

(6)   The copy of the auditor's report delivered to the registrar under this section must—
    (a)   state the name of the auditor and (where the auditor is a firm) the name of the person who signed it as senior statutory auditor, or
    (b)   if the conditions in section 506 (circumstances in which names may be omitted) are met, state that a determination has been made and notified to the Secretary of State in accordance with that section.

(7)   This section does not apply to LLPs within section 444 (filing obligations of LLPs subject to the small LLPs regime)."

(2)   Until section 1068 comes fully into force, for subsections (5) and (6) of section 445 as applied to LLPs by paragraph (1) substitute—

"(5)   The copy of the balance sheet delivered to the registrar under this section must—
    (a)   state the name of the person who signed it on behalf of the members under section 414, and
    (b)   be signed on behalf of the members by a designated member.

(6)   The copy of the auditor's report delivered to the registrar under this section must—
    (a)   state the name of the auditor and (where the auditor is a firm) the name of the person who signed it as senior statutory auditor, and
    (b)   be signed by the auditor or (where the auditor is a firm) in the name of the firm by a person authorised to sign on its behalf,

or, if the conditions in section 506 (circumstances in which names may be omitted) are met, state that a determination has been made and notified to the Secretary of State in accordance with that section."

[4186]

NOTES
    Commencement: 1 October 2008.

---

19   Filing obligations of large LLPs

(1)   Section 446 applies to LLPs, modified so as to read as follows—

"446   Filing obligations of large LLPs

(1)   The designated members of an LLP that does not qualify as small or medium-sized must deliver to the registrar for each financial year of the LLP a copy of the LLP's annual accounts.

(2)   The designated members must also deliver to the registrar a copy of the auditor's report on those accounts.

(3)   The copy of the balance sheet delivered to the registrar under this section must state the name of the person who signed it on behalf of the members.

(4)   The copy of the auditor's report delivered to the registrar under this section must—
    (a)   state the name of the auditor and (where the auditor is a firm) the name of the person who signed it as senior statutory auditor, or
    (b)   if the conditions in section 506 (circumstances in which names may be omitted) are met, state that a determination has been made and notified to the Secretary of State in accordance with that section.

(5)   This section does not apply to LLPs within—
    (a)   section 444 (filing obligations of LLPs subject to the small LLPs regime), or
    (b)   section 445 (filing obligations of medium-sized LLPs)."

(2)   Until section 1068 comes fully into force, for subsections (3) and (4) of section 446 as applied to LLPs by paragraph (1) substitute—

"(3)   The copy of the balance sheet delivered to the registrar under this section must—
    (a)   state the name of the person who signed it on behalf of the members under section 414, and
    (b)   be signed on behalf of the members by a designated member.

(4)   The copy of the auditor's report delivered to the registrar under this section must—
    (a)   state the name of the auditor and (where the auditor is a firm) the name of the person who signed it as senior statutory auditor, and
    (b)   be signed by the auditor or (where the auditor is a firm) in the name of the firm by a person authorised to sign on its behalf,

or, if the conditions in section 506 (circumstances in which names may be omitted) are met, state that a determination has been made and notified to the Secretary of State in accordance with that section."

[4187]

NOTES
Commencement: 1 October 2008.

20 Requirements where abbreviated accounts delivered

(1)   Section 449 applies to LLPs, modified so that it reads as follow—

"449   Special auditor's report where abbreviated accounts delivered

(1)   This section applies where—
- (a)   the designated members of an LLP deliver abbreviated accounts to the registrar, and
- (b)   the LLP is not exempt from audit (or the members have not taken advantage of any such exemption).

(2)   The designated members must also deliver to the registrar a copy of a special report of the LLP's auditor stating that in his opinion—
- (a)   the LLP is entitled to deliver abbreviated accounts in accordance with the section in question, and
- (b)   the abbreviated accounts to be delivered are properly prepared in accordance with—
  - (i)   regulation 5 of the Small Limited Liability Partnerships (Accounts) Regulations 2008 (SI 2008/1912), or
  - (ii)   regulation 4 of the Large and Medium-sized Limited Liability Partnerships (Accounts) Regulations 2008 (SI 2008/1913).

(3)   The auditor's report on the LLP's annual accounts need not be delivered, but—
- (a)   if that report was qualified, the special report must set out that report in full together with any further material necessary to understand the qualification, and
- (b)   if that report contained a statement under—
  - (i)   section 498(2)(a) or (b) (accounts, records or returns inadequate or accounts not agreeing with records and returns), or
  - (ii)   section 498(3) (failure to obtain necessary information and explanations),

the special report must set out that statement in full.

(4)   The provisions of—
- sections 503 to 506 (signature of auditor's report), and
- sections 507 to 509 (offences in connection with auditor's report),

apply to a special report under this section as they apply to an auditor's report on the LLP's annual accounts prepared under Part 16.

(5)   If abbreviated accounts are delivered to the registrar, the references in section 434 or 435 (requirements in connection with publication of accounts) to the auditor's report on the LLP's annual accounts shall be read as references to the special auditor's report required by this section."

(2)   Until section 1068 comes fully into force, after subsection (4) of section 449 as applied to LLPs by paragraph (1) insert—

"(4A) The copy of the special report delivered to the registrar under this section must—
- (a)   be signed by the auditor or (where the auditor is a firm) in the name of the firm by a person authorised to sign on its behalf, or
- (b)   if the conditions in section 506 (circumstances in which names may be omitted) are met, state that a determination has been made and notified to the Secretary of State in accordance with that section."

[4188]

NOTES
Commencement: 1 October 2008.

21 Approval and signing of abbreviated accounts

Section 450 is applied to LLPs, modified so as to read as follows—

"450   Approval and signing of abbreviated accounts

(1)   Abbreviated accounts must be approved by the members and signed on behalf of all the members by a designated member.

(2)   The signature must be on the balance sheet.

(3)   The balance sheet must contain in a prominent position above the signature a statement to the effect that it is prepared in accordance with the special provisions of this Act relating (as the case may be) to LLPs subject to the small LLPs regime or to medium-sized LLPs.

(4)   If abbreviated accounts are approved that do not comply with the requirements of regulation 5 of the Small Limited Liability Partnerships (Accounts) Regulations 2008 (SI 2008/1912), or (as the case may be) regulation 4 of the Large and Medium-sized Limited Liability Partnerships (Accounts) Regulations 2008 (SI 2008/1913), every member of the LLP who—

    (a)   knew that they did not comply, or was reckless as to whether they complied, and

    (b)   failed to take reasonable steps to prevent them from being approved,

commits an offence.

(5)   A person guilty of an offence under subsection (4) is liable—

    (a)   on conviction on indictment, to a fine;

    (b)   on summary conviction, to a fine not exceeding the statutory maximum."

[4189]

NOTES

Commencement: 1 October 2008.

22   Failure to file accounts and auditor's report

(1)   Sections 451 to 453 apply to LLPs, modified so that they read as follow—

"451   Default in filing accounts and auditor's report: offences

(1)   If the requirements of section 441 (duty to file accounts and auditor's report) are not complied with in relation to an LLP's accounts for a financial year and the auditor's report on those accounts before the end of the period for filing those accounts and that report, every person who immediately before the end of that period was a designated member of the LLP commits an offence.

(2)   It is a defence for a person charged with such an offence to prove that he took all reasonable steps for securing that those requirements would be complied with before the end of that period.

(3)   It is not a defence to prove that the documents in question were not in fact prepared as required by this Part.

(4)   A person guilty of an offence under this section is liable on summary conviction to a fine not exceeding level 5 on the standard scale and, for continued contravention, a daily default fine not exceeding one-tenth of level 5 on the standard scale.

452   Default in filing accounts and auditor's report: court order

(1)   If—

    (a)   the requirements of section 441 (duty to file accounts and auditor's report) are not complied with in relation to an LLP's accounts for a financial year and the auditor's report on those accounts before the end of the period for filing those accounts and that report, and

    (b)   the designated members of the LLP fail to make good the default within 14 days after the service of a notice on them requiring compliance,

the court may, on the application of any member or creditor of the LLP or of the registrar, make an order directing the designated members (or any of them) to make good the default within such time as may be specified in the order.

(2)   The court's order may provide that all costs (in Scotland, expenses) of and incidental to the application are to be borne by the members.

453   Civil penalty for failure to file accounts and auditor's report

(1)   Where the requirements of section 441 are not complied with in relation to an LLP's accounts for a financial year and the auditor's report on those accounts before the end of the period for filing those accounts and that report, the LLP is liable to a civil penalty.

This is in addition to any liability of the designated members under section 451.

(2)   Regulations 1(3) and 4(2) and (3) of the Companies (Late Filing Penalties) and Limited Liability Partnerships (Filing Periods and Late Filing Penalties) Regulations 2008 (SI 2008/497) apply to LLPs with the following modifications—

    (a)   references to a company or private company include references to an LLP;

    (b)   references to 6th April 2008 are to be read as references to 1st October 2008; and

    (c)   the second column of the table in regulation 4(2) (penalties for public companies) is omitted.

PART III
STATUTORY INSTRUMENTS

(3)　The penalty may be recovered by the registrar and is to be paid into the Consolidated Fund.

(4)　It is not a defence in proceedings under this section to prove that the documents in question were not in fact prepared as required by this Part."

(2)　(*Amends the Companies (Late Filing Penalties) and Limited Liability Partnerships (Filing Periods and Late Filing Penalties) Regulations 2008, SI 2008/497, reg 6.*)

[4190]

NOTES
Commencement: 1 October 2008.

PART 8
REVISION OF DEFECTIVE ACCOUNTS

23　Revision of defective accounts

Sections 454 to 456 apply to LLPs, modified so that they read as follows—

"**454**—(1)　If it appears to the members of an LLP that the LLP's annual accounts did not comply with the requirements of this Act, they may prepare revised accounts.

(2)　Where copies of the previous accounts have been sent out to members or delivered to the registrar, the revisions must be confined to—
(a)　the correction of those respects in which the previous accounts did not comply with the requirements of this Act, and
(b)　the making of any necessary consequential alterations.

(3)　The Companies (Revision of Defective Accounts and Reports) Regulations 2008 (SI 2008/373) apply for the purposes of this section with the following modifications—
(a)　references to a company include references to an LLP; and
(b)　references to a director or to an officer of a company include references to a member of an LLP.

455　Secretary of State's notice in respect of accounts

(1)　This section applies where copies of an LLP's annual accounts have been delivered to the registrar, and it appears to the Secretary of State that there is, or may be, a question whether the accounts comply with the requirements of this Act.

(2)　The Secretary of State may give notice to the members of the LLP indicating the respects in which it appears that such a question arises or may arise.

(3)　The notice must specify a period of not less than one month for the members to give an explanation of the accounts or prepare revised accounts.

(4)　If at the end of the specified period, or such longer period as the Secretary of State may allow, it appears to the Secretary of State that the members have not—
(a)　given a satisfactory explanation of the accounts, or
(b)　revised the accounts so as to comply with the requirements of this Act,
the Secretary of State may apply to the court.

(5)　The provisions of this section apply equally to revised annual accounts, in which case they have effect as if the references to revised accounts were references to further revised accounts.

456　Application to court in respect of defective accounts

(1)　An application may be made to the court—
(a)　by the Secretary of State, after having complied with section 455, or
(b)　by the Financial Reporting Review Panel,
for a declaration (in Scotland, a declarator) that the annual accounts of an LLP do not comply with the requirements of this Act and for an order requiring the members of the LLP to prepare revised accounts.

(2)　Notice of the application, together with a general statement of the matters at issue in the proceedings, shall be given by the applicant to the registrar for registration.

(3)　If the court orders the preparation of revised accounts, it may give directions as to—
(a)　the auditing of the accounts, and
(b)　the taking of steps by the members to bring the making of the order to the notice of persons likely to rely on the previous accounts,
and such other matters as the court thinks fit.

(4)　If the court finds that the accounts did not comply with the requirements of this Act it may order that all or part of—

    (a)   the costs (in Scotland, expenses) of and incidental to the application, and

    (b)   any reasonable expenses incurred by the LLP in connection with or in consequence of the preparation of revised accounts,

are to be borne by such of the members as were party to the approval of the defective accounts.

For this purpose every member of the LLP at the time of the approval of the accounts shall be taken to have been a party to the approval unless he shows that he took all reasonable steps to prevent that approval.

(5)   Where the court makes an order under subsection (4) it shall have regard to whether the members party to the approval of the defective accounts knew or ought to have known that the accounts did not comply with the requirements of this Act, and it may exclude one or more members from the order or order the payment of different amounts by different members.

(6)   On the conclusion of proceedings on an application under this section, the applicant must send to the registrar for registration a copy of the court order or, as the case may be, give notice to the registrar that the application has failed or been withdrawn.

(7)   The provisions of this section apply equally to revised annual accounts, in which case they have effect as if the references to revised accounts were references to further revised accounts."

[4191]

NOTES

    Commencement: 1 October 2008.

24 Disclosure of information

Sections 458 to 461 apply to LLPs, modified so that they read as follows—

"458 Disclosure of information by tax authorities

(1)   The Commissioners for Her Majesty's Revenue and Customs may disclose information to the Financial Reporting Review Panel for the purpose of facilitating—

    (a)   the taking of steps by the Financial Reporting Review Panel to discover whether there are grounds for an application to the court under section 456 (application in respect of defective accounts etc), or

    (b)   a decision by the Financial Reporting Review Panel whether to make such an application.

(2)   This section applies despite any statutory or other restriction on the disclosure of information.

Provided that, in the case of personal data within the meaning of the Data Protection Act 1998 (c.29), information is not to be disclosed in contravention of that Act.

(3)   Information disclosed to the Financial Reporting Review Panel under this section—

    (a)   may not be used except in or in connection with—

        (i)   taking steps to discover whether there are grounds for an application to the court under section 456, or

        (ii)   deciding whether or not to make such an application,

    or in, or in connection with, proceedings on such an application; and

    (b)   must not be further disclosed except—

        (i)   to the person to whom the information relates, or

        (ii)   in, or in connection with, proceedings on any such application to the court.

(4)   A person who contravenes subsection (3) commits an offence unless—

    (a)   he did not know, and had no reason to suspect, that the information had been disclosed under this section, or

    (b)   he took all reasonable steps and exercised all due diligence to avoid the commission of the offence.

(5)   A person guilty of an offence under subsection (4) is liable—

    (a)   on conviction on indictment, to imprisonment for a term not exceeding two years or a fine (or both);

    (b)   on summary conviction—

        (i)   in England and Wales, to imprisonment for a term not exceeding twelve months or to a fine not exceeding the statutory maximum (or both);

        (ii)   in Scotland or Northern Ireland, to imprisonment for a term not exceeding six months, or to a fine not exceeding the statutory maximum (or both).

(6)   Where an offence under this section is committed by a body corporate, every officer of the body who is in default also commits the offence.

For this purpose—

(a)   any person who purports to act as director, manager or secretary of the body is treated as an officer of the body, and

(b)   if the body is a company, any shadow director is treated as an officer of the company.

459 Power of the Financial Reporting Review Panel to require documents, information and explanations

(1)   This section applies where it appears to the Financial Reporting Review Panel that there is, or may be, a question whether an LLP's annual accounts comply with the requirements of this Act.

(2)   The Financial Reporting Review Panel may require any of the persons mentioned in subsection (3) to produce any document, or to provide him with any information or explanations, that he may reasonably require for the purpose of—

(a)   discovering whether there are grounds for an application to the court under section 456, or

(b)   deciding whether to make such an application.

(3)   Those persons are—

(a)   the LLP;

(b)   any member, employee, or auditor of the LLP;

(c)   any persons who fell within paragraph (b) at a time to which the document or information required by the Financial Reporting Review Panel relates.

(4)   If a person fails to comply with such a requirement, the Financial Reporting Review Panel may apply to the court.

(5)   If it appears to the court that the person has failed to comply with a requirement under subsection (2), it may order the person to take such steps as it directs for securing that the documents are produced or the information or explanations are provided.

(6)   A statement made by a person in response to a requirement under subsection (2) or an order under subsection (5) may not be used in evidence against him in any criminal proceedings.

(7)   Nothing in this section compels any person to disclose documents or information in respect of which a claim to legal professional privilege (in Scotland, to confidentiality of communications) could be maintained in legal proceedings.

(8)   In this section "document" includes information recorded in any form.

460 Restrictions on disclosure of information obtained under compulsory powers

(1)   This section applies to information (in whatever form) obtained in pursuance of a requirement or order under section 459 (power of Financial Reporting Review Panel to require documents etc) that relates to the private affairs of an individual or to any particular business.

(2)   No such information may, during the lifetime of that individual or so long as that business continues to be carried on, be disclosed without the consent of that individual or the person for the time being carrying on that business.

(3)   This does not apply—

(a)   to disclosure permitted by section 461 (permitted disclosure of information obtained under compulsory powers), or

(b)   to the disclosure of information that is or has been available to the public from another source.

(4)   A person who discloses information in contravention of this section commits an offence, unless—

(a)   he did not know, and had no reason to suspect, that the information had been disclosed under section 459, or

(b)   he took all reasonable steps and exercised all due diligence to avoid the commission of the offence.

(5)   A person guilty of an offence under this section is liable—

(a)   on conviction on indictment, to imprisonment for a term not exceeding two years or a fine (or both);

(b)   on summary conviction—

(i)   in England and Wales, to imprisonment for a term not exceeding twelve months or to a fine not exceeding the statutory maximum (or both);

(ii)   in Scotland or Northern Ireland, to imprisonment for a term not exceeding six months, or to a fine not exceeding the statutory maximum (or both).

(6)   Where an offence under this section is committed by a body corporate, every officer of the body who is in default also commits the offence.

For this purpose—

(a)   any person who purports to act as director, manager or secretary of the body is treated as an officer of the body, and

(b)   if the body is a company, any shadow director is treated as an officer of the company.

461   Permitted disclosure of information obtained under compulsory powers

(1)   The prohibition in section 460 of the disclosure of information obtained in pursuance of a requirement or order under section 459 (power of Financial Reporting Review Panel to require documents etc) that relates to the private affairs of an individual or to any particular business has effect subject to the following exceptions.

(2)   It does not apply to the disclosure of information for the purpose of facilitating the carrying out by the Financial Reporting Review Panel of its functions under section 456.

(3)   It does not apply to disclosure to—
(a)   the Secretary of State,
(b)   the Department of Enterprise, Trade and Investment for Northern Ireland,
(c)   the Treasury,
(d)   the Bank of England,
(e)   the Financial Services Authority, or
(f)   the Commissioners for Her Majesty's Revenue and Customs.

(4)   It does not apply to disclosure—
(a)   for the purpose of assisting the body known as the Professional Oversight Board established under the articles of association of the Financial Reporting Council Limited (registered number 02486368) to exercise its functions under Part 42 of this Act;
(b)   with a view to the institution of, or otherwise for the purposes of, disciplinary proceedings relating to the performance by an accountant or auditor of his professional duties;
(c)   for the purpose of enabling or assisting the Secretary of State or the Treasury to exercise any of their functions under any of the following—
(i)   the Companies Acts,
(ii)   Part 5 of the Criminal Justice Act 1993 (c.36) (insider dealing),
(iii) the Insolvency Act 1986 (c.45) or the Insolvency (Northern Ireland) Order 1989 (SI 1989/2405 (NI 19)),
(iv)   the Company Directors Disqualification Act 1986 (c.46) or the Company Directors Disqualification (Northern Ireland) Order 2002 (SI 2002/3150 (NI 4)),
(v)   the Financial Services and Markets Act 2000 (c.8);
(d)   for the purpose of enabling or assisting the Department of Enterprise, Trade and Investment for Northern Ireland to exercise any powers conferred on it by the enactments relating to companies, directors' disqualification or insolvency;
(e)   for the purpose of enabling or assisting the Bank of England to exercise its functions;
(f)   for the purpose of enabling or assisting the Commissioners for Her Majesty's Revenue and Customs to exercise their functions;
(g)   for the purpose of enabling or assisting the Financial Services Authority to exercise its functions under any of the following—
(i)   the legislation relating to friendly societies or to industrial and provident societies,
(ii)   the Building Societies Act 1986 (c.53),
(iii) Part 7 of the Companies Act 1989 (c.40),
(iv)   the Financial Services and Markets Act 2000; or
(h)   in pursuance of any Community obligation.

(5)   It does not apply to disclosure to a body exercising functions of a public nature under legislation in any country or territory outside the United Kingdom that appear to the Financial Reporting Review Panel to be similar to its functions under section 456 for the purpose of enabling or assisting that body to exercise those functions.

(6)   In determining whether to disclose information to a body in accordance with subsection (5), the Financial Reporting Review Panel must have regard to the following considerations—
(a)   whether the use which the body is likely to make of the information is sufficiently important to justify making the disclosure;
(b)   whether the body has adequate arrangements to prevent the information from being used or further disclosed other than—
(i)   for the purposes of carrying out the functions mentioned in that subsection, or

(ii) for other purposes substantially similar to those for which information disclosed to the Financial Reporting Review Panel could be used or further disclosed.

(7) Nothing in this section authorises the making of a disclosure in contravention of the Data Protection Act 1998 (c.29)."

[4192]

NOTES

Commencement: 1 October 2008.

PART 9

ACCOUNTS: SUPPLEMENTARY PROVISIONS

25 Accounting standards

Section 464 applies to LLPs, modified so that it reads as follows—

"464 Accounting standards

(1) In this Part "accounting standards" means statements of standard accounting practice issued by the body known as the Accounting Standards Board, as prescribed by the Accounting Standards (Prescribed Body) Regulations 2008 (SI 2008/651).

(2) References in this Part to accounting standards applicable to an LLP's annual accounts are to such standards as are, in accordance with their terms, relevant to the LLP's circumstances and to the accounts."

[4193]

NOTES

Commencement: 1 October 2008.

26 Medium-sized LLPs

Sections 465 to 467 apply to LLPs, modified so that they read as follows—

"465 LLPs qualifying as medium-sized: general

(1) An LLP qualifies as medium-sized in relation to its first financial year if the qualifying conditions are met in that year.

(2) An LLP qualifies as medium-sized in relation to a subsequent financial year—
(a) if the qualifying conditions are met in that year and the preceding financial year;
(b) if the qualifying conditions are met in that year and the LLP qualified as medium-sized in relation to the preceding financial year;
(c) if the qualifying conditions were met in the preceding financial year and the LLP qualified as medium-sized in relation to that year.

(3) The qualifying conditions are met by an LLP in a year in which it satisfies two or more of the following requirements—

1. Turnover	Not more than £25.9 million
2. Balance sheet total	Not more than £12.9 million
3. Number of employees	Not more than 250

(4) For a period that is an LLP's financial year but not in fact a year the maximum figures for turnover must be proportionately adjusted.

(5) The balance sheet total means the aggregate of the amounts shown as assets in the LLP's balance sheet.

(6) The number of employees means the average number of persons employed by the LLP in the year, determined as follows—

(a) find for each month in the financial year the number of persons employed under contracts of service by the LLP in that month (whether throughout the month or not),
(b) add together the monthly totals, and
(c) divide by the number of months in the financial year.

(7) This section is subject to section 466 (LLPs qualifying as medium-sized: parent LLPs).

466   LLPs qualifying as medium-sized: parent LLPs

(1)   A parent LLP qualifies as a medium-sized LLP in relation to a financial year only if the group headed by it qualifies as a medium-sized group.

(2)   A group qualifies as medium-sized in relation to the parent LLP's first financial year if the qualifying conditions are met in that year.

(3)   A group qualifies as medium-sized in relation to a subsequent financial year of the parent LLP—
    (a)   if the qualifying conditions are met in that year and the preceding financial year;
    (b)   if the qualifying conditions are met in that year and the group qualified as medium-sized in relation to the preceding financial year;
    (c)   if the qualifying conditions were met in the preceding financial year and the group qualified as medium-sized in relation to that year.

(4)   The qualifying conditions are met by a group in a year in which it satisfies two or more of the following requirements—

1. Aggregate turnover	Not more than £25.9 million net (or £31.1 million gross)
2. Aggregate balance sheet total	Not more than £12.9 million net (or £15.5 million gross)
3. Aggregate number of employees	Not more than 250

(5)   The aggregate figures are ascertained by aggregating the relevant figures determined in accordance with section 465 for each member of the group.

(6)   In relation to the aggregate figures for turnover and balance sheet total—

"net" means after any set-offs and other adjustments made to eliminate group transactions—
            (a)   in the case of non-IAS accounts, in accordance with Schedule 3 to the Large and Medium-sized Limited Liability Partnerships (Accounts) Regulations 2008 (SI 2008/1913),
    (b)   in the case of IAS accounts, in accordance with international accounting standards; and
"gross" means without those set-offs and other adjustments.

An LLP may satisfy any relevant requirement on the basis of either the net or the gross figure.

(7)   The figures for each subsidiary undertaking shall be those included in its individual accounts for the relevant financial year, that is—
    (a)   if its financial year ends with that of the parent LLP, that financial year, and
    (b)   if not, its financial year ending last before the end of the financial year of the parent LLP.

If those figures cannot be obtained without disproportionate expense or undue delay, the latest available figures shall be taken.

467   LLPs excluded from being treated as medium-sized

(1)   An LLP is not entitled to take advantage of any of the provisions of this Part relating to LLPs qualifying as medium-sized if it was at any time within the financial year in question—
    (a)   an LLP whose securities are admitted to trading on a regulated market in an EEA State,
    (b)   an LLP that—
            (i)   has permission under Part 4 of the Financial Services and Markets Act 2000 (c.8) to carry on a regulated activity, or
            (ii)   carries on insurance market activity, or
    (c)   a member of an ineligible group.

(2)   A group is ineligible if any of its members is—
    (a)   a public company,
    (b)   a body corporate (other than a company) whose shares are admitted to trading on a regulated market,
    (c)   a person (other than a small company or small LLP) who has permission under Part 4 of the Financial Services and Markets Act 2000 to carry on a regulated activity,

(d)   a small company or small LLP that is an authorised insurance company, a banking company or banking LLP, an e-money issuer, a MiFID investment firm or a UCITS management company, or

(e)   a person who carries on insurance market activity.

(3)   An LLP is a small LLP for the purposes of subsection (2) if it qualified as small in relation to its last financial year ending on or before the end of the financial year in question."

[4194]

NOTES

Commencement: 1 October 2008.

---

27 General power to make further provision about accounts

Section 468 applies to LLPs, modified so that it reads as follows—

"468 General power to make further provision about accounts

(1)   The Secretary of State may make provision by regulations about—

   (a)   the accounts that LLPs are required to prepare;

   (b)   the categories of LLPs required to prepare accounts of any description;

   (c)   the form and content of the accounts that LLPs are required to prepare;

   (d)   the obligations of LLPs and others as regards—

      (i)   the approval of accounts,

      (ii)   the sending of accounts to members and others,

      (iii)   the delivery of copies of accounts to the registrar, and

      (iv)   the publication of accounts.

(2)   The regulations may amend this Part by adding, altering or repealing provisions.

(3)   But they must not amend (other than consequentially)—

   (a)   section 393 (accounts to give true and fair view), or

   (b)   the provisions of Chapter 11 (revision of defective accounts and reports).

(4)   The regulations may create criminal offences in cases corresponding to those in which an offence is created by an existing provision of this Part.

The maximum penalty for any such offence may not be greater than is provided in relation to an offence under the existing provision.

(5)   The regulations may provide for civil penalties in circumstances corresponding to those within section 453(1) (civil penalty for failure to file accounts and reports).

The provisions of section 453(3) and (4) apply in relation to any such penalty."

[4195]

NOTES

Commencement: 1 October 2008.

---

28 Other supplementary provisions

Section 469 applies to LLPs, modified so that it reads as follows—

"469 Preparation and filing of accounts in euros

(1)   The amounts set out in the annual accounts of an LLP may also be shown in the same accounts translated into euros.

(2)   When complying with section 441 (duty to file accounts and auditor's report), the designated members of an LLP may deliver to the registrar an additional copy of the LLP's annual accounts in which the amounts have been translated into euros.

(3)   In both cases—

   (a)   the amounts must have been translated at the exchange rate prevailing on the date to which the balance sheet is made up, and

   (b)   that rate must be disclosed in the notes to the accounts.

(4)   For the purposes of sections 434 and 435 (requirements in connection with published accounts) any additional copy of the LLP's annual accounts delivered to the registrar under subsection (2) above shall be treated as statutory accounts of the LLP.

In the case of such a copy, references in those sections to the auditor's report on the LLP's annual accounts shall be read as references to the auditor's report on the annual accounts of which it is a copy."

[4196]

NOTES

Commencement: 1 October 2008.

29 Meaning of "annual accounts"

Section 471 applies to LLPs, modified so that it reads as follows—

"471 Meaning of "annual accounts" and related expressions

(1) In this Part an LLP's "annual accounts", in relation to a financial year, means—

(a) the LLP's individual accounts for that year (see section 394), and

(b) any group accounts prepared by the LLP for that year (see sections 398 and 399).

This is subject to section 408 (option to omit individual profit and loss account from annual accounts where information given in group accounts).

(2) In this Part an LLP's "annual accounts and auditor's report" for a financial year are—

(a) its annual accounts,

(b) the auditor's report on those accounts (unless the LLP is exempt from audit)."

[4197]

NOTES

Commencement: 1 October 2008.

30 Notes to the accounts

Section 472 applies to LLPs, modified so that it reads as follows—

"472 Notes to the accounts

(1) Information required by this Part to be given in notes to an LLP's annual accounts may be contained in the accounts or in a separate document annexed to the accounts.

(2) References in this Part to an LLP's annual accounts, or to a balance sheet or profit and loss account, include notes to the accounts giving information which is required by any provision of this Act or international accounting standards, and required or allowed by any such provision to be given in a note to LLP accounts."

[4198]

NOTES

Commencement: 1 October 2008.

31 Parliamentary procedure for regulations under section 468

Section 473 applies to LLPs, modified so that it reads as follows—

"473 Parliamentary procedure for regulations under section 468

(1) This section applies to regulations under section 468 (general power to make further provision about accounts).

(2) Any such regulations may make consequential amendments or repeals in other provisions of this Act, or in other enactments.

(3) Regulations that—

(a) restrict the classes of LLP which have the benefit of any exemption, exception or special provision,

(b) require additional matter to be included in a document of any class, or

(c) otherwise render the requirements of this Part more onerous,

are subject to affirmative resolution procedure.

(4) Otherwise, the regulations are subject to negative resolution procedure."

[4199]

NOTES

Commencement: 1 October 2008.

32 Minor definitions

Section 474 applies to LLPs, modified so that it reads as follows—

"474 Minor definitions

(1) In this Part—

"authorised insurance company" means a person (whether incorporated or not) who has permission under Part 4 of the Financial Services and Markets Act 2000 (c.8) to effect or carry out contracts of insurance, but does not include a friendly society within the meaning of the Friendly Societies Act 1992 (c.40);

"banking company" means a person who has permission under Part 4 of the Financial Services and Markets Act 2000 to accept deposits, other than—

(a) a person who is not a company, and

(b)   a person who has such permission only for the purpose of carrying on another regulated activity in accordance with permission under that Part;

"banking LLP" means an LLP which has permission under Part 4 of the Financial Services and Markets Act 2000 to accept deposits (but does not include such an LLP which has permission to accept deposits only for the purpose of carrying on another regulated activity in accordance with that permission);

"e-money issuer" means a person who has permission under Part 4 of the Financial Services and Markets Act 2000 to carry on the activity of issuing electronic money within the meaning of article 9B of the Financial Services and Markets Act 2000 (Regulated Activities) Order 2001 (SI 2001/544);

"Financial Reporting Review Panel" means the body known as the Financial Reporting Review Panel established under the articles of association of the Financial Reporting Council Limited (registered number 02486368);

"group" means a parent undertaking and its subsidiary undertakings;

"IAS Regulation" means EC Regulation No. 1606/2002 of the European Parliament and of the Council of 19 July 2002 on the application of international accounting standards;

"included in the consolidation", in relation to group accounts, or "included in consolidated group accounts", means that the undertaking is included in the accounts by the method of full (and not proportional) consolidation, and references to an undertaking excluded from consolidation shall be construed accordingly;

"insurance company" means—

   (a)   an authorised insurance company, or

   (b)   any other person (whether incorporated or not) who—

      (i)   carries on insurance market activity (within the meaning of section 316(3) of the Financial Services and Markets Act 2000), or

      (ii) may effect or carry out contracts of insurance under which the benefits provided by that person are exclusively or primarily benefits in kind in the event of accident to or breakdown of a vehicle,

but does not include a friendly society within the meaning of the Friendly Societies Act 1992;

"international accounting standards" means the international accounting standards, within the meaning of the IAS Regulation, adopted from time to time by the European Commission in accordance with that Regulation;

"LLP" means a limited liability partnership formed and registered under the Limited Liability Partnerships Act 2000 (c.12) or the Limited Liability Partnerships Act (NI) 2002 (2002 (NI) (c.12));

"MiFID investment firm" means an investment firm within the meaning of Article 4.1.1 of Directive 2004/39/EC of the European Parliament and of the Council of 21 April 2004 on markets in financial instruments other than—

   (a)   an LLP to which that Directive does not apply by virtue of Article 2 of that Directive,

   (b)   an LLP which is an exempt investment firm within the meaning of regulation 4A(3) of the Financial Services and Markets Act 2000 (Markets in Financial Instruments) Regulations 2007 (SI 2007/126), and

   (c)   any other LLP which fulfils all the requirements set out in regulation 4C(3) of those Regulations;

"profit and loss account", in relation to an LLP that prepares IAS accounts, includes an income statement or other equivalent financial statement required to be prepared by international accounting standards;

"regulated activity" has the meaning given in section 22 of the Financial Services and Markets Act 2000, except that it does not include activities of the kind specified in any of the following provisions of the Financial Services and Markets Act 2000 (Regulated Activities) Order 2001 (SI 2001/544)—

   (a)   article 25A (arranging regulated mortgage contracts),

   (b)   article 25B (arranging regulated home reversion plans),

   (c)   article 25C (arranging regulated home purchase plans),

   (d)   article 39A (assisting administration and performance of a contract of insurance),

   (e)   article 53A (advising on regulated mortgage contracts),

   (f)   article 53B (advising on regulated home reversion plans),

   (g)   article 53C (advising on regulated home purchase plans),

   (h)   article 21 (dealing as agent), article 25 (arranging deals in investments) or article 53 (advising on investments) where the activity concerns relevant investments that are not contractually based investments (within the meaning of article 3 of that Order), or

     (i)   article 64 (agreeing to carry on a regulated activity of the kind mentioned in paragraphs (a) to (h));

"turnover", in relation to an LLP, means the amounts derived from the provision of goods and services falling within the LLP's ordinary activities, after deduction of—

     (a)   trade discounts,

     (b)   value added tax, and

     (c)   any other taxes based on the amounts so derived;

"UCITS management company" has the meaning given by the Glossary forming part of the Handbook made by the Financial Services Authority under the Financial Services and Markets Act 2000 (c.8);

"wholly-owned subsidiary" has the meaning given in section 1159(2) of this Act.

(2)   In subsection (1)—

     (a)   the definitions of "banking company" and "banking LLP", and

     (b)   references in the definition of "insurance company" to contracts of insurance and to the effecting or carrying out of such contracts,

    must be read with—

          (i)   section 22 of the Financial Services and Markets Act 2000,

         (ii)   the Financial Services and Markets Act 2000 (Regulated Activities) Order 2001 (SI 2001/544), and

       (iii)   Schedule 2 to that Act."

                                                      [4200]

NOTES

Commencement: 1 October 2008.

PART 10
AUDIT REQUIREMENT

33   Requirement for audited accounts

Section 475 applies to LLPs, modified so that it reads as follows—

"475   Requirement for audited accounts

(1)   An LLP's annual accounts for a financial year must be audited in accordance with this Part unless the LLP is exempt from audit under—

     (a)   section 477 (small LLPs), or

     (b)   section 480 (dormant LLPs).

(2)   An LLP is not entitled to any such exemption unless its balance sheet contains a statement by the members to that effect.

(3)   An LLP is not entitled to exemption under any of the provisions mentioned in subsection (1)(a) unless its balance sheet contains a statement by the members to the effect that the members acknowledge their responsibilities for complying with the requirements of this Act with respect to accounting records and the preparation of accounts.

(4)   The statement required by subsection (2) or (3) must appear on the balance sheet above the signature required by section 414."

                                                      [4201]

NOTES

Commencement: 1 October 2008.

---

34   Exemption from audit: small LLPs

Sections 477 to 479 apply to LLPs, modified so that they read as follows—

"477   Small LLPs: conditions for exemption from audit

(1)   An LLP that meets the following conditions in respect of a financial year is exempt from the requirements of this Act relating to the audit of accounts for that year.

(2)   The conditions are—

     (a)   that the LLP qualifies as a small LLP in relation to that year,

     (b)   that its turnover in that year is not more than £6.5 million, and

     (c)   that its balance sheet total for that year is not more than £3.26 million.

(3)   For a period which is an LLP's financial year but not in fact a year the maximum figure for turnover shall be proportionately adjusted.

(4)   For the purposes of this section—

     (a)   whether an LLP qualifies as a small LLP shall be determined in accordance with section 382(1) to (6), and

(b) "balance sheet total" has the same meaning as in that section.

(5) This section has effect subject to—
- section 475(2) and (3) (requirements as to statements to be contained in balance sheet),
- section 478 (LLPs excluded from small LLPs exemption), and
- section 479 (availability of small LLPs exemption in case of group LLP).

478 LLPs excluded from small LLPs exemption

An LLP is not entitled to the exemption conferred by section 477 (small LLPs) if it was at any time within the financial year in question—

(a) an LLP whose securities are admitted to trading on a regulated market in an EEA State,

(b) an LLP that—
   (i) is an authorised insurance company, a banking LLP, an e-money issuer, a MiFID investment firm or a UCITS management company, or
   (ii) carries on insurance market activity, or

(c) an employers' association as defined in section 122 of the Trade Union and Labour Relations (Consolidation) Act 1992 (c.52) or Article 4 of the Industrial Relations (Northern Ireland) Order 1992 (SI 1992/807 (NI 5)).

479 Availability of small LLPs exemption in case of group LLP

(1) An LLP is not entitled to the exemption conferred by section 477 (small LLPs) in respect of a financial year during any part of which it was a group LLP unless—

(a) the conditions specified in subsection (2) below are met, or

(b) subsection (3) applies.

(2) The conditions are—

(a) that the group—
   (i) qualifies as a small group in relation to that financial year, and
   (ii) was not at any time in that year an ineligible group;

(b) that the group's aggregate turnover in that year is not more than £6.5 million net (or £7.8 million gross);

(c) that the group's aggregate balance sheet total for that year is not more than £3.26 million net (or £3.9 million gross).

(3) An LLP is not excluded by subsection (1) if, throughout the whole of the period or periods during the financial year when it was a group LLP, it was both a subsidiary undertaking and dormant.

(4) In this section—

(a) "group LLP" means an LLP that is a parent LLP or a subsidiary undertaking, and

(b) "the group", in relation to a group LLP, means that LLP together with all its associated undertakings.

For this purpose undertakings are associated if one is a subsidiary undertaking of the other or both are subsidiary undertakings of a third undertaking.

(5) For the purposes of this section—

(a) whether a group qualifies as small shall be determined in accordance with section 383 (LLPs qualifying as small: parent LLPs);

(b) "ineligible group" has the meaning given by section 384(2) and (3);

(c) a group's aggregate turnover and aggregate balance sheet total shall be determined as for the purposes of section 383;

(d) "net" and "gross" have the same meaning as in that section;

(e) an LLP may meet any relevant requirement on the basis of either the gross or the net figure.

(6) The provisions mentioned in subsection (5) apply for the purposes of this section as if all the bodies corporate in the group were LLPs or companies."

[4202]

NOTES

Commencement: 1 October 2008.

35 Exemption from audit: dormant LLPs

Sections 480 and 481 apply to LLPs, modified so that they read as follows—

"480 Dormant LLPS: conditions for exemption from audit

(1) An LLP is exempt from the requirements of this Act relating to the audit of accounts in respect of a financial year if—

(a) it has been dormant since its formation, or

    (b)   it has been dormant since the end of the previous financial year and the following conditions are met.

(2)   The conditions are that the LLP—

    (a)   as regards its individual accounts for the financial year in question—

        (i)   is entitled to prepare accounts in accordance with the small LLPs regime (see sections 381 to 384), or

        (ii)   would be so entitled but for having been a member of an ineligible group, and

    (b)   is not required to prepare group accounts for that year.

(3)   This section has effect subject to—

-     section 475(2) and (3) (requirements as to statements to be contained in balance sheet), and
-     section 481 (LLPs excluded from dormant LLPs exemption).

481   LLPs excluded from dormant LLPs exemption

An LLP is not entitled to the exemption conferred by section 480 (dormant LLPs) if it was at any time within the financial year in question an LLP that—

    (a)   is an authorised insurance company, a banking LLP, an e-money issuer, a MiFID investment firm or a UCITS management company, or

    (b)   carries on insurance market activity."

[4203]

NOTES

Commencement: 1 October 2008.

PART 11
APPOINTMENT OF AUDITORS

36   Appointment of auditors

Sections 485 to 488 apply to LLPs, modified so that they read as follows—

"485   Appointment of auditors: general

(1)   An auditor or auditors of an LLP must be appointed for each financial year of the LLP, unless the designated members reasonably determine otherwise on the ground that audited accounts are unlikely to be required.

(2)   For each financial year for which an auditor or auditors is or are to be appointed (other than the LLP's first financial year), the appointment must be made before the end of the period of 28 days beginning with—

    (a)   the end of the time allowed for sending out copies of the LLP's annual accounts and auditor's report for the previous financial year (see section 423), or

    (b)   if earlier, the day on which copies of the LLP's annual accounts and auditor's report for the previous financial year are sent out under section 423.

This is the "period for appointing auditors".

(3)   The designated members may appoint an auditor or auditors—

    (a)   at any time before the LLP's first period for appointing auditors,

    (b)   following a period during which the LLP (being exempt from audit) did not have any auditor, at any time before the LLP's next period for appointing auditors, or

    (c)   to fill a casual vacancy in the office of auditor.

(4)   The members may appoint an auditor or auditors—

    (a)   during a period for appointing auditors,

    (b)   if the LLP should have appointed an auditor or auditors during a period for appointing auditors but failed to do so, or

    (c)   where the designated members had power to appoint under subsection (3) but have failed to make an appointment.

(5)   An auditor or auditors of an LLP may only be appointed—

    (a)   in accordance with this section, or

    (b)   in accordance with section 486 (default power of Secretary of State).

This is without prejudice to any deemed re-appointment under section 487.

486   Appointment of auditor: default power of Secretary of State

(1)   If an LLP fails to appoint an auditor or auditors in accordance with section 485, the Secretary of State may appoint one or more persons to fill the vacancy.

(2) Where subsection (2) of that section applies and the LLP fails to make the necessary appointment before the end of the period for appointing auditors, the LLP must within one week of the end of that period give notice to the Secretary of State of his power having become exercisable.

(3) If an LLP fails to give the notice required by this section, an offence is committed by—

    (a) the LLP, and

    (b) every designated member who is in default.

(4) A person guilty of an offence under this section is liable on summary conviction to a fine not exceeding level 3 on the standard scale and, for continued contravention, a daily default fine not exceeding one-tenth of level 3 on the standard scale.

487 Term of office of auditors

(1) An auditor or auditors of an LLP hold office in accordance with the terms of their appointment, subject to the requirements that—

    (a) they do not take office until any previous auditor or auditors cease to hold office, and

    (b) they cease to hold office at the end of the next period for appointing auditors unless re-appointed.

(2) Where no auditor has been appointed by the end of the next period for appointing auditors, any auditor in office immediately before that time is deemed to be re-appointed at that time, unless—

    (a) the LLP agreement requires actual re-appointment, or

    (b) the deemed re-appointment is prevented by the members under section 488, or

    (c) the members have determined that he should not be re-appointed, or

    (d) the designated members have determined that no auditor or auditors should be appointed for the financial year in question.

(3) This is without prejudice to the provisions of this Part as to removal and resignation of auditors.

(4) No account shall be taken of any loss of the opportunity of deemed reappointment under this section in ascertaining the amount of any compensation or damages payable to an auditor on his ceasing to hold office for any reason.

488 Prevention by members of deemed re-appointment of auditor

(1) An auditor of an LLP is not deemed to be re-appointed under section 487(2) if the LLP has received notices under this section from members representing at least the requisite percentage of the total voting rights in the LLP that the auditor should not be re-appointed.

(2) The "requisite percentage" is 5%, or such lower percentage as is specified for this purpose in the LLP agreement.

(3) A notice under this section—

    (a) may be in hard copy or electronic form,

    (b) must be authenticated by the person or persons giving it, and

    (c) must be received by the LLP before the end of the accounting reference period immediately preceding the time when the deemed reappointment would have effect."

[4204]

NOTES

Commencement: 1 October 2008.

---

37 Fixing of auditor remuneration

Section 492 applies to LLPs, modified so that it reads as follows—

"492 Fixing of auditor's remuneration

(1) The remuneration of an auditor appointed by the LLP must be fixed by the designated members or in such manner as the members of the LLP may determine.

(2) The remuneration of an auditor appointed by the Secretary of State must be fixed by the Secretary of State.

(3) For the purposes of this section "remuneration" includes sums paid in respect of expenses.

(4) This section applies in relation to benefits in kind as to payments of money."

[4205]

NOTES
Commencement: 1 October 2008.

38   Disclosure of auditor remuneration

Section 494 applies to LLPs, modified so that it reads as follows—

> **"494   Disclosure of services provided by auditor or associates and related remuneration**
>
> Parts 1 and 2 of the Companies (Disclosure of Auditor Remuneration and Liability Limitation Agreements) Regulations 2008 (SI 2008/489) apply to LLPs with the following modifications—
>
> (a)   in regulation 3(1), omit the definition of "principal terms";
>
> (b)   references to 6th April 2008 are to be read as references to 1st October 2008;
>
> (c)   references to a company include references to an LLP; and
>
> (d)   except in paragraph 3 of Schedule 1, references to a director or to an officer of a company include references to a member of an LLP."

[4206]

NOTES
Commencement: 1 October 2008.

PART 12
FUNCTIONS OF AUDITOR

39   Auditor's report

Section 495 applies to LLPs, modified so that it reads as follows—

> **"495   Auditor's report on LLP's annual accounts**
>
> (1)   An LLP's auditor must make a report to the LLP's members on all annual accounts of the LLP of which copies are, during his tenure of office to be sent out to members under section 423.
>
> (2)   The auditor's report must include—
>
> (a)   an introduction identifying the annual accounts that are the subject of the audit and the financial reporting framework that has been applied in their preparation, and
>
> (b)   a description of the scope of the audit identifying the auditing standards in accordance with which the audit was conducted.
>
> (3)   The report must state clearly whether, in the auditor's opinion, the annual accounts—
>
> (a)   give a true and fair view—
>
>> (i)   in the case of an individual balance sheet, of the state of affairs of the LLP as at the end of the financial year,
>>
>> (ii)   in the case of an individual profit and loss account, of the profit or loss of the LLP for the financial year,
>>
>> (iii)   in the case of group accounts, of the state of affairs as at the end of the financial year and of the profit or loss for the financial year of the undertakings included in the consolidation as a whole, so far as concerns members of the LLP;
>
> (b)   have been properly prepared in accordance with the relevant financial reporting framework; and
>
> (c)   have been prepared in accordance with the requirements of this Act.
>
> Expressions used in this subsection that are defined for the purposes of Part 15 (see section 474) have the same meaning as in that Part.
>
> (4)   The auditor's report—
>
> (a)   must be either unqualified or qualified, and
>
> (b)   must include a reference to any matters to which the auditor wishes to draw attention by way of emphasis without qualifying the report."

[4207]

NOTES
Commencement: 1 October 2008.

40   Duties and rights of auditors

Sections 498 to 502 apply to LLPs, modified so that they read as follows—

> **"498   Duties of auditor**
>
> (1)   An LLP's auditor, in preparing his report, must carry out such investigations as will enable him to form an opinion as to—

    (a)   whether adequate accounting records have been kept by the LLP and returns adequate for their audit have been received from branches not visited by him, and

    (b)   whether the LLP's individual accounts are in agreement with the accounting records and returns.

(2)   If the auditor is of the opinion—

    (a)   that adequate accounting records have not been kept, or that returns adequate for their audit have not been received from branches not visited by him, or

    (b)   that the LLP's individual accounts are not in agreement with the accounting records and returns,

the auditor shall state that fact in his report.

(3)   If the auditor fails to obtain all the information and explanations which, to the best of his knowledge and belief, are necessary for the purposes of his audit, he shall state that fact in his report.

(4)   If the members of the LLP have prepared accounts in accordance with the small LLPs regime and in the auditor's opinion they were not entitled so to do, the auditor shall state that fact in his report.

499 Auditor's general right to information

(1)   An auditor of an LLP—

    (a)   has a right of access at all times to the LLP's books, accounts and vouchers (in whatever form they are held), and

    (b)   may require any of the following persons to provide him with such information or explanations as he thinks necessary for the performance of his duties as auditor.

(2)   Those persons are—

    (a)   any member or employee of the LLP;

    (b)   any person holding or accountable for any of the LLP's books, accounts or vouchers;

    (c)   any subsidiary undertaking of the LLP which is a body corporate incorporated in the United Kingdom;

    (d)   any officer, employee or auditor of any such subsidiary undertaking or any person holding or accountable for any books, accounts or vouchers of any such subsidiary undertaking;

    (e)   any person who fell within any of paragraphs (a) to (d) at a time to which the information or explanations required by the auditor relates or relate.

(3)   A statement made by a person in response to a requirement under this section may not be used in evidence against him in criminal proceedings except proceedings for an offence under section 501.

(4)   Nothing in this section compels a person to disclose information in respect of which a claim to legal professional privilege (in Scotland, to confidentiality of communications) could be maintained in legal proceedings.

500 Auditor's right to information from overseas subsidiaries

(1)   Where a parent LLP has a subsidiary undertaking that is not a body corporate incorporated in the United Kingdom, the auditor of the parent LLP may require it to obtain from any of the following persons such information or explanations as he may reasonably require for the purposes of his duties as auditor.

(2)   Those persons are—

    (a)   the undertaking;

    (b)   any officer, employee or auditor of the undertaking;

    (c)   any person holding or accountable for any of the undertaking's books, accounts or vouchers;

    (d)   any person who fell within paragraph (b) or (c) at a time to which the information or explanations relates or relate.

(3)   If so required, the parent LLP must take all such steps as are reasonably open to it to obtain the information or explanations from the person concerned.

(4)   A statement made by a person in response to a requirement under this section may not be used in evidence against him in criminal proceedings except proceedings for an offence under section 501.

(5)   Nothing in this section compels a person to disclose information in respect of which a claim to legal professional privilege (in Scotland, to confidentiality of communications) could be maintained in legal proceedings.

501   Auditor's right to information: offences

(1)   A person commits an offence who knowingly or recklessly makes to an auditor of an LLP a statement (oral or written) that—

(a)   conveys or purports to convey any information or explanations which the auditor requires, or is entitled to require, under section 499, and

(b)   is misleading, false or deceptive in a material particular.

(2)   A person guilty of an offence under subsection (1) is liable—

(a)   on conviction on indictment, to imprisonment for a term not exceeding two years or a fine (or both);

(b)   on summary conviction—

(i)   in England and Wales, to imprisonment for a term not exceeding twelve months or to a fine not exceeding the statutory maximum (or both);

(ii)   in Scotland or Northern Ireland, to imprisonment for a term not exceeding six months or to a fine not exceeding the statutory maximum (or both).

(3)   A person who fails to comply with a requirement under section 499 without delay commits an offence unless it was not reasonably practicable for him to provide the required information or explanations.

(4)   If a parent LLP fails to comply with section 500, an offence is committed by—

(a)   the LLP, and

(b)   every member of the LLP who is in default.

(5)   A person guilty of an offence under subsection (3) or (4) is liable on summary conviction to a fine not exceeding level 3 on the standard scale.

(6)   Nothing in this section affects any right of an auditor to apply for an injunction (in Scotland, an interdict or an order for specific performance) to enforce any of his rights under section 499 or 500.

502   Auditor's rights in relation to meetings

(1)   An LLP's auditor is entitled—

(a)   to receive all notices of, and other communications relating to, any meeting which a member of the LLP is entitled to receive, where any part of the business of the meeting concerns them as auditors,

(b)   to attend any meeting of the LLP where any part of the business of the meeting concerns them as auditors, and

(c)   to be heard at any meeting which he attends on any part of the business of the meeting which concerns him as auditor.

(2)   Where the auditor is a firm, the right to attend or be heard at a meeting is exercisable by an individual authorised by the firm in writing to act as its representative at the meeting."

[4208]

NOTES

Commencement: 1 October 2008.

---

41   Signature of auditor's report

Sections 503 to 506 apply to LLPs, modified so that they read as follows—

"503   Signature of auditor's report

(1)   The auditor's report must state the name of the auditor and be signed and dated.

(2)   Where the auditor is an individual, the report must be signed by him.

(3)   Where the auditor is a firm, the report must be signed by the senior statutory auditor in his own name, for and on behalf of the auditor.

504   Senior statutory auditor

(1)   The senior statutory auditor means the individual identified by the firm as senior statutory auditor in relation to the audit in accordance with—

(a)   standards issued by the European Commission, or

(b)   if there is no applicable standard so issued, any relevant guidance issued by—

(i)   the Secretary of State, or

(ii)   a body appointed by order of the Secretary of State.

(2)   The person identified as senior statutory auditor must be eligible for appointment as auditor of the LLP in question (see Chapter 2 of Part 42 of this Act).

(3)   The senior statutory auditor is not, by reason of being named or identified as senior statutory auditor or by reason of his having signed the auditor's report, subject to any civil liability to which he would not otherwise be subject.

(4)   An order appointing a body for the purpose of subsection (1)(b)(ii) is subject to negative resolution procedure.

505   Names to be stated in published copies of auditor's report

(1)   Every copy of the auditor's report that is published by or on behalf of the LLP must—
  (a)   state the name of the auditor and (where the auditor is a firm) the name of the person who signed it as senior statutory auditor, or
  (b)   if the conditions in section 506 (circumstances in which names may be omitted) are met, state that a determination has been made and notified to the Secretary of State in accordance with that section.

(2)   For the purposes of this section an LLP is regarded as publishing the report if it publishes, issues or circulates it or otherwise makes it available for public inspection in a manner calculated to invite members of the public generally, or any class of members of the public, to read it.

(3)   If a copy of the auditor's report is published without the statement required by this section, an offence is committed by—
  (a)   the LLP, and
  (b)   every designated member of the LLP who is in default.

(4)   A person guilty of an offence under this section is liable on summary conviction to a fine not exceeding level 3 on the standard scale.

506   Circumstances in which names may be omitted

(1)   The auditor's name and, where the auditor is a firm, the name of the person who signed the report as senior statutory auditor, may be omitted from—
  (a)   published copies of the report, and
  (b)   the copy of the report delivered to the registrar under Chapter 10 of Part 15 (filing of accounts and reports),
if the following conditions are met.

(2)   The conditions are that the LLP—
  (a)   considering on reasonable grounds that statement of the name would create or be likely to create a serious risk that the auditor or senior statutory auditor, or any other person, would be subject to violence or intimidation, has determined that the name should not be stated, and
  (b)   has given notice of the determination to the Secretary of State, stating—
    (i)   the name and registered number of the LLP,
    (ii)   the financial year of the LLP to which the report relates, and
    (iii) the name of the auditor and (where the auditor is a firm) the name of the person who signed the report as senior statutory auditor."

[4209]

NOTES
Commencement: 1 October 2008.

---

42   Offences in connection with auditor's report

Sections 507 to 509 apply to LLPs, modified so that they read as follows—

"507   Offences in connection with auditor's report

(1)   A person to whom this section applies commits an offence if he knowingly or recklessly causes a report under section 495 (auditor's report on LLP's annual accounts) to include any matter that is misleading, false or deceptive in a material particular.

(2)   A person to whom this section applies commits an offence if he knowingly or recklessly causes such a report to omit a statement required by—
  (a)   section 498(2)(b) (statement that LLP's accounts do not agree with accounting records and returns),
  (b)   section 498(3) (statement that necessary information and explanations not obtained), or
  (c)   section 498(4) (statement that members wrongly prepared accounts in accordance with the small LLPs regime).

(3)   This section applies to—
  (a)   where the auditor is an individual, that individual and any employee or agent of his who is eligible for appointment as auditor of the LLP;
  (b)   where the auditor is a firm, any director, member, employee or agent of the firm who is eligible for appointment as auditor of the LLP.

(4)   A person guilty of an offence under this section is liable—
  (a)   on conviction on indictment, to a fine;

(b)   on summary conviction, to a fine not exceeding the statutory maximum.

508 Guidance for regulatory and prosecuting authorities: England, Wales and Northern Ireland

(1)   The Secretary of State may issue guidance for the purpose of helping relevant regulatory and prosecuting authorities to determine how they should carry out their functions in cases where behaviour occurs that—

(a)   appears to involve the commission of an offence under section 507 (offences in connection with auditor's report), and

(b)   has been, is being or may be investigated pursuant to arrangements—

   (i)   under paragraph 15 of Schedule 10 (investigation of complaints against auditors and supervisory bodies), or

   (ii)   of a kind mentioned in paragraph 24 of that Schedule (independent investigation for disciplinary purposes of public interest cases).

(2)   The Secretary of State must obtain the consent of the Attorney General before issuing any such guidance.

(3)   In this section "relevant regulatory and prosecuting authorities" means—

(a)   supervisory bodies within the meaning of Part 42 of this Act,

(b)   bodies to which the Secretary of State may make grants under section 16(1) of the Companies (Audit, Investigations and Community Enterprise) Act 2004 (c.27) (bodies concerned with accounting standards etc),

(c)   the Director of the Serious Fraud Office,

(d)   the Director of Public Prosecutions or the Director of Public Prosecutions for Northern Ireland, and

(e)   the Secretary of State.

(4)   This section does not apply to Scotland.

509 Guidance for regulatory authorities: Scotland

(1)   The Lord Advocate may issue guidance for the purpose of helping relevant regulatory authorities to determine how they should carry out their functions in cases where behaviour occurs that—

(a)   appears to involve the commission of an offence under section 507 (offences in connection with auditor's report), and

(b)   has been, is being or may be investigated pursuant to arrangements—

   (i)   under paragraph 15 of Schedule 10 (investigation of complaints against auditors and supervisory bodies), or

   (ii)   of a kind mentioned in paragraph 24 of that Schedule (independent investigation for disciplinary purposes of public interest cases).

(2)   The Lord Advocate must consult the Secretary of State before issuing any such guidance.

(3)   In this section "relevant regulatory authorities" means—

(a)   supervisory bodies within the meaning of Part 42 of this Act,

(b)   bodies to which the Secretary of State may make grants under section 16(1) of the Companies (Audit, Investigations and Community Enterprise) Act 2004 (c.27) (bodies concerned with accounting standards etc), and

(c)   the Secretary of State.

(4)   This section applies only to Scotland."

[4210]

NOTES

Commencement: 1 October 2008.

PART 13
REMOVAL, RESIGNATION, ETC OF AUDITORS

43 Removal, resignation, etc of auditors

(1)   Sections 510 to 512 apply to LLPs, modified so that they read as follows—

"510 Removal of auditor

(1)   The members of an LLP may remove an auditor from office at any time.

(2)   Nothing in this section is to be taken as depriving the person removed of compensation or damages payable to him in respect of the termination—

(a)   of his appointment as auditor, or

(b)   of any appointment terminating with that as auditor.

(3)   An auditor may not be removed from office before the expiration of his term of office except under this section.

511   Notice of removal of auditor

(1)   No determination to remove an auditor before the expiration of his term of office may be made under section 510 unless the LLP has given 7 days' prior notice to any auditor whom it is proposed to remove

(2)   The auditor proposed to be removed may make with respect to the proposal representations in writing to the LLP (not exceeding a reasonable length) and request their notification to members of the LLP.

(3)   The LLP must upon receipt send a copy of the representations to every member.

(4)   Copies of the representations need not be sent out if, on the application either of the LLP or of any other person claiming to be aggrieved, the court is satisfied that the auditor is using the provisions of this section to secure needless publicity for defamatory matter.

The court may order the LLP's costs (in Scotland, expenses) on the application to be paid in whole or in part by the auditor, notwithstanding that he is not a party to the application.

512   Notice to registrar of determination removing auditor from office

(1)   Where the members of an LLP have removed an auditor from office under section 510, the LLP must give notice of that fact to the registrar within 14 days.

(2)   If the LLP fails to give the notice required by this section, an offence is committed by the LLP and every designated member who is in default.

(3)   A person guilty of an offence under this section is liable on summary conviction to a fine not exceeding level 3 on the standard scale and, for continued contravention, a daily default fine not exceeding one-tenth of level 3 on the standard scale."

(2)   Until section 1068(1) comes into force, the notice referred to in section 512(1) as applied to LLPs by paragraph (1) must be in the form prescribed for the purposes of section 391(2) of the 1985 Act or Article 399(2) of the 1986 Order as applied to LLPs.

[4211]

NOTES
Commencement: 1 October 2008.

44   Rights of auditor removed from office

(1)   Section 513 applies to LLPs, modified so that it reads as follows—

"513   Rights of auditor who has been removed from office

(1)   An auditor who has been removed has, notwithstanding his removal, the rights conferred by section 502(1) in relation to any meeting of the LLP—
   (a)   at which his term of office would otherwise have expired, or
   (b)   at which it is proposed to fill the vacancy caused by his removal.

(2)   In such a case the references in that section to matters concerning the auditor as auditor shall be construed as references to matters concerning him as a former auditor."

(2)   In section 513 (applied to LLPs by paragraph (1)) as it applies in relation to an auditor appointed before 1st October 2008, the reference to rights under section 502(1) shall be read as a reference to rights under section 390(1) of the 1985 Act or Article 398(1) of the 1986 Order as applied to LLPs.

[4212]

NOTES
Commencement: 1 October 2008.

45   Rights of auditor not re-appointed

(1)   Sections 515 to 518 apply to LLPs, modified so that they read as follows—

"515   Failure to re-appoint auditor: rights of auditor who is not re-appointed

(1)   No person may be appointed as auditor in place of a person (the "outgoing auditor") whose term of office has ended or is to end at the end of the period for appointing auditors unless the LLP has given 7 days' prior notice to the outgoing auditor.

(2)   The outgoing auditor may make with respect to the proposal representations in writing to the LLP (not exceeding a reasonable length) and request their notification to members of the LLP.

(3)   The LLP must upon receipt send a copy of the representations to every member.

(4)   Copies of the representations need not be sent out if, on the application either of the LLP or of any other person claiming to be aggrieved, the court is satisfied that the auditor is using the provisions of this section to secure needless publicity for defamatory matter.

The court may order the LLP's costs (in Scotland, expenses) on the application to be paid in whole or in part by the auditor, notwithstanding that he is not a party to the application.

516   Resignation of auditor

(1)   An auditor of an LLP may resign his office by depositing a notice in writing to that effect at the LLP's registered office.

(2)   The notice is not effective unless it is accompanied by the statement required by section 519.

(3)   An effective notice of resignation operates to bring the auditor's term of office to an end as of the date on which the notice is deposited or on such later date as may be specified in it.

517   Notice to registrar of resignation of auditor

(1)   Where an auditor resigns the LLP must within 14 days of the deposit of a notice of resignation send a copy of the notice to the registrar of companies.

(2)   If default is made in complying with this section, an offence is committed by—
    (a)   the LLP, and
    (b)   every designated member of the LLP who is in default.

(3)   A person guilty of an offence under this section is liable—
    (a)   on conviction on indictment, to a fine;
    (b)   on summary conviction, to a fine not exceeding the statutory maximum and, for continued contravention, a daily default fine not exceeding one-tenth of the statutory maximum.

518   Rights of resigning auditor

(1)   This section applies where an auditor's notice of resignation is accompanied by a statement of the circumstances connected with his resignation (see section 519).

(2)   He may deposit with the notice a signed requisition calling on the designated members of the LLP forthwith duly to convene a meeting of the members of the LLP for the purpose of receiving and considering such explanation of the circumstances connected with his resignation as he may wish to place before the meeting.

(3)   He may request the LLP to circulate to its members before the meeting convened on his requisition, a statement in writing (not exceeding a reasonable length) of the circumstances connected with his resignation.

(4)   The LLP must (unless the statement is received too late for it to comply)—
    (a)   in any notice of the meeting given to members of the LLP, state the fact of the statement having been made, and
    (b)   send a copy of the statement to every member of the LLP to whom notice of the meeting is or has been sent.

(5)   The designated members must within 21 days from the date of the deposit of a requisition under this section proceed duly to convene a meeting for a day not more than 28 days after the date on which the notice convening the meeting is given.

(6)   If default is made in complying with subsection (5), every designated member who failed to take all reasonable steps to secure that a meeting was convened commits an offence.

(7)   A person guilty of an offence under this section is liable—
    (a)   on conviction on indictment, to a fine;
    (b)   on summary conviction to a fine not exceeding the statutory maximum.

(8)   If a copy of the statement mentioned above is not sent out as required because received too late or because of the LLP's default, the auditor may (without prejudice to his right to be heard orally) require that the statement be read out at the meeting.

(9)   Copies of a statement need not be sent out and the statement need not be read out at the meeting if, on the application either of the LLP or of any other person who claims to be aggrieved, the court is satisfied that the auditor is using the provisions of this section to secure needless publicity for defamatory matter.

The court may order the LLP's costs (in Scotland, expenses) on such an application to be paid in whole or in part by the auditor, notwithstanding that he is not a party to the application.

(10)   An auditor who has resigned has, notwithstanding his resignation, the rights conferred by section 502(1) in relation to any such meeting of the LLP as is mentioned in subsection (3).

In such a case the references in that section to matters concerning the auditor as auditor shall be construed as references to matters concerning him as a former auditor."

(2)   In section 518 (applied to LLPs by paragraph (1)) as it applies in relation to an auditor appointed before 1st October 2008, the reference to rights under section 502(1) shall be read as a reference to rights under section 390(1) of the 1985 Act or Article 398(1) of the 1986 Order as applied to LLPs.

[4213]

NOTES
Commencement: 1 October 2008.

46   Auditor statements

Sections 519 to 526 apply to LLPs, modified so that they read as follows—

"519   Statement by auditor to be deposited with LLP

(1)   Where an auditor of an LLP ceases for any reason to hold office, he must deposit at the LLP's registered office a statement of the circumstances connected with his ceasing to hold office, unless he considers that there are no circumstances in connection with his ceasing to hold office that need to be brought to the attention of members or creditors of the LLP.

(2)   If he considers that there are no circumstances in connection with his ceasing to hold office that need to be brought to the attention of members or creditors of the LLP, he must deposit at the LLP's registered office a statement to that effect.

(3)   The statement required by this section must be deposited—
(a)   in the case of resignation, along with the notice of resignation;
(b)   in the case of failure to seek re-appointment, not less than 14 days before the end of the time allowed for next appointing an auditor;
(c)   in any other case, not later than the end of the period of 14 days beginning with the date on which he ceases to hold office.

(4)   A person ceasing to hold office as auditor who fails to comply with this section commits an offence.

(5)   In proceedings for such an offence it is a defence for the person charged to show that he took all reasonable steps and exercised all due diligence to avoid the commission of the offence.

(6)   A person guilty of an offence under this section is liable—
(a)   on conviction on indictment, to a fine;
(b)   on summary conviction, to a fine not exceeding the statutory maximum.

(7)   Where an offence under this section is committed by a body corporate, every officer of the body who is in default also commits the offence.

For this purpose—
(a)   any person who acts as director, manager or secretary of the body is treated as an officer of the body, and
(b)   if the body is a company, any shadow director is treated as an officer of the company.

520   LLP's duties in relation to statement

(1)   This section applies where the statement deposited under section 519 states the circumstances connected with the auditor's ceasing to hold office.

(2)   The LLP must within 14 days of the deposit of the statement either—
(a)   send a copy of it to every person who under section 423 is entitled to be sent copies of the accounts, or
(b)   apply to the court.

(3)   If it applies to the court, the LLP must notify the auditor of the application.

(4)   If the court is satisfied that the auditor is using the provisions of section 519 to secure needless publicity for defamatory matter—
(a)   it shall direct that copies of the statement need not be sent out, and
(b)   it may further order the LLP's costs (in Scotland, expenses) on the application to be paid in whole or in part by the auditor, even if he is not a party to the application.

The LLP must within 14 days of the court's decision send to the persons mentioned in subsection (2)(a) a statement setting out the effect of the order.

(5)   If no such direction is made the LLP must send copies of the statement to the persons mentioned in subsection (2)(a) within 14 days of the court's decision or, as the case may be, of the discontinuance of the proceedings.

(6)   In the event of default in complying with this section an offence is committed by every designated member of the LLP who is in default.

(7)   In proceedings for such an offence it is a defence for the person charged to show that he took all reasonable steps and exercised all due diligence to avoid the commission of the offence.

(8)   A person guilty of an offence under this section is liable—
    (a)   on conviction on indictment, to a fine;
    (b)   on summary conviction, to a fine not exceeding the statutory maximum.

521   Copy of statement to be sent to registrar

(1)   Unless within 21 days beginning with the day on which he deposited the statement under section 519 the auditor receives notice of an application to the court under section 520, he must within a further seven days send a copy of the statement to the registrar.

(2)   If an application to the court is made under section 520 and the auditor subsequently receives notice under subsection (5) of that section, he must within seven days of receiving the notice send a copy of the statement to the registrar.

(3)   An auditor who fails to comply with subsection (1) or (2) commits an offence.

(4)   In proceedings for such an offence it is a defence for the person charged to show that he took all reasonable steps and exercised all due diligence to avoid the commission of the offence.

(5)   A person guilty of an offence under this section is liable—
    (a)   on conviction on indictment, to a fine;
    (b)   on summary conviction, to a fine not exceeding the statutory maximum.

(6)   Where an offence under this section is committed by a body corporate, every officer of the body who is in default also commits the offence.

For this purpose—
    (a)   any person who acts as director, manager or secretary of the body is treated as an officer of the body, and
    (b)   if the body is a company, any shadow director is treated as an officer of the company.

522   Duty of auditor to notify appropriate audit authority

(1)   Where—
    (a)   in the case of a major audit, an auditor ceases for any reason to hold office, or
    (b)   in the case of an audit that is not a major audit, an auditor ceases to hold office before the end of his term of office,
the auditor ceasing to hold office must notify the appropriate audit authority.

(2)   The notice must—
    (a)   inform the appropriate audit authority that he has ceased to hold office, and
    (b)   be accompanied by a copy of the statement deposited by him at the LLP's registered office in accordance with section 519.

(3)   If the statement so deposited is to the effect that he considers that there are no circumstances in connection with his ceasing to hold office that need to be brought to the attention of members or creditors of the LLP, the notice must also be accompanied by a statement of the reasons for his ceasing to hold office.

(4)   The auditor must comply with this section—
    (a)   in the case of a major audit, at the same time as he deposits a statement at the LLP's registered office in accordance with section 519;
    (b)   in the case of an audit that is not a major audit, at such time (not being earlier than the time mentioned in paragraph (a)) as the appropriate audit authority may require.

(5)   A person ceasing to hold office as auditor who fails to comply with this section commits an offence.

(6)   If that person is a firm an offence is committed by—
    (a)   the firm, and
    (b)   every officer of the firm who is in default.

(7)   In proceedings for an offence under this section it is a defence for the person charged to show that he took all reasonable steps and exercised all due diligence to avoid the commission of the offence.

(8)   A person guilty of an offence under this section is liable—
    (a)   on conviction on indictment, to a fine;
    (b)   on summary conviction, to a fine not exceeding the statutory maximum.

523 Duty of LLP to notify appropriate audit authority

(1)   Where an auditor ceases to hold office before the end of his term of office, the LLP must notify the appropriate audit authority.

(2)   The notice must—
(a)   inform the appropriate audit authority that the auditor has ceased to hold office, and
(b)   be accompanied by—
(i)   a statement by the LLP of the reasons for his ceasing to hold office, or
(ii)   if the copy of the statement deposited by the auditor at the LLP's registered office in accordance with section 519 contains a statement of circumstances in connection with his ceasing to hold office that need to be brought to the attention of members or creditors of the LLP, a copy of that statement.

(3)   The LLP must give notice under this section not later than 14 days after the date on which the auditor's statement is deposited at the LLP's registered office in accordance with section 519.

(4)   If an LLP fails to comply with this section, an offence is committed by—
(a)   the LLP, and
(b)   every designated member of the LLP who is in default.

(5)   In proceedings for such an offence it is a defence for the person charged to show that he took all reasonable steps and exercised all due diligence to avoid the commission of the offence.

(6)   A person guilty of an offence under this section is liable—
(a)   on conviction on indictment, to a fine;
(b)   on summary conviction, to a fine not exceeding the statutory maximum.

524 Information to be given to accounting authorities

(1)   The appropriate audit authority on receiving notice under section 522 or 523 of an auditor's ceasing to hold office—
(a)   must inform the accounting authorities, and
(b)   may if it thinks fit forward to those authorities a copy of the statement or statements accompanying the notice.

(2)   The accounting authorities are—
(a)   the Secretary of State, and
(b)   the body known as the Financial Reporting Review Panel established under the articles of association of the Financial Reporting Council Limited (registered number 02486368).

(3)   If either of the accounting authorities is also the appropriate audit authority it is only necessary to comply with this section as regards any other accounting authority.

(4)   If the court has made an order under section 520(4) directing that copies of the statement need not be sent out by the LLP, sections 460 and 461 (restriction on further disclosure) apply in relation to the copies sent to the accounting authorities as they apply to information obtained under section 459 (power to require documents etc).

525 Meaning of "appropriate audit authority" and "major audit"

(1)   In sections 522, 523 and 524 "appropriate audit authority" means—
(a)   in the case of a major audit (other than one conducted by an Auditor General), the body known as the Professional Oversight Board established under the articles of association of the Financial Reporting Council Limited (registered number 02486368);
(b)   in the case of an audit (other than one conducted by an Auditor General) that is not a major audit, the relevant supervisory body;
(c)   in the case of an audit conducted by an Auditor General, the Independent Supervisor.

"Supervisory body" and "Independent Supervisor" have the same meaning as in Part 42 (statutory auditors) (see sections 1217 and 1228).

(2)   In section 522 and this section "major audit" means a statutory audit conducted in respect of—
(a)   an LLP any of whose securities have been admitted to the official list (within the meaning of Part 6 of the Financial Services and Markets Act 2000 (c.8)), or
(b)   any other person in whose financial condition there is a major public interest.

(3)   In determining whether an audit is a major audit within subsection (2)(b), regard shall be had to any guidance issued by any of the authorities mentioned in subsection (1).

526   Effect of casual vacancies

If an auditor ceases to hold office for any reason, any surviving or continuing auditor or auditors may continue to act."

[4214]

NOTES
Commencement: 1 October 2008.

PART 14
LLP AUDIT: SUPPLEMENTARY PROVISIONS

47   Minor definitions

Section 539 applies to LLPs, modified so that it reads as follows—

"539   Minor definitions

In this Part—
   "e-money issuer" means a person who has permission under Part 4 of the Financial
      Services and Markets Act 2000 (c.8) to carry on the activity of issuing electronic
      money within the meaning of article 9B of the Financial Services and Markets
      Act 2000 (Regulated Activities) Order 2001 (SI 2001/544);
   "LLP agreement" means any agreement express or implied between the members of the
      LLP or between the LLP and the members of the LLP which determines the mutual
      rights and duties of the members, and their rights and duties in relation to the LLP;
   "MiFID investment firm" means an investment firm within the meaning of Article 4.1.1
      of Directive 2004/39/EEC of the European Parliament and of the Council of 21 April
      2004 on markets in financial instruments, other than—
      (a)   an LLP to which that Directive does not apply by virtue of Article 2 of
            that Directive,
      (b)   an LLP which is an exempt investment firm within the meaning of
            regulation 4A(3) of the Financial Services and Markets Act 2000
            (Markets in Financial Instruments) Regulations 2007, and
      (c)   any other LLP which fulfils all the requirements set out in
            regulation 4C(3) of those Regulations;
   "qualified", in relation to an auditor's report (or a statement contained in an auditor's
      report), means that the report or statement does not state the auditor's unqualified
      opinion that the accounts have been properly prepared in accordance with this Act or,
      in the case of an undertaking not required to prepare accounts in accordance with this
      Act, under any corresponding legislation under which it is required to prepare
      accounts;
   "turnover", in relation to an LLP, means the amounts derived from the provision of goods
      and services falling within the LLP's ordinary activities, after deduction of—
      (a)   trade discounts,
      (b)   value added tax, and
      (c)   any other taxes based on the amounts so derived;
   "UCITS management company" has the meaning given by the Glossary forming part of
      the Handbook made by the Financial Services Authority under the Financial Services
      and Markets Act 2000."

[4215]

NOTES
Commencement: 1 October 2008.

PART 15
STATUTORY AUDITORS

48   Extension of Part 42

For the purposes of section 1210(1)(h) (meaning of "statutory auditor")—
   (a)   an LLP is a prescribed person, and
   (b)   Part 16 of the Companies Act 2006 as applied to LLPs is a prescribed enactment,

(and accordingly a person appointed as auditor of an LLP under Part 16 of that Act as applied to LLPs by these Regulations is a statutory auditor).

[4216]

NOTES
Commencement: 1 October 2008.

PART 16
OFFENCES

49 Liability of member in default

Sections 1121 and 1122 apply to LLPs, modified so that they read as follows—

"1121 Liability of member in default

(1) This section has effect for the purposes of any provision of the Companies Acts to the effect that, in the event of contravention of an enactment in relation to an LLP, an offence is committed by every member or, as the case may be, every designated member of the LLP who is in default.

(2) A member or designated member is "in default" for the purposes of the provision if he authorises or permits, participates in, or fails to take all reasonable steps to prevent, the contravention.

1122 Liability of company as member in default

(1) Where a company is a member or designated member of an LLP, it does not commit an offence as a member or designated member in default unless one of its officers is in default.

(2) Where any such offence is committed by a company the officer in question also commits the offence and is liable to be proceeded against and punished accordingly.

(3) In this section—
  (a) officer" includes any director, manager or secretary, and
  (b) an officer is "in default" for the purposes of the provision if he authorises or permits, participates in, or fails to take all reasonable steps to prevent, the contravention."

[4217]

NOTES

Commencement: 1 October 2008.

50 General provisions

Sections 1125 to 1132 apply to LLPs, modified so that they read as follows—

"1125 Meaning of "daily default fine

(1) This section defines what is meant in the Companies Acts where it is provided that a person guilty of an offence is liable on summary conviction to a fine not exceeding a specified amount "and, for continued contravention, a daily default fine" not exceeding a specified amount.

(2) This means that the person is liable on a second or subsequent summary conviction of the offence to a fine not exceeding the latter amount for each day on which the contravention is continued (instead of being liable to a fine not exceeding the former amount).

1126 Consents required for certain prosecutions

(1) This section applies to proceedings for an offence under section 458 or 460 of this Act.

(2) No such proceedings are to be brought in England and Wales except by or with the consent of the Secretary of State or the Director of Public Prosecutions.

(3) No such proceedings are to be brought in Northern Ireland except by or with the consent of the Secretary of State or the Director of Public Prosecutions for Northern Ireland.

1127 Summary proceedings: venue

(1) Summary proceedings for any offence under the Companies Acts may be taken—
  (a) against a body corporate, at any place at which the body has a place of business, and
  (b) against any other person, at any place at which he is for the time being.

(2) This is without prejudice to any jurisdiction exercisable apart from this section.

1128 Summary proceedings: time limit for proceedings

(1) An information relating to an offence under the Companies Acts that is triable by a magistrates' court in England and Wales may be so tried if it is laid—
  (a) at any time within three years after the commission of the offence, and
  (b) within twelve months after the date on which evidence sufficient in the opinion of the Director of Public Prosecutions or the Secretary of State (as the case may be) to justify the proceedings comes to his knowledge.

(2) Summary proceedings in Scotland for an offence under the Companies Acts—

(a) must not be commenced after the expiration of three years from the commission of the offence;

(b) subject to that, may be commenced at any time—

(i) within twelve months after the date on which evidence sufficient in the Lord Advocate's opinion to justify the proceedings came to his knowledge, or

(ii) where such evidence was reported to him by the Secretary of State, within twelve months after the date on which it came to the knowledge of the latter.

Section 136(3) of the Criminal Procedure (Scotland) Act 1995 (c.46) (date when proceedings deemed to be commenced) applies for the purposes of this subsection as for the purposes of that section.

(3) A magistrates' court in Northern Ireland has jurisdiction to hear and determine a complaint charging the commission of a summary offence under the Companies Acts provided that the complaint is made—

(a) within three years from the time when the offence was committed, and

(b) within twelve months from the date on which evidence sufficient in the opinion of the Director of Public Prosecutions for Northern Ireland or the Secretary of State (as the case may be) to justify the proceedings comes to his knowledge.

(4) For the purposes of this section a certificate of the Director of Public Prosecutions, the Lord Advocate, the Director of Public Prosecutions for Northern Ireland or the Secretary of State (as the case may be) as to the date on which such evidence as is referred to above came to his notice is conclusive evidence.

1129 Legal professional privilege

In proceedings against a person for an offence under the Companies Acts, nothing in those Acts is to be taken to require any person to disclose any information that he is entitled to refuse to disclose on grounds of legal professional privilege (in Scotland, confidentiality of communications).

1130 Proceedings against unincorporated bodies

(1) Proceedings for an offence under the Companies Acts alleged to have been committed by an unincorporated body must be brought in the name of the body (and not in that of any of its members).

(2) For the purposes of such proceedings—

(a) any rules of court relating to the service of documents have effect as if the body were a body corporate, and

(b) the following provisions apply as they apply in relation to a body corporate—

(i) in England and Wales, section 33 of the Criminal Justice Act 1925 (c.86) and Schedule 3 to the Magistrates' Courts Act 1980 (c.43),

(ii) in Scotland, sections 70 and 143 of the Criminal Procedure (Scotland) Act 1995 (c.46),

(iii) in Northern Ireland, section 18 of the Criminal Justice Act (Northern Ireland) 1945 (c.15 (NI)) and Article 166 of and Schedule 4 to the Magistrates' Courts (Northern Ireland) Order 1981 (SI 1981/1675 (NI 26)).

(3) A fine imposed on an unincorporated body on its conviction of an offence under the Companies Acts must be paid out of the funds of the body.

1131 Imprisonment on summary conviction in England and Wales: transitory provision

(1) This section applies to any provision of the Companies Acts that provides that a person guilty of an offence is liable on summary conviction in England and Wales to imprisonment for a term not exceeding twelve months.

(2) In relation to an offence committed before the commencement of section 154(1) of the Criminal Justice Act 2003 (c.44), for "twelve months" substitute "six months".

1132 Production and inspection of documents where offence suspected

(1) An application under this section may be made—

(a) in England and Wales, to a judge of the High Court by the Director of Public Prosecutions, the Secretary of State or a chief officer of police;

(b) in Scotland, to one of the Lords Commissioners of Justiciary by the Lord Advocate;

(c) in Northern Ireland, to the High Court by the Director of Public Prosecutions for Northern Ireland, the Department of Enterprise, Trade and Investment or a chief superintendent of the Police Service of Northern Ireland.

(2) If on an application under this section there is shown to be reasonable cause to believe—

    (a)   that any person has, while a member of an LLP, committed an offence in connection with the management of the LLP's affairs, and

    (b)   that evidence of the commission of the offence is to be found in any documents in the possession or control of the LLP, an order under this section may be made.

(3) The order may—

    (a)   authorise any person named in it to inspect the documents in question, or any of them, for the purpose of investigating and obtaining evidence of the offence, or

    (b)   require such member of the LLP as may be named in the order, to produce the documents (or any of them) to a person named in the order at a place so named.

(4) This section applies also in relation to documents in the possession or control of a person carrying on the business of banking, so far as they relate to the LLP's affairs, as it applies to documents in the possession or control of the LLP, except that no such order as is referred to in subsection (3)(b) may be made by virtue of this subsection."

The decision under this section of a judge of the High Court, any of the Lords Commissioners of Justiciary or the High Court is not appealable.

In this section "document" includes information recorded in any form.

[4218]

NOTES
Commencement: 1 October 2008.

PART 17
LLPS: SUPPLEMENTARY AND INTERPRETATION

51 Courts and legal proceedings

Section 1157 applies to LLPs, modified so that it reads as follows—

"1157 Power of court to grant relief in certain cases

(1) If in proceedings for negligence, default, breach of duty or breach of trust against—

    (a)   a member of an LLP, or

    (b)   a person employed by an LLP as auditor,

it appears to the court hearing the case that the member or person is or may be liable but that he acted honestly and reasonably, and that having regard to all the circumstances of the case (including those connected with his appointment) he ought fairly to be excused, the court may relieve him, either wholly or in part, from his liability on such terms as it thinks fit.

(2) If any such member or person has reason to apprehend that a claim will or might be made against him in respect of negligence, default, breach of duty or breach of trust—

    (a)   he may apply to the court for relief, and

    (b)   the court has the same power to relieve him as it would have had if it had been a court before which proceedings against him for negligence, default, breach of duty or breach of trust had been brought.

(3) Where a case to which subsection (1) applies is being tried by a judge with a jury, the judge, after hearing the evidence, may, if he is satisfied that the defendant (in Scotland, the defender) ought in pursuance of that subsection to be relieved either in whole or in part from the liability sought to be enforced against him, withdraw the case from the jury and forthwith direct judgment to be entered for the defendant (in Scotland, grant decree of absolvitor) on such terms as to costs (in Scotland, expenses) or otherwise as the judge may think proper."

[4219]

NOTES
Commencement: 1 October 2008.

52 Meaning of "undertaking" and related expressions

Sections 1161 and 1162 and Schedule 7 apply to LLPs, modified so that they read as follows—

"1161 Meaning of "undertaking" and related expressions

(1) In this Act "undertaking" means—

    (a)   a body corporate or partnership, or

    (b)   an unincorporated association carrying on a trade or business, with or without a view to profit.

(2) In this Act references to shares—

(a)   in relation to an undertaking with capital but no share capital, are to rights to share in the capital of the undertaking; and

(b)   in relation to an undertaking without capital, are to interests—

    (i)   conferring any right to share in the profits or liability to contribute to the losses of the undertaking, or

    (ii)   giving rise to an obligation to contribute to the debts or expenses of the undertaking in the event of a winding up.

(3)   Other expressions appropriate to companies shall be construed, in relation to an undertaking which is not a company, as references to the corresponding persons, officers, documents or organs, as the case may be, appropriate to undertakings of that description.

This is subject to provision in any specific context providing for the translation of such expressions.

(4)   References in this Act to "fellow subsidiary undertakings" are to undertakings which are subsidiary undertakings of the same parent undertaking but are not parent undertakings or subsidiary undertakings of each other.

(5)   In this Act "group undertaking", in relation to an undertaking, means an undertaking which is—

(a)   a parent undertaking or subsidiary undertaking of that undertaking, or

(b)   a subsidiary undertaking of any parent undertaking of that undertaking.

1162   Parent and subsidiary undertakings

(1)   This section (together with Schedule 7) defines "parent undertaking" and "subsidiary undertaking" for the purposes of this Act.

(2)   An undertaking is a parent undertaking in relation to another undertaking, a subsidiary undertaking, if—

(a)   it holds a majority of the voting rights in the undertaking, or

(b)   it is a member of the undertaking and has the right to appoint or remove a majority of its board of directors, or

(c)   it has the right to exercise a dominant influence over the undertaking—

    (i)   by virtue of provisions contained in the undertaking's articles or in an LLP Agreement, or

    (ii)   by virtue of a control contract, or

(d)   it is a member of the undertaking and controls alone, pursuant to an agreement with other shareholders or members, a majority of the voting rights in the undertaking.

(3)   For the purposes of subsection (2) an undertaking shall be treated as a member of another undertaking—

(a)   if any of its subsidiary undertakings is a member of that undertaking, or

(b)   if any shares in that other undertaking are held by a person acting on behalf of the undertaking or any of its subsidiary undertakings.

(4)   An undertaking is also a parent undertaking in relation to another undertaking, a subsidiary undertaking, if—

(a)   it has the power to exercise, or actually exercises, dominant influence or control over it, or

(b)   it and the subsidiary undertaking are managed on a unified basis.

(5)   A parent undertaking shall be treated as the parent undertaking of undertakings in relation to which any of its subsidiary undertakings are, or are to be treated as, parent undertakings; and references to its subsidiary undertakings shall be construed accordingly.

(6)   Schedule 7 contains provisions explaining expressions used in this section and otherwise supplementing this section.

(7)   In this section and that Schedule references to shares, in relation to an undertaking, are to allotted shares."

"SCHEDULE 7

PARENT AND SUBSIDIARY UNDERTAKINGS: SUPPLEMENTARY PROVISIONS

Introduction

1.   The provisions of this Schedule explain expressions used in section 1162 (parent and subsidiary undertakings) and otherwise supplement that section.

Voting rights in an undertaking

2.—(1)   In section 1162(2)(a) and (d) the references to the voting rights in an undertaking are to the rights conferred on shareholders in respect of their shares or, in the case of an

PART III

STATUTORY INSTRUMENTS

undertaking not having a share capital, on members, to vote at general meetings of the undertaking on all, or substantially all, matters.

(2) In relation to an undertaking which does not have general meetings at which matters are decided by the exercise of voting rights the references to holding a majority of the voting rights in the undertaking are to be construed as references to having the right under the constitution of the undertaking to direct the overall policy of the undertaking or to alter the terms of its constitution.

Right to appoint or remove a majority of members or directors

3.—(1) In section 1162(2)(b) the reference to the right to appoint or remove a majority of the board of directors is to the right to appoint or remove directors holding a majority of the voting rights at meetings of the board on all, or substantially all, matters.

(2) An undertaking shall be treated as having the right to appoint to a directorship if—
 (a) a person's appointment to it follows necessarily from his appointment as director of the undertaking, or
 (b) the directorship is held by the undertaking itself.

(3) A right to appoint or remove which is exercisable only with the consent or concurrence of another person shall be left out of account unless no other person has a right to appoint or, as the case may be, remove in relation to that directorship.

(4) (4) In relation to an undertaking the business of which is managed by the members, references to the board of directors or directors are to be construed as references to members.

Right to exercise dominant influence

4.—(1) For the purposes of section 1162(2)(c) an undertaking shall not be regarded as having the right to exercise a dominant influence over another undertaking unless it has a right to give directions with respect to the operating and financial policies of that other undertaking which its directors are obliged to comply with whether or not they are for the benefit of that other undertaking.

(2) A "control contract" means a contract in writing conferring such a right which—
 (a) is of a kind authorised by the articles of the undertaking or by the LLP agreement of the LLP in relation to which the right is exercisable, and
 (b) is permitted by the law under which that undertaking is established.

(3) In relation to an undertaking the business of which is managed by the members, references to directors are to be construed as references to members.

(4) This paragraph shall not be read as affecting the construction of section 1162(4)(a).

Rights exercisable only in certain circumstances or temporarily incapable of exercise

5.—(1) Rights which are exercisable only in certain circumstances shall be taken into account only—
 (a) when the circumstances have arisen, and for so long as they continue to obtain, or
 (b) when the circumstances are within the control of the person having the rights.

(2) Rights which are normally exercisable but are temporarily incapable of exercise shall continue to be taken into account.

Rights held by one person on behalf of another

6. Rights held by a person in a fiduciary capacity shall be treated as not held by him.

7.—(1) Rights held by a person as nominee for another shall be treated as held by the other.

(2) Rights shall be regarded as held as nominee for another if they are exercisable only on his instructions or with his consent or concurrence.

Rights attached to shares held by way of security

8. Rights attached to shares held by way of security shall be treated as held by the person providing the security—
 (a) where apart from the right to exercise them for the purpose of preserving the value of the security, or of realising it, the rights are exercisable only in accordance with his instructions, and
 (b) where the shares are held in connection with the granting of loans as part of normal business activities and apart from the right to exercise them for the purpose of preserving the value of the security, or of realising it, the rights are exercisable only in his interests.

Rights attributed to parent undertaking

9.—(1) Rights shall be treated as held by a parent undertaking if they are held by any of its subsidiary undertakings.

(2) Nothing in paragraph 7 or 8 shall be construed as requiring rights held by a parent undertaking to be treated as held by any of its subsidiary undertakings.

(3) For the purposes of paragraph 8 rights shall be treated as being exercisable in accordance with the instructions or in the interests of an undertaking if they are exercisable in accordance with the instructions of or, as the case may be, in the interests of any group undertaking.

Disregard of certain rights

10. The voting rights in an undertaking shall be reduced by any rights held by the undertaking itself.

Supplementary

11. References in any provision of paragraphs 6 to 10 to rights held by a person include rights falling to be treated as held by him by virtue of any other provision of those paragraphs but not rights which by virtue of any such provision are to be treated as not held by him."

[4220]

NOTES
Commencement: 1 October 2008.

---

53 Meaning of "dormant"

Section 1169 applies to LLPs, modified so that it reads as follows—

"1169 Dormant LLPs

(1) For the purposes of this Act an LLP is "dormant" during any period in which it has no significant accounting transaction.

(2) A "significant accounting transaction" means a transaction that is required by section 386 to be entered in the LLP's accounting records.

(3) In determining whether or when an LLP is dormant, there shall be disregarded any transaction consisting of the payment of—
  (a) a fee to the registrar on a change of the LLP's name,
  (b) a penalty under section 453 (penalty for failure to file accounts), or
  (c) a fee to the registrar for the registration of an annual return."

[4221]

NOTES
Commencement: 1 October 2008.

---

54 Requirements of this Act

Section 1172 applies to LLPs, modified so that it reads as follows—

"1172 References to requirements of this Act

References in the provisions of this Act applied to LLPs to the requirements of this Act include the requirements of regulations and orders made under it."

[4222]

NOTES
Commencement: 1 October 2008.

---

55 Minor definitions

Section 1173 applies to LLPs, modified so that it reads as follows—

"1173 Minor definitions: general

(1) In this Act—
  "body corporate" includes a body incorporated outside the United Kingdom, but does not include—
  (a) a corporation sole, or
  (b) a partnership that, whether or not a legal person, is not regarded as a body corporate under the law by which it is governed;
  "EEA undertaking" means an undertaking governed by the law of an EEA State.
  "parent LLP" means an LLP that is a parent undertaking (see section 1162 and Schedule 7);

"regulated activity" has the meaning given by section 22 of the Financial Services and Markets Act 2000 (c.8);

"regulated market" has the same meaning as in Directive 2004/39/EC of the European Parliament and of the Council on markets in financial instruments (see Article 4.1(14)).

(2) In relation to an EEA State that has not implemented Directive 2004/39/EC of the European Parliament and of the Council on markets in financial instruments, the following definition of "regulated market" has effect in place of that in subsection (1)—

"regulated market" has the same meaning as it has in Council Directive 93/22/EEC on investment services in the securities field."

[4223]

NOTES

Commencement: 1 October 2008.

56 Regulations

Sections 1288 to 1290 apply to LLPs, modified so that they read as follows—

"1288 Regulations: statutory instrument

Except as otherwise provided, regulations under this Act shall be made by statutory instrument.

1289 Regulations: negative resolution procedure

Where regulations under this Act are subject to "negative resolution procedure" the statutory instrument containing the regulations or order shall be subject to annulment in pursuance of a resolution of either House of Parliament.

1290 Regulations: affirmative resolution procedure

Where regulations under this Act are subject to "affirmative resolution procedure" the regulations must not be made unless a draft of the statutory instrument containing them has been laid before Parliament and approved by a resolution of each House of Parliament."

[4224]

NOTES

Commencement: 1 October 2008.

57 Section 1292 applies to LLPs, modified so that it reads as follows—

"1292 Regulations and orders: supplementary

(1) Regulations under this Act may—
  (a) make different provision for different cases or circumstances,
  (b) include supplementary, incidental and consequential provision, and
  (c) make transitional provision and savings.

(2) Any provision that may be made by regulations under this Act subject to negative resolution procedure may be made by regulations subject to affirmative resolution procedure."

[4225]

NOTES

Commencement: 1 October 2008.

PART 18
FINAL PROVISIONS

58 Revocation and transitional provisions

(1) Subject to paragraphs (3) to (11), the following provisions of the Limited Liability Partnerships Regulations 2001 are revoked—
  (a) regulation 3 and Schedule 1,
  (b) in Schedule 2, the entries relating to sections 384, 385, 387, 388, 388A, 389A, 390, 390A, 390B, 391, 391A, 392, 392A, 394, 394A and 742, and
  (c) entries 1, 2, 3 and 6 in Part I of Schedule 6.

(2) Subject to paragraphs (3) to (11), the following provisions of the Limited Liability Partnerships Regulations (Northern Ireland) 2004 are revoked—
  (a) regulation 3 and Schedule 1,
  (b) in Schedule 2, the entries relating to Articles 10, 392, 393, 395, 396, 396A, 397A, 398, 398A, 398B, 399, 399A, 400, 400A, 401A and 401B, and
  (c) entries 1, 2, 3 and 6 in Part I of Schedule 5.

(3)   The provisions specified in paragraphs (1)(a) and (c) and (2)(a) and (c), and the entries specified in paragraphs (1)(b) and (2)(b) relating to section 742 of the 1985 Act or Article 10 of the 1986 Order, continue to apply to accounts for, and otherwise as regards, financial years beginning before 1st October 2008.

(4)   The entries specified in paragraphs (1)(b) and (2)(b) relating to sections 384, 385, 387, 388 and 388A of the 1985 Act or Articles 392, 393, 395, 396 and 396A of the 1986 Order continue to apply in relation to appointments of auditors for financial years beginning before 1st October 2008, and section 388(2) of the 1985 Act or Article 396(2) of the 1986 Order as applied to LLPs continues to apply where the vacancy occurs before that date.

(5)   The entries specified in paragraphs (1)(b) and (2)(b) relating to section 389A of the 1985 Act or Article 397A of the 1986 Order continue to apply as regards financial years beginning before 1st October 2008.

(6)   The entries specified in paragraphs (1)(b) and (2)(b) relating to section 390 of the 1985 Act or Article 398 of the 1986 Order continue to apply to auditors appointed before 1st October 2008.

(7)   The entries specified in paragraphs (1)(b) and (2)(b) relating to sections 390A and 390B of the 1985 Act or Articles 398A and 398B of the 1986 Order continue to apply to auditors appointed for financial years beginning before 1st October 2008.

(8)   The entries specified in paragraphs (1)(b) and (2)(b) relating to sections 391 and 391A of the 1985 Act or Articles 399 and 399A of the 1986 Order continue to apply as respects removal of auditors where notice is given to the auditor before 1st October 2008.

(9)   The entries specified in paragraphs (1)(b) and (2)(b) relating to section 391A of the 1985 Act or Article 399A of the 1986 Order continue to apply as regards failure to re-appoint an auditor to appointments for financial years beginning before 1st October 2008.

(10)   The entries specified in paragraphs (1)(b) and (2)(b) relating to sections 392 and 392A of the 1985 Act or Articles 400 and 400A of the 1986 Order continue to apply to resignations occurring before 1st October 2008.

(11)   The entries specified in paragraphs (1)(b) and (2)(b) relating to sections 394 and 394A of the 1985 Act or Articles 401A and 401B of the 1986 Order continue to apply where the auditor ceases to hold office before 1st October 2008.

[4226]

NOTES
Commencement: 1 October 2008.

PROCEEDS OF CRIME ACT 2002 (INVESTIGATIVE POWERS OF PROSECUTORS IN ENGLAND, WALES AND NORTHERN IRELAND: CODE OF PRACTICE) ORDER 2008

(SI 2008/1978)

NOTES
Made: 21 July 2008.
Authority: Proceeds of Crime Act 2002, s 377A(5).
Commencement: 22 July 2008.
As of 1 February 2009, this Order had not been amended.

1   This Order may be cited as the Proceeds of Crime Act 2002 (Investigative Powers of Prosecutors in England, Wales and Northern Ireland: Code of Practice) Order 2008 and shall come into force on the day after the day on which it is made.

[4226A]

NOTES
Commencement: 22 July 2008.

2   The code of practice entitled "Code of Practice issued under section 377A of the Proceeds of Crime Act 2002" laid before Parliament on 18 June 2008 shall come into operation on the day after the day on which this Order is made.

[4226B]

NOTES
Commencement: 22 July 2008.

BRADFORD & BINGLEY PLC TRANSFER OF SECURITIES AND PROPERTY ETC ORDER 2008

(SI 2008/2546)

NOTES
Made: 29 September 2008 (7.30 am).
Authority: Banking (Special Provisions) Act 2008, ss 3, 4, 8, 12, 13(2), Sch 1.
Commencement: 29 September 2008 (8.00 am).

As of 1 February 2009, this Order had not been amended.

ARRANGEMENT OF ARTICLES

PART 1
GENERAL

PART 2
THE FIRST TRANSFER AND RELATED PROVISIONS

PART 3
MEMBERS, MEETINGS, DIRECTORS AND PROCEEDINGS

PART 4
DE-LISTING, APPROVAL ETC

PART 5
THE SECOND TRANSFER

PART 6
FINANCIAL SERVICES COMPENSATION SCHEME

PART 1
GENERAL

1   Citation and commencement

(1)   This Order may be cited as the Bradford & Bingley plc Transfer of Securities and Property etc Order 2008.

(2)   This Order comes into force at 8.00 am on 29th September 2008.

[4227]

NOTES
Commencement: 29 September 2008 (8.00 am).

2   Interpretation: general

In this Order—
      "the 1985 Act" means the Companies Act 1985;
      "the 2000 Act" means the Financial Services and Markets Act 2000;
      "the 2006 Act" means the Companies Act 2006;
      "Abbey" means Abbey National plc, company registered number 2294747;
      "the Act" means the Banking (Special Provisions) Act 2008;
      "the Authority" means the Financial Services Authority;
      "the Bank" means the Governor and Company of the Bank of England;
      "Bradford & Bingley" means Bradford & Bingley plc, company registered number 3938288;
      "Bradford & Bingley International" means Bradford & Bingley International Limited, a company registered in the Isle of Man, company number 052221C;
      "Bradford & Bingley's registrar" means the person appointed by Bradford & Bingley, as its agent, among other things to maintain its register of members;
      "the COMP Sourcebook" means the Compensation Sourcebook made by the Authority under the 2000 Act;
      "the Companies Acts" has the meaning given by section 2 of the 2006 Act;
      "the dated subordinated notes" means the following debt issued by Bradford & Bingley—
            (a)   the £125,000,000 7.625 per cent subordinated notes due February 2010;
            (b)   the £125,000,000 6.625 per cent subordinated notes due 16 June 2023;
            (c)   the £200,000,000 fixed-rate step-up subordinated notes due 2022;
            (d)   the £150,000,000 floating rate dated subordinated notes due March 2054;
            (e)   the £250,000,000 fixed rate/floating rate callable step-up subordinated notes due January 2018; and
            (f)   any further subordinated debt which ranks or is expressed to rank *pari passu* with any of the notes referred to in (a) to (e);
      "eligible claimant" has the meaning given in rule 4.2.1 of the COMP Sourcebook;

"the FEES 6 Chapter" means Chapter 6 (Financial Services Compensation Scheme Funding) of the Fees Manual made by the Authority under the 2000 Act;

"the Financial Services Compensation Scheme" means the scheme established by the Authority under Part 15 (the financial services compensation scheme) of the 2000 Act;

"the first transfer" means the transfer effected by article 3;

"the first transfer time" has the meaning given by article 3(2);

"FSCS" means the body corporate established by the Authority under section 212 (the scheme manager) of the 2000 Act;

"protected deposit" has the meaning given in rule 5.3.1 of the COMP Sourcebook;

"qualifying claimant" means an eligible claimant who immediately before the first transfer time had a claim against Bradford & Bingley for a protected deposit;

"relevant undertaking" means Bradford & Bingley or any of its UK subsidiary undertakings;

"retail deposits" means liabilities represented by amounts standing to the credit of retail deposit accounts including instant access accounts, fixed term and notice savings accounts, savings bonds and individual savings accounts, together with interest and other sums accruing to the benefit of such accounts;

"the second transfer" means the transfer effected by article 16;

"the second transfer time" has the meaning given by article 16(2);

"shares in Bradford & Bingley" means the ordinary shares issued by Bradford & Bingley;

"the transitional period" means the period of 18 months beginning with the date of this Order;

"the Treasury Solicitor" has the same meaning as in the Treasury Solicitor Act 1876 and whose address is One Kemble Street, London WC2B 4TS;

"UK subsidiary undertaking" means a subsidiary undertaking of Bradford & Bingley that is a body corporate incorporated, or a partnership established, under the law of any part of the United Kingdom; and

"the USRs" means the Uncertificated Securities Regulations 2001.

[4228]

NOTES

Commencement: 29 September 2008 (8.00 am).

PART 2
THE FIRST TRANSFER AND RELATED PROVISIONS

3 The first transfer

(1) By virtue of this Order, the shares in Bradford & Bingley are transferred to the Treasury Solicitor as nominee of the Treasury.

(2) The transfer under paragraph (1) takes place at the time this Order comes into force ("the first transfer time").

(3) The transfer of the shares effected under paragraph (1) shall vest title in the Treasury Solicitor—

    (a) free from all trusts, liabilities and incumbrances; and

    (b) together with all rights, benefits or privileges which attach or accrue to or arise from such shares on or after the first transfer time.

[4229]

NOTES

Commencement: 29 September 2008 (8.00 am).

4 Registration of shares and issue of certificates

(1) The Treasury Solicitor is entitled with effect from the first transfer time to be entered in the register of members of Bradford & Bingley as holder of the shares in Bradford & Bingley without the need for delivery of any instrument of transfer or other instrument or document and notwithstanding—

    (a) the absence of any required consent or concurrence to or with the transfer; and

    (b) any other restriction relating to the transfer.

(2) The operator of a relevant system in which any shares in Bradford & Bingley are held immediately prior to the first transfer time ("relevant shares") shall forthwith after the first transfer time—

    (a) withdraw his permission for title to the relevant shares to be transferred by means of the relevant system with effect from the first transfer time; and

    (b) inform all the system-members and Bradford & Bingley's registrar of the date and time the relevant shares ceased to be securities participating in the system.

(3) Bradford & Bingley shall procure that Bradford & Bingley's registrar shall forthwith after the first transfer time—

(a)   take such action as the operator of a relevant system may require to convert any relevant shares held in such a system immediately prior to the first transfer time into certificated form; and

(b)   register in Bradford & Bingley's register of members (including its issuer register of members) the Treasury Solicitor as the holder of shares in Bradford & Bingley.

(4)   The operator of a relevant system in which any relevant shares are held immediately prior to the first transfer time, Bradford & Bingley and Bradford & Bingley's registrar shall each—

(a)   provide each other with such information as shall be necessary to comply with this article; and

(b)   co-operate to ensure that the issuer register of members of Bradford & Bingley reconciles with the operator register of members of Bradford & Bingley immediately prior to the first transfer time.

(5)   From the first transfer time and until the Treasury Solicitor is entered in Bradford & Bingley's register of members (including its issuer register of members)—

(a)   he is deemed for all purposes (including for the purposes of the Companies Acts and the USRs) to be—

    (i)   the sole member of Bradford & Bingley; and

    (ii)   entered as holder on the operator register of members of Bradford & Bingley and in Bradford & Bingley's register of members (including its issuer register of members); and

(b)   no other person may exercise or purport to exercise in respect of Bradford & Bingley any right deriving from any shares in Bradford & Bingley.

(6)   The Treasury Solicitor is entitled from the first transfer time to all the rights and advantages of a member of Bradford & Bingley to the exclusion of all other persons, notwithstanding that he is not entered in either Bradford & Bingley's register of members (including its issuer register of members) or the operator register of members of Bradford & Bingley.

(7)   Part 21 of the 2006 Act (certification and transfer of securities) applies to Bradford & Bingley with the following modifications—

(a)   the transfer effected by article 3(1) is deemed to be a transfer falling within section 776(2)(a) (duty of company as to issue of certificates etc on transfer); and

(b)   sections 776(3) and (4), 777 (issue of certificates etc: cases within the Stock Transfer Act 1982) and 778 (issue of certificates etc: allotment or transfer to financial institution) do not apply.

(8)   In this article "certificated", "issuer register of members", "operator", "operator register of members", "relevant system" and "system-member" have the meanings given in the USRs.

[4230]

NOTES

Commencement: 29 September 2008 (8.00 am).

---

5   Extinguishment of rights in relation to shares in Bradford & Bingley

By virtue of this Order, with effect from the first transfer time, any right or entitlement of a person to receive shares in Bradford & Bingley (whether by subscription, conversion or otherwise) is extinguished if the right or entitlement was granted by—

(a)   a relevant undertaking; or

(b)   a person not within sub-paragraph (a) and is enjoyed by reason of or in connection with—

    (i)   any person's office or employment with a relevant undertaking; or

    (ii)   the services provided by any person to a relevant undertaking.

[4231]

NOTES

Commencement: 29 September 2008 (8.00 am).

---

6   Modification of interests, rights and liabilities associated with the dated subordinated notes

(1)   This article applies, with effect from the first transfer time, in respect of the dated subordinated notes.

(2)   By virtue of this Order, the rights and liabilities associated with the dated subordinated notes shall be modified in accordance with paragraph (3).

(3)   A default in the payment of any principal due in respect of a dated subordinated note—

(a)   shall not constitute an event of default under the note; and

(b)   shall not give rise to the consequences specified in paragraph (3) of article 7 in respect of any relevant instrument under that article.

[4232]

NOTES
Commencement: 29 September 2008 (8.00 am).

7 Modification of rights in relevant instruments

(1)   The consequences specified in paragraph (3) shall not arise in respect of any relevant instrument as a result of the first transfer, or any other thing done, or matter arising, by virtue of or in connection with the first transfer.

(2)   Any circumstances which, but for paragraph (1), would give rise to the consequences specified in paragraph (3) shall be taken not to have arisen for the purposes of any relevant instrument.

(3)   The consequences are—
(a)   the termination of the relevant instrument or any rights or obligations under it;
(b)   any right to terminate the relevant instrument or any right or obligation under it becoming exercisable;
(c)   any amount becoming due and payable or capable of being declared due and payable;
(d)   any other change in the amount or timing of any payment falling to be made or due to be received by any person;
(e)   any right to withhold, net or set off any payment becoming exercisable;
(f)   any event of default or breach of any right arising;
(g)   any right not to advance any amount becoming exercisable;
(h)   any obligation to provide or transfer any deposit or collateral;
(i)   any right to give or withhold any consent or approval; or
(j)   any other right or remedy (whether or not similar in kind to those referred to in paragraphs (a) to (i)) arising or becoming exercisable.

(4)   Without prejudice to paragraph (3), any provision in a relevant instrument that, as a result of the first transfer or any other thing done, or matter arising, by virtue of or in connection with the first transfer, provides for an obligation not to be created, suspends or extinguishes (in whole or in part) such an obligation or renders such an obligation subject to conditions, shall be of no effect.

(5)   This article does not apply to any action taken by the Treasury under article 10.

(6)   In this article, "relevant instrument" has the meaning given in paragraph 4(3) of Schedule 1 to the Act and the specified connection referred to in paragraph 4(3)(c) of that Schedule is between Bradford & Bingley and those undertakings whose assets and liabilities, profits and losses are consolidated in the consolidated accounts of Bradford & Bingley.

[4233]

NOTES
Commencement: 29 September 2008 (8.00 am).

PART 3
MEMBERS, MEETINGS, DIRECTORS AND PROCEEDINGS

8 Minimum membership for carrying on business

(1)   While Bradford & Bingley is wholly owned by the Treasury, section 24 of the 1985 Act (minimum membership for carrying on business) shall not apply in relation to Bradford & Bingley or any member of Bradford & Bingley.

(2)   While Bradford & Bingley is wholly owned by the Treasury, no petition shall be presented for the winding up of Bradford & Bingley on the ground that the number of its members is less than the number required by law, nor shall any person be liable on that ground as a member of the company for the payment of any of its debts.

[4234]

NOTES
Commencement: 29 September 2008 (8.00 am).

9 Resolutions and meetings

(1)   While Bradford & Bingley is wholly owned by the Treasury, any meeting of members of Bradford & Bingley shall, if the Treasury Solicitor is present in person, by proxy or authorises a corporate representative to attend, be deemed to be a duly constituted general meeting of the company notwithstanding that it may not have been properly called, or notice of it may not have been properly given, or any quorum required by Bradford & Bingley's articles of association may not be present.

(2)   Notwithstanding any provision in the articles of association of Bradford & Bingley, an appointment of a proxy for the Treasury Solicitor—

(a) may be in any written form (including in an electronic communication);
(b) need not be given with any period of notice;
(c) shall not require the approval of the board of Bradford & Bingley; and
(d) is deemed to be given in accordance with the articles of association.

(3) A resolution of the company adopted after the first transfer time is effective notwithstanding that special notice (notice of intention to move it given to company at least 28 days before the meeting at which it is moved) of the resolution is required by any provision of the 1985 Act or 2006 Act but has not been given.

[4235]

NOTES

Commencement: 29 September 2008 (8.00 am).

10 Removal of directors

(1) While Bradford & Bingley is wholly owned by the Treasury, the Treasury may in accordance with this article—
(a) remove any person as a director of a relevant undertaking;
(b) terminate a director's service contract with any relevant undertaking.

(2) For the purposes of any contract or arrangement between a person and a relevant undertaking, action taken under paragraph (1) shall be treated as having been carried out by the relevant undertaking and, in the case of paragraph (1)(a), under and in accordance with its articles of association.

(3) The Treasury may remove a person as a director of a relevant undertaking and may terminate his service contract by written notice to the relevant undertaking.

(4) Any notice given in accordance with paragraph (3) shall take effect from the date specified in the notice.

(5) A relevant undertaking which receives notice under paragraph (3) shall notify the person to whom the notice relates of that fact as soon as reasonably practicable.

(6) A person—
(a) removed as director of a relevant undertaking, or
(b) whose service contract with a relevant undertaking is terminated,
in accordance with this article shall not have any right or claim against the Treasury or any company wholly owned by the Treasury (other than a relevant undertaking) in consequence of the Treasury's actions under this article.

(7) This article does not—
(a) deprive any person removed under it of compensation or damages payable to him by a relevant undertaking in respect of—
(i) the termination of his appointment as director or of any appointment terminating with that as director; or
(ii) the termination of his service contract; or
(b) derogate from any power to remove a director or to terminate a director's service contract that may exist apart from this article.

(8) In this article and in article 11, "service contract" has the meaning given by section 227 of the 2006 Act (directors' service contracts).

[4236]

NOTES

Commencement: 29 September 2008 (8.00 am).

11 Appointment of directors

(1) While Bradford & Bingley is wholly owned by the Treasury, the Treasury may appoint one or more directors of a relevant undertaking in accordance with this article and notwithstanding any provision in the articles of association of the relevant undertaking.

(2) The Treasury may appoint a director of a relevant undertaking by written notice to the relevant undertaking provided the appointee has agreed to act in such a capacity.

(3) The appointment shall take effect from the date specified in the notice.

(4) The Treasury may determine the terms (including remuneration) of the service contract of a person appointed as a director under this article in whatever written form they see fit.

(5) Any appointment, contract or arrangement which is made or the terms of which are determined under this article is to be treated as made or entered into by the relevant undertaking in question.

(6)   This article does not derogate from any power to appoint a director or determine the remuneration and other terms and conditions of a director's service contract that may exist apart from this article.

[4237]

NOTES
Commencement: 29 September 2008 (8.00 am).

12   Proceedings against directors

(1)   No director of a relevant undertaking shall be liable for any act or omission of the director, acting in such capacity, which occurs while Bradford & Bingley is wholly owned by the Treasury and accordingly no proceedings may be brought (or in Scotland, raised) against any such director in respect of such matters.

(2)   The Treasury may in writing—
    (a)   disapply paragraph (1), and
    (b)   give consent to bring (or in Scotland, raise) such proceedings against such directors.

(3)   Where paragraph (1) applies, section 232 of the 2006 Act (provisions protecting directors from liability) shall not apply to a relevant undertaking.

(4)   In this article—
"proceedings" includes proceedings under Part 11 of the 2006 Act (derivative claims and proceedings by members);
"director" means—
    (a)   a person who is appointed as a director while Bradford & Bingley is wholly owned by the Treasury, whether or not he has ceased to be a director when proceedings in respect of that liability commenced;
    (b)   a person who was a director immediately before the first transfer time and whose continuing appointment as director while Bradford & Bingley is wholly owned by the Treasury, the Treasury approves in writing, whether or not he has ceased to be a director at the time when proceedings in respect of that liability commenced; and
    (c)   an alternate director of a person falling within sub-paragraph (a) or (b).

[4238]

NOTES
Commencement: 29 September 2008 (8.00 am).

13   Shadow directorship

(1)   While Bradford & Bingley is wholly owned by the Treasury, for the purposes of the provisions listed in Schedule 1 to this Order, none of the persons listed in paragraph (3) shall be regarded as a shadow director of or (unless otherwise appointed as a director) a person discharging managerial responsibilities of a relevant undertaking.

(2)   For the purposes of the definition of "director" in section 417 of the 2000 Act (definitions), while Bradford & Bingley is wholly owned by the Treasury, none of the persons listed in paragraph (3) shall be regarded as a person in accordance with whose directions or instructions (not being advice given in a professional capacity) the directors of a relevant undertaking are accustomed to act.

(3)   The persons are—
    (a)   a Minister of the Crown;
    (b)   the Treasury;
    (c)   the Treasury Solicitor;
    (d)   the Bank;
    (e)   persons—
        (i)   employed by or under; or
        (ii)   acting on behalf of,
any of the persons specified in sub-paragraphs (a) to (d).

[4239]

NOTES
Commencement: 29 September 2008 (8.00 am).

PART 4
DE-LISTING, APPROVAL ETC

14   De-listing

(1)   By virtue of this Order, the listing of any shares of Bradford & Bingley is discontinued with effect from the first transfer time without the need for any notice to, or consent of, Bradford & Bingley or any other person.

(2)   In paragraph (1), "listing" has the meaning given in section 74 of the 2000 Act (the official list).

[4240]

NOTES
Commencement: 29 September 2008 (8.00 am).

15   Approved persons

(1)   While Bradford & Bingley is wholly owned by the Treasury, the requirements imposed on a relevant undertaking by section 59 of the 2000 Act (approval for particular arrangements) in relation to directors (including non-executive directors) and the chief executive officer shall be deemed to be satisfied in relation to the relevant undertaking, provided that at all material times the Authority is satisfied that at least two individuals who effectively direct the business of the relevant undertaking are of sufficiently good repute and have sufficient experience to perform controlled functions in that respect.

(2)   The Treasury may give written notice to the Authority that paragraph (1) is no longer to apply in respect of a relevant undertaking.

(3)   At least one month prior to giving a notice under paragraph (2) the Treasury shall give written notice to the relevant undertaking of their intention to give a notice to the Authority under that paragraph.

(4)   In paragraph (1), "controlled functions" has the meaning given in section 59(3) of the 2000 Act.

[4241]

NOTES
Commencement: 29 September 2008 (8.00 am).

PART 5
THE SECOND TRANSFER

16   The second transfer

(1)   By virtue of this Order—
(a)   the rights and liabilities of Bradford & Bingley specified in paragraph 1 of Schedule 2;
(b)   the property specified in paragraph 3 of Schedule 2;
(c)   the contracts, agreements and other arrangements specified in paragraph 4 of Schedule 2;
(d)   the personal property specified in paragraph 5 of Schedule 2; and
(e)   the intellectual property specified in paragraph 6 of Schedule 2,
are transferred to Abbey.

(2)   The transfer under paragraph (1) takes place immediately after the first transfer time ("the second transfer time").

[4242]

NOTES
Commencement: 29 September 2008 (8.00 am).

17   Isle of Man deposits

(1)   Subject to the prior approval of the Financial Services Commission of the Isle of Man of the proposed change of control of Bradford & Bingley International, as soon as practicable after the second transfer time, Bradford & Bingley shall—
(a)   transfer the Bradford & Bingley International shares to Abbey; and
(b)   take such steps as are reasonably necessary to ensure that—
(i)   the transfer in sub-paragraph (a) is effective under Manx law (including but not limited to duly executing requisite transfers, paying related Manx taxes such as stamp duty and delivering the relevant share certificates to Abbey);
(ii)   the Bradford & Bingley International shares are transferred to Abbey free from all trusts, liabilities and incumbrances;

(iii)   any right or other entitlement to receive shares in Bradford & Bingley International (whether by subscription, conversion or otherwise) is extinguished with effect from the relevant time; and

(iv)   Abbey is entered in the register of members of Bradford & Bingley International.

(2)   By virtue of this Order—

   (a)   the intercompany undertaking is terminated from the relevant time, except in relation to liabilities arising from or in respect of a breach of contract or other duty or of any legal or regulatory requirement occurring before the relevant time; and

   (b)   subject to sub-paragraph (a) any interests, rights, entitlements or claims that have accrued in connection with the intercompany undertaking are extinguished.

(3)   Articles 18 to 22 apply to any transfer made under this article as they apply to the second transfer.

(4)   In this article—

"the Bradford & Bingley International shares" means all shares in Bradford & Bingley International held by or on behalf of Bradford & Bingley at the relevant time;

"the intercompany undertaking" means the undertaking by Bradford & Bingley, dated 4 December 2000, to discharge the liabilities of Bradford & Bingley International;

"the relevant time" means the time at which the transfer under paragraph (1) is effected.

[4243]

NOTES
Commencement: 29 September 2008 (8.00 am).

18 No consent or concurrence required

The second transfer is effective despite the absence of any required consent or concurrence to or with the transfer.

[4244]

NOTES
Commencement: 29 September 2008 (8.00 am).

19 Associated liability and interference

(1)   The second transfer takes effect as if—

   (a)   no associated liability existed in respect of any failure to comply with any requirement in respect of the transfer; and

   (b)   there were no associated interference with the property, rights and liabilities transferred.

(2)   In this article, "associated liability" and "associated interference" have the meanings given in paragraph 2(2) of Schedule 2 to the Act.

[4245]

NOTES
Commencement: 29 September 2008 (8.00 am).

20 Termination etc of interest or right

(1)   Subject to paragraph (2)—

   (a)   from the coming into force of this Order until the second transfer time, no person is entitled to terminate, modify, acquire or claim any interest or right to be transferred by article 16, or to treat such an interest or right as terminated or modified; and

   (b)   any purported termination, modification, acquisition or claim in contravention of sub-paragraph (a), and any action taken in consequence of a contravention of that sub-paragraph, shall have no effect.

(2)   This article shall not apply to the ordinary course of dealings by a depositor in relation to his retail deposit.

[4246]

NOTES
Commencement: 29 September 2008 (8.00 am).

21 Interests, rights and liabilities of third parties relating to property, rights and liabilities transferred

(1)   No interest or right of any third party relating to any property, right or liability of Bradford & Bingley, whether or not it is transferred by article 16, shall arise or become exercisable by virtue of or in connection with the second transfer.

(2)   Save as otherwise provided in this Order, no third party shall, by virtue of or in connection with the second transfer, incur any liability or be subject to any obligation relating to any property, right or liability of Bradford & Bingley, whether or not it is transferred by article 16.

(3)   Without prejudice to the generality of paragraphs (1) and (2)—
(a)   the consequences specified in paragraph (4) shall not arise in respect of any relevant instrument as a result of the second transfer or any other thing done, or matter arising, by virtue of or in connection with that transfer; and
(b)   any circumstances which, but for sub-paragraph (a), would give rise to the consequences specified in paragraph (4) shall be taken not to have arisen for the purposes of any relevant instrument.

(4)   The consequences are—
(a)   the termination of a relevant instrument or any rights or obligations under it;
(b)   any right to terminate a relevant instrument or any right or obligation under it becoming exercisable;
(c)   any amount becoming due and payable or capable of being declared due and payable;
(d)   any other change in the amount or timing of any payment falling to be made or due to be received by any person;
(e)   any right to withhold, net or set off any payment becoming exercisable;
(f)   any event of default or breach of any right arising;
(g)   any right not to advance any amount becoming exercisable;
(h)   any obligation to provide or transfer any deposit or collateral;
(i)   any right to give or withhold any consent or approval; or
(j)   any other right or remedy (whether or not similar in kind to those referred to in sub-paragraphs (a) to (i)) arising or becoming exercisable.

(5)   Without prejudice to paragraph (4), any provision in a relevant instrument that, as a result of the second transfer or any other thing done, or matter arising, by virtue of or in connection with that transfer, provides for an obligation not to be created, suspends or extinguishes (in whole or in part) such an obligation or renders such an obligation subject to conditions, shall be of no effect.

(6)   In this article—
"relevant instrument" has the same meaning as in paragraph 4(3) of Schedule 1 to the Act and the specified connection referred to in paragraph 4(3)(c) of that Schedule is between Bradford & Bingley and those undertakings whose assets and liabilities, profits and losses are consolidated in the consolidated accounts of Bradford & Bingley; and
"third party" shall be construed in accordance with paragraph 2(3) of Schedule 2 to the Act.

[4247]

NOTES
Commencement: 29 September 2008 (8.00 am).

22   Modification of rights and liabilities transferred

(1)   Where a transferred obligation conflicts with an obligation of Abbey existing at the second transfer time, the transferred obligation is modified to the extent required to avoid that conflict.

(2)   No person shall be entitled to acquire, claim, modify or terminate any interest or right by virtue of or in connection with paragraph (1).

(3)   In this article a "transferred obligation" means an obligation, covenant, undertaking or restriction under a contract, agreement or arrangement transferred to Abbey under article 16(1)(c) or treated as made or done by or in relation to Abbey in accordance with article 25(a).

[4248]

NOTES
Commencement: 29 September 2008 (8.00 am).

23   Foreign property etc

Bradford & Bingley must take such steps as are reasonably requested by Abbey for securing the vesting in Abbey under the relevant foreign law of any foreign property, foreign rights or liabilities expressed to be transferred by article 16.

[4249]

NOTES
Commencement: 29 September 2008 (8.00 am).

24   Subsequent transactions

(1)   To the extent that any property, rights or liabilities—
(a)   transferred by Bradford & Bingley to Abbey in connection with the second transfer do

not relate mainly to the retail deposit business or to any property, rights or liabilities transferred to Abbey by article 16(1)(b) or (d); or

(b) retained by Bradford & Bingley after the second transfer time relate mainly to the retail deposit business or to any property, rights or liabilities transferred to Abbey by article 16(1)(b) or (d),

the Treasury Solicitor and Abbey shall procure that such property, rights and liabilities are promptly transferred for no further consideration to Bradford & Bingley or Abbey as appropriate.

(2) This article shall not apply to any contract of employment or qualifying financial contract.

(3) Articles 18 to 22 apply to any transfer made under this article as they apply to the second transfer.

(4) For the purposes of this article "qualifying financial contract" means any agreement entered into either with the purpose of borrowing or lending money (not being a retail deposit), or in connection with a transaction on the financial markets, including (howsoever documented) any loan agreement, securities contract, derivative contract, commodities contract, forward contract, repurchase contract, swap agreement, margin lending agreement and master agreement.

[4250]

NOTES

Commencement: 29 September 2008 (8.00 am).

25 Construction of documents etc

As from the second transfer time, and save as otherwise provided in this Order—

(a) agreements made or other things done by or in relation to Bradford & Bingley shall be treated, so far as may be necessary for the purposes of or in connection with the second transfer, but not otherwise, as made or done by or in relation to Abbey, as the case may be; and

(b) references to Bradford & Bingley, or to any officer or employee of Bradford & Bingley, in instruments or documents relating to the property, rights and liabilities transferred by or under article 16 shall have effect as if they were references to Abbey, or to any officer or employee of Abbey, as the case may be.

[4251]

NOTES

Commencement: 29 September 2008 (8.00 am).

26 Pensions

Schedule 3 shall have effect.

[4252]

NOTES

Commencement: 29 September 2008 (8.00 am).

27 Employees

(1) The Transfer of Undertakings (Protection of Employment) Regulations 2006 (the "transfer regulations") and sections 257 and 258 of the Pensions Act 2004 shall apply upon the second transfer on the basis that any individual other than a director of Bradford & Bingley who is employed by a relevant undertaking and—

(a) whose work relates wholly or mainly to—

(i) the retail deposit business of Bradford and Bingley; or

(ii) any property, rights or liabilities transferred to Abbey by article 16(1)(b) or (d); or

(b) whose normal place of work is any real property transferred by article 16(1)(b),

is assigned to the organised grouping of resources or employees that is subject to the relevant transfer.

(2) Paragraph (1) is without prejudice to the application of the transfer regulations or sections 257 and 258 of the Pensions Act 2004 in respect of any individual not referred to in that paragraph.

[4253]

NOTES

Commencement: 29 September 2008 (8.00 am).

PART 6
FINANCIAL SERVICES COMPENSATION SCHEME

28   Sums to be paid to Abbey following the second transfer

(1)   The following liabilities arise on the occurrence of the second transfer—

  (a)   the FSCS is liable to pay, as soon as practicable, to Abbey an amount equal to the amount that qualifying claimants would, immediately before the first transfer time, have been entitled to claim from the FSCS in respect of claims against Bradford & Bingley for protected deposits; and

  (b)   the Treasury are liable to pay, as soon as practicable, to Abbey an amount equal to the aggregate amount of the liabilities transferred to Abbey under article 16(1)(a) less the amount specified in sub-paragraph (a) and less £612,000,000,

and the Treasury shall subsequently make the necessary adjustments such that Bradford & Bingley obtains the benefit of the reduction of £612,000,000 referred to in sub-paragraph (b).

(2)   For the purposes of paragraph (1)(a), if the quantification date for a claim would have been a date other than the date on which Bradford & Bingley was determined to be in default for the purposes of section 6.3 of the COMP Sourcebook, the amount that a qualifying claimant would have been entitled to claim from the FSCS is the lesser of—

  (a)   the amount which the FSCS quantifies as being the value of that claim as at immediately before the first transfer time; and

  (b)   the amount that would have been payable at the quantification date, if different, for that claim.

(3)   In paragraph (2), "quantification date" has the meaning given in rule 12.3.1 of the COMP Sourcebook.

(4)   Immediately after the second transfer time—

  (a)   Bradford & Bingley shall estimate the aggregate amount of the liabilities transferred to Abbey under article 16(1)(a);

  (b)   the FSCS shall pay to Abbey the amount it is liable to pay under paragraph (1)(a) as estimated by the Authority; and

  (c)   the Treasury shall pay to Abbey an amount equal to the amount estimated by Bradford & Bingley in accordance with sub-paragraph (a) less the amount estimated by the Authority in accordance with sub-paragraph (b) and less £612,000,000.

(5)   From time to time—

  (a)   the FSCS may revise the estimate of its liability under paragraph (1)(a); and

  (b)   Bradford & Bingley may revise the estimate of the aggregate amount of the liabilities transferred to Abbey under article 16(1)(a),

and the FSCS, the Treasury and Abbey shall make such corresponding payments to each other as are necessary to ensure that the FSCS and the Treasury have each paid to Abbey the amount required to meet their liability under paragraph (1) (and no more than such amount).

(6)   The liability referred to in paragraph (1)(a) shall be assessed by the FSCS and, in doing so, the FSCS may calculate, by any methodology or approach it considers appropriate, the total amounts of compensation that would have been paid to all qualifying claimants, if (and to the extent that) it considers that the costs of ascertaining the entitlement to and amount of compensation by reference to each qualifying claimant would exceed or be disproportionate to the benefit of doing so.

[4254]

NOTES

Commencement: 29 September 2008 (8.00 am).

---

29   Payment to Abbey to constitute payment of compensation for the purposes of the Financial Services Compensation Scheme

For the purposes of Part 15 (the financial services compensation scheme) of the 2000 Act, the COMP Sourcebook and the FEES 6 Chapter (including, without limitation, the power of the FSCS to impose levies)—

  (a)   all payments by the FSCS to Abbey under article 28 shall constitute the payment of compensation to each qualifying claimant under the Financial Services Compensation Scheme in accordance with their respective entitlements in respect of claims against Bradford & Bingley for protected deposits;

  (b)   each qualifying claimant—

    (i)   is deemed to have made an application for compensation for the purposes of rule 3.2.1(1) of the COMP Sourcebook; and

    (ii)   is deemed to have accepted an offer of compensation made by the FSCS and to have received payment of such compensation for the purposes of rule 11.2.1 of the COMP Sourcebook, and, accordingly, a qualifying claimant has no right to claim, and the FSCS has no obligation to pay, for a protected deposit any further compensation under the Financial Services Compensation Scheme in respect of the default of Bradford & Bingley determined by the Authority under section 6.3 of the COMP Sourcebook.

[4255]

NOTES
Commencement: 29 September 2008 (8.00 am).

30 Liability of Bradford & Bingley to the FSCS and the Treasury

(1)   Bradford & Bingley is liable to the FSCS in respect of an amount equal to the aggregate of—
- (a)   the amount which the FSCS is liable to pay under article 28(1)(a); and
- (b)   the amount which the Treasury are liable to pay under article 28(1)(b).

(2)   Bradford & Bingley, the FSCS and the Treasury shall agree terms on which, subject to paragraph (6), the amount of Bradford & Bingley's liability to the FSCS under paragraph (1) is to be reduced out of excess cash flow and other proceeds.

(3)   The FSCS shall determine the proportion of any amount which it receives or recovers from Bradford & Bingley which is properly attributable to each type of liability described below and shall promptly on receipt account to the Treasury as follows—
- (a)   in full, where the liability is a liability which has been transferred under article 16(1)(a) and the person to whom such transferred liability is owed would not have been entitled to make a claim for compensation from the FSCS immediately before the first transfer time; and
- (b)   up to the amount of the excess, where the liability is a liability owed by Bradford & Bingley to a qualifying claimant and the amount of such liability exceeds the maximum compensation that the qualifying claimant would have been entitled to claim from the FSCS immediately before the first transfer time,

and, where the liability is a liability owed by Bradford and Bingley to a qualifying claimant and the amount of such liability is equal to or less than the maximum compensation that the qualifying claimant would have been entitled to claim from the FSCS immediately before the first transfer time, that amount shall be for the account of the FSCS.

(4)   Once all the assets of Bradford & Bingley have been realised and distributed, if the claim of the FSCS against Bradford & Bingley has not been satisfied in full, Bradford & Bingley's liability for the shortfall shall be extinguished, without prejudice to any claim the FSCS may have against any other party.

(5)   The FSCS shall not take or join in any corporate action or other steps or legal proceedings for the winding-up, dissolution or re-organisation or for the appointment of an administrator, liquidator or similar appointment in respect of Bradford & Bingley, or any analogous step or proceeding in any other jurisdiction.

(6)   Nothing in this Part shall have the effect that the FSCS recovers less than it would have recovered if this Order had not been made and Bradford and Bingley had gone into liquidation following the declaration of default by the Authority in relation to Bradford and Bingley for the purposes of section 6.3 of the COMP Sourcebook.

[4256]

NOTES
Commencement: 29 September 2008 (8.00 am).

31 Co-operation with the FSCS

(1)   Bradford & Bingley and Abbey must each—
- (a)   comply with any request of the FSCS for the provision of information; and
- (b)   provide the FSCS with any other information which Bradford & Bingley or Abbey, as the case may be, considers may be useful for the purpose of co-operating in the fulfilment of the FSCS's functions under the COMP Sourcebook and the FEES 6 Chapter.

(2)   Nothing in this article affects the power of the FSCS to require information under section 219 of the 2000 Act (scheme manager's power to require information).

[4257]

NOTES
Commencement: 29 September 2008 (8.00 am).

32   Statutory immunity

For the purposes of section 222 (statutory immunity) of the 2000 Act the scheme manager's functions shall include any acts or omissions carried out by the FSCS pursuant to or in connection with this Order.

[4258]

NOTES
  Commencement: 29 September 2008 (8.00 am).

PART 7
TRANSITIONAL PROVISIONS

33   Services and facilities

The agreement dated 29th September 2009 between the Treasury and Abbey relating to the provision of transitional services by Bradford & Bingley and Abbey to one another shall bind Bradford & Bingley as if it were a party.

[4259]

NOTES
  Commencement: 29 September 2008 (8.00 am).

34   Use of the Bradford & Bingley brand by Abbey

Bradford & Bingley shall grant to Abbey a non-exclusive royalty-free licence for a period of three years to use the Bradford & Bingley brand for the purposes of carrying on the business transferred to Abbey by the second transfer.

[4260]

NOTES
  Commencement: 29 September 2008 (8.00 am).

35   Termination etc of interest or right

  (1)   Except with the consent of the Treasury or the permission of the court, during the transitional period—
  (a)   no person is entitled—
    (i)   to terminate or modify any contract or agreement, or any right or obligation under any contract or agreement where such contract or agreement is for the services and facilities reasonably required by—
        (aa)   Bradford & Bingley to carry on the business retained by it after the second transfer; or
        (bb)   Abbey to carry on the retail deposit business, or
    (ii)   to treat such a contract, agreement, right, obligation or interest as terminated or modified,
  by virtue of or in connection with the first or second transfer; and
  (b)   any counterparty to such contract or agreement must perform their obligations in accordance with that contract or agreement.

  (2)   Any purported termination or modification of any contract, agreement, right, obligation or interest in contravention of paragraph (1), and any action taken in consequence of any such purported termination or modification, shall have no effect.

  (3)   Paragraph (1) does not apply where—
  (a)   Bradford & Bingley or Abbey, as the case may be, has failed to perform its payment obligations under the relevant contract or agreement and such non-payment is not remedied within 7 days of Bradford & Bingley becoming aware of the non-performance; or
  (b)   Bradford & Bingley or Abbey, as the case may be, fails to notify the counterparty to the relevant contract or agreement within 14 days of his becoming aware of the request for consent to such termination, modification or non-performance of an obligation, that such consent has been withheld.

  (4)   Without prejudice to the generality of paragraph (1), neither the first nor second transfer shall have the effect of terminating or otherwise changing the terms of Bradford & Bingley's membership of any payment system, including, in particular, BACS, CHAPS and the LINK payments systems.

  (5)   This article is subject to any requirement of Community law.

[4261]

PART III
STATUTORY INSTRUMENTS

NOTES
Commencement: 29 September 2008 (8.00 am).

36 Provision of information

Bradford & Bingley shall provide Abbey with such information as is reasonably requested by Abbey in relation to anything transferred by or under article 16.

[4262]

NOTES
Commencement: 29 September 2008 (8.00 am).

PART 8
SUPPLEMENTARY

37 Modification to Authority's rule-making power

(1) Subsections (1) and (1A) of section 138 of the 2000 Act (general rule-making power) have effect as if modified by inserting after "protecting the interests of consumers"—

"or for the purposes of, to facilitate or in consequence of, a transfer under section 3 or 8 of the Banking (Special Provisions) Act 2008".

(2) Section 148(2) of the 2000 Act (modification or waiver of rules) shall also apply in relation to a relevant undertaking—
    (a) in the absence of an application by a person subject to rules made by the Authority; and
    (b) without any requirement for the consent of such a person.

(3) Section 148(4) of the 2000 Act shall not prevent the Authority from modifying or waiving rules in relation to a relevant undertaking under section 148 of that Act provided that the Authority is satisfied that the modification or waiver is necessary for the purposes of, to facilitate or in consequence of the first or second transfer.

[4263]

NOTES
Commencement: 29 September 2008 (8.00 am).

38 Modification to Authority's duty to consult on rule changes

(1) Section 155(7) of the 2000 Act (consultation) has effect as if modified by adding at the end—

"or if it is making rules for the purposes of, or to facilitate or in consequence of, a transfer under section 3 or 8 of the Banking (Special Provisions) Act 2008."

(2) Section 157 of the 2000 Act (guidance) has effect as if modified by adding after subsection (3)—

"(3A) Section 155(7) applies to proposed guidance as it applies to proposed rules with the modification made by article 39(1) of the Bradford & Bingley plc Transfer of Securities and Property etc Order 2008.".

[4264]

NOTES
Commencement: 29 September 2008 (8.00 am).

39 Modification of provision on liability in relation to operator's functions

(1) Section 291 of the 2000 Act (liability in relation to recognised body's regulatory functions) shall have effect for the purposes of this Order as if the following modifications are made.

(2) In subsection (1)—
    (a) after "its officers and staff" add "and an operator and its officers and staff";
    (b) after "recognised body's" add "or the operator's".

(3) In subsection (3) at the end add—

"and the functions of the operator so far as relating to, or matters arising out of, the obligations to which the operator is subject under the Bradford & Bingley plc Transfer of Securities and Property etc Order 2008.

(4) In this section, "operator" has the meaning given in the Uncertificated Securities Regulations 2001.".

[4265]

NOTES
Commencement: 29 September 2008 (8.00 am).

40 Enterprise Act 2002

Part 3 of the Enterprise Act 2002 (mergers) shall not apply to the first or second transfer save insofar as it gives effect to an obligation under Community law.

[4266]

NOTES
Commencement: 29 September 2008 (8.00 am).

41 Freedom of information

For the purposes of section 3 of the Freedom of Information Act 2000 (public authorities), while Bradford & Bingley is wholly owned by the Treasury, a relevant undertaking shall be deemed—
  (a)   not to be a publicly-owned company for the purposes of subsection (1)(b);
  (b)   not to hold information on behalf of the Treasury for the purposes of subsection (2)(b).

[4267]

NOTES
Commencement: 29 September 2008 (8.00 am).

42 Notification requirement

  (1)   The Treasury must notify the Authority of the making of this Order.

  (2)   A notification under paragraph (1)—
  (a)   may be given by such means as the Treasury consider appropriate;
  (b)   must be given to the Authority as soon as reasonably practicable after the first transfer time.

[4268]

NOTES
Commencement: 29 September 2008 (8.00 am).

SCHEDULES

SCHEDULE 1
SHADOW DIRECTORSHIP

Article 13

1.   The following provisions of the Insolvency Act 1986—
  (a)   section 288 (register of directors);
  (b)   section 305 (directors' names on correspondence, etc);
  (c)   section 317 (disclosure of interests in contracts).

2.   The following provisions of the 2006 Act—
  (a)   section 84 (criminal consequences of failure to make required disclosure);
  (b)   section 162 (register of directors);
  (c)   section 165 (register of directors' residential addresses);
  (d)   section 167 (duty to notify registrar of changes);
  (e)   sections 170 to 177 (general duties of directors);
  (f)   sections 182 to 186 (declaration of interest in existing transaction) as applied to shadow directors by section 187;
  (g)   sections 188 and 189 (directors' service contracts);
  (h)   sections 190 to 196 (substantial property transactions);
  (i)   sections 197 to 214 (loans etc to directors);
  (j)   sections 215 to 222 (payments for loss of office) as applied to shadow directors by section 223(2);
  (k)   sections 227 to 230 (directors' service contracts);
  (l)   section 231 (contracts with sole members who are directors);
  (m)   sections 260 to 269 (derivative claims in England and Wales and Northern Ireland);
  (n)   sections 854 to 859 (annual return).

3.   The following provisions of the 1986 Act—
  (a)   section 214 (wrongful trading);
  (b)   section 249 ("connected" with a company).

4. The following provisions of the 2000 Act—
    (a) section 96A (disclosure of information requirements);
    (b) section 96B (disclosure rules: persons responsible for compliance).

[4269]

NOTES
Commencement: 29 September 2008 (8.00 am).
Drafting error: it is believed that the sections listed in para 1 above (ie, section 288 (register of directors); section 305 (directors' names on correspondence, etc); section 317 (disclosure of interests in contracts)) are actually the following sections of the Companies Act 1985, and not the Insolvency Act 1986 as stated in the introductory wording of that paragraph—
*   Section 288 (Register of directors and secretaries).
*   Section 305 (Directors' names on company correspondence, etc).
*   Section 317 (Directors to disclosure interest in contracts)

All three sections were repealed by the Companies Act 2006 as from 1 October 2008, subject to savings in the Companies Act 2006 (Commencement No 8, Transitional Provisions and Savings) Order 2008, SI 2008/2860.

SCHEDULE 2
PROPERTY, RIGHTS AND LIABILITIES OF BRADFORD & BINGLEY TRANSFERRED TO ABBEY

Article 16

1. Subject to paragraph 2, all rights and liabilities in respect of retail deposits with Bradford & Bingley.

2. The liabilities referred to in paragraph 1 shall not include any liability in respect of any breach of a contract with or other duty in relation to any customer of the retail deposit business arising before the second transfer time.

3. All freehold and leasehold real property of a relevant undertaking relating to—
    (a) all retail deposit branches of Bradford & Bingley;
    (b) the operation of any branch-type agency of Bradford & Bingley; and
    (c) any other properties, including call-centres, which mainly relate to the operation of the retail deposit business of Bradford & Bingley.

4. All contracts, agreements and other arrangements of Bradford & Bingley or a relevant undertaking which relate mainly to—
    (a) the retail deposit business of Bradford & Bingley; or
    (b) any property, rights or liabilities transferred to Abbey by article 16(1)(b) or (d), but excluding any contract of employment,

but excluding any qualifying financial contract within the meaning of article 24(4).

5. Any personal property of a relevant undertaking—
    (a) situated within any real property transferred by article 16(1)(b); or
    (b) relating mainly to the retail deposit business of Bradford & Bingley.

6. All intellectual property which relate to the operation of the retail deposit business of Bradford & Bingley except the Bradford & Bingley brand.

[4270]

NOTES
Commencement: 29 September 2008 (8.00 am).

SCHEDULE 3
PENSIONS

Article 26

1. With effect from the segregation time the provisions of the pension scheme shall be modified so as to include a section ("the international section") which is divided from the remainder of the pension scheme ("the remaining section") such that—
    (a) the only employer in the international section shall be Bradford & Bingley International;
    (b) all members of the pension scheme who are in pensionable service with Bradford & Bingley International at the segregation time shall become members of the international section immediately following the segregation time;
    (c) the contributions payable by Bradford & Bingley International and the members of the international section to the pension scheme shall be allocated to the international section; and
    (d) the assets attributable to the international section cannot be used for the purposes of, or to meet any liabilities arising under, any other part of the pension scheme.

2. The liabilities of the international section shall be—
    (a) the liabilities of the pension scheme existing at the segregation time that are attributable

to pensionable service with Bradford & Bingley International including any liabilities attributable to a transfer received by the pension scheme during that pensionable service; and

(b)   any liabilities arising after the segregation time by reason of—
    (i)   the continued pensionable service of the active members referred to in paragraph 1(b); or
    (ii)   the admission of new members after the segregation time in accordance with the terms of the international section from time to time.

3.   At the segregation time, the following assets shall be allocated to the international section—
   (a)   the assets representing the value of any rights to money purchase benefits which are comprised within the liabilities mentioned in paragraph 2(a); and
   (b)   a proportion of the assets of the pension scheme determined in accordance with paragraph 4 at the segregation time.

4.   The proportion shall be—
   (a)   comprised of a selection of assets of the pension scheme (excluding any assets representing the value of any rights to money purchase benefits) that the actuary reasonably considers to be representative of those assets; and
   (b)   equal in value to such proportion of the pension scheme's assets as the amount of the liabilities in paragraph 2(a) bears to the total amount of the pension scheme's liabilities.

5.   For the purposes of paragraph 4(b)—
   (a)   any liabilities or assets representing the value of any rights to money purchase benefits under the pension scheme are to be left out of account;
   (b)   the value of any other liabilities is to be determined by the actuary—
    (i)   using the method and assumptions used to calculate the pension scheme's technical provisions for the purposes of Part 3 of the Pensions Act 2004; and
    (ii)   updating any economic and financial assumptions which are based on yields, rates or indices to take account of those yields, rates or indices as at the segregation time (or the latest practicable time prior to the segregation time); and
   (c)   the value of any asset is to be determined by such method as the actuary reasonably considers to be a proper means of providing a market value of that asset at the segregation time.

6.   At the segregation time—
   (a)   Bradford & Bingley International shall cease to be an employer in the remaining section; and
   (b)   if it would otherwise apply, section 75 of the Pensions Act 1995 shall not apply to that cessation.

7.—(1)   Following the segregation time Bradford & Bingley International shall have no liability, including any liability arising by virtue of sections 38 and 43 of the Pensions Act 2004, with regard to the liabilities of any part of the pension scheme (other than the international section) by reason of any fact, matter or circumstance occurring or existing prior to the second transfer time and accordingly no proceedings may be brought in respect of such matters.

(2)   The Treasury may in writing—
   (a)   disapply sub-paragraph (1); and
   (b)   give consent to bring such proceedings.

8.   Subject to this Schedule, the provisions of the international section (including any provisions as to amendment or termination) at the segregation time shall be identical to those of the remaining section, save that any reference in the pension scheme to Bradford & Bingley shall, in relation only to the international section, be taken to be a reference to Bradford & Bingley International.

9.   No provision of the pension scheme shall apply if it would otherwise have the effect of requiring Bradford & Bingley International to cease participation in the scheme when it ceases to be associated with Bradford & Bingley.

10.   The Treasury shall give a guarantee or make other arrangements for the purposes of securing that the assets of the remaining section are sufficient to meet its liabilities.

11.   Unless otherwise stated or provided in the guarantee or arrangements mentioned in paragraph 10—
   (a)   that guarantee or those arrangements shall for the purposes of determining the application of any provision of pensions legislation be deemed to have been given or made at the guarantee time; and
   (b)   from the guarantee time until the time that such guarantee or arrangements have been given or made the following provisions shall not apply to the remaining section—
    (i)   section 75 of the Pensions Act 1995;
    (ii)   sections 38, 43 and 52 of the Pensions Act 2004; and
    (iii)   Part 3 (scheme funding) of the Pensions Act 2004.

12. Except as expressly provided in this Schedule, or to the extent necessary to give effect to article 27, or to the extent necessary to give effect to the Transfer of Undertakings (Protection of Employment) Regulations 2006—

    (a)   nothing in Part 7 transfers to Abbey, or to any party associated or connected with Abbey, any rights or liabilities in connection with any occupational pension scheme operated by any relevant undertaking; and

    (b)   article 23 shall not apply to any agreements, instruments, documents or other things related to any such scheme.

13. In this Schedule—

    "the actuary" means the actuary appointed for the pension scheme in pursuance of subsection (1)(b) of section 47 of the Pensions Act 1995;

    "the guarantee time" means the time immediately before the second transfer time;

    "money purchase benefits" shall have the meaning given in section 181 of the Pension Schemes Act 1993;

    "pensions legislation" shall have the meaning given in section 13 of the Pensions Act 2004;

    "the pension scheme" means the Bradford & Bingley Staff Pension Scheme established by a trust deed and rules dated 24 April 1967;

    "the segregation time" means the time immediately before the guarantee time.

[4271]

NOTES

Commencement: 29 September 2008 (8.00 am).

HERITABLE BANK PLC TRANSFER OF CERTAIN RIGHTS AND LIABILITIES ORDER 2008

(SI 2008/2644)

NOTES

Made: 7 October 2008 (9.27 am).

Authority: Banking (Special Provisions) Act 2008, ss 6, 12, 13(2), Sch 2.

Commencement: 7 October 2008 (9.30 am).

This Order is reproduced as amended by: the Transfer of Rights and Liabilities to ING Order 2008, SI 2008/2666.

See also the Transfer of Rights and Liabilities to ING Order 2008, SI 2008/2666 at **[4306]**. That Order is also made under the Banking (Special Provisions) Act 2008 and provides for certain rights and liabilities to be transferred to ING. The transferred rights and liabilities are those, relating to certain accounts, which were transferred to Deposits Management (Holding) by virtue of this Order.

ARRANGEMENT OF ARTICLES

PART 1
GENERAL

PART 2
THE TRANSFER

PART 3
FINANCIAL SERVICES COMPENSATION SCHEME

PART 1
GENERAL

1 Citation and commencement

(1)   This Order may be cited as the Heritable Bank plc Transfer of Certain Rights and Liabilities Order 2008.

(2)   This Order comes into force at 9.30 am on 7 October 2008.

[4272]

NOTES

Commencement: 7 October 2008 (9.30 am).

---

2 Interpretation

In this Order—

"the Act" means the Banking (Special Provisions) Act 2008;

"the 1986 Act" means the Insolvency Act 1986;

"the 2000 Act" means the Financial Services and Markets Act 2000;

"administrator" means—

    (a)   an administrator appointed under paragraph 14 or 22 of Schedule B1 (Administration) to the 1986 Act or on an administration application made to the court (and if more than one administrator is appointed, the reference to "the administrator" is to any administrator so appointed); or

    (b)   any person on whom a discretion is conferred under an interim order made under paragraph 13(1)(d) of Schedule B1 to the 1986 Act;

"the Authority" means the Financial Services Authority;

"the Bank" means the Bank of England;

"Community law" means—

    (c)   all the rights, powers, liabilities, obligations and restrictions from time to time created or arising by or under the Community Treaties; and

    (d)   all the remedies and procedures from time to time provided for by or under the Community Treaties;

"the COMP Sourcebook" means the Compensation Sourcebook made by the Authority under the 2000 Act;

"Deposits Management (Heritable)" means Deposits Management (Heritable) Limited, company registered number 6690442, a company which is for the purposes of the Act wholly owned by the Treasury;

"the effective time" means the time this Order comes into force;

"eligible claimant" has the meaning given in rule 4.2.1 of the COMP Sourcebook;

"the FEES 6 Chapter" means Chapter 6 (Financial Services Compensation Scheme Funding) of the Fees Manual made by the Authority under the 2000 Act;

"the Financial Services Compensation Scheme" means the scheme established by the Authority under Part 15 of the 2000 Act (The Financial Services Compensation Scheme);

"FSCS" means the body corporate established by the Authority under section 212 of the 2000 Act (the Scheme Manager);

"Heritable" means Heritable Bank plc, company registered in Scotland number SC000717;

"protected deposit" has the meaning given in rule 5.3.1 of the COMP Sourcebook;

"relevant protected deposit" means a protected deposit which relates to a transferred account;

"the transfer" means the transfer effected by article 3;

"transferred accounts" means the accounts to which the transferred rights and liabilities relate;

"transferred liabilities" means the liabilities transferred by article 3(1);

"transferred rights" means the rights transferred by article 3(2);

"the transitional period" means the period of 6 months following the effective time.

[4273]

NOTES

Commencement: 7 October 2008 (9.30 am).

PART 2
THE TRANSFER

3 Transfer

(1) Subject to paragraph (3), by virtue of this Order the liabilities of Heritable to depositors in respect of the principal of, and accrued interest on, relevant deposit accounts are transferred to Deposits Management (Heritable).

(2) From the effective time, Deposits Management (Heritable) shall have the same rights in relation to depositors in relation to the transferred accounts as it would have if Heritable's relevant terms of business applied.

(3) Paragraph (1) does not apply to any liability in respect of any breach of contract or other duty which arose before the effective time.

(4) In paragraph (1), "relevant deposit accounts" means any of the following accounts operated by Heritable—

   (a)   1 Year Fixed Rate Bond;
   (b)   2 Year Fixed Rate Bond;
   (c)   3 Year Fixed Rate Bond;
   (d)   4 Year Fixed Rate Bond;
   (e)   5 Year Fixed Rate Bond;
   (f)   50 Plus Saver;
   (g)   60 Day Notice;
   (h)   90 Day Notice;
   (i)   120 Day Notice;
   (j)   Easy Access;
   (k)   Online Saver;
   (l)   Direct Saver.

(5) The transfer under paragraph (1) takes place at the time this Order comes into force.

[4274]

NOTES

Commencement: 7 October 2008 (9.30 am).

4 No consent or concurrence required

The transfer is effective despite the absence of any required consent or concurrence to, or in connection with, the transfer.

[4275]

NOTES

Commencement: 7 October 2008 (9.30 am).

5 Associated liability and interference

(1) The transfer takes effect as if—

   (a)   no associated liability existed in respect of any failure to comply with any requirement in respect of the transfer; and
   (b)   there were no associated interference with the transferred rights and liabilities.

(2)   In this article "associated liability" and "associated interference" have the meanings given in paragraph 2(2) of Schedule 2 to the Act.

[4276]

NOTES
Commencement: 7 October 2008 (9.30 am).

6   Interests, rights and liabilities of third parties relating to transferred rights and liabilities

(1)   No interest or right of any third party relating to any of the transferred rights and liabilities shall arise or become exercisable by virtue of or in connection with this Order.

(2)   Save as otherwise provided in this Order, no third party shall incur any liability, or be subject to any obligation, relating to any of the transferred rights and liabilities, by virtue of or in connection with this Order.

(3)   Without prejudice to the generality of paragraphs (1) and (2)—
  (a)   the consequences specified in paragraph (4) shall not arise in respect of any relevant instrument as a result of the transfer or any other thing done, or matter arising, by virtue of or in connection with article 3 of this Order;
  (b)   any circumstances which, but for sub-paragraph (a), would give rise to the consequences specified in paragraph (4) shall not be taken to have arisen for the purposes of any relevant instrument.

(4)   The consequences are—
  (a)   the termination of a relevant instrument or any rights or obligations under it;
  (b)   any right to terminate a relevant instrument or any right or obligation under it becoming exercisable;
  (c)   any amount becoming due and payable or capable of being declared due and payable;
  (d)   any other change in the amount or timing of any payment falling to be made or due to be received by any person;
  (e)   any right to withhold, net or set off any payment becoming exercisable;
  (f)   any event of default or breach of any right arising;
  (g)   any right not to advance any amount becoming exercisable;
  (h)   any obligation to provide or transfer any deposit or collateral;
  (i)   any right to give or withhold any consent or approval; or
  (j)   any other right or remedy (whether or not similar in kind to those referred to in paragraphs (a) to (i)) arising or becoming exercisable.

(5)   Without prejudice to paragraph (4), any provision in a relevant instrument that, as a result of the transfer or any other thing done, or matter arising, by virtue of or in connection with article 3 of this Order, provides for an obligation not to be created, suspends or extinguishes (in whole or in part) such an obligation or renders such an obligation subject to conditions, shall be of no effect.

(6)   In this article—
  "relevant instrument" has same meaning as in paragraph 4(3) of Schedule 1 to the Act and the specified connection referred to in paragraph 4(3)(c) of that Schedule is between Heritable and those undertakings whose assets and liabilities, profits and losses are consolidated in the consolidated accounts of Heritable;
  "third party" shall be construed in accordance with paragraph 2(3) of Schedule 2 to the Act.

[4277]

NOTES
Commencement: 7 October 2008 (9.30 am).

7   Payment of transferred liabilities

(1)   Deposits Management (Heritable) may without penalty or other charge pay any transferred liability prior to the due date for payment.

(2)   Where Deposits Management (Heritable), in pursuance of paragraph (1), pays a transferred liability prior to the due date for payment, Deposits Management (Heritable) may not rely on any transferred right or any other term of business of Heritable to reduce or modify the transferred liability by reason of the fact that payment is being made prior to the due date for payment.

(3)   Deposits Management (Heritable) shall not be obliged to pay any transferred liability sooner than is reasonably practicable.

[4278]

NOTES
Commencement: 7 October 2008 (9.30 am).

PART III
STATUTORY INSTRUMENTS

8 Construction of documents etc

As from the effective time and save as otherwise provided in this Order—
  (a)   agreements made or other things done by or in relation to Heritable shall be treated, so far as may be necessary for the purposes of or in connection with the transfer (but not otherwise) as made or done by or in relation to Deposits Management (Heritable), as the case may be;
  (b)   references to Heritable or to any officer or employee of Heritable in instruments or documents relating to the transferred rights and liabilities, shall have effect as if they were references to Deposits Management (Heritable), or to any officer or employee of Deposits Management (Heritable), as the case may be.

[4279]

NOTES
  Commencement: 7 October 2008 (9.30 am).

9 Validity of acts done by Deposits Management (Heritable)

Anything done by or in relation to Deposits Management (Heritable) after the effective time for the purposes of or in connection with this Order which would have been effective had it been done by or in relation to Heritable prior to the effective time shall be effective.

[4280]

NOTES
  Commencement: 7 October 2008 (9.30 am).

10 Exemption of Deposits Management (Heritable) Limited

Deposits Management (Heritable) is an exempt person for the purposes of the 2000 Act in respect of any regulated activity of the kind specified by article 5 of the Financial Services and Markets Act 2000 (Regulated Activities) Order 2001(accepting deposits).

[4281]

NOTES
  Commencement: 7 October 2008 (9.30 am).

11 Provision of information and assistance

  (1)   Heritable shall provide Deposits Management (Heritable) with such information and assistance as is reasonably requested by Deposits Management (Heritable)—
  (a)   in relation to the transferred rights and liabilities;
  (b)   for any purpose relating to this Order; or
  (c)   for any purpose relating to any other function of Deposits Management (Heritable) which relate to its functions under this Order.

  (2)   Heritable shall provide the Treasury with such information and assistance as is requested by the Treasury for any purposes relating to this Order.

[4282]

NOTES
  Commencement: 7 October 2008 (9.30 am).

PART 3
FINANCIAL SERVICES COMPENSATION SCHEME

12 Application of Part 3

This Part applies where, before the effective time, Heritable is in default for the purposes of rule 6.3.1 of the COMP Sourcebook.

[4283]

NOTES
  Commencement: 7 October 2008 (9.30 am).

13 Sums to be paid to Deposits Management (Heritable) following the transfer

  (1)   The following liabilities arise at the effective time—
  (a)   the FSCS is liable to pay (as soon as practicable) to Deposits Management (Heritable) an amount equal to the amount that eligible claimants would, immediately before the effective time, have been entitled to claim from the FSCS in respect of claims against Heritable in relation to relevant protected deposits; and

(b)   the Treasury are liable to pay (as soon as practicable) to Deposits Management (Heritable) an amount equal to the aggregate amount of the liabilities transferred to Deposits Management (Heritable) under article 3 less the amount specified in sub-paragraph (a).

(2)   For the purposes of paragraph (1)(a), if the quantification date for a claim would have been a date other than the date on which Heritable was determined to be in default for the purposes of section 6.3 of the COMP Sourcebook, the amount that an eligible claimant would have been entitled to claim from the FSCS is the lesser of—

(a)   the amount which the FSCS quantifies as being the value of that claim as at immediately before the effective time; and

(b)   the amount that would have been payable at the quantification date, if different, for that claim.

(3)   In paragraph (2), "quantification date" has the meaning given in rule 12.3.1 of the COMP Sourcebook.

(4)   As soon as practicable after the effective time—

(a)   Heritable shall estimate the aggregate amount of the transferred liabilities;

(b)   the FSCS shall pay to Deposits Management (Heritable) the amount it is liable to pay under paragraph (1)(a) as estimated by the Authority; and

(c)   the Treasury shall pay to Deposits Management (Heritable) an amount equal to the amount estimated by Heritable in accordance with sub-paragraph (a) less the amount estimated by the Authority in accordance with sub-paragraph (b).

(5)   From time to time—

(a)   the FSCS may revise the estimate of its liability under paragraph (1)(a); and

(b)   Heritable may revise the estimate of the aggregate amount of the transferred liabilities,

and the FSCS, the Treasury and Deposits Management (Heritable) shall make such corresponding payments to each other as are necessary to ensure that the FSCS and the Treasury have each paid to Deposits Management (Heritable) the amount required (and no more than the required amount) to meet their liability under paragraph (1).

(6)   If at any time after the effective time Heritable is placed into administration or an interim order is made in relation to Heritable under paragraph 13(1)(d) of Schedule B1 to the 1986 Act, the references to Heritable in paragraphs (4) and (5) are to be treated as references to the administrator.

[(7)   The liability referred to in paragraph (1)(a) shall be assessed by the FSCS and, in so doing, the FSCS may calculate, by any methodology or approach it considers appropriate, the total amounts of compensation that would have been paid to all eligible claimants, if (and to the extent that) it considers that the costs of ascertaining the entitlement to and amount of compensation by reference to each qualifying claimant would exceed or be disproportionate to the benefit of doing so.]

[4284]

NOTES

Commencement: 7 October 2008 (9.30 am).

Para (7): added by the Transfer of Rights and Liabilities to ING Order 2008, SI 2008/2666, art 10(1), (2), as from 10.10 am on 8 October 2008.

---

14   Payment to Deposits Management (Heritable) to constitute payment of compensation for the purposes of the Financial Services Compensation Scheme

For the purposes of Part 15 (the financial services compensation scheme) of the 2000 Act, the COMP Sourcebook and the FEES 6 Chapter (including, without limitation, the power of the FSCS to impose levies)—

(a)   all payments by the FSCS to Deposits Management (Heritable) under article 13 shall constitute the payment of compensation to each eligible claimant under the Financial Services Compensation Scheme in accordance with their respective entitlements in respect of claims against Heritable for relevant protected deposits;

(b)   each eligible claimant—

(i)   is deemed to have made an application for compensation for the purposes of rule 3.2.1(1) of the COMP Sourcebook; and

(ii)   is deemed to have accepted an offer of compensation made by the FSCS and to have received payment of such compensation for the purposes of rule 11.2.1 of the COMP Sourcebook,

and, accordingly, an eligible claimant has no right to claim, and the FSCS has no obligation to pay, for a relevant protected deposit any further compensation under the Financial Services Compensation Scheme in respect of the default of Heritable determined by the Authority under section 6.3 of the COMP Sourcebook.

[4285]

NOTES
Commencement: 7 October 2008 (9.30 am).

15 Liability of Heritable to the FSCS and the Treasury

(1) Heritable is liable to the FSCS in respect of an amount equal to the amount which would have been provable in the administration of Heritable in respect of the transferred liabilities had this Order not been made and had Heritable been placed in administration immediately before the effective date.

(2) The FSCS shall pursue recoveries from Heritable in respect of the liability incurred under paragraph (1) to the extent reasonably practicable.

(3) Subject to paragraph (4), if an eligible claimant had, in relation to a relevant protected deposit, a liability to Heritable which would have been capable of being set-off against a liability of Heritable to that claimant in an administration [or liquidation] of Heritable (if that liability had not been transferred), the amount which [the FSCS is entitled to recover] in the administration [or liquidation] shall for the purposes of paragraph (1) be taken to be the sum of—

   (a)   the amount of the reduction in the depositor's liability to Heritable as a result of the application of set-off; and

   (b)   the amount which would have been recovered in respect of the balance of the claim (if any) provable in the administration [or liquidation] of Heritable.

(4) Paragraph (3) applies only to the extent that its application does not have the effect that the other creditors of Heritable are in a worse position than they would have been had the set-off been applied.

(5) The FSCS shall determine the proportion of any amount which it receives or recovers from Heritable which is properly attributable to each type of liability described below and shall promptly on receipt account for that receipt or recovery as follows—

   (a)   in full to the Treasury, to the extent that—

      (i)   the receipt is attributable to a transferred liability; and

      (ii)   the person to whom such transferred liability is owed would not have been entitled to make a claim for compensation from the FSCS immediately before the effective time;

   (b)   to the Treasury by reference to the relevant proportion, to the extent that—

      (i)   the receipt is attributable to a transferred liability;

      (ii)   the person to whom such transferred liability is owed is an eligible claimant; and

      (iii)   the amount of such liability exceeds the maximum compensation that the eligible claimant would have been entitled to claim from the FSCS immediately before the effective time;

   (c)   for the account of the FSCS, to the extent that—

      (i)   the receipt is attributable to a transferred liability owed to an eligible claimant; and

      (ii)   the amount of such liability is equal to or less than the maximum compensation that the eligible claimant would have been entitled to claim from the FSCS immediately before the effective time.

(6) In paragraph (5), the "relevant proportion" is the proportion of the total liabilities which arise under article 13(1) for which the Treasury are liable.

(7) If Heritable is in administration or an interim order has been made in relation to Heritable under paragraph 13(1)(d) of Schedule B1 to the 1986 Act, the liability incurred under paragraph (1) shall not be treated as an expense of the administration under paragraph 99(3) of Schedule B1 of the 1986 Act, rule 2.67 of the Insolvency Rules 1986 or any analogous provision of the Insolvency (Scotland) Rules 1986.

(8) Nothing in this Part shall have the effect that the FSCS recovers less than it would have recovered if this Order had not been made.

[4286]

NOTES
Commencement: 7 October 2008 (9.30 am).
Para (7): words in first, third and final pairs of square brackets inserted, and words in second pair of square brackets substituted, by the Transfer of Rights and Liabilities to ING Order 2008, SI 2008/2666, art 10(1), (3), as from 10.10 am on 8 October 2008.

16 FSCS's power to require information

(1) The FSCS may, by notice in writing given to Deposits Management (Heritable), require it—

   (a)   to provide specified information or information of a specified description; or

   (b)   to produce specified documents or documents of a specified description.

(2)   Paragraph (1) only applies to information and documents the provision or production of which the FSCS considers to be necessary (or likely to be necessary) for the exercise of its functions under or by virtue of this Order.

(3)   Subsections (2), (4), (5) and (7) of section 219 of the 2000 Act (scheme manager's power to require information) apply to a requirement imposed under paragraph (1) as if it were a requirement imposed under that section.

[4287]

NOTES
Commencement: 7 October 2008 (9.30 am).

17 Statutory immunity

For the purposes of section 222 (statutory immunity) of the 2000 Act the scheme manager's functions shall include any acts or omissions carried out by the FSCS pursuant to or in connection with this Order.

[4288]

NOTES
Commencement: 7 October 2008 (9.30 am).

PART 4
THE ADMINISTRATOR AND TRANSITIONAL PROVISIONS

18 Application of this Part

This Part applies if after the effective time—
  (a)   Heritable is placed into administration; or
  (b)   an interim order in made in relation to Heritable under paragraph 13(1)(d) of Schedule B1 to the 1986 Act.

[4289]

NOTES
Commencement: 7 October 2008 (9.30 am).

19 The administration

The relevant provisions of the 1986 Act, the Insolvency Rules 1986 and the Insolvency (Scotland) Rules 1986 shall apply to Heritable subject to the provisions of this Part.

[4290]

NOTES
Commencement: 7 October 2008 (9.30 am).

20 Objectives etc of the administrator

  (1)   This article only applies during the transitional period.

  (2)   The administrator must perform his or her functions with the objectives ("the overriding objectives") of—
  (a)   ensuring that Heritable provides, and managing the affairs, business and property of Heritable to enable it to provide, the services and facilities reasonably required by Deposits Management (Heritable) to carry on its functions in relation to the transferred rights and liabilities; and
  (b)   ensuring that Heritable performs the other obligations imposed on it by or under this Order.

  (3)   The administrator shall only perform his or her functions with the objective determined in accordance with paragraph 3 of Schedule B1 to the 1986 Act to the extent that such objective is not inconsistent with and does not interfere with the achievement of the overriding objectives.

  (4)   Paragraph 3(2) of Schedule B1 to the 1986 Act only applies to the performance of the functions of the administrator to the extent that it is not inconsistent with and does not interfere with the achievement of the overriding objectives.

  (5)   The Treasury may, by notice in writing, give a direction to the administrator specifying that an act (or omission) is required for the overriding objectives.

  (6)   The Treasury may also, by notice in writing, give a direction to the administrator requiring him or her to act (or not act) if the Treasury consider that it is necessary to give such a direction for the purposes of—
  (a)   protecting or enhancing the stability of the financial systems of the United Kingdom;

(b)   protecting or enhancing public confidence in the stability of the banking system of the United Kingdom; or

(c)   protecting depositors.

(7)   The administrator must comply with any directions given under paragraph (5) or (6).

(8)   The services and facilities to which paragraph (2)(a) applies include (but are not limited to) the services and facilities specified in Schedule 1.

(9)   The administrator shall not be required to include any proposals for achieving the overriding objectives in any statement he or she makes under paragraph 49 (administrator's proposals) or paragraph 54 (revision of administrator's proposals) of Schedule B1 to the 1986 Act or to obtain approval of such proposals at any creditors' meeting or from the court.

(10)   The administrator shall not enter into a transaction or a series of transactions (whether related or not) to sell, lease, transfer or otherwise dispose of any property or right of Heritable having a value of more than £50 million at any time unless—

(a)   the court orders otherwise;

(b)   the Treasury gives its consent to the transaction; or

(c)   the sale, lease, transfer or disposal has been specifically approved at a meeting of creditors summoned under paragraph 51(1), 54(2) or 62 of Schedule B1 to the 1986 Act or by a creditors' committee constituted in accordance with rule 2.50 of the Insolvency Rules 1986 or any analogous provision of the Insolvency (Scotland) Rules 1986.

(11)   In this article, "court" means—

(a)   in England and Wales, the High Court;

(b)   in Scotland, the Court of Session;

(c)   in Northern Ireland, the High Court.

[4291]

NOTES
Commencement: 7 October 2008 (9.30 am).

21   Insolvency rules etc

Nothing in the 1986 Act, the Insolvency Rules 1986, the Insolvency (Scotland) Rules 1986 or any other enactment or rule of law shall operate to invalidate or prejudice any act or omission done under or pursuant to this Order or give rise to a claim against or impose any liability on Heritable or the administrator for any act or omission so done.

[4292]

NOTES
Commencement: 7 October 2008 (9.30 am).

22   Use of the Heritable brand

Heritable shall grant to Deposits Management (Heritable) a licence to use the Heritable brand during the transitional period for the purposes of Deposits Management (Heritable) carrying on its business in relation to the transferred rights and liabilities.

[4293]

NOTES
Commencement: 7 October 2008 (9.30 am).

23   Compensation payable to Heritable

(1)   The Treasury shall reimburse Heritable for the costs and expenses (including fees) properly incurred by the administrator during the transitional period in fulfilling his or her obligations under article 20(1).

(2)   Paragraph (1) does not apply to any cost or expense which would have been incurred even if this Order had not been made.

[4294]

NOTES
Commencement: 7 October 2008 (9.30 am).

24   Continuity

(1)   During the transitional period, any person wishing to terminate or modify (or treat as terminated or modified) any contract or agreement with Heritable for services and facilities or any right or obligation under such a contract or agreement must give not less than 14 days prior written notice to the administrator and to Deposits Management (Heritable).

(2)   Except with the consent of the Treasury or the permission of the court, during the transitional period—

(a)   no person is entitled—

(i)   to terminate or modify any contract or agreement with Heritable for services and facilities, or any right or obligation under such a contract or agreement, where the contract or agreement or right or obligation relates to services or facilities which are reasonably required by—

(aa)   Heritable to perform its duties under or pursuant to this Order;

(bb)   the administrator to perform his or her duties under or pursuant to this Order; or

(cc)   Deposits Management (Heritable) to carry on its functions in relation to the transferred rights and liabilities, or

(ii)   to treat such a contract, agreement, right or obligation as terminated or modified, by virtue of or in connection with the transfer, the commencement of the administration in relation to Heritable or the making of an interim order in relation to Heritable under paragraph 13(1)(d) of Schedule B1 to the 1986 Act; and

(b)   any counterparty to such a contract or agreement must perform his or her obligations in accordance with that contract or agreement.

(3)   The services and facilities to which paragraphs (1) and (2) apply include (but are not limited to) the services and facilities specified in Schedule 1.

(4)   Any purported termination or modification of any contract, agreement, right or obligation in contravention of paragraph (1) or (2), and any action taken in consequence of any such purported termination or modification, shall have no effect.

(5)   Paragraph (2) does not apply where—

(a)   Heritable, Deposits Management (Heritable) or the administrator, as the case may be, has failed to perform its payment obligations under the relevant contract or agreement and such non-payment is not remedied within 14 days of that person becoming aware of the non-performance; or

(b)   Heritable, Deposits Management (Heritable) or the administrator, as the case may be, fails to notify the counterparty to the relevant contract or agreement within 14 days of its becoming aware of the request for consent to such termination, modification or non-performance of an obligation, that such consent has been withheld.

(6)   Without prejudice to the generality of paragraph (2), the transfer shall not have the effect of terminating or otherwise changing the terms of Heritable's membership (if any) of any payment system, including, in particular, BACS, CHAPS and the LINK payments systems.

(7)   This article is subject to any requirement of Community law.

[4295]

NOTES
Commencement: 7 October 2008 (9.30 am).

---

25   Financial Ombudsman Scheme

For the purposes of section 227(2) (voluntary jurisdiction) of the 2000 Act, Deposits Management (Heritable) is deemed to be carrying on an activity to which the voluntary jurisdiction rules apply and is deemed to be participating in the ombudsman scheme.

[4296]

NOTES
Commencement: 7 October 2008 (9.30 am).

PART 5
MISCELLANEOUS

26   Shadow directorship

(1)   While Deposits Management (Heritable) is wholly owned by the Treasury (or to be regarded as wholly owned by the Treasury for the purposes of the Act), for the purposes of the provisions listed in Schedule 2 to this Order, none of the persons listed in paragraph (3) shall be regarded as a shadow director or (unless otherwise appointed as a director) a person discharging managerial responsibilities of Deposits Management (Heritable).

(2)   For the purposes of the definition of "director" in section 417 of the 2000 Act (definitions), none of the persons listed in paragraph (3) shall be regarded as a person in accordance with whose directions or instructions (not being advice given in a professional capacity) the directors of a relevant undertaking are accustomed to act while Deposits Management (Heritable) is wholly owned by the Treasury.

PART III
STATUTORY INSTRUMENTS

(3)   The persons are—
    (a)   a Minister of the Crown;
    (b)   the Treasury;
    (c)   the Treasury Solicitor;
    (d)   the Bank;
    (e)   persons—
        (i)   employed by or under; or
        (ii)   acting on behalf of,
any of the persons listed in sub-paragraph (a) to (d).

[4297]

NOTES
   Commencement: 7 October 2008 (9.30 am).

27   Modification to Authority's rule-making power

(1)   Subsections (1) and (1A) of section 138 of the 2000 Act (general rule-making power) have effect as if modified by inserting after "protecting the interests of consumers"—

"or for the purposes of, to facilitate or in consequence of, a transfer under section 6 of the Banking (Special Provisions) Act 2008".

(2)   Section 148(2) of the 2000 Act (modification or waiver of rules) shall also apply in relation to Heritable—
    (a)   in the absence of an application by a person subject to rules made by the Authority; and
    (b)   without any requirement for the consent of such a person.

(3)   Section 148(4) of the 2000 Act shall not prevent the Authority from modifying or waiving rules in relation to Heritable under section 148 of that Act provided that the Authority is satisfied that the modification or waiver is necessary for the purposes of, to facilitate or in consequence of the transfer.

[4298]

NOTES
   Commencement: 7 October 2008 (9.30 am).

28   Modification to Authority's duty to consult on rule changes

(1)   Section 155(7) of the 2000 Act (consultation) has effect as if modified by adding at the end—

"or if it is making rules for the purposes of, or to facilitate or in consequence of, a transfer under section 6 of the Banking (Special Provisions) Act 2008."

(2)   Section 157 of the 2000 Act (guidance) has effect as if modified by adding after subsection (3)—

"(3A)   Section 155(7) applies to proposed guidance as it applies to proposed rules with the modification made by article 28 of the Heritable Bank plc Transfer of Certain Rights and Liabilities Order 2008.".

[4299]

NOTES
   Commencement: 7 October 2008 (9.30 am).

29   Freedom of information

For the purposes of section 3 of the Freedom of Information Act 2000 (public authorities), Deposits Management (Heritable) shall be deemed—
    (a)   not to be a publicly-owned company for the purposes of subsection (1)(b);
    (b)   not to hold information on behalf of the Treasury or Treasury Solicitor for the purpose of subsection (2)(b).

[4300]

NOTES
   Commencement: 7 October 2008 (9.30 am).

30   Proceedings against directors

(1)   No director of—
    (a)   Heritable; or
    (b)   Deposits Management (Heritable),

shall be liable in connection with the transfer or any other provisions of this Order and accordingly no proceedings may be brought (or, in Scotland, raised) against any such director in respect of such matters.

(2)   The Treasury may in writing—
  (a)   waive the effect of paragraph (1), and
  (b)   give consent to bring (or, in Scotland, raise) such proceedings against such directors.

(3)   Where paragraph (1) applies, section 232 of the Companies Act 2006 (provisions protecting directors from liability) shall not apply to a relevant undertaking.

(4)   In this article—
  "director" means a person who was a director immediately before the effective time, whether or not he has ceased to be a director at the time when proceedings in respect of that liability commenced;
  "proceedings" includes proceedings under Part 11 of the Companies Act 2006 (derivative claims and proceedings by members).

[4301]

NOTES
Commencement: 7 October 2008 (9.30 am).

31   Notification requirement

(1)   The Treasury must notify the Authority of the making of this Order.

(2)   A notification under paragraph (1)—
  (a)   may be given by such means as the Treasury consider appropriate;
  (b)   must be given to the Authority as soon as reasonably practicable after the effective time.

(3)   On receiving a notification under paragraph (1), the Authority must in turn notify any relevant EEA authority of the making of the Order.

(4)   A notification under paragraph (3)—
  (a)   may be given by such means as the Authority considers appropriate;
  (b)   must be given to the relevant EEA authority as soon as reasonably practicable after the Authority is notified under paragraph (1).

(5)   "Relevant EEA authority" means any regulatory authority in an EEA state that exercises functions in relation to any office or branch of the authorised deposit-taker in question in that state.

[4302]

NOTES
Commencement: 7 October 2008 (9.30 am).

32   Transfer of data

Any transfer of data under this Order is not to be taken to breach any restriction on disclosure of information, however imposed.

[4303]

NOTES
Commencement: 7 October 2008 (9.30 am).

SCHEDULES

SCHEDULE 1
SERVICES AND FACILITIES

Article 20

1.   Website hosting services or facilities.

2.   Information technology services or facilities.

3.   Back office processing services or facilities.

4.   Call centre services or facilities.

5.   Payment and clearing services or facilities.

[4304]

NOTES
Commencement: 7 October 2008 (9.30 am).

SCHEDULE 2
SHADOW DIRECTORSHIP

Article 26

1. The following provisions of the Companies Act 1985—
    (a) section 317 of the (disclosure of interests in contracts);
    (b) section 733 (offences by bodies corporate).

2. The following provisions of the Companies Act 2006—
    (a) section 84 (criminal consequences of failure to make required disclosure);
    (b) section 162 (register of directors);
    (c) section 165 (register of directors' residential addresses);
    (d) section 167 (duty to notify registrar of changes);
    (e) sections 170 to 177 (general duties of directors);
    (f) sections 182 to 186 (declaration of interest in existing transaction) as applied to shadow directors by section 187;
    (g) sections 188 and 189 (directors' service contracts);
    (h) sections 190 to 196 (substantial property transactions);
    (i) sections 197 to 214 (loans etc to directors);
    (j) sections 215 to 222 (payments for loss of office) as applied to shadow directors by section 223(2);
    (k) sections 227 to 230 (directors' service contracts);
    (l) section 231 (contracts with sole members who are directors);
    (m) sections 260 to 269 (derivative claims in England and Wales and Northern Ireland);
    (n) sections 854 to 859 (annual return).

3. The following provisions of the Insolvency Act 1986—
    (a) section 214 (wrongful trading);
    (b) section 249 ("connected" with a company).

4. The following provisions of the 2000 Act—
    (a) section 96A (disclosure of information requirements);
    (b) section 96B (disclosure rules: persons responsible for compliance).

[4305]

NOTES
Commencement: 7 October 2008 (9.30 am).

TRANSFER OF RIGHTS AND LIABILITIES TO ING ORDER 2008

(SI 2008/2666)

NOTES
Made: 8 October 2008 (10.00 am).
Authority: Banking (Special Provisions) Act 2008, ss 6, 8, 12, 13(2), Sch 2.
Commencement: 8 October 2008 (10.10 am).

As of 1 February 2009, this Order had not been amended.

ARRANGEMENT OF ARTICLES

PART 1
GENERAL

PART 2
THE TRANSFER

PART 3
FINANCIAL SERVICES COMPENSATION SCHEME

PART 1

GENERAL

1 Citation and commencement

(1)   This Order may be cited as the Transfer of Rights and Liabilities to ING Order 2008.

(2)   This Order comes into force at 10.10 am on 8th October 2008.

[4306]

NOTES

Commencement: 8 October 2008 (10.10 am).

2 Interpretation: general

In this Order—

"the 2000 Act" means the Financial Services and Markets Act 2000;

"the Act" means the Banking (Special Provisions) Act 2008;

"the Authority" means the Financial Services Authority;

"the Companies Acts" has the meaning given by section 2 of the Companies Act 2006;

"Deposits Management (Heritable)" means Deposits Management (Heritable) Limited, company registered number 6690442, a company which is for the purposes of the Act wholly owned by the Treasury;

"the effective time" means the time this Order comes into force;

"the Financial Services Compensation Scheme" means the scheme established by the Authority under Part 15 (the financial services compensation scheme) of the 2000 Act;

"the first Order" means the Heritable Bank plc Transfer of Certain Rights and Liabilities Order 2008;

"FSCS" means the body corporate established by the Authority under section 212 (the scheme manager) of the 2000 Act;

"Heritable" means Heritable Bank plc, company registered in Scotland number SC000717;

"ING" means ING Direct NV, incorporated in the Netherlands and acting through its branch in the United Kingdom, branch reference number BR 7357;

"the transfer" means the transfer effected under article 3(1);

"the transitional period" means the period of 6 months beginning with the date of this Order.

[4307]

NOTES

Commencement: 8 October 2008 (10.10 am).

PART 2

THE TRANSFER

3 The transfer

(1)   By virtue of this Order all the rights and liabilities transferred to Deposits Management (Heritable) by article 3 of the first Order are transferred to ING.

(2)   From the effective time, ING shall—

(a)   have the same rights and obligations in relation to depositors in relation to the transferred accounts as it would have if Heritable's relevant terms of business applied; and

(b)   be liable to pay to depositors any accrued interest on the transferred accounts as at the time of coming into force of the first Order and any interest accruing after that time on those accounts.

(3)   In paragraph (2) "transferred accounts" has the same meaning as in the first Order.

(4)   Paragraph (1) does not apply to any liability in respect of any breach of contract or other duty which arose before the effective time.

(5)   The transfer under paragraph (1) takes place at the effective time.

[4308]

NOTES
Commencement: 8 October 2008 (10.10 am).

4   No consent or concurrence required

The transfer is effective despite the absence of any required consent or concurrence to or with the transfer.

[4309]

NOTES
Commencement: 8 October 2008 (10.10 am).

5   Associated liability and interference

(1)   The transfer takes effect as if—
   (a)   no associated liability existed in respect of any failure to comply with any requirement in respect of the transfer; and
   (b)   there were no associated interference with the rights and liabilities transferred.

(2)   In this article, "associated liability" and "associated interference" have the meanings given in paragraph 2(2) of Schedule 2 to the Act.

[4310]

NOTES
Commencement: 8 October 2008 (10.10 am).

6   Interests, rights and liabilities of third parties relating to property, rights and liabilities transferred

(1)   No interest or right of any third party relating to any right or liability transferred by article 3, shall arise or become exercisable by virtue of or in connection with this Order.

(2)   Save as otherwise provided in this Order, no third party shall, by virtue of or in connection with this Order, incur any liability or be subject to any obligation relating to any right or liability transferred by article 3.

(3)   Without prejudice to the generality of paragraphs (1) and (2)—
   (a)   the consequences specified in paragraph (4) shall not arise in respect of any relevant instrument as a result of the transfer or any other thing done, or matter arising, by virtue of or in connection with the transfer; and
   (b)   any circumstances which, but for sub-paragraph (a), would give rise to the consequences specified in paragraph (4) shall be taken not to have arisen for the purposes of any relevant instrument.

(4)   The consequences are—
   (a)   the termination of a relevant instrument or any rights or obligations under it;
   (b)   any right to terminate a relevant instrument or any right or obligation under it becoming exercisable;
   (c)   any amount becoming due and payable or capable of being declared due and payable;
   (d)   any other change in the amount or timing of any payment falling to be made or due to be received by any person;
   (e)   any right to withhold, net or set off any payment becoming exercisable;
   (f)   any event of default or breach of any right arising;
   (g)   any right not to advance any amount becoming exercisable;
   (h)   any obligation to provide or transfer any deposit or collateral;
   (i)   any right to give or withhold any consent or approval; or
   (j)   any other right or remedy (whether or not similar in kind to those referred to in sub-paragraphs (a) to (i)) arising or becoming exercisable.

(5)   Without prejudice to paragraph (4), any provision in a relevant instrument that, as a result of the transfer or any other thing done, or matter arising, by virtue of or in connection with the transfer, provides for an obligation not to be created, suspends or extinguishes (in whole or in part) such an obligation or renders such an obligation subject to conditions, shall be of no effect.

(6)   In this article—
   "relevant instrument" has the same meaning as in paragraph 4(3) of Schedule 1 to the Act and the specified connection referred to in paragraph 4(3)(c) of that Schedule is between

Heritable and those undertakings whose assets and liabilities, profits and losses are consolidated in the consolidated accounts of Heritable; and

"third party" shall be construed in accordance with paragraph 2(3) of Schedule 2 to the Act.

[4311]

NOTES

Commencement: 8 October 2008 (10.10 am).

7 Construction of documents etc

As from the effective time, and save as otherwise provided in this Order—

   (a)   agreements made or other things done by or in relation to Heritable shall be treated, so far as may be necessary for the purposes of or in connection with the transfer, but not otherwise, as made or done by or in relation to ING, as the case may be; and

   (b)   references to Heritable, or to any officer or employee of Heritable, in instruments or documents relating to the rights and liabilities transferred by or under article 3 shall have effect as if they were references to ING, or to any officer or employee of ING, as the case may be.

[4312]

NOTES

Commencement: 8 October 2008 (10.10 am).

8 Provision of information and assistance

Heritable shall provide ING with such information and assistance as is reasonably requested by ING—

   (a)   in relation to the rights and liabilities transferred by article 3;

   (b)   for any purpose relating to this Order;

   (c)   for any purpose relating to any other function of ING which relates to its functions under this Order.

[4313]

NOTES

Commencement: 8 October 2008 (10.10 am).

PART 3
FINANCIAL SERVICES COMPENSATION SCHEME

9 Sum to be paid to ING following the transfer

(1) Deposits Management (Heritable) is liable to pay (as soon as practicable after the effective time) to ING an amount equal to the aggregate amount of the liabilities transferred to ING under article 3 less £1,000,000.

(2) The Treasury shall subsequently make the necessary adjustments such that Heritable obtains the benefit of the reduction of £1,000,000 referred to in paragraph (1) less the total of all costs and liabilities incurred by Deposits Management (Heritable) in performing its obligations under this Order or the first Order.

[4314]

10 (*Amends the Heritable Bank plc Transfer of Certain Rights and Liabilities Order 2008, SI 2008/2644, arts 13, 15 at* **[4284]**, **[4286]**.)

11 Balancing payments

(1) Any payment which is required to be made pursuant to article 13(5) of the first Order by or to Deposits Management (Heritable) after the effective time shall be made by or, as the case may be, to ING.

(2) Deposits Management (Heritable) shall have no obligation to make or, as the case may be, right to receive any such payment.

[4315]

NOTES

Commencement: 8 October 2008 (10.10 am).

PART III
STATUTORY INSTRUMENTS

12 Payment by the FSCS to ING

Any payment by the FSCS to ING pursuant to article 11 shall for the purposes of article 14(a) of the first Order be deemed to be a payment by the FSCS to Deposits Management (Heritable) under article 13(5) of the first Order.

[4316]

NOTES

Commencement: 8 October 2008 (10.10 am).

13 FSCS power to require information

(1)   The FSCS may, by notice in writing given to ING, require it—
  (a)   to provide specified information or information of a specified description; or
  (b)   to produce specified documents or documents of a specified description.

(2)   Paragraph (1) only applies to information and documents the provision or production of which the FSCS considers to be necessary (or likely to be necessary) for the exercise of its functions under or by virtue of this Order or the first Order.

(3)   Subsections (2), (4), (5) and (7) of section 219 of the 2000 Act (scheme manager's power to require information) apply to a requirement imposed under paragraph (1) as if it were a requirement imposed under that section.

[4317]

NOTES

Commencement: 8 October 2008 (10.10 am).

14 Statutory immunity

For the purposes of section 222 (statutory immunity) of the 2000 Act the scheme manager's functions shall include any acts or omissions carried out by the FSCS pursuant to or in connection with this Order.

[4318]

NOTES

Commencement: 8 October 2008 (10.10 am).

PART 4
MISCELLANEOUS

15 Transitional provisions

Part 4 of the first Order (except for article 22) shall apply from the effective time with the substitution for references to Deposits Management (Heritable) of references to ING.

[4319]

NOTES

Commencement: 8 October 2008 (10.10 am).

16 Services and facilities

The agreement dated 8th October 2008 between the Treasury and ING relating to the provision of transitional services by Heritable to ING shall bind Heritable as if it were a party.

[4320]

NOTES

Commencement: 8 October 2008 (10.10 am).

17 Business continuity

(1)   During the transitional period, any person who provides to Heritable, pursuant to any contract or agreement, services or facilities which are reasonably required by Heritable to perform its duties under or pursuant to this Order or the agreement referred to in article 16 shall—
  (a)   provide such services to Heritable for the benefit of ING; or
  (b)   if so requested by Heritable, provide such services direct to ING.

(2)   No such person shall, without the consent of the Treasury or permission of the Court, during the transitional period, terminate or modify any such contract or agreement, or treat it as terminated or modified, by virtue or in connection with the requirement under this article to provide services or facilities to or for the benefit of ING.

[4321]

NOTES
Commencement: 8 October 2008 (10.10 am).

18 Modification to Authority's rule-making power

(1) Subsections (1) and (1A) of section 138 of the 2000 Act (general rule-making power) have effect as if modified by inserting after "protecting the interests of consumers"—

"or for the purposes of, to facilitate or in consequence of, a transfer under section 6 or 8 of the Banking (Special Provisions) Act 2008".

(2) Section 148(2) of the 2000 Act (modification or waiver of rules) shall also apply in relation to ING—

(a) in the absence of an application by a person subject to rules made by the Authority; and

(b) without any requirement for the consent of such a person.

(3) Section 148(4) of the 2000 Act shall not prevent the Authority from modifying or waiving rules in relation to ING under section 148 of that Act provided that the Authority is satisfied that the modification or waiver is necessary for the purposes of, to facilitate or in consequence of the transfer.

[4322]

NOTES
Commencement: 8 October 2008 (10.10 am).

19 Modification to Authority's duty to consult on rule changes

(1) Section 155(7) of the 2000 Act (consultation) has effect as if modified by adding at the end—

"or if it is making rules for the purposes of, or to facilitate or in consequence of, a transfer under section 6 or 8 of the Banking (Special Provisions) Act 2008."

(2) Section 157 of the 2000 Act (guidance) has effect as if modified by adding after subsection (3)—

"(3A) Section 155(7) applies to proposed guidance as it applies to proposed rules with the modification made by article 19 of the Transfer of Rights and Liabilities to ING Order 2008.".

[4323]

NOTES
Commencement: 8 October 2008 (10.10 am).

20 Transfer of data

Any transfer of data under this Order is not to be taken to breach any restriction on disclosure of information, however imposed.

[4324]

NOTES
Commencement: 8 October 2008 (10.10 am).

LANDSBANKI FREEZING ORDER 2008

(SI 2008/2668)

NOTES
Made: 8 October 2008 (10.00 am).
Authority: Anti-terrorism, Crime and Security Act 2001, ss 4, 14, Sch 3.
Commencement: 8 October 2008 (10.10 am).
This Order is reproduced as amended by: the Landsbanki Freezing (Amendment) Order 2008, SI 2008/2766.

ARRANGEMENT OF ARTICLES

1 Citation, commencement, extent and application

(1)   This Order may be cited as the Landsbanki Freezing Order 2008 and comes into force at 10.10 am on 8th October 2008.

(2)   [Subject to paragraph (3),] this Order extends to the United Kingdom.

(3)   [The prohibitions imposed by article 4 apply to the following persons]—
   (a)   any person in the United Kingdom;
   (b)   any person elsewhere who is—
      (i)   a British citizen, a British overseas territories citizen, a British National (Overseas) or a British Overseas citizen;
      (ii)   a person who under the British Nationality Act 1981 is a British subject;
      (iii) a British protected person within the meaning of that Act;
      (iv)   a body incorporated under the law of any part of the United Kingdom.

[4325]

NOTES

Commencement: 8 October 2008 (10.10 am).
Para (2): words in square brackets inserted by the Landsbanki Freezing (Amendment) Order 2008, SI 2008/2766, arts 2, 3(a), as from 21 October 2008.
Para (3): words in square brackets substituted by SI 2008/2766, arts 2, 3(b), as from 21 October 2008.

2 Interpretation

(1)   In this Order—
   "the 2000 Act" means the Financial Services and Markets Act 2000;
   "the Authorities" means—
      (a)   the Central Bank of Iceland, Kalkofnsvegi 1, 150 Reykjavik;
      (b)   the Icelandic Financial Services Authority (the Fjármálaeftirlitið); and
      (c)   the Landsbanki receivership committee established by the Icelandic Financial Services Authority;
   "body corporate" includes a Scottish partnership and "a body incorporated under the law of any part of the United Kingdom" is to be interpreted accordingly;
   "frozen funds" has the meaning given in article 4(1);
   "funds" means financial assets and economic benefits of any kind, including (but not limited to)—
      (a)   gold, cash, cheques, claims on money, drafts, money orders and other payment instruments;
      (b)   deposits with relevant institutions or other persons, balances on accounts, debts and debt obligations;
      (c)   publicly and privately traded securities and debt instruments, including stocks and shares, certificates representing securities, bonds, notes, warrants, debentures and derivative products;
      (d)   interest, dividends or other income on or value accruing from or generated by assets;
      (e)   credit, rights of set-off, guarantees, performance bonds or other financial commitments;
      (f)   letters of credit, bills of lading, bills of sale; and
      (g)   documents providing evidence of an interest in funds or financial resources;
   "Landsbanki" means Landsbanki Islands hf, a public limited company incorporated under the law of Iceland;
   "relevant institution" means—
      (h)   a person who has permission under Part 4 of the 2000 Act; and
      (i)   an EEA firm of the kind mentioned in paragraph 5(b) of Schedule 3 to the 2000 Act which has permission under paragraph 15 of that Schedule as a result of qualifying for authorisation under paragraph 12 of that Schedule to accept deposits.

(2)   The definition of "relevant institution" in paragraph (1) must be read with—
   (a)   section 22 of the 2000 Act;

(b) any relevant order under that section; and
(c) Schedule 2 to that Act.

[4326]

NOTES
Commencement: 8 October 2008 (10.10 am).

3 Specified persons

(1) The following are specified persons for the purposes of this Order [(being persons believed by the Treasury to have taken or be likely to take action to the detriment of the United Kingdom's economy (or part of it))]—
    (a) Landsbanki;
    (b) the Authorities; and
    (c) the Government of Iceland.

(2) If a specified person makes a written request, the Treasury must[, as soon as is practicable,] give it written reasons why it has been specified.

[4327]

NOTES
Commencement: 8 October 2008 (10.10 am).
Words in square brackets inserted by the Landsbanki Freezing (Amendment) Order 2008, SI 2008/2766, arts 2, 4, as from 21 October 2008.

4 Freezing prohibitions

(1) The provisions of this article apply in relation to the following funds ("frozen funds")—
    (a) funds owned, held or controlled by Landsbanki; and
    (b) funds relating to Landsbanki and owned, held or controlled by—
        (i) any of the Authorities; or
        (ii) the Government of Iceland.

(2) A person must not make frozen funds available to or for the benefit of a specified person.

(3) A person must not make frozen funds available at the direction or instruction of a specified person.

(4) A person must not deal with frozen funds.

(5) For the purposes of this article, making funds available to or for the benefit of a specified person includes—
    (a) allowing it to withdraw from an account;
    (b) honouring a cheque payable to it;
    (c) crediting its account with interest;
    (d) releasing documents of title (such as share certificates) held on its behalf;
    (e) making available the proceeds of realisation of its property; and
    (f) making a payment to or for its benefit.

(6) In this article, "deal with" means—
    (a) use, alter, move, allow access to or transfer;
    (b) deal with in any other way that would result in any change in volume, amount, location, ownership, possession, character or destination; or
    (c) make any other change that would enable use, including portfolio management.

[4328]

NOTES
Commencement: 8 October 2008 (10.10 am).

5 Freezing prohibitions: offences

(1) A person [referred to in article 1(3)] who fails to comply with a prohibition imposed by article 4 commits an offence.

(2) A person who engages in an activity knowing or intending that it will enable or facilitate the commission by another person of an offence under paragraph (1) commits an offence.

(3) It is a defence to the offences in this article for a person to prove that he or she did not know and had no reason to suppose that—
    (a) in relation to the prohibition in article 4(2) the person to whom or for whose benefit frozen funds were made available, or were to be made available;
    (b) in relation to the prohibition in article 4(3), the person at the direction or instruction of whom frozen funds were made available, or were to be made available;

(c)   in relation to the prohibition in article 4(4), the person who owned, held or controlled the frozen funds,

was a specified person.

[4329]

NOTES
Commencement: 8 October 2008 (10.10 am).
Para (1): words in square brackets inserted by the Landsbanki Freezing (Amendment) Order 2008, SI 2008/2766, arts 2, 5, as from 21 October 2008.

6 Licensing

(1)   The Treasury may, by licence, authorise frozen funds to be made available.

(2)   A licence may authorise a person to deal with frozen funds.

(3)   A licence granted under this article disapplies the prohibitions in article 4 in respect of frozen funds made available or dealt with in accordance with the licence.

(4)   A licence may be—
   (a)   of indefinite duration or subject to an expiry date;
   (b)   subject to conditions;
   (c)   granted generally or to a person or persons named or described in the licence;
   (d)   granted in relation to frozen funds generally or to funds of a description specified in the licence.

(5)   A licence may authorise frozen funds to be made available—
   (a)   generally or for purposes specified in the licence;
   (b)   to or for the benefit of persons generally or a person or persons named or described in the licence.

(6)   The Treasury may vary or revoke a licence at any time.

(7)   The Treasury, where they grant, vary or revoke a licence, must—
   (a)   in the case of a licence granted to a particular person, give written notice of the licence, variation or revocation to that person, and
   (b)   in the case of a general licence or a licence granted to a category of persons, take such steps as the Treasury consider appropriate to publicise the licence, variation or revocation.

[4330]

NOTES
Commencement: 8 October 2008 (10.10 am).

7 Licensing procedure

(1)   A person applying for a licence must—
   (a)   apply in writing; and
   (b)   include such documentation and information that may be required for taking the relevant licensing decision.

(2)   The Treasury—
   (a)   are not required to consider an application which is incomplete; but
   (b)   if an application is incomplete, must inform the applicant of the further documentation or information required.

(3)   The Treasury may grant a licence without an application having been made.

(4)   The Treasury may authorise a person to grant licences on their behalf.

(5)   A person who provides information, or produces a document, which he or she knows is false in a material particular with a view to obtaining a licence is guilty of an offence.

(6)   A person who recklessly provides information, or produces a document, which is false in a material particular with a view to obtaining a licence is guilty of an offence.

[4331]

NOTES
Commencement: 8 October 2008 (10.10 am).

8 Information

The Schedule (which contains provisions about information and documents, and their disclosure) has effect.

[4332]

NOTES
Commencement: 8 October 2008 (10.10 am).

9 Penalties

(1) A person guilty of an offence under article 5 is liable—
  (a) on summary conviction, to imprisonment for a term not exceeding 6 months or to a fine not exceeding the statutory maximum or to both;
  (b) on conviction on indictment, to imprisonment for a term not exceeding 2 years or to a fine or to both.

(2) A person guilty of an offence under article 7 or under [the Schedule] is liable on summary conviction to imprisonment for a term not exceeding 6 months or to a fine not exceeding level 5 on the standard scale or to both.

[4333]

NOTES
Commencement: 8 October 2008 (10.10 am).
Para (2): words in square brackets substituted by the Landsbanki Freezing (Amendment) Order 2008, SI 2008/2766, arts 2, 6, as from 21 October 2008.

10 Offences: procedure

(1) Proceedings for an offence under this Order are not to be instituted in England and Wales except by or with the consent of the Treasury or the Director of Public Prosecutions.

(2) Proceedings for an offence under this Order are not to be instituted in Northern Ireland except by or with the consent of the Treasury or the Director of Public Prosecutions for Northern Ireland.

(3) Despite anything in section 127(1) of the Magistrates' Courts Act 1980(information to be laid within 6 months of offence) an information relating to an offence under this Order which is triable by a magistrates' court in England and Wales may be so tried if it is laid at any time in the period of one year starting with the date of the commission of the offence.

(4) In Scotland summary proceedings for an offence under this Order may be commenced at any time in the period of one year starting with the date of the commission of the offence.

(5) In its application to an offence under this Order Article 19(1)(a) of the Magistrates' Courts (Northern Ireland) Order 1981 (time limit within which complaint charging offence must be made) is to have effect as if the reference to six months were a reference to twelve months.

[4334]

NOTES
Commencement: 8 October 2008 (10.10 am).

11 Offences by bodies corporate etc

(1) If an offence under this Order—
  (a) is committed by a body corporate, and
  (b) is proved to have been committed with the consent or connivance of an officer, or to be attributable to any neglect on his or her part,
he or she as well as the body corporate is guilty of the offence and liable to be proceeded against and punished accordingly.

(2) For the purpose of paragraph (1) these are officers of a body corporate—
  (a) a director, manager, secretary or other similar officer of the body;
  (b) any person purporting to act in any such capacity;
  (c) in the case of a Scottish partnership, a partner.

(3) If the affairs of a body corporate are managed by its members, paragraph (1) applies in relation to the acts and defaults of a member in connection with his or her functions of management as if he or she were an officer of the body.

[4335]

NOTES
Commencement: 8 October 2008 (10.10 am).

12 Notices

(1) This article has effect in relation to any notice to be given to a person by the Treasury under article 6.

(2) Any such notice may be given—

(a)   by posting it to his or her last known address; or

(b)   where the person is a body corporate, by posting it to the registered or principal office of the body corporate.

(3)   Where the Treasury do not have an address for the person, they must make arrangements for the notice to be given to him or her at the first available opportunity.

[4336]–[4337]

NOTES

Commencement: 8 October 2008 (10.10 am).

13   *(Revoked by the Landsbanki Freezing (Amendment) Order 2008, SI 2008/2766, arts 2, 7, as from 21 October 2008.)*

SCHEDULE

Article 8

1.—(1)   The Treasury may, in writing, request a person to provide information or produce documentation to them which they may reasonably need for the purpose of ascertaining whether an offence has been committed under this Order.

(2)   The request may be made by the Treasury or by a person authorised by the Treasury.

(3)   Any person to whom a request is made under sub-paragraph (1) must comply with it within 14 days and in such manner as may be specified in the request.

2.   A relevant institution must disclose [to the Treasury] information as soon as practicable if the conditions in paragraph 16 are satisfied.

3.—[(1)]   The conditions are that—

(a)   the relevant institution knows or suspects, or has grounds for knowing or suspecting, that a specified person—

(i)   is a customer or has been a customer of the institution at any time since this Order came into force, or

(ii)   is a person with whom it has dealings in the course of its business or has had such dealings at any time since this Order came into force.

(b)   the information—

(i)   on which the knowledge or suspicion of the [relevant institution] required to disclose is based, or

(ii)   which gives grounds for the knowledge or suspicion,

came to the [relevant institution] in the course of a business in the regulated sector.

(2)   For the purposes of this paragraph, Schedule 3A to the Terrorism Act 2000 is to have effect for the purpose of determining what is a business in the regulated sector.

4.   Disclosure of information in accordance with this Schedule is not to be taken to breach any restriction on the disclosure of information (however imposed).

5.—(1)   This Schedule does not require any person to provide information or produce documentation which is privileged.

(2)   Information and documentation is privileged if the person asked to provide or produce it would be entitled to refuse to do so on grounds of legal professional privilege in proceedings in the High Court or (in Scotland) on grounds of confidentiality of communications in proceedings in the Court of Session.

(3)   But information or documentation held with the intention of furthering a criminal purpose is not privileged.

6.—   … A person who—

(a)   fails without reasonable excuse to provide information, or to produce a document, in response to a requirement in or under this Schedule;

(b)   provides information, or produces a document, which he or she knows is false in a material particular in [response] to a requirement in or under this Schedule;

(c)   recklessly provides information, or produces a document, which is false in a material particular in response to a requirement in or under this Schedule;

(d)   fails without reasonable excuse to disclose information as required under paragraph 15,

is guilty of an offence.

7.   The Treasury may only disclose information given or documentation produced under this Order (including any copy or extract made of any such document)—

(a)   to a police officer;

(b)   to any person holding or acting in any office under or in the service of—

(i)   the Crown in respect of the Government of the United Kingdom;

(ii)   the Government of the Isle of Man;

(iii)   the States of Guernsey or Alderney or the Chief Pleas of Sark;

(iv)   the State of Jersey;

(v)   any British overseas territory;

(c)   for the purpose of giving assistance or cooperation to the Government of any country;

(d)   to the Financial Services Authority;

(e)   with a view to instituting, or otherwise for the purposes of, any proceedings—

    (i)   in the United Kingdom, for an offence under this Order; or

    (ii)   in any of the Channel Islands, the Isle of Man or any British overseas territory, for an offence under a similar provision in any such jurisdiction; or

(f)   with the consent of a person who, in his or her own right (and not merely in the capacity of servant or agent), is entitled to the information or to the possession of the document, to any third party.

8.   Where a person is convicted of an offence under paragraph 19 of this Schedule the court may make an order requiring that person, within such period as may be specified in the order, to give the requested information or to produce the requested document.

[4338]

NOTES

Commencement: 8 October 2008 (10.10 am).

Para 2: words in square brackets inserted by the Landsbanki Freezing (Amendment) Order 2008, SI 2008/2766, arts 2, 8(a), as from 21 October 2008.

Para 3: number "(1)" in square brackets inserted (to correct a drafting error), and words "relevant institution" in square brackets substituted, by SI 2008/2766, arts 2, 8(b), as from 21 October 2008.

Para 6: figure"(1)" (omitted) revoked (to correct a drafting error), and word "response" in square brackets substituted, by SI 2008/2766, arts 2, 8(c), as from 21 October 2008.

Note: in the original Queen's Printer's copy of this Order, the paragraphs in this Schedule were numbered as paragraphs 14–21. It is assumed that this was a drafting error made because the provision before this Schedule in the original Order was article 13 (now revoked). The Landsbanki Freezing (Amendment) Order 2008, SI 2008/2766 does not renumber the paragraphs of this Schedule, but it does specify that the amendments made to this Schedule are to paragraphs 2, 3 and 6 (and not paragraphs 14, 16 and 19). On this basis, this Schedule has been renumbered so that it begins at paragraph 1 and not paragraph 14 as in the original.

KAUPTHING SINGER & FRIEDLANDER LIMITED TRANSFER OF CERTAIN RIGHTS AND LIABILITIES ORDER 2008

(SI 2008/2674)

NOTES

Made: 8 October 2008 (12.05 pm).

Authority: Banking (Special Provisions) Act 2008, ss 6, 8, 12, 13(2), Sch 2.

Commencement: 8 October 2008 (12.15 pm).

As of 1 February 2009, this Order had not been amended.

ARRANGEMENT OF ARTICLES

PART 1
GENERAL

PART 2
THE FIRST TRANSFER

PART 3
THE SECOND TRANSFER

PART 4
FINANCIAL SERVICES COMPENSATION SCHEME

PART 5
THE ADMINISTRATOR AND TRANSITIONAL PROVISIONS

PART 6
MISCELLANEOUS

PART 1
GENERAL

1   Citation and commencement

(1)   This Order may be cited as the Kaupthing Singer & Friedlander Limited Transfer of Certain Rights and Liabilities Order 2008.

(2)   This Order comes into force at 12.15 pm on 8th October 2008.

[4339]

NOTES

Commencement: 8 October 2008 (12.15 pm).

2   Interpretation

In this Order—

"the 1986 Act" means the Insolvency Act 1986;
"the 2000 Act" means the Financial Services and Markets Act 2000;
"the Act" means the Banking (Special Provisions) Act 2008;
"administrator" means an administrator appointed under paragraph 13, 14 or 22 of Schedule B1 (Administration) to the 1986 Act or on an administration application made to the court (and if more than one administrator is appointed, the reference to "the administrator" is to any administrator so appointed);
"the Authority" means the Financial Services Authority;
"the Bank" means the Governor and Company of the Bank of England;
"Community law" means—

(a)   all the rights, powers, liabilities, obligations and restrictions from time to time created or arising by or under the Community Treaties; and

(b)   all the remedies and procedures from time to time provided for by or under the Community Treaties;

"the COMP Sourcebook" means the Compensation Sourcebook made by the Authority under the 2000 Act;
"Deposits Management (Edge)" means Frontpedal Limited (in the process of changing its name to Deposits Management (Edge) Limited), company registered number 6690432, a company which is for the purposes of the Act wholly owned by the Bank;
"Edge account" has the meaning given in article 3(4);

"the effective time" means the time this Order comes into force;

"eligible claimant" has the meaning given in rule 4.2.1 of the COMP Sourcebook;

"the FEES 6 Chapter" means Chapter 6 (Financial Services Compensation Scheme Funding) of the Fees Manual made by the Authority under the 2000 Act;

"the Financial Services Compensation Scheme" means the scheme established by the Authority under Part 15 of the 2000 Act (The Financial Services Compensation Scheme);

"the first transfer" means the transfer effected by article 3;

"FSCS" means the body corporate established by the Authority under section 212 of the 2000 Act (the Scheme Manager);

"ING" means ING Direct N.V, a limited liability company incorporated in the Netherlands acting through its branch in the United Kingdom with branch reference number BR7357;

"the Insolvency Rules" means the Insolvency Rules 1986;

"Kaupthing" means Kaupthing Singer & Friedlander Limited, company registered number 875947;

"protected deposit" has the meaning given in rule 5.3.1 of the COMP Sourcebook;

"relevant protected deposit" means a protected deposit which relates to a transferred right or liability;

"the second transfer" means the transfer effected by article 8;

"the second transfer time" has the meaning given in article 8(2);

"transferred accounts" means the accounts to which the transferred rights and liabilities relate;

"transferred liabilities" means the liabilities transferred by article 3(1);

"transferred rights" means the rights transferred by article 3(2);

"the transitional period" means the period of 6 months following the effective time.

[4340]

NOTES

Commencement: 8 October 2008 (12.15 pm).

PART 2

THE FIRST TRANSFER

3 The first transfer

(1)   Subject to paragraph (2), by virtue of this Order the liabilities of Kaupthing to holders of Edge accounts in respect of principal and accrued interest are transferred to Deposits Management (Edge).

(2)   From the effective time, Deposits Management (Edge) shall have the same rights in relation to each holder of an Edge account as it would have if Kaupthing's relevant terms of business applied.

(3)   Paragraph (1) does not apply to any liability in respect of any breach of contract or other duty which arose before the effective time.

(4)   In this article, "Edge account" means any of the following accounts held with Kaupthing—
   (a)   the accounts known as Kaupthing Edge Savings Accounts; and
   (b)   the accounts known as Kaupthing Edge fixed term deposit accounts.

(5)   The transfer under paragraph (1) takes place at the time this Order comes into force.

[4341]

NOTES

Commencement: 8 October 2008 (12.15 pm).

---

4 No consent or concurrence required

The first transfer is effective despite the absence of any required consent or concurrence to, or in connection with, the transfer.

[4342]

NOTES

Commencement: 8 October 2008 (12.15 pm).

---

5 Associated liability and interference

(1)   The first transfer takes effect as if—
   (a)   no associated liability existed in respect of any failure to comply with any requirement in respect of the transfer; and
   (b)   there were no associated interference with the transferred rights and liabilities.

(2)   In this article "associated liability" and "associated interference" have the meanings given in paragraph 2(2) of Schedule 2 to the Act.

[4343]

NOTES

Commencement: 8 October 2008 (12.15 pm).

6 Interests, rights and liabilities of third parties relating to transferred rights and liabilities

(1) No interest or right of any third party relating to any of the transferred rights and liabilities shall arise or become exercisable by virtue of or in connection with this Order.

(2) Save as otherwise provided in this Order, no third party shall incur any liability, or be subject to any obligation, relating to any of the transferred rights and liabilities, by virtue of or in connection with this Order.

(3) Without prejudice to the generality of paragraphs (1) and (2)—

    (a) the consequences specified in paragraph (4) shall not arise in respect of any relevant instrument as a result of the first transfer or any other thing done, or matter arising, by virtue of or in connection with the transfer;

    (b) any circumstances which, but for sub-paragraph (a), would give rise to the consequences specified in paragraph (4) shall not be taken to have arisen for the purposes of any relevant instrument.

(4) The consequences are—

    (a) the termination of a relevant instrument or any rights or obligations under it;

    (b) any right to terminate a relevant instrument or any right or obligation under it becoming exercisable;

    (c) any amount becoming due and payable or capable of being declared due and payable;

    (d) any other change in the amount or timing of any payment falling to be made or due to be received by any person;

    (e) any right to withhold, net or set off any payment becoming exercisable;

    (f) any event of default or breach of any right arising;

    (g) any right not to advance any amount becoming exercisable;

    (h) any obligation to provide or transfer any deposit or collateral;

    (i) any right to give or withhold any consent or approval; or

    (j) any other right or remedy (whether or not similar in kind to those referred to in paragraphs (a) to (i)) arising or becoming exercisable.

(5) Without prejudice to paragraph (4), any provision in a relevant instrument that, as a result of the first transfer or any other thing done, or matter arising, by virtue of or in connection with the transfer or this Order, provides for an obligation not to be created, suspends or extinguishes (in whole or in part) such an obligation or renders such an obligation subject to conditions, shall be of no effect.

(6) In this article—

    "relevant instrument" means an instrument which provides for interests or rights of third parties and in relation to which Kaupthing is a party or is bound;

    "third party" shall be construed in accordance with paragraph 2(3) of Schedule 2 to the Act.

[4344]

NOTES

Commencement: 8 October 2008 (12.15 pm).

7 Exemption of Deposits Management (Edge)

Deposits Management (Edge) is an exempt person for the purposes of the 2000 Act in respect of any regulated activity of the kind specified by article 5 of the Financial Services and Markets Act 2000 (Regulated Activities) Order 2001(accepting deposits).

[4345]

NOTES

Commencement: 8 October 2008 (12.15 pm).

PART 3
THE SECOND TRANSFER

8 The second transfer

(1) By virtue of this Order the transferred rights and liabilities are transferred to ING.

(2) The second transfer takes place immediately after the first transfer ("the second transfer time").

(3) From the second transfer time, ING shall—

    (a) be liable to pay depositors any accrued interest on the transferred accounts and any interest accruing at or after that time on those accounts;

(b)   have the same rights in relation to each holder of an Edge account as it would have if Kaupthing's relevant terms of business applied.

(4)   Paragraph (1) does not apply to any liability in respect of any breach of contract or other duty which arose before the second transfer time.

[4346]

NOTES
Commencement: 8 October 2008 (12.15 pm).

9   Provision of information and assistance

(1)   Kaupthing shall provide Deposits Management (Edge) and ING with such information and assistance as is reasonably requested by each of them, respectively—
(a)   in relation to the transferred rights and liabilities;
(b)   for any purpose relating to this Order; or
(c)   for any purpose relating to any other function of Deposits Management (Edge) or ING, as the case may be, which relates to its functions under this Order.

(2)   Kaupthing shall provide the Treasury with such information and assistance as is requested by the Treasury for any purposes relating to this Order.

[4347]

NOTES
Commencement: 8 October 2008 (12.15 pm).

10   No consent or concurrence required

The second transfer is effective despite the absence of any required consent or concurrence to, or in connection with, the transfer.

[4348]

NOTES
Commencement: 8 October 2008 (12.15 pm).

11   Associated liability and interference

(1)   The second transfer takes effect as if—
(a)   no associated liability existed in respect of any failure to comply with any requirement in respect of the transfer; and
(b)   there were no associated interference with the rights and liabilities transferred under the transfer.

(2)   In this article "associated liability" and "associated interference" have the meanings given in paragraph 2(2) of Schedule 2 to the Act.

[4349]

NOTES
Commencement: 8 October 2008 (12.15 pm).

12   Interests, rights and liabilities of third parties relating to transferred rights and liabilities

(1)   No interest or right of any third party relating to any of the rights and liabilities transferred under the second transfer shall arise or become exercisable by virtue of or in connection with this Order.

(2)   Save as otherwise provided in this Order, no third party shall incur any liability, or be subject to any obligation, relating to any of the rights and liabilities transferred under the second transfer, by virtue of or in connection with this Order.

(3)   Without prejudice to the generality of paragraphs (1) and (2)—
(a)   the consequences specified in paragraph (4) shall not arise in respect of any relevant instrument as a result of the second transfer or any other thing done, or matter arising, by virtue of or in connection with the second transfer;
(b)   any circumstances which, but for sub-paragraph (a), would give rise to the consequences specified in paragraph (4) shall not be taken to have arisen for the purposes of any relevant instrument.

(4)   The consequences are—
(a)   the termination of a relevant instrument or any rights or obligations under it;
(b)   any right to terminate a relevant instrument or any right or obligation under it becoming exercisable;
(c)   any amount becoming due and payable or capable of being declared due and payable;

    (d)   any other change in the amount or timing of any payment falling to be made or due to be received by any person;

    (e)   any right to withhold, net or set off any payment becoming exercisable;

    (f)   any event of default or breach of any right arising;

    (g)   any right not to advance any amount becoming exercisable;

    (h)   any obligation to provide or transfer any deposit or collateral;

    (i)   any right to give or withhold any consent or approval; or

    (j)   any other right or remedy (whether or not similar in kind to those referred to in paragraphs (a) to (i)) arising or becoming exercisable.

(5)   Without prejudice to paragraph (4), any provision in a relevant instrument that, as a result of the second transfer or any other thing done, or matter arising, by virtue of or in connection with the second transfer or this Order, provides for an obligation not to be created, suspends or extinguishes (in whole or in part) such an obligation or renders such an obligation subject to conditions, shall be of no effect.

(6)   In this article—

    "relevant instrument" means an instrument which provides for interests or rights of third parties and in relation to which Kaupthing is a party or is bound;

    "third party" shall be construed in accordance with paragraph 2(3) of Schedule 2 to the Act.

[4350]

NOTES

Commencement: 8 October 2008 (12.15 pm).

PART 4
FINANCIAL SERVICES COMPENSATION SCHEME

13 Application of Part 3

This Part applies where, before the effective time, Kaupthing is in default for the purposes of rule 6.3.1 of the COMP Sourcebook.

[4351]

NOTES

Commencement: 8 October 2008 (12.15 pm).

14 Sums to be paid to ING following the second transfer

(1)   The following liabilities arise at the second transfer time—

    (a)   the FSCS is liable to pay (as soon as practicable) to ING an amount equal to the amount that eligible claimants would, immediately before the effective time, have been entitled to claim from the FSCS in respect of claims against Kaupthing in relation to relevant protected deposits; and

    (b)   the Treasury are liable to pay (as soon as practicable) to ING an amount equal to the aggregate amount of the liabilities transferred to ING under the second transfer less the amount specified in sub-paragraph (a) and less £5,000,000,

and the Treasury shall subsequently make the necessary adjustment such that Kaupthing obtains the benefit (net of all costs and liabilities incurred by Deposits Management (Edge)) in connection with the first or second transfer or its obligations under this Order of the reduction of £5,000,000 referred to in sub-paragraph (b).

(2)   For the purposes of paragraph (1)(a), if the quantification date for a claim would have been a date other than the date on which Kaupthing was determined to be in default for the purposes of section 6.3 of the COMP Sourcebook, the amount that an eligible claimant would have been entitled to claim from the FSCS is the lesser of—

    (a)   the amount which the FSCS quantifies as being the value of that claim as at immediately before the effective time; and

    (b)   the amount which would have been payable at the quantification date, if different, for that claim.

(3)   In paragraph (2), "quantification date" has the meaning given in rule 12.3.1 of the COMP Sourcebook.

(4)   As soon as practicable after the second transfer time—

    (a)   Kaupthing shall estimate the aggregate amount of the transferred liabilities;

    (b)   the FSCS shall pay to ING the amount it is liable to pay under paragraph (1)(a) as estimated by the Authority; and

    (c)   the Treasury shall pay to ING an amount equal to the amount estimated by Kaupthing in accordance with sub-paragraph (a) less the amount estimated by the Authority in accordance with sub-paragraph (b) and less £5,000,000.

(5)　From time to time—

    (a)　the FSCS may revise the estimate of its liability under paragraph (1)(a); and

    (b)　Kaupthing may revise the estimate of the aggregate amount of the transferred liabilities.

(6)　In consequence of paragraph (5), the FSCS, the Treasury and ING shall make such corresponding payments to each other as are necessary to ensure that the FSCS and the Treasury have each paid to ING the amount required (and no more than the required amount) to meet their liability under paragraph (1).

(7)　If at any time after the effective time Kaupthing is placed into administration, the references to Kaupthing in paragraphs (4) and (5) are to be treated as references to the administrator.

(8)　The liability referred to in paragraph (1)(a) shall be assessed by the FSCS and, in doing so, the FSCS may calculate, by any methodology or approach it considers appropriate, the total amounts of compensation that would have been paid to all eligible claimants if (and to the extent that) it considers that the costs of ascertaining the entitlement to and the amount of compensation by reference to each eligible claimant would exceed or be disproportionate to the benefit of doing so.

[4352]

NOTES

Commencement: 8 October 2008 (12.15 pm).

15　Payment to ING to constitute payment of compensation for the purposes of the Financial Services Compensation Scheme

For the purposes of Part 15 of the 2000 Act (the financial services compensation scheme), the COMP Sourcebook and the FEES 6 Chapter (including, without limitation, the power of the FSCS to impose levies)—

    (a)　all payments by the FSCS to ING under article 14 shall constitute the payment of compensation to each eligible claimant under the Financial Services Compensation Scheme in accordance with their respective entitlements in respect of claims against Kaupthing for relevant protected deposits;

    (b)　in relation to a relevant protected deposit, each eligible claimant—

        (i)　is deemed to have made an application for compensation for the purposes of rule 3.2.1(1) of the COMP Sourcebook; and

        (ii)　is deemed to have accepted an offer of compensation made by the FSCS and to have received payment of such compensation for the purposes of rule 11.2.1 of the COMP Sourcebook,

and, accordingly, an eligible claimant has no right to claim, and the FSCS has no obligation to pay, for a relevant protected deposit any further compensation under the Financial Services Compensation Scheme in respect of the default of Kaupthing determined by the Authority under section 6.3 of the COMP Sourcebook.

[4353]

NOTES

Commencement: 8 October 2008 (12.15 pm).

16　Liability of Kaupthing to the FSCS and the Treasury

(1)　Kaupthing is liable to the FSCS in respect of an amount equal to the amount which would have been provable in the administration of Kaupthing in respect of the transferred liabilities had this Order not been made and had Kaupthing been placed in administration immediately before the effective time.

(2)　The FSCS shall pursue recoveries from Kaupthing in respect of the liability under paragraph (1) to the extent reasonably practicable.

(3)　Subject to paragraph (4), if an eligible claimant had, in relation to a relevant protected deposit, a liability to Kaupthing which would have been capable of being set-off against a liability of Kaupthing to that claimant in an administration or liquidation of Kaupthing (if that liability had not been transferred), the amount which the FSCS is entitled to recover in the administration or liquidation shall be taken to be the sum of—

    (a)　the amount of the reduction in the depositor's liability to Kaupthing as a result of the application of the set-off; and

    (b)　the amount which would have been recovered in respect of the balance of the claim (if any) provable in the administration or liquidation of Kaupthing.

(4)　Paragraph (3) applies only to the extent that its application does not have the effect that the other creditors of Kaupthing are in a worse position than they would have been had the set-off been applied.

(5)   The FSCS shall determine the proportion of any amount which it receives or recovers from Kaupthing which is properly attributable to each type of liability described below and shall promptly, on receipt, account for that receipt or recovery as follows—

 (a)   in full to the Treasury, to the extent that—
  (i)   the receipt is attributable to a transferred liability; and
  (ii)   the person to whom such a transferred liability is owed would not have been entitled to make a claim for compensation from the FSCS immediately before the effective time;
 (b)   by reference to the relevant proportion, to the extent that—
  (i)   the receipt is attributable to a transferred liability;
  (ii)   the person to whom such a transferred liability is an eligible claimant; and
  (iii)   the amount of such liability exceeds the maximum compensation that the eligible claimant would have been entitled to claim from the FSCS immediately before the effective time;

and where the receipt is attributable to a transferred liability owed to an eligible claimant in relation to a relevant qualifying deposit and the amount of such liability is equal to or less than the maximum compensation that the eligible claimant would have been entitled to claim from the FSCS immediately before the effective time that amount shall be for the account of the FSCS.

(6)   In paragraph (5), the "relevant proportion" is the proportion of the total liabilities which arise under article 14(1) for which the Treasury are liable.

(7)   If Kaupthing is in administration, the liability incurred under paragraph (1) shall not be treated as an expense of the administration under paragraph 99(3) of Schedule B1 of the 1986 Act or rule 2.67 of the Insolvency Rules.

(8)   Nothing in this Part shall have the effect that the FSCS recovers less than it would have recovered if this Order had not been made.

[4354]

NOTES
Commencement: 8 October 2008 (12.15 pm).

17   FSCS's power to require information

(1)   The FSCS may, by notice in writing given to ING, require it—
 (a)   to provide specified information or information of a specified description; or
 (b)   to produce specified documents or documents of a specified description.

(2)   Paragraph (1) only applies to information and documents the provision or production of which the FSCS considers to be necessary (or likely to be necessary) for the exercise of its functions under or by virtue of this Order.

(3)   Subsections (2), (4), (5) and (7) of section 219 of the 2000 Act (scheme manager's power to require information) apply to a requirement imposed under paragraph (1) as if it were a requirement imposed under that section.

[4355]

NOTES
Commencement: 8 October 2008 (12.15 pm).

18   Statutory immunity

For the purposes of section 222 of the 2000 Act (statutory immunity) the scheme manager's functions shall include any acts or omissions carried out by the FSCS pursuant to or in connection with this Order.

[4356]

NOTES
Commencement: 8 October 2008 (12.15 pm).

PART 5
THE ADMINISTRATOR AND TRANSITIONAL PROVISIONS

19   Application of this Part

This Part applies if Kaupthing is placed into administration after the effective time.

[4357]

NOTES
Commencement: 8 October 2008 (12.15 pm).

20 The administration

The relevant provisions of the 1986 Act and the Insolvency Rules shall apply to the administration of Kaupthing subject to the modifications set out in this Part.

[4358]

NOTES
Commencement: 8 October 2008 (12.15 pm).

21 Objectives etc of the administrator

(1) This article only applies during the transitional period.

(2) The administrator must perform his or her functions with the objectives ("the overriding objectives") of—

    (a) ensuring that Kaupthing provides, and managing the affairs, business and property of Kaupthing to enable it to provide, the services and facilities reasonably required by ING to discharge its obligations in respect of the rights and liabilities under the second transfer; and

    (b) ensuring that Kaupthing performs the other obligations imposed on it by or under this Order.

(3) The administrator shall only perform his or her functions with the objective determined in accordance with paragraph 3 of Schedule B1 to the 1986 Act to the extent that to do so is not inconsistent with and does not interfere with the achievement of the overriding objectives.

(4) Paragraph 3(2) of Schedule B1 to the 1986 Act only applies to the performance of the functions of the administrator to the extent that it is not inconsistent with and does not interfere with the achievement of the overriding objectives.

(5) The Treasury may, by notice in writing, give a direction to the administrator specifying that an act (or omission) is required for the overriding objectives.

(6) The Treasury may also, by notice in writing, give a direction to the administrator requiring him or her to act (or not act) if the Treasury consider that it is necessary to give such a direction for the purposes of—

    (a) protecting or enhancing the stability of the financial systems of the United Kingdom;

    (b) protecting or enhancing public confidence in the stability of the banking system of the United Kingdom; or

    (c) protecting depositors.

(7) The Treasury may also, by notice in writing, give a direction to the administrator that he or she need not perform his or her functions in accordance with the overriding objectives, either in relation to a particular matter or generally.

(8) The administrator must comply with any directions given under paragraph (5), (6) or (7).

(9) The services and facilities to which paragraph (2)(a) applies include (but are not limited to) the services and facilities specified in the Schedule.

(10) The administrator shall not be required to include any proposals for achieving the overriding objectives in any statement he or she makes under paragraph 49 (administrator's proposals) or paragraph 54 (revision of administrator's proposals) of Schedule B1 to the 1986 Act or to obtain approval of such proposals at any creditors' meeting or from the court.

(11) The administrator shall not enter into a transaction or a series of transactions (whether related or not) to sell, lease, transfer or otherwise dispose of any property or right of Kaupthing having in aggregate a value of more than £50 million at any time unless—

    (a) the court orders otherwise;

    (b) the Treasury gives its consent to the transaction; or

    (c) the sale, lease, transfer or disposal has been specifically approved at a meeting of creditors summoned under paragraph 51(1), 54(2) or 62 of Schedule B1 to the 1986 Act or by a creditors' committee constituted in accordance with rule 2.50 of the Insolvency Rules and the Treasury has consented to the sale, lease, transfer or disposal.

(12) In this article, "court" means—

    (a) in England and Wales, the High Court;

    (b) in Scotland, the Court of Session;

    (c) in Northern Ireland, the High Court.

[4359]

NOTES
Commencement: 8 October 2008 (12.15 pm).

22 Insolvency Act and Insolvency Rules etc

Nothing in the 1986 Act, the Insolvency Rules or any other enactment or rule of law shall operate to invalidate or prejudice any act or omission done under or pursuant to this Order or give rise to a claim against or impose any liability on Kaupthing or the administrator for any act or omission so done.

[4360]

NOTES
Commencement: 8 October 2008 (12.15 pm).

23 Services and facilities

The agreement dated 8th October 2008 between the Treasury and ING relating to the provision of transitional services by Kaupthing to ING shall bind Kaupthing as if it were a party.

[4361]

NOTES
Commencement: 8 October 2008 (12.15 pm).

24 Use of the Kaupthing brand

Kaupthing shall grant to ING a non-exclusive royalty-free licence to use the Kaupthing brand and the Edge brand and any relevant brands and sub-brands of Kaupthing during the transitional period for the purposes of ING carrying on its activities in relation to the rights and liabilities transferred under the second transfer.

[4362]

NOTES
Commencement: 8 October 2008 (12.15 pm).

25 Compensation payable to Kaupthing

(1) ING shall reimburse Kaupthing for the costs and expenses (including fees) properly incurred by the administrator during the transitional period in fulfilling his or her obligations under article 21.

(2) Paragraph (1) does not apply to any cost or expense which would have been incurred in the administration if this Order had not been made.

[4363]

NOTES
Commencement: 8 October 2008 (12.15 pm).

26 Continuity

(1) During the transitional period, any person wishing to terminate or modify (or treat as terminated or modified) any contract or agreement with Kaupthing for services and facilities or any right or obligation under such a contract or agreement must give not less than 14 days' prior written notice to the administrator and to ING.

(2) During the transitional period, any person who provides to Kaupthing, pursuant to any contract or agreement, services or facilities which are reasonably required by Kaupthing to perform its duties under or pursuant to this Order or the agreement dated 8th October 2008 between the Treasury and ING relating to the provision of transitional services by Kaupthing to ING shall, whether or not required pursuant to such contract or agreement, provide such services to Kaupthing for the benefit of ING or, at Kaupthing's request, directly to ING.

(3) Except with the consent of the Treasury or the permission of the court, during the transitional period—

    (a) no person is entitled—

        (i) to terminate or modify any contract or agreement with Kaupthing for services and facilities, or any right or obligation under such a contract or agreement, where the contract or agreement or right or obligation relates to services or facilities which are reasonably required by—

            (aa) Kaupthing to perform its duties under or pursuant to this Order;

            (bb) the administrator to perform his or her duties under or pursuant to this Order; or

            (cc) ING to carry on its functions in relation to the transferred rights and liabilities, or

        (ii) to treat such a contract, agreement, right or obligation as terminated or modified, by virtue of, or in connection with, the first transfer or the second transfer, the requirement to provide services or facilities to or for the benefit of ING under paragraph (2) or the commencement of the administration in relation to Kaupthing; and

(b)   any counterparty to such a contract or agreement must perform his or her obligations in accordance with that contract or agreement.

(4)   The services and facilities to which paragraphs (1), (2) and (3) apply include (but are not limited to) the services and facilities specified in the Schedule.

(5)   Any purported termination or modification of any contract, agreement, right or obligation in contravention of paragraph (1), (2) or (3), and any action taken in consequence of any such purported termination or modification, shall have no effect.

(6)   Paragraph (2) does not apply where—

(a)   Kaupthing, ING or the administrator, as the case may be, has failed to perform its payment obligations under the relevant contract or agreement and such non-payment is not remedied within 14 days of that person becoming aware of the non-performance; or

(b)   Kaupthing, ING or the administrator, as the case may be, fails to notify the counterparty to the relevant contract or agreement within 14 days of its becoming aware of the request for consent to such termination, modification or non-performance of an obligation, that such consent has been withheld.

(7)   Without prejudice to the generality of paragraph (3), the first transfer or the second transfer shall not have the effect of terminating or otherwise changing the terms of Kaupthing's membership (if any) of any payment system, including, in particular, BACS, CHAPS and the LINK payments systems.

(8)   "Court" has the meaning given by article 21(12).

(9)   This article is subject to any requirement of Community law.

[4364]

NOTES
Commencement: 8 October 2008 (12.15 pm).

27   Moratorium on payment to related companies

(1)   Kaupthing shall not make any payment, dispose of any property or modify or release any right or liability to or for the benefit of a related party without the prior consent of the Treasury, and any such purported payment, disposal, modification or release shall be void.

(2)   No related party shall exercise any right of set-off or combination of accounts in respect of any debt owing by Kaupthing without the consent of the Treasury, and any such purported exercise shall be void.

(3)   In this article, "related party" means any member of the same group as Kaupthing that is not a subsidiary undertaking of Kaupthing.

(4)   In paragraph (1), if Kaupthing is in administration, the reference to Kaupthing is to be treated as a reference to the administrator.

(5)   In paragraph (3), "group" has the meaning given by section 421 of the 2000 Act.

[4365]

NOTES
Commencement: 8 October 2008 (12.15 pm).

PART 6
MISCELLANEOUS

28   Construction of documents etc

As from the effective time and save as otherwise provided in this Order—

(a)   agreements made or other things done by or in relation to Kaupthing shall be treated, so far as may be necessary for the purposes of or in connection with the first transfer or the second transfer (but not otherwise) as made or done by or in relation to Deposits Management (Edge) or ING or both, as the case may be and as the context requires;

(b)   references to Kaupthing or to any officer or employee of Kaupthing in instruments or documents relating to the transferred rights and liabilities and rights and liabilities transferred under the second transfer, shall have effect as if they were references to Deposits Management (Edge) or ING or both, or to any officer or employee of Deposits Management (Edge) or ING, as the case may be and as the context requires.

[4366]

PART III
STATUTORY INSTRUMENTS

29 Modification to Authority's rule-making power

(1)   Subsections (1) and (1A) of section 138 of the 2000 Act (general rule-making power) have effect as if modified by inserting after "protecting the interests of consumers"—

"or for the purposes of, to facilitate or in consequence of, a transfer under section 6 or section 8 of the Banking (Special Provisions) Act 2008".

(2)   Section 148(2) of the 2000 Act (modification or waiver of rules) shall also apply in relation to Kaupthing—

(a)   in the absence of an application by a person subject to rules made by the Authority; and

(b)   without any requirement for the consent of such a person.

(3)   Section 148(4) of the 2000 Act shall not prevent the Authority from modifying or waiving rules in relation to Kaupthing under section 148 of that Act provided that the Authority is satisfied that the modification or waiver is necessary for the purposes of, to facilitate or in consequence of the first transfer or the second transfer.

[4367]

30 Modification to Authority's duty to consult on rule changes

(1)   Section 155(7) of the 2000 Act (consultation) has effect as if modified by adding at the end—

"or if it is making rules for the purposes of, or to facilitate or in consequence of, a transfer under section 6 or section 8 of the Banking (Special Provisions) Act 2008."

(2)   Section 157 of the 2000 Act (guidance) has effect as if modified by adding after subsection (3)—

"(3A)   Section 155(7) applies to proposed guidance as it applies to proposed rules with the modification made by article 30 of the Kaupthing Singer & Friedlander Limited Transfer of Certain Rights and Liabilities Order 2008.".

[4368]

31 Freedom of information

For the purposes of section 3(2)(b) of the Freedom of Information Act 2000 (public authorities), Deposits Management (Edge) shall be deemed not to hold information on behalf of the Bank.

[4369]

32 Proceedings against directors

(1)   No director of—

(a)   Kaupthing; or

(b)   Deposits Management (Edge),

shall be liable in connection with the first transfer or the second transfer or any other provisions of this Order and accordingly no proceedings may be brought (or, in Scotland, raised) against any such director in respect of such matters.

(2)   The Treasury may in writing—

(a)   waive the effect of paragraph (1), and

(b)   give consent to bring (or, in Scotland, raise) such proceedings against such directors.

(3)   Where paragraph (1) applies, section 232 of the Companies Act 2006 (provisions protecting directors from liability) shall not apply to a relevant undertaking.

(4)   In this article—

"director" means a person who was a director immediately before the effective time, whether or not he has ceased to be a director at the time when proceedings in respect of that liability commenced;

"proceedings" includes proceedings under Part 11 of the Companies Act 2006 (derivative claims and proceedings by members).

[4370]

NOTES
Commencement: 8 October 2008 (12.15 pm).

33 Immunity of Bank

(1)   The Bank has immunity in relation to action or inaction in relation to or pursuant to this Order.

(2)   In this article—
   (a)   a reference to the Bank is a reference to the Bank and anyone who acts or purports to act as a director, officer, servant or agent of the Bank;
   (b)   "immunity" means immunity from liability in damages.

(3)   The immunity does not extend to action taken—
   (a)   in bad faith, or
   (b)   in contravention of section 6(1) of the Human Rights Act 1998.

[4371]

NOTES
Commencement: 8 October 2008 (12.15 pm).

34 Transfer of data

Any transfer of data under this Order is not to be taken to breach any restriction on disclosure of information, however imposed.

[4372]

NOTES
Commencement: 8 October 2008 (12.15 pm).

SCHEDULE
SERVICES AND FACILITIES

Article 21

1.   Website hosting services or facilities.
2.   Information technology services or facilities.
3.   Back office processing services or facilities.
4.   Call centre services or facilities.
5.   Payment and clearing services or facilities.

[4373]

NOTES
Commencement: 8 October 2008 (12.15 pm).

TAKEOVER CODE (CONCERT PARTIES) REGULATIONS 2008

(SI 2008/3073)

NOTES
Made: 28 November 2008 (10.00 am).
Authority: European Communities Act 1972, s 2(2).
Commencement: 28 November 2008 (12.00 pm).

As of 1 February 2009, these Regulations had not been amended.

1   Citation, commencement and interpretation

(1)   These Regulations may be cited as the Takeover Code (Concert Parties) Regulations 2008 and come into force 12.00 pm on 28th November 2008.

(2)   In these Regulations—
   (a)   "the Takeover Code" means the rules made by the Panel on Takeovers and Mergers under section 943 of the Companies Act 2006 otherwise known as the City Code on Takeovers and Mergers;

(b) "shares" means equity securities within the meaning of section 560 of the Companies Act 2006 and other transferable securities carrying voting rights;

(c) "recapitalisation scheme" means the facility announced by the Chancellor of the Exchequer on 8 October 2008 to make available capital to certain financial institutions in order to strengthen their resources in the interests of financial stability;

(d) "UKFI" means UK Financial Investments Limited, company registered number 06720891.

[4374]

NOTES
Commencement: 28 November 2008 (12.00 pm).

2 Application of Rule 9 of the Takeover Code

(1) For the purposes of Rule 9 of the Takeover Code the following persons are not to be regarded as acting in concert with each other or the Treasury or the Secretary of State or UKFI by virtue of the Treasury holding (through a nominee or otherwise) shares in each of those persons—

(a) a person some or all of the shares in which are held by a nominee of the Treasury or a company wholly owned by the Treasury as a result of the exercise of powers under the Banking (Special Provisions) Act 2008;

(b) a person participating in the recapitalisation scheme.

(2) For the purposes of Rule 9 of the Takeover Code, the Treasury, the Secretary of State and UKFI are not to be regarded as acting in concert with each other by virtue of the Treasury's relationship with, and the Secretary of State's and UKFI's functions in relation to, a person listed in paragraph (1)(a) or (b).

[4375]

NOTES
Commencement: 28 November 2008 (12.00 pm).

BRADFORD & BINGLEY PLC COMPENSATION SCHEME ORDER 2008

(SI 2008/3249)

NOTES
Made: 18 December 2008.
Authority: Banking (Special Provisions) Act 2008, ss 5, 9, 12, 13(2).
Commencement: 19 December 2008.

As of 1 February 2009, this Order had not been amended.

ARRANGEMENT OF ARTICLES

1—(1) This Order may be cited as the Bradford & Bingley plc Compensation Scheme Order 2008.

(2) This Order comes into force on the day after the day on which it is made.

[4376]

NOTES
Commencement: 19 December 2008.

2 The Bradford & Bingley plc Compensation Scheme set out in the Schedule to this Order shall have effect.

[4377]

NOTES
Commencement: 19 December 2008.

SCHEDULE
THE BRADFORD & BINGLEY PLC COMPENSATION SCHEME
Article 2

PART 1
GENERAL PROVISIONS

1 Citation

This Scheme may be cited as the Bradford & Bingley plc Compensation Scheme.

2 Interpretation

In this Scheme—
"the Act" means the Banking (Special Provisions) Act 2008;
"assessment notice" means a notice issued under paragraph 10;
"Bradford & Bingley" means Bradford & Bingley plc, company registered number 3938288;
"revised assessment notice" means a notice issued under paragraph 11;
"shares in Bradford & Bingley" means the ordinary shares issued by Bradford & Bingley;
"the Transfer Order" means the Bradford & Bingley plc Transfer of Securities and Property etc
Order 2008;
"the transfer time" means 8.00 a.m. on 29th September 2008;
"the Tribunal" means the Financial Services and Markets Tribunal;
"valuer" means the independent valuer appointed by the Treasury in accordance with
paragraph 6.

[4378]

NOTES
Commencement: 19 December 2008.

PART 2
DETERMINATION OF AMOUNT OF COMPENSATION

3 Transfer of Bradford & Bingley shares

(1)   The amount of any compensation payable by the Treasury to persons who held shares in
Bradford & Bingley immediately before they were transferred by the Transfer Order shall be
determined in accordance with this paragraph.

(2)   The amount of compensation payable to a person shall be an amount equal to the value
immediately before the transfer time of all shares in Bradford & Bingley held immediately before
the transfer time by that person.

(3)   For the purposes of this Scheme, the holders of shares in Bradford & Bingley, and the class
and number of shares held by them, shall be identified by reference to—
  (a)   the Operator register of members of Bradford & Bingley; and
  (b)   the issuer register of members of Bradford & Bingley,
following the reconciliation required by article 4(4) of the Transfer Order.

(4)   In sub-paragraph (3) "issuer register of members" and "Operator register of members" have
the meanings given in the Uncertificated Securities Regulations 2001.

4 Extinguishment of subscription rights

(1)   The amount of any compensation payable by the Treasury to persons whose subscription
rights were extinguished by virtue of article 5 of the Transfer Order shall be determined in
accordance with this paragraph.

(2)   The amount of compensation payable to a person shall be an amount equal to the value
immediately before the transfer time of that person's subscription rights.

(3)   In this paragraph "subscription rights" means any right or other entitlement to receive
shares in Bradford & Bingley (whether by subscription, conversion or otherwise) granted by—
  (a)   a relevant undertaking; or
  (b)   a person not within paragraph (a), where the right or entitlement is enjoyed by reason of
        or in connection with—
    (i)   any individual's office or employment with a relevant undertaking; or
    (ii)   the services provided by any individual to a relevant undertaking.

(4)   In sub-paragraph (3) "relevant undertaking" means Bradford & Bingley or any of its UK subsidiary undertakings that is a body corporate incorporated, or a partnership established, under the law of any part of the United Kingdom.

5   Modification of interests, rights and liabilities in relevant instruments

(1)   Subject to sub-paragraph (4), the amount of any compensation payable by the Treasury to persons whose rights were extinguished by virtue of the provision made in article 6 or 7 of the Transfer Order (referred to in this paragraph as "consequential rights") shall be determined in accordance with this paragraph.

(2)   The amount of compensation payable to a person shall be such compensation as may be just in respect of that person's consequential rights.

(3)   The determination of any compensation in respect of consequential rights shall take into account—
    (a)   any diminution in the value of property; or
    (b)   any increase in the burden of any liability,
which is attributable to the consequences specified in article 7(3) of the Transfer Order not arising.

(4)   Compensation is payable in respect of a person's consequential rights only if such compensation is required to be paid to comply with the Convention rights (within the meaning given by section 1 of the Human Rights Act 1998).

[4379]

NOTES
Commencement: 19 December 2008.

PART 3
INDEPENDENT VALUER

6   Appointment of independent valuer

(1)   The Treasury shall appoint an independent valuer for the purposes of this Scheme.

(2)   The valuer so appointed shall determine the amount of any compensation payable by the Treasury in accordance with Part 2 of this Scheme.

(3)   The valuer is to hold and vacate office in accordance with the terms of his appointment.

(4)   The Treasury may remove the valuer only on the ground of incapacity or serious misbehaviour.

(5)   Before making any appointment under sub-paragraph (1) the Treasury must consult the Institute of Chartered Accountants in England and Wales.

7   Remuneration

The valuer shall be—
    (a)   paid such remuneration; and
    (b)   reimbursed such expenses;
as the Treasury may determine.

8   Appointment of staff

(1)   The valuer may appoint such staff as he or she may determine.

(2)   The valuer shall determine the remuneration and other conditions of service of the persons appointed under this paragraph.

(3)   The valuer may pay such pensions, allowances or gratuities to or in respect of the persons appointed under this paragraph as he or she may determine.

(4)   The references in sub-paragraph (3) to pensions, allowances or gratuities to or in respect of the persons appointed under this paragraph include reference to pensions, allowances or gratuities by way of compensation in respect of any of those persons who suffer loss of employment.

(5)   Any determination under sub-paragraphs (2) to (4) shall require the approval of the Treasury.

[4380]

NOTES
Commencement: 19 December 2008.

PART 4
ASSESSMENT OF COMPENSATION BY VALUER

9   Procedure

(1)   The valuer may make such rules as to the procedure in relation to the assessment of any compensation (including the procedure for the reconsideration of any decisions relating to the assessment of compensation) as he or she considers appropriate.

(2)   Rules made under sub-paragraph (1) may make different provision for different cases or circumstances.

10   Assessment notice

(1)   Where the valuer has assessed the amount of any compensation payable by the Treasury—
   (a)   to any person; or
   (b)   in respect of a class or description of shares or rights,
the valuer shall issue an assessment notice.

(2)   An assessment notice shall contain the following information—
   (a)   the date on which the notice is issued;
   (b)   the amount of any compensation determined by the valuer as being payable; and
   (c)   the reasons for the valuer's decision.

(3)   The valuer shall send a copy of the assessment notice to the Treasury.

11   Reconsideration of assessment notice

(1)   If—
   (a)   the Treasury; or
   (b)   any person who is affected by the determination of the amount of any compensation which is contained in an assessment notice,
are dissatisfied with the assessment notice, the Treasury or any such person may require the valuer to reconsider the determination.

(2)   Where the valuer is required to reconsider a determination in accordance with sub-paragraph (1) he or she shall issue a revised assessment notice.

(3)   A revised assessment notice shall contain the following information—
   (a)   the date on which the notice is issued;
   (b)   either—
      (i)   notification that the valuer has upheld the assessment notice; or
      (ii)   notification that the valuer has varied the assessment notice;
   (c)   the amount of any compensation determined by the valuer as being payable; and
   (d)   the reasons for the valuer's decision.

(4)   The valuer shall send a copy of the revised assessment notice to the Treasury.

12   Right to refer to the Tribunal

If—
   (a)   the Treasury; or
   (b)   any person who is affected by the determination of the amount of any compensation which is contained in the revised assessment notice,
are dissatisfied with the revised assessment notice, the Treasury or any such person may refer the matter to the Tribunal.

13   Payment of compensation

(1)   The Treasury shall pay the amount of any compensation determined by the valuer to be payable—
   (a)   to any person; or
   (b)   in respect of a class or description of shares or rights.

(2)   The Treasury shall not be required to make a payment in accordance with sub-paragraph (1) until—
   (a)   they have received a copy of the assessment notice or revised assessment notice, as the case may be; or
   (b)   if there is a reference to the Tribunal, the matter has been finally disposed of.

[4381]

NOTES
Commencement: 19 December 2008.

PART 5
REFERENCES TO THE TRIBUNAL

14   Application of FSMA 2000

(1)   The provisions of—
(a)   Part 9 (hearing and appeals) of, and Schedule 13 (the Financial Services and Markets Tribunal) to, FSMA 2000; and
(b)   the Financial Services and Markets Tribunal Rules 2001;

shall apply in respect of any reference made under paragraph 12, subject to the modifications set out in this Part.

Modification of FSMA 2000

15.   Part 9 of, and Schedule 13 to, FSMA 2000 are modified as follows.

16.   In section 133 (proceedings: general provisions) and Schedule 13, for "the Authority" in each place it occurs substitute "the independent valuer appointed under paragraph 6 of the Schedule to the Bradford & Bingley plc Compensation Scheme Order 2008".

17.   In section 133—
(i)   in subsection (1)(a) for "the decision notice or supervisory notice in question", substitute " the revised assessment notice issued by the valuer under paragraph 11(2) of the Schedule to the Bradford & Bingley plc Compensation Scheme Order 2008";
(ii)   for subsection (4) substitute—

"(4)   Where the Tribunal is satisfied that the decision as to the amount of compensation shown in the revised assessment notice was not a reasonable decision the Tribunal must remit the matter to the valuer for reconsideration in accordance with such directions (if any) as they consider appropriate.";
(iii)   omit subsections (5) to (9) and (12).

18.   Omit sections 134 to 136.

Modification of Financial Services and Markets Tribunal Rules 2001

19.   The Financial Services and Markets Tribunal Rules 2001 are modified as follows.

20.   In each place where it occurs (other than in rule 2)—
(a)   for "Authority" substitute "respondent";
(b)   for "Authority notice" substitute "revised assessment notice";
(c)   for "statement of case" substitute "response document".

21.   In rule 2 (interpretation)—
(a)   omit the definitions for "the Authority", "Authority notice", "further material", "protected item", "reply" and "statement of case";
(b)   in the definition of "party", for "Authority", in both places where it occurs, substitute "respondent";
(c)   in the definition of "referred action" for "the act (or proposed act) on the part of the Authority" substitute "the revised assessment notice";
(d)   for the definition of "response document" substitute ""response document" means a statement filed by the respondent under rule 5(1);"; and
(e)   in the appropriate place insert—
""respondent" means the independent valuer appointed under paragraph 6 of the Schedule to the Bradford & Bingley plc Compensation Scheme Order 2008;";
"revised assessment notice" means the revised assessment notice issued by the respondent under paragraph 11 of the Schedule to the Bradford & Bingley plc Compensation Scheme Order 2008;".

22.   In rule 4(6) (reference notice) omit ", a direction under rule 10(1)(e) (suspension of Authority's action) or".

23.   In rule 5 (Authority's statement of case)—
(a)   for paragraphs (1) and (2) substitute—

"(1)   The respondent shall file a written statement ("a response document") dealing with any issues arising out of the reference notice that the respondent wishes the Tribunal to consider so that it is received by the Tribunal no later than 28 days after the day on which the respondent received the information sent by the Secretary in accordance with rule 4(9)(b).

(2)   At the same time as it files the response document, the respondent shall send a copy to the applicant.";
(b)   omit paragraphs (3) and (4).

24.   Omit rules 6 (applicant's reply), 7 (secondary disclosure by the Authority), 8 (exceptions to disclosure), 11 (filling of subsequent notices in relation to the referred action), 12(2) (summoning of witnesses), 14(3)(c) (withdrawal of reference and unopposed references), 15 (references by third parties) and 23(4) (application for permission to appeal).

25.   In rule 10 (particular types of directions) omit paragraphs (1)(e), (2)(a), (6) and (8).

26.   After rule 10 (particular types of directions) insert—

"10A   Same issues proceedings

(1)   The President may, of his own motion or on application by a party, direct that a reference is heard as a lead case where—

(a)   two or more references under paragraph 12 of the Schedule to the Bradford & Bingley plc Compensation Scheme Order 2008 have been made, but have not yet been determined by the Tribunal; and

(b)   it appears to the President that those references give rise to common or related issues of fact or law ("same issues proceedings").

(2)   The President may—

(a)   make such further directions as he considers appropriate for determination of the lead case; and

(b)   direct that pending determination of the lead case all other same issues proceedings before the Tribunal shall be stayed.

(3)   All parties in same issue proceedings must be allowed to make representations prior to the President making a direction under paragraph (1) or (2).

(4)   Without prejudice generally to the parties' rights of appeal and to paragraphs (5) to (7), the Tribunal's determination of the same issues in the lead case shall be binding on the parties to each of the same issues proceedings unless the Tribunal or the President directs otherwise.

(5)   Any party to any of the same issues proceedings may apply to the President for a direction that the determination of the same issues in the lead case does not apply to that party's case.

(6)   An application under paragraph (5) must be made not later than 21 days after the date on which that party received notice of the determination of the same issues in the lead case.

(7)   Within 28 days beginning with the date of determination of the same issues in the lead case the President may make further directions in relation to—

(a)   the lead case and each of the same issues proceedings stayed pending the determination of the same issues in the lead case;

(b)   the extent to which the determination of the same issues in the lead case is binding on any subsequent proceedings; and

(c)   any further directions required as a result of an application under paragraph (5), including a direction as to any further hearing required in relation to those proceedings.

(8)   Where a direction has been made for any proceedings to be heard as a lead case and those proceedings are withdrawn or discontinued either before or during the hearing, the President may direct—

(a)   that one of the remaining same issues proceedings be substituted as the lead case; and

(b)   the extent to which any directions made prior to substitution shall be binding in relation to the substituted proceedings.

(9)   The Secretary must send notice of the directions to be made under paragraphs (1) and (2), a copy of the directions made under paragraphs (1), (2), (4), (5), (7) and (8) and the determination of the same issues in the lead case to all the parties to the same issues proceedings.

10B   Joining of parties to proceedings

If it appears to the President or the Chairman, whether on the application of a party or otherwise, that it is desirable that any person other than the respondent be made a party to any proceedings, he may direct that such person be joined as a party in the proceedings and may make such further directions for giving effect to, or in connection with, the direction as he thinks fit.".

27.   In rule 19(3) (procedure at hearings) omit "when taking the referred action".

[4382]

NOTES

Commencement: 19 December 2008.

KAUPTHING SINGER & FRIEDLANDER LIMITED (DETERMINATION OF COMPENSATION) ORDER 2008

(SI 2008/3250)

NOTES
Made: 18 December 2008.
Authority: Banking (Special Provisions) Act 2008, s 7(1)(a).
Commencement: 19 December 2008.

As of 1 February 2009, this Order had not been amended.

1—(1)   This Order may be cited as the Kaupthing Singer & Friedlander Limited (Determination of Compensation) Order 2008.

(2)   This Order comes into force on the day after the day on which it is made.

[4383]

NOTES
Commencement: 19 December 2008.

2—(1)   The amount of any compensation payable by the Treasury to Kaupthing in respect of the rights and liabilities transferred by the Kaupthing Singer & Friedlander Limited Transfer of Certain Rights and Liabilities Order 2008 is determined as nil.

(2)   In paragraph (1) "Kaupthing" means Kaupthing Singer & Friedlander Limited, company registered number 875947.

[4384]

NOTES
Commencement: 19 December 2008.

HERITABLE BANK PLC (DETERMINATION OF COMPENSATION) ORDER 2008

(SI 2008/3251)

NOTES
Made: 18 December 2008.
Authority: Banking (Special Provisions) Act 2008, s 7(1)(a).
Commencement: 19 December 2008.

As of 1 February 2009, this Order had not been amended.

1—(1)   This Order may be cited as the Heritable Bank plc (Determination of Compensation) Order 2008.

(2)   This Order comes into force on the day after the day on which it is made.

[4385]

NOTES
Commencement: 19 December 2008.

2—(1)   The amount of any compensation payable by the Treasury to Heritable in respect of the rights and liabilities transferred by the Heritable Bank plc Transfer of Certain Rights and Liabilities Order 2008 is determined as nil.

(2)   In paragraph (1) "Heritable" means Heritable Bank plc, company registered in Scotland number SC000717.

[4386]

NOTES
Commencement: 19 December 2008.

PAYMENT SERVICES REGULATIONS 2009

(SI 2009/209)

NOTES
Made: 9 February 2009.
Authority: European Communities Act 1972, s 2(2).
Commencement: see reg 1(2).

ARRANGEMENT OF REGULATIONS

PART 1
INTRODUCTORY PROVISIONS

PART 2
REGISTRATION

The register

Authorisation as a payment institution

Registration as a small payment institution

Common provisions

PART 3
AUTHORISED PAYMENT INSTITUTIONS

Exercise of passport rights

PART 4
PROVISIONS APPLICABLE TO AUTHORISED PAYMENT INSTITUTIONS AND SMALL
PAYMENT INSTITUTIONS

PART 7
THE AUTHORITY

The functions of the Authority

Supervision and enforcement

Miscellaneous

PART 8
ACCESS TO PAYMENT SYSTEMS

General

Supervision and enforcement

Miscellaneous

PART 9
GENERAL

Criminal Offences

PART 1

INTRODUCTORY PROVISIONS

1 Citation and commencement

(1)   These Regulations may be cited as the Payment Services Regulations 2009.

(2)   These Regulations come into force—
   (a)   on 2nd March 2009 for the purposes of regulations 25, 80, 92 to 94, 95 in respect of paragraphs 5 and 10 of Schedule 5, 119 and 126 in respect of paragraphs 1 and 6(g) of Schedule 6;
   (b)   on 1st May 2009 for the purposes of—
      (i)   enabling applications for authorisation as a payment institution and the variation of an authorisation to be made under regulation 5 and the Authority to determine such applications in accordance with regulations 6 to 9;
      (ii)   enabling applications for registration as a small payment institution and the variation of a registration to be made under regulation 12 and the Authority to determine such applications in accordance with regulation 13 and regulations 7 to 9 (as applied by regulation 14);
      (iii)   enabling applications for an agent to be included on the register under regulation 29 and the Authority to determine such applications in accordance with that regulation;
      (iv)   enabling the Authority to give directions as to the manner in which an application under regulation 5(1) or (2), 12(1) or (2) or 29(3) is to be made and enabling the Authority to require the applicant to provide further information in accordance with regulation 5(4), 12(4) or 29(3)(a)(iv), as the case may be;
      (v)   enabling the Authority to cancel an authorisation or registration or vary an authorisation or registration on its own initiative in accordance with regulation 10 or 11 (as applied, in the case of a registration, by regulation 14);
      (vi)   requiring a person who has made an application under regulation 5(1) or (2) or 12(1) or (2) to provide information to the Authority in accordance with regulation 16 and enabling the Authority to give directions under that regulation;
      (vii)   enabling a person to make a reference to the Tribunal under regulation 9(9), 10(4), 11(5), 24(4) or 29(11);
      (viii)   enabling an applicant for authorisation as a payment institution to give the Authority a notice of intention under regulation 23(1) and the Authority to give directions as to the manner in which such a notice is to be given and to inform the host state competent authority in accordance with regulation 23(2);
      (ix)   enabling the Authority to decide whether to register an EEA branch, or to cancel such a registration, under regulation 24(1);

(x) enabling the Authority to give directions under regulation 82 to a person whose application under regulation 5(1) or 12(1) has been granted before 1st November 2009 in respect of—

    (aa) its provision as from that date of payment services; and

    (bb) its compliance as from that date with requirements imposed by or under Parts 2 to 6 of these Regulations;

(xi) enabling the Authority to give directions under paragraph 7, 11, 12 or 16(3) of Schedule 3 to a person whose application under regulation 5(1) has been granted before 1st November 2009;

(xii) requiring a person whose application under regulation 5(1), 12(1) or 29(3) has been granted before 1st November 2009 to provide information to the Authority in accordance with regulation 32 and enabling the Authority to give directions under that regulation;

(xiii) regulations 95 in respect of paragraphs 2 and 7 to 9 of Schedule 5, 114 to 118, and 121, 124 and 125; and

(c) for all other purposes on 1st November 2009.

[4387]

NOTES

Commencement: these Regulations come into force on 2 March 2009 (for the purposes specified in reg 1(2)(a)), 1 May 2009 (for the purposes specified in reg 1(2)(b)), and 1 November 2009 (otherwise). See above.

2 Interpretation

(1) In these Regulations—

"the 2000 Act" means the Financial Services and Markets Act 2000;

"agent" means a person who acts on behalf of an authorised payment institution or a small payment institution in the provision of payment services;

"authorised payment institution" means—

    (a) a person included by the Authority in the register as an authorised payment institution pursuant to regulation 4(1)(a); or

    (b) a person deemed to have been granted authorisation by the Authority by virtue of regulation 121;

"the Authority" means the Financial Services Authority;

"the banking consolidation directive" means Directive 2006/48/EC of the European Parliament and of the Council of 14th June 2006 relating to the taking up and pursuit of the business of credit institutions;

"branch" means a place of business of an authorised payment institution, a small payment institution, or an EEA authorised payment institution, other than its head office, which forms a legally dependent part of the institution and which carries out directly all or some of the transactions inherent in its business; and, for the purposes of these Regulations, all places of business set up in the same EEA State other than the United Kingdom by an authorised payment institution are to be regarded as a single branch;

"business day" means any day on which the relevant payment service provider is open for business as required for the execution of a payment transaction;

"charity" means a body whose annual income is less than £1 million and is—

    (c) in England and Wales, a charity as defined by section 1(1) of the Charities Act 2006;

    (d) in Scotland, a charity as defined by section 106 of the Charities and Trustee Investment (Scotland) Act 2005;

    (e) in Northern Ireland, a charity as defined by section 1(1) of the Charities Act (Northern Ireland) 2008 or, until that section comes into force, a body which is recognised as a charity for tax purposes by Her Majesty's Revenue and Customs;

"the Commissioners" means the Commissioners for Her Majesty's Revenue and Customs;

"consumer" means an individual who, in contracts for payment services to which these Regulations apply, is acting for purposes other than a trade, business or profession;

"credit institution" has the meaning given in Article 4(1)(a) of the banking consolidation directive;

"direct debit" means a payment service for debiting the payer's payment account where a payment transaction is initiated by the payee on the basis of consent given by the payer to the payee, to the payee's payment service provider or to the payer's own payment service provider;

"durable medium" means any instrument which enables the payment service user to store information addressed personally to them in a way accessible for future reference for a period of time adequate for the purposes of the information and which allows the unchanged reproduction of the information stored;

"the EEA" means the European Economic Area;

"EEA agent" means an agent through which an authorised payment institution, in the exercise of its passport rights, provides payment services in an EEA State other than the United Kingdom;

"EEA authorised payment institution" means a person authorised in an EEA State other than the United Kingdom to provide payment services in accordance with the payment services directive;

"EEA branch" means a branch established by an authorised payment institution, in the exercise of its passport rights, to carry out payment services in an EEA State other than the United Kingdom;

"the electronic money directive" means Directive 2000/46/EC of the European Parliament and of the Council of 18th September 2000 on the taking up, pursuit and prudential supervision of the business of electronic money institutions;

"electronic money institution" has the meaning given in Article 1(3)(a) of the electronic money directive;

"framework contract" means a contract for payment services which governs the future execution of individual and successive payment transactions and which may contain the obligation and conditions for setting up a payment account;

"funds" means banknotes and coins, scriptural money, and electronic money as defined in Article 1(3)(b) of the electronic money directive;

"group" means a group of undertakings which consists of a parent undertaking, its subsidiary undertakings and the entities in which the parent undertaking or its subsidiary undertakings have a holding, as well as undertakings linked to each other by a relationship referred to in Article 12(1) of the Seventh Council Directive 83/349/EEC of 13th June 1983 based on Article 54(3)(g) of the Treaty on consolidated accounts;

"home state competent authority" means the competent authority designated in accordance with Article 20 of the payment services directive as being responsible for the authorisation and prudential supervision of an EEA authorised payment institution which is exercising (or intends to exercise) its passport rights in the United Kingdom;

"host state competent authority" means the competent authority designated in accordance with Article 20 of the payment services directive in an EEA State in which an authorised payment institution exercises (or intends to exercise) its passport rights;

"means of distance communication" means any means which, without the simultaneous physical presence of the payment service provider and the payment service user, may be used for the conclusion of a contract for payment services between those parties;

"micro-enterprise" means an enterprise which, at the time at which the contract for payment services is entered into, is an enterprise as defined in Article 1 and Article 2(1) and (3) of the Annex to Recommendation 2003/361/EC;

"the money laundering directive" means Directive 2005/60/EC of the European Parliament and of the Council of 26th October 2005 on the prevention of the use of the financial system for the purpose of money laundering and terrorist financing;

"money remittance" means a service for the transmission of money (or any representation of monetary value), without any payment accounts being created in the name of the payer or the payee, where—

    (a)   funds are received from a payer for the sole purpose of transferring a corresponding amount to a payee or to another payment service provider acting on behalf of the payee; or

    (b)   funds are received on behalf of, and made available to, the payee;

"notice" means a notice in writing;

"the OFT" means the Office of Fair Trading;

"parent undertaking" has the same meaning as in the Companies Acts (see section 1162 of, and Schedule 7 to, the Companies Act 2006);

"passport right" (except for the purposes of regulation 26(1)) means the entitlement of a person to establish a branch or provide services in an EEA State other than that in which they are authorised to provide payment services—

    (a)   in accordance with the Treaty establishing the European Community as applied in the EEA; and

    (b)   subject to the conditions of the payment services directive;

"payee" means a person who is the intended recipient of funds which have been the subject of a payment transaction;

"payer" means—

    (a)   a person who holds a payment account and initiates, or consents to the initiation of, a payment order from that payment account; or

    (b)   where there is no payment account, a person who gives a payment order;

"payment account" means an account held in the name of one or more payment service users which is used for the execution of payment transactions;

"payment instrument" means any—

    (a)   personalised device; or

(b)   personalised set of procedures agreed between the payment service user and the payment service provider,

used by the payment service user in order to initiate a payment order;

"payment order" means any instruction by—

(a)   a payer; or

(b)   a payee,

to their respective payment service provider requesting the execution of a payment transaction;

"payment services" means any of the activities specified in Part 1 of Schedule 1 when carried out as a regular occupation or business activity, other than any of the activities specified in Part 2 of that Schedule;

"payment services directive" means Directive 2007/64/EC of the European Parliament and of the Council of 13th November 2007 on payment services in the internal market;

"payment service provider" means any of the following persons when they carry out payment services—

(a)   authorised payment institutions;

(b)   small payment institutions;

(c)   EEA authorised payment institutions;

(d)   credit institutions;

(e)   electronic money institutions;

(f)   the Post Office Limited;

(g)   the Bank of England, the European Central Bank and the national central banks of EEA States other than the United Kingdom, other than when acting in their capacity as a monetary authority or carrying out other functions of a public nature; and

(h)   government departments and local authorities, other than when carrying out functions of a public nature;

"payment service user" means a person when making use of a payment service in the capacity of either payer or payee, or both;

"payment system" means a funds transfer system with formal and standardised arrangements and common rules for the processing, clearing and settlement of payment transactions;

"payment transaction" means an act, initiated by the payer or payee, of placing, transferring or withdrawing funds, irrespective of any underlying obligations between the payer and payee;

"qualifying holding" has the meaning given in article 4(11) of the banking consolidation directive;

"reference exchange rate" means the exchange rate which is used as the basis to calculate any currency exchange and which is made available by the payment service provider or comes from a publicly available source;

"reference interest rate" means the interest rate which is used as the basis for calculating any interest to be applied and which comes from a publicly available source which can be verified by both parties to a contract for payment services;

"the register" means the register maintained by the Authority under regulation 4;

"regulated agreement" has the meaning given by section 189(1) of the Consumer Credit Act 1974 (definitions);

"single payment service contract" means a contract for a single payment transaction not covered by a framework contract;

"small payment institution" means a person included by the Authority in the register pursuant to regulation 4(1)(b);

"subsidiary undertaking" has the same meaning as in the Companies Acts (see section 1162 of, and Schedule 7 to, the Companies Act 2006);

"the Tribunal" means the Financial Services and Markets Tribunal;

"unique identifier" means a combination of letters, numbers or symbols specified to the payment service user by the payment service provider and to be provided by the payment service user in relation to a payment transaction in order to identify unambiguously one or both of—

(a)   the other payment service user who is a party to the payment transaction;

(b)   the other payment service user's payment account;

"value date" means a reference time used by a payment service provider for the calculation of interest on the funds debited from or credited to a payment account.

(2)   In these Regulations references to amounts in euro include references to equivalent amounts in another currency.

(3)   Unless otherwise defined, expressions used in these Regulations which are also used in the payment services directive have the same meaning as in that directive.

(4)   Expressions used in these Regulations and in a modification to a provision in primary or secondary legislation applied by these Regulations have the same meaning as in these Regulations.

[4388]

PART III
STATUTORY INSTRUMENTS

NOTES
Commencement: these Regulations come into force on 2 March 2009 (for the purposes specified in reg 1(2)(a)), 1 May 2009 (for the purposes specified in reg 1(2)(b)), and 1 November 2009 (otherwise). See reg 1 at **[4387]**.

3 Exemption for certain bodies

(1)   Subject to paragraph (2) and regulation 4(1)(d), these Regulations do not apply to the following persons—
   (a)   credit unions;
   (b)   municipal banks; and
   (c)   the National Savings Bank.

(2)   Where municipal banks provide or propose to provide payment services they must give notice to the Authority.

(3)   In this regulation—
   "credit union" means a credit union within the meaning of—
      (a)   the Credit Unions Act 1979;
      (b)   the Credit Unions (Northern Ireland) Order 1985;
   "municipal bank" means a company which, immediately before 1st December 2001, fell within the definition in section 103 of the Banking Act 1987.

[4389]

NOTES
Commencement: these Regulations come into force on 2 March 2009 (for the purposes specified in reg 1(2)(a)), 1 May 2009 (for the purposes specified in reg 1(2)(b)), and 1 November 2009 (otherwise). See reg 1 at **[4387]**.

PART 2
REGISTRATION

The register

4 The register of certain payment service providers

(1)   The Authority must maintain a register of—
   (a)   authorised payment institutions and their EEA branches;
   (b)   small payment institutions;
   (c)   agents of authorised payment institutions and small payment institutions required to be registered under regulation 29; and
   (d)   the persons specified in regulation 3(1) where they provide payment services.

(2)   The Authority may include on the register any of the persons mentioned in paragraphs (c) to (h) of the definition of a payment service provider in regulation 2(1) where such persons provide payment services.

(3)   Where a person mentioned in paragraph (f), (g) or (h) of the definition of a payment service provider in regulation 2(1)—
   (a)   is not included on the register; and
   (b)   provides, or proposes to provide, payment services,
the person must give notice to the Authority.

(4)   The Authority may—
   (a)   keep the register in any form it thinks fit;
   (b)   include on it such information as the Authority considers appropriate, provided that the register identifies the payment services for which an institution is authorised or registered under this Part; and
   (c)   exploit commercially the information contained in the register, or any part of that information.

(5)   The Authority must—
   (a)   publish the register online and make it available for public inspection;
   (b)   update the register on a regular basis; and
   (c)   provide a certified copy of the register, or any part of it, to any person who asks for it—
      (i)   on payment of the fee (if any) fixed by the Authority; and
      (ii)   in a form (either written or electronic) in which it is legible to the person asking for it.

[4390]

NOTES
  Commencement: these Regulations come into force on 2 March 2009 (for the purposes specified in
reg 1(2)(a)), 1 May 2009 (for the purposes specified in reg 1(2)(b)), and 1 November 2009 (otherwise). See reg 1
at **[4387]**.

Authorisation as a payment institution

5 Application for authorisation as a payment institution or variation of an existing authorisation

(1)   An application for authorisation as a payment institution must contain or be accompanied by the information specified in Schedule 2.

(2)   An application for the variation of an authorisation as a payment institution must—
  (a)   contain a statement of the proposed variation;
  (b)   contain a statement of the payment services which the applicant proposes to carry on if the authorisation is varied; and
  (c)   contain, or be accompanied by, such other information as the Authority may reasonably require.

(3)   An application under paragraph (1) or (2) must be made in such manner as the Authority may direct.

(4)   At any time after receiving an application and before determining it, the Authority may require the applicant to provide it with such further information as it reasonably considers necessary to enable it to determine the application.

(5)   Different directions may be given, and different requirements imposed, in relation to different applications or categories of application.

[4391]

NOTES
  Commencement: these Regulations come into force on 2 March 2009 (for the purposes specified in
reg 1(2)(a)), 1 May 2009 (for the purposes specified in reg 1(2)(b)), and 1 November 2009 (otherwise). See reg 1
at **[4387]**.

6   Conditions for authorisation as a payment institution

(1)   The Authority may refuse to grant all or part of an application for authorisation as a payment institution only if any of the conditions set out in paragraphs (2) to (8) is not met.

(2)   The application must comply with the requirements of, and any requirements imposed under, regulation 5.

(3)   The applicant must immediately before the time of authorisation hold the amount of initial capital required in accordance with Part 1 of Schedule 3.

(4)   The applicant must be a body corporate constituted under the law of a part of the United Kingdom having—
  (a)   its head office, and
  (b)   if it has a registered office, that office,
in the United Kingdom.

(5)   The applicant must satisfy the Authority that, taking into account the need to ensure the sound and prudent conduct of the affairs of the institution, it has—
  (a)   robust governance arrangements for its payment service business, including a clear organisational structure with well-defined, transparent and consistent lines of responsibility;
  (b)   effective procedures to identify, manage, monitor and report any risks to which it might be exposed;
  (c)   adequate internal control mechanisms, including sound administrative, risk management and accounting procedures,
which are comprehensive and proportionate to the nature, scale and complexity of the payment services to be provided by the institution.

(6)   The applicant must satisfy the Authority that—
  (a)   any persons having a qualifying holding in it are fit and proper persons having regard to the need to ensure the sound and prudent conduct of the affairs of an authorised payment institution;
  (b)   the directors and persons responsible for the management of the institution and, where relevant, the persons responsible for the management of payment services, are of good repute and possess appropriate knowledge and experience to provide payment services;
  (c)   it has a business plan (including, for the first three years, a forecast budget calculation)

under which appropriate and proportionate systems, resources and procedures will be employed by the institution to operate soundly; and

(d)   it has taken adequate measures for the purpose of safeguarding payment service users' funds in accordance with regulation 19.

(7)   The applicant must comply with a requirement of the Money Laundering Regulations 2007 to be included in a register maintained under those Regulations where such a requirement applies to the applicant.

(8)   If the applicant has close links with another person ("CL") the applicant must satisfy the Authority—

(a)   that those links are not likely to prevent the Authority's effective supervision of the applicant; and

(b)   if it appears to the Authority that CL is subject to the laws, regulations or administrative provisions of a territory which is not an EEA State ("the foreign provisions"), that neither the foreign provisions, nor any deficiency in their enforcement, would prevent the Authority's effective supervision of the applicant.

(9)   For the purposes of paragraph (8), an applicant has close links with CL if—

(a)   CL is a parent undertaking of the applicant;

(b)   CL is a subsidiary undertaking of the applicant;

(c)   CL is a parent undertaking of a subsidiary undertaking of the applicant;

(d)   CL is a subsidiary undertaking of a parent undertaking of the applicant;

(e)   CL owns or controls 20% or more of the voting rights or capital of the applicant; or

(f)   the applicant owns or controls 20% or more of the voting rights or capital of CL.

[4392]

NOTES

Commencement: these Regulations come into force on 2 March 2009 (for the purposes specified in reg 1(2)(a)), 1 May 2009 (for the purposes specified in reg 1(2)(b)), and 1 November 2009 (otherwise). See reg 1 at **[4387]**.

7 Imposition of requirements

(1)   The Authority may include in an authorisation such requirements as it considers appropriate.

(2)   A requirement may, in particular, be imposed so as to require the person concerned to—

(a)   take a specified action;

(b)   refrain from taking a specified action.

(3)   A requirement may be imposed by reference to the person's relationship with its group or other members of its group.

(4)   Where—

(a)   an applicant for authorisation as a payment institution intends to carry on business activities other than the provision of payment services; and

(b)   the Authority considers that the carrying on of such other business activities will impair, or is likely to impair—

(i)   the financial soundness of the applicant, or

(ii)   the Authority's effective supervision of the applicant,

the Authority may require the applicant to establish a separate body corporate to carry on the payment service business.

(5)   A requirement expires at the end of such period as the Authority may specify in the authorisation.

(6)   Paragraph (5) does not affect the Authority's powers under regulation 8 or 11.

[4393]

NOTES

Commencement: these Regulations come into force on 2 March 2009 (for the purposes specified in reg 1(2)(a)), 1 May 2009 (for the purposes specified in reg 1(2)(b)), and 1 November 2009 (otherwise). See reg 1 at **[4387]**.

8 Variation etc at request of authorised payment institution

The Authority may, on the application of an authorised payment institution, vary that person's authorisation by—

(a)   adding a payment service to those for which it has granted authorisation;

(b)   removing a payment service from those for which it has granted authorisation;

(c)   imposing a requirement such as may, under regulation 7, be included in an authorisation;

(d)   cancelling a requirement included in the authorisation or previously imposed under paragraph (c); or

(e)   varying such a requirement,

provided that the conditions set out in regulation 6(4) to (8) and, if applicable, the requirement in regulation 18(1) to maintain own funds, will continue to be met.

[4394]

NOTES
Commencement: these Regulations come into force on 2 March 2009 (for the purposes specified in reg 1(2)(a)), 1 May 2009 (for the purposes specified in reg 1(2)(b)), and 1 November 2009 (otherwise). See reg 1 at **[4387]**.

9   Determination of application for authorisation or variation of authorisation

(1)   The Authority must determine an application for authorisation or the variation of an authorisation before the end of the period of three months beginning with the date on which it received the completed application.

(2)   The Authority may determine an incomplete application if it considers it appropriate to do so, and it must in any event determine any such application within 12 months beginning with the date on which it received the application.

(3)   The applicant may withdraw its application, by giving the Authority notice, at any time before the Authority determines it.

(4)   The Authority may grant authorisation to carry out the payment services to which the application relates or such of them as may be specified in the grant of the authorisation.

(5)   If the Authority decides to grant an application for authorisation, or for the variation of an authorisation, it must give the applicant notice of its decision specifying—
    (a)   the payment services for which authorisation has been granted; or
    (b)   the variation granted,
described in such manner as the Authority considers appropriate.

(6)   The notice must state the date on which the authorisation or variation takes effect.

(7)   If the Authority proposes to refuse an application or to impose a requirement it must give the applicant a warning notice.

(8)   The Authority must, having considered any representations made in response to the warning notice—
    (a)   if it decides to refuse the application or to impose a requirement, give the applicant a decision notice; or
    (b)   if it grants the application without imposing a requirement, give the applicant notice of its decision, stating the date on which the authorisation or variation takes effect.

(9)   If the Authority decides to refuse the application or to impose a requirement the applicant may refer the matter to the Tribunal.

(10)   If the Authority decides to authorise the applicant, or vary its authorisation, it must update the register as soon as practicable.

[4395]

NOTES
Commencement: these Regulations come into force on 2 March 2009 (for the purposes specified in reg 1(2)(a)), 1 May 2009 (for the purposes specified in reg 1(2)(b)), and 1 November 2009 (otherwise). See reg 1 at **[4387]**.

10   Cancellation of authorisation

(1)   The Authority may cancel a person's authorisation and remove the person from the register where—
    (a)   the person does not provide payment services within 12 months beginning with the date on which the authorisation took effect;
    (b)   the person requests, or consents to, the cancellation of the authorisation;
    (c)   the person ceases to engage in business activity for more than six months;
    (d)   the person has obtained authorisation through false statements or any other irregular means;
    (e)   the person no longer meets, or is unlikely to continue to meet, any of the conditions set out in regulation 6(4) to (8) or, if applicable, the requirement in regulation 18(1) to maintain own funds;
    (f)   the person has provided payment services other than in accordance with the authorisation granted to it;
    (g)   the person would constitute a threat to the stability of a payment system by continuing its payment services business;
    (h)   the cancellation is desirable in order to protect the interests of consumers; or
    (i)   the person's provision of payment services is otherwise unlawful.

(2)　Where the Authority proposes to cancel a person's authorisation, other than at the person's request, it must give the person a warning notice.

(3)　The Authority must, having considered any representations made in response to the warning notice—

　　(a)　if it decides to cancel the authorisation, give the person a decision notice; or

　　(b)　if it decides not to cancel the authorisation, give the person notice of its decision.

(4)　If the Authority decides to cancel the authorisation, other than at the person's request, the person may refer the matter to the Tribunal.

(5)　Where the period for a reference to the Tribunal has expired without a reference being made, the Authority must as soon as practicable update the register accordingly.

[4396]

NOTES

Commencement: these Regulations come into force on 2 March 2009 (for the purposes specified in reg 1(2)(a)), 1 May 2009 (for the purposes specified in reg 1(2)(b)), and 1 November 2009 (otherwise). See reg 1 at **[4387]**.

11　Variation of authorisation on Authority's own initiative

(1)　The Authority may vary a person's authorisation in any of the ways mentioned in regulation 8 if it appears to the Authority that—

　　(a)　the person no longer meets, or is unlikely to continue to meet, any of the conditions set out in regulation 6(4) to (8) or, if applicable, the requirement in regulation 18(1) to maintain own funds;

　　(b)　the person has provided a particular payment service or payment services other than in accordance with the authorisation granted to it;

　　(c)　the person would constitute a threat to the stability of a payment system by continuing to provide a particular payment service or payment services;

　　(d)　the variation is desirable in order to protect the interests of consumers; or

　　(e)　the person's provision of a particular payment service or payment services is otherwise unlawful.

(2)　A variation under this regulation takes effect—

　　(a)　immediately, if the notice given under paragraph (6) states that that is the case;

　　(b)　on such date as may be specified in the notice; or

　　(c)　if no date is specified in the notice, when the matter to which the notice relates is no longer open to review.

(3)　A variation may be expressed to take effect immediately or on a specified date only if the Authority, having regard to the ground on which it is exercising the power under paragraph (1), reasonably considers that it is necessary for the variation to take effect immediately or, as the case may be, on that date.

(4)　The Authority must as soon as practicable after the variation takes effect update the register accordingly.

(5)　A person who is aggrieved by the variation of their authorisation under this regulation may refer the matter to the Tribunal.

(6)　Where the Authority proposes to vary a person's authorisation under this regulation, it must give the person notice.

(7)　The notice must—

　　(a)　give details of the variation;

　　(b)　state the Authority's reasons for the variation and for its determination as to when the variation takes effect;

　　(c)　inform the person that they may make representations to the Authority within such period as may be specified in the notice (whether or not the person has referred the matter to the Tribunal);

　　(d)　inform the person of the date on which the variation takes effect; and

　　(e)　inform the person of their right to refer the matter to the Tribunal and the procedure for such a reference.

(8)　The Authority may extend the period allowed under the notice for making representations.

(9)　If, having considered any representations made by the person, the Authority decides—

　　(a)　to vary the authorisation in the way proposed, or

　　(b)　if the authorisation has been varied, not to rescind the variation,

it must give the person notice.

(10)　If, having considered any representations made by the person, the Authority decides—

　　(a)　not to vary the authorisation in the way proposed,

　　(b)　to vary the authorisation in a different way, or

(c) to rescind a variation which has taken effect,
it must give the person notice.

(11) A notice given under paragraph (9) must inform the person of their right to refer the matter to the Tribunal and the procedure for such a reference.

(12) A notice under paragraph (10)(b) must comply with paragraph (7).

(13) For the purposes of paragraph (2)(c), paragraphs (a) to (d) of section 391(8) of the 2000 Act (publication) apply to determine whether a matter is open to review.

[4397]

NOTES
Commencement: these Regulations come into force on 2 March 2009 (for the purposes specified in reg 1(2)(a)), 1 May 2009 (for the purposes specified in reg 1(2)(b)), and 1 November 2009 (otherwise). See reg 1 at **[4387]**.

Registration as a small payment institution

12 Application for registration as a small payment institution or variation of an existing registration

(1) An application for registration as a small payment institution must contain, or be accompanied by, such information as the Authority may reasonably require.

(2) An application for the variation of a registration as a small payment institution must—
  (a) contain a statement of the proposed variation;
  (b) contain a statement of the payment services which the applicant proposes to carry on if the registration is varied; and
  (c) contain, or be accompanied by, such other information as the Authority may reasonably require.

(3) An application under paragraph (1) or (2) must be made in such manner as the Authority may direct.

(4) At any time after receiving an application and before determining it, the Authority may require the applicant to provide it with such further information as it reasonably considers necessary to enable it to determine the application.

(5) Different directions may be given, and different requirements imposed, in relation to different applications or categories of application.

[4398]

NOTES
Commencement: these Regulations come into force on 2 March 2009 (for the purposes specified in reg 1(2)(a)), 1 May 2009 (for the purposes specified in reg 1(2)(b)), and 1 November 2009 (otherwise). See reg 1 at **[4387]**.

13 Conditions for registration as a small payment institution

(1) The Authority may refuse to register an applicant as a small payment institution only if any of the conditions set out in paragraphs (2) to (6) is not met.

(2) The application must comply with the requirements of, and any requirements imposed under, regulation 12.

(3) The monthly average over the period of 12 months preceding the application of the total amount of payment transactions executed by the applicant, including any of its agents in the United Kingdom, must not exceed 3 million euros.

(4) None of the individuals responsible for the management or operation of the business has been convicted of—
  (a) an offence under Part 7 of the Proceeds of Crime Act 2002 (money laundering) or under the Money Laundering Regulations 2007;
  (b) an offence under section 15 (fund-raising), 16 (use and possession), 17 (funding arrangements), 18 (money laundering) or 63 (terrorist finance: jurisdiction) of the Terrorism Act 2000;
  (c) an offence under the 2000 Act;
  (d) an offence under article 7, 8 or 10 of the Terrorism (United Nations Measures) Order 2006 or article 7, 8 or 10 of the Al-Qaida and Taliban (United Nations Measures) Order 2006;
  (e) an offence under these Regulations; or
  (f) any other financial crimes.

(5) The applicant's head office, registered office or place of residence, as the case may be, must be in the United Kingdom.

(6)   The applicant must comply with a requirement of the Money Laundering Regulations 2007 to be included in a register maintained under those Regulations where such a requirement applies to the applicant.

(7)   For the purposes of paragraph (3), where the applicant has yet to commence the provision of payment services, or has been providing payment services for less than 12 months, the monthly average may be based on the projected total amount of payment transactions over a 12 month period.

(8)   In paragraph (4) "financial crime" includes any offence involving fraud or dishonesty and, for this purpose, "offence" includes any act or omission which would be an offence if it had taken place in the United Kingdom.

[4399]

NOTES
Commencement: these Regulations come into force on 2 March 2009 (for the purposes specified in reg 1(2)(a)), 1 May 2009 (for the purposes specified in reg 1(2)(b)), and 1 November 2009 (otherwise). See reg 1 at [4387].

14   Supplementary provisions

Regulations 7 to 11 apply to registration as a small payment institution as they apply to authorisation as a payment institution with the following modifications—
  (a)   references to authorisation are to be treated as references to registration;
  (b)   omit regulation 7(4);
  (c)   in regulation 8 for "an authorised payment institution" substitute "small payment institution" and for "provided that" to the end substitute—

"provided that the conditions set out in regulation 13(4) to (6) will continue to be met and that the monthly average over any period of 12 months of the total amount of payment transactions executed by the institution, including any of its agents in the United Kingdom, continues not to exceed 3 million euro ("the financial limit").";
  (d)   in regulation 10 for paragraph (1)(e) substitute—
      "(e)   the person no longer meets, or is unlikely to continue to meet, any of the conditions set out in regulation 13(4) to (6) or the financial limit referred to in regulation 8;"; and
  (e)   in regulation 11 for paragraph (1)(a) substitute—
      "(a)   the person no longer meets, or is unlikely to continue to meet, any of the conditions set out in regulation 13(4) to (6) or the financial limit referred to in regulation 8;".

[4400]

NOTES
Commencement: these Regulations come into force on 2 March 2009 (for the purposes specified in reg 1(2)(a)), 1 May 2009 (for the purposes specified in reg 1(2)(b)), and 1 November 2009 (otherwise). See reg 1 at [4387].

15   Application for authorisation as a payment institution where the financial limit is exceeded

Where the financial limit referred to in regulation 8 (as applied by regulation 14(c)) is exceeded, the institution concerned must, within 30 days of becoming aware of the change in circumstances, apply for authorisation as a payment institution under regulation 5 if it intends to continue providing payment services in the United Kingdom.

[4401]

NOTES
Commencement: these Regulations come into force on 2 March 2009 (for the purposes specified in reg 1(2)(a)), 1 May 2009 (for the purposes specified in reg 1(2)(b)), and 1 November 2009 (otherwise). See reg 1 at [4387].

Common provisions

16   Duty to notify changes

(1)   If at any time after an applicant has provided the Authority with any information under regulation 5(1), (2), or (4), or 12(1), (2) or (4) and before the Authority has determined the application—
  (a)   there is, or is likely to be, a material change affecting any matter contained in that information; or
  (b)   it becomes apparent to the applicant that the information is incomplete or contains a material inaccuracy,

the applicant must provide the Authority with details of the change, the complete information or a correction of the inaccuracy (as the case may be) without undue delay, or, in the case of a material change which has not yet taken place, the applicant must provide details of the likely change as soon as the applicant is aware of such change.

(2)   The obligation in paragraph (1) also applies to material changes or significant inaccuracies affecting any matter contained in any supplementary information provided pursuant to that paragraph.

(3)   Any information to be provided to the Authority under this regulation must be in such form or verified in such manner as it may direct.

[4402]

NOTES

Commencement: these Regulations come into force on 2 March 2009 (for the purposes specified in reg 1(2)(a)), 1 May 2009 (for the purposes specified in reg 1(2)(b)), and 1 November 2009 (otherwise). See reg 1 at **[4387]**.

17 Authorised payment institutions and small payment institutions acting without permission

If an authorised payment institution or a small payment institution carries on a payment service in the United Kingdom, or purports to do so, other than in accordance with an authorisation or registration granted, or deemed to be granted under regulation 121, to it by the Authority under these Regulations, it is to be taken to have contravened a requirement imposed on it under these Regulations.

[4403]

NOTES

Commencement: these Regulations come into force on 2 March 2009 (for the purposes specified in reg 1(2)(a)), 1 May 2009 (for the purposes specified in reg 1(2)(b)), and 1 November 2009 (otherwise). See reg 1 at **[4387]**.

PART 3
AUTHORISED PAYMENT INSTITUTIONS

18 Capital requirements

(1)   Subject to paragraph (2), an authorised payment institution must maintain at all times own funds as defined for the purposes of Part 2 of Schedule 3 equal to or in excess of—
  (a)   the amount of initial capital specified in Part 1 of Schedule 3, or
  (b)   the amount of the own funds requirement calculated in accordance with paragraph 11 of Schedule 3 subject to any adjustment directed by the Authority under paragraph 12 of that Schedule,
whichever is greater.

(2)   Paragraph (1) does not apply to an authorised payment institution—
  (a)   which is included in the consolidated supervision of a parent credit institution pursuant to the banking consolidation directive; and
  (b)   in respect of which all of the conditions specified in Article 69(1) of the banking consolidation directive are met.

[4404]

NOTES

Commencement: these Regulations come into force on 2 March 2009 (for the purposes specified in reg 1(2)(a)), 1 May 2009 (for the purposes specified in reg 1(2)(b)), and 1 November 2009 (otherwise). See reg 1 at **[4387]**.

19 Safeguarding requirements

(1)   For the purposes of this regulation "relevant funds" comprise the following—
  (a)   sums received from, or for the benefit of, a payment service user for the execution of a payment transaction; and
  (b)   sums received from a payment service provider for the execution of a payment transaction on behalf of a payment service user.

(2)   Where—
  (a)   only a portion of the sums referred to in paragraph (1)(a) or (b) is to be used for the execution of a payment transaction (with the remainder being used for non-payment services); and
  (b)   the precise portion attributable to the execution of the payment transaction is variable or unknown in advance,

the relevant funds are such amount as may be reasonably estimated, on the basis of historical data and to the satisfaction of the Authority, to be representative of the portion attributable to the execution of the payment transaction.

(3)   Where the relevant funds in respect of a payment transaction exceed £50, an authorised payment institution must safeguard such funds in accordance with either—
    (a)   paragraphs (4) to (8); or
    (b)   paragraphs (9) and (10).

(4)   An authorised payment institution must keep relevant funds segregated from any other funds that it holds.

(5)   Where the authorised payment institution continues to hold the relevant funds at the end of the business day following the day on which they were received it must—
    (a)   place them in a separate account that it holds with an authorised credit institution; or
    (b)   invest the relevant funds in such secure, liquid assets as the Authority may approve ("relevant assets") and place those assets in a separate account with an authorised custodian.

(6)   An account in which relevant funds or relevant assets are placed under paragraph (5) must—
    (a)   be designated in such a way as to show that it is an account which is held for the purpose of safeguarding relevant funds or relevant assets in accordance with this regulation; and
    (b)   be used only for holding those funds or assets.

(7)   No person other than the authorised payment institution may have any interest in or right over the relevant funds or relevant assets placed in an account in accordance with paragraph (5)(a) or (b) except as provided by this regulation.

(8)   The authorised payment institution must keep a record of—
    (a)   any relevant funds segregated in accordance with paragraph (4);
    (b)   any relevant funds placed in an account in accordance with paragraph (5)(a); and
    (c)   any relevant assets placed in an account in accordance with paragraph (5)(b).

(9)   The authorised payment institution must ensure that—
    (a)   any relevant funds are covered by—
        (i)   an insurance policy with an authorised insurer;
        (ii)   a guarantee from an authorised insurer; or
        (iii)   a guarantee from an authorised credit institution; and
    (b)   the proceeds of any such insurance policy or guarantee are payable upon an insolvency event into a separate account held by the authorised payment institution which must—
        (i)   be designated in such a way as to show that it is an account which is held for the purpose of safeguarding relevant funds in accordance with this regulation; and
        (ii)   be used only for holding such proceeds.

(10)   No person other than the authorised payment institution may have any interest in or right over the proceeds placed in an account in accordance with paragraph (9)(b) except as provided by this regulation.

(11)   Subject to paragraph (12), where there is an insolvency event—
    (a)   the claims of payment service users are to be paid from the asset pool in priority to all other creditors; and
    (b)   until all the claims of payment service users have been paid, no right of set-off or security right may be exercised in respect of the asset pool except to the extent that the right of set-off relates to fees and expenses in relation to operating an account held in accordance with paragraph (5)(a) or (b) or (9)(b).

(12)   The claims referred to in paragraph (11)(a) shall not be subject to the priority of expenses of an insolvency proceeding except in respect of the costs of distributing the asset pool.

(13)   Paragraphs (11) and (12) shall apply to any relevant funds which a small payment institution (or an authorised payment institution in relation to relevant funds of £50 or less) voluntarily safeguards in accordance with either paragraphs (4) to (8) or paragraphs (9) and (10).

(14)   An authorised payment institution (and any small payment institution which voluntarily safeguards relevant funds) must maintain organisational arrangements sufficient to minimise the risk of the loss or diminution of relevant funds or relevant assets through fraud, misuse, negligence or poor administration.

(15)   In this regulation—
    "asset pool" means—
        (a)   any relevant funds segregated in accordance with paragraph (4);
        (b)   any relevant funds held in an account in accordance with paragraph (5)(a);
        (c)   any relevant assets held in an account in accordance with paragraph (5)(b); and
        (d)   any proceeds of an insurance policy or guarantee held in an account in accordance with paragraph (9)(b);

"authorised insurer" means a person authorised for the purposes of the 2000 Act to effect and carry out a contract of general insurance as principal or otherwise authorised in accordance with Article 6 of the First Council Directive 73/239/EEC of 24th July 1973 on the business of direct insurance other than life insurance, other than a person in the same group as the authorised payment institution;

"authorised credit institution" means a person authorised for the purposes of the 2000 Act to accept deposits or otherwise authorised as a credit institution in accordance with Article 6 of the banking consolidation directive other than a person in the same group as the authorised payment institution;

"authorised custodian" means a person authorised for the purposes of the 2000 Act to safeguard and administer investments or authorised as an investment firm under Article 5 of Directive 2004/39/EC of 12th April 2004 on markets in financial instruments which holds those investments under regulatory standards at least equivalent to those set out under Article 13 of that directive;

"insolvency event" means any of the following procedures in relation to an authorised payment institution or small payment institution—

    (e)   the making of a winding-up order;

    (f)   the passing of a resolution for voluntary winding-up;

    (g)   the entry of the institution into administration;

    (h)   the appointment of a receiver or manager of the institution's property;

    (i)   the approval of a proposed voluntary arrangement (being a composition in satisfaction of debts or a scheme of arrangement);

    (j)   the making of a bankruptcy order;

    (k)   in Scotland, the award of sequestration;

    (l)   the making of any deed of arrangement for the benefit of creditors or, in Scotland, the execution of a trust deed for creditors;

    (m)   the conclusion of any composition contract with creditors; or

    (n)   the making of an insolvency administration order or, in Scotland, sequestration, in respect of the estate of a deceased person;

"insolvency proceeding" means—

    (o)   winding-up, administration, receivership, bankruptcy or, in Scotland, sequestration;

    (p)   a voluntary arrangement, deed of arrangement or trust deed for the benefit of creditors; or

    (q)   the administration of the insolvent estate of a deceased person;

"security right" means—

    (r)   security for a debt owed by an authorised payment institution or a small payment institution and includes any charge, lien, mortgage or other security over the asset pool or any part of the asset pool; and

    (s)   any charge arising in respect of the expenses of a voluntary arrangement.

[4405]

NOTES

Commencement: these Regulations come into force on 2 March 2009 (for the purposes specified in reg 1(2)(a)), 1 May 2009 (for the purposes specified in reg 1(2)(b)), and 1 November 2009 (otherwise). See reg 1 at **[4387]**.

20   Accounting and statutory audit

(1)   Where an authorised payment institution carries on activities other than the provision of payment services, it must provide to the Authority separate accounting information in respect of its provision of payment services.

(2)   Such accounting information must be subject, where relevant, to an auditor's report prepared by the institution's statutory auditors or an audit firm (within the meaning of Directive 2006/43/EC of the European Parliament and of the Council of 17th May 2006 on statutory audits of annual accounts and consolidated accounts).

(3)   A statutory auditor or audit firm ("the auditor") must, in any of the circumstances referred to in paragraph (4), communicate to the Authority information on, or its opinion on, matters—

    (a)   of which it has become aware in its capacity as auditor of an authorised payment institution or of a person with close links to an authorised payment institution; and

    (b)   which relate to payment services provided by that institution.

(4)   The circumstances are that—

    (a)   the auditor reasonably believes that—

        (i)   there is or has been, or may be or may have been, a contravention of any requirement imposed on the authorised payment institution by or under these Regulations; and

PART III
STATUTORY INSTRUMENTS

(ii)   the contravention may be of material significance to the Authority in determining whether to exercise, in relation to that institution, any functions conferred on the Authority by these Regulations;

(b)   the auditor reasonably believes that the information on, or his opinion on, those matters may be of material significance to the Authority in determining whether the institution meets or will continue to meet the conditions set out in regulation 6(4) to (8) and, if applicable, the requirement in regulation 18(1) to maintain own funds;

(c)   the auditor reasonably believes that the institution is not, may not be or may cease to be, a going concern;

(d)   the auditor is precluded from stating in his report that the annual accounts have been properly prepared in accordance with the Companies Act 2006;

(e)   the auditor is precluded from stating in his report, where applicable, that the annual accounts give a true and fair view of the matters referred to in section 495 of the Companies Act 2006 (auditor's report on company's annual accounts) including as it is applied and modified by regulation 39 of the Limited Liability Partnerships (Accounts and Audit) (Application of Companies Act 2006) Regulations 2008 ("the LLP Regulations"); or

(f)   the auditor is required to state in his report in relation to the person concerned any of the facts referred to in subsection (2), (3) or (5) of section 498 of the Companies Act 2006 (duties of auditor) or, in the case of limited liability partnerships, subsection (2), (3) or (4) of section 498 as applied and modified by regulation 40 of the LLP Regulations.

(5)   In this regulation a person has close links with an authorised payment institution ("A") if that person is—

(a)   a parent undertaking of A;

(b)   a subsidiary undertaking of A;

(c)   a parent undertaking of a subsidiary undertaking of A; or

(d)   a subsidiary undertaking of a parent undertaking of A.

[4406]

NOTES

Commencement: these Regulations come into force on 2 March 2009 (for the purposes specified in reg 1(2)(a)), 1 May 2009 (for the purposes specified in reg 1(2)(b)), and 1 November 2009 (otherwise). See reg 1 at **[4387]**.

21 Outsourcing

(1)   An authorised payment institution must notify the Authority of its intention to enter into a contract with another person under which that other person will carry out any operational function relating to its provision of payment services ("outsourcing").

(2)   Where an authorised payment institution intends to outsource any important operational function, all of the following conditions must be met—

(a)   the outsourcing is not undertaken in such a way as to impair—

(i)   the quality of the authorised payment institution's internal control; or

(ii)   the ability of the Authority to monitor the authorised payment institution's compliance with these Regulations;

(b)   the outsourcing does not result in any delegation by the senior management of the authorised payment institution of responsibility for complying with the requirements imposed by or under these Regulations;

(c)   the relationship and obligations of the authorised payment institution towards its payment service users under these Regulations is not substantially altered;

(d)   compliance with the conditions which the authorised payment institution must observe in order to be authorised and remain so is not adversely affected; and

(e)   none of the conditions of the payment institution's authorisation requires removal or variation.

(3)   For the purposes of paragraph (2), an operational function is important if a defect or failure in its performance would materially impair—

(a)   compliance by the authorised payment institution with these Regulations and any requirements of its authorisation;

(b)   the financial performance of the authorised payment institution; or

(c)   the soundness or continuity of the authorised payment institution's payment services.

[4407]

NOTES

Commencement: these Regulations come into force on 2 March 2009 (for the purposes specified in reg 1(2)(a)), 1 May 2009 (for the purposes specified in reg 1(2)(b)), and 1 November 2009 (otherwise). See reg 1 at **[4387]**.

22　Record keeping

(1)　An authorised payment institution must maintain relevant records and keep them for at least five years from the date on which the record was created.

(2)　For the purposes of paragraph (1), records are relevant where they relate to the authorised payment institution's compliance with this Part and, in particular, would enable the Authority to supervise effectively such compliance.

[4408]

NOTES
Commencement: these Regulations come into force on 2 March 2009 (for the purposes specified in reg 1(2)(a)), 1 May 2009 (for the purposes specified in reg 1(2)(b)), and 1 November 2009 (otherwise). See reg 1 at **[4387]**.

Exercise of passport rights

23　Notice of intention

(1)　Where an authorised payment institution intends to exercise its passport rights for the first time in a particular EEA State it must give the Authority, in such manner as the Authority may direct, notice of its intention to do so ("a notice of intention") which—

    (a)　identifies the payment services which it seeks to carry on in exercise of those rights in that State;

    (b)　gives the names of those responsible for the management of a proposed EEA branch, if any; and

    (c)　provides details of the organisational structure of a proposed EEA branch, if any.

(2)　The Authority must, within one month beginning with the date on which it receives the notice of intention, inform the host state competent authority of—

    (a)　the name and address of the authorised payment institution; and

    (b)　the information contained in the notice of intention.

(3)　Where an authorised payment institution intends to exercise its passport rights through an EEA agent, the provisions of regulation 29 apply.

[4409]

NOTES
Commencement: these Regulations come into force on 2 March 2009 (for the purposes specified in reg 1(2)(a)), 1 May 2009 (for the purposes specified in reg 1(2)(b)), and 1 November 2009 (otherwise). See reg 1 at **[4387]**.

24　Registration of EEA branch

(1)　If the Authority, taking into account any information received from the host state competent authority, has reasonable grounds to suspect that, in connection with the establishment of an EEA branch by an authorised payment institution—

    (a)　money laundering or terrorist financing within the meaning of the money laundering directive is taking place, has taken place, or has been attempted; or

    (b)　the risk of such activities taking place would be increased,

the Authority may refuse to register the EEA branch or cancel any such registration already made and remove the branch from the register.

(2)　If the Authority proposes to refuse to register, or cancel the registration of, an EEA branch, it must give the relevant authorised payment institution a warning notice.

(3)　The Authority must, having considered any representations made in response to the warning notice—

    (a)　if it decides not to register the branch, or to cancel its registration, give the authorised payment institution a decision notice; or

    (b)　if it decides to register the branch, or not to cancel the registration, give the authorised payment institution notice of its decision.

(4)　If the Authority decides not to register the branch, or to cancel its registration, the authorised payment institution may refer the matter to the Tribunal.

(5)　If the Authority decides to register an EEA branch, it must update the register as soon as practicable.

(6)　If the Authority decides to cancel the registration, the Authority must, where the period for a reference to the Tribunal has expired without a reference being made, as soon as practicable update the register accordingly.

[4410]

NOTES
Commencement: these Regulations come into force on 2 March 2009 (for the purposes specified in reg 1(2)(a)), 1 May 2009 (for the purposes specified in reg 1(2)(b)), and 1 November 2009 (otherwise). See reg 1 at **[4387]**.

25 Supervision of firms exercising passport rights

(1) Without prejudice to the generality of regulation 119, the Authority must co-operate with the relevant host state competent authority or home state competent authority, as the case may be, in relation to the exercise of passport rights by any authorised payment institution or EEA authorised payment institution.

(2) The Authority must, in particular—
    (a)   notify the host state competent authority whenever it intends to carry out an on-site inspection in the host state competent authority's territory; and
    (b)   provide the host state competent authority or home state competent authority, as the case may be—
        (i)   on request, with all relevant information; and
        (ii) on its own initiative, with all essential information,

relating to the exercise of passport rights by an authorised payment institution or EEA authorised payment institution, including where there is an infringement or suspected infringement of these Regulations or of the provisions of the payment services directive by an agent, branch or entity carrying out activities on behalf of such an institution.

(3) Where the Authority and the home state competent authority agree, the Authority may carry out on-site inspections on behalf of the home state competent authority in respect of payment services provided by an EEA authorised payment institution exercising its passport rights.

(4) If the Authority has reasonable grounds to suspect that, in connection with the proposed establishment of a branch or the proposed provision of services by an EEA authorised payment institution—
    (a)   money laundering or terrorist financing within the meaning of the Money Laundering Regulations 2007 is taking place, has taken place, or has been attempted; or
    (b)   the risk of such activities taking place would be increased,

it must inform the relevant home state competent authority of its grounds for suspicion.

[4411]

NOTES
Commencement: these Regulations come into force on 2 March 2009 (for the purposes specified in reg 1(2)(a)), 1 May 2009 (for the purposes specified in reg 1(2)(b)), and 1 November 2009 (otherwise). See reg 1 at **[4387]**.

26 Carrying on of Consumer Credit Act business by EEA authorised payment institutions

(1) Sections 203 (power to prohibit the carrying on of Consumer Credit Act business) and 204 (power to restrict the carrying on of Consumer Credit Act business) of, and Schedule 16 (prohibitions and restrictions imposed by OFT) to, the 2000 Act apply in relation to EEA authorised payment institutions exercising passport rights in the United Kingdom under these Regulations as they apply in relation to EEA firms exercising passport rights under Part 2 of Schedule 3 to the 2000 Act (EEA passport rights) with the following modifications—
    (a)   in section 203(10)—
        (i)   for the definition of "a consumer credit EEA firm" substitute—
        ""a consumer credit EEA firm" means an EEA authorised payment institution (as defined by regulation 2(1) of the Payment Services Regulations 2009) which is exercising passport rights in the United Kingdom and is carrying on any Consumer Credit Act business;" and
        (ii) for the definition of "listed activity" substitute—
        ""listed activity" means an activity listed in the Annex to the payment services directive and any activity carried on in accordance with Article 16 of that directive;";
    (b)   in paragraph 2(5)(b) of Schedule 16, for "the firm's home state regulator" substitute "the home state competent authority (as defined by regulation 2(1) of the Payment Services Regulations 2009)".

(2) Sections 21 (businesses needing a licence) and 39(1) (offences against Part 3) of the Consumer Credit Act 1974 do not apply in relation to the carrying on by an EEA authorised payment institution of a payment service which is Consumer Credit Act business, unless the OFT has exercised the power conferred on it by section 203 of the 2000 Act, as applied with modifications by paragraph (1), in relation to that institution.

(3) In this regulation "Consumer Credit Act business" has the same meaning as in section 203 of the 2000 Act.

[4412]

NOTES
Commencement: these Regulations come into force on 2 March 2009 (for the purposes specified in reg 1(2)(a)), 1 May 2009 (for the purposes specified in reg 1(2)(b)), and 1 November 2009 (otherwise). See reg 1 at **[4387]**.

PART 4
PROVISIONS APPLICABLE TO AUTHORISED PAYMENT INSTITUTIONS AND SMALL PAYMENT INSTITUTIONS

27 Additional activities

(1) Authorised payment institutions and small payment institutions may, in addition to providing payment services, engage in the following activities—
- (a) the provision of operational and closely related ancillary services, including—
  - (i) ensuring the execution of payment transactions;
  - (ii) foreign exchange services;
  - (iii) safe-keeping activities; and
  - (iv) the storage and processing of data;
- (b) the operation of payment systems; and
- (c) business activities other than the provision of payment services, subject to any relevant Community or national law.

(2) Authorised payment institutions and small payment institutions may grant credit in relation to the provision of the payment services specified in paragraph 1(d), (e) and (g) of Schedule 1 only if—
- (a) such credit is ancillary and granted exclusively in connection with the execution of a payment transaction;
- (b) such credit is not granted from the funds received or held for the purposes of executing payment transactions;
- (c) in cases where such credit is granted by an authorised payment institution exercising its passport rights, there is an obligation upon the payment service user to repay the credit within a period not exceeding 12 months; and
- (d) in relation to an authorised payment institution, in the opinion of the Authority the institution's own funds (comprising the items specified in paragraph 3(a) to (j) of Schedule 3) are, and continue to be, adequate in the light of the overall amount of credit granted.

[4413]

NOTES
Commencement: these Regulations come into force on 2 March 2009 (for the purposes specified in reg 1(2)(a)), 1 May 2009 (for the purposes specified in reg 1(2)(b)), and 1 November 2009 (otherwise). See reg 1 at **[4387]**.

28 Payment accounts and sums received for the execution of payment transactions

Any payment account held by an authorised payment institution or a small payment institution must be used only in relation to payment transactions.

[4414]

NOTES
Commencement: these Regulations come into force on 2 March 2009 (for the purposes specified in reg 1(2)(a)), 1 May 2009 (for the purposes specified in reg 1(2)(b)), and 1 November 2009 (otherwise). See reg 1 at **[4387]**.

29 Use of agents

(1) Authorised payment institutions and small payment institutions may not provide payment services in the United Kingdom through an agent unless the agent is included on the register.

(2) Authorised payment institutions may not provide payment services in the exercise of their passport rights through an EEA agent unless the agent is included on the register.

(3) An application for an agent to be included on the register must—
- (a) contain, or be accompanied by, the following information—
  - (i) the name and address of the agent;
  - (ii) where relevant, a description of the internal control mechanisms that will be used by the agent—

          (aa)   in the case of an agent in the United Kingdom, to comply with the Money Laundering Regulations 2007; and

          (bb)   in the case of an EEA agent, to comply with provisions of the money laundering directive; and

     (iii)   in the case of an agent of an authorised payment institution, the identity of the directors and persons responsible for the management of the agent and evidence that they are fit and proper persons; and

     (iv)   such other information as the Authority may reasonably require; and

  (b)   be made in such manner as the Authority may direct.

(4)   Different directions may be given, and different requirements imposed, in relation to different applications or categories of application.

(5)   At any time after receiving an application and before determining it, the Authority may require the applicant to provide it with such further information as it reasonably considers necessary to enable it to determine the application.

(6)   The Authority may refuse to include the agent on the register only if—

  (a)   it has not received the information referred to in paragraph (3)(a), or is not satisfied that such information is correct;

  (b)   it is not satisfied that the directors and persons responsible for the management of the agent are fit and proper persons;

  (c)   it has reasonable grounds to suspect that, in connection with the provision of services through the agent—

     (i)   money laundering or terrorist financing within the meaning of the money laundering directive (or, in the United Kingdom, the Money Laundering Regulations 2007) is taking place, has taken place, or has been attempted; or

     (ii)   the risk of such activities taking place would be increased.

(7)   Where—

  (a)   an authorised payment institution intends to provide payment services through an EEA agent; and

  (b)   the Authority proposes to include the EEA agent on the register,

the Authority must inform the host state competent authority and take account of its opinion (if provided within such reasonable period as the Authority specifies) on any of the matters referred to in paragraph (6)(b) or (c).

(8)   The Authority must decide whether to include the agent on the register within a reasonable period of it having received a completed application.

(9)   If the Authority proposes to refuse to include the agent on the register, it must give the authorised payment institution or the small payment institution, as the case may be, a warning notice.

(10)   The Authority must, having considered any representations made in response to the warning notice—

  (a)   if it decides not to include the agent on the register, give the applicant a decision notice; or

  (b)   if it decides to include the agent on the register, give the applicant notice of its decision, stating the date on which the registration takes effect.

(11)   If the Authority decides not to include the agent on the register the applicant may refer the matter to the Tribunal.

(12)   If the Authority decides to include the agent on the register, it must update the register as soon as practicable.

(13)   An application under paragraph (3) may be combined with an application under regulation 5 or 12, in which case the application must be determined in the manner set out in regulation 9 (if relevant, as applied by regulation 14).

(14)   An authorised payment institution or a small payment institution must ensure that agents acting on its behalf inform payment service users of the agency arrangement.

[4415]

NOTES

Commencement: these Regulations come into force on 2 March 2009 (for the purposes specified in reg 1(2)(a)), 1 May 2009 (for the purposes specified in reg 1(2)(b)), and 1 November 2009 (otherwise). See reg 1 at **[4387]**.

---

30 Removal of agent from register

(1)   The Authority may remove an agent of an authorised payment institution or small payment institution from the register where—

(a) the authorised payment institution or small payment institution requests, or consents to, the agent's removal from the register;

(b) the authorised payment institution or small payment institution has obtained registration through false statements or any other irregular means;

(c) regulation 29(6)(b) or (c) applies;

(d) the removal is desirable in order to protect the interests of consumers; or

(e) the agent's provision of payment services is otherwise unlawful.

(2) Where the Authority proposes to remove an agent from the register, other than at the request of the authorised payment institution or small payment institution, it must give the authorised payment institution or small payment institution a warning notice.

(3) The Authority must, having considered any representations made in response to the warning notice—

(a) if it decides to remove the agent, give the authorised payment institution or small payment institution a decision notice; or

(b) if it decides not to remove the agent, give the authorised payment institution or small payment institution notice of its decision.

(4) If the Authority decides to remove the agent, other than at the request of the authorised payment institution or small payment institution, the institution concerned may refer the matter to the Tribunal.

(5) Where the period for a reference to the Tribunal has expired without a reference being made, the Authority must as soon as practicable update the register accordingly.

[4416]

NOTES

Commencement: these Regulations come into force on 2 March 2009 (for the purposes specified in reg 1(2)(a)), 1 May 2009 (for the purposes specified in reg 1(2)(b)), and 1 November 2009 (otherwise). See reg 1 at **[4387]**.

31 Reliance

(1) Where an authorised payment institution or a small payment institution relies on a third party for the performance of operational functions it must take all reasonable steps to ensure that these Regulations are complied with.

(2) Without prejudice to paragraph (1), an authorised payment institution or a small payment institution is responsible, to the same extent as if it had expressly permitted it, for anything done or omitted by any of its employees, any agent or branch providing payment services on its behalf, or any entity to which activities are outsourced.

[4417]

NOTES

Commencement: these Regulations come into force on 2 March 2009 (for the purposes specified in reg 1(2)(a)), 1 May 2009 (for the purposes specified in reg 1(2)(b)), and 1 November 2009 (otherwise). See reg 1 at **[4387]**.

32 Duty to notify change in circumstance

(1) Where it becomes apparent to an authorised payment institution or a small payment institution that there is, or is likely to be, a significant change in circumstances which is relevant to—

(a) in the case of an authorised payment institution—

(i) its fulfilment of any of the conditions set out in regulation 6(4) to (8) and, if applicable, the requirement in regulation 18(1) to maintain own funds;

(ii) the payment services which it seeks to carry on in exercise of its passport rights;

(b) in the case of a small payment institution, its fulfilment of any of the conditions set out in regulation 13(4) to (6) and compliance with the financial limit referred to in regulation 8 (as applied by regulation 14(c)); and

(c) in the case of the use of an agent to provide payment services, the matters referred to in regulation 29(6)(b) and (c),

it must provide the Authority with details of the change without undue delay, or, in the case of a substantial change in circumstances which has not yet taken place, details of the likely change a reasonable period before it takes place.

(2) Any information to be provided to the Authority under this regulation must be in such form or verified in such manner as it may direct.

[4418]

NOTES
Commencement: these Regulations come into force on 2 March 2009 (for the purposes specified in reg 1(2)(a)), 1 May 2009 (for the purposes specified in reg 1(2)(b)), and 1 November 2009 (otherwise). See reg 1 at **[4387]**.

PART 5
INFORMATION REQUIREMENTS FOR PAYMENT SERVICES
Application

33 Application of Part 5

(1)   This Part applies to a contract for payment services where—

(a)   the services are provided from an establishment maintained by a payment service provider or its agent in the United Kingdom;

(b)   the payment service providers of both the payer and the payee are located within the EEA; and

(c)   the payment services are carried out either in euro or in the currency of an EEA State that has not adopted the euro as its currency.

(2)   Regulations 36 to 39 apply to payment services provided under a single payment service contract.

(3)   Regulations 40 to 46 apply to payment services provided under a framework contract.

(4)   Except where the payment service user is—

(a)   a consumer,

(b)   a micro-enterprise, or

(c)   a charity,

the parties may agree that any or all of the provisions of this Part do not apply to a contract for payment services.

[4419]

NOTES
Commencement: these Regulations come into force on 2 March 2009 (for the purposes specified in reg 1(2)(a)), 1 May 2009 (for the purposes specified in reg 1(2)(b)), and 1 November 2009 (otherwise). See reg 1 at **[4387]**.

34 Disapplication of certain regulations in the case of consumer credit agreements

Where the contract under which a payment service is provided is, or would be, when entered into, a regulated agreement—

(a)   regulations 41, 42 and 43 do not apply;

(b)   the payment service provider is only required under regulation 40(1) to provide the information specified in paragraph 3(b) of Schedule 4; and

(c)   the payment service provider is only required under regulation 45(1) to provide the information specified in paragraph (2)(d) of regulation 45.

[4420]

NOTES
Commencement: these Regulations come into force on 2 March 2009 (for the purposes specified in reg 1(2)(a)), 1 May 2009 (for the purposes specified in reg 1(2)(b)), and 1 November 2009 (otherwise). See reg 1 at **[4387]**.

35 Disapplication of certain regulations in the case of low-value payment instruments

(1)   This regulation applies in respect of payment instruments which, under the framework contract governing their use—

(a)   can be used only to execute individual payment transactions of 30 euro or less, or in relation to payment transactions executed wholly within the United Kingdom, 60 euro or less;

(b)   have a spending limit of 150 euro, or where payment transactions must be executed wholly within the United Kingdom, 300 euro; or

(c)   store funds that do not exceed 500 euro at any time.

(2)   Where this regulation applies—

(a)   regulations 40 and 44 do not apply and the payment service provider is only required to provide the payer with information about the main characteristics of the payment service, including—

(i)   the way in which the payment instrument can be used;

(ii)   the liability of the payer, as set out in regulation 62;

(iii)   charges levied;

      (iv)   any other material information the payer might need to take an informed decision; and

      (v)   an indication of where the information specified in Schedule 4 is made available in an easily accessible manner;

  (b)   the parties may agree that regulations 45 and 46 do not apply and instead—

      (i)   the payment service provider must provide or make available a reference enabling the payment service user to identify—

         (aa)   the payment transaction;

         (bb)   the amount of the payment transaction;

         (cc)   any charges payable in respect of the payment transaction;

      (ii)   in the case of several payment transactions of the same kind made to the same payee, the payment service provider must provide or make available to the payment service user information about the total amount of the payment transactions and any charges for those payment transactions; or

      (iii)   where the payment instrument is used anonymously or the payment service provider is not otherwise technically able to provide or make available the information specified in paragraph (i) or (ii), the payment service provider must enable the payer to verify the amount of funds stored; and

  (c)   the parties may agree that regulation 47(1) does not apply to information provided or made available in accordance with regulation 42.

[4421]

NOTES

Commencement: these Regulations come into force on 2 March 2009 (for the purposes specified in reg 1(2)(a)), 1 May 2009 (for the purposes specified in reg 1(2)(b)), and 1 November 2009 (otherwise). See reg 1 at **[4387]**.

Single payment service contracts

36 Information required prior to the conclusion of a single payment service contract

(1)   A payment service provider must provide or make available to the payment service user the information specified in paragraph (2), whether by supplying a copy of the draft single payment service contract or supplying a copy of the draft payment order or otherwise, either—

  (a)   before the payment service user is bound by the single payment service contract; or

  (b)   immediately after the execution of the payment transaction, where the contract is concluded at the payment service user's request using a means of distance communication which does not enable provision of such information in accordance with sub-paragraph (a).

(2)   The information referred to in paragraph (1) is—

  (a)   the information or unique identifier that has to be provided by the payment service user in order for a payment order to be properly executed;

  (b)   the maximum time in which the payment service will be executed;

  (c)   the charges payable by the payment service user to the user's payment service provider and, where applicable, a breakdown of the amounts of such charges;

  (d)   where applicable, the actual or reference exchange rate to be applied to the payment transaction; and

  (e)   such of the information specified in Schedule 4 as is relevant to the single payment service contract in question.

[4422]

NOTES

Commencement: these Regulations come into force on 2 March 2009 (for the purposes specified in reg 1(2)(a)), 1 May 2009 (for the purposes specified in reg 1(2)(b)), and 1 November 2009 (otherwise). See reg 1 at **[4387]**.

37 Information required after receipt of the payment order

(1)   The payer's payment service provider must, immediately after receipt of the payment order, provide or make available to the payer the information specified in paragraph (2).

(2)   The information referred to in paragraph (1) is—

  (a)   a reference enabling the payer to identify the payment transaction and, where appropriate, information relating to the payee;

  (b)   the amount of the payment transaction in the currency used in the payment order;

  (c)   the amount of any charges for the payment transaction payable by the payer and, where applicable, a breakdown of the amounts of such charges;

  (d)   where an exchange rate is used in the payment transaction and the actual rate used in the payment transaction differs from the rate provided in accordance with regulation 36(2)(d), the actual rate used or a reference to it, and the amount of the payment transaction after that currency conversion; and

(e)   the date on which the payment service provider received the payment order.

[4423]

NOTES
Commencement: these Regulations come into force on 2 March 2009 (for the purposes specified in reg 1(2)(a)), 1 May 2009 (for the purposes specified in reg 1(2)(b)), and 1 November 2009 (otherwise). See reg 1 at **[4387]**.

38   Information for the payee after execution

(1)   The payee's payment service provider must, immediately after the execution of the payment transaction, provide or make available to the payee the information specified in paragraph (2).

(2)   The information referred to in paragraph (1) is—
(a)   a reference enabling the payee to identify the payment transaction and, where appropriate, the payer and any information transferred with the payment transaction;
(b)   the amount of the payment transaction in the currency in which the funds are at the payee's disposal;
(c)   the amount of any charges for the payment transaction payable by the payee and, where applicable, a breakdown of the amount of such charges;
(d)   where applicable, the exchange rate used in the payment transaction by the payee's payment service provider, and the amount of the payment transaction before that currency conversion; and
(e)   the credit value date.

[4424]

NOTES
Commencement: these Regulations come into force on 2 March 2009 (for the purposes specified in reg 1(2)(a)), 1 May 2009 (for the purposes specified in reg 1(2)(b)), and 1 November 2009 (otherwise). See reg 1 at **[4387]**.

39   Avoidance of duplication of information

Where a payment order for a single payment transaction is transmitted by way of a payment instrument issued under a framework contract, the payment service provider in respect of that single payment transaction need not provide or make available under regulations 36 to 38 information which has been provided or made available, or will be provided or made available, under regulations 40 to 45 by another payment service provider in respect of the framework contract.

[4425]

NOTES
Commencement: these Regulations come into force on 2 March 2009 (for the purposes specified in reg 1(2)(a)), 1 May 2009 (for the purposes specified in reg 1(2)(b)), and 1 November 2009 (otherwise). See reg 1 at **[4387]**.

Framework contracts

40   Prior general information for framework contracts

(1)   A payment service provider must provide to the payment service user the information specified in Schedule 4, either—
(a)   in good time before the payment service user is bound by the framework contract; or
(b)   where the contract is concluded at the payment service user's request using a means of distance communication which does not enable provision of such information in accordance with sub-paragraph (a), immediately after the conclusion of the contract.

(2)   The payment service provider may discharge the duty under paragraph (1) by supplying a copy of the draft framework contract provided that such contract includes the information specified in Schedule 4.

[4426]

NOTES
Commencement: these Regulations come into force on 2 March 2009 (for the purposes specified in reg 1(2)(a)), 1 May 2009 (for the purposes specified in reg 1(2)(b)), and 1 November 2009 (otherwise). See reg 1 at **[4387]**.

41 Information during period of contract

If the payment service user so requests at any time during the contractual relationship, the payment service provider must provide the information specified in Schedule 4 and the terms of the framework contract.

[4427]

NOTES
Commencement: these Regulations come into force on 2 March 2009 (for the purposes specified in reg 1(2)(a)), 1 May 2009 (for the purposes specified in reg 1(2)(b)), and 1 November 2009 (otherwise). See reg 1 at **[4387]**.

42 Changes in contractual information

(1)   Subject to paragraph (4), any proposed changes to—
   (a)   the existing terms of the framework contract; or
   (b)   the information specified in Schedule 4,
must be communicated by the payment service provider to the payment service user no later than two months before the date on which they are to take effect.

(2)   The framework contract may provide for any such proposed changes to be made unilaterally by the payment service provider where the payment service user does not, before the proposed date of entry into force of the changes, notify the payment service provider to the contrary.

(3)   Where paragraph (2) applies, the payment service provider must inform the payment service user that—
   (a)   the payment service user will be deemed to have accepted the changes in the circumstances referred to in that paragraph; and
   (b)   the payment service user has the right to terminate the framework contract immediately and without charge before the proposed date of their entry into force.

(4)   Changes in the interest or exchange rates may be applied immediately and without notice where—
   (a)   such a right is agreed under the framework contract and the changes are based on the reference interest or exchange rates information on which has been provided to the payment service user in accordance with this Part; or
   (b)   the changes are more favourable to the payment service user.

(5)   The payment service provider must inform the payment service user of any change to the interest rate as soon as possible unless the parties have agreed on a specific frequency or manner in which the information is to be provided or made available.

(6)   Any change in the interest or exchange rate used in payment transactions must be implemented and calculated in a neutral manner that does not discriminate against payment service users.

[4428]

NOTES
Commencement: these Regulations come into force on 2 March 2009 (for the purposes specified in reg 1(2)(a)), 1 May 2009 (for the purposes specified in reg 1(2)(b)), and 1 November 2009 (otherwise). See reg 1 at **[4387]**.

43 Termination of framework contract

(1)   The payment service user may terminate the framework contract at any time unless the parties have agreed on a period of notice not exceeding one month.

(2)   Subject to paragraph (3), any charges for the termination of the contract must reasonably correspond to the actual costs to the payment service provider of termination.

(3)   The payment service provider may not charge the payment service user for the termination, after the expiry of 12 months, of a framework contract concluded for a fixed period of more than 12 months or for an indefinite period.

(4)   The payment service provider may terminate a framework contract concluded for an indefinite period by giving at least two months' notice, if the contract so provides.

(5)   Notice of termination given in accordance with paragraph (4) must be provided in the same way as information is required by regulation 47(1) to be provided or made available.

(6)   Where charges for the payment service are levied on a regular basis, such charges must be apportioned up until the time of the termination of the contract and any charges paid in advance must be reimbursed proportionally.

(7)   This regulation does not affect any right of a party to the framework contract to treat it as unenforceable or void (including any right arising out of a breach of the contract).

[4429]

PART III
STATUTORY INSTRUMENTS

NOTES
Commencement: these Regulations come into force on 2 March 2009 (for the purposes specified in reg 1(2)(a)), 1 May 2009 (for the purposes specified in reg 1(2)(b)), and 1 November 2009 (otherwise). See reg 1 at **[4387]**.

44 Information prior to execution of individual payment transaction

Where an individual payment transaction under a framework contract is initiated by the payer, at the payer's request the payer's payment service provider must inform the payer of—
- (a) the maximum execution time;
- (b) the charges payable by the payer in respect of the payment transaction; and
- (c) where applicable, a breakdown of the amounts of such charges.

[4430]

NOTES
Commencement: these Regulations come into force on 2 March 2009 (for the purposes specified in reg 1(2)(a)), 1 May 2009 (for the purposes specified in reg 1(2)(b)), and 1 November 2009 (otherwise). See reg 1 at **[4387]**.

45 Information for the payer on individual payment transactions

(1) The payer's payment service provider under a framework contract must provide to the payer the information specified in paragraph (2) as soon as reasonably practicable either—
- (a) after the amount of an individual payment transaction is debited from the payer's payment account; or
- (b) where the payer does not use a payment account, after receipt of the payment order.

(2) The information referred to in paragraph (1) is—
- (a) a reference enabling the payer to identify each payment transaction and, where appropriate, information relating to the payee;
- (b) the amount of the payment transaction in the currency in which the payer's payment account is debited or in the currency used for the payment order;
- (c) the amount of any charges for the payment transaction and, where applicable, a breakdown of the amounts of such charges, or the interest payable by the payer;
- (d) where applicable, the exchange rate used in the payment transaction by the payer's payment service provider and the amount of the payment transaction after that currency conversion; and
- (e) the debit value date or the date of receipt of the payment order.

(3) A framework contract may include a condition that the information specified in paragraph (2) be provided or made available periodically at least once a month and in an agreed manner which enables the payer to store and reproduce the information unchanged.

[4431]

NOTES
Commencement: these Regulations come into force on 2 March 2009 (for the purposes specified in reg 1(2)(a)), 1 May 2009 (for the purposes specified in reg 1(2)(b)), and 1 November 2009 (otherwise). See reg 1 at **[4387]**.

46 Information for the payee on individual payment transactions

(1) As soon as reasonably practicable after the execution of an individual payment transaction under a framework contract, the payee's payment service provider must provide to the payee the information specified in paragraph (2).

(2) The information referred to in paragraph (1) is-
- (a) a reference enabling the payee to identify the payment transaction and, where appropriate, the payer, and any information transferred with the payment transaction;
- (b) the amount of the payment transaction in the currency in which the payee's payment account is credited;
- (c) the amount of any charges for the payment transaction and, where applicable, a breakdown of the amounts of such charges, or the interest payable by the payee;
- (d) where applicable, the exchange rate used in the payment transaction by the payee's payment service provider, and the amount of the payment transaction before that currency conversion; and
- (e) the credit value date.

(3) A framework contract may include a condition that the information specified in paragraph (2) is to be provided or made available periodically at least once a month and in an agreed manner which enables the payee to store and reproduce the information unchanged.

[4432]

NOTES
Commencement: these Regulations come into force on 2 March 2009 (for the purposes specified in reg 1(2)(a)), 1 May 2009 (for the purposes specified in reg 1(2)(b)), and 1 November 2009 (otherwise). See reg 1 at **[4387]**.

Common provisions

47 Communication of information

(1)   Subject to regulation 35(2)(c), any information provided or made available in accordance with this Part must be provided or made available—

(a)   in an easily accessible manner;

(b)   if the payment service user so requests, on paper or on another durable medium;

(c)   in easily understandable language and in a clear and comprehensible form; and

(d)   in English or in the language agreed by the parties.

(2)   Paragraph (1)(b) is subject to any agreement in accordance with regulation 45(3) or 46(3) as to the manner in which information is to be provided or made available.

[4433]

NOTES
Commencement: these Regulations come into force on 2 March 2009 (for the purposes specified in reg 1(2)(a)), 1 May 2009 (for the purposes specified in reg 1(2)(b)), and 1 November 2009 (otherwise). See reg 1 at **[4387]**.

48 Charges for information

(1)   A payment service provider may not charge for providing or making available information which is required to be provided or made available by this Part.

(2)   The payment service provider and the payment service user may agree on charges for any information which is provided at the request of the payment service user where such information is—

(a)   additional to the information required to be provided or made available by this Part;

(b)   provided more frequently than is specified in this Part; or

(c)   transmitted by means of communication other than those specified in the framework contract.

(3)   Any charges imposed under paragraph (2) must reasonably correspond to the payment service provider's actual costs.

[4434]

NOTES
Commencement: these Regulations come into force on 2 March 2009 (for the purposes specified in reg 1(2)(a)), 1 May 2009 (for the purposes specified in reg 1(2)(b)), and 1 November 2009 (otherwise). See reg 1 at **[4387]**.

49 Currency and currency conversion

(1)   Payment transactions must be executed in the currency agreed between the parties.

(2)   Where a currency conversion service is offered before the initiation of the payment transaction—

(a)   at the point of sale; or

(b)   by the payee,

the party offering the currency conversion service to the payer must disclose to the payer all charges as well as the exchange rate to be used for converting the payment transaction.

[4435]

NOTES
Commencement: these Regulations come into force on 2 March 2009 (for the purposes specified in reg 1(2)(a)), 1 May 2009 (for the purposes specified in reg 1(2)(b)), and 1 November 2009 (otherwise). See reg 1 at **[4387]**.

50 Information on additional charges or reductions

(1)   The payee must inform the payer of any charge requested or reduction offered by the payee for the use of a particular payment instrument before the initiation of the payment transaction.

(2)   The payment service provider, or any relevant third party, must inform the payment service user of any charge requested by the payment service provider or third party, as the case may be, for the use of a particular payment instrument before the initiation of the payment transaction.

[4436]

NOTES
Commencement: these Regulations come into force on 2 March 2009 (for the purposes specified in reg 1(2)(a)), 1 May 2009 (for the purposes specified in reg 1(2)(b)), and 1 November 2009 (otherwise). See reg 1 at **[4387]**.

PART 6
RIGHTS AND OBLIGATIONS IN RELATION TO THE PROVISION OF PAYMENT SERVICES

Application

51 Application of Part 6

(1) This Part applies to a contract for payment services where—
  (a) the services are provided from an establishment maintained by a payment service provider or its agent in the United Kingdom;
  (b) subject to paragraph (2), the payment service providers of both the payer and the payee are located within the EEA; and
  (c) where the payment services are carried out in euro or in the currency of an EEA State that has not adopted the euro as its currency.

(2) Regulation 73 applies whether or not the payment service providers of both the payer and the payee are located within the EEA.

(3) Except where the payment service user is a consumer, a micro-enterprise or a charity, the parties may agree that—
  (a) any or all of regulations 54(1), 55(2), 60, 62, 63, 64, 67, 75, 76 and 77 do not apply;
  (b) a different time period applies for the purposes of regulation 59(1).

[4437]

NOTES
Commencement: these Regulations come into force on 2 March 2009 (for the purposes specified in reg 1(2)(a)), 1 May 2009 (for the purposes specified in reg 1(2)(b)), and 1 November 2009 (otherwise). See reg 1 at **[4387]**.

52 Disapplication of certain regulations in the case of consumer credit agreements

The following provisions of the Consumer Credit Act 1974 shall apply in relation to contracts for the provision of payment services which are regulated agreements for the purposes of that Act in place of the following provisions of these Regulations—
  (a) section 51 (prohibition of unsolicited credit tokens) in place of regulation 58(1)(b);
  (b) sections 66 (acceptance of credit tokens) and 84 (misuse of credit tokens) in place of regulations 59, 61 and 62;
  (c) section 83 (liability for misuse of credit facilities) in place of regulations 59, 61 and 62;
  (d) sections 76 (duty to give notice before taking certain action) and 87 (need for default notice) in relation to the grounds mentioned in regulation 56(2) in place of regulation 56(3) to (6).

[4438]

NOTES
Commencement: these Regulations come into force on 2 March 2009 (for the purposes specified in reg 1(2)(a)), 1 May 2009 (for the purposes specified in reg 1(2)(b)), and 1 November 2009 (otherwise). See reg 1 at **[4387]**.

53 Disapplication of certain regulations in the case of low value payment instruments

(1) This regulation applies in respect of payment instruments which, under the framework contract governing their use—
  (a) can be used only to execute individual payment transactions of 30 euro or less, or in relation to payment transactions executed wholly within the United Kingdom, 60 euro or less;
  (b) have a spending limit of 150 euro, or where payment transactions must be executed wholly within the United Kingdom, 300 euro; or
  (c) store funds that do not exceed 500 euro at any time.

(2) Where this regulation applies the parties may agree that—
  (a) regulations 57(1)(b), 58(1)(c), (d) and (e) and 62(3) do not apply where the payment instrument does not allow for the stopping or prevention of its use;
  (b) regulations 60, 61 and 62(1) and (2) do not apply where the payment instrument is used anonymously or the payment service provider is not in a position, for other reasons concerning the payment instrument, to prove that a payment transaction was authorised;

(c) the payment service provider is not required under regulation 66(1) to notify the payment service user of the refusal of a payment order if the non-execution is apparent from the context;

(d) the payer may not revoke the payment order under regulation 67 after transmitting the payment order or giving their consent to execute the payment transaction to the payee;

(e) execution periods other than those provided by regulations 70 and 71 apply.

(3) Subject to paragraph (2)(b), regulations 61 and 62(1) and (2) apply to electronic money as defined in Article 1(3)(b) of the electronic money directive unless the payer's payment service provider does not have the ability under the contract to—

(a) freeze the payment account; or

(b) stop the use of the payment instrument.

[4439]

NOTES

Commencement: these Regulations come into force on 2 March 2009 (for the purposes specified in reg 1(2)(a)), 1 May 2009 (for the purposes specified in reg 1(2)(b)), and 1 November 2009 (otherwise). See reg 1 at **[4387]**.

Charges

54 Charges

(1) The payment service provider may only charge the payment service user for the fulfilment of any of its obligations under this Part—

(a) in accordance with regulation 66(3), 67(6) or 74(2)(b);

(b) where agreed between the parties; and

(c) where such charges reasonably correspond to the payment service provider's actual costs.

(2) Where a payment transaction does not involve any currency conversion, the respective payment service providers must ensure that—

(a) the payee pays any charges levied by the payee's payment service provider; and

(b) the payer pays any charges levied by the payer's payment service provider.

(3) The payee's payment service provider may not prevent the payee from—

(a) requiring payment of a charge by; or

(b) offering a reduction to,

the payer for the use of a particular payment instrument.

[4440]

NOTES

Commencement: these Regulations come into force on 2 March 2009 (for the purposes specified in reg 1(2)(a)), 1 May 2009 (for the purposes specified in reg 1(2)(b)), and 1 November 2009 (otherwise). See reg 1 at **[4387]**.

Authorisation of payment transactions

55 Consent and withdrawal of consent

(1) A payment transaction is to be regarded as having been authorised by the payer for the purposes of this Part only if the payer has given its consent to—

(a) the execution of the payment transaction; or

(b) the execution of a series of payment transactions of which that payment transaction forms part.

(2) Such consent—

(a) may be given before or, if agreed between the payer and its payment service provider, after the execution of the payment transaction; and

(b) must be given in the form, and in accordance with the procedure, agreed between the payer and its payment service provider.

(3) The payer may withdraw its consent to a payment transaction at any time before the point at which the payment order can no longer be revoked under regulation 67.

(4) Subject to regulation 67(3) to (5), the payer may withdraw its consent to the execution of a series of payment transactions at any time with the effect that any future payment transactions are not regarded as authorised for the purposes of this Part.

[4441]

NOTES

Commencement: these Regulations come into force on 2 March 2009 (for the purposes specified in reg 1(2)(a)), 1 May 2009 (for the purposes specified in reg 1(2)(b)), and 1 November 2009 (otherwise). See reg 1 at **[4387]**.

PART III
STATUTORY INSTRUMENTS

56 Limits on the use of payment instruments

(1)   Where a specific payment instrument is used for the purpose of giving consent to the execution of a payment transaction, the payer and its payment service provider may agree on spending limits for any payment transactions executed through that payment instrument.

(2)   A framework contract may provide for the payment service provider to have the right to stop the use of a payment instrument on reasonable grounds relating to—
  (a)   the security of the payment instrument;
  (b)   the suspected unauthorised or fraudulent use of the payment instrument; or
  (c)   in the case of a payment instrument with a credit line, a significantly increased risk that the payer may be unable to fulfil its liability to pay.

(3)   The payment service provider must, in the manner agreed between the payment service provider and the payer and before carrying out any measures to stop the use of the payment instrument—
  (a)   inform the payer that it intends to stop the use of the payment instrument; and
  (b)   give its reasons for doing so.

(4)   Where the payment service provider is unable to inform the payer in accordance with paragraph (3) before carrying out any measures to stop the use of the payment instrument, it must do so immediately after.

(5)   Paragraphs (3) and (4) do not apply where provision of the information in accordance with paragraph (3) would compromise reasonable security measures or is otherwise unlawful.

(6)   The payment service provider must allow the use of the payment instrument or replace it with a new payment instrument as soon as practicable after the reasons for stopping its use cease to exist.

[4442]

NOTES
Commencement: these Regulations come into force on 2 March 2009 (for the purposes specified in reg 1(2)(a)), 1 May 2009 (for the purposes specified in reg 1(2)(b)), and 1 November 2009 (otherwise). See reg 1 at **[4387]**.

57 Obligations of the payment service user in relation to payment instruments

(1)   A payment service user to whom a payment instrument has been issued must—
  (a)   use the payment instrument in accordance with the terms and conditions governing its issue and use; and
  (b)   notify the payment service provider in the agreed manner and without undue delay on becoming aware of the loss, theft, misappropriation or unauthorised use of the payment instrument.

(2)   The payment service user must on receiving a payment instrument take all reasonable steps to keep its personalised security features safe.

[4443]

NOTES
Commencement: these Regulations come into force on 2 March 2009 (for the purposes specified in reg 1(2)(a)), 1 May 2009 (for the purposes specified in reg 1(2)(b)), and 1 November 2009 (otherwise). See reg 1 at **[4387]**.

58 Obligations of the payment service provider in relation to payment instruments

(1)   A payment service provider issuing a payment instrument must—
  (a)   subject to regulation 57, ensure that the personalised security features of the payment instrument are not accessible to persons other than the payment service user to whom the payment instrument has been issued;
  (b)   not send an unsolicited payment instrument, except where a payment instrument already issued to a payment service user is to be replaced;
  (c)   ensure that appropriate means are available at all times to enable the payment service user to notify the payment service provider in accordance with regulation 57(1)(b) or to request that the use of the payment instrument is no longer stopped in accordance with regulation 56(6);
  (d)   on request, provide the payment service user at any time during a period of 18 months after the alleged date of notification under regulation 57(1)(b) with the means to prove that such notification to the payment service provider was made;
  (e)   prevent any use of the payment instrument once notification has been made under regulation 57(1)(b).

(2)   The payment service provider bears the risk of sending a payment instrument or any of its personalised security features to the payment service user.

[4444]

NOTES
Commencement: these Regulations come into force on 2 March 2009 (for the purposes specified in reg 1(2)(a)), 1 May 2009 (for the purposes specified in reg 1(2)(b)), and 1 November 2009 (otherwise). See reg 1 at **[4387]**.

59 Notification of unauthorised or incorrectly executed payment transactions

(1) A payment service user is entitled to redress under regulation 61, 75, 76 or 77 only if it notifies the payment service provider without undue delay, and in any event no later than 13 months after the debit date, on becoming aware of any unauthorised or incorrectly executed payment transaction.

(2) Where the payment service provider has failed to provide or make available information concerning the payment transaction in accordance with Part 5 of these Regulations, the payment service user is entitled to redress under the regulations referred to in paragraph (1) notwithstanding that the payment service user has failed to notify the payment service provider as mentioned in that paragraph.

[4445]

NOTES
Commencement: these Regulations come into force on 2 March 2009 (for the purposes specified in reg 1(2)(a)), 1 May 2009 (for the purposes specified in reg 1(2)(b)), and 1 November 2009 (otherwise). See reg 1 at **[4387]**.

60 Evidence on authentication and execution of payment transactions

(1) Where a payment service user—
   (a) denies having authorised an executed payment transaction; or
   (b) claims that a payment transaction has not been correctly executed,

it is for the payment service provider to prove that the payment transaction was authenticated, accurately recorded, entered in the payment service provider's accounts and not affected by a technical breakdown or some other deficiency.

(2) In paragraph (1) "authenticated" means the use of any procedure by which a payment service provider is able to verify the use of a specific payment instrument, including its personalised security features.

(3) Where a payment service user denies having authorised an executed payment transaction, the use of a payment instrument recorded by the payment service provider is not in itself necessarily sufficient to prove either that—
   (a) the payment transaction was authorised by the payer; or
   (b) the payer acted fraudulently or failed with intent or gross negligence to comply with regulation 57.

[4446]

NOTES
Commencement: these Regulations come into force on 2 March 2009 (for the purposes specified in reg 1(2)(a)), 1 May 2009 (for the purposes specified in reg 1(2)(b)), and 1 November 2009 (otherwise). See reg 1 at **[4387]**.

61 Payment service provider's liability for unauthorised payment transactions

Subject to regulations 59 and 60, where an executed payment transaction was not authorised in accordance with regulation 55, the payment service provider must immediately—
   (a) refund the amount of the unauthorised payment transaction to the payer; and
   (b) where applicable, restore the debited payment account to the state it would have been in had the unauthorised payment transaction not taken place.

[4447]

NOTES
Commencement: these Regulations come into force on 2 March 2009 (for the purposes specified in reg 1(2)(a)), 1 May 2009 (for the purposes specified in reg 1(2)(b)), and 1 November 2009 (otherwise). See reg 1 at **[4387]**.

62 Payer's liability for unauthorised payment transaction

(1) Subject to paragraphs (2) and (3), the payer is liable up to a maximum of £50 for any losses incurred in respect of unauthorised payment transactions arising—
   (a) from the use of a lost or stolen payment instrument; or
   (b) where the payer has failed to keep the personalised security features of the payment instrument safe, from the misappropriation of the payment instrument.

(2)   The payer is liable for all losses incurred in respect of an unauthorised payment transaction where the payer—

    (a)   has acted fraudulently; or

    (b)   has with intent or gross negligence failed to comply with regulation 57.

(3)   Except where the payer has acted fraudulently, the payer is not liable for any losses incurred in respect of an unauthorised payment transaction—

    (a)   arising after notification under regulation 57(1)(b);

    (b)   where the payment service provider has failed at any time to provide, in accordance with regulation 58(1)(c), appropriate means for notification; or

    (c)   where the payment instrument has been used in connection with a distance contract (other than an excepted contract).

(4)   In paragraph (3)(c) "distance contract" and "excepted contract" have the meanings given in the Consumer Protection (Distance Selling) Regulations 2000.

[4448]

NOTES

Commencement: these Regulations come into force on 2 March 2009 (for the purposes specified in reg 1(2)(a)), 1 May 2009 (for the purposes specified in reg 1(2)(b)), and 1 November 2009 (otherwise). See reg 1 at **[4387]**.

---

63   Refunds for payment transactions initiated by or through a payee

(1)   Where the conditions in paragraph (2) and the requirement in regulation 64(1) are satisfied, the payer is entitled to a refund from its payment service provider of the full amount of any authorised payment transaction initiated by or through the payee.

(2)   The conditions are that—

    (a)   the authorisation did not specify the exact amount of the payment transaction when the authorisation was given in accordance with regulation 55; and

    (b)   the amount of the payment transaction exceeded the amount that the payer could reasonably have expected taking into account the payer's previous spending pattern, the conditions of the framework contract and the circumstances of the case.

(3)   The payer and payment service provider may agree in the framework contract, in respect of direct debits, that the conditions in paragraph (2) need not be satisfied in order for the payer to be entitled to a refund.

(4)   For the purposes of paragraph (2)(b), the payer cannot rely on currency exchange fluctuations where the reference exchange rate provided under regulation 36(2)(d) or paragraph 3(b) of Schedule 4 was applied.

(5)   The payer and payment service provider may agree in the framework contract that the right to a refund does not apply where—

    (a)   the payer has given consent directly to the payment service provider for the payment transaction to be executed; and

    (b)   if applicable, information on the payment transaction was provided or made available in an agreed manner to the payer for at least four weeks before the due date by the payment service provider or by the payee.

[4449]

NOTES

Commencement: these Regulations come into force on 2 March 2009 (for the purposes specified in reg 1(2)(a)), 1 May 2009 (for the purposes specified in reg 1(2)(b)), and 1 November 2009 (otherwise). See reg 1 at **[4387]**.

---

64   Requests for refunds for payment transactions initiated by or through a payee

(1)   The payer must request a refund under regulation 63 from its payment service provider within 8 weeks from the date on which the funds were debited.

(2)   The payment service provider may require the payer to provide such information as is reasonably necessary to ascertain whether the conditions in regulation 63(2) are satisfied.

(3)   Subject to paragraph (4), the payment service provider must either—

    (a)   refund the full amount of the payment transaction; or

    (b)   provide justification for refusing to refund the payment transaction, indicating the bodies to which the payer may refer the matter if the payer does not accept the justification provided.

(4)   Where an agreement in accordance with regulation 63(3) applies, the payment service provider must, notwithstanding that a condition in regulation 63(2) is not satisfied, refund the full amount of the payment transaction.

(5)   Any refund or justification for refusing a refund must be provided within 10 business days of receiving a request for a refund or, where applicable, within 10 business days of receiving any further information requested under paragraph (2).

[4450]

NOTES
Commencement: these Regulations come into force on 2 March 2009 (for the purposes specified in reg 1(2)(a)), 1 May 2009 (for the purposes specified in reg 1(2)(b)), and 1 November 2009 (otherwise). See reg 1 at **[4387]**.

Execution of payment transactions

65   Receipt of payment orders

(1)   Subject to paragraphs (2) to (5), for the purposes of these Regulations the time of receipt of a payment order is the time at which the payment order, given directly by the payer or indirectly by or through a payee, is received by the payer's payment service provider.

(2)   If the time of receipt of a payment order does not fall on a business day for the payer's payment service provider, the payment order is deemed to have been received on the first business day thereafter.

(3)   The payment service provider may set a time towards the end of a business day after which any payment order received will be deemed to have been received on the following business day.

(4)   Where the payment service user initiating a payment order agrees with its payment service provider that execution of the payment order is to take place—
   (a)   on a specific day;
   (b)   on the last day of a certain period; or
   (c)   on the day on which the payer has put funds at the disposal of its payment service provider,
the time of receipt is deemed to be the day so agreed.

(5)   If the day agreed under paragraph (4) is not a business day for the payer's payment service provider, the payment order is deemed to have been received on the first business day thereafter.

[4451]

NOTES
Commencement: these Regulations come into force on 2 March 2009 (for the purposes specified in reg 1(2)(a)), 1 May 2009 (for the purposes specified in reg 1(2)(b)), and 1 November 2009 (otherwise). See reg 1 at **[4387]**.

66   Refusal of payment orders

(1)   Subject to paragraph (4), where a payment service provider refuses to execute a payment order, it must notify the payment service user of—
   (a)   the refusal;
   (b)   if possible, the reasons for such refusal; and
   (c)   the procedure for rectifying any factual errors that led to the refusal.

(2)   Any notification under paragraph (1) must be given or made available in an agreed manner and at the earliest opportunity, and in any event within the periods specified in regulation 70.

(3)   The framework contract may provide for the payment service provider to charge the payment service user for such notification where the refusal is reasonably justified.

(4)   The payment service provider is not required to notify the payment service user under paragraph (1) where such notification would be otherwise unlawful.

(5)   Where all the conditions set out in the payer's framework contract have been satisfied, the payment service provider may not refuse to execute an authorised payment order irrespective of whether the payment order is initiated by the payer or by or through a payee, unless such execution is otherwise unlawful.

(6)   For the purposes of regulations 70, 75 and 76 a payment order of which execution has been refused is deemed not to have been received.

[4452]

NOTES
Commencement: these Regulations come into force on 2 March 2009 (for the purposes specified in reg 1(2)(a)), 1 May 2009 (for the purposes specified in reg 1(2)(b)), and 1 November 2009 (otherwise). See reg 1 at **[4387]**.

67   Revocation of a payment order

(1)   Subject to paragraphs (2) to (5), a payment service user may not revoke a payment order after it has been received by the payer's payment service provider.

(2)   In the case of a payment transaction initiated by or through the payee, the payer may not revoke the payment order after transmitting the payment order or giving consent to execute the payment transaction to the payee.

(3)   In the case of a direct debit, the payer may not revoke the payment order after the end of the business day preceding the day agreed for debiting the funds.

(4)   Where a day is agreed under regulation 65(4), the payment service user may not revoke a payment order after the end of the business day preceding the agreed day.

(5)   At any time after the time limits for revocation set out in paragraphs (1) to (4), the payment order may only be revoked if the revocation is—

(a)   agreed between the payment service user and its payment service provider; and

(b)   in the case of a payment transaction initiated by or through the payee, including in the case of a direct debit, also agreed with the payee.

(6)   A framework contract may provide for the payment service provider to charge for revocation under this regulation.

[4453]

NOTES
   Commencement: these Regulations come into force on 2 March 2009 (for the purposes specified in reg 1(2)(a)), 1 May 2009 (for the purposes specified in reg 1(2)(b)), and 1 November 2009 (otherwise). See reg 1 at [4387].

68   Amounts transferred and amounts received

(1)   Subject to paragraph (2), the payment service providers of the payer and payee must ensure that the full amount of the payment transaction is transferred and that no charges are deducted from the amount transferred.

(2)   The payee and its payment service provider may agree for the payment service provider to deduct its charges from the amount transferred before crediting it to the payee provided that the full amount of the payment transaction and the amount of the charges are clearly stated in the information provided to the payee.

(3)   If charges other than those provided for by paragraph (2) are deducted from the amount transferred—

(a)   in the case of a payment transaction initiated by the payer, the payer's payment service provider must ensure that the payee receives the full amount of the payment transaction;

(b)   in the case of a payment transaction initiated by the payee, the payee's payment service provider must ensure that the payee receives the full amount of the payment transaction.

[4454]

NOTES
   Commencement: these Regulations come into force on 2 March 2009 (for the purposes specified in reg 1(2)(a)), 1 May 2009 (for the purposes specified in reg 1(2)(b)), and 1 November 2009 (otherwise). See reg 1 at [4387].

Execution time and value date

69   Application of regulations 70 to 72

(1)   Regulations 70 to 72 apply to any transaction—

(a)   in euro;

(b)   in sterling; or

(c)   involving only one currency conversion between the euro and sterling, provided that—

(i)   the currency conversion is carried out in the United Kingdom; and

(ii)   in the case of cross-border payment transactions, the cross-border transfer takes place in euro.

(2)   In respect of any other transaction, the payment service user may agree with the payment service provider that regulations 70 (other than regulation 70(4)) to 72 do not apply.

[4455]

NOTES
   Commencement: these Regulations come into force on 2 March 2009 (for the purposes specified in reg 1(2)(a)), 1 May 2009 (for the purposes specified in reg 1(2)(b)), and 1 November 2009 (otherwise). See reg 1 at [4387].

70   Payment transactions to a payment account

(1)   Subject to paragraphs (2), (3) and (4), the payer's payment service provider must ensure that the amount of the payment transaction is credited to the payee's payment service provider's account by the end of the business day following the time of receipt of the payment order.

(2)   Until 1st January 2012, the payer and their payment service provider may agree that the amount of the payment transaction is to be credited to the payee's payment service provider's account by the end of the third business day following the time of receipt of the payment order.

(3)   Where a payment transaction is initiated by way of a paper payment order—
   (a)   the reference in paragraph (1) to the end of the business day following the time of receipt of the payment order is to be treated as a reference to the end of the second business day following the time of receipt of the payment order; and
   (b)   the reference in paragraph (2) to the end of the third business day following the time of receipt of the payment order is to be treated as a reference to the end of the fourth business day following the time of receipt of the payment order.

(4)   Where a payment transaction—
   (a)   does not fall within paragraphs (a) to (c) of regulation 69(1); but
   (b)   is to be executed wholly within the EEA,
the payer's payment service provider must ensure that the amount of the payment transaction is credited to the payee's payment service provider's account by the end of the fourth business day following the time of receipt of the payment order.

(5)   The payee's payment service provider must value date and credit the amount of the payment transaction to the payee's payment account following its receipt of the funds.

(6)   The payee's payment service provider must transmit a payment order initiated by or through the payee to the payer's payment service provider within the time limits agreed between the payee and its payment service provider, enabling settlement in respect of a direct debit to occur on the agreed due date.

[4456]

NOTES
   Commencement: these Regulations come into force on 2 March 2009 (for the purposes specified in reg 1(2)(a)), 1 May 2009 (for the purposes specified in reg 1(2)(b)), and 1 November 2009 (otherwise). See reg 1 at **[4387]**.

71   Absence of payee's payment account with the payment service provider

(1)   Paragraph (2) applies where a payment service provider accepts funds on behalf of a payee who does not have a payment account with that payment service provider.

(2)   The payment service provider must make the funds available to the payee immediately after the funds have been credited to that payment service provider's account.

[4457]

NOTES
   Commencement: these Regulations come into force on 2 March 2009 (for the purposes specified in reg 1(2)(a)), 1 May 2009 (for the purposes specified in reg 1(2)(b)), and 1 November 2009 (otherwise). See reg 1 at **[4387]**.

72   Cash placed on a payment account

Where a payment service user places cash on its payment account with a payment service provider in the same currency as that payment account, the payment service provider must—
   (a)   if the user is a consumer, micro-enterprise or charity, ensure that the amount is made available and value dated immediately after the receipt of the funds;
   (b)   in any other case, ensure that the amount is made available and value dated no later than the end of the business day after the receipt of the funds.

[4458]

NOTES
   Commencement: these Regulations come into force on 2 March 2009 (for the purposes specified in reg 1(2)(a)), 1 May 2009 (for the purposes specified in reg 1(2)(b)), and 1 November 2009 (otherwise). See reg 1 at **[4387]**.

73   Value date and availability of funds

(1)   The credit value date for the payee's payment account must be no later than the business day on which the amount of the payment transaction is credited to the account of the payee's payment service provider.

(2)   The payee's payment service provider must ensure that the amount of the payment transaction is at the payee's disposal immediately after that amount has been credited to that payment service provider's account.

(3)   The debit value date for the payer's payment account must be no earlier than the time at which the amount of the payment transaction is debited to that payment account.

[4459]

NOTES

Commencement: these Regulations come into force on 2 March 2009 (for the purposes specified in reg 1(2)(a)), 1 May 2009 (for the purposes specified in reg 1(2)(b)), and 1 November 2009 (otherwise). See reg 1 at **[4387]**.

Liability

74 Incorrect unique identifiers

(1)   Where a payment order is executed in accordance with the unique identifier, the payment order is deemed to have been correctly executed by each payment service provider involved in executing the payment order with respect to the payee specified by the unique identifier.

(2)   Where the unique identifier provided by the payment service user is incorrect, the payment service provider is not liable under regulation 75 or 76 for non-execution or defective execution of the payment transaction, but the payment service provider—

(a)   must make reasonable efforts to recover the funds involved in the payment transaction; and

(b)   may, if agreed in the framework contract, charge the payment service user for any such recovery.

(3)   Where the payment service user provides information additional to that specified in regulation 36(2)(a) or paragraph 2(b) of Schedule 4, the payment service provider is liable only for the execution of payment transactions in accordance with the unique identifier provided by the payment service user.

[4460]

NOTES

Commencement: these Regulations come into force on 2 March 2009 (for the purposes specified in reg 1(2)(a)), 1 May 2009 (for the purposes specified in reg 1(2)(b)), and 1 November 2009 (otherwise). See reg 1 at **[4387]**.

75 Non-execution or defective execution of payment transactions initiated by the payer

(1)   This regulation applies where a payment order is initiated by the payer.

(2)   The payer's payment service provider is liable to the payer for the correct execution of the payment transaction unless it can prove to the payer and, where relevant, to the payee's payment service provider, that the payee's payment service provider received the amount of the payment transaction in accordance with regulation 70.

(3)   The payer's payment service provider must, on request, make immediate efforts to trace the payment transaction and notify the payer of the outcome.

(4)   Where the payer's payment service provider is liable under paragraph (2), it must without undue delay refund to the payer the amount of the non-executed or defective payment transaction and, where applicable, restore the debited payment account to the state in which it would have been had the defective payment transaction not taken place.

(5)   Where the payer's payment service provider can prove (as set out in paragraph (2)) that the payee's payment service provider received the amount of the payment transaction in accordance with regulation 70, the payee's payment service provider is liable to the payee for the correct execution of the payment transaction and must—

(a)   immediately make available the amount of the payment transaction to the payee; and

(b)   where applicable, credit the corresponding amount to the payee's payment account.

[4461]

NOTES

Commencement: these Regulations come into force on 2 March 2009 (for the purposes specified in reg 1(2)(a)), 1 May 2009 (for the purposes specified in reg 1(2)(b)), and 1 November 2009 (otherwise). See reg 1 at **[4387]**.

76 Non-execution or defective execution of payment transactions initiated by the payee

(1)   This regulation applies where a payment order is initiated by the payee.

(2)   The payee's payment service provider is liable to the payee for the correct transmission of the payment order to the payer's payment service provider in accordance with regulation 70(6).

(3)   Where the payee's payment service provider is liable under paragraph (2), it must immediately re-transmit the payment order in question to the payer's payment service provider.

(4)   The payee's payment service provider must, on request, make immediate efforts to trace the payment transaction and notify the payee of the outcome.

(5)　Where the payee's payment service provider can prove to the payee and, where relevant, to the payer's payment service provider, that it is not liable under paragraph (2) in respect of a non-executed or defectively executed payment transaction, the payer's payment service provider is liable to the payer and must, as appropriate and without undue delay—

(a)　refund to the payer the amount of the payment transaction; and

(b)　restore the debited payment account to the state in which it would have been had the defective payment transaction not taken place.

[4462]

NOTES

Commencement: these Regulations come into force on 2 March 2009 (for the purposes specified in reg 1(2)(a)), 1 May 2009 (for the purposes specified in reg 1(2)(b)), and 1 November 2009 (otherwise). See reg 1 at **[4387]**.

77　Liability of payment service provider for charges and interest

A payment service provider is liable to its payment service user for—

(a)　any charges for which the payment service user is responsible; and

(b)　any interest which the payment service user must pay,

as a consequence of the non-execution or defective execution of the payment transaction.

[4463]

NOTES

Commencement: these Regulations come into force on 2 March 2009 (for the purposes specified in reg 1(2)(a)), 1 May 2009 (for the purposes specified in reg 1(2)(b)), and 1 November 2009 (otherwise). See reg 1 at **[4387]**.

78　Right of recourse

Where the liability of a payment service provider ("the first provider") under regulation 75 or 76 is attributable to another payment service provider or an intermediary, the other payment service provider or intermediary must compensate the first provider for any losses incurred or sums paid pursuant to those regulations.

[4464]

NOTES

Commencement: these Regulations come into force on 2 March 2009 (for the purposes specified in reg 1(2)(a)), 1 May 2009 (for the purposes specified in reg 1(2)(b)), and 1 November 2009 (otherwise). See reg 1 at **[4387]**.

79　Force majeure

(1)　A person is not liable for any contravention of a requirement imposed on it by or under this Part where the contravention is due to abnormal and unforeseeable circumstances beyond the person's control, the consequences of which would have been unavoidable despite all efforts to the contrary.

(2)　A payment service provider is not liable for any contravention of a requirement imposed on it by or under this Part where the contravention is due to the obligations of the payment service provider under other provisions of Community or national law.

[4465]

NOTES

Commencement: these Regulations come into force on 2 March 2009 (for the purposes specified in reg 1(2)(a)), 1 May 2009 (for the purposes specified in reg 1(2)(b)), and 1 November 2009 (otherwise). See reg 1 at **[4387]**.

PART 7
THE AUTHORITY

The functions of the Authority

80　Functions of the Authority

(1)　The Authority is to have the functions conferred on it by these Regulations.

(2)　In discharging its function of determining the general policy and principles by reference to which it performs particular functions under these Regulations, the Authority must have regard to—

(a)　the need to use its resources in the most efficient and economic way;

(b)　the responsibilities of those who manage the affairs of payment service providers;

(c)　the principle that a burden or restriction which is imposed on a person, or on the carrying on of an activity, should be proportionate to the benefits, considered in general terms, which are expected to result from the imposition of that burden or restriction;

PART III
STATUTORY INSTRUMENTS

(d)   the desirability of facilitating innovation in connection with payment services;
(e)   the international character of financial services and markets and the desirability of maintaining the competitive position of the United Kingdom;
(f)   the need to minimise the adverse effects on competition that may arise from anything done in the discharge of those functions; and
(g)   the desirability of facilitating competition in relation to payment services.

[4466]

NOTES

Commencement: these Regulations come into force on 2 March 2009 (for the purposes specified in reg 1(2)(a)), 1 May 2009 (for the purposes specified in reg 1(2)(b)), and 1 November 2009 (otherwise). See reg 1 at [4387].

Supervision and enforcement

81 Monitoring and enforcement

(1)   The Authority must maintain arrangements designed to enable it to determine whether—
(a)   persons on whom requirements are imposed by or under Part 2, 3 or 4 of these Regulations are complying with them;
(b)   there has been any contravention of regulation 110(1), 111(1) or 114(1)(a) or (2).

(2)   The Authority may maintain arrangements designed to enable it to determine whether persons on whom requirements are imposed by or under Part 5 or 6 of these Regulations are complying with them.

(3)   The arrangements referred to in paragraphs (1) and (2) may provide for functions to be performed on behalf of the Authority by any body or person who is, in its opinion, competent to perform them.

(4)   The Authority must also maintain arrangements for enforcing the provisions of these Regulations.

(5)   Paragraph (3) does not affect the Authority's duty under paragraph (1).

[4467]

NOTES

Commencement: these Regulations come into force on 2 March 2009 (for the purposes specified in reg 1(2)(a)), 1 May 2009 (for the purposes specified in reg 1(2)(b)), and 1 November 2009 (otherwise). See reg 1 at [4387].

82 Reporting requirements

(1)   A payment service provider must give the Authority such information in respect of its provision of payment services and its compliance with requirements imposed by or under Parts 2 to 6 of these Regulations as the Authority may direct.

(2)   Information required under this regulation must be given at such times and in such form, and verified in such manner, as the Authority may direct.

[4468]

NOTES

Commencement: these Regulations come into force on 2 March 2009 (for the purposes specified in reg 1(2)(a)), 1 May 2009 (for the purposes specified in reg 1(2)(b)), and 1 November 2009 (otherwise). See reg 1 at [4387].

83 Entry, inspection without a warrant etc

(1)   Paragraph (2) applies where an officer has reasonable cause to believe that any premises are being used by—
(i)   an authorised payment institution, an EEA authorised payment institution or a small payment institution (including any of its branches) in connection with its business activities;
(ii)   an agent providing payment services on behalf of an authorised payment institution, an EEA authorised payment institution or a small payment institution; or
(iii) an entity to which an authorised payment institution or an EEA authorised payment institution has outsourced any of its business activities.

(2)   The officer may on producing evidence of authority at any reasonable time—
(a)   enter the premises;
(b)   inspect the premises;
(c)   observe the carrying on of business activities by the authorised payment institution, the EEA authorised payment institution or the small payment institution, as the case may be;
(d)   inspect any document found on the premises;

(e) require any person on the premises to provide an explanation of any document or to state where it may be found.

(3) An officer may take copies of, or make extracts from, any document found under paragraph (2).

(4) An officer may exercise powers under this regulation only if the information or document sought to be obtained as a result is reasonably required in connection with the exercise by the Authority of its functions under these Regulations.

(5) An officer may not exercise powers under this regulation in relation to information or documents in respect of which a claim to legal professional privilege (in Scotland, to confidentiality of communications) could be maintained in legal proceedings.

(6) In this regulation—
"document" includes information recorded in any form;
"officer" means an officer of the Authority and includes a member of the Authority's staff or an agent of the Authority;
"premises" means any premises other than premises used only as a dwelling.

[4469]

NOTES
Commencement: these Regulations come into force on 2 March 2009 (for the purposes specified in reg 1(2)(a)), 1 May 2009 (for the purposes specified in reg 1(2)(b)), and 1 November 2009 (otherwise). See reg 1 at **[4387]**.

84 Public censure

If the Authority considers that a payment service provider has contravened a requirement imposed on them by or under these Regulations the Authority may publish a statement to that effect.

[4470]

NOTES
Commencement: these Regulations come into force on 2 March 2009 (for the purposes specified in reg 1(2)(a)), 1 May 2009 (for the purposes specified in reg 1(2)(b)), and 1 November 2009 (otherwise). See reg 1 at **[4387]**.

85 Financial penalties

(1) The Authority may impose a penalty of such amount as it considers appropriate on—
(a) a payment service provider who has contravened a requirement imposed on them by or under these Regulations; or
(b) a person who has contravened regulation 110(1),111(1) or 114(1)(a) or (2).

(2) The Authority may not in respect of any contravention both require a person to pay a penalty under this regulation and cancel their authorisation as a payment institution or their registration as a small payment institution (as the case may be).

(3) A penalty under this regulation is a debt due from that person to the Authority, and is recoverable accordingly.

[4471]

NOTES
Commencement: these Regulations come into force on 2 March 2009 (for the purposes specified in reg 1(2)(a)), 1 May 2009 (for the purposes specified in reg 1(2)(b)), and 1 November 2009 (otherwise). See reg 1 at **[4387]**.

86 Proposal to take disciplinary measures

(1) Where the Authority proposes to publish a statement under regulation 84 or to impose a penalty under regulation 85, it must give the person concerned a warning notice.

(2) The warning notice must set out the terms of the proposed statement or state the amount of the proposed penalty.

(3) If, having considered any representations made in response to the warning notice, the Authority decides to publish a statement under regulation 84 or to impose a penalty under regulation 85, it must without delay give the person concerned a decision notice.

(4) The decision notice must set out the terms of the statement or state the amount of the penalty.

(5) If the Authority decides to publish a statement under regulation 84 or impose a penalty on a person under regulation 85, the person concerned may refer the matter to the Tribunal.

(6) Sections 210 (statements of policy) and 211 (statements of policy: procedure) of the 2000 Act apply in respect of the imposition of penalties under regulation 85 and the amount of such

penalties as they apply in respect of the imposition of penalties under Part 14 of the 2000 Act (disciplinary measures) and the amount of penalties under that Part of that Act.

(7)   After a statement under regulation 84 is published, the Authority must send a copy of it to the person concerned and to any person to whom a copy of the decision notice was given under section 393(4) of the 2000 Act (third party rights) (as applied by paragraph 7 of Schedule 5 to these Regulations).

[4472]

NOTES

Commencement: these Regulations come into force on 2 March 2009 (for the purposes specified in reg 1(2)(a)), 1 May 2009 (for the purposes specified in reg 1(2)(b)), and 1 November 2009 (otherwise). See reg 1 at **[4387]**.

87   Injunctions

(1)   If, on the application of the Authority, the court is satisfied—
  (a)   that there is a reasonable likelihood that any person will contravene a requirement imposed by or under these Regulations; or
  (b)   that any person has contravened such a requirement and that there is a reasonable likelihood that the contravention will continue or be repeated,

the court may make an order restraining (or in Scotland an interdict prohibiting) the contravention.

(2)   If, on the application of the Authority, the court is satisfied—
  (a)   that any person has contravened a requirement imposed by or under these Regulations, and
  (b)   that there are steps which could be taken for remedying the contravention,

the court may make an order requiring that person, and any other person who appears to have been knowingly concerned in the contravention, to take such steps as the court may direct to remedy it.

(3)   If, on the application of the Authority, the court is satisfied that any person may have—
  (a)   contravened a requirement imposed by or under these Regulations, or
  (b)   been knowingly concerned in the contravention of such a requirement,

it may make an order restraining (or in Scotland an interdict prohibiting) them from disposing of, or otherwise dealing with, any assets of theirs which it is satisfied they are reasonably likely to dispose of or otherwise deal with.

(4)   The jurisdiction conferred by this regulation is exercisable by the High Court and the Court of Session.

(5)   In paragraph (2), references to remedying a contravention include references to mitigating its effect.

[4473]

NOTES

Commencement: these Regulations come into force on 2 March 2009 (for the purposes specified in reg 1(2)(a)), 1 May 2009 (for the purposes specified in reg 1(2)(b)), and 1 November 2009 (otherwise). See reg 1 at **[4387]**.

88   Power of Authority to require restitution

(1)   The Authority may exercise the power in paragraph (2) if it is satisfied that a payment service provider (referred to in this regulation and regulation 89 as "the person concerned") has contravened a requirement imposed by or under these Regulations, or been knowingly concerned in the contravention of such a requirement, and that—
  (a)   profits have accrued to the person concerned as a result of the contravention; or
  (b)   one or more persons have suffered loss or been otherwise adversely affected as a result of the contravention.

(2)   The power referred to in paragraph (1) is a power to require the person concerned, in accordance with such arrangements as the Authority considers appropriate, to pay to the appropriate person or distribute among the appropriate persons such amount as appears to the Authority to be just having regard—
  (a)   in a case within sub-paragraph (a) of paragraph (1), to the profits appearing to the Authority to have accrued;
  (b)   in a case within sub-paragraph (b) of that paragraph, to the extent of the loss or other adverse effect;
  (c)   in a case within both of those paragraphs, to the profits appearing to the Authority to have accrued and to the extent of the loss or other adverse effect.

(3)   In paragraph (2) "appropriate person" means a person appearing to the Authority to be someone—

(a) to whom the profits mentioned in paragraph (1)(a) are attributable; or
(b) who has suffered the loss or adverse effect mentioned in paragraph (1)(b).

[4474]

NOTES
Commencement: these Regulations come into force on 2 March 2009 (for the purposes specified in reg 1(2)(a)), 1 May 2009 (for the purposes specified in reg 1(2)(b)), and 1 November 2009 (otherwise). See reg 1 at **[4387]**.

89 Proposal to require restitution

(1) If the Authority proposes to exercise the power under regulation 88(2), it must give the person concerned a warning notice.

(2) The warning notice must state the amount which the Authority propose to require the person concerned to pay or distribute as mentioned in regulation 88(2).

(3) If, having considered any representations made in response to the warning notice, the Authority decides to exercise the power under regulation 88(2), it must without delay give the person concerned a decision notice.

(4) The decision notice must—
    (a) state the amount that the person concerned is to pay or distribute;
    (b) identify the person or persons to whom that amount is to be paid or among whom that amount is to be distributed; and
    (c) state the arrangements in accordance with which the payment or distribution is to be made.

(5) If the Authority decides to exercise the power under regulation 88(2), the person concerned may refer the matter to the Tribunal.

[4475]

NOTES
Commencement: these Regulations come into force on 2 March 2009 (for the purposes specified in reg 1(2)(a)), 1 May 2009 (for the purposes specified in reg 1(2)(b)), and 1 November 2009 (otherwise). See reg 1 at **[4387]**.

90 Restitution orders

(1) The court may, on the application of the Authority, make an order under paragraph (2) if it is satisfied that a payment service provider has contravened a requirement imposed by or under these Regulations, or been knowingly concerned in the contravention of such a requirement, and that—
    (a) profits have accrued to them as a result of the contravention; or
    (b) one or more persons have suffered loss or been otherwise adversely affected as a result of the contravention.

(2) The court may order the person concerned to pay to the Authority such sum as appears to the court to be just having regard—
    (a) in a case within sub-paragraph (a) of paragraph (1), to the profits appearing to the court to have accrued;
    (b) in a case within sub-paragraph (b) of that paragraph, to the extent of the loss or other adverse effect;
    (c) in a case within both of those sub-paragraphs, to the profits appearing to the court to have accrued and to the extent of the loss or other adverse effect.

(3) Any amount paid to the Authority in pursuance of an order under paragraph (2) must be paid by it to such qualifying person or distributed by it among such qualifying persons as the court may direct.

(4) In paragraph (3), "qualifying person" means a person appearing to the court to be someone—
    (a) to whom the profits mentioned in paragraph (1)(a) are attributable; or
    (b) who has suffered the loss or adverse effect mentioned in paragraph (1)(b).

(5) On an application under paragraph (1) the court may require the person concerned to supply it with such accounts or other information as it may require for any one or more of the following purposes—
    (a) establishing whether any and, if so, what profits have accrued to them as mentioned in sub-paragraph (a) of that paragraph;
    (b) establishing whether any person or persons have suffered any loss or adverse effect as mentioned in sub-paragraph (b) of that paragraph; and
    (c) determining how any amounts are to be paid or distributed under paragraph (3).

PART III
STATUTORY INSTRUMENTS

(6)   The court may require any accounts or other information supplied under paragraph (5) to be verified in such manner as it may direct.

(7)   The jurisdiction conferred by this regulation is exercisable by the High Court and the Court of Session.

(8)   Nothing in this regulation affects the right of any person other than the Authority to bring proceedings in respect of the matters to which this regulation applies.

[4476]

NOTES
Commencement: these Regulations come into force on 2 March 2009 (for the purposes specified in reg 1(2)(a)), 1 May 2009 (for the purposes specified in reg 1(2)(b)), and 1 November 2009 (otherwise). See reg 1 at **[4387]**.

91   Complaints

(1)   The Authority must maintain arrangements designed to enable payment service users and other interested parties to submit complaints to it that a requirement imposed by or under Parts 2 to 6 of these Regulations has been breached by a payment service provider.

(2)   Where it considers it appropriate, the Authority must include in any reply to a complaint under paragraph (1) details of the ombudsman scheme established under Part 16 of the 2000 Act (the ombudsman scheme).

[4477]

NOTES
Commencement: these Regulations come into force on 2 March 2009 (for the purposes specified in reg 1(2)(a)), 1 May 2009 (for the purposes specified in reg 1(2)(b)), and 1 November 2009 (otherwise). See reg 1 at **[4387]**.

Miscellaneous

92   Costs of supervision

(1)   The functions of the Authority under these Regulations are to be treated for the purposes of paragraph 17 (fees) of Part 3 of Schedule 1 to the 2000 Act as functions conferred on the Authority under that Act with the following modifications—

(a)   section 2(3) of the 2000 Act (the Authority's general duties) does not apply to the making of rules under paragraph 17 by virtue of this regulation;

(b)   rules made under paragraph 17 by virtue of this regulation are not to be treated as regulating provisions for the purposes of section 159(1) of the 2000 Act (competition scrutiny);

(c)   paragraph 17(2) and (3) are omitted.

(2)   The Authority must apply amounts paid to it by way of penalties imposed under regulation 85 towards expenses incurred in carrying out its functions under these Regulations or for any incidental purpose.

[4478]

NOTES
Commencement: these Regulations come into force on 2 March 2009 (for the purposes specified in reg 1(2)(a)), 1 May 2009 (for the purposes specified in reg 1(2)(b)), and 1 November 2009 (otherwise). See reg 1 at **[4387]**.

93   Guidance

(1)   The Authority may give guidance consisting of such information and advice as it considers appropriate with respect to—

(a)   the operation of these Regulations;

(b)   any matters relating to the functions of the Authority under these Regulations;

(c)   any other matters about which it appears to the Authority to be desirable to give information or advice in connection with these Regulations.

(2)   The Authority may—

(a)   publish its guidance;

(b)   offer copies of its published guidance for sale at a reasonable price;

(c)   if it gives guidance in response to a request made by any person, make a reasonable charge for that guidance.

[4479]

NOTES
Commencement: these Regulations come into force on 2 March 2009 (for the purposes specified in reg 1(2)(a)), 1 May 2009 (for the purposes specified in reg 1(2)(b)), and 1 November 2009 (otherwise). See reg 1 at **[4387]**.

94 Authority's exemption from liability in damages

The functions of the Authority under these Regulations are to be treated for the purposes of paragraph 19 (exemption from liability in damages) of Part 4 of Schedule 1 to the 2000 Act as functions conferred on the Authority under that Act.

[4480]

NOTES
Commencement: these Regulations come into force on 2 March 2009 (for the purposes specified in reg 1(2)(a)), 1 May 2009 (for the purposes specified in reg 1(2)(b)), and 1 November 2009 (otherwise). See reg 1 at **[4387]**.

95 Application and modification of primary and secondary legislation

The provisions of primary and secondary legislation set out in Schedule 5 apply in respect of the Authority's functions under these Regulations with the modifications set out in that Schedule.

[4481]

NOTES
Commencement: these Regulations come into force on 2 March 2009 (for the purposes specified in reg 1(2)(a)), 1 May 2009 (for the purposes specified in reg 1(2)(b)), and 1 November 2009 (otherwise). See reg 1 at **[4387]**.

PART 8
ACCESS TO PAYMENT SYSTEMS

General

96 Application of Part 8

(1) This Part does not apply to the following kinds of payment systems—
  (a) a designated system;
  (b) a payment system consisting solely of payment service providers belonging to the same group where one of the payment service providers enjoys effective control over the others;
  (c) a payment system where the sole payment service provider (whether as a single entity or a group)—
    (i) acts or is able to act as the payment service provider for both the payer and the payee and is solely responsible for the management of the system; and
    (ii) licenses other payment service providers to participate in the system subject to their having no right to negotiate fees in respect of the system between or amongst themselves (although they may establish their own pricing in relation to payers and payees).

(2) In paragraph (1)(a), "designated system" means a system which is declared by a designation order for the time being in force under regulation 4 of the Financial Markets and Insolvency (Settlement Finality) Regulations 1999 to be a designated system for the purposes of those Regulations.

[4482]

NOTES
Commencement: these Regulations come into force on 2 March 2009 (for the purposes specified in reg 1(2)(a)), 1 May 2009 (for the purposes specified in reg 1(2)(b)), and 1 November 2009 (otherwise). See reg 1 at **[4387]**.

97 Prohibition on restrictive rules on access to payment systems

(1) Rules or conditions governing access to, or participation in, a payment system by authorised payment institutions, EEA authorised payment institutions and small payment institutions must—
  (a) be objective, proportionate and non-discriminatory; and
  (b) not prevent, restrict or inhibit access or participation more than is necessary to—
    (i) safeguard against specific risks such as settlement risk, operational risk or business risk; or
    (ii) protect the financial and operational stability of the payment system.

(2)   Paragraph (1) applies only to such small payment institutions as are legal persons.

(3)   Rules or conditions governing access to, or participation in, a payment system which, in respect of payment service providers, payment service users or other payment systems—

    (a)   restrict effective participation in other payment systems;

    (b)   discriminate (whether directly or indirectly) between—

        (i)   different authorised payment institutions, or

        (ii)   different small payment institutions,

in relation to the rights, obligations or entitlements of participants in the payment system; or

    (c)   impose any restrictions on the basis that a person is not of a particular institutional status,

are prohibited.

[4483]

NOTES

Commencement: these Regulations come into force on 2 March 2009 (for the purposes specified in reg 1(2)(a)), 1 May 2009 (for the purposes specified in reg 1(2)(b)), and 1 November 2009 (otherwise). See reg 1 at **[4387]**.

Supervision and enforcement

98   Power of OFT to investigate

(1)   The OFT may conduct an investigation where there are reasonable grounds for suspecting that any rule or condition governing access to, or participation in, a payment system contravenes regulation 97(1) or (3).

(2)   Where the investigation relates to a possible breach of regulation 97(1)(b)(ii), the OFT must consult the Bank of England and the Authority.

[4484]

NOTES

Commencement: these Regulations come into force on 2 March 2009 (for the purposes specified in reg 1(2)(a)), 1 May 2009 (for the purposes specified in reg 1(2)(b)), and 1 November 2009 (otherwise). See reg 1 at **[4387]**.

99   OFT power to require information

(1)   For the purposes of an investigation under regulation 98 the OFT may require any person—

    (a)   to produce to it or to a person appointed by it, at a specified time and place, any specified document, or

    (b)   to provide to it or to a person appointed by it, at a specified time and place, any specified information,

which the OFT considers relates to any matter relevant to the investigation.

(2)   The power conferred by paragraph (1) is to be exercised by a notice indicating the subject matter and purpose of the investigation.

(3)   Information required to be provided under paragraph (1) must be provided in the specified manner and form, or, if that is not possible, in the nearest equivalent manner and form.

(4)   The power conferred by paragraph (1) to require a person to produce a document includes power—

    (a)   to require them to provide an explanation of the document, or

    (b)   if the document is not produced, to require them to state, to the best of their knowledge and belief, where it is.

(5)   In this regulation—

"document" includes information recorded in any form;

"information" includes estimates and forecasts;

"specified" means—

    (a)   specified, or described, in the notice referred to in paragraph (2), or

    (b)   falling within a category which is specified, or described, in such notice.

[4485]

NOTES

Commencement: these Regulations come into force on 2 March 2009 (for the purposes specified in reg 1(2)(a)), 1 May 2009 (for the purposes specified in reg 1(2)(b)), and 1 November 2009 (otherwise). See reg 1 at **[4387]**.

100 Failure to comply with information requirement

(1) If, on an application made by the OFT, it appears to the court that a person (the "information defaulter") has failed to do something that they were required to do under regulation 99, the court may make an order under this regulation.

(2) An order under this regulation may require the information defaulter—
  (a) to do the thing that they failed to do within such period as may be specified in the order;
  (b) otherwise to take such steps to remedy the consequence of the failure as may be so specified.

(3) In this regulation, "the court" means—
  (a) in England and Wales and Northern Ireland, the High Court or the county court;
  (b) in Scotland, the Court of Session or the sheriff court.

[4486]

NOTES
Commencement: these Regulations come into force on 2 March 2009 (for the purposes specified in reg 1(2)(a)), 1 May 2009 (for the purposes specified in reg 1(2)(b)), and 1 November 2009 (otherwise). See reg 1 at **[4387]**.

101 Privileged communications

(1) A person is not required under regulation 99 to produce or disclose a privileged communication.

(2) In paragraph (1) "privileged communication" means a communication—
  (a) between a professional legal adviser and their client, or
  (b) made in connection with, or in contemplation of, legal proceedings and for the purposes of those proceedings,
which in proceedings in the High Court would be protected from disclosure on grounds of legal professional privilege.

(3) In the application of this regulation to Scotland the reference in paragraph (2) to—
  (a) proceedings in the High Court is to be read as a reference to legal proceedings generally; and
  (b) an entitlement on grounds of legal professional privilege is to be read as a reference to an entitlement on the grounds of confidentiality of communications.

[4487]

NOTES
Commencement: these Regulations come into force on 2 March 2009 (for the purposes specified in reg 1(2)(a)), 1 May 2009 (for the purposes specified in reg 1(2)(b)), and 1 November 2009 (otherwise). See reg 1 at **[4387]**.

102 Notice of OFT decision

Before the OFT, as the result of an investigation under regulation 98, makes a decision that any rules or conditions governing access to, or participation in, a payment system contravene regulation 97(1) or (3), the OFT must—
  (a) give notice to the person (or persons) who the OFT considers are responsible for the contravention, and
  (b) give that person (or those persons) an opportunity to make representations.

[4488]

NOTES
Commencement: these Regulations come into force on 2 March 2009 (for the purposes specified in reg 1(2)(a)), 1 May 2009 (for the purposes specified in reg 1(2)(b)), and 1 November 2009 (otherwise). See reg 1 at **[4387]**.

103 Publication of OFT decision

Where the OFT makes a decision after an investigation under regulation 98, the OFT must publish its decision, together with its reasons for making it.

[4489]

NOTES
Commencement: these Regulations come into force on 2 March 2009 (for the purposes specified in reg 1(2)(a)), 1 May 2009 (for the purposes specified in reg 1(2)(b)), and 1 November 2009 (otherwise). See reg 1 at **[4387]**.

PART III
STATUTORY INSTRUMENTS

104 Enforcement of decisions

(1) If the OFT makes a decision that any rules or conditions governing access to, or participation in, a payment system contravene regulation 97(1) or (3), the OFT may give such directions as the OFT considers appropriate to such person or persons as it considers appropriate.

(2) A direction under paragraph (1) may (in particular)—

(a) require the person concerned to change any rule or condition so that it no longer contravenes regulation 97(1) or (3); and

(b) relate to the conduct of the person in implementing any rule or condition.

(3) A direction under paragraph (1) must be given in writing.

(4) If a person fails, without reasonable excuse, to comply with a direction under paragraph (1), the OFT may apply to the High Court (or, in Scotland, the Court of Session) for an order requiring that person to comply with the direction within a time specified in the order.

(5) An order under paragraph (4) may provide for all of the costs of, or incidental to, the application for the order to be borne by the person in default.

[4490]

NOTES
Commencement: these Regulations come into force on 2 March 2009 (for the purposes specified in reg 1(2)(a)), 1 May 2009 (for the purposes specified in reg 1(2)(b)), and 1 November 2009 (otherwise). See reg 1 at **[4387]**.

105 Power of OFT to impose financial penalties

(1) Where the OFT is satisfied that any rules or conditions governing access to, or participation in, a payment system contravene regulation 97(1) or (3), the OFT may impose a penalty of such amount as it considers appropriate on such persons as it considers appropriate.

(2) The OFT may impose a penalty on a person under paragraph (1) only if the OFT is satisfied that the infringement has been committed intentionally or negligently by that person.

(3) Notice of a penalty under this regulation must—

(a) be in writing; and

(b) specify the date before which the penalty is required to be paid.

(4) The date specified must not be earlier than the end of the period within which an appeal against the notice may be brought under regulation 106.

(5) Any sums received by the OFT under this regulation are to be paid into the Consolidated Fund.

[4491]

NOTES
Commencement: these Regulations come into force on 2 March 2009 (for the purposes specified in reg 1(2)(a)), 1 May 2009 (for the purposes specified in reg 1(2)(b)), and 1 November 2009 (otherwise). See reg 1 at **[4387]**.

Miscellaneous

106 Appeal to the Competition Appeal Tribunal

(1) A person may appeal to the Competition Appeal Tribunal from a decision by the OFT to give a direction under regulation 104(1) to that person or to impose a penalty under regulation 105 on that person.

(2) In determining an appeal under paragraph (1) the Competition Appeal Tribunal shall apply the same principles as would be applied by a court on an application for judicial review.

(3) Sections 14 (constitution of tribunal) and 15 (tribunal rules) of the Enterprise Act 2002 apply in respect of appeals to the Competition Appeal Tribunal under paragraph (1) as they apply in respect of appeals to the Competition Appeal Tribunal under that Act.

[4492]

NOTES
Commencement: these Regulations come into force on 2 March 2009 (for the purposes specified in reg 1(2)(a)), 1 May 2009 (for the purposes specified in reg 1(2)(b)), and 1 November 2009 (otherwise). See reg 1 at **[4387]**.

107 Disclosure of information by OFT

Subject to regulation 119(2) and (3), Part 9 of the Enterprise Act 2002 (information) applies in respect of information which comes to the OFT by virtue of these Regulations as it applies in respect of information which is specified information for the purposes of Part 9.

[4493]

NOTES
Commencement: these Regulations come into force on 2 March 2009 (for the purposes specified in reg 1(2)(a)), 1 May 2009 (for the purposes specified in reg 1(2)(b)), and 1 November 2009 (otherwise). See reg 1 at **[4387]**.

108 Defamation

For the purposes of the law relating to defamation, absolute privilege attaches to any decision made or notice given by the OFT in the exercise of any of its functions under this Part.

[4494]

NOTES
Commencement: these Regulations come into force on 2 March 2009 (for the purposes specified in reg 1(2)(a)), 1 May 2009 (for the purposes specified in reg 1(2)(b)), and 1 November 2009 (otherwise). See reg 1 at **[4387]**.

109 Guidance

(1) The OFT may give guidance consisting of such information and advice as it considers appropriate with respect to the exercise of its functions under this Part.

(2) The OFT may—
  (a) publish its guidance;
  (b) if it gives guidance in response to a request made by any person, make a reasonable charge for that guidance.

[4495]

NOTES
Commencement: these Regulations come into force on 2 March 2009 (for the purposes specified in reg 1(2)(a)), 1 May 2009 (for the purposes specified in reg 1(2)(b)), and 1 November 2009 (otherwise). See reg 1 at **[4387]**.

PART 9
GENERAL

Criminal Offences

110 Prohibition on provision of payment services by persons other than payment service providers

(1) A person may not provide a payment service in the United Kingdom, or purport to do so, unless the person is—
  (a) an authorised payment institution;
  (b) a small payment institution;
  (c) an EEA authorised payment institution exercising its passport rights;
  (d) a person mentioned in any of paragraphs (d) to (h) of the definition in regulation 2(1) of a payment service provider, including, where relevant, such a person exercising an EEA right in accordance with Part 2 of Schedule 3 to the 2000 Act (exercise of passport rights by EEA firms); or
  (e) exempt under regulation 3.

(2) A person who contravenes paragraph (1) is guilty of an offence and is liable—
  (a) on summary conviction, to imprisonment for a term not exceeding three months or to a fine not exceeding the statutory maximum, or both;
  (b) on conviction on indictment, to imprisonment for a term not exceeding two years or to a fine, or both.

[4496]

NOTES
Commencement: these Regulations come into force on 2 March 2009 (for the purposes specified in reg 1(2)(a)), 1 May 2009 (for the purposes specified in reg 1(2)(b)), and 1 November 2009 (otherwise). See reg 1 at **[4387]**.

111 False claims to be a payment service provider or exempt

(1) A person who does not fall within any of sub-paragraphs (a) to (e) of regulation 110(1) may not—
  (a) describe themselves (in whatever terms) as a person falling within any of those sub-paragraphs; or
  (b) behave, or otherwise hold themselves out, in a manner which indicates (or which is reasonably likely to be understood as indicating) that they are such a person.

(2) A person who contravenes paragraph (1) is guilty of an offence and is liable on summary conviction to imprisonment for a term not exceeding three months or to a fine not exceeding level 5 on the standard scale, or both.

[4497]

NOTES

Commencement: these Regulations come into force on 2 March 2009 (for the purposes specified in reg 1(2)(a)), 1 May 2009 (for the purposes specified in reg 1(2)(b)), and 1 November 2009 (otherwise). See reg 1 at **[4387]**.

112 Defences

In proceedings for an offence under regulation 110 or 111 it is a defence for the accused to show that they took all reasonable precautions and exercised all due diligence to avoid committing the offence.

[4498]

NOTES

Commencement: these Regulations come into force on 2 March 2009 (for the purposes specified in reg 1(2)(a)), 1 May 2009 (for the purposes specified in reg 1(2)(b)), and 1 November 2009 (otherwise). See reg 1 at **[4387]**.

113 Contravention of regulations 49 and 50

(1) A person (not being a payment service provider) who contravenes regulation 49(2) or 50(2) is guilty of an offence and liable on summary conviction to a fine not exceeding level 5 on the standard scale.

(2) No offence is committed if the person took all reasonable steps and exercised all due diligence to ensure that the requirement imposed on the person by regulation 49(2) or 50(2), as the case may be, would be complied with.

[4499]

NOTES

Commencement: these Regulations come into force on 2 March 2009 (for the purposes specified in reg 1(2)(a)), 1 May 2009 (for the purposes specified in reg 1(2)(b)), and 1 November 2009 (otherwise). See reg 1 at **[4387]**.

114 Misleading the Authority or the OFT

(1) A person may not, in purported compliance with any requirement imposed by or under these Regulations, knowingly or recklessly give—
   (a) the Authority; or
   (b) the OFT,
information which is false or misleading in a material particular.

(2) A person may not—
   (a) provide any information to another person, knowing the information to be false or misleading in a material particular, or
   (b) recklessly provide to another person any information which is false or misleading in a material particular,
knowing that the information is to be used for the purpose of providing information to the Authority in connection with its functions under these Regulations.

(3) A person may not—
   (a) provide any information to another person, knowing the information to be false or misleading in a material particular, or
   (b) recklessly provide to another person any information which is false or misleading in a material particular,
knowing that the information is to be used for the purpose of providing information to the OFT in connection with their functions under these Regulations.

(4) A person who knows or suspects that an investigation by the OFT under regulation 98 is being or is likely to be conducted may not—
   (a) intentionally or recklessly destroy or otherwise dispose of, falsify or conceal a document (as defined by regulation 99(5)) which may be relevant to such an investigation; or
   (b) cause or permit its destruction, disposal, falsification or concealment.

(5) A person who contravenes paragraph (1), (2), (3) or (4) is guilty of an offence and is liable—
   (a) on summary conviction, to a fine not exceeding the statutory maximum;
   (b) on conviction on indictment, to a fine.

[4500]

NOTES
  Commencement: these Regulations come into force on 2 March 2009 (for the purposes specified in reg 1(2)(a)), 1 May 2009 (for the purposes specified in reg 1(2)(b)), and 1 November 2009 (otherwise). See reg 1 at **[4387]**.

115　Restriction on penalties

A person who is convicted of an offence under these Regulations is not liable to a penalty under regulation 85 or 105 in respect of the same contravention of a requirement imposed by or under these Regulations.

[4501]

NOTES
  Commencement: these Regulations come into force on 2 March 2009 (for the purposes specified in reg 1(2)(a)), 1 May 2009 (for the purposes specified in reg 1(2)(b)), and 1 November 2009 (otherwise). See reg 1 at **[4387]**.

116　Liability of officers of bodies corporate etc

  (1)　If an offence under these Regulations committed by a body corporate is shown—
    (a)　to have been committed with the consent or connivance of an officer, or
    (b)　to be attributable to any neglect on their part,
the officer as well as the body corporate is guilty of the offence and liable to be proceeded against and punished accordingly.

  (2)　If the affairs of a body corporate are managed by its members, paragraph (1) applies in relation to the acts and defaults of a member in connection with such member's functions of management as if the member were a director of the body.

  (3)　If an offence under these Regulations committed by a partnership is shown—
    (a)　to have been committed with the consent or connivance of a partner, or
    (b)　to be attributable to any neglect on their part,
the partner as well as the partnership is guilty of the offence and liable to be proceeded against and punished accordingly.

  (4)　If an offence under these Regulations committed by an unincorporated association (other than a partnership) is shown—
    (a)　to have been committed with the consent or connivance of an officer, or
    (b)　to be attributable to any neglect of such officer,
the officer as well as the association is guilty of the offence and liable to be proceeded against and punished accordingly.

  (5)　In this regulation—
  "officer"—
    (a)　in relation to a body corporate, means a director, manager, secretary, chief executive, member of the committee of management, or a person purporting to act in such a capacity; and
    (b)　in relation to an unincorporated association, means any officer of the association or any member of its governing body, or a person purporting to act in such capacity; and
  "partner" includes a person purporting to act as a partner.

[4502]

NOTES
  Commencement: these Regulations come into force on 2 March 2009 (for the purposes specified in reg 1(2)(a)), 1 May 2009 (for the purposes specified in reg 1(2)(b)), and 1 November 2009 (otherwise). See reg 1 at **[4387]**.

117　Prosecution of offences

  (1)　Proceedings for an offence under these Regulations may be instituted only—
    (a)　in respect of an offence under regulation 110, 111, 113, or 114(1)(a) or (2), by the Authority;
    (b)　in respect of an offence under regulation 114(1)(b), (3) or (4), by the OFT; or
    (c)　by or with the consent of the Director of Public Prosecutions.
  (2)　Paragraph (1) does not apply to proceedings in Scotland.

[4503]

PART III
STATUTORY INSTRUMENTS

NOTES
Commencement: these Regulations come into force on 2 March 2009 (for the purposes specified in reg 1(2)(a)), 1 May 2009 (for the purposes specified in reg 1(2)(b)), and 1 November 2009 (otherwise). See reg 1 at [4387].

118 Proceedings against unincorporated bodies

(1) Proceedings for an offence alleged to have been committed by a partnership or an unincorporated association must be brought in the name of the partnership or association (and not in that of its members).

(2) A fine imposed on the partnership or association on its conviction of an offence is to be paid out of the funds of the partnership or association.

(3) Rules of court relating to the service of documents are to have effect as if the partnership or association were a body corporate.

(4) In proceedings for an offence brought against the partnership or association—
- (a) section 33 of the Criminal Justice Act 1925 (procedure on charge of offence against corporation) and section 46 of and Schedule 3 to the Magistrates' Courts Act 1980 (corporations) apply as they do in relation to a body corporate;
- (b) section 70 of the Criminal Procedure (Scotland) Act 1995 (proceedings against bodies corporate) applies as it does in relation to a body corporate;
- (c) section 18 of the Criminal Justice (Northern Ireland) Act 1945 (procedure on charge) and Schedule 4 to the Magistrates' Courts (Northern Ireland) Order 1981 (corporations) apply as they do in relation to a body corporate.

(5) Summary proceedings for an offence under these Regulations may be taken—
- (a) against a body corporate or unincorporated association at any place at which it has a place of business;
- (b) against an individual at any place where they are for the time being.

(6) Paragraph (5) does not affect any jurisdiction exercisable apart from this regulation.

[4504]

NOTES
Commencement: these Regulations come into force on 2 March 2009 (for the purposes specified in reg 1(2)(a)), 1 May 2009 (for the purposes specified in reg 1(2)(b)), and 1 November 2009 (otherwise). See reg 1 at [4387].

Duties of the Authority, the Commissioners and the OFT to cooperate

119 Duty to co-operate and exchange of information

(1) The Authority, the Commissioners and the OFT must take such steps as they consider appropriate to co-operate with each other and—
- (a) the competent authorities designated under Article 20(1), or referred to in Article 82(1), of the payment services directive, of EEA States other than the United Kingdom;
- (b) the European Central Bank, the Bank of England and the national central banks of EEA States other than the United Kingdom; and
- (c) any other relevant competent authorities designated under Community law or the law of the United Kingdom or any other EEA State which is applicable to payment service providers,

for the purposes of the exercise by those bodies of their functions under the payment services directive and other relevant Community or national legislation.

(2) Subject to the requirements of the Data Protection Act 1998, sections 348 and 349 of the 2000 Act (as applied with modifications by paragraph 5 of Schedule 5 to these Regulations), regulation 49A of the Money Laundering Regulations 2007 (as inserted by paragraph 6(g) of Schedule 6 to these Regulations) and any other applicable restrictions on the disclosure of information, the Authority, the Commissioners and the OFT may provide information to each other and—
- (a) the bodies mentioned in paragraph (1)(a) and (c);
- (b) the European Central Bank, the Bank of England and the national central banks of EEA States other than the United Kingdom when acting in their capacity as monetary and oversight authorities;
- (c) where relevant, other public authorities responsible for the oversight of payment and settlement systems;

for the purposes of the exercise by those bodies of their functions under the payment services directive and other relevant Community or national legislation.

(3) Part 9 of the Enterprise Act 2002 does not prohibit disclosure by the OFT under paragraph (2) but the OFT must have regard to the considerations mentioned in section 244 of that Act (specified information: considerations relevant to disclosure) before making any such disclosure.

[4505]

NOTES

Commencement: these Regulations come into force on 2 March 2009 (for the purposes specified in reg 1(2)(a)), 1 May 2009 (for the purposes specified in reg 1(2)(b)), and 1 November 2009 (otherwise). See reg 1 at **[4387]**.

Actions for breach of requirements

120 Right to bring actions

(1) A contravention—
   (a)   which is to be taken to have occurred by virtue of regulation 17;
   (b)   of a requirement imposed by regulation 19; or
   (c)   of a requirement imposed by or under Part 5 or 6,

is actionable at the suit of a private person who suffers loss as a result of the contravention, subject to the defences and other incidents applying to actions for breach of statutory duty.

(2) A person acting in a fiduciary or representative capacity may bring an action under paragraph (1) on behalf of a private person if any remedy—
   (a)   will be exclusively for the benefit of the private person; and
   (b)   cannot be obtained by way of an action brought otherwise than at the suit of the fiduciary or representative.

(3) In this regulation "private person" means—
   (a)   any individual, except where the individual suffers the loss in question in the course of providing payment services; and
   (b)   any person who is not an individual, except where that person suffers the loss in question in the course of carrying on business of any kind;

but does not include a government, a local authority (in the United Kingdom or elsewhere) or an international organisation.

[4506]

NOTES

Commencement: these Regulations come into force on 2 March 2009 (for the purposes specified in reg 1(2)(a)), 1 May 2009 (for the purposes specified in reg 1(2)(b)), and 1 November 2009 (otherwise). See reg 1 at **[4387]**.

Transitional provisions

121 Transitional provisions: deemed authorisation

(1) Any financial institution (within the meaning of the banking consolidation directive) which—
   (a)   is constituted under the law of a part of the United Kingdom and has its head office and, if it has a registered office, that office, in the United Kingdom; and
   (b)   before 25th December 2007 had—
      (i)   lawfully provided payment services in the United Kingdom; and
      (ii)   met the condition in Article 24(1)(e) of the banking consolidation directive;

shall be deemed to have been granted authorisation by the Authority under regulation 9.

(2) An institution which is deemed to have been granted authorisation by virtue of paragraph (1) shall continue on or after 25th December 2009 to be deemed to have been granted authorisation only if it has by that date—
   (a)   notified the Authority of the payment services referred to in sub-paragraph (b)(i); and
   (b)   provided the Authority with the information specified in paragraph 1, 4, 7 to 9 and 12 of Schedule 2 ("the required information").

(3) Authorisation which continues on or after 25th December 2009 to be deemed to have been granted by virtue of paragraph (2) shall continue to be so deemed until such time as the Authority decides whether to include the institution in the register as an authorised payment institution.

(4) If the Authority decides to include the institution in the register as an authorised payment institution—
   (a)   it must as soon as practicable update the register accordingly; and
   (b)   the institution shall cease to be deemed to have been granted authorisation by virtue of paragraph (1) or (2).

(5) The Authority may decide that an institution is not to be included in the register as an authorised payment institution only if—

(a)   it has not received the required information; or
(b)   any of the conditions in regulation 6(4) to (6) (other than the condition that a person must be a body corporate) ("the required conditions") are not met in respect of that institution.

(6)   If the Authority is satisfied that—
(a)   it has received the required information; and
(b)   the required conditions are met,
it must give the institution notice of its decision.

(7)   If the Authority proposes to decide that—
(a)   it has not received the required information; or
(b)   any of the required conditions is not met,
it must give the institution a warning notice.

(8)   The Authority must, having considered any representations in response to the warning notice—
(a)   if it decides that it has not received the required information or that any of the required conditions is not met, give the institution a decision notice; or
(b)   if it decides that it has received the required information and that the required conditions have been met, give the institution notice of its decision.

(9)   If the Authority gives the institution a decision notice, the institution may refer the matter to the Tribunal.

(10)   Where the period for a reference to the Tribunal has expired without a reference being made, the institution shall cease to be deemed to have been granted authorisation by virtue of paragraph (1) or (2).

(11)   Where an institution is deemed to have been granted authorisation by virtue of paragraph (1) or (2)—
(a)   the duty to which the Authority is subject under regulation 4(1)(a) to maintain a register shall not apply in respect of it; and
(b)   Parts 3 and 4 shall not apply to it.

[4507]

NOTES
Commencement: these Regulations come into force on 2 March 2009 (for the purposes specified in reg 1(2)(a)), 1 May 2009 (for the purposes specified in reg 1(2)(b)), and 1 November 2009 (otherwise). See reg 1 at [4387].

122   Transitional provisions: requirement to be authorised as a payment institution

(1)   Any person which—
(a)   is a body corporate constituted under the law of a part of the United Kingdom and has its head office and, if it has a registered office, that office, in the United Kingdom;
(b)   is not a body—
(i)   mentioned in any of paragraphs (d) to (h) of the definition in regulation 2(1) of a payment service provider; or
(ii)   which is deemed to have been granted authorisation by virtue of regulation 121(1) or (2); and
(c)   immediately before 25th December 2007, was lawfully providing payment services in the United Kingdom,
may continue until 1st May 2011 to provide payment services in the United Kingdom notwithstanding that the person has not been granted authorisation by the Authority under regulation 9.

(2)   Parts 5 to 8 and regulation 110(1) apply to a person falling within paragraph (1) as if the person were an authorised payment institution.

[4508]

NOTES
Commencement: these Regulations come into force on 2 March 2009 (for the purposes specified in reg 1(2)(a)), 1 May 2009 (for the purposes specified in reg 1(2)(b)), and 1 November 2009 (otherwise). See reg 1 at [4387].

123   Transitional provisions: requirement to be registered as a small payment institution

(1)   Any person who—
(a)   immediately before 25th December 2007, was lawfully providing payment services in the United Kingdom;
(b)   is not a body—

      (i)   mentioned in any of paragraphs (d) to (h) of the definition in regulation 2(1) of a payment service provider; or

     (ii)   which is deemed to have been granted authorisation by virtue of regulation 121(1) or (2) or which falls within regulation 122(1); and

  (c)   meets the conditions set out in regulation 13(4) to (6) and complies with the financial limit referred to in regulation 8 (as applied by regulation 14(c)),

may continue until 25th December 2010 to provide payment services in the United Kingdom notwithstanding that the person has not been granted registration by the Authority under regulation 9 (as applied by regulation 14).

(2)   Parts 5 to 8 and regulation 110(1) apply to a person falling within paragraph (1) as if the person were a small payment institution.

[4509]

NOTES

Commencement: these Regulations come into force on 2 March 2009 (for the purposes specified in reg 1(2)(a)), 1 May 2009 (for the purposes specified in reg 1(2)(b)), and 1 November 2009 (otherwise). See reg 1 at **[4387]**.

---

124 Transitional provisions: early applications

(1)   Where an application is made under regulation 5(1) or (2) or 12(1) or (2) before 1st August 2009 and is a completed application, the Authority must determine it before 1st November 2009.

(2)   The requirement under regulation 23(2) for information to be given to the host state competent authority within one month of receipt by the Authority of a notice of intention does not apply where the notice of intention is received by the Authority before 1st November 2009.

(3)   Any requirement under these Regulations to update the register does not apply until 1st November 2009.

[4510]

NOTES

Commencement: these Regulations come into force on 2 March 2009 (for the purposes specified in reg 1(2)(a)), 1 May 2009 (for the purposes specified in reg 1(2)(b)), and 1 November 2009 (otherwise). See reg 1 at **[4387]**.

---

125 Transitional provisions: the ombudsman scheme

Part 16 of, and Schedule 17 to, the 2000 Act (the ombudsman scheme) shall apply as if persons who fall within regulation 122(1) or 123(1) were payment service providers within the meaning of these Regulations.

[4511]

NOTES

Commencement: these Regulations come into force on 2 March 2009 (for the purposes specified in reg 1(2)(a)), 1 May 2009 (for the purposes specified in reg 1(2)(b)), and 1 November 2009 (otherwise). See reg 1 at **[4387]**.

Amendments to primary and secondary legislation

126 Amendments to primary and secondary legislation

Schedule 6, which contains amendments to primary and secondary legislation, has effect.

[4512]

NOTES

Commencement: these Regulations come into force on 2 March 2009 (for the purposes specified in reg 1(2)(a)), 1 May 2009 (for the purposes specified in reg 1(2)(b)), and 1 November 2009 (otherwise). See reg 1 at **[4387]**.

SCHEDULES

SCHEDULE 1
PAYMENT SERVICES

Regulation 2(1)

PART 1
PAYMENT SERVICES

1.   Subject to Part 2, the following activities, when carried out as a regular occupation or business activity, are payment services—

(a)   services enabling cash to be placed on a payment account and all of the operations required for operating a payment account;
(b)   services enabling cash withdrawals from a payment account and all of the operations required for operating a payment account;
(c)   the execution of the following types of payment transaction—
    (i)   direct debits, including one-off direct debits;
    (ii)   payment transactions executed through a payment card or a similar device;
    (iii)   credit transfers, including standing orders;
(d)   the execution of the following types of payment transaction where the funds are covered by a credit line for the payment service user—
    (i)   direct debits, including one-off direct debits;
    (ii)   payment transactions executed through a payment card or a similar device;
    (iii)   credit transfers, including standing orders;
(e)   issuing payment instruments or acquiring payment transactions;
(f)   money remittance;
(g)   the execution of payment transactions where the consent of the payer to execute the payment transaction is given by means of any telecommunication, digital or IT device and the payment is made to the telecommunication, IT system or network operator acting only as an intermediary between the payment service user and the supplier of the goods or services.

[4513]

NOTES
Commencement: these Regulations come into force on 2 March 2009 (for the purposes specified in reg 1(2)(a)), 1 May 2009 (for the purposes specified in reg 1(2)(b)), and 1 November 2009 (otherwise). See reg 1 at **[4387]**.

PART 2
ACTIVITIES WHICH DO NOT CONSTITUTE PAYMENT SERVICES

2.   The following activities do not constitute payment services—
(a)   payment transactions executed wholly in cash and directly between the payer and the payee, without any intermediary intervention;
(b)   payment transactions between the payer and the payee through a commercial agent authorised to negotiate or conclude the sale or purchase of goods or services on behalf of the payer or the payee;
(c)   the professional physical transport of banknotes and coins, including their collection, processing and delivery;
(d)   payment transactions consisting of non-professional cash collection and delivery as part of a not-for-profit or charitable activity;
(e)   services where cash is provided by the payee to the payer as part of a payment transaction for the purchase of goods or services following an explicit request by the payer immediately before the execution of the payment transaction;
(f)   money exchange business consisting of cash-to-cash operations where the funds are not held on a payment account;
(g)   payment transactions based on any of the following documents drawn on the payment service provider with a view to placing funds at the disposal of the payee—
    (i)   paper cheques of any kind, including traveller's cheques;
    (ii)   bankers' drafts;
    (iii)   paper-based vouchers;
    (iv)   paper postal orders;
(h)   payment transactions carried out within a payment or securities settlement system between payment service providers and settlement agents, central counterparties, clearing houses, central banks or other participants in the system;
(i)   payment transactions related to securities asset servicing, including dividends, income or other distributions, or redemption or sale, carried out by persons referred to in sub-paragraph (h) or by investment firms, credit institutions, collective investment undertakings or asset management companies providing investment services or by any other entities allowed to have the custody of financial instruments;
(j)   services provided by technical service providers, which support the provision of payment services, without the provider entering at any time into possession of the funds to be transferred, including—
    (i)   the processing and storage of data;
    (ii)   trust and privacy protection services;
    (iii)   data and entity authentication;
    (iv)   information technology;
    (v)   communication network provision; and

        (vi)   the provision and maintenance of terminals and devices used for payment services;

   (k)   services based on instruments that can be used to acquire goods or services only—

        (i)   in or on the issuer's premises; or

        (ii)   under a commercial agreement with the issuer, either within a limited network of service providers or for a limited range of goods or services,

and for these purposes the "issuer" is the person who issues the instrument in question;

   (l)   payment transactions executed by means of any telecommunication, digital or IT device, where the goods or services purchased are delivered to and are to be used through a telecommunication, digital or IT device, provided that the telecommunication, digital or IT operator does not act only as an intermediary between the payment service user and the supplier of the goods and services;

   (m)   payment transactions carried out between payment service providers, or their agents or branches, for their own account;

   (n)   payment transactions between a parent undertaking and its subsidiary or between subsidiaries of the same parent undertaking, without any intermediary intervention by a payment service provider other than an undertaking belonging to the same group;

   (o)   services by providers to withdraw cash by means of automated teller machines acting on behalf of one or more card issuers, which are not party to the framework contract with the customer withdrawing money from a payment account, where no other payment service is conducted by the provider.

[4514]

NOTES

Commencement: these Regulations come into force on 2 March 2009 (for the purposes specified in reg 1(2)(a)), 1 May 2009 (for the purposes specified in reg 1(2)(b)), and 1 November 2009 (otherwise). See reg 1 at **[4387]**.

SCHEDULE 2

INFORMATION TO BE INCLUDED IN OR WITH AN APPLICATION
FOR AUTHORISATION

Regulation 5(1)

1.   A programme of operations setting out, in particular, the type of payment services envisaged.

2.   A business plan including a forecast budget calculation for the first three financial years which demonstrates that the applicant is able to employ appropriate and proportionate systems, resources and procedures to operate soundly.

3.   Evidence that the applicant holds initial capital for the purposes of regulation 6(3).

4.   Where regulation 19 applies, a description of the measures taken for safeguarding payment service users' funds in accordance with that regulation.

5.   A description of the applicant's governance arrangements and internal control mechanisms, including administrative risk management and accounting procedures, which demonstrates that such arrangements, mechanisms and procedures are proportionate, appropriate, sound and adequate.

6.   A description of the internal control mechanisms which the applicant has established in order to comply with the Money Laundering Regulations 2007 and Regulation (EC) No 1781/2006 of the European Parliament and of the Council of 15 November 2006 on information on the payer accompanying transfers of funds.

7.   A description of the applicant's structural organisation, including, where applicable, a description of the intended use of agents and branches and a description of outsourcing arrangements, and of its participation in a national or international payment system.

8.—(1)   In relation to each person holding, directly or indirectly, a qualifying holding in the applicant—

   (a)   the size and nature of their qualifying holding; and

   (b)   evidence of their suitability taking into account the need to ensure the sound and prudent management of a payment institution.

9.—(1)   The identity of directors and persons who are or will be responsible for the management of the applicant and, where relevant, persons who are or will be responsible for the management of the payment services activities of the applicant.

(2)   Evidence that the persons described in sub-paragraph (1) are of good repute and that they possess appropriate knowledge and experience to perform payment services.

10.   The identity of the auditors of the applicant, if any.

11.—(1)   The legal status of the applicant and, where the applicant is a limited company, its articles.

(2)   In this paragraph "articles" has the meaning given in section 7 of the Companies Act 1985 (articles prescribing regulations for companies) until the coming into force of section 18 of the Companies Act 2006 (articles of association) when it will have the meaning given by that section.

12.   The address of the head office of the applicant.

13.   For the purposes of paragraphs 4, 5 and 7, a description of the audit arrangements of the applicant and of the organisational arrangements the applicant has set up with a view to taking all reasonable steps to protect the interests of its payment service users and to ensure continuity and reliability in the performance of payment services.

[4515]

NOTES
Commencement: these Regulations come into force on 2 March 2009 (for the purposes specified in reg 1(2)(a)), 1 May 2009 (for the purposes specified in reg 1(2)(b)), and 1 November 2009 (otherwise). See reg 1 at **[4387]**.
Note: para 8 above is reproduced as it appears in the Queen's Printer's copy of these Regulations, ie, there is no sub-paragraph (2).

SCHEDULE 3
CAPITAL REQUIREMENTS

Regulations 6(3), 18

PART 1
INITIAL CAPITAL

1.   For the purposes of this Part, "initial capital" comprises the items specified in paragraph 3(a), (b) and (c) of this Schedule.

2.—(1)   An applicant for authorisation as a payment institution must hold the amount of initial capital specified in the second column of the table, corresponding to the payment services provided or to be provided (as specified in the first column).

(2)   Where more than one initial capital requirement applies, the applicant must hold initial capital of whichever is the greater amount.

Payment services	Initial capital requirement (euro)
Payment services specified in paragraph 127(f) of Schedule 1	20,000
Payment services specified in paragraph 127(g) of Schedule 1	50,000
Any of the payment services specified in paragraph 127(a) to (e) of Schedule 1	125,000

[4516]

NOTES
Commencement: these Regulations come into force on 2 March 2009 (for the purposes specified in reg 1(2)(a)), 1 May 2009 (for the purposes specified in reg 1(2)(b)), and 1 November 2009 (otherwise). See reg 1 at **[4387]**.
Note: para 8 above is reproduced as it appears in the Queen's Printer's copy of these Regulations, ie, there is no sub-paragraph (2).

PART 2
OWN FUNDS

Qualifying items

3.   For the purposes of this Part, "own funds" means the following items, subject to the deductions specified in paragraph 147 and to the limits specified in paragraph 149—

    (a)   paid up capital, including share premium accounts but excluding amounts arising in respect of cumulative preference shares;

    (b)   reserves other than—

        (i)   revaluation reserves;

        (ii)   fair value reserves related to gains or losses on cash flow hedges of financial instruments measured at amortised cost; and

        (iii)   that part of profit and loss reserves that arises from any gains on liabilities valued at fair value that are due to changes in the authorised payment institution's credit standing;

   (c)   profit or loss brought forward as a result of the application of the final profit or loss, provided that—

        (i)   interim profits may only be included if they are—

            (aa)   verified by persons responsible for the auditing of the authorised payment institution's accounts;

            (bb)   shown to the satisfaction of the Authority that the amount has been evaluated in accordance with the principles set out in directive 86/635/EEC of the Council of the 8th December 1986 on the annual accounts and consolidated accounts of banks and other financial institutions; and

            (cc)   net of any foreseeable charge or dividend;

        (ii)   in the case of an authorised payment institution which is the originator of a securitisation, net gains arising from the capitalisation of future income from the securitised assets and providing credit enhancement to positions in the securitisation are excluded;

   (d)   revaluation reserves;

   (e)   general or collective provisions if—

        (i)   they are freely available to the authorised payment institution to cover normal payment services risks where revenue or capital losses have not yet been identified;

        (ii)   their existence is disclosed in internal accounting records; and

        (iii)   their amount is determined by the management of the authorised payment institution, verified by a statutory auditor or audit firm (as defined by regulation 20(2)) and notified to the Authority;

   (f)   securities of indeterminate duration and other instruments that fulfil the following conditions—

        (i)   they may not be reimbursed on the bearer's initiative or without the prior agreement of the Authority;

        (ii)   the debt agreement provides for the authorised payment institution to have the option of deferring the payment of interest on the debt;

        (iii)   the lender's claim on the authorised payment institution is wholly subordinated to those of all non-subordinated creditors;

        (iv)   the documents governing the issue of the securities provide for debt and unpaid interest to be such as to absorb losses, whilst leaving the authorised payment institution in a position to continue trading;

provided that only fully paid-up amounts are to be taken into account;

   (g)   cumulative preferential shares, other than fixed-term cumulative preference shares referred to in paragraph (j);

   (h)   the commitments of the members of an authorised payment institution set up as a cooperative, comprising—

        (i)   that institution's uncalled capital; and

        (ii)   the legal commitments of the members of that institution to make additional non-refundable payments should the institution incur a loss provided that such payments can be demanded without delay;

   (i)   the joint and several commitments of the borrower in the case of an authorised payment institution organised as a fund, comprising—

        (i)   that institution's uncalled capital; and

        (ii)   the legal commitments of the borrowers of that institution to make additional non-refundable payments should the institution incur a loss provided that such payments can be demanded without delay;

   (j)   fixed-term cumulative preferential shares and subordinated loan capital if—

        (i)   binding agreements exist under which, in the event of the winding-up of the authorised payment institution, they rank after the claims of all other creditors and are not to be repaid until all other debts outstanding at the time have been settled; and

        (ii)   in the case of subordinated loan capital—

            (aa)   only fully paid-up funds are taken into account;

            (bb)   the loans involved have an original maturity of at least five years, after which they may be repaid;

            (cc)   the extent to which they may rank as own funds is gradually reduced during at least the last five years before the repayment date; and

            (dd)   the loan agreement does not include any clause providing that in specified circumstances, other than the winding-up of the authorised payment institution, the debt will become repayable before the agreed repayment date.

4.   The items specified in paragraph 144(a) to (d) must be—

   (a)   available to the authorised payment institution for unrestricted and immediate use to cover risks or losses as soon as these occur; and

(b)   net of any foreseeable tax charge at the moment of their calculation or be suitably adjusted in so far as such tax charges reduce the amount up to which these items may be applied to cover risks or losses.

5.   Own funds are not to include guarantees provided by the Crown or a local authority to a payment institution which is a public sector entity for the purposes of the banking consolidation directive.

Deductions from own funds

6.   The deductions from own funds are—
(a)   own shares at book value held by the authorised payment institution;
(b)   intangible assets;
(c)   material losses of the current financial year;
(d)   holdings of shares in credit institutions and financial institutions exceeding 10% of their capital;
(e)   if sub-paragraph (d) applies, the items specified in paragraph 144(f), (g) and (j) held in the relevant credit institution or financial institution;
(f)   holdings of shares or of the items specified in paragraph 3(f), (g) and (j) held in other credit institutions or financial institutions where—
   (i)   the holding has not been deducted in accordance with sub-paragraph (d) or (e) of this paragraph; and
   (ii)   the total amount of such holdings exceeds 10% of the authorised payment institution's own funds calculated before deduction of the items specified in this sub-paragraph and sub-paragraphs (d), (e), (g) and (h);
(g)   participations which the authorised payment institution holds in an insurance undertaking, reinsurance undertaking or insurance holding company; and
(h)   the following instruments held in an insurance undertaking, reinsurance undertaking or insurance holding company in which the authorised payment institution holds a participation—
   (i)   instruments referred to in article 16(3) of directive 73/239/EEC of the Council on the coordination of laws, regulations and administrative provisions relating to the taking-up and pursuit of the business of direct insurance other than life assurance;
   (ii)   instruments referred to in article 27(3) of directive 2002/83/EC of the European Parliament and of the Council of 5th November 2002 concerning life assurance.

7.   Where shares in another credit institution, financial institution, insurance undertaking, reinsurance undertaking or insurance holding company are held temporarily for the purposes of a financial assistance operation designed to reorganise and save that entity, the Authority may direct that any or all of the items specified in paragraph 147(d) to (h) are not to be deducted from own funds.

Limits on qualifying items

8.—(1)   The limits referred to in paragraph 144 are—
(a)   that A must not exceed B; and
(b)   that C must not exceed 50% of B.

(2)   After applying such limits—
(a)   50% of the total of the items specified in paragraph 6(d) to (h) must be deducted from A and the remaining 50% must be deducted from B; and
(b)   the amount, if any, by which the amount to be deducted from A exceeds A must be deducted from B.

(3)   In this paragraph—
(a)   "A" means the total of the items specified in paragraph 144(d) to (j);
(b)   "B" means the total of the items specified in paragraph 144(a) to (c) less the total of the items specified in paragraph 147(a) to (c); and
(c)   "C" means the total of the items specified in paragraph 144(h) to (j).

9.   The Authority may in temporary and exceptional circumstances direct that an authorised payment institution may exceed one or more of the limits described in paragraph 8(1).

10.   An authorised payment institution must not include in its own funds calculation any item—
(a)   used in an equivalent calculation by an authorised payment institution, credit institution, investment firm, asset management company or insurance undertaking in the same group; or
(b)   in the case of an authorised payment institution which carries out activities other than providing payment services, is used in carrying out those activities.

Own funds requirement

11.   An authorised payment institution must hold own funds calculated in accordance with such of Method A, Method B or Method C as the Authority may direct.

Adjustment by the Authority

12.   The Authority may direct that an authorised payment institution must hold own funds up to 20% higher, or up to 20% lower, than the amount which would result from paragraph 152.

13.   A direction made under paragraph 153 must be on the basis of an evaluation of the relevant authorised payment institution including, if available and where the Authority considers it appropriate, any risk-management processes, risk loss database or internal control mechanisms of the authorised payment institution.

14.   The Authority may make a reasonable charge for making an evaluation required under paragraph 154.

Provision for start-up payment institutions

15.   If an authorised payment institution has not completed a full financial year's business, references to a figure for the preceding financial year are to be read as the equivalent figure projected in the business plan provided in the payment institution's application for authorisation, subject to any adjustment to that plan required by the Authority.

Method A

16.—(1)   "Method A" means the calculation method set out in this paragraph.

(2)   The own funds requirement is 10% of the authorised payment institution's fixed overheads for the preceding financial year.

(3)   If a material change has occurred in an authorised payment institution's business since the preceding financial year, the Authority may direct that the own funds requirement is to be a higher or lower amount than that calculated in accordance with sub-paragraph (2).

Method B

17.—(1)   "Method B" means the calculation method set out in this paragraph.

(2)   The own funds requirement is the sum of the following elements multiplied by the scaling factor—
- (a)   4% of the first 5,000,000 euro of payment volume;
- (b)   2.5% of the next 5,000,000 euro of payment volume;
- (c)   1% of the next 90,000,000 euro of payment volume;
- (d)   0.5% of the next 150,000,000 euro of payment volume; and
- (e)   0.25% of any remaining payment volume.

(3)   "Payment volume" means the total amount of payment transactions executed by the authorised payment institution in the preceding financial year divided by the number of months in that year.

(4)   The "scaling factor" is—
- (a)   0.5 for a payment institution that is authorised to provide the payment service specified in paragraph 127(f) of Schedule 1;
- (b)   0.8 for a payment institution that is authorised to provide the payment service specified in paragraph 127(g) of Schedule 1; and
- (c)   1 for a payment institution that is authorised to provide any other payment service.

Method C

18.—(1)   "Method C" means the calculation method set out in this paragraph.

(2)   The own funds requirement is the relevant indicator multiplied by—
- (a)   the multiplication factor; and
- (b)   the scaling factor;

subject to the proviso in sub-paragraph (7).

(3)   The "relevant indicator" is the sum of the following elements—
- (a)   interest income;
- (b)   interest expenses;
- (c)   gross commissions and fees received; and
- (d)   gross other operating income.

(4)   For the purpose of calculating the relevant indicator—
- (a)   each element must be included in the sum with its positive or negative sign;
- (b)   income from extraordinary or irregular items may not be used;
- (c)   expenditure on the outsourcing of services rendered by third parties may reduce the relevant indicator if the expenditure is incurred from a payment service provider;
- (d)   the relevant indicator is calculated on the basis of the twelve-monthly observation at the end of the previous financial year;
- (e)   the relevant indicator must be calculated over the previous financial year; and

    (f)   audited figures must be used unless they are not available in which case business estimates may be used.

(5)   The "multiplication factor" is the sum of—
    (a)   10% of the first 2,500,000 euro of the relevant indicator;
    (b)   8% of the next 2,500,000 euro of the relevant indicator;
    (c)   6% of the next 20,000,000 euro of the relevant indicator;
    (d)   3% of the next 25,000,000 euro of the relevant indicator; and
    (e)   1.5% of any remaining amount of the relevant indicator.

(6)   "Scaling factor" has the meaning given in paragraph 158(4).

(7)   The proviso is that the own funds requirement must not be less than 80 % of the average of the previous three financial years for the relevant indicator.

Application of accounting standards

19.   Except where this Schedule provides for a different method of recognition, measurement or valuation, whenever a provision in this Schedule refers to an asset, liability, equity or income statement item, an authorised payment institution must, for the purpose of that provision, recognise the asset, liability, equity or income statement item and measure its value in accordance with whichever of the following are applicable for the purpose of the institution's external financial reporting—
    (a)   Financial Reporting Standards and Statements of Standard Accounting Practice issued or adopted by the Accounting Standards Board;
    (b)   Statements of Recommended Practice, issued by industry or sectoral bodies recognised for this purpose by the Accounting Standards Board;
    (c)   International Financial Reporting Standards and International Accounting Standards issued or adopted by the International Accounting Standards Board;
    (d)   International Standards on Auditing (United Kingdom and Ireland) issued by the Auditing Practices Board; and
    (e)   the Companies Act 2006.

                                                           [4517]

NOTES

Commencement: these Regulations come into force on 2 March 2009 (for the purposes specified in reg 1(2)(a)), 1 May 2009 (for the purposes specified in reg 1(2)(b)), and 1 November 2009 (otherwise). See reg 1 at **[4387]**.

SCHEDULE 4
PRIOR GENERAL INFORMATION FOR FRAMEWORK CONTRACTS

Regulations 36(2), 40(1)

1.   The following information about the payment service provider—
    (a)   the name of the payment service provider;
    (b)   the address and contact details of the payment service provider's head office;
    (c)   if different from the information under sub-paragraph (b), the address and contact details of the branch or agent from which the payment service is being provided;
    (d)   details of the payment service provider's regulators, including any reference or registration number of the payment service provider.

2.   The following information about the payment service—
    (a)   a description of the main characteristics of the payment service to be provided;
    (b)   the information or unique identifier that must be provided by the payment service user in order for a payment order to be properly executed;
    (c)   the form and procedure for giving consent to the execution of a payment transaction and for the withdrawal of consent in accordance with regulation 55;
    (d)   a reference to the time of receipt of a payment order, as defined in regulation 65, and the cut-off time, if any, established by the payment service provider;
    (e)   the maximum execution time for the payment services to be provided;
    (f)   whether spending limits for the use of a payment instrument may be agreed in accordance with regulation 56(1).

3.   The following information about charges, interest and exchange rates—
    (a)   details of all charges payable by the payment service user to the payment service provider and, where applicable, a breakdown of the amounts of any charges;
    (b)   where relevant, details of the interest and exchange rates to be applied or, if reference interest and exchange rates are to be used, the method of calculating the actual interest and the relevant date and index or base for determining such reference interest or exchange rates;

    (c)   if agreed, the immediate application of changes in reference interest or exchange rates and information requirements relating to the changes in accordance with regulation 42(4).

4.   The following information about communication—

    (a)   the means of communication agreed between the parties for the transmission of information or notifications under these Regulations including, where relevant, any technical requirements for the payment service user's equipment for receipt of the information or notifications;

    (b)   the manner in which and frequency with which information under these Regulations is to be provided or made available;

    (c)   the language or languages in which the framework contract will be concluded and in which any information or notifications under these Regulations will be communicated;

    (d)   the payment service user's right to receive the terms of the framework contract and information in accordance with regulation 41.

5.   The following information about safeguards and corrective measures—

    (a)   where relevant, a description of the steps that the payment service user is to take in order to keep safe a payment instrument and how to notify the payment service provider for the purposes of regulation 57(1)(b);

    (b)   where relevant, the conditions under which the payment service provider proposes to reserve the right to stop or prevent the use of a payment instrument in accordance with regulation 56;

    (c)   the payer's liability under regulation 62, including details of any limits on such liability;

    (d)   how and within what period of time the payment service user is to notify the payment service provider of any unauthorised or incorrectly executed payment transaction under regulation 59, and the payment service provider's liability for unauthorised payment transactions under regulation 61;

    (e)   the payment service provider's liability for the execution of payment transactions under regulation 75 or 76;

    (f)   the conditions for the payment of any refund under regulation 63.

6.   The following information about changes to and termination of the framework contract—

    (a)   where relevant, the proposed terms under which the payment service user will be deemed to have accepted changes to the framework contract in accordance with regulation 42(2), unless they notify the payment service provider that they do not accept such changes before the proposed date of their entry into force;

    (b)   the duration of the framework contract;

    (c)   the right of the payment service user to terminate the framework contract and any agreements relating to termination in accordance with regulation 43.

7.   The following information about redress—

    (a)   any contractual clause on—

        (i)   the law applicable to the framework contract;

        (ii)   the competent courts;

    (b)   the availability of out-of-court complaint and redress procedures for the payment service user and the methods for having access to them.

                [4518]

NOTES

Commencement: these Regulations come into force on 2 March 2009 (for the purposes specified in reg 1(2)(a)), 1 May 2009 (for the purposes specified in reg 1(2)(b)), and 1 November 2009 (otherwise). See reg 1 at **[4387]**.

SCHEDULE 5
APPLICATION AND MODIFICATION OF LEGISLATION
Regulation 95

PART 1
APPLICATION AND MODIFICATION OF THE 2000 ACT

Disciplinary powers

1.   Sections 66 (disciplinary powers) to 70 (statements of policy: procedure) of the 2000 Act apply with the following modifications to section 66—

    (a)   for subsection (2) substitute—

"(2)   A person is guilty of misconduct if, while a relevant person, he has been knowingly concerned in a contravention of the Payment Services Regulations 2009 by an authorised payment institution or a small payment institution.";

    (b)   for subsection (6) substitute—

"(6) "Relevant person" means any person responsible for the management of the authorised payment institution or small payment institution or, where relevant, any person responsible for the management of the institution's payment services activities."; and

(c) omit subsection (7).

The Tribunal

2. Part 9 of the 2000 Act (hearings and appeals) applies in respect of references to the Tribunal made under these Regulations as it applies in respect of references made to the Tribunal under that Act, with the following modifications to section 133 (proceedings: general provision)—

(a) in subsection (6) omit ", or as a result of section 338(2),";

(b) omit subsection (8); and

(c) in subsection (12) for "has the same meaning as in section 395" substitute "means a notice given under regulation 11(6), (9) or (10)(b) (including as applied by regulation 14) of the Payment Services Regulations 2009".

Information gathering and investigations

3. Part 11 of the 2000 Act (information gathering and investigations) applies with the following modifications—

(a) in section 165 (Authority's power to require information)—

    (i) for references to "an authorised person" substitute "an authorised payment institution, an EEA authorised payment institution or a small payment institution";

    (ii) in subsection (4), for "this Act" substitute "the Payment Services Regulations 2009"; and

    (iii) in subsection (7) omit paragraphs (b) and (c);

(b) in subsection (2)(a) of section 166 (reports by skilled persons), for "an authorised person" substitute "an authorised payment institution, an EEA authorised payment institution or a small payment institution";

(c) in section 167 (appointment of persons to carry out general investigations)—

    (i) in subsection (1)—

        (aa) omit "or the Secretary of State";

        (bb) in paragraph (a) for "a recognised investment exchange or an authorised person or of an appointed representative" substitute "an authorised payment institution, an EEA authorised payment institution or a small payment institution";

        (cc) in paragraph (c) for "a recognised investment exchange or an authorised person" substitute "an authorised payment institution, an EEA authorised payment institution or a small payment institution";

    (ii) in subsection (4)—

        (aa) for "in relation to a former authorised person (or appointed representative)" substitute "in relation to a former authorised payment institution, former EEA authorised payment institution or former small payment institution";

        (bb) in paragraph (a) for "he was an authorised person (or appointed representative)" substitute "it was an authorised payment institution, EEA authorised payment institution or small payment institution";

        (cc) for paragraph (b) substitute—

"(b) the ownership or control of a former authorised payment institution, former EEA authorised payment institution or former small payment institution at any time when it was an authorised payment institution, EEA authorised payment institution or small payment institution, as the case may be.";

    (iii) in subsection (5) for "regulated activities" substitute "payment services"; and

    (iv) omit subsection (6);

(d) in section 168 (appointment of persons to carry out investigations in particular cases)—

    (i) in subsection (1)—

        (aa) in paragraph (a) for "any regulation made under section 142" substitute "any requirement of or imposed under the Payment Services Regulations 2009";

        (bb) in paragraph (b) for "191" to the end substitute "or under regulation 110, 111, 113 or 114 of the Payment Services Regulations 2009";

    (ii) for subsection (2) substitute—

"(2) Subsection (3) also applies if it appears to an investigating authority that there are circumstances suggesting that a person may be guilty of an offence under, or has contravened a requirement of, the Money Laundering Regulations 2007.";

    (iii) omit subsections (4) and (5); and

    (iv) in subsection (6) omit "or the Secretary of State";

(e) in section 169 (investigations etc in support of overseas regulator)—

    (i)   in subsection (8) for "Part XXIII" substitute "sections 348, 349, 351 and 352, as applied with modifications by the Payment Services Regulations 2009"; and

    (ii)   in subsection (13) for "has the same meaning as in section 195" substitute "means a competent authority designated in accordance with Article 20 of the payment services directive";

  (f)   in section 170 (investigations: general)—

    (i)   in subsection (1) omit "or (5)";

    (ii)   in subsection (3)(a) omit "or (4)"; and

    (iii)   for subsection (10) substitute—

    "(10)   "Investigating authority" in relation to an investigator means the Authority.";

  (g)   in section 171 (powers of persons appointed under section 167), omit subsections (3A) and (7);

  (h)   in subsection (4) of section 172 (additional power of persons appointed as a result of section 168(1) or (4)), omit "or (4)";

  (i)   in section 174 (admissibility of statements made to investigators)—

    (i)   in subsection (2) omit "or in proceedings in relation to action to be taken against that person under section 123";

    (ii)   in subsection (3)(a) for "398" substitute "regulation 114 of the Payment Services Regulations 2009"; and

    (iii)   in subsection (4) omit "or (5)";

  (j)   in subsection (8) of section 175 (information and documents: supplemental provisions) omit "or (5)";

  (k)   in section 176(entry of premises under warrant)—

    (i)   in subsection (1)—

        (aa)   omit "the Secretary of State,"; and

        (bb)   for "the first, second or third" substitute "the first or second";

    (ii)   in subsection (3)(a) for "an authorised person or an appointed representative" substitute "an authorised payment institution, a small payment institution or an EEA authorised payment institution";

    (iii)   omit subsection (4);

    (iv)   in subsection (10) omit "or (5)";

    (v)   in subsection (11)(a) omit "87C, 87J,"; and

  (l)   in subsection (5)(a) of section 177 (offences), for "six months" substitute "three months".

Auditors and actuaries

4.   Sections 341 (access to books etc) to 346 (provision of false or misleading information to auditor or actuary) of the 2000 Act apply as though in sections 341(1), 342(1) to (3) and (7), 343(1) to (3), (7) and (8), 344(2), 345(1) and 346(1) and (2) the references to "an authorised person" were to "an authorised payment institution".

Restriction on disclosure of information

5.   Sections 348 (restrictions on disclosure of confidential information by Authority etc), 349 (exceptions from section 348), 351 (competition information) and 352 (offences) of the 2000 Act apply with the following modifications—

  (a)   in section 348—

    (i)   in subsection (2)(b) for the words from ", the competent authority" to the end substitute "under the Payment Services Regulations 2009";

    (ii)   in subsection (3)(a) for "this Act" substitute "the Payments Services Regulations 2009";

    (iii)   in subsection (5)—

        (aa)   for "this Part", substitute "the Payment Services Regulations 2009";

        (bb)   omit paragraphs (b) and (c);

        (cc)   in paragraph (e) for "paragraphs (a) to (c)" substitute "paragraph (a)";

    (iv)   in subsection (6)—

        (aa)   omit paragraphs (a) and (b); and

        (bb)   in paragraph (c) for "paragraph 6 of Schedule 1" substitute "regulation 81 of the Payment Services Regulations 2009"; and

  (b)   in section 349 omit subsections (3A) and (3B).

Insolvency

6.   Sections 359 (administration order), 367 (winding-up petitions) and 368 (winding-up petitions: EEA and Treaty firms) of the 2000 Act apply with the following modifications—

  (a)   for references to "an authorised person" substitute "an authorised payment institution or an EEA authorised payment institution";

  (b)   in section 359—

    (i)   omit subsections (1)(b), (3)(b) and (5);

      (ii)   for subsection (1)(c) substitute—

"(c) is providing or has provided payment services in contravention of regulation 110(1) of the Payment Services Regulations 2009.";

      (iii) in subsection (3)(a) omit "or partnership" and for "an agreement" substitute "a contract for payment services"; and

      (iv) in subsection (4) omit the definitions of "agreement", "authorised deposit taker" and "relevant deposit";

  (c)   in section 367—

      (i)   omit subsections (1)(b), (2), (5), (6) and (7);

      (ii)   for subsection (1)(c) substitute—

"(c) is providing or has provided payment services in contravention of regulation 110(1) of the Payment Services Regulations 2009."; and

      (iii) in subsection (4) for "an agreement" substitute "a contract for payment services"; and

  (d)   in section 368 for the words from "winding up" to the end substitute "winding up of an EEA authorised payment institution unless it has been asked to do so by the home state competent authority.".

Warning notices and decision notices

7.   Part 26 of the 2000 Act (notices) applies with the following modifications—
  (a)   omit section 388(2) (decision notices);
  (b)   in section 390 (final notices)—
      (i)   omit subsections (6) and (10); and
      (ii)   in subsection (8) omit "or (6)(c)";
  (c)   in section 391 (publication), in subsection (10) for "has the same meaning as in section 395" substitute "means a notice given under regulation 11(6), (9) or (10)(b) (including as applied by regulation 14) of the Payment Services Regulations 2009";
  (d)   for section 392 (application of sections 393 and 394) substitute—

    "**392.**   Sections 393 and 394 apply to—
    (a)   a warning notice given in accordance with regulations 10(2) (including as applied by regulation 14), 24(2) (in relation to the cancellation of a registration), 30(2), 86(1) or 89(1) of the Payment Services Regulations 2009;
    (b)   a decision notice given in accordance with regulations 10(3)(a) (including as applied by regulation 14), 24(3)(a) (in relation to the cancellation of a registration), 30(3)(a), 86(3) or 89(3) of the Payment Services Regulations 2009."; and
  (e)   in section 395 (the Authority's procedures) in subsection (13) for "in accordance with" to the end substitute "under regulation 11(6), (9) or (10)(b) (including as applied by regulation 14) of the Payment Services Regulations 2009".

Limitation on power to require documents

8.   Section 413 of the 2000 Act (protected items) applies for the purposes of these Regulations as it applies for the purposes of that Act.

[4519]

NOTES

  Commencement: these Regulations come into force on 2 March 2009 (for the purposes specified in reg 1(2)(a)), 1 May 2009 (for the purposes specified in reg 1(2)(b)), and 1 November 2009 (otherwise). See reg 1 at **[4387]**.

PART 2
APPLICATION AND MODIFICATION OF SECONDARY LEGISLATION

The Financial Services and Markets Act 2000 (Service of Notices) Regulations 2001

9.   The Financial Services and Markets Act 2000 (Service of Notices) Regulations 2001 applies to any notice, direction or document of any kind given by or to the Authority under these Regulations as it applies to any notice, direction or document of any kind under the 2000 Act.

The Financial Services and Markets Act 2000
(Disclosure of Confidential Information) Regulations 2001

10.   The Financial Services and Markets Act 2000 (Disclosure of Confidential Information) Regulations 2001 applies with the following modifications—
  (a)   in regulation 2—
      (i)   in the definition of "directive restrictions" for "and article 9 of the insurance mediation directive" substitute ", article 9 of the insurance mediation directive and Article 22 of the payment services directive";
      (ii)   in paragraph (a) of the definition of "overseas regulatory authority" after "of the

Act" insert "or any function conferred under national legislation in implementation of the payment services directive"; and

    (iii)   after the definition of "overseas regulatory authority" insert—

""payment services directive" means Directive 2007/64/EC of the European Parliament and of the Council of 13th November 2007 on payment services in the internal market;

"payment services directive information" means confidential information received by the Authority in the course of discharging its functions as the competent authority under the payment services directive;";

  (b)   in regulation 5(4)(a) for "an authorised person, former authorised person or former regulated person" substitute "an authorised payment institution, former authorised payment institution, small payment institution or former small payment institution";

  (c)   in regulation 5(6)(e) for "an authorised person, former authorised person or former regulated person" substitute "an authorised payment institution, former authorised payment institution, small payment institution or former small payment institution";

  (d)   in regulation 8 after sub-paragraph (b) insert—

"(c)   payment services directive information.";

  (e)   in regulation 9—

    (i)   in paragraph (1) for "(3) and (3A)" substitute "(3), (3A) and (4)"; and

    (ii)   after paragraph (3B) insert—

"(4)   Paragraph (1) does not permit disclosure to the persons specified in the first column in Part 5 of Schedule 1 unless the disclosure is of payment services directive information.";

  (f)   in regulation 11 after sub-paragraph (d) insert—

"(e)   payment services directive information.";

  (g)   in the second column in Part 1 of Schedule 1, in the list of functions beside—

    (i)   "An official receiver appointed under section 399 of the Insolvency Act 1986, or an official receiver for Northern Ireland appointed under article 355 of the Insolvency (Northern Ireland) Order 1989", after paragraph (ii) insert—

"or

    (iii)   payment service providers or former payment service providers";

    (ii)   "The Department of Enterprise, Trade and Investment in Northern Ireland", after paragraph (c)(ii) insert—

"or

    (iii)   payment service providers or former payment service providers";

    (iii)   "The Pensions Regulator", after paragraph (ii) insert—

"or

    (iii)   payment service providers or former payment service providers";

    (iv)   "The Charity Commissioners for England and Wales", after paragraph (ii) insert—

"or

    (iii)   payment service providers or former payment service providers"; and

  (h)   in Schedule 1, after Part 4 insert—

"PART 5

Person	Functions
The Commissioners for Her Majesty's Revenue and Customs	Their functions under the Money Laundering Regulations 2007"

[4520]–[5000]

NOTES

Commencement: these Regulations come into force on 2 March 2009 (for the purposes specified in reg 1(2)(a)), 1 May 2009 (for the purposes specified in reg 1(2)(b)), and 1 November 2009 (otherwise). See reg 1 at **[4387]**.

(Sch 6 (Amendments to Primary and Secondary Legislation) contains the following amendments: Sch 6, Pt 1 (Amendments to Primary Legislation) amends the Financial Services and Markets Act 2000, ss 226, 234, Sch 17, Pt III at **[254]**, **[261]**, **[493]**; *Sch 6, Pt 2 (Amendments to Secondary Legislation) revokes the Cross-Border Credit Transfers Regulations 1999, SI 1999/1876, and the Consumer Protection (Distance Selling) Regulations 2000, SI 2000/2334, reg 21, adds the Financial Services and Markets Act 2000 (Regulated Activities) Order 2001, SI 2001/544, arts 9AB, 9L (at* **[2020A]**, **[2030A]**), *amends the Financial Services (Distance Marketing) Regulations 2004, SI 2004/2095, regs 7, 8 (at* **[3898]**, **[3899]**) *and revokes reg 14 of those Regulations, and contain various amendments to the Money Laundering Regulations 2007, SI 2007/2157 (see* **[2877AA]** *et seq.)*

PART III STATUTORY INSTRUMENTS

PART IV
EC MATERIALS

COUNCIL DIRECTIVE

of 20 December 1985

to protect the consumer in respect of contracts negotiated away from business premises

(85/577/EEC)

NOTES

Date of publication in OJ: OJ L372, 31.12.1985, p 31. Notes are as in the original OJ version.

As of 1 February 2009, this Directive had not been amended (but see below).

Proposed repeal of this Directive: see the 2008 Proposal for a Directive of the European Parliament and of the Council on consumer rights[1] which proposes the repeal of this Directive (together with (i) Council Directive 93/13/EEC on unfair terms in consumer contracts, (ii) Directive 97/7/EC of the European Parliament and of the Council on the protection of consumers in respect of distance contracts, and (iii) Directive 1999/44/EC of the European Parliament and of the Council on certain aspects of the sale of consumer goods) and their replacement with a single Directive on consumer rights. The proposed Directive would cover all contracts for sales of goods and services from business to consumer including purchases made in a shop, at a distance or away from business premises. It would also include rules specific to particular situations (eg, providing for a right of withdrawal in the case of distance and off-premises contracts).

[1] Brussels, 8.10.2008, COM(2008) 614 final. Available on the Europa website.

THE COUNCIL OF THE EUROPEAN COMMUNITIES,

Having regard to the Treaty establishing the European Economic Community, and in particular Article 100 thereof,

Having regard to the proposal from the Commission,[1]

Having regard to the opinion of the European Parliament,[2]

Having regard to the opinion of the Economic and Social Committee,[3]

Whereas it is a common form of commercial practice in the Member States for the conclusion of a contract or a unilateral engagement between a trader and consumer to be made away from the business premises of the trader, and whereas such contracts and engagements are the subject of legislation which differs from one Member State to another;

Whereas any disparity between such legislation may directly affect the functioning of the common market; whereas it is therefore necessary to approximate laws in this field;

Whereas the preliminary programme of the European Economic Community for a consumer protection and information policy[4] provides inter alia, under paragraphs 24 and 25, that appropriate measures be taken to protect consumers against unfair commercial practices in respect of doorstep selling; whereas the second programme of the European Economic Community for a consumer protection and information policy[5] confirmed that the action and priorities defined in the preliminary programme would be pursued;

Whereas the special feature of contracts concluded away from the business premises of the trader is that as a rule it is the trader who initiates the contract negotiations, for which the consumer is unprepared or which he does not except; whereas the consumer is often unable to compare the quality and price of the offer with other offers; whereas this surprise element generally exists not only in contracts made at the doorstep but also in other forms of contract concluded by the trader away from his business premises;

Whereas the consumer should be given a right of cancellation over a period of at least seven days in order to enable him to assess the obligations arising under the contract;

Whereas appropriate measures should be taken to ensure that the consumer is informed in writing of this period for reflection;

Whereas the freedom of Member States to maintain or introduce a total or partial prohibition on the conclusion of contracts away from business premises, inasmuch as they consider this to be in the interest of consumers, must not be affected;

[5001]

NOTES

[1] OJ No C22, 29.1.1977, p 6; OJ No C127, 1.6.1978, p 6.
[2] OJ No C241, 10.10.1977, p 26.
[3] OJ No C180, 18.7.1977, p 39.
[4] OJ No C92, 25.4.1975, p 2.
[5] OJ No C133, 3.6.1981, p 1.

HAS ADOPTED THIS DIRECTIVE:

Article 1

1. This Directive shall apply to contracts under which a trader supplies goods or services to a consumer and which are concluded:

— during an excursion organized by the trader away from his business premises, or
— during a visit by a trader
    (i)   to the consumer's home or to that of another consumer;
    (ii) to the consumer's place of work;
where the visit does not take place at the express request of the consumer.

2. This Directive shall also apply to contracts for the supply of goods or services other than those concerning which the consumer requested the visit of the trader, provided that when he requested the visit the consumer did not know, or could not reasonably have known, that the supply of those other goods or services formed part of the trader's commercial or professional activities.

3. This Directive shall also apply to contracts in respect of which an offer was made by the consumer under conditions similar to those described in paragraph 1 or paragraph 2 although the consumer was not bound by that offer before its acceptance by the trader.

4. This Directive shall also apply to offers made contractually by the consumer under conditions similar to those described in paragraph 1 or paragraph 2 where the consumer is bound by his offer.

[5001A]

Article 2

For the purposes of this Directive:
"consumer" means a natural person who, in transactions covered by this Directive, is acting for purposes which can be regarded as outside his trade or profession;
"trader" means a natural or legal person who, for the transaction in question, acts in his commercial or professional capacity, and anyone acting in the name or on behalf of a trader.

[5001B]

Article 3

1. The Member States may decide that this Directive shall apply only to contracts for which the payment to be made by the consumer exceeds a specified amount. This amount may not exceed 60 ECU.

The Council, acting on a proposal from the Commission, shall examine and, if necessary, revise this amount for the first time no later than four years after notification of the Directive and thereafter every two years, taking into account economic and monetary developments in the Community.

2. This Directive shall not apply to:
  (a)   contracts for the construction, sale and rental of immovable property or contracts concerning other rights relating to immovable property.
       Contracts for the supply of goods and for their incorporation in immovable property or contracts for repairing immovable property shall fall within the scope of this Directive;
  (b)   contracts for the supply of foodstuffs or beverages or other goods intended for current consumption in the household and supplied by regular roundsmen;
  (c)   contracts for the supply of goods or services, provided that all three of the following conditions are met:
      (i)   the contract is concluded on the basis of a trader's catalogue which the consumer has a proper opportunity of reading in the absence of the trader's representative,
      (ii) there is intended to be continuity of contact between the trader's representative and the consumer in relation to that or any subsequent transaction,
      (iii) both the catalogue and the contract clearly inform the consumer of his right to return goods to the supplier within a period of not less than seven days of receipt or otherwise to cancel the contract within that period without obligation of any kind other than to take reasonable care of the goods;
  (d)   insurance contracts;
  (e)   contracts for securities.

3. By way of derogation from Article 1(2), Member States may refrain from applying this Directive to contracts for the supply of goods or services having a direct connection with the goods or services concerning which the consumer requested the visit of the trader.

[5001C]

Article 4

In the case of transactions within the scope of Article 1, traders shall be required to give consumers written notice of their right of cancellation within the period laid down in Article 5, together with the name and address of a person against whom that right may be exercised.

Such notice shall be dated and shall state particulars enabling the contract to be identified. It shall be given to the consumer:
  (a)   in the case of Article 1(1), at the time of conclusion of the contract;
  (b)   in the case of Article 1(2), not later than the time of conclusion of the contract;
  (c)   in the case of Article 1(3) and 1(4), when the offer is made by the consumer.

Member States shall ensure that their national legislation lays down appropriate consumer protection measures in cases where the information referred to in this Article is not supplied.

[5001D]

Article 5

1. The consumer shall have the right to renounce the effects of his undertaking by sending notice within a period of not less than seven days from receipt by the consumer of the notice referred to in Article 4, in accordance with the procedure laid down by national law. It shall be sufficient if the notice is dispatched before the end of such period.

2. The giving of the notice shall have the effect of releasing the consumer from any obligations under the cancelled contract.

[5001E]

Article 6

The consumer may not waive the rights conferred on him by this Directive.

[5001F]

Article 7

If the consumer exercises his right of renunciation, the legal effects of such renunciation shall be governed by national laws, particularly regarding the reimbursement of payments for goods or services provided and the return of goods received.

[5001G]

Article 8

This Directive shall not prevent Member States from adopting or maintaining more favourable provisions to protect consumers in the field which it covers.

[5001H]

Article 9

1. Member States shall take the measures necessary to comply with this Directive within 24 months of its notification.[1] They shall forthwith inform the Commission thereof.

2. Member States shall ensure that the texts of the main provisions of national law which they adopt in the field covered by this Directive are communicated to the Commission.

[5001I]

NOTES

1   This Directive was notified to the Member States on 23 December 1985.

Article 10

This Directive is addressed to the Member States.

[5001J]

COUNCIL DIRECTIVE

of 20 December 1985

on the coordination of laws, regulations and administrative provisions relating to undertakings for collective investment in transferable securities (UCITS)

(85/611/EEC)

NOTES

Date of publication in OJ: OJ L375, 31.12.85, p 3. Notes are as in the original OJ version.

This Directive is reproduced as amended by: European Parliament and Council Directive 95/26/EC (OJ L168, 18.7.95, p 7); European Parliament and Council Directive 2000/64/EC (OJ L290, 17.11.2000, p 27); European Parliament and Council Directive 2001/107/EC (OJ L41, 13.2.2002, p 20); European Parliament and Council Directive 2001/108/EC (OJ L41, 13.2.2002, p 35); European Parliament and Council Directive 2004/39/EC (OJ L145, 30.04.2004, p 1); European Parliament and Council Directive 2005/1/EC (OJ L79, 24.3.2005, p 9); European Parliament and Council Directive 2008/18/EC (OJ L76, 19.3.2008, p 42).Amendments made by Council Directive 88/220/EEC (OJ L100, 19.4.88, p 31) have been superseded by the amendments listed above.

THE COUNCIL OF THE EUROPEAN COMMUNITIES,

Having regard to the Treaty establishing the European Economic Community, and in particular Article 57(2) thereof,

Having regard to the proposal from the Commission,[1]

Having regard to the opinion of the European Parliament,[2]

Having regard to the opinion of the Economic and Social Committee,[3]

Whereas the laws of the Member States relating to collective investment undertakings differ appreciably from one state to another, particularly as regards the obligations and controls which are imposed on those undertakings; whereas those differences distort the conditions of competition between those undertakings and do not ensure equivalent protection for unit-holders;

Whereas national laws governing collective investment undertakings should be coordinated with a view to approximating the conditions of competition between those undertakings at Community level, while at the same time ensuring more effective and more uniform protection for unit-holders; whereas such coordination will make it easier for a collective investment undertaking situated in one Member State to market its units in other Member States;

Whereas the attainment of these objectives will facilitate the removal of the restrictions on the free circulation of the units of collective investment undertakings in the Community, and such coordination will help to bring about a European capital market;

Whereas, having regard to these objectives, it is desirable that common basic rules be established for the authorisation, supervision, structure and activities of collective investment undertakings situated in the Member States and the information they must publish;

Whereas the application of these common rules is a sufficient guarantee to permit collective investment undertakings situated in Member States, subject to the applicable provisions relating to capital movements, to market their units in other Member States without those Member States' being able to subject those undertakings or their units to any provision whatsoever other than provisions which, in those states, do not fall within the field covered by this Directive; whereas, nevertheless, if a collective investment undertaking situated in one Member State markets its units in a different Member State it must take all necessary steps to ensure that unit-holders in that other Member State can exercise their financial rights there with ease and are provided with the necessary information;

Whereas the coordination of the laws of the Member States should be confined initially to collective investment undertakings other than of the closed-ended type which promote the sale of their units to the public in the Community and the sole object of which is investment in transferable securities (which are essentially transferable securities officially listed on stock exchanges or similar regulated markets); whereas regulation of the collective investment undertakings not covered by the Directive poses a variety of problems which must be dealt with by means of other provisions, and such undertakings will accordingly be the subject of coordination at a later stage; whereas pending such coordination any Member State may, *inter alia*, prescribe those categories of undertakings for collective investment in transferable securities (UCITS) excluded from this Directive's scope on account of their investment and borrowing policies and lay down those specific rules to which such UCITS are subject in carrying on their business within its territory;

Whereas the free marketing of the units issued by UCITS authorised to invest up to 100% of their assets in transferable securities issued by the same body (State, local authority, etc) may not have the direct or indirect effect of disturbing the functioning of the capital market or the financing of the Member States or of creating economic situations similar to those which Article 68(3) of the Treaty seeks to prevent;

Whereas account should be taken of the special situations of the Hellenic Republic's and Portuguese Republic's financial markets by allowing those countries an additional period in which to implement this Directive,

[5002]

NOTES

1   OJ C1, 26.7.76, p 1.
2   OJ C57, 7.3.77, p 31.
3   OJ C75, 26.3.77, p 10.

HAS ADOPTED THIS DIRECTIVE—

SECTION I
GENERAL PROVISIONS AND SCOPE

Article 1

1.   The Member States shall apply this Directive to undertakings for collective investment in transferable securities (hereinafter referred to as UCITS) situated within their territories.

2.   For the purposes of this Directive, and subject to Article 2, UCITS shall be undertakings—
    [—   the sole object of which is the collective investment in transferable securities and/or in other liquid financial assets referred to in Article 19(1) of capital raised from the public and which operates on the principle of risk-spreading and]
    —   the units of which are, at the request of holders, re-purchased or redeemed, directly or

indirectly, out of these undertakings' assets. Action taken by a UCITS to ensure that the stock exchange value of its units does not significantly vary from their net asset value shall be regarded as equivalent to such re-purchase or redemption.

3. Such undertakings may be constituted according to law, either under the law of contract (as common funds managed by management companies) or trust law (as unit trusts) or under statute (as investment companies).

For the purposes of this Directive "common funds" shall also include unit trusts.

4. Investment companies the assets of which are invested through the intermediary of subsidiary companies mainly otherwise than in transferable securities shall not, however, be subject to this Directive.

5. The Member States shall prohibit UCITS which are subject to this Directive from transforming themselves into collective investment undertakings which are not covered by this Directive.

6. Subject to the provisions governing capital movements and to Articles 44, 45 and 52(2) no Member State may apply any other provisions whatsoever in the field covered by this Directive to UCITS situated in another Member State or to the units issued by such UCITS, where they market their units within its territory.

7. Without prejudice to paragraph 6, a Member State may apply to UCITS situated within its territory requirements which are stricter than or additional to those laid down in Article 4 *et seq* of this Directive, provided that they are of general application and do not conflict with the provisions of this Directive.

[8. For the purposes of this Directive, "transferable securities" shall mean—
—   shares in companies and other securities equivalent to shares in companies ("shares"),
—   bonds and other forms of securitised debt ("debt securities"),
—   any other negotiable securities which carry the right to acquire any such transferable securities by subscription or exchange,

excluding the techniques and instruments referred to in Article 21.

9. For the purposes of this Directive "money market instruments" shall mean instruments normally dealt in on the money market which are liquid, and have a value which can be accurately determined at any time.]

[5002A]

NOTES

Para 2: words in square brackets substituted by European Parliament and Council Directive 2001/108/EC, Art 1(1), as from 13 February 2002.

Paras 8, 9: added by European Parliament and Council Directive 2001/108/EC, Art 1(2), as from 13 February 2002.

[Article 1a

For the purposes of this Directive—

1.   "depositary" shall mean any institution entrusted with the duties mentioned in Articles 7 and 14 and subject to the other provisions laid down in Sections IIIa and IVa;

2.   "management company" shall mean any company, the regular business of which is the management of UCITS in the form of unit trusts/common funds and/or of investment companies (collective portfolio management of UCITS); this includes the functions mentioned in Annex II;

3.   a "management company's home Member State" shall mean the Member State, in which the management company's registered office is situated;

4.   a "management company's host Member State" shall mean the Member State, other than the home Member State, within the territory of which a management company has a branch or provides services;

5.   a "UCITS home Member State" shall mean—
    (a)   with regard to a UCITS constituted as unit trust/common fund, the Member State in which the management company's registered office is situated,
    (b)   with regard to a UCITS constituted as investment company, the Member State in which the investment company's registered office is situated;

6.   a "UCITS host Member State" shall mean the Member State, other than the UCITS home Member State, in which the units of the common fund/unit trust or of the investment company are marketed;

7.   "branch" shall mean a place of business which is a part of the management company, which has no legal personality and which provides the services for which the management company has been authorised; all the places of business set up in the same Member State by a management company with headquarters in another Member State shall be regarded as a single branch;

8. "competent authorities" shall mean the authorities which each Member State designates under Article 49 of this Directive;
9. "close links" shall mean a situation as defined in Article 2(1) of Directive 95/26/EC;[1]
10. "qualifying holdings" shall mean any direct or indirect holding in a management company which represents 10% or more of the capital or of the voting rights or which makes it possible to exercise a significant influence over the management of the management company in which that holding subsists.
    For the purpose of this definition, the voting rights referred to in Article 7 of Directive 88/627/EEC[2] shall be taken into account;
11. "ISD" shall mean Council Directive 93/22/EEC of 10 May 1993 on investment services in the securities field;[3]
12. "parent undertaking" shall mean a parent undertaking as defined in Articles 1 and 2 of Directive 83/ 349/EEC;[4]
13. "subsidiary" shall mean a subsidiary undertaking as defined in Articles 1 and 2 of Directive 83/349/EEC; any subsidiary of a subsidiary undertaking shall also be regarded as a subsidiary of the parent undertaking which is the ultimate parent of those undertakings;
14. "initial capital" shall mean capital as defined in items 1 and 2 of Article 34(2) of Directive 2000/12/EC;[5]
15. "own funds" shall mean own funds as defined in Title V, Chapter 2, Section 1 of Directive 2000/12/EC; this definition may, however, be amended in the circumstances described in Annex V of Directive 93/ 6/EEC.[6]]

[5002B]

NOTES

Inserted by European Parliament and Council Directive 2001/107/EC, Art 1(1), as from 13 February 2002.

[1] OJ L168, 18.7.1995, p 7.
[2] OJ L348, 17.12.1988, p 62.
[3] OJ L141, 11.6.1993, p 27. Directive as last amended by Directive 2000/64/EC (OJ L290, 17.11.2000, p 27).
[4] OJ L193, 18.7.1983, p 1. Directive as last amended by the 1994 Act of Accession.
[5] OJ L126, 26.5.2000, p 1. Directive as amended by Directive 2000/28/EC of the European Parliament and of the Council (OJ L275, 27.10.2000, p 37).
[6] OJ L141, 11.6.1993, p 1. Directive as last amended by Directive 98/33/EC of the European Parliament and of the Council (OJ L204, 21.7.1998, p 29).

Article 2

1. The following shall not be UCITS subject to this Directive—
    — UCITS of the closed-ended type;
    — UCITS which raise capital without promoting the sale of their units to the public within the Community or any part of it;
    — UCITS the units of which, under the fund rules or the investment company's instruments of incorporation, may be sold only to the public in non-member countries;
    — categories of UCITS prescribed by the regulations of the Member States in which such UCITS are situated, for which the rules laid down in Section V and Article 36 are inappropriate in view of their investment and borrowing policies.

2. Five years after the implementation of this Directive the Commission shall submit to the Council a report on the implementation of paragraph 1 and, in particular, of its fourth indent. If necessary, it shall propose suitable measures to extend the scope.

[5003]

Article 3

For the purposes of this Directive, a UCITS shall be deemed to be situated in the Member State in which the investment company or the management company of the unit trust has its registered office; the Member States must require that the head office be situated in the same Member State as the registered office.

[5004]

SECTION II
AUTHORISATION OF UCITS

Article 4

1. No UCITS shall carry on activities as such unless it has been authorised by the competent authorities of the Member State in which it is situated, hereinafter referred to as "the competent authorities".

Such authorisation shall be valid for all Member States.

2. A unit trust shall be authorised only if the competent authorities have approved the management company, the fund rules and the choice of depositary. An investment company shall be authorised only if the competent authorities have approved both its instruments of incorporation and the choice of depositary.

[3. The competent authorities may not authorise a UCITS if the management company or the investment company do not comply with the preconditions laid down in this Directive, in Sections III and IV respectively.

Moreover the competent authorities may not authorise a UCITS if the directors of the depositary are not of sufficiently good repute or are not sufficiently experienced also in relation to the type of UCITS to be managed. To that end, the names of the directors of the depositary and of every person succeeding them in office must be communicated forthwith to the competent authorities.

Directors shall mean those persons who, under the law or the instruments of incorporation, represent the depositary, or who effectively determine the policy of the depositary.

3a. The competent authorities shall not grant authorisation if the UCITS is legally prevented (e g through a provision in the fund rules or instruments of incorporation) from marketing its units or shares in its home Member State.]

4. Neither the management company nor the depositary may be replaced, nor may the fund rules or the investment company's instruments of incorporation be amended, without the approval of the competent authorities.

[5005]

NOTES

Paras 3, 3a: substituted, for original para 3, by European Parliament and Council Directive 2001/107/EC, Art 1(2), as from 13 February 2002.

[SECTION III
OBLIGATIONS REGARDING MANAGEMENT COMPANIES

TITLE A

Conditions for taking up business

Article 5

1. Access to the business of management companies is subject to prior official authorisation to be granted by the home Member State's competent authorities. Authorisation granted under this Directive to a management company shall be valid for all Member States.

2. No management company may engage in activities other than the management of UCITS authorised according to this Directive except the additional management of other collective investment undertakings which are not covered by this Directive and for which the management company is subject to prudential supervision but which cannot be marketed in other Member States under this Directive.

The activity of management of unit trusts/common funds and of investment companies includes, for the purpose of this Directive, the functions mentioned in Annex II which are not exhaustive.

3. By way of derogation from paragraph 2, Member States may authorise management companies to provide, in addition to the management of unit trusts/common funds and of investment companies, the following services—

    (a)   management of portfolios of investments, including those owned by pension funds, in accordance with mandates given by investors on a discretionary, client-by-client basis, where such portfolios include one or more of the instruments listed in Section B of the Annex to the ISD,

    (b)   as non-core services:

        —   investment advice concerning one or more of the instruments listed in Section B of the Annex to the ISD,

        —   safekeeping and administration in relation to units of collective investment undertakings.

Management companies may in no case be authorised under this Directive to provide only the services mentioned in this paragraph or to provide non-core services without being authorised for the service referred to in point (a).

[4. Articles 2(2), 12, 13 and 19 of Directive 2004/39/EC of the European Parliament and of the Council of 21 April 2004 on markets in financial instruments, shall apply to the provision of the services referred to in paragraph 3 of this Article by management companies.]]

[5006]

NOTES

Substituted, together with preceding headings and Arts 5a–5h, 6, 6a–6c for original Arts 5, 6, by European Parliament and Council Directive 2001/107/EC, Art 1(3), as from 13 February 2002.

Para 4: substituted by European Parliament and Council Directive 2004/39/EC, Art 66, as from 30 April 2004.

[Article 5a

1. Without prejudice to other conditions of general application laid down by national law, the competent authorities shall not grant authorisation to a management company unless—

    (a)   the management company has an initial capital of at least EUR 125,000—

         —   When the value of the portfolios of the management company, exceeds EUR 250,000 000, the management company shall be required to provide an additional amount of own funds. This additional amount of own funds shall be equal to 0,02% of the amount by which the value of the portfolios of the management company exceeds EUR 250,000,000. The required total of the initial capital and the additional amount shall not, however, exceed EUR 10,000,000.

         —   For the purpose of this paragraph, the following portfolios shall be deemed to be the portfolios of the management company—

            (i)   unit trusts/common funds managed by the management company including portfolios for which it has delegated the management function but excluding portfolios that it is managing under delegation;

            (ii)   investment companies for which the management company is the designated management company;

            (iii)   other collective investment undertakings managed by the management company including portfolios for which it has delegated the management function but excluding portfolios that it is managing under delegation.

         —   Irrespective of the amount of these requirements, the own funds of the management company shall never be less than the amount prescribed in Annex IV of Directive 93/6/EEC.

         —   Member States may authorise management companies not to provide up to 50% of the additional amount of own funds referred to in the first indent if they benefit from a guarantee of the same amount given by a credit institution or an insurance undertaking. The credit institution or insurance undertaking must have its registered office in a Member State, or in a non-Member State provided that it is subject to prudential rules considered by the competent authorities as equivalent to those laid down in Community law.

         —   No later than 13 February 2005, the Commission shall present a report to the European Parliament and the Council on the application of this capital requirement, accompanied where appropriate by proposals for its revision;

    (b)   the persons who effectively conduct the business of a management company are of sufficiently good repute and are sufficiently experienced also in relation to the type of UCITS managed by the management company. To that end, the names of these persons and of every person succeeding them in office must be communicated forthwith to the competent authorities. The conduct of a management company's business must be decided by at least two persons meeting such conditions;

    (c)   the application for authorisation is accompanied by a programme of activity setting out, *inter alia*, the organisational structure of the management company;

    (d)   both its head office and its registered office are located in the same Member State.

2. Moreover where close links exist between the management company and other natural or legal persons, the competent authorities shall grant authorisation only if those do not prevent the effective exercise of their supervisory functions.

The competent authorities shall also refuse authorisation if the laws, regulations or administrative provisions of a non-member country governing one or more natural or legal persons with which the management company has close links, or difficulties involved in their enforcement, prevent the effective exercise of their supervisory functions.

The competent authorities shall require management companies to provide them with the information they require to monitor compliance with the conditions referred to in this paragraph on a continuous basis.

3. An applicant shall be informed, within six months of the submission of a complete application, whether or not authorisation has been granted. Reasons shall be given whenever an authorisation is refused.

4. A management company may start business as soon as authorisation has been granted.

5. The competent authorities may withdraw the authorisation issued to a management company subject to this Directive only where that company—

    (a)   does not make use of the authorisation within 12 months, expressly renounces the authorisation or has ceased the activity covered by this Directive more than six months previously unless the Member State concerned has provided for authorisation to lapse in such cases;

(b) has obtained the authorisation by making false statements or by any other irregular means;

(c) no longer fulfils the conditions under which authorisation was granted;

(d) no longer complies with Directive 93/6/EEC if its authorisation also covers the discretionary portfolio management service referred to in Article 5(3)(a) of this Directive;

(e) has seriously and/or systematically infringed the provisions adopted pursuant to this Directive; or

(f) falls within any of the cases where national law provides for withdrawal.]

[5007]

NOTES
Substituted as noted to Article 5 at **[5006]**.

[Article 5b

1. The competent authorities shall not grant authorisation to take up the business of management companies until they have been informed of the identities of the shareholders or members, whether direct or indirect, natural or legal persons, that have qualifying holdings and of the amounts of those holdings.

The competent authorities shall refuse authorisation if, taking into account the need to ensure the sound and prudent management of a management company, they are not satisfied as to the suitability of the aforementioned shareholders or members.

2. In the case of branches of management companies that have registered offices outside the European Union and are starting or carrying on business, the Member States shall not apply provisions that result in treatment more favourable than that accorded to branches of management companies that have registered offices in Member States.

3. The competent authorities of the other Member State involved shall be consulted beforehand on the authorisation of any management company which is—

(a) a subsidiary of another management company, an investment firm, a credit institution or an insurance undertaking authorised in another Member State,

(b) a subsidiary of the parent undertaking of another management company, an investment firm, a credit institution or an insurance undertaking authorised in another Member State, or

(c) controlled by the same natural or legal persons as control another management company, an investment firm, a credit institution or an insurance undertaking authorised in another Member State.]

[5008]

NOTES
Substituted as noted to Article 5 at **[5006]**.

[TITLE B

Relations with third countries

Article 5c

1. Relations with third countries shall be regulated in accordance with the relevant rules laid down in Article 7 of the ISD.

For the purpose of this Directive, the expressions "firm/investment firm" and "investment firms" contained in Article 7 of the ISD shall be construed respectively as "management company" and "management companies"; the expression "providing investment services" in Article 7(2) of the ISD shall be construed as "providing services".

2. The Member States shall also inform the Commission of any general difficulties which UCITS encounter in marketing their units in any third country.]

[5009]

NOTES
Substituted as noted to Article 5 at **[5006]**.

[TITLE C
Operating conditions

Article 5d

1. The competent authorities of the management company's home Member State shall require that the management company which they have authorised complies at all times with the conditions laid down in Article 5 and Article 5a(1) and (2) of this Directive. The own funds of a management company may not fall below the level specified in Article 5a(1)(a). If they do, however, the competent authorities may, where the circumstances justify it, allow such firms a limited period in which to rectify their situations or cease their activities.

2. The prudential supervision of a management company shall be the responsibility of the competent authorities of the home Member State, whether the management company establishes a branch or provides services in another Member State or not, without prejudice to those provisions of this Directive which give responsibility to the authorities of the host country.]

[5010]

NOTES
Substituted as noted to Article 5 at **[5006]**.

[Article 5e

1. Qualifying holdings in management companies shall be subject to the same rules as those laid down in Article 9 of the ISD.

2. For the purpose of this Directive, the expressions "firm/investment firm" and "investment firms" contained in Article 9 of the ISD shall be construed respectively as "management company" and "management companies".]

[5011]

NOTES
Substituted as noted to Article 5 at **[5006]**.

[Article 5f

1. Each home Member State shall draw up prudential rules which management companies, with regard to the activity of management of UCITS authorised according to this Directive, shall observe at all times.

In particular, the competent authorities of the home Member State having regard also to the nature of the UCITS managed by a management company, shall require that each such company—

(a) has sound administrative and accounting procedures, control and safeguard arrangements for electronic data processing and adequate internal control mechanisms including, in particular, rules for personal transactions by its employees or for the holding or management of investments in financial instruments in order to invest own funds and ensuring, *inter alia*, that each transaction involving the fund may be reconstructed according to its origin, the parties to it, its nature, and the time and place at which it was effected and that the assets of the unit trusts/common funds or of the investment companies managed by the management company are invested according to the fund rules or the instruments of incorporation and the legal provisions in force;

(b) is structured and organised in such a way as to minimise the risk of UCITS' or clients' interests being prejudiced by conflicts of interest between the company and its clients, between one of its clients and another, between one of its clients and a UCITS or between two UCITS. Nevertheless, where a branch is set up, the organisational arrangements may not conflict with the rules of conduct laid down by the host Member State to cover conflicts of interest.

2. Each management company the authorisation of which also covers the discretionary portfolio management service mentioned in Article 5(3)(a)—

— shall not be permitted to invest all or a part of the investor's portfolio in units of unit trusts/common funds or of investment companies it manages, unless it receives prior general approval from the client,

— shall be subject with regard to the services referred to in Article 5(3) to the provisions laid down in Directive 97/9/EC of the European Parliament and of the Council of 3 March 1997 on investor-compensation schemes.[1]]

[5012]

NOTES
Substituted as noted to Article 5 at **[5006]**.
[1]   OJ L84, 26.3.1997, p 22.

[Article 5g

1.   If Member States permit management companies to delegate to third parties for the purpose of a more efficient conduct of the companies' business to carry out on their behalf one or more of their own functions the following preconditions have to be complied with—

    (a)   the competent authority must be informed in an appropriate manner;

    (b)   the mandate shall not prevent the effectiveness of supervision over the management company, and in particular it must not prevent the management company from acting, or the UCITS from being managed, in the best interests of its investors;

    (c)   when the delegation concerns the investment management, the mandate may only be given to undertakings which are authorised or registered for the purpose of asset management and subject to prudential supervision; the delegation must be in accordance with investment-allocation criteria periodically laid down by the management companies;

    (d)   where the mandate concerns the investment management and is given to a third-country undertaking, cooperation between the supervisory authorities concerned must be ensured;

    (e)   a mandate with regard to the core function of investment management shall not be given to the depositary or to any other undertaking whose interests may conflict with those of the management company or the unit-holders;

    (f)   measures shall exist which enable the persons who conduct the business of the management company to monitor effectively at any time the activity of the undertaking to which the mandate is given;

    (g)   the mandate shall not prevent the persons who conduct the business of the management company to give at any time further instructions to the under-taking to which functions are delegated and to withdraw the mandate with immediate effect when this is in the interest of investors;

    (h)   having regard to the nature of the functions to be delegated, the undertaking to which functions will be delegated must be qualified and capable of undertaking the functions in question, and

    (i)   the UCITS' prospectuses list the functions which the management company has been permitted to delegate.

2.   In no case shall the management company's and the depositary's liability be affected by the fact that the management company delegated any functions to third parties, nor shall the management company delegate its functions to the extent that it becomes a letter box entity.]

[5013]

NOTES
    Substituted as noted to Article 5 at **[5006]**.

[Article 5h

Each Member State shall draw up rules of conduct which management companies authorised in that Member State shall observe at all times. Such rules must implement at least the principles set out in the following indents. These principles shall ensure that a management company—

    (a)   acts honestly and fairly in conducting its business activities in the best interests of the UCITS it manages and the integrity of the market;

    (b)   acts with due skill, care and diligence, in the best interests of the UCITS it manages and the integrity of the market;

    (c)   has and employs effectively the resources and procedures that are necessary for the proper performance of its business activities;

    (d)   tries to avoid conflicts of interests and, when they cannot be avoided, ensures that the UCITS it manages are fairly treated, and

    (e)   complies with all regulatory requirements applicable to the conduct of its business activities so as to promote the best interests of its investors and the integrity of the market.]

[5014]

NOTES
    Substituted as noted to Article 5 at **[5006]**.

[TITLE D

The right of establishment and the freedom to provide services

Article 6

1.   Member States shall ensure that a management company, authorised in accordance with this Directive by the competent authorities of another Member State, may carry on within their territories the activity for which it has been authorised, either by the establishment of a branch or under the freedom to provide services.

2.   Member States may not make the establishment of a branch or the provision of the services subject to any authorisation requirement, to any requirement to provide endowment capital or to any other measure having equivalent effect.]

[5015]

NOTES
   Substituted as noted to Art 5 at [5006].

[Article 6a

1.   In addition to meeting the conditions imposed in Articles 5 and 5a, any management company wishing to establish a branch within the territory of another Member State shall notify the competent authorities of its home Member State.

2.   Member States shall require every management company wishing to establish a branch within the territory of another Member State to provide the following information and documents, when effecting the notification provided for in paragraph 1—
   (a)   the Member State within the territory of which the management company plans to establish a branch;
   (b)   a programme of operations setting out the activities and services according to Article 5(2) and (3) envisaged and the organisational structure of the branch;
   (c)   the address in the host Member State from which documents may be obtained;
   (d)   the names of those responsible for the management of the branch.

Unless the competent authorities of the home Member State have reason to doubt the adequacy of the administrative structure or the financial situation of a management company, taking into account the activities envisaged, they shall, within three months of receiving all the information referred to in paragraph 2, communicate that information to the competent authorities of the host Member State and shall inform the management company accordingly. They shall also communicate details of any compensation scheme intended to protect investors.

Where the competent authorities of the home Member State refuse to communicate the information referred to in paragraph 2 to the competent authorities of the host Member State, they shall give reasons for their refusal to the management company concerned within two months of receiving all the information. That refusal or failure to reply shall be subject to the right to apply to the courts in the home Member State.

4.   Before the branch of a management company starts business, the competent authorities of the host Member State shall, within two months of receiving the information referred to in paragraph 2, prepare for the supervision of the management company and, if necessary, indicate the conditions, including the rules mentioned in Articles 44 and 45 in force in the host Member State and the rules of conduct to be respected in the case of provision of the portfolio management service mentioned in Article 5(3) and of investment advisory services and custody, under which, in the interest of the general good, that business must be carried on in the host Member State.

5.   On receipt of a communication from the competent authorities of the host Member State or on the expiry of the period provided for in paragraph 4 without receipt of any communication from those authorities, the branch may be established and start business. From that moment the management company may also begin distributing the units of the unit trusts/common funds and of the investment companies subject to this Directive which it manages, unless the competent authorities of the host Member State establish, in a reasoned decision taken before the expiry of that period of two months—to be communicated to the competent authorities of the home Member State—that the arrangements made for the marketing of the units do not comply with the provisions referred to in Article 44(1) and Article 45.

6.   In the event of change of any particulars communicated in accordance with paragraphs 2(b), (c) or (d), a management company shall give written notice of that change to the competent authorities of the home and host Member States at least one month before implementing the change so that the competent authorities of the home Member State may take a decision on the change under paragraph 3 and the competent authorities of the host Member State may do so under paragraph 4.

7. In the event of a change in the particulars communicated in accordance with the first subparagraph of paragraph 3, the authorities of the home Member State shall inform the authorities of the host Member State accordingly.]

[5016]

NOTES
Substituted as noted to Art 5 at [5006].

[Article 6b

1. Any management company wishing to carry on business within the territory of another Member State for the first time under the freedom to provide services shall communicate the following information to the competent authorities of its home Member State—
    (a) the Member State within the territory of which the management company intends to operate;
    (b) a programme of operations stating the activities and services referred to in Article 5(2) and (3) envisaged.

2. The competent authorities of the home Member State shall, within one month of receiving the information referred to in paragraph 1, forward it to the competent authorities of the host Member State.

They shall also communicate details of any applicable compensation scheme intended to protect investors.

3. The management company may then start business in the host Member State notwithstanding the provisions of Article 46.

When appropriate, the competent authorities of the host Member State shall, on receipt of the information referred to in paragraph 1, indicate to the management company the conditions, including the rules of conduct to be respected in the case of provision of the portfolio management service mentioned in Article 5(3) and of investment advisory services and custody, with which, in the interest of the general good, the management company must comply in the host Member State.

4. Should the content of the information communicated in accordance with paragraph 1(b) be amended, the management company shall give notice of the amendment in writing to the competent authorities of the home Member State and of the host Member State before implementing the change, so that the competent authorities of the host Member State may, if necessary, inform the company of any change or addition to be made to the information communicated under paragraph 3.

5. A management company shall also be subject to the notification procedure laid down in this Article in cases where it entrusts a third party with the marketing of the units in a host Member State.]

[5017]

NOTES
Substituted as noted to Art 5 at [5006].

[Article 6c

1. Host Member States may, for statistical purposes, require all management companies with branches within their territories to report periodically on their activities in those host Member States to the competent authorities of those host Member States.

2. In discharging their responsibilities under this Directive, host Member States may require branches of management companies to provide the same particulars as national management companies for that purpose.

Host Member States may require management companies, carrying on business within their territories under the freedom to provide services, to provide the information necessary for the monitoring of their compliance with the standards set by the host Member State that apply to them, although those requirements may not be more stringent than those which the same Member State imposes on established management companies for the monitoring of their compliance with the same standards.

3. Where the competent authorities of a host Member State ascertain that a management company that has a branch or provides services within its territory is in breach of the legal or regulatory provisions adopted in that State pursuant to those provisions of this Directive which confer powers on the host Member State's competent authorities, those authorities shall require the management company concerned to put an end to its irregular situation.

4. If the management company concerned fails to take the necessary steps, the competent authorities of the host Member State shall inform the competent authorities of the home Member State accordingly. The latter shall, at the earliest opportunity, take all appropriate measures to ensure

that the management company concerned puts an end to its irregular situation. The nature of those measures shall be communicated to the competent authorities of the host Member State.

5.   If, despite the measures taken by the home Member State or because such measures prove inadequate or are not available in the Member State in question, the management company persists in breaching the legal or regulatory provisions referred to in paragraph 2 in force in the host Member State, the latter may, after informing the competent authorities of the home Member State, take appropriate measures to prevent or to penalise further irregularities and, insofar as necessary, to prevent that management company from initiating any further transaction within its territory. The Member States shall ensure that within their territories it is possible to serve the legal documents necessary for those measures on management companies.

6.   The foregoing provisions shall not affect the powers of host Member States to take appropriate measures to prevent or to penalise irregularities committed within their territories which are contrary to legal or regulatory provisions adopted in the interest of the general good. This shall include the possibility of preventing offending management companies from initiating any further transactions within their territories.

7.   Any measure adopted pursuant to paragraphs 4, 5 or 6 involving penalties or restrictions on the activities of a management company must be properly justified and communicated to the management company concerned. Every such measure shall be subject to the right to apply to the courts in the Member State which adopted it.

8.   Before following the procedure laid down in paragraphs 3, 4 or 5 the competent authorities of the host Member State may, in emergencies, take any precautionary measures necessary to protect the interests of investors and others for whom services are provided. The Commission and the competent authorities of the other Member States concerned must be informed of such measures at the earliest opportunity.

After consulting the competent authorities of the Member States concerned, the Commission may decide that the Member State in question must amend or abolish those measures.

9.   In the event of the withdrawal of authorisation, the competent authorities of the host Member State shall be informed and shall take appropriate measures to prevent the management company concerned from initiating any further transactions within its territory and to safeguard investors' interests. [Every two years the Commission shall issue a report on such cases.]

10.   The Member States shall inform the Commission of the number and type of cases in which there have been refusals pursuant to Article 6a or measures have been taken in accordance with paragraph 5. [Every two years the Commission shall issue a report on such cases.]]

[5018]

NOTES

Substituted as noted to Art 5 at **[5006]**.
Paras 9, 10: words in square brackets substituted by European Parliament and Council Directive 2005/1/EC, Art 9(1), as from 13 April 2005.

[SECTION IIIA
OBLIGATIONS REGARDING THE DEPOSITARY]

NOTES

Section heading: inserted by European Parliament and Council Directive 2001/107/EC, Art 1(4), as from 13 February 2002.

Article 7

1.   A unit trust's assets must be entrusted to a depositary for safe-keeping.

2.   A depositary's liability as referred to in Article 9 shall not be affected by the fact that it has entrusted to a third party all or some of the assets in its safe-keeping.

3.   A depositary must, moreover—
(a)   ensure that the sale, issue, re-purchase, redemption and cancellation of units effected on behalf of a unit trust or by a management company are carried out in accordance with the law and the fund rules;
(b)   ensure that the value of units is calculated in accordance with the law and the fund rules;
(c)   carry out the instructions of the management company, unless they conflict with the law or the fund rules;
(d)   ensure that in transactions involving a unit trust's assets any consideration is remitted to it within the usual time limits;
(e)   ensure that a unit trust's income is applied in accordance with the law and the fund rules.

[5019]

Article 8

1. A depositary must either have its registered office in the same Member State as that of the management company or be established in that Member State if its registered office is in another Member State.

2. A depositary must be an institution which is subject to public control. It must also furnish sufficient financial and professional guarantees to be able effectively to pursue its business as depositary and meet the commitments inherent in that function.

3. The Member States shall determine which of the categories of institutions referred to in paragraph 2 shall be eligible to be depositaries.

[5020]

Article 9

A depositary shall, in accordance with the national law of the State in which the management company's registered office is situated, be liable to the management company and the unit-holders for any loss suffered by them as a result of its unjustifiable failure to perform its obligations or its improper performance of them. Liability to unit-holders may be invoked either directly or indirectly through the management company, depending on the legal nature of the relationship between the depositary, the management company and the unit-holders.

[5021]

Article 10

1. No single company shall act as both management company and depositary.

2. In the context of their respective roles the management company and the depositary must act independently and solely in the interest of the unit-holders.

[5022]

Article 11

The law or the fund rules shall lay down the conditions for the replacement of the management company and the depositary and rules to ensure the protection of unit-holders in the event of such replacement.

[5023]

[SECTION IV
OBLIGATIONS REGARDING INVESTMENT COMPANIES

TITLE A

Conditions for taking up business

Article 12

Access to the business of investment companies shall be subject to prior official authorisation to be granted by the home Member States competent authorities.

The Member States shall determine the legal form which an investment company must take.]

[5024]

NOTES

Substituted, together with preceding section heading, by European Parliament and Council Directive 2001/107/EC, Art 1(5), as from 13 February 2002.

Article 13

No investment company may engage in activities other than those referred to in Article 1(2).

[5025]

[Article 13a

1. Without prejudice to other conditions of general application laid down by national law, the competent authorities shall not grant authorisation to an investment company that has not designated a management company unless the investment company has a sufficient initial capital of at least EUR 300,000.

In addition, when an investment company has not designated a management company authorised pursuant to this Directive—

— the authorisation shall not be granted unless the application for authorisation is accompanied by a programme of activity setting out, *inter alia*, the organisational structure of the investment company;

— the directors of the investment company shall be of sufficiently good repute and be sufficiently experienced also in relation to the type of business carried out by the investment company. To that end, the names of the directors and of every person succeeding them in office must be communicated forthwith to the competent authorities. The conduct of an investment company's business must be decided by at least two persons meeting such conditions. Directors shall mean those persons who, under the law or the instruments of incorporation, represent the investment company, or who effectively determine the policy of the company;

— moreover, where close links exist between the investment company and other natural or legal persons, the competent authorities shall grant authorisation only if those do not prevent the effective exercise of their supervisory functions.

The competent authorities shall also refuse authorisation if the laws, regulations or administrative provisions of a non-member country governing one or more natural or legal persons with which the investment company has close links, or difficulties involved in their enforcement, prevent the effective exercise of their supervisory functions.

The competent authorities shall require investment companies to provide them with the information they require.

2. An applicant shall be informed, within six months of the submission of a complete application, whether or not authorisation has been granted. Reasons shall be given whenever an authorisation is refused.

3. An investment company may start business as soon as authorisation has been granted.

4. The competent authorities may withdraw the authorisation issued to an investment company subject to this Directive only where that company—

(a) does not make use of the authorisation within 12 months, expressly renounces the authorisation or has ceased the activity covered by this Directive more than 6 months previously unless the Member State concerned has provided for authorisation to lapse in such cases;

(b) has obtained the authorisation by making false statements or by any other irregular means;

(c) no longer fulfils the conditions under which authorisation was granted;

(d) has seriously and/or systematically infringed the provisions adopted pursuant to this Directive; or

(e) falls within any of the cases where national law provides for withdrawal.]

[5026]

NOTES
Inserted, together with Arts 13b (and preceding heading), and 13c, by European Parliament and Council Directive 2001/107/EC, Art 1(6), as from 13 February 2002.

[TITLE B

Operating conditions

Article 13b

Articles 5g and 5h shall apply to investment companies that have not designated a management company authorised pursuant to this Directive. For the purpose of this Article "management company" shall be construed as "investment company".

Investment companies may only manage assets of their own portfolio and may not, under any circumstances, receive any mandate to manage assets on behalf of a third party.]

[5027]

NOTES
Inserted as noted to Article 13a at **[5026]**.

[**Article 13c**

Each home Member State shall draw up prudential rules which shall be observed at all times by investment companies that have not designated a management company authorised pursuant to this Directive.

In particular, the competent authorities of the home Member State, having regard also to the nature of the investment company, shall require that the company has sound administrative and accounting procedures, control and safeguard arrangements for electronic data processing and adequate internal control mechanisms including, in particular, rules for personal transactions by its employees or for the holding or management of investments in financial instruments in order to invest its initial capital and ensuring, *inter alia*, that each transaction involving the company may be reconstructed according to its origin, the parties to it, its nature, and the time and place at which it was effected and that the assets of the investment company are invested according to the instruments of incorporation and the legal provisions in force.]

[5028]

NOTES
Inserted as noted to Article 13a at **[5026]**.

[SECTION IVA
OBLIGATIONS REGARDING THE DEPOSITARY]

NOTES
Section heading inserted by European Parliament and Council Directive 2001/107/EC, Art 1(7), as from 13 February 2002.

Article 14

1.   An investment company's assets must be entrusted to a depositary for safe-keeping.

2.   A depositary's liability as referred to in Article 16 shall not be affected by the fact that it has entrusted to a third party all or some of the assets in its safe-keeping.

3.   A depositary must, moreover—
    (a)   ensure that the sale, issue, re-purchase, redemption and cancellation of units effected by or on behalf of a company are carried out in accordance with the law and with the company's instruments of incorporation;
    (b)   ensure that in transactions involving a company's assets any consideration is remitted to it within the usual time limits;
    (c)   ensure that a company's income is applied in accordance with the law and its instruments of incorporation.

4.   A Member State may decide that investment companies situated within its territory which market their units exclusively through one or more stock exchanges on which their units are admitted to official listing shall not be required to have depositaries within the meaning of this Directive.

Articles 34, 37 and 38 shall not apply to such companies. However, the rules for the valuation of such companies' assets must be stated in law or in their instruments of incorporation.

5.   A Member State may decide that investment companies situated within its territory which market at least 80% of their units through one or more stock exchanges designated in their instruments of incorporation shall not be required to have depositaries within the meaning of this Directive provided that their units are admitted to official listing on the stock exchanges of those Member States within the territories of which the units are marketed, and that any transactions which such a company may effect outwith stock exchanges are effected at stock exchange prices only. A company's instruments of incorporation must specify the stock exchange in the country of marketing the prices on which shall determine the prices at which that company will effect any transactions outwith stock exchanges in that country.

A Member State shall avail itself of the option provided for in the preceding subparagraph only if it considers that unit-holders have protection equivalent to that of unit-holders in UCITS which have depositaries within the meaning of this Directive.

In particular, such companies and the companies referred to in paragraph 4, must—
    (a)   in the absence of provision in law, state in their instruments of incorporation the methods of calculation of the net asset values of their units;
    (b)   intervene on the market to prevent the stock exchange values of their units from deviating by more than 5% from their net asset values;
    (c)   establish the net asset values of their units, communicate them to the competent authorities at least twice a week and publish them twice a month.

At least twice a month, an independent auditor must ensure that the calculation of the value of units is effected in accordance with the law and the company's instruments of incorporation. On such occasions, the auditor must make sure that the company's assets are invested in accordance with the rules laid down by law and the company's instruments of incorporation.

6.   The Member States shall inform the Commission of the identities of the companies benefiting from the derogations provided for in paragraphs 4 and 5.

...

[5029]

NOTES
Para 6: words omitted repealed by European Parliament and Council Directive 2005/1/EC, Art 9(2), as from 13 April 2005.

Article 15

1.   A depositary must either have its registered office in the same Member State as that of the investment company or be established in that Member State if its registered office is in another Member State.

2.   A depositary must be an institution which is subject to public control. It must also furnish sufficient financial and professional guarantees to be able effectively to pursue its business as depositary and meet the commitments inherent in that function.

3.   The Member States shall determine which of the categories of institutions referred to in paragraph 2 shall be eligible to be depositaries.

[5030]

Article 16

A depositary shall, in accordance with the national law of the State in which the investment company's registered office is situated, be liable to the investment company and the unit-holders for any loss suffered by them as a result of its unjustifiable failure to perform its obligations, or its improper performance of them.

[5031]

Article 17

1.   No single company shall act as both investment company and depositary.

2.   In carrying out its role as depositary, the depositary must act solely in the interests of the unit-holders.

[5032]

Article 18

The law or the investment company's instruments of incorporation shall lay down the conditions for the replacement of the depositary and rules to ensure the protection of unit-holders in the event of such replacement.

[5033]

SECTION V
OBLIGATIONS CONCERNING THE INVESTMENT POLICIES OF UCITS

Article 19

1.   The investments of a unit trust or of an investment company must consist solely of—
   [(a)   transferable securities and money market instruments admitted to or dealt in on a regulated market within the meaning of Article 1(13) of the ISD, and/or;]
   (b)   transferable securities [and money market instruments] dealt in on another regulated market in a Member State which operates regularly and is recognised and open to the public and/or;
   (c)   transferable securities [and money market instruments] admitted to official listing on a stock exchange in a non-member State or dealt in on another regulated market in a non-member State which operates regularly and is recognised and open to the public provided that the choice of stock exchange or market has been approved by the competent authorities or is provided for in law or the fund rules or the investment company's instruments of incorporation and/or;
   (d)   recently issued transferable securities, provided that—
      —   the terms of issue include an undertaking that application will be made for admission to official listing on a stock exchange or to another regulated market which operates regularly and is recognised and open to the public, provided that the choice of stock exchange or market has been approved by the competent authorities or is provided for in law or the fund rules or the investment company's instruments of incorporation;
      —   such admission is secured within a year of issue; [and/or]
   [(e)   units of UCITS authorised according to this Directive and/or other collective investment undertakings within the meaning of the first and second indent of Article 1(2), should they be situated in a Member State or not, provided that—
      —   such other collective investment undertakings are authorised under laws which provide that they are subject to supervision considered by the UCITS' competent authorities to be equivalent to that laid down in Community law, and that cooperation between authorities is sufficiently ensured,
      —   the level of protection for unit-holders in the other collective investment undertakings is equivalent to that provided for unit-holders in a UCITS, and in particular that the rules on assets segregation, borrowing, lending, and uncovered sales of transferable securities and money market instruments are equivalent to the requirements of this Directive,

    — the business of the other collective investment undertakings is reported in half-yearly and annual reports to enable an assessment to be made of the assets and liabilities, income and operations over the reporting period,

    — no more than 10% of the UCITS' or the other collective investment undertakings' assets, whose acquisition is contemplated, can, according to their fund rules or instruments of incorporation, be invested in aggregate in units of other UCITS or other collective investment undertakings, and/or

(f) deposits with credit institutions which are repayable on demand or have the right to be withdrawn, and maturing in no more than 12 months, provided that the credit institution has its registered office in a Member State or, if the registered office of the credit institution is situated in a non-Member State, provided that it is subject to prudential rules considered by the UCITS' competent authorities as equivalent to those laid down in Community law, and/or

(g) financial derivative instruments, including equivalent cash-settled instruments, dealt in on a regulated market referred to in subparagraphs (a), (b) and (c); and/or financial derivative instruments dealt in over-the-counter ("OTC derivatives"), provided that—

    — the underlying consists of instruments covered by this paragraph, financial indices, interest rates, foreign exchange rates or currencies, in which the UCITS may invest according to its investment objectives as stated in the UCITS' fund rules or instruments of incorporation,

    — the counterparties to OTC derivative transactions are institutions subject to prudential supervision, and belonging to the categories approved by the UCITS' competent authorities, and

    — the OTC derivatives are subject to reliable and verifiable valuation on a daily basis and can be sold, liquidated or closed by an offsetting transaction at any time at their fair value at the UCITS' initiative, and/or

(h) money market instruments other than those dealt in on a regulated market, which fall under Article 1(9), if the issue or issuer of such instruments is itself regulated for the purpose of protecting investors and savings, and provided that they are—

    — issued or guaranteed by a central, regional or local authority or central bank of a Member State, the European Central Bank, the European Union or the European Investment Bank, a non-Member State or, in the case of a Federal State, by one of the members making up the federation, or by a public international body to which one or more Member States belong, or

    — issued by an undertaking any securities of which are dealt in on regulated markets referred to in subparagraphs (a), (b) or (c), or

    — issued or guaranteed by an establishment subject to prudential supervision, in accordance with criteria defined by Community law, or by an establishment which is subject to and complies with prudential rules considered by the competent authorities to be at least as stringent as those laid down by Community law; or

    — issued by other bodies belonging to the categories approved by the UCITS' competent authorities provided that investments in such instruments are subject to investor protection equivalent to that laid down in the first, the second or the third indent and provided that the issuer is a company whose capital and reserves amount to at least EUR 10 million and which presents and publishes its annual accounts in accordance with Directive 78/660/EEC,[1] is an entity which, within a group of companies which includes one or several listed companies, is dedicated to the financing of the group or is an entity which is dedicated to the financing of securitisation vehicles which benefit from a banking liquidity line.]

2. However—

    (a) a UCITS may invest no more than 10% of its assets in transferable securities [and money market instruments] other than those referred to in paragraph 1;

    (b) …

    (c) an investment company may acquire movable and immovable property which is essential for the direct pursuit of its business;

    (d) a UCITS may not acquire either precious metals or certificates representing them.

3. …

4. Unit trusts and investment companies may hold ancillary liquid assets.

[5034]

NOTES

Para 1: point (a) substituted, words in square brackets in points (b)–(d) inserted, and points (e)–(h) added, by European Parliament and Council Directive 2001/108/EC, Art 1(3)–(5), as from 13 February 2002.

Para 2: words in square brackets in point (a) inserted, and point (b) repealed, by European Parliament and Council Directive 2001/108/EC, Art 1(6), (7), as from 13 February 2002.

Para 3: repealed by European Parliament and Council Directive 2001/108/EC, Art 1(7), as from 13 February 2002.

¹ Fourth Council Directive 78/660/EEC based on Article 54(3)(g) of the Treaty on the annual accounts of certain types of companies (OJ L222, 14.8.1978, p 11). Directive as last amended by Directive 1999/60/EC (OJ L162, 26.6.1999, p 65).

Article 20

(Repealed by European Parliament and Council Directive 2001/108/EC, Art 1(8), as from 13 February 2002.)

[Article 21

1. The management or investment company must employ a risk-management process which enables it to monitor and measure at any time the risk of the positions and their contribution to the overall risk profile of the portfolio; it must employ a process for accurate and independent assessment of the value of OTC derivative instruments. It must communicate to the competent authorities regularly and in accordance with the detailed rules they shall define, the types of derivative instruments, the underlying risks, the quantitative limits and the methods which are chosen in order to estimate the risks associated with transactions in derivative instruments regarding each managed UCITS.

2. The Member States may authorise UCITS to employ techniques and instruments relating to transferable securities and money market instruments under the conditions and within the limits which they lay down provided that such techniques and instruments are used for the purpose of efficient portfolio management. When these operations concern the use of derivative instruments, these conditions and limits shall conform to the provisions laid down in this Directive.

Under no circumstances shall these operations cause the UCITS to diverge from its investment objectives as laid down in the UCITS' fund rules, instruments of incorporation or prospectus.

3. A UCITS shall ensure that its global exposure relating to derivative instruments does not exceed the total net value of its portfolio.

The exposure is calculated taking into account the current value of the underlying assets, the counterparty risk, future market movements and the time available to liquidate the positions. This shall also apply to the following subparagraphs.

A UCITS may invest, as a part of its investment policy and within the limit laid down in Article 22(5), in financial derivative instruments provided that the exposure to the underlying assets does not exceed in aggregate the investment limits laid down in Article 22. The Member States may allow that, when a UCITS invests in index-based financial derivative instruments, these investments do not have to be combined to the limits laid down in Article 22.

When a transferable security or money market instrument embeds a derivative, the latter must be taken into account when complying with the requirements of this Article.

4. The Member States shall send the Commission full information and any subsequent changes in their regulation concerning the methods used to calculate the risk exposures mentioned in paragraph 3, including the risk exposure to a counterpart in OTC derivative transactions, no later than 13 February 2004. The Commission shall forward that information to the other Member States. [Such information shall be the subject of exchanges of views within the European Securities Committee.]]

[5035]

NOTES

Substituted by European Parliament and Council Directive 2001/108/EC, Art 1(9), as from 13 February 2002.
Para 4: words in square brackets substituted by European Parliament and Council Directive 2005/1/EC, Art 9(3), as from 13 April 2005.

[Article 22

1. A UCITS may invest no more than 5% of its assets in transferable securities or money market instruments issued by the same body. A UCITS may not invest more than 20% of its assets in deposits made with the same body.

The risk exposure to a counterparty of the UCITS in an OTC derivative transaction may not exceed—

— 10% of its assets when the counterpart is a credit institution referred to in Article 19(1)(f), or

— 5% of its assets, in other cases.

2. Member States may raise the 5% limit laid down in the first sentence of paragraph 1 to a maximum of 10%. However, the total value of the transferable securities and the money market instruments held by the UCITS in the issuing bodies in each of which it invests more than 5% of its

assets must not then exceed 40% of the value of its assets. This limitation does not apply to deposits and OTC derivative transactions made with financial institutions subject to prudential supervision.

Notwithstanding the individual limits laid down in paragraph 1, a UCITS may not combine—
— investments in transferable securities or money market instruments issued by,
— deposits made with, and/or
— exposures arising from OTC derivative transactions undertaken with a single body in excess of 20% of its assets.

3. The Member States may raise the 5% limit laid down in the first sentence of paragraph 1 to a maximum of 35% if the transferable securities or money market instruments are issued or guaranteed by a Member State, by its local authorities, by a non-member State or by public international bodies to which one or more Member States belong.

4. Member States may raise the 5% limit laid down in the first sentence of paragraph 1 to a maximum of 25% in the case of certain bonds when these are issued by a credit institution which has its registered office in a Member State and is subject by law to special public supervision designed to protect bond-holders. In particular, sums deriving from the issue of these bonds must be invested in conformity with the law in assets which, during the whole period of validity of the bonds, are capable of covering claims attaching to the bonds and which, in the event of failure of the issuer, would be used on a priority basis for the reimbursement of the principal and payment of the accrued interest.

When a UCITS invests more than 5% of its assets in the bonds referred to in the first subparagraph and issued by one issuer, the total value of these investments may not exceed 80% of the value of the assets of the UCITS.

The Member States shall send the Commission a list of the aforementioned categories of bonds together with the categories of issuers authorised, in accordance with the laws and supervisory arrangements mentioned in the first subparagraph, to issue bonds complying with the criteria set out above. A notice specifying the status of the guarantees offered shall be attached to these lists. The Commission shall immediately forward that information to the other Member States together with any comments which it considers appropriate, and shall make the information available to the public. [Such communications may be the subject of exchanges of views within the European Securities Committee.]

5. The transferable securities and money market instruments referred to in paragraphs 3 and 4 shall not be taken into account for the purpose of applying the limit of 40% referred to in paragraph 2.

The limits provided for in paragraphs 1, 2, 3 and 4 may not be combined, and thus investments in transferable securities or money market instruments issued by the same body or in deposits or derivative instruments made with this body carried out in accordance with paragraphs 1, 2, 3 and 4 shall under no circumstances exceed in total 35% of the assets of the UCITS.

Companies which are included in the same group for the purposes of consolidated accounts, as defined in accordance with Directive 83/349/EEC[1] or in accordance with recognised international accounting rules, are regarded as a single body for the purpose of calculating the limits contained in this Article.

Member States may allow cumulative investment in transferable securities and money market instruments within the same group up to a limit of 20%.

[5036]

NOTES
Substituted by European Parliament and Council Directive 2001/108/EC, Art 1(10), as from 13 February 2002.
Para 4: words in square brackets substituted by European Parliament and Council Directive 2005/1/EC, Art 9(4), as from 13 April 2005.
[1] Seventh Council Directive 83/349/EEC based on the Article 54(3)(g) of the Treaty on consolidated accounts (OJ L193, 18.7.1983, p 1). Directive as last amended by the 1994 Act of Accession.

[**Article 22a**

1. Without prejudice to the limits laid down in Article 25, the Member States may raise the limits laid down in Article 22 to a maximum of 20% for investment in shares and/or debt securities issued by the same body when, according to the fund rules or instruments of incorporation, the aim of the UCITS' investment policy is to replicate the composition of a certain stock or debt securities index which is recognised by the competent authorities, on the following basis—
— its composition is sufficiently diversified,
— the index represents an adequate benchmark for the market to which it refers,
— it is published in an appropriate manner.

2. Member States may raise the limit laid down in paragraph 1 to a maximum of 35% where that proves to be justified by exceptional market conditions in particular in regulated markets where certain transferable securities or money market instruments are highly dominant. The investment up to this limit is only permitted for a single issuer.]

[5037]

NOTES
Inserted by European Parliament and Council Directive 2001/108/EC, Art 1(11), as from 13 February 2002.

Article 23

1. By way of derogation from Article 22 and without prejudice to Article 68(3) of the Treaty, the Member States may authorise UCITS to invest in accordance with the principle of risk-spreading up to 100% of their assets in different transferable securities [and money market instruments] issued or guaranteed by any Member State, its local authorities, a non-member State or public international bodies of which one or more Member States are members.

The competent authorities shall grant such a derogation only if they consider that unit-holders in the UCITS have protection equivalent to that of unit-holders in UCITS complying with the limits laid down in Article 22.

Such a UCITS must hold securities from at least six different issues, but securities from any one issue may not account for more than 30% of its total assets.

2. The UCITS referred to in paragraph 1 must make express mention in the fund rules or in the investment company's instruments of incorporation of the States, local authorities or public international bodies issuing or guaranteeing securities in which they intend to invest more than 35% of their assets; such fund rules or instruments of incorporation must be approved by the competent authorities.

3. In addition each such UCITS referred to in paragraph 1 must include a prominent statement in its prospectus and any promotional literature drawing attention to such authorisation and indicating the States, local authorities and/or public international bodies in the securities of which it intends to invest or has invested more than 35% of its assets.

[5038]

NOTES
Para 1: words in square brackets inserted by European Parliament and Council Directive 2001/108/EC, Art 1(12), as from 13 February 2002.

[Article 24

1. A UCITS may acquire the units of UCITS and/or other collective investment undertakings referred to in Article 19(1)(e), provided that no more than 10% of its assets are invested in units of a single UCITS or other collective investment undertaking. The Member States may raise the limit to a maximum of 20%.

2. Investments made in units of collective investment undertakings other than UCITS may not exceed, in aggregate, 30% of the assets of the UCITS.

The Member States may allow that, when a UCITS has acquired units of UCITS and/or other collective investment undertakings, the assets of the respective UCITS or other collective investment undertakings do not have to be combined for the purposes of the limits laid down in Article 22.

3. When a UCITS invests in the units of other UCITS and/or other collective investment undertakings that are managed, directly or by delegation, by the same management company or by any other company with which the management company is linked by common management or control, or by a substantial direct or indirect holding, that management company or other company may not charge subscription or redemption fees on account of the UCITS's investment in the units of such other UCITS and/or collective investment undertakings.

A UCITS that invests a substantial proportion of its assets in other UCITS and/or collective investment undertakings shall disclose in its prospectus the maximum level of the management fees that may be charged both to the UCITS itself and to the other UCITS and/or collective investment undertakings in which it intends to invest. In its annual report it shall indicate the maximum proportion of management fees charged both to the UCITS itself and to the UCITS and/or other collective investment undertaking in which it invests.]

[5039]

NOTES
Substituted by European Parliament and Council Directive 2001/108/EC, Art 1(13), as from 13 February 2002.

[Article 24a

1.   The prospectus shall indicate in which categories of assets a UCITS is authorised to invest. It shall mention if transactions in financial derivative instruments are authorised; in this event, it must include a prominent statement indicating if these operations may be carried out for the purpose of hedging or with the aim of meeting investment goals, and the possible outcome of the use of financial derivative instruments on the risk profile.

2.   When a UCITS invests principally in any category of assets defined in Article 19 other than transferable securities and money market instruments or replicates a stock or debt securities index in accordance with Article 22a, its prospectus and, where necessary, any other promotional literature must include a prominent statement drawing attention to the investment policy.

3.   When the net asset value of a UCITS is likely to have a high volatility due to its portfolio composition or the portfolio management techniques that may be used, its prospectus and, where necessary, any other promotional literature must include a prominent statement drawing attention to this characteristic.

4.   Upon request of an investor, the management company must also provide supplementary information relating to the quantitative limits that apply in the risk management of the UCITS, to the methods chosen to this end and to the recent evolution of the main instrument categories' risks and yields.]

[5040]

NOTES

Inserted by European Parliament and Council Directive 2001/108/EC, Art 1(14), as from 13 February 2002.

Article 25

1.   An investment company or a management company acting in connection with all of the unit trusts which it manages and which fall within the scope of this Directive may not acquire any shares carrying voting rights which would enable it to exercise significant influence over the management of an issuing body.

Pending further co-ordination, the Member States shall take account of existing rules defining the principle stated in the first subparagraph under other Member States' legislation.

2.   Moreover, an investment company or unit trust may acquire no more than—
—   10% of the non-voting shares of any single issuing body;
—   10% of the debt securities of any single issuing body;
[—   25% of the units of any single UCITS and/or other collective investment undertaking within the meaning of the first and second indent of Article 1(2),]
[—   10% of the money market instruments of any single issuing body,]

[The limits laid down in the second, third and fourth indents may be disregarded at the time of acquisition if at that time the gross amount of the debt securities or of the money market instruments, or the net amount of the securities in issue, cannot be calculated.]

3.   A Member State may waive application of paragraphs 1 and 2 as regards—
(a)   transferable securities [and money market instruments] issued or guaranteed by a Member State or its local authorities;
(b)   transferable securities [and money market instruments] issued or guaranteed by a non-member State;
(c)   transferable securities [and money market instruments] issued by public international bodies of which one or more Member States are members;
(d)   shares held by a UCITS in the capital of a company incorporated in a non-member State investing its assets mainly in the securities of issuing bodies having their registered offices in that State, where under the legislation of that State such a holding represents the only way in which the UCITS can invest in the securities of issuing bodies of that State. This derogation, however, shall apply only if in its investment policy the company from the non-member State complies with the limits laid down in Articles 22, 24 and 25(1) and (2). Where the limits set in Articles 22 and 24 are exceeded, Article 26 shall apply *mutatis mutandis*;
[(e)   shares held by an investment company or investment companies in the capital of subsidiary companies carrying on only the business of management, advice or marketing in the country where the subsidiary is located, in regard to the repurchase of units at unit-holders' request exclusively on its or their behalf.]

[5041]

NOTES

Para 2: words in first and third pairs of square brackets substituted, and words in second pair of square brackets inserted, by European Parliament and Council Directive 2001/108/EC, Art 1(15), (16), as from 13 February 2002.

Para 3: words in square brackets in points (a)–(c) inserted, and point (e) substituted, by European Parliament and Council Directive 2001/108/EC, Art 1(17), (18), as from 13 February 2002.

Article 26

[1. UCITS need not comply with the limits laid down in this section when exercising subscription rights attaching to transferable securities or money market instruments which form part of their assets.

While ensuring observance of the principle of risk spreading, the Member States may allow recently authorised UCITS to derogate from Articles 22, 22a, 23 and 24 for six months following the date of their authorisation.]

2. If the limits referred to in paragraph 1 are exceeded for reasons beyond the control of a UCITS or as a result of the exercise of subscription rights, that UCITS must adopt as a priority objective for its sales transactions the remedying of that situation, taking due account of the interests of its unit-holders.

[5042]

NOTES

Para 1: substituted by European Parliament and Council Directive 2001/108/EC, Art 1(19), as from 13 February 2002.

SECTION VI
OBLIGATIONS CONCERNING INFORMATION TO BE
SUPPLIED TO UNIT-HOLDERS

A. PUBLICATION OF A PROSPECTUS AND PERIODICAL REPORTS

Article 27

[1. An investment company and, for each of the unit trusts and common funds it manages, a management company, must publish—
— a simplified prospectus,
— a full prospectus,
— a annual report for each financial year, and
— a half-yearly report covering the first six months of the financial year.]

2. The annual and half-yearly reports must be published within the following time limits, with effect from the ends of the periods to which they relate—
— four months in the case of the annual report,
— two months in the case of the half-yearly report.

[5043]

NOTES

Para 1: substituted by European Parliament and Council Directive 2001/107/EC, Art 1(8), as from 13 February 2002.

[Article 28

1. Both the simplified and the full prospectuses must include the information necessary for investors to be able to make an informed judgement of the investment proposed to them, and, in particular, of the risks attached thereto. The latter shall include, independent of the instruments invested in, a clear and easily understandable explanation of the fund's risk profile.

2. The full prospectus shall contain at least the information provided for in Schedule A, Annex I to this Directive, in so far as that information does not already appear in the fund rules or instruments of incorporation annexed to the full prospectus in accordance with Article 29(1).

3. The simplified prospectus shall contain in summary form the key information provided for in Schedule C, Annex I to this Directive. It shall be structured and written in such a way that it can be easily understood by the average investor. Member States may permit that the simplified prospectus be attached to the full prospectus as a removable part of it. The simplified prospectus can be used as a marketing tool designed to be used in all Member States without alterations except translation. Member States may therefore not require any further documents or additional information to be added.

4. Both the full and the simplified prospectus may be incorporated in a written document or in any durable medium having an equivalent legal status approved by the competent authorities.

5. The annual report must include a balance-sheet or a statement of assets and liabilities, a detailed income and expenditure account for the financial year, a report on the activities of the financial year and the other information provided for in Schedule B, Annex I to this Directive, as

well as any significant information which will enable investors to make an informed judgment on the development of the activities of the UCITS and its results.

6.   The half-yearly report must include at least the information provided for in Chapters I to IV of Schedule B, Annex I to this Directive; where a UCITS has paid or proposes to pay an interim dividend, the figures must indicate the results after tax for the half-year concerned and the interim dividend paid or proposed.]

[5044]

NOTES

Substituted by European Parliament and Council Directive 2001/107/EC, Art 1(9), as from 13 February 2002.

[Article 29

1.   The fund rules or an investment company's instruments of incorporation shall form an integral part of the full prospectus and must be annexed thereto.

2.   The documents referred to in paragraph 1 need not, however, be annexed to the full prospectus provided that the unit-holder is informed that on request he or she will be sent those documents or be apprised of the place where, in each Member State in which the units are placed on the market, he or she may consult them.]

[5045]

NOTES

Substituted by European Parliament and Council Directive 2001/107/EC, Art 1(10), as from 13 February 2002.

[Article 30

The essential elements of the simplified and the full prospectuses must be kept up to date.]

[5046]

NOTES

Substituted by European Parliament and Council Directive 2001/107/EC, Art 1(11), as from 13 February 2002.

Article 31

The accounting information given in the annual report must be audited by one or more persons empowered by law to audit accounts in accordance with Council Directive 84/253 EEC of 10 April 1984 based on Article 54(3)(g) of the EEC Treaty on the approval of persons responsible for carrying out the statutory audits of accounting documents.[1] The auditor's report, including any qualifications, shall be reproduced in full in the annual report.

[5047]

NOTES

[1]   OJ L126, 12.5.84, p 20.

[Article 32

UCITS must send their simplified and full prospectuses and any amendments thereto, as well as their annual and half-yearly reports, to the competent authorities.]

[5048]

NOTES

Substituted by European Parliament and Council Directive 2001/107/EC, Art 1(12), as from 13 February 2002.

[Article 33

1.   The simplified prospectus must be offered to subscribers free of charge before the conclusion of the contract.

In addition, the full prospectus and the latest published annual and half-yearly reports shall be supplied to subscribers free of charge on request.

2.   The annual and half-yearly reports shall be supplied to unit-holders free of charge on request.

3.   The annual and half-yearly reports must be available to the public at the places, or through other means approved by the competent authorities, specified in the full and simplified prospectus.]

[5049]

NOTES

Substituted by European Parliament and Council Directive 2001/107/EC, Art 1(13), as from 13 February 2002.

B. PUBLICATION OF OTHER INFORMATION

Article 34

A UCITS must make public in an appropriate manner the issue, sale, re-purchase or redemption price of its units each time it issues, sells, re-purchases or redeems them, and at least twice a month. The competent authorities may, however, permit a UCITS to reduce the frequency to once a month on condition that such a derogation does not prejudice the interests of the unit-holders.

[5050]

[Article 35

All publicity comprising an invitation to purchase the units of UCITS must indicate that prospectuses exist and the places where they may be obtained by the public or how the public may have access to them.]

[5051]

NOTES

Substituted by European Parliament and Council Directive 2001/107/EC, Art 1(14), as from 13 February 2002.

SECTION VII
THE GENERAL OBLIGATIONS OF UCITS

Article 36

1. Neither—
   — an investment company, nor
   — a management company or depositary acting on behalf of a unit trust,

may borrow.

However, a UCITS may acquire foreign currency by means of a "back-to-back" loan.

2. By way of derogation from paragraph 1, a Member State may authorise a UCITS to borrow—
   (a) up to 10%
      — of its assets, in the case of an investment company, or
      — of the value of the fund, in the case of a unit trust,
   provided that the borrowing is on a temporary basis;
   (b) up to 10% of its assets, in the case of an investment company, provided that the borrowing is to make possible the acquisition of immovable property essential for the direct pursuit of its business; in this case the borrowing and that referred to in subparagraph (a) may not in any case in total exceed 15% of the borrower's assets.

[5052]

Article 37

1. A UCITS must re-purchase or redeem its units at the request of any unit-holder.

2. By way of derogation from paragraph 1—
   (a) a UCITS may, in the cases and according to the procedures provided for by law, the fund rules or the investment company's instruments of incorporation, temporarily suspend the re-purchase or redemption of its units. Suspension may be provided for only in exceptional cases where circumstances so require, and suspension is justified having regard to the interests of the unit-holders;
   (b) the Member States may allow the competent authorities to require the suspension of the re-purchase or redemption of units in the interest of the unit-holders or of the public.

3. In the cases mentioned in paragraph 2(a), a UCITS must without delay communicate its decision to the competent authorities and to the authorities of all Member States in which it markets its units.

[5053]

Article 38

The rules for the valuation of assets and the rules for calculating the sale or issue price and the re-purchase or redemption price of the units of a UCITS must be laid down in the law, in the fund rules or in the investment company's instruments of incorporation.

[5054]

Article 39

The distribution or reinvestment of the income of a unit trust or of an investment company shall be effected in accordance with the law and with the fund rules or the investment company's instruments of incorporation.

[5055]

Article 40

A UCITS unit may not be issued unless the equivalent of the net issue price is paid into the assets of the UCITS within the usual time limits. This provision shall not preclude the distribution of bonus units.

[5056]

Article 41

1.   Without prejudice to the application of Articles 19 and 21, neither—
     —   an investment company, nor
     —   a management company or depositary acting on behalf of a unit trust

may grant loans or act as a guarantor on behalf of third parties.

[2.   Paragraph 1 shall not prevent such undertakings from acquiring transferable securities, money market instruments or other financial instruments referred to in Article 19(1)(e), (g) and (h) which are not fully paid.]

[5057]

NOTES

Para 2: substituted by European Parliament and Council Directive 2001/108/EC, Art 1(20), as from 13 February 2002.

[Article 42

Neither—
     —   an investment company, nor
     —   a management company or depositary acting on behalf of a unit trust

may carry out uncovered sales of transferable securities, money market instruments or other financial instruments referred to in Article 19(1)(e), (g) and (h).]

[5058]

NOTES

Substituted by European Parliament and Council Directive 2001/108/EC, Art 1(21), as from 13 February 2002.

Article 43

The law or the fund rules must prescribe the remuneration and the expenditure which a management company is empowered to charge to a unit trust and the method of calculation of such remuneration.

The law or an investment company's instruments of incorporation must prescribe the nature of the cost to be borne by the company.

[5059]

SECTION VIII
SPECIAL PROVISIONS APPLICABLE TO UCITS WHICH MARKET THEIR UNITS IN MEMBER STATES OTHER THAN THOSE IN WHICH THEY ARE SITUATED

Article 44

1.   A UCITS which markets its units in another Member State must comply with the laws, regulations and administrative provisions in force in that State which do not fall within the field governed by this Directive.

2.   Any UCITS may advertise its units in the Member State in which they are marketed. It must comply with the provisions governing advertising in that State.

3.   The provisions referred to in paragraphs 1 and 2 must be applied without discrimination.

[5060]

Article 45

In the case referred to in Article 44, the UCITS must, *inter alia*, in accordance with the laws, regulations and administrative provisions in force in the Member State of marketing, take the measures necessary to ensure that facilities are available in that State for making payments to unit-holders, re-purchasing or redeeming units and making available the information which UCITS are obliged to provide.

[5061]

[Article 46

If a UCITS proposes to market its units in a Member State other than that in which it is situated, it must first inform the competent authorities of that other Member State accordingly. It must simultaneously send the latter authorities—

— an attestation by the competent authorities to the effect that it fulfils the conditions imposed by this Directive,
— its fund rules or its instruments of incorporation,
— its full and simplified prospectuses,
— where appropriate, its latest annual report and any subsequent half-yearly report, and
— details of the arrangements made of the marketing of its units in that other Member State.

An investment company or a management company may begin to market its units in that other Member State two months after such communication, unless the authorities of the Member States concerned establish, in a reasoned decision taken before the expiry of that period of two months, that the arrangements made for the marketing of units do not comply with the provisions referred to in Article 44(1) and Article 45.]

[5062]

NOTES
Substituted by the European Parliament and Council Directive 2001/107/EC, Art 1(15), as from 13 February 2002.

[Article 47

If a UCITS markets its units in a Member State other than that in which it is situated, it must distribute in that other Member State, in accordance with the same procedures as those provided for in the home Member State, the full and simplified prospectuses, the annual and half-yearly reports and the other information provided for in Articles 29 and 30.

These documents shall be provided in the or one of the official languages of the host Member State or in a language approved by the competent authorities of the host Member State.]

[5063]

NOTES
Substituted by European Parliament and Council Directive 2001/107/EC, Art 1(16), as from 13 February 2002.

Article 48

For the purpose of carrying on its activities, a UCITS may use the same generic name (such as investment company or unit trust) in the Community as it uses in the Member State in which it is situated. In the event of any danger of confusion, the host Member State may, for the purpose of clarification, require that the name be accompanied by certain explanatory particulars.

[5064]

SECTION IX
PROVISIONS CONCERNING THE AUTHORITIES RESPONSIBLE FOR AUTHORISATION AND SUPERVISION

Article 49

1. The Member States shall designate the authorities which are to carry out the duties provided for in this Directive. They shall inform the Commission thereof, indicating any division of duties.

2. The authorities referred to in paragraph 1 must be public authorities or bodies appointed by public authorities.

3. The authorities of the State in which a UCITS is situated shall be competent to supervise that UCITS. However, the authorities of the State in which a UCITS markets its units in accordance with Article 44 shall be competent to supervise compliance with Section VIII.

4. The authorities concerned must be granted all the powers necessary to carry out their task.

[5065]

Article 50

1. The authorities of the Member States referred to in Article 49 shall collaborate closely in order to carry out their task and must for that purpose alone communicate to each other all information required.

[2. Member States shall provide that all persons who work or who have worked for the competent authorities, as well as auditors and experts instructed by the competent authorities, shall be bound by the obligation of professional secrecy. Such secrecy implies that no confidential information which they may receive in the course of their duties may be divulged to any person or authority whatsoever, save in summary or aggregate form such that UCITS and management companies and depositaries (hereinafter referred to as undertakings contributing towards their business activity) cannot be individually identified, without prejudice to cases covered by criminal law.

Nevertheless, when an UCITS or an undertaking contributing towards its business activity has been declared bankrupt or is being compulsorily wound up, confidential information which does not concern third parties involved in rescue attempts may be divulged in civil or commercial proceedings.

3.   Paragraph 2 shall not prevent the competent authorities of the various Member States from exchanging information in accordance with this Directive or other Directives applicable to UCITS or to undertakings contributing towards their business activity. That information shall be subject to the conditions of professional secrecy imposed in paragraph 2.

[4.   Member States may conclude cooperation agreements providing for exchange of information with the competent authorities of third countries or with authorities or bodies of third countries as defined in paragraphs 6 and 7 only if the information disclosed is subject to guarantees of professional secrecy at least equivalent to those referred to in this Article. Such exchange of information must be intended for the performance of the supervisory task of the authorities or bodies mentioned. Where the information originates in another Member State, it may not be disclosed without the express agreement of the competent authorities which have disclosed it and, where appropriate, solely for the purposes for which those authorities gave their agreement.]

5.   Competent authorities receiving confidential information under paragraphs 2 or 3 may use it only in the course of their duties—
—   to check that the conditions governing the taking-up of the business of UCITS or of undertakings contributing towards their business activity are met and to facilitate the monitoring of the conduct of that business, administrative and accounting procedures and internal-control mechanisms,
—   to impose sanctions,
—   in administrative appeals against decisions by the competent authorities, or
—   in court proceedings initiated under Article 51(2).

6.   Paragraphs 2 and 5 shall not preclude the exchange of information—
(a)   within a Member State, where there are two or more competent authorities; or
(b)   within a Member State or between Member States, between competent authorities; and
—   authorities with public responsibility for the supervision of credit institutions, investment undertakings, insurance undertakings and other undertaking for collective investment in transferable securities (UCITS) or an undertaking contributing towards its business activity and the authorities responsible for the supervision of financial markets,
—   bodies involved in the liquidation or bankruptcy of UCITS and other similar procedures and of undertakings contributing towards their business activity,
—   persons responsible for carrying out statutory audits of the accounts of insurance undertakings, credit institutions, investment undertakings and other financial institutions, in the performance of their supervisory functions, or the disclosure to bodies which administer compensation schemes of information necessary for the performance of their functions. Such information shall be subject to the conditions of professional secrecy imposed in paragraph 2.

7.   Notwithstanding paragraphs 2 to 5, Member States may authorise exchanges of information between the competent authorities and—
—   the authorities responsible for overseeing the bodies involved in the liquidation and bankruptcy of undertakings for collective investment in transferable securities (UCITS) or undertakings contributing towards their business activities and other similar procedures, or
—   the authorities responsible for overseeing persons charged with carrying out statutory audits of the accounts of insurance undertakings, credit institutions, investment firms and other financial institutions.

Member States which have recourse to the option provided for in the first subparagraph shall require at least that the following conditions are met—
—   the information shall be for the purpose of performing the task of overseeing referred to in the first subparagraph,
—   information received in this context shall be subject to the conditions of professional secrecy imposed in paragraph 2,
—   where the information originates in another Member State, it may not be disclosed without the express agreement of the competent authorities which have disclosed it and, where appropriate, solely for the purposes for which those authorities gave their agreement.

Member States shall communicate to the Commission and to the other Member States the names of the authorities which may receive information pursuant to this paragraph.

8. Notwithstanding paragraphs 2 to 5, Member States may, with the aim of strengthening the stability, including integrity, of the financial system, authorise the exchange of information between the competent authorities and the authorities or bodies responsible under the law for the detection and investigation of breaches of company law.

Member States which have recourse to the option provided for in the first subparagraph shall require at least that the following conditions are met—

— the information shall be for the purpose of performing the task referred to in the first subparagraph,

— information received in this context shall be subject to the conditions of professional secrecy imposed in paragraph 2,

— where the information originates in another Member State, it may not be disclosed without the express agreement of the competent authorities which have disclosed it and, where appropriate, solely for the purposes for which these authorities gave their agreement.

Where, in a Member State, the authorities or bodies referred to in the first subparagraph perform their task of detection or investigation with the aid, in view of their specific competence, of persons appointed for that purpose and not employed in the public sector, the possibility of exchanging information provided for in the first subparagraph may be extended to such persons under the conditions stipulated in the second subparagraph.

In order to implement the final indent of the second subparagraph, the authorities or bodies referred to in the first subparagraph shall communicate to the competent authorities which have disclosed the information the names and precise responsibilities of the persons to whom it is to be sent.

Member States shall communicate to the Commission and to the other Member States the names of the authorities or bodies which may receive information pursuant to this paragraph.

Before 31 December 2000, the Commission shall draw up a report on the application of this paragraph.

9. This Article shall not prevent a competent authority from transmitting to central banks and other bodies with a similar function in their capacity as monetary authorities information intended for the performance of their tasks, nor shall it prevent such authorities or bodies from communicating to the competent authorities such information as they may need for the purposes of paragraph 5. Information received in this context shall be subject to the conditions of professional secrecy imposed in this Article.

10. This Article shall not prevent the competent authorities from communicating the information referred to in paragraphs 2 to 5 to a clearing house or other similar body recognised under national law for the provision of clearing or settlement services for one of their Member State's markets if they consider that it is necessary to communicate the information in order to ensure the proper functioning of those bodies in relation to defaults or potential defaults by market participants. The information received in this context shall be subject to the conditions of professional secrecy imposed in paragraph 2. Member States shall, however, ensure that information received under paragraph 3 may not be disclosed in the circumstances referred to in this paragraph without the express consent of the competent authorities which disclosed it.

11. In addition, notwithstanding the provisions referred to in paragraphs 2 and 5, Member States may, by virtue of provisions laid down by law, authorise the disclosure of certain information to other departments of their central government administrations responsible for legislation on the supervision of UCITS and of undertakings contributing towards their business activity, credit institutions, financial institutions, investment undertakings and insurance undertakings and to inspectors instructed by those departments.

Such disclosures may, however, be made only where necessary for reasons of prudential control.

Member States shall, however, provide that information received under paragraphs 3 and 6 may never be disclosed in the circumstances referred to in this paragraph except with the express agreement of the competent authorities which disclosed the information.]

[5066]

NOTES

Paras 2–11: substituted, for original paras 2–4, by European Parliament and Council Directive 95/26/EC, Arts 1, 4(7), as from 29 June 1995.

Para 4: further substituted by European Parliament and Council Directive 2000/64/EC, Art 1, as from 17 November 2000.

[Article 50a

1. Member States shall provide at least that—

(a)   any person authorised within the meaning of Directive 84/253/EEC,[1] performing in an undertaking for collective investment in transferable securities (UCITS) or an undertaking contributing towards its business activity the task described in Article 51 of Directive 78/660/EEC,[2] Article 37 of Directive 83/349/EEC or Article 31 of Directive 85/611/EEC or any other statutory task, shall have a duty to report promptly to the competent authorities any fact or decision concerning that undertaking of which he has become aware while carrying out that task which is liable to—

—   constitute a material breach of the laws, regulations or administrative provisions which lay down the conditions governing authorisation or which specifically govern pursuit of the activities of undertakings for collective investment in transferable securities (UCITS) or undertakings contributing towards their business activities, or

—   affect the continuous functioning of the undertaking for collective investment in transferable securities (UCITS) or an undertaking contributing towards its business activity, or

—   lead to refusal to certify the accounts or to the expression of reservations;

(b)   that person shall likewise have a duty to report any facts and decisions of which he becomes aware in the course of carrying out a task as described in (a) in an undertaking having close links resulting from a control relationship with the undertaking for collective investment in transferable securities (UCITS) or an undertaking contributing towards its business activity within which he is carrying out the abovementioned task.

2.   The disclosure in good faith to the competent authorities, by persons authorised within the meaning of Directive 84/253/EEC, of any fact or decision referred to in paragraph 1 shall not constitute a breach of any restriction on disclosure of information imposed by contract of by any legislative, regulatory or administrative provision and shall not invoice such persons in liability of any kind.]

[5067]

NOTES

Inserted by European Parliament and Council Directive 95/26/EC, Arts 1, 5, as from 29 June 1995.
[1]   Directive 84/253/EEC: OJ L126, 12.5.84, p 20.
[2]   Directive 78/660/EEC: OJ L222, 14.8.78, p 11, as last amended by Directive 90/605/EEC, OJ L317, 16.11.90, p 60.

Article 51

1.   The authorities referred to in Article 49 must give reasons for any decision to refuse authorisation, and any negative decision taken in implementation of the general measures adopted in application of this Directive, and communicate them to applicants.

2.   The Member States shall provide that decisions taken in respect of a UCITS pursuant to laws, regulations and administrative provisions adopted in accordance with this Directive are subject to the right to apply to the courts; the same shall apply if no decision is taken within six months of its submission on an authorisation application made by a UCITS which includes all the information required under the provisions in force.

[5068]

Article 52

1.   Only the authorities of the Member State in which a UCITS is situated shall have the power to take action against it if it infringes any law, regulation or administrative provision or any regulation laid down in the fund rules or in the investment company's instruments of incorporation.

2.   Nevertheless, the authorities of the Member State in which the units of a UCITS are marketed may take action against it if it infringes the provisions referred to in Section VIII.

3.   Any decision to withdraw authorisation, or any other serious measure taken against a UCITS, or any suspension of re-purchase or redemption imposed upon it, must be communicated without delay by the authorities of the Member State in which the UCITS in question is situated to the authorities of the other Member States in which its units are marketed.

[5069]

[Article 52a

1.   Where, through the provision of services or by the establishment of branches, a management company operates in one or more host Member States, the competent authorities of all the Member States concerned shall collaborate closely.

They shall supply one another on request with all the information concerning the management and ownership of such management companies that is likely to facilitate their supervision and all information likely to facilitate the monitoring of such companies. In particular, the authorities of the home Member State shall cooperate to ensure that the authorities of the host Member State collect the particulars referred to in Article 6c(2).

2. Insofar as it is necessary for the purpose of exercising their powers of supervision, the competent authorities of the home Member State shall be informed by the competent authorities of the host Member State of any measures taken by the host Member State pursuant to Article 6c(6) which involve penalties imposed on a management company or restrictions on a management company's activities.]

[5070]

NOTES
  Inserted, together with Art 52b, by European Parliament and Council Directive 2001/107/EC, Art 1(17), as from 13 February 2002.

[Article 52b

1. Each host Member State shall ensure that, where a management company authorised in another Member State carries on business within its territory through a branch, the competent authorities of the management company's home Member State may, after informing the competent authorities of the host Member State, themselves or through the intermediary of persons they instruct for the purpose, carry out on-the-spot verification of the information referred to in Article 52a.

2. The competent authorities of the management company's home Member State may also ask the competent authorities of the management company's host Member State to have such verification carried out. Authorities which receive such requests must, within the framework of their powers, act upon them by carrying out the verifications themselves, by allowing the authorities who have requested them to carry them out or by allowing auditors or experts to do so.

3. This Article shall not affect the right of the competent authorities of the host Member State, in discharging their responsibilities under this Directive, to carry out on-the-spot verifications of branches established within their territory.]

[5071]

NOTES
  Inserted as noted to Article 52a at **[5070]**.

SECTION X
[EUROPEAN SECURITIES COMMITTEE]

NOTES
  Section heading: words in square brackets substituted by European Parliament and Council Directive 2005/1/EC, Art 9(5), as from 13 April 2005.

Article 53

(*Repealed by European Parliament and Council Directive 2005/1/EC, Art 9(6), as from 13 April 2005.*)

[Article 53a

The Commission shall adopt technical amendments to this Directive in the following areas:
  (a) clarification of the definitions in order to ensure uniform application of this Directive throughout the Community;
  (b) alignment of terminology and the framing of definitions in accordance with subsequent acts on UCITS and related matters.

Those measures, designed to amend non-essential elements of this Directive, shall be adopted in accordance with the regulatory procedure with scrutiny referred to in Article 53b(2).]

[5072]

NOTES
  Inserted by European Parliament and Council Directive 2001/108/EC, Art 1(22), as from 13 February 2002.
  Substituted by European Parliament and Council Directive 2008/18/EC, Art 1, as from 20 March 2008.

[Article 53b

1. The Commission shall be assisted by the European Securities Committee instituted by Commission Decision 2001/528/EC.[1]

2. Where reference is made to this paragraph, Article 5a(1) to (4) and Article 7 of Decision 1999/468/EC shall apply, having regard to the provisions of Article 8 thereof.]

[5073]

NOTES
   Inserted by European Parliament and Council Directive 2005/1/EC, Art 9(8), as from 13 April 2005.
   Substituted by European Parliament and Council Directive 2008/18/EC, Art 1, as from 20 March 2008.
   ¹   OJ L191, 13.7.2001, p 45. Decision as amended by Decision 2004/8/EC (OJ L3, 7.1.2004, p 33).

SECTION XI
TRANSITIONAL PROVISIONS, DEROGATIONS AND FINAL PROVISIONS

Article 54

Solely for the purpose of Danish UCITS, *pantebreve* issued in Denmark shall be treated as equivalent to the transferable securities referred to in Article 19(1)(b).

[5074]

Article 55

By way of derogation from Articles 7(1) and 14(1), the competent authorities may authorise those UCITS which, on the date of adoption of this Directive, had two or more depositaries in accordance with their national law to maintain that number of depositaries if those authorities have guarantees that the functions to be performed under Articles 7(3) and 14(3) will be performed in practice.

[5075]

Article 56

   1.   By way of derogation from Article 6, the Member States may authorise management companies to issue bearer certificates representing the registered securities of other companies.

   2.   The Member States may authorise those management companies which, on the date of adoption of this Directive, also carry on activities other than those provided for in Article 6 to continue those other activities for five years after that date.

[5076]

Article 57

   1.   The Member States shall bring into force no later than 1 October 1989 the measures necessary for them to comply with this Directive. They shall forthwith inform the Commission thereof.

   2.   The Member States may grant UCITS existing on the date of implementation of this Directive a period of not more than 12 months from that date in order to comply with the new national legislation.

   3.   The Hellenic Republic and the Portuguese Republic shall be authorised to postpone the implementation of this Directive until 1 April 1992 at the latest.

One year before that date the Commission shall report to the Council on progress in implementing the Directive and on any difficulties which the Hellenic Republic or the Portuguese Republic may encounter in implementing the Directive by the date referred to in the first subparagraph.

The Commission shall, if necessary, propose that the Council extend the postponement by up to four years.

[5077]

Article 58

The Member States shall ensure that the Commission is informed of the texts of the main laws, regulations and administrative provisions which they adopt in the field covered by this Directive.

[5078]

Article 59

This Directive is addressed to the Member States.

[5079]

[ANNEX I]

NOTES
   Original Annex renumbered as Annex I by the European Parliament and Council Directive 2001/107/EC, Art 1(18), as from 13 February 2002.

SCHEDULE A
MINIMUM INFORMATION TO BE INCLUDED IN PROSPECTUS

1. Information concerning the unit trust	1. Information concerning the management company	1. Information concerning the investment company
1.1. Name	1.1. Name or style, form in law, registered office and head office if different from the registered office.	1.1. Name or style, form in law, registered office and head office if different from the registered office.
1.2. Date of establishment of the unit trust. Indication of duration, if limited.	1.2. Date of the incorporation of the company. Indication of duration if limited.	1.2. Date of the incorporation of the company. Indication of duration, if limited.
	1.3. If the company manages other unit trusts, indication of those other trusts.	[1.3. In the case of investment companies having different investment compartments, the indication of the compartments.]
1.4. Statement of the place where the fund rules, if they are not annexed, and periodic reports may be obtained.		1.4. Statement of the place where the instruments of incorporation, if they are not annexed, and periodical reports may be obtained.
1.5. Brief indications relevant to unit-holders of the tax system applicable to the unit trust. Details of whether deductions are made at source from the income and capital gains paid by the trust to unit-holders.		1.5. Brief indications relevant to unit-holders of the tax system applicable to the company. Details of whether deductions are made at source from the income and capital gains paid by the company to unit-holders.
1.6. Accounting and distribution dates.		1.6. Accounting and distribution dates.
1.7. Names of the persons responsible for auditing the accounting information referred to in Article 31.		1.7. Names of the persons responsible for auditing the accounting information referred to in Article 31.
	1.8. Names and positions in the company of the members of the administrative, management and supervisory bodies. Details of their main activities outside the company where these are of significance with respect to that company.	1.8. Names and positions in the company of the members of the administrative, management and supervisory bodies. Details of their main activities outside the company where these are of significance with respect to that company.
	1.9. Amount of the subscribed capital with an indication of the capital paid-up.	1.9. Capital.
1.10. Details of the types and main characteristics of the units and in particular—		1.10. Details of the types and main characteristics of the units and in particular—
— the nature of the right (real, personal or other) represented by the unit,		— original securities or certificates providing evidence of title; entry in a register or in an account,
— original securities or certificates providing evidence of title; entry in a register or in an account,		— characteristics of the units: registered or bearer. Indication of any denominations which may be provided for,

1. Information concerning the unit trust	1. Information concerning the management company	1. Information concerning the investment company
— characteristics of the units: registered or bearer. Indication of any denominations which may be provided for,		
— indication of unit-holders' voting rights,		— indication of unit-holders' voting rights,
if these exist,		
— circumstances in which winding-up of the unit trust can be decided on and winding-up procedure, in particular as regards the rights of unit-holders.		— circumstances in which winding-up of the investment company can be decided on and winding-up procedure, in particular as regards the rights of unit-holders.
1.11. Where applicable, indication of stock exchanges or markets where the units are listed or dealt in.		1.11. Where applicable, indication of stock exchanges or markets where the units are listed or dealt in.
1.12. Procedures and conditions of issue and sale of units.		1.12. Procedures and conditions of issue and sale of units.
1.13. Procedures and conditions for re-purchase or redemption of units, and circumstances in which repurchase or redemption may be suspended.		1.13. Procedures and conditions for re-purchase or redemption of units, and circumstances in which repurchase or redemption may be suspended. [In the case of investment companies having different investment compartments, information on how a unit-holder may pass from one compartment into another and the charges applicable in such cases.]
1.14. Description of rules for determining and applying income.		1.14. Description of rules for determining and applying income.
1.15. Description of the unit trust's investment objectives, including its financial objectives (e g capital growth or income), investment policy (e g specialisation in geographical or industrial sectors), any limitations on that investment policy and an indication of any techniques and instruments or borrowing powers which may be used in the management of the unit trust.		1.15. Description of the company's investment objectives, including its financial objectives (e g capital growth or income), investment policy (e g specialisation in geographical or industrial sectors), any limitations on that investment policy and an indication of any techniques and instruments or borrowing powers which may be used in the management of the company.
1.16. Rules for the valuation of assets.		1.16. Rules for the valuation of assets.
1.17. Determination of the sale or issue price and the re-purchase or redemption price of units, in particular—		1.17. Determination of the sale or issue price and the repurchase or redemption price of units, in particular—

1. Information concerning the unit trust	1. Information concerning the management company	1. Information concerning the investment company
— the method and frequency of the calculation of those prices,		— the method and frequency of the calculation of those prices,
— information concerning the charges relating to the sale or issue and there-purchase or redemption of units,		— information concerning the charges relating to the sale or issue and there-purchase or redemption of units,
— the means, places and frequency of the publication of those prices.		— the means, places and frequency of the publication of those prices[1]
1.18. Information concerning the manner, amount and calculation of remuneration payable by the unit trust to the management company, the depositary or third parties, and reimbursement of costs by the unit trust to the management company, to the depository or to third parties.		1.18. Information concerning the manner, amount and calculation of remuneration paid by the company to its directors, and members of the administrative, management and supervisory bodies, to the depositary, or to third parties, and reimbursement of costs by the company to its directors, to the depositary or to third parties.

2. Information concerning the depositary—

   2.1   Name or style, form in law, registered office and head office if different from the registered office;

   2.2   Main activity.

3. Information concerning the advisory firms or external investment advisers who give advice under contract which is paid for out of the assets of the UCITS—

   3.1   Name or style of the firm or name of the adviser;

   3.2   Material provisions of the contract with the management company or the investment company which may be relevant to the unit-holders, excluding those relating to remuneration;

   3.3   Other significant activities.

4. Information concerning the arrangements for making payments to unit-holders, re-purchasing or redeeming units and making available information concerning the UCITS. Such information must in any case be given in the Member State in which the UCITS is situated. In addition, where units are marketed in another Member State, such information shall be given in respect of that Member State in the prospectus published there.

   [5.   Other investment information

   5.1.   Historical performance of the unit trust/common fund or of the investment company (where applicable) such information may be either included in or attached to the prospectus;

   5.2.   Profile of the typical investor for whom the unit trust/common fund or the investment company is designed.

6. Economic information

   6.1.   Possible expenses or fees, other than the charges mentioned in paragraph 1.17, distinguishing between those to be paid by the unit-holder and those to be paid out of the unit trust's/common fund's or of the investment company's assets.]

[5080]

NOTES

Para 1: words in square brackets inserted by European Parliament and Council Directive 2001/107/EC, Art 1(19)(1), (2), as from 13 February 2002.

Paras 5, 6: inserted by European Parliament and Council Directive 2001/107/EC, Art 1(19)(3), as from 13 February 2002.

[1]   Investment companies within the meaning of Article 14(5) of the Directive shall also indicate—

   —   the method and frequency of calculation of the net asset value of units,

   —   the means, place and frequency of the publication of that value,

—   the stock exchange in the country of marketing the price on which determines the price of transactions effected outwith stock exchanges in that country.

SCHEDULE B
INFORMATION TO BE INCLUDED IN THE PERIODIC REPORTS

I.   Statement of assets and liabilities
—   transferable securities,
—   debt instruments of the type referred to in Article 19(2)(b),
—   bank balances,
—   other assets,
—   total assets,
—   liabilities,
—   net asset value.

II.   Number of units in circulation

III.   Net asset value per unit

IV.   Portfolio, distinguishing between—
(a)   transferable securities admitted to official stock exchange listing;
(b)   transferable securities dealt in on another regulated market;
(c)   recently issued transferable securities of the type referred to in Article 19(1)(d);
(d)   other transferable securities of the type referred to in Article 19(2)(a);
(e)   debt instruments treated as equivalent in accordance with Article 19(2)(b);

and analysed in accordance with the most appropriate criteria in the light of the investment policy of the UCITS (e g in accordance with economic, geographical or currency criteria) as a percentage of net assets; for each of the above investments the proportion it represents of the total assets of the UCITS should be stated.

V.   Statement of the developments concerning the assets of the UCITS during the reference period including the following—
—   income from investments,
—   other income,
—   management charges,
—   depositary's charges,
—   other charges and taxes,
—   net income,
—   distributions and income reinvested,
—   changes in capital account,
—   appreciation or depreciation of investments,
—   any other changes affecting the assets and liabilities of the UCITS.

VI.   A comparative table covering the last three financial years and including, for each financial year, at the end of the financial year—
—   the total net asset value,
—   the net asset value per unit.

VII.   Details, by category of transaction within the meaning of Article 21 carried out by the UCITS during the reference period, of the resulting amount of commitments.

[5081]

[SCHEDULE C
CONTENTS OF THE SIMPLIFIED PROSPECTUS

Brief presentation of the UCITS
—   when the unit trust/common fund or the investment company was created and indication of the Member State where the unit trust/common fund or the investment company has been registered/incorporated,
—   in the case of UCITS having different investment compartments, the indication of this circumstance, management company (when applicable),
—   expected period of existence (when applicable),
—   depositary,
—   auditors,
—   financial group (e g a bank) promoting the UCITS.

Investment information
—   short definition of the UCITS' objectives,
—   the unit trust's/common fund's or the investment company's investment policy and a brief assessment of the fund's risk profile (including, if applicable, information according to Article 24a and by investment compartment),
—   historical performance of the unit trust/common fund/investment company (where

applicable) and a warning that this is not an indicator of future performance such information may be either included in or attached to the prospectus,

— profile of the typical investor the unit trust/common fund or the investment company is designed for.

Economic information
— tax regime,
— entry and exit commissions,
— other possible expenses or fees, distinguishing between those to be paid by the unit-holder and those to be paid out of the unit trust's/common fund's or the investment company's assets.

Commercial information
— how to buy the units,
— how to sell the units,
— in the case of UCITS having different investment compartments how to pass from one investment compartment into another and the charges applicable in such cases,
— when and how dividends on units or shares of the UCITS (if applicable) are distributed,
— frequency and where/how prices are published or made available.

Additional information
— statement that, on request, the full prospectus, the annual and half-yearly reports may be obtained free of charge before the conclusion of the contract and afterwards,
— competent authority,
— indication of a contact point (person/department, timing, etc) where additional explanations may be obtained if needed,
— publishing date of the prospectus.]

[5082]

NOTES
  Inserted by European Parliament and Council Directive 2001/107/EC, Art 1(20), Annex I, as from 13 February 2002.

[ANNEX II

Functions included in the activity of collective portfolio management—
— Investment management.
— Administration—
    (a)   legal and fund management accounting services;
    (b)   customer inquiries;
    (c)   valuation and pricing (including tax returns);
    (d)   regulatory compliance monitoring;
    (e)   maintenance of unit-holder register;
    (f)   distribution of income;
    (g)   unit issues and redemptions;
    (h)   contract settlements (including certificate dispatch);
    (i)   record keeping.
— Marketing.]

[5083]

NOTES
  Inserted by European Parliament and Council Directive 2001/107/EC, Art 1(21), Annex II, as from 13 February 2002.

COUNCIL DIRECTIVE

of 10 June 1991

on prevention of the use of the financial system for the purpose of money laundering

(91/308/EEC)

NOTES
  Date of publication in OJ: OJ L166, 28.6.91, p 77. Notes are as in the original OJ version.
  Repeal of this Directive: this Directive was repealed and replaced by European Parliament and Council Directive 2005/60/EC at **[5722]** but has been retained here for historical reasons. The 2005 Directive entered into

force on 15 December 2005 (see Art 46 at **[5767]**) and has been transposed as the Money Laundering Regulations 2007, SI 2007/2157 at **[2877AA]** with effect from 15 December 2007.

This Directive is reproduced as amended by: European Parliament and Council Directive 2001/97/EC (OJ L344, 28.12.2001, p 76).

THE COUNCIL OF THE EUROPEAN COMMUNITIES,

Having regard to the Treaty establishing the European Economic Community, and in particular Article 57(2), first and third sentences, and Article 100a thereof,

Having regard to the proposal from the Commission,[1]

In cooperation with the European Parliament,[2]

Having regard to the opinion of the Economic and Social Committee,[3]

Whereas when credit and financial institutions are used to launder proceeds from criminal activities (hereinafter referred to as 'money laundering'), the soundness and stability of the institution concerned and confidence in the financial system as a whole could be seriously jeopardised, thereby losing the trust of the public;

Whereas lack of Community action against money laundering could lead Member States, for the purpose of protecting their financial systems, to adopt measures which could be inconsistent with completion of the single market; whereas, in order to facilitate their criminal activities, launderers could try to take advantage of the freedom of capital movement and freedom to supply financial services which the integrated financial areas involves, if certain coordinating measures are not adopted at Community level;

Whereas money laundering has an evident influence on the rise of organised crime in general and drug trafficking in particular; whereas there is more and more awareness that combating money laundering is one of the most effective means of opposing this form of criminal activity, which constitutes a particular threat to Member States' societies;

Whereas money laundering must be combated mainly by penal means and within the framework of international cooperation among judicial and law enforcement authorities, as has been undertaken, in the field of drugs, by the United Nations Convention Against Illicit Traffic in Narcotic Drugs and Psychotropic Substances, adopted on 19 December 1988 in Vienna (hereinafter referred to as the 'Vienna Convention') and more generally in relation to all criminal activities, by the Council of Europe Convention on laundering, tracing, seizure and confiscation of proceeds of crime, opened for signature on 8 November 1990 in Strasbourg;

Whereas a penal approach should, however, not be the only way to combat money laundering, since the financial system can play a highly effective role; whereas reference must be made in this context to the recommendation of the Council of Europe of 27 June 1980 and to the declaration of principles adopted in December 1988 in Basle by the banking supervisory authorities of the Group of Ten, both of which constitute major steps towards preventing the use of the financial system for money laundering;

Whereas money laundering is usually carried out in an international context so that the criminal origin of the funds can be better disguised; whereas measures exclusively adopted at a national level, without taking account of international coordination and cooperation, would have very limited effects;

Whereas any measures adopted by the Community in this field should be consistent with other action undertaken in other international fora; whereas in this respect any Community action should take particular account of the recommendations adopted by the financial action task force on money laundering, set up in July 1989 by the Paris summit of the seven most developed countries;

Whereas the European Parliament has requested, in several resolutions, the establishment of a global Community programme to combat drug trafficking, including provisions on prevention of money laundering;

Whereas for the purposes of this Directive the definition of money laundering is taken from that adopted in the Vienna Convention; whereas, however, since money laundering occurs not only in relation to the proceeds of drug-related offences but also in relation to the proceeds of other criminal activities (such as organised crime and terrorism), the Member States should, within the meaning of their legislation, extend the effects of the Directive to include the proceeds of such activities, to the extent that they are likely to result in laundering operations justifying sanctions on that basis;

Whereas prohibition of money laundering in Member States' legislation backed by appropriate measures and penalties is a necessary condition for combating this phenomenon;

Whereas ensuring that credit and financial institutions require identification of their customers when entering into business relations or conducting transactions, exceeding certain thresholds, are necessary to avoid launderers' taking advantage of anonymity to carry out their criminal activities; whereas such provisions must also be extended, as far as possible, to any beneficial owners;

Whereas credit and financial institutions must keep for at least five years copies or references of the identification documents required as well as supporting evidence and records consisting of documents relating to transactions or copies thereof similarly admissible in court proceedings under the applicable national legislation for use as evidence in any investigation into money laundering;

Whereas ensuring that credit and financial institutions examine with special attention any transaction which they regard as particularly likely, by its nature, to be related to money laundering is necessary in order to preserve the soundness and integrity of the financial system as well as to contribute to combating this phenomenon; whereas to this end they should pay special attention to transactions with third countries which do not apply comparable standards against money laundering to those established by the Community or to other equivalent standards set out by international fora and endorsed by the Community;

Whereas, for those purposes, Member States may ask credit and financial institutions to record in writing the results of the examination they are required to carry out and to ensure that those results are available to the authorities responsible for efforts to eliminate money laundering;

Whereas preventing the financial system from being used for money laundering is a task which cannot be carried out by the authorities responsible for combating this phenomenon without the cooperation of credit and financial institutions and their supervisory authorities; whereas banking secrecy must be lifted in such cases; whereas a mandatory system of reporting suspicious transactions which ensures that information is transmitted to the above mentioned authorities without alerting the customers concerned, is the most effective way to accomplish such cooperation; whereas a special protection clause is necessary to exempt credit and financial institutions, their employees and their directors from responsibility for breaching restrictions on disclosure of information;

Whereas the information received by the authorities pursuant to this Directive may be used only in connection with combating money laundering; whereas Member States may nevertheless provide that this information may be used for other purposes;

Whereas establishment by credit and financial institutions of procedures of internal control and training programmes in this field are complementary provisions without which the other measures contained in this Directive could become ineffective;

Whereas, since money laundering can be carried out not only through credit and financial institutions but also through other types of professions and categories of undertakings, Member States must extend the provisions of this Directive in whole or in part, to include those professions and undertakings whose activities are particularly likely to be used for money laundering purposes;

Whereas it is important that the Member States should take particular care to ensure that coordinated action is taken in the Community where there are strong grounds for believing that professions or activities the conditions governing the pursuit of which have been harmonised at Community level are being used for laundering money;

Whereas the effectiveness of efforts to eliminate money laundering is particularly dependent on the close coordination and harmonisation of national implementing measures; whereas such coordination and harmonisation which is being carried out in various international bodies requires, in the Community context, cooperation between Member States and the Commission in the framework of a contact committee;

Whereas it is for each Member State to adopt appropriate measures and to penalise infringement of such measures in an appropriate manner to ensure full application of this Directive,

[5084]

NOTES

1   OJ C106, 24.4.90, p 6; and OJ C319, 19.12.90, p 9.
2   OJ C324, 24.12.90, p 264; and OJ C129, 20.5.91.
3   OJ C332, 31.12.90, p 86.

HAS ADOPTED THIS DIRECTIVE—

[Article 1

For the purpose of this Directive—

(A) "Credit institution" means a "credit institution", as defined in Article 1(1) first subparagraph of Directive 2000/12/EC[1] and includes branches within the meaning of Article 1(3) of that Directive and located in the Community, of credit institutions having their head-offices inside or outside the Community;

(B) "Financial institution" means—

    1.   an undertaking other than a credit institution whose principal activity is to carry out one or more of the operations included in numbers 2 to 12 and number 14 of the list set out in Annex I to Directive 2000/12/EC; these include the activities of currency exchange offices (bureaux de change) and of money transmission/remittance offices;

    2.   an insurance company duly authorised in accordance with Directive 79/267/EEC,[2] insofar as it carries out activities covered by that Directive;

    3.   an investment firm as defined in Article 1(2) of Directive 93/22/EEC;[3]

    4.   a collective investment undertaking marketing its units or shares.

This definition of financial institution includes branches located in the Community of financial institutions, whose head offices are inside or outside the Community,

(C) *"Money laundering" means the following conduct when committed intentionally—*

— *the conversion or transfer of property, knowing that such property is derived from criminal activity or from an act of participation in such activity, for the purpose of concealing or disguising the illicit origin of the property or of assisting any person who is involved in the commission of such activity to evade the legal consequences of his action;*

— *the concealment or disguise of the true nature, source, location, disposition, movement, rights with respect to, or ownership of property, knowing that such property is derived from criminal activity or from an act of participation in such activity;*

— *the acquisition, possession or use of property, knowing, at the time of receipt, that such property was derived from criminal activity or from an act of participation in such activity;*

— *participation in, association to commit, attempts to commit and aiding, abetting, facilitating and counselling the commission of any of the actions mentioned in the foregoing indents.*

Knowledge, intent or purpose required as an element of the abovementioned activities may be inferred from objective factual circumstances.

Money laundering shall be regarded as such even where the activities which generated the property to be laundered were carried out in the territory of another Member State or in that of a third country.

(D) *"Property" means assets of every kind, whether corporeal or incorporeal, movable or immovable, tangible or intangible, and legal documents or instruments evidencing title to or interests in such assets.*

(E) *"Criminal activity" means any kind of criminal involvement in the commission of a serious crime.*

Serious crimes are, at least—

— *any of the offences defined in Article 3(1)(a) of the Vienna Convention;*

— *the activities of criminal organisations as defined in Article 1 of Joint Action 98/733/JHA;[4]*

— *fraud, at least serious, as defined in Article 1(1) and Article 2 of the Convention on the protection of the European Communities' financial interests;[5]*

— *corruption;*

— *a offence which may generate substantial proceeds and which is punishable by a severe sentence of imprisonment in accordance with the penal law of the Member State.*

Member States shall before 15 December 2004 amend the definition provided for in this indent in order to bring this definition into line with the definition of serious crime of Joint Action 98/699/JHA. The Council invites the Commission to present before 15 December 2004 a proposal for a Directive amending in that respect this Directive.

Member States may designate any other offence as a criminal activity for the purposes of this Directive.

(F) *"Competent authorities" means the national authorities empowered by law or regulation to supervise the activity of any of the institutions or persons subject to this Directive.]*

[5084A]

NOTES

Repealed as noted at the beginning of this Directive.

Substituted by European Parliament and Council Directive 2001/97/EC, Art 1(1), as from 28 December 2001.

1   OJ L126, 26.5.2000, p 1. Directive as amended by Directive 2000/28/EC (OJ L275, 27.10.2000, p 37).
2   OJ L63, 13.3.1979, p 1. Directive as last amended by Directive 95/26/EC of the European Parliament and of the Council (OJ L168, 18.7.1995, p 7).
3   OJ L141, 11.6.1993, p 27. Directive as last amended by Directive 97/9/EC of the European Parliament and of the Council (OJ L84, 26.3.1997, p 22).
4   OJ L351, 29.12.1998, p 1.
5   OJ C316, 27.11.1995, p 48.

Article 2

Member States shall ensure that money laundering as defined in this Directive is prohibited.

[5085]

NOTES

Repealed as noted at the beginning of this Directive.

[Article 2a

Member States shall ensure that the obligations laid down in this Directive are imposed on the following institutions—

1.   credit institutions as defined in point A of Article 1;

2.   *financial institutions as defined in point B of Article 1;*

and on the following legal or natural persons acting in the exercise of their professional activities—

3.   *auditors, external accountants and tax advisors;*

4.   *real estate agents;*

5.   *notaries and other independent legal professionals, when they participate, whether—*

   (a)   *by assisting in the planning or execution of transactions for their client concerning the*

      (i)   *buying and selling of real property or business entities;*

      (ii)   *managing of client money, securities or other assets;*

      (iii)   *opening or management of bank, savings or securities accounts;*

      (iv)   *organisation of contributions necessary for the creation, operation or management of companies;*

      (v)   *creation, operation or management of trusts, companies or similar structures;*

   (b)   *or by acting on behalf of and for their client in any financial or real estate transaction;*

6.   *dealers in high-value goods, such as precious stones or metals, or works of art, auctioneers, whenever payment is made in cash, and in an amount of EUR 15,000 or more;*

7.   *casinos.]*

[5086]

NOTES

Inserted by European Parliament and Council Directive 2001/97/EC, Art 1(2), as from 28 December 2001. Repealed as noted at the beginning of this Directive.

[Article 3

1.   Member States shall ensure that the institutions and persons subject to this Directive require identification of their customers by means of supporting evidence when entering into business relations, particularly, in the case of the institutions, when opening an account or savings accounts, or when offering safe custody facilities.

2.   The identification requirement shall also apply for any transaction with customers other than those referred to in paragraph 1, involving a sum amounting to EUR 15,000 or more, whether the transaction is carried out in a single operation or in several operations which seem to be linked. Where the sum is not known at the time when the transaction is undertaken, the institution or person concerned shall proceed with identification as soon as it or he is apprised of the sum and establishes that the threshold has been reached.

3.   By way of derogation from the preceding paragraphs, the identification requirements with regard to insurance policies written by insurance undertakings within the meaning of Council Directive 92/96/EEC of 10 November 1992 on the coordination of laws, regulations and administrative provisions relating to direct life assurance (third life assurance Directive),[1] where they perform activities which fall within the scope of that Directive shall not be required where the periodic premium amount or amounts to be paid in any given year does or do not exceed EUR 1,000 or where a single premium is paid amounting to EUR 2 500 or less. If the periodic premium amount or amounts to be paid in any given year is or are increased so as to exceed the EUR 1,000 threshold, identification shall be required.

4.   Member States may provide that the identification requirement is not compulsory for insurance policies in respect of pension schemes taken out by virtue of a contract of employment or the insured's occupation, provided that such policies contain no surrender clause and may not be used as collateral for a loan.

5.   By way of derogation from the preceding paragraphs, all casino customers shall be identified if they purchase or sell gambling chips with a value of EUR 1,000 or more.

6.   Casinos subject to State supervision shall be deemed in any event to have complied with the identification requirement laid down in this Directive if they register and identify their customers immediately on entry, regardless of the number of gambling chips purchased.

7.   In the event of doubt as to whether the customers referred to in the above paragraphs are acting on their own behalf, or where it is certain that they are not acting on their own behalf, the institutions and persons subject to this Directive shall take reasonable measures to obtain information as to the real identity of the persons on whose behalf those customers are acting.

8.   The institutions and persons subject to this Directive shall carry out such identification, even where the amount of the transaction is lower than the threshold laid down, wherever there is suspicion of money laundering.

9.   The institutions and persons subject to this Directive shall not be subject to the identification requirements provided for in this Article where the customer is a credit or financial institution covered by this Directive or a credit or financial institution situated in a third country which imposes, in the opinion of the relevant Member States, equivalent requirements to those laid down by this Directive.

10. Member States may provide that the identification requirements regarding transactions referred to in paragraphs 3 and 4 are fulfilled when it is established that the payment for the transaction is to be debited from an account opened in the customer's name with a credit institution subject to this Directive according to the requirements of paragraph 1.

11. Member States shall, in any case, ensure that the institutions and persons subject to this Directive take specific and adequate measures necessary to compensate for the greater risk of money laundering which arises when establishing business relations or entering into a transaction with a customer who has not been physically present for identification purposes (non-face to face operations). Such measures shall ensure that the customer's identity is established, for example, by requiring additional documentary evidence, or supplementary measures to verify or certify the documents supplied, or confirmatory certification by an institution subject to this Directive, or by requiring that the first payment of the operations is carried out through an account opened in the customer's name with a credit institution subject to this Directive. The internal control procedures laid down in Article 11(1) shall take specific account of these measures.]

[5087]

NOTES
  Substituted by European Parliament and Council Directive 2001/97/EC, Art 1(3), as from 28 December 2001. Repealed as noted at the beginning of this Directive.
  [1]   OJ L360, 9.12.1992, p 1. Directive as last amended by Directive 2000/64/EC of the European Parliament and of the Council (OJ L290, 17.11.2000, p 27.)

Article 4

Member States shall ensure that [the institutions and persons subject to this Directive] keep the following for use as evidence in any investigation into money laundering—
  —   *in the case of identification, a copy or the references of the evidence required, for a period of at least five years after the relationship with their customer has ended,*
  —   *in the case of transactions, the supporting evidence and records, consisting of the original documents or copies admissible in court proceedings under the applicable national legislation for a period of at least five years following execution of the transactions.*

[5088]

NOTES
  Repealed as noted at the beginning of this Directive.
  Words in square brackets substituted by European Parliament and Council Directive 2001/97/EC, Art 1(4), as from 28 December 2001.

Article 5

Member States shall ensure that [the institutions and persons subject to this Directive] examine with special attention any transaction which they regard as particularly likely, by its nature, to be related to money laundering.

[5089]

NOTES
  Repealed as noted at the beginning of this Directive.
  Words in square brackets substituted by European Parliament and Council Directive 2001/97/EC, Art 1(4), as from 28 December 2001.

[Article 6

1. Member States shall ensure that the institutions and persons subject to this Directive and their directors and employees cooperate fully with the authorities responsible for combating money laundering—
  (a)   by informing those authorities, on their own initiative, of any fact which might be an indication of money laundering;
  (b)   by furnishing those authorities, at their request, with all necessary information, in accordance with the procedures established by the applicable legislation.

2. The information referred to in paragraph 1 shall be forwarded to the authorities responsible for combating money laundering of the Member State in whose territory the institution or person forwarding the information is situated. The person or persons designated by the institutions and persons in accordance with the procedures provided for in Article 11(1)(a) shall normally forward the information.

3.   *In the case of the notaries and independent legal professionals referred to in Article 2a(5), Member States may designate an appropriate self-regulatory body of the profession concerned as the authority to be informed of the facts referred to in paragraph 1(a) and in such case shall lay down the appropriate forms of cooperation between that body and the authorities responsible for combating money laundering.*

Member States shall not be obliged to apply the obligations laid down in paragraph 1 to notaries, independent legal professionals, auditors, external accountants and tax advisors with regard to information they receive from or obtain on one of their clients, in the course of ascertaining the legal position for their client or performing their task of defending or representing that client in, or concerning judicial proceedings, including advice on instituting or avoiding proceedings, whether such information is received or obtained before, during or after such proceedings.]

[5090]

NOTES
   Substituted by European Parliament and Council Directive 2001/97/EC, Art 1(5), as from 28 December 2001.
   Repealed as noted at the beginning of this Directive.

[Article 7

Member States shall ensure that the institutions and persons subject to this Directive refrain from carrying out transactions which they know or suspect to be related to money laundering until they have apprised the authorities referred to in Article 6. Those authorities may, under conditions determined by their national legislation, give instructions not to execute the operation. Where such a transaction is suspected of giving rise to money laundering and where to refrain in such manner is impossible or is likely to frustrate efforts to pursue the beneficiaries of a suspected money-laundering operation, the institutions and persons concerned shall apprise the authorities immediately afterwards.]

[5091]

NOTES
   Substituted by European Parliament and Council Directive 2001/97/EC, Art 1(6), as from 28 December 2001.
   Repealed as noted at the beginning of this Directive.

Article 8

[1.]   [The institutions and persons subject to this Directive] and their directors and employees shall not disclose to the customer concerned nor to other third persons that information has been transmitted to the authorities in accordance with Articles 6 and 7 or that a money laundering investigation is being carried out.

[2.   Member States shall not be obliged under this Directive to apply the obligation laid down in paragraph 1 to the professions mentioned in the second paragraph of Article 6(3).]

[5092]

NOTES
   Repealed as noted at the beginning of this Directive.
   Para 1 numbered as such, words in square brackets in that paragraph substituted, and para 2 added, by European Parliament and Council Directive 2001/97/EC, Art 1(4), (7), as from 28 December 2001.

[Article 9

The disclosure in good faith to the authorities responsible for combating money laundering by an institution or person subject to this Directive or by an employee or director of such an institution or person of the information referred to in Articles 6 and 7 shall not constitute a breach of any restriction on disclosure of information imposed by contract or by any legislative, regulatory or administrative provision, and shall not involve the institution or person or its directors or employees in liability of any kind.]

[5093]

NOTES
   Substituted by European Parliament and Council Directive 2001/97/EC, Art 1(8), as from 28 December 2001.
   Repealed as noted at the beginning of this Directive.

Article 10

Member States shall ensure that if, in the course of inspections carried out in [the institutions and persons subject to this Directive] by the competent authorities, or in any other way, those authorities discover facts that could constitute evidence of money laundering, they inform the authorities responsible for combating money laundering.

[Member States shall ensure that supervisory bodies empowered by law or regulation to oversee the stock, foreign exchange and financial derivatives markets inform the authorities responsible for combating money laundering if they discover facts that could constitute evidence of money laundering.]

[5094]

NOTES
Repealed as noted at the beginning of this Directive.
Words in first pair of square brackets substituted, and words in second pair of square brackets inserted, by European Parliament and Council Directive 2001/97/EC, Art 1(4), (9), as from 28 December 2001.

[Article 11

1.   *Member States shall ensure that the institutions and persons subject to this Directive—*
     (a)   *establish adequate procedures of internal control and communication in order to forestall and prevent operations related to money laundering;*
     (b)   *take appropriate measures so that their employees are aware of the provisions contained in this Directive. These measures shall include participation of their relevant employees in special training programmes to help them recognise operations which may be related to money laundering as well as to instruct them as to how to proceed in such cases.*

Where a natural person falling within any of Article 2a(3) to (7) undertakes his professional activities as an employee of a legal person, the obligations in this Article shall apply to that legal person rather than to the natural person.

2.   *Member States shall ensure that the institutions and persons subject to this Directive have access to up-to-date information on the practices of money launderers and on indications leading to the recognition of suspicious transactions.]*

[5095]

NOTES
Substituted by European Parliament and Council Directive 2001/97/EC, Art 1(10), as from 28 December 2001.
Repealed as noted at the beginning of this Directive.

Article 12

Member States shall ensure that the provisions of this Directive are extended in whole or in part to professions and to categories of undertakings, other than the [institutions and persons referred to in Article 2a], which engage in activities which are particularly likely to be used for money-laundering purposes.

[5096]

NOTES
Repealed as noted at the beginning of this Directive.
Words in square brackets substituted by European Parliament and Council Directive 2001/97/EC, Art 1(11), as from 28 December 2001.

Article 13

1.   *A contact committee (hereinafter referred to as "the Committee") shall be set up under the aegis of the Commission. Its function shall be—*
     (a)   *without prejudice to Articles 169 and 170 of the Treaty, to facilitate harmonised implementation of this Directive through regular consultation on any practical problems arising from its application and on which exchanges of view are deemed useful;*
     (b)   *to facilitate consultation between the Member States on the more stringent or additional conditions and obligations which they may lay down at national level;*
     (c)   *to advise the Commission, if necessary, on any supplements or amendments to be made to this Directive or on any adjustments deemed necessary, in particular to harmonise the effects of Article 12;*
     (d)   *to examine whether a profession or a category of undertaking should be included in the scope of Article 12 where it has been established that such profession or category of undertaking has been used in a Member State for money laundering.*

2.   *It shall not be the function of the Committee to appraise the merits of decisions taken by the competent authorities in individual cases.*

3.   *The Committee shall be composed of persons appointed by the Member States and of representatives of the Commission. The secretariat shall be provided by the Commission. The chairman shall be a representative of the Commission. It shall be convened by its chairman, either on his own initiative or at the request of the delegation of a Member State.*

[5097]

NOTES

Repealed as noted at the beginning of this Directive.

Article 14

Each Member State shall take appropriate measures to ensure full application of all the provisions of this Directive and shall in particular determine the penalties to be applied for infringement of the measures adopted pursuant to this Directive.

[5098]

NOTES

Repealed as noted at the beginning of this Directive.

Article 15

The Member States may adopt or retain in force stricter provisions in the field covered by this Directive to prevent money laundering.

[5099]

NOTES

Repealed as noted at the beginning of this Directive.

Article 16

1.   Member States shall bring into force the laws, regulations and administrative decisions necessary to comply with this Directive before 1 January 1993 at the latest.

2.   Where Member States adopt these measures, they shall contain a reference to this Directive or shall be accompanied by such reference on the occasion of their official publication. The methods of making such a reference shall be laid down by the Member States.

3.   Member States shall communicate to the Commission the text of the main provisions of national law which they adopt in the field governed by this Directive.

[5100]

NOTES

Repealed as noted at the beginning of this Directive.

Article 17

One year after 1 January 1993, whenever necessary and at least at three yearly intervals thereafter, the Commission shall draw up a report on the implementation of this Directive and submit it to the European Parliament and the Council.

[5101]

NOTES

Repealed as noted at the beginning of this Directive.

Article 18

This Directive is addressed to the Member States.

[5102]

NOTES

Repealed as noted at the beginning of this Directive.

STATEMENT BY THE REPRESENTATIVES OF THE GOVERNMENTS OF THE MEMBER STATES MEETING WITHIN THE COUNCIL

The representatives of the Governments of the Member States, meeting within the Council,

Recalling that the Member States signed the United Nations Convention against illicit traffic in narcotic drugs and psychotropic substances, adopted on 19 December 1988 in Vienna;

Recalling also that most Member States have already signed the Council of Europe Convention on laundering, tracing, seizure and confiscation of proceeds of crime on 8 November 1990 in Strasbourg;

Conscious of the fact that the descriptions of money laundering contained in Article 1 of Council Directive 91/308/EEC[1] derives its wording from the relevant provisions of the aforementioned Conventions;

Hereby undertake to take all necessary steps by 31 December 1992 at the latest to enact criminal legislation enabling them to comply with their obligations under the aforementioned instruments.

[5103]

NOTES
Repealed as noted at the beginning of this Directive.
[1]   OJ L166, 28.91, p 77.

COUNCIL DIRECTIVE

of 15 March 1993

on the capital adequacy of investment firms and credit institutions (Note)

(93/6/EEC)

NOTES
Date of publication in OJ: OJ L141, 11.6.1993, p 1.
Due to the large number of amendments made to this Directive it has been recast. It is repealed and replaced by European Parliament and Council Directive 2006/49/EC on the capital adequacy of investment firms and credit institutions (recast) (at **[5847]**). See, in particular, recital (1) of Directive 2006/49/EC which provides that it also contains new provisions. As to the repeal of this Directive, see Art 52 of the 2006 Directive at **[5898]**, and as to the entry into force of 2006/49/EC (on 20 July 2006), see Art 53 at **[5899]**.

[5104]–[5127]

COUNCIL DIRECTIVE

of 5 April 1993

on unfair terms in consumer contracts

(93/13/EEC)

NOTES
Date of publication in OJ: OJ L95, 21.4.1993, p 29. Notes are as in the original OJ version.
As of 1 February 2009, this Directive had not been amended (but see below).
Proposed repeal of this Directive: see the 2008 Proposal for a Directive of the European Parliament and of the Council on consumer rights[1] which proposes the repeal of this Directive (together with (i) Council Directive 85/577/EEC to protect the consumer in respect of contracts negotiated away from business premises, (ii) Directive 97/7/EC of the European Parliament and of the Council on the protection of consumers in respect of distance contracts, and (iii) Directive 1999/44/EC of the European Parliament and of the Council on certain aspects of the sale of consumer goods) and their replacement with a single Directive on consumer rights. The proposed Directive would cover all contracts for sales of goods and services from business to consumer including purchases made in a shop, at a distance or away from business premises. It would also include rules specific to particular situations (eg, providing for a right of withdrawal in the case of distance and off-premises contracts).
[1]   Brussels, 8.10.2008, COM(2008) 614 final. Available on the Europa website.

THE COUNCIL OF THE EUROPEAN COMMUNITIES,
   Having regard to the Treaty establishing the European Economic Community, and in particular Article 100A thereof,
   Having regard to the proposal from the Commission,[1]
   In cooperation with the European Parliament,[2]
   Having regard to the opinion of the Economic and Social Committee,[3]
   Whereas it is necessary to adopt measures with the aim of progressively establishing the internal market before 31 December 1992; whereas the internal market comprises an area without internal frontiers in which goods, persons, services and capital move freely;
   Whereas the laws of Member States relating to the terms of contract between the seller of goods or supplier of services, on the one hand, and the consumer of them, on the other hand, show many disparities, with the result that the national markets for the sale of goods and services to consumers differ from each other and that distortions of competition may arise amongst the sellers and suppliers, notably when they sell and supply in other Member States;

Whereas, in particular, the laws of Member States relating to unfair terms in consumer contracts show marked divergences;

Whereas it is the responsibility of the Member States to ensure that contracts concluded with consumers do not contain unfair terms;

Whereas, generally speaking, consumers do not know the rules of law which, in Member States other than their own, govern contracts for the sale of goods or services; whereas this lack of awareness may deter them from direct transactions for the purchase of goods or services in another Member State;

Whereas, in order to facilitate the establishment of the internal market and to safeguard the citizen in his role as consumer when acquiring goods and services under contracts which are governed by the laws of Member States other than his own, it is essential to remove unfair terms from those contracts;

Whereas sellers of goods and suppliers of services will thereby be helped in their task of selling goods and supplying services, both at home and throughout the internal market; whereas competition will thus be stimulated, so contributing to increased choice for Community citizens as consumers;

Whereas the two Community programmes for a consumer protection and information policy[4] underlined the importance of safeguarding consumers in the matter of unfair terms of contract; whereas this protection ought to be provided by laws and regulations which are either harmonized at Community level or adopted directly at that level;

Whereas in accordance with the principle laid down under the heading 'Protection of the economic interests of the consumers', as stated in those programmes: 'acquirers of goods and services should be protected against the abuse of power by the seller or supplier, in particular against one-sided standard contracts and the unfair exclusion of essential rights in contracts';

Whereas more effective protection of the consumer can be achieved by adopting uniform rules of law in the matter of unfair terms; whereas those rules should apply to all contracts concluded between sellers or suppliers and consumers; whereas as a result inter alia contracts relating to employment, contracts relating to succession rights, contracts relating to rights under family law and contracts relating to the incorporation and organization of companies or partnership agreements must be excluded from this Directive;

Whereas the consumer must receive equal protection under contracts concluded by word of mouth and written contracts regardless, in the latter case, of whether the terms of the contract are contained in one or more documents;

Whereas, however, as they now stand, national laws allow only partial harmonization to be envisaged; whereas, in particular, only contractual terms which have not been individually negotiated are covered by this Directive; whereas Member States should have the option, with due regard for the Treaty, to afford consumers a higher level of protection through national provisions that are more stringent than those of this Directive;

Whereas the statutory or regulatory provisions of the Member States which directly or indirectly determine the terms of consumer contracts are presumed not to contain unfair terms; whereas, therefore, it does not appear to be necessary to subject the terms which reflect mandatory statutory or regulatory provisions and the principles or provisions of international conventions to which the Member States or the Community are party; whereas in that respect the wording 'mandatory statutory or regulatory provisions' in Article 1(2) also covers rules which, according to the law, shall apply between the contracting parties provided that no other arrangements have been established;

Whereas Member States must however ensure that unfair terms are not included, particularly because this Directive also applies to trades, business or professions of a public nature;

Whereas it is necessary to fix in a general way the criteria for assessing the unfair character of contract terms;

Whereas the assessment, according to the general criteria chosen, of the unfair character of terms, in particular in sale or supply activities of a public nature providing collective services which take account of solidarity among users, must be supplemented by a means of making an overall evaluation of the different interests involved; whereas this constitutes the requirement of good faith; whereas, in making an assessment of good faith, particular regard shall be had to the strength of the bargaining positions of the parties, whether the consumer had an inducement to agree to the term and whether the goods or services were sold or supplied to the special order of the consumer; whereas the requirement of good faith may be satisfied by the seller or supplier where he deals fairly and equitably with the other party whose legitimate interests he has to take into account;

Whereas, for the purposes of this Directive, the annexed list of terms can be of indicative value only and, because of the cause of the minimal character of the Directive, the scope of these terms may be the subject of amplification or more restrictive editing by the Member States in their national laws;

Whereas the nature of goods or services should have an influence on assessing the unfairness of contractual terms;

Whereas, for the purposes of this Directive, assessment of unfair character shall not be made of terms which describe the main subject matter of the contract nor the quality/price ratio of the goods or services supplied; whereas the main subject matter of the contract and the price/quality ratio may nevertheless be taken into account in assessing the fairness of other terms; whereas it follows, inter alia, that in insurance contracts, the terms which clearly define or circumscribe the insured risk and the insurer's liability shall not be subject to such assessment since these restrictions are taken into account in calculating the premium paid by the consumer;

Whereas contracts should be drafted in plain, intelligible language, the consumer should actually be given an opportunity to examine all the terms and, if in doubt, the interpretation most favourable to the consumer should prevail;

Whereas Member States should ensure that unfair terms are not used in contracts concluded with consumers by a seller or supplier and that if, nevertheless, such terms are so used, they will not bind the consumer, and the contract will continue to bind the parties upon those terms if it is capable of continuing in existence without the unfair provisions;

Whereas there is a risk that, in certain cases, the consumer may be deprived of protection under this Directive by designating the law of a non-Member country as the law applicable to the contract; whereas provisions should therefore be included in this Directive designed to avert this risk;

Whereas persons or organizations, if regarded under the law of a Member State as having a legitimate interest in the matter, must have facilities for initiating proceedings concerning terms of contract drawn up for general use in contracts concluded with consumers, and in particular unfair terms, either before a court or before an administrative authority competent to decide upon complaints or to initiate appropriate legal proceedings; whereas this possibility does not, however, entail prior verification of the general conditions obtaining in individual economic sectors;

Whereas the courts or administrative authorities of the Member States must have at their disposal adequate and effective means of preventing the continued application of unfair terms in consumer contracts,

[5128]

NOTES
1   OJ C73, 24.3.1992, p 7.
2   OJ C326, 16.12.1991, p 108 and OJ C21, 25.1.1993.
3   OJ C159, 17.6.1991, p 34.
4   OJ C92, 25.4.1975, p 1 and OJ C133, 3.6.1981, p 1.

HAS ADOPTED THIS DIRECTIVE:

Article 1

1.   The purpose of this Directive is to approximate the laws, regulations and administrative provisions of the Member States relating to unfair terms in contracts concluded between a seller or supplier and a consumer.

2.   The contractual terms which reflect mandatory statutory or regulatory provisions and the provisions or principles of international conventions to which the Member States or the Community are party, particularly in the transport area, shall not be subject to the provisions of this Directive.

[5128A]

Article 2

For the purposes of this Directive:
   (a)   'unfair terms' means the contractual terms defined in Article 3
   (b)   'consumer' means any natural person who, in contracts covered by this Directive, is acting for purposes which are outside his trade, business or profession;
   (c)   'seller or supplier' means any natural or legal person who, in contracts covered by this Directive, is acting for purposes relating to his trade, business or profession, whether publicly owned or privately owned.

[5129]

Article 3

1.   A contractual term which has not been individually negotiated shall be regarded as unfair if, contrary to the requirement of good faith, it causes a significant imbalance in the parties' rights and obligations arising under the contract, to the detriment of the consumer.

2.   A term shall always be regarded as not individually negotiated where it has been drafted in advance and the consumer has therefore not been able to influence the substance of the term, particularly in the context of a pre-formulated standard contract.

The fact that certain aspects of a term or one specific term have been individually negotiated shall not exclude the application of this Article to the rest of a contract if an overall assessment of the contract indicates that it is nevertheless a pre-formulated standard contract.

Where any seller or supplier claims that a standard term has been individually negotiated, the burden of proof in this respect shall be incumbent on him.

3. The Annex shall contain an indicative and non-exhaustive list of the terms which may be regarded as unfair.

[5130]

Article 4

1. Without prejudice to Article 7, the unfairness of a contractual term shall be assessed, taking into account the nature of the goods or services for which the contract was concluded and by referring, at the time of conclusion of the contract, to all the circumstances attending the conclusion of the contract and to all the other terms of the contract or of another contract on which it is dependent.

2. Assessment of the unfair nature of the terms shall relate neither to the definition of the main subject matter of the contract nor to the adequacy of the price and remuneration, on the one hand, as against the services or goods supplies in exchange, on the other, in so far as these terms are in plain intelligible language.

[5131]

Article 5

In the case of contracts where all or certain terms offered to the consumer are in writing, these terms must always be drafted in plain, intelligible language. Where there is doubt about the meaning of a term, the interpretation most favourable to the consumer shall prevail. This rule on interpretation shall not apply in the context of the procedures laid down in Article 7(2).

[5132]

Article 6

1. Member States shall lay down that unfair terms used in a contract concluded with a consumer by a seller or supplier shall, as provided for under their national law, not be binding on the consumer and that the contract shall continue to bind the parties upon those terms if it is capable of continuing in existence without the unfair terms.

2. Member States shall take the necessary measures to ensure that the consumer does not lose the protection granted by this Directive by virtue of the choice of the law of a non-Member country as the law applicable to the contract if the latter has a close connection with the territory of the Member States.

[5133]

Article 7

1. Member States shall ensure that, in the interests of consumers and of competitors, adequate and effective means exist to prevent the continued use of unfair terms in contracts concluded with consumers by sellers or suppliers.

2. The means referred to in paragraph 1 shall include provisions whereby persons or organizations, having a legitimate interest under national law in protecting consumers, may take action according to the national law concerned before the courts or before competent administrative bodies for a decision as to whether contractual terms drawn up for general use are unfair, so that they can apply appropriate and effective means to prevent the continued use of such terms.

3. With due regard for national laws, the legal remedies referred to in paragraph 2 may be directed separately or jointly against a number of sellers or suppliers from the same economic sector or their associations which use or recommend the use of the same general contractual terms or similar terms.

[5134]

Article 8

Member States may adopt or retain the most stringent provisions compatible with the Treaty in the area covered by this Directive, to ensure a maximum degree of protection for the consumer.

[5135]

Article 9

The Commission shall present a report to the European Parliament and to the Council concerning the application of this Directive five years at the latest after the date in Article 10(1).

[5136]

Article 10

1. Member States shall bring into force the laws, regulations and administrative provisions necessary to comply with this Directive no later than 31 December 1994. They shall forthwith inform the Commission thereof.

These provisions shall be applicable to all contracts concluded after 31 December 1994.

2. When Member States adopt these measures, they shall contain a reference to this Directive or shall be accompanied by such reference on the occasion of their official publication. The methods of making such a reference shall be laid down by the Member States.

3.   Member States shall communicate the main provisions of national law which they adopt in the field covered by this Directive to the Commission.

[5137]

Article 11

This Directive is addressed to the Member States.

[5138]

ANNEX
TERMS REFERRED TO IN ARTICLE 3(3)

1.   Terms which have the object or effect of:

    (a)   excluding or limiting the legal liability of a seller or supplier in the event of the death of a consumer or personal injury to the latter resulting from an act or omission of that seller or supplier;

    (b)   inappropriately excluding or limiting the legal rights of the consumer vis-à-vis the seller or supplier or another party in the event of total or partial non-performance or inadequate performance by the seller or supplier of any of the contractual obligations, including the option of offsetting a debt owed to the seller or supplier against any claim which the consumer may have against him;

    (c)   making an agreement binding on the consumer whereas provision of services by the seller or supplier is subject to a condition whose realization depends on his own will alone;

    (d)   permitting the seller or supplier to retain sums paid by the consumer where the latter decides not to conclude or perform the contract, without providing for the consumer to receive compensation of an equivalent amount from the seller or supplier where the latter is the party cancelling the contract;

    (e)   requiring any consumer who fails to fulfil his obligation to pay a disproportionately high sum in compensation;

    (f)   authorizing the seller or supplier to dissolve the contract on a discretionary basis where the same facility is not granted to the consumer, or permitting the seller or supplier to retain the sums paid for services not yet supplied by him where it is the seller or supplier himself who dissolves the contract;

    (g)   enabling the seller or supplier to terminate a contract of indeterminate duration without reasonable notice except where there are serious grounds for doing so;

    (h)   automatically extending a contract of fixed duration where the consumer does not indicate otherwise, when the deadline fixed for the consumer to express this desire not to extend the contract is unreasonably early;

    (i)   irrevocably binding the consumer to terms with which he had no real opportunity of becoming acquainted before the conclusion of the contract;

    (j)   enabling the seller or supplier to alter the terms of the contract unilaterally without a valid reason which is specified in the contract;

    (k)   enabling the seller or supplier to alter unilaterally without a valid reason any characteristics of the product or service to be provided;

    (l)   providing for the price of goods to be determined at the time of delivery or allowing a seller of goods or supplier of services to increase their price without in both cases giving the consumer the corresponding right to cancel the contract if the final price is too high in relation to the price agreed when the contract was concluded;

    (m)   giving the seller or supplier the right to determine whether the goods or services supplied are in conformity with the contract, or giving him the exclusive right to interpret any term of the contract;

    (n)   limiting the seller's or supplier's obligation to respect commitments undertaken by his agents or making his commitments subject to compliance with a particular formality;

    (o)   obliging the consumer to fulfil all his obligations where the seller or supplier does not perform his;

    (p)   giving the seller or supplier the possibility of transferring his rights and obligations under the contract, where this may serve to reduce the guarantees for the consumer, without the latter's agreement;

    (q)   excluding or hindering the consumer's right to take legal action or exercise any other legal remedy, particularly by requiring the consumer to take disputes exclusively to arbitration not covered by legal provisions, unduly restricting the evidence available to him or imposing on him a burden of proof which, according to the applicable law, should lie with another party to the contract.

2.   Scope of subparagraphs (g), (j) and (l)

    (a)   Subparagraph (g) is without hindrance to terms by which a supplier of financial services reserves the right to terminate unilaterally a contract of indeterminate duration without notice where there is a valid reason, provided that the supplier is required to inform the other contracting party or parties thereof immediately.

(b)　Subparagraph (j) is without hindrance to terms under which a supplier of financial services reserves the right to alter the rate of interest payable by the consumer or due to the latter, or the amount of other charges for financial services without notice where there is a valid reason, provided that the supplier is required to inform the other contracting party or parties thereof at the earliest opportunity and that the latter are free to dissolve the contract immediately.

Subparagraph (j) is also without hindrance to terms under which a seller or supplier reserves the right to alter unilaterally the conditions of a contract of indeterminate duration, provided that he is required to inform the consumer with reasonable notice and that the consumer is free to dissolve the contract.

(c)　Subparagraphs (g), (j) and (l) do not apply to:
— transactions in transferable securities, financial instruments and other products or services where the price is linked to fluctuations in a stock exchange quotation or index or a financial market rate that the seller or supplier does not control;
— contracts for the purchase or sale of foreign currency, traveller's cheques or international money orders denominated in foreign currency;

(d)　Subparagraph (l) is without hindrance to price-indexation clauses, where lawful, provided that the method by which prices vary is explicitly described.

[5139]

COUNCIL DIRECTIVE

of 10 May 1993

on investment services in the securities field (Note)

(93/22/EEC)

NOTES

Date of publication in OJ: OJ L141, 11.6.93, p 27.

This Directive was repealed by European Parliament and Council Directive 2004/39/EC, Art 69 (at **[5590]**), as from 1 November 2007; for transitional provisions see Art 71 of the 2004 Directive at **[5592]**.

[5140]–[5174]

DIRECTIVE OF THE EUROPEAN PARLIAMENT AND OF THE COUNCIL

of 3 March 1997

on investor-compensation schemes

(97/9/EC)

NOTES

Date of publication in OJ: OJ L84, 26.3.97, p 22. Notes are as in the original OJ version.

As of 1 February 2009, this Directive had not been amended.

THE EUROPEAN PARLIAMENT AND THE COUNCIL OF THE EUROPEAN UNION,

Having regard to the Treaty establishing the European Community, and in particular Article 87(2) thereof,

Having regard to the proposal from the Commission,[1]

Having regard to the opinion of the Economic and Social Committee,[2]

Having regard to the opinion of the European Monetary Institute,[3]

Acting in accordance with the procedure laid down in Article 189b of the Treaty[4] in the light of the joint text approved by the Conciliation Committee on 18 December 1996,

(1)　Whereas on 10 May 1993 the Council adopted Directive 93/22/EEC on investment services in the securities field;[5] whereas that Directive is an essential instrument for the achievement of the internal market for investment firms

(2)　Whereas Directive 93/22/EEC lays down prudential rules which investment firms must observe at all times, including rules the purpose of which is to protect as far as possible investor's rights in respect of money or instruments belonging to them

(3) Whereas, however, no system of supervision can provide complete protection, particularly where acts of fraud are committed

(4) Whereas the protection of investors and the maintenance of confidence in the financial system are an important aspect of the completion and proper functioning of the internal market in this area; whereas to that end it is therefore essential that each Member State should have an investor-compensation scheme that guarantees a harmonised minimum level of protection at least for the small investor in the event of an investment firm being unable to meet its obligations to its investor clients

(5) Whereas small investors will therefore be able to purchase investment services from branches of Community investment firms or on the basis of the cross-border provision of services as confidently as from domestic investment firms, in the knowledge that a harmonised minimum level of protection would be available to them in the event of an investment firm being unable to meet its obligations to its investor clients

(6) Whereas, in the absence of such minimum harmonisation, a host Member State might consider itself justified, by considerations of investor protection, in requiring membership of its compensation scheme when a Community investment firm operating through a branch or under the freedom to provide services either belonged to no investor-compensation scheme in its home Member State or belonged to a scheme which was not regarded as offering equivalent protection; whereas such a requirement might prejudice the operation of the internal market

(7) Whereas although most Member States currently have some investor-compensation arrangements those arrangements do not in general cover all investment firms that hold the single authorisation provided for in Directive 93/22/EEC

(8) Whereas, therefore, every Member State should be required to have an investor-compensation scheme or schemes to which every such investment firm would belong; whereas each scheme must cover money and instruments held by an investment firm in connection with an investor's investment operations which, where an investment firm is unable to meet its obligations to its investor clients, cannot be returned to the investor; whereas this is entirely without prejudice to the rules and procedures applicable in each Member State as regards the decisions to be taken in the event of the insolvency or winding-up of an investment firm

(9) Whereas the definition of investment firm includes credit institutions which are authorised to provide investment services; whereas every such credit institution must also be required to belong to an investor-compensation scheme to cover its investment business; whereas, however, it is not necessary to require such a credit institution to belong to two separate schemes where a single scheme meets the requirements both of this Directive and of Directive 94/19/EC of the European Parliament and of the Council of 30 May 1994 on deposit-guarantee schemes;[6] whereas, however, in the case of investment firms which are credit institutions it may in certain cases be difficult to distinguish between deposits covered by Directive 94/19/EC and money held in connection with investment business; whereas Member States should be allowed to determine which Directive shall apply to such claims

(10) Whereas Directive 94/19/EC allows a Member State to exempt a credit institution from the obligation to belong to a deposit-guarantee scheme where that credit institution belongs to a system which protects the credit institution itself and, in particular, ensures its solvency; whereas, where a credit institution belonging to such a system is also an investment firm, a Member State should also be allowed, subject to certain conditions, to exempt it from the obligation to belong to an investor-compensation scheme

(11) Whereas a harmonised minimum level of compensation of ECU 20,000 for each investor should be sufficient to protect the interests of the small investor where an investment firm is unable to meet its obligations to its investor clients; whereas it would therefore appear reasonable to set the harmonised minimum level of compensation at ECU 20,000; whereas, as in Directive 94/19/EC, limited transitional provisions might be required to enable compensation schemes to comply with that figure since this applies equally to Member States which, when this Directive is adopted, do not have any such scheme

(12) Whereas the same figure was adopted in Directive 94/19/EC

(13) Whereas in order to encourage investors to take due care in their choice of investment firms it is reasonable to allow Member States to require investors to bear a proportion of any loss; whereas, however, an investor must be covered for at least 90% of any loss as long as the compensation paid is less than the Community minimum

(14) Whereas certain Member States' schemes offer levels of cover higher than the harmonised minimum level of protection under this Directive; whereas, however, it does not seem desirable to require any change in those schemes in that respect

(15) Whereas the retention in the Community of schemes providing levels of cover higher than the harmonised minimum may, within the same territory, lead to disparities in compensation and unequal conditions of competition between national investment firms and branches of firms from other Member States; whereas, in order to counteract those disadvantages, branches should be authorised to join their host countries' schemes so that they may offer their investors the same cover as is provided by the schemes of the countries in which they are located; whereas it is appropriate that, in its report on the application of this Directive, the Commission should indicate the extent to

which branches have exercised that option and any difficulties which they or the investor-compensation schemes may have encountered in implementing those provisions; whereas the possibility that home Member States' schemes should themselves offer such supplementary cover, subject to the conditions such schemes may lay down, is not ruled out

(16) Whereas market disturbances could be caused by branches of investment firms established in Member States other than their Member States of origin which offer levels of cover higher than those offered by investment firms authorised in their host Member States; whereas it is not appropriate that the level or scope of cover offered by compensation schemes should become an instrument of competition; whereas it is therefore necessary, at least during an initial period, to stipulate that neither the level nor the scope of cover offered by a home Member State's scheme to investors at branches located in another Member State should exceed the maximum level or scope offered by the corresponding scheme in the host Member State; whereas any market disturbances should be reviewed at an early date, on the basis of the experience acquired and in the light of developments in the financial sector

(17) Whereas a Member State must be able to exclude certain categories of specifically listed investments or investors, if it does not consider that they need special protection from the cover afforded by investor-compensation schemes

(18) Whereas some Member States have investor-compensation schemes under the responsibility of professional organisations; whereas in other Member States there are schemes that have been set up and are regulated on a statutory basis; whereas that diversity of status poses a problem only with regard to compulsory membership of and exclusion from schemes; whereas it is therefore necessary to take steps to limit the powers of schemes in that area

(19) Whereas the investor must be compensated without excessive delay once the validity of his claim has been established; whereas the compensation scheme itself must be able to fix a reasonable period for the presentation of claims; whereas, however, the fact that such a period has expired may not be invoked against an investor who for good reason has not been able to present his claim within the time allowed

(20) Whereas informing investors of compensation arrangements is an essential element of investor protection; whereas Article 12 of Directive 93/22/EEC required investment firms to inform investors, before doing business with them, of the possible application of a compensation scheme; whereas, therefore, this Directive should lay down rules on informing such intending investors regarding the compensation schemes covering their investment business

(21) Whereas, however, the unregulated use in advertising of references to the amount and scope of a compensation scheme could affect the stability of the financial system or investor confidence; whereas Member States should therefore lay down rules to limit such references

(22) Whereas in principle this Directive requires every investment firm to join an investor-compensation scheme; whereas the Directives governing the admission of any investment firm the head office of which is in a non-member country, and in particular Directive 93/22/EEC, allow Member States to decide whether and subject to what conditions to permit branches of such investment firms to operate within their territories; whereas such branches will not enjoy the freedom to provide services under the second paragraph of Article 59 of the Treaty, or the right of establishment in Member States other than those in which they are established; whereas, accordingly, a Member State admitting such branches must decide how to apply the principles of this Directive to such branches in accordance with Article 5 of Directive 93/22/EEC and with the need to protect investors and maintain the integrity of the financial system; whereas it is essential that investors at such branches should be fully aware of the compensation arrangements applicable to them

(23) Whereas it is not indispensable in this Directive to harmonise the ways in which investor-compensation schemes are to be financed given, on the one hand, that the cost of financing such schemes must, in principle, be borne by investment firms themselves and, on the other hand, that the financing capacities of such schemes must be in proportion to their liabilities; whereas that must not, however, jeopardise the stability of the financial system of the Member State concerned

(24) Whereas this Directive may not result in the Member States or their competent authorities being made liable in respect of investors if they have ensured that one or more schemes for the compensation or protection of investors under the conditions prescribed in this Directive have been introduced and officially recognised

(25) Whereas, in conclusion, a minimum degree of harmonisation of investor-compensation arrangements is necessary for the completion of the internal market for investment firms since it will make it possible for investors to do business with such firms with greater confidence, especially firms from other Member States, and make it possible to avoid any difficulties caused by host Member States applying national investor-protection rules that are not coordinated at Community level; whereas a binding Community Directive is the only appropriate instrument for the achievement of the desired objective in the general absence of investor-compensation arrangements corresponding to the coverage of Directive 93/22/EEC; whereas this Directive effects only the

minimum harmonisation required, allows Member States to prescribe wider or higher coverage if they desire and gives Member States the necessary latitude as regards the organisation and financing of investor-compensation schemes,

[5175]

NOTES
1   OJ C321, 27.11 93, p 15 and OJ C382, 31.11.94, p 27.
2   OJ C127, 7.5.94, p 1.
3   Opinion delivered on 28 July 1995.
4   European Parliament opinion of 19 April 1994 (OJ C128, 9.5.94, p 85). Council common position of 23 October 1995 (OJ C320, 30.11.95, p 9) and European Parliament Decision of 12 March 1996 (OJ C96, 1.4.96, p 28). Decision of the Council of 17 February 1997 and Decision of the European Parliament of 19 February 1997 (OJ C85, 17.3.97).
5   OJ L141, 11.6.93, p 27.
6   OJ L135, 31.5.94, p 5.

HAVE ADOPTED THIS DIRECTIVE—

Article 1
For the purposes of this Directive—
    1.   "investment firm" shall mean an investment firm as defined in Article 1(2) of Directive 93/22/EEC
        —   authorised in accordance with Article 3 of Directive 93/22/EEC, or
        —   authorised as a credit institution in accordance with Council Directive 77/780/EEC and Council Directive 89/646/EEC, the authorisation of which covers one or more of the investment services listed in Section A of the Annex to Directive 93/22/EEC;
    2.   "investment business" shall mean any investment service as defined in Article 1(1) of Directive 93/22/EEC and the service referred to in point 1 of Section C of the Annex to that Directive,
    3.   "instruments" shall mean the instruments listed in Section B of the Annex to Directive 93/22/EEC;
    4.   "investor" shall mean any person who has entrusted money or instruments to an investment firm in connection with investment business;
    5.   "branch" shall mean a place of business which is a part of an investment firm, which has no legal personality and which provides investment services for which the investment firm has been authorised; all the places of business set up in the same Member State by an investment firm with headquarters in another Member State shall be regarded as a single branch;
    6.   "joint investment business" shall mean investment business carried out for the account of two or more persons or over which two or more persons have rights that may be exercised by means of the signature of one or more of those persons;
    7.   "competent authorities" shall mean the authorities defined in Article 22 of Directive 93/22/EEC; those authorities may, if appropriate, be those defined in Article 1 of Council Directive 92/30/EEC of 6 April 1992 on the supervision of credit institutions on a consolidated basis.

[5175A]

Article 2
    1.   Each Member State shall ensure that within its territory one or more investor-compensation schemes are introduced and officially recognised. Except in the circumstances envisaged in the second subparagraph and in Article 5(3), no investment firm authorised in that Member State may carry on investment business unless it belongs to such a scheme.

    A Member State may, however, exempt a credit institution to which this Directive applies from the obligation to belong to an investor-compensation scheme where that credit institution is already exempt under Article 3(1) of Directive 94/19/EC from the obligation to belong to a deposit-guarantee scheme, provided that the protection and information given to depositors are also given to investors on the same terms and investors thus enjoy protection at least equivalent to that afforded by an investor-compensation scheme.

    Any Member State that avails itself of that option shall inform the Commission accordingly; it shall, in particular, disclose the characteristics of the protective systems in question and the credit institutions covered by them for the purposes of this Directive, as well as any subsequent changes to the information supplied. The Commission shall inform the Council thereof.

    2.   A scheme shall provide cover for investors in accordance with Article 4 where either—
        —   the competent authorities have determined that in their view an instrument firm appears,

for the time being, for reasons directly related to its financial circumstances, to be unable to meet its obligations arising out of investors' claims and has no early prospect of being able to do so,

or

— a judicial authority has made a ruling, for reasons directly related to an investment firm's financial circumstances, which has the effect of suspending investors' ability to make claims against it,

whichever is the earlier.

Cover shall be provided for claims arising out of an investment firm's inability to—

— repay money owed to or belonging to investors and held on their behalf in connection with investment business,

or

— return to investors any instruments belonging to them and held, administered or managed on their behalf in connection with investment business.

in accordance with the legal and contractual conditions applicable.

3. Any claim under paragraph 2 on a credit institution which, in a given Member State, would be subject both to this Directive and to Directive 94/19/EC shall be directed by that Member State to a scheme under one or other of those Directives as that Member State shall consider appropriate. No claim shall be eligible for compensation more than once under those Directives.

4. The amount of an investor's claim shall be calculated in accordance with the legal and contractual conditions, in particular those concerning set off and counterclaims, that are applicable to the assessment, on the date of the determination or ruling referred to in paragraph 2, of the amount of the money or the value, determined where possible by reference to the market value, of the instruments belonging to the investor which the investment firm is unable to repay or return.

[5176]

Article 3

Claims arising out of transactions in connection with which a criminal conviction has been obtained for money laundering, as defined in Article 1 of Council Directive 91/308/EEC of 10 June 1991 on prevention of the use of the financial system for the purpose of money laundering,[1] shall be excluded from any compensation under investor-compensation schemes.

[5177]

NOTES

[1] OJ L166, 28.6.91, p 77.

Article 4

1. Member States shall ensure that schemes provide for cover of not less than ECU 20,000 for each investor in respect of the claims referred to in Article 2(2).

Until 31 December 1999 Member States in which, when this Directive is adopted, cover is less than ECU 20,000 may retain that lower level of cover, provided it is not less than ECU 15,000. That option shall also be available to Member States to which the transitional provisions of the second subparagraph of Article 7(1) of Directive 94/19/EC apply.

2. A Member State may provide that certain investors shall be excluded from cover by schemes or shall be granted a lower level of cover. Those exclusions shall be as listed in Annex 1.

3. This Article shall not preclude the retention or adoption of provisions which afford greater or more comprehensive cover to investors.

4. A Member State may limit the cover provided for in paragraph 1 or that referred to in paragraph 3 to a specified percentage of an investor's claim. The percentage covered must, however, be equal to or exceed 90% of the claim as long as the amount to be paid under the scheme is less than ECU 20,000.

[5178]

Article 5

1. If an investment firm required by Article 2(1) to belong to a scheme does not meet the obligations incumbent on it as a member of that scheme, the competent authorities which issued its authorisation shall be notified and, in cooperation with the compensation scheme, shall take all measures appropriate, including the imposition of penalties, to ensure that the investment firm meets its obligations.

2. If those measures fail to secure compliance on the part of the investment firm, the scheme may, where national law permits the exclusion of a member, with the express consent of the competent authorities, give not less than 12 months' notice of its intention of excluding the investment firm from membership of the scheme. The scheme shall continue to provide cover under

the second subparagraph of Article 2(2) in respect of investment business transacted during that period. If, on expiry of the period of notice, the investment firm has not met its obligations, the compensation scheme may, again having obtained the express consent of the competent authorities, exclude it.

3.   Where national law permits, and with the express consent of the competent authorities which issued its authorisation, an investment firm excluded from an investor-compensation scheme may continue to provide investment services if, before its exclusion, it made alternative compensation arrangements which ensure that investors will enjoy cover that is at least equivalent to that offered by the officially recognised scheme and has characteristics equivalent to those of that scheme.

4.   If an investment firm the exclusion of which is proposed under paragraph 2 is unable to make alternative arrangements which comply with the conditions imposed in paragraph 3, the competent authorities which issued its authorisation shall withdraw it forthwith.

[5179]

Article 6

After the withdrawal of an investment firm's authorisation, cover under the second subparagraph of Article 2(2) shall continue to be provided in respect of investment business transacted up to the time of that withdrawal.

[5180]

Article 7

1.   Investor-compensation schemes introduced and officially recognised in a Member State in accordance with Article 2(1) shall also cover investors at branches set up by investment firms in other Member States.

Until 31 December 1999, neither the level nor the scope, including the percentage, of the cover provided for may exceed the maximum level or scope of the cover offered by the corresponding compensation scheme within the territory of the host Member State. Before that date the Commission shall draw up a report on the basis of the experience acquired in applying this subparagraph and Article 4(1) of Directive 94/19/EC referred to above and shall consider the need to continue those provisions. If appropriate, the Commission shall submit a proposal for a Directive to the European Parliament and the Council, with a view to the extension of their validity.

Where the level or scope, including the percentage, of the cover offered by the host Member State's investor-compensation scheme exceeds the level or scope of the cover provided in the Member State in which an investment firm is authorised, the host Member State shall ensure that there is an officially recognised scheme within its territory which a branch may join voluntarily in order to supplement the cover which its investors already enjoy by virtue of its membership of its home Member State's scheme.

If a branch joins such a scheme, that scheme shall be one that covers the category of institution to which the branch belongs or most closely corresponds in its host Member State.

Member States shall ensure that objective and generally applied conditions are established concerning branches' membership of all investor-compensation schemes. Admission shall be conditional on a branch meeting the relevant membership obligations, including in particular the payment of all contributions and other charges. Member States shall follow the guiding principles set out in Annex II in implementing this paragraph.

If a branch which has exercised the option of voluntary membership under paragraph 1 does not meet the obligations incumbent on it as a member of an investor-compensation scheme, the competent authorities which issued its authorisation shall be notified and, in cooperation with the compensation scheme, shall take all measures necessary to ensure that the branch meets the aforementioned obligations.

If those measures fail to ensure that the branch meets the obligations referred to in this Article, after an appropriate period of notice of not less than 12 months the compensation scheme may, with the consent of the competent authorities which issued the authorisation, exclude the branch. Investment business transacted before the date of exclusion shall continue to be covered after that date by the compensation scheme of which the branch was a voluntary member. Investors shall be informed of the withdrawal of the supplementary cover and of the date on which it takes effect.

[5181]

Article 8

1.   The cover provided for in Article 4(1), (3) and (4) shall apply to the investor's aggregate claim on the same investment firm under this Directive irrespective of the number of accounts, the currency and location within the Community.

Member States may, however, provide that funds in currencies other than those of the Member States and the ecu shall be excluded from cover or be subject to lower cover. This option shall not apply to instruments.

2. Each investor's share in joint investment business shall be taken into account in calculating the cover provided for in Article 4(1), (3) and (4).

In the absence of special provisions, claims shall be divided equally amongst investors.

Member States may provide that claims relating to joint investment business to which two or more persons are entitled as members of a business partnership, association or grouping of a similar nature which has no legal personality may, for the purpose of calculating the limits provided for in Article 4(1), (3) and (4), be aggregated and treated as if arising from an investment made by a single investor.

3. Where an investor is not absolutely entitled to the sums or securities held, the person who is absolutely entitled shall receive the compensation, provided that that person has been or can be identified before the date of the determination or ruling referred to in Article 2(2).

If two or more persons are absolutely entitled, the share of each under the arrangements subject to which the sums or the securities are managed shall be taken into account when the limits laid down in Article 4(1), (3) and (4) are calculated.

This provision shall not apply to collective-investment undertakings.

[5182]

Article 9

1. The compensation scheme shall take appropriate measures to inform investors of the determination or ruling referred to in Article 2(2) and, if they are to be compensated, to compensate them as soon as possible. It may fix a period during which investors shall be required to submit their claims. That period may not be less than five months from the date of the aforementioned determination or ruling or from the date on which that determination or ruling is made public.

The fact that that period has expired may not, however, be invoked by the scheme to deny cover to an investor who has been unable to assert his right to compensation in time.

2. The scheme shall be in a position to pay an investor's claim as soon as possible and at the latest within three months of the establishment of the eligibility and the amount of the claim.

In wholly exceptional circumstances and in special cases a compensation scheme may apply to the competent authorities for an extension of the time limit. No such extension may exceed three months.

3. Notwithstanding the time limit laid down in paragraph 2, where an investor or any other person entitled to or having an interest in investment business has been charged with an offence arising out of or in relation to money laundering as defined in Article 1 of Directive 91/308/EEC, the compensation scheme may suspend any payment pending the judgment of the court.

[5183]

Article 10

1. Member States shall ensure that each investment firm takes appropriate measures to make available to actual and intending investors the information necessary for the identification of the investor-compensation scheme of which the investment firm and its branches within the Community are members or any alternative arrangement provided for under the second subparagraph of Article 2(1) or Article 5(3). Investors shall be informed of the provisions of the investor-compensation scheme or any alternative arrangement applicable, including the amount and scope of the cover offered by the compensation scheme and any rules laid down by the Member States pursuant to Article 2(3). That information shall be made available in a readily comprehensible manner.

Information shall also be given on request concerning the conditions governing compensation and the formalities which must be completed to obtain compensation.

2. The information provided for in paragraph 1 shall be made available in the manner prescribed by national law in the official language or languages of the Member State in which a branch is established.

3. Member States shall establish rules limiting the use in advertising of the information referred to in paragraph 1 in order to prevent such use from affecting the stability of the financial system or investor confidence. In particular, a Member State may restrict such advertising to a factual reference to the scheme to which an investment firm belonged.

[5184]

Article 11

1. Each Member State shall check whether branches established by an investment firm the head office of which is outwith the Community have cover equivalent to that prescribed in this Directive. Failing such cover, a Member State may, subject to Article 5 of Directive 93/22/EEC, stipulate that branches established by an investment firm the head office of which is outwith the Community shall join investor-compensation schemes in operation within its territory.

2. Actual and intending investors at branches established by an investment firm the head office of which is outwith the Community shall be provided by that investment firm with all relevant information concerning the compensation arrangements which cover their investments.

3. The information provided for in paragraph 2 shall be made available in the manner prescribed by national law in the official language or languages of the Member State in which a branch is established and shall be drafted in a clear and comprehensible form.

[5185]

Article 12

Without prejudice to any other rights which they may have under national law, schemes which make payments in order to compensate investors shall have the right of subrogation to the rights of those investors in liquidation proceedings for amounts equal to their payments.

[5186]

Article 13

Member States shall ensure that an investor's right to compensation may be the subject of an action by the investor against the compensation scheme.

[5187]

Article 14

No later than 31 December 1999 the Commission shall submit a report to the European Parliament and to the Council on the application of this Directive together, where appropriate, with proposals for its revision.

[5188]

Article 15

1. The Member States shall bring into force the laws, regulations and administrative provisions necessary for them to comply with this Directive no later than 26 September 1998. They shall forthwith inform the Commission thereof.

When the Member States adopt those measures, they shall contain references to this Directive or shall be accompanied by such references on the occasion of their official publication. The methods of making such references shall be laid down by the Member States.

2. The Member States shall communicate to the Commission the texts of the main provisions of national law which they adopt in the field covered by this Directive.

[5189]

Article 16

(*Repeals Directive 93/22/EEC, Art 12, as from 26 September 1998.*)

Article 17

This Directive shall enter into force on the day of its publication in the *Official Journal of the European Communities.*

[5190]

Article 18

This Directive is addressed to the Member States.

[5191]

ANNEX I
LIST OF EXCLUSIONS REFERRED TO IN ARTICLE 4(2)

1. Professional and institutional investors, including:
   — investment firms as defined in Article 1(2) of Directive 93/22/EEC,
   — credit institutions as defined in the first indent of Article 1 of Council Directive 77/780/EEC,
   — financial institutions as defined in Article 1(6) of Council Directive 89/646/EEC,
   — insurance undertakings,
   — collective-investment undertakings,
   — pension and retirement funds.

Other professional and institutional investors.

2. Supranational institutions, government and central administrative authorities.

3. Provincial, regional, local and municipal authorities.

4. Directors, managers and personally liable members of investment firms, persons holding 5% or more of the capital of such investment firms, persons responsible for carrying out the statutory audits of investment firms' accounting documents and investors with similar status in other firms within the same group as such a firm.

5. Close relatives and third parties acting on behalf of the investors referred to in point 4.

6. Other firms in the same group.

7. Investors who have any responsibility for or have taken advantage of certain facts relating to an investment firm which gave rise to the firm's financial difficulties or contributed to the deterioration of its financial situation.

8. Companies which are of such a size that they are not permitted to draw up abridged balance sheets under Article 11 of the Fourth Council Directive 78/660/EEC of 25 July 1978 based on Article 54(3)(g) of the Treaty on the annual accounts of certain types of companies.[1]

[5192]

NOTES

[1]   OJ L222, 14.8.1978, p 11. Directive as last amended by Directive 94/8/EC (OJ L82, 25.3.1994, p 33).

ANNEX II
GUIDING PRINCIPLES (REFERRED TO IN THE FIFTH
SUBPARAGRAPH OF ARTICLE 7(1))

Where a branch applies to join a host Member State's scheme for supplementary cover, the host Member State's scheme will bilaterally establish with the home Member State's scheme appropriate rules and procedures for the payment of compensation to investors at that branch. The following principles will apply both to the drawing up of those procedures and in the framing of the membership conditions applicable to that branch (as referred to in Article 7(1)):

(a)   the host Member State's scheme will retain full rights to impose its objective and generally applied rules on participating investment firms; it will be able to require the provision of relevant information and be entitled to verify such information with the home Member State's competent authorities;

(b)   the host Member State's scheme will meet claims for supplementary compensation after it has been informed by the home Member State's competent authorities of the determination or ruling referred to in Article 2(2). The host Member State's scheme will retain full rights to verify an investor's entitlement according to its own standards and procedures before paying supplementary compensation;

(c)   the host Member State's and the home Member State's schemes will cooperate fully with each other to ensure that investors receive compensation promptly and in the correct amounts. In particular, they will agree on how the existence of a counterclaim which may give rise to set-off under either scheme will affect the compensation paid to the investor by each scheme;

(d)   the host Member State's scheme will be entitled to charge branches for supplementary cover on an appropriate basis which takes into account the cover funded by the home Member State's scheme. To facilitate charging, the host Member State's scheme will be entitled to assume that its liability will in all circumstances be limited to the excess of the cover it has offered over the cover offered by the home Member State regardless of whether the home Member State actually pays any compensation in respect of claims by investors within the host Member State's territory.

[5193]

DIRECTIVE OF THE EUROPEAN PARLIAMENT
AND OF THE COUNCIL

of 19 May 1998

on settlement finality in payment and securities settlement systems

(98/26/EC)

NOTES

Date of publication in OJ: OJ L166, 11.6.1998, p 45. Notes are as in the original OJ version.

As of 1 February 2009, this Directive had not been amended.

Proposed amendment of this Directive: see the Proposal for a Directive of the European Parliament and of the Council amending Directive 98/26/EC on settlement finality in payment and securities settlement systems and Directive 2002/47/EC on financial collateral arrangements as regards linked systems and credit claims.[1]

[1]   Brussels, 23.4.2008, COM(2008) 213 final. Available on the Europa website.

THE EUROPEAN PARLIAMENT AND THE COUNCIL OF THE EUROPEAN UNION,

Having regard to the Treaty establishing the European Community, and in particular Article 100a thereof,

Having regard to the proposal from the Commission,[1]

Having regard to the opinion of the European Monetary Institute,[2]

Having regard to the opinion of the Economic and Social Committee,[3]

Acting in accordance with the procedure laid down in Article 189b of the Treaty,[4]

(1) Whereas the Lamfalussy report of 1990 to the Governors of the central banks of the Group of Ten Countries demonstrated the important systemic risk inherent in payment systems which operate on the basis of several legal types of payment netting, in particular multilateral netting; whereas the reduction of legal risks associated with participation in real time gross settlement systems is of paramount importance, given the increasing development of these systems;

(2) Whereas it is also of the utmost importance to reduce the risk associated with participation in securities settlement systems, in particular where there is a close connection between such systems and payment systems;

(3) Whereas this Directive aims at contributing to the efficient and cost effective operation of cross-border payment and securities settlement arrangements in the Community, which reinforces the freedom of movement of capital in the internal market; whereas this Directive thereby follows up the progress made towards completion of the internal market, in particular towards the freedom to provide services and liberalisation of capital movements, with a view to the realisation of Economic and Monetary Union;

(4) Whereas it is desirable that the laws of the Member States should aim to minimise the disruption to a system caused by insolvency proceedings against a participant in that system;

(5) Whereas a proposal for a Directive on the reorganisation and winding-up of credit institutions submitted in 1985 and amended on 8 February 1988 is still pending before the Council; whereas the Convention on Insolvency Proceedings drawn up on 23 November 1995 by the Member States meeting within the Council explicitly excludes insurance undertakings, credit institutions and investment firms;

(6) Whereas this Directive is intended to cover payment and securities settlement systems of a domestic as well as of a cross-border nature; whereas the Directive is applicable to Community systems and to collateral security constituted by their participants, be they Community or third country participants, in connection with participation in these systems;

(7) Whereas Member States may apply the provisions of this Directive to their domestic institutions which participate directly in third country systems and to collateral security provided in connection with participation in such systems;

(8) Whereas Member States should be allowed to designate as a system covered by this Directive a system whose main activity is the settlement of securities even if the system to a limited extent also deals with commodity derivatives;

(9) Whereas the reduction of systemic risk requires in particular the finality of settlement and the enforceability of collateral security; whereas collateral security is meant to comprise all means provided by a participant to the other participants in the payment and/or securities settlement systems to secure rights and obligations in connection with that system, including repurchase agreements, statutory liens and fiduciary transfers; whereas regulation in national law of the kind of collateral security which can be used should not be affected by the definition of collateral security in this Directive;

(10) Whereas this Directive, by covering collateral security provided in connection with operations of the central banks of the Member States functioning as central banks, including monetary policy operations, assists the European Monetary Institute in its task of promoting the efficiency of cross-border payments with a view to the preparation of the third stage of Economic and Monetary Union and thereby contributes to developing the necessary legal framework in which the future European central bank may develop its policy;

(11) Whereas transfer orders and their netting should be legally enforceable under all Member States' jurisdictions and binding on third parties;

(12) Whereas rules on finality of netting should not prevent systems testing, before the netting takes place, whether orders that have entered the system comply with the rules of that system and allow the settlement of that system to take place;

(13) Whereas nothing in this Directive should prevent a participant or a third party from exercising any right or claim resulting from the underlying transaction which they may have in law to recovery or restitution in respect of a transfer order which has entered a system, eg in case of fraud or technical error, as long as this leads neither to the unwinding of netting nor to the revocation of the transfer order in the system;

(14) Whereas it is necessary to ensure that transfer orders cannot be revoked after a moment defined by the rules of the system;

(15) Whereas it is necessary that a Member State should immediately notify other Member States of the opening of insolvency proceedings against a participant in the system;

(16) Whereas insolvency proceedings should not have a retroactive effect on the rights and obligations of participants in a system;

(17) Whereas, in the event of insolvency proceedings against a participant in a system, this Directive furthermore aims at determining which insolvency law is applicable to the rights and obligations of that participant in connection with its participation in a system;

(18) Whereas collateral security should be insulated from the effects of the insolvency law applicable to the insolvent participant;

(19) Whereas the provisions of Article 9(2) should only apply to a register, account or centralized deposit system which evidences the existence of proprietary rights in or for the delivery or transfer of the securities concerned;

(20) Whereas the provisions of Article 9(2) are intended to ensure that if the participant, the central bank of a Member State or the future European central bank has a valid and effective collateral security as determined under the law of the Member State where the relevant register, account or centralized deposit system is located, then the validity and enforceability of that collateral security as against that system (and the operator thereof) and against any other person claiming directly or indirectly through it, should be determined solely under the law of that Member State;

(21) Whereas the provisions of Article 9(2) are not intended to prejudice the operation and effect of the law of the Member State under which the securities are constituted or of the law of the Member State where the securities may otherwise be located (including, without limitation, the law concerning the creation, ownership or transfer of such securities or of rights in such securities) and should not be interpreted to mean that any such collateral security will be directly enforceable or be capable of being recognised in any such Member State otherwise than in accordance with the law of that Member State;

(22) Whereas it is desirable that Member States endeavour to establish sufficient links between all the securities settlement systems covered by this Directive with a view towards promoting maximum transparency and legal certainty of transactions relating to securities;

(23) Whereas the adoption of this Directive constitutes the most appropriate way of realising the abovementioned objectives and does not go beyond what is necessary to achieve them,

[5194]

NOTES

¹   OJ C207, 18.7.1996, p 13, and OJ C259, 26.8.1997, p 6.
²   Opinion delivered on 21 November 1996.
³   OJ C56, 24.2.1997, p 1.
⁴   Opinion of the European Parliament of 9 April 1997 (OJ C132, 28.4.1997, p 74), Council Common Position of 13 October 1997 (OJ C375, 10.12.1997, p 34) and Decision of the European Parliament of 29 January 1998 (OJ C56, 23.2.1998). Council Decision of 27 April 1998.

HAVE ADOPTED THIS DIRECTIVE—

SECTION I
SCOPE AND DEFINITIONS

Article 1

The provisions of this Directive shall apply to:
  (a)   any system as defined in Article 2(a), governed by the law of a Member State and operating in any currency, the ecu or in various currencies which the system converts one against another;
  (b)   any participant in such a system;
  (c)   collateral security provided in connection with:
      —   participation in a system, or
      —   operations of the central banks of the Member States in their functions as central banks.

[5194A]

Article 2

For the purpose of this Directive:
  (a)   'system' shall mean a formal arrangement:
      —   between three or more participants, without counting a possible settlement agent, a possible central counterparty, a possible clearing house or a possible indirect participant, with common rules and standardised arrangements for the execution of transfer orders between the participants,
      —   governed by the law of a Member State chosen by the participants; the participants may, however, only choose the law of a Member State in which at least one of them has its head office, and
      —   designated, without prejudice to other more stringent conditions of general application laid down by national law, as a system and notified to the Commission

by the Member State whose law is applicable, after that Member State is satisfied as to the adequacy of the rules of the system.

Subject to the conditions in the first subparagraph, a Member State may designate as a system such a formal arrangement whose business consists of the execution of transfer orders as defined in the second indent of (i) and which to a limited extent executes orders relating to other financial instruments, when that Member State considers that such a designation is warranted on grounds of systemic risk.

A Member State may also on a case-by-case basis designate as a system such a formal arrangement between two participants, without counting a possible settlement agent, a possible central counterparty, a possible clearing house or a possible indirect participant, when that Member State considers that such a designation is warranted on grounds of systemic risk;

(b) 'institution' shall mean:
  — a credit institution as defined in the first indent of Article 1 of Directive 77/780/EEC[1] including the institutions set out in the list in Article 2(2) thereof, or
  — an investment firm as defined in point 2 of Article 1 of Directive 93/22/EEC[2] excluding the institutions set out in the list in Article 2(2)(a) to (k) thereof, or
  — public authorities and publicly guaranteed undertakings, or
  — any undertaking whose head office is outside the Community and whose functions correspond to those of the Community credit institutions or investment firms as defined in the first and second indent,

which participates in a system and which is responsible for discharging the financial obligations arising from transfer orders within that system.

If a system is supervised in accordance with national legislation and only executes transfer orders as defined in the second indent of (i), as well as payments resulting from such orders, a Member State may decide that undertakings which participate in such a system and which have responsibility for discharging the financial obligations arising from transfer orders within this system, can be considered institutions, provided that at least three participants of this system are covered by the categories referred to in the first subparagraph and that such a decision is warranted on grounds of systemic risk;

(c) 'central counterparty' shall mean an entity which is interposed between the institutions in a system and which acts as the exclusive counterparty of these institutions with regard to their transfer orders;

(d) 'settlement agent' shall mean an entity providing to institutions and/or a central counterparty participating in systems, settlement accounts through which transfer orders within such systems are settled and, as the case may be, extending credit to those institutions and/or central counterparties for settlement purposes;

(e) 'clearing house' shall mean an entity responsible for the calculation of the net positions of institutions, a possible central counterparty and/or a possible settlement agent;

(f) 'participant' shall mean an institution, a central counterparty, a settlement agent or a clearing house.

According to the rules of the system, the same participant may act as a central counterparty, a settlement agent or a clearing house or carry out part or all of these tasks.

A Member State may decide that for the purposes of this Directive an indirect participant may be considered a participant if it is warranted on the grounds of systemic risk and on condition that the indirect participant is known to the system;

(g) 'indirect participant' shall mean a credit institution as defined in the first indent of (b) with a contractual relationship with an institution participating in a system executing transfer orders as defined in the first indent of (i) which enables the abovementioned credit institution to pass transfer orders through the system;

(h) 'securities' shall mean all instruments referred to in section B of the Annex to Directive 93/22/EEC;

(i) 'transfer order' shall mean:
  — any instruction by a participant to place at the disposal of a recipient an amount of money by means of a book entry on the accounts of a credit institution, a central bank or a settlement agent, or any instruction which results in the assumption or discharge of a payment obligation as defined by the rules of the system, or
  — an instruction by a participant to transfer the title to, or interest in, a security or securities by means of a book entry on a register, or otherwise;

(j) 'insolvency proceedings' shall mean any collective measure provided for in the law of a Member State, or a third country, either to wind up the participant or to reorganise it, where such measure involves the suspending of, or imposing limitations on, transfers or payments;

(k) 'netting' shall mean the conversion into one net claim or one net obligation of claims and obligations resulting from transfer orders which a participant or participants either issue to, or receive from, one or more other participants with the result that only a net claim can be demanded or a net obligation be owed;

(l) 'settlement account' shall mean an account at a central bank, a settlement agent or a central counterparty used to hold funds and securities and to settle transactions between participants in a system;

(m) 'collateral security' shall mean all realisable assets provided under a pledge (including money provided under a pledge), a repurchase or similar agreement, or otherwise, for the purpose of securing rights and obligations potentially arising in connection with a system, or provided to central banks of the Member States or to the future European central bank.

[5195]

NOTES

¹ First Council Directive 77/780/EEC of 12 December 1977 on the coordination of the laws, regulations and administrative provisions relating to the taking up and pursuit of the business of credit institutions (OJ L322, 17.12.1977, p 30). Directive as last amended by Directive 96/13/EC (OJ L66, 16.3.1996, p 15).
² Council Directive 93/22/EEC of 10 May 1993 on investment services in the securities field (OJ L141, 11.6.1993, p 27). Directive as last amended by Directive 97/9/EC (OJ L84, 26.3.1997, p 22).

SECTION II
NETTING AND TRANSFER ORDERS

Article 3

1. Transfer orders and netting shall be legally enforceable and, even in the event of insolvency proceedings against a participant, shall be binding on third parties, provided that transfer orders were entered into a system before the moment of opening of such insolvency proceedings as defined in Article 6(1).

Where, exceptionally, transfer orders are entered into a system after the moment of opening of insolvency proceedings and are carried out on the day of opening of such proceedings, they shall be legally enforceable and binding on third parties only if, after the time of settlement, the settlement agent, the central counterparty or the clearing house can prove that they were not aware, nor should have been aware, of the opening of such proceedings.

2. No law, regulation, rule or practice on the setting aside of contracts and transactions concluded before the moment of opening of insolvency proceedings, as defined in Article 6(1) shall lead to the unwinding of a netting.

3. The moment of entry of a transfer order into a system shall be defined by the rules of that system. If there are conditions laid down in the national law governing the system as to the moment of entry, the rules of that system must be in accordance with such conditions.

[5196]

Article 4

Member States may provide that the opening of insolvency proceedings against a participant shall not prevent funds or securities available on the settlement account of that participant from being used to fulfil that participant's obligations in the system on the day of the opening of the insolvency proceedings. Furthermore, Member States may also provide that such a participant's credit facility connected to the system be used against available, existing collateral security to fulfil that participant's obligations in the system.

[5197]

Article 5

A transfer order may not be revoked by a participant in a system, nor by a third party, from the moment defined by the rules of that system.

[5198]

SECTION III
PROVISIONS CONCERNING INSOLVENCY PROCEEDINGS

Article 6

1. For the purpose of this Directive, the moment of opening of insolvency proceedings shall be the moment when the relevant judicial or administrative authority handed down its decision.

2. When a decision has been taken in accordance with paragraph 1, the relevant judicial or administrative authority shall immediately notify that decision to the appropriate authority chosen by its Member State.

3. The Member State referred to in paragraph 2 shall immediately notify other Member States.

[5199]

Article 7

Insolvency proceedings shall not have retroactive effects on the rights and obligations of a participant arising from, or in connection with, its participation in a system earlier than the moment of opening of such proceedings as defined in Article 6(1).

[5200]

Article 8

In the event of insolvency proceedings being opened against a participant in a system, the rights and obligations arising from, or in connection with, the participation of that participant shall be determined by the law governing that system.

[5201]

SECTION IV
INSULATION OF THE RIGHTS OF HOLDERS OF COLLATERAL SECURITY FROM THE EFFECTS OF THE INSOLVENCY OF THE PROVIDER

Article 9

1. The rights of:
   —   a participant to collateral security provided to it in connection with a system, and
   —   central banks of the Member States or the future European central bank to collateral security provided to them,

shall not be affected by insolvency proceedings against the participant or counterparty to central banks of the Member States or the future European central bank which provided the collateral security. Such collateral security may be realised for the satisfaction of these rights.

2.   Where securities (including rights in securities) are provided as collateral security to participants and/or central banks of the Member States or the future European central bank as described in paragraph 1, and their right (or that of any nominee, agent or third party acting on their behalf) with respect to the securities is legally recorded on a register, account or centralised deposit system located in a Member State, the determination of the rights of such entities as holders of collateral security in relation to those securities shall be governed by the law of that Member State.

[5202]

SECTION V
FINAL PROVISIONS

Article 10

Member States shall specify the systems which are to be included in the scope of this Directive and shall notify them to the Commission and inform the Commission of the authorities they have chosen in accordance with Article 6(2).

The system shall indicate to the Member State whose law is applicable the participants in the system, including any possible indirect participants, as well as any change in them.

In addition to the indication provided for in the second subparagraph, Member States may impose supervision or authorisation requirements on systems which fall under their jurisdiction.

Anyone with a legitimate interest may require an institution to inform him of the systems in which it participates and to provide information about the main rules governing the functioning of those systems.

[5203]

Article 11

1.   Member States shall bring into force the laws, regulations and administrative provisions necessary to comply with this Directive before 11 December 1999. They shall forthwith inform the Commission thereof.

When Member States adopt these measures, they shall contain a reference to this Directive or shall be accompanied by such reference on the occasion of their official publication. The methods of making such a reference shall be laid down by the Member States.

2.   Member States shall communicate to the Commission the text of the provisions of domestic law which they adopt in the field governed by this Directive. In this Communication, Member States shall provide a table of correspondence showing the national provisions which exist or are introduced in respect of each Article of this Directive.

[5204]

PART IV
EC MATERIALS

Article 12

No later than three years after the date mentioned in Article 11(1), the Commission shall present a report to the European Parliament and the Council on the application of this Directive, accompanied where appropriate by proposals for its revision.

[5205]

Article 13

This Directive shall enter into force on the day of its publication in the Official Journal of the European Communities.

[5206]

Article 14

This Directive is addressed to the Member States.

[5207]

DIRECTIVE OF THE EUROPEAN PARLIAMENT AND OF THE COUNCIL

of 20 March 2000

relating to the taking up and pursuit of the business of credit institutions (Note)

(2000/12/EC)

NOTES

Date of publication in OJ: OJ L126, 26.5.2000, p 1.

Due to the large number of amendments made to this Directive it has been recast. It is repealed and replaced by European Parliament and Council Directive 2006/48/EC relating to the taking up and pursuit of the business of credit institutions (recast) (at **[5784]**). See, in particular, recital (1) of Directive 2006/48/EC which provides that it also contains new provisions. As to the repeal of this Directive, see Art 158 of the 2006 Directive at **[5841]**, and as to the entry into force of 2006/48/EC (on 20 July 2006), see Art 159 at **[5842]**.

[5208]–[5249]

DIRECTIVE OF THE EUROPEAN PARLIAMENT AND OF THE COUNCIL

of 18 September 2000

on the taking up, pursuit of and prudential supervision of the business of electronic money institutions

(2000/46/EC)

NOTES

Date of publication in OJ: L275, 27.10.2000, p 39. Notes are as in the original OJ version.

As of 1 February 2009, this Directive had not been amended (but see below).

Proposed repeal of this Directive: see the 2008 Proposal for a Directive of the European Parliament and of the Council on the taking up, pursuit and prudential supervision of the business of electronic money institutions, amending Directives 2005/60/EC and 2006/48/EC and repealing Directive 2000/46/EC.[1]

[1]   Brussels, 9.10.2008, COM(2008) 627 final. Available on the Europa website.

THE EUROPEAN PARLIAMENT AND THE COUNCIL OF THE EUROPEAN UNION,

Having regard to the Treaty establishing the European Community, and in particular the first and third sentences of Article 47(2) thereof,

Having regard to the proposal from the Commission,[1]

Having regard to the opinion of the Economic and Social Committee,[2]

Having regard to the opinion of the European Central Bank,[3]

Acting in accordance with the procedure laid down in Article 251 of the Treaty,[4]

Whereas—

(1)   Credit institutions within the meaning of Article 1, point 1, first subparagraph (b) of Directive 2000/12/EC[5] are limited in the scope of their activities.

(2) It is necessary to take account of the specific characteristics of these institutions and to provide the appropriate measures necessary to coordinate and harmonise Member States' laws, regulations and administrative provisions relating to the taking up, pursuit and prudential supervision of the business of electronic money institutions.

(3) For the purposes of this Directive, electronic money can be considered an electronic surrogate for coins and banknotes, which is stored on an electronic device such as a chip card or computer memory and which is generally intended for the purpose of effecting electronic payments of limited amounts.

(4) The approach adopted is appropriate to achieve only the essential harmonisation necessary and sufficient to secure the mutual recognition of authorisation and prudential supervision of electronic money institutions, making possible the granting of a single licence recognised throughout the Community and designed to ensure bearer confidence and the application of the principle of home Member State prudential supervision.

(5) Within the wider context of the rapidly evolving electronic commerce it is desirable to provide a regulatory framework that assists electronic money in delivering its full potential benefits and that avoids hampering technological innovation in particular. Therefore, this Directive introduces a technology-neutral legal framework that harmonises the prudential supervision of electronic money institutions to the extent necessary for ensuring their sound and prudent operation and their financial integrity in particular.

(6) Credit institutions, by virtue of point 5 of Annex I to Directive 2000/12/EC, are already allowed to issue and administer means of payment including electronic money and to carry on such activities Community-wide subject to mutual recognition and to the comprehensive prudential supervisory system applying to them in accordance with the European banking Directives.

(7) The introduction of a separate prudential supervisory regime for electronic money institutions, which, although calibrated on the prudential supervisory regime applying to other credit institutions and Directive 2000/12/EC except Title V, Chapters 2 and 3 thereof in particular, differs from that regime, is justified and desirable because the issuance of electronic money does not constitute in itself, in view of its specific character as an electronic surrogate for coins and banknotes, a deposit-taking activity pursuant to Article 3 of Directive 2000/12/EC, if the received funds are immediately exchanged for electronic money.

(8) The receipt of funds from the public in exchange for electronic money, which results in a credit balance left on account with the issuing institution, constitutes the receipt of deposits or other repayable funds for the purpose of Directive 2000/12/EC.

(9) It is necessary for electronic money to be redeemable to ensure bearer confidence. Redeemability does not imply, in itself, that the funds received in exchange for electronic money shall be regarded as deposits or other repayable funds for the purpose of Directive 2000/12/EC.

(10) Redeemability should always be understood to be at par value.

(11) In order to respond to the specific risks associated with the issuance of electronic money this prudential supervisory regime must be more targeted and, accordingly, less cumbersome than the prudential supervisory regime applying to credit institutions, notably as regards reduced initial capital requirements and the non-application of Directive 93/6/EEC[6] and Title V, Chapter 2, Sections II and III of Directive 2000/12/EC.

(12) However, it is necessary to preserve a level playing field between electronic money institutions and other credit institutions issuing electronic money and, thus, to ensure fair competition among a wider range of institutions to the benefit of bearers. This is achieved since the abovementioned less cumbersome features of the prudential supervisory regime applying to electronic money institutions are balanced by provisions that are more stringent than those applying to other credit institutions, notably as regards restrictions on the business activities which electronic money institutions may carry on and, particularly, prudent limitations of their investments aimed at ensuring that their financial liabilities related to outstanding electronic money are backed at all times by sufficiently liquid low risk assets.

(13) Pending the harmonisation of prudential supervision of outsourced activities for credit institutions it is appropriate that electronic money institutions have sound and prudent management and control procedures. With a view to the possibility of operational and other ancillary functions related to the issuance of electronic money being performed by undertakings which are not subject to prudential supervision it is essential that electronic money institutions have in place internal structures which should respond to the financial and non-financial risks to which they are exposed.

(14) The issuance of electronic money may affect the stability of the financial system and the smooth operation of payments systems. Close cooperation in assessing the integrity of electronic money schemes is called for.

(15) It is appropriate to afford competent authorities the possibility of waiving some or all of the requirements imposed by this Directive for electronic money institutions which operate only within the territories of the respective Member States.

(16) Adoption of this Directive constitutes the most appropriate means of achieving the desired objectives. This Directive is limited to the minimum necessary to achieve these objectives and does not go beyond what is necessary for this purpose.

(17)   Provision should be made for the review of this Directive in the light of experience of developments in the market and the protection of bearers of electronic money.

(18)   The Banking Advisory Committee has been consulted on the adoption of this Directive,

[5250]

NOTES

1   OJ C317, 15.10.1998, p 7.
2   OJ C101, 12.4.1999, p 64.
3   OJ C189, 6.7.1999, p 7.
4   Opinion of the European Parliament of 15 April 1999 (OJ C219, 30.7.1999, p 415), confirmed on 27 October 1999, Council Common Position of 29 November 1999 (OJ C26, 28.1.2000, p 1) and Decision of the European Parliament of 11 April 2000 (not yet published in the Official Journal). Decision of the Council of 16 June 2000.
5   Directive 2000/12/EC of the European Parliament and of the Council of 20 March 2000 relating to the taking up and pursuit of the business of credit institutions (OJ L126, 26.5.2000, p 1). Directive as last amended by Directive 2000/28/EC (see page 37 of this Official Journal).
6   Council Directive 93/6/EEC of 15 March 1993 on the capital adequacy of investment firms and credit institutions (OJ L141, 11.6.1993, p 1). Directive as last amended by Directive 98/33/EC (OJ L204, 21.7.1998, p 29).

HAVE ADOPTED THIS DIRECTIVE—

Article 1
Scope, definitions and restriction of activities

1.   This Directive shall apply to electronic money institutions.

2.   It shall not apply to the institutions referred to in Article 2(3) of Directive 2000/12/EC.

3.   For the purposes of this Directive—
   (a)   "electronic money institution" shall mean an undertaking or any other legal person, other than a credit institution as defined in Article 1, point 1, first subparagraph (a) of Directive 2000/12/EC which issues means of payment in the form of electronic money;
   (b)   "electronic money" shall mean monetary value as represented by a claim on the issuer which is—
      (i)   stored on an electronic device;
      (ii)   issued on receipt of funds of an amount not less in value than the monetary value issued;
      (iii)   accepted as means of payment by undertakings other than the issuer.

4.   Member States shall prohibit persons or undertakings that are not credit institutions, as defined in Article 1, point 1, first subparagraph of Directive 2000/12/EC, from carrying on the business of issuing electronic money.

5.   The business activities of electronic money institutions other than the issuing of electronic money shall be restricted to—
   (a)   the provision of closely related financial and non-financial services such as the administering of electronic money by the performance of operational and other ancillary functions related to its issuance, and the issuing and administering of other means of payment but excluding the granting of any form of credit; and
   (b)   the storing of data on the electronic device on behalf of other undertakings or public institutions.

Electronic money institutions shall not have any holdings in other undertakings except where these undertakings perform operational or other ancillary functions related to electronic money issued or distributed by the institution concerned.

[5250A]

Article 2
Application of Banking Directives

1.   Save where otherwise expressly provided for, only references to credit institutions in Directive 91/308/EEC[1] and Directive 2000/12/EC except Title V, Chapter 2 thereof shall apply to electronic money institutions.

2.   Articles 5, 11, 13, 19, 20(7), 51 and 59 of Directive 2000/12/EC shall not apply. The mutual recognition arrangements provided for in Directive 2000/12/EC shall not apply to electronic money institutions' business activities other than the issuance of electronic money.

3.   The receipt of funds within the meaning of Article 1(3)(b)(ii) does not constitute a deposit or other repayable funds according to Article 3 of Directive 2000/12/EC, if the funds received are immediately exchanged for electronic money.

[5251]

NOTES

1   Council Directive 91/308/EEC of 10 June 1991 on prevention of the use of the financial system for the purpose of money laundering (OJ L166, 28.6.1991, p 77).

Article 3
Redeemability

1.   A bearer of electronic money may, during the period of validity, ask the issuer to redeem it at par value in coins and bank notes or by a transfer to an account free of charges other than those strictly necessary to carry out that operation.

2.   The contract between the issuer and the bearer shall clearly state the conditions of redemption.

3.   The contract may stipulate a minimum threshold for redemption. The threshold may not exceed EUR 10.

[5252]

Article 4
Initial capital and ongoing own funds requirements

1.   Electronic money institutions shall have an initial capital, as defined in Article 34(2), subparagraphs (1) and (2) of Directive 2000/12/EC, of not less than EUR 1 million. Notwithstanding paragraphs 2 and 3, their own funds, as defined in Directive 2000/12/EC, shall not fall below that amount.

2.   Electronic money institutions shall have at all times own funds which are equal to or above 2% of the higher of the current amount or the average of the preceding six months' total amount of their financial liabilities related to outstanding electronic money.

3.   Where an electronic money institution has not completed a six months' period of business, including the day it starts up, it shall have own funds which are equal to or above 2% of the higher of the current amount or the six months' target total amount of its financial liabilities related to outstanding electronic money. The six months' target total amount of the institution's financial liabilities related to outstanding electronic money shall be evidenced by its business plan subject to any adjustment to that plan having been required by the competent authorities.

[5253]

Article 5
Limitations of investments

1.   Electronic money institutions shall have investments of an amount of no less than their financial liabilities related to outstanding electronic money in the following assets only—
    (a)   asset items which according to Article 43(1)(a) (1), (2), (3) and (4) and Article 44(1) of Directive 2000/12/EC attract a zero credit risk weighting and which are sufficiently liquid;
    (b)   sight deposits held with Zone A credit institutions as defined in Directive 2000/12/EC; and
    (c)   debt instruments which are—
       (i)   sufficiently liquid;
       (ii)   not covered by paragraph 1(a);
       (iii)   recognised by competent authorities as qualifying items within the meaning of Article 2(12) of Directive 93/6/EEC; and
       (iv)   issued by undertakings other than undertakings which have a qualifying holding, as defined in Article 1 of Directive 2000/12/EC, in the electronic money institution concerned or which must be included in those undertakings' consolidated accounts.

2.   Investments referred to in paragraph 1(b) and (c) may not exceed 20 times the own funds of the electronic money institution concerned and shall be subject to limitations which are at least as stringent as those applying to credit institutions in accordance with Title V, Chapter 2, Section III of Directive 2000/12/EC.

3.   For the purpose of hedging market risks arising from the issuance of electronic money and from the investments referred to in paragraph 1, electronic money institutions may use sufficiently liquid interest-rate and foreign-exchange-related off balance-sheet items in the form of exchange-traded (ie not OTC) derivative instruments where they are subject to daily margin requirements or foreign exchange contracts with an original maturity of 14 calendar days or less. The use of derivative instruments according to the first sentence is permissible only if the full elimination of market risks is intended and, to the extent possible, achieved.

4.   Member States shall impose appropriate limitations on the market risks electronic money institutions may incur from the investments referred to in paragraph 1.

PART IV
EC MATERIALS

5.   For the purpose of applying paragraph 1, assets shall be valued at the lower of cost or market value.

6.   If the value of the assets referred to in paragraph 1 falls below the amount of financial liabilities related to outstanding electronic money, the competent authorities shall ensure that the electronic money institution in question takes appropriate measures to remedy that situation promptly. To this end, and for a temporary period only, the competent authorities may allow the institution's financial liabilities related to outstanding electronic money to be backed by assets other than those referred to in paragraph 1 up to a amount not exceeding the lower of 5% of these liabilities or the institution's total amount of own funds.

[5254]

Article 6
Verification of specific requirements by the competent authorities

The competent authorities shall ensure that the calculations justifying compliance with Articles 4 and 5 are made, not less than twice each year, either by electronic money institutions themselves, which shall communicate them, and any component data required, to the competent authorities, or by competent authorities, using data supplied by the electronic money institutions.

[5255]

Article 7
Sound and prudent operation

Electronic money institutions shall have sound and prudent management, administrative and accounting procedures and adequate internal control mechanisms. These should respond to the financial and non-financial risks to which the institution is exposed including technical and procedural risks as well as risks connected to its cooperation with any undertaking performing operational or other ancillary functions related to its business activities.

[5256]

Article 8
Waiver

1.   Member States may allow their competent authorities to waive the application of some or all of the provisions of this Directive and the application of Directive 2000/12/EC to electronic money institutions in cases where either—

(a)   the total business activities of the type referred to in Article 1(3)(a) of this Directive of the institution generate a total amount of financial liabilities related to outstanding electronic money that normally does not exceed EUR 5 million and never exceeds EUR 6 million; or

(b)   the electronic money issued by the institution is accepted as a means of payment only by any subsidiaries of the institution which perform operational or other ancillary functions related to electronic money issued or distributed by the institution, any parent undertaking of the institution or any other subsidiaries of that parent undertaking; or

(c)   electronic money issued by the institution is accepted as payment only by a limited number of undertakings, which can be clearly distinguished by—

    (i)   their location in the same premises or other limited local area; or

    (ii)   their close financial or business relationship with the issuing institution, such as a common marketing or distribution scheme.

The underlying contractual arrangements must provide that the electronic storage device at the disposal of bearers for the purpose of making payments is subject to a maximum storage amount of not more than EUR 150.

2.   An electronic money institution for which a waiver has been granted under paragraph 1 shall not benefit from the mutual recognition arrangements provided for in Directive 2000/12/EC.

3.   Member States shall require that all electronic money institutions to which the application of this Directive and Directive 2000/12/EC has been waived report periodically on their activities including the total amount of financial liabilities related to electronic money.

[5257]

Article 9
Grandfathering

Electronic money institutions subject to this Directive which have commenced their activity in accordance with the provisions in force in the Member State in which they have their head office before the date of entry into force of the provisions adopted in implementation of this Directive or the date referred to in Article 10(1), whichever date is earlier, shall be presumed to be authorised. The Member States shall oblige such electronic money institutions to submit all relevant information to the competent authorities in order to allow them to assess within six months from the date of entry into force of the provisions adopted in implementation of this Directive, whether the institutions comply with the requirements pursuant to this Directive, which measures need to be taken in order to ensure compliance, or whether a withdrawal of authorisation is appropriate. If compliance is not ensured within six months from the date referred to in Article 10(1), the electronic money institution shall not benefit from mutual recognition after that time.

[5258]

Article 10
Implementation

1. Member States shall bring into force the laws, regulations and administrative provisions necessary to comply with this Directive not later than 27 April 2002. They shall immediately inform the Commission thereof.

When Member States adopt these measures, they shall contain a reference to this Directive or shall be accompanied by such reference on the occasion of their official publication. The methods of making such a reference shall be laid down by the Member States.

2. Member States shall communicate to the Commission the text of the main provisions of national law, which they adopt in the field covered by this Directive.

[5259]

Article 11
Review

Not later than 27 April 2005 the Commission shall present a report to the European Parliament and the Council on the application of this Directive, in particular on—
— the measures to protect the bearers of electronic money, including the possible need to introduce a guarantee scheme,
— capital requirements,
— waivers, and
— the possible need to prohibit interest being paid on funds received in exchange for electronic money,
accompanied where appropriate by a proposal for its revision.

[5260]

Article 12
Entry into force

This Directive shall enter into force on the day of its publication in the *Official Journal of the European Communities*.

[5261]

Article 13

This Directive is addressed to the Member States.

[5262]

DIRECTIVE OF THE EUROPEAN PARLIAMENT
AND OF THE COUNCIL

of 28 May 2001

on the admission of securities to official stock exchange listing and on information to be published on those securities

(2001/34/EC)

NOTES
Date of publication in OJ: OJ L184, 6.7.2001, p 1. Notes are as in the original OJ version.
This Directive is reproduced as amended by: European Parliament and Council Directive 2003/6/EC (OJ L96, 12.4.2003, p 16); European Parliament and Council Directive 2003/71/EC (OJ L345, 31.12.2003, p 64); European Parliament and Council Directive 2004/109/EC (OJ L390, 31.12.2004, p 38); European Parliament and Council Directive 2005/1/EC (OJ L79, 24.3.2005, p 9).

THE EUROPEAN PARLIAMENT AND THE COUNCIL OF THE EUROPEAN UNION,
Having regard to the Treaty establishing the European Economic Community, and in particular Articles 44 and 95 thereof,
Having regard to the proposal from the Commission,
Having regard to the Opinion of the Economic and Social Committee,[1]
Acting in accordance with the procedure laid down in Article 251 of the Treaty,[2]
Whereas—

(1) Council Directive 79/279/EEC of 5 March 1979 coordinating the conditions for the admission of securities to official stock exchange listing,[3] Council Directive 80/390/EEC of 17 March 1980 coordinating the requirements for the drawing up, scrutiny and distribution of the listing particulars to be published for the admission of securities to official stock exchange listing,[4] Council Directive 82/121/EEC of 15 February 1982 on information to be published on a regular basis by companies the shares of which have been admitted to official stock-exchange listing[5] and Council Directive 88/627/EEC of 12 December 1988 on the information to be published when a major holding in a listed company is acquired or disposed of[6] have been substantially amended several times. In the interests of clarity and rationality, the said Directives should therefore be codified by grouping them together in a single text.

(2) The coordination of the conditions for the admission of securities to official listing on stock exchanges situated or operating in the Member States is likely to provide equivalent protection for investors at Community level, because of the more uniform guarantees offered to investors in the various Member States, it will facilitate both the admission to official stock exchange listing, in each such State, of securities from other Member States and the listing of any given security on a number of stock exchanges in the Community; it will accordingly make for greater interpenetration of national securities markets by removing those obstacles that may prudently be removed and therefore contribute to the prospect of establishing a European capital market.

(3) Such coordination must therefore apply to securities, independently of the legal status of their issuers, and must therefore also apply to securities issued by non-member States or their regional or local authorities or international public bodies; this Directive therefore covers entities not covered by the second paragraph of Article 48 of the Treaty.

(4) There should be the possibility of a right to apply to the courts against decisions by the competent national authorities in respect of the application of this Directive, concerning the admission of securities to official listing, although such right to apply must not be allowed to restrict the discretion of these authorities.

(5) Initially, this coordination of the conditions for admission of securities to official listing should be sufficiently flexible to enable account to be taken of present differences in the structures of securities markets in the Member States and to enable the Member States to take account of any specific situations with which they may be confronted.

(6) For this reason, coordination should first be limited to the establishment of minimum conditions for the admission of securities to official listing on stock exchanges situated or operating in the Member States, without however giving issuers any right to listing.

(7) This partial coordination of the conditions for admission to official listing constitutes a first step towards subsequent closer alignment of the rules of Member States in this field.

(8) The market in which undertakings operate has been enlarged to embrace the whole Community and this enlargement involves a corresponding increase in their financial requirements and extension of the capital markets on which they must call to satisfy them; admission to official listing on stock exchanges of Member States of securities issued by undertakings constitutes an important means of access to these capital markets; furthermore exchange restrictions on the purchase of securities traded on the stock exchanges of another Member State have been eliminated as part of the liberalisation of capital movements.

(9) Safeguards for the protection of the interests of actual and potential investors are required in most Member States of undertakings offering their securities to the public, either at the time of their offer or of their admission to official stock exchange listing; such safeguards require the provision of information which is sufficient and as objective as possible concerning the financial circumstances of the issuer and particulars of the securities for which admission to official listing is requested; the form under which this information is required usually consists of the publication of listing particulars.

(10) The safeguards required differ from Member State to Member State, both as regards the contents and the layout of the listing particulars and the efficacy, methods and timing of the check on the information given therein; the effect of these differences is not only to make it more difficult for undertakings to obtain admission of securities to official listing on stock exchanges of several Member States but also to hinder the acquisition by investors residing in one Member State of securities listed on stock exchanges of other Member States and thus to inhibit the financing of the undertakings and investment throughout the Community.

(11) These differences should be eliminated by coordinating the rules and regulations without necessarily making them completely uniform, in order to achieve an adequate degree of equivalence in the safeguards required in each Member State to ensure the provision of information which is sufficient and as objective as possible for actual or potential security holders.

(12) Such coordination must apply to securities independently of the legal status of the issuing undertaking; this Directive applies to entities to which no reference is made in the second paragraph of Article 48 of the Treaty.

(13) Mutual recognition of listing particulars to be published for the admission of securities to official listing represents an important step forward in the creation of the Community's internal market.

(14) In this connection, it is necessary to specify which authorities are competent to check and approve listing particulars to be published for the admission of securities to official listing in the event of simultaneous applications for admission to official listing in two or more Member States.

(15) Article 21 of Council Directive 89/298/EEC of 17 April 1989 coordinating the requirements for the drawing-up, scrutiny and distribution of the prospectus to be published when transferable securities are offered to the public[7] provides that where public offers are made simultaneously or within short intervals of one another in two or more Member States, a public-offer prospectus drawn up and approved in accordance with Article 7, 8 or 12 of that Directive must be recognised as a public-offer prospectus in the other Member States concerned on the basis of mutual recognition.

(16) It is also desirable to provide the recognition of a public-offer prospectus as listing particulars where admission to official stock-exchange listing is requested within a short period of the public offer.

(17) The mutual recognition of a public-offer prospectus and admission to official listings does not in itself confer a right to admissions.

(18) It is advisable to provide for the extension, by means of agreements to be concluded by the Community with non-member countries, of the recognition of listing particulars for admission to official listings from those countries on a reciprocal basis.

(19) It seems appropriate to provide for the possibility for the Member State in which admission to official listing is sought in certain cases to grant partial or complete exemption from the obligation to publish listing particulars for admission to official listings to issuers the securities of which have already been admitted to official stock-exchange listing in another Member State.

(20) Companies which have already been listed in the Community for some time and are of high quality and international standing are the most likely candidates for cross-border listing. Those companies are generally well known in most Member States: information concerning them is widely circulated and available.

(21) The aim of this Directive is to ensure that sufficient information is provided for investors; therefore, when such a company seeks to have its securities admitted to listing in a host Member State, investors operating on the market in that country may be sufficiently protected by receiving only simplified information rather than full listing particulars.

(22) Member States may find it useful to establish non-discriminatory minimum quantitative criteria, such as the current equity market capitalisation, which issuers must fulfil to be eligible to benefit from the possibilities for exemption provided for in this Directive; given the increasing integration of securities markets, it should equally be open to the competent authorities to give smaller companies similar treatment.

(23) Furthermore, many stock exchanges have second-tier markets in order to deal in shares of companies not admitted to official listing; in some cases the second-tier markets are regulated and supervised by authorities recognised by public bodies that impose on companies disclosure requirements equivalent in substance to those imposed on officially listed companies; therefore, the principle underlying Article 23 of this Directive could also be applied when such companies seek to have their securities admitted to official listing.

(24) In order to protect investors the documents intended to be made available to the public must first be sent to the competent authorities in the Member State in which admission to official listing is sought; it is for that Member State to decide whether those documents should be scrutinised by its competent authorities and to determine, if necessary, the nature and the manner in which that scrutiny should be carried out.

(25) In the case of securities admitted to official stock-exchange listing, the protection of investors requires that the latter be supplied with appropriate regular information throughout the entire period during which the securities are listed; coordination of requirements for this regular information has similar objectives to those envisaged for the listing particulars, namely to improve such protection and to make it more equivalent, to facilitate the listing of these securities on more than one stock exchange in the Community, and in so doing to contribute towards the establishment of a genuine Community capital market by permitting a fuller inter-penetration of securities markets.

(26) Under this Directive, listed companies must as soon as possible make available to investors their annual accounts and report giving information on the company for the whole of the financial year; whereas the Fourth Council Directive 78/660/EEC[8] has coordinated the laws, regulations and administrative provisions of the Member States concerning the annual accounts of certain types of companies.

(27) Companies should also, at least once during each financial year, make available to investors reports on their activities; this Directive can, consequently, be confined to coordinating the content and distribution of a single report covering the first six months of the financial year.

(28) However, in the case of ordinary debentures, because of the rights they confer on their holders, the protection of investors by means of the publication of a half-yearly report is not essential; by virtue of this Directive, convertible or exchangeable debentures and debentures with warrants may be admitted to official listing only if the related shares are already listed on the same stock exchange or on another regulated, regularly operating, recognised open market or are so

admitted simultaneously; the Member States may derogate from this principle only if their competent authorities are satisfied that holders have at their disposal all the information necessary to form an opinion concerning the value of the shares to which these debentures relate; consequently, regular information needs to be coordinated only for companies whose shares are admitted to official stock-exchange listing.

(29) The half-yearly report must enable investors to make an informed appraisal of the general development of the company's activities during the period covered by the report; however, this report need contain only the essential details on the financial position and general progress of the business of the company in question.

(30) So as to ensure the effective protection of investors and the proper operation of stock exchanges, the rules relating to regular information to be published by companies, the shares of which are admitted to official stock-exchange listing within the Community, should apply not only to companies from Member States, but also to companies from non-member countries.

(31) A policy of adequate information of investors in the field of transferable securities is likely to improve investor protection, to increase investors' confidence in securities markets and thus to ensure that securities markets function correctly.

(32) By making such protection more equivalent, coordination of that policy at Community level is likely to make for greater inter-penetration of the Member States' transferable securities markets and therefore help to establish a true European capital market.

(33) To that end investors should be informed of major holdings and of changes in those holdings in Community companies the shares of which are officially listed on stock exchanges situated or operating within the Community.

(34) Coordinated rules should be laid down concerning the detailed content and the procedure for applying that requirement.

(35) Companies, the shares of which are officially listed on a Community stock exchange, can inform the public of changes in major holdings only if they have been informed of such changes by the holders of those holdings.

(36) Most Member States do not subject holders to such a requirement and where such a requirement exists there are appreciable differences in the procedures for applying it; coordinated rules should therefore be adopted at Community level in this field.

(37) This Directive should not affect the obligations of the Member States concerning the deadlines for transposition set out in Annex II, Part B,

[5263]

NOTES

1. OJ C116, 20.4.2001, p 69.
2. Opinion of the European Parliament of 14 March 2001 (not yet published in the Official Journal) and Council Decision of 7 May 2001.
3. OJ L66, 16.3.1979, p 21. Directive as last amended by Directive 88/627/EEC (OJ L348, 17.12.1988, p 62).
4. OJ L100, 17.4.1980, p 1. Directive as last amended by European Parliament and Council Directive 94/18/EC (OJ L135, 31.5.1994, p 1).
5. OJ L48, 20.2.1982, p 26.
6. OJ L348, 17.12.1988, p 62.
7. OJ L124, 5.5.1989, p 8.
8. OJ L222, 14.8.1978, p 11. Directive as last amended by Directive 1999/60/EC (OJ L162, 26.6.1999, p 65).

HAVE ADOPTED THIS DIRECTIVE—

TITLE I
DEFINITIONS AND SCOPE OF APPLICATION

CHAPTER I
DEFINITIONS

Article 1

For the purposes of this Directive—

    (a)   "issuers" shall mean companies and other legal persons and any undertaking whose securities are the subject of an application for admission to official listing on a stock exchange;

    (b)   "collective investment undertakings other than the closed-end type" shall mean unit trusts and investment companies—

        (i)   the object of which is the collective investment of capital provided by the public, and which operate on the principle of risk spreading, and

        (ii)   the units of which are, at the holders' request, repurchased or redeemed, directly or indirectly, out of the assets of these undertakings. Action taken by such undertakings to ensure that the stock exchange value of its units does not significantly vary from their net asset value shall be regarded as equivalent to such repurchase or redemption;

(c) for the purposes of this Directive "investment companies other than those of the closed-end type" shall mean investment companies—

  (i) the object of which is the collective investment of capital provided by the public, and which operate on the principle of risk spreading, and

  (ii) the shares of which are, at the holders' request, repurchased or redeemed, directly or indirectly, out of those companies' assets. Action taken by such companies to ensure that the stock exchange value operating of their shares does not significantly vary from their net asset value shall be regarded as equivalent to such repurchase or redemption;

(d) "credit institution" shall mean an undertaking whose business is to receive deposits or other repayable funds from the public and to grant credits for its own account;

(e) "units of a collective investment undertaking" shall mean securities issued by a collective investment undertaking as representing the rights of participants in the assets of such undertaking;

(f) "participating interest" shall mean rights in the capital of other undertakings, whether or not represented by certificates, which, by creating a durable link with those undertakings, are intended to contribute to the activities of the undertaking which holds these rights;

(g), (h) ...

                             [5263A]

NOTES

Points (g), (h) repealed by European Parliament and Council Directive 2004/109/EC, Art 32(1), as from 20 January 2007.

CHAPTER II
SCOPE OF APPLICATION

Article 2

 1. Articles 5 to 19, 42 to 69, and 78 to 84 shall apply to securities which are admitted to official listing or are the subject of an application for admission to official listing on a stock exchange situated or operating within a Member State.

 2. Member States may decide not to apply the provisions mentioned in paragraph 1 to—

 (a) units issued by collective investment undertakings other than the closed-end type,

 (b) securities issued by a Member State or its regional or local authorities.

                          [5264]–[5265]

Articles 3, 4

(Article 3 repealed by European Parliament and Council Directive 2003/71/EC, Art 27(2), as from 1 July 2005; Article 4 repealed by European Parliament and Council Directive 2004/109/EC, Art 32(2), as from 20 January 2007.)

TITLE II
GENERAL PROVISIONS CONCERNING THE OFFICIAL LISTING OF SECURITIES

CHAPTER I
GENERAL CONDITIONS FOR ADMISSION

Article 5

Member States shall ensure—

 (a) securities may not be admitted to official listing on any stock exchange situated or operating within their territory unless the conditions laid down by this Directive are satisfied, and

 (b) that issuers of securities admitted to such official listing, to regardless of the date on which this admission takes place, are subject to the obligations provided for by this Directive.

                          [5266]

Article 6

 1. The admission of securities to official listing shall be subject to the conditions set out in Articles 42 to 51, or 52 to 63, relating to shares and debt securities respectively.

 2. ...

3.   Certificates representing shares may be admitted to official listing only if the issuer of the shares represented fulfils the conditions set out in Articles 42 to 44 and the obligations set out in Articles 64 to 69 and if the certificates fulfil the conditions set out in Articles 45 to 50.

[5267]

NOTES
Para 2: repealed by European Parliament and Council Directive 2004/109/EC, Art 32(3), as from 20 January 2007.

Article 7

Member States may not make the admission to official listing of securities issued by companies or other legal persons which are nationals of another Member State subject to the condition that the securities must already have been admitted to official listing on a stock exchange situated or operating in one of the Member States.

[5268]

CHAPTER II
MORE STRINGENT OR ADDITIONAL CONDITIONS AND OBLIGATIONS

Article 8

1.   Subject to the prohibitions provided for in Article 7 and in Articles 42 to 63, the Member States may make the admission of securities to official listing subject to more stringent conditions than those set out in Articles 42 to 63 or to additional conditions, provided that these more stringent and additional conditions apply generally for all issuers or for individual classes of issuer and that they have been published before application for admission of such securities is made.

[2.   Member States may make the issuers of securities admitted to official listing subject to additional obligations, provided that those additional obligations apply generally for all issuers or for individual classes of issuers.]

3.   Member States may, under the same conditions as those laid down in Article 9, authorise derogations from the additional or more stringent conditions and obligations referred to in paragraphs 1 and 2 hereof.

4.   Member States may, in accordance with the applicable national rules require issuers of securities admitted to official listing to inform the public on a regular basis of their financial position and the general course of their business.

[5269]

NOTES
Para 2: substituted by European Parliament and Council Directive 2004/109/EC, Art 32(4), as from 20 January 2007.

CHAPTER III
DEROGATIONS

Article 9

Any derogations from the conditions for the admission of securities to official listing which may be authorised in accordance with Articles 42 to 63 must apply generally for all issuers where the circumstances justifying them are similar.

[5270]

Article 10

Member States may decide not to apply the conditions set out in Articles 52 to 63 and the obligations set out in Article 81(1) and (3) in respect of applications for admission to official listing of debt securities issued by companies and other legal persons which are nationals of a Member State and which are set up by, governed by or managed pursuant to a special law where repayments and interest payments in respect of those securities are guaranteed by a Member State or one of its federal states.

[5271]

CHAPTER IV
POWERS OF THE NATIONAL COMPETENT AUTHORITIES

SECTION 1
DECISION OF ADMISSION

Article 11

1.   The competent authorities referred to in Article 105 shall decide on the admission of securities to official listing on a stock exchange situated or operating within their territories.

2. Without prejudice to the other powers conferred upon them, the competent authorities may reject an application for the admission of a security to official listing if, in their opinion, the issuer's situation is such that admission would be detrimental to investors' interests.

[5272]

Article 12

By way of derogation from Article 8, Member States may, solely in the interests of protecting the investors, give the competent authorities power to make the admission of a security to official listing subject to any special condition which the competent authorities consider appropriate and of which they have explicitly informed the applicant.

[5273]

Article 13

1. Where applications are to be made simultaneously or within short intervals of one another for admission of the same securities to official listing on stock exchanges situated or operating in more than one Member State, or where an application for admission is made in respect of a security already listed on a stock exchange in another Member State, the competent authorities shall communicate with each other and make such arrangements as may be necessary to expedite the procedure and simplify as far as possible the formalities and any additional conditions required for admission of the security concerned.

2. In order to facilitate the work of the competent authorities, any application for the admission of a security to official listing on a stock exchange situated or operating in a Member State must state whether a similar application is being or has been made in another Member State, or will be made in the near future.

[5274]

Article 14

The competent authorities may refuse to admit to official listing a security already officially listed in another Member State where the issuer fails to comply with the obligations resulting from admission in that Member State.

[5275]

Article 15

Where an application for admission to official listing relates to certificates representing shares, the application shall be considered only if the competent authorities are of the opinion that the issuer of the certificates is offering adequate safeguards for the protection of investors.

[5276]

SECTION 2
INFORMATION REQUESTED BY THE COMPETENT AUTHORITIES

Article 16

1. An issuer whose securities are admitted to official listing shall provide the competent authorities with all the information which the latter consider appropriate in order to protect investors or ensure the smooth operation of the market.

2. Where protection of investors or the smooth operation of the market so requires, an issuer may be required by the competent authorities to publish such information in such a form and within such time limits as they consider appropriate. Should the issuer fail to comply with such requirement, the competent authorities may themselves publish such information after having heard the issuer.

[5277]

SECTION 3
ACTION AGAINST AN ISSUER FAILING TO COMPLY WITH THE OBLIGATIONS
RESULTING FROM ADMISSION

Article 17

Without prejudice to any other action or penalties which they may contemplate in the event of failure on the part of the issuer to comply with the obligations resulting from admission to official listing, the competent authorities may make public the fact that an issuer is failing to comply with those obligations.

[5278]

PART IV
EC MATERIALS

SECTION 4
SUSPENSION AND DISCONTINUANCE

Article 18

1. The competent authorities may decide to suspend the listing of a security where the smooth operation of the market is, or may be, temporarily jeopardised or where protection of investors so requires.

2. The competent authorities may decide that the listing of the security be discontinued where they are satisfied that, owing to special circumstances, normal regular dealings in a security are no longer possible.

[5279]

SECTION 5
RIGHT TO APPLY TO THE COURTS IN CASE OF REFUSAL OF ADMISSION OR DISCONTINUANCE

Article 19

1. Member States shall ensure decisions of the competent authorities refusing the admission of a security to official listing or discontinuing such a listing shall be subject to the right to apply to the courts.

2. An applicant shall be notified of a decision regarding his application for admission to official listing within six months of receipt of the application or, should the competent authority require any further information within that period, within six months of the applicant's supplying such information.

3. Failure to give a decision within the time limit specified in paragraph 2 shall be deemed a rejection of the application. Such rejection shall give rise to the right to apply to the courts provided for in paragraph 1.

[5280]

TITLE III
PARTICULAR CONDITIONS RELATING TO OFFICIAL LISTINGS OF SECURITIES

Articles 20–41

(Articles 20–41 (Chapter I) repealed by European Parliament and Council Directive 2003/71/EC, Art 27(1), as from 1 July 2005.)

CHAPTER II
SPECIFIC CONDITIONS FOR THE ADMISSION OF SHARES

SECTION 1
CONDITIONS RELATING TO COMPANIES FOR THE SHARES OF WHICH ADMISSION TO OFFICIAL LISTING IS SOUGHT

Article 42

The legal position of the company must be in conformity with the laws and Regulations to which it is subject, as regards both its formation and its operation under its statutes.

[5281]

Article 43

1. The foreseeable market capitalisation of the shares for which admission to official listing is sought or, if this cannot be assessed, the company's capital and reserves, including profit or loss, from the last financial year, must be at least one million euro.

2. Member States may provide for admission to official listing, even when this condition is not fulfilled, provided that the competent authorities are satisfied that there will be an adequate market for the shares concerned.

3. A higher foreseeable market capitalisation or higher capital and reserves may be required by a Member State for admission to official listing only if another regulated, regularly operating, recognised open market exists in that State and the requirements for it are equal to or less than those referred to in paragraph 1.

4. The condition set out in paragraph 1 shall not be applicable for the admission to official listing of a further block of shares of the same class as those already admitted.

5. The equivalent in national currency of one million euro shall initially be the equivalent in national currency of one million European units of account that were applicable on 5 March 1979.

6. If, as a result of adjustment of the equivalent of the euro in national currency, the market capitalisation expressed in national currency remains for a period of one year at least 10% more or

less than the value of one million euro the Member state must, within the 12 months following the expiry of that period, adjust its laws, regulations or administrative provisions to comply with paragraph 1.

[5282]

Article 44

A company must have published or filed its annual accounts in accordance with national law for the three financial years preceding the application for official listing. By way of exception, the competent authorities may derogate from this condition where such derogation is desirable in the interests of the company or of investors and where the competent authorities are satisfied that investors have the necessary information available to be able to arrive at an informed judgement on the company and the shares for which admission to official listing is sought.

[5283]

SECTION 2
CONDITIONS RELATING TO THE SHARES FOR WHICH ADMISSION IS SOUGHT

Article 45

The legal position of the shares must be in conformity with the laws and regulations to which they are subject.

[5284]

Article 46

1. The shares must be freely negotiable.

2. The competent authorities may treat shares which are not fully paid up as freely negotiable, if arrangements have been made to ensure that the negotiability of such shares is not restricted and that dealing is made open and proper by providing the public with all appropriate information.

3. The competent authorities may, in the case of the admission to official listing of shares which may be acquired only subject to approval, derogate from paragraph 1 only if the use of the approval clause does not disturb the market.

[5285]

Article 47

Where public issue precedes admission to official listing, the first listing may be made only after the end of the period during which subscription applications may be submitted.

[5286]

Article 48

1. A sufficient number of shares must be distributed to the public in one or more Member States not later than the time of admission.

2. The condition set out in paragraph 1 shall not apply where shares are to be distributed to the public through the stock exchange. In that event, admission to official listing may be granted only if the competent authorities are satisfied that a sufficient number of shares will be distributed through the stock exchange within a short period.

3. Where admission to official listing is sought for a further block of shares of the same class, the competent authorities may assess whether a sufficient number of shares has been distributed to the public in relation to all the shares issued and not only in relation to this further block.

4. By way of derogation from paragraph 1, if the shares are admitted to official listing in one or more non-member countries, the competent authorities may provide for their admission to official listing if a sufficient number of shares is distributed to the public in the non-Member State or States where they are listed.

5. A sufficient number of shares shall be deemed to have been distributed either when the shares in respect of which application for admission has been made are in the hands of the public to the extent of a least 25% of the subscribed capital represented by the class of shares concerned or when, in view of the large number of shares of the same class and the extent of their distribution to the public, the market will operate properly with a lower percentage.

[5287]

Article 49

1. The application for admission to official listing must cover all the shares of the same class already issued.

2. Member States may provide that this condition shall not apply to applications for admission not covering all the shares of the same class already issued where the shares of that class for which admission is not sought belong to blocks serving to maintain control of the company or are not negotiable for a certain time under agreements, provided that the public is informed of such

situations and that there is no danger of such situations prejudicing the interests of the holders of the shares for which admission to official listing is sought.

[5288]

Article 50

1. For the admission to official listing of shares issued by companies which are nationals of another Member State and which shares have a physical form it is necessary and sufficient that their physical form comply with the standards laid down in that other Member State. Where the physical form does not conform to the standards in force in the Member State in which admission to official listing is applied for, the competent authorities of that state shall make that fact known to the public.

2. The physical form of shares issued by companies which are nationals of a non-member country must afford sufficient safeguard for the protection of the investors.

[5289]

Article 51

If the shares issued by a company which is a national of a non-member country are not listed in either the country of origin or in the country in which the major proportion of the shares is held, they may not be admitted to official listing unless the competent authorities are satisfied that the absence of a listing the in the country of origin or in the country in which the major proportion is held is not due to the need to protect investors.

[5290]

CHAPTER III
PARTICULAR CONDITIONS RELATING TO THE ADMISSION TO OFFICIAL LISTING OF DEBT SECURITIES ISSUED BY AN UNDERTAKING

SECTION 1
CONDITIONS RELATING TO UNDERTAKINGS FOR THE DEBT SECURITIES OF WHICH ADMISSION TO OFFICIAL LISTING IS SOUGHT

Article 52

The legal position of the undertaking must be in conformity with the laws and regulations to which it is subject, as regards both its formation and its operation under its statutes.

[5291]

SECTION 2
CONDITIONS RELATING TO THE DEBT SECURITIES FOR WHICH ADMISSION TO OFFICIAL LISTING IS SOUGHT

Article 53

The legal position of the debt securities must be in conformity with the laws and regulations to which they are subject.

[5292]

Article 54

1. The debt securities must be freely negotiable.

2. The competent authorities may treat debt securities which are not fully paid up as freely negotiable if arrangements have been made to ensure that the negotiability of these debt securities is not restricted and that dealing is made open and proper by providing the public with all appropriate information.

[5293]

Article 55

Where public issue precedes admission to official listing, the first listing may be made only after the end of the period during which subscription applications may be submitted. This provision shall not apply in the case of tap issues of debt securities when the closing date for subscription is not fixed.

[5294]

Article 56

The application for admission to official listing must cover all debt securities ranking *pari passu*.

[5295]

Article 57

1. For the admission to official listing of debt securities issued by undertakings which are nationals of another Member State and which debt securities have a physical form, it is necessary and sufficient that their physical form comply with the standards laid down in that other Member

State. Where the physical form does not conform to the standards in force in the Member State in which admission to official listing is applied for, the competent authorities of that State shall make that fact known to the public.

2. The physical form of debt securities issued in a single Member State must conform to the standards in force in that State.

3. The physical form of debt securities issued by undertakings which are nationals of a non-member country must afford sufficient safeguard for the protection of the investors.

[5296]

SECTION 3
OTHER CONDITIONS

Article 58

1. The amount of the loan may not be less than EUR 200,000. This provision shall not be applicable in the case of tap issues where the amount of the loan is not fixed.

2. Member States may provide for admission to official listing even when this condition is not fulfilled, where the competent authorities are satisfied that there will be a sufficient market for the debt securities concerned.

3. The equivalent in national currency of EUR 200,000 shall initially be the equivalent in national currency of 200,000 units of account that were applicable on 5 March 1979.

4. If as a result of adjustment of the equivalent of the euro in national currency the minimum amount of the loan expressed in national currency remains, for a period of one year, at least 10% less than the value of EUR 200,000 the Member State must, within the 12 months following the expiry of that period, amend its laws, regulations and administrative provisions to comply with paragraph 1.

[5297]

Article 59

1. Convertible or exchangeable debentures and debentures with warrants may be admitted to official listing only if the related shares are already listed on the same stock exchange or on another regulated, regularly operating, recognised open market or are so admitted simultaneously.

2. Member States may, by way of derogation from paragraph 1, provide for the admission to official listing of convertible or exchangeable debentures or debentures with warrants, if the competent authorities are satisfied that holders have at their disposal all the information necessary to form an opinion concerning the value of the shares to which these debt securities relate.

[5298]

CHAPTER IV
PARTICULAR CONDITIONS RELATING TO THE ADMISSION TO OFFICIAL LISTING OF DEBT SECURITIES ISSUED BY A STATE, ITS REGIONAL OR LOCAL AUTHORITIES OR A PUBLIC INTERNATIONAL BODY

Article 60

The debt securities must be freely negotiable.

[5299]

Article 61

Where public issue precedes admission to official listing, the first listing may be made only after the end of the period during which subscription applications may be submitted. This provision shall not apply where the closing date for subscription is not fixed.

[5300]

Article 62

The application for admission to official listing must cover all the securities ranking *pari passu*.

[5301]

Article 63

1. For the admission to official listing of debt securities which are issued by a Member State or its regional or local authorities in a physical form, it is necessary and sufficient that such physical form comply with the standards in force in that Member State. Where the physical form does not comply with the standards in force in the Member State where admission to official listing is applied for, the competent authorities of that state shall bring this situation to the attention of the public.

2. The physical form of debt securities issued by non-member countries or their regional or local authorities or by public international bodies must afford sufficient safeguard for the protection of the investors.

[5302]

TITLE IV
OBLIGATIONS RELATING TO SECURITIES ADMITTED TO OFFICIAL LISTING

CHAPTER I
OBLIGATIONS OF COMPANIES WHOSE SHARES ARE ADMITTED TO OFFICIAL LISTING

SECTION 1
LISTING OF NEWLY ISSUED SHARES OF THE SAME CLASS

Article 64

Without prejudice to Article 49(2), in the case of a new public issue of shares of the same class as those already officially listed, the company shall be required, where the new shares are not automatically admitted, to apply for their admission to the same listing, either not more than a year after their issue or when they become freely negotiable.

[5303]–[5338]

Articles 65–104

(*Articles 65–97 (Title IV, Chapter I, Sections 2–8, Chapters II, III) repealed by European Parliament and Council Directive 2004/109/EC, Art 32(5), as from 20 January 2007 (Articles 68(1), 81(1) had been repealed previously by European Parliament and Council Directive 2003/6/EC, as from 12 April 2003); Articles 98–104 (Title V) repealed by European Parliament and Council Directive 2003/71/EC, Art 27(2), as from 1 July 2005, and European Parliament and Council Directive 2004/109/EC, Art 32(6), as from 20 January 2007.*)

TITLE VI
COMPETENT AUTHORITIES AND COOPERATION BETWEEN MEMBER STATES

Article 105

1. Member States shall ensure that this Directive is applied and shall appoint one or more competent authorities for the purposes of the Directive. They shall notify the Commission thereof, giving details of any division of powers among them.

2. Member States shall ensure that the competent authorities have the powers necessary for them to carry out their task.

3. This Directive shall not affect the competent authorities' liability, which shall continue to be governed solely by national law.

[5339]

Article 106

The competent authorities shall cooperate whenever necessary for the purpose of carrying out their duties and shall exchange any information useful for that purpose.

[5340]

Article 107

1. Member States shall provide that all persons employed or formerly employed by the competent authorities shall be bound by professional secrecy. This means that any confidential information received in the course of their duties may not be divulged to any person or authority except by virtue of provisions laid down by law.

2. Paragraph 1 shall not, however, preclude the competent authorities of the various Member States from exchanging information as provided for in this Directive. Information thus exchanged shall be covered by the obligation of professional secrecy to which the persons employed or formerly employed by the competent authorities receiving the information are subject.

3. ...

[5341]

NOTES

Para 3: repealed by a combination of European Parliament and Council Directive 2003/71/EC, Art 27(2), as from 1 July 2005, and European Parliament and Council Directive 2004/109/EC, Art 32(7), as from 20 January 2007.

TITLE VII
CONTACT COMMITTEE

CHAPTER I
COMPOSITION, WORKING AND TASKS OF THE COMMITTEE

Article 108

(Repealed by European Parliament and Council Directive 2005/1/EC, Art 10(1), as from 13 April 2005.)

CHAPTER II
ADAPTATION OF THE AMOUNT OF EQUITY MARKET CAPITALISATION

[Article 109

1.   For the purpose of adjusting, in the light of the requirements of the economic situation, the minimum amount of the foreseeable market capitalisation laid down in Article 43(1), the Commission shall submit to the European Securities Committee instituted by Commission Decision 2001/528/EC of 6 June 2001¹ a draft of the measures to be taken.

2.   Where reference is made to this paragraph, Articles 5 and 7 of Council Decision 1999/468/EC of 28 June 1999 laying down the procedures for the exercise of implementing powers conferred on the Commission² shall apply, having regard to Article 8 thereof.

The period laid down in Article 5(6) of Decision 1999/468/EC shall be set at three months.

3.   The Committee shall adopt its rules of procedure.]

[5342]

NOTES

Substituted by European Parliament and Council Directive 2005/1/EC, Art 10(2), as from 13 April 2005.

¹   OJ L191, 13.7.2001, p 45. Decision as amended by Decision 2004/8/EC (OJ L3, 7.1.2004, p 33).
²   OJ L184, 17.7.1999, p 23.

TITLE VIII
FINAL PROVISIONS

Article 110

The Member States shall communicate to the Commission the texts of the main laws, regulations and administrative provisions which they adopt in the field covered by this Directive.

[5343]

Article 111

1.   Directives 79/279/EEC, 80/390/EEC, 82/121/EEC and 88/627/EEC, as amended by the acts listed in Annex II Part A, are hereby repealed without prejudice to the obligations of the Member States concerning the time-limits for transposition set out in Annex II Part B.

2.   References to the repealed Directives shall be construed as references to this Directive and should be read in accordance with the correlation table shown in Annex III.

[5344]

Article 112

This Directive shall enter into force the twentieth day following that of its publication in the *Official Journal of the European Communities*.

[5345]

Article 113

This Directive is addressed to the Member States.

[5346]

(Annex I repealed by European Parliament and Council Directive 2003/71/EC, Art 27(4), as from 1 July 2005.)

ANNEX II

PART A
REPEALED DIRECTIVES AND THEIR SUCCESSIVE AMENDMENTS
(REFERRED TO IN ARTICLE 111)

Council Directive 79/279/EEC	(OJ L66, 16.3.1979, p 21)
Council Directive 82/148/EEC	(OJ L62, 5.3.1982, p 22)
Council Directive 88/627/EEC	(OJ L348, 17.12.1988, p 62)
Council Directive 80/390/EEC	(OJ L100, 17.4.1980, p 1)
Council Directive 82/148/EEC	(OJ L62, 5.3.1982, p 22)
Council Directive 87/345/EEC	(OJ L185, 4.7.1987, p 81)
Council Directive 90/211/EEC	(OJ L112, 3.5.1990, p 24)
European Parliament and Council Directive 94/18/EC	(OJ L135, 31.5.1994, p 1)
Council Directive 82/121/EEC	(OJ L48, 20.2.1982, p 26)
Council Directive 88/627/EEC	(OJ L348, 17.12.1988, p 62)

[5347]

PART B
TIME-LIMITS FOR TRANSPOSITION INTO NATIONAL LAW
(REFERRED TO IN ARTICLE 111)

Directive	*Time-limit for transposition*
79/279/EEC	8 March 1981[1, 2]
80/390/EEC	19 September 1982[2]
82/121/EEC; 82/148/EEC	30 June 1983[3]
87/345/EEC	1 January 1990 1 January 1991 for Spain 1 January 1992 for Portugal
88/627/EEC	1 January 1991
90/211/EEC; 94/18/EC	17 April 1991

[5348]

NOTES
[1]   8.3.1982 for the Member States which introduce simultaneously Directives 79/279/EEC and 80/390/EEC.
[2]   30.6.1983 for the Member States which introduce simultaneously Directives 79/279/EEC, 80/390/EEC and 82/121/EEC.
[3]   Time-limit for application: 30.6.1986.

(Annex III (Correlation Table) not reproduced.)

DIRECTIVE OF THE EUROPEAN PARLIAMENT AND OF THE COUNCIL

of 21 January 2002

amending Council Directive 85/611/EEC on the coordination of laws, regulations and administrative provisions relating to undertakings for collective investment in transferable securities (UCITS) with a view to regulating management companies and simplified prospectuses (Note)

(2001/107/EC)

NOTES
Date of publication in OJ: OJ L41, 13.2.2002, p 20.
As of 1 February 2009, this Directive had not been amended.
This Directive amends Council Directive 85/611/EEC at **[5002]**.

[5349]

DIRECTIVE OF THE EUROPEAN PARLIAMENT AND OF THE COUNCIL

of 21 January 2002

amending Council Directive 85/611/EEC on the coordination of laws, regulations and administrative provisions relating to undertakings for collective investment in transferable securities (UCITS) with regard to investments of UCITS (Note)

(2001/108/EC)

NOTES
Date of publication in OJ: OJ L41, 13.2.2002, p 35.
As of 1 February 2009, this Directive had not been amended.
This Directive amends Council Directive 85/611/EEC at **[5002]**.

[5350]

DIRECTIVE OF THE EUROPEAN PARLIAMENT AND OF THE COUNCIL

of 6 June 2002

on financial collateral arrangements

(2002/47/EC)

NOTES
Date of publication in OJ: OJ L168, 27.6.02, p 43. Notes are as in the original OJ version.
As of 1 February 2009, this Directive had not been amended.
Proposed amendment of this Directive: see the Proposal for a Directive of the European Parliament and of the Council amending Directive 98/26/EC on settlement finality in payment and securities settlement systems and Directive 2002/47/EC on financial collateral arrangements as regards linked systems and credit claims.[1]
[1]　Brussels, 23.4.2008, COM(2008) 213 final. Available on the Europa website.

THE EUROPEAN PARLIAMENT AND THE COUNCIL OF THE EUROPEAN UNION,

Having regard to the Treaty establishing the European Community, and in particular Article 95 thereof,

Having regard to the proposal from the Commission,[1]

Having regard to the opinion of the European Central Bank,[2]

Having regard to the opinion of the Economic and Social Committee,[3]

Acting in accordance with the procedure laid down in Article 251 of the Treaty,[4]

Whereas:

(1)   Directive 98/26/EC of the European Parliament and of the Council of 19 May 1998 on settlement finality in payment and securities settlement systems[5] constituted a milestone in establishing a sound legal framework for payment and securities settlement systems. Implementation of that Directive has demonstrated the importance of limiting systemic risk inherent in such systems stemming from the different influence of several jurisdictions, and the benefits of common rules in relation to collateral constituted to such systems.

(2)   In its communication of 11 May 1999 to the European Parliament and to the Council on financial services: implementing the framework for financial markets: action plan, the Commission undertook, after consultation with market experts and national authorities, to work on further proposals for legislative action on collateral urging further progress in the field of collateral, beyond Directive 98/26/EC.

(3)   A Community regime should be created for the provision of securities and cash as collateral under both security interest and title transfer structures including repurchase agreements (repos). This will contribute to the integration and cost-efficiency of the financial market as well as to the stability of the financial system in the Community, thereby supporting the freedom to provide services and the free movement of capital in the single market in financial services. This Directive focuses on bilateral financial collateral arrangements.

(4)   This Directive is adopted in a European legal context which consists in particular of the said Directive 98/ 26/EC as well as Directive 2001/24/EC of the European Parliament and of the Council of 4 April 2001 on the reorganisation and winding up of credit institutions,[6] Directive 2001/17/EC of the European Parliament and of the Council of 19 March 2001 on the reorganisation and winding-up of insurance undertakings[7] and Council Regulation (EC) No 1346/2000 of 29 May 2000 on insolvency proceedings.[8] This Directive is in line with the general pattern of these previous legal acts and is not opposed to it. Indeed, this Directive complements these existing legal acts by dealing with further issues and going beyond them in connection with particular matters already dealt with by these legal acts.

(5)   In order to improve the legal certainty of financial collateral arrangements, Member States should ensure that certain provisions of insolvency law do not apply to such arrangements, in particular, those that would inhibit the effective realisation of financial collateral or cast doubt on the validity of current techniques such as bilateral close-out netting, the provision of additional collateral in the form of top-up collateral and substitution of collateral.

(6)   This Directive does not address rights which any person may have in respect of assets provided as financial collateral, and which arise otherwise than under the terms of the financial collateral arrangement and otherwise than on the basis of any legal provision or rule of law arising by reason of the commencement or continuation of winding-up proceedings or reorganisation measures, such as restitution arising from mistake, error or lack of capacity.

(7)   The principle in Directive 98/26/EC, whereby the law applicable to book entry securities provided as collateral is the law of the jurisdiction where the relevant register, account or centralised deposit system is located, should be extended in order to create legal certainty regarding the use of such securities held in a cross-border context and used as financial collateral under the scope of this Directive.

(8)   The *lex rei sitae* rule, according to which the applicable law for determining whether a financial collateral arrangement is properly perfected and therefore good against third parties is the law of the country where the financial collateral is located, is currently recognised by all Member States. Without affecting the application of this Directive to directly-held securities, the location of book entry securities provided as financial collateral and held through one or more intermediaries should be determined. If the collateral taker has a valid and effective collateral arrangement according to the governing law of the country in which the relevant account is maintained, then the validity against any competing title or interest and the enforceability of the collateral should be governed solely by the law of that country, thus preventing legal uncertainty as a result of other unforeseen legislation.

(9)   In order to limit the administrative burdens for parties using financial collateral under the scope of this Directive, the only perfection requirement which national law may impose in respect of financial collateral should be that the financial collateral is delivered, transferred, held, registered or otherwise designated so as to be in the possession or under the control of the collateral taker or of a person acting on the collateral taker's behalf while not excluding collateral techniques where the collateral provider is allowed to substitute collateral or to withdraw excess collateral.

(10)   For the same reasons, the creation, validity, perfection, enforceability or admissibility in evidence of a financial collateral arrangement, or the provision of financial collateral under a financial collateral arrangement, should not be made dependent on the performance of any formal act such as the execution of any document in a specific form or in a particular manner, the making of any filing with an official or public body or registration in a public register, advertisement in a newspaper or journal, in an official register or publication or in any other matter, notification to a public officer or the provision of evidence in a particular form as to the date of execution of a document or instrument, the amount of the relevant financial obligations or any other matter. This Directive must however provide a balance between market efficiency and the safety of the parties to the arrangement and third parties, thereby avoiding *inter alia* the risk of fraud. This balance should

be achieved through the scope of this Directive covering only those financial collateral arrangements which provide for some form of dispossession, i e the provision of the financial collateral, and where the provision of the financial collateral can be evidenced in writing or in a durable medium, ensuring thereby the traceability of that collateral. For the purpose of this Directive, acts required-under the law of a Member State as conditions for transferring or creating a security interest on financial instruments, other than book entry securities, such as endorsement in the case of instruments to order, or recording on the issuer's register in the case of registered instruments, should not be considered as formal acts.

(11) Moreover, this Directive should protect only financial collateral arrangements which can be evidenced. Such evidence can be given in writing or in any other legally enforceable manner provided by the law which is applicable to the financial collateral arrangement.

(12) The simplification of the use of financial collateral through the limitation of administrative burdens promotes the efficiency of the cross-border operations of the European Central Bank and the national central banks of Member States participating in the economic and monetary union, necessary for the implementation of the common monetary policy. Furthermore, the provision of limited protection of financial collateral arrangements from some rules of insolvency law in addition supports the wider aspect of the common monetary policy, where the participants in the money market balance the overall amount of liquidity in the market among themselves, by cross-border transactions backed by collateral.

(13) This Directive seeks to protect the validity of financial collateral arrangements which are based upon the transfer of the full ownership of the financial collateral, such as by eliminating the so-called re-characterisation of such financial collateral arrangements (including repurchase agreements) as security interests.

(14) The enforceability of bilateral close-out netting should be protected, not only as an enforcement mechanism for title transfer financial collateral arrangements including repurchase agreements but more widely, where close-out netting forms part of a financial collateral arrangement. Sound risk management practices commonly used in the financial market should be protected by enabling participants to manage and reduce their credit exposures arising from all kinds of financial transactions on a net basis, where the credit exposure is calculated by combining the estimated current exposures under all outstanding transactions with a counterparty, setting off reciprocal items to produce a single aggregated amount that is compared with the current value of the collateral.

(15) This Directive should be without prejudice to any restrictions or requirements under national law on bringing into account claims, on obligations to set-off, or on netting, for example relating to their reciprocity or the fact that they have been concluded prior to when the collateral taker knew or ought to have known of the commencement (or of any mandatory legal act leading to the commencement) of winding-up proceedings or reorganisation measures in respect of the collateral provider.

(16) The sound market practice favoured by regulators whereby participants in the financial market use top-up financial collateral arrangements to manage and limit their credit risk to each other by mark-to-market calculations of the current market value of the credit exposure and the value of the financial collateral and accordingly ask for top-up financial collateral or return the surplus of financial collateral should be protected against certain automatic avoidance rules. The same applies to the possibility of substituting for assets provided as financial collateral other assets of the same value. The intention is merely that the provision of top-up or substitution financial collateral cannot be questioned on the sole basis that the relevant financial obligations existed before that financial collateral was provided, or that the financial collateral was provided during a prescribed-period. However, this does not prejudice the possibility of questioning under national law the financial collateral arrangement and the provision of financial collateral as part of the initial provision, top-up or substitution of financial collateral, for example where this has been intentionally done to the detriment of the other creditors (this covers *inter alia* actions based on fraud or similar avoidance rules which may apply in a prescribed period).

(17) This Directive provides for rapid and non-formalistic enforcement procedures in order to safeguard financial stability and limit contagion effects in case of a default of a party to a financial collateral arrangement. However, this Directive balances the latter objectives with the protection of the collateral provider and third-parties by explicitly confirming the possibility for Member States to keep or introduce in their national legislation an *a posteriori* control which the Courts can exercise in relation to the realisation or valuation of financial collateral and the calculation of the relevant financial obligations. Such control should allow for the judicial authorities to verify that the realisation or valuation has been conducted in a commercially reasonable manner.

(18) It should be possible to provide cash as collateral under both title transfer and secured structures respectively protected by the recognition of netting or by the pledge of cash collateral. Cash refers only to money which is represented by a credit to an account, or similar claims on repayment of money (such as money market deposits), thus explicitly excluding banknotes.

(19) This Directive provides for a right of use in case of security financial collateral arrangements, which increases liquidity in the financial market stemming from such reuse of

pledged securities. This reuse however should be without prejudice to national legislation about separation of assets and unfair treatment of creditors.

(20) This Directive does not prejudice the operation and effect of the contractual terms of financial instruments provided as financial collateral, such as rights and obligations and other conditions contained in the terms of issue and any other rights and obligations and other conditions which apply between the issuers and holders of such instruments.

(21) This Act complies with the fundamental rights and follows the principles laid down in particular in the Charter of Fundamental Rights of the European Union.

(22) Since the objective of the proposed action, namely to create a minimum regime relating to the use of financial collateral, cannot be sufficiently achieved by the Member States and can therefore, by reason of the scale and effects of the action, be better achieved at Community level, the Community may adopt measures, in accordance with the principle of subsidiarity as set out in Article 5 of the Treaty. In accordance with the principle of proportionality, as set out in that Article, this Directive does not go beyond what is necessary in order to achieve that objective,

[5351]

NOTES
1   OJ C180 E, 26.6.2001, p 312.
2   OJ C196, 12.7.2001, p 10.
3   OJ C48, 21.2.2002, p 1.
4   Opinion of the European Parliament of 13 December 2001 (not yet published in the Official Journal), Council Common Position of 5 March 2002 (not yet published in the Official Journal) and Decision of the European Parliament of 15 May 2002.
5   OJ L166, 11.6.1998, p 45.
6   OJ L125, 5.5.2001, p 15.
7   OJ L110, 20.4.2001, p 28.
8   OJ L160, 30.6.2000, p 1.

HAVE ADOPTED THIS DIRECTIVE:

Article 1
Subject matter and scope

1. This Directive lays down a Community regime applicable to financial collateral arrangements which satisfy the requirements set out in paragraphs 2 and 5 and to financial collateral in accordance with the conditions set out in paragraphs 4 and 5.

2. The collateral taker and the collateral provider must each belong to one of the following categories:
    (a) a public authority (excluding publicly guaranteed undertakings unless they fall under points (b) to (e)) including:
        (i) public sector bodies of Member States charged with or intervening in the management of public debt, and
        (ii) public sector bodies of Member States authorised to hold accounts for customers;
    (b) a central bank, the European Central Bank, the Bank for International Settlements, a multilateral development bank as defined in Article 1(19) of Directive 2000/12/EC of the European Parliament and of the Council of 20 March 2000 relating to the taking up and pursuit of the business of credit institutions,[1] the International Monetary Fund and the European Investment Bank;
    (c) a financial institution subject to prudential supervision including:
        (i) a credit institution as defined in Article 1(1) of Directive 2000/12/EC, including the institutions listed in Article 2(3) of that Directive;
        (ii) an investment firm as defined in Article 1(2) of Council Directive 93/22/EEC of 10 May 1993 on investment services in the securities field;[2]
        (iii) a financial institution as defined in Article 1(5) of Directive 2000/12/EC;
        (iv) an insurance undertaking as defined in Article 1(a) of Council Directive 92/49/EEC of 18 June 1992 on the coordination of laws, regulations and administrative provisions relating to direct insurance other than life assurance[3] and a life assurance undertaking as defined in Article 1(a) of Council Directive 92/96/EEC of 10 November 1992 on the coordination of laws, regulations and administrative provisions relating to direct life assurance;[4]
        (v) an undertaking for collective investment in transferable securities (UCITS) as defined in Article 1(2) of Council Directive 85/611/EEC of 20 December 1985 on the coordination of laws, regulations and administrative provisions relating to undertakings for collective investment in transferable securities (UCITS);[5]
        (vi) a management company as defined in Article 1a(2) of Directive 85/611/EEC;
    (d) a central counterparty, settlement agent or clearing house, as defined respectively in Article 2(c), (d) and (e) of Directive 98/26/EC, including similar institutions regulated under national law acting in the futures, options and derivatives markets to the extent not

covered by that Directive, and a person, other than a natural person, who acts in a trust or representative capacity on behalf of any one or more persons that includes any bondholders or holders of other forms of securitised debt or any institution as defined in points (a) to (d);

(e)   a person other than a natural person, including unincorporated firms and partnerships, provided that the other party is an institution as defined in points (a) to (d).

If they make use of this option Member States shall inform the Commission which shall inform the other Member States thereof.

3.   Member States may exclude from the scope of this Directive financial collateral arrangements where one of the parties is a person mentioned in paragraph 2(e).

4.

(a)   The financial collateral to be provided must consist of cash or financial instruments.

(b)   Member States may exclude from the scope of this Directive financial collateral consisting of the collateral provider's own shares, shares in affiliated undertakings within the meaning of seventh Council Directive 83/ 349/EEC of 13 June 1983 on consolidated accounts,[6] and shares in undertakings whose exclusive purpose is to own means of production that are essential for the collateral provider's business or to own real property.

5.   This Directive applies to financial collateral once it has been provided and if that provision can be evidenced in writing.

The evidencing of the provision of financial collateral must allow for the identification of the financial collateral to which it applies. For this purpose, it is sufficient to prove that the book entry securities collateral has been credited to, or forms a credit in, the relevant account and that the cash collateral has been credited to, or forms a credit in, a designated account.

This Directive applies to financial collateral arrangements if that arrangement can be evidenced in writing or in a legally equivalent manner.

[5351A]

NOTES

[1]   OJ L126, 26.5.2000, p 1. Directive as amended by Directive 2000/28/EC (OJ L275, 27.10.2000, p 37).
[2]   OJ L141, 11.6.1993, p 27. Directive as last amended by Directive 2000/64/EC of the European Parliament and of the Council (OJ L290, 17.11.2000, p 27).
[3]   OJ L228, 11.8.1992, p 1. Directive as last amended by Directive 2000/64/EC of the European Parliament and of the Council.
[4]   OJ L360, 9.12.1992, p 1. Directive as last amended by Directive 2000/64/EC of the European Parliament and of the Council.
[5]   OJ L375, 31.12.1985, p 3. Directive as last amended by Directive 2001/108/EC of the European Parliament and of the Council. (OJ L41, 13.2.2002, p 35).
[6]   OJ L193, 18.7.1983, p 1. Directive as last amended by Directive 2001/65/EC of the European Parliament and of the Council (OJ L283, 27.10.2001, p 28).

Article 2
Definitions

1.   For the purpose of this Directive:

(a)   financial collateral arrangement means a title transfer financial collateral arrangement or a security financial collateral arrangement whether or not these are covered by a master agreement or general terms and conditions;

(b)   title transfer financial collateral arrangement means an arrangement, including repurchase agreements, under which a collateral provider transfers full ownership of financial collateral to a collateral taker for the purpose of securing or otherwise covering the performance of relevant financial obligations;

(c)   security financial collateral arrangement means an arrangement under which a collateral provider provides financial collateral by way of security in favour of, or to, a collateral taker, and where the full ownership of the financial collateral remains with the collateral provider when the security right is established;

(d)   cash means money credited to an account in any currency, or similar claims for the repayment of money, such as money market deposits;

(e)   financial instruments means shares in companies and other securities equivalent to shares in companies and bonds and other forms of debt instruments if these are negotiable on the capital market, and any other securities which are normally dealt in and which give the right to acquire any such shares, bonds or other securities by subscription, purchase or exchange or which give rise to a cash settlement (excluding instruments of payment), including units in collective investment undertakings, money market instruments and claims relating to or rights in or in respect of any of the foregoing;

(f)   relevant financial obligations means the obligations which are secured by a financial collateral arrangement and which give a right to cash settlement and/or delivery of financial instruments.

Relevant financial obligations may consist of or include:
  (i)   present or future, actual or contingent or prospective obligations (including such obligations arising under a master agreement or similar arrangement);
  (ii)   obligations owed to the collateral taker by a person other than the collateral provider; or
  (iii) obligations of a specified class or kind arising from time to time;

(g)   book entry securities collateral means financial collateral provided under a financial collateral arrangement which consists of financial instruments, title to which is evidenced by entries in a register or account maintained by or on behalf of an intermediary;

(h)   relevant account means in relation to book entry securities collateral which is subject to a financial collateral arrangement, the register or account which may be maintained by the collateral taker i which the entries are made by which that book entry securities collateral is provided to the collateral taker;

(i)   equivalent collateral:
  (i)   in relation to cash, means a payment of the same amount and in the same currency;
  (ii)   in relation to financial instruments, means financial instruments of the same issuer or debtor, forming part of the same issue or class and of the same nominal amount, currency and description or, where a financial collateral arrangement provides for the transfer of other assets following the occurrence of any event relating to or affecting any financial instruments provided as financial collateral, those other assets;

(j)   winding-up proceedings means collective proceedings involving realisation of the assets and distribution of the proceeds among the creditors, shareholders or members as appropriate, which involve any intervention by administrative or judicial authorities, including where the collective proceedings are terminated by a composition or other analogous measure, whether or not they are founded on insolvency or are voluntary or compulsory;

(k)   reorganisation measures means measures which involve any intervention by administrative or judicial authorities which are intended to preserve or restore the financial situation and which affect pre-existing rights of third-parties, including but not limited to measures involving a suspension of payments, suspension of enforcement measures or reduction of claims;

(l)   enforcement event means an event of default or any similar event as agreed between the parties on the occurrence of which, under the terms of a financial collateral arrangement or by operation of law, the collateral taker is entitled to realise or appropriate financial collateral or a close-out netting provision comes into effect;

(m)   right of use means the right of the collateral taker to use and dispose of financial collateral provided under a security financial collateral arrangement as the owner of it in accordance with the terms of the security financial collateral arrangement;

(n)   close-out netting provision means a provision of a financial collateral arrangement, or of an arrangement of which a financial collateral arrangement forms part, or, in the absence of any such provision, any statutory rule by which, on the occurrence of an enforcement event, whether through the operation of netting or set-off or otherwise:
  (i)   the obligations of the parties are accelerated so as to be immediately due and expressed as an obligation to pay an amount representing their estimated current value, or are terminated and replaced by an obligation to pay such an amount; and/or
  (ii)   an account is taken of what is due from each party to the other in respect of such obligations, and a net sum equal to the balance of the account is payable by the party from whom the larger amount is due to the other party.

2.   References in this Directive to financial collateral being provided , or to the provision of financial collateral, are to the financial collateral being delivered, transferred, held, registered or otherwise designated so as to be in the possession or under the control of the collateral taker or of a person acting on the collateral taker's behalf. Any right of substitution or to withdraw excess financial collateral in favour of the collateral provider shall not prejudice the financial collateral having been provided to the collateral taker as mentioned in this Directive.

3.   References in this Directive to writing include recording by electronic means and any other durable medium.

Article 3
Formal requirements

1.   Member States shall not require that the creation, validity, perfection, enforceability or admissibility in evidence of a financial collateral arrangement or the provision of financial collateral under a financial collateral arrangement be dependent on the performance of any formal act.

2.   Paragraph 1 is without prejudice to the application of this Directive to financial collateral only once it has been provided and if that provision can be evidenced in writing and where the financial collateral arrangement can be evidenced in writing or in a legally equivalent manner.

[5353]

Article 4
Enforcement of financial collateral arrangements

1.   Member States shall ensure that on the occurrence of an enforcement event, the collateral taker shall be able to realise in the following manners, any financial collateral provided under, and subject to the terms agreed in, a security financial collateral arrangement:

    (a)   financial instruments by sale or appropriation and by setting off their value against, or applying their value in discharge of, the relevant financial obligations;

    (b)   cash by setting off the amount against or applying it in discharge of the relevant financial obligations.

2.   Appropriation is possible only if:

    (a)   this has been agreed by the parties in the security financial collateral arrangement; and

    (b)   the parties have agreed in the security financial collateral arrangement on the valuation of the financial instruments.

3.   Member States which do not allow appropriation on 27 June 2002 are not obliged to recognise it.

If they make use of this option, Member States shall inform the Commission which in turn shall inform the other Member States thereof.

4.   The manners of realising the financial collateral referred to in paragraph 1 shall, subject to the terms agreed in the security financial collateral arrangement, be without any requirement to the effect that:

    (a)   prior notice of the intention to realise must have been given;

    (b)   the terms of the realisation be approved by any court, public officer or other person;

    (c)   the realisation be conducted by public auction or in any other prescribed manner; or

    (d)   any additional time period must have elapsed.

5.   Member States shall ensure that a financial collateral arrangement can take effect in accordance with its terms notwithstanding the commencement or continuation of winding-up proceedings or reorganisation measures in respect of the collateral provider or collateral taker.

6.   This Article and Articles 5, 6 and 7 shall be without prejudice to any requirements under national law to the effect that the realisation or valuation of financial collateral and the calculation of the relevant financial obligations must be conducted in a commercially reasonable manner.

[5354]

Article 5
Right of use of financial collateral under security financial collateral arrangements

1.   If and to the extent that the terms of a security financial collateral arrangement so provide, Member States shall ensure that the collateral taker is entitled to exercise a right of use in relation to financial collateral provided under the security financial collateral arrangement.

2.   Where a collateral taker exercises a right of use, he thereby incurs an obligation to transfer equivalent collateral to replace the original financial collateral at the latest on the due date for the performance of the relevant financial obligations covered by the security financial collateral arrangement.

Alternatively, the collateral taker shall, on the due date for the performance of the relevant financial obligations, either transfer equivalent collateral, or, if and to the extent that the terms of a security financial collateral arrangement so provide, set off the value of the equivalent collateral against or apply it in discharge of the relevant financial obligations.

3.   The equivalent collateral transferred in discharge of an obligation as described in paragraph 2, first subparagraph, shall be subject to the same security financial collateral agreement to which the original financial collateral was subject and shall be treated as having been provided under the security financial collateral arrangement at the same time as the original financial collateral was first provided.

4.   Member States shall ensure that the use of financial collateral by the collateral taker according to this Article does not render invalid or unenforceable the rights of the collateral taker under the security financial collateral arrangement in relation to the financial collateral transferred by the collateral taker in discharge of an obligation as described in paragraph 2, first subparagraph.

5. If an enforcement event occurs while an obligation as described in paragraph 2 first subparagraph remains outstanding, the obligation may be the subject of a close-out netting provision.

[5355]

Article 6
Recognition of title transfer financial collateral arrangements

1. Member States shall ensure that a title transfer financial collateral arrangement can take effect in accordance with its terms.

2. If an enforcement event occurs while any obligation of the collateral taker to transfer equivalent collateral under a title transfer financial collateral arrangement remains outstanding, the obligation may be the subject of a close-out netting provision.

[5356]

Article 7
Recognition of close-out netting provisions

1. Member States shall ensure that a close-out netting provision can take effect in accordance with its terms:
   (a) notwithstanding the commencement or continuation of winding-up proceedings or reorganisation measures in respect of the collateral provider and/or the collateral taker; and/or
   (b) notwithstanding any purported assignment, judicial or other attachment or other disposition of or in respect of such rights.

2. Member States shall ensure that the operation of a close-out netting provision may not be subject to any of the requirements that are mentioned in Article 4(4), unless otherwise agreed by the parties.

[5357]

Article 8
Certain insolvency provisions disapplied

1. Member States shall ensure that a financial collateral arrangement, as well as the provision of financial collateral under such arrangement, may not be declared invalid or void or be reversed on the sole basis that the financial collateral arrangement has come into existence, or the financial collateral has been provided:
   (a) on the day of the commencement of winding-up proceedings or reorganisation measures, but prior to the order or decree making that commencement; or
   (b) in a prescribed period prior to, and defined by reference to, the commencement of such proceedings or measures or by reference to the making of any order or decree or the taking of any other action or occurrence of any other event in the course of such proceedings or measures.

2. Member States shall ensure that where a financial collateral arrangement or a relevant financial obligation has come into existence, or financial collateral has been provided on the day of, but after the moment of the commencement of, winding-up proceedings or reorganisation measures, it shall be legally enforceable and binding on third parties if the collateral taker can prove that he was not aware, nor should have been aware, of the commencement of such proceedings or measures.

3. Where a financial collateral arrangement contains:
   (a) an obligation to provide financial collateral or additional financial collateral in order to take account of changes in the value of the financial collateral or in the amount of the relevant financial obligations, or
   (b) a right to withdraw financial collateral on providing, by way of substitution or exchange, financial collateral of substantially the same value,

Member States shall ensure that the provision of financial collateral, additional financial collateral or substitute or replacement financial collateral under such an obligation or right shall not be treated as invalid or reversed or declared void on the sole basis that:
   (i) such provision was made on the day of the commencement of winding-up proceedings or reorganisation measures, but prior to the order or decree making that commencement or in a prescribed period prior to, and defined by reference to, the commencement of winding-up proceedings or reorganisation measures or by reference to the making of any order or decree or the taking of any other action or occurrence of any other event in the course of such proceedings or measures; and/or
   (ii) the relevant financial obligations were incurred prior to the date of the provision of the financial collateral, additional financial collateral or substitute or replacement financial collateral.

4.   Without prejudice to paragraphs 1, 2 and 3, this Directive leaves unaffected the general rules of national insolvency law in relation to the violence of transactions entered into during the prescribed period referred to in paragraph 1(b) and in paragraph 3(i).

[5358]

Article 9
Conflict of laws

1.   Any question with respect to any of the matters specified in paragraph 2 arising in relation to book entry securities collateral shall be governed by the law of the country in which the relevant account is maintained. The reference to the law of a country is a reference to its domestic law, disregarding any rule under which, in deciding the relevant question, reference should be made to the law of another country.

2.   The matters referred to in paragraph 1 are:
- (a)   the legal nature and proprietary effects of book entry securities collateral;
- (b)   the requirements for perfecting a financial collateral arrangement relating to book entry securities collateral and the provision of book entry securities collateral under such an arrangement, and more generally the completion of the steps necessary to render such an arrangement and provision effective against third parties;
- (c)   whether a person's title to or interest in such book entry securities collateral is overridden by or subordinated to a competing title or interest, or a good faith acquisition has occurred;
- (d)   the steps required for the realisation of book entry securities collateral following the occurrence of an enforcement event.

[5359]

Article 10
Report by the Commission

Not later than 27 December 2006, the Commission shall present a report to the European Parliament and the Council on the application of this Directive, in particular on the application of Article 1(3), Article 4(3) and Article 5, accompanied where appropriate by proposals for its revision.

[5360]

Article 11
Implementation

Member States shall bring into force the laws, regulations and administrative provisions necessary to comply with this Directive by 27 December 2003 at the latest. They shall forthwith inform the Commission thereof.

When Member States adopt those provisions, they shall contain a reference to this Directive or be accompanied by such reference on the occasion of their official publication. Member States shall determine how such reference is to be made.

[5361]

Article 12
Entry into force

This Directive shall enter into force on the day of its publication in the *Official Journal of the European Communities*.

[5362]

Article 13
Addressees

This Directive is addressed to the Member States.

[5363]

DIRECTIVE OF THE EUROPEAN PARLIAMENT
AND OF THE COUNCIL

of 23 September 2002

concerning the distance marketing of consumer financial services and amending Council Directive 90/619/EEC and Directives 97/7/EC and 98/27/EC

(2002/65/EC)

NOTES

Date of publication in OJ: OJ L271, 9.10.2002, p 16. Notes are as in the original OJ version.

This Directive is reproduced as amended by: European Parliament and Council Directive 2005/29/EC (OJ L149, 11.6.2005, p 22); European Parliament and Council Directive 2007/64/EC (OJ L319, 5.12.2007, p 1).
Council Directive 90/619/EEC: repealed by European Parliament and Council Directive 2002/83/EC, Annex V, Pt A, as from 19 December 2002.

THE EUROPEAN PARLIAMENT AND THE COUNCIL OF THE EUROPEAN UNION,

Having regard to the Treaty establishing the European Community, and in particular Article 47(2), Article 55 and Article 95 thereof,

Having regard to the proposal from the Commission,[1]

Having regard to the opinion of the Economic and Social Committee,[2]

Acting in accordance with the procedure laid down in Article 251 of the Treaty,[3]

Whereas:

(1) It is important, in the context of achieving the aims of the single market, to adopt measures designed to consolidate progressively this market and those measures must contribute to attaining a high level of consumer protection, in accordance with Articles 95 and 153 of the Treaty.

(2) Both for consumers and suppliers of financial services, the distance marketing of financial services will constitute one of the main tangible results of the completion of the internal market.

(3) Within the framework of the internal market, it is in the interest of consumers to have access without discrimination to the widest possible range of financial services available in the Community so that they can choose those that are best suited to their needs. In order to safeguard freedom of choice, which is an essential consumer right, a high degree of consumer protection is required in order to enhance consumer confidence in distance selling.

(4) It is essential to the smooth operation of the internal market for consumers to be able to negotiate and conclude contracts with a supplier established in other Member States, regardless of whether the supplier is also established in the Member State in which the consumer resides.

(5) Because of their intangible nature, financial services are particularly suited to distance selling and the establishment of a legal framework governing the distance marketing of financial services should increase consumer confidence in the use of new techniques for the distance marketing of financial services, such as electronic commerce.

(6) This Directive should be applied in conformity with the Treaty and with secondary law, including Directive 2000/31/EC[4] on electronic commerce, the latter being applicable solely to the transactions which it covers.

(7) This Directive aims to achieve the objectives set forth above without prejudice to Community or national law governing freedom to provide services or, where applicable, host Member State control and/or authorisation or supervision systems in the Member States where this is compatible with Community legislation.

(8) Moreover, this Directive, and in particular its provisions relating to information about any contractual clause on law applicable to the contract and/or on the competent court does not affect the applicability to the distance marketing of consumer financial services of Council Regulation (EC) No 44/2001 of 22 December 2000 on jurisdiction and the recognition and enforcement of judgements in civil and commercial matters[5] or of the 1980 Rome Convention on the law applicable to contractual obligations.

(9) The achievement of the objectives of the Financial Services Action Plan requires a higher level of consumer protection in certain areas. This implies a greater convergence, in particular, in non harmonised collective investment funds, rules of conduct applicable to investment services and consumer credits. Pending the achievement of the above convergence, a high level of consumer protection should be maintained.

(10) Directive 97/7/EC of the European Parliament and of the Council of 20 May 1997 on the protection of consumers in respect of distance contracts,[6] lays down the main rules applicable to distance contracts for goods or services concluded between a supplier and a consumer. However, that Directive does not cover financial services.

(11) In the context of the analysis conducted by the Commission with a view to ascertaining the need for specific measures in the field of financial services, the Commission invited all the interested parties to transmit their comments, notably in connection with the preparation of its Green Paper entitled 'Financial Services—Meeting Consumers' Expectations'. The consultations in this context showed that there is a need to strengthen consumer protection in this area. The Commission therefore decided to present a specific proposal concerning the distance marketing of financial services.

(12) The adoption by the Member States of conflicting or different consumer protection rules governing the distance marketing of consumer financial services could impede the functioning of the internal market and competition between firms in the market. It is therefore necessary to enact common rules at Community level in this area, consistent with no reduction in overall consumer protection in the Member States.

(13) A high level of consumer protection should be guaranteed by this Directive, with a view to ensuring the free movement of financial services. Member States should not be able to adopt provisions other than those laid down in this Directive in the fields it harmonises, unless otherwise specifically indicated in it.

(14)   This Directive covers all financial services liable to be provided at a distance. However, certain financial services are governed by specific provisions of Community legislation which continue to apply to those financial services. However, principles governing the distance marketing of such services should be laid down.

(15)   Contracts negotiated at a distance involve the use of means of distance communication which are used as part of a distance sales or service-provision scheme not involving the simultaneous presence of the supplier and the consumer. The constant development of those means of communication requires principles to be defined that are valid even for those means which are not yet in widespread use. Therefore, distance contracts are those the offer, negotiation and conclusion of which are carried out at a distance.

(16)   A single contract involving successive operations or separate operations of the same nature performed over time may be subject to different legal treatment in the different Member States, but it is important that this Directive be applied in the same way in all the Member States. To that end, it is appropriate that this Directive should be considered to apply to the first of a series of successive operations or separate operations of the same nature performed over time which may be considered as forming a whole, irrespective of whether that operation or series of operations is the subject of a single contract or several successive contracts.

(17)   An 'initial service agreement' may be considered to be for example the opening of a bank account, acquiring a credit card, concluding a portfolio management contract, and 'operations' may be considered to be for example the deposit or withdrawal of funds to or from the bank account, payment by credit card, transactions made within the framework of a portfolio management contract. Adding new elements to an initial service agreement, such as a possibility to use an electronic payment instrument together with one's existing bank account, does not constitute an 'operation' but an additional contract to which this Directive applies. The subscription to new units of the same collective investment fund is considered to be one of 'successive operations of the same nature'.

(18)   By covering a service-provision scheme organised by the financial services provider, this Directive aims to exclude from its scope services provided on a strictly occasional basis and outside a commercial structure dedicated to the conclusion of distance contracts.

(19)   The supplier is the person providing services at a distance. This Directive should however also apply when one of the marketing stages involves an intermediary. Having regard to the nature and degree of that involvement, the pertinent provisions of this Directive should apply to such an intermediary, irrespective of his or her legal status.

(20)   Durable mediums include in particular floppy discs, CD-ROMs, DVDs and the hard drive of the consumer's computer on which the electronic mail is stored, but they do not include Internet websites unless they fulfil the criteria contained in the definition of a durable medium.

(21)   The use of means of distance communications should not lead to an unwarranted restriction on the information provided to the client. In the interests of transparency this Directive lays down the requirements needed to ensure that an appropriate level of information is provided to the consumer both before and after conclusion of the contract. The consumer should receive, before conclusion of the contract, the prior information needed so as to properly appraise the financial service offered to him and hence make a well-informed choice. The supplier should specify how long his offer applies as it stands.

(22)   Information items listed in this Directive cover information of a general nature applicable to all kinds of financial services. Other information requirements concerning a given financial service, such as the coverage of an insurance policy, are not solely specified in this Directive. This kind of information should be provided in accordance, where applicable, with relevant Community legislation or national legislation in conformity with Community law.

(23)   With a view to optimum protection of the consumer, it is important that the consumer is adequately informed of the provisions of this Directive and of any codes of conduct existing in this area and that he has a right of withdrawal.

(24)   When the right of withdrawal does not apply because the consumer has expressly requested the performance of a contract, the supplier should inform the consumer of this fact.

(25)   Consumers should be protected against unsolicited services. Consumers should be exempt from any obligation in the case of unsolicited services, the absence of a reply not being construed as signifying consent on their part. However, this rule should be without prejudice to the tacit renewal of contracts validly concluded between the parties whenever the law of the Member States permits such tacit renewal.

(26)   Member States should take appropriate measures to protect effectively consumers who do not wish to be contacted through certain means of communication or at certain times. This Directive should be without prejudice to the particular safeguards available to consumers under Community legislation concerning the protection of personal data and privacy.

(27)   With a view to protecting consumers, there is a need for suitable and effective complaint and redress procedures in the Member States with a view to settling potential disputes between suppliers and consumers, by using, where appropriate, existing procedures.

(28)   Member States should encourage public or private bodies established with a view to settling disputes out of court to cooperate in resolving cross-border disputes. Such cooperation

could in particular entail allowing consumers to submit to extra-judicial bodies in the Member State of their residence complaints concerning suppliers established in other Member States. The establishment of FIN-NET offers increased assistance to consumers when using cross-border services.

(29)   This Directive is without prejudice to extension by Member States, in accordance with Community law, of the protection provided by this Directive to non-profit organisations and persons making use of financial services in order to become entrepreneurs.

(30)   This Directive should also cover cases where the national legislation includes the concept of a consumer making a binding contractual statement.

(31)   The provisions in this Directive on the supplier's choice of language should be without prejudice to provisions of national legislation, adopted in conformity with Community law governing the choice of language.

(32)   The Community and the Member States have entered into commitments in the context of the General Agreement on Trade in Services (GATS) concerning the possibility for consumers to purchase banking and investment services abroad. The GATS entitles Member States to adopt measures for prudential reasons, including measures to protect investors, depositors, policy-holders and persons to whom a financial service is owed by the supplier of the financial service. Such measures should not impose restrictions going beyond what is required to ensure the protection of consumers.

(33)   In view of the adoption of this Directive, the scope of Directive 97/7/EC and Directive 98/27/EC of the European Parliament and of the Council of 19 May 1998 on injunctions for the protection of consumers' interests[7] and the scope of the cancellation period in Council Directive 90/619/EEC of 8 November 1990 on the coordination of laws, regulations and administrative provisions relating to direct life assurance, laying down provisions to facilitate the effective exercise of freedom to provide services[8] should be adapted.

(34)   Since the objectives of this Directive, namely the establishment of common rules on the distance marketing of consumer financial services cannot be sufficiently achieved by the Member States and can therefore be better achieved at Community level, the Community may adopt measures, in accordance with the principles of subsidiarity as set out in Article 5 of the Treaty. In accordance with the principle of proportionality, as set out in that Article, this Directive does not go beyond what is necessary to achieve that objective,

[5364]

NOTES

1   OJ C385, 11.12.1998, p 10 and OJ C177E, 27.6.2000, p 21.
2   OJ C169, 16.6.1999, p 43.
3   Opinion of the European Parliament of 5 May 1999 (OJ C279, 1.10.1999, p 207), Council Common Position of 19 December 2001 (OJ C58E, 5.3.2002, p 32) and Decision of the European Parliament of 14 May 2002 (not yet published in the Official Journal). Council Decision of 26 June 2002 (not yet published in the Official Journal).
4   OJ L178, 17.7.2000, p 1.
5   OJ L12, 16.1.2001, p 1.
6   OJ L144, 4.6.1997, p 19.
7   OJ L166, 11.6.1998, p 51. Directive as last amended by Directive 2000/31/EC (OJ L178, 17.7.2001, p 1).
8   OJ L330, 29.11.1990, p 50. Directive as last amended by Directive 92/96/EEC (OJ L360, 9.12.1992, p 1).

HAVE ADOPTED THIS DIRECTIVE:

Article 1
Object and scope

1.   The object of this Directive is to approximate the laws, regulations and administrative provisions of the Member States concerning the distance marketing of consumer financial services.

2.   In the case of contracts for financial services comprising an initial service agreement followed by successive operations or a series of separate operations of the same nature performed over time, the provisions of this Directive shall apply only to the initial agreement.

In case there is no initial service agreement but the successive operations or the separate operations of the same nature performed over time are performed between the same contractual parties, Articles 3 and 4 apply only when the first operation is performed. Where, however, no operation of the same nature is performed for more than one year, the next operation will be deemed to be the first in a new series of operations and, accordingly, Articles 3 and 4 shall apply.

[5364A]

Article 2
Definitions

For the purposes of this Directive:
   (a)   'distance contract' means any contract concerning financial services concluded between a supplier and a consumer under an organised distance sales or service-provision scheme

run by the supplier, who, for the purpose of that contract, makes exclusive use of one or more means of distance communication up to and including the time at which the contract is concluded;

(b)   'financial service' means any service of a banking, credit, insurance, personal pension, investment or payment nature;

(c)   'supplier' means any natural or legal person, public or private, who, acting in his commercial or professional capacity, is the contractual provider of services subject to distance contracts;

(d)   'consumer' means any natural person who, in distance contracts covered by this Directive, is acting for purposes which are outside his trade, business or profession;

(e)   'means of distance communication' refers to any means which, without the simultaneous physical presence of the supplier and the consumer, may be used for the distance marketing of a service between those parties;

(f)   'durable medium' means any instrument which enables the consumer to store information addressed personally to him in a way accessible for future reference for a period of time adequate for the purposes of the information and which allows the unchanged reproduction of the information stored;

(g)   'operator or supplier of a means of distance communication' means any public or private, natural or legal person whose trade, business or profession involves making one or more means of distance communication available to suppliers.

[5365]

Article 3
Information to the consumer prior to the conclusion of the distance contract

1.   In good time before the consumer is bound by any distance contract or offer, he shall be provided with the following information concerning:

(1)   the supplier

      (a)   the identity and the main business of the supplier, the geographical address at which the supplier is established and any other geographical address relevant for the customer's relations with the supplier;

      (b)   the identity of the representative of the supplier established in the consumer's Member State of residence and the geographical address relevant for the customer's relations with the representative, if such a representative exists;

      (c)   when the consumer's dealings are with any professional other than the supplier, the identity of this professional, the capacity in which he is acting vis-à-vis the consumer, and the geographical address relevant for the customer's relations with this professional;

      (d)   where the supplier is registered in a trade or similar public register, the trade register in which the supplier is entered and his registration number or an equivalent means of identification in that register;

      (e)   where the supplier's activity is subject to an authorisation scheme, the particulars of the relevant supervisory authority;

(2)   the financial service

      (a)   a description of the main characteristics of the financial service;

      (b)   the total price to be paid by the consumer to the supplier for the financial service, including all related fees, charges and expenses, and all taxes paid via the supplier or, when an exact price cannot be indicated, the basis for the calculation of the price enabling the consumer to verify it;

      (c)   where relevant notice indicating that the financial service is related to instruments involving special risks related to their specific features or the operations to be executed or whose price depends on fluctuations in the financial markets outside the supplier's control and that historical performances are no indicators for future performances;

      (d)   notice of the possibility that other taxes and/or costs may exist that are not paid via the supplier or imposed by him;

      (e)   any limitations of the period for which the information provided is valid;

      (f)   the arrangements for payment and for performance;

      (g)   any specific additional cost for the consumer of using the means of distance communication, if such additional cost is charged;

(3)   the distance contract

      (a)   the existence or absence of a right of withdrawal in accordance with Article 6 and, where the right of withdrawal exists, its duration and the conditions for exercising it, including information on the amount which the consumer may be required to pay on the basis of Article 7(1), as well as the consequences of non-exercise of that right;

      (b)   the minimum duration of the distance contract in the case of financial services to be performed permanently or recurrently;

      (c)   information on any rights the parties may have to terminate the contract early or unilaterally by virtue of the terms of the distance contract, including any penalties imposed by the contract in such cases;

      (d)   practical instructions for exercising the right of withdrawal indicating, *inter alia*, the address to which the notification of a withdrawal should be sent;

      (e)   the Member State or States whose laws are taken by the supplier as a basis for the establishment of relations with the consumer prior to the conclusion of the distance contract;

      (f)   any contractual clause on law applicable to the distance contract and/or on competent court;

      (g)   in which language, or languages, the contractual terms and conditions, and the prior information referred to in this Article are supplied, and furthermore in which language, or languages, the supplier, with the agreement of the consumer, undertakes to communicate during the duration of this distance contract;

  (4)   redress

      (a)   whether or not there is an out-of-court complaint and redress mechanism for the consumer that is party to the distance contract and, if so, the methods for having access to it;

      (b)   the existence of guarantee funds or other compensation arrangements, not covered by Directive 94/19/EC of the European Parliament and of the Council of 30 May 1994 on deposit guarantee schemes[1] and Directive 97/9/EC of the European Parliament and of the Council of 3 March 1997 on investor compensation schemes.[2]

  2.   The information referred to in paragraph 1, the commercial purpose of which must be made clear, shall be provided in a clear and comprehensible manner in any way appropriate to the means of distance communication used, with due regard, in particular, to the principles of good faith in commercial transactions, and the principles governing the protection of those who are unable, pursuant to the legislation of the Member States, to give their consent, such as minors.

  3.   In the case of voice telephony communications

      (a)   the identity of the supplier and the commercial purpose of the call initiated by the supplier shall be made explicitly clear at the beginning of any conversation with the consumer;

      (b)   subject to the explicit consent of the consumer only the following information needs to be given:

         —   the identity of the person in contact with the consumer and his link with the supplier,

         —   a description of the main characteristics of the financial service,

         —   the total price to be paid by the consumer to the supplier for the financial service including all taxes paid via the supplier or, when an exact price cannot be indicated, the basis for the calculation of the price enabling the consumer to verify it,

         —   notice of the possibility that other taxes and/or costs may exist that are not paid via the supplier or imposed by him,

         —   the existence or absence of a right of withdrawal in accordance with Article 6 and, where the right of withdrawal exists, its duration and the conditions for exercising it, including information on the amount which the consumer may be required to pay on the basis of Article 7(1).

  The supplier shall inform the consumer that other information is available on request and of what nature this information is. In any case the supplier shall provide the full information when he fulfils his obligations under Article 5.

  4.   Information on contractual obligations, to be communicated to the consumer during the pre-contractual phase, shall be in conformity with the contractual obligations which would result from the law presumed to be applicable to the distance contract if the latter were concluded.

                                                            [5366]

NOTES
  [1]   OJ L135, 31.5.1994, p 5.
  [2]   OJ L84, 26.3.1997, p 22.

Article 4
Additional information requirements

  1.   Where there are provisions in the Community legislation governing financial services which contain prior information requirements additional to those listed in Article 3(1), these requirements shall continue to apply.

2.   Pending further harmonisation, Member States may maintain or introduce more stringent provisions on prior information requirements when the provisions are in conformity with Community law.

3.   Member States shall communicate to the Commission national provisions on prior information requirements under paragraphs 1 and 2 of this Article when these requirements are additional to those listed in Article 3(1). The Commission shall take account of the communicated national provisions when drawing up the report referred to in Article 20(2).

4.   The Commission shall, with a view to creating a high level of transparency by all appropriate means, ensure that information, on the national provisions communicated to it, is made available to consumers and suppliers.

[5.   Where Directive 2007/64/EC of the European Parliament and of the Council of 13 November 2007 on payment services in the internal market[1] is also applicable, the information provisions under Article 3(1) of this Directive, with the exception of paragraphs (2)(c) to (g), (3)(a), (d) and (e), and (4)(b), shall be replaced with Articles 36, 37, 41 and 42 of that Directive.]

[5367]

NOTES
    Para 5: added by European Parliament and Council Directive 2007/64/EC, Art 90(1), as from 25 December 2007. Note that 2007/64/EC has a transposition date of 1 November 2009 (see Art 94 at **[6179]**) and for transitional provisions see Art 88 at **[6177]**.
    [1]   OJ L319, 5.12.2007, p 1.

Article 5
Communication of the contractual terms and conditions and of the prior information

1.   The supplier shall communicate to the consumer all the contractual terms and conditions and the information referred to in Article 3(1) and Article 4 on paper or on another durable medium available and accessible to the consumer in good time before the consumer is bound by any distance contract or offer.

2.   The supplier shall fulfil his obligation under paragraph 1 immediately after the conclusion of the contract, if the contract has been concluded at the consumer's request using a means of distance communication which does not enable providing the contractual terms and conditions and the information in conformity with paragraph 1.

3.   At any time during the contractual relationship the consumer is entitled, at his request, to receive the contractual terms and conditions on paper. In addition, the consumer is entitled to change the means of distance communication used, unless this is incompatible with the contract concluded or the nature of the financial service provided.

[5368]

Article 6
Right of withdrawal

1.   The Member States shall ensure that the consumer shall have a period of 14 calendar days to withdraw from the contract without penalty and without giving any reason. However, this period shall be extended to 30 calendar days in distance contracts relating to life insurance covered by Directive 90/619/EEC and personal pension operations.

The period for withdrawal shall begin:
- — either from the day of the conclusion of the distance contract, except in respect of the said life assurance, where the time limit will begin from the time when the consumer is informed that the distance contract has been concluded, or
- — from the day on which the consumer receives the contractual terms and conditions and the information in accordance with Article 5(1) or (2), if that is later than the date referred to in the first indent.

Member States, in addition to the right of withdrawal, may provide that the enforceability of contracts relating to investment services is suspended for the same period provided for in this paragraph.

2.   The right of withdrawal shall not apply to:
   (a)   financial services whose price depends on fluctuations in the financial market outside the suppliers control, which may occur during the withdrawal period, such as services related to:
   - — foreign exchange,
   - — money market instruments,
   - — transferable securities,
   - — units in collective investment undertakings,
   - — financial-futures contracts, including equivalent cash-settled instruments,
   - — forward interest-rate agreements (FRAs),

—   interest-rate, currency and equity swaps,
—   options to acquire or dispose of any instruments referred to in this point including equivalent cash-settled instruments. This category includes in particular options on currency and on interest rates;

(b)   travel and baggage insurance policies or similar short-term insurance policies of less than one month's duration;

(c)   contracts whose performance has been fully completed by both parties at the consumer's express request before the consumer exercises his right of withdrawal.

3.   Member States may provide that the right of withdrawal shall not apply to:

(a)   any credit intended primarily for the purpose of acquiring or retaining property rights in land or in an existing or projected building, or for the purpose of renovating or improving a building, or

(b)   any credit secured either by mortgage on immovable property or by a right related to immovable property, or

(c)   declarations by consumers using the services of an official, provided that the official confirms that the consumer is guaranteed the rights under Article 5(1).

This paragraph shall be without prejudice to the right to a reflection time to the benefit of the consumers that are resident in those Member States where it exists, at the time of the adoption of this Directive.

4.   Member States making use of the possibility set out in paragraph 3 shall communicate it to the Commission.

5.   The Commission shall make available the information communicated by Member States to the European Parliament and the Council and shall ensure that it is also available to consumers and suppliers who request it.

6.   If the consumer exercises his right of withdrawal he shall, before the expiry of the relevant deadline, notify this following the practical instructions given to him in accordance with Article 3(1)(3)(d) by means which can be proved in accordance with national law. The deadline shall be deemed to have been observed if the notification, if it is on paper or on another durable medium available and accessible to the recipient, is dispatched before the deadline expires.

7.   This Article does not apply to credit agreements cancelled under the conditions of Article 6(4) of Directive 97/7/EC or Article 7 of Directive 94/47/EC of the European Parliament and of the Council of 26 October 1994 on the protection of purchasers in respect of certain aspects of contracts relating to the purchase of the right to use immovable properties on a timeshare basis.[1]

If to a distance contract of a given financial service another distance contract has been attached concerning services provided by the supplier or by a third party on the basis of an agreement between the third party and the supplier, this additional distance contract shall be cancelled, without any penalty, if the consumer exercises his right of withdrawal as provided for in Article 6(1).

8.   The provisions of this Article are without prejudice to the Member States' laws and regulations governing the cancellation or termination or non-enforceability of a distance contract or the right of a consumer to fulfil his contractual obligations before the time fixed in the distance contract. This applies irrespective of the conditions for and the legal effects of the winding-up of the contract.

[5369]

NOTES
[1]   OJ L280, 29.10.1994, p 83.

Article 7
Payment of the service provided before withdrawal

1.   When the consumer exercises his right of withdrawal under Article 6(1) he may only be required to pay, without any undue delay, for the service actually provided by the supplier in accordance with the contract. The performance of the contract may only begin after the consumer has given his approval. The amount payable shall not:

—   exceed an amount which is in proportion to the extent of the service already provided in comparison with the full coverage of the contract,
—   in any case be such that it could be construed as a penalty.

2.   Member States may provide that the consumer cannot be required to pay any amount when withdrawing from an insurance contract.

3.   The supplier may not require the consumer to pay any amount on the basis of paragraph 1 unless he can prove that the consumer was duly informed about the amount payable, in conformity with Article 3(1)(3)(a). However, in no case may he require such payment if he has commenced the performance of the contract before the expiry of the withdrawal period provided for in Article 6(1) without the consumer's prior request.

4. The supplier shall, without any undue delay and no later than within 30 calendar days, return to the consumer any sums he has received from him in accordance with the distance contract, except for the amount referred to in paragraph 1. This period shall begin from the day on which the supplier receives the notification of withdrawal.

5. The consumer shall return to the supplier any sums and/or property he has received from the supplier without any undue delay and no later than within 30 calendar days. This period shall begin from the day on which the consumer dispatches the notification of withdrawal.

[5370]

Article 8
Payment by card

Member States shall ensure that appropriate measures exist to allow a consumer:
— *to request cancellation of a payment where fraudulent use has been made of his payment card in connection with distance contracts,*
— *in the event of such fraudulent use, to be re-credited with the sum paid or have them returned.*

[5371]

NOTES
  Repealed by European Parliament and Council Directive 2007/64/EC, Art 90(2), as from 25 December 2007. Note that 2007/64/EC has a transposition date of 1 November 2009 (see Art 94 at **[6179]**) and for transitional provisions see Art 88 at **[6177]**.

[Article 9

Given the prohibition of inertia selling practices laid down in Directive 2005/29/EC of 11 May 2005 of the European Parliament and of the Council concerning unfair business-to-consumer commercial practices in the internal market[1] and without prejudice to the provisions of Member States' legislation on the tacit renewal of distance contracts, when such rules permit tacit renewal, Member States shall take measures to exempt the consumer from any obligation in the event of unsolicited supplies, the absence of a reply not constituting consent.]

[5372]

NOTES
  Substituted by European Parliament and Council Directive 2005/29/EC, Art 15(2), as from 12 June 2005.
  [1]   OJ L149, 11.6.2005, p 22.

Article 10
Unsolicited communications

1. The use by a supplier of the following distance communication techniques shall require the consumer's prior consent:
  (a)   automated calling systems without human intervention (automatic calling machines);
  (b)   fax machines.

2. Member States shall ensure that means of distance communication other than those referred to in paragraph 1, when they allow individual communications:
  (a)   shall not be authorised unless the consent of the consumers concerned has been obtained, or
  (b)   may only be used if the consumer has not expressed his manifest objection.

3. The measures referred to in paragraphs 1 and 2 shall not entail costs for consumers.

[5373]

Article 11
Sanctions

Member States shall provide for appropriate sanctions in the event of the supplier's failure to comply with national provisions adopted pursuant to this Directive.

They may provide for this purpose in particular that the consumer may cancel the contract at any time, free of charge and without penalty.

These sanctions must be effective, proportional and dissuasive.

[5374]

Article 12
Imperative nature of this Directive's provisions

1. Consumers may not waive the rights conferred on them by this Directive.

2. Member States shall take the measures needed to ensure that the consumer does not lose the protection granted by this Directive by virtue of the choice of the law of a non-member country as the law applicable to the contract, if this contract has a close link with the territory of one or more Member States.

[5375]

Article 13
Judicial and administrative redress

1. Member States shall ensure that adequate and effective means exist to ensure compliance with this Directive in the interests of consumers.

2. The means referred to in paragraph 1 shall include provisions whereby one or more of the following bodies, as determined by national law, may take action in accordance with national law before the courts or competent administrative bodies to ensure that the national provisions for the implementation of this Directive are applied:

    (a) public bodies or their representatives;
    (b) consumer organisations having a legitimate interest in protecting consumers;
    (c) professional organisations having a legitimate interest in acting.

3. Member States shall take the measures necessary to ensure that operators and suppliers of means of distance communication put an end to practices that have been declared to be contrary to this Directive, on the basis of a judicial decision, an administrative decision or a decision issued by a supervisory authority notified to them, where those operators or suppliers are in a position to do so.

[5376]

Article 14
Out-of-court redress

1. Member States shall promote the setting up or development of adequate and effective out-of-court complaints and redress procedures for the settlement of consumer disputes concerning financial services provided at distance.

2. Member States shall, in particular, encourage the bodies responsible for out-of-court settlement of disputes to cooperate in the resolution of cross-border disputes concerning financial services provided at distance.

[5377]

Article 15
Burden of proof

Without prejudice to Article 7(3), Member States may stipulate that the burden of proof in respect of the supplier's obligations to inform the consumer and the consumer's consent to conclusion of the contract and, where appropriate, its performance, can be placed on the supplier.

Any contractual term or condition providing that the burden of proof of the respect by the supplier of all or part of the obligations incumbent on him pursuant to this Directive should lie with the consumer shall be an unfair term within the meaning of Council Directive 93/13/EEC of 5 April 1993 on unfair terms in consumer contracts.[1]

[5378]

NOTES
  [1] OJ L95, 21.4.1993, p 29.

Article 16
Transitional measures

Member States may impose national rules which are in conformity with this Directive on suppliers established in a Member State which has not yet transposed this Directive and whose law has no obligations corresponding to those provided for in this Directive.

[5379]

Articles 17–19

(*Amend Council Directive 90/619/EC (repealed), European Parliament and Council Directive 97/7/EC, and European Parliament and Council Directive 98/27/EC.*)

Article 20
Review

1. Following the implementation of this Directive, the Commission shall examine the functioning of the internal market in financial services in respect of the marketing of those services. It should seek to analyse and detail the difficulties that are, or might be faced by both consumers and suppliers, in particular arising from differences between national provisions regarding information and right of withdrawal.

2. Not later than 9 April 2006 the Commission shall report to the European Parliament and the Council on the problems facing both consumers and suppliers seeking to buy and sell financial services, and shall submit, where appropriate, proposals to amend and/or further harmonise the information and right of withdrawal provisions in Community legislation concerning financial services and/or those covered in Article 3.

[5380]

Article 21
Transposition

1. Member States shall bring into force the laws, regulations and administrative provisions necessary to comply with this Directive not later than 9 October 2004. They shall forthwith inform the Commission thereof.

When Member States adopt these measures, they shall contain a reference to this Directive or shall be accompanied by such a reference on the occasion of their official publication. The methods of making such reference shall be laid down by Member States.

2. Member States shall communicate to the Commission the text of the main provisions of national law which they adopt in the field governed by this Directive together with a table showing how the provisions of this Directive correspond to the national provisions adopted.

[5381]

Article 22
Entry into force

This Directive shall enter into force on the day of its publication in the *Official Journal of the European Communities*.

[5382]

Article 23
Addressees

This Directive is addressed to the Member States.

[5383]

DIRECTIVE OF THE EUROPEAN PARLIAMENT
AND OF THE COUNCIL

of 16 December 2002

on the supplementary supervision of credit institutions, insurance undertakings and investment firms in a financial conglomerate and amending Council Directives 73/239/EEC, 79/267/EEC, 92/49/EEC, 92/96/EEC, 93/6/EEC and 93/22/EEC, and Directives 98/78/EC and 2000/12/EC of the European Parliament and of the Council

(2002/87/EC)

NOTES

Date of publication in OJ: OJ 035, 11.02.2003, p 1. Notes are as in the original OJ version.

This Directive is reproduced as amended by: European Parliament and Council Directive 2005/1/EC (OJ L79, 24.3.2005, p 9); European Parliament and Council Directive 2006/48/EC (OJ L177, 30.6.2006, p 1); European Parliament and Council Directive 2006/49/EC (OJ L177, 30.6.2006, p 201); European Parliament and Council Directive 2008/25/EC (OJ L81, 20.3.2008, p 40).

Council Directive 79/267/EEC, Council Directive 92/96/EEC: repealed by European Parliament and Council Directive 2002/83/EC.

Council Directive 93/6/EEC: repealed by European Parliament and Council Directive 2006/49/EC.

Council Directive 93/22/EEC: repealed by European Parliament and Council Directive 2004/39/EC.

Council Directive 2000/12/EC: repealed by European Parliament and Council Directive 2006/48/EC.

THE EUROPEAN PARLIAMENT AND THE COUNCIL OF THE EUROPEAN UNION,

Having regard to the Treaty establishing the European Community, and in particular Article 47(2) thereof,

Having regard to the proposal from the Commission,[1]

Having regard to the opinion of the Economic and Social Committee,[2]

After consulting the Committee of the Regions,

Having regard to the opinion of the European Central Bank,[3]

Acting in accordance with the procedure laid down in Article 251 of the Treaty,[4]

Whereas:

(1)   The current Community legislation provides for a comprehensive set of rules on the prudential supervision of credit institutions, insurance undertakings and investment firms on a stand alone basis and credit institutions, insurance undertakings and investment firms which are part of respectively a banking/investment firm group or an insurance group, ie groups with homogeneous financial activities.

(2)   New developments in financial markets have led to the creation of financial groups which provide services and products in different sectors of the financial markets, called financial conglomerates. Until now, there has been no form of prudential supervision on a group-wide basis of credit institutions, insurance undertakings and investment firms which are part of such a conglomerate, in particular as regards the solvency position and risk concentration at the level of the conglomerate, the intra-group transactions, the internal risk management processes at conglomerate level, and the fit and proper character of the management. Some of these conglomerates are among the biggest financial groups which are active in the financial markets and provide services on a global basis. If such conglomerates, and in particular credit institutions, insurance undertakings and investment firms which are part of such a conglomerate, were to face financial difficulties, these could seriously destabilise the financial system and affect individual depositors, insurance policy holders and investors.

(3)   The Commission Action Plan for Financial Services identifies a series of actions which are needed to complete the Single Market in Financial Services, and announces the development of supplementary prudential legislation for financial conglomerates which will address loopholes in the present sectoral legislation and additional prudential risks to ensure sound supervisory arrangements with regard to financial groups with cross-sectoral financial activities. Such an ambitious objective can only be attained in stages. The establishment of the supplementary supervision of credit institutions, insurance undertakings and investment firms in a financial conglomerate is one such stage.

(4)   Other international forums have also identified the need for the development of appropriate supervisory concepts with regard to financial conglomerates.

(5)   In order to be effective, the supplementary supervision of credit institutions, insurance undertakings and investment firms in a financial conglomerate should be applied to all such conglomerates, the cross-sectoral financial activities of which are significant, which is the case when certain thresholds are reached, no matter how they are structured. Supplementary supervision should cover all financial activities identified by the sectoral financial legislation and all entities principally engaged in such activities should be included in the scope of the supplementary supervision, including asset management companies.

(6)   Decisions not to include a particular entity in the scope of supplementary supervision should be taken, bearing in mind inter alia whether or not such entity is included in the group-wide supervision under sectoral rules.

(7)   The competent authorities should be able to assess at a group-wide level the financial situation of credit institutions, insurance undertakings and investment firms which are part of a financial conglomerate, in particular as regards solvency (including the elimination of multiple gearing of own funds instruments), risk concentration and intra-group transactions.

(8)   Financial conglomerates are often managed on a business-line basis which does not fully coincide with the conglomerate's legal structures. In order to take account of this trend, the requirements for management should be further extended, in particular as regards the management of the mixed financial holding company.

(9)   All financial conglomerates subject to supplementary supervision should have a coordinator appointed from among the competent authorities involved.

(10)   The tasks of the coordinator should not affect the tasks and responsibilities of the competent authorities as provided for by the sectoral rules.

(11)   The competent authorities involved, and especially the coordinator, should have the means of obtaining from the entities within a financial conglomerate, or from other competent authorities, the information necessary for the performance of their supplementary supervision.

(12)   There is a pressing need for increased collaboration between authorities responsible for the supervision of credit institutions, insurance undertakings and investment firms, including the development of ad hoc cooperation arrangements between the authorities involved in the supervision of entities belonging to the same financial conglomerate.

(13)   Credit institutions, insurance undertakings and investment firms which have their head office in the Community can be part of a financial conglomerate, the head of which is outside the Community. These regulated entities should also be subject to equivalent and appropriate supplementary supervisory arrangements which achieve objectives and results similar to those pursued by the provisions of this Directive. To this end, transparency of rules and exchange of information with third-country authorities on all relevant circumstances are of great importance.

(14)   Equivalent and appropriate supplementary supervisory arrangements can only be assumed to exist if the third-country supervisory authorities have agreed to cooperate with the competent authorities concerned on the means and objectives of exercising supplementary supervision of the regulated entities of a financial conglomerate.

(15) This Directive does not require the disclosure by competent authorities to a financial conglomerates committee of information which is subject to an obligation of confidentiality under this Directive or other sectoral directives.

(16) Since the objective of the proposed action, namely the establishment of rules on the supplementary supervision of credit institutions, insurance undertakings and investment firms in a financial conglomerate, cannot be sufficiently achieved by the Member States and can therefore, by reason of the scale and the effects of the action, be better achieved at Community level, the Community may adopt measures, in accordance with the principle of subsidiarity as set out in Article 5 of the Treaty. In accordance with the principle of proportionality, as set out in that Article, this Directive does not go beyond what is necessary in order to achieve this objective. Since this Directive defines minimum standards, Member States may lay down stricter rules.

(17) This Directive respects the fundamental rights and observes the principles recognised in particular by the Charter of Fundamental Rights of the European Union.

(18) The measures necessary for the implementation of this Directive should be adopted in accordance with Council Decision 1999/468/EC of 28 June 1999 laying down the procedures for the exercise of implementing powers conferred on the Commission.[5]

(19) Technical guidance and implementing measures for the rules laid down in this Directive may from time to time be necessary to take account of new developments on financial markets. The Commission should accordingly be empowered to adopt implementing measures, provided that these do not modify the essential elements of this Directive.

(20) The existing sectoral rules for credit institutions, insurance undertakings and investment firms should be supplemented to a minimum level, in particular to avoid regulatory arbitrage between the sectoral rules and those for financial conglomerates. Therefore, First Council Directive 73/239/EEC of 24 July 1973 on the coordination of laws, regulations and administrative provisions relating to the taking up and pursuit of the business of direct insurance other than life assurance,[6] First Council Directive 79/267/EEC of 5 March 1979 on the coordination of laws, regulations and administrative provisions relating to the taking up and pursuit of the business of direct life assurance,[7] Council Directive 92/49/EEC of 18 June 1992 on the coordination of laws, regulations and administrative provisions relating to direct insurance other than life insurance (third non-life insurance Directive),[8] Council Directive 92/96/EEC of 10 November 1992 on the coordination of laws, regulations and administrative provisions relating to direct life assurance (third life insurance Directive),[9] Council Directive 93/6/EEC of 15 March 1993 on the capital adequacy of investments firms and credit institutions[10] and Council Directive 93/22/EEC of 10 May 1993 on investment services in the securities field,[11] as well as Directive 98/78/EC of the European Parliament and of the Council of 27 October 1998 on the supplementary supervision of insurance undertakings in an insurance group[12] and Directive 2000/12/EC of the European Parliament and of the Council of 20 March 2000 relating to the taking up and pursuit of the business of credit institutions[13] should be amended accordingly. The objective of further harmonisation can, however, only be achieved by stages and needs to be based on careful analysis.

(21) In order to assess the need for and prepare any possible future harmonisation of the treatment of asset management companies under sectoral rules, the Commission should report on Member States' practices in this field,

[5384]

NOTES

[1] OJ C213E, 31.7.2001, p 227.
[2] OJ C36, 8.2.2002, p 1.
[3] OJ C271, 26.9.2001, p 10.
[4] Opinion of the European Parliament of 14 March 2002 (not yet published in the Official Journal), Council Common Position of 12 September 2002 (OJ C253E, 22.10.2002, p 1) and Decision of the European Parliament of 20 November 2002 (not yet published in the Official Journal).
[5] OJ L184, 17.7.1999, p 23.
[6] OJ L228, 16.8.1973, p 3. Directive as last amended by Directive 2002/13/EC of the European Parliament and of the Council (OJ L77, 20.3.2002, p 17).
[7] OJ L63, 13.3.1979, p 1. Directive as last amended by Directive 2002/12/EC of the European Parliament and of the Council (OJ L77, 20.3.2002, p 11).
[8] OJ L228, 11.8.1992, p 1. Directive as last amended by Directive 2000/64/EC of the European Parliament and of the Council (OJ L290, 17.11.2000, p 27).
[9] OJ L360, 9.12.1992, p 1. Directive as last amended by Directive 2000/64/EC.
[10] OJ L141, 11.6.1993, p 1. Directive as last amended by Directive 98/33/EC of the European Parliament and of the Council (OJ L204, 21.7.1998, p 29).
[11] OJ L141, 11.6.1993, p 27. Directive as last amended by Directive 2000/64/EC.
[12] OJ L330, 5.12.1998, p 1.
[13] OJ L126, 26.5.2000, p 1. Directive as amended by Directive 2000/28/EC (OJ L275, 27.10.2000, p 37).

HAVE ADOPTED THIS DIRECTIVE:

CHAPTER I
OBJECTIVE AND DEFINITIONS

Article 1
Objective

This Directive lays down rules for supplementary supervision of regulated entities which have obtained an authorisation pursuant to Article 6 of Directive 73/239/EEC, Article 6 of Directive 79/267/EEC, Article 3(1) of Directive 93/22/EEC or Article 4 of Directive 2000/12/EC, and which are part of a financial conglomerate. It also amends the relevant sectoral rules which apply to entities regulated by the Directives referred to above.

[5384A]

Article 2
Definitions

For the purposes of this Directive:

1. "credit institution" shall mean a credit institution within the meaning of the second subparagraph of Article 1(1) of Directive 2000/12/EC;

2. "insurance undertaking" shall mean an insurance undertaking within the meaning of Article 6 of Directive 73/239/EEC, Article 6 of Directive 79/267/EEC or Article 1(b) of Directive 98/78/EC;

3. "investment firm" shall mean an investment firm within the meaning of Article 1(2) of Directive 93/22/EEC, including the undertakings referred to in Article 2(4) of Directive 93/6/EEC;

4. "regulated entity" shall mean a credit institution, an insurance undertaking or an investment firm;

5. "asset management company" shall mean a management company within the meaning of Article 1a(2) of Council Directive 85/611/EEC of 20 December 1985 on the coordination of laws, regulations and administrative provisions relating to undertakings for collective investment in transferable securities (UCITS),[1] as well as an undertaking the registered office of which is outside the Community and which would require authorisation in accordance with Article 5(1) of that Directive if it had its registered office within the Community;

6. "reinsurance undertaking" shall mean a reinsurance undertaking within the meaning of Article 1(c) of Directive 98/78/EC;

7. "sectoral rules" shall mean the Community legislation relating to the prudential supervision of regulated entities, in particular laid down in Directives 73/239/EEC, 79/267/EEC, 98/78/EC, 93/6/EEC, 93/22/EEC and 2000/12/EC;

8. "financial sector" shall mean a sector composed of one or more of the following entities:
   (a) a credit institution, a financial institution or an ancillary banking services undertaking within the meaning of Article 1(5) and (23) of Directive 2000/12/EC (the banking sector);
   (b) an insurance undertaking, a reinsurance undertaking or an insurance holding company within the meaning of Article 1(i) of Directive 98/78/EC (the insurance sector);
   (c) an investment firm or a financial institution within the meaning of Article 2(7) of Directive 93/6/EEC (the investment services sector);
   (d) a mixed financial holding company;

9. "parent undertaking" shall mean a parent undertaking within the meaning of Article 1 of Seventh Council Directive 83/349/EEC of 13 June 1983 on consolidated accounts[2] and any undertaking which, in the opinion of the competent authorities, effectively exercises a dominant influence over another undertaking;

10. "subsidiary undertaking" shall mean a subsidiary undertaking within the meaning of Article 1 of Directive 83/349/EEC and any undertaking over which, in the opinion of the competent authorities, a parent undertaking effectively exercises a dominant influence; all subsidiary undertakings of subsidiary undertakings shall also be considered as subsidiary undertakings of the parent undertaking;

11. "participation" shall mean a participation within the meaning of the first sentence of Article 17 of Fourth Council Directive 78/660/EEC of 25 July 1978 on the annual accounts of certain types of companies,[3] or the direct or indirect ownership of 20% or more of the voting rights or capital of an undertaking;

12. "group" shall mean a group of undertakings, which consists of a parent undertaking, its subsidiaries and the entities in which the parent undertaking or its subsidiaries hold a participation, as well as undertakings linked to each other by a relationship within the meaning of Article 12(1) of Directive 83/349/EEC;

13. "close links" shall mean a situation in which two or more natural or legal persons are linked by:
   (a) "participation", which shall mean the ownership, direct or by way of control, of 20% or more of the voting rights or capital of an undertaking; or
   (b) "control", which shall mean the relationship between a parent undertaking and a subsidiary, in all the cases referred to in Article 1(1) and (2) of Directive 83/349/EEC, or a similar relationship between any natural or legal person and an undertaking; any subsidiary undertaking of a subsidiary undertaking shall also be considered a subsidiary of the parent undertaking which is at the head of those undertakings.

A situation in which two or more natural or legal persons are permanently linked to one and the same person by a control relationship shall also be regarded as constituting a close link between such persons;

14. "financial conglomerate" shall mean a group which meets, subject to Article 3, the following conditions:
   (a) a regulated entity within the meaning of Article 1 is at the head of the group or at least one of the subsidiaries in the group is a regulated entity within the meaning of Article 1;
   (b) where there is a regulated entity within the meaning of Article 1 at the head of the group, it is either a parent undertaking of an entity in the financial sector, an entity which holds a participation in an entity in the financial sector, or an entity linked with an entity in the financial sector by a relationship within the meaning of Article 12(1) of Directive 83/349/EEC;
   (c) where there is no regulated entity within the meaning of Article 1 at the head of the group, the group's activities mainly occur in the financial sector within the meaning of Article 3(1);
   (d) at least one of the entities in the group is within the insurance sector and at least one is within the banking or investment services sector;
   (e) the consolidated and/or aggregated activities of the entities in the group within the insurance sector and the consolidated and/or aggregated activities of the entities within the banking and investment services sector are both significant within the meaning of Article 3(2) or (3).

Any subgroup of a group within the meaning of point 12 which meets the criteria in this point shall be considered as a financial conglomerate;

15. "mixed financial holding company" shall mean a parent undertaking, other than a regulated entity, which together with its subsidiaries, at least one of which is a regulated entity which has its head office in the Community, and other entities, constitutes a financial conglomerate;

16. "competent authorities" shall mean the national authorities of the Member States which are empowered by law or regulation to supervise credit institutions, and/or insurance undertakings and/or investment firms whether on an individual or a group-wide basis;

17. "relevant competent authorities" shall mean:
   (a) Member States' competent authorities responsible for the sectoral group-wide supervision of any of the regulated entities in a financial conglomerate;
   (b) the coordinator appointed in accordance with Article 10 if different from the authorities referred to in (a);
   (c) other competent authorities concerned, where relevant, in the opinion of the authorities referred to in (a) and (b); this opinion shall especially take into account the market share of the regulated entities of the conglomerate in other Member States, in particular if it exceeds 5%, and the importance in the conglomerate of any regulated entity established in another Member State;

18. "intra-group transactions" shall mean all transactions by which regulated entities within a financial conglomerate rely either directly or indirectly upon other undertakings within the same group or upon any natural or legal person linked to the undertakings within that group by "close links", for the fulfilment of an obligation, whether or not contractual, and whether or not for payment;

19. "risk concentration" shall mean all exposures with a loss potential borne by entities within a financial conglomerate, which are large enough to threaten the solvency or the financial position in general of the regulated entities in the financial conglomerate; such exposures may be caused by counterparty risk/credit risk, investment risk, insurance risk, market risk, other risks, or a combination or interaction of these risks.

[5385]

NOTES

1. OJ L375, 31.12.1985, p 3. Directive as last amended by Directive 2001/108/EC of the European Parliament and of the Council (OJ L41, 13.2.2002, p 35).

² OJ L193, 18.7.1983, p 1. Directive as last amended by Directive 2001/65/EC of the European Parliament and of the Council (OJ L283, 27.10.2001, p 28).
³ OJ L222, 14.8.1978, p 11. Directive as last amended by Directive 2001/65/EC.

Article 3
Thresholds for identifying a financial conglomerate

1. For the purposes of determining whether the activities of a group mainly occur in the financial sector, within the meaning of Article 2(14)(c), the ratio of the balance sheet total of the regulated and non-regulated financial sector entities in the group to the balance sheet total of the group as a whole should exceed 40%.

2. For the purposes of determining whether activities in different financial sectors are significant within the meaning of Article 2(14)(e), for each financial sector the average of the ratio of the balance sheet total of that financial sector to the balance sheet total of the financial sector entities in the group and the ratio of the solvency requirements of the same financial sector to the total solvency requirements of the financial sector entities in the group should exceed 10%.

For the purposes of this Directive, the smallest financial sector in a financial conglomerate is the sector with the smallest average and the most important financial sector in a financial conglomerate is the sector with the highest average. For the purposes of calculating the average and for the measurement of the smallest and the most important financial sectors, the banking sector and the investment services sector shall be considered together.

3. Cross-sectoral activities shall also be presumed to be significant within the meaning of Article 2(14)(e) if the balance sheet total of the smallest financial sector in the group exceeds EUR 6 billion. If the group does not reach the threshold referred to in paragraph 2, the relevant competent authorities may decide by common agreement not to regard the group as a financial conglomerate, or not to apply the provisions of Articles 7, 8 or 9, if they are of the opinion that the inclusion of the group in the scope of this Directive or the application of such provisions is not necessary or would be inappropriate or misleading with respect to the objectives of supplementary supervision, taking into account, for instance, the fact that:
   (a) the relative size of its smallest financial sector does not exceed 5%, measured either in terms of the average referred to in paragraph 2 or in terms of the balance sheet total or the solvency requirements of such financial sector; or
   (b) the market share does not exceed 5% in any Member State, measured in terms of the balance sheet total in the banking or investment services sectors and in terms of gross premiums written in the insurance sector.

Decisions taken in accordance with this paragraph shall be notified to the other competent authorities concerned.

4. For the application of paragraphs 1, 2 and 3, the relevant competent authorities may by common agreement:
   (a) exclude an entity when calculating the ratios, in the cases referred to in Article 6(5);
   (b) take into account compliance with the thresholds envisaged in paragraphs 1 and 2 for three consecutive years so as to avoid sudden regime shifts, and disregard such compliance if there are significant changes in the group's structure.

Where a financial conglomerate has been identified according to paragraphs 1, 2 and 3, the decisions referred to in the first subparagraph of this paragraph shall be taken on the basis of a proposal made by the coordinator of that financial conglomerate.

5. For the application of paragraphs 1 and 2, the relevant competent authorities may, in exceptional cases and by common agreement, replace the criterion based on balance sheet total with one or both of the following parameters or add one or both of these parameters, if they are of the opinion that these parameters are of particular relevance for the purposes of supplementary supervision under this Directive: income structure, off-balance-sheet activities.

6. For the application of paragraphs 1 and 2, if the ratios referred to in those paragraphs fall below 40% and 10% respectively for conglomerates already subject to supplementary supervision, a lower ratio of 35% and 8% respectively shall apply for the following three years to avoid sudden regime shifts.

Similarly, for the application of paragraph 3, if the balance sheet total of the smallest financial sector in the group falls below EUR 6 billion for conglomerates already subject to supplementary supervision, a lower figure of EUR 5 billion shall apply for the following three years to avoid sudden regime shifts.

During the period referred to in this paragraph, the coordinator may, with the agreement of the other relevant competent authorities, decide that the lower ratios or the lower amount referred to in this paragraph shall cease to apply.

7. The calculations referred to in this Article regarding the balance sheet shall be made on the basis of the aggregated balance sheet total of the entities of the group, according to their annual

accounts. For the purposes of this calculation, undertakings in which a participation is held shall be taken into account as regards the amount of their balance sheet total corresponding to the aggregated proportional share held by the group. However, where consolidated accounts are available, they shall be used instead of aggregated accounts.

The solvency requirements referred to in paragraphs 2 and 3 shall be calculated in accordance with the provisions of the relevant sectoral rules.

[5386]

Article 4
Identifying a financial conglomerate

1. Competent authorities which have authorised regulated entities shall, on the basis of Articles 2, 3 and 5, identify any group that falls under the scope of this Directive.

For this purpose:
— competent authorities which have authorised regulated entities in the group shall, where necessary, cooperate closely,
— if a competent authority is of the opinion that a regulated entity authorised by that competent authority is a member of a group which may be a financial conglomerate, which has not already been identified according to this Directive, the competent authority shall communicate its view to the other competent authorities concerned.

2. The coordinator appointed in accordance with Article 10 shall inform the parent undertaking at the head of a group or, in the absence of a parent undertaking, the regulated entity with the largest balance sheet total in the most important financial sector in a group, that the group has been identified as a financial conglomerate and of the appointment of the coordinator. The coordinator shall also inform the competent authorities which have authorised regulated entities in the group and the competent authorities of the Member State in which the mixed financial holding company has its head office, as well as the Commission.

[5387]

CHAPTER II
SUPPLEMENTARY SUPERVISION

SECTION 1
SCOPE

Article 5
Scope of supplementary supervision of regulated entities referred to in Article 1

1. Without prejudice to the provisions on supervision contained in the sectoral rules, Member States shall provide for the supplementary supervision of the regulated entities referred to in Article 1, to the extent and in the manner prescribed in this Directive.

2. The following regulated entities shall be subject to supplementary supervision at the level of the financial conglomerate in accordance with Articles 6 to 17:
    (a) every regulated entity which is at the head of a financial conglomerate;
    (b) every regulated entity, the parent undertaking of which is a mixed financial holding company which has its head office in the Community;
    (c) every regulated entity linked with another financial sector entity by a relationship within the meaning of Article 12(1) of Directive 83/349/EEC.

Where a financial conglomerate is a subgroup of another financial conglomerate which meets the requirements of the first subparagraph, Member States may apply Articles 6 to 17 to the regulated entities within the latter group only and any reference in the Directive to the terms group and financial conglomerate will then be understood as referring to that latter group.

3. Every regulated entity which is not subject to supplementary supervision in accordance with paragraph 2, the parent undertaking of which is a regulated entity or a mixed financial holding company, having its head office outside the Community, shall be subject to supplementary supervision at the level of the financial conglomerate to the extent and in the manner prescribed in Article 18.

4. Where persons hold participations or capital ties in one or more regulated entities or exercise significant influence over such entities without holding a participation or capital ties, other than the cases referred to in paragraphs 2 and 3, the relevant competent authorities shall, by common agreement and in conformity with national law, determine whether and to what extent supplementary supervision of the regulated entities is to be carried out, as if they constitute a financial conglomerate.

In order to apply such supplementary supervision, at least one of the entities must be a regulated entity as referred to in Article 1 and the conditions set out in Article 2(14)(d) and (e) must be met. The relevant competent authorities shall take their decision, taking into account the objectives of the supplementary supervision as provided for by this Directive.

For the purposes of applying the first subparagraph to "cooperative groups", the competent authorities must take into account the public financial commitment of these groups with respect to other financial entities.

5.   Without prejudice to Article 13, the exercise of supplementary supervision at the level of the financial conglomerate shall in no way imply that the competent authorities are required to play a supervisory role in relation to mixed financial holding companies, third-country regulated entities in a financial conglomerate or unregulated entities in a financial conglomerate, on a stand-alone basis.

[5388]

SECTION 2
FINANCIAL POSITION

Article 6
Capital adequacy

1.   Without prejudice to the sectoral rules, supplementary supervision of the capital adequacy of the regulated entities in a financial conglomerate shall be exercised in accordance with the rules laid down in Article 9(2) to (5), in Section 3 of this Chapter, and in Annex I.

2.   The Member States shall require regulated entities in a financial conglomerate to ensure that own funds are available at the level of the financial conglomerate which are always at least equal to the capital adequacy requirements as calculated in accordance with Annex I.

The Member States shall also require regulated entities to have in place adequate capital adequacy policies at the level of the financial conglomerate.

The requirements referred to in the first and second subparagraphs shall be subject to supervisory overview by the coordinator in accordance with Section 3.

The coordinator shall ensure that the calculation referred to in the first subparagraph is carried out at least once a year, either by the regulated entities or by the mixed financial holding company.

The results of the calculation and the relevant data for the calculation shall be submitted to the coordinator by the regulated entity within the meaning of Article 1 which is at the head of the financial conglomerate, or, where the financial conglomerate is not headed by a regulated entity within the meaning of Article 1, by the mixed financial holding company or by the regulated entity in the financial conglomerate identified by the coordinator after consultation with the other relevant competent authorities and with the financial conglomerate.

3.   For the purposes of calculating the capital adequacy requirements referred to in the first subparagraph of paragraph 2, the following entities shall be included in the scope of supplementary supervision in the manner and to the extent defined in Annex I:
   (a)   a credit institution, a financial institution or an ancillary banking services undertaking within the meaning of Article 1(5) and (23) of Directive 2000/12/EC;
   (b)   an insurance undertaking, a reinsurance undertaking or an insurance holding company within the meaning of Article 1(i) of Directive 98/78/EC;
   (c)   an investment firm or a financial institution within the meaning of Article 2(7) of Directive 93/6/EEC;
   (d)   mixed financial holding companies.

4.   When calculating the supplementary capital adequacy requirements with regard to a financial conglomerate by applying method 1 (Accounting consolidation) referred to in Annex I, the own funds and the solvency requirements of the entities in the group shall be calculated by applying the corresponding sectoral rules on the form and extent of consolidation as laid down in particular in Article 54 of Directive 2000/12/EC and Annex I.1.B. of Directive 98/78/EC.

When applying methods 2 or 3 (Deduction and aggregation, Book value/Requirement deduction) referred to in Annex I, the calculation shall take account of the proportional share held by the parent undertaking or undertaking which holds a participation in another entity of the group. "Proportional share" means the proportion of the subscribed capital which is held, directly or indirectly, by that undertaking.

5.   The coordinator may decide not to include a particular entity in the scope when calculating the supplementary capital adequacy requirements in the following cases:
   (a)   if the entity is situated in a third country where there are legal impediments to the transfer of the necessary information, without prejudice to the sectoral rules regarding the obligation of competent authorities to refuse authorisation where the effective exercise of their supervisory functions is prevented;
   (b)   if the entity is of negligible interest with respect to the objectives of the supplementary supervision of regulated entities in a financial conglomerate;
   (c)   if the inclusion of the entity would be inappropriate or misleading with respect to the objectives of supplementary supervision.

However, if several entities are to be excluded pursuant to (b) of the first subparagraph, they must nevertheless be included when collectively they are of non-negligible interest.

In the case mentioned in (c) of the first subparagraph the coordinator shall, except in cases of urgency, consult the other relevant competent authorities before taking a decision.

When the coordinator does not include a regulated entity in the scope under one of the cases provided for in (b) and (c) of the first subparagraph, the competent authorities of the Member State in which that entity is situated may ask the entity which is at the head of the financial conglomerate for information which may facilitate their supervision of the regulated entity.

[5389]

Article 7
Risk concentration

1. Without prejudice to the sectoral rules, supplementary supervision of the risk concentration of regulated entities in a financial conglomerate shall be exercised in accordance with the rules laid down in Article 9(2) to (4), in Section 3 of this Chapter and in Annex II.

2. The Member States shall require regulated entities or mixed financial holding companies to report on a regular basis and at least annually to the coordinator any significant risk concentration at the level of the financial conglomerate, in accordance with the rules laid down in this Article and in Annex II. The necessary information shall be submitted to the coordinator by the regulated entity within the meaning of Article 1 which is at the head of the financial conglomerate or, where the financial conglomerate is not headed by a regulated entity within the meaning of Article 1, by the mixed financial holding company or by the regulated entity in the financial conglomerate identified by the coordinator after consultation with the other relevant competent authorities and with the financial conglomerate.

These risk concentrations shall be subject to supervisory overview by the coordinator in accordance with Section 3.

3. Pending further coordination of Community legislation, Member States may set quantitative limits or allow their competent authorities to set quantitative limits, or take other supervisory measures which would achieve the objectives of supplementary supervision, with regard to any risk concentration at the level of a financial conglomerate.

4. Where a financial conglomerate is headed by a mixed financial holding company, the sectoral rules regarding risk concentration of the most important financial sector in the financial conglomerate, if any, shall apply to that sector as a whole, including the mixed financial holding company.

[5390]

Article 8
Intra-group transactions

1. Without prejudice to the sectoral rules, supplementary supervision of intra-group transactions of regulated entities in a financial conglomerate shall be exercised in accordance with the rules laid down in Article 9(2) to (4), in Section 3 of this Chapter, and in Annex II.

2. The Member States shall require regulated entities or mixed financial holding companies to report, on a regular basis and at least annually, to the coordinator all significant intra-group transactions of regulated entities within a financial conglomerate, in accordance with the rules laid down in this Article and in Annex II. Insofar as no definition of the thresholds referred to in the last sentence of the first paragraph of Annex II has been drawn up, an intra-group transaction shall be presumed to be significant if its amount exceeds at least 5% of the total amount of capital adequacy requirements at the level of a financial conglomerate.

The necessary information shall be submitted to the coordinator by the regulated entity within the meaning of Article 1 which is at the head of the financial conglomerate or, where the financial conglomerate is not headed by a regulated entity within the meaning of Article 1, by the mixed financial holding company or by the regulated entity in the financial conglomerate identified by the coordinator after consultation with the other relevant competent authorities and with the financial conglomerate.

These intra-group transactions shall be subject to supervisory overview by the coordinator.

3. Pending further coordination of Community legislation, Member States may set quantitative limits and qualitative requirements or allow their competent authorities to set quantitative limits and qualitative requirements, or take other supervisory measures that would achieve the objectives of supplementary supervision, with regard to intra-group transactions of regulated entities within a financial conglomerate.

4. Where a financial conglomerate is headed by a mixed financial holding company, the sectoral rules regarding intra-group transactions of the most important financial sector in the financial conglomerate shall apply to that sector as a whole, including the mixed financial holding company.

[5391]

Article 9
Internal control mechanisms and risk management processes

1. The Member States shall require regulated entities to have, in place at the level of the financial conglomerate, adequate risk management processes and internal control mechanisms, including sound administrative and accounting procedures.

2. The risk management processes shall include:
    (a) sound governance and management with the approval and periodical review of the strategies and policies by the appropriate governing bodies at the level of the financial conglomerate with respect to all the risks they assume;
    (b) adequate capital adequacy policies in order to anticipate the impact of their business strategy on risk profile and capital requirements as determined in accordance with Article 6 and Annex I;
    (c) adequate procedures to ensure that their risk monitoring systems are well integrated into their organisation and that all measures are taken to ensure that the systems implemented in all the undertakings included in the scope of supplementary supervision are consistent so that the risks can be measured, monitored and controlled at the level of the financial conglomerate.

3. The internal control mechanisms shall include:
    (a) adequate mechanisms as regards capital adequacy to identify and measure all material risks incurred and to appropriately relate own funds to risks;
    (b) sound reporting and accounting procedures to identify, measure, monitor and control the intra-group transactions and the risk concentration.

4. The Member States shall ensure that, in all undertakings included in the scope of supplementary supervision pursuant to Article 5, there are adequate internal control mechanisms for the production of any data and information which would be relevant for the purposes of the supplementary supervision.

5. The processes and mechanisms referred to in paragraphs 1 to 4 shall be subject to supervisory overview by the coordinator.

[5392]

SECTION 3
MEASURES TO FACILITATE SUPPLEMENTARY SUPERVISION

Article 10
Competent authority responsible for exercising supplementary supervision (the coordinator)

1. In order to ensure proper supplementary supervision of the regulated entities in a financial conglomerate, a single coordinator, responsible for coordination and exercise of supplementary supervision, shall be appointed from among the competent authorities of the Member States concerned, including those of the Member State in which the mixed financial holding company has its head office.

2. The appointment shall be based on the following criteria:
    (a) where a financial conglomerate is headed by a regulated entity, the task of coordinator shall be exercised by the competent authority which has authorised that regulated entity pursuant to the relevant sectoral rules;
    (b) where a financial conglomerate is not headed by a regulated entity, the task of coordinator shall be exercised by the competent authority identified in accordance with the following principles:
        (i) where the parent of a regulated entity is a mixed financial holding company, the task of coordinator shall be exercised by the competent authority which has authorised that regulated entity pursuant to the relevant sectoral rules;
        (ii) where more than one regulated entity with a head office in the Community have as their parent the same mixed financial holding company, and one of these entities has been authorised in the Member State in which the mixed financial holding company has its head office, the task of coordinator shall be exercised by the competent authority of the regulated entity authorised in that Member State.
        Where more than one regulated entity, being active in different financial sectors, have been authorised in the Member State in which the mixed financial holding company has its head office, the task of coordinator shall be exercised by the competent authority of the regulated entity active in the most important financial sector.
        Where the financial conglomerate is headed by more than one mixed financial holding company with a head office in different Member States and there is a regulated entity in each of these States, the task of coordinator shall be exercised by the competent authority of the regulated entity with the largest balance sheet total if these entities are in the same financial sector, or by the competent authority of the regulated entity in the most important financial sector;
        (iii) where more than one regulated entity with a head office in the Community have

as their parent the same mixed financial holding company and none of these entities has been authorised in the Member State in which the mixed financial holding company has its head office, the task of coordinator shall be exercised by the competent authority which authorised the regulated entity with the largest balance sheet total in the most important financial sector;

(iv)   where the financial conglomerate is a group without a parent undertaking at the top, or in any other case, the task of coordinator shall be exercised by the competent authority which authorised the regulated entity with the largest balance sheet total in the most important financial sector.

3.   In particular cases, the relevant competent authorities may by common agreement waive the criteria referred to in paragraph 2 if their application would be inappropriate, taking into account the structure of the conglomerate and the relative importance of its activities in different countries, and appoint a different competent authority as coordinator. In these cases, before taking their decision, the competent authorities shall give the conglomerate an opportunity to state its opinion on that decision.

[5393]

Article 11
Tasks of the coordinator

1.   The tasks to be carried out by the coordinator with regard to supplementary supervision shall include:

(a)   coordination of the gathering and dissemination of relevant or essential information in going concern and emergency situations, including the dissemination of information which is of importance for a competent authority's supervisory task under sectoral rules;

(b)   supervisory overview and assessment of the financial situation of a financial conglomerate;

(c)   assessment of compliance with the rules on capital adequacy and of risk concentration and intra-group transactions as set out in Articles 6, 7 and 8;

(d)   assessment of the financial conglomerate's structure, organisation and internal control system as set out in Article 9;

(e)   planning and coordination of supervisory activities in going concern as well as in emergency situations, in cooperation with the relevant competent authorities involved;

(f)   other tasks, measures and decisions assigned to the coordinator by this Directive or deriving from the application of this Directive.

In order to facilitate and establish supplementary supervision on a broad legal basis, the coordinator and the other relevant competent authorities, and where necessary other competent authorities concerned, shall have coordination arrangements in place. The coordination arrangements may entrust additional tasks to the coordinator and may specify the procedures for the decision-making process among the relevant competent authorities as referred to in Articles 3, 4, 5(4), 6, 12(2), 16 and 18, and for cooperation with other competent authorities.

2.   The coordinator should, when it needs information which has already been given to another competent authority in accordance with the sectoral rules, contact this authority whenever possible in order to prevent duplication of reporting to the various authorities involved in supervision.

3.   Without prejudice to the possibility of delegating specific supervisory competences and responsibilities as provided for by Community legislation, the presence of a coordinator entrusted with specific tasks concerning the supplementary supervision of regulated entities in a financial conglomerate shall not affect the tasks and responsibilities of the competent authorities as provided for by the sectoral rules.

[5394]

Article 12
Cooperation and exchange of information between competent authorities

1.   The competent authorities responsible for the supervision of regulated entities in a financial conglomerate and the competent authority appointed as the coordinator for that financial conglomerate shall cooperate closely with each other. Without prejudice to their respective responsibilities as defined under sectoral rules, these authorities, whether or not established in the same Member State, shall provide one another with any information which is essential or relevant for the exercise of the other authorities' supervisory tasks under the sectoral rules and this Directive. In this regard, the competent authorities and the coordinator shall communicate on request all relevant information and shall communicate on their own initiative all essential information.

This cooperation shall at least provide for the gathering and the exchange of information with regard to the following items:

(a)   identification of the group structure of all major entities belonging to the financial conglomerate, as well as of the competent authorities of the regulated entities in the group;

(b)   the financial conglomerate's strategic policies;

(c)   the financial situation of the financial conglomerate, in particular on capital adequacy, intra-group transactions, risk concentration and profitability;

(d)   the financial conglomerate's major shareholders and management;

(e)   the organisation, risk management and internal control systems at financial conglomerate level;

(f)   procedures for the collection of information from the entities in a financial conglomerate, and the verification of that information;

(g)   adverse developments in regulated entities or in other entities of the financial conglomerate which could seriously affect the regulated entities;

(h)   major sanctions and exceptional measures taken by competent authorities in accordance with sectoral rules or this Directive.

The competent authorities may also exchange with the following authorities such information as may be needed for the performance of their respective tasks, regarding regulated entities in a financial conglomerate, in line with the provisions laid down in the sectoral rules: central banks, the European System of Central Banks and the European Central Bank.

2.   Without prejudice to their respective responsibilities as defined under sectoral rules, the competent authorities concerned shall, prior to their decision, consult each other with regard to the following items, where these decisions are of importance for other competent authorities' supervisory tasks:

(a)   changes in the shareholder, organisational or management structure of regulated entities in a financial conglomerate, which require the approval or authorisation of competent authorities;

(b)   major sanctions or exceptional measures taken by competent authorities.

A competent authority may decide not to consult in cases of urgency or where such consultation may jeopardise the effectiveness of the decisions. In this case, the competent authority shall, without delay, inform the other competent authorities.

3.   The coordinator may invite the competent authorities of the Member State in which a parent undertaking has its head office, and which do not themselves exercise the supplementary supervision pursuant to Article 10, to ask the parent undertaking for any information which would be relevant for the exercise of its coordination tasks as laid down in Article 11, and to transmit that information to the coordinator.

Where the information referred to in Article 14(2) has already been given to a competent authority in accordance with sectoral rules, the competent authorities responsible for exercising supplementary supervision may apply to the first-mentioned authority to obtain the information.

4.   Member States shall authorise the exchange of the information between their competent authorities and between their competent authorities and other authorities, as referred to in paragraphs 1, 2 and 3. The collection or possession of information with regard to an entity within a financial conglomerate which is not a regulated entity shall not in any way imply that the competent authorities are required to play a supervisory role in relation to these entities on a stand-alone basis.

Information received in the framework of supplementary supervision, and in particular any exchange of information between competent authorities and between competent authorities and other authorities which is provided for in this Directive, shall be subject to the provisions on professional secrecy and communication of confidential information laid down in the sectoral rules.

[5395]

Article 13
Management body of mixed financial holding companies

Member States shall require that persons who effectively direct the business of a mixed financial holding company are of sufficiently good repute and have sufficient experience to perform those duties.

[5396]

Article 14
Access to information

1.   Member States shall ensure that there are no legal impediments within their jurisdiction preventing the natural and legal persons included within the scope of supplementary supervision, whether or not a regulated entity, from exchanging amongst themselves any information which would be relevant for the purposes of supplementary supervision.

2.   Member States shall provide that, when approaching the entities in a financial conglomerate, whether or not a regulated entity, either directly or indirectly, their competent authorities responsible for exercising supplementary supervision shall have access to any information which would be relevant for the purposes of supplementary supervision.

[5397]

Article 15
Verification

Where, in applying this Directive, competent authorities wish in specific cases to verify the information concerning an entity, whether or not regulated, which is part of a financial conglomerate and is situated in another Member State, they shall ask the competent authorities of that other Member State to have the verification carried out.

The authorities which receive such a request shall, within the framework of their competences, act upon it either by carrying out the verification themselves, by allowing an auditor or expert to carry it out, or by allowing the authority which made the request to carry it out itself.

The competent authority which made the request may, if it so wishes, participate in the verification when it does not carry out the verification itself.

[5398]

Article 16
Enforcement measures

If the regulated entities in a financial conglomerate do not comply with the requirements referred to in Articles 6 to 9 or where the requirements are met but solvency may nevertheless be jeopardised or where the intra-group transactions or the risk concentrations are a threat to the regulated entities' financial position, the necessary measures shall be required in order to rectify the situation as soon as possible:

—   by the coordinator with respect to the mixed financial holding company,
—   by the competent authorities with respect to the regulated entities; to that end, the coordinator shall inform those competent authorities of its findings.

Without prejudice to Article 17(2), Member States may determine what measures may be taken by their competent authorities with respect to mixed financial holding companies.

The competent authorities involved, including the coordinator, shall where appropriate coordinate their supervisory actions.

[5399]

Article 17
Additional powers of the competent authorities

1.   Pending further harmonisation between sectoral rules, the Member States shall provide that their competent authorities shall have the power to take any supervisory measure deemed necessary in order to avoid or to deal with the circumvention of sectoral rules by regulated entities in a financial conglomerate.

2.   Without prejudice to their criminal law provisions, Member States shall ensure that penalties or measures aimed at ending observed breaches or the causes of such breaches may be imposed on mixed financial holding companies, or their effective managers, which infringe laws, regulations or administrative provisions enacted to implement this Directive. In certain cases, such measures may require the intervention of the courts. The competent authorities shall cooperate closely to ensure that such penalties or measures produce the desired results.

[5400]

SECTION 4
THIRD COUNTRIES

Article 18
Parent undertakings outside the Community

1.   Without prejudice to the sectoral rules, in the case referred to in Article 5(3), competent authorities shall verify whether the regulated entities, the parent undertaking of which has its head office outside the Community, are subject to supervision by a third-country competent authority, which is equivalent to that provided for by the provisions of this Directive on the supplementary supervision of regulated entities referred to in Article 5(2). The verification shall be carried out by the competent authority which would be the coordinator if the criteria set out in Article 10(2) were to apply, on the request of the parent undertaking or of any of the regulated entities authorised in the Community or on its own initiative. That competent authority shall consult the other relevant competent authorities, and shall take into account any applicable guidance prepared by the Financial Conglomerates Committee in accordance with Article 21(5). For this purpose the competent authority shall consult the Committee before taking a decision.

2.   In the absence of equivalent supervision referred to in paragraph 1, Member States shall apply to the regulated entities, by analogy, the provisions concerning the supplementary supervision of regulated entities referred to in Article 5(2). As an alternative, competent authorities may apply one of the methods set out in paragraph 3.

3.   Member States shall allow their competent authorities to apply other methods which ensure appropriate supplementary supervision of the regulated entities in a financial conglomerate. These

methods must be agreed by the coordinator, after consultation with the other relevant competent authorities. The competent authorities may in particular require the establishment of a mixed financial holding company which has its head office in the Community, and apply this Directive to the regulated entities in the financial conglomerate headed by that holding company. The methods must achieve the objectives of the supplementary supervision as defined in this Directive and must be notified to the other competent authorities involved and the Commission.

[5401]

Article 19
Cooperation with third-country competent authorities

1. Article 25(1) and (2) of Directive 2000/12/EC and Article 10a of Directive 98/78/EC shall apply mutatis mutandis to the negotiation of agreements with one or more third countries regarding the means of exercising supplementary supervision of regulated entities in a financial conglomerate.

[2. Without prejudice to Article 300(1) and (2) of the Treaty, the Commission shall, with the assistance of the European Banking Committee, the European Insurance and Occupational Pensions Committee and the Financial Conglomerates Committee, examine the outcome of the negotiations referred to in paragraph 1 and the resulting situation.]

[5402]

NOTES
Para 2: substituted by European Parliament and Council Directive 2005/1/EC, Art 11, as from 13 April 2005.

CHAPTER III
POWERS CONFERRED ON THE COMMISSION AND COMMITTEE PROCEDURE

Article 20
Powers conferred on the Commission

1. The Commission shall adopt ... the technical adaptations to be made to this Directive in the following areas:
   (a) a more precise formulation of the definitions referred to in Article 2 in order to take account of developments in financial markets in the application of this Directive;
   (b) a more precise formulation of the definitions referred to in Article 2 in order to ensure uniform application of this Directive in the Community;
   (c) the alignment of terminology and the framing of definitions in the Directive in accordance with subsequent Community acts on regulated entities and related matters;
   (d) a more precise definition of the calculation methods set out in Annex I in order to take account of developments on financial markets and prudential techniques;
   (e) coordination of the provisions adopted pursuant to Articles 7 and 8 and Annex II with a view to encouraging uniform application within the Community.

[Those measures, designed to amend non-essential elements of this Directive, inter alia, by supplementing it, shall be adopted in accordance with the regulatory procedure with scrutiny referred to in Article 21(2).]

2. The Commission shall inform the public of any proposal presented in accordance with this Article and will consult interested parties prior to submitting the draft measures to the Financial Conglomerates Committee referred to in Article 21.

[5403]

NOTES
Para 1: words omitted repealed, and words in square brackets substituted, by European Parliament and Council Directive 2008/25/EC, Art 1(1), as from 21 March 2008.

Article 21
Committee

1. The Commission shall be assisted by a Financial Conglomerates Committee, hereinafter referred to as the "Committee".

[2. Where reference is made to this paragraph, Article 5a(1) to (4) and Article 7 of Decision 1999/468/EC shall apply, having regard to the provisions of Article 8 thereof.]

[3. By 31 December 2010, and, thereafter, at least every three years, the Commission shall review the provisions concerning its implementing powers and present a report to the European Parliament and to the Council on the functioning of those powers. The report shall examine, in particular, the need for the Commission to propose amendments to this Directive in order to ensure the appropriate scope of the implementing powers conferred on the Commission. The conclusion as to whether or not amendment is necessary shall be accompanied by a detailed statement of reasons. If necessary, the report shall be accompanied by a legislative proposal to amend the provisions conferring implementing powers on the Commission.]

5.   The Committee may give general guidance as to whether the supplementary supervision arrangements of competent authorities in third countries are likely to achieve the objectives of the supplementary supervision as defined in this Directive, in relation to the regulated entities in a financial conglomerate, the head of which has its head office outside the Community. The Committee shall keep any such guidance under review and take into account any changes to the supplementary supervision carried out by such competent authorities.

6.   The Committee shall be kept informed by Member States of the principles they apply concerning the supervision of intra-group transactions and risk concentration.

[5404]

NOTES

Para 2 substituted, and para 3 substituted (for original paras 3, 4), by European Parliament and Council Directive 2008/25/EC, Art 1(2), as from 21 March 2008.

Articles 22–29

((*Chap IV*) *amend Council Directive 73/239/EEC, Council Directive 79/267/EEC (repealed), Council Directive 92/49/EEC, Council Directive 92/96/EEC (repealed), Council Directive 93/6/EEC (repealed), Council Directive 93/22/EEC (repealed), and European Parliament and Council Directives 98/78/EC and 2000/12/EC (repealed). Note that Art 26 (which amended Council Directive 93/6/EEC) was repealed by Council Directive 2006/49/EC, as from 20 July 2006. Note also that Art 29(1)(a), (b), (2), (4)(a), (b), (5)–(11) (which amended European Parliament and Council Directive 2000/12/EC) was repealed by Council Directive 2006/48/EC, as from 20 July 2006.*)

CHAPTER V
ASSET MANAGEMENT COMPANIES

Article 30
Asset management companies

Pending further coordination of sectoral rules, Member States shall provide for the inclusion of asset management companies:

(a)   in the scope of consolidated supervision of credit institutions and investment firms, and/or in the scope of supplementary supervision of insurance undertakings in an insurance group; and

(b)   where the group is a financial conglomerate, in the scope of supplementary supervision within the meaning of this Directive.

For the application of the first paragraph, Member States shall provide, or give their competent authorities the power to decide, according to which sectoral rules (banking sector, insurance sector or investment services sector) asset management companies shall be included in the consolidated and/or supplementary supervision referred to in (a) of the first paragraph. For the purposes of this provision, the relevant sectoral rules regarding the form and extent of the inclusion of financial institutions (where asset management companies are included in the scope of consolidated supervision of credit institutions and investment firms) and of reinsurance undertakings (where asset management companies are included in the scope of supplementary supervision of insurance undertakings) shall apply mutatis mutandis to asset management companies. For the purposes of supplementary supervision referred to in (b) of the first paragraph, the asset management company shall be treated as part of whichever sector it is included in by virtue of (a) of the first paragraph.

Where an asset management company is part of a financial conglomerate, any reference to the notion of regulated entity and any reference to the notion of competent authorities and relevant competent authorities shall therefore, for the purposes of this Directive, be understood as including, respectively, asset management companies and the competent authorities responsible for the supervision of asset management companies. This applies mutatis mutandis as regards groups referred to in (a) of the first paragraph.

[5405]

CHAPTER VI
TRANSITIONAL AND FINAL PROVISIONS

Article 31
Report by the Commission

1.   By 11 August 2007, the Commission shall submit to the Financial Conglomerates Committee referred to in Article 21 a report on Member States' practices, and, if necessary, on the need for further harmonisation, with regard to

—   the inclusion of asset management companies in group-wide supervision,

—   the choice and the application of the capital adequacy methods set out in Annex I,

—   the definition of significant intra-group transactions and significant risk concentration and the supervision of intra-group transactions and risk concentration referred to in Annex II, in particular regarding the introduction of quantitative limits and qualitative requirements for this purpose,

— the intervals at which financial conglomerates shall carry out the calculations of capital adequacy requirements as set out in Article 6(2) and report to the coordinator on significant risk concentration as set out in Article 7(2).

The Commission shall consult the Committee before making its proposals.

2. Within one year of agreement being reached at international level on the rules for eliminating the double gearing of own funds in financial groups, the Commission shall examine how to bring the provisions of this Directive into line with those international agreements and, if necessary, make appropriate proposals.

[5406]

Article 32
Transposition

Member States shall bring into force the laws, regulations and administrative provisions necessary to comply with this Directive before 11 August 2004. They shall forthwith inform the Commission thereof.

Member States shall provide that the provisions referred to in the first subparagraph shall first apply to the supervision of accounts for the financial year beginning on 1 January 2005 or during that calendar year.

When Member States adopt these measures, they shall contain a reference to this Directive or shall be accompanied by such reference on the occasion of their official publication. The methods of making such reference shall be laid down by Member States.

[5407]

Article 33
Entry into force

This Directive shall enter into force on the day of its publication in the Official Journal of the European Union.

[5408]

Article 34
Addressees

This Directive is addressed to the Member States.

[5409]

ANNEX I
CAPITAL ADEQUACY

The calculation of the supplementary capital adequacy requirements of the regulated entities in a financial conglomerate referred to in Article 6(1) shall be carried out in accordance with the technical principles and one of the methods described in this Annex.

Without prejudice to the provisions of the next paragraph, Member States shall allow their competent authorities, where they assume the role of coordinator with regard to a particular financial conglomerate, to decide, after consultation with the other relevant competent authorities and the conglomerate itself, which method shall be applied by that financial conglomerate.

Member States may require that the calculation be carried out according to one particular method among those described in this Annex if a financial conglomerate is headed by a regulated entity which has been authorised in that Member State. Where a financial conglomerate is not headed by a regulated entity within the meaning of Article 1, Member States shall authorise the application of any of the methods described in this Annex, except in situations where the relevant competent authorities are located in the same Member State, in which case that Member State may require the application of one of the methods.

I. TECHNICAL PRINCIPLES

1. Extent and form of the supplementary capital adequacy requirements calculation

Whichever method is used, when the entity is a subsidiary undertaking and has a solvency deficit, or, in the case of a non-regulated financial sector entity, a notional solvency deficit, the total solvency deficit of the subsidiary has to be taken into account. Where in this case, in the opinion of the coordinator, the responsibility of the parent undertaking owning a share of the capital is limited strictly and unambiguously to that share of the capital, the coordinator may give permission for the solvency deficit of the subsidiary undertaking to be taken into account on a proportional basis.

Where there are no capital ties between entities in a financial conglomerate, the coordinator, after consultation with the other relevant competent authorities, shall determine which proportional share will have to be taken into account, bearing in mind the liability to which the existing relationship gives rise.

2. Other technical principles

Regardless of the method used for the calculation of the supplementary capital adequacy requirements of regulated entities in a financial conglomerate as laid down in Section II of this Annex, the coordinator, and where necessary other competent authorities concerned, shall ensure that the following principles will apply:

    (i)   the multiple use of elements eligible for the calculation of own funds at the level of the financial conglomerate (multiple gearing) as well as any inappropriate intra-group creation of own funds must be eliminated; in order to ensure the elimination of multiple gearing and the intra-group creation of own funds, competent authorities shall apply by analogy the relevant principles laid down in the relevant sectoral rules;

    (ii)   pending further harmonisation of sectoral rules, the solvency requirements for each different financial sector represented in a financial conglomerate shall be covered by own funds elements in accordance with the corresponding sectoral rules; when there is a deficit of own funds at the financial conglomerate level, only own funds elements which are eligible according to each of the sectoral rules (cross-sector capital) shall qualify for verification of compliance with the additional solvency requirements;

where sectoral rules provide for limits on the eligibility of certain own funds instruments, which would qualify as cross-sector capital, these limits would apply mutatis mutandis when calculating own funds at the level of the financial conglomerate;

when calculating own funds at the level of the financial conglomerate, competent authorities shall also take into account the effectiveness of the transferability and availability of the own funds across the different legal entities in the group, given the objectives of the capital adequacy rules;

where, in the case of a non-regulated financial sector entity, a notional solvency requirement is calculated in accordance with section II of this Annex, notional solvency requirement means the capital requirement with which such an entity would have to comply under the relevant sectoral rules as if it were a regulated entity of that particular financial sector; in the case of asset management companies, solvency requirement means the capital requirement set out in Article 5a(1)(a) of Directive 85/611/EEC; the notional solvency requirement of a mixed financial holding company shall be calculated according to the sectoral rules of the most important financial sector in the financial conglomerate.

II. TECHNICAL CALCULATION METHODS

Method 1: "Accounting consolidation" method

The calculation of the supplementary capital adequacy requirements of the regulated entities in a financial conglomerate shall be carried out on the basis of the consolidated accounts.

The supplementary capital adequacy requirements shall be calculated as the difference between:

    (i)   the own funds of the financial conglomerate calculated on the basis of the consolidated position of the group; the elements eligible are those that qualify in accordance with the relevant sectoral rules;

    and

    (ii)   the sum of the solvency requirements for each different financial sector represented in the group; the solvency requirements for each different financial sector are calculated in accordance with the corresponding sectoral rules.

The sectoral rules referred to are in particular Directives 2000/12/EC, Title V, Chapter 3, as regards credit institutions, 98/78/EC as regards insurance undertakings, and 93/6/EEC as regards credit institutions and investment firms.

In the case of non-regulated financial sector entities which are not included in the aforementioned sectoral solvency requirement calculations, a notional solvency requirement shall be calculated.

The difference shall not be negative.

Method 2: "Deduction and aggregation" method

The calculation of the supplementary capital adequacy requirements of the regulated entities in a financial conglomerate shall be carried out on the basis of the accounts of each of the entities in the group.

The supplementary capital adequacy requirements shall be calculated as the difference between:

    (i)   the sum of the own funds of each regulated and non-regulated financial sector entity in the financial conglomerate; the elements eligible are those which qualify in accordance with the relevant sectoral rules;

    and

(ii) the sum of
  —   the solvency requirements for each regulated and non-regulated financial sector
       entity in the group; the solvency requirements shall be calculated in accordance
       with the relevant sectoral rules, and
  —   the book value of the participations in other entities of the group.

In the case of non-regulated financial sector entities, a notional solvency requirement shall be calculated. Own funds and solvency requirements shall be taken into account for their proportional share as provided for in Article 6(4) and in accordance with Section I of this Annex.

The difference shall not be negative.

Method 3: "Book value/Requirement deduction" method

The calculation of the supplementary capital adequacy requirements of the regulated entities in a financial conglomerate shall be carried out on the basis of the accounts of each of the entities in the group.

The supplementary capital adequacy requirements shall be calculated as the difference between:
  (i) the own funds of the parent undertaking or the entity at the head of the financial
       conglomerate; the elements eligible are those which qualify in accordance with the
       relevant sectoral rules;
and
  (ii) the sum of
  —   the solvency requirement of the parent undertaking or the head referred to in (i),
       and
  —   the higher of the book value of the former's participation in other entities in the
       group and these entities' solvency requirements; the solvency requirements of the
       latter shall be taken into account for their proportional share as provided for in
       Article 6(4) and in accordance with Section I of this Annex.

In the case of non-regulated financial sector entities, a notional solvency requirement shall be calculated. When valuing the elements eligible for the calculation of the supplementary capital adequacy requirements, participations may be valued by the equity method in accordance with the option set out in Article 59(2)(b) of Directive 78/660/EEC.

The difference shall not be negative.

Method 4: Combination of methods 1, 2 and 3

Competent authorities may allow a combination of methods 1, 2 and 3, or a combination of two of these methods.

[5410]

ANNEX II
TECHNICAL APPLICATION OF THE PROVISIONS ON INTRA-GROUP TRANSACTIONS AND RISK CONCENTRATION

The coordinator, after consultation with the other relevant competent authorities, shall identify the type of transactions and risks regulated entities in a particular financial conglomerate shall report in accordance with the provisions of Article 7(2) and Article 8(2) on the reporting of intra-group transactions and risk concentration. When defining or giving their opinion about the type of transactions and risks, the coordinator and the relevant competent authorities shall take into account the specific group and risk management structure of the financial conglomerate. In order to identify significant intra-group transactions and significant risk concentration to be reported in accordance with the provisions of Articles 7 and 8, the coordinator, after consultation with the other relevant competent authorities and the conglomerate itself, shall define appropriate thresholds based on regulatory own funds and/or technical provisions.

When overviewing the intra-group transactions and risk concentrations, the coordinator shall in particular monitor the possible risk of contagion in the financial conglomerate, the risk of a conflict of interests, the risk of circumvention of sectoral rules, and the level or volume of risks.

Member States may allow their competent authorities to apply at the level of the financial conglomerate the provisions of the sectoral rules on intra-group transactions and risk concentration, in particular to avoid circumvention of the sectoral rules.

[5411]

HAVE ADOPTED THIS DIRECTIVE:

CHAPTER I
SCOPE AND DEFINITIONS

Article 1
Scope

1.   This Directive lays down rules for the taking-up and pursuit of the activities of insurance and reinsurance mediation by natural and legal persons which are established in a Member State or which wish to become established there.

2.   This Directive shall not apply to persons providing mediation services for insurance contracts if all the following conditions are met:
    (a)   the insurance contract only requires knowledge of the insurance cover that is provided;
    (b)   the insurance contract is not a life assurance contract;
    (c)   the insurance contract does not cover any liability risks;
    (d)   the principal professional activity of the person is other than insurance mediation;
    (e)   the insurance is complementary to the product or service supplied by any provider, where such insurance covers:
        (i)   the risk of breakdown, loss of or damage to goods supplied by that provider, or
        (ii)   damage to or loss of baggage and other risks linked to the travel booked with that provider, even if the insurance covers life assurance or liability risks, provided that the cover is ancillary to the main cover for the risks linked to that travel;
    (f)   the amount of the annual premium does not exceed EUR 500 and the total duration of the insurance contract, including any renewals, does not exceed five years.

3.   This Directive shall not apply to insurance and reinsurance mediation services provided in relation to risks and commitments located outside the Community.

This Directive shall not affect a Member State's law in respect of insurance mediation business pursued by insurance and reinsurance intermediaries established in a third country and operating on its territory under the principle of freedom to provide services, provided that equal treatment is guaranteed to all persons carrying out or authorised to carry out insurance mediation activities on that market.

This Directive shall not regulate insurance mediation activities carried out in third countries nor activities of Community insurance or reinsurance undertakings, as defined in First Council Directive 73/239/EEC of 24 July 1973 on the coordination of laws, regulations and administrative provisions relating to the taking-up and pursuit of the business of direct insurance other than life assurance[1] and First Council Directive 79/267/EEC of 5 March 1979 on the coordination of laws, regulations and administrative provisions relating to the taking-up and pursuit of the business of direct life assurance,[2] carried out through insurance intermediaries in third countries.

[5412A]

NOTES
[1]   OJ L228, 16.8.1973, p 3. Directive as last amended by Directive 2002/13/EC of the European Parliament and of the Council (OJ L77, 20.3.2002, p 17).
[2]   OJ L63, 13.3.1979, p 1. Directive as last amended by Directive 2002/12/EC of the European Parliament and of the Council (OJ L77, 20.3.2002, p 11).

Article 2
Definitions

For the purpose of this Directive:
    1.   'insurance undertaking' means an undertaking which has received official authorisation in accordance with Article 6 of Directive 73/239/EEC or Article 6 of Directive 79/267/EEC;
    2.   'reinsurance undertaking' means an undertaking, other than an insurance undertaking or a non-member-country insurance undertaking, the main business of which consists in accepting risks ceded by an insurance undertaking, a non-member-country insurance undertaking or other reinsurance undertakings;
    3.   'insurance mediation' means the activities of introducing, proposing or carrying out other work preparatory to the conclusion of contracts of insurance, or of concluding such contracts, or of assisting in the administration and performance of such contracts, in particular in the event of a claim.

These activities when undertaken by an insurance undertaking or an employee of an insurance undertaking who is acting under the responsibility of the insurance undertaking shall not be considered as insurance mediation.

The provision of information on an incidental basis in the context of another professional activity provided that the purpose of that activity is not to assist the customer in concluding or performing an insurance contract, the management of claims of an insurance undertaking on a professional basis, and loss adjusting and expert appraisal of claims shall also not be considered as insurance mediation;

4. 'reinsurance mediation' means the activities of introducing, proposing or carrying out other work preparatory to the conclusion of contracts of reinsurance, or of concluding such contracts, or of assisting in the administration and performance of such contracts, in particular in the event of a claim.

These activities when undertaken by a reinsurance undertaking or an employee of a reinsurance undertaking who is acting under the responsibility of the reinsurance undertaking are not considered as reinsurance mediation.

The provision of information on an incidental basis in the context of another professional activity provided that the purpose of that activity is not to assist the customer in concluding or performing a reinsurance contract, the management of claims of a reinsurance undertaking on a professional basis, and loss adjusting and expert appraisal of claims shall also not be considered as reinsurance mediation;

5. 'insurance intermediary' means any natural or legal person who, for remuneration, takes up or pursues insurance mediation;

6. 'reinsurance intermediary' means any natural or legal person who, for remuneration, takes up or pursues reinsurance mediation;

7. 'tied insurance intermediary' means any person who carries on the activity of insurance mediation for and on behalf of one or more insurance undertakings in the case of insurance products which are not in competition but does not collect premiums or amounts intended for the customer and who acts under the full responsibility of those insurance undertakings for the products which concern them respectively.

Any person who carries on the activity of insurance mediation in addition to his principal professional activity is also considered as a tied insurance intermediary acting under the responsibility of one or several insurance undertakings for the products which concern them respectively if the insurance is complementary to the goods or services supplied in the framework of this principal professional activity and the person does not collect premiums or amounts intended for the customer;

8. 'large risks' shall be as defined by Article 5(d) of Directive 73/239/EEC;

9. 'home Member State' means:
   (a) where the intermediary is a natural person, the Member State in which his residence is situated and in which he carries on business;
   (b) where the intermediary is a legal person, the Member State in which its registered office is situated or, if under its national law it has no registered office, the Member State in which its head office is situated;

10. 'host Member State' means the Member State in which an insurance or reinsurance intermediary has a branch or provides services;

11. 'competent authorities' means the authorities which each Member State designates under Article 7;

12. 'durable medium' means any instrument which enables the customer to store information addressed personally to him in a way accessible for future reference for a period of time adequate to the purposes of the information and which allows the unchanged reproduction of the information stored.

In particular, durable medium covers floppy disks, CD-ROMs, DVDs and hard drives of personal computers on which electronic mail is stored, but it excludes Internet sites, unless such sites meet the criteria specified in the first paragraph.

[5413]

CHAPTER II
REGISTRATION REQUIREMENTS

Article 3
Registration

1. Insurance and reinsurance intermediaries shall be registered with a competent authority as defined in Article 7(2), in their home Member State.

Without prejudice to the first subparagraph, Member States may stipulate that insurance and reinsurance undertakings and other bodies may collaborate with the competent authorities in registering insurance and reinsurance intermediaries and in the application of the requirements of Article 4 to such intermediaries. In particular, in the case of tied insurance intermediaries, they may be registered by an insurance undertaking or by an association of insurance undertakings under the supervision of a competent authority.

The insurance or reinsurance intermediary may start business one month after the date on which he was informed by the competent authorities of the home Member State of the notification referred to in the second subparagraph. However, that intermediary may start business immediately if the host Member State does not wish to be informed of the fact.

2. Member States shall notify the Commission of their wish to be informed in accordance with paragraph 1. The Commission shall in turn notify all the Member States of this.

3. The competent authorities of the host Member State may take the necessary steps to ensure appropriate publication of the conditions under which, in the interest of the general good, the business concerned must be carried on in their territories.

[5417]

Article 7
Competent authorities

1. Member States shall designate the competent authorities empowered to ensure implementation of this Directive. They shall inform the Commission thereof, indicating any division of those duties.

2. The authorities referred to in paragraph 1 shall be either public authorities or bodies recognised by national law or by public authorities expressly empowered for that purpose by national law. They shall not be insurance or reinsurance undertakings.

3. The competent authorities shall possess all the powers necessary for the performance of their duties. Where there is more than one competent authority on its territory, a Member State shall ensure that those authorities collaborate closely so that they can discharge their respective duties effectively.

[5418]

Article 8
Sanctions

1. Member States shall provide for appropriate sanctions in the event that a person exercising the activity of insurance or reinsurance mediation is not registered in a Member State and is not referred to in Article 1(2).

2. Member States shall provide for appropriate sanctions against insurance or reinsurance undertakings which use the insurance or reinsurance mediation services of persons who are not registered in a Member State and who are not referred to in Article 1(2).

3. Member States shall provide for appropriate sanctions in the event of an insurance or reinsurance intermediary's failure to comply with national provisions adopted pursuant to this Directive.

4. This Directive shall not affect the power of the host Member States to take appropriate measures to prevent or to penalise irregularities committed within their territories which are contrary to legal or regulatory provisions adopted in the interest of the general good. This shall include the possibility of preventing offending insurance or reinsurance intermediaries from initiating any further activities within their territories.

5. Any measure adopted involving sanctions or restrictions on the activities of an insurance or reinsurance intermediary must be properly justified and communicated to the intermediary concerned. Every such measure shall be subject to the right to apply to the courts in the Member State which adopted it.

[5419]

Article 9
Exchange of information between Member States

1. The competent authorities of the various Member States shall cooperate in order to ensure the proper application of the provisions of this Directive.

2. The competent authorities shall exchange information on insurance and reinsurance intermediaries if they have been subject to a sanction referred to in Article 8(3) or a measure referred to in Article 8(4) and such information is likely to lead to removal from the register of such intermediaries. The competent authorities may also exchange any relevant information at the request of an authority.

3. All persons required to receive or divulge information in connection with this Directive shall be bound by professional secrecy, in the same manner as is laid down in Article 16 of Council Directive 92/49/EEC of 18 June 1992 on the coordination of laws, regulations and administrative provisions relating to direct insurance other than life assurance and amending Directives 73/239/EEC and 88/357/EEC (third non-life insurance Directive)[1] and Article 15 of Council Directive 92/96/EEC of 10 November 1992 on the coordination of laws, regulations and administrative provisions relating to direct life assurance and amending Directives 79/267/EEC and 90/619/EEC (third life assurance Directive).[2]

[5420]

NOTES

¹   OJ L228, 11.8.1992, p 1. Directive as last amended by Directive 2000/64/EC of the European Parliament and of the Council (OJ L290, 17.11.2000, p 27).

²   OJ L360, 9.12.1992, p 1. Directive as last amended by Directive 2000/64/EC of the European Parliament and of the Council.

Article 10
Complaints

Member States shall ensure that procedures are set up which allow customers and other interested parties, especially consumer associations, to register complaints about insurance and reinsurance intermediaries. In all cases complaints shall receive replies.

[5421]

Article 11
Out-of-court redress

1.   Member States shall encourage the setting-up of appropriate and effective complaints and redress procedures for the out-of-court settlement of disputes between insurance intermediaries and customers, using existing bodies where appropriate.

2.   Member States shall encourage these bodies to cooperate in the resolution of cross-border disputes.

[5422]

CHAPTER III
INFORMATION REQUIREMENTS FOR INTERMEDIARIES

Article 12
Information provided by the insurance intermediary

1.   Prior to the conclusion of any initial insurance contract, and, if necessary, upon amendment or renewal thereof, an insurance intermediary shall provide the customer with at least the following information:

(a)   his identity and address;

(b)   the register in which he has been included and the means for verifying that he has been registered;

(c)   whether he has a holding, direct or indirect, representing more than 10% of the voting rights or of the capital in a given insurance undertaking;

(d)   whether a given insurance undertaking or parent undertaking of a given insurance undertaking has a holding, direct or indirect, representing more than 10% of the voting rights or of the capital in the insurance intermediary;

(e)   the procedures referred to in Article 10 allowing customers and other interested parties to register complaints about insurance and reinsurance intermediaries and, if appropriate, about the out-of-court complaint and redress procedures referred to in Article 11.

In addition, an insurance intermediary shall inform the customer, concerning the contract that is provided, whether:

(i)   he gives advice based on the obligation in paragraph 2 to provide a fair analysis, or

(ii)   he is under a contractual obligation to conduct insurance mediation business exclusively with one or more insurance undertakings. In that case, he shall, at the customer's request provide the names of those insurance undertakings, or

(iii)   he is not under a contractual obligation to conduct insurance mediation business exclusively with one or more insurance undertakings and does not give advice based on the obligation in paragraph 2 to provide a fair analysis. In that case, he shall, at the customer's request provide the names of the insurance undertakings with which he may and does conduct business.

In those cases where information is to be provided solely at the customer's request, the customer shall be informed that he has the right to request such information.

2.   When the insurance intermediary informs the customer that he gives his advice on the basis of a fair analysis, he is obliged to give that advice on the basis of an analysis of a sufficiently large number of insurance contracts available on the market, to enable him to make a recommendation, in accordance with professional criteria, regarding which insurance contract would be adequate to meet the customer's needs.

3.   Prior to the conclusion of any specific contract, the insurance intermediary shall at least specify, in particular on the basis of information provided by the customer, the demands and the

needs of that customer as well as the underlying reasons for any advice given to the customer on a given insurance product. These details shall be modulated according to the complexity of the insurance contract being proposed.

4. The information referred to in paragraphs 1, 2 and 3 need not be given when the insurance intermediary mediates in the insurance of large risks, nor in the case of mediation by reinsurance intermediaries.

5. Member States may maintain or adopt stricter provisions regarding the information requirements referred to in paragraph 1, provided that such provisions comply with Community law.

Member States shall communicate to the Commission the national provisions set out in the first subparagraph.

In order to establish a high level of transparency by all appropriate means, the Commission shall ensure that the information it receives relating to national provisions is also communicated to consumers and insurance intermediaries.

[5423]

Article 13
Information conditions

1. All information to be provided to customers in accordance with Article 12 shall be communicated:
   (a) on paper or on any other durable medium available and accessible to the customer;
   (b) in a clear and accurate manner, comprehensible to the customer;
   (c) in an official language of the Member State of the commitment or in any other language agreed by the parties.

2. By way of derogation from paragraph 1(a), the information referred to in Article 12 may be provided orally where the customer requests it, or where immediate cover is necessary. In those cases, the information shall be provided to the customer in accordance with paragraph 1 immediately after the conclusion of the insurance contract.

3. In the case of telephone selling, the prior information given to the customer shall be in accordance with Community rules applicable to the distance marketing of consumer financial services. Moreover, information shall be provided to the customer in accordance with paragraph 1 immediately after the conclusion of the insurance contract.

[5424]

CHAPTER IV
FINAL PROVISIONS

Article 14
Right to apply to the courts

Member States shall ensure that decisions taken in respect of an insurance intermediary, reinsurance intermediary or an insurance undertaking under the laws, regulations and administrative provisions adopted in accordance with this Directive may be subject to the right to apply to the courts.

[5425]

Article 15
Repeal

Directive 77/92/EEC is hereby repealed with effect from the date referred to in Article 16(1).

[5426]

Article 16
Transposition

1. Member States shall bring into force the laws, regulations and administrative provisions necessary to comply with this Directive before 15 January 2005. They shall forthwith inform the Commission thereof.

These measures shall contain a reference to this Directive or shall be accompanied by such reference on the occasion of their official publication. The methods of making such reference shall be laid down by the Member States.

2. Member States shall communicate to the Commission the text of the laws, regulations and administrative provisions which they adopt in the field governed by this Directive. In that communication they shall provide a table indicating the national provisions corresponding to this Directive.

[5427]

Article 17
Entry into force

This Directive shall enter into force on the day of its publication in the *Official Journal of the European Communities*.

[5428]

Article 18
Addressees

This Directive is addressed to the Member States.

[5429]

DIRECTIVE OF THE EUROPEAN PARLIAMENT AND OF THE COUNCIL

of 28 January 2003

on insider dealing and market manipulation
(market abuse)

(2003/6/EC)

NOTES

Date of publication in OJ: OJ L96, 12.4.2003, p 16. Notes are as in the original OJ version.
This Directive is reproduced as amended by: European Parliament and Council Directive 2008/26/EC (OJ L81, 20.3.2008, p 42).

THE EUROPEAN PARLIAMENT AND THE COUNCIL OF THE EUROPEAN UNION,

Having regard to the Treaty establishing the European Community, and in particular Article 95 thereof,

Having regard to the proposal from the Commission,[1]

Having regard to the opinion of the European Economic and Social Committee,[2]

Having regard to the opinion of the European Central Bank,[3]

Acting in accordance with the procedure laid down in Article 251,[4]

Whereas:

(1) A genuine Single Market for financial services is crucial for economic growth and job creation in the Community.

(2) An integrated and efficient financial market requires market integrity. The smooth functioning of securities markets and public confidence in markets are prerequisites for economic growth and wealth. Market abuse harms the integrity of financial markets and public confidence in securities and derivatives.

(3) The Commission Communication of 11 May 1999 entitled "Implementing the framework for financial markets: action plan" identifies a series of actions that are needed in order to complete the single market for financial services. The Lisbon European Council of April 2000 called for the implementation of that action plan by 2005. The action plan stresses the need to draw up a Directive against market manipulation.

(4) At its meeting on 17 July 2000, the Council set up the Committee of Wise Men on the Regulation of European Securities Markets. In its final report, the Committee of Wise Men proposed the introduction of new legislative techniques based on a four-level approach, namely framework principles, implementing measures, cooperation and enforcement. Level 1, the Directive, should confine itself to broad general "framework" principles while Level 2 should contain technical implementing measures to be adopted by the Commission with the assistance of a committee.

(5) The Resolution adopted by the Stockholm European Council of March 2001 endorsed the final report of the Committee of Wise Men and the proposed four-level approach to make the regulatory process for Community securities legislation more efficient and transparent.

(6) The Resolution of the European Parliament of 5 February 2002 on the implementation of financial services legislation also endorsed the Committee of Wise Men's report, on the basis of the solemn declaration made before Parliament the same day by the Commission and the letter of 2 October 2001 addressed by the Internal Market Commissioner to the chairman of Parliament's Committee on Economic and Monetary Affairs with regard to the safeguards for the European Parliament's role in this process.

(7) The measures necessary for the implementation of this Directive should be adopted in accordance with Council Decision 1999/468/EC of 28 June 1999 laying down the procedures for the exercise of implementing powers conferred on the Commission.[5]

(8) According to the Stockholm European Council, Level 2 implementing measures should be used more frequently, to ensure that technical provisions can be kept up to date with market and supervisory developments, and deadlines should be set for all stages of Level 2 work.

(9) The European Parliament should be given a period of three months from the first transmission of draft implementing measures to allow it to examine them and to give its opinion. However, in urgent and duly justified cases, this period may be shortened. If, within that period, a resolution is passed by the European Parliament, the Commission should re-examine the draft measures.

(10) New financial and technical developments enhance the incentives, means and opportunities for market abuse: through new products, new technologies, increasing cross-border activities and the Internet.

(11) The existing Community legal framework to protect market integrity is incomplete. Legal requirements vary from one Member State to another, leaving economic actors often uncertain over concepts, definitions and enforcement. In some Member States there is no legislation addressing the issues of price manipulation and the dissemination of misleading information.

(12) Market abuse consists of insider dealing and market manipulation. The objective of legislation against insider dealing is the same as that of legislation against market manipulation: to ensure the integrity of Community financial markets and to enhance investor confidence in those markets. It is therefore advisable to adopt combined rules to combat both insider dealing and market manipulation. A single Directive will ensure throughout the Community the same framework for allocation of responsibilities, enforcement and cooperation.

(13) Given the changes in financial markets and in Community legislation since the adoption of Council Directive 89/592/EEC of 13 November 1989 coordinating regulations on insider dealing,[6] that Directive should now be replaced, to ensure consistency with legislation against market manipulation. A new Directive is also needed to avoid loopholes in Community legislation which could be used for wrongful conduct and which would undermine public confidence and therefore prejudice the smooth functioning of the markets.

(14) This Directive meets the concerns expressed by the Member States following the terrorist attacks on 11 September 2001 as regards the fight against financing terrorist activities.

(15) Insider dealing and market manipulation prevent full and proper market transparency, which is a prerequisite for trading for all economic actors in integrated financial markets.

(16) Inside information is any information of a precise nature which has not been made public, relating, directly or indirectly, to one or more issuers of financial instruments or to one or more financial instruments. Information which could have a significant effect on the evolution and forming of the prices of a regulated market as such could be considered as information which indirectly relates to one or more issuers of financial instruments or to one or more related derivative financial instruments.

(17) As regards insider dealing, account should be taken of cases where inside information originates not from a profession or function but from criminal activities, the preparation or execution of which could have a significant effect on the prices of one or more financial instruments or on price formation in the regulated market as such.

(18) Use of inside information can consist in the acquisition or disposal of financial instruments by a person who knows, or ought to have known, that the information possessed is inside information. In this respect, the competent authorities should consider what a normal and reasonable person would know or should have known in the circumstances. Moreover, the mere fact that market-makers, bodies authorised to act as counterparties, or persons authorised to execute orders on behalf of third parties with inside information confine themselves, in the first two cases, to pursuing their legitimate business of buying or selling financial instruments or, in the last case, to carrying out an order dutifully, should not in itself be deemed to constitute use of such inside information.

(19) Member States should tackle the practice known as "front running", including "front running" in commodity derivatives, where it constitutes market abuse under the definitions contained in this Directive.

(20) A person who enters into transactions or issues orders to trade which are constitutive of market manipulation may be able to establish that his reasons for entering into such transactions or issuing orders to trade were legitimate and that the transactions and orders to trade were in conformity with accepted practice on the regulated market concerned. A sanction could still be imposed if the competent authority established that there was another, illegitimate, reason behind these transactions or orders to trade.

(21) The competent authority may issue guidance on matters covered by this Directive, e g definition of inside information in relation to derivatives on commodities or implementation of the definition of accepted market practices relating to the definition of market manipulation. This guidance should be in conformity with the provisions of the Directive and the implementing measures adopted in accordance with the comitology procedure.

(22) Member States should be able to choose the most appropriate way to regulate persons producing or disseminating research concerning financial instruments or issuers of financial

instruments or persons producing or disseminating other information recommending or suggesting investment strategy, including appropriate mechanisms for self-regulation, which should be notified to the Commission.

(23) Posting of inside information by issuers on their internet sites should be in accordance with the rules on transfer of personal data to third countries as laid down in Directive 95/46/EC of the European Parliament and of the Council of 24 October 1995 on the protection of individuals with regard to the processing of personal data and on the movement of such data.[7]

(24) Prompt and fair disclosure of information to the public enhances market integrity, whereas selective disclosure by issuers can lead to a loss of investor confidence in the integrity of financial markets. Professional economic actors should contribute to market integrity by various means. Such measures could include, for instance, the creation of "grey lists", the application of "window trading" to sensitive categories of personnel, the application of internal codes of conduct and the establishment of "Chinese walls". Such preventive measures may contribute to combating market abuse only if they are enforced with determination and are dutifully controlled. Adequate enforcement control would imply for instance the designation of compliance officers within the bodies concerned and periodic checks conducted by independent auditors.

(25) Modern communication methods make it possible for financial market professionals and private investors to have more equal access to financial information, but also increase the risk of the spread of false or misleading information.

(26) Greater transparency of transactions conducted by persons discharging managerial responsibilities within issuers and, where applicable, persons closely associated with them, constitutes a preventive measure against market abuse. The publication of those transactions on at least an individual basis can also be a highly valuable source of information to investors.

(27) Market operators should contribute to the prevention of market abuse and adopt structural provisions aimed at preventing and detecting market manipulation practices. Such provisions may include requirements concerning transparency of transactions concluded, total disclosure of price-regularisation agreements, a fair system of order pairing, introduction of an effective atypical-order detection scheme, sufficiently robust financial instrument reference price-fixing schemes and clarity of rules on the suspension of transactions.

(28) This Directive should be interpreted, and implemented by Member States, in a manner consistent with the requirements for effective regulation in order to protect the interests of holders of transferable securities carrying voting rights in a company (or which may carry such rights as a consequence of the exercise of rights or conversion) when the company is subject to a public take-over bid or other proposed change of control. In particular, this Directive does not in any way prevent a Member State from putting or having in place such measures as it sees fit for these purposes.

(29) Having access to inside information relating to another company and using it in the context of a public take-over bid for the purpose of gaining control of that company or proposing a merger with that company should not in itself be deemed to constitute insider dealing.

(30) Since the acquisition or disposal of financial instruments necessarily involves a prior decision to acquire or dispose taken by the person who undertakes one or other of these operations, the carrying out of this acquisition or disposal should not be deemed in itself to constitute the use of inside information.

(31) Research and estimates developed from publicly available data should not be regarded as inside information and, therefore, any transaction carried out on the basis of such research or estimates should not be deemed in itself to constitute insider dealing within the meaning of this Directive.

(32) Member States and the European System of Central Banks, national central banks or any other officially designated body, or any person acting on their behalf, should not be restricted in carrying out monetary, exchange-rate or public debt management policy.

(33) Stabilisation of financial instruments or trading in own shares in buy-back programmes can be legitimate, in certain circumstances, for economic reasons and should not, therefore, in themselves be regarded as market abuse. Common standards should be developed to provide practical guidance.

(34) The widening scope of financial markets, the rapid change and the range of new products and developments require a wide application of this Directive to financial instruments and techniques involved, in order to guarantee the integrity of Community financial markets.

(35) Establishing a level playing field in Community financial markets requires wide geographical application of the provisions covered by this Directive. As regards derivative instruments not admitted to trading but falling within the scope of this Directive, each Member State should be competent to sanction actions carried out on its territory or abroad which concern underlying financial instruments admitted to trading on a regulated market situated or operating within its territory or for which a request for admission to trading on such a regulated market has been made. Each Member State should also be competent to sanction actions carried out on its territory which concern underlying financial instruments admitted to trading on a regulated market in a Member State or for which a request for admission to trading on such a market has been made.

(36)   A variety of competent authorities in Member States, having different responsibilities, may create confusion among economic actors. A single competent authority should be designated in each Member State to assume at least final responsibility for supervising compliance with the provisions adopted pursuant to this Directive, as well as international collaboration. Such an authority should be of an administrative nature guaranteeing its independence of economic actors and avoiding conflicts of interest. In accordance with national law, Member States should ensure appropriate financing of the competent authority. That authority should have adequate arrangements for consultation concerning possible changes in national legislation such as a consultative committee composed of representatives of issuers, financial services providers and consumers, so as to be fully informed of their views and concerns.

(37)   A common minimum set of effective tools and powers for the competent authority of each Member State will guarantee supervisory effectiveness. Market undertakings and all economic actors should also contribute at their level to market integrity. In this sense, the designation of a single competent authority for market abuse does not exclude collaboration links or delegation under the responsibility of the competent authority, between that authority and market undertakings with a view to guaranteeing efficient supervision of compliance with the provisions adopted pursuant to this Directive.

(38)   In order to ensure that a Community framework against market abuse is sufficient, any infringement of the prohibitions or requirements laid down pursuant to this Directive will have to be promptly detected and sanctioned. To this end, sanctions should be sufficiently dissuasive and proportionate to the gravity of the infringement and to the gains realised and should be consistently applied.

(39)   Member States should remain alert, in determining the administrative measures and sanctions, to the need to ensure a degree of uniformity of regulation from one Member State to another.

(40)   Increasing cross-border activities require improved cooperation and a comprehensive set of provisions for the exchange of information between national competent authorities. The organisation of supervision and of investigatory powers in each Member State should not hinder cooperation between the competent national authorities.

(41)   Since the objective of the proposed action, namely to prevent market abuse in the form of insider dealing and market manipulation, cannot be sufficiently achieved by the Member States and can therefore, by reason of the scale and effects of the measures, be better achieved at Community level, the Community may adopt measures, in accordance with the principle of subsidiarity as set out in Article 5 of the Treaty. In accordance with the principle of proportionality, as set out in that Article, this Directive does not go beyond what is necessary in order to achieve that objective.

(42)   Technical guidance and implementing measures for the rules laid down in this Directive may from time to time be necessary to take account of new developments on financial markets. The Commission should accordingly be empowered to adopt implementing measures, provided that these do not modify the essential elements of this Directive and the Commission acts according to the principles set out in this Directive, after consulting the European Securities Committee established by Commission Decision 2001/528/EC.[8]

(43)   In exercising its implementing powers in accordance with this Directive, the Commission should respect the following principles:

—   the need to ensure confidence in financial markets among investors by promoting high standards of transparency in financial markets,

—   the need to provide investors with a wide range of competing investments and a level of disclosure and protection tailored to their circumstances,

—   the need to ensure that independent regulatory authorities enforce the rules consistently, especially as regards the fight against economic crime,

—   the need for high levels of transparency and consultation with all market participants and with the European Parliament and the Council,

—   the need to encourage innovation in financial markets if they are to be dynamic and efficient,

—   the need to ensure market integrity by close and reactive monitoring of financial innovation,

—   the importance of reducing the cost of, and increasing access to, capital,

—   the balance of costs and benefits to market participants on a long-term basis (including small and medium-sized businesses and small investors) in any implementing measures,

—   the need to foster the international competitiveness of EU financial markets without prejudice to a much-needed extension of international cooperation,

—   the need to achieve a level playing field for all market participants by establishing EU-wide regulations every time it is appropriate,

—   the need to respect differences in national markets where these do not unduly impinge on the coherence of the single market,

—   the need to ensure coherence with other Community legislation in this area, as imbalances in information and a lack of transparency may jeopardise the operation of the markets and above all harm consumers and small investors.

(44)   This Directive respects the fundamental rights and observes the principles recognised in particular by the Charter of Fundamental Rights of the European Union and in particular by Article 11 thereof and Article 10 of the European Convention on Human Rights. In this regard, this Directive does not in any way prevent Member States from applying their constitutional rules relating to freedom of the press and freedom of expression in the media,

[5430]

NOTES

1   OJ C240E, 28.8.2001, p 265.
2   OJ C80, 3.4.2002, p 61.
3   OJ C24, 26.1.2002, p 8.
4   Opinion of the European Parliament of 14 March 2002 (not yet published in the Official Journal), Council Common Position of 19 July 2002 (OJ C228E, 25.9.2002, p 19) and Decision of the European Parliament of 24 October 2002 (not yet published in the Official Journal).
5   OJ L184, 17.7.1999, p 23.
6   OJ L334, 18.11.1989, p 30.
7   OJ L281, 23.11.1995, p 31.
8   OJ L191, 13.7.2001, p 45.

HAVE ADOPTED THIS DIRECTIVE:

Article 1

For the purposes of this Directive:

1.   "Inside information" shall mean information of a precise nature which has not been made public, relating, directly or indirectly, to one or more issuers of financial instruments or to one or more financial instruments and which, if it were made public, would be likely to have a significant effect on the prices of those financial instruments or on the price of related derivative financial instruments.

In relation to derivatives on commodities, "inside information" shall mean information of a precise nature which has not been made public, relating, directly or indirectly, to one or more such derivatives and which users of markets on which such derivatives are traded would expect to receive in accordance with accepted market practices on those markets.

For persons charged with the execution of orders concerning financial instruments, "inside information" shall also mean information conveyed by a client and related to the client's pending orders, which is of a precise nature, which relates directly or indirectly to one or more issuers of financial instruments or to one or more financial instruments, and which, if it were made public, would be likely to have a significant effect on the prices of those financial instruments or on the price of related derivative financial instruments.

2.   "Market manipulation" shall mean:
    (a)   transactions or orders to trade:
        —   which give, or are likely to give, false or misleading signals as to the supply of, demand for or price of financial instruments, or
        —   which secure, by a person, or persons acting in collaboration, the price of one or several financial instruments at an abnormal or artificial level,
    unless the person who entered into the transactions or issued the orders to trade establishes that his reasons for so doing are legitimate and that these transactions or orders to trade conform to accepted market practices on the regulated market concerned;
    (b)   transactions or orders to trade which employ fictitious devices or any other form of deception or contrivance;
    (c)   dissemination of information through the media, including the Internet, or by any other means, which gives, or is likely to give, false or misleading signals as to financial instruments, including the dissemination of rumours and false or misleading news, where the person who made the dissemination knew, or ought to have known, that the information was false or misleading. In respect of journalists when they act in their professional capacity such dissemination of information is to be assessed, without prejudice to Article 11, taking into account the rules governing their profession, unless those persons derive, directly or indirectly, an advantage or profits from the dissemination of the information in question.

In particular, the following instances are derived from the core definition given in points (a), (b) and (c) above:
    —   conduct by a person, or persons acting in collaboration, to secure a dominant position over the supply of or demand for a financial instrument which has the effect of fixing, directly or indirectly, purchase or sale prices or creating other unfair trading conditions,
    —   the buying or selling of financial instruments at the close of the market with the effect of misleading investors acting on the basis of closing prices,
    —   taking advantage of occasional or regular access to the traditional or electronic media by voicing an opinion about a financial instrument (or indirectly about its issuer) while

having previously taken positions on that financial instrument and profiting subsequently from the impact of the opinions voiced on the price of that instrument, without having simultaneously disclosed that conflict of interest to the public in a proper and effective way.

The definitions of market manipulation shall be adapted so as to ensure that new patterns of activity that in practice constitute market manipulation can be included.

3.   "Financial instrument" shall mean:
—   transferable securities as defined in Council Directive 93/22/EEC of 10 May 1993 on investment services in the securities field,[1]
—   units in collective investment undertakings,
—   money-market instruments,
—   financial-futures contracts, including equivalent cash-settled instruments,
—   forward interest-rate agreements,
—   interest-rate, currency and equity swaps,
—   options to acquire or dispose of any instrument falling into these categories, including equivalent cash-settled instruments. This category includes in particular options on currency and on interest rates,
—   derivatives on commodities,
—   any other instrument admitted to trading on a regulated market in a Member State or for which a request for admission to trading on such a market has been made.

4.   "Regulated market" shall mean a market as defined by Article 1(13) of Directive 93/22/EEC.

[5.   "Accepted market practices" shall mean practices that are reasonably expected in one or more financial markets and are accepted by the competent authority in accordance with guidelines adopted by the Commission in accordance with the regulatory procedure with scrutiny laid down in Article 17(2a).]

6.   "Person" shall mean any natural or legal person.

7.   "Competent authority" shall mean the competent authority designated in accordance with Article 11.

In order to take account of developments on financial markets and to ensure uniform application of this Directive in the Community, the Commission, ... shall adopt implementing measures concerning points 1, 2 and 3 of this Article. [Those measures, designed to amend non-essential elements of this Directive by supplementing it, shall be adopted in accordance with the regulatory procedure with scrutiny referred to in Article 17(2a).]

[5430A]

NOTES

Point 5 substituted, words omitted repealed, and final words in square brackets inserted, by European Parliament and Council Directive 2008/26/EC, Art 1(1), as from 21 March 2008.

[1]   OJ L141, 11.6.1993, p 27. Directive as last amended by European Parliament and Council Directive 2000/64/EC (OJ L290, 17.11.2000, p. 27).

Article 2

1.   Member States shall prohibit any person referred to in the second subparagraph who possesses inside information from using that information by acquiring or disposing of, or by trying to acquire or dispose of, for his own account or for the account of a third party, either directly or indirectly, financial instruments to which that information relates.

The first subparagraph shall apply to any person who possesses that information:
(a)   by virtue of his membership of the administrative, management or supervisory bodies of the issuer; or
(b)   by virtue of his holding in the capital of the issuer; or
(c)   by virtue of his having access to the information through the exercise of his employment, profession or duties; or
(d)   by virtue of his criminal activities.

2.   Where the person referred to in paragraph 1 is a legal person, the prohibition laid down in that paragraph shall also apply to the natural persons who take part in the decision to carry out the transaction for the account of the legal person concerned.

3.   This Article shall not apply to transactions conducted in the discharge of an obligation that has become due to acquire or dispose of financial instruments where that obligation results from an agreement concluded before the person concerned possessed inside information.

[5431]

Article 3

Member States shall prohibit any person subject to the prohibition laid down in Article 2 from:

    (a)   disclosing inside information to any other person unless such disclosure is made in the normal course of the exercise of his employment, profession or duties;

    (b)   recommending or inducing another person, on the basis of inside information, to acquire or dispose of financial instruments to which that information relates.

[5432]

Article 4

Member States shall ensure that Articles 2 and 3 also apply to any person, other than the persons referred to in those Articles, who possesses inside information while that person knows, or ought to have known, that it is inside information.

[5433]

Article 5

Member States shall prohibit any person from engaging in market manipulation.

[5434]

Article 6

1.   Member States shall ensure that issuers of financial instruments inform the public as soon as possible of inside information which directly concerns the said issuers.

Without prejudice to any measures taken to comply with the provisions of the first subparagraph, Member States shall ensure that issuers, for an appropriate period, post on their Internet sites all inside information that they are required to disclose publicly.

2.   An issuer may under his own responsibility delay the public disclosure of inside information, as referred to in paragraph 1, such as not to prejudice his legitimate interests provided that such omission would not be likely to mislead the public and provided that the issuer is able to ensure the confidentiality of that information. Member States may require that an issuer shall without delay inform the competent authority of the decision to delay the public disclosure of inside information.

3.   Member States shall require that, whenever an issuer, or a person acting on his behalf or for his account, discloses any inside information to any third party in the normal exercise of his employment, profession or duties, as referred to in Article 3(a), he must make complete and effective public disclosure of that information, simultaneously in the case of an intentional disclosure and promptly in the case of a non-intentional disclosure.

The provisions of the first subparagraph shall not apply if the person receiving the information owes a duty of confidentiality, regardless of whether such duty is based on a law, on regulations, on articles of association or on a contract.

Member States shall require that issuers, or persons acting on their behalf or for their account, draw up a list of those persons working for them, under a contract of employment or otherwise, who have access to inside information. Issuers and persons acting on their behalf or for their account shall regularly update this list and transmit it to the competent authority whenever the latter requests it.

4.   Persons discharging managerial responsibilities within an issuer of financial instruments and, where applicable, persons closely associated with them, shall, at least, notify to the competent authority the existence of transactions conducted on their own account relating to shares of the said issuer, or to derivatives or other financial instruments linked to them. Member States shall ensure that public access to information concerning such transactions, on at least an individual basis, is readily available as soon as possible.

5.   Member States shall ensure that there is appropriate regulation in place to ensure that persons who produce or disseminate research concerning financial instruments or issuers of financial instruments and persons who produce or disseminate other information recommending or suggesting investment strategy, intended for distribution channels or for the public, take reasonable care to ensure that such information is fairly presented and disclose their interests or indicate conflicts of interest concerning the financial instruments to which that information relates. Details of such regulation shall be notified to the Commission.

6.   Member States shall ensure that market operators adopt structural provisions aimed at preventing and detecting market manipulation practices.

7.   With a view to ensuring compliance with paragraphs 1 to 5, the competent authority may take all necessary measures to ensure that the public is correctly informed.

8.   Public institutions disseminating statistics liable to have a significant effect on financial markets shall disseminate them in a fair and transparent way.

9.   Member States shall require that any person professionally arranging transactions in financial instruments who reasonably suspects that a transaction might constitute insider dealing or market manipulation shall notify the competent authority without delay.

10. In order to take account of technical developments on financial markets and to ensure uniform application of this Directive, the Commission shall adopt, ... implementing measures concerning:

— the technical modalities for appropriate public disclosure of inside information as referred to in paragraphs 1 and 3,

— the technical modalities for delaying the public disclosure of inside information as referred to in paragraph 2,

— the technical modalities designed to favour a common approach in the implementation of the second sentence of paragraph 2,

— the conditions under which issuers, or entities acting on their behalf, are to draw up a list of those persons working for them and having access to inside information, as referred to in paragraph 3, together with the conditions under which such lists are to be updated,

— the categories of persons who are subject to a duty of disclosure as referred to in paragraph 4 and the characteristics of a transaction, including its size, which trigger that duty, and the technical arrangements for disclosure to the competent authority,

— technical arrangements, for the various categories of person referred to in paragraph 5, for fair presentation of research and other information recommending investment strategy and for disclosure of particular interests or conflicts of interest as referred to in paragraph 5. Such arrangements shall take into account the rules, including self-regulation, governing the profession of journalist,

— technical arrangements governing notification to the competent authority by the persons referred to in paragraph 9.

[Those measures, designed to amend non-essential elements of this Directive by supplementing it, shall be adopted in accordance with the regulatory procedure with scrutiny referred to in Article 17(2a).]

[5435]

NOTES

Para 10: words omitted repealed, and words in square brackets inserted, by European Parliament and Council Directive 2008/26/EC, Art 1(2), as from 21 March 2008.

Article 7

This Directive shall not apply to transactions carried out in pursuit of monetary, exchange-rate or public debt-management policy by a Member State, by the European System of Central Banks, by a national central bank or by any other officially designated body, or by any person acting on their behalf. Member States may extend this exemption to their federated States or similar local authorities in respect of the management of their public debt.

[5436]

Article 8

The prohibitions provided for in this Directive shall not apply to trading in own shares in "buy-back" programmes or to the stabilisation of a financial instrument provided such trading is carried out in accordance with implementing measures ...

[Those measures, designed to amend non-essential elements of this Directive by supplementing it, shall be adopted in accordance with the regulatory procedure with scrutiny referred to in Article 17(2a).]

[5437]

NOTES

Words omitted repealed, and words in square brackets inserted, by European Parliament and Council Directive 2008/26/EC, Art 1(3), as from 21 March 2008.

Article 9

This Directive shall apply to any financial instrument admitted to trading on a regulated market in at least one Member State, or for which a request for admission to trading on such a market has been made, irrespective of whether or not the transaction itself actually takes place on that market.

Articles 2, 3 and 4 shall also apply to any financial instrument not admitted to trading on a regulated market in a Member State, but whose value depends on a financial instrument as referred to in paragraph 1.

Article 6(1) to (3) shall not apply to issuers who have not requested or approved admission of their financial instruments to trading on a regulated market in a Member State.

[5438]

Article 10

Each Member State shall apply the prohibitions and requirements provided for in this Directive to:

(a) actions carried out on its territory or abroad concerning financial instruments that are admitted to trading on a regulated market situated or operating within its territory or for which a request for admission to trading on such market has been made;

(b)   actions carried out on its territory concerning financial instruments that are admitted to trading on a regulated market in a Member State or for which a request for admission to trading on such market has been made.

[5439]

Article 11

Without prejudice to the competences of the judicial authorities, each Member State shall designate a single administrative authority competent to ensure that the provisions adopted pursuant to this Directive are applied.

Member States shall establish effective consultative arrangements and procedures with market participants concerning possible changes in national legislation. These arrangements may include consultative committees within each competent authority, the membership of which should reflect as far as possible the diversity of market participants, be they issuers, providers of financial services or consumers.

[5440]

Article 12

1.   The competent authority shall be given all supervisory and investigatory powers that are necessary for the exercise of its functions. It shall exercise such powers:

(a)   directly; or

(b)   in collaboration with other authorities or with the market undertakings; or

(c)   under its responsibility by delegation to such authorities or to the market undertakings; or

(d)   by application to the competent judicial authorities.

2.   Without prejudice to Article 6(7), the powers referred to in paragraph 1 of this Article shall be exercised in conformity with national law and shall include at least the right to:

(a)   have access to any document in any form whatsoever, and to receive a copy of it;

(b)   demand information from any person, including those who are successively involved in the transmission of orders or conduct of the operations concerned, as well as their principals, and if necessary, to summon and hear any such person;

(c)   carry out on-site inspections;

(d)   require existing telephone and existing data traffic records;

(e)   require the cessation of any practice that is contrary to the provisions adopted in the implementation of this Directive;

(f)   suspend trading of the financial instruments concerned;

(g)   request the freezing and/or sequestration of assets;

(h)   request temporary prohibition of professional activity.

3.   This Article shall be without prejudice to national legal provisions on professional secrecy.

[5441]

Article 13

The obligation of professional secrecy shall apply to all persons who work or who have worked for the competent authority or for any authority or market undertaking to whom the competent authority has delegated its powers, including auditors and experts instructed by the competent authority. Information covered by professional secrecy may not be disclosed to any other person or authority except by virtue of provisions laid down by law.

[5442]

Article 14

1.   Without prejudice to the right of Member States to impose criminal sanctions, Member States shall ensure, in conformity with their national law, that the appropriate administrative measures can be taken or administrative sanctions be imposed against the persons responsible where the provisions adopted in the implementation of this Directive have not been complied with. Member States shall ensure that these measures are effective, proportionate and dissuasive.

2.   In accordance with the procedure laid down in Article 17(2), the Commission shall, for information, draw up a list of the administrative measures and sanctions referred to in paragraph 1.

3.   Member States shall determine the sanctions to be applied for failure to cooperate in an investigation covered by Article 12.

4.   Member States shall provide that the competent authority may disclose to the public every measure or sanction that will be imposed for infringement of the provisions adopted in the implementation of this Directive, unless such disclosure would seriously jeopardise the financial markets or cause disproportionate damage to the parties involved.

[5443]

Article 15

Member States shall ensure that an appeal may be brought before a court against the decisions taken by the competent authority.

[5444]

Article 16

1.   Competent authorities shall cooperate with each other whenever necessary for the purpose of carrying out their duties, making use of their powers whether set out in this Directive or in national law. Competent authorities shall render assistance to competent authorities of other Member States. In particular, they shall exchange information and cooperate in investigation activities.

2.   Competent authorities shall, on request, immediately supply any information required for the purpose referred to in paragraph 1. Where necessary, the competent authorities receiving any such request shall immediately take the necessary measures in order to gather the required information. If the requested competent authority is not able to supply the required information immediately, it shall notify the requesting competent authority of the reasons. Information thus supplied shall be covered by the obligation of professional secrecy to which the persons employed or formerly employed by the competent authorities receiving the information are subject.

The competent authorities may refuse to act on a request for information where:
—   communication might adversely affect the sovereignty, security or public policy of the Member State addressed,
—   judicial proceedings have already been initiated in respect of the same actions and against the same persons before the authorities of the Member State addressed, or
—   where a final judgment has already been delivered in relation to such persons for the same actions in the Member State addressed.

In any such case, they shall notify the requesting competent authority accordingly, providing as detailed information as possible on those proceedings or the judgment.

Without prejudice to Article 226 of the Treaty, a competent authority whose request for information is not acted upon within a reasonable time or whose request for information is rejected may bring that non-compliance to the attention of the Committee of European Securities Regulators, where discussion will take place in order to reach a rapid and effective solution.

Without prejudice to the obligations to which they are subject in judicial proceedings under criminal law, the competent authorities which receive information pursuant to paragraph 1 may use it only for the exercise of their functions within the scope of this Directive and in the context of administrative or judicial proceedings specifically related to the exercise of those functions. However, where the competent authority communicating information consents thereto, the authority receiving the information may use it for other purposes or forward it to other States' competent authorities.

3.   Where a competent authority is convinced that acts contrary to the provisions of this Directive are being, or have been, carried out on the territory of another Member State or that acts are affecting financial instruments traded on a regulated market situated in another Member State, it shall give notice of that fact in as specific a manner as possible to the competent authority of the other Member State. The competent authority of the other Member State shall take appropriate action. It shall inform the notifying competent authority of the outcome and, so far as possible, of significant interim developments. This paragraph shall not prejudice the competences of the competent authority that has forwarded the information. The competent authorities of the various Member States that are competent for the purposes of Article 10 shall consult each other on the proposed follow-up to their action.

4.   A competent authority of one Member State may request that an investigation be carried out by the competent authority of another Member State, on the latter's territory.

It may further request that members of its own personnel be allowed to accompany the personnel of the competent authority of that other Member State during the course of the investigation.

The investigation shall, however, be subject throughout to the overall control of the Member State on whose territory it is conducted.

The competent authorities may refuse to act on a request for an investigation to be conducted as provided for in the first subparagraph, or on a request for its personnel to be accompanied by personnel of the competent authority of another Member State as provided for in the second subparagraph, where such an investigation might adversely affect the sovereignty, security or public policy of the State addressed, or where judicial proceedings have already been initiated in respect of the same actions and against the same persons before the authorities of the State addressed or where a final judgment has already been delivered in relation to such persons for the same actions in the State addressed. In such case, they shall notify the requesting competent authority accordingly, providing information, as detailed as possible, on those proceedings or judgment.

Without prejudice to the provisions of Article 226 of the Treaty, a competent authority whose application to open an inquiry or whose request for authorisation for its officials to accompany those of the other Member State's competent authority is not acted upon within a reasonable time or is rejected may bring that non-compliance to the attention of the Committee of European Securities Regulators, where discussion will take place in order to reach a rapid and effective solution.

[5. In accordance with the regulatory procedure laid down in Article 17(2), the Commission shall adopt implementing measures on the working procedures for exchange of information and cross-border inspections as referred to in this Article.]

[5445]

NOTES

Para 5: substituted by European Parliament and Council Directive 2008/26/EC, Art 1(4), as from 21 March 2008.

Article 17

1. The Commission shall be assisted by the European Securities Committee instituted by Decision 2001/528/EC (hereinafter referred to as the "Committee").

2. Where reference is made to this paragraph, Articles 5 and 7 of Decision 1999/468/EC shall apply, having regard to the provisions of Article 8 thereof, provided that the implementing measures adopted according to this procedure do not modify the essential provisions of this Directive.

The period laid down in Article 5(6) of Decision 1999/468/EC shall be set at three months.

[2a. Where reference is made to this paragraph, Article 5a(1) to (4) and Article 7 of Decision 1999/468/EC shall apply, having regard to the provisions of Article 8 thereof.]

[3. By 31 December 2010, and, thereafter, at least every three years, the Commission shall review the provisions concerning its implementing powers and present a report to the European Parliament and to the Council on the functioning of those powers. The report shall examine, in particular, the need for the Commission to propose amendments to this Directive in order to ensure the appropriate scope of the implementing powers conferred on the Commission. The conclusion as to whether or not amendment is necessary shall be accompanied by a detailed statement of reasons. If necessary, the report shall be accompanied by a legislative proposal to amend the provisions conferring implementing powers on the Commission.]

[5446]

NOTES

Para 2a inserted, and para 3 substituted (for original paras 3, 4), by European Parliament and Council Directive 2008/26/EC, Art 1(5), as from 21 March 2008.

Article 18

Member States shall bring into force the laws, regulations and administrative provisions necessary to comply with this Directive not later than 12 October 2004. They shall forthwith inform the Commission thereof.

When Member States adopt those measures, they shall contain a reference to this Directive or be accompanied by such a reference on the occasion of their official publication. Member States shall determine how such reference is to be made.

[5447]

Article 19

Article 11 shall not prejudice the possibility for a Member State to make separate legal and administrative arrangements for overseas European territories for whose external relations that Member State is responsible.

[5448]

Article 20

Directive 89/592/EEC and Article 68(1) and Article 81(1) of Directive 2001/34/EC of the European Parliament and of the Council of 28 May 2001 on the admission of securities to official stock exchange listing and on information to be published on those securities[1] shall be repealed with effect from the date of entry into force of this Directive.

[5449]

NOTES

[1]   OJ L184, 6.7.2001, p 1.

Article 21

This Directive shall enter into force on the day of its publication in the Official Journal of the European Union.

[5450]

Article 22

This Directive is addressed to the Member States.

DIRECTIVE OF THE EUROPEAN PARLIAMENT AND OF THE COUNCIL

of 4 November 2003

on the prospectus to be published when securities are offered to the public or admitted to trading and amending Directive 2001/34/EC

(2003/71/EC)

(Text with EEA relevance)

NOTES

Date of publication in OJ: OJ L345, 31.12.2003, p 64. Notes are as in the original OJ version.

This Directive is reproduced as amended by: European Parliament and Council Directive 2008/11/EC (OJ L76, 19.3.2008, p 37).

THE EUROPEAN PARLIAMENT AND THE COUNCIL OF THE EUROPEAN UNION,

Having regard to the Treaty establishing the European Community, and in particular Articles 44 and 95 thereof,

Having regard to the proposal from the Commission,[1]

Having regard to the opinion of the European Economic and Social Committee,[2]

Having regard to the opinion of the European Central Bank,[3]

Acting in accordance with the procedure laid down in Article 251 of the Treaty,[4]

Whereas:

(1) Council Directives 80/390/EEC of 17 March 1980 coordinating the requirements for the drawing up, scrutiny and distribution of the listing particulars to be published for the admission of securities to official stock exchange listing[5] and 89/298/EEC of 17 April 1989 coordinating the requirements for the drawing up, scrutiny and distribution of the prospectus to be published when transferable securities are offered to the public[6] were adopted several years ago introducing a partial and complex mutual recognition mechanism which is unable to achieve the objective of the single passport provided for by this Directive. Those directives should be upgraded, updated and grouped together into a single text.

(2) Meanwhile, Directive 80/390/EEC was integrated into Directive 2001/34/EC of the European Parliament and of the Council of 28 May 2001 on the admission of securities to official stock exchange listing and on information to be published on those securities,[7] which codifies several directives in the field of listed securities.

(3) For reasons of consistency, however, it is appropriate to regroup the provisions of Directive 2001/34/EC which stem from Directive 80/390/EEC together with Directive 89/298/EEC and to amend Directive 2001/34/EC accordingly.

(4) This Directive constitutes an instrument essential to the achievement of the internal market as set out in timetable form in the Commission communications 'Risk capital action plan' and 'Implementing the framework for financial market: Action Plan' facilitating the widest possible access to investment capital on a Community-wide basis, including for small and medium-sized enterprises (SMEs) and start-ups, by granting a single passport to the issuer.

(5) On 17 July 2000, the Council set up the Committee of Wise Men on the regulation of European securities markets. In its initial report of 9 November 2000 the Committee stresses the lack of an agreed definition of public offer of securities, with the result that the same operation is regarded as a private placement in some Member States and not in others; the current system discourages firms from raising capital on a Community-wide basis and therefore from having real access to a large, liquid and integrated financial market.

(6) In its final report of 15 February 2001 the Committee of Wise Men proposed the introduction of new legislative techniques based on a four-level approach, namely framework principles, implementing measures, cooperation and enforcement. Level 1, the directive, should confine itself to broad, general 'framework' principles, while Level 2 should contain technical implementing measures to be adopted by the Commission with the assistance of a committee.

(7) The Stockholm European Council of 23 and 24 March 2001 endorsed the final report of the Committee of Wise Men and the proposed four-level approach to make the regulatory process for Community securities legislation more efficient and transparent.

(8) The resolution of the European Parliament of 5 February 2002 on the implementation of financial services legislation also endorsed the Committee of Wise Men's final report, on the basis

of the solemn declaration made before Parliament the same day by the Commission and the letter of 2 October 2001 addressed by the Internal Market Commissioner to the chairman of Parliament's Committee on Economic and Monetary Affairs with regard to the safeguards for the European Parliament's role in this process.

(9)   According to the Stockholm European Council, Level 2 implementing measures should be used more frequently to ensure that technical provisions can be kept up to date with market and supervisory developments and deadlines should be set for all stages of Level 2.

(10)   The aim of this Directive and its implementing measures is to ensure investor protection and market efficiency, in accordance with high regulatory standards adopted in the relevant international fora.

(11)   Non-equity securities issued by a Member State or by one of a Member State's regional or local authorities, by public international bodies of which one or more Member States are members, by the European Central Bank or by the central banks of the Member States are not covered by this Directive and thus remain unaffected by this Directive; the abovementioned issuers of such securities may, however, if they so choose, draw up a prospectus in accordance with this Directive.

(12)   Full coverage of equity and non-equity securities offered to the public or admitted to trading on regulated markets as defined by Council Directive 93/22/EEC of 10 May 1993 on investment services in the securities field,[8] and not only securities which have been admitted to the official lists of stock exchanges, is also needed to ensure investor protection. The wide definition of securities in this Directive, which includes warrants and covered warrants and certificates, is only valid for this Directive and consequently in no way affects the various definitions of financial instruments used in national legislation for other purposes, such as taxation. Some of the securities defined in this Directive entitle the holder to acquire transferable securities or to receive a cash amount through a cash settlement determined by reference to other instruments, notably transferable securities, currencies, interest rates or yields, commodities or other indices or measures. Depositary receipts and convertible notes, e g securities convertible at the option of the investor, fall within the definition of non-equity securities set out in this Directive.

(13)   Issuance of securities having a similar type and/or class in the case of non-equity securities issued on the basis of an offering programme, including warrants and certificates in any form, as well as the case of securities issued in a continuous or repeated manner, should be understood as covering not only identical securities but also securities that belong in general terms to one category. These securities may include different products, such as debt securities, certificates and warrants, or the same product under the same programme, and may have different features notably in terms of seniority, types of underlying, or the basis on which to determine the redemption amount or coupon payment.

(14)   The grant to the issuer of a single passport, valid throughout the Community, and the application of the country of origin principle require the identification of the home Member State as the one best placed to regulate the issuer for the purposes of this Directive.

(15)   The disclosure requirements of the present Directive do not prevent a Member State or a competent authority or an exchange through its rule book to impose other particular requirements in the context of admission to trading of securities on a regulated market (notably regarding corporate governance). Such requirements may not directly or indirectly restrict the drawing up, the content and the dissemination of a prospectus approved by a competent authority.

(16)   One of the objectives of this Directive is to protect investors. It is therefore appropriate to take account of the different requirements for protection of the various categories of investors and their level of expertise. Disclosure provided by the prospectus is not required for offers limited to qualified investors. In contrast, any resale to the public or public trading through admission to trading on a regulated market requires the publication of a prospectus.

(17)   Issuers, offerors or persons asking for the admission to trading on a regulated market of securities which are exempted from the obligation to publish a prospectus will benefit from the single passport if they comply with this Directive.

(18)   The provision of full information concerning securities and issuers of those securities promotes, together with rules on the conduct of business, the protection of investors. Moreover, such information provides an effective means of increasing confidence in securities and thus of contributing to the proper functioning and development of securities markets. The appropriate way to make this information available is to publish a prospectus.

(19)   Investment in securities, like any other form of investment, involves risk. Safeguards for the protection of the interests of actual and potential investors are required in all Member States in order to enable them to make an informed assessment of such risks and thus to take investment decisions in full knowledge of the facts.

(20)   Such information, which needs to be sufficient and as objective as possible as regards the financial circumstances of the issuer and the rights attaching to the securities, should be provided in an easily analysable and comprehensible form. Harmonisation of the information contained in the prospectus should provide equivalent investor protection at Community level.

(21)   Information is a key factor in investor protection; a summary conveying the essential characteristics of, and risks associated with, the issuer, any guarantor and the securities should be

included in the prospectus. To ensure easy access to this information, the summary should be written in non-technical language and normally should not exceed 2,500 words in the language in which the prospectus was originally drawn up.

(22)   Best practices have been adopted at international level in order to allow cross-border offers of equities to be made using a single set of disclosure standards established by the International Organisation of Securities Commissions (IOSCO); the IOSCO disclosure standards[9] will upgrade information available for the markets and investors and at the same time will simplify the procedure for Community issuers wishing to raise capital in third countries. The Directive also calls for tailored disclosure standards to be adopted for other types of securities and issuers.

(23)   Fast-track procedures for issuers admitted to trading on a regulated market and frequently raising capital on these markets require the introduction at Community level of a new format of prospectuses for offering programmes or mortgage bonds and a new registration document system. Issuers may choose not to use those formats and therefore to draft the prospectus as a single document.

(24)   The content of a base prospectus should, in particular, take into account the need for flexibility in relation to the information to be provided about the securities.

(25)   Omission of sensitive information to be included in a prospectus should be allowed through a derogation granted by the competent authority in certain circumstances in order to avoid detrimental situations for an issuer.

(26)   A clear time limit should be set for the validity of a prospectus in order to avoid outdated information.

(27)   Investors should be protected by ensuring publication of reliable information. The issuers whose securities are admitted to trading on a regulated market are subject to an ongoing disclosure obligation but are not required to publish updated information regularly. Further to this obligation, issuers should, at least annually, list all relevant information published or made available to the public over the preceding 12 months, including information provided to the various reporting requirements laid down in other Community legislation. This should make it possible to ensure the publication of consistent and easily understandable information on a regular basis. To avoid excessive burdens for certain issuers, issuers of non-equity securities with high minimum denomination should not be required to meet this obligation.

(28)   It is necessary for the annual information to be provided by issuers whose securities are admitted to trading on a regulated market to be appropriately monitored by Member States in accordance with their obligations under the provisions of Community and national law concerning the regulation of securities, issuers of securities and securities markets.

(29)   The opportunity of allowing issuers to incorporate by reference documents containing the information to be disclosed in a prospectus—provided that the documents incorporated by reference have been previously filed with or accepted by the competent authority—should facilitate the procedure of drawing up a prospectus and lower the costs for the issuers without endangering investor protection.

(30)   Differences regarding the efficiency, methods and timing of the checking of the information given in a prospectus not only make it more difficult for undertakings to raise capital or to obtain admission to trading on a regulated market in more than one Member State but also hinder the acquisition by investors established in one Member State of securities offered by an issuer established in another Member State or admitted to trading in another Member State. These differences should be eliminated by harmonising the rules and regulations in order to achieve an adequate degree of equivalence of the safeguards required in each Member State to ensure the provision of information which is sufficient and as objective as possible for actual or potential securities holders.

(31)   To facilitate circulation of the various documents making up the prospectus, the use of electronic communication facilities such as the Internet should be encouraged. The prospectus should always be delivered in paper form, free of charge to investors on request.

(32)   The prospectus should be filed with the relevant competent authority and be made available to the public by the issuer, the offeror or the person asking for admission to trading on a regulated market, subject to European Union provisions relating to data protection.

(33)   It is also necessary, in order to avoid loopholes in Community legislation which would undermine public confidence and therefore prejudice the proper functioning of financial markets, to harmonise advertisements.

(34)   Any new matter liable to influence the assessment of the investment, arising after the publication of the prospectus but before the closing of the offer or the start of trading on a regulated market, should be properly evaluated by investors and therefore requires the approval and dissemination of a supplement to the prospectus.

(35)   The obligation for an issuer to translate the full prospectus into all the relevant official languages discourages cross-border offers or multiple trading. To facilitate cross-border offers, where the prospectus is drawn up in a language that is customary in the sphere of international finance, the host or home Member State should only be entitled to require a summary in its official language(s).

(36)   The competent authority of the host Member State should be entitled to receive a certificate from the competent authority of the home Member State which states that the prospectus has been drawn up in accordance with this Directive. In order to ensure that the purposes of this Directive will be fully achieved, it is also necessary to include within its scope securities issued by issuers governed by the laws of third countries.

(37)   A variety of competent authorities in Member States, having different responsibilities, may create unnecessary costs and overlapping of responsibilities without providing any additional benefit. In each Member State one single competent authority should be designated to approve prospectuses and to assume responsibility for supervising compliance with this Directive. Under strict conditions, a Member State should be allowed to designate more than one competent authority, but only one will assume the duties for international cooperation. Such an authority or authorities should be established as an administrative authority and in such a form that their independence from economic actors is guaranteed and conflicts of interest are avoided. The designation of a competent authority for prospectus approval should not exclude cooperation between that authority and other entities, with a view to guaranteeing efficient scrutiny and approval of prospectuses in the interest of issuers, investors, markets participants and markets alike. Any delegation of tasks relating to the obligations provided for in this Directive and in its implementing measures should be reviewed, in accordance with Article 31, five years after the date of entry into force of this Directive and should, except for publication on the Internet of approved prospectuses, and the filing of prospectuses as mentioned in Article 14, end eight years after the entry into force of this Directive.

(38)   A common minimum set of powers for the competent authorities will guarantee the effectiveness of their supervision. The flow of information to the markets required by Directive 2001/34/EC should be ensured and action against breaches should be taken by competent authorities.

(39)   For the purposes of carrying out their duties, cooperation between competent authorities of the Member States is required.

(40)   Technical guidance and implementing measures for the rules laid down in this Directive may from time to time be necessary to take into account developments on financial markets. The Commission should accordingly be empowered to adopt implementing measures, provided that these do not modify the essential elements of this Directive and provided that the Commission acts in accordance with the principles set out in this Directive, after consulting the European Securities Committee established by Commission Decision 2001/528/EC.[10]

(41)   In exercising its implementing powers in accordance with this Directive, the Commission should respect the following principles:

—   the need to ensure confidence in financial markets among small investors and small and medium-sized enterprises (SMEs) by promoting high standards of transparency in financial markets,

—   the need to provide investors with a wide range of competing investment opportunities and a level of disclosure and protection tailored to their circumstances,

—   the need to ensure that independent regulatory authorities enforce the rules consistently, especially as regards the fight against white-collar crime,

—   the need for a high level of transparency and consultation with all market participants and with the European Parliament and the Council,

—   the need to encourage innovation in financial markets if they are to be dynamic and efficient,

—   the need to ensure systemic stability of the financial system by close and reactive monitoring of financial innovation,

—   the importance of reducing the cost of, and increasing access to, capital,

—   the need to balance, on a long-term basis, the costs and benefits to market participants (including SMEs and small investors) of any implementing measures,

—   the need to foster the international competitiveness of the Community's financial markets without prejudice to a much-needed extension of international cooperation,

—   the need to achieve a level playing field for all market participants by establishing Community legislation every time it is appropriate,

—   the need to respect differences in national financial markets where these do not unduly impinge on the coherence of the single market,

—   the need to ensure coherence with other Community legislation in this area, as imbalances in information and a lack of transparency may jeopardise the operation of the markets and above all harm consumers and small investors.

(42)   The European Parliament should be given a period of three months from the first transmission of draft implementing measures to allow it to examine them and to give its opinion. However, in urgent and duly justified cases, this period may be shortened. If, within that period, a resolution is passed by the European Parliament, the Commission should re-examine the draft measures.

(43)   Member States should lay down a system of sanctions for breaches of the national provisions adopted pursuant to this Directive and should take all the measures necessary to ensure that these sanctions are applied. The sanctions thus provided for should be effective, proportional and dissuasive.

(44)   Provision should be made for the right of judicial review of decisions taken by Member States' competent authorities in respect of the application of this Directive.

(45)   In accordance with the principle of proportionality, it is necessary and appropriate for the achievement of the basic objective of ensuring the completion of a single securities market to lay down rules on a single passport for issuers. This Directive does not go beyond what is necessary in order to achieve the objectives pursued in accordance with the third paragraph of Article 5 of the Treaty.

(46)   The assessment made by the Commission of the application of this Directive should focus in particular on the process of approval of prospectuses by the competent authorities of the Member States, and more generally on the application of the home-country principle, and whether or not problems of investor protection and market efficiency might result from this application; the Commission should also examine the functioning of Article 10.

(47)   For future developments of this Directive, consideration should be given to the matter of deciding which approval mechanism should be adopted to enhance further the uniform application of Community legislation on prospectuses, including the possible establishment of a European Securities Unit.

(48)   This Directive respects the fundamental rights and observes the principles recognised in particular by the Charter of Fundamental Rights of the European Union.

(49)   The measures necessary for the implementation of this Directive should be adopted in accordance with Council Decision 1999/468/EC of 28 June 1999 laying down the procedures for the exercise of implementing powers conferred on the Commission,[11]

[5452]

NOTES

[1]   OJ C240E, 28.8.2001, p 272 and OJ C20E, 28.1.2003, p 122.
[2]   OJ C80, 3.4.2002, p 52.
[3]   OJ C344, 6.12.2001, p 4.
[4]   Opinion of the European Parliament of 14 March 2002 (OJ C47E, 27.2.2003, p 417), Council Common Position of 24 March 2003 (OJ C125E, 27.5.2003, p 21) and Position of the European Parliament of 2 July 2003 (not yet published in the Official Journal). Decision of the Council of 15 July 2003.
[5]   OJ L100, 17.4.1980, p 1. Directive as last amended by Directive of the European Parliament and of the Council 94/18/EC (OJ L135, 31.5.1994, p 1).
[6]   OJ L124, 5.5.1989, p 8.
[7]   OJ L184, 6.7.2001, p 1.
[8]   OJ L141, 11.6.1993, p 27. Directive as last amended by Directive 2000/64/EC of the European Parliament and of the Council (OJ L290, 17.11.2000, p 27).
[9]   International disclosure standards for cross-border offering and initial listings by foreign issuers, Part I, International Organisation of Securities Commissions, September 1998.
[10]   OJ L191, 13.7.2001, p 45.
[11]   OJ L184, 17.7.1999, p 23.

HAVE ADOPTED THIS DIRECTIVE:

CHAPTER I
GENERAL PROVISIONS

Article 1
Purpose and scope

1.   The purpose of this Directive is to harmonise requirements for the drawing up, approval and distribution of the prospectus to be published when securities are offered to the public or admitted to trading on a regulated market situated or operating within a Member State.

2.   This Directive shall not apply to:
   (a)   units issued by collective investment undertakings other than the closed-end type;
   (b)   non-equity securities issued by a Member State or by one of a Member State's regional or local authorities, by public international bodies of which one or more Member States are members, by the European Central Bank or by the central banks of the Member States;
   (c)   shares in the capital of central banks of the Member States;
   (d)   securities unconditionally and irrevocably guaranteed by a Member State or by one of a Member State's regional or local authorities;
   (e)   securities issued by associations with legal status or non-profit-making bodies, recognised by a Member State, with a view to their obtaining the means necessary to achieve their non-profit-making objectives;

(f) non-equity securities issued in a continuous or repeated manner by credit institutions provided that these securities:
  (i) are not subordinated, convertible or exchangeable;
  (ii) do not give a right to subscribe to or acquire other types of securities and that they are not linked to a derivative instrument;
  (iii) materialise reception of repayable deposits;
  (iv) are covered by a deposit guarantee scheme under Directive 94/19/EC of the European Parliament and of the Council on deposit-guarantee schemes;[1]
(g) non-fungible shares of capital whose main purpose is to provide the holder with a right to occupy an apartment, or other form of immovable property or a part thereof and where the shares cannot be sold on without this right being given up;
(h) securities included in an offer where the total consideration of the offer is less than EUR 2,500,000, which limit shall be calculated over a period of 12 months;
(i) 'bostadsobligationer' issued repeatedly by credit institutions in Sweden whose main purpose is to grant mortgage loans, provided that
  (i) the 'bostadsobligationer' issued are of the same series;
  (ii) the 'bostadsobligationer' are issued on tap during a specified issuing period;
  (iii) the terms and conditions of the 'bostadsobligationer' are not changed during the issuing period;
  (iv) the sums deriving from the issue of the said 'bostadsobligationer', in accordance with the articles of association of the issuer, are placed in assets which provide sufficient coverage for the liability deriving from securities;
(j) non-equity securities issued in a continuous or repeated manner by credit institutions where the total consideration of the offer is less than EUR 50,000,000, which limit shall be calculated over a period of 12 months, provided that these securities:
  (i) are not subordinated, convertible or exchangeable;
  (ii) do not give a right to subscribe to or acquire other types of securities and that they are not linked to a derivative instrument.

3. Notwithstanding paragraph 2(b), (d), (h), (i) and (j), an issuer, an offeror or a person asking for admission to trading on a regulated market shall be entitled to draw up a prospectus in accordance with this Directive when securities are offered to the public or admitted to trading.

[5453]

NOTES
[1] OJ L135, 31.5.1994, p 5.

Article 2
Definitions

1. For the purposes of this Directive, the following definitions shall apply:
  (a) 'securities' means transferable securities as defined by Article 1(4) of Directive 93/22/EEC with the exception of money market instruments as defined by Article 1(5) of Directive 93/22/EEC, having a maturity of less than 12 months. For these instruments national legislation may be applicable;
  (b) 'equity securities' means shares and other transferable securities equivalent to shares in companies, as well as any other type of transferable securities giving the right to acquire any of the aforementioned securities as a consequence of their being converted or the rights conferred by them being exercised, provided that securities of the latter type are issued by the issuer of the underlying shares or by an entity belonging to the group of the said issuer;
  (c) 'non-equity securities' means all securities that are not equity securities;
  (d) 'offer of securities to the public' means a communication to persons in any form and by any means, presenting sufficient information on the terms of the offer and the securities to be offered, so as to enable an investor to decide to purchase or subscribe to these securities. This definition shall also be applicable to the placing of securities through financial intermediaries;
  (e) 'qualified investors' means:
    (i) legal entities which are authorised or regulated to operate in the financial markets, including: credit institutions, investment firms, other authorised or regulated financial institutions, insurance companies, collective investment schemes and their management companies, pension funds and their management companies, commodity dealers, as well as entities not so authorised or regulated whose corporate purpose is solely to invest in securities;
    (ii) national and regional governments, central banks, international and supranational institutions such as the International Monetary Fund, the European Central Bank, the European Investment Bank and other similar international organisations;

(iii)   other legal entities which do not meet two of the three criteria set out in paragraph (f);

(iv)   certain natural persons: subject to mutual recognition, a Member State may choose to authorise natural persons who are resident in the Member State and who expressly ask to be considered as qualified investors if these persons meet at least two of the criteria set out in paragraph 2;

(v)   certain SMEs: subject to mutual recognition, a Member State may choose to authorise SMEs which have their registered office in that Member State and who expressly ask to be considered as qualified investors;

(f)   'small and medium-sized enterprises' means companies, which, according to their last annual or consolidated accounts, meet at least two of the following three criteria: an average number of employees during the financial year of less than 250, a total balance sheet not exceeding EUR 43,000,000 and an annual net turnover not exceeding EUR 50,000,000;

(g)   'credit institution' means an undertaking as defined by Article 1(1)(a) of Directive 2000/12/EC of the European Parliament and of the Council of 20 March 2000 relating to the taking up and pursuit of the business of credit institutions;[1]

(h)   'issuer' means a legal entity which issues or proposes to issue securities;

(i)   'person making an offer' (or 'offeror') means a legal entity or individual which offers securities to the public;

(j)   'regulated market' means a market as defined by Article 1(13) of Directive 93/22/EEC;

(k)   'offering programme' means a plan which would permit the issuance of non-equity securities, including warrants in any form, having a similar type and/or class, in a continuous or repeated manner during a specified issuing period;

(l)   'securities issued in a continuous or repeated manner' means issues on tap or at least two separate issues of securities of a similar type and/or class over a period of 12 months;

(m)   'home Member State' means:

    (i)   for all Community issuers of securities which are not mentioned in (ii), the Member State where the issuer has its registered office;

    (ii)   for any issues of non-equity securities whose denomination per unit amounts to at least EUR 1,000, and for any issues of non-equity securities giving the right to acquire any transferable securities or to receive a cash amount, as a consequence of their being converted or the rights conferred by them being exercised, provided that the issuer of the non-equity securities is not the issuer of the underlying securities or an entity belonging to the group of the latter issuer, the Member State where the issuer has its registered office, or where the securities were or are to be admitted to trading on a regulated market or where the securities are offered to the public, at the choice of the issuer, the offeror or the person asking for admission, as the case may be. The same regime shall be applicable to non-equity securities in a currency other than euro, provided that the value of such minimum denomination is nearly equivalent to EUR 1,000;

    (iii)   for all issuers of securities incorporated in a third country, which are not mentioned in (ii), the Member State where the securities are intended to be offered to the public for the first time after the date of entry into force of this Directive or where the first application for admission to trading on a regulated market is made, at the choice of the issuer, the offeror or the person asking for admission, as the case may be, subject to a subsequent election by issuers incorporated in a third country if the home Member State was not determined by their choice;

(n)   'host Member State' means the State where an offer to the public is made or admission to trading is sought, when different from the home Member State;

(o)   'collective investment undertaking other than the closed-end type' means unit trusts and investment companies:

    (i)   the object of which is the collective investment of capital provided by the public, and which operate on the principle of risk-spreading;

    (ii)   the units of which are, at the holder's request, repurchased or redeemed, directly or indirectly, out of the assets of these undertakings;

(p)   'units of a collective investment undertaking' mean securities issued by a collective investment undertaking as representing the rights of the participants in such an undertaking over its assets;

(q)   'approval' means the positive act at the outcome of the scrutiny of the completeness of the prospectus by the home Member State's competent authority including the consistency of the information given and its comprehensibility;

(r)   'base prospectus' means a prospectus containing all relevant information as specified in Articles 5, 7 and 16 in case there is a supplement, concerning the issuer and the securities to be offered to the public or admitted to trading, and, at the choice of the issuer, the final terms of the offering.

2. For the purposes of paragraph 1(e)(iv) the criteria are as follows:

(a) the investor has carried out transactions of a significant size on securities markets at an average frequency of, at least, 10 per quarter over the previous four quarters;

(b) the size of the investor's securities portfolio exceeds EUR 0.5 million;

(c) the investor works or has worked for at least one year in the financial sector in a professional position which requires knowledge of securities investment.

3. For the purposes of paragraphs 1(e)(iv) and (v) the following shall apply:

Each competent authority shall ensure that appropriate mechanisms are in place for a register of natural persons and SMEs considered as qualified investors, taking into account the need to ensure an adequate level of data protection. The register shall be available to all issuers. Each natural person or SME wishing to be considered as a qualified investor shall register and each registered investor may decide to opt out at any moment.

4. In order to take account of technical developments on financial markets and to ensure uniform application of this Directive, the Commission shall ... adopt implementing measures concerning the definitions referred to in paragraph 1, including adjustment of the figures used for the definition of SMEs, taking into account Community legislation and recommendations as well as economic developments and disclosure measures relating to the registration of individual qualified investors. [Those measures, designed to amend non-essential elements of this Directive by supplementing it, shall be adopted in accordance with the regulatory procedure with scrutiny referred to in Article 24(2a).]

[5454]

NOTES

Para 4: words omitted repealed, and words in square brackets added, by European Parliament and Council Directive 2008/11/EC, Art 1(1) as from 20 March 2008. Note that Art 1(1)(a) of the 2008 Directive actually provides that the words "in accordance with the procedure referred to in Article 24(2)" shall be deleted from para 4 above. The omitted words in para 4 were "in accordance with the procedure *set out* in Article 24(2)". It is assumed that this is a drafting error and the words have been deleted accordingly.

¹ OJ L126, 26.5.2000, p 1. Directive as last amended by Directive 2000/28/EC (OJ L275, 27.10.2000, p 37).

Article 3
Obligation to publish a prospectus

1. Member States shall not allow any offer of securities to be made to the public within their territories without prior publication of a prospectus.

2. The obligation to publish a prospectus shall not apply to the following types of offer:

(a) an offer of securities addressed solely to qualified investors; and/or

(b) an offer of securities addressed to fewer than 100 natural or legal persons per Member State, other than qualified investors; and/or

(c) an offer of securities addressed to investors who acquire securities for a total consideration of at least EUR 50,000 per investor, for each separate offer; and/or

(d) an offer of securities whose denomination per unit amounts to at least EUR 50,000; and/or

(e) an offer of securities with a total consideration of less than EUR 100,000, which limit shall be calculated over a period of 12 months.

However, any subsequent resale of securities which were previously the subject of one or more of the types of offer mentioned in this paragraph shall be regarded as a separate offer and the definition set out in Article 2(1)(d) shall apply for the purpose of deciding whether that resale is an offer of securities to the public. The placement of securities through financial intermediaries shall be subject to publication of a prospectus if none of the conditions (a) to (e) are met for the final placement.

3. Member States shall ensure that any admission of securities to trading on a regulated market situated or operating within their territories is subject to the publication of a prospectus.

[5455]

Article 4
Exemptions from the obligation to publish a prospectus

1. The obligation to publish a prospectus shall not apply to offers of securities to the public of the following types of securities:

(a) shares issued in substitution for shares of the same class already issued, if the issuing of such new shares does not involve any increase in the issued capital;

(b) securities offered in connection with a takeover by means of an exchange offer, provided that a document is available containing information which is regarded by the competent authority as being equivalent to that of the prospectus, taking into account the requirements of Community legislation;

(c) securities offered, allotted or to be allotted in connection with a merger, provided that a document is available containing information which is regarded by the competent authority as being equivalent to that of the prospectus, taking into account the requirements of Community legislation;

(d) shares offered, allotted or to be allotted free of charge to existing shareholders, and dividends paid out in the form of shares of the same class as the shares in respect of which such dividends are paid, provided that a document is made available containing information on the number and nature of the shares and the reasons for and details of the offer;

(e) securities offered, allotted or to be allotted to existing or former directors or employees by their employer which has securities already admitted to trading on a regulated market or by an affiliated undertaking, provided that a document is made available containing information on the number and nature of the securities and the reasons for and details of the offer.

2. The obligation to publish a prospectus shall not apply to the admission to trading on a regulated market of the following types of securities:

(a) shares representing, over a period of 12 months, less than 10 per cent of the number of shares of the same class already admitted to trading on the same regulated market;

(b) shares issued in substitution for shares of the same class already admitted to trading on the same regulated market, if the issuing of such shares does not involve any increase in the issued capital;

(c) securities offered in connection with a takeover by means of an exchange offer, provided that a document is available containing information which is regarded by the competent authority as being equivalent to that of the prospectus, taking into account the requirements of Community legislation;

(d) securities offered, allotted or to be allotted in connection with a merger, provided that a document is available containing information which is regarded by the competent authority as being equivalent to that of the prospectus, taking into account the requirements of Community legislation;

(e) shares offered, allotted or to be allotted free of charge to existing shareholders, and dividends paid out in the form of shares of the same class as the shares in respect of which such dividends are paid, provided that the said shares are of the same class as the shares already admitted to trading on the same regulated market and that a document is made available containing information on the number and nature of the shares and the reasons for and details of the offer;

(f) securities offered, allotted or to be allotted to existing or former directors or employees by their employer or an affiliated undertaking, provided that the said securities are of the same class as the securities already admitted to trading on the same regulated market and that a document is made available containing information on the number and nature of the securities and the reasons for and detail of the offer;

(g) shares resulting from the conversion or exchange of other securities or from the exercise of the rights conferred by other securities, provided that the said shares are of the same class as the shares already admitted to trading on the same regulated market;

(h) securities already admitted to trading on another regulated market, on the following conditions:

    (i) that these securities, or securities of the same class, have been admitted to trading on that other regulated market for more than 18 months;

    (ii) that, for securities first admitted to trading on a regulated market after the date of entry into force of this Directive, the admission to trading on that other regulated market was associated with an approved prospectus made available to the public in conformity with Article 14;

    (iii) that, except where (ii) applies, for securities first admitted to listing after 30 June 1983, listing particulars were approved in accordance with the requirements of Directive 80/390/EEC or Directive 2001/34/EC;

    (iv) that the ongoing obligations for trading on that other regulated market have been fulfilled;

    (v) that the person seeking the admission of a security to trading on a regulated market under this exemption makes a summary document available to the public in a language accepted by the competent authority of the Member State of the regulated market where admission is sought;

    (vi) that the summary document referred to in (v) is made available to the public in the Member State of the regulated market where admission to trading is sought in the manner set out in Article 14(2); and

    (vii) that the contents of the summary document shall comply with Article 5(2). Furthermore the document shall state where the most recent prospectus can be obtained and where the financial information published by the issuer pursuant to his ongoing disclosure obligations is available.

3. In order to take account of technical developments on financial markets and to ensure uniform application of this Directive, the Commission shall ... adopt implementing measures concerning paragraphs 1(b), 1(c), 2(c) and 2(d), notably in relation to the meaning of equivalence. [Those measures, designed to amend non-essential elements of this Directive by supplementing it, shall be adopted in accordance with the regulatory procedure with scrutiny referred to in Article 24(2a).]

[5456]

NOTES
Para 3: words omitted repealed, and words in square brackets added, by European Parliament and Council Directive 2008/11/EC, Art 1(1) as from 20 March 2008.

CHAPTER II
DRAWING UP OF THE PROSPECTUS

Article 5
The prospectus

1. Without prejudice to Article 8(2), the prospectus shall contain all information which, according to the particular nature of the issuer and of the securities offered to the public or admitted to trading on a regulated market, is necessary to enable investors to make an informed assessment of the assets and liabilities, financial position, profit and losses, and prospects of the issuer and of any guarantor, and of the rights attaching to such securities. This information shall be presented in an easily analysable and comprehensible form.

2. The prospectus shall contain information concerning the issuer and the securities to be offered to the public or to be admitted to trading on a regulated market. It shall also include a summary. The summary shall, in a brief manner and in non-technical language, convey the essential characteristics and risks associated with the issuer, any guarantor and the securities, in the language in which the prospectus was originally drawn up. The summary shall also contain a warning that:
   (a) it should be read as an introduction to the prospectus;
   (b) any decision to invest in the securities should be based on consideration of the prospectus as a whole by the investor;
   (c) where a claim relating to the information contained in a prospectus is brought before a court, the plaintiff investor might, under the national legislation of the Member States, have to bear the costs of translating the prospectus before the legal proceedings are initiated; and
   (d) civil liability attaches to those persons who have tabled the summary including any translation thereof, and applied for its notification, but only if the summary is misleading, inaccurate or inconsistent when read together with the other parts of the prospectus.

Where the prospectus relates to the admission to trading on a regulated market of non-equity securities having a denomination of at least EUR 50,000, there shall be no requirement to provide a summary except when requested by a Member State as provided for in Article 19(4).

3. Subject to paragraph 4, the issuer, offeror or person asking for the admission to trading on a regulated market may draw up the prospectus as a single document or separate documents. A prospectus composed of separate documents shall divide the required information into a registration document, a securities note and a summary note. The registration document shall contain the information relating to the issuer. The securities note shall contain the information concerning the securities offered to the public or to be admitted to trading on a regulated market.

4. For the following types of securities, the prospectus can, at the choice of the issuer, offeror or person asking for the admission to trading on a regulated market consist of a base prospectus containing all relevant information concerning the issuer and the securities offered to the public or to be admitted to trading on a regulated market:
   (a) non-equity securities, including warrants in any form, issued under an offering programme;
   (b) non-equity securities issued in a continuous or repeated manner by credit institutions,
      (i) where the sums deriving from the issue of the said securities, under national legislation, are placed in assets which provide sufficient coverage for the liability deriving from securities until their maturity date;
      (ii) where, in the event of the insolvency of the related credit institution, the said sums are intended, as a priority, to repay the capital and interest falling due, without prejudice to the provisions of Directive 2001/24/EC of the European Parliament and of the Council of 4 April 2001 on the reorganisation and winding up of credit institutions.[1]

The information given in the base prospectus shall be supplemented, if necessary, in accordance with Article 16, with updated information on the issuer and on the securities to be offered to the public or to be admitted to trading on a regulated market.

If the final terms of the offer are not included in either the base prospectus or a supplement, the final terms shall be provided to investors and filed with the competent authority when each public offer is made as soon as practicable and if possible in advance of the beginning of the offer. The provisions of Article 8(1)(a) shall be applicable in any such case.

5. In order to take account of technical developments on financial markets and to ensure uniform application of this Directive, the Commission shall ... adopt implementing measures concerning the format of the prospectus or base prospectus and supplements. [Those measures, designed to amend non-essential elements of this Directive by supplementing it, shall be adopted in accordance with the regulatory procedure with scrutiny referred to in Article 24(2a).]

[5457]

NOTES

Para 5: words omitted repealed, and words in square brackets added, by European Parliament and Council Directive 2008/11/EC, Art 1(1) as from 20 March 2008.

¹   OJ L125, 5.5.2001, p 15.

Article 6
Responsibility attaching to the prospectus

1. Member States shall ensure that responsibility for the information given in a prospectus attaches at least to the issuer or its administrative, management or supervisory bodies, the offeror, the person asking for the admission to trading on a regulated market or the guarantor, as the case may be. The persons responsible shall be clearly identified in the prospectus by their names and functions or, in the case of legal persons, their names and registered offices, as well as declarations by them that, to the best of their knowledge, the information contained in the prospectus is in accordance with the facts and that the prospectus makes no omission likely to affect its import.

2. Member States shall ensure that their laws, regulation and administrative provisions on civil liability apply to those persons responsible for the information given in a prospectus.

However, Member States shall ensure that no civil liability shall attach to any person solely on the basis of the summary, including any translation thereof, unless it is misleading, inaccurate or inconsistent when read together with the other parts of the prospectus.

[5458]

Article 7
Minimum information

1. Detailed implementing measures regarding the specific information which must be included in a prospectus, avoiding duplication of information when a prospectus is composed of separate documents, shall be adopted by the Commission ... . The first set of implementing measures shall be adopted by 1 July 2004. [Those measures, designed to amend non-essential elements of this Directive by supplementing it, shall be adopted in accordance with the regulatory procedure with scrutiny referred to in Article 24(2a).]

2. In particular, for the elaboration of the various models of prospectuses, account shall be taken of the following:
- (a) the various types of information needed by investors relating to equity securities as compared with non-equity securities; a consistent approach shall be taken with regard to information required in a prospectus for securities which have a similar economic rationale, notably derivative securities;
- (b) the various types and characteristics of offers and admissions to trading on a regulated market of non-equity securities. The information required in a prospectus shall be appropriate from the point of view of the investors concerned for non-equity securities having a denomination per unit of at least EUR 50,000;
- (c) the format used and the information required in prospectuses relating to non-equity securities, including warrants in any form, issued under an offering programme;
- (d) the format used and the information required in prospectuses relating to non-equity securities, in so far as these securities are not subordinated, convertible, exchangeable, subject to subscription or acquisition rights or linked to derivative instruments, issued in a continuous or repeated manner by entities authorised or regulated to operate in the financial markets within the European Economic Area;
- (e) the various activities and size of the issuer, in particular SMEs. For such companies the information shall be adapted to their size and, where appropriate, to their shorter track record;
- (f) if applicable, the public nature of the issuer.

3. The implementing measures referred to in paragraph 1 shall be based on the standards in the field of financial and non-financial information set out by international securities commission organisations, and in particular by IOSCO and on the indicative Annexes to this Directive.

[5459]

NOTES
Para 1: words omitted repealed, and words in square brackets added, by European Parliament and Council Directive 2008/11/EC, Art 1(1) as from 20 March 2008.

Article 8
Omission of information

1. Member States shall ensure that where the final offer price and amount of securities which will be offered to the public cannot be included in the prospectus:
   (a) the criteria, and/or the conditions in accordance with which the above elements will be determined or, in the case of price, the maximum price, are disclosed in the prospectus; or
   (b) the acceptances of the purchase or subscription of securities may be withdrawn for not less than two working days after the final offer price and amount of securities which will be offered to the public have been filed.

The final offer price and amount of securities shall be filed with the competent authority of the home Member State and published in accordance with the arrangements provided for in Article 14(2).

2. The competent authority of the home Member State may authorise the omission from the prospectus of certain information provided for in this Directive or in the implementing measures referred to in Article 7(1), if it considers that:
   (a) disclosure of such information would be contrary to the public interest; or
   (b) disclosure of such information would be seriously detrimental to the issuer, provided that the omission would not be likely to mislead the public with regard to facts and circumstances essential for an informed assessment of the issuer, offeror or guarantor, if any, and of the rights attached to the securities to which the prospectus relates; or
   (c) such information is of minor importance only for a specific offer or admission to trading on a regulated market and is not such as will influence the assessment of the financial position and prospects of the issuer, offeror or guarantor, if any.

3. Without prejudice to the adequate information of investors, where, exceptionally, certain information required by implementing measures referred to in Article 7(1) to be included in a prospectus is inappropriate to the issuer's sphere of activity or to the legal form of the issuer or to the securities to which the prospectus relates, the prospectus shall contain information equivalent to the required information. If there is no such information, this requirement shall not apply.

4. In order to take account of technical developments on financial markets and to ensure uniform application of this Directive, the Commission shall … adopt implementing measures concerning paragraph 2. [Those measures, designed to amend non-essential elements of this Directive by supplementing it, shall be adopted in accordance with the regulatory procedure with scrutiny referred to in Article 24(2a).]

[5460]

NOTES
Para 4: words omitted repealed, and words in square brackets added, by European Parliament and Council Directive 2008/11/EC, Art 1(1) as from 20 March 2008.

Article 9
Validity of a prospectus, base prospectus and registration document

1. A prospectus shall be valid for 12 months after its publication for offers to the public or admissions to trading on a regulated market, provided that the prospectus is completed by any supplements required pursuant to Article 16.

2. In the case of an offering programme, the base prospectus, previously filed, shall be valid for a period of up to 12 months.

3. In the case of non-equity securities referred to in Article 5(4)(b), the prospectus shall be valid until no more of the securities concerned are issued in a continuous or repeated manner.

4. A registration document, as referred to in Article 5(3), previously filed, shall be valid for a period of up to 12 months provided that it has been updated in accordance with Article 10(1). The registration document accompanied by the securities note, updated if applicable in accordance with Article 12, and the summary note shall be considered to constitute a valid prospectus.

[5461]

Article 10
Information

1.   Issuers whose securities are admitted to trading on a regulated market shall at least annually provide a document that contains or refers to all information that they have published or made available to the public over the preceding 12 months in one or more Member States and in third countries in compliance with their obligations under Community and national laws and rules dealing with the regulation of securities, issuers of securities and securities markets. Issuers shall refer at least to the information required pursuant to company law directives, Directive 2001/34/EC and Regulation (EC) No 1606/2002 of the European Parliament and of the Council of 19 July 2002 on the application of international accounting standards.[1]

2.   The document shall be filed with the competent authority of the home Member State after the publication of the financial statement. Where the document refers to information, it shall be stated where the information can be obtained.

3.   The obligation set out in paragraph 1 shall not apply to issuers of non-equity securities whose denomination per unit amounts to at least EUR 50,000.

4.   In order to take account of technical developments on financial markets and to ensure uniform application of this Directive, the Commission may, in accordance with the procedure referred to in Article 24(2), adopt implementing measures concerning paragraph 1. These measures will relate only to the method of publication of the disclosure requirements mentioned in paragraph 1 and will not entail new disclosure requirements. The first set of implementing measures shall be adopted by 1 July 2004.

[5462]

NOTES
   [1]   OJ L243, 11.9.2002, p 1.

Article 11
Incorporation by reference

1.   Member States shall allow information to be incorporated in the prospectus by reference to one or more previously or simultaneously published documents that have been approved by the competent authority of the home Member State or filed with it in accordance with this Directive, in particular pursuant to Article 10, or with Titles IV and V of Directive 2001/34/EC. This information shall be the latest available to the issuer. The summary shall not incorporate information by reference.

2.   When information is incorporated by reference, a cross-reference list must be provided in order to enable investors to identify easily specific items of information.

3.   In order to take account of technical developments on financial markets and to ensure uniform application of this Directive, the Commission shall … adopt implementing measures concerning the information to be incorporated by reference. The first set of implementing measures shall be adopted by 1 July 2004. [Those measures, designed to amend non-essential elements of this Directive by supplementing it, shall be adopted in accordance with the regulatory procedure with scrutiny referred to in Article 24(2a).]

[5463]

NOTES
   Para 3: words omitted repealed, and words in square brackets added, by European Parliament and Council Directive 2008/11/EC, Art 1(1) as from 20 March 2008.

Article 12
Prospectuses consisting of separate documents

1.   An issuer which already has a registration document approved by the competent authority shall be required to draw up only the securities note and the summary note when securities are offered to the public or admitted to trading on a regulated market.

2.   In this case, the securities note shall provide information that would normally be provided in the registration document if there has been a material change or recent development which could affect investors' assessments since the latest updated registration document or any supplement as provided for in Article 16 was approved. The securities and summary notes shall be subject to a separate approval.

3.   Where an issuer has only filed a registration document without approval, the entire documentation, including updated information, shall be subject to approval.

[5464]

CHAPTER III
ARRANGEMENTS FOR APPROVAL AND PUBLICATION OF THE PROSPECTUS

Article 13
Approval of the prospectus

1.   No prospectus shall be published until it has been approved by the competent authority of the home Member State.

2.   This competent authority shall notify the issuer, the offeror or the person asking for admission to trading on a regulated market, as the case may be, of its decision regarding the approval of the prospectus within 10 working days of the submission of the draft prospectus.

If the competent authority fails to give a decision on the prospectus within the time limits laid down in this paragraph and paragraph 3, this shall not be deemed to constitute approval of the application.

3.   The time limit referred to in paragraph 2 shall be extended to 20 working days if the public offer involves securities issued by an issuer which does not have any securities admitted to trading on a regulated market and who has not previously offered securities to the public.

4.   If the competent authority finds, on reasonable grounds, that the documents submitted to it are incomplete or that supplementary information is needed, the time limits referred to in paragraphs 2 and 3 shall apply only from the date on which such information is provided by the issuer, the offeror or the person asking for admission to trading on a regulated market.

In the case referred to in paragraph 2 the competent authority should notify the issuer if the documents are incomplete within 10 working days of the submission of the application.

5.   The competent authority of the home Member State may transfer the approval of a prospectus to the competent authority of another Member State, subject to the agreement of that authority. Furthermore, this transfer shall be notified to the issuer, the offeror or the person asking for admission to trading on a regulated market within three working days from the date of the decision taken by the competent authority of the home Member State. The time limit referred to in paragraph 2 shall apply from that date.

6.   This Directive shall not affect the competent authority's liability, which shall continue to be governed solely by national law.

Member States shall ensure that their national provisions on the liability of competent authorities apply only to approvals of prospectuses by their competent authority or authorities.

7.   In order to take account of technical developments on financial markets and to ensure uniform application of this Directive, the Commission may … adopt implementing measures concerning the conditions in accordance with which time limits may be adjusted. [Those measures, designed to amend non-essential elements of this Directive by supplementing it, shall be adopted in accordance with the regulatory procedure with scrutiny referred to in Article 24(2a).]

[5465]

NOTES
Para 7: words omitted repealed, and words in square brackets added, by European Parliament and Council Directive 2008/11/EC, Art 1(1) as from 20 March 2008.

Article 14
Publication of the prospectus

1.   Once approved, the prospectus shall be filed with the competent authority of the home Member State and shall be made available to the public by the issuer, offeror or person asking for admission to trading on a regulated market as soon as practicable and in any case, at a reasonable time in advance of, and at the latest at the beginning of, the offer to the public or the admission to trading of the securities involved. In addition, in the case of an initial public offer of a class of shares not already admitted to trading on a regulated market that is to be admitted to trading for the first time, the prospectus shall be available at least six working days before the end of the offer.

2.   The prospectus shall be deemed available to the public when published either:
   (a)   by insertion in one or more newspapers circulated throughout, or widely circulated in, the Member States in which the offer to the public is made or the admission to trading is sought; or
   (b)   in a printed form to be made available, free of charge, to the public at the offices of the market on which the securities are being admitted to trading, or at the registered office of the issuer and at the offices of the financial intermediaries placing or selling the securities, including paying agents; or
   (c)   in an electronic form on the issuer's website and, if applicable, on the website of the financial intermediaries placing or selling the securities, including paying agents; or
   (d)   in an electronic form on the website of the regulated market where the admission to trading is sought; or

   (e)   in electronic form on the website of the competent authority of the home Member State if the said authority has decided to offer this service.

A home Member State may require issuers which publish their prospectus in accordance with (a) or (b) also to publish their prospectus in an electronic form in accordance with (c).

3.   In addition, a home Member State may require publication of a notice stating how the prospectus has been made available and where it can be obtained by the public.

4.   The competent authority of the home Member State shall publish on its website over a period of 12 months, at its choice, all the prospectuses approved, or at least the list of prospectuses approved in accordance with Article 13, including, if applicable, a hyperlink to the prospectus published on the website of the issuer, or on the website of the regulated market.

5.   In the case of a prospectus comprising several documents and/or incorporating information by reference, the documents and information making up the prospectus may be published and circulated separately provided that the said documents are made available, free of charge, to the public, in accordance with the arrangements established in paragraph 2. Each document shall indicate where the other constituent documents of the full prospectus may be obtained.

6.   The text and the format of the prospectus, and/or the supplements to the prospectus, published or made available to the public, shall at all times be identical to the original version approved by the competent authority of the home Member State.

7.   Where the prospectus is made available by publication in electronic form, a paper copy must nevertheless be delivered to the investor, upon his request and free of charge, by the issuer, the offeror, the person asking for admission to trading or the financial intermediaries placing or selling the securities.

8.   In order to take account of technical developments on financial markets and to ensure uniform application of the Directive, the Commission shall ... adopt implementing measures concerning paragraphs 1, 2, 3 and 4. The first set of implementing measures shall be adopted by 1 July 2004. [Those measures, designed to amend non-essential elements of this Directive by supplementing it, shall be adopted in accordance with the regulatory procedure with scrutiny referred to in Article 24(2a).]

[5466]

NOTES

Para 8: words omitted repealed, and words in square brackets added, by European Parliament and Council Directive 2008/11/EC, Art 1(1) as from 20 March 2008.

Article 15
Advertisements

1.   Any type of advertisements relating either to an offer to the public of securities or to an admission to trading on a regulated market shall observe the principles contained in paragraphs 2 to 5. Paragraphs 2 to 4 shall apply only to cases where the issuer, the offeror or the person applying for admission to trading is covered by the obligation to draw up a prospectus.

2.   Advertisements shall state that a prospectus has been or will be published and indicate where investors are or will be able to obtain it.

3.   Advertisements shall be clearly recognisable as such. The information contained in an advertisement shall not be inaccurate, or misleading. This information shall also be consistent with the information contained in the prospectus, if already published, or with the information required to be in the prospectus, if the prospectus is published afterwards.

4.   In any case, all information concerning the offer to the public or the admission to trading on a regulated market disclosed in an oral or written form, even if not for advertising purposes, shall be consistent with that contained in the prospectus.

5.   When according to this Directive no prospectus is required, material information provided by an issuer or an offeror and addressed to qualified investors or special categories of investors, including information disclosed in the context of meetings relating to offers of securities, shall be disclosed to all qualified investors or special categories of investors to whom the offer is exclusively addressed. Where a prospectus is required to be published, such information shall be included in the prospectus or in a supplement to the prospectus in accordance with Article 16(1).

6.   The competent authority of the home Member State shall have the power to exercise control over the compliance of advertising activity, relating to a public offer of securities or an admission to trading on a regulated market, with the principles referred to in paragraphs 2 to 5.

7.   In order to take account of technical developments on financial markets and to ensure uniform application of this Directive, the Commission shall ... adopt implementing measures concerning the dissemination of advertisements announcing the intention to offer securities to the public or the admission to trading on a regulated market, in particular before the prospectus has been made available to the public or before the opening of the subscription, and concerning paragraph 4.

The first set of implementing measures shall be adopted by the Commission by 1 July 2004. [Those measures, designed to amend non-essential elements of this Directive by supplementing it, shall be adopted in accordance with the regulatory procedure with scrutiny referred to in Article 24(2a).]

[5467]

NOTES

Para 7: words omitted repealed, and words in square brackets added, by European Parliament and Council Directive 2008/11/EC, Art 1(1) as from 20 March 2008.

Article 16
Supplements to the prospectus

1. Every significant new factor, material mistake or inaccuracy relating to the information included in the prospectus which is capable of affecting the assessment of the securities and which arises or is noted between the time when the prospectus is approved and the final closing of the offer to the public or, as the case may be, the time when trading on a regulated market begins, shall be mentioned in a supplement to the prospectus. Such a supplement shall be approved in the same way in a maximum of seven working days and published in accordance with at least the same arrangements as were applied when the original prospectus was published. The summary, and any translations thereof, shall also be supplemented, if necessary to take into account the new information included in the supplement.

2. Investors who have already agreed to purchase or subscribe for the securities before the supplement is published shall have the right, exercisable within a time limit which shall not be shorter than two working days after the publication of the supplement, to withdraw their acceptances.

[5468]

CHAPTER IV
CROSS-BORDER OFFERS AND ADMISSION TO TRADING

Article 17
Community scope of approvals of prospectuses

1. Without prejudice to Article 23, where an offer to the public or admission to trading on a regulated market is provided for in one or more Member States, or in a Member State other than the home Member State, the prospectus approved by the home Member State and any supplements thereto shall be valid for the public offer or the admission to trading in any number of host Member States, provided that the competent authority of each host Member State is notified in accordance with Article 18. Competent authorities of host Member States shall not undertake any approval or administrative procedures relating to prospectuses.

2. If there are significant new factors, material mistakes or inaccuracies, as referred to in Article 16, arising since the approval of the prospectus, the competent authority of the home Member State shall require the publication of a supplement to be approved as provided for in Article 13(1). The competent authority of the host Member State may draw the attention of the competent authority of the home Member State to the need for any new information.

[5469]

Article 18
Notification

1. The competent authority of the home Member State shall, at the request of the issuer or the person responsible for drawing up the prospectus and within three working days following that request or, if the request is submitted together with the draft prospectus, within one working day after the approval of the prospectus provide the competent authority of the host Member State with a certificate of approval attesting that the prospectus has been drawn up in accordance with this Directive and with a copy of the said prospectus. If applicable, this notification shall be accompanied by a translation of the summary produced under the responsibility of the issuer or person responsible for drawing up the prospectus. The same procedure shall be followed for any supplement to the prospectus.

2. The application of the provisions of Article 8(2) and (3) shall be stated in the certificate, as well as its justification.

[5470]

CHAPTER V
USE OF LANGUAGES AND ISSUERS INCORPORATED IN THIRD COUNTRIES

Article 19
Use of languages

1.　Where an offer to the public is made or admission to trading on a regulated market is sought only in the home Member State, the prospectus shall be drawn up in a language accepted by the competent authority of the home Member State.

2.　Where an offer to the public is made or admission to trading on a regulated market is sought in one or more Member States excluding the home Member State, the prospectus shall be drawn up either in a language accepted by the competent authorities of those Member States or in a language customary in the sphere of international finance, at the choice of the issuer, offeror or person asking for admission, as the case may be. The competent authority of each host Member State may only require that the summary be translated into its official language(s).

For the purpose of the scrutiny by the competent authority of the home Member State, the prospectus shall be drawn up either in a language accepted by this authority or in a language customary in the sphere of international finance, at the choice of the issuer, offeror or person asking for admission to trading, as the case may be.

3.　Where an offer to the public is made or admission to trading on a regulated market is sought in more than one Member State including the home Member State, the prospectus shall be drawn up in a language accepted by the competent authority of the home Member State and shall also be made available either in a language accepted by the competent authorities of each host Member State or in a language customary in the sphere of international finance, at the choice of the issuer, offeror, or person asking for admission to trading, as the case may be. The competent authority of each host Member State may only require that the summary referred to in Article 5(2) be translated into its official language(s).

4.　Where admission to trading on a regulated market of non-equity securities whose denomination per unit amounts to at least EUR 50,000 is sought in one or more Member States, the prospectus shall be drawn up either in a language accepted by the competent authorities of the home and host Member States or in a language customary in the sphere of international finance, at the choice of the issuer, offeror or person asking for admission to trading, as the case may be. Member States may choose to require in their national legislation that a summary be drawn up in their official language(s).

[5471]

Article 20
Issuers incorporated in third countries

1.　The competent authority of the home Member State of issuers having their registered office in a third country may approve a prospectus for an offer to the public or for admission to trading on a regulated market, drawn up in accordance with the legislation of a third country, provided that:

    (a)　the prospectus has been drawn up in accordance with international standards set by international securities commission organisations, including the IOSCO disclosure standards;

    (b)　the information requirements, including information of a financial nature, are equivalent to the requirements under this Directive.

2.　In the case of an offer to the public or admission to trading on a regulated market of securities, issued by an issuer incorporated in a third country, in a Member State other than the home Member State, the requirements set out in Articles 17, 18 and 19 shall apply.

[3.　In order to ensure uniform application of this Directive, the Commission shall adopt implementing measures aimed at establishing general equivalence criteria, based on the requirements laid down in Articles 5 and 7. Those measures, designed to amend non-essential elements of this Directive by supplementing it, shall be adopted in accordance with the regulatory procedure with scrutiny referred to in Article 24(2a).

On the basis of the above criteria, the Commission may adopt implementing measures in accordance with the regulatory procedure referred to in Article 24(2), stating that a third country ensures the equivalence of prospectuses drawn up in that country with this Directive by reason of its national law or of practices or procedures based on international standards set by international organisations, including the IOSCO disclosure standards.]

[5472]

NOTES

Para 3: substituted by European Parliament and Council Directive 2008/11/EC, Art 1(2) as from 20 March 2008.

CHAPTER VI
COMPETENT AUTHORITIES

Article 21
Powers

1. Each Member State shall designate a central competent administrative authority responsible for carrying out the obligations provided for in this Directive and for ensuring that the provisions adopted pursuant to this Directive are applied.

However, a Member State may, if so required by national law, designate other administrative authorities to apply Chapter III.

These competent authorities shall be completely independent from all market participants.

If an offer of securities is made to the public or admission to trading on a regulated market is sought in a Member State other than the home Member State, only the central competent administrative authority designated by each Member State shall be entitled to approve the prospectus.

2. Member States may allow their competent authority or authorities to delegate tasks. Except for delegation of the publication on the Internet of approved prospectuses and the filing of prospectuses as mentioned in Article 14, any delegation of tasks relating to the obligations provided for in this Directive and in its implementing measures shall be reviewed, in accordance with Article 31 by 31 December 2008, and shall end on 31 December 2011. Any delegation of tasks to entities other than the authorities referred to in paragraph 1 shall be made in a specific manner stating the tasks to be undertaken and the conditions under which they are to be carried out.

These conditions shall include a clause obliging the entity in question to act and be organised in such a manner as to avoid conflict of interest and so that information obtained from carrying out the delegated tasks is not used unfairly or to prevent competition. In any case, the final responsibility for supervising compliance with this Directive and with its implementing measures and for approving the prospectus shall lie with the competent authority or authorities designated in accordance with paragraph 1.

Member States shall inform the Commission and the competent authorities of other Member States of any arrangements entered into with regard to delegation of tasks, including the precise conditions regulating such delegation.

3. Each competent authority shall have all the powers necessary for the performance of its functions. A competent authority that has received an application for approving a prospectus shall be empowered at least to:
(a) require issuers, offerors or persons asking for admission to trading on a regulated market to include in the prospectus supplementary information, if necessary for investor protection;
(b) require issuers, offerors or persons asking for admission to trading on a regulated market, and the persons that control them or are controlled by them, to provide information and documents;
(c) require auditors and managers of the issuer, offeror or person asking for admission to trading on a regulated market, as well as financial intermediaries commissioned to carry out the offer to the public or ask for admission to trading, to provide information;
(d) suspend a public offer or admission to trading for a maximum of 10 consecutive working days on any single occasion if it has reasonable grounds for suspecting that the provisions of this Directive have been infringed;
(e) prohibit or suspend advertisements for a maximum of 10 consecutive working days on any single occasion if it has reasonable grounds for believing that the provisions of this Directive have been infringed;
(f) prohibit a public offer if it finds that the provisions of this Directive have been infringed or if it has reasonable grounds for suspecting that they would be infringed;
(g) suspend or ask the relevant regulated markets to suspend trading on a regulated market for a maximum of 10 consecutive working days on any single occasion if it has reasonable grounds for believing that the provisions of this Directive have been infringed;
(h) prohibit trading on a regulated market if it finds that the provisions of this Directive have been infringed;
(i) make public the fact that an issuer is failing to comply with its obligations.

Where necessary under national law, the competent authority may ask the relevant judicial authority to decide on the use of the powers referred to in points (d) to (h) above.

4. Each competent authority shall also, once the securities have been admitted to trading on a regulated market, be empowered to:
(a) require the issuer to disclose all material information which may have an effect on the

assessment of the securities admitted to trading on regulated markets in order to ensure investor protection or the smooth operation of the market;

(b) suspend or ask the relevant regulated market to suspend the securities from trading if, in its opinion, the issuer's situation is such that trading would be detrimental to investors' interests;

(c) ensure that issuers whose securities are traded on regulated markets comply with the obligations provided for in Articles 102 and 103 of Directive 2001/34/EC and that equivalent information is provided to investors and equivalent treatment is granted by the issuer to all securities holders who are in the same position, in all Member States where the offer to the public is made or the securities are admitted to trading;

(d) carry out on-site inspections in its territory in accordance with national law, in order to verify compliance with the provisions of this Directive and its implementing measures. Where necessary under national law, the competent authority or authorities may use this power by applying to the relevant judicial authority and/or in cooperation with other authorities.

5. Paragraphs 1 to 4 shall be without prejudice to the possibility for a Member State to make separate legal and administrative arrangements for overseas European territories for whose external relations that Member State is responsible.

[5473]

Article 22
Professional secrecy and cooperation between authorities

1. The obligation of professional secrecy shall apply to all persons who work or have worked for the competent authority and for entities to which competent authorities may have delegated certain tasks. Information covered by professional secrecy may not be disclosed to any other person or authority except in accordance with provisions laid down by law.

2. Competent authorities of Member States shall cooperate with each other whenever necessary for the purpose of carrying out their duties and making use of their powers. Competent authorities shall render assistance to competent authorities of other Member States. In particular, they shall exchange information and cooperate when an issuer has more than one home competent authority because of its various classes of securities, or where the approval of a prospectus has been transferred to the competent authority of another Member State pursuant to Article 13(5). They shall also closely cooperate when requiring suspension or prohibition of trading for securities traded in various Member States in order to ensure a level playing field between trading venues and protection of investors. Where appropriate, the competent authority of the host Member State may request the assistance of the competent authority of the home Member State from the stage at which the case is scrutinised, in particular as regards a new type or rare forms of securities. The competent authority of the home Member State may ask for information from the competent authority of the host Member State on any items specific to the relevant market.

Without prejudice to Article 21, the competent authorities of Member States may consult with operators of regulated markets as necessary and, in particular, when deciding to suspend, or to ask a regulated market to suspend or prohibit trading.

3. Paragraph 1 shall not prevent the competent authorities from exchanging confidential information. Information thus exchanged shall be covered by the obligation of professional secrecy, to which the persons employed or formerly employed by the competent authorities receiving the information are subject.

[5474]

Article 23
Precautionary measures

1. Where the competent authority of the host Member State finds that irregularities have been committed by the issuer or by the financial institutions in charge of the public offer or that breaches have been committed of the obligations attaching to the issuer by reason of the fact that the securities are admitted to trading on a regulated market, it shall refer these findings to the competent authority of the home Member State.

2. If, despite the measures taken by the competent authority of the home Member State or because such measures prove inadequate, the issuer or the financial institution in charge of the public offer persists in breaching the relevant legal or regulatory provisions, the competent authority of the host Member State, after informing the competent authority of the home Member State, shall take all the appropriate measures in order to protect investors. The Commission shall be informed of such measures at the earliest opportunity.

[5475]

PART IV
EC MATERIALS

CHAPTER VII
IMPLEMENTING MEASURES

Article 24
Committee procedure

1. The Commission shall be assisted by the European Securities Committee, instituted by Decision 2001/528/EC (hereinafter referred to as 'the Committee').

2. Where reference is made to this paragraph, Articles 5 and 7 of Decision 1999/468/EC shall apply, having regard to the provisions of Article 8 thereof and provided that the implementing measures adopted in accordance with this procedure do not modify the essential provisions of this Directive.

The period laid down in Article 5(6) of Decision 1999/468/EC shall be set at three months.

[2a. Where reference is made to this paragraph, Article 5a(1) to (4) and Article 7 of Decision 1999/468/EC shall apply, having regard to the provisions of Article 8 thereof.]

[3. By 31 December 2010 and, thereafter, at least every three years, the Commission shall review the provisions concerning its implementing powers and present a report to the European Parliament and to the Council on the functioning of those powers. The report shall examine, in particular, the need for the Commission to propose amendments to this Directive in order to ensure the appropriate scope of the implementing powers conferred on the Commission. The conclusion as to whether or not amendment is necessary shall be accompanied by a detailed statement of reasons. If necessary, the report shall be accompanied by a legislative proposal to amend the provisions conferring implementing powers on the Commission.]

[5476]

NOTES

Para 2a inserted, and para 3 substituted (for original paras 3, 4) by European Parliament and Council Directive 2008/11/EC, Art 1(3) as from 20 March 2008.

Article 25
Sanctions

1. Without prejudice to the right of Member States to impose criminal sanctions and without prejudice to their civil liability regime, Member States shall ensure, in conformity with their national law, that the appropriate administrative measures can be taken or administrative sanctions be imposed against the persons responsible, where the provisions adopted in the implementation of this Directive have not been complied with. Member States shall ensure that these measures are effective, proportionate and dissuasive.

2. Member States shall provide that the competent authority may disclose to the public every measure or sanction that has been imposed for infringement of the provisions adopted pursuant to this Directive, unless the disclosure would seriously jeopardise the financial markets or cause disproportionate damage to the parties involved.

[5477]

Article 26
Right of appeal

Member States shall ensure that decisions taken pursuant to laws, regulations and administrative provisions adopted in accordance with this Directive are subject to the right to appeal to the courts.

[5478]

CHAPTER VIII
TRANSITIONAL AND FINAL PROVISIONS

Article 27
Amendments

With effect from the date set out in Article 29, Directive 2001/34/EC is hereby amended as follows:
1. Articles 3, 20 to 41, 98 to 101, 104 and 108(2)(c)(ii) shall be deleted;
2. in Article 107(3), the first subparagraph shall be deleted;
3. in Article 108(2)(a), the words 'the conditions of establishment, the control and circulation of listing particulars to be published for admission' shall be deleted;
4. Annex I shall be deleted.

[5479]

Article 28
Repeal

With effect from the date indicated in Article 29, Directive 89/298/EEC shall be repealed. References to the repealed Directive shall be construed as references to this Directive.

[5480]

Article 29
Transposition

Member States shall bring into force the laws, regulations and administrative provisions necessary to comply with this Directive not later than 1 July 2005. They shall forthwith inform the Commission thereof. When Member States adopt those measures they shall contain a reference to this Directive or shall be accompanied by such a reference on the occasion of their official publication. The methods for making such reference shall be laid down by Member States.

[5481]

Article 30
Transitional provision

1. Issuers which are incorporated in a third country and whose securities have already been admitted to trading on a regulated market shall choose their competent authority in accordance with Article 2(1)(m)(iii) and notify their decision to the competent authority of their chosen home Member State by 31 December 2005.

2. By way of derogation from Article 3, Member States which have used the exemption in Article 5(a) of Directive 89/298/EEC may continue to allow credit institutions or other financial institutions equivalent to credit institutions which are not covered by Article 1(2)(j) of this Directive to offer debt securities or other transferable securities equivalent to debt securities issued in a continuous or repeated manner within their territory for five years following the date of entry into force of this Directive.

3. By way of derogation from Article 29, the Federal Republic of Germany shall comply with Article 21(1) by 31 December 2008.

[5482]

Article 31
Review

Five years after the date of entry into force of this Directive, the Commission shall make an assessment of the application of this Directive and present a report to the European Parliament and the Council, accompanied where appropriate by proposals for its review.

[5483]

Article 32
Entry into force

This Directive shall enter into force on the day of its publication in the *Official Journal of the European Union.*

[5484]

Article 33
Addressees

This Directive is addressed to the Member States.

[5485]

ANNEX I
PROSPECTUS

I. SUMMARY

The summary shall provide in a few pages the most important information included in the prospectus, covering at least the following items:

    A.   identity of directors, senior management, advisers and auditors
    B.   offer statistics and expected timetable
    C.   key information concerning selected financial data; capitalisation and indebtedness; reasons for the offer and use of proceeds; risk factors
    D.   information concerning the issuer
        —   history and development of the issuer
        —   business overview
    E.   operating and financial review and prospects
        —   research and development, patents and licences, etc
        —   trends
    F.   directors, senior management and employees
    G.   major shareholders and related-party transactions
    H.   financial information
        —   consolidated statement and other financial information
        —   significant changes
    I.   details of the offer and admission to trading
        —   offer and admission to trading

- — plan for distribution
- — markets
- — selling shareholders
- — dilution (equity securities only)
- — expenses of the issue

J. additional information
- — share capital
- — memorandum and articles of association
- — documents on display

II. IDENTITY OF DIRECTORS, SENIOR MANAGEMENT, ADVISERS AND AUDITORS

The purpose is to identify the company representatives and other individuals involved in the company's offer or admission to trading; these are the persons responsible for drawing up the prospectus as required by Article 5 of the Directive and those responsible for auditing the financial statements.

III. OFFER STATISTICS AND EXPECTED TIMETABLE

The purpose is to provide key information regarding the conduct of any offer and the identification of important dates relating to that offer.

A. Offer statistics
B. Method and expected timetable

IV. KEY INFORMATION

The purpose is to summarise key information about the company's financial condition, capitalisation and risk factors. If the financial statements included in the document are restated to reflect material changes in the company's group structure or accounting policies, the selected financial data must also be restated.

A. Selected financial data
B. Capitalisation and indebtedness
C. Reasons for the offer and use of proceeds
D. Risk factors

V. INFORMATION ON THE COMPANY

The purpose is to provide information about the company's business operations, the products it makes or the services it provides, and the factors which affect the business. It is also intended to provide information regarding the adequacy and suitability of the company's properties, plant and equipment, as well as its plans for future capacity increases or decreases.

A. History and development of the company
B. Business overview
C. Organisational structure
D. Property, plant and equipment

VI. OPERATING AND FINANCIAL REVIEW AND PROSPECTS

The purpose is to provide the management's explanation of factors that have affected the company's financial condition and results of operations for the historical periods covered by the financial statements, and management's assessment of factors and trends which are expected to have a material effect on the company's financial condition and results of operations in future periods.

A. Operating results
B. Liquidity and capital resources
C. Research and development, patents and licences, etc
D. Trends

VII. DIRECTORS, SENIOR MANAGEMENT AND EMPLOYEES

The purpose is to provide information concerning the company's directors and managers that will allow investors to assess their experience, qualifications and levels of remuneration, as well as their relationship with the company.

A. Directors and senior management
B. Remuneration
C. Board practices
D. Employees
E. Share ownership

VIII. MAJOR SHAREHOLDERS AND RELATED-PARTY TRANSACTIONS

The purpose is to provide information regarding the major shareholders and others that may control or have an influence on the company. It also provides information regarding transactions the company has entered into with persons affiliated with the company and whether the terms of such transactions are fair to the company.

    A.   Major shareholders
    B.   Related-party transactions
    C.   Interests of experts and advisers

IX. FINANCIAL INFORMATION

The purpose is to specify which financial statements must be included in the document, as well as the periods to be covered, the age of the financial statements and other information of a financial nature. The accounting and auditing principles that will be accepted for use in preparation and audit of the financial statements will be determined in accordance with international accounting and auditing standards.

    A.   Consolidated statements and other financial information
    B.   Significant changes

X. DETAILS OF THE OFFER AND ADMISSION TO TRADING DETAILS

The purpose is to provide information regarding the offer and the admission to trading of securities, the plan for distribution of the securities and related matters.

    A.   Offer and admission to trading
    B.   Plan for distribution
    C.   Markets
    D.   Holders of securities who are selling
    E.   Dilution (for equity securities only)
    F.   Expenses of the issue

XI. ADDITIONAL INFORMATION

The purpose is to provide information, most of which is of a statutory nature, that is not covered elsewhere in the prospectus.

    A.   Share capital
    B.   Memorandum and articles of association
    C.   Material contracts
    D.   Exchange controls
    E.   Taxation
    F.   Dividends and paying agents
    G.   Statement by experts
    H.   Documents on display
    I.   Subsidiary information

[5486]

ANNEX II
REGISTRATION DOCUMENT

I. IDENTITY OF DIRECTORS, SENIOR MANAGEMENT, ADVISERS AND AUDITORS

The purpose is to identify the company representatives and other individuals involved in the company's offer or admission to trading; these are the persons responsible for drawing up the prospectus and those responsible for auditing the financial statements.

II. KEY INFORMATION ABOUT THE ISSUER

The purpose is to summarise key information about the company's financial condition, capitalisation and risk factors. If the financial statements included in the document are restated to reflect material changes in the company's group structure or accounting policies, the selected financial data must also be restated.

    A.   Selected financial data
    B.   Capitalisation and indebtedness
    C.   Risk factors

III. INFORMATION ON THE COMPANY

The purpose is to provide information about the company's business operations, the products it makes or the services it provides and the factors which affect the business. It is also intended to provide information regarding the adequacy and suitability of the company's properties, plants and equipment, as well as its plans for future capacity increases or decreases.

    A.   History and development of the company
    B.   Business overview
    C.   Organisational structure
    D.   Property, plants and equipment

IV. OPERATING AND FINANCIAL REVIEW AND PROSPECTS

The purpose is to provide the management's explanation of factors that have affected the company's financial condition and results of operations for the historical periods covered by the financial statements, and management's assessment of factors and trends which are expected to have a material effect on the company's financial condition and results of operations in future periods.

    A.   Operating results
    B.   Liquidity and capital resources
    C.   Research and development, patents and licences, etc
    D.   Trends

V. DIRECTORS, SENIOR MANAGEMENT AND EMPLOYEES

The purpose is to provide information concerning the company's directors and managers that will allow investors to assess their experience, qualifications and levels of remuneration, as well as their relationship with the company.

    A.   Directors and senior management
    B.   Remuneration
    C.   Board practices
    D.   Employees
    E.   Share ownership

VI. MAJOR SHAREHOLDERS AND RELATED-PARTY TRANSACTIONS

The purpose is to provide information regarding the major shareholders and others that may control or have an influence on the company. It also provides information regarding transactions the company has entered into with persons affiliated with the company and whether the terms of such transactions are fair to the company.

    A.   Major shareholders
    B.   Related-party transactions
    C.   Interests of experts and advisers

VII. FINANCIAL INFORMATION

The purpose is to specify which financial statements must be included in the document, as well as the periods to be covered, the age of the financial statements and other information of a financial nature. The accounting and auditing principles that will be accepted for use in preparation and audit of the financial statements will be determined in accordance with international accounting and auditing standards.

    A.   Consolidated statements and other financial information
    B.   Significant changes

VIII. ADDITIONAL INFORMATION

The purpose is to provide information, most of which is of a statutory nature, that is not covered elsewhere in the prospectus.

    A.   Share capital
    B.   Memorandum and articles of association
    C.   Material contracts
    D.   Statement by experts
    E.   Documents on display
    F.   Subsidiary information

[5487]

ANNEX III
SECURITIES NOTE

I. IDENTITY OF DIRECTORS, SENIOR MANAGEMENT, ADVISERS AND AUDITORS

The purpose is to identify the company representatives and other individuals involved in the company's offer or admission to trading; these are the persons responsible for drawing up the prospectus and those responsible for auditing the financial statements.

II. OFFER STATISTICS AND EXPECTED TIMETABLE

The purpose is to provide key information regarding the conduct of any offer and the identification of important dates relating to that offer.

    A.   Offer statistics
    B.   Method and expected timetable

III. KEY INFORMATION ABOUT THE ISSUER

The purpose is to summarise key information about the company's financial condition, capitalisation and risk factors. If the financial statements included in the document are restated to reflect material changes in the company's group structure or accounting policies, the selected financial data must also be restated.

A.   Capitalisation and indebtedness
B.   Reasons for the offer and use of proceeds
C.   Risk factors

IV. INTERESTS OF EXPERTS

The purpose is to provide information regarding transactions the company has entered into with experts or advisers employed on a contingent basis.

V. DETAILS OF THE OFFER AND ADMISSION TO TRADING

The purpose is to provide information regarding the offer and the admission to trading of securities, the plan for distribution of the securities and related matters.

A.   Offer and admission to trading
B.   Plan for distribution
C.   Markets
D.   Selling securities holders
E.   Dilution (for equity securities only)
F.   Expenses of the issue

VI. ADDITIONAL INFORMATION

The purpose is to provide information, most of which is of a statutory nature, that is not covered elsewhere in the prospectus.

A.   Exchange controls
B.   Taxation
C.   Dividends and paying agents
D.   Statement by experts
E.   Documents on display

[5488]

ANNEX IV
SUMMARY NOTE

The summary note shall provide in a few pages the most important information included in the prospectus, covering at least the following items:

—   identity of directors, senior management, advisers and auditors
—   offer statistics and expected timetable
—   key information concerning selected financial data; capitalisation and indebtedness; reasons for the offer and use of proceeds; risk factors
—   information concerning the issuer
    —   history and development of the issuer
    —   business overview
—   operating and financial review and prospects
    —   research and development, patents and licences, etc
    —   trends
—   directors, senior management and employees
—   major shareholders and related-party transactions
—   financial information
    —   consolidated statement and other financial information
    —   significant changes
—   details on the offer and admission to trading
    —   offer and admission to trading
    —   plan for distribution
    —   markets
    —   selling shareholders
    —   dilution (for equity securities only)
    —   expenses of the issue
—   additional information
    —   share capital
    —   memorandum and articles of incorporation
    —   documents available for inspection

[5489]

COMMISSION REGULATION

of 22 December 2003

implementing Directive 2003/6/EC of the European Parliament and of the Council as regards exemptions for buy-back programmes and stabilisation of financial instruments

(2273/2003/EC)

(Text with EEA relevance)

NOTES

Date of publication in OJ: OJ L336, 23.12.2003, p 33. Notes are as in the original OJ version.
As of 1 February 2009, this Regulation had not been amended.

THE COMMISSION OF THE EUROPEAN COMMUNITIES,
Having regard to the Treaty establishing the European Community,
Having regard to Directive 2003/6/EC of the European Parliament and the Council of 28 January 2003 on insider dealing and market manipulation (market abuse),[1] and in particular Article 8 thereof,
After consulting the Committee of European Securities Regulators (CESR)[2] for technical advice, Whereas:

(1) Article 8 of Directive 2003/6/EC provides that the prohibitions provided therein shall not apply to trading in own shares in 'buy back' programmes or to the stabilisation of a financial instrument, provided such trading is carried out in accordance with implementing measures adopted to that effect.

(2) Activities of trading in own shares in 'buy-back' programmes and of stabilisation of a financial instrument which would not benefit from the exemption of the prohibitions of Directive 2003/6/EC as provided for by Article 8 thereof, should not in themselves be deemed to constitute market abuse.

(3) On the other hand, the exemptions created by this Regulation only cover behaviour directly related to the purpose of the buy-back and stabilisation activities. Behaviour which is not directly related to the purpose of the buy-back and stabilisation activities shall therefore be considered as any other action covered by Directive 2003/6/EC and may be the object of administrative measures or sanctions, if the competent authority establishes that the action in question constitutes market abuse.

(4) As regards trading in own shares in 'buy-back' programmes, the rules provided for by this Regulation are without prejudice to the application of Council Directive 77/91/EEC on coordination of safeguards which, for the protection of the interests of members and others, are required by Member States of companies within the meaning of the second paragraph of Article 58 of the Treaty, in respect of the formation of public limited liability companies and the maintenance and alteration of their capital, with a view to making such safeguards equivalent.[3]

(5) Allowable 'buy back' activities in order to benefit from the exemption of the prohibitions of Directive 2003/6/EC include issuers needing the possibility to reduce their capital, to meet obligations arising from debt financial instruments exchangeable into equity instruments, and to meet obligations arising from allocations of shares to employees.

(6) Transparency is a prerequisite for prevention of market abuse. To this end Member States may officially appoint mechanisms to be used for public disclosure of information required to be publicly disclosed under this Regulation.

(7) Issuers having adopted 'buy-back' programmes shall inform their competent authority and, wherever required, the public.

(8) Trading in own shares in 'buy-back' programmes may be carried out through derivative financial instruments.

(9) In order to prevent market abuse, the daily volume of trading in own shares in 'buy-back' programmes shall be limited. However, some flexibility is necessary in order to respond to given market conditions such as a low level of transactions.

(10) Particular attention has to be paid to the selling of own shares during the life of a 'buy-back' programme, to the possible existence of closed periods within issuers during which transactions are prohibited and to the fact that an issuer may have legitimate reasons to delay public disclosure of inside information.

(11) Stabilisation transactions mainly have the effect of providing support for the price of an offering of relevant securities during a limited time period if they come under selling pressure, thus alleviating sales pressure generated by short term investors and maintaining an orderly market in the relevant securities. This is in the interest of those investors having subscribed or purchased those relevant securities in the context of a significant distribution, and of issuers. In this way, stabilisation can contribute to greater confidence of investors and issuers in the financial markets.

(12)   Stabilisation activity may be carried out either on or off a regulated market and may be carried out by use of financial instruments other than those admitted or to be admitted to the regulated market which may influence the price of the instrument admitted or to be admitted to trading on a regulated market.

(13)   Relevant securities shall include financial instruments that become fungible after an initial period because they are substantially the same, although they have different initial dividend or interest payment rights.

(14)   In relation to stabilisation, block trades shall not be considered as a significant distribution of relevant securities as they are strictly private transactions.

(15)   When Member States permit, in the context of an initial public offer, trading prior to the beginning of the official trading on a regulated market, the permission covers 'when issued trading'.

(16)   Market integrity requires the adequate public disclosure of stabilisation activity by issuers or by entities undertaking stabilisation, acting or not on behalf of these issuers. Methods used for adequate public disclosure of such information should be efficient and can take into account market practices accepted by competent authorities.

(17)   There should be adequate coordination in place between all investment firms and credit institutions undertaking stabilisation. During stabilisation, one investment firm or credit institution shall act as a central point of inquiry for any regulatory intervention by the competent authority in each Member State concerned.

(18)   In order to avoid confusion of market participants, stabilisation activity should be carried out by taking into account the market conditions and the offering price of the relevant security and transactions to liquidate positions established as a result of stabilisation activity should be undertaken to minimise market impact having due regard to prevailing market conditions.

(19)   Overallotment facilities and 'greenshoe options' are closely related to stabilisation, by providing resources and hedging for stabilisation activity.

(20)   Particular attention should be paid to the exercise of an overallotment facility by an investment firm or a credit institution for the purpose of stabilisation when it results in a position uncovered by the 'greenshoe option'.

(21)   The measures provided for in this Regulation are in accordance with the opinion of the European Securities Committee,

[5490]

NOTES

1   OJ L96, 12.4.2003, p 16.
2   CESR was established by Commission Decision 2001/527/EC (OJ L191,13.7.2001, p 43).
3   OJ L26, 31.1.1977, p 1.

HAS ADOPTED THIS REGULATION:

CHAPTER I
DEFINITIONS

Article 1
Subject matter

This Regulation lays down the conditions to be met by buyback programmes and the stabilisation of financial instruments in order to benefit from the exemption provided for in Article 8 of Directive 2003/6/EC.

[5490A]

Article 2
Definitions

For the purposes of this Regulation, the following definitions shall apply in addition to those laid down in Directive 2003/6/EC:

1.   'investment firm' means any legal person as defined in point (2) of Article 1 of Council Directive 93/22/EEC;[1]

2.   'credit institution' means a legal person as defined in Article 1(1) of Directive 2000/12/EC of the European Parliament and the Council;[2]

3.   'buy-back programmes' means trading in own shares in accordance with Articles 19 to 24 of Council Directive 77/91/EEC;

4.   'time-scheduled "buy-back" programme' means a 'buy-back' programme where the dates and quantities of securities to be traded during the time period of the programme are set out at the time of the public disclosure of the 'buy-back' programme;

5.   'adequate public disclosure' means disclosure made in accordance with the procedure laid down in Articles 102(1) and 103 of Directive 2001/34/EC of the European Parliament and of the Council;[3]

6.   'relevant securities' means transferable securities as defined in Directive 93/22/EEC,

which are admitted to trading on a regulated market or for which a request for admission to trading on such a market has been made, and which are the subject of a significant distribution;

7. 'stabilisation' means any purchase or offer to purchase relevant securities, or any transaction in associated instruments equivalent thereto, by investment firms or credit institutions, which is undertaken in the context of a significant distribution of such relevant securities exclusively for supporting the market price of these relevant securities for a predetermined period of time, due to a selling pressure in such securities;

8. 'associated instruments' means the following financial instruments (including those which are not admitted to trading on a regulated market, or for which a request for admission to trading on such a market has not been made, provided that the relevant competent authorities have agreed to standards of transparency for transactions in such financial instruments):
   (a) contracts or rights to subscribe for, acquire or dispose of relevant securities;
   (b) financial derivatives on relevant securities;
   (c) where the relevant securities are convertible or exchangeable debt instruments, the securities into which such convertible or exchangeable debt instruments may be converted or exchanged;
   (d) instruments which are issued or guaranteed by the issuer or guarantor of the relevant securities and whose market price is likely to materially influence the price of the relevant securities, or vice versa;
   (e) where the relevant securities are securities equivalent to shares, the shares represented by those securities (and any other securities equivalent to those shares).

9. 'significant distribution' means an initial or secondary offer of relevant securities, publicly announced and distinct from ordinary trading both in terms of the amount in value of the securities offered and the selling methods employed;

10. 'offeror' means the prior holders of, or the entity issuing, the relevant securities;

11. 'allotment' means the process or processes by which the number of relevant securities to be received by investors who have previously subscribed or applied for them is determined;

12. 'ancillary stabilisation' means the exercise of an overallotment facility or of a greenshoe option by investment firms or credit institutions, in the context of a significant distribution of relevant securities, exclusively for facilitating stabilisation activity;

13. 'overallotment facility' means a clause in the underwriting agreement or lead management agreement which permits acceptance of subscriptions or offers to purchase a greater number of relevant securities than originally offered;

14. 'greenshoe option' means an option granted by the offeror in favour of the investment firm(s) or credit institution(s) involved in the offer for the purpose of covering overallotments, under the terms of which such firm(s) or institution(s) may purchase up to a certain amount of relevant securities at the offer price for a certain period of time after the offer of the relevant securities.

[5491]

NOTES
1   OJ L141, 11.6.1993, p 27.
2   OJ L126, 26.5.2000, p 1.
3   OJ L184, 6.7.2001, p 1.

CHAPTER II
'BUY-BACK' PROGRAMMES

Article 3
Objectives of buy-back programmes

In order to benefit from the exemption provided for in Article 8 of Directive 2003/6/EC, a buy-back programme must comply with Articles 4, 5 and 6 of this Regulation and the sole purpose of that buy-back programme must be to reduce the capital of an issuer (in value or in number of shares) or to meet obligations arising from any of the following:
   (a) debt financial instruments exchangeable into equity instruments;
   (b) employee share option programmes or other allocations of shares to employees of the issuer or of an associate company.

[5492]

Article 4
Conditions for 'buy-back' programmes and disclosure

1.   The 'buy-back' programme must comply with the conditions laid down by Article 19(1) of Directive 77/91/EEC.

2. Prior to the start of trading, full details of the programme approved in accordance with Article 19(1) of Directive 77/91/EEC must be adequately disclosed to the public in Member States in which an issuer has requested admission of its shares to trading on a regulated market.

Those details must include the objective of the programme as referred to in Article 3, the maximum consideration, the maximum number of shares to be acquired and the duration of the period for which authorisation for the programme has been given.

Subsequent changes to the programme must be subject to adequate public disclosure in Member States.

3. The issuer must have in place the mechanisms ensuring that it fulfils trade reporting obligations to the competent authority of the regulated market on which the shares have been admitted to trading. These mechanisms must record each transaction related to 'buy-back' programmes, including the information specified in Article 20(1) of Directive 93/22/EEC.

4. The issuer must publicly disclose details of all transactions as referred to in paragraph 3 no later than the end of the seventh daily market session following the date of execution of such transactions.

[5493]

Article 5
Conditions for trading

1. In so far as prices are concerned, the issuer must not, when executing trades under a 'buy-back' programme, purchase shares at a price higher than the higher of the price of the last independent trade and the highest current independent bid on the trading venues where the purchase is carried out.

If the trading venue is not a regulated market, the price of the last independent trade or the highest current independent bid taken in reference shall be the one of the regulated market of the Member State in which the purchase is carried out.

Where the issuer carries out the purchase of own shares through derivative financial instruments, the exercise price of those derivative financial instruments shall not be above the higher of the price of the last independent trade and the highest current independent bid.

2. In so far as volume is concerned, the issuer must not purchase more than 25% of the average daily volume of the shares in any one day on the regulated market on which the purchase is carried out.

The average daily volume figure must be based on the average daily volume traded in the month preceding the month of public disclosure of that programme and fixed on that basis for the authorised period of the programme.

Where the programme makes no reference to that volume, the average daily volume figure must be based on the average daily volume traded in the 20 trading days preceding the date of purchase.

3. For the purposes of paragraph 2, in cases of extreme low liquidity on the relevant market, the issuer may exceed the 25% limit, provided that the following conditions are met:
   (a) the issuer informs the competent authority of the relevant market, in advance, of its intention to deviate from the 25% limit;
   (b) the issuer discloses adequately to the public the fact that it may deviate from the 25% limit;
   (c) the issuer does not exceed 50% of the average daily volume.

[5494]

Article 6
Restrictions

1. In order to benefit from the exemption provided by Article 8 of Directive 2003/6/EC, the issuer shall not, during its participation in a buy-back programme, engage in the following trading:
   (a) selling of own shares during the life of the programme;
   (b) trading during a period which, under the law of the Member State in which trading takes place, is a closed period;
   (c) trading where the issuer has decided to delay the public disclosure of inside information in accordance with Article 6(2) of Directive 2003/6/EC.

2. Paragraph 1(a) shall not apply if the issuer is an investment firm or credit institution and has established effective information barriers (Chinese Walls) subject to supervision by the competent authority, between those responsible for the handling of inside information related directly or indirectly to the issuer and those responsible for any decision relating to the trading of own shares (including the trading of own shares on behalf of clients), when trading in own shares on the basis of such any decision.

Paragraphs 1(b) and (c) shall not apply if the issuer is an investment firm or credit institution and has established effective information barriers (Chinese Walls) subject to supervision by the competent authority, between those responsible for the handling of inside information related directly or indirectly to the issuer (including trading decisions under the 'buy-back' programme) and those responsible for the trading of own shares on behalf of clients, when trading in own shares on behalf of those clients.

3. Paragraph 1 shall not apply if:
    (a)   the issuer has in place a time-scheduled 'buy-back' programme; or
    (b)   the 'buy-back' programme is lead-managed by an investment firm or a credit institution which makes its trading decisions in relation to the issuer's shares independently of, and without influence by, the issuer with regard to the timing of the purchases.

[5495]

CHAPTER III
STABILISATION OF A FINANCIAL INSTRUMENT

Article 7
Conditions for stabilisation

In order to benefit from the exemption provided for in Article 8 of Directive 2003/6/EC, stabilisation of a financial instrument must be carried out in accordance with Articles 8, 9 and 10 of this Regulation.

[5496]

Article 8
Time-related conditions for stabilisation

1. Stabilisation shall be carried out only for a limited time period.

2. In respect of shares and other securities equivalent to shares, the time period referred to in paragraph 1 shall, in the case of an initial offer publicly announced, start on the date of commencement of trading of the relevant securities on the regulated market and end no later than 30 calendar days thereafter.

Where the initial offer publicly announced takes place in a Member State that permits trading prior to the commencement of trading on a regulated market, the time period referred to in paragraph 1 shall start on the date of adequate public disclosure of the final price of the relevant securities and end no later than 30 calendar days thereafter, provided that any such trading is carried out in compliance with the rules, if any, of the regulated market on which the relevant securities are to be admitted to trading, including any rules concerning public disclosure and trade reporting.

3. In respect of shares and other securities equivalent to shares, the time period referred to in paragraph 1 shall, in the case of a secondary offer, start on the date of adequate public disclosure of the final price of the relevant securities and end no later than 30 calendar days after the date of allotment.

4. In respect of bonds and other forms of securitised debt (which are not convertible or exchangeable into shares or into other securities equivalent to shares), the time period referred to in paragraph 1 shall start on the date of adequate public disclosure of the terms of the offer of the relevant securities(ie including the spread to the benchmark, if any, once it has been fixed) and end, whatever is earlier, either no later than 30 calendar days after the date on which the issuer of the instruments received the proceeds of the issue, or no later than 60 calendar days after the date of allotment of the relevant securities.

5. In respect of securitised debt convertible or exchangeable into shares or into other securities equivalent to shares, the time period referred to in paragraph 1 shall start on the date of adequate public disclosure of the final terms of the offer of the relevant securities and end, whatever is earlier, either no later than 30 calendar days after the date on which the issuer of the instruments received the proceeds of the issue, or no later than 60 calendar days after the date of allotment of the relevant securities.

[5497]

Article 9
Disclosure and reporting conditions for stabilisation

1. The following information shall be adequately publicly disclosed by issuers, offerors, or entities undertaking the stabilisation acting, or not, on behalf of such persons, before the opening of the offer period of the relevant securities:
    (a)   the fact that stabilisation may be undertaken, that there is no assurance that it will be undertaken and that it may be stopped at any time;
    (b)   the fact that stabilisation transactions are aimed to support the market price of the relevant securities;
    (c)   the beginning and end of the period during which stabilisation may occur;
    (d)   the identity of the stabilisation manager, unless this is not known at the time of publication in which case it must be publicly disclosed before any stabilisation activity begins;

(e)   the existence and maximum size of any overallotment facility or greenshoe option, the exercise period of the greenshoe option and any conditions for the use of the overallotment facility or exercise of the greenshoe option.

The application of the provisions of this paragraph shall be suspended for offers under the scope of application of the measures implementing Directive 2003/71/EC (prospectus Directive), from the date of application of these measures.

2.   Without prejudice to Article 12(1)(c) of Directive 2003/6/EC, the details of all stabilisation transactions must be notified by issuers, offerors, or entities undertaking the stabilisation acting, or not, on behalf of such persons, to the competent authority of the relevant market no later than the end of the seventh daily market session following the date of execution of such transactions.

3.   Within one week of the end of the stabilisation period, the following information must be adequately disclosed to the public by issuers, offerors, or entities undertaking the stabilisation acting, or not, on behalf of such persons:
   (a)   whether or not stabilisation was undertaken;
   (b)   the date at which stabilisation started;
   (c)   the date at which stabilisation last occurred;
   (d)   the price range within which stabilisation was carried out, for each of the dates during which stabilisation transactions were carried out.

4.   Issuers, offerors, or entities undertaking the stabilisation, acting or not, on behalf of such persons, must record each stabilisation order or transaction with, as a minimum, the information specified in Article 20(1) of Directive 93/22/EEC extended to financial instruments other than those admitted or going to be admitted to the regulated market.

5.   Where several investment firms or credit institutions undertake the stabilisation acting, or not, on behalf of the issuer or offeror, one of those persons shall act as central point of inquiry for any request from the competent authority of the regulated market on which the relevant securities have been admitted to trading.

[5498]

Article 10
Specific price conditions

1.   In the case of an offer of shares or other securities equivalent to shares, stabilisation of the relevant securities shall not in any circumstances be executed above the offering price.

2.   In the case of an offer of securitised debt convertible or exchangeable into instruments as referred to in paragraph 1, stabilisation of those instruments shall not in any circumstances be executed above the market price of those instruments at the time of the public disclosure of the final terms of the new offer.

[5499]

Article 11
Conditions for ancillary stabilisation

In order to benefit from the exemption provided for in Article 8 of Directive 2003/6/EC, ancillary stabilisation must be undertaken in accordance with Article 9 of this Regulation and with the following:
   (a)   relevant securities may be overallotted only during the subscription period and at the offer price;
   (b)   a position resulting from the exercise of an overallotment facility by an investment firm or credit institution which is not covered by the greenshoe option may not exceed 5% of the original offer;
   (c)   the greenshoe option may be exercised by the beneficiaries of such an option only where relevant securities have been overallotted;
   (d)   the greenshoe option may not amount to more than 15% of the original offer;
   (e)   the exercise period of the greenshoe option must be the same as the stabilisation period required under Article 8;
   (f)   the exercise of the greenshoe option must be disclosed to the public promptly, together with all appropriate details, including in particular the date of exercise and the number and nature of relevant securities involved.

[5500]

CHAPTER IV
FINAL PROVISION

Article 12
Entry into force

This Regulation shall enter into force in Member States on the day of its publication in the *Official Journal of the European Union*.

This Regulation shall be binding in its entirety and directly applicable in all Member States.

[5501]

COMMISSION DIRECTIVE

of 22 December 2003

implementing Directive 2003/6/EC of the European Parliament and of the Council as regards the definition and public disclosure of inside information and the definition of market manipulation

(2003/124/EC)

(Text with EEA relevance)

NOTES

Date of publication in OJ: OJ L339, 24.12.2003, p 70. Notes are as in the original OJ version.
As of 1 February 2009, this Directive had not been amended.

THE COMMISSION OF THE EUROPEAN COMMUNITIES,
Having regard to the Treaty establishing the European Community,
Having regard to Directive 2003/6/EC of the European Parliament and of the Council of 28 January 2003 on insider dealing and market manipulation (market abuse),[1] and in particular the second paragraph of Article 1 and the first, second and third indents of Article 6(10) thereof,
After consulting the Committee of European Securities Regulators (CESR)[2] for technical advice, Whereas:
(1) Reasonable investors base their investment decisions on information already available to them, that is to say, on *ex ante* available information. Therefore, the question whether, in making an investment decision, a reasonable investor would be likely to take into account a particular piece of information should be appraised on the basis of the *ex ante* available information. Such an assessment has to take into consideration the anticipated impact of the information in light of the totality of the related issuer's activity, the reliability of the source of information and any other market variables likely to affect the related financial instrument or derivative financial instrument related thereto in the given circumstances.
(2) *Ex post* information may be used to check the presumption that the *ex ante* information was price sensitive, but should not be used to take action against someone who drew reasonable conclusions from *ex ante* information available to him.
(3) Legal certainty for market participants should be enhanced through a closer definition of two of the elements essential to the definition of inside information, namely the precise nature of that information and the significance of its potential effect on the prices of financial instruments or related derivative financial instruments.
(4) Not only does the protection of investors require timely public disclosure of inside information by issuers, it also requires such disclosure to be as fast and as synchronised as possible between all categories of investors in all Member States in which the issuer has requested or approved admission of its financial instruments to trading on a regulated market, in order to guarantee at Community level equal access of investors to such information and to prevent insider dealing. To this end Member States may officially appoint mechanisms to be used for such disclosure.
(5) In order to protect the legitimate interests of issuers, it should be permissible, in closely defined specific circumstances, to delay public disclosure of inside information. However, the protection of investors requires that in such cases the information be kept confidential in order to prevent insider dealing.
(6) In order to guide both market participants and competent authorities, signals have to be taken into account when examining possibly manipulative behaviours.
(7) The measures provided for in this Directive are in accordance with the opinion of the European Securities Committee,

[5502]

NOTES
1   OJ L96, 12.4.2003, p 16.
2   CESR was established by Commission Decision 2001/527/EC (OJ L191;13.7.2001, p 43).

HAS ADOPTED THIS DIRECTIVE:

Article 1
Inside information

1.   For the purposes of applying point 1 of Article 1 of Directive 2003/6/EC, information shall be deemed to be of a precise nature if it indicates a set of circumstances which exists or may reasonably be expected to come into existence or an event which has occurred or may reasonably be expected to do so and if it is specific enough to enable a conclusion to be drawn as to the possible effect of that set of circumstances or event on the prices of financial instruments or related derivative financial instruments.

2.   For the purposes of applying point 1 of Article 1 of Directive 2003/6/EC, 'information which, if it were made public, would be likely to have a significant effect on the prices of financial instruments or related derivative financial instruments' shall mean information a reasonable investor would be likely to use as part of the basis of his investment decisions.

[5502A]

Article 2
Means and time-limits for public disclosure of inside information

1.   For the purposes of applying Article 6(1) of Directive 2003/6/EC, Articles 102(1) and Article 103 of Directive 2001/34/EC of the European Parliament and of the Council[1] shall apply.

Furthermore, Member States shall ensure that the inside information is made public by the issuer in a manner which enables fast access and complete, correct and timely assessment of the information by the public.

In addition, Member States shall ensure that the issuer does not combine, in a manner likely to be misleading, the provision of inside information to the public with the marketing of its activities.

2.   Member States shall ensure that issuers are deemed to have complied with the first subparagraph of Article 6(1) of Directive 2003/6/EC where, upon the coming into existence of a set of circumstances or the occurrence of an event, albeit not yet formalised, the issuers have promptly informed the public thereof.

3.   Any significant changes concerning already publicly disclosed inside information shall be publicly disclosed promptly after these changes occur, through the same channel as the one used for public disclosure of the original information.

4.   Member States shall require issuers to take reasonable care to ensure that the disclosure of inside information to the public is synchronised as closely as possible between all categories of investors in all Member States in which those issuers have requested or approved the admission to trading of their financial instruments on a regulated market.

[5503]

NOTES
1   OJ L184, 6.7.2001, p 1.

Article 3
Legitimate interests for delaying public disclosure and confidentiality

1.   For the purposes of applying Article 6(2) of Directive 2003/6/EC, legitimate interests may, in particular, relate to the following non-exhaustive circumstances:

    (a)   negotiations in course, or related elements, where the outcome or normal pattern of those negotiations would be likely to be affected by public disclosure. In particular, in the event that the financial viability of the issuer is in grave and imminent danger, although not within the scope of the applicable insolvency law, public disclosure of information may be delayed for a limited period where such a public disclosure would seriously jeopardise the interest of existing and potential shareholders by undermining the conclusion of specific negotiations designed to ensure the long-term financial recovery of the issuer;

    (b)   decisions taken or contracts made by the management body of an issuer which need the approval of another body of the issuer in order to become effective, where the organisation of such an issuer requires the separation between these bodies, provided that a public disclosure of the information before such approval together with the simultaneous announcement that this approval is still pending would jeopardise the correct assessment of the information by the public.

PART IV
EC MATERIALS

2. For the purposes of applying Article 6(2) of Directive 2003/6/EC, Member States shall require that, in order to be able to ensure the confidentiality of inside information, an issuer controls access to such information and, in particular, that:

    (a)   the issuer has established effective arrangements to deny access to such information to persons other than those who require it for the exercise of their functions within the issuer;

    (b)   the issuer has taken the necessary measures to ensure that any person with access to such information acknowledges the legal and regulatory duties entailed and is aware of the sanctions attaching to the misuse or improper circulation of such information;

    (c)   the issuer has in place measures which allow immediate public disclosure in case the issuer was not able to ensure the confidentiality of the relevant inside information, without prejudice to the second subparagraph of Article 6(3) of Directive 2003/6/EC.

[5504]

Article 4
Manipulative behaviour related to false or misleading signals and to price securing

For the purposes of applying point 2(a) of Article 1 of Directive 2003/6/EC, and without prejudice to the examples set out in the second paragraph of point 2 thereof, Member States shall ensure that the following non-exhaustive signals, which should not necessarily be deemed in themselves to constitute market manipulation, are taken into account when transactions or orders to trade are-examined by market participants and competent authorities:

    (a)   the extent to which orders to trade given or transactions undertaken represent a significant proportion of the daily volume of transactions in the relevant financial instrument on the regulated market concerned, in particular when these activities lead to a significant change in the price of the financial instrument;

    (b)   the extent to which orders to trade given or transactions undertaken by persons with a significant buying or selling position in a financial instrument lead to significant changes in the price of the financial instrument or related derivative or underlying asset admitted to trading on a regulated market;

    (c)   whether transactions undertaken lead to no change in beneficial ownership of a financial instrument admitted to trading on a regulated market;

    (d)   the extent to which orders to trade given or transactions undertaken include position reversals in a short period and represent a significant proportion of the daily volume of transactions in the relevant financial instrument on the regulated market concerned, and might be associated with significant changes in the price of a financial instrument admitted to trading on a regulated market;

    (e)   the extent to which orders to trade given or transactions undertaken are concentrated within a short time span in the trading session and lead to a price change which is subsequently reversed;

    (f)   the extent to which orders to trade given change the representation of the best bid or offer prices in a financial instrument admitted to trading on a regulated market, or more generally the representation of the order book available to market participants, and are removed before they are executed;

    (g)   the extent to which orders to trade are given or transactions are undertaken at or around a specific time when reference prices, settlement prices and valuations are calculated and lead to price changes which have an effect on such prices and valuations.

[5505]

Article 5
Manipulative behaviours related to the employment of fictitious devices or any other form of deception or contrivance

For the purposes of applying point 2(b) of Article 1 of Directive 2003/6/EC, and without prejudice to the examples set out in the second paragraph of point 2 thereof, Member States shall ensure that the following non-exhaustive signals, which should not necessarily be deemed in themselves to constitute market manipulation, are taken into account when transactions or orders to trade are-examined by market participants and competent authorities:

    (a)   whether orders to trade given or transactions undertaken by persons are preceded or followed by dissemination of false or misleading information by the same persons or persons linked to them;

    (b)   whether orders to trade are given or transactions are undertaken by persons before or after the same persons or persons linked to them produce or disseminate research or investment recommendations which are erroneous or biased or demonstrably influenced by material interest.

[5506]

Article 6
Transposition

1. Member States shall bring into force the laws, regulations and administrative provisions necessary to comply with this Directive by 12 October 2004 at the latest. They shall forthwith communicate to the Commission the text of the provisions and a correlation table between those provisions and this Directive.

When Member States adopt those provisions, they shall contain a reference to this Directive or be accompanied by such a reference on the occasion of their official publication. Member States shall determine how such reference is to be made.

2. Member States shall communicate to the Commission the text of the main provisions of national law which they adopt in the field covered by this Directive.

[5507]

Article 7
Entry into force

This Directive shall enter into force on the day of its publication in the *Official Journal of the European Union*.

[5508]

Article 8
Addressees

This Directive is addressed to the Member States.

[5509]

COMMISSION DIRECTIVE

of 22 December 2003

implementing Directive 2003/6/EC of the European Parliament and of the Council as regards the fair presentation of investment recommendations and the disclosure of conflicts of interest

(2003/125/EC)

(Text with EEA relevance)

NOTES
Date of publication in OJ: OJ L339, 24.12.2003, p 73. Notes are as in the original OJ version.
As of 1 February 2009, this Directive had not been amended.

THE COMMISSION OF THE EUROPEAN COMMUNITIES,

Having regard to the Treaty establishing the European Community,

Having regard to Directive 2003/6/EC of the European Parliament and of the Council of 28 January 2003 on insider dealing and market manipulation (market abuse),[1] and in particular the sixth indent of Article 6(10) thereof,

After consulting the Committee of European Securities Regulators (CESR)[2] for technical advice,

Whereas:

(1) Harmonised standards are necessary for the fair, clear and accurate presentation of information and disclosure of interests and conflicts of interest, to be complied with by persons producing or disseminating information recommending or suggesting an investment strategy, intended for distribution channels or for the public. In particular, market integrity requires high standards of fairness, probity and transparency when information recommending or suggesting an investment strategy is presented.

(2) Recommending or suggesting an investment strategy is either done explicitly (such as 'buy', 'hold' or 'sell' recommendations) or implicitly (by reference to a price target or otherwise).

(3) Investment advice, through the provision of a personal recommendation to a client in respect of one or more transactions relating to financial instruments (in particular informal short-term investment recommendations originating from inside the sales or trading departments of an investment firm or a credit institution expressed to their clients), which are not likely to become publicly available, should not be considered in themselves as recommendations within the meaning of this Directive.

(4) Investment recommendations that constitute a possible basis for investment decisions should be produced and disseminated in accordance with high standards of care in order to avoid misleading market participants.

(5)   The identity of the producer of investment recommendations, his conduct of business rules and the identity of his competent authority should be disclosed, since it may be a valuable piece of information for investors to consider in relation to their investment decisions.

(6)   Recommendations should be presented clearly and accurately.

(7)   Own interests or conflicts of interest of persons recommending or suggesting investment strategy may influence the opinion that they express in investment recommendations. In order to ensure that the objectivity and reliability of the information can be evaluated, appropriate disclosure should be made of significant financial interests in any financial instrument which is the subject of the information recommending investment strategies, or of any conflicts of interest or control relationship with respect to the issuer to whom the information relates, directly or indirectly. However, this Directive should not require relevant persons producing investment recommendations to breach effective information barriers put in place in order to prevent and avoid conflicts of interest.

(8)   Investment recommendations may be disseminated in unaltered, altered or summarised form by a person other than the producer. The way in which disseminators handle such recommendations may have an important impact on the evaluation of those recommendations by investors. In particular, the knowledge of the identity of the disseminator of investment recommendations, his conduct of business rules or the extent of alteration of the original recommendation can be a valuable piece of information for investors when considering their investment decisions.

(9)   Posting of investment recommendations on internet sites should be in accordance with the rules on transfer of personal data to third countries as laid down in Directive 95/46/EC of the European Parliament and of the Council of 24 October 1995 on the protection of individuals with regard to the processing of personal data and on the movement of such data.[3]

(10)   Credit rating agencies issue opinions on the creditworthiness of a particular issuer or financial instrument as of a given date. As such, these opinions do not constitute a recommendation within the meaning of this Directive. However, credit rating agencies should consider adopting internal policies and procedures designed to ensure that credit ratings published by them are fairly presented and that they appropriately disclose any significant interests or conflicts of interest concerning the financial instruments or the issuers to which their credit ratings relate.

(11)   This Directive respects the fundamental rights and observes the principles recognised in particular by the Charter of Fundamental Rights of the European Union and in particular by Article 11 thereof and Article 10 of the European Convention on Human Rights. In this regard, this Directive does not in any way prevent Member States from applying their constitutional rules relating to freedom of the press and freedom of expression in the media.

(12)   The measures provided for in this Directive are in accordance with the opinion of the European Securities Committee,

[5510]

NOTES

[1]   OJ L96, 12.4.2003, p 16.
[2]   CESR was established by Commission Decision 2001/527/EC (OJ L191,13.7.2001, p 43).
[3]   OJ L281, 23.11.1995, p 31.

HAS ADOPTED THIS DIRECTIVE:

CHAPTER I
DEFINITIONS

Article 1
Definitions

For the purposes of this Directive, the following definitions shall apply in addition to those laid down in Directive 2003/6/EC:

1.   'investment firm' means any person as defined in Article 1(2) of Council Directive 93/22/EEC;[1]

2.   'credit institution' means any person as defined in Article 1(1) of Directive 2000/12/EC of the European Parliament and of the Council;[2]

3.   'recommendation' means research or other information recommending or suggesting an investment strategy, explicitly or implicitly, concerning one or several financial instruments or the issuers of financial instruments, including any opinion as to the present or future value or price of such instruments, intended for distribution channels or for the public;

4.   'research or other information recommending or suggesting investment strategy' means:

    (a)   information produced by an independent analyst, an investment firm, a credit institution, any other person whose main business is to produce recommendations or a natural person working for them under a contract of employment or otherwise, that, directly or indirectly, expresses a particular investment recommendation in respect of a financial instrument or an issuer of financial instruments;

    (b)   information produced by persons other than the persons referred to in (a) which directly recommends a particular investment decision in respect of a financial instrument;

5.   'relevant person' means a natural or legal person producing or disseminating recommendations in the exercise of his profession or the conduct of his business;

6.   'issuer' means the issuer of a financial instrument to which a recommendation relates, directly or indirectly;

7.   'distribution channels' shall mean a channel through which information is, or is likely to become, publicly available. 'Likely to become publicly available information' shall mean information to which a large number of persons have access;

8.   'appropriate regulation' shall mean any regulation, including self-regulation, in place in Member States as referred to by Directive 2003/6/EC.

[5510A]

NOTES

1   OJ L141, 11.6.1993, p 27.
2   OJ L126, 26.5.2000, p 1.

CHAPTER II
PRODUCTION OF RECOMMENDATIONS

Article 2
Identity of producers of recommendations

1.   Member States shall ensure that there is appropriate regulation in place to ensure that any recommendation discloses clearly and prominently the identity of the person responsible for its production, in particular, the name and job title of the individual who prepared the recommendation and the name of the legal person responsible for its production.

2.   Where the relevant person is an investment firm or a credit institution, Member States shall require that the identity of the relevant competent authority be disclosed.

Where the relevant person is neither an investment firm nor a credit institution, but is subject to self-regulatory standards or codes of conduct, Member States shall ensure that a reference to those standards or codes is disclosed.

3.   Member States shall ensure that there is appropriate regulation in place to ensure that the requirements laid down in paragraphs 1 and 2 are adapted in order not to be disproportionate in the case of non-written recommendations. Such adaptation may include a reference to the place where such disclosures can be directly and easily accessed by the public, such as an appropriate internet site of the relevant person.

4.   Paragraphs 1 and 2 shall not apply to journalists subject to equivalent appropriate regulation, including equivalent appropriate self regulation, in the Member States, provided that such regulation achieves similar effects as those of paragraphs 1 and 2.

[5511]

Article 3
General standard for fair presentation of recommendations

1.   Member States shall ensure that there is appropriate regulation in place to ensure that all relevant persons take reasonable care to ensure that:

    (a)   facts are clearly distinguished from interpretations, estimates, opinions and other types of non-factual information;

    (b)   all sources are reliable or, where there is any doubt as to whether a source is reliable, this is clearly indicated;

    (c)   all projections, forecasts and price targets are clearly labelled as such and that the material assumptions made in producing or using them are indicated.

2.   Member States shall ensure that there is appropriate regulation in place to ensure that the requirements laid down in paragraph 1 are adapted in order not to be disproportionate in the case of non-written recommendations.

3.   Member States shall require that all relevant persons take reasonable care to ensure that any recommendation can be substantiated as reasonable, upon request by the competent authorities.

4.   Paragraphs 1 and 3 shall not apply to journalists subject to equivalent appropriate regulation in the Member States, including equivalent appropriate self regulation, provided that such regulation achieves similar effects as those of paragraphs 1 and 3.

[5512]

Article 4
Additional obligations in relation to fair presentation of recommendations

1.   In addition to the obligations laid down in Article 3, where the relevant person is an independent analyst, an investment firm, a credit institution, any related legal person, any other relevant person whose main business is to produce recommendations, or a natural person working for them under a contract of employment or otherwise, Member States shall ensure that there is appropriate regulation in place to ensure that person to take reasonable care to ensure that at least:

(a)   all substantially material sources are indicated, as appropriate, including the relevant issuer, together with the fact whether the recommendation has been disclosed to that issuer and amended following this disclosure before its dissemination;

(b)   any basis of valuation or methodology used to evaluate a financial instrument or an issuer of a financial instrument, or to set a price target for a financial instrument, is adequately summarised;

(c)   the meaning of any recommendation made, such as buy, sell or hold, which may include the time horizon of the investment to which the recommendation relates, is adequately explained and any appropriate risk warning, including a sensitivity analysis of the relevant assumptions, indicated;

(d)   reference is made to the planned frequency, if any, of updates of the recommendation and to any major changes in the coverage policy previously announced;

(e)   the date at which the recommendation was first released for distribution is indicated clearly and prominently, as well as the relevant date and time for any financial instrument price mentioned;

(f)   where a recommendation differs from a recommendation concerning the same financial instrument or issuer, issued during the 12-month period immediately preceding its release, this change and the date of the earlier recommendation are indicated clearly and prominently.

2.   Member States shall ensure that, where the requirements laid down in points (a), (b) or (c) of paragraph 1 would be disproportionate in relation to the length of the recommendation distributed, it shall suffice to make clear and prominent reference in the recommendation itself to the place where the required information can be directly and easily accessed by the public, such as a direct Internet link to that information on an appropriate internet site of the relevant person, provided that there has been no change in the methodology or basis of valuation used.

3.   Member States shall ensure that there is appropriate regulation in place to ensure that, in the case of non-written recommendations, the requirements of paragraph 1 are adapted so that they are not disproportionate.

[5513]

Article 5
General standard for disclosure of interests and conflicts of interest

1.   Member States shall ensure that there is appropriate regulation in place to ensure that relevant persons disclose all relationships and circumstances that may reasonably be expected to impair the objectivity of the recommendation, in particular where relevant persons have a significant financial interest in one or more of the financial instruments which are the subject of the recommendation, or a significant conflict of interest with respect to an issuer to which the recommendation relates.

Where the relevant person is a legal person, that requirement shall apply also to any legal or natural person working for it, under a contract of employment or otherwise, who was involved in preparing the recommendation.

2.   Where the relevant person is a legal person, the information to be disclosed in accordance with paragraph 1 shall at least include the following:

(a)   any interests or conflicts of interest of the relevant person or of related legal persons that are accessible or reasonably expected to be accessible to the persons involved in the preparation of the recommendation;

(b)   any interests or conflicts of interest of the relevant person or of related legal persons known to persons who, although not involved in the preparation of the recommendation, had or could reasonably be expected to have access to the recommendation prior to its dissemination to customers or the public.

3.   Member States shall ensure that there is appropriate regulation in place to ensure that the recommendation itself shall include the disclosures provided for in paragraphs 1 and 2. Where such disclosures would be disproportionate in relation to the length of the recommendation distributed, it shall suffice to make clear and prominent reference in the recommendation itself to the place where such disclosures can be directly and easily accessed by the public, such as a direct Internet link to the disclosure on an appropriate internet site of the relevant person.

4. Member States shall ensure that there is appropriate regulation in place to ensure that the requirements laid down in paragraph 1 are adapted in order not to be disproportionate in the case of non-written recommendations.

5. Paragraphs 1 to 3 shall not apply to journalists subject to equivalent appropriate regulation, including equivalent appropriate self regulation, in the Member States, provided that such regulation achieves similar effects as those of paragraphs 1 to 3.

[5514]

Article 6
Additional obligations in relation to disclosure of interests or conflicts of interest

1. In addition to the obligations laid down in Article 5, Member States shall require that any recommendation produced by an independent analyst, an investment firm, a credit institution, any related legal person, or any other relevant person whose main business is to produce recommendations, discloses clearly and prominently the following information on their interests and conflicts of interest:

(a) major shareholdings that exist between the relevant person or any related legal person on the one hand and the issuer on the other hand. These major shareholdings include at least the following instances:

  — when shareholdings exceeding 5% of the total issued share capital in the issuer are held by the relevant person or any related legal person, or

  — when shareholdings exceeding 5% of the total issued share capital of the relevant person or any related legal person are held by the issuer.

  Member States may provide for lower thresholds than the 5% threshold as provided for in these two instances;

(b) other significant financial interests held by the relevant person or any related legal person in relation to the issuer;

(c) where applicable, a statement that the relevant person or any related legal person is a market maker or liquidity provider in the financial instruments of the issuer;

(d) where applicable, a statement that the relevant person or any related legal person has been lead manager or co-lead manager over the previous 12 months of any publicly disclosed offer of financial instruments of the issuer;

(e) where applicable, a statement that the relevant person or any related legal person is party to any other agreement with the issuer relating to the provision of investment banking services, provided that this would not entail the disclosure of any confidential commercial information and that the agreement has been in effect over the previous 12 months or has given rise during the same period to the payment of a compensation or to the promise to get a compensation paid;

(f) where applicable, a statement that the relevant person or any related legal person is party to an agreement with the issuer relating to the production of the recommendation.

2. Member States shall require disclosure, in general terms, of the effective organisational and administrative arrangements set up within the investment firm or the credit institution for the prevention and avoidance of conflicts of interest with respect to recommendations, including information barriers.

3. Member States shall require that for natural or legal persons working for an investment firm or a credit institution, under a contract of employment or otherwise, and who were involved in preparing the recommendation, the requirement under the second subparagraph of paragraph 1 of Article 5 shall include, in particular, disclosure of whether the remuneration of such persons is tied to investment banking transactions performed by the investment firm or credit institution or any related legal person.

Where those natural persons receive or purchase the shares of the issuers prior to a public offering of such shares, the price at which the shares were acquired and the date of acquisition shall also be disclosed.

4. Member States shall require that investment firms and credit institutions disclose, on a quarterly basis, the proportion of all recommendations that are 'buy', 'hold', 'sell' or equivalent terms, as well as the proportion of issuers corresponding to each of these categories to which the investment firm or the credit institution has supplied material investment banking services over the previous 12 months.

5. Member States shall ensure that the recommendation itself includes the disclosures required by paragraphs 1 to 4. Where the requirements under paragraphs 1 to 4 would be disproportionate in relation to the length of the recommendation distributed, it shall suffice to make clear and prominent reference in the recommendation itself to the place where such disclosure can be directly and easily accessed by the public, such as a direct Internet link to the disclosure on an appropriate internet site of the investment firm or credit institution.

PART IV
EC MATERIALS

6.   Member States shall ensure that there is appropriate regulation in place to ensure that, in the case of non-written recommendations, the requirements of paragraph 1 are adapted so that they are not disproportionate.

[5515]

CHAPTER III
DISSEMINATION OF RECOMMENDATIONS PRODUCED BY THIRD PARTIES

Article 7
Identity of disseminators of recommendations

Member States shall ensure that there is appropriate regulation in place to ensure that, whenever a relevant person under his own responsibility disseminates a recommendation produced by a third party, the recommendation indicates clearly and prominently the identity of that relevant person.

[5516]

Article 8
General standard for dissemination of recommendations

Member States shall ensure that there is appropriate regulation in place to ensure that whenever a recommendation produced by a third party is substantially altered within disseminated information, that information clearly indicates the substantial alteration in detail. Member States shall ensure that whenever the substantial alteration consists of a change of the direction of the recommendation (such as changing a 'buy' recommendation into a 'hold' or 'sell' recommendation or vice versa), the requirements laid down in Articles 2 to 5 on producers are met by the disseminator, to the extent of the substantial alteration.

In addition, Member States shall ensure that there is appropriate regulation in place to ensure that relevant legal persons who themselves, or through natural persons, disseminate a substantially altered recommendation have a formal written policy so that the persons receiving the information may be directed to where they can have access to the identity of the producer of the recommendation, the recommendation itself and the disclosure of the producer's interests or conflicts of interest, provided that these elements are publicly available.

The first and second paragraphs do not apply to news reporting on recommendations produced by a third party where the substance of the recommendation is not altered.

In case of dissemination of a summary of a recommendation produced by a third party, the relevant persons disseminating such summary shall ensure that the summary is clear and not misleading, mentioning the source document and where the disclosures related to the source document can be directly and easily accessed by the public provided that they are publicly available.

[5517]

Article 9
Additional obligations for investment firms and credit institutions

In addition to the obligations laid down in Articles 7 and 8, whenever the relevant person is an investment firm, a credit institution or a natural person working for such persons under a contract of employment or otherwise, and disseminates recommendations produced by a third party, Member States shall require that:

    (a)   the name of the competent authority of the investment firm or credit institution is clearly and prominently indicated;

    (b)   if the producer of the recommendation has not already disseminated it through a distribution channel, the requirements laid down in Article 6 on producers are met by the disseminator;

    (c)   if the investment firm or credit institution has substantially altered the recommendation, the requirements laid down in Articles 2 to 6 on producers are met.

[5518]

CHAPTER IV
FINAL PROVISIONS

Article 10
Transposition

1.   Member States shall bring into force the laws, regulations and administrative provisions necessary to comply with this Directive by 12 October 2004 at the latest. They shall forthwith communicate to the Commission the text of those provisions and a correlation table between these provisions and this Directive.

When Member States adopt those provisions, they shall contain a reference to this Directive or be accompanied by such a reference on the occasion of their official publication. Member States shall determine how such reference is to be made.

2. Member States shall communicate to the Commission the text of the main provisions of national law which they adopt in the field covered by this Directive.

[5519]

Article 11
Entry into force

This Directive shall enter into force on the day of its publication in the *Official Journal of the European Union*.

[5520]

Article 12
Addressees

This Directive is addressed to the Member States.

[5521]

DIRECTIVE OF THE EUROPEAN PARLIAMENT
AND OF THE COUNCIL

of 21 April 2004

on markets in financial instruments amending Council Directives 85/611/EEC and 93/6/EEC and Directive 2000/12/EC of the European Parliament and of the Council and repealing Council Directive 93/22/EEC

(2004/39/EC)

NOTES
Date of Publication in OJ: OJ L145, 30.4.2004, p 1. The text of this Directive incorporates the corrigendum published in OJ L45, 16.2.2005, p 18. Notes are as in the original OJ version.
This Directive is reproduced as amended by: European Parliament and Council Directive 2006/31/EC (OJ L114, 27.4.2006, p 60) (at [5781]); European Parliament and Council Directive 2006/48/EC (OJ L177, 30.6.2006, p 1) (at [5784]); European Parliament and Council Directive 2006/49/EC (OJ L177, 30.6.2006, p 201) (at [5847]); European Parliament and Council Directive 2007/44/EC (OJ L247, 21.9.2007, p 1); European Parliament and Council Directive 2008/10/EC (OJ L76, 19.03.2008, p 33).
Note: the proposed transposition of MiFID (originally 30 April 2006) has been subject to certain delays. See now the amendments made to this Directive by Directive 2006/31/EC and, in particular, Art 70 at [5591].
Council Directive 93/6/EEC: repealed by European Parliament and Council Directive 2006/49/EC.
Council Directive 2000/12/EC: repealed by European Parliament and Council Directive 2006/48/EC.

THE EUROPEAN PARLIAMENT AND THE COUNCIL OF THE EUROPEAN UNION,

Having regard to the Treaty establishing the European Community, and in particular Article 47(2) thereof,

Having regard to the proposal from the Commission,[1]

Having regard to the Opinion of the European Economic and Social Committee,[2]

Having regard to the opinion of the European Central Bank,[3]

Acting in accordance with the procedure laid down in Article 251 of the Treaty,[4]

Whereas:

(1) Council Directive 93/22/EEC of 10 May 1993 on investment services in the securities field[5] sought to establish the conditions under which authorised investment firms and banks could provide specified services or establish branches in other Member States on the basis of home country authorisation and supervision. To this end, that Directive aimed to harmonise the initial authorisation and operating requirements for investment firms including conduct of business rules. It also provided for the harmonisation of some conditions governing the operation of regulated markets.

(2) In recent years more investors have become active in the financial markets and are offered an even more complex wide-ranging set of services and instruments. In view of these developments the legal framework of the Community should encompass the full range of investor-oriented activities. To this end, it is necessary to provide for the degree of harmonisation needed to offer investors a high level of protection and to allow investment firms to provide services throughout the Community, being a Single Market, on the basis of home country supervision. In view of the preceding, Directive 93/22/EEC should be replaced by a new Directive.

(3) Due to the increasing dependence of investors on personal recommendations, it is appropriate to include the provision of investment advice as an investment service requiring authorisation.

(4)   It is appropriate to include in the list of financial instruments certain commodity derivatives and others which are constituted and traded in such a manner as to give rise to regulatory issues comparable to traditional financial instruments.

(5)   It is necessary to establish a comprehensive regulatory regime governing the execution of transactions in financial instruments irrespective of the trading methods used to conclude those transactions so as to ensure a high quality of execution of investor transactions and to uphold the integrity and overall efficiency of the financial system. A coherent and risk sensitive framework for regulating the main types of order-execution arrangement currently active in the European financial marketplace should be provided for. It is necessary to recognise the emergence of a new generation of organised trading systems alongside regulated markets which should be subjected to obligations designed to preserve the efficient and orderly functioning of financial markets. With a view to establishing a proportionate regulatory new investment framework provision should be made for the inclusion of a service which relates to the operation of an MTF.

(6)   Definitions of regulated market and MTF should be introduced and closely aligned with each other to reflect the fact that they represent the same organised trading functionality. The definitions should exclude bilateral systems where an investment firm enters into every trade on own account and not as a riskless counterparty interposed between the buyer and seller. The term 'system' encompasses all those markets that are composed of a set of rules and a trading platform as well as those that only function on the basis of a set of rules. Regulated markets and MTFs are not obliged to operate a 'technical' system for matching orders. A market which is only composed of a set of rules that governs aspects related to membership, admission of instruments to trading, trading between members, reporting and, where applicable, transparency obligations is a regulated market or an MTF within the meaning of this Directive and the transactions concluded under those rules are considered to be concluded under the systems of a regulated market or an MTF. The term 'buying and selling interests' is to be understood in a broad sense and includes orders, quotes and indications of interest. The requirement that the interests be brought together in the system by means of non-discretionary rules set by the system operator means that they are brought together under the system's rules or by means of the system's protocols or internal operating procedures (including procedures embodied in computer software). The term 'non-discretionary rules' means that these rules leave the investment firm operating an MTF with no discretion as to how interests may interact. The definitions require that interests be brought together in such a way as to result in a contract, meaning that execution takes place under the system's rules or by means of the system's protocols or internal operating procedures.

(7)   The purpose of this Directive is to cover undertakings the regular occupation or business of which is to provide investment services and/or perform investment activities on a professional basis. Its scope should not therefore cover any person with a different professional activity.

(8)   Persons administering their own assets and undertakings, who do not provide investment services and/or perform investment activities other than dealing on own account unless they are market makers or they deal on own account outside a regulated market or an MTF on an organised, frequent and systematic basis, by providing a system accessible to third parties in order to engage in dealings with them should not be covered by the scope of this Directive.

(9)   References in the text to persons should be understood as including both natural and legal persons.

(10)   Insurance or assurance undertakings the activities of which are subject to appropriate monitoring by the competent prudential-supervision authorities and which are subject to Council Directive 64/225/EEC of 25 February 1964 on the abolition of restrictions on freedom of establishment and freedom to provide services in respect of reinsurance and retrocession,[6] First Council Directive 73/239/EEC of 24 July 1973 on the coordination of laws, regulations and administrative provisions relating to the taking up and pursuit of direct insurance other than life assurance[7] and Council Directive 2002/83/EC of 5 November 2002 concerning life assurance[8] should be excluded.

(11)   Persons who do not provide services for third parties but whose business consists in providing investment services solely for their parent undertakings, for their subsidiaries, or for other subsidiaries of their parent undertakings should not be covered by this Directive.

(12)   Persons who provide investment services only on an incidental basis in the course of professional activity should also be excluded from the scope of this Directive, provided that activity is regulated and the relevant rules do not prohibit the provision, on an incidental basis, of investment services.

(13)   Persons who provide investment services consisting exclusively in the administration of employee participation schemes and who therefore do not provide investment services for third parties should not be covered by this Directive.

(14)   It is necessary to exclude from the scope of this Directive central banks and other bodies performing similar functions as well as public bodies charged with or intervening in the management of the public debt, which concept covers the investment thereof, with the exception of bodies that are partly or wholly State-owned the role of which is commercial or linked to the acquisition of holdings.

(15) It is necessary to exclude from the scope of this Directive collective investment undertakings and pension funds whether or not coordinated at Community level, and the depositaries or managers of such undertakings, since they are subject to specific rules directly adapted to their activities.

(16) In order to benefit from the exemptions from this Directive the person concerned should comply on a continuous basis with the conditions laid down for such exemptions. In particular, if a person provides investment services or performs investment activities and is exempted from this Directive because such services or activities are ancillary to his main business, when considered on a group basis, he should no longer be covered by the exemption related to ancillary services where the provision of those services or activities ceases to be ancillary to his main business.

(17) Persons who provide the investment services and/or perform investment activities covered by this Directive should be subject to authorisation by their home Member States in order to protect investors and the stability of the financial system.

(18) Credit institutions that are authorised under Directive 2000/12/EC of the European Parliament and of the Council of 20 March 2000 relating to the taking up and pursuit of the business of credit institutions[9] should not need another authorisation under this Directive in order to provide investment services or perform investment activities. When a credit institution decides to provide investment services or perform investment activities the competent authorities, before granting an authorisation, should verify that it complies with the relevant provisions of this Directive.

(19) In cases where an investment firm provides one or more investment services not covered by its authorisation, or performs one or more investment activities not covered by its authorisation, on a non-regular basis it should not need an additional authorisation under this Directive.

(20) For the purposes of this Directive, the business of the reception and transmission of orders should also include bringing together two or more investors thereby bringing about a transaction between those investors.

(21) In the context of the forthcoming revision of the Capital Adequacy framework in Basel II, Member States recognise the need to re-examine whether or not investment firms who execute client orders on a matched principal basis are to be regarded as acting as principals, and thereby be subject to additional regulatory capital requirements.

(22) The principles of mutual recognition and of home Member State supervision require that the Member States' competent authorities should not grant or should withdraw authorisation where factors such as the content of programmes of operations, the geographical distribution or the activities actually carried on indicate clearly that an investment firm has opted for the legal system of one Member State for the purpose of evading the stricter standards in force in another Member State within the territory of which it intends to carry on or does carry on the greater part of its activities. An investment firm which is a legal person should be authorised in the Member State in which it has its registered office. An investment firm which is not a legal person should be authorised in the Member State in which it has its head office. In addition, Member States should require that an investment firm's head office must always be situated in its home Member State and that it actually operates there.

(23) An investment firm authorised in its home Member State should be entitled to provide investment services or perform investment activities throughout the Community without the need to seek a separate authorisation from the competent authority in the Member State in which it wishes to provide such services or perform such activities.

(24) Since certain investment firms are exempted from certain obligations imposed by Council Directive 93/6/EEC of 15 March 1993 on the capital adequacy of investment firms and credit institutions,[10] they should be obliged to hold either a minimum amount of capital or professional indemnity insurance or a combination of both. The adjustments of the amounts of that insurance should take into account adjustments made in the framework of Directive 2002/92/EC of the European Parliament and of the Council of 9 December 2002 on insurance mediation.[11] This particular treatment for the purposes of capital adequacy should be without prejudice to any decisions regarding the appropriate treatment of these firms under future changes to Community legislation on capital adequacy.

(25) Since the scope of prudential regulation should be limited to those entities which, by virtue of running a trading book on a professional basis, represent a source of counterparty risk to other market participants, entities which deal on own account in financial instruments, including those commodity derivatives covered by this Directive, as well as those that provide investment services in commodity derivatives to the clients of their main business on an ancillary basis to their main business when considered on a group basis, provided that this main business is not the provision of investment services within the meaning of this Directive, should be excluded from the scope of this Directive.

(26) In order to protect an investor's ownership and other similar rights in respect of securities and his rights in respect of funds entrusted to a firm those rights should in particular be kept distinct from those of the firm. This principle should not, however, prevent a firm from doing business in its name but on behalf of the investor, where that is required by the very nature of the transaction and the investor is in agreement, for example stock lending.

(27)   Where a client, in line with Community legislation and in particular Directive 2002/47/EC of the European Parliament and of the Council of 6 June 2002 on financial collateral arrangements,[12] transfers full ownership of financial instruments or funds to an investment firm for the purpose of securing or otherwise covering present or future, actual or contingent or prospective obligations, such financial instruments or funds should likewise no longer be regarded as belonging to the client.

(28)   The procedures for the authorisation, within the Community, of branches of investment firms authorised in third countries should continue to apply to such firms. Those branches should not enjoy the freedom to provide services under the second paragraph of Article 49 of the Treaty or the right of establishment in Member States other than those in which they are established. In view of cases where the Community is not bound by any bilateral or multilateral obligations it is appropriate to provide for a procedure intended to ensure that Community investment firms receive reciprocal treatment in the third countries concerned.

(29)   The expanding range of activities that many investment firms undertake simultaneously has increased potential for conflicts of interest between those different activities and the interests of their clients. It is therefore necessary to provide for rules to ensure that such conflicts do not adversely affect the interests of their clients.

(30)   A service should be considered to be provided at the initiative of a client unless the client demands it in response to a personalised communication from or on behalf of the firm to that particular client, which contains an invitation or is intended to influence the client in respect of a specific financial instrument or specific transaction. A service can be considered to be provided at the initiative of the client notwithstanding that the client demands it on the basis of any communication containing a promotion or offer of financial instruments made by any means that by its very nature is general and addressed to the public or a larger group or category of clients or potential clients.

(31)   One of the objectives of this Directive is to protect investors. Measures to protect investors should be adapted to the particularities of each category of investors (retail, professional and counterparties).

(32)   By way of derogation from the principle of home country authorisation, supervision and enforcement of obligations in respect of the operation of branches, it is appropriate for the competent authority of the host Member State to assume responsibility for enforcing certain obligations specified in this Directive in relation to business conducted through a branch within the territory where the branch is located, since that authority is closest to the branch, and is better placed to detect and intervene in respect of infringements of rules governing the operations of the branch.

(33)   It is necessary to impose an effective 'best execution' obligation to ensure that investment firms execute client orders on terms that are most favourable to the client. This obligation should apply to the firm which owes contractual or agency obligations to the client.

(34)   Fair competition requires that market participants and investors be able to compare the prices that trading venues (i.e. regulated markets, MTFs and intermediaries) are required to publish. To this end, it is recommended that Member States remove any obstacles which may prevent the consolidation at European level of the relevant information and its publication.

(35)   When establishing the business relationship with the client the investment firm might ask the client or potential client to consent at the same time to the execution policy as well as to the possibility that his orders may be executed outside a regulated market or an MTF.

(36)   Persons who provide investment services on behalf of more than one investment firm should not be considered as tied agents but as investment firms when they fall under the definition provided in this Directive, with the exception of certain persons who may be exempted.

(37)   This Directive should be without prejudice to the right of tied agents to undertake activities covered by other Directives and related activities in respect of financial services or products not covered by this Directive, including on behalf of parts of the same financial group.

(38)   The conditions for conducting activities outside the premises of the investment firm (door-to-door selling) should not be covered by this Directive.

(39)   Member States' competent authorities should not register or should withdraw the registration where the activities actually carried on indicate clearly that a tied agent has opted for the legal system of one Member State for the purpose of evading the stricter standards in force in another Member State within the territory of which it intends to carry on or does carry on the greater part of its activities.

(40)   For the purposes of this Directive eligible counterparties should be considered as acting as clients.

(41)   For the purposes of ensuring that conduct of business rules (including rules on best execution and handling of client orders) are enforced in respect of those investors most in need of these protections, and to reflect well-established market practice throughout the Community, it is appropriate to clarify that conduct of business rules may be waived in the case of transactions entered into or brought about between eligible counterparties.

(42)   In respect of transactions executed between eligible counterparties, the obligation to disclose client limit orders should only apply where the counter party is explicitly sending a limit order to an investment firm for its execution.

(43) Member States shall protect the right to privacy of natural persons with respect to the processing of personal data in accordance with Directive 95/46/EC of the European Parliament and of the Council of 24 October 1995 on the protection of individuals with regard to the processing of personal data and of the free movement of such data.[13]

(44) With the two fold aim of protecting investors and ensuring the smooth operation of securities markets, it is necessary to ensure that transparency of transactions is achieved and that the rules laid down for that purpose apply to investment firms when they operate on the markets. In order to enable investors or market participants to assess at any time the terms of a transaction in shares that they are considering and to verify afterwards the conditions in which it was carried out, common rules should be established for the publication of details of completed transactions in shares and for the disclosure of details of current opportunities to trade in shares. These rules are needed to ensure the effective integration of Member State equity markets, to promote the efficiency of the overall price formation process for equity instruments, and to assist the effective operation of 'best execution' obligations. These considerations require a comprehensive transparency regime applicable to all transactions in shares irrespective of their execution by an investment firm on a bilateral basis or through regulated markets or MTFs. The obligations for investment firms under this Directive to quote a bid and offer price and to execute an order at the quoted price do not relieve investment firms of the obligation to route an order to another execution venue when such internalisation could prevent the firm from complying with 'best execution' obligations.

(45) Member States should be able to apply transaction reporting obligations of the Directive to financial instruments that are not admitted to trading on a regulated market.

(46) A Member State may decide to apply the pre- and post-trade transparency requirements laid down in this Directive to financial instruments other than shares. In that case those requirements should apply to all investment firms for which that Member State is the home Member State for their operations within the territory of that Member State and those carried out cross border through the freedom to provide services. They should also apply to the operations carried out within the territory of that Member State by the branches established in its territory of investment firms authorised in another Member State.

(47) Investment firms should all have the same opportunities of joining or having access to regulated markets throughout the Community. Regardless of the manner in which transactions are at present organised in the Member States, it is important to abolish the technical and legal restrictions on access to regulated markets.

(48) In order to facilitate the finalisation of cross-border transactions, it is appropriate to provide for access to clearing and settlement systems throughout the Community by investment firms, irrespective of whether transactions have been concluded through regulated markets in the Member State concerned. Investment firms which wish to participate directly in other Member States' settlement systems should comply with the relevant operational and commercial requirements for membership and the prudential measures to uphold the smooth and orderly functioning of the financial markets.

(49) The authorisation to operate a regulated market should extend to all activities which are directly related to the display, processing, execution, confirmation and reporting of orders from the point at which such orders are received by the regulated market to the point at which they are transmitted for subsequent finalisation, and to activities related to the admission of financial instruments to trading. This should also include transactions concluded through the medium of designated market makers appointed by the regulated market which are undertaken under its systems and in accordance with the rules that govern those systems. Not all transactions concluded by members or participants of the regulated market or MTF are to be considered as concluded within the systems of a regulated market or MTF. Transactions which members or participants conclude on a bilateral basis and which do not comply with all the obligations established for a regulated market or an MTF under this Directive should be considered as transactions concluded outside a regulated market or an MTF for the purposes of the definition of systematic internaliser. In such a case the obligation for investment firms to make public firm quotes should apply if the conditions established by this Directive are met.

(50) Systematic internalisers might decide to give access to their quotes only to retail clients, only to professional clients, or to both. They should not be allowed to discriminate within those categories of clients.

(51) Article 27 does not oblige systematic internalisers to publish firm quotes in relation to transactions above standard market size.

(52) Where an investment firm is a systematic internaliser both in shares and in other financial instruments, the obligation to quote should only apply in respect of shares without prejudice to Recital 46.

(53) It is not the intention of this Directive to require the application of pre-trade transparency rules to transactions carried out on an OTC basis, the characteristics of which include that they are ad-hoc and irregular and are carried out with wholesale counterparties and are part of a business relationship which is itself characterised by dealings above standard market size, and where the deals are carried out outside the systems usually used by the firm concerned for its business as a systematic internaliser.

(54)   The standard market size for any class of share should not be significantly disproportionate to any share included in that class.

(55)   Revision of Directive 93/6/EEC should fix the minimum capital requirements with which regulated markets should comply in order to be authorised, and in so doing should take into account the specific nature of the risks associated with such markets.

(56)   Operators of a regulated market should also be able to operate an MTF in accordance with the relevant provisions of this Directive.

(57)   The provisions of this Directive concerning the admission of instruments to trading under the rules enforced by the regulated market should be without prejudice to the application of Directive 2001/34/EC of the European Parliament and of the Council of 28 May 2001 on the admission of securities to official stock exchange listing and on information to be published on those securities.[14] A regulated market should not be prevented from applying more demanding requirements in respect of the issuers of securities or instruments which it is considering for admission to trading than are imposed pursuant to this Directive.

(58)   Member States should be able to designate different competent authorities to enforce the wide-ranging obligations laid down in this Directive. Such authorities should be of a public nature guaranteeing their independence from economic actors and avoiding conflicts of interest. In accordance with national law, Member States should ensure appropriate financing of the competent authority. The designation of public authorities should not exclude delegation under the responsibility of the competent authority.

(59)   Any confidential information received by the contact point of one Member State through the contact point of another Member State should not be regarded as purely domestic.

(60)   It is necessary to enhance convergence of powers at the disposal of competent authorities so as to pave the way towards an equivalent intensity of enforcement across the integrated financial market. A common minimum set of powers coupled with adequate resources should guarantee supervisory effectiveness.

(61)   With a view to protecting clients and without prejudice to the right of customers to bring their action before the courts, it is appropriate that Member States encourage public or private bodies established with a view to settling disputes out-of-court, to cooperate in resolving cross border disputes, taking into account Commission Recommendation 98/257/EC of 30 March 1998 on the principles applicable to the bodies responsible for out-of-court settlement of consumer disputes.[15] When implementing provisions on complaints and redress procedures for out of court settlements, Member States should be encouraged to use existing cross-border cooperation mechanisms, notably the Financial Services Complaints Network (FIN Net).

(62)   Any exchange or transmission of information between competent authorities, other authorities, bodies or persons should be in accordance with the rules on transfer of personal data to third countries as laid down in Directive 95/46/EC.

(63)   It is necessary to reinforce provisions on exchange of information between national competent authorities and to strengthen the duties of assistance and cooperation which they owe to each other. Due to increasing cross-border activity, competent authorities should provide each other with the relevant information for the exercise of their functions, so as to ensure the effective enforcement of this Directive, including in situations where infringements or suspected infringements may be of concern to authorities in two or more Member States. In the exchange of information, strict professional secrecy is needed to ensure the smooth transmission of that information and the protection of particular rights.

(64)   At its meeting on 17 July 2000, the Council set up the Committee of Wise Men on the Regulation of European Securities Markets. In its final report, the Committee of Wise Men proposed the introduction of new legislative techniques based on a four-level approach, namely framework principles, implementing measures, cooperation and enforcement. Level 1, the Directive, should confine itself to broad general 'framework' principles while Level 2 should contain technical implementing measures to be adopted by the Commission with the assistance of a committee.

(65)   The Resolution adopted by the Stockholm European Council of 23 March 2001 endorsed the final report of the Committee of Wise Men and the proposed four-level approach to make the regulatory process for Community securities legislation more efficient and transparent.

(66)   According to the Stockholm European Council, Level 2 implementing measures should be used more frequently, to ensure that technical provisions can be kept up to date with market and supervisory developments, and deadlines should be set for all stages of Level 2 work.

(67)   The Resolution of the European Parliament of 5 February 2002 on the implementation of financial services legislation also endorsed the Committee of Wise Men's report, on the basis of the solemn declaration made before Parliament the same day by the Commission and the letter of 2 October 2001 addressed by the Internal Market Commissioner to the chairman of Parliament's Committee on Economic and Monetary Affairs with regard to the safeguards for the European Parliament's role in this process.

(68)   The measures necessary for the implementation of this Directive should be adopted in accordance with Council Decision 1999/468/EC of 28 June 1999 laying down the procedures for the exercise of implementing powers conferred on the Commission.[16]

[(69) The European Parliament should be given a period of three months from the first transmission of draft amendments and implementing measures to allow it to examine them and to give its opinion. However, in urgent and duly justified cases, it should be possible to shorten that period. If, within that period, a resolution is adopted by the European Parliament, the Commission should re-examine the draft amendments or measures.]

(70) With a view to taking into account further developments in the financial markets the Commission should submit reports to the European Parliament and the Council on the application of the provisions concerning professional indemnity insurance, the scope of the transparency rules and the possible authorisation of specialised dealers in commodity derivatives as investment firms.

(71) The objective of creating an integrated financial market, in which investors are effectively protected and the efficiency and integrity of the overall market are safeguarded, requires the establishment of common regulatory requirements relating to investment firms wherever they are authorised in the Community and governing the functioning of regulated markets and other trading systems so as to prevent opacity or disruption on one market from undermining the efficient operation of the European financial system as a whole. Since this objective may be better achieved at Community level, the Community may adopt measures in accordance with the principle of subsidiarity as set out in Article 5 of the Treaty. In accordance with the principle of proportionality, as set out in that Article, this Directive does not go beyond what is necessary in order to achieve this objective,

[5522]

NOTES

Recital 69 substituted by European Parliament and Council Directive 2006/31/EC, Art 1(1), as from 28 April 2006.

1   OJ C71E, 25.3.2003, p 62.
2   OJ C220, 16.9.2003, p 1.
3   OJ C144, 20.6.2003, p 6.
4   Opinion of the European Parliament of 25 September 2003 (not yet published in the Official Journal), Council Common Position of 8 December 2003 (OJ C60E, 9.3.2004, p 1), Position of the European Parliament of 30 March 2004 (not yet published in the Official Journal) and Decision of the Council of 7 April 2004.
5   OJ L141, 11.6.1993, p 27. Directive as last amended by Directive 2002/87/EC of the European Parliament and of the Council (OJ L35, 11.2.2003, p 1).
6   OJ 56, 4.4. 1964, p 878/64. Directive as amended by the 1972 Act of Accession.
7   OJ L228, 16.8.1973, p 3. Directive as last amended by Directive 2002/87/EC.
8   OJ L345, 19.12.2002, p 1.
9   OJ L126, 26.5.2000, p 1. Directive as last amended by Directive 2002/87/EC.
10   OJ L141, 11.6.1993, p 1. Directive as last amended by Directive 2002/87/EC.
11   OJ L9, 15.1.2003, p 3.
12   OJ L168, 27.6.2002, p 43.
13   OJ L281, 23.11.1995, p 31.
14   OJ L184, 6.7.2001, p 1. Directive as last amended by European Parliament and Council Directive 2003/71/EC (OJ L345, 31.12.2003, p 64.).
15   OJ L115, 17.4.1998, p 31.
16   OJ L184, 17.7.1999, p 23.

HAVE ADOPTED THIS DIRECTIVE:

TITLE I
DEFINITIONS AND SCOPE

Article 1
Scope

1. This Directive shall apply to investment firms and regulated markets.

2. The following provisions shall also apply to credit institutions authorised under Directive 2000/12/EC, when providing one or more investment services and/or performing investment activities:

— Articles 2(2), 11, 13 and 14,
— Chapter II of Title II excluding Article 23(2) second sub-paragraph,
— Chapter III of Title II excluding Articles 31(2) to 31(4) and 32(2) to 32(6), 32(8) and 32(9),
— Articles 48 to 53, 57, 61 and 62, and
— Article 71(1).

[5522A]

Article 2
Exemptions

1. This Directive shall not apply to:
(a) insurance undertakings as defined in Article 1 of Directive 73/239/EEC or assurance

undertakings as defined in Article 1 of Directive 2002/83/EC or undertakings carrying on the reinsurance and retrocession activities referred to in Directive 64/225/EEC;

(b) persons which provide investment services exclusively for their parent undertakings, for their subsidiaries or for other subsidiaries of their parent undertakings;

(c) persons providing an investment service where that service is provided in an incidental manner in the course of a professional activity and that activity is regulated by legal or regulatory provisions or a code of ethics governing the profession which do not exclude the provision of that service;

(d) persons who do not provide any investment services or activities other than dealing on own account unless they are market makers or deal on own account outside a regulated market or an MTF on an organised, frequent and systematic basis by providing a system accessible to third parties in order to engage in dealings with them;

(e) persons which provide investment services consisting exclusively in the administration of employee-participation schemes;

(f) persons which provide investment services which only involve both administration of employee-participation schemes and the provision of investment services exclusively for their parent undertakings, for their subsidiaries or for other subsidiaries of their parent undertakings;

(g) the members of the European System of Central Banks and other national bodies performing similar functions and other public bodies charged with or intervening in the management of the public debt;

(h) collective investment undertakings and pension funds whether coordinated at Community level or not and the depositaries and managers of such undertakings;

(i) persons dealing on own account in financial instruments, or providing investment services in commodity derivatives or derivative contracts included in Annex I, Section C 10 to the clients of their main business, provided this is an ancillary activity to their main business, when considered on a group basis, and that main business is not the provision of investment services within the meaning of this Directive or banking services under Directive 2000/12/EC;

(j) persons providing investment advice in the course of providing another professional activity not covered by this Directive provided that the provision of such advice is not specifically remunerated;

(k) persons whose main business consists of dealing on own account in commodities and/or commodity derivatives. This exception shall not apply where the persons that deal on own account in commodities and/or commodity derivatives are part of a group the main business of which is the provision of other investment services within the meaning of this Directive or banking services under Directive 2000/12/EC;

(l) firms which provide investment services and/or perform investment activities consisting exclusively in dealing on own account on markets in financial futures or options or other derivatives and on cash markets for the sole purpose of hedging positions on derivatives markets or which deal for the accounts of other members of those markets or make prices for them and which are guaranteed by clearing members of the same markets, where responsibility for ensuring the performance of contracts entered into by such firms is assumed by clearing members of the same markets;

(m) associations set up by Danish and Finnish pension funds with the sole aim of managing the assets of pension funds that are members of those associations;

(n) 'agenti di cambio' whose activities and functions are governed by Article 201 of Italian Legislative Decree No 58 of 24 February 1998.

2. The rights conferred by this Directive shall not extend to the provision of services as counterparty in transactions carried out by public bodies dealing with public debt or by members of the European System of Central Banks performing their tasks as provided for by the Treaty and the Statute of the European System of Central Banks and of the European Central Bank or performing equivalent functions under national provisions.

3. In order to take account of developments on financial markets, and to ensure the uniform application of this Directive, the Commission, ... may, in respect of exemptions (c)(i), and (k) define the criteria for determining when an activity is to be considered as ancillary to the main business on a group level as well as for determining when an activity is provided in an incidental manner. [Those measures, designed to amend non-essential elements of this Directive by supplementing it, shall be adopted in accordance with the regulatory procedure with scrutiny referred to in Article 64(2).]

[5523]

NOTES

Para 3: words omitted repealed, and words in square brackets added, by European Parliament and Council Directive 2008/10/EC, Art 1(1), as from 20 March 2008.

Article 3
Optional exemptions

1. Member States may choose not to apply this Directive to any persons for which they are the home Member State that:

— are not allowed to hold clients' funds or securities and which for that reason are not allowed at any time to place themselves in debit with their clients, and

— are not allowed to provide any investment service except the reception and transmission of orders in transferable securities and units in collective investment undertakings and the provision of investment advice in relation to such financial instruments, and

— in the course of providing that service, are allowed to transmit orders only to:

    (i) investment firms authorised in accordance with this Directive;

    (ii) credit institutions authorised in accordance with Directive 2000/12/EC;

    (iii) branches of investment firms or of credit institutions which are authorised in a third country and which are subject to and comply with prudential rules considered by the competent authorities to be at least as stringent as those laid down in this Directive, in Directive 2000/12/EC or in Directive 93/6/EEC;

    (iv) collective investment undertakings authorised under the law of a Member State to market units to the public and to the managers of such undertakings;

    (v) investment companies with fixed capital, as defined in Article 15(4) of Second Council Directive 77/91/EEC of 13 December 1976 on coordination of safeguards which, for the protection of the interests of members and others, are required by Member States of companies within the meaning of the second paragraph of Article 58 of the Treaty, in respect of the formation of public limited liability companies and the maintenance and alteration of their capital, with a view to making such safeguards equivalent,[1] the securities of which are listed or dealt in on a regulated market in a Member State;

provided that the activities of those persons are regulated at national level.

2. Persons excluded from the scope of this Directive according to paragraph 1 cannot benefit from the freedom to provide services and/or activities or to establish branches as provided for in Articles 31 and 32 respectively.

[5524]

NOTES

[1] OJ L26, 31.1.1977, p 1. Directive as last amended by the 1994 Act of Accession.

Article 4
Definitions

1. For the purposes of this Directive, the following definitions shall apply:

  1) 'Investment firm' means any legal person whose regular occupation or business is the provision of one or more investment services to third parties and/or the performance of one or more investment activities on a professional basis;

Member States may include in the definition of investment firms undertakings which are not legal persons, provided that:

    (a) their legal status ensures a level of protection for third parties' interests equivalent to that afforded by legal persons, and

    (b) they are subject to equivalent prudential supervision appropriate to their legal form.

However, where a natural person provides services involving the holding of third parties' funds or transferable securities, he may be considered as an investment firm for the purposes of this Directive only if, without prejudice to the other requirements imposed in this Directive and in Directive 93/6/EEC, he complies with the following conditions:

    (a) the ownership rights of third parties in instruments and funds must be safeguarded, especially in the event of the insolvency of the firm or of its proprietors, seizure, set-off or any other action by creditors of the firm or of its proprietors;

    (b) the firm must be subject to rules designed to monitor the firm's solvency and that of its proprietors;

    (c) the firm's annual accounts must be audited by one or more persons empowered, under national law, to audit accounts;

    (d) where the firm has only one proprietor, he must make provision for the protection of investors in the event of the firm's cessation of business following his death, his incapacity or any other such event;

  2) 'Investment services and activities' means any of the services and activities listed in Section A of Annex I relating to any of the instruments listed in Section C of Annex I; The Commission shall determine, ...:

— the derivative contracts mentioned in Section C 7 of Annex I that have the characteristics of other derivative financial instruments, having regard to whether, inter alia, they are cleared and settled through recognised clearing houses or are subject to regular margin calls

— the derivative contracts mentioned in Section C 10 of Annex I that have the characteristics of other derivative financial instruments, having regard to whether, inter alia, they are traded on a regulated market or an MTF, are cleared and settled through recognised clearing houses or are subject to regular margin calls;

3) 'Ancillary service' means any of the services listed in Section B of Annex I;

4) 'Investment advice' means the provision of personal recommendations to a client, either upon its request or at the initiative of the investment firm, in respect of one or more transactions relating to financial instruments;

5) 'Execution of orders on behalf of clients' means acting to conclude agreements to buy or sell one or more financial instruments on behalf of clients;

6) 'Dealing on own account' means trading against proprietary capital resulting in the conclusion of transactions in one or more financial instruments;

7) 'Systematic internaliser' means an investment firm which, on an organised, frequent and systematic basis, deals on own account by executing client orders outside a regulated market or an MTF;

8) 'Market maker' means a person who holds himself out on the financial markets on a continuous basis as being willing to deal on own account by buying and selling financial instruments against his proprietary capital at prices defined by him;

9) 'Portfolio management' means managing portfolios in accordance with mandates given by clients on a discretionary client-by-client basis where such portfolios include one or more financial instruments;

10) 'Client' means any natural or legal person to whom an investment firm provides investment and/or ancillary services;

11) 'Professional client' means a client meeting the criteria laid down in Annex II;

12) 'Retail client' means a client who is not a professional client;

13) 'Market operator' means a person or persons who manages and/or operates the business of a regulated market. The market operator may be the regulated market itself;

14) 'Regulated market' means a multilateral system operated and/or managed by a market operator, which brings together or facilitates the bringing together of multiple third party buying and selling interests in financial instruments – in the system and in accordance with its non-discretionary rules – in a way that results in a contract, in respect of the financial instruments admitted to trading under its rules and/or systems, and which is authorised and functions regularly and in accordance with the provisions of Title III;

15) 'Multilateral trading facility (MTF)' means a multilateral system, operated by an investment firm or a market operator, which brings together multiple third-party buying and selling interests in financial instruments – in the system and in accordance with non discretionary rules – in a way that results in a contract in accordance with the provisions of Title II;

16) 'Limit order' means an order to buy or sell a financial instrument at its specified price limit or better and for a specified size;

17) 'Financial instrument' means those instruments specified in Section C of Annex I;

18) 'Transferable securities' means those classes of securities which are negotiable on the capital market, with the exception of instruments of payment, such as:

(a) shares in companies and other securities equivalent to shares in companies, partnerships or other entities, and depositary receipts in respect of shares;

(b) bonds or other forms of securitised debt, including depositary receipts in respect of such securities;

(c) any other securities giving the right to acquire or sell any such transferable securities or giving rise to a cash settlement determined by reference to transferable securities, currencies, interest rates or yields, commodities or other indices or measures;

19) 'Money-market instruments' means those classes of instruments which are normally dealt in on the money market, such as treasury bills, certificates of deposit and commercial papers and excluding instruments of payment;

20) 'Home Member State' means:

(a) in the case of investment firms:

    (i) if the investment firm is a natural person, the Member State in which its head office is situated;

    (ii) if the investment firm is a legal person, the Member State in which its registered office is situated;

    (iii) if the investment firm has, under its national law, no registered office, the Member State in which its head office is situated;

(b) in the case of a regulated market, the Member State in which the regulated market is registered or, if under the law of that Member State it has no registered office, the Member State in which the head office of the regulated market is situated;

21) 'Host Member State' means the Member State, other than the home Member State, in which an investment firm has a branch or performs services and/or activities or the Member State in which a regulated market provides appropriate arrangements so as to facilitate access to trading on its system by remote members or participants established in that same Member State;

22) 'Competent authority' means the authority, designated by each Member State in accordance with Article 48, unless otherwise specified in this Directive;

23) 'Credit institutions' means credit institutions as defined under Directive 2000/12/EC;

24) 'UCITS management company' means a management company as defined in Council Directive 85/611/EEC of 20 December 1985, on the coordination of laws, regulations and administrative provisions relating to undertakings for collective investment in transferable securities (UCITS);[1]

25) 'Tied agent' means a natural or legal person who, under the full and unconditional responsibility of only one investment firm on whose behalf it acts, promotes investment and/or ancillary services to clients or prospective clients, receives and transmits instructions or orders from the client in respect of investment services or financial instruments, places financial instruments and/or provides advice to clients or prospective clients in respect of those financial instruments or services;

26) 'Branch' means a place of business other than the head office which is a part of an investment firm, which has no legal personality and which provides investment services and/or activities and which may also perform ancillary services for which the investment firm has been authorised; all the places of business set up in the same Member State by an investment firm with headquarters in another Member State shall be regarded as a single branch;

[27) 'Qualifying holding' means any direct or indirect holding in an investment firm which represents 10% or more of the capital or of the voting rights, as set out in Articles 9 and 10 of Directive 2004/109/EC,* taking into account the conditions regarding aggregation thereof laid down in Article 12(4) and (5) of that Directive, or which makes it possible to exercise a significant influence over the management of the investment firm in which that holding subsists;]

28) 'Parent undertaking' means a parent undertaking as defined in Articles 1 and 2 of Seventh Council Directive 83/349/EEC of 13 June 1983 on consolidated accounts;[2]

29) 'Subsidiary' means a subsidiary undertaking as defined in Articles 1 and 2 of Directive 83/349/EEC, including any subsidiary of a subsidiary undertaking of an ultimate parent undertaking;

30) 'Control' means control as defined in Article 1 of Directive 83/349/EEC;

31) 'Close links' means a situation in which two or more natural or legal persons are linked by:
(a) participation which means the ownership, direct or by way of control, of 20% or more of the voting rights or capital of an undertaking,
(b) control which means the relationship between a parent undertaking and a subsidiary, in all the cases referred to in Article 1(1) and (2) of Directive 83/349/EEC, or a similar relationship between any natural or legal person and an undertaking, any subsidiary undertaking of a subsidiary undertaking also being considered a subsidiary of the parent undertaking which is at the head of those undertakings.

A situation in which two or more natural or legal persons are permanently linked to one and the same person by a control relationship shall also be regarded as constituting a close link between such persons.

2. In order to take account of developments on financial markets, and to ensure the uniform application of this Directive, the Commission, ... may clarify the definitions laid down in paragraph 1 of this Article.

[The measures referred to in this Article, designed to amend non-essential elements of this Directive by supplementing it, shall be adopted in accordance with the regulatory procedure with scrutiny referred to in Article 64(2).]

[5525]

PART IV
EC MATERIALS

NOTES

Para 1 is amended as follows

Words omitted from point 2) repealed by European Parliament and Council Directive 2008/10/EC, Art 1(2)(a), as from 20 March 2008.

Point 27) substituted by European Parliament and Council Directive 2007/44/EC, Art 3(1), as from 21 September 2007. Note that the 2007 Directive has a transposition date of 21 March 2009, and that the original point 27) read as follows—

"27) 'Qualifying holding' means any direct or indirect holding in an investment firm which represents

10% or more of the capital or of the voting rights, as set out in Article 92 of Directive 2001/34/EC, or which makes it possible to exercise a significant influence over the management of the investment firm in which that holding subsists;".

Para 2: words omitted repealed, and words in square brackets added, by European Parliament and Council Directive 2008/10/EC, Art 1(2)(b), as from 20 March 2008.

¹   OJ L375, 31.12.1985, p 3. Directive as last amended by Directive 2001/108/EC of the European Parliament and of the Council (OJ L41, 13.2.2002, p 35).
*   Directive 2004/109/EC of the European Parliament and of the Council of 15 December 2004 on the harmonisation of transparency requirements in relation to information about issuers whose securities are admitted to trading on a regulated market (OJ L390, 31.12.2004, p 38).
²   OJ L193, 18.7.1983, p 1. Directive as last amended by Directive 2003/51/EC of the European Parliament and of the Council (OJ L178, 17.7.2003, p 16).

TITLE II
AUTHORISATION AND OPERATING CONDITIONS FOR INVESTMENT FIRMS

CHAPTER I
CONDITIONS AND PROCEDURES FOR AUTHORISATION

Article 5
Requirement for authorisation

1.   Each Member State shall require that the performance of investment services or activities as a regular occupation or business on a professional basis be subject to prior authorisation in accordance with the provisions of this Chapter. Such authorisation shall be granted by the home Member State competent authority designated in accordance with Article 48.

2.   By way of derogation from paragraph 1, Member States shall allow any market operator to operate an MTF, subject to the prior verification of their compliance with the provisions of this Chapter, excluding Articles 11 and 15.

3.   Member States shall establish a register of all investment firms. This register shall be publicly accessible and shall contain information on the services and/or activities for which the investment firm is authorised. It shall be updated on a regular basis.

4.   Each Member State shall require that:
—   any investment firm which is a legal person have its head office in the same Member State as its registered office,
—   any investment firm which is not a legal person or any investment firm which is a legal person but under its national law has no registered office have its head office in the Member State in which it actually carries on its business.

5.   In the case of investment firms which provide only investment advice or the service of reception and transmission of orders under the conditions established in Article 3, Member States may allow the competent authority to delegate administrative, preparatory or ancillary tasks related to the granting of an authorisation, in accordance with the conditions laid down in Article 48(2).

[5526]

Article 6
Scope of authorisation

1.   The home Member State shall ensure that the authorisation specifies the investment services or activities which the investment firm is authorised to provide. The authorisation may cover one or more of the ancillary services set out in Section B of Annex I. Authorisation shall in no case be granted solely for the provision of ancillary services.

2.   An investment firm seeking authorisation to extend its business to additional investment services or activities or ancillary services not foreseen at the time of initial authorisation shall submit a request for extension of its authorisation.

3.   The authorisation shall be valid for the entire Community and shall allow an investment firm to provide the services or perform the activities, for which it has been authorised, throughout the Community, either through the establishment of a branch or the free provision of services.

[5527]

Article 7
Procedures for granting and refusing requests for authorisation

1.   The competent authority shall not grant authorisation unless and until such time as it is fully satisfied that the applicant complies with all requirements under the provisions adopted pursuant to this Directive.

2.   The investment firm shall provide all information, including a programme of operations setting out inter alia the types of business envisaged and the organisational structure, necessary to

enable the competent authority to satisfy itself that the investment firm has established, at the time of initial authorisation, all the necessary arrangements to meet its obligations under the provisions of this Chapter.

3. An applicant shall be informed, within six months of the submission of a complete application, whether or not authorisation has been granted.

[5528]

Article 8
Withdrawal of authorisations

The competent authority may withdraw the authorisation issued to an investment firm where such an investment firm:

(a) does not make use of the authorisation within 12 months, expressly renounces the authorisation or has provided no investment services or performed no investment activity for the preceding six months, unless the Member State concerned has provided for authorisation to lapse in such cases;

(b) has obtained the authorisation by making false statements or by any other irregular means;

(c) no longer meets the conditions under which authorisation was granted, such as compliance with the conditions set out in Directive 93/6/EEC;

(d) has seriously and systematically infringed the provisions adopted pursuant to this Directive governing the operating conditions for investment firms;

(e) falls within any of the cases where national law, in respect of matters outside the scope of this Directive, provides for withdrawal.

[5529]

Article 9
Persons who effectively direct the business

1. Member States shall require the persons who effectively direct the business of an investment firm to be of sufficiently good repute and sufficiently experienced as to ensure the sound and prudent management of the investment firm.

Where the market operator that seeks authorisation to operate an MTF and the persons that effectively direct the business of the MTF are the same as those that effectively direct the business of the regulated market, those persons are deemed to comply with the requirements laid down in the first subparagraph.

2. Member States shall require the investment firm to notify the competent authority of any changes to its management, along with all information needed to assess whether the new staff appointed to manage the firm are of sufficiently good repute and sufficiently experienced.

3. The competent authority shall refuse authorisation if it is not satisfied that the persons who will effectively direct the business of the investment firm are of sufficiently good repute or sufficiently experienced, or if there are objective and demonstrable grounds for believing that proposed changes to the management of the firm pose a threat to its sound and prudent management.

4. Member States shall require that the management of investment firms is undertaken by at least two persons meeting the requirements laid down in paragraph 1.

By way of derogation from the first subparagraph, Member States may grant authorisation to investment firms that are natural persons or to investment firms that are legal persons managed by a single natural person in accordance with their constitutive rules and national laws. Member States shall nevertheless require that alternative arrangements be in place which ensure the sound and prudent management of such investment firms.

[5530]

Article 10
Shareholders and members with qualifying holdings

1. The competent authorities shall not authorise the performance of investment services or activities by an investment firm until they have been informed of the identities of the shareholders or members, whether direct or indirect, natural or legal persons, that have qualifying holdings and the amounts of those holdings.

The competent authorities shall refuse authorisation if, taking into account the need to ensure the sound and prudent management of an investment firm, they are not satisfied as to the suitability of the shareholders or members that have qualifying holdings.

Where close links exist between the investment firm and other natural or legal persons, the competent authority shall grant authorisation only if those links do not prevent the effective exercise of the supervisory functions of the competent authority.

2. The competent authority shall refuse authorisation if the laws, regulations or administrative provisions of a third country governing one or more natural or legal persons with which the undertaking has close links, or difficulties involved in their enforcement, prevent the effective exercise of its supervisory functions.

[3. Member States shall require any natural or legal person or such persons acting in concert (hereinafter referred to as the proposed acquirer), who have taken a decision either to acquire, directly or indirectly, a qualifying holding in an investment firm or to further increase, directly or indirectly, such a qualifying holding in an investment firm as a result of which the proportion of the voting rights or of the capital held would reach or exceed 20%, 30% or 50% or so that the investment firm would become its subsidiary (hereinafter referred to as the proposed acquisition), first to notify in writing the competent authorities of the investment firm in which they are seeking to acquire or increase a qualifying holding, indicating the size of the intended holding and relevant information, as referred to in Article 10b(4).

Member States shall require any natural or legal person who has taken a decision to dispose, directly or indirectly, of a qualifying holding in an investment firm first to notify in writing the competent authorities, indicating the size of the intended holding. Such a person shall likewise notify the competent authorities if he has taken a decision to reduce his qualifying holding so that the proportion of the voting rights or of the capital held would fall below 20%, 30% or 50% or so that the investment firm would cease to be his subsidiary.

Member States need not apply the 30% threshold where, in accordance with Article 9(3)(a) of Directive 2004/109/EC, they apply a threshold of one-third.

In determining whether the criteria for a qualifying holding referred to in this Article are fulfilled, Member States shall not take into account voting rights or shares which investment firms or credit institutions may hold as a result of providing the underwriting of financial instruments and/or placing of financial instruments on a firm commitment basis included under point 6 of Section A of Annex I, provided that those rights are, on the one hand, not exercised or otherwise used to intervene in the management of the issuer and, on the other, disposed of within one year of acquisition.

4. The relevant competent authorities shall work in full consultation with each other when carrying out the assessment provided for in Article 10b(1) (hereinafter referred to as the assessment) if the proposed acquirer is one of the following:

(a) a credit institution, assurance undertaking, insurance undertaking, reinsurance undertaking, investment firm or UCITS management company authorised in another Member State or in a sector other than that in which the acquisition is proposed;

(b) the parent undertaking of a credit institution, assurance undertaking, insurance undertaking, reinsurance undertaking, investment firm or UCITS management company authorised in another Member State or in a sector other than that in which the acquisition is proposed; or

(c) a natural or legal person controlling a credit institution, assurance undertaking, insurance undertaking, reinsurance undertaking, investment firm or UCITS management company authorised in another Member State or in a sector other than that in which the acquisition is proposed.

The competent authorities shall, without undue delay, provide each other with any information which is essential or relevant for the assessment. In this regard, the competent authorities shall communicate to each other upon request all relevant information and shall communicate on their own initiative all essential information. A decision by the competent authority that has authorised the investment firm in which the acquisition is proposed shall indicate any views or reservations expressed by the competent authority responsible for the proposed acquirer.]

5. Member States shall require that, if an investment firm becomes aware of any acquisitions or disposals of holdings in its capital that cause holdings to exceed or fall below any of the thresholds referred to in the first subparagraph of paragraph 3, that investment firm is to inform the competent authority without delay.

At least once a year, investment firms shall also inform the competent authority of the names of shareholders and members possessing qualifying holdings and the sizes of such holdings as shown, for example, by the information received at annual general meetings of shareholders and members or as a result of compliance with the regulations applicable to companies whose transferable securities are admitted to trading on a regulated market.

6. Member States shall require that, where the influence exercised by the persons referred to in the first subparagraph of paragraph 1 is likely to be prejudicial to the sound and prudent management of an investment firm, the competent authority take appropriate measures to put an end to that situation.

Such measures may consist in applications for judicial orders and/or the imposition of sanctions against directors and those responsible for management, or suspension of the exercise of the voting rights attaching to the shares held by the shareholders or members in question.

Similar measures shall be taken in respect of persons who fail to comply with the obligation to provide prior information in relation to the acquisition or increase of a qualifying holding. If a holding is acquired despite the opposition of the competent authorities, the Member States shall, regardless of any other sanctions to be adopted, provide either for exercise of the corresponding voting rights to be suspended, for the nullity of the votes cast or for the possibility of their annulment.

[5531]

NOTES

Paras 3, 4: substituted by European Parliament and Council Directive 2007/44/EC, Art 3(2), as from 21 September 2007. Note that the 2007 Directive has a transposition date of 21 March 2009, and that the original paragraphs read as follows—

"3. Member States shall require any natural or legal person that proposes to acquire or sell, directly or indirectly, a qualifying holding in an investment firm, first to notify, in accordance with the second subparagraph, the competent authority of the size of the resulting holding. Such persons shall likewise be required to notify the competent authority if they propose to increase or reduce their qualifying holding, if in consequence the proportion of the voting rights or of the capital that they hold would reach or fall below or exceed 20%, 33% or 50% or the investment firm would become or cease to be their subsidiary.

Without prejudice to paragraph 4, the competent authority shall have up to three months from the date of the notification of a proposed acquisition provided for in the first subparagraph to oppose such a plan if, in view of the need to ensure sound and prudent management of the investment firm, it is not satisfied as to the suitability of the persons referred to in the first subparagraph. If the competent authority does not oppose the plan, it may fix a deadline for its implementation.

4. If the acquirer of any holding referred to in paragraph 3 is an investment firm, a credit institution, an insurance under-taking or a UCITS management company authorised in another Member State, or the parent undertaking of an investment firm, credit institution, insurance undertaking or a UCITS management company authorised in another Member State, or a person controlling an investment firm, credit institution, insurance undertaking or a UCITS management company authorised in another Member State, and if, as a result of that acquisition, the undertaking would become the acquirer's subsidiary or come under his control, the assessment of the acquisition shall be subject to the prior consultation provided for in Article 60.".

[Article 10a
Assessment period

1. The competent authorities shall, promptly and in any event within two working days following receipt of the notification required under the first subparagraph of Article 10(3), as well as following the possible subsequent receipt of the information referred to in paragraph 2 of this Article, acknowledge receipt thereof in writing to the proposed acquirer.

The competent authorities shall have a maximum of sixty working days as from the date of the written acknowledgement of receipt of the notification and all documents required by the Member State to be attached to the notification on the basis of the list referred to in Article 10b(4) (hereinafter referred to as the assessment period), to carry out the assessment.

The competent authorities shall inform the proposed acquirer of the date of the expiry of the assessment period at the time of acknowledging receipt.

2. The competent authorities may, during the assessment period, if necessary, and no later than on the 50th working day of the assessment period, request any further information that is necessary to complete the assessment. Such request shall be made in writing and shall specify the additional information needed.

For the period between the date of request for information by the competent authorities and the receipt of a response thereto by the proposed acquirer, the assessment period shall be interrupted. The interruption shall not exceed 20 working days. Any further requests by the competent authorities for completion or clarification of the information shall be at their discretion but may not result in an interruption of the assessment period.

3. The competent authorities may extend the interruption referred to in the second subparagraph of paragraph 2 up to 30 working days if the proposed acquirer is:
    (a)   situated or regulated outside the Community; or
    (b)   a natural or legal person not subject to supervision under this Directive or Directives 85/611/EEC,[1] 92/49/EEC,[2] 2002/83/EC,[3] 2005/68/EC[4] or 2006/48/EC.[5]

4. If the competent authorities, upon completion of the assessment, decide to oppose the proposed acquisition, they shall, within two working days, and not exceeding the assessment period, inform the proposed acquirer in writing and provide the reasons for that decision. Subject to national law, an appropriate statement of the reasons for the decision may be made accessible to the public at the request of the proposed acquirer. This shall not prevent a Member State from allowing the competent authority to make such disclosure in the absence of a request by the proposed acquirer.

5. If the competent authorities do not oppose the proposed acquisition within the assessment period in writing, it shall be deemed to be approved.

6.   The competent authorities may fix a maximum period for concluding the proposed acquisition and extend it where appropriate.

7.   Member States may not impose requirements for the notification to and approval by the competent authorities of direct or indirect acquisitions of voting rights or capital that are more stringent than those set out in this Directive.]

[5531A]

NOTES
Inserted by European Parliament and Council Directive 2007/44/EC, Art 3(3), as from 21 September 2007. Note that the 2007 Directive has a transposition date of 21 March 2009.

[1]   Council Directive 85/611/EEC of 20 December 1985 on the coordination of laws, regulations and administrative provisions relating to undertakings for collective investment in transferable securities (UCITS) (OJ L375, 31.12.1985, p 3). Directive as last amended by Directive 2005/1/EC.

[2]   Council Directive 92/49/EEC of 18 June 1992 on the coordination of laws, regulations and administrative provisions relating to direct insurance other than life assurance (third non-life insurance Directive) (OJ L228, 11.8.1992, p 1). Directive as last amended by Directive 2007/44/EC.

[3]   Directive 2002/83/EC of the European Parliament and of the Council of 5 November 2002 concerning life assurance (OJ L345, 19.12.2002, p 1). Directive as last amended by Directive 2007/44/EC.

[4]   Directive 2005/68/EC of the European Parliament and of the Council of 16 November 2005 on reinsurance (OJ L323, 9.12.2005, p 1). Directive as amended by Directive 2007/44/EC.

[5]   Directive 2006/48/EC of the European Parliament and of the Council of 14 June 2006 relating to the taking up and pursuit of the business of credit institutions (recast) (OJ L177, 30.6.2006, p 1). Directive as last amended by Directive 2007/44/EC.

[Article 10b
Assessment

1.   In assessing the notification provided for in Article 10(3) and the information referred to in Article 10a(2), the competent authorities shall, in order to ensure the sound and prudent management of the investment firm in which an acquisition is proposed, and having regard to the likely influence of the proposed acquirer on the investment firm, appraise the suitability of the proposed acquirer and the financial soundness of the proposed acquisition against all of the following criteria:

(a)   the reputation of the proposed acquirer;

(b)   the reputation and experience of any person who will direct the business of the investment firm as a result of the proposed acquisition;

(c)   the financial soundness of the proposed acquirer, in particular in relation to the type of business pursued and envisaged in the investment firm in which the acquisition is proposed;

(d)   whether the investment firm will be able to comply and continue to comply with the prudential requirements based on this Directive and, where applicable, other Directives, notably, Directives 2002/87/EC[1] and 2006/49/EC,[2] in particular, whether the group of which it will become a part has a structure that makes it possible to exercise effective supervision, effectively exchange information among the competent authorities and determine the allocation of responsibilities among the competent authorities;

(e)   whether there are reasonable grounds to suspect that, in connection with the proposed acquisition, money laundering or terrorist financing within the meaning of Article 1 of Directive 2005/60/EC[3] is being or has been committed or attempted, or that the proposed acquisition could increase the risk thereof.

In order to take account of future developments and to ensure the uniform application of this Directive, the Commission, acting in accordance with the procedure referred to in Article 64(2), may adopt implementing measures which adjust the criteria set out in the first subparagraph of this paragraph.

2.   The competent authorities may oppose the proposed acquisition only if there are reasonable grounds for doing so on the basis of the criteria set out in paragraph 1 or if the information provided by the proposed acquirer is incomplete.

3.   Member States shall neither impose any prior conditions in respect of the level of holding that must be acquired nor allow their competent authorities to examine the proposed acquisition in terms of the economic needs of the market.

4.   Member States shall make publicly available a list specifying the information that is necessary to carry out the assessment and that must be provided to the competent authorities at the time of notification referred to in Article 10(3). The information required shall be proportionate and adapted to the nature of the proposed acquirer and the proposed acquisition. Member States shall not require information that is not relevant for a prudential assessment.

5.   Notwithstanding Article 10a(1), (2) and (3), where two or more proposals to acquire or increase qualifying holdings in the same investment firm have been notified to the competent authority, the latter shall treat the proposed acquirers in a non-discriminatory manner.]

[5531B]

NOTES
   Inserted by European Parliament and Council Directive 2007/44/EC, Art 3(3), as from 21 September 2007. Note that the 2007 Directive has a transposition date of 21 March 2009.
1   Directive 2002/87/EC of the European Parliament and of the Council of 16 December 2002 on the supplementary supervision of credit institutions, insurance undertakings and investment firms in a financial conglomerate (OJ L359, 11.2.2003, p 1). Directive as amended by Directive 2005/1/EC (OJ L79, 24.3.2005, p 9).
2   Directive 2006/49/EC of the European Parliament and of the Council of 14 June 2006 on the capital adequacy of investment firms and credit institutions (recast) (OJ L177, 30.6.2006, p 201).
3   Directive 2005/60/EC of the European Parliament and of the Council of 26 October 2005 on the prevention of the use of financial system for the purpose of money laundering and terrorist financing (OJ L309, 25.11.2005, p 15).

Article 11
Membership of an authorised Investor Compensation Scheme

The competent authority shall verify that any entity seeking authorisation as an investment firm meets its obligations under Directive 97/9/EC of the European Parliament and of the Council of 3 March 1997 on investor-compensation schemes[1] at the time of authorisation.

[5532]

NOTES
1   OJ L84, 26.3.1997, p. 22.

Article 12
Initial capital endowment

Member States shall ensure that the competent authorities do not grant authorisation unless the investment firm has sufficient initial capital in accordance with the requirements of Directive 93/6/EEC having regard to the nature of the investment service or activity in question.

Pending the revision of Directive 93/6/EEC, the investment firms provided for in Article 67 shall be subject to the capital requirements laid down in that Article.

[5533]

Article 13
Organisational requirements

1.   The home Member State shall require that investment firms comply with the organisational requirements set out in paragraphs 2 to 8.

2.   An investment firm shall establish adequate policies and procedures sufficient to ensure compliance of the firm including its managers, employees and tied agents with its obligations under the provisions of this Directive as well as appropriate rules governing personal transactions by such persons.

3.   An investment firm shall maintain and operate effective organisational and administrative arrangements with a view to taking all reasonable steps designed to prevent conflicts of interest as defined in Article 18 from adversely affecting the interests of its clients.

4.   An investment firm shall take reasonable steps to ensure continuity and regularity in the performance of investment services and activities. To this end the investment firm shall employ appropriate and proportionate systems, resources and procedures.

5.   An investment firm shall ensure, when relying on a third party for the performance of operational functions which are critical for the provision of continuous and satisfactory service to clients and the performance of investment activities on a continuous and satisfactory basis, that it takes reasonable steps to avoid undue additional operational risk. Outsourcing of important operational functions may not be undertaken in such a way as to impair materially the quality of its internal control and the ability of the supervisor to monitor the firm's compliance with all obligations.

An investment firm shall have sound administrative and accounting procedures, internal control mechanisms, effective procedures for risk assessment, and effective control and safeguard arrangements for information processing systems.

6.   An investment firm shall arrange for records to be kept of all services and transactions undertaken by it which shall be sufficient to enable the competent authority to monitor compliance with the requirements under this Directive, and in particular to ascertain that the investment firm has complied with all obligations with respect to clients or potential clients.

PART IV
EC MATERIALS

7.   An investment firm shall, when holding financial instruments belonging to clients, make adequate arrangements so as to safeguard clients' ownership rights, especially in the event of the investment firm's insolvency, and to prevent the use of a client's instruments on own account except with the client's express consent.

8.   An investment firm shall, when holding funds belonging to clients, make adequate arrangements to safeguard the clients' rights and, except in the case of credit institutions, prevent the use of client funds for its own account.

9.   In the case of branches of investment firms, the competent authority of the Member State in which the branch is located shall, without prejudice to the possibility of the competent authority of the home Member State of the investment firm to have direct access to those records, enforce the obligation laid down in paragraph 6 with regard to transactions undertaken by the branch.

10.   In order to take account of technical developments on financial markets and to ensure the uniform application of paragraphs 2 to 9, the Commission shall adopt, … implementing measures which specify the concrete organisational requirements to be imposed on investment firms performing different investment services and/or activities and ancillary services or combinations thereof. [Those measures, designed to amend non-essential elements of this Directive by supplementing it, shall be adopted in accordance with the regulatory procedure with scrutiny referred to in Article 64(2).]

[5534]

NOTES

Para 10: words omitted repealed, and words in square brackets added, by European Parliament and Council Directive 2008/10/EC, Art 1(3), as from 20 March 2008.

Article 14
Trading process and finalisation of transactions in an MTF

1.   Member States shall require that investment firms or market operators operating an MTF, in addition to meeting the requirements laid down in Article 13, establish transparent and non-discretionary rules and procedures for fair and orderly trading and establish objective criteria for the efficient execution of orders.

2.   Member States shall require that investment firms or market operators operating an MTF establish transparent rules regarding the criteria for determining the financial instruments that can be traded under its systems.

Member States shall require that, where applicable, investment firms or market operators operating an MTF provide, or are satisfied that there is access to, sufficient publicly available information to enable its users to form an investment judgement, taking into account both the nature of the users and the types of instruments traded.

3.   Member States shall ensure that Articles 19, 21 and 22 are not applicable to the transactions concluded under the rules governing an MTF between its members or participants or between the MTF and its members or participants in relation to the use of the MTF. However, the members of or participants in the MTF shall comply with the obligations provided for in Articles 19, 21 and 22 with respect to their clients when, acting on behalf of their clients, they execute their orders through the systems of an MTF.

4.   Member States shall require that investment firms or market operators operating an MTF establish and maintain transparent rules, based on objective criteria, governing access to its facility. These rules shall comply with the conditions established in Article 42(3).

5.   Member States shall require that investment firms or market operators operating an MTF clearly inform its users of their respective responsibilities for the settlement of the transactions executed in that facility. Member States shall require that investment firms or market operators operating an MTF have put in place the necessary arrangements to facilitate the efficient settlement of the transactions concluded under the systems of the MTF.

6.   Where a transferable security, which has been admitted to trading on a regulated market, is also traded on an MTF without the consent of the issuer, the issuer shall not be subject to any obligation relating to initial, ongoing or ad hoc financial disclosure with regard to that MTF.

7.   Member States shall require that any investment firm or market operator operating an MTF comply immediately with any instruction from its competent authority pursuant to Article 50(1) to suspend or remove a financial instrument from trading.

[5535]

Article 15
Relations with third countries

1.   Member States shall inform the Commission of any general difficulties which their investment firms encounter in establishing themselves or providing investment services and/or performing investment activities in any third country.

2. Whenever it appears to the Commission, on the basis of information submitted to it under paragraph 1, that a third country does not grant Community investment firms effective market access comparable to that granted by the Community to investment firms from that third country, the Commission may submit proposals to the Council for an appropriate mandate for negotiation with a view to obtaining comparable competitive opportunities for Community investment firms. The Council shall act by a qualified majority.

3. Whenever it appears to the Commission, on the basis of information submitted to it under paragraph 1, that Community investment firms in a third country are not granted national treatment affording the same competitive opportunities as are available to domestic investment firms and that the conditions of effective market access are not fulfilled, the Commission may initiate negotiations in order to remedy the situation.

In the circumstances referred to in the first subparagraph, the Commission may decide, [in accordance with the regulatory procedure referred to in Article 64(3),] at any time and in addition to the initiation of negotiations, that the competent authorities of the Member States must limit or suspend their decisions regarding requests pending or future requests for authorisation and the acquisition of holdings by direct or indirect parent undertakings governed by the law of the third country in question. Such limitations or suspensions may not be applied to the setting-up of subsidiaries by investment firms duly authorised in the Community or by their subsidiaries, or to the acquisition of holdings in Community investment firms by such firms or subsidiaries. The duration of such measures may not exceed three months.

Before the end of the three-month period referred to in the second subparagraph and in the light of the results of the negotiations, the Commission may decide, [in accordance with the regulatory procedure referred to in Article 64(3),] to extend these measures.

4. Whenever it appears to the Commission that one of the situations referred to in paragraphs 2 and 3 obtains, the Member States shall inform it at its request:
    (a)   of any application for the authorisation of any firm which is the direct or indirect subsidiary of a parent undertaking governed by the law of the third country in question;
    (b)   whenever they are informed in accordance with Article 10(3) that such a parent undertaking proposes to acquire a holding in a Community investment firm, in consequence of which the latter would become its subsidiary.

That obligation to provide information shall lapse whenever agreement is reached with the third country concerned or when the measures referred to in the second and third subparagraphs of paragraph 3 cease to apply.

5. Measures taken under this Article shall comply with the Community's obligations under any international agreements, bilateral or multilateral, governing the taking-up or pursuit of the business of investment firms.

[5536]

NOTES
    Para 3: words in square brackets substituted by European Parliament and Council Directive 2008/10/EC, Art 1(4), as from 20 March 2008.

CHAPTER II
OPERATING CONDITIONS FOR INVESTMENT FIRMS

SECTION 1
GENERAL PROVISIONS

Article 16
Regular review of conditions for initial authorisation

1. Member States shall require that an investment firm authorised in their territory comply at all times with the conditions for initial authorisation established in Chapter I of this Title.

2. Member States shall require competent authorities to establish the appropriate methods to monitor that investment firms comply with their obligation under paragraph 1. They shall require investment firms to notify the competent authorities of any material changes to the conditions for initial authorisation.

3. In the case of investment firms which provide only investment advice, Member States may allow the competent authority to delegate administrative, preparatory or ancillary tasks related to the review of the conditions for initial authorisation, in accordance with the conditions laid down in Article 48(2).

[5537]

Article 17
General obligation in respect of on-going supervision

1. Member States shall ensure that the competent authorities monitor the activities of investment firms so as to assess compliance with the operating conditions provided for in this Directive. Member States shall ensure that the appropriate measures are in place to enable the competent authorities to obtain the information needed to assess the compliance of investment firms with those obligations.

2. In the case of investment firms which provide only investment advice, Member States may allow the competent authority to delegate administrative, preparatory or ancillary tasks related to the regular monitoring of operational requirements, in accordance with the conditions laid down in Article 48(2).

[5538]

Article 18
Conflicts of interest

1. Member States shall require investment firms to take all reasonable steps to identify conflicts of interest between themselves, including their managers, employees and tied agents, or any person directly or indirectly linked to them by control and their clients or between one client and another that arise in the course of providing any investment and ancillary services, or combinations thereof.

2. Where organisational or administrative arrangements made by the investment firm in accordance with Article 13(3) to manage conflicts of interest are not sufficient to ensure, with reasonable confidence, that risks of damage to client interests will be prevented, the investment firm shall clearly disclose the general nature and/or sources of conflicts of interest to the client before undertaking business on its behalf.

3. In order to take account of technical developments on financial markets and to ensure uniform application of paragraphs 1 and 2, the Commission shall adopt, ... implementing measures to:
  (a) define the steps that investment firms might reasonably be expected to take to identify, prevent, manage and/or disclose conflicts of interest when providing various investment and ancillary services and combinations thereof;
  (b) establish appropriate criteria for determining the types of conflict of interest whose existence may damage the interests of the clients or potential clients of the investment firm.

[The measures referred to in the first subparagraph, designed to amend non-essential elements of this Directive by supplementing it, shall be adopted in accordance with the regulatory procedure with scrutiny referred to in Article 64(2).]

[5539]

NOTES

Para 3: words omitted repealed, and words in square brackets added, by European Parliament and Council Directive 2008/10/EC, Art 1(5), as from 20 March 2008.

SECTION 2
PROVISIONS TO ENSURE INVESTOR PROTECTION

Article 19
Conduct of business obligations when providing investment services to clients

1. Member States shall require that, when providing investment services and/or, where appropriate, ancillary services to clients, an investment firm act honestly, fairly and professionally in accordance with the best interests of its clients and comply, in particular, with the principles set out in paragraphs 2 to 8.

2. All information, including marketing communications, addressed by the investment firm to clients or potential clients shall be fair, clear and not misleading. Marketing communications shall be clearly identifiable as such.

3. Appropriate information shall be provided in a comprehensible form to clients or potential clients about:
  — the investment firm and its services,
  — financial instruments and proposed investment strategies; this should include appropriate guidance on and warnings of the risks associated with investments in those instruments or in respect of particular investment strategies,
  — execution venues, and
  — costs and associated charges

so that they are reasonably able to understand the nature and risks of the investment service and of the specific type of financial instrument that is being offered and, consequently, to take investment decisions on an informed basis. This information may be provided in a standardised format.

4.   When providing investment advice or portfolio management the investment firm shall obtain the necessary information regarding the client's or potential client's knowledge and experience in the investment field relevant to the specific type of product or service, his financial situation and his investment objectives so as to enable the firm to recommend to the client or potential client the investment services and financial instruments that are suitable for him.

5.   Member States shall ensure that investment firms, when providing investment services other than those referred to in paragraph 4, ask the client or potential client to provide information regarding his knowledge and experience in the investment field relevant to the specific type of product or service offered or demanded so as to enable the investment firm to assess whether the investment service or product envisaged is appropriate for the client.

In case the investment firm considers, on the basis of the information received under the previous subparagraph, that the product or service is not appropriate to the client or potential client, the investment firm shall warn the client or potential client. This warning may be provided in a standardised format.

In cases where the client or potential client elects not to provide the information referred to under the first subparagraph, or where he provides insufficient information regarding his knowledge and experience, the investment firm shall warn the client or potential client that such a decision will not allow the firm to determine whether the service or product envisaged is appropriate for him. This warning may be provided in a standardised format.

6.   Member States shall allow investment firms when providing investment services that only consist of execution and/or the reception and transmission of client orders with or without ancillary services to provide those investment services to their clients without the need to obtain the information or make the determination provided for in paragraph 5 where all the following conditions are met:

—   the above services relate to shares admitted to trading on a regulated market or in an equivalent third country market, money market instruments, bonds or other forms of securitised debt (excluding those bonds or securitised debt that embed a derivative), UCITS and other non-complex financial instruments. A third country market shall be considered as equivalent to a regulated market if it complies with equivalent requirements to those established under Title III. The Commission shall publish a list of those markets that are to be considered as equivalent. This list shall be updated periodically,

—   the service is provided at the initiative of the client or potential client,

—   the client or potential client has been clearly informed that in the provision of this service the investment firm is not required to assess the suitability of the instrument or service provided or offered and that therefore he does not benefit from the corresponding protection of the relevant conduct of business rules; this warning may be provided in a standardised format,

—   the investment firm complies with its obligations under Article 18.

7.   The investment firm shall establish a record that includes the document or documents agreed between the firm and the client that set out the rights and obligations of the parties, and the other terms on which the firm will provide services to the client. The rights and duties of the parties to the contract may be incorporated by reference to other documents or legal texts.

8.   The client must receive from the investment firm adequate reports on the service provided to its clients. These reports shall include, where applicable, the costs associated with the transactions and services undertaken on behalf of the client.

9.   In cases where an investment service is offered as part of a financial product which is already subject to other provisions of Community legislation or common European standards related to credit institutions and consumer credits with respect to risk assessment of clients and/or information requirements, this service shall not be additionally subject to the obligations set out in this Article.

10.   In order to ensure the necessary protection of investors and the uniform application of paragraphs 1 to 8, the Commission shall adopt, … implementing measures to ensure that investment firms comply with the principles set out therein when providing investment or ancillary services to their clients. Those implementing measures shall take into account:

(a)   the nature of the service(s) offered or provided to the client or potential client, taking into account the type, object, size and frequency of the transactions;

(b)   the nature of the financial instruments being offered or considered;

(c)   the retail or professional nature of the client or potential clients.

[The measures referred to in the first subparagraph, designed to amend non-essential elements of this Directive by supplementing it, shall be adopted in accordance with the regulatory procedure with scrutiny referred to in Article 64(2).]

NOTES

Para 10: words omitted repealed, and words in square brackets added, by European Parliament and Council Directive 2008/10/EC, Art 1(6), as from 20 March 2008.

Article 20
Provision of services through the medium of another investment firm

Member States shall allow an investment firm receiving an instruction to perform investment or ancillary services on behalf of a client through the medium of another investment firm to rely on client information transmitted by the latter firm. The investment firm which mediates the instructions will remain responsible for the completeness and accuracy of the information transmitted.

The investment firm which receives an instruction to undertake services on behalf of a client in this way shall also be able to rely on any recommendations in respect of the service or transaction that have been provided to the client by another investment firm. The investment firm which mediates the instructions will remain responsible for the appropriateness for the client of the recommendations or advice provided.

The investment firm which receives client instructions or orders through the medium of another investment firm shall remain responsible for concluding the service or transaction, based on any such information or recommendations, in accordance with the relevant provisions of this Title.

[5541]

Article 21
Obligation to execute orders on terms most favourable to the client

1. Member States shall require that investment firms take all reasonable steps to obtain, when executing orders, the best possible result for their clients taking into account price, costs, speed, likelihood of execution and settlement, size, nature or any other consideration relevant to the execution of the order. Nevertheless, whenever there is a specific instruction from the client the investment firm shall execute the order following the specific instruction.

2. Member States shall require investment firms to establish and implement effective arrangements for complying with paragraph 1. In particular Member States shall require investment firms to establish and implement an order execution policy to allow them to obtain, for their client orders, the best possible result in accordance with paragraph 1.

3. The order execution policy shall include, in respect of each class of instruments, information on the different venues where the investment firm executes its client orders and the factors affecting the choice of execution venue. It shall at least include those venues that enable the investment firm to obtain on a consistent basis the best possible result for the execution of client orders.

Member States shall require that investment firms provide appropriate information to their clients on their order execution policy. Member States shall require that investment firms obtain the prior consent of their clients to the execution policy.

Member States shall require that, where the order execution policy provides for the possibility that client orders may be executed outside a regulated market or an MTF, the investment firm shall, in particular, inform its clients about this possibility. Member States shall require that investment firms obtain the prior express consent of their clients before proceeding to execute their orders outside a regulated market or an MTF. Investment firms may obtain this consent either in the form of a general agreement or in respect of individual transactions.

4. Member States shall require investment firms to monitor the effectiveness of their order execution arrangements and execution policy in order to identify and, where appropriate, correct any deficiencies. In particular, they shall assess, on a regular basis, whether the execution venues included in the order execution policy provide for the best possible result for the client or whether they need to make changes to their execution arrangements. Member States shall require investment firms to notify clients of any material changes to their order execution arrangements or execution policy.

5. Member States shall require investment firms to be able to demonstrate to their clients, at their request, that they have executed their orders in accordance with the firm's execution policy.

6. In order to ensure the protection necessary for investors, the fair and orderly functioning of markets, and to ensure the uniform application of paragraphs 1, 3 and 4, the Commission shall, … adopt implementing measures concerning:

    (a) the criteria for determining the relative importance of the different factors that, pursuant to paragraph 1, may be taken into account for determining the best possible result taking into account the size and type of order and the retail or professional nature of the client;

    (b) factors that may be taken into account by an investment firm when reviewing its execution arrangements and the circumstances under which changes to such arrangements may be appropriate. In particular, the factors for determining which venues enable investment firms to obtain on a consistent basis the best possible result for executing the client orders;

(c) the nature and extent of the information to be provided to clients on their execution policies, pursuant to paragraph 3.

[The measures referred to in the first subparagraph, designed to amend non-essential elements of this Directive by supplementing it, shall be adopted in accordance with the regulatory procedure with scrutiny referred to in Article 64(2).]

[5542]

NOTES
Para 6: words omitted repealed, and words in square brackets added, by European Parliament and Council Directive 2008/10/EC, Art 1(7), as from 20 March 2008.

Article 22
Client order handling rules

1. Member States shall require that investment firms authorised to execute orders on behalf of clients implement procedures and arrangements which provide for the prompt, fair and expeditious execution of client orders, relative to other client orders or the trading interests of the investment firm.

These procedures or arrangements shall allow for the execution of otherwise comparable client orders in accordance with the time of their reception by the investment firm.

2. Member States shall require that, in the case of a client limit order in respect of shares admitted to trading on a regulated market which are not immediately executed under prevailing market conditions, investment firms are, unless the client expressly instructs otherwise, to take measures to facilitate the earliest possible execution of that order by making public immediately that client limit order in a manner which is easily accessible to other market participants. Member States may decide that investment firms comply with this obligation by transmitting the client limit order to a regulated market and/or MTF. Member States shall provide that the competent authorities may waive the obligation to make public a limit order that is large in scale compared with normal market size as determined under Article 44(2).

3. In order to ensure that measures for the protection of investors and fair and orderly functioning of markets take account of technical developments in financial markets, and to ensure the uniform application of paragraphs 1 and 2, the Commission shall adopt, … implementing measures which define:

(a) the conditions and nature of the procedures and arrangements which result in the prompt, fair and expeditious execution of client orders and the situations in which or types of transaction for which investment firms may reasonably deviate from prompt execution so as to obtain more favourable terms for clients;

(b) the different methods through which an investment firm can be deemed to have met its obligation to disclose not immediately executable client limit orders to the market.

[The measures referred to in the first subparagraph, designed to amend non-essential elements of this Directive by supplementing it, shall be adopted in accordance with the regulatory procedure with scrutiny referred to in Article 64(2).]

[5543]

NOTES
Para 3: words omitted repealed, and words in square brackets added, by European Parliament and Council Directive 2008/10/EC, Art 1(8), as from 20 March 2008.

Article 23
Obligations of investment firms when appointing tied agents

1. Member States may decide to allow an investment firm to appoint tied agents for the purposes of promoting the services of the investment firm, soliciting business or receiving orders from clients or potential clients and transmitting them, placing financial instruments and providing advice in respect of such financial instruments and services offered by that investment firm.

2. Member States shall require that where an investment firm decides to appoint a tied agent it remains fully and unconditionally responsible for any action or omission on the part of the tied agent when acting on behalf of the firm. Member States shall require the investment firm to ensure that a tied agent discloses the capacity in which he is acting and the firm which he is representing when contacting or before dealing with any client or potential client.

Member States may allow, in accordance with Article 13(6), (7) and (8), tied agents registered in their territory to handle clients' money and/or financial instruments on behalf and under the full responsibility of the investment firm for which they are acting within their territory or, in the case of a cross border operation, in the territory of a Member State which allows a tied agent to handle clients' money.

Member States shall require the investment firms to monitor the activities of their tied agents so as to ensure that they continue to comply with this Directive when acting through tied agents.

3. Member States that decide to allow investment firms to appoint tied agents shall establish a public register. Tied agents shall be registered in the public register in the Member State where they are established.

Where the Member State in which the tied agent is established has decided, in accordance with paragraph 1, not to allow the investment firms authorised by their competent authorities to appoint tied agents, those tied agents shall be registered with the competent authority of the home Member State of the investment firm on whose behalf it acts.

Member States shall ensure that tied agents are only admitted to the public register if it has been established that they are of sufficiently good repute and that they possess appropriate general, commercial and professional knowledge so as to be able to communicate accurately all relevant information regarding the proposed service to the client or potential client.

Member States may decide that investment firms can verify whether the tied agents which they have appointed are of sufficiently good repute and possess the knowledge as referred to in the third subparagraph.

The register shall be updated on a regular basis. It shall be publicly available for consultation.

4. Member States shall require that investment firms appointing tied agents take adequate measures in order to avoid any negative impact that the activities of the tied agent not covered by the scope of this Directive could have on the activities carried out by the tied agent on behalf of the investment firm.

Member States may allow competent authorities to collaborate with investment firms and credit institutions, their associations and other entities in registering tied agents and in monitoring compliance of tied agents with the requirements of paragraph 3. In particular, tied agents may be registered by an investment firm, credit institution or their associations and other entities under the supervision of the competent authority.

5. Member States shall require that investment firms appoint only tied agents entered in the public registers referred to in paragraph 3.

6. Member States may reinforce the requirements set out in this Article or add other requirements for tied agents registered within their jurisdiction.

[5544]

Article 24
Transactions executed with eligible counterparties

1. Member States shall ensure that investment firms authorised to execute orders on behalf of clients and/or to deal on own account and/or to receive and transmit orders, may bring about or enter into transactions with eligible counterparties without being obliged to comply with the obligations under Articles 19, 21 and 22(1) in respect of those transactions or in respect of any ancillary service directly related to those transactions.

2. Member States shall recognise as eligible counterparties for the purposes of this Article investment firms, credit institutions, insurance companies, UCITS and their management companies, pension funds and their management companies, other financial institutions authorised or regulated under Community legislation or the national law of a Member State, undertakings exempted from the application of this Directive under Article 2(1)(k) and (l), national governments and their corresponding offices including public bodies that deal with public debt, central banks and supranational organisations.

Classification as an eligible counterparty under the first subparagraph shall be without prejudice to the right of such entities to request, either on a general form or on a trade-by-trade basis, treatment as clients whose business with the investment firm is subject to Articles 19, 21 and 22.

3. Member States may also recognise as eligible counterparties other undertakings meeting pre-determined proportionate requirements, including quantitative thresholds. In the event of a transaction where the prospective counterparties are located in different jurisdictions, the investment firm shall defer to the status of the other undertaking as determined by the law or measures of the Member State in which that undertaking is established.

Member States shall ensure that the investment firm, when it enters into transactions in accordance with paragraph 1 with such undertakings, obtains the express confirmation from the prospective counterparty that it agrees to be treated as an eligible counterparty. Member States shall allow the investment firm to obtain this confirmation either in the form of a general agreement or in respect of each individual transaction.

4.   Member States may recognise as eligible counterparties third country entities equivalent to those categories of entities mentioned in paragraph 2.

Member States may also recognise as eligible counterparties third country undertakings such as those mentioned in paragraph 3 on the same conditions and subject to the same requirements as those laid down at paragraph 3.

5.   In order to ensure the uniform application of paragraphs 2, 3 and 4 in the light of changing market practice and to facilitate the effective operation of the single market, the Commission may adopt,… implementing measures which define:

    (a)   the procedures for requesting treatment as clients under paragraph 2;

    (b)   the procedures for obtaining the express confirmation from prospective counterparties under paragraph 3;

    (c)   the predetermined proportionate requirements, including quantitative thresholds that would allow an undertaking to be considered as an eligible counterparty under paragraph 3.

[The measures referred to in the first subparagraph, designed to amend non-essential elements of this Directive by supplementing it, shall be adopted in accordance with the regulatory procedure with scrutiny referred to in Article 64(2).]

                                                        [5545]

NOTES

Para 5: words omitted repealed, and words in square brackets added, by European Parliament and Council Directive 2008/10/EC, Art 1(9), as from 20 March 2008.

SECTION 3
MARKET TRANSPARENCY AND INTEGRITY

Article 25
Obligation to uphold integrity of markets, report transactions and maintain records

1.   Without prejudice to the allocation of responsibilities for enforcing the provisions of Directive 2003/6/EC of the European Parliament and of the Council of 28 January 2003 on insider dealing and market manipulation (market abuse),[1] Member States shall ensure that appropriate measures are in place to enable the competent authority to monitor the activities of investment firms to ensure that they act honestly, fairly and professionally and in a manner which promotes the integrity of the market.

2.   Member States shall require investment firms to keep at the disposal of the competent authority, for at least five years, the relevant data relating to all transactions in financial instruments which they have carried out, whether on own account or on behalf of a client. In the case of transactions carried out on behalf of clients, the records shall contain all the information and details of the identity of the client, and the information required under Council Directive 91/308/EEC of 10 June 1991 on prevention of the use of the financial system for the purpose of money laundering.[2]

3.   Member States shall require investment firms which execute transactions in any financial instruments admitted to trading on a regulated market to report details of such transactions to the competent authority as quickly as possible, and no later than the close of the following working day. This obligation shall apply whether or not such transactions were carried out on a regulated market.

The competent authorities shall, in accordance with Article 58, establish the necessary arrangements in order to ensure that the competent authority of the most relevant market in terms of liquidity for those financial instruments also receives this information.

4.   The reports shall, in particular, include details of the names and numbers of the instruments bought or sold, the quantity, the dates and times of execution and the transaction prices and means of identifying the investment firms concerned.

5.   Member States shall provide for the reports to be made to the competent authority either by the investment firm itself, a third party acting on its behalf or by a trade-matching or reporting system approved by the competent authority or by the regulated market or MTF through whose systems the transaction was completed. In cases where transactions are reported directly to the competent authority by a regulated market, an MTF, or a trade-matching or reporting system approved by the competent authority, the obligation on the investment firm laid down in paragraph 3 may be waived.

6.   When, in accordance with Article 32(7), reports provided for under this Article are transmitted to the competent authority of the host Member State, it shall transmit this information to the competent authorities of the home Member State of the investment firm, unless they decide that they do not want to receive this information.

7.   In order to ensure that measures for the protection of market integrity are modified to take account of technical developments in financial markets, and to ensure the uniform application of paragraphs 1 to 5, the Commission may adopt, … implementing measures which define the methods

and arrangements for reporting financial transactions, the form and content of these reports and the criteria for defining a relevant market in accordance with paragraph 3. [Those measures, designed to amend non-essential elements of this Directive by supplementing it, shall be adopted in accordance with the regulatory procedure with scrutiny referred to in Article 64(2).]

[5546]

NOTES

Para 7: words omitted repealed, and words in square brackets added, by European Parliament and Council Directive 2008/10/EC, Art 1(10), as from 20 March 2008.

1   OJ L96, 12.4.2003, p 16.
2   OJ L166, 28.6.1991, p 77. Directive as last amended by Directive 2001/97/EC of the European Parliament and of the Council (OJ L344, 28.12.2001, p 76).

Article 26
Monitoring of compliance with the rules of the MTF and with other legal obligations

1.   Member States shall require that investment firms and market operators operating an MTF establish and maintain effective arrangements and procedures, relevant to the MTF, for the regular monitoring of the compliance by its users with its rules. Investment firms and market operators operating an MTF shall monitor the transactions undertaken by their users under their systems in order to identify breaches of those rules, disorderly trading conditions or conduct that may involve market abuse.

2.   Member States shall require investment firms and market operators operating an MTF to report significant breaches of its rules or disorderly trading conditions or conduct that may involve market abuse to the competent authority. Member States shall also require investment firms and market operators operating an MTF to supply the relevant information without delay to the authority competent for the investigation and prosecution of market abuse and to provide full assistance to the latter in investigating and prosecuting market abuse occurring on or through its systems.

[5547]

Article 27
Obligation for investment firms to make public firm quotes

1.   Member States shall require systematic internalisers in shares to publish a firm quote in those shares admitted to trading on a regulated market for which they are systematic internalisers and for which there is a liquid market. In the case of shares for which there is not a liquid market, systematic internalisers shall disclose quotes to their clients on request.

The provisions of this Article shall be applicable to systematic internalisers when dealing for sizes up to standard market size. Systematic internalisers that only deal in sizes above standard market size shall not be subject to the provisions of this Article.

Systematic internalisers may decide the size or sizes at which they will quote. For a particular share each quote shall include a firm bid and/or offer price or prices for a size or sizes which could be up to standard market size for the class of shares to which the share belongs. The price or prices shall also reflect the prevailing market conditions for that share.

Shares shall be grouped in classes on the basis of the arithmetic average value of the orders executed in the market for that share. The standard market size for each class of shares shall be a size representative of the arithmetic average value of the orders executed in the market for the shares included in each class of shares.

The market for each share shall be comprised of all orders executed in the European Union in respect of that share excluding those large in scale compared to normal market size for that share.

2.   The competent authority of the most relevant market in terms of liquidity as defined in Article 25 for each share shall determine at least annually, on the basis of the arithmetic average value of the orders executed in the market in respect of that share, the class of shares to which it belongs. This information shall be made public to all market participants.

3.   Systematic internalisers shall make public their quotes on a regular and continuous basis during normal trading hours. They shall be entitled to update their quotes at any time. They shall also be allowed, under exceptional market conditions, to withdraw their quotes.

The quote shall be made public in a manner which is easily accessible to other market participants on a reasonable commercial basis.

Systematic internalisers shall, while complying with the provisions set down in Article 21, execute the orders they receive from their retail clients in relation to the shares for which they are systematic internalisers at the quoted prices at the time of reception of the order.

Systematic internalisers shall execute the orders they receive from their professional clients in relation to the shares for which they are systematic internalisers at the quoted price at the time of reception of the order. However, they may execute those orders at a better price in justified cases provided that this price falls within a public range close to market conditions and provided that the orders are of a size bigger than the size customarily undertaken by a retail investor.

Furthermore, systematic internalisers may execute orders they receive from their professional clients at prices different than their quoted ones without having to comply with the conditions established in the fourth subparagraph, in respect of transactions where execution in several securities is part of one transaction or in respect of orders that are subject to conditions other than the current market price.

Where a systematic internaliser who quotes only one quote or whose highest quote is lower than the standard market size receives an order from a client of a size bigger than its quotation size, but lower than the standard market size, it may decide to execute that part of the order which exceeds its quotation size, provided that it is executed at the quoted price, except where otherwise permitted under the conditions of the previous two subparagraphs. Where the systematic internaliser is quoting in different sizes and receives an order between those sizes, which it chooses to execute, it shall execute the order at one of the quoted prices in compliance with the provisions of Article 22, except where otherwise permitted under the conditions of the previous two subparagraphs.

4.   The competent authorities shall check:
  (a)   that investment firms regularly update bid and/or offer prices published in accordance with paragraph 1 and maintain prices which reflect the prevailing market conditions;
  (b)   that investment firms comply with the conditions for price improvement laid down in the fourth subparagraph of paragraph 3.

5.   Systematic internalisers shall be allowed to decide, on the basis of their commercial policy and in an objective non-discriminatory way, the investors to whom they give access to their quotes. To that end there shall be clear standards for governing access to their quotes. Systematic internalisers may refuse to enter into or discontinue business relationships with investors on the basis of commercial considerations such as the investor credit status, the counterparty risk and the final settlement of the transaction.

6.   In order to limit the risk of being exposed to multiple transactions from the same client systematic internalisers shall be allowed to limit in a non-discriminatory way the number of transactions from the same client which they undertake to enter at the published conditions. They shall also be allowed, in a non-discriminatory way and in accordance with the provisions of Article 22, to limit the total number of transactions from different clients at the same time provided that this is allowable only where the number and/or volume of orders sought by clients considerably exceeds the norm.

7.   In order to ensure the uniform application of paragraphs 1 to 6, in a manner which supports the efficient valuation of shares and maximises the possibility of investment firms of obtaining the best deal for their clients, the Commission shall, … adopt implementing measures which:
  (a)   specify the criteria for application of paragraphs 1 and 2;
  (b)   specify the criteria determining when a quote is published on a regular and continuous basis and is easily accessible as well as the means by which investment firms may comply with their obligation to make public their quotes, which shall include the following possibilities:
      (i)   through the facilities of any regulated market which has admitted the instrument in question to trading;
      (ii)   through the offices of a third party;
      (iii)   through proprietary arrangements;
  (c)   specify the general criteria for determining those transactions where execution in several securities is part of one transaction or orders that are subject to conditions other than current market price;
  (d)   specify the general criteria for determining what can be considered as exceptional market circumstances that allow for the withdrawal of quotes as well as conditions for updating quotes;
  (e)   specify the criteria for determining what is a size customarily undertaken by a retail investor.
  (f)   specify the criteria for determining what constitutes considerably exceeding the norm as set down in paragraph 6;
  (g)   specify the criteria for determining when prices fall within a public range close to market conditions.

[The measures referred to in the first subparagraph, designed to amend non-essential elements of this Directive by supplementing it, shall be adopted in accordance with the regulatory procedure with scrutiny referred to in Article 64(2).]

[5548]

NOTES
  Para 7: words omitted repealed, and words in square brackets added, by European Parliament and Council Directive 2008/10/EC, Art 1(11), as from 20 March 2008.

Article 28
Post-trade disclosure by investment firms

1. Member States shall, at least, require investment firms which, either on own account or on behalf of clients, conclude transactions in shares admitted to trading on a regulated market outside a regulated market or MTF, to make public the volume and price of those transactions and the time at which they were concluded. This information shall be made public as close to real-time as possible, on a reasonable commercial basis, and in a manner which is easily accessible to other market participants.

2. Member States shall require that the information which is made public in accordance with paragraph 1 and the time-limits within which it is published comply with the requirements adopted pursuant to Article 45. Where the measures adopted pursuant to Article 45 provide for deferred reporting for certain categories of transaction in shares, this possibility shall apply mutatis mutandis to those transactions when undertaken outside regulated markets or MTFs.

3. In order to ensure the transparent and orderly functioning of markets and the uniform application of paragraph 1, the Commission shall adopt, ... implementing measures which:
  (a) specify the means by which investment firms may comply with their obligations under paragraph 1 including the following possibilities:
    (i) through the facilities of any regulated market which has admitted the instrument in question to trading or through the facilities of an MTF in which the share in question is traded;
    (ii) through the offices of a third party;
    (iii) through proprietary arrangements;
  (b) clarify the application of the obligation under paragraph 1 to transactions involving the use of shares for collateral, lending or other purposes where the exchange of shares is determined by factors other than the current market valuation of the share.

[The measures referred to in the first subparagraph, designed to amend non-essential elements of this Directive by supplementing it, shall be adopted in accordance with the regulatory procedure with scrutiny referred to in Article 64(2).]

[5549]

NOTES
  Para 3: words omitted repealed, and words in square brackets added, by European Parliament and Council Directive 2008/10/EC, Art 1(12), as from 20 March 2008.

Article 29
Pre-trade transparency requirements for MTFs

1. Member States shall, at least, require that investment firms and market operators operating an MTF make public current bid and offer prices and the depth of trading interests at these prices which are advertised through their systems in respect of shares admitted to trading on a regulated market. Member States shall provide for this information to be made available to the public on reasonable commercial terms and on a continuous basis during normal trading hours.

2. Member States shall provide for the competent authorities to be able to waive the obligation for investment firms or market operators operating an MTF to make public the information referred to in paragraph 1 based on the market model or the type and size of orders in the cases defined in accordance with paragraph 3. In particular, the competent authorities shall be able to waive the obligation in respect of transactions that are large in scale compared with normal market size for the share or type of share in question.

3. In order to ensure the uniform application of paragraphs 1 and 2, the Commission shall, ... adopt implementing measures as regards:
  (a) the range of bid and offers or designated market-maker quotes, and the depth of trading interest at those prices, to be made public;
  (b) the size or type of orders for which pre-trade disclosure may be waived under paragraph 2;
  (c) the market model for which pre-trade disclosure may be waived under paragraph 2 and in particular, the applicability of the obligation to trading methods operated by an MTF which conclude transactions under their rules by reference to prices established outside the systems of the MTF or by periodic auction.

Except where justified by the specific nature of the MTF, the content of these implementing measures shall be equal to that of the implementing measures provided for in Article 44 for regulated markets.

[The measures referred to in the first subparagraph, designed to amend non-essential elements of this Directive by supplementing it, shall be adopted in accordance with the regulatory procedure with scrutiny referred to in Article 64(2).]

[5550]

Article 30
Post-trade transparency requirements for MTFs

1.   Member States shall, at least, require that investment firms and market operators operating
an MTF make public the price, volume and time of the transactions executed under its systems in
respect of shares which are admitted to trading on a regulated market. Member States shall require
that details of all such transactions be made public, on a reasonable commercial basis, as close to
real-time as possible. This requirement shall not apply to details of trades executed on an MTF that
are made public under the systems of a regulated market.

2.   Member States shall provide that the competent authority may authorise investment firms or
market operators operating an MTF to provide for deferred publication of the details of transactions
based on their type or size. In particular, the competent authorities may authorise the deferred
publication in respect of transactions that are large in scale compared with the normal market size
for that share or that class of shares. Member States shall require MTFs to obtain the competent
authority's prior approval to proposed arrangements for deferred trade-publication, and shall require
that these arrangements be clearly disclosed to market participants and the investing public.

3.   In order to provide for the efficient and orderly functioning of financial markets, and to
ensure the uniform application of paragraphs 1 and 2, the Commission shall, ... adopt implementing
measures in respect of:
    (a)   the scope and content of the information to be made available to the public;
    (b)   the conditions under which investment firms or market operators operating an MTF may
           provide for deferred publication of trades and the criteria to be applied when deciding
           the transactions for which, due to their size or the type of share involved, deferred
           publication is allowed.

Except where justified by the specific nature of the MTF, the content of these implementing
measures shall be equal to that of the implementing measures provided for in Article 45 for
regulated markets.

[The measures referred to in the first subparagraph, designed to amend non-essential elements of
this Directive by supplementing it, shall be adopted in accordance with the regulatory procedure
with scrutiny referred to in Article 64(2).]

[5551]

CHAPTER III
RIGHTS OF INVESTMENT FIRMS

Article 31
Freedom to provide investment services and activities

1.   Member States shall ensure that any investment firm authorised and supervised by the
competent authorities of another Member State in accordance with this Directive, and in respect of
credit institutions in accordance with Directive 2000/12/EC, may freely perform investment services
and/or activities as well as ancillary services within their territories, provided that such services and
activities are covered by its authorisation. Ancillary services may only be provided together with an
investment service and/or activity.

Member States shall not impose any additional requirements on such an investment firm or credit
institution in respect of the matters covered by this Directive.

2.   Any investment firm wishing to provide services or activities within the territory of another
Member State for the first time, or which wishes to change the range of services or activities so
provided, shall communicate the following information to the competent authorities of its home
Member State:
    (a)   the Member State in which it intends to operate;
    (b)   a programme of operations stating in particular the investment services and/or activities
           as well as ancillary services which it intends to perform and whether it intends to use
           tied agents in the territory of the Member States in which it intends to provide services.

In cases where the investment firm intends to use tied agents, the competent authority of the
home Member State of the investment firm shall, at the request of the competent authority of the

host Member State and within a reasonable time, communicate the identity of the tied agents that the investment firm intends to use in that Member State. The host Member State may make public such information.

3. The competent authority of the home Member State shall, within one month of receiving the information, forward it to the competent authority of the host Member State designated as contact point in accordance with Article 56(1). The investment firm may then start to provide the investment service or services concerned in the host Member State.

4. In the event of a change in any of the particulars communicated in accordance with paragraph 2, an investment firm shall give written notice of that change to the competent authority of the home Member State at least one month before implementing the change. The competent authority of the home Member State shall inform the competent authority of the host Member State of those changes.

5. Member States shall, without further legal or administrative requirement, allow investment firms and market operators operating MTFs from other Member States to provide appropriate arrangements on their territory so as to facilitate access to and use of their systems by remote users or participants established in their territory.

6. The investment firm or the market operator that operates an MTF shall communicate to the competent authority of its home Member State the Member State in which it intends to provide such arrangements. The competent authority of the home Member State of the MTF shall communicate, within one month, this information to the Member State in which the MTF intends to provide such arrangements.

The competent authority of the home Member State of the MTF shall, on the request of the competent authority of the host Member State of the MTF and within a reasonable delay, communicate the identity of the members or participants of the MTF established in that Member State.

[5552]

Article 32
Establishment of a branch

1. Member States shall ensure that investment services and/or activities as well as ancillary services may be provided within their territories in accordance with this Directive and Directive 2000/12/EC through the establishment of a branch provided that those services and activities are covered by the authorisation granted to the investment firm or the credit institution in the home Member State. Ancillary services may only be provided together with an investment service and/or activity.

Member States shall not impose any additional requirements save those allowed under paragraph 7, on the organisation and operation of the branch in respect of the matters covered by this Directive.

2. Member States shall require any investment firm wishing to establish a branch within the territory of another Member State first to notify the competent authority of its home Member State and to provide it with the following information:
   (a) the Member States within the territory of which it plans to establish a branch;
   (b) a programme of operations setting out inter alia the investment services and/or activities as well as the ancillary services to be offered and the organisational structure of the branch and indicating whether the branch intends to use tied agents;
   (c) the address in the host Member State from which documents may be obtained;
   (d) the names of those responsible for the management of the branch.

In cases where an investment firm uses a tied agent established in a Member State outside its home Member State, such tied agent shall be assimilated to the branch and shall be subject to the provisions of this Directive relating to branches.

3. Unless the competent authority of the home Member State has reason to doubt the adequacy of the administrative structure or the financial situation of an investment firm, taking into account the activities envisaged, it shall, within three months of receiving all the information, communicate that information to the competent authority of the host Member State designated as contact point in accordance with Article 56(1) and inform the investment firm concerned accordingly.

4. In addition to the information referred to in paragraph 2, the competent authority of the home Member State shall communicate details of the accredited compensation scheme of which the investment firm is a member in accordance with Directive 97/9/EC to the competent authority of the host Member State. In the event of a change in the particulars, the competent authority of the home Member State shall inform the competent authority of the host Member State accordingly.

5. Where the competent authority of the home Member State refuses to communicate the information to the competent authority of the host Member State, it shall give reasons for its refusal to the investment firm concerned within three months of receiving all the information.

6. On receipt of a communication from the competent authority of the host Member State, or failing such communication from the latter at the latest after two months from the date of transmission of the communication by the competent authority of the home Member State, the branch may be established and commence business.

7. The competent authority of the Member State in which the branch is located shall assume responsibility for ensuring that the services provided by the branch within its territory comply with the obligations laid down in Articles 19, 21, 22, 25, 27 and 28 and in measures adopted pursuant thereto.

The competent authority of the Member State in which the branch is located shall have the right to examine branch arrangements and to request such changes as are strictly needed to enable the competent authority to enforce the obligations under Articles 19, 21, 22, 25, 27 and 28 and measures adopted pursuant thereto with respect to the services and/or activities provided by the branch within its territory.

8. Each Member State shall provide that, where an investment firm authorised in another Member State has established a branch within its territory, the competent authority of the home Member State of the investment firm, in the exercise of its responsibilities and after informing the competent authority of the host Member State, may carry out on-site inspections in that branch.

9. In the event of a change in any of the information communicated in accordance with paragraph 2, an investment firm shall give written notice of that change to the competent authority of the home Member State at least one month before implementing the change. The competent authority of the host Member State shall also be informed of that change by the competent authority of the home Member State.

[5553]

Article 33
Access to regulated markets

1. Member States shall require that investment firms from other Member States which are authorised to execute client orders or to deal on own account have the right of member-ship or have access to regulated markets established in their territory by means of any of the following arrangements:
   (a) directly, by setting up branches in the host Member States;
   (b) by becoming remote members of or having remote access to the regulated market without having to be established in the home Member State of the regulated market, where the trading procedures and systems of the market in question do not require a physical presence for conclusion of transactions on the market.

2. Member States shall not impose any additional regulatory or administrative requirements, in respect of matters covered by this Directive, on investment firms exercising the right conferred by paragraph 1.

[5554]

Article 34
Access to central counterparty, clearing and settlement facilities and right to designate settlement system

1. Member States shall require that investment firms from other Member States have the right of access to central counterparty, clearing and settlement systems in their territory for the purposes of finalising or arranging the finalisation of transactions in financial instruments.

Member States shall require that access of those investment firms to such facilities be subject to the same non-discriminatory, transparent and objective criteria as apply to local participants. Member States shall not restrict the use of those facilities to the clearing and settlement of transactions in financial instruments undertaken on a regulated market or MTF in their territory.

2. Member States shall require that regulated markets in their territory offer all their members or participants the right to designate the system for the settlement of transactions in financial instruments undertaken on that regulated market, subject to:
   (a) such links and arrangements between the designated settlement system and any other system or facility as are necessary to ensure the efficient and economic settlement of the transaction in question; and
   (b) agreement by the competent authority responsible for the supervision of the regulated market that technical conditions for settlement of transactions concluded on the regulated market through a settlement system other than that designated by the regulated market are such as to allow the smooth and orderly functioning of financial markets.

This assessment of the competent authority of the regulated market shall be without prejudice to the competencies of the national central banks as overseers of settlement systems or other supervisory authorities on such systems. The competent authority shall take into account the oversight/supervision already exercised by those institutions in order to avoid undue duplication of control.

3.   The rights of investment firms under paragraphs 1 and 2 shall be without prejudice to the right of operators of central counterparty, clearing or securities settlement systems to refuse on legitimate commercial grounds to make the requested services available.

[5555]

Article 35
Provisions regarding central counterparty, clearing and settlement arrangements in respect of MTFs

1.   Member States shall not prevent investment firms and market operators operating an MTF from entering into appropriate arrangements with a central counterparty or clearing house and a settlement system of another Member State with a view to providing for the clearing and/or settlement of some or all trades concluded by market participants under their systems.

2.   The competent authority of investment firms and market operators operating an MTF may not oppose the use of central counterparty, clearing houses and/or settlement systems in another Member State except where this is demonstrably necessary in order to maintain the orderly functioning of that MTF and taking into account the conditions for settlement systems established in Article 34(2).

In order to avoid undue duplication of control, the competent authority shall take into account the oversight/supervision of the clearing and settlement system already exercised by the national central banks as overseers of clearing and settlement systems or by other supervisory authorities with a competence in such systems.

[5556]

TITLE III
REGULATED MARKETS

Article 36
Authorisation and applicable law

1.   Member States shall reserve authorisation as a regulated market to those systems which comply with the provisions of this Title.

Authorisation as a regulated market shall be granted only where the competent authority is satisfied that both the market operator and the systems of the regulated market comply at least with the requirements laid down in this Title.

In the case of a regulated market that is a legal person and that is managed or operated by a market operator other than the regulated market itself, Member States shall establish how the different obligations imposed on the market operator under this Directive are to be allocated between the regulated market and the market operator.

The operator of the regulated market shall provide all information, including a programme of operations setting out inter alia the types of business envisaged and the organisational structure, necessary to enable the competent authority to satisfy itself that the regulated market has established, at the time of initial authorisation, all the necessary arrangements to meet its obligations under the provisions of this Title.

2.   Member States shall require the operator of the regulated market to perform tasks relating to the organisation and operation of the regulated market under the supervision of the competent authority. Member States shall ensure that competent authorities keep under regular review the compliance of regulated markets with the provisions of this Title. They shall also ensure that competent authorities monitor that regulated markets comply at all times with the conditions for initial authorisation established under this Title.

3.   Member States shall ensure that the market operator is responsible for ensuring that the regulated market that he manages complies with all requirements under this Title.

Member States shall also ensure that the market operator is entitled to exercise the rights that correspond to the regulated market that he manages by virtue of this Directive.

4.   Without prejudice to any relevant provisions of Directive 2003/6/EC, the public law governing the trading conducted under the systems of the regulated market shall be that of the home Member State of the regulated market.

5.   The competent authority may withdraw the authorisation issued to a regulated market where it:
   (a)   does not make use of the authorisation within 12 months, expressly renounces the authorisation or has not operated for the preceding six months, unless the Member State concerned has provided for authorisation to lapse in such cases;
   (b)   has obtained the authorisation by making false statements or by any other irregular means;
   (c)   no longer meets the conditions under which authorisation was granted;

(d)　has seriously and systematically infringed the provisions adopted pursuant to this Directive;

(e)　falls within any of the cases where national law provides for withdrawal.

[5557]

Article 37
Requirements for the management of the regulated market

1.　Member States shall require the persons who effectively direct the business and the operations of the regulated market to be of sufficiently good repute and sufficiently experienced as to ensure the sound and prudent management and operation of the regulated market. Member States shall also require the operator of the regulated market to inform the competent authority of the identity and any other subsequent changes of the persons who effectively direct the business and the operations of the regulated market.

The competent authority shall refuse to approve proposed changes where there are objective and demonstrable grounds for believing that they pose a material threat to the sound and prudent management and operation of the regulated market.

2.　Member States shall ensure that, in the process of authorisation of a regulated market, the person or persons who effectively direct the business and the operations of an already authorised regulated market in accordance with the conditions of this Directive are deemed to comply with the requirements laid down in paragraph 1.

[5558]

Article 38
Requirements relating to persons exercising significant influence over the management of the regulated market

1.　Member States shall require the persons who are in a position to exercise, directly or indirectly, significant influence over the management of the regulated market to be suitable.

2.　Member States shall require the operator of the regulated market:
(a)　to provide the competent authority with, and to make public, information regarding the ownership of the regulated market and/or the market operator, and in particular, the identity and scale of interests of any parties in a position to exercise significant influence over the management;
(b)　to inform the competent authority of and to make public any transfer of ownership which gives rise to a change in the identity of the persons exercising significant influence over the operation of the regulated market.

3.　The competent authority shall refuse to approve proposed changes to the controlling interests of the regulated market and/or the market operator where there are objective and demonstrable grounds for believing that they would pose a threat to the sound and prudent management of the regulated market.

[5559]

Article 39
Organisational requirements

Member States shall require the regulated market:
(a)　to have arrangements to identify clearly and manage the potential adverse consequences, for the operation of the regulated market or for its participants, of any conflict of interest between the interest of the regulated market, its owners or its operator and the sound functioning of the regulated market, and in particular where such conflicts of interest might prove prejudicial to the accomplishment of any functions delegated to the regulated market by the competent authority;
(b)　to be adequately equipped to manage the risks to which it is exposed, to implement appropriate arrangements and systems to identify all significant risks to its operation, and to put in place effective measures to mitigate those risks;
(c)　to have arrangements for the sound management of the technical operations of the system, including the establishment of effective contingency arrangements to cope with risks of systems disruptions;
(d)　to have transparent and non-discretionary rules and procedures that provide for fair and orderly trading and establish objective criteria for the efficient execution of orders;
(e)　to have effective arrangements to facilitate the efficient and timely finalisation of the transactions executed under its systems;
(f)　to have available, at the time of authorisation and on an ongoing basis, sufficient financial resources to facilitate its orderly functioning, having regard to the nature and extent of the transactions concluded on the market and the range and degree of the risks to which it is exposed.

[5560]

PART IV
EC MATERIALS

Article 40

Admission of financial instruments to trading

1. Member States shall require that regulated markets have clear and transparent rules regarding the admission of financial instruments to trading.

Those rules shall ensure that any financial instruments admitted to trading in a regulated market are capable of being traded in a fair, orderly and efficient manner and, in the case of transferable securities, are freely negotiable.

2. In the case of derivatives, the rules shall ensure in particular that the design of the derivative contract allows for its orderly pricing as well as for the existence of effective settlement conditions.

3. In addition to the obligations set out in paragraphs 1 and 2, Member States shall require the regulated market to establish and maintain effective arrangements to verify that issuers of transferable securities that are admitted to trading on the regulated market comply with their obligations under Community law in respect of initial, ongoing or ad hoc disclosure obligations.

Member States shall ensure that the regulated market establishes arrangements which facilitate its members or participants in obtaining access to information which has been made public under Community law.

4. Member States shall ensure that regulated markets have established the necessary arrangements to review regularly the compliance with the admission requirements of the financial instruments which they admit to trading.

5. A transferable security that has been admitted to trading on a regulated market can subsequently be admitted to trading on other regulated markets, even without the consent of the issuer and in compliance with the relevant provisions of Directive 2003/71/EC of the European Parliament and of the Council of 4 November 2003 on the prospectus to be published when securities are offered to the public or admitted to trading and amending Directive 2001/34/EC.[1] The issuer shall be informed by the regulated market of the fact that its securities are traded on that regulated market. The issuer shall not be subject to any obligation to provide information required under paragraph 3 directly to any regulated market which has admitted the issuer's securities to trading without its consent.

6. In order to ensure the uniform application of paragraphs 1 to 5, the Commission shall, … adopt implementing measures which:

(a) specify the characteristics of different classes of instruments to be taken into account by the regulated market when assessing whether an instrument is issued in a manner consistent with the conditions laid down in the second subparagraph of paragraph 1 for admission to trading on the different market segments which it operates;

(b) clarify the arrangements that the regulated market is to implement so as to be considered to have fulfilled its obligation to verify that the issuer of a transferable security complies with its obligations under Community law in respect of initial, ongoing or ad hoc disclosure obligations;

(c) clarify the arrangements that the regulated market has to establish pursuant to paragraph 3 in order to facilitate its members or participants in obtaining access to information which has been made public under the conditions established by Community law.

[The measures referred to in the first subparagraph, designed to amend non-essential elements of this Directive by supplementing it, shall be adopted in accordance with the regulatory procedure with scrutiny referred to in Article 64(2).]

[5561]

NOTES

Para 6: words omitted repealed, and words in square brackets added, by European Parliament and Council Directive 2008/10/EC, Art 1(15), as from 20 March 2008.

[1] OJ L345, 31.12.2003, p 64.

Article 41

Suspension and removal of instruments from trading

1. Without prejudice to the right of the competent authority under Article 50(2)(j) and (k) to demand suspension or removal of an instrument from trading, the operator of the regulated market may suspend or remove from trading a financial instrument which no longer complies with the rules of the regulated market unless such a step would be likely to cause significant damage to the investors' interests or the orderly functioning of the market.

Notwithstanding the possibility for the operators of regulated markets to inform directly the operators of other regulated markets, Member States shall require that an operator of a regulated market that suspends or removes from trading a financial instrument make public this decision and communicates relevant information to the competent authority. The competent authority shall inform the competent authorities of the other Member States.

2. A competent authority which demands the suspension or removal of a financial instrument from trading on one or more regulated markets shall immediately make public its decision and inform the competent authorities of the other Member States. Except where it could cause significant damage to the investors' interests or the orderly functioning of the market the competent authorities of the other Member States shall demand the suspension or removal of that financial instrument from trading on the regulated markets and MTFs that operate under their authority.

[5562]

Article 42
Access to the regulated market

1. Member States shall require the regulated market to establish and maintain transparent and non-discriminatory rules, based on objective criteria, governing access to or membership of the regulated market.

2. Those rules shall specify any obligations for the members or participants arising from:
   (a) the constitution and administration of the regulated market;
   (b) rules relating to transactions on the market;
   (c) professional standards imposed on the staff of the investment firms or credit institutions that are operating on the market;
   (d) the conditions established, for members or participants other than investment firms and credit institutions, under paragraph 3;
   (e) the rules and procedures for the clearing and settlement of transactions concluded on the regulated market.

3. Regulated markets may admit as members or participants investment firms, credit institutions authorised under Directive 2000/12/EC and other persons who:
   (a) are fit and proper;
   (b) have a sufficient level of trading ability and competence;
   (c) have, where applicable, adequate organisational arrangements;
   (d) have sufficient resources for the role they are to perform, taking into account the different financial arrangements that the regulated market may have established in order to guarantee the adequate settlement of transactions.

4. Member States shall ensure that, for the transactions concluded on a regulated market, members and participants are not obliged to apply to each other the obligations laid down in Articles 19, 21 and 22. However, the members or participants of the regulated market shall apply the obligations provided for in Articles 19, 21 and 22 with respect to their clients when they, acting on behalf of their clients, execute their orders on a regulated market.

5. Member States shall ensure that the rules on access to or membership of the regulated market provide for the direct or remote participation of investment firms and credit institutions.

6. Member States shall, without further legal or administrative requirements, allow regulated markets from other Member States to provide appropriate arrangements on their territory so as to facilitate access to and trading on those markets by remote members or participants established in their territory.

The regulated market shall communicate to the competent authority of its home Member State the Member State in which it intends to provide such arrangements. The competent authority of the home Member State shall communicate, within one month, this information to the Member State in which the regulated market intends to provide such arrangements.

The competent authority of the home Member State of the regulated market shall, on the request of the competent authority of the host Member State and within a reasonable time, communicate the identity of the members or participants of the regulated market established in that Member State.

7. Member States shall require the operator of the regulated market to communicate, on a regular basis, the list of the members and participants of the regulated market to the competent authority of the regulated market.

[5563]

Article 43
Monitoring of compliance with the rules of the regulated market and with other legal obligations

1. Member States shall require that regulated markets establish and maintain effective arrangements and procedures for the regular monitoring of the compliance by their members or participants with their rules. Regulated markets shall monitor the transactions undertaken by their members or participants under their systems in order to identify breaches of those rules, disorderly trading conditions or conduct that may involve market abuse.

2. Member States shall require the operators of the regulated markets to report significant breaches of their rules or disorderly trading conditions or conduct that may involve market abuse to the competent authority of the regulated market. Member States shall also require the operator of the regulated market to supply the relevant information without delay to the authority competent for the investigation and prosecution of market abuse on the regulated market and to provide full assistance to the latter in investigating and prosecuting market abuse occurring on or through the systems of the regulated market.

[5564]

Article 44
Pre-trade transparency requirements for regulated markets

1. Member States shall, at least, require regulated markets to make public current bid and offer prices and the depth of trading interests at those prices which are advertised through their systems for shares admitted to trading. Member States shall require this information to be made available to the public on reasonable commercial terms and on a continuous basis during normal trading hours.

Regulated markets may give access, on reasonable commercial terms and on a non-discriminatory basis, to the arrangements they employ for making public the information under the first subparagraph to investment firms which are obliged to publish their quotes in shares pursuant to Article 27.

2. Member States shall provide that the competent authorities are to be able to waive the obligation for regulated markets to make public the information referred to in paragraph 1 based on the market model or the type and size of orders in the cases defined in accordance with paragraph 3. In particular, the competent authorities shall be able to waive the obligation in respect of transactions that are large in scale compared with normal market size for the share or type of share in question.

3. In order to ensure the uniform application of paragraphs 1 and 2, the Commission shall, … adopt implementing measures as regards:
   (a)   the range of bid and offers or designated market maker quotes, and the depth of trading interest at those prices, to be made public;
   (b)   the size or type of orders for which pre trade disclosure may be waived under paragraph 2;
   (c)   the market model for which pre-trade disclosure may be waived under paragraph 2, and in particular, the applicability of the obligation to trading methods operated by regulated markets which conclude transactions under their rules by reference to prices established outside the regulated market or by periodic auction.

[The measures referred to in the first subparagraph, designed to amend non-essential elements of this Directive by supplementing it, shall be adopted in accordance with the regulatory procedure with scrutiny referred to in Article 64(2).]

[5565]

NOTES
Para 3: words omitted repealed, and words in square brackets added, by European Parliament and Council Directive 2008/10/EC, Art 1(16), as from 20 March 2008.

Article 45
Post-trade transparency requirements for regulated markets

1. Member States shall, at least, require regulated markets to make public the price, volume and time of the transactions executed in respect of shares admitted to trading. Member States shall require details of all such transactions to be made public, on a reasonable commercial basis and as close to real time as possible.

Regulated markets may give access, on reasonable commercial terms and on a non-discriminatory basis, to the arrangements they employ for making public the information under the first subparagraph to investment firms which are obliged to publish the details of their transactions in shares pursuant to Article 28.

2. Member States shall provide that the competent authority may authorise regulated markets to provide for deferred publication of the details of transactions based on their type or size. In particular, the competent authorities may authorise the deferred publication in respect of transactions that are large in scale compared with the normal market size for that share or that class of shares. Member States shall require regulated markets to obtain the competent authority's prior approval of proposed arrangements for deferred trade-publication, and shall require that these arrangements be clearly disclosed to market participants and the investing public.

3. In order to provide for the efficient and orderly functioning of financial markets, and to ensure the uniform application of paragraphs 1 and 2, the Commission shall, … adopt implementing measures in respect of:
   (a)   the scope and content of the information to be made available to the public;

(b)   the conditions under which a regulated market may provide for deferred publication of trades and the criteria to be applied when deciding the transactions for which, due to their size or the type of share involved, deferred publication is allowed.

[The measures referred to in the first subparagraph, designed to amend non-essential elements of this Directive by supplementing it, shall be adopted in accordance with the regulatory procedure with scrutiny referred to in Article 64(2).]

[5566]

NOTES

Para 3: words omitted repealed, and words in square brackets added, by European Parliament and Council Directive 2008/10/EC, Art 1(17), as from 20 March 2008.

Article 46
Provisions regarding central counterparty and clearing and settlement arrangements

1.   Member States shall not prevent regulated markets from entering into appropriate arrangements with a central counterparty or clearing house and a settlement system of another Member State with a view to providing for the clearing and/or settlement of some or all trades concluded by market participants under their systems.

2.   The competent authority of a regulated market may not oppose the use of central counterparty, clearing houses and/or settlement systems in another Member State except where this is demonstrably necessary in order to maintain the orderly functioning of that regulated market and taking into account the conditions for settlement systems established in Article 34(2).

In order to avoid undue duplication of control, the competent authority shall take into account the oversight/supervision of the clearing and settlement system already exercised by the national central banks as overseers of clearing and settlement systems or by other supervisory authorities with competence in relation to such systems.

[5567]

Article 47
List of regulated markets

Each Member State shall draw up a list of the regulated markets for which it is the home Member State and shall forward that list to the other Member States and the Commission. A similar communication shall be effected in respect of each change to that list. The Commission shall publish a list of all regulated markets in the *Official Journal of the European Union* and update it at least once a year. The Commission shall also publish and update the list at its website, each time the Member States communicate changes to their lists.

[5568]

TITLE IV
COMPETENT AUTHORITIES

CHAPTER I
DESIGNATION, POWERS AND REDRESS PROCEDURES

Article 48
Designation of competent authorities

1.   Each Member State shall designate the competent authorities which are to carry out each of the duties provided for under the different provisions of this Directive. Member States shall inform the Commission and the competent authorities of other Member States of the identity of the competent authorities responsible for enforcement of each of those duties, and of any division of those duties.

2.   The competent authorities referred to in paragraph 1 shall be public authorities, without prejudice to the possibility of delegating tasks to other entities where that is expressly provided for in Articles 5(5), 16(3), 17(2) and 23(4).

Any delegation of tasks to entities other than the authorities referred to in paragraph 1 may not involve either the exercise of public authority or the use of discretionary powers of judgement. Member States shall require that, prior to delegation, competent authorities take all reasonable steps to ensure that the entity to which tasks are to be delegated has the capacity and resources to effectively execute all tasks and that the delegation takes place only if a clearly defined and documented framework for the exercise of any delegated tasks has been established stating the tasks to be undertaken and the conditions under which they are to be carried out. These conditions shall include a clause obliging the entity in question to act and be organised in such a manner as to avoid conflict of interest and so that information obtained from carrying out the delegated tasks is not used unfairly or to prevent competition. In any case, the final responsibility for supervising compliance with this Directive and with its implementing measures shall lie with the competent authority or authorities designated in accordance with paragraph 1.

Member States shall inform the Commission and the competent authorities of other Member States of any arrangements entered into with regard to delegation of tasks, including the precise conditions regulating such delegation.

3. The Commission shall publish a list of the competent authorities referred to in paragraphs 1 and 2 in the *Official Journal of the European Union* at least once a year and update it continuously on its website.

[5569]

Article 49
Cooperation between authorities in the same Member State

If a Member State designates more than one competent authority to enforce a provision of this Directive, their respective roles shall be clearly defined and they shall cooperate closely.

Each Member State shall require that such cooperation also take place between the competent authorities for the purposes of this Directive and the competent authorities responsible in that Member State for the supervision of credit and other financial institutions, pension funds, UCITS, insurance and reinsurance intermediaries and insurance undertakings.

Member States shall require that competent authorities exchange any information which is essential or relevant to the exercise of their functions and duties.

[5570]

Article 50
Powers to be made available to competent authorities

1. Competent authorities shall be given all supervisory and investigatory powers that are necessary for the exercise of their functions. Within the limits provided for in their national legal frameworks they shall exercise such powers:
   (a) directly; or
   (b) in collaboration with other authorities; or
   (c) under their responsibility by delegation to entities to which tasks have been delegated according to Article 48(2); or
   (d) by application to the competent judicial authorities.

2. The powers referred to in paragraph 1 shall be exercised in conformity with national law and shall include, at least, the rights to:
   (a) have access to any document in any form whatsoever and to receive a copy of it;
   (b) demand information from any person and if necessary to summon and question a person with a view to obtaining information;
   (c) carry out on-site inspections;
   (d) require existing telephone and existing data traffic records;
   (e) require the cessation of any practice that is contrary to the provisions adopted in the implementation of this Directive;
   (f) request the freezing and/or the sequestration of assets;
   (g) request temporary prohibition of professional activity;
   (h) require authorised investment firms and regulated markets' auditors to provide information;
   (i) adopt any type of measure to ensure that investment firms and regulated markets continue to comply with legal requirements;
   (j) require the suspension of trading in a financial instrument;
   (k) require the removal of a financial instrument from trading, whether on a regulated market or under other trading arrangements;
   (l) refer matters for criminal prosecution;
   (m) allow auditors or experts to carry out verifications or investigations.

[5571]

Article 51
Administrative sanctions

1. Without prejudice to the procedures for the withdrawal of authorisation or to the right of Member States to impose criminal sanctions, Member States shall ensure, in conformity with their national law, that the appropriate administrative measures can be taken or administrative sanctions be imposed against the persons responsible where the provisions adopted in the implementation of this Directive have not been complied with. Member States shall ensure that these measures are effective, proportionate and dissuasive.

2. Member States shall determine the sanctions to be applied for failure to cooperate in an investigation covered by Article 50.

3. Member States shall provide that the competent authority may disclose to the public any measure or sanction that will be imposed for infringement of the provisions adopted in the

implementation of this Directive, unless such disclosure would seriously jeopardise the financial markets or cause disproportionate damage to the parties involved.

[5572]

Article 52
Right of appeal

1. Member States shall ensure that any decision taken under laws, regulations or administrative provisions adopted in accordance with this Directive is properly reasoned and is subject to the right to apply to the courts. The right to apply to the courts shall also apply where, in respect of an application for authorisation which provides all the information required, no decision is taken within six months of its submission.

2. Member States shall provide that one or more of the following bodies, as determined by national law, may, in the interests of consumers and in accordance with national law, take action before the courts or competent administrative bodies to ensure that the national provisions for the implementation of this Directive are applied:
   - (a) public bodies or their representatives;
   - (b) consumer organisations having a legitimate interest in protecting consumers;
   - (c) professional organisations having a legitimate interest in acting to protect their members.

[5573]

Article 53
Extra-judicial mechanism for investors' complaints

1. Member States shall encourage the setting-up of efficient and effective complaints and redress procedures for the out-of-court settlement of consumer disputes concerning the provision of investment and ancillary services provided by investment firms, using existing bodies where appropriate.

2. Member States shall ensure that those bodies are not prevented by legal or regulatory provisions from cooperating effectively in the resolution of cross-border disputes.

[5574]

Article 54
Professional secrecy

1. Member States shall ensure that competent authorities, all persons who work or who have worked for the competent authorities or entities to whom tasks are delegated pursuant to Article 48(2), as well as auditors and experts instructed by the competent authorities, are bound by the obligation of professional secrecy. No confidential information which they may receive in the course of their duties may be divulged to any person or authority whatsoever, save in summary or aggregate form such that individual investment firms, market operators, regulated markets or any other person cannot be identified, without prejudice to cases covered by criminal law or the other provisions of this Directive.

2. Where an investment firm, market operator or regulated market has been declared bankrupt or is being compulsorily wound up, confidential information which does not concern third parties may be divulged in civil or commercial proceedings if necessary for carrying out the proceeding.

3. Without prejudice to cases covered by criminal law, the competent authorities, bodies or natural or legal persons other than competent authorities which receive confidential information pursuant to this Directive may use it only in the performance of their duties and for the exercise of their functions, in the case of the competent authorities, within the scope of this Directive or, in the case of other authorities, bodies or natural or legal persons, for the purpose for which such information was provided to them and/or in the context of administrative or judicial proceedings specifically related to the exercise of those functions. However, where the competent authority or other authority, body or person communicating information consents thereto, the authority receiving the information may use it for other purposes.

4. Any confidential information received, exchanged or transmitted pursuant to this Directive shall be subject to the conditions of professional secrecy laid down in this Article. Nevertheless, this Article shall not prevent the competent authorities from exchanging or transmitting confidential information in accordance with this Directive and with other Directives applicable to investment firms, credit institutions, pension funds, UCITS, insurance and reinsurance intermediaries, insurance undertakings regulated markets or market operators or otherwise with the consent of the competent authority or other authority or body or natural or legal person that communicated the information.

5. This Article shall not prevent the competent authorities from exchanging or transmitting in accordance with national law, confidential information that has not been received from a competent authority of another Member State.

[5575]

Article 55
Relations with auditors

1. Member States shall provide, at least, that any person authorised within the meaning of Eighth Council Directive 84/253/EEC of 10 April 1984 on the approval of persons responsible for carrying out the statutory audits of accounting documents,[1] performing in an investment firm the task described in Article 51 of Fourth Council Directive 78/660/EEC of 25 July 1978 on the annual accounts of certain types of companies,[2] Article 37 of Directive 83/349/EEC or Article 31 of Directive 85/611/EEC or any other task prescribed by law, shall have a duty to report promptly to the competent authorities any fact or decision concerning that undertaking of which that person has become aware while carrying out that task and which is liable to:

    (a)   constitute a material breach of the laws, regulations or administrative provisions which lay down the conditions governing authorisation or which specifically govern pursuit of the activities of investment firms;

    (b)   affect the continuous functioning of the investment firm;

    (c)   lead to refusal to certify the accounts or to the expression of reservations.

That person shall also have a duty to report any facts and decisions of which the person becomes aware in the course of carrying out one of the tasks referred to in the first subparagraph in an undertaking having close links with the investment firm within which he is carrying out that task.

2. The disclosure in good faith to the competent authorities, by persons authorised within the meaning of Directive 84/253/EEC, of any fact or decision referred to in paragraph 1 shall not constitute a breach of any contractual or legal restriction on disclosure of information and shall not involve such persons in liability of any kind.

[5576]

NOTES

[1]   OJ L126, 12.5.1984, p 20.

[2]   OJ L222, 14.8.1978, p 11. Directive as last amended by Directive 2003/51/EC of the European Parliament and of the Council (OJ L178, 17.7.2003, p 16).

CHAPTER II
COOPERATION BETWEEN COMPETENT AUTHORITIES OF DIFFERENT
MEMBER STATES

Article 56
Obligation to cooperate

1. Competent authorities of different Member States shall cooperate with each other whenever necessary for the purpose of carrying out their duties under this Directive, making use of their powers whether set out in this Directive or in national law.

Competent authorities shall render assistance to competent authorities of the other Member States. In particular, they shall exchange information and cooperate in any investigation or supervisory activities.

In order to facilitate and accelerate cooperation, and more particularly exchange of information, Member States shall designate one single competent authority as a contact point for the purposes of this Directive. Member States shall communicate to the Commission and to the other Member States the names of the authorities which are designated to receive requests for exchange of information or cooperation pursuant to this paragraph.

2. When, taking into account the situation of the securities markets in the host Member State, the operations of a regulated market that has established arrangements in a host Member State have become of substantial importance for the functioning of the securities markets and the protection of the investors in that host Member State, the home and host competent authorities of the regulated market shall establish proportionate cooperation arrangements.

3. Member States shall take the necessary administrative and organisational measures to facilitate the assistance provided for in paragraph 1.

Competent authorities may use their powers for the purpose of cooperation, even in cases where the conduct under investigation does not constitute an infringement of any regulation in force in that Member State.

4. Where a competent authority has good reasons to suspect that acts contrary to the provisions of this Directive, carried out by entities not subject to its supervision, are being or have been carried out on the territory of another Member State, it shall notify this in as specific a manner as possible to the competent authority of the other Member State. The latter authority shall take appropriate action. It shall inform the notifying competent authority of the outcome of the action and, to the extent possible, of significant interim developments. This paragraph shall be without prejudice to the competences of the competent authority that has forwarded the information.

5.   In order to ensure the uniform application of paragraph 2 the Commission may adopt, ... implementing measures to establish the criteria under which the operations of a regulated market in a host Member State could be considered as of substantial importance for the functioning of the securities markets and the protection of the investors in that host Member State. [Those measures, designed to amend non-essential elements of this Directive by supplementing it, shall be adopted in accordance with the regulatory procedure with scrutiny referred to in Article 64(2).]

[5577]

NOTES

Para 5: words omitted repealed, and words in square brackets added, by European Parliament and Council Directive 2008/10/EC, Art 1(18), as from 20 March 2008.

Article 57
Cooperation in supervisory activities, on-the-spot verifications or in investigations

A competent authority of one Member State may request the cooperation of the competent authority of another Member State in a supervisory activity or for an on-the-spot verification or in an investigation. In the case of investment firms that are remote members of a regulated market the competent authority of the regulated market may choose to address them directly, in which case it shall inform the competent authority of the home Member State of the remote member accordingly.

Where a competent authority receives a request with respect to an on-the-spot verification or an investigation, it shall, within the framework of its powers:

(a)   carry out the verifications or investigations itself; or

(b)   allow the requesting authority to carry out the verification or investigation; or

(c)   allow auditors or experts to carry out the verification or investigation.

[5578]

Article 58
Exchange of information

1.   Competent authorities of Member States having been designated as contact points for the purposes of this Directive in accordance with Article 56(1) shall immediately supply one another with the information required for the purposes of carrying out the duties of the competent authorities, designated in accordance to Article 48(1), set out in the provisions adopted pursuant to this Directive.

Competent authorities exchanging information with other competent authorities under this Directive may indicate at the time of communication that such information must not be disclosed without their express agreement, in which case such information may be exchanged solely for the purposes for which those authorities gave their agreement.

2.   The competent authority having been designated as the contact point may transmit the information received under paragraph 1 and Articles 55 and 63 to the authorities referred to in Article 49. They shall not transmit it to other bodies or natural or legal persons without the express agreement of the competent authorities which disclosed it and solely for the purposes for which those authorities gave their agreement, except in duly justified circumstances. In this last case, the contact point shall immediately inform the contact point that sent the information.

3.   Authorities as referred to in Article 49 as well as other bodies or natural and legal persons receiving confidential information under paragraph 1 of this Article or under Articles 55 and 63 may use it only in the course of their duties, in particular:

(a)   to check that the conditions governing the taking-up of the business of investment firms are met and to facilitate the monitoring, on a non-consolidated or consolidated basis, of the conduct of that business, especially with regard to the capital adequacy requirements imposed by Directive 93/6/EEC, administrative and accounting procedures and internal-control mechanisms;

(b)   to monitor the proper functioning of trading venues;

(c)   to impose sanctions;

(d)   in administrative appeals against decisions by the competent authorities;

(e)   in court proceedings initiated under Article 52; or

(f)   in the extra-judicial mechanism for investors' complaints provided for in Article 53.

4.   The Commission may adopt, [in accordance with the regulatory procedure referred to in Article 64(3),] implementing measures concerning procedures for the exchange of information between competent authorities.

5.   Articles 54, 58 and 63 shall not prevent a competent authority from transmitting to central banks, the European System of Central Banks and the European Central Bank, in their capacity as monetary authorities, and, where appropriate, to other public authorities responsible for overseeing payment and settlement systems, confidential information intended for the performance of their

tasks; likewise such authorities or bodies shall not be prevented from communicating to the competent authorities such information as they may need for the purpose of performing their functions provided for in this Directive.

[5579]

NOTES
Para 4: words in square brackets substituted by European Parliament and Council Directive 2008/10/EC, Art 1(19), as from 20 March 2008.

Article 59
Refusal to cooperate

A competent authority may refuse to act on a request for cooperation in carrying out an investigation, on-the-spot verification or supervisory activity as provided for in Article 57 or to exchange information as provided for in Article 58 only where:

(a) such an investigation, on-the-spot verification, supervisory activity or exchange of information might adversely affect the sovereignty, security or public policy of the State addressed;

(b) judicial proceedings have already been initiated in respect of the same actions and the same persons before the authorities of the Member State addressed;

(c) final judgment has already been delivered in the Member State addressed in respect of the same persons and the same actions.

In the case of such a refusal, the competent authority shall notify the requesting competent authority accordingly, providing as detailed information as possible.

[5580]

Article 60
Inter-authority consultation prior to authorisation

1. The competent authorities of the other Member State involved shall be consulted prior to granting authorisation to an investment firm which is:

(a) a subsidiary of an investment firm or credit institution authorised in another Member State; or

(b) a subsidiary of the parent undertaking of an investment firm or credit institution authorised in another Member State; or

(c) controlled by the same natural or legal persons as control an investment firm or credit institution authorised in another Member State.

2. The competent authority of the Member State responsible for the supervision of credit institutions or insurance under-takings shall be consulted prior to granting an authorisation to an investment firm which is:

(a) a subsidiary of a credit institution or insurance undertaking authorised in the Community; or

(b) a subsidiary of the parent undertaking of a credit institution or insurance undertaking authorised in the Community; or

(c) controlled by the same person, whether natural or legal, who controls a credit institution or insurance undertaking authorised in the Community.

3. The relevant competent authorities referred to in paragraphs 1 and 2 shall in particular consult each other when assessing the suitability of the shareholders or members and the reputation and experience of persons who effectively direct the business involved in the management of another entity of the same group. They shall exchange all information regarding the suitability of shareholders or members and the reputation and experience of persons who effectively direct the business that is of relevance to the other competent authorities involved, for the granting of an authorisation as well as for the ongoing assessment of compliance with operating conditions.

[5581]

Article 61
Powers for host Member States

1. Host Member States may, for statistical purposes, require all investment firms with branches within their territories to report to them periodically on the activities of those branches.

2. In discharging their responsibilities under this Directive, host Member States may require branches of investment firms to provide the information necessary for the monitoring of their compliance with the standards set by the host Member State that apply to them for the cases provided for in Article 32(7). Those requirements may not be more stringent than those which the same Member State imposes on established firms for the monitoring of their compliance with the same standards.

[5582]

Article 62
Precautionary measures to be taken by host Member States

1. Where the competent authority of the host Member State has clear and demonstrable grounds for believing that an investment firm acting within its territory under the freedom to provide services is in breach of the obligations arising from the provisions adopted pursuant to this Directive or that an investment firm that has a branch within its territory is in breach of the obligations arising from the provisions adopted pursuant to this Directive which do not confer powers on the competent authority of the host Member State, it shall refer those findings to the competent authority of the home Member State.

If, despite the measures taken by the competent authority of the home Member State or because such measures prove inadequate, the investment firm persists in acting in a manner that is clearly prejudicial to the interests of host Member State investors or the orderly functioning of markets, the competent authority of the host Member State, after informing the competent authority of the home Member State shall take all the appropriate measures needed in order to protect investors and the proper functioning of the markets. This shall include the possibility of preventing offending investment firms from initiating any further transactions within their territories. The Commission shall be informed of such measures without delay.

2. Where the competent authorities of a host Member State ascertain that an investment firm that has a branch within its territory is in breach of the legal or regulatory provisions adopted in that State pursuant to those provisions of this Directive which confer powers on the host Member State's competent authorities, those authorities shall require the investment firm concerned to put an end to its irregular situation.

If the investment firm concerned fails to take the necessary steps, the competent authorities of the host Member State shall take all appropriate measures to ensure that the investment firm concerned puts an end to its irregular situation. The nature of those measures shall be communicated to the competent authorities of the home Member State.

If, despite the measures taken by the host Member State, the investment firm persists in breaching the legal or regulatory provisions referred to in the first subparagraph in force in the host Member State, the latter may, after informing the competent authorities of the home Member State, take appropriate measures to prevent or to penalise further irregularities and, in so far as necessary, to prevent that investment firm from initiating any further transactions within its territory. The Commission shall be informed of such measures without delay.

3. Where the competent authority of the host Member State of a regulated market or an MTF has clear and demonstrable grounds for believing that such regulated market or MTF is in breach of the obligations arising from the provisions adopted pursuant to this Directive, it shall refer those findings to the competent authority of the home Member State of the regulated market or the MTF.

If, despite the measures taken by the competent authority of the home Member State or because such measures prove inadequate, the said regulated market or the MTF persists in acting in a manner that is clearly prejudicial to the interests of host Member State investors or the orderly functioning of markets, the competent authority of the host Member State, after informing the competent authority of the home Member State, shall take all the appropriate measures needed in order to protect investors and the proper functioning of the markets. This shall include the possibility of preventing the said regulated market or the MTF from making their arrangements available to remote members or participants established in the host Member State. The Commission shall be informed of such measures without delay.

4. Any measure adopted pursuant to paragraphs 1, 2 or 3 involving sanctions or restrictions on the activities of an investment firm or of a regulated market shall be properly justified and communicated to the investment firm or to the regulated market concerned.

[5583]

CHAPTER III
COOPERATION WITH THIRD COUNTRIES

Article 63
Exchange of information with third countries

1. Member States may conclude cooperation agreements providing for the exchange of information with the competent authorities of third countries only if the information disclosed is subject to guarantees of professional secrecy at least equivalent to those required under Article 54. Such exchange of information must be intended for the performance of the tasks of those competent authorities.

Member States may transfer personal data to a third country in accordance to Chapter IV of Directive 95/46/EC.

Member States may also conclude cooperation agreements providing for the exchange of information with third country authorities, bodies and natural or legal persons responsible for:

(i)   the supervision of credit institutions, other financial organisations, insurance undertakings and the supervision of financial markets;

(ii)   the liquidation and bankruptcy of investment firms and other similar procedures;

(iii)   carrying out statutory audits of the accounts of investment firms and other financial institutions, credit institutions and insurance undertakings, in the performance of their supervisory functions, or which administer compensation schemes, in the performance of their functions;

(iv)   overseeing the bodies involved in the liquidation and bankruptcy of investment firms and other similar procedures;

(v)   overseeing persons charged with carrying out statutory audits of the accounts of insurance undertakings, credit institutions, investment firms and other financial institutions,

only if the information disclosed is subject to guarantees of professional secrecy at least equivalent to those required under Article 54. Such exchange of information must be intended for the performance of the tasks of those authorities or bodies or natural or legal persons.

2.   Where the information originates in another Member State, it may not be disclosed without the express agreement of the competent authorities which have transmitted it and, where appropriate, solely for the purposes for which those authorities gave their agreement. The same provision applies to information provided by third country competent authorities.

[5584]

TITLE V
FINAL PROVISIONS

Article 64
Committee procedure

1.   The Commission shall be assisted by the European Securities Committee established by Commission Decision 2001/528/EC[1] (hereinafter referred to as the Committee).

[2.   Where reference is made to this paragraph, Article 5a(1) to (4) and Article 7 of Decision 1999/468/EC shall apply, having regard to the provisions of Article 8 thereof.]

[2a.   None of the implementing measures enacted may change the essential provisions of this Directive.]

[3.   Where reference is made to this paragraph, Articles 5 and 7 of Decision 1999/468/EC shall apply, having regard to the provisions of Article 8 thereof.

The period laid down in Article 5(6) of Decision 1999/468/EC shall be set at three months.]

[4.   By 31 December 2010, and, thereafter, at least every three years, the Commission shall review the provisions concerning its implementing powers and present a report to the European Parliament and to the Council on the functioning of those powers. The report shall examine, in particular, the need for the Commission to propose amendments to this Directive in order to ensure the appropriate scope of the implementing powers conferred on the Commission. The conclusion as to whether or not amendment is necessary shall be accompanied by a detailed statement of reasons. If necessary, the report shall be accompanied by a legislative proposal to amend the provisions conferring implementing powers on the Commission.]

[5585]

NOTES

Paras 2, 3: substituted by European Parliament and Council Directive 2008/10/EC, Art 1(20)(a), (b), as from 20 March 2008.

Para 2a: inserted by European Parliament and Council Directive 2006/31/EC, Art 1(2), as from 28 April 2006.

Para 4: added by European Parliament and Council Directive 2008/10/EC, Art 1(20)(c), as from 20 March 2008.

[1]   OJ L191, 13.7.2001, p 45.

[Article 65
Reports and review

1.   By 31 October 2007, the Commission shall, on the basis of public consultation and in the light of discussions with competent authorities, report to the European Parliament and to the Council on the possible extension of the scope of the provisions of this Directive concerning pre and post-trade transparency obligations to transactions in classes of financial instruments other than shares.

2.   By 31 October 2008, the Commission shall present the European Parliament and the Council with a report on the application of Article 27.

3.   By 30 April 2008, the Commission shall, on the basis of public consultations and in the light of discussions with competent authorities, report to the European Parliament and to the Council on:

    (a)   the continued appropriateness of the exemption provided for in Article 2(1)(k) for undertakings whose main business is dealing on own account in commodity derivatives;

    (b)   the content and form of proportionate requirements for the authorisation and supervision of such undertakings as investment firms within the meaning of this Directive;

    (c)   the appropriateness of rules concerning the appointment of tied agents in performing investment services and/or activities, in particular with respect to the supervision of them;

    (d)   the continued appropriateness of the exemption provided for in Article 2(1)(i).

4.   By 30 April 2008, the Commission shall present the European Parliament and the Council with a report on the state of the removal of the obstacles which may prevent the consolidation at European level of the information that trading venues are required to publish.

5.   On the basis of the reports referred to in paragraphs 1 to 4, the Commission may submit proposals for related amendments to this Directive.

6.   By 31 October 2006, the Commission shall, in the light of discussions with competent authorities, report to the European Parliament and to the Council on the continued appropriateness of the requirements for professional indemnity insurance imposed on intermediaries under Community law.]

[5586]

NOTES

    Substituted by European Parliament and Council Directive 2006/31/EC, Art 1(3), as from 28 April 2006.

Article 66
Amendment of Directive 85/611/EEC

In Article 5 of Directive 85/611/EEC, paragraph 4 shall be replaced by the following:

    "4.   Articles 2(2), 12, 13 and 19 of Directive 2004/39/EC of the European Parliament and of the Council of 21 April 2004 on markets in financial instruments,[1] shall apply to the provision of the services referred to in paragraph 3 of this Article by management companies.".

[5587]–[5589]

NOTES

    [1]   OJ L145, 30.4.2004, p 1.

Articles 67, 68

(*Article 67 repealed by European Parliament and Council Directive 2006/49/EC, Art 52, Annex VIII, as from 20 July 2006; Article 68 repealed by European Parliament and Council Directive 2006/48/EC, Art 158, Annex XIII, as from 20 July 2006.*)

[Article 69
Repeal of Directive 93/22/EEC

Directive 93/22/EEC shall be repealed with effect from 1 November 2007. References to Directive 93/22/EEC shall be construed as references to this Directive. References to terms defined in, or Articles of, Directive 93/22/EEC shall be construed as references to the equivalent term defined in, or Article of, this Directive.]

[5590]

NOTES

    Substituted by European Parliament and Council Directive 2006/31/EC, Art 1(4), as from 28 April 2006.

Article 70
Transposition

[Member States shall adopt the laws, regulations and administrative provisions necessary to comply with this Directive by 31 January 2007. They shall forthwith inform the Commission thereof.

    They shall apply these measures from 1 November 2007.]

    When Member States adopt these measures, they shall contain a reference to this Directive or shall be accompanied by such reference on the occasion of their official publication. The methods of making such reference shall be laid down by the Member States.

[5591]

NOTES

    Words in square brackets substituted by European Parliament and Council Directive 2006/31/EC, Art 1(5), as from 28 April 2006.

Article 71
Transitional provisions

[1. Investment firms already authorised in their home Member State to provide investment services before 1 November 2007 shall be deemed to be so authorised for the purposes of this Directive if the laws of that Member State provide that to take up such activities they must comply with conditions comparable to those provided for in Articles 9 to 14.

2. A regulated market or a market operator already authorised in its home Member State before 1 November 2007 shall be deemed to be so authorised for the purposes of this Directive if the laws of that Member State provide that the regulated market or market operator, as the case may be, must comply with conditions comparable to those provided for in Title III.

3. Tied agents already entered in a public register before 1 November 2007 shall be deemed to be so registered for the purposes of this Directive if the laws of Member States concerned provide that tied agents must comply with conditions comparable to those provided for in Article 23.

4. Information communicated before 1 November 2007 for the purposes of Articles 17, 18 or 30 of Directive 93/22/EEC shall be deemed to have been communicated for the purposes of Articles 31 and 32 of this Directive.

5. Any existing system falling under the definition of an MTF operated by a market operator of a regulated market shall, at the request of the market operator of the regulated market, be authorised as an MTF, provided that it complies with rules equivalent to those required by this Directive for the authorisation and operation of MTFs and that the request concerned is made within eighteen months following 1 November 2007.]

6. Investment firms shall be authorised to continue considering existing professional clients as such provided that this categorisation has been granted by the investment firm on the basis of an adequate assessment of the expertise, experience and knowledge of the client which gives reasonable assurance, in light of the nature of the transactions or services envisaged, that the client is capable of making his own investment decisions and understands the risks involved. Those investment firms shall inform their clients about the conditions established in the Directive for the categorisation of clients.

[5592]

NOTES
    Paras 1–5: substituted by European Parliament and Council Directive 2006/31/EC, Art 1(6), as from 28 April 2006.

Article 72
Entry into force

This Directive shall enter into force on the day of its publication in the *Official Journal of the European Union*.

[5593]

Article 73
Addressees

This Directive is addressed to the Member States.

[5594]

ANNEX I
LIST OF SERVICES AND ACTIVITIES AND FINANCIAL INSTRUMENTS

SECTION A
INVESTMENT SERVICES AND ACTIVITIES

(1) Reception and transmission of orders in relation to one or more financial instruments.

(2) Execution of orders on behalf of clients.

(3) Dealing on own account.

(4) Portfolio management.

(5) Investment advice.

(6) Underwriting of financial instruments and/or placing of financial instruments on a firm commitment basis.

(7) Placing of financial instruments without a firm commitment basis

(8) Operation of Multilateral Trading Facilities.

SECTION B
ANCILLARY SERVICES

(1)   Safekeeping and administration of financial instruments for the account of clients, including custodianship and related services such as cash/collateral management;

(2)   Granting credits or loans to an investor to allow him to carry out a transaction in one or more financial instruments, where the firm granting the credit or loan is involved in the transaction;

(3)   Advice to undertakings on capital structure, industrial strategy and related matters and advice and services relating to mergers and the purchase of undertakings;

(4)   Foreign exchange services where these are connected to the provision of investment services;

(5)   Investment research and financial analysis or other forms of general recommendation relating to transactions in financial instruments;

(6)   Services related to underwriting.

(7)   Investment services and activities as well as ancillary services of the type included under Section A or B of Annex 1 related to the underlying of the derivatives included under Section C – 5, 6, 7 and 10 – where these are connected to the provision of investment or ancillary services.

SECTION C
FINANCIAL INSTRUMENTS

(1)   Transferable securities;

(2)   Money-market instruments;

(3)   Units in collective investment undertakings;

(4)   Options, futures, swaps, forward rate agreements and any other derivative contracts relating to securities, currencies, interest rates or yields, or other derivatives instruments, financial indices or financial measures which may be settled physically or in cash;

(5)   Options, futures, swaps, forward rate agreements and any other derivative contracts relating to commodities that must be settled in cash or may be settled in cash at the option of one of the parties (otherwise than by reason of a default or other termination event);

(6)   Options, futures, swaps, and any other derivative contract relating to commodities that can be physically settled provided that they are traded on a regulated market and/or an MTF;

(7)   Options, futures, swaps, forwards and any other derivative contracts relating to commodities, that can be physically settled not otherwise mentioned in C.6 and not being for commercial purposes, which have the characteristics of other derivative financial instruments, having regard to whether, inter alia, they are cleared and settled through recognised clearing houses or are subject to regular margin calls;

(8)   Derivative instruments for the transfer of credit risk;

(9)   Financial contracts for differences.

(10)   Options, futures, swaps, forward rate agreements and any other derivative contracts relating to climatic variables, freight rates, emission allowances or inflation rates or other official economic statistics that must be settled in cash or may be settled in cash at the option of one of the parties (otherwise than by reason of a default or other termination event), as well as any other derivative contracts relating to assets, rights, obligations, indices and measures not otherwise mentioned in this Section, which have the characteristics of other derivative financial instruments, having regard to whether, inter alia, they are traded on a regulated market or an MTF, are cleared and settled through recognised clearing houses or are subject to regular margin calls.

[5595]

ANNEX II
PROFESSIONAL CLIENTS FOR THE PURPOSE OF THIS DIRECTIVE

Professional client is a client who possesses the experience, knowledge and expertise to make its own investment decisions and properly assess the risks that it incurs. In order to be considered a professional client, the client must comply with the following criteria:

I. Categories of client who are considered to be professionals

The following should all be regarded as professionals in all investment services and activities and financial instruments for the purposes of the Directive.

(1)   Entities which are required to be authorised or regulated to operate in the financial markets. The list below should be understood as including all authorised entities carrying out the characteristic activities of the entities mentioned: entities authorised by a Member State under a Directive, entities authorised or regulated by a Member State without reference to a Directive, and entities authorised or regulated by a non-Member State:

    (a)   Credit institutions
    (b)   Investment firms
    (c)   Other authorised or regulated financial institutions
    (d)   Insurance companies
    (e)   Collective investment schemes and management companies of such schemes
    (f)   Pension funds and management companies of such funds
    (g)   Commodity and commodity derivatives dealers
    (h)   Locals
    (i)   Other institutional investors

(2)   Large undertakings meeting two of the following size requirements on a company basis:
— balance sheet total: EUR 20,000,000,
— net turnover: EUR 40,000,000,
— own funds: EUR 2,000,000.

(3)   National and regional governments, public bodies that manage public debt, Central Banks, international and supranational institutions such as the World Bank, the IMF, the ECB, the EIB and other similar international organisations.

(4)   Other institutional investors whose main activity is to invest in financial instruments, including entities dedicated to the securitisation of assets or other financing transactions.

The entities mentioned above are considered to be professionals. They must however be allowed to request non-professional treatment and investment firms may agree to provide a higher level of protection. Where the client of an investment firm is an undertaking referred to above, the investment firm must inform it prior to any provision of services that, on the basis of the information available to the firm, the client is deemed to be a professional client, and will be treated as such unless the firm and the client agree otherwise. The firm must also inform the customer that he can request a variation of the terms of the agreement in order to secure a higher degree of protection.

It is the responsibility of the client, considered to be a professional client, to ask for a higher level of protection when it deems it is unable to properly assess or manage the risks involved.

This higher level of protection will be provided when a client who is considered to be a professional enters into a written agreement with the investment firm to the effect that it shall not be treated as a professional for the purposes of the applicable conduct of business regime. Such agreement should specify whether this applies to one or more particular services or transactions, or to one or more types of product or transaction.

II. Clients who may be treated as professionals on request
II.1. Identification criteria

Clients other than those mentioned in section I, including public sector bodies and private individual investors, may also be allowed to waive some of the protections afforded by the conduct of business rules.

Investment firms should therefore be allowed to treat any of the above clients as professionals provided the relevant criteria and procedure mentioned below are fulfilled. These clients should not, however, be presumed to possess market knowledge and experience comparable to that of the categories listed in section I.

Any such waiver of the protection afforded by the standard conduct of business regime shall be considered valid only if an adequate assessment of the expertise, experience and knowledge of the client, undertaken by the investment firm, gives reasonable assurance, in light of the nature of the transactions or services envisaged, that the client is capable of making his own investment decisions and understanding the risks involved.

The fitness test applied to managers and directors of entities licensed under Directives in the financial field could be regarded as an example of the assessment of expertise and knowledge. In the case of small entities, the person subject to the above assessment should be the person authorised to carry out transactions on behalf of the entity.

In the course of the above assessment, as a minimum, two of the following criteria should be satisfied:
— the client has carried out transactions, in significant size, on the relevant market at an average frequency of 10 per quarter over the previous four quarters,
— the size of the client's financial instrument portfolio, defined as including cash deposits and financial instruments exceeds EUR 500,000,
— the client works or has worked in the financial sector for at least one year in a professional position, which requires knowledge of the transactions or services envisaged.

II.2. Procedure

The clients defined above may waive the benefit of the detailed rules of conduct only where the following procedure is followed:
— they must state in writing to the investment firm that they wish to be treated as a professional client, either generally or in respect of a particular investment service or transaction, or type of transaction or product,

—   the investment firm must give them a clear written warning of the protections and investor compensation rights they may lose;

—   they must state in writing, in a separate document from the contract, that they are aware of the consequences of losing such protections.

Before deciding to accept any request for waiver, investment firms must be required to take all reasonable steps to ensure that the client requesting to be treated as a professional client meets the relevant requirements stated in Section II.1 above.

However, if clients have already been categorised as professionals under parameters and procedures similar to those above, it is not intended that their relationships with investment firms should be affected by any new rules adopted pursuant to this Annex.

Firms must implement appropriate written internal policies and procedures to categorise clients. Professional clients are responsible for keeping the firm informed about any change, which could affect their current categorisation. Should the investment firm become aware however that the client no longer fulfils the initial conditions, which made him eligible for a professional treatment, the investment firm must take appropriate action.

[5596]

COMMISSION DIRECTIVE

of 29 April 2004

implementing Directive 2003/6/EC of the European Parliament and of the Council as regards accepted market practices, the definition of inside information in relation to derivatives on commodities, the drawing up of lists of insiders, the notification of managers' transactions and the notification of suspicious transactions

(2004/72/EC)

(Text with EEA relevance)

NOTES
   Date of publication in OJ: OJ L162, 30.4.2004, p 70. Notes are as in the original OJ version.
   As of 1 February 2009, this Directive had not been amended.

THE COMMISSION OF THE EUROPEAN COMMUNITIES,

   Having regard to the Treaty establishing the European Community,

   Having regard to Directive 2003/6/EC of the European Parliament and of the Council of 28 January 2003 on insider dealing and market manipulation (market abuse)[1], and in particular the second paragraph of point 1 and point 2(a) of Article 1 and the fourth, fifth and seventh indents of Article 6(10) thereof,

   After consulting the Committee of European Securities Regulators (CESR)[2] for technical advice,

   Whereas:

   (1)   Practising fairness and efficiency by market participants is required in order not to create prejudice to normal market activity and market integrity. In particular, market practices inhibiting the interaction of supply and demand by limiting the opportunities for other market participants to respond to transactions can create higher risks for market integrity and are, therefore, less likely to be accepted by competent authorities. On the other hand, market practices which enhance liquidity are more likely to be accepted than those practices reducing them. Market practices breaching rules and regulations designed to prevent market abuse, or codes of conduct, are less likely to be accepted by competent authorities. Since market practices change rapidly in order to meet investors' needs, competent authorities need to be alert to new and emerging market practice.

   (2)   Transparency of market practices by market participants is crucial for considering whether a particular market practice can be accepted by competent authorities. The less transparent a practice is, the more likely it is not to be accepted. However, practices on non regulated markets might for structural reasons be less transparent than similar practices on regulated markets. Such practices should not be in themselves considered as unacceptable by competent authorities.

   (3)   Particular market practices in a given market should not put at risk market integrity of other, directly or indirectly, related markets throughout the Community, whether those markets be regulated or not. Therefore, the higher the risk for market integrity on such a related market within the Community, the less those practices are likely to be accepted by competent authorities.

   (4)   Competent authorities, while considering the acceptance of a particular market practice, should consult other competent authorities, particularly for cases where there exist comparable markets to the one under scrutiny. However, there might be circumstances in which a market practice can be deemed to be acceptable on one particular market and unacceptable on another comparable market within the Community. In case of discrepancies between market practices which

are accepted in one Member State and not in another one, discussion could take place in the Committee of European Securities Regulators in order to find a solution. With regard to their decisions about such acceptance, competent authorities should ensure a high degree of consultation and transparency vis-à-vis market participants and end-users.

(5)   It is essential for market participants on derivative markets the underlying of which is not a financial instrument, to get greater legal certainty on what constitutes inside information.

(6)   The establishment, by issuers or persons acting on their behalf or for their account, of lists of persons working for them under a contract of employment or otherwise and having access to inside information relating, directly or indirectly, to the issuer, is a valuable measure for protecting market integrity. These lists may serve issuers or such persons to control the flow of such inside information and thereby manage their confidentiality duties. Moreover, these lists may also constitute a useful tool for competent authorities when monitoring the application of market abuse legislation. Identifying inside information to which any insider has access and the date on which it gained access thereto is necessary for issuers and competent authorities. Access to inside information relating, directly or indirectly, to the issuer by persons included on such a list is without prejudice to their duty to refrain from insider dealing on the basis of any inside information as defined in Directive 2003/6/EC.

(7)   The notification of transactions conducted by persons discharging managerial responsibilities within an issuer on their own account, or by persons closely associated with them, is not only a valuable information for market participants, but also constitutes an additional means for competent authorities to supervise markets. The obligation by senior executives to notify transactions is without prejudice to their duty to refrain from insider dealing on the basis of any inside information as defined in Directive 2003/6/EC.

(8)   Notification of transactions should be in accordance with the rules on transfer of personal data laid down in Directive 95/46/EC[3] of the European Parliament and of the Council of 24 October 1995 on the protection of individuals with regard to the processing of personal data and on the movement of such data.

(9)   Notification of suspicious transactions by persons professionally arranging transactions in financial instruments to the competent authority requires sufficient indications that the transactions might constitute market abuse, ie transactions which give reasonable ground for suspecting that insider dealing or market manipulation is involved. Certain transactions by themselves may seem completely void of anything suspicious, but might deliver such indications of possible market abuse, when seen in perspective with other transactions, certain behaviour or other information.

(10)   This Directive respects the fundamental rights and observes the principles recognised in particular by the Charta of Fundamental Rights of the European Union and in particular by Article 8 of the European Convention on Human Rights.

(11)   The measures provided for in this Directive are in accordance with the opinion of the European Securities Committee,

[5597]

NOTES

[1]   OJ L96, 12.4.2003, p 16.
[2]   CESR was established by Commission Decision 2001/527/EC of 6 June 2001 (OJ L191, 13.7.2001, p 43).
[3]   OJ L281, 23.11.1995, p 31.

HAS ADOPTED THIS DIRECTIVE:

Article 1
Definitions

For the purpose of applying Article 6(10) of Directive 2003/6/EC:

   1.   'Person discharging managerial responsibilities within an issuer' shall mean a person who is
         (a)   a member of the administrative, management or supervisory bodies of the issuer;
         (b)   a senior executive, who is not a member of the bodies as referred to in point (a), having regular access to inside information relating, directly or indirectly, to the issuer, and the power to make managerial decisions affecting the future developments and business prospects of this issuer.
   2.   'Person closely associated with a person discharging managerial responsibilities within an issuer of financial instruments' shall mean:
         (a)   the spouse of the person discharging managerial responsibilities, or any partner of that person considered by national law as equivalent to the spouse;
         (b)   according to national law, dependent children of the person discharging managerial responsibilities;
         (c)   other relatives of the person discharging managerial responsibilities, who have shared the same household as that person for at least one year on the date of the transaction concerned;

(d)   any legal person, trust or partnership, whose managerial responsibilities are discharged by a person referred to in point 1 of this Article or in letters (a), (b) and (c) of this point, or which is directly or indirectly controlled by such a person, or that is set up for the benefit of such a person, or whose economic interests are substantially equivalent to those of such person.

3.   'Person professionally arranging transactions' shall mean at least an investment firm or a credit institution.

4.   'Investment firm' shall mean any person as defined in Article 1(2) of Council Directive 93/22/EEC;[1]

5.   'Credit institution' shall mean any person as defined in Article 1(1) of Directive 2000/12/EC of the European Parliament and of the Council;[2]

6.   'Competent authority' shall mean the competent authority as defined in Article 1(7) of Directive 2003/6/EC.

[5597A]

NOTES
[1]   OJ L141, 11.6.1993, p 27.
[2]   OJ L126, 26.5.2000, p 1.

Article 2
Factors to be taken into account when considering market practices

1.   For the purposes of applying paragraph 2 of point 1 and point 2(a) of Article 1 of Directive 2003/6/EC, Member States shall ensure that the following non exhaustive factors are taken into account by competent authorities, without prejudice to collaboration with other authorities, when assessing whether they can accept a particular market practice:

(a)   the level of transparency of the relevant market practice to the whole market;
(b)   the need to safeguard the operation of market forces and the proper interplay of the forces of supply and demand.;
(c)   the degree to which the relevant market practice has an impact on market liquidity and efficiency;
(d)   the degree to which the relevant practice takes into account the trading mechanism of the relevant market and enables market participants to react properly and in a timely manner to the new market situation created by that practice;
(e)   the risk inherent in the relevant practice for the integrity of, directly or indirectly, related markets, whether regulated or not, in the relevant financial instrument within the whole Community;
(f)   the outcome of any investigation of the relevant market practice by any competent authority or other authority mentioned in Article 12(1) of Directive 2003/6/EC, in particular whether the relevant market practice breached rules or regulations designed to prevent market abuse, or codes of conduct, be it on the market in question or on directly or indirectly related markets within the Community;
(g)   the structural characteristics of the relevant market including whether it is regulated or not, the types of financial instruments traded and the type of market participants, including the extent of retail investors participation in the relevant market.

Member States shall ensure that competent authorities shall, when considering the need for safeguard referred to in point (b) of the first subparagraph, in particular analyse the impact of the relevant market practice against the main market parameters, such as the specific market conditions before carrying out the relevant market practice, the weighted average price of a single session or the daily closing price.

2.   Member States shall ensure that practices, in particular new or emerging market practices are not assumed to be unacceptable by the competent authority simply because they have not been previously accepted by it.

3.   Member States shall ensure that competent authorities review regularly the market practices they have accepted, in particular taking into account significant changes to the relevant market environment, such as changes to trading rules or to market infrastructure.

[5598]

Article 3
Consultation procedures and disclosure of decisions

1.   For the purposes of applying paragraph 2 of point 1 and point 2(a) of Article 1 of Directive 2003/6/EC, Member States shall ensure that the procedures set out in paragraphs 2 and 3 of this Article are observed by competent authorities when considering whether to accept or continue to accept a particular market practice.

PART IV
EC MATERIALS

2.   Without prejudice to Article 11(2) of Directive 2003/6/EC, Member States shall ensure that competent authorities, before accepting or not the market practice concerned, consult as appropriate relevant bodies such as representatives of issuers, financial services providers, consumers, other authorities and market operators.

The consultation procedure shall include consultation of other competent authorities, in particular where there exist comparable markets, i e in structures, volume, type of transactions.

3.   Member States shall ensure that competent authorities publicly disclose their decisions regarding the acceptability of the market practice concerned, including appropriate descriptions of such practices. Member States shall further ensure that competent authorities transmit their decisions as soon as possible to the Committee of European Securities Regulators which shall make them immediately available on its website.

The disclosure shall include a description of the factors taken into account in determining whether the relevant practice is regarded as acceptable, in particular where different conclusions have been reached regarding the acceptability of the same practice on different Member States markets.

4.   When investigatory actions on specific cases have already started, the consultation procedures set out in paragraphs 1 to 3 may be delayed until the end of such investigation and possible related sanctions.

5.   A market practice which was accepted following the consultation procedures set out in paragraphs 1 to 3 shall not be changed without using the same consultation procedures.

[5599]

Article 4
Inside information in relation to derivatives on commodities

For the purposes of applying the second paragraph of point 1 of Article 1 of Directive 2003/6/EC, users of markets on which derivatives on commodities are traded, are deemed to expect to receive information relating, directly or indirectly, to one or more such derivatives which is:
   (a)   routinely made available to the users of those markets, or
   (b)   required to be disclosed in accordance with legal or regulatory provisions, market rules, contracts or customs on the relevant underlying commodity market or commodity derivatives market.

[5600]

Article 5
Lists of insiders

1.   For the purposes of applying the third subparagraph of Article 6(3) of Directive 2003/6/EC, Member States shall ensure that lists of insiders include all persons covered by that Article who have access to inside information relating, directly or indirectly, to the issuer, whether on a regular or occasional basis.

2.   Lists of insiders shall state at least:
   (a)   the identity of any person having access to inside information;
   (b)   the reason why any such person is on the list;
   (c)   the date at which the list of insiders was created and updated.

3.   Lists of insiders shall be promptly updated
   (a)   whenever there is a change in the reason why any person is already on the list;
   (b)   whenever any new person has to be added to the list;
   (c)   by mentioning whether and when any person already on the list has no longer access to inside information.

4.   Member States shall ensure that lists of insiders will be kept for at least five years after being drawn up or updated.

5.   Member States shall ensure that the persons required to draw up lists of insiders take the necessary measures to ensure that any person on such a list that has access to inside information acknowledges the legal and regulatory duties entailed and is aware of the sanctions attaching to the misuse or improper circulation of such information.

[5601]

Article 6
Managers' Transactions

1.   For the purposes of applying Article 6(4) of Directive 2003/6/EC, and without prejudice to the right of Member States to provide for other notification obligations than those covered by that Article, Member States shall ensure that all transactions related to shares admitted to trading on a regulated market, or to derivatives or other financial instruments linked to them, conducted on the own account of persons referred to in Article 1 points 1 and 2 above, are notified to the competent authorities. The rules of notification to which those persons have to comply with shall be those of the Member State where the issuer is registered. The notification shall be made within five working

days of the transaction date to the competent authority of that Member State. When the issuer is not registered in a Member State, this notification shall be made to the competent authority of the Member State in which it is required to file the annual information in relation to the shares in accordance with Article 10 of Directive 2003/71/EC.

2. Member States may decide that, until the total amount of transactions has reached five thousand Euros at the end of a calendar year, no notification is required or notification may be delayed until the 31 January of the following year. The total amount of transactions shall be computed by summing up the transactions conducted on the own account of persons referred to in Article 1 point 1 with the transactions conducted on the own account of persons referred to in Article 1 point 2.

3. The notification shall contain the following information:
   (a) name of the person discharging managerial responsibilities within the issuer, or, where applicable, name of the person closely associated with such a person,
   (b) reason for responsibility to notify,
   (c) name of the relevant issuer,
   (d) description of the financial instrument,
   (e) nature of the transaction (e g acquisition or disposal),
   (f) date and place of the transaction
   (g) price and volume of the transaction.

[5602]

Article 7
Suspicious transactions to be notified

For the purposes of applying Article 6(9) of Directive 2003/6/EC, Member States shall ensure that persons referred to in Article 1 point 3 above shall decide on a case-by-case basis whether there are reasonable grounds for suspecting that a transaction involves insider dealing or market manipulation, taking into account the elements constituting insider dealing or market manipulation, referred to in Articles 1 to 5 of Directive 2003/6/EC, in Commission Directive 2003/124/EC[1] implementing Directive 2003/6/EC as regards the definition and public disclosure of inside information and the definition of market manipulation, and in Article 4 of this Directive. Without prejudice to Article 10 of Directive 2003/6/EC, persons professionally arranging transactions shall be subject to the rules of notification of the Member State in which they are registered or have their head office, or in the case of a branch, the Member State where the branch is situated. The notification shall be addressed to the competent authority of this Member State.

Member States shall ensure that competent authorities receiving the notification of suspicious transactions transmit such information immediately to the competent authorities of the regulated markets concerned.

[5603]

NOTES
1 OJ L339, 24.12.2003, p 70.

Article 8
Timeframe for notification

Member States shall ensure that in the event that persons, as referred to in Article 1 point 3, become aware of a fact or information that gives reasonable ground for suspicion concerning the relevant transaction, make a notification without delay.

[5604]

Article 9
Content of notification

1. Member States shall ensure that persons subject to the notification obligation transmit to the competent authority the following information:
   (a) description of the transactions, including the type of order (such as limit order, market order or other characteristics of the order) and the type of trading market (such as block trade);
   (b) reasons for suspicion that the transactions might constitute market abuse;
   (c) means for identification of the persons on behalf of whom the transactions have been carried out, and of other persons involved in the relevant transactions;
   (d) capacity in which the person subject to the notification obligation operates (such as for own account or on behalf of third parties);
   (e) any information which may have significance in reviewing the suspicious transactions.

2. Where that information is not available at the time of notification, the notification shall include at least the reasons why the notifying persons suspect that the transactions might constitute

insider dealing or market manipulation. All remaining information shall be provided to the competent authority as soon as it becomes available.

[5605]

Article 10
Means of notification

Member States shall ensure that notification to the competent authority can be done by mail, electronic mail, telecopy or telephone, provided that in the latter case confirmation is notified by any written form upon request by the competent authority.

[5606]

Article 11
Liability and professional secrecy

1. Member States shall ensure that the person notifying to the competent authority as referred to in Articles 7 to 10 shall not inform any other person, in particular the persons on behalf of whom the transactions have been carried out or parties related to those persons, of this notification, except by virtue of provisions laid down by law. The fulfilment of this requirement shall not involve the notifying person in liability of any kind, providing the notifying person acts in good faith.

2. Member States shall ensure that competent authorities do not disclose to any person the identity of the person having notified these transactions, if disclosure would, or would be likely to harm the person having notified the transactions. This provision is without prejudice to the requirements of the enforcement and the sanctioning regimes under Directive 2003/6/EC and to the rules on transfer of personal data laid down in Directive 95/46/EC.

3. The notification in good faith to the competent authority as referred to in Articles 7 to 10 shall not constitute a breach of any restriction on disclosure of information imposed by contract or by any legislative, regulatory or administrative provision, and shall not involve the person notifying in liability of any kind related to such notification.

[5607]

Article 12
Transposition

1. Member States shall bring into force the laws, regulations and administrative provisions necessary to comply with this Directive by 12 October 2004 at the latest. They shall forthwith communicate to the Commission the text of the provisions and a correlation table between those provisions and this Directive.

When Member States adopt those provisions, they shall contain a reference to this Directive or be accompanied by such a reference on the occasion of their official publication. Member States shall determine how such reference is to be made.

2. Member States shall communicate to the Commission the text of the main provisions of national law which they adopt in the field covered by this Directive.

[5608]

Article 13
Entry into force

This Directive shall enter into force on the day of its publication in the *Official Journal of the European Union*.

[5609]

Article 14
Addressees

This Directive is addressed to the Member States.

[5610]

COMMISSION REGULATION

of 29 April 2004

implementing Directive 2003/71/EC of the European Parliament and of the Council as regards information contained in prospectuses as well as the format, incorporation by reference and publication of such prospectuses and dissemination of advertisements

(809/2004/EC)

(Text with EEA relevance)

NOTES

Date of publication in OJ: this Regulation originally appeared in OJ L149, 30.4.2004, p 1. Note that a corrigendum was published in OJ L215, 16.6.2004, p 3; that corrigendum set out the whole of the Regulation (with changes incorporated) and it is the version from that corrigendum that is reproduced here (notes are as in the OJ version).

This Regulation is reproduced as amended by: Commission Regulation 1787/2006/EC (OJ L337, 5.12.2006, p 17); Commission Regulation 211/2007/EC (OJ L61, 28.2.2007, p 24); Commission Regulation 1289/2008/EC (OJ L340, 19.12.2008, p 17).

THE COMMISSION OF THE EUROPEAN COMMUNITIES,

Having regard to the Treaty establishing the European Community,

Having regard to Directive 2003/71/EC of the European Parliament and the Council of 4 November 2003 on the prospectus to be published when securities are offered to the public or admitted to trading and amending Directive 2001/34/EC,[1] and in particular Article 5(5), Article 7, Article 10(4), Article 11(3), Article 14(8) and Article 15(7) thereof,

After consulting the Committee of European Securities Regulators (CESR)[2] for technical advice,

Whereas:

(1) Directive 2003/71/EC lays down principles to be observed when drawing up prospectuses. These principles need to be supplemented as far as the information to be given therein, the format and aspects of publication, the information to be incorporated by reference in a prospectus and dissemination of advertisements are concerned.

(2) Depending on the type of issuer and securities involved, a typology of minimum information requirements should be established corresponding to those schedules that are in practice most frequently applied. The schedules should be based on the information items required in the IOSCO "Disclosure Standards for cross-border offering and initial listings" (part I) and on the existing schedules of Directive 2001/34/EC of the European Parliament and of the Council of 28 May on the admission of securities to official stock exchange listing and on information to be published on those securities.[3]

(3) Information given by the issuer, the offeror or the person asking for admission to trading on a regulated market, according to this Regulation, should be subject to European Union provisions relating to data protection.

(4) Care should be taken that, in those cases where a prospectus is composed of separate documents, duplication of information is avoided; to this end separate detailed schedules for the registration document and for the securities note, adapted to the particular type of issuer and the securities concerned, should be laid down in order to cover each type of security.

(5) The issuer, the offeror or the person asking for admission to trading on a regulated market are entitled to include in a prospectus or base prospectus additional information going beyond the information items provided for in the schedules and building blocks. Any additional information provided should be appropriate to the type of securities or the nature of the issuer involved.

(6) In most cases, given the variety of issuers, the types of securities, the involvement or not of a third party as a guarantor, whether or not there is a listing etc, one single schedule will not give the appropriate information for an investor to make his investment decision. Therefore the combination of various schedules should be possible. A non exhaustive table of combinations, providing for different possible combinations of schedules and "building blocks" for most of the different type of securities, should be set up in order to assist issuers when drafting their prospectus.

(7) The share registration document schedule should be applicable to shares and other transferable securities equivalent to shares but also to other securities giving access to the capital of the issuer by way of conversion or exchange. In the latter case this schedule should not be used where the underlying shares to be delivered have already been issued before the issuance of the securities giving access to the capital of the issuer; however this schedule should be used where the underlying shares to be delivered have already been issued but are not yet admitted to trading on a regulated market.

(8) Voluntary disclosure of profit forecasts in a share registration document should be presented in a consistent and comparable manner and accompanied by a statement prepared by independent accountants or auditors. This information should not be confused with the disclosure of known

trends or other factual data with material impact on the issuers' prospects. Moreover, they should provide an explanation of any changes in disclosure policy relating to profit forecasts when supplementing a prospectus or drafting a new prospectus.

(9) Pro forma financial information is needed in case of significant gross change, i. e. a variation of more than 25% relative to one or more indicators of the size of the issuer's business, in the situation of an issuer due to a particular transaction, with the exception of those situations where merger accounting is required.

(10) The schedule for the share securities note should be applicable to any class of share since it considers information regarding a description of the rights attached to the securities and the procedure for the exercise of any rights attached to the securities.

(11) Some debt securities such as structured bonds incorporate certain elements of a derivative security, therefore additional disclosure requirements related to the derivative component in the interest payment should be included in the securities note schedule for debt securities.

(12) The additional "building block" related to guarantee should apply to any obligation in relation to any kind of security.

(13) The asset backed securities registration document should not apply to mortgage bonds as provided for in Article 5(4)(b) of Directive 2003/71/EC and other covered bonds. The same should apply for the asset backed securities additional "building block" that has to be combined with the securities note for debt securities.

(14) Wholesale investors should be able to make their investment decision on other elements than those taken into consideration by retail investors. Therefore a differentiated content of prospectus is necessary for debt and derivative securities aimed at those investors who purchase debt or derivative securities with a denomination per unit of at least EUR 50,000 or a denomination in another currency provided that the value of such minimum denomination when converted to EURO amounts to at least EURO 50,000.

(15) In the context of depository receipts, emphasis should be put on the issuer of the underlying shares and not on the issuer of the depository receipt. Where there is legal recourse to the depository over and above a breach of its fiduciary or agency duties, the risk factors section in the prospectus should contain full information on this fact and on the circumstances of such recourse. Where a prospectus is drafted as a tripartite document (i.e. registration document, securities note and summary), the registration document should be limited to the information on the depository.

(16) The banks registration document schedule should be applicable to banks from third countries which do not fall under the definition of credit institution provided for in Article 1(1)(a) of Directive 2000/12/EC of the European Parliament and of the Council of 20 March 2000 relating to the taking up and pursuit of the business of credit institutions[4] but have their registered office in a state which is a member of the OECD.

(17) If a special purpose vehicle issues debt and derivative securities guaranteed by a bank, it should not use the banks registration document schedule.

(18) The schedule "securities note for derivative securities" should be applicable to securities which are not covered by the other schedules and building blocks. The scope of this schedule is determined by reference to the other two generic categories of shares and debt securities. In order to provide a clear and comprehensive explanation to help investors understand how the value of their investment is affected by the value of the underlying, issuers should be able to use appropriate examples on a voluntary basis. For instance, for some complex derivatives securities, examples might be the most effective way to explain the nature of those securities.

(19) The additional information "building block" on the underlying share for certain equity securities should be added to the securities note for debt securities or substitute the item referring to "information required in respect of the underlying" of the schedule securities note for derivative securities, depending on the characteristics of the securities being issued.

(20) Member States and their regional or local authorities are outside the scope of Directive 2003/71/EC. However, they may choose to produce a prospectus in accordance with this Directive. Third country sovereign issuers and their regional or local authorities are not outside the scope of Directive 2003/71/EC and are obliged to produce a prospectus if they wish to make a public offer of securities in the Community or wish their securities to be admitted to trading on a regulated market. For those cases, particular schedules should be used for the securities issued by States, their regional and local authorities and by public international bodies.

(21) A base prospectus and its final terms should contain the same information as a prospectus. All the general principles applicable to a prospectus are applicable also to the final terms. Nevertheless, where the final terms are not included in the base prospectus they do not have to be approved by the competent authority.

(22) For some categories of issuers the competent authority should be entitled to require adapted information going beyond the information items included in the schedules and building blocks because of the particular nature of the activities carried out by those issuers. A precise and restrictive list of issuers for which adapted information may be required is necessary. The adapted information requirements for each category of issuers included in this list should be appropriate and proportionate to the type of business involved. The Committee of European Securities Regulators

could actively try to reach convergence on these information requirements within the Community. Inclusion of new categories in the list should be restricted to those cases where this can be duly justified.

(23) In the case of completely new types of securities which cannot be covered by the existing schedules or any of their combinations, the issuer should still have the possibility to apply for approval for a prospectus. In those cases he should be able to discuss the content of the information to be provided with the competent authority. The prospectus approved by the competent authority under those circumstances should benefit from the single passport established in Directive 2003/71/EC. The competent authority should always try to find similarities and make use as much as possible of existing schedules. Any additional information requirements should be proportionate and appropriate to the type of securities involved.

(24) Certain information items required in the schedules and building blocks or equivalent information items are not relevant to a particular security and thus may be inapplicable in some specific cases; in those cases the issuer should have the possibility to omit this information.

(25) The enhanced flexibility in the articulation of the base prospectus with its final terms compared to a single issue prospectus should not hamper the easy access to material information for investors.

(26) With respect to base prospectuses, it should be set out in an easily identifiable manner which kind of information will have to be included as final terms. This requirement should be able to be satisfied in a number of different ways, for example, if the base prospectus contains blanks for any information to be inserted in the final terms or if the base prospectus contains a list of the missing information.

(27) Where a single document includes more than one base prospectus and each base prospectus would require approval by a different home competent authority, the respective competent authorities should act in cooperation and, where appropriate, transfer the approval of the prospectus in accordance with Article 13(5) of Directive 2003/71/EC, so that the approval by only one competent authority is sufficient for the entire document.

(28) Historical financial information as required in the schedules should principally be presented in accordance with Regulation (EC) No 1606/2002 of the European Parliament and of the Council of 19 July 2002 on the application of international accounting standard[5] or Member States' accounting standards. Specific requirements should, however, be laid down for third country issuers.

(29) For the purposes of publication of the document referred to in Article 10 of Directive 2003/71/EC, issuers should be allowed to choose the method of publication they consider adequate among those referred to in Article 14 of that Directive. In selecting the method of publication they should consider the objective of the document and that it should permit investors a fast and cost-efficient access to that information.

(30) The aim of incorporation by reference, as provided for in Article 11 of Directive 2003/71/EC, is to simplify and reduce the costs of drafting a prospectus; however this aim should not be achieved to the detriment of other interests the prospectus is meant to protect. For instance, the fact that the natural location of the information required is the prospectus, and that the information should be presented in an easily and comprehensible form, should also be considered. Particular attention should be granted to the language used for information incorporated by reference and its consistency with the prospectus itself. Information incorporated by reference may refer to historical data, however if this information is no more relevant due to material change, this should be clearly stated in the prospectus and the updated information should also be provided.

(31) Where a prospectus is published in electronic form, additional safety measures compared to traditional means of publication, using best practices available, are necessary in order to maintain the integrity of the information, to avoid manipulation or modification from unauthorised persons, to avoid altering its comprehensibility and to escape from possible adverse consequences from different approaches on offer of securities to the public in third countries.

(32) The newspaper chosen for the publication of a prospectus should have a wide area of distribution and a high circulation.

(33) A home Member State should be able to require publication of a notice stating how the prospectus has been made available and where it can be obtained by the public. Where a home Member State requires publication of notices in its legislation, the content of such a notice should be kept to the necessary items information to avoid duplication with the summary. These home Member States may also require that an additional notice in relation to the final terms of a base prospectus is to be published.

(34) In order to facilitate centralising useful information for investors a mention should be included in the list of approved prospectuses posted in the web-site of the competent authority of the home Member State, indicating how a prospectus has been published and where it can be obtained.

(35) Member States should ensure effective compliance of advertising rules concerning public offers and admission to trading on a regulated market. Proper co-ordination between competent authorities should be achieved in cross-border offerings or cross-border admission to trading.

(36) In view of the interval between the entry into force of Regulation (EC) No 1606/2002 and the production of certain of its effects, a number of transitional arrangements for historical financial information to be included in a prospectus should be provided for, in order to prevent excessive

burden on issuers and enable them to adapt the way they prepare and present historical financial information within a reasonable period of time after the entry into force of Directive 2003/71/EC.

(37) The obligation to restate in a prospectus historical financial information according to Regulation (EC) No 1606/2002 does not cover securities with a denomination per unit of at least EUR 50,000; consequently such transitional arrangements are not necessary for such securities.

(38) For reasons of coherence it is appropriate that this Regulation applies from the date of transposition of Directive 2003/71/EC.

(39) Whereas the measures provided for in this Regulation are in accordance with the opinion of the European Securities Committee,

[5611]

NOTES

1 OJ L345, 31.12.2003, p 64.
2 CESR was established by Commission Decision 2001/527/EC of 6 June 2001, OJ L191, 13 July 2001, p 43.
3 OJ L184, 6.7.2001, p 1. Directive as last amended by Directive 2003/71/EC.
4 OJ L126, 26.5.2000, p 1. Directive as last amended by the 2003 Act of Accession.
5 OJ L243, 11.9.2002, p 1.

HAS ADOPTED THIS REGULATION:

CHAPTER I
SUBJECT MATTER AND DEFINITIONS

Article 1
Subject matter

This Regulation lays down:

1. the format of prospectus referred to in Article 5 of Directive 2003/71/EC;

2. the minimum information requirements to be included in a prospectus provided for in Article 7 of Directive 2003/71/EC;

3. the method of publication referred to in Article 10 of Directive 2003/71/EC;

4. the modalities according to which information can be incorporated by reference in a prospectus provided for in Article 11 of Directive 2003/71/EC;

5. the publication methods of a prospectus in order to ensure that a prospectus is publicly available according to Article 14 of Directive 2003/71/EC;

6. the methods of dissemination of advertisements referred to in Article 15 of Directive 2003/71/EC.

[5611A]

Article 2
Definitions

For the purposes of this Regulation, the following definitions shall apply in addition to those laid down in Directive 2003/71/EC:

1. "schedule" means a list of minimum information requirements adapted to the particular nature of the different types of issuers and/or the different securities involved;

2. "building block" means a list of additional information requirements, not included in one of the schedules, to be added to one or more schedules, as the case may be, depending on the type of instrument and/or transaction for which a prospectus or base prospectus is drawn up;

3. "risk factors" means a list of risks which are specific to the situation of the issuer and/or the securities and which are material for taking investment decisions;

4. "special purpose vehicle" means an issuer whose objects and purposes are primarily the issue of securities;

5. "asset backed securities" means securities which:
    (a) represent an interest in assets, including any rights intended to assure servicing, or the receipt or timeliness of receipts by holders of assets of amounts payable there under; or
    (b) are secured by assets and the terms of which provide for payments which relate to payments or reasonable projections of payments calculated by reference to identified or identifiable assets;

6. "umbrella collective investment undertaking" means a collective investment undertaking invested in one or more collective investment undertakings, the asset of which is composed of separate class(es) or designation(s) of securities;

7. "property collective investment undertaking" means a collective investment undertaking whose investment objective is the participation in the holding of property in the long term;

8. "public international body" means a legal entity of public nature established by an international treaty between sovereign States and of which one or more Member States are members;

9. "advertisement" means announcements:
   (a) relating to an specific offer to the public of securities or to an admission to trading on a regulated market; and
   (b) aiming to specifically promote the potential subscription or acquisition of securities.

10. "profit forecast" means a form of words which expressly states or by implication indicates a figure or a minimum or maximum figure for the likely level of profits or losses for the current financial period and/or financial periods subsequent to that period, or contains data from which a calculation of such a figure for future profits or losses may be made, even if no particular figure is mentioned and the word "profit" is not used.

11. "profit estimate" means a profit forecast for a financial period which has expired and for which results have not yet been published.

12. "regulated information" means all information which the issuer, or any person who has applied for the admission of securities to trading on a regulated market without the issuer's consent, is required to disclose under Directive 2001/34/EC or under Article 6 of Directive 2003/6/EC of the European Parliament and of the Council.[1]

[5612]

NOTES
[1]   OJ L96, 12.4.2003, p 16.

CHAPTER II
MINIMUM INFORMATION

Article 3
Minimum information to be included in a prospectus

A prospectus shall be drawn up by using one or a combination of the following schedules and building blocks set out in Articles 4 to 20, according to the combinations for various types of securities provided for in Article 21.

A prospectus shall contain the information items required in Annexes I to XVII depending on the type of issuer and securities involved, provided for in the schedules and building blocks set out in Articles 4 to 20. [Subject to Article 4a(1), a competent authority shall not request that a prospectus contain information items which are not included in Annexes I to XVII.]

In order to ensure conformity with the obligation referred to in Article 5(1) of Directive 2003/71/EC, the competent authority of the home Member State, when approving a prospectus in accordance with Article 13 of that Directive, may require that the information provided by the issuer, the offeror or the person asking for admission to trading on a regulated market be completed, for each of the information items, on a case by case basis.

[5613]

NOTES
Words in square brackets substituted by Commission Regulation 211/2007/EC, Art 1(1), as from 1 March 2007.

Article 4
Share registration document schedule

1. For the share registration document information shall be given in accordance with the schedule set out in Annex I.

2. The schedule set out in paragraph 1 shall apply to the following:
   (1) shares and other transferable securities equivalent to shares;
   (2) other securities which comply with the following conditions:
      (a) they can be converted or exchanged into shares or other transferable securities equivalent to shares, at the issuer's or at the investor's discretion, or on the basis of the conditions established a the moment of the issue, or give, in any other way, the possibility to acquire shares or other transferable securities equivalent to shares; and
      (b) provided that these shares or other transferable securities equivalent to shares are or will be issued by the issuer of the security and are not yet traded on a regulated market or an equivalent market outside the Community at the time of the approval

of the prospectus covering the securities, and that the underlying shares or other transferable securities equivalent to shares can be delivered with physical settlement.

[5614]

[Article 4a
Share registration document schedule in cases of complex financial history or significant financial commitment

1. Where the issuer of a security covered by Article 4(2) has a complex financial history, or has made a significant financial commitment, and in consequence the inclusion in the registration document of certain items of financial information relating to an entity other than the issuer is necessary in order to satisfy the obligation laid down in Article 5(1) of Directive 2003/71/EC, those items of financial information shall be deemed to relate to the issuer. The competent authority of the home Member State shall in such cases request that the issuer, the offeror or the person asking for admission to trading include those items of information in the registration document.

Those items of financial information may include pro forma information prepared in accordance with Annex II. In this context, where the issuer has made a significant financial commitment any such pro forma information shall illustrate the anticipated effects of the transaction that the issuer has agreed to undertake, and references in Annex II to "the transaction" shall be read accordingly.

2. The competent authority shall base any request pursuant to paragraph 1 on the requirements set out in item 20.1 of Annex I as regards the content of financial information and the applicable accounting and auditing principles, subject to any modification which is appropriate in view of any of the following factors:
  (a)   the nature of the securities;
  (b)   the nature and range of information already included in the prospectus, and the existence of financial information relating to an entity other than the issuer in a form that might be included in a prospectus without modification;
  (c)   the facts of the case, including the economic substance of the transactions by which the issuer has acquired or disposed of its business undertaking or any part of it, and the specific nature of that undertaking;
  (d)   the ability of the issuer to obtain financial information relating to another entity with reasonable effort.

Where, in the individual case, the obligation laid down in Article 5(1) of Directive 2003/71/EC may be satisfied in more than one way, preference shall be given to the way that is the least costly or onerous.

3. Paragraph 1 is without prejudice to the responsibility under national law of any other person, including the persons referred to in Article 6(1) of Directive 2003/71/EC, for the information contained in the prospectus. In particular, those persons shall be responsible for the inclusion in the registration document of any items of information requested by the competent authority pursuant to paragraph 1.

4. For the purposes of paragraph 1, an issuer shall be treated as having a complex financial history if all of the following conditions apply:
  (a)   its entire business undertaking at the time that the prospectus is drawn up is not accurately represented in the historical financial information which it is required to provide under item 20.1 of Annex I;
  (b)   that inaccuracy will affect the ability of an investor to make an informed assessment as mentioned in Article 5(1) of Directive 2003/71/EC; and
  (c)   information relating to its business undertaking that is necessary for an investor to make such an assessment is included in financial information relating to another entity.

5. For the purposes of paragraph 1, an issuer shall be treated as having made a significant financial commitment if it has entered into a binding agreement to undertake a transaction which, on completion, is likely to give rise to a significant gross change.

In this context, the fact that an agreement makes completion of the transaction subject to conditions, including approval by a regulatory authority, shall not prevent that agreement from being treated as binding if it is reasonably certain that those conditions will be fulfilled.

In particular, an agreement shall be treated as binding where it makes the completion of the transaction conditional on the outcome of the offer of the securities that are the subject matter of the prospectus or, in the case of a proposed takeover, if the offer of securities that are the subject matter of the prospectus has the objective of funding that takeover.

6. For the purposes of paragraph 5 of this Article, and of item 20.2 of Annex I, a significant gross change means a variation of more than 25%, relative to one or more indicators of the size of the issuer's business, in the situation of an issuer.]

[5614A]

NOTES

Inserted by Commission Regulation 211/2007/EC, Art 1(2), as from 1 March 2007.

Article 5
Pro-forma financial information building block

For pro forma financial information, information shall be given in accordance with the building block set out in Annex II.

Pro forma financial information should be preceded by an introductory explanatory paragraph that states in clear terms the purpose of including this information in the prospectus.

[5615]

Article 6
Share securities note schedule

1. For the share securities note information is necessary to be given in accordance with the schedule set out in Annex III.

2. The schedule shall apply to shares and other transferable securities equivalent to shares.

[5616]

Article 7
Debt and derivative securities registration document schedule for securities with a denomination per unit of less than EUR 50,000

For the debt and derivative securities registration document concerning securities which are not covered in Article 4 with a denomination per unit of less than EUR 50,000 or, where there is no individual denomination, securities that can only be acquired on issue for less than EUR 50,000 per security, information shall be given in accordance with the schedule set out in Annex IV.

[5617]

Article 8
Securities note schedule for debt securities with a denomination per unit of less than EUR 50,000

1. For the securities note for debt securities with a denomination per unit of less than EUR 50,000 information shall be given in accordance with the schedule set out in Annex V.

2. The schedule shall apply to debt where the issuer has an obligation arising on issue to pay the investor 100% of the nominal value in addition to which there may be also an interest payment.

[5618]

Article 9
Guarantees building block

For guarantees information shall be given in accordance with the building block set out in Annex VI.

[5619]

Article 10
Asset backed securities registration document schedule

For the asset backed securities registration document information shall be given in accordance with the schedule set out in Annex VII.

[5620]

Article 11
Asset backed securities building block

For the additional information building block to the securities note for asset backed securities information shall be given in accordance with the building block set out in Annex VIII.

[5621]

Article 12
Debt and derivative securities registration document schedule for securities with a denomination per unit of at least EUR 50,000

For the debt and derivative securities registration document concerning securities which are not covered in Article 4 with a denomination per unit of at least EUR 50,000 or, where there is no individual denomination, securities that can only be acquired on issue for at least EUR 50,000 per security, information shall be given in accordance with the schedule set out in Annex IX.

[5622]

PART IV
EC MATERIALS

Article 13
Depository receipts schedule

For depository receipts issued over shares information shall be given in accordance with the schedule set out in Annex X.

[5623]

Article 14
Banks registration document schedule

1.   For the banks registration document for debt and derivative securities and those securities which are not covered by Article 4 information shall be given in accordance with the schedule set out in Annex XI.

2.   The schedule set out in paragraph 1 shall apply to credit institutions as defined in point (a) of Article 1(1) of Directive 2000/12/EC as well as to third country credit institutions which do not fall under that definition but have their registered office in a state which is a member of the OECD.

These entities may also use alternatively the registration document schedules provided for under in Articles 7 and 12.

[5624]

Article 15
Securities note schedule for derivative securities

1.   For the securities note for derivative securities information shall be given in accordance with the schedule set out in Annex XII.

2.   The schedule shall apply to securities which are not in the scope of application of the other securities note schedules referred to in Articles 6, 8 and 16, including certain securities where the payment and/or delivery obligations are linked to an underlying.

[5625]

Article 16
Securities note schedule for debt securities with a denomination per unit of at least EUR 50,000

1.   For the securities note for debt securities with a denomination per unit of at least EUR 50,000 information shall be given in accordance with the schedule set out in Annex XIII.

2.   The schedule shall apply to debt where the issuer has an obligation arising on issue to pay the investor 100% of the nominal value in addition to which there may be also an interest payment.

[5626]

Article 17
Additional information building block on the underlying share

1.   For the additional information on the underlying share, the description of the underlying share shall be given in accordance with the building block set out in Annex XIV.

In addition, if the issuer of the underlying share is an entity belonging to the same group, the information required by the schedule referred to in Article 4 shall be given in respect of that issuer.

2.   The additional information referred to in the first subparagraph of paragraph 1 shall only apply to those securities which comply with both of the following conditions:
  (1)   they can be converted or exchanged into shares or other transferable securities equivalent to shares, at the issuer's or at the investor's discretion, or on the basis of the conditions established a the moment of the issue or give, in any other way, the possibility to acquire shares or other transferable securities equivalent to shares; and
  (2)   provided that these shares or other transferable securities equivalent to shares are or will be issued by the issuer of the security or by an entity belonging to the group of that issuer and are not yet traded on a regulated market or an equivalent market outside the Community at the time of the approval of the prospectus covering the securities, and that the underlying shares or other transferable securities equivalent to shares can be delivered with physical settlement.

[5627]

Article 18
Registration document schedule for collective investment undertakings of the closed-end type

1.   In addition to the information required pursuant to items 1, 2, 3, 4, 5.1, 7, 9.1, 9.2.1, 9.2.3, 10.4, 13, 14, 15, 16, 17.2, 18, 19, 20, 21, 22, 23, 24, 25 of Annex I, for the registration document for securities issued by collective investment undertakings of the closed-end type information shall be given in accordance with the schedule set out in Annex XV.

2.   The schedule shall apply to collective investment undertakings of the closed-end type holding a portfolio of assets on behalf of investors that:
  (1)   are recognised by national law in the Member State in which it is incorporated as a collective investment undertaking of the closed end type; or

(2)   do not take or seek to take legal or management control of any of the issuers of its underlying investments. In such a case, legal control and/or participation in the administrative, management or supervisory bodies of the underlying issuer(s) may be taken where such action is incidental to the primary investment objective, necessary for the protection of shareholders and only in circumstances where the collective investment undertaking will not exercise significant management control over the operations of that underlying issuer(s).

[5628]

Article 19
Registration document schedule for Member States, third countries and their regional and local authorities

1.   For the registration document for securities issued by Member States, third countries and their regional and local authorities information shall be given in accordance with the schedule set out in Annex XVI.

2.   The schedule shall apply to all types of securities issued by Member States, third countries and their regional and local authorities.

[5629]

Article 20
Registration document schedule for public international bodies and for issuers of debt securities guaranteed by a member state of the OECD

1.   For the registration document for securities issued by public international bodies and for securities unconditionally and irrevocably guaranteed, on the basis of national legislation, by a state which is member of the OECD information shall be given in accordance with the schedule set out in Annex XVII.

2.   The schedule shall apply to:
—   all types of securities issued by public international bodies,
—   to debt securities unconditionally and irrevocably guaranteed, on the basis of national legislation, by a state which is member of the OECD.

[5630]

Article 21
Combination of schedules and building blocks

1.   The use of the combinations provided for in the table set out in Annex XVIII shall be mandatory when drawing up prospectuses for the types of securities to which those combinations correspond according to this table.

However, for securities not covered by those combinations further combinations may be used.

2.   The most comprehensive and stringent registration document schedule, ie the most demanding schedule in term of number of information items and the extent of the information included in them, may always be used to issue securities for which a less comprehensive and stringent registration document schedule is provided for, according to the following ranking of schedules:
(1)   share registration document schedule;
(2)   debt and derivative securities registration document schedule for securities with a denomination per unit of less than EUR 50,000 ;
(3)   debt and derivative securities registration document schedule for securities with a denomination per unit at least EUR 50,000.

[5631]

Article 22
Minimum information to be included in a base prospectus and its related final terms

1.   A base prospectus shall be drawn up by using one or a combination of schedules and building blocks provided for in Articles 4 to 20 according to the combinations for various types of securities set out in Annex XVIII.

A base prospectus shall contain the information items required in Annexes I to XVII depending on the type of issuer and securities involved, provided for in the schedules and building blocks set out in Articles 4 to 20. A competent authority shall not request that a base prospectus contains information items which are not included in Annexes I to XVII.

In order to ensure conformity with the obligation referred to in Article 5(1) of Directive 2003/71/EC, the competent authority of the home Member State, when approving a base prospectus in accordance with Article 13 of that Directive, may require that the information provided by the issuer, the offeror or the person asking for admission to trading on a regulated market be completed, for each of the information items, on a case by case basis.

2. The issuer, the offeror or the person asking for admission to trading on a regulated market may omit information items which are not known when the base prospectus is approved and which can only be determined at the time of the individual issue.

3. The use of the combinations provided for in the table in Annex XVIII shall be mandatory when drawing up base prospectuses for the types of securities to which those combinations correspond according to this table.

However, for securities not covered by those combinations further combinations may be used.

4. The final terms attached to a base prospectus shall only contain the information items from the various securities note schedules according to which the base prospectus is drawn up.

5. In addition to the information items set out in the schedules and building blocks referred to in Articles 4 to 20 the following information shall be included in a base prospectus:
   (1) indication on the information that will be included in the final terms;
   (2) the method of publication of the final terms; if the issuer is not in a position to determine, at the time of the approval of the prospectus, the method of publication of the final terms, an indication of how the public will be informed about which method will be used for the publication of the final terms;
   (3) in the case of issues of non equity securities according to point (a) of Article 5(4) of Directive 2003/71/EC, a general description of the programme.

6. Only the following categories of securities may be contained in a base prospectus and its related final terms covering issues of various types of securities:
   (1) asset backed securities;
   (2) warrants falling under Article 17;
   (3) non-equity securities provided for under point (b) of Article 5(4) of Directive 2003/71/EC;
   (4) all other non-equity securities including warrants with the exception of those mentioned in (2).

In drawing up a base prospectus the issuer, the offeror or the person asking for admission to trading on a regulated market shall clearly segregate the specific information on each of the different securities included in these categories.

7. Where an event envisaged under Article 16(1) of Directive 2003/71/EC occurs between the time that the base prospectus has been approved and the final closing of the offer of each issue of securities under the base prospectus or, as the case may be, the time that trading on a regulated market of those securities begins, the issuer, the offeror or the person asking for admission to trading on a regulated market shall publish a supplement prior to the final closing of the offer or the admission of those securities to trading.

[5632]

Article 23
Adaptations to the minimum information given in prospectuses and base prospectuses

1. Notwithstanding Articles 3 second paragraph and 22(1) second subparagraph, where the issuer's activities fall under one of the categories included in Annex XIX, the competent authority of the home Member State, taking into consideration the specific nature of the activities involved, may ask for adapted information, in addition to the information items included in the schedules and building blocks set out in Articles 4 to 20, including, where appropriate, a valuation or other expert's report on the assets of the issuer, in order to comply with the obligation referred to in Article 5(1) of Directive 2003/71/EC. The competent authority shall forthwith inform the Commission thereof.

In order to obtain the inclusion of a new category in Annex XIX a Member State shall notify its request to the Commission. The Commission shall update this list following the Committee procedure provided for in Article 24 of Directive 2003/71/EC.

2. By way of derogation of Articles 3 to 22, where an issuer, an offeror or a person asking for admission to trading on a regulated market applies for approval of a prospectus or a base prospectus for a security which is not the same but comparable to the various types of securities mentioned in the table of combinations set out in Annex XVIII, the issuer, the offeror or the person asking for admission to trading on a regulated market shall add the relevant information items from another securities note schedule provided for in Articles 4 to 20 to the main securities note schedule chosen. This addition shall be done in accordance with the main characteristics of the securities being offered to the public or admitted to trading on a regulated market.

3. By way of derogation of Articles 3 to 22, where an issuer, an offeror or a person asking for admission to trading on a regulated market applies for approval of a prospectus or a base prospectus for a new type of security, the issuer, the offeror or the person asking for admission to trading on a regulated market shall notify a draft prospectus or base prospectus to the competent authority of the home Member State.

The competent authority shall decide, in consultation with the issuer, the offeror or the person asking for admission to trading on a regulated market, what information shall be included in the prospectus or base prospectus in order to comply with the obligation referred to in Article 5(1) of Directive 2003/71/EC. The competent authority shall forthwith inform the Commission thereof.

The derogation referred to in the first subparagraph shall only apply in case of a new type of security which has features completely different from the various types of securities mentioned in Annex XVIII, if the characteristics of this new security are such that a combination of the different information items referred to in the schedules and building blocks provided for in Articles 4 to 20 is not pertinent.

4.   By way of derogation of Articles 3 to 22, in the cases where one of the information items required in one of the schedules or building blocks referred to in 4 to 20 or equivalent information is not pertinent to the issuer, to the offer or to the securities to which the prospectus relates, that information may be omitted.

[5633]

Article 24
Content of the summary of prospectus and base prospectus

The issuer, the offeror or the person asking for admission to trading on a regulated market shall determine on its own the detailed content of the summary to the prospectus or base prospectus referred to in Article 5(2) of Directive 2003/71/EC.

[5634]

CHAPTER III
FORMAT OF THE PROSPECTUS, BASE PROSPECTUS
AND SUPPLEMENTS

Article 25
Format of the prospectus

1.   Where an issuer, an offeror or a person asking for the admission to trading on a regulated market chooses, according to Article 5(3) of Directive 2003/71/EC to draw up a prospectus as a single document, the prospectus shall be composed of the following parts in the following order:
   (1)   a clear and detailed table of contents;
   (2)   the summary provided for in Article 5 (2) of Directive 2003/71/EC;
   (3)   the risk factors linked to the issuer and the type of security covered by the issue;
   (4)   the other information items included in the schedules and building blocks according to which the prospectus is drawn up.

2.   Where an issuer, an offeror or a person asking for the admission to trading on a regulated market chooses, according to in Article 5(3) of Directive 2003/71/EC, to draw up a prospectus composed of separate documents, the securities note and the registration document shall be each composed of the following parts in the following order:
   (1)   a clear and detailed table of content;
   (2)   as the case may be, the risk factors linked to the issuer and the type of security covered by the issue;
   (3)   the other information items included in the schedules and building blocks according to which the prospectus is drawn up.

3.   In the cases mentioned in paragraphs 1 and 2, the issuer, the offeror or the person asking for admission to trading on a regulated market shall be free in defining the order in the presentation of the required information items included in the schedules and building blocks according to which the prospectus is drawn up.

4.   Where the order of the items does not coincide with the order of the information provided for in the schedules and building blocks according to which the prospectus is drawn up, the competent authority of the home Member State may ask the issuer, the offeror or the person asking for the admission to trading on a regulated market to provide a cross reference list for the purpose of checking the prospectus before its approval. Such list shall identify the pages where each item can be found in the prospectus.

5.   Where the summary of a prospectus must be supplemented according to Article 16(1) of Directive 2003/71/EC, the issuer, the offeror or the person asking for admission to trading on a regulated market shall decide on a case-by-case basis whether to integrate the new information in the original summary by producing a new summary, or to produce a supplement to the summary.

If the new information is integrated in the original summary, the issuer, the offeror or the person asking for admission to trading on a regulated market shall ensure that investors can easily identify the changes, in particular by way of footnotes.

[5635]

PART IV
EC MATERIALS

Article 26
Format of the base prospectus and its related final terms

1. Where an issuer, an offeror or a person asking for the admission to trading on a regulated market chooses, according to Article 5 (4) of Directive 2003/71/EC to draw up a base prospectus, the base prospectus shall be composed of the following parts in the following order:

(1) a clear and detailed table of contents;

(2) the summary provided for in Article 5 (2) of Directive 2003/71/EC;

(3) the risk factors linked to the issuer and the type of security or securities covered by the issue(s);

(4) the other information items included in the schedules and building blocks according to which the prospectus is drawn up.

2. Notwithstanding paragraph 1, the issuer, the offeror or the person asking for admission to trading on a regulated market shall be free in defining the order in the presentation of the required information items included in the schedules and building blocks according to which the prospectus is drawn up. The information on the different securities contained in the base prospectus shall be clearly segregated.

3. Where the order of the items does not coincide with the order of the information provided for by the schedules and building blocks according to which the prospectus is drawn up, the home competent authority may ask the issuer, the offeror or the person asking for admission to trading on a regulated market to provide a cross reference list for the purpose of checking the prospectus before its approval. Such list should identify the pages where each item can be found in the prospectus.

4. In case the issuer, the offeror or the person asking for admission to trading on a regulated market has previously filed a registration document for a particular type of security and, at a later stage, chooses to draw up base prospectus in conformity with the conditions provided for in points (a) and (b) of Article 5(4) of Directive 2003/71/EC, the base prospectus shall contain:

(1) the information contained in the previously or simultaneously filed and approved registration document which shall be incorporated by reference, following the conditions provided for in Article 28 of this Regulation;

(2) the information which would otherwise be contained in the relevant securities note less the final terms where the final terms are not included in the base prospectus.

5. The final terms attached to a base prospectus shall be presented in the form of a separate document containing only the final terms or by inclusion of the final terms into the base prospectus.

In the case that the final terms are included in a separate document containing only the final terms, they may replicate some information which has been included in the approved base prospectus according to the relevant securities note schedule that has been used for drawing up the base prospectus. In this case the final terms have to be presented in such a way that they can be easily identified as such.

A clear and prominent statement shall be inserted in the final terms indicating that the full information on the issuer and on the offer is only available on the basis of the combination of base prospectus and final terms and where the base prospectus is available.

6. Where a base prospectus relates to different securities, the issuer, the offeror or the person asking for admission to trading on a regulated market shall include a single summary in the base prospectus for all securities. The information on the different securities contained in the summary, however, shall be clearly segregated.

7. Where the summary of a base prospectus must be supplemented according to Article 16(1) of Directive 2003/71/EC, the issuer, the offeror or the person asking for admission to trading on a regulated market shall decide on a case-by-case basis whether to integrate the new information in the original summary by producing a new summary, or by producing a supplement to the summary.

If the new information is integrated in the original summary of the base prospectus by producing a new summary, the issuer, the offeror or the person asking for admission to trading on a regulated market shall ensure that investors can easily identify the changes, in particular by way of footnotes.

8. Issuers, offerors or persons asking for admission to trading on a regulated market may compile in one single document two or more different base prospectuses.

[5636]

CHAPTER IV
INFORMATION AND INCORPORATION BY REFERENCE

Article 27
Publication of the document referred to in Article 10(1) of Directive 2003/71/EC

1. The document referred to in Article 10(1) of Directive 2003/71/EC shall be made available to the public, at the choice of the issuer, the offeror or the person asking for admission to trading on a regulated market, through one of the means permitted under Article 14 of that Directive in the home Member State of the issuer.

2.   The document shall be filed with the competent authority of the home Member State and made available to the public at the latest 20 working days after the publication of the annual financial statements in the home Member State.

3.   The document shall include a statement indicating that some information may be out-of-date, if such is the case.

[5637]

Article 28
Arrangements for incorporation by reference

1.   Information may be incorporated by reference in a prospectus or base prospectus, notably if it is contained in one the following documents:
   (1)   annual and interim financial information;
   (2)   documents prepared on the occasion of a specific transaction such as a merger or de-merger;
   (3)   audit reports and financial statements;
   (4)   memorandum and articles of association;
   (5)   earlier approved and published prospectuses and/or base prospectuses;
   (6)   regulated information;
   (7)   circulars to security holders.

2.   The documents containing information that may be incorporated by reference in a prospectus or base prospectus or in the documents composing it shall be drawn up following the provisions of Article 19 of Directive 2003/71/EC.

3.   If a document which may be incorporated by reference contains information which has undergone material changes, the prospectus or base prospectus shall clearly state such a circumstance and shall give the updated information.

4.   The issuer, the offeror or the person asking for admission to trading on a regulated market may incorporate information in a prospectus or base prospectus by making reference only to certain parts of a document, provided that it states that the non-incorporated parts are either not relevant for the investor or covered elsewhere in the prospectus.

5.   When incorporating information by reference, issuers, offerors or persons asking for admission to trading on a regulated market shall endeavour not to endanger investor protection in terms of comprehensibility and accessibility of the information.

[5638]

CHAPTER V
PUBLICATION AND DISSEMINATION OF ADVERTISEMENTS

Article 29
Publication in electronic form

1.   The publication of the prospectus or base prospectus in electronic form, either pursuant to points (c) (d) and (e) of Article 14(2) of Directive 2003/71/EC, or as an additional means of availability, shall be subject to the following requirements:
   (1)   the prospectus or base prospectus shall be easily accessible when entering the web-site;
   (2)   the file format shall be such that the prospectus or base prospectus cannot be modified;
   (3)   the prospectus or base prospectus shall not contain hyper-links, with exception of links to the electronic addresses where information incorporated by reference is available;
   (4)   the investors shall have the possibility of downloading and printing the prospectus or base prospectus.

The exception referred to in point 3 of the first subparagraph shall only be valid for documents incorporated by reference; those documents shall be available with easy and immediate technical arrangements.

2.   If a prospectus or base prospectus for offer of securities to the public is made available on the web-sites of issuers and financial intermediaries or of regulated markets, these shall take measures, to avoid targeting residents in Members States or third countries where the offer of securities to the public does not take place, such as the insertion of a disclaimer as to who are the addressees of the offer.

[5639]

Article 30
Publication in newspapers

1.   In order to comply with point (a) of Article 14(2) of Directive 2003/71/EC the publication of a prospectus or a base prospectus shall be made in a general or financial information newspaper having national or supra-regional scope;

2.   If the competent authority is of the opinion that the newspaper chosen for publication does not comply with the requirements set out in paragraph 1, it shall determine a newspaper whose

circulation is deemed appropriate for this purpose taking into account, in particular, the geographic area, number of inhabitants and reading habits in each Member State.

[5640]

Article 31
Publication of the notice

1. If a Member State makes use of the option, referred to in Article 14(3) of Directive 2003/71/EC, to require the publication of a notice stating how the prospectus or base prospectus has been made available and where it can be obtained by the public, that notice shall be published in a newspaper that fulfils the requirements for publication of prospectuses according to Article 30 of this Regulation.

If the notice relates to a prospectus or base prospectus published for the only purpose of admission of securities to trading on a regulated market where securities of the same class are already admitted, it may alternatively be inserted in the gazette of that regulated market, irrespective of whether that gazette is in paper copy or electronic form.

2. The notice shall be published no later than the next working day following the date of publication of the prospectus or base prospectus pursuant to Article 14(1) of Directive 2003/71/EC.

3. The notice shall contain the following information:
   (1) the identification of the issuer;
   (2) the type, class and amount of the securities to be offered and/or in respect of which admission to trading is sought, provided that these elements are known at the time of the publication of the notice;
   (3) the intended time schedule of the offer/admission to trading;
   (4) a statement that a prospectus or base prospectus has been published and where it can be obtained;
   (5) if the prospectus or base prospectus has been published in a printed form, the addresses where and the period of time during which such printed forms are available to the public;
   (6) if the prospectus or base prospectus has been published in electronic form, the addresses to which investors shall refer to ask for a paper copy;
   (7) the date of the notice.

[5641]

Article 32
List of approved prospectuses

The list of the approved prospectuses and base prospectuses published on the web-site of the competent authority, in accordance with Article 14(4) of Directive 2003/71/EC, shall mention how such prospectuses have been made available and where they can be obtained.

[5642]

Article 33
Publication of the final terms of base prospectuses

The publication method for final terms related to a base prospectus does not have to be the same as the one used for the base prospectus as long as the publication method used is one of the publication methods indicated in Article 14 of the Directive 2003/71/EC.

[5643]

Article 34
Dissemination of advertisements

Advertisements related to an offer to the public of securities or to an admission to trading on a regulated market may be disseminated to the public by interested parties, such as issuer, offeror or person asking for admission, the financial intermediaries that participate in the placing and/or underwriting of securities, notably by one of the following means of communication:
   (1) addressed or unaddressed printed matter;
   (2) electronic message or advertisement received via a mobile telephone or pager;
   (3) standard letter;
   (4) Press advertising with or without order form;
   (5) catalogue;
   (6) telephone with or without human intervention;
   (7) seminars and presentations;
   (8) radio;
   (9) videophone;
   (10) videotext;
   (11) electronic mail;
   (12) facsimile machine (fax);
   (13) television;
   (14) notice;

(15) bill;
(16) poster;
(17) brochure;
(18) web posting including internet banners.

[5644]

CHAPTER VI
TRANSITIONAL AND FINAL PROVISIONS

Article 35
Historical financial information

1.   The obligation for Community issuers to restate in a prospectus historical financial information according to Regulation (EC) No 1606/2002, set out in Annex I item 20.1, Annex IV item 13.1, Annex VII items 8.2, Annex X items 20.1 and Annex XI item 11.1 shall not apply to any period earlier than 1 January 2004 or, where an issuer has securities admitted to trading on a regulated market on 1 July 2005 , until the issuer has published its first consolidated annual accounts with accordance with Regulation (EC) No 1606/2002.

2.   Where a Community issuer is subject to transitional national provisions adopted pursuant Article 9 of Regulation (EC) No 1606/2002, the obligation to restate in a prospectus historical financial information does not apply to any period earlier than 1 January 2006 or, where an issuer has securities admitted to trading on a regulated market on 1 July 2005 , until the issuer has published its first consolidated annual accounts with accordance with Regulation (EC) No 1606/2002.

3.   Until 1 January 2007 the obligation to restate in a prospectus historical financial information according to Regulation (EC) No 1606/2002, set out in Annex I item 20.1, Annex IV item 13.1, Annex VII items 8.2, Annex X items 20.1 and Annex XI item 11.1 shall not apply to issuers from third countries:
   (1)   who have their securities admitted to trading on a regulated market on 1 January 2007; and
   (2)   who have presented and prepared historical financial information according to the national accounting standards of a third country.

In this case, historical financial information shall be accompanied with more detailed and/or additional information if the financial statements included in the prospectus do not give a true and fair view of the issuer's assets and liabilities, financial position and profit and loss.

4.   Third country issuers having prepared historical financial information according to internationally accepted standards as referred to in Article 9 of Regulation (EC) No 1606/2002 may use that information in any prospectus filed before 1 January 2007 , without being subject to restatement obligations.

[5.   From 1 January 2009, third country issuers shall present their historical financial information in accordance either with one of the following accounting standards:
   (a)   International Financial Reporting Standards adopted pursuant to Regulation (EC) No 1606/2002;
   (b)   International Financial Reporting Standards provided that the notes to the audited financial statements that form part of the historical financial information contain an explicit and unreserved statement that these financial statements comply with International Financial Reporting Standards in accordance with IAS 1 Presentation of Financial Statements;
   (c)   Generally Accepted Accounting Principles of Japan;
   (d)   Generally Accepted Accounting Principles of the United States of America.

5a.   Third country issuers are not subject to a requirement, under Annex I, item 20.1; Annex IV, item 13.1; Annex VII, item 8.2; Annex X, item 20.1 or Annex XI, item 11.1, to restate historical financial information, included in a prospectus and relevant for the financial years prior to financial years starting on or after 1 January 2012, or to a requirement under Annex VII, item 8.2.bis; Annex IX, item 11.1; or Annex X, item 20.1.bis, to provide a narrative description of the differences between International Financial Reporting Standards adopted pursuant to Regulation (EC) No 1606/2002 and the accounting principles in accordance with which such information is drawn up relating to the financial years prior to financial years starting on or after 1 January 2012, provided that the historical financial information is prepared in accordance with the Generally Accepted Accounting Principles of the People's Republic of China, Canada, the Republic of Korea or the Republic of India.]

[5b.–5e. ...]

6.   The provisions of this Article shall also apply to Annex VI, item 3.

[5645]

NOTES

Paras 5, 5a: substituted by Commission Regulation 1289/2008/EC, Art 1(1), as from 1 January 2009 (para 5a was previously inserted by Commission Regulation 1787/2006/EC, Art 1, as from 8 December 2006).

Paras 5b–5e: inserted by Commission Regulation 1787/2006/EC, Art 1, as from 8 December 2006, and repealed by Commission Regulation 1289/2008/EC, Art 1(2), as from 1 January 2009.

Note that Articles 2 and 3 of Commission Regulation 1289/2008/EC provide as follows—

"Article 2

The Commission shall continue to monitor, with the technical assistance of the CESR, the efforts made by third countries towards a changeover to IFRS and pursue an active dialogue with authorities during the convergence process. The Commission shall submit a report on progress made in this regard to the European Parliament and the European Securities Committee (ESC) during 2009. The Commission shall also report expeditiously to Council and the European Parliament if situations arise where EU issuers in the future are required to reconcile their financial statements to the national GAAP of the foreign jurisdiction concerned.

Article 3

The dates announced publicly by third countries in relation to a changeover to IFRS shall serve as reference dates for the abolition of equivalence recognition for those third countries.".

Article 36
Entry into force

This Regulation shall enter into force in Member States on the twentieth day after its publication in the *Official Journal of the European Union*.

It shall apply from 1 July 2005.

This Regulation shall be binding in its entirety and directly applicable in all Member States.

[5646]

ANNEXES

Annexes I to XVII: Schedules and building blocks

Annex XVIII: Table of combinations of schedules and building blocks

Annex XIX: List of specialist issuers

ANNEX I
MINIMUM DISCLOSURE REQUIREMENTS FOR THE SHARE REGISTRATION DOCUMENT (SCHEDULE)

1. PERSONS RESPONSIBLE

1.1. All persons responsible for the information given in the Registration Document and, as the case may be, for certain parts of it, with, in the latter case, an indication of such parts. In the case of natural persons including members of the issuer's administrative, management or supervisory bodies indicate the name and function of the person; in case of legal persons indicate the name and registered office.

1.2. A declaration by those responsible for the registration document that, having taken all reasonable care to ensure that such is the case, the information contained in the registration document is, to the best of their knowledge, in accordance with the facts and contains no omission likely to affect its import. As the case may be, a declaration by those responsible for certain parts of the registration document that, having taken all reasonable care to ensure that such is the case, the information contained in the part of the registration document for which they are responsible is, to the best of their knowledge, in accordance with the facts and contains no omission likely to affect its import.

2. STATUTORY AUDITORS

2.1. Names and addresses of the issuer's auditors for the period covered by the historical financial information (together with their membership in a professional body).

2.2. If auditors have resigned, been removed or not been re-appointed during the period covered by the historical financial information, indicate details if material.

3. SELECTED FINANCIAL INFORMATION

3.1. Selected historical financial information regarding the issuer, presented for each financial year for the period covered by the historical financial information, and any subsequent interim financial period, in the same currency as the financial information.

The selected historical financial information must provide the key figures that summarise the financial condition of the issuer.

3.2. If selected financial information for interim periods is provided, comparative data from the same period in the prior financial year must also be provided, except that the requirement for comparative balance sheet information is satisfied by presenting the year end balance sheet information.

4. RISK FACTORS

Prominent disclosure of risk factors that are specific to the issuer or its industry in a section headed "Risk Factors".

5. INFORMATION ABOUT THE ISSUER

5.1. *History and development of the issuer*

5.1.1. The legal and commercial name of the issuer

5.1.2. The place of registration of the issuer and its registration number

5.1.3. The date of incorporation and the length of life of the issuer, except where indefinite

5.1.4. The domicile and legal form of the issuer, the legislation under which the issuer operates, its country of incorporation, and the address and telephone number of its registered office (or principal place of business if different from its registered office)

5.1.5. The important events in the development of the issuer's business.

5.2. *Investments*

5.2.1. A description, (including the amount) of the issuer's principal investments for each financial year for the period covered by the historical financial information up to the date of the registration document

5.2.2. A description of the issuer's principal investments that are in progress, including the geographic distribution of these investments (home and abroad) and the method of financing (internal or external)

5.2.3. Information concerning the issuer's principal future investments on which its management bodies have already made firm commitments.

6. BUSINESS OVERVIEW

6.1. *Principal Activities*

6.1.1. A description of, and key factors relating to, the nature of the issuer's operations and its principal activities, stating the main categories of products sold and/or services performed for each financial year for the period covered by the historical financial information; and

6.1.2. An indication of any significant new products and/or services that have been introduced and, to the extent the development of new products or services has been publicly disclosed, give the status of development.

6.2. *Principal Markets*

A description of the principal markets in which the issuer competes, including a breakdown of total revenues by category of activity and geographic market for each financial year for the period covered by the historical financial information.

6.3. Where the information given pursuant to items 6.1 and 6.2 has been influenced by exceptional factors, mention that fact.

6.4. If material to the issuer's business or profitability, a summary information regarding the extent to which the issuer is dependent, on patents or licences, industrial, commercial or financial contracts or new manufacturing processes.

6.5. The basis for any statements made by the issuer regarding its competitive position.

7. ORGANISATIONAL STRUCTURE

7.1. If the issuer is part of a group, a brief description of the group and the issuer's position within the group.

7.2. A list of the issuer's significant subsidiaries, including name, country of incorporation or residence, proportion of ownership interest and, if different, proportion of voting power held.

8. PROPERTY, PLANTS AND EQUIPMENT

8.1. Information regarding any existing or planned material tangible fixed assets, including leased properties, and any major encumbrances thereon.

8.2. A description of any environmental issues that may affect the issuer's utilisation of the tangible fixed assets.

9. OPERATING AND FINANCIAL REVIEW

9.1. *Financial condition*

To the extent not covered elsewhere in the registration document, provide a description of the issuer's financial condition, changes in financial condition and results of operations for each year and interim period, for which historical financial information is required, including the causes of material changes from year to year in the financial information to the extent necessary for an understanding of the issuer's business as a whole.

9.2. *Operating results*

9.2.1. Information regarding significant factors, including unusual or infrequent events or new developments, materially affecting the issuer's income from operations, indicating the extent to which income was so affected.

9.2.2. Where the financial statements disclose material changes in net sales or revenues, provide a narrative discussion of the reasons for such changes.

9.2.3. Information regarding any governmental, economic, fiscal, monetary or political policies or factors that have materially affected, or could materially affect, directly or indirectly, the issuer's operations.

10. CAPITAL RESOURCES

10.1. Information concerning the issuer's capital resources (both short and long term);

10.2. An explanation of the sources and amounts of and a narrative description of the issuer's cash flows;

10.3. Information on the borrowing requirements and funding structure of the issuer;

10.4. Information regarding any restrictions on the use of capital resources that have materially affected, or could materially affect, directly or indirectly, the issuer's operations.

10.5. Information regarding the anticipated sources of funds needed to fulfil commitments referred to in items 5.2.3 and 8.1.

11. RESEARCH AND DEVELOPMENT, PATENTS AND LICENCES

Where material, provide a description of the issuer's research and development policies for each financial year for the period covered by the historical financial information, including the amount spent on issuer-sponsored research and development activities.

12. TREND INFORMATION

12.1. The most significant recent trends in production, sales and inventory, and costs and selling prices since the end of the last financial year to the date of the registration document.

12.2. Information on any known trends, uncertainties, demands, commitments or events that are reasonably likely to have a material effect on the issuer's prospects for at least the current financial year.

13. PROFIT FORECASTS OR ESTIMATES

If an issuer chooses to include a profit forecast or a profit estimate the registration document must contain the information set out in items 13.1 and 13.2:

13.1. A statement setting out the principal assumptions upon which the issuer has based its forecast, or estimate.

There must be a clear distinction between assumptions about factors which the members of the administrative, management or supervisory bodies can influence and assumptions about factors which are exclusively outside the influence of the members of the administrative, management or supervisory bodies; the assumptions must be readily understandable by investors, be specific and precise and not relate to the general accuracy of the estimates underlying the forecast.

13.2. A report prepared by independent accountants or auditors stating that in the opinion of the independent accountants or auditors the forecast or estimate has been properly compiled on the basis stated and that the basis of accounting used for the profit forecast or estimate is consistent with the accounting policies of the issuer.

13.3. The profit forecast or estimate must be prepared on a basis comparable with the historical financial information.

13.4. If a profit forecast in a prospectus has been published which is still outstanding, then provide a statement setting out whether or not that forecast is still correct as at the time of the registration document, and an explanation of why such forecast is no longer valid if that is the case.

14. ADMINISTRATIVE, MANAGEMENT, AND SUPERVISORY BODIES AND SENIOR MANAGEMENT

14.1.   Names, business addresses and functions in the issuer of the following persons and an indication of the principal activities performed by them outside that issuer where these are significant with respect to that issuer:

(a)   members of the administrative, management or supervisory bodies;

(b)   partners with unlimited liability, in the case of a limited partnership with a share capital;

(c)   founders, if the issuer has been established for fewer than five years; and

(d)   any senior manager who is relevant to establishing that the issuer has the appropriate expertise and experience for the management of the issuer's business.

The nature of any family relationship between any of those persons.

In the case of each member of the administrative, management or supervisory bodies of the issuer and of each person mentioned in points (b) and (d) of the first subparagraph, details of that person's relevant management expertise and experience and the following information:

(a)   the names of all companies and partnerships of which such person has been a member of the administrative, management or supervisory bodies or partner at any time in the previous five years, indicating whether or not the individual is still a member of the administrative, management or supervisory bodies or partner. It is not necessary to list all the subsidiaries of an issuer of which the person is also a member of the administrative, management or supervisory bodies;

(b)   any convictions in relation to fraudulent offences for at least the previous five years;

(c)   details of any bankruptcies, receiverships or liquidations with which a person described in (a) and (d) of the first subparagraph who was acting in the capacity of any of the positions set out in (a) and (d) of the first subparagraph was associated for at least the previous five years;

(d)   details of any official public incrimination and/or sanctions of such person by statutory or regulatory authorities (including designated professional bodies) and whether such person has ever been disqualified by a court from acting as a member of the administrative, management or supervisory bodies of an issuer or from acting in the management or conduct of the affairs of any issuer for at least the previous five years.

If there is no such information to be disclosed, a statement to that effect is to be made.

14.2.   Administrative, management, and supervisory bodies' and senior management conflicts of interests

Potential conflicts of interests between any duties to the issuer, of the persons referred to in item 14.1 and their private interests and or other duties must be clearly stated. In the event that there are no such conflicts, a statement to that effect must be made.

Any arrangement or understanding with major shareholders, customers, suppliers or others, pursuant to which any person referred to in item 14.1 was selected as a member of the administrative, management or supervisory bodies or member of senior management.

Details of any restrictions agreed by the persons referred to in item 14.1 on the disposal within a certain period of time of their holdings in the issuer's securities.

15. REMUNERATION AND BENEFITS

In relation to the last full financial year for those persons referred to in points (a) and (d) of the first subparagraph of item 14.1:

15.1.   The amount of remuneration paid (including any contingent or deferred compensation), and benefits in kind granted to such persons by the issuer and its subsidiaries for services in all capacities to the issuer and its subsidiaries by any person.

That information must be provided on an individual basis unless individual disclosure is not required in the issuer's home country and is not otherwise publicly disclosed by the issuer.

15.2.   The total amounts set aside or accrued by the issuer or its subsidiaries to provide pension, retirement or similar benefits.

16. BOARD PRACTICES

In relation to the issuer's last completed financial year, and unless otherwise specified, with respect to those persons referred to in point (a) of the first subparagraph of 14.1:

16.1.   Date of expiration of the current term of office, if applicable, and the period during which the person has served in that office.

16.2.   Information about members of the administrative, management or supervisory bodies' service contracts with the issuer or any of its subsidiaries providing for benefits upon termination of employment, or an appropriate negative statement.

PART IV
EC MATERIALS

16.3. Information about the issuer's audit committee and remuneration committee, including the names of committee members and a summary of the terms of reference under which the committee operates.

16.4. A statement as to whether or not the issuer complies with its country's of incorporation corporate governance regime(s). In the event that the issuer does not comply with such a regime, a statement to that effect must be included together with an explanation regarding why the issuer does not comply with such regime.

17. EMPLOYEES

17.1. Either the number of employees at the end of the period or the average for each financial year for the period covered by the historical financial information up to the date of the registration document (and changes in such numbers, if material) and, if possible and material, a breakdown of persons employed by main category of activity and geographic location. If the issuer employs a significant number of temporary employees, include disclosure of the number of temporary employees on average during the most recent financial year.

17.2. Shareholdings and stock options

With respect to each person referred to in points (a) and (d) of the first subparagraph of item 14.1. provide information as to their share ownership and any options over such shares in the issuer as of the most recent practicable date.

17.3. Description of any arrangements for involving the employees in the capital of the issuer.

18. MAJOR SHAREHOLDERS

18.1. In so far as is known to the issuer, the name of any person other than a member of the administrative, management or supervisory bodies who, directly or indirectly, has an interest in the issuer's capital or voting rights which is notifiable under the issuer's national law, together with the amount of each such person's interest or, if there are no such persons, an appropriate negative statement.

18.2. Whether the issuer's major shareholders have different voting rights, or an appropriate negative statement.

18.3. To the extent known to the issuer, state whether the issuer is directly or indirectly owned or controlled and by whom and describe the nature of such control and describe the measures in place to ensure that such control is not abused.

18.4. A description of any arrangements, known to the issuer, the operation of which may at a subsequent date result in a change in control of the issuer.

19. RELATED PARTY TRANSACTIONS

Details of related party transactions (which for these purposes are those set out in the Standards adopted according to the Regulation (EC) No 1606/2002), that the issuer has entered into during the period covered by the historical financial information and up to the date of the registration document, must be disclosed in accordance with the respective standard adopted according to Regulation (EC) No 1606/2002 if applicable.

If such standards do not apply to the issuer the following information must be disclosed:
- (a) the nature and extent of any transactions which are – as a single transaction or in their entirety – material to the issuer. Where such related party transactions are not concluded at arm's length provide an explanation of why these transactions were not concluded at arms length. In the case of outstanding loans including guarantees of any kind indicate the amount outstanding;
- (b) the amount or the percentage to which related party transactions form part of the turnover of the issuer.

20. FINANCIAL INFORMATION CONCERNING THE ISSUER'S ASSETS AND LIABILITIES, FINANCIAL POSITION AND PROFITS AND LOSSES

20.1. *Historical financial information*

Audited historical financial information covering the latest three financial years (or such shorter period that the issuer has been in operation), and the audit report in respect of each year. [If the issuer has changed its accounting reference date during the period for which historical financial information is required, the audited historical information shall cover at least 36 months, or the entire period for which the issuer has been in operation, whichever is the shorter.] Such financial information must be prepared according to Regulation (EC) No 1606/2002, or if not applicable to a Member State national accounting standards for issuers from the Community. For third country issuers, such financial information must be prepared according to the international accounting standards adopted pursuant to the procedure of Article 3 of Regulation (EC) No 1606/2002 or to a third country's national accounting standards equivalent to these standards. If such financial information is not equivalent to these standards, it must be presented in the form of restated financial statements.

The last two years audited historical financial information must be presented and prepared in a form consistent with that which will be adopted in the issuer's next published annual financial statements having regard to accounting standards and policies and legislation applicable to such annual financial statements.

If the issuer has been operating in its current sphere of economic activity for less than one year, the audited historical financial information covering that period must be prepared in accordance with the standards applicable to annual financial statements under the Regulation (EC) No 1606/2002, or if not applicable to a Member State national accounting standards where the issuer is an issuer from the Community. For third country issuers, the historical financial information must be prepared according to the international accounting standards adopted pursuant to the procedure of Article 3 of Regulation (EC) No 1606/2002 or to a third country's national accounting standards equivalent to these standards. This historical financial information must be audited.

If the audited financial information is prepared according to national accounting standards, the financial information required under this heading must include at least:

(a) balance sheet;
(b) income statement;
(c) a statement showing either all changes in equity or changes in equity other than those arising from capital transactions with owners and distributions to owners;
(d) cash flow statement;
(e) accounting policies and explanatory notes.

The historical annual financial information must be independently audited or reported on as to whether or not, for the purposes of the registration document, it gives a true and fair view, in accordance with auditing standards applicable in a Member State or an equivalent standard.

20.2. *Pro forma financial information*

In the case of a significant gross change, a description of how the transaction might have affected the assets and liabilities and earnings of the issuer, had the transaction been undertaken at the commencement of the period being reported on or at the date reported.

This requirement will normally be satisfied by the inclusion of pro forma financial information.

This pro forma financial information is to be presented as set out in Annex II and must include the information indicated therein.

Pro forma financial information must be accompanied by a report prepared by independent accountants or auditors.

20.3. *Financial statements*

If the issuer prepares both own and consolidated annual financial statements, include at least the consolidated annual financial statements in the registration document.

20.4. *Auditing of historical annual financial information*

20.4.1. A statement that the historical financial information has been audited. If audit reports on the historical financial information have been refused by the statutory auditors or if they contain qualifications or disclaimers, such refusal or such qualifications or disclaimers must be reproduced in full and the reasons given.

20.4.2. Indication of other information in the registration document which has been audited by the auditors.

20.4.3. Where financial data in the registration document is not extracted from the issuer's audited financial statements state the source of the data and state that the data is unaudited.

20.5. *Age of latest financial information*

20.5.1. The last year of audited financial information may not be older than one of the following:

(a) 18 months from the date of the registration document if the issuer includes audited interim financial statements in the registration document;
(b) 15 months from the date of the registration document if the issuer includes unaudited interim financial statements in the registration document.

20.6. *Interim and other financial information*

20.6.1. If the issuer has published quarterly or half yearly financial information since the date of its last audited financial statements, these must be included in the registration document. If the quarterly or half yearly financial information has been reviewed or audited, the audit or review report must also be included. If the quarterly or half yearly financial information is unaudited or has not been reviewed state that fact.

20.6.2. If the registration document is dated more than nine months after the end of the last audited financial year, it must contain interim financial information, which may be unaudited (in which case that fact must be stated) covering at least the first six months of the financial year.

The interim financial information must include comparative statements for the same period in the prior financial year, except that the requirement for comparative balance sheet information may be satisfied by presenting the years end balance sheet.

20.7. *Dividend policy*

A description of the issuer's policy on dividend distributions and any restrictions thereon.

20.7.1. The amount of the dividend per share for each financial year for the period covered by the historical financial information adjusted, where the number of shares in the issuer has changed, to make it comparable.

20.8. *Legal and arbitration proceedings*

Information on any governmental, legal or arbitration proceedings (including any such proceedings which are pending or threatened of which the issuer is aware), during a period covering at least the previous 12 months which may have, or have had in the recent past significant effects on the issuer and/or group's financial position or profitability, or provide an appropriate negative statement.

20.9. *Significant change in the issuer's financial or trading position*

A description of any significant change in the financial or trading position of the group which has occurred since the end of the last financial period for which either audited financial information or interim financial information have been published, or provide an appropriate negative statement.

21. ADDITIONAL INFORMATION

21.1. *Share capital*

The following information as of the date of the most recent balance sheet included in the historical financial information:

21.1.1. The amount of issued capital, and for each class of share capital:
- (a) the number of shares authorised;
- (b) the number of shares issued and fully paid and issued but not fully paid;
- (c) the par value per share, or that the shares have no par value; and
- (d) a reconciliation of the number of shares outstanding at the beginning and end of the year. If more than 10% of capital has been paid for with assets other than cash within the period covered by the historical financial information, state that fact.

21.1.2. If there are shares not representing capital, state the number and main characteristics of such shares.

21.1.3. The number, book value and face value of shares in the issuer held by or on behalf of the issuer itself or by subsidiaries of the issuer.

21.1.4. The amount of any convertible securities, exchangeable securities or securities with warrants, with an indication of the conditions governing and the procedures for conversion, exchange or subscription.

21.1.5. Information about and terms of any acquisition rights and or obligations over authorised but unissued capital or an undertaking to increase the capital.

21.1.6. Information about any capital of any member of the group which is under option or agreed conditionally or unconditionally to be put under option and details of such options including those persons to whom such options relate.

21.1.7. A history of share capital, highlighting information about any changes, for the period covered by the historical financial information.

21.2. *Memorandum and Articles of Association*

21.2.1. A description of the issuer's objects and purposes and where they can be found in the memorandum and articles of association.

21.2.2. A summary of any provisions of the issuer's articles of association, statutes, charter or bylaws with respect to the members of the administrative, management and supervisory bodies.

21.2.3. A description of the rights, preferences and restrictions attaching to each class of the existing shares.

21.2.4. A description of what action is necessary to change the rights of holders of the shares, indicating where the conditions are more significant than is required by law.

21.2.5. A description of the conditions governing the manner in which annual general meetings and extraordinary general meetings of shareholders are called including the conditions of admission.

21.2.6. A brief description of any provision of the issuer's articles of association, statutes, charter or bylaws that would have an effect of delaying, deferring or preventing a change in control of the issuer.

21.2.7. An indication of the articles of association, statutes, charter or bylaw provisions, if any, governing the ownership threshold above which shareholder ownership must be disclosed.

21.2.8.   A description of the conditions imposed by the memorandum and articles of association statutes, charter or bylaw governing changes in the capital, where such conditions are more stringent than is required by law.

22. MATERIAL CONTRACTS

A summary of each material contract, other than contracts entered into in the ordinary course of business, to which the issuer or any member of the group is a party, for the two years immediately preceding publication of the registration document.

A summary of any other contract (not being a contract entered into in the ordinary course of business) entered into by any member of the group which contains any provision under which any member of the group has any obligation or entitlement which is material to the group as at the date of the registration document.

23. THIRD PARTY INFORMATION AND STATEMENT BY EXPERTS AND DECLARATIONS OF ANY INTEREST

23.1.   Where a statement or report attributed to a person as an expert is included in the registration document, provide such person's name, business address, qualifications and material interest if any in the issuer. If the report has been produced at the issuer's request a statement to the effect that such statement or report is included, in the form and context in which it is included, with the consent of the person who has authorised the contents of that part of the registration document.

23.2.   Where information has been sourced from a third party, provide a confirmation that this information has been accurately reproduced and that as far as the issuer is aware and is able to ascertain from information published by that third party, no facts have been omitted which would render the reproduced information inaccurate or misleading. In addition, identify the source(s) of the information.

24. DOCUMENTS ON DISPLAY

A statement that for the life of the registration document the following documents (or copies thereof), where applicable, may be inspected:
  (a)   the memorandum and articles of association of the issuer;
  (b)   all reports, letters, and other documents, historical financial information, valuations and statements prepared by any expert at the issuer's request any part of which is included or referred to in the registration document;
  (c)   the historical financial information of the issuer or, in the case of a group, the historical financial information for the issuer and its subsidiary undertakings for each of the two financial years preceding the publication of the registration document.

An indication of where the documents on display may be inspected, by physical or electronic means.

25. INFORMATION ON HOLDINGS

Information relating to the undertakings in which the issuer holds a proportion of the capital likely to have a significant effect on the assessment of its own assets and liabilities, financial position or profits and losses.

[5647]

NOTES

Words in square brackets in item 20.1 inserted by Commission Regulation 211/2007/EC, Art 1(3), as from 1 March 2007.

ANNEX II
PRO FORMA FINANCIAL INFORMATION BUILDING BLOCK

1.   The pro forma information must include a description of the transaction, the businesses or entities involved and the period to which it refers, and must clearly state the following:
  (a)   the purpose to which it has been prepared;
  (b)   the fact that it has been prepared for illustrative purposes only;
  (c)   the fact that because of its nature, the pro forma financial information addresses a hypothetical situation and, therefore, does not represent the company's actual financial position or results.

2.   In order to present pro forma financial information, a balance sheet and profit and loss account, and accompanying explanatory notes, depending on the circumstances may be included.

3.   Pro forma financial information must normally be presented in columnar format, composed of:
  (a)   the historical unadjusted information;
  (b)   the pro forma adjustments; and
  (c)   the resulting pro forma financial information in the final column.

The sources of the pro forma financial information have to be stated and, if applicable, the financial statements of the acquired businesses or entities must be included in the prospectus

4. The pro forma information must be prepared in a manner consistent with the accounting policies adopted by the issuer in its last or next financial statements and shall identify the following:
   (a) the basis upon which it is prepared;
   (b) the source of each item of information and adjustment.

5. Pro forma information may only be published in respect of:
   (a) the current financial period;
   (b) the most recently completed financial period;
   and/or
   (c) the most recent interim period for which relevant unadjusted information has been or will be published or is being published in the same document.

6. Pro forma adjustments related to the pro forma financial information must be:
   (a) clearly shown and explained;
   (b) directly attributable to the transaction;
   (c) factually supportable.

In addition, in respect of a pro forma profit and loss or cash flow statement, they must be clearly identified as to those expected to have a continuing impact on the issuer and those which are not.

7. The report prepared by the independent accountants or auditors must state that in their opinion:
   (a) the pro forma financial information has been properly compiled on the basis stated;
   (b) that basis is consistent with the accounting policies of the issuer.

[5648]

ANNEX III
MINIMUM DISCLOSURE REQUIREMENTS FOR THE SHARE SECURITIES NOTE (SCHEDULE)

1. PERSONS RESPONSIBLE

1.1. All persons responsible for the information given in the prospectus and, as the case may be, for certain parts of it, with, in the latter case, an indication of such parts. In the case of natural persons including members of the issuer's administrative, management or supervisory bodies indicate the name and function of the person; in case of legal persons indicate the name and registered office.

1.2. A declaration by those responsible for the prospectus that, having taken all reasonable care to ensure that such is the case the information contained in the prospectus is, to the best of their knowledge, in accordance with the facts and contains no omission likely to affect its import. As the case may be, declaration by those responsible for certain parts of the prospectus that, having taken all reasonable care to ensure that such is the case the information contained in the part of the prospectus for which they are responsible is, to the best of their knowledge, in accordance with the facts and contains no omission likely to affect its import.

2. RISK FACTORS

Prominent disclosure of risk factors that are material to the securities being offered and/or admitted to trading in order to assess the market risk associated with these securities in a section headed "Risk Factors".

3. KEY INFORMATION

3.1. *Working capital statement*

Statement by the issuer that, in its opinion, the working capital is sufficient for the issuer's present requirements or, if not, how it proposes to provide the additional working capital needed.

3.2. *Capitalisation and indebtedness*

A statement of capitalisation and indebtedness (distinguishing between guaranteed and unguaranteed, secured and unsecured indebtedness) as of a date no earlier than 90 days prior to the date of the document. Indebtedness also includes indirect and contingent indebtedness.

3.3. *Interest of natural and legal persons involved in the issue/offer*

A description of any interest, including conflicting ones that is material to the issue/offer, detailing the persons involved and the nature of the interest.

3.4. *Reasons for the offer and use of proceeds*

Reasons for the offer and, where applicable, the estimated net amount of the proceeds broken into each principal intended use and presented by order of priority of such uses. If the issuer is aware that the anticipated proceeds will not be sufficient to fund all the proposed uses, state the amount and sources of other funds needed. Details must be given with regard to the use of the proceeds, in particular when they are being used to acquire assets, other than in the ordinary course of business, to finance announced acquisitions of other business, or to discharge, reduce or retire indebtedness.

4. INFORMATION CONCERNING THE SECURITIES TO BE OFFERED/ADMITTED TO TRADING

4.1.   A description of the type and the class of the securities being offered and/or admitted to trading, including the ISIN (international security identification number) or other such security identification code.

4.2.   Legislation under which the securities have been created.

4.3.   An indication whether the securities are in registered form or bearer form and whether the securities are in certificated form or book-entry form. In the latter case, name and address of the entity in charge of keeping the records.

4.4.   Currency of the securities issue.

4.5.   A description of the rights attached to the securities, including any limitations of those rights, and procedure for the exercise of those rights.
  Dividend rights:
—   fixed date(s) on which the entitlement arises,
—   time limit after which entitlement to dividend lapses and an indication of the person in whose favour the lapse operates,
—   dividend restrictions and procedures for non-resident holders,
—   rate of dividend or method of its calculation, periodicity and cumulative or non-cumulative nature of payments.
  Voting rights.
  Pre-emption rights in offers for subscription of securities of the same class.
  Right to share in the issuer's profits.
  Rights to share in any surplus in the event of liquidation.
—   Redemption provisions.
—   Conversion provisions.

4.6.   In the case of new issues, a statement of the resolutions, authorisations and approvals by virtue of which the securities have been or will be created and/or issued.

4.7.   In the case of new issues, the expected issue date of the securities.

4.8.   A description of any restrictions on the free transferability of the securities.

4.9.   An indication of the existence of any mandatory takeover bids and/or squeeze-out and sell-out rules in relation to the securities.

4.10.   An indication of public takeover bids by third parties in respect of the issuer's equity, which have occurred during the last financial year and the current financial year. The price or exchange terms attaching to such offers and the outcome thereof must be stated.

4.11.   In respect of the country of registered office of the issuer and the country(ies) where the offer is being made or admission to trading is being sought:
—   information on taxes on the income from the securities withheld at source,
—   indication as to whether the issuer assumes responsibility for the withholding of taxes at the source.

5. TERMS AND CONDITIONS OF THE OFFER

5.1.   *Conditions, offer statistics, expected timetable and action required to apply for the offer*

5.1.1.   Conditions to which the offer is subject.

5.1.2.   Total amount of the issue/offer, distinguishing the securities offered for sale and those offered for subscription; if the amount is not fixed, description of the arrangements and time for announcing to the public the definitive amount of the offer.

5.1.3.   The time period, including any possible amendments, during which the offer will be open and description of the application process.

5.1.4.   An indication of when, and under which circumstances, the offer may be revoked or suspended and whether revocation can occur after dealing has begun.

5.1.5.   A description of the possibility to reduce subscriptions and the manner for refunding excess amount paid by applicants.

5.1.6.   Details of the minimum and/or maximum amount of application (whether in number of securities or aggregate amount to invest).

5.1.7.   An indication of the period during which an application may be withdrawn, provided that investors are allowed to withdraw their subscription.

5.1.8.   Method and time limits for paying up the securities and for delivery of the securities.

5.1.9.   A full description of the manner and date in which results of the offer are to be made public.

5.1.10.   The procedure for the exercise of any right of pre-emption, the negotiability of subscription rights and the treatment of subscription rights not exercised.

5.2.   *Plan of distribution and allotment*

5.2.1.   The various categories of potential investors to which the securities are offered. If the offer is being made simultaneously in the markets of two or more countries and if a tranche has been or is being reserved for certain of these, indicate any such tranche.

5.2.2.   To the extent known to the issuer, an indication of whether major shareholders or members of the issuer's management, supervisory or administrative bodies intended to subscribe in the offer, or whether any person intends to subscribe for more than five per cent of the offer.

5.2.3.   Pre-allotment disclosure:
  (a)   the division into tranches of the offer including the institutional, retail and issuer's employee tranches and any other tranches;
  (b)   the conditions under which the clawback may be used, the maximum size of such claw back and any applicable minimum percentages for individual tranches;
  (c)   the allotment method or methods to be used for the retail and issuer's employee tranche in the event of an over-subscription of these tranches;
  (d)   a description of any pre-determined preferential treatment to be accorded to certain classes of investors or certain affinity groups (including friends and family programmes) in the allotment, the percentage of the offer reserved for such preferential treatment and the criteria for inclusion in such classes or groups;
  (e)   whether the treatment of subscriptions or bids to subscribe in the allotment may be determined on the basis of which firm they are made through or by;
  (f)   a target minimum individual allotment if any within the retail tranche;
  (g)   the conditions for the closing of the offer as well as the date on which the offer may be closed at the earliest;
  (h)   whether or not multiple subscriptions are admitted, and where they are not, how any multiple subscriptions will be handled.

5.2.4.   Process for notification to applicants of the amount allotted and indication whether dealing may begin before notification is made.

5.2.5.   Over-allotment and "green shoe" :
  (a)   the existence and size of any over-allotment facility and/or "green shoe".
  (b)   the existence period of the over-allotment facility and/or "green shoe".
  (c)   any conditions for the use of the over-allotment facility or exercise of the "green shoe".

5.3.   *Pricing*

5.3.1.   An indication of the price at which the securities will be offered. If the price is not known or if there is no established and/or liquid market for the securities, indicate the method for determining the offer price, including a statement as to who has set the criteria or is formally responsible for the determination. Indication of the amount of any expenses and taxes specifically charged to the subscriber or purchaser.

5.3.2.   Process for the disclosure of the offer price.

5.3.3.   If the issuer's equity holders have pre-emptive purchase rights and this right is restricted or withdrawn, indication of the basis for the issue price if the issue is for cash, together with the reasons for and beneficiaries of such restriction or withdrawal.

5.3.4.   Where there is or could be a material disparity between the public offer price and the effective cash cost to members of the administrative, management or supervisory bodies or senior management, or affiliated persons, of securities acquired by them in transactions during the past year, or which they have the right to acquire, include a comparison of the public contribution in the proposed public offer and the effective cash contributions of such persons.

5.4.   *Placing and underwriting*

5.4.1.   Name and address of the coordinator(s) of the global offer and of single parts of the offer and, to the extend known to the issuer or to the offeror, of the placers in the various countries where the offer takes place.

5.4.2.   Name and address of any paying agents and depository agents in each country.

5.4.3.   Name and address of the entities agreeing to underwrite the issue on a firm commitment basis, and name and address of the entities agreeing to place the issue without a firm commitment or under "best efforts" arrangements. Indication of the material features of the agreements, including the quotas. Where not all of the issue is underwritten, a statement of the portion not covered. Indication of the overall amount of the underwriting commission and of the placing commission.

5.4.4.   When the underwriting agreement has been or will be reached.

6. ADMISSION TO TRADING AND DEALING ARRANGEMENTS

6.1.   An indication as to whether the securities offered are or will be the object of an application for admission to trading, with a view to their distribution in a regulated market or other equivalent markets with indication of the markets in question. This circumstance must be mentioned, without creating the impression that the admission to trading will necessarily be approved. If known, the earliest dates on which the securities will be admitted to trading.

6.2.   All the regulated markets or equivalent markets on which, to the knowledge of the issuer, securities of the same class of the securities to be offered or admitted to trading are already admitted to trading.

6.3.   If simultaneously or almost simultaneously with the creation of the securities for which admission to a regulated market is being sought securities of the same class are subscribed for or placed privately or if securities of other classes are created for public or private placing, give details of the nature of such operations and of the number and characteristics of the securities to which they relate.

6.4.   Details of the entities which have a firm commitment to act as intermediaries in secondary trading, providing liquidity through bid and offer rates and description of the main terms of their commitment.

6.5.   Stabilisation: where an issuer or a selling shareholder has granted an over-allotment option or it is otherwise proposed that price stabilising activities may be entered into in connection with an offer:

6.5.1.   The fact that stabilisation may be undertaken, that there is no assurance that it will be undertaken and that it may be stopped at any time,

6.5.2.   The beginning and the end of the period during which stabilisation may occur,

6.5.3.   The identity of the stabilisation manager for each relevant jurisdiction unless this is not known at the time of publication,

6.5.4.   The fact that stabilisation transactions may result in a market price that is higher than would otherwise prevail.

7. SELLING SECURITIES HOLDERS

7.1.   Name and business address of the person or entity offering to sell the securities, the nature of any position office or other material relationship that the selling persons has had within the past three years with the issuer or any of its predecessors or affiliates.

7.2.   The number and class of securities being offered by each of the selling security holders.

7.3.   Lock-up agreements
The parties involved.
Content and exceptions of the agreement.
Indication of the period of the lock up.

8. EXPENSE OF THE ISSUE/OFFER

8.1.   The total net proceeds and an estimate of the total expenses of the issue/offer.

9. DILUTION

9.1.   The amount and percentage of immediate dilution resulting from the offer.

9.2.   In the case of a subscription offer to existing equity holders, the amount and percentage of immediate dilution if they do not subscribe to the new offer.

10. ADDITIONAL INFORMATION

10.1.   If advisors connected with an issue are mentioned in the Securities Note, a statement of the capacity in which the advisors have acted.

10.2.   An indication of other information in the Securities Note which has been audited or reviewed by statutory auditors and where auditors have produced a report. Reproduction of the report or, with permission of the competent authority, a summary of the report.

10.3.   Where a statement or report attributed to a person as an expert is included in the Securities Note, provide such persons' name, business address, qualifications and material interest if any in the issuer. If the report has been produced at the issuer's request a statement to the effect that such statement or report is included, in the form and context in which it is included, with the consent of the person who has authorised the contents of that part of the Securities Note.

10.4.   Where information has been sourced from a third party, provide a confirmation that this information has been accurately reproduced and that as far as the issuer is aware and is able to ascertain from information published by that third party, no facts have been omitted which would render the reproduced information inaccurate or misleading. In addition, identify the source(s) of the information.

ANNEX IV
MINIMUM DISCLOSURE REQUIREMENTS FOR THE DEBT AND DERIVATIVE SECURITIES REGISTRATION DOCUMENT (SCHEDULE)

(Debt and derivative securities with a denomination per unit of less than EUR 50,000)

1. PERSONS RESPONSIBLE

1.1. All persons responsible for the information given in the registration document and, as the case may be, for certain parts of it, with, in the latter case, an indication of such parts. In the case of natural persons including members of the issuer's administrative, management or supervisory bodies indicate the name and function of the person; in case of legal persons indicate the name and registered office.

1.2. A declaration by those responsible for the registration document that, having taken all reasonable care to ensure that such is the case the information contained in the registration document is, to the best of their knowledge, in accordance with the facts and contains no omission likely to affect its import. As the case may be, declaration by those responsible for certain parts of the registration document that, having taken all reasonable care to ensure that such is the case, the information contained in the part of the registration document for which they are responsible is, to the best of their knowledge, in accordance with the facts and contains no omission likely to affect its import.

2. STATUTORY AUDITORS

2.1. Names and addresses of the issuer's auditors for the period covered by the historical financial information (together with their membership in a professional body).

2.2. If auditors have resigned, been removed or not been re-appointed during the period covered by the historical financial information, details if material.

3. SELECTED FINANCIAL INFORMATION

3.1. Selected historical financial information regarding the issuer, presented, for each financial year for the period covered by the historical financial information, and any subsequent interim financial period, in the same currency as the financial information.

The selected historical financial information must provide key figures that summarise the financial condition of the issuer.

3.2. If selected financial information for interim periods is provided, comparative data from the same period in the prior financial year must also be provided, except that the requirement for comparative balance sheet data is satisfied by presenting the year end balance sheet information.

4. RISK FACTORS

Prominent disclosure of risk factors that may affect the issuer's ability to fulfil its obligations under the securities to investors in a section headed "Risk Factors".

5. INFORMATION ABOUT THE ISSUER

5.1. *History and development of the issuer*

5.1.1. the legal and commercial name of the issuer;

5.1.2. the place of registration of the issuer and its registration number;

5.1.3. the date of incorporation and the length of life of the issuer, except where indefinite;

5.1.4. the domicile and legal form of the issuer, the legislation under which the issuer operates, its country of incorporation, and the address and telephone number of its registered office (or principal place of business if different from its registered office);

5.1.5. any recent events particular to the issuer which are to a material extent relevant to the evaluation of the issuer's solvency.

5.2. *Investments*

5.2.1. A description of the principal investments made since the date of the last published financial statements.

5.2.2. Information concerning the issuer's principal future investments, on which its management bodies have already made firm commitments.

5.2.3. Information regarding the anticipated sources of funds needed to fulfil commitments referred to in item 5.2.2.

6. BUSINESS OVERVIEW

6.1. *Principal activities*

6.1.1. A description of the issuer's principal activities stating the main categories of products sold and/or services performed; and

6.1.2.   an indication of any significant new products and/or activities.

6.2.   *Principal markets*

A brief description of the principal markets in which the issuer competes.

6.3.   The basis for any statements made by the issuer regarding its competitive position.

7. ORGANISATIONAL STRUCTURE

7.1.   If the issuer is part of a group, a brief description of the group and of the issuer's position within it.

7.2.   If the issuer is dependent upon other entities within the group, this must be clearly stated together with an explanation of this dependence.

8. TREND INFORMATION

8.1.   Include a statement that there has been no material adverse change in the prospects of the issuer since the date of its last published audited financial statements.

In the event that the issuer is unable to make such a statement, provide details of this material adverse change.

8.2.   Information on any known trends, uncertainties, demands, commitments or events that are reasonably likely to have a material effect on the issuer's prospects for at least the current financial year.

9. PROFIT FORECASTS OR ESTIMATES

If an issuer chooses to include a profit forecast or a profit estimate, the registration document must contain the information items 9.1 and 9.2:

9.1.   A statement setting out the principal assumptions upon which the issuer has based its forecast, or estimate.

There must be a clear distinction between assumptions about factors which the members of the administrative, management or supervisory bodies can influence and assumptions about factors which are exclusively outside the influence of the members of the administrative, management or supervisory bodies; the assumptions must be readily understandable by investors, be specific and precise and not relate to the general accuracy of the estimates underlying the forecast.

9.2.   A report prepared by independent accountants or auditors must be included stating that in the opinion of the independent accountants or auditors the forecast or estimate has been properly compiled on the basis stated and that the basis of accounting used for the profit forecast or estimate is consistent with the accounting policies of the issuer.

9.3.   The profit forecast or estimate must be prepared on a basis comparable with the historical financial information.

10. ADMINISTRATIVE, MANAGEMENT, AND SUPERVISORY BODIES

10.1.   Names, business addresses and functions in the issuer of the following persons, and an indication of the principal activities performed by them outside the issuer where these are significant with respect to that issuer:
- (a)   members of the administrative, management or supervisory bodies;
- (b)   partners with unlimited liability, in the case of a limited partnership with a share capital.

10.2.   Administrative, management, and supervisory bodies' conflicts of interests

Potential conflicts of interests between any duties to the issuing entity of the persons referred to in item 10.1 and their private interests and or other duties must be clearly stated. In the event that there are no such conflicts, make a statement to that effect.

11. BOARD PRACTICES

11.1.   Details relating to the issuer's audit committee, including the names of committee members and a summary of the terms of reference under which the committee operates.

11.2.   A statement as to whether or not the issuer complies with its country's of incorporation corporate governance regime(s). In the event that the issuer does not comply with such a regime a statement to that effect must be included together with an explanation regarding why the issuer does not comply with such regime.

12. MAJOR SHAREHOLDERS

12.1.   To the extent known to the issuer, state whether the issuer is directly or indirectly owned or controlled and by whom and describe the nature of such control, and describe the measures in place to ensure that such control is not abused.

12.2.   A description of any arrangements, known to the issuer, the operation of which may at a subsequent date result in a change in control of the issuer.

13. FINANCIAL INFORMATION CONCERNING THE ISSUER'S ASSETS AND LIABILITIES, FINANCIAL POSITION AND PROFITS AND LOSSES

13.1. *Historical financial information*

Audited historical financial information covering the latest 2 financial years (or such shorter period that the issuer has been in operation), and the audit report in respect of each year. [If the issuer has changed its accounting reference date during the period for which historical financial information is required, the audited historical information shall cover at least 24 months, or the entire period for which the issuer has been in operation, whichever is the shorter.] Such financial information must be prepared according to Regulation (EC) No 1606/2002, or if not applicable to a Member States national accounting standards for issuers from the Community. For third country issuers, such financial information must be prepared according to the international accounting standards adopted pursuant to the procedure of Article 3 of Regulation (EC) No 1606/2002 or to a third country's national accounting standards equivalent to these standards. If such financial information is not equivalent to these standards, it must be presented in the form of restated financial statements.

The most recent year's historical financial information must be presented and prepared in a form consistent with that which will be adopted in the issuer's next published annual financial statements having regard to accounting standards and policies and legislation applicable to such annual financial statements.

If the issuer has been operating in its current sphere of economic activity for less than one year, the audited historical financial information covering that period must be prepared in accordance with the standards applicable to annual financial statements under the Regulation (EC) No 1606/2002, or if not applicable to a Member States national accounting standards where the issuer is an issuer from the Community. For third country issuers, the historical financial information must be prepared according to the international accounting standards adopted pursuant to the procedure of Article 3 of Regulation (EC) No 1606/2002 or to a third country's national accounting standards equivalent to these standards. This historical financial information must be audited.

If the audited financial information is prepared according to national accounting standards, the financial information required under this heading must include at least:
  (a)   balance sheet;
  (b)   income statement;
  (c)   cash flow statement; and
  (d)   accounting policies and explanatory notes

The historical annual financial information must have been independently audited or reported on as to whether or not, for the purposes of the registration document, it gives a true and fair view, in accordance with auditing standards applicable in a Member State or an equivalent standard.

13.2. *Financial statements*

If the issuer prepares both own and consolidated financial statements, include at least the consolidated financial statements in the registration document.

13.3. *Auditing of historical annual financial information*

13.3.1.   A statement that the historical financial information has been audited. If audit reports on the historical financial information have been refused by the statutory auditors or if they contain qualifications or disclaimers, such refusal or such qualifications or disclaimers must be reproduced in full and the reasons given.

13.3.2.   An indication of other information in the registration document which has been audited by the auditors.

13.3.3.   Where financial data in the registration document is not extracted from the issuer's audited financial statements state the source of the data and state that the data is unaudited.

13.4. *Age of latest financial information*

13.4.1.   The last year of audited financial information may not be older than 18 months from the date of the registration document.

13.5. *Interim and other financial information*

13.5.1.   If the issuer has published quarterly or half yearly financial information since the date of its last audited financial statements, these must be included in the registration document. If the quarterly or half yearly financial information has been reviewed or audited the audit or review report must also be included. If the quarterly or half yearly financial information is unaudited or has not been reviewed state that fact.

13.5.2.   If the registration document is dated more than nine months after the end of the last audited financial year, it must contain interim financial information, covering at least the first six months of the financial year. If the interim financial information is un-audited state that fact.

The interim financial information must include comparative statements for the same period in the prior financial year, except that the requirement for comparative balance sheet information may be satisfied by presenting the years end balance sheet.

13.6. *Legal and arbitration proceedings*

Information on any governmental, legal or arbitration proceedings (including any such proceedings which are pending or threatened of which the issuer is aware), during a period covering at least the previous 12 months which may have, or have had in the recent past, significant effects on the issuer and/or group's financial position or profitability, or provide an appropriate negative statement.

13.7. *Significant change in the issuer's financial or trading position*

A description of any significant change in the financial or trading position of the group which has occurred since the end of the last financial period for which either audited financial information or interim financial information have been published, or an appropriate negative statement.

14. ADDITIONAL INFORMATION

14.1. *Share capital*

14.1.1. The amount of the issued capital, the number and classes of the shares of which it is composed with details of their principal characteristics, the part of the issued capital still to be paid up, with an indication of the number, or total nominal value, and the type of the shares not yet fully paid up, broken down where applicable according to the extent to which they have been paid up.

14.2. *Memorandum and Articles of Association*

14.2.1. The register and the entry number therein, if applicable, and a description of the issuer's objects and purposes and where they can be found in the memorandum and articles of association.

15. MATERIAL CONTRACTS

A brief summary of all material contracts that are not entered into in the ordinary course of the issuer's business, which could result in any group member being under an obligation or entitlement that is material to the issuer's ability to meet its obligation to security holders in respect of the securities being issued.

16. THIRD PARTY INFORMATION AND STATEMENT BY EXPERTS AND DECLARATIONS OF ANY INTEREST

16.1. Where a statement or report attributed to a person as an expert is included in the registration document, provide such person's name, business address, qualifications and material interest if any in the issuer. If the report has been produced at the issuer's request a statement to that effect that such statement or report is included, in the form and context in which it is included, with the consent of that person who has authorised the contents of that part of the registration document.

16.2. Where information has been sourced from a third party, provide a confirmation that this information has been accurately reproduced and that as far as the issuer is aware and is able to ascertain from information published by that third party, no facts have been omitted which would render the reproduced information inaccurate or misleading. In addition, the issuer shall identify the source(s) of the information.

17. DOCUMENTS ON DISPLAY

A statement that for the life of the registration document the following documents (or copies thereof), where applicable, may be inspected:

(a) the memorandum and articles of association of the issuer;
(b) all reports, letters, and other documents, historical financial information, valuations and statements prepared by any expert at the issuer's request any part of which is included or referred to in the registration document;
(c) the historical financial information of the issuer or, in the case of a group, the historical financial information of the issuer and its subsidiary undertakings for each of the two financial years preceding the publication of the registration document.

An indication of where the documents on display may be inspected, by physical or electronic means.

[5650]

NOTES

Words in square brackets in item 13.1 inserted by Commission Regulation 211/2007/EC, Art 1(4), as from 1 March 2007.

ANNEX V
MINIMUM DISCLOSURE REQUIREMENTS FOR THE SECURITIES NOTE RELATED TO DEBT SECURITIES (SCHEDULE)

(Debt securities with a denomination per unit of less than EUR 50,000)

1. PERSONS RESPONSIBLE

1.1.   All persons responsible for the information given in the prospectus and, as the case may be, for certain parts of it, with, in the latter case, an indication of such parts. In the case of natural persons including members of the issuer's administrative, management or supervisory bodies indicate the name and function of the person; in case of legal persons indicate the name and registered office.

1.2.   A declaration by those responsible for the prospectus that, having taken all reasonable care to ensure that such is the case, the information contained in the prospectus is, to the best of their knowledge, in accordance with the facts and contains no omission likely to affect its import. As the case may be, declaration by those responsible for certain parts of the prospectus that the information contained in the part of the prospectus for which they are responsible is, to the best of their knowledge, in accordance with the facts and contains no omission likely to affect its import.

2. RISK FACTORS

2.1.   Prominent disclosure of risk factors that are material to the securities being offered and/or admitted to trading in order to assess the market risk associated with these securities in a section headed "Risk Factors".

3. KEY INFORMATION

3.1.   *Interest of natural and legal persons involved in the issue/offer*

A description of any interest, including conflicting ones, that is material to the issue/offer, detailing the persons involved and the nature of the interest.

3.2.   *Reasons for the offer and use of proceeds*

Reasons for the offer if different from making profit and/or hedging certain risks. Where applicable, disclosure of the estimated total expenses of the issue/offer and the estimated net amount of the proceeds. These expenses and proceeds shall be broken into each principal intended use and presented by order of priority of such uses. If the issuer is aware that the anticipated proceeds will not be sufficient to fund all the proposed uses, state the amount and sources of other funds needed.

4. INFORMATION CONCERNING THE SECURITIES TO BE OFFERED/ADMITTED TO TRADING

4.1.   A description of the type and the class of the securities being offered and/or admitted to trading, including the ISIN (International Security Identification Number) or other such security identification code.

4.2.   Legislation under which the securities have been created.

4.3.   An indication of whether the securities are in registered form or bearer form and whether the securities are in certificated form or book-entry form. In the latter case, name and address of the entity in charge of keeping the records.

4.4.   Currency of the securities issue.

4.5.   Ranking of the securities being offered and/or admitted to trading, including summaries of any clauses that are intended to affect ranking or subordinate the security to any present or future liabilities of the issuer.

4.6.   A description of the rights attached to the securities, including any limitations of those rights, and procedure for the exercise of those rights.

4.7.   The nominal interest rate and provisions relating to interest payable.
—   The date from which interest becomes payable and the due dates for interest
—   The time limit on the validity of claims to interest and repayment of principal.

Where the rate is not fixed, description of the underlying on which it is based and of the method used to relate the two and an indication where information about the past and the further performance of the underlying and its volatility can be obtained.
—   A description of any market disruption or settlement disruption events that affect the underlying
—   Adjustment rules with relation to events concerning the underlying
—   Name of the calculation agent.

If the security has a derivative component in the interest payment, provide a clear and comprehensive explanation to help investors understand how the value of their investment is affected by the value of the underlying instrument(s), especially under the circumstances when the risks are most evident.

4.8.   Maturity date and arrangements for the amortisation of the loan, including the repayment procedures. Where advance amortisation is contemplated, on the initiative of the issuer or of the holder, it shall be described, stipulating amortisation terms and conditions.

4.9.   An indication of yield. Describe the method whereby that yield is calculated in summary form.

4.10.   Representation of debt security holders including an identification of the organisation representing the investors and provisions applying to such representation. Indication of where the public may have access to the contracts relating to these forms of representation.

4.11.   In the case of new issues, a statement of the resolutions, authorisations and approvals by virtue of which the securities have been or will be created and/or issued.

4.12.   In the case of new issues, the expected issue date of the securities.

4.13.   A description of any restrictions on the free transferability of the securities.

4.14.   In respect of the country of registered office of the issuer and the country(ies) where the offer being made or admission to trading is being sought:
—   information on taxes on the income from the securities withheld at source;
—   indication as to whether the issuer assumes responsibility for the withholding of taxes at the source.

5. TERMS AND CONDITIONS OF THE OFFER

5.1.   *Conditions, offer statistics, expected timetable and action required to apply for the offer*

5.1.1.   Conditions to which the offer is subject.

5.1.2.   Total amount of the issue/offer; if the amount is not fixed, description of the arrangements and time for announcing to the public the definitive amount of the offer.

5.1.3.   The time period, including any possible amendments, during which the offer will be open and description of the application process.

5.1.4.   A description of the possibility to reduce subscriptions and the manner for refunding excess amount paid by applicants.

5.1.5.   Details of the minimum and/or maximum amount of application, (whether in number of securities or aggregate amount to invest).

5.1.6.   Method and time limits for paying up the securities and for delivery of the securities.

5.1.7.   A full description of the manner and date in which results of the offer are to be made public.

5.1.8.   The procedure for the exercise of any right of pre-emption, the negotiability of subscription rights and the treatment of subscription rights not exercised.

5.2.   *Plan of distribution and allotment*

5.2.1.   The various categories of potential investors to which the securities are offered. If the offer is being made simultaneously in the markets of two or more countries and if a tranche has been or is being reserved for certain of these, indicate any such tranche.

5.2.2.   Process for notification to applicants of the amount allotted and indication whether dealing may begin before notification is made.

5.3.   *Pricing*

5.3.1.   An indication of the expected price at which the securities will be offered or the method of determining the price and the process for its disclosure. Indicate the amount of any expenses and taxes specifically charged to the subscriber or purchaser.

5.4.   *Placing and underwriting*

5.4.1.   Name and address of the co-ordinator(s) of the global offer and of single parts of the offer and, to the extend known to the issuer or to the offeror, of the placers in the various countries where the offer takes place.

5.4.2.   Name and address of any paying agents and depository agents in each country.

5.4.3.   Name and address of the entities agreeing to underwrite the issue on a firm commitment basis, and name and address of the entities agreeing to place the issue without a firm commitment or under "best efforts" arrangements. Indication of the material features of the agreements, including the quotas. Where not all of the issue is underwritten, a statement of the portion not covered. Indication of the overall amount of the underwriting commission and of the placing commission.

5.4.4.   When the underwriting agreement has been or will be reached.

6. ADMISSION TO TRADING AND DEALING ARRANGEMENTS

6.1.   An indication as to whether the securities offered are or will be the object of an application for admission to trading, with a view to their distribution in a regulated market or other equivalent markets with indication of the markets in question. This circumstance must be mentioned, without creating the impression that the admission to trading will necessarily be approved. If known, give the earliest dates on which the securities will be admitted to trading.

6.2.   All the regulated markets or equivalent markets on which, to the knowledge of the issuer, securities of the same class of the securities to be offered or admitted to trading are already admitted to trading.

6.3.   Name and address of the entities which have a firm commitment to act as intermediaries in secondary trading, providing liquidity through bid and offer rates and description of the main terms of their commitment.

7. ADDITIONAL INFORMATION

7.1.   If advisors connected with an issue are mentioned in the Securities Note, a statement of the capacity in which the advisors have acted.

7.2.   An indication of other information in the Securities Note which has been audited or reviewed by statutory auditors and where auditors have produced a report. Reproduction of the report or, with permission of the competent authority, a summary of the report.

7.3.   Where a statement or report attributed to a person as an expert is included in the Securities Note, provide such persons' name, business address, qualifications and material interest if any in the issuer. If the report has been produced at the issuer's request a statement to that effect that such statement or report is included, in the form and context in which it is included, with the consent of that person who has authorised the contents of that part of the Securities Note.

7.4.   Where information has been sourced from a third party, provide a confirmation that this information has been accurately reproduced and that as far as the issuer is aware and is able to ascertain from information published by that third party, no facts have been omitted which would render the reproduced information inaccurate or misleading. In addition, identify the source(s) of the information.

7.5.   Credit ratings assigned to an issuer or its debt securities at the request or with the co-operation of the issuer in the rating process. A brief explanation of the meaning of the ratings if this has previously been published by the rating provider.

[5651]

ANNEX VI
MINIMUM DISCLOSURE REQUIREMENTS FOR GUARANTEES
(ADDITIONAL BUILDING BLOCK)

1. Nature of the guarantee

A description of any arrangement intended to ensure that any obligation material to the issue will be duly serviced, whether in the form of guarantee, surety, Keep well Agreement, Mono-line Insurance policy or other equivalent commitment (hereafter referred to generically as "guarantees" and their provider as "guarantor" for convenience).

Without prejudice to the generality of the foregoing, such arrangements encompass commitments to ensure obligations to repay debt securities and/or the payment of interest and the description shall set out how the arrangement is intended to ensure that the guaranteed payments will be duly serviced.

2. Scope of the guarantee

Details shall be disclosed about the terms and conditions and scope of the guarantee. Without prejudice to the generality of the foregoing, these details should cover any conditionality on the application of the guarantee in the event of any default under the terms of the security and the material terms of any mono-line insurance or keep well agreement between the issuer and the guarantor. Details must also be disclosed of any guarantor's power of veto in relation to changes to the security holder's rights, such as is often found in Mono-line Insurance.

3. Information to be disclosed about the guarantor

The guarantor must disclose information about itself as if it were the issuer of that same type of security that is the subject of the guarantee.

4. Documents on display

Indication of the places where the public may have access to the material contracts and other documents relating to the guarantee.

[5652]

ANNEX VII
MINIMUM DISCLOSURE REQUIREMENTS FOR ASSET BACKED SECURITIES
REGISTRATION DOCUMENT (SCHEDULE)

1. PERSONS RESPONSIBLE

1.1.　All persons responsible for the information given in the registration document and, as the case may be, for certain parts of it, with, in the latter case, an indication of such parts. In the case of natural persons including members of the issuer's administrative, management or supervisory bodies indicate the name and function of the person; in case of legal persons indicate the name and registered office.

1.2.　A declaration by those responsible for the registration document that, having taken all reasonable care to ensure that such is the case, the information given in the registration document is, to the best of their knowledge, in accordance with the facts and does not omit anything likely to affect its import. As the case may be, declaration by those responsible for certain parts of the registration document that having taken all reasonable care to ensure that such is the case, the information contained in that part of the registration document for which they are responsible is, to the best of their knowledge, in accordance with the facts and contains no omission likely to affect its import.

2. STATUTORY AUDITORS

2.1.　Names and addresses of the issuer's auditors for the period covered by the historical financial information (together with any membership of any relevant professional body).

3. RISK FACTORS

3.1.　The document must prominently disclose risk factors in a section headed "Risk Factors" that are specific to the issuer and its industry.

4. INFORMATION ABOUT THE ISSUER:

4.1.　A statement whether the issuer has been established as a special purpose vehicle or entity for the purpose of issuing asset backed securities;

4.2.　The legal and commercial name of the issuer;

4.3.　The place of registration of the issuer and its registration number;

4.4.　The date of incorporation and the length of life of the issuer, except where indefinite;

4.5.　The domicile and legal form of the issuer, the legislation under which the issuer operates its country of incorporation and the address and telephone number of its registered office (or principal place of business if different from its registered office).

4.6.　Description of the amount of the issuer's authorised and issued capital and the amount of any capital agreed to be issued, the number and classes of the securities of which it is composed.

5. BUSINESS OVERVIEW

5.1.　A brief description of the issuer's principal activities.

5.2.　A global overview of the parties to the securitisation program including information on the direct or indirect ownership or control between those parties.

6. ADMINISTRATIVE, MANAGEMENT AND SUPERVISORY BODIES

6.1.　Names, business addresses and functions in the issuer of the following persons, and an indication of the principal activities performed by them outside the issuer where these are significant with respect to that issuer:
   (a)　members of the administrative, management or supervisory bodies;
   (b)　partners with unlimited liability, in the case of a limited partnership with a share capital.

7. MAJOR SHAREHOLDERS

7.1.　To the extent known to the issuer, state whether the issuer is directly or indirectly owned or controlled and by whom, and describe the nature of such control and describe the measures in place to ensure that such control is not abused.

8. FINANCIAL INFORMATION CONCERNING THE ISSUER'S ASSETS AND LIABILITIES, FINANCIAL POSITION, AND PROFITS AND LOSSES

8.1.　Where, since the date of incorporation or establishment, an issuer has not commenced operations and no financial statements have been made up as at the date of the registration document, a statement to that effect shall be provided in the registration document.

8.2.　*Historical financial information*

Where, since the date of incorporation or establishment, an issuer has commenced operations and financial statements have been made up, the registration document must contain audited historical financial information covering the latest 2 financial years (or shorter period that the issuer has been in operation) and the audit report in respect of each year. [If the issuer has changed its accounting reference date during the period for which historical financial information is required, the audited historical information shall cover at least 24 months, or the entire period for which the issuer has been in operation, whichever is the shorter.] Such financial information must be prepared according to Regulation (EC) No 1606/2002, or if not applicable to a Member's State national accounting standards for issuers from the Community. For third country issuers, such financial information must be prepared according to the international accounting standards adopted pursuant to the procedure of Article 3 of Regulation (EC) No 1606/2002 or to a third country's national accounting standards equivalent to these standards. If such financial information is not equivalent to these standards, it must be presented in the form of restated financial statements.

The most recent year's historical financial information must be presented and prepared in a form consistent with that which will be adopted in the issuer's next annual published financial statements having regard to accounting standards and policies and legislation applicable to such annual financial statements.

If the issuer has been operating in its current sphere of economic activity for less than one year, the audited historical financial information covering that period must be prepared in accordance with the standards applicable to annual financial statements under Regulation (EC) No 1606/2002, or if not applicable to a Member States national accounting standards where the issuer is from the Community. For third country issuers, the historical financial information must be prepared according to the international accounting standards adopted pursuant to the procedure of Article 3 of Regulation (EC) No 1606/2002 or to a third country's national accounting standards equivalent to these standards. This historical financial information must be audited.

If the audited financial information is prepared according to national accounting standards, the financial information required under this heading must include at least the following:
   (a)   the balance sheet;
   (b)   the income statement;
   (c)   the accounting policies and explanatory notes.

The historical annual financial information must be independently audited or reported on as to whether or not, for the purposes of the registration document, it gives a true and fair view, in accordance with auditing standards applicable in a Member State or an equivalent standard.

8.2a.   This paragraph may be used only for issues of asset backed securities having a denomination per unit of at least EUR 50,000.

Where, since the date of incorporation or establishment, an issuer has commenced operations and financial statements have been made up, the registration document must contain audited historical financial information covering the latest 2 financial years (or shorter period that the issuer has been in operation) and the audit report in respect of each year. [If the issuer has changed its accounting reference date during the period for which historical financial information is required, the audited historical information shall cover at least 24 months, or the entire period for which the issuer has been in operation, whichever is the shorter.] Such financial information must be prepared according to Regulation (EC) No 1606/2002 or, if not applicable, to a Member's State national accounting standards for issuers from the Community. For third country issuers, such financial information must be prepared according to the international accounting standards adopted pursuant to the procedure of Article 3 of Regulation (EC) No 1606/2002 or to a third country's national accounting standards equivalent to these standards. Otherwise, the following information must be included in the registration document:
   (a)   a prominent statement that the financial information included in the registration document has not been prepared in accordance with the international accounting standards adopted pursuant to the procedure of Article 3 of Regulation (EC) No 1606/2002 and that there may be material differences in the financial information had Regulation (EC) No 1606/2002 been applied to the historical financial information;
   (b)   immediately following the historical financial information a narrative description of the differences between the international accounting standards adopted pursuant to the procedure of Article 3 of Regulation (EC) No 1606/2002 and the accounting principles adopted by the issuer in preparing its annual financial statements.

The most recent year's historical financial information must be presented and prepared in a form consistent with that which will be adopted in the issuer's next annual financial statements having regard to accounting standards and policies and legislation applicable to such annual financial statements.

If the audited financial information is prepared according to national accounting standards, the financial information required under this heading must include at least the following:
   (a)   the balance sheet;
   (b)   the income statement;
   (c)   the accounting policies and explanatory notes.

The historical annual financial information must be independently audited or reported on as to whether or not, for the purposes of the registration document, it gives a true and fair view, in

accordance with auditing standards applicable in a Member State or an equivalent standard. Otherwise, the following information must be included in the registration document:
(a)   a prominent statement disclosing which auditing standards have been applied;
(b)   an explanation of any significant departures from International Standards on Auditing.

8.3.   *Legal and arbitration proceedings*

Information on any governmental, legal or arbitration proceedings (including any such proceedings which are pending or threatened of which the company is aware), during a period covering at least the previous 12 months, which may have, or have had in the recent past, significant effects on the issuer and/or group's financial position or profitability, or provide an appropriate negative statement.

8.4.   *Material adverse change in the issuer's financial position*

Where an issuer has prepared financial statements, include a statement that there has been no material adverse change in the financial position or prospects of the issuer since the date of its last published audited financial statements. Where a material adverse change has occurred, this must be disclosed in the registration document.

9. THIRD PARTY INFORMATION AND STATEMENT BY EXPERTS AND DECLARATIONS OF ANY INTEREST

9.1.   Where a statement or report attributed to a person as an expert is included in the registration document, provide such person's name, business address, qualifications and material interest if any in the issuer. If the report has been produced at the issuer's request a statement to that effect that such statement or report is included, in the form and context in which it is included, with the consent of that person who has authorised the contents of that part of the registration document.

9.2.   Where information has been sourced from a third party, provide a confirmation that this information has been accurately reproduced and that as far as the issuer is aware and is able to ascertain from information published by that third party, no facts have been omitted which would render the reproduced information inaccurate or misleading In addition, the issuer shall identify the source(s) of the information.

10. DOCUMENTS ON DISPLAY

10.1.   A statement that for the life of the registration document the following documents (or copies thereof), where applicable, may be inspected:
(a)   the memorandum and articles of association of the issuer;
(b)   all reports, letters, and other documents, historical financial information, valuations and statements prepared by any expert at the issuer's request any part of which is included or referred to in the registration document;
(c)   the historical financial information of the issuer or, in the case of a group, the historical financial information of the issuer and its subsidiary undertakings for each of the two financial years preceding the publication of the registration document.

An indication of where the documents on display may be inspected, by physical or electronic means.

[5653]

NOTES
Words in square brackets in items 8.2, and 8.2a inserted by Commission Regulation 211/2007/EC, Art 1(4), as from 1 March 2007.

ANNEX VIII
MINIMUM DISCLOSURE REQUIREMENTS FOR THE ASSET-BACKED SECURITIES ADDITIONAL BUILDING BLOCK

1. THE SECURITIES

1.1.   The minimum denomination of an issue.

1.2.   Where information is disclosed about an undertaking/obligor which is not involved in the issue, provide a confirmation that the information relating to the undertaking/obligor has been accurately reproduced from information published by the undertaking/obligor. So far as the issuer is aware and is able to ascertain from information published by the undertaking/obligor no facts have been omitted which would render the reproduced information misleading.

In addition, identify the source(s) of information in the Securities Note that has been reproduced from information published by an undertaking/obligor.

2. THE UNDERLYING ASSETS

2.1.   Confirmation that the securitised assets backing the issue have characteristics that demonstrate capacity to produce funds to service any payments due and payable on the securities.

2.2.   In respect of a pool of discrete assets backing the issue:

2.2.1.   The legal jurisdiction by which the pool of assets is governed

2.2.2.

(a)   In the case of a small number of easily identifiable obligors, a general description of each obligor.

(b)   In all other cases, a description of: the general characteristics of the obligors; and the economic environment, as well as global statistical data referred to the securitised assets.

2.2.3.   The legal nature of the assets;

2.2.4.   the expiry or maturity date(s) of the assets;

2.2.5.   the amount of the assets;

2.2.6.   loan to value ratio or level of collateralisation;

2.2.7.   the method of origination or creation of the assets, and for loans and credit agreements, the principal lending criteria and an indication of any loans which do not meet these criteria and any rights or obligations to make further advances;

2.2.8.   an indication of significant representations and collaterals given to the issuer relating to the assets;

2.2.9.   any rights to substitute the assets and a description of the manner in which and the type of assets which may be so substituted; if there is any capacity to substitute assets with a different class or quality of assets a statement to that effect together with a description of the impact of such substitution;

2.2.10.   a description of any relevant insurance policies relating to the assets. Any concentration with one insurer must be disclosed if it is material to the transaction.

2.2.11.   Where the assets comprise obligations of 5 or fewer obligors which are legal persons or where an obligor accounts for 20% or more of the assets, or where an obligor accounts for a material portion of the assets, so far as the issuer is aware and/or is able to ascertain from information published by the obligor(s) indicate either of the following:

(a)   information relating to each obligor as if it were an issuer drafting a registration document for debt and derivative securities with an individual denomination of at least EUR 50,000;

(b)   if an obligor or guarantor has securities already admitted to trading on a regulated or equivalent market or the obligations are guaranteed by an entity admitted to trading on a regulated or equivalent market, the name, address, country of incorporation, nature of business and name of the market in which its securities are admitted.

2.2.12.   If a relationship exists that is material to the issue, between the issuer, guarantor and obligor, details of the principal terms of that relationship.

2.2.13.   Where the assets comprise obligations that are not traded on a regulated or equivalent market, a description of the principal terms and conditions of the obligations.

2.2.14.   Where the assets comprise equity securities that are admitted to trading on a regulated or equivalent market indicate the following:

(a)   a description of the securities;

(b)   a description of the market on which they are traded including its date of establishment, how price information is published, an indication of daily trading volumes, information as to the standing of the market in the country and the name of the market's regulatory authority;

(c)   the frequency with which prices of the relevant securities, are published.

2.2.15.   Where more than ten (10) per cent of the assets comprise equity securities that are not traded on a regulated or equivalent market, a description of those equity securities and equivalent information to that contained in the schedule for share registration document in respect of each issuer of those securities.

2.2.16.   Where a material portion of the assets are secured on or backed by real property, a valuation report relating to the property setting out both the valuation of the property and cash flow/income streams.

Compliance with this disclosure is not required if the issue is of securities backed by mortgage loans with property as security, where there has been no revaluation of the properties for the purpose of the issue, and it is clearly stated that the valuations quoted are as at the date of the original initial mortgage loan origination.

2.3.   In respect of an actively managed pool of assets backing the issue:

2.3.1.   equivalent information to that contained in items 2.1 and 2.2 to allow an assessment of the type, quality, sufficiency and liquidity of the asset types in the portfolio which will secure the issue;

2.3.2.   the parameters within which investments can be made, the name and description of the entity responsible for such management including a description of that entity's expertise and experience, a summary of the provisions relating to the termination of the appointment of such entity and the appointment of an alternative management entity, and a description of that entity's relationship with any other parties to the issue.

2.4. Where an issuer proposes to issue further securities backed by the same assets, a prominent statement to that effect and unless those further securities are fungible with or are subordinated to those classes of existing debt, a description of how the holders of that class will be informed.

3. STRUCTURE AND CASH FLOW

3.1. Description of the structure of the transaction, including, if necessary, a structure diagram.

3.2. Description of the entities participating in the issue and description of the functions to be performed by them.

3.3. Description of the method and date of the sale, transfer, novation or assignment of the assets or of any rights and/or obligations in the assets to the issuer or, where applicable, the manner and time period in which the proceeds from the issue will be fully invested by the issuer.

3.4. An explanation of the flow of funds including:

3.4.1. how the cash flow from the assets will meet the issuer's obligations to holders of the securities, including, if necessary, a financial service table and a description of the assumptions used in developing the table;

3.4.2. information on any credit enhancements, an indication of where material potential liquidity shortfalls may occur and the availability of any liquidity supports and indication of provisions designed to cover interest/principal shortfall risks;

3.4.3. without prejudice to item 3.4.2, details of any subordinated debt finance;

3.4.4. an indication of any investment parameters for the investment of temporary liquidity surpluses and description of the parties responsible for such investment;

3.4.5. how payments are collected in respect of the assets;

3.4.6. the order of priority of payments made by the issuer to the holders of the class of securities in question;

3.4.7. details of any other arrangements upon which payments of interest and principal to investors are dependent.

3.5. The name, address and significant business activities of the originators of the securitised assets.

3.6. Where the return on, and/or repayment of the security is linked to the performance or credit of other assets which are not assets of the issuer, items 2.2 and 2.3 are necessary.

3.7. The name, address and significant business activities of the administrator, calculation agent or equivalent, together with a summary of the administrator's/calculation agents responsibilities, their relationship with the originator or the creator of the assets and a summary of the provisions relating to the termination of the appointment of the administrator/calculation agent and the appointment of an alternative administrator/calculation agent.

3.8. The names and addresses and brief description of:
    (a)   any swap counterparties and any providers of other material forms of credit/liquidity enhancement;
    (b)   the banks with which the main accounts relating to the transaction are held.

4. POST ISSUANCE REPORTING

4.1. Indication in the prospectus whether or not it intends to provide post-issuance transaction information regarding securities to be admitted to trading and the performance of the underlying collateral. Where the issuer has indicated that it intends to report such information, specify in the prospectus what information will be reported, where such information can be obtained, and the frequency with which such information will be reported.

[5654]

ANNEX IX
MINIMUM DISCLOSURE REQUIREMENTS FOR THE DEBT AND DERIVATIVE
SECURITIES REGISTRATION DOCUMENT (SCHEDULE)

(Debt and derivative securities with a denomination per unit of at least EUR 50,000)

1. PERSONS RESPONSIBLE

1.1. All persons responsible for the information given in the registration document and, as the case may be, for certain parts of it, with, in the latter case, an indication of such parts. In the case of natural persons including members of the issuer's administrative, management or supervisory bodies indicate the name and function of the person; in case of legal persons indicate the name and registered office.

1.2. A declaration by those responsible for the registration document that, having taken all reasonable care to ensure that such is the case, the information contained in the registration document is, to the best of their knowledge, in accordance with the facts and contains no omission likely to affect its import. As the case may be, declaration by those responsible for certain parts of the registration document that, having taken all reasonable care to ensure that such is the case, the information contained in the part of the registration document for which they are responsible is, to the best of their knowledge, in accordance with the facts and contains no omission likely to affect its import.

2. STATUTORY AUDITORS

2.1. Names and addresses of the issuer's auditors for the period covered by the historical financial information (together with their membership in a professional body).

2.2. If auditors have resigned, been removed or not been re-appointed during the period covered by the historical financial information, details if material.

3. RISK FACTORS

3.1. Prominent disclosure of risk factors that may affect the issuer's ability to fulfil its obligations under the securities to investors in a section headed "Risk Factors".

4. INFORMATION ABOUT THE ISSUER

4.1. *History and development of the issuer*

4.1.1. the legal and commercial name of the issuer;

4.1.2. the place of registration of the issuer and its registration number;

4.1.3. the date of incorporation and the length of life of the issuer, except where indefinite;

4.1.4. the domicile and legal form of the issuer, the legislation under which the issuer operates, its country of incorporation, and the address and telephone number of its registered office (or principal place of business if different from its registered office;

4.1.5. any recent events particular to the issuer and which are to a material extent relevant to the evaluation of the issuer's solvency.

5. BUSINESS OVERVIEW

5.1. *Principal activities:*

5.1.1. A brief description of the issuer's principal activities stating the main categories of products sold and/or services performed;

5.1.2. The basis for any statements in the registration document made by the issuer regarding its competitive position.

6. ORGANISATIONAL STRUCTURE

6.1. If the issuer is part of a group, a brief description of the group and of the issuer's position within it.

6.2. If the issuer is dependent upon other entities within the group, this must be clearly stated together with an explanation of this dependence.

7. TREND INFORMATION

7.1. Include a statement that there has been no material adverse change in the prospects of the issuer since the date of its last published audited financial statements.

In the event that the issuer is unable to make such a statement, provide details of this material adverse change.

8. PROFIT FORECASTS OR ESTIMATES

If an issuer chooses to include a profit forecast or a profit estimate, the registration document must contain the information items 8.1 and 8.2 the following:

8.1. A statement setting out the principal assumptions upon which the issuer has based its forecast, or estimate.

There must be a clear distinction between assumptions about factors which the members of the administrative, management or supervisory bodies can influence and assumptions about factors which are exclusively outside the influence of the members of the administrative, management or supervisory bodies; be readily understandable by investors; be specific and precise; and not relate to the general accuracy of the estimates underlying the forecast.

8.2. Any profit forecast set out in the registration document must be accompanied by a statement confirming that the said forecast has been properly prepared on the basis stated and that the basis of accounting is consistent with the accounting policies of the issuer.

8.3. The profit forecast or estimate must be prepared on a basis comparable with the historical financial information.

9. ADMINISTRATIVE, MANAGEMENT, AND SUPERVISORY BODIES

9.1.   Names, business addresses and functions in the issuer of the following persons, and an indication of the principal activities performed by them outside the issuer where these are significant with respect to that issuer:

(a)   members of the administrative, management or supervisory bodies;

(b)   partners with unlimited liability, in the case of a limited partnership with a share capital.

9.2.   *Administrative, management, and supervisory bodies' conflicts of interests*

Potential conflicts of interests between any duties to the issuing entity of the persons referred to in item 9.1 and their private interests and or other duties must be clearly stated. In the event that there are no such conflicts, a statement to that effect.

10. MAJOR SHAREHOLDERS

10.1.   To the extent known to the issuer, state whether the issuer is directly or indirectly owned or controlled and by whom, and describe the nature of such control, and describe the measures in place to ensure that such control is not abused.

10.2.   A description of any arrangements, known to the issuer, the operation of which may at a subsequent date result in a change in control of the issuer.

11. FINANCIAL INFORMATION CONCERNING THE ISSUER'S ASSETS AND LIABILITIES, FINANCIAL POSITION AND PROFITS AND LOSSES

11.1.   *Historical financial information*

Audited historical financial information covering the latest two financial years (or such shorter period that the issuer has been in operation), and the audit report in respect of each year. [If the issuer has changed its accounting reference date during the period for which historical financial information is required, the audited historical information shall cover at least 24 months, or the entire period for which the issuer has been in operation, whichever is the shorter.] Such financial information must be prepared according to Regulation (EC) No 1606/2002, or if not applicable to a Member's State national accounting standards for issuers from the Community. For third country issuers, such financial information must be prepared according to the international accounting standards adopted pursuant to the procedure of Article 3 of Regulation (EC) No 1606/2002 or to a third country's national accounting standards equivalent to these standards. Otherwise, the following information must be included in the registration document:

(a)   a prominent statement that the financial information included in the registration document has not been prepared in accordance with the international accounting standards adopted pursuant to the procedure of Article 3 of Regulation (EC) No 1606/2002 and that there may be material differences in the financial information had Regulation (EC) No 1606/2002 been applied to the historical financial information;

(b)   immediately following the historical financial information a narrative description of the differences between the international accounting standards adopted pursuant to the procedure of Article 3 of Regulation (EC) No 1606/2002 and the accounting principles adopted by the issuer in preparing its annual financial statements.

The most recent year's historical financial information must be presented and prepared in a form consistent with that which will be adopted in the issuer's next published annual financial statements having regard to accounting standards and policies and legislation applicable to such annual financial statements.

If the audited financial information is prepared according to national accounting standards, the financial information required under this heading must include at least the following:

(a)   the balance sheet;

(b)   the income statement;

(c)   the accounting policies and explanatory notes.

The historical annual financial information must be independently audited or reported on as to whether or not, for the purposes of the registration document, it gives a true and fair view, in accordance with auditing standards applicable in a Member State or an equivalent standard. Otherwise, the following information must be included in the registration document:

(a)   a prominent statement disclosing which auditing standards have been applied;

(b)   an explanation of any significant departures from international standards on auditing.

11.2.   *Financial statements*

If the issuer prepares both own and consolidated financial statements, include at least the consolidated financial statements in the registration document.

11.3.   *Auditing of historical annual financial information*

11.3.1.   A statement that the historical financial information has been audited. If audit reports on the historical financial information have been refused by the statutory auditors or if they contain qualifications or disclaimers, such refusal or such qualifications or disclaimers must be reproduced in full and the reasons given.

11.3.2.   An indication of other information in the registration document which has been audited by the auditors.

11.3.3.   Where financial data in the registration document is not extracted from the issuer's audited financial statements, state the source of the data and state that the data is unaudited.

11.4.   *Age of latest financial information*

11.4.1.   The last year of audited financial information may not be older than 18 months from the date of the registration document.

11.5.   *Legal and arbitration proceedings*

Information on any governmental, legal or arbitration proceedings (including any such proceedings which are pending or threatened of which the issuer is aware), during a period covering at least the previous 12 months which may have, or have had in the recent past, significant effects on the issuer and/or group's financial position or profitability, or provide an appropriate negative statement.

11.6.   *Significant change in the issuer's financial or trading position*

A description of any significant change in the financial or trading position of the group which has occurred since the end of the last financial period for which either audited financial information or interim financial information have been published, or an appropriate negative statement.

12. MATERIAL CONTRACTS

A brief summary of all material contracts that are not entered into in the ordinary course of the issuer's business, which could result in any group member being under an obligation or entitlement that is material to the issuer's ability to meet its obligation to security holders in respect of the securities being issued.

13. THIRD PARTY INFORMATION AND STATEMENT BY EXPERTS AND DECLARATIONS OF ANY INTEREST

13.1.   Where a statement or report attributed to a person as an expert is included in the registration document, provide such person's name, business address, qualifications and material interest if any in the issuer. If the report has been produced at the issuer's request a statement to that effect that such statement or report is included, in the form and context in which it is included, with the consent of that person who has authorised the contents of that part of the registration document.

13.2.   *Third party information*

Where information has been sourced from a third party, provide a confirmation that this information has been accurately reproduced and that as far as the issuer is aware and is able to ascertain from information published by that third party, no facts have been omitted which would render the reproduced information inaccurate or misleading; in addition, identify the source(s) of the information.

14. DOCUMENTS ON DISPLAY

A statement that for the life of the registration document the following documents (or copies thereof), where applicable, may be inspected:

(a)   the memorandum and articles of association of the issuer;

(b)   all reports, letters, and other documents, historical financial information, valuations and statements prepared by any expert at the issuer's request any part of which is included or referred to in the registration document;

(c)   the historical financial information of the issuer or, in the case of a group, the historical financial information of the issuer and its subsidiary undertakings for each of the two financial years preceding the publication of the registration document.

An indication of where the documents on display may be inspected, by physical or electronic means.

[5655]

NOTES

Words in square brackets in item 11.1 inserted by Commission Regulation 211/2007/EC, Art 1(4), as from 1 March 2007.

ANNEX X
MINIMUM DISCLOSURE REQUIREMENTS FOR THE DEPOSITORY RECEIPTS ISSUED OVER SHARES (SCHEDULE)

Information about the Issuer of the Underlying Shares

1. PERSONS RESPONSIBLE

1.1.   All persons responsible for the information given in the prospectus and, as the case may be, for certain parts of it, with, in the latter case, an indication of such parts. In the case of natural persons including members of the issuer's administrative, management or supervisory bodies indicate the name and function of the person; in case of legal persons indicate the name and registered office.

1.2.   A declaration by those responsible for the prospectus that, having taken all reasonable care to ensure that such is the case, the information contained in the prospectus is, to the best of their knowledge, in accordance with the facts and contains no omission likely to affect its import. As the case may be, declaration by those responsible for certain parts of the prospectus that, having taken all reasonable care to ensure that such is the case, the information contained in the part of the prospectus for which they are responsible is, to the best of their knowledge, in accordance with the facts and contains no omission likely to affect its import.

2. STATUTORY AUDITORS

2.1.   Names and addresses of the issuer's auditors for the period covered by the historical financial information (together with their membership in a professional body).

2.2.   If auditors have resigned, been removed or not been re-appointed during the period covered by the historical financial information, indicate details if material.

3. SELECTED FINANCIAL INFORMATION

3.1.   Selected historical financial information regarding the issuer, presented for each financial year for the period covered by the historical financial information, and any subsequent interim financial period, in the same currency as the financial information.

The selected historical financial information must provide the key figures that summarise the financial condition of the issuer.

3.2.   If selected financial information for interim periods is provided, comparative data from the same period in the prior financial year shall also be provided, except that the requirement for comparative balance sheet information is satisfied by presenting the year end balance sheet information.

4. RISK FACTORS

Prominent disclosure of risk factors that are specific to the issuer or its industry in a section headed "Risk Factors".

5. INFORMATION ABOUT THE ISSUER

5.1.   *History and development of the issuer*

5.1.1.   the legal and commercial name of the issuer;

5.1.2.   the place of registration of the issuer and its registration number;

5.1.3.   the date of incorporation and the length of life of the issuer, except where indefinite;

5.1.4.   the domicile and legal form of the issuer, the legislation under which the issuer operates, its country of incorporation, and the address and telephone number of its registered office (or principal place of business if different from its registered office);

5.1.5.   the important events in the development of the issuer's business.

5.2.   *Investments*

5.2.1.   A description, (including the amount) of the issuer's principal investments for each financial year for the period covered by the historical financial information up to the date of the prospectus;

5.2.2.   A description of the issuer's principal investments that are currently in progress, including the distribution of these investments geographically (home and abroad) and the method of financing (internal or external);

5.2.3.   Information concerning the issuer's principal future investments on which its management bodies have already made firm commitments.

6. BUSINESS OVERVIEW

6.1.   *Principal activities*

6.1.1.   A description of, and key factors relating to, the nature of the issuer's operations and its principal activities, stating the main categories of products sold and/or services performed for each financial year for the period covered by the historical financial information.

6.1.2.   An indication of any significant new products and/or services that have been introduced and, to the extent the development of new products or services has been publicly disclosed, give the status of development.

6.2.   *Principal markets*

A description of the principal markets in which the issuer competes, including a breakdown of total revenues by category of activity and geographic market for each financial year for the period covered by the historical financial information.

6.3.   Where the information given pursuant to items 6.1 and 6.2 has been influenced by exceptional factors, mention that fact.

6.4.   If material to the issuer's business or profitability, disclose summary information regarding the extent to which the issuer is dependent, on patents or licences, industrial, commercial or financial contracts or new manufacturing processes.

6.5.   The basis for any statements made by the issuer regarding its competitive position.

7. ORGANISATIONAL STRUCTURE

7.1.   If the issuer is part of a group, a brief description of the group and the issuer's position within the group.

7.2.   A list of the issuer's significant subsidiaries, including name, country of incorporation or residence, proportion of ownership interest and, if different, proportion of voting power held.

8. PROPERTY, PLANTS AND EQUIPMENT

8.1.   Information regarding any existing or planned material tangible fixed assets, including leased properties, and any major encumbrances thereon.

8.2.   A description of any environmental issues that may affect the issuer's utilisation of the tangible fixed assets.

9. OPERATING AND FINANCIAL REVIEW

9.1.   *Financial condition*

To the extent not covered elsewhere in the prospectus, provide a description of the issuer's financial condition, changes in financial condition and results of operations for each year and interim period, for which historical financial information is required, including the causes of material changes from year to year in the financial information to the extent necessary for an understanding of the issuer's business as a whole.

9.2.   *Operating results*

9.2.1.   Information regarding significant factors, including unusual or infrequent events or new developments, materially affecting the issuer's income from operations, indicating the extent to which income was so affected.

9.2.2.   Where the financial statements disclose material changes in net sales or revenues, provide a narrative discussion of the reasons for such changes.

9.2.3.   Information regarding any governmental, economic, fiscal, monetary or political policies or factors that have materially affected, or could materially affect, directly or indirectly, the issuer's operations.

10. CAPITAL RESOURCES

10.1.   Information concerning the issuer's capital resources (both short and long term).

10.2.   An explanation of the sources and amounts of and a narrative description of the issuer's cash flows.

10.3.   Information on the borrowing requirements and funding structure of the issuer.

10.4.   Information regarding any restrictions on the use of capital resources that have materially affected, or could materially affect, directly or indirectly, the issuer's operations.

10.5.   Information regarding the anticipated sources of funds needed to fulfil commitments referred to in items 5.2.3 and 8.1.

11. RESEARCH AND DEVELOPMENT, PATENTS AND LICENCES

Where material, provide a description of the issuer's research and development policies for each financial year for the period covered by the historical financial information, including the amount spent on issuer-sponsored research and development activities.

12. TREND INFORMATION

12.1.   The most significant recent trends in production, sales and inventory, and costs and selling prices since the end of the last financial year to the date of the prospectus.

12.2.   Information on any known trends, uncertainties, demands, commitments or events that are reasonably likely to have a material effect on the issuer's prospects for at least the current financial year.

13. PROFIT FORECASTS OR ESTIMATES

If an issuer chooses to include a profit forecast or a profit estimate the prospectus must contain the information items 13.1 and 13.2.

13.1.   A statement setting out the principal assumptions upon which the issuer has based its forecast, or estimate.

There must be a clear distinction between assumptions about factors which the members of the administrative, management or supervisory bodies can influence and assumptions about factors which are exclusively outside the influence of the members of the administrative, management or supervisory bodies; the assumptions must be readily understandable by investors, be specific and precise and not relate to the general accuracy of the estimates underlying the forecast.

13.2.   A report prepared by independent accountants or auditors stating that in the opinion of the independent accountants or auditors the forecast or estimate has been properly compiled on the basis stated and that the basis of accounting used for the profit forecast or estimate is consistent with the accounting policies of the issuer.

13.3.   The profit forecast or estimate prepared on a basis comparable with the historical financial information.

13.4.   If the issuer has published a profit forecast in a prospectus which is still outstanding, provide a statement setting out whether or not that forecast is still correct as at the time of the prospectus, and an explanation of why such forecast is no longer valid if that is the case.

14. ADMINISTRATIVE, MANAGEMENT, AND SUPERVISORY BODIES AND SENIOR MANAGEMENT

14.1.   Names, business addresses and functions in the issuer of the following persons and an indication of the principal activities performed by them outside that issuer where these are significant with respect to that issuer:

(a)   members of the administrative, management or supervisory bodies;

(b)   partners with unlimited liability, in the case of a limited partnership with a share capital;

(c)   founders, if the issuer has been established for fewer than five years;

(d)   any senior manager who is relevant to establishing that the issuer has the appropriate expertise and experience for the management of the issuer's business.

The nature of any family relationship between any of those persons.

In the case of each member of the administrative, management or supervisory bodies of the issuer and person described in points (b) and (d) of the first subparagraph, details of that person's relevant management expertise and experience and the following information:

(a)   the names of all companies and partnerships of which such person has been a member of the administrative, management or supervisory bodies or partner at any time in the previous five years, indicating whether or not the individual is still a member of the administrative, management or supervisory bodies or partner. It is not necessary to list all the subsidiaries of an issuer of which the person is also a member of the administrative, management or supervisory bodies;

(b)   any convictions in relation to fraudulent offences for at least the previous five years;

(c)   details of any bankruptcies, receiverships or liquidations with which a person described in points (a) and (d) of the first subparagraph who was acting in the capacity of any of the positions set out in points (a) and (d) of the first subparagraph member of the administrative, management or supervisory bodies was associated for at least the previous five years;

(d)   details of any official public incrimination and/or sanctions of such person by statutory or regulatory authorities (including designated professional bodies) and whether such person has ever been disqualified by a court from acting as a member of the administrative, management or supervisory bodies of an issuer or from acting in the management or conduct of the affairs of any issuer for at least the previous five years.

If there is no such information to be disclosed, a statement to that effect must be made.

14.2.   *Administrative, management, and supervisory bodies' and senior management conflicts of interests*

Potential conflicts of interests between any duties to the issuer of the persons referred to in the first subparagraph of item 14.1 and their private interests and or other duties must be clearly stated. In the event that there are no such conflicts, make a statement to that effect.

Any arrangement or understanding with major shareholders, customers, suppliers or others, pursuant to which any person referred to in the first subparagraph of item 14.1 was selected as a member of the administrative, management or supervisory bodies or member of senior management.

15. REMUNERATION AND BENEFITS

In relation to the last full financial year for those persons referred to in points (a) and (d) of the first subparagraph of item 14.1:

15.1.   The amount of remuneration paid (including any contingent or deferred compensation), and benefits in kind granted, to such persons by the issuer and its subsidiaries for services in all capacities to the issuer and its subsidiaries by any person.

This information must be provided on an individual basis unless individual disclosure is not required in the issuer's home country and is not otherwise publicly disclosed by the issuer.

15.2. The total amounts set aside or accrued by the issuer or its subsidiaries to provide pension, retirement or similar benefits.

16. BOARD PRACTICES

In relation to the issuer's last completed financial year, and unless otherwise specified, with respect to those persons referred to in point (a) of the first subparagraph of item 14.1.

16.1. Date of expiration of the current term of office, if applicable, and the period during which the person has served in that office.

16.2. Information about members of the administrative, management or supervisory bodies' service contracts with the issuer or any of its subsidiaries providing for benefits upon termination of employment, or an appropriate negative statement.

16.3. Information about the issuer's audit committee and remuneration committee, including the names of committee members and a summary of the terms of reference under which the committee operates.

16.4. A statement as to whether or not the issuer complies with its country's of incorporation corporate governance regime(s). In the event that the issuer does not comply with such a regime, a statement to that effect together with an explanation regarding why the issuer does not comply with such regime.

17. EMPLOYEES

17.1. Either the number of employees at the end of the period or the average for each financial year for the period covered by the historical financial information up to the date of the prospectus (and changes in such numbers, if material) and, if possible and material, a breakdown of persons employed by main category of activity and geographic location. If the issuer employs a significant number of temporary employees, include disclosure of the number of temporary employees on average during the most recent financial year.

17.2. Shareholdings and stock options

With respect to each person referred to in points (a) and (b) of the first subparagraph of item 14.1, provide information as to their share ownership and any options over such shares in the issuer as of the most recent practicable date.

17.3. Description of any arrangements for involving the employees in the capital of the issuer.

18. MAJOR SHAREHOLDERS

18.1. In so far as is known to the issuer, the name of any person other than a member of the administrative, management or supervisory bodies who, directly or indirectly, has an interest notifiable under the issuer's national law in the issuer's capital or voting rights, together with the amount of each such person's interest or, if there are no such persons, an appropriate negative statement.

18.2. Whether the issuer's major shareholders have different voting rights, or an appropriate negative statement.

18.3. To the extent known to the issuer, state whether the issuer is directly or indirectly owned or controlled and by whom and describe the nature of such control and describe the measures in place to ensure that such control is not abused.

18.4. A description of any arrangements, known to the issuer, the operation of which may at a subsequent date result in a change in control of the issuer.

19. RELATED PARTY TRANSACTIONS

Details of related party transactions (which for these purposes are those set out in the Standards adopted according to Regulation (EC) No 1606/2002), that the issuer has entered into during the period covered by the historical financial information and up to the date of the prospectus must be disclosed in accordance with the respective standard adopted according to Regulation (EC) No 1606/2002 if applicable.

If such standards do not apply to the issuer the following information must be disclosed:
(a) the nature and extent of any transactions which are – as a single transaction or in their entirety – material to the issuer. Where such related party transactions are not concluded at arm's length provide an explanation of why these transactions were not concluded at arms length. In the case of outstanding loans including guarantees of any kind indicate the amount outstanding;
(b) the amount or the percentage to which related party transactions form part of the turnover of the issuer.

20. FINANCIAL INFORMATION CONCERNING THE ISSUER'S ASSETS AND LIABILITIES, FINANCIAL POSITION AND PROFITS AND LOSSES

20.1. *Historical financial information*

Audited historical financial information covering the latest 3 financial years (or such shorter period that the issuer has been in operation), and the audit report in respect of each year. [If the issuer has changed its accounting reference date during the period for which historical financial information is required, the audited historical information shall cover at least 36 months, or the entire period for which the issuer has been in operation, whichever is the shorter.] Such financial information must be prepared according to Regulation (EC) No 1606/2002, or if not applicable to a Member States national accounting standards for issuers from the Community. For third country issuers, such financial information must be prepared according to the international accounting standards adopted pursuant to the procedure of Article 3 of Regulation (EC) No 1606/2002 or to a third country's national accounting standards equivalent to these standards. If such financial information is not equivalent to these standards, it must be presented in the form of restated financial statements.

The last two years audited historical financial information must be presented and prepared in a form consistent with that which will be adopted in the issuer's next published annual financial statements having regard to accounting standards and policies and legislation applicable to such annual financial statements.

If the issuer has been operating in its current sphere of economic activity for less than one year, the audited historical financial information covering that period must be prepared in accordance with the standards applicable to annual financial statements under Regulation (EC) No 1606/2002, or if not applicable to a Member States national accounting standards where the issuer is an issuer from the Community. For third country issuers, the historical financial information must be prepared according to the international accounting standards adopted pursuant to the procedure of Article 3 of Regulation (EC) No 1606/2002 or to a third country's national accounting standards equivalent to these standards. This historical financial information must be audited.

If the audited financial information is prepared according to national accounting standards, the financial information required under this heading must include at least the following:
(a)   the balance sheet;
(b)   the income statement;
(c)   a statement showing either all changes in equity or changes in equity other than those arising from capital transactions with owners and distributions to owners;
(d)   the cash flow statement;
(e)   the accounting policies and explanatory notes.

The historical annual financial information must be independently audited or reported on as to whether or not, for the purposes of the prospectus, it gives a true and fair view, in accordance with auditing standards applicable in a Member State or an equivalent standard.

20.1a.   *This paragraph may be used only for issues of depository receipts having a denomination per unit of at least EUR 50,000.*

Audited historical financial information covering the latest three financial years (or such shorter period that the issuer has been in operation), and the audit report in respect of each year. [If the issuer has changed its accounting reference date during the period for which historical financial information is required, the audited historical information shall cover at least 36 months, or the entire period for which the issuer has been in operation, whichever is the shorter.] Such financial information must be prepared according to Regulation (EC) No 1606/2002, or if not applicable to a Member State's national accounting standards for issuers from the Community. For third country issuers, such financial information must be prepared according to the international accounting standards adopted pursuant to the procedure of Article 3 of Regulation (EC) No 1606/2002 or to a third country's national accounting standards equivalent to these standards. Otherwise, the following information must be included in the prospectus:
(a)   a prominent statement that the financial information included in the registration document has not been prepared in accordance with the international accounting standards adopted pursuant to the procedure of Article 3 of Regulation (EC) No 1606/2002 and that there may be material differences in the financial information had Regulation (EC) No 1606/2002 been applied to the historical financial information;
(b)   immediately following the historical financial information a narrative description of the differences between the international accounting standards adopted pursuant to the procedure of Article 3 of Regulation (EC) No 1606/2002 and the accounting principles adopted by the issuer in preparing its annual financial statements.

The last two years audited historical financial information must be presented and prepared in a form consistent with that which will be adopted in the issuer's next published annual financial statements having regard to accounting standards and policies and legislation applicable to such annual financial statements.

If the audited financial information is prepared according to national accounting standards, the financial information required under this heading must include at least the following:

(a)   the balance sheet;

(b)   the income statement;

(c)   a statement showing either all changes in equity or changes in equity other than those arising from capital transactions with owners and distributions to owners;

(d)   the cash flow statement;

(e)   the accounting policies and explanatory notes.

The historical annual financial information must be independently audited or reported on as to whether or not, for the purposes of the prospectus, it gives a true and fair view, in accordance with auditing standards applicable in a Member State or an equivalent standard. Otherwise, the following information must be included in the prospectus:

(a)   a prominent statement disclosing which auditing standards have been applied;

(b)   an explanation of any significant departures from international standards on auditing.

20.2.   *Financial statements*

If the issuer prepares both own and consolidated annual financial statements, include at least the consolidated annual financial statements in the prospectus.

20.3.   *Auditing of historical annual financial information*

20.3.1.   A statement that the historical financial information has been audited. If audit reports on the historical financial information have been refused by the statutory auditors or if they contain qualifications or disclaimers, such refusal or such qualifications or disclaimers must be reproduced in full and the reasons given.

20.3.2.   Indication of other information in the prospectus which has been audited by the auditors.

20.3.3.   Where financial data in the prospectus is not extracted from the issuer's audited financial statements state the source of the data and state that the data is unaudited.

20.4.   *Age of latest financial information*

20.4.1.   The last year of audited financial information may not be older than:

(a)   18 months from the date of the prospectus if the issuer includes audited interim financial statements in the prospectus;

(b)   15 months from the date of the prospectus if the issuer includes unaudited interim financial statements in the prospectus.

20.5.   *Interim and other financial information*

20.5.1.   If the issuer has published quarterly or half yearly financial information since the date of its last audited financial statements, these must be included in the prospectus. If the quarterly or half yearly financial information has been reviewed or audited the audit or review report must also be included. If the quarterly or half yearly financial information is unaudited or has not been reviewed, state that fact.

20.5.2.   If the prospectus is dated more than nine months after the end of the last audited financial year, it must contain interim financial information, which may be unaudited (in which case that fact shall be stated) covering at least the first six months of the financial year.

The interim financial information must include comparative statements for the same period in the prior financial year, except that the requirement for comparative balance sheet information may be satisfied by presenting the years end balance sheet.

20.6.   *Dividend policy*

A description of the issuer's policy on dividend distributions and any restrictions thereon.

20.6.1.   The amount of the dividend per share for each financial year for the period covered by the historical financial information adjusted, where the number of shares in the issuer has changed, to make it comparable.

20.7.   *Legal and arbitration proceedings*

Information on any governmental, legal or arbitration proceedings (including any such proceedings which are pending or threatened of which the issuer is aware), during a period covering at least the previous 12 months which may have, or have had in the recent past significant effects on the issuer and/or group's financial position or profitability, or provide an appropriate negative statement.

20.8.   *Significant change in the issuer's financial or trading position*

A description of any significant change in the financial or trading position of the group which has occurred since the end of the last financial period for which either audited financial information or interim financial information have been published, or provide an appropriate negative statement.

21. ADDITIONAL INFORMATION

21.1.   *Share capital*

The following information as of the date of the most recent balance sheet included in the historical financial information:

21.1.1.   The amount of issued capital, and for each class of share capital:
  (a)   the number of shares authorised;
  (b)   the number of shares issued and fully paid and issued but not fully paid;
  (c)   the par value per share, or that the shares have no par value;
  (d)   a reconciliation of the number of shares outstanding at the beginning and end of the year. If more than 10% of capital has been paid for with assets other than cash within the period covered by the historical financial information, state that fact.

21.1.2.   If there are shares not representing capital, state the number and main characteristics of such shares.

21.1.3.   The number, book value and face value of shares in the issuer held by or on behalf of the issuer itself or by subsidiaries of the issuer.

21.1.4.   The amount of any convertible securities, exchangeable securities or securities with warrants, with an indication of the conditions governing and the procedures for conversion, exchange or subscription.

21.1.5.   Information about and terms of any acquisition rights and or obligations over authorised but unissued capital or an undertaking to increase the capital.

21.1.6.   Information about any capital of any member of the group which is under option or agreed conditionally or unconditionally to be put under option and details of such options including those persons to whom such options relate.

21.1.7.   A history of share capital, highlighting information about any changes, for the period covered by the historical financial information.

21.2.   *Memorandum and Articles of Association*

21.2.1.   A description of the issuer's objects and purposes and where they can be found in the memorandum and articles of association.

21.2.2.   A summary of any provisions of the issuer's articles of association, statutes or charter and bylaws with respect to the members of the administrative, management and supervisory bodies.

21.2.3.   A description of the rights, preferences and restrictions attaching to each class of the existing shares.

21.2.4.   A description of what action is necessary to change the rights of holders of the shares, indicating where the conditions are more significant than is required by law.

21.2.5.   A description of the conditions governing the manner in which annual general meetings and extraordinary general meetings of shareholders are called including the conditions of admission.

21.2.6.   A brief description of any provision of the issuer's articles of association, statutes, charter or bylaws that would have an effect of delaying, deferring or preventing a change in control of the issuer.

21.2.7.   An indication of the articles of association, statutes, charter or bylaws provisions, if any, governing the ownership threshold above which shareholder ownership must be disclosed.

21.2.8.   A description of the conditions imposed by the memorandum and articles of association statutes, charter or bylaws governing changes in the capital, where such conditions are more stringent than is required by law.

22. MATERIAL CONTRACTS

A summary of each material contract, other than contracts entered into in the ordinary course of business, to which the issuer or any member of the group is a party, for the two years immediately preceding publication of the prospectus.

A summary of any other contract (not being a contract entered into in the ordinary course of business) entered into by any member of the group which contains any provision under which any member of the group has any obligation or entitlement which is material to the group as at the date of the prospectus.

23. THIRD PARTY INFORMATION, STATEMENT BY EXPERTS AND DECLARATIONS OF ANY INTEREST

23.1.   Where a statement or report attributed to a person as an expert is included in the prospectus provide such person's name, business address, qualifications and material interest if any in the issuer. If the report has been produced at the issuer's request a statement to that effect that such statement or report is included, in the form and context in which it is included, with the consent of that person who has authorised the contents of that part of the prospectus.

23.2.   Where information has been sourced from a third party, provide a confirmation that this information has been accurately reproduced and that as far as the issuer is aware and is able to ascertain from information published by that third party, no facts have been omitted which would render the reproduced information inaccurate or misleading. In addition, the issuer shall identify the source(s) of the information.

24. DOCUMENTS ON DISPLAY

A statement that for the life of the prospectus the following documents (or copies thereof), where applicable, may be inspected:
- (a)   the memorandum and articles of association of the issuer;
- (b)   all reports, letters, and other documents, historical financial information, valuations and statements prepared by any expert at the issuer's request any part of which is included or referred to in the prospectus;
- (c)   the historical financial information of the issuer or, in the case of a group, the historical financial information for the issuer and its subsidiary undertakings for each of the two financial years preceding the publication of the prospectus.

An indication of where the documents on display may be inspected, by physical or electronic means.

25. INFORMATION ON HOLDINGS

25.1.   Information relating to the undertakings in which the issuer holds a proportion of the capital likely to have a significant effect on the assessment of its own assets and liabilities, financial position or profits and losses.

26. INFORMATION ABOUT THE ISSUER OF THE DEPOSITORY RECEIPTS

26.1.   Name, registered office and principal administrative establishment if different from the registered office.

26.2.   Date of incorporation and length of life of the issuer, except where indefinite.

26.3.   Legislation under which the issuer operates and legal form which it has adopted under that legislation.

27. INFORMATION ABOUT THE UNDERLYING SHARES

27.1.   A description of the type and the class of the underlying shares, including the ISIN (International Security Identification Number) or other such security identification code.

27.2.   Legislation under which the underlying shares have been created.

27.3.   An indication whether the underlying shares are in registered form or bearer form and whether the underlying shares are in certificated form or book-entry form. In the latter case, name and address of the entity in charge of keeping the records.

27.4.   Currency of the underlying shares.

27.5.   A description of the rights, including any limitations of these, attached to the underlying shares and procedure for the exercise of said rights.

27.6.   Dividend rights:
- (a)   fixed date(s) on which the entitlement arises;
- (b)   time limit after which entitlement to dividend lapses and an indication of the person in whose favour the lapse operates;
- (c)   dividend restrictions and procedures for non-resident holders;
- (d)   rate of dividend or method of its calculation, periodicity and cumulative or non-cumulative nature of payments.

27.7.   Voting rights
Pre-emption rights in offers for subscription of securities of the same class
Right to share in the issuer's profits
Rights to share in any surplus in the event of liquidation
Redemption provisions
Conversion provisions.

27.8.   The issue date of the underlying shares if new underlying shares are being created for the issue of the depository receipts and they are not in existence at the time of issue of the depository receipts.

27.9.   If new underlying shares are being created for the issue of the depository receipts, state the resolutions, authorisations and approvals by virtue of which the new underlying shares have been or will be created and/or issued.

27.10.   A description of any restrictions on the free transferability of the underlying shares.

27.11.   In respect of the country of registered office of the issuer and the country(ies) where the offer is being made or admission to trading is being sought:

(a)   information on taxes on the income from the underlying shares withheld at source;

(b)   indication as to whether the issuer assumes responsibility for the withholding of taxes at the source.

27.12.   An indication of the existence of any mandatory takeover bids and/or squeeze-out and sell-out rules in relation to the underlying shares.

27.13.   An indication of public takeover bids by third parties in respect of the issuer's equity, which have occurred during the last financial year and the current financial year. The price or exchange terms attaching to such offers and the outcome thereof must be stated.

27.14.   Lock up agreements:

—   the parties involved,

—   content and exceptions of the agreement,

—   indication of the period of the lock up.

27.15.   *Information about selling share holders if any*

27.15.1.   Name and business address of the person or entity offering to sell the underlying shares, the nature of any position office or other material relationship that the selling persons has had within the past three years with the issuer of the underlying shares or any of its predecessors or affiliates.

27.16.   *Dilution*

27.16.1.   Amount and percentage of immediate dilution resulting from the offer of the depository receipts.

27.16.2.   In the case of a subscription offer of the depository receipts to existing shareholders, disclose the amount and percentage of immediate dilutions if they do not subscribe to the offer of depository receipts.

27.17.   *Additional information where there is a simultaneous or almost simultaneous offer or admission to trading of the same class of underlying shares as those underlying shares over which the depository receipts are being issued.*

27.17.1.   If simultaneously or almost simultaneously with the creation of the depository receipts for which admission to a regulated market is being sought underlying shares of the same class as those over which the depository receipts are being issued are subscribed for or placed privately, details are to be given of the nature of such operations and of the number and characteristics of the underlying shares to which they relate.

27.17.2.   Disclose all regulated markets or equivalent markets on which, to the knowledge of the issuer of the depository receipts, underlying shares of the same class of those over which the depository receipts are being issued are offered or admitted to trading.

27.17.3.   To the extent known to the issuer of the depository receipts, indicate whether major shareholders, members of the administrative, management or supervisory bodies intended to subscribe in the offer, or whether any person intends to subscribe for more than five per cent of the offer.

28. INFORMATION REGARDING THE DEPOSITORY RECEIPTS

28.1.   A description of the type and class of depository receipts being offered and/or admitted to trading.

28.2.   Legislation under which the depository receipts have been created.

28.3.   An indication whether the depository receipts are in registered or bearer form and whether the depository receipts are in certificated or book-entry form. In the latter case, include the name and address of the entity in charge of keeping the records.

28.4.   Currency of the depository receipts.

28.5.   Describe the rights attaching to the depository receipts, including any limitations of these attached to the depository receipts and the procedure if any for the exercise of these rights.

28.6.   If the dividend rights attaching to depository receipts are different from the dividend rights disclosed in relation to the underlying disclose the following about the dividend rights:

(a)   fixed date(s) on which the entitlement arises;

(b)   time limit after which entitlement to dividend lapses and an indication of the person in whose favour the lapse operates;

(c)   dividend restrictions and procedures for non-resident holders;

(d)   rate of dividend or method of its calculation, periodicity and cumulative or non-cumulative nature of payments.

28.7.   If the voting rights attaching to the depository receipts are different from the voting rights disclosed in relation to the underlying shares disclose the following about those rights:

—   voting rights.

—   pre-emption rights in offers for subscription of securities of the same class.

—   right to share in the issuer's profits.

— rights to share in any surplus in the event of liquidation.
— redemption provisions.
— conversion provisions.

28.8.   Describe the exercise of and benefit from the rights attaching to the underlying shares, in particular voting rights, the conditions on which the issuer of the depository receipts may exercise such rights, and measures envisaged to obtain the instructions of the depository receipt holders – and the right to share in profits and any liquidation surplus which are not passed on to the holder of the depository receipt.

28.9.   The expected issue date of the depository receipts.

28.10.   A description of any restrictions on the free transferability of the depository receipts.

28.11.   In respect of the country of registered office of the issuer and the country(ies) where the offer is being made or admission to trading is being sought:
(a) information on taxes on the income from the depository receipts withheld at source;
(b) indication as to whether the issuer assumes responsibility for the withholding of taxes at the source.

28.12.   Bank or other guarantees attached to the depository receipts and intended to underwrite the issuer's obligations.

28.13.   Possibility of obtaining the delivery of the depository receipts into original shares and procedure for such delivery.

29. INFORMATION ABOUT THE TERMS AND CONDITIONS OF THE OFFER OF THE DEPOSITORY RECEIPTS

29.1.   *Conditions, offer statistics, expected timetable and action required to apply for the offer*

29.1.1.   Total amount of the issue/offer, distinguishing the securities offered for sale and those offered for subscription; if the amount is not fixed, description of the arrangements and time for announcing to the public the definitive amount of the offer.

29.1.2.   The time period, including any possible amendments, during which the offer will be open and description of the application process.

29.1.3.   An indication of when, and under what circumstances, the offer may be revoked or suspended and whether revocation can occur after dealing has begun.

29.1.4.   A description of the possibility to reduce subscriptions and the manner for refunding excess amount paid by applicants.

29.1.5.   Details of the minimum and/or maximum amount of application (whether in number of securities or aggregate amount to invest).

29.1.6.   An indication of the period during which an application may be withdrawn, provided that investors are allowed to withdraw their subscription.

29.1.7.   Method and time limits for paying up the securities and for delivery of the securities.

29.1.8.   A full description of the manner and date in which results of the offer are to be made public.

29.1.9.   The procedure for the exercise of any right of pre-emption, the negotiability of subscription rights and the treatment of subscription rights not exercised.

29.2.   *Plan of distribution and allotment*

29.2.1.   The various categories of potential investors to which the securities are offered. If the offer is being made simultaneously in the markets of two or more countries and if a tranche has been or is being reserved for certain of these, indicate any such tranche.

29.2.2.   To the extent known to the issuer, indicate whether major shareholders or members of the issuer's management, supervisory or administrative bodies intended to subscribe in the offer, or whether any person intends to subscribe for more than five per cent of the offer.

29.2.3.   Pre-allotment disclosure:

29.2.3.1.   The division into tranches of the offer including the institutional, retail and issuer's employee tranches and any other tranches.

29.2.3.2.   The conditions under which the claw-back may be used, the maximum size of such claw back and any applicable minimum percentages for individual tranches.

29.2.3.3.   The allotment method or methods to be used for the retail and issuer's employee tranche in the event of an over-subscription of these tranches.

29.2.3.4.   A description of any pre-determined preferential treatment to be accorded to certain classes of investors or certain affinity groups (including friends and family programmes) in the allotment, the percentage of the offer reserved for such preferential treatment and the criteria for inclusion in such classes or groups.

29.2.3.5. Whether the treatment of subscriptions or bids to subscribe in the allotment may be determined on the basis of which firm they are made through or by.

29.2.3.6. A target minimum individual allotment if any within the retail tranche.

29.2.3.7. The conditions for the closing of the offer as well as the date on which the offer may be closed at the earliest;

29.2.3.8. Whether or not multiple subscriptions are admitted, and where they are not, how any multiple subscriptions will be handled.

29.2.3.9. Process for notification to applicants of the amount allotted and indication whether dealing may begin before notification is made.

29.2.4. Over-allotment and "green shoe" :

29.2.4.1. The existence and size of any over-allotment facility and/or "green shoe".

29.2.4.2. The existence period of the over-allotment facility and/or "green shoe".

29.2.4.3. Any conditions for the use of the over-allotment facility or exercise of the "green shoe".

29.3. *Pricing*

29.3.1. An indication of the price at which the securities will be offered. When the price is not known or when there is not an established and/or liquid market for the securities, indicate the method for determination of the offer price, including who has set the criteria or is formally responsible for its determination. Indication of the amount of any expenses and taxes specifically charged to the subscriber or purchaser.

29.3.2. Process for the disclosure of the offer price.

29.3.3. Where there is or could be a material disparity between the public offer price and the effective cash cost to members of the administrative, management or supervisory bodies or senior management, or affiliated persons, of securities acquired by them in transactions during the past year, or which they have the right to acquire, include a comparison of the public contribution in the proposed public offer and the effective cash contributions of such persons.

29.4. *Placing and underwriting*

29.4.1. Name and address of the co-coordinator(s) of the global offer and of single parts of the offer and, to the extend known to the issuer, of the placers in the various countries where the offer takes place.

29.4.2. Name and address of any paying agents and depository agents in each country.

29.4.3. Name and address of the entities agreeing to underwrite the issue on a firm commitment basis, and name and address of the entities agreeing to place the issue without a firm commitment or under "best efforts" arrangements. Indication of the material features of the agreements, including the quotas. Where not all of the issue is underwritten, a statement of the portion not covered. Indication of the overall amount of the underwriting commission and of the placing commission.

29.4.4. When the underwriting agreement has been or will be reached.

30. ADMISSION TO TRADING AND DEALING ARRANGEMENTS IN THE DEPOSITORY RECEIPTS

30.1. An indication as to whether the securities offered are or will be the object of an application for admission to trading, with a view to their distribution in a regulated market or other equivalent markets with indication of the markets in question. This circumstance must be mentioned, without creating the impression that the admission to trading necessarily will be approved. If known, the earliest dates on which the securities will be admitted to trading must be given.

30.2. All the regulated markets or equivalent markets on which, to the knowledge of the issuer, securities of the same class of the securities to be offered or admitted to trading are already admitted to trading.

30.3. If simultaneously or almost simultaneously with the creation of the securities for which admission to a regulated market is being sought securities of the same class are subscribed for or placed privately or if securities of other classes are created for public or private placing, details must be given of the nature of such operations and of the number and characteristics of the securities to which they relate.

30.4. Name and address of the entities which have a firm commitment to act as intermediaries in secondary trading, providing liquidity through bid and offer rates and description of the main terms of their commitment.

30.5. Stabilisation: where an issuer or a selling shareholder has granted an over-allotment option or it is otherwise proposed that price stabilising activities may be entered into in connection with an offer:

30.6.   The fact that stabilisation may be undertaken, that there is no assurance that it will be undertaken and that it may be stopped at any time.

30.7.   The beginning and the end of the period during which stabilisation may occur.

30.8.   The identity of the stabilisation manager for each relevant jurisdiction unless this is not known at the time of publication.

30.9.   The fact that stabilisation transactions may result in a market price that is higher than would otherwise prevail.

31. KEY INFORMATION ABOUT THE ISSUE OF THE DEPOSITORY RECEIPTS

31.1.   *Reasons for the offer and use of proceeds*

31.1.1.   Reasons for the offer and, where applicable, the estimated net amount of the proceeds broken into each principal intended use and presented by order of priority of such uses. If the issuer is aware that the anticipated proceeds will not be sufficient to fund all the proposed uses, state the amount and sources of other funds needed. Details must be given with regard to the use of the proceeds, in particular when they are being used to acquire assets, other than in the ordinary course of business, to finance announced acquisitions of other business, or to discharge, reduce or retire indebtedness.

31.2.   *Interest of natural and legal persons involved in the issue/offer*

31.2.1.   A description of any interest, including conflicting ones, that is material to the issue/offer, detailing the persons involved and the nature of the interest.

31.3.   *Risk factors*

31.3.1.   Prominent disclosure of risk factors that are material to the securities being offered and/or admitted to trading in order to assess the market risk associated with these securities in a section headed "Risk factors".

32. EXPENSE OF THE ISSUE/OFFER OF THE DEPOSITORY RECEIPTS

32.1.   The total net proceeds and an estimate of the total expenses of the issue/offer.

[5656]

NOTES
Words in square brackets in items 20.1 and 20.1a inserted by Commission Regulation 211/2007/EC, Art 1(3), as from 1 March 2007.

ANNEX XI
MINIMUM DISCLOSURE REQUIREMENTS FOR THE BANKS REGISTRATION
DOCUMENT (SCHEDULE)

1. PERSONS RESPONSIBLE

1.1.   All persons responsible for the information given in the registration document and, as the case may be, for certain parts of it, with, in the latter case, an indication of such parts. In the case of natural persons including members of the issuer's administrative, management or supervisory bodies indicate the name and function of the person; in case of legal persons indicate the name and registered office.

1.2.   A declaration by those responsible for the registration document that, having taken all reasonable care to ensure that such is the case, the information contained in the registration document is, to the best of their knowledge, in accordance with the facts and contains no omission likely to affect its import. As the case may be, declaration by those responsible for certain parts of the registration document that, having taken all reasonable care to ensure that such is the case, the information contained in the part of the registration document for which they are responsible is, to the best of their knowledge, in accordance with the facts and contains no omission likely to affect its import.

2. STATUTORY AUDITORS

2.1.   Names and addresses of the issuer's auditors for the period covered by the historical financial information (together with their membership in a professional body).

2.2.   If auditors have resigned, been removed or not been reappointed during the period covered by the historical financial information, details if material.

3. RISK FACTORS

3.1.   Prominent disclosure of risk factors that may affect the issuer's ability to fulfil its obligations under the securities to investors in a section headed "Risk factors".

4. INFORMATION ABOUT THE ISSUER

4.1.   *History and development of the Issuer*

4.1.1.   the legal and commercial name of the issuer;

4.1.2.   the place of registration of the issuer and its registration number;

4.1.3.   the date of incorporation and the length of life of the issuer, except where indefinite;

4.1.4.   the domicile and legal form of the issuer, the legislation under which the issuer operates, its country of incorporation, and the address and telephone number of its registered office (or principal place of business if different from its registered office);

4.1.5.   any recent events particular to the issuer which are to a material extent relevant to the evaluation of the issuer's solvency.

5. BUSINESS OVERVIEW

5.1.   *Principal activities:*

5.1.1.   A brief description of the issuer's principal activities stating the main categories of products sold and/or services performed;

5.1.2.   An indication of any significant new products and/or activities.

5.1.3.   Principal markets

A brief description of the principal markets in which the issuer competes.

5.1.4.   The basis for any statements in the registration document made by the issuer regarding its competitive position.

6. ORGANISATIONAL STRUCTURE

6.1.   If the issuer is part of a group, a brief description of the group and of the issuer's position within it.

6.2.   If the issuer is dependent upon other entities within the group, this must be clearly stated together with an explanation of this dependence.

7. TREND INFORMATION

7.1.   Include a statement that there has been no material adverse change in the prospects of the issuer since the date of its last published audited financial statements.

In the event that the issuer is unable to make such a statement, provide details of this material adverse change.

7.2.   Information on any known trends, uncertainties, demands, commitments or events that are reasonably likely to have a material effect on the issuer's prospects for at least the current financial year.

8. PROFIT FORECASTS OR ESTIMATES

If an issuer chooses to include a profit forecast or a profit estimate the registration document must contain the information items 8.1 and 8.2.

8.1.   A statement setting out the principal assumptions upon which the issuer has based its forecast, or estimate.

There must be a clear distinction between assumptions about factors which the members of the administrative, management or supervisory bodies can influence and assumptions about factors which are exclusively outside the influence of the members of the administrative, management or supervisory bodies; be readily understandable by investors; be specific and precise; and not relate to the general accuracy of the estimates underlying the forecast.

8.2.   A report prepared by independent accountants or auditors stating that in the opinion of the independent accountants or auditors the forecast or estimate has been properly compiled on the basis stated and that the basis of accounting used for the profit forecast or estimate is consistent with the accounting policies of the issuer.

8.3.   The profit forecast or estimate must be prepared on a basis comparable with the historical financial information.

9. ADMINISTRATIVE, MANAGEMENT, AND SUPERVISORY BODIES

9.1.   Names, business addresses and functions in the issuer of the following persons, and an indication of the principal activities performed by them outside the issuer where these are significant with respect to that issuer:

    (a)   members of the administrative, management or supervisory bodies;

    (b)   partners with unlimited liability, in the case of a limited partnership with a share capital.

9.2.   *Administrative, Management, and Supervisory bodies conflicts of interests*

Potential conflicts of interests between any duties to the issuing entity of the persons referred to in item 9.1 and their private interests and or other duties must be clearly stated. In the event that there are no such conflicts, make a statement to that effect.

10. MAJOR SHAREHOLDERS

10.1.   To the extent known to the issuer, state whether the issuer is directly or indirectly owned or controlled and by whom, and describe the nature of such control, and describe the measures in place to ensure that such control is not abused.

10.2.   A description of any arrangements, known to the issuer, the operation of which may at a subsequent date result in a change in control of the issuer.

11. FINANCIAL INFORMATION CONCERNING THE ISSUER'S ASSETS AND LIABILITIES, FINANCIAL POSITION AND PROFITS AND LOSSES

11.1.   *Historical Financial Information*

Audited historical financial information covering the latest two financial years (or such shorter period that the issuer has been in operation), and the audit report in respect of each year. [If the issuer has changed its accounting reference date during the period for which historical financial information is required, the audited historical information shall cover at least 24 months, or the entire period for which the issuer has been in operation, whichever is the shorter.] Such financial information must be prepared according to Regulation (EC) No 1606/2002, or if not applicable to a Member State national accounting standards for issuers from the Community. For third country issuers, such financial information must be prepared according to the international accounting standards adopted pursuant to the procedure of Article 3 of Regulation (EC) No 1606/2002 or to a third country's national accounting standards equivalent to these standards. If such financial information is not equivalent to these standards, it must be presented in the form of restated financial statements.

The most recent year's audited historical financial information must be presented and prepared in a form consistent with that which will be adopted in the issuer's next published annual financial statements having regard to accounting standards and policies and legislation applicable to such annual financial statements.

If the issuer has been operating in its current sphere of economic activity for less than one year, the audited historical financial information covering that period must be prepared in accordance with the standards applicable to annual financial statements under Regulation (EC) No 1606/2002, or if not applicable to a Member State national accounting standards where the issuer is an issuer from the Community. For third country issuers, the historical financial information must be prepared according to the international accounting standards adopted pursuant to the procedure of Article 3 of Regulation (EC) No 1606/2002 or to a third country's national accounting standards equivalent to these standards. This historical financial information must be audited.

If the audited financial information is prepared according to national accounting standards, the financial information required under this heading must include at least the following:
(a)   the balance sheet;
(b)   the income statement;
(c)   in the case of an admission of securities to trading on a regulated market only, a cash flow statement;
(d)   the accounting policies and explanatory notes.

The historical annual financial information must be independently audited or reported on as to whether or not, for the purposes of the registration document, it gives a true and fair view, in accordance with auditing standards applicable in a Member State or an equivalent standard.

11.2.   *Financial statements*

If the issuer prepares both own and consolidated financial statements, include at least the consolidated financial statements in the registration document.

11.3.   *Auditing of historical annual financial information*

11.3.1.   A statement that the historical financial information has been audited. If audit reports on the historical financial information have been refused by the statutory auditors or if they contain qualifications or disclaimers, such refusal or such qualifications or disclaimers must be reproduced in full and the reasons given.

11.3.2.   An indication of other information in the registration document which has been audited by the auditors.

11.3.3.   Where financial data in the registration document is not extracted from the issuer's audited financial statements state the source of the data and state that the data is unaudited.

11.4.   *Age of latest financial information*

11.4.1.   The last year of audited financial information may not be older than 18 months from the date of the registration document.

11.5.   *Interim and other financial information*

11.5.1.   If the issuer has published quarterly or half yearly financial information since the date of its last audited financial statements, these must be included in the registration document. If the quarterly or half yearly financial information has been reviewed or audited the audit or review report must also be included. If the quarterly or half yearly financial information is unaudited or has not been reviewed state that fact.

11.5.2. If the registration document is dated more than nine months after the end of the last audited financial year, it must contain interim financial information, covering at least the first six months of the financial year. If the interim financial information is un-audited state that fact.

The interim financial information must include comparative statements for the same period in the prior financial year, except that the requirement for comparative balance sheet information may be satisfied by presenting the years-end balance sheet.

11.6. *Legal and arbitration proceedings*

Information on any governmental, legal or arbitration proceedings (including any such proceedings which are pending or threatened of which the issuer is aware), during a period covering at least the previous 12 months which may have, or have had in the recent past, significant effects on the issuer and/or group's financial position or profitability, or provide an appropriate negative statement.

11.7. *Significant change in the issuer's financial position*

A description of any significant change in the financial position of the group which has occurred since the end of the last financial period for which either audited financial information or interim financial information have been published, or an appropriate negative statement.

12. MATERIAL CONTRACTS

A brief summary of all material contracts that are not entered into in the ordinary course of the issuer's business, which could result in any group member being under an obligation or entitlement that is material to the issuer's ability to meet its obligation to security holders in respect of the securities being issued.

13. THIRD PARTY INFORMATION AND STATEMENT BY EXPERTS AND DECLARATIONS OF ANY INTEREST

13.1. Where a statement or report attributed to a person as an expert is included in the registration document, provide such person's name, business address, qualifications and material interest if any in the issuer. If the report has been produced at the issuer's request a statement to that effect that such statement or report is included, in the form and context in which it is included, with the consent of that person who has authorised the contents of that part of the registration document.

13.2. Where information has been sourced from a third party, provide a confirmation that this information has been accurately reproduced and that as far as the issuer is aware and is able to ascertain from information published by that third party, no facts have been omitted which would render the reproduced information inaccurate or misleading In addition, the issuer shall identify the source(s) of the information.

14. DOCUMENTS ON DISPLAY

A statement that for the life of the registration document the following documents (or copies thereof), where applicable, may be inspected:
    (a)   the memorandum and articles of association of the issuer;
    (b)   all reports, letters, and other documents, historical financial information, valuations and statements prepared by any expert at the issuer's request any part of which is included or referred to in the registration document;
    (c)   the historical financial information of the issuer or, in the case of a group, the historical financial information of the issuer and its subsidiary undertakings for each of the two financial years preceding the publication of the registration document.

An indication of where the documents on display may be inspected, by physical or electronic means.

[5657]

NOTES

Words in square brackets in item 11.1 inserted by Commission Regulation 211/2007/EC, Art 1(4), as from 1 March 2007.

ANNEX XII
MINIMUM DISCLOSURE REQUIREMENTS FOR THE SECURITIES NOTE FOR DERIVATIVE SECURITIES (SCHEDULE)

1. PERSONS RESPONSIBLE

1.1. All persons responsible for the information given in the prospectus and, as the case may be, for certain parts of it, with, in the latter case, an indication of such parts. In the case of natural persons including members of the issuer's administrative, management or supervisory bodies indicate the name and function of the person; in case of legal persons indicate the name and registered office.

1.2. A declaration by those responsible for the prospectus that, having taken all reasonable care to ensure that such is the case, the information contained in the prospectus is, to the best of their knowledge, in accordance with the facts and contains no omission likely to affect its import. As the case may be, declaration by those responsible for certain parts of the prospectus that, having taken all reasonable care to ensure that such is the case, the information contained in the part of the prospectus for which they are responsible is, to the best of their knowledge, in accordance with the facts and contains no omission likely to affect its import.

2. RISK FACTORS

Prominent disclosure of risk factors that are material to the securities being offered and/or admitted to trading in order to assess the market risk associated with these securities in a section headed "risk factors". This must include a risk warning to the effect that investors may lose the value of their entire investment or part of it, as the case may be, and/or, if the investor's liability is not limited to the value of his investment, a statement of that fact, together with a description of the circumstances in which such additional liability arises and the likely financial effect.

3. KEY INFORMATION

3.1. *Interest of natural and legal persons involved in the issue/offer*

A description of any interest, including conflicting ones that is material to the issue/offer, detailing the persons involved and the nature of the interest.

3.2. *Reasons for the offer and use of proceeds when different from making profit and/or hedging certain risks*

If reasons for the offer and use of proceeds are disclosed provide the total net proceeds and an estimate of the total expenses of the issue/offer.

4. INFORMATION CONCERNING THE SECURITIES TO BE OFFERED/ADMITTED TO TRADING

4.1. *Information concerning the securities*

4.1.1. A description of the type and the class of the securities being offered and/or admitted to trading, including the ISIN (International security identification number) or other such security identification code.

4.1.2. A clear and comprehensive explanation to help investors understand how the value of their investment is affected by the value of the underlying instrument(s), especially under the circumstances when the risks are most evident unless the securities have a denomination per unit of at least EUR 50,000 or can only be acquired for at least EUR 50,000 per security.

4.1.3. Legislation under which the securities have been created.

4.1.4. An indication whether the securities are in registered form or bearer form and whether the securities are in certificated form or book-entry form. In the latter case, name and address of the entity in charge of keeping the records.

4.1.5. Currency of the securities issue.

4.1.6. Ranking of the securities being offered and/or admitted to trading, including summaries of any clauses that are intended to affect ranking or subordinate the security to any present or future liabilities of the issuer.

4.1.7. A description of the rights, including any limitations of these, attached to the securities and procedure for the exercise of said rights.

4.1.8. In the case of new issues, a statement of the resolutions, authorisations and approvals by virtue of which the securities have been or will be created and/or issued.

4.1.9. The issue date of the securities.

4.1.10. A description of any restrictions on the free transferability of the securities.

4.1.11.
— The expiration or maturity date of the derivative securities.
— The exercise date or final reference date.

4.1.12. A description of the settlement procedure of the derivative securities.

4.1.13. A description of how any return on derivative securities takes place, the payment or delivery date, and the way it is calculated.

4.1.14. In respect of the country of registered office of the issuer and the country(ies) where the offer is being made or admission to trading is being sought:
(a) information on taxes on the income from the securities withheld at source;

(b)   indication as to whether the issuer assumes responsibility for the withholding of taxes at the source.

4.2.   *Information concerning the underlying*

4.2.1.   The exercise price or the final reference price of the underlying.

4.2.2.   A statement setting out the type of the underlying and details of where information on the underlying can be obtained:

—   an indication where information about the past and the further performance of the underlying and its volatility can be obtained,

—   where the underlying is a security,

     —   the name of the issuer of the security,

     —   the ISIN (international security identification number) or other such security identification code,

—   where the underlying is an index,

     —   the name of the index and a description of the index if it is composed by the issuer. If the index is not composed by the issuer, where information about the index can be obtained,

—   where the underlying is an interest rate,

     —   a description of the interest rate,

—   others:

     —   Where the underlying does not fall within the categories specified above the securities note shall contain equivalent information.

—   where the underlying is a basket of underlyings,

     —   disclosure of the relevant weightings of each underlying in the basket.

4.2.3.   A description of any market disruption or settlement disruption events that affect the underlying.

4.2.4.   Adjustment rules with relation to events concerning the underlying.

5. TERMS AND CONDITIONS OF THE OFFER

5.1.   *Conditions, offer statistics, expected timetable and action required to apply for the offer*

5.1.1.   Conditions to which the offer is subject.

5.1.2.   Total amount of the issue/offer; if the amount is not fixed, description of the arrangements and time for announcing to the public the amount of the offer.

5.1.3.   The period of time , including any possible amendments, during which the offer will be open and description of the application process.

5.1.4.   Details of the minimum and/or maximum amount of application, (whether in number of securities or aggregate amount to invest).

5.1.5.   Method and time limits for paying up the securities and for delivery of the securities.

5.1.6.   A full description of the manner and date in which results of the offer are to be made public.

5.2.   *Plan of distribution and allotment*

5.2.1.   The various categories of potential investors to which the securities are offered. If the offer is being made simultaneously in the markets of two or more countries and if a tranche has been or is being reserved for certain of these, indicate any such tranche.

5.2.2.   Process for notification to applicants of the amount allotted and indication whether dealing may begin before notification is made.

5.3.   *Pricing*

Indication of the expected price at which the securities will be offered or the method of determining the price and the process for its disclosure. Indicate the amount of any expenses and taxes specifically charged to the subscriber or purchaser.

5.4.   *Placing and underwriting*

5.4.1.   Name and address of the coordinator(s) of the global offer and of single parts of the offer and, to the extend known to the issuer or to the offeror, of the placers in the various countries where the offer takes place.

5.4.2.   Name and address of any paying agents and depository agents in each country.

5.4.3.   Entities agreeing to underwrite the issue on a firm commitment basis, and entities agreeing to place the issue without a firm commitment or under "best efforts" arrangements. Where not all of the issue is underwritten, a statement of the portion not covered.

5.4.4.   When the underwriting agreement has been or will be reached.

5.4.5.   Name and address of a calculation agent.

6. ADMISSION TO TRADING AND DEALING ARRANGEMENTS

6.1.   An indication as to whether the securities offered are or will be the object of an application for admission to trading, with a view to their distribution in a regulated market or other equivalent markets with indication of the markets in question. This circumstance shall be mentioned, without creating the impression that the admission to trading necessarily will be approved. If known, the earliest dates on which the securities will be admitted to trading shall be given.

6.2.   All the regulated markets or equivalent markets on which, to the knowledge of the issuer, securities of the same class of the securities to be offered or admitted to trading are already admitted to trading.

6.3.   Name and address of the entities which have a firm commitment to act as intermediaries in secondary trading, providing liquidity through bid and offer rates and description of the main terms of their commitment.

7. ADDITIONAL INFORMATION

7.1.   If advisors connected with an issue are mentioned in the Securities Note, a statement of the capacity in which the advisors have acted.

7.2.   An indication of other information in the Securities Note which has been audited or reviewed by statutory auditors and where auditors have produced a report. Reproduction of the report or, with permission of the competent authority, a summary of the report.

7.3.   Where a statement or report attributed to a person as an expert is included in the Securities Note, provide such person's name, business address, qualifications and material interest, if any, in the issuer. If the report has been produced at the issuer's request a statement to that effect that such statement or report is included, in the form and context in which it is included, with the consent of that person who has authorised the contents of that part of the Securities Note.

7.4.   Where information has been sourced from a third party, provide a confirmation that this information has been accurately reproduced and that as far as the issuer is aware and is able to ascertain from information published by that third party, no facts have been omitted which would render the reproduced information inaccurate or misleading. In addition, the issuer shall identify the source(s) of the information.

7.5.   An indication in the prospectus whether or not the issuer intends to provide post-issuance information. Where the issuer has indicated that it intends to report such information, the issuer shall specify in the prospectus what information will be reported and where such information can be obtained.

[5658]

ANNEX XIII
MINIMUM DISCLOSURE REQUIREMENTS FOR THE SECURITIES NOTE
FOR DEBT SECURITIES WITH A DENOMINATION PER UNIT OF AT LEAST
EUR 50,000 (SCHEDULE)

1. PERSONS RESPONSIBLE

1.1.   All persons responsible for the information given in the prospectus and, as the case may be, for certain parts of it, with, in the latter case, an indication of such parts. In case of natural persons including members of the issuer's administrative, management or supervisory bodies indicate the name and function of the person; in case of legal persons indicate the name and registered office.

1.2.   A declaration by those responsible for the prospectus that, having taken all reasonable care to ensure that such is the case, the information contained in the prospectus is, to the best of their knowledge, in accordance with the facts and contains no omission likely to affect its import. As the case may be, declaration by those responsible for certain parts of the prospectus that the information contained in the part of the prospectus for which they are responsible is, to the best of their knowledge, in accordance with the facts and contains no omission likely to affect its import.

2. RISK FACTORS

Prominent disclosure of risk factors that are material to the securities admitted to trading in order to assess the market risk associated with these securities in a section headed "Risk factors".

3. KEY INFORMATION

Interest of natural and legal persons involved in the issue

A description of any interest, including conflicting ones, that is material to the issue, detailing the persons involved and the nature of the interest.

4. INFORMATION CONCERNING THE SECURITIES TO BE ADMITTED TO TRADING

4.1.   Total amount of securities being admitted to trading.

4.2.   A description of the type and the class of the securities being admitted to trading, including the ISIN (international security identification number) or other such security identification code.

4.3.   Legislation under which the securities have been created.

4.4.   An indication of whether the securities are in registered or bearer form and whether the securities are in certificated or book-entry form. In the latter case, name and address of the entity in charge of keeping the records.

4.5.   Currency of the securities issue.

4.6.   Ranking of the securities being admitted to trading, including summaries of any clauses that are intended to affect ranking or subordinate the security to any present or future liabilities of the issuer.

4.7.   A description of the rights, including any limitations of these, attached to the securities and procedure for the exercise of said rights.

4.8.   The nominal interest rate and provisions relating to interest payable:
—   The date from which interest becomes payable and the due dates for interest.
—   The time limit on the validity of claims to interest and repayment of principal.

Where the rate is not fixed, description of the underlying on which it is based and of the method used to relate the two:
—   A description of any market disruption or settlement disruption events that affect the underlying.
—   Adjustment rules with relation to events concerning the underlying.
—   Name of the calculation agent.

4.9.   Maturity date and arrangements for the amortisation of the loan, including the repayment procedures. Where advance amortisation is contemplated, on the initiative of the issuer or of the holder, it must be described, stipulating amortisation terms and conditions.

4.10.   An indication of yield.

4.11.   Representation of debt security holders including an identification of the organisation representing the investors and provisions applying to such representation. Indication of where investors may have access to the contracts relating to these forms of representation.

4.12.   A statement of the resolutions, authorisations and approvals by virtue of which the securities have been created and/or issued.

4.13.   The issue date of the securities.

4.14.   A description of any restrictions on the free transferability of the securities.

5. ADMISSION TO TRADING AND DEALING ARRANGEMENTS

5.1.   Indication of the market where the securities will be traded and for which prospectus has been published. If known, give the earliest dates on which the securities will be admitted to trading.

5.2.   Name and address of any paying agents and depository agents in each country.

6. EXPENSE OF THE ADMISSION TO TRADING

An estimate of the total expenses related to the admission to trading.

7. ADDITIONAL INFORMATION

7.1.   If advisors are mentioned in the Securities Note, a statement of the capacity in which the advisors have acted.

7.2.   An indication of other information in the Securities Note which has been audited or reviewed by auditors and where auditors have produced a report. Reproduction of the report or, with permission of the competent authority, a summary of the report.

7.3.   Where a statement or report attributed to a person as an expert is included in the Securities Note, provide such person's name, business address, qualifications and material interest if any in the issuer. If the report has been produced at the issuer's request a statement to that effect that such statement or report is included, in the form and context in which it is included, with the consent of that person who has authorised the contents of that part of the Securities Note.

7.4.   Where information has been sourced from a third party, provide a confirmation that this information has been accurately reproduced and that as far as the issuer is aware and is able to ascertain from information published by that third party, no facts have been omitted which would render the reproduced information inaccurate or misleading. In addition, identify the source(s) of the information.

7.5.   Credit ratings assigned to an issuer or its debt securities at the request or with the cooperation of the issuer in the rating process.

ANNEX XIV
ADDITIONAL INFORMATION BUILDING BLOCK ON UNDERLYING SHARE FOR SOME EQUITY SECURITIES

1. Description of the underlying share
   1.1. Describe the type and the class of the shares
   1.2. Legislation under which the shares have been or will be created
   1.3. Indication whether the securities are in registered form or bearer form and whether the securities are in certificated form or book-entry form. In the latter case, name and address of the entity in charge of keeping the records
   1.4. Indication of the currency of the shares issue
   1.5. A description of the rights, including any limitations of these, attached to the securities and procedure for the exercise of those rights:
       — Dividend rights:
           — fixed date(s) on which the entitlement arises,
           — time limit after which entitlement to dividend lapses and an indication of the person in whose favour the lapse operates,
           — dividend restrictions and procedures for non resident holders,
           — rate of dividend or method of its calculation, periodicity and cumulative or non-cumulative nature of payments.
       — Voting rights.
       — pre-emption rights in offers for subscription of securities of the same class.
       — right to share in the issuer's profits.
       — rights to share in any surplus in the event of liquidation.
       — redemption provisions.
       — conversion provisions.
   1.6. In the case of new issues, a statement of the resolutions, authorisations and approvals by virtue of which the shares have been or will be created and/or issued and indication of the issue date.
   1.7. Where and when the shares will be or have been admitted to trading.
   1.8. Description of any restrictions on the free transferability of the shares.
   1.9. Indication of the existence of any mandatory takeover bids/or squeeze-out and sell-out rules in relation to the shares.
   1.10. Indication of public takeover bids by third parties in respect of the issuer's equity, which have occurred during the last financial year and the current financial year. The price or exchange terms attaching to such offers and the outcome thereof must be stated.
   1.11. Impact on the issuer of the underlying share of the exercise of the right and potential dilution effect for the shareholders.

2. When the issuer of the underlying is an entity belonging to the same group, the information to provide on this issuer is the one required by the share registration document schedule.

[5660]

ANNEX XV
MINIMUM DISCLOSURE REQUIREMENTS FOR THE REGISTRATION DOCUMENT FOR SECURITIES ISSUED BY COLLECTIVE INVESTMENT UNDERTAKINGS OF THE CLOSED-END TYPE (SCHEDULE)

In addition to the information required in this schedule, the collective investment undertaking must provide the following information as required under paragraphs and items 1, 2, 3, 4, 5.1, 7, 9.1, 9.2.1, 9.2.3, 10.4, 13, 14, 15, 16, 17.2, 18, 19, 20, 21, 22, 23, 24, 25 in Annex I (minimum disclosure requirements for the share registration document schedule).

1. Investment objective and policy

1.1. A detailed description of the investment objective and policy which the collective investment undertaking will pursue and a description of how that investment objectives and policy may be varied including any circumstances in which such variation requires the approval of investors. A description of any techniques and instruments that may be used in the management of the collective investment undertaking.

1.2. The borrowing and/or leverage limits of the collective investment undertaking. If there are no such limits, include a statement to that effect.

1.3. The regulatory status of the collective investment undertaking together with the name of any regulator in its country of incorporation.

1.4. The profile of a typical investor for whom the collective investment undertaking is designed.

2. Investment restrictions

2.1. A statement of the investment restrictions which apply to the collective investment undertaking, if any, and an indication of how the holders of securities will be informed of the actions that the investment manager will take in the event of a breach.

2.2.   Where more than 20% of the gross assets of any collective investment undertaking (except where items 2.3 or 2.5 apply) may be:

    (a)   invested in, either directly or indirectly, or lent to any single underlying issuer (including the underlying issuer's subsidiaries or affiliates); or

    (b)   invested in one or more collective investment undertakings which may invest in excess of 20% of its gross assets in other collective investment undertakings (open-end and/or closed-end type); or

    (c)   exposed to the creditworthiness or solvency of any one counterparty (including its subsidiaries or affiliates);

the following information must be disclosed:

    (i)   information relating to each underlying issuer/collective investment undertaking/ counterparty as if it were an issuer for the purposes of the minimum disclosure requirements for the share registration document schedule (in the case of (a)) or minimum disclosure requirements for the registration document schedule for securities issued by collective investment undertaking of the closed-end type (in the case of (b)) or the minimum disclosure requirements for the debt and derivative securities with an individual denomination per unit of at least EUR 50,000 registration document schedule (in the case of (c)); or

    (ii)   if the securities issued by the underlying issuer/collective investment undertaking/ counterparty have already been admitted to trading on a regulated or equivalent market or the obligations are guaranteed by an entity admitted to trading on a regulated or equivalent market, the name, address, country of incorporation, nature of business and name of the market in which its securities are admitted.

This requirement shall not apply where the 20% is exceeded due to appreciations or depreciations, changes in exchange rates, or by reason of the receipt of rights, bonuses, benefits in the nature of capital or by reason of any other action affecting every holder of that investment, provided the investment manager has regard to the threshold when considering changes in the investment portfolio.

2.3.   Where a collective investment undertaking may invest in excess of 20% of its gross assets in other collective investment undertakings (open ended and/or closed ended), a description of if and how risk is spread in relation to those investments. In addition, item 2.2 shall apply, in aggregate, to its underlying investments as if those investments had been made directly.

2.4.   With reference to point (c) of item 2.2, if collateral is advanced to cover that portion of the exposure to any one counterparty in excess of 20% of the gross assets of the collective investment undertaking, details of such collateral arrangements.

2.5.   Where a collective investment undertaking may invest in excess of 40% of its gross assets in another collective investment undertaking either of the following must be disclosed:

    (a)   information relating to each underlying collective investment undertaking as if it were an issuer under minimum disclosure requirements for the registration document schedule for securities issued by collective investment undertaking of the closed-end type;

    (b)   if securities issued by an underlying collective investment undertaking have already been admitted to trading on a regulated or equivalent market or the obligations are guaranteed by an entity admitted to trading on a regulated or equivalent market, the name, address, country of incorporation, nature of business and name of the market in which its securities are admitted.

2.6.   *Physical commodities*

Where a collective investment undertaking invests directly in physical commodities a disclosure of that fact and the percentage that will be so invested.

2.7.   *Property collective investment undertakings*

Where a collective investment undertaking is a property collective investment undertaking, disclosure of that fact, the percentage of the portfolio that is to be invested in the property, as well as a description of the property and any material costs relating to the acquisition and holding of such property. In addition, a valuation report relating to the properties must be included.

Disclosure of item 4.1. applies to:

    (a)   the valuation entity;

    (b)   any other entity responsible for the administration of the property.

2.8.   *Derivatives financial instruments/money market instruments/currencies*

Where a collective investment undertaking invests in derivatives financial instruments, money market instruments or currencies other than for the purposes of efficient portfolio management (i.e. solely for the purpose of reducing, transferring or eliminating investment risk in the underlying investments of a collective investment undertaking, including any technique or instrument used to provide protection against exchange and credit risks), a statement whether those investments are used for hedging or for investment purposes, and a description of if and how risk is spread in relation to those investments.

2.9.   Item 2.2 does not apply to investment in securities issued or guaranteed by a government, government agency or instrumentality of any Member State, its regional or local authorities, or OECD Member State.

2.10.   Point (a) of item 2.2 does not apply to a collective investment undertaking whose investment objective is to track, without material modification, that of a broadly based and recognised published index. A description of the composition of the index must be provided.

3.   The applicant's service providers

3.1.   The actual or estimated maximum amount of all material fees payable directly or indirectly by the collective investment undertaking for any services under arrangements entered into on or prior to the date of the registration document and a description of how these fees are calculated.

3.2.   A description of any fee payable directly or indirectly by the collective investment undertaking which cannot be quantified under item 3.1 and which is or may be material.

3.3.   If any service provider to the collective investment undertaking is in receipt of any benefits from third parties (other than the collective investment undertaking) by virtue of providing any services to the collective investment undertaking, and those benefits may not accrue to the collective investment undertaking, a statement of that fact, the name of that third party, if available, and a description of the nature of the benefits.

3.4.   The name of the service provider which is responsible for the determination and calculation of the net asset value of the collective investment undertaking.

3.5.   A description of any material potential conflicts of interest which any of the service providers to the collective investment undertaking may have as between their duty to the collective investment undertaking and duties owed by them to third parties and their other interests. A description of any arrangements which are in place to address such potential conflicts.

4.   Investment manager/advisers

4.1.   In respect of any investment manager such information as is required to be disclosed under items 5.1.1 to 5.1.4 and, if material, under item 5.1.5 of Annex I together with a description of its regulatory status and experience.

4.2.   In respect of any entity providing investment advice in relation to the assets of the collective investment undertaking, the name and a brief description of such entity.

5.   Custody

5.1.   A full description of how the assets of the collective investment undertaking will be held and by whom and any fiduciary or similar relationship between the collective investment undertaking and any third party in relation to custody:

Where a custodian, trustee, or other fiduciary is appointed:
   (a)   such information as is required to be disclosed under items 5.1.1 to 5.1.4 and, if material, under item 5.1.5 of Annex I;
   (b)   a description of the obligations of such party under the custody or similar agreement;
   (c)   any delegated custody arrangements;
   (d)   the regulatory status of such party and delegates.

5.2.   Where any entity other than those entities mentioned in item 5.1, holds any assets of the collective investment undertaking, a description of how these assets are held together with a description of any additional risks.

6.   Valuation

6.1.   A description of how often, and the valuation principles and the method by which, the net asset value of the collective investment undertaking will be determined, distinguishing between categories of investments and a statement of how such net asset value will be communicated to investors.

6.2.   Details of all circumstances in which valuations may be suspended and a statement of how such suspension will be communicated or made available to investors.

7.   Cross liabilities

7.1.   In the case of an umbrella collective investment undertaking, a statement of any cross liability that may occur between classes or investments in other collective investment undertakings and any action taken to limit such liability.

8.   Financial information

8.1.   Where, since the date of incorporation or establishment, a collective investment undertaking has not commenced operations and no financial statements have been made up as at the date of the registration document, a statement to that effect.

Where a collective investment undertaking has commenced operations, the provisions of item 20 of Annex I on the Minimum Disclosure Requirements for the share registration document apply.

8.2. A comprehensive and meaningful analysis of the collective investment undertaking's portfolio (if unaudited, clearly marked as such).

8.3. An indication of the most recent net asset value per security must be included in the securities note schedule (and, if un-audited, clearly marked as such).

[5661]

ANNEX XVI
MINIMUM DISCLOSURE REQUIREMENTS FOR THE REGISTRATION DOCUMENT FOR SECURITIES ISSUED BY MEMBER STATES, THIRD COUNTRIES AND THEIR REGIONAL AND LOCAL AUTHORITIES (SCHEDULE)

1. PERSONS RESPONSIBLE

1.1. All persons responsible for the information given in the registration document and, as the case may be, for certain parts of it, with, in the latter case, an indication of such parts. In the case of natural persons including members of the issuer's administrative, management or supervisory bodies indicate the name and function of the person; in case of legal persons indicate the name and registered office.

1.2. A declaration by those responsible for the registration document that, having taken all reasonable care to ensure that such is the case, the information contained in the registration document is, to the best of their knowledge in accordance with the facts and contains no omission likely to affect its import. As the case may be, declaration by those responsible for certain parts of the registration document that, having taken all reasonable care to ensure that such is the case the information contained in the part of the registration document for which they are responsible is, to the best of their knowledge, in accordance with the facts and contains no omission likely to affect its import.

2. RISK FACTORS

Prominent disclosure of risk factors that may affect the issuer's ability to fulfil its obligations under the securities to investors in a section headed "Risk factors".

3. INFORMATION ABOUT THE ISSUER

3.1. The legal name of the issuer and a brief description of the issuer's position within the national governmental framework.

3.2. The domicile or geographical location and legal form of the issuer and its contact address and telephone number.

3.3. Any recent events relevant to the evaluation of the issuer's solvency.

3.4. A description of the issuer's economy including:
   (a) the structure of the economy with details of the main sectors of the economy;
   (b) gross domestic product with a breakdown by the issuer's economic sectors over for the previous two fiscal years.

3.5. A general description of the issuer's political system and government including details of the governing body of the issuer.

4. PUBLIC FINANCE AND TRADE

Information on the following for the two fiscal years prior to the date of the registration document:
   (a) the tax and budgetary systems;
   (b) gross public debt including a summary of the debt, the maturity structure of outstanding debt (particularly noting debt with a residual maturity of less than one year) and debt payment record, and of the parts of debt denominated in the domestic currency of the issuer and in foreign currencies;
   (c) foreign trade and balance of payment figures;
   (d) foreign exchange reserves including any potential encumbrances to such foreign exchange reserves as forward contracts or derivatives;
   (e) financial position and resources including liquid deposits available in domestic currency;
   (f) income and expenditure figures.

Description of any auditing or independent review procedures on the accounts of the issuer.

5. SIGNIFICANT CHANGE

5.1. Details of any significant changes to the information provided pursuant to item 4 which have occurred since the end of the last fiscal year, or an appropriate negative statement.

6. LEGAL AND ARBITRATION PROCEEDINGS

6.1. Information on any governmental, legal or arbitration proceedings (including any such proceedings which are pending or threatened of which the issuer is aware), during a period covering

PART IV
EC MATERIALS

at least the previous 12 months which may have, or have had in the recent past, significant effects on the issuer financial position, or provide an appropriate negative statement.

6.2.   Information on any immunity the issuer may have from legal proceedings.

7. STATEMENT BY EXPERTS AND DECLARATIONS OF ANY INTEREST

Where a statement or report attributed to a person as an expert is included in the registration document, provide such person's name, business address and qualifications. If the report has been produced at the issuer's request a statement to that effect, that such statement or report is included, in the form and context in which it is included, with the consent of that person, who has authorised the contents of that part of the registration document.

To the extent known to the issuer, provide information in respect of any interest relating to such expert which may have an effect on the independence of the expert in the preparation of the report.

8. DOCUMENTS ON DISPLAY

A statement that for the life of the registration document the following documents (or copies thereof), where applicable, may be inspected:

(a)   financial and audit reports for the issuer covering the last two fiscal years and the budget for the current fiscal year;

(b)   all reports, letters, and other documents, valuations and statements prepared by any expert at the issuer's request any part of which is included or referred to in the registration document.

An indication of where the documents on display may be inspected, by physical or electronic means.

[5662]

ANNEX XVII
MINIMUM DISCLOSURE REQUIREMENTS FOR THE REGISTRATION DOCUMENT FOR SECURITIES ISSUED BY PUBLIC INTERNATIONAL BODIES AND FOR DEBT SECURITIES GUARANTEED BY A MEMBER STATE OF THE OECD (SCHEDULE)

1. PERSONS RESPONSIBLE

1.1.   All persons responsible for the information given in the registration document and, as the case may be, for certain parts of it, with, in the latter case, an indication of such parts. In the case of natural persons including members of the issuer's administrative, management or supervisory bodies indicate the name and function of the person; in case of legal persons indicate the name and registered office.

1.2.   A declaration by those responsible for the registration document, that, having taken all reasonable care to ensure that such is the case, the information contained in the registration document is, to the best of their knowledge, in accordance with the facts and contains no omission likely to materially affect its import. As the case may be, declaration by those responsible for certain parts of the registration document that, having taken all reasonable care to ensure that such is the case the information contained in the part of the registration document for which they are responsible is, to the best of their knowledge, in accordance with the facts and contains no omission likely to affect its import.

2. RISK FACTORS

Prominent disclosure of risk factors that may affect the issuer's ability to fulfil its obligations under the securities to investors in a section headed "Risk factors".

3. INFORMATION ABOUT THE ISSUER

3.1.   The legal name of the issuer and a brief description of the issuer's legal status.

3.2.   The location of the principal office and the legal form of the issuer and its contact address and telephone number.

3.3.   Details of the governing body of the issuer and a description of its governance arrangements, if any.

3.4.   A brief description of the issuer's purpose and functions.

3.5.   The sources of funding, guarantees and other obligations owed to the issuer by its members.

3.6.   Any recent events relevant to the evaluation of the issuer's solvency.

3.7.   A list of the issuer's members.

4. FINANCIAL INFORMATION

4.1.   The two most recently published audited annual financial statements prepared in accordance with the accounting and auditing principles adopted by the issuer, and a brief description of those accounting and auditing principles.

Details of any significant changes to the issuer's financial position which has occurred since the end of the latest published audited annual financial statement, or an appropriate negative statement.

5. LEGAL AND ARBITRATION PROCEEDINGS

5.1.   Information on any governmental, legal or arbitration proceedings (including any such proceedings which are pending or threatened of which the issuer is aware), during a period covering at least the previous 12 months which are likely to have, or have had in the recent past, significant effects on the issuer's financial position, or provide an appropriate negative statement.

5.2.   Information on any immunity the issuer may have from legal proceedings pursuant to its constituent document.

6. STATEMENT BY EXPERTS AND DECLARATION OF ANY INTERESTS

Where a statement or report attributed to a person as an expert is included in the registration document, provide such person's name, business address and qualifications. If the report has been produced at the issuer's request a statement to that effect, that such statement or report is included, in the form and context in which it is included, with the consent of that person.

To the extent known to the issuer, provide information in respect of any conflict of interests relating to such expert which may have an effect on the independence of the expert in the preparation of the report.

7. DOCUMENT ON DISPLAY

A statement that for the life of the registration document the following documents (or copies thereof), where applicable, will be made available on request:
(a)   annual and audit reports of the issuer for each of the last two financial years prepared in accordance with the accounting and auditing principles adopted by the issuer;
(b)   all reports, letters, and other documents, valuations and statements prepared by any expert at the issuer's request any part of which is included or referred to in the registration document;
(c)   the issuer's constituent document.

An indication of where the documents on display may be inspected, by physical or electronic means.

[5663]

ANNEX XVIII
TABLE OF COMBINATIONS

ANNEX XVIII TYPES OF SECURITIES	REGISTRATION DOCUMENT					BUILDING BLOCK
	SCHEDULES					PRO FORMA INFORMATION
	SHARE	DEBT and DERIVATIVE (<EUR 50000)	DEBT and DERIVATIVE (> or = EUR 50000)	ASSET BACKED SEC.	BANKS DEBT and DERIVATIVE	
Shares (preference shares, redeemable shares, shares with preferential subscription rights; etc…)						
Bonds (vanilla bonds, income bonds, structured bonds, etc …) with a denomination of less than EUR 50 000		OR			OR	
Bonds (vanilla bonds, income bonds, structured bonds, etc …) with a denomination of at least EUR 50 000			OR		OR	
Debt securities guaranteed by a third party		OR	OR		OR	
Derivative sec. guaranteed by a third party		OR	OR		OR	
Asset backed securities						
Bonds exchangeable or convertible into third party shares or issuers' or group shares which are admitted on a regulated market		OR	OR		OR	
Bonds exchangeable or convertible into the issuer's shares not admitted on a regulated market						
Bonds exchangeable or convertible into group's shares not admitted on a regulated market		OR	OR		OR	
Bonds with warrants to acquire the issuer's shares not admitted to trading on a regulated market						
Shares with warrants to acquire the issuer's shares not admitted to trading on a regulated market						
Derivatives sec. giving the right to subscribe or to acquire the issuer's shares not admitted on a regulated market						
Derivatives sec, giving the right to acquire group's shares not admitted on a regulated market		OR	OR		OR	
Derivatives sec. giving the right to subscribe or to acquire issuer's or group shares which are admitted on a regulated market and derivatives sec. linked to any other underlying than issuer's or group shares which are not admitted on a regulated market (including any derivatives sec. entitling to cash settlement)		OR	OR		OR	

ANNEX XVIII	REGISTRATION DOCUMENT		
	SCHEDULES		
TYPES OF SECURITIES	COLLECTIVE INVESTMENT UNDERTAKING OF THE CLOSED-END TYPE	STATES AND THEIR REGIONAL AND LOCAL AUTHORITIES	PUBLIC INTERNATIONAL BODIES/Debt Securities guaranteed by a Member State of the OECD
Shares (preference shares, redeemable shares, shares with preferential subscription rights; etc…)			
Bonds (vanilla bonds, income bonds, structured bonds, etc …) with a denomination of less than EUR 50 000			
Bonds (vanilla bonds, income bonds, structured bonds, etc …) with a denomination of at least EUR 50 000			
Debt securities guaranteed by a third party			
Derivative sec. guaranteed by a third party			
Asset backed securities			
Bonds exchangeable or convertible into third party shares or issuers' or group shares which are admitted on a regulated market			
Bonds exchangeable or convertible into the issuer's shares not admitted on a regulated market			
Bonds exchangeable or convertible into group's shares not admitted on a regulated market			
Bonds with warrants to acquire the issuer's shares not admitted to trading on a regulated market			
Shares with warrants to acquire the issuer's shares not admitted to trading on a regulated market			
Derivatives sec. giving the right to subscribe or to acquire the issuer's shares not admitted on a regulated market			
Derivatives sec, giving the right to acquire group's shares not admitted on a regulated market			
Derivatives sec. giving the right to subscribe or to acquire issuer's or group shares which are admitted on a regulated market and derivatives sec. linked to any other underlying than issuer's or group shares which are not admitted on a regulated market (including any derivatives sec. entitling to cash settlement)			

ANNEX XVIII	SECURITIES NOTE						
	SCHEDULES				ADDITIONAL BUILDING BLOCKS		
TYPES OF SECURITIES	SHARE	DEBT (<EUR 50000)	DEBT (> or = EUR 50000)	DERIVATIVES SEC.	GUARANTEES	ASSET BACKED SEC.	UNDERLYING SHARE
Shares (preference shares, redeemable shares, shares with preferential subscription rights; etc...)	■						
Bonds (vanilla bonds, income bonds, structured bonds, etc ...) with a denomination of less than EUR 50 000		■					
Bonds (vanilla bonds, income bonds, structured bonds, etc ...) with a denomination of at least EUR 50 000			■				
Debt securities guaranteed by a third party		OR	OR		■		
Derivative sec. guaranteed by a third party				■	■		
Asset backed securities		OR	OR			■	
Bonds exchangeable or convertible into third party shares or issuers' or group shares which are admitted on a regulated market		OR	OR	only item 4.2.2			■
Bonds exchangeable or convertible into the issuer's shares not admitted on a regulated market		OR	OR	■			■
Bonds exchangeable or convertible into group's shares not admitted on a regulated market		OR	OR	■			■
Bonds with warrants to acquire the issuer's shares not admitted to trading on a regulated market		OR	OR	AND except item 4.2.2			■
Shares with warrants to acquire the issuer's shares not admitted to trading on a regulated market	■			AND except item 4.2.2			■
Derivatives sec. giving the right to subscribe or to acquire the issuer's shares not admitted on a regulated market				except item 4.2.2			■
Derivatives sec, giving the right to acquire group's shares not admitted on a regulated market				except item 4.2.2			■
Derivatives sec. giving the right to subscribe or to acquire issuer's or group shares which are admitted on a regulated market and derivatives sec. linked to any other underlying than issuer's or group shares which are not admitted on a regulated market (including any derivatives sec. entitling to cash settlement)				■			

ANNEX XIX
LIST OF SPECIALIST ISSUERS

— Property companies
— Mineral companies
— Investment companies
— Scientific research based companies
— Companies with less than three years of existence (start-up companies)
— shipping companies.

[5665]

DIRECTIVE OF THE EUROPEAN PARLIAMENT AND OF THE COUNCIL

of 15 December 2004

on the harmonisation of transparency requirements in relation to information about issuers whose securities are admitted to trading on a regulated market and amending Directive 2001/34/EC

(2004/109/EC)

NOTES
Date of publication in OJ: OJ L390, 31.12.2004, p 38. Notes are as in the original OJ version.
This Directive is reproduced as amended by: European Parliament and Council Directive 2008/22/EC (OJ L76, 19.3.2008, p 50).

THE EUROPEAN PARLIAMENT AND THE COUNCIL OF THE EUROPEAN UNION,
Having regard to the Treaty establishing the European Community, and in particular Articles 44 and 95 thereof,
Having regard to the proposal from the Commission,
Having regard to the opinion of the European Economic and Social Committee,[1]
Having regard to the opinion of the European Central Bank,[2]
Acting in accordance with the procedure laid down in Article 251 of the Treaty,[3]
Whereas:
(1) Efficient, transparent and integrated securities markets contribute to a genuine single market in the Community and foster growth and job creation by better allocation of capital and by reducing costs. The disclosure of accurate, comprehensive and timely information about security issuers builds sustained investor confidence and allows an informed assessment of their business performance and assets. This enhances both investor protection and market efficiency.
(2) To that end, security issuers should ensure appropriate transparency for investors through a regular flow of information. To the same end, shareholders, or natural persons or legal entities holding voting rights or financial instruments that result in an entitlement to acquire existing shares with voting rights, should also inform issuers of the acquisition of or other changes in major holdings in companies so that the latter are in a position to keep the public informed.
(3) The Commission Communication of 11 May 1999, entitled "Implementing the framework for financial markets: Action Plan", identifies a series of actions that are needed in order to complete the single market for financial services. The Lisbon European Council of March 2000 calls for the implementation of that Action Plan by 2005. The Action Plan stresses the need to draw up a Directive upgrading transparency requirements. That need was confirmed by the Barcelona European Council of March 2002.
(4) This Directive should be compatible with the tasks and duties conferred upon the European System of Central Banks (ESCB) and the Member States' central banks by the Treaty and the Statute of the European System of Central Banks and of the European Central Bank; particular attention in this regard needs to be given to the Member States' central banks whose shares are currently admitted to trading on a regulated market, in order to guarantee the pursuit of primary Community law objectives.
(5) Greater harmonisation of provisions of national law on periodic and ongoing information requirements for security issuers should lead to a high level of investor protection throughout the Community. However, this Directive does not affect existing Community legislation on units issued by collective investment undertakings other than the closed-end type, or on units acquired or disposed of in such undertakings.
(6) Supervision of an issuer of shares, or of debt securities the denomination per unit of which is less than EUR 1,000, for the purposes of this Directive, would be best effected by the Member

PART IV
EC MATERIALS

State in which the issuer has its registered office. In that respect, it is vital to ensure consistency with Directive 2003/71/EC of the European Parliament and of the Council of 4 November 2003 on the prospectus to be published when securities are offered to the public or admitted to trading.[4] Along the same lines, some flexibility should be introduced allowing third country issuers and Community companies issuing only securities other than those mentioned above a choice of home Member State.

(7) A high level of investor protection throughout the Community would enable barriers to the admission of securities to regulated markets situated or operating within a Member State to be removed. Member States other than the home Member State should no longer be allowed to restrict admission of securities to their regulated markets by imposing more stringent requirements on periodic and ongoing information about issuers whose securities are admitted to trading on a regulated market.

(8) The removal of barriers on the basis of the home Member State principle under this Directive should not affect areas not covered by this Directive, such as rights of shareholders to intervene in the management of an issuer. Nor should it affect the home Member State's right to request the issuer to publish, in addition, parts of or all regulated information through newspapers.

(9) Regulation (EC) No 1606/2002 of the European Parliament and of the Council of 19 July 2002 on the application of international accounting standards[5] has already paved the way for a convergence of financial reporting standards throughout the Community for issuers whose securities are admitted to trading on a regulated market and who are required to prepare consolidated accounts. Thus, a specific regime for security issuers beyond the general system for all companies, as laid down in the Company Law Directives, is already established. This Directive builds on this approach with regard to annual and interim financial reporting, including the principle of providing a true and fair view of an issuer's assets, liabilities, financial position and profit or loss. A condensed set of financial statements, as part of a half-yearly financial report, also represents a sufficient basis for giving such a true and fair view of the first six months of an issuer's financial year.

(10) An annual financial report should ensure information over the years once the issuer's securities have been admitted to a regulated market. Making it easier to compare annual financial reports is only of use to investors in securities markets if they can be sure that this information will be published within a certain time after the end of the financial year. As regards debt securities admitted to trading on a regulated market prior to 1 January 2005 and issued by issuers incorporated in a third country, the home Member State may under certain conditions allow issuers not to prepare annual financial reports in accordance with the standards required under this Directive.

(11) This Directive introduces more comprehensive half-yearly financial reports for issuers of shares admitted to trading on a regulated market. This should allow investors to make a more informed assessment of the issuer's situation.

(12) A home Member State may provide for exemptions from half-yearly reporting by issuers of debt securities in the case of:
— credit institutions acting as small-size issuers of debt securities, or
— issuers already existing on the date of the entry into force of this Directive who exclusively issue debt securities unconditionally and irrevocably guaranteed by the home Member State or by one of its regional or local authorities, or
— during a transitional period of ten years, only in respect of those debt securities admitted to trading on a regulated market prior to 1 January 2005 which may be purchased by professional investors only. If such an exemption is given by the home Member State, it may not be extended in respect of any debt securities admitted to a regulated market thereafter.

(13) The European Parliament and the Council welcome the Commission's commitment rapidly to consider enhancing the transparency of the remuneration policies, total remuneration paid, including any contingent or deferred compensation, and benefits in kind granted to each member of administrative, management or supervisory bodies under its Action Plan for "Modernising Company Law and Enhancing Corporate Governance in the European Union" of 21 May 2003 and the Commission's intention to make a Recommendation on this topic in the near future.

(14) The home Member State should encourage issuers whose shares are admitted to trading on a regulated market and whose principal activities lie in the extractive industry to disclose payments to governments in their annual financial report. The home Member State should also encourage an increase in the transparency of such payments within the framework established at various international financial fora.

(15) This Directive will also make half-yearly reporting mandatory for issuers of only debt securities on regulated markets. Exemptions should only be provided for wholesale markets on the basis of a denomination per unit starting at EUR 50,000, as under Directive 2003/71/EC. Where debt securities are issued in another currency, exemptions should only be possible where the denomination per unit in such a currency is, at the date of the issue, at least equivalent to EUR 50,000.

(16) More timely and more reliable information about the share issuer's performance over the financial year also requires a higher frequency of interim information. A requirement should

therefore be introduced to publish an interim management statement during the first six months and a second interim management statement during the second six months of a financial year. Share issuers who already publish quarterly financial reports should not be required to publish interim management statements.

(17) Appropriate liability rules, as laid down by each Member State under its national law or regulations, should be applicable to the issuer, its administrative, management or supervisory bodies, or persons responsible within the issuer. Member States should remain free to determine the extent of the liability.

(18) The public should be informed of changes to major holdings in issuers whose shares are traded on a regulated market situated or operating within the Community. This information should enable investors to acquire or dispose of shares in full knowledge of changes in the voting structure; it should also enhance effective control of share issuers and overall market transparency of important capital movements. Information about shares or financial instruments as determined by Article 13, lodged as collateral, should be provided in certain circumstances.

(19) Articles 9 and 10(c) should not apply to shares provided to or by the members of the ESCB in carrying out their functions as monetary authorities provided that the voting rights attached to such shares are not exercised; the reference to a "short period" in Article 11 should be understood with reference to credit operations carried out in accordance with the Treaty and the European Central Bank (ECB) legal acts, in particular the ECB Guidelines on monetary policy instruments and procedures and TARGET, and to credit operations for the purpose of performing equivalent functions in accordance with national provisions.

(20) In order to avoid unnecessary burdens for certain market participants and to clarify who actually exercises influence over an issuer, there is no need to require notification of major holdings of shares, or other financial instruments as determined by Article 13 that result in an entitlement to acquire shares with regard to market makers or custodians, or of holdings of shares or such financial instruments acquired solely for clearing and settlement purposes, within limits and guarantees to be applied throughout the Community. The home Member State should be allowed to provide limited exemptions as regards holdings of shares in trading books of credit institutions and investment firms.

(21) In order to clarify who is actually a major holder of shares or other financial instruments in the same issuer throughout the Community, parent undertakings should not be required to aggregate their own holdings with those managed by undertakings for collective investment in transferable securities (UCITS) or investment firms, provided that such undertakings or firms exercise voting rights independently from their parent undertakings and fulfil certain further conditions.

(22) Ongoing information to holders of securities admitted to trading on a regulated market should continue to be based on the principle of equal treatment. Such equal treatment only relates to shareholders in the same position and does not therefore prejudice the issue of how many voting rights may be attached to a particular share. By the same token, holders of debt securities ranking pari passu should continue to benefit from equal treatment, even in the case of sovereign debt. Information to holders of shares and/or debt securities in general meetings should be facilitated. In particular, holders of shares and/or debt securities situated abroad should be more actively involved in that they should be able to mandate proxies to act on their behalf. For the same reasons, it should be decided in a general meeting of holders of shares and/or debt securities whether the use of modern information and communication technologies should become a reality. In that case, issuers should put in place arrangements in order effectively to inform holders of their shares and/or debt securities, insofar as it is possible for them to identify those holders.

(23) Removal of barriers and effective enforcement of new Community information requirements also require adequate control by the competent authority of the home Member State. This Directive should at least provide for a minimum guarantee for the timely availability of such information. For this reason, at least one filing and storage system should exist in each Member State.

(24) Any obligation for an issuer to translate all ongoing and periodic information into all the relevant languages in all the Member States where its securities are admitted to trading does not foster integration of securities markets, but has deterrent effects on cross-border admission of securities to trading on regulated markets. Therefore, the issuer should in certain cases be entitled to provide information drawn up in a language that is customary in the sphere of international finance. Since a particular effort is needed to attract investors from other Member States and third countries, Member States should no longer prevent shareholders, persons exercising voting rights, or holders of financial instruments, from making the required notifications to the issuer in a language that is customary in the sphere of international finance.

(25) Access for investors to information about issuers should be more organised at a Community level in order to actively promote integration of European capital markets. Investors who are not situated in the issuer's home Member State should be put on an equal footing with investors situated in the issuer's home Member State, when seeking access to such information. This could be achieved if the home Member State ensures compliance with minimum quality standards for disseminating information throughout the Community, in a fast manner on a non-discriminatory basis and depending on the type of regulated information in question. In addition, information which

has been disseminated should be available in the home Member State in a centralised way allowing a European network to be built up, accessible at affordable prices for retail investors, while not leading to unnecessary duplication of filing requirements for issuers. Issuers should benefit from free competition when choosing the media or operators for disseminating information under this Directive.

(26) In order to further simplify investor access to corporate information across Member States, it should be left to the national supervisory authorities to formulate guidelines for setting up electronic networks, in close consultation with the other parties concerned, in particular security issuers, investors, market participants, operators of regulated markets and financial information providers.

(27) So as to ensure the effective protection of investors and the proper operation of regulated markets, the rules relating to information to be published by issuers whose securities are admitted to trading on a regulated market should also apply to issuers which do not have a registered office in a Member State and which do not fall within the scope of Article 48 of the Treaty. It should also be ensured that any additional relevant information about Community issuers or third country issuers, disclosure of which is required in a third country but not in a Member State, is made available to the public in the Community.

(28) A single competent authority should be designated in each Member State to assume final responsibility for supervising compliance with the provisions adopted pursuant to this Directive, as well as for international cooperation. Such an authority should be of an administrative nature, and its independence from economic players should be ensured in order to avoid conflicts of interest. Member States may however designate another competent authority for examining that information referred to in this Directive is drawn up in accordance with the relevant reporting framework and taking appropriate measures in case of discovered infringements; such an authority need not be of an administrative nature.

(29) Increasing cross-border activities require improved cooperation between national competent authorities, including a comprehensive set of provisions for the exchange of information and for precautionary measures. The organisation of the regulatory and supervisory tasks in each Member State should not hinder efficient cooperation between the competent national authorities.

(30) At its meeting on 17 July 2000, the Council set up the Committee of Wise Men on the Regulation of European securities markets. In its final report, that Committee proposed the introduction of new legislative techniques based on a four-level approach, namely essential principles, technical implementing measures, cooperation amongst national securities regulators, and enforcement of Community law. This Directive should confine itself to broad "framework" principles, while implementing measures to be adopted by the Commission with the assistance of the European Securities Committee established by Commission Decision 2001/528/EC[6] should lay down the technical details.

(31) The Resolution adopted by the Stockholm European Council of March 2001 endorsed the final report of the Committee of Wise Men and the proposed four-level approach to make the regulatory process for Community securities legislation more efficient and transparent.

(32) According to that Resolution, implementing measures should be used more frequently, to ensure that technical provisions can be kept up to date with market and supervisory developments, and deadlines should be set for all stages of implementing rules.

(33) The Resolution of the European Parliament of 5 February 2002 on the implementation of financial services legislation also endorsed the Committee of Wise Men's report, on the basis of the solemn declaration made before the European Parliament the same day by the President of the Commission and the letter of 2 October 2001 addressed by the Internal Market Commissioner to the Chairman of the Parliament's Committee on Economic and Monetary Affairs with regard to safeguards for the European Parliament's role in this process.

(34) The European Parliament should be given a period of three months from the first transmission of draft implementing measures to allow it to examine them and to give its opinion. However, in urgent and duly justified cases, that period may be shortened. If, within that period, a Resolution is passed by the European Parliament, the Commission should re-examine the draft measures.

(35) Technical implementing measures for the rules laid down in this Directive may be necessary to take account of new developments on securities markets. The Commission should accordingly be empowered to adopt implementing measures, provided that they do not modify the essential elements of this Directive and provided that the Commission acts in accordance with the principles set out therein, after consulting the European Securities Committee.

(36) In exercising its implementing powers in accordance with this Directive, the Commission should respect the following principles:

— the need to ensure confidence in financial markets among investors by promoting high standards of transparency in financial markets;

— the need to provide investors with a wide range of competing investments and a level of disclosure and protection tailored to their circumstances;

— the need to ensure that independent regulatory authorities enforce the rules consistently, especially as regards the fight against economic crime;

— the need for high levels of transparency and consultation with all market participants and with the European Parliament and the Council;

— the need to encourage innovation in financial markets if they are to be dynamic and efficient;

— the need to ensure market integrity by close and reactive monitoring of financial innovation;

— the importance of reducing the cost of, and increasing access to, capital;

— the balance of costs and benefits to market participants on a long-term basis, including small and medium-sized businesses and small investors, in any implementing measures;

— the need to foster the international competitiveness of Community financial markets without prejudice to a much-needed extension of international cooperation;

— the need to achieve a level playing field for all market participants by establishing Community-wide regulations wherever appropriate;

— the need to respect differences in national markets where these do not unduly impinge on the coherence of the single market;

— the need to ensure coherence with other Community legislation in this area, as imbalances in information and a lack of transparency may jeopardise the operation of the markets and above all harm consumers and small investors.

(37)   In order to ensure that the requirements set out in this Directive or the measures implementing this Directive are fulfilled, any infringement of those requirements or measures should be promptly detected and, if necessary, subject to penalties. To that end, measures and penalties should be sufficiently dissuasive, proportionate and consistently enforced. Member States should ensure that decisions taken by the competent national authorities are subject to the right of appeal to the courts.

(38)   This Directive aims to upgrade the current transparency requirements for security issuers and investors acquiring or disposing of major holdings in issuers whose shares are admitted to trading on a regulated market. This Directive replaces some of the requirements set out in Directive 2001/34/EC of the European Parliament and of the Council of 28 May 2001 on the admission of securities to official stock exchange listing and on information to be published on those securities.[7] In order to gather transparency requirements in a single act it is necessary to amend it accordingly. Such an amendment however should not affect the ability of Member States to impose additional requirements under Articles 42 to 63 of Directive 2001/34/EC, which remain valid.

(39)   This Directive is in line with Directive 95/46/EC of the European Parliament and of the Council of 24 October 1995 on the protection of individuals with regard to the processing of personal data and on the free movement of such data.[8]

(40)   This Directive respects fundamental rights and observes the principles recognised in particular by the Charter of the Fundamental Rights of the European Union.

(41)   Since the objectives of this Directive, namely to ensure investor confidence through equivalent transparency throughout the Community and thereby to complete the internal market, cannot be sufficiently achieved by the Member States on the basis of the existing Community legislation and can therefore be better achieved at Community level, the Community may adopt measures, in accordance with the principle of subsidiarity as set out in Article 5 of the Treaty. In accordance with the principle of proportionality, as set out in that Article, this Directive does not go beyond what is necessary in order to achieve these objectives.

(42)   The measures necessary for implementing this Directive should be adopted in accordance with Council Decision 1999/468/EC of 28 June 1999 laying down the procedures for the exercise of implementing powers conferred on the Commission,[9]

[5666]

NOTES

1   OJ C80, 30.3.2004, p 128.
2   OJ C242, 9.10.2003, p 6.
3   Opinion of the European Parliament of 30 March 2004 (not yet published in the Official Journal) and Council Decision of 2 December 2004.
4   OJ L345, 31.12.2003, p 64.
5   OJ L243, 11.9.2002, p 1.
6   OJ L191, 13.7.2001, p 45. Decision as amended by Decision 2004/8/EC (OJ L3, 7.1.2004, p 33).
7   OJ L184, 6.7.2001, p 1. Directive as last amended by Directive 2003/71/EC.
8   OJ L281, 23.11.1995, p 31. Directive as amended by Regulation (EC) No 1882/2003 (OJ L284, 31.10.2003, p 1).
9   OJ L184, 17.7.1999, p 23.

HAVE ADOPTED THIS DIRECTIVE:

CHAPTER I
GENERAL PROVISIONS

Article 1
Subject matter and scope

1.   This Directive establishes requirements in relation to the disclosure of periodic and ongoing information about issuers whose securities are already admitted to trading on a regulated market situated or operating within a Member State.

2.   This Directive shall not apply to units issued by collective investment undertakings other than the closed-end type, or to units acquired or disposed of in such collective investment undertakings.

3.   Member States may decide not to apply the provisions mentioned in Article 16(3) and in paragraphs 2, 3 and 4 of Article 18 to securities which are admitted to trading on a regulated market issued by them or their regional or local authorities.

4.   Member States may decide not to apply Article 17 to their national central banks in their capacity as issuers of shares admitted to trading on a regulated market if this admission took place before 20 January 2005.

[5666A]

Article 2
Definitions

1.   For the purposes of this Directive the following definitions shall apply:

(a)   "securities" means transferable securities as defined in Article 4(1), point 18, of Directive 2004/39/EC of the European Parliament and of the Council of 21 April 2004 on markets in financial instruments[1] with the exception of money-market instruments, as defined in Article 4(1), point 19, of that Directive having a maturity of less than 12 months, for which national legislation may be applicable;

(b)   "debt securities" means bonds or other forms of transferable securitised debts, with the exception of securities which are equivalent to shares in companies or which, if converted or if the rights conferred by them are exercised, give rise to a right to acquire shares or securities equivalent to shares;

(c)   "regulated market" means a market as defined in Article 4(1), point 14, of Directive 2004/39/EC;

(d)   "issuer" means a legal entity governed by private or public law, including a State, whose securities are admitted to trading on a regulated market, the issuer being, in the case of depository receipts representing securities, the issuer of the securities represented;

(e)   "shareholder" means any natural person or legal entity governed by private or public law, who holds, directly or indirectly:

(i)   shares of the issuer in its own name and on its own account;

(ii)   shares of the issuer in its own name, but on behalf of another natural person or legal entity;

(iii) depository receipts, in which case the holder of the depository receipt shall be considered as the shareholder of the underlying shares represented by the depository receipts;

(f)   "controlled undertaking" means any undertaking

(i)   in which a natural person or legal entity has a majority of the voting rights; or

(ii)   of which a natural person or legal entity has the right to appoint or remove a majority of the members of the administrative, management or supervisory body and is at the same time a shareholder in, or member of, the undertaking in question; or

(iii) of which a natural person or legal entity is a shareholder or member and alone controls a majority of the shareholders' or members' voting rights, respectively, pursuant to an agreement entered into with other shareholders or members of the undertaking in question; or

(iv)   over which a natural person or legal entity has the power to exercise, or actually exercises, dominant influence or control;

(g)   "collective investment undertaking other than the closed-end type" means unit trusts and investment companies:

(i)   the object of which is the collective investment of capital provided by the public, and which operate on the principle of risk spreading; and

(ii)   the units of which are, at the request of the holder of such units, repurchased or redeemed, directly or indirectly, out of the assets of those undertakings;

(h)   "units of a collective investment undertaking" means securities issued by a collective investment undertaking and representing rights of the participants in such an undertaking over its assets;

(i)   "home Member State" means
    (i)   in the case of an issuer of debt securities the denomination per unit of which is less than EUR 1,000 or an issuer of shares:

        — where the issuer is incorporated in the Community, the Member State in which it has its registered office;

        — where the issuer is incorporated in a third country, the Member State in which it is required to file the annual information with the competent authority in accordance with Article 10 of Directive 2003/71/EC.

The definition of "home" Member State shall be applicable to debt securities in a currency other than Euro, provided that the value of such denomination per unit is, at the date of the issue, less than EUR 1,000, unless it is nearly equivalent to EUR 1,000;

    (ii)   for any issuer not covered by (i), the Member State chosen by the issuer from among the Member State in which the issuer has its registered office and those Member States which have admitted its securities to trading on a regulated market on their territory. The issuer may choose only one Member State as its home Member State. Its choice shall remain valid for at least three years unless its securities are no longer admitted to trading on any regulated market in the Community;

(j)   "host Member State" means a Member State in which securities are admitted to trading on a regulated market, if different from the home Member State;

(k)   "regulated information" means all information which the issuer, or any other person who has applied for the admission of securities to trading on a regulated market without the issuer's consent, is required to disclose under this Directive, under Article 6 of Directive 2003/6/EC of the European Parliament and of the Council of 28 January 2003 on insider dealing and market manipulation (market abuse),[2] or under the laws, regulations or administrative provisions of a Member State adopted under Article 3(1) of this Directive;

(l)   "electronic means" are means of electronic equipment for the processing (including digital compression), storage and transmission of data, employing wires, radio, optical technologies, or any other electromagnetic means;

(m)   "management company" means a company as defined in Article 1a(2) of Council Directive 85/611/EEC of 20 December 1985 on the coordination of laws, regulations and administrative provisions relating to undertakings for collective investment in transferable securities (UCITS);[3]

(n)   "market maker" means a person who holds himself out on the financial markets on a continuous basis as being willing to deal on own account by buying and selling financial instruments against his proprietary capital at prices defined by him;

(o)   "credit institution" means an undertaking as defined in Article 1(1)(a) of Directive 2000/12/EC of the European Parliament and of the Council of 20 March 2000 relating to the taking up and pursuit of the business of credit institutions;[4]

(p)   "securities issued in a continuous or repeated manner" means debt securities of the same issuer on tap or at least two separate issues of securities of a similar type and/or class.

2.   For the purposes of the definition of "controlled undertaking" in paragraph 1(f)(ii), the holder's rights in relation to voting, appointment and removal shall include the rights of any other undertaking controlled by the shareholder and those of any natural person or legal entity acting, albeit in its own name, on behalf of the shareholder or of any other undertaking controlled by the shareholder.

[3.   In order to take account of technical developments on financial markets and to ensure the uniform application of paragraph 1, the Commission shall, in accordance with the procedures referred to in Article 27(2) and (2a), adopt implementing measures concerning the definitions set out in paragraph 1.

The Commission shall, in particular:

(a)   establish, for the purposes of paragraph 1(i)(ii), the procedural arrangements in accordance with which an issuer may make the choice of the home Member State;

(b)   adjust, where appropriate for the purposes of the choice of the home Member State referred to in paragraph 1(i)(ii), the three-year period in relation to the issuer's track record in the light of any new requirement under Community law concerning admission to trading on a regulated market; and

(c)   establish, for the purposes of paragraph 1(l), an indicative list of means which are not to be considered as electronic means, thereby taking into account Annex V to Directive 98/34/EC of the European Parliament and of the Council of 22 June 1998 laying down a procedure for the provision of information in the field of technical standards and regulations and of rules on Information Society services[5] in accordance with the regulatory procedure referred to in Article 27(2).

The measures referred to in points (a) and (b) of the second subparagraph, designed to amend non-essential elements of this Directive by supplementing it, shall be adopted in accordance with the regulatory procedure with scrutiny referred to in Article 27(2a).]

[5667]

NOTES

Para 3: substituted by European Parliament and Council Directive 2008/22/EC, Art 1(1), as from 20 March 2008.

¹   OJ L145, 30.4.2004, p 1.
²   OJ L96, 12.4.2003, p 16.
³   OJ L375, 31.12.1985, p 3. Directive as last amended by Directive 2004/39/EC.
⁴   OJ L126, 26.5.2000, p 1. Directive as last amended by Commission Directive 2004/69/EC (OJ L125, 28.4.2004, p 44).
⁵   OJ L 204, 21.7.1998, p. 37. Directive as last amended by Council Directive 2006/96/EC (OJ L 363, 20.12.2006, p. 81).

Article 3
Integration of securities markets

1.   The home Member State may make an issuer subject to requirements more stringent than those laid down in this Directive.

The home Member State may also make a holder of shares, or a natural person or legal entity referred to in Articles 10 or 13, subject to requirements more stringent than those laid down in this Directive.

2.   A host Member State may not:
    (a)   as regards the admission of securities to a regulated market in its territory, impose disclosure requirements more stringent than those laid down in this Directive or in Article 6 of Directive 2003/6/EC;
    (b)   as regards the notification of information, make a holder of shares, or a natural person or legal entity referred to in Articles 10 or 13, subject to requirements more stringent than those laid down in this Directive.

[5668]

CHAPTER II
PERIODIC INFORMATION

Article 4
Annual financial reports

1.   The issuer shall make public its annual financial report at the latest four months after the end of each financial year and shall ensure that it remains publicly available for at least five years.

2.   The annual financial report shall comprise:
    (a)   the audited financial statements;
    (b)   the management report; and
    (c)   statements made by the persons responsible within the issuer, whose names and functions shall be clearly indicated, to the effect that, to the best of their knowledge, the financial statements prepared in accordance with the applicable set of accounting standards give a true and fair view of the assets, liabilities, financial position and profit or loss of the issuer and the undertakings included in the consolidation taken as a whole and that the management report includes a fair review of the development and performance of the business and the position of the issuer and the undertakings included in the consolidation taken as a whole, together with a description of the principal risks and uncertainties that they face.

3.   Where the issuer is required to prepare consolidated accounts according to the Seventh Council Directive 83/349/EEC of 13 June 1983 on consolidated accounts,¹ the audited financial statements shall comprise such consolidated accounts drawn up in accordance with Regulation (EC) No 1606/2002 and the annual accounts of the parent company drawn up in accordance with the national law of the Member State in which the parent company is incorporated.

Where the issuer is not required to prepare consolidated accounts, the audited financial statements shall comprise the accounts prepared in accordance with the national law of the Member State in which the company is incorporated.

4.   The financial statements shall be audited in accordance with Articles 51 and 51a of the Fourth Council Directive 78/660/EEC of 25 July 1978 on the annual accounts of certain types of companies² and, if the issuer is required to prepare consolidated accounts, in accordance with Article 37 of Directive 83/349/EEC.

The audit report, signed by the person or persons responsible for auditing the financial statements, shall be disclosed in full to the public together with the annual financial report.

5. The management report shall be drawn up in accordance with Article 46 of Directive 78/660/EEC and, if the issuer is required to prepare consolidated accounts, in accordance with Article 36 of Directive 83/349/EEC.

6. The Commission shall, in accordance with the procedure referred to in Article 27(2), adopt implementing measures in order to take account of technical developments in financial markets and to ensure the uniform application of paragraph 1. The Commission shall in particular specify the technical conditions under which a published annual financial report, including the audit report, is to remain available to the public. Where appropriate, the Commission may also adapt the five-year period referred to in paragraph 1.

[5669]

NOTES

1   OJ L193, 18.7.1983, p 1. Directive as last amended by Directive 2003/51/EC of the European Parliament and of the Council (OJ L178, 17.7.2003, p 16).
2   OJ L222, 14.8.1978, p 11. Directive as last amended by Directive 2003/51/EC.

Article 5
Half-yearly financial reports

1. The issuer of shares or debt securities shall make public a half-yearly financial report covering the first six months of the financial year as soon as possible after the end of the relevant period, but at the latest two months thereafter. The issuer shall ensure that the half-yearly financial report remains available to the public for at least five years.

2. The half-yearly financial report shall comprise:
   (a) the condensed set of financial statements;
   (b) an interim management report; and
   (c) statements made by the persons responsible within the issuer, whose names and functions shall be clearly indicated, to the effect that, to the best of their knowledge, the condensed set of financial statements which has been prepared in accordance with the applicable set of accounting standards gives a true and fair view of the assets, liabilities, financial position and profit or loss of the issuer, or the undertakings included in the consolidation as a whole as required under paragraph 3, and that the interim management report includes a fair review of the information required under paragraph 4.

3. Where the issuer is required to prepare consolidated accounts, the condensed set of financial statements shall be prepared in accordance with the international accounting standard applicable to the interim financial reporting adopted pursuant to the procedure provided for under Article 6 of Regulation (EC) No 1606/2002.

Where the issuer is not required to prepare consolidated accounts, the condensed set of financial statements shall at least contain a condensed balance sheet, a condensed profit and loss account and explanatory notes on these accounts. In preparing the condensed balance sheet and the condensed profit and loss account, the issuer shall follow the same principles for recognising and measuring as when preparing annual financial reports.

4. The interim management report shall include at least an indication of important events that have occurred during the first six months of the financial year, and their impact on the condensed set of financial statements, together with a description of the principal risks and uncertainties for the remaining six months of the financial year. For issuers of shares, the interim management report shall also include major related parties transactions.

5. If the half-yearly financial report has been audited, the audit report shall be reproduced in full. The same shall apply in the case of an auditors' review. If the half-yearly financial report has not been audited or reviewed by auditors, the issuer shall make a statement to that effect in its report.

6. The Commission shall … adopt implementing measures in order to take account of technical developments on financial markets and to ensure the uniform application of paragraphs 1 to 5 of this Article.

The Commission shall, in particular:
   (a) specify the technical conditions under which a published half-yearly financial report, including the auditors' review, is to remain available to the public;
   (b) clarify the nature of the auditors' review;
   (c) specify the minimum content of the condensed balance sheet and profit and loss accounts and explanatory notes on these accounts, where they are not prepared in accordance with the international accounting standards adopted pursuant to the procedure provided for under Article 6 of Regulation (EC) No 1606/2002.

[The measures referred to in point (a) shall be adopted in accordance with the regulatory procedure referred to in Article 27(2). The measures referred to in points (b) and (c), designed to amend non-essential elements of this Directive by supplementing it, shall be adopted in accordance with the regulatory procedure with scrutiny referred to in Article 27(2a).

Where appropriate, the Commission may also adapt the five-year period referred to in paragraph 1. That measure, designed to amend non-essential elements of this Directive, shall be adopted in accordance with the regulatory procedure with scrutiny referred to in Article 27(2a).]

[5670]

NOTES

Para 6: words omitted repealed, and words in square brackets substituted, by European Parliament and Council Directive 2008/22/EC, Art 1(2), as from 20 March 2008.

Article 6
Interim management statements

1. Without prejudice to Article 6 of Directive 2003/6/EC, an issuer whose shares are admitted to trading on a regulated market shall make public a statement by its management during the first six-month period of the financial year and another statement by its management during the second six-month period of the financial year. Such statement shall be made in a period between ten weeks after the beginning and six weeks before the end of the relevant six-month period. It shall contain information covering the period between the beginning of the relevant six-month period and the date of publication of the statement. Such a statement shall provide:

— an explanation of material events and transactions that have taken place during the relevant period and their impact on the financial position of the issuer and its controlled undertakings, and

— a general description of the financial position and performance of the issuer and its controlled undertakings during the relevant period.

2. Issuers which, under either national legislation or the rules of the regulated market or of their own initiative, publish quarterly financial reports in accordance with such legislation or rules shall not be required to make public statements by the management provided for in paragraph 1.

3. The Commission shall provide a report to the European Parliament and the Council by 20 January 2010 on the transparency of quarterly financial reporting and statements by the management of issuers to examine whether the information provided meets the objective of allowing investors to make an informed assessment of the financial position of the issuer. Such a report shall include an impact assessment on areas where the Commission considers proposing amendments to this Article.

[5671]

Article 7
Responsibility and liability

Member States shall ensure that responsibility for the information to be drawn up and made public in accordance with Articles 4, 5, 6 and 16 lies at least with the issuer or its administrative, management or supervisory bodies and shall ensure that their laws, regulations and administrative provisions on liability apply to the issuers, the bodies referred to in this Article or the persons responsible within the issuers.

[5672]

Article 8
Exemptions

1. Articles 4, 5 and 6 shall not apply to the following issuers:

(a) a State, a regional or local authority of a State, a public international body of which at least one Member State is a member, the ECB, and Member States' national central banks whether or not they issue shares or other securities; and

(b) an issuer exclusively of debt securities admitted to trading on a regulated market, the denomination per unit of which is at least EUR 50,000 or, in the case of debt securities denominated in a currency other than Euro, the value of such denomination per unit is, at the date of the issue, equivalent to at least EUR 50,000.

2. The home Member State may choose not to apply Article 5 to credit institutions whose shares are not admitted to trading on a regulated market and which have, in a continuous or repeated manner, only issued debt securities provided that the total nominal amount of all such debt securities remains below EUR 100,000,000 and that they have not published a prospectus under Directive 2003/71/EC.

3. The home Member State may choose not to apply Article 5 to issuers already existing at the date of the entry into force of Directive 2003/71/EC which exclusively issue debt securities unconditionally and irrevocably guaranteed by the home Member State or by one of its regional or local authorities, on a regulated market.

[5673]

CHAPTER III
ONGOING INFORMATION

SECTION I
INFORMATION ABOUT MAJOR HOLDINGS

Article 9
Notification of the acquisition or disposal of major holdings

1. The home Member State shall ensure that, where a shareholder acquires or disposes of shares of an issuer whose shares are admitted to trading on a regulated market and to which voting rights are attached, such shareholder notifies the issuer of the proportion of voting rights of the issuer held by the shareholder as a result of the acquisition or disposal where that proportion reaches, exceeds or falls below the thresholds of 5%, 10%, 15%, 20%, 25%, 30%, 50% and 75%.

The voting rights shall be calculated on the basis of all the shares to which voting rights are attached even if the exercise thereof is suspended. Moreover this information shall also be given in respect of all the shares which are in the same class and to which voting rights are attached.

2. The home Member States shall ensure that the shareholders notify the issuer of the proportion of voting rights, where that proportion reaches, exceeds or falls below the thresholds provided for in paragraph 1, as a result of events changing the breakdown of voting rights, and on the basis of the information disclosed pursuant to Article 15. Where the issuer is incorporated in a third country, the notification shall be made for equivalent events.

3. The home Member State need not apply:
    (a)   the 30% threshold, where it applies a threshold of one-third;
    (b)   the 75% threshold, where it applies a threshold of two-thirds.

4. This Article shall not apply to shares acquired for the sole purpose of clearing and settling within the usual short settlement cycle, or to custodians holding shares in their custodian capacity provided such custodians can only exercise the voting rights attached to such shares under instructions given in writing or by electronic means.

5. This Article shall not apply to the acquisition or disposal of a major holding reaching or crossing the 5% threshold by a market maker acting in its capacity of a market maker, provided that:
    (a)   it is authorised by its home Member State under Directive 2004/39/EC; and
    (b)   it neither intervenes in the management of the issuer concerned nor exerts any influence on the issuer to buy such shares or back the share price.

6. Home Member States under Article 2(1)(i) may provide that voting rights held in the trading book, as defined in Article 2(6) of Council Directive 93/6/EEC of 15 March 1993 on the capital adequacy of investment firms and credit institutions,[1] of a credit institution or investment firm shall not be counted for the purposes of this Article provided that:
    (a)   the voting rights held in the trading book do not exceed 5%, and
    (b)   the credit institution or investment firm ensures that the voting rights attaching to shares held in the trading book are not exercised nor otherwise used to intervene in the management of the issuer.

[7. The Commission shall adopt implementing measures in order to take account of technical developments on financial markets and to ensure the uniform application of paragraphs 2, 4 and 5. Those measures, designed to amend non-essential elements of this Directive by supplementing it, shall be adopted in accordance with the regulatory procedure with scrutiny referred to in Article 27(2a).

The Commission shall specify the maximum length of the "short settlement cycle" referred to in paragraph 4 of this Article, as well as the appropriate control mechanisms by the competent authority of the home Member State. Those measures, designed to amend non-essential elements of this Directive by supplementing it, shall be adopted in accordance with the regulatory procedure with scrutiny referred to in Article 27(2a).

In addition, the Commission may draw up a list of the events referred to in paragraph 2 of this Article, in accordance with the regulatory procedure referred to in Article 27(2).]

[5674]

NOTES
   Para 7: substituted by European Parliament and Council Directive 2008/22/EC, Art 1(3), as from 20 March 2008.
   [1]   OJ L141, 11.6.1993, p 1. Directive as last amended by Directive 2004/39/EC.

Article 10
Acquisition or disposal of major proportions of voting rights

The notification requirements defined in paragraphs 1 and 2 of Article 9 shall also apply to a natural person or legal entity to the extent it is entitled to acquire, to dispose of, or to exercise voting rights in any of the following cases or a combination of them:

(a) voting rights held by a third party with whom that person or entity has concluded an agreement, which obliges them to adopt, by concerted exercise of the voting rights they hold, a lasting common policy towards the management of the issuer in question;

(b) voting rights held by a third party under an agreement concluded with that person or entity providing for the temporary transfer for consideration of the voting rights in question;

(c) voting rights attaching to shares which are lodged as collateral with that person or entity, provided the person or entity controls the voting rights and declares its intention of exercising them;

(d) voting rights attaching to shares in which that person or entity has the life interest;

(e) voting rights which are held, or may be exercised within the meaning of points (a) to (d), by an undertaking controlled by that person or entity;

(f) voting rights attaching to shares deposited with that person or entity which the person or entity can exercise at its discretion in the absence of specific instructions from the shareholders;

(g) voting rights held by a third party in its own name on behalf of that person or entity;

(h) voting rights which that person or entity may exercise as a proxy where the person or entity can exercise the voting rights at its discretion in the absence of specific instructions from the shareholders.

[5675]

Article 11

1. Articles 9 and 10(c) shall not apply to shares provided to or by the members of the ESCB in carrying out their functions as monetary authorities, including shares provided to or by members of the ESCB under a pledge or repurchase or similar agreement for liquidity granted for monetary policy purposes or within a payment system.

2. The exemption shall apply to the above transactions lasting for a short period and provided that the voting rights attaching to such shares are not exercised.

[5676]

Article 12
Procedures on the notification and disclosure of major holdings

1. The notification required under Articles 9 and 10 shall include the following information:

(a) the resulting situation in terms of voting rights;

(b) the chain of controlled undertakings through which voting rights are effectively held, if applicable;

(c) the date on which the threshold was reached or crossed; and

(d) the identity of the shareholder, even if that shareholder is not entitled to exercise voting rights under the conditions laid down in Article 10, and of the natural person or legal entity entitled to exercise voting rights on behalf of that shareholder.

2. The notification to the issuer shall be effected as soon as possible, but not later than four trading days, the first of which shall be the day after the date on which the shareholder, or the natural person or legal entity referred to in Article 10,

(a) learns of the acquisition or disposal or of the possibility of exercising voting rights, or on which, having regard to the circumstances, should have learned of it, regardless of the date on which the acquisition, disposal or possibility of exercising voting rights takes effect; or

(b) is informed about the event mentioned in Article 9(2).

3. An undertaking shall be exempted from making the required notification in accordance with paragraph 1 if the notification is made by the parent undertaking or, where the parent undertaking is itself a controlled undertaking, by its own parent undertaking.

4. The parent undertaking of a management company shall not be required to aggregate its holdings under Articles 9 and 10 with the holdings managed by the management company under the conditions laid down in Directive 85/611/EEC, provided such management company exercises its voting rights independently from the parent undertaking.

However, Articles 9 and 10 shall apply where the parent undertaking, or another controlled undertaking of the parent undertaking, has invested in holdings managed by such management company and the management company has no discretion to exercise the voting rights attached to such holdings and may only exercise such voting rights under direct or indirect instructions from the parent or another controlled undertaking of the parent undertaking.

5.　The parent undertaking of an investment firm authorised under Directive 2004/39/EC shall not be required to aggregate its holdings under Articles 9 and 10 with the holdings which such investment firm manages on a client-by-client basis within the meaning of Article 4(1), point 9, of Directive 2004/39/EC, provided that:

— the investment firm is authorised to provide such portfolio management under point 4 of Section A of Annex I to Directive 2004/39/EC;

— it may only exercise the voting rights attached to such shares under instructions given in writing or by electronic means or it ensures that individual portfolio management services are conducted independently of any other services under conditions equivalent to those provided for under Directive 85/611/EEC by putting into place appropriate mechanisms; and

— the investment firm exercises its voting rights independently from the parent undertaking.

However, Articles 9 and 10 shall apply where the parent undertaking, or another controlled undertaking of the parent undertaking, has invested in holdings managed by such investment firm and the investment firm has no discretion to exercise the voting rights attached to such holdings and may only exercise such voting rights under direct or indirect instructions from the parent or another controlled undertaking of the parent undertaking.

6.　Upon receipt of the notification under paragraph 1, but no later than three trading days thereafter, the issuer shall make public all the information contained in the notification.

7.　A home Member State may exempt issuers from the requirement in paragraph 6 if the information contained in the notification is made public by its competent authority, under the conditions laid down in Article 21, upon receipt of the notification, but no later than three trading days thereafter.

8.　In order to take account of technical developments on financial markets and to ensure the uniform application of paragraphs 1, 2, 4, 5 and 6 of this Article, the Commission shall ... adopt implementing measures:

(a)　to establish a standard form to be used throughout the Community when notifying the required information to the issuer under paragraph 1 or when filing information under Article 19(3);

(b)　to determine a calendar of "trading days" for all Member States;

(c)　to establish in which cases the shareholder, or the natural person or legal entity referred to in Article 10, or both, shall effect the necessary notification to the issuer;

(d)　to clarify the circumstances under which the shareholder, or the natural person or legal entity referred to in Article 10, should have learned of the acquisition or disposal;

(e)　to clarify the conditions of independence to be complied with by management companies and their parent undertakings or by investment firms and their parent undertakings to benefit from the exemptions in paragraphs 4 and 5.

[Those measures, designed to amend non-essential elements of this Directive by supplementing it, shall be adopted in accordance with the regulatory procedure with scrutiny referred to in Article 27(2a).]

[5677]

NOTES

Para 8: words omitted repealed, and words in square brackets inserted, by European Parliament and Council Directive 2008/22/EC, Art 1(4), as from 20 March 2008.

Article 13

1.　The notification requirements laid down in Article 9 shall also apply to a natural person or legal entity who holds, directly or indirectly, financial instruments that result in an entitlement to acquire, on such holder's own initiative alone, under a formal agreement, shares to which voting rights are attached, already issued, of an issuer whose shares are admitted to trading on a regulated market.

2.　The Commission shall ... adopt implementing measures in order to take account of technical developments in financial markets and to ensure the uniform application of paragraph 1. It shall in particular determine:

(a)　the types of financial instruments referred to in paragraph 1 and their aggregation;

(b)　the nature of the formal agreement referred to in paragraph 1;

(c)　the contents of the notification to be made, establishing a standard form to be used throughout the Community for that purpose;

(d)　the notification period;

(e)　to whom the notification is to be made.

[Those measures, designed to amend non-essential elements of this Directive by supplementing it, shall be adopted in accordance with the regulatory procedure with scrutiny referred to in Article 27(2a).]

[5678]

NOTES

Para 2: words omitted repealed, and words in square brackets inserted, by European Parliament and Council Directive 2008/22/EC, Art 1(5), as from 20 March 2008.

Article 14

1. Where an issuer of shares admitted to trading on a regulated market acquires or disposes of its own shares, either itself or through a person acting in his own name but on the issuer's behalf, the home Member State shall ensure that the issuer makes public the proportion of its own shares as soon as possible, but not later than four trading days following such acquisition or disposal where that proportion reaches, exceeds or falls below the thresholds of 5% or 10% of the voting rights. The proportion shall be calculated on the basis of the total number of shares to which voting rights are attached.

2. The Commission shall ... adopt implementing measures in order to take account of technical developments in financial markets and to ensure the uniform application of paragraph 1.

[Those measures, designed to amend non-essential elements of this Directive by supplementing it, shall be adopted in accordance with the regulatory procedure with scrutiny referred to in Article 27(2a).]

[5679]

NOTES

Para 2: words omitted repealed, and words in square brackets added, by European Parliament and Council Directive 2008/22/EC, Art 1(6), as from 20 March 2008.

Article 15

For the purpose of calculating the thresholds provided for in Article 9, the home Member State shall at least require the disclosure to the public by the issuer of the total number of voting rights and capital at the end of each calendar month during which an increase or decrease of such total number has occurred.

[5680]

Article 16
Additional information

1. The issuer of shares admitted to trading on a regulated market shall make public without delay any change in the rights attaching to the various classes of shares, including changes in the rights attaching to derivative securities issued by the issuer itself and giving access to the shares of that issuer.

2. The issuer of securities, other than shares admitted to trading on a regulated market, shall make public without delay any changes in the rights of holders of securities other than shares, including changes in the terms and conditions of these securities which could indirectly affect those rights, resulting in particular from a change in loan terms or in interest rates.

3. The issuer of securities admitted to trading on a regulated market shall make public without delay of new loan issues and in particular of any guarantee or security in respect thereof. Without prejudice to Directive 2003/6/EC, this paragraph shall not apply to a public international body of which at least one Member State is member.

[5681]

SECTION II
INFORMATION FOR HOLDERS OF SECURITIES ADMITTED TO TRADING ON A REGULATED MARKET

Article 17
Information requirements for issuers whose shares are admitted to trading on a regulated market

1. The issuer of shares admitted to trading on a regulated market shall ensure equal treatment for all holders of shares who are in the same position.

2. The issuer shall ensure that all the facilities and information necessary to enable holders of shares to exercise their rights are available in the home Member State and that the integrity of data is preserved. Shareholders shall not be prevented from exercising their rights by proxy, subject to the law of the country in which the issuer is incorporated. In particular, the issuer shall:
   (a)   provide information on the place, time and agenda of meetings, the total number of shares and voting rights and the rights of holders to participate in meetings;

(b)   make available a proxy form, on paper or, where applicable, by electronic means, to each person entitled to vote at a shareholders' meeting, together with the notice concerning the meeting or, on request, after an announcement of the meeting;

(c)   designate as its agent a financial institution through which shareholders may exercise their financial rights; and

(d)   publish notices or distribute circulars concerning the allocation and payment of dividends and the issue of new shares, including information on any arrangements for allotment, subscription, cancellation or conversion.

3.   For the purposes of conveying information to shareholders, the home Member State shall allow issuers the use of electronic means, provided such a decision is taken in a general meeting and meets at least the following conditions:

(a)   the use of electronic means shall in no way depend upon the location of the seat or residence of the shareholder or, in the cases referred to in Article 10(a) to (h), of the natural persons or legal entities;

(b)   identification arrangements shall be put in place so that the shareholders, or the natural persons or legal entities entitled to exercise or to direct the exercise of voting rights, are effectively informed;

(c)   shareholders, or in the cases referred to in Article 10(a) to (e) the natural persons or legal entities entitled to acquire, dispose of or exercise voting rights, shall be contacted in writing to request their consent for the use of electronic means for conveying information and, if they do not object within a reasonable period of time, their consent shall be deemed to be given. They shall be able to request, at any time in the future, that information be conveyed in writing, and

(d)   any apportionment of the costs entailed in the conveyance of such information by electronic means shall be determined by the issuer in compliance with the principle of equal treatment laid down in paragraph 1.

4.   The Commission shall … adopt implementing measures in order to take account of technical developments in financial markets, to take account of developments in information and communication technology and to ensure the uniform application of paragraphs 1, 2 and 3. It shall, in particular, specify the types of financial institution through which a shareholder may exercise the financial rights provided for in paragraph 2(c).

[Those measures, designed to amend non-essential elements of this Directive by supplementing it, shall be adopted in accordance with the regulatory procedure with scrutiny referred to in Article 27(2a).]

[5682]

NOTES

   Para 4: words omitted repealed, and words in square brackets inserted, by European Parliament and Council Directive 2008/22/EC, Art 1(6), as from 20 March 2008. Note that Art 1(6) provides that the words ", in accordance with the procedure referred to in Article 27(2)," should be deleted from this paragraph, but the actual words in the original read ", in accordance with the procedure provided for in Article 27(2),". It is assumed that this is a drafting error and the amendment has been incorporated.

Article 18
Information requirements for issuers whose debt securities are admitted to trading on a regulated market

1.   The issuer of debt securities admitted to trading on a regulated market shall ensure that all holders of debt securities ranking pari passu are given equal treatment in respect of all the rights attaching to those debt securities.

2.   The issuer shall ensure that all the facilities and information necessary to enable debt securities holders to exercise their rights are publicly available in the home Member State and that the integrity of data is preserved. Debt securities holders shall not be prevented from exercising their rights by proxy, subject to the law of country in which the issuer is incorporated. In particular, the issuer shall:

(a)   publish notices, or distribute circulars, concerning the place, time and agenda of meetings of debt securities holders, the payment of interest, the exercise of any conversion, exchange, subscription or cancellation rights, and repayment, as well as the right of those holders to participate therein;

(b)   make available a proxy form on paper or, where applicable, by electronic means, to each person entitled to vote at a meeting of debt securities holders, together with the notice concerning the meeting or, on request, after an announcement of the meeting; and

(c)   designate as its agent a financial institution through which debt securities holders may exercise their financial rights.

3.   If only holders of debt securities whose denomination per unit amounts to at least EUR 50,000 or, in the case of debt securities denominated in a currency other than Euro whose denomination per unit is, at the date of the issue, equivalent to at least EUR 50,000, are to be invited

to a meeting, the issuer may choose as venue any Member State, provided that all the facilities and information necessary to enable such holders to exercise their rights are made available in that Member State.

4.   For the purposes of conveying information to debt securities holders, the home Member State, or the Member State chosen by the issuer pursuant to paragraph 3, shall allow issuers the use of electronic means, provided such a decision is taken in a general meeting and meets at least the following conditions:

(a)   the use of electronic means shall in no way depend upon the location of the seat or residence of the debt security holder or of a proxy representing that holder;

(b)   identification arrangements shall be put in place so that debt securities holders are effectively informed;

(c)   debt securities holders shall be contacted in writing to request their consent for the use of electronic means for conveying information and if they do not object within a reasonable period of time, their consent shall be deemed to be given. They shall be able to request, at any time in the future, that information be conveyed in writing; and

(d)   any apportionment of the costs entailed in the conveyance of information by electronic means shall be determined by the issuer in compliance with the principle of equal treatment laid down in paragraph 1.

5.   The Commission shall … adopt implementing measures in order to take account of technical developments in financial markets, to take account of developments in information and communication technology and to ensure the uniform application of paragraphs 1 to 4. It shall, in particular, specify the types of financial institution through which a debt security holder may exercise the financial rights provided for in paragraph 2(c).

[Those measures, designed to amend non-essential elements of this Directive by supplementing it, shall be adopted in accordance with the regulatory procedure with scrutiny referred to in Article 27(2a).]

[5683]

NOTES

Para 5: words omitted repealed, and words in square brackets inserted, by European Parliament and Council Directive 2008/22/EC, Art 1(6), as from 20 March 2008. Note that Art 1(6) provides that the words ", in accordance with the procedure referred to in Article 27(2),"should be deleted from this paragraph, but the actual words in the original read ", in accordance with the procedure provided for in Article 27(2),". It is assumed that this is a drafting error and the amendment has been incorporated.

CHAPTER IV
GENERAL OBLIGATIONS

Article 19
Home Member State control

1.   Whenever the issuer, or any person having requested, without the issuer's consent, the admission of its securities to trading on a regulated market, discloses regulated information, it shall at the same time file that information with the competent authority of its home Member State. That competent authority may decide to publish such filed information on its Internet site.

Where an issuer proposes to amend its instrument of incorporation or statutes, it shall communicate the draft amendment to the competent authority of the home Member State and to the regulated market to which its securities have been admitted to trading. Such communication shall be effected without delay, but at the latest on the date of calling the general meeting which is to vote on, or be informed of, the amendment.

2.   The home Member State may exempt an issuer from the requirement under paragraph 1 in respect of information disclosed in accordance with Article 6 of Directive 2003/6/EC or Article 12(6) of this Directive.

3.   Information to be notified to the issuer in accordance with Articles 9, 10, 12 and 13 shall at the same time be filed with the competent authority of the home Member State.

4.   In order to ensure the uniform application of paragraphs 1, 2 and 3, the Commission shall … adopt implementing measures.

The Commission shall, in particular, specify the procedure in accordance with which an issuer, a holder of shares or other financial instruments, or a person or entity referred to in Article 10, is to file information with the competent authority of the home Member State under paragraphs 1 or 3, respectively, in order to:

(a)   enable filing by electronic means in the home Member State;

(b)   coordinate the filing of the annual financial report referred to in Article 4 of this Directive with the filing of the annual information referred to in Article 10 of Directive 2003/71/EC.

[The measures referred to in the first and second subparagraphs, designed to amend non-essential elements of this Directive by supplementing it, shall be adopted in accordance with the regulatory procedure with scrutiny referred to in Article 27(2a).]

[5684]

NOTES

Para 4: words omitted repealed, and words in square brackets added, by European Parliament and Council Directive 2008/22/EC, Art 1(7), as from 20 March 2008.

Article 20
Languages

1. Where securities are admitted to trading on a regulated market only in the home Member State, regulated information shall be disclosed in a language accepted by the competent authority in the home Member State.

2. Where securities are admitted to trading on a regulated market both in the home Member State and in one or more host Member States, regulated information shall be disclosed:
   (a) in a language accepted by the competent authority in the home Member State; and
   (b) depending on the choice of the issuer, either in a language accepted by the competent authorities of those host Member States or in a language customary in the sphere of international finance.

3. Where securities are admitted to trading on a regulated market in one or more host Member States, but not in the home Member State, regulated information shall, depending on the choice of the issuer, be disclosed either in a language accepted by the competent authorities of those host Member States or in a language customary in the sphere of international finance.

In addition, the home Member State may lay down in its law, regulations or administrative provisions that the regulated information shall, depending on the choice of the issuer, be disclosed either in a language accepted by its competent authority or in a language customary in the sphere of international finance.

4. Where securities are admitted to trading on a regulated market without the issuer's consent, the obligations under paragraphs 1, 2 and 3 shall be incumbent not upon the issuer, but upon the person who, without the issuer's consent, has requested such admission.

5. Member States shall allow shareholders and the natural person or legal entity referred to in Articles 9, 10 and 13 to notify information to an issuer under this Directive only in a language customary in the sphere of international finance. If the issuer receives such a notification, Member States may not require the issuer to provide a translation into a language accepted by the competent authorities.

6. By way of derogation from paragraphs 1 to 4, where securities whose denomination per unit amounts to at least EUR 50,000 or, in the case of debt securities denominated in a currency other than Euro equivalent to at least EUR 50,000 at the date of the issue, are admitted to trading on a regulated market in one or more Member States, regulated information shall be disclosed to the public either in a language accepted by the competent authorities of the home and host Member States or in a language customary in the sphere of international finance, at the choice of the issuer or of the person who, without the issuer's consent, has requested such admission.

7. If an action concerning the content of regulated information is brought before a court or tribunal in a Member State, responsibility for the payment of costs incurred in the translation of that information for the purposes of the proceedings shall be decided in accordance with the law of that Member State.

[5685]

Article 21
Access to regulated information

1. The home Member State shall ensure that the issuer, or the person who has applied for admission to trading on a regulated market without the issuer's consent, discloses regulated information in a manner ensuring fast access to such information on a non-discriminatory basis and makes it available to the officially appointed mechanism referred to in paragraph 2. The issuer, or the person who has applied for admission to trading on a regulated market without the issuer's consent, may not charge investors any specific cost for providing the information. The home Member State shall require the issuer to use such media as may reasonably be relied upon for the effective dissemination of information to the public throughout the Community. The home Member State may not impose an obligation to use only media whose operators are established on its territory.

2. The home Member State shall ensure that there is at least one officially appointed mechanism for the central storage of regulated information. These mechanisms should comply with minimum quality standards of security, certainty as to the information source, time recording and easy access by end users and shall be aligned with the filing procedure under Article 19(1).

PART IV
EC MATERIALS

3. Where securities are admitted to trading on a regulated market in only one host Member State and not in the home Member State, the host Member State shall ensure disclosure of regulated information in accordance with the requirements referred to in paragraph 1.

4. In order to take account of technical developments in financial markets, to take account of developments in information and communication technology and to ensure the uniform application of paragraphs 1, 2 and 3, the Commission shall adopt implementing measures …

The Commission shall in particular specify:
   (a)   minimum standards for the dissemination of regulated information, as referred to in paragraph 1;
   (b)   minimum standards for the central storage mechanism as referred to in paragraph 2.

The Commission may also specify and update a list of media for the dissemination of information to the public.

[The measures referred to in the first, second and third subparagraphs, designed to amend non-essential elements of this Directive by supplementing it, shall be adopted in accordance with the regulatory procedure with scrutiny referred to in Article 27(2a).]

[5686]

NOTES
   Para 4: words omitted repealed, and words in square brackets inserted, by European Parliament and Council Directive 2008/22/EC, Art 1(8), as from 20 March 2008.

Article 22
Guidelines

1. The competent authorities of the Member States shall draw up appropriate guidelines with a view to further facilitating public access to information to be disclosed under Directive 2003/6/EC, Directive 2003/71/EC and this Directive.

The aim of those guidelines shall be the creation of:
   (a)   an electronic network to be set up at national level between national securities regulators, operators of regulated markets and national company registers covered by the First Council Directive 68/151/EEC of 9 March 1968 on coordination of safeguards which, for the protection of the interests of members and others, are required by Member States of companies within the meaning of the second paragraph of Article 48[1] of the Treaty, with a view to making such safeguards equivalent throughout the Community;[2] and
   (b)   a single electronic network, or a platform of electronic networks across Member States.

2. The Commission shall review the results achieved under paragraph 1 by 31 December 2006 and may, in accordance with the procedure referred to in Article 27(2), adopt implementing measures to facilitate compliance with Articles 19 and 21.

[5687]

NOTES
   [1]   The title has been adjusted to take account of the renumbering of the Articles of the Treaty establishing the European Community in accordance with Article 12 of the Treaty of Amsterdam; the original reference was to Article 58 of the Treaty.
   [2]   OJ L65, 14.3.1968, p 8. Directive as last amended by Directive 2003/58/EC of the European Parliament and of the Council (OJ L221, 4.9.2003, p 13).

Article 23
Third countries

1. Where the registered office of an issuer is in a third country, the competent authority of the home Member State may exempt that issuer from requirements under Articles 4 to 7 and Articles 12(6), 14, 15 and 16 to 18, provided that the law of the third country in question lays down equivalent requirements or such an issuer complies with requirements of the law of a third country that the competent authority of the home Member State considers as equivalent.

However, the information covered by the requirements laid down in the third country shall be filed in accordance with Article 19 and disclosed in accordance with Articles 20 and 21.

2. By way of derogation from paragraph 1, an issuer whose registered office is in a third country shall be exempted from preparing its financial statement in accordance with Article 4 or Article 5 prior to the financial year starting on or after 1 January 2007, provided such issuer prepares its financial statements in accordance with internationally accepted standards referred to in Article 9 of Regulation (EC) No 1606/2002.

3.   The competent authority of the home Member State shall ensure that information disclosed in a third country which may be of importance for the public in the Community is disclosed in accordance with Articles 20 and 21, even if such information is not regulated information within the meaning of Article 2(1)(k).

4.   In order to ensure the uniform application of paragraph 1, the Commission shall, in accordance with the procedure referred to in Article 27(2), adopt implementing measures

    (i)   setting up a mechanism ensuring the establishment of equivalence of information required under this Directive, including financial statements and information, including financial statements, required under the law, regulations or administrative provisions of a third country;

    (ii) stating that, by reason of its domestic law, regulations, administrative provisions, or of the practices or procedures based on the international standards set by international organisations, the third country where the issuer is registered ensures the equivalence of the information requirements provided for in this Directive.

[In the context of point (ii) of the first subparagraph, the Commission shall also adopt implementing measures concerning the assessment of standards relevant to the issuers of more than one country. Those measures, designed to amend non-essential elements of this Directive by supplementing it, shall be adopted in accordance with the regulatory procedure with scrutiny referred to in Article 27(2a).]

The Commission shall, in accordance with the procedure referred to in Article 27(2), take the necessary decisions on the equivalence of accounting standards which are used by third country issuers under the conditions set out in Article 30(3) at the latest five years following the date referred to in Article 31. If the Commission decides that the accounting standards of a third country are not equivalent, it may allow the issuers concerned to continue using such accounting standards during an appropriate transitional period.

[In the context of the previous subparagraph, the Commission shall also adopt implementing measures aimed at establishing general equivalence criteria regarding accounting standards relevant to issuers of more than one country. Those measures, designed to amend non-essential elements of this Directive by supplementing it, shall be adopted in accordance with the regulatory procedure with scrutiny referred to in Article 27(2a).]

5.   In order to ensure uniform application of paragraph 2, the Commission may ... adopt implementing measures defining the type of information disclosed in a third country that is of importance to the public in the Community. [Those measures, designed to amend non-essential elements of this Directive by supplementing it, shall be adopted in accordance with the regulatory procedure with scrutiny referred to in Article 27(2a).]

6.   Undertakings whose registered office is in a third country which would have required an authorisation in accordance with Article 5(1) of Directive 85/611/EEC or, with regard to portfolio management under point 4 of section A of Annex I to Directive 2004/39/EC if it had its registered office or, only in the case of an investment firm, its head office within the Community, shall also be exempted from aggregating holdings with the holdings of its parent undertaking under the requirements laid down in Article 12(4) and (5) provided that they comply with equivalent conditions of independence as management companies or investment firms.

7.   In order to take account of technical developments in financial markets and to ensure the uniform application of paragraph 6, the Commission shall, in accordance with the procedure referred to in Article 27(2), adopt implementing measures stating that, by reason of its domestic law, regulations, or administrative provisions, a third country ensures the equivalence of the independence requirements provided for under this Directive and its implementing measures.

[The Commission shall also adopt implementing measures aimed at establishing general equivalence criteria for the purpose of the first subparagraph. Those measures, designed to amend non-essential elements of this Directive by supplementing it, shall be adopted in accordance with the regulatory procedure with scrutiny referred to in Article 27(2a).]

[5688]

NOTES

   Words omitted repealed, and words in square brackets inserted, by European Parliament and Council Directive 2008/22/EC, Art 1(9), as from 20 March 2008.

CHAPTER V
COMPETENT AUTHORITIES

Article 24
Competent authorities and their powers

1.   Each Member State shall designate the central authority referred to in Article 21(1) of Directive 2003/71/EC as central competent administrative authority responsible for carrying out the

obligations provided for in this Directive and for ensuring that the provisions adopted pursuant to this Directive are applied. Member States shall inform the Commission accordingly.

However, for the purpose of paragraph 4(h) Member States may designate a competent authority other than the central competent authority referred to in the first subparagraph.

2. Member States may allow their central competent authority to delegate tasks. Except for the tasks referred to in paragraph 4(h), any delegation of tasks relating to the obligations provided for in this Directive and in its implementing measures shall be reviewed five years after the entry into force of this Directive and shall end eight years after the entry into force of this Directive. Any delegation of tasks shall be made in a specific manner stating the tasks to be undertaken and the conditions under which they are to be carried out.

Those conditions shall include a clause requiring the entity in question to be organised in a manner such that conflicts of interest are avoided and information obtained from carrying out the delegated tasks is not used unfairly or to prevent competition. In any case, the final responsibility for supervising compliance with the provisions of this Directive and implementing measures adopted pursuant thereto shall lie with the competent authority designated in accordance with paragraph 1.

3. Member States shall inform the Commission and competent authorities of other Member States of any arrangements entered into with regard to the delegation of tasks, including the precise conditions for regulating the delegations.

4. Each competent authority shall have all the powers necessary for the performance of its functions. It shall at least be empowered to:
    (a)   require auditors, issuers, holders of shares or other financial instruments, or persons or entities referred to in Articles 10 or 13, and the persons that control them or are controlled by them, to provide information and documents;
    (b)   require the issuer to disclose the information required under point (a) to the public by the means and within the time limits the authority considers necessary. It may publish such information on its own initiative in the event that the issuer, or the persons that control it or are controlled by it, fail to do so and after having heard the issuer;
    (c)   require managers of the issuers and of the holders of shares or other financial instruments, or of persons or entities referred to in Articles 10 or 13, to notify the information required under this Directive, or under national law adopted in accordance with this Directive, and, if necessary, to provide further information and documents;
    (d)   suspend, or request the relevant regulated market to suspend, trading in securities for a maximum of ten days at a time if it has reasonable grounds for suspecting that the provisions of this Directive, or of national law adopted in accordance with this Directive, have been infringed by the issuer;
    (e)   prohibit trading on a regulated market if it finds that the provisions of this Directive, or of national law adopted in accordance with this Directive, have been infringed, or if it has reasonable grounds for suspecting that the provisions of this Directive have been infringed;
    (f)   monitor that the issuer discloses timely information with the objective of ensuring effective and equal access to the public in all Member States where the securities are traded and take appropriate action if that is not the case;
    (g)   make public the fact that an issuer, or a holder of shares or other financial instruments, or a person or entity referred to in Articles 10 or 13, is failing to comply with its obligations;
    (h)   examine that information referred to in this Directive is drawn up in accordance with the relevant reporting framework and take appropriate measures in case of discovered infringements; and
    (i)   carry out on-site inspections in its territory in accordance with national law, in order to verify compliance with the provisions of this Directive and its implementing measures. Where necessary under national law, the competent authority or authorities may use this power by applying to the relevant judicial authority and/or in cooperation with other authorities.

5. Paragraphs 1 to 4 shall be without prejudice to the possibility for a Member State to make separate legal and administrative arrangements for overseas European territories for whose external relations that Member State is responsible.

6. The disclosure to competent authorities by the auditors of any fact or decision related to the requests made by the competent authority under paragraph (4)(a) shall not constitute a breach of any restriction on disclosure of information imposed by contract or by any law, regulation or administrative provision and shall not involve such auditors in liability of any kind.

[5689]

Article 25
Professional secrecy and cooperation between Member States

1.   The obligation of professional secrecy shall apply to all persons who work or who have worked for the competent authority and for entities to which competent authorities may have delegated certain tasks. Information covered by professional secrecy may not be disclosed to any other person or authority except by virtue of the laws, regulations or administrative provisions of a Member State.

2.   Competent authorities of the Member States shall cooperate with each other, whenever necessary, for the purpose of carrying out their duties and making use of their powers, whether set out in this Directive or in national law adopted pursuant to this Directive. Competent authorities shall render assistance to competent authorities of other Member States.

3.   Paragraph 1 shall not prevent the competent authorities from exchanging confidential information. Information thus exchanged shall be covered by the obligation of professional secrecy to which the persons employed or formerly employed by the competent authorities receiving the information are subject.

4.   Member States may conclude cooperation agreements providing for the exchange of information with the competent authorities or bodies of third countries enabled by their respective legislation to carry out any of the tasks assigned by this Directive to the competent authorities in accordance with Article 24. Such an exchange of information is subject to guarantees of professional secrecy at least equivalent to those referred to in this Article. Such exchange of information shall be intended for the performance of the supervisory task of the authorities or bodies mentioned. Where the information originates in another Member State, it may not be disclosed without the express agreement of the competent authorities which have disclosed it and, where appropriate, solely for the purposes for which those authorities gave their agreement.

[5690]

Article 26
Precautionary measures

1.   Where the competent authority of a host Member State finds that the issuer or the holder of shares or other financial instruments, or the person or entity referred to in Article 10, has committed irregularities or infringed its obligations, it shall refer its findings to the competent authority of the home Member State.

2.   If, despite the measures taken by the competent authority of the home Member State, or because such measures prove inadequate, the issuer or the security holder persists in infringing the relevant legal or regulatory provisions, the competent authority of the host Member State shall, after informing the competent authority of the home Member State, take, in accordance with Article 3(2), all the appropriate measures in order to protect investors. The Commission shall be informed of such measures at the earliest opportunity.

[5691]

CHAPTER VI
IMPLEMENTING MEASURES

Article 27
Committee procedure

1.   The Commission shall be assisted by the European Securities Committee, instituted by Article 1 of Decision 2001/528/EC.

2.   Where reference is made to this paragraph, Articles 5 and 7 of Decision 1999/468/EC shall apply, having regard to the provisions of Article 8 thereof, provided that the implementing measures adopted in accordance with that procedure do not modify the essential provisions of this Directive.

The period laid down in Article 5(6) of Decision 1999/468/EC shall be set at three months.

[2a.   Where reference is made to this paragraph, Article 5a(1) to (4) and Article 7 of Decision 1999/468/EC shall apply, having regard to the provisions of Article 8 thereof.]

[3.   By 31 December 2010, and, thereafter, at least every three years, the Commission shall review the provisions concerning its implementing powers and present a report to the European Parliament and to the Council on the functioning of those powers. The report shall examine, in particular, the need for the Commission to propose amendments to this Directive in order to ensure the appropriate scope of the implementing powers conferred on the Commission. The conclusion as to whether or not amendment is necessary shall be accompanied by a detailed statement of reasons. If necessary, the report shall be accompanied by a legislative proposal to amend the provisions conferring implementing powers on the Commission.]

[5692]

NOTES

Para 2a inserted, and para 3 substituted (for original paras 3, 4), by European Parliament and Council Directive 2008/22/EC, Art 1(10), as from 20 March 2008.

Article 28
Penalties

1. Without prejudice to the right of Member States to impose criminal penalties, Member States shall ensure, in conformity with their national law, that at least the appropriate administrative measures may be taken or civil and/or administrative penalties imposed in respect of the persons responsible, where the provisions adopted in accordance with this Directive have not been complied with. Member States shall ensure that those measures are effective, proportionate and dissuasive.

2. Member States shall provide that the competent authority may disclose to the public every measure taken or penalty imposed for infringement of the provisions adopted in accordance with this Directive, save where such disclosure would seriously jeopardise the financial markets or cause disproportionate damage to the parties involved.

[5693]

Article 29
Right of appeal

Member States shall ensure that decisions taken under laws, regulations, and administrative provisions adopted in accordance with this Directive are subject to the right of appeal to the courts.

[5694]

CHAPTER VII
TRANSITIONAL AND FINAL PROVISIONS

Article 30
Transitional provisions

1. By way of derogation from Article 5(3) of this Directive, the home Member State may exempt from disclosing financial statements in accordance with Regulation (EC) No 1606/2002 issuers referred to in Article 9 of that Regulation for the financial year starting on or after 1 January 2006.

2. Notwithstanding Article 12(2), a shareholder shall notify the issuer at the latest two months after the date in Article 31(1) of the proportion of voting rights and capital it holds, in accordance with Articles 9, 10 and 13, with issuers at that date, unless it has already made a notification containing equivalent information before that date.

Notwithstanding Article 12(6), an issuer shall in turn disclose the information received in those notifications no later than three months after the date in Article 31(1).

3. Where an issuer is incorporated in a third country, the home Member State may exempt such issuer only in respect of those debt securities which have already been admitted to trading on a regulated market in the Community prior to 1 January 2005 from drawing up its financial statements in accordance with Article 4(3) and its management report in accordance with Article 4(5) as long as

(a) the competent authority of the home Member State acknowledges that annual financial statements prepared by issuers from such a third country give a true and fair view of the issuer's assets and liabilities, financial position and results;

(b) the third country where the issuer is incorporated has not made mandatory the application of international accounting standards referred to in Article 2 of Regulation (EC) No 1606/2002; and

(c) the Commission has not taken any decision in accordance with Article 23(4)(ii) as to whether there is an equivalence between the abovementioned accounting standards and

— the accounting standards laid down in the law, regulations or administrative provisions of the third country where the issuer is incorporated, or

— the accounting standards of a third country such an issuer has elected to comply with.

4. The home Member State may exempt issuers only in respect of those debt securities which have already been admitted to trading on a regulated market in the Community prior to 1 January 2005 from disclosing half-yearly financial report in accordance with Article 5 for 10 years following 1 January 2005, provided that the home Member State had decided to allow such issuers to benefit from the provisions of Article 27 of Directive 2001/34/EC at the point of admission of those debt securities.

[5695]

Article 31
Transposition

1.   Member States shall take the necessary measures to comply with this Directive by 20 January 2007. They shall forthwith inform the Commission thereof.

When Member States adopt these measures, they shall contain a reference to this Directive or shall be accompanied by such reference on the occasion of their official publication. The methods of making such reference shall be laid down by Member States.

2.   Where Member States adopt measures pursuant to Articles 3(1), 8(2), 8(3), 9(6) or 30, they shall immediately communicate those measures to the Commission and to the other Member States.

[5696]

Article 32
Amendments

With effect from the date specified in Article 31(1), Directive 2001/34/EC shall be amended as follows:
(1)   In Article 1, points (g) and (h) shall be deleted;
(2)   Article 4 shall be deleted;
(3)   In Article 6, paragraph 2 shall be deleted;
(4)   In Article 8, paragraph 2 shall be replaced by the following:

   "2.   Member States may make the issuers of securities admitted to official listing subject to additional obligations, provided that those additional obligations apply generally for all issuers or for individual classes of issuers.".
(5)   Articles 65 to 97 shall be deleted;
(6)   Articles 102 and 103 shall be deleted;
(7)   In Article 107(3), the second subparagraph shall be deleted;
(8)   In Article 108, paragraph 2 shall be amended as follows:
   (a)   in point (a), the words "periodic information to be published by the companies of which shares are admitted" shall be deleted;
   (b)   point (b) shall be deleted;
   (c)   point (c)(iii) shall be deleted;
   (d)   point (d) shall be deleted.

References made to the repealed provisions shall be construed as being made to the provisions of this Directive.

[5697]

Article 33
Review

The Commission shall by 30 June 2009 report on the operation of this Directive to the European Parliament and to the Council including the appropriateness of ending the exemption for existing debt securities after the 10-year period as provided for by Article 30(4) and its potential impact on the European financial markets.

[5698]

Article 34
Entry into force

This Directive shall enter into force on the twentieth day following that of its publication in the Official Journal of the European Union.

[5699]

Article 35
Addressees

This Directive is addressed to the Member States.

[5700]–[5721]

DIRECTIVE OF THE EUROPEAN PARLIAMENT AND OF THE COUNCIL

of 26 October 2005

on the prevention of the use of the financial system for the purpose of money laundering and terrorist financing

(2005/60/EC)

(Text with EEA relevance)

NOTES

Date of publication in OJ: OJ L309, 25.11.2005, p 15. Notes are as in the original OJ version.

This Directive is reproduced as amended by: European Parliament and Council Directive 2007/64/EC (OJ L319, 5.12.2007, p 1); European Parliament and Council Directive 2008/20/EC (OJ L76, 19.3.2008, p 46).

Proposed amendment of this Directive: see the 2008 Proposal for a Directive of the European Parliament and of the Council on the taking up, pursuit and prudential supervision of the business of electronic money institutions, amending Directives 2005/60/EC and 2006/48/EC and repealing Directive 2000/46/EC.[1]

[1] Brussels, 9.10.2008, COM(2008) 627 final. Available on the Europa website.

THE EUROPEAN PARLIAMENT AND THE COUNCIL OF THE EUROPEAN UNION,

Having regard to the Treaty establishing the European Community, and in particular Article 47(2), first and third sentences, and Article 95 thereof,

Having regard to the proposal from the Commission,

Having regard to the opinion of the European Economic and Social Committee,[1]

Having regard to the opinion of the European Central Bank,[2]

Acting in accordance with the procedure laid down in Article 251 of the Treaty,[3]

Whereas:

(1) Massive flows of dirty money can damage the stability and reputation of the financial sector and threaten the single market, and terrorism shakes the very foundations of our society. In addition to the criminal law approach, a preventive effort via the financial system can produce results.

(2) The soundness, integrity and stability of credit and financial institutions and confidence in the financial system as a whole could be seriously jeopardised by the efforts of criminals and their associates either to disguise the origin of criminal proceeds or to channel lawful or unlawful money for terrorist purposes. In order to avoid Member States' adopting measures to protect their financial systems which could be inconsistent with the functioning of the internal market and with the prescriptions of the rule of law and Community public policy, Community action in this area is necessary.

(3) In order to facilitate their criminal activities, money launderers and terrorist financers could try to take advantage of the freedom of capital movements and the freedom to supply financial services which the integrated financial area entails, if certain coordinating measures are not adopted at Community level.

(4) In order to respond to these concerns in the field of money laundering, Council Directive 91/308/EEC of 10 June 1991 on prevention of the use of the financial system for the purpose of money laundering[4] was adopted. It required Member States to prohibit money laundering and to oblige the financial sector, comprising credit institutions and a wide range of other financial institutions, to identify their customers, keep appropriate records, establish internal procedures to train staff and guard against money laundering and to report any indications of money laundering to the competent authorities.

(5) Money laundering and terrorist financing are frequently carried out in an international context. Measures adopted solely at national or even Community level, without taking account of international coordination and cooperation, would have very limited effects. The measures adopted by the Community in this field should therefore be consistent with other action undertaken in other international fora. The Community action should continue to take particular account of the Recommendations of the Financial Action Task Force (hereinafter referred to as the FATF), which constitutes the foremost international body active in the fight against money laundering and terrorist financing. Since the FATF Recommendations were substantially revised and expanded in 2003, this Directive should be in line with that new international standard.

(6) The General Agreement on Trade in Services (GATS) allows Members to adopt measures necessary to protect public morals and prevent fraud and adopt measures for prudential reasons, including for ensuring the stability and integrity of the financial system.

(7) Although initially limited to drugs offences, there has been a trend in recent years towards a much wider definition of money laundering based on a broader range of predicate offences. A wider range of predicate offences facilitates the reporting of suspicious transactions and international cooperation in this area. Therefore, the definition of serious crime should be brought into line with

the definition of serious crime in Council Framework Decision 2001/500/JHA of 26 June 2001 on money laundering, the identification, tracing, freezing, seizing and confiscation of instrumentalities and the proceeds of crime.[5]

(8)   Furthermore, the misuse of the financial system to channel criminal or even clean money to terrorist purposes poses a clear risk to the integrity, proper functioning, reputation and stability of the financial system. Accordingly, the preventive measures of this Directive should cover not only the manipulation of money derived from crime but also the collection of money or property for terrorist purposes.

(9)   Directive 91/308/EEC, though imposing a customer identification obligation, contained relatively little detail on the relevant procedures. In view of the crucial importance of this aspect of the prevention of money laundering and terrorist financing, it is appropriate, in accordance with the new international standards, to introduce more specific and detailed provisions relating to the identification of the customer and of any beneficial owner and the verification of their identity. To that end a precise definition of "beneficial owner" is essential. Where the individual beneficiaries of a legal entity or arrangement such as a foundation or trust are yet to be determined, and it is therefore impossible to identify an individual as the beneficial owner, it would suffice to identify the class of persons intended to be the beneficiaries of the foundation or trust. This requirement should not include the identification of the individuals within that class of persons.

(10)   The institutions and persons covered by this Directive should, in conformity with this Directive, identify and verify the identity of the beneficial owner. To fulfil this requirement, it should be left to those institutions and persons whether they make use of public records of beneficial owners, ask their clients for relevant data or obtain the information otherwise, taking into account the fact that the extent of such customer due diligence measures relates to the risk of money laundering and terrorist financing, which depends on the type of customer, business relationship, product or transaction.

(11)   Credit agreements in which the credit account serves exclusively to settle the loan and the repayment of the loan is effected from an account which was opened in the name of the customer with a credit institution covered by this Directive pursuant to Article 8(1)(a) to (c) should generally be considered as an example of types of less risky transactions.

(12)   To the extent that the providers of the property of a legal entity or arrangement have significant control over the use of the property they should be identified as a beneficial owner.

(13)   Trust relationships are widely used in commercial products as an internationally recognised feature of the comprehensively supervised wholesale financial markets. An obligation to identify the beneficial owner does not arise from the fact alone that there is a trust relationship in this particular case.

(14)   This Directive should also apply to those activities of the institutions and persons covered hereunder which are performed on the Internet.

(15)   As the tightening of controls in the financial sector has prompted money launderers and terrorist financers to seek alternative methods for concealing the origin of the proceeds of crime and as such channels can be used for terrorist financing, the anti-money laundering and anti-terrorist financing obligations should cover life insurance intermediaries and trust and company service providers.

(16)   Entities already falling under the legal responsibility of an insurance undertaking, and therefore falling within the scope of this Directive, should not be included within the category of insurance intermediary.

(17)   Acting as a company director or secretary does not of itself make someone a trust and company service provider. For that reason, the definition covers only those persons that act as a company director or secretary for a third party and by way of business.

(18)   The use of large cash payments has repeatedly proven to be very vulnerable to money laundering and terrorist financing. Therefore, in those Member States that allow cash payments above the established threshold, all natural or legal persons trading in goods by way of business should be covered by this Directive when accepting such cash payments. Dealers in high-value goods, such as precious stones or metals, or works of art, and auctioneers are in any event covered by this Directive to the extent that payments to them are made in cash in an amount of EUR 15,000 or more. To ensure effective monitoring of compliance with this Directive by that potentially wide group of institutions and persons, Member States may focus their monitoring activities in particular on those natural and legal persons trading in goods that are exposed to a relatively high risk of money laundering or terrorist financing, in accordance with the principle of risk-based supervision. In view of the different situations in the various Member States, Member States may decide to adopt stricter provisions, in order to properly address the risk involved with large cash payments.

(19)   Directive 91/308/EEC brought notaries and other independent legal professionals within the scope of the Community anti-money laundering regime; this coverage should be maintained unchanged in this Directive; these legal professionals, as defined by the Member States, are subject to the provisions of this Directive when participating in financial or corporate transactions, including providing tax advice, where there is the greatest risk of the services of those legal professionals being misused for the purpose of laundering the proceeds of criminal activity or for the purpose of terrorist financing.

PART IV
EC MATERIALS

(20) Where independent members of professions providing legal advice which are legally recognised and controlled, such as lawyers, are ascertaining the legal position of a client or representing a client in legal proceedings, it would not be appropriate under this Directive to put those legal professionals in respect of these activities under an obligation to report suspicions of money laundering or terrorist financing. There must be exemptions from any obligation to report information obtained either before, during or after judicial proceedings, or in the course of ascertaining the legal position for a client. Thus, legal advice shall remain subject to the obligation of professional secrecy unless the legal counsellor is taking part in money laundering or terrorist financing, the legal advice is provided for money laundering or terrorist financing purposes or the lawyer knows that the client is seeking legal advice for money laundering or terrorist financing purposes.

(21) Directly comparable services need to be treated in the same manner when provided by any of the professionals covered by this Directive. In order to ensure the respect of the rights laid down in the European Convention for the Protection of Human Rights and Fundamental Freedoms and the Treaty on European Union, in the case of auditors, external accountants and tax advisors, who, in some Member States, may defend or represent a client in the context of judicial proceedings or ascertain a client's legal position, the information they obtain in the performance of those tasks should not be subject to the reporting obligations in accordance with this Directive.

(22) It should be recognised that the risk of money laundering and terrorist financing is not the same in every case. In line with a risk-based approach, the principle should be introduced into Community legislation that simplified customer due diligence is allowed in appropriate cases.

(23) The derogation concerning the identification of beneficial owners of pooled accounts held by notaries or other independent legal professionals should be without prejudice to the obligations that those notaries or other independent legal professionals have pursuant to this Directive. Those obligations include the need for such notaries or other independent legal professionals themselves to identify the beneficial owners of the pooled accounts held by them.

(24) Equally, Community legislation should recognise that certain situations present a greater risk of money laundering or terrorist financing. Although the identity and business profile of all customers should be established, there are cases where particularly rigorous customer identification and verification procedures are required.

(25) This is particularly true of business relationships with individuals holding, or having held, important public positions, particularly those from countries where corruption is widespread. Such relationships may expose the financial sector in particular to significant reputational and/or legal risks. The international effort to combat corruption also justifies the need to pay special attention to such cases and to apply the complete normal customer due diligence measures in respect of domestic politically exposed persons or enhanced customer due diligence measures in respect of politically exposed persons residing in another Member State or in a third country.

(26) Obtaining approval from senior management for establishing business relationships should not imply obtaining approval from the board of directors but from the immediate higher level of the hierarchy of the person seeking such approval.

(27) In order to avoid repeated customer identification procedures, leading to delays and inefficiency in business, it is appropriate, subject to suitable safeguards, to allow customers to be introduced whose identification has been carried out elsewhere. Where an institution or person covered by this Directive relies on a third party, the ultimate responsibility for the customer due diligence procedure remains with the institution or person to whom the customer is introduced. The third party, or introducer, also retains his own responsibility for all the requirements in this Directive, including the requirement to report suspicious transactions and maintain records, to the extent that he has a relationship with the customer that is covered by this Directive.

(28) In the case of agency or outsourcing relationships on a contractual basis between institutions or persons covered by this Directive and external natural or legal persons not covered hereby, any anti-money laundering and anti-terrorist financing obligations for those agents or outsourcing service providers as part of the institutions or persons covered by this Directive, may only arise from contract and not from this Directive. The responsibility for complying with this Directive should remain with the institution or person covered hereby.

(29) Suspicious transactions should be reported to the financial intelligence unit (FIU), which serves as a national centre for receiving, analysing and disseminating to the competent authorities suspicious transaction reports and other information regarding potential money laundering or terrorist financing. This should not compel Member States to change their existing reporting systems where the reporting is done through a public prosecutor or other law enforcement authorities, as long as the information is forwarded promptly and unfiltered to FIUs, allowing them to conduct their business properly, including international cooperation with other FIUs.

(30) By way of derogation from the general prohibition on executing suspicious transactions, the institutions and persons covered by this Directive may execute suspicious transactions before informing the competent authorities, where refraining from the execution thereof is impossible or likely to frustrate efforts to pursue the beneficiaries of a suspected money laundering or terrorist financing operation. This, however, should be without prejudice to the international obligations

accepted by the Member States to freeze without delay funds or other assets of terrorists, terrorist organisations or those who finance terrorism, in accordance with the relevant United Nations Security Council resolutions.

(31) Where a Member State decides to make use of the exemptions provided for in Article 23(2), it may allow or require the self-regulatory body representing the persons referred to therein not to transmit to the FIU any information obtained from those persons in the circumstances referred to in that Article.

(32) There has been a number of cases of employees who report their suspicions of money laundering being subjected to threats or hostile action. Although this Directive cannot interfere with Member States' judicial procedures, this is a crucial issue for the effectiveness of the anti-money laundering and anti-terrorist financing system. Member States should be aware of this problem and should do whatever they can to protect employees from such threats or hostile action.

(33) Disclosure of information as referred to in Article 28 should be in accordance with the rules on transfer of personal data to third countries as laid down in Directive 95/46/EC of the European Parliament and of the Council of 24 October 1995 on the protection of individuals with regard to the processing of personal data and on the free movement of such data.[6] Moreover, Article 28 cannot interfere with national data protection and professional secrecy legislation.

(34) Persons who merely convert paper documents into electronic data and are acting under a contract with a credit institution or a financial institution do not fall within the scope of this Directive, nor does any natural or legal person that provides credit or financial institutions solely with a message or other support systems for transmitting funds or with clearing and settlement systems.

(35) Money laundering and terrorist financing are international problems and the effort to combat them should be global. Where Community credit and financial institutions have branches and subsidiaries located in third countries where the legislation in this area is deficient, they should, in order to avoid the application of very different standards within an institution or group of institutions, apply the Community standard or notify the competent authorities of the home Member State if this application is impossible.

(36) It is important that credit and financial institutions should be able to respond rapidly to requests for information on whether they maintain business relationships with named persons. For the purpose of identifying such business relationships in order to be able to provide that information quickly, credit and financial institutions should have effective systems in place which are commensurate with the size and nature of their business. In particular it would be appropriate for credit institutions and larger financial institutions to have electronic systems at their disposal. This provision is of particular importance in the context of procedures leading to measures such as the freezing or seizing of assets (including terrorist assets), pursuant to applicable national or Community legislation with a view to combating terrorism.

(37) This Directive establishes detailed rules for customer due diligence, including enhanced customer due diligence for high-risk customers or business relationships, such as appropriate procedures to determine whether a person is a politically exposed person, and certain additional, more detailed requirements, such as the existence of compliance management procedures and policies. All these requirements are to be met by each of the institutions and persons covered by this Directive, while Member States are expected to tailor the detailed implementation of those provisions to the particularities of the various professions and to the differences in scale and size of the institutions and persons covered by this Directive.

(38) In order to ensure that the institutions and others subject to Community legislation in this field remain committed, feedback should, where practicable, be made available to them on the usefulness and follow-up of the reports they present. To make this possible, and to be able to review the effectiveness of their systems to combat money laundering and terrorist financing Member States should keep and improve the relevant statistics.

(39) When registering or licensing a currency exchange office, a trust and company service provider or a casino nationally, competent authorities should ensure that the persons who effectively direct or will direct the business of such entities and the beneficial owners of such entities are fit and proper persons. The criteria for determining whether or not a person is fit and proper should be established in conformity with national law. As a minimum, such criteria should reflect the need to protect such entities from being misused by their managers or beneficial owners for criminal purposes.

(40) Taking into account the international character of money laundering and terrorist financing, coordination and cooperation between FIUs as referred to in Council Decision 2000/642/JHA of 17 October 2000 concerning arrangements for cooperation between financial intelligence units of the Member States in respect of exchanging information,[7] including the establishment of an EU FIU-net, should be encouraged to the greatest possible extent. To that end, the Commission should lend such assistance as may be needed to facilitate such coordination, including financial assistance.

(41) The importance of combating money laundering and terrorist financing should lead Member States to lay down effective, proportionate and dissuasive penalties in national law for failure to respect the national provisions adopted pursuant to this Directive. Provision should be

made for penalties in respect of natural and legal persons. Since legal persons are often involved in complex money laundering or terrorist financing operations, sanctions should also be adjusted in line with the activity carried on by legal persons.

(42)   Natural persons exercising any of the activities referred to in Article 2(1)(3)(a) and (b) within the structure of a legal person, but on an independent basis, should be independently responsible for compliance with the provisions of this Directive, with the exception of Article 35.

(43)   Clarification of the technical aspects of the rules laid down in this Directive may be necessary to ensure an effective and sufficiently consistent implementation of this Directive, taking into account the different financial instruments, professions and risks in the different Member States and the technical developments in the fight against money laundering and terrorist financing. The Commission should accordingly be empowered to adopt implementing measures, such as certain criteria for identifying low and high risk situations in which simplified due diligence could suffice or enhanced due diligence would be appropriate, provided that they do not modify the essential elements of this Directive and provided that the Commission acts in accordance with the principles set out herein, after consulting the Committee on the Prevention of Money Laundering and Terrorist Financing.

(44)   The measures necessary for the implementation of this Directive should be adopted in accordance with Council Decision 1999/468/EC of 28 June 1999 laying down the procedures for the exercise of implementing powers conferred on the Commission.[8] To that end a new Committee on the Prevention of Money Laundering and Terrorist Financing, replacing the Money Laundering Contact Committee set up by Directive 91/308/EEC, should be established.

(45)   In view of the very substantial amendments that would need to be made to Directive 91/308/EEC, it should be repealed for reasons of clarity.

(46)   Since the objective of this Directive, namely the prevention of the use of the financial system for the purpose of money laundering and terrorist financing, cannot be sufficiently achieved by the Member States and can therefore, by reason of the scale and effects of the action, be better achieved at Community level, the Community may adopt measures, in accordance with the principle of subsidiarity as set out in Article 5 of the Treaty. In accordance with the principle of proportionality, as set out in that Article, this Directive does not go beyond what is necessary in order to achieve that objective.

(47)   In exercising its implementing powers in accordance with this Directive, the Commission should respect the following principles: the need for high levels of transparency and consultation with institutions and persons covered by this Directive and with the European Parliament and the Council; the need to ensure that competent authorities will be able to ensure compliance with the rules consistently; the balance of costs and benefits to institutions and persons covered by this Directive on a long-term basis in any implementing measures; the need to respect the necessary flexibility in the application of the implementing measures in accordance with a risk-sensitive approach; the need to ensure coherence with other Community legislation in this area; the need to protect the Community, its Member States and their citizens from the consequences of money laundering and terrorist financing.

(48)   This Directive respects the fundamental rights and observes the principles recognised in particular by the Charter of Fundamental Rights of the European Union. Nothing in this Directive should be interpreted or implemented in a manner that is inconsistent with the European Convention on Human Rights,

[5722]

NOTES

1   Opinion delivered on 11 May 2005 (not yet published in the Official Journal).
2   OJ C40, 17.2.2005, p 9.
3   Opinion of the European Parliament of 26 May 2005 (not yet published in the Official Journal) and Council Decision of 19 September 2005.
4   OJ L166, 28.6.1991, p 77. Directive as amended by Directive 2001/97/EC of the European Parliament and of the Council (OJ L344, 28.12.2001, p 76).
5   OJ L182, 5.7.2001, p 1.
6   OJ L281, 23.11.1995, p 31. Directive as amended by Regulation (EC) No 1882/2003 (OJ L284, 31.10.2003, p 1).
7   OJ L271, 24.10.2000, p 4.
8   OJ L184, 17.7.1999, p 23.

HAVE ADOPTED THIS DIRECTIVE:

CHAPTER I
SUBJECT MATTER, SCOPE AND DEFINITIONS

Article 1

1.   Member States shall ensure that money laundering and terrorist financing are prohibited.

2.   For the purposes of this Directive, the following conduct, when committed intentionally, shall be regarded as money laundering:

(a)   the conversion or transfer of property, knowing that such property is derived from criminal activity or from an act of participation in such activity, for the purpose of concealing or disguising the illicit origin of the property or of assisting any person who is involved in the commission of such activity to evade the legal consequences of his action;

(b)   the concealment or disguise of the true nature, source, location, disposition, movement, rights with respect to, or ownership of property, knowing that such property is derived from criminal activity or from an act of participation in such activity;

(c)   the acquisition, possession or use of property, knowing, at the time of receipt, that such property was derived from criminal activity or from an act of participation in such activity;

(d)   participation in, association to commit, attempts to commit and aiding, abetting, facilitating and counselling the commission of any of the actions mentioned in the foregoing points.

3.   Money laundering shall be regarded as such even where the activities which generated the property to be laundered were carried out in the territory of another Member State or in that of a third country.

4.   For the purposes of this Directive, "terrorist financing" means the provision or collection of funds, by any means, directly or indirectly, with the intention that they should be used or in the knowledge that they are to be used, in full or in part, in order to carry out any of the offences within the meaning of Articles 1 to 4 of Council Framework Decision 2002/475/JHA of 13 June 2002 on combating terrorism.[1]

5.   Knowledge, intent or purpose required as an element of the activities mentioned in paragraphs 2 and 4 may be inferred from objective factual circumstances.

[5722A]

NOTES
[1]   OJ L164, 22.6.2002, p 3.

Article 2

1.   This Directive shall apply to:

(1)   credit institutions;

(2)   financial institutions;

(3)   the following legal or natural persons acting in the exercise of their professional activities:

(a)   auditors, external accountants and tax advisors;

(b)   notaries and other independent legal professionals, when they participate, whether by acting on behalf of and for their client in any financial or real estate transaction, or by assisting in the planning or execution of transactions for their client concerning the:

(i)   buying and selling of real property or business entities;

(ii)   managing of client money, securities or other assets;

(iii)   opening or management of bank, savings or securities accounts;

(iv)   organisation of contributions necessary for the creation, operation or management of companies;

(v)   creation, operation or management of trusts, companies or similar structures;

(c)   trust or company service providers not already covered under points (a) or (b);

(d)   real estate agents;

(e)   other natural or legal persons trading in goods, only to the extent that payments are made in cash in an amount of EUR 15,000 or more, whether the transaction is executed in a single operation or in several operations which appear to be linked;

(f)   casinos.

2.   Member States may decide that legal and natural persons who engage in a financial activity on an occasional or very limited basis and where there is little risk of money laundering or terrorist financing occurring do not fall within the scope of Article 3(1) or (2).

[5723]

Article 3

For the purposes of this Directive the following definitions shall apply:

(1)   "credit institution" means a credit institution, as defined in the first subparagraph of Article 1(1) of Directive 2000/12/EC of the European Parliament and of the Council of 20 March 2000 relating to the taking up and pursuit of the business of credit

institutions,[1] including branches within the meaning of Article 1(3) of that Directive located in the Community of credit institutions having their head offices inside or outside the Community;

(2) "financial institution" means:

[(a) an undertaking other than a credit institution which carries out one or more of the activities listed in points 2 to 12 and 14 of Annex I to Directive 2006/48/EC, including the activities of currency exchange offices (bureaux de change);]

(b) an insurance company duly authorised in accordance with Directive 2002/83/EC of the European Parliament and of the Council of 5 November 2002 concerning life assurance,[2] insofar as it carries out activities covered by that Directive;

(c) an investment firm as defined in point 1 of Article 4(1) of Directive 2004/39/EC of the European Parliament and of the Council of 21 April 2004 on markets in financial instruments;[3]

(d) a collective investment undertaking marketing its units or shares;

(e) an insurance intermediary as defined in Article 2(5) of Directive 2002/92/EC of the European Parliament and of the Council of 9 December 2002 on insurance mediation,[4] with the exception of intermediaries as mentioned in Article 2(7) of that Directive, when they act in respect of life insurance and other investment related services;

(f) branches, when located in the Community, of financial institutions as referred to in points (a) to (e), whose head offices are inside or outside the Community;

(3) "property" means assets of every kind, whether corporeal or incorporeal, movable or immovable, tangible or intangible, and legal documents or instruments in any form including electronic or digital, evidencing title to or an interest in such assets;

(4) "criminal activity" means any kind of criminal involvement in the commission of a serious crime;

(5) "serious crimes" means, at least:

(a) acts as defined in Articles 1 to 4 of Framework Decision 2002/475/JHA;

(b) any of the offences defined in Article 3(1)(a) of the 1988 United Nations Convention against Illicit Traffic in Narcotic Drugs and Psychotropic Substances;

(c) the activities of criminal organisations as defined in Article 1 of Council Joint Action 98/733/JHA of 21 December 1998 on making it a criminal offence to participate in a criminal organisation in the Member States of the European Union;[5]

(d) fraud, at least serious, as defined in Article 1(1) and Article 2 of the Convention on the Protection of the European Communities' Financial Interests;[6]

(e) corruption;

(f) all offences which are punishable by deprivation of liberty or a detention order for a maximum of more than one year or, as regards those States which have a minimum threshold for offences in their legal system, all offences punishable by deprivation of liberty or a detention order for a minimum of more than six months;

(6) "beneficial owner" means the natural person(s) who ultimately owns or controls the customer and/or the natural person on whose behalf a transaction or activity is being conducted. The beneficial owner shall at least include:

(a) in the case of corporate entities:

(i) the natural person(s) who ultimately owns or controls a legal entity through direct or indirect ownership or control over a sufficient percentage of the shares or voting rights in that legal entity, including through bearer share holdings, other than a company listed on a regulated market that is subject to disclosure requirements consistent with Community legislation or subject to equivalent international standards; a percentage of 25% plus one share shall be deemed sufficient to meet this criterion;

(ii) the natural person(s) who otherwise exercises control over the management of a legal entity:

(b) in the case of legal entities, such as foundations, and legal arrangements, such as trusts, which administer and distribute funds:

(i) where the future beneficiaries have already been determined, the natural person(s) who is the beneficiary of 25% or more of the property of a legal arrangement or entity;

(ii) where the individuals that benefit from the legal arrangement or entity have yet to be determined, the class of persons in whose main interest the legal arrangement or entity is set up or operates;

(iii) the natural person(s) who exercises control over 25% or more of the property of a legal arrangement or entity;

(7) "trust and company service providers" means any natural or legal person which by way of business provides any of the following services to third parties:

(a)   forming companies or other legal persons;

(b)   acting as or arranging for another person to act as a director or secretary of a company, a partner of a partnership, or a similar position in relation to other legal persons;

(c)   providing a registered office, business address, correspondence or administrative address and other related services for a company, a partnership or any other legal person or arrangement;

(d)   acting as or arranging for another person to act as a trustee of an express trust or a similar legal arrangement;

(e)   acting as or arranging for another person to act as a nominee shareholder for another person other than a company listed on a regulated market that is subject to disclosure requirements in conformity with Community legislation or subject to equivalent international standards;

(8)   "politically exposed persons" means natural persons who are or have been entrusted with prominent public functions and immediate family members, or persons known to be close associates, of such persons;

(9)   "business relationship" means a business, professional or commercial relationship which is connected with the professional activities of the institutions and persons covered by this Directive and which is expected, at the time when the contact is established, to have an element of duration;

(10)   "shell bank" means a credit institution, or an institution engaged in equivalent activities, incorporated in a jurisdiction in which it has no physical presence, involving meaningful mind and management, and which is unaffiliated with a regulated financial group.

[5724]

NOTES

Para (2): point (a) substituted by European Parliament and Council Directive 2007/64/EC, Art 91(1), as from 25 December 2007 (for transitional provisions see Art 88 of that Directive at **[6177]**). Note that 2007/64/EC has a transposition date of 1 November 2009 (see Art 94 at **[6179]**) and that the original point (a) read as follows—

    "(a)   an undertaking other than a credit institution which carries out one or more of the operations included in points 2 to 12 and 14 of Annex I to Directive 2000/12/EC, including the activities of currency exchange offices (bureaux de change) and of money transmission or remittance offices;".

1   OJ L126, 26.5.2000, p 1. Directive as last amended by Directive 2005/1/EC (OJ L79, 24.3.2005, p 9).
2   OJ L345, 19.12.2002, p 1. Directive as last amended by Directive 2005/1/EC.
3   OJ L145, 30.4.2004, p 1.
4   OJ L9, 15.1.2003, p 3.
5   OJ L351, 29.12.1998, p 1.
6   OJ C316, 27.11.1995, p 49.

Article 4

1.   Member States shall ensure that the provisions of this Directive are extended in whole or in part to professions and to categories of undertakings, other than the institutions and persons referred to in Article 2(1), which engage in activities which are particularly likely to be used for money laundering or terrorist financing purposes.

2.   Where a Member State decides to extend the provisions of this Directive to professions and to categories of undertakings other than those referred to in Article 2(1), it shall inform the Commission thereof.

[5725]

Article 5

The Member States may adopt or retain in force stricter provisions in the field covered by this Directive to prevent money laundering and terrorist financing.

[5726]

CHAPTER II
CUSTOMER DUE DILIGENCE

SECTION 1
GENERAL PROVISIONS

Article 6

Member States shall prohibit their credit and financial institutions from keeping anonymous accounts or anonymous passbooks. By way of derogation from Article 9(6), Member States shall in all cases require that the owners and beneficiaries of existing anonymous accounts or anonymous passbooks be made the subject of customer due diligence measures as soon as possible and in any event before such accounts or passbooks are used in any way.

[5727]

Article 7

The institutions and persons covered by this Directive shall apply customer due diligence measures in the following cases:
- (a)   when establishing a business relationship;
- (b)   when carrying out occasional transactions amounting to EUR 15,000 or more, whether the transaction is carried out in a single operation or in several operations which appear to be linked;
- (c)   when there is a suspicion of money laundering or terrorist financing, regardless of any derogation, exemption or threshold;
- (d)   when there are doubts about the veracity or adequacy of previously obtained customer identification data.

[5728]

Article 8

1.   Customer due diligence measures shall comprise:
- (a)   identifying the customer and verifying the customer's identity on the basis of documents, data or information obtained from a reliable and independent source;
- (b)   identifying, where applicable, the beneficial owner and taking risk-based and adequate measures to verify his identity so that the institution or person covered by this Directive is satisfied that it knows who the beneficial owner is, including, as regards legal persons, trusts and similar legal arrangements, taking risk-based and adequate measures to understand the ownership and control structure of the customer;
- (c)   obtaining information on the purpose and intended nature of the business relationship;
- (d)   conducting ongoing monitoring of the business relationship including scrutiny of transactions undertaken throughout the course of that relationship to ensure that the transactions being conducted are consistent with the institution's or person's knowledge of the customer, the business and risk profile, including, where necessary, the source of funds and ensuring that the documents, data or information held are kept up-to-date.

2.   The institutions and persons covered by this Directive shall apply each of the customer due diligence requirements set out in paragraph 1, but may determine the extent of such measures on a risk-sensitive basis depending on the type of customer, business relationship, product or transaction. The institutions and persons covered by this Directive shall be able to demonstrate to the competent authorities mentioned in Article 37, including self-regulatory bodies, that the extent of the measures is appropriate in view of the risks of money laundering and terrorist financing.

[5729]

Article 9

1.   Member States shall require that the verification of the identity of the customer and the beneficial owner takes place before the establishment of a business relationship or the carrying-out of the transaction.

2.   By way of derogation from paragraph 1, Member States may allow the verification of the identity of the customer and the beneficial owner to be completed during the establishment of a business relationship if this is necessary not to interrupt the normal conduct of business and where there is little risk of money laundering or terrorist financing occurring. In such situations these procedures shall be completed as soon as practicable after the initial contact.

3.   By way of derogation from paragraphs 1 and 2, Member States may, in relation to life insurance business, allow the verification of the identity of the beneficiary under the policy to take place after the business relationship has been established. In that case, verification shall take place at or before the time of payout or at or before the time the beneficiary intends to exercise rights vested under the policy.

4.   By way of derogation from paragraphs 1 and 2, Member States may allow the opening of a bank account provided that there are adequate safeguards in place to ensure that transactions are not carried out by the customer or on its behalf until full compliance with the aforementioned provisions is obtained.

5.   Member States shall require that, where the institution or person concerned is unable to comply with points (a), (b) and (c) of Article 8(1), it may not carry out a transaction through a bank account, establish a business relationship or carry out the transaction, or shall terminate the business relationship, and shall consider making a report to the financial intelligence unit (FIU) in accordance with Article 22 in relation to the customer.

Member States shall not be obliged to apply the previous subparagraph in situations when notaries, independent legal professionals, auditors, external accountants and tax advisors are in the course of ascertaining the legal position for their client or performing their task of defending or representing that client in, or concerning judicial proceedings, including advice on instituting or avoiding proceedings.

6.   Member States shall require that institutions and persons covered by this Directive apply the customer due diligence procedures not only to all new customers but also at appropriate times to existing customers on a risk-sensitive basis.

[5730]

Article 10

1.   Member States shall require that all casino customers be identified and their identity verified if they purchase or exchange gambling chips with a value of EUR 2,000 or more.

2.   Casinos subject to State supervision shall be deemed in any event to have satisfied the customer due diligence requirements if they register, identify and verify the identity of their customers immediately on or before entry, regardless of the amount of gambling chips purchased.

[5731]

SECTION 2
SIMPLIFIED CUSTOMER DUE DILIGENCE

Article 11

1.   By way of derogation from Articles 7(a), (b) and (d), 8 and 9(1), the institutions and persons covered by this Directive shall not be subject to the requirements provided for in those Articles where the customer is a credit or financial institution covered by this Directive, or a credit or financial institution situated in a third country which imposes requirements equivalent to those laid down in this Directive and supervised for compliance with those requirements.

2.   By way of derogation from Articles 7(a), (b) and (d), 8 and 9(1) Member States may allow the institutions and persons covered by this Directive not to apply customer due diligence in respect of:

(a)   listed companies whose securities are admitted to trading on a regulated market within the meaning of Directive 2004/39/EC in one or more Member States and listed companies from third countries which are subject to disclosure requirements consistent with Community legislation;

(b)   beneficial owners of pooled accounts held by notaries and other independent legal professionals from the Member States, or from third countries provided that they are subject to requirements to combat money laundering or terrorist financing consistent with international standards and are supervised for compliance with those requirements and provided that the information on the identity of the beneficial owner is available, on request, to the institutions that act as depository institutions for the pooled accounts;

(c)   domestic public authorities,

or in respect of any other customer representing a low risk of money laundering or terrorist financing which meets the technical criteria established in accordance with Article 40(1)(b).

3.   In the cases mentioned in paragraphs 1 and 2, institutions and persons covered by this Directive shall in any case gather sufficient information to establish if the customer qualifies for an exemption as mentioned in these paragraphs.

4.   The Member States shall inform each other and the Commission of cases where they consider that a third country meets the conditions laid down in paragraphs 1 or 2 or in other situations which meet the technical criteria established in accordance with Article 40(1)(b).

5.   By way of derogation from Articles 7(a), (b) and (d), 8 and 9(1), Member States may allow the institutions and persons covered by this Directive not to apply customer due diligence in respect of:

(a)   life insurance policies where the annual premium is no more than EUR 1,000 or the single premium is no more than EUR 2500;

(b)   insurance policies for pension schemes if there is no surrender clause and the policy cannot be used as collateral;

(c)   a pension, superannuation or similar scheme that provides retirement benefits to employees, where contributions are made by way of deduction from wages and the scheme rules do not permit the assignment of a member's interest under the scheme;

(d)   electronic money, as defined in Article 1(3)(b) of Directive 2000/46/EC of the European Parliament and of the Council of 18 September 2000 on the taking up, pursuit of and prudential supervision of the business of electronic money institutions,[1] where, if the device cannot be recharged, the maximum amount stored in the device is no more than EUR 150, or where, if the device can be recharged, a limit of EUR 2500 is imposed on the total amount transacted in a calendar year, except when an amount of EUR 1,000 or more is redeemed in that same calendar year by the bearer as referred to in Article 3 of Directive 2000/46/EC,

or in respect of any other product or transaction representing a low risk of money laundering or terrorist financing which meets the technical criteria established in accordance with Article 40(1)(b).

[5732]

PART IV
EC MATERIALS

NOTES

1   OJ L275, 27.10.2000, p 39.

Article 12

Where the Commission adopts a decision pursuant to Article 40(4), the Member States shall prohibit the institutions and persons covered by this Directive from applying simplified due diligence to credit and financial institutions or listed companies from the third country concerned or other entities following from situations which meet the technical criteria established in accordance with Article 40(1)(b).

[5733]

SECTION 3
ENHANCED CUSTOMER DUE DILIGENCE

Article 13

1.   Member States shall require the institutions and persons covered by this Directive to apply, on a risk-sensitive basis, enhanced customer due diligence measures, in addition to the measures referred to in Articles 7, 8 and 9(6), in situations which by their nature can present a higher risk of money laundering or terrorist financing, and at least in the situations set out in paragraphs 2, 3, 4 and in other situations representing a high risk of money laundering or terrorist financing which meet the technical criteria established in accordance with Article 40(1)(c).

2.   Where the customer has not been physically present for identification purposes, Member States shall require those institutions and persons to take specific and adequate measures to compensate for the higher risk, for example by applying one or more of the following measures:
   (a)   ensuring that the customer's identity is established by additional documents, data or information;
   (b)   supplementary measures to verify or certify the documents supplied, or requiring confirmatory certification by a credit or financial institution covered by this Directive;
   (c)   ensuring that the first payment of the operations is carried out through an account opened in the customer's name with a credit institution.

3.   In respect of cross-frontier correspondent banking relationships with respondent institutions from third countries, Member States shall require their credit institutions to:
   (a)   gather sufficient information about a respondent institution to understand fully the nature of the respondent's business and to determine from publicly available information the reputation of the institution and the quality of supervision;
   (b)   assess the respondent institution's anti-money laundering and anti-terrorist financing controls;
   (c)   obtain approval from senior management before establishing new correspondent banking relationships;
   (d)   document the respective responsibilities of each institution;
   (e)   with respect to payable-through accounts, be satisfied that the respondent credit institution has verified the identity of and performed ongoing due diligence on the customers having direct access to accounts of the correspondent and that it is able to provide relevant customer due diligence data to the correspondent institution, upon request.

4.   In respect of transactions or business relationships with politically exposed persons residing in another Member State or in a third country, Member States shall require those institutions and persons covered by this Directive to:
   (a)   have appropriate risk-based procedures to determine whether the customer is a politically exposed person;
   (b)   have senior management approval for establishing business relationships with such customers;
   (c)   take adequate measures to establish the source of wealth and source of funds that are involved in the business relationship or transaction;
   (d)   conduct enhanced ongoing monitoring of the business relationship.

5.   Member States shall prohibit credit institutions from entering into or continuing a correspondent banking relationship with a shell bank and shall require that credit institutions take appropriate measures to ensure that they do not engage in or continue correspondent banking relationships with a bank that is known to permit its accounts to be used by a shell bank.

6.   Member States shall ensure that the institutions and persons covered by this Directive pay special attention to any money laundering or terrorist financing threat that may arise from products or transactions that might favour anonymity, and take measures, if needed, to prevent their use for money laundering or terrorist financing purposes.

[5734]

SECTION 4
PERFORMANCE BY THIRD PARTIES

Article 14

Member States may permit the institutions and persons covered by this Directive to rely on third parties to meet the requirements laid down in Article 8(1)(a) to (c). However, the ultimate responsibility for meeting those requirements shall remain with the institution or person covered by this Directive which relies on the third party.

[5735]

Article 15

[1. Where a Member State permits credit and financial institutions referred to in Article 2(1)(1) or (2) situated in its territory to be relied on as a third party domestically, that Member State shall in any case permit institutions and persons referred to in Article 2(1) situated in its territory to recognise and accept, in accordance with Article 14, the outcome of the customer due diligence requirements laid down in Article 8(1)(a) to (c), carried out in accordance with this Directive by an institution referred to in Article 2(1)(1) or (2) in another Member State, with the exception of currency exchange offices and payment institutions as defined in Article 4(4) of Directive 2007/64/EC of the European Parliament and of the Council of 13 November 2007 on payment services in the internal market,[1] which mainly provide the payment service listed in point 6 of the Annex to that Directive, including natural and legal persons benefiting from a waiver under Article 26 of that Directive, and meeting the requirements laid down in Articles 16 and 18 of this Directive, even if the documents or data on which these requirements have been based are different to those required in the Member State to which the customer is being referred.

2. Where a Member State permits currency exchange offices referred to in Article 3(2)(a) and payment institutions as defined in Article 4(4) of Directive 2007/64/EC, which mainly provide the payment service listed in point 6 of the Annex to that Directive, situated in its territory to be relied on as a third party domestically, that Member State shall in any case permit them to recognise and accept, in accordance with Article 14 of this Directive, the outcome of the customer due diligence requirements laid down in Article 8(1)(a) to (c), carried out in accordance with this Directive by the same category of institution in another Member State and meeting the requirements laid down in Articles 16 and 18 of this Directive, even if the documents or data on which these requirements have been based are different to those required in the Member State to which the customer is being referred.]

3. Where a Member State permits persons referred to in Article 2(1)(3)(a) to (c) situated in its territory to be relied on as a third party domestically, that Member State shall in any case permit them to recognise and accept, in accordance with Article 14, the outcome of the customer due diligence requirements laid down in Article 8(1)(a) to (c), carried out in accordance with this Directive by a person referred to in Article 2(1)(3)(a) to (c) in another Member State and meeting the requirements laid down in Articles 16 and 18, even if the documents or data on which these requirements have been based are different to those required in the Member State to which the customer is being referred.

[5736]

NOTES

Paras 1, 2: substituted by European Parliament and Council Directive 2007/64/EC, Art 91(2), as from 25 December 2007 (for transitional provisions see Art 88 of that Directive at **[6177]**). Note that 2007/64/EC has a transposition date of 1 November 2009 (see Art 94 at **[6179]**) and that the original paragraphs read as follows—

"1. Where a Member State permits credit and financial institutions referred to in Article 2(1)(1) or (2) situated in its territory to be relied on as a third party domestically, that Member State shall in any case permit institutions and persons referred to in Article 2(1) situated in its territory to recognise and accept, in accordance with the provisions laid down in Article 14, the outcome of the customer due diligence requirements laid down in Article 8(1)(a) to (c), carried out in accordance with this Directive by an institution referred to in Article 2(1)(1) or (2) in another Member State, with the exception of currency exchange offices and money transmission or remittance offices, and meeting the requirements laid down in Articles 16 and 18, even if the documents or data on which these requirements have been based are different to those required in the Member State to which the customer is being referred.

2. Where a Member State permits currency exchange offices and money transmission or remittance offices referred to in Article 3(2)(a) situated in its territory to be relied on as a third party domestically, that Member State shall in any case permit them to recognise and accept, in accordance with Article 14, the outcome of the customer due diligence requirements laid down in Article 8(1)(a) to (c), carried out in accordance with this Directive by the same category of institution in another Member State and meeting the requirements laid down in Articles 16 and 18, even if the documents or data on which these requirements have been based are different to those required in the Member State to which the customer is being referred.".

[1] OJ L319, 5.12.2007, p 1."

Article 16

1. For the purposes of this Section, "third parties" shall mean institutions and persons who are listed in Article 2, or equivalent institutions and persons situated in a third country, who meet the following requirements:

(a) they are subject to mandatory professional registration, recognised by law;

(b) they apply customer due diligence requirements and record keeping requirements as laid down or equivalent to those laid down in this Directive and their compliance with the requirements of this Directive is supervised in accordance with Section 2 of Chapter V, or they are situated in a third country which imposes equivalent requirements to those laid down in this Directive.

2. Member States shall inform each other and the Commission of cases where they consider that a third country meets the conditions laid down in paragraph 1(b).

[5737]

Article 17

Where the Commission adopts a decision pursuant to Article 40(4), Member States shall prohibit the institutions and persons covered by this Directive from relying on third parties from the third country concerned to meet the requirements laid down in Article 8(1)(a) to (c).

[5738]

Article 18

1. Third parties shall make information requested in accordance with the requirements laid down in Article 8(1)(a) to (c) immediately available to the institution or person covered by this Directive to which the customer is being referred.

2. Relevant copies of identification and verification data and other relevant documentation on the identity of the customer or the beneficial owner shall immediately be forwarded, on request, by the third party to the institution or person covered by this Directive to which the customer is being referred.

[5739]

Article 19

This Section shall not apply to outsourcing or agency relationships where, on the basis of a contractual arrangement, the outsourcing service provider or agent is to be regarded as part of the institution or person covered by this Directive.

[5740]

CHAPTER III
REPORTING OBLIGATIONS

SECTION 1
GENERAL PROVISIONS

Article 20

Member States shall require that the institutions and persons covered by this Directive pay special attention to any activity which they regard as particularly likely, by its nature, to be related to money laundering or terrorist financing and in particular complex or unusually large transactions and all unusual patterns of transactions which have no apparent economic or visible lawful purpose.

[5741]

Article 21

1. Each Member State shall establish a FIU in order effectively to combat money laundering and terrorist financing.

2. That FIU shall be established as a central national unit. It shall be responsible for receiving (and to the extent permitted, requesting), analysing and disseminating to the competent authorities, disclosures of information which concern potential money laundering, potential terrorist financing or are required by national legislation or regulation. It shall be provided with adequate resources in order to fulfil its tasks.

3. Member States shall ensure that the FIU has access, directly or indirectly, on a timely basis, to the financial, administrative and law enforcement information that it requires to properly fulfil its tasks.

[5742]

Article 22

1. Member States shall require the institutions and persons covered by this Directive, and where applicable their directors and employees, to cooperate fully:

(a) by promptly informing the FIU, on their own initiative, where the institution or person covered by this Directive knows, suspects or has reasonable grounds to suspect that money laundering or terrorist financing is being or has been committed or attempted;

(b) by promptly furnishing the FIU, at its request, with all necessary information, in accordance with the procedures established by the applicable legislation.

2. The information referred to in paragraph 1 shall be forwarded to the FIU of the Member State in whose territory the institution or person forwarding the information is situated. The person or persons designated in accordance with the procedures provided for in Article 34 shall normally forward the information.

[5743]

Article 23

1. By way of derogation from Article 22(1), Member States may, in the case of the persons referred to in Article 2(1)(3)(a) and (b), designate an appropriate self-regulatory body of the profession concerned as the authority to be informed in the first instance in place of the FIU. Without prejudice to paragraph 2, the designated self-regulatory body shall in such cases forward the information to the FIU promptly and unfiltered.

2. Member States shall not be obliged to apply the obligations laid down in Article 22(1) to notaries, independent legal professionals, auditors, external accountants and tax advisors with regard to information they receive from or obtain on one of their clients, in the course of ascertaining the legal position for their client or performing their task of defending or representing that client in, or concerning judicial proceedings, including advice on instituting or avoiding proceedings, whether such information is received or obtained before, during or after such proceedings.

[5744]

Article 24

1. Member States shall require the institutions and persons covered by this Directive to refrain from carrying out transactions which they know or suspect to be related to money laundering or terrorist financing until they have completed the necessary action in accordance with Article 22(1)(a). In conformity with the legislation of the Member States, instructions may be given not to carry out the transaction.

2. Where such a transaction is suspected of giving rise to money laundering or terrorist financing and where to refrain in such manner is impossible or is likely to frustrate efforts to pursue the beneficiaries of a suspected money laundering or terrorist financing operation, the institutions and persons concerned shall inform the FIU immediately afterwards.

[5745]

Article 25

1. Member States shall ensure that if, in the course of inspections carried out in the institutions and persons covered by this Directive by the competent authorities referred to in Article 37, or in any other way, those authorities discover facts that could be related to money laundering or terrorist financing, they shall promptly inform the FIU.

2. Member States shall ensure that supervisory bodies empowered by law or regulation to oversee the stock, foreign exchange and financial derivatives markets inform the FIU if they discover facts that could be related to money laundering or terrorist financing.

[5746]

Article 26

The disclosure in good faith as foreseen in Articles 22(1) and 23 by an institution or person covered by this Directive or by an employee or director of such an institution or person of the information referred to in Articles 22 and 23 shall not constitute a breach of any restriction on disclosure of information imposed by contract or by any legislative, regulatory or administrative provision, and shall not involve the institution or person or its directors or employees in liability of any kind.

[5747]

Article 27

Member States shall take all appropriate measures in order to protect employees of the institutions or persons covered by this Directive who report suspicions of money laundering or terrorist financing either internally or to the FIU from being exposed to threats or hostile action.

[5748]

SECTION 2

PROHIBITION OF DISCLOSURE

Article 28

1. The institutions and persons covered by this Directive and their directors and employees shall not disclose to the customer concerned or to other third persons the fact that information has

been transmitted in accordance with Articles 22 and 23 or that a money laundering or terrorist financing investigation is being or may be carried out.

2.   The prohibition laid down in paragraph 1 shall not include disclosure to the competent authorities referred to in Article 37, including the self-regulatory bodies, or disclosure for law enforcement purposes.

3.   The prohibition laid down in paragraph 1 shall not prevent disclosure between institutions from Member States, or from third countries provided that they meet the conditions laid down in Article 11(1), belonging to the same group as defined by Article 2(12) of Directive 2002/87/EC of the European Parliament and of the Council of 16 December 2002 on the supplementary supervision of credit institutions, insurance undertakings and investment firms in a financial conglomerate.[1]

4.   The prohibition laid down in paragraph 1 shall not prevent disclosure between persons referred to in Article 2(1)(3)(a) and (b) from Member States, or from third countries which impose requirements equivalent to those laid down in this Directive, who perform their professional activities, whether as employees or not, within the same legal person or a network. For the purposes of this Article, a "network" means the larger structure to which the person belongs and which shares common ownership, management or compliance control.

5.   For institutions or persons referred to in Article 2(1)(1), (2) and (3)(a) and (b) in cases related to the same customer and the same transaction involving two or more institutions or persons, the prohibition laid down in paragraph 1 shall not prevent disclosure between the relevant institutions or persons provided that they are situated in a Member State, or in a third country which imposes requirements equivalent to those laid down in this Directive, and that they are from the same professional category and are subject to equivalent obligations as regards professional secrecy and personal data protection. The information exchanged shall be used exclusively for the purposes of the prevention of money laundering and terrorist financing.

6.   Where the persons referred to in Article 2(1)(3)(a) and (b) seek to dissuade a client from engaging in illegal activity, this shall not constitute a disclosure within the meaning of the paragraph 1.

7.   The Member States shall inform each other and the Commission of cases where they consider that a third country meets the conditions laid down in paragraphs 3, 4 or 5.

[5749]

NOTES
¹   OJ L35, 11.2.2003, p 1.

Article 29

Where the Commission adopts a decision pursuant to Article 40(4), the Member States shall prohibit the disclosure between institutions and persons covered by this Directive and institutions and persons from the third country concerned.

[5750]

CHAPTER IV
RECORD KEEPING AND STATISTICAL DATA

Article 30

Member States shall require the institutions and persons covered by this Directive to keep the following documents and information for use in any investigation into, or analysis of, possible money laundering or terrorist financing by the FIU or by other competent authorities in accordance with national law:
  (a)   in the case of the customer due diligence, a copy or the references of the evidence required, for a period of at least five years after the business relationship with their customer has ended;
  (b)   in the case of business relationships and transactions, the supporting evidence and records, consisting of the original documents or copies admissible in court proceedings under the applicable national legislation for a period of at least five years following the carrying-out of the transactions or the end of the business relationship.

[5751]

Article 31

1.   Member States shall require the credit and financial institutions covered by this Directive to apply, where applicable, in their branches and majority-owned subsidiaries located in third countries measures at least equivalent to those laid down in this Directive with regard to customer due diligence and record keeping.

Where the legislation of the third country does not permit application of such equivalent measures, the Member States shall require the credit and financial institutions concerned to inform the competent authorities of the relevant home Member State accordingly.

2.   Member States and the Commission shall inform each other of cases where the legislation of the third country does not permit application of the measures required under the first subparagraph of paragraph 1 and coordinated action could be taken to pursue a solution.

3.   Member States shall require that, where the legislation of the third country does not permit application of the measures required under the first subparagraph of paragraph 1, credit or financial institutions take additional measures to effectively handle the risk of money laundering or terrorist financing.

[5752]

Article 32

Member States shall require that their credit and financial institutions have systems in place that enable them to respond fully and rapidly to enquiries from the FIU, or from other authorities, in accordance with their national law, as to whether they maintain or have maintained during the previous five years a business relationship with specified natural or legal persons and on the nature of that relationship.

[5753]

Article 33

1.   Member States shall ensure that they are able to review the effectiveness of their systems to combat money laundering or terrorist financing by maintaining comprehensive statistics on matters relevant to the effectiveness of such systems.

2.   Such statistics shall as a minimum cover the number of suspicious transaction reports made to the FIU, the follow-up given to these reports and indicate on an annual basis the number of cases investigated, the number of persons prosecuted, the number of persons convicted for money laundering or terrorist financing offences and how much property has been frozen, seized or confiscated.

3.   Member States shall ensure that a consolidated review of these statistical reports is published.

[5754]

CHAPTER V
ENFORCEMENT MEASURES

SECTION 1
INTERNAL PROCEDURES, TRAINING AND FEEDBACK

Article 34

1.   Member States shall require that the institutions and persons covered by this Directive establish adequate and appropriate policies and procedures of customer due diligence, reporting, record keeping, internal control, risk assessment, risk management, compliance management and communication in order to forestall and prevent operations related to money laundering or terrorist financing.

2.   Member States shall require that credit and financial institutions covered by this Directive communicate relevant policies and procedures where applicable to branches and majority-owned subsidiaries in third countries.

[5755]

Article 35

1.   Member States shall require that the institutions and persons covered by this Directive take appropriate measures so that their relevant employees are aware of the provisions in force on the basis of this Directive.

These measures shall include participation of their relevant employees in special ongoing training programmes to help them recognise operations which may be related to money laundering or terrorist financing and to instruct them as to how to proceed in such cases.

Where a natural person falling within any of the categories listed in Article 2(1)(3) performs his professional activities as an employee of a legal person, the obligations in this Section shall apply to that legal person rather than to the natural person.

2.   Member States shall ensure that the institutions and persons covered by this Directive have access to up-to-date information on the practices of money launderers and terrorist financers and on indications leading to the recognition of suspicious transactions.

3.   Member States shall ensure that, wherever practicable, timely feedback on the effectiveness of and follow-up to reports of suspected money laundering or terrorist financing is provided.

[5756]

SECTION 2
SUPERVISION

Article 36

1.   Member States shall provide that currency exchange offices and trust and company service providers shall be licensed or registered and casinos be licensed in order to operate their business legally. ...

2.   Member States shall require competent authorities to refuse licensing or registration of the entities referred to in paragraph 1 if they are not satisfied that the persons who effectively direct or will direct the business of such entities or the beneficial owners of such entities are fit and proper persons.

[5757]

NOTES
Para 1: words omitted repealed by European Parliament and Council Directive 2007/64/EC, Art 91(3), as from 25 December 2007 (for transitional provisions see Art 88 of that Directive at **[6177]**). Note that 2007/64/EC has a transposition date of 1 November 2009 (see Art 94 at **[6179]**) and that the original words read as follows: "Without prejudice to future Community legislation, Member States shall provide that money transmission or remittance offices shall be licensed or registered in order to operate their business legally.".

Article 37

1.   Member States shall require the competent authorities at least to effectively monitor and to take the necessary measures with a view to ensuring compliance with the requirements of this Directive by all the institutions and persons covered by this Directive.

2.   Member States shall ensure that the competent authorities have adequate powers, including the power to compel the production of any information that is relevant to monitoring compliance and perform checks, and have adequate resources to perform their functions.

3.   In the case of credit and financial institutions and casinos, competent authorities shall have enhanced supervisory powers, notably the possibility to conduct on-site inspections.

4.   In the case of the natural and legal persons referred to in Article 2(1)(3)(a) to (e), Member States may allow the functions referred to in paragraph 1 to be performed on a risk-sensitive basis.

5.   In the case of the persons referred to in Article 2(1)(3)(a) and (b), Member States may allow the functions referred to in paragraph 1 to be performed by self-regulatory bodies, provided that they comply with paragraph 2.

[5758]

SECTION 3
COOPERATION

Article 38

The Commission shall lend such assistance as may be needed to facilitate coordination, including the exchange of information between FIUs within the Community.

[5759]

SECTION 4
PENALTIES

Article 39

1.   Member States shall ensure that natural and legal persons covered by this Directive can be held liable for infringements of the national provisions adopted pursuant to this Directive. The penalties must be effective, proportionate and dissuasive.

2.   Without prejudice to the right of Member States to impose criminal penalties, Member States shall ensure, in conformity with their national law, that the appropriate administrative measures can be taken or administrative sanctions can be imposed against credit and financial institutions for infringements of the national provisions adopted pursuant to this Directive. Member States shall ensure that these measures or sanctions are effective, proportionate and dissuasive.

3.   In the case of legal persons, Member States shall ensure that at least they can be held liable for infringements referred to in paragraph 1 which are committed for their benefit by any person, acting either individually or as part of an organ of the legal person, who has a leading position within the legal person, based on:

(a)   a power of representation of the legal person;

    (b)   an authority to take decisions on behalf of the legal person, or

    (c)   an authority to exercise control within the legal person.

4.   In addition to the cases already provided for in paragraph 3, Member States shall ensure that legal persons can be held liable where the lack of supervision or control by a person referred to in paragraph 3 has made possible the commission of the infringements referred to in paragraph 1 for the benefit of a legal person by a person under its authority.

[5760]

CHAPTER VI
IMPLEMENTING MEASURES

Article 40

1.   In order to take account of technical developments in the fight against money laundering or terrorist financing and to ensure uniform implementation of this Directive, the Commission may … adopt the following implementing measures:

    (a)   clarification of the technical aspects of the definitions in Article 3(2)(a) and (d), (6), (7), (8), (9) and (10);

    (b)   establishment of technical criteria for assessing whether situations represent a low risk of money laundering or terrorist financing as referred to in Article 11(2) and (5);

    (c)   establishment of technical criteria for assessing whether situations represent a high risk of money laundering or terrorist financing as referred to in Article 13;

    (d)   establishment of technical criteria for assessing whether, in accordance with Article 2(2), it is justified not to apply this Directive to certain legal or natural persons carrying out a financial activity on an occasional or very limited basis.

[The measures referred to in the first subparagraph, designed to amend non-essential elements of this Directive, inter alia by supplementing it, shall be adopted in accordance with the regulatory procedure with scrutiny referred to in Article 41(2a).]

2.   In any event, the Commission shall adopt the first implementing measures to give effect to paragraphs 1(b) and 1(d) by 15 June 2006.

3.   The Commission shall … adapt the amounts referred to in Articles 2(1)(3)(e), 7(b), 10(1) and 11(5)(a) and (d) taking into account Community legislation, economic developments and changes in international standards.

[The measures referred to in the first subparagraph, designed to amend non-essential elements of this Directive, shall be adopted in accordance with the regulatory procedure with scrutiny referred to in Article 41(2a).]

4.   Where the Commission finds that a third country does not meet the conditions laid down in Article 11(1) or (2), Article 28(3), (4) or (5), or in the measures established in accordance with paragraph 1(b) of this Article or in Article 16(1)(b), or that the legislation of that third country does not permit application of the measures required under the first subparagraph of Article 31(1), it shall adopt a decision so stating in accordance with the procedure referred to in Article 41(2).

[5761]

NOTES

Words omitted repealed, and words in square brackets inserted, by European Parliament and Council Directive 2008/20/EC, Art 1(1), (2), as from 20 March 2008.

Article 41

1.   The Commission shall be assisted by a Committee on the Prevention of Money Laundering and Terrorist Financing, hereinafter "the Committee".

2.   Where reference is made to this paragraph, Articles 5 and 7 of Decision 1999/468/EC shall apply, having regard to the provisions of Article 8 thereof and provided that the implementing measures adopted in accordance with this procedure do not modify the essential provisions of this Directive.

The period laid down in Article 5(6) of Decision 1999/468/EC shall be set at three months.

[2a.   Where reference is made to this paragraph, Article 5a(1) to (4) and Article 7 of Decision 1999/468/EC shall apply, having regard to the provisions of Article 8 thereof.]

[3.   By 31 December 2010, and thereafter at least every three years, the Commission shall review the provisions concerning its implementing powers and present a report to the European Parliament and to the Council on the functioning of those powers. The report shall examine, in particular, the need for the Commission to propose amendments to this Directive in order to ensure the appropriate scope of the implementing powers conferred on the Commission. The conclusion as to whether or not an amendment is necessary shall be accompanied by a detailed statement of reasons. If necessary, the report shall be accompanied by a legislative proposal to amend the provisions conferring implementing powers on the Commission.]

PART IV
EC MATERIALS

4. Without prejudice to the implementing measures already adopted, the implementation of the provisions of this Directive concerning the adoption of technical rules and decisions in accordance with the procedure referred to in paragraph 2 shall be suspended four years after the entry into force of this Directive. On a proposal from the Commission, the European Parliament and the Council may renew the provisions concerned in accordance with the procedure laid down in Article 251 of the Treaty and, to that end, shall review them prior to the expiry of the four-year period.

[5762]

NOTES

Para 2a: inserted by European Parliament and Council Directive 2008/20/EC, Art 1(3)(a), as from 20 March 2008.

Para 3: substituted, for original paras 3, 4, by European Parliament and Council Directive 2008/20/EC, Art 1(3)(b), as from 20 March 2008.

CHAPTER VII
FINAL PROVISIONS

Article 42

By 15 December 2009, and at least at three-yearly intervals thereafter, the Commission shall draw up a report on the implementation of this Directive and submit it to the European Parliament and the Council. For the first such report, the Commission shall include a specific examination of the treatment of lawyers and other independent legal professionals.

[5763]

Article 43

By 15 December 2010, the Commission shall present a report to the European Parliament and to the Council on the threshold percentages in Article 3(6), paying particular attention to the possible expediency and consequences of a reduction of the percentage in points (a)(i), (b)(i) and (b)(iii) of Article 3(6) from 25% to 20%. On the basis of the report the Commission may submit a proposal for amendments to this Directive.

[5764]

Article 44

Directive 91/308/EEC is hereby repealed.

References made to the repealed Directive shall be construed as being made to this Directive and should be read in accordance with the correlation table set out in the Annex.

[5765]

Article 45

1. Member States shall bring into force the laws, regulations and administrative provisions necessary to comply with this Directive by 15 December 2007. They shall forthwith communicate to the Commission the text of those provisions together with a table showing how the provisions of this Directive correspond to the national provisions adopted.

When Member States adopt those measures, they shall contain a reference to this Directive or be accompanied by such a reference on the occasion of their official publication. The methods of making such reference shall be laid down by Member States.

2. Member States shall communicate to the Commission the text of the main provisions of national law which they adopt in the field covered by this Directive.

[5766]

Article 46

This Directive shall enter into force on the 20th day after its publication in the Official Journal of the European Union.

[5767]

Article 47

This Directive is addressed to the Member States.

[5768]

ANNEX

CORRELATION TABLE

This Directive	Directive 91/308/EEC
Article 1(1)	Article 2
Article 1(2)	Article 1(C)
Article 1(2)(a)	Article 1(C) first point
Article 1(2)(b)	Article 1(C) second point
Article 1(2)(c)	Article 1(C) third point
Article 1(2)(d)	Article 1(C) fourth point
Article 1(3)	Article 1(C), third paragraph
Article 1(4)	
Article 1(5)	Article 1(C), second paragraph
Article 2(1)(1)	Article 2a(1)
Article 2(1)(2)	Article 2a(2)
Article 2(1)(3)(a), (b) and (d) to (f)	Article 2a(3) to (7)
Article 2(1)(3)(c)	
Article 2(2)	
Article 3(1)	Article 1(A)
Article 3(2)(a)	Article 1(B)(1)
Article 3(2)(b)	Article 1(B)(2)
Article 3(2)(c)	Article 1(B)(3)
Article 3(2)(d)	Article 1(B)(4)
Article 3(2)(e)	
Article 3(2)(f)	Article 1(B), second paragraph
Article 3(3)	Article 1(D)
Article 3(4)	Article 1(E), first paragraph
Article 3(5)	Article 1(E), second paragraph
Article 3(5)(a)	
Article 3(5)(b)	Article 1(E), first indent
Article 3(5)(c)	Article 1(E), second indent
Article 3(5)(d)	Article 1(E), third indent
Article 3(5)(e)	Article 1(E), fourth indent
Article 3(5)(f)	Article 1(E), fifth indent, and third paragraph
Article 3(6)	
Article 3(7)	
Article 3(8)	
Article 3(9)	
Article 3(10)	
Article 4	Article 12
Article 5	Article 15
Article 6	
Article 7(a)	Article 3(1)
Article 7(b)	Article 3(2)
Article 7(c)	Article 3(8)

This Directive	Directive 91/308/EEC
Article 7(d)	Article 3(7)
Article 8(1)(a)	Article 3(1)
Article 8(1)(b) to (d)	
Article 8(2)	
Article 9(1)	Article 3(1)
Article 9(2) to (6)	
Article 10	Article 3(5) and (6)
Article 11(1)	Article 3(9)
Article 11(2)	
Article 11(3) and (4)	
Article 11(5)(a)	Article 3(3)
Article 11(5)(b)	Article 3(4)
Article 11(5)(c)	Article 3(4)
Article 11(5)(d)	
Article 12	
Article 13(1) and (2)	Article 3(10) and (11)
Article 13(3) to (5)	
Article 13(6)	Article 5
Article 14	
Article 15	
Article 16	
Article 17	
Article 18	
Article 19	
Article 20	Article 5
Article 21	
Article 22	Article 6(1) and (2)
Article 23	Article 6(3)
Article 24	Article 7
Article 25	Article 10
Article 26	Article 9
Article 27	
Article 28(1)	Article 8(1)
Article 28(2) to (7)	
Article 29	
Article 30(a)	Article 4, first indent
Article 30(b)	Article 4, second indent
Article 31	
Article 32	
Article 33	
Article 34(1)	Article 11(1)(a)
Article 34(2)	
Article 35(1), first paragraph	Article 11(1)(b), first sentence
Article 35(1), second paragraph	Article 11(1)(b) second sentence
Article 35(1), third paragraph	Article 11(1), second paragraph

This Directive	Directive 91/308/EEC
Article 35(2)	
Article 35(3)	
Article 36	
Article 37	
Article 38	
Article 39(1)	Article 14
Article 39(2) to (4)	
Article 40	
Article 41	
Article 42	Article 17
Article 43	
Article 44	
Article 45	Article 16
Article 46	Article 16

[5769]

EUROPEAN PARLIAMENT AND COUNCIL REGULATION

of 26 October 2005

on controls of cash entering or leaving the Community

(1889/2005/EC)

NOTES

Date of publication in OJ: OJ L309, 25.11.2005, p 9. Notes are as in the original OJ version.
As of 1 February 2009, this Regulation had not been amended.

THE EUROPEAN PARLIAMENT AND THE COUNCIL OF THE EUROPEAN UNION,

Having regard to the Treaty establishing the European Community, and in particular Articles 95 and 135 thereof,

Having regard to the proposal from the Commission,[1]

After consulting the European Economic and Social Committee,

Acting in accordance with the procedure referred to in Article 251 of the Treaty,[2]

Whereas:

(1) One of the Community's tasks is to promote harmonious, balanced and sustainable development of economic activities throughout the Community by establishing a common market and an economic and monetary union. To that end the internal market comprises an area without internal frontiers in which the free movement of goods, persons, services and capital is ensured.

(2) The introduction of the proceeds of illegal activities into the financial system and their investment after laundering are detrimental to sound and sustainable economic development. Accordingly, Council Directive 91/308/EEC of 10 June 1991 on prevention of the use of the financial system for the purpose of money laundering[3] introduced a Community mechanism to prevent money laundering by monitoring transactions through credit and financial institutions and certain types of professions. As there is a risk that the application of that mechanism will lead to an increase in cash movements for illicit purposes, Directive 91/308/EEC should be supplemented by a control system on cash entering or leaving the Community.

(3) At present such control systems are applied by only a few Member States, acting under national legislation. The disparities in legislation are detrimental to the proper functioning of the internal market. The basic elements should therefore be harmonised at Community level to ensure an equivalent level of control on movements of cash crossing the borders of the Community. Such harmonisation should not, however, affect the possibility for Member States to apply, in accordance with the existing provisions of the Treaty, national controls on movements of cash within the Community.

(4)   Account should also be taken of complementary activities carried out in other international fora, in particular those of the Financial Action Task Force on Money Laundering (FATF), which was established by the G7 Summit held in Paris in 1989. Special Recommendation IX of 22 October 2004 of the FATF calls on governments to take measures to detect physical cash movements, including a declaration system or other disclosure obligation.

(5)   Accordingly, cash carried by any natural person entering or leaving the Community should be subject to the principle of obligatory declaration. This principle would enable the customs authorities to gather information on such cash movements and, where appropriate, transmit that information to other authorities. Customs authorities are present at the borders of the Community, where controls are most effective, and some have already built up practical experience in the matter. Use should be made of Council Regulation (EC) No 515/97 of 13 March 1997 on mutual assistance between the administrative authorities of the Member States and cooperation between the latter and the Commission to ensure the correct application of the law on customs and agricultural matters.[4] This mutual assistance should ensure both the correct application of cash controls and the transmission of information that might help to achieve the objectives of Directive 91/308/EEC.

(6)   In view of its preventive purpose and deterrent character, the obligation to declare should be fulfilled upon entering or leaving the Community. However, in order to focus the authorities' action on significant movements of cash, only those movements of EUR 10,000 or more should be subject to such an obligation. Also, it should be specified that the obligation to declare applies to the natural person carrying the cash, regardless of whether that person is the owner.

(7)   Use should be made of a common standard for the information to be provided. This will enable competent authorities to exchange information more easily.

(8)   It is desirable to establish the definitions needed for a uniform interpretation of this Regulation.

(9)   Information gathered under this Regulation by the competent authorities should be passed on to the authorities referred to in Article 6(1) of Directive 91/308/EEC.

(10)   Directive 95/46/EC of the European Parliament and of the Council of 24 October 1995 on the protection of individuals with regard to the processing of personal data and on the free movement of such data[5] and Regulation (EC) No 45/2001 of the European Parliament and of the Council of 18 December 2000 on the protection of individuals with regard to the processing of personal data by the Community institutions and bodies and on the free movement of such data[6] apply to the processing of personal data by the competent authorities of the Member States pursuant to this Regulation.

(11)   Where there are indications that the sums of cash are related to any illegal activity, associated with the movement of cash, as referred to in Directive 91/308/EEC, information gathered under this Regulation by the competent authorities may be passed on to competent authorities in other Member States and/or to the Commission. Similarly, provision should be made for certain information to be transmitted whenever there are indications of cash movements involving sums lower than the threshold laid down in this Regulation.

(12)   Competent authorities should be vested with the powers needed to exercise effective control on movements of cash.

(13)   The powers of the competent authorities should be supplemented by an obligation on the Member States to lay down penalties. However, penalties should be imposed only for failure to make a declaration in accordance with this Regulation.

(14)   Since the objective of this Regulation cannot be sufficiently achieved by the Member States and can therefore, by reason of the transnational scale of money laundering in the internal market, be better achieved at Community level, the Community may adopt measures, in accordance with the principle of subsidiarity as set out in Article 5 of the Treaty. In accordance with the principle of proportionality, as set out in that Article, this Regulation does not go beyond what is necessary in order to achieve that objective.

(15)   This Regulation respects the fundamental rights and observes the principles recognised in Article 6(2) of the Treaty on European Union and reflected in the Charter of Fundamental Rights of the European Union, in particular in Article 8 thereof,

[5770]

NOTES
1   OJ C227E, 24.9.2002, p 574.
2   Opinion of the European Parliament of 15 May 2003 (OJ C67E, 17.3.2004, p 259), Council Common Position of 17 February 2005 (OJ C144E, 14.6.2005, p 1), Position of the European Parliament of 8 June 2005 and Council Decision of 12 July 2005.
3   OJ L166, 28.6.1991, p 77. Directive as amended by Directive 2001/97/EC of the European Parliament and of the Council (OJ L344, 28.12.2001, p 76).
4   OJ L82, 22.3.1997, p 1. Regulation as amended by Regulation (EC) No 807/2003 (OJ L122, 16.5.2003, p 36).
5   OJ L281, 23.11.1995, p 31. Directive as amended by Regulation (EC) No 1882/2003 (OJ L284, 31.10.2003, p 1).
6   OJ L8, 12.1.2001, p 1.

HAVE ADOPTED THIS REGULATION:

Article 1
Objective

1.   This Regulation complements the provisions of Directive 91/308/EEC concerning transactions through financial and credit institutions and certain professions by laying down harmonised rules for the control, by the competent authorities, of cash entering or leaving the Community.

2.   This Regulation shall be without prejudice to national measures to control cash movements within the Community, where such measures are taken in accordance with Article 58 of the Treaty.

[5770A]

Article 2
Definitions

For the purposes of this Regulation:
   1.   "competent authorities" means the customs authorities of the Member States or any other authorities empowered by Member States to apply this Regulation;
   2.   "cash" means:
      (a)   bearer-negotiable instruments including monetary instruments in bearer form such as travellers cheques, negotiable instruments (including cheques, promissory notes and money orders) that are either in bearer form, endorsed without restriction, made out to a fictitious payee, or otherwise in such form that title thereto passes upon delivery and incomplete instruments (including cheques, promissory notes and money orders) signed, but with the payee's name omitted;
      (b)   currency (banknotes and coins that are in circulation as a medium of exchange).

[5771]

Article 3
Obligation to declare

1.   Any natural person entering or leaving the Community and carrying cash of a value of EUR 10,000 or more shall declare that sum to the competent authorities of the Member State through which he is entering or leaving the Community in accordance with this Regulation. The obligation to declare shall not have been fulfilled if the information provided is incorrect or incomplete.

2.   The declaration referred to in paragraph 1 shall contain details of:
   (a)   the declarant, including full name, date and place of birth and nationality;
   (b)   the owner of the cash;
   (c)   the intended recipient of the cash;
   (d)   the amount and nature of the cash;
   (e)   the provenance and intended use of the cash;
   (f)   the transport route;
   (g)   the means of transport.

3.   Information shall be provided in writing, orally or electronically, to be determined by the Member State referred to in paragraph 1. However, where the declarant so requests, he shall be entitled to provide the information in writing. Where a written declaration has been lodged, an endorsed copy shall be delivered to the declarant upon request.

[5772]

Article 4
Powers of the competent authorities

1.   In order to check compliance with the obligation to declare laid down in Article 3, officials of the competent authorities shall be empowered, in accordance with the conditions laid down under national legislation, to carry out controls on natural persons, their baggage and their means of transport.

2.   In the event of failure to comply with the obligation to declare laid down in Article 3, cash may be detained by administrative decision in accordance with the conditions laid down under national legislation.

[5773]

Article 5
Recording and processing of information

1.   The information obtained under Article 3 and/or Article 4 shall be recorded and processed by the competent authorities of the Member State referred to in Article 3(1) and shall be made available to the authorities referred to in Article 6(1) of Directive 91/308/EEC of that Member State.

2.   Where it appears from the controls provided for in Article 4 that a natural person is entering or leaving the Community with sums of cash lower than the threshold fixed in Article 3 and where

there are indications of illegal activities associated with the movement of cash, as referred to in Directive 91/308/EEC, that information, the full name, date and place of birth and nationality of that person and details of the means of transport used may also be recorded and processed by the competent authorities of the Member State referred to in Article 3(1) and be made available to the authorities referred to in Article 6(1) of Directive 91/308/EEC of that Member State.

[5774]

Article 6
Exchange of information

1. Where there are indications that the sums of cash are related to any illegal activity associated with the movement of cash, as referred to in Directive 91/308/EEC, the information obtained through the declaration provided for in Article 3 or the controls provided for in Article 4 may be transmitted to competent authorities in other Member States.

Regulation (EC) No 515/97 shall apply *mutatis mutandis*.

2. Where there are indications that the sums of cash involve the proceeds of fraud or any other illegal activity adversely affecting the financial interests of the Community, the information shall also be transmitted to the Commission.

[5775]

Article 7
Exchange of information with third countries

In the framework of mutual administrative assistance, the information obtained under this Regulation may be communicated by Member States or by the Commission to a third country, subject to the consent of the competent authorities which obtained the information pursuant to Article 3 and/or Article 4 and to compliance with the relevant national and Community provisions on the transfer of personal data to third countries. Member States shall notify the Commission of such exchanges of information where particularly relevant for the implementation of this Regulation.

[5776]

Article 8
Duty of professional secrecy

All information which is by nature confidential or which is provided on a confidential basis shall be covered by the duty of professional secrecy. It shall not be disclosed by the competent authorities without the express permission of the person or authority providing it. The communication of information shall, however, be permitted where the competent authorities are obliged to do so pursuant to the provisions in force, particularly in connection with legal proceedings. Any disclosure or communication of information shall fully comply with prevailing data protection provisions, in particular Directive 95/46/EC and Regulation (EC) No 45/2001.

[5777]

Article 9
Penalties

1. Each Member State shall introduce penalties to apply in the event of failure to comply with the obligation to declare laid down in Article 3. Such penalties shall be effective, proportionate and dissuasive.

2. By 15 June 2007, Member States shall notify the Commission of the penalties applicable in the event of failure to comply with the obligation to declare laid down in Article 3.

[5778]

Article 10
Evaluation

The Commission shall submit to the European Parliament and the Council a report on the application of this Regulation four years after its entry into force.

[5779]

Article 11
Entry into force

This Regulation shall enter into force on the twentieth day following that of its publication in the *Official Journal of the European Union*.

It shall apply from 15 June 2007.

This Regulation shall be binding in its entirety and directly applicable in all Member States.

[5780]

DIRECTIVE OF THE EUROPEAN PARLIAMENT AND OF THE COUNCIL

of 5 April 2006

amending directive 2004/39/EC on markets in financial instruments, as regards certain deadlines

(2006/31/EC)

(Text with EEA relevance)

NOTES

Date of Publication in OJ: OJ L114, 27.4.2006, p 60. Notes are as in the original OJ version.
As of 1 February 2009, this Directive had not been amended.

THE EUROPEAN PARLIAMENT AND THE COUNCIL OF THE EUROPEAN UNION,

Having regard to the Treaty establishing the European Community, and in particular Article 47(2) thereof,

Having regard to the proposal from the Commission,

After consulting the European Economic and Social Committee,

Having regard to the opinion of European Central Bank,[1]

Acting in accordance with the procedure laid down in Article 251 of the Treaty,[2]

Whereas:

(1) Directive 2004/39/EC of the European Parliament and of the Council of 21 April 2004 on markets in financial instruments[3] introduces a comprehensive regulatory regime to ensure a high quality of execution of investor transactions.

(2) Directive 2004/39/EC provides that Member States are to adopt the laws, regulations and administrative provisions necessary to comply with it by 30 April 2006. In order to ensure uniform application in the Member States, a significant number of complex provisions of that Directive need to be supplemented by implementing measures, to be adopted by the Commission during the period for transposition by Member States. Because Member States cannot fully prepare and finalise their national laws until the content of the implementing measures is clear, they may have difficulty in meeting the current transposition deadline.

(3) In order to comply with the requirements of Directive 2004/39/EC and national implementing legislation, investment firms and other regulated entities may have to introduce new information technology systems, new organisational structures, and reporting and recordkeeping procedures, or to make significant modifications to existing systems and practices. This can only be done once the contents of the implementing measures to be adopted by the Commission and of the national legislation transposing the Directive are settled.

(4) It is also necessary that Directive 2004/39/EC and its implementing measures be transposed into national law or apply directly in Member States simultaneously for the Directive to produce its full effect.

(5) It is therefore appropriate to extend the deadline for Member States to transpose Directive 2004/39/EC into national law. Similarly, the deadline for investment firms and credit institutions to comply with the new requirements should be postponed for a period after the transposition into national law has been completed by the Member States.

(6) Given the interaction between the different provisions of Directive 2004/39/EC, it is appropriate that any extension of those deadlines apply to all the provisions of that Directive. Any extension of the transposition and application deadlines should be proportionate to, and not exceed, the needs of the Member States and regulated entities. In order to avoid fragmentation that could hamper the functioning of the internal market in securities, Member States should apply the provisions of Directive 2004/39/EC at the same time.

(7) In its Resolution of 5 February 2002 on the implementation of financial services legislation,[4] the European Parliament requested that it and the Council should have an equal role in supervising the way in which the Commission exercises its executive role in order to reflect the legislative powers of the European Parliament under Article 251 of the Treaty. In the solemn declaration made before the European Parliament the same day by its President, the Commission supported that request. On 11 December 2002, the Commission proposed amendments to Council Decision 1999/468/ EC of 28 June 1999 laying down the procedures for the exercise of implementing powers conferred on the Commission,[5] and then submitted an amended proposal on 22 April 2004. The European Parliament does not consider that this proposal preserves its legislative prerogatives. In the view of the European Parliament, it and the Council should have the opportunity of evaluating the conferral of implementing powers on the Commission within a determined period. It is therefore appropriate to limit the period during which the Commission may adopt implementing measures.

(8) The European Parliament should be given a period of three months from the first transmission of draft amendments and implementing measures to allow it to examine them and to give its opinion. However, in urgent and duly justified cases, it should be possible to shorten that period. If, within that period, a resolution is adopted by the European Parliament, the Commission should re-examine the draft amendments or measures.

(9) Further consequential amendments are necessary to postpone the dates for the repeal of Council Directive 93/22/EEC of 10 May 1993 on investment services in the securities field[6] and for the transitional provisions laid down in Directive 2004/39/EC, and to extend the timetable for the Commission's reporting obligations.

(10) Given the postponed deadline between the obligation for Member States to transpose Directive 2004/39/EC into national law and the deadline for investment firms and credit institutions to comply with the new requirements, the provisions of Directive 2004/39/EC will remain ineffective until 1 November 2007; it is therefore appropriate to repeal Directive 93/22/EEC with effect from 1 November 2007.

(11) Directive 2004/39/EC should therefore be amended accordingly,

[5781]

NOTES
1   OJ C323, 20.12.2005, p 31.
2   Opinion of the European Parliament of 13 December 2005 (not yet published in the Official Journal) and Council Decision of 10 March 2006.
3   OJ L145, 30.4.2004, p 1.
4   OJ C284E, 21.11.2002, p 115.
5   OJ L184, 17.7.1999, p 23.
6   OJ L141, 11.6.1993, p 27. Directive as last amended by Directive 2002/87/EC of the European Parliament and of the Council (OJ L35, 11.2.2003, p 1).

HAVE ADOPTED THIS DIRECTIVE:

Article 1

(Amends Directive 2004/39/EC, Arts 64, 70, 71 at **[5585]**, **[5591]**, **[5592]** *(and the recitals to that Directive at* **[5522]**)*, and substitutes Arts 65, 69 at* **[5586]**, **[5590]**.)

Article 2

1. Member States shall adopt the laws, regulations and administrative provisions necessary to comply with this Directive by 31 January 2007. They shall forthwith inform the Commission thereof. They shall apply these measures from 1 November 2007.

2. When Member States adopt these measures, they shall contain a reference to this Directive or shall be accompanied by such reference on the occasion of their official publication. The methods of making such reference shall be laid down by Member States.

[5781A]

Article 3

This Directive shall enter into force on the day following that of its publication in the Official Journal of the European Union.

[5782]

Article 4

This Directive is addressed to the Member States.

[5783]

DIRECTIVE OF THE EUROPEAN PARLIAMENT AND OF THE COUNCIL

of 14 June 2006

relating to the taking up and pursuit of the business of credit institutions (recast)

(2006/48/EC)

(Text with EEA relevance)

NOTES
Date of publication in OJ: OJ L177, 30.6.2006, p 1. Notes are as in the original OJ version.

This Directive is reproduced as amended by: Commission Directive 2007/18/EC (OJ L87, 28.3.2007, p 9); European Parliament and Council Directive 2007/44/EC (OJ L247, 21.9.2007, p 1); European Parliament and Council Directive 2007/64/EC (OJ L319, 5.12.2007, p 1); European Parliament and Council Directive 2008/24/EC (OJ L81, 20.3.2008, p 38).

Proposed amendments of this Directive: see the 2008 Proposal for a Directive of the European Parliament and of the Council on the taking up, pursuit and prudential supervision of the business of electronic money institutions, amending Directives 2005/60/EC and 2006/48/EC and repealing Directive 2000/46/EC.[1]

See also the 2008 Proposal for a Directive of the European Parliament and of the Council amending Directives 2006/48/EC and 2006/49/EC as regards banks affiliated to central institutions, certain own funds items, large exposures, supervisory arrangements, and crisis management.[2]

[1]   Brussels, 9.10.2008, COM(2008) 627 final. Available on the Europa website.
[2]   Brussels, 1.10.2008, COM(2008) 602 final. Available on the Europa website.

THE EUROPEAN PARLIAMENT AND THE COUNCIL OF THE EUROPEAN UNION,

Having regard to the Treaty establishing the European Community, and in particular the first and third sentences of Article 47(2) thereof,

Having regard to the proposal from the Commission,

Having regard to the Opinion of the European Economic and Social Committee,[1]

Having regard to the Opinion of the European Central Bank,[2]

Acting in accordance with the procedure laid down in Article 251 of the Treaty,[3]

Whereas:

(1)   Directive 2000/12/EC of the European Parliament and of the Council of 20 March 2000 relating to the taking up and pursuit of the business of credit institutions[4] has been significantly amended on several occasions. Now that new amendments are being made to the said Directive, it is desirable, in order to clarify matters, that it should be recast.

(2)   In order to make it easier to take up and pursue the business of credit institutions, it is necessary to eliminate the most obstructive differences between the laws of the Member States as regards the rules to which these institutions are subject.

(3)   This Directive constitutes the essential instrument for the achievement of the internal market from the point of view of both the freedom of establishment and the freedom to provide financial services, in the field of credit institutions.

(4)   The Commission Communication of 11 May 1999 entitled "Implementing the framework for financial markets: Action plan", listed a number of goals that need to be achieved in order to complete the internal market in financial services. The Lisbon European Council of 23 and 24 March 2000 set the goal of implementing the action plan by 2005. Recasting of the provisions on own funds is a key element of the action plan.

(5)   Measures to coordinate credit institutions should, both in order to protect savings and to create equal conditions of competition between these institutions, apply to all of them. Due regard should however be had to the objective differences in their statutes and their proper aims as laid down by national laws.

(6)   The scope of those measures should therefore be as broad as possible, covering all institutions whose business is to receive repayable funds from the public, whether in the form of deposits or in other forms such as the continuing issue of bonds and other comparable securities and to grant credits for their own account. Exceptions should be provided for in the case of certain credit institutions to which this Directive cannot apply. The provisions of this Directive should not prejudice the application of national laws which provide for special supplementary authorisations permitting credit institutions to carry on specific activities or undertake specific kinds of operations.

(7)   It is appropriate to effect only the essential harmonisation necessary and sufficient to secure the mutual recognition of authorisation and of prudential supervision systems, making possible the granting of a single licence recognised throughout the Community and the application of the principle of home Member State prudential supervision. Therefore, the requirement that a programme of operations be produced should be seen merely as a factor enabling the competent authorities to decide on the basis of more precise information using objective criteria. A measure of flexibility should nonetheless be possible as regards the requirements on the legal form of credit institutions concerning the protection of banking names.

(8)   Since the objectives of this Directive, namely the introduction of rules concerning the taking up and pursuit of the business of credit institutions, and their prudential supervision, cannot be sufficiently achieved by the Member States and can therefore, by reason of the scale and the effects of the proposed action, be better achieved at Community level, the Community may adopt measures, in accordance with the principle of subsidiarity as set out in Article 5 of the Treaty. In accordance with the principle of proportionality, as set out in that Article, this Directive does not go beyond what is necessary in order to achieve those objectives.

(9)   Equivalent financial requirements for credit institutions are necessary to ensure similar safeguards for savers and fair conditions of competition between comparable groups of credit institutions. Pending further coordination, appropriate structural ratios should be formulated making it possible within the framework of cooperation between national authorities to observe, in accordance with standard methods, the position of comparable types of credit institutions. This procedure should help to bring about the gradual approximation of the systems of coefficients

established and applied by the Member States. It is necessary, however to make a distinction between coefficients intended to ensure the sound management of credit institutions and those established for the purposes of economic and monetary policy.

(10) The principles of mutual recognition and home Member State supervision require that Member States' competent authorities should not grant or should withdraw an authorisation where factors such as the content of the activities programmes, the geographical distribution of activities or the activities actually carried on indicate clearly that a credit institution has opted for the legal system of one Member State for the purpose of evading the stricter standards in force in another Member State within whose territory it carries on or intends to carry on the greater Part of its activities. Where there is no such clear indication, but the majority of the total assets of the entities in a banking group are located in another Member State the competent authorities of which are responsible for exercising supervision on a consolidated basis, in the context of Articles 125 and 126 responsibility for exercising supervision on a consolidated basis should be changed only with the agreement of those competent authorities. A credit institution which is a legal person should be authorised in the Member State in which it has its registered office. A credit institution which is not a legal person should have its head office in the Member State in which it has been authorised. In addition, Member States should require that a credit institution's head office always be situated in its home Member State and that it actually operates there.

(11) The competent authorities should not authorise or continue the authorisation of a credit institution where they are liable to be prevented from effectively exercising their supervisory functions by the close links between that institution and other natural or legal persons. Credit institutions already authorised should also satisfy the competent authorities in that respect.

(12) The reference to the supervisory authorities' effective exercise of their supervisory functions covers supervision on a consolidated basis which should be exercised over a credit institution where the provisions of Community law so provide. In such cases, the authorities applied to for authorisation should be able to identify the authorities competent to exercise supervision on a consolidated basis over that credit institution.

(13) This Directive enables Member States and/or competent authorities to apply capital requirements on a solo and consolidated basis, and to disapply solo where they deem this appropriate. Solo, consolidated and cross-border consolidated supervision are useful tools in overseeing credit institutions. This Directive enables competent authorities to support cross border institutions by facilitating cooperation between them. In particular, the competent authorities should continue to make use of Articles 42, 131 and 141 to coordinate their activities and information requests.

(14) Credit institutions authorised in their home Member States should be allowed to carry on, throughout the Community, any or all of the activities listed in Annex I by establishing branches or by providing services.

(15) The Member States may also establish stricter rules than those laid down in Article 9(1), first subparagraph, Article 9(2) and Articles 12, 19 to 21, 44 to 52, 75 and 120 to 122 for credit institutions authorised by their competent authorities. The Member States may also require that Article 123 be complied with on an individual or other basis, and that the sub-consolidation described in Article 73(2) be applied to other levels within a group.

(16) It is appropriate to extend mutual recognition to the activities listed in Annex I when they are carried on by financial institutions which are subsidiaries of credit institutions, provided that such subsidiaries are covered by the consolidated supervision of their parent undertakings and meet certain strict conditions.

(17) The host Member State should be able, in connection with the exercise of the right of establishment and the freedom to provide services, to require compliance with specific provisions of its own national laws or regulations on the Part of institutions not authorised as credit institutions in their home Member States and with regard to activities not listed in Annex I provided that, on the one hand, such provisions are compatible with Community law and are intended to protect the general good and that, on the other hand, such institutions or such activities are not subject to equivalent rules under this legislation or regulations of their home Member States.

(18) The Member States should ensure that there are no obstacles to carrying on activities receiving mutual recognition in the same manner as in the home Member State, as long as the latter do not conflict with legal provisions protecting the general good in the host Member State.

(19) The rules governing branches of credit institutions having their head office outside the Community should be analogous in all Member States. It is important to provide that such rules may not be more favourable than those for branches of institutions from another Member State. The Community should be able to conclude agreements with third countries providing for the application of rules which accord such branches the same treatment throughout its territory. The branches of credit institutions authorised in third countries should not enjoy the freedom to provide services under the second paragraph of Article 49 of the Treaty or the freedom of establishment in Member States other than those in which they are established.

(20) Agreement should be reached, on the basis of reciprocity, between the Community and third countries with a view to allowing the practical exercise of consolidated supervision over the largest possible geographical area.

(21) Responsibility for supervising the financial soundness of a credit institution, and in particular its solvency, should lay with its home Member State. The host Member State's competent authorities should be responsible for the supervision of the liquidity of the branches and monetary policies. The supervision of market risk should be the subject of close cooperation between the competent authorities of the home and host Member States.

(22) The smooth operation of the internal banking market requires not only legal rules but also close and regular cooperation and significantly enhanced convergence of regulatory and supervisory practices between the competent authorities of the Member States. To this end, in particular, consideration of problems concerning individual credit institutions and the mutual exchange of information should take place in the Committee of European Banking Supervisors set up by Commission Decision 2004/5/EC.[5] That mutual information procedure should not in any case replace bilateral cooperation. Without prejudice to their own powers of control, the competent authorities of the host Member States should be able, in an emergency, on their own initiative or following the initiative of the competent authorities of home Member State, to verify that the activities of a credit institution established within their territories comply with the relevant laws and with the principles of sound administrative and accounting procedures and adequate internal control.

(23) It is appropriate to allow the exchange of information between the competent authorities and authorities or bodies which, by virtue of their function, help to strengthen the stability of the financial system. In order to preserve the confidential nature of the information forwarded, the list of addressees should remain within strict limits.

(24) Certain behaviour, such as fraud and insider offences, is liable to affect the stability, including the integrity, of the financial system, even when involving institutions other than credit institutions. It is necessary to specify the conditions under which exchange of information in such cases is authorised.

(25) Where it is stipulated that information may be disclosed only with the express agreement of the competent authorities, these should be able, where appropriate, to make their agreement subject to compliance with strict conditions.

(26) Exchanges of information between, on the one hand, the competent authorities and, on the other, central banks and other bodies with a similar function in their capacity as monetary authorities and, where appropriate, other public authorities responsible for supervising payment systems should also be authorised.

(27) For the purpose of strengthening the prudential supervision of credit institutions and the protection of clients of credit institutions, auditors should have a duty to report promptly to the competent authorities, wherever, during the performance of their tasks, they become aware of certain facts which are liable to have a serious effect on the financial situation or the administrative and accounting organisation of a credit institution. For the same reason Member States should also provide that such a duty applies in all circumstances where such facts are discovered by an auditor during the performance of his tasks in an undertaking which has close links with a credit institution. The duty of auditors to communicate, where appropriate, to the competent authorities certain facts and decisions concerning a credit institution which they discover during the performance of their tasks in a non-financial undertaking should not in itself change the nature of their tasks in that undertaking nor the manner in which they should perform those tasks in that undertaking.

(28) This Directive specifies that for certain own funds items qualifying criteria should be specified, without prejudice to the possibility of Member States to apply more stringent provisions.

(29) According to the nature of the items constituting own funds, this Directive distinguishes between on the one hand, items constituting original own funds and, on the other, those constituting additional own funds.

(30) To reflect the fact that items constituting additional own funds are not of the same nature as those constituting original own funds, the amount of the former included in own funds should not exceed the original own funds. Moreover, the amount of certain items of additional own funds included should not exceed one half of the original own funds.

(31) In order to avoid distortions of competition, public credit institutions should not include in their own funds guarantees granted them by the Member States or local authorities.

(32) Whenever in the course of supervision it is necessary to determine the amount of the consolidated own funds of a group of credit institutions, the calculation should be effected in accordance with this Directive.

(33) The precise accounting technique to be used for the calculation of own funds, their adequacy for the risk to which a credit institution is exposed, and for the assessment of the concentration of exposures should take account of the provisions of Council Directive 86/635/EEC of 8 December 1986 on the annual accounts and consolidated accounts of banks and other financial institutions,[6] which incorporates certain adaptations of the provisions of Seventh Council Directive 83/349/EEC of 13 June 1983 on consolidated accounts[7] or of Regulation (EC) No 1606/2002 of the European Parliament and of the Council of 19 July 2002 on the application of international accounting standards,[8] whichever governs the accounting of the credit institutions under national law.

(34) Minimum capital requirements play a central role in the supervision of credit institutions and in the mutual recognition of supervisory techniques. In that respect, the provisions on minimum

capital requirements should be considered in conjunction with other specific instruments also harmonising the fundamental techniques for the supervision of credit institutions.

(35)   In order to prevent distortions of competition and to strengthen the banking system in the internal market, it is appropriate to lay down common minimum capital requirements.

(36)   For the purposes of ensuring adequate solvency it is important to lay down minimum capital requirements which weight assets and off-balance-sheet items according to the degree of risk.

(37)   On this point, on 26 June 2004 the Basel Committee on Banking Supervision adopted a framework agreement on the international convergence of capital measurement and capital requirements. The provisions in this Directive on the minimum capital requirements of credit institutions, and the minimum capital provisions in Directive 2006/49/EC of the European Parliament and of the Council of 14 June 2006 on the capital adequacy of investment firms and credit institutions,[9] form an equivalent to the provisions of the Basel framework agreement.

(38)   It is essential to take account of the diversity of credit institutions in the Community by providing alternative approaches to the calculation of minimum capital requirements for credit risk incorporating different levels of risk-sensitivity and requiring different degrees of sophistication. Use of external ratings and credit institutions' own estimates of individual credit risk parameters represents a significant enhancement in the risk-sensitivity and prudential soundness of the credit risk rules. There should be appropriate incentives for credit institutions to move towards the more risk-sensitive approaches. In producing the estimates needed to apply the approaches to credit risk of this Directive, credit institutions will have to adjust their data processing needs to their clients' legitimate data protection interests as governed by the existing Community legislation on data protection, while enhancing credit risk measurement and management processes of credit institutions to make methods for determining credit institutions' regulatory own funds requirements available that reflect the sophistication of individual credit institutions' processes. The processing of data should be in accordance with the rules on transfer of personal data laid down in Directive 95/46/EC of the European Parliament and of the Council of 24 October 1995 on the protection of individuals with regard to the processing of personal data and on the free movement of such data.[10] In this regard, the processing of data in connection with the incurring and management of exposures to customers should be considered to include the development and validation of credit risk management and measurement systems. That serves not only to fulfil the legitimate interest of credit institutions but also the purpose of this Directive, to use better methods for risk measurement and management and also use them for regulatory own funds purposes.

(39)   With regard to the use of both external and an institution's own estimates or internal ratings, account should be taken of the fact that, at present, only the latter are drawn up by an entity — the financial institution itself — which is subject to a Community authorisation process. In the case of external ratings use is made of the products of what are known as recognised rating agencies, which in the Community are not currently subject to an authorisation process. In view of the importance of external ratings in connection with the calculation of capital requirements under this Directive, appropriate future authorisation and supervisory process for rating agencies need to be kept under review.

(40)   The minimum capital requirements should be proportionate to the risks addressed. In particular the reduction in risk levels deriving from having a large number of relatively small exposures should be reflected in the requirements.

(41)   The provisions of this Directive respect the principle of proportionality, having regard in particular to the diversity in size and scale of operations and to the range of activities of credit institutions. Respect of the principle of proportionality also means that the simplest possible rating procedures, even in the Internal Ratings Based Approach ("IRB Approach"), are recognised for retail exposures.

(42)   The "evolutionary" nature of this Directive enables credit institutions to choose amongst three approaches of varying complexity. In order to allow especially small credit institutions to opt for the more risk-sensitive IRB Approach, the competent authorities should implement the provisions of Article 89(1)(a) and (b) whenever appropriate. Those provisions should be read as such that exposure classes referred to in Article 86(1)(a) and (b) include all exposures that are, directly or indirectly, put on a par with them throughout this Directive. As a general rule, the competent authorities should not discriminate between the three approaches with regard to the Supervisory Review Process, ie credit institutions operating according to the provisions of the Standardised Approach should not for that reason alone be supervised on a stricter basis.

(43)   Increased recognition should be given to techniques of credit risk mitigation within a framework of rules designed to ensure that solvency is not undermined by undue recognition. The relevant Member States' current customary banking collateral for mitigating credit risks should wherever possible be recognised in the Standardised Approach, but also in the other approaches.

(44)   In order to ensure that the risks and risk reductions arising from credit institutions' securitisation activities and investments are appropriately reflected in the minimum capital requirements of credit institutions it is necessary to include rules providing for a risk-sensitive and prudentially sound treatment of such activities and investments.

(45) Operational risk is a significant risk faced by credit institutions requiring coverage by own funds. It is essential to take account of the diversity of credit institutions in the Community by providing alternative approaches to the calculation of operational risk requirements incorporating different levels of risk-sensitivity and requiring different degrees of sophistication. There should be appropriate incentives for credit institutions to move towards the more risk-sensitive approaches. In view of the emerging state of the art for the measurement and management of operational risk the rules should be kept under review and updated as appropriate including in relation to the charges for different business lines and the recognition of risk mitigation techniques. Particular attention should be paid in this regard to taking insurance into account in the simple approaches to calculating capital requirements for operational risk.

(46) In order to ensure adequate solvency of credit institutions within a group it is essential that the minimum capital requirements apply on the basis of the consolidated financial situation of the group. In order to ensure that own funds are appropriately distributed within the group and available to protect savings where needed, the minimum capital requirements should apply to individual credit institutions within a group, unless this objective can be effectively otherwise achieved.

(47) The essential rules for monitoring large exposures of credit institutions should be harmonised. Member States should still be able to adopt provisions more stringent than those provided for by this Directive.

(48) The monitoring and control of a credit institution's exposures should be an integral Part of its supervision. Therefore, excessive concentration of exposures to a single client or group of connected clients may result in an unacceptable risk of loss. Such a situation can be considered prejudicial to the solvency of a credit institution.

(49) Since credit institutions in the internal market are engaged in direct competition, monitoring requirements should be equivalent throughout the Community.

(50) While it is appropriate to base the definition of exposures for the purposes of limits to large exposures on that provided for the purposes of minimum own funds requirements for credit risk, it is not appropriate to refer on principle to the weightings or degrees of risk. Those weightings and degrees of risk were devised for the purpose of establishing a general solvency requirement to cover the credit risk of credit institutions. In order to limit the maximum loss that a credit institution may incur through any single client or group of connected clients it is appropriate to adopt rules for the determination of large exposures which take account of the nominal value of the exposure without applying weightings or degrees of risk.

(51) While it is desirable, pending further review of the large exposures provisions, to permit the recognition of the effects of credit risk mitigation in a manner similar to that permitted for minimum capital requirement purposes in order to limit the calculation requirements, the rules on credit risk mitigation were designed in the context of the general diversified credit risk arising from exposures to a large number of counterparties. Accordingly, recognition of the effects of such techniques for the purposes of limits to large exposures designed to limit the maximum loss that may be incurred through any single client or group of connected clients should be subject to prudential safeguards.

(52) When a credit institution incurs an exposure to its own parent undertaking or to other subsidiaries of its parent undertaking, particular prudence is necessary. The management of exposures incurred by credit institutions should be carried out in a fully autonomous manner, in accordance with the principles of sound banking management, without regard to any other considerations. Where the influence exercised by persons directly or indirectly holding a qualifying participation in a credit institution is likely to operate to the detriment of the sound and prudent management of that institution, the competent authorities should take appropriate measures to put an end to that situation. In the field of large exposures, specific standards, including more stringent restrictions, should be laid down for exposures incurred by a credit institution to its own group. Such standards need not, however be applied where the parent undertaking is a financial holding company or a credit institution or where the other subsidiaries are either credit or financial institutions or undertakings offering ancillary services, provided that all such undertakings are covered by the supervision of the credit institution on a consolidated basis.

(53) Credit institutions should ensure that they have internal capital that, having regard to the risks to which they are or may be exposed, is adequate in quantity, quality and distribution. Accordingly, credit institutions should have strategies and processes in place for assessing and maintaining the adequacy of their internal capital.

(54) Competent authorities have responsibility to be satisfied that credit institutions have good organisation and adequate own funds, having regard to the risks to which the credit institutions are or might be exposed.

(55) In order for the internal banking market to operate effectively the Committee of European Banking Supervisors should contribute to the consistent application of this Directive and to the convergence of supervisory practices throughout the Community, and should report on a yearly basis to the Community institutions on progress made.

(56) For the same reason, and to ensure that Community credit institutions which are active in several Member States are not disproportionately burdened as a result of the continued responsibilities of individual Member State competent authorities for authorisation and supervision,

it is essential to significantly enhance the cooperation between competent authorities. In this context, the role of the consolidating supervisor should be strengthened. The Committee of European Banking Supervisors should support and enhance such cooperation.

(57) Supervision of credit institutions on a consolidated basis aims at, in particular, protecting the interests of the depositors of credit institutions and at ensuring the stability of the financial system.

(58) In order to be effective, supervision on a consolidated basis should therefore be applied to all banking groups, including those the parent undertakings of which are not credit institutions. The competent authorities should hold the necessary legal instruments to be able to exercise such supervision.

(59) In the case of groups with diversified activities where parent undertakings control at least one credit institution subsidiary, the competent authorities should be able to assess the financial situation of a credit institution in such a group. The competent authorities should at least have the means of obtaining from all undertakings within a group the information necessary for the performance of their function. Cooperation between the authorities responsible for the supervision of different financial sectors should be established in the case of groups of undertakings carrying on a range of financial activities. Pending subsequent coordination, the Member States should be able to lay down appropriate methods of consolidation for the achievement of the objective of this Directive.

(60) The Member States should be able to refuse or withdraw banking authorisation in the case of certain group structures considered inappropriate for carrying on banking activities, in particular because such structures could not be supervised effectively. In this respect the competent authorities should have the necessary powers to ensure the sound and prudent management of credit institutions.

(61) In order for the internal banking market to operate with increasing effectiveness and for citizens of the Community to be afforded adequate levels of transparency, it is necessary that competent authorities disclose publicly and in a way which allows for meaningful comparison the manner in which this Directive is implemented.

(62) In order to strengthen market discipline and stimulate credit institutions to improve their market strategy, risk control and internal management organization, appropriate public disclosure by credit institutions should be provided for.

(63) The examination of problems connected with matters covered by this Directive, as well as by other Directives on the business of credit institutions, requires cooperation between the competent authorities and the Commission, particularly when conducted with a view to closer coordination.

(64) The measures necessary for the implementation of this Directive should be adopted in accordance with Council Decision 1999/468/EC of 28 June 1999 laying down the procedures for the exercise of implementing powers conferred on the Commission.[11]

(65) In its resolution of 5 February 2002 on the implementation of financial services legislation[12] the Parliament requested that it and the Council should have an equal role in supervising the way in which the Commission exercises its executive role in order to reflect the legislative powers of Parliament under Article 251 of the Treaty. In the solemn declaration made before the Parliament the same day by its President, the Commission supported this request. On 11 December 2002 the Commission proposed amendments to Decision 1999/468/EC, and then submitted an amended proposal on 22 April 2004. The Parliament does not consider that this proposal preserves its legislative prerogatives. In the view of the Parliament, it and the Council should have the opportunity of evaluating the conferral of implementing powers on the Commission within a determined period. It is therefore appropriate to limit the period during which the Commission may adopt implementing measures.

(66) The Parliament should be given a period of three months from the first transmission of draft amendments and implementing measures to allow it to examine them and to give its opinion. However, in urgent and duly justified cases, it should be possible to shorten this period. If, within that period, a resolution is adopted by the Parliament, the Commission should re-examine the draft amendments or measures.

(67) In order to avoid disruption to markets and to ensure continuity in overall levels of own funds it is appropriate to provide for specific transitional arrangements.

(68) In view of the risk-sensitivity of the rules relating to minimum capital requirements, it is desirable to keep under review whether these have significant effects on the economic cycle. The Commission, taking into account the contribution of the European Central Bank should report on these aspects to the European Parliament and to the Council.

(69) The arrangements necessary for the supervision of liquidity risks should also be harmonised.

(70) This Directive respects fundamental rights and observes the principles recognised in particular by the Charter of Fundamental Rights of the European Union as general principles of Community law.

(71) The obligation to transpose this Directive into national law should be confined to those provisions which represent a substantive change as compared with earlier directives. The obligation to transpose the provisions which are unchanged exists under the earlier directives.

(72) This Directive should be without prejudice to the obligations of the Member States relating to the time-limits for transposition into national law of the Directives set out in Annex XIII, Part B,

[5784]

NOTES

1   OJ C234, 22.9.2005, p 8.
2   OJ C52, 2.3.2005, p 37.
3   Opinion of the European Parliament of 28 September 2005 (not yet published in the OJ) and Decision of the Council of 7 June 2006.
4   OJ L126, 26.5.2000, p 1. Directive as last amended by Directive 2006/29/EC (OJ L70, 9.3.2006, p 50).
5   OJ L3, 7.1.2004, p 28.
6   OJ L372, 31.12.1986, p 1. Directive as last amended by Directive 2003/51/EC of the European Parliament and of the Council (OJ L178, 17.7.2003, p 16).
7   OJ L193, 18.7.1983, p 1. Directive as last amended by Directive 2003/51/EC.
8   OJ L243, 11.9.2002, p 1.
9   See page 201 of this Official Journal.
10   OJ L281, 23.11.1995, p 31. Directive as amended by Regulation (EC) No 1882/2003 (OJ L284, 31.10.2003, p 1).
11   OJ L184, 17.7.1999, p 23.
12   OJ C284E, 21.11.2002, p 115.

HAVE ADOPTED THIS DIRECTIVE—

TITLE I
SUBJECT MATTER, SCOPE AND DEFINITIONS

Article 1

1. This Directive lays down rules concerning the taking up and pursuit of the business of credit institutions, and their prudential supervision.

2. Article 39 and Title V, Chapter 4, Section 1 shall apply to financial holding companies and mixed-activity holding companies which have their head offices in the Community.

3. The institutions permanently excluded pursuant to Article 2, with the exception, however, of the central banks of the Member States, shall be treated as financial institutions for the purposes of Article 39 and Title V, Chapter 4, Section 1.

[5784A]

Article 2

This Directive shall not apply to the following:
—   the central banks of Member States,
—   post office giro institutions,
—   in Belgium, the "Institut de Réescompte et de Garantie/Herdiscontering- en Waarborginstituut",
[—   in Denmark, the "Dansk Eksportfinansieringsfond", the "Danmarks Skibskredit A/S" and the "KommuneKredit",]
—   in Germany, the "Kreditanstalt für Wiederaufbau", undertakings which are recognised under the "Wohnungsgemeinnützigkeitsgesetz" as bodies of State housing policy and are not mainly engaged in banking transactions, and undertakings recognised under that law as non-profit housing undertakings,
—   in Greece, the "Ταμείο Παρακαταθηκών και Δανείων" (Tamio Parakatathikon kai Danion),
—   in Spain, the "Instituto de Crédito Oficial",
—   in France, the "Caisse des dépôts et consignations",
—   in Ireland, credit unions and the friendly societies,
—   in Italy, the "Cassa depositi e prestiti",
—   in Latvia, the "krājaizdevu sabiedrības", undertakings that are recognised under the "krājaizdevu sabiedrību likums" as cooperative undertakings rendering financial services solely to their members,
—   in Lithuania, the "kredito unijos" other than the "Centrinė kredito unija",
—   in Hungary, the "Magyar Fejlesztési Bank Rt." and the "Magyar Export-Import Bank Rt.",
—   in the Netherlands, the "Nederlandse Investeringsbank voor Ontwikkelingslanden NV", the "NV Noordelijke Ontwikkelingsmaatschappij", the "NV Industriebank Limburgs Instituut voor Ontwikkeling en Financiering" and the "Overijsselse Ontwikkelingsmaatschappij NV",

— in Austria, undertakings recognised as housing associations in the public interest and the "Österreichische Kontrollbank AG",

— in Poland, the "Spółdzielcze Kasy Oszczędnościowo — Kreditowe" and the "Bank Gospodarstwa Krajowego",

— in Portugal, "Caixas Económicas" existing on 1 January 1986 with the exception of those incorporated as limited companies and of the "Caixa Económica Montepio Geral",

— in Finland, the "Teollisen yhteistyön rahasto Oy/Fonden för industriellt samarbete AB", and the "Finnvera Oyj/Finnvera Abp",

— in Sweden, the "Svenska Skeppshypotekskassan",

— in the United Kingdom, the National Savings Bank, the Commonwealth Development Finance Company Ltd, the Agricultural Mortgage Corporation Ltd, the Scottish Agricultural Securities Corporation Ltd, the Crown Agents for overseas governments and administrations, credit unions and municipal banks.

[5785]

NOTES

Entry relating to Denmark substituted by Commission Directive 2007/18/EC, Art 1(1), as from 17 April 2007.

Article 3

1. One or more credit institutions situated in the same Member State and which are permanently affiliated, on 15 December 1977, to a central body which supervises them and which is established in the same Member State, may be exempted from the requirements of Articles 7 and 11(1) if, no later than 15 December 1979, national law provides that:

    (a)   the commitments of the central body and affiliated institutions are joint and several liabilities or the commitments of its affiliated institutions are entirely guaranteed by the central body;

    (b)   the solvency and liquidity of the central body and of all the affiliated institutions are monitored as a whole on the basis of consolidated accounts; and

    (c)   the management of the central body is empowered to issue instructions to the management of the affiliated institutions.

Credit institutions operating locally which are permanently affiliated, subsequent to 15 December 1977, to a central body within the meaning of the first subparagraph, may benefit from the conditions laid down therein if they constitute normal additions to the network belonging to that central body.

In the case of credit institutions other than those which are set up in areas newly reclaimed from the sea or have resulted from scission or mergers of existing institutions dependent or answerable to the central body, the Commission, pursuant to the procedure referred to in Article 151(2) may lay down additional rules for the application of the second subparagraph including the repeal of exemptions provided for in the first subparagraph, where it is of the opinion that the affiliation of new institutions benefiting from the arrangements laid down in the second subparagraph might have an adverse effect on competition.

2. A credit institution referred to in the first subparagraph of paragraph 1, may also be exempted from the provisions of Articles 9 and 10, and also Title V, Chapter 2, Sections 2, 3, 4, 5 and 6 and Chapter 3 provided that, without prejudice to the application of those provisions to the central body, the whole as constituted by the central body together with its affiliated institutions is subject to those provisions on a consolidated basis.

In case of exemption, Articles 16, 23, 24, 25, 26(1) to (3) and 28 to 37 shall apply to the whole as constituted by the central body together with its affiliated institutions.

[5786]

Article 4

For the purposes of this Directive, the following definitions shall apply:

  (1) "credit institution" means:

    (a)   an undertaking whose business is to receive deposits or other repayable funds from the public and to grant credits for its own account; or

    (b)   an electronic money institution within the meaning of Directive 2000/46/EC;[1]

  (2) "authorisation" means an instrument issued in any form by the authorities by which the right to carry on the business of a credit institution is granted;

  (3) "branch" means a place of business which forms a legally dependent Part of a credit institution and which carries out directly all or some of the transactions inherent in the business of credit institutions;

  (4) "competent authorities" means the national authorities which are empowered by law or regulation to supervise credit institutions;

(5) "financial institution" means an undertaking other than a credit institution, the principal activity of which is to acquire holdings or to carry on one or more of the activities listed in points 2 to 12 of Annex I;

(6) "institutions", for the purposes of Sections 2 and 3 of Title V, Chapter 2, means institutions as defined in Article 3(1)(c) of Directive 2006/49/EC;

(7) "home Member State" means the Member State in which a credit institution has been authorised in accordance with Articles 6 to 9 and 11 to 14;

(8) "host Member State" means the Member State in which a credit institution has a branch or in which it provides services;

(9) "control" means the relationship between a parent undertaking and a subsidiary, as defined in Article 1 of Directive 83/349/EEC, or a similar relationship between any natural or legal person and an undertaking;

(10) "participation" for the purposes of points (o) and (p) of Article 57, Articles 71 to 73 and Title V, Chapter 4 means participation within the meaning of the first sentence of Article 17 of Fourth Council Directive 78/660/EEC of 25 July 1978 on the annual accounts of certain types of companies,[2] or the ownership, direct or indirect, of 20% or more of the voting rights or capital of an undertaking;

(11) "qualifying holding" means a direct or indirect holding in an undertaking which represents 10% or more of the capital or of the voting rights or which makes it possible to exercise a significant influence over the management of that undertaking;

(12) "parent undertaking" means:
   (a) a parent undertaking as defined in Articles 1 and 2 of Directive 83/349/EEC; or
   (b) for the purposes of Articles 71 to 73, Title V, Chapter 2, Section 5 and Chapter 4, a parent undertaking within the meaning of Article 1(1) of Directive 83/349/EEC and any undertaking which, in the opinion of the competent authorities, effectively exercises a dominant influence over another undertaking;

(13) "subsidiary" means:
   (a) a subsidiary undertaking as defined in Articles 1 and 2 of Directive 83/349/EEC; or
   (b) for the purposes of Articles 71 to 73, Title V, Chapter 2, Section 5, and Chapter 4 a subsidiary undertaking within the meaning of Article 1(1) of Directive 83/349/EEC and any undertaking over which, in the opinion of the competent authorities, a parent undertaking effectively exercises a dominant influence.

All subsidiaries of subsidiary undertakings shall also be considered subsidiaries of the undertaking that is their original parent;

(14) "parent credit institution in a Member State" means a credit institution which has a credit institution or a financial institution as a subsidiary or which holds a participation in such an institution, and which is not itself a subsidiary of another credit institution authorised in the same Member State, or of a financial holding company set up in the same Member State;

(15) "parent financial holding company in a Member State" means a financial holding company which is not itself a subsidiary of a credit institution authorised in the same Member State, or of a financial holding company set up in the same Member State;

(16) "EU parent credit institution" means a parent credit institution in a Member State which is not a subsidiary of another credit institution authorised in any Member State, or of a financial holding company set up in any Member State;

(17) "EU parent financial holding company" means a parent financial holding company in a Member State which is not a subsidiary of a credit institution authorised in any Member State or of another financial holding company set up in any Member State;

(18) "public sector entities" means non-commercial administrative bodies responsible to central governments, regional governments or local authorities, or authorities that in the view of the competent authorities exercise the same responsibilities as regional and local authorities, or non-commercial undertakings owned by central governments that have explicit guarantee arrangements, and may include self administered bodies governed by law that are under public supervision;

(19) "financial holding company" means a financial institution, the subsidiary undertakings of which are either exclusively or mainly credit institutions or financial institutions, at least one of such subsidiaries being a credit institution, and which is not a mixed financial holding company within the meaning of Article 2(15) of Directive 2002/87/EC;[3]

(20) "mixed-activity holding company" means a parent undertaking, other than a financial holding company or a credit institution or a mixed financial holding company within the meaning of Article 2(15) of Directive 2002/87/EC, the subsidiaries of which include at least one credit institution;

(21) "ancillary services undertaking" means an undertaking the principal activity of which consists in owning or managing property, managing data-processing services, or any other similar activity which is ancillary to the principal activity of one or more credit institutions;

(22) "operational risk" means the risk of loss resulting from inadequate or failed internal processes, people and systems or from external events, and includes legal risk;

(23) "central banks" include the European Central Bank unless otherwise indicated;

(24) "dilution risk" means the risk that an amount receivable is reduced through cash or non-cash credits to the obligor;

(25) "probability of default" means the probability of default of a counterparty over a one year period;

(26) "loss", for the purposes of Title V, Chapter 2, Section 3, means economic loss, including material discount effects, and material direct and indirect costs associated with collecting on the instrument;

(27) "loss given default (LGD)" means the ratio of the loss on an exposure due to the default of a counterparty to the amount outstanding at default;

(28) "conversion factor" means the ratio of the currently undrawn amount of a commitment that will be drawn and outstanding at default to the currently undrawn amount of the commitment, the extent of the commitment shall be determined by the advised limit, unless the unadvised limit is higher;

(29) "expected loss (EL)", for the purposes of Title V, Chapter 2, Section 3, shall mean the ratio of the amount expected to be lost on an exposure from a potential default of a counterparty or dilution over a one year period to the amount outstanding at default;

(30) "credit risk mitigation" means a technique used by a credit institution to reduce the credit risk associated with an exposure or exposures which the credit institution continues to hold;

(31) "funded credit protection" means a technique of credit risk mitigation where the reduction of the credit risk on the exposure of a credit institution derives from the right of the credit institution — in the event of the default of the counterparty or on the occurrence of other specified credit events relating to the counterparty — to liquidate, or to obtain transfer or appropriation of, or to retain certain assets or amounts, or to reduce the amount of the exposure to, or to replace it with, the amount of the difference between the amount of the exposure and the amount of a claim on the credit institution;

(32) "unfunded credit protection" means a technique of credit risk mitigation where the reduction of the credit risk on the exposure of a credit institution derives from the undertaking of a third party to pay an amount in the event of the default of the borrower or on the occurrence of other specified credit events;

(33) "repurchase transaction" means any transaction governed by an agreement falling within the definition of "repurchase agreement" or "reverse repurchase agreement" as defined in Article 3(1)(m) of Directive 2006/49/EC;

(34) "securities or commodities lending or borrowing transaction" means any transaction falling within the definition of "securities or commodities lending" or "securities or commodities borrowing" as defined in Article 3(1)(n) of Directive 2006/49/EC;

(35) "cash assimilated instrument" means a certificate of deposit or other similar instrument issued by the lending credit institution;

(36) "securitisation" means a transaction or scheme, whereby the credit risk associated with an exposure or pool of exposures is tranched, having the following characteristics:
  (a)   payments in the transaction or scheme are dependent upon the performance of the exposure or pool of exposures; and
  (b)   the subordination of tranches determines the distribution of losses during the ongoing life of the transaction or scheme;

(37) "traditional securitisation" means a securitisation involving the economic transfer of the exposures being securitised to a securitisation special purpose entity which issues securities. This shall be accomplished by the transfer of ownership of the securitised exposures from the originator credit institution or through sub-participation. The securities issued do not represent payment obligations of the originator credit institution;

(38) "synthetic securitisation" means a securitisation where the tranching is achieved by the use of credit derivatives or guarantees, and the pool of exposures is not removed from the balance sheet of the originator credit institution;

(39) "tranche" means a contractually established segment of the credit risk associated with an exposure or number of exposures, where a position in the segment entails a risk of credit loss greater

than or less than a position of the same amount in each other such segment, without taking account of credit protection provided by third parties directly to the holders of positions in the segment or in other segments;

(40) "securitisation position" shall mean an exposure to a securitisation;

(41) "originator" means either of the following:
   (a) an entity which, either itself or through related entities, directly or indirectly, was involved in the original agreement which created the obligations or potential obligations of the debtor or potential debtor giving rise to the exposure being securitised; or
   (b) an entity which purchases a third party's exposures onto its balance sheet and then securitises them;

(42) "sponsor" means a credit institution other than an originator credit institution that establishes and manages an asset-backed commercial paper programme or other securitisation scheme that purchases exposures from third party entities;

(43) "credit enhancement" means a contractual arrangement whereby the credit quality of a position in a securitisation is improved in relation to what it would have been if the enhancement had not been provided, including the enhancement provided by more junior tranches in the securitisation and other types of credit protection;

(44) "securitisation special purpose entity (SSPE)" means a corporation trust or other entity, other than a credit institution, organised for carrying on a securitisation or securitisations, the activities of which are limited to those appropriate to accomplishing that objective, the structure of which is intended to isolate the obligations of the SSPE from those of the originator credit institution, and the holders of the beneficial interests in which have the right to pledge or exchange those interests without restriction;

(45) "group of connected clients" means:
   (a) two or more natural or legal persons who, unless it is shown otherwise, constitute a single risk because one of them, directly or indirectly, has control over the other or others; or
   (b) two or more natural or legal persons between whom there is no relationship of control as set out in point (a) but who are to be regarded as constituting a single risk because they are so interconnected that, if one of them were to experience financial problems, the other or all of the others would be likely to encounter repayment difficulties;

(46) "close links" means a situation in which two or more natural or legal persons are linked in any of the following ways:
   (a) participation in the form of ownership, direct or by way of control, of 20% or more of the voting rights or capital of an undertaking;
   (b) control; or
   (c) the fact that both or all are permanently linked to one and the same third person by a control relationship;

(47) "recognised exchanges" means exchanges which are recognised as such by the competent authorities and which meet the following conditions:
   (a) they function regularly;
   (b) they have rules, issued or approved by the appropriate authorities of the home country of the exchange, defining the conditions for the operation of the exchange, the conditions of access to the exchange as well as the conditions that shall be satisfied by a contract before it can effectively be dealt on the exchange; and
   (c) they have a clearing mechanism whereby contracts listed in Annex IV are subject to daily margin requirements which, in the opinion of the competent authorities, provide appropriate protection.

[5787]

NOTES

[1] Directive 2000/46/EC of the European Parliament and of the Council of 18 September 2000 on the taking up, pursuit of and prudential supervision of the business of electronic money institutions (OJ L275, 27.10.2000, p 39).

[2] OJ L222, 14.8.1978, p 11. Directive as last amended by Directive 2003/51/EC.

[3] Directive 2002/87/EC of the European Parliament and of the Council of 16 December 2002 on the supplementary supervision of credit institutions, insurance undertakings and investment firms in a financial conglomerate (OJ L35, 11.2.2003, p 1). Directive as amended by Directive 2005/1/EC.

Article 5

Member States shall prohibit persons or undertakings that are not credit institutions from carrying on the business of taking deposits or other repayable funds from the public.

The first paragraph shall not apply to the taking of deposits or other funds repayable by a Member State or by a Member State's regional or local authorities or by public international bodies of which one or more Member States are members or to cases expressly covered by national or Community legislation, provided that those activities are subject to regulations and controls intended to protect depositors and investors and applicable to those cases.

[5788]

TITLE II
REQUIREMENTS FOR ACCESS TO THE TAKING UP AND PURSUIT OF THE BUSINESS OF CREDIT INSTITUTIONS

Article 6

Member States shall require credit institutions to obtain authorisation before commencing their activities. Without prejudice to Articles 7 to 12, they shall lay down the requirements for such authorisation and notify them to the Commission.

[5789]

Article 7

Member States shall require applications for authorisation to be accompanied by a programme of operations setting out, inter alia, the types of business envisaged and the structural organisation of the credit institution.

[5790]

Article 8

Member States may not require the application for authorisation to be examined in terms of the economic needs of the market.

[5791]

Article 9

1. Without prejudice to other general conditions laid down by national law, the competent authorities shall not grant authorisation when the credit institution does not possess separate own funds or in cases where initial capital is less than EUR 5 million.

"Initial capital" shall comprise capital and reserves as referred to in Article 57(a) and (b).

Member States may decide that credit institutions which do not fulfil the requirement of separate own funds and which were in existence on 15 December 1979 may continue to carry on their business. They may exempt such credit institutions from complying with the requirement contained in the first subparagraph of Article 11(1).

2. Member States may, subject to the following conditions, grant authorisation to particular categories of credit institutions the initial capital of which is less than that specified in paragraph 1:
    (a) the initial capital shall be no less than EUR 1 million;
    (b) the Member States concerned shall notify the Commission of their reasons for exercising this option; and
    (c) the name of each credit institution that does not have the minimum capital specified in paragraph 1 shall be annotated to that effect in the list referred to in Article 14.

[5792]

Article 10

1. A credit institution's own funds may not fall below the amount of initial capital required under Article 9 at the time of its authorisation.

2. Member States may decide that credit institutions already in existence on 1 January 1993, the own funds of which do not attain the levels specified for initial capital in Article 9, may continue to carry on their activities. In that event, their own funds may not fall below the highest level reached with effect from 22 December 1989.

3. If control of a credit institution falling within the category referred to in paragraph 2 is taken by a natural or legal person other than the person who controlled the institution previously, the own funds of that credit institution shall attain at least the level specified for initial capital in Article 9.

4. In certain specific circumstances and with the consent of the competent authorities, where there is a merger of two or more credit institutions falling within the category referred to in paragraph 2, the own funds of the credit institution resulting from the merger may not fall below the total own funds of the merged credit institutions at the time of the merger, as long as the appropriate levels specified in Article 9 have not been attained.

5. If, in the cases referred to in paragraphs 1, 2 and 4, the own funds should be reduced, the competent authorities may, where the circumstances justify it, allow a credit institution a limited period in which to rectify its situation or cease its activities.

[5793]

Article 11

1. The competent authorities shall grant an authorisation to the credit institution only when there are at least two persons who effectively direct the business of the credit institution.

They shall not grant authorisation if these persons are not of sufficiently good repute or lack sufficient experience to perform such duties.

2. Each Member State shall require that:
   (a) any credit institution which is a legal person and which, under its national law, has a registered office shall have its head office in the same Member State as its registered office; and
   (b) any other credit institution shall have its head office in the Member State which granted its authorisation and in which it actually carries on its business.

[5794]

Article 12

1. The competent authorities shall not grant authorisation for the taking-up of the business of credit institutions unless they have been informed of the identities of the shareholders or members, whether direct or indirect, natural or legal persons, that have qualifying holdings, and of the amounts of those holdings.

[In determining whether the criteria for a qualifying holding in the context of this Article are fulfilled, the voting rights referred to in Articles 9 and 10 of Directive 2004/109/EC,[1] as well as the conditions regarding aggregation thereof laid down in Article 12(4) and (5) of that Directive shall be taken into account.

Member States shall not take into account voting rights or shares which investment firms or credit institutions may hold as a result of providing the underwriting of financial instruments and/or placing of financial instruments on a firm commitment basis included under point 6 of Section A of Annex I to Directive 2004/39/EC,[2] provided that those rights are, on the one hand, not exercised or otherwise used to intervene in the management of the issuer and, on the other, disposed of within one year of acquisition.]

2. The competent authorities shall not grant authorisation if, taking into account the need to ensure the sound and prudent management of a credit institution, they are not satisfied as to the suitability of the shareholders or members.

3. Where close links exist between the credit institution and other natural or legal persons, the competent authorities shall grant authorisation only if those links do not prevent the effective exercise of their supervisory functions.

The competent authorities shall also not grant authorisation if the laws, regulations or administrative provisions of a third country governing one or more natural or legal persons with which the credit institution has close links, or difficulties involved in the enforcement of those laws, regulations or administrative provisions, prevent the effective exercise of their supervisory functions.

The competent authorities shall require credit institutions to provide them with the information they require to monitor compliance with the conditions referred to in this paragraph on a continuous basis.

[5795]

NOTES

Para 1: words in square brackets substituted by European Parliament and Council Directive 2007/44/EC, Art 5(1), as from 21 September 2007. Note that the 2007 Directive has a transposition date of 21 March 2009, and that the original words read as follows—

"In determining a qualifying holding in the context of this Article, the voting rights referred to in Article 92 of Directive 2001/34/EC of the European Parliament and of the Council of 28 May 2001 on the admission of securities to official stock exchange listing and on information to be published on those securities shall be taken into consideration.".

[1] Directive 2004/109/EC of the European Parliament and of the Council of 15 December 2004 on the harmonisation of transparency requirements in relation to information about issuers whose securities are admitted to trading on a regulated market (OJ L390, 31.12.2004, p 38).

[2] Directive 2004/39/EC of the European Parliament and of the Council of 21 April 2004 on markets in financial instruments (OJ L145, 30.4.2004, p 1). Directive as last amended by Directive 2007/44/EC (OJ L247, 21.9.2007, p 1).

Article 13

Reasons shall be given whenever a decision not to grant an authorisation is taken and the applicant shall be notified thereof within six months of receipt of the application or, should the latter be incomplete, within six months of the applicant's sending the information required for the decision. A decision shall, in any case, be taken within 12 months of the receipt of the application.

[5796]

Article 14

Every authorisation shall be notified to the Commission.

The name of each credit institution to which authorisation has been granted shall be entered in a list. The Commission shall publish that list in the Official Journal of the European Union and shall keep it up to date.

[5797]

Article 15

1. The competent authority shall, before granting authorisation to a credit institution, consult the competent authorities of the other Member State involved in the following cases:
   (a) the credit institution concerned is a subsidiary of a credit institution authorised in another Member State;
   (b) the credit institution concerned is a subsidiary of the parent undertaking of a credit institution authorised in another Member State; or
   (c) the credit institution concerned is controlled by the same persons, whether natural or legal, as control a credit institution authorised in another Member State.

2. The competent authority shall, before granting authorisation to a credit institution, consult the competent authority of a Member State involved, responsible for the supervision of insurance undertakings or investment firms in the following cases:
   (a) the credit institution concerned is a subsidiary of an insurance undertaking or investment firm authorised in the Community;
   (b) the credit institution concerned is a subsidiary of the parent undertaking of an insurance undertaking or investment firm authorised in the Community; or
   (c) the credit institution concerned is controlled by the same person, whether natural or legal, as controls an insurance undertaking or investment firm authorised in the Community.

3. The relevant competent authorities referred to in paragraphs 1 and 2 shall in particular consult each other when assessing the suitability of the shareholders and the reputation and experience of directors involved in the management of another entity of the same group. They shall exchange any information regarding the suitability of shareholders and the reputation and experience of directors which is of relevance for the granting of an authorisation as well as for the ongoing assessment of compliance with operating conditions.

[5798]

Article 16

Host Member States may not require authorisation or endowment capital for branches of credit institutions authorised in other Member States. The establishment and supervision of such branches shall be effected in accordance with Articles 22, 25, 26(1) to (3), 29 to 37 and 40.

[5799]

Article 17

1. The competent authorities may withdraw the authorisation granted to a credit institution only where such an institution:
   (a) does not make use of the authorisation within 12 months, expressly renounces the authorisation or has ceased to engage in business for more than six months, if the Member State concerned has made no provision for the authorisation to lapse in such cases;
   (b) has obtained the authorisation through false statements or any other irregular means;
   (c) no longer fulfils the conditions under which authorisation was granted;
   (d) no longer possesses sufficient own funds or can no longer be relied on to fulfil its obligations towards its creditors, and in particular no longer provides security for the assets entrusted to it; or
   (e) falls within one of the other cases where national law provides for withdrawal of authorisation.

2. Reasons shall be given for any withdrawal of authorisation and those concerned informed thereof. Such withdrawal shall be notified to the Commission.

[5800]

Article 18

For the purposes of exercising their activities, credit institutions may, notwithstanding any provisions in the host Member State concerning the use of the words "bank", "savings bank" or other banking names, use throughout the territory of the Community the same name as they use in the Member State in which their head office is situated. In the event of there being any danger of confusion, the host Member State may, for the purposes of clarification, require that the name be accompanied by certain explanatory particulars.

[5801]

[Article 19

1. Member States shall require any natural or legal person or such persons acting in concert (hereinafter referred to as the proposed acquirer), who have taken a decision either to acquire, directly or indirectly, a qualifying holding in a credit institution or to further increase, directly or indirectly, such a qualifying holding in a credit institution as a result of which the proportion of the voting rights or of the capital held would reach or exceed 20%, 30% or 50% or so that the credit institution would become its subsidiary (hereinafter referred to as the proposed acquisition), first to notify in writing the competent authorities of the credit institution in which they are seeking to acquire or increase a qualifying holding, indicating the size of the intended holding and relevant information, as referred to in Article 19a(4). Member States need not apply the 30% threshold where, in accordance with Article 9(3)(a) of Directive 2004/109/EC, they apply a threshold of one-third.

2. The competent authorities shall, promptly and in any event within two working days following receipt of the notification, as well as following the possible subsequent receipt of the information referred to in paragraph 3, acknowledge receipt thereof in writing to the proposed acquirer.

The competent authorities shall have a maximum of sixty working days as from the date of the written acknowledgement of receipt of the notification and all documents required by the Member State to be attached to the notification on the basis of the list referred to in Article 19a(4) (hereinafter referred to as the assessment period), to carry out the assessment provided for in Article 19a(1) (hereinafter referred to as the assessment).

The competent authorities shall inform the proposed acquirer of the date of the expiry of the assessment period at the time of acknowledging receipt.

3. The competent authorities may, during the assessment period, if necessary, and no later than on the 50th working day of the assessment period, request any further information that is necessary to complete the assessment. Such request shall be made in writing and shall specify the additional information needed.

For the period between the date of request for information by the competent authorities and the receipt of a response thereto by the proposed acquirer, the assessment period shall be interrupted. The interruption shall not exceed 20 working days. Any further requests by the competent authorities for completion or clarification of the information shall be at their discretion but may not result in an interruption of the assessment period.

4. The competent authorities may extend the interruption referred to in the second subparagraph of paragraph 3 up to thirty working days if the proposed acquirer is:
 (a) situated or regulated outside the Community; or
 (b) a natural or legal person not subject to supervision under this Directive or Directives 85/611/EEC,[1] 92/49/EEC,[2] 2002/83/EC,[3] 2004/39/EC or 2005/68/EC.[4]

5. If the competent authorities, upon completion of the assessment, decide to oppose the proposed acquisition, they shall, within two working days, and not exceeding the assessment period, inform the proposed acquirer in writing and provide the reasons for that decision. Subject to national law, an appropriate statement of the reasons for the decision may be made accessible to the public at the request of the proposed acquirer. This shall not prevent a Member State from allowing the competent authority to make such disclosure in the absence of a request by the proposed acquirer.

6. If the competent authorities do not oppose the proposed acquisition within the assessment period in writing, it shall be deemed to be approved.

7. The competent authorities may fix a maximum period for concluding the proposed acquisition and extend it where appropriate.

8. Member States may not impose requirements for notification to and approval by the competent authorities of direct or indirect acquisitions of voting rights or capital that are more stringent than those set out in this Directive.]

[5802]

NOTES

Substituted by European Parliament and Council Directive 2007/44/EC, Art 5(2), as from 21 September 2007. Note that the 2007 Directive has a transposition date of 21 March 2009 and the original Article read as follows—

"Article 19

1. The Member States shall require any natural or legal person who proposes to hold, directly or indirectly, a qualifying holding in a credit institution first to inform the competent authorities, telling them of the size of the intended holding. Such a person shall likewise inform the competent authorities if he proposes to increase his qualifying holding so that the proportion of the voting rights or of the capital held by him would reach or exceed 20%, 33% or 50% or so that the credit institution would become his subsidiary.

Without prejudice to paragraph 2, the competent authorities shall have a maximum of three months from the date of the notification provided for in the first and second subparagraphs to oppose such a plan if, in view of the need to ensure sound and prudent management of the credit institution, they are not satisfied as to the suitability of the person concerned. If they do not oppose the plan, they may fix a maximum period for its implementation.

2.   If the person proposing to acquire the holdings referred to in paragraph 1 is a credit institution, insurance undertaking or investment firm authorised in another Member State or the parent undertaking of a credit institution, insurance undertaking or investment firm authorised in another Member State or a natural or legal person controlling a credit institution, insurance undertaking or investment firm authorised in another Member State, and if, as a result of that acquisition, the credit institution in which the acquirer proposes to hold a holding would become a subsidiary or subject to the control of the acquirer, the assessment of the acquisition shall be subject to the prior consultation provided for in Article 15.".

1   Council Directive 85/611/EEC of 20 December 1985 on the coordination of laws, regulations and administrative provisions relating to undertakings for collective investment in transferable securities (UCITS) (OJ L375, 31.12.1985, p 3). Directive as last amended by Directive 2005/1/EC.
2   Council Directive 92/49/EEC of 18 June 1992 on the coordination of laws, regulations and administrative provisions relating to direct insurance other than life assurance (third non-life insurance Directive) (OJ L228, 11.8.1992, p 1). Directive as last amended by Directive 2007/44/EC.
3   Directive 2002/83/EC of the European Parliament and of the Council of 5 November 2002 concerning life assurance (OJ L345, 19.12.2002, p 1). Directive as last amended by Directive 2007/44/EC.
4   Directive 2005/68/EC of the European Parliament and of the Council of 16 November 2005 on reinsurance (OJ L323, 9.12.2005, p 1). Directive as amended by Directive 2007/44/EC.

[Article 19a

1.   In assessing the notification provided for in Article 19(1) and the information referred to in Article 19(3), the competent authorities shall, in order to ensure the sound and prudent management of the credit institution in which an acquisition is proposed, and having regard to the likely influence of the proposed acquirer on the credit institution, appraise the suitability of the proposed acquirer and the financial soundness of the proposed acquisition against all of the following criteria:
   (a)   the reputation of the proposed acquirer;
   (b)   the reputation and experience of any person who will direct the business of the credit institution as a result of the proposed acquisition;
   (c)   the financial soundness of the proposed acquirer, in particular in relation to the type of business pursued and envisaged in the credit institution in which the acquisition is proposed;
   (d)   whether the credit institution will be able to comply and continue to comply with the prudential requirements based on this Directive and, where applicable, other Directives, notably, Directives 2000/46/EC, 2002/87/EC and 2006/49/EC, in particular, whether the group of which it will become a part has a structure that makes it possible to exercise effective supervision, effectively exchange information among the competent authorities and determine the allocation of responsibilities among the competent authorities;
   (e)   whether there are reasonable grounds to suspect that, in connection with the proposed acquisition, money laundering or terrorist financing within the meaning of Article 1 of Directive 2005/60/EC[1] is being or has been committed or attempted, or that the proposed acquisition could increase the risk thereof.

2.   The competent authorities may oppose the proposed acquisition only if there are reasonable grounds for doing so on the basis of the criteria set out in paragraph 1 or if the information provided by the proposed acquirer is incomplete.

3.   Member States shall neither impose any prior conditions in respect of the level of holding that must be acquired nor allow their competent authorities to examine the proposed acquisition in terms of the economic needs of the market.

4.   Member States shall make publicly available a list specifying the information that is necessary to carry out the assessment and that must be provided to the competent authorities at the time of notification referred to in Article 19(1). The information required shall be proportionate and adapted to the nature of the proposed acquirer and the proposed acquisition. Member States shall not require information that is not relevant for a prudential assessment.

5.   Notwithstanding Article 19(2), (3) and (4), where two or more proposals to acquire or increase qualifying holdings in the same credit institution have been notified to the competent authority, the latter shall treat the proposed acquirers in a non-discriminatory manner.]

[5802A]

NOTES

Inserted by European Parliament and Council Directive 2007/44/EC, Art 5(3), as from 21 September 2007. Note that the 2007 Directive has a transposition date of 21 March 2009.

1   Directive 2005/60/EC of the European Parliament and of the Council of 26 October 2005 on the prevention of the use of financial system for the purpose of money laundering and terrorist financing (OJ L309, 25.11.2005, p 15).

[Article 19b

1. The relevant competent authorities shall work in full consultation with each other when carrying out the assessment if the proposed acquirer is one of the following:

(a) a credit institution, assurance undertaking, insurance undertaking, reinsurance undertaking, investment firm or management company within the meaning of Article 1a, point 2 of Directive 85/611/EEC (hereinafter referred to as the UCITS management company) authorised in another Member State or in a sector other than that in which the acquisition is proposed;

(b) the parent undertaking of a credit institution, assurance undertaking, insurance undertaking, reinsurance undertaking, investment firm or UCITS management company authorised in another Member State or in a sector other than that in which the acquisition is proposed; or

(c) a natural or legal person controlling a credit institution, assurance undertaking, insurance undertaking, reinsurance undertaking, investment firm or UCITS management company authorised in another Member State or in a sector other than that in which the acquisition is proposed.

2. The competent authorities shall, without undue delay, provide each other with any information which is essential or relevant for the assessment. In this regard, the competent authorities shall communicate to each other upon request all relevant information and shall communicate on their own initiative all essential information. A decision by the competent authority that has authorised the credit institution in which the acquisition is proposed shall indicate any views or reservations expressed by the competent authority responsible for the proposed acquirer.]

[5802B]

NOTES

Inserted by European Parliament and Council Directive 2007/44/EC, Art 5(3), as from 21 September 2007. Note that the 2007 Directive has a transposition date of 21 March 2009.

[Article 20

The Member States shall require any natural or legal person who has taken a decision to dispose, directly or indirectly, of a qualifying holding in a credit institution first to notify in writing the competent authorities, indicating the size of his intended holding. Such a person shall likewise notify the competent authorities if he has taken a decision to reduce his qualifying holding so that the proportion of the voting rights or of the capital held would fall below 20%, 30% or 50% or so that the credit institution would cease to be his subsidiary. Member States need not apply the 30% threshold where, in accordance with Article 9(3)(a) of Directive 2004/109/EC, they apply a threshold of one-third.]

[5803]

NOTES

Substituted by European Parliament and Council Directive 2007/44/EC, Art 5(4), as from 21 September 2007. Note that the 2007 Directive has a transposition date of 21 March 2009 and the original Article read as follows—

"Article 20

The Member States shall require any natural or legal person who proposes to dispose, directly or indirectly, of a qualifying holding in a credit institution first to inform the competent authorities, telling them of the size of his intended holding. Such a person shall likewise inform the competent authorities if he proposes to reduce his qualifying holding so that the proportion of the voting rights or of the capital held by him would fall below 20%, 33% or 50% or so that the credit institution would cease to be his subsidiary.".

Article 21

1. Credit institutions shall, on becoming aware of any acquisitions or disposals of holdings in their capital that cause holdings to exceed or fall below one of the thresholds referred to in Article 19(1) and Article 20, inform the competent authorities of those acquisitions or disposals.

They shall also, at least once a year, inform the competent authorities of the names of shareholders and members possessing qualifying holdings and the sizes of such holdings as shown, for example, by the information received at the annual general meetings of shareholders and members or as a result of compliance with the regulations relating to companies listed on stock exchanges.

2. The Member States shall require that, where the influence exercised by the persons referred to in Article 19(1) is likely to operate to the detriment of the prudent and sound management of the institution, the competent authorities shall take appropriate measures to put an end to that situation. Such measures may consist in injunctions, sanctions against directors and managers, or the suspension of the exercise of the voting rights attaching to the shares held by the shareholders or members in question.

Similar measures shall apply to natural or legal persons who fail to comply with the obligation to provide prior information, as laid down in Article 19(1).

If a holding is acquired despite the opposition of the competent authorities, the Member States shall, regardless of any other sanctions to be adopted, provide either for exercise of the corresponding voting rights to be suspended, or for the nullity of votes cast or for the possibility of their annulment.

[3. In determining whether the criteria for a qualifying holding in the context of Articles 19 and 20 and this Article are fulfilled, the voting rights referred to in Articles 9 and 10 of Directive 2004/109/EC, as well as the conditions regarding aggregation thereof laid down in Article 12(4) and (5) of that Directive, shall be taken into account.

In determining whether the criteria for a qualifying holding referred to in this Article are fulfilled, Member States shall not take into account voting rights or shares which investment firms or credit institutions may hold as a result of providing the underwriting of financial instruments and/or placing of financial instruments on a firm commitment basis included under point 6 of Section A of Annex I to Directive 2004/39/EC, provided that those rights are, on the one hand, not exercised or otherwise used to intervene in the management of the issuer and, on the other, disposed of within one year of acquisition.]

[5804]

NOTES

Para 3: substituted by European Parliament and Council Directive 2007/44/EC, Art 5(5), as from 21 September 2007. Note that the 2007 Directive has a transposition date of 21 March 2009 and the original paragraph read as follows—

"3. In determining a qualifying holding and other levels of holding referred to in this Article, the voting rights referred to in Article 92 of Directive 2001/34/EC shall be taken into consideration.".

Article 22

1. Home Member State competent authorities shall require that every credit institution have robust governance arrangements, which include a clear organisational structure with well defined, transparent and consistent lines of responsibility, effective processes to identify, manage, monitor and report the risks it is or might be exposed to, and adequate internal control mechanisms, including sound administrative and accounting procedures.

2. The arrangements, processes and mechanisms referred to in paragraph 1 shall be comprehensive and proportionate to the nature, scale and complexity of the credit institution's activities. The technical criteria laid down in Annex V shall be taken into account.

[5805]

TITLE III
PROVISIONS CONCERNING THE FREEDOM OF ESTABLISHMENT AND THE FREEDOM TO PROVIDE SERVICES

SECTION 1
CREDIT INSTITUTIONS

Article 23

The Member States shall provide that the activities listed in Annex I may be carried on within their territories, in accordance with Articles 25, 26(1) to (3), 28(1) and (2) and 29 to 37 either by the establishment of a branch or by way of the provision of services, by any credit institution authorised and supervised by the competent authorities of another Member State, provided that such activities are covered by the authorisation.

[5806]

SECTION 2
FINANCIAL INSTITUTIONS

Article 24

1. The Member States shall provide that the activities listed in Annex I may be carried on within their territories, in accordance with Articles 25, 26(1) to (3), 28(1) and (2) and 29 to 37 either by the establishment of a branch or by way of the provision of services, by any financial institution from another Member State, whether a subsidiary of a credit institution or the jointly-owned subsidiary of two or more credit institutions, the memorandum and Article of association of which permit the carrying on of those activities and which fulfils each of the following conditions:

    (a)   the parent undertaking or undertakings shall be authorised as credit institutions in the Member State by the law of which the financial institution is governed;

    (b)   the activities in question shall actually be carried on within the territory of the same Member State;

(c)   the parent undertaking or undertakings shall hold 90% or more of the voting rights attaching to shares in the capital of the financial institution;

(d)   the parent undertaking or undertakings shall satisfy the competent authorities regarding the prudent management of the financial institution and shall have declared, with the consent of the relevant home Member State competent authorities, that they jointly and severally guarantee the commitments entered into by the financial institution; and

(e)   the financial institution shall be effectively included, for the activities in question in particular, in the consolidated supervision of the parent undertaking, or of each of the parent undertakings, in accordance with Title V, Chapter 4, Section 1, in particular for the purposes of the minimum own funds requirements set out in Article 75 for the control of large exposures and for purposes of the limitation of holdings provided for in Articles 120 to 122.

Compliance with these conditions shall be verified by the competent authorities of the home Member State and the latter shall supply the financial institution with a certificate of compliance which shall form Part of the notification referred to in Articles 25 and 28.

The competent authorities of the home Member State shall ensure the supervision of the financial institution in accordance with Articles 10(1), 19 to 22, 40, 42 to 52 and 54.

2.   If a financial institution as referred to in the first subparagraph of paragraph 1 ceases to fulfil any of the conditions imposed, the home Member State shall notify the competent authorities of the host Member State and the activities carried on by that financial institution in the host Member State shall become subject to the legislation of the host Member State.

3.   Paragraphs 1 and 2 shall apply mutatis mutandis to subsidiaries of a financial institution as referred to in the first subparagraph of paragraph 1.

[5807]

SECTION 3
EXERCISE OF THE RIGHT OF ESTABLISHMENT

Article 25

1.   A credit institution wishing to establish a branch within the territory of another Member State shall notify the competent authorities of its home Member State.

2.   Member States shall require every credit institution wishing to establish a branch in another Member State to provide the following information when effecting the notification referred to in paragraph 1:

(a)   the Member State within the territory of which it plans to establish a branch;

(b)   a programme of operations setting out, inter alia, the types of business envisaged and the structural organisation of the branch;

(c)   the address in the host Member State from which documents may be obtained; and

(d)   the names of those to be responsible for the management of the branch.

3.   Unless the competent authorities of the home Member State have reason to doubt the adequacy of the administrative structure or the financial situation of the credit institution, taking into account the activities envisaged, they shall within three months of receipt of the information referred to in paragraph 2 communicate that information to the competent authorities of the host Member State and shall inform the credit institution accordingly.

The home Member State's competent authorities shall also communicate the amount of own funds and the sum of the capital requirements under Article 75 of the credit institution.

By way of derogation from the second subparagraph, in the case referred to in Article 24, the home Member State's competent authorities shall communicate the amount of own funds of the financial institution and the sum of the consolidated own funds and consolidated capital requirements under Article 75 of the credit institution which is its parent undertaking.

4.   Where the competent authorities of the home Member State refuse to communicate the information referred to in paragraph 2 to the competent authorities of the host Member State, they shall give reasons for their refusal to the credit institution concerned within three months of receipt of all the information.

That refusal or a failure to reply, shall be subject to a right to apply to the courts in the home Member State.

[5808]

Article 26

1.   Before the branch of a credit institution commences its activities the competent authorities of the host Member State shall, within two months of receiving the information referred to in Article 25, prepare for the supervision of the credit institution in accordance with Section 5 and if necessary indicate the conditions under which, in the interest of the general good, those activities shall be carried on in the host Member State.

PART IV
EC MATERIALS

2.   On receipt of a communication from the competent authorities of the host Member State, or in the event of the expiry of the period provided for in paragraph 1 without receipt of any communication from the latter, the branch may be established and may commence its activities.

3.   In the event of a change in any of the particulars communicated pursuant to points (b), (c) or (d) of Article 25(2), a credit institution shall give written notice of the change in question to the competent authorities of the home and host Member States at least one month before making the change so as to enable the competent authorities of the home Member State to take a decision pursuant to Article 25 and the competent authorities of the host Member State to take a decision on the change pursuant to paragraph 1 of this Article.

4.   Branches which have commenced their activities, in accordance with the provisions in force in their host Member States, before 1 January 1993, shall be presumed to have been subject to the procedure laid down in Article 25 and in paragraphs 1 and 2 of this Article. They shall be governed, from 1 January 1993, by paragraph 3 of this Article and by Articles 23 and 43 as well as Sections 2 and 5.

[5809]

Article 27

Any number of places of business set up in the same Member State by a credit institution with headquarters in another Member State shall be regarded as a single branch.

[5810]

SECTION 4
EXERCISE OF THE FREEDOM TO PROVIDE SERVICES

Article 28

1.   Any credit institution wishing to exercise the freedom to provide services by carrying on its activities within the territory of another Member State for the first time shall notify the competent authorities of the home Member State, of the activities on the list in Annex I which it intends to carry on.

2.   The competent authorities of the home Member State shall, within one month of receipt of the notification provided for in paragraph 1, send that notification to the competent authorities of the host Member State.

3.   This Article shall not affect rights acquired by credit institutions providing services before 1 January 1993.

[5811]

SECTION 5
POWERS OF THE COMPETENT AUTHORITIES OF THE HOST MEMBER STATE

Article 29

Host Member States may, for statistical purposes, require that all credit institutions having branches within their territories shall report periodically on their activities in those host Member States to the competent authorities of those host Member States.

In discharging the responsibilities imposed on them in Article 41, host Member States may require that branches of credit institutions from other Member States provide the same information as they require from national credit institutions for that purpose.

[5812]

Article 30

1.   Where the competent authorities of a host Member State ascertain that a credit institution having a branch or providing services within its territory is not complying with the legal provisions adopted in that State pursuant to the provisions of this Directive involving powers of the host Member State's competent authorities, those authorities shall require the credit institution concerned to put an end to that irregular situation.

2.   If the credit institution concerned fails to take the necessary steps, the competent authorities of the host Member State shall inform the competent authorities of the home Member State accordingly.

The competent authorities of the home Member State shall, at the earliest opportunity, take all appropriate measures to ensure that the credit institution concerned puts an end to that irregular situation. The nature of those measures shall be communicated to the competent authorities of the host Member State.

3.   If, despite the measures taken by the home Member State or because such measures prove inadequate or are not available in the Member State in question, the credit institution persists in violating the legal rules referred to in paragraph 1 in force in the host Member State, the latter State may, after informing the competent authorities of the home Member State, take appropriate

measures to prevent or to punish further irregularities and, in so far as is necessary, to prevent that credit institution from initiating further transactions within its territory. The Member States shall ensure that within their territories it is possible to serve the legal documents necessary for these measures on credit institutions.

[5813]

Article 31

Articles 29 and 30 shall not affect the power of host Member States to take appropriate measures to prevent or to punish irregularities committed within their territories which are contrary to the legal rules they have adopted in the interests of the general good. This shall include the possibility of preventing offending credit institutions from initiating further transactions within their territories.

[5814]

Article 32

Any measure taken pursuant to Article 30(2) and (3), or Article 31 involving penalties or restrictions on the exercise of the freedom to provide services shall be properly justified and communicated to the credit institution concerned. Every such measure shall be subject to a right of appeal to the courts in the Member State in which it was taken.

[5815]

Article 33

Before following the procedure provided for in Article 30, the competent authorities of the host Member State may, in emergencies, take any precautionary measures necessary to protect the interests of depositors, investors and others to whom services are provided. The Commission and the competent authorities of the other Member States concerned shall be informed of such measures at the earliest opportunity.

The Commission may, after consulting the competent authorities of the Member States concerned, decide that the Member State in question shall amend or abolish those measures.

[5816]

Article 34

Host Member States may exercise the powers conferred on them under this Directive by taking appropriate measures to prevent or to punish irregularities committed within their territories. This shall include the possibility of preventing offending credit institutions from initiating further transactions within their territories.

[5817]

Article 35

In the event of the withdrawal of authorisation, the competent authorities of the host Member State shall be informed and shall take appropriate measures to prevent the credit institution concerned from initiating further transactions within its territory and to safeguard the interests of depositors.

[5818]

Article 36

The Member States shall inform the Commission of the number and type of cases in which there has been a refusal pursuant to Articles 25 and 26(1) to (3) or in which measures have been taken in accordance with Article 30(3).

[5819]

Article 37

This Section shall not prevent credit institutions with head offices in other Member States from advertising their services through all available means of communication in the host Member State, subject to any rules governing the form and the content of such advertising adopted in the interests of the general good.

[5820]

TITLE IV
RELATIONS WITH THIRD COUNTRIES

SECTION 1
NOTIFICATION IN RELATION TO THIRD COUNTRIES' UNDERTAKINGS AND
CONDITIONS OF ACCESS TO THE MARKETS OF THESE COUNTRIES

Article 38

1. Member States shall not apply to branches of credit institutions having their head office outside the Community, when commencing or carrying on their business, provisions which result in more favourable treatment than that accorded to branches of credit institutions having their head office in the Community.

2. The competent authorities shall notify the Commission and the European Banking Committee of all authorisations for branches granted to credit institutions having their head office outside the Community.

3. Without prejudice to paragraph 1, the Community may, through agreements concluded with one or more third countries, agree to apply provisions which accord to branches of a credit institution having its head office outside the Community identical treatment throughout the territory of the Community.

[5821]

SECTION 2
COOPERATION WITH THIRD COUNTRIES' COMPETENT AUTHORITIES REGARDING SUPERVISION ON A CONSOLIDATED BASIS

Article 39

1. The Commission may submit proposals to the Council, either at the request of a Member State or on its own initiative, for the negotiation of agreements with one or more third countries regarding the means of exercising supervision on a consolidated basis over the following:
   (a) credit institutions the parent undertakings of which have their head offices in a third country; or
   (b) credit institutions situated in third countries the parent undertakings of which, whether credit institutions or financial holding companies, have their head offices in the Community.

2. The agreements referred to in paragraph 1 shall, in particular, seek to ensure the following:
   (a) that the competent authorities of the Member States are able to obtain the information necessary for the supervision, on the basis of their consolidated financial situations, of credit institutions or financial holding companies situated in the Community and which have as subsidiaries credit institutions or financial institutions situated outside the Community, or holding participation in such institutions; and
   (b) that the competent authorities of third countries are able to obtain the information necessary for the supervision of parent undertakings the head offices of which are situated within their territories and which have as subsidiaries credit institutions or financial institutions situated in one or more Member States or holding participation in such institutions.

3. Without prejudice to Article 300(1) and (2) of the Treaty, the Commission shall, with the assistance of the European Banking Committee, examine the outcome of the negotiations referred to in paragraph 1 and the resulting situation.

[5822]

TITLE V
PRINCIPLES AND TECHNICAL INSTRUMENTS FOR PRUDENTIAL SUPERVISION AND DISCLOSURE

CHAPTER 1
PRINCIPLES OF PRUDENTIAL SUPERVISION

SECTION 1
COMPETENCE OF HOME AND HOST MEMBER STATE

Article 40

1. The prudential supervision of a credit institution, including that of the activities it carries on accordance with Articles 23 and 24, shall be the responsibility of the competent authorities of the home Member State, without prejudice to those provisions of this Directive which give responsibility to the competent authorities of the host Member State.

2. Paragraph 1 shall not prevent supervision on a consolidated basis pursuant to this Directive.

[5823]

Article 41

Host Member States shall, pending further coordination, retain responsibility in cooperation with the competent authorities of the home Member State for the supervision of the liquidity of the branches of credit institutions.

Without prejudice to the measures necessary for the reinforcement of the European Monetary System, host Member States shall retain complete responsibility for the measures resulting from the implementation of their monetary policies.

Such measures may not provide for discriminatory or restrictive treatment based on the fact that a credit institution is authorised in another Member State.

[5824]

Article 42

The competent authorities of the Member States concerned shall collaborate closely in order to supervise the activities of credit institutions operating, in particular through a branch, in one or more Member States other than that in which their head offices are situated. They shall supply one another with all information concerning the management and ownership of such credit institutions that is likely to facilitate their supervision and the examination of the conditions for their authorisation, and all information likely to facilitate the monitoring of such institutions, in particular with regard to liquidity, solvency, deposit guarantees, the limiting of large exposures, administrative and accounting procedures and internal control mechanisms.

[5825]

Article 43

1.　Host Member States shall provide that, where a credit institution authorised in another Member State carries on its activities through a branch, the competent authorities of the home Member State may, after having first informed the competent authorities of the host Member State, carry out themselves or through the intermediary of persons they appoint for that purpose on-the-spot verification of the information referred to in Article 42.

2.　The competent authorities of the home Member State may also, for purposes of the verification of branches, have recourse to one of the other procedures laid down in Article 141.

3.　Paragraphs 1 and 2 shall not affect the right of the competent authorities of the host Member State to carry out, in the discharge of their responsibilities under this Directive, on-the-spot verifications of branches established within their territory.

[5826]

SECTION 2
EXCHANGE OF INFORMATION AND PROFESSIONAL SECRECY

Article 44

1.　Member States shall provide that all persons working for or who have worked for the competent authorities, as well as auditors or experts acting on behalf of the competent authorities, shall be bound by the obligation of professional secrecy.

No confidential information which they may receive in the course of their duties may be divulged to any person or authority whatsoever, except in summary or collective form, such that individual credit institutions cannot be identified, without prejudice to cases covered by criminal law.

Nevertheless, where a credit institution has been declared bankrupt or is being compulsorily wound up, confidential information which does not concern third parties involved in attempts to rescue that credit institution may be divulged in civil or commercial proceedings.

2.　Paragraph 1 shall not prevent the competent authorities of the various Member States from exchanging information in accordance with this Directive and with other Directives applicable to credit institutions. That information shall be subject to the conditions of professional secrecy indicated in paragraph 1.

[5827]

Article 45

Competent authorities receiving confidential information under Article 44 may use it only in the course of their duties and only for the following purposes:
- (a)　to check that the conditions governing the taking-up of the business of credit institutions are met and to facilitate monitoring, on a non-consolidated or consolidated basis, of the conduct of such business, especially with regard to the monitoring of liquidity, solvency, large exposures, and administrative and accounting procedures and internal control mechanisms;
- (b)　to impose penalties;
- (c)　in an administrative appeal against a decision of the competent authority; or
- (d)　in court proceedings initiated pursuant to Article 55 or to special provisions provided for in this in other Directives adopted in the field of credit institutions.

[5828]

Article 46

Member States may conclude cooperation agreements, providing for exchanges of information, with the competent authorities of third countries or with authorities or bodies of third countries as defined in Articles 47 and 48(1) only if the information disclosed is subject to guarantees of professional secrecy at least equivalent to those referred to in Article 44(1). Such exchange of information shall be for the purpose of performing the supervisory task of the authorities or bodies mentioned.

Where the information originates in another Member State, it may not be disclosed without the express agreement of the competent authorities which have disclosed it and, where appropriate, solely for the purposes for which those authorities gave their agreement.

[5829]

Article 47

Articles 44(1) and 45 shall not preclude the exchange of information within a Member State, where there are two or more competent authorities in the same Member State, or between Member States, between competent authorities and the following:

(a) authorities entrusted with the public duty of supervising other financial organisations and insurance companies and the authorities responsible for the supervision of financial markets;

(b) bodies involved in the liquidation and bankruptcy of credit institutions and in other similar procedures; and

(c) persons responsible for carrying out statutory audits of the accounts of credit institutions and other financial institutions;

in the discharge of their supervisory functions.

Articles 44(1) and 45 shall not preclude the disclosure to bodies which administer deposit-guarantee schemes of information necessary to the exercise of their functions.

In both cases, the information received shall be subject to the conditions of professional secrecy specified in Article 44(1).

[5830]

Article 48

1. Notwithstanding Articles 44 to 46, Member States may authorise exchange of information between the competent authorities and the following:

(a) the authorities responsible for overseeing the bodies involved in the liquidation and bankruptcy of credit institutions and in other similar procedures; and

(b) the authorities responsible for overseeing persons charged with carrying out statutory audits of the accounts of insurance undertakings, credit institutions, investment firms and other financial institutions.

In such cases, Member States shall require fulfilment of at least the following conditions:

(a) the information shall be for the purpose of performing the supervisory task referred to in the first subparagraph;

(b) information received in this context shall be subject to the conditions of professional secrecy specified in Article 44(1); and

(c) where the information originates in another Member State, it may not be disclosed without the express agreement of the competent authorities which have disclosed it and, where appropriate, solely for the purposes for which those authorities gave their agreement.

Member States shall communicate to the Commission and to the other Member States the names of the authorities which may receive information pursuant to this paragraph.

2. Notwithstanding Articles 44 to 46, Member States may, with the aim of strengthening the stability, including integrity, of the financial system, authorise the exchange of information between the competent authorities and the authorities or bodies responsible under law for the detection and investigation of breaches of company law.

In such cases Member States shall require fulfilment of at least the following conditions:

(a) the information is for the purpose of performing the task referred to in the first subparagraph;

(b) information received in this context is subject to the conditions of professional secrecy specified in Article 44(1); and

(c) where the information originates in another Member State, it may not be disclosed without the express agreement of the competent authorities which have disclosed it and, where appropriate, solely for the purposes for which those authorities gave their agreement.

Where, in a Member State, the authorities or bodies referred to in the first subparagraph perform their task of detection or investigation with the aid, in view of their specific competence, of persons appointed for that purpose and not employed in the public sector, the possibility of exchanging information provided for in the first subparagraph may be extended to such persons under the conditions specified in the second subparagraph.

In order to implement the third subparagraph, the authorities or bodies referred to in the first subparagraph shall communicate to the competent authorities which have disclosed the information, the names and precise responsibilities of the persons to whom it is to be sent.

Member States shall communicate to the Commission and to the other Member States the names of the authorities or bodies which may receive information pursuant to this Article.

The Commission shall draw up a report on the application of the provisions of this Article.

[5831]

Article 49

This Section shall not prevent a competent authority from transmitting information to the following for the purposes of their tasks:

(a)   central banks and other bodies with a similar function in their capacity as monetary authorities; and

(b)   where appropriate, to other public authorities responsible for overseeing payment systems.

This Section shall not prevent such authorities or bodies from communicating to the competent authorities such information as they may need for the purposes of Article 45.

Information received in this context shall be subject to the conditions of professional secrecy specified in Article 44(1).

[5832]

Article 50

Notwithstanding Articles 44(1) and 45, the Member States may, by virtue of provisions laid down by law, authorise the disclosure of certain information to other departments of their central government administrations responsible for legislation on the supervision of credit institutions, financial institutions, investment services and insurance companies and to inspectors acting on behalf of those departments.

However, such disclosures may be made only where necessary for reasons of prudential control.

[5833]

Article 51

The Member States shall provide that information received under Articles 44(2) and 47 and information obtained by means of the on-the-spot verification referred to in Article 43(1) and (2) may never be disclosed in the cases referred to in Article 50 except with the express consent of the competent authorities which disclosed the information or of the competent authorities of the Member State in which on-the-spot verification was carried out.

[5834]

Article 52

This Section shall not prevent the competent authorities of a Member State from communicating the information referred to in Articles 44 to 46 to a clearing house or other similar body recognised under national law for the provision of clearing or settlement services for one of their national markets if they consider that it is necessary to communicate the information in order to ensure the proper functioning of those bodies in relation to defaults or potential defaults by market participants. The information received in this context shall be subject to the conditions of professional secrecy specified in Article 44(1).

The Member States shall, however, ensure that information received under Article 44(2) may not be disclosed in the circumstances referred to in this Article without the express consent of the competent authorities which disclosed it.

[5835]

SECTION 3
DUTY OF PERSONS RESPONSIBLE FOR THE LEGAL CONTROL OF ANNUAL AND CONSOLIDATED ACCOUNTS

Article 53

1.   Member States shall provide at least that any person authorised within the meaning of Directive 84/253/EEC[1] performing in a credit institution the task described in Article 51 of Directive 78/660/EEC, Article 37 of Directive 83/349/EEC or Article 31 of Directive 85/611/EEC,[2] or any other statutory task, shall have a duty to report promptly to the competent authorities any fact or decision concerning that credit institution of which he has become aware while carrying out that task which is liable to:

(a)   constitute a material breach of the laws, regulations or administrative provisions which lay down the conditions governing authorisation or which specifically govern pursuit of the activities of credit institutions;

(b)   affect the continuous functioning of the credit institution; or

(c)   lead to refusal to certify the accounts or to the expression of reservations.

Member States shall provide at least that that person shall likewise have a duty to report any fact or decision of which he becomes aware in the course of carrying out a task as described in the first sub-paragraph in an undertaking having close links resulting from a control relationship with the credit institution within which he is carrying out that task.

2.   The disclosure in good faith to the competent authorities, by persons authorised within the meaning of Directive 84/253/EEC, of any fact or decision referred to in paragraph 1 shall not constitute a breach of any restriction on disclosure of information imposed by contract or by any legislative, regulatory or administrative provision and shall not involve such persons in liability of any kind.

[5836]

NOTES

¹   Eighth Council Directive 84/253/EEC of 10 April 1984 on the approval of persons responsible for carrying out the statutory audits of accounting documents (OJ L126, 12.5.1984, p 20).
²   Council Directive 85/611/EEC of 20 December 1985 on the coordination of laws, regulations and administrative provisions relating to undertakings for collective investment in transferable securities (UCITS) (OJ L375, 31.12.1985, p 3). Directive as last amended by Directive 2005/1/EC.

SECTION 4
POWER OF SANCTION AND RIGHT TO APPLY TO THE COURTS

Article 54

Without prejudice to the procedures for the withdrawal of authorisations and the provisions of criminal law, the Member States shall provide that their respective competent authorities may, as against credit institutions, or those who effectively control the business of credit institutions, which breach laws, regulations or administrative provisions concerning the supervision or pursuit of their activities, adopt or impose penalties or measures aimed specifically at ending the observed breaches or the causes of such breaches.

[5837]

Article 55

Member States shall ensure that decisions taken in respect of a credit institution in pursuance of laws, regulations and administrative provisions adopted in accordance with this Directive may be subject to the right to apply to the courts. The same shall apply where no decision is taken, within six months of its submission, in respect of an application for authorisation which contains all the information required under the provisions in force.

[5838]

CHAPTER 2
TECHNICAL INSTRUMENTS OF PRUDENTIAL SUPERVISION

SECTION 1
OWN FUNDS

Article 56

Wherever a Member State lays down by law, regulation or administrative action a provision in implementation of Community legislation concerning the prudential supervision of an operative credit institution which uses the term or refers to the concept of own funds, it shall bring this term or concept into line with the definition given in Articles 57 to 61 and Articles 63 to 66.

[5838A]

Article 57

Subject to the limits imposed in Article 66, the unconsolidated own funds of credit institutions shall consist of the following items:
(a)   capital within the meaning of Article 22 of Directive 86/635/EEC, in so far as it has been paid up, plus share premium accounts but excluding cumulative preferential shares;
(b)   reserves within the meaning of Article 23 of Directive 86/635/EEC and profits and losses brought forward as a result of the application of the final profit or loss;
(c)   funds for general banking risks within the meaning of Article 38 of Directive 86/635/EEC;
(d)   revaluation reserves within the meaning of Article 33 of Directive 78/660/EEC;
(e)   value adjustments within the meaning of Article 37(2) of Directive 86/635/EEC;
(f)   other items within the meaning of Article 63;
(g)   the commitments of the members of credit institutions set up as cooperative societies and the joint and several commitments of the borrowers of certain institutions organised as funds, as referred to in Article 64(1); and
(h)   fixed-term cumulative preferential shares and subordinated loan capital as referred to in Article 64(3).

The following items shall be deducted in accordance with Article 66:
(i)   own shares at book value held by a credit institution;
(j)   intangible assets within the meaning of Article 4(9) ("Assets") of Directive 86/635/EEC;
(k)   material losses of the current financial year;
(l)   holdings in other credit and financial institutions amounting to more than 10% of their capital;
(m)   subordinated claims and instruments referred to in Article 63 and Article 64(3) which a credit institution holds in respect of credit and financial institutions in which it has holdings exceeding 10% of the capital in each case;
(n)   holdings in other credit and financial institutions of up to 10% of their capital, the subordinated claims and the instruments referred to in Article 63 and Article 64(3) which a credit institution holds in respect of credit and financial institutions other than those referred to in points (l) and (m) in respect of the amount of the total of such holdings, subordinated claims and instruments which exceed 10% of that credit institution's own funds calculated before the deduction of items in points (l) to (p);
(o)   participations within the meaning of Article 4(10) which a credit institution holds in:
     (i)   insurance undertakings within the meaning of Article 6 of Directive 73/239/EEC,[1] Article 4 of Directive 2002/83/EC[2] or Article 1(b) of Directive 98/78/EC,[3]
     (ii)   reinsurance undertakings within the meaning of Article 1(c) of Directive 98/78/EC, or
     (iii)   insurance holding companies within the meaning of Article 1(i) of Directive 98/78/EC;
(p)   each of the following items which the credit institution holds in respect of the entities defined in point (o) in which it holds a participation:
     (i)   instruments referred to in Article 16(3) of Directive 73/239/EEC, and
     (ii)   instruments referred to in Article 27(3) of Directive 2002/83/EC;
(q)   for credit institutions calculating risk-weighted exposure amounts under Section 3, Subsection 2, negative amounts resulting from the calculation in Annex VII, Part 1, point 36 and expected loss amounts calculated in accordance with Annex VII, Part 1 points 32 and 33; and
(r)   the exposure amount of securitisation positions which receive a risk weight of 1250% under Annex IX, Part 4, calculated in the manner there specified.

For the purposes of point (b), the Member States may permit inclusion of interim profits before a formal decision has been taken only if these profits have been verified by persons responsible for the auditing of the accounts and if it is proved to the satisfaction of the competent authorities that the amount thereof has been evaluated in accordance with the principles set out in Directive 86/635/EEC and is net of any foreseeable charge or dividend.

In the case of a credit institution which is the originator of a securitisation, net gains arising from the capitalisation of future income from the securitised assets and providing credit enhancement to positions in the securitisation shall be excluded from the item specified in point (b).

[5838B]

NOTES

[1]   First Council Directive 73/239/EEC of 24 July 1973 on the coordination of laws, regulations and administrative provisions relating to the taking-up and pursuit of the business of direct insurance other than life assurance (OJ L228, 16.8.1973, p 3). Directive as last amended by Directive 2005/1/EC.
[2]   Directive 2002/83/EC of the European Parliament and of the Council of 5 November 2002 concerning life assurance (OJ L345, 19.12.2002, p 1). Directive as last amended by Directive 2005/1/EC.
[3]   Directive 98/78/EC of the European Parliament and of the Council of 27 October 1998 on the supplementary supervision of insurance undertakings in an insurance group (OJ L330, 5.12.1998, p 1). Directive as last amended by Directive 2005/1/EC.

Article 58

Where shares in another credit institution, financial institution, insurance or reinsurance undertaking or insurance holding company are held temporarily for the purposes of a financial assistance operation designed to reorganise and save that entity, the competent authority may waive the provisions on deduction referred to in points (l) to (p) of Article 57.

[5838C]

Article 59

As an alternative to the deduction of the items referred to in points (o) and (p) of Article 57, Member States may allow their credit institutions to apply mutatis mutandis methods 1, 2 or 3 of Annex I to Directive 2002/87/EC. Method 1 (accounting consolidation) may be applied only if the competent authority is confident about the level of integrated management and internal control regarding the entities which would be included in the scope of consolidation. The method chosen shall be applied in a consistent manner over time.

[5838D]

Article 60

Member States may provide that for the calculation of own funds on a stand-alone basis, credit institutions subject to supervision on a consolidated basis in accordance with Chapter 4, Section 1, or to supplementary supervision in accordance with Directive 2002/87/EC, need not deduct the items referred to in points (l) to (p) of Article 57 which are held in credit institutions, financial institutions, insurance or reinsurance undertakings or insurance holding companies, which are included in the scope of consolidated or supplementary supervision.

This provision shall apply to all the prudential rules harmonised by Community acts.

[5838E]

Article 61

The concept of own funds as defined in points (a) to (h) of Article 57 embodies a maximum number of items and amounts. The use of those items and the fixing of lower ceilings, and the deduction of items other than those listed in points (i) to (r) of Article 57 shall be left to the discretion of the Member States.

The items listed in points (a) to (e) of Article 57 shall be available to a credit institution for unrestricted and immediate use to cover risks or losses as soon as these occur. The amount shall be net of any foreseeable tax charge at the moment of its calculation or be suitably adjusted in so far as such tax charges reduce the amount up to which these items may be applied to cover risks or losses.

[5838F]

Article 62

Member States may report to the Commission on the progress achieved in convergence with a view to a common definition of own funds. On the basis of these reports the Commission shall, if appropriate, by 1 January 2009, submit a proposal to the European Parliament and to the Council for amendment of this Section.

[5838G]

Article 63

1. The concept of own funds used by a Member State may include other items provided that, whatever their legal or accounting designations might be, they have the following characteristics:
   (a) they are freely available to the credit institution to cover normal banking risks where revenue or capital losses have not yet been identified;
   (b) their existence is disclosed in internal accounting records; and
   (c) their amount is determined by the management of the credit institution, verified by independent auditors, made known to the competent authorities and placed under the supervision of the latter.

2. Securities of indeterminate duration and other instruments that fulfil the following conditions may also be accepted as other items:
   (a) they may not be reimbursed on the bearer's initiative or without the prior agreement of the competent authority;
   (b) the debt agreement shall provide for the credit institution to have the option of deferring the payment of interest on the debt;
   (c) the lender's claims on the credit institution shall be wholly subordinated to those of all non-subordinated creditors;
   (d) the documents governing the issue of the securities shall provide for debt and unpaid interest to be such as to absorb losses, whilst leaving the credit institution in a position to continue trading; and
   (e) only fully paid-up amounts shall be taken into account.

   To these securities and other instruments may be added cumulative preferential shares other than those referred to in point (h) of Article 57.

3. For credit institutions calculating risk-weighted exposure amounts under Section 3, Subsection 2, positive amounts resulting from the calculation in Annex VII, Part 1, point 36, may, up to 0.6% of risk weighted exposure amounts calculated under Subsection 2, be accepted as other items. For these credit institutions value adjustments and provisions included in the calculation referred to in Annex VII, Part 1, point 36 and value adjustments and provisions for exposures referred to in point (e) of Article 57 shall not be included in own funds other than in accordance with this paragraph. For these purposes, risk-weighted exposure amounts shall not include those calculated in respect of securitisation positions which have a risk weight of 1250%.

[5838H]

Article 64

1. The commitments of the members of credit institutions set up as cooperative societies referred to in point (g) of Article 57, shall comprise those societies' uncalled capital, together with

the legal commitments of the members of those cooperative societies to make additional non-refundable payments should the credit institution incur a loss, in which case it shall be possible to demand those payments without delay.

The joint and several commitments of borrowers in the case of credit institutions organised as funds shall be treated in the same way as the preceding items.

All such items may be included in own funds in so far as they are counted as the own funds of institutions of this category under national law.

2.   Member States shall not include in the own funds of public credit institutions guarantees which they or their local authorities extend to such entities.

3.   Member States or the competent authorities may include fixed-term cumulative preferential shares referred to in point (h) of Article 57 and subordinated loan capital referred to in that provision in own funds, if binding agreements exist under which, in the event of the bankruptcy or liquidation of the credit institution, they rank after the claims of all other creditors and are not to be repaid until all other debts outstanding at the time have been settled.

Subordinated loan capital shall fulfil the following additional criteria:
- (a)   only fully paid-up funds may be taken into account;
- (b)   the loans involved shall have an original maturity of at least five years, after which they may be repaid;
- (c)   the extent to which they may rank as own funds shall be gradually reduced during at least the last five years before the repayment date; and
- (d)   the loan agreement shall not include any clause providing that in specified circumstances, other than the winding-up of the credit institution, the debt shall become repayable before the agreed repayment date.

For the purposes of point (b) of the second subparagraph, if the maturity of the debt is not fixed, the loans involved shall be repayable only subject to five years' notice unless the loans are no longer considered as own funds or unless the prior consent of the competent authorities is specifically required for early repayment. The competent authorities may grant permission for the early repayment of such loans provided the request is made at the initiative of the issuer and the solvency of the credit institution in question is not affected.

4.   Credit institutions shall not include in own funds either the fair value reserves related to gains or losses on cash flow hedges of financial instruments measured at amortised cost, or any gains or losses on their liabilities valued at fair value that are due to changes in the credit institutions' own credit standing.

[5838I]

Article 65

1.   Where the calculation is to be made on a consolidated basis, the consolidated amounts relating to the items listed under Article 57 shall be used in accordance with the rules laid down in Chapter 4, Section 1. Moreover, the following may, when they are credit ("negative") items, be regarded as consolidated reserves for the calculation of own funds:
- (a)   any minority interests within the meaning of Article 21 of Directive 83/349/EEC, where the global integration method is used;
- (b)   the first consolidation difference within the meaning of Articles 19, 30 and 31 of Directive 83/349/EEC;
- (c)   the translation differences included in consolidated reserves in accordance with Article 39(6) of Directive 86/635/EEC; and
- (d)   any difference resulting from the inclusion of certain participating interests in accordance with the method prescribed in Article 33 of Directive 83/349/EEC.

2.   Where the items referred to in points (a) to (d) of paragraph 1 are debit ("positive") items, they shall be deducted in the calculation of consolidated own funds.

[5838J]

Article 66

1.   The items referred to in points (d) to (h) of Article 57, shall be subject to the following limits:
- (a)   the total of the items in points (d) to (h) may not exceed a maximum of 100% of the items in points (a) plus (b) and (c) minus (i) to (k); and
- (b)   the total of the items in points (g) to (h) may not exceed a maximum of 50% of the items in points (a) plus (b) and (c) minus (i) to (k).

2.   The total of the items in points (l) to (r) of Article 57 shall be deducted half from the total of the items (a) to (c) minus (i) to (k), and half from the total of the items (d) to (h) of Article 57, after application of the limits laid down in paragraph 1 of this Article. To the extent that half of the total of the items (l) to (r) exceeds the total of the items (d) to (h) of Article 57, the excess shall be deducted from the total of the items (a) to (c) minus (i) to (k) of Article 57. Items in point (r) of

Article 57 shall not be deducted if they have been included in the calculation of risk-weighted exposure amounts for the purposes of Article 75 as specified in Annex IX, Part 4.

3. For the purposes of Sections 5 and 6, the provisions laid down in this Section shall be read without taking into account the items referred to in points (q) and (r) of Article 57 and Article 63(3).

4. The competent authorities may authorise credit institutions to exceed the limits laid down in paragraph 1 in temporary and exceptional circumstances.

[5838K]

Article 67

Compliance with the conditions laid down in this Section shall be proved to the satisfaction of the competent authorities.

[5838L]

SECTION 2
PROVISION AGAINST RISKS

SUBSECTION 1
LEVEL OF APPLICATION

Article 68

1. Credit institutions shall comply with the obligations laid down in Articles 22 and 75 and Section 5 on an individual basis.

2. Every credit institution which is neither a subsidiary in the Member State where it is authorised and supervised, nor a parent undertaking, and every credit institution not included in the consolidation pursuant to Article 73, shall comply with the obligations laid down in Articles 120 and 123 on an individual basis.

3. Every credit institution which is neither a parent undertaking, nor a subsidiary, and every credit institution not included in the consolidation pursuant to Article 73, shall comply with the obligations laid down in Chapter 5 on an individual basis.

[5838M]

Article 69

1. The Member States may choose not to apply Article 68(1) to any subsidiary of a credit institution, where both the subsidiary and the credit institution are subject to authorisation and supervision by the Member State concerned, and the subsidiary is included in the supervision on a consolidated basis of the credit institution which is the parent undertaking, and all of the following conditions are satisfied, in order to ensure that own funds are distributed adequately among the parent undertaking and the subsidiaries:

(a) there is no current or foreseen material practical or legal impediment to the prompt transfer of own funds or repayment of liabilities by its parent undertaking;

(b) either the parent undertaking satisfies the competent authority regarding the prudent management of the subsidiary and has declared, with the consent of the competent authority, that it guarantees the commitments entered into by the subsidiary, or the risks in the subsidiary are of negligible interest;

(c) the risk evaluation, measurement and control procedures of the parent undertaking cover the subsidiary; and

(d) the parent undertaking holds more than 50% of the voting rights attaching to shares in the capital of the subsidiary and/or has the right to appoint or remove a majority of the members of the management body of the subsidiary described in Article 11.

2. The Member States may exercise the option provided for in paragraph 1 where the parent undertaking is a financial holding company set up in the same Member State as the credit institution, provided that it is subject to the same supervision as that exercised over credit institutions, and in particular to the standards laid down in Article 71(1).

3. The Member States may choose not to apply Article 68(1) to a parent credit institution in a Member State where that credit institution is subject to authorisation and supervision by the Member State concerned, and it is included in the supervision on a consolidated basis, and all the following conditions are satisfied, in order to ensure that own funds are distributed adequately among the parent undertaking and the subsidiaries:

(a) there is no current or foreseen material practical or legal impediment to the prompt transfer of own funds or repayment of liabilities to the parent credit institution in a Member State; and

(b) the risk evaluation, measurement and control procedures relevant for consolidated supervision cover the parent credit institution in a Member State.

The competent authority which makes use of this paragraph shall inform the competent authorities of all other Member States.

4. Without prejudice to the generality of Article 144, the competent authority of the Member States exercising the discretion laid down in paragraph 3 shall publicly disclose, in the manner indicated in Article 144:

(a) criteria it applies to determine that there is no current or foreseen material practical or legal impediment to the prompt transfer of own funds or repayment of liabilities;

(b) the number of parent credit institutions which benefit from the exercise of the discretion laid down in paragraph 3 and the number of these which incorporate subsidiaries in a third country; and

(c) on an aggregate basis for the Member State:

    (i) the total amount of own funds on the consolidated basis of the parent credit institution in a Member State, which benefits from the exercise of the discretion laid down in paragraph 3, which are held in subsidiaries in a third country;

    (ii) the percentage of total own funds on the consolidated basis of parent credit institutions in a Member State which benefits from the exercise of the discretion laid down in paragraph 3, represented by own funds which are held in subsidiaries in a third country; and

    (iii) the percentage of total minimum own funds required under Article 75 on the consolidated basis of parent credit institutions in a Member State, which benefits from the exercise of the discretion laid down in paragraph 3, represented by own funds which are held in subsidiaries in a third country.

[5838N]

Article 70

1. Subject to paragraphs 2 to 4 of this Article, the competent authorities may allow on a case by case basis parent credit institutions to incorporate in the calculation of their requirement under Article 68(1) subsidiaries which meet the conditions laid down in points (c) and (d) of Article 69(1), and whose material exposures or material liabilities are to that parent credit institution.

2. The treatment in paragraph 1 shall be allowed only where the parent credit institution demonstrates fully to the competent authorities the circumstances and arrangements, including legal arrangements, by virtue of which there is no material practical or legal impediment, and none are foreseen, to the prompt transfer of own funds, or repayment of liabilities when due by the subsidiary to its parent undertaking.

3. Where a competent authority exercises the discretion laid down in paragraph 1, it shall on a regular basis and not less than once a year inform the competent authorities of all the other Member States of the use made of paragraph 1 and of the circumstances and arrangements referred to in paragraph 2. Where the subsidiary is in a third country, the competent authorities shall provide the same information to the competent authorities of that third country as well.

4. Without prejudice to the generality of Article 144, a competent authority which exercises the discretion laid down in paragraph 1 shall publicly disclose, in the manner indicated in Article 144:

(a) the criteria it applies to determine that there is no current or foreseen material practical or legal impediment to the prompt transfer of own funds or repayment of liabilities;

(b) the number of parent credit institutions which benefit from the exercise of the discretion laid down in paragraph 1 and the number of these which incorporate subsidiaries in a third country; and

(c) on an aggregate basis for the Member State:

    (i) the total amount of own funds of parent credit institutions which benefit from the exercise of the discretion laid down in paragraph 1 which are held in subsidiaries in a third country;

    (ii) the percentage of total own funds of parent credit institutions which benefit from the exercise of the discretion laid down in paragraph 1 represented by own funds which are held in subsidiaries in a third country; and

    (iii) the percentage of total minimum own funds required under Article 75 of parent credit institutions which benefit from the exercise of the discretion laid down in paragraph 1 represented by own funds which are held in subsidiaries in a third country.

[5838O]

Article 71

1. Without prejudice to Articles 68 to 70, parent credit institutions in a Member State shall comply, to the extent and in the manner prescribed in Article 133, with the obligations laid down in Articles 75, 120, 123 and Section 5 on the basis of their consolidated financial situation.

2. Without prejudice to Articles 68 to 70, credit institutions controlled by a parent financial holding company in a Member State shall comply, to the extent and in the manner prescribed in Article 133, with the obligations laid down in Articles 75, 120, 123 and Section 5 on the basis of the consolidated financial situation of that financial holding company.

Where more than one credit institution is controlled by a parent financial holding company in a Member State, the first subparagraph shall apply only to the credit institution to which supervision on a consolidated basis applies in accordance with Articles 125 and 126.

[5838P]

Article 72

1. EU parent credit institutions shall comply with the obligations laid down in Chapter 5 on the basis of their consolidated financial situation.

Significant subsidiaries of EU parent credit institutions shall disclose the information specified in Annex XII, Part 1, point 5, on an individual or sub-consolidated basis.

2. Credit institutions controlled by an EU parent financial holding company shall comply with the obligations laid down in Chapter 5 on the basis of the consolidated financial situation of that financial holding company.

Significant subsidiaries of EU parent financial holding companies shall disclose the information specified in Annex XII, Part 1, point 5, on an individual or sub-consolidated basis.

3. The competent authorities responsible for exercising supervision on a consolidated basis pursuant to Articles 125 and 126 may decide not to apply in full or in part paragraphs 1 and 2 to the credit institutions which are included within comparable disclosures provided on a consolidated basis by a parent undertaking established in a third country.

[5838Q]

Article 73

1. The Member States or the competent authorities responsible for exercising supervision on a consolidated basis pursuant to Articles 125 and 126 may decide in the following cases that a credit institution, financial institution or ancillary services undertaking which is a subsidiary or in which a participation is held need not be included in the consolidation:

    (a)   where the undertaking concerned is situated in a third country where there are legal impediments to the transfer of the necessary information;

    (b)   where, in the opinion of the competent authorities, the undertaking concerned is of negligible interest only with respect to the objectives of monitoring credit institutions and in any event where the balance-sheet total of the undertaking concerned is less than the smaller of the following two amounts:

        (i)   EUR 10 million, or

        (ii)   1% of the balance-sheet total of the parent undertaking or the undertaking that holds the participation,

    (c)   where, in the opinion of the competent authorities responsible for exercising supervision on a consolidated basis, the consolidation of the financial situation of the undertaking concerned would be inappropriate or misleading as far as the objectives of the supervision of credit institutions are concerned.

If, in the cases referred to in point (b) of the first subparagraph, several undertakings meet the above criteria set out therein, they shall nevertheless be included in the consolidation where collectively they are of non-negligible interest with respect to the specified objectives.

2. Competent authorities shall require subsidiary credit institutions to apply the requirements laid down in Articles 75, 120 and 123 and Section 5 on a sub-consolidated basis if those credit institutions, or the parent undertaking where it is a financial holding company, have a credit institution or a financial institution or an asset management company as defined in Article 2(5) of Directive 2002/87/EC as a subsidiary in a third country, or hold a participation in such an undertaking.

3. Competent authorities shall require the parent undertakings and subsidiaries subject to this Directive to meet the obligations laid down in Article 22 on a consolidated or sub-consolidated basis, to ensure that their arrangements, processes and mechanisms are consistent and well-integrated and that any data and information relevant to the purpose of supervision can be produced.

[5838R]

SUBSECTION 2
CALCULATION OF REQUIREMENTS

Article 74

1. Save where otherwise provided, the valuation of assets and off-balance-sheet items shall be effected in accordance with the accounting framework to which the credit institution is subject under Regulation (EC) No 1606/2002 and Directive 86/635/EEC.

2. Notwithstanding the requirements laid down in Articles 68 to 72, the calculations to verify the compliance of credit institutions with the obligations laid down in Article 75 shall be carried out not less than twice each year.

The credit institutions shall communicate the results and any component data required to the competent authorities.

[5838S]

SUBSECTION 3
MINIMUM LEVEL OF OWN FUNDS

Article 75

Without prejudice to Article 136, Member States shall require credit institutions to provide own funds which are at all times more than or equal to the sum of the following capital requirements:

    (a)   for credit risk and dilution risk in respect of all of their business activities with the exception of their trading book business and illiquid assets if deducted from own funds under Article 13(2)(d) of Directive 2006/49/EC, 8% of the total of their risk-weighted exposure amounts calculated in accordance with Section 3;

    (b)   in respect of their trading-book business, for position risk, settlement and counter-party risk and, in so far as the limits laid down in Articles 111 to 117 are authorised to be exceeded, for large exposures exceeding such limits, the capital requirements determined in accordance with Article 18 and Chapter V, Section 4 of Directive 2006/49/EC;

    (c)   in respect of all of their business activities, for foreign-exchange risk and for commodities risk, the capital requirements determined according to Article 18 of Directive 2006/49/EC; and

    (d)   in respect of all of their business activities, for operational risk, the capital requirements determined in accordance with Section 4.

[5838T]

SECTION 3
MINIMUM OWN FUNDS REQUIREMENTS FOR CREDIT RISK

Article 76

Credit institutions shall apply either the Standardised Approach provided for in Articles 78 to 83 or, if permitted by the competent authorities in accordance with Article 84, the Internal Ratings Based Approach provided for in Articles 84 to 89 to calculate their risk-weighted exposure amounts for the purposes of Article 75(a).

[5838U]

Article 77

"Exposure" for the purposes of this Section means an asset or off-balance sheet item.

[5838V]

SUBSECTION 1
STANDARDISED APPROACH

Article 78

    1.   Subject to paragraph 2, the exposure value of an asset item shall be its balance-sheet value and the exposure value of an off-balance sheet item listed in Annex II shall be the following percentage of its value: 100% if it is a full-risk item, 50% if it is a medium-risk item, 20% if it is a medium/low-risk item, 0% if it is a low-risk item. The off-balance sheet items referred to in the first sentence of this paragraph shall be assigned to risk categories as indicated in Annex II. In the case of a credit institution using the Financial Collateral Comprehensive Method under Annex VIII, Part 3, where an exposure takes the form of securities or commodities sold, posted or lent under a repurchase transaction or under a securities or commodities lending or borrowing transaction, and margin lending transactions the exposure value shall be increased by the volatility adjustment appropriate to such securities or commodities as prescribed in Annex VIII, Part 3, points 34 to 59.

    2.   The exposure value of a derivative instrument listed in Annex IV shall be determined in accordance with Annex III with the effects of contracts of novation and other netting agreements taken into account for the purposes of those methods in accordance with Annex III. The exposure value of repurchase transactions, securities or commodities lending or borrowing transactions, long settlement transactions and margin lending transactions may be determined either in accordance with Annex III or Annex VIII.

    3.   Where an exposure is subject to funded credit protection, the exposure value applicable to that item may be modified in accordance with Subsection 3.

    4.   Notwithstanding paragraph 2, the exposure value of credit risk exposures outstanding, as determined by the competent authorities, with a central counterparty shall be determined in accordance with Annex III, Part 2, point 6, provided that the central counterparty's counterparty credit risk exposures with all participants in its arrangements are fully collateralised on a daily basis.

[5838W]

Article 79

1. Each exposure shall be assigned to one of the following exposure classes:
   (a) claims or contingent claims on central governments or central banks;
   (b) claims or contingent claims on regional governments or local authorities;
   (c) claims or contingent claims on administrative bodies and non-commercial undertakings;
   (d) claims or contingent claims on multilateral development banks;
   (e) claims or contingent claims on international organisations;
   (f) claims or contingent claims on institutions;
   (g) claims or contingent claims on corporates;
   (h) retail claims or contingent retail claims;
   (i) claims or contingent claims secured on real estate property;
   (j) past due items;
   (k) items belonging to regulatory high-risk categories;
   (l) claims in the form of covered bonds;
   (m) securitisation positions;
   (n) short-term claims on institutions and corporate;
   (o) claims in the form of collective investment undertakings ("CIU"); or
   (p) other items.

2. To be eligible for the retail exposure class referred to in point (h) of paragraph 1, an exposure shall meet the following conditions:
   (a) the exposure shall be either to an individual person or persons, or to a small or medium sized entity;
   (b) the exposure shall be one of a significant number of exposures with similar characteristics such that the risks associated with such lending are substantially reduced; and
   (c) the total amount owed to the credit institution and parent undertakings and its subsidiaries, including any past due exposure, by the obligor client or group of connected clients, but excluding claims or contingent claims secured on residential real estate collateral, shall not, to the knowledge of the credit institution, exceed EUR 1 million. The credit institution shall take reasonable steps to acquire this knowledge.

   Securities shall not be eligible for the retail exposure class.

(3) The present value of retail minimum lease payments is eligible for the retail exposure class.

[5838X]

Article 80

1. To calculate risk-weighted exposure amounts, risk weights shall be applied to all exposures, unless deducted from own funds, in accordance with the provisions of Annex VI, Part 1. The application of risk weights shall be based on the exposure class to which the exposure is assigned and, to the extent specified in Annex VI, Part 1, its credit quality. Credit quality may be determined by reference to the credit assessments of External Credit Assessment Institutions ("ECAIs") in accordance with the provisions of Articles 81 to 83 or the credit assessments of Export Credit Agencies as described in Annex VI, Part 1.

2. For the purposes of applying a risk weight, as referred to in paragraph 1, the exposure value shall be multiplied by the risk weight specified or determined in accordance with this Subsection.

3. For the purposes of calculating risk-weighted exposure amounts for exposures to institutions, Member States shall decide whether to adopt the method based on the credit quality of the central government of the jurisdiction in which the institution is incorporated or the method based on the credit quality of the counterparty institution in accordance with Annex VI.

4. Notwithstanding paragraph 1, where an exposure is subject to credit protection the risk weight applicable to that item may be modified in accordance with Subsection 3.

5. Risk-weighted exposure amounts for securitised exposures shall be calculated in accordance with Subsection 4.

6. Exposures the calculation of risk-weighted exposure amounts for which is not otherwise provided for under this Subsection shall be assigned a risk-weight of 100%.

7. With the exception of exposures giving rise to liabilities in the form of the items referred to in paragraphs (a) to (h) of Article 57, competent authorities may exempt from the requirements of paragraph 1 of this Article the exposures of a credit institution to a counterparty which is its parent undertaking, its subsidiary, a subsidiary of its parent undertaking or an undertaking linked by a relationship within the meaning of Article 12(1) of Directive 83/349/EEC, provided that the following conditions are met:
   (a) the counterparty is an institution or a financial holding company, financial institution, asset management company or ancillary services undertaking subject to appropriate prudential requirements;

(b)   the counterparty is included in the same consolidation as the credit institution on a full basis;

(c)   the counterparty is subject to the same risk evaluation, measurement and control procedures as the credit institution;

(d)   the counterparty is established in the same Member State as the credit institution; and

(e)   there is no current or foreseen material practical or legal impediment to the prompt transfer of own funds or repayment of liabilities from the counterparty to the credit institution.

In such a case, a risk weight of 0% shall be assigned.

8.   With the exception of exposures giving rise to liabilities in the form of the items referred to in points (a) to (h) of Article 57, competent authorities may exempt from the requirements of paragraph 1 of this Article the exposures to counterparties which are members of the same institutional protection scheme as the lending credit institution, provided that the following conditions are met:

(a)   the requirements set out in points (a), (d) and (e) of paragraph 7;

(b)   the credit institution and the counterparty have entered into a contractual or statutory liability arrangement which protects those institutions and in particular ensures their liquidity and solvency to avoid bankruptcy in case it becomes necessary (referred to below as an institutional protection scheme);

(c)   the arrangements ensure that the institutional protection scheme will be able to grant support necessary under its commitment from funds readily available to it;

(d)   the institutional protection scheme disposes of suitable and uniformly stipulated systems for the monitoring and classification of risk (which gives a complete overview of the risk situations of all the individual members and the institutional protection scheme as a whole) with corresponding possibilities to take influence; those systems shall suitably monitor defaulted exposures in accordance with Annex VII, Part 4, point 44;

(e)   the institutional protection scheme conducts its own risk review which is communicated to the individual members;

(f)   the institutional protection scheme draws up and publishes once in a year either, a consolidated report comprising the balance sheet, the profit-and-loss account, the situation report and the risk report, concerning the institutional protection scheme as a whole, or a report comprising the aggregated balance sheet, the aggregated profit-and-loss account, the situation report and the risk report, concerning the institutional protection scheme as a whole;

(g)   members of the institutional protection scheme are obliged to give advance notice of at least 24 months if they wish to end the arrangements;

(h)   the multiple use of elements eligible for the calculation of own funds ("multiple gearing") as well as any inappropriate creation of own funds between the members of the institutional protection scheme shall be eliminated;

(i)   the institutional protection scheme shall be based on a broad membership of credit institutions of a predominantly homogeneous business profile; and

(j)   the adequacy of the systems referred to in point (d) is approved and monitored at regular intervals by the relevant competent authorities.

In such a case, a risk weight of 0% shall be assigned.

                                                         [5838Y]

Article 81

1.   An external credit assessment may be used to determine the risk weight of an exposure in accordance with Article 80 only if the ECAI which provides it has been recognised as eligible for those purposes by the competent authorities ("an eligible ECAI" for the purposes of this Subsection).

2.   Competent authorities shall recognise an ECAI as eligible for the purposes of Article 80 only if they are satisfied that its assessment methodology complies with the requirements of objectivity, independence, ongoing review and transparency, and that the resulting credit assessments meet the requirements of credibility and transparency. For those purposes, the competent authorities shall take into account the technical criteria set out in Annex VI, Part 2.

3.   If an ECAI has been recognised as eligible by the competent authorities of a Member State, the competent authorities of other Member States may recognise that ECAI as eligible without carrying out their own evaluation process.

4.   Competent authorities shall make publicly available an explanation of the recognition process, and a list of eligible ECAIs.

                                                              [5838Z]

Article 82

1.   The competent authorities shall determine, taking into account the technical criteria set out in Annex VI, Part 2, with which of the credit quality steps set out in Part 1 of that Annex the relevant credit assessments of an eligible ECAI are to be associated. Those determinations shall be objective and consistent.

2.   When the competent authorities of a Member State have made a determination under paragraph 1, the competent authorities of other Member States may recognise that determination without carrying out their own determination process.

[5839]

Article 83

1.   The use of ECAI credit assessments for the calculation of a credit institution's risk-weighted exposure amounts shall be consistent and in accordance with Annex VI, Part 3. Credit assessments shall not be used selectively.

2.   Credit institutions shall use solicited credit assessments. However, with the permission of the relevant competent authority, they may use unsolicited assessments.

[5839A]

SUBSECTION 2
INTERNAL RATINGS BASED APPROACH

Article 84

1.   In accordance with this Subsection, the competent authorities may permit credit institutions to calculate their risk-weighted exposure amounts using the Internal Ratings Based Approach ("IRB Approach"). Explicit permission shall be required in the case of each credit institution.

2.   Permission shall be given only if the competent authority is satisfied that the credit institution's systems for the management and rating of credit risk exposures are sound and implemented with integrity and, in particular, that they meet the following standards in accordance with Annex VII, Part 4:

    (a)   the credit institution's rating systems provide for a meaningful assessment of obligor and transaction characteristics, a meaningful differentiation of risk and accurate and consistent quantitative estimates of risk;

    (b)   internal ratings and default and loss estimates used in the calculation of capital requirements and associated systems and processes play an essential role in the risk management and decision-making process, and in the credit approval, internal capital allocation and corporate governance functions of the credit institution;

    (c)   the credit institution has a credit risk control unit responsible for its rating systems that is appropriately independent and free from undue influence;

    (d)   the credit institution collects and stores all relevant data to provide effective support to its credit risk measurement and management process; and

    (e)   the credit institution documents its rating systems and the rationale for their design and validates its rating systems.

Where an EU parent credit institution and its subsidiaries or an EU parent financial holding company and its subsidiaries use the IRB Approach on a unified basis, the competent authorities may allow minimum requirements of Annex VII, Part 4 to be met by the parent and its subsidiaries considered together.

3.   A credit institution applying for the use of the IRB Approach shall demonstrate that it has been using for the IRB exposure classes in question rating systems that were broadly in line with the minimum requirements set out in Annex VII, Part 4 for internal risk measurement and management purposes for at least three years prior to its qualification to use the IRB Approach.

4.   A credit institution applying for the use of own estimates of LGDs and/or conversion factors shall demonstrate that it has been estimating and employing own estimates of LGDs and/or conversion factors in a manner that was broadly consistent with the minimum requirements for use of own estimates of those parameters set out in Annex VII, Part 4 for at least three years prior to qualification to use own estimates of LGDs and/or conversion factors.

5.   If a credit institution ceases to comply with the requirements set out in this Subsection, it shall either present to the competent authority a plan for a timely return to compliance or demonstrate that the effect of non-compliance is immaterial.

6.   When the IRB Approach is intended to be used by the EU parent credit institution and its subsidiaries, or by the EU parent financial holding company and its subsidiaries, the competent authorities of the different legal entities shall cooperate closely as provided for in Articles 129 to 132.

[5839B]

Article 85

1.   Without prejudice to Article 89, credit institutions and any parent undertaking and its subsidiaries shall implement the IRB Approach for all exposures.

Subject to the approval of the competent authorities, implementation may be carried out sequentially across the different exposure classes, referred to in Article 86, within the same business unit, across different business units in the same group or for the use of own estimates of LGDs or conversion factors for the calculation of risk weights for exposures to corporates, institutions, and central governments and central banks.

In the case of the retail exposure class referred to in Article 86, implementation may be carried out sequentially across the categories of exposures to which the different correlations in Annex VII, Part 1, points 10 to 13 correspond.

2.   Implementation as referred to in paragraph 1 shall be carried out within a reasonable period of time to be agreed with the competent authorities. The implementation shall be carried out subject to strict conditions determined by the competent authorities. Those conditions shall be designed to ensure that the flexibility under paragraph 1 is not used selectively with the purpose of achieving reduced minimum capital requirements in respect of those exposure classes or business units that are yet to be included in the IRB Approach or in the use of own estimates of LGDs and/or conversion factors.

3.   Credit institutions using the IRB Approach for any exposure class shall at the same time use the IRB Approach for the equity exposure class.

4.   Subject to paragraphs 1 to 3 of this Article and Article 89, credit institutions which have obtained permission under Article 84 to use the IRB Approach shall not revert to the use of Subsection 1 for the calculation of risk-weighted exposure amounts except for demonstrated good cause and subject to the approval of the competent authorities.

5.   Subject to paragraphs 1 and 2 of this Article and Article 89, credit institutions which have obtained permission under Article 87(9) to use own estimates of LGDs and conversion factors, shall not revert to the use of LGD values and conversion factors referred to in Article 87(8) except for demonstrated good cause and subject to the approval of the competent authorities.

[5839C]

Article 86

1.   Each exposure shall be assigned to one of the following exposure classes:
    (a)   claims or contingent claims on central governments and central banks;
    (b)   claims or contingent claims on institutions;
    (c)   claims or contingent claims on corporates;
    (d)   retail claims or contingent retail claims;
    (e)   equity claims;
    (f)   securitisation positions; or
    (g)   other non credit-obligation assets.

2.   The following exposures shall be treated as exposures to central governments and central banks:
    (a)   exposures to regional governments, local authorities or public sector entities which are treated as exposures to central governments under Subsection 1; and
    (b)   exposures to Multilateral Development Banks and International Organisations which attract a risk weight of 0% under Subsection 1.

3.   The following exposures shall be treated as exposures to institutions:
    (a)   exposures to regional governments and local authorities which are not treated as exposures to central governments under Subsection 1;
    (b)   exposures to Public Sector Entities which are treated as exposures to institutions under the Subsection 1; and
    (c)   exposures to Multilateral Development Banks which do not attract a 0% risk weight under Subsection 1.

4.   To be eligible for the retail exposure class referred to in point (d) of paragraph 1, exposures shall meet the following criteria:
    (a)   they shall be either to an individual person or persons, or to a small or medium sized entity, provided in the latter case that the total amount owed to the credit institution and parent undertakings and its subsidiaries, including any past due exposure, by the obligor client or group of connected clients, but excluding claims or contingent claims secured on residential real estate collateral, shall not, to the knowledge of the credit institution, which shall have taken reasonable steps to confirm the situation, exceed EUR 1 million;
    (b)   they are treated by the credit institution in its risk management consistently over time and in a similar manner;
    (c)   they are not managed just as individually as exposures in the corporate exposure class; and

(d)   they each represent one of a significant number of similarly managed exposures.

The present value of retail minimum lease payments is eligible for the retail exposure class.

5.   The following exposures shall be classed as equity exposures:
  (a)   non-debt exposures conveying a subordinated, residual claim on the assets or income of the issuer; and
  (b)   debt exposures the economic substance of which is similar to the exposures specified in point (a).

6.   Within the corporate exposure class, credit institutions shall separately identify as specialised lending exposures, exposures which possess the following characteristics:
  (a)   the exposure is to an entity which was created specifically to finance and/or operate physical assets;
  (b)   the contractual arrangements give the lender a substantial degree of control over the assets and the income that they generate; and
  (c)   the primary source of repayment of the obligation is the income generated by the assets being financed, rather than the independent capacity of a broader commercial enterprise.

7.   Any credit obligation not assigned to the exposure classes referred to in points (a), (b) and (d) to (f) of paragraph 1 shall be assigned to the exposure class referred to in point (c) of that paragraph.

8.   The exposure class referred to in point (g) of paragraph 1 shall include the residual value of leased properties if not included in the lease exposure as defined in Annex VII, Part 3, paragraph 4.

9.   The methodology used by the credit institution for assigning exposures to different exposure classes shall be appropriate and consistent over time.

[5839D]
Article 87

1.   The risk-weighted exposure amounts for credit risk for exposures belonging to one of the exposure classes referred to in points (a) to (e) or (g) of Article 86(1) shall, unless deducted from own funds, be calculated in accordance with Annex VII, Part 1, points 1 to 27.

2.   The risk-weighted exposure amounts for dilution risk for purchased receivables shall be calculated according to Annex VII, Part 1, point 28. Where a credit institution has full recourse in respect of purchased receivables for default risk and for dilution risk, to the seller of the purchased receivables, the provisions of Articles 87 and 88 in relation to purchased receivables need not be applied. The exposure may instead be treated as a collateralised exposure.

3.   The calculation of risk-weighted exposure amounts for credit risk and dilution risk shall be based on the relevant parameters associated with the exposure in question. These shall include probability of default (PD), LGD, maturity (M) and exposure value of the exposure. PD and LGD may be considered separately or jointly, in accordance with Annex VII, Part 2.

4.   Notwithstanding paragraph 3, the calculation of risk-weighted exposure amounts for credit risk for all exposures belonging to the exposure class referred to in point (e) of Article 86(1) shall be calculated in accordance with Annex VII, Part 1, points 17 to 26 subject to approval of the competent authorities. Competent authorities shall only allow a credit institution to use the approach set out in Annex VII, Part 1, points 25 and 26 if the credit institution meets the minimum requirements set out in Annex VII, Part 4, points 115 to 123.

5.   Notwithstanding paragraph 3, the calculation of risk weighted exposure amounts for credit risk for specialised lending exposures may be calculated in accordance with Annex VII, Part 1, point 6. Competent authorities shall publish guidance on how credit institutions should assign risk weights to specialised lending exposures under Annex VII, Part 1, point 6 and shall approve credit institution assignment methodologies.

6.   For exposures belonging to the exposure classes referred to in points (a) to (d) of Article 86(1), credit institutions shall provide their own estimates of PDs in accordance with Article 84 and Annex VII, Part 4.

7.   For exposures belonging to the exposure class referred to in point (d) of Article 86(1), credit institutions shall provide own estimates of LGDs and conversion factors in accordance with Article 84 and Annex VII, Part 4.

8.   For exposures belonging to the exposure classes referred to in points (a) to (c) of Article 86(1), credit institutions shall apply the LGD values set out in Annex VII, Part 2, point 8, and the conversion factors set out in Annex VII, Part 3, point 9(a) to (d).

9.   Notwithstanding paragraph 8, for all exposures belonging to the exposure classes referred to in points (a) to (c) of Article 86(1), competent authorities may permit credit institutions to use own estimates of LGDs and conversion factors in accordance with Article 84 and Annex VII, Part 4.

10.   The risk-weighted exposure amounts for securitised exposures and for exposures belonging to the exposure class referred to in point (f) of Article 86(1) shall be calculated in accordance with Subsection 4.

11.   Where exposures in the form of a collective investment undertaking (CIU) meet the criteria set out in Annex VI, Part 1, points 77 and 78 and the credit institution is aware of all of the underlying exposures of the CIU, the credit institution shall look through to those underlying exposures in order to calculate risk-weighted exposure amounts and expected loss amounts in accordance with the methods set out in this Subsection.

Where the credit institution does not meet the conditions for using the methods set out in this Subsection, risk weighted exposure amounts and expected loss amounts shall be calculated in accordance with the following approaches:

(a)   for exposures belonging to the exposure class referred to in point (e) of Article 86(1), the approach set out in Annex VII, Part 1, points 19 to 21. If, for those purposes, the credit institution is unable to differentiate between private equity, exchange-traded and other equity exposures, it shall treat the exposures concerned as other equity exposures;

(b)   for all other underlying exposures, the approach set out in Subsection 1, subject to the following modifications:

     (i)   the exposures are assigned to the appropriate exposure class and attributed the risk weight of the credit quality step immediately above the credit quality step that would normally be assigned to the exposure, and

     (ii)   exposures assigned to the higher credit quality steps, to which a risk weight of 150% would normally be attributed, are assigned a risk weight of 200%.

12.   Where exposures in the form of a CIU do not meet the criteria set out in Annex VI, Part 1, points 77 and 78, or the credit institution is not aware of all of the underlying exposures of the CIU, the credit institution shall look through to the underlying exposures and calculate risk-weighted exposure amounts and expected loss amounts in accordance with the approach set out in Annex VII, Part 1, points 19 to 21. If, for those purposes, the credit institution is unable to differentiate between private equity, exchange-traded and other equity exposures, it shall treat the exposures concerned as other equity exposures. For these purposes, non equity exposures are assigned to one of the classes (private equity, exchange traded equity or other equity) set out in Annex VII, Part 1, point 19 and unknown exposures are assigned to other equity class.

Alternatively to the method described above, credit institutions may calculate themselves or may rely on a third party to calculate and report the average risk weighted exposure amounts based on the CIU's underlying exposures in accordance with the following approaches, provided that the correctness of the calculation and the report is adequately ensured:

(a)   for exposures belonging to the exposure class referred to in point (e) of Article 86(1), the approach set out in Annex VII, Part 1, points 19 to 21. If, for those purposes, the credit institution is unable to differentiate between private equity, exchange-traded and other equity exposures, it shall treat the exposures concerned as other equity exposures; or

(b)   for all other underlying exposures, the approach set out in Subsection 1, subject to the following modifications:

     (i)   the exposures are assigned to the appropriate exposure class and attributed the risk weight of the credit quality step immediately above the credit quality step that would normally be assigned to the exposure, and

     (ii)   exposures assigned to the higher credit quality steps, to which a risk weight of 150% would normally be attributed, are assigned a risk weight of 200%.

                                                           [5839E]

Article 88

1.   The expected loss amounts for exposures belonging to one of the exposure classes referred to in points (a) to (e) of Article 86(1) shall be calculated in accordance with the methods set out in Annex VII, Part 1, points 29 to 35.

2.   The calculation of expected loss amounts in accordance with Annex VII, Part 1, points 29 to 35 shall be based on the same input figures of PD, LGD and the exposure value for each exposure as being used for the calculation of risk-weighted exposure amounts in accordance with Article 87. For defaulted exposures, where credit institutions use own estimates of LGDs, expected loss ("EL") shall be the credit institution's best estimate of EL ("ELBE,") for the defaulted exposure, in accordance with Annex VII, Part 4, point 80.

3.   The expected loss amounts for securitised exposures shall be calculated in accordance with Subsection 4.

4.   The expected loss amount for exposures belonging to the exposure class referred to in point (g) of Article 86(1) shall be zero.

5.   The expected loss amounts for dilution risk of purchased receivables shall be calculated in accordance with the methods set out in Annex VII, Part 1, point 35.

6.   The expected loss amounts for exposures referred to in Article 87(11) and (12) shall be calculated in accordance with the methods set out in Annex VII, Part 1, points 29 to 35.

                                                            [5839F]

Article 89

1.   Subject to the approval of the competent authorities, credit institutions permitted to use the IRB Approach in the calculation of risk-weighted exposure amounts and expected loss amounts for one or more exposure classes may apply Subsection 1 for the following:

(a)   the exposure class referred to in point (a) of Article 86(1), where the number of material counterparties is limited and it would be unduly burdensome for the credit institution to implement a rating system for these counterparties;

(b)   the exposure class referred to in point (b) of Article 86(1), where the number of material counterparties is limited and it would be unduly burdensome for the credit institution to implement a rating system for these counterparties;

(c)   exposures in non-significant business units as well as exposure classes that are immaterial in terms of size and perceived risk profile;

(d)   exposures to central governments of the home Member State and to their regional governments, local authorities and administrative bodies, provided that:

(i)   there is no difference in risk between the exposures to that central government and those other exposures because of specific public arrangements, and

(ii)   exposures to the central government are assigned a 0% risk weight under Subsection 1;

(e)   exposures of a credit institution to a counterparty which is its parent undertaking, its subsidiary or a subsidiary of its parent undertaking provided that the counterparty is an institution or a financial holding company, financial institution, asset management company or ancillary services undertaking subject to appropriate prudential requirements or an undertaking linked by a relationship within the meaning of Article 12(1) of Directive 83/349/EEC and exposures between credit institutions which meet the requirements set out in Article 80(8);

(f)   equity exposures to entities whose credit obligations qualify for a 0% risk weight under Subsection 1 (including those publicly sponsored entities where a zero risk weight can be applied);

(g)   equity exposures incurred under legislative programmes to promote specified sectors of the economy that provide significant subsidies for the investment to the credit institution and involve some form of government oversight and restrictions on the equity investments. This exclusion is limited to an aggregate of 10% of original own funds plus additional own funds;

(h)   the exposures identified in Annex VI, Part 1, point 40 meeting the conditions specified therein; or

(i)   State and State-reinsured guarantees pursuant to Annex VIII, Part 2, point 19.

This paragraph shall not prevent the competent authorities of other Member States to allow the application of the rules of Subsection 1 for equity exposures which have been allowed for this treatment in other Member States.

2.   For the purposes of paragraph 1, the equity exposure class of a credit institution shall be considered material if their aggregate value, excluding equity exposures incurred under legislative programmes as referred to in paragraph 1, point (g), exceeds, on average over the preceding year, 10% of the credit institution's own funds. If the number of those equity exposures is less than 10 individual holdings, that threshold shall be 5% of the credit institution's own funds.

[5839G]

SUBSECTION 3
CREDIT RISK MITIGATION

Article 90

For the purposes of this Subsection, "lending credit institution" shall mean the credit institution which has the exposure in question, whether or not deriving from a loan.

[5839H]

Article 91

Credit institutions using the Standardised Approach under Articles 78 to 83 or using the IRB Approach under Articles 84 to 89, but not using their own estimates of LGD and conversion factors under Articles 87 and 88, may recognise credit risk mitigation in accordance with this Subsection in the calculation of risk-weighted exposure amounts for the purposes of Article 75 point (a) or as relevant expected loss amounts for the purposes of the calculation referred to in point (q) of Article 57, and Article 63(3).

[5839I]

an agreed limit, and an early amortisation provision shall be a contractual clause which requires, on the occurrence of defined events, investors' positions to be redeemed before the originally stated maturity of the securities issued.

[5839R]

Article 101

1.   An originator credit institution which, in respect of a securitisation, has made use of Article 95 in the calculation of risk-weighted exposure amounts or a sponsor credit institution shall not, with a view to reducing potential or actual losses to investors, provide support to the securitisation beyond its contractual obligations.

2.   If an originator credit institution or a sponsor credit institution fails to comply with paragraph 1 in respect of a securitisation, the competent authority shall require it at a minimum, to hold capital against all of the securitised exposures as if they had not been securitised. The credit institution shall disclose publicly that it has provided non-contractual support and the regulatory capital impact of having done so.

[5839S]

SECTION 4
MINIMUM OWN FUNDS REQUIREMENTS FOR OPERATIONAL RISK

Article 102

1.   Competent authorities shall require credit institutions to hold own funds against operational risk in accordance with the approaches set out in Articles 103, 104 and 105.

2.   Without prejudice to paragraph 4, credit institutions that use the approach set out in Article 104 shall not revert to the use of the approach set out in Article 103, except for demonstrated good cause and subject to approval by the competent authorities.

3.   Without prejudice to paragraph 4, credit institutions that use the approach set out in Article 105 shall not revert to the use of the approaches set out in Articles 103 or 104 except for demonstrated good cause and subject to approval by the competent authorities.

4.   Competent authorities may allow credit institutions to use a combination of approaches in accordance with Annex X, Part 4.

[5839T]

Article 103

The capital requirement for operational risk under the Basic Indicator Approach shall be a certain percentage of a relevant indicator, in accordance with the parameters set out in Annex X, Part 1.

[5839U]

Article 104

1.   Under the Standardised Approach, credit institutions shall divide their activities into a number of business lines as set out in Annex X, Part 2.

2.   For each business line, credit institutions shall calculate a capital requirement for operational risk as a certain percentage of a relevant indicator, in accordance with the parameters set out in Annex X, Part 2.

3.   For certain business lines, the competent authorities may under certain conditions authorise a credit institution to use an alternative relevant indicator for determining its capital requirement for operational risk as set out in Annex X, Part 2, points 5 to 11.

4.   The capital requirement for operational risk under the Standardised Approach shall be the sum of the capital requirements for operational risk across all individual business lines.

5.   The parameters for the Standardised Approach are set out in Annex X, Part 2.

6.   To qualify for use of the Standardised Approach, credit institutions shall meet the criteria set out in Annex X, Part 2.

[5839V]

Article 105

1.   Credit institutions may use Advanced Measurement Approaches based on their own operational risk measurement systems, provided that the competent authority expressly approves the use of the models concerned for calculating the own funds requirement.

2.   Credit institutions shall satisfy their competent authorities that they meet the qualifying criteria set out in Annex X, Part 3.

3.   When an Advanced Measurement Approach is intended to be used by an EU parent credit institution and its subsidiaries or by the subsidiaries of an EU parent financial holding company, the competent authorities of the different legal entities shall cooperate closely as provided for in Articles 129 to 132. The application shall include the elements listed in Annex X, Part 3.

PART IV
EC MATERIALS

4.   Where an EU parent credit institution and its subsidiaries or the subsidiaries of an EU parent financial holding company use an Advanced Measurement Approach on a unified basis, the competent authorities may allow the qualifying criteria set out in Annex X, Part 3 to be met by the parent and its subsidiaries considered together.

[5839W]

SECTION 5
LARGE EXPOSURES

Article 106

1.   "Exposures", for the purposes of this Section, shall mean any asset or off-balance-sheet item referred to in Section 3, Subsection 1, without application of the risk weights or degrees of risk there provided for.

Exposures arising from the items referred to in Annex IV shall be calculated in accordance with one of the methods set out in Annex III. For the purposes of this Section, Annex III, Part 2, point 2 shall also apply.

All elements entirely covered by own funds may, with the agreement of the competent authorities, be excluded from the determination of exposures, provided that such own funds are not included in the credit institution's own funds for the purposes of Article 75 or in the calculation of other monitoring ratios provided for in this Directive and in other Community acts.

2.   Exposures shall not include either of the following:
   (a)   in the case of foreign exchange transactions, exposures incurred in the ordinary course of settlement during the 48 hours following payment; or
   (b)   in the case of transactions for the purchase or sale of securities, exposures incurred in the ordinary course of settlement during the five working days following payment or delivery of the securities, whichever is the earlier.

[5839X]

Article 107

For the purposes of applying this Section, the term "credit institution" shall cover the following:
   (a)   a credit institution, including its branches in third countries; and
   (b)   any private or public undertaking, including its branches, which meets the definition of "credit institution" and has been authorised in a third country.

[5839Y]

Article 108

A credit institution's exposure to a client or group of connected clients shall be considered a large exposure where its value is equal to or exceeds 10% of its own funds.

[5839Z]

Article 109

The competent authorities shall require that every credit institution have sound administrative and accounting procedures and adequate internal control mechanisms for the purposes of identifying and recording all large exposures and subsequent changes to them, in accordance with this Directive, and for that of monitoring those exposures in the light of each credit institution's own exposure policies.

[5840]

Article 110

1.   A credit institution shall report every large exposure to the competent authorities.

Member States shall provide that reporting is to be carried out, at their discretion, in accordance with one of the following two methods:
   (a)   reporting of all large exposures at least once a year, combined with reporting during the year of all new large exposures and any increases in existing large exposures of at least 20% with respect to the previous communication; or
   (b)   reporting of all large exposures at least four times a year.

2.   Except in the case of credit institutions relying on Article 114 for the recognition of collateral in calculating the value of exposures for the purposes of paragraphs 1, 2 and 3 of Article 111, exposures exempted under Article 113(3)(a) to (d) and (f) to (h) need not be reported as laid down in paragraph 1 and the reporting frequency laid down in point (b) of paragraph 1 of this Article may be reduced to twice a year for the exposures referred to in Article 113(3)(e) and (i), and in Articles 115 and 116.

Where a credit institution invokes this paragraph, it shall keep a record of the grounds advanced for at least one year after the event giving rise to the dispensation, so that the competent authorities may establish whether it is justified.

3. Member States may require credit institutions to analyse their exposures to collateral issuers for possible concentrations and where appropriate take action or report any significant findings to their competent authority.

[5840A]

Article 111

1. A credit institution may not incur an exposure to a client or group of connected clients the value of which exceed 25% of its own funds.

2. Where that client or group of connected clients is the parent undertaking or subsidiary of the credit institution and/or one or more subsidiaries of that parent undertaking, the percentage laid down in paragraph 1 shall be reduced to 20%. Member States may, however, exempt the exposures incurred to such clients from the 20% limit if they provide for specific monitoring of such exposures by other measures or procedures. They shall inform the Commission and the European Banking Committee of the content of such measures or procedures.

3. A credit institution may not incur large exposures which in total exceed 800% of its own funds.

4. A credit institution shall at all times comply with the limits laid down in paragraphs 1, 2 and 3 in respect of its exposures. If in an exceptional case exposures exceed those limits, that fact shall be reported without delay to the competent authorities which may, where the circumstances warrant it, allow the credit institution a limited period of time in which to comply with the limits.

[5840B]

Article 112

1. For the purposes of Articles 113 to 117, the term "guarantee" shall include credit derivatives recognised under Articles 90 to 93 other than credit linked notes.

2. Subject to paragraph 3, where, under Articles 113 to 117, the recognition of funded or unfunded credit protection may be permitted, this shall be subject to compliance with the eligibility requirements and other minimum requirements, set out under Articles 90 to 93 for the purposes of calculating risk-weighted exposure amounts under Articles 78 to 83.

3. Where a credit institution relies upon Article 114(2), the recognition of funded credit protection shall be subject to the relevant requirements under Articles 84 to 89.

[5840C]

Article 113

1. Member States may impose limits more stringent than those laid down in Article 111.

2. Member States may fully or partially exempt from the application of Article 111(1), (2) and (3) exposures incurred by a credit institution to its parent undertaking, to other subsidiaries of that parent undertaking or to its own subsidiaries, in so far as those undertakings are covered by the supervision on a consolidated basis to which the credit institution itself is subject, in accordance with this Directive or with equivalent standards in force in a third country.

3. Member States may fully or partially exempt the following exposures from the application of Article 111:

(a) asset items constituting claims on central governments or central banks which, unsecured, would be assigned a 0% risk weight under Articles 78 to 83;

(b) asset items constituting claims on international organisations or multilateral development banks which, unsecured, would be assigned a 0% risk weight under Articles 78 to 83;

(c) asset items constituting claims carrying the explicit guarantees of central governments, central banks, international organisations, multilateral development banks or public sector entities, where unsecured claims on the entity providing the guarantee would be assigned a 0% risk weight under Articles 78 to 83;

(d) other exposures attributable to, or guaranteed by, central governments, central banks, international organisations, multilateral development banks or public sector entities, where unsecured claims on the entity to which the exposure is attributable or by which it is guaranteed would be assigned a 0% risk weight under Articles 78 to 83;

(e) asset items constituting claims on and other exposures to central governments or central banks not mentioned in point (a) which are denominated and, where applicable, funded in the national currencies of the borrowers;

(f) asset items and other exposures secured, to the satisfaction of the competent authorities, by collateral in the form of debt securities issued by central governments or central banks, international organisations, multilateral development banks, Member States' regional governments, local authorities or public sector entities, which securities constitute claims on their issuer which would be assigned a 0% risk weighting under Articles 78 to 83;

(g) asset items and other exposures secured, to the satisfaction of the competent authorities, by collateral in the form of cash deposits placed with the lending credit institution or with a credit institution which is the parent undertaking or a subsidiary of the lending institution;

(h) asset items and other exposures secured, to the satisfaction of the competent authorities, by collateral in the form of certificates of deposit issued by the lending credit institution or by a credit institution which is the parent undertaking or a subsidiary of the lending credit institution and lodged with either of them;

(i) asset items constituting claims on and other exposures to institutions, with a maturity of one year or less, but not constituting such institutions" own funds;

(j) asset items constituting claims on and other exposures to those institutions which are not credit institutions but which fulfil the conditions referred to in Annex VI, Part 1, point 85, with a maturity of one year or less, and secured in accordance with the same point;

(k) bills of trade and other similar bills, with a maturity of one year or less, bearing the signatures of other credit institutions;

(l) covered bonds falling within the terms of Annex VI, Part 1, points 68 to 70;

(m) pending subsequent coordination, holdings in the insurance companies referred to in Article 122(1) up to 40% of the own funds of the credit institution acquiring such a holding;

(n) asset items constituting claims on regional or central credit institutions with which the lending credit institution is associated in a network in accordance with legal or statutory provisions and which are responsible, under those provisions, for cash-clearing operations within the network;

(o) exposures secured, to the satisfaction of the competent authorities, by collateral in the form of securities other than those referred to in point (f);

(p) loans secured, to the satisfaction of the competent authorities, by mortgages on residential property or by shares in Finnish residential housing companies, operating in accordance with the Finnish Housing Company Act of 1991 or subsequent equivalent legislation and leasing transactions under which the lessor retains full ownership of the residential property leased for as long as the lessee has not exercised his option to purchase, in all cases up to 50% of the value of the residential property concerned;

(q) the following, where they would receive a 50% risk weight under Articles 78 to 83, and only up to 50% of the value of the property concerned:

    (i) exposures secured by mortgages on offices or other commercial premises, or by shares in Finnish housing companies, operating in accordance with the Finnish Housing Company Act of 1991 or subsequent equivalent legislation, in respect of offices or other commercial premises; and

    (ii) exposures related to property leasing transactions concerning offices or other commercial premises;

for the purposes of point (ii), until 31 December 2011, the competent authorities of each Member State may allow credit institutions to recognise 100% of the value of the property concerned. At the end of this period, this treatment shall be reviewed. Member States shall inform the Commission of the use they make of this preferential treatment;

(r) 50% of the medium/low-risk off-balance-sheet items referred to in Annex II;

(s) subject to the competent authorities' agreement, guarantees other than loan guarantees which have a legal or regulatory basis and are given for their members by mutual guarantee schemes possessing the status of credit institutions, subject to a weighting of 20% of their amount; and

(t) the low-risk off-balance-sheet items referred to in Annex II, to the extent that an agreement has been concluded with the client or group of connected clients under which the exposure may be incurred only if it has been ascertained that it will not cause the limits applicable under Article 111(1) to (3) to be exceeded.

Cash received under a credit linked note issued by the credit institution and loans and deposits of a counterparty to or with the credit institution which are subject to an on-balance sheet netting agreement recognised under Articles 90 to 93 shall be deemed to fall under point (g).

For the purposes of point (o), the securities used as collateral shall be valued at market price, have a value that exceeds the exposures guaranteed and be either traded on a stock exchange or effectively negotiable and regularly quoted on a market operated under the auspices of recognised professional operators and allowing, to the satisfaction of the competent authorities of the Member State of origin of the credit institution, for the establishment of an objective price such that the excess value of the securities may be verified at any time. The excess value required shall be 100%. It shall, however, be 150% in the case of shares and 50% in the case of debt securities issued by institutions, Member State regional governments or local authorities other than those referred to in sub-point (f), and in the case of debt securities issued by multilateral development banks other than those assigned a 0% risk weight under Articles 78 to 83. Where there is a mismatch between the maturity of the exposure and the maturity of the credit protection, the collateral shall not be recognised. Securities used as collateral may not constitute credit institutions' own funds.

For the purposes of point (p), the value of the property shall be calculated, to the satisfaction of the competent authorities, on the basis of strict valuation standards laid down by law, regulation or administrative provisions. Valuation shall be carried out at least once a year. For the purposes of point (p), residential property shall mean a residence to be occupied or let by the borrower.

Member States shall inform the Commission of any exemption granted under point (s) in order to ensure that it does not result in a distortion of competition.

[5840D]

Article 114

1. Subject to paragraph 3, for the purposes of calculating the value of exposures for the purposes of Article 111(1) to (3) Member States may, in respect of credit institutions using the Financial Collateral Comprehensive Method under Articles 90 to 93, in the alternative to availing of the full or partial exemptions permitted under points (f), (g), (h), and (o) of Article 113(3), permit such credit institutions to use a value lower than the value of the exposure, but no lower than the total of the fully-adjusted exposure values of their exposures to the client or group of connected clients.

For these purposes, "fully adjusted exposure value" means that calculated under Articles 90 to 93 taking into account the credit risk mitigation, volatility adjustments, and any maturity mismatch (E*).

Where this paragraph is applied to a credit institution, points (f), (g), (h), and (o) of Article 113(3) shall not apply to the credit institution in question.

2. Subject to paragraph 3, a credit institution permitted to use own estimates of LGDs and conversion factors for an exposure class under Articles 84 to 89 may be permitted, where it is able to the satisfaction of the competent authorities to estimate the effects of financial collateral on their exposures separately from other LGD-relevant aspects, to recognise such effects in calculating the value of exposures for the purposes of Article 111(1) to (3).

Competent authorities shall be satisfied as to the suitability of the estimates produced by the credit institution for use for the reduction of the exposure value for the purposes of compliance with the provisions of Article 111.

Where a credit institution is permitted to use its own estimates of the effects of financial collateral, it shall do so on a basis consistent with the approach adopted in the calculation of capital requirements.

Credit institutions permitted to use own estimates of LGDs and conversion factors for an exposure class under Articles 84 to 89 which do not calculate the value of their exposures using the method referred to in the first subparagraph may be permitted to use the approach set out in paragraph 1 or the exemption set out in Article 113(3)(o) for calculating the value of exposures. A credit institution shall use only one of these two methods.

3. A credit institution that is permitted to use the methods described in paragraphs 1 and 2 in calculating the value of exposures for the purposes of Article 111(1) to (3), shall conduct periodic stress tests of their credit-risk concentrations, including in relation to the realisable value of any collateral taken.

These periodic stress tests shall address risks arising from potential changes in market conditions that could adversely impact the credit institutions' adequacy of own funds and risks arising from the realisation of collateral in stressed situations.

The credit institution shall satisfy the competent authorities that the stress tests carried out are adequate and appropriate for the assessment of such risks.

In the event that such a stress test indicates a lower realisable value of collateral taken than would be permitted to be taken into account under paragraphs 1 and 2 as appropriate, the value of collateral permitted to be recognised in calculating the value of exposures for the purposes of Article 111(1) to (3) shall be reduced accordingly.

Such credit institutions shall include the following in their strategies to address concentration risk:

(a)   policies and procedures to address risks arising from maturity mismatches between exposures and any credit protection on those exposures;

(b)   policies and procedures in the event that a stress test indicates a lower realisable value of collateral than taken into account under paragraphs 1 and 2; and

(c)   policies and procedures relating to concentration risk arising from the application of credit risk mitigation techniques, and in particular large indirect credit exposures, for example to a single issuer of securities taken as collateral.

4. Where the effects of collateral are recognised under the terms of paragraphs 1 or 2, Member States may treat any covered Part of the exposure as having been incurred to the collateral issuer rather than to the client.

[5840E]

Article 115

1.   For the purposes of Article 111(1) to (3), Member States may assign a weighting of 20% to asset items constituting claims on Member States' regional governments and local authorities where those claims would be assigned a 20% risk weight under Articles 78 to 83 and to other exposures to or guaranteed by such governments and authorities claims on which are assigned a 20% risk weight under Articles 78 to 83. However, Member States may reduce that rate to 0% in respect of asset items constituting claims on Member States' regional governments and local authorities where those claims would be assigned a 0% risk weight under Article 78 to 83 and to other exposures to or guaranteed by such governments and authorities claims on which are assigned a 0% risk weight under Articles 78 to 83.

2.   For the purposes of Article 111(1) to (3), Member States may assign a weighting of 20% to asset items constituting claims on and other exposures to institutions with a maturity of more than one but not more than three years and a weighting of 50% to asset items constituting claims on institutions with a maturity of more than three years, provided that the latter are represented by debt instruments that were issued by a institution and that those debt instruments are, in the opinion of the competent authorities, effectively negotiable on a market made up of professional operators and are subject to daily quotation on that market, or the issue of which was authorised by the competent authorities of the Member State of origin of the issuing institutions. In no case may any of these items constitute own funds.

[5840F]

Article 116

By way of derogation from Article 113(3)(i) and Article 115(2), Member States may assign a weighting of 20% to asset items constituting claims on and other exposures to institutions, regardless of their maturity.

[5840G]

Article 117

1.   Where an exposure to a client is guaranteed by a third party, or by collateral in the form of securities issued by a third party under the conditions laid down in Article 113(3)(o), Member States may:

(a)   treat the exposure as having been incurred to the guarantor rather than to the client; or
(b)   treat the exposure as having been incurred to the third party rather than to the client, if the exposure defined in Article 113(3)(o) is guaranteed by collateral under the conditions there laid down.

2.   Where Member States apply the treatment provided for in point (a) of paragraph 1:

(a)   where the guarantee is denominated in a currency different from that in which the exposure is denominated the amount of the exposure deemed to be covered will be calculated in accordance with the provisions on the treatment of currency mismatch for unfunded credit protection in Annex VIII;
(b)   a mismatch between the maturity of the exposure and the maturity of the protection will be treated in accordance with the provisions on the treatment of maturity mismatch in Annex VIII; and
(c)   partial coverage may be recognised in accordance with the treatment set out in Annex VIII.

[5840H]

Article 118

Where compliance by a credit institution on an individual or sub-consolidated basis with the obligations imposed in this Section is disapplied under Article 69(1), or the provisions of Article 70 are applied in the case of parent credit institutions in a Member State, measures must be taken to ensure the satisfactory allocation of risks within the group.

[5840I]

Article 119

By 31 December 2007, the Commission shall submit to the European Parliament and to the Council a report on the functioning of this Section, together with any appropriate proposals.

[5840J]

SECTION 6
QUALIFYING HOLDINGS OUTSIDE THE FINANCIAL SECTOR

Article 120

1.   No credit institution may have a qualifying holding the amount of which exceeds 15% of its own funds in an undertaking which is neither a credit institution, nor a financial institution, nor an undertaking carrying on activities which are a direct extension of banking or concern services

ancillary to banking, such as leasing, factoring, the management of unit trusts, the management of data processing services or any other similar activity.

2. The total amount of a credit institution's qualifying holdings in undertakings other than credit institutions, financial institutions or undertakings carrying on activities which are a direct extension of banking or concern services ancillary to banking, such as leasing, factoring, the management of unit trusts, the management of data processing services, or any other similar activity may not exceed 60% of its own funds.

3. The limits laid down in paragraphs 1 and 2 may be exceeded only in exceptional circumstances. In such cases, however, the competent authorities shall require a credit institution either to increase its own funds or to take other equivalent measures.

[5840K]

Article 121

Shares held temporarily during a financial reconstruction or rescue operation or during the normal course of underwriting or in an institution's own name on behalf of others shall not be counted as qualifying holdings for the purpose of calculating the limits laid down in Articles 120(1) and (2). Shares which are not financial fixed assets as defined in Article 35(2) of Directive 86/635/EEC shall not be included in the calculation.

[5840L]

Article 122

1. The Member States need not apply the limits laid down in Articles 120(1) and (2) to holdings in insurance companies as defined in Directives 73/239/EEC and 2002/83/EC, or in reinsurance companies as defined in Directive 98/78/EC.

2. The Member States may provide that the competent authorities are not to apply the limits laid down in Article 120(1) and (2) if they provide that 100% of the amounts by which a credit institution's qualifying holdings exceed those limits shall be covered by own funds and that the latter shall not be included in the calculation required under Article 75. If both the limits laid down in Article 120(1) and (2) are exceeded, the amount to be covered by own funds shall be the greater of the excess amounts.

[5840M]

CHAPTER 3
CREDIT INSTITUTIONS' ASSESSMENT PROCESS

Article 123

Credit institutions shall have in place sound, effective and complete strategies and processes to assess and maintain on an ongoing basis the amounts, types and distribution of internal capital that they consider adequate to cover the nature and level of the risks to which they are or might be exposed.

These strategies and processes shall be subject to regular internal review to ensure that they remain comprehensive and proportionate to the nature, scale and complexity of the activities of the credit institution concerned.

[5840N]

CHAPTER 4
SUPERVISION AND DISCLOSURE BY COMPETENT AUTHORITIES

SECTION 1
SUPERVISION

Article 124

1. Taking into account the technical criteria set out in Annex XI, the competent authorities shall review the arrangements, strategies, processes and mechanisms implemented by the credit institutions to comply with this Directive and evaluate the risks to which the credit institutions are or might be exposed.

2. The scope of the review and evaluation referred to in paragraph 1 shall be that of the requirements of this Directive.

3. On the basis of the review and evaluation referred to in paragraph 1, the competent authorities shall determine whether the arrangements, strategies, processes and mechanisms implemented by the credit institutions and the own funds held by these ensure a sound management and coverage of their risks.

4. Competent authorities shall establish the frequency and intensity of the review and evaluation referred to in paragraph 1 having regard to the size, systemic importance, nature, scale

and complexity of the activities of the credit institution concerned and taking into account the principle of proportionality. The review and evaluation shall be updated at least on an annual basis.

5.   The review and evaluation performed by competent authorities shall include the exposure of credit institutions to the interest rate risk arising from non-trading activities. Measures shall be required in the case of institutions whose economic value declines by more than 20% of their own funds as a result of a sudden and unexpected change in interest rates the size of which shall be prescribed by the competent authorities and shall not differ between credit institutions.

[5840O]

Article 125

1.   Where a parent undertaking is a parent credit institution in a Member State or an EU parent credit institution, supervision on a consolidated basis shall be exercised by the competent authorities that authorised it under Article 6.

2.   Where the parent of a credit institution is a parent financial holding company in a Member State or an EU parent financial holding company, supervision on a consolidated basis shall be exercised by the competent authorities that authorised that credit institution under Article 6.

[5840P]

Article 126

1.   Where credit institutions authorised in two or more Member States have as their parent the same parent financial holding company in a Member State or the same EU parent financial holding company, supervision on a consolidated basis shall be exercised by the competent authorities of the credit institution authorised in the Member State in which the financial holding company was set up.

Where the parents of credit institutions authorised in two or more Member States comprise more than one financial holding company with head offices in different Member States and there is a credit institution in each of these States, supervision on a consolidated basis shall be exercised by the competent authority of the credit institution with the largest balance sheet total.

2.   Where more than one credit institution authorised in the Community has as its parent the same financial holding company and none of these credit institutions has been authorised in the Member State in which the financial holding company was set up, supervision on a consolidated basis shall be exercised by the competent authority that authorised the credit institution with the largest balance sheet total, which shall be considered, for the purposes of this Directive, as the credit institution controlled by an EU parent financial holding company.

3.   In particular cases, the competent authorities may by common agreement waive the criteria referred to in paragraphs 1 and 2 if their application would be inappropriate, taking into account the credit institutions and the relative importance of their activities in different countries, and appoint a different competent authority to exercise supervision on a consolidated basis. In these cases, before taking their decision, the competent authorities shall give the EU parent credit institution, or EU parent financial holding company, or credit institution with the largest balance sheet total, as appropriate, an opportunity to state its opinion on that decision.

4.   The competent authorities shall notify the Commission of any agreement falling within paragraph 3.

[5840Q]

Article 127

1.   Member States shall adopt any measures necessary, where appropriate, to include financial holding companies in consolidated supervision. Without prejudice to Article 135, the consolidation of the financial situation of the financial holding company shall not in any way imply that the competent authorities are required to play a supervisory role in relation to the financial holding company on a stand-alone basis.

2.   When the competent authorities of a Member State do not include a credit institution subsidiary in supervision on a consolidated basis under one of the cases provided for in points (b) and (c) of Article 73(1), the competent authorities of the Member State in which that credit institution subsidiary is situated may ask the parent undertaking for information which may facilitate their supervision of that credit institution.

3.   Member States shall provide that their competent authorities responsible for exercising supervision on a consolidated basis may ask the subsidiaries of a credit institution or a financial holding company, which are not included within the scope of supervision on a consolidated basis for the information referred to in Article 137. In such a case, the procedures for transmitting and verifying the information laid down in that Article shall apply.

[5840R]

Article 128

Where Member States have more than one competent authority for the prudential supervision of credit institutions and financial institutions, Member States shall take the requisite measures to organise coordination between such authorities.

[5840S]

Article 129

1.   In addition to the obligations imposed by the provisions of this Directive, the competent authority responsible for the exercise of supervision on a consolidated basis of EU parent credit institutions and credit institutions controlled by EU parent financial holding companies shall carry out the following tasks:

   (a)   coordination of the gathering and dissemination of relevant or essential information in going concern and emergency situations; and

   (b)   planning and coordination of supervisory activities in going concern as well as in emergency situations, including in relation to the activities in Article 124, in cooperation with the competent authorities involved.

2.   In the case of applications for the permissions referred to in Articles 84(1), 87(9) and 105 and in Annex III, Part 6, respectively, submitted by an EU parent credit institution and its subsidiaries, or jointly by the subsidiaries of an EU parent financial holding company, the competent authorities shall work together, in full consultation, to decide whether or not to grant the permission sought and to determine the terms and conditions, if any, to which such permission should be subject.

An application as referred to in the first subparagraph shall be submitted only to the competent authority referred to in paragraph 1.

The competent authorities shall do everything within their power to reach a joint decision on the application within six months. This joint decision shall be set out in a document containing the fully reasoned decision which shall be provided to the applicant by the competent authority referred to in paragraph 1.

The period referred to in subparagraph 3 shall begin on the date of receipt of the complete application by the competent authority referred to in paragraph 1. The competent authority referred to in paragraph 1 shall forward the complete application to the other competent authorities without delay.

In the absence of a joint decision between the competent authorities within six months, the competent authority referred to in paragraph 1 shall make its own decision on the application. The decision shall be set out in a document containing the fully reasoned decision and shall take into account the views and reservations of the other competent authorities expressed during the six months period. The decision shall be provided to the applicant and the other competent authorities by the competent authority referred to in paragraph 1.

The decisions referred to in the third and fifth subparagraphs shall be recognised as determinative and applied by the competent authorities in the Member States concerned.

[5840T]

Article 130

1.   Where an emergency situation arises within a banking group which potentially jeopardises the stability of the financial system in any of the Member States where entities of a group have been authorised, the competent authority responsible for the exercise of supervision on a consolidated basis shall alert as soon as is practicable, subject to Chapter 1, Section 2, the authorities referred to in Article 49(a) and Article 50. This obligation shall apply to all competent authorities identified under Articles 125 and 126 in relation to a particular group, and to the competent authority identified under Article 129(1). Where possible, the competent authority shall use existing defined channels of communication.

2.   The competent authority responsible for supervision on a consolidated basis shall, when it needs information which has already been given to another competent authority, contact this authority whenever possible in order to prevent duplication of reporting to the various authorities involved in supervision.

[5840U]

Article 131

In order to facilitate and establish effective supervision, the competent authority responsible for supervision on a consolidated basis and the other competent authorities shall have written coordination and cooperation arrangements in place.

Under these arrangements additional tasks may be entrusted to the competent authority responsible for supervision on a consolidated basis and procedures for the decision-making process and for cooperation with other competent authorities, may be specified.

The competent authorities responsible for authorising the subsidiary of a parent undertaking which is a credit institution may, by bilateral agreement, delegate their responsibility for supervision to the competent authorities which authorised and supervise the parent undertaking so that they assume responsibility for supervising the subsidiary in accordance with this Directive. The Commission shall be kept informed of the existence and content of such agreements. It shall forward such information to the competent authorities of the other Member States and to the European Banking Committee.

[5840V]

Article 132

1. The competent authorities shall cooperate closely with each other. They shall provide one another with any information which is essential or relevant for the exercise of the other authorities' supervisory tasks under this Directive. In this regard, the competent authorities shall communicate on request all relevant information and shall communicate on their own initiative all essential information.

Information referred to in the first subparagraph shall be regarded as essential if it could materially influence the assessment of the financial soundness of a credit institution or financial institution in another Member State.

In particular, competent authorities responsible for consolidated supervision of EU parent credit institutions and credit institutions controlled by EU parent financial holding companies shall provide the competent authorities in other Member States who supervise subsidiaries of these parents with all relevant information. In determining the extent of relevant information, the importance of these subsidiaries within the financial system in those Member States shall be taken into account.

The essential information referred to in the first subparagraph shall include, in particular, the following items:
(a) identification of the group structure of all major credit institutions in a group, as well as of the competent authorities of the credit institutions in the group;
(b) procedures for the collection of information from the credit institutions in a group, and the verification of that information;
(c) adverse developments in credit institutions or in other entities of a group, which could seriously affect the credit institutions; and
(d) major sanctions and exceptional measures taken by competent authorities in accordance with this Directive, including the imposition of an additional capital charge under Article 136 and the imposition of any limitation on the use of the Advanced Measurement Approach for the calculation of the own funds requirements under Article 105.

2. The competent authorities responsible for the supervision of credit institutions controlled by an EU parent credit institution shall whenever possible contact the competent authority referred to in Article 129(1) when they need information regarding the implementation of approaches and methodologies set out in this Directive that may already be available to that competent authority.

3. The competent authorities concerned shall, prior to their decision, consult each other with regard to the following items, where these decisions are of importance for other competent authorities' supervisory tasks:
(a) changes in the shareholder, organisational or management structure of credit institutions in a group, which require the approval or authorisation of competent authorities; and
(b) major sanctions or exceptional measures taken by competent authorities, including the imposition of an additional capital charge under Article 136 and the imposition of any limitation on the use of the Advances Measurement Approaches for the calculation of the own funds requirements under Article 105.

For the purposes of point (b), the competent authority responsible for supervision on a consolidated basis shall always be consulted.

However, a competent authority may decide not to consult in cases of urgency or where such consultation may jeopardise the effectiveness of the decisions. In this case, the competent authority shall, without delay, inform the other competent authorities.

[5840W]

Article 133

1. The competent authorities responsible for supervision on a consolidated basis shall, for the purposes of supervision, require full consolidation of all the credit institutions and financial institutions which are subsidiaries of a parent undertaking.

However, the competent authorities may require only proportional consolidation where, in their opinion, the liability of a parent undertaking holding a share of the capital is limited to that share of the capital in view of the liability of the other shareholders or members whose solvency is satisfactory. The liability of the other shareholders and members shall be clearly established, if necessary by means of formal signed commitments.

In the case where undertakings are linked by a relationship within the meaning of Article 12(1) of Directive 83/349/EEC, the competent authorities shall determine how consolidation is to be carried out.

2. The competent authorities responsible for supervision on a consolidated basis shall require the proportional consolidation of participations in credit institutions and financial institutions managed by an undertaking included in the consolidation together with one or more undertakings not included in the consolidation, where those undertakings' liability is limited to the share of the capital they hold.

3. In the case of participations or capital ties other than those referred to in paragraphs 1 and 2, the competent authorities shall determine whether and how consolidation is to be carried out. In particular, they may permit or require use of the equity method. That method shall not, however, constitute inclusion of the undertakings concerned in supervision on a consolidated basis.

[5840X]

Article 134

1. Without prejudice to Article 133, the competent authorities shall determine whether and how consolidation is to be carried out in the following cases:

   (a) where, in the opinion of the competent authorities, a credit institution exercises a significant influence over one or more credit institutions or financial institutions, but without holding a participation or other capital ties in these institutions; and

   (b) where two or more credit institutions or financial institutions are placed under single management other than pursuant to a contract or clauses of their memoranda or Articles of association.

In particular, the competent authorities may permit, or require use of, the method provided for in Article 12 of Directive 83/349/EEC. That method shall not, however, constitute inclusion of the undertakings concerned in consolidated supervision.

2. Where consolidated supervision is required pursuant to Articles 125 and 126, ancillary services undertakings and asset management companies as defined in Directive 2002/87/EC shall be included in consolidations in the cases, and in accordance with the methods, laid down in Article 133 and paragraph 1 of this Article.

[5840Y]

Article 135

The Member States shall require that persons who effectively direct the business of a financial holding company be of sufficiently good repute and have sufficient experience to perform those duties.

[5840Z]

Article 136

1. Competent authorities shall require any credit institution that does not meet the requirements of this Directive to take the necessary actions or steps at an early stage to address the situation.

For those purposes, the measures available to the competent authorities shall include the following:

   (a) obliging credit institutions to hold own funds in excess of the minimum level laid down in Article 75;

   (b) requiring the reinforcement of the arrangements, processes, mechanisms and strategies implemented to comply with Articles 22 and 123;

   (c) requiring credit institutions to apply a specific provisioning policy or treatment of assets in terms of own funds requirements;

   (d) restricting or limiting the business, operations or network of credit institutions; and

   (e) requiring the reduction of the risk inherent in the activities, products and systems of credit institutions.

The adoption of these measures shall be subject to Chapter 1, Section 2.

2. A specific own funds requirement in excess of the minimum level laid down in Article 75 shall be imposed by the competent authorities at least on the credit institutions which do not meet the requirements laid down in Articles 22, 109 and 123, or in respect of which a negative determination has been made on the issue described in Article 124, paragraph 3, if the sole application of other measures is unlikely to improve the arrangements, processes, mechanisms and strategies sufficiently within an appropriate timeframe.

[5841]

Article 137

1. Pending further coordination of consolidation methods, Member States shall provide that, where the parent undertaking of one or more credit institutions is a mixed-activity holding company, the competent authorities responsible for the authorisation and supervision of those credit

institutions shall, by approaching the mixed-activity holding company and its subsidiaries either directly or via credit institution subsidiaries, require them to supply any information which would be relevant for the purpose of supervising the credit institution subsidiaries.

2.   Member States shall provide that their competent authorities may carry out, or have carried out by external inspectors, on-the-spot inspections to verify information received from mixed-activity holding companies and their subsidiaries. If the mixed-activity holding company or one of its subsidiaries is an insurance undertaking, the procedure laid down in Article 140(1) may also be used. If a mixed-activity holding company or one of its subsidiaries is situated in a Member State other than that in which the credit institution subsidiary is situated, on-the-spot verification of information shall be carried out in accordance with the procedure laid down in Article 141.

[5841A]

Article 138

1.   Without prejudice to Chapter 2, Section 5, Member States shall provide that, where the parent undertaking of one or more credit institutions is a mixed-activity holding company, the competent authorities responsible for the supervision of these credit institutions shall exercise general supervision over transactions between the credit institution and the mixed-activity holding company and its subsidiaries.

2.   Competent authorities shall require credit institutions to have in place adequate risk management processes and internal control mechanisms, including sound reporting and accounting procedures, in order to identify, measure, monitor and control transactions with their parent mixed-activity holding company and its subsidiaries appropriately. Competent authorities shall require the reporting by the credit institution of any significant transaction with these entities other than the one referred to in Article 110. These procedures and significant transactions shall be subject to overview by the competent authorities.

Where these intra-group transactions are a threat to a credit institution's financial position, the competent authority responsible for the supervision of the institution shall take appropriate measures.

[5841B]

Article 139

1.   Member States shall take the necessary steps to ensure that there are no legal impediments preventing the exchange, as between undertakings included within the scope of supervision on a consolidated basis, mixed-activity holding companies and their subsidiaries, or subsidiaries of the kind covered in Article 127(3), of any information which would be relevant for the purposes of supervision in accordance with Articles 124 to 138 and this Article.

2.   Where a parent undertaking and any of its subsidiaries that are credit institutions are situated in different Member States, the competent authorities of each Member State shall communicate to each other all relevant information which may allow or aid the exercise of supervision on a consolidated basis.

Where the competent authorities of the Member State in which a parent undertaking is situated do not themselves exercise supervision on a consolidated basis pursuant to Articles 125 and 126, they may be invited by the competent authorities responsible for exercising such supervision to ask the parent undertaking for any information which would be relevant for the purposes of supervision on a consolidated basis and to transmit it to these authorities.

3.   Member States shall authorise the exchange between their competent authorities of the information referred to in paragraph 2, on the understanding that, in the case of financial holding companies, financial institutions or ancillary services undertakings, the collection or possession of information shall not in any way imply that the competent authorities are required to play a supervisory role in relation to those institutions or undertakings standing alone.

Similarly, Member States shall authorise their competent authorities to exchange the information referred to in Article 137 on the understanding that the collection or possession of information does not in any way imply that the competent authorities play a supervisory role in relation to the mixed-activity holding company and those of its subsidiaries which are not credit institutions, or to subsidiaries of the kind covered in Article 127(3).

[5841C]

Article 140

1.   Where a credit institution, financial holding company or a mixed-activity holding company controls one or more subsidiaries which are insurance companies or other undertakings providing investment services which are subject to authorisation, the competent authorities and the authorities entrusted with the public task of supervising insurance undertakings or those other undertakings providing investment services shall cooperate closely. Without prejudice to their respective responsibilities, those authorities shall provide one another with any information likely to simplify their task and to allow supervision of the activity and overall financial situation of the undertakings they supervise.

2. Information received, in the framework of supervision on a consolidated basis, and in particular any exchange of information between competent authorities which is provided for in this Directive, shall be subject to the obligation of professional secrecy defined in Chapter 1, Section 2.

3. The competent authorities responsible for supervision on a consolidated basis shall establish lists of the financial holding companies referred to in Article 71(2). Those lists shall be communicated to the competent authorities of the other Member States and to the Commission.

[5841D]

Article 141

Where, in applying this Directive, the competent authorities of one Member State wish in specific cases to verify the information concerning a credit institution, a financial holding company, a financial institution, an ancillary services undertaking, a mixed-activity holding company, a subsidiary of the kind covered in Article 137 or a subsidiary of the kind covered in Article 127(3), situated in another Member State, they shall ask the competent authorities of that other Member State to have that verification carried out. The authorities which receive such a request shall, within the framework of their competence, act upon it either by carrying out the verification themselves, by allowing the authorities who made the request to carry it out, or by allowing an auditor or expert to carry it out. The competent authority which made the request may, if it so wishes, participate in the verification when it does not carry out the verification itself.

[5841E]

Article 142

Without prejudice to their criminal law provisions, Member States shall ensure that penalties or measures aimed at ending observed breaches or the causes of such breaches may be imposed on financial holding companies and mixed-activity holding companies, or their effective managers, that infringe laws, regulation or administrative provisions enacted to implement Articles 124 to 141 and this Article. The competent authorities shall cooperate closely to ensure that those penalties or measures produce the desired results, especially when the central administration or main establishment of a financial holding company or of a mixed-activity holding company is not located at its head office.

[5841F]

Article 143

1. Where a credit institution, the parent undertaking of which is a credit institution or a financial holding company, the head office of which is in a third country, is not subject to consolidated supervision under Articles 125 and 126, the competent authorities shall verify whether the credit institution is subject to consolidated supervision by a third-country competent authority which is equivalent to that governed by the principles laid down in this Directive.

The verification shall be carried out by the competent authority which would be responsible for consolidated supervision if paragraph 3 were to apply, at the request of the parent undertaking or of any of the regulated entities authorised in the Community or on its own initiative. That competent authority shall consult the other competent authorities involved.

2. The Commission may request the European Banking Committee to give general guidance as to whether the consolidated supervision arrangements of competent authorities in third countries are likely to achieve the objectives of consolidated supervision as defined in this Chapter, in relation to credit institutions, the parent undertaking of which has its head office in a third country. The Committee shall keep any such guidance under review and take into account any changes to the consolidated supervision arrangements applied by such competent authorities.

The competent authority carrying out the verification specified in the first subparagraph of paragraph 1 shall take into account any such guidance. For this purpose the competent authority shall consult the Committee before taking a decision.

3. In the absence of such equivalent supervision, Member States shall apply the provisions of this Directive to the credit institution by analogy or shall allow their competent authorities to apply other appropriate supervisory techniques which achieve the objectives of supervision on a consolidated basis of credit institutions.

Those supervisory techniques shall, after consultation with the other competent authorities involved, be agreed upon by the competent authority which would be responsible for consolidated supervision.

Competent authorities may in particular require the establishment of a financial holding company which has its head office in the Community, and apply the provisions on consolidated supervision to the consolidated position of that financial holding company.

The supervisory techniques shall be designed to achieve the objectives of consolidated supervision as defined in this Chapter and shall be notified to the other competent authorities involved and the Commission.

[5841G]

PART IV
EC MATERIALS

SECTION 2
DISCLOSURE BY COMPETENT AUTHORITIES

Article 144

Competent authorities shall disclose the following information:

    (a)   the texts of laws, regulations, administrative rules and general guidance adopted in their Member State in the field of prudential regulation;

    (b)   the manner of exercise of the options and discretions available in Community legislation;

    (c)   the general criteria and methodologies they use in the review and evaluation referred to in Article 124; and

    (d)   without prejudice to the provisions laid down in Chapter 1, Section 2, aggregate statistical data on key aspects of the implementation of the prudential framework in each Member State.

The disclosures provided for in the first subparagraph shall be sufficient to enable a meaningful comparison of the approaches adopted by the competent authorities of the different Member States. The disclosures shall be published with a common format, and updated regularly. The disclosures shall be accessible at a single electronic location.

[5841H]

CHAPTER 5
DISCLOSURE BY CREDIT INSTITUTIONS

Article 145

1.   For the purposes of this Directive, credit institutions shall publicly disclose the information laid down in Annex XII, Part 2, subject to the provisions laid down in Article 146.

2.   Recognition by the competent authorities under Chapter 2, Section 3, Subsections 2 and 3 and Article 105 of the instruments and methodologies referred to in Annex XII, Part 3 shall be subject to the public disclosure by credit institutions of the information laid down therein.

3.   Credit institutions shall adopt a formal policy to comply with the disclosure requirements laid down in paragraphs 1 and 2, and have policies for assessing the appropriateness of their disclosures, including their verification and frequency.

4.   Credit institutions should, if requested, explain their rating decisions to SMEs and other corporate applicants for loans, providing an explanation in writing when asked. Should a voluntary undertaking by the sector in this regard prove inadequate, national measures shall be adopted. The administrative costs of the explanation have to be at an appropriate rate to the size of the loan.

[5841I]

Article 146

1.   Notwithstanding Article 145, credit institutions may omit one or more of the disclosures listed in Annex XII, Part 2 if the information provided by such disclosures is not, in the light of the criterion specified in Annex XII, Part 1, point 1, regarded as material.

2.   Notwithstanding Article 145, credit institutions may omit one or more items of information included in the disclosures listed in Annex XII, Parts 2 and 3 if those items include information which, in the light of the criteria specified in Annex XII, Part 1, points 2 and 3, is regarded as proprietary or confidential.

3.   In the exceptional cases referred to in paragraph 2, the credit institution concerned shall state in its disclosures the fact that the specific items of information are not disclosed, the reason for non-disclosure, and publish more general information about the subject matter of the disclosure requirement, except where these are to be classified as proprietary or confidential under the criteria set out in Annex XII, Part 1, points 2 and 3.

[5841J]

Article 147

1.   Credit institutions shall publish the disclosures required under Article 145 on an annual basis at a minimum. Disclosures shall be published as soon as practicable.

2.   Credit institutions shall also determine whether more frequent publication than is provided for in paragraph 1 is necessary in the light of the criteria set out in Annex XII, Part 1, point 4.

[5841K]

Article 148

1.   Credit institutions may determine the appropriate medium, location and means of verification to comply effectively with the disclosure requirements laid down in Article 145. To the degree feasible, all disclosures shall be provided in one medium or location.

2. Equivalent disclosures made by credit institutions under accounting, listing or other requirements may be deemed to constitute compliance with Article 145. If disclosures are not included in the financial statements, credit institutions shall indicate where they can be found.

[5841L]

Article 149

Notwithstanding Articles 146 to 148, Member States shall empower the competent authorities to require credit institutions:

    (a)   to make one or more of the disclosures referred to in Annex XII, Parts 2 and 3;

    (b)   to publish one or more disclosures more frequently than annually, and to set deadlines for publication;

    (c)   to use specific media and locations for disclosures other than the financial statements; and

    (d)   to use specific means of verification for the disclosures not covered by statutory audit.

[5841M]

TITLE VI

POWERS OF EXECUTION

Article 150

[1. Without prejudice, as regards own funds, to the proposal that the Commission is to submit pursuant to Article 62, the technical adjustments designed to amend non-essential elements of this Directive in the following areas shall be adopted in accordance with the regulatory procedure with scrutiny referred to in Article 151(2):]

    (a)   clarification of the definitions in order to take account, in the application of this Directive, of developments on financial markets;

    (b)   clarification of the definitions to ensure uniform application of this Directive;

    (c)   the alignment of terminology on, and the framing of definitions in accordance with, subsequent acts on credit institutions and related matters;

    (d)   technical adjustments to the list in Article 2;

    (e)   alteration of the amount of initial capital prescribed in Article 9 to take account of developments in the economic and monetary field;

    (f)   expansion of the content of the list referred to in Articles 23 and 24 and set out in Annex I or adaptation of the terminology used in that list to take account of developments on financial markets;

    (g)   the areas in which the competent authorities shall exchange information as listed in Article 42;

    (h)   technical adjustments in Articles 56 to 67 and in Article 74 as a result of developments in accounting standards or requirements which take account of Community legislation or with regard to convergence of supervisory practices;

    (i)   amendment of the list of exposure classes in Articles 79 and 86 in order to take account of developments on financial markets;

    (j)   the amount specified in Article 79(2)(c), Article 86(4)(a), Annex VII, Part 1, point 5 and Annex VII, Part 2, point 15 to take into account the effects of inflation;

    (k)   the list and classification of off-balance-sheet items in Annexes II and IV and their treatment in the determination of exposure values for the purposes of Title V, Chapter 2, Section 3; or

    (l)   adjustment of the provisions in Annexes V to XII in order to take account of developments on financial markets (in particular new financial products) or in accounting standards or requirements which take account of Community legislation, or with regard to convergence of supervisory practice.

2. The Commission may adopt the following implementing measures ... :

    (a)   specification of the size of sudden and unexpected changes in the interest rates referred to in Article 124(5);

    (b)   a temporary reduction in the minimum level of own funds laid down in Article 75 and/or the risk weights laid down in Title V, Chapter 2, Section 3 in order to take account of specific circumstances;

    (c)   without prejudice to the report referred to in Article 119, clarification of exemptions provided for in Articles 111(4), 113, 115 and 116;

    (d)   specification of the key aspects on which aggregate statistical data are to be disclosed under Article 144(1)(d); or

    (e)   specification of the format, structure, contents list and annual publication date of the disclosures provided for in Article 144;

    [(f)   adjustments of the criteria set out in Article 19a(1), in order to take account of future developments and to ensure the uniform application of this Directive].

[The measures referred to in points (a), (b), (c) and (f), designed to amend non-essential elements of this Directive by supplementing it, shall be adopted in accordance with the regulatory procedure with scrutiny referred to in Article 151(2). The measures referred to in points (d) and (e) shall be adopted in accordance with the regulatory procedure referred to in Article 151(2a).]

3, 4. ...

[5841N]

NOTES
Words in square brackets in para 1 substituted, words omitted from para 2 repealed, words in final pair of square brackets in that paragraph added, and paras 3, 4 repealed, by European Parliament and Council Directive 2008/24/EC, Art 1(1), as from 21 March 2008.
Point (f) in para 2 inserted by European Parliament and Council Directive 2007/44/EC, Art 5(6), as from 21 September 2007. Note that the 2007 Directive has a transposition date of 21 March 2009.

Article 151

1. The Commission shall be assisted by the European Banking Committee established by Commission Decision 2004/10/EC.[1]

[2. Where reference is made to this paragraph, Article 5a(1) to (4) and Article 7 of Decision 1999/468/EC shall apply, having regard to the provisions of Article 8 thereof.]

[2a. Where reference is made to this paragraph, Articles 5 and 7 of Decision 1999/468/EC shall apply, having regard to the provisions of Article 8 thereof.

The period laid down in Article 5(6) of Decision 1999/468/EC shall be set at three months.]

[3. By 31 December 2010, and, thereafter, at least every three years, the Commission shall review the provisions concerning its implementing powers and present a report to the European Parliament and to the Council on the functioning of those powers. This report shall examine, in particular, the need for the Commission to propose amendments to this Directive in order to ensure the appropriate scope of the implementing powers conferred on the Commission. The conclusion as to whether or not amendment is necessary shall be accompanied by a detailed statement of reasons. If necessary, the report shall be accompanied by a legislative proposal to amend the provisions conferring implementing powers on the Commission.]

[5841O]

NOTES
Paras 2, 3 substituted, and para 2a inserted, by European Parliament and Council Directive 2008/24/EC, Art 1(1), as from 21 March 2008.
[1]   OJ L3, 7.1.2004, p 36.

TITLE VII
TRANSITIONAL AND FINAL PROVISIONS

CHAPTER 1
TRANSITIONAL PROVISIONS

Article 152

1. Credit institutions calculating risk-weighted exposure amounts in accordance with Articles 84 to 89 shall during the first, second and third twelve-month periods after 31 December 2006 provide own funds which are at all times more than or equal to the amounts indicated in paragraphs 3, 4 and 5.

2. Credit institutions using the Advanced Measurement Approaches as specified in Article 105 for the calculation of their capital requirements for operational risk shall, during the second and third twelve-month periods after 31 December 2006, provide own funds which are at all times more than or equal to the amounts indicated in paragraphs 4 and 5.

3. For the first twelve-month period referred to in paragraph 1, the amount of own funds shall be 95% of the total minimum amount of own funds that would be required to be held during that period by the credit institution under Article 4 of Council Directive 93/6/EEC of 15 March 1993 on the capital adequacy of investment firms and credit institutions[1] as that Directive and Directive 2000/12/EC stood prior to 1 January 2007.

4. For the second twelve-month period referred to in paragraph 1, the amount of own funds shall be 90% of the total minimum amount of own funds that would be required to be held during that period by the credit institution under Article 4 of Directive 93/6/EEC as that Directive and Directive 2000/12/EC stood prior to 1 January 2007.

5. For the third twelve-month period referred to in paragraph 1, the amount of own funds shall be 80% of the total minimum amount of own funds that would be required to be held during that period by the credit institution under Article 4 of Directive 93/6/EEC as that Directive and Directive 2000/12/EC stood prior to 1 January 2007.

6. Compliance with the requirements of paragraphs 1 to 5 shall be on the basis of amounts of own funds fully adjusted to reflect differences in the calculation of own funds under Directive 2000/12/EC and Directive 93/6/EEC as those Directives stood prior to 1 January 2007 and the calculation of own funds under this Directive deriving from the separate treatments of expected loss and unexpected loss under Articles 84 to 89 of this Directive.

7. For the purposes of paragraphs 1 to 6 of this Article, Articles 68 to 73 shall apply.

8. Until 1 January 2008 credit institutions may treat the Articles constituting the Standardised Approach set out in Title V, Chapter 2, Section 3, Subsection 1 as being replaced by Articles 42 to 46 of Directive 2000/12/EC as those Articles stood prior to 1 January 2007.

9. Where the discretion referred to in paragraph 8 is exercised, the following shall apply concerning the provisions of Directive 2000/12/EC:

(a) the provisions of that Directive referred to in Articles 42 to 46 shall apply as they stood prior to 1 January 2007;

(b) "risk-adjusted value" as referred to in Article 42(1) of that Directive shall mean "risk-weighted exposure amount";

(c) the figures produced by Article 42(2) of that Directive shall be considered risk-weighted exposure amounts;

(d) "credit derivatives" shall be included in the list of "Full risk" items in Annex II of that Directive; and

(e) the treatment set out in Article 43(3) of that Directive shall apply to derivative instruments listed in Annex IV of that Directive whether on- or off-balance sheet and the figures produced by the treatment set out in Annex III shall be considered risk-weighted exposure amounts.

10. Where the discretion referred to in paragraph 8 is exercised, the following shall apply in relation to the treatment of exposures for which the Standardised Approach is used:

(a) Title V, Chapter 2, Section 3, Subsection 3 relating to the recognition of credit risk mitigation shall not apply;

(b) Title V, Chapter 2, Section 3, Subsection 4 concerning the treatment of securitisation may be disapplied by competent authorities.

11. Where the discretion referred to in paragraph 8 is exercised, the capital requirement for operational risk under Article 75(d) shall be reduced by the percentage representing the ratio of the value of the credit institution's exposures for which risk-weighted exposure amounts are calculated in accordance with the discretion referred to in paragraph 8 to the total value of its exposures.

12. Where a credit institution calculates risk-weighted exposure amounts for all of its exposures in accordance with the discretion referred to in paragraph 8, Articles 48 to 50 of Directive 2000/12/EC relating to large exposures may apply as they stood prior to 1 January 2007.

13. Where the discretion referred to in paragraph 8 is exercised, references to Articles 78 to 83 of this Directive shall be read as references to Articles 42 to 46 of Directive 2000/12/EC as those Articles stood prior to 1 January 2007.

14. If the discretion referred to in paragraph 8 is exercised, Articles 123, 124, 145 and 149 shall not apply before the date referred to therein.

[5841P]

NOTES

¹ OJ L141, 11.6.1993, p 1. Directive as last amended by 2005/1/EC.

Article 153

In the calculation of risk-weighted exposure amounts for exposures arising from property leasing transactions concerning offices or other commercial premises situated in their territory and meeting the criteria set out in Annex VI, Part 1, point 54, the competent authorities may, until 31 December 2012 allow a 50% risk weight to be assigned without the application of Annex VI, Part 1, points 55 and 56.

Until 31 December 2010, competent authorities may, for the purpose of defining the secured portion of a past due loan for the purposes of Annex VI, recognise collateral other than eligible collateral as set out under Articles 90 to 93.

In the calculation of risk weighted exposure amounts for the purposes of Annex VI, Part 1, point 4, until 31 December 2012 the same risk weight shall be assigned in relation to exposures to Member States' central governments or central banks denominated and funded in the domestic currency of any Member State as would be applied to such exposures denominated and funded in their domestic currency.

[5841Q]

Article 154

1. Until 31 December 2011, the competent authorities of each Member State may, for the purposes of Annex VI, Part 1, point 61, set the number of days past due up to a figure of 180 for exposures indicated in Annex VI, Part 1, points 12 to 17 and 41 to 43, to counterparties situated in their territory, if local conditions make it appropriate. The specific number may differ across product lines.

Competent authorities which do not exercise the discretion provided for in the first subparagraph in relation to exposures to counterparties situated in their territory may set a higher number of days for exposures to counterparties situated in the territories of other Member States, the competent authorities of which have exercised that discretion. The specific number shall fall within 90 days and such figures as the other competent authorities have set for exposures to such counterparties within their territory.

2. For credit institutions applying for the use of the IRB Approach before 2010, subject to the approval of the competent authorities, the three-years' use requirement prescribed in Article 84(3) may be reduced to a period no shorter than one year until 31 December 2009.

3. For credit institutions applying for the use of own estimates of LGDs and/or conversion factors, the three year use requirement prescribed in Article 84(4) may be reduced to two years until 31 December 2008.

4. Until 31 December 2012, the competent authorities of each Member State may allow credit institutions to continue to apply to participations of the type set out in Article 57(o) acquired before 20 July 2006 the treatment set out in Article 38 of Directive 2000/12/EC as that article stood prior to 1 January 2007.

5. Until 31 December 2010 the exposure weighted average LGD for all retail exposures secured by residential properties and not benefiting from guarantees from central governments shall not be lower than 10%.

6. Until 31 December 2017, the competent authorities of the Member States may exempt from the IRB treatment certain equity exposures held by credit institutions and EU subsidiaries of credit institutions in that Member State at 31 December 2007.

The exempted position shall be measured as the number of shares as of 31 December 2007 and any additional share arising directly as a result of owning those holdings, as long as they do not increase the proportional share of ownership in a portfolio company.

If an acquisition increases the proportional share of ownership in a specific holding the exceeding Part of the holding shall not be subject to the exemption. Nor shall the exemption apply to holdings that were originally subject to the exemption, but have been sold and then bought back.

Equity exposures covered by this transitional provision shall be subject to the capital requirements calculated in accordance with Title V, Chapter 2, Section 3, Subsection 1.

7. Until 31 December 2011, for corporate exposures, the competent authorities of each Member State may set the number of days past due that all credit institutions in its jurisdiction shall abide by under the definition of "default" set out in Annex VII, Part 4, point 44 for exposures to such counterparts situated within this Member State. The specific number shall fall within 90 up to a figure of 180 days if local conditions make it appropriate. For exposures to such counterparts situated in the territories of other Member States, the competent authorities shall set a number of days past due which is not higher than the number set by the competent authority of the respective Member State.

[5841R]

Article 155

Until 31 December 2012, for credit institutions the relevant indicator for the trading and sales business line of which represents at least 50% of the total of the relevant indicators for all of its business lines accordance with Annex X, Part 2, points 1 to 4, Member States may apply a percentage of 15% to the business line "trading and sales".

[5841S]

CHAPTER 2
FINAL PROVISIONS

Article 156

The Commission, in cooperation with Member States, and taking into account the contribution of the European Central Bank, shall periodically monitor whether this Directive taken as a whole, together with Directive 2006/49/EC, has significant effects on the economic cycle and, in the light of that examination, shall consider whether any remedial measures are justified.

Based on that analysis and taking into account the contribution of the European Central Bank, the Commission shall draw up a biennial report and submit it to the European Parliament and to the

Council, together with any appropriate proposals. Contributions from credit taking and credit lending parties shall be adequately acknowledged when the report is drawn up.

By 1 January 2012 the Commission shall, review and report on the application of this Directive with particular attention to all aspects of Articles 68 to 73, 80(7), 80(8) and 129, and shall submit this report to the Parliament and the Council together with any appropriate proposals.

[5841T]

Article 157

1. By 31 December 2006 Member States shall adopt and publish the laws, regulations and administrative provisions necessary to comply with Articles 4, 22, 57, 61 to 64, 66, 68 to 106, 108, 110 to 115, 117 to 119, 123 to 127, 129 to 132, 133, 136, 144 to 149 and 152 to 155, and Annexes II, III and V to XII. They shall forthwith communicate to the Commission the text of those provisions and a correlation table between those provisions and this Directive.

Notwithstanding paragraph 3, Member States shall apply those provisions from 1 January 2007.

When Member States adopt those provisions, they shall contain a reference to this Directive or be accompanied by such a reference on the occasion of their official publication. They shall also include a statement that references in existing laws, regulations and administrative provisions to the directives repealed by this Directive shall be construed as references to this Directive. Member States shall determine how such reference is to be made and how that statement is to be formulated.

2. Member States shall communicate to the Commission the text of the main provisions of national law which they adopt in the field covered by this Directive.

3. Member States shall apply, from 1 January 2008, and no earlier, the laws regulations and administrative provisions necessary to comply with Articles 87(9) and 105.

[5841U]

Article 158

1. Directive 2000/12/EC as amended by the Directives set out in Annex XIII, Part A, is hereby repealed without prejudice to the obligations of the Member States concerning the deadlines for transposition of the said Directives listed in Annex XIII, Part B.

2. References to the repealed Directives shall be construed as being made to this Directive and should be read in accordance with the correlation table in Annex XIV.

[5841V]

Article 159

This Directive shall enter into force on the 20th day following its publication in the Official Journal of the European Union.

[5841W]

Article 160

This Directive is addressed to the Member States.

[5841X]

ANNEX I

LIST OF ACTIVITIES SUBJECT TO MUTUAL RECOGNITION

1. Acceptance of deposits and other repayable funds

2. Lending including, inter alia: consumer credit, mortgage credit, factoring, with or without recourse, financing of commercial transactions (including forfeiting)

3. Financial leasing

[4. Payment services as defined in Article 4(3) of Directive 2007/64/EC of the European Parliament and of the Council of 13 November 2007 on payment services in the internal market.[1]

5. Issuing and administering other means of payment (e g travellers' cheques and bankers' drafts) insofar as this activity is not covered by point 4.]

6. Guarantees and commitments

7. Trading for own account or for account of customers in:
  (a) money market instruments (cheques, bills, certificates of deposit, etc.);
  (b) foreign exchange;
  (c) financial futures and options;
  (d) exchange and interest-rate instruments; or
  (e) transferable securities.

8. Participation in securities issues and the provision of services related to such issues

9. Advice to undertakings on capital structure, industrial strategy and related questions and advice as well as services relating to mergers and the purchase of undertakings

10. Money broking
11. Portfolio management and advice
12. Safekeeping and administration of securities
13. Credit reference services
14. Safe custody services

The services and activities provided for in Sections A and B of Annex I to Directive 2004/39/EC of the European Parliament and of the Council of 21 April 2004 on markets in financial instruments,[2] when referring to the financial instruments provided for in Section C of Annex I of that Directive, are subject to mutual recognition according to this Directive.

[5841Y]

NOTES

Points 4, 5: substituted by European Parliament and Council Directive 2007/64/EC, Art 92, as from 25 December 2007 (for transitional provisions see Art 88 of that Directive at **[6177]**). Note that 2007/64/EC has a transposition date of 1 November 2009 (see Art 94 at **[6179]**) and that the original points read as follows—

"4. Money transmission services

5. Issuing and administering means of payment (e g credit cards, travellers' cheques and bankers' drafts).".

[1]   OJ L319, 5.12.2007, p 1.
[2]   OJ L145, 30.4.2004, p 1. Directive as amended by Directive 2006/31/EC (OJ L114, 27.4.2006, p 60). [Note that this footnote was footnote 1 in the original OJ version but has been renumbered following the substitution of points 4, 5 as noted above.]

ANNEX II
CLASSIFICATION OF OFF-BALANCE-SHEET ITEMS

Full risk:
—   Guarantees having the character of credit substitutes,
—   Credit derivatives,
—   Acceptances,
—   Endorsements on bills not bearing the name of another credit institution,
—   Transactions with recourse,
—   Irrevocable standby letters of credit having the character of credit substitutes,
—   Assets purchased under outright forward purchase agreements,
—   Forward forward deposits,
—   The unpaid portion of partly-paid shares and securities,
—   Asset sale and repurchase agreements as defined in Article 12(3) and (5) of Directive 86/635/EEC, and
—   Other items also carrying full risk.

Medium risk:
—   Documentary credits issued and confirmed (see also "Medium/low risk"),
—   Warranties and indemnities (including tender, performance, customs and tax bonds) and guarantees not having the character of credit substitutes,
—   Irrevocable standby letters of credit not having the character of credit substitutes,
—   Undrawn credit facilities (agreements to lend, purchase securities, provide guarantees or acceptance facilities) with an original maturity of more than one year,
—   Note issuance facilities (NIFs) and revolving underwriting facilities (RUFs), and
—   Other items also carrying medium risk and as communicated to the Commission.

Medium/low risk:
—   Documentary credits in which underlying shipment acts as collateral and other self-liquidating transactions,
—   Undrawn credit facilities (agreements to lend, purchase securities, provide guarantees or acceptance facilities) with an original maturity of up to and including one year which may not be cancelled unconditionally at any time without notice or that do not effectively provide for automatic cancellation due to deterioration in a borrower's creditworthiness, and
—   Other items also carrying medium/low risk and as communicated to the Commission.

Low risk:
—   Undrawn credit facilities (agreements to lend, purchase securities, provide guarantees or acceptance facilities) which may be cancelled unconditionally at any time without notice, or that do effectively provide for automatic cancellation due to deterioration in a borrower's creditworthiness. Retail credit lines may be considered as unconditionally cancellable if the terms permit the credit institution to cancel them to the full extent allowable under consumer protection and related legislation, and
—   Other items also carrying low risk and as communicated to the Commission.

[5841Z]

ANNEX III
THE TREATMENT OF COUNTERPARTY CREDIT RISK OF DERIVATIVE INSTRUMENTS, REPURCHASE TRANSACTIONS, SECURITIES OR COMMODITIES LENDING OR BORROWING TRANSACTIONS, LONG SETTLEMENT TRANSACTIONS AND MARGIN LENDING TRANSACTIONS

PART 1
DEFINITIONS

For the purposes of this Annex the following definitions shall apply:

General terms

1. "Counterparty Credit Risk (CCR)" means the risk that the counterparty to a transaction could default before the final settlement of the transaction's cash flows.

2. "Central counterparty" means an entity that legally interposes itself between counterparties to contracts traded within one or more financial markets, becoming the buyer to every seller and the seller to every buyer.

Transaction types

3. "Long Settlement Transactions" mean transactions where a counterparty undertakes to deliver a security, a commodity, or a foreign exchange amount against cash, other financial instruments, or commodities, or vice versa, at a settlement or delivery date that is contractually specified as more than the lower of the market standard for this particular transaction and five business days after the date on which the credit institution enters into the transaction.

4. "Margin Lending Transactions" mean transactions in which a credit institution extends credit in connection with the purchase, sale, carrying or trading of securities. Margin lending transactions do not include other loans that happen to be secured by securities collateral.

Netting sets, hedging sets, and related terms

5. "Netting Set" means a group of transactions with a single counterparty that are subject to a legally enforceable bilateral netting arrangement and for which netting is recognised under Part 7 of this Annex and Articles 90 to 93. Each transaction that is not subject to a legally enforceable bilateral netting arrangement, which is recognised under Part 7 of this Annex, should be interpreted as its own netting set for the purpose of this Annex.

6. "Risk Position" means a risk number that is assigned to a transaction under the Standardised Method set out in Part 5 following a predetermined algorithm.

7. "Hedging Set" means a group of risk positions from the transactions within a single netting set for which only their balance is relevant for determining the exposure value under the Standardised Method set out in Part 5.

8. "Margin Agreement" means a contractual agreement or provisions of an agreement under which one counterparty shall supply collateral to a second counterparty when an exposure of that second counterparty to the first counterparty exceeds a specified level.

9. "Margin Threshold" means the largest amount of an exposure that remains outstanding until one party has the right to call for collateral.

10. "Margin Period of Risk" means the time period from the last exchange of collateral covering a netting set of transactions with a defaulting counterpart until that counterpart is closed out and the resulting market risk is re-hedged.

11. "Effective Maturity under the Internal Model Method, for a netting set with maturity greater than one year" means the ratio of the sum of expected exposure over the life of the transactions in the netting set discounted at the risk-free rate of return divided by the sum of expected exposure over one year in a netting set discounted at the risk-free rate. This effective maturity may be adjusted to reflect rollover risk by replacing expected exposure with effective expected exposure for forecasting horizons under one year.

12. "Cross-Product Netting" means the inclusion of transactions of different product categories within the same netting set pursuant to the Cross-Product Netting rules set out in this Annex.

13. For the purposes of Part 5, "Current Market Value (CMV)" refers to the net market value of the portfolio of transactions within the netting set with the counterparty. Both positive and negative market values are used in computing CMV.

Distributions

14. "Distribution of Market Values" means the forecast of the probability distribution of net market values of transactions within a netting set for some future date (the forecasting horizon), given the realised market value of those transactions up to the present time.

15. "Distribution of Exposures" means the forecast of the probability distribution of market values that is generated by setting forecast instances of negative net market values equal to zero.

16. "Risk-Neutral Distribution" means a distribution of market values or exposures at a future time period where the distribution is calculated using market implied values such as implied volatilities.

17. "Actual Distribution" means a distribution of market values or exposures at a future time period where the distribution is calculated using historic or realised values such as volatilities calculated using past price or rate changes.

Exposure measures and adjustments

18. "Current Exposure" means the larger of zero or the market value of a transaction or portfolio of transactions within a netting set with a counterparty that would be lost upon the default of the counterparty, assuming no recovery on the value of those transactions in bankruptcy.

19. "Peak Exposure" means a high percentile of the distribution of exposures at any particular future date before the maturity date of the longest transaction in the netting set.

20. "Expected Exposure (EE)" means the average of the distribution of exposures at any particular future date before the longest maturity transaction in the netting set matures.

21. "Effective Expected Exposure (Effective EE) at a specific date" means the maximum expected exposure that occurs at that date or any prior date. Alternatively, it may be defined for a specific date as the greater of the expected exposure at that date, or the effective exposure at the previous date.

22. "Expected Positive Exposure (EPE)" means the weighted average over time of expected exposures where the weights are the proportion that an individual expected exposure represents of the entire time interval. When calculating the minimum capital requirement, the average is taken over the first year or, if all the contracts within the netting set mature within less than one year, over the time period of the longest maturity contract in the netting set.

23. "Effective Expected Positive Exposure (Effective EPE)" means the weighted average over time of effective expected exposure over the first year, or, if all the contracts within the netting set mature within less than one year, over the time period of the longest maturity contract in the netting set, where the weights are the proportion that an individual expected exposure represents of the entire time interval.

24. "Credit Valuation Adjustment" means an adjustment to the mid-market valuation of the portfolio of transactions with a counterparty. This adjustment reflects the market value of the credit risk due to any failure to perform on contractual agreements with a counterparty. This adjustment may reflect the market value of the credit risk of the counterparty or the market value of the credit risk of both the credit institution and the counterparty.

25. "One-Sided Credit Valuation Adjustment" means a credit valuation adjustment that reflects the market value of the credit risk of the counterparty to the credit institution, but does not reflect the market value of the credit risk of the credit institution to the counterparty.

CCR related risks

26. "Rollover Risk" means the amount by which expected positive exposure is understated when future transactions with a counterpart are expected to be conducted on an ongoing basis. The additional exposure generated by those future transactions is not included in calculation of EPE.

27. "General Wrong-Way Risk" arises when the PD of counterparties is positively correlated with general market risk factors.

28. "Specific Wrong-Way Risk" arises when the exposure to a particular counterparty is positively correlated with the PD of the counterparty due to the nature of the transactions with the counterparty. A credit institution shall be considered to be exposed to Specific Wrong-Way Risk if the future exposure to a specific counterparty is expected to be high when the counterparty's PD is also high.

PART 2
CHOICE OF THE METHOD

1. Subject to paragraphs 2 to 7, credit institutions shall determine the exposure value for the contracts listed in Annex IV with one of the methods set out in Parts 3 to 6. Credit institutions which are not eligible for the treatment set out in Article 18(2) of Directive 2006/49/EC are not permitted to use the method set out in Part 4. To determine the exposure value for the contracts listed in point 3 of Annex IV, credit institutions are not permitted to use the method set out in Part 4.

The combined use of the methods set out in Parts 3 to 6 shall be permitted on a permanent basis within a group, but not within a single legal entity. Combined use of the methods set out in Parts 3 and 5 within a legal entity shall be permitted where one of the methods is used for the cases set out in Part 5, point 19.

2. Subject to the approval of the competent authorities, credit institutions may determine the exposure value for:

    (i) the contracts listed in Annex IV,

    (ii) repurchase transactions,

    (iii) securities or commodities lending or borrowing transactions,

    (iv) margin lending transactions, and

    (v) long settlement transactions

using the Internal Model Method as set out in Part 6.

3. When a credit institution purchases credit derivative protection against a non-trading book exposure, or against a CCR exposure, it may compute its capital requirement for the hedged asset in accordance with Annex VIII, Part 3, points 83 to 92, or subject to the approval of the competent authorities, in accordance with Annex VII, Part 1, point 4 or Annex VII, Part 4, points 96 to 104. In these cases, the exposure value for CCR for these credit derivatives is set to zero.

4. The exposure value for CCR from sold credit default swaps in the non-trading book, where they are treated as credit protection provided by the credit institution and subject to a capital requirement for credit risk for the full notional amount, is set to zero.

5. Under all methods set out in Parts 3 to 6, the exposure value for a given counterparty is equal to the sum of the exposure values calculated for each netting set with that counterparty.

6. An exposure value of zero for CCR can be attributed to derivative contracts, or repurchase transactions, securities or commodities lending or borrowing transactions, long settlement transactions and margin lending transactions outstanding with a central counterparty and that have not been rejected by the central counterparty. Furthermore, an exposure value of zero can be attributed to credit risk exposures to central counterparties that result from the derivative contracts, repurchase transactions, securities or commodities lending or borrowing transactions, long settlement transactions and margin lending transactions or other exposures, as determined by the competent authorities, that the credit institution has outstanding with the central counterparty. The central counterparty CCR exposures with all participants in its arrangements shall be fully collateralised on a daily basis.

7. Exposures arising from long settlement transactions can be determined using any of the methods set out in Parts 3 to 6, regardless of the methods chosen for treating OTC derivatives and repurchase transactions, securities or commodities lending or borrowing transactions, and margin lending transactions. In calculating capital requirements for long settlement transactions, credit institutions that use the approach set out in Articles 84 to 89 may assign the risk weights under the approach set out in Articles 78 to 83 on a permanent basis and irrespective of the materiality of such positions.

8. For the methods set out in Parts 3 and 4 the competent authorities must ensure that the notional amount to be taken into account is an appropriate yardstick for the risk inherent in the contract. Where, for instance, the contract provides for a multiplication of cash flows, the notional amount must be adjusted in order to take into account the effects of the multiplication on the risk structure of that contract.

PART 3
MARK-TO-MARKET METHOD

Step (a): by attaching current market values to contracts (mark-to-market), the current replacement cost of all contracts with positive values is obtained.

Step (b): to obtain a figure for future credit exposure, except in the case of single-currency "floating/floating" interest rate swaps in which only the current replacement cost will be calculated, the notional principal amounts or underlying values are multiplied by the percentages in Table 1:

Table 1[1, 2]

Residual maturity[3]	Interest-rate contracts	Contracts concerning foreign-exchange rates and gold	Contracts concerning equities	Contracts concerning precious metals except gold	Contracts concerning commodities other than precious metals
One year or less	0%	1%	6%	7%	10%
Over one year, not exceeding five years	0.5%	5%	8%	7%	12%
Over five years	1.5%	7.5%	10%	8%	15%

For the purpose of calculating the potential future credit exposure in accordance with step (b) the competent authorities may allow credit institutions to apply the percentages in Table 2 instead of those prescribed in Table 1 provided that the institutions make use of the option set out in Annex IV, point 21 to Directive 2006/49/EC for contracts relating to commodities other than gold within the meaning of paragraph 3 of Annex IV, to this Directive:

Table 2

Residual maturity	Precious metals (except gold)	Base metals	Agricultural products (softs)	Other, including energy products
One year or less	2%	2.5%	3%	4%
Over one year, not exceeding five years	5%	4%	5%	6%
Over five years	7.5%	8%	9%	10%

Step (c): the sum of current replacement cost and potential future credit exposure is the exposure value.

NOTES

[1] Contracts which do not fall within one of the five categories indicated in this table shall be treated as contracts concerning commodities other than precious metals.

[2] For contracts with multiple exchanges of principal, the percentages have to be multiplied by the number of remaining payments still to be made according to the contract.

[3] For contracts that are structured to settle outstanding exposure following specified payment dates and where the terms are reset such that the market value of the contract is zero on these specified dates, the residual maturity would be equal to the time until the next reset date. In the case of interest-rate contracts that meet these criteria and have a remaining maturity of over one year, the percentage shall be no lower than 0.5%.

PART 4
ORIGINAL EXPOSURE METHOD

Step (a): the notional principal amount of each instrument is multiplied by the percentages given in Table 3.

Table 3

Original maturity[1]	Interest-rate contracts	Contracts concerning foreign-exchange rates and gold
One year or less	0.5%	2%
Over one year, not exceeding two years	1%	5%
Additional allowance for each additional year	1%	3%

Step (b): the original exposure thus obtained shall be the exposure value.

NOTES

  [1]   In the case of interest-rate contracts, credit institutions may, subject to the consent of their competent authorities, choose either original or residual maturity.

PART 5
STANDARDISED METHOD

1. The Standardised Method (SM) can be used only for OTC derivatives and long settlement transactions. The exposure value shall be calculated separately for each netting set. It shall be determined net of collateral, as follows:

exposure value =

$$\beta^* \max\left(CMV - CMC; \sum_j \left| \sum_i RPT_{ij} - \sum_l RPC_{lj} \right|^* CCRM_j \right)$$

where:

CMV = current market value of the portfolio of transactions within the netting set with a counterparty gross of collateral, that is, where:

$$CMV = \sum_i CMV_i$$

where:

CMV_i = the current market value of transaction i;

CMC = the current market value of the collateral assigned to the netting set, that is, where:

$$CMC = \sum_l CMC_l$$

where

CMC_l = the current market value of collateral l;

i = index designating transaction;

l = index designating collateral;

j = index designating hedging set category. These hedging sets correspond to risk factors for which risk positions of opposite sign can be offset to yield a net risk position on which the exposure measure is then based;

RPT_{ij} = risk position from transaction i with respect to hedging set j;

RPC_{lj} = risk position from collateral l with respect to hedging set j;

$CCRM_j$ = CCR Multiplier set out in Table 5 with respect to hedging set j;

β = 1.4.

Collateral received from a counterparty has a positive sign and collateral posted to a counterparty has a negative sign.

Collateral that is recognised for this method is confined to the collateral that is eligible under point 11 of Part 1 of Annex VIII to this Directive and point 9 of Annex II to Directive 2006/49/EC.

2. When an OTC derivative transaction with a linear risk profile stipulates the exchange of a financial instrument for a payment, the payment Part is referred to as the payment leg. Transactions that stipulate the exchange of payment against payment consist of two payment legs. The payment

legs consist of the contractually agreed gross payments, including the notional amount of the transaction. Credit institutions may disregard the interest rate risk from payment legs with a remaining maturity of less than one year for the purposes of the following calculations. Credit institutions may treat transactions that consist of two payment legs that are denominated in the same currency, such as interest rate swaps, as a single aggregate transaction. The treatment for payment legs applies to the aggregate transaction.

3. Transactions with a linear risk profile with equities (including equity indices), gold, other precious metals or other commodities as the underlying financial instruments are mapped to a risk position in the respective equity (or equity index) or commodity (including gold and other precious metals) and an interest rate risk position for the payment leg. If the payment leg is denominated in a foreign currency, it is additionally mapped to a risk position in the respective currency.

4. Transactions with a linear risk profile with a debt instrument as the underlying instrument are mapped to an interest rate risk position for the debt instrument and another interest rate risk position for the payment leg. Transactions with a linear risk profile that stipulate the exchange of payment against payment, including foreign exchange forwards, are mapped to an interest rate risk position for each of the payment legs. If the underlying debt instrument is denominated in a foreign currency, the debt instrument is mapped to a risk position in this currency. If a payment leg is denominated in foreign currency, the payment leg is again mapped to a risk position in this currency. The exposure value assigned to a foreign exchange basis swap transaction is zero.

5. The size of a risk position from a transaction with linear risk profile is the effective notional value (market price multiplied by quantity) of the underlying financial instruments (including commodities) converted to the credit institution's domestic currency, except for debt instruments.

6. For debt instruments and for payment legs, the size of the risk position is the effective notional value of the outstanding gross payments (including the notional amount) converted to the credit institution's domestic currency, multiplied by the modified duration of the debt instrument, or payment leg, respectively.

7. The size of a risk position from a credit default swap is the notional value of the reference debt instrument multiplied by the remaining maturity of the credit default swap.

8. The size of a risk position from an OTC derivative with a non-linear risk profile, including options and swaptions, is equal to the delta equivalent effective notional value of the financial instrument that underlies the transaction, except in the case of an underlying debt instrument.

9. The size of a risk position from an OTC derivative with a non-linear risk profile, including options and swaptions, of which the underlying is a debt instrument or a payment leg, is equal to the delta equivalent effective notional value of the financial instrument or payment leg multiplied by the modified duration of the debt instrument, or payment leg, respectively.

10. For the determination of risk positions, collateral received from a counterparty is to be treated as a claim on the counterparty under a derivative contract (long position) that is due today, while collateral posted is to be treated like an obligation to the counterparty (short position) that is due today.

11. Credit institutions may use the following formulae to determine the size and sign of a risk position:

for all instruments other than debt instruments:

effective notional value, or

delta equivalent notional value =

$$P_{ref} \frac{\delta V}{\delta p}$$

where:

P_{ref} = price of the underlying instrument, expressed in the reference currency;

V = value of the financial instrument (in the case of an option this is the option price and in the case of a transaction with a linear risk profile this is the value of the underlying instrument itself);

p = price of the underlying instrument, expressed in the same currency as V;

for debt instruments and the payment legs of all transactions:

effective notional value multiplied by the modified duration, or

delta equivalent in notional value multiplied by the modified duration

$$\frac{\delta V}{\delta r}$$

where:

V = value of the financial instrument (in the case of an option this is the option price and in the case of a transaction with a linear risk profile this is the value of the underlying instrument itself or of the payment leg, respectively);

r = interest rate level.

If V is denominated in a currency other than the reference currency, the derivative must be converted into the reference currency by multiplication with the relevant exchange rate.

12. The risk positions are to be grouped into hedging sets. For each hedging set, the absolute value amount of the sum of the resulting risk positions is computed. This sum is termed the "net risk position" and is represented by:

$$\left| \sum_i RPT_{ij} - \sum_l RPC_{lj} \right|$$

in the formulae set out in paragraph 1.

13. For interest rate risk positions from money deposits received from the counterparty as collateral, from payment legs and from underlying debt instruments, to which according to Table 1 of Annex I to Directive 2006/49/EC a capital charge of 1.60% or less applies, there are six hedging sets for each currency, as set out in Table 4 below. Hedging sets are defined by a combination of the criteria "maturity" and "referenced interest rates".

Table 4

	Government referenced interest rates	Non-government referenced interest rates
Maturity	← 1 year	← 1 year
Maturity	>1 — ← 5 years	>1 — ← 5 years
Maturity	> 5 years	> 5 years

14. For interest rate risk positions from underlying debt instruments or payment legs for which the interest rate is linked to a reference interest rate that represents a general market interest level, the remaining maturity is the length of the time interval up to the next re-adjustment of the interest rate. In all other cases, it is the remaining life of the underlying debt instrument or in the case of a payment leg, the remaining life of the transaction.

15. There is one hedging set for each issuer of a reference debt instrument that underlies a credit default swap.

16. For interest rate risk positions from money deposits that are posted with a counterparty as collateral when that counterparty does not have debt obligations of low specific risk outstanding and from underlying debt instruments, to which according to Table 1 of Annex I to Directive 2006/49/EC a capital charge of more than 1.60% applies, there is one hedging set for each issuer. When a payment leg emulates such a debt instrument, there is also one hedging set for each issuer of the reference debt instrument. Credit institutions may assign risk positions that arise from debt instruments of a certain issuer, or from reference debt instruments of the same issuer that are emulated by payment legs, or that underlie a credit default swap, to the same hedging set.

17. Underlying financial instruments other than debt instruments shall be assigned to the same respective hedging sets only if they are identical or similar instruments. In all other cases they shall be assigned to separate hedging sets. The similarity of instruments is established as follows:

—   for equities, similar instruments are those of the same issuer. An equity index is treated as a separate issuer;

—   for precious metals, similar instruments are those of the same metal. A precious metal index is treated as a separate precious metal;

—   for electric power, similar instruments are those delivery rights and obligations that refer to the same peak or off-peak load time interval within any 24-hour interval; and

—   for commodities, similar instruments are those of the same commodity. A commodity index is treated as a separate commodity.

18. The CCR multipliers (CCRM) for the different hedging set categories are set out in Table 5 below:

Table 5

	Hedging set categories	CCRM
1.	Interest Rates	0.2%
2.	Interest Rates for risk positions from a reference debt instrument that underlies a credit default swap and to which a capital charge of 1.60%, or less, applies under Table 1 of Annex I to Directive 2006/49/EC	0.3%
3.	Interest Rates for risk positions from a debt instrument or reference debt instrument to which a capital charge of more than 1.60% applies under Table 1 of Annex I to Directive 2006/49/EC	0.6%
4.	Exchange Rates	2.5%
5.	Electric Power	4%
6.	Gold	5%
7.	Equity	7%
8.	Precious Metals (except gold)	8.5%
9.	Other Commodities (excluding precious metals and electricity power)	10%
10.	Underlying instruments of OTC derivatives that are not in any of the above categories	10%

Underlying instruments of OTC derivatives, as referred to in point 10 of Table 5, shall be assigned to separate individual hedging sets for each category of underlying instrument.

19. For transactions with a non-linear risk profile or for payment legs and transactions with debt instruments as underlying for which the credit institution cannot determine the delta or the modified duration, respectively, with an instrument model that the competent authority has approved for the purposes of determining the minimum capital requirements for market risk, the competent authority shall determine the size of the risk positions and the applicable CCRMjs conservatively. Alternatively, competent authorities may require the use of the method set out in Part 3. Netting shall not be recognised (that is, the exposure value shall be determined as if there were a netting set that comprises just the individual transaction).

20. A credit institution shall have internal procedures to verify that, prior to including a transaction in a hedging set, the transaction is covered by a legally enforceable netting contract that meets the requirements set out in Part 7.

21. A credit institution that makes use of collateral to mitigate its CCR shall have internal procedures to verify that, prior to recognising the effect of collateral in its calculations, the collateral meets the legal certainty standards set out in Annex VIII.

PART 6
INTERNAL MODEL METHOD

1. Subject to the approval of the competent authorities, a credit institution may use the Internal Model Method (IMM) to calculate the exposure value for the transactions in Part 2, paragraph 2(i), or for the transactions in Part 2, point 2(ii), (iii) and (iv), or for the transactions in Part 2, point 2(i) to (iv). In each of these cases the transactions in Part 2, point 2(v) may be included as well. Notwithstanding Part 2, point 1, second paragraph, credit institutions may choose not to apply this method to exposures that are immaterial in size and risk. To apply the IMM, a credit institution shall meet the requirements set out in this Part.

2. Subject to the approval of the competent authorities, implementation of the IMM may be carried out sequentially across different transaction types, and during this period a credit institution may use the methods set out in Part 3 or Part 5. Notwithstanding the remainder of this Part, credit institutions shall not be required to use a specific type of model.

3. For all OTC derivative transactions and for long settlement transactions for which a credit institution has not received approval to use the IMM, the credit institution shall use the methods set out in Part 3 or Part 5. Combined use of these two methods is permitted on a permanent basis within a group. Combined use of these two methods within a legal entity is only permitted where one of the methods is used for the cases set out in Part 5, point 19.

4. Credit institutions which have obtained permission to use the IMM shall not revert to the use of the methods set out in Part 3 or Part 5 except for demonstrated good cause and subject to approval

of the competent authorities. If a credit institution ceases to comply with the requirements set out in this Part, it shall either present to the competent authority a plan for a timely return to compliance or demonstrate that the effect of non-compliance is immaterial.

Exposure value

5.   The exposure value shall be measured at the level of the netting set. The model shall specify the forecasting distribution for changes in the market value of the netting set attributable to changes in market variables, such as interest rates, foreign exchange rates. The model shall then compute the exposure value for the netting set at each future date given the changes in the market variables. For margined counterparties, the model may also capture future collateral movements.

6.   Credit institutions may include eligible financial collateral as defined in point 11 of Part 1 of Annex VIII to this Directive and point 9 of Annex II to Directive 2006/49/EC in their forecasting distributions for changes in the market value of the netting set, if the quantitative, qualitative and data requirements for the IMM are met for the collateral.

7.   The exposure value shall be calculated as the product of α times Effective EPE, as follows:

Exposure value = $\alpha \times$ Effective EPE

where:

alpha (α) shall be 1.4, but competent authorities may require a higher α, and Effective EPE shall be computed by estimating expected exposure (EEt) as the average exposure at future date t, where the average is taken across possible future values of relevant market risk factors. The model estimates EE at a series of future dates t1, t2, t3, etc.

8.   Effective EE shall be computed recursively as:

Effective EEtk = max(Effective EEtk-1; EEtk)

where:

the current date is denoted as t0 and Effective EEt0 equals current exposure.

9.   In this regard, Effective EPE is the average Effective EE during the first year of future exposure. If all contracts in the netting set mature within less than one year, EPE is the average of EE until all contracts in the netting set mature. Effective EPE is computed as a weighted average of Effective EE:

$$Effective\ EPE = \sum_{k=1}^{min(1\,year;maturity)} Effective\ EE_{tk}{}^* \Delta t_k$$

where:

the weights $\Delta tk = tk - tk\text{-}1$ allow for the case when future exposure is calculated at dates that are not equally spaced over time.

10.   EE or peak exposure measures shall be calculated based on a distribution of exposures that accounts for the possible non-normality of the distribution of exposures.

11.   Credit institutions may use a measure that is more conservative than α multiplied by Effective EPE as calculated according to the equation above for every counterparty.

12.   Notwithstanding point 7, competent authorities may permit credit institutions to use their own estimates of α, subject to a floor of 1,2, where α shall equal the ratio of internal capital from a full simulation of CCR exposure across counterparties (numerator) and internal capital based on EPE (denominator). In the denominator, EPE shall be used as if it were a fixed outstanding amount. Credit institutions shall demonstrate that their internal estimates of α capture in the numerator material sources of stochastic dependency of distribution of market values of transactions or of portfolios of transactions across counterparties. Internal estimates of α shall take account of the granularity of portfolios.

13.   A credit institution shall ensure that the numerator and denominator of α are computed in a consistent fashion with respect to the modelling methodology, parameter specifications and portfolio composition. The approach used shall be based on the credit institution's internal capital approach, be well documented and be subject to independent validation. In addition, credit institutions shall review their estimates on at least a quarterly basis, and more frequently when the composition of the portfolio varies over time. Credit institutions shall also assess the model risk.

14.   Where appropriate, volatilities and correlations of market risk factors used in the joint simulation of market and credit risk should be conditioned on the credit risk factor to reflect potential increases in volatility or correlation in an economic downturn.

15.   If the netting set is subject to a margin agreement, credit institutions shall use one of the following EPE measures:

(a)   Effective EPE without taking into account the margin agreement;

(b)   the threshold, if positive, under the margin agreement plus an add-on that reflects the potential increase in exposure over the margin period of risk. The add-on is computed as the expected increase in the netting set's exposure beginning from a current exposure of zero over the margin period of risk. A floor of five business days for netting sets consisting only of repo-style transactions subject to daily remargining and daily mark-to-market, and ten business days for all other netting sets is imposed on the margin period of risk used for this purpose; or

(c)   if the model captures the effects of margining when estimating EE, the model's EE measure may be used directly in the equation in point 8 subject to the approval of the competent authorities.

Minimum requirements for EPE models

16.   A credit institution's EPE model shall meet the operational requirements set out in points 17 to 41.

CCR control

17.   The credit institution shall have a control unit that is responsible for the design and implementation of its CCR management system, including the initial and on-going validation of the model. This unit shall control input data integrity and produce and analyse reports on the output of the credit institution's risk measurement model, including an evaluation of the relationship between measures of risk exposure and credit and trading limits. This unit shall be independent from units responsible for originating, renewing or trading exposures and free from undue influence; it shall be adequately staffed; it shall report directly to the senior management of the credit institution. The work of this unit shall be closely integrated into the day-to-day credit risk management process of the credit institution. Its output shall, accordingly, be an integral Part of the process of planning, monitoring and controlling the credit institution's credit and overall risk profile.

18.   A credit institution shall have CCR management policies, processes and systems that are conceptually sound and implemented with integrity. A sound CCR management framework shall include the identification, measurement, management, approval and internal reporting of CCR.

19.   A credit institution's risk management policies shall take account of market, liquidity, and legal and operational risks that can be associated with CCR. The credit institution shall not undertake business with a counterparty without assessing its creditworthiness and shall take due account of settlement and pre-settlement credit risk. These risks shall be managed as comprehensively as practicable at the counterparty level (aggregating CCR exposures with other credit exposures) and at the firm-wide level.

20.   A credit institution's board of directors and senior management shall be actively involved in the CCR control process and shall regard this as an essential aspect of the business to which significant resources need to be devoted. Senior management shall be aware of the limitations and assumptions of the model used and the impact these can have on the reliability of the output. Senior management shall also consider the uncertainties of the market environment and operational issues and be aware of how these are reflected in the model.

21.   The daily reports prepared on a credit institution's exposures to CCR shall be reviewed by a level of management with sufficient seniority and authority to enforce both reductions of positions taken by individual credit managers or traders and reductions in the credit institution's overall CCR exposure.

22.   A credit institution's CCR management system shall be used in conjunction with internal credit and trading limits. Credit and trading limits shall be related to the credit institution's risk measurement model in a manner that is consistent over time and that is well understood by credit managers, traders and senior management.

23.   A credit institution's measurement of CCR shall include measuring daily and intra-day usage of credit lines. The credit institution shall measure current exposure gross and net of collateral. At portfolio and counterparty level, the credit institution shall calculate and monitor peak exposure or PFE at the confidence interval chosen by the credit institution. The credit institution shall take account of large or concentrated positions, including by groups of related counterparties, by industry, by market, etc.

24.   A credit institution shall have a routine and rigorous program of stress testing in place as a supplement to the CCR analysis based on the day-to-day output of the credit institution's risk measurement model. The results of this stress testing shall be reviewed periodically by senior management and shall be reflected in the CCR policies and limits set by management and the board of directors. Where stress tests reveal particular vulnerability to a given set of circumstances, prompt steps shall be taken to manage those risks appropriately.

25.   A credit institution shall have a routine in place for ensuring compliance with a documented set of internal policies, controls and procedures concerning the operation of the CCR management

system. The credit institution's CCR management system shall be well documented and shall provide an explanation of the empirical techniques used to measure CCR.

26. A credit institution shall conduct an independent review of its CCR management system regularly through its own internal auditing process. This review shall include both the activities of the business units referred to in point 17 and of the independent CCR control unit. A review of the overall CCR management process shall take place at regular intervals and shall specifically address, at a minimum:

    (a)   the adequacy of the documentation of the CCR management system and process;
    (b)   the organisation of the CCR control unit;
    (c)   the integration of CCR measures into daily risk management;
    (d)   the approval process for risk pricing models and valuation systems used by front and back-office personnel;
    (e)   the validation of any significant change in the CCR measurement process;
    (f)   the scope of CCR captured by the risk measurement model;
    (g)   the integrity of the management information system;
    (h)   the accuracy and completeness of CCR data;
    (i)   the verification of the consistency, timeliness and reliability of data sources used to run models, including the independence of such data sources;
    (j)   the accuracy and appropriateness of volatility and correlation assumptions;
    (k)   the accuracy of valuation and risk transformation calculations; and
    (l)   the verification of the model's accuracy through frequent back-testing.

Use test

27. The distribution of exposures generated by the model used to calculate effective EPE shall be closely integrated into the day-to-day CCR management process of the credit institution. The model's output shall accordingly play an essential role in the credit approval, CCR management, internal capital allocation and corporate governance of the credit institution.

28. A credit institution shall have a track record in the use of models that generate a distribution of exposures to CCR. Thus, the credit institution shall demonstrate that it has been using a model to calculate the distributions of exposures upon which the EPE calculation is based that meets, broadly, the minimum requirements set out in this Part for at least one year prior to approval by the competent authorities.

29. The model used to generate a distribution of exposures to CCR shall be Part of a CCR management framework that includes the identification, measurement, management, approval and internal reporting of CCR. This framework shall include the measurement of usage of credit lines (aggregating CCR exposures with other credit exposures) and internal capital allocation. In addition to EPE, a credit institution shall measure and manage current exposures. Where appropriate, the credit institution shall measure current exposure gross and net of collateral. The use test is satisfied if a credit institution uses other CCR measures, such as peak exposure or (PFE), based on the distribution of exposures generated by the same model to compute EPE.

30. A credit institution shall have the systems capability to estimate EE daily if necessary, unless it demonstrates to its competent authorities that its exposures to CCR warrant less frequent calculation. The credit institution shall compute EE along a time profile of forecasting horizons that adequately reflects the time structure of future cash flows and maturity of the contracts and in a manner that is consistent with the materiality and composition of the exposures.

31. Exposure shall be measured, monitored and controlled over the life of all contracts in the netting set (not just to the one year horizon). The credit institution shall have procedures in place to identify and control the risks for counterparties where the exposure rises beyond the one-year horizon. The forecast increase in exposure shall be an input into the credit institution's internal capital model.

Stress testing

32. A credit institution shall have in place sound stress testing processes for use in the assessment of capital adequacy for CCR. These stress measures shall be compared with the measure of EPE and considered by the credit institution as Part of the process set out in Article 123. Stress testing shall also involve identifying possible events or future changes in economic conditions that could have unfavourable effects on a credit institution's credit exposures and an assessment of the credit institution's ability to withstand such changes.

33. The credit institution shall stress test its CCR exposures, including jointly stressing market and credit risk factors. Stress tests of CCR shall consider concentration risk (to a single counterparty or groups of counterparties), correlation risk across market and credit risk, and the risk that liquidating the counterparty's positions could move the market. Stress tests shall also consider the impact on the credit institution's own positions of such market moves and integrate that impact in its assessment of CCR.

Wrong-Way Risk

34. Credit institutions shall give due consideration to exposures that give rise to a significant degree of General Wrong-Way Risk.

35. Credit institutions shall have procedures in place to identify, monitor and control cases of Specific Wrong-Way Risk, beginning at the inception of a transaction and continuing through the life of the transaction.

Integrity of the modelling process

36. The model shall reflect transaction terms and specifications in a timely, complete, and conservative fashion. Such terms shall include at least contract notional amounts, maturity, reference assets, margining arrangements, netting arrangements. The terms and specifications shall be maintained in a database that is subject to formal and periodic audit. The process for recognising netting arrangements shall require signoff by legal staff to verify the legal enforceability of netting and be input into the database by an independent unit. The transmission of transaction terms and specifications data to the model shall also be subject to internal audit and formal reconciliation processes shall be in place between the model and source data systems to verify on an ongoing basis that transaction terms and specifications are being reflected in EPE correctly or at least conservatively.

37. The model shall employ current market data to compute current exposures. When using historical data to estimate volatility and correlations, at least three years of historical data shall be used and shall be updated quarterly or more frequently if market conditions warrant. The data shall cover a full range of economic conditions, such as a full business cycle. A unit independent from the business unit shall validate the price supplied by the business unit. The data shall be acquired independently of the lines of business, fed into the model in a timely and complete fashion, and maintained in a database subject to formal and periodic audit. A credit institution shall also have a well-developed data integrity process to clean the data of erroneous and/or anomalous observations. To the extent that the model relies on proxy market data, including, for new products, where three years of historical data may not be available, internal policies shall identify suitable proxies and the credit institution shall demonstrate empirically that the proxy provides a conservative representation of the underlying risk under adverse market conditions. If the model includes the effect of collateral on changes in the market value of the netting set, the credit institution shall have adequate historical data to model the volatility of the collateral.

38. The model shall be subject to a validation process. The process shall be clearly articulated in credit institutions' policies and procedures. The validation process shall specify the kind of testing needed to ensure model integrity and identify conditions under which assumptions are violated and may result in an understatement of EPE. The validation process shall include a review of the comprehensiveness of the model.

39. A credit institution shall monitor the appropriate risks and have processes in place to adjust its estimation of EPE when those risks become significant. This includes the following:
    (a) the credit institution shall identify and manage its exposures to specific wrong-way risk;
    (b) for exposures with a rising risk profile after one year, the credit institution shall compare on a regular basis the estimate of EPE over one year with EPE over the life of the exposure; and
    (c) for exposures with a residual maturity below one year, the credit institution shall compare on a regular basis the replacement cost (current exposure) and the realised exposure profile, and/or store data that would allow such a comparison.

40. A credit institution shall have internal procedures to verify that, prior to including a transaction in a netting set, the transaction is covered by a legally enforceable netting contract that meets the requirements set out in Part 7.

41. A credit institution that makes use of collateral to mitigate its CCR shall have internal procedures to verify that, prior to recognising the effect of collateral in its calculations, the collateral meets the legal certainty standards set out in Annex VIII.

Validation requirements for EPE models

42. A credit institution's EPE model shall meet the following validation requirements:
    (a) the qualitative validation requirements set out in Annex V to Directive 2006/49/EC;
    (b) interest rates, foreign exchange rates, equity prices, commodities, and other market risk factors shall be forecast over long time horizons for measuring CCR exposure. The performance of the forecasting model for market risk factors shall be validated over a long time horizon;
    (c) the pricing models used to calculate CCR exposure for a given scenario of future shocks to market risk factors shall be tested as Part of the model validation process. Pricing models for options shall account for the nonlinearity of option value with respect to market risk factors;
    (d) the EPE model shall capture transaction-specific information in order to aggregate

exposures at the level of the netting set. A credit institution shall verify that transactions are assigned to the appropriate netting set within the model;

(e) the EPE model shall also include transaction-specific information to capture the effects of margining. It shall take into account both the current amount of margin and margin that would be passed between counterparties in the future. Such a model shall account for the nature of margin agreements (unilateral or bilateral), the frequency of margin calls, the margin period of risk, the minimum threshold of unmargined exposure the credit institution is willing to accept, and the minimum transfer amount. Such a model shall either model the mark-to-market change in the value of collateral posted or apply the rules set out in Annex VIII; and

(f) static, historical back-testing on representative counterparty portfolios shall be Part of the model validation process. At regular intervals, a credit institution shall conduct such back-testing on a number of representative counterparty portfolios (actual or hypothetical). These representative portfolios shall be chosen based on their sensitivity to the material risk factors and correlations to which the credit institution is exposed.

If back-testing indicates that the model is not sufficiently accurate, the competent authorities shall revoke the model approval or impose appropriate measures to ensure that the model is improved promptly. They may also require additional own funds to be held by credit institutions pursuant to Article 136.

PART 7
CONTRACTUAL NETTING (CONTRACTS FOR NOVATION AND OTHER NETTING AGREEMENTS)

(a) Types of netting that competent authorities may recognise

For the purpose of this Part, "counterparty" means any entity (including natural persons)   that has the power to conclude a contractual netting agreement and "contractual cross product netting agreement" means a written bilateral agreement between a credit institution and a counterparty which creates a single legal obligation covering all included bilateral master agreements and transactions belonging to different product categories. Contractual cross product netting agreements do not cover netting other than on a bilateral basis.

For the purposes of cross product netting, the following are considered different product categories:

(i)   repurchase transactions, reverse repurchase transactions, securities and commodities lending and borrowing transactions,

(ii) margin lending transactions, and

(iii) the contracts listed in Annex IV.

The competent authorities may recognise as risk-reducing the following types of contractual netting:

(i)   bilateral contracts for novation between a credit institution and its counterparty under which mutual claims and obligations are automatically amalgamated in such a way that this novation fixes one single net amount each time novation applies and thus creates a legally binding, single new contract extinguishing former contracts,

(ii) other bilateral agreements between a credit institution and its counterparty, and

(iii) contractual cross product netting agreements for credit institutions that have received approval by their competent authorities to use the method set out in Part 6, for transactions falling under the scope of that method. Netting across transactions entered by members of a group is not recognised for the purposes of calculating capital requirements.

(b) Conditions for recognition

The competent authorities may recognise contractual netting as risk-reducing only under the following conditions:

(i)   a credit institution must have a contractual netting agreement with its counterparty which creates a single legal obligation, covering all included transactions, such that, in the event of a counterparty's failure to perform owing to default, bankruptcy, liquidation or any other similar circumstance, the credit institution would have a claim to receive or an obligation to pay only the net sum of the positive and negative mark-to-market values of included individual transactions,

(ii) a credit institution must have made available to the competent authorities written and reasoned legal opinions to the effect that, in the event of a legal challenge, the relevant courts and administrative authorities would, in the cases described under (i), find that the credit institution's claims and obligations would be limited to the net sum, as described in (i), under:

—   the law of the jurisdiction in which the counterparty is incorporated and, if a foreign branch of an undertaking is involved, also under the law of the jurisdiction in which the branch is located,

— the law that governs the individual transactions included, and
— the law that governs any contract or agreement necessary to effect the contractual netting,

(iii) a credit institution must have procedures in place to ensure that the legal validity of its contractual netting is kept under review in the light of possible changes in the relevant laws,

(iv) the credit institution maintains all required documentation in its files,

(v) the effects of netting shall be factored into the credit institution's measurement of each counterparty's aggregate credit risk exposure and the credit institution manages its CCR on such a basis, and

(vi) credit risk to each counterparty is aggregated to arrive at a single legal exposure across transactions. This aggregation shall be factored into credit limit purposes and internal capital purposes.

The competent authorities must be satisfied, if necessary after consulting the other competent authorities concerned, that the contractual netting is legally valid under the law of each of the relevant jurisdictions. If any of the competent authorities are not satisfied in that respect, the contractual netting agreement will not be recognised as risk-reducing for either of the counterparties.

The competent authorities may accept reasoned legal opinions drawn up by types of contractual netting.

No contract containing a provision which permits a non-defaulting counterparty to make limited payments only, or no payments at all, to the estate of the defaulter, even if the defaulter is a net creditor (a "walkaway" clause), may be recognised as risk-reducing.

In addition, for contractual cross-product netting agreements the following criteria shall be met:

(a) the net sum referred to in subpoint (b)(i) of this Part shall be the net sum of the positive and negative close out values of any included individual bilateral master agreement and of the positive and negative mark-to-market value of the individual transactions (the "Cross-Product Net Amount");

(b) the written and reasoned legal opinions referred to in subpoint (b)(ii) of this Part shall address the validity and enforceability of the entire contractual cross-product netting agreement under its terms and the impact of the netting arrangement on the material provisions of any included individual bilateral master agreement. A legal opinion shall be generally recognised as such by the legal community in the Member State in which the credit institution is authorised or a memorandum of law that addresses all relevant issues in a reasoned manner;

(c) the credit institution shall have procedures in place under subpoint (b)(iii) of this Part to verify that any transaction which is to be included in a netting set is covered by a legal opinion; and

(d) taking into account the contractual cross product netting agreement, the credit institution shall continue to comply with the requirements for the recognition of bilateral netting and the requirements of Articles 90 to 93 for the recognition of credit risk mitigation, as applicable, with respect to each included individual bilateral master agreement and transaction.

(c) Effects of recognition

Netting for the purposes of Parts 5 and 6 shall be recognised as set out therein.

(i) Contracts for novation

The single net amounts fixed by contracts for novation, rather than the gross amounts involved, may be weighted. Thus, in the application of Part 3, in:

— step (a): the current replacement cost, and in
— step (b): the notional principal amounts or underlying values

may be obtained taking account of the contract for novation. In the application of Part 4, in step (a) the notional principal amount may be calculated taking account of the contract for novation; the percentages of Table 3 must apply.

(ii) Other netting agreements

In application of Part 3:

— in step (a) the current replacement cost for the contracts included in a netting agreement may be obtained by taking account of the actual hypothetical net replacement cost which results from the agreement; in the case where netting leads to a net obligation for the credit institution calculating the net replacement cost, the current replacement cost is calculated as "0", and

— in step (b) the figure for potential future credit exposure for all contracts included in a netting agreement may be reduced according to the following formula:

$$PCE_{red} = 0.4^*PCE_{gross} + 0.6^*NGR^*PCE_{gross}$$

where:

— PCEred = the reduced figure for potential future credit exposure for all contracts with a given counterparty included in a legally valid bilateral netting agreement

— PCEgross = the sum of the figures for potential future credit exposure for all contracts with a given counterparty which are included in a legally valid bilateral netting agreement and are calculated by multiplying their notional principal amounts by the percentages set out in Table 1

— NGR = "net to gross ratio": at the discretion of the competent authorities either:

(i) separate calculation: the quotient of the net replacement cost for all contracts included in a legally valid bilateral netting agreement with a given counterparty (numerator) and the gross replacement cost for all contracts included in a legally valid bilateral netting agreement with that counterparty (denominator), or

(ii) aggregate calculation: the quotient of the sum of the net replacement cost calculated on a bilateral basis for all counterparties taking into account the contracts included in legally valid netting agreements (numerator) and the gross replacement cost for all contracts included in legally valid netting agreements (denominator).

If Member States permit credit institutions a choice of methods, the method chosen is to be used consistently.

For the calculation of the potential future credit exposure according to the above formula perfectly matching contracts included in the netting agreement may be taken into account as a single contract with a notional principal equivalent to the net receipts. Perfectly matching contracts are forward foreign-exchange contracts or similar contracts in which a notional principal is equivalent to cash flows if the cash flows fall due on the same value date and fully or partly in the same currency.

In the application of Part 4, in step (a)

— perfectly matching contracts included in the netting agreement may be taken into account as a single contract with a notional principal equivalent to the net receipts, the notional principal amounts are multiplied by the percentages given in Table 3, and

— for all other contracts included in a netting agreement, the percentages applicable may be reduced as indicated in Table 6:

Table 6

Original maturity[1]	Interest-rate contracts	Foreign-exchange contracts
One year or less	0.35%	1.50%
More than one year but not more than two years	0.75%	3.75%
Additional allowance for each additional year	0.75%	2.25%

[5842]

NOTES

[1]   In the case of interest-rate contracts, credit institutions may, subject to the consent of their competent authorities, choose either original or residual maturity.

ANNEX IV
TYPES OF DERIVATIVES

1. Interest-rate contracts:
    (a) single-currency interest rate swaps;
    (b) basis-swaps;
    (c) forward rate agreements;
    (d) interest-rate futures;
    (e) interest-rate options purchased; and
    (f) other contracts of similar nature.

2. Foreign-exchange contracts and contracts concerning gold:
    (a) cross-currency interest-rate swaps;
    (b) forward foreign-exchange contracts;
    (c) currency futures;
    (d) currency options purchased;
    (e) other contracts of a similar nature; and
    (f) contracts concerning gold of a nature similar to (a) to (e).

3. Contracts of a nature similar to those in points 1(a) to (e) and 2(a) to (d) concerning other reference items or indices. This includes as a minimum all instruments specified in points 4 to 7, 9 and 10 of Section C of Annex I to Directive 2004/39/EC not otherwise included in points 1 or 2.

[5842A]

ANNEX V
TECHNICAL CRITERIA CONCERNING THE ORGANISATION AND TREATMENT OF RISKS

1. GOVERNANCE

1. Arrangements shall be defined by the management body described in Article 11 concerning the segregation of duties in the organisation and the prevention of conflicts of interest.

2. TREATMENT OF RISKS

2. The management body described in Article 11 shall approve and periodically review the strategies and policies for taking up, managing, monitoring and mitigating the risks the credit institution is or might be exposed to, including those posed by the macroeconomic environment in which it operates in relation to the status of the business cycle.

3. CREDIT AND COUNTERPARTY RISK

3. Credit-granting shall be based on sound and well-defined criteria. The process for approving, amending, renewing, and re-financing credits shall be clearly established.

4. The ongoing administration and monitoring of their various credit risk-bearing portfolios and exposures, including for identifying and managing problem credits and for making adequate value adjustments and provisions, shall be operated through effective systems.

5. Diversification of credit portfolios shall be adequate given the credit institution's target markets and overall credit strategy.

4. RESIDUAL RISK

6. The risk that recognised credit risk mitigation techniques used by the credit institution prove less effective than expected shall be addressed and controlled by means of written policies and procedures.

5. CONCENTRATION RISK

7. The concentration risk arising from exposures to counterparties, groups of connected counterparties, and counterparties in the same economic sector, geographic region or from the same activity or commodity, the application of credit risk mitigation techniques, and including in particular risks associated with large indirect credit exposures (e g to a single collateral issuer), shall be addressed and controlled by means of written policies and procedures.

6. SECURITISATION RISK

8. The risks arising from securitisation transactions in relation to which the credit institutions are originator or sponsor shall be evaluated and addressed through appropriate policies and procedures, to ensure in particular that the economic substance of the transaction is fully reflected in the risk assessment and management decisions.

9. Liquidity plans to address the implications of both scheduled and early amortization shall exist at credit institutions which are originators of revolving securitisation transactions involving early amortisation provisions.

7. MARKET RISK

10. Policies and processes for the measurement and management of all material sources and effects of market risks shall be implemented.

8. INTEREST RATE RISK ARISING FROM NON-TRADING ACTIVITIES

11. Systems shall be implemented to evaluate and manage the risk arising from potential changes in interest rates as they affect a credit institution's non-trading activities.

9. OPERATIONAL RISK

12. Policies and processes to evaluate and manage the exposure to operational risk, including to low-frequency high-severity events, shall be implemented. Without prejudice to the definition laid down in Article 4(22), credit institutions shall articulate what constitutes operational risk for the purposes of those policies and procedures.

13.   Contingency and business continuity plans shall be in place to ensure a credit institution's ability to operate on an ongoing basis and limit losses in the event of severe business disruption.

10. LIQUIDITY RISK

14.   Policies and processes for the measurement and management of their net funding position and requirements on an ongoing and forward-looking basis shall exist. Alternative scenarios shall be considered and the assumptions underpinning decisions concerning the net funding position shall be reviewed regularly.

15.   Contingency plans to deal with liquidity crises shall be in place.

[5842B]

ANNEX VI
STANDARDISED APPROACH

PART 1
RISK WEIGHTS

1. EXPOSURES TO CENTRAL GOVERNMENTS OR CENTRAL BANKS

1.1. Treatment

1.   Without prejudice to points 2 to 7, exposures to central governments and central banks shall be assigned a 100% risk weight.

2.   Subject to point 3, exposures to central governments and central banks for which a credit assessment by a nominated ECAI is available shall be assigned a risk weight according to Table 1 in accordance with the assignment by the competent authorities of the credit assessments of eligible ECAIs to six steps in a credit quality assessment scale.

Table 1

Credit quality step	1	2	3	4	5	6
Risk weight	0%	20%	50%	100%	100%	150%

3.   Exposures to the European Central Bank shall be assigned a 0% risk weight.

1.2. Exposures in the national currency of the borrower

4.   Exposures to Member States' central governments and central banks denominated and funded in the domestic currency of that central government and central bank shall be assigned a risk weight of 0%.

5.   When the competent authorities of a third country which apply supervisory and regulatory arrangements at least equivalent to those applied in the Community assign a risk weight which is lower than that indicated in point 1 to 2 to exposures to their central government and central bank denominated and funded in the domestic currency, Member States may allow their credit institutions to risk weight such exposures in the same manner.

1.3. Use of credit assessments by Export Credit Agencies

6.   Export Credit Agency credit assessments shall be recognised by the competent authorities if either of the following conditions is met:

(a)   it is a consensus risk score from Export Credit Agencies participating in the OECD "Arrangement on Guidelines for Officially Supported Export Credits"; or

(b)   the Export Credit Agency publishes its credit assessments, and the Export Credit Agency subscribes to the OECD agreed methodology, and the credit assessment is associated with one of the eight minimum export insurance premiums (MEIP) that the OECD agreed methodology establishes.

7.   Exposures for which a credit assessment by an Export Credit Agency is recognised for risk weighting purposes shall be assigned a risk weight according to Table 2.

Table 2

MEIP	0	1	2	3	4	5	6	7
Risk weight	0%	0%	20%	50%	100%	100%	100%	150%

2. EXPOSURES TO REGIONAL GOVERNMENTS OR LOCAL AUTHORITIES

8.   Without prejudice to points 9 to 11, exposures to regional governments and local authorities shall be risk weighted as exposures to institutions. This treatment is independent of the exercise of discretion as specified in Article 80(3). The preferential treatment for short-term exposures specified in points 31, 32 and 37 shall not be applied.

9.   Exposures to regional governments and local authorities shall be treated as exposures to the central government in whose jurisdiction they are established where there is no difference in risk between such exposures because of the specific revenue-raising powers of the former, and the existence of specific institutional arrangements the effect of which is to reduce their risk of default.

Competent authorities shall draw up and make public the list of the regional governments and local authorities to be risk-weighted like central governments.

10.   Exposures to churches and religious communities constituted in the form of a legal person under public law shall, in so far as they raise taxes in accordance with legislation conferring on them the right to do so, be treated as exposures to regional governments and local authorities, except that point 9 shall not apply. In this case for the purposes of Article 89(1)(a), permission to apply Title V, Chapter 2, Section 3, Subsection 1 shall not be excluded.

11.   When competent authorities of a third country jurisdiction which apply supervisory and regulatory arrangements at least equivalent to those applied in the Community treat exposures to regional governments and local authorities as exposures to their central government, Member States may allow their credit institutions to risk weight exposures to such regional governments and local authorities in the same manner.

3. EXPOSURES TO ADMINISTRATIVE BODIES AND NON-COMMERCIAL UNDERTAKINGS

3.1. Treatment

12.   Without prejudice to points 13 to 17, exposures to administrative bodies and non-commercial undertakings shall be assigned a 100% risk weight.

3.2. Public Sector Entities

13.   Without prejudice to points 14 to 17, exposures to public sector entities shall be assigned a 100% risk weight.

14.   Subject to the discretion of competent authorities, exposures to public sector entities may be treated as exposures to institutions. Exercise of this discretion by competent authorities is independent of the exercise of discretion as specified in Article 80(3). The preferential treatment for short-term exposures specified in points 31, 32 and 37 shall not be applied.

15.   In exceptional circumstances, exposures to public-sector entities may be treated as exposures to the central government in whose jurisdiction they are established where in the opinion of the competent authorities there is no difference in risk between such exposures because of the existence of an appropriate guarantee by the central government.

16.   When the discretion to treat exposures to public-sector entities as exposures to institutions or as exposures to the central government in whose jurisdiction they are established is exercised by the competent authorities of one Member State, the competent authorities of another Member State shall allow their credit institutions to risk-weight exposures to such public-sector entities in the same manner.

17.   When competent authorities of a third country jurisdiction, which apply supervisory and regulatory arrangements at least equivalent to those applied in the Community, treat exposures to public sector entities as exposures to institutions, Member States may allow their credit institutions to risk weight exposures to such public sector entities in the same manner.

4. EXPOSURES TO MULTILATERAL DEVELOPMENT BANKS

4.1. Scope

18.   For the purposes of Articles 78 to 83, the Inter-American Investment Corporation, the Black Sea Trade and Development Bank and the Central American Bank for Economic Integration are considered to be Multilateral Development Banks (MDB).

4.2. Treatment

19.   Without prejudice to points 20 and 21, exposures to multilateral development banks shall be treated in the same manner as exposures to institutions in accordance with points 29 to 32. The preferential treatment for short-term exposures as specified in points 31, 32 and 37 shall not apply.

[20.   Exposures to the following multilateral development banks shall be assigned a 0% risk weight:

(a)   the International Bank for Reconstruction and Development;
(b)   the International Finance Corporation;
(c)   the Inter-American Development Bank;
(d)   the Asian Development Bank;
(e)   the African Development Bank;
(f)   the Council of Europe Development Bank;
(g)   the Nordic Investment Bank;
(h)   the Caribbean Development Bank;
(i)   the European Bank for Reconstruction and Development;
(j)   the European Investment Bank;
(k)   the European Investment Fund;
(l)   the Multilateral Investment Guarantee Agency;
(m)   the International Finance Facility for Immunisation; and
(n)   the Islamic Development Bank.]

21.   A risk weight of 20% shall be assigned to the portion of unpaid capital subscribed to the European Investment Fund.

5. EXPOSURES TO INTERNATIONAL ORGANISATIONS

22.   Exposures to the following international organisations shall be assigned a 0% risk weight:
(a)   the European Community;
(b)   the International Monetary Fund;
(c)   the Bank for International Settlements.

6. EXPOSURES TO INSTITUTIONS

6.1. Treatment

23.   One of the two methods described in points 26 to 27 and 29 to 32 shall apply in determining the risk weights for exposures to institutions.

24.   Without prejudice to the other provisions of points 23 to 39, exposures to financial institutions authorised and supervised by the competent authorities responsible for the authorisation and supervision of credit institutions and subject to prudential requirements equivalent to those applied to credit institutions shall be risk-weighted as exposures to institutions.

6.2. Risk-weight floor on exposures to unrated institutions

25.   Exposures to an unrated institution shall not be assigned a risk weight lower than that applied to exposures to its central government.

6.3. Central government risk weight based method

26.   Exposures to institutions shall be assigned a risk weight according to the credit quality step to which exposures to the central government of the jurisdiction in which the institution is incorporated are assigned in accordance with Table 3.

Table 3

Credit quality step to which central government is assigned	1	2	3	4	5	6
Risk weight of exposure	20%	50%	100%	100%	100%	150%

27.   For exposures to institutions incorporated in countries where the central government is unrated, the risk weight shall be not more than 100%.

28.   For exposures to institutions with an original effective maturity of three months or less, the risk weight shall be 20%.

6.4. Credit assessment based method

29.   Exposures to institutions with an original effective maturity of more than three months for which a credit assessment by a nominated ECAI is available shall be assigned a risk weight

according to Table 4 in accordance with the assignment by the competent authorities of the credit assessments of eligible ECAIs to six steps in a credit quality assessment scale.

Table 4

Credit quality step	1	2	3	4	5	6
Risk weight	20%	50%	50%	100%	100%	150%

30. Exposures to unrated institutions shall be assigned a risk weight of 50%.

31. Exposures to an institution with an original effective maturity of three months or less for which a credit assessment by a nominated ECAI is available shall be assigned a risk weight according to Table 5 in accordance with the assignment by the competent authorities of the credit assessments of eligible ECAIs to six steps in a credit quality assessment scale:

Table 5

Credit quality step	1	2	3	4	5	6
Risk weight	20%	20%	20%	50%	50%	150%

32. Exposures to unrated institutions having an original effective maturity of three months or less shall be assigned a 20% risk weight.

6.5. Interaction with short-term credit assessments

33. If the method specified in points 29 to 32 is applied to exposures to institutions, then the interaction with specific short-term assessments shall be as follows.

34. If there is no short-term exposure assessment, the general preferential treatment for short-term exposures as specified in point 31 shall apply to all exposures to institutions of up to three months residual maturity.

35. If there is a short-term assessment and such an assessment determines the application of a more favourable or identical risk weight than the use of the general preferential treatment for short-term exposures, as specified in point 31, then the short-term assessment shall be used for that specific exposure only. Other short-term exposures shall follow the general preferential treatment for short-term exposures, as specified in point 31.

36. If there is a short-term assessment and such an assessment determines a less favourable risk weight than the use of the general preferential treatment for short-term exposures, as specified in point 31, then the general preferential treatment for short-term exposures shall not be used and all unrated short-term claims shall be assigned the same risk weight as that applied by the specific short-term assessment.

6.6. Short-term exposures in the national currency of the borrower

37. Exposures to institutions of a residual maturity of 3 months or less denominated and funded in the national currency may, subject to the discretion of the competent authority, be assigned, under both methods described in points 26 to 27 and 29 to 32, a risk weight that is one category less favourable than the preferential risk weight, as described in points 4 and 5, assigned to exposures to its central government.

38. No exposures of a residual maturity of 3 months or less denominated and funded in the national currency of the borrower shall be assigned a risk weight less than 20%.

6.7 Investments in regulatory capital instruments

39. Investments in equity or regulatory capital instruments issued by institutions shall be risk weighted at 100%, unless deducted from the own funds.

6.8 Minimum reserves required by the ECB

40. Where an exposure to an institution is in the form of minimum reserves required by the ECB or by the central bank of a Member State to be held by the credit institution, Member States may permit the assignment of the risk weight that would be assigned to exposures to the central bank of the Member State in question provided:

(a) the reserves are held in accordance with Regulation (EC) No 1745/2003 of the European Central Bank of 12 September 2003 on the application of minimum reserves[1] or a subsequent replacement regulation or in accordance with national requirements in all material respects equivalent to that Regulation; and

    (b)   in the event of the bankruptcy or insolvency of the institution where the reserves are held, the reserves are fully repaid to the credit institution in a timely manner and are not made available to meet other liabilities of the institution.

7. EXPOSURES TO CORPORATES

7.1. Treatment

41.   Exposures for which a credit assessment by a nominated ECAI is available shall be assigned a risk weight according to Table 6 in accordance with the assignment by the competent authorities of the credit assessments of eligible ECAIs to six steps in a credit quality assessment scale.

Table 6

Credit quality step	1	2	3	4	5	6
Risk weight	20%	50%	100%	100%	150%	150%

42.   Exposures for which such a credit assessment is not available shall be assigned a 100% risk weight or the risk weight of its central government, whichever is the higher.

8. RETAIL EXPOSURES

43.   Exposures that comply with the criteria listed in Article 79(2) shall be assigned a risk weight of 75%.

9. EXPOSURES SECURED BY REAL ESTATE PROPERTY

44.   Without prejudice to points 45 to 60, exposures fully secured by real estate property shall be assigned a risk weight of 100%.

9.1. Exposures secured by mortgages on residential property

45.   Exposures or any part of an exposure fully and completely secured, to the satisfaction of the competent authorities, by mortgages on residential property which is or shall be occupied or let by the owner, or the beneficial owner in the case of personal investment companies, shall be assigned a risk weight of 35%.

46.   Exposures fully and completely secured, to the satisfaction of the competent authorities, by shares in Finnish residential housing companies, operating in accordance with the Finnish Housing Company Act of 1991 or subsequent equivalent legislation, in respect of residential property which is or shall be occupied or let by the owner shall be assigned a risk weight of 35%.

47.   Exposures to a tenant under a property leasing transaction concerning residential property under which the credit institution is the lessor and the tenant has an option to purchase, shall be assigned a risk weight of 35% provided that the competent authorities are satisfied that the exposure of the credit institution is fully and completely secured by its ownership of the property.

48.   In the exercise of their judgement for the purposes of points 45 to 47, competent authorities shall be satisfied only if the following conditions are met:

    (a)   the value of the property does not materially depend upon the credit quality of the obligor. This requirement does not preclude situations where purely macro-economic factors affect both the value of the property and the performance of the borrower;

    (b)   the risk of the borrower does not materially depend upon the performance of the underlying property or project, but rather on the underlying capacity of the borrower to repay the debt from other sources. As such, repayment of the facility does not materially depend on any cash flow generated by the underlying property serving as collateral;

    (c)   the minimum requirements set out in Annex VIII, Part 2, point 8 and the valuation rules set out in Annex VIII, Part 3, points 62 to 65 are met; and

    (d)   the value of the property exceeds the exposures by a substantial margin.

49.   Competent authorities may dispense with the condition contained in point 48(b) for exposures fully and completely secured by mortgages on residential property which is situated within their territory, if they have evidence that a well-developed and long-established residential real estate market is present in their territory with loss rates which are sufficiently low to justify such treatment.

50.   When the discretion contained in point 49 is exercised by the competent authorities of a Member State, the competent authorities of another Member State may allow their credit institutions to assign a risk weight of 35% to such exposures fully and completely secured by mortgages on residential property.

9.2. Exposures secured by mortgages on commercial real estate

51.   Subject to the discretion of the competent authorities, exposures or any part of an exposure fully and completely secured, to the satisfaction of the competent authorities, by mortgages on offices or other commercial premises situated within their territory may be assigned a risk weight of 50%.

52.   Subject to the discretion of the competent authorities, exposures fully and completely secured, to the satisfaction of the competent authorities, by shares in Finnish housing companies, operating in accordance with the Finnish Housing Company Act of 1991 or subsequent equivalent legislation, in respect of offices or other commercial premises may be assigned a risk weight of 50%.

53.   Subject to the discretion of the competent authorities, exposures related to property leasing transactions concerning offices or other commercial premises situated in their territories under which the credit institution is the lessor and the tenant has an option to purchase may be assigned a risk weight of 50% provided that the exposure of the credit institution is fully and completely secured to the satisfaction of the competent authorities by its ownership of the property.

54.   The application of points 51 to 53 is subject to the following conditions:
   (a)   the value of the property must not materially depend upon the credit quality of the obligor. This requirement does not preclude situations where purely macro-economic factors affect both the value of the property and the performance of the borrower;
   (b)   the risk of the borrower must not materially depend upon the performance of the underlying property or project, but rather on the underlying capacity of the borrower to repay the debt from other sources. As such, repayment of the facility must not materially depend on any cash flow generated by the underlying property serving as collateral; and
   (c)   the minimum requirements set out in Annex VIII, Part 2, point 8, and the valuation rules set out in Annex VIII, Part 3, points 62 to 65 are met.

55.   The 50% risk weight shall be assigned to the Part of the loan that does not exceed a limit calculated according to either of the following conditions:
   (a)   50% of the market value of the property in question;
   (b)   50% of the market value of the property or 60% of the mortgage lending value, whichever is lower, in those Member States that have laid down rigorous criteria for the assessment of the mortgage lending value in statutory or regulatory provisions.

56.   A 100% risk weigh shall be assigned to the Part of the loan that exceeds the limits set out in point 55.

57.   When the discretion contained in points 51 to 53 is exercised by the competent authorities of one Member State, the competent authorities of another Member State may allow their credit institutions to risk weight at 50% such exposures fully and completely secured by mortgages on commercial property.

58.   Competent authorities may dispense with the condition contained in point 54(b) for exposures fully and completely secured by mortgages on commercial property which is situated within their territory, if they have evidence that a well-developed and long-established commercial real estate market is present in their territory with loss-rates which do not exceed the following limits:
   (a)   losses stemming from lending collateralised by commercial real estate property up to 50% of the market value (or where applicable and if lower 60% of the mortgage lending value (MLV)) do not exceed 0.3% of the outstanding loans collateralised by commercial real estate property in any given year; and
   (b)   overall losses stemming from lending collateralised by commercial real estate property must not exceed 0.5% of the outstanding loans collateralised by commercial real estate property in any given year.

59.   If either of the limits referred to in point 58 is not satisfied in a given year, the eligibility to use point 58 shall cease and the condition contained in point 54(b) shall apply until the conditions in point 58 are satisfied in a subsequent year.

60.   When the discretion contained in point 58 is exercised by the competent authorities of a Member State, the competent authorities of another Member State may allow their credit institutions to assign a risk weight of 50% to such exposures fully and completely secured by mortgages on commercial property.

10. PAST DUE ITEMS

61.   Without prejudice to the provisions contained in points 62 to 65, the unsecured part of any item that is past due for more than 90 days and which is above a threshold defined by the competent authorities and which reflects a reasonable level of risk shall be assigned a risk weight of:
   (a)   150%, if value adjustments are less than 20% of the unsecured part of the exposure gross of value adjustments; and

    (b)   100%, if value adjustments are no less than 20% of the unsecured part of the exposure gross of value adjustments.

62.   For the purpose of defining the secured part of the past due item, eligible collateral and guarantees shall be those eligible for credit risk mitigation purposes.

63.   Nonetheless, where a past due item is fully secured by forms of collateral other then those eligible for credit risk mitigation purposes, a 100% risk weight may be assigned subject to the discretion of competent authorities based upon strict operational criteria to ensure the good quality of the collateral when value adjustments reach 15% of the exposure gross of value adjustments.

64.   Exposures indicated in points 45 to 50 shall be assigned a risk weight of 100% net of value adjustments if they are past due for more than 90 days. If value adjustments are no less than 20% of the exposure gross of value adjustments, the risk weight to be assigned to the remainder of the exposure may be reduced to 50% at the discretion of competent authorities.

65.   Exposures indicated in points 51 to 60 shall be assigned a risk weight of 100% if they are past due for more than 90 days.

11. ITEMS BELONGING TO REGULATORY HIGH-RISK CATEGORIES

66.   Subject to the discretion of competent authorities, exposures associated with particularly high risks such as investments in venture capital firms and private equity investments shall be assigned a risk weight of 150%.

67.   Competent authorities may permit non past due items to be assigned a 150% risk weight according to the provisions of this Part and for which value adjustments have been established to be assigned a risk weight of:
    (a)   100%, if value adjustments are no less than 20% of the exposure value gross of value adjustments; and
    (b)   50%, if value adjustments are no less than 50% of the exposure value gross of value adjustments.

12. EXPOSURES IN THE FORM OF COVERED BONDS

68.   "Covered bonds", shall mean bonds as defined in Article 22(4) of Directive 85/611/EEC and collateralised by any of the following eligible assets:
    (a)   exposures to or guaranteed by central governments, central banks, public sector entities, regional governments and local authorities in the EU;
    (b)   exposures to or guaranteed by non-EU central governments, non-EU central banks, multilateral development banks, international organisations that qualify for the credit quality step 1 as set out in this Annex, and exposures to or guaranteed by non-EU public sector entities, non-EU regional governments and non-EU local authorities that are risk weighted as exposures to institutions or central governments and central banks according to points 8, 9, 14 or 15 respectively and that qualify for the credit quality step 1 as set out in this Annex, and exposures in the sense of this point that qualify as a minimum for the credit quality step 2 as set out in this Annex, provided that they do not exceed 20% of the nominal amount of outstanding covered bonds of issuing institutions;
    (c)   exposures to institutions that qualify for the credit quality step 1 as set out in this Annex. The total exposure of this kind shall not exceed 15% of the nominal amount of outstanding covered bonds of the issuing credit institution. Exposures caused by transmission and management of payments of the obligors of, or liquidation proceeds in respect of, loans secured by real estate to the holders of covered bonds shall not be comprised by the 15% limit. Exposures to institutions in the EU with a maturity not exceeding 100 days shall not be comprised by the step 1 requirement but those institutions must as a minimum qualify for credit quality step 2 as set out in this Annex;
    (d)   loans secured by residential real estate or shares in Finnish residential housing companies as referred to in point 46 up to the lesser of the principal amount of the liens that are combined with any prior liens and 80% of the value of the pledged properties or by senior units issued by French Fonds Communs de Créances or by equivalent securitisation entities governed by the laws of a Member State securitising residential real estate exposures provided that at least 90% of the assets of such Fonds Communs de Créances or of equivalent securitisation entities governed by the laws of a Member State are composed of mortgages that are combined with any prior liens up to the lesser of the principal amounts due under the units, the principal amounts of the liens, and 80% of the value of the pledged properties and the units qualify for the credit quality step 1 as set out in this Annex where such units do not exceed 20% of the nominal amount of the outstanding issue. Exposures caused by transmission and management of payments of the obligors of, or liquidation proceeds in respect of, loans secured by pledged properties of the senior units or debt securities shall not be comprised in calculating the 90% limit;
    (e)   loans secured by commercial real estate or shares in Finnish housing companies as referred to in point 52 up to the lesser of the principal amount of the liens that are

combined with any prior liens and 60% of the value of the pledged properties or by senior units issued by French Fonds Communs de Créances or by equivalent securitisation entities governed by the laws of a Member State securitising commercial real estate exposures provided that, at least, 90% of the assets of such Fonds Communs de Créances or of equivalent securitisation entities governed by the laws of a Member State are composed of mortgages that are combined with any prior liens up to the lesser of the principal amounts due under the units, the principal amounts of the liens, and 60% of the value of the pledged properties and the units qualify for the credit quality step 1 as set out in this Annex where such units do not exceed 20% of the nominal amount of the outstanding issue. The competent authorities may recognise loans secured by commercial real estate as eligible where the Loan to Value ratio of 60% is exceeded up to a maximum level of 70% if the value of the total assets pledged as collateral for the covered bonds exceed the nominal amount outstanding on the covered bond by at least 10%, and the bondholders' claim meets the legal certainty requirements set out in Annex VIII. The bondholders' claim must take priority over all other claims on the collateral. Exposures caused by transmission and management of payments of the obligors of, or liquidation proceeds in respect of, loans secured by pledged properties of the senior units or debt securities shall not be comprised in calculating the 90% limit; or

(f)   loans secured by ships where only liens that are combined with any prior liens within 60% of the value of the pledged ship.

For these purposes "collateralised" includes situations where the assets as described in subpoints (a) to (f) are exclusively dedicated in law to the protection of the bond-holders against losses.

Until 31 December 2010 the 20% limit for senior units issued by French Fonds Communs de Créances or by equivalent securitisation entities as specified in subpoints (d) and (e) does not apply, provided that those senior units have a credit assessment by a nominated ECAI which is the most favourable category of credit assessment made by the ECAI in respect of covered bonds. Before the end of this period this derogation shall be reviewed and consequent to such review the Commission may as appropriate extend this period in accordance with the procedure referred to in Article 151(2) with or without a further review clause.

Until 31 December 2010 the figure of 60% indicated in subpoint (f) can be replaced with a figure of 70%. Before the end of this period this derogation shall be reviewed and consequent to such review the Commission may as appropriate extend this period in accordance with the procedure referred to in Article 151(2) with or without a further review clause.

69.   Credit institutions shall for real estate collateralising covered bonds meet the minimum requirements set out in Annex VIII Part 2, point 8 and the valuation rules set out in Annex VIII, Part 3, points 62 to 65.

70.   Notwithstanding points 68 and 69, covered bonds meeting the definition of Article 22(4) of Directive 85/611/EEC and issued before 31 December 2007 are also eligible for the preferential treatment until their maturity.

71.   Covered bonds shall be assigned a risk weight on the basis of the risk weight assigned to senior unsecured exposures to the credit institution which issues them. The following correspondence between risk weights shall apply:
(a)   if the exposures to the institution are assigned a risk weight of 20%, the covered bond shall be assigned a risk weight of 10%;
(b)   if the exposures to the institution are assigned a risk weight of 50%, the covered bond shall be assigned a risk weight of 20%;
(c)   if the exposures to the institution are assigned a risk weight of 100%, the covered bond shall be assigned a risk weight of 50%; and
(d)   if the exposures to the institution are assigned a risk weight of 150%, the covered bond shall be assigned a risk weight of 100%.

13. ITEMS REPRESENTING SECURITISATION POSITIONS

72.   Risk weight exposure amounts for securitisation positions shall be determined in accordance with Articles 94 to 101.

14. SHORT-TERM EXPOSURES TO INSTITUTIONS AND CORPORATES

73.   Short-term exposures to an institution or corporate for which a credit assessment by a nominated ECAI is available shall be assigned a risk weight according to Table 7 as follows, in accordance with the mapping by the competent authorities of the credit assessments of eligible ECAIs to six steps in a credit quality assessment scale:

Table 7

Credit Quality Step	1	2	3	4	5	6
Risk weight	20%	50%	100%	150%	150%	150%

15. EXPOSURES IN THE FORM OF COLLECTIVE INVESTMENT UNDERTAKINGS (CIUS)

74.   Without prejudice to points 75 to 81, exposures in collective investment undertakings (CIUs) shall be assigned a risk weight of 100%.

75.   Exposures in the form of CIUs for which a credit assessment by a nominated ECAI is available shall be assigned a risk weight according to Table 8, in accordance with the assignment by the competent authorities of the credit assessments of eligible ECAIs to six steps in a credit quality assessment scale.

Table 8

Credit quality step	1	2	3	4	5	6
Risk weight	20%	50%	100%	100%	150%	150%

76.   Where competent authorities consider that a position in a CIU is associated with particularly high risks they shall require that that position is assigned a risk weight of 150%.

77.   Credit institutions may determine the risk weight for a CIU as set out in points 79 to 81, if the following eligibility criteria are met:

   (a)   the CIU is managed by a company which is subject to supervision in a Member State or, subject to approval of the credit institution's competent authority, if:
   (i)   the CIU is managed by a company which is subject to supervision that is considered equivalent to that laid down in Community law; and
   (ii)   cooperation between competent authorities is sufficiently ensured;
   (b)   the CIU's prospectus or equivalent document includes:
   (i)   the categories of assets in which the CIU is authorised to invest; and
   (ii)   if investment limits apply, the relative limits and the methodologies to calculate them; and
   (c)   the business of the CIU is reported on at least an annual basis to enable an assessment to be made of the assets and liabilities, income and operations over the reporting period.

78.   If a competent authority approves a third country CIU as eligible, as set out in point 77(a), then a competent authority in another Member State may make use of this recognition without conducting its own assessment.

79.   Where the credit institution is aware of the underlying exposures of a CIU, it may look through to those underlying exposures in order to calculate an average risk weight for the CIU in accordance with the methods set out in Article 78 to 83.

80.   Where the credit institution is not aware of the underlying exposures of a CIU, it may calculate an average risk weight for the CIU in accordance with the methods set out in Articles 78 to 83 subject to the following rules: it will be assumed that the CIU first invests, to the maximum extent allowed under its mandate, in the exposure classes attracting the highest capital requirement, and then continues making investments in descending order until the maximum total investment limit is reached.

81.   Credit institutions may rely on a third party to calculate and report, in accordance with the methods set out in points 79 and 80, a risk weight for the CIU provided that the correctness of the calculation and report shall be adequately ensured.

16. OTHER ITEMS

16.1. Treatment

82.   Tangible assets within the meaning of Article 4(10) of Directive 86/635/EEC shall be assigned a risk weight of 100%.

83.   Prepayments and accrued income for which an institution is unable to determine the counterparty in accordance with Directive 86/635/EEC, shall be assigned a risk weight of 100%.

84.   Cash items in the process of collection shall be assigned a 20% risk weight. Cash in hand and equivalent cash items shall be assigned a 0% risk weight.

85.   Member States may allow a risk weight of 10% for exposures to institutions specialising in the inter-bank and public-debt markets in their home Member States and subject to close supervision by the competent authorities where those asset items are fully and completely secured, to the satisfaction of the competent authorities of the home Member States, by a items assigned a 0% or a 20% risk weight and recognised by the latter as constituting adequate collateral.

86.   Holdings of equity and other participations, except where deducted from own funds, shall be assigned a risk weight of at least 100%.

87.   Gold bullion held in own vaults or on an allocated basis to the extent backed by bullion liabilities shall be assigned a 0% risk weight.

88.   In the case of asset sale and repurchase agreements and outright forward purchases, the risk weight shall be that assigned to the assets in question and not to the counterparties to the transactions.

89.   Where a credit institution provides credit protection for a number of exposures under terms that the nth default among the exposures shall trigger payment and that this credit event shall terminate the contract, and where the product has an external credit assessment from an eligible ECAI, the risk weights prescribed in Articles 94 to 101 shall be assigned. If the product is not rated by an eligible ECAI, the risk weights of the exposures included in the basket will be aggregated, excluding n-1 exposures, up to a maximum of 1250% and multiplied by the nominal amount of the protection provided by the credit derivative to obtain the risk weighted asset amount. The n-1 exposures to be excluded from the aggregation shall be determined on the basis that they shall include those exposures each of which produces a lower risk-weighted exposure amount than the risk-weighted exposure amount of any of the exposures included in the aggregation.

PART 2
RECOGNITION OF ECAIS AND MAPPING OF THEIR CREDIT ASSESSMENTS

1. METHODOLOGY

1.1. Objectivity

1.   Competent authorities shall verify that the methodology for assigning credit assessments is rigorous, systematic, continuous and subject to validation based on historical experience.

1.2. Independence

2.   Competent authorities shall verify that the methodology is free from external political influences or constraints, and from economic pressures that may influence the credit assessment.

3.   Independence of the ECAI's methodology shall be assessed by competent authorities according to factors such as the following:
   (a)   ownership and organisation structure of the ECAI;
   (b)   financial resources of the ECAI;
   (c)   staffing and expertise of the ECAI; and
   (d)   corporate governance of the ECAI.

1.3. Ongoing review

4.   Competent authorities shall verify that ECAI's credit assessments are subject to ongoing review and shall be responsive to changes in the financial conditions. Such review shall take place after all significant events and at least annually.

5.   Before any recognition, competent authorities shall verify that the assessment methodology for each market segment is established according to standards such as the following:
   (a)   the back-testing must be established for at least one year;
   (b)   the regularity of the review process by the ECAI must be monitored by the competent authorities; and
   (c)   the competent authorities must be able to receive from the ECAI the extent of its contacts with the senior management of the entities which it rates.

6.   Competent authorities shall take the necessary measures to be promptly informed by ECAIs of any material changes in the methodology they use for assigning credit assessments.

1.4. Transparency and disclosure

7.   Competent authorities shall take the necessary measures to assure that the principles of the methodology employed by the ECAI for the formulation of its credit assessments are publicly available as to allow all potential users to decide whether they are derived in a reasonable way.

2. INDIVIDUAL CREDIT ASSESSMENTS

2.1. Credibility and market acceptance

8. Competent authorities shall verify that ECAIs' individual credit assessments are recognised in the market as credible and reliable by the users of such credit assessments.

9. Credibility shall be assessed by competent authorities according to factors such as the following:

    (a)   market share of the ECAI;

    (b)   revenues generated by the ECAI, and more in general financial resources of the ECAI;

    (c)   whether there is any pricing on the basis of the rating; and

    (d)   at least two credit institutions use the ECAI's individual credit assessment for bond issuing and/or assessing credit risks.

2.2. Transparency and Disclosure

10. Competent authorities shall verify that individual credit assessments are accessible at equivalent terms at least to all credit institutions having a legitimate interest in these individual credit assessments.

11. In particular, competent authorities shall verify that individual credit assessments are available to non-domestic parties on equivalent terms as to domestic credit institutions having a legitimate interest in these individual credit assessments.

3. "MAPPING"

12. In order to differentiate between the relative degrees of risk expressed by each credit assessment, competent authorities shall consider quantitative factors such as the long-term default rate associated with all items assigned the same credit assessment. For recently established ECAIs and for those that have compiled only a short record of default data, competent authorities shall ask the ECAI what it believes to be the long-term default rate associated with all items assigned the same credit assessment.

13. In order to differentiate between the relative degrees of risk expressed by each credit assessment, competent authorities shall consider qualitative factors such as the pool of issuers that the ECAI covers, the range of credit assessments that the ECAI assigns, each credit assessment meaning and the ECAI's definition of default.

14. Competent authorities shall compare default rates experienced for each credit assessment of a particular ECAI and compare them with a benchmark built on the basis of default rates experienced by other ECAIs on a population of issuers that the competent authorities believes to present an equivalent level of credit risk.

15. When competent authorities believe that the default rates experienced for the credit assessment of a particular ECAI are materially and systematically higher then the benchmark, competent authorities shall assign a higher credit quality step in the credit quality assessment scale to the ECAI credit assessment.

16. When competent authorities have increased the associated risk weight for a specific credit assessment of a particular ECAI, if the ECAI demonstrates that the default rates experienced for its credit assessment are no longer materially and systematically higher than the benchmark, competent authorities may decide to restore the original credit quality step in the credit quality assessment scale for the ECAI credit assessment.

PART 3
USE OF ECAIS' CREDIT ASSESSMENTS FOR THE DETERMINATION OF RISK WEIGHTS

1. TREATMENT

1. A credit institution may nominate one or more eligible ECAIs to be used for the determination of risk weights to be assigned to asset and off-balance sheet items.

2. A credit institution which decides to use the credit assessments produced by an eligible ECAI for a certain class of items must use those credit assessments consistently for all exposures belonging to that class.

3. A credit institution which decides to use the credit assessments produced by an eligible ECAI must use them in a continuous and consistent way over time.

4. A credit institution can only use ECAIs credit assessments that take into account all amounts both in principal and in interest owed to it.

5. If only one credit assessment is available from a nominated ECAI for a rated item, that credit assessment shall be used to determine the risk weight for that item.

6. If two credit assessments are available from nominated ECAIs and the two correspond to different risk weights for a rated item, the higher risk weight shall be assigned.

7.   If more than two credit assessments are available from nominated ECAIs for a rated item, the two assessments generating the two lowest risk weights shall be referred to. If the two lowest risk weights are different, the higher risk weight shall be assigned. If the two lowest risk weights are the same, that risk weight shall be assigned.

2. ISSUER AND ISSUE CREDIT ASSESSMENT

8.   Where a credit assessment exists for a specific issuing program or facility to which the item constituting the exposure belongs, this credit assessment shall be used to determine the risk weight to be assigned to that item.

9.   Where no directly applicable credit assessment exists for a certain item, but a credit assessment exists for a specific issuing program or facility to which the item constituting the exposure does not belong or a general credit assessment exists for the issuer, then that credit assessment shall be used if it produces a higher risk weight than would other wise be the case or if it produces a lower risk weight and the exposure in question ranks pari passu or senior in all respects to the specific issuing program or facility or to senior unsecured exposures of that issuer, as relevant.

10.   Points 8 and 9 are not to prevent the application of points 68 to 71 of Part 1.

11.   Credit assessments for issuers within a corporate group cannot be used as credit assessment of another issuer within the same corporate group.

3. LONG-TERM AND SHORT-TERM CREDIT ASSESSMENTS

12.   Short-term credit assessments may only be used for short-term asset and off-balance sheet items constituting exposures to institutions and corporates.

13.   Any short-term credit assessment shall only apply to the item the short-term credit assessment refers to, and it shall not be used to derive risk weights for any other item.

14.   Notwithstanding point 13, if a short-term rated facility is assigned a 150% risk weight, then all unrated unsecured exposures on that obligor whether short-term or long-term shall also be assigned a 150% risk weight.

15.   Notwithstanding point 13, if a short-term rated facility is assigned a 50% risk-weight, no unrated short-term exposure shall be assigned a risk weight lower than 100%.

4. DOMESTIC AND FOREIGN CURRENCY ITEMS

16.   A credit assessment that refers to an item denominated in the obligor's domestic currency cannot be used to derive a risk weight for another exposure on that same obligor that is denominated in a foreign currency.

17.   Notwithstanding point 16, when an exposure arises through a credit institution's participation in a loan that has been extended by a Multilateral Development Bank whose preferred creditor status is recognised in the market, competent authorities may allow the credit assessment on the obligors' domestic currency item to be used for risk weighting purposes.

[5842C]

NOTES
  Part 1, point 20: substituted by Commission Directive 2007/18/EC, Art 1(2), as from 17 April 2007.
  [1]   OJ L250, 2.10.2003, p 10.

ANNEX VII
INTERNAL RATINGS BASED APPROACH

PART 1
RISK WEIGHTED EXPOSURE AMOUNTS AND EXPECTED LOSS AMOUNTS

1. CALCULATION OF RISK WEIGHTED EXPOSURE AMOUNTS FOR CREDIT RISK

1.   Unless noted otherwise, the input parameters PD, LGD, and maturity value (M) shall be determined as set out in Part 2 and the exposure value shall be determined as set out in Part 3.

2.   The risk weighted exposure amount for each exposure shall be calculated in accordance with the following formulae.

1.1. Risk weighted exposure amounts for exposures to corporates, institutions and central governments and central banks.

3.   Subject to points 5 to 9, the risk weighted exposure amounts for exposures to corporates, institutions and central governments and central banks shall be calculated according to the following formulae:

Correlation (R) =

$$0.12 \times (1 - \text{EXP}(-50^*\text{PD}))/(1 - \text{EXP}(-50)) + 0.24^*[1 - (1 - \text{EXP}(-50^*\text{PD}))/(1 - \text{EXP}(-50))]$$

Looptijdfactor (b) = $(0.11852 - 0.05478^*\ln(\text{PD}))^2$

$(\text{LGD}^*\text{N}[(1-\text{R})^{-0.5}{}^*\text{G}(\text{PD})+(\text{R}/(1-\text{R}))^{0.5}{}^*\text{G}(0.999)]-\text{PD}^*\text{LDG})^*(1-1.5^*\text{b})^{-1}{}^*(1+(\text{M}-2.5)^*\text{b})^*12.5^*1.06$

N(x) denotes the cumulative distribution function for a standard normal random variable (ie the probability that a normal random variable with mean zero and variance of one is less than or equal to x). G (Z) denotes the inverse cumulative distribution function for a standard normal random variable (ie the value x such that N(x) z)

For PD = 0, RW shall be 0.

For PD = 1:

— for defaulted exposures where credit institutions apply the LGD values set out in Part 2, point 8, RW shall be 0; and

— for defaulted exposures where credit institutions use own estimates of LGDs, RW shall be

$$\text{Max}\{0, \ 12.5^*(\text{LGD} - \text{EL}_{\text{BE}})\}$$

where EL_{BE} shall be the credit institution's best estimate of expected loss for the defaulted exposure according to point 80 of Part 4.

Risk-weighted exposure amount = RW * exposure value.

4. The risk weighted exposure amount for each exposure which meets the requirements set out in Annex VIII, Part 1, point 29 and Annex VIII, Part 2, point 22 may be adjusted according to the following formula:

Risk-weighted exposure amount = RW * exposure value * ((0.15 + 160*PDpp)]

where:

PDpp = PD of the protection provider.

RW shall be calculated using the relevant risk weight formula set out in point 3 for the exposure, the PD of the obligor and the LGD of a comparable direct exposure to the protection provider. The maturity factor (b) shall be calculated using the lower of the PD of the protection provider and the PD of the obligor.

5. For exposures to companies where the total annual sales for the consolidated group of which the firm is a Part is less than EUR 50 million, credit institutions may use the following correlation formula for the calculation of risk weights for corporate exposures. In this formula S is expressed as total annual sales in millions of Euros with EUR 5 million <= S <= EUR 50 million. Reported sales of less than EUR 5 million shall be treated as if they were equivalent to EUR 5 million. For purchased receivables the total annual sales shall be the weighted average by individual exposures of the pool.

Correlation (R) =

$$0.12 \times (1 - \text{EXP}(-50^*\text{PD}))/(1 - \text{EXP}(-50)) + 0.24^*[1 - (1 - \text{EXP}(-50^*\text{PD}))/(1 - \text{EXP}(-50))]$$
$$- 0.04^*(1 - (\text{S} - 5)/45)$$

Credit institutions shall substitute total assets of the consolidated group for total annual sales when total annual sales are not a meaningful indicator of firm size and total assets are a more meaningful indicator than total annual sales.

6. For specialised lending exposures in respect of which a credit institution cannot demonstrate that its PD estimates meet the minimum requirements set out in Part 4 it shall assign risk weights to these exposures according to Table 1, as follows:

Table 1

Remaining Maturity	Category 1	Category 2	Category 3	Category 4	Category 5
Less than 2.5 years	50%	70%	115%	250%	0%
Equal or more than 2.5 years	70%	90%	115%	250%	0%

The competent authorities may authorise a credit institution generally to assign preferential risk weights of 50% to exposures in category 1, and a 70% risk weight to exposures in category 2, provided the credit institution's underwriting characteristics and other risk characteristics are substantially strong for the relevant category.

In assigning risk weights to specialised lending exposures credit institutions shall take into account the following factors: financial strength, political and legal environment, transaction and/or asset characteristics, strength of the sponsor and developer, including any public private partnership income stream, and security package.

7.   For their purchased corporate receivables credit institutions shall comply with the minimum requirements set out in points 105 to 109 of Part 4. For purchased corporate receivables that comply in addition with the conditions set out in point 14, and where it would be unduly burdensome for a credit institution to use the risk quantification standards for corporate exposures as set out in Part 4 for these receivables, the risk quantification standards for retail exposures as set out in Part 4 may be used.

8.   For purchased corporate receivables, refundable purchase discounts, collateral or partial guarantees that provide first-loss protection for default losses, dilution losses, or both, may be treated as first-loss positions under the IRB securitisation framework.

9.   Where an institution provides credit protection for a number of exposures under terms that the nth default among the exposures shall trigger payment and that this credit event shall terminate the contract, if the product has an external credit assessment from an eligible ECAI the risk weights set out in Articles 94 to 101 will be applied. If the product is not rated by an eligible ECAI, the risk weights of the exposures included in the basket will be aggregated, excluding n-1 exposures where the sum of the expected loss amount multiplied by 12.5 and the risk weighted exposure amount shall not exceed the nominal amount of the protection provided by the credit derivative multiplied by 12.5. The n-1 exposures to be excluded from the aggregation shall be determined on the basis that they shall include those exposures each of which produces a lower risk-weighted exposure amount than the risk-weighted exposure amount of any of the exposures included in the aggregation.

1.2. Risk weighted exposure amounts for retail exposures

10.   Subject to points 12 and 13, the risk weighted exposure amounts for retail exposures shall be calculated according to the following formulae:

Correlation (R) =

$$0.03 \times (1 - EXP(-35^*PD))/(1 - EXP(-35)) + 0.16^*[1 - (1 - EXP - 35^*PD)/(1 - EXP(-35))]$$

Risk weighted (RW)

$$(LGD^*N\{(1-R)^{-0.5}G(PD) + (R/(1-R))^{0.5}G(0.999)\} - PD^*12.5^*1.06)$$

N(x) denotes the cumulative distribution function for a standard normal random variable (ie the probability that a normal random variable with mean zero and variance of one is less than or equal to x). G (Z) denotes the inverse cumulative distribution function for a standard normal random variable (ie the value x such that N(x) = z).

For PD = 1 (defaulted exposure), RW shall be

$$Max\{0, \ 12.5^*(LGD - EL_{BE})\}$$

where EL_{BE} shall be the credit institution's best estimate of expected loss for the defaulted exposure according to point 80 of Part 4.

Risk-weighted exposure amount = RW * exposure value.

11.   The risk weighted exposure amount for each exposure to small and medium sized entities as defined in Article 86(4) which meets the requirements set out in Annex VIII, Part 1, point 29 and Annex VIII, Part 2, point 22 may be calculated according to point 4.

12.   For retail exposures secured by real estate collateral a correlation (R) of 0.15 shall replace the figure produced by the correlation formula in point 10.

13.   For qualifying revolving retail exposures as defined in points (a) to (e), a correlation (R) of 0.04 shall replace the figure produced by the correlation formula in point 10.

Exposures shall qualify as qualifying revolving retail exposures if they meet the following conditions:

(a)   The exposures are to individuals;

(b)   The exposures are revolving, unsecured, and to the extent they are not drawn immediately and unconditionally, cancellable by the credit institution. (In this context revolving exposures are defined as those where customers' outstanding balances are permitted to fluctuate based on their decisions to borrow and repay, up to a limit established by the credit institution.). Undrawn commitments may be considered as unconditionally cancellable if the terms permit the credit institution to cancel them to the full extent allowable under consumer protection and related legislation;

(c) The maximum exposure to a single individual in the sub-portfolio is EUR 100,000 or less;

(d) The credit institution can demonstrate that the use of the correlation of this point is limited to portfolios that have exhibited low volatility of loss rates, relative to their average level of loss rates, especially within the low PD bands. Competent authorities shall review the relative volatility of loss rates across the qualifying revolving retail sub-portfolios, as well the aggregate qualifying revolving retail portfolio, and intend to share information on the typical characteristics of qualifying revolving retail loss rates across jurisdictions; and

(e) The competent authority concurs that treatment as a qualifying revolving retail exposure is consistent with the underlying risk characteristics of the sub-portfolio.

By way of derogation from point (b), competent authorities may waive the requirement that the exposure be unsecured in respect of collateralised credit facilities linked to a wage account. In this case amounts recovered from the collateral shall not be taken into account in the LGD estimate.

14. To be eligible for the retail treatment, purchased receivables shall comply with the minimum requirements set out in Part 4, points 105 to 109 and the following conditions:

(a) The credit institution has purchased the receivables from unrelated, third party sellers, and its exposure to the obligor of the receivable does not include any exposures that are directly or indirectly originated by the credit institution itself;

(b) The purchased receivables shall be generated on an arm's-length basis between the seller and the obligor. As such, inter-company accounts receivables and receivables subject to contra-accounts between firms that buy and sell to each other are ineligible;

(c) The purchasing credit institution has a claim on all proceeds from the purchased receivables or a pro-rata interest in the proceeds; and

(d) The portfolio of purchased receivables is sufficiently diversified.

15. For purchased receivables, refundable purchase discounts, collateral or partial guarantees that provide first-loss protection for default losses, dilution losses, or both, may be treated as first-loss positions under the IRB securitisation framework.

16. For hybrid pools of purchased retail receivables where purchasing credit institutions cannot separate exposures secured by real estate collateral and qualifying revolving retail exposures from other retail exposures, the retail risk weight function producing the highest capital requirements for those exposures shall apply.

1.3. Risk weighted exposure amounts for equity exposures

17. A credit institution may employ different approaches to different portfolios where the credit institution itself uses different approaches internally. Where a credit institution uses different approaches, the credit institution shall demonstrate to the competent authorities that the choice is made consistently and is not determined by regulatory arbitrage considerations.

18. Notwithstanding point 17, competent authorities may allow the attribution of risk weighted exposure amounts for equity exposures to ancillary services undertakings according to the treatment of other non credit-obligation assets.

1.3.1. Simple risk weight approach

19. The risk weighted exposure amount shall be calculated according to the following formula:

Risk weight (RW) = 190% for private equity exposures in sufficiently diversified portfolios.

Risk weight (RW) = 290% for exchange traded equity exposures.

Risk weight (RW) = 370% for all other equity exposures.

Risk-weighted exposure amount = RW * exposure value.

20. Short cash positions and derivative instruments held in the non-trading book are permitted to offset long positions in the same individual stocks provided that these instruments have been explicitly designated as hedges of specific equity exposures and that they provide a hedge for at least another year. Other short positions are to be treated as if they are long positions with the relevant risk weight assigned to the absolute value of each position. In the context of maturity mismatched positions, the method is that for corporate exposures as set out in point 16 of Annex VII, Part 2.

21. Credit institutions may recognise unfunded credit protection obtained on an equity exposure in accordance with the methods set out in Articles 90 to 93.

PART IV
EC MATERIALS

1.3.2. PD/LGD approach

22. The risk weighted exposure amounts shall be calculated according to the formulas in point 3. If credit institutions do not have sufficient information to use the definition of default set out in points 44 to 48 of Part 4, a scaling factor of 1.5 shall be assigned to the risk weights.

23. At the individual exposure level the sum of the expected loss amount multiplied by 12.5 and the risk weighted exposure amount shall not exceed the exposure value multiplied by 12.5.

24. Credit institutions may recognise unfunded credit protection obtained on an equity exposure in accordance with the methods set out in Articles 90 to 93. This shall be subject to an LGD of 90% on the exposure to the provider of the hedge. For private equity exposures in sufficiently diversified portfolios an LGD of 65% may be used. For these purposes M shall be 5 years.

1.3.3. Internal models approach

25. The risk weighted exposure amount shall be the potential loss on the credit institution's equity exposures as derived using internal value-at-risk models subject to the 99th percentile, one-tailed confidence interval of the difference between quarterly returns and an appropriate risk-free rate computed over a long-term sample period, multiplied by 12.5. The risk weighted exposure amounts at the individual exposure level shall not be less than the sum of minimum risk weighted exposure amounts required under the PD/LGD Approach and the corresponding expected loss amounts multiplied by 12.5 and calculated on the basis of the PD values set out in Part 2, point 24(a) and the corresponding LGD values set out in Part 2, points 25 and 26.

26. Credit institutions may recognise unfunded credit protection obtained on an equity position.

1.4. Risk weighted exposure amounts for other non credit-obligation assets

27. The risk weighted exposure amounts shall be calculated according to the formula:

Risk-weighted exposure amount = 100% * exposure value,

except for when the exposure is a residual value in which case it should be provisioned for each year and will be calculated as follows:

1/t * 100% * exposure value,

where t is the number of years of the lease contract term.

2. CALCULATION OF RISK WEIGHTED EXPOSURE AMOUNTS FOR DILUTION RISK OF PURCHASED RECEIVABLES

28. Risk weights for dilution risk of purchased corporate and retail receivables:

The risk weights shall be calculated according to the formula in point 3. The input parameters PD and LGD shall be determined as set out in Part 2, the exposure value shall be determined as set out in Part 3 and M shall be 1 year. If credit institutions can demonstrate to the competent authorities that dilution risk is immaterial, it need not be recognised.

3. CALCULATION OF EXPECTED LOSS AMOUNTS

29. Unless noted otherwise, the input parameters PD and LGD shall be determined as set out in Part 2 and the exposure value shall be determined as set out in Part 3.

30. The expected loss amounts for exposures to corporates, institutions, central governments and central banks and retail exposures shall be calculated according to the following formulae:
Expected loss (EL) = PD × LGD.
Expected loss amount = EL × exposure value.

For defaulted exposures (PD = 1) where credit institutions use own estimates of LGDs, EL shall be EL_{BE}, the credit institution's best estimate of expected loss for the defaulted exposure according to Part 4, point 80.

For exposures subject to the treatment set out in Part 1, point 4, EL shall be 0.

31. The EL values for specialised lending exposures where credit institutions use the methods set out in point 6 for assigning risk weights shall be assigned according to Table 2.

Table 2

Remaining Maturity	Category 1	Category 2	Category 3	Category 4	Category 5
Less than 2.5 years	0%	0.4%	2.8%	8%	50%
Equal to or more than 2.5 years	0.4%	0.8%	2.8%	8%	50%

Where competent authorities have authorised a credit institution generally to assign preferential risk weights of 50% to exposures in category 1, and 70% to exposures in category 2, the EL value for exposures in category 1 shall be 0%, and for exposures in category 2 shall be 0.4%.

32.   The expected loss amounts for equity exposures where the risk weighted exposure amounts are calculated according to the methods set out in points 19 to 21, shall be calculated according to the following formula:

Expected loss amount = EL × exposure value

The EL values shall be the following:

Expected loss (EL) = 0.8% for private equity exposures in sufficiently diversified portfolios

Expected loss (EL) = 0.8% for exchange traded equity exposures

Expected loss (EL) = 2.4% for all other equity exposures.

33.   The expected loss amounts for equity exposures where the risk weighted exposure amounts are calculated according to the methods set out in points 22 to 24 shall be calculated according to the following formulae:

Expected loss (EL) = PD × LGD and

Expected loss amount = EL × exposure value

34.   The expected loss amounts for equity exposures where the risk weighted exposure amounts are calculated according to the methods set out in points 25 to 26 shall be 0%.

35.   The expected loss amounts for dilution risk of purchased receivables shall be calculated according to the following formula:

Expected loss (EL) = PD × LGD and

Expected loss amount = EL × exposure value

4. TREATMENT OF EXPECTED LOSS AMOUNTS

36.   The expected loss amounts calculated in accordance with points 30, 31 and 35 shall be subtracted from the sum of value adjustments and provisions related to these exposures. Discounts on balance sheet exposures purchased when in default according to Part 3, point 1 shall be treated in the same manner as value adjustments. Expected loss amounts for securitised exposures and value adjustments and provisions related to these exposures shall not be included in this calculation.

PART 2
PD, LGD AND MATURITY

1.   The input parameters PD, LGD and maturity value (M) into the calculation of risk weighted exposure amounts and expected loss amounts specified in Part 1 shall be those estimated by the credit institution in accordance with Part 4, subject to the following provisions.

1. EXPOSURES TO CORPORATES, INSTITUTIONS AND CENTRAL GOVERNMENTS AND CENTRAL BANKS

1.1. PD

2.   The PD of an exposure to a corporate or an institution shall be at least 0.03%.

3.   For purchased corporate receivables in respect of which a credit institution cannot demonstrate that its PD estimates meet the minimum requirements set out in Part 4, the PDs for these exposures shall be determined according to the following methods: for senior claims on purchased corporate receivables PD shall be the credit institutions estimate of EL divided by LGD for these receivables. For subordinated claims on purchased corporate receivables PD shall be the credit institution's estimate of EL. If a credit institution is permitted to use own LGD estimates for corporate exposures and it can decompose its EL estimates for purchased corporate receivables into PDs and LGDs in a reliable manner, the PD estimate may be used

4.   The PD of obligors in default shall be 100%.

5.   Credit institutions may recognise unfunded credit protection in the PD in accordance with the provisions of Articles 90 to 93. For dilution risk, however, competent authorities may recognise as eligible unfunded credit protection providers other than those indicated in Annex VIII, Part 1.

6.   Credit institutions using own LGD estimates may recognise unfunded credit protection by adjusting PDs subject to point 10.

7.   For dilution risk of purchased corporate receivables, PD shall be set equal to EL estimate for dilution risk. If a credit institution is permitted to use own LGD estimates for corporate exposures and it can decompose its EL estimates for dilution risk of purchased corporate receivables into PDs and LGDs in a reliable manner, the PD estimate may be used. Credit institutions may recognise unfunded credit protection in the PD in accordance with the provisions of Articles 90 to 93. Competent authorities may recognise as eligible unfunded credit protection providers other than those indicated in Annex VIII, Part 1. If a credit institution is permitted to use own LGD estimates for dilution risk of purchased corporate receivables, it may recognise unfunded credit protection by adjusting PDs subject of point 10.

1.2. LGD

8.   Credit institutions shall use the following LGD values:

(a)   Senior exposures without eligible collateral: 45%;

(b)   Subordinated exposures without eligible collateral: 75%;

(c)   Credit institutions may recognise funded and unfunded credit protection in the LGD in accordance with Articles 90 to 93;

(d)   Covered bonds as defined in Annex VI, Part 1, points 68 to 70 may be assigned an LGD value of 12.5%;

(e)   For senior purchased corporate receivables exposures where a credit institution cannot demonstrate that its PD estimates meet the minimum requirements set out in Part 4: 45%;

(f)   For subordinated purchased corporate receivables exposures where a credit institution cannot demonstrate that its PD estimates meet the minimum requirements set out in Part 4: 100%; and

(g)   For dilution risk of purchased corporate receivables: 75%.

Until 31 December 2010, covered bonds as defined in Annex VI, Part 1, points 68 to 70 may be assigned an LGD value of 11.25% if:

—   assets as set out in Annex VI, Part 1, point 68(a) to (c) collateralising the bonds all qualify for credit quality step 1 as set out in that Annex;

—   where assets set out in Annex VI, Part 1, point 68(d) and (e) are used as collateral, the respective upper limits laid down in each of those points is 10% of the nominal amount of the outstanding issue;

—   assets as set out in Annex VI, Part 1, point 68(f) are not used as collateral; or

—   the covered bonds are the subject of a credit assessment by a nominated ECAI, and the ECAI places them in the most favourable category of credit assessment that the ECAI could make in respect of covered bonds.

By 31 December 2010, this derogation shall be reviewed and consequent to such review the Commission may make proposals in accordance with the procedure referred to in Article 151(2).

9.   Notwithstanding point 8, for dilution and default risk if a credit institution is permitted to use own LGD estimates for corporate exposures and it can decompose its EL estimates for purchased corporate receivables into PDs and LGDs in a reliable manner, the LGD estimate for purchased corporate receivables may be used.

10.   Notwithstanding point 8, if a credit institution is permitted to use own LGD estimates for exposures to corporates, institutions, central governments and central banks, unfunded credit protection may be recognised by adjusting PD and/or LGD subject to minimum requirements as specified in Part 4 and approval of competent authorities. A credit institution shall not assign guaranteed exposures an adjusted PD or LGD such that the adjusted risk weight would be lower than that of a comparable, direct exposure to the guarantor.

11.   Notwithstanding points 8 and 10, for the purposes of Part 1, point 4, the LGD of a comparable direct exposure to the protection provider shall either be the LGD associated with an unhedged facility to the guarantor or the unhedged facility of the obligor, depending upon whether in the event both the guarantor and obligor default during the life of the hedged transaction, available evidence and the structure of the guarantee indicate that the amount recovered would depend on the financial condition of the guarantor or obligor, respectively.

1.3. Maturity

12.   Subject to point 13, credit institutions shall assign to exposures arising from repurchase transactions or securities or commodities lending or borrowing transactions a maturity value (M)

of 0.5 years and to all other exposures an M of 2.5 years. Competent authorities may require all credit institutions in their jurisdiction to use M for each exposure as set out under point 13.

13.   Credit institutions permitted to use own LGDs and/or own conversion factors for exposures to corporates, institutions or central governments and central banks shall calculate M for each of these exposures as set out in (a) to (e) and subject to points 14 to 16. In all cases, M shall be no greater than 5 years:

(a)   For an instrument subject to a cash flow schedule, M shall be calculated according to the following formula:

$$M = MAX\left\{ 1; MIN\left\{ \sum_t t^* CF_t / \sum_t CF_t, 5 \right\} \right\}$$

where CF_t denotes the cash flows (principal, interest payments and fees) contractually payable by the obligor in period t;

(b)   For derivatives subject to a master netting agreement, M shall be the weighted average remaining maturity of the exposure, where M shall be at least 1 year. The notional amount of each exposure shall be used for weighting the maturity;

(c)   For exposures arising from fully or nearly-fully collateralised derivative instruments (listed in Annex IV) transactions and fully or nearly-fully collateralised margin lending transactions which are subject to a master netting agreement, M shall be the weighted average remaining maturity of the transactions where M shall be at least 10 days. The notional amount of each transaction shall be used for weighting the maturity;

(d)   If a credit institution is permitted to use own PD estimates for purchased corporate receivables, for drawn amounts M shall equal the purchased receivables exposure weighted average maturity, where M shall be at least 90 days. This same value of M shall also be used for undrawn amounts under a committed purchase facility provided the facility contains effective covenants, early amortisation triggers, or other features that protect the purchasing credit institution against a significant deterioration in the quality of the future receivables it is required to purchase over the facility's term. Absent such effective protections, M for undrawn amounts shall be calculated as the sum of the longest-dated potential receivable under the purchase agreement and the remaining maturity of the purchase facility, where M shall be at least 90 days;

(e)   For any other instrument than those mentioned in this point or when a credit institution is not in a position to calculate M as set out in (a), M shall be the maximum remaining time (in years) that the obligor is permitted to take to fully discharge its contractual obligations, where M shall be at least 1 year;

(f)   for credit institutions using the Internal Model Method set out in Annex III, Part 6 to calculate the exposure values, M shall be calculated for exposures to which they apply this method and for which the maturity of the longest-dated contract contained in the netting set is greater than one year according to the following formula:

$$M = MIN\left(\frac{\sum_{k=1}^{tk \leq 1\,year} EffectiveEE_k^* \Delta t_k^* df_k + \sum_{tk > 1\,year}^{maturity} EE_k^* \Delta t_k^* df_k}{\sum_{k=1}^{tk \leq 1\,year} EffectiveEE_k^* \Delta t_k^* df_k} ; 5 \right)$$

where:
df = the risk-free discount factor for future time period tk and the remaining symbols are defined in Annex III, Part 6.

Notwithstanding the first paragraph of point 13(f), a credit institution that uses an internal model to calculate a one-sided credit valuation adjustment (CVA) may use, subject to the approval of the competent authorities, the effective credit duration estimated by the internal model as M.

Subject to paragraph 14, for netting sets in which all contracts have an original maturity of less than one year the formula in point (a) shall apply; and

(g)   for the purposes of Part 1, point 4, M shall be the effective maturity of the credit protection but at least 1 year.

14.   Notwithstanding point 13(a), (b), (d) and (e), M shall be at least one-day for:
—   fully or nearly-fully collateralised derivative instruments listed in Annex IV;
—   fully or nearly-fully collateralised margin lending transactions; and
—   repurchase transactions, securities or commodities lending or borrowing transactions

provided the documentation requires daily re-margining and daily revaluation and includes provisions that allow for the prompt liquidation or setoff of collateral in the event of default or failure to re-margin.

In addition, for other short-term exposures specified by the competent authorities which are not Part of the credit institution's ongoing financing of the obligor, M shall be at least one-day. A careful review of the particular circumstances shall be made in each case.

15. The competent authorities may allow for exposures to corporates situated in the Community and having consolidated sales and consolidated assets of less than EUR 500 million the use of M as set out in point 12. Competent authorities may replace EUR 500 million total assets with EUR 1000 million total assets for corporates which primarily invest in real estate.

16. Maturity mismatches shall be treated as specified in Articles 90 to 93.

2. RETAIL EXPOSURES

2.1. PD

17. The PD of an exposure shall be at least 0.03%.

18. The PD of obligors or, where an obligation approach is used, of exposures in default shall be 100%.

19. For dilution risk of purchased receivables PD shall be set equal to EL estimates for dilution risk. If a credit institution can decompose its EL estimates for dilution risk of purchased receivables into PDs and LGDs in a reliable manner, the PD estimate may be used.

20. Unfunded credit protection may be recognised as eligible by adjusting PDs subject to point 22. For dilution risk, where credit institutions do not use own estimates of LGDs, this shall be subject to compliance with Articles 90 to 93; for this purpose competent authorities may recognise as eligible unfunded protection providers other than those indicated in Annex VIII, Part 1.

2.2. LGD

21. Credit institutions shall provide own estimates of LGDs subject to minimum requirements as specified in Part 4 and approval of competent authorities. For dilution risk of purchased receivables, an LGD value of 75% shall be used. If a credit institution can decompose its EL estimates for dilution risk of purchased receivables into PDs and LGDs in a reliable manner, the LGD estimate may be used.

22. Unfunded credit protection may be recognised as eligible by adjusting PD or LGD estimates subject to minimum requirements as specified in Part 4, points 99 to 104 and approval of competent authorities either in support of an individual exposure or a pool of exposures. A credit institution shall not assign guaranteed exposures an adjusted PD or LGD such that the adjusted risk weight would be lower than that of a comparable, direct exposure to the guarantor.

23. Notwithstanding point 22, for the purposes of Part 1, point 11 the LGD of a comparable direct exposure to the protection provider shall either be the LGD associated with an unhedged facility to the guarantor or the unhedged facility of the obligor, depending upon whether, in the event both the guarantor and obligor default during the life of the hedged transaction, available evidence and the structure of the guarantee indicate that the amount recovered would depend on the financial condition of the guarantor or obligor, respectively.

3. EQUITY EXPOSURES SUBJECT TO PD/LGD METHOD

3.1. PD

24. PDs shall be determined according to the methods for corporate exposures.
   (a) 0.09% for exchange traded equity exposures where the investment is part of a long-term customer relationship;
   (b) 0.09% for non-exchange traded equity exposures where the returns on the investment are based on regular and periodic cash flows not derived from capital gains;
   (c) 0.40% for exchange traded equity exposures including other short positions as set out in part 1, point 20; and
   (d) 1.25% for all other equity exposures including other short positions as set out in Part 1, point 20.

3.2. LGD

25. Private equity exposures in sufficiently diversified portfolios may be assigned an LGD of 65%.

26. All other exposures shall be assigned an LGD of 90%.

3.3. Maturity

27. M assigned to all exposures shall be 5 years.

PART 3
EXPOSURE VALUE

1. EXPOSURES TO CORPORATES, INSTITUTIONS, CENTRAL GOVERNMENTS AND CENTRAL BANKS AND RETAIL EXPOSURES.

1. Unless noted otherwise, the exposure value of on-balance sheet exposures shall be measured gross of value adjustments. This rule also applies to assets purchased at a price different than the amount owed. For purchased assets, the difference between the amount owed and the net value recorded on the balance-sheet of credit institutions is denoted discount if the amount owed is larger, and premium if it is smaller.

2. Where credit institutions use Master netting agreements in relation to repurchase transactions or securities or commodities lending or borrowing transactions, the exposure value shall be calculated in accordance with Articles 90 to 93.

3. For on-balance sheet netting of loans and deposits, credit institutions shall apply for the calculation of the exposure value the methods set out in Articles 90 to 93.

4. The exposure value for leases shall be the discounted minimum lease payments.

"Minimum lease payments" are the payments over the lease term that the lessee is or can be required to make and any bargain option (i e option the exercise of which is reasonably certain). Any guaranteed residual value fulfilling the set of conditions in Annex VIII, Part 1, points 26 to 28 regarding the eligibility of protection providers as well as the minimum requirements for recognising other types of guarantees provided in Annex VIII, Part 2, points 14 to 19 should also be included in the minimum lease payments.

5. In the case of any item listed in Annex IV, the exposure value shall be determined by the methods set out in Annex III.

6. The exposure value for the calculation of risk weighted exposure amounts of purchased receivables shall be the outstanding amount minus the capital requirements for dilution risk prior to credit risk mitigation.

7. Where an exposure takes the form of securities or commodities sold, posted or lent under repurchase transactions or securities or commodities lending or borrowing transactions, long settlement transactions and margin lending transactions, the exposure value shall be the value of the securities or commodities determined in accordance with Article 74. Where the Financial Collateral Comprehensive Method as set out under Annex VIII, Part 3 is used, the exposure value shall be increased by the volatility adjustment appropriate to such securities or commodities, as set out therein. The exposure value of repurchase transactions, securities or commodities lending or borrowing transactions, long settlement transactions and margin lending transactions may be determined either in accordance with Annex III or Annex VIII, Part 3, points 12 to 21.

8. Notwithstanding point 7, the exposure value of credit risk exposures outstanding, as determined by the competent authorities, with a central counterparty shall be determined in accordance with Annex III, Part 2, point 6, provided that the central counterparty's counterparty credit risk exposures with all participants in its arrangements are fully collateralised on a daily basis.

9. The exposure value for the following items shall be calculated as the committed but undrawn amount multiplied by a conversion factor.

Credit institutions shall use the following conversion factors:
- (a) for credit lines which are uncommitted, that are unconditionally cancellable at any time by the credit institution without prior notice, or that effectively provide for automatic cancellation due to deterioration in a borrower's credit worthiness, a conversion factor of 0% shall apply. To apply a conversion factor of 0%, credit institutions shall actively monitor the financial condition of the obligor, and their internal control systems shall enable them to immediately detect a deterioration in the credit quality of the obligor. Undrawn retail credit lines may be considered as unconditionally cancellable if the terms permit the credit institution to cancel them to the full extent allowable under consumer protection and related legislation;
- (b) for short-term letters of credit arising from the movement of goods, a conversion factor of 20% shall apply for both the issuing and confirming institutions;
- (c) for undrawn purchase commitments for revolving purchased receivables that are unconditionally cancellable or that effectively provide for automatic cancellation at any time by the institution without prior notice, a conversion factor of 0% shall apply. To apply a conversion factor of 0%, credit institutions shall actively monitor the financial condition of the obligor, and their internal control systems shall enable them to immediately detect a deterioration in the credit quality of the obligor;
- (d) for other credit lines, note issuance facilities (NIFs), and revolving underwriting facilities (RUFs), a conversion factor of 75% shall apply; and
- (e) credit institutions which meet the minimum requirements for the use of own estimates of

conversion factors as specified in Part 4 may use their own estimates of conversion factors across different product types as mentioned in points (a) to (d), subject to approval of the competent authorities.

10.   Where a commitment refers to the extension of another commitment, the lower of the two conversion factors associated with the individual commitment shall be used.

11.   For all off-balance sheet items other than those mentioned in points 1 to 9, the exposure value shall be the following percentage of its value:

—   100% if it is a full risk item,
—   50% if it is a medium-risk item,
—   20% if it is a medium/low-risk item, and
—   0% if it is a low-risk item.

For the purposes of this point the off-balance sheet items shall be assigned to risk categories as indicated in Annex II.

2. EQUITY EXPOSURES

12.   The exposure value shall be the value presented in the financial statements. Admissible equity exposure measures are the following:

(a)   For investments held at fair value with changes in value flowing directly through income and into own funds, the exposure value is the fair value presented in the balance sheet;

(b)   For investments held at fair value with changes in value not flowing through income but into a tax-adjusted separate component of equity, the exposure value is the fair value presented in the balance sheet; and

(c)   For investments held at cost or at the lower of cost or market, the exposure value is the cost or market value presented in the balance sheet.

3. OTHER NON CREDIT-OBLIGATION ASSETS

13.   The exposure value of other non credit-obligation assets shall be the value presented in the financial statements.

PART 4
MINIMUM REQUIREMENTS FOR IRB APPROACH

1. RATING SYSTEMS

1.   A "rating system" shall comprise all of the methods, processes, controls, data collection and IT systems that support the assessment of credit risk, the assignment of exposures to grades or pools (rating), and the quantification of default and loss estimates for a certain type of exposure.

2.   If a credit institution uses multiple rating systems, the rationale for assigning an obligor or a transaction to a rating system shall be documented and applied in a manner that appropriately reflects the level of risk.

3.   Assignment criteria and processes shall be periodically reviewed to determine whether they remain appropriate for the current portfolio and external conditions.

1.1. Structure of rating systems

4.   Where a credit institution uses direct estimates of risk parameters these may be seen as the outputs of grades on a continuous rating scale.

1.1.1. Exposures to corporates, institutions and central governments and central banks

5.   A rating system shall take into account obligor and transaction risk characteristics.

6.   A rating system shall have an obligor rating scale which reflects exclusively quantification of the risk of obligor default. The obligor rating scale shall have a minimum of 7 grades for non-defaulted obligors and one for defaulted obligors.

7.   An "obligor grade" shall mean a risk category within a rating system's obligor rating scale, to which obligors are assigned on the basis of a specified and distinct set of rating criteria, from which estimates of PD are derived. A credit institution shall document the relationship between obligor grades in terms of the level of default risk each grade implies and the criteria used to distinguish that level of default risk.

8.   Credit institutions with portfolios concentrated in a particular market segment and range of default risk shall have enough obligor grades within that range to avoid undue concentrations of obligors in a particular grade. Significant concentrations within a single grade shall be supported by convincing empirical evidence that the obligor grade covers a reasonably narrow PD band and that the default risk posed by all obligors in the grade falls within that band.

9.   To qualify for recognition by the competent authorities of the use for capital requirement calculation of own estimates of LGDs, a rating system shall incorporate a distinct facility rating scale which exclusively reflects LGD-related transaction characteristics.

10.   A "facility grade" shall mean a risk category within a rating system's facility scale, to which exposures are assigned on the basis of a specified and distinct set of rating criteria from which own estimates of LGDs are derived. The grade definition shall include both a description of how exposures are assigned to the grade and of the criteria used to distinguish the level of risk across grades.

11.   Significant concentrations within a single facility grade shall be supported by convincing empirical evidence that the facility grade covers a reasonably narrow LGD band, respectively, and that the risk posed by all exposures in the grade falls within that band.

12.   Credit institutions using the methods set out in Part 1, point 6 for assigning risk weights for specialised lending exposures are exempt from the requirement to have an obligor rating scale which reflects exclusively quantification of the risk of obligor default for these exposures. Notwithstanding point 6, these institutions shall have for these exposures at least 4 grades for non-defaulted obligors and at least one grade for defaulted obligors.

1.1.2. Retail exposures

13.   Rating systems shall reflect both obligor and transaction risk, and shall capture all relevant obligor and transaction characteristics.

14.   The level of risk differentiation shall ensure that the number of exposures in a given grade or pool is sufficient to allow for meaningful quantification and validation of the loss characteristics at the grade or pool level. The distribution of exposures and obligors across grades or pools shall be such as to avoid excessive concentrations.

15.   Credit institutions shall demonstrate that the process of assigning exposures to grades or pools provides for a meaningful differentiation of risk, provides for a grouping of sufficiently homogenous exposures, and allows for accurate and consistent estimation of loss characteristics at grade or pool level. For purchased receivables the grouping shall reflect the seller's underwriting practices and the heterogeneity of its customers.

16.   Credit institutions shall consider the following risk drivers when assigning exposures to grades or pools.
   (a)   Obligor risk characteristics;
   (b)   Transaction risk characteristics, including product or collateral types or both. Credit institutions shall explicitly address cases where several exposures benefit from the same collateral; and
   (c)   Delinquency, unless the credit institution demonstrates to its competent authority that delinquency is not a material risk drivers for the exposure;

1.2. Assignment to grades or pools

17.   A credit institution shall have specific definitions, processes and criteria for assigning exposures to grades or pools within a rating system.
   (a)   The grade or pool definitions and criteria shall be sufficiently detailed to allow those charged with assigning ratings to consistently assign obligors or facilities posing similar risk to the same grade or pool. This consistency shall exist across lines of business, departments and geographic locations;
   (b)   The documentation of the rating process shall allow third parties to understand the assignments of exposures to grades or pools, to replicate grade and pool assignments and to evaluate the appropriateness of the assignments to a grade or a pool; and
   (c)   The criteria shall also be consistent with the credit institution's internal lending standards and its policies for handling troubled obligors and facilities.

18.   A credit institution shall take all relevant information into account in assigning obligors and facilities to grades or pools. Information shall be current and shall enable the credit institution to forecast the future performance of the exposure. The less information a credit institution has, the more conservative shall be its assignments of exposures to obligor and facility grades or pools. If a credit institution uses an external rating as a primary factor determining an internal rating assignment, the credit institution shall ensure that it considers other relevant information.

1.3. Assignment of exposures

1.3.1. Exposures to corporates, institutions and central governments and central banks

19.   Each obligor shall be assigned to an obligor grade as Part of the credit approval process.

20.   For those credit institutions permitted to use own estimates of LGDs and/or conversion factors, each exposure shall also be assigned to a facility grade as Part of the credit approval process.

21.   Credit institutions using the methods set out in Part 1, point 6 for assigning risk weights for specialised lending exposures shall assign each of these exposures to a grade in accordance with point 12.

22. Each separate legal entity to which the credit institution is exposed shall be separately rated. A credit institution shall demonstrate to its competent authority that it has acceptable policies regarding the treatment of individual obligor clients and groups of connected clients.

23. Separate exposures to the same obligor shall be assigned to the same obligor grade, irrespective of any differences in the nature of each specific transaction. Exceptions, where separate exposures are allowed to result in multiple grades for the same obligor are:

(a) country transfer risk, this being dependent on whether the exposures are denominated in local or foreign currency;

(b) where the treatment of associated guarantees to an exposure may be reflected in an adjusted assignment to an obligor grade; and

(c) where consumer protection, bank secrecy or other legislation prohibit the exchange of client data.

1.3.2. Retail exposures

24. Each exposure shall be assigned to a grade or a pool as part of the credit approval process.

1.3.3. Overrides

25. For grade and pool assignments credit institutions shall document the situations in which human judgement may override the inputs or outputs of the assignment process and the personnel responsible for approving these overrides. Credit institutions shall document these overrides and the personnel responsible. Credit institutions shall analyse the performance of the exposures whose assignments have been overridden. This analysis shall include assessment of the performance of exposures whose rating has been overridden by a particular person, accounting for all the responsible personnel.

1.4. Integrity of assignment process

1.4.1. Exposures to corporates, institutions and central governments and central banks

26. Assignments and periodic reviews of assignments shall be completed or approved by an independent party that does not directly benefit from decisions to extend the credit.

27. Credit institutions shall update assignments at least annually. High risk obligors and problem exposures shall be subject to more frequent review. Credit institutions shall undertake a new assignment if material information on the obligor or exposure becomes available.

28. A credit institution shall have an effective process to obtain and update relevant information on obligor characteristics that affect PDs, and on transaction characteristics that affect LGDs and/or conversion factors.

1.4.2. Retail exposures

29. A credit institution shall at least annually update obligor and facility assignments or review the loss characteristics and delinquency status of each identified risk pool, whichever applicable. A credit institution shall also at least annually review in a representative sample the status of individual exposures within each pool as a means of ensuring that exposures continue to be assigned to the correct pool.

1.5. Use of models

30. If a credit institution uses statistical models and other mechanical methods to assign exposures to obligors or facilities grades or pools, then:

(a) the credit institution shall demonstrate to its competent authority that the model has good predictive power and that capital requirements are not distorted as a result of its use. The input variables shall form a reasonable and effective basis for the resulting predictions. The model shall not have material biases;

(b) the credit institution shall have in place a process for vetting data inputs into the model, which includes an assessment of the accuracy, completeness and appropriateness of the data;

(c) the credit institution shall demonstrate that the data used to build the model is representative of the population of the credit institution's actual obligors or exposures;

(d) the credit institution shall have a regular cycle of model validation that includes monitoring of model performance and stability; review of model specification; and testing of model outputs against outcomes; and

(e) the credit institution shall complement the statistical model by human judgement and human oversight to review model-based assignments and to ensure that the models are used appropriately. Review procedures shall aim at finding and limiting errors associated with model weaknesses. Human judgements shall take into account all relevant information not considered by the model. The credit institution shall document how human judgement and model results are to be combined.

1.6. Documentation of rating systems

31.   The credit institutions shall document the design and operational details of its rating systems. The documentation shall evidence compliance with the minimum requirements in this part, and address topics including portfolio differentiation, rating criteria, responsibilities of parties that rate obligors and exposures, frequency of assignment reviews, and management oversight of the rating process.

32.   The credit institution shall document the rationale for and analysis supporting its choice of rating criteria. A credit institution shall document all major changes in the risk rating process, and such documentation shall support identification of changes made to the risk rating process subsequent to the last review by the competent authorities. The organisation of rating assignment including the rating assignment process and the internal control structure shall also be documented.

33.   The credit institutions shall document the specific definitions of default and loss used internally and demonstrate consistency with the definitions set out in this Directive.

34.   If the credit institution employs statistical models in the rating process, the credit institution shall document their methodologies. This material shall:
- (a)   provide a detailed outline of the theory, assumptions and/or mathematical and empirical basis of the assignment of estimates to grades, individual obligors, exposures, or pools, and the data source(s) used to estimate the model;
- (b)   establish a rigorous statistical process (including out-of-time and out-of-sample performance tests) for validating the model; and
- (c)   indicate any circumstances under which the model does not work effectively.

35.   Use of a model obtained from a third-party vendor that claims proprietary technology is not a justification for exemption from documentation or any other of the requirements for rating systems. The burden is on the credit institution to satisfy competent authorities.

1.7. Data maintenance

36.   Credit institutions shall collect and store data on aspects of their internal ratings as required under Articles 145 to 149.

1.7.1. Exposures to corporates, institutions and central governments and central banks

37.   Credit institutions shall collect and store:
- (a)   complete rating histories on obligors and recognised guarantors;
- (b)   the dates the ratings were assigned;
- (c)   the key data and methodology used to derive the rating;
- (d)   the person responsible for the rating assignment;
- (e)   the identity of obligors and exposures that defaulted;
- (f)   the date and circumstances of such defaults; and
- (g)   data on the PDs and realised default rates associated with rating grades and ratings migration;

Credit institutions not using own estimates of LGDs and/or conversion factors shall collect and store data on comparisons of realised LGDs to the values as set out in Part 2, point 8 and realised conversion factors to the values as set out in Part 3, point 9.

38.   Credit institutions using own estimates of LGDs and/or conversion factors shall collect and store:
- (a)   complete histories of data on the facility ratings and LGD and conversion factor estimates associated with each rating scale;
- (b)   the dates the ratings were assigned and the estimates were done;
- (c)   the key data and methodology used to derive the facility ratings and LGD and conversion factor estimates;
- (d)   the person who assigned the facility rating and the person who provided LGD and conversion factor estimates;
- (e)   data on the estimated and realised LGDs and conversion factors associated with each defaulted exposure;
- (f)   data on the LGD of the exposure before and after evaluation of the effects of a guarantee/or credit derivative, for those credit institutions that reflect the credit risk mitigating effects of guarantees or credit derivatives through LGD; and
- (g)   data on the components of loss for each defaulted exposure.

1.7.2. Retail exposures

39.   Credit institutions shall collect and store:
- (a)   data used in the process of allocating exposures to grades or pools;
- (b)   data on the estimated PDs, LGDs and conversion factors associated with grades or pools of exposures;
- (c)   the identity of obligors and exposures that defaulted;

(d)   for defaulted exposures, data on the grades or pools to which the exposure was assigned over the year prior to default and the realised outcomes on LGD and conversion factor; and

(e)   data on loss rates for qualifying revolving retail exposures.

1.8. Stress tests used in assessment of capital adequacy

40.   A credit institution shall have in place sound stress testing processes for use in the assessment of its capital adequacy. Stress testing shall involve identifying possible events or future changes in economic conditions that could have unfavourable effects on a credit institution's credit exposures and assessment of the credit institution's ability to withstand such changes.

41.   A credit institution shall regularly perform a credit risk stress test to assess the effect of certain specific conditions on its total capital requirements for credit risk. The test shall be one chosen by the credit institution, subject to supervisory review. The test to be employed shall be meaningful and reasonably conservative, considering at least the effect of mild recession scenarios. A credit institution shall assess migration in its ratings under the stress test scenarios. Stressed portfolios shall contain the vast majority of a credit institution's total exposure.

42.   Credit institutions using the treatment set out in Part 1, point 4 shall consider as Part of their stress testing framework the impact of a deterioration in the credit quality of protection providers, in particular the impact of protection providers falling outside the eligibility criteria.

2. RISK QUANTIFICATION

43.   In determining the risk parameters to be associated with rating grades or pools, credit institutions shall apply the following requirements.

2.1. Definition of default

44.   A "default" shall be considered to have occurred with regard to a particular obligor when either or both of the two following events has taken place:

(a)   the credit institution considers that the obligor is unlikely to pay its credit obligations to the credit institution, the parent undertaking or any of its subsidiaries in full, without recourse by the credit institution to actions such as realising security (if held);

(b)   the obligor is past due more than 90 days on any material credit obligation to the credit institution, the parent undertaking or any of its subsidiaries.

For overdrafts, days past due commence once an obligor has breached an advised limit, has been advised a limit smaller than current outstandings, or has drawn credit without authorisation and the underlying amount is material.

An "advised limit" shall mean a limit which has been brought to the knowledge of the obligor.

Days past due for credit cards commence on the minimum payment due date.

In the case of retail exposures and exposures to public sector entities (PSE) the competent authorities shall set a number of days past due as specified in point 48.

In the case of corporate exposures the competent authorities may set a number of days past due as specified in Article 154(7).

In the case of retail exposures credit institutions may apply the definition of default at a facility level.

In all cases, the exposure past due shall be above a threshold defined by the competent authorities and which reflects a reasonable level of risk.

45.   Elements to be taken as indications of unlikeliness to pay shall include:

(a)   The credit institution puts the credit obligation on non-accrued status,

(b)   The credit institution makes a value adjustment resulting from a significant perceived decline in credit quality subsequent to the credit institution taking on the exposure,

(c)   The credit institution sells the credit obligation at a material credit-related economic loss,

(d)   The credit institution consents to a distressed restructuring of the credit obligation where this is likely to result in a diminished financial obligation caused by the material forgiveness, or postponement, of principal, interest or (where relevant) fees. This includes, in the case of equity exposures assessed under a PD/LGD Approach, distressed restructuring of the equity itself,

(e)   The credit institution has filed for the obligor's bankruptcy or a similar order in respect of an obligor's credit obligation to the credit institution, the parent undertaking or any of its subsidiaries, and

(f)   The obligor has sought or has been placed in bankruptcy or similar protection where this would avoid or delay repayment of a credit obligation to the credit institution, the parent undertaking or any of its subsidiaries.

46. Credit institutions that use external data that is not itself consistent with the definition of default, shall demonstrate to their competent authorities that appropriate adjustments have been made to achieve broad equivalence with the definition of default.

47. If the credit institution considers that a previously defaulted exposure is such that no trigger of default continues to apply, the credit institution shall rate the obligor or facility as they would for a non-defaulted exposure. Should the definition of default subsequently be triggered, another default would be deemed to have occurred.

48. For retail and PSE exposures, the competent authorities of each Member State shall set the exact number of days past due that all credit institutions in its jurisdiction shall abide by under the definition of default set out in point 44, for exposures to such counterparts situated within this Member State. The specific number shall fall within 90–180 days and may differ across product lines. For exposures to such counterparts situated in the territories of other Member States, the competent authorities shall set a number of days past due which is not higher than the number set by the competent authority of the respective Member State.

2.2. Overall requirements for estimation

49. A credit institution's own estimates of the risk parameters PD, LGD, conversion factor and EL shall incorporate all relevant data, information and methods. The estimates shall be derived using both historical experience and empirical evidence, and not based purely on judgemental considerations. The estimates shall be plausible and intuitive and shall be based on the material drivers of the respective risk parameters. The less data a credit institution has, the more conservative it shall be in its estimation.

50. The credit institution shall be able to provide a breakdown of its loss experience in terms of default frequency, LGD, conversion factor, or loss where EL estimates are used, by the factors it sees as the drivers of the respective risk parameters. The credit institution shall demonstrate that its estimates are representative of long run experience.

51. Any changes in lending practice or the process for pursuing recoveries over the observation periods referred to in points 66, 71, 82, 86, 93 and 95 shall be taken into account. A credit institution's estimates shall reflect the implications of technical advances and new data and other information, as it becomes available. Credit institutions shall review their estimates when new information comes to light but at least on an annual basis.

52. The population of exposures represented in the data used for estimation, the lending standards used when the data was generated and other relevant characteristics shall be comparable with those of the credit institution's exposures and standards. The credit institution shall also demonstrate that the economic or market conditions that underlie the data are relevant to current and foreseeable conditions. The number of exposures in the sample and the data period used for quantification shall be sufficient to provide the credit institution with confidence in the accuracy and robustness of its estimates.

53. For purchased receivables the estimates shall reflect all relevant information available to the purchasing credit institution regarding the quality of the underlying receivables, including data for similar pools provided by the seller, by the purchasing credit institution, or by external sources. The purchasing credit institution shall evaluate any data relied upon which is provided by the seller.

54. A credit institution shall add to its estimates a margin of conservatism that is related to the expected range of estimation errors. Where methods and data are less satisfactory and the expected range of errors is larger, the margin of conservatism shall be larger.

55. If credit institutions use different estimates for the calculation of risk weights and for internal purposes, it shall be documented and their reasonableness shall be demonstrated to the competent authority.

56. If credit institutions can demonstrate to their competent authorities that for data that have been collected prior to the date of implementation of this Directive appropriate adjustments have been made to achieve broad equivalence with the definitions of default or loss, competent authorities may allow the credit institutions some flexibility in the application of the required standards for data.

57. If a credit institution uses data that is pooled across credit institutions it shall demonstrate that:
   (a)   the rating systems and criteria of other credit institutions in the pool are similar with its own;
   (b)   the pool is representative of the portfolio for which the pooled data is used; and
   (c)   the pooled data is used consistently over time by the credit institution for its estimates.

58. If a credit institution uses data that is pooled across credit institutions, it shall remain responsible for the integrity of its rating systems. The credit institution shall demonstrate to the competent authority that it has sufficient in-house understanding of its rating systems, including effective ability to monitor and audit the rating process.

2.2.1. Requirements specific to PD estimation

Exposures to corporates, institutions and central governments and central banks

59.   Credit institutions shall estimate PDs by obligor grade from long run averages of one-year default rates.

60.   For purchased corporate receivables credit institutions may estimate ELs by obligor grade from long run averages of one-year realised default rates.

61.   If a credit institution derives long run average estimates of PDs and LGDs for purchased corporate receivables from an estimate of EL, and an appropriate estimate of PD or LGD, the process for estimating total losses shall meet the overall standards for estimation of PD and LGD set out in this part, and the outcome shall be consistent with the concept of LGD as set out in point 73.

62.   Credit institutions shall use PD estimation techniques only with supporting analysis. Credit institutions shall recognise the importance of judgmental considerations in combining results of techniques and in making adjustments for limitations of techniques and information.

63.   To the extent that a credit institution uses data on internal default experience for the estimation of PDs, it shall demonstrate in its analysis that the estimates are reflective of underwriting standards and of any differences in the rating system that generated the data and the current rating system. Where underwriting standards or rating systems have changed, the credit institution shall add a greater margin of conservatism in its estimate of PD.

64.   To the extent that a credit institution associates or maps its internal grades to the scale used by an ECAI or similar organisations and then attributes the default rate observed for the external organisation's grades to the credit institution's grades, mappings shall be based on a comparison of internal rating criteria to the criteria used by the external organisation and on a comparison of the internal and external ratings of any common obligors. Biases or inconsistencies in the mapping approach or underlying data shall be avoided. The external organisation's criteria underlying the data used for quantification shall be oriented to default risk only and not reflect transaction characteristics. The credit institution's analysis shall include a comparison of the default definitions used, subject to the requirements in points 44 to 48. The credit institution shall document the basis for the mapping.

65.   To the extent that a credit institution uses statistical default prediction models it is allowed to estimate PDs as the simple average of default-probability estimates for individual obligors in a given grade. The credit institution's use of default probability models for this purpose shall meet the standards specified in point 30.

66.   Irrespective of whether a credit institution is using external, internal, or pooled data sources, or a combination of the three, for its PD estimation, the length of the underlying historical observation period used shall be at least five years for at least one source. If the available observation period spans a longer period for any source, and this data is relevant, this longer period shall be used. This point also applies to the PD/LGD Approach to equity. Member States may allow credit institutions which are not permitted to use own estimates of LGDs or conversion factors to have, when they implement the IRB Approach, relevant data covering a period of two years. The period to be covered shall increase by one year each year until relevant data cover a period of five years.

Retail exposures

67.   Credit institutions shall estimate PDs by obligor grade or pool from long run averages of one-year default rates.

68.   Notwithstanding point 67, PD estimates may also be derived from realised losses and appropriate estimates of LGDs.

69.   Credit institutions shall regard internal data for assigning exposures to grades or pools as the primary source of information for estimating loss characteristics. Credit institutions are permitted to use external data (including pooled data) or statistical models for quantification provided a strong link can be demonstrated between:

    (a)   the credit institution's process of assigning exposures to grades or pools and the process used by the external data source; and

    (b)   the credit institution's internal risk profile and the composition of the external data.

For purchased retail receivables, credit institutions may use external and internal reference data. Credit institutions shall use all relevant data sources as points of comparison.

70.   If a credit institution derives long run average estimates of PD and LGD for retail from an estimate of total losses and an appropriate estimate of PD or LGD, the process for estimating total losses shall meet the overall standards for estimation of PD and LGD set out in this part, and the outcome shall be consistent with the concept of LGD as set out in point 73.

71.   Irrespective of whether a credit institution is using external, internal or pooled data sources or a combination of the three, for their estimation of loss characteristics, the length of the underlying historical observation period used shall be at least five years for at least one source. If the available

observation spans a longer period for any source, and these data are relevant, this longer period shall be used. A credit institution need not give equal importance to historic data if it can convince its competent authority that more recent data is a better predictor of loss rates. Member States may allow credit institutions to have, when they implement the IRB Approach, relevant data covering a period of two years. The period to be covered shall increase by one year each year until relevant data cover a period of five years.

72.   Credit institutions shall identify and analyse expected changes of risk parameters over the life of credit exposures (seasoning effects).

2.2.2. Requirements specific to own-LGD estimates

73.   Credit institutions shall estimate LGDs by facility grade or pool on the basis of the average realised LGDs by facility grade or pool using all observed defaults within the data sources (default weighted average).

74.   Credit institutions shall use LGD estimates that are appropriate for an economic downturn if those are more conservative than the long-run average. To the extent a rating system is expected to deliver realised LGDs at a constant level by grade or pool over time, credit institutions shall make adjustments to their estimates of risk parameters by grade or pool to limit the capital impact of an economic downturn.

75.   A credit institution shall consider the extent of any dependence between the risk of the obligor with that of the collateral or collateral provider. Cases where there is a significant degree of dependence shall be addressed in a conservative manner.

76.   Currency mismatches between the underlying obligation and the collateral shall be treated conservatively in the credit institution's assessment of LGD.

77.   To the extent that LGD estimates take into account the existence of collateral, these estimates shall not solely be based on the collateral's estimated market value. LGD estimates shall take into account the effect of the potential inability of credit institutions to expeditiously gain control of their collateral and liquidate it.

78.   To the extent that LGD estimates take into account the existence of collateral, credit institutions must establish internal requirements for collateral management, legal certainty and risk management that are generally consistent with those set out in Annex VIII, Part 2.

79.   To the extent that a credit institution recognises collateral for determining the exposure value for counterparty credit risk according to Annex III, Part 5 or 6, any amount expected to be recovered from the collateral shall not be taken into account in the LGD estimates.

80.   For the specific case of exposures already in default, the credit institution shall use the sum of its best estimate of expected loss for each exposure given current economic circumstances and exposure status and the possibility of additional unexpected losses during the recovery period.

81.   To the extent that unpaid late fees have been capitalised in the credit institution's income statement, they shall be added to the credit institution's measure of exposure and loss.

Exposures to corporates, institutions and central governments and central banks

82.   Estimates of LGD shall be based on data over a minimum of five years, increasing by one year each year after implementation until a minimum of seven years is reached, for at least one data source. If the available observation period spans a longer period for any source, and the data is relevant, this longer period shall be used.

Retail exposures

83.   Notwithstanding point 73, LGD estimates may be derived from realised losses and appropriate estimates of PDs.

84.   Notwithstanding point 89, credit institutions may reflect future drawings either in their conversion factors or in their LGD estimates.

85.   For purchased retail receivables credit institutions may use external and internal reference data to estimate LGDs.

86.   Estimates of LGD shall be based on data over a minimum of five years. Notwithstanding point 73, a credit institution needs not give equal importance to historic data if it can demonstrate to its competent authority that more recent data is a better predictor of loss rates. Member States may allow credit institutions to have, when they implement the IRB Approach, relevant data covering a period of two years. The period to be covered shall increase by one year each year until relevant data cover a period of five years.

2.2.3. Requirements specific to own-conversion factor estimates

87.   Credit institutions shall estimate conversion factors by facility grade or pool on the basis of the average realised conversion factors by facility grade or pool using all observed defaults within the data sources (default weighted average).

88.   Credit institutions shall use conversion factor estimates that are appropriate for an economic downturn if those are more conservative than the long-run average. To the extent a rating system is expected to deliver realised conversion factors at a constant level by grade or pool over time, credit institutions shall make adjustments to their estimates of risk parameters by grade or pool to limit the capital impact of an economic downturn.

89.   Credit institutions' estimates of conversion factors shall reflect the possibility of additional drawings by the obligor up to and after the time a default event is triggered.

The conversion factor estimate shall incorporate a larger margin of conservatism where a stronger positive correlation can reasonably be expected between the default frequency and the magnitude of conversion factor.

90.   In arriving at estimates of conversion factors credit institutions shall consider their specific policies and strategies adopted in respect of account monitoring and payment processing. Credit institutions shall also consider their ability and willingness to prevent further drawings in circumstances short of payment default, such as covenant violations or other technical default events.

91.   Credit institutions shall have adequate systems and procedures in place to monitor facility amounts, current outstandings against committed lines and changes in outstandings per obligor and per grade. The credit institution shall be able to monitor outstanding balances on a daily basis.

92.   If credit institutions use different estimates of conversion factors for the calculation of risk weighted exposure amounts and internal purposes it shall be documented and their reasonableness shall be demonstrated to the competent authority.

Exposures to corporates, institutions and central governments and central banks

93.   Estimates of conversion factors shall be based on data over a minimum of five years, increasing by one year each year after implementation until a minimum of seven years is reached, for at least one data source. If the available observation period spans a longer period for any source, and the data is relevant, this longer period shall be used.

Retail exposures

94.   Notwithstanding point 89, credit institutions may reflect future drawings either in their conversion factors or in their LGD estimates.

95.   Estimates of conversion factors shall be based on data over a minimum of five years. Notwithstanding point 87, a credit institution need not give equal importance to historic data if it can demonstrate to its competent authority that more recent data is a better predictor of draw downs. Member States may allow credit institutions to have, when they implement the IRB Approach, relevant data covering a period of two years. The period to be covered shall increase by one year each year until relevant data cover a period of five years.

2.2.4. Minimum requirements for assessing the effect of guarantees and credit derivatives

Exposures to corporates, institutions and central governments and central banks where own estimates of LGD are used and retail exposures

96.   The requirements in points 97 to 104 shall not apply for guarantees provided by institutions and central governments and central banks if the credit institution has received approval to apply the rules of Articles 78 to 83 for exposures to such entities. In this case the requirements of Articles 90 to 93 shall apply.

97.   For retail guarantees, these requirements also apply to the assignment of exposures to grades or pools, and the estimation of PD.

Eligible guarantors and guarantees

98.   Credit institutions shall have clearly specified criteria for the types of guarantors they recognise for the calculation of risk weighted exposure amounts.

99.   For recognised guarantors the same rules as for obligors as set out in points 17 to 29 shall apply.

100.   The guarantee shall be evidenced in writing, non-cancellable on the part of the guarantor, in force until the obligation is satisfied in full (to the extent of the amount and tenor of the guarantee) and legally enforceable against the guarantor in a jurisdiction where the guarantor has assets to attach and enforce a judgement. Guarantees prescribing conditions under which the guarantor may not be obliged to perform (conditional guarantees) may be recognised subject to approval of competent authorities. The credit institution shall demonstrate that the assignment criteria adequately address any potential reduction in the risk mitigation effect.

Adjustment criteria

101.   A credit institution shall have clearly specified criteria for adjusting grades, pools or LGD estimates, and, in the case of retail and eligible purchased receivables, the process of allocating

exposures to grades or pools, to reflect the impact of guarantees for the calculation of risk weighted exposure amounts. These criteria shall comply with the minimum requirements set out in points 17 to 29.

102.   The criteria shall be plausible and intuitive. They shall address the guarantor's ability and willingness to perform under the guarantee, the likely timing of any payments from the guarantor, the degree to which the guarantor's ability to perform under the guarantee is correlated with the obligor's ability to repay, and the extent to which residual risk to the obligor remains.

Credit derivatives

103.   The minimum requirements for guarantees in this part shall apply also for single-name credit derivatives. In relation to a mismatch between the underlying obligation and the reference obligation of the credit derivative or the obligation used for determining whether a credit event has occurred, the requirements set out under Annex VIII Part 2, point 21 shall apply. For retail exposures and eligible purchased receivables, this point applies to the process of allocating exposures to grades or pools.

104.   The criteria shall address the payout structure of the credit derivative and conservatively assess the impact this has on the level and timing of recoveries. The credit institution shall consider the extent to which other forms of residual risk remain.

2.2.5. Minimum requirements for purchased receivables

Legal certainty

105.   The structure of the facility shall ensure that under all foreseeable circumstances the credit institution has effective ownership and control of all cash remittances from the receivables. When the obligor makes payments directly to a seller or servicer, the credit institution shall verify regularly that payments are forwarded completely and within the contractually agreed terms. "Servicer" shall mean an entity that manages a pool of purchased receivables or the underlying credit exposures on a day-to-day basis. Credit institutions shall have procedures to ensure that ownership over the receivables and cash receipts is protected against bankruptcy stays or legal challenges that could materially delay the lender's ability to liquidate or assign the receivables or retain control over cash receipts.

Effectiveness of monitoring systems

106.   The credit institution shall monitor both the quality of the purchased receivables and the financial condition of the seller and servicer. In particular:
- (a)   the credit institution shall assess the correlation among the quality of the purchased receivables and the financial condition of both the seller and servicer, and have in place internal policies and procedures that provide adequate safeguards to protect against any contingencies, including the assignment of an internal risk rating for each seller and servicer;
- (b)   the credit institution shall have clear and effective policies and procedures for determining seller and servicer eligibility. The credit institution or its agent shall conduct periodic reviews of sellers and servicers in order to verify the accuracy of reports from the seller or servicer, detect fraud or operational weaknesses, and verify the quality of the seller's credit policies and servicer's collection policies and procedures. The findings of these reviews shall be documented;
- (c)   the credit institution shall assess the characteristics of the purchased receivables pools, including over-advances; history of the seller's arrears, bad debts, and bad debt allowances; payment terms, and potential contra accounts;
- (d)   the credit institution shall have effective policies and procedures for monitoring on an aggregate basis single-obligor concentrations both within and across purchased receivables pools; and
- (e)   the credit institution shall ensure that it receives from the servicer timely and sufficiently detailed reports of receivables ageings and dilutions to ensure compliance with the credit institution's eligibility criteria and advancing policies governing purchased receivables, and provide an effective means with which to monitor and confirm the seller's terms of sale and dilution.

Effectiveness of work-out systems

107.   The credit institution shall have systems and procedures for detecting deteriorations in the seller's financial condition and purchased receivables quality at an early stage, and for addressing emerging problems pro-actively. In particular, the credit institution shall have clear and effective policies, procedures, and information systems to monitor covenant violations, and clear and effective policies and procedures for initiating legal actions and dealing with problem purchased receivables.

Effectiveness of systems for controlling collateral, credit availability, and cash

108.   The credit institution shall have clear and effective policies and procedures governing the control of purchased receivables, credit, and cash. In particular, written internal policies shall specify all material elements of the receivables purchase programme, including the advancing rates, eligible collateral, necessary documentation, concentration limits, and the way cash receipts are to be handled. These elements shall take appropriate account of all relevant and material factors, including the seller and servicer's financial condition, risk concentrations, and trends in the quality of the purchased receivables and the seller's customer base, and internal systems shall ensure that funds are advanced only against specified supporting collateral and documentation.

Compliance with the credit institution's internal policies and procedures

109.   The credit institution shall have an effective internal process for assessing compliance with all internal policies and procedures. The process shall include regular audits of all critical phases of the credit institution's receivables purchase programme, verification of the separation of duties between firstly the assessment of the seller and servicer and the assessment of the obligor and secondly between the assessment of the seller and servicer and the field audit of the seller and servicer, and evaluations of back office operations, with particular focus on qualifications, experience, staffing levels, and supporting automation systems.

3. VALIDATION OF INTERNAL ESTIMATES

110.   Credit institutions shall have robust systems in place to validate the accuracy and consistency of rating systems, processes, and the estimation of all relevant risk parameters. A credit institution shall demonstrate to its competent authority that the internal validation process enables it to assess the performance of internal rating and risk estimation systems consistently and meaningfully.

111.   Credit institutions shall regularly compare realised default rates with estimated PDs for each grade and, where realised default rates are outside the expected range for that grade, credit institutions shall specifically analyse the reasons for the deviation. Credit institutions using own estimates of LGDs and/or conversion factors shall also perform analogous analysis for these estimates. Such comparisons shall make use of historical data that cover as long a period as possible. The credit institution shall document the methods and data used in such comparisons. This analysis and documentation shall be updated at least annually.

112.   Credit institutions shall also use other quantitative validation tools and comparisons with relevant external data sources. The analysis shall be based on data that are appropriate to the portfolio, are updated regularly, and cover a relevant observation period. Credit institutions' internal assessments of the performance of their rating systems shall be based on as long a period as possible.

113.   The methods and data used for quantitative validation shall be consistent through time. Changes in estimation and validation methods and data (both data sources and periods covered) shall be documented.

114.   Credit institutions shall have sound internal standards for situations where deviations in realised PDs, LGDs, conversion factors and total losses, where EL is used, from expectations, become significant enough to call the validity of the estimates into question. These standards shall take account of business cycles and similar systematic variability in default experience. Where realised values continue to be higher than expected values, credit institutions shall revise estimates upward to reflect their default and loss experience.

4. CALCULATION OF RISK WEIGHTED EXPOSURE AMOUNTS FOR EQUITY EXPOSURES UNDER THE INTERNAL MODELS APPROACH

4.1. Capital requirement and risk quantification

115.   For the purpose of calculating capital requirements credit institutions shall meet the following standards:

   (a)   the estimate of potential loss shall be robust to adverse market movements relevant to the long-term risk profile of the credit institution's specific holdings. The data used to represent return distributions shall reflect the longest sample period for which data is available and meaningful in representing the risk profile of the credit institution's specific equity exposures. The data used shall be sufficient to provide conservative, statistically reliable and robust loss estimates that are not based purely on subjective or judgmental considerations. Credit institutions shall demonstrate to competent authorities that the shock employed provides a conservative estimate of potential losses over a relevant long-term market or business cycle. The credit institution shall combine empirical analysis of available data with adjustments based on a variety of factors in order to attain model outputs that achieve appropriate realism and conservatism. In constructing Value at Risk (VaR) models estimating potential quarterly losses, credit institutions may use quarterly data or convert shorter horizon period data to a quarterly equivalent using an analytically appropriate method supported by empirical evidence and through a well-developed and documented thought process and analysis. Such an approach shall be applied conservatively and consistently over time. Where only limited relevant data is available the credit institution shall add appropriate margins of conservatism;

(b)   the models used shall be able to capture adequately all of the material risks embodied in equity returns including both the general market risk and specific risk exposure of the credit institution's equity portfolio. The internal models shall adequately explain historical price variation, capture both the magnitude and changes in the composition of potential concentrations, and be robust to adverse market environments. The population of risk exposures represented in the data used for estimation shall be closely matched to or at least comparable with those of the credit institution's equity exposures;

(c)   the internal model shall be appropriate for the risk profile and complexity of a credit institution's equity portfolio. Where a credit institution has material holdings with values that are highly non-linear in nature the internal models shall be designed to capture appropriately the risks associated with such instruments;

(d)   mapping of individual positions to proxies, market indices, and risk factors shall be plausible, intuitive, and conceptually sound;

(e)   credit institutions shall demonstrate through empirical analyses the appropriateness of risk factors, including their ability to cover both general and specific risk;

(f)   the estimates of the return volatility of equity exposures shall incorporate relevant and available data, information, and methods. Independently reviewed internal data or data from external sources (including pooled data) shall be used; and

(g)   a rigorous and comprehensive stress-testing programme shall be in place;

4.2. Risk management process and controls

116.   With regard to the development and use of internal models for capital requirement purposes, credit institutions shall establish policies, procedures, and controls to ensure the integrity of the model and modelling process. These policies, procedures, and controls shall include the following:

(a)   full integration of the internal model into the overall management information systems of the credit institution and in the management of the non-trading book equity portfolio. Internal models shall be fully integrated into the credit institution's risk management infrastructure if they are particularly used in measuring and assessing equity portfolio performance (including the risk-adjusted performance), allocating economic capital to equity exposures and evaluating overall capital adequacy and the investment management process;

(b)   established management systems, procedures, and control functions for ensuring the periodic and independent review of all elements of the internal modelling process, including approval of model revisions, vetting of model inputs, and review of model results, such as direct verification of risk computations. These reviews shall assess the accuracy, completeness, and appropriateness of model inputs and results and focus on both finding and limiting potential errors associated with known weaknesses and identifying unknown model weaknesses. Such reviews may be conducted by an internal independent unit, or by an independent external third party;

(c)   adequate systems and procedures for monitoring investment limits and the risk exposures of equity exposures;

(d)   the units responsible for the design and application of the model shall be functionally independent from the units responsible for managing individual investments; and

(e)   parties responsible for any aspect of the modelling process shall be adequately qualified. Management shall allocate sufficient skilled and competent resources to the modelling function.

4.3. Validation and documentation

117.   Credit institutions shall have a robust system in place to validate the accuracy and consistency of their internal models and modelling processes. All material elements of the internal models and the modelling process and validation shall be documented.

118.   Credit institutions shall use the internal validation process to assess the performance of its internal models and processes in a consistent and meaningful way.

119.   The methods and data used for quantitative validation shall be consistent through time. Changes in estimation and validation methods and data (both data sources and periods covered) shall be documented.

120.   Credit institutions shall regularly compare actual equity returns (computed using realised and unrealised gains and losses) with modelled estimates. Such comparisons shall make use of

historical data that cover as long a period as possible. The credit institution shall document the methods and data used in such comparisons. This analysis and documentation shall be updated at least annually.

121. Credit institutions shall make use of other quantitative validation tools and comparisons with external data sources. The analysis shall be based on data that are appropriate to the portfolio, are updated regularly, and cover a relevant observation period. Credit institutions' internal assessments of the performance of their models shall be based on as long a period as possible.

122. Credit institutions shall have sound internal standards for situations where comparison of actual equity returns with the models estimates calls the validity of the estimates or of the models as such into question. These standards shall take account of business cycles and similar systematic variability in equity returns. All adjustments made to internal models in response to model reviews shall be documented and consistent with the credit institution's model review standards.

123. The internal model and the modelling process shall be documented, including the responsibilities of parties involved in the modelling, and the model approval and model review processes.

5. CORPORATE GOVERNANCE AND OVERSIGHT

5.1. Corporate Governance

124. All material aspects of the rating and estimation processes shall be approved by the credit institution's management body described in Article 11 or a designated committee thereof and senior management. These parties shall possess a general understanding of the credit institution's rating systems and detailed comprehension of its associated management reports.

125. Senior management shall provide notice to the management body described in Article 11 or a designated committee thereof of material changes or exceptions from established policies that will materially impact the operations of the credit institution's rating systems.

126. Senior management shall have a good understanding of the rating systems designs and operations. Senior management shall ensure, on an ongoing basis that the rating systems are operating properly. Senior management shall be regularly informed by the credit risk control units about the performance of the rating process, areas needing improvement, and the status of efforts to improve previously identified deficiencies.

127. Internal ratings-based analysis of the credit institution's credit risk profile shall be an essential part of the management reporting to these parties. Reporting shall include at least risk profile by grade, migration across grades, estimation of the relevant parameters per grade, and comparison of realised default rates, and to the extent that own estimates are used of realised LGDs and realised conversion factors against expectations and stress-test results. Reporting frequencies shall depend on the significance and type of information and the level of the recipient.

5.2. Credit risk control

128. The credit risk control unit shall be independent from the personnel and management functions responsible for originating or renewing exposures and report directly to senior management. The unit shall be responsible for the design or selection, implementation, oversight and performance of the rating systems. It shall regularly produce and analyse reports on the output of the rating systems.

129. The areas of responsibility for the credit risk control unit(s) shall include:
  (a) testing and monitoring grades and pools;
  (b) production and analysis of summary reports from the credit institution's rating systems;
  (c) implementing procedures to verify that grade and pool definitions are consistently applied across departments and geographic areas;
  (d) reviewing and documenting any changes to the rating process, including the reasons for the changes;
  (e) reviewing the rating criteria to evaluate if they remain predictive of risk. Changes to the rating process, criteria or individual rating parameters shall be documented and retained;
  (f) active participation in the design or selection, implementation and validation of models used in the rating process;
  (g) oversight and supervision of models used in the rating process; and
  (h) ongoing review and alterations to models used in the rating process.

130. Notwithstanding point 129, credit institutions using pooled data according to points 57 and 58 may outsource the following tasks:
  (a) production of information relevant to testing and monitoring grades and pools;
  (b) production of summary reports from the credit institution's rating systems;
  (c) production of information relevant to review of the rating criteria to evaluate if they remain predictive of risk;
  (d) documentation of changes to the rating process, criteria or individual rating parameters; and

(e)   production of information relevant to ongoing review and alterations to models used in the rating process.

Credit institutions making use of this point shall ensure that the competent authorities have access to all relevant information from the third party that is necessary for examining compliance with the minimum requirements and that the competent authorities may perform on-site examinations to the same extent as within the credit institution.

5.3. Internal Audit

131.   Internal audit or another comparable independent auditing unit shall review at least annually the credit institution's rating systems and its operations, including the operations of the credit function and the estimation of PDs, LGDs, ELs and conversion factors. Areas of review shall include adherence to all applicable minimum requirements.

[5842D]

ANNEX VIII
CREDIT RISK MITIGATION

PART 1
ELIGIBILITY

1.   This part sets out eligible forms of credit risk mitigation for the purposes of Article 92.

2.   "Secured lending transaction" shall mean any transaction giving rise to an exposure secured by collateral which does not include a provision conferring upon the credit institution the right to receive margin frequently.

"Capital market-driven transaction" shall mean any transaction giving rise to an exposure secured by collateral which includes a provision conferring upon the credit institution the right to receive margin frequently.

1. FUNDED CREDIT PROTECTION

1.1. On-balance sheet netting

3.   The on-balance sheet netting of mutual claims between the credit institution and its counterparty may be recognised as eligible.

4.   Without prejudice to point 5, eligibility is limited to reciprocal cash balances between the credit institution and the counterparty. Only loans and deposits of the lending credit institution may be subject to a modification of risk-weighted exposure amounts and, as relevant, expected loss amounts as a result of an on-balance sheet netting agreement.

1.2. Master netting agreements covering repurchase transactions and/or securities or commodities lending or borrowing transactions and/or other capital market-driven transactions

5.   For credit institutions adopting the Financial Collateral Comprehensive Method under Part 3, the effects of bilateral netting contracts covering repurchase transactions, securities or commodities lending or borrowing transactions, and/or other capital market-driven transactions with a counterparty may be recognised. Without prejudice to Annex II to Directive 2006/49/EC to be recognised the collateral taken and securities or commodities borrowed within such agreements must comply with the eligibility requirements for collateral set out at points 7 to 11.

1.3. Collateral

6.   Where the credit risk mitigation technique used relies on the right of the credit institution to liquidate or retain assets, eligibility depends upon whether risk-weighted exposure amounts, and, as relevant, expected loss amounts, are calculated under Articles 78 to 83 or Articles 84 to 89. Eligibility further depends upon whether the Financial Collateral Simple Method is used or the Financial Collateral Comprehensive Method under Part 3. In relation to repurchase transactions and securities or commodities lending or borrowing transactions, eligibility also depends upon whether the transaction is booked in the non-trading book or the trading book.

1.3.1. Eligibility under all approaches and methods

7.   The following financial items may be recognised as eligible collateral under all approaches and methods:
(a)   cash on deposit with, or cash assimilated instruments held by, the lending credit institution;
(b)   debt securities issued by central governments or central banks, which securities have a credit assessment by an ECAI or export credit agency recognised as eligible for the purposes of Articles 78 to 83 which has been determined by the competent authority to

be associated with credit quality step 4 or above under the rules for the risk weighting of exposures to central governments and central banks under Articles 78 to 83;

(c)   debt securities issued by institutions, which securities have a credit assessment by an eligible ECAI which has been determined by the competent authority to be associated with credit quality step 3 or above under the rules for the risk weighting of exposures to credit institutions under Articles 78 to 83;

(d)   debt securities issued by other entities, which securities have a credit assessment by an eligible ECAI which has been determined by the competent authority to be associated with credit quality step 3 or above under the rules for the risk weighting of exposures to corporates under Articles 78 to 83;

(e)   debt securities with a short-term credit assessment by an eligible ECAI which has been determined by the competent authority to be associated with credit quality step 3 or above under the rules for the risk weighting of short term exposures under Articles 78 to 83;

(f)   equities or convertible bonds that are included in a main index; and

(g)   gold.

For the purposes of point (b), "debt securities issued by central governments or central banks" shall include:

(i)   debt securities issued by regional governments or local authorities, exposures to which are treated as exposures to the central government in whose jurisdiction they are established under Articles 78 to 83;

(ii)   debt securities issued by public sector entities which are treated as exposures to central governments in accordance with point 15 of Part 1 of Annex VI;

(iii)   debt securities issued by multilateral development banks to which a 0% risk weight is assigned under Articles 78 to 83; and

(iv)   debt securities issued by international organisations which are assigned a 0% risk weight under Articles 78 to 83.

For the purposes of point (c), "debt securities issued by institutions" include:

(i)   debt securities issued by regional governments or local authorities other than those exposures to which are treated as exposures to the central government in whose jurisdiction they are established under Articles 78 to 83;

(ii)   debt securities issued by public sector entities, exposures to which are treated as exposures to credit institutions under Articles 78 to 83; and

(iii)   debt securities issued by multilateral development banks other than those to which a 0% risk weight is assigned under Articles 78 to 83.

8.   Debt securities issued by institutions which securities do not have a credit assessment by an eligible ECAI may be recognised as eligible collateral if they fulfil the following criteria:

(a)   they are listed on a recognised exchange;

(b)   they qualify as senior debt;

(c)   all other rated issues by the issuing institution of the same seniority have a credit assessment by an eligible ECAI which has been determined by the competent authorities to be associated with credit quality step 3 or above under the rules for the risk weighting of exposures to institutions or short term exposures under Articles 78 to 83;

(d)   the lending credit institution has no information to suggest that the issue would justify a credit assessment below that indicated in (c); and

(e)   the credit institution can demonstrate to the competent authorities that the market liquidity of the instrument is sufficient for these purposes.

9.   Units in collective investment undertakings may be recognised as eligible collateral if the following conditions are satisfied:

(a)   they have a daily public price quote; and

(b)   the collective investment undertaking is limited to investing in instruments that are eligible for recognition under points 7 and 8.

The use (or potential use) by a collective investment undertaking of derivative instruments to hedge permitted investments shall not prevent units in that undertaking from being eligible.

10.   In relation to points (b) to (e) of point 7, where a security has two credit assessments by eligible ECAIs, the less favourable assessment shall be deemed to apply. In cases where a security has more than two credit assessments by eligible ECAIs, the two most favourable assessments shall be deemed to apply. If the two most favourable credit assessments are different, the less favourable of the two shall be deemed to apply.

1.3.2. Additional eligibility under the Financial Collateral Comprehensive Method

11.   In addition to the collateral set out in points 7 to 10, where a credit institution uses the Financial Collateral Comprehensive Method under Part 3, the following financial items may be recognised as eligible collateral:

(a) equities or convertible bonds not included in a main index but traded on a recognised exchange; and

(b) units in collective investment undertakings if the following conditions are met:
  (i) they have a daily public price quote; and
  (ii) the collective investment undertaking is limited to investing in instruments that are eligible for recognition under point 7 and 8 and the items mentioned in point (a) of this point.

The use (or potential use) by a collective investment undertaking of derivative instruments to hedge permitted investments shall not prevent units in that undertaking from being eligible.

1.3.3. Additional eligibility for calculations under Articles 84 to 89

12. In addition to the collateral set out above the provisions of points 13 to 22 apply where a credit institution calculates risk-weighted exposure amounts and expected loss amounts under the approach set out in Articles 84 to 89:

(a) Real estate collateral

13. Residential real estate property which is or will be occupied or let by the owner, or the beneficial owner in the case of personal investment companies, and commercial real estate property, that is, offices and other commercial premises, may be recognised as eligible collateral where the following conditions are met:

(a) the value of the property does not materially depend upon the credit quality of the obligor. This requirement does not preclude situations where purely macro-economic factors affect both the value of the property and the performance of the borrower; and

(b) the risk of the borrower does not materially depend upon the performance of the underlying property or project, but rather on the underlying capacity of the borrower to repay the debt from other sources. As such, repayment of the facility does not materially depend on any cash flow generated by the underlying property serving as collateral.

14. Credit institutions may also recognise as eligible collateral shares in Finnish residential housing companies operating in accordance with the Finnish Housing Company Act of 1991 or subsequent equivalent legislation in respect of residential property which is or will be occupied or let by the owner, as residential real estate collateral, provided that these conditions are met.

15. The competent authorities may also authorise their credit institutions to recognise as eligible collateral shares in Finnish housing companies operating in accordance with the Finnish Housing Company Act of 1991 or subsequent equivalent legislation as commercial real estate collateral, provided that these conditions are met.

16. The competent authorities may waive the requirement for their credit institutions to comply with condition (b) in point 13 for exposures secured by residential real estate property situated within the territory of that Member State, if the competent authorities have evidence that the relevant market is well-developed and long-established with loss-rates which are sufficiently low to justify such action. This shall not prevent the competent authorities of a Member State, which do not use this waiver from recognising as eligible residential real estate property recognised as eligible in another Member State by virtue of the waiver. Member States shall disclose publicly the use they make of this waiver.

17. The competent authorities of the Member States may waive the requirement for their credit institutions to comply with the condition in point 13(b) for commercial real estate property situated within the territory of that Member State, if the competent authorities have evidence that the relevant market is well-developed and long-established and that loss-rates stemming from lending secured by commercial real estate property satisfy the following conditions:

(a) losses stemming from loans collateralised by commercial real estate property up to 50% of the market value (or where applicable and if lower 60% of the mortgage-lending-value) do not exceed 0.3% of the outstanding loans collateralised by commercial real estate property in any given year; and

(b) overall losses stemming from loans collateralised by commercial real estate property do not exceed 0.5% of the outstanding loans collateralised by commercial real estate property in any given year.

18. If either of these conditions is not satisfied in a given year, the eligibility to use this treatment will cease until the conditions are satisfied in a subsequent year.

19. The competent authorities of a Member State may recognise as eligible collateral commercial real estate property recognised as eligible collateral in another Member State by virtue of the waiver provided for in point 17.

(b) Receivables

20. The competent authorities may recognise as eligible collateral amounts receivable linked to a commercial transaction or transactions with an original maturity of less than or equal to one year. Eligible receivables do not include those associated with securitisations, sub-participations or credit derivatives or amounts owed by affiliated parties.

(c) Other physical collateral

21. The competent authorities may recognise as eligible collateral physical items of a type other than those types indicated in points 13 to 19 if satisfied as to the following:
- (a) the existence of liquid markets for disposal of the collateral in an expeditious and economically efficient manner; and
- (b) the existence of well-established publicly available market prices for the collateral. The credit institution must be able to demonstrate that there is no evidence that the net prices it receives when collateral is realised deviates significantly from these market prices.

(d) Leasing

22. Subject to the provisions of Part 3, point 72, where the requirements set out in Part 2, point 11 are met, exposures arising from transactions whereby a credit institution leases property to a third party will be treated the same as loans collateralised by the type of property leased.

1.4. Other funded credit protection

1.4.1. Cash on deposit with, or cash assimilated instruments held by, a third party institution.

23. Cash on deposit with, or cash assimilated instruments held by, a third party institution in a non-custodial arrangement and pledged to the lending credit institution may be recognised as eligible credit protection.

1.4.2. Life insurance policies pledged to the lending credit institution

24. Life insurance policies pledged to the lending credit institution may be recognised as eligible credit protection.

1.4.3. Institution instruments repurchased on request

25. Instruments issued by third party institutions which will be repurchased by that institution on request may be recognised as eligible credit protection.

2. UNFUNDED CREDIT PROTECTION

2.1. Eligibility of protection providers under all approaches

26. The following parties may be recognised as eligible providers of unfunded credit protection:
- (a) central governments and central banks;
- (b) regional governments or local authorities;
- (c) multilateral development banks;
- (d) international organisations exposures to which a 0% risk weight under Articles 78 to 83 is assigned;
- (e) public sector entities, claims on which are treated by the competent authorities as claims on institutions or central governments under Articles 78 to 83;
- (f) institutions; and
- (g) other corporate entities, including parent, subsidiary and affiliate corporate entities of the credit institution, that:
  - (i) have a credit assessment by a recognised ECAI which has been determined by the competent authorities to be associated with credit quality step 2 or above under the rules for the risk weighting of exposures to corporates under Articles 78 to 83; and
  - (ii) in the case of credit institutions calculating risk-weighted exposure amounts and expected loss amounts under Articles 84 to 89, do not have a credit assessment by a recognised ECAI and are internally rated as having a PD equivalent to that associated with the credit assessments of ECAIs determined by the competent authorities to be associated with credit quality step 2 or above under the rules for the risk weighting of exposures to corporate under Articles 78 to 83.

27. Where risk-weighted exposure amounts and expected loss amounts are calculated under Articles 84 to 89, to be eligible a guarantor must be internally rated by the credit institution in accordance with the provisions of Annex VII, Part 4.

28. By way of derogation from point 26, the Member States may also recognise as eligible providers of unfunded credit protection, other financial institutions authorised and supervised by the competent authorities responsible for the authorisation and supervision of credit institutions and subject to prudential requirements equivalent to those applied to credit institutions.

2.2 Eligibility of protection providers under the IRB Approach which qualify for the treatment set out in Annex VII, Part 1, point 4.

29. Institutions, insurance and reinsurance undertakings and export credit agencies which fulfil the following conditions may be recognised as eligible providers of unfunded credit protection which qualify for the treatment set out in Annex VII, Part 1, point 4:

— the protection provider has sufficient expertise in providing unfunded credit protection;

— the protection provider is regulated in a manner equivalent to the rules laid down in this Directive, or had, at the time the credit protection was provided, a credit assessment by a recognised ECAI which had been determined by the competent authorities to be associated with credit quality step 3, or above, under the rules for the risk weighting of exposures to corporate under Articles 78 to 83;

— the protection provider had, at the time the credit protection was provided, or for any period of time thereafter, an internal rating with a PD equivalent to or lower than that associated with credit quality step 2 or above under the rules for the risk weighting of exposures to corporates under Articles 78 to 83; and

— the provider has an internal rating with a PD equivalent to or lower than that associated with credit quality step 3 or above under the rules for the risk weighting of exposures to corporates under Articles 78 to 83.

For the purpose of this point, credit protection provided by export credit agencies shall not benefit from any explicit central government counter-guarantee.

3. TYPES OF CREDIT DERIVATIVES

30. The following types of credit derivatives, and instruments that may be composed of such credit derivatives or that are economically effectively similar, may be recognised as eligible:

(a) credit default swaps;

(b) total return swaps; and

(c) credit linked notes to the extent of their cash funding.

31. Where a credit institution buys credit protection through a total return swap and records the net payments received on the swap as net income, but does not record offsetting deterioration in the value of the asset that is protected (either through reductions in fair value or by an addition to reserves), the credit protection shall not be recognised as eligible.

3.1. Internal hedges

32. When a credit institution conducts an internal hedge using a credit derivative — i e hedges the credit risk of an exposure in the non-trading book with a credit derivative booked in the trading book — in order for the protection to be recognised as eligible for the purposes of this Annex the credit risk transferred to the trading book shall be transferred out to a third party or parties. In such circumstances, subject to the compliance of such transfer with the requirements for the recognition of credit risk mitigation set out in this Annex, the rules set out in Parts 3 to 6 for the calculation of risk-weighted exposure amounts and expected loss amounts where unfunded credit protection is acquired shall be applied.

PART 2
MINIMUM REQUIREMENTS

1. The credit institution must satisfy the competent authorities that it has adequate risk management processes to control those risks to which the credit institution may be exposed as a result of carrying out credit risk mitigation practices.

2. Notwithstanding the presence of credit risk mitigation taken into account for the purposes of calculating risk-weighted exposure amounts and as relevant expected loss amounts, credit institutions shall continue to undertake full credit risk assessment of the underlying exposure and be in a position to demonstrate the fulfilment of this requirement to the competent authorities. In the case of repurchase transactions and/or securities or commodities lending or borrowing transactions the underlying exposure shall, for the purposes of this point only, be deemed to be the net amount of the exposure.

1. FUNDED CREDIT PROTECTION

1.1. On-balance sheet netting agreements (other than master netting agreements covering repurchase transactions, securities or commodities lending or borrowing transactions and/or other capital market-driven transactions).

3. For on-balance sheet netting agreements — other than master netting agreements covering repurchase transactions, securities or commodities lending or borrowing transactions and/or other capital market-driven transactions — to be recognised for the purposes of Articles 90 to 93, the following conditions shall be satisfied:

(a) they must be legally effective and enforceable in all relevant jurisdictions, including in the event of the insolvency or bankruptcy of a counterparty;

(b) the credit institution must be able to determine at any time those assets and liabilities that are subject to the on-balance sheet netting agreement;

(c) the credit institution must monitor and control the risks associated with the termination of the credit protection; and

(d) the credit institution must monitor and control the relevant exposures on a net basis.

1.2. Master netting agreements covering repurchase transactions and/or securities or commodities lending or borrowing transactions and/or other capital market driven transactions

4. For master netting agreements covering repurchase transactions and/or securities or commodities lending or borrowing transactions and/or other capital market driven transactions to be recognised for the purposes of Articles 90 to 93, they shall:

(a) be legally effective and enforceable in all relevant jurisdictions, including in the event of the bankruptcy or insolvency of the counterparty;

(b) give the non-defaulting party the right to terminate and close-out in a timely manner all transactions under the agreement upon the event of default, including in the event of the bankruptcy or insolvency of the counterparty; and

(c) provide for the netting of gains and losses on transactions closed out under a master agreement so that a single net amount is owed by one party to the other.

5. In addition, the minimum requirements for the recognition of financial collateral under the Financial Collateral Comprehensive Method set out in point 6 shall be fulfilled.

1.3. Financial collateral

1.3.1. Minimum requirements for the recognition of financial collateral under all Approaches and Methods

6. For the recognition of financial collateral and gold, the following conditions shall be met.

(a) Low correlation

The credit quality of the obligor and the value of the collateral must not have a material positive correlation.

Securities issued by the obligor, or any related group entity, are not eligible. This notwithstanding, the obligor's own issues of covered bonds falling within the terms of Annex VI, Part 1, points 68 to 70 may be recognised as eligible when they are posted as collateral for repurchase transactions, provided that the first paragraph of this point is complied with.

(b) Legal certainty

Credit institutions shall fulfil any contractual and statutory requirements in respect of, and take all steps necessary to ensure, the enforceability of the collateral arrangements under the law applicable to their interest in the collateral.

Credit institutions shall have conducted sufficient legal review confirming the enforceability of the collateral arrangements in all relevant jurisdictions. They shall re-conduct such review as necessary to ensure continuing enforceability.

(c) Operational requirements

The collateral arrangements shall be properly documented, with a clear and robust procedure for the timely liquidation of collateral.

Credit institutions shall employ robust procedures and processes to control risks arising from the use of collateral — including risks of failed or reduced credit protection, valuation risks, risks associated with the termination of the credit protection, concentration risk arising from the use of collateral and the interaction with the credit institution's overall risk profile.

The credit institution shall have documented policies and practices concerning the types and amounts of collateral accepted.

Credit institutions shall calculate the market value of the collateral, and revalue it accordingly, with a minimum frequency of once every six months and whenever the credit institution has reason to believe that there has occurred a significant decrease in its market value.

Where the collateral is held by a third party, credit institutions must take reasonable steps to ensure that the third party segregates the collateral from its own assets.

1.3.2. Additional minimum requirements for the recognition of financial collateral under the Financial Collateral Simple Method

7. In addition to the requirements set out in point 6, for the recognition of financial collateral under the Financial Collateral Simple Method the residual maturity of the protection must be at least as long as the residual maturity of the exposure.

1.4. Minimum requirements for the recognition of real estate collateral

8. For the recognition of real estate collateral the following conditions shall be met.

(a) Legal certainty

The mortgage or charge shall be enforceable in all jurisdictions which are relevant at the time of the conclusion of the credit agreement, and the mortgage or charge shall be properly filed on a timely basis. The arrangements shall reflect a perfected lien (i e all legal requirements for establishing the pledge shall been fulfilled). The protection agreement and the legal process underpinning it shall enable the credit institution to realise the value of the protection within a reasonable timeframe.

(b) Monitoring of property values

The value of the property shall be monitored on a frequent basis and at a minimum once every year for commercial real estate and once every three years for residential real estate. More frequent monitoring shall be carried out where the market is subject to significant changes in conditions. Statistical methods may be used to monitor the value of the property and to identify property that needs revaluation. The property valuation shall be reviewed by an independent valuer when information indicates that the value of the property may have declined materially relative to general market prices. For loans exceeding EUR 3 million or 5% of the own funds of the credit institution, the property valuation shall be reviewed by an independent valuer at least every three years.

"Independent valuer" shall mean a person who possesses the necessary qualifications, ability and experience to execute a valuation and who is independent from the credit decision process.

(c) Documentation

The types of residential and commercial real estate accepted by the credit institution and its lending policies in this regard shall be clearly documented.

(d) Insurance

The credit institution shall have procedures to monitor that the property taken as protection is adequately insured against damage.

1.5. Minimum requirements for the recognition of receivables as collateral

9. For the recognition of receivables as collateral the following conditions shall be met:

(a) Legal certainty
   (i) The legal mechanism by which the collateral is provided shall be robust and effective and ensure that the lender has clear rights over the proceeds;
   (ii) Credit institutions must take all steps necessary to fulfil local requirements in respect of the enforceability of security interest. There shall be a framework which allows the lender to have a first priority claim over the collateral subject to national discretion to allow such claims to be subject to the claims of preferential creditors provided for in legislative or implementing provisions;
   (iii) Credit institutions shall have conducted sufficient legal review confirming the enforceability of the collateral arrangements in all relevant jurisdictions; and
   (iv) The collateral arrangements must be properly documented, with a clear and robust procedure for the timely collection of collateral. Credit institution's procedures shall ensure that any legal conditions required for declaring the default of the borrower and timely collection of collateral are observed. In the event of the borrower's financial distress or default, the credit institution shall have legal authority to sell or assign the receivables to other parties without consent of the receivables obligors.

(b) Risk management
   (i) The credit institution must have a sound process for determining the credit risk associated with the receivables. Such a process shall include, among other things, analyses of the borrower's business and industry and the types of customers with whom the borrower does business. Where the credit institution relies on the borrower to ascertain the credit risk of the customers, the credit institution must review the borrower's credit practices to ascertain their soundness and credibility;
   (ii) The margin between the amount of the exposure and the value of the receivables must reflect all appropriate factors, including the cost of collection, concentration within the receivables pool pledged by an individual borrower, and potential concentration risk within the credit institution's total exposures beyond that controlled by the credit institution's general methodology. The credit institution must maintain a continuous monitoring process appropriate to the receivables. Additionally, compliance with loan covenants, environmental restrictions, and other legal requirements shall be reviewed on a regular basis;
   (iii) The receivables pledged by a borrower shall be diversified and not be unduly correlated with the borrower. Where there is material positive correlation, the attendant risks shall be taken into account in the setting of margins for the collateral pool as a whole;
   (iv) Receivables from affiliates of the borrower (including subsidiaries and employees) shall not be recognised as risk mitigants; and
   (v) The credit institution shall have a documented process for collecting receivable

payments in distressed situations. The requisite facilities for collection shall be in place, even when the credit institution normally looks to the borrower for collections.

1.6. Minimum requirements for the recognition of other physical collateral

10. For the recognition of other physical collateral the following conditions shall be met:

(a) the collateral arrangement shall be legally effective and enforceable in all relevant jurisdictions and shall enable the credit institution to realise the value of the property within a reasonable timeframe;

(b) with the sole exception of permissible prior claims referred to in point 9(a)(ii), only first liens on, or charges over, collateral are permissible. As such, the credit institution shall have priority over all other lenders to the realised proceeds of the collateral;

(c) the value of the property shall be monitored on a frequent basis and at a minimum once every year. More frequent monitoring shall be required where the market is subject to significant changes in conditions;

(d) the loan agreement shall include detailed descriptions of the collateral plus detailed specifications of the manner and frequency of revaluation;

(e) the types of physical collateral accepted by the credit institution and policies and practices in respect of the appropriate amount of each type of collateral relative to the exposure amount shall be clearly documented in internal credit policies and procedures available for examination;

(f) the credit institution's credit policies with regard to the transaction structure shall address appropriate collateral requirements relative to the exposure amount, the ability to liquidate the collateral readily, the ability to establish objectively a price or market value, the frequency with which the value can readily be obtained (including a professional appraisal or valuation), and the volatility or a proxy of the volatility of the value of the collateral;

(g) both initial valuation and revaluation shall take fully into account any deterioration or obsolescence of the collateral. Particular attention must be paid in valuation and revaluation to the effects of the passage of time on fashion- or date-sensitive collateral;

(h) the credit institution must have the right to physically inspect the property. It shall have policies and procedures addressing its exercise of the right to physical inspection; and

(i) the credit institution must have procedures to monitor that the property taken as protection is adequately insured against damage.

1.7. Minimum requirements for treating lease exposures as collateralised

11. For the exposures arising from leasing transactions to be treated as collateralised by the type of property leased, the following conditions shall be met:

(a) the conditions set out in points 8 or 10 as appropriate for the recognition as collateral of the type of property leased shall be met;

(b) there shall be robust risk management on the part of the lessor with respect to the use to which the leased asset is put, its age and the planned duration of its use, including appropriate monitoring of the value of the security;

(c) there shall be in place a robust legal framework establishing the lessor's legal ownership of the asset and its ability to exercise its rights as owner in a timely fashion; and

(d) where this has not already been ascertained in calculating the LGD level, the difference between the value of the unamortised amount and the market value of the security must not be so large as to overstate the credit risk mitigation attributed to the leased assets.

1.8. Minimum requirements for the recognition of other funded credit protection

1.8.1. Cash on deposit with, or cash assimilated instruments held by, a third party institution

12. To be eligible for the treatment set out at Part 3, point 79, the protection referred to in Part 1, point 23 must satisfy the following conditions:

(a) the borrower's claim against the third party institution is openly pledged or assigned to the lending credit institution and such pledge or assignment is legally effective and enforceable in all relevant jurisdictions;

(b) the third party institution is notified of the pledge or assignment;

(c) as a result of the notification, the third party institution is able to make payments solely to the lending credit institution or to other parties with the lending credit institution's consent; and

(d) the pledge or assignment is unconditional and irrevocable.

1.8.2. Life insurance policies pledged to the lending credit institution.

13. For life insurance policies pledged to the lending credit institution to be recognised the following conditions shall be met:

(a) the company providing the life insurance may be recognised as an eligible unfunded credit protection provider under Part 1, point 26;

(b) the life insurance policy is openly pledged or assigned to the lending credit institution;

(c) the company providing the life insurance is notified of the pledge or assignment and as a result may not pay amounts payable under the contract without the consent of the lending credit institution;

(d) the declared surrender value of the policy is non-reducible;

(e) the lending credit institution must have the right to cancel the policy and receive the surrender value in a timely way in the event of the default of the borrower;

(f) the lending credit institution is informed of any non-payments under the policy by the policy-holder;

(g) the credit protection must be provided for the maturity of the loan. Where this is not possible because the insurance relationship ends before the loan relationship expires, the credit institution must ensure that the amount deriving from the insurance contract serves the credit institution as security until the end of the duration of the credit agreement; and

(h) the pledge or assignment must be legally effective and enforceable in all jurisdictions which are relevant at the time of the conclusion of the credit agreement.

2. UNFUNDED CREDIT PROTECTION AND CREDIT LINKED NOTES

2.1. Requirements common to guarantees and credit derivatives

14. Subject to point 16, for the credit protection deriving from a guarantee or credit derivative to be recognised the following conditions shall be met:

(a) the credit protection shall be direct;

(b) the extent of the credit protection shall be clearly defined and incontrovertible;

(c) the credit protection contract shall not contain any clause, the fulfilment of which is outside the direct control of the lender, that:

    (i) would allow the protection provider unilaterally to cancel the protection;

    (ii) would increase the effective cost of protection as a result of deteriorating credit quality of the protected exposure;

    (iii) could prevent the protection provider from being obliged to pay out in a timely manner in the event that the original obligor fails to make any payments due; or

    (iv) could allow the maturity of the credit protection to be reduced by the protection provider; and

(d) it must be legally effective and enforceable in all jurisdictions which are relevant at the time of the conclusion of the credit agreement.

2.1.1. Operational requirements

15. The credit institution shall satisfy the competent authority that it has systems in place to manage potential concentration of risk arising from the credit institution's use of guarantees and credit derivatives. The credit institution must be able to demonstrate how its strategy in respect of its use of credit derivatives and guarantees interacts with its management of its overall risk profile.

2.2. Sovereign and other public sector counter-guarantees

16. Where an exposure is protected by a guarantee which is counter-guaranteed by a central government or central bank, a regional government or local authority, a public sector entity, claims on which are treated as claims on the central government in whose jurisdiction they are established under Articles 78 to 83, a multi-lateral development bank to which a 0% risk weight is assigned under or by virtue of Articles 78 to 83, or a public sector entity, claims on which are treated as claims on credit institutions under Articles 78 to 83, the exposure may be treated as protected by a guarantee provided by the entity in question, provided the following conditions are satisfied:

(a) the counter-guarantee covers all credit risk elements of the claim;

(b) both the original guarantee and the counter-guarantee meet the requirements for guarantees set out in points 14, 15 and 18, except that the counter-guarantee need not be direct; and

(c) the competent authority is satisfied that the cover is robust and that nothing in the historical evidence suggests that the coverage of the counter-guarantee is less than effectively equivalent to that of a direct guarantee by the entity in question.

17. The treatment set out in point 16 also applies to an exposure which is not counter-guaranteed by an entity listed in that point if that exposure's counter-guarantee is in turn directly guaranteed by one of the listed entities and the conditions listed in that point are satisfied.

2.3. Additional requirements for guarantees

18. For a guarantee to be recognised the following conditions shall also be met:

(a) on the qualifying default of and/or non-payment by the counterparty, the lending credit institution shall have the right to pursue, in a timely manner, the guarantor for any monies due under the claim in respect of which the protection is provided. Payment by the guarantor shall not be subject to the lending credit institution first having to pursue the obligor.

In the case of unfunded credit protection covering residential mortgage loans, the requirements in point 14(c)(iii) and in the first subparagraph of this point have only to be satisfied within 24 months;

(b)   the guarantee shall be an explicitly documented obligation assumed by the guarantor; and

(c)   subject to the following sentence, the guarantee shall cover all types of payments the obligor is expected to make in respect of the claim. Where certain types of payment are excluded from the guarantee, the recognised value of the guarantee shall be adjusted to reflect the limited coverage.

19.   In the case of guarantees provided in the context of mutual guarantee schemes recognised for these purposes by the competent authorities or provided by or counter-guaranteed by entities referred to in point 16, the requirements in point 18(a) shall be considered to be satisfied where either of the following conditions are met:

(a)   the lending credit institution has the right to obtain in a timely manner a provisional payment by the guarantor calculated to represent a robust estimate of the amount of the economic loss, including losses resulting from the non-payment of interest and other types of payment which the borrower is obliged to make, likely to be incurred by the lending credit institution proportional to the coverage of the guarantee; or

(b)   the lending credit institution can demonstrate that the loss-protecting effects of the guarantee, including losses resulting from the non-payment of interest and other types of payments which the borrower is obliged to make, justify such treatment.

2.4. Additional requirements for credit derivatives

20.   For a credit derivative to be recognised the following conditions shall also be met:

(a)   subject to point (b), the credit events specified under the credit derivative shall at a minimum include:

    (i)   the failure to pay the amounts due under the terms of the underlying obligation that are in effect at the time of such failure (with a grace period that is closely in line with or shorter than the grace period in the underlying obligation);

    (ii)   the bankruptcy, insolvency or inability of the obligor to pay its debts, or its failure or admission in writing of its inability generally to pay its debts as they become due, and analogous events; and

    (iii)   the restructuring of the underlying obligation involving forgiveness or postponement of principal, interest or fees that results in a credit loss event (ie value adjustment or other similar debit to the profit and loss account);

(b)   where the credit events specified under the credit derivative do not include restructuring of the underlying obligation as described in point (a)(iii), the credit protection may nonetheless be recognised subject to a reduction in the recognised value as specified in point 83 of Part 3;

(c)   in the case of credit derivatives allowing for cash settlement, a robust valuation process shall be in place in order to estimate loss reliably. There shall be a clearly specified period for obtaining post-credit-event valuations of the underlying obligation;

(d)   if the protection purchaser's right and ability to transfer the underlying obligation to the protection provider is required for settlement, the terms of the underlying obligation shall provide that any required consent to such transfer may not be unreasonably withheld; and

(e)   the identity of the parties responsible for determining whether a credit event has occurred shall be clearly defined. This determination shall not be the sole responsibility of the protection provider. The protection buyer shall have the right/ability to inform the protection provider of the occurrence of a credit event.

21.   A mismatch between the underlying obligation and the reference obligation under the credit derivative (ie the obligation used for the purposes of determining cash settlement value or the deliverable obligation) or between the underlying obligation and the obligation used for purposes of determining whether a credit event has occurred is permissible only if the following conditions are met:

(a)   the reference obligation or the obligation used for purposes of determining whether a credit event has occurred, as the case may be, ranks pari passu with or is junior to the underlying obligation; and

(b)   the underlying obligation and the reference obligation or the obligation used for purposes of determining whether a credit event has occurred, as the case may be, share the same obligor (ie, the same legal entity) and there are in place legally enforceable cross-default or cross-acceleration clauses.

2.5. Requirements to qualify for the treatment set out in Annex VII, Part 1, point 4

22.   To be eligible for the treatment set out in Annex VII, Part 1, point 4, credit protection deriving from a guarantee or credit derivative shall meet the following conditions:
    (a)   the underlying obligation shall be to:
        —   a corporate exposure as defined in Article 86, excluding insurance and reinsurance undertakings;
        —   an exposure to a regional government, local authority or Public Sector Entity which is not treated as an exposure to a central government or a central bank according to Article 86; or
        —   an exposure to a small or medium sized entity, classified as a retail exposure according to Article 86(4);
    (b)   the underlying obligors shall not be members of the same group as the protection provider;
    (c)   the exposure shall be hedged by one of the following instruments:
        —   single-name unfunded credit derivatives or single-name guarantees,
        —   first-to-default basket products — the treatment shall be applied to the asset within the basket with the lowest risk-weighted exposure amount, or
        — n^{th}-to-default basket products — the protection obtained is only eligible for consideration under this framework if eligible (n-1)th default protection has also be obtained or where (n-1) of the assets within the basket has/have already defaulted. Where this is the case the treatment shall be applied to the asset within the basket with the lowest risk-weighted exposure amount;
    (d)   the credit protection meets the requirements set out in points 14, 15, 18, 20 and 21;
    (e)   the risk weight that is associated with the exposure prior to the application of the treatment in Annex VII, Part 1, point 4, does not already factor in any aspect of the credit protection;
    (f)   a credit institution shall have the right and expectation to receive payment from the protection provider without having to take legal action in order to pursue the counterparty for payment. To the extent possible, a credit institution shall take steps to satisfy itself that the protection provider is willing to pay promptly should a credit event occur;
    (g)   the purchased credit protection shall absorb all credit losses incurred on the hedged portion of an exposure that arise due to the occurrence of credit events outlined in the contract;
    (h)   if the payout structure provides for physical settlement, then there shall be legal certainty with respect to the deliverability of a loan, bond, or contingent liability. If a credit institution intends to deliver an obligation other than the underlying exposure, it shall ensure that the deliverable obligation is sufficiently liquid so that the credit institution would have the ability to purchase it for delivery in accordance with the contract;
    (i)   the terms and conditions of credit protection arrangements shall be legally confirmed in writing by both the protection provider and the credit institution;
    (j)   credit institutions shall have a process in place to detect excessive correlation between the creditworthiness of a protection provider and the obligor of the underlying exposure due to their performance being dependent on common factors beyond the systematic risk factor; and
    (k)   in the case of protection against dilution risk, the seller of purchased receivables shall not be a member of the same group as the protection provider.

PART 3
CALCULATING THE EFFECTS OF CREDIT RISK MITIGATION

1.   Subject to Parts 4 to 6, where the provisions in Parts 1 and 2 are satisfied, the calculation of risk-weighted exposure amounts under Articles 78 to 83 and the calculation of risk-weighted exposure amounts and expected loss amounts under Articles 84 to 89 may be modified in accordance with the provisions of this Part.

2.   Cash, securities or commodities purchased, borrowed or received under a repurchase transaction or securities or commodities lending or borrowing transaction shall be treated as collateral.

1. FUNDED CREDIT PROTECTION

1.1. Credit linked notes

3.   Investments in credit linked notes issued by the lending credit institution may be treated as cash collateral.

1.2. On-balance sheet netting

4.   Loans and deposits with the lending credit institution subject to on-balance sheet netting are to be treated as cash collateral.

1.3. Master netting agreements covering repurchase transactions and/or securities or commodities lending or borrowing transactions and/or other capital market-driven transactions

1.3.1. Calculation of the fully-adjusted exposure value

(a) Using the "Supervisory" volatility adjustments or the "Own Estimates" volatility adjustments approaches

5. Subject to points 12 to 21, in calculating the "fully adjusted exposure value" (E*) for the exposures subject to an eligible master netting agreement covering repurchase transactions and/or securities or commodities lending or borrowing transactions and/or other capital market-driven transactions, the volatility adjustments to be applied shall be calculated either using the Supervisory Volatility Adjustments Approach or the Own Estimates Volatility Adjustments Approach as set out in points 30 to 61 for the Financial Collateral Comprehensive Method. For the use of the Own estimates approach, the same conditions and requirements shall apply as apply under the Financial Collateral Comprehensive Method.

6. The net position in each "type of security" or commodity shall be calculated by subtracting from the total value of the securities or commodities of that type lent, sold or provided under the master netting agreement, the total value of securities or commodities of that type borrowed, purchased or received under the agreement.

7. For the purposes of point 6, "type of security" means securities which are issued by the same entity, have the same issue date, the same maturity and are subject to the same terms and conditions and are subject to the same liquidation periods as indicated in points 34 to 59.

8. The net position in each currency, other than the settlement currency of the master netting agreement, shall be calculated by subtracting from the total value of securities denominated in that currency lent, sold or provided under the master netting agreement added to the amount of cash in that currency lent or transferred under the agreement, the total value of securities denominated in that currency borrowed, purchased or received under the agreement added to the amount of cash in that currency borrowed or received under the agreement.

9. The volatility adjustment appropriate to a given type of security or cash position shall be applied to the absolute value of the positive or negative net position in the securities of that type.

10. The foreign exchange risk (fx) volatility adjustment shall be applied to the net positive or negative position in each currency other than the settlement currency of the master netting agreement.

11. E* shall be calculated according to the following formula:

$$E^* = \max\left\{0, \left[\left(\sum(E) - \sum(C)\right) + \sum\left(\left|\text{nettopositie in elk effect}\right| \times \text{Hsec}\right) + \left(\sum\left|\text{Efx}\right| \times \text{Hfx}\right)\right]\right\}$$

Where risk-weighted exposure amounts are calculated under Articles 78 to 83, E is the exposure value for each separate exposure under the agreement that would apply in the absence of the credit protection.

Where risk-weighted exposure amounts and expected loss amounts are calculated under Articles 84 to 89, E is the exposure value for each separate exposure under the agreement that would apply in the absence of the credit protection.

C is the value of the securities or commodities borrowed, purchased or received or the cash borrowed or received in respect of each such exposure.

S(E) is the sum of all Es under the agreement.

S(C) is the sum of all Cs under the agreement.

E_{fx} is the net position (positive or negative) in a given currency other than the settlement currency of the agreement as calculated under point 8.

H_{sec} is the volatility adjustment appropriate to a particular type of security.

H_{fx} is the foreign exchange volatility adjustment.

E* is the fully adjusted exposure value.

(b) Using the Internal Models approach

12. As an alternative to using the Supervisory volatility adjustments approach or the Own Estimates volatility adjustments approach in calculating the fully adjusted exposure value (E*) resulting from the application of an eligible master netting agreement covering repurchase transactions, securities or commodities lending or borrowing transactions, and/or other capital market driven transactions other than derivative transactions, credit institutions may be permitted to use an internal models approach which takes into account correlation effects between security positions subject to the master netting agreement as well as the liquidity of the instruments concerned. Internal models used in this approach shall provide estimates of the potential change in value of the unsecured exposure amount ($\Sigma E - \Sigma C$). Subject to the approval of the competent

authorities, credit institutions may also use their internal models for margin lending transactions, if the transactions are covered under a bilateral master netting agreement that meets the requirements set out in Annex III, Part 7.

13. A credit institution may choose to use an internal models approach independently of the choice it has made between Articles 78 to 83 and Articles 84 to 89 for the calculation of risk-weighted exposure amounts. However, if a credit institution seeks to use an internal models approach, it must do so for all counterparties and securities, excluding immaterial portfolios where it may use the Supervisory volatility adjustments approach or the Own estimates volatility adjustments approach as set out in points 5 to 11.

14. The internal models approach is available to credit institutions that have received recognition for an internal risk-management model under Annex V to Directive 2006/49/EC.

15. Credit institutions which have not received supervisory recognition for use of such a model under Directive 2006/49/EC, may apply to the competent authorities for recognition of an internal risk-measurement model for the purposes of points 12 to 21.

16. Recognition shall only be given if the competent authority is satisfied that the credit institution's risk management system for managing the risks arising on the transactions covered by the master netting agreement is conceptually sound and implemented with integrity and that, in particular, the following qualitative standards are met:

(a) the internal risk-measurement model used for calculation of potential price volatility for the transactions is closely integrated into the daily risk-management process of the credit institution and serves as the basis for reporting risk exposures to senior management of the credit institution;

(b) the credit institution has a risk control unit that is independent from business trading units and reports directly to senior management. The unit must be responsible for designing and implementing the credit institution's risk-management system. It shall produce and analyse daily reports on the output of the risk-measurement model and on the appropriate measures to be taken in terms of position limits;

(c) the daily reports produced by the risk-control unit are reviewed by a level of management with sufficient authority to enforce reductions of positions taken and of overall risk exposure;

(d) the credit institution has sufficient staff skilled in the use of sophisticated models in the risk control unit;

(e) the credit institution has established procedures for monitoring and ensuring compliance with a documented set of internal policies and controls concerning the overall operation of the risk-measurement system;

(f) the credit institution's models have a proven track record of reasonable accuracy in measuring risks demonstrated through the back-testing of its output using at least one year of data;

(g) the credit institution frequently conducts a rigorous programme of stress testing and the results of these tests are reviewed by senior management and reflected in the policies and limits it sets;

(h) the credit institution must conduct, as Part of its regular internal auditing process, an independent review of its risk-measurement system. This review must include both the activities of the business trading units and of the independent risk-control unit;

(i) at least once a year, the credit institution must conduct a review of its risk-management system; and

(j) the internal model shall meet the requirements set out in Annex III, Part 6, points 40 to 42.

17. The calculation of the potential change in value shall be subject to the following minimum standards:

(a) at least daily calculation of the potential change in value;

(b) a 99th percentile, one-tailed confidence interval;

(c) a 5-day equivalent liquidation period, except in the case of transactions other than securities repurchase transactions or securities lending or borrowing transactions where a 10-day equivalent liquidation period shall be used;

(d) an effective historical observation period of at least one year except where a shorter observation period is justified by a significant upsurge in price volatility; and

(e) three-monthly data set updates.

18. The competent authorities shall require that the internal risk-measurement model captures a sufficient number of risk factors in order to capture all material price risks.

19. The competent authorities may allow credit institutions to use empirical correlations within risk categories and across risk categories if they are satisfied that the credit institution's system for measuring correlations is sound and implemented with integrity.

20.   The fully adjusted exposure value (E*) for credit institutions using the Internal models approach shall be calculated according to the following formula:

$$E^* = \max\left\{0, \left[\left(\sum E - \sum C\right) + (\text{uitkomst van het interne model})\right]\right\}$$

Where risk-weighted exposure amounts are calculated under Articles 78 to 83, E is the exposure value for each separate exposure under the agreement that would apply in the absence of the credit protection.

Where risk-weighted exposure amounts and expected loss amounts are calculated under Articles 84 to 89, E is the exposure value for each separate exposure under the agreement that would apply in the absence of the credit protection.

C is the value of the securities borrowed, purchased or received or the cash borrowed or received in respect of each such exposure.

$\Sigma(E)$ is the sum of all Es under the agreement.

$\Sigma(C)$ is the sum of all Cs under the agreement.

21.   In calculating risk-weighted exposure amounts using internal models, credit institutions shall use the previous business day's model output.

1.3.2. Calculating risk-weighted exposure amounts and expected loss amounts for repurchase transactions and/or securities or commodities lending or borrowing transactions and/or other capital market-driven transactions covered by master netting agreements

Standardised Approach

22.   E* as calculated under points 5 to 21 shall be taken as the exposure value of the exposure to the counterparty arising from the transactions subject to the master netting agreement for the purposes of Article 80.

IRB Approach

23.   E* as calculated under points 5 to 21 shall be taken as the exposure value of the exposure to the counterparty arising from the transactions subject to the master netting agreement for the purposes of Annex VII.

1.4. Financial collateral

1.4.1. Financial Collateral Simple Method

24.   The Financial Collateral Simple Method shall be available only where risk-weighted exposure amounts are calculated under Articles 78 to 83. A credit institution shall not use both the Financial Collateral Simple Method and the Financial Collateral Comprehensive Method.

Valuation

25.   Under this method, recognised financial collateral is assigned a value equal to its market value as determined in accordance with Part 2, point 6.

Calculating risk-weighted exposure amounts

26.   The risk weight that would be assigned under Articles 78 to 83 if the lender had a direct exposure to the collateral instrument shall be assigned to those portions of claims collateralised by the market value of recognised collateral. The risk weight of the collateralised portion shall be a minimum of 20% except as specified in points 27 to 29. The remainder of the exposure shall receive the risk weight that would be assigned to an unsecured exposure to the counterparty under Articles 78 to 83.

Repurchase transactions and securities lending or borrowing transactions

27.   A risk weight of 0% shall be assigned to the collateralised portion of the exposure arising from transactions which fulfil the criteria enumerated in points 58 and 59. If the counterparty to the transaction is not a core market participant a risk weight of 10% shall be assigned.

OTC derivative transactions subject to daily mark-to-market

28.   A risk weight of 0% shall, to the extent of the collateralisation, be assigned to the exposure values determined under Annex III for the derivative instruments listed in Annex IV and subject to daily marking-to-market, collateralised by cash or cash-assimilated instruments where there is no currency mismatch. A risk weight of 10% shall be assigned to the extent of the collateralisation to the exposure values of such transactions collateralised by debt securities issued by central governments or central banks which are assigned a 0% risk weight under Articles 78 to 83.

For the purposes of this point debt securities issued by central governments or central banks shall include:—

(a)   debt securities issued by regional governments or local authorities exposures to which are treated as exposures to the central government in whose jurisdiction they are established under Articles 78 to 83;

(b)   debt securities issued by multilateral development banks to which a 0% risk weight is assigned under or by virtue of Articles 78 to 83; and

(c)   debt securities issued by international organisations which are assigned a 0% risk weight under Articles 78 to 83.

Other transactions

29.   A 0% risk weight may be assigned where the exposure and the collateral are denominated in the same currency, and either:

(a)   the collateral is cash on deposit or a cash assimilated instrument; or

(b)   the collateral is in the form of debt securities issued by central governments or central banks eligible for a 0% risk weight under Articles 78 to 83, and its market value has been discounted by 20%.

For the purposes of this point "debt securities issued by central governments or central banks" shall to include those indicated under point 28.

1.4.2. Financial Collateral Comprehensive Method

30.   In valuing financial collateral for the purposes of the Financial Collateral Comprehensive Method, "volatility adjustments" shall be applied to the market value of collateral, as set out in points 34 to 59 below, in order to take account of price volatility.

31.   Subject to the treatment for currency mismatches in the case of OTC derivatives transactions set out in point 32, where collateral is denominated in a currency that differs from that in which the underlying exposure is denominated, an adjustment reflecting currency volatility shall be added to the volatility adjustment appropriate to the collateral as set out in points 34 to 59.

32.   In the case of OTC derivatives transactions covered by netting agreements recognised by the competent authorities under Annex III, a volatility adjustment reflecting currency volatility shall be applied when there is a mismatch between the collateral currency and the settlement currency. Even in the case where multiple currencies are involved in the transactions covered by the netting agreement, only a single volatility adjustment shall be applied.

(a) Calculating adjusted values

33.   The volatility-adjusted value of the collateral to be taken into account is calculated as follows in the case of all transactions except those transactions subject to recognised master netting agreements to which the provisions set out in points 5 to 23 are applied:

$$C_{VA} = C \times (1 - H_C - H_{FX})$$

The volatility-adjusted value of the exposure to be taken into account is calculated as follows:

$$E_{VA} = E \times (1 + H_E)$$, and, in the case of OTC derivative transactions, $E_{VA} = E$.

The fully adjusted value of the exposure, taking into account both volatility and the risk-mitigating effects of collateral is calculated as follows:

$$E^* = \max \{0, [E_{VA} - C_{VAM}]\}$$

Where:

E is the exposure value as would be determined under Articles 78 to 83 or Articles 84 to 89 as appropriate if the exposure was not collateralised. For this purpose, for credit institutions calculating risk-weighted exposure amounts under Articles 78 to 83, the exposure value of off-balance sheet items listed in Annex II shall be 100% of its value rather than the percentages indicated in Article 78(1), and for credit institutions calculating risk-weighted exposure amounts under Articles 84 to 89, the exposure value of the items listed in Annex VII, Part 3, points 9 to 11 shall be calculated using a conversion factor of 100% rather than the conversion factors or percentages indicated in those points.

E_{VA} is the volatility-adjusted exposure amount.

$C_{VA}A$ is the volatility-adjusted value of the collateral.

C_{VAM} is C_{VA} further adjusted for any maturity mismatch in accordance with the provisions of Part 4.

H_E is the volatility adjustment appropriate to the exposure (E), as calculated under points 34 to 59.

H_C is the volatility adjustment appropriate to the collateral, as calculated under points 34 to 59.

H_{FX} is the volatility adjustment appropriate to currency mismatch, as calculated under points 34 to 59.

E^* is the fully adjusted exposure value taking into account volatility and the risk-mitigating effects of the collateral.

(b) Calculation of volatility adjustments to be applied

34. Volatility adjustments may be calculated in two ways: the Supervisory volatility adjustments approach and the Own estimates of volatility adjustments approach (the "Own estimates" approach).

35. A credit institution may choose to use the Supervisory volatility adjustments approach or the Own estimates approach independently of the choice it has made between the Articles 78 to 83 and Articles 84 to 89 for the calculation of risk-weighted exposure amounts. However, if credit institutions seek to use the Own estimates approach, they must do so for the full range of instrument types, excluding immaterial portfolios where they may use the Supervisory volatility adjustments approach.

Where the collateral consists of a number of recognised items, the volatility adjustment shall be:

$$H = \sum_i \alpha_i H_i$$

where α_i is the proportion of an item to the collateral as a whole and Hi is the volatility adjustment applicable to that item.

(i) Supervisory volatility adjustments

36. The volatility adjustments to be applied under the Supervisory volatility adjustments approach (assuming daily revaluation) shall be those set out in Tables 1 to 4.

Volatility Adjustments

Table 1

Credit quality step with which the credit assessment of the debt security is associated	Residual Maturity	Volatility adjustments for debt securities issued by entities described in Part 1, point 7(b)			Volatility adjustments for debt securities issued by entities described in Part 1, point 7(c) and (d)		
		20-day liquid-ation period (%)	10-day liquid-ation period (%)	5-day liquid-ation period (%)	20-day liquid-ation period (%)	10-day liquid-ation period (%)	5-day liquid-ation period (%)
1	≤ 1 year	0.707	0.5	0.354	1.414	1	0.707
	>1 ≤ 5 years	2.828	2	1.414	5.657	4	2.828
	> 5 years	5.657	4	2.828	11.314	8	5.657
2–3	≤ 1 year	1.414	1	0.707	2.828	2	1.414
	>1 ≤ 5 years	4.243	3	2.121	8.485	6	4.243
	> 5 years	8.485	6	4.243	16.971	12	8.485
4	≤ 1 year	21.213	15	10.607	N/A	N/A	N/A
	>1 ≤ 5 years	21.213	15	10.607	N/A	N/A	N/A
	> 5 years	21.213	15	10.607	N/A	N/A	N/A

Table 2

Credit quality step with which the credit assessment of a short term debt security is associated	Volatility adjustments for debt securities issued by entities described in Part 1, point 7(b) with short-term credit assessments			Volatility adjustments for debt securities issued by entities described in Part 1, point 7(c) and (d) with short-term credit assessments		
	20-day liquid- ation period (%)	10-day liquid- ation period (%)	5-day liquid- ation period (%)	20-day liquid- ation period (%)	10-day liquid- ation period (%)	5-day liquid- ation period (%)
1	0.707	0.5	0.354	1.414	1	0.707
2–3	1.414	1	0.707	2.828	2	1.414

Table 3

Other collateral or exposure types	0-day liquidation period (%)	10-day liquidation period (%)	5-day liquidation period (%)
Main Index Equities, Main Index Convertible Bonds	21.213	15	10.607
Other Equities or Convertible Bonds listed on a recognised exchange	35.355	25	17.678
Cash	0	0	0
Gold	21.213	15	10.607

Table 4

Volatility adjustment for currency mismatch		
20-day liquidation period (%)	10-day liquidation period (%)	5-day liquidation period)
11.314	8	5.657

37. For secured lending transactions the liquidation period shall be 20 business days. For repurchase transactions (except insofar as such transactions involve the transfer of commodities or guaranteed rights relating to title to commodities) and securities lending or borrowing transactions the liquidation period shall be 5 business days. For other capital market driven transactions, the liquidation period shall be 10 business days.

38. In Tables 1 to 4 and in points 39 to 41, the credit quality step with which a credit assessment of the debt security is associated is the credit quality step with which the credit assessment is determined by the competent authorities to be associated under Articles 78 to 83. For the purpose of this point, Part 1, point 10 also applies.

39. For non-eligible securities or for commodities lent or sold under repurchase transactions or securities or commodities lending or borrowing transactions, the volatility adjustment is the same as for non-main index equities listed on a recognised exchange.

40. For eligible units in collective investment undertakings the volatility adjustment is the weighted average volatility adjustments that would apply, having regard to the liquidation period of the transaction as specified in point 37, to the assets in which the fund has invested. If the assets in which the fund has invested are not known to the credit institution, the volatility adjustment is the highest volatility adjustment that would apply to any of the assets in which the fund has the right to invest.

41. For unrated debt securities issued by institutions and satisfying the eligibility criteria in Part 1, point 8 the volatility adjustments shall be the same as for securities issued by institutions or corporates with an external credit assessment associated with credit quality steps 2 or 3.

(ii) Own estimates of volatility adjustments

42.　The competent authorities shall permit credit institutions complying with the requirements set out in points 47 to 56 to use their own volatility estimates for calculating the volatility adjustments to be applied to collateral and exposures.

43.　When debt securities have a credit assessment from a recognised ECAI equivalent to investment grade or better, the competent authorities may allow credit institutions to calculate a volatility estimate for each category of security.

44.　In determining relevant categories, credit institutions shall take into account the type of issuer of the security the external credit assessment of the securities, their residual maturity, and their modified duration. Volatility estimates must be representative of the securities included in the category by the credit institution.

45.　For debt securities having a credit assessment from a recognised ECAI equivalent to below investment grade, and for other eligible collateral, the volatility adjustments must be calculated for each individual item.

46.　Credit institutions using the Own estimates approach must estimate volatility of the collateral or foreign exchange mismatch without taking into account any correlations between the unsecured exposure, collateral and/or exchange rates.

Quantitative Criteria

47.　In calculating the volatility adjustments, a 99th percentile one-tailed confidence interval shall be used.

48.　The liquidation period shall be 20 business days for secured lending transactions; 5 business days for repurchase transactions, except insofar as such transactions involve the transfer of commodities or guaranteed rights relating to title to commodities and securities lending or borrowing transactions, and 10 business days for other capital market driven transactions.

49.　Credit institutions may use volatility adjustment numbers calculated according to shorter or longer liquidation periods, scaled up or down to the liquidation period set out in point 48 for the type of transaction in question, using the square root of time formula:

$$HM = HN\sqrt{T_M/T_N}$$

where T_M is the relevant liquidation period;

H_M is the volatility adjustment under T_M and

H_N is the volatility adjustment based on the liquidation period T_N.

50.　Credit institutions shall take into account the illiquidity of lower-quality assets. The liquidation period shall be adjusted upwards in cases where there is doubt concerning the liquidity of the collateral. They shall also identify where historical data may understate potential volatility, eg, a pegged currency. Such cases shall be dealt with by means of a stress scenario.

51.　The historical observation period (sample period) for calculating volatility adjustments shall be a minimum length of one year. For credit institutions that use a weighting scheme or other methods for the historical observation period, the effective observation period shall be at least one year (that is, the weighted average time lag of the individual observations shall not be less than 6 months). The competent authorities may also require a credit institution to calculate its volatility adjustments using a shorter observation period if, in the competent authorities' judgement, this is justified by a significant upsurge in price volatility.

52.　Credit institutions shall update their data sets at least once every three months and shall also reassess them whenever market prices are subject to material changes. This implies that volatility adjustments shall be computed at least every three months.

Qualitative Criteria

53.　The volatility estimates shall be used in the day-to-day risk management process of the credit institution including in relation to its internal exposure limits.

54.　If the liquidation period used by the credit institution in its day-to-day risk management process is longer than that set out in this Part for the type of transaction in question, the credit institution's volatility adjustments shall be scaled up in accordance with the square root of time formula set out in point 49.

55.　The credit institution shall have established procedures for monitoring and ensuring compliance with a documented set of policies and controls for the operation of its system for the estimation of volatility adjustments and for the integration of such estimations into its risk management process.

56.　An independent review of the credit institution's system for the estimation of volatility adjustments shall be carried out regularly in the credit institution's own internal auditing process. A review of the overall system for the estimation of volatility adjustments and for integration of those adjustments into the credit institution's risk management process shall take place at least once a year and shall specifically address, at a minimum:

(a)   the integration of estimated volatility adjustments into daily risk management;
(b)   the validation of any significant change in the process for the estimation of volatility adjustments;
(c)   the verification of the consistency, timeliness and reliability of data sources used to run the system for the estimation of volatility adjustments, including the independence of such data sources; and
(d)   the accuracy and appropriateness of the volatility assumptions.

(iii) Scaling up of volatility adjustments

57.   The volatility adjustments set out in points 36 to 41 are the volatility adjustments to be applied where there is daily revaluation. Similarly, where a credit institution uses its own estimates of the volatility adjustments in accordance with points 42 to 56, these must be calculated in the first instance on the basis of daily revaluation. If the frequency of revaluation is less than daily, larger volatility adjustments shall be applied. These shall be calculated by scaling up the daily revaluation volatility adjustments, using the following "square root of time" formula:

$$H = H_M \sqrt{\frac{N_R + (T_M - 1)}{T_M}}$$

where:

H is the volatility adjustment to be applied

H_M is the volatility adjustment where there is daily revaluation

N_R is the actual number of business days between revaluations

T_M is the liquidation period for the type of transaction in question.

(iv) Conditions for applying a 0% volatility adjustment

58.   In relation to repurchase transactions and securities lending or borrowing transactions, where a credit institution uses the Supervisory Volatility Adjustments Approach or the Own Estimates Approach and where the conditions set out in points (a) to (h) are satisfied, credit institutions may, instead of applying the volatility adjustments calculated under points 34 to 57, apply a 0% volatility adjustment. This option is not available in respect of credit institutions using the internal models approach set out in points 12 to 21:

(a)   Both the exposure and the collateral are cash or debt securities issued by central governments or central banks within the meaning of Part 1, point 7(b) and eligible for a 0% risk weight under Articles 78 to 83,
(b)   Both the exposure and the collateral are denominated in the same currency,
(c)   Either the maturity of the transaction is no more than one day or both the exposure and the collateral are subject to daily marking-to-market or daily remargining,
(d)   It is considered that the time between the last marking-to-market before a failure to remargin by the counterparty and the liquidation of the collateral shall be no more than four business days,
(e)   The transaction is settled across a settlement system proven for that type of transaction,
(f)   The documentation covering the agreement is standard market documentation for repurchase transactions or securities lending or borrowing transactions in the securities concerned,
(g)   The transaction is governed by documentation specifying that if the counterparty fails to satisfy an obligation to deliver cash or securities or to deliver margin or otherwise defaults, then the transaction is immediately terminable, and
(h)   The counterparty is considered a "core market participant" by the competent authorities. Core market participants shall include the following entities:
—   the entities mentioned in point 7(b) of Part 1 exposures to which are assigned a 0% risk weight under Articles 78 to 83;
—   institutions;
—   other financial companies (including insurance companies) exposures to which are assigned a 20% risk weight under Articles 78 to 83 or which, in the case of credit institutions calculating risk-weighted exposure amounts and expected loss amounts under Articles 83 to 89, do not have a credit assessment by a recognised ECAI and are internally rated as having a PD equivalent to that associated with the credit assessments of ECAIs determined by the competent authorities to be associated with credit quality step 2 or above under the rules for the risk weighting of exposures to corporates under Articles 78 to 83;

    —   regulated collective investment undertakings that are subject to capital or leverage
           requirements;
    —   regulated pension funds; and
    —   recognised clearing organisations.

59.   Where a competent authority permits the treatment set out in point 58 to be applied in the case of repurchase transactions or securities lending or borrowing transactions in securities issued by its domestic government, then other competent authorities may choose to allow credit institutions incorporated in their jurisdiction to adopt the same approach to the same transactions.

(c) Calculating risk-weighted exposure amounts and expected loss amounts

Standardised Approach

60.   E* as calculated under point 33 shall be taken as the exposure value for the purposes of Article 80. In the case of off-balance sheet items listed in Annex II, E* shall be taken as the value at which the percentages indicated in Article 78(1) shall be applied to arrive at the exposure value.

IRB Approach

61.   LGD* (the effective LGD) calculated as set out in this point shall be taken as the LGD for the purposes of Annex VII.

LGD* = LGD x (E*/E)

where:

LGD is the LGD that would apply to the exposure under Articles 84 to 89 if the exposure was not collateralised;

E is the exposure value as described under point 33;

E* is as calculated under point 33.

1.5. Other eligible collateral for Articles 84 to 89

1.5.1. Valuation

(a) Real estate collateral

62.   The property shall be valued by an independent valuer at or less than the market value. In those Member States that have laid down rigorous criteria for the assessment of the mortgage lending value in statutory or regulatory provisions the property may instead be valued by an independent valuer at or less than the mortgage lending value.

63.   "Market value" means the estimated amount for which the property should exchange on the date of valuation between a willing buyer and a willing seller in an arm's-length transaction after proper marketing wherein the parties had each acted knowledgeably, prudently and without compulsion. The market value shall be documented in a transparent and clear manner.

64.   "Mortgage lending value" means the value of the property as determined by a prudent assessment of the future marketability of the property taking into account long-term sustainable aspects of the property, the normal and local market conditions, the current use and alternative appropriate uses of the property. Speculative elements shall not be taken into account in the assessment of the mortgage lending value. The mortgage lending value shall be documented in a transparent and clear manner.

65.   The value of the collateral shall be the market value or mortgage lending value reduced as appropriate to reflect the results of the monitoring required under Part 2, point 8 and to take account of the any prior claims on the property.

(b) Receivables

66.   The value of receivables shall be the amount receivable.

(c) Other physical collateral

67.   The property shall be valued at its market value — that is the estimated amount for which the property would exchange on the date of valuation between a willing buyer and a willing seller in an arm's-length transaction.

1.5.2. Calculating risk-weighted exposure amounts and expected loss amounts

(a) General treatment

68.   LGD* calculated as set out in points 69 to 72 shall be taken as the LGD for the purposes of Annex VII.

69.   Where the ratio of the value of the collateral (C) to the exposure value (E) is below a threshold level of C* (the required minimum collateralisation level for the exposure) as laid down in Table 5, LGD* shall be the LGD laid down in Annex VII for uncollateralised exposures to the counterparty.

70. Where the ratio of the value of the collateral to the exposure value exceeds a second, higher threshold level of C** (ie the required level of collateralisation to receive full LGD recognition) as laid down in Table 5, LGD* shall be that prescribed in Table 5.

71. Where the required level of collateralisation C** is not achieved in respect of the exposure as a whole, the exposure shall be considered to be two exposures — that part in respect of which the required level of collateralisation C** is achieved and the remainder.

72. Table 5 sets out the applicable LGD* and required collateralisation levels for the secured parts of exposures.

Table 5
Minimum LGD for secured parts of exposures

	LGD* for senior claims or contingent claims	LGD* for subordinated claims or contingent claims	Required minimum collateralisation level of the exposure (C*)	Required minimum collateralisation level of the exposure (C**)
Receivables	35%	65%	0%	125%
Residential real estate/commercial real estate	35%	65%	30%	140%
Other collateral	40%	70%	30%	140%

By way of derogation, until 31 December 2012 the competent authorities may, subject to the levels of collateralisation indicated in Table 5:

(a) allow credit institutions to assign a 30% LGD for senior exposures in the form of Commercial Real Estate leasing;

(b) allow credit institutions to assign a 35% LGD for senior exposures in the form of equipment leasing; and

(c) allow credit institutions to assign a 30% LGD for senior exposures secured by residential or commercial real estate.

At the end of this period, this derogation shall be reviewed.

(b) Alternative treatment for real estate collateral

73. Subject to the requirements of this point and point 74 and as an alternative to the treatment in points 68 to 72, the competent authorities of a Member State may authorise credit institutions to assign a 50% risk weight to the Part of the exposure fully collateralised by residential real estate property or commercial real estate property situated within the territory of the Member State if they have evidence that the relevant markets are well-developed and long-established with loss-rates from lending collateralised by residential real estate property or commercial real estate property respectively that do not exceed the following limits:

(a) losses stemming from lending collateralised by residential real estate property or commercial real estate property respectively up to 50% of the market value (or where applicable and if lower 60% of the mortgage-lending-value) do not exceed 0.3% of the outstanding loans collateralised by that form of real estate property in any given year; and

(b) overall losses stemming from lending collateralised by residential real estate property or commercial real estate property respectively do not exceed 0.5% of the outstanding loans collateralised by that form of real estate property in any given year.

74. If either of the conditions in point 73 is not satisfied in a given year, the eligibility to use this treatment shall cease until the conditions are satisfied in a subsequent year.

75. The competent authorities, which do not authorise the treatment in point 73, may authorise credit institutions to assign the risk weights permitted under this treatment in respect of exposures collateralised by residential real estate property of commercial real estate property respectively located in the territory of those Member States the competent authorities of which authorise this treatment subject to the same conditions as apply in that Member State.

1.6. Calculating risk-weighted exposure amounts and expected loss amounts in the case of mixed pools of collateral

76.   Where risk-weighted exposure amounts and expected loss amounts are calculated under Articles 84 to 89, and an exposure is collateralised by both financial collateral and other eligible collateral, LGD*, to be taken as the LGD for the purposes of Annex VII, shall be calculated as follows.

77.   The credit institution shall be required to subdivide the volatility-adjusted value of the exposure (ie the value after the application of the volatility adjustment as set out in point 33) into parts each covered by only one type of collateral. That is, the credit institution must divide the exposure into the part covered by eligible financial collateral, the portion covered by receivables, the portions covered by commercial real estate property collateral and/or residential real estate property collateral, the part covered by other eligible collateral, and the unsecured portion, as relevant.

78.   LGD* for each part of exposure shall be calculated separately in accordance with the relevant provisions of this Annex.

1.7. Other funded credit protection

1.7.1. Deposits with third party institutions

79.   Where the conditions set out in Part 2, point 12 are satisfied, credit protection falling within the terms of Part 1, point 23 may be treated as a guarantee by the third party institution.

1.7.2. Life insurance policies pledged to the lending credit institution

80.   Where the conditions set out in Part 2, point 13 are satisfied, credit protection falling within the terms of Part 1, point 24 may be treated as a guarantee by the company providing the life insurance. The value of the credit protection recognised shall be the surrender value of the life insurance policy.

1.7.3. Institution instruments repurchased on request

81.   Instruments eligible under Part 1, point 25 may be treated as a guarantee by the issuing institution.

82.   The value of the credit protection recognised shall be the following:
  (a)   where the instrument will be repurchased at its face value, the value of the protection shall be that amount;
  (b)   where the instrument will be repurchased at market price, the value of the protection shall be the value of the instrument valued in the same way as the debt securities specified in Part 1, point 8.

2. UNFUNDED CREDIT PROTECTION

2.1. Valuation

83.   The value of unfunded credit protection (G) shall be the amount that the protection provider has undertaken to pay in the event of the default or non-payment of the borrower or on the occurrence of other specified credit events. In the case of credit derivatives which do not include as a credit event restructuring of the underlying obligation involving forgiveness or postponement of principal, interest or fees that result in a credit loss event (eg value adjustment, the making of a value adjustment or other similar debit to the profit and loss account),
  (a)   where the amount that the protection provider has undertaken to pay is not higher than the exposure value, the value of the credit protection calculated under the first sentence of this point shall be reduced by 40%; or
  (b)   where the amount that the protection provider has undertaken to pay is higher than the exposure value, the value of the credit protection shall be no higher than 60% of the exposure value.

84.   Where unfunded credit protection is denominated in a currency different from that in which the exposure is denominated (a currency mismatch) the value of the credit protection shall be reduced by the application of a volatility adjustment H_{FX} as follows:

$$G^* = G \times (1 - H_{FX})$$

where:

G is the nominal amount of the credit protection,

G* is G adjusted for any foreign exchange risk, and

H_{fx} is the volatility adjustment for any currency mismatch between the credit protection and the underlying obligation.

Where there is no currency mismatch

$$G^* = G$$

85.   The volatility adjustments for any currency mismatch may be calculated based on the Supervisory volatility adjustments approach or the Own estimates approach as set out in points 34 to 57.

2.2. Calculating risk-weighted exposure amounts and expected loss amounts

2.2.1. Partial protection — tranching

86.   Where the credit institution transfers a part of the risk of a loan in one or more tranches, the rules set out in Articles 94 to 101 shall apply. Materiality thresholds on payments below which no payment shall be made in the event of loss are considered to be equivalent to retained first loss positions and to give rise to a tranched transfer of risk.

2.2.2. Standardised Approach

(a) Full protection

87.   For the purposes of Article 80, g shall be the risk weight to be assigned to an exposure which is fully protected by unfunded protection (G_A), where:

g is the risk weight of exposures to the protection provider as specified under Articles 78 to 83; and

G_A is the value of G* as calculated under point 84 further adjusted for any maturity mismatch as laid down in Part 4.

(b) Partial protection — equal seniority

88.   Where the protected amount is less than the exposure value and the protected and unprotected parts are of equal seniority — ie the credit institution and the protection provider share losses on a pro-rata basis, proportional regulatory capital relief shall be afforded. For the purposes of Article 80, risk-weighted exposure amounts shall be calculated in accordance with the following formula:

$(E-G_A) \times r + G_A \times g$

where:

E is the exposure value;

G_A is the value of G* as calculated under point 84 further adjusted for any maturity mismatch as laid down in Part 4;

r is the risk weight of exposures to the obligor as specified under Articles 78 to 83; and

g is the risk weight of exposures to the protection provider as specified under Articles 78 to 83.

(c) Sovereign guarantees

89.   The competent authorities may extend the treatment provided for in Annex VI, Part 1, points 4 and 5 to exposures or parts of exposures guaranteed by the central government or central bank, where the guarantee is denominated in the domestic currency of the borrower and the exposure is funded in that currency.

2.2.3. IRB Approach

Full protection/Partial protection — equal seniority

90.   For the covered portion of the exposure (based on the adjusted value of the credit protection G_A), the PD for the purposes of Annex VII, Part 2 may be the PD of the protection provider, or a PD between that of the borrower and that of the guarantor if a full substitution is deemed not to be warranted. In the case of subordinated exposures and non-subordinated unfunded protection, the LGD to be applied for the purposes of Annex VII, Part 2 may be that associated with senior claims.

91.   For any uncovered portion of the exposure the PD shall be that of the borrower and the LGD shall be that of the underlying exposure.

92. G_A is the value of G* as calculated under point 84 further adjusted for any maturity mismatch as laid down in Part 4.

PART 4
MATURITY MISMATCHES

1.   For the purposes of calculating risk-weighted exposure amounts, a maturity mismatch occurs when the residual maturity of the credit protection is less than that of the protected exposure. Protection of less than three months residual maturity, the maturity of which is less than the maturity of the underlying exposure, shall not be recognised.

2.   Where there is a maturity mismatch the credit protection shall not be recognised where:
    (a)   the original maturity of the protection is less than 1 year; or

(b) the exposure is a short term exposure specified by the competent authorities as being subject to a one-day floor rather than a one-year floor in respect of the maturity value (M) under Annex VII, Part 2, point 14.

1. DEFINITION OF MATURITY

3. Subject to a maximum of 5 years, the effective maturity of the underlying shall be the longest possible remaining time before the obligor is scheduled to fulfil its obligations. Subject to point 4, the maturity of the credit protection shall be the time to the earliest date at which the protection may terminate or be terminated.

4. Where there is an option to terminate the protection which is at the discretion of the protection seller, the maturity of the protection shall be taken to be the time to the earliest date at which that option may be exercised. Where there is an option to terminate the protection which is at the discretion of the protection buyer and the terms of the arrangement at origination of the protection contain a positive incentive for the credit institution to call the transaction before contractual maturity, the maturity of the protection shall be taken to be the time to the earliest date at which that option may be exercised; otherwise such an option may be considered not to affect the maturity of the protection.

5. Where a credit derivative is not prevented from terminating prior to expiration of any grace period required for a default on the underlying obligation to occur as a result of a failure to pay the maturity of the protection shall be reduced by the amount of the grace period.

2. VALUATION OF PROTECTION

2.1. Transactions subject to funded credit protection — Financial Collateral Simple Method

6. Where there is a mismatch between the maturity of the exposure and the maturity of the protection, the collateral shall not be recognised.

2.2. Transactions subject to funded credit protection — Financial Collateral Comprehensive Method

7. The maturity of the credit protection and that of the exposure must be reflected in the adjusted value of the collateral according to the following formula:

$$C_{VAM} = C_{VA} \times (t - t^*)/(T - t^*)$$

where:

C_{VA} is the volatility adjusted value of the collateral as specified in Part 3, point 33 or the amount of the exposure, whichever is the lowest;

t is the number of years remaining to the maturity date of the credit protection calculated in accordance with points 3 to 5, or the value of T, whichever is the lower;

T is the number of years remaining to the maturity date of the exposure calculated in accordance with points 3 to 5, or 5 years, whichever is the lower; and

t^* is 0.25.

C_{VAM} shall be taken as C_{VA} further adjusted for maturity mismatch to be included in the formula for the calculation of the fully adjusted value of the exposure (E*) set out at Part 3, point 33.

2.3. Transactions subject to unfunded credit protection

8. The maturity of the credit protection and that of the exposure must be reflected in the adjusted value of the credit protection according to the following formula:

$$G_A = G^* \times (t - t^*)/(T - t^*)$$

where:

G* is the amount of the protection adjusted for any currency mismatch

G_A is G* adjusted for any maturity mismatch

t is the number of years remaining to the maturity date of the credit protection calculated in accordance with points 3 to 5, or the value of T, whichever is the lower;

T is the number of years remaining to the maturity date of the exposure calculated in accordance with points 3 to 5, or 5 years, whichever is the lower; and

t^* is 0.25.

G_A is then taken as the value of the protection for the purposes of Part 3, points 83 to 92.

PART 5
COMBINATIONS OF CREDIT RISK MITIGATION IN THE STANDARDISED APPROACH

1. In the case where a credit institution calculating risk-weighted exposure amounts under Articles 78 to 83 has more than one form of credit risk mitigation covering a single exposure (eg a

credit institution has both collateral and a guarantee partially covering an exposure), the credit institution shall be required to subdivide the exposure into parts covered by each type of credit risk mitigation tool (e g a part covered by collateral and a portion covered by guarantee) and the risk-weighted exposure amount for each portion must be calculated separately in accordance with the provisions of Articles 78 to 83 and this Annex.

2. When credit protection provided by a single protection provider has differing maturities, a similar approach to that described in point 1 shall be applied.

PART 6
BASKET CRM TECHNIQUES

1. FIRST-TO-DEFAULT CREDIT DERIVATIVES

1. Where a credit institution obtains credit protection for a number of exposures under terms that the first default among the exposures shall trigger payment and that this credit event shall terminate the contract, the credit institution may modify the calculation of the risk-weighted exposure amount and, as relevant, the expected loss amount of the exposure which would, in the absence of the credit protection, produce the lowest risk-weighted exposure amount under Articles 78 to 83 or Articles 84 to 89 as appropriate in accordance with this Annex, but only if the exposure value is less than or equal to the value of the credit protection.

2. N NTH-TO-DEFAULT CREDIT DERIVATIVES

2. Where the nth default among the exposures triggers payment under the credit protection, the credit institution purchasing the protection may only recognise the protection for the calculation of risk-weighted exposure amounts and, as relevant, expected loss amounts if protection has also been obtained for defaults 1 to n-1 or when n-1 defaults have already occurred. In such cases, the methodology shall follow that set out in point 1 for first-to-default derivatives appropriately modified for nth-to-default products.

[5842E]

ANNEX IX
SECURITISATION

PART 1
DEFINITIONS FOR THE PURPOSES OF ANNEX IX

1. For the purposes of this Annex:
— "Excess spread" means finance charge collections and other fee income received in respect of the securitised exposures net of costs and expenses;
— "Clean-up call option" means a contractual option for the originator to repurchase or extinguish the securitisation positions before all of the underlying exposures have been repaid, when the amount of outstanding exposures falls below a specified level;
— "Liquidity facility" means the securitisation position arising from a contractual agreement to provide funding to ensure timeliness of cash flows to investors;
— "Kirb" means 8% of the risk-weighted exposure amounts that would be calculated under Articles 84 to 89 in respect of the securitised exposures, had they not been securitised, plus the amount of expected losses associated with those exposures calculated under those Articles;
— "Ratings based method" means the method of calculating risk-weighted exposure amounts for securitisation positions in accordance with Part 4, points 46 to 51;
— "Supervisory formula method" means the method of calculating risk-weighted exposure amounts for securitisation positions in accordance with Part 4, points 52 to 54;
— "Unrated position" means a securitisation position which does not have an eligible credit assessment by an eligible ECAI as defined in Article 97;
— "Rated position" means a securitisation position which has an eligible credit assessment by an eligible ECAI as defined in Article 97; and
— "Asset-backed commercial paper (ABCP) programme" means a programme of securitisations the securities issued by which predominantly take the form of commercial paper with an original maturity of one year or less.

PART 2
MINIMUM REQUIREMENTS FOR RECOGNITION OF SIGNIFICANT CREDIT RISK TRANSFER AND CALCULATION OF RISK-WEIGHTED EXPOSURE AMOUNTS AND EXPECTED LOSS AMOUNTS FOR SECURITISED EXPOSURES

1. MINIMUM REQUIREMENTS FOR RECOGNITION OF SIGNIFICANT CREDIT RISK TRANSFER IN A TRADITIONAL SECURITISATION

1. The originator credit institution of a traditional securitisation may exclude securitised exposures from the calculation of risk-weighted exposure amounts and expected loss amounts if

significant credit risk associated with the securitised exposures has been transferred to third parties and the transfer complies with the following conditions:

(a) The securitisation documentation reflects the economic substance of the transaction;

(b) The securitised exposures are put beyond the reach of the originator credit institution and its creditors, including in bankruptcy and receivership. This shall be supported by the opinion of qualified legal counsel;

(c) The securities issued do not represent payment obligations of the originator credit institution;

(d) The transferee is a securitisation special-purpose entity (SSPE);

(e) The originator credit institution does not maintain effective or indirect control over the transferred exposures. An originator shall be considered to have maintained effective control over the transferred exposures if it has the right to repurchase from the transferee the previously transferred exposures in order to realise their benefits or if it is obligated to re-assume transferred risk. The originator credit institution's retention of servicing rights or obligations in respect of the exposures shall not of itself constitute indirect control of the exposures;

(f) Where there is a clean-up call option, the following conditions are satisfied:

   (i) The clean-up call option is exercisable at the discretion of the originator credit institution;

   (ii) The clean-up call option may only be exercised when 10% or less of the original value of the exposures securitised remains unamortised; and

   (iii) The clean-up call option is not structured to avoid allocating losses to credit enhancement positions or other positions held by investors and is not otherwise structured to provide credit enhancement; and

(g) The securitisation documentation does not contain clauses that

   (i) other than in the case of early amortisation provisions, require positions in the securitisation to be improved by the originator credit institution including but not limited to altering the underlying credit exposures or increasing the yield payable to investors in response to a deterioration in the credit quality of the securitised exposures; or

   (ii) increase the yield payable to holders of positions in the securitisation in response to a deterioration in the credit quality of the underlying pool.

2. MINIMUM REQUIREMENTS FOR RECOGNITION OF SIGNIFICANT CREDIT RISK TRANSFER IN A SYNTHETIC SECURITISATION

2. An originator credit institution of a synthetic securitisation may calculate risk-weighted exposure amounts, and, as relevant, expected loss amounts, for the securitised exposures in accordance with points 3 and 4 below, if significant credit risk has been transferred to third parties either through funded or unfunded credit protection and the transfer complies with the following conditions:

(a) The securitisation documentation reflects the economic substance of the transaction;

(b) The credit protection by which the credit risk is transferred complies with the eligibility and other requirements under Articles 90 to 93 for the recognition of such credit protection. For the purposes of this point, special purpose entities shall not be recognised as eligible unfunded protection providers.

(c) The instruments used to transfer credit risk do not contain terms or conditions that:

   (i) impose significant materiality thresholds below which credit protection is deemed not to be triggered if a credit event occurs;

   (ii) allow for the termination of the protection due to deterioration of the credit quality of the underlying exposures;

   (iii) other than in the case of early amortisation provisions, require positions in the securitisation to be improved by the originator credit institution;

   (iv) increase the credit institutions' cost of credit protection or the yield payable to holders of positions in the securitisation in response to a deterioration in the credit quality of the underlying pool; and

(d) An opinion is obtained from qualified legal counsel confirming the enforceability of the credit protection in all relevant jurisdictions.

3. ORIGINATOR CREDIT INSTITUTIONS' CALCULATION OF RISK-WEIGHTED EXPOSURE AMOUNTS FOR EXPOSURES SECURITISED IN A SYNTHETIC SECURITISATION

3. In calculating risk-weighted exposure amounts for the securitised exposures, where the conditions in point 2 are met, the originator credit institution of a synthetic securitisation shall, subject to points 5 to 7, use the relevant calculation methodologies set out in Part 4 and not those set out in Articles 78 to 89. For credit institutions calculating risk-weighted exposure amounts and expected loss amounts under Articles 84 to 89, the expected loss amount in respect of such exposures shall be zero.

4.   For clarity, point 3 refers to the entire pool of exposures included in the securitisation. Subject to points 5 to 7, the originator credit institution is required to calculate risk-weighted exposure amounts in respect of all tranches in the securitisation in accordance with the provisions of Part 4 including those relating to the recognition of credit risk mitigation. For example, where a tranche is transferred by means of unfunded credit protection to a third party, the risk weight of that third party shall be applied to the tranche in the calculation of the originator credit institution's risk-weighted exposure amounts.

3.1. Treatment of maturity mismatches in synthetic securitisations

5.   For the purposes of calculating risk-weighted exposure amounts in accordance with point 3, any maturity mismatch between the credit protection by which the tranching is achieved and the securitised exposures shall be taken into consideration in accordance with points 6 to 7.

6.   The maturity of the securitised exposures shall be taken to be the longest maturity of any of those exposures subject to a maximum of five years. The maturity of the credit protection shall be determined in accordance with Annex VIII.

7.   An originator credit institution shall ignore any maturity mismatch in calculating risk-weighted exposure amounts for tranches appearing pursuant to Part 4 with a risk weighting of 1250%. For all other tranches, the maturity mismatch treatment set out in Annex VIII shall be applied in accordance with the following formula:

$$RW^* \text{ is } [RW(SP) \times (t - t^*)/(T - t^*)] + [RW(Ass) \times (T - t)/(T - t^*)]$$

Where:

RW^* is Risk-weighted exposure amounts for the purposes of Article 75(a) ;

$RW(Ass)$ is Risk-weighted exposure amounts for exposures if they had not been securitised, calculated on a pro-rata basis;

$RW(SP)$ is Risk-weighted exposure amounts calculated under point 3 if there was no maturity mismatch;

T is maturity of the underlying exposures expressed in years;

t is maturity of credit protection. expressed in years; and

t^* is 0.25.

PART 3

EXTERNAL CREDIT ASSESSMENTS

1. REQUIREMENTS TO BE MET BY THE CREDIT ASSESSMENTS OF ECAIS

1.   To be used for the purposes of calculating risk-weighted exposure amounts under Part 4, a credit assessment of an eligible ECAI shall comply with the following conditions.

    (a)   There shall be no mismatch between the types of payments reflected in the credit assessment and the types of payment to which the credit institution is entitled under the contract giving rise to the securitisation position in question; and

    (b)   The credit assessments shall be available publicly to the market. Credit assessments are considered to be publicly available only if they have been published in a publicly accessible forum and they are included in the ECAI's transition matrix. Credit assessments that are made available only to a limited number of entities shall not be considered to be publicly available.

2. USE OF CREDIT ASSESSMENTS

2.   A credit institution may nominate one or more eligible ECAIs the credit assessments of which shall be used in the calculation of its risk-weighted exposure amounts under Articles 94 to 101 (a "nominated ECAI").

3.   Subject to points 5 to 7 below, a credit institution must use credit assessments from nominated ECAIs consistently in respect of its securitisation positions.

4.   Subject to points 5 and 6, a credit institution may not use an ECAI's credit assessments for its positions in some tranches and another ECAI's credit assessments for its positions in other tranches within the same structure that may or may not be rated by the first ECAI.

5.   Where a position has two credit assessments by nominated ECAIs, the credit institution shall use the less favourable credit assessment.

6.   Where a position has more than two credit assessments by nominated ECAIs, the two most favourable credit assessments shall be used. If the two most favourable assessments are different, the least favourable of the two shall be used.

7.   Where credit protection eligible under Articles 90 to 93 is provided directly to the SSPE, and that protection is reflected in the credit assessment of a position by a nominated ECAI, the risk weight associated with that credit assessment may be used. If the protection is not eligible under

Articles 90 to 93, the credit assessment shall not be recognised. In the situation where the credit protection is not provided to the SSPE but rather directly to a securitisation position, the credit assessment shall not be recognised.

3. MAPPING

8.   The competent authorities shall determine with which credit quality step in the tables set out in Part 4 each credit assessment of an eligible ECAI shall be associated. In doing so the competent authorities shall differentiate between the relative degrees of risk expressed by each assessment. They shall consider quantitative factors, such as default and/or loss rates, and qualitative factors such as the range of transactions assessed by the ECAI and the meaning of the credit assessment.

9.   The competent authorities shall seek to ensure that securitisation positions to which the same risk weight is applied on the basis of the credit assessments of eligible ECAIs are subject to equivalent degrees of credit risk. This shall include modifying their determination as to the credit quality step with which a particular credit assessment shall be associated, as appropriate.

PART 4
CALCULATION

1. CALCULATION OF RISK-WEIGHTED EXPOSURE AMOUNTS

1.   For the purposes of Article 96, the risk-weighted exposure amount of a securitisation position shall be calculated by applying to the exposure value of the position the relevant risk weight as set out in this Part.

2.   Subject to point 3:
   (a)   where a credit institution calculates risk-weighted exposure amounts under points 6 to 36, the exposure value of an on-balance sheet securitisation position shall be its balance sheet value;
   (b)   where a credit institution calculates risk-weighted exposure amounts under points 37 to 76, the exposure value of an on-balance sheet securitisation position shall be measured gross of value adjustments; and
   (c)   the exposure value of an off-balance sheet securitisation position shall be its nominal value multiplied by a conversion figure as prescribed in this Annex. This conversion figure shall be 100% unless otherwise specified.

3.   The exposure value of a securitisation position arising from a derivative instrument listed in Annex IV, shall be determined in accordance with Annex III.

4.   Where a securitisation position is subject to funded credit protection, the exposure value of that position may be modified in accordance with and subject to the requirements in Annex VIII as further specified in this Annex.

5.   Where a credit institution has two or more overlapping positions in a securitisation, it will be required to the extent that they overlap to include in its calculation of risk-weighted exposure amounts only the position or portion of a position producing the higher risk-weighted exposure amounts. For the purpose of this point "overlapping" means that the positions, wholly or partially, represent an exposure to the same risk such that to the extent of the overlap there is a single exposure.

2. CALCULATION OF RISK-WEIGHTED EXPOSURE AMOUNTS UNDER THE STANDARDISED APPROACH

6.   Subject to point 8, the risk-weighted exposure amount of a rated securitisation position shall be calculated by applying to the exposure value the risk weight associated with the credit quality step with which the credit assessment has been determined to be associated by the competent authorities in accordance with Article 98 as laid down in Tables 1 and 2.

Table 1
Positions other than ones with short-term credit assessments

Credit quality step	1	2	3	4	5 and below
Risk weight	20%	50%	100%	350%	1250%

Table 2
Positions with short-term credit assessments

Credit quality step	1	2	3	All other credit assessments
Risk weight	20%	50%	100%	1250%

7.　Subject to points 10 to 15, the risk-weighted exposure amount of an unrated securitisation position shall be calculated by applying a risk weight of 1250%.

2.1. Originator and sponsor credit institutions

8.　For an originator credit institution or sponsor credit institution, the risk-weighted exposure amounts calculated in respect of its positions in a securitisation may be limited to the risk-weighted exposure amounts which would be calculated for the securitised exposures had they not been securitised subject to the presumed application of a 150% risk weight to all past due items and items belonging to "regulatory high risk categories" amongst the securitised exposures.

2.2. Treatment of unrated positions

9.　Credit institutions having an unrated securitisation position may apply the treatment set out in point 10 for calculating the risk-weighted exposure amount for that position provided the composition of the pool of exposures securitised is known at all times.

10.　A credit institution may apply the weighted-average risk weight that would be applied to the securitised exposures under Articles 78 to 83 by a credit institution holding the exposures, multiplied by a concentration ratio. This concentration ratio is equal to the sum of the nominal amounts of all the tranches divided by the sum of the nominal amounts of the tranches junior to or pari passu with the tranche in which the position is held including that tranche itself. The resulting risk weight shall not be higher than 1250% or lower than any risk weight applicable to a rated more senior tranche. Where the credit institution is unable to determine the risk weights that would be applied to the securitised exposures under Articles 78 to 83, it shall apply a risk weight of 1250% to the position.

2.3. Treatment of securitisation positions in a second loss tranche or better in an ABCP programme

11.　Subject to the availability of a more favourable treatment by virtue of the provisions concerning liquidity facilities in points 13 to 15, a credit institution may apply to securitisation positions meeting the conditions set out in point 12 a risk weight that is the greater of 100% or the highest of the risk weights that would be applied to any of the securitised exposures under Articles 78 to 83 by a credit institution holding the exposures.

12.　For the treatment set out in point 11 to be available, the securitisation position shall be:

(a)　in a tranche which is economically in a second loss position or better in the securitisation and the first loss tranche must provide meaningful credit enhancement to the second loss tranche;

(b)　of a quality the equivalent of investment grade or better; and

(c)　held by a credit institution which does not hold a position in the first loss tranche.

2.4. Treatment of unrated liquidity facilities

2.4.1. Eligible liquidity facilities

13.　When the following conditions are met, to determine its exposure value a conversion figure of 20% may be applied to the nominal amount of a liquidity facility with an original maturity of one year or less and a conversion figure of 50% may be applied to the nominal amount of a liquidity facility with an original maturity of more than one year:

(a)　The liquidity facility documentation shall clearly identify and limit the circumstances under which the facility may be drawn;

(b)　It shall not be possible for the facility to be drawn so as to provide credit support by covering losses already incurred at the time of draw — for example, by providing liquidity in respect of exposures in default at the time of draw or by acquiring assets at more than fair value;

(c)　The facility shall not be used to provide permanent or regular funding for the securitisation;

(d)　Repayment of draws on the facility shall not be subordinated to the claims of investors other than to claims arising in respect of interest rate or currency derivative contracts, fees or other such payments, nor be subject to waiver or deferral;

(e) It shall not be possible for the facility to be drawn after all applicable credit enhancements from which the liquidity facility would benefit are exhausted; and

(f) The facility must include a provision that results in an automatic reduction in the amount that can be drawn by the amount of exposures that are in default, where "default" has the meaning given to it under Articles 84 to 89, or where the pool of securitised exposures consists of rated instruments, that terminates the facility if the average quality of the pool falls below investment grade.

The risk weight to be applied shall be the highest risk weight that would be applied to any of the securitised exposures under Articles 78 to 83 by a credit institution holding the exposures.

2.4.2. Liquidity facilities that may be drawn only in the event of a general market disruption

14. To determine its exposure value, a conversion figure of 0% may be applied to the nominal amount of a liquidity facility that may be drawn only in the event of a general market disruption (ie where more than one SPE across different transactions are unable to roll over maturing commercial paper and that inability is not the result of an impairment of the SPE's credit quality or of the credit quality of the securitised exposures), provided that the conditions set out in point 13 are satisfied.

2.4.3. Cash advance facilities

15. To determine its exposure value, a conversion figure of 0% may be applied to the nominal amount of a liquidity facility that is unconditionally cancellable provided that the conditions set out at point 13 are satisfied and that repayment of draws on the facility are senior to any other claims on the cash flows arising from the securitised exposures.

2.5. Additional capital requirements for securitisations of revolving exposures with early amortisation provisions

16. In addition to the risk-weighted exposure amounts calculated in respect of its securitisation positions, an originator credit institution shall calculate a risk-weighted exposure amount according to the method set out in points 17 to 33 when it sells revolving exposures into a securitisation that contains an early amortisation provision.

17. The credit institution shall calculate a risk-weighted exposure amount in respect of the sum of the originator's interest and the investors' interest.

18. For securitisation structures where the securitised exposures comprise revolving and non-revolving exposures, an originator credit institution shall apply the treatment set out in point 19 to 31 to that portion of the underlying pool containing revolving exposures.

19. For the purposes of point 16 to 31, "originator's interest" means the exposure value of that notional Part of a pool of drawn amounts sold into a securitisation, the proportion of which in relation to the amount of the total pool sold into the structure determines the proportion of the cash flows generated by principal and interest collections and other associated amounts which are not available to make payments to those having securitisation positions in the securitisation.

To qualify as such, the originator's interest may not be subordinate to the investors' interest.

"Investors' interest" means the exposure value of the remaining notional Part of the pool of drawn amounts.

20. The exposure of the originator credit institution, associated with its rights in respect of the originator's interest, shall not be considered a securitisation position but as a pro rata exposure to the securitised exposures as if they had not been securitised.

2.5.1. Exemptions from early amortisation treatment

21. Originators of the following types of securitisation are exempt from the capital requirement in point 16:

(a) securitisations of revolving exposures whereby investors remain fully exposed to all future draws by borrowers so that the risk on the underlying facilities does not return to the originator credit institution even after an early amortisation event has occurred, and

(b) securitisations where any early amortisation provision is solely triggered by events not related to the performance of the securitised assets or the originator credit institution, such as material changes in tax laws or regulations.

2.5.2. Maximum capital requirement

22. For an originator credit institution subject to the capital requirement in point 16 the total of the risk-weighted exposure amounts in respect of its positions in the investors' interest and the risk-weighted exposure amounts calculated under point 16 shall be no greater than the greater of:

(a) the risk-weighted exposure amounts calculated in respect of its positions in the investors' interest; and

(b) the risk-weighted exposure amounts that would be calculated in respect of the securitised exposures by a credit institution holding the exposures as if they had not been securitised in an amount equal to the investors' interest.

23. Deduction of net gains, if any, arising from the capitalisation of future income required under Article 57, shall be treated outside the maximum amount indicated in point 22.

2.5.3. Calculation of risk-weighted exposure amounts

24. The risk-weighted exposure amount to be calculated in accordance with point 16 shall be determined by multiplying the amount of the investors' interest by the product of the appropriate conversion figure as indicated in points 26 to 33 and the weighted average risk weight that would apply to the securitised exposures if the exposures had not been securitised.

25. An early amortisation provision shall be considered to be "controlled" where the following conditions are met:

(a) the originator credit institution has an appropriate capital/liquidity plan in place to ensure that it has sufficient capital and liquidity available in the event of an early amortisation;

(b) throughout the duration of the transaction there is pro-rata sharing between the originator's interest and the investor's interest of payments of interest and principal, expenses, losses and recoveries based on the balance of receivables outstanding at one or more reference points during each month;

(c) the amortisation period is considered sufficient for 90% of the total debt (originator's and investors' interest) outstanding at the beginning of the early amortisation period to have been repaid or recognised as in default; and

(d) the speed of repayment is no more rapid than would be achieved by straight-line amortisation over the period set out in point (c).

26. In the case of securitisations subject to an early amortisation provision of retail exposures which are uncommitted and unconditionally cancellable without prior notice, where the early amortisation is triggered by the excess spread level falling to a specified level, credit institutions shall compare the three-month average excess spread level with the excess spread levels at which excess spread is required to be trapped.

27. Where the securitisation does not require excess spread to be trapped, the trapping point is deemed to be 4.5 percentage points greater than the excess spread level at which an early amortisation is triggered.

28. The conversion figure to be applied shall be determined by the level of the actual three month average excess spread in accordance with Table 3.

Table 3

	Securitisations subject to a controlled early amortisation provision	Securitisations subject to a non-controlled early amortisation provision
3 months average excess spread	Conversion figure	Conversion figure
Above level A	0%	0%
Level A	1%	5%
Level B	2%	15%
Level C	10%	50%
Level D	20%	100%
Level E	40%	100%

29. In Table 3, "Level A" means levels of excess spread less than 133.33% of the trapping level of excess spread but not less than 100% of that trapping level, "Level B" means levels of excess spread less than 100% of the trapping level of excess spread but not less than 75% of that trapping level, "Level C" means levels of excess spread less than 75% of the trapping level of excess spread but not less than 50% of that trapping level, "Level D" means levels of excess spread less than 50% of the trapping level of excess spread but not less than 25% of that trapping level and "Level E" means levels of excess spread less than 25% of the trapping level of excess spread.

30. In the case of securitisations subject to an early amortisation provision of retail exposures which are uncommitted and unconditionally cancellable without prior notice and where the early amortisation is triggered by a quantitative value in respect of something other than the three months

average excess spread, the competent authorities may apply a treatment which approximates closely to that prescribed in points 26 to 29 for determining the conversion figure indicated.

31. Where a competent authority intends to apply a treatment in accordance with point 30 in respect of a particular securitisation, it shall first inform the relevant competent authorities of all the other Member States. Before the application of such a treatment becomes Part of the general policy approach of the competent authority to securitisations containing early amortisation clauses of the type in question, the competent authority shall consult the relevant competent authorities of all the other Member States and take into consideration the views expressed. The views expressed in such consultation and the treatment applied shall be publicly disclosed by the competent authority in question.

32. All other securitisations subject to a controlled early amortisation provision of revolving exposures shall be subject to a conversion figure of 90%.

33. All other securitisations subject to a non-controlled early amortisation provision of revolving exposures shall be subject to a conversion figure of 100%.

2.6. Recognition of credit risk mitigation on securitisation positions

34. Where credit protection is obtained on a securitisation position, the calculation of risk-weighted exposure amounts may be modified in accordance with Annex VIII.

2.7. Reduction in risk-weighted exposure amounts

35. As provided in Article 66(2), in respect of a securitisation position in respect of which a 1250% risk weight is assigned, credit institutions may, as an alternative to including the position in their calculation of risk-weighted exposure amounts, deduct from own funds the exposure value of the position. For these purposes, the calculation of the exposure value may reflect eligible funded credit protection in a manner consistent with point 34.

36. Where a credit institution makes use of the alternative indicated in point 35, 12.5 times the amount deducted in accordance with that point shall, for the purposes of point 8, be subtracted from the amount specified in point 8 as the maximum risk-weighted exposure amount to be calculated by the credit institutions there indicated.

3. CALCULATION OF RISK-WEIGHTED EXPOSURE AMOUNTS UNDER THE INTERNAL RATINGS BASED APPROACH

3.1. Hierarchy of methods

37. For the purposes of Article 96, the risk-weighted exposure amount of a securitisation positions shall be calculated in accordance with points 38 to 76.

38. For a rated position or a position in respect of which an inferred rating may be used, the Ratings Based Method set out in points 46 to 51 shall be used to calculate the risk-weighted exposure amount.

39. For an unrated position the Supervisory Formula Method set out in points 52 to 54 shall be used except where the Internal Assessment Approach is permitted to be used as set out in points 43 and 44.

40. A credit institution other than an originator credit institution or a sponsor credit institution may only use the Supervisory Formula Method with the approval of the competent authorities.

41. In the case of an originator or sponsor credit institution unable to calculate Kirb and which has not obtained approval to use the Internal Assessment Approach for positions in ABCP programmes, and in the case of other credit institutions where they have not obtained approval to use the Supervisory Formula Method or, for positions in ABCP programmes, the Internal Assessment Approach, a risk weight of 1250% shall be assigned to securitisation positions which are unrated and in respect of which an inferred rating may not be used.

3.1.1. Use of inferred ratings

42. When the following minimum operational requirements are satisfied, an institution shall attribute to an unrated position an inferred credit assessment equivalent to the credit assessment of those rated positions (the "reference positions") which are the most senior positions which are in all respects subordinate to the unrated securitisation position in question:

   (a) the reference positions must be subordinate in all respects to the unrated securitisation position;
   (b) the maturity of the reference positions must be equal to or longer than that of the unrated position in question; and
   (c) on an ongoing basis, any inferred rating must be updated to reflect any changes in the credit assessment of the reference positions.

3.1.2. The "Internal Assessment Approach" for positions in ABCP programmes

43.   Subject to the approval of the competent authorities, when the following conditions are satisfied a credit institution may attribute to an unrated position in an ABCP programme a derived rating as laid down in point 44:

(a)   positions in the commercial paper issued from the ABCP programme shall be rated positions;

(b)   the credit institution shall satisfy the competent authorities that its internal assessment of the credit quality of the position reflects the publicly available assessment methodology of one or more eligible ECAIs, for the rating of securities backed by the exposures of the type securitised;

(c)   the ECAIs, the methodology of which shall be reflected as required by the point (b), shall include those ECAIs which have provided an external rating for the commercial paper issued from the ABCP programme. Quantitative elements, such as stress factors, used in assessing the position to a particular credit quality must be at least as conservative as those used in the relevant assessment methodology of the ECAIs in question;

(d)   in developing its internal assessment methodology the credit institution shall take into consideration relevant published ratings methodologies of the eligible ECAIs that rate the commercial paper of the ABCP programme. This consideration shall be documented by the credit institution and updated regularly, as outlined in point (g);

(e)   the credit institution's internal assessment methodology shall include rating grades. There shall be a correspondence between such rating grades and the credit assessments of eligible ECAIs. This correspondence shall be explicitly documented;

(f)   the internal assessment methodology shall be used in the credit institution's internal risk management processes, including its decision making, management information and capital allocation processes;

(g)   internal or external auditors, an ECAI, or the credit institution's internal credit review or risk management function shall perform regular reviews of the internal assessment process and the quality of the internal assessments of the credit quality of the credit institution's exposures to an ABCP programme. If the credit institution's internal audit, credit review, or risk management functions perform the review, then these functions shall be independent of the ABCP programme business line, as well as the customer relationship;

(h)   the credit institution shall track the performance of its internal ratings over time to evaluate the performance of its internal assessment methodology and shall make adjustments, as necessary, to that methodology when the performance of the exposures routinely diverges from that indicated by the internal ratings;

(i)   the ABCP programme shall incorporate underwriting standards in the form of credit and investment guidelines. In deciding on an asset purchase, the ABCP programme administrator shall consider the type of asset being purchased, the type and monetary value of the exposures arising from the provision of liquidity facilities and credit enhancements, the loss distribution, and the legal and economic isolation of the transferred assets from the entity selling the assets. A credit analysis of the asset seller's risk profile shall be performed and shall include analysis of past and expected future financial performance, current market position, expected future competitiveness, leverage, cash flow, interest coverage and debt rating. In addition, a review of the seller's underwriting standards, servicing capabilities, and collection processes shall be performed;

(j)   the ABCP programme's underwriting standards shall establish minimum asset eligibility criteria that, in particular:

    (i)   exclude the purchase of assets that are significantly past due or defaulted;

    (ii)   limit excess concentration to individual obligor or geographic area; and

    (iii)   limits the tenor of the assets to be purchased;

(k)   the ABCP programme shall have collections policies and processes that take into account the operational capability and credit quality of the servicer. The ABCP programme shall mitigate seller/servicer risk through various methods, such as triggers based on current credit quality that would preclude commingling of funds;

(l)   the aggregated estimate of loss on an asset pool that the ABCP programme is considering purchasing must take into account all sources of potential risk, such as credit and dilution risk. If the seller-provided credit enhancement is sized based only on credit-related losses, then a separate reserve shall be established for dilution risk, if dilution risk is material for the particular exposure pool. In addition, in sizing the required enhancement level, the program shall review several years of historical information, including losses, delinquencies, dilutions, and the turnover rate of the receivables; and

(m) the ABCP programme shall incorporate structural features — for example wind down triggers — into the purchase of exposures in order to mitigate potential credit deterioration of the underlying portfolio.

The requirement for the assessment methodology of the ECAI to be publicly available may be waived by the competent authorities where they are satisfied that due to the specific features of the securitisation — for example its unique structure — there is as yet no publicly available ECAI assessment methodology.

44. The unrated position shall be assigned by the credit institution to one of the rating grades described in point 43. The position shall be attributed a derived rating the same as the credit assessments corresponding to that rating grade as laid down in point 43. Where this derived rating is, at the inception of the securitisation, at the level of investment grade or better, it shall be considered the same as an eligible credit assessment by an eligible ECAI for the purposes of calculating risk-weighted exposure amounts.

3.2. Maximum risk-weighted exposure amounts

45. For an originator credit institution, a sponsor credit institution, or for other credit institutions which can calculate KIRB, the risk-weighted exposure amounts calculated in respect of its positions in a securitisation may be limited to that which would produce a capital requirement under Article 75(a) equal to the sum of 8% of the risk-weighted exposure amounts which would be produced if the securitised assets had not been securitised and were on the balance sheet of the credit institution plus the expected loss amounts of those exposures.

3.3. Ratings Based Method

46. Under the Ratings Based Method, the risk-weighted exposure amount of a rated securitisation position shall be calculated by applying to the exposure value the risk weight associated with the credit quality step with which the credit assessment has been determined to be associated by the competent authorities in accordance with Article 98, as set out in the Tables 4 and 5, multiplied by 1.06.

Table 4
Positions other than ones with short-term credit assessments

Credit Quality Step (CQS)	Risk weight		
	A	B	C
CQS 1	7%	12%	20%
CQS 2	8%	15%	25%
CQS 3	10%	18%	35%
CQS 4	12%	20%	35%
CQS 5	20%	35%	35%
CQS 6	35%	50%	50%
CQS 7	60%	75%	75%
CQS 8	100%	100%	100%
CQS 9	250%	250%	250%
CQS 10	425%	425%	425%
CQS 11	650%	650%	650%
Below CQS 11	1250%	1250%	1250%

Table 5
Positions with short term credit assessments

Credit Quality Step (CQS)	Risk weight		
	A	B	C
CQS 1	7%	12%	20%
CQS 2	12%	20%	35%
CQS 3	60%	75%	75%
All other credit assessments	1250%	1250%	1250%

47.　Subject to points 48 and 49, the risk weights in column A of each table shall be applied where the position is in the most senior tranche of a securitisation. When determining whether a tranche is the most senior, it is not required to take into consideration amounts due under interest rate or currency derivative contracts, fees due, or other similar payments.

48.　A risk weight of 6% may be applied to a position in the most senior tranche of a securitisation where that tranche is senior in all respects to another tranche of the securitisation positions which would receive a risk weight of 7% under point 46, provided that:

(a)　the competent authority is satisfied that this is justified due to the loss absorption qualities of subordinate tranches in the securitisation; and

(b)　either the position has an external credit assessment which has been determined to be associated with credit quality step 1 in Table 4 or 5 or, if it is unrated, requirements (a) to (c) in point 42 are satisfied where "reference positions" are taken to mean positions in the subordinate tranche which would receive a risk weight of 7% under point 46.

49.　The risk weights in column C of each table shall be applied where the position is in a securitisation where the effective number of exposures securitised is less than six. In calculating the effective number of exposures securitised multiple exposures to one obligor must be treated as one exposure. The effective number of exposures is calculated as:

$$N = \frac{\left(\sum_i EAD_i \right)^2}{\sum_i EAD_i^2}$$

where EAD_i represents the sum of the exposure values of all exposures to the ith obligor. In the case of resecuritisation (securitisation of securitisation exposures), the credit institution must look at the number of securitisation exposures in the pool and not the number of underlying exposures in the original pools from which the underlying securitisation exposures stem. If the portfolio share associated with the largest exposure, C_1, is available, the credit institution may compute N as $1/C_1$.

50.　The risk weights in Column B shall be applied to all other positions.

51.　Credit risk mitigation on securitisation positions may be recognised in accordance with points 60 to 62.

3.4. Supervisory Formula Method

52.　Subject to points 58 and 59, under the Supervisory Formula Method, the risk weight for a securitisation position shall be the greater of 7% or the risk weight to be applied in accordance with point 53.

53.　Subject to points 58 and 59, the risk weight to be applied to the exposure amount shall be:

$12.5 \times (S[L+T] - S[L])/T$

where:

$$S[x] = \left\{ \begin{array}{l} x \qquad\qquad \text{when } x \leq Kirbr \\ Kirbr + K[x] - K[Kirbr] + (d \cdot Kirbr/\omega)(1 - e^{\omega(Kirbr-x)/Kirbr}) \text{ when } Kirbr < x \end{array} \right\}$$

where:

$h = (1 - Kirbr/ELGD)^N$

$c = Kirbr/(1 - h)$

$$v = \frac{(ELGD - Kirbr)Kirbr + 0.25(1 - ELGD)Kirbr}{N}$$

$$f = \left(\frac{v + Kirbr^2}{1 - h} - c^2\right) + \frac{(1 - Kirbr)Kirbr - v}{(1 - h)\tau}$$

$$g = \frac{(1 - c)c}{f} - 1$$

$a = g \cdot c$

$b = g \cdot (1 - c)$

$d = 1 - (1 - h) \cdot (1 - Beta[Kirbr;a,b])$

$K[x] = (1 - h) \cdot ((1 - Beta[x;a,b]x + Beta[x;a + 1,b]c)$

$\tau = 1000$, and

$\omega = 20$.

In these expressions, Beta $[x; a, b]$ refers to the cumulative beta distribution with parameters a and b evaluated at x.

T (the thickness of the tranche in which the position is held) is measured as the ratio of (a) the nominal amount of the tranche to (b) the sum of the exposure values of the exposures that have been securitised. For the purposes of calculating T the exposure value of a derivative instrument listed in Annex IV shall, where the current replacement cost is not a positive value, be the potential future credit exposure calculated in accordance with Annex III.

Kirbr is the ratio of (a) Kirb to (b) the sum of the exposure values of the exposures that have been securitised. Kirbr is expressed in decimal form (e g Kirb equal to 15% of the pool would be expressed as Kirbr of 0.15).

L (the credit enhancement level) is measured as the ratio of the nominal amount of all tranches subordinate to the tranche in which the position is held to the sum of the exposure values of the exposures that have been securitised. Capitalised future income shall not be included in the measured L. Amounts due by counterparties to derivative instruments listed in Annex IV that represent tranches more junior than the tranche in question may be measured at their current replacement cost (without the potential future credit exposures) in calculating the enhancement level.

N is the effective number of exposures calculated in accordance with point 49.

ELGD, the exposure-weighted average loss-given-default, is calculated as follows:

$$ELGD = \frac{\sum_i LGD_i \cdot EAD_i}{\sum_i EAD_i}$$

where LGD_i represents the average LGD associated with all exposures to the ith obligor, where LGD is determined in accordance with Articles 84 to 89. In the case of resecuritisation, an LGD of 100% shall be applied to the securitised positions. When default and dilution risk for purchased receivables are treated in an aggregate manner within a securitisation (e g a single reserve or over-collateralisation is available to cover losses from either source), the LGDi input shall be constructed as a weighted average of the LGD for credit risk and the 75% LGD for dilution risk. The weights shall be the stand-alone capital charges for credit risk and dilution risk respectively.

Simplified inputs

If the exposure value of the largest securitised exposure, C_1, is no more than 3% of the sum of the exposure values of the securitised exposures, then, for the purposes of the Supervisory Formula Method, the credit institution may set LGD= 50% and N equal to either:

$$N = \left(C_1C_m + \left(\frac{C_m - C_1}{m - 1}\right)\max\{1 - mC_1, 0\}\right)^{-1}$$

or

$N = 1/C_1$.

C_m is the ratio of the sum of the exposure values of the largest "m" exposures to the sum of the exposure values of the exposures securitised. The level of "m" may be set by the credit institution.

For securitisations involving retail exposures, the competent authorities may permit the Supervisory Formula Method to be implemented using the simplifications: h = 0 and v = 0.

54.   Credit risk mitigation on securitisation positions may be recognised in accordance with points 60, 61 and 63 to 67.

3.5. Liquidity Facilities

55.   The provisions in points 56 to 59 apply for the purposes of determining the exposure value of an unrated securitisation position in the form of certain types of liquidity facility.

3.5.1. Liquidity Facilities Only Available in the Event of General Market Disruption

56.   A conversion figure of 20% may be applied to the nominal amount of a liquidity facility that may only be drawn in the event of a general market disruption and that meets the conditions to be an "eligible liquidity facility" set out in point 13.

3.5.2. Cash advance facilities

57.   A conversion figure of 0% may be applied to the nominal amount of a liquidity facility that meets the conditions set out in point 15.

3.5.3. Exceptional treatment where K_{irb} cannot be calculated.

58.   When it is not practical for the credit institution to calculate the risk-weighted exposure amounts for the securitised exposures as if they had not been securitised, a credit institution may, on an exceptional basis and subject to the consent of the competent authorities, temporarily be allowed to apply the method set out in point 59 for the calculation of risk-weighted exposure amounts for an unrated securitisation position in the form of a liquidity facility that meets the conditions to be an "eligible liquidity facility" set out in point 13 or that falls within the terms of point 56.

59.   The highest risk weight that would be applied under Articles 78 to 83 to any of the securitised exposures, had they not been securitised, may be applied to the securitisation position represented by the liquidity facility. To determine the exposure value of the position a conversion figure of 50% may be applied to the nominal amount of the liquidity facility if the facility has an original maturity of one year or less. If the liquidity facility complies with the conditions in point 56 a conversion figure of 20% may be applied. In other cases a conversion factor of 100% shall be applied.

3.6. Recognition of credit risk mitigation in respect of securitisation positions

3.6.1. Funded credit protection

60.   Eligible funded protection is limited to that which is eligible for the calculation of risk-weighted exposure amounts under Articles 78 to 83 as laid down under Articles 90 to 93 and recognition is subject to compliance with the relevant minimum requirements as laid down under those Articles.

3.6.2. Unfunded credit protection

61.   Eligible unfunded credit protection and unfunded protection providers are limited to those which are eligible under Articles 90 to 93 and recognition is subject to compliance with the relevant minimum requirements laid down under those Articles.

3.6.3. Calculation of capital requirements for securitisation positions with credit risk mitigation

Ratings Based Method

62.   Where risk-weighted exposure amounts are calculated using the Ratings Based Method, the exposure value and/or the risk-weighted exposure amount for a securitisation position in respect of which credit protection has been obtained may be modified in accordance with the provisions of Annex VIII as they apply for the calculation of risk-weighted exposure amounts under Articles 78 to 83.

Supervisory Formula Method — full credit protection

63.   Where risk-weighted exposure amounts are calculated using the Supervisory Formula Method, the credit institution shall determine the "effective risk weight" of the position. It shall do this by dividing the risk-weighted exposure amount of the position by the exposure value of the position and multiplying the result by 100.

64.   In the case of funded credit protection, the risk-weighted exposure amount of the securitisation position shall be calculated by multiplying the funded protection-adjusted exposure amount of the position (E*, as calculated under Articles 90 to 93 for the calculation of risk-weighted exposure amounts under Articles 78 to 83 taking the amount of the securitisation position to be E) by the effective risk weight.

65.   In the case of unfunded credit protection, the risk-weighted exposure amount of the securitisation position shall be calculated by multiplying GA (the amount of the protection adjusted for any currency mismatch and maturity mismatch in accordance with the provisions of Annex VIII) by the risk weight of the protection provider; and adding this to the amount arrived at by multiplying the amount of the securitisation position minus GA by the effective risk weight.

Supervisory formula method — partial protection

66. If the credit risk mitigation covers the "first loss" or losses on a proportional basis on the securitisation position, the credit institution may apply points 63 to 65.

67. In other cases, the credit institution shall treat the securitisation position as two or more positions with the uncovered portion being considered the position with the lower credit quality. For the purposes of calculating the risk-weighted exposure amount for this position, the provisions in points 52 to 54 shall apply subject to the modifications that "T" shall be adjusted to e* in the case of funded credit protection; and to T-g in the case of unfunded credit protection, where e* denotes the ratio of E* to the total notional amount of the underlying pool, where E* is the adjusted exposure amount of the securitisation position calculated in accordance with the provisions of Annex VIII as they apply for the calculation of risk-weighted exposure amounts under Articles 78 to 83 taking the amount of the securitisation position to be E; and g is the ratio of the nominal amount of credit protection (adjusted for any currency or maturity mismatch in accordance with the provisions of Annex VIII) to the sum of the exposure amounts of the securitised exposures. In the case of unfunded credit protection the risk weight of the protection provider shall be applied to that portion of the position not falling within the adjusted value of "T".

3.7. Additional capital requirements for securitisations of revolving exposures with early amortisation provisions

68. In addition to the risk-weighted exposure amounts calculated in respect of its securitisation positions, an originator credit institution shall be required to calculate a risk-weighted exposure amount according to the methodology set out in points 16 to 33 when it sells revolving exposures into a securitisation that contains an early amortisation provision.

69. For the purposes of point 68, points 70 and 71 shall replace points 19 and 20.

70. For the purposes of these provisions, "originators interest" shall be the sum of:

(a) the exposure value of that notional Part of a pool of drawn amounts sold into a securitisation, the proportion of which in relation to the amount of the total pool sold into the structure determines the proportion of the cash flows generated by principal and interest collections and other associated amounts which are not available to make payments to those having securitisation positions in the securitisation; plus

(b) the exposure value of that Part of the pool of undrawn amounts of the credit lines, the drawn amounts of which have been sold into the securitisation, the proportion of which to the total amount of such undrawn amounts is the same as the proportion of the exposure value described in point (a) to the exposure value of the pool of drawn amounts sold into the securitisation.

To qualify as such, the originator's interest may not be subordinate to the investors' interest.

"Investors' interest" means the exposure value of the notional part of the pool of drawn amounts not falling within point (a) plus the exposure value of that part of the pool of undrawn amounts of credit lines, the drawn amounts of which have been sold into the securitisation, not falling within point (b).

71. The exposure of the originator credit institution associated with its rights in respect of that Part of the originator's interest described in point 70(a) shall not be considered a securitisation position but as a pro rata exposure to the securitised drawn amounts exposures as if they had not been securitised in an amount equal to that described in point 70(a). The originator credit institution shall also be considered to have a pro rata exposure to the undrawn amounts of the credit lines, the drawn amounts of which have been sold into the securitisation, in an amount equal to that described in point 70(b).

3.8. Reduction in risk-weighted exposure amounts

72. The risk-weighted exposure amount of a securitisation position to which a 1250% risk weight is assigned may be reduced by 12.5 times the amount of any value adjustments made by the credit institution in respect of the securitised exposures. To the extent that value adjustments are taken account of for this purpose they shall not be taken account of for the purposes of the calculation indicated in Annex VII, Part 1, point 36.

73. The risk-weighted exposure amount of a securitisation position may be reduced by 12.5 times the amount of any value adjustments made by the credit institution in respect of the position.

74. As provided in Article 66(2), in respect of a securitisation position in respect of which a 1250% risk weight applies, credit institutions may, as an alternative to including the position in their calculation of risk-weighted exposure amounts, deduct from own funds the exposure value of the position.

75. For the purposes of point 74:

(a) the exposure value of the position may be derived from the risk-weighted exposure amounts taking into account any reductions made in accordance with points 72 and 73;

(b) the calculation of the exposure value may reflect eligible funded protection in a manner consistent with the methodology prescribed in points 60 to 67; and

(c) where the Supervisory Formula Method is used to calculate risk-weighted exposure amounts and $L \leq K_{IRBR}$ and $[L+T] > K_{IRBR}$ the position may be treated as two positions with L equal to K_{IRBR} for the more senior of the positions.

76. Where a credit institution makes use of the alternative indicated in point 74, 12.5 times the amount deducted in accordance with that point shall, for the purposes of point 45, be subtracted from the amount specified in point 45 as the maximum risk-weighted exposure amount to be calculated by the credit institutions there indicated.

[5842F]

ANNEX X
OPERATIONAL RISK

PART 1
BASIC INDICATOR APPROACH

1. CAPITAL REQUIREMENT

1. Under the Basic Indicator Approach, the capital requirement for operational risk is equal to 15% of the relevant indicator defined in points 2 to 9.

2. RELEVANT INDICATOR

2. The relevant indicator is the average over three years of the sum of net interest income and net non-interest income.

3. The three-year average is calculated on the basis of the last three twelve-monthly observations at the end of the financial year. When audited figures are not available, business estimates may be used.

4. If for any given observation, the sum of net interest income and net non-interest income is negative or equal to zero, this figure shall not be taken into account in the calculation of the three-year average. The relevant indicator shall be calculated as the sum of positive figures divided by the number of positive figures.

2.1. Credit institutions subject to Directive 86/635/EEC

5. Based on the accounting categories for the profit and loss account of credit institutions under Article 27 of Directive 86/635/EEC, the relevant indicator shall be expressed as the sum of the elements listed in Table 1. Each element shall be included in the sum with its positive or negative sign.

6. These elements may need to be adjusted to reflect the qualifications in points 7 and 8.

Table 1

1	Interest receivable and similar income
2	Interest payable and similar charges
3	Income from shares and other variable/fixed-yield securities
4	Commissions/fees receivable
5	Commissions/fees payable
6	Net profit or net loss on financial operations
7	Other operating income

2.1.1. Qualifications

7. The indicator shall be calculated before the deduction of any provisions and operating expenses. Operating expenses shall include fees paid for outsourcing services rendered by third parties which are not a parent or subsidiary of the credit institution or a subsidiary of a parent which is also the parent of the credit institution. Expenditure on the outsourcing of services rendered by third parties may reduce the relevant indicator if the expenditure is incurred from an undertaking subject to supervision under, or equivalent to, this Directive.

8. The following elements shall not be used in the calculation of the relevant indicator:

(a) Realised profits/losses from the sale of non-trading book items;

(b) Income from extraordinary or irregular items;

(c) Income derived from insurance.

When revaluation of trading items is part of the profit and loss statement, revaluation could be included. When Article 36(2) of Directive 86/635/EEC is applied, revaluation booked in the profit and loss account should be included.

2.2. Credit institutions subject to a different accounting framework

9. When credit institutions are subject to an accounting framework different from the one established by Directive 86/635/EEC, they should calculate the relevant indicator on the basis of data that best reflect the definition set out in points 2 to 8.

PART 2
STANDARDISED APPROACH

1. CAPITAL REQUIREMENT

1. Under the Standardised Approach, the capital requirement for operational risk is the average over three years of the risk-weighted relevant indicators calculated each year across the business lines referred to in Table 2. In each year, a negative capital requirement in one business line, resulting from a negative relevant indicator may be imputed to the whole. However, where the aggregate capital charge across all business lines within a given year is negative, then the input to the average for that year shall be zero.

2. The three-year average is calculated on the basis of the last three twelve-monthly observations at the end of the financial year. When audited figures are not available, business estimates may be used.

Table 2

Business line	List of activities	Percentage
Corporate finance	Underwriting of financial instruments and/or placing of financial instruments on a firm commitment basis Services related to underwriting Investment advice Advice to undertakings on capital structure, industrial strategy and related matters and advice and services relating to the mergers and the purchase of undertakings Investment research and financial analysis and other forms of general recommendation relating to transactions in financial instruments	18%
Trading and sales	Dealing on own account Money broking Reception and transmission of orders in relation to one or more financial instruments Execution of orders on behalf of clients Placing of financial instruments without a firm commitment basis Operation of Multilateral Trading Facilities	18%
Retail brokerage (Activities with a individual physical persons or with small and medium sized entities meeting the criteria set out in Article 79 for the retail exposure class)	Reception and transmission of orders in relation to one or more financial instruments Execution of orders on behalf of clients Placing of financial instruments without a firm commitment basis	12%
Commercial banking	Acceptance of deposits and other repayable funds Lending Financial leasing Guarantees and commitments	15%

Retail banking (Activities with a individual physical persons or with small and medium sized entities meeting the criteria set out in Article 79 for the retail exposure class)	Acceptance of deposits and other repayable funds Lending Financial leasing Guarantees and commitments	12%
Payment and settlement	Money transmission services, Issuing and administering means of payment	18%
Agency services	Safekeeping and administration of financial instruments for the account of clients, including custodianship and related services such as cash/collateral management	15%
Asset management	Portfolio management Managing of UCITS Other forms of asset management	12%

3. Competent authorities may authorise a credit institution to calculate its capital requirement for operational risk using an alternative standardised approach, as set out in points 5 to 11.

2. PRINCIPLES FOR BUSINESS LINE MAPPING

4. Credit institutions must develop and document specific policies and criteria for mapping the relevant indicator for current business lines and activities into the standardised framework. The criteria must be reviewed and adjusted as appropriate for new or changing business activities and risks. The principles for business line mapping are:

(a) all activities must be mapped into the business lines in a mutually exclusive and jointly exhaustive manner;

(b) any activity which cannot be readily mapped into the business line framework, but which represents an ancillary function to an activity included in the framework, must be allocated to the business line it supports. If more than one business line is supported through the ancillary activity, an objective-mapping criterion must be used;

(c) if an activity cannot be mapped into a particular business line then the business line yielding the highest percentage must be used. The same business line equally applies to any associated ancillary activity;

(d) credit institutions may use internal pricing methods to allocate the relevant indicator between business lines. Costs generated in one business line which are imputable to a different business line may be reallocated to the business line to which they pertain, for instance by using a treatment based on internal transfer costs between the two business lines;

(e) the mapping of activities into business lines for operational risk capital purposes must be consistent with the categories used for credit and market risks;

(f) senior management is responsible for the mapping policy under the control of the governing bodies of the credit institution; and

(g) the mapping process to business lines must be subject to independent review.

3. ALTERNATIVE INDICATORS FOR CERTAIN BUSINESS LINES

3.1. Modalities

5. The competent authorities may authorise the credit institution to use an alternative relevant indicator for the business lines: retail banking and commercial banking.

6. For these business lines, the relevant indicator shall be a normalised income indicator equal to the three-year average of the total nominal amount of loans and advances multiplied by 0.035.

7. For the retail and/or commercial banking business lines, the loans and advances shall consist of the total drawn amounts in the corresponding credit portfolios. For the commercial banking business line, securities held in the non trading book shall also be included.

3.2. Conditions

8. The authorisation to use alternative relevant indicators shall be subject to the conditions in points 9 to 11.

3.2.1. General condition

9. The credit institution meets the qualifying criteria set out in point 12.

3.2.2. Conditions specific to retail banking and commercial banking

10.   The credit institution is overwhelmingly active in retail and/or commercial banking activities, which shall account for at least 90% of its income.

11.   The credit institution is able to demonstrate to the competent authorities that a significant proportion of its retail and/or commercial banking activities comprise loans associated with a high PD, and that the alternative standardised approach provides an improved basis for assessing the operational risk.

4. QUALIFYING CRITERIA

12.   Credit institutions must meet the qualifying criteria listed below, in addition to the general risk management standards set out in Article 22 and Annex V. Satisfaction of these criteria shall be determined having regard to the size and scale of activities of the credit institution and to the principle of proportionality.

(a)   Credit institutions shall have a well-documented assessment and management system for operational risk with clear responsibilities assigned for this system. They shall identify their exposures to operational risk and track relevant operational risk data, including material loss data. This system shall be subject to regular independent review.

(b)   The operational risk assessment system must be closely integrated into the risk management processes of the credit institution. Its output must be an integral Part of the process of monitoring and controlling the credit institution's operational risk profile.

(c)   Credit institutions shall implement a system of management reporting that provides operational risk reports to relevant functions within the credit institution. Credit institutions shall have procedures for taking appropriate action according to the information within the management reports.

PART 3
ADVANCED MEASUREMENT APPROACHES

1. QUALIFYING CRITERIA

1.   To be eligible for an Advanced Measurement Approach, credit institutions must satisfy the competent authorities that they meet the qualifying criteria below, in addition to the general risk management standards in Article 22 and Annex V.

1.1. Qualitative Standards

2.   The credit institution's internal operational risk measurement system shall be closely integrated into its day-to-day risk management processes.

3.   The credit institution must have an independent risk management function for operational risk.

4.   There must be regular reporting of operational risk exposures and loss experience. The credit institution shall have procedures for taking appropriate corrective action.

5.   The credit institution's risk management system must be well documented. The credit institution shall have routines in place for ensuring compliance and policies for the treatment of non-compliance.

6.   The operational risk management processes and measurement systems shall be subject to regular reviews performed by internal and/or external auditors.

7.   The validation of the operational risk measurement system by the competent authorities shall include the following elements:

(a)   verifying that the internal validation processes are operating in a satisfactory manner;

(b)   making sure that data flows and processes associated with the risk measurement system are transparent and accessible.

1.2. Quantitative Standards

1.2.1. Process

8.   Credit institutions shall calculate their capital requirement as comprising both expected loss and unexpected loss, unless they can demonstrate that expected loss is adequately captured in their internal business practices. The operational risk measure must capture potentially severe tail events, achieving a soundness standard comparable to a 99.9% confidence interval over a one year period.

9.   The operational risk measurement system of a credit institution must have certain key elements to meet the soundness standard set out in point 8. These elements must include the use of internal data, external data, scenario analysis and factors reflecting the business environment and internal control systems as set out in points 13 to 24. A credit institution needs to have a well documented approach for weighting the use of these four elements in its overall operational risk measurement system.

10. The risk measurement system shall capture the major drivers of risk affecting the shape of the tail of the loss estimates.

11. Correlations in operational risk losses across individual operational risk estimates may be recognised only if credit institutions can demonstrate to the satisfaction of the competent authorities that their systems for measuring correlations are sound, implemented with integrity, and take into account the uncertainty surrounding any such correlation estimates, particularly in periods of stress. The credit institution must validate its correlation assumptions using appropriate quantitative and qualitative techniques.

12. The risk measurement system shall be internally consistent and shall avoid the multiple counting of qualitative assessments or risk mitigation techniques recognised in other areas of the capital adequacy framework.

1.2.2. Internal data

13. Internally generated operational risk measures shall be based on a minimum historical observation period of five years. When a credit institution first moves to an Advanced Measurement Approach, a three-year historical observation period is acceptable.

14. Credit institutions must be able to map their historical internal loss data into the business lines defined in Part 2 and into the event types defined in Part 5, and to provide these data to competent authorities upon request. There must be documented, objective criteria for allocating losses to the specified business lines and event types. The operational risk losses that are related to credit risk and have historically been included in the internal credit risk databases must be recorded in the operational risk databases and be separately identified. Such losses will not be subject to the operational risk charge, as long as they continue to be treated as credit risk for the purposes of calculating minimum capital requirements. Operational risk losses that are related to market risks shall be included in the scope of the capital requirement for operational risk.

15. The credit institution's internal loss data must be comprehensive in that it captures all material activities and exposures from all appropriate sub-systems and geographic locations. Credit institutions must be able to justify that any excluded activities or exposures, both individually and in combination, would not have a material impact on the overall risk estimates. Appropriate minimum loss thresholds for internal loss data collection must be defined.

16. Aside from information on gross loss amounts, credit institutions shall collect information about the date of the event, any recoveries of gross loss amounts, as well as some descriptive information about the drivers or causes of the loss event.

17. There shall be specific criteria for assigning loss data arising from an event in a centralised function or an activity that spans more than one business line, as well as from related events over time.

18. Credit institutions must have documented procedures for assessing the on-going relevance of historical loss data, including those situations in which judgement overrides, scaling, or other adjustments may be used, to what extent they may be used and who is authorised to make such decisions.

1.2.3. External data

19. The credit institution's operational risk measurement system shall use relevant external data, especially when there is reason to believe that the credit institution is exposed to infrequent, yet potentially severe, losses. A credit institution must have a systematic process for determining the situations for which external data must be used and the methodologies used to incorporate the data in its measurement system. The conditions and practices for external data use must be regularly reviewed, documented and subject to periodic independent review.

1.2.4. Scenario analysis

20. The credit institution shall use scenario analysis of expert opinion in conjunction with external data to evaluate its exposure to high severity events. Over time, such assessments need to be validated and re-assessed through comparison to actual loss experience to ensure their reasonableness.

1.2.5. Business environment and internal control factors

21. The credit institution's firm-wide risk assessment methodology must capture key business environment and internal control factors that can change its operational risk profile.

22. The choice of each factor needs to be justified as a meaningful driver of risk, based on experience and involving the expert judgment of the affected business areas.

23. The sensitivity of risk estimates to changes in the factors and the relative weighting of the various factors need to be well reasoned. In addition to capturing changes in risk due to

improvements in risk controls, the framework must also capture potential increases in risk due to greater complexity of activities or increased business volume.

24. This framework must be documented and subject to independent review within the credit institution and by competent authorities. Over time, the process and the outcomes need to be validated and re-assessed through comparison to actual internal loss experience and relevant external data.

2. IMPACT OF INSURANCE AND OTHER RISK TRANSFER MECHANISMS

25. Credit institutions shall be able to recognise the impact of insurance subject to the conditions set out in points 26 to 29 and other risk transfer mechanisms where the credit institution can demonstrate to the satisfaction of the competent authorities that a noticeable risk mitigating effect is achieved.

26. The provider is authorised to provide insurance or re-insurance and the provider has a minimum claims paying ability rating by an eligible ECAI which has been determined by the competent authority to be associated with credit quality step 3 or above under the rules for the risk weighting of exposures to credit institutions under Articles 78 to 83.

27. The insurance and the credit institutions' insurance framework shall meet the following conditions:
- (a) the insurance policy must have an initial term of no less than one year. For policies with a residual term of less than one year, the credit institution must make appropriate haircuts reflecting the declining residual term of the policy, up to a full 100% haircut for policies with a residual term of 90 days or less;
- (b) the insurance policy has a minimum notice period for cancellation of the contract of 90 days;
- (c) the insurance policy has no exclusions or limitations triggered by supervisory actions or, in the case of a failed credit institution, that preclude the credit institution receiver or liquidator, from recovering for damages suffered or expenses incurred by the credit institution, except in respect of events occurring after the initiation of receivership or liquidation proceedings in respect of the credit institution; provided that the insurance policy may exclude any fine, penalty, or punitive damages resulting from actions by the competent authorities;
- (d) the risk mitigation calculations must reflect the insurance coverage in a manner that is transparent in its relationship to, and consistent with, the actual likelihood and impact of loss used in the overall determination of operational risk capital;
- (e) the insurance is provided by a third party entity. In the case of insurance through captives and affiliates, the exposure has to be laid off to an independent third party entity, for example through re-insurance, that meets the eligibility criteria; and
- (f) the framework for recognising insurance is well reasoned and documented.

28. The methodology for recognising insurance shall capture the following elements through discounts or haircuts in the amount of insurance recognition:
- (a) the residual term of an insurance policy, where less than one year, as noted above;
- (b) a policy's cancellation terms, where less than one year; and
- (c) the uncertainty of payment as well as mismatches in coverage of insurance policies.

29. The capital alleviation arising from the recognition of insurance shall not exceed 20% of the capital requirement for operational risk before the recognition of risk-mitigation techniques.

3. APPLICATION TO USE AN ADVANCED MEASUREMENT APPROACH ON A GROUP-WIDE BASIS

30. When an Advanced Measurement Approach is intended to be used by the EU parent credit institution and its subsidiaries, or by the subsidiaries of an EU parent financial holding company, the application shall include a description of the methodology used for allocating operational risk capital between the different entities of the group.

31. The application shall indicate whether and how diversification effects are intended to be factored in the risk measurement system.

PART 4
COMBINED USE OF DIFFERENT METHODOLOGIES

1. USE OF AN ADVANCED MEASUREMENT APPROACH IN COMBINATION WITH OTHER APPROACHES

1. A credit institution may use an Advanced Measurement Approach in combination with either the Basic Indicator Approach or the Standardised Approach, subject to the following conditions:
- (a) all operational risks of the credit institution are captured. The competent authority shall be satisfied with the methodology used to cover different activities, geographical locations, legal structures or other relevant divisions determined on an internal basis; and

    (b)   the qualifying criteria set out in Parts 2 and 3 are fulfilled for the Part of activities covered by the Standardised Approach and Advanced Measurement Approaches respectively.

2.   On a case-by case basis, the competent authority may impose the following additional conditions:

    (a)   on the date of implementation of an Advanced Measurement Approach, a significant part of the credit institution's operational risks are captured by the Advanced Measurement Approach; and

    (b)   the credit institution takes a commitment to roll out the Advanced Measurement Approach across a material Part of its operations within a time schedule agreed with its competent authorities.

2. COMBINED USE OF THE BASIC INDICATOR APPROACH AND OF THE STANDARDISED APPROACH

3.   A credit institution may use a combination of the Basic Indicator Approach and the Standardised Approach only in exceptional circumstances such as the recent acquisition of new business which may require a transition period for the roll out of the Standardised Approach.

4.   The combined use of the Basic Indicator Approach and the Standardised Approach shall be conditional upon a commitment by the credit institution to roll out the Standardised Approach within a time schedule agreed with the competent authorities.

PART 5
LOSS EVENT TYPE CLASSIFICATION

Table 3

Event-Type Category	Definition
Internal fraud	Losses due to acts of a type intended to defraud, misappropriate property or circumvent regulations, the law or company policy, excluding diversity/discrimination events, which involves at least one internal party
External fraud	Losses due to acts of a type intended to defraud, misappropriate property or circumvent the law, by a third party
Employment Practices and Workplace Safety	Losses arising from acts inconsistent with employment, health or safety laws or agreements, from payment of personal injury claims, or from diversity/discrimination events
Clients, Products & Business Practices	Losses arising from an unintentional or negligent failure to meet a professional obligation to specific clients (including fiduciary and suitability requirements), or from the nature or design of a product
Damage to Physical Assets	Losses arising from loss or damage to physical assets from natural disaster or other events
Business disruption and system failures	Losses arising from disruption of business or system failures
Execution, Delivery & Process Management	Losses from failed transaction processing or process management, from relations with trade counterparties and vendors

[5843]

ANNEX XI
TECHNICAL CRITERIA ON REVIEW AND EVALUATION BY THE COMPETENT AUTHORITIES

1.   In addition to credit, market and operational risks, the review and evaluation performed by competent authorities pursuant to Article 124 shall include the following:

    (a)   the results of the stress test carried out by the credit institutions applying an IRB approach;

    (b)   the exposure to and management of concentration risk by the credit institutions, including their compliance with the requirements laid down in Articles 108 to 118;

    (c)   the robustness, suitability and manner of application of the policies and procedures implemented by credit institutions for the management of the residual risk associated with the use of recognized credit risk mitigation techniques;

(d) the extent to which the own funds held by a credit institution in respect of assets which it has securitised are adequate having regard to the economic substance of the transaction, including the degree of risk transfer achieved;

(e) the exposure to and management of liquidity risk by the credit institutions;

(f) the impact of diversification effects and how such effects are factored into the risk measurement system; and

(g) the results of stress tests carried out by institutions using an internal model to calculate market risk capital requirements under Annex V to Directive 2006/49/EC.

2. Competent authorities shall monitor whether a credit institution has provided implicit support to a securitisation. If a credit institution is found to have provided implicit support on more than one occasion the competent authority shall take appropriate measures reflective of the increased expectation that it will provide future support to its securitisation thus failing to achieve a significant transfer of risk.

3. For the purposes of the determination to be made under Article 124(3), competent authorities shall consider whether the value adjustments and provisions taken for positions/portfolios in the trading book, as set out in Part B of Annex VII to Directive 2006/49/EC, enable the credit institution to sell or hedge out its positions within a short period without incurring material losses under normal market conditions.

[5844]

ANNEX XII
TECHNICAL CRITERIA ON DISCLOSURE

PART 1
GENERAL CRITERIA

1. Information shall be regarded as material in disclosures if its omission or misstatement could change or influence the assessment or decision of a user relying on that information for the purpose of making economic decisions.

2. Information shall be regarded as proprietary to a credit institution if sharing that information with the public would undermine its competitive position. It may include information on products or systems which, if shared with competitors, would render a credit institution's investments therein less valuable.

3. Information shall be regarded as confidential if there are obligations to customers or other counterparty relationships binding a credit institution to confidentiality.

4. Competent authorities shall require credit institution to assess the need to publish some or all disclosures more frequently than annually in the light of the relevant characteristics of their business such as scale of operations, range of activities, presence in different countries, involvement in different financial sectors, and participation in international financial markets and payment, settlement and clearing systems. That assessment shall pay particular attention to the possible need for more frequent disclosure of items of information laid down in Part 2, points 3(b) and 3(e) and 4(b) to 4(e), and information on risk exposure and other items prone to rapid change.

5. The disclosure requirement in Part 2, points 3 and 4 shall be provided pursuant to Article 72(1) and (2).

PART 2
GENERAL REQUIREMENTS

1. The risk management objectives and policies of the credit institution shall be disclosed for each separate category of risk, including the risks referred to under points 1 to 14. These disclosures shall include:

(a) the strategies and processes to manage those risks;

(b) the structure and organisation of the relevant risk management function or other appropriate arrangements;

(c) the scope and nature of risk reporting and measurement systems; and

(d) the policies for hedging and mitigating risk, and the strategies and processes for monitoring the continuing effectiveness of hedges and mitigants.

2. The following information shall be disclosed regarding the scope of application of the requirements of this Directive:

(a) the name of the credit institution to which the requirements of this Directive apply;

(b) an outline of the differences in the basis of consolidation for accounting and prudential purposes, with a brief description of the entities that are:
   (i) fully consolidated;
   (ii) proportionally consolidated;
   (iii) deducted from own funds; or

      (iv)   neither consolidated nor deducted;

(c)   any current or foreseen material practical or legal impediment to the prompt transfer of own funds or repayment of liabilities among the parent undertaking and its subsidiaries;

(d)   the aggregate amount by which the actual own funds are less than the required minimum in all subsidiaries not included in the consolidation, and the name or names of such subsidiaries; and

(e)   if applicable, the circumstance of making use of the provisions laid down in Articles 69 and 70.

3.   The following information shall be disclosed by the credit institutions regarding their own funds:

(a)   summary information on the terms and conditions of the main features of all own funds items and components thereof;

(b)   the amount of the original own funds, with separate disclosure of all positive items and deductions;

(c)   the total amount of additional own funds, and own funds as defined in Chapter IV of Directive 2006/49/EC,

(d)   deductions from original and additional own funds pursuant to Article 66(2), with separate disclosure of items referred to in Article 57(q); and

(e)   total eligible own funds, net of deductions and limits laid down in Article 66.

4.   The following information shall be disclosed regarding the compliance by the credit institution with the requirements laid down in Articles 75 and 123:

(a)   a summary of the credit institution's approach to assessing the adequacy of its internal capital to support current and future activities;

(b)   for credit institutions calculating the risk-weighted exposure amounts in accordance with Articles 78 to 83, 8 per cent of the risk-weighted exposure amounts for each of the exposure classes specified in Article 79;

(c)   for credit institutions calculating risk-weighted exposure amounts in accordance with Articles 84 to 89, 8 per cent of the risk-weighted exposure amounts for each of the exposure classes specified in Article 86. For the retail exposure class, this requirement applies to each of the categories of exposures to which the different correlations in Annex VII, Part 1, points 10 to 13 correspond. For the equity exposure class, this requirement applies to:

      (i)   each of the approaches provided in Annex VII, Part 1, points 17 to 26;

      (ii)   exchange traded exposures, private equity exposures in sufficiently diversified portfolios, and other exposures;

      (iii)   exposures subject to supervisory transition regarding capital requirements; and

      (iv)   exposures subject to grandfathering provisions regarding capital requirements;

(d)   minimum capital requirements calculated in accordance with Article 75, points (b) and (c); and

(e)   minimum capital requirements calculated in accordance with Articles 103 to 105, and disclosed separately.

5.   The following information shall be disclosed regarding the credit institution's exposure to counterparty credit risk as defined in Annex III, Part 1:

(a)   a discussion of the methodology used to assign internal capital and credit limits for counterparty credit exposures;

(b)   a discussion of policies for securing collateral and establishing credit reserves;

(c)   a discussion of policies with respect to wrong-way risk exposures;

(d)   a discussion of the impact of the amount of collateral the credit institution would have to provide given a downgrade in its credit rating;

(e)   gross positive fair value of contracts, netting benefits, netted current credit exposure, collateral held and net derivatives credit exposure. Net derivatives credit exposure is the credit exposure on derivatives transactions after considering both the benefits from legally enforceable netting agreements and collateral arrangements;

(f)   measures for exposure value under the methods set out in Parts 3 to 6 of Annex III, whichever method is applicable;

(g)   the notional value of credit derivative hedges, and the distribution of current credit exposure by types of credit exposure;

(h)   credit derivative transactions (notional), segregated between use for the credit institution's own credit portfolio, as well as in its intermediation activities, including the distribution of the credit derivatives products used, broken down further by protection bought and sold within each product group; and

(i)   the estimate of α if the credit institution has received the approval of the competent authorities to estimate α.

6.   The following information shall be disclosed regarding the credit institution's exposure to credit risk and dilution risk:

(a)   the definitions for accounting purposes of "past due" and "impaired";

(b) a description of the approaches and methods adopted for determining value adjustments and provisions;

(c) the total amount of exposures after accounting offsets and without taking into account the effects of credit risk mitigation, and the average amount of the exposures over the period broken down by different types of exposure classes;

(d) the geographic distribution of the exposures, broken down in significant areas by material exposure classes, and further detailed if appropriate;

(e) the distribution of the exposures by industry or counterparty type, broken down by exposure classes, and further detailed if appropriate;

(f) the residual maturity breakdown of all the exposures, broken down by exposure classes, and further detailed if appropriate;

(g) by significant industry or counterparty type, the amount of:
    (i) impaired exposures and past due exposures, provided separately;
    (ii) value adjustments and provisions; and
    (iii) charges for value adjustments and provisions during the period;

(h) the amount of the impaired exposures and past due exposures, provided separately, broken down by significant geographical areas including, if practical, the amounts of value adjustments and provisions related to each geographical area;

(i) the reconciliation of changes in the value adjustments and provisions for impaired exposures, shown separately. The information shall comprise:
    (i) a description of the type of value adjustments and provisions;
    (ii) the opening balances;
    (iii) the amounts taken against the provisions during the period;
    (iv) the amounts set aside or reversed for estimated probable losses on exposures during the period, any other adjustments including those determined by exchange rate differences, business combinations, acquisitions and disposals of subsidiaries, and transfers between provisions; and
    (v) the closing balances.

Value adjustments and recoveries recorded directly to the income statement shall be disclosed separately.

7. For credit institutions calculating the risk-weighted exposure amounts in accordance with Articles 78 to 83, the following information shall be disclosed for each of the exposure classes specified in Article 79:

(a) the names of the nominated ECAIs and ECAs and the reasons for any changes;

(b) the exposure classes for which each ECAI or ECA is used;

(c) a description of the process used to transfer the issuer and issue credit assessments onto items not included in the trading book;

(d) the association of the external rating of each nominated ECAI or ECA with the credit quality steps prescribed in Annex VI, taking into account that this information needs not be disclosed if the credit institution complies with the standard association published by the competent authority; and

(e) the exposure values and the exposure values after credit risk mitigation associated with each credit quality step prescribed in Annex VI, as well as those deducted from own funds.

8. The credit institutions calculating the risk-weighted exposure amounts in accordance with Annex VII, Part 1, points 6 or 19 to 21 shall disclose the exposures assigned to each category in Table 1 in point 6 of Annex VII, Part 1, or to each risk weight mentioned in points 19 to 21 of Annex VII, Part 1.

9. The credit institutions calculating their capital requirements in accordance with Article 75, points (b) and (c) shall disclose those requirements separately for each risk referred to in those provisions.

10. The following information shall be disclosed by each credit institution which calculates its capital requirements in accordance with Annex V to Directive 2006/49/EC:

(a) for each sub-portfolio covered:
    (i) the characteristics of the models used;
    (ii) a description of stress testing applied to the sub-portfolio;
    (iii) a description of the approaches used for back-testing and validating the accuracy and consistency of the internal models and modelling processes;

(b) the scope of acceptance by the competent authority; and

(c) a description of the extent and methodologies for compliance with the requirements set out in Annex VII, Part B to Directive 2006/49/EC.

11. The following information shall be disclosed by the credit institutions on operational risk:

(a) the approaches for the assessment of own funds requirements for operational risk that the credit institution qualifies for; and

(b) a description of the methodology set out in Article 105, if used by the credit institution, including a discussion of relevant internal and external factors considered in the credit institution's measurement approach. In the case of partial use, the scope and coverage of the different methodologies used.

12.　The following information shall be disclosed regarding the exposures in equities not included in the trading book:

(a)　the differentiation between exposures based on their objectives, including for capital gains relationship and strategic reasons, and an overview of the accounting techniques and valuation methodologies used, including key assumptions and practices affecting valuation and any significant changes in these practices;

(b)　the balance sheet value, the fair value and, for those exchange-traded, a comparison to the market price where it is materially different from the fair value;

(c)　the types, nature and amounts of exchange-traded exposures, private equity exposures in sufficiently diversified portfolios, and other exposures;

(d)　the cumulative realised gains or losses arising from sales and liquidations in the period; and

(e)　the total unrealised gains or losses, the total latent revaluation gains or losses, and any of these amounts included in the original or additional own funds.

13.　The following information shall be disclosed by credit institutions on their exposure to interest rate risk on positions not included in the trading book:

(a)　the nature of the interest rate risk and the key assumptions (including assumptions regarding loan prepayments and behaviour of non-maturity deposits), and frequency of measurement of the interest rate risk; and

(b)　the variation in earnings, economic value or other relevant measure used by the management for upward and downward rate shocks according to management's method for measuring the interest rate risk, broken down by currency.

14.　The credit institutions calculating risk weighted exposure amounts in accordance with Articles 94 to 101 shall disclose the following information:

(a)　a description of the credit institution's objectives in relation to securitisation activity;

(b)　the roles played by the credit institution in the securitisation process;

(c)　an indication of the extent of the credit institution's involvement in each of them;

(d)　the approaches to calculating risk weighted exposure amounts that the credit institution follows for its securitisation activities;

(e)　a summary of the credit institution's accounting policies for securitisation activities, including:

　(i)　whether the transactions are treated as sales or financings;

　(ii)　the recognition of gains on sales;

　(iii)　the key assumptions for valuing retained interests; and

　(iv)　the treatment of synthetic securitisations if this is not covered by other accounting policies;

(f)　the names of the ECAIs used for securitisations and the types of exposure for which each agency is used;

(g)　the total outstanding amount of exposures securitised by the credit institution and subject to the securitisation framework (broken down into traditional and synthetic), by exposure type;

(h)　for exposures securitised by the credit institution and subject to the securitisation framework, a breakdown by exposure type of the amount of impaired and past due exposures securitised, and the losses recognised by the credit institution during the period;

(i)　the aggregate amount of securitisation positions retained or purchased, broken down by exposure type;

(j)　the aggregate amount of securitisation positions retained or purchased, broken down into a meaningful number of risk weight bands. Positions that have been risk weighted at 1250% or deducted shall be disclosed separately;

(k)　the aggregate outstanding amount of securitised revolving exposures segregated by the originator's interest and the investors' interest; and

(l)　a summary of the securitisation activity in the period, including the amount of exposures securitised (by exposure type), and recognised gain or loss on sale by exposure type.

PART 3
QUALIFYING REQUIREMENTS FOR THE USE OF PARTICULAR INSTRUMENTS OR METHODOLOGIES

1.　The credit institutions calculating the risk-weighted exposure amounts in accordance with Articles 84 to 89 shall disclose the following information:

(a)　the competent authority's acceptance of approach or approved transition;

(b)　an explanation and review of:

(i) the structure of internal rating systems and relation between internal and external ratings;

(ii) the use of internal estimates other than for calculating risk-weighted exposure amounts in accordance with Articles 84 to 89;

(iii) the process for managing and recognising credit risk mitigation; and

(iv) the control mechanisms for rating systems including a description of independence, accountability, and rating systems review;

(c) a description of the internal ratings process, provided separately for the following exposure classes:

(i) central governments and central banks;

(ii) institutions;

(iii) corporate, including SMEs, specialised lending and purchased corporate receivables;

(iv) retail, for each of the categories of exposures to which the different correlations in Annex VII, Part 1, points 10 to 13 correspond; and

(v) equities;

(d) the exposure values for each of the exposure classes specified in Article 86. Exposures to central governments and central banks, institutions and corporates where credit institutions use own estimates of LGDs or conversion factors for the calculation of risk-weighted exposure amounts shall be disclosed separately from exposures for which the credit institutions do not use such estimates;

(e) for each of the exposure classes central governments and central banks, institutions, corporate and equity, and across a sufficient number of obligor grades (including default) to allow for a meaningful differentiation of credit risk, credit institutions shall disclose:

(i) the total exposures (for the exposure classes central governments and central banks, institutions and corporate, the sum of outstanding loans and exposure values for undrawn commitments; for equities, the outstanding amount);

(ii) for the credit institutions using own LGD estimates for the calculation of risk-weighted exposure amounts, the exposure-weighted average LGD in percentage;

(iii) the exposure-weighted average risk weight; and

(iv) for the credit institutions using own estimates of conversion factors for the calculation of risk-weighted exposure amounts, the amount of undrawn commitments and exposure-weighted average exposure values for each exposure class;

(f) for the retail exposure class and for each of the categories as defined under point (c)(iv), either the disclosures outlined under (e) above (if applicable, on a pooled basis), or an analysis of exposures (outstanding loans and exposure values for undrawn commitments) against a sufficient number of EL grades to allow for a meaningful differentiation of credit risk (if applicable, on a pooled basis);

(g) the actual value adjustments in the preceding period for each exposure class (for retail, for each of the categories as defined under point (c)(iv) and how they differ from past experience;

(h) a description of the factors that impacted on the loss experience in the preceding period (for example, has the credit institution experienced higher than average default rates, or higher than average LGDs and conversion factors); and

(i) the credit institution's estimates against actual outcomes over a longer period. At a minimum, this shall include information on estimates of losses against actual losses in each exposure class (for retail, for each of the categories as defined under point (c)(iv) over a period sufficient to allow for a meaningful assessment of the performance of the internal rating processes for each exposure class (for retail for each of the categories as defined under point (c)(iv). Where appropriate, the credit institutions shall further decompose this to provide analysis of PD and, for the credit institutions using own estimates of LGDs and/or conversion factors, LGD and conversion factor outcomes against estimates provided in the quantitative risk assessment disclosures above.

For the purposes of point (c), the description shall include the types of exposure included in the exposure class, the definitions, methods and data for estimation and validation of PD and, if applicable, LGD and conversion factors, including assumptions employed in the derivation of these variables, and the descriptions of material deviations from the definition of default as set out in Annex VII, Part 4, points 44 to 48, including the broad segments affected by such deviations.

2. The credit institutions applying credit risk mitigation techniques shall disclose the following information:

(a) the policies and processes for, and an indication of the extent to which the entity makes use of, on- and off-balance sheet netting;

(b) the policies and processes for collateral valuation and management;

(c) a description of the main types of collateral taken by the credit institution;

(d)   the main types of guarantor and credit derivative counterparty and their creditworthiness;

(e)   information about market or credit risk concentrations within the credit mitigation taken;

(f)   for credit institutions calculating risk-weighted exposure amounts in accordance with Articles 78 to 83 or 84 to 89, but not providing own estimates of LGDs or conversion factors in respect of the exposure class, separately for each exposure class, the total exposure value (after, where applicable, on- or off-balance sheet netting) that is covered — after the application of volatility adjustments — by eligible financial collateral, and other eligible collateral; and

(g)   for credit institutions calculating risk-weighted exposure amounts in accordance with Articles 78 to 83 or 84 to 89, separately for each exposure class, the total exposure (after, where applicable, on- or off-balance sheet netting) that is covered by guarantees or credit derivatives. For the equity exposure class, this requirement applies to each of the approaches provided in Annex VII, Part 1, points 17 to 26.

3.   The credit institutions using the approach set out in Article 105 for the calculation of their own funds requirements for operational risk shall disclose a description of the use of insurance for the purpose of mitigating the risk.

[5845]

ANNEX XIII

PART A
REPEALED DIRECTIVES TOGETHER WITH THEIR SUCCESSIVE AMENDMENTS
(REFERRED TO IN ARTICLE 158)

Directive 2000/12/EC of the European Parliament and of the Council of 20 March 2000 relating to the taking up and pursuit of the business of credit institutions

Directive 2000/28/EC of the European Parliament and of the Council of 18 September 2000 amending Directive 2000/12/EC relating to the taking up and pursuit of the business of credit institutions

Directive 2002/87/EC of the European Parliament and of the Council of 16 December 2002 on the supplementary supervision of credit institutions, insurance undertakings and investment firms in a financial conglomerate and amending Council Directives 73/239/EEC, 79/267/EEC, 92/49/EEC, 92/96/EEC, 93/6/EEC and 93/22/EEC, and Directives 98/78/EC and 2000/12/EC of the European Parliament and of the Council

Only Art 29.1(a)(b), Art 29.2, Art 29.4(a)(b), Art 29.5, Art 29.6, Art 29.7, Art 29.8, Art 29.9, Art 29.10, Art 29.11

Directive 2004/39/EC of the European Parliament and of the Council of 21 April 2004 on markets in financial instruments amending Council Directives 85/611/EEC and 93/6/EEC and Directive 2000/12/EC of the European Parliament and of the Council and repealing Council Directive 93/22/EEC

Only Art 68

Commission Directive 2004/69/EC of 27 April 2004 amending Directive 2000/12/EC of the European Parliament and of the Council as regards the definition of "multilateral development banks"

Directive 2005/1/EC of the European Parliament and of the Council of 9 March 2005 amending Council Directives 73/239/EEC, 85/611/EEC, 91/675/EEC, 92/49/EEC and 93/6/EEC and Directives 94/19/EC, 98/78/EC, 2000/12/EC, 2001/34/EC, 2002/83/EC and 2002/87/EC in order to establish a new organisational structure for financial services committees

Only Art 3

NON-REPEALED MODIFICATIONS

Act of Accession 2003

PART B
DEADLINES FOR TRANSPOSITION (REFERRED TO IN ARTICLE 158)

Directive		Deadline for transposition
Directive 2000/12/EC		—
Directive 2000/28/EC		27.4.2002
Directive 2002/87/EC		11.8.2004

Directive		Deadline for transposition
Directive 2004/39/EC		30.04.2006/31.1.2007
Directive 2004/69/EC		30.6.2004
Directive 2005/1/EC		13.5.2005

[5845A]

ANNEX XIV
CORRELATION TABLE

This Directive	Directive 2000/12/EC	Directive 2000/28/EC	Directive 2002/87/EC	Directive 2004/39/EC	Directive 2005/1/EC
Article 1	Art 2(1) and (2)				
Article 2	Art 2(3) Act of Accession				
Article 2	Art 2(4)				
Article 3	Art 2(5) and (6)				
Article 3(1), third subparagraph					Art 3(2)
Article 4(1)	Art 1(1)				
Article 4(2) to (5)		Art 1(2) to (5)			
Article 4(7) to (9)		Art 1(6) to (8)			
Article 4(10)			Art 29(1)(a)		
Article 4(11) to (14)	Art 1(10), (12) and (13)				
Article 4(21) and 22)			Art 29(1)(b)		
Article 4(23)	Art 1(23)				
Article 4(45) to (47)	Art 1(25) to (27)				
Article 5					
Article 6	Art 4				
Article 7	Art 8				
Article 8	Art 9				
Article 9(1)	Art 5(1) and 1(11)				
Article 9(2)	Art 5(2)				
Article 10	Art 5(3) to (7)				
Article 11	Art 6				
Article 12	Art 7				
Article 13	Art 10				
Article 14	Art 11				
Article 15(1)	Art 12				
Article 15(2) and (3)			Art 29(2)		

This Directive	Directive 2000/12/EC	Directive 2000/28/EC	Directive 2002/87/EC	Directive 2004/39/EC	Directive 2005/1/EC
Article 16	Art 13				
Article 17	Art 14				
Article 18	Art 15				
Article 19(1)	Art 16(1)				
Article 19(2)			Art 29(3)		
Article 20	Art 16(3)				
Article 21	Art 16(4) to (6)				
Article 22	Art 17				
Article 23	Art 18				
Article 24(1)	Art 19(1) to (3)				
Article 24(2)	Art 19(6)				
Article 24(3)	Art 19(4)				
Article 25(1) to (3)	Art 20(1) to (3), first and second subparagraphs				
Article 25(3)	Art 19(5)				
Article 25(4)	Art 20(3) third subparagraph				
Article 26	Art 20(4) to (7)				
Article 27	Art 1(3), second sentence				
Article 28	Art 21				
Article 29	Art 22				
Article 30	Art 22(2) to (4)				
Article 31	Art 22(5)				
Article 32	Art 22(6)				
Article 33	Art 22(7)				
Article 34	Art 22(8)				
Article 35	Art 22(9)				
Article 36	Art 22(10)				
Article 37	Art 22(11)				
Article 38	Art 24				
Article 39(1) and (2)	Art 25				
Article 39(3)					Art 3(8)
Article 40	Art 26				
Article 41	Art 27				
Article 42	Art 28				
Article 43	Art 29				
Article 44	Art 30(1) to (3)				
Article 45	Art 30(4)				

PART IV
EC MATERIALS

This Directive	Directive 2000/12/EC	Directive 2000/28/EC	Directive 2002/87/EC	Directive 2004/39/EC	Directive 2005/1/EC
Article 46	Art 30(3)				
Article 47	Art 30(5)				
Article 48	Art 30(6) and (7)				
Article 49	Art 30(8)				
Article 50	Art 30(9), first and second subparagraphs				
Article 51	Art 30(9), third subparagraph				
Article 52	Art 30(10)				
Article 53	Art 31				
Article 54	Art 32				
Article 55	Art 33				
Article 56	Art 34(1)				
Article 57	Art 34(2), first subparagraph; and Art 34(2), point 2, second sentence		Art 29(4)(a)		
Article 58			Art 29(4)(b)		
Article 59			Art 29(4)(b)		
Article 60			Art 29(4)(b)		
Article 61	Art 34(3) and (4)				
Article 63	Art 35				
Article 64	Art 36				
Article 65	Art 37				
Article 66(1) and (2)	Art 38(1) and (2)				
Article 67	Art 39				
Article 73	Art 52(3)				
Article 106	Art 1(24)				
Article 107	Art 1(1), third subparagraph				
Article 108	Art 48(1)				
Article 109	Art 48(4), first subparagraph				
Article 110	Art 48(2) to (4), second subparagraph				
Article 111	Art 49(1) to (5)				
Article 113	Art 49(4), (6) and (7)				
Article 115	Art 49(8) and (9)				

This Directive	Directive 2000/12/EC	Directive 2000/28/EC	Directive 2002/87/EC	Directive 2004/39/EC	Directive 2005/1/EC
Article 116	Art 49(10)				
Article 117	Art 49(11)				
Article 118	Art 50				
Article 120	Art 51(1), (2) and (5)				
Article 121	Art 51(4)				
Article 122(1) and (2)	Art 51(6)		Art 29(5)		
Article 125	Art 53(1) and (2)				
Article 126	Art 53(3)				
Article 128	Art 53(5)				
Article 133(1)	Art 54(1)		Art 29(7)(a)		
Article 133(2) and (3)	Art 54(2) and (3)				
Article 134(1)	Art 54(4), first subparagraph				
Article 134(2)	Art 54(4), second subparagraph				
Article 135			Art 29(8)		
Article 137	Art 55				
Article 138			Art 29(9)		
Article 139	Art 56(1) to (3)				
Article 140	Art 56(4) to (6)				
Article 141	Art 56(7)		Art 29(10)		
Article 142	Art 56(8)				
Article 143			Art 29(11)		Art 3(10)
Article 150	Art 60(1)				
Article 151	Art 60(2)				Art 3(10)
Article 158	Art 67				
Article 159	Art 68				
Article 160	Art 69				
Annex I, points 1 to 14, excluding the final paragraph	Annex I				
Annex I, final paragraph				Art 68	
Annex II	Annex II				
Annex III	Annex III				
Annex IV	Annex IV				

DIRECTIVE OF THE EUROPEAN PARLIAMENT AND OF THE COUNCIL

of 14 June 2006

on the capital adequacy of investment firms and credit institutions (recast)

(2006/49/EC)

NOTES

Date of publication in OJ: OJ L177, 30.6.2006, p 201. Notes are as in the original OJ version.

This Directive is reproduced as amended by: European Parliament and Council Directive 2008/23/EC (OJ L76, 19.3.2008, p 54).

Proposed amendments of this Directive: see the 2008 Proposal for a Directive of the European Parliament and of the Council amending Directives 2006/48/EC and 2006/49/EC as regards banks affiliated to central institutions, certain own funds items, large exposures, supervisory arrangements, and crisis management.[1]

1   Brussels, 1.10.2008, COM(2008) 602 final. Available on the Europa website.

THE EUROPEAN PARLIAMENT AND THE COUNCIL OF THE EUROPEAN UNION,

Having regard to the Treaty establishing the European Community, and in particular Article 47(2) thereof,

Having regard to the proposal from the Commission,

Having regard to the Opinion of the European Economic and Social Committee,[1]

Having regard to the Opinion of the European Central Bank,[2]

After consulting the Committee of the Regions,

Acting in accordance with the procedure laid down in Article 251 of the Treaty,[3]

Whereas:

(1)   Council Directive 93/6/EEC of 15 March 1993 on the capital adequacy of investment firms and credit institutions[4] has been significantly amended on several occasions. Now that new amendments are being made to the said Directive, it is desirable, in order to clarify matters, that it should be recast.

(2)   One of the objectives of Directive 2004/39/EC of the European Parliament and of the Council of 21 April 2004 on markets in financial instruments[5] is to allow investment firms authorised by the competent authorities of their home Member State and supervised by the same authorities to establish branches and provide services freely in other Member States. That Directive accordingly provides for the coordination of the rules governing the authorisation and pursuit of the business of investment firms.

(3)   Directive 2004/39/EC does not, however, establish common standards for the own funds of investment firms nor indeed does it establish the amounts of the initial capital of such firms or a common framework for monitoring the risks incurred by them.

(4)   It is appropriate to effect only the essential harmonisation that is necessary and sufficient to secure the mutual recognition of authorisation and of prudential supervision systems; in order to achieve mutual recognition within the framework of the internal financial market, measures should be laid down to coordinate the definition of the own funds of investment firms, the establishment of the amounts of their initial capital and the establishment of a common framework for monitoring the risks incurred by investment firms.

(5)   Since the objectives of this Directive, namely the establishment of the capital adequacy requirements applying to investment firms and credit institutions, the rules for their calculation and the rules for their prudential supervision, cannot be sufficiently achieved by the Member States and can therefore, by reason of the scale and the effects of the proposed action, be better achieved at Community level, the Community may adopt measures, in accordance with the principle of subsidiarity as set out in Article 5 of the Treaty. In accordance with the principle of proportionality, as set out in that Article, this Directive does not go beyond what is necessary in order to achieve its objectives.

(6)   It is appropriate to establish different amounts of initial capital depending on the range of activities that investment firms are authorised to undertake.

(7)   Existing investment firms should be permitted, under certain conditions, to continue their business even if they do not comply with the minimum amount of initial capital fixed for new investment firms.

(8)   Member States should be able to establish rules stricter than those provided for in this Directive.

(9)   The smooth operation of the internal market requires not only legal rules but also close and regular cooperation and significantly enhanced convergence of regulatory and supervisory practices between the competent authorities of the Member States.

(10)   The Commission Communication of 11 May 1999 entitled "Implementing the framework for financial markets: Action Plan" listed a number of goals that need to be achieved in order to

complete the internal market in financial services. The Lisbon European Council of 23 and 24 March 2000 set the goal of implementing the action plan by 2005. Recasting of the provisions on own funds is a key element of the action plan.

(11) Since investment firms face in respect of their trading book business the same risks as credit institutions, it is appropriate for the pertinent provisions of Directive 2006/48/EC of the European Parliament and of the Council of 14 June 2006 relating to the taking up and pursuit of the business of credit institutions[6] to apply equally to investment firms.

(12) The own funds of investment firms or credit institutions (hereinafter referred to collectively as "institutions") can serve to absorb losses which are not matched by a sufficient volume of profits, to ensure the continuity of institutions and to protect investors. The own funds also serve as an important yardstick for the competent authorities, in particular for the assessment of the solvency of institutions and for other prudential purposes. Furthermore, institutions, engage in direct competition with each other in the internal market. Therefore, in order to strengthen the Community financial system and to prevent distortions of competition, it is appropriate to lay down common basic standards for own funds.

(13) For the purposes of recital (12), it is appropriate for the definition of own funds as laid down in Directive 2006/48/EC to serve as a basis, and to provide for supplementary specific rules which take into account the different scope of market risk related capital requirements.

(14) As regards credit institutions, common standards have already been established for the supervision and monitoring of different types of risks by Directive 2000/12/EC.

(15) In that respect, the provisions on minimum capital requirements should be considered in conjunction with other specific instruments which also harmonise the fundamental techniques of the supervision of institutions.

(16) It is necessary to develop common standards for market risks incurred by credit institutions and provide a complementary framework for the supervision of the risks incurred by institutions, in particular market risks, and more especially position risks, counterparty/settlement risks and foreign-exchange risks.

(17) It is necessary to provide for the concept of a "trading book" comprising positions in securities and other financial instruments which are held for trading purposes and which are subject mainly to market risks and exposures relating to certain financial services provided to customers.

(18) With a view to reducing the administrative burden for institutions with negligible trading-book business in both absolute and relative terms, such institutions should be able to apply Directive 2006/48/EC, rather than the requirements laid down in Annexes I and II to this Directive.

(19) It is important that monitoring of settlement/delivery risks should take account of the existence of systems offering adequate protection reducing those risks.

(20) In any case, institutions should comply with this Directive as regards the coverage of the foreign-exchange risks on their overall business. Lower capital requirements should be imposed for positions in closely correlated currencies, whether statistically confirmed or arising out of binding intergovernmental agreements.

(21) The capital requirements for commodity dealers, including those dealers currently exempt from the requirements of Directive 2004/39/EC, will be reviewed as appropriate in conjunction with the review of that exemption as set out in Article 65(3) of that Directive.

(22) The goal of liberalisation of gas and electricity markets is both economically and politically important for the Community. With this in mind, the capital requirements and other prudential rules to be applied to firms active in those markets should be proportionate and should not unduly interfere with achievement of the goal of liberalisation. This goal should, in particular, be kept in mind when the reviews referred to in recital 21 are carried out.

(23) The existence of internal systems for monitoring and controlling interest-rate risks on all business of institutions is a particularly important way of minimising such risks. Consequently, such systems should be supervised by the competent authorities.

(24) Since Directive 2006/48/EC does not establish common rules for the monitoring and control of large exposures in activities which are principally subject to market risks, it is therefore appropriate to provide for such rules.

(25) Operational risk is a significant risk faced by institutions and requires coverage by own funds. It is essential to take account of the diversity of institutions in the EU by providing alternative approaches.

(26) Directive 2006/48/EC states the principle of consolidation. It does not establish common rules for the consolidation of financial institutions which are involved in activities principally subject to market risks.

(27) In order to ensure adequate solvency of institutions within a group, it is essential that the minimum capital requirements apply on the basis of the consolidated financial situation of the group. In order to ensure that own funds are appropriately distributed within the group and are available to protect investments where needed, the minimum capital requirements should apply to individual institutions within a group, unless this objective can be effectively achieved by other means.

(28)   Directive 2006/48/EC does not apply to groups which include one or more investment firms but no credit institutions. A common framework for the introduction of the supervision of investment firms on a consolidated basis should therefore be provided for.

(29)   Institutions should ensure that they have internal capital which, having regard to the risks to which they are or might be exposed, is adequate in quantity, quality and distribution. Accordingly, institutions should have strategies and processes in place for assessing and maintaining the adequacy of their internal capital.

(30)   Competent authorities should evaluate the adequacy of own funds of institutions, having regard to the risks to which the latter are exposed.

(31)   In order for the internal banking market to operate effectively, the Committee of European Banking Supervisors should contribute to the consistent application of this Directive and to the convergence of supervisory practices throughout the Community, and should report on a yearly basis to the Community Institutions on progress made.

(32)   In order for the internal market to operate with increasing effectiveness it is essential that there should be significantly enhanced convergence in the implementation and application of the provisions of harmonising Community legislation.

(33)   For the same reason, and to ensure that Community institutions which are active in several Member States are not disproportionately burdened as a result of the continued responsibilities of individual Member State competent authorities for authorisation and supervision, it is essential significantly to enhance the cooperation between competent authorities. In this context the role of the consolidating supervisor should be strengthened.

(34)   In order for the internal market to operate with increasing effectiveness and for citizens of the Union to be afforded adequate levels of transparency, it is necessary that competent authorities disclose publicly and in a way which allows for meaningful comparison the manner in which the requirements of this Directive are implemented.

(35)   In order to strengthen market discipline and stimulate institutions to improve their market strategy, risk control and internal management organisation, appropriate public disclosures by institutions should be provided for.

(36) The measures necessary for the implementation of this Directive should be adopted in accordance with Council Decision 1999/468/EC of 28 June 1999 laying down the procedures for the exercise of implementing powers conferred on the Commission.[7]

(37)   In its Resolution of 5 February 2002 on the implementation of financial services legislation,[8] the Parliament requested that the Parliament and the Council should have an equal role in supervising the way in which the Commission exercises its executive role in order to reflect the legislative powers of Parliament under Article 251 of the Treaty. In the solemn declaration made before the Parliament the same day, by its President, the Commission supported this request. On 11 December 2002, the Commission proposed amendments to Decision 1999/468/EC and then submitted an amended proposal on 22 April 2004. The Parliament considers that this proposal does not preserve its legislative prerogatives. In the Parliament's view, the Parliament and the Council should have the opportunity of evaluating the conferral of implementing powers on the Commission within a determined period. It is therefore appropriate to limit the period during which the Commission may adopt implementing measures.

(38)   The Parliament should be given a period of three months from the first transmission of draft amendments and implementing measures to allow it to examine them and to give its opinion. However, in urgent and duly justified cases, it should be possible to shorten this period. If, within that period, a resolution is adopted by the Parliament, the Commission should re-examine the draft amendments or measures.

(39)   In order to avoid disruption to markets and to ensure continuity in overall levels of own funds, it is appropriate to provide for specific transitional arrangements.

(40)   This Directive respects fundamental rights and observes the principles recognised in particular by the Charter of Fundamental Rights of the European Union as general principles of Community law.

(41)   The obligation to transpose this Directive into national law should be confined to those provisions that represent a substantive change compared to earlier directives. The obligation to transpose the provisions that remain unchanged exists under the earlier directives.

(42)   This Directive should be without prejudice to the obligations of the Member States relating to the time-limits for transposition into national law of the Directives set out in Part B of Annex VIII,

[5847]

NOTES
1   OJ C234, 22.9.2005, p 8.
2   OJ C52, 2.3.2005, p 37.
3   Opinion of the European Parliament of 28 September 2005 (not yet published in the OJ) and Decision of the Council of 7 June 2006.
4   OJ L141, 11.6.1993, p 1. Directive as last amended by Directive 2005/1/EC of the European Parliament and of the Council (OJ L79, 24.3.2005, p 9).
5   OJ L145, 30.4.2004, p 1.

6   See page 1 of this official Journal.
7   OJ L184, 17.7.1999, p 23.
8   OJ C284E, 21.11.2002, p 115.

HAVE ADOPTED THIS DIRECTIVE:

CHAPTER I
SUBJECT MATTER, SCOPE AND DEFINITIONS

SECTION 1
SUBJECT MATTER AND SCOPE

Article 1

1. This Directive lays down the capital adequacy requirements applying to investment firms and credit institutions, the rules for their calculation and the rules for their prudential supervision. Member States shall apply the requirements of this Directive to investment firms and credit institutions as defined in Article 3.

2. A Member State may impose additional or more stringent requirements on those investment firms and credit institutions that it has authorised.

[5847A]

Article 2

1. Subject to Articles 18, 20, 22 to 32, 34 and 39 of this Directive, Articles 68 to 73 of Directive 2006/48/EC shall apply mutatis mutandis to investment firms. In applying Articles 70 to 72 of Directive 2006/48/EC to investment firms, every reference to a parent credit institution in a Member State shall be construed as a reference to a parent investment firm in a Member State and every reference to an EU parent credit institution shall be construed as a reference to an EU parent investment firm.

Where a credit institution has as a parent undertaking a parent investment firm in a Member State, only that parent investment firm shall be subject to requirements on a consolidated basis in accordance with Articles 71 to 73 of Directive 2006/48/EC.

Where an investment firm has as a parent undertaking a parent credit institution in a Member State, only that parent credit institution shall be subject to requirements on a consolidated basis in accordance with Articles 71 to 73 of Directive 2006/48/EC.

Where a financial holding company has as a subsidiary both a credit institution and an investment firm, requirements on the basis of the consolidated financial situation of the financial holding company shall apply to the credit institution.

2. When a group covered by paragraph 1 does not include a credit institution, Directive 2006/48/EC shall apply, subject to the following:
   (a)   every reference to credit institutions shall be construed as a reference to investment firms;
   (b)   in Articles 125 and 140(2) of Directive 2006/48/EC, each reference to other articles of that Directive shall be construed as a reference to Directive 2004/39/EC;
   (c)   for the purposes of Article 39(3) of Directive 2006/48/EC, references to the European Banking Committee shall be construed as references to the Council and the Commission; and
   (d)   by way of derogation from Article 140(1) of Directive 2006/48/EC, where a group does not include a credit institution, the first sentence of that Article shall be replaced by the following: "Where an investment firm, a financial holding company or a mixed-activity holding company controls one or more subsidiaries which are insurance companies, the competent authorities and the authorities entrusted with the public task of supervising insurance undertakings shall cooperate closely".

[5848]

SECTION 2
DEFINITIONS

Article 3

1. For the purposes of this Directive the following definitions shall apply:
   (a)   "credit institutions" means credit institutions as defined in Article 4(1) of Directive 2006/48/EC;
   (b)   "investment firms" means institutions as defined in Article 4(1)(1) of Directive 2004/39/EC, which are subject to the requirements imposed by that Directive, excluding:
      (i)   credit institutions;

    (ii)   local firms as defined in point (p); and

    (iii) firms which are only authorised to provide the service of investment advice and/or receive and transmit orders from investors without holding money or securities belonging to their clients and which for that reason may not at any time place themselves in debt with those clients;

(c)   "institutions" means credit institutions and investment firms;

(d)   "recognised third-country investment firms" means firms meeting the following conditions:

    (i)   firms which, if they were established within the Community, would be covered by the definition of investment firm;

    (ii)   firms which are authorised in a third country; and

    (iii) firms which are subject to and comply with prudential rules considered by the competent authorities as at least as stringent as those laid down by this Directive;

(e)   "financial instruments" means any contract that gives rise to both a financial asset of one party and a financial liability or equity instrument of another party;

(f)   "parent investment firm in a Member State" means an investment firm which has an institution or financial institution as a subsidiary or which holds a participation in one or both such entities, and which is not itself a subsidiary of another institution authorised in the same Member State or of a financial holding company set up in the same Member State;

(g)   "EU parent investment firm" means a parent investment firm in a Member State which is not a subsidiary of another institution authorised in any Member State or of a financial holding company set up in any Member State;

(h)   "over-the-counter (OTC) derivative instruments" means the items falling within the list in Annex IV to Directive 2006/48/EC other than those items to which an exposure value of zero is attributed under point 6 of Part 2 of Annex III to that Directive;

(i)   "regulated market" means a market as defined in Article 4(1)(14) of Directive 2004/39/EC;

(j)   "convertible" means a security which, at the option of the holder, may be exchanged for another security;

(k)   "warrant" means a security which gives the holder the right to purchase an underlying asset at a stipulated price until or at the expiry date of the warrant and which may be settled by the delivery of the underlying itself or by cash settlement;

(l)   "stock financing" means positions where physical stock has been sold forward and the cost of funding has been locked in until the date of the forward sale;

(m)   "repurchase agreement" and "reverse repurchase agreement" mean any agreement in which an institution or its counterparty transfers securities or commodities or guaranteed rights relating to title – to securities or commodities where that guarantee is issued by a recognised exchange which holds the rights to the securities or commodities and the agreement does not allow an institution to transfer or pledge a particular security or commodity to more than one counterparty at one time, subject to a commitment to repurchase them – or substituted securities or commodities of the same description – at a specified price on a future date specified, or to be specified, by the transferor, being a repurchase agreement for the institution selling the securities or commodities and a reverse repurchase agreement for the institution buying them;

(n)   "securities or commodities lending" and "securities or commodities borrowing" mean any transaction in which an institution or its counterparty transfers securities or commodities against appropriate collateral, subject to a commitment that the borrower will return equivalent securities or commodities at some future date or when requested to do so by the transferor, that transaction being securities or commodities lending for the institution transferring the securities or commodities and being securities or commodities borrowing for the institution to which they are transferred;

(o)   "clearing member" means a member of the exchange or the clearing house which has a direct contractual relationship with the central counterparty (market guarantor);

(p)   "local firm" means a firm dealing for its own account on markets in financial futures or options or other derivatives and on cash markets for the sole purpose of hedging positions on derivatives markets, or dealing for the accounts of other members of those markets and being guaranteed by clearing members of the same markets, where responsibility for ensuring the performance of contracts entered into by such a firm is assumed by clearing members of the same markets;

(q)   "delta" means the expected change in an option price as a proportion of a small change in the price of the instrument underlying the option;

(r)   "own funds" means own funds as defined in Directive 2006/48/EC; and

(s)   "capital" means own funds.

For the purposes of applying supervision on a consolidated basis, the term "investment firm" shall include third-country investment firms.

For the purposes of point (e), financial instruments shall include both primary financial instruments or cash instruments and derivative financial instruments the value of which is derived from the price of an underlying financial instrument, a rate, an index or the price of another underlying item, and include as a minimum the instruments specified in Section C of Annex I to Directive 2004/39/EC.

2. The terms "parent undertaking", "subsidiary undertaking", "asset management company" and "financial institution" shall cover undertakings defined in Article 4 of Directive 2006/48/EC.

The terms "financial holding company", "parent financial holding company in a Member State", "EU parent financial holding company" and "ancillary services undertaking" shall cover undertakings defined in Article 4 of Directive 2006/48/EC, save that every reference to credit institutions shall be read as a reference to institutions.

3. For the purposes of applying Directive 2006/48/EC to groups covered by Article 2(1) which do not include a credit institution, the following definitions shall apply:

(a) "financial holding company" means a financial institution the subsidiary undertakings of which are either exclusively or mainly investment firms or other financial institutions, at least one of which is an investment firm, and which is not a mixed financial holding company within the meaning of Directive 2002/87/EC of the European Parliament and of the Council of 16 December 2002 on the supplementary supervision of credit institutions, insurance undertakings and investment firms in a financial conglomerate;[1]

(b) "mixed-activity holding company" means a parent undertaking, other than a financial holding company or an investment firm or a mixed financial holding company within the meaning of Directive 2002/87/EC, the subsidiaries of which include at least one investment firm; and

(c) "competent authorities" means the national authorities which are empowered by law or regulation to supervise investment firms.

[5849]

NOTES

   [1]   OJ L35, 11.2.2003, p 1. Directive as amended by Directive 2005/1/EC.

CHAPTER II
INITIAL CAPITAL

Article 4

For the purposes of this Directive, "initial capital" shall be comprised of the items referred to in Article 57(a) and (b) of Directive 2006/48/EC.

[5850]

Article 5

1. An investment firm that does not deal in any financial instruments for its own account or underwrite issues of financial instruments on a firm commitment basis, but which holds clients' money and/or securities and which offers one or more of the following services, shall have initial capital of EUR 125,000:

(a) the reception and transmission of investors' orders for financial instruments;

(b) the execution of investors' orders for financial instruments; or

(c) the management of individual portfolios of investments in financial instruments.

2. The competent authorities may allow an investment firm which executes investors' orders for financial instruments to hold such instruments for its own account if the following conditions are met:

(a) such positions arise only as a result of the firm's failure to match investors' orders precisely;

(b) the total market value of all such positions is subject to a ceiling of 15% of the firm's initial capital;

(c) the firm meets the requirements laid down in Articles 18, 20 and 28; and

(d) such positions are incidental and provisional in nature and strictly limited to the time required to carry out the transaction in question.

The holding of non-trading-book positions in financial instruments in order to invest own funds shall not be considered as dealing in relation to the services set out in paragraph 1 or for the purposes of paragraph 3.

3. Member States may reduce the amount referred to in paragraph 1 to EUR 50,000 where a firm is not authorised to hold clients' money or securities, to deal for its own account, or to underwrite issues on a firm commitment basis.

[5851]

Article 6

Local firms shall have initial capital of EUR 50,000 insofar as they benefit from the freedom of establishment or to provide services specified in Articles 31 and 32 of Directive 2004/39/EC.

[5852]

Article 7

Coverage for the firms referred to in Article 3(1)(b)(iii) shall take one of the following forms:
  (a) initial capital of EUR 50,000;
  (b) professional indemnity insurance covering the whole territory of the Community or some other comparable guarantee against liability arising from professional negligence, representing at least EUR 1,000,000 applying to each claim and in aggregate EUR 1,500,000 per year for all claims; or
  (c) a combination of initial capital and professional indemnity insurance in a form resulting in a level of coverage equivalent to that referred to in points (a) or (b).

The amounts referred to in the first sub-paragraph shall be periodically reviewed by the Commission in order to take account of changes in the European Index of Consumer Prices as published by Eurostat, in line with and at the same time as the adjustments made under Article 4(7) of Directive 2002/92/EC of the European Parliament and of the Council of 9 December 2002 on insurance mediation.[1]

[5853]

NOTES

[1]   OJ L9, 15.1.2003, p 3.

Article 8

If a firm as referred to in Article 3(1)(b)(iii) is also registered under Directive 2002/92/EC, it shall comply with Article 4(3) of that Directive and have coverage in one of the following forms:
  (a) initial capital of EUR 25,000;
  (b) professional indemnity insurance covering the whole territory of the Community or some other comparable guarantee against liability arising from professional negligence, representing at least EUR 500,000 applying to each claim and in aggregate EUR 750,000 per year for all claims; or
  (c) a combination of initial capital and professional indemnity insurance in a form resulting in a level of coverage equivalent to that referred to in points (a) or (b).

[5854]

Article 9

All investment firms other than those referred to in Articles 5 to 8 shall have initial capital of EUR 730,000.

[5855]

Article 10

1.   By way of derogation from Articles 5(1), 5(3), 6 and 9, Member States may continue an authorisation of investment firms and firms covered by Article 6 which was in existence before 31 December 1995, the own funds of which firms or investment firms are less than the initial capital levels specified for them in Articles 5(1), 5(3), 6 and 9.

The own funds of such firms or investment firms shall not fall below the highest reference level calculated after the date of notification contained in Directive 93/6/EEC. That reference level shall be the average daily level of own funds calculated over a six-month period preceding the date of calculation. It shall be calculated every six months in respect of the corresponding preceding period.

2.   If control of a firm covered by paragraph 1 is taken by a natural or legal person other than the person who controlled it previously, the own funds of that firm shall attain at least the level specified for them in Articles 5(1), 5(3), 6 and 9, except in the case of a first transfer by inheritance made after 31 December 1995, subject to the competent authorities' approval and for a period of not more than 10 years from the date of that transfer.

3.   In certain specific circumstances, and with the approval of the competent authorities, in the event of a merger of two or more investment firms and/or firms covered by Article 6, the own funds of the firm produced by the merger need not attain the level specified in Articles 5(1), 5(3), 6 and 9. Nevertheless, during any period when the level specified in Articles 5(1), 5(3), 6 and 9 has not been attained, the own funds of the new firm may not fall below the merged firms' total own funds at the time of the merger.

4.   The own funds of investment firms and firms covered by Article 6 may not fall below the level specified in Articles 5(1), 5(3), 6 and 9 and paragraphs 1 and 3 of this Article.

In the event that the own funds of such firms and investment firms fall below that level, the competent authorities may, where the circumstances justify it, allow such firms a limited period in which to rectify their situations or cease their activities.

[5856]

CHAPTER III
TRADING BOOK

Article 11

1. The trading book of an institution shall consist of all positions in financial instruments and commodities held either with trading intent or in order to hedge other elements of the trading book and which are either free of any restrictive covenants on their tradability or able to be hedged.

2. Positions held with trading intent are those held intentionally for short-term resale and/or with the intention of benefiting from actual or expected short-term price differences between buying and selling prices or from other price or interest rate variations. The term "positions" shall include proprietary positions and positions arising from client servicing and market making.

3. Trading intent shall be evidenced on the basis of the strategies, policies and procedures set up by the institution to manage the position or portfolio in accordance with Part A of Annex VII.

4. Institutions shall establish and maintain systems and controls to manage their trading book in accordance with Parts B and D of Annex VII.

5. Internal hedges may be included in the trading book, in which case Part C of Annex VII shall apply.

[5857]

CHAPTER IV
OWN FUNDS

Article 12

"Original own funds" means the sum of points (a) to (c), less the sum of points (i) to (k) of Article 57 of Directive 2006/48/EC.

The Commission shall, by 1 January 2009, submit an appropriate proposal to the European Parliament and to the Council for amendment of this Chapter.

[5858]

Article 13

1. Subject to paragraphs 2 to 5 of this Article and Articles 14 to 17, the own funds of investment firms and credit institutions shall be determined in accordance with Directive 2006/48/EC.

In addition, the first subparagraph applies to investment firms which do not have one of the legal forms referred to in Article 1(1) of the Fourth Council Directive 78/660/EEC of 25 July 1978 based on Article 54(3) of the Treaty on the annual accounts of certain types of companies.[1]

2. By way of derogation from paragraph 1, the competent authorities may permit those institutions which are obliged to meet the capital requirements calculated in accordance with Articles 21 and 28 to 32 and Annexes I and III to VI to use, for that purpose only, an alternative determination of own funds. No part of the own funds used for that purpose may be used simultaneously to meet other capital requirements.

Such an alternative determination shall be the sum of the items set out in points (a) to (c) of this subparagraph, minus the item set out in point (d), with the deduction of that last item being left to the discretion of the competent authorities:

   (a)   own funds as defined in Directive 2006/48/EC, excluding only points (l) to (p) of Article 57 of that Directive for those investment firms which are required to deduct item (d) of this paragraph from the total of items (a) to (c);

   (b)   an institution's net trading-book profits net of any foreseeable charges or dividends, less net losses on its other business, provided that none of those amounts has already been included in item (a) of this paragraph as one of the items set out in points (b) or (k) of Article 57 of Directive 2006/48/EC;

   (c)   subordinated loan capital and/or the items referred to in paragraph 5 of this Article, subject to the conditions set out in paragraphs 3 and 4 of this Article and in Article 14; and

   (d)   illiquid assets as specified in Article 15.

3. The subordinated loan capital referred to in point (c) of the second subparagraph of paragraph 2 shall have an initial maturity of at least two years. It shall be fully paid up and the loan agreement shall not include any clause providing that in specified circumstances, other than the winding up of the institution, the debt will become repayable before the agreed repayment date, unless the competent authorities approve the repayment. Neither the principal nor the interest on

such subordinated loan capital may be repaid if such repayment would mean that the own funds of the institution in question would then amount to less than 100% of that institution's overall capital requirements.

In addition, an institution shall notify the competent authorities of all repayments on such subordinated loan capital as soon as its own funds fall below 120% of its overall capital requirements.

4.   The subordinated loan capital referred to in point (c) of the second subparagraph of paragraph 2 may not exceed a maximum of 150% of the original own funds left to meet the requirements calculated in accordance with Articles 21 and 28 to 32 and Annexes I to VI and may approach that maximum only in particular circumstances acceptable to the competent authorities.

5.   The competent authorities may permit institutions to replace the subordinated loan capital referred to in point (c) of the second subparagraph of paragraph 2 with points (d) to (h) of Article 57 of Directive 2006/48/EC.

[5859]

NOTES

1   OJ L222, 14.8.1978, p 11. Directive as last amended by Directive 2003/51/EC of the European Parliament and of the Council (OJ L178, 17.7.2003, p 16).

Article 14

1.   The competent authorities may permit investment firms to exceed the ceiling for subordinated loan capital set out in Article 13(4) if they judge it prudentially adequate and provided that the total of such subordinated loan capital and the items referred to in Article 13(5) does not exceed 200% of the original own funds left to meet the requirements calculated in accordance with Articles 21 and 28 to 32 and Annexes I and III to VI, or 250% of the same amount where investment firms deduct the item set out in Article 13(2)(d) when calculating own funds.

2.   The competent authorities may permit the ceiling for subordinated loan capital set out in Article 13(4) to be exceeded by a credit institution if they judge it prudentially adequate and provided that the total of such subordinated loan capital and points (d) to (h) of Article 57 of Directive 2006/48/EC does not exceed 250% of the original own funds left to meet the requirements calculated in accordance with Articles 28 to 32 and Annexes I and III to VI to this Directive.

[5860]

Article 15

Illiquid assets as referred to in point (d) of the second subparagraph of Article 13(2) shall include the following:

(a)   tangible fixed assets, except to the extent that land and buildings may be allowed to count against the loans which they are securing;

(b)   holdings in, including subordinated claims on, credit or financial institutions which may be included in the own funds of those institutions, unless they have been deducted under points (l) to (p) of Article 57 of Directive 2006/48/EC or under Article 16(d) of this Directive;

(c)   holdings and other investments in undertakings other than credit or financial institutions, which are not readily marketable;

(d)   deficiencies in subsidiaries;

(e)   deposits made, other than those which are available for repayment within 90 days, and also excluding payments in connection with margined futures or options contracts;

(f)   loans and other amounts due, other than those due to be repaid within 90 days; and

(g)   physical stocks, unless they are already subject to capital requirements at least as stringent as those set out in Articles 18 and 20.

For the purposes of point (b), where shares in a credit or financial institution are held temporarily for the purpose of a financial assistance operation designed to reorganise and save that institution, the competent authorities may waive the application of this Article. They may also waive it in respect of those shares which are included in an investment firm's trading book.

[5861]

Article 16

Investment firms included in a group which has been granted the waiver provided for in Article 22 shall calculate their own funds in accordance with Articles 13 to 15, subject to the following:

(a)   the illiquid assets referred to in Article 13(2)(d) shall be deducted;

(b)   the exclusion referred to in point (a) of Article 13(2) shall not cover those components of points (l) to (p) of Article 57 of Directive 2006/48/EC which an investment firm holds in respect of undertakings included in the scope of consolidation as defined in Article 2(1) of this Directive;

(c)   the limits referred to in points (a) and (b) of Article 66(1) of Directive 2006/48/EC shall be calculated with reference to the original own funds less the components of points (l) to (p) of Article 57 of that Directive as referred to in point (b) of this Article which are elements of the original own funds of those undertakings; and

(d)   the components of points (l) to (p) of Article 57 of Directive 2006/48/EC referred to in point (c) of this Article shall be deducted from the original own funds rather than from the total of all items as laid down in Article 66(2) of that Directive for the purposes in particular of Articles 13(4), 13(5) and 14 of this Directive.

[5862]

Article 17

1.   Where an institution calculates risk-weighted exposure amounts for the purposes of Annex II to this Directive in accordance with Articles 84 to 89 of Directive 2006/48/EC, then for the purposes of the calculation provided for in point 4 of Part 1 of Annex VII to Directive 2006/48/EC, the following shall apply:

(a)   value adjustments made to take account of the credit quality of the counterparty may be included in the sum of value adjustments and provisions made for the exposures indicated in Annex II; and

(b)   subject to the approval of the competent authorities, if the credit risk of the counterparty is adequately taken into account in the valuation of a position included in the trading book, the expected loss amount for the counterparty risk exposure shall be zero.

For the purposes of point (a), for such institutions, such value adjustments shall not be included in own funds other than in accordance with the provisions of this paragraph.

2.   For the purposes of this Article, Article 153 and 154 of Directive 2006/48/EC shall apply.

[5863]

CHAPTER V

SECTION 1
PROVISIONS AGAINST RISKS

Article 18

1.   Institutions shall have own funds which are always more than or equal to the sum of the following:

(a)   the capital requirements, calculated in accordance with the methods and options laid down in Articles 28 to 32 and Annexes I, II and VI and, as appropriate, Annex V, for their trading-book business; and

(b)   the capital requirements, calculated in accordance with the methods and options laid down in Annexes III and IV and, as appropriate, Annex V, for all of their business activities.

2.   By way of derogation from paragraph 1, the competent authorities may allow institutions to calculate the capital requirements for their trading book business in accordance with Article 75(a) of Directive 2006/48/EC and points 6, 7, and 9 of Annex II to this Directive, where the size of the trading book business meets the following requirements:

(a)   the trading-book business of such institutions does not normally exceed 5% of their total business;

(b)   their total trading-book positions do not normally exceed EUR 15 million; and

(c)   the trading-book business of such institutions never exceeds 6% of their total business and their total trading-book positions never exceed EUR 20 million.

3.   In order to calculate the proportion that trading-book business bears to total business for the purposes of points (a) and (c) of paragraph 2, the competent authorities may refer either to the size of the combined on- and off-balance-sheet business, to the profit and loss account or to the own funds of the institutions in question, or to a combination of those measures. When the size of on- and off-balance-sheet business is assessed, debt instruments shall be valued at their market prices or their principal values, equities at their market prices and derivatives according to the nominal or market values of the instruments underlying them. Long positions and short positions shall be summed regardless of their signs.

4.   If an institution should happen for more than a short period to exceed either or both of the limits imposed in paragraph 2(a) and (b) or either or both of the limits imposed in paragraph 2(c), it shall be required to meet the requirements imposed in paragraph 1(a) in respect of its trading-book business and to notify the competent authority thereof.

[5864]

Article 19

1.   For the purposes of point 14 of Annex I, subject to the discretion of the national authorities, a 0% weighting can be assigned to debt securities issued by the entities listed in Table 1 of Annex I, where these debt securities are denominated and funded in domestic currency.

PART IV
EC MATERIALS

2. By way of derogation from points 13 and 14 of Annex I, Member States may set a specific risk requirement for any bonds falling within points 68 to 70 of Part 1 of Annex VI to Directive 2006/48/EC which shall be equal to the specific risk requirement for a qualifying item with the same residual maturity as such bonds and reduced in accordance with the percentages given in point 71 of Part 1 to Annex VI to that Directive.

3. If, as set out in point 52 of Annex I, a competent authority approves a third country's collective investment undertaking (CIU) as eligible, a competent authority in another Member State may make use of this approval without conducting its own assessment.

[5865]

Article 20

1. Subject to paragraphs 2, 3 and 4 of this Article, and Article 34 of this Directive, the requirements in Article 75 of Directive 2006/48/EC shall apply to investment firms.

2. By way of derogation from paragraph 1, competent authorities may allow investment firms that are not authorised to provide the investment services listed in points 3 and 6 of Section A of Annex I to Directive 2004/39/EC to provide own funds which are always more than or equal to the higher of the following:
   (a) the sum of the capital requirements contained in points (a) to (c) of Article 75 of Directive 2006/48/EC; and
   (b) the amount laid down in Article 21 of this Directive.

3. By way of derogation from paragraph 1, competent authorities may allow investment firms which hold initial capital as set out in Article 9, but which fall within the following categories, to provide own funds which are always more than or equal to the sum of the capital requirements calculated in accordance with the requirements contained in points (a) to (c) of Article 75 of Directive 2006/48/EC and the amount laid down in Article 21 of this Directive:
   (a) investment firms that deal on own account only for the purpose of fulfilling or executing a client order or for the purpose of gaining entrance to a clearing and settlement system or a recognised exchange when acting in an agency capacity or executing a client order; and
   (b) investment firms:
       (i) that do not hold client money or securities;
       (ii) that undertake only dealing on own account;
       (iii) that have no external customers;
       (iv) the execution and settlement of whose transactions takes place under the responsibility of a clearing institution and are guaranteed by that clearing institution.

4. Investment firms referred to in paragraphs 2 and 3 shall remain subject to all other provisions regarding operational risk set out in Annex V of Directive 2006/48/EC.

5. Article 21 shall apply only to investment firms to which paragraphs (2) or (3) or Article 46 apply and in the manner specified therein.

[5866]

Article 21

Investment firms shall be required to hold own funds equivalent to one quarter of their preceding year's fixed overheads.

The competent authorities may adjust that requirement in the event of a material change in a firm's business since the preceding year.

Where a firm has not completed a year's business, starting from the day it starts up, the requirement shall be a quarter of the fixed overheads projected in its business plan, unless an adjustment to that plan is required by the competent authorities.

[5867]

SECTION 2
APPLICATION OF REQUIREMENTS ON A CONSOLIDATED BASIS

Article 22

1. The competent authorities required or mandated to exercise supervision of groups covered by Article 2 on a consolidated basis may waive, on a case-by-case basis, the application of capital requirements on a consolidated basis provided that:
   (a) each EU investment firm in such a group uses the calculation of own funds set out in Article 16;
   (b) all investment firms in such a group fall within the categories in Article 20(2) and (3);
   (c) each EU investment firm in such a group meets the requirements imposed in Articles 18 and 20 on an individual basis and at the same time deducts from its own funds any

contingent liability in favour of investment firms, financial institutions, asset management companies and ancillary services undertakings, which would otherwise be consolidated and;

(d) any financial holding company which is the parent financial holding company in a Member State of any investment firm in such a group holds at least as much capital, defined here as the sum of points (a) to (h) of Article 57 of Directive 2006/48/EC, as the sum of the full book value of any holdings, subordinated claims and instruments as referred to in Article 57 of that Directive in investment firms, financial institutions, asset management companies and ancillary services undertakings which would otherwise be consolidated, and the total amount of any contingent liability in favour of investment firms, financial institutions, asset management companies and ancillary services undertakings which would otherwise be consolidated.

Where the criteria in the first subparagraph are met, each EU investment firm shall have in place systems to monitor and control the sources of capital and funding of all financial holding companies, investment firms, financial institutions, asset management companies and ancillary services undertakings within the group.

2. By way of derogation from paragraph 1, competent authorities may permit financial holding companies which are the parent financial holding company in a Member State of an investment firm in such a group to use a value lower than the value calculated under paragraph 1(d), but no lower than the sum of the requirements imposed in Articles 18 and 20 on an individual basis to investment firms, financial institutions, asset management companies and ancillary services undertakings which would otherwise be consolidated and the total amount of any contingent liability in favour of investment firms, financial institutions, asset management companies and ancillary services undertakings which would otherwise be consolidated. For the purposes of this paragraph, the capital requirement for investment undertakings of third countries, financial institutions, asset management companies and ancillary services undertakings is a notional capital requirement.

[5868]

Article 23

The competent authorities shall require investment firms in a group which has been granted the waiver provided for in Article 22 to notify them of the risks which could undermine their financial positions, including those associated with the composition and sources of their capital and funding. If the competent authorities then consider that the financial positions of those investment firms is not adequately protected, they shall require them to take measures including, if necessary, limitations on the transfer of capital from such firms to group entities.

Where the competent authorities waive the obligation of supervision on a consolidated basis provided for in Article 22, they shall take other appropriate measures to monitor the risks, namely large exposures, of the whole group, including any undertakings not located in a Member State.

Where the competent authorities waive the application of capital requirements on a consolidated basis provided for in Article 22, the requirements of Article 123 and Chapter 5 of Title V of Directive 2006/48/EC shall apply on an individual basis, and the requirements of Article 124 of that Directive shall apply to the supervision of investment firms on an individual basis.

[5869]

Article 24

1. By way of derogation from Article 2(2), competent authorities may exempt investment firms from the consolidated capital requirement established in that Article, provided that all the investment firms in the group are covered by Article 20(2) and the group does not include credit institutions.

2. Where the requirements of paragraph 1 are met, a parent investment firm in a Member State shall be required to provide own funds at a consolidated level which are always more than or equal to the higher of the following two amounts, calculated on the basis of the parent investment firm's consolidated financial position and in compliance with Section 3 of this Chapter:

(a) the sum of the capital requirements contained in points (a) to (c) of Article 75 of Directive 2006/48/EC; and

(b) the amount prescribed in Article 21 of this Directive.

3. Where the requirements of paragraph 1 are met, an investment firm controlled by a financial holding company shall be required to provide own funds at a consolidated level which are always more than or equal to the higher of the following two amounts, calculated on the basis of the financial holding company's consolidated financial position and in compliance with Section 3 of this Chapter:

(a) the sum of the capital requirements contained in points (a) to (c) of Article 75 of Directive 2006/48/EC; and

(b) the amount prescribed in Article 21 of this Directive.

[5870]

Article 25

By way of derogation from Article 2(2), competent authorities may exempt investment firms from the consolidated capital requirement established in that Article, provided that all the investment firms in the group fall within the investment firms referred to in Article 20(2) and (3), and the group does not include credit institutions.

Where the requirements of the first paragraph are met, a parent investment firm in a Member State shall be required to provide own funds at a consolidated level which are always more than or equal to the sum of the requirements contained in points (a) to (c) of Article 75 of Directive 2006/48/EC and the amount prescribed in Article 21 of this Directive, calculated on the basis of the parent investment firm's consolidated financial position and in compliance with Section 3 of this Chapter.

Where the requirements of the first paragraph are met, an investment firm controlled by a financial holding company shall be required to provide own funds at a consolidated level which are always more than or equal to the sum of the requirements contained in points (a) to (c) of Article 75 of Directive 2006/48/EC and the amount prescribed in Article 21 of this Directive, calculated on the basis of the financial holding company's consolidated financial position and in compliance with Section 3 of this Chapter.

[5871]

SECTION 3
CALCULATION OF CONSOLIDATED REQUIREMENTS

Article 26

1. Where the waiver provided for in Article 22 is not exercised, the competent authorities may, for the purpose of calculating the capital requirements set out in Annexes I and V and the exposures to clients set out in Articles 28 to 32 and Annex VI on a consolidated basis, permit positions in the trading book of one institution to offset positions in the trading book of another institution according to the rules set out in Articles 28 to 32 Annexes I, V and VI.

In addition, the competent authorities may allow foreign-exchange positions in one institution to offset foreign-exchange positions in another institution in accordance with the rules set out in Annex III and/or Annex V. They may also allow commodities positions in one institution to offset commodities positions in another institution in accordance with the rules set out in Annex IV and/or Annex V.

2. The competent authorities may permit offsetting of the trading book and of the foreign-exchange and commodities positions, respectively, of undertakings located in third countries, subject to the simultaneous fulfilment of the following conditions:

(a) such undertakings have been authorised in a third country and either satisfy the definition of credit institution set out in Article 4(1) of Directive 2006/48/EC or are recognised third-country investment firms;

(b) such undertakings comply, on an individual basis, with capital adequacy rules equivalent to those laid down in this Directive; and

(c) no regulations exist in the third countries in question which might significantly affect the transfer of funds within the group.

3. The competent authorities may also allow the offsetting provided for in paragraph 1 between institutions within a group that have been authorised in the Member State in question, provided that:

(a) there is a satisfactory allocation of capital within the group; and

(b) the regulatory, legal or contractual framework in which the institutions operate is such as to guarantee mutual financial support within the group.

4. Furthermore, the competent authorities may allow the offsetting provided for in paragraph 1 between institutions within a group that fulfil the conditions imposed in paragraph 3 and any institution included in the same group which has been authorised in another Member State provided that that institution is obliged to fulfil the capital requirements imposed in Articles 18, 20 and 28 on an individual basis.

[5872]

Article 27

1. In the calculation of own funds on a consolidated basis Article 65 of Directive 2006/48/EC shall apply.

2. The competent authorities responsible for exercising supervision on a consolidated basis may recognise the validity of the specific own-funds definitions applicable to the institutions concerned under Chapter IV in the calculation of their consolidated own funds.

[5873]

SECTION 4
MONITORING AND CONTROL OF LARGE EXPOSURES

Article 28

1. Institutions shall monitor and control their large exposures in accordance with Articles 106 to 118 of Directive 2006/48/EC.

2. By way of derogation from paragraph 1, institutions which calculate the capital requirements for their trading-book business in accordance with Annexes I and II, and, as appropriate, Annex V to this Directive, shall monitor and control their large exposures in accordance with Articles 106 to 118 of Directive 2006/48/EC subject to the amendments laid down in Articles 29 to 32 of this Directive.

3. By 31 December 2007, the Commission shall submit to the European Parliament and to the Council a report on the functioning of this Section, together with any appropriate proposals.

[5874]

Article 29

1. The exposures to individual clients which arise on the trading book shall be calculated by summing the following items:
    (a) the excess – where positive – of an institution's long positions over its short positions in all the financial instruments issued by the client in question, the net position in each of the different instruments being calculated according to the methods laid down in Annex I;
    (b) the net exposure, in the case of the underwriting of a debt or an equity instrument; and
    (c) the exposures due to the transactions, agreements and contracts referred to in Annex II with the client in question, such exposures being calculated in the manner laid down in that Annex, for the calculation of exposure values.

For the purposes of point (b), the net exposure is calculated by deducting those underwriting positions which are subscribed or sub-underwritten by third parties on the basis of a formal agreement reduced by the factors set out in point 41 of Annex I.

For the purposes of point (b), pending further coordination, the competent authorities shall require institutions to set up systems to monitor and control their underwriting exposures between the time of the initial commitment and working day one in the light of the nature of the risks incurred in the markets in question.

For the purposes of point (c), Articles 84 to 89 of Directive 2006/48/EC shall be excluded from the reference in point 6 of Annex II to this Directive.

2. The exposures to groups of connected clients on the trading book shall be calculated by summing the exposures to individual clients in a group, as calculated in paragraph 1.

[5875]

Article 30

1. The overall exposures to individual clients or groups of connected clients shall be calculated by summing the exposures which arise on the trading book and the exposures which arise on the non-trading book, taking into account Article 112 to 117 of Directive 2006/48/EC.

In order to calculate the exposure which arises on the non-trading book, institutions shall take the exposure arising from assets which are deducted from their own funds by virtue of point (d) of the second subparagraph of Article 13(2) to be zero.

2. Institutions' overall exposures to individual clients and groups of connected clients calculated in accordance with paragraph 4 shall be reported in accordance with Article 110 of Directive 2006/48/EC.

Other than in relation to repurchase transactions, securities or commodities lending or borrowing transactions, the calculation of large exposures to individual clients and groups of connected clients for reporting purposes shall not include the recognition of credit risk mitigation.

3. The sum of the exposures to an individual client or group of connected clients in paragraph 1 shall be limited in accordance with Articles 111 to 117 of Directive 2006/48/EC.

4. By derogation from paragraph 3 competent authorities may allow assets constituting claims and other exposures on recognised third-country investment firms and recognised clearing houses and exchanges in financial instruments to be subject to the same treatment accorded to those on institutions laid out in Articles 113(3)(i), 115(2) and 116 of Directive 2006/48/EC.

[5876]

Article 31

The competent authorities may authorise the limits laid down in Articles 111 to 117 of Directive 2006/48/EC to be exceeded if the following conditions are met:
    (a) the exposure on the non-trading book to the client or group of clients in question does not exceed the limits laid down in Articles 111 to 117 of Directive 2006/48/EC, those

limits being calculated with reference to own funds as specified in that Directive, so that the excess arises entirely on the trading book;

(b) the institution meets an additional capital requirement on the excess in respect of the limits laid down in Article 111(1) and (2) of Directive 2006/48/EC, that additional capital requirement being calculated in accordance with Annex VI to that Directive;

(c) where 10 days or less has elapsed since the excess occurred, the trading-book exposure to the client or group of connected clients in question shall not exceed 500% of the institution's own funds;

(d) any excesses that have persisted for more than 10 days must not, in aggregate, exceed 600% of the institution's own funds; and

(e) institutions shall report to the competent authorities every three months all cases where the limits laid down in Article 111(1) and (2) of Directive 2006/48/EC have been exceeded during the preceding three months.

In relation to point (e), in each case in which the limits have been exceeded the amount of the excess and the name of the client concerned shall be reported.

[5877]

Article 32

1. The competent authorities shall establish procedures to prevent institutions from deliberately avoiding the additional capital requirements that they would otherwise incur, on exposures exceeding the limits laid down in Article 111(1) and (2) of Directive 2006/48/EC once those exposures have been maintained for more than 10 days, by means of temporarily transferring the exposures in question to another company, whether within the same group or not, and/or by undertaking artificial transactions to close out the exposure during the 10-day period and create a new exposure.

The competent authorities shall notify the Council and the Commission of those procedures.

Institutions shall maintain systems which ensure that any transfer which has the effect referred to in the first subparagraph is immediately reported to the competent authorities.

2. The competent authorities may permit institutions which are allowed to use the alternative determination of own funds under Article 13(2) to use that determination for the purposes of Articles 30(2), 30(3) and 31 provided that the institutions concerned are required to meet all of the obligations set out in Articles 110 to 117 of Directive 2006/48/EC, in respect of the exposures which arise outside their trading books by using own funds as defined in that Directive.

[5878]

SECTION 5
VALUATION OF POSITIONS FOR REPORTING PURPOSES

Article 33

1. All trading book positions shall be subject to prudent valuation rules as specified in Annex VII, Part B. These rules shall require institutions to ensure that the value applied to each of its trading book positions appropriately reflects the current market value. The former value shall contain an appropriate degree of certainty having regard to the dynamic nature of trading book positions, the demands of prudential soundness and the mode of operation and purpose of capital requirements in respect of trading book positions.

2. Trading book positions shall be re-valued at least daily.

3. In the absence of readily available market prices, the competent authorities may waive the requirement imposed in paragraphs 1 and 2 and shall require institutions to use alternative methods of valuation provided that those methods are sufficiently prudent and have been approved by competent authorities.

[5879]

SECTION 6
RISK MANAGEMENT AND CAPITAL ASSESSMENT

Article 34

Competent authorities shall require that every investment firm, as well as meeting the requirements set out in Article 13 of Directive 2004/39/EC, shall meet the requirements set out in Articles 22 and 123 of Directive 2006/48/EC, subject to the provisions on level of application set out in Articles 68 to 73 of that Directive.

[5880]

SECTION 7
REPORTING REQUIREMENTS

Article 35

1. Member States shall require that investment firms and credit institutions provide the competent authorities of their home Member States with all the information necessary for the assessment of their compliance with the rules adopted in accordance with this Directive. Member States shall also ensure that internal control mechanisms and administrative and accounting procedures of the institutions permit the verification of their compliance with such rules at all times.

2. Investment firms shall report to the competent authorities in the manner specified by the latter at least once every month in the case of firms covered by Article 9, at least once every three months in the case of firms covered by Article 5(1) and at least once every six months in the case of firms covered by Article 5(3).

3. Notwithstanding paragraph 2, investment firms covered by Articles 5(1) and 9 shall be required to provide the information on a consolidated or sub-consolidated basis only once every six months.

4. Credit institutions shall be obliged to report in the manner specified by the competent authorities as often as they are obliged to report under Directive 2006/48/EC.

5. The competent authorities shall oblige institutions to report to them immediately any case in which their counter parties in repurchase and reverse repurchase agreements or securities and commodities-lending and securities and commodities-borrowing transactions default on their obligations.

[5881]

CHAPTER VI

SECTION 1
COMPETENT AUTHORITIES

Article 36

1. Member States shall designate the authorities which are competent to carry out the duties provided for in this Directive. They shall inform the Commission thereof, indicating any division of duties.

2. The competent authorities shall be public authorities or bodies officially recognized by national law or by public authorities as part of the supervisory system in operation in the Member State concerned.

3. The competent authorities shall be granted all the powers necessary for the performance of their tasks, and in particular that of overseeing the constitution of trading books.

[5882]

SECTION 2
SUPERVISION

Article 37

1. Chapter 4 of Title V of Directive 2006/48/EC shall apply mutatis mutandis to the supervision of investment firms in accordance with the following:
   (a) references to Article 6 of Directive 2006/48/EC shall be construed as references to Article 5 of Directive 2004/39/EC;
   (b) references to Article 22 and 123 of Directive 2006/48/EC shall be construed s references to Article 34 of this Directive; and
   (c) references to Articles 44 to 52 of Directive 2006/48/EC shall be construed as references to Articles 54 and 58 of Directive 2004/39/EC.

Where an EU parent financial holding company has as subsidiary both a credit institution and an investment firm, Title V, Chapter 4 of Directive 2006/48/EC shall apply to the supervision of institutions as if references to credit institutions were to institutions.

2. Article 129(2) of Directive 2006/48/EC shall also apply to the recognition of internal models of institutions under Annex V to this Directive where the application is submitted by an EU parent credit institution and its subsidiaries or an EU parent investment firm and its subsidiaries, or jointly by the subsidiaries of an EU parent financial holding company.

The period for the recognition referred to in the first sub-paragraph shall be six months.

[5883]

Article 38

1. The competent authorities of the Member States shall cooperate closely in the performance of the duties provided for in this Directive, particularly where investment services are provided on the basis of the freedom to provide services or through the establishment of branches.

The competent authorities shall on request supply one another with all information likely to facilitate the supervision of the capital adequacy of institutions, in particular the verification of their compliance with the rules laid down in this Directive.

2. Any exchange of information between competent authorities which is provided for in this Directive shall be subject to the following obligations of professional secrecy:
    (a) for investment firms, those imposed in Article 54 and 58 of Directive 2004/39/EC; and
    (b) for credit institutions, those imposed in Articles 44 to 52 of Directive 2006/48/EC.

[5884]

CHAPTER VII
DISCLOSURE

Article 39

The requirements set out in Title V, Chapter 5 of Directive 2006/48/EC shall apply to investment firms.

[5885]

CHAPTER VIII

SECTION 1

Article 40

For the purposes of the calculation of minimum capital requirements for counterparty risk under this Directive, and for the calculation of minimum capital requirements for credit risk under Directive 2006/48/EC, and without prejudice to the provisions of Part 2, point 6 of Annex III to that Directive, exposures to recognised third-country investment firms and exposures to recognised clearing houses and exchanges shall be treated as exposures to institutions.

[5886]

SECTION 2
POWERS OF EXECUTION

Article 41

1. The Commission shall decide on any technical adaptations in the following areas ...
    (a) clarification of the definitions in Article 3 in order to ensure uniform application of this Directive;
    (b) clarification of the definitions in Article 3 to take account of developments on financial markets;
    (c) adjustment of the amounts of initial capital prescribed in Articles 5 to 9 and the amount referred to in Article 18(2) to take account of developments in the economic and monetary field;
    (d) adjustment of the categories of investment firms in Article 20(2) and (3) to take account of developments on financial markets;
    (e) clarification of the requirement laid down in Article 21 to ensure uniform application of this Directive;
    (f) alignment of terminology on and the framing of definitions in accordance with subsequent acts on institutions and related matters;
    (g) adjustment of the technical provisions in Annexes I to VII as a result of developments on financial markets, risk measurement, accounting standards or requirements which take account of Community legislation or which have regard to convergence of supervisory practices; or
    (h) technical adaptations to take account of the outcome of the review referred to in Article 65(3) of Directive 2004/39/EC.

[2. The measures referred to in paragraph 1, designed to amend non-essential elements of this Directive, shall be adopted in accordance with the regulatory procedure with scrutiny referred to in Article 42(2).]

[5887]

NOTES

Words omitted from para 1 repealed, and para 2 substituted, by European Parliament and Council Directive 2008/23/EC, Art 1(1), as from 20 March 2008.

Note that this Article is numbered as Article 22 in the original OJ version. It is assumed that this is an error.

Article 42

1. The Commission shall be assisted by the European Banking Committee established by Commission Decision 2004/10/EC[1] of 5 November 2003 (hereinafter referred to as "the Committee").

[2. Where reference is made to this paragraph, Article 5a(1) to (4) and Article 7 of Decision 1999/468/EC shall apply, having regard to the provisions of Article 8 thereof.]

[3. By 31 December 2010, and, thereafter, at least every three years, the Commission shall review the provisions concerning its implementing powers and present a report to the European Parliament and to the Council on the functioning of those powers. The report shall examine, in particular, the need for the Commission to propose amendments to this Directive in order to ensure the appropriate scope of the implementing powers conferred on the Commission. The conclusion as to whether or not amendment is necessary shall be accompanied by a detailed statement of reasons. If necessary, the report shall be accompanied by a legislative proposal to amend the provisions conferring implementing powers on the Commission.]

[5888]

NOTES

Para 2 substituted, and para 3 substituted (for original paras 3, 4), by European Parliament and Council Directive 2008/23/EC, Art 1(2), as from 20 March 2008.

1   OJ L3, 7.1.2004, p 36.

SECTION 3

TRANSITIONAL PROVISIONS

Article 43

Article 152(1) to (7) of Directive 2006/48/EC shall apply, in accordance with Article 2 and Chapter V, Sections 2 and 3 of this Directive, to investment firms calculating risk-weighted exposure amounts, for the purposes of Annex II to this Directive, in accordance with Articles 84 to 89 of Directive 2006/48/EC, or using the Advanced Measurement Approach as specified in Article 105 of that Directive for the calculation of their capital requirements for operational risk.

[5889]

Article 44

Until 31 December 2012, for investment firms the relevant indicator for the trading and sales business line of which represents at least 50% of the total of relevant indicators for all of their business lines calculated in accordance with Article 20 of this Directive and points 1 to 4 of Part 2 of Annex X to Directive 2006/48/EC, Member States may apply a percentage of 15% to the business line "trading and sales".

[5890]

Article 45

1. Competent authorities may permit investment firms to exceed the limits concerning large exposures set out in Article 111 of Directive 2006/48/EC. Investment firms need not include any excesses in their calculation of capital requirements exceeding such limits, as set out in Article 75(b) of that Directive. This discretion is available until 31 December 2010 or the date of entry into force of any modifications consequent to the treatment of large exposures pursuant to Article 119 of Directive 2006/48/EC, whichever is the earlier. For this discretion to be exercised, the following conditions shall be met:

   (a)   the investment firm provides investment services or investment activities related to the financial instruments listed in points 5, 6, 7, 9 and 10 of Section C of Annex I to Directive 2004/39/EC;

   (b)   the investment firm does not provide such investment services or undertake such investment activities for, or on behalf of, retail clients;

   (c)   breaches of the limits referred to in the introductory part of this paragraph arise in connection with exposures resulting from contracts that are financial instruments as listed in point (a) and relate to commodities or underlyings within the meaning of point 10 of Section C of Annex I to Directive 2004/39/EC (MiFID) and are calculated in accordance with Annexes III and IV of Directive 2006/48/EC, or in connection with exposures resulting from contracts concerning the delivery of commodities or emission allowances; and

   (d)   the investment firm has a documented strategy for managing and, in particular, for controlling and limiting risks arising from the concentration of exposures. The investment firm shall inform the competent authorities of this strategy and all material changes to it without delay. The investment firm shall make appropriate arrangements to ensure a continuous monitoring of the creditworthiness of borrowers, according to their impact on concentration risk. These arrangements shall enable the investment firm to react adequately and sufficiently promptly to any deterioration in that creditworthiness.

2. Where an investment firm exceeds the internal limits set according to the strategy referred to in point (d) of paragraph 1, it shall notify the competent authority without delay of the size and nature of the excess and of the counterparty.

[5891]

Article 46

By way of derogation from Article 20(1), until 31 December 2011 competent authorities may choose, on a case-by-case basis, not to apply the capital requirements arising from point (d) of Article 75 of Directive 2006/48/EC in respect of investment firms to which Article 20(2) and (3) do not apply, whose total trading book positions never exceed EUR 50 million and whose average number of relevant employees during the financial year does not exceed 100.

Instead, the capital requirement in relation to those investment firms shall be at least the lower of:
 (a) the capital requirements arising from point (d) of Article 75 of Directive 2006/48/EC; and
 (b) 12/88 of the higher of the following:
  (i) the sum of the capital requirements contained in points (a) to (c) of Article 75 of Directive 2006/48/EC; and
  (ii) the amount laid down in Article 21 of this Directive, notwithstanding Article 20(5).

If point (b) applies, an incremental increase shall be applied on at least an annual basis.

Applying this derogation shall not result in a reduction in the overall level of capital requirements for an investment firm, in comparison to the requirements as at 31 December 2006, unless such a reduction is prudentially justified by a reduction in the size of the investment firm's business.

[5892]

Article 47

Until 31 December 2009 or any earlier date specified by the competent authorities on a case-by-case basis, institutions that have received specific risk model recognition prior to 1 January 2007 in accordance with point 1 of Annex V may, for that existing recognition, treat points 4 and 8 of Annex V to Directive 93/6/EEC as those points stood prior to 1 January 2007.

[5893]

Article 48

1. The provisions on capital requirements as laid down in this Directive and Directive 2006/48/EC shall not apply to investment firms whose main business consists exclusively of the provision of investment services or activities in relation to the financial instruments set out in points 5, 6, 7, 9 and 10 of Section C of Annex I to Directive 2004/39/EC and to whom Directive 93/22/EEC[1] did not apply on 31 December 2006. This exemption is available until 31 December 2010 or the date of entry into force of any modifications pursuant to paragraphs 2 and 3, whichever is the earlier.

2. As part of the review required by Article 65(3) of Directive 2004/39/EC, the Commission shall, on the basis of public consultations and in the light of discussions with the competent authorities, report to the Parliament and the Council on:
 (a) an appropriate regime for the prudential supervision of investment firms whose main business consists exclusively of the provision of investment services or activities in relation to the commodity derivatives or derivatives contracts set out in points 5, 6, 7, 9 and 10 of Section C of Annex I to Directive 2004/39/EC; and
 (b) the desirability of amending Directive 2004/39/EC to create a further category of investment firm whose main business consists exclusively of the provision of investment services or activities in relation to the financial instruments set out in points 5, 6, 7, 9 and 10 of Section C of Annex I to Directive 2004/39/EC relating to energy supplies (including electricity, coal, gas and oil).

3. On the basis of the report referred to in paragraph 2, the Commission may submit proposals for amendments to this Directive and to Directive 2006/48/EC.

[5894]

NOTES
[1] Council Directive 93/22/EEC of 10 May 1993 on investment services in the securities field (OJ L141, 11.6.1993, p 27). Directive as last amended by Directive 2002/87/EC.

SECTION 4
FINAL PROVISIONS

Article 49

1. Member States shall adopt and publish, by 31 December 2006, the laws, regulations and administrative provisions necessary to comply with Articles 2, 3, 11, 13, 17, 18, 19, 20, 22, 23, 24, 25, 29, 30, 33, 34, 35, 37, 39, 40, 41, 43, 44, 50 and the Annexes I, II, III, V, VII. They shall forthwith communicate to the Commission the text of those provisions and a correlation table between those provisions and this Directive.

They shall apply those provisions from 1 January 2007.

When Member States adopt those measures, they shall contain a reference to this Directive or be accompanied by such a reference on the occasion of their official publication. They shall also include a statement that references in existing laws, regulations and administrative provisions to the directives repealed by this Directive shall be construed as references to this Directive.

2. Member States shall communicate to the Commission the text of the main provisions of national law which they adopt in the field covered by this Directive.

[5895]

Article 50

1. Article 152(8) to (14) of Directive 2006/48/EC shall apply mutatis mutandis for the purposes of this Directive subject to the following provisions which shall apply where the discretion referred to in Article 152(8) of Directive 2006/48/EC is exercised:

(a) references in point 7 of Annex II to this Directive to Directive 2006/48/EC shall be read as references to Directive 2000/12/EC as that Directive stood prior to 1 January 2007; and

(b) point 4 of Annex II to this Directive shall apply as it stood prior to 1 January 2007.

2. Article 157(3) of Directive 2006/48/EC shall apply mutatis mutandis for the purposes of Articles 18 and 20 of this Directive.

[5896]

Article 51

By 1 January 2011, the Commission shall review and report on the application of this Directive and submit its report to the Parliament and the Council together with any appropriate proposals for amendment.

[5897]

Article 52

Directive 93/6/EEC, as amended by the Directives listed in Annex VIII, Part A, is repealed, without prejudice to the obligations of the Member States relating to the time-limits for transposition into national law of the Directives set out in Annex VIII, Part B.

References made to the repealed directives shall be construed as being made to this Directive and should be read in accordance with the correspondence table set out in Annex IX.

[5898]

Article 53

This Directive shall enter into force on the twentieth day following that of its publication in the Official Journal of the European Union.

[5899]

Article 54

This Directive is addressed to the Member States.

[5900]

ANNEX I
CALCULATING CAPITAL REQUIREMENTS FOR POSITION RISK

GENERAL PROVISIONS

Netting

1. The excess of an institution's long (short) positions over its short (long) positions in the same equity, debt and convertible issues and identical financial futures, options, warrants and covered warrants shall be its net position in each of those different instruments. In calculating the net position the competent authorities shall allow positions in derivative instruments to be treated, as laid down in points 4 to 7, as positions in the underlying (or notional) security or securities. Institutions' holdings of their own debt instruments shall be disregarded in calculating specific risk under point 14.

2. No netting shall be allowed between a convertible and an offsetting position in the instrument underlying it, unless the competent authorities adopt an approach under which the likelihood of a particular convertible's being converted is taken into account or have a capital requirement to cover any loss which conversion might entail.

3. All net positions, irrespective of their signs, must be converted on a daily basis into the institution's reporting currency at the prevailing spot exchange rate before their aggregation.

Particular instruments

4. Interest-rate futures, forward-rate agreements (FRAs) and forward commitments to buy or sell debt instruments shall be treated as combinations of long and short positions. Thus a long interest-rate futures position shall be treated as a combination of a borrowing maturing on the delivery date of the futures contract and a holding of an asset with maturity date equal to that of the instrument or notional position underlying the futures contract in question. Similarly a sold FRA will be treated as a long position with a maturity date equal to the settlement date plus the contract period, and a short position with maturity equal to the settlement date. Both the borrowing and the asset holding shall be included in the first category set out in Table 1 in point 14 in order to calculate the capital required against specific risk for interest-rate futures and FRAs. A forward commitment to buy a debt instrument shall be treated as a combination of a borrowing maturing on the delivery date and a long (spot) position in the debt instrument itself. The borrowing shall be included in the first category set out in Table 1 in point 14 for purposes of specific risk, and the debt instrument under whichever column is appropriate for it in the same table.

The competent authorities may allow the capital requirement for an exchange-traded future to be equal to the margin required by the exchange if they are fully satisfied that it provides an accurate measure of the risk associated with the future and that it is at least equal to the capital requirement for a future that would result from a calculation made using the method set out in this Annex or applying the internal models method described in Annex V. The competent authorities may also allow the capital requirement for an OTC derivatives contract of the type referred to in this point cleared by a clearing house recognised by them to be equal to the margin required by the clearing house if they are fully satisfied that it provides an accurate measure of the risk associated with the derivatives contract and that it is at least equal to the capital requirement for the contract in question that would result from a calculation made using the method set out in the this Annex or applying the internal models method described in Annex V.

For the purposes of this point, "long position" means a position in which an institution has fixed the interest rate it will receive at some time in the future, and "short position" means a position in which it has fixed the interest rate it will pay at some time in the future.

5. Options on interest rates, debt instruments, equities, equity indices, financial futures, swaps and foreign currencies shall be treated as if they were positions equal in value to the amount of the underlying instrument to which the option refers, multiplied by its delta for the purposes of this Annex. The latter positions may be netted off against any offsetting positions in the identical underlying securities or derivatives. The delta used shall be that of the exchange concerned, that calculated by the competent authorities or, where that is not available or for OTC-options, that calculated by the institution itself, subject to the competent authorities being satisfied that the model used by the institution is reasonable.

However, the competent authorities may also prescribe that institutions calculate their deltas using a methodology specified by the competent authorities.

Other risks, apart from the delta risk, associated with options shall be safeguarded against. The competent authorities may allow the requirement against a written exchange-traded option to be equal to the margin required by the exchange if they are fully satisfied that it provides an accurate measure of the risk associated with the option and that it is at least equal to the capital requirement against an option that would result from a calculation made using the method set out in the remainder of this Annex or applying the internal models method described in Annex V. The competent authorities may also allow the capital requirement for an OTC option cleared by a clearing house recognised by them to be equal to the margin required by the clearing house if they are fully satisfied that it provides an accurate measure of the risk associated with the option and that it is at least equal to the capital requirement for an OTC option that would result from a calculation made using the method set out in the remainder of this Annex or applying the internal models method described in Annex V. In addition they may allow the requirement on a bought exchange-traded or OTC option to be the same as that for the instrument underlying it, subject to the constraint that the resulting requirement does not exceed the market value of the option. The requirement against a written OTC option shall be set in relation to the instrument underlying it.

6. Warrants relating to debt instruments and equities shall be treated in the same way as options under point 5.

7. Swaps shall be treated for interest-rate risk purposes on the same basis as on-balance-sheet instruments. Thus, an interest-rate swap under which an institution receives floating-rate interest and pays fixed-rate interest shall be treated as equivalent to a long position in a floating-rate instrument

of maturity equivalent to the period until the next interest fixing and a short position in a fixed-rate instrument with the same maturity as the swap itself.

A. TREATMENT OF THE PROTECTION SELLER

8.   When calculating the capital requirement for market risk of the party who assumes the credit risk (the 'protection seller'), unless specified differently, the notional amount of the credit derivative contract must be used. For the purpose of calculating the specific risk charge, other than for total return swaps, the maturity of the credit derivative contract is applicable instead of the maturity of the obligation. Positions are determined as follows:

(i)   A total return swap creates a long position in the general market risk of the reference obligation and a short position in the general market risk of a government bond with a maturity equivalent to the period until the next interest fixing and which is assigned a 0% risk weight under Annex VI of Directive 2006/48/EC. It also creates a long position in the specific risk of the reference obligation.

(ii)   A credit default swap does not create a position for general market risk. For the purposes of specific risk, the institution must record a synthetic long position in an obligation of the reference entity, unless the derivative is rated externally and meets the conditions for a qualifying debt item, in which case a long position in the derivative is recorded. If premium or interest payments are due under the product, these cash flows must be represented as notional positions in government bonds.

(iii)   A single name credit linked note creates a long position in the general market risk of the note itself, as an interest rate product. For the purpose of specific risk, a synthetic long position is created in an obligation of the reference entity. An additional long position is created in the issuer of the note. Where the credit linked note has an external rating and meets the conditions for a qualifying debt item, a single long position with the specific risk of the note need only be recorded.

(iv)   In addition to a long position in the specific risk of the issuer of the note, a multiple name credit linked note providing proportional protection creates a position in each reference entity, with the total notional amount of the contract assigned across the positions according to the proportion of the total notional amount that each exposure to a reference entity represents. Where more than one obligation of a reference entity can be selected, the obligation with the highest risk weighting determines the specific risk.

Where a multiple name credit linked note has an external rating and meets the conditions for a qualifying debt item, a single long position with the specific risk of the note need only be recorded.

(v)   A first-asset-to-default credit derivative creates a position for the notional amount in an obligation of each reference entity. If the size of the maximum credit event payment is lower than the capital requirement under the method in the first sentence of this point, the maximum payment amount may be taken as the capital requirement for specific risk.

A second-asset-to-default credit derivative creates a position for the notional amount in an obligation of each reference entity less one (that with the lowest specific risk capital requirement). If the size of the maximum credit event payment is lower than the capital requirement under the method in the first sentence of this point, this amount may be taken as the capital requirement for specific risk.

If a first or second-asset to default derivative is externally rated and meets the conditions for a qualifying debt item, then the protection seller need only calculate one specific risk charge reflecting the rating of the derivative.

B. TREATMENT OF THE PROTECTION BUYER

For the party who transfers credit risk (the "protection buyer"), the positions are determined as the mirror image of the protection seller, with the exception of a credit linked note (which entails no short position in the issuer). If at a given moment there is a call option in combination with a step-up, such moment is treated as the maturity of the protection. In the case of nth to default credit derivatives, protection buyers are allowed to off-set specific risk for n-1 of the underlyings (ie, the n-1 assets with the lowest specific risk charge).

9.   Institutions which mark to market and manage the interest-rate risk on the derivative instruments covered in points 4 to 7 on a discounted-cash-flow basis may use sensitivity models to calculate the positions referred to in those points and may use them for any bond which is amortised over its residual life rather than via one final repayment of principal. Both the model and its use by the institution must be approved by the competent authorities. These models should generate positions which have the same sensitivity to interest-rate changes as the underlying cash flows. This sensitivity must be assessed with reference to independent movements in sample rates across the yield curve, with at least one sensitivity point in each of the maturity bands set out in Table 2 of point 20. The positions shall be included in the calculation of capital requirements according to the provisions laid down in points 17 to 32.

10. Institutions which do not use models under point 9 may, with the approval of the competent authorities, treat as fully offsetting any positions in derivative instruments covered in points 4 to 7 which meet the following conditions at least:

(a)   the positions are of the same value and denominated in the same currency;

(b)   the reference rate (for floating-rate positions) or coupon (for fixed-rate positions) is closely matched; and

(c)   the next interest-fixing date or, for fixed coupon positions, residual maturity corresponds with the following limits:

(i)   less than one month hence: same day;

(ii)   between one month and one year hence: within seven days; and

(iii)   over one year hence: within 30 days.

11. The transferor of securities or guaranteed rights relating to title to securities in a repurchase agreement and the lender of securities in a securities lending shall include these securities in the calculation of its capital requirement under this Annex provided that such securities meet the criteria laid down in Article 11.

Specific and general risks

12. The position risk on a traded debt instrument or equity (or debt or equity derivative) shall be divided into two components in order to calculate the capital required against it. The first shall be its specific-risk component – this is the risk of a price change in the instrument concerned due to factors related to its issuer or, in the case of a derivative, the issuer of the underlying instrument. The second component shall cover its general risk – this is the risk of a price change in the instrument due (in the case of a traded debt instrument or debt derivative) to a change in the level of interest rates or (in the case of an equity or equity derivative) to a broad equity-market movement unrelated to any specific attributes of individual securities.

TRADED DEBT INSTRUMENTS

13. Net positions shall be classified according to the currency in which they are denominated and shall calculate the capital requirement for general and specific risk in each individual currency separately.

Specific risk

14. The institution shall assign its net positions in the trading book, as calculated in accordance with point 1 to the appropriate categories in Table 1 on the basis of their issuer/obligor, external or internal credit assessment, and residual maturity, and then multiply them by the weightings shown in that table. It shall sum its weighted positions (regardless of whether they are long or short) in order to calculate its capital requirement against specific risk.

Table 1

Categories	Specific risk capital charge
Debt securities issued or guaranteed by central governments, issued by central banks, international organisations, multilateral development banks or Member States' regional government or local authorities which would qualify for credit quality step 1 or which would receive a 0% risk weight under the rules for the risk weighting of exposures under Articles 78 to 83 of Directive 2006/48/EC.	0%

Categories	Specific risk capital charge
Debt securities issued or guaranteed by central governments, issued by central banks, international organisations, multilateral development banks or Member States' regional governments or local authorities which would qualify for credit quality step 2 or 3 under the rules for the risk weighting of exposures under Articles 78 to 83 of Directive 2006/48/EC, and debt securities issued or guaranteed by institutions which would qualify for credit quality step 1 or 2 under the rules for the risk weighting of exposures under Articles 78 to 83 of Directive 2006/48/EC, and debt securities issued or guaranteed by institutions which would qualify for credit quality step 3 under the rules for the risk weighting of exposures under point 28, Part 1 of Annex VI to Directive 2006/48/EC, and debt securities issued or guaranteed by corporates which would qualify for credit quality step 1 or 2 under the rules for the risk weighting of exposures under Articles 78 to 83 of Directive 2006/48/EC. Other qualifying items as defined in point 15.	0,25% (residual term to final maturity 6 months or less) 1,00% (residual term to final maturity greater than 6 and up to and including 24 months) 1,60% (residual term to final maturity exceeding 24 months)
Debt securities issued or guaranteed by central governments, issued by central banks, international organisations, multilateral development banks or Member States' regional governments or local authorities or institutions which would qualify for credit quality step 4 or 5 under the rules for the risk weighting of exposures under Articles 78 to 83 of Directive 2006/48/EC, and debt securities issued or guaranteed by institutions which would qualify for credit quality step 3 under the rules for the risk weighting of exposures under point 26 of Part 1 of Annex VI to Directive 2006/48/EC, and debt securities issued or guaranteed by corporates which would qualify for credit quality step 3 or 4 under the rules for the risk weighting of exposures under Articles 78 to 83 of Directive 2006/48/EC. Exposures for which a credit assessment by a nominated ECAI is not available.	8,00%
Debt securities issued or guaranteed by central governments, issued by central banks, international organisations, multilateral development banks or Member States' regional governments or local authorities or institutions which would qualify for credit quality step 6 under the rules for the risk weighting of exposures under Articles 78 to 83 of Directive 2006/48/EC, and debt securities issued or guaranteed by corporates which would qualify for credit quality step 5 or 6 under the rules for the risk weighting of exposures under Articles 78 to 83 of Directive 2006/48/EC.	12,00%

For institutions which apply the rules for the risk weighting of exposures under Articles 84 to 89 of Directive 2006/48/EC, to qualify for a credit quality step the obligor of the exposure shall have an internal rating with a PD equivalent to or lower than that associated with the appropriate credit quality step under the rules for the risk weighting of exposures to corporates under Articles 78 to 83 of that Directive.

Instruments issued by a non-qualifying issuer shall receive a specific risk capital charge of 8% or 12% according to Table 1. Competent authorities may require institutions to apply a higher specific risk charge to such instruments and/or to disallow offsetting for the purposes of defining the extent of general market risk between such instruments and any other debt instruments.

Securitisation exposures that would be subject to a deduction treatment as set out in Article 66(2) of Directive 2006/48/EC, or risk-weighted at 1,250% as set out in Part 4 of Annex IX to that Directive, shall be subject to a capital charge that is no less than that set out under those treatments. Unrated liquidity facilities shall be subject to a capital charge that is no less than that set out in Part 4 of Annex IX to Directive 2006/48/EC.

15.   For the purposes of point 14 qualifying items shall include:

(a)   long and short positions in assets qualifying for a credit quality step corresponding at least to investment grade in the mapping process described in Title V, Chapter 2, Section 3, Sub-section 1 of Directive 2006/48/EC;

(b)   long and short positions in assets which, because of the solvency of the issuer, have a PD which is not higher than that of the assets referred to under (a), under the approach described in Title V, Chapter 2, Section 3, Sub-section 2 of Directive 2006/48/EC;

(c) long and short positions in assets for which a credit assessment by a nominated external credit assessment institution is not available and which meet the following conditions:
  (i) they are considered by the institutions concerned to be sufficiently liquid;
  (ii) their investment quality is, according to the institution's own discretion, at least equivalent to that of the assets referred to under point (a); and
  (iii) they are listed on at least one regulated market in a Member State or on a stock exchange in a third country provided that the exchange is recognised by the competent authorities of the relevant Member State;

(d) long and short positions in assets issued by institutions subject to the capital adequacy requirements set out in Directive 2006/48/EC which are considered by the institutions concerned to be sufficiently liquid and whose investment quality is, according to the institution's own discretion, at least equivalent to that of the assets referred to under point (a); and

(e) securities issued by institutions that are deemed to be of equivalent, or higher, credit quality than those associated with credit quality step 2 under the rules for the risk weighting of exposures to institutions set out in Articles 78 to 83 of Directive 2006/48/EC and that are subject to supervisory and regulatory arrangements comparable to those under this Directive.

The manner in which the debt instruments are assessed shall be subject to scrutiny by the competent authorities, which shall overturn the judgment of the institution if they consider that the instruments concerned are subject to too high a degree of specific risk to be qualifying items.

16. The competent authorities shall require the institution to apply the maximum weighting shown in Table 1 to point 14 to instruments that show a particular risk because of the insufficient solvency of the issuer.

General risk

(a) Maturity-based

17. The procedure for calculating capital requirements against general risk involves two basic steps. First, all positions shall be weighted according to maturity (as explained in point 18), in order to compute the amount of capital required against them. Second, allowance shall be made for this requirement to be reduced when a weighted position is held alongside an opposite weighted position within the same maturity band. A reduction in the requirement shall also be allowed when the opposite weighted positions fall into different maturity bands, with the size of this reduction depending both on whether the two positions fall into the same zone, or not, and on the particular zones they fall into. There are three zones (groups of maturity bands) altogether.

18. The institution shall assign its net positions to the appropriate maturity bands in column 2 or 3, as appropriate, in Table 2 in point 20. It shall do so on the basis of residual maturity in the case of fixed-rate instruments and on the basis of the period until the interest rate is next set in the case of instruments on which the interest rate is variable before final maturity. It shall also distinguish between debt instruments with a coupon of 3% or more and those with a coupon of less than 3% and thus allocate them to column 2 or column 3 in Table 2. It shall then multiply each of them by the weighing for the maturity band in question in column 4 in Table 2.

19. It shall then work out the sum of the weighted long positions and the sum of the weighted short positions in each maturity band. The amount of the former which are matched by the latter in a given maturity band shall be the matched weighted position in that band, while the residual long or short position shall be the unmatched weighted position for the same band. The total of the matched weighted positions in all bands shall then be calculated.

20. The institution shall compute the totals of the unmatched weighted long positions for the bands included in each of the zones in Table 2 in order to derive the unmatched weighted long position for each zone. Similarly the sum of the unmatched weighted short positions for each band in a particular zone shall be summed to compute the unmatched weighted short position for that zone. That part of the unmatched weighted long position for a given zone that is matched by the unmatched weighted short position for the same zone shall be the matched weighted position for that zone. That part of the unmatched weighted long or unmatched weighted short position for a zone that cannot be thus matched shall be the unmatched weighted position for that zone.

Table 2

Zone	Maturity band		Weighting (in %)	Assumed interest rate change (in %)
	Coupon of 3% or more	Coupon of less than 3%		
One	0 ≤ 1 month	0 ≤ 1 month	0,00	
	> 1 ≤ 3 months	> 1 ≤ 3 months	0,20	1,00
	> 3 ≤ 6 months	> 3 ≤ 6 months	0,40	1,00
	> 6 ≤ 12 months	> 6 ≤ 12 months	0,70	1,00
	> 1 ≤ 2 years	>1,0 ≤ 1,9 years	1,25	0,90
Two	> 2 ≤ 3 years	> 1,9 ≤ 2,8 years	1,75	0,80
	> 3 ≤ 4 years	> 2,8 ≤ 3,6 years	2,25	0,75
	> 4 ≤ 5 years	> 3,6 ≤ 4,3 years	2,75	0,75
	> 5 ≤ 7 years	> 4,3 ≤ 5,7 years	3,25	0,70
	> 7 ≤ 10 years	> 5,7 ≤ 7,3 years	3,75	0,65
	> 10 ≤ 15 years	>7,3 ≤ 9,3 years	4,50	0,60
Three	> 15 ≤ 20 years	> 9,3 ≤ 10,6 years	5,25	0,60
	> 20 years	> 10,6 ≤ 12,0 years	6,00	0,60
		> 12,0 ≤ 20,0 years	8,00	0,60
		> 20,0 years	12,50	0,60

21. The amount of the unmatched weighted long (short) position in zone one which is matched by the unmatched weighted short (long) position in zone two shall then be computed. This shall be referred to in point 25 as the matched weighted position between zones one and two. The same calculation shall then be undertaken with regard to that part of the unmatched weighted position in zone two which is left over and the unmatched weighted position in zone three in order to calculate the matched weighted position between zones two and three.

22. The institution may, if it wishes, reverse the order in point 21 so as to calculate the matched weighted position between zones two and three before calculating that position between zones one and two.

23. The remainder of the unmatched weighted position in zone one shall then be matched with what remains of that for zone three after the latter's matching with zone two in order to derive the matched weighted position between zones one and three.

24. Residual positions, following the three separate matching calculations in points 21, 22 and 23, shall be summed.

25. The institution's capital requirement shall be calculated as the sum of:

    (a)   10% of the sum of the matched weighted positions in all maturity bands;
    (b)   40% of the matched weighted position in zone one;
    (c)   30% of the matched weighted position in zone two;
    (d)   30% of the matched weighted position in zone three;
    (e)   40% of the matched weighted position between zones one and two and between zones two and three (see point 21);
    (f)   150% of the matched weighted position between zones one and three; and
    (g)   100% of the residual unmatched weighted positions.

(b) Duration-based

26. The competent authorities may allow institutions in general or on an individual basis to use a system for calculating the capital requirement for the general risk on traded debt instruments which reflects duration, instead of the system set out in points 17 to 25, provided that the institution does so on a consistent basis.

27. Under a system referred to in point 26 the institution shall take the market value of each fixed-rate debt instrument and thence calculate its yield to maturity, which is implied discount rate for that instrument. In the case of floating-rate instruments, the institution shall take the market value of each instrument and thence calculate its yield on the assumption that the principal is due when the interest rate can next be changed.

28.   The institution shall then calculate the modified duration of each debt instrument on the basis of the following formula: modified duration = ((duration (D))/(1 + r)), where:

$$D = \left(\left(\sum\nolimits_{t=1}^{m} \left((tC_t) / \left((1 + r)^t \right) \right) \right) / \left(\sum\nolimits_{t=1}^{m} \left((C_t) / \left((1 + r)^t \right) \right) \right) \right)$$

where:

R = yield to maturity (see point 25),

C_t = cash payment in time t,

M = total maturity (see point 25).

29.   The institution shall then allocate each debt instrument to the appropriate zone in Table 3. It shall do so on the basis of the modified duration of each instrument.

Table 3

Zone	Modified duration (in years)	Assumed interest (change in %)
One	> 0 ≤ 1,0	1,0
Two	> 1,0 ≤ 3,6	0,85
Three	> 3,6	0,7

30.   The institution shall then calculate the duration-weighted position for each instrument by multiplying its market price by its modified duration and by the assumed interest-rate change for an instrument with that particular modified duration (see column 3 in Table 3).

31.   The institution shall calculate its duration-weighted long and its duration-weighted short positions within each zone. The amount of the former which are matched by the latter within each zone shall be the matched duration-weighted position for that zone.

The institution shall then calculate the unmatched duration-weighted positions for each zone. It shall then follow the procedures laid down for unmatched weighted positions in points 21 to 24.

32.   The institution's capital requirement shall then be calculated as the sum of:

(a)   2% of the matched duration-weighted position for each zone;
(b)   40% of the matched duration-weighted positions between zones one and two and between zones two and three;
(c)   150% of the matched duration-weighted position between zones one and three; and
(d)   100% of the residual unmatched duration-weighted positions.

EQUITIES

33.   The institution shall sum all its net long positions and all its net short positions in accordance with point 1. The sum of the two figures shall be its overall gross position. The difference between them shall be its overall net position.

Specific risk

34.   The institution shall sum all its net long positions and all its net short positions in accordance with point 1. It shall multiply its overall gross position by 4% in order to calculate its capital requirement against specific risk.

35.   By derogation from point 34, the competent authorities may allow the capital requirement against specific risk to be 2% rather than 4% for those portfolios of equities that an institution holds which meet the following conditions:

(a)   the equities shall not be those of issuers which have issued only traded debt instruments that currently attract an 8% or 12% requirement in Table 1 to point 14 or that attract a lower requirement only because they are guaranteed or secured;
(b)   the equities must be adjudged highly liquid by the competent authorities according to objective criteria; and
(c)   no individual position shall comprise more than 5% of the value of the institution's whole equity portfolio.

For the purpose of point (c), the competent authorities may authorise individual positions of up to 10% provided that the total of such positions does not exceed 50% of the portfolio.

General risk

36.   Its capital requirement against general risk shall be its overall net position multiplied by 8%.

Stock-index futures

37. Stock-index futures, the delta-weighted equivalents of options in stock-index futures and stock indices collectively referred to hereafter as "stock-index futures", may be broken down into positions in each of their constituent equities. These positions may be treated as underlying positions in the equities in question, and may, subject to the approval of the competent authorities, be netted against opposite positions in the underlying equities themselves.

38. The competent authorities shall ensure that any institution which has netted off its positions in one or more of the equities constituting a stock-index future against one or more positions in the stock-index future itself has adequate capital to cover the risk of loss caused by the future's values not moving fully in line with that of its constituent equities; they shall also do this when an institution holds opposite positions in stock-index futures which are not identical in respect of either their maturity or their composition or both.

39. By derogation from points 37 and 38, stock-index futures which are exchange traded and – in the opinion of the competent authorities – represent broadly diversified indices shall attract a capital requirement against general risk of 8%, but no capital requirement against specific risk. Such stock-index futures shall be included in the calculation of the overall net position in point 33, but disregarded in the calculation of the overall gross position in the same point.

40. If a stock-index future is not broken down into its underlying positions, it shall be treated as if it were an individual equity. However, the specific risk on this individual equity can be ignored if the stock-index future in question is exchange traded and, in the opinion of the competent authorities, represents a broadly diversified index.

UNDERWRITING

41. In the case of the underwriting of debt and equity instruments, the competent authorities may allow an institution to use the following procedure in calculating its capital requirements. Firstly, it shall calculate the net positions by deducting the underwriting positions which are subscribed or sub-underwritten by third parties on the basis of formal agreements. Secondly, it shall reduce the net positions by the following reduction factors in Table 4:

Table 4

working day 0:	100%
working day 1:	90%
working days 2 to 3:	75%
working day 4:	50%
working day 5:	25%
after working day 5:	0%

"Working day zero" shall be the working day on which the institution becomes unconditionally committed to accepting a known quantity of securities at an agreed price.

Thirdly, it shall calculate its capital requirements using the reduced underwriting positions.

The competent authorities shall ensure that the institution holds sufficient capital against the risk of loss which exists between the time of the initial commitment and working day 1.

SPECIFIC RISK CAPITAL CHARGES FOR TRADING BOOK POSITIONS HEDGED BY CREDIT DERIVATIVES

42. An allowance shall be given for protection provided by credit derivatives, in accordance with the principles set out in points 43 to 46.

43. Full allowance shall be given when the value of two legs always move in the opposite direction and broadly to the same extent. This will be the case in the following situations:

(a) the two legs consist of completely identical instruments; or

(b) a long cash position is hedged by a total rate of return swap (or vice versa) and there is an exact match between the reference obligation and the underlying exposure (ie, the cash position). The maturity of the swap itself may be different from that of the underlying exposure.

In these situations, a specific risk capital charge should not be applied to either side of the position.

44. An 80% offset will be applied when the value of two legs always move in the opposite direction and where there is an exact match in terms of the reference obligation, the maturity of both the reference obligation and the credit derivative, and the currency of the underlying exposure. In

addition, key features of the credit derivative contract should not cause the price movement of the credit derivative to materially deviate from the price movements of the cash position. To the extent that the transaction transfers risk, an 80% specific risk offset will be applied to the side of the transaction with the higher capital charge, while the specific risk requirements on the other side shall be zero.

45.   Partial allowance shall be given when the value of two legs usually move in the opposite direction. This would be the case in the following situations:
    (a)   the position falls under point 43(b) but there is an asset mismatch between the reference obligation and the underlying exposure. However, the positions meet the following requirements:
        (i)   the reference obligation ranks pari passu with or is junior to the underlying obligation; and
        (ii)   the underlying obligation and reference obligation share the same obligor and have legally enforceable cross-default or cross-acceleration clauses;
    (b)   the position falls under point 43(a) or point 44 but there is a currency or maturity mismatch between the credit protection and the underlying asset (currency mismatches should be included in the normal reporting foreign exchange risk under Annex III); or
    (c)   the position falls under point 44 but there is an asset mismatch between the cash position and the credit derivative. However, the underlying asset is included in the (deliverable) obligations in the credit derivative documentation.

In each of those situations, rather than adding the specific risk capital requirements for each side of the transaction, only the higher of the two capital requirements shall apply.

46.   In all situations not falling under points 43 to 45, a specific risk capital charge will be assessed against both sides of the positions.

Capital charges for CIUs in the trading book

47.   The capital requirements for positions in CIUs which meet the conditions specified in Article 11 for a trading book capital treatment shall be calculated in accordance with the methods set out in points 48 to 56.

48.   Without prejudice to other provisions in this section, positions in CIUs shall be subject to a capital requirement for position risk (specific and general) of 32%. Without prejudice to the provisions of the fourth paragraph of point 2.1 of Annex III or the sixth paragraph of point 12 of Annex V (commodity risk) taken together with the fourth paragraph of point 2.1 of Annex III, where the modified gold treatment set out in those points is used, positions in CIUs shall be subject to a capital requirement for position risk (specific and general) and foreign-exchange risk of no more than 40%.

49.   Institutions may determine the capital requirement for positions in CIUs which meet the criteria set out in point 51, by the methods set out in points 53 to 56.

50.   Unless noted otherwise, no netting is permitted between the underlying investments of a CIU and other positions held by the institution.

GENERAL CRITERIA

51.   The general eligibility criteria for using the methods in points 53 to 56, for CIUs issued by companies supervised or incorporated within the Community are that:
    (a)   the CIU's prospectus or equivalent document shall include:
        (i)   the categories of assets the CIU is authorised to invest in;
        (ii)   if investment limits apply, the relative limits and the methodologies to calculate them;
        (iii)   if leverage is allowed, the maximum level of leverage; and
        (iv)   if investment in OTC financial derivatives or repo-style transactions are allowed, a policy to limit counterparty risk arising from these transactions;
    (b)   the business of the CIU shall be reported in half-yearly and annual reports to enable an assessment to be made of the assets and liabilities, income and operations over the reporting period;
    (c)   the units/shares of the CIU are redeemable in cash, out of the undertaking's assets, on a daily basis at the request of the unit holder;
    (d)   investments in the CIU shall be segregated from the assets of the CIU manager; and
    (e)   there shall be adequate risk assessment of the CIU, by the investing institution.

52.   Third country CIUs may be eligible if the requirements in points (a) to (e) of point 51 are met, subject to the approval of the institution's competent authority.

SPECIFIC METHODS

53.   Where the institution is aware of the underlying investments of the CIU on a daily basis, the institution may look through to those underlying investments in order to calculate the capital requirements for position risk (general and specific) for those positions in accordance with the

methods set out in this Annex or, if permission has been granted, in accordance with the methods set out in Annex V. Under this approach, positions in CIUs shall be treated as positions in the underlying investments of the CIU. Netting is permitted between positions in the underlying investments of the CIU and other positions held by the institution, as long as the institution holds a sufficient quantity of units to allow for redemption/creation in exchange for the underlying investments.

54.   Institutions may calculate the capital requirements for position risk (general and specific) for positions in CIUs in accordance with the methods set out in this Annex or, if permission has been granted, in accordance with the methods set out in Annex V, to assumed positions representing those necessary to replicate the composition and performance of the externally generated index or fixed basket of equities or debt securities referred to in (a), subject to the following conditions:

(a)   the purpose of the CIU's mandate is to replicate the composition and performance of an externally generated index or fixed basket of equities or debt securities; and

(b)   a minimum correlation of 0.9 between daily price movements of the CIU and the index or basket of equities or debt securities it tracks can be clearly established over a minimum period of six months. "Correlation" in this context means the correlation coefficient between daily returns on the CIU and the index or basket of equities or debt securities it tracks.

55.   Where the institution is not aware of the underlying investments of the CIU on a daily basis, the institution may calculate the capital requirements for position risk (general and specific) in accordance with the methods set out in this Annex, subject to the following conditions:

(a)   it will be assumed that the CIU first invests to the maximum extent allowed under its mandate in the asset classes attracting the highest capital requirement for position risk (general and specific), and then continues making investments in descending order until the maximum total investment limit is reached. The position in the CIU will be treated as a direct holding in the assumed position;

(b)   institutions shall take account of the maximum indirect exposure that they could achieve by taking leveraged positions through the CIU when calculating their capital requirement for position risk, by proportionally increasing the position in the CIU up to the maximum exposure to the underlying investment items resulting from the mandate; and

(c)   should the capital requirement for position risk (general and specific) according to this point exceed that set out in point 48, the capital requirement shall be capped at that level.

56.   Institutions may rely on a third party to calculate and report capital requirements for position risk (general and specific) for positions in CIUs falling under points 53 and 55, in accordance with the methods set out in this Annex, provided that the correctness of the calculation and the report is adequately ensured.

[5901]

ANNEX II
CALCULATING CAPITAL REQUIREMENTS FOR SETTLEMENT AND COUNTERPARTY CREDIT RISK

SETTLEMENT/DELIVERY RISK

1.   In the case of transactions in which debt instruments, equities, foreign currencies and commodities (excluding repurchase and reverse repurchase agreements and securities or commodities lending and securities or commodities borrowing) are unsettled after their due delivery dates, an institution must calculate the price difference to which it is exposed. This is the difference between the agreed settlement price for the debt instrument, equity, foreign currency or commodity in question and its current market value, where the difference could involve a loss for the institution. It must multiply this difference by the appropriate factor in column A of Table 1 in order to calculate its capital requirement.

Table 1

Number of working days after due settlement date	(%)
5–15	8
16–30	50
31–45	75
46 or more	100

FREE DELIVERIES

2. An institution shall be required to hold own funds, as set out in Table 2, if:

    (a)   it has paid for securities, foreign currencies or commodities before receiving them or it has delivered securities, foreign currencies or commodities before receiving payment for them; and

    (b)   in the case of cross-border transactions, one day or more has elapsed since it made that payment or delivery.

Table 2
Capital treatment for free deliveries

Transaction Type	Up to first contractual payment or delivery leg	From first contractual payment or delivery leg up to four days after second contractual payment or delivery leg	From 5 business days post second contractual payment or delivery leg until extinction of the transaction
Free delivery	No capital charge	Treat as an exposure	Deduct value transferred plus current positive exposure from own funds

3. In applying a risk weight to free delivery exposures treated according to column 3 of Table 2, institutions using the approach set out in Articles 84 to 89 of Directive 2006/48/EC, may assign PDs to counterparties, for which they have no other non-trading book exposure, on the basis of the counterparty's external rating. Institutions using own estimates of loss given defaults ("LGDs") may apply the LGD set out in point 8 of Part 2 of Annex VII to Directive 2006/48/EC to free delivery exposures treated according to column 3 of Table 2 provided that they apply it to all such exposures. Alternatively, institutions using the approach set out in Articles 84 to 89 of Directive 2006/48/EC may apply the risk weights, as set out in Articles 78 to 83 of that Directive provided that they apply them to all such exposures or may apply a 100% risk weight to all such exposures.

If the amount of positive exposure resulting from free delivery transactions is not material, institutions may apply a risk weight of 100% to these exposures.

4. In cases of a system wide failure of a settlement or clearing system, competent authorities may waive the capital requirements calculated as set out in points 1 and 2 until the situation is rectified. In this case, the failure of a counterparty to settle a trade shall not be deemed a default for purposes of credit risk.

COUNTERPARTY CREDIT RISK (CCR)

5. An institution shall be required to hold capital against the CCR arising from exposures due to the following:

    (a)   OTC derivative instruments and credit derivatives;

    (b)   Repurchase agreements, reverse repurchase agreements, securities or commodities lending or borrowing transactions based on securities or commodities included in the trading book;

    (c)   margin lending transactions based on securities or commodities; and

    (d)   long settlement transactions.

6. Subject to the provisions of points 7 to 10, exposure values and risk-weighted exposure amounts for such exposures shall be calculated in accordance with the provisions of Section 3 of Chapter 2 of Title V of Directive 2006/48/EC with references to "credit institutions" in that Section interpreted as references to "institutions", references to "parent credit institutions" interpreted as references to "parent institutions", and with concomitant terms interpreted accordingly.

7. For the purposes of point 6:

Annex IV to Directive 2006/48/EC shall be considered to be amended to include point 8 of Section C of Annex I to Directive 2004/39/EC;

Annex III to Directive 2006/48/EC shall be considered to be amended to include, after the footnotes of Table 1, the following text:

'To obtain a figure for potential future credit exposure in the case of total return swap credit derivatives and credit default swap credit derivatives, the nominal amount of the instrument is multiplied by the following percentages:

    —   where the reference obligation is one that if it gave rise to a direct exposure of the institution it would be a qualifying item for the purposes of Annex I: 5%; and

— where the reference obligation is one that if it gave rise to a direct exposure of the institution it would not be a qualifying item for the purposes of Annex I: 10%.

However, in the case of a credit default swap, an institution the exposure of which arising from the swap represents a long position in the underlying shall be permitted to use a figure of 0% for potential future credit exposure, unless the credit default swap is subject to closeout upon the insolvency of the entity the exposure of which arising from the swap represents a short position in the underlying, even though the underlying has not defaulted.".

Where the credit derivative provides protection in relation to "n^{th} to default" amongst a number of underlying obligations, which of the percentage figures prescribed above is to be applied is determined by the obligation with the nth lowest credit quality determined by whether it is one that if incurred by the institution would be a qualifying item for the purposes of Annex I.

8. For the purposes of point 6, in calculating risk-weighted exposure amounts institutions shall not be permitted to use the Financial Collateral Simple Method, set out in points 24 to 29, Part 3, Annex VIII to Directive 2006/48/EC, for the recognition of the effects of financial collateral.

9. For the purposes of point 6, in the case of repurchase transactions and securities or commodities lending or borrowing transactions booked in the trading book, all financial instruments and commodities that are eligible to be included in the trading book may be recognised as eligible collateral. For exposures due to OTC derivative instruments booked in the trading book, commodities that are eligible to be included in the trading book may also be recognised as eligible collateral. For the purposes of calculating volatility adjustments where such financial instruments or commodities which are not eligible under Annex VIII of Directive 2006/48/EC are lent, sold or provided, or borrowed, purchased or received by way of collateral or otherwise under such a transaction, and the institution is using the Supervisory volatility adjustments approach under Part 3 of Annex VIII to that Directive, such instruments and commodities shall be treated in the same way as non-main index equities listed on a recognised exchange.

Where institutions are using the Own Estimates of Volatility adjustments approach under Part 3 of Annex VIII to Directive 2006/48/EC in respect of financial instruments or commodities which are not eligible under Annex VIII of that Directive, volatility adjustments must be calculated for each individual item. Where institutions are using the Internal Models Approach defined in Part 3 of Annex VIII to Directive 2006/48/EC, they may also apply this approach in the trading book.

10. For the purposes of point 6, in relation to the recognition of master netting agreements covering repurchase transactions and/or securities or commodities lending or borrowing transactions and/or other capital market-driven transactions netting across positions in the trading book and the non-trading book will only be recognised when the netted transactions fulfil the following conditions:
  (a) all transactions are marked to market daily; and
  (b) any items borrowed, purchased or received under the transactions may be recognised as eligible financial collateral under Title V, Chapter 2, Section 3, Subsection 3 of Directive 2006/48/EC without the application of point 9 of this Annex.

11. Where a credit derivative included in the trading book forms part of an internal hedge and the credit protection is recognised under Directive 2006/48/EC, there shall be deemed not to be counterparty risk arising from the position in the credit derivative.

12. The capital requirement shall be 8% of the total risk-weighted exposure amounts.

[5902]

ANNEX III
CALCULATING CAPITAL REQUIREMENTS FOR FOREIGN-EXCHANGE RISK

1. If the sum of an institution's overall net foreign-exchange position and its net gold position, calculated in accordance with the procedure set out in point 2, exceeds 2% of its total own funds, it shall multiply the sum of its net foreign-exchange position and its net gold position by 8% in order to calculate its own-funds requirement against foreign-exchange risk.

2. A two-stage calculation shall be used for capital requirements for foreign-exchange risk.

2.1. Firstly, the institution's net open position in each currency (including the reporting currency) and in gold shall be calculated.

This net open position shall consist of the sum of the following elements (positive or negative):
  (a) the net spot position (ie all asset items less all liability items, including accrued interest, in the currency in question or, for gold, the net spot position in gold);
  (b) the net forward position (ie all amounts to be received less all amounts to be paid under forward exchange and gold transactions, including currency and gold futures and the principal on currency swaps not included in the spot position);
  (c) irrevocable guarantees (and similar instruments) that are certain to be called and likely to be irrecoverable;
  (d) net future income/expenses not yet accrued but already fully hedged (at the discretion of the reporting institution and with the prior consent of the competent authorities, net

future income/expenses not yet entered in accounting records but already fully hedged by forward foreign-exchange transactions may be included here). Such discretion must be exercised on a consistent basis;

(e)   the net delta (or delta-based) equivalent of the total book of foreign-currency and gold options; and

(f)   the market value of other (i e non-foreign-currency and non-gold) options.

Any positions which an institution has deliberately taken in order to hedge against the adverse effect of the exchange rate on its capital ratio may be excluded from the calculation of net open currency positions. Such positions should be of a non-trading or structural nature and their exclusion, and any variation of the terms of their exclusion, shall require the consent of the competent authorities. The same treatment subject to the same conditions as above may be applied to positions which an institution has which relate to items that are already deducted in the calculation of own funds.

For the purposes of the calculation referred to in the first paragraph, in respect of CIUs the actual foreign exchange positions of the CIU shall be taken into account. Institutions may rely on third party reporting of the foreign exchange positions in the CIU, where the correctness of this report is adequately ensured. If an institution is not aware of the foreign exchange positions in a CIU, it shall be assumed that the CIU is invested up to the maximum extent allowed under the CIU's mandate in foreign exchange and institutions shall, for trading book positions, take account of the maximum indirect exposure that they could achieve by taking leveraged positions through the CIU when calculating their capital requirement for foreign exchange risk. This shall be done by proportionally increasing the position in the CIU up to the maximum exposure to the underlying investment items resulting from the investment mandate. The assumed position of the CIU in foreign exchange shall be treated as a separate currency according to the treatment of investments in gold, subject to the modification that, if the direction of the CIU's investment is available, the total long position may be added to the total long open foreign exchange position and the total short position may be added to the total short open foreign exchange position. There would be no netting allowed between such positions prior to the calculation.

The competent authorities shall have the discretion to allow institutions to use the net present value when calculating the net open position in each currency and in gold.

2.2.   Secondly, net short and long positions in each currency other than the reporting currency and the net long or short position in gold shall be converted at spot rates into the reporting currency. They shall then be summed separately to form the total of the net short positions and the total of the net long positions respectively. The higher of these two totals shall be the institution's overall net foreign-exchange position.

3.   By derogation from points 1 and 2 and pending further coordination, the competent authorities may prescribe or allow institutions to use the following procedures for the purposes of this Annex.

3.1.   The competent authorities may allow institutions to provide lower capital requirements against positions in closely correlated currencies than those which would result from applying points 1 and 2 to them. The competent authorities may deem a pair of currencies to be closely correlated only if the likelihood of a loss – calculated on the basis of daily exchange-rate data for the preceding three or five years – occurring on equal and opposite positions in such currencies over the following 10 working days, which is 4% or less of the value of the matched position in question (valued in terms of the reporting currency) has a probability of at least 99%, when an observation period of three years is used, or 95%, when an observation period of five years is used. The own-funds requirement on the matched position in two closely correlated currencies shall be 4% multiplied by the value of the matched position. The capital requirement on unmatched positions in closely correlated currencies, and all positions in other currencies, shall be 8%, multiplied by the higher of the sum of the net short or the net long positions in those currencies after the removal of matched positions in closely correlated currencies.

3.2.   The competent authorities may allow institutions to remove positions in any currency which is subject to a legally binding intergovernmental agreement to limit its variation relative to other currencies covered by the same agreement from whichever of the methods described in points 1, 2 and 3.1 that they apply. Institutions shall calculate their matched positions in such currencies and subject them to a capital requirement no lower than half of the maximum permissible variation laid down in the intergovernmental agreement in question in respect of the currencies concerned. Unmatched positions in those currencies shall be treated in the same way as other currencies.

By derogation from the first paragraph, the competent authorities may allow the capital requirement on the matched positions in currencies of Member States participating in the second stage of the economic and monetary union to be 1,6%, multiplied by the value of such matched positions.

4.   Net positions in composite currencies may be broken down into the component currencies according to the quotas in force.

ANNEX IV
CALCULATING CAPITAL REQUIREMENTS FOR COMMODITIES RISK

1. Each position in commodities or commodity derivatives shall be expressed in terms of the standard unit of measurement. The spot price in each commodity shall be expressed in the reporting currency.

2. Positions in gold or gold derivatives shall be considered as being subject to foreign-exchange risk and treated according to Annex III or Annex V, as appropriate, for the purpose of calculating market risk.

3. For the purposes of this Annex, positions which are purely stock financing may be excluded from the commodities risk calculation only.

4. The interest-rate and foreign-exchange risks not covered by other provisions of this Annex shall be included in the calculation of general risk for traded debt instruments and in the calculation of foreign-exchange risk.

5. When the short position falls due before the long position, institutions shall also guard against the risk of a shortage of liquidity which may exist in some markets.

6. For the purpose of point 19, the excess of an institution's long (short) positions over its short (long) positions in the same commodity and identical commodity futures, options and warrants shall be its net position in each commodity.

The competent authorities shall allow positions in derivative instruments to be treated, as laid down in points 8, 9 and 10, as positions in the underlying commodity.

7. The competent authorities may regard the following positions as positions in the same commodity:
  (a) positions in different sub-categories of commodities in cases where the sub-categories are deliverable against each other; and
  (b) positions in similar commodities if they are close substitutes and if a minimum correlation of 0,9 between price movements can be clearly established over a minimum period of one year.

Particular instruments

8. Commodity futures and forward commitments to buy or sell individual commodities shall be incorporated in the measurement system as notional amounts in terms of the standard unit of measurement and assigned a maturity with reference to expiry date.

The competent authorities may allow the capital requirement for an exchange-traded future to be equal to the margin required by the exchange if they are fully satisfied that it provides an accurate measure of the risk associated with the future and that it is at least equal to the capital requirement for a future that would result from a calculation made using the method set out in the remainder of this Annex or applying the internal models method described in Annex V.

The competent authorities may also allow the capital requirement for an OTC commodity derivatives contract of the type referred to in this point cleared by a clearing house recognised by them to be equal to the margin required by the clearing house if they are fully satisfied that it provides an accurate measure of the risk associated with the derivatives contract and that it is at least equal to the capital requirement for the contract in question that would result from a calculation made using the method set out in the remainder of this Annex or applying the internal models method described in Annex V.

9. Commodity swaps where one side of the transaction is a fixed price and the other the current market price shall be incorporated into the maturity ladder approach, as set out in points 13 to 18, as a series of positions equal to the notional amount of the contract, with one position corresponding with each payment on the swap and slotted into the maturity ladder set out in Table 1 to point 13. The positions would be long positions if the institution is paying a fixed price and receiving a floating price and short positions if the institution is receiving a fixed price and paying a floating price.

Commodity swaps where the sides of the transaction are in different commodities are to be reported in the relevant reporting ladder for the maturity ladder approach.

10. Options on commodities or on commodity derivatives shall be treated as if they were positions equal in value to the amount of the underlying to which the option refers, multiplied by its delta for the purposes of this Annex. The latter positions may be netted off against any offsetting positions in the identical underlying commodity or commodity derivative. The delta used shall be that of the exchange concerned, that calculated by the competent authorities or, where none of those is available, or for OTC options, that calculated by the institution itself, subject to the competent authorities being satisfied that the model used by the institution is reasonable.

However, the competent authorities may also prescribe that institutions calculate their deltas using a methodology specified by the competent authorities.

Other risks, apart from the delta risk, associated with commodity options shall be safeguarded against.

The competent authorities may allow the requirement for a written exchange-traded commodity option to be equal to the margin required by the exchange if they are fully satisfied that it provides an accurate measure of the risk associated with the option and that it is at least equal to the capital requirement against an option that would result from a calculation made using the method set out in the remainder of this Annex or applying the internal models method described in Annex V.

The competent authorities may also allow the capital requirement for an OTC commodity option cleared by a clearing house recognised by them to be equal to the margin required by the clearing house if they are fully satisfied that it provides an accurate measure of the risk associated with the option and that it is at least equal to the capital requirement for an OTC option that would result from a calculation made using the method set out in the remainder of this Annex or applying the internal models method described in Annex V.

In addition they may allow the requirement on a bought exchange-traded or OTC commodity option to be the same as that for the commodity underlying it, subject to the constraint that the resulting requirement does not exceed the market value of the option. The requirement for a written OTC option shall be set in relation to the commodity underlying it.

11.   Warrants relating to commodities shall be treated in the same way as commodity options referred to in point 10.

12.   The transferor of commodities or guaranteed rights relating to title to commodities in a repurchase agreement and the lender of commodities in a commodities lending agreement shall include such commodities in the calculation of its capital requirement under this Annex.

(a) Maturity ladder approach

13.   The institution shall use a separate maturity ladder in line with Table 1 for each commodity. All positions in that commodity and all positions which are regarded as positions in the same commodity pursuant to point 7 shall be assigned to the appropriate maturity bands. Physical stocks shall be assigned to the first maturity band.

Table 1

Maturity band (1)	Spread rate (in %) (2)
$0 \leq 1$ month	1,50
$> 1 \leq 3$ months	1,50
$> 3 \leq 6$ months	1,50
$> 6 \leq 12$ months	1,50
$> 1 \leq 2$ years	1,50
$> 2 \leq 3$ years	1,50
> 3 years	1,50

14.   Competent authorities may allow positions which are, or are regarded pursuant to point 7 as, positions in the same commodity to be offset and assigned to the appropriate maturity bands on a net basis for the following:

(a)   positions in contracts maturing on the same date; and
(b)   positions in contracts maturing within 10 days of each other if the contracts are traded on markets which have daily delivery dates.

15.   The institution shall then calculate the sum of the long positions and the sum of the short positions in each maturity band. The amount of the former (latter) which are matched by the latter (former) in a given maturity band shall be the matched positions in that band, while the residual long or short position shall be the unmatched position for the same band.

16.   That part of the unmatched long (short) position for a given maturity band that is matched by the unmatched short (long) position for a maturity band further out shall be the matched position between two maturity bands. That part of the unmatched long or unmatched short position that cannot be thus matched shall be the unmatched position.

17.   The institution's capital requirement for each commodity shall be calculated on the basis of the relevant maturity ladder as the sum of the following:
(a)   the sum of the matched long and short positions, multiplied by the appropriate spread rate as indicated in the second column of Table 1 to point 13 for each maturity band and by the spot price for the commodity;

(b)   the matched position between two maturity bands for each maturity band into which an unmatched position is carried forward, multiplied by 0,6% (carry rate) and by the spot price for the commodity; and

(c)   the residual unmatched positions, multiplied by 15% (outright rate) and by the spot price for the commodity.

18.   The institution's overall capital requirement for commodities risk shall be calculated as the sum of the capital requirements calculated for each commodity according to point 17.

(b) Simplified approach

19.   The institution's capital requirement for each commodity shall be calculated as the sum of:

(a)   15% of the net position, long or short, multiplied by the spot price for the commodity; and

(b)   3% of the gross position, long plus short, multiplied by the spot price for the commodity.

20.   The institution's overall capital requirement for commodities risk shall be calculated as the sum of the capital requirements calculated for each commodity according to point 19.

(c) Extended Maturity ladder approach

21.   Competent authorities may authorise institutions to use the minimum spread, carry and outright rates set out in the following table (Table 2) instead of those indicated in points 13, 14, 17 and 18 provided that the institutions, in the opinion of their competent authorities:

(a)   undertake significant commodities business;

(b)   have a diversified commodities portfolio; and

(c)   are not yet in a position to use internal models for the purpose of calculating the capital requirement on commodities risk in accordance with Annex V.

Table 2

	Precious metals (except gold)	Base metals	Agricultural products (softs)	Other, including energy products
Spread rate (%)	1,0	1,2	1,5	1,5
Carry rate (%)	0,3	0,5	0,6	0,6
Outright rate (%)	8	10	12	15

[5904]

ANNEX V
USE OF INTERNAL MODELS TO CALCULATE CAPITAL REQUIREMENTS

1.   The competent authorities may, subject to the conditions laid down in this Annex, allow institutions to calculate their capital requirements for position risk, foreign-exchange risk and/or commodities risk using their own internal risk-management models instead of or in combination with the methods described in Annexes I, III and IV. Explicit recognition by the competent authorities of the use of models for supervisory capital purposes shall be required in each case.

2.   Recognition shall only be given if the competent authority is satisfied that the institution's risk-management system is conceptually sound and implemented with integrity and that, in particular, the following qualitative standards are met:

(a)   the internal risk-measurement model is closely integrated into the daily risk-management process of the institution and serves as the basis for reporting risk exposures to senior management of the institution;

(b)   the institution has a risk control unit that is independent from business trading units and reports directly to senior management. The unit must be responsible for designing and implementing the institution's risk-management system. It shall produce and analyse daily reports on the output of the risk-measurement model and on the appropriate measures to be taken in terms of trading limits. The unit shall also conduct the initial and on-going validation of the internal model;

(c)   the institution's board of directors and senior management are actively involved in the risk-control process and the daily reports produced by the risk-control unit are reviewed by a level of management with sufficient authority to enforce both reductions of positions taken by individual traders as well as in the institution's overall risk exposure;

(d)   the institution has sufficient numbers of staff skilled in the use of sophisticated models in the trading, risk-control, audit and back-office areas;

(e) the institution has established procedures for monitoring and ensuring compliance with a documented set of internal policies and controls concerning the overall operation of the risk-measurement system;

(f) the institution's model has a proven track record of reasonable accuracy in measuring risks;

(g) the institution frequently conducts a rigorous programme of stress testing and the results of these tests are reviewed by senior management and reflected in the policies and limits it sets. This process shall particularly address illiquidity of markets in stressed market conditions, concentration risk, one way markets, event and jump-to-default risks, non-linearity of products, deep out-of-the-money positions, positions subject to the gapping of prices and other risks that may not be captured appropriately in the internal models. The shocks applied shall reflect the nature of the portfolios and the time it could take to hedge out or manage risks under severe market conditions; and

(h) the institution must conduct, as part of its regular internal auditing process, an independent review of its risk-measurement system.

The review referred to in point (h) of the first paragraph shall include both the activities of the business trading units and of the independent risk-control unit. At least once a year, the institution must conduct a review of its overall risk-management process.

The review shall consider the following:

(a) the adequacy of the documentation of the risk-management system and process and the organisation of the risk-control unit;

(b) the integration of market risk measures into daily risk management and the integrity of the management information system;

(c) the process the institution employs for approving risk-pricing models and valuation systems that are used by front and back-office personnel;

(d) the scope of market risks captured by the risk-measurement model and the validation of any significant changes in the risk-measurement process;

(e) the accuracy and completeness of position data, the accuracy and appropriateness of volatility and correlation assumptions, and the accuracy of valuation and risk sensitivity calculations;

(f) the verification process the institution employs to evaluate the consistency, timeliness and reliability of data sources used to run internal models, including the independence of such data sources; and

(g) the verification process the institution uses to evaluate back-testing that is conducted to assess the models' accuracy.

3.   Institutions shall have processes in place to ensure that their internal models have been adequately validated by suitably qualified parties independent of the development process to ensure that they are conceptually sound and adequately capture all material risks. The validation shall be conducted when the internal model is initially developed and when any significant changes are made to the internal model. The validation shall also be conducted on a periodic basis but especially where there have been any significant structural changes in the market or changes to the composition of the portfolio which might lead to the internal model no longer being adequate. As techniques and best practices evolve, institutions shall avail themselves of these advances. Internal model validation shall not be limited to back-testing, but shall, at a minimum, also include the following:

(a) tests to demonstrate that any assumptions made within the internal model are appropriate and do not underestimate or overestimate the risk;

(b) in addition to the regulatory back-testing programmes, institutions shall carry out their own internal model validation tests in relation to the risks and structures of their portfolios; and

(c) the use of hypothetical portfolios to ensure that the internal model is able to account for particular structural features that may arise, for example material basis risks and concentration risk.

4.   The institution shall monitor the accuracy and performance of its model by conducting a back-testing programme. The back-testing has to provide for each business day a comparison of the one-day value-at-risk measure generated by the institution's model for the portfolio's end-of-day positions to the one-day change of the portfolio's value by the end of the subsequent business day.

Competent authorities shall examine the institution's capability to perform back-testing on both actual and hypothetical changes in the portfolio's value. Back-testing on hypothetical changes in the portfolio's value is based on a comparison between the portfolio's end-of-day value and, assuming unchanged positions, its value at the end of the subsequent day. Competent authorities shall require institutions to take appropriate measures to improve their back-testing programme if deemed deficient. Competent authorities may require institutions to perform back-testing on either hypothetical (using changes in portfolio value that would occur were end-of-day positions to remain unchanged), or actual trading (excluding fees, commissions, and net interest income) outcomes, or both.

5.   For the purpose of calculating capital requirements for specific risk associated with traded debt and equity positions, the competent authorities may recognise the use of an institution's internal model if, in addition to compliance with the conditions in the remainder of this Annex, the internal model meets the following conditions:

    (a)   it explains the historical price variation in the portfolio;

    (b)   it captures concentration in terms of magnitude and changes of composition of the portfolio;

    (c)   it is robust to an adverse environment;

    (d)   it is validated through back-testing aimed at assessing whether specific risk is being accurately captured. If competent authorities allow this back-testing to be performed on the basis of relevant sub-portfolios, these must be chosen in a consistent manner;

    (e)   it captures name-related basis risk, that is institutions shall demonstrate that the internal model is sensitive to material idiosyncratic differences between similar but not identical positions; and

    (f)   it captures event risk.

The institution shall also meet the following conditions:

—   where an institution is subject to event risk that is not reflected in its value-at-risk measure, because it is beyond the 10-day holding period and 99 percent confidence interval (low probability and high severity events), the institution shall ensure that the impact of such events is factored in to its internal capital assessment; and

—   the institution's internal model shall conservatively assess the risk arising from less liquid positions and positions with limited price transparency under realistic market scenarios. In addition, the internal model shall meet minimum data standards. Proxies shall be appropriately conservative and may be used only where available data is insufficient or is not reflective of the true volatility of a position or portfolio.

Further, as techniques and best practices evolve, institutions shall avail themselves of these advances.

In addition, the institution shall have an approach in place to capture, in the calculation of its capital requirements, the default risk of its trading book positions that is incremental to the default risk captured by the value-at-risk measure as specified in the previous requirements of this point. To avoid double counting, an institution may, when calculating its incremental default risk charge, take into account the extent to which default risk has already been incorporated into the value-at-risk measure, especially for risk positions that could and would be closed within 10 days in the event of adverse market conditions or other indications of deterioration in the credit environment. Where an institution captures its incremental default risk through a surcharge, it shall have in place methodologies for validating the measure.

The institution shall demonstrate that its approach meets soundness standards comparable to the approach set out in Articles 84 to 89 of Directive 2006/48/EC, under the assumption of a constant level of risk, and adjusted where appropriate to reflect the impact of liquidity, concentrations, hedging and optionality.

An institution that does not capture the incremental default risk through an internally developed approach shall calculate the surcharge through an approach consistent with the either the approach set out in Articles 78 to 83 of Directive 2006/48/EC or the approach set out in Articles 84 to 89 of that Directive.

With respect to cash or synthetic securitisation exposures that would be subject to a deduction treatment under the treatment set out in Article 66(2) of Directive 2006/48/EC, or risk-weighted at 1,250% as set out in Part 4 of Annex IX to that Directive, these positions shall be subject to a capital charge that is no less than set forth under that treatment. Institutions that are dealers in these exposures may apply a different treatment where they can demonstrate to their competent authorities, in addition to trading intent, that a liquid two-way market exists for the securitisation exposures or, in the case of synthetic securitisations that rely solely on credit derivatives, for the securitisation exposures themselves or all their constituent risk components. For the purposes of this section a two-way market is deemed to exist where there are independent good faith offers to buy and sell so that a price reasonably related to the last sales price or current good faith competitive bid and offer quotations can be determined within one day and settled at such a price within a relatively short time conforming to trade custom. For an institution to apply a different treatment, it shall have sufficient market data to ensure that it fully captures the concentrated default risk of these exposures in its internal approach for measuring the incremental default risk in accordance with the standards set out above.

6.   Institutions using internal models which are not recognised in accordance with point 4 shall be subject to a separate capital charge for specific risk as calculated according to Annex I.

7.   For the purposes of point 9(b), the results of the institution's own calculation shall be scaled up by a multiplication factor of at least 3.

8.   The multiplication factor shall be increased by a plus-factor of between 0 and 1 in accordance with Table 1, depending on the number of overshootings for the most recent 250

business days as evidenced by the institution's back-testing. Competent authorities shall require the institutions to calculate overshootings consistently on the basis of back-testing either on actual or on hypothetical changes in the portfolio's value. An overshooting is a one-day change in the portfolio's value that exceeds the related one-day value-at-risk measure generated by the institution's model. For the purpose of determining the plus-factor the number of overshootings shall be assessed at least quarterly.

Table 1

Number of overshootings	Plus-factor
Fewer than 5	0,00
5	0,40
6	0,50
7	0,65
8	0,75
9	0,85
10 or more	1,00

The competent authorities may, in individual cases and owing to an exceptional situation, waive the requirement to increase the multiplication factor by the "plus-factor" in accordance with Table 1, if the institution has demonstrated to the satisfaction of the competent authorities that such an increase is unjustified and that the model is basically sound.

If numerous overshootings indicate that the model is not sufficiently accurate, the competent authorities shall revoke the model's recognition or impose appropriate measures to ensure that the model is improved promptly.

In order to allow competent authorities to monitor the appropriateness of the plus-factor on an ongoing basis, institutions shall notify promptly, and in any case no later than within five working days, the competent authorities of overshootings that result form their back-testing programme and that would according to the above table imply an increase of a plus-factor.

9.   Each institution must meet a capital requirement expressed as the higher of:

(a)   its previous day's value-at-risk measure according to the parameters specified in this Annex plus, where appropriate, the incremental default risk charge required under point 5; or

(b)   an average of the daily value-at-risk measures on each of the preceding 60 business days, multiplied by the factor mentioned in point 7, adjusted by the factor referred to in point 8 plus, where appropriate, the incremental default risk charge required under point 5.

10.   The calculation of the value-at-risk measure shall be subject to the following minimum standards:

(a)   at least daily calculation of the value-at-risk measure;

(b)   a 99th percentile, one-tailed confidence interval;

(c)   a 10-day equivalent holding period;

(d)   an effective historical observation period of at least one year except where a shorter observation period is justified by a significant upsurge in price volatility; and

(e)   three-monthly data set updates.

11.   The competent authorities shall require that the model captures accurately all the material price risks of options or option-like positions and that any other risks not captured by the model are covered adequately by own funds.

12.   The risk-measurement model shall capture a sufficient number of risk factors, depending on the level of activity of the institution in the respective markets and in particular the following.

Interest rate risk

The risk-measurement system shall incorporate a set of risk factors corresponding to the interest rates in each currency in which the institution has interest rate sensitive on- or off-balance sheet positions. The institution shall model the yield curves using one of the generally accepted approaches. For material exposures to interest-rate risk in the major currencies and markets, the yield curve shall be divided into a minimum of six maturity segments, to capture the variations of volatility of rates along the yield curve. The risk-measurement system must also capture the risk of less than perfectly correlated movements between different yield curves.

Foreign-exchange risk

The risk-measurement system shall incorporate risk factors corresponding to gold and to the individual foreign currencies in which the institution's positions are denominated.

For CIUs the actual foreign exchange positions of the CIU shall be taken into account. Institutions may rely on third party reporting of the foreign exchange position of the CIU, where the correctness of this report is adequately ensured. If an institution is not aware of the foreign exchange positions of a CIU, this position should be carved out and treated in accordance with the fourth paragraph of point 2.1 of Annex III.

Equity risk

The risk-measurement system shall use a separate risk factor at least for each of the equity markets in which the institution holds significant positions.

Commodity risk

The risk-measurement system shall use a separate risk factor at least for each commodity in which the institution holds significant positions. The risk-measurement system must also capture the risk of less than perfectly correlated movements between similar, but not identical, commodities and the exposure to changes in forward prices arising from maturity mismatches. It shall also take account of market characteristics, notably delivery dates and the scope provided to traders to close out positions.

13.　The competent authorities may allow institutions to use empirical correlations within risk categories and across risk categories if they are satisfied that the institution's system for measuring correlations is sound and implemented with integrity.

[5905]

ANNEX VI

CALCULATING CAPITAL REQUIREMENTS FOR LARGE EXPOSURES

1.　The excess referred to in Article 31(b) shall be calculated by selecting those components of the total trading exposure to the client or group of clients in question which attract the highest specific-risk requirements in Annex I and/or requirements in Annex II, the sum of which equals the amount of the excess referred to in Article 31(a).

2.　Where the excess has not persisted for more than 10 days, the additional capital requirement shall be 200% of the requirements referred to in point 1, on these components.

3.　As from 10 days after the excess has occurred, the components of the excess, selected in accordance with point 1, shall be allocated to the appropriate line in column 1 of Table 1 in ascending order of specific-risk requirements in Annex I and/or requirements in Annex II. The additional capital requirement shall be equal to the sum of the specific-risk requirements in Annex I and/or the Annex II requirements on these components, multiplied by the corresponding factor in column 2 of Table 1.

Table 1

Excess over the limits (on the basis of a percentage of own funds)	Factors
Up to 40%	200%
From 40% to 60%	300%
From 60% to 80%	400%
From 80% to 100%	500%
From 100% to 250%	600%
Over 250%	900%

[5906]

ANNEX VII

TRADING

PART A

TRADING INTENT

1.　Positions/portfolios held with trading intent shall comply with the following requirements:

(a)   there must be a clearly documented trading strategy for the position/instrument or portfolios, approved by senior management, which shall include expected holding horizon;

(b)   there must be clearly defined policies and procedures for the active management of the position, which shall include the following:

    (i)   positions entered into on a trading desk;

    (ii)   position limits are set and monitored for appropriateness;

    (iii)   dealers have the autonomy to enter into/manage the position within agreed limits and according to the approved strategy;

    (iv)   positions are reported to senior management as an integral part of the institution's risk management process; and

    (v)   positions are actively monitored with reference to market information sources and an assessment made of the marketability or hedge-ability of the position or its component risks, including the assessment of, the quality and availability of market inputs to the valuation process, level of market turnover, sizes of positions traded in the market; and

(c)   there must be clearly defined policy and procedures to monitor the position against the institution's trading strategy including the monitoring of turnover and stale positions in the institution's trading book.

PART B
SYSTEMS AND CONTROLS

1.   Institutions shall establish and maintain systems and controls sufficient to provide prudent and reliable valuation estimates.

2.   Systems and controls shall include at least the following elements:

(a)   documented policies and procedures for the process of valuation. This includes clearly defined responsibilities of the various areas involved in the determination of the valuation, sources of market information and review of their appropriateness, frequency of independent valuation, timing of closing prices, procedures for adjusting valuations, month end and ad-hoc verification procedures; and

(b)   reporting lines for the department accountable for the valuation process that are clear and independent of the front office.

The reporting line shall ultimately be to a main board executive director.

Prudent Valuation Methods

3.   Marking to market is the at least daily valuation of positions at readily available close out prices that are sourced independently. Examples include exchange prices, screen prices, or quotes from several independent reputable brokers.

4.   When marking to market, the more prudent side of bid/offer shall be used unless the institution is a significant market maker in the particular type of financial instrument or commodity in question and it can close out at mid market.

5.   Where marking to market is not possible, institutions must mark to model their positions/ portfolios before applying trading book capital treatment. Marking to model is defined as any valuation which has to be benchmarked, extrapolated or otherwise calculated from a market input.

6.   The following requirements must be complied with when marking to model:

(a)   senior management shall be aware of the elements of the trading book which are subject to mark to model and shall understand the materiality of the uncertainty this creates in the reporting of the risk/performance of the business;

(b)   market inputs shall be sourced, where possible, in line with market prices, and the appropriateness of the market inputs of the particular position being valued and the parameters of the model shall be assessed on a frequent basis;

(c)   where available, valuation methodologies which are accepted market practice for particular financial instruments or commodities shall be used;

(d)   where the model is developed by the institution itself, it shall be based on appropriate assumptions, which have been assessed and challenged by suitably qualified parties independent of the development process;

(e)   there shall be formal change control procedures in place and a secure copy of the model shall be held and periodically used to check valuations;

(f)   risk management shall be aware of the weaknesses of the models used and how best to reflect those in the valuation output; and

(g)   the model shall be subject to periodic review to determine the accuracy of its performance (eg assessing the continued appropriateness of assumptions, analysis of profit and loss versus risk factors, comparison of actual close out values to model outputs).

For the purposes of point (d), the model shall be developed or approved independently of the front office and shall be independently tested, including validation of the mathematics, assumptions and software implementation.

7.   Independent price verification should be performed in addition to daily marking to market or marking to model. This is the process by which market prices or model inputs are regularly verified for accuracy and independence. While daily marking to market may be performed by dealers, verification of market prices and model inputs should be performed by a unit independent of the dealing room, at least monthly (or, depending on the nature of the market/trading activity, more frequently). Where independent pricing sources are not available or pricing sources are more subjective, prudent measures such as valuation adjustments may be appropriate.

Valuation adjustments or reserves

8.   Institutions shall establish and maintain procedures for considering valuation adjustments/ reserves.

General standards

9.   The competent authorities shall require the following valuation adjustments/reserves to be formally considered: unearned credit spreads, close-out costs, operational risks, early termination, investing and funding costs, future administrative costs and, where relevant, model risk.

Standards for less liquid positions

10.   Less liquid positions could arise from both market events and institution-related situations e g concentrated positions and/or stale positions.

11.   Institutions shall consider several factors when determining whether a valuation reserve is necessary for less liquid positions. These factors include the amount of time it would take to hedge out the position/risks within the position, the volatility and average of bid/offer spreads, the availability of market quotes (number and identity of market makers) and the volatility and average of trading volumes, market concentrations, the aging of positions, the extent to which valuation relies on marking-to-model, and the impact of other model risks.

12.   When using third party valuations or marking to model, institutions shall consider whether to apply a valuation adjustment. In addition, institutions shall consider the need for establishing reserves for less liquid positions and on an ongoing basis review their continued suitability.

13.   When valuation adjustments/reserves give rise to material losses of the current financial year, these shall be deducted from an institution's original own funds according to point (k) of Article 57 of Directive 2006/48/EC.

14.   Other profits/losses originating from valuation adjustments/reserves shall be included in the calculation of "net trading book profits" mentioned in point (b) of Article 13(2) and be added to/deducted from the additional own funds eligible to cover market risk requirements according to such provisions.

15.   Valuation adjustments/reserves which exceed those made under the accounting framework to which the institution is subject shall be treated in accordance with point 13 if they give rise to material losses, or point 14 otherwise.

PART C
INTERNAL HEDGES

1.   An internal hedge is a position that materially or completely offsets the component risk element of a non-trading book position or a set of positions. Positions arising from internal hedges are eligible for trading book capital treatment, provided that they are held with trading intent and that the general criteria on trading intent and prudent valuation specified in Parts A and B are met. In particular:

   (a)   internal hedges shall not be primarily intended to avoid or reduce capital requirements;
   (b)   internal hedges shall be properly documented and subject to particular internal approval and audit procedures;
   (c)   the internal transaction shall be dealt with at market conditions;
   (d)   the bulk of the market risk that is generated by the internal hedge shall be dynamically managed in the trading book within the authorised limits; and
   (e)   internal transactions shall be carefully monitored.

Monitoring must be ensured by adequate procedures.

2.   The treatment referred to in point 1 applies without prejudice to the capital requirements applicable to the "non-trading book leg" of the internal hedge.

3.   Notwithstanding points 1 and 2, when an institution hedges a non-trading book credit risk exposure using a credit derivative booked in its trading book (using an internal hedge), the non-trading book exposure is not deemed to be hedged for the purposes of calculating capital

requirements unless the institution purchases from an eligible third party protection provider a credit derivative meeting the requirements set out in point 19 of Part 2 of Annex VIII to Directive 2006/48/EC with regard to the non-trading book exposure. Where such third party protection is purchased and is recognised as a hedge of a non-trading book exposure for the purposes of calculating capital requirements, neither the internal nor external credit derivative hedge shall be included in the trading book for the purposes of calculating capital requirements.

PART D
INCLUSION IN THE TRADING BOOK

1. Institutions shall have clearly defined policies and procedures for determining which position to include in the trading book for the purposes of calculating their capital requirements, consistent with the criteria set out in Article 11 and taking into account the institution's risk management capabilities and practices. Compliance with these policies and procedures shall be fully documented and subject to periodic internal audit.

2. Institutions shall have clearly defined policies and procedures for overall management of the trading book. At a minimum these policies and procedures shall address:
   (a) the activities the institution considers to be trading and as constituting part of the trading book for capital requirement purposes;
   (b) the extent to which a position can be marked-to-market daily by reference to an active, liquid two-way market;
   (c) for positions that are marked-to-model, the extent to which the institution can:
       (i) identify all material risks of the position;
       (ii) hedge all material risks of the position with instruments for which an active, liquid two-way market exists; and
       (iii) derive reliable estimates for the key assumptions and parameters used in the model;
   (d) the extent to which the institution can, and is required to, generate valuations for the position that can be validated externally in a consistent manner;
   (e) the extent to which legal restrictions or other operational requirements would impede the institution's ability to effect a liquidation or hedge of the position in the short term;
   (f) the extent to which the institution can, and is required to, actively risk manage the position within its trading operation; and
   (g) the extent to which the institution may transfer risk or positions between the non-trading and trading books and the criteria for such transfers.

3. Competent authorities may allow institutions to treat positions that are holdings in the trading book as set out in Article 57(l), (m) and (n) of Directive 2006/48/EC as equity or debt instruments, as appropriate, where an institution demonstrates that it is an active market maker in these positions. In this case, the institution shall have adequate systems and controls surrounding the trading of eligible own funds instruments.

4. Term trading-related repo-style transactions that an institution accounts for in its non-trading book may be included in the trading book for capital requirement purposes so long as all such repo-style transactions are included. For this purpose, trading-related repo-style transactions are defined as those that meet the requirements of Article 11(2) and of Annex VII, Part A, and both legs are in the form of either cash or securities includable in the trading book. Regardless of where they are booked, all repo-style transactions are subject to a non-trading book counterparty credit risk charge.

[5907]

ANNEX VIII
REPEALED DIRECTIVES

PART A
REPEALED DIRECTIVES TOGETHER WITH THEIR SUCCESSIVE AMENDMENTS
(REFERRED TO IN ARTICLE 52)

Council Directive 93/6/EEC of 15 March 1993 on the capital adequacy of investments firms and credit institutions

Directive 98/31/EC of the European Parliament and of the Council of 22 June 1998 amending Council Directive 93/6/EEC on the capital adequacy of investment firms and credit institutions

Directive 98/33/EC of the European Parliament and of the Council of 22 June 1998 amending Article 12 of Council Directive 77/780/EEC on the taking up and pursuit of the business of credit institutions, Articles 2, 5, 6, 7, 8 of and Annexes II and III to Council Directive 89/647/EEC on a solvency ratio for credit institutions and Article 2 of and Annex II to Council Directive 93/6/EEC on the capital adequacy of investment firms and credit institutions

Directive 2002/87/EC of the European Parliament and of the Council of 16 December 2002 on the supplementary supervision of credit institutions, insurance undertakings and investment firms in a financial conglomerate and amending Council Directives 73/239/EEC, 79/267/EEC, 92/49/EEC, 92/96/EEC, 93/6/EEC and 93/22/EEC, and Directives 98/78/EC and 2000/12/EC of the European Parliament and of the Council:

Only Article 26

Directive 2004/39/EC of the European Parliament and of the Council of 21 April 2004 on markets in financial instruments amending Council Directives 85/611/EEC and 93/6/EEC and Directive 2000/12/EC of the European Parliament and of the Council and repealing Council Directive 93/22/EEC:

Only Article 67

PART B
DEADLINES FOR TRANSPOSITION
(REFERRED TO IN ARTICLE 52)

Directive	Deadline for transposition
Council Directive 93/6/EEC	1.7.1995
Directive 98/31/EC	21.7.2000
Directive 98/33/EC	21.7.2000
Directive 2002/87/EC	11.8.2004
Directive 2004/39/EC	30.4.2006/31.1.2007
Directive 2005/1/EC	13.5.2005

[5908]

ANNEX IX
CORRELATION TABLE

This Directive	Directive 93/6/EEC	Directive 98/31/EC	Directive 98/33/EC	Directive 2002/87/EC	Directive 2004/39/EC
Article 1(1) first sentence					
Article 1(1) second sentence and (2)	Art 1				
Article 2(1)					
Article 2(2)	Art 7(3)				
Article 3(1)(a)	Art 2(1)				
Article 3(1)(b)	Art 2(2)				Art 67(1)
Article 3(1)(c) to (e)	Art 2(3) to (5)				
Article 3(1)(f) and (g)					
Article 3(1)(h)	Art 2(10)				
Article 3(1)(i)	Art 2(11)		Art 3(1)		
Article 3(1)(j)	Art 2(14)				
Article 3(1)(k) and (l)	Art 2(15) and (16)	Art 1(1)(b)			
Article 3(1)(m)	Art 2(17)	Art 1(1)(c)			
Article 3(1)(n)	Art 2(18)	Art 1(1)(d)			

This Directive	Directive 93/6/EEC	Directive 98/31/EC	Directive 98/33/EC	Directive 2002/87/EC	Directive 2004/39/EC
Article 3(1)(o) to (q)	Art 2(19) to (21)				
Article 3(1)(r)	Art 2(23)				
Article 3(1)(s)	Art 2(26)				
Article 3(2)	Art 2(7) and (8)				
Article 3(3)(a) and (b)	Art 7(3)			Art 26	
Article 3(3)(c)	Art 7(3)				
Article 4	Art 2(24)				
Article 5	Art 3(1) and (2)				
Article 6	Art 3(4)				Art 67(2)
Article 7	Art 3(4a)				Art 67(3)
Article 8	Art 3(4b)				Art 67(3)
Article 9	Art 3(3)				
Article 10	Art 3(5) to (8)				
Article 11	Art 2(6)				
Article 12 first paragraph	Art 2(25)				
Article 12 second paragraph					
Article 13(1) first sub-paragraph	Annex V(1) first sub-paragraph				
Article 13(1) second sub-paragraph and (2) to (5)	Annex V(1) second sub-paragraph and (2) to (5)	Art 1(7) and Annex 4(a)(b)			
Article 14	Annex V(6) and (7)	Annex 4(c)			
Article 15	Annex V(8)				
Article 16	Annex V(9)				
Article 17					
Article 18(1) first sub-paragraph	Art 4(1) first sub-paragraph				
Article 18(1)(a) and (b)	Art 4(1)(i) and (ii)	Art 1(2)			
Article 18(2) to (4)	Art 4(6) to (8)				
Article 19(1)					
Article 19(2)	Art 11(2)				
Article 19(3)					
Article 20					

This Directive	Directive 93/6/EEC	Directive 98/31/EC	Directive 98/33/EC	Directive 2002/87/EC	Directive 2004/39/EC
Article 21	Annex IV				
Article 22					
Article 23 first and second paragraph	Art 7(5) and (6)				
Article 23 third paragraph					
Article 24					
Article 25					
Article 26(1)	Art 7(10)	Art 1(4)			
Article 26(2) to (4)	Art 7(11) to (13)				
Article 27	Art 7(14) and (15)				
Article 28(1)	Art 5(1)				
Article 28(2)	Art 5(2)	Art 1(3)			
Article 28(3)					
Article 29(1)(a) to (c) and next two sub-paragraphs	Annex VI(2)				
Article 29(1) last sub-paragraph					
Article 29(2)	Annex VI(3)				
Article 30(1) and (2) first sub-paragraph	Annex VI(4) and (5)				
Article 30(2) second sub-paragraph					
Article 30(3) and (4)	Annex VI(6) and (7)				
Article 31	Annex VI(8)(1), (2) first sentence, (3) to (5)				
Article 32	Annex VI(9) and (10)				
Article 33(1) and (2)					
Article 33(3)	Art 6(2)				
Article 34					
Article 35(1) to (4)	Art 8(1) to (4)				
Article 35(5)	Art 8(5) first sentence	Art 1(5)			

This Directive	Directive 93/6/EEC	Directive 98/31/EC	Directive 98/33/EC	Directive 2002/87/EC	Directive 2004/39/EC
Article 36	Art 9(1) to (3)				
Article 37					
Article 38	Art 9(4)				
Article 39					
Article 40	Art 2(9)				
Article 41(1)(a) to (c)	Art 10 first, second and third indents				
Article 41(1)(d) and (e)					
Article 41(1)(f)	Art 10 fourth indent				
Article 41(1)(g)					
Article 42					
Article 43					
Article 44					
Article 45					
Article 46	Art 12				
Article 47					
Article 48					
Article 49					
Article 50	Art 15				
Annex I(1) to (4)	Annex I(1) to (4)				
Annex I(4) last paragraph	Art 2(22)				
Annex I(5) to (7)	Annex I(5) to (7)				
Annex I(8)					
Annex I(9) to (11)	Annex I(8) to (10)				
Annex I(12) to (14)	Annex I(12) to (14)				
Annex I(15) and (16)	Art 2(12)				
Annex I(17) to (41)	Annex I(15) to (39)				
Annex I(42) to (56)					
Annex II(1) and (2)	Annex II(1) and (2)				
Annex II(3) to (10)					
Annex III(1)	Annex III(1) first sub-paragraph	Art 1(7) and Annex 3(a)			

This Directive	Directive 93/6/EEC	Directive 98/31/EC	Directive 98/33/EC	Directive 2002/87/EC	Directive 2004/39/EC
Annex III(2)	Annex III(2)				
Annex III(2.1) first to third paragraphs	Annex III(3.1)	Art 1(7) and Annex 3(b)			
Annex III(2.1) fourth paragraph					
Annex III(2.1) fifth paragraph	Annex III(3.2)	Art 1(7) and Annex 3(b)			
Annex III(2.2), (3), (3.1)	Annex III(4) to (6)	Art 1(7) and Annex 3(c)			
Annex III(3.2)	Annex III(8)				
Annex III(4)	Annex III(11)				
Annex IV(1) to (20)	Annex VII(1) to (20)	Art 1(7) and Annex 5			
Annex IV(21)	Art 11a	Art 1(6)			
Annex V(1) to (12) fourth paragraph	Annex VIII(1) to (13)(ii)	Art 1(7) and Annex 5			
Annex V(12) fifth paragraph					
Annex V(12) sixth paragraph to (13)	Annex VIII(13)(iii) to (14)	Art 1(7) and Annex 5			
Annex VI	Annex VI(8)(2) after the first sentence				
Annex VII					
Annex VIII					
Annex IX					

[5909]

COUNCIL DECISION

of 17 July 2006

amending Decision 1999/468/EC laying down the procedures for the exercise of implementing powers conferred on the Commission

(2006/512/EC)

NOTES
    Date of publication in OJ: OJ L200, 22.7.2006, p 11. Notes are as in the original OJ version.
    As of 1 February 2009, this Decision had not been amended.

THE COUNCIL OF THE EUROPEAN UNION,

Having regard to the Treaty establishing the European Community, and in particular the third indent of Article 202 thereof,

Having regard to the proposal from the Commission,

Having regard to the Opinion of the European Parliament,[1]

Whereas:

(1)   The Council adopted Decision 1999/468/EC of 28 June 1999 laying down the procedures for the exercise of implementing powers conferred on the Commission.[2] That Decision provided for a limited number of procedures for the exercise of such powers.

(2)   That Decision should be amended in order to introduce a new type of procedure for the exercise of implementing powers, the regulatory procedure with scrutiny, which allows the legislator to oppose the adoption of draft measures where it indicates that the draft exceeds the implementing powers provided for in the basic instrument, or that the draft is incompatible with the aim or the content of that instrument or fails to respect the principles of subsidiarity or proportionality.

(3)   It is necessary to follow the new regulatory procedure with scrutiny for measures of general scope designed to amend non-essential elements of a basic instrument adopted in accordance with the procedure referred to in Article 251 of the Treaty, including by deleting some of those elements or by supplementing the instrument by the addition of new non-essential elements.

(4)   In this same framework, it should be ensured that the European Parliament receives better information on the work of committees,

[5909A]

NOTES

[1]   Not yet published in the Official Journal.

[2]   OJ L184, 17.7.1999, p 23.

HAS DECIDED AS FOLLOWS:

Article 1

Decision 1999/468/EC is hereby amended as follows:

1.   at the end of recital 5, the following shall be added:

'with the exception of those governing the regulatory procedure with scrutiny';

2.   after recital (7), the following recital shall be inserted:

'(7a)   It is necessary to follow the regulatory procedure with scrutiny as regards measures of general scope which seek to amend non-essential elements of a basic instrument adopted in accordance with the procedure referred to in Article 251 of the Treaty, inter alia by deleting some of those elements or by supplementing the instrument by the addition of new nonessential elements. This procedure should enable the two arms of the legislative authority to scrutinise such measures before they are adopted. The essential elements of a legislative act may only be amended by the legislator on the basis of the Treaty;';

3.   recital (10) shall be replaced by the following:

'(10) The third purpose of this Decision is to improve information to the European Parliament by providing that the Commission should inform it on a regular basis of committee proceedings, that the Commission should transmit to it documents related to activities of committees and inform it whenever the Commission transmits to the Council measures or proposals for measures to be taken; particular attention will be paid to the provision of information to the European Parliament on the proceedings of committees in the framework of the regulatory procedure with scrutiny, so as to ensure that the European Parliament takes a decision within the stipulated deadline.';

4.   in Article 1:

'5a' shall be inserted between '5' and 'and 6' in the last line;

5.   in Article 2:

(a)   in the first paragraph the words '1. Without prejudice to paragraph 2,' shall be inserted at the beginning of the text;

(b)   the following paragraph shall be added:

'2.   Where a basic instrument, adopted in accordance with the procedure referred to in Article 251 of the Treaty, provides for the adoption of measures of general scope designed to amend non-essential elements of that instrument, inter alia by deleting some of those elements or by supplementing the instrument by the addition of new non-essential elements, those measures shall be adopted in accordance with the regulatory procedure with scrutiny.';

6.   in Article 4(2) and Article 5(2), the terms 'and (4)' shall be added after 'Article 205(2)';

7.   after Article 5, the following Article shall be inserted:

'Article 5a
Regulatory procedure with scrutiny

1.   The Commission shall be assisted by a Regulatory Procedure with Scrutiny Committee composed of the representatives of the Member States and chaired by the representative of the Commission.

2.   The representative of the Commission shall submit to the Committee a draft of the measures to be taken. The Committee shall deliver its opinion on the draft within a time-limit which the chairman may lay down according to the urgency of the matter. The opinion shall be delivered by the majority laid down in Article 205(2) and (4) of the Treaty in the case of decisions which the Council is required to adopt on a proposal from the Commission. The votes of the representatives of the Member States within the Committee shall be weighted in the manner set out in that Article. The chairman shall not vote.

3.   If the measures envisaged by the Commission are in accordance with the opinion of the Committee, the following procedure shall apply:

    (a)   the Commission shall without delay submit the draft measures for scrutiny by the European Parliament and the Council;

    (b)   the European Parliament, acting by a majority of its component members, or the Council, acting by a qualified majority, may oppose the adoption of the said draft by the Commission, justifying their opposition by indicating that the draft measures proposed by the Commission exceed the implementing powers provided for in the basic instrument or that the draft is not compatible with the aim or the content of the basic instrument or does not respect the principles of subsidiarity or proportionality;

    (c)   if, within three months from the date of referral to them, the European Parliament or the Council opposes the draft measures, the latter shall not be adopted by the Commission. In that event, the Commission may submit to the Committee an amended draft of the measures or present a legislative proposal on the basis of the Treaty;

    (d)   if, on expiry of that period, neither the European Parliament nor the Council has opposed the draft measures, the latter shall be adopted by the Commission.

4.   If the measures envisaged by the Commission are not in accordance with the opinion of the Committee, or if no opinion is delivered, the following procedure shall apply:

    (a)   the Commission shall without delay submit a proposal relating to the measures to be taken to the Council and shall forward it to the European Parliament at the same time;

    (b)   the Council shall act on the proposal by a qualified majority within two months from the date of referral to it;

    (c)   if, within that period, the Council opposes the proposed measures by a qualified majority, the measures shall not be adopted. In that event, the Commission may submit to the Council an amended proposal or present a legislative proposal on the basis of the Treaty;

    (d)   if the Council envisages adopting the proposed measures, it shall without delay submit them to the European Parliament. If the Council does not act within the two-month period, the Commission shall without delay submit the measures for scrutiny by the European Parliament;

    (e)   the European Parliament, acting by a majority of its component members within four months from the forwarding of the proposal in accordance with point (a), may oppose the adoption of the measures in question, justifying their opposition by indicating that the proposed measures exceed the implementing powers provided for in the basic instrument or are not compatible with the aim or the content of the basic instrument or do not respect the principles of subsidiarity or proportionality;

    (f)   if, within that period, the European Parliament opposes the proposed measures, the latter shall not be adopted. In that event, the Commission may submit to the Committee an amended draft of the measures or present a legislative proposal on the basis of the Treaty;

    (g)   if, on expiry of that period, the European Parliament has not opposed the proposed measures, the latter shall be adopted by the Council or by the Commission, as the case may be.

5.   By way of derogation from paragraphs 3 and 4, a basic instrument may in duly substantiated exceptional cases provide:

    (a)   that the time-limits laid down in paragraphs 3(c), 4(b) and 4(e) shall be extended by an additional month, when justified by the complexity of the measures; or

    (b)   that the time-limits laid down in paragraphs 3(c), 4(b) and 4(e) shall be curtailed where justified on the grounds of efficiency.

6.   A basic instrument may provide that if, on imperative grounds of urgency, the timelimits for the regulatory procedure with scrutiny referred to in paragraphs 3, 4 and 5 cannot be complied with, the following procedure shall apply:

(a)   if the measures envisaged by the Commission are in accordance with the opinion of the Committee, the Commission shall adopt the measures, which shall immediately be implemented. The Commission shall without delay communicate them to the European Parliament and to the Council;

(b)   within a time-limit of one month following that communication, the European Parliament, acting by a majority of its component members, or the Council, acting by a qualified majority, may oppose the measures adopted by the Commission, on the grounds that the measures exceed the implementing powers provided for in the basic instrument or are not compatible with the aim or the content of the basic instrument or do not respect the principles of subsidiarity or proportionality;

(c)   in the event of opposition by the European Parliament or the Council, the Commission shall repeal the measures. It may however provisionally maintain the measures in force if warranted on health protection, safety or environmental grounds. In that event, it shall without delay submit to the Committee an amended draft of the measures or a legislative proposal on the basis of the Treaty. The provisional measures shall remain in force until they are replaced by a definitive instrument.'.

8.   In Article 7(3) at the end of the first sentence, the following shall be added:

'following arrangements which ensure that the transmission system is transparent and that the information forwarded and the various stages of the procedure are identified.'.

[5909B]

Article 2

This Decision shall take effect on the day following that of its publication in the Official Journal of the European Union.

[5909C]

EUROPEAN PARLIAMENT
COUNCIL
COMMISSION

Statement by the European Parliament, the Council and the Commission concerning the Council Decision of 17 July 2006 amending Decision 1999/468/EC laying down the procedures for the exercise of implementing powers conferred on the Commission (2006/512/EC)

(2006/C255/01)

NOTES

Date of publication in OJ: OJ C255, 21.10.2006, p 1. Notes are as in the original OJ version.
As of 1 February 2009, this document had not been amended.

1.   The European Parliament, the Council and the Commission welcome the forthcoming adoption of the Council Decision amending the Council Decision of 28 June 1999 laying down the procedures for the exercise of implementing powers conferred on the Commission.[1] The inclusion in the 1999 Decision of a new procedure, known as the 'regulatory procedure with scrutiny', will enable the legislator to scrutinise the adoption of 'quasi-legislative' measures implementing an instrument adopted by codecision.

2.   The European Parliament, the Council and the Commission emphasise that, in the context of the existing Treaty, this Decision provides a horizontal and satisfactory solution to the European Parliament's wish to scrutinise the implementation of instruments adopted under the codecision procedure.

3.   Without prejudice to the rights of the legislative authorities, the European Parliament and the Council recognise that the principles of good legislation require that implementing powers be conferred on the Commission without time-limit. However, where an adaptation is necessary within a specified period, the European Parliament, the Council and the Commission consider that a clause requesting the Commission to submit a proposal to revise or abrogate the provisions concerning the delegation of implementing powers could strengthen the scrutiny exercised by the legislator.

4.   This new procedure will apply following its entry into force to the quasi-legislative measures provided for in instruments adopted in accordance with the codecision procedure, including those provided for in instruments to be adopted in future in the financial services field (Lamfalussy instruments). However, for it to be applicable to instruments adopted by codecision which are already in force, those instruments must be adjusted in accordance with the applicable procedures, so as to replace the regulatory procedure laid down in Article 5 of Decision 1999/468/EC by the regulatory procedure with scrutiny, wherever there are measures which fall within its scope.

5.   The European Parliament, the Council and the Commission consider that the following instruments should be adjusted as a matter of urgency:

(a)   Regulation of the European Parliament and of the Council on nutrition and health claims made on foods (not yet published in the Official Journal)

(b)   Directive of the European Parliament and of the Council re-casting Council Directive 93/6/EEC of 15 March 1993 on the capital adequacy of investment firms and credit institutions (not yet published in the Official Journal)

(c)   Directive of the European Parliament and of the Council re-casting Directive 2000/12/EC of the European Parliament and of the Council of 20 March 2000 relating to the taking up and pursuit of the business of credit institutions (not yet published in the Official Journal)

(d)   Directive 2006/43/EC of the European Parliament and of the Council of 17 May 2006 on statutory audits of annual accounts and consolidated accounts, amending Council Directives 78/660/EEC and 83/349/EEC and repealing Council Directive 84/253/EEC (OJ L157, 9.6.2006, p 87)

(e)   Regulation (EC) No 562/2006 of the European Parliament and of the Council of 15 March 2006 establishing a Community Code on the rules governing the movement of persons across borders (Schengen Borders Code) (OJ L105, 13.4.2006, p 1)

(f)   Directive 2005/60/EC of the European Parliament and of the Council of 26 October 2005 on the prevention of the use of the financial system for the purpose of money laundering and terrorist financing (OJ L309, 25.11.2005, p 15)

(g)   Directive 2005/32/EC of the European Parliament and of the Council of 6 July 2005 establishing a framework for the setting of ecodesign requirements for energy-using products and amending Council Directive 92/42/EEC and Directives 96/57/EC and 2000/55/EC of the European Parliament and of the Council (OJ L191, 22.7.2005, p 29)

(h)   Directive 2005/1/EC of the European Parliament and of the Council of 9 March 2005 amending Council Directives 73/239/EEC, 85/611/EEC, 91/675/EEC, 92/49/EEC and 93/6/EEC and Directives 94/19/EC, 98/78/EC, 2000/12/EC, 2001/34/EC, 2002/83/EC and 2002/87/EC in order to establish a new organisational structure for financial services committees (OJ L79, 24.3.2005, p 9)

(i)   Regulation (EC) No 396/2005 of the European Parliament and of the Council of 23 February 2005 on maximum residue levels of pesticides in or on food and feed of plant and animal origin and amending Council Directive 91/414/EEC (OJ L70, 16.3.2005, p 1)

(j)   Directive 2004/109/EC of the European Parliament and of the Council of 15 December 2004 on the harmonisation of transparency requirements in relation to information about issuers whose securities are admitted to trading on a regulated market and amending Directive 2001/34/EC (OJ L390, 31.12.2004, p 38)

(k)   Directive 2004/39/EC of the European Parliament and of the Council of 21 April 2004 on markets in financial instruments amending Council Directives 85/611/EEC and 93/6/EEC and Directive 2000/12/EC of the European Parliament and of the Council and repealing Council Directive 93/22/EEC (OJ L145, 30.4.2004, p 1)

(l)   Directive 2003/71/EC of the European Parliament and of the Council of 4 November 2003 on the prospectus to be published when securities are offered to the public or admitted to trading and amending Directive 2001/34/EC (OJ L345, 31.12.2003, p 64)

(m)   Regulation (EC) No 1829/2003 of the European Parliament and of the Council of 22 September 2003 on genetically modified food and feed (OJ L268, 18.10.2003, p 1)

(n)   Directive 2003/41/EC of the European Parliament and of the Council of 3 June 2003 on the activities and supervision of institutions for occupational retirement provision (OJ L235, 23.9.2003, p 10)

(o)   Directive 2003/6/EC of the European Parliament and of the Council of 28 January 2003 on insider dealing and market manipulation (market abuse) (OJ L96, 12.4.2003, p 16) C255/2 EN Official Journal of the European Union 21.10.2006

(p)   Directive 2002/96/EC of the European Parliament and of the Council of 27 January 2003 on waste electrical and electronic equipment (WEEE) (OJ L37, 13.2.2003, p 24)

(q)   Directive 2002/95/EC of the European Parliament and of the Council of 27 January 2003 on the restriction of the use of certain hazardous substances in electrical and electronic equipment (OJ L37, 13.2.2003, p 19)

(r)   Directive 2002/87/EC of the European Parliament and of the Council of 16 December 2002 on the supplementary supervision of credit institutions, insurance undertakings and

PART IV
EC MATERIALS

investment firms in a financial conglomerate and amending Council Directives 73/239/EEC, 79/267/EEC, 92/49/EEC, 92/96/EEC, 93/6/EEC and 93/22/EEC, and Directives 98/78/EC and 2000/12/EC of the European Parliament and of the Council (OJ L35, 11.2.2003, p 1)

(s) Regulation (EC) No 1606/2002 of the European Parliament and of the Council of 19 July 2002 on the application of international accounting standards (OJ L243, 11.9.2002, p 1)

(t) Directive 2001/107/EC of the European Parliament and of the Council of 21 January 2002 amending Council Directive 85/611/EEC on the coordination of laws, regulations and administrative provisions relating to undertakings for collective investment in transferable securities (UCITS) with a view to regulating management companies and simplified prospectuses (OJ L41, 13.2.2002, p 20)

(u) Directive 2001/83/EC of the European Parliament and of the Council of 6 November 2001 on the Community code relating to medicinal products for human use (OJ L311, 28.11.2001, p 67)

(v) Directive 2001/18/EC of the European Parliament and of the Council of 12 March 2001 on the deliberate release into the environment of genetically modified organisms and repealing Council Directive 90/220/EEC (OJ L106, 17.4.2001, p 1)

(w) Directive 2000/60/EC of the European Parliament and of the Council of 23 October 2000 establishing a framework for Community action in the field of water policy (OJ L327, 22.12.2000, p 1)

(x) Directive 2000/53/EC of the European Parliament and of the Council of 18 September 2000 on end-of life vehicles (OJ L269, 21.10.2000, p 34)

(y) Directive 98/8/EC of the European Parliament and of the Council of 16 February 1998 concerning the placing of biocidal products on the market (OJ L123, 24.4.1998, p 1).

To this end, the Commission has indicated that it will shortly submit proposals to the European Parliament and the Council for the amendment of the instruments referred to above, so as to introduce the regulatory procedure with scrutiny and consequently repeal any provisions of these instruments that provide for a time-limit on the delegation of implementing powers to the Commission. The European Parliament and the Council will ensure that the proposals are adopted as rapidly as possible.

6. In accordance with the Interinstitutional Agreement on better law-making (OJ 2003 C321/01), the European Parliament, the Council and the Commission draw attention to the important role played by implementing measures in legislation. In addition, they consider that the general principles of the Interinstitutional Agreement on common guidelines for the quality of drafting of Community legislation (OJ 1999/C73/01) should apply in any event to measures of general scope adopted under the new regulatory procedure with scrutiny.

[5909D]

NOTES
1   OJ L184, 17.7.1999, p 23.

COMMISSION DIRECTIVE

of 1 August 2006

laying down implementing measures for Directive 2005/60/EC of the European Parliament and of the Council as regards the definition of politically exposed person and the technical criteria for simplified customer due diligence procedures and for exemption on grounds of a financial activity conducted on an occasional or very limited basis

(2006/70/EC)

NOTES
Date of publication in OJ: OJ L214, 4.8.2006, p 29. Notes are as in the original OJ version.
As of 1 February 2009, this Directive had not been amended.

THE COMMISSION OF THE EUROPEAN COMMUNITIES,
    Having regard to the Treaty establishing the European Community,
    Having regard to Directive 2005/60/EC of the European Parliament and of the Council of 26 October 2005 on the prevention of the use of the financial system for the purpose of money laundering and terrorist financing,[1] and in particular points (a), (b) and (d) of Article 40(1) thereof,
    Whereas:

(1)   Directive 2005/60/EC requires institutions and persons covered to apply, on a risk-sensitive basis, enhanced customer due diligence measures in respect of transactions or business relationships with politically exposed persons residing in another Member State or in a third country. In the context of this risk analysis, it is appropriate for the resources of the institutions and persons covered to be focused in particular on products and transactions that are characterised by a high risk of money laundering. Politically exposed persons are understood to be persons entrusted with prominent public functions, their immediate family members or persons known to be close associates of such persons. In order to provide for a coherent application of the concept of politically exposed person, when determining the groups of persons covered, it is essential to take into consideration the social, political and economic differences between countries concerned.

(2)   Institutions and persons covered by Directive 2005/60/EC may fail to identify a customer as falling within one of the politically exposed person categories, despite having taken reasonable and adequate measures in this regard. In those circumstances, Member States, when exercising their powers in relation to the application of that Directive, should give due consideration to the need to ensure that those persons do not automatically incur liability for such failure. Member States should also consider facilitating compliance with that Directive by providing the necessary guidance to institutions and persons in this connection.

(3)   Public functions exercised at levels lower than national should normally not be considered prominent. However, where their political exposure is comparable to that of similar positions at national level, institutions and persons covered by this Directive should consider, on a risk-sensitive basis, whether persons exercising those public functions should be considered as politically exposed persons.

(4)   Where Directive 2005/60/EC requires institutions and persons covered to identify close associates of natural persons who are entrusted with prominent public functions, this requirement applies to the extent that the relation with the associate is publicly known or that the institution or person has reasons to believe that such relation exists. Thus it does not presuppose active research on the part of the institutions and persons covered by the Directive.

(5)   Persons falling under the concept of politically exposed persons should not be considered as such after they have ceased to exercise prominent public functions, subject to a minimum period.

(6)   Since the adaptation, on a risk-sensitive basis, of the general customer due diligence procedures to low-risk situations is the normal tool under Directive 2005/60/EC, and given the fact that simplified customer due diligence procedures require adequate checks and balances elsewhere in the system aiming at preventing money laundering and terrorist financing, the application of simplified customer due diligence procedures should be restricted to a limited number of cases. In these cases, the requirements for institutions and persons covered by that Directive do not disappear, and these are expected to, inter alia, conduct ongoing monitoring of the business relations, in order to be able to detect complex or unusually large transactions which have no apparent economic or visible lawful purpose.

(7)   Domestic public authorities are generally considered as low-risk customers within their own Member State and, in accordance with Directive 2005/60/EC, may be subject to simplified customer due diligence procedures. However, none of the Community institutions, bodies, offices or agencies, including the European Central Bank (ECB), directly qualify in the Directive for simplified customer due diligence under the "domestic public authority" category or, in the case of the ECB, under the "credit and financial institution" category. However, since these entities do not appear to present a high risk of money laundering or terrorist financing, they should be recognised as low-risk customers and benefit from the simplified customer due diligence procedures provided that appropriate criteria are fulfilled.

(8)   Furthermore, it should be possible to apply simplified customer due diligence procedures in the case of legal entities undertaking financial activities which do not fall under the definition of financial institution under Directive 2005/60/EC but which are subject to national legislation pursuant to that Directive and comply with requirements concerning sufficient transparency as to their identity and adequate control mechanisms, in particular enhanced supervision. This could be the case for undertakings providing general insurance services.

(9)   It should be possible to apply simplified customer due diligence procedures to products and related transactions in limited circumstances, for example where the benefits of the financial product in question cannot generally be realised for the benefit of third parties and those benefits are only realisable in the long term, such as some investment insurance policies or savings products, or where the financial product aims at financing physical assets in the form of leasing agreements in which the legal and beneficial title of the underlying asset remains with the leasing company or in the form of low value consumer credit, provided the transactions are carried out through bank accounts and are below an appropriate threshold. State controlled products which are generally addressed to specific categories of clients, such as savings products for the benefit of children, should benefit from simplified customer due diligence procedures even if not all the criteria are fulfilled. State control should be understood as an activity beyond normal supervision on financial markets and should not be construed as covering products, such as debt securities, issued directly by the State.

(10)   Before allowing use of simplified customer due diligence procedures, Member States should assess whether the customers or the products and related transactions represent a low-risk of

money laundering or terrorist financing, notably by paying special attention to any activity of these customers or to any type of products or transactions which may be regarded as particularly likely, by their nature, to be used or abused for money laundering or terrorist financing purposes. In particular, any attempt by customers in relation to low-risk products to act anonymously or hide their identity should be considered as a risk factor and as potentially suspicious.

(11)   In certain circumstances, natural persons or legal entities may conduct financial activities on an occasional or very limited basis, as a complement to other non-financial activities, such as hotels that provide currency exchange services to their clients. Directive 2005/60/EC allows Member States to decide that financial activities of that kind fall outside its scope. The assessment of the occasional or very limited nature of the activity should be made by reference to quantitative thresholds in relation to the transactions and the turnover of the business concerned. These thresholds should be decided at national level, depending on the type of financial activity, in order to take account of differences between countries.

(12)   Moreover, a person engaging in a financial activity on an occasional or very limited basis should not provide a full range of financial services to the public but only those needed for improving the performance of its main business. When the main business of the person relates to an activity covered by Directive 2005/60/EC, the exemption for occasional or limited financial activities should not be granted, except in relation to traders in goods.

(13)   Some financial activities, such as money transmission or remittance services, are more likely to be used or abused for money laundering or terrorist financing purposes. It is therefore necessary to ensure that these or similar financial activities are not exempted from the scope of Directive 2005/60/EC.

(14)   Provision should be made for decisions pursuant to Article 2(2) of Directive 2005/60/EC to be withdrawn as quickly as possible if necessary.

(15)   Member States should ensure that the exemption decisions are not abused for money laundering or terrorist financing purposes. They notably should avoid adopting decisions under Article 2(2) of Directive 2005/60/EC in cases where monitoring or enforcement activities by national authorities present special difficulties as a result of overlapping competences between more than one Member State, such as the provision of financial services on board ships providing transport services between ports situated in different Member States.

(16)   The application of this Directive is without prejudice to the application of Council Regulation (EC) No 2580/2001 of 27 December 2001 on specific restrictive measures directed against certain persons and entities with a view to combating terrorism[2] and Council Regulation (EC) No 881/2002 of 27 May 2002 imposing certain specific restrictive measures directed against certain persons and entities associated with Usama bin Laden, the Al-Qaida network and the Taliban, and repealing Council Regulation (EC) No 467/2001 prohibiting the export of certain goods and services to Afghanistan, strengthening the flight ban and extending the freeze of funds and other financial resources in respect of the Taliban of Afghanistan.[3]

(17)   The measures provided for in this Directive are in accordance with the opinion of the Committee on the Prevention of Money Laundering and Terrorist Financing,

[5910]

NOTES
[1]   OJ L309, 25.11.2005, p 15.
[2]   OJ L344, 28.12.2001, p 70. Regulation as last amended by Decision 2006/379/EC (OJ L144, 31.5.2006, p 21).
[3]   OJ L139, 29.5.2002, p 9. Regulation as last amended by Commission Regulation (EC) No 674/2006 (OJ L116, 29.4.2006, p 58).

HAS ADOPTED THIS DIRECTIVE:

Article 1
Subject-matter

This Directive lays down implementing measures for Directive 2005/60/EC as regards the following:

1.   the technical aspects of the definition of politically exposed persons set out in Article 3(8) of that Directive;

2.   technical criteria for assessing whether situations represent a low risk of money laundering or terrorist financing as referred to in Article 11(2) and (5) of that Directive;

3.   technical criteria for assessing whether, in accordance with Article 2(2) of Directive 2005/60/EC, it is justified not to apply that Directive to certain legal or natural persons carrying out a financial activity on an occasional or very limited basis.

[5910A]

Article 2
Politically exposed persons

1. For the purposes of Article 3(8) of Directive 2005/60/EC, "natural persons who are or have been entrusted with prominent public functions" shall include the following:

(a) heads of State, heads of government, ministers and deputy or assistant ministers;

(b) members of parliaments;

(c) members of supreme courts, of constitutional courts or of other high-level judicial bodies whose decisions are not subject to further appeal, except in exceptional circumstances;

(d) members of courts of auditors or of the boards of central banks;

(e) ambassadors, chargés d'affaires and high-ranking officers in the armed forces;

(f) members of the administrative, management or supervisory bodies of State-owned enterprises.

None of the categories set out in points (a) to (f) of the first subparagraph shall be understood as covering middle ranking or more junior officials.

The categories set out in points (a) to (e) of the first subparagraph shall, where applicable, include positions at Community and international level.

2. For the purposes of Article 3(8) of Directive 2005/60/EC, "immediate family members" shall include the following:

(a) the spouse;

(b) any partner considered by national law as equivalent to the spouse;

(c) the children and their spouses or partners;

(d) the parents.

3. For the purposes of Article 3(8) of Directive 2005/60/EC, "persons known to be close associates" shall include the following:

(a) any natural person who is known to have joint beneficial ownership of legal entities or legal arrangements, or any other close business relations, with a person referred to in paragraph 1;

(b) any natural person who has sole beneficial ownership of a legal entity or legal arrangement which is known to have been set up for the benefit de facto of the person referred to in paragraph 1.

4. Without prejudice to the application, on a risk-sensitive basis, of enhanced customer due diligence measures, where a person has ceased to be entrusted with a prominent public function within the meaning of paragraph 1 of this Article for a period of at least one year, institutions and persons referred to in Article 2(1) of Directive 2005/60/EC shall not be obliged to consider such a person as politically exposed.

[5911]

Article 3
Simplified customer due diligence

1. For the purposes of Article 11(2) of Directive 2005/60/EC, Member States may, subject to paragraph 4 of this Article, consider customers who are public authorities or public bodies and who fulfil all the following criteria as customers representing a low risk of money laundering or terrorist financing:

(a) the customer has been entrusted with public functions pursuant to the Treaty on European Union, the Treaties on the Communities or Community secondary legislation;

(b) the customer's identity is publicly available, transparent and certain;

(c) the activities of the customer, as well as its accounting practices, are transparent;

(d) either the customer is accountable to a Community institution or to the authorities of a Member State, or appropriate check and balance procedures exist ensuring control of the customer's activity.

2. For the purposes of Article 11(2) of Directive 2005/60/EC, Member States may, subject to paragraph 4 of this Article, consider customers who are legal entities which do not enjoy the status of public authority or public body but which fulfil all the following criteria as customers representing a low risk of money laundering or terrorist financing:

(a) the customer is an entity that undertakes financial activities outside the scope of Article 2 of Directive 2005/60/EC but to which national legislation has extended the obligations of that Directive pursuant to Article 4 thereof;

(b) the identity of the customer is publicly available, transparent and certain;

(c) the customer is subject to a mandatory licensing requirement under national law for the undertaking of financial activities and licensing may be refused if the competent authorities are not satisfied that the persons who effectively direct or will direct the business of such an entity, or its beneficial owner, are fit and proper persons;

(d) the customer is subject to supervision, within the meaning of Article 37(3) of Directive

2005/60/EC, by competent authorities as regards compliance with the national legislation transposing that Directive and, where applicable, additional obligations under national legislation;

(e) failure by the customer to comply with the obligations referred to in point (a) is subject to effective, proportionate and dissuasive sanctions including the possibility of appropriate administrative measures or the imposition of administrative sanctions.

Entity, as referred to in point (a) of the first subparagraph, shall include subsidiaries only in so far as the obligations of Directive 2005/60/EC have been extended to them on their own account.

For the purposes of point (c) of the first subparagraph, the activity conducted by the customer shall be supervised by competent authorities. Supervision is to be understood in this context as meaning the type of supervisory activity with the highest supervisory powers, including the possibility of conducting on-site inspections. Such inspections shall include the review of policies, procedures, books and records, and shall extend to sample testing.

3. For the purposes of Article 11(5) of Directive 2005/60/EC, Member States may, subject to paragraph 4 of this Article, allow the institutions and persons covered by that Directive to consider products which fulfil all the following criteria, or transactions related to such products, as representing a low risk of money laundering or terrorist financing:

(a) the product has a written contractual base;

(b) the related transactions are carried out through an account of the customer with a credit institution covered by Directive 2005/60/EC or a credit institution situated in a third country which imposes requirements equivalent to those laid down in that Directive;

(c) the product or related transactions are not anonymous and their nature is such that it allows for the timely application of Article 7(c) of Directive 2005/60/EC;

(d) the product is subject to a predetermined maximum threshold;

(e) the benefits of the product or related transactions cannot be realised for the benefit of third parties, except in the case of death, disablement, survival to a predetermined advanced age, or similar events;

(f) in the case of products or related transactions allowing for the investment of funds in financial assets or claims, including insurance or other kind of contingent claims:

    (i) the benefits of the product or related transactions are only realisable in the long term;

    (ii) the product or related transactions cannot be used as collateral;

    (iii) during the contractual relationship, no accelerated payments are made, no surrender clauses are used and no early termination takes place.

For the purposes of point (d) of the first subparagraph, the thresholds established in Article 11(5)(a) of Directive 2005/60/EC shall apply in the case of insurance policies or savings products of similar nature. Without prejudice to the third subparagraph, in the other cases the maximum threshold shall be EUR 15,000. Member States may derogate from that threshold in the case of products which are related to the financing of physical assets and where the legal and beneficial title of the assets is not transferred to the customer until termination of the contractual relationship, provided that the threshold established by the Member State for the transactions related to this type of product, whether the transaction is carried out in a single operation or in several operations which appear to be linked, does not exceed EUR 15,000 per year.

Member States may derogate from the criteria set out in points (e) and (f) of the first subparagraph in the case of products the characteristics of which are determined by their relevant domestic public authorities for purposes of general interest, which benefit from specific advantages from the State in the form of direct grants or tax rebates, and the use of which is subject to control by those authorities, provided that the benefits of the product are realisable only in the long term and that the threshold established for the purposes of point (d) of the first subparagraph is sufficiently low. Where appropriate, that threshold may be set as a maximum annual amount.

4. In assessing whether the customers or products and transactions referred to in paragraphs 1, 2 and 3 represent a low risk of money laundering or terrorist financing, Member States shall pay special attention to any activity of those customers or to any type of product or transaction which may be regarded as particularly likely, by its nature, to be used or abused for money laundering or terrorist financing purposes.

Member States shall not consider that customers or products and transactions referred to in paragraphs 1, 2 and 3 represent a low risk of money laundering or terrorist financing if there is information available to suggest that the risk of money laundering or terrorist financing may not be low.

[5912]

Article 4
Financial activity on an occasional or very limited basis

1.   For the purposes of Article 2(2) of Directive 2005/60/EC, Member States may, subject to paragraph 2 of this Article, consider legal or natural persons who engage in a financial activity which fulfils all the following criteria as not falling within the scope of Article 3(1) or (2) of that Directive:

(a)   the financial activity is limited in absolute terms;

(b)   the financial activity is limited on a transaction basis;

(c)   the financial activity is not the main activity;

(d)   the financial activity is ancillary and directly related to the main activity;

(e)   with the exception of the activity referred to in point (3)(e) of Article 2(1) of Directive 2005/60/EC, the main activity is not an activity mentioned in Article 2(1) of that Directive;

(f)   the financial activity is provided only to the customers of the main activity and is not generally offered to the public.

For the purposes of point (a) of the first subparagraph, the total turnover of the financial activity may not exceed a threshold which must be sufficiently low. That threshold shall be established at national level, depending on the type of financial activity.

For the purposes of point (b) of the first subparagraph, Member States shall apply a maximum threshold per customer and single transaction, whether the transaction is carried out in a single operation or in several operations which appear to be linked. That threshold shall be established at national level, depending on the type of financial activity. It shall be sufficiently low in order to ensure that the types of transactions in question are an impractical and inefficient method for laundering money or for terrorist financing, and shall not exceed EUR 1,000.

For the purposes of point (c) of the first subparagraph, Member States shall require that the turnover of the financial activity does not exceed 5% of the total turnover of the legal or natural person concerned.

2.   In assessing the risk of money laundering or terrorist financing occurring for the purposes of Article 2(2) of Directive 2005/60/EC, Member States shall pay special attention to any financial activity which is regarded as particularly likely, by its nature, to be used or abused for money laundering or terrorist financing purposes.

Member States shall not consider that the financial activities referred to in paragraph 1 represent a low risk of money laundering or terrorist financing if there is information available to suggest that the risk of money laundering or terrorist financing may not be low.

3.   Any decision pursuant to Article 2(2) of Directive 2005/60/EC shall state the reasons on which it is based. Member States shall provide for the possibility of withdrawing that decision should circumstances change.

4.   Member States shall establish risk-based monitoring activities or take any other adequate measures to ensure that the exemption granted by decisions pursuant to Article 2(2) of Directive 2005/60/EC is not abused by possible money launderers or financers of terrorism.

[5913]

Article 5
Transposition

1.   Member States shall bring into force the laws, regulations and administrative provisions necessary to comply with this Directive by 15 December 2007 at the latest. They shall forthwith communicate to the Commission the text of those provisions and a correlation table between those provisions and this Directive.

When Member States adopt those provisions, they shall contain a reference to this Directive or be accompanied by such a reference on the occasion of their official publication. Member States shall determine how such reference is to be made.

2.   Member States shall communicate to the Commission the text of the main provisions of national law which they adopt in the field covered by this Directive.

[5914]

Article 6

This Directive shall enter into force on the 20th day following its publication in the Official Journal of the European Union.

[5915]

Article 7

This Directive is addressed to the Member States.

[5916]

COMMISSION REGULATION

of 10 August 2006

implementing Directive 2004/39/EC of the European Parliament and of the Council as regards record-keeping obligations for investment firms, transaction reporting, market transparency, admission of financial instruments to trading, and defined terms for the purposes of that Directive

(1287/2006/EC)

(Text with EEA relevance)

NOTES

Date of publication in OJ: OJ L241, 2.9.2006, p 1. Notes are as in the original OJ version.
As of 1 February 2009, this Regulation had not been amended.

THE COMMISSION OF THE EUROPEAN COMMUNITIES,

Having regard to the Treaty establishing the European Community,

Having regard to Directive 2004/39/EC of the European Parliament and of the Council of 21 April 2004 on markets in financial instruments amending Council Directives 85/611/EEC and 93/6/EEC and Directive 2000/12/EC of the European Parliament and of the Council and repealing Council Directive 93/22/EEC,[1] and in particular Articles 4(1)(2), 4(1)(7) and 4(2), Article 13(10), Article 25(7), Article 27(7), Article 28(3), Article 29(3), Article 30(3), Article 40(6), Article 44(3), Article 45(3), Article 56(5), and Article 58(4) thereof,

Whereas:

(1) Directive 2004/39/EC establishes the general framework for a regulatory regime for financial markets in the Community, setting out, among other matters: operating conditions relating to the performance by investment firms of investment and ancillary services, and investment activities; organisational requirements (including record-keeping obligations) for investment firms performing such services and activities on a professional basis, and for regulated markets; transaction reporting requirements in respect of transactions in financial instruments, and transparency requirements in respect of transactions in shares.

(2) It is appropriate that the provisions of this Regulation take that legislative form in order to ensure a harmonised regime in all Member States, to promote market integration and the cross-border provision of investment and ancillary services, and to facilitate the further consolidation of the single market. Provisions relating to certain aspects of record-keeping, and to transaction reporting, transparency and commodity derivatives have few interfaces with national law and with detailed laws governing client relationships.

(3) Detailed and fully harmonised transparency requirements and rules regulating transaction reporting are appropriate so as to ensure equivalent market conditions and the smooth operation of securities markets throughout the Community, and to facilitate the effective integration of those markets. Certain aspects of record-keeping are closely allied as they make use of the same concepts as are defined for transaction reporting and transparency purposes.

(4) The regime established by Directive 2004/39/EC governing transaction reporting requirements in respect of transactions in financial instruments aims to ensure that relevant competent authorities are properly informed about transactions in which they have a supervisory interest. For those purposes it is necessary to ensure that a single data set is collected from all investment firms with a minimum of variation between Member States, so as to minimise the extent to which businesses operating across borders are subject to different reporting obligations, and so as to maximise the proportion of data held by a competent authority that can be shared with other competent authorities. The measures are also designed to ensure that competent authorities are in a position to carry out their obligations under that Directive as expeditiously and efficiently as possible.

(5) The regime established by Directive 2004/39/EC governing transparency requirements in respect of transactions in shares admitted to trading on a regulated market aims to ensure that investors are adequately informed as to the true level of actual and potential transactions in such shares, whether those transactions take place on regulated markets, multilateral trading facilities, hereinafter "MTFs", systematic internalisers, or outside those trading venues. Those requirements are part of a broader framework of rules designed to promote competition between trading venues for execution services so as to increase investor choice, encourage innovation, lower transaction costs, and increase the efficiency of the price formation process on a pan-Community basis. A high degree of transparency is an essential part of this framework, so as to ensure a level playing field between trading venues so that the price discovery mechanism in respect of particular shares is not impaired by the fragmentation of liquidity, and investors are not thereby penalised. On the other hand, that Directive recognises that there may be circumstances where exemptions from pre-trade transparency obligations, or deferral of post-trade transparency obligations, may be necessary. This

Regulation sets out details of those circumstances, bearing in mind the need both to ensure a high level of transparency, and to ensure that liquidity on trading venues and elsewhere is not impaired as an unintended consequence of obligations to disclose transactions and thereby to make public risk positions.

(6)　For the purposes of the provisions on record-keeping, a reference to the type of the order should be understood as referring to its status as a limit order, market order, or other specific type of order. For the purposes of the provisions on record-keeping, a reference to the nature of the order or transaction should be understood as referring to orders to subscribe for securities or the subscription of securities, or to exercise an option or the exercise of an option, or similar client orders or transactions.

(7)　It is not necessary at this stage to specify or prescribe in detail the type, nature and sophistication of the arrangements for the exchange of information between competent authorities.

(8)　Where a notification made by a competent authority relating to the alternative determination of the most relevant market in terms of liquidity is not acted upon within a reasonable time, or where a competent authority does not agree with the calculation made by the other authority, the competent authorities concerned should seek to find a solution. It is open to the competent authorities, where appropriate, to discuss the matter in the Committee of European Securities Regulators.

(9)　The competent authorities should coordinate the design and establishment of arrangements for the exchange of transaction information between themselves. Again it is open to the competent authorities to discuss those matters in the Committee of European Securities Regulators. Competent authorities should report to the Commission which should inform the European Securities Committee of those arrangements. In carrying out the coordination, competent authorities should consider the need to monitor the activities of investment firms effectively, so as to ensure that they act honestly, fairly and professionally and in a manner which promotes the integrity of the market in the Community, the need for decisions to be based on a thorough cost-benefit analysis, the need to ensure that transaction information is used only for the proper discharge of the functions of competent authorities and finally the need to have effective and accountable governance arrangements for any common system that might be considered necessary.

(10)　It is appropriate to set the criteria for determining when the operations of a regulated market are of substantial importance in a host Member State and the consequences of that status in such a way as to avoid creating an obligation on a regulated market to deal with or be made subject to more than one competent authority where otherwise there would be no such obligation.

(11)　ISO 10962 (Classification of financial instruments code) is an example of a uniform internationally accepted standard for financial instrument classification.

(12)　If granting waivers in relation to pre-trade transparency requirements, or authorising the deferral of post-trade transparency obligations, competent authorities should treat all regulated markets and MTFs equally and in a non-discriminatory manner, so that a waiver or deferral is granted either to all regulated markets and MTFs that they authorise under Directive 2004/39/EC, or to none. Competent authorities which grant the waivers or deferrals should not impose additional requirements.

(13)　It is appropriate to consider that a trading algorithm operated by a regulated market or MTF usually should seek to maximise the volume traded, but other trading algorithms should be possible.

(14)　A waiver from pre-trade transparency obligations arising under Articles 29 or 44 of Directive 2004/39/EC conferred by a competent authority should not enable investment firms to avoid such obligations in respect of those transactions in liquid shares which they conclude on a bilateral basis under the rules of a regulated market or an MTF where, if carried out outside the rules of the regulated market or MTF, those transactions would be subject to the requirements to publish quotes set out in Article 27 of that Directive.

(15)　An activity should be considered as having a material commercial role for an investment firm if the activity is a significant source of revenue, or a significant source of cost. An assessment of significance for these purposes should, in every case, take into account the extent to which the activity is conducted or organised separately, the monetary value of the activity, and its comparative significance by reference both to the overall business of the firm and to its overall activity in the market for the share concerned in which the firm operates. It should be possible to consider an activity to be a significant source of revenue for a firm even if only one or two of the factors mentioned is relevant in a particular case.

(16)　Shares not traded daily should not be considered as having a liquid market for the purposes of Directive 2004/39/EC. However, if, for exceptional reasons, trading in a share is suspended for reasons related to the preservation of an orderly market or force majeure and therefore a share is not traded during some trading days, this should not mean that the share cannot be considered to have a liquid market.

(17)　The requirement to make certain quotes, orders or transactions public pursuant to Articles 27, 28, 29, 30, 44 and 45 of Directive 2004/39/EC and this Regulation should not prevent regulated markets and MTFs from requiring their members or participants to make public other such information.

(18)   Information which is required to be made available as close to real time as possible should be made available as close to instantaneously as technically possible, assuming a reasonable level of efficiency and of expenditure on systems on the part of the person concerned. The information should only be published close to the three minute maximum limit in exceptional cases where the systems available do not allow for a publication in a shorter period of time.

(19)   For the purposes of the provisions of this Regulation as to the admission to trading on a regulated market of a transferable security as defined in Article 4(1)(18)(c) of Directive 2004/39/EC, in the case of a security within the meaning of Directive 2003/71/EC of the European Parliament and of the Council of 4 November 2003 on the prospectus to be published when securities are offered to the public or admitted to trading and amending Directive 2001/34/EC[2] there should be considered to be sufficient information publicly available of a kind needed to value that financial instrument.

(20)   The admission to trading on a regulated market of units issued by undertakings for collective investment in transferable securities should not allow the avoidance of the relevant provisions of Council Directive 85/611/EEC of 20 December 1985 on the coordination of laws, regulations and administrative provisions relating to undertakings for collective investment in transferable securities (UCITS)[3] and in particular Articles 44 to 48 of that Directive.

(21)   A derivative contract should only be considered to be a financial instrument under Section C(7) of Annex I to Directive 2004/39/EC if it relates to a commodity and meets the criteria in this Regulation for determining whether a contract should be considered as having the characteristics of other derivative financial instruments and as not being for commercial purposes. A derivative contract should only be considered to be a financial instrument under Section C(10) of that Annex if it relates to an underlying specified in Section C(10) or in this Regulation and meets the criteria in this Regulation for determining whether it should be considered as having the characteristics of other derivative financial instruments.

(22)   The exemptions in Directive 2004/39/EC that relate to dealing on own account or to dealing or providing other investment services in relation to commodity derivatives covered by Sections C(5), C(6) and C(7) of Annex I to that Directive or derivatives covered by Section C(10) of that Annex I could be expected to exclude significant numbers of commercial producers and consumers of energy and other commodities, including energy suppliers, commodity merchants and their subsidiaries from the scope of that Directive, and therefore such participants will not be required to apply the tests in this Regulation to determine if the contracts they deal in are financial instruments.

(23)   In accordance with Section B(7) of Annex I to Directive 2004/39/EC, investment firms may exercise the freedom to provide ancillary services in a Member State other than their home Member State, by performing investment services and activities and ancillary services of the type included under Section A or B of that Annex related to the underlying of the derivatives included under Sections C(5), (6), (7) and (10) of that Annex, where these are connected to the provision of investment or ancillary services. On this basis, a firm performing investment services or activities, and connected trading in spot contracts, should be capable to take advantage of the freedom to provide ancillary services in respect of that connected trading.

(24)   The definition of a commodity should not affect any other definition of that term in national legislation and other community legislation. The tests for determining whether a contract should be considered as having the characteristics of other derivative financial instruments and not being for commercial purposes are only intended to be used for the purposes of determining whether contracts fall within Section C(7) or C(10) of Annex I to Directive 2004/39/EC.

(25)   A derivative contract should be understood as relating to a commodity or to another factor where there is a direct link between that contract and the relevant underlying commodity or factor. A derivative contract on the price of a commodity should therefore be regarded as a derivative contract relating to the commodity, while a derivative contract on the transportation costs for the commodity should not be regarded as a derivative contract relating to the commodity. A derivative that relates to a commodity derivative, such as an option on a commodity future (a derivative relating to a derivative) would constitute an indirect investment in commodities and should therefore still be regarded as a commodity derivative for the purposes of Directive 2004/39/EC.

(26)   The concept of commodity should not include services or other items that are not goods, such as currencies or rights in real estate, or that are entirely intangible.

(27)   The Committee of European Securities Regulators, established by Commission Decision 2001/527/EC[4] has been consulted for technical advice.

(28)   The measures provided for in this Regulation are in accordance with the opinion of the European Securities Committee,

[5917]

NOTES

1   OJ L145, 30.4.2004, p 1. Directive as amended by Directive 2006/31/EC (OJ L114, 27.4.2006, p 60).
2   OJ L345, 31.12.2003, p 64.

³   OJ L375, 31.12.1985, p 3. Directive as last amended by Directive 2005/1/EC of the European Parliament
     and of the Council (OJ L79, 24.3.2005, p 9).
⁴   OJ L191, 13.7.2001, p 43.

HAS ADOPTED THIS REGULATION—

CHAPTER I
GENERAL

Article 1
Subject-matter and scope

1.   This Regulation lays down the detailed rules for the implementation of Articles 4(1)(2), 4(1)(7), 13(6), 25, 27, 28, 29, 30, 40, 44, 45, 56 and 58 of Directive 2004/39/EC.

2.   Articles 7 and 8 shall apply to management companies in accordance with Article 5(4) of Directive 85/611/EEC.

[5917A]

Article 2
Definitions

For the purposes of this Regulation, the following definitions shall apply:

(1)   "commodity" means any goods of a fungible nature that are capable of being delivered, including metals and their ores and alloys, agricultural products, and energy such as electricity;

(2)   "issuer" means an entity which issues transferable securities and, where appropriate, other financial instruments;

(3)   "Community issuer" means an issuer which has its registered office in the Community;

(4)   "third country issuer" means an issuer which is not a Community issuer;

(5)   "normal trading hours" for a trading venue or an investment firm means those hours which the trading venue or investment firm establishes in advance and makes public as its trading hours;

(6)   "portfolio trade" means a transaction in more than one security where those securities are grouped and traded as a single lot against a specific reference price;

(7)   "relevant competent authority" for a financial instrument means the competent authority of the most relevant market in terms of liquidity for that financial instrument;

(8)   "trading venue" means a regulated market, MTF or systematic internaliser acting in its capacity as such, and, where appropriate, a system outside the Community with similar functions to a regulated market or MTF;

(9)   "turnover", in relation to a financial instrument, means the sum of the results of multiplying the number of units of that instrument exchanged between buyers and sellers in a defined period of time, pursuant to transactions taking place on a trading venue or otherwise, by the unit price applicable to each such transaction;

(10) "securities financing transaction" means an instance of stock lending or stock borrowing or the lending or borrowing of other financial instruments, a repurchase or reverse repurchase transaction, or a buy-sell back or sell-buy back transaction.

[5918]

Article 3
Transactions related to an individual share in a portfolio trade and volume weighted average price transactions

1.   A transaction related to an individual share in a portfolio trade shall be considered, for the purposes of Article 18(1)(b)(ii), as a transaction subject to conditions other than the current market price.

It shall also be considered, for the purposes of Article 27(1)(b), as a transaction where the exchange of shares is determined by factors other than the current market valuation of the share.

2.   A volume weighted average price transaction shall be considered, for the purposes of Article 18(1)(b)(ii), as a transaction subject to conditions other than the current market price and, for the purposes of Article 25, as an order subject to conditions other than the current market price.

It shall also be considered, for the purposes of Article 27(1)(b), as a transaction where the exchange of shares is determined by factors other than the current market valuation of the share.

[5919]

Article 4
References to trading day

1.   A reference to a trading day in relation to a trading venue, or in relation to post-trade information to be made public under Article 30 or 45 of Directive 2004/39/EC in relation to a share, shall be a reference to any day during which the trading venue concerned is open for trading.

PART IV
EC MATERIALS

A reference to the opening of the trading day shall be a reference to the commencement of the normal trading hours of the trading venue.

A reference to noon on the trading day shall be a reference to noon in the time zone where the trading venue is established.

A reference to the end of the trading day shall be a reference to the end of its normal trading hours.

2. A reference to a trading day in relation to the most relevant market in terms of liquidity for a share, or in relation to post-trade information to be made public under Article 28 of Directive 2004/39/EC in relation to a share, shall be a reference to any day of normal trading on trading venues in that market.

A reference to the opening of the trading day shall be a reference to the earliest commencement of normal trading in that share on trading venues in that market.

A reference to noon on the trading day shall be a reference to noon in the time zone of that market.

A reference to the end of the trading day shall be a reference to the latest cessation of normal trading in that share on trading venues in that market.

3. A reference to a trading day in relation to a spot contract, within the meaning of Article 38(2), shall be a reference to any day of normal trading of that contract on trading venues.

[5920]

Article 5
References to transaction

For the purposes of this Regulation, a reference to a transaction is a reference only to the purchase and sale of a financial instrument. For the purposes of this Regulation, other than Chapter II, the purchase and sale of a financial instrument does not include any of the following:

    (a)   securities financing transactions;

    (b)   the exercise of options or of covered warrants;

    (c)   primary market transactions (such as issuance, allotment or subscription) in financial instruments falling within Article 4(1)(18)(a) and (b) of Directive 2004/39/EC.

[5921]

Article 6
First admission to trading of a share on a regulated market

For the purposes of this Regulation, the first admission to trading of a share on a regulated market referred to in Article 40 of Directive 2004/39/EC shall be considered to take place at a time when one of the following conditions applies:

    (a)   the share has not previously been admitted to trading on a regulated market;

    (b)   the share has previously been admitted to trading on a regulated market but the share is removed from trading on every regulated market which has so admitted it.

[5922]

CHAPTER II
RECORD-KEEPING: CLIENT ORDERS AND TRANSACTIONS

Article 7
Record-keeping of client orders and decisions to deal
(*Article 13(6) of Directive 2004/39/EC*)

An investment firm shall, in relation to every order received from a client, and in relation to every decision to deal taken in providing the service of portfolio management, immediately make a record of the following details, to the extent they are applicable to the order or decision to deal in question:

    (a)   the name or other designation of the client;

    (b)   the name or other designation of any relevant person acting on behalf of the client;

    (c)   the details specified in points 4, 6 and 16 to 19, of Table 1 of Annex I;

    (d)   the nature of the order if other than buy or sell;

    (e)   the type of the order;

    (f)   any other details, conditions and particular instructions from the client that specify how the order must be carried out;

    (g)   the date and exact time of the receipt of the order, or of the decision to deal, by the investment firm.

[5923]

Article 8
Record-keeping of transactions
(*Article 13(6) of Directive 2004/39/EC*)

1.   Immediately after executing a client order, or, in the case of investment firms that transmit orders to another person for execution, immediately after receiving confirmation that an order has been executed, investment firms shall record the following details of the transaction in question:
   (a)   the name or other designation of the client;
   (b)   the details specified in points 2, 3, 4, 6 and 16 to 21, of Table 1 of Annex I;
   (c)   the total price, being the product of the unit price and the quantity;
   (d)   the nature of the transaction if other than buy or sell;
   (e)   the natural person who executed the transaction or who is responsible for the execution.

2.   If an investment firm transmits an order to another person for execution, the investment firm shall immediately record the following details after making the transmission:
   (a)   the name or other designation of the client whose order has been transmitted;
   (b)   the name or other designation of the person to whom the order was transmitted;
   (c)   the terms of the order transmitted;
   (d)   the date and exact time of transmission.

                                                [5924]

CHAPTER III
TRANSACTION REPORTING

Article 9
Determination of the most relevant market in terms of liquidity
(*Second subparagraph of Article 25(3) of Directive 2004/39/EC*)

1.   The most relevant market in terms of liquidity for a financial instrument which is admitted to trading on a regulated market, hereinafter "the most relevant market", shall be determined in accordance with paragraphs 2 to 8.

2.   In the case of a share or other transferable security covered by Article 4(1)(18)(a) of Directive 2004/39/EC or of a unit in a collective investment undertaking, the most relevant market shall be the Member State where the share or the unit was first admitted to trading on a regulated market.

3.   In the case of a bond or other transferable security covered by Article 4(1)(18)(b) of Directive 2004/39/EC or of a money market instrument which, in either case, is issued by a subsidiary, within the meaning of Seventh Council Directive 83/349/EEC of 13 June 1983 on consolidated accounts,[1] of an entity which has its registered office in a Member State, the most relevant market shall be the Member State where the registered office of the parent entity is situated.

4.   In the case of a bond or other transferable security covered by Article 4(1)(18)(b) of Directive 2004/39/EC or of a money market instrument which, in either case, is issued by a Community issuer and which is not covered by paragraph 3 of this Article, the most relevant market shall be the Member State where the registered office of the issuer is situated.

5.   In the case of a bond or other transferable security covered by Article 4(1)(18)(b) of Directive 2004/39/EC or a money market instrument which, in either case, is issued by a third country issuer and which is not covered by paragraph 3 of this Article, the most relevant market shall be the Member State where that security was first admitted to trading on a regulated market.

6.   In the case of a derivative contract or a financial contract for differences or a transferable security covered by Article 4(1)(18)(c) of Directive 2004/39/EC, the most relevant market shall be:
   (a)   where the underlying security is a share or other transferable security covered by Article 4(1)(18)(a) of Directive 2004/39/EC which is admitted to trading on a regulated market, the Member State deemed to be the most relevant market in terms of liquidity for the underlying security, in accordance with paragraph 2;
   (b)   where the underlying security is a bond or other transferable security covered by Article 4(1)(18)(b) of Directive 2004/39/EC or a money market instrument which is admitted to trading on a regulated market, the Member State deemed to be the most relevant market in terms of liquidity for that underlying security, in accordance with paragraphs 3, 4 or 5;
   (c)   where the underlying is an index composed of shares all of which are traded on a particular regulated market, the Member State where that regulated market is situated.

7.   In any case not covered by paragraphs 2 to 6, the most relevant market shall be the Member State where the regulated market that first admitted the transferable security or derivative contract or financial contract for differences to trading is located.

8.   Where a financial instrument covered by paragraphs 2, 5 or 7, or the underlying financial instrument of a financial instrument covered by paragraph 6 to which one of paragraphs 2, 5 or 7 is

PART IV
EC MATERIALS

relevant, was first admitted to trading on more than one regulated market simultaneously, and all those regulated markets share the same home Member State, that Member State shall be the most relevant market.

Where the regulated markets concerned do not share the same home Member State, the most relevant market in terms of liquidity for that instrument shall be the market where the turnover of that instrument is highest.

For the purposes of determining the most relevant market where the turnover of the instrument is highest, each competent authority that has authorised one of the regulated markets concerned shall calculate the turnover for that instrument in its respective market for the previous calendar year, provided that the instrument was admitted to trading at the beginning of that year.

Where the turnover for the relevant financial instrument cannot be calculated by reason of insufficient or non-existent data and the issuer has its registered office in a Member State, the most relevant market shall be the market of the Member State where the registered office of the issuer is situated.

However, where issuer does not have its registered office in a Member State, the most relevant market for that instrument shall be the market where the turnover of the relevant instrument class is the highest. For the purposes of determining that market, each competent authority that has authorised one of the regulated markets concerned shall calculate the turnover for the instruments of the same class in its respective market for the preceding calendar year.

The relevant classes of financial instrument are the following:
   (a)   shares;
   (b)   bonds or other forms of securitised debt;
   (c)   any other financial instruments.

[5925]

NOTES
   1   OJ L193, 18. 7.1983, p 1.

Article 10
Alternative determination of most relevant market in terms of liquidity
(*Second subparagraph of Article 25(3) of Directive 2004/39/EC*)

1.   A competent authority may, in January every year, notify the relevant competent authority for a particular financial instrument that it intends to contest the determination, made in accordance with Article 9, of the most relevant market for that instrument.

2.   Within four weeks of the sending of the notification, both authorities shall calculate the turnover for that financial instrument in their respective markets over the period of the previous calendar year.

If the results of that calculation indicate that the turnover is higher in the market of the contesting competent authority, that market shall be the most relevant market for that financial instrument. Where that financial instrument is of a type specified in Article 9(6)(a) or (b), that market shall also be the most relevant market for any derivative contract or financial contract for differences or transferable security which is covered by Article 4(1)(18)(c) of Directive 2004/39/EC and in respect of which that financial instrument is the underlying.

[5926]

Article 11
List of financial instruments
(*Article 25(3) of Directive 2004/39/EC*)

The relevant competent authority for one or more financial instruments shall ensure that there is established and maintained an updated list of those financial instruments. That list shall be made available to the single competent authority designated as a contact point by each Member State in accordance with Article 56 of Directive 2004/39/EC. That list shall be made available for the first time on the first trading day in June 2007.

In order to assist competent authorities to comply with the first subparagraph, each regulated market shall submit identifying reference data on each financial instrument admitted to trading in an electronic and standardised format to its home competent authority. This information shall be submitted for each financial instrument before trading commences in that particular instrument. The home competent authority shall ensure the data is transmitted to the relevant competent authority for the financial instrument concerned. The reference data shall be updated whenever there are changes to the data with respect to an instrument. The requirements in this subparagraph may be waived if the relevant competent authority for that financial instrument obtains the relevant reference data by other means.

[5927]

Article 12
Reporting channels
(*Article 25(5) of Directive 2004/39/EC*)

1.   The reports of transactions in financial instruments shall be made in an electronic form except under exceptional circumstances, when they may be made in a medium which allows for the storing of the information in a way accessible for future reference by the competent authorities other than an electronic form, and the methods by which those reports are made shall satisfy the following conditions:

(a)   they ensure the security and confidentiality of the data reported;
(b)   they incorporate mechanisms for identifying and correcting errors in a transaction report;
(c)   they incorporate mechanisms for authenticating the source of the transaction report;
(d)   they include appropriate precautionary measures to enable the timely resumption of reporting in the case of system failure;
(e)   they are capable of reporting the information required under Article 13 in the format required by the competent authority and in accordance with this paragraph, within the time limits set out in Article 25(3) of Directive 2004/39/EC.

2.   A trade-matching or reporting system shall be approved by the competent authority for the purposes of Article 25(5) of Directive 2004/39/EC if the arrangements for reporting transactions established by that system comply with paragraph 1 of this Article and are subject to monitoring by a competent authority in respect of their continuing compliance.

[5928]

Article 13
Content of the transaction report
(*Article 25(3) and (5) of Directive 2004/39/EC*)

1.   The reports of transactions referred to in Article 25(3) and (5) of Directive 2004/39/EC shall contain the information specified in Table 1 of Annex I to this Regulation which is relevant to the type of financial instrument in question and which the competent authority declares is not already in its possession or is not available to it by other means.

2.   For the purposes of the identification of a counterparty to the transaction which is a regulated market, an MTF or other central counterparty, as specified in Table 1 of Annex I, each competent authority shall make publicly available a list of identification codes of the regulated markets and MTFs for which, in each case, it is the competent authority of the home Member State, and of any entities which act as central counterparties for such regulated markets and MTFs.

3.   Member States may require reports made in accordance with Article 25(3) and (5) of Directive 2004/39/EC to contain information related to the transactions in question which is additional to that specified in Table 1 of Annex I where that information is necessary to enable the competent authority to monitor the activities of investment firms to ensure that they act honestly, fairly and professionally and in a manner that promotes the integrity of the market, and provided that one of the following criteria is met:

(a)   the financial instrument which is the subject of the report has characteristics which are specific to an instrument of that kind and which are not covered by the information items specified in that table;
(b)   trading methods which are specific to the trading venue where the transaction took place involve features which are not covered by the information items specified in that table.

4.   Member States may also require a report of a transaction made in accordance with Article 25(3) and (5) of Directive 2004/39/EC to identify the clients on whose behalf the investment firm has executed that transaction.

[5929]

Article 14
Exchange of information on transactions
(*Article 25(3) and (5) of Directive 2004/39/EC*)

1.   The competent authorities shall establish arrangements designed to ensure that the information received in accordance with Article 25(3) and (5) of Directive 2004/39/EC is made available to the following:

(a)   the relevant competent authority for the financial instrument in question;
(b)   in the case of branches, the competent authority that has authorised the investment firm providing the information, without prejudice to its right not to receive this information in accordance with Article 25(6) of Directive 2004/39/EC;
(c)   any other competent authority that requests the information for the proper discharge of its supervisory duties under Article 25(1) of Directive 2004/39/EC.

2.   The information to be made available in accordance with paragraph 1 shall contain the information items described in Tables 1 and 2 of Annex I.

3. The information referred to in paragraph 1 shall be made available as soon as possible.

With effect from 1 November 2008 that information shall be made available no later than the close of the next working day of the competent authority that received the information or the request following the day on which the competent authority has received the information or the request.

4. The competent authorities shall coordinate the following:
   (a) the design and establishment of arrangements for the exchange of transaction information between the competent authorities as required by Directive 2004/39/EC and this Regulation;
   (b) any future upgrading of the arrangements.

5. Before 1 February 2007, the competent authorities shall report to the Commission, which shall inform the European Securities Committee, on the design of the arrangements to be established in accordance with paragraph 1.

They shall also report to the Commission, which shall inform the European Securities Committee, whenever significant changes to those arrangements are proposed.

[5930]

Article 15
Request for cooperation and exchange of information
(Article 58(1) of Directive 2004/39/EC)

1. Where a competent authority wishes another competent authority to supply or exchange information in accordance with Article 58(1) of Directive 2004/39/EC, it shall submit a written request to that competent authority containing sufficient detail to enable it to provide the information requested.

However, in a case of urgency, the request may be transmitted orally provided that it is confirmed in writing.

The competent authority which receives a request shall acknowledge receipt as soon as practicable.

2. Where the information requested under paragraph 1 is internally available to the competent authority that receives the request, that authority shall transmit the requested information without delay to the competent authority which made the request.

However, if the competent authority that receives the request does not possess or control the information requested, it shall immediately take the necessary steps to obtain that information and to comply fully with the request. That competent authority shall also inform the competent authority that made the request of the reasons for not sending immediately the information requested.

[5931]

Article 16
Determination of the substantial importance of a regulated market's operations in a host Member State
(Article 56(2) of Directive 2004/39/EC)

The operations of a regulated market in a host Member State shall be considered to be of substantial importance for the functioning of the securities markets and the protection of investors in that host State where one of the following criteria is met:
   (a) the host Member State has formerly been the home Member State of the regulated market in question;
   (b) the regulated market in question has acquired through merger, takeover, or any other form of transfer the business of a regulated market which had its registered office or head office in the host Member State.

[5932]

CHAPTER IV
MARKET TRANSPARENCY

SECTION 1
PRE-TRADE TRANSPARENCY FOR REGULATED MARKETS AND MTFS

Article 17
Pre-trade transparency obligations
(Articles 29 and 44 of Directive 2004/39/EC)

1. An investment firm or market operator operating an MTF or a regulated market shall, in respect of each share admitted to trading on a regulated market that is traded within a system operated by it and specified in Table 1 of Annex II, make public the information set out in paragraphs 2 to 6.

2. Where one of the entities referred to in paragraph 1 operates a continuous auction order book trading system, it shall, for each share as specified in paragraph 1, make public continuously

throughout its normal trading hours the aggregate number of orders and of the shares those orders represent at each price level, for the five best bid and offer price levels.

3. Where one of the entities referred to in paragraph 1 operates a quote-driven trading system, it shall, for each share as specified in paragraph 1, make public continuously throughout its normal trading hours the best bid and offer by price of each market maker in that share, together with the volumes attaching to those prices.

The quotes made public shall be those that represent binding commitments to buy and sell the shares and which indicate the price and volume of shares in which the registered market makers are prepared to buy or sell.

In exceptional market conditions, however, indicative or one-way prices may be allowed for a limited time.

4. Where one of the entities referred to in paragraph 1 operates a periodic auction trading system, it shall, for each share specified in paragraph 1, make public continuously throughout its normal trading hours the price that would best satisfy the system's trading algorithm and the volume that would potentially be executable at that price by participants in that system.

5. Where one of the entities referred to in paragraph 1 operates a trading system which is not wholly covered by paragraph 2 or 3 or 4, either because it is a hybrid system falling under more than one of those paragraphs or because the price determination process is of a different nature, it shall maintain a standard of pre-trade transparency that ensures that adequate information is made public as to the price level of orders or quotes for each share specified in paragraph 1, as well as the level of trading interest in that share.

In particular, the five best bid and offer price levels and/or two-way quotes of each market maker in that share shall be made public, if the characteristics of the price discovery mechanism permit it.

6. A summary of the information to be made public in accordance with paragraphs 2 to 5 is specified in Table 1 of Annex II.

[5933]

Article 18
Waivers based on market model and type of order or transaction
(*Articles 29(2) and 44(2) of Directive 2004/39/EC*)

1. Waivers in accordance with Article 29(2) and 44(2) of Directive 2004/39/EC may be granted by the competent authorities for systems operated by an MTF or a regulated market, if those systems satisfy one of the following criteria:
    (a) they must be based on a trading methodology by which the price is determined in accordance with a reference price generated by another system, where that reference price is widely published and is regarded generally by market participants as a reliable reference price;
    (b) they formalise negotiated transactions, each of which meets one of the following criteria:
        (i) it is made at or within the current volume weighted spread reflected on the order book or the quotes of the market makers of the regulated market or MTF operating that system or, where the share is not traded continuously, within a percentage of a suitable reference price, being a percentage and a reference price set in advance by the system operator;
        (ii) it is subject to conditions other than the current market price of the share.

For the purposes of point (b), the other conditions specified in the rules of the regulated market or MTF for a transaction of this kind must also have been fulfilled.

In the case of systems having functionality other than as described in points (a) or (b), the waiver shall not apply to that other functionality.

2. Waivers in accordance with Articles 29(2) and 44(2) of Directive 2004/39/EC based on the type of orders may be granted only in relation to orders held in an order management facility maintained by the regulated market or the MTF pending their being disclosed to the market.

[5934]

Article 19
References to negotiated transaction
(*Articles 29(2) and 44(2) of Directive 2004/39/EC*)

For the purpose of Article 18(1)(b) a negotiated transaction shall mean a transaction involving members or participants of a regulated market or an MTF which is negotiated privately but executed within the regulated market or MTF and where that member or participant in doing so undertakes one of the following tasks:
    (a) dealing on own account with another member or participant who acts for the account of a client;
    (b) dealing with another member or participant, where both are executing orders on own account;

(c) acting for the account of both the buyer and seller;
(d) acting for the account of the buyer, where another member or participant acts for the account of the seller;
(e) trading for own account against a client order.

[5935]

Article 20
Waivers in relation to transactions which are large in scale
(Articles 29(2) and 44(2), and fifth subparagraph of Article 27(1) of Directive 2004/39/EC)

An order shall be considered to be large in scale compared with normal market size if it is equal to or larger than the minimum size of order specified in Table 2 in Annex II. For the purposes of determining whether an order is large in scale compared to normal market size, all shares admitted to trading on a regulated market shall be classified in accordance with their average daily turnover, which shall be calculated in accordance with the procedure set out in Article 33.

[5936]

SECTION 2
PRE-TRADE TRANSPARENCY FOR SYSTEMATIC INTERNALISERS

Article 21
Criteria for determining whether an investment firm is a systematic internaliser
(Article 4(1)(7) of Directive 2004/39/EC)

1. Where an investment firm deals on own account by executing client orders outside a regulated market or an MTF, it shall be treated as a systematic internaliser if it meets the following criteria indicating that it performs that activity on an organised, frequent and systematic basis:
   (a) the activity has a material commercial role for the firm, and is carried on in accordance with non-discretionary rules and procedures;
   (b) the activity is carried on by personnel, or by means of an automated technical system, assigned to that purpose, irrespective of whether those personnel or that system are used exclusively for that purpose;
   (c) the activity is available to clients on a regular or continuous basis.

2. An investment firm shall cease to be a systematic internaliser in one or more shares if it ceases to carry on the activity specified in paragraph 1 in respect of those shares, provided that it has announced in advance that it intends to cease that activity using the same publication channels for that announcement as it uses to publish its quotes or, where that is not possible, using a channel which is equally accessible to its clients and other market participants.

3. The activity of dealing on own account by executing client orders shall not be treated as performed on an organised, frequent and systematic basis where the following conditions apply:
   (a) the activity is performed on an ad hoc and irregular bilateral basis with wholesale counterparties as part of business relationships which are themselves characterised by dealings above standard market size;
   (b) the transactions are carried out outside the systems habitually used by the firm concerned for any business that it carries out in the capacity of a systematic internaliser.

4. Each competent authority shall ensure the maintenance and publication of a list of all systematic internalisers, in respect of shares admitted to trading on a regulated market, which it has authorised as investment firms.

It shall ensure that the list is current by reviewing it at least annually.

The list shall be made available to the Committee of European Securities Regulators. It shall be considered as published when it is published by the Committee of European Securities Regulators in accordance with Article 34(5).

[5937]

Article 22
Determination of liquid shares
(Article 27 of Directive 2004/39/EC)

1. A share admitted to trading on a regulated market shall be considered to have a liquid market if the share is traded daily, with a free float not less than EUR 500 million, and one of the following conditions is satisfied:
   (a) the average daily number of transactions in the share is not less than 500;
   (b) the average daily turnover for the share is not less than EUR 2 million.

However, a Member State may, in respect of shares for which it is the most relevant market, specify by notice that both of those conditions are to apply. That notice shall be made public.

2. A Member State may specify the minimum number of liquid shares for that Member State. The minimum number shall be no greater than five. The specification shall be made public.

3. Where, pursuant to paragraph 1, a Member State would be the most relevant market for fewer liquid shares than the minimum number specified in accordance with paragraph 2, the competent authority for that Member State may designate one or more additional liquid shares, provided that the total number of shares which are considered in consequence to be liquid shares for which that Member State is the most relevant market does not exceed the minimum number specified by that Member State.

The competent authority shall designate the additional liquid shares successively in decreasing order of average daily turnover from among the shares for which it is the relevant competent authority that are admitted to trading on a regulated market and are traded daily.

4. For the purposes of the first subparagraph of paragraph 1, the calculation of the free float of a share shall exclude holdings exceeding 5% of the total voting rights of the issuer, unless such a holding is held by a collective investment undertaking or a pension fund.

Voting rights shall be calculated on the basis of all the shares to which voting rights are attached, even if the exercise of such a right is suspended.

5. A share shall not be considered to have a liquid market for the purposes of Article 27 of Directive 2004/39/EC until six weeks after its first admission to trading on a regulated market, if the estimate of the total market capitalisation for that share at the start of the first day's trading after that admission, provided in accordance with Article 33(3), is less than EUR 500 million.

6. Each competent authority shall ensure the maintenance and publication of a list of all liquid shares for which it is the relevant competent authority.

It shall ensure that the list is current by reviewing it at least annually.

The list shall be made available to the Committee of European Securities Regulators. It shall be considered as published when it is published by the Committee of European Securities Regulators in accordance with Article 34(5).

[5938]

Article 23
Standard market size
(Fourth subparagraph of Article 27(1) of Directive 2004/39/EC)

In order to determine the standard market size for liquid shares, those shares shall be grouped into classes in terms of the average value of orders executed in accordance with Table 3 in Annex II.

[5939]

Article 24
Quotes reflecting prevailing market conditions
(Article 27(1) of Directive 2004/39/EC)

A systematic internaliser shall, for each liquid share for which it is a systematic internaliser, maintain the following:

(a) a quote or quotes which are close in price to comparable quotes for the same share in other trading venues;

(b) a record of its quoted prices, which it shall retain for a period of 12 months or such longer period as it considers appropriate.

The obligation laid down in point (b) is without prejudice to the obligation of the investment firm under Article 25(2) of Directive 2004/39/EC to keep at the disposal of the competent authority for at least five years the relevant data relating to all transactions it has carried out.

[5940]

Article 25
Execution of orders by systematic internalisers
(Fifth subparagraph of Article 27(3) and Article 27(6) of Directive 2004/39/EC)

1. For the purposes of the fifth subparagraph of Article 27(3) of Directive 2004/39/EC, execution in several securities shall be regarded as part of one transaction if that one transaction is a portfolio trade that involves 10 or more securities.

For the same purposes, an order subject to conditions other than the current market price means any order which is neither an order for the execution of a transaction in shares at the prevailing market price, nor a limit order.

2. For the purposes of Article 27(6) of Directive 2004/39/EC, the number or volume of orders shall be regarded as considerably exceeding the norm if a systematic internaliser cannot execute those orders without exposing itself to undue risk.

In order to identify the number and volume of orders that it can execute without exposing itself to undue risk, a systematic internaliser shall maintain and implement as part of its risk management policy under Article 7 of Commission Directive 2006/73/EC[1] a non-discriminatory policy which takes into account the volume of the transactions, the capital that the firm has available to cover the risk for that type of trade, and the prevailing conditions in the market in which the firm is operating.

3.   Where, in accordance with Article 27(6) of Directive 2004/39/EC, an investment firm limits the number or volume of orders it undertakes to execute, it shall set out in writing, and make available to clients and potential clients, the arrangements designed to ensure that such a limitation does not result in the discriminatory treatment of clients.

[5941]

NOTES
   [1]   OJ L241, 2.9.2006, p 26.

Article 26
Retail size
(*Fourth subparagraph Article 27(3) of Directive 2004/39/EC*)

For the purposes of the fourth subparagraph of Article 27(3) of Directive 2004/39/EC, an order shall be regarded as being of a size bigger than the size customarily undertaken by a retail investor if it exceeds EUR 7500.

[5942]

SECTION 3
POST-TRADE TRANSPARENCY FOR REGULATED MARKETS, MTFS AND INVESTMENT FIRMS

Article 27
Post-trade transparency obligation
(*Articles 28, 30 and 45 of Directive 2004/39/EC*)

1.   Investment firms, regulated markets, and investment firms and market operators operating an MTF shall, with regard to transactions in respect of shares admitted to trading on regulated markets concluded by them or, in the case of regulated markets or MTFs, within their systems, make public the following details:
  (a)   the details specified in points 2, 3, 6, 16, 17, 18, and 21 of Table 1 in Annex I;
  (b)   an indication that the exchange of shares is determined by factors other than the current market valuation of the share, where applicable;
  (c)   an indication that the trade was a negotiated trade, where applicable;
  (d)   any amendments to previously disclosed information, where applicable.

Those details shall be made public either by reference to each transaction or in a form aggregating the volume and price of all transactions in the same share taking place at the same price at the same time.

2.   By way of exception, a systematic internaliser shall be entitled to use the acronym "SI" instead of the venue identification referred to in paragraph 1(a) in respect of a transaction in a share that is executed in its capacity as a systematic internaliser in respect of that share.

The systematic internaliser may exercise that right only as long as it makes available to the public aggregate quarterly data as to the transactions executed in its capacity as a systematic internaliser in respect of that share relating to the most recent calendar quarter, or part of a calendar quarter, during which the firm acted as a systematic internaliser in respect of that share. That data shall be made available no later than one month after the end of each calendar quarter.

It may also exercise that right during the period between the date specified in Article 41(2), or the date on which the firm commences to be a systematic internaliser in relation to a share, whichever is the later, and the date that aggregate quarterly data in relation to a share is first due to be published.

3.   The aggregated quarterly data referred to in the second subparagraph of paragraph 2 shall contain the following information for the share in respect of each trading day of the calendar quarter concerned:
  (a)   the highest price;
  (b)   the lowest price;
  (c)   the average price;
  (d)   the total number of shares traded;
  (e)   the total number of transactions;
  (f)   such other information as the systematic internaliser decides to make available.

4.   Where the transaction is executed outside the rules of a regulated market or an MTF, one of the following investment firms shall, by agreement between the parties, arrange to make the information public:
  (a)   the investment firm that sells the share concerned;
  (b)   the investment firm that acts on behalf of or arranges the transaction for the seller;
  (c)   the investment firm that acts on behalf of or arranges the transaction for the buyer;
  (d)   the investment firm that buys the share concerned.

In the absence of such an agreement, the information shall be made public by the investment firm determined by proceeding sequentially from point (a) to point (d) until the first point that applies to the case in question.

The parties shall take all reasonable steps to ensure that the transaction is made public as a single transaction. For those purposes two matching trades entered at the same time and price with a single party interposed shall be considered to be a single transaction.

[5943]

Article 28
Deferred publication of large transactions
(Articles 28, 30 and 45 of Directive 2004/39/EC)

The deferred publication of information in respect of transactions may be authorised, for a period no longer than the period specified in Table 4 in Annex II for the class of share and transaction concerned, provided that the following criteria are satisfied:

(a)   the transaction is between an investment firm dealing on own account and a client of that firm;

(b)   the size of the transaction is equal to or exceeds the relevant minimum qualifying size, as specified in Table 4 in Annex II.

In order to determine the relevant minimum qualifying size for the purposes of point (b), all shares admitted to trading on a regulated market shall be classified in accordance with their average daily turnover to be calculated in accordance with Article 33.

[5944]

SECTION 4
PROVISIONS COMMON TO PRE- AND POST-TRADE TRANSPARENCY

Article 29
Publication and availability of pre- and post-trade transparency data
(Articles 27(3), 28(1), 29(1), 44(1) and 45(1) of Directive 2004/39/EC)

1.   A regulated market, MTF or systematic internaliser shall be considered to publish pre-trade information on a continuous basis during normal trading hours if that information is published as soon as it becomes available during the normal trading hours of the regulated market, MTF or systematic internaliser concerned, and remains available until it is updated.

2.   Pre-trade information, and post-trade information relating to transactions taking place on trading venues and within normal trading hours, shall be made available as close to real time as possible. Post-trade information relating to such transactions shall be made available in any case within three minutes of the relevant transaction.

3.   Information relating to a portfolio trade shall be made available with respect to each constituent transaction as close to real time as possible, having regard to the need to allocate prices to particular shares. Each constituent transaction shall be assessed separately for the purposes of determining whether deferred publication in respect of that transaction is available under Article 28.

4.   Post-trade information relating to transactions taking place on a trading venue but outside its normal trading hours shall be made public before the opening of the next trading day of the trading venue on which the transaction took place.

5.   For transactions that take place outside a trading venue, post-trade information shall be made public:

(a)   if the transaction takes place during a trading day of the most relevant market for the share concerned, or during the investment firm's normal trading hours, as close to real time as possible. Post-trade information relating to such transactions shall be made available in any case within three minutes of the relevant transaction;

(b)   in a case not covered by point (a), immediately upon the commencement of the investment firm's normal trading hours or at the latest before the opening of the next trading day in the most relevant market for that share.

[5945]

Article 30
Public availability of pre- and post-trade information
(Articles 27, 28, 29, 30, 44 and 45 of Directive 2004/39/EC)

For the purposes of Articles 27, 28, 29, 30, 44 and 45 of Directive 2004/39/EC and of this Regulation, pre- and post-trade information shall be considered to be made public or available to the public if it is made available generally through one of the following to investors located in the Community:

(a)   the facilities of a regulated market or an MTF;

(b)   the facilities of a third party;

(c)   proprietary arrangements.

[5946]

PART IV
EC MATERIALS

Article 31
Disclosure of client limit orders
(*Article 22(2) of Directive 2004/39/EC*)

An investment firm shall be considered to disclose client limit orders that are not immediately executable if it transmits the order to a regulated market or MTF that operates an order book trading system, or ensures that the order is made public and can be easily executed as soon as market conditions allow.

[5947]

Article 32
Arrangements for making information public
(*Article 22(2), 27, 28, 29, 30, 44 and 45 of Directive 2004/39/EC*)

Any arrangement to make information public, adopted for the purposes of Articles 30 and 31, shall satisfy the following conditions:

(a) it must include all reasonable steps necessary to ensure that the information to be published is reliable, monitored continuously for errors, and corrected as soon as errors are detected;

(b) it must facilitate the consolidation of the data with similar data from other sources;

(c) it must make the information available to the public on a non-discriminatory commercial basis at a reasonable cost.

[5948]

Article 33
Calculations and estimates for shares admitted to trading on a regulated market
(*Articles 27, 28, 29, 30, 44 and 45 of Directive 2004/39/EC*)

1. In respect of each share that is admitted to trading on a regulated market, the relevant competent authority for that share shall ensure that the following calculations are made in respect of that share promptly after the end of each calendar year:

(a) the average daily turnover;

(b) the average daily number of transactions;

(c) for those shares which satisfy the conditions laid down in Article 22(1)(a) or (b) (as applicable), the free float as at 31 December;

(d) if the share is a liquid share, the average value of the orders executed.

This paragraph and paragraph 2 shall not apply to a share which is first admitted to trading on a regulated market four weeks or less before the end of the calendar year.

2. The calculation of the average daily turnover, average value of the orders executed and average daily number of transactions shall take into account all the orders executed in the Community in respect of the share in question between 1 January and 31 December of the preceding year, or, where applicable, that part of the year during which the share was admitted to trading on a regulated market and was not suspended from trading on a regulated market.

In the calculations of the average daily turnover, average value of the orders executed and average daily number of transactions of a share, non-trading days in the Member State of the relevant competent authority for that share shall be excluded.

3. Before the first admission of a share to trading on a regulated market, the relevant competent authority for that share shall ensure that estimates are provided, in respect of that share, of the average daily turnover, the market capitalisation as it will stand at the start of the first day of trading and, where the estimate of the market capitalisation is EUR 500 million or more:

(a) the average daily number of transactions and, for those shares which satisfy the conditions laid down in Article 22(1)(a) or (b) (as applicable), the free float;

(b) in the case of a share that is estimated to be a liquid share, the average value of the orders executed.

The estimates shall relate to the six-week period following admission to trading, or the end of that period, as applicable, and shall take account of any previous trading history of the share, as well as that of shares that are considered to have similar characteristics.

4. After the first admission of a share to trading on a regulated market, the relevant competent authority for that share shall ensure that, in respect of that share, the figures referred to in points (a) to (d) of paragraph 1 are calculated, using data relating to the first four weeks' trading, as if a reference in point (c) of paragraph 1 to 31 December were a reference to the end of the first four weeks' trading, as soon as practicable after those data are available, and in any case before the end of the six-week period referred to in Article 22(5).

5. During the course of a calendar year, the relevant competent authorities shall ensure the review and where necessary the recalculation of the average daily turnover, average value of the orders executed, average daily number of transactions executed and the free float whenever there is a change in relation to the share or the issuer which significantly affects the previous calculations on an ongoing basis.

6.   The calculations referred to in paragraphs 1 to 5 which are to be published on or before the first trading day in March 2009 shall be made on the basis of the data relating to the regulated market or markets of the Member State which is the most relevant market in terms of liquidity for the share in question. For those purposes, negotiated transactions within the meaning of Article 19 shall be excluded from the calculations.

[5949]

Article 34
Publication and effect of results of required calculations and estimates
(*Articles 27, 28, 29, 30, 44 and 45 of Directive 2004/39/EC*)

1.   On the first trading day of March of each year, each competent authority shall, in relation to each share for which it is the relevant competent authority that was admitted to trading on a regulated market at the end of the preceding calendar year, ensure the publication of the following information:
   (a)   the average daily turnover and average daily number of transactions, as calculated in accordance with Article 33(1) and (2);
   (b)   the free float and average value of the orders executed, where calculated in accordance with Article 33(1) and (2).

This paragraph shall not apply to shares to which the second subparagraph of Article 33(1) applies.

2.   The results of the estimates and calculations required under Article 33(3), (4) or (5) shall be published as soon as practicable after the calculation or estimate is completed.

3.   The information referred to in paragraphs 1 or 2 shall be considered as published when it is published by the Committee of European Securities Regulators in accordance with paragraph 5.

4.   For the purposes of this Regulation, the following shall apply:
   (a)   the classification based on the publication referred to in paragraph 1 shall apply for the 12-month period starting on 1 April following publication and ending on the following 31 March;
   (b)   the classification based on the estimates provided for in Article 33(3) shall apply from the relevant first admission to trading until the end of the six-week period referred to in Article 22(5);
   (c)   the classification based on the calculations specified in Article 33(4) shall apply from the end of the six-week period referred to in Article 22(5), until:
       (i)   where the end of that six-week period falls between 15 January and 31 March (both inclusive) in a given year, 31 March of the following year;
       (ii)   otherwise, the following 31 March after the end of that period.

However, the classification based on the recalculations specified in Article 33(5) shall apply from the date of publication and, unless further recalculated under Article 33(5), until the following 31 March.

5.   The Committee of European Securities Regulators shall, on the basis of data supplied to it by or on behalf of competent authorities, publish on its website consolidated and regularly updated lists of:
   (a)   every systematic internaliser in respect of a share admitted to trading on a regulated market;
   (b)   every share admitted to trading on a regulated market, specifying:
       (i)   the average daily turnover, average daily number of transactions and, for those shares which satisfy the conditions laid down in Article 22(1)(a) or (b) (as applicable), the free float;
       (ii)   in the case of a liquid share, the average value of the orders executed and the standard market size for that share;
       (iii) in the case of a liquid share which has been designated as an additional liquid share in accordance with Article 22(3), the name of the competent authority that so designated it; and
       (iv)   the relevant competent authority.

6.   Each competent authority shall ensure the first publication of the details referred to in points (a) and (b) of paragraph 1 on the first trading day in July 2007, based on the reference period 1 April 2006 to 31 March 2007. By way of derogation from paragraph 4, the classification based on that publication shall apply for the five-month period starting on 1 November 2007 and ending on 31 March 2008.

[5950]

CHAPTER V
ADMISSION OF FINANCIAL INSTRUMENTS TO TRADING

Article 35
Transferable securities
(Article 40(1) of Directive 2004/39/EC)

1. Transferable securities shall be considered freely negotiable for the purposes of Article 40(1) of Directive 2004/39/EC if they can be traded between the parties to a transaction, and subsequently transferred without restriction, and if all securities within the same class as the security in question are fungible.

2. Transferable securities which are subject to a restriction on transfer shall not be considered as freely negotiable unless that restriction is not likely to disturb the market.

3. Transferable securities that are not fully paid may be considered as freely negotiable if arrangements have been made to ensure that the negotiability of such securities is not restricted and that adequate information concerning the fact that the securities are not fully paid, and the implications of that fact for shareholders, is publicly available.

4. When exercising its discretion whether to admit a share to trading, a regulated market shall, in assessing whether the share is capable of being traded in a fair, orderly and efficient manner, take into account the following:
    (a) the distribution of those shares to the public;
    (b) such historical financial information, information about the issuer, and information providing a business overview as is required to be prepared under Directive 2003/71/EC, or is or will be otherwise publicly available.

5. A transferable security that is officially listed in accordance with Directive 2001/34/EC of the European Parliament and of the Council,[1] and the listing of which is not suspended, shall be deemed to be freely negotiable and capable of being traded in a fair, orderly and efficient manner.

6. For the purposes of Article 40(1) of Directive 2004/39/EC, when assessing whether a transferable security referred to in Article 4(1)(18)(c) of that Directive is capable of being traded in a fair, orderly and efficient manner, the regulated market shall take into account, depending on the nature of the security being admitted, whether the following criteria are satisfied:
    (a) the terms of the security are clear and unambiguous and allow for a correlation between the price of the security and the price or other value measure of the underlying;
    (b) the price or other value measure of the underlying is reliable and publicly available;
    (c) there is sufficient information publicly available of a kind needed to value the security;
    (d) the arrangements for determining the settlement price of the security ensure that this price properly reflects the price or other value measure of the underlying;
    (e) where the settlement of the security requires or provides for the possibility of the delivery of an underlying security or asset rather than cash settlement, there are adequate settlement and delivery procedures for that underlying as well as adequate arrangements to obtain relevant information about that underlying.

[5951]

NOTES
1 OJ L184, 6.7.2001, p 1. Directive as last amended by Directive 2005/1/EC.

Article 36
Units in collective investment undertakings
(Article 40(1) of Directive 2004/39/EC)

1. A regulated market shall, when admitting to trading units in a collective investment undertaking, whether or not that undertaking is constituted in accordance with Directive 85/611/EEC, satisfy itself that the collective investment undertaking complies or has complied with the registration, notification or other procedures which are a necessary precondition for the marketing of the collective investment undertaking in the jurisdiction of the regulated market.

2. Without prejudice to Directive 85/611/EEC or any other Community legislation or national law relating to collective investment undertakings, Member States may provide that compliance with the requirements referred to in paragraph 1 is not a necessary precondition for the admission of units in a collective investment undertaking to trading on a regulated market.

3. When assessing whether units in an open-ended collective investment undertaking are capable of being traded in a fair, orderly and efficient manner in accordance with Article 40(1) of Directive 2004/39/EC, the regulated market shall take the following aspects into account:
    (a) the distribution of those units to the public;
    (b) whether there are appropriate market-making arrangements, or whether the management company of the scheme provides appropriate alternative arrangements for investors to redeem the units;

(c)   whether the value of the units is made sufficiently transparent to investors by means of the periodic publication of the net asset value.

4.   When assessing whether units in a closed-end collective investment undertaking are capable of being traded in a fair, orderly and efficient manner in accordance with Article 40(1) of Directive 2004/39/EC, the regulated market shall take the following aspects into account:
(a)   the distribution of those units to the public;
(b)   whether the value of the units is made sufficiently transparent to investors, either by publication of information on the fund's investment strategy or by the periodic publication of net asset value.

[5952]

Article 37
Derivatives
(Article 40(1) and (2) of Directive 2004/39/EC)

1.   When admitting to trading a financial instrument of a kind listed in points of Sections C(4) to (10) of Annex I to Directive 2004/39/EC, regulated markets shall verify that the following conditions are satisfied:
(a)   the terms of the contract establishing the financial instrument must be clear and unambiguous, and enable a correlation between the price of the financial instrument and the price or other value measure of the underlying;
(b)   the price or other value measure of the underlying must be reliable and publicly available;
(c)   sufficient information of a kind needed to value the derivative must be publicly available;
(d)   the arrangements for determining the settlement price of the contract must be such that the price properly reflects the price or other value measure of the underlying;
(e)   where the settlement of the derivative requires or provides for the possibility of the delivery of an underlying security or asset rather than cash settlement, there must be adequate arrangements to enable market participants to obtain relevant information about that underlying as well as adequate settlement and delivery procedures for the underlying.

2.   Where the financial instruments concerned are of a kind listed in Sections C (5), (6), (7) or (10) of Annex I to Directive 2004/39/EC, point (b) of paragraph 1 shall not apply if the following conditions are satisfied:
(a)   the contract establishing that instrument must be likely to provide a means of disclosing to the market, or enabling the market to assess, the price or other value measure of the underlying, where the price or value measure is not otherwise publicly available;
(b)   the regulated market must ensure that appropriate supervisory arrangements are in place to monitor trading and settlement in such financial instruments;
(c)   the regulated market must ensure that settlement and delivery, whether physical delivery or by cash settlement, can be effected in accordance with the contract terms and conditions of those financial instruments.

[5953]

CHAPTER VI
DERIVATIVE FINANCIAL INSTRUMENTS

Article 38
Characteristics of other derivative financial instruments
(Article 4(1)(2) of Directive 2004/39/EC)

1.   For the purposes of Section C(7) of Annex I to Directive 2004/39/EC, a contract which is not a spot contract within the meaning of paragraph 2 of this Article and which is not covered by paragraph 4 shall be considered as having the characteristics of other derivative financial instruments and not being for commercial purposes if it satisfies the following conditions:
(a)   it meets one of the following sets of criteria:
    (i)   it is traded on a third country trading facility that performs a similar function to a regulated market or an MTF;
    (ii)   it is expressly stated to be traded on, or is subject to the rules of, a regulated market, an MTF or such a third country trading facility;
    (iii) it is expressly stated to be equivalent to a contract traded on a regulated market, MTF or such a third country trading facility;
(b)   it is cleared by a clearing house or other entity carrying out the same functions as a central counterparty, or there are arrangements for the payment or provision of margin in relation to the contract;
(c)   it is standardised so that, in particular, the price, the lot, the delivery date or other terms are determined principally by reference to regularly published prices, standard lots or standard delivery dates.

2. A spot contract for the purposes of paragraph 1 means a contract for the sale of a commodity, asset or right, under the terms of which delivery is scheduled to be made within the longer of the following periods:

    (a)   two trading days;

    (b)   the period generally accepted in the market for that commodity, asset or right as the standard delivery period.

However, a contract is not a spot contract if, irrespective of its explicit terms, there is an understanding between the parties to the contract that delivery of the underlying is to be postponed and not to be performed within the period mentioned in the first subparagraph.

3. For the purposes of Section C(10) of Annex I to Directive 2004/39/EC, a derivative contract relating to an underlying referred to in that Section or in Article 39 shall be considered to have the characteristics of other derivative financial instruments if one of the following conditions is satisfied:

    (a)   that contract is settled in cash or may be settled in cash at the option of one or more of the parties, otherwise than by reason of a default or other termination event;

    (b)   that contract is traded on a regulated market or an MTF;

    (c)   the conditions laid down in paragraph 1 are satisfied in relation to that contract.

4. A contract shall be considered to be for commercial purposes for the purposes of Section C(7) of Annex I to Directive 2004/39/EC, and as not having the characteristics of other derivative financial instruments for the purposes of Sections C(7) and (10) of that Annex, if it is entered into with or by an operator or administrator of an energy transmission grid, energy balancing mechanism or pipeline network, and it is necessary to keep in balance the supplies and uses of energy at a given time.

[5954]

Article 39
Derivatives within Section C(10) of Annex I to Directive 2004/39/EC
(Article 4(1)(2) of Directive 2004/39/EC)

In addition to derivative contracts of a kind referred to in Section C(10) of Annex I to Directive 2004/39/EC, a derivative contract relating to any of the following shall fall within that Section if it meets the criteria set out in that Section and in Article 38(3):

    (a)   telecommunications bandwidth;

    (b)   commodity storage capacity;

    (c)   transmission or transportation capacity relating to commodities, whether cable, pipeline or other means;

    (d)   an allowance, credit, permit, right or similar asset which is directly linked to the supply, distribution or consumption of energy derived from renewable resources;

    (e)   a geological, environmental or other physical variable;

    (f)   any other asset or right of a fungible nature, other than a right to receive a service, that is capable of being transferred;

    (g)   an index or measure related to the price or value of, or volume of transactions in any asset, right, service or obligation.

[5955]

CHAPTER VII
FINAL PROVISIONS

Article 40
Re-examinations

1. At least once every two years, and after consulting the Committee of European Securities Regulators, the Commission shall re-examine the definition of "transaction" for the purposes of this Regulation, the Tables included in Annex II, as well as the criteria for determination of liquid shares contained in Article 22.

2. The Commission shall, after consulting the Committee of European Securities Regulators, re-examine the provisions of Articles 38 and 39 relating to criteria for determining which instruments are to be treated as having the characteristics of other derivative financial instruments, or as being for commercial purposes, or which fall within Section C(10) of Annex I to Directive 2004/39/EC if the other criteria set out in that Section are satisfied in relation to them.

The Commission shall report to the European Parliament and to the Council at the same time that it makes its reports under Article 65(3)(a) and (d) of Directive 2004/39/EC.

3. The Commission shall, no later than two years after the date of application of this Regulation, after consulting the Committee of European Securities Regulators, re-examine Table 4 of Annex II and report on the results of this re-examination to the European Parliament and the Council.

[5956]

Article 41
Entry into force

This Regulation shall enter into force on the 20th day following its publication in the Official Journal of the European Union.

This Regulation shall apply from 1 November 2007, except Article 11 and Article 34(5) and (6), which shall apply from 1 June 2007.

This Regulation shall be binding in its entirety and directly applicable in all Member States.

[5957]

ANNEX I

| Table 1: List of fields for reporting purposes ||
Field Identifier	Description
1. Reporting firm identification	A unique code to identify the firm which executed the transaction.
2. Trading day	The trading day on which the transaction was executed.
3. Trading time	The time at which the transaction was executed, reported in the local time of the competent authority to which the transaction will be reported, and the basis in which the transaction is reported expressed as Coordinated Universal Time (UTC) +/- hours.
4. Buy/sell indicator	Identifies whether the transaction was a buy or sell from the perspective of the reporting investment firm or, in the case of a report to a client, of the client.
5. Trading capacity	Identifies whether the firm executed the transaction: — on its own account (either on its own behalf or on behalf of a client), — for the account, and on behalf, of a client.
6. Instrument identification	This shall consist of: — a unique code, to be decided by the competent authority (if any) to which the report is made identifying the financial instrument which is the subject of the transaction, — if the financial instrument in question does not have a unique identification code, the report must include the name of the instrument or, in the case of a derivative contract, the characteristics of the contract.
7. Instrument code type	The code type used to report the instrument.
8. Underlying instrument identification	The instrument identification applicable to the security that is the underlying asset in a derivative contract as well as the transferable security falling within Article 4(1)(18)(c) of Directive 2004/39/EC.
9. Underlying instrument identification code type	The code type used to report the underlying instrument.
10. Instrument type	The harmonised classification of the financial instrument that is the subject of the transaction. The description must at least indicate whether the instrument belongs to one of the top level categories as provided by a uniform internationally accepted standard for financial instrument classification.
11. Maturity date	The maturity date of a bond or other form of securitised debt, or the exercise date/maturity date of a derivative contract.
12. Derivative type	The harmonised description of the derivative type should be done according to one of the top level categories as provided by a uniform internationally accepted standard for financial instrument classification.
13. Put/call	Specification whether an option or any other financial instrument is a put or a call.
14. Strike price	The strike price of an option or other financial instrument.

Table 1: List of fields for reporting purposes	
Field Identifier	**Description**
15. Price multiplier	The number of units of the financial instrument in question which are contained in a trading lot; for example, the number of derivatives or securities represented by one contract.
16. Unit price	The price per security or derivative contract excluding commission and (where relevant) accrued interest. In the case of a debt instrument, the price may be expressed either in terms of currency or as a percentage.
17. Price notation	The currency in which the price is expressed. If, in the case of a bond or other form of securitised debt, the price is expressed as a percentage, that percentage shall be included.
18. Quantity	The number of units of the financial instruments, the nominal value of bonds, or the number of derivative contracts included in the transaction.
19. Quantity notation	An indication as to whether the quantity is the number of units of financial instruments, the nominal value of bonds or the number of derivative contracts.
20. Counterparty	Identification of the counterparty to the transaction. That identification shall consist of: — where the counterparty is an investment firm, a unique code for that firm, to be determined by the competent authority (if any) to which the report is made, — where the counterparty is a regulated market or MTF or an entity acting as its central counterparty, the unique harmonised identification code for that market, MTF or entity acting as central counterparty, as specified in the list published by the competent authority of the home Member State of that entity in accordance with Article 13(2), — where the counterparty is not an investment firm, a regulated market, an MTF or an entity acting as central counterparty, it should be identified as "customer/client" of the investment firm which executed the transaction.
21. Venue identification	Identification of the venue where the transaction was executed. That identification shall consist in: — where the venue is a trading venue: its unique harmonised identification code, — otherwise: the code "OTC".
22. Transaction reference number	A unique identification number for the transaction provided by the investment firm or a third party reporting on its behalf.
23. Cancellation flag	An indication as to whether the transaction was cancelled.

Table 2: Further details for use of competent authorities	
Field Identifier	**Description**
1. Reporting firm identification	If a unique code as referred to in Table 1 of Annex I is not sufficient to identify the counterparty, competent authorities should develop adequate measures that ensure the identification of the counterparty.
6. Instrument identification	The unique code, agreed between all the competent authorities, applicable to the financial instrument in question shall be used.
20. Counterparty	If a unique code, or unique harmonised identification code as referred to in Table 1 of Annex 1 is not sufficient to identify the counterparty, competent authorities should develop adequate measures that ensure the identification of the counterparty.

ANNEX II

Table 1: Information to be made public in accordance with Article 17		
Type of system	**Description of system**	**Summary of information to be made public, in accordance with Article 17**
Continuous auction order book trading system	A system that by means of an order book and a trading algorithm operated without human intervention matches sell orders with matching buy orders on the basis of the best available price on a continuous basis.	The aggregate number of orders and the shares they represent at each price level, for at least the five best bid and offer price levels.
Quote-driven trading system	A system where transactions are concluded on the basis of firm quotes that are continuously made available to participants, which requires the market makers to maintain quotes in a size that balances the needs of members and participants to deal in a commercial size and the risk to which the market maker exposes itself.	The best bid and offer by price of each market maker in that share, together with the volumes attaching to those prices.
Periodic auction trading system	A system that matches orders on the basis of a periodic auction and a trading algorithm operated without human intervention.	The price at which the auction trading system would best satisfy its trading algorithm and the volume that would potentially be executable at that price.
Trading system not covered by first three rows	A hybrid system falling into two or more of the first three rows or a system where the price determination process is of a different nature than that applicable to the types of system covered by first three rows.	Adequate information as to the level of orders or quotes and of trading interest; in particular, the five best bid and offer price levels and/or two-way quotes of each market maker in the share, if the characteristics of the price discovery mechanism so permit.

Table 2: Orders large in scale compared with normal market size (*in EUR*)					
Class in terms of average daily turnover (ADT)	ADT < 500,000	500,000 ≤ ADT < 1,000,000	1,000,000 ≤ ADT < 25,000,000	25,000,000 ≤ ADT < 50,000,000	ADT ≥ 50,000,000
Minimum size of order qualifying as large in scale compared with normal market size	50,000	100,000	250,000	400,000	500,000

Table 3: Standard market sizes (*in EUR*)								
Class in terms of average value of transactions (AVT)	AVT < 10,000	10,000 ≤ AVT < 20,000	20,000 ≤ AVT < 30,000	30,000 ≤ AVT < 40,000	40,000 ≤ AVT < 50,000	50,000 ≤ AVT < 70,000	70,000 ≤ AVT < 90,000	Etc.
Standard market size	7,500	15,000	25,000	35,000	45,000	60,000	80,000	Etc.

Table 4: Deferred publication thresholds and delays

The table below shows, for each permitted delay for publication and each class of shares in terms of average daily turnover (ADT), the minimum qualifying size of transaction that will qualify for that delay in respect of a share of that type.

		Class of shares in terms of average daily turnover (ADT)			
		ADT < EUR 100,000	EUR 100,000 ≤ ADT < EUR 1,000,000	EUR 1,000,000 ≤ ADT < EUR 50,000,000	ADT ≥ EUR 50,000,000
		Minimum qualifying size of transaction for permitted delay			
Permitted delay for publication	60 minutes	EUR 10,000	Greater of 5% of ADT and EUR 25,000	Lower of 10% of ADT and EUR 3,500,000	Lower of 10% of ADT and EUR 7,500,000
	180 minutes	EUR 25,000	Greater of 15% of ADT and EUR 75,000	Lower of 15% of ADT and EUR 5,000,000	Lower of 20% of ADT and EUR 15,000,000
	Until end of trading day (or roll-over to noon of next trading day if trade undertaken in final two hours of trading day)	EUR 45,000	Greater of 25% of ADT and EUR 100,000	Lower of 25% of ADT and EUR 10,000,000	Lower of 30% of ADT and EUR 30,000,000
	Until end of trading day next after trade	EUR 60,000	Greater of 50% of ADT and EUR 100,000	Greater of 50% of ADT and EUR 1,000,000	100% of ADT
	Until end of second trading day next after trade	EUR 80,000	100% of ADT	100% of ADT	250% of ADT
	Until end of third trading day next after trade		250% of ADT	250% of ADT	

[5959]

COMMISSION DIRECTIVE

of 10 August 2006

implementing Directive 2004/39/EC of the European Parliament and of the Council as regards organisational requirements and operating conditions for investment firms and defined terms for the purposes of that Directive

(2006/73/EC)

(Text with EEA relevance)

NOTES
Date of publication in OJ: OJ L241, 2.9.2006, p 26. Notes are as in the original OJ version
As of 1 February 2009, this Directive had not been amended.

THE COMMISSION OF THE EUROPEAN COMMUNITIES,
Having regard to the Treaty establishing the European Community,
Having regard to Directive 2004/39/EC of the European Parliament and of the Council of 21 April 2004 on markets in financial instruments amending Council Directives 85/611/EEC and 93/6/EEC and Directive 2000/12/EC of the European Parliament and of the Council and repealing Council Directive 93/22/EEC,[1] and in particular Article 4(2), Article 13(10), Article 18(3), Article 19(10), Article 21(6), Article 22(3) and Article 24(5) thereof,
Whereas:

(1) Directive 2004/39/EC establishes the framework for a regulatory regime for financial markets in the Community, governing, among other matters, operating conditions relating to the performance by investment firms of investment services and, where appropriate, ancillary services and investment activities; organisational requirements for investment firms performing such services and activities, and for regulated markets; reporting requirements in respect of transactions in financial instruments; and transparency requirements in respect of transactions in shares admitted to trading on a regulated market.

(2) The rules for the implementation of the regime governing organisational requirements for investment firms performing investment services and, where appropriate, ancillary services and investment activities on a professional basis, and for regulated markets, should be consistent with the aim of Directive 2004/39/EC. They should be designed to ensure a high level of integrity, competence and soundness among investment firms and entities that operate regulated markets or MTFs, and to be applied in a uniform manner.

(3) It is necessary to specify concrete organisational requirements and procedures for investment firms performing such services or activities. In particular, rigorous procedures should be provided for with regard to matters such as compliance, risk management, complaints handling, personal transactions, outsourcing and the identification, management and disclosure of conflicts of interest.

(4) The organisational requirements and conditions for authorisation for investment firms should be set out in the form of a set of rules that ensures the uniform application of the relevant provisions of Directive 2004/39/EC. This is necessary in order to ensure that investment firms have equal access on equivalent terms to all markets in the Community and to eliminate obstacles, linked to authorisation procedures, to cross-border activities in the field of investment services.

(5) The rules for the implementation of the regime governing operating conditions for the performance of investment and ancillary services and investment activities should reflect the aim underlying that regime. That is to say, they should be designed to ensure a high level of investor protection to be applied in a uniform manner through the introduction of clear standards and requirements governing the relationship between an investment firm and its client. On the other hand, as regards investor protection, and in particular the provision of investors with information or the seeking of information from investors, the retail or professional nature of the client or potential client concerned should be taken into account.

(6) The form of a Directive is necessary in order to enable the implementing provisions to be adjusted to the specificities of the particular market and legal system in each Member State.

(7) In order to ensure the uniform application of the various provisions of Directive 2004/39/EC, it is necessary to establish a harmonised set of organisational requirements and operating conditions for investment firms. Consequently, Member States and competent authorities should not add supplementary binding rules when transposing and applying the rules specified in this Directive, save where this Directive makes express provision to this effect.

(8) However, in exceptional circumstances, it should be possible for Member States to impose requirements on investment firms additional to those laid down in the implementing rules. However, such intervention should be restricted to those cases where specific risks to investor protection or to market integrity including those related to the stability of the financial system have not been adequately addressed by the Community legislation, and it should be strictly proportionate.

(9) Any additional requirements retained or imposed by Member States in conformity with this Directive must not restrict or otherwise affect the rights of investment firms under Articles 31 and 32 of Directive 2004/39/EC.

(10) The specific risks addressed by any additional requirements retained by Member States at the date of application of this Directive should be of particular importance to the market structure of the State in question, including the behaviour of firms and consumers in that market. The assessment of those specific risks should be made in the context of the regulatory regime put in place by Directive 2004/39/EC and its detailed implementing rules. Any decision to retain additional requirements should be made with proper regard to the objectives of that Directive to remove barriers to the cross-border provision of investment service by harmonising the initial authorisation and operating requirements for investment firms.

(11) Investment firms vary widely in their size, their structure and the nature of their business. A regulatory regime should be adapted to that diversity while imposing certain fundamental regulatory requirements which are appropriate for all firms. Regulated entities should comply with their high level obligations and design and adopt measures that are best suited to their particular nature and circumstances.

(12) However, a regulatory regime which entails too much uncertainty for investment firms may reduce efficiency. Competent authorities are expected to issue interpretative guidance on provisions on this Directive, with a view in particular to clarifying the practical application of the requirements of this Directive to particular kinds of firms and circumstances. Non-binding guidance of this kind might, among other things, clarify how the provisions of this Directive and Directive 2004/39/EC apply in the light of market developments. To ensure a uniform application of this Directive and Directive 2004/39/EC, the Commission may issue guidance by way of interpretative

communications or other means. Furthermore, the Committee of European Securities Regulators may issue guidance in order to secure convergent application of this Directive and Directive 2004/39/EC by competent authorities.

(13) The organisational requirements established under Directive 2004/39/EC are without prejudice to systems established by national law for the registration of individuals working within investment firms.

(14) For the purposes of the provisions of this Directive requiring an investment firm to establish, implement and maintain an adequate risk management policy, the risks relating to the firm's activities, processes and systems should include the risks associated with the outsourcing of critical or important functions or of investment services or activities. Such risks should include those associated with the firm's relationship with the service provider, and the potential risks posed where the outsourced activities of multiple investment firms or other regulated entities are concentrated within a limited number of service providers.

(15) The fact that risk management and compliance functions are performed by the same person does not necessarily jeopardise the independent functioning of each function. The conditions that persons involved in the compliance function should not also be involved in the performance of the functions that they monitor, and that the method of determining the remuneration of such persons should not be likely to compromise their objectivity, may not be proportionate in the case of small investment firms. However, they would only be disproportionate for larger firms in exceptional circumstances.

(16) A number of the provisions of Directive 2004/39/EC require investment firms to collect and maintain information relating to clients and services provided to clients. Where those requirements involve the collection and processing of personal data, firms should ensure that they comply with national measures implementing Directive 95/46/EC of the European Parliament and of the Council of 24 October 1995[2] on the protection of individuals with regard to the processing of personal data and on the free movement of such data.

(17) Where successive personal transactions are carried out on behalf of a person in accordance with prior instructions given by that person, the obligations under the provisions of this Directive relating to personal transactions should not apply separately to each such successive transaction if those instructions remain in force and unchanged. Similarly, those obligations should not apply to the termination or withdrawal of such instructions, provided that any financial instruments which had previously been acquired pursuant to the instructions are not disposed of at the same time as the instructions terminate or are withdrawn. However, those obligations should apply in relation to a personal transaction, or the commencement of successive personal transactions, carried out on behalf of the same person if those instructions are changed or if new instructions are issued.

(18) Competent authorities should not make the authorisation to provide investment services or activities subject to a general prohibition on the outsourcing of one or more critical or important functions or investment services or activities. Investment firms should be allowed to outsource such activities if the outsourcing arrangements established by the firm comply with certain conditions.

(19) For the purposes of the provisions of this Directive setting out conditions for outsourcing critical or important operational functions or investment services or activities, an outsourcing that would involve the delegation of functions to the extent that the firm becomes a letter box entity should be considered to undermine the conditions with which the investment firm must comply in order to be and remain authorised in accordance with Article 5 of Directive 2004/39/EC.

(20) The outsourcing of investment services or activities or critical and important functions is capable of constituting a material change of the conditions for the authorisation of the investment firm, as referred to in Article 16(2) of Directive 2004/39/EC. If such outsourcing arrangements are to be put in place after the investment firm has obtained an authorisation according to the provisions included in Chapter I of Title II of Directive 2004/39/EC, those arrangements should be notified to the competent authority where required by Article 16(2) of Directive 2004/39/EC.

(21) Investment firms are required by this Directive to give the responsible competent authority prior notification of any arrangement for the outsourcing of the management of retail client portfolios that it proposes to enter into with a service provider located in a third country, where certain specified conditions are not met. However, competent authorities are not expected to authorise or otherwise approve any such arrangement or its terms. The purpose of the notification, rather, is to ensure that the competent authority has the opportunity to intervene in appropriate cases. It is the responsibility of the investment firm to negotiate the terms of any outsourcing arrangement, and to ensure that those terms are consistent with the obligations of the firm under this Directive and Directive 2004/39/EC, without the formal intervention of the competent authority.

(22) For the purposes of regulatory transparency, and in order to ensure an appropriate level of certainty for investment firms, this Directive requires each competent authority to publish a statement of its policy in relation to the outsourcing of retail portfolio management to service providers located in third countries. That statement must set out examples of cases where the competent authority is unlikely to object to such outsourcing, and must include an explanation of why outsourcing in such cases is unlikely to impair the ability of the firm to comply with the general conditions for outsourcing under this Directive. In providing that explanation, a competent authority should always indicate the reasons why outsourcing in the cases in question would not impede the

effectiveness of its access to all the information relating to the outsourced service that is necessary for the authority to carry out its regulatory functions in respect of the investment firm.

(23) Where an investment firm deposits funds it holds on behalf of a client with a qualifying money market fund, the units in that money market fund should be held in accordance with the requirements for holding financial instruments belonging to clients.

(24) The circumstances which should be treated as giving rise to a conflict of interest should cover cases where there is a conflict between the interests of the firm or certain persons connected to the firm or the firm's group and the duty the firm owes to a client; or between the differing interests of two or more of its clients, to whom the firm owes in each case a duty. It is not enough that the firm may gain a benefit if there is not also a possible disadvantage to a client, or that one client to whom the firm owes a duty may make a gain or avoid a loss without there being a concomitant possible loss to another such client.

(25) Conflicts of interest should be regulated only where an investment service or ancillary service is provided by an investment firm. The status of the client to whom the service is provided – as either retail, professional or eligible counterparty – is irrelevant for this purpose.

(26) In complying with its obligation to draw up a conflict of interest policy under Directive 2004/39/EC which identifies circumstances which constitute or may give rise to a conflict of interest, the investment firm should pay special attention to the activities of investment research and advice, proprietary trading, portfolio management and corporate finance business, including underwriting or selling in an offering of securities and advising on mergers and acquisitions. In particular, such special attention is appropriate where the firm or a person directly or indirectly linked by control to the firm performs a combination of two or more of those activities.

(27) Investment firms should aim to identify and manage the conflicts of interest arising in relation to their various business lines and their group's activities under a comprehensive conflicts of interest policy. In particular, the disclosure of conflicts of interest by an investment firm should not exempt it from the obligation to maintain and operate the effective organisational and administrative arrangements required under Article 13(3) of Directive 2004/39/EC. While disclosure of specific conflicts of interest is required by Article 18(2) of Directive 2004/39/EC, an over-reliance on disclosure without adequate consideration as to how conflicts may appropriately be managed is not permitted.

(28) Investment research should be a sub-category of the type of information defined as a recommendation in Commission Directive 2003/125/EC of 22 December 2003 implementing Directive 2003/6/EC of the European Parliament and of the Council as regards the fair presentation of investment recommendations and the disclosure of conflicts of interest,[3] but it applies to financial instruments as defined in Directive 2004/39/EC. Recommendations, of the type so defined, which do not constitute investment research as defined in this Directive are nevertheless subject to the provisions of Directive 2003/125/EC as to the fair presentation of investment recommendations and the disclosure of conflicts of interest.

(29) The measures and arrangements adopted by an investment firm to manage the conflicts of interests that might arise from the production and dissemination of material that is presented as investment research should be appropriate to protect the objectivity and independence of financial analysts and of the investment research they produce. Those measures and arrangements should ensure that financial analysts enjoy an adequate degree of independence from the interests of persons whose responsibilities or business interests may reasonably be considered to conflict with the interests of the persons to whom the investment research is disseminated.

(30) Persons whose responsibilities or business interests may reasonably be considered to conflict with the interests of the persons to whom investment research is disseminated should include corporate finance personnel and persons involved in sales and trading on behalf of clients or the firm.

(31) Exceptional circumstances in which financial analysts and other persons connected with the investment firm who are involved in the production of investment research may, with prior written approval, undertake personal transactions in instruments to which the research relates should include those circumstances where, for personal reasons relating to financial hardship, the financial analyst or other person is required to liquidate a position.

(32) Small gifts or minor hospitality below a level specified in the firm's conflicts of interest policy and mentioned in the summary description of that policy that is made available to clients should not be considered as inducements for the purposes of the provisions relating to investment research.

(33) The concept of dissemination of investment research to clients or the public should not include dissemination exclusively to persons within the group of the investment firm.

(34) Current recommendations should be considered to be those recommendations contained in investment research which have not been withdrawn and which have not lapsed.

(35) The same requirements should apply to the substantial alteration of investment research produced by a third party as apply to the production of research.

(36) Financial analysts should not become involved in activities other than the preparation of investment research where such involvement is inconsistent with the maintenance of that person's objectivity. The following involvements should ordinarily be considered as inconsistent with the

maintenance of that person's objectivity: participating in investment banking activities such as corporate finance business and underwriting, participating in "pitches" for new business or "road shows" for new issues of financial instruments; or being otherwise involved in the preparation of issuer marketing.

(37) Without prejudice to the provisions of this Directive relating to the production or dissemination of investment research, it is recommended that producers of investment research that are not investment firms should consider adopting internal policies and procedures designed to ensure that they also comply with the principles set out in this Directive as to the protection of the independence and objectivity of that research.

(38) Requirements imposed by this Directive, including those relating to personal transactions, to dealing with knowledge of investment research and to the production or dissemination of investment research, apply without prejudice to other requirements of Directive 2004/39/EC and Directive 2003/6/EC of the European parliament and of the Council of 28 January 2003 on insider dealing and market manipulation (market abuse)[4] and their respective implementing measures.

(39) For the purposes of the provisions of this Directive concerning inducements, the receipt by an investment firm of a commission in connection with investment advice or general recommendations, in circumstances where the advice or recommendations are not biased as a result of the receipt of commission, should be considered as designed to enhance the quality of the investment advice to the client.

(40) This Directive permits investment firms to give or receive certain inducements only subject to specific conditions, and provided they are disclosed to the client, or are given to or by the client or a person on behalf of the client.

(41) This Directive requires investment firms that provide investment services other than investment advice to new retail clients to enter into a written basic agreement with the client, setting out the essential rights and obligations of the firm and the client. However, it imposes no other obligations as to the form, content and performance of contracts for the provisions of investment or ancillary services.

(42) This Directive sets out requirements for marketing communications only with respect to the obligation in Article 19(2) of Directive 2004/39/EC that information addressed to clients, including marketing communications, should be fair, clear and not misleading.

(43) Nothing in this Directive requires competent authorities to approve the content and form of marketing communications. However, neither does it prevent them from doing so, insofar as any such pre-approval is based only on compliance with the obligation in Directive 2004/39/EC that information to clients, including marketing communications, should be fair, clear and not misleading.

(44) Appropriate and proportionate information requirements should be established which take account of the status of a client as either retail or professional. An objective of Directive 2004/39/EC is to ensure a proportionate balance between investor protection and the disclosure obligations which apply to investment firms. To this end, it is appropriate that less stringent specific information requirements be included in this Directive with respect to professional clients than apply to retail clients. Professional clients should, subject to limited exceptions, be able to identify for themselves the information that is necessary for them to make an informed decision, and to ask the investment firm to provide that information. Where such information requests are reasonable and proportionate investment firms should provide additional information.

(45) Investment firms should provide clients or potential clients with adequate information on the nature of financial instruments and the risks associated with investing in them so that their clients can take each investment decision on a properly informed basis. The level of detail of this information may vary according to the client's categorisation as either a retail client or a professional client and the nature and risk profile of the financial instruments that are being offered, but should never be so general as to omit any essential elements. It is possible that for some financial instruments only the information referring to the type of an instrument will be sufficient whereas for some others the information will need to be product-specific.

(46) The conditions with which information addressed by investment firms to clients and potential clients must comply in order to be fair, clear and not misleading should apply to communications intended for retail clients in a way that is appropriate and proportionate, taking into account, for example, the means of communication, and the information that the communication is intended to convey to the clients or potential clients. In particular, it would not be appropriate to apply such conditions to marketing communications which consist only of one or more of the following: the name of the firm, a logo or other image associated with the firm, a contact point, a reference to the types of investment services provided by the firm, or to its fees or commissions.

(47) For the purposes of Directive 2004/39/EC and of this Directive, information should be considered to be misleading if it has a tendency to mislead the person or persons to whom it is addressed or by whom it is likely to be received, whether or not the person who provides the information considers or intends it to be misleading.

(48) In determining what constitutes the provision of information in good time before a time specified in this Directive, an investment firm should take into account, having regard to the urgency of the situation and the time necessary for the client to absorb and react to the specific information

provided, the client's need for sufficient time to read and understand it before taking an investment decision. A client is likely to require less time to review information about a simple or standardised product or service, or a product or service of a kind he has purchased previously, than he would require for a more complex or unfamiliar product or service.

(49) Nothing in this Directive obliges investment firms to provide all required information about the investment firm, financial instruments, costs and associated charges, or concerning the safeguarding of client financial instruments or client funds immediately and at the same time, provided that they comply with the general obligation to provide the relevant information in good time before the time specified in this Directive. Provided that the information is communicated to the client in good time before the provision of the service, nothing in this Directive obliges firms to provide it either separately, as part of a marketing communication, or by incorporating the information in a client agreement.

(50) In cases where an investment firm is required to provide information to a client before the provision of a service, each transaction in respect of the same type of financial instrument should not be considered as the provision of a new or different service.

(51) In cases where an investment firm providing portfolio management services is required to provide to retail clients or potential retail clients information on the types of financial instruments that may be included in the client portfolio and the types of transactions that may be carried out in such instruments, such information should state separately whether the investment firm will be mandated to invest in financial instruments not admitted to trading on a regulated market, in derivatives, or in illiquid or highly volatile instruments; or to undertake short sales, purchases with borrowed funds, securities financing transactions, or any transactions involving margin payments, deposit of collateral or foreign exchange risk.

(52) The provision by an investment firm to a client of a copy of a prospectus that has been drawn up and published in accordance with Directive 2003/71/EC of the European Parliament and of the Council of 4 November 2003 on the prospectus to be published when securities are offered to the public or admitted to trading[5] should not be treated as the provision by the firm of information to a client for the purposes of the operating conditions under Directive 2004/39/EC which relate to the quality and contents of such information, if the firm is not responsible under that directive for the information given in the prospectus.

(53) The information which an investment firm is required to give to a retail client concerning costs and associated charges includes information about the arrangements for payment or performance of the agreement for the provision of investment services and any other agreement relating to a financial instrument that is being offered. For this purpose, arrangements for payment will generally be relevant where a financial instrument contract is terminated by cash settlement. Arrangements for performance will generally be relevant where, upon termination, a financial instrument requires the delivery of shares, bonds, a warrant, bullion or another instrument or commodity.

(54) As regards collective investment undertakings covered by Council Directive 85/611/EEC of 20 December 1985 on the coordination of laws, regulations and administrative provisions relating to undertakings for collective investment in transferable securities (UCITS),[6] it is not the purpose of this Directive to regulate the content of the simplified prospectus as defined by Article 28 of Directive 85/611/EEC. No information should be added to the simplified prospectus as a result of the implementation of this Directive.

(55) The simplified prospectus provides, notably, sufficient information in relation to the costs and associated charges in respect to the UCITS itself. However, investment firms distributing units in UCITS should additionally inform their clients about all the other costs and associated charges related to their provision of investment services in relation to units in UCITS.

(56) It is necessary to make different provision for the application of the suitability test in Article 19(4) of Directive 2004/39/EC and the appropriateness test in Article 19(5) of that Directive. These tests have different scope with regards to the investment services to which they relate, and have different functions and characteristics.

(57) For the purposes of Article 19(4) of Directive 2004/39/EC, a transaction may be unsuitable for the client or potential client because of the risks of the financial instruments involved, the type of transaction, the characteristics of the order or the frequency of the trading. A series of transactions that are each suitable when viewed in isolation may be unsuitable if the recommendation or the decisions to trade are made with a frequency that is not in the best interests of the client. In the case of portfolio management, a transaction might also be unsuitable if it would result in an unsuitable portfolio.

(58) In accordance with Article 19(4) of Directive 2004/39/EC, a firm is required to assess the suitability of investment services and financial instruments to a client only when it is providing investment advice or portfolio management to that client. In the case of other investment services, the firm is required by Article 19(5) of that Directive to assess the appropriateness of an investment service or product for a client, and then only if the product is not offered on an execution-only basis under Article 19(6) of that Directive (which applies to non-complex products).

(59) For the purposes of the provisions of this Directive requiring investment firms to assess the appropriateness of investment services or products offered or demanded, a client who has engaged

in a course of dealings involving a specific type of product or service beginning before the date of application of Directive 2004/39/EC should be presumed to have the necessary experience and knowledge in order to understand the risks involved in relation to that product or investment service. Where a client engages in a course of dealings of that kind through the services of an investment firm, beginning after the date of application of that Directive, the firm is not required to make a new assessment on the occasion of each separate transaction. It complies with its duty under Article 19(5) of that Directive provided that it makes the necessary assessment of appropriateness before beginning that service.

(60)   A recommendation or request made, or advice given, by a portfolio manager to a client to the effect that the client should give or alter a mandate to the portfolio manager that defines the limits of the portfolio manager's discretion should be considered a recommendation within the meaning of Article 19(4) of Directive 2004/39/EC.

(61)   For the purposes of determining whether a unit in a collective investment undertaking which does not comply with the requirements of Directive 85/611/EC, that has been authorised for marketing to the public, should be considered as non-complex, the circumstances in which valuation systems will be independent of the issuer should include where they are overseen by a depositary that is regulated as a provider of depositary services in a Member State.

(62)   Nothing in this Directive requires competent authorities to approve the content of the basic agreement between an investment firm and its retail clients. However, neither does it prevent them from doing so, insofar as any such approval is based only on the firm's compliance with its obligations under Directive 2004/39/EC to act honestly, fairly and professionally in accordance with the best interests of its clients, and to establish a record that sets out the rights and obligations of investment firms and their clients, and the other terms on which firms will provide services to their clients.

(63)   The records an investment firm is required to keep should be adapted to the type of business and the range of investment services and activities performed, provided that the record-keeping obligations set out in Directive 2004/39/EC and this Directive are fulfilled. For the purposes of the reporting obligations in respect of portfolio management, a contingent liability transaction is one that involves any actual or potential liability for the client that exceeds the cost of acquiring the instrument.

(64)   For the purposes of the provisions on reporting to clients, a reference to the type of the order should be understood as referring to its status as a limit order, market order, or other specific type of order.

(65)   For the purposes of the provisions on reporting to clients, a reference to the nature of the order should be understood as referring to orders to subscribe for securities, or to exercise an option, or similar client order.

(66)   When establishing its execution policy in accordance with Article 21(2) of Directive 2004/39/EC, an investment firm should determine the relative importance of the factors mentioned in Article 21(1) of that Directive, or at least establish the process by which it determines the relative importance of these factors, so that it can deliver the best possible result to its clients. In order to give effect to that policy, an investment firm should select the execution venues that enable it to obtain on a consistent basis the best possible result for the execution of client orders. An investment firm should apply its execution policy to each client order that it executes with a view to obtaining the best possible result for the client in accordance with that policy. The obligation under Directive 2004/39/EC to take all reasonable steps to obtain the best possible result for the client should not be treated as requiring an investment firm to include in its execution policy all available execution venues.

(67)   For the purposes of ensuring that an investment firm obtains the best possible result for the client when executing a retail client order in the absence of specific client instructions, the firm should take into consideration all factors that will allow it to deliver the best possible result in terms of the total consideration, representing the price of the financial instrument and the costs related to execution. Speed, likelihood of execution and settlement, the size and nature of the order, market impact and any other implicit transaction costs may be given precedence over the immediate price and cost consideration only insofar as they are instrumental in delivering the best possible result in terms of the total consideration to the retail client.

(68)   When an investment firm executes an order following specific instructions from the client, it should be treated as having satisfied its best execution obligations only in respect of the part or aspect of the order to which the client instructions relate. The fact that the client has given specific instructions which cover one part or aspect of the order should not be treated as releasing the investment firm from its best execution obligations in respect of any other parts or aspects of the client order that are not covered by such instructions. An investment firm should not induce a client to instruct it to execute an order in a particular way, by expressly indicating or implicitly suggesting the content of the instruction to the client, when the firm ought reasonably to know that an instruction to that effect is likely to prevent it from obtaining the best possible result for that client. However, this should not prevent a firm inviting a client to choose between two or more specified trading venues, provided that those venues are consistent with the execution policy of the firm.

(69) Dealing on own account with clients by an investment firm should be considered as the execution of client orders, and therefore subject to the requirements under Directive 2004/39/EC and this Directive and, in particular, those obligations in relation to best execution. However, if an investment firm provides a quote to a client and that quote would meet the investment firm's obligations under Article 21(1) of Directive 2004/39/EC if the firm executed that quote at the time the quote was provided, then the firm will meet those same obligations if it executes its quote after the client accepts it, provided that, taking into account the changing market conditions and the time elapsed between the offer and acceptance of the quote, the quote is not manifestly out of date.

(70) The obligation to deliver the best possible result when executing client orders applies in relation to all types of financial instruments. However, given the differences in market structures or the structure of financial instruments, it may be difficult to identify and apply a uniform standard of and procedure for best execution that would be valid and effective for all classes of instrument. Best execution obligations should therefore be applied in a manner that takes into account the different circumstances associated with the execution of orders related to particular types of financial instruments. For example, transactions involving a customised OTC financial instrument that involve a unique contractual relationship tailored to the circumstances of the client and the investment firm may not be comparable for best execution purposes with transactions involving shares traded on centralised execution venues.

(71) For the purposes of determining best execution when executing retail client orders, the costs related to execution should include an investment firm's own commissions or fees charged to the client for limited purposes, in cases where more than one venue listed in the firm's execution policy is capable of executing a particular order. In such cases, the firm's own commissions and costs for executing the order on each of the eligible execution venues should be taken into account in order to assess and compare the results for the client that would be achieved by executing the order on each such venue. However, it is not intended to require a firm to compare the results that would be achieved for its client on the basis of its own execution policy and its own commissions and fees, with results that might be achieved for the same client by any other investment firm on the basis of a different execution policy or a different structure of commissions or fees. Nor is it intended to require a firm to compare the differences in its own commissions which are attributable to differences in the nature of the services that the firm provides to clients.

(72) The provisions of this Directive that provide that costs of execution should include an investment firm's own commissions or fees charged to the client for the provision of an investment service should not apply for the purpose of determining what execution venues must be included in the firm's execution policy for the purposes of Article 21(3) of Directive 2004/39/EC.

(73) It should be considered that an investment firm structures or charges its commissions in a way which discriminates unfairly between execution venues if it charges a different commission or spread to clients for execution on different execution venues and that difference does not reflect actual differences in the cost to the firm of executing on those venues.

(74) The provisions of this Directive as to execution policy are without prejudice to the general obligation of an investment firm under Article 21(4) of Directive 2004/39/EC to monitor the effectiveness of its order execution arrangements and policy and assess the venues in its execution policy on a regular basis.

(75) This Directive is not intended to require a duplication of effort as to best execution between an investment firm which provides the service of reception and transmission of order or portfolio management and any investment firm to which that investment firm transmits its orders for execution.

(76) The best execution obligation under Directive 2004/39/EC requires investment firms to take all reasonable steps to obtain the best possible result for their clients. The quality of execution, which includes aspects such as the speed and likelihood of execution (fill rate) and the availability and incidence of price improvement, is an important factor in the delivery of best execution. Availability, comparability and consolidation of data related to execution quality provided by the various execution venues is crucial in enabling investment firms and investors to identify those execution venues that deliver the highest quality of execution for their clients. This Directive does not mandate the publication by execution venues of their execution quality data, as execution venues and data providers should be permitted to develop solutions concerning the provision of execution quality data. The Commission should submit a report by 1 November 2008 on the market-led developments in this area with a view to assessing availability, comparability and consolidation at a European level of information concerning execution quality.

(77) For the purposes of the provisions of this Directive concerning client order handling, the reallocation of transactions should be considered as detrimental to a client if, as an effect of that reallocation, unfair precedence is given to the investment firm or to any particular client.

(78) Without prejudice to Directive 2003/6/EC, for the purposes of the provisions of this Directive concerning client order handling, client orders should not be treated as otherwise comparable if they are received by different media and it would not be practicable for them to be treated sequentially. For the further purposes of those provisions, any use by an investment firm of information relating to a pending client order in order to deal on own account in the financial instruments to which the client order relates, or in related financial instruments, should be

considered a misuse of that information. However, the mere fact that market makers or bodies authorised to act as counterparties confine themselves to pursuing their legitimate business of buying and selling financial instruments, or that persons authorised to execute orders on behalf of third parties confine themselves to carrying out an order dutifully, should not in itself be deemed to constitute a misuse of information.

(79)   Advice about financial instruments given in a newspaper, journal, magazine or any other publication addressed to the general public (including by means of the internet), or in any television or radio broadcast, should not be considered as a personal recommendation for the purposes of the definition of "investment advice" in Directive 2004/39/EC.

(80)   This Directive respects the fundamental rights and observes the principles recognised in particular by the Charter of Fundamental Rights of the European Union and in particular by Article 11 thereof and Article 10 of the European Convention on Human Rights. In this regard, this Directive does not in any way prevent Member States from applying their constitutional rules relating to freedom of the press and freedom of expression in the media.

(81)   Generic advice about a type of financial instrument is not investment advice for the purposes of Directive 2004/39/EC, because this Directive specifies that, for the purposes of Directive 2004/39/EC, investment advice is restricted to advice on particular financial instruments. However, if an investment firm provides generic advice to a client about a type of financial instrument which it presents as suitable for, or based on a consideration of the circumstances of, that client, and that advice is not in fact suitable for the client, or is not based on a consideration of his circumstances, depending on the circumstances of the particular case, the firm is likely to be acting in contravention of Article 19(1) or (2) of Directive 2004/39/EC. In particular, a firm which gives a client such advice would be likely to contravene the requirement of Article 19(1) to act honestly, fairly and professionally in accordance with the best interests of its clients. Similarly or alternatively, such advice would be likely to contravene the requirement of Article 19(2) that information addressed by a firm to a client should be fair, clear and not misleading.

(82)   Acts carried out by an investment firm that are preparatory to the provision of an investment service or carrying out an investment activity should be considered as an integral part of that service or activity. This would include, for example, the provision of generic advice by an investment firm to clients or potential clients prior to or in the course of the provision of investment advice or any other investment service or activity.

(83)   The provision of a general recommendation (that is, one which is intended for distribution channels or the public) about a transaction in a financial instrument or a type of financial instrument constitutes the provision of an ancillary service within Section B(5) of Annex I of Directive 2004/39/EC, and consequently Directive 2004/39/EC and its protections apply to the provision of that recommendation.

(84)   The Committee of European Securities Regulators, established by Commission Decision 2001/527/EC[7] has been consulted for technical advice.

(85)   The measures provided for in this Directive are in accordance with the opinion of the European Securities Committee,

[5960]

NOTES

[1]   OJ L145, 30.4.2004, p 1. Directive as amended by Directive 2006/31/EC (OJ L114, 27.4.2006, p 60).
[2]   OJ L281, 23.11.1995, p 31. Directive as amended by Regulation (EC) No 1882/2003 (OJ L284, 31.10.2003, p 1).
[3]   OJ L339, 24.12.2003, p 73.
[4]   OJ L96, 12.4.2003, p 16.
[5]   OJ L345, 31.12.2003, p 64.
[6]   OJ L375, 31.12.1985, p 3. Directive as last amended by Directive 2005/1/EC of the European Parliament and of the Council (OJ L79, 24.3.2005, p 9).
[7]   OJ L191, 13.7.2001, p 43.

HAS ADOPTED THIS DIRECTIVE:

CHAPTER I
SCOPE AND DEFINITIONS

Article 1
Subject-matter and scope

1.   This Directive lays down the detailed rules for the implementation of Article 4(1)(4) and 4(2), Article 13(2) to (8), Article 18, Article 19(1) to (6), Article 19(8), and Articles 21, 22 and 24 of Directive 2004/39/EC.

2. Chapter II and Sections 1 to 4, Article 45 and Sections 6 and 8 of Chapter III and, to the extent they relate to those provisions, Chapter I and Section 9 of Chapter III and Chapter IV of this Directive shall apply to management companies in accordance with Article 5(4) of Directive 85/611/EEC.

[5961]

Article 2
Definitions

For the purposes of this Directive, the following definitions shall apply:

(1) "distribution channels" means distribution channels within the meaning of Article 1(7) of Commission Directive 2003/125/EC;

(2) "durable medium" means any instrument which enables a client to store information addressed personally to that client in a way accessible for future reference for a period of time adequate for the purposes of the information and which allows the unchanged reproduction of the information stored;

(3) "relevant person" in relation to an investment firm, means any of the following:

  (a) a director, partner or equivalent, manager or tied agent of the firm;

  (b) a director, partner or equivalent, or manager of any tied agent of the firm;

  (c) an employee of the firm or of a tied agent of the firm, as well as any other natural person whose services are placed at the disposal and under the control of the firm or a tied agent of the firm and who is involved in the provision by the firm of investment services and activities;

  (d) a natural person who is directly involved in the provision of services to the investment firm or to its tied agent under an outsourcing arrangement for the purpose of the provision by the firm of investment services and activities;

(4) "financial analyst" means a relevant person who produces the substance of investment research;

(5) "group", in relation to an investment firm, means the group of which that firm forms a part, consisting of a parent undertaking, its subsidiaries and the entities in which the parent undertaking or its subsidiaries hold a participation, as well as undertakings linked to each other by a relationship within the meaning of Article 12(1) of Council Directive 83/349/EEC on consolidated accounts;[1]

(6) "outsourcing" means an arrangement of any form between an investment firm and a service provider by which that service provider performs a process, a service or an activity which would otherwise be undertaken by the investment firm itself;

(7) "person with whom a relevant person has a family relationship" means any of the following:

  (a) the spouse of the relevant person or any partner of that person considered by national law as equivalent to a spouse;

  (b) a dependent child or stepchild of the relevant person;

  (c) any other relative of the relevant person who has shared the same household as that person for at least one year on the date of the personal transaction concerned;

(8) "securities financing transaction" has the meaning given in Commission Regulation (EC) No 1287/2006;[2]

(9) "senior management" means the person or persons who effectively direct the business of the investment firm as referred to in Article 9(1) of Directive 2004/39/EC.

[5962]

NOTES

[1] OJ L193, 18.7.1983, p 1.

[2] See page 1 of this Official Journal.

Article 3
Conditions applying to the provision of information

1. Where, for the purposes of this Directive, information is required to be provided in a durable medium, Member States shall permit investment firms to provide that information in a durable medium other than on paper only if:

  (a) the provision of that information in that medium is appropriate to the context in which the business between the firm and the client is, or is to be, carried on; and

  (b) the person to whom the information is to be provided, when offered the choice between information on paper or in that other durable medium, specifically chooses the provision of the information in that other medium.

2. Where, pursuant to Article 29, 30, 31, 32, 33 or 46(2) of this Directive, an investment firm provides information to a client by means of a website and that information is not addressed personally to the client, Member States shall ensure that the following conditions are satisfied:

(a)   the provision of that information in that medium is appropriate to the context in which the business between the firm and the client is, or is to be, carried on;

(b)   the client must specifically consent to the provision of that information in that form;

(c)   the client must be notified electronically of the address of the website, and the place on the website where the information may be accessed;

(d)   the information must be up to date;

(e)   the information must be accessible continuously by means of that website for such period of time as the client may reasonably need to inspect it.

3.   For the purposes of this Article, the provision of information by means of electronic communications shall be treated as appropriate to the context in which the business between the firm and the client is, or is to be, carried on if there is evidence that the client has regular access to the internet. The provision by the client of an e-mail address for the purposes of the carrying on of that business shall be treated as such evidence.

[5963]

Article 4
Additional requirements on investment firms in certain cases

1.   Member States may retain or impose requirements additional to those in this Directive only in those exceptional cases where such requirements are objectively justified and proportionate so as to address specific risks to investor protection or to market integrity that are not adequately addressed by this Directive, and provided that one of the following conditions is met:

(a)   the specific risks addressed by the requirements are of particular importance in the circumstances of the market structure of that Member State;

(b)   the requirement addresses risks or issues that emerge or become evident after the date of application of this Directive and that are not otherwise regulated by or under Community measures.

2.   Any requirements imposed under paragraph 1 shall not restrict or otherwise affect the rights of investment firms under Articles 31 and 32 of Directive 2004/39/EC.

3.   Member States shall notify to the Commission:

(a)   any requirement which it intends to retain in accordance with paragraph 1 before the date of transposition of this Directive; and

(b)   any requirement which it intends to impose in accordance with paragraph 1 at least one month before the date appointed for that requirement to come into force.

In each case, the notification shall include a justification for that requirement.

The Commission shall communicate to Member States and make public on its website the notifications it receives in accordance with this paragraph.

4.   By 31 December 2009 the Commission shall report to the European Parliament and the Council on the application of this Article.

[5964]

CHAPTER II
ORGANISATIONAL REQUIREMENTS

SECTION 1
ORGANISATION

Article 5
General organisational requirements
(Article 13(2) to (8) of Directive 2004/39/EC)

1.   Member States shall require investment firms to comply with the following requirements:

(a)   to establish, implement and maintain decision-making procedures and an organisational structure which clearly and in documented manner specifies reporting lines and allocates functions and responsibilities;

(b)   to ensure that their relevant persons are aware of the procedures which must be followed for the proper discharge of their responsibilities;

(c)   to establish, implement and maintain adequate internal control mechanisms designed to secure compliance with decisions and procedures at all levels of the investment firm;

(d)   to employ personnel with the skills, knowledge and expertise necessary for the discharge of the responsibilities allocated to them;

(e)   to establish, implement and maintain effective internal reporting and communication of information at all relevant levels of the investment firm;

(f)   to maintain adequate and orderly records of their business and internal organisation;

(g)   to ensure that the performance of multiple functions by their relevant persons does not and is not likely to prevent those persons from discharging any particular function soundly, honestly, and professionally.

Member States shall ensure that, for those purposes, investment firms take into account the nature, scale and complexity of the business of the firm, and the nature and range of investment services and activities undertaken in the course of that business.

2. Member States shall require investment firms to establish, implement and maintain systems and procedures that are adequate to safeguard the security, integrity and confidentiality of information, taking into account the nature of the information in question.

3. Member States shall require investment firms to establish, implement and maintain an adequate business continuity policy aimed at ensuring, in the case of an interruption to their systems and procedures, the preservation of essential data and functions, and the maintenance of investment services and activities, or, where that is not possible, the timely recovery of such data and functions and the timely resumption of their investment services and activities.

4. Member States shall require investment firms to establish, implement and maintain accounting policies and procedures that enable them, at the request of the competent authority, to deliver in a timely manner to the competent authority financial reports which reflect a true and fair view of their financial position and which comply with all applicable accounting standards and rules.

5. Member States shall require investment firms to monitor and, on a regular basis, to evaluate the adequacy and effectiveness of their systems, internal control mechanisms and arrangements established in accordance with paragraphs 1 to 4, and to take appropriate measures to address any deficiencies.

[5965]

Article 6
Compliance
(*Article 13(2) of Directive 2004/39/EC*)

1. Member States shall ensure that investment firms establish, implement and maintain adequate policies and procedures designed to detect any risk of failure by the firm to comply with its obligations under Directive 2004/39/EC, as well as the associated risks, and put in place adequate measures and procedures designed to minimise such risk and to enable the competent authorities to exercise their powers effectively under that Directive.

Member States shall ensure that, for those purposes, investment firms take into account the nature, scale and complexity of the business of the firm, and the nature and range of investment services and activities undertaken in the course of that business.

2. Member States shall require investment firms to establish and maintain a permanent and effective compliance function which operates independently and which has the following responsibilities:

    (a)   to monitor and, on a regular basis, to assess the adequacy and effectiveness of the measures and procedures put in place in accordance with the first subparagraph of paragraph 1, and the actions taken to address any deficiencies in the firm's compliance with its obligations;

    (b)   to advise and assist the relevant persons responsible for carrying out investment services and activities to comply with the firm's obligations under Directive 2004/39/EC.

3. In order to enable the compliance function to discharge its responsibilities properly and independently, Member States shall require investment firms to ensure that the following conditions are satisfied:

    (a)   the compliance function must have the necessary authority, resources, expertise and access to all relevant information;

    (b)   a compliance officer must be appointed and must be responsible for the compliance function and for any reporting as to compliance required by Article 9(2);

    (c)   the relevant persons involved in the compliance function must not be involved in the performance of services or activities they monitor;

    (d)   the method of determining the remuneration of the relevant persons involved in the compliance function must not compromise their objectivity and must not be likely to do so.

However, an investment firm shall not be required to comply with point (c) or point (d) if it is able to demonstrate that in view of the nature, scale and complexity of its business, and the nature and range of investment services and activities, the requirement under that point is not proportionate and that its compliance function continues to be effective.

[5966]

Article 7
Risk management
(*second subparagraph of Article 13(5) of Directive 2004/39/EC*)

1. Member States shall require investment firms to take the following actions:

    (a)   to establish, implement and maintain adequate risk management policies and procedures which identify the risks relating to the firm's activities, processes and systems, and where appropriate, set the level of risk tolerated by the firm;

    (b)   to adopt effective arrangements, processes and mechanisms to manage the risks relating to the firm's activities, processes and systems, in light of that level of risk tolerance;

    (c)   to monitor the following:

        (i)   the adequacy and effectiveness of the investment firm's risk management policies and procedures;

        (ii)   the level of compliance by the investment firm and its relevant persons with the arrangements, processes and mechanisms adopted in accordance with point (b);

        (iii)   the adequacy and effectiveness of measures taken to address any deficiencies in those policies, procedures, arrangements, processes and mechanisms, including failures by the relevant persons to comply with such arrangements, processes and mechanisms or follow such policies and procedures.

2.   Member States shall require investment firms, where appropriate and proportionate in view of the nature, scale and complexity of their business and the nature and range of the investment services and activities undertaken in the course of that business, to establish and maintain a risk management function that operates independently and carries out the following tasks:

    (a)   implementation of the policy and procedures referred to in paragraph 1;

    (b)   provision of reports and advice to senior management in accordance with Article 9(2).

Where an investment firm is not required under the first sub-paragraph to establish and maintain a risk management function that functions independently, it must nevertheless be able to demonstrate that the policies and procedures which it is has adopted in accordance with paragraph 1 satisfy the requirements of that paragraph and are consistently effective.

[5967]

Article 8
Internal audit
(second subparagraph of Article 13(5) of Directive 2004/39/EC)

Member States shall require investment firms, where appropriate and proportionate in view of the nature, scale and complexity of their business and the nature and range of investment services and activities undertaken in the course of that business, to establish and maintain an internal audit function which is separate and independent from the other functions and activities of the investment firm and which has the following responsibilities:

    (a)   to establish, implement and maintain an audit plan to examine and evaluate the adequacy and effectiveness of the investment firm's systems, internal control mechanisms and arrangements;

    (b)   to issue recommendations based on the result of work carried out in accordance with point (a);

    (c)   to verify compliance with those recommendations;

    (d)   to report in relation to internal audit matters in accordance with Article 9(2).

[5968]

Article 9
Responsibility of senior management
(Article 13(2) of Directive 2004/39/EC)

1.   Member States shall require investment firms, when allocating functions internally, to ensure that senior management, and, where appropriate, the supervisory function, are responsible for ensuring that the firm complies with its obligations under Directive 2004/39/EC.

In particular, senior management and, where appropriate, the supervisory function shall be required to assess and periodically to review the effectiveness of the policies, arrangements and procedures put in place to comply with the obligations under Directive 2004/39/EC and to take appropriate measures to address any deficiencies.

2.   Member States shall require investment firms to ensure that their senior management receive on a frequent basis, and at least annually, written reports on the matters covered by Articles 6, 7 and 8 indicating in particular whether the appropriate remedial measures have been taken in the event of any deficiencies.

3.   Member States shall require investment firms to ensure that the supervisory function, if any, receives on a regular basis written reports on the same matters.

4.   For the purposes of this Article, "supervisory function" means the function within an investment firm responsible for the supervision of its senior management.

[5969]

Article 10
Complaints handling
(*Article 13(2) of Directive 2004/39/EC*)

Member States shall require investment firms to establish, implement and maintain effective and transparent procedures for the reasonable and prompt handling of complaints received from retail clients or potential retail clients, and to keep a record of each complaint and the measures taken for its resolution.

[5970]

Article 11
Meaning of personal transaction
(*Article 13(2) of Directive 2004/39/EC*)

For the purposes of Article 12 and Article 25, personal transaction means a trade in a financial instrument effected by or on behalf of a relevant person, where at least one of the following criteria are met:

    (a)   that relevant person is acting outside the scope of the activities he carries out in that capacity;

    (b)   the trade is carried out for the account of any of the following persons:

        (i)   the relevant person;

        (ii)   any person with whom he has a family relationship, or with whom he has close links;

        (iii)   a person whose relationship with the relevant person is such that the relevant person has a direct or indirect material interest in the outcome of the trade, other than a fee or commission for the execution of the trade.

[5971]

Article 12
Personal transactions
(*Article 13(2) of Directive 2004/39/EC*)

    1.   Member States shall require investment firms to establish, implement and maintain adequate arrangements aimed at preventing the following activities in the case of any relevant person who is involved in activities that may give rise to a conflict of interest, or who has access to inside information within the meaning of Article 1(1) of Directive 2003/6/EC or to other confidential information relating to clients or transactions with or for clients by virtue of an activity carried out by him on behalf of the firm:

    (a)   entering into a personal transaction which meets at least one of the following criteria:

        (i)   that person is prohibited from entering into it under Directive 2003/6/EC;

        (ii)   it involves the misuse or improper disclosure of that confidential information;

        (iii)   it conflicts or is likely to conflict with an obligation of the investment firm under Directive 2004/39/EC;

    (b)   advising or procuring, other than in the proper course of his employment or contract for services, any other person to enter into a transaction in financial instruments which, if a personal transaction of the relevant person, would be covered by point (a) or Article 25(2)(a) or (b) or Article 47(3);

    (c)   without prejudice to Article 3(a) of Directive 2003/6/EC, disclosing, other than in the normal course of his employment or contract for services, any information or opinion to any other person if the relevant person knows, or reasonably ought to know, that as a result of that disclosure that other person will or would be likely to take either of the following steps:

        (i)   to enter into a transaction in financial instruments which, if a personal transaction of the relevant person, would be covered by point (a) or Article 25(2)(a) or (b) or Article 47(3);

        (ii)   to advise or procure another person to enter into such a transaction.

    2.   The arrangements required under paragraph 1 must in particular be designed to ensure that:

    (a)   each relevant person covered by paragraph 1 is aware of the restrictions on personal transactions, and of the measures established by the investment firm in connection with personal transactions and disclosure, in accordance with paragraph 1;

    (b)   the firm is informed promptly of any personal transaction entered into by a relevant person, either by notification of that transaction or by other procedures enabling the firm to identify such transactions;

    In the case of outsourcing arrangements the investment firm must ensure that the firm to which the activity is outsourced maintains a record of personal transactions entered into by any relevant person and provides that information to the investment firm promptly on request.

    (c)   a record is kept of the personal transaction notified to the firm or identified by it, including any authorisation or prohibition in connection with such a transaction.

    3.   Paragraphs 1 and 2 shall not apply to the following kinds of personal transaction:

(a) personal transactions effected under a discretionary portfolio management service where there is no prior communication in connection with the transaction between the portfolio manager and the relevant person or other person for whose account the transaction is executed;

(b) personal transactions in units in collective undertakings that comply with the conditions necessary to enjoy the rights conferred by Directive 85/611/EEC or are subject to supervision under the law of a Member State which requires an equivalent level of risk spreading in their assets, where the relevant person and any other person for whose account the transactions are effected are not involved in the management of that undertaking.

[5972]

SECTION 2
OUTSOURCING

Article 13
Meaning of critical and important operational functions
(Article 13(2) and first subparagraph of Article 13(5) of Directive 2004/39/EC)

1. For the purposes of the first subparagraph of Article 13(5) of Directive 2004/39/EC, an operational function shall be regarded as critical or important if a defect or failure in its performance would materially impair the continuing compliance of an investment firm with the conditions and obligations of its authorisation or its other obligations under Directive 2004/39/EC, or its financial performance, or the soundness or the continuity of its investment services and activities.

2. Without prejudice to the status of any other function, the following functions shall not be considered as critical or important for the purposes of paragraph 1:

(a) the provision to the firm of advisory services, and other services which do not form part of the investment business of the firm, including the provision of legal advice to the firm, the training of personnel of the firm, billing services and the security of the firm's premises and personnel;

(b) the purchase of standardised services, including market information services and the provision of price feeds.

[5973]

Article 14
Conditions for outsourcing critical or important operational functions or investment services or activities
(Article 13(2) and first subparagraph of Article 13(5) of Directive 2004/39/EC)

1. Member States shall ensure that, when investment firms outsource critical or important operational functions or any investment services or activities, the firms remain fully responsible for discharging all of their obligations under Directive 2004/39/EC and comply, in particular, with the following conditions:

(a) the outsourcing must not result in the delegation by senior management of its responsibility;

(b) the relationship and obligations of the investment firm towards its clients under the terms of Directive 2004/39/EC must not be altered;

(c) the conditions with which the investment firm must comply in order to be authorised in accordance with Article 5 of Directive 2004/39/EC, and to remain so, must not be undermined;

(d) none of the other conditions subject to which the firm's authorisation was granted must be removed or modified.

2. Member States shall require investment firms to exercise due skill, care and diligence when entering into, managing or terminating any arrangement for the outsourcing to a service provider of critical or important operational functions or of any investment services or activities.

Investment firms shall in particular take the necessary steps to ensure that the following conditions are satisfied:

(a) the service provider must have the ability, capacity, and any authorisation required by law to perform the outsourced functions, services or activities reliably and professionally;

(b) the service provider must carry out the outsourced services effectively, and to this end the firm must establish methods for assessing the standard of performance of the service provider;

(c) the service provider must properly supervise the carrying out of the outsourced functions, and adequately manage the risks associated with the outsourcing;

(d) appropriate action must be taken if it appears that the service provider may not be carrying out the functions effectively and in compliance with applicable laws and regulatory requirements;

(e) the investment firm must retain the necessary expertise to supervise the outsourced functions effectively and manage the risks associated with the outsourcing and must supervise those functions and manage those risks;

(f)　the service provider must disclose to the investment firm any development that may have a material impact on its ability to carry out the outsourced functions effectively and in compliance with applicable laws and regulatory requirements;

(g)　the investment firm must be able to terminate the arrangement for outsourcing where necessary without detriment to the continuity and quality of its provision of services to clients;

(h)　the service provider must cooperate with the competent authorities of the investment firm in connection with the outsourced activities;

(i)　the investment firm, its auditors and the relevant competent authorities must have effective access to data related to the outsourced activities, as well as to the business premises of the service provider; and the competent authorities must be able to exercise those rights of access;

(j)　the service provider must protect any confidential information relating to the investment firm and its clients;

(k)　the investment firm and the service provider must establish, implement and maintain a contingency plan for disaster recovery and periodic testing of backup facilities, where that is necessary having regard to the function, service or activity that has been outsourced.

3.　Member States shall require the respective rights and obligations of the investment firms and of the service provider to be clearly allocated and set out in a written agreement.

4.　Member States shall provide that, where the investment firm and the service provider are members of the same group, the investment firm may, for the purposes of complying with this Article and Article 15, take into account the extent to which the firm controls the service provider or has the ability to influence its actions.

5.　Member States shall require investment firms to make available on request to the competent authority all information necessary to enable the authority to supervise the compliance of the performance of the outsourced activities with the requirements of this Directive.

[5974]

Article 15
Service providers located in third countries
(Article 13(2) and first subparagraph of Article 13(5) of Directive 2004/39/EC)

1.　In addition to the requirements set out in Article 14, Member States shall require that, where an investment firm outsources the investment service of portfolio management provided to retail clients to a service provider located in a third country, that investment firm ensures that the following conditions are satisfied:

(a)　the service provider must be authorised or registered in its home country to provide that service and must be subject to prudential supervision;

(b)　there must be an appropriate cooperation agreement between the competent authority of the investment firm and the supervisory authority of the service provider.

2.　Where one or both of those conditions mentioned in paragraph 1 are not satisfied, an investment firm may outsource investment services to a service provider located in a third country only if the firm gives prior notification to its competent authority about the outsourcing arrangement and the competent authority does not object to that arrangement within a reasonable time following receipt of that notification.

3.　Without prejudice to paragraph 2, Member States shall publish or require competent authorities to publish a statement of policy in relation to outsourcing covered by paragraph 2. That statement shall set out examples of cases where the competent authority would not, or would be likely not to, object to an outsourcing under paragraph 2 where one or both of the conditions in points (a) and (b) of paragraph 1 are not met. It shall include a clear explanation as to why the competent authority considers that in such cases outsourcing would not impair the ability of investment firms to fulfil their obligations under Article 14.

4.　Nothing in this article limits the obligations on investment firms to comply with the requirements in Article 14.

5.　Competent authorities shall publish a list of the supervisory authorities in third countries with which they have cooperation agreements that are appropriate for the purposes of point (b) of paragraph 1.

[5975]

SECTION 3
SAFEGUARDING OF CLIENT ASSETS

Article 16
Safeguarding of client financial instruments and funds
(*Article 13(7) and (8) of Directive 2004/39/EC*)

1.   Member States shall require that, for the purposes of safeguarding clients' rights in relation to financial instruments and funds belonging to them, investment firms comply with the following requirements:

   (a)   they must keep such records and accounts as are necessary to enable them at any time and without delay to distinguish assets held for one client from assets held for any other client, and from their own assets;

   (b)   they must maintain their records and accounts in a way that ensures their accuracy, and in particular their correspondence to the financial instruments and funds held for clients;

   (c)   they must conduct, on a regular basis, reconciliations between their internal accounts and records and those of any third parties by whom those assets are held;

   (d)   they must take the necessary steps to ensure that any client financial instruments deposited with a third party, in accordance with Article 17, are identifiable separately from the financial instruments belonging to the investment firm and from financial instruments belonging to that third party, by means of differently titled accounts on the books of the third party or other equivalent measures that achieve the same level of protection;

   (e)   they must take the necessary steps to ensure that client funds deposited, in accordance with Article 18, in a central bank, a credit institution or a bank authorised in a third country or a qualifying money market fund are held in an account or accounts identified separately from any accounts used to hold funds belonging to the investment firm;

   (f)   they must introduce adequate organisational arrangements to minimise the risk of the loss or diminution of client assets, or of rights in connection with those assets, as a result of misuse of the assets, fraud, poor administration, inadequate record-keeping or negligence.

2.   If, for reasons of the applicable law, including in particular the law relating to property or insolvency, the arrangements made by investment firms in compliance with paragraph 1 to safeguard clients' rights are not sufficient to satisfy the requirements of Article 13(7) and (8) of Directive 2004/39/EC, Member States shall prescribe the measures that investment firms must take in order to comply with those obligations.

3.   If the applicable law of the jurisdiction in which the client funds or financial instruments are held prevents investment firms from complying with points (d) or (e) of paragraph 1, Member States shall prescribe requirements which have an equivalent effect in terms of safeguarding clients' rights.

[5976]

Article 17
Depositing client financial instruments
(*Article 13(7) of Directive 2004/39/EC*)

1.   Member States shall permit investment firms to deposit financial instruments held by them on behalf of their clients into an account or accounts opened with a third party provided that the firms exercise all due skill, care and diligence in the selection, appointment and periodic review of the third party and of the arrangements for the holding and safekeeping of those financial instruments.

In particular, Member States shall require investment firms to take into account the expertise and market reputation of the third party as well as any legal requirements or market practices related to the holding of those financial instruments that could adversely affect clients' rights.

2.   Member States shall ensure that, if the safekeeping of financial instruments for the account of another person is subject to specific regulation and supervision in a jurisdiction where an investment firm proposes to deposit client financial instruments with a third party, the investment firm does not deposit those financial instruments in that jurisdiction with a third party which is not subject to such regulation and supervision.

3.   Member States shall ensure that investment firms do not deposit financial instruments held on behalf of clients with a third party in a third country that does not regulate the holding and safekeeping of financial instruments for the account of another person unless one of the following conditions is met:

   (a)   the nature of the financial instruments or of the investment services connected with those instruments requires them to be deposited with a third party in that third country;

   (b)   where the financial instruments are held on behalf of a professional client, that client requests the firm in writing to deposit them with a third party in that third country.

[5977]

Article 18
Depositing client funds
(*Article 13(8) of Directive 2004/39/EC*)

1. Member States shall require investment firms, on receiving any client funds, promptly to place those funds into one or more accounts opened with any of the following:
(a) a central bank;
(b) a credit institution authorised in accordance with Directive 2000/12/EC;
(c) a bank authorised in a third country;
(d) a qualifying money market fund.

The first subparagraph shall not apply to a credit institution authorised under Directive 2006/48/EC of the European Parliament and of the Council of 14 June 2006 relating to the taking up and pursuit of the business of credit institutions (recast)[1] in relation to deposits within the meaning of that Directive held by that institution.

2. For the purposes of point (d) of paragraph 1, and of Article 16(1)(e), a "qualifying money market fund" means a collective investment undertaking authorised under Directive 85/611/EEC, or which is subject to supervision and, if applicable, authorised by an authority under the national law of a Member State, and which satisfies the following conditions:
(a) its primary investment objective must be to maintain the net asset value of the undertaking either constant at par (net of earnings), or at the value of the investors' initial capital plus earnings;
(b) it must, with a view to achieving that primary investment objective, invest exclusively in high quality money market instruments with a maturity or residual maturity of no more than 397 days, or regular yield adjustments consistent with such a maturity, and with a weighted average maturity of 60 days. It may also achieve this objective by investing on an ancillary basis in deposits with credit institutions;
(c) it must provide liquidity through same day or next day settlement.

For the purposes of point (b), a money market instrument shall be considered to be of high quality if it has been awarded the highest available credit rating by each competent rating agency which has rated that instrument. An instrument that is not rated by any competent rating agency shall not be considered to be of high quality.

For the purposes of the second subparagraph, a rating agency shall be considered to be competent if it issues credit ratings in respect of money market funds regularly and on a professional basis and is an eligible ECAI within the meaning of Article 81(1) of Directive 2006/48/EC.

3. Member States shall require that, where investment firms do not deposit client funds with a central bank, they exercise all due skill, care and diligence in the selection, appointment and periodic review of the credit institution, bank or money market fund where the funds are placed and the arrangements for the holding of those funds.

Member States shall ensure, in particular, that investment firms take into account the expertise and market reputation of such institutions or money market funds with a view to ensuring the protection of clients' rights, as well as any legal or regulatory requirements or market practices related to the holding of client funds that could adversely affect clients' rights.

Member States shall ensure that clients have the right to oppose the placement of their funds in a qualifying money market fund.

[5978]

NOTES
[1] OJ L177, 30.6.2006, p 1.

Article 19
Use of client financial instruments
(*Article 13(7) of Directive 2004/39/EC*)

1. Member States shall not allow investment firms to enter into arrangements for securities financing transactions in respect of financial instruments held by them on behalf of a client, or otherwise use such financial instruments for their own account or the account of another client of the firm, unless the following conditions are met:
(a) the client must have given his prior express consent to the use of the instruments on specified terms, as evidenced, in the case of a retail client, by his signature or equivalent alternative mechanism;
(b) the use of that client's financial instruments must be restricted to the specified terms to which the client consents.

2. Member States may not allow investment firms to enter into arrangements for securities financing transactions in respect of financial instruments which are held on behalf of a client in an omnibus account maintained by a third party, or otherwise use financial instruments held in such an

account for their own account or for the account of another client unless, in addition to the conditions set out in paragraph 1, at least one of the following conditions is met:

(a) each client whose financial instruments are held together in an omnibus account must have given prior express consent in accordance with point (a) of paragraph 1;

(b) the investment firm must have in place systems and controls which ensure that only financial instruments belonging to clients who have given prior express consent in accordance with point (a) of paragraph 1 are so used.

The records of the investment firm shall include details of the client on whose instructions the use of the financial instruments has been effected, as well as the number of financial instruments used belonging to each client who has given his consent, so as to enable the correct allocation of any loss.

[5979]

Article 20
Reports by external auditors
(Article 13(7) and (8) of Directive 2004/39/EC)

Member States shall require investment firms to ensure that their external auditors report at least annually to the competent authority of the home Member State of the firm on the adequacy of the firm's arrangements under Articles 13(7) and (8) of Directive 2004/39/EC and this Section.

[5980]

SECTION 4
CONFLICTS OF INTEREST

Article 21
Conflicts of interest potentially detrimental to a client
(Articles 13(3) and 18 of Directive 2004/39/EC)

Member States shall ensure that, for the purposes of identifying the types of conflict of interest that arise in the course of providing investment and ancillary services or a combination thereof and whose existence may damage the interests of a client, investment firms take into account, by way of minimum criteria, the question of whether the investment firm or a relevant person, or a person directly or indirectly linked by control to the firm, is in any of the following situations, whether as a result of providing investment or ancillary services or investment activities or otherwise:

(a) the firm or that person is likely to make a financial gain, or avoid a financial loss, at the expense of the client;

(b) the firm or that person has an interest in the outcome of a service provided to the client or of a transaction carried out on behalf of the client, which is distinct from the client's interest in that outcome;

(c) the firm or that person has a financial or other incentive to favour the interest of another client or group of clients over the interests of the client;

(d) the firm or that person carries on the same business as the client;

(e) the firm or that person receives or will receive from a person other than the client an inducement in relation to a service provided to the client, in the form of monies, goods or services, other than the standard commission or fee for that service.

[5981]

Article 22
Conflicts of interest policy
(Articles 13(3) and 18(1) of Directive 2004/39/EC)

1. Member States shall require investment firms to establish, implement and maintain an effective conflicts of interest policy set out in writing and appropriate to the size and organisation of the firm and the nature, scale and complexity of its business.

Where the firm is a member of a group, the policy must also take into account any circumstances, of which the firm is or should be aware, which may give rise to a conflict of interest arising as a result of the structure and business activities of other members of the group.

2. The conflicts of interest policy established in accordance with paragraph 1 shall include the following content:

(a) it must identify, with reference to the specific investment services and activities and ancillary services carried out by or on behalf of the investment firm, the circumstances which constitute or may give rise to a conflict of interest entailing a material risk of damage to the interests of one or more clients;

(b) it must specify procedures to be followed and measures to be adopted in order to manage such conflicts.

3. Member States shall ensure that the procedures and measures provided for in paragraph 2(b) are designed to ensure that relevant persons engaged in different business activities involving a conflict of interest of the kind specified in paragraph 2(a) carry on those activities at a level of independence appropriate to the size and activities of the investment firm and of the group to which it belongs, and to the materiality of the risk of damage to the interests of clients.

For the purposes of paragraph 2(b), the procedures to be followed and measures to be adopted shall include such of the following as are necessary and appropriate for the firm to ensure the requisite degree of independence:

(a) effective procedures to prevent or control the exchange of information between relevant persons engaged in activities involving a risk of a conflict of interest where the exchange of that information may harm the interests of one or more clients;

(b) the separate supervision of relevant persons whose principal functions involve carrying out activities on behalf of, or providing services to, clients whose interests may conflict, or who otherwise represent different interests that may conflict, including those of the firm;

(c) the removal of any direct link between the remuneration of relevant persons principally engaged in one activity and the remuneration of, or revenues generated by, different relevant persons principally engaged in another activity, where a conflict of interest may arise in relation to those activities;

(d) measures to prevent or limit any person from exercising inappropriate influence over the way in which a relevant person carries out investment or ancillary services or activities;

(e) measures to prevent or control the simultaneous or sequential involvement of a relevant person in separate investment or ancillary services or activities where such involvement may impair the proper management of conflicts of interest.

If the adoption or the practice of one or more of those measures and procedures does not ensure the requisite degree of independence, Member States shall require investment firms to adopt such alternative or additional measures and procedures as are necessary and appropriate for those purposes.

4. Member States shall ensure that disclosure to clients, pursuant to Article 18(2) of Directive 2004/39/EC, is made in a durable medium and includes sufficient detail, taking into account the nature of the client, to enable that client to take an informed decision with respect to the investment or ancillary service in the context of which the conflict of interest arises.

[5982]

Article 23
Record of services or activities giving rise to detrimental conflict of interest
(Article 13(6) of Directive 2004/39/EC)

Member States shall require investment firms to keep and regularly to update a record of the kinds of investment or ancillary service or investment activity carried out by or on behalf of the firm in which a conflict of interest entailing a material risk of damage to the interests of one or more clients has arisen or, in the case of an ongoing service or activity, may arise.

[5983]

Article 24
Investment research
(Article 19(2) of Directive 2004/39/EC)

1. For the purposes of Article 25, "investment research" means research or other information recommending or suggesting an investment strategy, explicitly or implicitly, concerning one or several financial instruments or the issuers of financial instruments, including any opinion as to the present or future value or price of such instruments, intended for distribution channels or for the public, and in relation to which the following conditions are met:

(a) it is labelled or described as investment research or in similar terms, or is otherwise presented as an objective or independent explanation of the matters contained in the recommendation;

(b) if the recommendation in question were made by an investment firm to a client, it would not constitute the provision of investment advice for the purposes of Directive 2004/39/EC.

2. A recommendation of the type covered by Article 1(3) of Directive 2003/125/EC but relating to financial instruments as defined in Directive 2004/39/EC that does not meet the conditions set out in paragraph 1 shall be treated as a marketing communication for the purposes of Directive 2004/39/EC and Member States shall require any investment firm that produces or disseminates the recommendation to ensure that it is clearly identified as such.

Additionally, Member States shall require those firms to ensure that any such recommendation contains a clear and prominent statement that (or, in the case of an oral recommendation, to the effect that) it has not been prepared in accordance with legal requirements designed to promote the independence of investment research, and that it is not subject to any prohibition on dealing ahead of the dissemination of investment research.

[5984]

Article 25
Additional organisational requirements where a firm produces and disseminates investment research
(*Article 13(3) of Directive 2004/39/EC*)

1.   Member States shall require investment firms which produce, or arrange for the production of, investment research that is intended or likely to be subsequently disseminated to clients of the firm or to the public, under their own responsibility or that of a member of their group, to ensure the implementation of all the measures set out in Article 22(3) in relation to the financial analysts involved in the production of the investment research and other relevant persons whose responsibilities or business interests may conflict with the interests of the persons to whom the investment research is disseminated.

2.   Member States shall require investment firms covered by paragraph 1 to have in place arrangements designed to ensure that the following conditions are satisfied:
  (a)   financial analysts and other relevant persons must not undertake personal transactions or trade, other than as market makers acting in good faith and in the ordinary course of market making or in the execution of an unsolicited client order, on behalf of any other person, including the investment firm, in financial instruments to which investment research relates, or in any related financial instruments, with knowledge of the likely timing or content of that investment research which is not publicly available or available to clients and cannot readily be inferred from information that is so available, until the recipients of the investment research have had a reasonable opportunity to act on it;
  (b)   in circumstances not covered by point (a), financial analysts and any other relevant persons involved in the production of investment research must not undertake personal transactions in financial instruments to which the investment research relates, or in any related financial instruments, contrary to current recommendations, except in exceptional circumstances and with the prior approval of a member of the firm's legal or compliance function;
  (c)   the investment firms themselves, financial analysts, and other relevant persons involved in the production of the investment research must not accept inducements from those with a material interest in the subject-matter of the investment research;
  (d)   the investment firms themselves, financial analysts, and other relevant persons involved in the production of the investment research must not promise issuers favourable research coverage;
  (e)   issuers, relevant persons other than financial analysts, and any other persons must not before the dissemination of investment research be permitted to review a draft of the investment research for the purpose of verifying the accuracy of factual statements made in that research, or for any other purpose other than verifying compliance with the firm's legal obligations, if the draft includes a recommendation or a target price.

For the purposes of this paragraph, "related financial instrument" means a financial instrument the price of which is closely affected by price movements in another financial instrument which is the subject of investment research, and includes a derivative on that other financial instrument.

3.   Member States shall exempt investment firms which disseminate investment research produced by another person to the public or to clients from complying with paragraph 1 if the following criteria are met:
  (a)   the person that produces the investment research is not a member of the group to which the investment firm belongs;
  (b)   the investment firm does not substantially alter the recommendations within the investment research;
  (c)   the investment firm does not present the investment research as having been produced by it;
  (d)   the investment firm verifies that the producer of the research is subject to requirements equivalent to the requirements under this Directive in relation to the production of that research, or has established a policy setting such requirements.

[5985]

CHAPTER III
OPERATING CONDITIONS FOR INVESTMENT FIRMS

SECTION 1
INDUCEMENTS

Article 26
Inducements
(*Article 19(1) of Directive 2004/39/EC*)

Member States shall ensure that investment firms are not regarded as acting honestly, fairly and professionally in accordance with the best interests of a client if, in relation to the provision of an investment or ancillary service to the client, they pay or are paid any fee or commission, or provide or are provided with any non-monetary benefit, other than the following:

    (a)   a fee, commission or non-monetary benefit paid or provided to or by the client or a person on behalf of the client;

    (b)   a fee, commission or non-monetary benefit paid or provided to or by a third party or a person acting on behalf of a third party, where the following conditions are satisfied:

        (i)   the existence, nature and amount of the fee, commission or benefit, or, where the amount cannot be ascertained, the method of calculating that amount, must be clearly disclosed to the client, in a manner that is comprehensive, accurate and understandable, prior to the provision of the relevant investment or ancillary service;

        (ii)   the payment of the fee or commission, or the provision of the non-monetary benefit must be designed to enhance the quality of the relevant service to the client and not impair compliance with the firm's duty to act in the best interests of the client;

    (c)   proper fees which enable or are necessary for the provision of investment services, such as custody costs, settlement and exchange fees, regulatory levies or legal fees, and which, by their nature, cannot give rise to conflicts with the firm's duties to act honestly, fairly and professionally in accordance with the best interests of its clients.

Member States shall permit an investment firm, for the purposes of point (b)(i), to disclose the essential terms of the arrangements relating to the fee, commission or non-monetary benefit in summary form, provided that it undertakes to disclose further details at the request of the client and provided that it honours that undertaking.

[5986]

SECTION 2
INFORMATION TO CLIENTS AND POTENTIAL CLIENTS

Article 27
Conditions with which information must comply in order to be fair, clear and not misleading
(*Article 19(2) of Directive 2004/39/EC*)

    1.   Member States shall require investment firms to ensure that all information they address to, or disseminate in such a way that it is likely to be received by, retail clients or potential retail clients, including marketing communications, satisfies the conditions laid down in paragraphs 2 to 8.

    2.   The information referred to in paragraph 1 shall include the name of the investment firm.

It shall be accurate and in particular shall not emphasise any potential benefits of an investment service or financial instrument without also giving a fair and prominent indication of any relevant risks.

It shall be sufficient for, and presented in a way that is likely to be understood by, the average member of the group to whom it is directed, or by whom it is likely to be received.

It shall not disguise, diminish or obscure important items, statements or warnings.

    3.   Where the information compares investment or ancillary services, financial instruments, or persons providing investment or ancillary services, the following conditions shall be satisfied:

    (a)   the comparison must be meaningful and presented in a fair and balanced way;

    (b)   the sources of the information used for the comparison must be specified;

    (c)   the key facts and assumptions used to make the comparison must be included.

    4.   Where the information contains an indication of past performance of a financial instrument, a financial index or an investment service, the following conditions shall be satisfied:

    (a)   that indication must not be the most prominent feature of the communication;

    (b)   the information must include appropriate performance information which covers the immediately preceding 5 years, or the whole period for which the financial instrument has been offered, the financial index has been established, or the investment service has been provided if less than five years, or such longer period as the firm may decide, and in every case that performance information must be based on complete 12-month periods;

    (c)   the reference period and the source of information must be clearly stated;

    (d)   the information must contain a prominent warning that the figures refer to the past and that past performance is not a reliable indicator of future results;

    (e)   where the indication relies on figures denominated in a currency other than that of the Member State in which the retail client or potential retail client is resident, the currency must be clearly stated, together with a warning that the return may increase or decrease as a result of currency fluctuations;

    (f)   where the indication is based on gross performance, the effect of commissions, fees or other charges must be disclosed.

5. Where the information includes or refers to simulated past performance, it must relate to a financial instrument or a financial index, and the following conditions shall be satisfied:

(a) the simulated past performance must be based on the actual past performance of one or more financial instruments or financial indices which are the same as, or underlie, the financial instrument concerned;

(b) in respect of the actual past performance referred to in point (a), the conditions set out in points (a) to (c), (e) and (f) of paragraph 4 must be complied with;

(c) the information must contain a prominent warning that the figures refer to simulated past performance and that past performance is not a reliable indicator of future performance.

6. Where the information contains information on future performance, the following conditions shall be satisfied:

(a) the information must not be based on or refer to simulated past performance;

(b) it must be based on reasonable assumptions supported by objective data;

(c) where the information is based on gross performance, the effect of commissions, fees or other charges must be disclosed;

(d) it must contain a prominent warning that such forecasts are not a reliable indicator of future performance.

7. Where the information refers to a particular tax treatment, it shall prominently state that the tax treatment depends on the individual circumstances of each client and may be subject to change in the future.

8. The information shall not use the name of any competent authority in such a way that would indicate or suggest endorsement or approval by that authority of the products or services of the investment firm.

[5987]

Article 28
Information concerning client categorisation
(Article 19(3) of Directive 2004/39/EC)

1. Member States shall ensure that investment firms notify new clients, and existing clients that the investment firm has newly categorised as required by Directive 2004/39/EC, of their categorisation as a retail client, a professional client or an eligible counterparty in accordance with that Directive.

2. Member States shall ensure that investment firms inform clients in a durable medium about any right that client has to request a different categorisation and about any limitations to the level of client protection that it would entail.

3. Member States shall permit investment firms, either on their own initiative or at the request of the client concerned:

(a) to treat as a professional or retail client a client that might otherwise be classified as an eligible counterparty pursuant to Article 24(2) of Directive 2004/39/EC;

(b) to treat as a retail client a client that is considered as a professional client pursuant to Section I of Annex II to Directive 2004/39/EC.

[5988]

Article 29
General requirements for information to clients
(Article 19(3) of Directive 2004/39/EC)

1. Member States shall require investment firms, in good time before a retail client or potential retail client is bound by any agreement for the provision of investment services or ancillary services or before the provision of those services, whichever is the earlier, to provide that client or potential client with the following information:

(a) the terms of any such agreement;

(b) the information required by Article 30 relating to that agreement or to those investment or ancillary services.

2. Member States shall require investment firms, in good time before the provision of investment services or ancillary services to retail clients or potential retail clients, to provide the information required under Articles 30 to 33.

3. Member States shall require investment firms to provide professional clients with the information referred to in Article 32(5) and (6) in good time before the provision of the service concerned.

4. The information referred to in paragraphs 1 to 3 shall be provided in a durable medium or by means of a website (where that does not constitute a durable medium) provided that the conditions specified in Article 3(2) are satisfied.

5. By way of exception to paragraphs 1 and 2, Member States shall permit investment firms, in the following circumstances, to provide the information required under paragraph 1 to a retail client

immediately after that client is bound by any agreement for the provision of investment services or ancillary services, and the information required under paragraph 2 immediately after starting to provide the service:

(a)   the firm was unable to comply with the time limits specified in paragraphs 1 and 2 because, at the request of the client, the agreement was concluded using a means of distance communication which prevents the firm from providing the information in accordance with paragraph 1 or 2;

(b)   in any case where Article 3(3) of Directive 2002/65/EC of the European Parliament and of the Council of 23 September 2002 concerning the distance marketing of consumer financial services and amending Council Directive 90/619/EEC and Directives 97/7/EC and 98/27/EC[1] does not otherwise apply, the investment firm complies with the requirements of that Article in relation to the retail client or potential retail client, as if that client or potential client were a "consumer" and the investment firm were a "supplier" within the meaning of that Directive.

6.   Member State shall ensure that investment firms notify a client in good time about any material change to the information provided under Articles 30 to 33 which is relevant to a service that the firm is providing to that client. That notification shall be given in a durable medium if the information to which it relates is given in a durable medium.

7.   Member States shall require investment firms to ensure that information contained in a marketing communication is consistent with any information the firm provides to clients in the course of carrying on investment and ancillary services.

8.   Member States shall ensure that, where a marketing communication contains an offer or invitation of the following nature and specifies the manner of response or includes a form by which any response may be made, it includes such of the information referred to in Articles 30 to 33 as is relevant to that offer or invitation:

(a)   an offer to enter into an agreement in relation to a financial instrument or investment service or ancillary service with any person who responds to the communication;

(b)   an invitation to any person who responds to the communication to make an offer to enter into an agreement in relation to a financial instrument or investment service or ancillary service.

However, the first subparagraph shall not apply if, in order to respond to an offer or invitation contained in the marketing communication, the potential retail client must refer to another document or documents, which, alone or in combination, contain that information.

[5989]

NOTES
    [1]   OJ L271, 9.10.2002, p 16.

Article 30
Information about the investment firm and its services for retail clients and potential retail clients
(first indent of Article 19(3) of Directive 2004/39/EC)

1.   Member States shall require investment firms to provide retail clients or potential retail clients with the following general information, where relevant:

(a)   the name and address of the investment firm, and the contact details necessary to enable clients to communicate effectively with the firm;

(b)   the languages in which the client may communicate with the investment firm, and receive documents and other information from the firm;

(c)   the methods of communication to be used between the investment firm and the client including, where relevant, those for the sending and reception of orders;

(d)   a statement of the fact that the investment firm is authorised and the name and contact address of the competent authority that has authorised it;

(e)   where the investment firm is acting through a tied agent, a statement of this fact specifying the Member State in which that agent is registered;

(f)   the nature, frequency and timing of the reports on the performance of the service to be provided by the investment firm to the client in accordance with Article 19(8) of Directive 2004/39/EC;

(g)   if the investment firm holds client financial instruments or client funds, a summary description of the steps which it takes to ensure their protection, including summary details of any relevant investor compensation or deposit guarantee scheme which applies to the firm by virtue of its activities in a Member State;

(h)   a description, which may be provided in summary form, of the conflicts of interest policy maintained by the firm in accordance with Article 22;

(i)   at any time that the client requests it, further details of that conflicts of interest policy in a durable medium or by means of a website (where that does not constitute a durable medium) provided that the conditions specified in Article 3(2) are satisfied.

2. Member States shall ensure that, when providing the service of portfolio management, investment firms establish an appropriate method of evaluation and comparison such as a meaningful benchmark, based on the investment objectives of the client and the types of financial instruments included in the client portfolio, so as to enable the client for whom the service is provided to assess the firm's performance.

3. Member States shall require that where investment firms propose to provide portfolio management services to a retail client or potential retail client, they provide the client, in addition to the information required under paragraph 1, with such of the following information as is applicable:
   (a) information on the method and frequency of valuation of the financial instruments in the client portfolio;
   (b) details of any delegation of the discretionary management of all or part of the financial instruments or funds in the client portfolio;
   (c) a specification of any benchmark against which the performance of the client portfolio will be compared;
   (d) the types of financial instrument that may be included in the client portfolio and types of transaction that may be carried out in such instruments, including any limits;
   (e) the management objectives, the level of risk to be reflected in the manager's exercise of discretion, and any specific constraints on that discretion.

[5990]

Article 31
Information about financial instruments
(*second indent of Article 19(3) of Directive 2004/39/EC*)

1. Member States shall require investment firms to provide clients or potential clients with a general description of the nature and risks of financial instruments, taking into account, in particular, the client's categorisation as either a retail client or a professional client. That description must explain the nature of the specific type of instrument concerned, as well as the risks particular to that specific type of instrument in sufficient detail to enable the client to take investment decisions on an informed basis.

2. The description of risks shall include, where relevant to the specific type of instrument concerned and the status and level of knowledge of the client, the following elements:
   (a) the risks associated with that type of financial instrument including an explanation of leverage and its effects and the risk of losing the entire investment;
   (b) the volatility of the price of such instruments and any limitations on the available market for such instruments;
   (c) the fact that an investor might assume, as a result of transactions in such instruments, financial commitments and other additional obligations, including contingent liabilities, additional to the cost of acquiring the instruments;
   (d) any margin requirements or similar obligations, applicable to instruments of that type.

Member States may specify the precise terms, or the contents, of the description of risks required under this paragraph.

3. If an investment firm provides a retail client or potential retail client with information about a financial instrument that is the subject of a current offer to the public and a prospectus has been published in connection with that offer in accordance with Directive 2003/71/EC, that firm shall inform the client or potential client where that prospectus is made available to the public.

4. Where the risks associated with a financial instrument composed of two or more different financial instruments or services are likely to be greater than the risks associated with any of the components, the investment firm shall provide an adequate description of the components of that instrument and the way in which its interaction increases the risks.

5. In the case of financial instruments that incorporate a guarantee by a third party, the information about the guarantee shall include sufficient detail about the guarantor and the guarantee to enable the retail client or potential retail client to make a fair assessment of the guarantee.

[5991]

Article 32
Information requirements concerning safeguarding of client financial instruments or client funds
(*first indent of Article 19(3) of Directive 2004/39/EC*)

1. Member States shall ensure that, where investment firms hold financial instruments or funds belonging to retail clients, they provide those retail clients or potential retail clients with such of the information specified in paragraphs 2 to 7 as is relevant.

2. The investment firm shall inform the retail client or potential retail client where the financial instruments or funds of that client may be held by a third party on behalf of the investment firm and

of the responsibility of the investment firm under the applicable national law for any acts or omissions of the third party and the consequences for the client of the insolvency of the third party.

3. Where financial instruments of the retail client or potential retail client may, if permitted by national law, be held in an omnibus account by a third party, the investment firm shall inform the client of this fact and shall provide a prominent warning of the resulting risks.

4. The investment firm shall inform the retail client or potential retail client where it is not possible under national law for client financial instruments held with a third party to be separately identifiable from the proprietary financial instruments of that third party or of the investment firm and shall provide a prominent warning of the resulting risks.

5. The investment firm shall inform the client or potential client where accounts that contain financial instruments or funds belonging to that client or potential client are or will be subject to the law of a jurisdiction other than that of a Member State and shall indicate that the rights of the client or potential client relating to those financial instruments or funds may differ accordingly.

6. An investment firm shall inform the client about the existence and the terms of any security interest or lien which the firm has or may have over the client's financial instruments or funds, or any right of set-off it holds in relation to those instruments or funds. Where applicable, it shall also inform the client of the fact that a depository may have a security interest or lien over, or right of set-off in relation to those instruments or funds.

7. An investment firm, before entering into securities financing transactions in relation to financial instruments held by it on behalf of a retail client, or before otherwise using such financial instruments for its own account or the account of another client, shall in good time before the use of those instruments provide the retail client, in a durable medium, with clear, full and accurate information on the obligations and responsibilities of the investment firm with respect to the use of those financial instruments, including the terms for their restitution, and on the risks involved.

[5992]

Article 33
Information about costs and associated charges
(*fourth indent of Article 19(3) of Directive 2004/39/EC*)

Member States shall require investment firms to provide their retail clients and potential retail clients with information on costs and associated charges that includes such of the following elements as are relevant:

    (a)   the total price to be paid by the client in connection with the financial instrument or the investment service or ancillary service, including all related fees, commissions, charges and expenses, and all taxes payable via the investment firm or, if an exact price cannot be indicated, the basis for the calculation of the total price so that the client can verify it;

    (b)   where any part of the total price referred to in point (a) is to be paid in or represents an amount of foreign currency, an indication of the currency involved and the applicable currency conversion rates and costs;

    (c)   notice of the possibility that other costs, including taxes, related to transactions in connection with the financial instrument or the investment service may arise for the client that are not paid via the investment firm or imposed by it;

    (d)   the arrangements for payment or other performance.

For the purposes of point (a), the commissions charged by the firm shall be itemised separately in every case.

[5993]

Article 34
Information drawn up in accordance with Directive 85/611/EEC
(*second and fourth indent of Article 19(3) of Directive 2004/39/EC*)

1. Member States shall ensure that in respect of units in a collective investment undertaking covered by Directive 85/611/EEC, a simplified prospectus complying with Article 28 of that Directive is regarded as appropriate information for the purposes of the second indent of Article 19(3) of Directive 2004/39/EC.

2. Member States shall ensure that in respect of units in a collective investment undertaking covered by Directive 85/611/EEC, a simplified prospectus complying with Article 28 of that Directive is regarded as appropriate information for the purposes of the fourth indent of Article 19(3) of Directive 2004/39/EC with respect to the costs and associated charges related to the UCITS itself, including the exit and entry commissions.

[5994]

SECTION 3
ASSESSMENT OF SUITABILITY AND APPROPRIATENESS

Article 35
Assessment of suitability
(Article 19(4) of Directive 2004/39/EC)

1. Member States shall ensure that investment firms obtain from clients or potential clients such information as is necessary for the firm to understand the essential facts about the client and to have a reasonable basis for believing, giving due consideration to the nature and extent of the service provided, that the specific transaction to be recommended, or entered into in the course of providing a portfolio management service, satisfies the following criteria:

    (a)   it meets the investment objectives of the client in question;
    (b)   it is such that the client is able financially to bear any related investment risks consistent with his investment objectives;
    (c)   it is such that the client has the necessary experience and knowledge in order to understand the risks involved in the transaction or in the management of his portfolio.

2. Where an investment firm provides an investment service to a professional client it shall be entitled to assume that, in relation to the products, transactions and services for which it is so classified, the client has the necessary level of experience and knowledge for the purposes of paragraph 1(c).

Where that investment service consists in the provision of investment advice to a professional client covered by Section 1 of Annex II to Directive 2004/39/EC, the investment firm shall be entitled to assume for the purposes of paragraph 1(b) that the client is able financially to bear any related investment risks consistent with the investment objectives of that client.

3. The information regarding the financial situation of the client or potential client shall include, where relevant, information on the source and extent of his regular income, his assets, including liquid assets, investments and real property, and his regular financial commitments.

4. The information regarding the investment objectives of the client or potential client shall include, where relevant, information on the length of time for which the client wishes to hold the investment, his preferences regarding risk taking, his risk profile, and the purposes of the investment.

5. Where, when providing the investment service of investment advice or portfolio management, an investment firm does not obtain the information required under Article 19(4) of Directive 2004/39/EC, the firm shall not recommend investment services or financial instruments to the client or potential client.

[5995]

Article 36
Assessment of appropriateness
(Article 19(5) of Directive 2004/39/EC)

Member States shall require investment firms, when assessing whether an investment service as referred to in Article 19(5) of Directive 2004/39/EC is appropriate for a client, to determine whether that client has the necessary experience and knowledge in order to understand the risks involved in relation to the product or investment service offered or demanded.

For those purposes, an investment firm shall be entitled to assume that a professional client has the necessary experience and knowledge in order to understand the risks involved in relation to those particular investment services or transactions, or types of transaction or product, for which the client is classified as a professional client.

[5996]

Article 37
Provisions common to the assessment of suitability or appropriateness
(Article 19(4) and (5) of Directive 2004/39/EC)

1. Member States shall ensure that the information regarding a client's or potential client's knowledge and experience in the investment field includes the following, to the extent appropriate to the nature of the client, the nature and extent of the service to be provided and the type of product or transaction envisaged, including their complexity and the risks involved:

    (a)   the types of service, transaction and financial instrument with which the client is familiar;
    (b)   the nature, volume, and frequency of the client's transactions in financial instruments and the period over which they have been carried out;
    (c)   the level of education, and profession or relevant former profession of the client or potential client.

2. An investment firm shall not encourage a client or potential client not to provide information required for the purposes of Article 19(4) and (5) of Directive 2004/39/EC.

3.   An investment firm shall be entitled to rely on the information provided by its clients or potential clients unless it is aware or ought to be aware that the information is manifestly out of date, inaccurate or incomplete.

[5997]

Article 38
Provision of services in non-complex instruments
(*first indent of Article 19(6) of Directive 2004/39/EC*)

A financial instrument which is not specified in the first indent of Article 19(6) of Directive 2004/39/EC shall be considered as non-complex if it satisfies the following criteria:
-   (a)   it does not fall within Article 4(1)(18)(c) of, or points (4) to (10) of Section C of Annex I to, Directive 2004/39/EC;
-   (b)   there are frequent opportunities to dispose of, redeem, or otherwise realise that instrument at prices that are publicly available to market participants and that are either market prices or prices made available, or validated, by valuation systems independent of the issuer;
-   (c)   it does not involve any actual or potential liability for the client that exceeds the cost of acquiring the instrument;
-   (d)   adequately comprehensive information on its characteristics is publicly available and is likely to be readily understood so as to enable the average retail client to make an informed judgment as to whether to enter into a transaction in that instrument.

[5998]

Article 39
Retail client agreement
(*Article 19(1) and 19(7) of Directive 2004/39/EC*)

Member States shall require an investment firm that provides an investment service other than investment advice to a new retail client for the first time after the date of application of this Directive to enter into a written basic agreement, in paper or another durable medium, with the client setting out the essential rights and obligations of the firm and the client.

The rights and duties of the parties to the agreement may be incorporated by reference to other documents or legal texts.

[5999]

SECTION 4
REPORTING TO CLIENTS

Article 40
Reporting obligations in respect of execution of orders other than for portfolio management
(*Article 19(8) of Directive 2004/39/EC*)

1.   Member States shall ensure that where investment firms have carried out an order, other than for portfolio management, on behalf of a client, they take the following action in respect of that order:
-   (a)   the investment firm must promptly provide the client, in a durable medium, with the essential information concerning the execution of that order;
-   (b)   in the case of a retail client, the investment firm must send the client a notice in a durable medium confirming execution of the order as soon as possible and no later than the first business day following execution or, if the confirmation is received by the investment firm from a third party, no later than the first business day following receipt of the confirmation from the third party.

Point (b) shall not apply where the confirmation would contain the same information as a confirmation that is to be promptly dispatched to the retail client by another person.

Points (a) and (b) shall not apply where orders executed on behalf of clients relate to bonds funding mortgage loan agreements with the said clients, in which case the report on the transaction shall be made at the same time as the terms of the mortgage loan are communicated, but no later than one month after the execution of the order.

2.   In addition to the requirements under paragraph 1, Member States shall require investment firms to supply the client, on request, with information about the status of his order.

3.   Member States shall ensure that, in the case of orders for a retail clients relating to units or shares in a collective investment undertaking which are executed periodically, investment firms either take the action specified in point (b) of paragraph 1 or provide the retail client, at least once every six months, with the information listed in paragraph 4 in respect of those transactions.

4.   The notice referred to in point (b) of paragraph 1 shall include such of the following information as is applicable and, where relevant, in accordance with Table 1 of Annex I to Regulation (EC) No 1287/2006:

(a)   the reporting firm identification;
(b)   the name or other designation of the client;
(c)   the trading day;
(d)   the trading time;
(e)   the type of the order;
(f)   the venue identification;
(g)   the instrument identification;
(h)   the buy/sell indicator;
(i)   the nature of the order if other than buy/sell;
(j)   the quantity;
(k)   the unit price;
(l)   the total consideration;
(m)   a total sum of the commissions and expenses charged and, where the retail client so requests, an itemised breakdown;
(n)   the client's responsibilities in relation to the settlement of the transaction, including the time limit for payment or delivery as well as the appropriate account details where these details and responsibilities have not previously been notified to the client;
(o)   if the client's counterparty was the investment firm itself or any person in the investment firm's group or another client of the investment firm, the fact that this was the case unless the order was executed through a trading system that facilitates anonymous trading.

For the purposes of point (k), where the order is executed in tranches, the investment firm may supply the client with information about the price of each tranche or the average price. Where the average price is provided, the investment firm shall supply the retail client with information about the price of each tranche upon request.

5.   The investment firm may provide the client with the information referred to in paragraph 4 using standard codes if it also provides an explanation of the codes used.

[6000]

Article 41
Reporting obligations in respect of portfolio management
(*Article 19(8) of Directive 2004/39/EC*)

1.   Member States shall require investments firms which provide the service of portfolio management to clients to provide each such client with a periodic statement in a durable medium of the portfolio management activities carried out on behalf of that client unless such a statement is provided by another person.

2.   In the case of retail clients, the periodic statement required under paragraph 1 shall include, where relevant, the following information:
(a)   the name of the investment firm;
(b)   the name or other designation of the retail client's account;
(c)   a statement of the contents and the valuation of the portfolio, including details of each financial instrument held, its market value, or fair value if market value is unavailable and the cash balance at the beginning and at the end of the reporting period, and the performance of the portfolio during the reporting period;
(d)   the total amount of fees and charges incurred during the reporting period, itemising at least total management fees and total costs associated with execution, and including, where relevant, a statement that a more detailed breakdown will be provided on request;
(e)   a comparison of performance during the period covered by the statement with the investment performance benchmark (if any) agreed between the investment firm and the client;
(f)   the total amount of dividends, interest and other payments received during the reporting period in relation to the client's portfolio;
(g)   information about other corporate actions giving rights in relation to financial instruments held in the portfolio;
(h)   for each transaction executed during the period, the information referred to in Article 40(4)(c) to (l) where relevant, unless the client elects to receive information about executed transactions on a transaction-by-transaction basis, in which case paragraph 4 of this Article shall apply.

3.   In the case of retail clients, the periodic statement referred to in paragraph 1 shall be provided once every six months, except in the following cases:
(a)   where the client so requests, the periodic statement must be provided every three months;
(b)   in cases where paragraph 4 applies, the periodic statement must be provided at least once every 12 months;

   (c)   where the agreement between an investment firm and a retail client for a portfolio management service authorises a leveraged portfolio, the periodic statement must be provided at least once a month.

Investment firms shall inform retail clients that they have the right to make requests for the purposes of point (a).

However, the exception provided for in point (b) shall not apply in the case of transactions in financial instruments covered by Article 4(1)(18)(c) of, or any of points 4 to 10 of Section C in Annex I to, Directive 2004/39/EC.

4.   Member States shall require investment firms, in cases where the client elects to receive information about executed transactions on a transaction-by-transaction basis, to provide promptly to the client, on the execution of a transaction by the portfolio manager, the essential information concerning that transaction in a durable medium.

Where the client concerned is a retail client, the investment firm must send him a notice confirming the transaction and containing the information referred to in Article 40(4) no later than the first business day following that execution or, if the confirmation is received by the investment firm from a third party, no later than the first business day following receipt of the confirmation from the third party.

The second subparagraph shall not apply where the confirmation would contain the same information as a confirmation that is to be promptly dispatched to the retail client by another person.

[6001]

Article 42
Additional reporting obligations for portfolio management or contingent liability transactions
(Article 19(8) of Directive 2004/39/EC)

Member States shall ensure that where investment firms provide portfolio management transactions for retail clients or operate retail client accounts that include an uncovered open position in a contingent liability transaction, they also report to the retail client any losses exceeding any predetermined threshold, agreed between the firm and the client, no later than the end of the business day in which the threshold is exceeded or, in a case where the threshold is exceeded on a non-business day, the close of the next business day.

[6002]

Article 43
Statements of client financial instruments or client funds
(Article 19(8) of Directive 2004/39/EC)

1.   Member States shall require investment firms that hold client financial instruments or client funds to send at least once a year, to each client for whom they hold financial instruments or funds, a statement in a durable medium of those financial instruments or funds unless such a statement has been provided in any other periodic statement.

The first subparagraph shall not apply to a credit institution authorised under Directive 2000/12/EC in respect of deposits within the meaning of that Directive held by that institution.

2.   The statement of client assets referred to in paragraph 1 shall include the following information:

   (a)   details of all the financial instruments or funds held by the investment firm for the client at the end of the period covered by the statement;

   (b)   the extent to which any client financial instruments or client funds have been the subject of securities financing transactions;

   (c)   the extent of any benefit that has accrued to the client by virtue of participation in any securities financing transactions, and the basis on which that benefit has accrued.

In cases where the portfolio of a client includes the proceeds of one or more unsettled transactions, the information referred to in point (a) may be based either on the trade date or the settlement date, provided that the same basis is applied consistently to all such information in the statement.

3.   Member States shall permit investment firms which hold financial instruments or funds and which carry out the service of portfolio management for a client to include the statement of client assets referred to in paragraph 1 in the periodic statement it provides to that client pursuant to Article 41(1).

[6003]

SECTION 5
BEST EXECUTION

Article 44
Best execution criteria
(Articles 21(1) and 19(1) of Directive 2004/39/EC)

1. Member States shall ensure that, when executing client orders, investment firms take into account the following criteria for determining the relative importance of the factors referred to in Article 21(1) of Directive 2004/39/EC:

    (a)   the characteristics of the client including the categorisation of the client as retail or professional;

    (b)   the characteristics of the client order;

    (c)   the characteristics of financial instruments that are the subject of that order;

    (d)   the characteristics of the execution venues to which that order can be directed.

For the purposes of this Article and Article 46, "execution venue" means a regulated market, an MTF, a systematic internaliser, or a market maker or other liquidity provider or an entity that performs a similar function in a third country to the functions performed by any of the foregoing.

2. An investment firm satisfies its obligation under Article 21(1) of Directive 2004/39/EC to take all reasonable steps to obtain the best possible result for a client to the extent that it executes an order or a specific aspect of an order following specific instructions from the client relating to the order or the specific aspect of the order.

3. Where an investment firm executes an order on behalf of a retail client, the best possible result shall be determined in terms of the total consideration, representing the price of the financial instrument and the costs related to execution, which shall include all expenses incurred by the client which are directly related to the execution of the order, including execution venue fees, clearing and settlement fees and any other fees paid to third parties involved in the execution of the order.

For the purposes of delivering best execution where there is more than one competing venue to execute an order for a financial instrument, in order to assess and compare the results for the client that would be achieved by executing the order on each of the execution venues listed in the firm's order execution policy that is capable of executing that order, the firm's own commissions and costs for executing the order on each of the eligible execution venues shall be taken into account in that assessment.

4. Member States shall require that investment firms do not structure or charge their commissions in such a way as to discriminate unfairly between execution venues.

5. Before 1 November 2008 the Commission shall present a report to the European Parliament and to the Council on the availability, comparability and consolidation of information concerning the quality of execution of various execution venues.

[6004]

Article 45
Duty of investment firms carrying out portfolio management and reception and transmission of orders to act in the best interests of the client
(Article 19(1) of Directive 2004/39/EC)

1. Member States shall require investment firms, when providing the service of portfolio management, to comply with the obligation under Article 19(1) of Directive 2004/39/EC to act in accordance with the best interests of their clients when placing orders with other entities for execution that result from decisions by the investment firm to deal in financial instruments on behalf of its client.

2. Member States shall require investment firms, when providing the service of reception and transmission of orders, to comply with the obligation under Article 19(1) of Directive 2004/39/EC to act in accordance with the best interests of their clients when transmitting client orders to other entities for execution.

3. Member States shall ensure that, in order to comply with paragraphs 1 or 2, investment firms take the actions mentioned in paragraphs 4 to 6.

4. Investment firms shall take all reasonable steps to obtain the best possible result for their clients taking into account the factors referred to in Article 21(1) of Directive 2004/39/EC. The relative importance of these factors shall be determined by reference to the criteria set out in Article 44(1)and, for retail clients, to the requirement under Article 44(3).

An investment firm satisfies its obligations under paragraph 1 or 2, and is not required to take the steps mentioned in this paragraph, to the extent that it follows specific instructions from its client when placing an order with, or transmitting an order to, another entity for execution.

5. Investment firms shall establish and implement a policy to enable them to comply with the obligation in paragraph 4. The policy shall identify, in respect of each class of instruments, the entities with which the orders are placed or to which the investment firm transmits orders for

execution. The entities identified must have execution arrangements that enable the investment firm to comply with its obligations under this Article when it places or transmits orders to that entity for execution.

Investment firms shall provide appropriate information to their clients on the policy established in accordance with this paragraph.

6. Investment firms shall monitor on a regular basis the effectiveness of the policy established in accordance with paragraph 5 and, in particular, the execution quality of the entities identified in that policy and, where appropriate, correct any deficiencies.

In addition, investment firms shall review the policy annually. Such a review shall also be carried out whenever a material change occurs that affects the firm's ability to continue to obtain the best possible result for their clients.

7. This Article shall not apply when the investment firm that provides the service of portfolio management and/or reception and transmission of orders also executes the orders received or the decisions to deal on behalf of its client's portfolio. In those cases Article 21 of Directive 2004/39/EC applies.

[6005]

Article 46
Execution policy
(Article 21(3) and (4) of Directive 2004/39/EC)

1. Member States shall ensure that investment firms review annually the execution policy established pursuant to Article 21(2) of Directive 2004/39/EC, as well as their order execution arrangements.

Such a review shall also be carried out whenever a material change occurs that affects the firm's ability to continue to obtain the best possible result for the execution of its client orders on a consistent basis using the venues included in its execution policy.

2. Investment firms shall provide retail clients with the following details on their execution policy in good time prior to the provision of the service:

(a) an account of the relative importance the investment firm assigns, in accordance with the criteria specified in Article 44(1), to the factors referred to in Article 21(1) of Directive 2004/39/EC, or the process by which the firm determines the relative importance of those factors;

(b) a list of the execution venues on which the firm places significant reliance in meeting its obligation to take all reasonable steps to obtain on a consistent basis the best possible result for the execution of client orders;

(c) a clear and prominent warning that any specific instructions from a client may prevent the firm from taking the steps that it has designed and implemented in its execution policy to obtain the best possible result for the execution of those orders in respect of the elements covered by those instructions.

That information shall be provided in a durable medium, or by means of a website (where that does not constitute a durable medium) provided that the conditions specified in Article 3(2) are satisfied.

[6006]

SECTION 6
CLIENT ORDER HANDLING

Article 47
General principles
(Articles 22(1) and 19(1) of Directive 2004/39/EC)

1. Member States shall require investment firms to satisfy the following conditions when carrying out client orders:

(a) they must ensure that orders executed on behalf of clients are promptly and accurately recorded and allocated;

(b) they must carry out otherwise comparable client orders sequentially and promptly unless the characteristics of the order or prevailing market conditions make this impracticable, or the interests of the client require otherwise;

(c) they must inform a retail client about any material difficulty relevant to the proper carrying out of orders promptly upon becoming aware of the difficulty.

2. Where an investment firm is responsible for overseeing or arranging the settlement of an executed order, it shall take all reasonable steps to ensure that any client financial instruments or client funds received in settlement of that executed order are promptly and correctly delivered to the account of the appropriate client.

PART IV
EC MATERIALS

3.   An investment firm shall not misuse information relating to pending client orders, and shall take all reasonable steps to prevent the misuse of such information by any of its relevant persons.

[6007]

Article 48
Aggregation and allocation of orders
(Articles 22(1) and 19(1) of Directive 2004/39/EC)

1.   Member States shall not permit investment firms to carry out a client order or a transaction for own account in aggregation with another client order unless the following conditions are met:

(a)   it must be unlikely that the aggregation of orders and transactions will work overall to the disadvantage of any client whose order is to be aggregated;

(b)   it must be disclosed to each client whose order is to be aggregated that the effect of aggregation may work to its disadvantage in relation to a particular order;

(c)   an order allocation policy must be established and effectively implemented, providing in sufficiently precise terms for the fair allocation of aggregated orders and transactions, including how the volume and price of orders determines allocations and the treatment of partial executions.

2.   Member States shall ensure that where an investment firm aggregates an order with one or more other client orders and the aggregated order is partially executed, it allocates the related trades in accordance with its order allocation policy.

[6008]

Article 49
Aggregation and allocation of transactions for own account
(Articles 22(1) and 19(1) of Directive 2004/39/EC)

1.   Member States shall ensure that investment firms which have aggregated transactions for own account with one or more client orders do not allocate the related trades in a way that is detrimental to a client.

2.   Member States shall require that, where an investment firm aggregates a client order with a transaction for own account and the aggregated order is partially executed, it allocates the related trades to the client in priority to the firm.

However, if the firm is able to demonstrate on reasonable grounds that without the combination it would not have been able to carry out the order on such advantageous terms, or at all, it may allocate the transaction for own account proportionally, in accordance with its order allocation policy referred to in Article 48(1)(c).

3.   Member States shall require investment firms, as part of the order allocation policy referred to in Article 48(1)(c), to put in place procedures designed to prevent the reallocation, in a way that is detrimental to the client, of transactions for own account which are executed in combination with client orders.

[6009]

SECTION 7
ELIGIBLE COUNTERPARTIES

Article 50
Eligible counterparties
(Article 24(3) of Directive 2004/39/EC)

1.   Member States may recognise an undertaking as an eligible counterparty if that undertaking falls within a category of clients who are to be considered professional clients in accordance with paragraphs 1, 2 and 3 of Section I of Annex II to Directive 2004/39/EC, excluding any category which is explicitly mentioned in Article 24(2) of that Directive.

On request, Member States may also recognise as eligible counterparties undertakings which fall within a category of clients who are to be considered professional clients in accordance with Section II of Annex II to Directive 2004/39/EC. In such cases, however, the undertaking concerned shall be recognised as an eligible counterparty only in respect of the services or transactions for which it could be treated as a professional client.

2.   Where, pursuant to the second subparagraph of Article 24(2) of Directive 2004/39/EC, an eligible counterparty requests treatment as a client whose business with an investment firm is subject to Articles 19, 21 and 22 of that Directive, but does not expressly request treatment as a retail client, and the investment firm agrees to that request, the firm shall treat that eligible counterparty as a professional client.

However, where that eligible counterparty expressly requests treatment as a retail client, the provisions in respect of requests of non-professional treatment specified in the second, third and fourth sub-paragraphs of Section I of Annex II to Directive 2004/39/EC shall apply.

[6010]

SECTION 8
RECORD-KEEPING

Article 51
Retention of records
(*Article 13(6) of Directive 2004/39EC*)

1.   Member States shall require investment firms to retain all the records required under Directive 2004/39/EC and its implementing measures for a period of at least five years.

Additionally, records which set out the respective rights and obligations of the investment firm and the client under an agreement to provide services, or the terms on which the firm provides services to the client, shall be retained for at least the duration of the relationship with the client.

However, competent authorities may, in exceptional circumstances, require investment firms to retain any or all of those records for such longer period as is justified by the nature of the instrument or transaction, if that is necessary to enable the authority to exercise its supervisory functions under Directive 2004/39/EC.

Following the termination of the authorisation of an investment firm, Member States or competent authorities may require the firm to retain records for the outstanding term of the five year period required under the first subparagraph.

2.   The records shall be retained in a medium that allows the storage of information in a way accessible for future reference by the competent authority, and in such a form and manner that the following conditions are met:

(a)   the competent authority must be able to access them readily and to reconstitute each key stage of the processing of each transaction;

(b)   it must be possible for any corrections or other amendments, and the contents of the records prior to such corrections or amendments, to be easily ascertained;

(c)   it must not be possible for the records otherwise to be manipulated or altered.

3.   The competent authority of each Member State shall draw up and maintain a list of the minimum records investment firms are required to keep under Directive 2004/39/EC and its implementing measures.

4.   Record-keeping obligations under Directive 2004/39/EC and in this Directive are without prejudice to the right of Member States to impose obligations on investment firms relating to the recording of telephone conversations or electronic communications involving client orders.

5.   Before 31 December 2009 the Commission shall, in the light of discussions with the Committee of European Securities Regulators, report to the European Parliament and the Council on the continued appropriateness of the provisions of paragraph 4.

[6011]

SECTION 9
DEFINED TERMS FOR THE PURPOSES OF DIRECTIVE 2004/39/EC

Article 52
Investment advice
(*Article 4(1)(4) of Directive 2004/39/EC*)

For the purposes of the definition of "investment advice" in Article 4(1)(4) of Directive 2004/39/EC, a personal recommendation is a recommendation that is made to a person in his capacity as an investor or potential investor, or in his capacity as an agent for an investor or potential investor.

That recommendation must be presented as suitable for that person, or must be based on a consideration of the circumstances of that person, and must constitute a recommendation to take one of the following sets of steps:

(a)   to buy, sell, subscribe for, exchange, redeem, hold or underwrite a particular financial instrument;

(b)   to exercise or not to exercise any right conferred by a particular financial instrument to buy, sell, subscribe for, exchange, or redeem a financial instrument.

A recommendation is not a personal recommendation if it is issued exclusively through distribution channels or to the public.

[6012]

PART IV
EC MATERIALS

CHAPTER IV
FINAL PROVISIONS

Article 53
Transposition

1. Member States shall adopt and publish, by 31 January 2007 at the latest, the laws, regulations and administrative provisions necessary to comply with this Directive. They shall forthwith communicate to the Commission the text of those provisions and a correlation table between those provisions and this Directive.

2. Member States shall apply those provisions from 1 November 2007.

3. When Member States adopt those provisions, they shall contain a reference to this Directive or be accompanied by such a reference on the occasion of their official publication. Member States shall determine how such reference is to be made.

4. Member States shall communicate to the Commission the text of the main provisions of national law which they adopt in the field covered by this Directive.

[6013]

Article 54
Entry into force

This Directive shall enter into force on the 20th day following its publication in the Official Journal of the European Union.

[6014]

Article 55
Addressees

This Directive is addressed to the Member States.

[6015]

EUROPEAN PARLIAMENT AND COUNCIL REGULATION

of 15 November 2006

on information on the payer accompanying transfers of funds

(1781/2006/EC)

(Text with EEA relevance)

NOTES
Date of publication in OJ: OJ L345, 8.12.2006, p 1. The text of this Regulation incorporates the corrigendum published in OJ L323, 8.12.2007, p 59. Notes are as in the original OJ version.
As of 1 February 2009, this Regulation had not been amended.

THE EUROPEAN PARLIAMENT AND THE COUNCIL OF THE EUROPEAN UNION,
    Having regard to the Treaty establishing the European Community, and in particular Article 95 thereof,
    Having regard to the proposal from the Commission,
    Having regard to the opinion of the European Central Bank,[1]
    Acting in accordance with the procedure laid down in Article 251 of the Treaty,[2]
    Whereas:
    (1) Flows of dirty money through transfers of funds can damage the stability and reputation of the financial sector and threaten the internal market. Terrorism shakes the very foundations of our society. The soundness, integrity and stability of the system of transfers of funds and confidence in the financial system as a whole could be seriously jeopardised by the efforts of criminals and their associates either to disguise the origin of criminal proceeds or to transfer funds for terrorist purposes.
    (2) In order to facilitate their criminal activities, money launderers and terrorist financers could try to take advantage of the freedom of capital movements entailed by the integrated financial area, unless certain coordinating measures are adopted at Community level. By its scale, Community action should ensure that Special Recommendation VII on wire transfers (SR VII) of the Financial Action Task Force (FATF) established by the Paris G7 Summit of 1989 is transposed uniformly throughout the European Union, and, in particular, that there is no discrimination between national payments within a Member State and cross-border payments between Member States.

Uncoordinated action by Member States alone in the field of cross-border transfers of funds could have a significant impact on the smooth functioning of payment systems at EU level, and therefore damage the internal market in the field of financial services.

(3) In the wake of the terrorist attacks in the USA on 11 September 2001, the extraordinary European Council on 21 September 2001 reiterated that the fight against terrorism is a key objective of the European Union. The European Council approved a plan of action dealing with enhanced police and judicial cooperation, developing international legal instruments against terrorism, preventing terrorist funding, strengthening air security and greater consistency between all relevant policies. This plan of action was revised by the European Council following the terrorist attacks of 11 March 2004 in Madrid, and now specifically addresses the need to ensure that the legislative framework created by the Community for the purpose of combating terrorism and improving judicial cooperation is adapted to the nine Special Recommendations against Terrorist Financing adopted by the FATF.

(4) In order to prevent terrorist funding, measures aimed at the freezing of funds and economic resources of certain persons, groups and entities have been taken, including Regulation (EC) No 2580/2001,[3] and Council Regulation (EC) No 881/2002.[4] To that same end, measures aimed at protecting the financial system against the channelling of funds and economic resources for terrorist purposes have been taken. Directive 2005/60/EC of the European Parliament and of the Council[5] contains a number of measures aimed at combating the misuse of the financial system for the purpose of money laundering and terrorist financing. Those measures do not, however, fully prevent terrorists and other criminals from having access to payment systems for moving their funds.

(5) In order to foster a coherent approach in the international context in the field of combating money laundering and terrorist financing, further Community action should take account of developments at that level, namely the nine Special Recommendations against Terrorist Financing adopted by the FATF, and in particular SR VII and the revised interpretative note for its implementation.

(6) The full traceability of transfers of funds can be a particularly important and valuable tool in the prevention, investigation and detection of money laundering or terrorist financing. It is therefore appropriate, in order to ensure the transmission of information on the payer throughout the payment chain, to provide for a system imposing the obligation on payment service providers to have transfers of funds accompanied by accurate and meaningful information on the payer.

(7) The provisions of this Regulation apply without prejudice to Directive 95/46/EC of the European Parliament and of the Council.[6] For example, information collected and kept for the purpose of this Regulation should not be used for commercial purposes.

(8) Persons who merely convert paper documents into electronic data and are acting under a contract with a payment service provider do not fall within the scope of this Regulation; the same applies to any natural or legal person who provides payment service providers solely with messaging or other support systems for transmitting funds or with clearing and settlement systems.

(9) It is appropriate to exclude from the scope of this Regulation transfers of funds that represent a low risk of money laundering or terrorist financing. Such exclusions should cover credit or debit cards, Automated Teller Machine (ATM) withdrawals, direct debits, truncated cheques, payments of taxes, fines or other levies, and transfers of funds where both the payer and the payee are payment service providers acting on their own behalf. In addition, in order to reflect the special characteristics of national payment systems, Member States may exempt electronic giro payments, provided that it is always possible to trace the transfer of funds back to the payer. Where Member States have applied the derogation for electronic money in Directive 2005/60/EC, it should be applied under this Regulation, provided the amount transacted does not exceed EUR 1,000.

(10) The exemption for electronic money, as defined by Directive 2000/46/EC of the European Parliament and of the Council,[7] covers electronic money irrespective of whether the issuer of such money benefits from a waiver under Article 8 of that Directive.

(11) In order not to impair the efficiency of payment systems, the verification requirements for transfers of funds made from an account should be separate from those for transfers of funds not made from an account. In order to balance the risk of driving transactions underground by imposing overly strict identification requirements against the potential terrorist threat posed by small transfers of funds, the obligation to check whether the information on the payer is accurate should, in the case of transfers of funds not made from an account, be imposed only in respect of individual transfers of funds that exceed EUR 1,000, without prejudice to the obligations under Directive 2005/60/EC. For transfers of funds made from an account, payment service providers should not be required to verify information on the payer accompanying each transfer of funds, where the obligations under Directive 2005/60/EC have been met.

(12) Against the background of Regulation (EC) No 2560/2001 of the European Parliament and of the Council[8] and the Commission Communication "A New Legal Framework for Payments in the Internal Market", it is sufficient to provide for simplified information on the payer to accompany transfers of funds within the Community.

(13) In order to allow the authorities responsible for combating money laundering or terrorist financing in third countries to trace the source of funds used for those purposes, transfers of funds from the Community to outside the Community should carry complete information on the payer.

Those authorities should be granted access to complete information on the payer only for the purposes of preventing, investigating and detecting money laundering or terrorist financing.

(14) For transfers of funds from a single payer to several payees to be sent in an inexpensive way in batch files containing individual transfers from the Community to outside the Community, provision should be made for such individual transfers to carry only the account number of the payer or a unique identifier provided that the batch file contains complete information on the payer.

(15) In order to check whether the required information on the payer accompanies transfers of funds, and to help to identify suspicious transactions, the payment service provider of the payee should have effective procedures in place in order to detect whether information on the payer is missing.

(16) Owing to the potential terrorist financing threat posed by anonymous transfers, it is appropriate to enable the payment service provider of the payee to avoid or correct such situations when it becomes aware that information on the payer is missing or incomplete. In this regard, flexibility should be allowed as concerns the extent of information on the payer on a risk-sensitive basis. In addition, the accuracy and completeness of information on the payer should remain the responsibility of the payment service provider of the payer. Where the payment service provider of the payer is situated outside the territory of the Community, enhanced customer due diligence should be applied, in accordance with Directive 2005/60/EC, in respect of cross-border correspondent banking relationships with that payment service provider.

(17) Where guidance is given by national competent authorities as regards the obligations either to reject all transfers from a payment service provider which regularly fails to supply the required information on the payer or to decide whether or not to restrict or terminate a business relationship with that payment service provider, it should inter alia be based on the convergence of best practices and should also take into account the fact that the revised interpretative note to SR VII of the FATF allows third countries to set a threshold of EUR 1,000 or USD 1,000 for the obligation to send information on the payer, without prejudice to the objective of efficiently combating money laundering and terrorist financing.

(18) In any event, the payment service provider of the payee should exercise special vigilance, assessing the risks, when it becomes aware that information on the payer is missing or incomplete, and should report suspicious transactions to the competent authorities, in accordance with the reporting obligations set out in Directive 2005/60/EC and national implementing measures.

(19) The provisions on transfers of funds where information on the payer is missing or incomplete apply without prejudice to any obligations on payment service providers to suspend and/or reject transfers of funds which violate provisions of civil, administrative or criminal law.

(20) Until technical limitations that may prevent intermediary payment service providers from satisfying the obligation to transmit all the information they receive on the payer are removed, those intermediary payment service providers should keep records of that information. Such technical limitations should be removed as soon as payment systems are upgraded.

(21) Since in criminal investigations it may not be possible to identify the data required or the individuals involved until many months, or even years, after the original transfer of funds, it is appropriate to require payment service providers to keep records of information on the payer for the purposes of preventing, investigating and detecting money laundering or terrorist financing. This period should be limited.

(22) To enable prompt action to be taken in the fight against terrorism, payment service providers should respond promptly to requests for information on the payer from the authorities responsible for combating money laundering or terrorist financing in the Member State where they are situated.

(23) The number of working days in the Member State of the payment service provider of the payer determines the number of days to respond to requests for information on the payer.

(24) Given the importance of the fight against money laundering and terrorist financing, Member States should lay down effective, proportionate and dissuasive penalties in national law for failure to comply with this Regulation.

(25) The measures necessary for the implementation of this Regulation should be adopted in accordance with Council Decision 1999/468/EC of 28 June 1999 laying down the procedures for the exercise of implementing powers conferred on the Commission.[9]

(26) A number of countries and territories which do not form part of the territory of the Community share a monetary union with a Member State, form part of the currency area of a Member State or have signed a monetary convention with the European Community represented by a Member State, and have payment service providers that participate directly or indirectly in the payment and settlement systems of that Member State. In order to avoid the application of this Regulation to transfers of funds between the Member States concerned and those countries or territories having a significant negative effect on the economies of those countries or territories, it is appropriate to provide for the possibility for such transfers of funds to be treated as transfers of funds within the Member States concerned.

(27) In order not to discourage donations for charitable purposes, it is appropriate to authorise Member States to exempt payment services providers situated in their territory from collecting, verifying, recording, or sending information on the payer for transfers of funds up to a maximum

amount of EUR 150 executed within the territory of that Member State. It is also appropriate to make this option conditional upon requirements to be met by non-profit organisations, in order to allow Member States to ensure that this exemption does not give rise to abuse by terrorists as a cover for or a means of facilitating the financing of their activities.

(28) Since the objectives of this Regulation cannot be sufficiently achieved by the Member States and can therefore, by reason of the scale or effects of the action, be better achieved at Community level, the Community may adopt measures, in accordance with the principle of subsidiarity as set out in Article 5 of the Treaty. In accordance with the principle of proportionality, as set out in that Article, this Regulation does not go beyond what is necessary in order to achieve those objectives.

(29) In order to establish a coherent approach in the field of combating money laundering and terrorist financing, the main provisions of this Regulation should apply from the same date as the relevant provisions adopted at international level,

[6016]

NOTES
1   OJ C336, 31.12.2005, p 109.
2   Opinion of the European Parliament delivered on 6 July 2006 (not yet published in the Official Journal) and Council Decision delivered on 7 November 2006.
3   OJ L344, 28.12.2001, p 70. Regulation as last amended by Commission Regulation (EC) No 1461/2006 (OJ L272, 3.10.2006, p 11).
4   OJ L139, 29.5.2002, p 9. Regulation as last amended by Commission Regulation (EC) No 1508/2006 (OJ L280, 12.10.2006, p 12).
5   OJ L309, 25.11.2005, p 15.
6   OJ L281, 23.11.1995, p 31. Directive as amended by Regulation (EC) No 1882/2003 (OJ L284, 31.10.2003, p 1).
7   OJ L275, 27.10.2000, p 39.
8   Regulation as corrected by OJ L344, 28.12.2001, p 13.
9   OJ L184, 17.7.1999, p 23. Decision as last amended by Decision 2006/512/EC (OJ L200, 22.7.2006, p 11).

HAVE ADOPTED THIS REGULATION:

CHAPTER I
SUBJECT MATTER, DEFINITIONS AND SCOPE

Article 1
Subject matter

This Regulation lays down rules on information on the payer to accompany transfers of funds for the purposes of the prevention, investigation and detection of money laundering and terrorist financing.

[6017]

Article 2
Definitions

For the purposes of this Regulation, the following definitions shall apply:
(1)   "terrorist financing" means the provision or collection of funds within the meaning of Article 1(4) of Directive 2005/60/EC;
(2)   "money laundering" means any conduct which, when committed intentionally, is regarded as money laundering for the purposes of Article 1(2) or (3) of Directive 2005/60/EC;
(3)   "payer" means either a natural or legal person who holds an account and allows a transfer of funds from that account, or, where there is no account, a natural or legal person who places an order for a transfer of funds;
(4)   "payee" means a natural or legal person who is the intended final recipient of transferred funds;
(5)   "payment service provider" means a natural or legal person whose business includes the provision of transfer of funds services;
(6)   "intermediary payment service provider" means a payment service provider, neither of the payer nor of the payee, that participates in the execution of transfers of funds;
(7)   "transfer of funds" means any transaction carried out on behalf of a payer through a payment service provider by electronic means, with a view to making funds available to a payee at a payment service provider, irrespective of whether the payer and the payee are the same person;
(8)   "batch file transfer" means several individual transfers of funds which are bundled together for transmission;
(9)   "unique identifier" means a combination of letters, numbers or symbols, determined by the payment service provider, in accordance with the protocols of the payment and settlement system or messaging system used to effect the transfer of funds.

[6018]

Article 3
Scope

1.   This Regulation shall apply to transfers of funds, in any currency, which are sent or received by a payment service provider established in the Community.

2.   This Regulation shall not apply to transfers of funds carried out using a credit or debit card, provided that:
   (a)   the payee has an agreement with the payment service provider permitting payment for the provision of goods and services;
   and
   (b)   a unique identifier, allowing the transaction to be traced back to the payer, accompanies such transfer of funds.

3.   Where a Member State chooses to apply the derogation set out in Article 11(5)(d) of Directive 2005/60/EC, this Regulation shall not apply to transfers of funds using electronic money covered by that derogation, except where the amount transferred exceeds EUR 1,000.

4.   Without prejudice to paragraph 3, this Regulation shall not apply to transfers of funds carried out by means of a mobile telephone or any other digital or Information Technology (IT) device, when such transfers are pre-paid and do not exceed EUR 150.

5.   This Regulation shall not apply to transfers of funds carried out by means of a mobile telephone or any other digital or IT device, when such transfers are post-paid and meet all of the following conditions:
   (a)   the payee has an agreement with the payment service provider permitting payment for the provision of goods and services;
   (b)   a unique identifier, allowing the transaction to be traced back to the payer, accompanies the transfer of funds;
   and
   (c)   the payment service provider is subject to the obligations set out in Directive 2005/60/EC.

6.   Member States may decide not to apply this Regulation to transfers of funds within that Member State to a payee account permitting payment for the provision of goods or services if:
   (a)   the payment service provider of the payee is subject to the obligations set out in Directive 2005/60/EC;
   (b)   the payment service provider of the payee is able by means of a unique reference number to trace back, through the payee, the transfer of funds from the natural or legal person who has an agreement with the payee for the provision of goods and services;
   and
   (c)   the amount transacted is EUR 1,000 or less.

Member States making use of this derogation shall inform the Commission thereof.

7.   This Regulation shall not apply to transfers of funds:
   (a)   where the payer withdraws cash from his or her own account;
   (b)   where there is a debit transfer authorisation between two parties permitting payments between them through accounts, provided that a unique identifier accompanies the transfer of funds, enabling the natural or legal person to be traced back;
   (c)   where truncated cheques are used;
   (d)   to public authorities for taxes, fines or other levies within a Member State;
   (e)   where both the payer and the payee are payment service providers acting on their own behalf.

[6019]

CHAPTER II
OBLIGATIONS ON THE PAYMENT SERVICE PROVIDER OF THE PAYER

Article 4
Complete information on the payer

1.   Complete information on the payer shall consist of his name, address and account number.

2.   The address may be substituted with the date and place of birth of the payer, his customer identification number or national identity number.

3.   Where the payer does not have an account number, the payment service provider of the payer shall substitute it by a unique identifier which allows the transaction to be traced back to the payer.

[6020]

Article 5
Information accompanying transfers of funds and record keeping

1.   Payment service providers shall ensure that transfers of funds are accompanied by complete information on the payer.

2.   The payment service provider of the payer shall, before transferring the funds, verify the complete information on the payer on the basis of documents, data or information obtained from a reliable and independent source.

3.   In the case of transfers of funds from an account, verification may be deemed to have taken place if:

    (a)   a payer's identity has been verified in connection with the opening of the account and the information obtained by this verification has been stored in accordance with the obligations set out in Articles 8(2) and 30(a) of Directive 2005/60/EC;

    or

    (b)   the payer falls within the scope of Article 9(6) of Directive 2005/60/EC.

4.   However, without prejudice to Article 7(c) of Directive 2005/60/EC, in the case of transfers of funds not made from an account, the payment service provider of the payer shall verify the information on the payer only where the amount exceeds EUR 1,000, unless the transaction is carried out in several operations that appear to be linked and together exceed EUR 1,000.

5.   The payment service provider of the payer shall for five years keep records of complete information on the payer which accompanies transfers of funds.

[6021]

Article 6
Transfers of funds within the Community

1.   By way of derogation from Article 5(1), transfers of funds, where both the payment service provider of the payer and the payment service provider of the payee are situated in the Community, shall only be required to be accompanied by the account number of the payer or a unique identifier allowing the transaction to be traced back to the payer.

2.   However, if so requested by the payment service provider of the payee, the payment service provider of the payer shall make available to the payment service provider of the payee complete information on the payer, within three working days of receiving that request.

[6022]

Article 7
Transfers of funds from the Community to outside the Community

1.   Transfers of funds where the payment service provider of the payee is situated outside the Community shall be accompanied by complete information on the payer.

2.   In the case of batch file transfers from a single payer where the payment service providers of the payees are situated outside the Community, paragraph 1 shall not apply to the individual transfers bundled together therein, provided that the batch file contains that information and that the individual transfers carry the account number of the payer or a unique identifier.

[6023]

CHAPTER III
OBLIGATIONS ON THE PAYMENT SERVICE PROVIDER OF THE PAYEE

Article 8
Detection of missing information on the payer

The payment service provider of the payee shall detect whether, in the messaging or payment and settlement system used to effect a transfer of funds, the fields relating to the information on the payer have been completed using the characters or inputs admissible within the conventions of that messaging or payment and settlement system. Such provider shall have effective procedures in place in order to detect whether the following information on the payer is missing:

    (a)   for transfers of funds where the payment service provider of the payer is situated in the Community, the information required under Article 6;

    (b)   for transfers of funds where the payment service provider of the payer is situated outside the Community, complete information on the payer as referred to in Article 4, or where applicable, the information required under Article 13;

    and

    (c)   for batch file transfers where the payment service provider of the payer is situated outside the Community, complete information on the payer as referred to in Article 4 in the batch file transfer only, but not in the individual transfers bundled therein.

[6024]

Article 9
Transfers of funds with missing or incomplete information on the payer

1.   If the payment service provider of the payee becomes aware, when receiving transfers of funds, that information on the payer required under this Regulation is missing or incomplete, it shall either reject the transfer or ask for complete information on the payer. In any event, the payment service provider of the payee shall comply with any applicable law or administrative provisions

relating to money laundering and terrorist financing, in particular, Regulations (EC) No 2580/2001 and (EC) No 881/2002, Directive 2005/60/EC and any national implementing measures.

2.   Where a payment service provider regularly fails to supply the required information on the payer, the payment service provider of the payee shall take steps, which may initially include the issuing of warnings and setting of deadlines, before either rejecting any future transfers of funds from that payment service provider or deciding whether or not to restrict or terminate its business relationship with that payment service provider.

The payment service provider of the payee shall report that fact to the authorities responsible for combating money laundering or terrorist financing.

[6025]

Article 10
Risk-based assessment

The payment service provider of the payee shall consider missing or incomplete information on the payer as a factor in assessing whether the transfer of funds, or any related transaction, is suspicious, and whether it must be reported, in accordance with the obligations set out in Chapter III of Directive 2005/60/EC, to the authorities responsible for combating money laundering or terrorist financing.

[6026]

Article 11
Record keeping

The payment service provider of the payee shall for five years keep records of any information received on the payer.

[6027]

CHAPTER IV
OBLIGATIONS ON INTERMEDIARY PAYMENT SERVICE PROVIDERS

Article 12
Keeping information on the payer with the transfer

Intermediary payment service providers shall ensure that all information received on the payer that accompanies a transfer of funds is kept with the transfer.

[6028]

Article 13
Technical limitations

1.   This Article shall apply where the payment service provider of the payer is situated outside the Community and the intermediary payment service provider is situated within the Community.

2.   Unless the intermediary payment service provider becomes aware, when receiving a transfer of funds, that information on the payer required under this Regulation is missing or incomplete, it may use a payment system with technical limitations which prevents information on the payer from accompanying the transfer of funds to send transfers of funds to the payment service provider of the payee.

3.   Where the intermediary payment service provider becomes aware, when receiving a transfer of funds, that information on the payer required under this Regulation is missing or incomplete, it shall only use a payment system with technical limitations if it is able to inform the payment service provider of the payee thereof, either within a messaging or payment system that provides for communication of this fact or through another procedure, provided that the manner of communication is accepted by, or agreed between, both payment service providers.

4.   Where the intermediary payment service provider uses a payment system with technical limitations, the intermediary payment service provider shall, upon request from the payment service provider of the payee, make available to that payment service provider all the information on the payer which it has received, irrespective of whether it is complete or not, within three working days of receiving that request.

5.   In the cases referred to in paragraphs 2 and 3, the intermediary payment service provider shall for five years keep records of all information received.

[6029]

CHAPTER V
GENERAL OBLIGATIONS AND IMPLEMENTING POWERS

Article 14
Cooperation obligations

Payment service providers shall respond fully and without delay, in accordance with the procedural requirements established in the national law of the Member State in which they are situated, to enquiries from the authorities responsible for combating money laundering or terrorist financing of that Member State concerning the information on the payer accompanying transfers of funds and corresponding records.

Without prejudice to national criminal law and the protection of fundamental rights, those authorities may use that information only for the purposes of preventing, investigating or detecting money laundering or terrorist financing.

[6030]

Article 15
Penalties and monitoring

1.   Member States shall lay down the rules on penalties applicable to infringements of the provisions of this Regulation and shall take all measures necessary to ensure that they are implemented. Such penalties shall be effective, proportionate and dissuasive. They shall apply from 15 December 2007.

2.   Member States shall notify the Commission of the rules referred to in paragraph 1 and the authorities responsible for their application by 14 December 2007 at the latest, and shall notify it without delay of any subsequent amendment affecting them.

3.   Member States shall require competent authorities to effectively monitor, and take necessary measures with a view to ensuring, compliance with the requirements of this Regulation.

[6031]

Article 16
Committee procedure

1.   The Commission shall be assisted by the Committee on the Prevention of Money Laundering and Terrorist Financing established by Directive 2005/60/EC, hereinafter referred to as "the Committee".

2.   Where reference is made to this paragraph, Articles 5 and 7 of Decision 1999/468/EC shall apply, having regard to the provisions of Article 8 thereof and provided that the implementing measures adopted in accordance with this procedure do not modify the essential provisions of this Regulation.

The period laid down in Article 5(6) of Decision 1999/468/EC shall be set at three months.

[6032]

CHAPTER VI
DEROGATIONS

Article 17
Agreements with territories or countries which do not form part of the territory of the Community

1.   The Commission may authorise any Member State to conclude agreements, under national arrangements, with a country or territory which does not form part of the territory of the Community as determined in accordance with Article 299 of the Treaty, which contain derogations from this Regulation, in order to allow for transfers of funds between that country or territory and the Member State concerned to be treated as transfers of funds within that Member State.

Such agreements may be authorised only if:

    (a)   the country or territory concerned shares a monetary union with the Member State concerned, forms part of the currency area of that Member State or has signed a Monetary Convention with the European Community represented by a Member State;

    (b)   payment service providers in the country or territory concerned participate directly or indirectly in payment and settlement systems in that Member State;

    and

    (c)   the country or territory concerned requires payment service providers under its jurisdiction to apply the same rules as those established under this Regulation.

2.   Any Member State wishing to conclude an agreement as referred to in paragraph 1 shall send an application to the Commission and provide it with all the necessary information.

Upon receipt by the Commission of an application from a Member State, transfers of funds between that Member State and the country or territory concerned shall be provisionally treated as transfers of funds within that Member State, until a decision is reached in accordance with the procedure set out in this Article.

If the Commission considers that it does not have all the necessary information, it shall contact the Member State concerned within two months of receipt of the application and specify the additional information required.

Once the Commission has all the information it considers necessary for appraisal of the request, it shall within one month notify the requesting Member State accordingly and shall transmit the request to the other Member States.

3.   Within three months of the notification referred to in the fourth subparagraph of paragraph 2, the Commission shall decide, in accordance with the procedure referred to in Article 16(2), whether to authorise the Member State concerned to conclude the agreement referred to in paragraph 1 of this Article.

In any event, a decision as referred to in the first subparagraph shall be adopted within eighteen months of receipt of the application by the Commission.

[6033]

Article 18
Transfers of funds to non-profit organisations within a Member State

1.   Member States may exempt payment service providers situated in their territory from the obligations set out in Article 5, as regards transfers of funds to organisations carrying out activities for non-profit charitable, religious, cultural, educational, social, scientific or fraternal purposes, provided that those organisations are subject to reporting and external audit requirements or supervision by a public authority or self-regulatory body recognised under national law and that those transfers of funds are limited to a maximum amount of EUR 150 per transfer and take place exclusively within the territory of that Member State.

2.   Member States making use of this Article shall communicate to the Commission the measures that they have adopted for applying the option provided for in paragraph 1, including a list of organisations covered by the exemption, the names of the natural persons who ultimately control those organisations and an explanation of how the list will be updated. That information shall also be made available to the authorities responsible for combating money laundering and terrorist financing.

3.   An up-to-date list of organisations covered by the exemption shall be communicated by the Member State concerned to the payment service providers operating in that Member State.

[6034]

Article 19
Review clause

1.   By 28 December 2011 the Commission shall present a report to the European Parliament and to the Council giving a full economic and legal assessment of the application of this Regulation, accompanied, if appropriate, by a proposal for its modification or repeal.

2.   That report shall in particular review:
   (a)   the application of Article 3 with regard to further experience of the possible misuse of electronic money, as defined in Article 1(3) of Directive 2000/46/EC, and other newly-developed means of payment, for the purposes of money laundering and terrorist financing. Should there be a risk of such misuse, the Commission shall submit a proposal to amend this Regulation;
   (b)   the application of Article 13 with regard to the technical limitations which may prevent complete information on the payer from being transmitted to the payment service provider of the payee. Should it be possible to overcome such technical limitations in the light of new developments in the payments area, and taking into account related costs for payment service providers, the Commission shall submit a proposal to amend this Regulation.

[6035]

CHAPTER VII
FINAL PROVISIONS

Article 20
Entry into force

This Regulation shall enter into force on the 20th day following the day of its publication in the *Official Journal of the European Union*, but in any event not before 1 January 2007.

This Regulation shall be binding in its entirety and directly applicable in all Member States.

[6036]

COMMUNICATION FROM THE COMMISSION TO THE COUNCIL AND THE EUROPEAN PARLIAMENT

Investment research and financial analysts

(Text with EEA relevance)

{SEC (2006) 1655}

NOTES

Brussels, 12.12.2006; COM(2006) 789 final. Notes are as per the original.
As of 1 February 2009 this document had not been amended.

---

1. INTRODUCTION

The purpose of this Communication is to take stock of, and to provide stakeholders with practical guidance on, the provisions of recent European legislation relating to investment research and financial analysts, and to respond to the report of the Forum Group on Financial Analysts,[1] which helped inform the drafting of that legislation.

For the most part, this Communication deals with the issue of conflicts of interest, and describes the main European legislation specifically addressing that topic. In the final section, other issues are addressed (analyst registration, independent research, issuer relations with analysts and investor education).

[6037]

NOTES

[1]   Forum Group, Financial Analysts: Best practices in an integrated European financial market September 2003). See
http://europa.eu.int/comm/internal_market/en/finances/mobil/finanalysts/index_en.htm.

---

2. BACKGROUND

2.1. THE ROLE OF INVESTMENT RESEARCH

The ready availability of various types of financial information ensures appropriate pricing, helps issuers to raise debt and equity capital in primary markets, and ensures deep and liquid secondary markets for financial instruments.

The financial analysts who prepare investment research play an important role in the financial information 'ecosystem' that nourishes financial markets. Analysts synthesise raw information into more readily digestible research pieces. In turn the research will be used by investors to help them make their investment decisions, or by intermediaries to produce investment research, investment advice, or marketing communications.

Regulation of investment research and of the financial analysts who create it therefore needs to be sensitive to, and appropriate for, the many roles research plays. It is also of prime importance to ensure that any such regulation limit as little as possible the flow of information of potential value to investors.

2.2. REGULATORY SCRUTINY OF INVESTMENT RESEARCH

Since the collapse of the 'new economy' bubble in 2000 and several subsequent high-profile corporate collapses, the value and integrity of investment research, has been under increased regulatory scrutiny globally.

In Europe, the informal meeting of Economics and Finance Ministers in Oviedo in April 2002 discussed policy issues related to the Enron collapse in particular, and among other initiatives asked the Commission to consider possible regulatory action on investment research.

The Commission subsequently convened the Forum Group on Financial Analysts, composed of private sector practitioners, independent consultants, regulators and professional bodies, to consider the issue. The Group's report was released in September 2003 and was subject to subsequent public consultation.

This Communication constitutes the Commission's response to the Forum Group report and the public consultation. Before responding, it was first necessary to complete the European legislation dealing with research. This finally took place in September 2006, with the adoption of the implementing measures for the Markets in Financial Instruments Directive.[2]

Also in September 2003, the International Organization of Securities Commissioners' Technical Committee (IOSCO) published a report[3] and a statement of principles[4] on analyst conflicts of interest. These documents are discussed further below.

The Forum Group's report and the IOSCO report and statement of principles have helped to shape the regulatory debate on financial analysts. That debate has largely focused on the potential for poor conflicts management within firms that produce investment research to lead to biased research.

Research analysts face a variety of potential conflicts which can impair their objectivity. They may be exposed to interests of the firm, or of certain groups of clients, that conflict with the interests of those to whom the research is directed. Some examples of such interests include the interests of issuers in disposing of their securities, and of corporate financiers in attracting and keeping issuance and placement-related business. The firm itself, if it is a proprietary trader, will have an interest in selling financial instruments. Where the firm conducts agency business such as equities broking on a commission basis, it will have a commercial incentive to generate orders. All these interests can impair the analyst's objectivity.

2.2.1. The Forum Group's report

The focus of the Forum Group's report was also on the prevention, management, monitoring and disclosure of conflicts of interest relating to investment research. The recommendations were focused in particular on: conflicts of interest resulting from analysts' involvement in securities offerings and other corporate finance work; best practice for companies issuing securities; remuneration of analysts; securities dealing by analysts; qualifications; and the distribution of investment research to the retail market. **Annex 1**[5] sets out the Forum Group's recommendations in more detail.

After the Commission invited comment on the Forum Group's recommendations, there was broad support for the principles-based approach suggested by the Forum Group, and for many of the Group's specific recommendations, including those focusing on the management of conflicts of interest. Some support was expressed for a European framework laying down minimum standards; however, the desire was also expressed that European standards should as far as possible be compatible with those adopted in other major jurisdictions.[6]

2.2.2. The IOSCO Report and Statement of Principles

While not legally binding on Member States or the Community as a whole,[7] IOSCO principles are nevertheless of persuasive force. They represent an attempt by IOSCO member regulators to reach consensus, at the level of principle, on important securities regulatory issues. In the field of investment research, where many research providers operate on a global basis, it is particularly desirable if regulators can implement consistent rules.

The Principles devised by IOSCO's Technical Committee focus on:
- the identification and elimination, avoidance, management or disclosure of conflicts of interest faced by analysts;
- the integrity of analysts and their research; and
- the education of investors concerning the actual and potential conflicts of interest analysts face.

The principles, and the respective core measures to implement those principles, are set out in **Annex 2**.

Although the principles focus on the activities of equity sell-side analysts (ie those working in integrated investment banks or broker-dealers), it is specifically mentioned that "sell-side analysts are by no means alone in facing such conflicts of interest and concepts developed in this work could be used in other areas";[8] and the accompanying report does mention specifically "the conflicts of interest faced by sell-side analysts in the production of equity research and by the firms that employ them".[9]

[6038]

NOTES
2   See section 5 below.
3   IOSCO Technical Committee, Report on Analyst Conflicts of Interest (September 2003) at http://www.iosco.org/pubdocs/pdf/IOSCOPD152.pdf
4   IOSCO Technical Committee, Statement of Principles for Addressing Sell-Side Securities Analyst Conflicts of Interest (September 2003) at http://www.iosco.org/pubdocs/pdf/IOSCOPD150.pdf
5   All Annexes referred to in this Communication are contained in the Commission Staff Working Document "Investment research and financial analysts – Annexes" (reference SEC(2006) 1655) (available only in English).
6   For more details, see the summary of responses at http://ec.europa.eu/internal_market/securities/docs/analysts/contributions/contributions-summary_en.pdf
7   It is important to note in this connection that Europe is represented at IOSCO only at the level of regulators of certain Member States.
8   See paragraph 2 of the IOSCO Statement of Principles.
9   Section V, p 14 of the IOSCO Report.

3. EUROPEAN LEGISLATION ADDRESSING CONFLICTS OF INTEREST IN INVESTMENT RESEARCH

Two major pieces of European legislation include provisions that address the issue of conflicts of interest relating to investment research. These are the Market Abuse Directive[10] and the Markets in Financial Instruments Directive[11] (the MiFID). The Market Abuse Directive and its implementing measures have come into force in all Member States. The MiFID and its implementing measures are due to be transposed by Member States by 31 January 2007 and applied to firms as from 1 November 2007.

3.1. MARKET ABUSE DIRECTIVE

Article 6(5) of the Market Abuse Directive contains a requirement that persons who produce or disseminate information recommending or suggesting an investment strategy, intended for distribution channels or for the public, take reasonable care to ensure that such information is fairly presented and disclose their interests or indicate conflicts of interest concerning the financial instruments to which that information relates.

Directive 2003/125/EC,[12] which implements Article 6(5) of the Market Abuse Directive, sets out a comprehensive disclosure regime for conflicts of interest relating to research recommendations (see **Annex 3** for a summary).

The Market Abuse Directive and its implementing Directives 2003/124/EC[13] and 2004/72/EC,[14] also restrict issuers from disclosing price-sensitive information to selected analysts ahead of its release to the rest of the market place.

The Market Abuse Directive and its implementing measures are not restricted to investment firms within the meaning of MiFID[15] and affect other producers of recommendations, such as independent research houses, credit institutions and the like.

3.2. THE MIFID

The MiFID sets out *inter alia* organisational and operating conditions for authorised investment firms. Where an investment firm provides investment services on a professional basis to third parties, it will normally need to be authorised under the MiFID and comply with all its requirements. This also covers the provision of ancillary services such as that of 'investment research and financial analysis or other forms of general recommendation relating to transactions in financial instruments'.[16] The provisions that relate specifically to investment research are contained in an implementing Directive under the MiFID (the MiFID implementing Directive).[17]

3.2.1. Conflicts of interest – general

MiFID tackles the issue of conflicts of interest generally by requiring investment firms to:

- take all reasonable steps to identify relevant conflicts of interest arising in the course of providing investment or ancillary services;[18]
- maintain and operate effective organisational and administrative arrangements with a view to taking all reasonable steps designed to prevent conflicts of interest from adversely affecting the interests of their clients;[19]
- where those organisational arrangements are not sufficient to ensure, with reasonable confidence, that risks of damage to client interests will be prevented, to clearly disclose the general nature and/or sources of conflicts of interest to the client before undertaking business on its behalf.[20]

The MiFID implementing Directive specifies that investment firms should adopt a written policy in relation to conflicts of interest setting out the methods by which they propose to manage conflicts of interest arising in the course of their various investment and ancillary activities, including the provision of investment research.[21] A further key requirement is the need to ensure an appropriate level of independence between persons engaged in different business activities involving a conflict of interest entailing a risk of damage to the interests of a client.[22] The Directive also sets out a series of organisational measures to ensure the requisite degree of independence in appropriate cases, such as the separation of supervision or remuneration between different activities.[23]

3.2.2. Conflicts of interest – investment research

Apart from these general provisions, the MIFID implementing Directive contains specific rules[24] relating to the provision of investment research. They apply to investment firms which produce or arrange for the production of investment research that is intended or likely to be subsequently disseminated to clients or to the public under their own responsibility or that of group members.

Investment research is defined[25] as a sub-category of recommendations as defined in Article 1(3) of Directive 2003/125/EC. In order to qualify as investment research, such recommendations must be labelled or described as investment research, or otherwise presented as objective or independent, and must not constitute investment advice (ie, the provision of personal recommendations, which are presented as suitable for the recipient, or based on a consideration of the circumstances of that person).[26]

Where the provisions apply, there are two consequences:
- the investment firm must ensure that it implements all the organisational measures set out in the MiFID implementing Directive in relation to analysts and other persons[27] whose responsibilities or business interests may conflict with the interests of recipients of the research; those measures require effective separation between business functions that serve different client or business interests;[28] and
- investment firms should take other specified steps designed to ensure the objectivity of the investment research. Importantly, the firm must prevent certain dealings in financial instruments by relevant persons[29] who have knowledge of the timing or contents of relevant investment research that is not public;[30] as well as certain personal transactions contrary to outstanding recommendations.[31] There are also restrictions[32] on the acceptance of inducements in relation to investment research, the promising of favourable research coverage, and on who may review drafts of investment research and for what purposes.

The requirements which apply to the production of research also apply to the substantial alteration of investment research produced by a third party.[33] However, a firm which simply disseminates research which has been produced by a third party is not bound by the consequences mentioned above, provided that the disseminating firm does not substantially alter the research, and verifies that the producer of the research is subject to requirements, or has established a policy, equivalent to the requirements of the MiFID implementing Directive.[34]

3.2.3. Disclosure of conflicts and relation to the Market Abuse Directive regime

As regards disclosure of research conflicts, the MiFID supplements the detailed regime in the Market Abuse Directive by requiring:
- disclosure where organisational arrangements are not sufficient to ensure, with reasonable confidence, that risks of damage to client interests will be prevented;[35] and
- disclosure of the conflicts of interest policy of the investment firm.[36]

It is intended that the MiFID and the Market Abuse Directive should operate together seamlessly. The field of "recommendations" within the meaning of the Directive 2003/125/EC (where produced by an investment firm) should exclusively contain investment research for MiFID purposes or marketing communications for MiFID purposes. Recommendations of an investment firm that do not constitute investment research must be clearly identifiable as marketing communications[37] and must contain a clear and prominent statement that (or, in the case of oral recommendations, to the effect that) they have not been prepared in accordance with standards designed to promote the objectivity of investment research.[38]

The diagram in **Annex 4** explains the relationship between recommendations, marketing communications, investment advice and investment research.

[6039]

NOTES

[10] Directive 2003/6/EC of the European Parliament and of the Council of 28 January 2003 on insider dealing and market manipulation (market abuse). OJ L96, 12.04.2003, p 16.

[11] Directive 2004/39/EC of the European Parliament and of the Council of 21 April 2004 on markets in financial instruments amending Council Directives 85/611/EEC and 93/6/EEC and Directive 2000/12/EC of the European Parliament and of the Council and repealing Council Directive 93/22/EEC. OJ L145, 30.4.2004, p 1. As amended by Directive 2006/31/EC of the European Parliament and of the Council of 5 April 2006 amending directive 2004/39/EC on markets in financial instruments, as regards certain deadlines. OJ L114, 27.04.2006, p 60.

[12] Commission Directive 2003/125/EC of 22 December 2003 implementing Directive 2003/6/EC of the European Parliament and of the Council as regards the fair presentation of investment recommendations and the disclosure of conflicts of interest, OJ L339, 24.12.2003, p 73.

[13] Commission Directive 2003/124/EC of 22 December 2003 implementing Directive 2003/6/EC of the European Parliament and of the Council as regards the definition and public disclosure of inside information and the definition of market manipulation, OJ L339, 24.12.2003, p 70.

[14] Commission Directive 2004/72/EC of 29 April 2004 implementing Directive 2003/6/EC of the European Parliament and of the Council as regards accepted market practices, the definition of inside information in relation to derivatives on commodities, the drawing up of lists of insiders, the notification of managers' transactions and the notification of suspicious transactions, OJ L162, 30.4.2004, p 70.

[15] As defined in Article 4(1)(1) of MiFID.

[16] Investment services are those services set out in Section A of Annex 1 to the MiFID. Ancillary services are those set out in Section B of that Annex.

[17] Commission Directive 2006/73/EC implementing Directive 2004/39/EC of the European Parliament and of the Council as regards organisational requirements and operating conditions for investment firms, and defined terms for the purposes of that Directive. OJ L241, 2.9.2006, p 26.

[18] Article 18(1).

[19] Article 13(3)

[20] Article 18(2).

[21] Article 22 of the implementing Directive.

[22] Article 22(3) of the implementing Directive.

[23] Article 22(3) of the implementing Directive.

24   Article 25 of the implementing Directive.
25   Article 24 of the implementing Directive.
26   Article 4(1)(4) of MiFID and Article 52 of the MiFID implementing Directive.
27   Recital 30 of the implementing Directive explains that those other persons should include corporate finance personnel and persons involved in sales and trading on behalf of clients or the firm.
28   Article 22(3) and Recital 36 of the implementing Directive.
29   This term is defined in Article 2(3) of the implementing Directive.
30   Article 25(2)(a) of the implementing Directive.
31   Article 25(2)(b) of the implementing Directive.
32   Article 25(2)(c)–(e) of the implementing Directive.
33   Recital 35 of the implementing Directive.
34   Article 25(3) of the implementing Directive.
35   Article 18(2) of the MiFID.
36   Article 19(3) of the MiFID and Article 30(1) of the implementing Directive.
37   Article 19(2) of MiFID.
38   Article 24(2) of the implementing Directive.

4. OTHER ISSUES

The main outstanding issues arising from the Forum Group's report and the IOSCO Principles are:

- the possibility of mandatory analyst registration, possibly linked to qualifications;
- the regulatory and competitive position of independent research firms vis-à-vis the provision of research by investment banks;
- the desirability for best practice codes or corporate governance rules covering issuer relations with analysts; and
- the important role of investor education in addressing the problem of conflicts of interest in investment research.

4.1. ANALYST REGISTRATION

The Commission has decided not to propose at this stage mandatory registration of analysts linked to qualifications. The Forum Group was divided on the need to subject analysts to mandatory minimum qualification requirements.[39] There is insufficient evidence that problems of analyst bias derive from a lack of qualifications. Rather, it seems evident that they derive from failures by firms properly to manage the conflicts of interest arising in their production of investment research. These issues are addressed by the MiFID.[40] Moreover, mandatory registration of analysts is not one of the IOSCO core measures.

4.2. INDEPENDENT RESEARCH

The Commission does not consider that there are necessarily inherent quality differences between research produced by independent research firms and that produced by investment firms. Nevertheless, whereas independent firms need to cover their costs by charging clients, much research produced by investment banks is paid for by institutional investors (and, through them, by their underlying clients) only indirectly. This process can often be somewhat opaque and accountability is not always clear.

To a large extent, these issues are addressed in the MiFID and its implementing measures. In particular, implementing measures relating to inducements permit inducements to be accepted by investment firms (such as portfolio managers) from third parties (such as their brokers) only if they are fully disclosed to their clients and only if they are designed to improve the quality of the provision of the investment or ancillary service concerned to the client, and do not impair compliance with the firm's duty to act in the best interests of the client.[41] These measures are particularly relevant to 'bundled' or 'softed' services[42] that are received by portfolio managers from or on behalf of brokerage houses.[43] The receipt and provision of 'softed' and 'bundled' research can continue beyond implementation of the MiFID, only if it can be duly justified and shown to pass the strict tests in the legislation. This ensures that research produced in-house by banks, and research produced by independent investment houses under so-called commission-sharing arrangements, remains on an equal competitive footing.[44]

4.3. ISSUER RELATIONS WITH ANALYSTS

The Commission notes that the consultation on the Forum Group's report demonstrated support for some form of best practice code or corporate governance rules covering **issuer relations with analysts**.

The MiFID and the Market Abuse Directive, with their strict rules on conflicts management and disclosure and presentation of research, will prevent issuers from having undue editorial influence over research prepared by investment firms. They will also prohibit issuers from disclosing price-sensitive information to analysts ahead of its release to the rest of the marketplace, except where they are made insiders and subjected to confidentiality obligations.

The Commission believes that best practice codes of professional or trade associations can help to promote more professional relations between issuers and analysts.[45] Such codes address issues such as retaliation by issuers against analysts that produce negative or 'sell' recommendations.

Against this background, the Commission does not propose to bring forward a legislative proposal in this area at this stage.

4.4. INVESTOR EDUCATION

The IOSCO Technical Committee stated that investor education should play an important role in managing analyst conflicts of interest.

The Commission agrees that investors should be aware of the potential for conflicts of interest to affect investment research, and about the meaning of disclosures as to conflicts. This is an area that we consider especially well suited for action by Member States, by trade associations, and of course by investment firms themselves.

The Commission for its part is committed, as part of its health and consumer protection strategy, to ensure better informed and educated consumers.[46] In this context, the Commission plans a conference for Spring 2007 to bring together examples of best practice in consumer education and improving consumer financial literacy. The outcome of this conference will drive further reflection by the Commission on what further role, if any, it should play in the field of consumer financial education.

4.5. OTHER MATERIAL CONTAINED IN THE FORUM GROUP'S RECOMMENDATIONS AND THE IOSCO PRINCIPLES

To the extent that the Forum Group recommendations or the IOSCO principles for independence of analysts are not specifically addressed in the legislative measures mentioned, they will nevertheless be useful to assist:

- investment firms in framing their conflicts of interest policies under the MiFID and the text of their required disclosures under the Market Abuse Directive;
- analysts, issuers and investment firms in drawing up codes of conduct and other self-regulatory measures to ensure adequate management and disclosure of conflicts of interest and other issues affecting research quality and integrity.

[6040]

NOTES

[39] at p 50 of the Forum Group's report (cited at footnote 1)

[40] See the provisions mentioned in section 3.2 above.

[41] Article 26 of the Implementing Directive.

[42] 'Bundled services' refers to those services provided by investment firms to their clients (for example, institutional investors) as part of a total package of services for which a single fee, usually a commission, is paid. 'Softed services' refers to those services which are provided to the client as part of a package for which a single fee is payable, but which are not provided by the investment firm in question but by another party under an arrangement with it.

[43] This applies to providers authorised under MiFID who provide individual portfolio management, and also to UCITS managers by virtue of Article 5.3 of Directive UCITS Directive (Council Directive 85/611/EEC of 20 December 1985 on the coordination of laws, regulations and administrative provisions relating to undertakings for collective investment in transferable securities (UCITS), OJ L375, 31.12.1985, p 3.

[44] See also Recital 37 of the implementing Directive, which recommends independent research houses adopt MiFID-like standards of conflicts management and disclosure.

[45] Examples of such codes include the Charter for Financial Communications (drawn up jointly by the Cercle de Liaison des Informateurs Financiers en France (CLIFF) and the Société Française des Analystes Financiers (SFAF)) at http://www.cliff.asso.fr/en-GB/iso_album/charter.pdf. See also the best practice guidelines drawn up by the Association of Investment Management and Research and the National Investor Relations Institute at http://www.cfainstitute.org/standards/ethics/aimrniricomment.html. See also the Principles of Ethical Conduct of the Association of Certified International Analysts at http://tinyurl.com/lxsq2.

[46] See Healthier, Safer, More Confident Citizens: a Health and Consumer Protection Strategy, COM(2005) 115 final; 2005/0042 (COD), at paragraph 4.2.4.

5. CONCLUSION

Taken together, the MiFID and the Market Abuse Directive and their implementing measures will represent a significant step forward in creating a European-level regulatory framework for avoiding, managing and disclosing conflicts of interest in all investment and ancillary services, including investment research. All such measures need to be implemented by Member States within agreed timetables to be fully effective. Where appropriate, regulators should also consider issuing guidance to ensure convergent, commonsense application of the legislative measures.

At this point, the Commission does not consider that it is needed to adopt further specific legislation in this field. Nevertheless, the Commission will continue to carefully monitor the application of these measures, including their effect on the market for investment research. This experience will be valuable in reviewing the legislative measures for their continued appropriateness. In line with the principle of Better Regulation, should existing measures prove insufficient, then the Commission will consider bringing forward further proposals (legislative or other). Any such proposals would be subject to consultation and regulatory impact assessment.

[6041]

ANNEXES

NOTES

The following Annexes are taken from a separate document entitled "Annexes to the Communication from the Commission to the Council and the European Parliament on Investment research and financial analysts" {COM (2006) 789 final}. They have been combined here for convenience.

ANNEX 1
FORUM GROUP KEY PRINCIPLES AND RECOMMENDATIONS

Clarity: Research should be fair, clear and not misleading.

1. Firms should put in place mechanisms preventing the capacity of a firm's Investment Banking department, its staff, or a firm's management from influencing research recommendations improperly.

2. Companies should not seek to influence an analyst's recommendation or engage in retaliatory action in the event of an unfavourable assessment.

3. Companies should be permitted, at the discretion of the research analyst (other than in the case of corporate finance transactions subject to their own set of rules) to review research before publication for factual accuracy, but in no case should companies be informed of the recommendation or valuation.

4. Companies should encourage and not restrict the attendance of analysts at financial information meetings organised in connection with an offering (for example by making attendance conditional on agreement not to publish or to submit research for review by the issuer), nor discriminate in terms of provision of information to analysts.

5. Companies should develop their own governance rules covering relations with analysts.

6. Listing authorities should consider making adherence to issuer best practice codes a listing requirement.

7. Research analysts should adhere to the highest ethical standards.

Competence, conduct and personal integrity: Research should be produced by competent analysts with skill, care, diligence and integrity; and it should reflect the opinion of its author(s).

8. Analysts should receive on going training in market practice and in relevant regional laws and regulation.

9. Firms should review their internal procedures regularly to ensure compliance with relevant regulatory requirements and with the ethical principles set out by relevant professional and industry bodies and to ensure consistency with this report's recommendations.

Suitability and market integrity: Research should be distributed taking into account the different categories of its intended recipients and the need to maintain market integrity.

10. Respecting all legal requirements on selective disclosure of market sensitive information, disseminators of research should take reasonable care to ensure that research is not distributed to investors other than the intended audience and that market integrity is not compromised.

11. Producers of research who target both retail and institutional investors should disclose any earlier publication targeting institutional investors.

Conflict avoidance, prevention and management: Analysts' firms should have in place systems and controls to identify and avoid, prevent or manage personal and corporate conflicts of interest.

12. Consistent with either agreed or proposed Community legislation (including the Market Abuse and Investment Services Directives and relevant implementing measures), firms must identify conflicts of interest between investment banking and research departments and, as appropriate, avoid, prevent, manage, disclose, record and monitor such conflicts.

13. Regulators should ensure that firms' internal procedures for managing conflicts of interest are adequate and effective; and properly implemented and adhered to.

14. Integrated firms should ensure that they have in place effective and appropriate procedures to control the flow of information between investment banking and research departments, and those analysts, including research management, should never report directly or indirectly to investment banking.

15. Firms should bring analysts 'over the wall' only in specific circumstances, documented and agreed by the Compliance and Research departments.

16. Where analysts are involved in investment banking business and are producing published research, strict controls should be in place, in particular to prevent or control the flow of non public, sensitive information to the analyst.

17. Where an analyst has access to non public market sensitive information, s/he should not subsequently publish or otherwise disseminate research, recommendations or opinions on the subject company to investment clients unless and until any non public information with which s/he has been provided is in the public domain.

18. Research by selling syndicate analysts should be subject to a quiet period immediately after an offering has been priced. Quiet periods should be uniform throughout the EU.

19. Quiet periods may be waived in certain specific circumstances, in a manner compatible with the Prospectus Directive, to facilitate the discussion of specific material developments that may occur during the offering period and its immediate aftermath.

20. There should be no restrictions on the provision of written and oral research and recommendations on new issues by unaffiliated and non syndicate analysts (including the consumer facing units of universal banks or integrated firms).

21. Either (a) analysts ('covered persons') and connected persons should not own securities in sectors on which they are producing research; or (b) where analysts or connected persons trade or acquire such securities, other than through a managed portfolio or mutual fund, their employers should have in place effective written policies covering such activities and monitoring and enforcement procedures, to be notified to all covered employees.

22. Firms should not link analyst remuneration to individual investment banking or other banking transactions. Consideration should be given to the objective measurement of research related performance.

23. Investment banking departments should have no involvement in determining analysts' remuneration.

Disclosure: Conflicts of interest, whether corporate or personal, should be prominently disclosed.

24. Any research distributed by firms that are selling syndicate members, either prior to an offering or during the quiet period after an offering has been priced, must include prominent disclosures of relevant investment banking relationships; and should not contain recommendations or price targets unless previously published.

25. Investment research produced and disseminated in the European Union should comply with the principles and standards advocated in this report regardless of the location of the subject compan(y)(ies) covered in the research.

26. Subject to the requirements of Community and national legislation, where relevant, the dissemination of investment research produced under equivalent rules of non-European jurisdictions should be permitted. Where the dissemination of research from third countries that is not produced to equivalent standards is permitted, this should be prominently disclosed.

27. The Commission should seek acceptance of European standards relating to the production and dissemination of research in other jurisdictions.

28. Buy side analysts and portfolio managers making recommendations to a public audience should be subject to the Group's recommendations drawn up for sell side analysts.

29. The same ethical principles and internal rules applying to analysts and firms producing research concerning equity markets should be appropriately observed in fixed income and other non equity securities markets, with adaptations reflecting market structure and internal organisational differences.

30. Education of retail investors – and particularly of fiduciaries responsible for retail collective investment vehicles – should be encouraged.

31. Analysts in independent houses should be appropriately and proportionately required to respect the Principles of this report.

[6042]

ANNEX 2
IOSCO PRINCIPLES AND CORE MEASURES

1. ANALYST TRADING AND FINANCIAL INTERESTS

Principle 1: Mechanisms should exist so that analysts' trading activities or financial interests do not prejudice their research and recommendations.

Core Measures

— Prohibiting analysts from trading in securities or related derivatives of an issuer they review in a manner contrary to their outstanding recommendations, except in special circumstances subject to pre-approval by compliance or legal personnel;

— Prohibiting analysts from covering an issuer, where the analyst serves as an officer, director or member of the issuer's supervisory board and requiring disclosure of any such relationship involving individuals related to or associated with the analyst; in the alternative, requiring analysts covering an issuer to disclose if they, or individuals related to or associated with them, serve as officers, directors or members of the issuer's supervisory board;

— Prohibiting analysts from trading securities or related derivatives ahead of publishing research on the issuer of those securities; and,

— Requiring analysts or firms employing the analysts to publicly disclose if the analysts have investment positions or otherwise have financial interests in issuers that the analysts review.

2. FIRM FINANCIAL INTERESTS AND BUSINESS RELATIONSHIPS

Principle 2.1: Mechanisms should exist so that analysts' research and recommendations are not prejudiced by the trading activities or financial interests of the firms that employ them.

Core Measures

— Requiring analysts, or firms employing analysts, to publicly disclose if an analyst's firm makes a market for securities of an issuer that the analyst reviews or if the firm has a significant financial interest in the issuer;

— Requiring analysts or the firms employing analysts to publicly disclose if individuals employed by or associated with the firm serve as officers, directors, or members of the supervisory board of an issuer that the analysts review; and

— Prohibiting firms that employ analysts from improperly trading securities or related derivatives ahead of the analyst publishing research on the issuer of those securities.

Principle 2.2: Mechanisms should exist so that analysts' research and recommendations are not prejudiced by the business relationships of the firms that employ them.

Core Measures

— Establishing robust information barriers between analysts and a firm's other divisions in order to limit the potential for conflicts of interest and prevent other individuals in the firm from attempting to influence analysts' research;

— Prohibiting firms that employ analysts from promising issuers favourable research coverage, specific ratings, or specific target prices in return for a future or continued business relationship, service or investment; and,

— Prohibiting analysts from participating in investment banking sales pitches and road shows.

3. ANALYSTS' REPORTING LINES AND COMPENSATION

Principle 3: Reporting lines for analysts and their compensation arrangements should be structured to eliminate or severely limit actual and potential conflicts of interest.

Core Measures

— Prohibiting analysts from reporting to the investment banking function;

— Prohibiting analyst compensation from being directly linked to specific investment banking transactions;

— Adopting mechanisms within firms to safeguard reporting line and compensation structures to protect analysts' independence; and,

— Prohibiting the investment banking function from pre-approving analyst reports or recommendations, except in circumstances subject to oversight by compliance or legal personnel where investment banking personnel review a research report for factual accuracy prior to publication.

4. FIRM COMPLIANCE SYSTEMS AND SENIOR MANAGEMENT RESPONSIBILITY

Principle 4: Firms that employ analysts should establish written internal procedures or controls to identify and eliminate, manage or disclose actual and potential analyst conflicts of interest.

Core Measures

— Requiring firms that employ analysts to have written internal procedures for addressing actual and potential analyst conflicts of interest.

5. OUTSIDE INFLUENCE

Principle 5: The undue influence of issuers, institutional investors and other outside parties upon analysts should be eliminated or managed.

Core Measures

— Requiring that analysts, or the firms that employ analysts, publicly disclose whether the issuer or other third party provided any compensation or other benefit in connection with a research report; and,
— Prohibiting issuers from selectively disclosing material information to one analyst and not other analysts, except as specifically permitted by law or regulations.

[6043]

ANNEX 3
DISCLOSURES REQUIRED BY DIRECTIVE 2003/125/EC IMPLEMENTING THE MARKET ABUSE DIRECTIVE[1]

This Directive contains implementing measures for the purposes of Article 6(5) of the Market Abuse Directive. In general, it covers 'relevant persons', ie those natural or legal persons producing or disseminating recommendations in the exercise of their profession or the conduct of their business. Some provisions, notably Articles 4 and 6, only apply to independent analysts, investment firms, credit institutions, related legal persons, or other relevant persons whose main business is to produce recommendations

Article 2 contains requirements for the disclosure of the identity of the person preparing the recommendation and of the legal person responsible for the recommendation; and the relevant competent authority (for investment firms or credit institutions) or applicable self-regulatory code standards or code of conduct.

Article 3 contains substantive requirements for the presentation of recommendations, ensuring for example that facts are clearly distinguished from non-factual information, the reliability of sources is indicated, and assumptions are indicated.

Article 4 sets out additional disclosure obligations for recommendations, including matters such as indication of sources, valuation bases, explanation of the meaning of the recommendations used, the recommendation's release date and update frequency, and changes of recommendations.

Article 5 sets out the general standard for the disclosure of conflicts of interest by relevant persons. It requires that all relationships and circumstances be disclosed that may reasonably be expected to impair the objectivity of the recommendation, particularly financial interests in the instruments covered, or significant conflicts with respect to covered issuers.

Article 6 sets out more detailed requirements as to the disclosure of research conflicts. In general terms, it requires disclosure of the effective organisational and administrative arrangements set up within the investment firm or the credit institution for the prevention and avoidance of conflicts of interest with respect to recommendations, including information barriers. It also requires clear and prominent disclosure of:

- major shareholdings of the relevant person or related legal persons in the issuer covered;
- other significant financial interests held by the relevant person or any related legal person in relation to the issuer;
- where applicable, a statement that the relevant person or any related legal person is a market maker or liquidity provider in the financial instruments of the issuer;
- where applicable, a statement that the relevant person or any related legal person has been lead manager or co-lead manager over the previous 12 months of any publicly disclosed offer of financial instruments of the issuer;
- where applicable, a statement that the relevant person or any related legal person is party to any other agreement with the issuer relating to the provision of investment banking services, with exceptions for cases of confidentiality; and
- where applicable, a statement that the relevant person or any related legal person is party to an agreement with the issuer relating to the production of the recommendation.

Article 6 also requires credit institutions and investment firms to disclose:

- whether the remuneration of analysts is tied to investment banking transactions;
- details of any pre-issuance share acquisitions by analysts; and

- a quarterly breakdown of the proportions of buy, sell and hold recommendations overall, and for those issuers to which material investment banking services have been provided over the previous 12 months.

Articles 7, 8 and 9 contain further disclosure and substantive requirements for research that is disseminated by relevant persons but produced by third parties.

The Directive contains provisions allowing for the inclusion of some disclosures by way of hyperlinks, where inclusion in the body of the research recommendations would be disproportionate. There is also provision for adaptation of the requirements to the case of oral recommendations.

[6044]

NOTES

¹   Note: the following is an overview only and does not purport to be definitive or exhaustive; affected firms should consult the text of the Directive itself and/or seek legal advice as to their particular circumstances.

ANNEX 4
RELATIONSHIP BETWEEN MIFID AND MARKET ABUSE REGIMES: RECOMMENDATIONS AND INVESTMENT RESEARCH

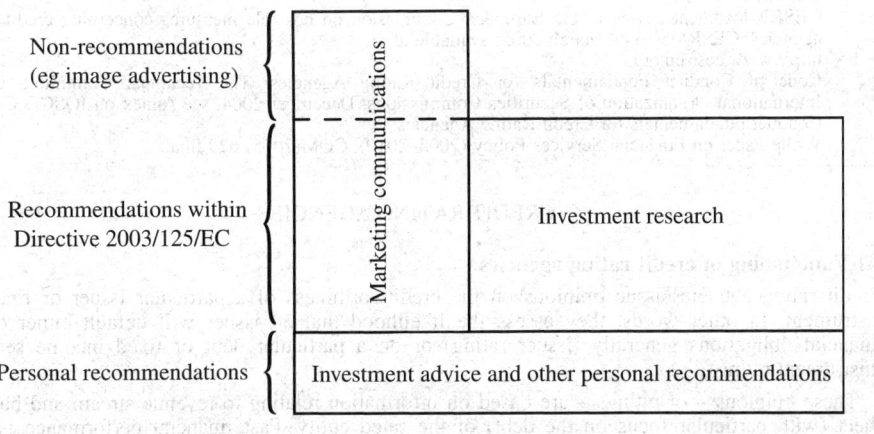

[6045]

COMMUNICATION FROM THE COUNCIL

on Credit Rating Agencies

(2006/C59/02)

(Text with EEA relevance)

NOTES

Date of publication in OJ: OJ C59, 11.3.2006, p 2. Notes are as per the original.
As of 1 February 2009, this document had not been amended.

1. INTRODUCTION

Credit rating agencies play a vital role in global securities and banking markets. It is essential, therefore, that they consistently provide ratings which are independent, objective and of the highest possible quality.

The Commission made a commitment to analyse the issue of credit rating agencies at the Oviedo Informal ECOFIN Council (April 2002), in the aftermath of the Enron scandal. The European Parliament then adopted (February 2004) a Resolution on credit rating agencies,¹ following an own initiative report from its Committee on Economic and Monetary Affairs,² calling on the Commission to produce an assessment of the need (if any) for legislative intervention in this field. In March 2004, following the Parmalat scandal, the Commission identified, in cooperation with the European Parliament and the Member States, the main regulatory issues of concern with regard to credit rating agencies. In July 2004, the Commission asked the Committee of European Securities Regulators ("CESR") to provide the Commission with technical analysis and advice to assess the need for introducing European legislation or other solutions. CESR provided its advice to the Commission in March 2005.[3] Meanwhile, a number of key EU legislative measures with major implications for credit rating agencies have been adopted as part of the Commission's Financial Services Action Plan (FSAP). Moreover, the International Organisation of Securities Commissions ("IOSCO") published in December 2004 its Code of Conduct Fundamentals for credit rating agencies ("IOSCO Code").[4]

The purpose of this Communication is to report back to the Council and European Parliament on the Commission's regulatory approach towards credit rating agencies, bearing in mind these latest developments. In developing this approach, the Commission has been guided by the advice provided by CESR. It has also sought to adhere to the principles of "Better Regulation" to which the Commission has committed itself as part of the drive to boost growth and employment in the Union and which form a crucial part of its approach to financial services policy set out in its recent White Paper.[5]

[6045A]

NOTES

[1]   European Parliament resolution on Role and methods of rating agencies (2003/2081(INI)), available at: http://www.europarl.eu.int/registre/seance_pleniere/textes_adoptes/definitif/2004/0210/0080/ P5_TA(2004)0080_EN.pdf.

[2]   Report of the Committee on Economic and Monetary Affairs (A5–0040/2004); rapporteur Giorgos Katiforis.

[3]   CESR's technical advice to the European Commission on possible measures concerning credit rating agencies, CESR/05/139b, March 2005, available at: http://www.cesr-eu.org.

[4]   Code of Conduct Fundamentals for Credit Rating Agencies, The Technical Committee of the International Organization of Securities Commissions, December 2004, see Annex on IOSCO Code of Conduct Fundamentals for Credit Rating Agencies.

[5]   White Paper on Financial Services Policy (2005–2010), COM(2005) 629 final.

2. CREDIT RATING AGENCIES

2.1 Functioning of credit rating agencies

Credit rating agencies issue opinions on the creditworthiness of a particular issuer or financial instrument. In other words, they assess the likelihood that an issuer will default either on its financial obligations generally (issuer rating) or on a particular debt or fixed income security (instrument rating).

These opinions – or ratings – are based on information relating to revenue stream and balance sheet (with particular focus on the debt) of the rated entity. Past financial performance is also considered. They only give an indication as to the situation at a given time and must therefore be periodically confirmed or revised to take account of recent economic or other developments. The credit ratings effectively categorise issuers into corresponding grades, depending on whether they are considered as more or less default-prone. Credit rating agencies employ comprehensive creditworthiness scales, with the critical border line running between the so-called investment grade (low-risk) and speculative grade (high-risk), reflecting the risks related to the security (ie the likelihood of default).

Ratings are usually requested – and paid for – by the issuers themselves. In these cases, they are based on both publicly available data and information which is not accessible to the public but which is voluntarily disclosed by the rated entity (eg by means of interviews with senior financial officials of the rated entity). However, credit rating agencies sometimes issue unsolicited ratings (ie ratings which have not been requested by an issuer). These are usually prepared without access to non-public information.

Although the provision of ratings is obviously their core activity, many credit rating agencies make use of their expertise in risk assessment to provide other financial services (eg investment advice) to issuers (either directly or through related entities).

2.2 Impact on the financial markets

Credit ratings carry considerable weight in financial markets. There are two basic reasons for this. First, although they are based on complex assessments they can be easily and instantly assimilated by investors regardless of their expertise and profile. Secondly, credit rating agencies enjoy a good reputation and are seen by market participants to be providing unbiased data analysis.

The importance of credit rating agencies in recent years can be observed in both business practice and regulatory requirements. On the one hand, the commercial success of most debt instrument issues largely depends on the rating granted. A rating has become a pre-requisite for seeking external financing in the securities markets (especially when issuers do not have an established presence on the debt markets).The credit rating of an issuer determines the interest rates that they will have to offer in order to obtain external financing. Moreover, credit ratings are increasingly used in contractual provisions regarding the termination of credit availability, acceleration of debt repayment or modification of other crediting conditions.

On the other hand, several jurisdictions now insist that certain types of investment products can only be sold if the issuer can demonstrate a certain grade of creditworthiness reflected in a rating issued by a recognised credit rating agency. Credit rating agencies are also increasingly involved in the assessment of the risks associated with assets held by financial institutions which are subject to capital adequacy requirements.

The role which credit rating agencies play in the markets is generally very positive for both investors and issuers. They provide investors with information which helps them to assess the risks related to a security. And they help to lower the costs of raising capital for issuers (or at least for those issuers who receive a favourable rating).

2.3 Issues of concern

The Resolution of the European Parliament does not call into question the positive role that credit rating agencies can and generally do play. However, it identifies a number of issues of concern which require serious attention in order to ensure that all credit rating agencies exercise their functions responsibly at all times.[6]

Concern centres on the quality of credit ratings provided by credit rating agencies. Credit rating agencies must base their ratings on a diligent analysis of the available information and control continuously the integrity of their information sources. This means that credit ratings must be regularly updated, if necessary. Credit rating agencies must also be more open about the way in which their ratings are arrived at. In addition, it is important that credit rating agencies are independent and entirely objective in their approach. The position of credit rating agencies must not be compromised by the relationships which they have with issuers. There are also concerns relating to the access which credit rating agencies have to inside information of issuers. It is important that credit rating agencies are prevented from using this information for other activities. Finally, the European Parliament expressed concern about the degree of concentration in the ratings industry and its possible anti-competitive effects.

[6045B]

NOTES
   6   See footnote 1.

---

3. RELEVANT REGULATION

The issues relating to credit rating agencies are serious and must be tackled. Both the new EU-level legislative framework and the IOSCO Code seek to do this. The EU legislation applies only to credit rating agencies operating in the EU. The Code, on the other hand, is expected to be applied by credit rating agencies in all jurisdictions where they operate. In terms of content, the Code complements the EU legislation. While the Directives are legally binding, the Code works on a "comply or explain" basis – ie credit rating agencies are expected to incorporate all the provisions of the IOSCO Code into their own internal Codes of Conduct. Where they choose not to do this, they must explain how their Code nevertheless gives effect to the provisions of the IOSCO Code.

3.1 EU legislation

The aim of the FSAP was to create open, integrated and efficient financial markets in the EU – where competitive forces maximise investors' returns – but where investors are not subject to excessive risk. It therefore sought to minimise the regulatory burden on firms while at the same time maintaining an effective level of regulatory control and a high level of investor protection.

There are three FSAP Directives which are relevant to credit rating agencies. The most important is the **Market Abuse Directive** ("MAD") which – together with its implementing Regulation and Directives[7] – tackles the issue of insider dealing and market manipulation (market abuse) in order to ensure the integrity of Community financial markets and to enhance investor confidence in those markets. Insider dealing and market manipulation prevent full market transparency, which is important for trading for all economic actors in integrated financial markets. In the field of conflicts of interest, fair presentation of investment recommendations and the access to inside information, the provisions of the Market Abuse Directives constitute a comprehensive legal framework for credit rating agencies while, at the same time, acknowledging their specific role and the differences between credit ratings and investment recommendations.

In order to prevent insider dealing and market manipulation, the Directive 2003/125/EC addresses the fair presentation of investment recommendations and the disclosure of conflicts of interest. For the purposes of the said Directive, credit ratings do not constitute a recommendation but they are regarded as opinions on the creditworthiness of a particular issuer or financial instrument. Nevertheless, it is stipulated that credit rating agencies should consider adopting internal policies and procedures designed to ensure that credit ratings published by them are fairly presented. Moreover, it is stated that a credit rating agency discloses any significant interests or conflicts of interest concerning the financial instruments or the issuers to which their credit ratings relate.[8] Additionally, it follows from the Directive 2003/6/EC that, in case a credit rating agency knew, or ought to have known, that the credit rating was false or misleading, the prohibition to disseminate false or misleading information, constituting market manipulation, may apply to credit ratings.[9] Considering these provisions, it is clear that credit rating agencies need to implement internal procedures and policies to ensure objective, independent and accurate credit ratings which will benefit investor confidence. It is of major importance for the Commission that credit rating agencies will effectively enforce their procedures to ensure high quality of credit ratings.

With respect to the legal treatment of credit rating agencies' access to inside information, the Directive 2003/6/EC prohibits any person possessing inside information from using that information by acquiring or disposing of financial instruments to which that information relates. Inside information is defined as information of a precise nature which has not been made public, relating, directly or indirectly, to one or more issuers of financial instruments and which, if it were made public, would be likely to have a significant effect on the price of those financial instruments or on the price of related derivative financial instruments.[10] As a rule, an issuer must disclose inside information as soon as possible. Consequently, there will be few circumstances in which an issuer can legitimately be in possession of inside information that has not already been disclosed to the market. If an issuer decides to allow a credit rating agency access to inside information, the credit rating agency would owe a duty of confidentiality as required by Article 6(3) of Directive 2003/6/EC.

As a result, a credit rating agency or an employee who has access to inside information of any sort is prohibited from any trading using inside information. Moreover, it is not allowed to disclose this inside information to anyone else except in the normal course of employment, profession or duties. In this respect, Article 6(3), third subparagraph of Directive 2003/6/EC states that issuers, or persons acting on their behalf or for their account, draw up list of persons working for them who have access to inside information. This provision allows Member States to require credit rating agencies to draw up lists of insiders. These lists must regularly be updated and transmitted to the competent authority whenever the latter requests it.

In addition to having access to inside information of the issuer, it is possible that a credit rating itself constitutes inside information, in particular when the credit rating agency has access to non-public information of the issuer. This implies that using the unpublished rating for trading or disclosing this information to anyone else, except in the normal course of employment, profession or duties, is prohibited. However, a credit rating agency communicating an imminent rating publication to the issuer on a confidential basis for the purpose of checking the accuracy of the information it is based on would be allowed.

The Commission believes that the provisions of the Market Abuse Directives provide a comprehensive set of rules for the activities of credit rating agencies in the area of market abuse concerns. The specific role of credit rating agencies in the financial markets requires diligent application of these provisions. Consequently, the Commission will monitor actively the implementation and enforcement of these provisions in the Market Abuse Directives in relation to credit rating agencies.

The second item of EU legislation which is relevant to credit rating agencies is the **Capital Requirements Directive** ("CRD") which introduces a new capital requirements framework for banks and investment firms.[11] The CRD is based on the new international capital requirements framework agreed by the Basel Committee on Banking Supervision ("Basel II") in 2004.

The CRD provides for the use of external credit assessments in the determination of risk weights (and consequential capital requirements) applied to a bank or investment firm's exposures. Only the use of assessments provided by recognised External Credit Assessment Institutions ("ECAIs"), mainly credit rating agencies, will be acceptable to the competent authorities. A recognition mechanism is also outlined in the Directive.

The CRD sets out a number of requirements which ECAIs should meet before the competent authority grant them recognition. For example, their ratings must be objectively and independently assigned and reviewed on an ongoing basis. In addition, their rating procedures should be sufficiently transparent. In addition, the competent authorities should assess whether individual credit assessments are recognised in the market as credible and reliable by the users of such credit assessments and accessible at equivalent terms to all interested parties.

Building on the CRD, the Committee of European Banking Supervisors ("CEBS") is working to promote convergence of the recognition processes of ECAIs across the EU by defining a common understanding on the criteria necessary to implement the recognition requirements laid down in the CRD.[12]

Clearly, the CRD does not constitute a form of regulation of credit rating agencies on how to do business but focuses predominantly on the weighting of capital requirements. Consequently, the recognition process of ECAIs does not address the broader conduct of business issues concerning credit rating agencies in general. Moreover, credit rating agencies may choose not to become ECAIs under the CRD and therefore the CRD may not cover the entire population of credit rating agencies. However, the objectives and effects of the ECAI recognition system cannot be seen separately from the aims of other legislation and supervisory standards applicable to credit rating agencies since the CRD affirms the meaningful function of credit rating agencies. To this end, the Commission will closely monitor developments with regard to the recognition of ECAIs and assess whether credit rating agencies perform their important role adequately under the CRD. Hence, competent authorities should ensure that the effects of recognition are shared with all stakeholders in order to assess whether the ECAI recognition criteria could be used in the future for conduct of business regulation of credit rating agencies, if this appears to be necessary.

The final piece of relevant legislation is the **Markets in Financial Instruments Directive** ("MiFID").[13] MiFID and its future implementing measures are not applicable to the rating process of credit rating agencies in the case where the rating process itself does not involve the firm undertaking investment services and activities as defined in the MiFID. In other words, the issuing of a credit rating will normally not result in the credit rating agency also providing 'investment advice' within the meaning of Annex I to the MiFID. But credit rating agencies should be aware of the precise limits of this activity in order to continue to operate outside MiFID regulation. However, credit rating agencies that also provide investment services and activities on a professional basis may require authorisation. In such cases, the MiFID provisions regarding conduct of business and organisational requirements will apply to the firm and its undertaking of investment services and activities. Where, for example, a credit rating agency provides investment services (such as investment advice) to clients that fall under the MiFID, the provisions on conflicts of interest will apply to protect the interest of those who receive these services. The provisions on conflicts of interest may require an appropriate degree of separation of investment services from the credit rating process so that ancillary services may not interfere with the quality and objectivity of credit ratings.[14]

This comprehensive legal framework is now being put in place by the Member States. All Directives must be correctly implemented. Consequently, the transposition of the Directives is actively monitored by the Commission. It may initiate infringement procedures on the grounds of incorrect or non-transposition of the Directives, where necessary.

Another area of Community law which is potentially important for credit rating agencies is **competition law**. The Commission does not share the European Parliament's concerns about the degree of concentration in the ratings industry. There is no indication of any anti-competitive practices in this industry but any evidence to the contrary will be examined thoroughly. The Commission does not therefore see the need for action in this area at the moment. Moreover, one could conceive that in this particular industry, excessive market fragmentation could have adverse consequences (ie credit rating agencies may face undue pressure to issue favourable ratings in order to attract clients).

NOTES

7   Directive 2003/6/EC of 28/01/03 (OJ 2003 L96/16); Commission Directive 2003/124/EC of 22/12/03 (OJ 2003 L339/70); Commission Directive 2003/125/EC of 22/12/03 (OJ 2003 L339/73); Commission Directive 2004/72/EC of 29/04/04 (OJ 2003 L162/70) and Commission Regulation (EC) No 2273/2003 of 22/12/03 (OJ 2003 L336/33).

8   See Article 1(8) and recital 10 of Directive 2003/125/EC.

9   Article 1(2) under c stipulates that *"market manipulation shall mean: dissemination of information through the media, including the Internet, or by any other means, which gives, or is likely to give, false or misleading signals as to financial instruments, including the dissemination of rumours and false or misleading news, where the person knew, or ought to have known, that the information was false or misleading.(…)"*

10   Article 1(1) and 2(1) of Directive 2003/6/EC.

11   Re-casting Directive 2000/12/EC of the European Parliament and of the Council of 20 March 2000 relating to the taking up and pursuit of the business of credit institutions and Council Directive 93/6/EEC of 15 March 1993 on the capital adequacy of investment firms and credit institutions.

12   CEBS Consultation paper on the recognition of External Credit Assessment Institutions, 29 June 2005, available at http://www.c-ebs.org/pdfs/CP07.pdf

13   Directive 2004/39/EC of 21/04/04 (OJ 2004 L145/1).

14   See Articles 13(3), 13(10) and 18 of the MiFID.

3.2 The IOSCO Code

In September 2003, IOSCO published its Principles Regarding the Activities of Credit Rating Agencies ("IOSCO Principles"),[15] setting high-level objectives for credit rating agencies, securities regulators, issuers and other market participants to improve investor protection and market fairness, efficiency and transparency and to reduce systemic risk. In response to comments on these principles, IOSCO developed the IOSCO Code of Conduct Fundamentals for credit rating agencies (see Annex).

Reflecting the global nature of the market for credit rating agencies, the IOSCO Code is meant to be applied by rating agencies of all sizes and business models and in every jurisdiction. The Commission notes that the IOSCO Code has not been implemented into the national law of Member

Sates. However, credit rating agencies are expected to give full effect to the provisions of the IOSCO Code – as long as these provisions are consistent with the EU Directives. This requires that credit rating agencies incorporate the IOSCO Standards in their procedures. Recent market developments show that several credit rating agencies have set up their own Codes of Conduct along the lines of the IOSCO Code which proves that the latter provides a useful set of standards for self-regulation of the credit rating industry.

It is very important that credit rating agencies not only incorporate the IOSCO Code in their own Code of Conduct but fully comply with the IOSCO Code by enforcing their Code of Conduct in daily practice. Credit rating agencies need to inform regularly in the coming years all stakeholders about their compliance with their Codes of Conduct. To this end, the Commission recommends to analyse the effects of the IOSCO Code on a regular basis.

[6045C]

NOTES

15   IOSCO's Principles Regarding the Activities of Credit Rating Agencies, available at: www.iosco.org/IOSCOPD151.

4. CONCLUSION

Following the request by the European Parliament, the Commission has considered very carefully whether or not fresh legislative proposals are required to regulate the activities of credit rating agencies.

Its conclusion is that at present no new legislative initiatives are needed. One of the central principles of "Better Regulation" is that legislative solutions should be applied only where they are strictly necessary for the achievement of public policy objectives. The Commission believes that the case for new legislation in this area remains unproven.

There are already three new financial services Directives which cover credit rating agencies. The Commission is confident that these Directives – when combined with self regulation by the credit rating agencies themselves on the basis of the newly adopted IOSCO Code – will provide an answer to all the major issues of concern raised by the European Parliament.

In its advice to the Commission, CESR also indicated that the right balance between legislation and self-regulation had been struck and that no further regulatory initiatives were needed for the time being.

However, the Commission is continuing to monitor developments in this area very carefully. It is clear that the new arrangements will only produce the desired results if credit rating agencies take the task of regulating themselves sufficiently seriously. They must be scrupulous in implementing the provisions of the IOSCO Code. And they must be open and transparent about the way in which they are doing it.

It is encouraging that many credit rating agencies have established their own Codes of Conduct based on the IOSCO Code. But establishing these Codes in itself is not enough; they must also be implemented in practice on a day to day basis. The Commission intends to ask CESR to monitor compliance with the IOSCO Code and to report back to it on an annual basis. It will also consider how best to gauge the opinions of market participants, especially those purchasing complex financial instruments. This might include the setting up of an informal expert group. The ratings industry should be aware that the Commission may have to take legislative action if it becomes clear that compliance with EU rules or the Code is unsatisfactory and damaging EU capital markets.

The Commission will also consider introducing legislative proposals if new circumstances arise – including serious problems of market failure.

Finally, the Commission intends to monitor the global development of the rating business. If there are significant changes in the way credit rating agencies are regulated in other parts of the world, it may be necessary for the Commission to re-evaluate its approach.

[6045D]

COMMISSION DIRECTIVE

of 8 March 2007

laying down detailed rules for the implementation of certain provisions of Directive 2004/109/EC on the harmonisation of transparency requirements in relation to information about issuers whose securities are admitted to trading on a regulated market

(2007/14/EC)

NOTES
Date of publication in OJ: OJ L69, 9.3.2007, p 27. Notes are as in the original OJ version.
As of 1 February 2009, this Directive had not been amended.

THE COMMISSION OF THE EUROPEAN COMMUNITIES,

Having regard to the Treaty establishing the European Community,

Having regard to Directive 2004/109/EC of the European Parliament and of the Council of 15 December 2004 on the harmonisation of transparency requirements in relation to information about issuers whose securities are admitted to trading on a regulated market and amending Directive 2001/34/EC,[1] and in particular Articles 2(3)(a), 5(6), first subparagraph, and 5(6)(c), 9(7), 12(8)(b) to (e), 13(2), 14(2), 21(4)(a), 23(4)(ii) and 23(7) thereof,

After consulting the Committee of European Securities Regulators (CESR)[2] for technical advice,

Whereas:

(1) Directive 2004/109/EC establishes the general principles for the harmonisation of transparency requirements in respect of the holding of voting rights or financial instruments that result in an entitlement to acquire existing shares with voting rights. It seeks to ensure that, through the disclosure of accurate, comprehensive and timely information about security issuers, investor confidence is built up and sustained. By the same token, by requiring issuers to be informed of movements affecting major holdings in companies, it seeks to ensure that the latter are in a position to keep the public informed.

(2) The rules for the implementation of the rules governing transparency requirements should likewise be designed to ensure a high level of investor protection, to enhance market efficiency, and to be applied in a uniform manner.

(3) As regards the procedural arrangements in accordance with which investors are to be informed of the issuer's choice of home Member State, it is appropriate that such choices be disclosed in accordance with the same procedure as regulated information under Directive 2004/109/EC.

(4) As regards the minimum content of the condensed set of half-yearly financial statements, where that set is not prepared in accordance with international accounting standards, this should be such as to avoid giving a misleading view of the assets, liabilities, financial position and profit or loss of the issuer. The content of half-yearly reports should be such as to ensure appropriate transparency for investors through a regular flow of information about the performance of the issuer, and that information should be presented in such a way that it is easy to compare it with the information provided in the annual report of the preceding year.

(5) Issuers of shares who prepare consolidated accounts in accordance with International Accounting Standards (IAS) and International Financial Reporting Standards (IFRS) should apply the same definition of related party transactions in annual and half-yearly reports under Directive 2004/109/EC. Issuers of shares who do not prepare consolidated accounts and are not required to apply IAS and IFRS should, in their half-yearly reports under Directive 2004/109/EC, apply the definition of related party transactions set out in Council Directive 78/660/EEC of 25 July 1978 based on Article 54(3)(g) of the Treaty on the annual accounts of certain types of companies.[3]

(6) For the purposes of benefiting from the exemption from the notification of major holdings under Directive 2004/109/EC in the case of shares acquired for the sole purpose of clearing and settling, the maximum length of the "short settlement cycle" should be as short as possible.

(7) In order for the relevant competent authority to be able to monitor compliance as regards the derogation for market makers with respect to the notification of information about major holdings, the market maker seeking to benefit from that derogation should make known that it is acting or intends to act as market maker and for which shares or financial instruments.

(8) Conducting market making activities in full transparency is particularly important. Thus, the market maker should be capable upon request from the relevant competent authority of identifying the activities conducted in relation to the issuer in question, and in particular the shares or financial instruments held for market making activities purposes.

(9) As regards the calendar of trading days, it is appropriate, for the sake of ease of operation, that time limits be calculated by reference to the trading days in the Member State of the issuer. However, in order to enhance transparency, provision should be made for each competent authority to inform investors and market participants of the calendar of trading days applicable for the various regulated markets situated or operating on its territory.

(10)   As regards the circumstances in which notification of major holdings is to be made, it is appropriate to determine when that obligation is triggered either individually or collectively, and how that obligation is to be complied with in the case of proxies.

(11)   It is reasonable to assume that natural persons or legal entities exercise a high duty of care when acquiring or disposing of major holdings. It follows that such persons or entities will very quickly become aware of such acquisitions or disposals, or of the possibility to exercise voting rights, and it is therefore appropriate to specify only a very short period following the relevant transaction as the period after which they are deemed to have knowledge.

(12)   The exemption from the obligation to aggregate major holdings should be available only to parent undertakings that can demonstrate that their subsidiary management companies or investment firms fulfil adequate conditions of independence. To ensure full transparency, a statement to that effect should be notified ex ante to the relevant competent authority. In this regard, it is important that the notification mentions the competent authority supervising the management companies' activities under the conditions laid down pursuant to Council Directive 85/611/EEC of 20 December 1985 on the coordination of laws, regulations and administrative provisions relating to undertakings for collective investment in transferable securities (UCITS),[4] irrespective of whether or not they are authorised under that Directive, provided in the latter case that they are supervised under national legislation.

(13)   For the purposes of Directive 2004/109/EC, financial instruments should be taken into account in the context of notifying major holdings, to the extent that such instruments give the holder an unconditional right to acquire the underlying shares or discretion as to whether to acquire the underlying shares or cash on maturity. Consequently, financial instruments should not be considered to include instruments entitling the holder to receive shares depending on the price of the underlying share reaching a certain level at a certain moment in time. Nor should they be considered to cover those instruments that allow the instrument issuer or a third party to give shares or cash to the instrument holder on maturity.

(14)   The financial instruments in Section C of Annex I of Directive 2004/39/EC of the European Parliament and of the Council[5] which are not mentioned in Article 11(1) of this Commission directive do not qualify as financial instruments within the meaning of Article 13(1) of Directive 2004/109/EC.

(15)   Directive 2004/109/EC sets high-level requirements in the area of dissemination of regulated information. The mere availability of information, which means that investors must actively seek it out, is therefore not sufficient for the purposes of that Directive. Accordingly, dissemination should involve the active distribution of information from the issuers to the media, with a view to reaching investors.

(16)   Minimum quality standards for the dissemination of regulated information are necessary to ensure that investors, even if situated in a Member State other than that of the issuer, have equal access to regulated information. Issuers should ensure that those minimum standards are met, whether by disseminating the regulated information themselves or by entrusting a third party to do so on their behalf. In the latter case, the third party should be capable of dissemination in adequate conditions and have adequate mechanisms in place to ensure that the regulated information it receives emanates from the relevant issuer and that there is no significant risk of data corruption or of unauthorised access to unpublished inside information. Where the third party provides other services or performs other functions, such as media, competent authorities, stock exchanges or the entity in charge of the officially appointed storage mechanism, such services or functions should be kept clearly separated from the services and functions relating to the dissemination of regulated information. When communicating information to the media, issuers or third parties should give priority to the use of electronic means and industry standard formats so as to facilitate and accelerate the processing of the information.

(17)   Additionally, by way of minimum standards, regulated information should be disseminated in a way that ensures the widest possible public access, and where possible reaching the public simultaneously inside and outside the issuer's home Member State. That is without prejudice to the right of Member States to request issuers to publish parts or all regulated information through newspapers, and to the possibility for issuers to make regulated information available on their own or other websites accessible to investors.

(18)   Equivalence should be able to be declared when general disclosure rules of third countries provide users with understandable and broadly equivalent assessment of issuers' position that enable them to make similar decisions as if they were provided with the information according to requirements under Directive 2004/109/EC, even if the requirements are not identical. However, equivalence should be limited to the substance of the relevant information and no exception as regards the time limits set by Directive 2004/109/EC should be accepted.

(19)   In order to establish whether or not a third country issuer is meeting equivalent requirements to those laid down in Article 4(3) of Directive 2004/109/EC, it is important to ensure that there is consistency with Commission Regulation (EC) No 809/2004 of 29 April 2004 implementing Directive 2003/71/EC of the European Parliament and of the Council as regards information contained in prospectuses as well as the format, incorporation by reference and publication of such prospectuses and dissemination of advertisements,[6] in particular the items dealing with Historical Financial Information to be included in a prospectus.

(20)   As regards the equivalence of independence requirements, a parent undertaking of a management company or investment firm registered in a third country should be able to benefit from the exemption under Article 12(4) or (5) of Directive 2004/109/EC, independently of whether the authorisation is required by the law of the third country for the controlled management company or investment firm to conduct management activities or portfolio management activities, provided that certain conditions of independence are respected.

(21)   The measures provided for in this Directive are in accordance with the opinion of the European Securities Committee,

[6046]

NOTES

1   OJ L390, 31.12.2004, p 38.
2   CESR was established by Commission Decision 2001/527/EC of 6 June 2001 (OJ L191, 13.7.2001, p 43).
3   OJ L222, 14.8.1978, p 11. Directive as last amended by Directive 2006/46/EC of the European Parliament and of the Council (OJ L224, 16.8.2006, p 1).
4   OJ L375, 31.12.1985, p 3, Directive as last amended by Directive 2005/1/EC of the European Parliament and of the Council (OJ L79, 24.3.2005, p 9).
5   OJ L145, 30.4.2004, p 1. Directive as amended by Directive 2006/31/EC (OJ L114, 27.4.2006, p 60).
6   OJ L149, 30.4.2004, p 1, as corrected by OJ L215, 16.6.2004, p 3. Regulation as amended by Regulation (EC) No 1787/2006 (OJ L337, 5.12.2006, p 17).

HAS ADOPTED THIS DIRECTIVE:

Article 1
Subject matter

This Directive lays down detailed rules for the implementation of Article 2(1)(i)(ii), the second subparagraph of Article 5(3), the second sentence of Article 5(4), Article 9(1), (2) and (4), Article 10, Article 12(1), (2), (4), (5) and (6), Article 12(2)(a), Article 13(1), Article 21(1), Article 23(1) and (6) of Directive 2004/109/EC.

[6047]

Article 2
Procedural arrangements for the choice of the home Member State
(*Article 2(1)(i)(ii) of Directive 2004/109/EC*)

Where the issuer makes a choice of home Member State, that choice shall be disclosed in accordance with the same procedure as regulated information.

[6048]

Article 3
Minimum content of half-yearly non-consolidated financial statements
(*Article 5(3), second subparagraph, of Directive 2004/109/EC*)

1.   The minimum content of the condensed set of half-yearly financial statements, where that set is not prepared in accordance with international accounting standards adopted pursuant to the procedure provided for under Article 6 of Regulation (EC) No 1606/2002, shall be in accordance with paragraphs 2 and 3 of this Article.

2.   The condensed balance sheet and the condensed profit and loss account shall show each of the headings and subtotals included in the most recent annual financial statements of the issuer. Additional line items shall be included if, as a result of their omission, the half-yearly financial statements would give a misleading view of the assets, liabilities, financial position and profit or loss of the issuer.

In addition, the following comparative information shall be included:

    (a)   balance sheet as at the end of the first six months of the current financial year and comparative balance sheet as at the end of the immediate preceding financial year;

    (b)   profit and loss account for the first six months of the current financial year with, from two years after the date of entry into force of this Directive, comparative information for the comparable period for the preceding financial year.

3.   The explanatory notes shall include the following:

    (a)   sufficient information to ensure the comparability of the condensed half-yearly financial statements with the annual financial statements;

    (b)   sufficient information and explanations to ensure a user's proper understanding of any material changes in amounts and of any developments in the half-year period concerned, which are reflected in the balance sheet and the profit and loss account.

[6049]

Article 4
Major related parties' transactions
(Article 5(4), second sentence, of Directive 2004/109/EC)

1. In the interim management reports, issuers of shares shall disclose as major related parties' transactions, as a minimum, the following:
    (a) related parties' transactions that have taken place in the first six months of the current financial year and that have materially affected the financial position or the performance of the enterprise during that period;
    (b) any changes in the related parties' transactions described in the last annual report that could have a material effect on the financial position or performance of the enterprise in the first six months of the current financial year.

2. Where the issuer of shares is not required to prepare consolidated accounts, it shall disclose, as a minimum, the related parties' transactions referred to in Article 43(1)(7b) of Directive 78/660/EEC.

[6050]

Article 5
Maximum length of the usual "short settlement cycle"
(Article 9(4) of Directive 2004/109/EC)

The maximum length of the usual "short settlement cycle" shall be three trading days following the transaction.

[6051]

Article 6
Control mechanisms by competent authorities as regards market makers
(Article 9(5) of Directive 2004/109/EC)

1. The market maker seeking to benefit from the exemption provided for in Article 9(5) of Directive 2004/109/EC shall notify to the competent authority of the Home Member State of the issuer, at the latest within the time limit laid down in Article 12(2) of Directive 2004/109/EC, that it conducts or intends to conduct market making activities on a particular issuer.

Where the market maker ceases to conduct market making activities on the issuer concerned, it shall notify that competent authority accordingly.

2. Without prejudice to the application of Article 24 of Directive 2004/109/EC, where in case the market maker seeking to benefit from the exemption provided for in Article 9(5) of that Directive is requested by the competent authority of the issuer to identify the shares or financial instruments held for market making activity purposes, that market maker shall be allowed to make such identification by any verifiable means. Only if the market maker is not able to identify the shares or financial instruments concerned, he may be required to hold them in a separate account for the purposes of that identification.

3. Without prejudice to the application of Article 24(4)(a) of Directive 2004/109/EC, if a market-making agreement between the market maker and the stock exchange and/or the issuer is required under national law, the market maker shall upon request of the relevant competent authority provide the agreement to such authority.

[6052]

Article 7
Calendar of trading days
(Article 12(2) and (6), and Article 14(1), of Directive 2004/109/EC)

1. For the purposes of Article 12(2) and (6), and Article 14(1), of Directive 2004/109/EC, the calendar of trading days of the home Member State of the issuer shall apply.

2. Each competent authority shall publish in its Internet site the calendar of trading days of the different regulated markets situated or operating on the territory within its jurisdiction.

[6053]

Article 8
Shareholders and natural persons or legal entities referred to in Article 10 of the Transparency Directive required to make the notification of major holdings
(Article 12(2) of Directive 2004/109/EC)

1. For the purposes of Article 12(2) of Directive 2004/109/EC, the notification obligation which arises as soon as the proportion of voting rights held reaches, exceeds or falls below the applicable thresholds following transactions of the type referred to in Article 10 of Directive 2004/109/EC shall be an individual obligation incumbent upon each shareholder, or each natural person or legal entity as referred to in Article 10 of that Directive, or both in case the proportion of voting rights held by each party reaches, exceeds or falls below the applicable threshold.

In the circumstances referred to in point (a) of Article 10 of the Directive 2004/109/EC, the notification obligation shall be a collective obligation shared by all parties to the agreement.

2.   In the circumstances referred to in point (h) of Article 10 of Directive 2004/109/EC, if a shareholder gives the proxy in relation to one shareholder meeting, notification may be made by means of a single notification at the moment of giving the proxy provided that it is made clear in the notification what the resulting situation in terms of voting rights will be when the proxy may no longer exercise the voting rights at its discretion.

If, in the circumstances referred to in point (h) of Article 10, the proxy holder receives one or several proxies in relation to one shareholder meeting, notification may be made by means of a single notification at the moment of receiving the proxies provided that it is made clear in the notification what the resulting situation in terms of voting rights will be when the proxy may no longer exercise the voting rights at its discretion.

3.   Where the duty to make a notification lies with more than one natural person or legal entity, notification may be made by means of a single common notification.

However, use of a single common notification may not be deemed to release any of the natural persons or legal entities concerned from their responsibility in relation to notification.

[6054]

Article 9
Circumstances under which the notifying person should have learned of acquisition or disposal or of possibility to exercise voting rights
(Article 12(2) of Directive 2004/109/EC)

For the purposes of point (a) of Article 12(2) of Directive 2004/109/EC, the shareholder, or the natural person or legal entity referred to in Article 10 of that Directive, shall be deemed to have knowledge of the acquisition, disposal or possibility to exercise voting rights no later than two trading days following the transaction.

[6055]

Article 10
Conditions of independence to be complied with by management companies and investment firms involved in individual portfolio management
(Article 12(4), first subparagraph, and Article 12(5), first subparagraph, of Directive 2004/109/EC)

1.   For the purposes of the exemption to the aggregation of holdings provided for in the first subparagraphs of Article 12(4) and (5) of Directive 2004/109/EC, a parent undertaking of a management company or of an investment firm shall comply with the following conditions:

    (a)   it must not interfere by giving direct or indirect instructions or in any other way in the exercise of the voting rights held by that management company or investment firm;

    (b)   that management company or investment firm must be free to exercise, independently of the parent undertaking, the voting rights attached to the assets it manages.

2.   A parent undertaking which wishes to make use of the exemption shall, without delay, notify the following to the competent authority of the home Member State of issuers whose voting rights are attached to holdings managed by the management companies or investment firms:

    (a)   a list of the names of those management companies and investment firms, indicating the competent authorities that supervise them or that no competent authority supervises them, but with no reference to the issuers concerned;

    (b)   a statement that, in the case of each such management company or investment firm, the parent undertaking complies with the conditions laid down in paragraph 1.

The parent undertaking shall update the list referred to in point (a) on an ongoing basis.

3.   Where the parent undertaking intends to benefit from the exemptions only in relation to the financial instruments referred to in Article 13 of Directive 2004/109/EC, it shall notify to the competent authority of the home Member State of the issuer only the list referred to in point (a) of paragraph 2.

4.   Without prejudice to the application of Article 24 of Directive 2004/109/EC, a parent undertaking of a management company or of an investment firm shall be able to demonstrate to the competent authority of the home Member State of the issuer on request that:

    (a)   the organisational structures of the parent undertaking and the management company or investment firm are such that the voting rights are exercised independently of the parent undertaking;

    (b)   the persons who decide how the voting rights are to be exercised act independently;

    (c)   if the parent undertaking is a client of its management company or investment firm or has holding in the assets managed by the management company or investment firm, there is a clear written mandate for an arms-length customer relationship between the parent undertaking and the management company or investment firm.

The requirement in point (a) shall imply as a minimum that the parent undertaking and the management company or investment firm must established written policies and procedures reasonably designed to prevent the distribution of information between the parent undertaking and the management company or investment firm in relation to the exercise of voting rights.

5. For the purposes of point (a) of paragraph 1, "direct instruction" means any instruction given by the parent undertaking, or another controlled undertaking of the parent undertaking, specifying how the voting rights are to be exercised by the management company or investment firm in particular cases.

"Indirect instruction" means any general or particular instruction, regardless of the form, given by the parent undertaking, or another controlled undertaking of the parent undertaking, that limits the discretion of the management company or investment firm in relation to the exercise of the voting rights in order to serve specific business interests of the parent undertaking or another controlled undertaking of the parent undertaking.

[6056]

Article 11
Types of financial instruments that result in an entitlement to acquire, on the holder's own initiative alone, shares to which voting rights are attached
(Article 13(1) of Directive 2004/109/EC)

1. For the purposes of Article 13(1) of Directive 2004/109/EC, transferable securities; and options, futures, swaps, forward rate agreements and any other derivative contracts, as referred to in Section C of Annex I of Directive 2004/39/EC, shall be considered to be financial instruments, provided that they result in an entitlement to acquire, on the holder's own initiative alone, under a formal agreement, shares to which voting rights are attached, already issued, of an issuer whose shares are admitted to trading on a regulated market.

The instrument holder must enjoy, on maturity, either the unconditional right to acquire the underlying shares or the discretion as to his right to acquire such shares or not.

A formal agreement means an agreement which is binding under the applicable law.

2. For the purposes of Article 13(1) of Directive 2004/109/EC, the holder shall aggregate and notify all financial instruments within the meaning of paragraph 1 relating to the same underlying issuer.

3. The notification required under Article 13(1) of Directive 2004/109/EC shall include the following information:
   (a) the resulting situation in terms of voting rights;
   (b) if applicable, the chain of controlled undertakings through which financial instruments are effectively held;
   (c) the date on which the threshold was reached or crossed;
   (d) for instruments with an exercise period, an indication of the date or time period where shares will or can be acquired, if applicable;
   (e) date of maturity or expiration of the instrument;
   (f) identity of the holder;
   (g) name of the underlying issuer.

For the purposes of point (a), the percentage of voting rights shall be calculated by reference to the total number of voting rights and capital as last disclosed by the issuer under Article 15 of Directive 2004/109/EC.

4. The notification period shall be the same as laid down in Article 12(2) of Directive 2004/109/EC and the related implementing provisions.

5. The notification shall be made to the issuer of the underlying share and to the competent authority of the home Member States of such issuer.

If a financial instrument relates to more than one underlying share, a separate notification shall be made to each issuer of the underlying shares.

[6057]

Article 12
Minimum Standards
(Article 21(1) of Directive 2004/109/EC)

1. The dissemination of regulated information for the purposes of Article 21(1) of Directive 2004/109/EC shall be carried out in compliance with the minimum standards set out in paragraphs 2 to 5.

2. Regulated information shall be disseminated in a manner ensuring that it is capable of being disseminated to as wide a public as possible, and as close to simultaneously as possible in the home Member State, or the Member State referred to in Article 21(3) of Directive 2004/109/EC, and in the other Member States.

3. Regulated information shall be communicated to the media in unedited full text.

However, in the case of the reports and statements referred to in Articles 4, 5 and 6 of Directive 2004/109/EC, this requirement shall be deemed fulfilled if the announcement relating to the regulated information is communicated to the media and indicates on which website, in addition to the officially appointed mechanism for the central storage of regulated information referred to in Article 21 of that Directive, the relevant documents are available.

4. Regulated information shall be communicated to the media in a manner which ensures the security of the communication, minimises the risk of data corruption and unauthorised access, and provides certainty as to the source of the regulated information.

Security of receipt shall be ensured by remedying as soon as possible any failure or disruption in the communication of regulated information.

The issuer or the person who has applied for admission to trading on a regulated market without the issuer's consent shall not be responsible for systemic errors or shortcomings in the media to which the regulated information has been communicated.

5. Regulated information shall be communicated to the media in a way which makes clear that the information is regulated information, identifies clearly the issuer concerned, the subject matter of the regulated information and the time and date of the communication of the information by the issuer or the person who has applied for admission to trading on a regulated market without the issuer's consent.

Upon request, the issuer or the person who has applied for admission to trading on a regulated market without the issuer's consent shall be able to communicate to the competent authority, in relation to any disclosure of regulated information, the following:

    (a)   the name of the person who communicated the information to the media;
    (b)   the security validation details;
    (c)   the time and date on which the information was communicated to the media;
    (d)   the medium in which the information was communicated;
    (e)   if applicable, details of any embargo placed by the issuer on the regulated information.

[6058]

Article 13
Requirements equivalent to Article 4(2)(b) of Directive 2004/109/EC
(*Article 23(1) of Directive 2004/109/EC*)

A third country shall be deemed to set requirements equivalent to those set out in Article 4(2)(b) of Directive 2004/109/EC where, under the law of that country, the annual management report is required to include at least the following information:

    (a)   a fair review of the development and performance of the issuer's business and of its position, together with a description of the principal risks and uncertainties that it faces, such that the review presents a balanced and comprehensive analysis of the development and performance of the issuer's business and of its position, consistent with the size and complexity of the business;
    (b)   an indication of any important events that have occurred since the end of the financial year;
    (c)   indications of the issuer's likely future development.

The analysis referred to in point (a) shall, to the extent necessary for an understanding of the issuer's development, performance or position, include both financial and, where appropriate, non-financial key performance indicators relevant to the particular business.

[6059]

Article 14
Requirements equivalent to Article 5(4) of Directive 2004/109/EC
(*Article 23(1) of Directive 2004/109/EC*)

A third country shall be deemed to set requirements equivalent to those set out in Article 5(4) of Directive 2004/109/EC where, under the law of that country, a condensed set of financial statements is required in addition to the interim management report, and the interim management report is required to include at least the following information:

    (a)   review of the period covered;
    (b)   indications of the issuer's likely future development for the remaining six months of the financial year;
    (c)   for issuers of shares and if already not disclosed on an ongoing basis, major related parties transactions.

[6060]

Article 15
Requirements equivalent to Articles 4(2) and 5(2)(c) of Directive 2004/109/EC
(*Article 23(1) of Directive 2004/109/EC*)

A third country shall be deemed to set requirements equivalent to those set out in Articles 4(2)(c) and 5(2)(c) of Directive 2004/109/EC where, under the law of that country, a person or persons within the issuer are responsible for the annual and half-yearly financial information, and in particular for the following:

(a)   the compliance of the financial statements with the applicable reporting framework or set of accounting standards;

(b)   the fairness of the management review included in the management report.

[6061]

Article 16
Requirements equivalent to Article 6 of Directive 2004/109/EC
(Article 23(1) of Directive 2004/109/EC)

A third country shall be deemed to set requirements equivalent to those set out in Article 6 of Directive 2004/109/EC where, under the law of that country, an issuer is required to publish quarterly financial reports.

[6062]

Article 17
Requirements equivalent to Article 4(3) of Directive 2004/109/EC
(Article 23(1) of Directive 2004/109/EC)

A third country shall be deemed to set requirements equivalent to those set out in the first subparagraph of Article 4(3) of Directive 2004/109/EC where, under the law of that country, the provision of individual accounts by the parent company is not required but the issuer whose registered office is in that third country is required, in preparing consolidated accounts, to include the following information:

(a)   for issuers of shares, dividends computation and ability to pay dividends;

(b)   for all issuers, where applicable, minimum capital and equity requirements and liquidity issues.

For the purposes of equivalence, the issuer must also be able to provide the competent authority of the home Member State with additional audited disclosures giving information on the individual accounts of the issuer as a standalone, relevant to the elements of information referred to under points (a) and (b). Those disclosures may be prepared under the accounting standards of the third country.

[6063]

Article 18
Requirements equivalent to Article 4(3), second subparagraph, of Directive 2004/109/EC
(Article 23(1) of Directive 2004/109/EC)

A third country shall be deemed to set requirements equivalent to those set out in the second subparagraph of Article 4(3) of Directive 2004/109/EC in relation to individual accounts where, under the law of a third country, an issuer whose registered office is in that third country is not required to prepare consolidated accounts but is required to prepare its individual accounts in accordance with international accounting standards recognised pursuant to Article 3 of Regulation (EC) No 1606/2002 of the European Parliament and of the Council[1] as applicable within the Community or with third country national accounting standards equivalent to those standards.

For the purposes of equivalence, if such financial information is not in line with those standards, it must be presented in the form of restated financial statements.

In addition, the individual accounts must be audited independently.

[6064]

NOTES
1   OJ L243, 11.9.2002, p 1.

Article 19
Requirements equivalent to Article 12(6) of Directive 2004/109/EC
(Article 23(1) of Directive 2004/109/EC)

A third country shall be deemed to set requirements equivalent to those set out in Article 12(6) of Directive 2004/109/EC where, under the law of that country, the time period within which an issuer whose registered office is in that third country must be notified of major holdings and within which it must disclose to the public those major holdings is in total equal to or shorter than seven trading days.

The time frames for the notification to the issuer and for the subsequent disclosure to the public by the issuer may be different from those set out in Articles 12(2) and 12(6) of Directive 2004/109/EC.

[6065]

Article 20
Requirements equivalent to Article 14 of Directive 2004/109/EC
(Article 23(1) of Directive 2004/109/EC)

A third country shall be deemed to set requirements equivalent to those set out in Article 14 of Directive 2004/109/EC where, under the law of that country, an issuer whose registered office is in that third country is required to comply with the following conditions:

    (a)   in the case of an issuer allowed to hold up to a maximum of 5% of its own shares to which voting rights are attached, it must make a notification whenever that threshold is reached or crossed;

    (b)   in the case of an issuer allowed to hold up to a maximum of between 5% and 10% of its own shares to which voting rights are attached, it must make a notification whenever a 5% threshold or that maximum threshold is reached or crossed;

    (c)   in the case of an issuer allowed to hold more than 10% of its own shares to which voting rights are attached, it must make a notification whenever the 5% threshold or the 10% threshold is reached or crossed.

For the purposes of equivalence, notification above the 10% threshold need not be required.

[6066]

Article 21
Requirements equivalent to Article 15 of Directive 2004/109/EC
(Article 23(1) of Directive 2004/109/EC)

A third country shall be deemed to set requirements equivalent to those set out in Article 15 of Directive 2004/109/EC where, under the law of that country, an issuer whose registered office is in that third country is required to disclose to the public the total number of voting rights and capital within 30 calendar days after an increase or decrease of such total number has occurred.

[6067]

Article 22
Requirements equivalent to Articles 17(2)(a) and 18(2)(a) of Directive 2004/109/EC
(Article 23(1) of Directive 2004/109/EC)

A third country shall be deemed to set requirements equivalent to those set out in Article 17(2)(a) and 18(2)(a) of Directive 2004/109/EC, as far as the content of the information about meetings is concerned, where, under the law of that country, an issuer whose registered office is in that third country is required to provide at least information on the place, time and agenda of meetings.

[6068]

Article 23
Equivalence in relation to the test of independence for parent undertakings of management companies and investment firms
(Article 23(6) of Directive 2004/109/EC)

    1.   A third country shall be deemed to set conditions of independence equivalent to those set out in Article 12(4) and (5) of that Directive where, under the law of that country, a management company or investment firm as referred to in Article 23(6) of Directive 2004/109/EC is required to meet the following conditions:

    (a)   the management company or investment firm must be free in all situations to exercise, independently of its parent undertaking, the voting rights attached to the assets it manages;

    (b)   the management company or investment firm must disregard the interests of the parent undertaking or of any other controlled undertaking of the parent undertaking whenever conflicts of interest arise.

    2.   The parent undertaking shall comply with the notification requirements laid down in Article 10(2)(a) and (3) of this Directive.

In addition, it shall make a statement that, in the case of each management company or investment firm concerned, the parent undertaking complies with the conditions laid down in paragraph 1 of this Article.

    3.   Without prejudice to the application of Article 24 of Directive 2004/109/EC, the parent undertaking shall be able to demonstrate to the competent authority of the home Member State of the issuer on request that the requirements laid down in Article 10(4) of this Directive are respected.

[6069]

Article 24
Transposition

    1.   Member States shall bring into force the laws, regulations and administrative provisions necessary to comply with this Directive by 12 months after date of adoption at the latest. They shall forthwith communicate to the Commission the text of those provisions and a correlation table between those provisions and this Directive.

When Member States adopt those provisions, they shall contain a reference to this Directive or be accompanied by such a reference on the occasion of their official publication. Member States shall determine how such reference is to be made.

2. Member States shall communicate to the Commission the text of the main provisions of national law which they adopt in the field covered by this Directive.

[6070]

Article 25

This Directive shall enter into force on the 20th day following its publication in the Official Journal of the European Union.

[6071]

Article 26

This Directive is addressed to the Member States.

[6072]

COMMISSION DIRECTIVE

of 19 March 2007

implementing Council Directive 85/611/EEC on the coordination of laws, regulations and administrative provisions relating to undertakings for collective investment in transferable securities (UCITS) as regards the clarification of certain definitions

(Text with EEA relevance)

(2007/16/EC)

NOTES

Date of publication in OJ: OJ L79, 20.03.2007, p 11. Notes are as in the original OJ version.
As of 1 February 2009, this Directive had not been amended.

THE COMMISSION OF THE EUROPEAN COMMUNITIES,

Having regard to the Treaty establishing the European Community,

Having regard to Council Directive 85/611/EEC of 20 December 1985 on the coordination of laws, regulations and administrative provisions relating to undertakings for collective investment in transferable securities (UCITS),[1] and in particular point (a) of Article 53a thereof,

Whereas:

(1) Directive 85/611/EEC contains several definitions, sometimes interlinked, related to the assets which are eligible for investment by undertakings for collective investment in transferable securities, hereinafter "UCITS", such as a definition of transferable securities and a definition of money market instruments.

(2) Since the adoption of Directive 85/611/EEC, the variety of financial instruments traded on financial markets has increased considerably, leading to uncertainty in determining whether certain categories of financial instruments are encompassed by those definitions. Uncertainty in applying the definitions gives rise to divergent interpretations of the Directive.

(3) In order to ensure a uniform application of Directive 85/611/EEC, to help Member States to develop a common understanding as to whether a given asset category is eligible for a UCITS and to ensure that the definitions are understood in a manner consistent with the principles underlying Directive 85/611/EEC, such as those governing risk-diversification and limits to exposure, the ability of the UCITS to redeem its units at the request of the unit-holders and to calculate its net asset value whenever units are issued or redeemed, it is necessary to provide competent authorities and market participants with more certainty in this respect. Greater certainty will also facilitate a better functioning of the notification procedure for the cross-border distribution of UCITS.

(4) The clarifications provided by this Directive do not of themselves give rise to any new behavioural or operational obligations for competent authorities or market participants. Rather than establishing exhaustive lists of financial instruments and transactions, they elucidate basic criteria as an aid in assessing whether or not a class of financial instrument is covered by the various definitions.

(5) The eligibility of an asset for a UCITS must be assessed not only with regard to whether it falls within the scope of the definitions as clarified by this text but also with regard to the other requirements of Directive 85/611/EEC. National competent authorities could work together through the Committee of European Securities Regulators (CESR) to develop common approaches on the practical, day-to-day application of those clarifications in the context of their supervisory duties, notably in connection with other requirements of Directive 85/611/EEC such as control or risk management procedures, and to ensure the smooth functioning of the product passport.

(6) Directive 85/611/EEC defines transferable securities exclusively from a formal/legal point of view. Accordingly the definition of transferable securities is applicable to a wide range of financial products with differing features and different levels of liquidity. For each of those financial products, consistency between the definition of transferable securities and other provisions of the Directive should be ensured.

(7) Closed end funds constitute an asset class which is not explicitly referred to as an eligible asset for a UCITS under Directive 85/611/EEC. However, the units of closed end funds are often treated as transferable securities and their admission to trading on a regulated market often gives grounds for such a treatment. It is therefore necessary to provide market participants and competent authorities with certainty as to whether units of closed end funds are covered by the definition of transferable securities. National competent authorities could work together through the CESR to develop common approaches as regards the practical, day-to-day application of the criteria applicable to closed end funds, notably in respect of minimum core standards in relation to corporate governance mechanisms.

(8) Additional legal certainty is also necessary with regard to the categorisation, as transferable securities, of financial instruments which are linked to the performance of other assets, including assets which are not referred to by Directive 85/611/EEC itself, or which are backed by such assets. It should be made clear that if the linkage to the underlying or to another component of the instrument amounts to an element which has to be considered as an embedded derivative, the financial instrument falls in the subcategory of transferable securities embedding a derivative element. This has the consequence that the criteria for derivatives under Directive 85/611/EEC have to be applied in respect of that element.

(9) In order to be covered by the definition of money market instruments in Directive 85/611/EEC, a financial instrument should fulfil certain criteria, notably it must normally be dealt in on the money market, it must be liquid and it must have a value which can be accurately determined at any time. It is necessary to ensure a uniform application of those criteria taking into account certain market practices. It is also necessary to clarify that the criteria have to be understood in coherence with other principles of Directive 85/611/EEC. The definition of money market instruments should extend to financial instruments which are not admitted to or dealt in on a regulated market and for which Directive 85/611/EEC sets out criteria in addition to the general criteria for money market instruments. It was therefore equally necessary to clarify those criteria in the light of investor protection requirements and taking into account principles of the Directive such as portfolio liquidity, as resulting from Article 37 thereof.

(10) Under Directive 85/611/EEC financial derivative instruments are to be considered as liquid financial assets if they fulfil the criteria set out in that Directive. It is necessary to ensure a uniform application of those criteria and it is also necessary to make clear that the criteria have to be understood in a way which is consistent with other provisions of the Directive. It should also be made clear that if credit derivatives comply with those criteria, they are financial derivative instruments within the meaning of Directive 85/611/EEC and hence eligible for treatment as liquid financial assets.

(11) The need for clarification is particularly pressing for derivatives on financial indices. There is currently a wide range of financial indices which function as the underlying for a derivative instrument. These indices may vary as regards their composition or the weighting of their components. In all cases it has to be ensured that the UCITS is able to fulfil its obligations as regards portfolio liquidity, as resulting from Article 37 of Directive 85/611/EEC, and the calculation of the net asset value and that those obligations are not negatively affected by the features of the underlying of a derivative. It should be clarified that derivatives on financial indices whose composition is sufficiently diversified, which represent an adequate benchmark to the market to which they refer and which are subject to appropriate information regarding the index composition and calculation fall under the category of derivatives as liquid financial assets. National competent authorities could work together through the CESR to develop common approaches as regards the practical, day-to-day application of those criteria in respect of indices based on assets which are not individually identified as eligible assets in the Directive.

(12) Directive 85/611/EEC recognises as a sub-category of transferable securities and money market instruments those which embed a derivative element. Embedding a derivative element into a transferable security or money market instrument does not transform the whole financial instrument into a financial derivative instrument which would fall outside the definitions of transferable security or money market instrument. Therefore, it is necessary to make clear whether a financial derivative can be considered embedded in another instrument. In addition, embedding a derivative into a transferable security or money market instrument entails the risk that the rules for derivatives imposed by Directive 85/611/EEC are bypassed. For that reason, the Directive requires identification of the embedded derivative element and compliance with those rules. Given the level of financial innovation, the identification of an embedded derivative element is not always evident. In order to achieve more certainty in this respect, criteria for identifying such elements should be laid down.

(13) Pursuant to Directive 85/611/EEC, techniques and instruments relating to transferable securities or money market instruments for the purpose of efficient portfolio management do not fall under the definitions of transferable securities and money market instruments. To clarify the boundaries of those definitions it is necessary to set out criteria to identify the transactions which

would fall under those techniques and instruments. It is also necessary to recall that those techniques and instruments have to be understood in coherence with the other obligations of a UCITS, particularly as regards its risk profile. That is to say, they must be consistent with the rules laid down by Directive 85/611/EEC on risk management and on risk diversification, as well as with its restrictions on short sales and borrowing.

(14) Directive 85/611/EEC sets out criteria to define UCITS which replicate bond or share indices. UCITS which comply with those criteria are subject to a more flexible treatment as regards issuer concentration limits. It is therefore necessary to develop a clear understanding of those criteria and to ensure their uniform application in all Member States. That entails giving further clarification as to whether a UCITS can be considered to be an index-replicating UCITS, and thus more certainty about the conditions which justify the preferential treatment of index-replicating UCITS.

(15) The Committee of European Securities Regulators has been consulted for technical advice.

(16) The measures provided for in this Directive are in accordance with the opinion of the European Securities Committee,

[6073]

NOTES

¹ OJ L375, 31.12.1985, p 3. Directive as last amended by Directive 2005/1/EC of the European Parliament and of the Council (OJ L79, 24.3.2005, p 9).

HAS ADOPTED THIS DIRECTIVE:

Article 1
Subject matter

This Directive lays down rules clarifying, for the purposes of their uniform application, the following terms:

1.   transferable securities, as defined in Article 1(8) of Directive 85/611/EEC;
2.   money market instruments, as defined in Article 1(9) of Directive 85/611/EEC;
3.   liquid financial assets, as referred to in the definition of UCITS laid down in Article 1(2) of Directive 85/611/EEC, with respect to financial derivative instruments;
4.   transferable securities and money market instruments embedding derivatives, as referred to in the fourth subparagraph of Article 21(3) of Directive 85/611/EEC;
5.   techniques and instruments for the purpose of efficient portfolio management, as referred to in Article 21(2) of Directive 85/611/EEC;
6.   index-replicating UCITS, as referred to in Article 22a(1) of Directive 85/611/EEC.

[6074]

Article 2
Article 1(8) of Directive 85/611/EEC Transferable securities

1.   The reference in Article 1(8) of Directive 85/611/EEC to transferable securities shall be understood as a reference to financial instruments which fulfil the following criteria:

(a)   the potential loss which the UCITS may incur with respect to holding those instruments is limited to the amount paid for them;

(b)   their liquidity does not compromise the ability of the UCITS to comply with Article 37 of Directive 85/611/EEC;

(c)   reliable valuation is available for them as follows:

(i)   in the case of securities admitted to or dealt in on a regulated market as referred to in points (a) to (d) of Article 19(1) of Directive 85/611/EEC, in the form of accurate, reliable and regular prices which are either market prices or prices made available by valuation systems independent from issuers;

(ii)   in the case of other securities as referred to in Article 19(2) of Directive 85/611/EEC, in the form of a valuation on a periodic basis which is derived from information from the issuer of the security or from competent investment research;

(d)   appropriate information is available for them as follows:

(i)   in the case of securities admitted to or dealt in on a regulated market as referred to in points (a) to (d) of Article 19(1) of Directive 85/611/EEC, in the form of regular, accurate and comprehensive information to the market on the security or, where relevant, on the portfolio of the security;

(ii)   in the case of other securities as referred to in Article 19(2) of Directive 85/611/EEC, in the form of regular and accurate information to the UCITS on the security or, where relevant, on the portfolio of the security;

(e)   they are negotiable;

(f)   their acquisition is consistent with the investment objectives or the investment policy, or both, of the UCITS pursuant to Directive 85/611/EEC;

(g)   their risks are adequately captured by the risk management process of the UCITS.

For the purposes of points (b) and (e) of the first subparagraph, and unless there is information available to the UCITS that would lead to a different determination, financial instruments which are admitted or dealt in on a regulated market in accordance with points (a), (b) or (c) of Article 19(1) of Directive 85/611/EEC shall be presumed not to compromise the ability of the UCITS to comply with Article 37 of Directive 85/611/EEC and shall also be presumed to be negotiable.

2.　Transferable securities as referred to in Article 1(8) of Directive 85/611/EEC shall be taken to include the following:

   (a)　units in closed end funds constituted as investment companies or as unit trusts which fulfil the following criteria:
      (i)　they fulfil the criteria set out in paragraph 1;
      (ii)　they are subject to corporate governance mechanisms applied to companies;
      (iii)　where asset management activity is carried out by another entity on behalf of the closed end fund, that entity is subject to national regulation for the purpose of investor protection;

   (b)　units in closed end funds constituted under the law of contract which fulfil the following criteria:
      (i)　they fulfil the criteria set out in paragraph 1;
      (ii)　they are subject to corporate governance mechanisms equivalent to those applied to companies as referred to in point (a)(ii);
      (iii)　they are managed by an entity which is subject to national regulation for the purpose of investor protection;

   (c)　financial instruments which fulfil the following criteria:
      (i)　they fulfil the criteria set out in paragraph 1;
      (ii)　they are backed by, or linked to the performance of, other assets, which may differ from those referred to in Article 19(1) of Directive 85/611/EEC.

3.　Where a financial instrument covered by point (c) of paragraph 2 contains an embedded derivative component as referred to in Article 10 of this Directive, the requirements of Article 21 of Directive 85/611/EEC shall apply to that component.

[6075]

Article 3
Instruments normally dealt in on the money market
(Article 1(9) of Directive 85/611/EEC)

1.　The reference in Article 1(9) of Directive 85/611/EEC to money market instruments as instruments shall be understood as a reference to the following:

   (a)　financial instruments which are admitted to trading or dealt in on a regulated market in accordance with points (a), (b) and (c) of Article 19(1) of Directive 85/611/EEC;
   (b)　financial instruments which are not admitted to trading.

2.　The reference in Article 1(9) of Directive 85/611/EEC to money market instruments as instruments normally dealt in on the money market shall be understood as a reference to financial instruments which fulfil one of the following criteria:

   (a)　they have a maturity at issuance of up to and including 397 days;
   (b)　they have a residual maturity of up to and including 397 days;
   (c)　they undergo regular yield adjustments in line with money market conditions at least every 397 days;
   (d)　their risk profile, including credit and interest rate risks, corresponds to that of financial instruments which have a maturity as referred to in points (a) or (b), or are subject to a yield adjustment as referred to in point (c).

[6076]

Article 4
Liquid instruments with a value which can be accurately determined at any time
(Article 1(9) of Directive 85/611/EEC)

1.　The reference in Article 1(9) of Directive 85/611/EEC to money market instruments as instruments which are liquid shall be understood as a reference to financial instruments which can be sold at limited cost in an adequately short time frame, taking into account the obligation of the UCITS to repurchase or redeem its units at the request of any unit holder.

2.　The reference in Article 1(9) of Directive 85/611/EEC to money market instruments as instruments which have a value which can be accurately determined at any time shall be understood as a reference to financial instruments for which accurate and reliable valuations systems, which fulfil the following criteria, are available:

   (a)　they enable the UCITS to calculate a net asset value in accordance with the value at which the financial instrument held in the portfolio could be exchanged between knowledgeable willing parties in an arm's length transaction;
   (b)　they are based either on market data or on valuation models including systems based on amortised costs.

3.   The criteria referred to in paragraphs 1 and 2 shall be presumed to be fulfilled in the case of financial instruments which are normally dealt in on the money market for the purposes of Article 1(9) of Directive 85/611/EEC and which are admitted to, or dealt in on, a regulated market in accordance with points (a), (b) or (c) of Article 19(1) thereof, unless there is information available to the UCITS that would lead to a different determination.

[6077]

Article 5
Instruments of which the issue or issuer is regulated for the purpose of protecting investors and savings
(Article 19(1)(h) of Directive 85/611/EEC)

1.   The reference in Article 19(1)(h) of Directive 85/611/EEC to money market instruments, other than those dealt in on a regulated market, of which the issue or the issuer is itself regulated for the purpose of protecting investors and savings, shall be understood as a reference to financial instruments which fulfil the following criteria:
   (a)   they fulfil one of the criteria set out in Article 3(2) and all the criteria set out in Article 4(1) and (2);
   (b)   appropriate information is available for them, including information which allows an appropriate assessment of the credit risks related to the investment in such instruments, taking into account paragraphs 2, 3 and 4 of this Article;
   (c)   they are freely transferable.

2.   For money market instruments covered by the second and the fourth indents of Article 19(1)(h) of Directive 85/611/EEC, or for those which are issued by a local or regional authority of a Member State or by a public international body but are not guaranteed by a Member State or, in the case of a federal State which is a Member State, by one of the members making up the federation, appropriate information as referred to in point (b) of paragraph 1 of this Article shall consist in the following:
   (a)   information on both the issue or the issuance programme and the legal and financial situation of the issuer prior to the issue of the money market instrument;
   (b)   updates of the information referred to in point (a) on a regular basis and whenever a significant event occurs;
   (c)   the information referred to in point (a), verified by appropriately qualified third parties not subject to instructions from the issuer;
   (d)   available and reliable statistics on the issue or the issuance programme.

3.   For money market instruments covered by the third indent of Article 19(1)(h) of Directive 85/611/EEC, appropriate information as referred to in point (b) of paragraph 1 of this Article shall consist in the following:
   (a)   information on the issue or the issuance programme or on the legal and financial situation of the issuer prior to the issue of the money market instrument;
   (b)   updates of the information referred to in point (a) on a regular basis and whenever a significant event occurs;
   (c)   available and reliable statistics on the issue or the issuance programme or other data enabling an appropriate assessment of the credit risks related to the investment in such instruments.

4.   For all money market instruments covered by the first indent of Article 19(1)(h) of Directive 85/611/EEC except those referred to in paragraph 2 of this Article and those issued by the European Central Bank or by a central bank from a Member State, appropriate information as referred to in point (b) of paragraph 1 of this Article shall consist in information on the issue or the issuance programme or on the legal and financial situation of the issuer prior to the issue of the money market instrument.

[6078]

Article 6
Establishment which is subject to and complies with prudential rules considered by the competent authorities to be at least as stringent as those laid down by Community law
(Article 19(1)(h) of Directive 85/611/EEC)

The reference in the third indent of Article 19(1)(h) of Directive 85/611/EEC to an establishment which is subject to and complies with prudential rules considered by the competent authorities to be at least as stringent as those laid down by Community law shall be understood as a reference to an issuer which is subject to and complies with prudential rules and fulfils one of the following criteria:
   1.   it is located in the European Economic Area;
   2.   it is located in the OECD countries belonging to the Group of Ten;
   3.   it has at least investment grade rating;
   4.   it can be demonstrated on the basis of an in-depth analysis of the issuer that the prudential rules applicable to that issuer are at least as stringent as those laid down by Community law.

[6079]

Article 7
Securitisation vehicles which benefit from a banking liquidity line
(Article 19(1)(h) of Directive 85/611/EEC)

1.   The reference in the fourth indent of Article 19(1)(h) of Directive 85/611/EEC to securitisation vehicles shall be understood as a reference to structures, whether in corporate, trust or contractual form, set up for the purpose of securitisation operations.

2.   The reference in the fourth indent of Article 19(1)(h) of Directive 85/611/EEC to banking liquidity lines shall be understood as a reference to banking facilities secured by a financial institution which itself complies with the third indent of Article 19(1)(h) of Directive 85/611/EEC.

[6080]

Article 8
Liquid financial assets with respect to financial derivative instruments
(Articles 1(2) and 19(1)(g) of Directive 85/611/EEC)

1.   The reference in Article 1(2) of Directive 85/611/EEC to liquid financial assets shall be understood, with respect to financial derivative instruments, as a reference to financial derivative instruments which fulfil the following criteria:
    (a)   their underlyings consist in one or more of the following:
        (i)   assets as listed in Article 19(1) of Directive 85/611/EEC including financial instruments having one or several characteristics of those assets;
        (ii)   interest rates;
        (iii)   foreign exchange rates or currencies;
        (iv)   financial indices;
    (b)   in the case of OTC derivatives, they comply with the conditions set out in the second and third indents of Article 19(1)(g) of Directive 85/611/EEC.

2.   Financial derivative instruments as referred to in Article 19(1)(g) of Directive 85/611/EEC shall be taken to include instruments which fulfil the following criteria:
    (a)   they allow the transfer of the credit risk of an asset as referred to in point (a) of paragraph 1 of this Article independently from the other risks associated with that asset;
    (b)   they do not result in the delivery or in the transfer, including in the form of cash, of assets other than those referred to in Article 19(1) and (2) of Directive 85/611/EEC;
    (c)   they comply with the criteria for OTC-derivatives laid down in the second and third indents of Article 19(1)(g) of Directive 85/611/EEC and in paragraphs 3 and 4 of this Article;
    (d)   their risks are adequately captured by the risk management process of the UCITS, and by its internal control mechanisms in the case of risks of asymmetry of information between the UCITS and the counterparty to the credit derivative resulting from potential access of the counterparty to non-public information on firms the assets of which are used as underlyings by credit derivatives.

3.   For the purposes of the third indent of Article 19(1)(g) of Directive 85/611/EEC, the reference to fair value shall be understood as a reference to the amount for which an asset could be exchanged, or a liability settled, between knowledgeable, willing parties in an arm's length transaction.

4.   For the purposes of the third indent of Article 19(1)(g) of Directive 85/611/EEC, the reference to reliable and verifiable valuation shall be understood as a reference to a valuation, by the UCITS, corresponding to the fair value as referred to in paragraph 3 of this Article, which does not rely only on market quotations by the counterparty and which fulfils the following criteria:
    (a)   the basis for the valuation is either a reliable up-to-date market value of the instrument, or, if such a value is not available, a pricing model using an adequate recognised methodology;
    (b)   verification of the valuation is carried out by one of the following:
        (i)   an appropriate third party which is independent from the counterparty of the OTC-derivative, at an adequate frequency and in such a way that the UCITS is able to check it;
        (ii)   a unit within the UCITS which is independent from the department in charge of managing the assets and which is adequately equipped for such purpose.

5.   The reference in Articles 1(2) and 19(1)(g) of Directive 85/611/EEC to liquid financial assets shall be understood as excluding derivatives on commodities.

[6081]

Article 9
Financial indices
(Article 19(1)(g) of Directive 85/611/EEC)

1.   The reference in point (g) of Article 19(1) of Directive 85/611/EEC to financial indices shall be understood as a reference to indices which fulfil the following criteria:
    (a)   they are sufficiently diversified, in that the following criteria are fulfilled:

      (i)   the index is composed in such a way that price movements or trading activities regarding one component do not unduly influence the performance of the whole index;

      (ii)   where the index is composed of assets referred to in Article 19(1) of Directive 85/611/EEC, its composition is at least diversified in accordance with Article 22a of that Directive;

      (iii) where the index is composed of assets other than those referred to in Article 19(1) of Directive 85/611/EEC, it is diversified in a way which is equivalent to that provided for in Article 22a of that Directive;

   (b)   they represent an adequate benchmark for the market to which they refer, in that the following criteria are fulfilled:

      (i)   the index measures the performance of a representative group of underlyings in a relevant and appropriate way;

      (ii)   the index is revised or rebalanced periodically to ensure that it continues to reflect the markets to which it refers following criteria which are publicly available;

      (iii) the underlyings are sufficiently liquid, which allows users to replicate the index, if necessary;

   (c)   they are published in an appropriate manner, in that the following criteria are fulfilled:

      (i)   their publication process relies on sound procedures to collect prices and to calculate and to subsequently publish the index value, including pricing procedures for components where a market price is not available;

      (ii)   material information on matters such as index calculation, rebalancing methodologies, index changes or any operational difficulties in providing timely or accurate information is provided on a wide and timely basis.

2.   Where the composition of assets which are used as underlyings by financial derivatives in accordance with Article 19(1) of Directive 85/611/EEC does not fulfil the criteria set out in paragraph 1 of this Article, those financial derivatives shall, where they comply with the criteria set out in Article 8(1) of this Directive, be regarded as financial derivatives on a combination of the assets referred to in points (i), (ii) and (iii) of Article 8(1)(a).

[6082]

Article 10
Transferable securities and money market instruments embedding derivatives
(Article 21(3) of Directive 85/611/EEC, fourth subparagraph)

1.   The reference in the fourth subparagraph of Article 21(3) of Directive 85/611/EEC to transferable securities embedding a derivative shall be understood as a reference to financial instruments which fulfil the criteria set out in Article 2(1) of this Directive and which contain a component which fulfils the following criteria:

   (a)   by virtue of that component some or all of the cash flows that otherwise would be required by the transferable security which functions as host contract can be modified according to a specified interest rate, financial instrument price, foreign exchange rate, index of prices or rates, credit rating or credit index, or other variable, and therefore vary in a way similar to a stand-alone derivative;

   (b)   its economic characteristics and risks are not closely related to the economic characteristics and risks of the host contract;

   (c)   it has a significant impact on the risk profile and pricing of the transferable security.

2.   Money market instruments which fulfil one of the criteria set out in Article 3(2) and all the criteria set out in Article 4(1) and (2) thereof and which contain a component which fulfils the criteria set out in paragraph 1 of this Article shall be regarded as money market instruments embedding a derivative.

3.   A transferable security or a money market instrument shall not be regarded as embedding a derivative where it contains a component which is contractually transferable independently of the transferable security or the money market instrument. Such a component shall be deemed to be a separate financial instrument.

[6083]

Article 11
Techniques and instruments for the purpose of efficient portfolio management
(Article 21(2) of Directive 85/611/EEC)

1.   The reference in Article 21(2) of Directive 85/611/EEC to techniques and instruments which relate to transferable securities and which are used for the purpose of efficient portfolio management shall be understood as a reference to techniques and instruments which fulfil the following criteria:

   (a)   they are economically appropriate in that they are realised in a cost-effective way;

   (b)   they are entered into for one or more of the following specific aims:

      (i)   reduction of risk;

      (ii)   reduction of cost;

      (iii) generation of additional capital or income for the UCITS with a level of risk which is consistent with the risk profile of the UCITS and the risk diversification rules laid down in Article 22 of Directive 85/611/EEC;

(c)   their risks are adequately captured by the risk management process of the UCITS.

2.   Techniques and instruments which comply with the criteria set out in paragraph 1 and which relate to money market instruments shall be regarded as techniques and instruments relating to money market instruments for the purpose of efficient portfolio management as referred to in Article 21(2) of Directive 85/611/EEC.

[6084]

Article 12
Index replicating UCITS
(*Article 22a(1) of Directive 85/611/EEC*)

1.   The reference in Article 22a(1) of Directive 85/611/EEC to replicating the composition of a stock or debt securities index shall be understood as a reference to replication of the composition of the underlying assets of the index, including the use of derivatives or other techniques and instruments as referred to in Article 21(2) of Directive 85/611/EEC and Article 11 of this Directive.

2.   The reference in the first indent of Article 22a(1) of Directive 85/611/EEC to an index whose composition is sufficiently diversified shall be understood as a reference to an index which complies with the risk diversification rules of Article 22a of that Directive.

3.   The reference in the second indent of Article 22a(1) of Directive 85/611/EEC to an index which represents an adequate benchmark shall be understood as a reference to an index whose provider uses a recognised methodology which generally does not result in the exclusion of a major issuer of the market to which it refers.

4.   The reference in the third indent of Article 22a(1) of Directive 85/611/EEC to an index which is published in an appropriate manner shall be understood as a reference to an index which fulfils the following criteria:

(a) it is accessible to the public;

(b) the index provider is independent from the index-replicating UCITS.

Point (b) shall not preclude index providers and the UCITS forming part of the same economic group, provided that effective arrangements for the management of conflicts of interest are in place.

[6085]

Article 13
Transposition

1.   Member States shall adopt and publish, by 23 March 2008 at the latest, the laws, regulations and administrative provisions necessary to comply with this Directive. They shall forthwith communicate to the Commission the text of those provisions and a correlation table between those provisions and this Directive.

They shall apply those provisions from 23 July 2008.

When Member States adopt those provisions, they shall contain a reference to this Directive or be accompanied by such a reference on the occasion of their official publication. Member States shall determine how such reference is to be made.

2.   Member States shall communicate to the Commission the text of the main provisions of national law which they adopt in the field covered by this Directive.

[6086]

Article 14
Entry into force

This Directive shall enter into force on the third day following its publication in the Official Journal of the European Union.

[6087]

Article 15
Addressees

This Directive is addressed to the Member States.

[6088]

COMMISSION RECOMMENDATION

of 11 October 2007

on the electronic network of officially appointed mechanisms for the central storage of regulated information referred to in Directive 2004/109/EC of the European Parliament and of the Council

(notified under document number C(2007) 4607)

(Text with EEA relevance)

(2007/657/EC)

NOTES

Date of publication in OJ: OJ L267, 12.10.2007, p 16. Notes are as in the original OJ version.
As of 1 February 2009, this document had not been amended.

THE COMMISSION OF THE EUROPEAN COMMUNITIES,

Having regard to the Treaty establishing the European Community, and in particular second indent of Article 211 thereof,

Whereas:

(1)   Directive 2004/109/EC of the European Parliament and of the Council of 15 December 2004 on the harmonisation of transparency requirements in relation to information about issuers whose securities are admitted to trading on a regulated market and amending Directive 2001/34/EC[1] requires that the access for investors to information about issuers is more organised at a Community level in order to actively promote the integration of European capital markets.

(2)   Directive 2004/109/EC obliges the competent authorities of the Member States to draw up guidelines with a view to further facilitate public access to information to be disclosed under Directive 2003/6/EC of the European Parliament and of the Council of 28 January 2003 on insider dealing and market manipulation (market abuse),[2] Directive 2003/71/EC of the European Parliament and of the Council of 4 November 2003 on the prospectus to be published when securities are offered tot he public or admitted to trading and amending directive 2001/34/EC[3] and Directive 2004/109/EC of the European Parliament and of the Council and to create a single electronic network (hereinafter "the electronic network") or a platform of electronic networks across Member States linking the different mechanisms appointed at national level for the storage of such information (hereinafter "the storage mechanisms").

(3)   The competent authorities of the Member States adopted, within Committee of European Securities Regulators (CESR) established by Commission Decision 2001/527/EC,[4] an opinion to the Commission on 30 June 2006, in which they expressed a preference for a simple electronic network mode linking the storage mechanisms. Such network could be accessed via a common interface which would contain a list of all listed companies in the Community and would redirect the user to the site of the relevant storage mechanism. The relevant data would thus remain stored at national level without any need to establish a common infrastructure replicating all the relevant information contained at national level and incurring excessive additional costs.

(4)   It is appropriate to provide at this stage for voluntary standards giving the necessary flexibility to the storage mechanisms to adapt themselves to the functioning of the electronic network.

(5)   It is desirable that the storage mechanisms are able to interconnect electronically to each other, so that investors and interested parties can easily accede to financial information on listed companies in the Community. In order to provide for a rapid establishment of such an electronic network, it should be based on simple conditions such as those suggested by the competent authorities of the Member States. A simple network should also allow for the provision of added value services to investors.

(6)   For the purposes of facilitating the access of investors to financial information on listed companies, storage mechanisms should be invited to integrate, wherever possible, related financial information disclosed by issuers in accordance with other Community or national acts.

(7)   In order to enable effective launching of the electronic network, the competent authorities of the Member States, within CESR and in close association with the storage mechanisms, should be invited to prepare a network governance agreement containing the essential conditions for the creation, functioning and funding of the electronic network and notably the appointment of a body that should be charged with the daily management of the network.

(8)   It is important that the storage mechanisms remain free to decide on their own pricing policy so as to secure their own financial viability. At the same time, they should not discriminate in their pricing policy between the users of electronic network and the users who have access to the storage mechanism at national level.

(9)   For the proper functioning of the electronic network, and in order to make sure that comparable services are offered to the users of that network within the Community, minimum

quality standards for the storage of regulated information at the national level are necessary. It is important that sufficient security as regards the communication, storage and access to data is guaranteed by the storage mechanisms. It is equally important to establish systems providing for certainty as to the source and the content of the information filed with the storage mechanisms. In order to facilitate the automatic electronic docketing, date and time stamping and further processing of information filed, storage mechanisms should consider imposing the use of appropriate formats and templates. Additionally, in order to facilitate the access to the information stored by end users, appropriate searching facilities and service support should be provided. For the purposes of coherence of the system, the standards should be, to the extent possible, identical for the storage mechanisms participating in the network and for the body designed to manage the network platform on a daily basis.

(10)   A gradual approach appears necessary in order to ensure that the electronic network of storage mechanisms will be able to meet the expectations of issuers and investors in the long term, notably the possibility of a virtual one-stop-shop for accessing financial information disclosed by listed companies. Therefore, it is appropriate to provide for an examination of possible solutions to enhance this network in the future. In order to ensure coherence with the initial establishment of the network, such examination should be undertaken by the competent authorities of the Member States within the CESR. This work should at least include an examination of the possibility to link this electronic network with the electronic network which is being developed by the national company registries covered by the First Council Directive 68/151/EEC of 9 March 1968 on coordination of safeguards which, for the protection of the interests of members and others, are required by Member States of companies within the meaning of the second paragraph of Article 58 of the Treaty, with a view to making such safeguards equivalent throughout the Community.[5]

(11)   In order to allow the Commission to monitor closely the situation and to assess the need for further measures, including the possibility to adopt implementing measures in accordance with Article 22(2) of Directive 2004/109/EC, the Member States should be invited to provide the Commission with the relevant information,

[6088A]

NOTES
[1]   OJ L390, 31.12.2004, p 38.
[2]   OJ L96, 12.4.2003, p 16.
[3]   OJ L345, 31.12.2003, p 64.
[4]   OJ L191, 13.7.2001, p 43.
[5]   OJ L65, 14.3.1968, p 8. Directive as last amended by Directive 2006/99/EC (OJ L363, 20.12.2006, p 137).

HEREBY RECOMMENDS:

CHAPTER I
SUBJECT MATTER

1.   The objective of this Recommendation is to encourage the Member States to ensure that the necessary steps are taken in order to effectively interconnect the officially appointed mechanisms for the central storage of regulated information, as referred to in Article 21(2) of Directive 2004/109/EC (hereinafter "the storage mechanisms"), in a single electronic network within the Community, as referred to in point (b) of second subparagraph of Article 22(1) of that Directive (hereinafter "the electronic network").

[6088B]

CHAPTER II
THE ELECTRONIC NETWORK

2. The agreement on governance of the electronic network

2.1.   Member States should facilitate the establishment and development of the electronic network in its initial stage by mandating the competent authorities referred to in Article 24 of Directive 2004/109/EC to prepare within the Committee of European Securities Regulators (CESR) established by Decision 2001/527/EC, an agreement on the governance of the electronic network (hereinafter "the governance agreement"). The storage mechanisms should be closely associated to the preparation of that agreement.

Member States should designate the entity empowered to conclude this agreement. In doing so, they should take into account the respective powers of the storage mechanisms, the competent authorities or other appropriate entity.

2.2.   The governance agreement should address at least the following issues:
   (a)   the creation of a network platform;
   (b)   the conditions to join the electronic network;
   (c)   the consequences of non-compliance with the conditions of participation and how to enforce these conditions;

(d) the appointment of a body that manages the network platform on a daily basis and the main conditions applicable to this management;

(e) the mechanism to decide on the upgrades of the electronic network, which should take into account, where appropriate, the views of all stakeholders, including end users;

(f) the funding conditions;

(g) the dispute resolution system;

(h) the mechanism for the modification of the agreement itself.

2.3. Member States should take appropriate measures to ensure that the storage mechanisms comply with the governance agreement.

3. The conditions as regards technical interoperability of the electronic network

The electronic network, established under the governance agreement, should, at least, contain the following functionalities:

(a) a central application server and a central database containing a list of all issuers with a common interface and allowing, for each issuer, to link the end user to the storage mechanism which holds regulated information relating to that issuer;

(b) a single access point for end users, which could be either achieved at a central point or at each storage mechanism individually;

(c) an interface language directory available to end users at the single access point with the communication languages accepted nationally by the storage mechanisms participating in the electronic network;

(d) access to all documents available nationally in the storage mechanisms participating in the electronic network, including, when available, information disclosed by issuers pursuant to Directive 2003/06/EC, Directive 2003/71/EC and other Community acts or national law;

(e) the possibility of the further use of data accessible through the electronic network, where possible.

4. Pricing of access to the information contained in the electronic network

4.1. Storage mechanisms should be free to establish their own pricing policy. However, they should not discriminate in their pricing policy between end users accessing to their information directly through their respective national access point and those accessing indirectly through the single access point provided by the electronic network.

4.2. Storage mechanisms should consider granting free of charge access to investors or interested parties in relation to the regulated information, at least during a certain period following its filing by the issuer.

4.3. Points 4.1 and 4.2 do not concern the provision of added value services by the storage mechanisms or by any third party using the information accessible through the electronic network.

[6088C]

CHAPTER III
THE MINIMUM QUALITY STANDARDS

Section 1
General

5. Member States should ensure that the storage mechanisms participating in the electronic network comply with standards equivalent to the model standards laid down in this chapter.

The Member States should also ensure that the body referred to in point 2.2(d) appointed pursuant to the governance agreement complies with the standards laid down in Sections 2 and 3.

6. Member States should ensure that the same standards applying to issuers as defined in point 1(d) of Article 2 of Directive 2004/109/EC apply also to persons who have applied for admission to trading on a regulated market without the issuer's consent, as referred to in Article 21(1) of that Directive.

Section 2
Security

7. Security of communication

7.1. The storage mechanism should have in place sound security mechanisms designed to ensure the security of the means of communication used to link the issuer with the mechanism, and to provide certainty as to the source of the information being filed.

7.2. The storage mechanism should be, for security reasons, entitled to limit the means of communication to be used but it should be able, at least, to receive electronic filings through a system accessible to the issuer.

In any event, the types of means of communication to be used should be easily accessible, commonly used and widely available at a low cost.

8. Integrity of stored regulated information

8.1.   The storage mechanism should store the information in a secure electronic format and should have in place appropriate security mechanisms designed to minimise the risks of data corruption and unauthorised access.

8.2.   The storage mechanism should ensure that the regulated information it holds as received from the issuer is complete and that the content of the regulated information is not editable while stored.

In case that the storage mechanism accepts the filing of information using means of communication other than electronic, the storage mechanism should ensure, when converting the documents into electronic documents, that the content of the information is complete and unedited as originally sent by the issuer the information.

8.3.   Information that has been sent to the storage mechanism and displayed should not be taken out of the storage mechanism. If an addition or correction is necessary, then the correcting or additional piece of information should identify the item it modifies and should be identified as a correction or addendum.

9. Validation

9.1.   The storage mechanism should be able to validate the information filed, meaning that the mechanism should enable an automatic inspection of the filed documents for technical adherence to standards required, completeness and accuracy of their formats.

9.2.   The storage mechanism should have systems in place to detect interruptions of the electronic feed and to request the re-transmission of any data that it fails to receive from the sender.

10. Reliable access to services

10.1.   The storage mechanism should have security systems in place so as to ensure that its services can be accessed by issuers and end users, without disruption, 24 hours a day and seven days a week.

Each storage mechanism should define its own requirements, based on the characteristics of its systems and the particular conditions in which it operates.

The capacity of the systems, namely, the capacity of its servers and the bandwidth available, should be sufficient to support the expected requests from issuers, as regards filing of information, and end users, as regards access to stored information.

10.2.   The storage mechanism should be entitled to prevent access to its systems for brief periods when necessary in order to perform essential maintenance or in order to upgrade its services. Where possible, such interruptions should be announced in advance.

11. Acceptance of waivers and recovery

The storage mechanism should have an evaluation process for reviewing and accepting or denying waivers for late filings due to technical issues of the storage mechanism and non-standard submissions. The mechanism should also provide recovery tools that allow the issuer to use other mechanisms of filing in place of the prescribed one when this is out of order. However, there should be an obligation on the issuer to re-file the information through the main mechanism when restored.

12. Back-up systems

12.1.   The storage mechanism should be technologically independent and have sufficient back-up facilities in place in order to maintain and to re-establish its services in a reasonable timeframe.

12.2.   The nature of these back-up systems will need to be evaluated by each storage mechanism taking into consideration the specific characteristics of the systems in place.

Section 3
Certainty as to the Information Source

13. Certainty as to the source of information and the authenticity of origin

13.1.   The storage mechanism should have in place sound systems designed to provide certainty as to the source of the information being filed. The storage mechanism should have certainty that the information it receives is from an authentic source. The storage mechanism should verify that any regulated financial information it receives directly originates from the person or entity that has the filing obligation or from a person or entity authorised to on its behalf.

13.2.   The storage mechanism should be able to electronically acknowledge receipt of documents. The storage mechanism should either confirm validation of filing or reject a submission with an explanation for the rejection and it should have a "non-repudiation" function.

14. User Authentication

The security measures of the storage mechanism should be designed to establish the validity of the originator, or a means of verifying an individual's authorization to send specific information. The storage mechanism should be entitled to impose the use of digital signatures, access codes or any other appropriate measure providing with sufficient certainty.

15. Need to ensure integrity of the content of regulated information

The storage mechanism should assure that there is no significant risk of corruption or change of original information either accidentally or maliciously and to ascertain any alteration.

Section 4
Time Recording

16. Electronic docketing and date and time stamp

16.1.   The storage mechanism should be able to automatically docket electronic filings and add a date and time stamp.

16.2.   The storage mechanism should be entitled to impose the filing of information in pre-determined formats and templates allowing for the use of straight-through processing technology.

If particular formats are imposed, the storage mechanism should nevertheless use open architecture systems for the filing of information and should, at least, accept:
   (a)   file formats and transmission protocols that are non-proprietary and that obviate single vendor software applications;
   (b)   commonly used and generally accepted proprietary formats.

If templates are imposed, the storage mechanism should ensure that they are easily accessible and, where available, they should be aligned with those used for filing the same regulated information with the competent authority.

16.3.   The information should be date and time stamped as it enters into the storage mechanism, irrespective of whether the information is checked by the competent authority before (ex ante control) or will be checked after (ex post control) it enters in the storage mechanism.

Section 5
Easy Access by End Users

17. Presentation of the information

When presenting its services to the end users, the storage mechanism should distinguish between regulated financial information filed pursuant to a legal obligation and any additional valued-added service offered by the storage mechanism.

18. Language regime

18.1.   The storage mechanism should file and facilitate access to all the available linguistic versions of the information as submitted by the issuer. However, access to all the linguistic versions does not mean that the information should be translated by the storage mechanism into languages other than those submitted by the issuer.

18.2.   The searching facilities in the storage mechanism should be available in the language accepted by the competent authorities in the home Member State and, at least, in a language customary in the sphere of international finance.

19. Technical accessibility

19.1.   The storage mechanism should use open architecture systems for the access to the stored information. In designing the systems, the storage mechanism should ensure that its systems allow or are capable of allowing for technical interoperability with other storage mechanisms in the same or in other Member States.

19.2.   Information should be accessible to end users by the storage mechanism as soon as technically feasible from its filing, taking into consideration the structures and operating procedures of the storage mechanism. The storage mechanism should not deliberately delay the process.

19.3.   The storage mechanism should provide end users with access to all stored regulated information on a continuous basis, in accordance with the conditions described in point 10.

19.4.   The storage mechanism should offer service support for its users. The level of support that each storage mechanism decides to provide needs to be decided at national level.

20. Format of the information that can be accessed by end users

20.1.   Regulated information held by the storage mechanism should be held in a format that enables users to view, download and print, in a straightforward manner, the full content of regulated information from wherever the user is located. However, access to the regulated information does not mean that printed copies of this information should be made available by the storage mechanism.

20.2.   The storage mechanism should offer end users the possibility to search, order and interrogate regulated information stored.

20.3.   The storage mechanism should record sufficient reference information relating to the regulated information it receives. Such reference information should, at least, include the following items:

(a)   identify the information as regulated information;
(b)   the name of the issuer from which the regulated information originated;
(c)   the title of the document;
(d)   the time and date on which the regulated information was disseminated;
(e)   the language of the document;
(f)   the type of regulated information.

The storage mechanism should organise and categorise regulated information in accordance with, at least, the items listed in the first subparagraph.

The storage mechanism should be allowed to require issuers to provide the necessary reference information when filing regulated information.

The storage mechanism should align these categories with the other storage mechanisms, in particular in relation to the type of regulated information, in accordance with the agreement referred to in chapter II of this Recommendation.

20.4.   The storage mechanism should be allowed to require issuers to use predetermined file formats and templates. In any event, the storage mechanism should, at least, accept:

(a)   file formats and transmission protocols that are non-proprietary and that obviate single vendor software applications;
(b)   commonly used and generally accepted proprietary formats.

If templates are imposed, the storage mechanism should ensure that they are easily accessible and they should be aligned with those used for filing the same regulated information with the competent authority.

[6088D]

CHAPTER IV
GUIDELINES FOR FUTURE DEVELOPMENT OF ELECTRONIC NETWORK

21.   The Member States should encourage the competent authorities to draw up, by 30 September 2010, within CESR, appropriate guidelines for the future development of the electronic network.

22.   Those guidelines should in particular examine the feasibility, including a cost/benefit analysis, to require:

(a)   the use, in all the access points to the electronic network, of harmonised searching facilities based on a set of common search keys and reference data items, thus harmonising the methods of classifying and identifying the information to store;
(b)   the use of common input formats and standards for the submission of regulated information to the storage mechanisms;
(c)   the use by the storage mechanism of a common list of types of regulated information;
(d)   the technical interconnection with the electronic network developed by the national company registries covered by the Directive 68/151/EEC;
(e)   entrusting the supervision of the services provided by any legal entity operating the common elements of the electronic network to a single body composed of representatives of the competent authorities referred to in Article 24 of Directive 2004/109/EC.

The harmonised searching facilities referred to in point (a) of the first subparagraph should at least provide for the possibility of making:

(a)   searches using common category labels attached to the regulated financial information when filed with the storage mechanisms, such as: issuer name; date of filing; country of issuer; title of document; industry/branch of trade and type of regulated information;
(b)   dynamic or chain searches;
(c)   multiple-country searches with a single request.

The guidelines should also develop common lists for the purposes of establishing sub-category labels with regard to industry/branch of trade and type of regulated information.

[6088E]

CHAPTER V
FOLLOW-UP AND ADDRESSEES

23.   Member States are invited to inform the Commission of the steps taken in the light of this Recommendation by 31 December 2008.

24.   This recommendation is addressed to the Member States.

[6088F]

DIRECTIVE OF THE EUROPEAN PARLIAMENT AND OF THE COUNCIL

of 13 November 2007

on payment services in the internal market amending Directives 97/7/EC, 2002/65/EC, 2005/60/EC and 2006/48/EC and repealing Directive 97/5/EC

(2007/64/EC)

(Text with EEA relevance)

NOTES
Date of publication in OJ: L319, 5.12.2007, p 1. Notes are as in the original OJ version.
As of 1 February 2009, this Directive had not been amended.

THE EUROPEAN PARLIAMENT AND THE COUNCIL OF THE EUROPEAN UNION,

Having regard to the Treaty establishing the European Community, and in particular the first and third sentences of Article 47(2) and Article 95 thereof,

Having regard to the proposal from the Commission,

Having consulted the European Economic and Social Committee,

Having regard to the opinion of the European Central Bank,[1]

Acting in accordance with the procedure laid down in Article 251 of the Treaty,[2]

Whereas:

(1)   It is essential for the establishment of the internal market that all internal frontiers in the Community be dismantled so as to enable the free movement of goods, persons, services and capital. The proper operation of the single market in payment services is therefore vital. At present, however, the lack of harmonisation in this area hinders the operation of that market.

(2)   Currently, the payment services markets of the Member States are organised separately, along national lines and the legal framework for payment services is fragmented into 27 national legal systems.

(3)   Several Community acts have already been adopted in this area, namely Directive 97/5/EC of the European Parliament and of the Council of 27 January 1997 on cross-border credit transfers[3] and Regulation (EC) No 2560/2001 of the European Parliament and of the Council of 19 December 2001 on cross-border payments in euro,[4] but these have not sufficiently remedied this situation any more than have Commission Recommendation 87/598/EEC of 8 December 1987 on a European Code of Conduct relating to electronic payment (relations between financial institutions, traders and service establishments, and consumers),[5] Commission Recommendation 88/590/EEC of 17 November 1988 concerning payment systems, and in particular the relationship between cardholder and card issuer,[6] or Commission Recommendation 97/489/EC of 30 July 1997 concerning transactions by electronic payment instruments and in particular the relationship between issuer and holder.[7] These measures continue to be insufficient. The co-existence of national provisions and an incomplete Community framework gives rise to confusion and a lack of legal certainty.

(4)   It is vital, therefore, to establish at Community level a modern and coherent legal framework for payment services, whether or not the services are compatible with the system resulting from the financial sector initiative for a single euro payments area, which is neutral so as to ensure a level playing field for all payment systems, in order to maintain consumer choice, which should mean a considerable step forward in terms of consumer cost, safety and efficiency, as compared with the present national systems.

(5)   That legal framework should ensure the coordination of national provisions on prudential requirements, the access of new payment service providers to the market, information requirements, and the respective rights and obligations of payment services users and providers. Within that framework, the provisions of Regulation (EC) No 2560/2001, which created a single market for euro payments as far as prices are concerned, should be maintained. The provisions of Directive 97/5/EC and the recommendations made in Recommendations 87/598/EEC, 88/590/EEC and 97/489/EC should be integrated in a single act with binding force.

(6)   However, it is not appropriate for that legal framework to be fully comprehensive. Its application should be confined to payment service providers whose main activity consists in the

provision of payment services to payment service users. Nor is it appropriate for it to apply to services where the transfer of funds from the payer to the payee or their transport is executed solely in bank notes and coins or where the transfer is based on a paper cheque, paper-based bill of exchange, promissory note or other instrument, paper-based vouchers or cards drawn upon a payment service provider or other party with a view to placing funds at the disposal of the payee. Furthermore, a differentiation should be made in the case of means offered by telecommunication, information technology or network operators to facilitate purchasing of digital goods or services, such as ring tones, music or digital newspapers, besides traditional voice services and their distribution to digital devices. The content of these goods or services may be produced either by a third party or by the operator, who may add intrinsic value to them in the form of access, distribution or search facilities. In the latter case, where the goods or services are distributed by one of those operators, or, for technical reasons, by a third party, and where they can be used only through digital devices, such as mobile phones or computers, that legal framework should not apply as the activity of the operator goes beyond a mere payment transaction. However, it is appropriate for that legal framework to apply to cases where the operator acts only as an intermediary who simply arranges for payment to be made to a third-party supplier.

(7) Money remittance is a simple payment service that is usually based on cash provided by a payer to a payment service provider, which remits the corresponding amount, for example via communication network, to a payee or to another payment service provider acting on behalf of the payee. In some Member States supermarkets, merchants and other retailers provide to the public a corresponding service enabling the payment of utility and other regular household bills. Those bill-paying services should be treated as money remittance as defined in this Directive, unless the competent authorities consider the activity to fall under another payment service listed in the Annex.

(8) It is necessary to specify the categories of payment service providers which may legitimately provide payment services throughout the Community, namely, credit institutions which take deposits from users that can be used to fund payment transactions and which should continue to be subject to the prudential requirements under Directive 2006/48/EC of the European Parliament and of the Council of 14 June 2006 relating to the taking up and pursuit of the business of credit institutions,[8] electronic money institutions which issue electronic money that can be used to fund payment transactions and which should continue to be subject to the prudential requirements under Directive 2000/46/EC of the European Parliament and of the Council of 18 September 2000 on the taking-up, pursuit and prudential supervision of the business of electronic money institutions,[9] and post office giro institutions which are so entitled under national law.

(9) This Directive should lay down rules on the execution of payment transactions where the funds are electronic money, as defined in Article 1(3)(b) of Directive 2000/46/EC. This Directive should, however, neither regulate issuance of electronic money nor amend the prudential regulation of electronic money institutions as provided for in Directive 2000/46/EC. Therefore, payment institutions should not be allowed to issue electronic money.

(10) However, in order to remove legal barriers to market entry, it is necessary to establish a single licence for all providers of payment services which are not connected to taking deposits or issuing electronic money. It is appropriate, therefore, to introduce a new category of payment service providers, "payment institutions", by providing for the authorisation, subject to a set of strict and comprehensive conditions, of legal persons outside the existing categories to provide payment services throughout the Community. Thus, the same conditions would apply Community-wide to such services.

(11) The conditions for granting and maintaining authorisation as payment institutions should include prudential requirements proportionate to the operational and financial risks faced by such bodies in the course of their business. In this connection, there is a need for a sound regime of initial capital combined with ongoing capital which could be elaborated in a more sophisticated way in due course depending on the needs of the market. Due to the range of variety in the payments services area, this Directive should allow various methods combined with a certain range of supervisory discretion to ensure that the same risks are treated the same way for all payment service providers. The requirements for the payment institutions should reflect the fact that payment institutions engage in more specialised and limited activities, thus generating risks that are narrower and easier to monitor and control than those that arise across the broader spectrum of activities of credit institutions. In particular, payment institutions should be prohibited from accepting deposits from users and permitted to use funds received from users only for rendering payment services. Provision should be made for client funds to be kept separate from the payment institution's funds for other business activities. Payment institutions should also be made subject to effective anti-money laundering and anti-terrorist financing requirements.

(12) Payment institutions should draw up their annual and consolidated accounts in accordance with Council Directive 78/660/EEC of 25 July 1978 on the annual accounts of certain types of companies[10] and, where applicable, Council Directive 83/349/EEC of 13 June 1983 on consolidated accounts[11] and Council Directive 86/635/EEC of 8 December 1986 on the annual accounts and consolidated accounts of banks and other financial institutions.[12] The annual accounts and consolidated accounts should be audited, unless the payment institution is exempted from this obligation under Directive 78/660/EEC and, where applicable, Directives 83/349/EEC and 86/635/EEC.

PART IV
EC MATERIALS

(13)   This Directive should regulate the granting of credit by payment institutions, ie the granting of credit lines and the issuance of credit cards, only where it is closely linked to payment services. Only if credit is granted in order to facilitate payment services and such credit is of a short-term nature and is granted for a period not exceeding twelve months, including on a revolving basis, is it appropriate to allow payment institutions to grant such credit with regard to their cross-border activities, on condition that it is refinanced using mainly the payment institution's own funds, as well as other funds from the capital markets, but not the funds held on behalf of clients for payment services. The above should be without prejudice to Council Directive 87/102/EEC of 22 December 1986 for the approximation of the laws, regulations and administrative provisions of the Member States concerning consumer credit[13] or other relevant Community or national legislation regarding conditions for granting credit to consumers not harmonised by this Directive.

(14)   It is necessary for the Member States to designate the authorities responsible for granting authorisations to payment institutions, carrying out controls and deciding on the withdrawal of those authorisations. In order to ensure equality of treatment, Member States should apply to payment institutions no requirements other than those provided for in this Directive. However, all decisions made by the competent authorities should be contestable before the courts. In addition, the tasks of the competent authorities should be without prejudice to the oversight of payment systems, which, in line with the fourth indent of Article 105(2) of the Treaty, is a task to be carried out by the European System of Central Banks.

(15)   Given the desirability of registering the identity and whereabouts of all persons providing remittance services and of according them all a measure of acceptance, irrespective of whether they are able to meet the full range of conditions for authorisation as payment institutions, so that none are forced into the black economy and bring all persons providing remittance service within the ambit of certain minimum legal and regulatory requirements, it is appropriate and in line with the rationale of Special Recommendation VI of the Financial Action Task Force on Money Laundering to provide a mechanism whereby payment service providers unable to meet all those conditions may nevertheless be treated as payment institutions. For those purposes, Member States should enter such persons in the register of payment institutions while not applying all or part of the conditions for authorisation. However, it is essential to make the possibility of waiver subject to strict requirements relating to the volume of payment transactions. Payment institutions benefiting from a waiver should have neither the right of establishment nor the freedom to provide services, nor should they indirectly exercise those rights when being a member of a payment system.

(16)   It is essential for any payment service provider to be able to access the services of technical infrastructures of payment systems. Such access should, however, be subject to appropriate requirements in order to ensure integrity and stability of those systems. Each payment service provider applying for a participation in a payment system should furnish proof to the participants of the payment system that its internal arrangements are sufficiently robust against all kinds of risk. These payment systems typically include e g the four-party card schemes as well as major systems processing credit transfers and direct debits. In order to ensure equality of treatment throughout the Community as between the different categories of authorised payment service providers, according to the terms of their licence, it is necessary to clarify the rules concerning access to the provision of payment services and access to payment systems. Provision should be made for the non-discriminatory treatment of authorised payment institutions and credit institutions so that any payment service provider competing in the internal market is able to use the services of the technical infrastructures of these payment systems under the same conditions. It is appropriate to provide for different treatment for authorised payment service providers and for those benefiting from a waiver under this Directive as well as from the waiver under the Article 8 of the Directive 2000/46/EC, due to the differences in their prudential framework. In any case differences in price conditions should be allowed only when this is motivated by differences in costs induced by the payment service providers. This should be without prejudice to Member States' right to limit access to systemically important systems in accordance with Directive 98/26/EC of the European Parliament and of the Council of 19 May 1998 on settlement finality in payment and securities settlement systems[14] and without prejudice to the competence of the European Central Bank and the European System of Central Banks (ESCB), as laid down in Article 105(2) of the Treaty and Article 3(1) and Article 22 of the Statute of the ESCB, concerning access to payment systems.

(17)   The provisions of the access to payment systems should not apply to systems set up and operated by a single payment service provider. Those payment systems can operate either in direct competition to payment systems, or, more typically, in a market niche not adequately covered by payment systems. They typically cover three-party schemes, such as three party card schemes, payment services offered by telecommunication providers or money remittance services where the scheme operator is the payment service provider to both the payer and payee as well as internal systems of banking groups. In order to stimulate the competition that can be provided by such payment systems to established mainstream payment systems, it should in principle not be appropriate to grant third parties access to these payment systems. Nevertheless, such systems should always be subject to Community and national competition rules which may require that access be granted to the schemes in order to maintain effective competition in payments markets.

(18)   A set of rules should be established in order to ensure transparency of conditions and information requirements for payment services.

(19) This Directive should apply neither to payment transactions made in cash since a single payments market for cash already exists nor to payment transactions based on paper cheques since, by their nature, they cannot be processed as efficiently as other means of payment. Good practice in this area should, however, be based on the principles set out in this Directive.

(20) As consumers and enterprises are not in the same position, they do not need the same level of protection. While it is important to guarantee consumers' rights by provisions which cannot be derogated from by contract, it is reasonable to let enterprises and organisations agree otherwise. However, Member States should have the possibility to provide that micro-enterprises, as defined by Commission Recommendation 2003/361/EC of 6 May 2003 concerning the definition of micro, small and medium-sized enterprises,[15] should be treated in the same way as consumers. In any case, certain core provisions of this Directive should always be applicable irrespective of the status of the user.

(21) This Directive should specify the obligations on payment service providers as regards the provision of information to the payment service users who should receive the same high level of clear information about payment services in order to make well-informed choices and be able to shop around within the EU. In the interest of transparency this Directive should lay down the harmonised requirements needed to ensure that necessary and sufficient information is given to the payment service users with regard to the payment service contract and the payment transactions. In order to promote smooth functioning of the single market in payment services, Member States should be able to adopt only those information provisions laid down in this Directive.

(22) Consumers should be protected against unfair and misleading practices in line with Directive 2005/29/EC of the European Parliament and the Council of 11 May 2005 concerning unfair business-to-consumer commercial practices in the Internal Market[16] as well as Directive 2000/31/EC of the European Parliament and the Council of 8 June 2000 on certain legal aspects of information society services, in particular electronic commerce, in the Internal Market (Directive on electronic commerce)[17] and Directive 2002/65/EC of the European Parliament and the Council of 23 September 2002 concerning the distance marketing of consumer financial services.[18] The additional provisions in those Directives continue to be applicable. However, the relationship of the pre-contractual information requirements between this Directive and Directive 2002/65/EC should, in particular, be clarified.

(23) The information required should be proportionate to the needs of users and communicated in a standard manner. However, the information requirements for a single payment transaction should be different from those of a framework contract which provides for the series of payment transactions.

(24) In practice, framework contracts and the payment transactions covered by them are far more common and economically important than single payment transactions. If there is a payment account or a specific payment instrument, a framework contract is required. Therefore, the requirements for prior information on framework contracts should be quite comprehensive and information should always be provided on paper or on another durable medium, such as printouts by account printers, floppy disks, CD-ROMs, DVDs and hard drives of personal computers on which electronic mail can be stored, and Internet sites, as long as such sites are accessible for future reference for a period of time adequate for the purposes of information and allow the unchanged reproduction of the information stored. However, it should be possible for the payment service provider and the payment service user to agree in the framework contract on the manner in which subsequent information on executed payment transactions is given, for instance, that in Internet banking all information on the payment account is made available online.

(25) In single payment transactions only the essential information should always be given on the payment service provider's own initiative. As the payer is usually present when he gives the payment order, it is not necessary to require that information should in every case be provided on paper or on another durable medium. The payment service provider may give information orally over the counter or make it otherwise easily accessible, for example by keeping the conditions on a notice board on the premises. Information should also be given on where other more detailed information is available (e g the address of the website). However, if the consumer so requests, the essential information should be given on paper or on another durable medium.

(26) This Directive should provide for the consumer's right to receive relevant information free of charge before he is bound by any payment service contract. The consumer should also be able to request prior information as well as the framework contract, on paper, free of charge at any time during the contractual relationship, so as to enable him to compare payment service providers' services and their conditions and in case of any dispute verify his contractual rights and obligations. Those provisions should be compatible with Directive 2002/65/EC. The explicit provisions on free information in this Directive should not have the effect of allowing charges to be imposed for the provision of information to consumers under other applicable Directives.

(27) The way in which the required information is to be given by the payment service provider to the payment service user should take into account the needs of the latter as well as practical technical aspects and cost-efficiency depending on the situation with regard to the agreement in the respective payment service contract. Thus, this Directive should distinguish between two ways in which information is to be given by the payment service provider: either the information should be provided, i e actively communicated by the payment service provider at the appropriate time as required by this Directive without further prompting by the payment service user, or the information

should be made available to the payment service user, taking into account any request he may have for further information. In the latter case, the payment service user should take some active steps in order to obtain the information, such as requesting it explicitly from the payment service provider, logging into bank account mail box or inserting a bank card into printer for account statements. For such purposes the payment service provider should ensure that access to the information is possible and that the information is available to the payment service user.

(28) In addition, the consumer should receive basic information on executed payment transactions for no additional charge. In the case of a single payment transaction the payment service provider should not charge separately for this information. Similarly, the subsequent monthly information on payment transactions under a framework contract should be given free of charge. However, taking into account the importance of transparency in pricing and differing customer needs, the parties should be able to agree on charges for more frequent or additional information. In order to take into account different national practices, Member States should be allowed to set rules requiring that monthly paper-based statements of payment accounts are always to be given free of charge.

(29) In order to facilitate customer mobility, it should be possible for consumers to terminate a framework contract after the expiry of a year without incurring charges. For consumers, the period of notice agreed should be no longer than a month, and for payment service providers no shorter than two months. This Directive should be without prejudice to the payment service provider's obligation to terminate the payment service contract in exceptional circumstances under other relevant Community or national legislation, such as legislation on money laundering and terrorist financing, any action targeting the freezing of funds, or any specific measure linked to the prevention and investigation of crimes.

(30) Low value payment instruments should be a cheap and easy-to-use alternative in the case of low-priced goods and services and should not be overburdened by excessive requirements. The relevant information requirements and rules on their execution should therefore be limited to essential information, taking also into account technical capabilities that can justifiably be expected from instruments dedicated to low value payments. Despite the lighter regime payment service users should benefit from adequate protection considering the limited risks posed by those payment instruments, especially with regard to prepaid payment instruments.

(31) In order to reduce the risks and consequences of unauthorised or incorrectly executed payment transactions the payment service user should inform the payment service provider as soon as possible about any contestations concerning allegedly unauthorised or incorrectly executed payment transactions provided that the payment service provider has fulfilled his information obligations under this Directive. If the notification deadline is met by the payment service user, he should be able to pursue those claims within the prescription periods pursuant to national law. This Directive should not affect other claims between payment service users and payment service providers.

(32) In order to provide an incentive for the payment service user to notify, without undue delay, his provider of any theft or loss of a payment instrument and thus to reduce the risk of unauthorised payment transactions, the user should be liable only for a limited amount, unless the payment service user has acted fraudulently or with gross negligence. Moreover, once a user has notified a payment service provider that his payment instrument may have been compromised, the user should not be required to cover any further losses stemming from unauthorised use of that instrument. This Directive should be without prejudice to the payment service providers' responsibility for technical security of their own products.

(33) In order to assess possible negligence by the payment service user, account should be taken of all the circumstances. The evidence and degree of alleged negligence should be evaluated according to national law. Contractual terms and conditions relating to the provision and use of a payment instrument, the effect of which would be to increase the burden of proof on the consumer or to reduce the burden of proof on the issuer should be considered null and void.

(34) However, Member States should be able to establish less stringent rules than mentioned above in order to maintain existing levels of consumer protection and promote trust in the safe usage of electronic payment instruments. The fact that different payment instruments involve different risks should be taken into account accordingly thus promoting the issuance of safer instruments. Member States should be allowed to reduce or completely waive the payer's liability except where the payer has acted fraudulently.

(35) Provisions should be made for the allocation of losses in the case of unauthorised payment transactions. Different provisions may apply to payment service users who are not consumers, since such users are normally in a better position to assess the risk of fraud and take countervailing measures.

(36) This Directive should lay down rules for a refund to protect the consumer when the executed payment transaction exceeds the amount which could reasonably have been expected. Payment service providers should be able to provide even more favourable terms to their customers and, for example, refund any disputed payment transactions. In cases where the user makes a claim for the refund of a payment transaction refund rights should affect neither the liability of the payer *vis-à-vis* the payee from the underlying relationship, e g for goods or services ordered, consumed or legitimately charged, nor the users rights with regard to revocation of a payment order.

(37) For financial planning and the fulfilment of payment obligations in due time, consumers and enterprises need to have certainty on the length of time that the execution of a payment order takes. Therefore, this Directive should introduce a point in time at which rights and obligations take effect, namely, when the payment service provider receives the payment order, including when he has had the opportunity to receive it through the means of communication agreed in the payment service contract, notwithstanding any prior involvement in the process leading up to the creation and transmission of the payment order, e g security and availability of funds checks, information on the use of the personal identity number or issuance of a payment promise. Furthermore, the receipt of a payment order should occur when the payer's payment service provider receives the payment order to be debited from the payer's account. The day or moment in time when a payee transmits to his service provider payment orders for the collection e g of card payment or of direct debits or when the payee is granted a pre-financing on the related amounts by his payment service provider (by way of a contingent credit to his account) should have no relevance in this respect. Users should be able to rely on the proper execution of a complete and valid payment order if the payment service provider has no contractual or statutory ground for refusal. If the payment service provider refuses a payment order, the refusal and the reason therefore should be communicated to the payment service user at the earliest opportunity subject to the requirements of Community and national law.

(38) In view of the speed with which modern fully automated payment systems process payment transactions, which means that after a certain point in time payment orders cannot be revoked without high manual intervention costs, it is necessary to specify a clear deadline for payment revocations. However, depending on the type of the payment service and the payment order, the point in time may be varied by agreement between the parties. Revocation, in this context, is applicable only to the relationship between a payment service user and payment service provider, thus being without prejudice to the irrevocability and finality of payment transactions in payment systems.

(39) Such irrevocability should not affect a payment service provider's right or obligation under the laws of some Member States, based on the payer's framework contract or national laws, regulations, administrative provisions or guidelines, to reimburse the payer with the amount of the executed payment transaction in the event of a dispute between the payer and the payee. Such reimbursement should be considered to be a new payment order. Except for those cases, legal disputes arising within the relationship underlying the payment order should be settled only between the payer and the payee.

(40) It is essential, for the fully integrated straight-through processing of payments and for legal certainty with respect to the fulfilment of any underlying obligation between payment service users, that the full amount transferred by the payer should be credited to the account of the payee. Accordingly, it should not be possible for any of the intermediaries involved in the execution of payment transactions to make deductions from the amount transferred. However, it should be possible for the payee to enter into an agreement with his payment service provider under which the latter may deduct his own charges. Nevertheless, in order to enable the payee to verify that the amount due is correctly paid, subsequent information provided on the payment transaction should indicate not only the full amount of funds transferred but also the amount of any charges.

(41) With regard to charges, experience has shown that the sharing of charges between a payer and a payee is the most efficient system since it facilitates the straight-through processing of payments. Provision should therefore be made for charges to be levied, in the normal course, directly on the payer and the payee by their respective payment service providers. However, that should apply only where the payment transaction does not require currency exchange. The amount of any charges levied may also be zero as the provisions of this Directive do not affect the practice whereby the payment service provider does not charge consumers for crediting their accounts. Similarly, depending on the contract terms, a payment service provider may charge only the payee (merchant) for the use of the payment service, which has the effect that no charges are imposed on the payer. The charging of the payment systems may be in the form of a subscription fee. The provisions on the amount transferred or any charges levied have no direct impact on pricing between payment service providers or any intermediaries.

(42) In order to promote transparency and competition, the payment service provider should not prevent the payee from requesting a charge from the payer for using a specific payment instrument. While the payee should be free to levy charges for the use of a certain payment instrument, Member States may decide whether they forbid or limit any such practice where, in their view, this may be warranted in view of abusive pricing or pricing which may have a negative impact on the use of a certain payment instrument taking into account the need to encourage competition and the use of efficient payment instruments.

(43) In order to improve the efficiency of payments throughout the Community, all payment orders initiated by the payer and denominated in euro or the currency of a Member State outside the euro area, including credit transfers and money remittances, should be subject to a maximum one-day execution time. For all other payments, such as payments initiated by or through a payee, including direct debits and card payments, in the absence of an explicit agreement between the payment service provider and the payer setting a longer execution time, the same one-day execution time should apply. The periods above could be extended by an additional business day, if a payment order is given on paper. This allows the continued provision of payment services for those consumers who are used to paper documents only. When a direct debit scheme is used the payee's

payment service provider should transmit the collection order within the time limits agreed between the payee and his payment service provider, enabling settlement at the agreed due date. In view of the fact that national payment infrastructures are often highly efficient and in order to prevent any deterioration in current service levels, Member States should be allowed to maintain or set rules specifying an execution time shorter than one business day, where appropriate.

(44) The provisions on execution for the full amount and execution time should constitute good practice where one of the service providers is not located in the Community.

(45) It is essential for payment service users to know the real costs and charges of payment services in order to make their choice. Accordingly, the use of non-transparent pricing methods should not be allowed, since it is commonly accepted that those methods make it extremely difficult for users to establish the real price of the payment service. Specifically, the use of value dating to the disadvantage of the user should not be permitted.

(46) The smooth and efficient functioning of the payment system depends on the user being able to rely on the payment service provider executing the payment transaction correctly and within the agreed time. Usually, the provider is in the position to assess the risks involved in the payment transaction. It is the provider that provides the payments system, makes arrangements to recall misplaced or wrongly allocated funds and decides in most cases on the intermediaries involved in the execution of a payment transaction. In view of all those considerations, it is entirely appropriate, except under abnormal and unforeseeable circumstances, to impose liability on the payment service provider in respect of execution of a payment transaction accepted from the user, except for the payee's payment service provider's acts and omissions for whose selection solely the payee is responsible. However, in order not to leave the payer unprotected in unlikely constellations where it may remain open (*non liquet*) whether the payment amount was duly received by the payee's payment service provider or not, the corresponding burden of proof should lie upon the payer's payment service provider. As a rule, it can be expected that the intermediary institution, usually a "neutral" body like a central bank or a clearing house, transferring the payment amount from the sending to the receiving payment service provider will store the account data and be able to furnish the latter whenever this may be necessary. Whenever the payment amount has been credited to the receiving payment service provider's account, the payee should immediately have a claim against his payment service provider for credit to his account.

(47) The payer's payment service provider should assume liability for correct payment execution, including, in particular the full amount of the payment transaction and execution time, and full responsibility for any failure by other parties in the payment chain up to the account of the payee. As a result of that liability the payment service provider of the payer should, where the full amount is not credited to the payee's payment service provider, correct the payment transaction or without undue delay refund to the payer the relevant amount of that transaction, without prejudice to any other claims which may be made in accordance with national law. This Directive should concern only contractual obligations and responsibilities between the payment service user and his payment service provider. However, the proper functioning of credit transfers and other payment services requires that payment service providers and their intermediaries, such as processors, have contracts where their mutual rights and obligations are agreed upon. Questions related to liabilities form an essential part of these uniform contracts. To ensure the reliability among payment service providers and intermediaries taking part in a payment transaction, legal certainty is necessary to the effect that a non-responsible payment service provider is compensated for losses incurred or sums paid under the provisions of this Directive relating to liability. Further rights and details of content of recourse and how to handle claims towards the payment service provider or intermediary attributable to a defective payment transaction should be left to be defined by contractual arrangements.

(48) It should be possible for the payment service provider to specify unambiguously the information required to execute a payment order correctly. On the other hand, however, in order to avoid fragmentation and jeopardising the setting-up of integrated payment systems in the Community, Member States should not be allowed to require a particular identifier to be used for payment transactions. However, this should not prevent Member States from requiring the payment service provider of the payer to act in due diligence and verify, where technically possible and without requiring manual intervention, the coherence of the unique identifier, and where the unique identifier is found to be incoherent, to refuse the payment order and inform the payer thereof. The liability of the payment service provider should be limited to the correct execution of the payment transaction in accordance with the payment order of the payment service user.

(49) In order to facilitate effective fraud prevention and combat payment fraud across the Community, provision should be made for the efficient exchange of data between payment service providers who should be allowed to collect, process and exchange personal data relating to persons involved in payment fraud. All those activities should be conducted in compliance with Directive 95/46/EC of the European Parliament and of the Council of 24 October 1995 on the protection of individuals with regard to the processing of personal data and on the free movement of such data.[19]

(50) It is necessary to ensure the effective enforcement of the provisions of national law adopted pursuant to this Directive. Appropriate procedures should therefore be established by means of which it will be possible to pursue complaints against payment service providers which do not comply with those provisions and to ensure that, where appropriate, effective, proportionate and dissuasive penalties are imposed.

(51) Without prejudice to the right of customers to bring action in the courts, Member States should ensure an easily accessible and cost-sensitive out-of-court resolution of conflicts between payment service providers and consumers arising from the rights and obligations set out in this Directive. Article 5(2) of the Rome Convention on the law applicable to contractual obligations[20] ensures that the protection afforded to consumers by the mandatory rules of the law of the country in which they have their habitual residence may not be undermined by any contractual terms on law applicable.

(52) Member States should determine whether the competent authorities designated for granting authorisation to payment institutions might also be the competent authorities with regard to out-of-court complaint and redress procedures.

(53) This Directive should be without prejudice to provisions of national law relating to the consequences as regards liability of inaccuracy in the expression or transmission of a statement.

(54) Since it is necessary to review the efficient functioning of this Directive and to monitor progress on the establishment of a single payment market, the Commission should be required to produce a report three years after the end of the transposition period of this Directive. With regard to the global integration of financial services and harmonised consumer protection also beyond the efficient functioning of this Directive focal points of the review should be the possible need to expand the scope of application with regard to non-EU currencies and to payment transactions where only one payment service provider concerned is located in the Community.

(55) Since the provisions of this Directive replace those of Directive 97/5/EC, that Directive should be repealed.

(56) It is necessary to lay down more detailed rules concerning the fraudulent use of payment cards, an area currently covered by Directive 97/7/EC of the European Parliament and of the Council of 20 May 1997 on the protection of consumers in respect of distance contracts[21] and Directive 2002/65/EC. Those Directives should therefore be amended accordingly.

(57) Since, pursuant to Directive 2006/48/EC, financial institutions are not subject to the rules applicable to credit institutions, they should be made subject to the same requirements as payment institutions so that they are able to provide payment services throughout the Community. Directive 2006/48/EC should therefore be amended accordingly.

(58) Since money remittance is defined in this Directive as a payment service which requires an authorisation for a payment institution or a registration for some natural or legal persons benefiting from a waiver clause under certain circumstances specified in the provisions of this Directive, Directive 2005/60/EC of the European Parliament and of the Council of 26 October 2005 on the prevention of the use of the financial system for the purpose of money laundering and terrorist financing[22] should be amended accordingly.

(59) In the interests of legal certainty, it is appropriate to make transitional arrangements in accordance with which persons who have commenced the activities of payment institutions in accordance with the national law in force before the entry into force of this Directive may continue those activities within the Member State concerned for a specified period.

(60) Since the objective of this Directive, namely, the establishment of a single market in payment services, cannot be sufficiently achieved by the Member States because it requires the harmonisation of a multitude of different rules currently existing in the legal systems of the various Member States and can therefore be better achieved at Community level, the Community may adopt measures, in accordance with the principle of subsidiarity as set out in Article 5 of the Treaty. In accordance with the principle of proportionality, as set out in that Article, this Directive does not go beyond what is necessary in order to achieve that objective.

(61) The measures necessary for the implementation of this Directive should be adopted in accordance with Council Decision 1999/468/EC of 28 June 1999 laying down the procedures for the exercise of implementing powers conferred on the Commission.[23]

(62) In particular, the Commission should be empowered to adopt implementing provisions in order to take account of technological and market developments. Since those measures are of general scope and are designed to amend non-essential elements of this Directive, they must be adopted in accordance with the regulatory procedure with scrutiny provided for in Article 5a of Decision 1999/468/EC.

(63) In accordance with point 34 of the Interinstitutional Agreement on better law-making,[24] Member States are encouraged to draw up, for themselves and in the interest of the Community, their own tables illustrating, as far as possible, the correlation between this Directive and the transposition measures, and to make them public,

[6089]

NOTES

1. OJ C109, 9.5.2006, p 10.
2. Opinion of the European Parliament of 24 April 2007 (not yet published in the Official Journal) and Council Decision of 15 October 2007.
3. OJ L43, 14.2.1997, p 25.
4. OJ L344, 28.12.2001, p 13.
5. OJ L365, 24.12.1987, p 72.
6. OJ L317, 24.11.1988, p 55.
7. OJ L208, 2.8.1997, p 52.

8   OJ L177, 30.6.2006, p 1. Directive as amended by Commission Directive 2007/44/EC (OJ L247, 21.9.2007, p 1).
9   OJ L275, 27.10.2000, p 39.
10   OJ L222, 14.8.1978, p 11. Directive as last amended by Directive 2006/46/EC of the European Parliament and of the Council (OJ L224, 16.8.2006, p 1).
11   OJ L193, 18.7.1983, p 1. Directive as last amended by Directive 2006/99/EC (OJ L363, 20.12.2006, p 137).
12   OJ L372, 31.12.1986, p 1. Directive as last amended by Directive 2006/46/EC.
13   OJ L42, 12.2.1987, p 48. Directive as last amended by Directive 98/7/EC of the European Parliament and of the Council (OJ L101, 1.4.1998, p 17).
14   OJ L166, 11.6.1998, p 45.
15   OJ L124, 20.5.2003, p 36.
16   OJ L149, 11.6.2005, p 22.
17   OJ L178, 17.7.2000, p 1.
18   OJ L271, 9.10.2002, p 16. Directive as amended by Directive 2005/29/EC.
19   OJ L281, 23.11.1995, p 31. Directive as amended by Regulation (EC) No 1882/2003 (OJ L284, 31.10.2003, p 1).
20   OJ C27, 26.1.1998, p 34.
21   OJ L144, 4.6.1997, p 19. Directive as last amended by Directive 2005/29/EC.
22   OJ L309, 25.11.2005, p 15.
23   OJ L184, 17.7.1999, p 23. Decision as amended by Decision 2006/512/EC (OJ L200, 22.7.2006, p 11).
24   OJ C321, 31.12.2003, p 1.

HAVE ADOPTED THIS DIRECTIVE:

TITLE I
SUBJECT MATTER, SCOPE AND DEFINITIONS

Article 1
Subject matter

1.   This Directive lays down the rules in accordance with which Member States shall distinguish the following six categories of payment service provider:

(a)   credit institutions within the meaning of Article 4(1)(a) of Directive 2006/48/EC;

(b)   electronic money institutions within the meaning of Article 1(3)(a) of Directive 2000/46/EC;

(c)   post office giro institutions which are entitled under national law to provide payment services;

(d)   payment institutions within the meaning of this Directive;

(e)   the European Central Bank and national central banks when not acting in their capacity as monetary authority or other public authorities;

(f)   Member States or their regional or local authorities when not acting in their capacity as public authorities.

2.   This Directive also lays down rules concerning transparency of conditions and information requirements for payment services, and the respective rights and obligations of payment service users and payment service providers in relation to the provision of payment services as a regular occupation or business activity.

[6090]

Article 2
Scope

1.   This Directive shall apply to payment services provided within the Community. However, with the exception of Article 73, Titles III and IV shall apply only where both the payer's payment service provider and the payee's payment service provider are, or the sole payment service provider in the payment transaction is, located in the Community.

2.   Titles III and IV shall apply to payment services made in euro or the currency of a Member State outside the euro area.

3.   Member States may waive the application of all or part of the provisions of this Directive to the institutions referred to in Article 2 of Directive 2006/48/EC, with the exception of those referred to in the first and second indent of that article.

[6091]

Article 3
Negative scope

This Directive shall apply to none of the following:

(a)   payment transactions made exclusively in cash directly from the payer to the payee, without any intermediary intervention;

(b)   payment transactions from the payer to the payee through a commercial agent authorised to negotiate or conclude the sale or purchase of goods or services on behalf of the payer or the payee;

(c) professional physical transport of banknotes and coins, including their collection, processing and delivery;

(d) payment transactions consisting of the non-professional cash collection and delivery within the framework of a non-profit or charitable activity;

(e) services where cash is provided by the payee to the payer as part of a payment transaction following an explicit request by the payment service user just before the execution of the payment transaction through a payment for the purchase of goods or services;

(f) money exchange business, that is to say, cash-to-cash operations, where the funds are not held on a payment account;

(g) payment transactions based on any of the following documents drawn on the payment service provider with a view to placing funds at the disposal of the payee:

 (i) paper cheques in accordance with the Geneva Convention of 19 March 1931 providing a uniform law for cheques;

 (ii) paper cheques similar to those referred to in point (i) and governed by the laws of Member States which are not party to the Geneva Convention of 19 March 1931 providing a uniform law for cheques;

 (iii) paper-based drafts in accordance with the Geneva Convention of 7 June 1930 providing a uniform law for bills of exchange and promissory notes;

 (iv) paper-based drafts similar to those referred to in point (iii) and governed by the laws of Member States which are not party to the Geneva Convention of 7 June 1930 providing a uniform law for bills of exchange and promissory notes;

 (v) paper-based vouchers;

 (vi) paper-based traveller's cheques; or

 (vii) paper-based postal money orders as defined by the Universal Postal Union;

(h) payment transactions carried out within a payment or securities settlement system between settlement agents, central counterparties, clearing houses and/or central banks and other participants of the system, and payment service providers, without prejudice to Article 28;

(i) payment transactions related to securities asset servicing, including dividends, income or other distributions, or redemption or sale, carried out by persons referred to in point (h) or by investment firms, credit institutions, collective investment undertakings or asset management companies providing investment services and any other entities allowed to have the custody of financial instruments;

(j) services provided by technical service providers, which support the provision of payment services, without them entering at any time into possession of the funds to be transferred, including processing and storage of data, trust and privacy protection services, data and entity authentication, information technology (IT) and communication network provision, provision and maintenance of terminals and devices used for payment services;

(k) services based on instruments that can be used to acquire goods or services only in the premises used by the issuer or under a commercial agreement with the issuer either within a limited network of service providers or for a limited range of goods or services;

(l) payment transactions executed by means of any telecommunication, digital or IT device, where the goods or services purchased are delivered to and are to be used through a telecommunication, digital or IT device, provided that the telecommunication, digital or IT operator does not act only as an intermediary between the payment service user and the supplier of the goods and services;

(m) payment transactions carried out between payment service providers, their agents or branches for their own account;

(n) payment transactions between a parent undertaking and its subsidiary or between subsidiaries of the same parent undertaking, without any intermediary intervention by a payment service provider other than an undertaking belonging to the same group; or

(o) services by providers to withdraw cash by means of automated teller machines acting on behalf of one or more card issuers, which are not a party to the framework contract with the customer withdrawing money from a payment account, on condition that these providers do not conduct other payment services as listed in the Annex.

[6092]

Article 4
Definitions

For the purposes of this Directive, the following definitions shall apply:

1. "home Member State" means either of the following:

 (i) the Member State in which the registered office of the payment service provider is situated; or

 (ii) if the payment service provider has, under its national law, no registered office, the Member State in which its head office is situated;

2. "host Member State" means the Member State other than the home Member State in which a payment service provider has an agent or a branch or provides payment services;

3. "payment service" means any business activity listed in the Annex;

4. "payment institution" means a legal person that has been granted authorisation in accordance with Article 10 to provide and execute payment services throughout the Community;

5. "payment transaction" means an act, initiated by the payer or by the payee, of placing, transferring or withdrawing funds, irrespective of any underlying obligations between the payer and the payee;

6. "payment system" means a funds transfer system with formal and standardised arrangements and common rules for the processing, clearing and/or settlement of payment transactions;

7. "payer" means a natural or legal person who holds a payment account and allows a payment order from that payment account, or, where there is no payment account, a natural or legal person who gives a payment order;

8. "payee" means a natural or legal person who is the intended recipient of funds which have been the subject of a payment transaction;

9. "payment service provider" means bodies referred to in Article 1(1) and legal and natural persons benefiting from the waiver under Article 26;

10. "payment service user" means a natural or legal person making use of a payment service in the capacity of either payer or payee, or both;

11. "consumer" means a natural person who, in payment service contracts covered by this Directive, is acting for purposes other than his trade, business or profession;

12. "framework contract" means a payment service contract which governs the future execution of individual and successive payment transactions and which may contain the obligation and conditions for setting up a payment account;

13. "money remittance" means a payment service where funds are received from a payer, without any payment accounts being created in the name of the payer or the payee, for the sole purpose of transferring a corresponding amount to a payee or to another payment service provider acting on behalf of the payee, and/or where such funds are received on behalf of and made available to the payee;

14. "payment account" means an account held in the name of one or more payment service users which is used for the execution of payment transactions;

15. "funds" means banknotes and coins, scriptural money and electronic money as defined in Article 1(3)(b) of Directive 2000/46/EC;

16. "payment order" means any instruction by a payer or payee to his payment service provider requesting the execution of a payment transaction;

17. "value date" means a reference time used by a payment service provider for the calculation of interest on the funds debited from or credited to a payment account;

18. "reference exchange rate" means the exchange rate which is used as the basis to calculate any currency exchange and which is made available by the payment service provider or comes from a publicly available source;

19. "authentication" means a procedure which allows the payment service provider to verify the use of a specific payment instrument, including its personalised security features;

20. "reference interest rate" means the interest rate which is used as the basis for calculating any interest to be applied and which comes from a publicly available source which can be verified by both parties to a payment service contract;

21. "unique identifier" means a combination of letters, numbers or symbols specified to the payment service user by the payment service provider and to be provided by the payment service user to identify unambiguously the other payment service user and/or his payment account for a payment transaction;

22. "agent" means a natural or legal person which acts on behalf of a payment institution in providing payment services;

23. "payment instrument" means any personalised device(s) and/or set of procedures agreed between the payment service user and the payment service provider and used by the payment service user in order to initiate a payment order;

24. "means of distance communication" refers to any means which, without the simultaneous physical presence of the payment service provider and the payment service user, may be used for the conclusion of a payment services contract;

25. "durable medium" means any instrument which enables the payment service user to store information addressed personally to him in a way accessible for future reference for a period of time adequate to the purposes of the information and which allows the unchanged reproduction of the information stored;

26. "micro-enterprise" means an enterprise, which at the time of conclusion of the payment service contract, is an enterprise as defined in Article 1 and Article 2(1) and (3) of the Annex to Recommendation 2003/361/EC;

27. "business day" means a day on which the relevant payment service provider of the payer or the payment service provider of the payee involved in the execution of a payment transaction is open for business as required for the execution of a payment transaction;

28. "direct debit" means a payment service for debiting a payer's payment account, where a payment transaction is initiated by the payee on the basis of the payer's consent given to the payee, to the payee's payment service provider or to the payer's own payment service provider;

29. "branch" means a place of business other than the head office which is a part of a payment institution, which has no legal personality and which carries out directly some or all of the transactions inherent in the business of a payment institution; all the places of business set up in the same Member State by a payment institution with a head office in another Member State shall be regarded as a single branch;

30. "group" means a group of undertakings, which consists of a parent undertaking, its subsidiaries and the entities in which the parent undertaking or its subsidiaries have a holding as well as undertakings linked to each other by a relationship referred to in Article 12(1) of Directive 83/349/EEC.

[6093]

TITLE II
PAYMENT SERVICE PROVIDERS

CHAPTER 1
PAYMENT INSTITUTIONS

Section 1
General rules

Article 5
Applications for authorisation

For authorisation as a payment institution, an application shall be submitted to the competent authorities of the home Member State, together with the following:

(a)   a programme of operations, setting out in particular the type of payment services envisaged;

(b)   a business plan including a forecast budget calculation for the first three financial years which demonstrates that the applicant is able to employ the appropriate and proportionate systems, resources and procedures to operate soundly;

(c)   evidence that the payment institution holds initial capital provided for in Article 6;

(d)   for the payment institutions referred to in Article 9(1), a description of the measures taken for safeguarding payment service users' funds in accordance with Article 9;

(e)   a description of the applicant's governance arrangements and internal control mechanisms, including administrative, risk management and accounting procedures, which demonstrates that these governance arrangements, control mechanisms and procedures are proportionate, appropriate, sound and adequate;

(f)   a description of the internal control mechanisms which the applicant has established in order to comply with obligations in relation to money laundering and terrorist financing under Directive 2005/60/EC and Regulation (EC) No 1781/2006 of the European Parliament and of the Council of 15 November 2006 on information on the payer accompanying transfers of funds;[1]

(g)   a description of the applicant's structural organisation, including, where applicable, a description of the intended use of agents and branches and a description of outsourcing arrangements, and of its participation in a national or international payment system;

(h)   the identity of persons holding in the applicant, directly or indirectly, qualifying holdings within the meaning of Article 4(11) of Directive 2006/48/EC, the size of their holdings and evidence of their suitability taking into account the need to ensure the sound and prudent management of a payment institution;

(i)   the identity of directors and persons responsible for the management of the payment institution and, where relevant, persons responsible for the management of the payment services activities of the payment institution, as well as evidence that they are of good repute and possess appropriate knowledge and experience to perform payment services as determined by the home Member State of the payment institution;

(j)   where applicable, the identity of statutory auditors and audit firms as defined in

Directive 2006/43/EC of the European Parliament and of the Council of 17 May 2006 on statutory audits of annual accounts and consolidated accounts;[2]
(k) the applicant's legal status and articles of association;
(l) the address of the applicant's head office.

For the purposes of points (d), (e) and (g), the applicant shall provide a description of its audit arrangements and the organisational arrangements it has set up with a view to taking all reasonable steps to protect the interests of its users and to ensure continuity and reliability in the performance of payment services.

[6094]

NOTES
[1] OJ L345, 8.12.2006, p 1.
[2] OJ L157, 9.6.2006, p 87.

Article 6
Initial capital

Member States shall require payment institutions to hold, at the time of authorisation, initial capital, comprised of the items defined in Article 57(a) and (b) of Directive 2006/48/EC as follows:
(a) where the payment institution provides only the payment service listed in point 6 of the Annex, its capital shall at no time be less than EUR 20000;
(b) where the payment institution provides the payment service listed in point 7 of the Annex, its capital shall at no time be less than EUR 50000; and
(c) where the payment institution provides any of the payment services listed in points 1 to 5 of the Annex, its capital shall at no time be less than EUR 125000.

[6095]

Article 7
Own funds

1. The payment institution's own funds, as defined in Articles 57 to 61, 63, 64 and 66 of Directive 2006/48/EC, may not fall below the amount required under Articles 6 or 8 of this Directive, whichever the higher.

2. Member States shall take the necessary measures to prevent the multiple use of elements eligible for own funds where the payment institution belongs to the same group as another payment institution, credit institution, investment firm, asset management company or insurance undertaking. This paragraph shall also apply where a payment institution has a hybrid character and carries out activities other than providing payment services listed in the Annex.

3. If the conditions laid down in Article 69 of Directive 2006/48/EC are met, Member States or their competent authorities may choose not to apply Article 8 of this Directive to payment institutions which are included in the consolidated supervision of the parent credit institution pursuant to Directive 2006/48/EC.

[6096]

Article 8
Calculation of own funds

1. Notwithstanding the initial capital requirements set out in Article 6, Member States shall require payment institutions to hold, at all times, own funds calculated in accordance with one of the following three methods, as determined by the competent authorities in accordance with national legislation:

Method A

The payment institution's own funds shall amount to at least 10% of its fixed overheads of the preceding year. The competent authorities may adjust that requirement in the event of a material change in a payment institution's business since the preceding year. Where a payment institution has not completed a full year's business at the date of the calculation, the requirement shall be that its own funds amount to at least 10% of the corresponding fixed overheads as projected in its business plan, unless an adjustment to that plan is required by the competent authorities.

Method B

The payment institution's own funds shall amount to at least the sum of the following elements multiplied by the scaling factor k defined in paragraph 2, where payment volume (PV) represents one twelfth of the total amount of payment transactions executed by the payment institution in the preceding year:
(a) 4,0% of the slice of PV up to EUR 5 million,
plus
(b) 2,5% of the slice of PV above EUR 5 million up to EUR 10 million,
plus

(c)   1% of the slice of PV above EUR 10 million up to EUR 100 million, plus

(d)   0,5% of the slice of PV above EUR 100 million up to EUR 250 million, plus

(e)   0,25% of the slice of PV above EUR 250 million.

Method C

The payment institution's own funds shall amount to at least the relevant indicator defined in point (a), multiplied by the multiplication factor defined in point (b) and by the scaling factor k defined in paragraph 2.

(a)   The relevant indicator is the sum of the following:
  —   interest income,
  —   interest expenses,
  —   commissions and fees received, and
  —   other operating income.

Each element shall be included in the sum with its positive or negative sign. Income from extraordinary or irregular items may not be used in the calculation of the relevant indicator. Expenditure on the outsourcing of services rendered by third parties may reduce the relevant indicator if the expenditure is incurred from an undertaking subject to supervision under this Directive. The relevant indicator is calculated on the basis of the twelve-monthly observation at the end of the previous financial year. The relevant indicator shall be calculated over the previous financial year. Nevertheless own funds calculated according to Method C shall not fall below 80% of the average of the previous three financial years for the relevant indicator. When audited figures are not available, business estimates may be used.

(b)   The multiplication factor shall be:
  (i)   10% of the slice of the relevant indicator up to EUR 2,5 million;
  (ii)   8% of the slice of the relevant indicator from EUR 2,5 million up to EUR 5 million;
  (iii)   6% of the slice of the relevant indicator from EUR 5 million up to EUR 25 million;
  (iv)   3% of the slice of the relevant indicator from EUR 25 million up to 50 million;
  (v)   1,5% above EUR 50 million.

2.   The scaling factor k to be used in Methods B and C shall be:
  (a)   0,5 where the payment institution provides only the payment service listed in point 6 of the Annex;
  (b)   0,8 where the payment institution provides the payment service listed in point 7 of the Annex;
  (c)   1 where the payment institution provides any of the payment services listed in points 1 to 5 of the Annex.

3.   The competent authorities may, based on an evaluation of the risk-management processes, risk loss data base and internal control mechanisms of the payment institution, require the payment institution to hold an amount of own funds which is up to 20% higher than the amount which would result from the application of the method chosen in accordance with paragraph 1, or permit the payment institution to hold an amount of own funds which is up to 20% lower than the amount which would result from the application of the method chosen in accordance with paragraph 1.

[6097]

Article 9
Safeguarding requirements

1.   The Member States or competent authorities shall require a payment institution which provides any of the payment services listed in the Annex and, at the same time, is engaged in other business activities referred to in Article 16(1)(c) to safeguard funds which have been received from the payment service users or through another payment service provider for the execution of payment transactions, as follows:

either:

  (a)   they shall not be commingled at any time with the funds of any natural or legal person other than payment service users on whose behalf the funds are held and, where they are still held by the payment institution and not yet delivered to the payee or transferred to another payment service provider by the end of the business day following the day when the funds have been received, they shall be deposited in a separate account in a credit institution or invested in secure, liquid low-risk assets as defined by the competent authorities of the home Member State; and

  (b)   they shall be insulated in accordance with national law in the interest of the payment service users against the claims of other creditors of the payment institution, in particular in the event of insolvency;

or

  (c)   they shall be covered by an insurance policy or some other comparable guarantee from an insurance company or a credit institution, which does not belong to the same group as the payment institution itself, for an amount equivalent to that which would have been segregated in the absence of the insurance policy or other comparable guarantee, payable in the event that the payment institution is unable to meet its financial obligations.

2.   Where a payment institution is required to safeguard funds under paragraph 1 and a portion of those funds is to be used for future payment transactions with the remaining amount to be used for non-payment services, that portion of the funds to be used for future payment transactions shall also be subject to the requirements under paragraph 1. Where that portion is variable or unknown in advance, Member States may allow payment institutions to apply this paragraph on the basis of a representative portion assumed to be used for payment services provided such a representative portion can be reasonably estimated on the basis of historical data to the satisfaction of the competent authorities.

3.   The Member States or competent authorities may require that payment institutions which are not engaged in other business activities referred to in Article 16(1)(c) shall also comply with the safeguarding requirements under paragraph 1 of this Article.

4.   The Member States or competent authorities may also limit such safeguarding requirements to funds of those payment service users whose funds individually exceed a threshold of EUR 600.

[6098]

Article 10
Granting of authorisation

1.   Member States shall require undertakings other than those referred to in Article 1(1)(a) to (c), (e) and (f) and other than legal or natural persons benefiting from a waiver under Article 26, who intend to provide payment services, to obtain authorisation as a payment institution before commencing the provision of payment services. An authorisation shall only be granted to a legal person established in a Member State.

2.   An authorisation shall be granted if the information and evidence accompanying the application complies with all the requirements under Article 5 and if the competent authorities' overall assessment, having scrutinised the application, is favourable. Before an authorisation is granted, the competent authorities may, where relevant, consult the national central bank or other relevant public authorities.

3.   A payment institution which under the national law of its home Member State is required to have a registered office, shall have its head office in the same Member State as its registered office.

4.   The competent authorities shall grant an authorisation only if, taking into account the need to ensure the sound and prudent management of a payment institution, the payment institution has robust governance arrangements for its payment services business, which include a clear organisational structure with well-defined, transparent and consistent lines of responsibility, effective procedures to identify, manage, monitor and report the risks to which it is or might be exposed, and adequate internal control mechanisms, including sound administrative and accounting procedures; those arrangements, procedures and mechanisms shall be comprehensive and proportionate to the nature, scale and complexity of the payment services provided by the payment institution.

5.   Where a payment institution provides any of the payment services listed in the Annex and, at the same time, is engaged in other business activities, the competent authorities may require the establishment of a separate entity for the payment services business, where the non-payment services activities of the payment institution impair or are likely to impair either the financial soundness of the payment institution or the ability of the competent authorities to monitor the payment institution's compliance with all obligations laid down by this Directive.

6.   The competent authorities shall refuse to grant an authorisation if, taking into account the need to ensure the sound and prudent management of a payment institution, they are not satisfied as to the suitability of the shareholders or members that have qualifying holdings.

7.   Where close links as defined in Article 4(46) of Directive 2006/48/EC exist between the payment institution and other natural or legal persons, the competent authorities shall grant an authorisation only if those links do not prevent the effective exercise of their supervisory functions.

8.   The competent authorities shall grant an authorisation only if the laws, regulations or administrative provisions of a third country governing one or more natural or legal persons with which the payment institution has close links, or difficulties involved in the enforcement of those laws, regulations or administrative provisions, do not prevent the effective exercise of their supervisory functions.

9.   An authorisation shall be valid in all Member States and shall allow the payment institution concerned to provide payment services throughout the Community, either under the freedom to provide services or the freedom of establishment, provided that such services are covered by the authorisation.

[6099]

Article 11
Communication of the decision

Within three months of receipt of an application or, should the application be incomplete, of all the information required for the decision, the competent authorities shall inform the applicant whether the authorisation has been granted or refused. Reasons shall be given whenever an authorisation is refused.

[6100]

Article 12
Withdrawal of authorisation

1. The competent authorities may withdraw an authorisation issued to a payment institution only where the institution:
   (a) does not make use of the authorisation within 12 months, expressly renounces the authorisation or has ceased to engage in business for more than six months, if the Member State concerned has made no provision for the authorisation to lapse in such cases;
   (b) has obtained the authorisation through false statements or any other irregular means;
   (c) no longer fulfils the conditions for granting the authorisation;
   (d) would constitute a threat to the stability of the payment system by continuing its payment services business; or
   (e) falls within one of the other cases where national law provides for withdrawal of an authorisation.

2. Reasons shall be given for any withdrawal of an authorisation and those concerned shall be informed accordingly.

3. The withdrawal of an authorisation shall be made public.

[6101]

Article 13
Registration

Member States shall establish a public register of authorised payment institutions, their agents and branches, as well as of natural and legal persons, their agents and branches, benefiting from a waiver under Article 26, and of the institutions referred to in Article 2(3) that are entitled under national law to provide payment services. They shall be entered in the register of the home Member State.

This register shall identify the payment services for which the payment institution is authorised or for which the natural or legal person has been registered. Authorised payment institutions shall be listed in the register separately from natural and legal persons that have been registered in accordance with Article 26. The register shall be publicly available for consultation, accessible online, and updated on a regular basis.

[6102]

Article 14
Maintenance of authorisation

Where any change affects the accuracy of information and evidence provided in accordance with Article 5, the payment institution shall without undue delay inform the competent authorities of its home Member State accordingly.

[6103]

Article 15
Accounting and statutory audit

1. Directive 78/660/EEC and, where applicable, Directives 83/349/EEC and 86/635/EEC and Regulation (EC) 1606/2002 of the European Parliament and of the Council of 19 July 2002 on the application of international accounting standards[1] shall apply to payment institutions *mutatis mutandis*.

2. Unless exempted under Directive 78/660/EEC and, where applicable, Directives 83/349/EEC and 86/635/EEC, the annual accounts and consolidated accounts of payment institutions shall be audited by statutory auditors or audit firms within the meaning of Directive 2006/43/EC.

3. For supervisory purposes, Member States shall require that payment institutions provide separate accounting information for payment services listed in the Annex and activities referred to in Article 16(1), which shall be subject to an auditor's report. That report shall be prepared, where applicable, by the statutory auditors or an audit firm.

4. The obligations established in Article 53 of Directive 2006/48/EC shall apply mutatis mutandis to the statutory auditors or audit firms of payment institutions in respect of payment services activities.

[6104]

PART IV
EC MATERIALS

NOTES

¹ OJ L243, 11.9.2002, p 1.

Article 16
Activities

1.   Apart from the provision of payment services listed in the Annex payment institutions shall be entitled to engage in the following activities:

(a)   the provision of operational and closely related ancillary services such as ensuring the execution of payment transactions, foreign exchange services, safekeeping activities, and the storage and processing of data;

(b)   the operation of payment systems, without prejudice to Article 28;

(c)   business activities other than the provision of payment services, having regard to applicable Community and national law.

2.   When payment institutions engage in the provision of one or more of the payment services listed in the Annex, they may hold only payment accounts used exclusively for payment transactions. Any funds received by payment institutions from payment service users with a view to the provision of payment services shall not constitute a deposit or other repayable funds within the meaning of Article 5 of Directive 2006/48/EC, or electronic money within the meaning of Article 1(3) of Directive 2000/46/EC.

3.   Payment institutions may grant credit related to payment services referred to in points 4, 5 or 7 of the Annex only if the following conditions are met:

(a)   the credit shall be ancillary and granted exclusively in connection with the execution of a payment transaction;

(b)   notwithstanding national rules on providing credit by credit cards, the credit granted in connection with a payment and executed in accordance with Article 10(9) and Article 25 shall be repaid within a short period which shall in no case exceed twelve months;

(c)   such credit shall not be granted from the funds received or held for the purpose of executing a payment transaction; and

(d)   the own funds of the payment institution shall at all times and to the satisfaction of the supervisory authorities be appropriate in view of the overall amount of credit granted.

4.   Payment institutions shall not conduct the business of taking deposits or other repayable funds within the meaning of Article 5 of Directive 2006/48/EC.

5.   This Directive shall be without prejudice to national measures implementing Directive 87/102/EEC. This Directive shall also be without prejudice to other relevant Community or national legislation regarding conditions for granting credit to consumers not harmonised by this Directive that are in conformity with Community law.

[6105]

Section 2
Other requirements

Article 17
Use of agents, branches or entities to which activities are outsourced

1.   When a payment institution intends to provide payment services through an agent it shall communicate the following information to the competent authorities in its home Member State:

(a)   the name and address of the agent;

(b)   a description of the internal control mechanisms that will be used by agents in order to comply with the obligations in relation to money laundering and terrorist financing under Directive 2005/60/EC; and

(c)   the identity of directors and persons responsible for the management of the agent to be used in the provision of payment services and evidence that they are fit and proper persons.

2.   When the competent authorities receive the information in accordance with paragraph 1 then they may list the agent in the register provided for in Article 13.

3.   Before listing the agent in the register, the competent authorities may, if they consider that the information provided to them is incorrect, take further action to verify the information.

4.   If, after taking action to verify the information, the competent authorities are not satisfied that the information provided to them pursuant to paragraph 1 is correct, they shall refuse to list the agent in the register provided for in Article 13.

5.   If the payment institution wishes to provide payment services in another Member State by engaging an agent it shall follow the procedures set out in Article 25. In that case, before the agent may be registered under this Article, the competent authorities of the home Member State shall inform the competent authorities of the host Member State of their intention to register the agent and take their opinion into account.

6.   If the competent authorities of the host Member State have reasonable grounds to suspect that, in connection with the intended engagement of the agent or establishment of the branch, money laundering or terrorist financing within the meaning of Directive 2005/60/EC is taking place, has taken place or been attempted, or that the engagement of such agent or establishment of such branch could increase the risk of money laundering or terrorist financing, they shall so inform the competent authorities of the home Member State, which may refuse to register the agent or branch, or may withdraw the registration, if already made, of the agent or branch.

7.   Where a payment institution intends to outsource operational functions of payment services, it shall inform the competent authorities of its home Member State accordingly.

Outsourcing of important operational functions may not be undertaken in such way as to impair materially the quality of the payment institution's internal control and the ability of the competent authorities to monitor the payment institution's compliance with all obligations laid down in this Directive.

For the purposes of the second subparagraph, an operational function shall be regarded as important if a defect or failure in its performance would materially impair the continuing compliance of a payment institution with the requirements of its authorisation requested under this Title or its other obligations under this Directive, or its financial performance, or the soundness or the continuity of its payment services. Member States shall ensure that when payment institutions outsource important operational functions, the payment institutions comply with the following conditions:

(a)   the outsourcing shall not result in the delegation by senior management of its responsibility;

(b)   the relationship and obligations of the payment institution towards its payment service users under this Directive shall not be altered;

(c)   the conditions with which the payment institution is to comply in order to be authorised and remain so in accordance with this Title shall not be undermined; and

(d)   none of the other conditions subject to which the payment institution's authorisation was granted shall be removed or modified.

8.   Payment institutions shall ensure that agents or branches acting on their behalf inform payment service users of this fact.

[6106]

Article 18
Liability

1.   Member States shall ensure that, where payment institutions rely on third parties for the performance of operational functions, those payment institutions take reasonable steps to ensure that the requirements of this Directive are complied with.

2.   Member States shall require that payment institutions remain fully liable for any acts of their employees, or any agent, branch or entity to which activities are outsourced.

[6107]

Article 19
Record-keeping

Member States shall require payment institutions to keep all appropriate records for the purpose of this Title for at least five years, without prejudice to Directive 2005/60/EC or other relevant Community or national legislation.

[6108]

Section 3
Competent authorities and supervision

Article 20
Designation of competent authorities

1.   Member States shall designate as the competent authorities responsible for the authorisation and prudential supervision of payment institutions which are to carry out the duties provided for under this Title either public authorities, or bodies recognised by national law or by public authorities expressly empowered for that purpose by national law, including national central banks.

The competent authorities shall guarantee independence from economic bodies and avoid conflicts of interest. Without prejudice to the first subparagraph, payment institutions, credit institutions, electronic money institutions, or post office giro institutions shall not be designated as competent authorities.

The Member States shall inform the Commission accordingly.

2.   Member States shall ensure that the competent authorities designated under paragraph 1 possess all the powers necessary for the performance of their duties.

3.   Where there is more than one competent authority for matters covered by this Title on its territory, Member States shall ensure that those authorities cooperate closely so that they can

discharge their respective duties effectively. The same applies in cases where the authorities competent for matters covered by this Title are not the competent authorities responsible for the supervision of credit institutions.

4.　The tasks of the competent authorities designated under paragraph 1 shall be the responsibility of the competent authorities of the home Member State.

5.　Paragraph 1 shall not imply that the competent authorities are required to supervise business activities of the payment institutions other than the provision of payment services listed in the Annex and the activities listed in Article 16(1)(a).

[6109]

Article 21
Supervision

1.　Member States shall ensure that the controls exercised by the competent authorities for checking continued compliance with this Title are proportionate, adequate and responsive to the risks to which payment institutions are exposed.

In order to check compliance with this Title, the competent authorities shall be entitled to take the following steps, in particular:
- (a)　to require the payment institution to provide any information needed to monitor compliance;
- (b)　to carry out on-site inspections at the payment institution, at any agent or branch providing payment services under the responsibility of the payment institution, or at any entity to which activities are outsourced;
- (c)　to issue recommendations, guidelines and, if applicable, binding administrative provisions; and
- (d)　to suspend or withdraw authorisation in cases referred to in Article 12.

2.　Without prejudice to the procedures for the withdrawal of authorisations and the provisions of criminal law, the Member States shall provide that their respective competent authorities, may, as against payment institutions or those who effectively control the business of payment institutions which breach laws, regulations or administrative provisions concerning the supervision or pursuit of their payment service business, adopt or impose in respect of them penalties or measures aimed specifically at ending observed breaches or the causes of such breaches.

3.　Notwithstanding the requirements of Article 6, Article 7(1) and (2) and Article 8, Member States shall ensure that the competent authorities are entitled to take steps described under paragraph 1 of this Article to ensure sufficient capital for payment services, in particular where the non-payment services activities of the payment institution impair or are likely to impair the financial soundness of the payment institution.

[6110]

Article 22
Professional secrecy

1.　Member States shall ensure that all persons working or who have worked for the competent authorities, as well as experts acting on behalf of the competent authorities, are bound by the obligation of professional secrecy, without prejudice to cases covered by criminal law.

2.　In the exchange of information in accordance with Article 24, professional secrecy shall be strictly applied to ensure the protection of individual and business rights.

3.　Member States may apply this Article taking into account, mutatis mutandis, Articles 44 to 52 of Directive 2006/48/EC.

[6111]

Article 23
Right to apply to the courts

1.　Member States shall ensure that decisions taken by the competent authorities in respect of a payment institution pursuant to the laws, regulations and administrative provisions adopted in accordance with this Directive may be contested before the courts.

2.　Paragraph 1 shall apply also in respect of failure to act.

[6112]

Article 24
Exchange of information

1.　The competent authorities of the different Member States shall cooperate with each other and, where appropriate, with the European Central Bank and the national central banks of the Member States and other relevant competent authorities designated under Community or national legislation applicable to payment service providers.

2.　Member States shall, in addition, allow the exchange of information between their competent authorities and the following:

(a) the competent authorities of other Member States responsible for the authorisation and supervision of payment institutions;

(b) the European Central Bank and the national central banks of Member States, in their capacity as monetary and oversight authorities, and, where appropriate, other public authorities responsible for overseeing payment and settlement systems;

(c) other relevant authorities designated under this Directive, Directive 95/46/EC, Directive 2005/60/EC and other Community legislation applicable to payment service providers, such as legislation applicable to the protection of individuals with regard to the processing of personal data as well as money laundering and terrorist financing.

[6113]

Article 25
Exercise of the right of establishment and freedom to provide services

1. Any authorised payment institution wishing to provide payment services for the first time in a Member State other than its home Member State, in exercise of the right of establishment or the freedom to provide services, shall so inform the competent authorities in its home Member State.

Within one month of receiving that information, the competent authorities of the home Member State shall inform the competent authorities of the host Member State of the name and address of the payment institution, the names of those responsible for the management of the branch, its organisational structure and of the kind of payment services it intends to provide in the territory of the host Member State.

2. In order to carry out the controls and take the necessary steps provided for in Article 21 in respect of the agent, branch or entity to which activities are outsourced of a payment institution located in the territory of another Member State, the competent authorities of the home Member State shall cooperate with the competent authorities of the host Member State.

3. By way of cooperation in accordance with paragraphs 1 and 2, the competent authorities of the home Member State shall notify the competent authorities of the host Member State whenever they intend to carry out an on-site inspection in the territory of the latter.

However, if they so wish, the competent authorities of the home Member State may delegate to the competent authorities of the host Member State the task of carrying out on-site inspections of the institution concerned.

4. The competent authorities shall provide each other with all essential and/or relevant information, in particular in the case of infringements or suspected infringements by an agent, a branch or an entity to which activities are outsourced. In this regard, the competent authorities shall communicate, upon request, all relevant information and, on their own initiative, all essential information.

5. Paragraphs 1 to 4 shall be without prejudice to the obligation of competent authorities under Directive 2005/60/EC and Regulation (EC) No 1781/2006, in particular under Article 37(1) of Directive 2005/60/EC and Article 15(3) of Regulation (EC) No 1781/2006 to supervise or monitor the compliance with the requirements laid down in those instruments.

[6114]

Section 4
Waiver

Article 26
Conditions

1. Notwithstanding Article 13, Member States may waive or allow their competent authorities to waive the application of all or part of the procedure and conditions set out in Sections 1 to 3, with the exception of Articles 20, 22, 23 and 24, and allow natural or legal persons to be entered in the register provided for in Article 13, where:

(a) the average of the preceding 12 months' total amount of payment transactions executed by the person concerned, including any agent for which it assumes full responsibility, does not exceed EUR 3 million per month. That requirement shall be assessed on the projected total amount of payment transactions in its business plan, unless an adjustment to that plan is required by the competent authorities; and

(b) none of the natural persons responsible for the management or operation of the business has been convicted of offences relating to money laundering or terrorist financing or other financial crimes.

2. Any natural or legal person registered in accordance with paragraph 1 shall be required to have its head office or place of residence in the Member State in which it actually carries on its business.

3. The persons referred to in paragraph 1 shall be treated as payment institutions, save that Article 10(9) and Article 25 shall not apply to them.

4. Member States may also provide that any natural or legal person registered in accordance with paragraph 1 may engage only in certain activities listed in Article 16.

5.   The persons referred to in paragraph 1 shall notify the competent authorities of any change in their situation which is relevant to the conditions specified in that paragraph. Member States shall take the necessary steps to ensure that where the conditions set out in paragraphs 1, 2 and 4 are no longer fulfilled, the persons concerned shall seek authorisation within 30 calendar days in accordance with the procedure laid down in Article 10.

6.   This Article shall not be applied in respect of provisions of Directive 2005/60/EC or national anti-money-laundering provisions.

[6115]

Article 27
Notification and information

If a Member State avails itself of the waiver provided for in Article 26, it shall notify the Commission accordingly by 1 November 2009 and it shall notify the Commission forthwith of any subsequent change. In addition, the Member State shall inform the Commission of the number of natural and legal persons concerned and, on an annual basis, of the total amount of payment transactions executed as of 31 December of each calendar year, as referred to in Article 26(1)(a).

[6116]

CHAPTER 2
COMMON PROVISIONS

Article 28
Access to payment systems

1.   Member States shall ensure that the rules on access of authorised or registered payment service providers that are legal persons to payment systems shall be objective, non-discriminatory and proportionate and that those rules do not inhibit access more than is necessary to safeguard against specific risks such as settlement risk, operational risk and business risk and to protect the financial and operational stability of the payment system.

Payment systems shall impose on payment service providers, on payment service users or on other payment systems none of the following requirements:
(a)   any restrictive rule on effective participation in other payment systems;
(b)   any rule which discriminates between authorised payment service providers or between registered payment service providers in relation to the rights, obligations and entitlements of participants; or
(c)   any restriction on the basis of institutional status.

2.   Paragraph 1 shall not apply to:
(a)   payment systems designated under Directive 98/26/EC;
(b)   payment systems composed exclusively of payment service providers belonging to a group composed of entities linked by capital where one of the linked entities enjoys effective control over the other linked entities; or
(c)   payment systems where a sole payment service provider (whether as a single entity or as a group):
—   acts or can act as the payment service provider for both the payer and the payee and is exclusively responsible for the management of the system, and
—   licenses other payment service providers to participate in the system and the latter have no right to negotiate fees between or amongst themselves in relation to the payment system although they may establish their own pricing in relation to payers and payees.

[6117]

Article 29
Prohibition for persons other than payment service providers to provide payment services

Member States shall prohibit natural or legal persons that are neither payment service providers nor explicitly excluded from the scope of this Directive from providing the payment services listed in the Annex.

[6118]

TITLE III
TRANSPARENCY OF CONDITIONS AND INFORMATION REQUIREMENTS FOR
PAYMENT SERVICES

CHAPTER 1
GENERAL RULES

Article 30
Scope

1.   This Title shall apply to single payment transactions, framework contracts and payment transactions covered by them. The parties may agree that it shall not apply in whole or in part when the payment service user is not a consumer.

2.   Member States may provide that the provisions in this Title shall be applied to micro enterprises in the same way as to consumers.

3.   This Directive shall be without prejudice to national measures implementing Directive 87/102/EEC. This Directive shall also be without prejudice to other relevant Community or national legislation regarding conditions for granting credit to consumers not harmonised by this Directive that are in conformity with Community law.

[6119]

Article 31
Other provisions in Community legislation

The provisions of this Title are without prejudice to any Community legislation containing additional requirements on prior information.

However, where Directive 2002/65/EC is also applicable, the information requirements set out in Article 3(1) of that Directive, with the exception of points (2)(c) to (g), (3)(a), (d) and (e), and (4)(b) of that paragraph shall be replaced by Articles 36, 37, 41 and 42 of this Directive.

[6120]

Article 32
Charges for information

1.   The payment service provider shall not charge the payment service user for providing information under this Title.

2.   The payment service provider and the payment service user may agree on charges for additional or more frequent information, or transmission by means of communication other than those specified in the framework contract, provided at the payment service user's request.

3.   Where the payment service provider may impose charges for information in accordance with paragraph 2, they shall be appropriate and in line with the payment service provider's actual costs.

[6121]

Article 33
Burden of proof on information requirements

Member States may stipulate that the burden of proof shall lie with the payment service provider to prove that it has complied with the information requirements set out in this Title.

[6122]

Article 34
Derogation from information requirements for low-value payment instruments and electronic money

1.   In cases of payment instruments which, according to the framework contract, concern only individual payment transactions that do not exceed EUR 30 or that either have a spending limit of EUR 150 or store funds that do not exceed EUR 150 at any time:

(a)   by way of derogation from Articles 41, 42 and 46, the payment service provider shall provide the payer only with information on the main characteristics of the payment service, including the way in which the payment instrument can be used, liability, charges levied and other material information needed to take an informed decision as well as an indication of where any other information and conditions specified in Article 42 are made available in an easily accessible manner;

(b)   it may be agreed that, by way of derogation from Article 44, the payment service provider shall not be required to propose changes in the conditions of the framework contract in the same way as provided for in Article 41(1);

(c)   it may be agreed that, by way of derogation from Articles 47 and 48, after the execution of a payment transaction:

(i)   the payment service provider shall provide or make available only a reference enabling the payment service user to identify the payment transaction, the amount of the payment transaction, any charges and/or, in the case of several payment transactions of the same kind made to the same payee, information on the total amount and charges for those payment transactions;

(ii)   the payment service provider shall not be required to provide or make available information referred to in point (i) if the payment instrument is used anonymously or if the payment service provider is not otherwise technically in a position to provide it. However, the payment service provider shall provide the payer with a possibility to verify the amount of funds stored.

2.   For national payment transactions, Member States or their competent authorities may reduce or double the amounts referred to in paragraph 1. For prepaid payment instruments, Member States may increase those amounts up to EUR 500.

[6123]

CHAPTER 2
SINGLE PAYMENT TRANSACTIONS

Article 35
Scope

1.   This Chapter shall apply to single payment transactions not covered by a framework contract.

2.   When a payment order for a single payment transaction is transmitted by a payment instrument covered by a framework contract, the payment service provider shall not be obliged to provide or make available information which is already given to the payment service user on the basis of a framework contract with another payment service provider or which will be given to him according to that framework contract.

[6124]

Article 36
Prior general information

1.   Member States shall require that before the payment service user is bound by any single payment service contract or offer, the payment service provider, in an easily accessible manner, makes available to the payment service user the information and conditions specified in Article 37. At the payment service user's request, the payment service provider shall provide the information and conditions on paper or on another durable medium. The information and conditions shall be given in easily understandable words and in a clear and comprehensible form, in an official language of the Member State where the payment service is offered or in any other language agreed between the parties.

2.   If the single payment service contract has been concluded at the request of the payment service user using a means of distance communication which does not enable the payment service provider to comply with paragraph 1, the payment service provider shall fulfil its obligations under that paragraph immediately after the execution of the payment transaction.

3.   The obligations under paragraph 1 may also be discharged by supplying a copy of the draft single payment service contract or the draft payment order including the information and conditions specified in Article 37.

[6125]

Article 37
Information and conditions

1.   Member States shall ensure that the following information and conditions are provided or made available to the payment service user:

(a)   a specification of the information or unique identifier that has to be provided by the payment service user in order for a payment order to be properly executed;

(b)   the maximum execution time for the payment service to be provided;

(c)   all charges payable by the payment service user to his payment service provider and, where applicable, the breakdown of the amounts of any charges;

(d)   where applicable, the actual or reference exchange rate to be applied to the payment transaction.

2.   Where applicable, any other relevant information and conditions specified in Article 42 shall be made available to the payment service user in an easily accessible manner.

[6126]

Article 38
Information for the payer after receipt of the payment order

Immediately after receipt of the payment order, the payer's payment service provider shall provide or make available to the payer, in the same way as provided for in Article 36(1), the following information:

(a)   a reference enabling the payer to identify the payment transaction and, where appropriate, information relating to the payee;

   (b)   the amount of the payment transaction in the currency used in the payment order;

   (c)   the amount of any charges for the payment transaction payable by the payer and, where applicable, a breakdown of the amounts of such charges;

   (d)   where applicable, the exchange rate used in the payment transaction by the payer's payment service provider or a reference thereto, when different from the rate provided in accordance with Article 37(1)(d), and the amount of the payment transaction after that currency conversion; and

   (e)   the date of receipt of the payment order.

[6127]

Article 39
Information for the payee after execution

Immediately after the execution of the payment transaction, the payee's payment service provider shall provide or make available to the payee, in the same way as provided for in Article 36(1), the following information:

   (a)   the reference enabling the payee to identify the payment transaction and, where appropriate, the payer and any information transferred with the payment transaction;

   (b)   the amount of the payment transaction in the currency in which the funds are at the payee's disposal;

   (c)   the amount of any charges for the payment transaction payable by the payee and, where applicable, a breakdown of the amount of such charges;

   (d)   where applicable, the exchange rate used in the payment transaction by the payee's payment service provider, and the amount of the payment transaction before that currency conversion; and

   (e)   the credit value date.

[6128]

CHAPTER 3
FRAMEWORK CONTRACTS

Article 40
Scope

This Chapter applies to payment transactions covered by a framework contract.

[6129]

Article 41
Prior general information

1.   Member States shall require that, in good time before the payment service user is bound by any framework contract or offer, the payment service provider provide the payment service user on paper or on another durable medium with the information and conditions specified in Article 42. The information and conditions shall be given in easily understandable words and in a clear and comprehensible form, in an official language of the Member State where the payment service is offered or in any other language agreed between the parties.

2.   If the framework contract has been concluded at the request of the payment service user using a means of distance communication which does not enable the payment service provider to comply with paragraph 1, the payment service provider shall fulfil its obligations under that paragraph immediately after the conclusion of the framework contract.

3.   The obligations under paragraph 1 may also be discharged by supplying a copy of the draft framework contract including the information and conditions specified in Article 42.

[6130]

Article 42
Information and conditions

Member States shall ensure that the following information and conditions are provided to the payment service user:

1.   on the payment service provider:

   (a)   the name of the payment service provider, the geographical address of its head office and, where applicable, the geographical address of its agent or branch established in the Member State where the payment service is offered, and any other address, including electronic mail address, relevant for communication with the payment service provider; and

   (b)   the particulars of the relevant supervisory authorities and of the register provided for in Article 13 or of any other relevant public register of authorisation of the payment service provider and the registration number, or equivalent means of identification in that register;

2.   on use of the payment service:

   (a)   a description of the main characteristics of the payment service to be provided;

(b)   a specification of the information or unique identifier that has to be provided by the payment service user in order for a payment order to be properly executed;

(c)   the form of and procedure for giving consent to execute a payment transaction and withdrawal of such consent in accordance with Articles 54 and 66;

(d)   a reference to the point in time of receipt of a payment order as defined in Article 64 and the cut-off time, if any, established by the payment service provider;

(e)   the maximum execution time for the payment services to be provided; and

(f)   whether there is a possibility to agree on spending limits for the use of the payment instrument in accordance with Article 55(1);

3.   on charges, interest and exchange rates:

(a)   all charges payable by the payment service user to the payment service provider and, where applicable, the breakdown of the amounts of any charges;

(b)   where applicable, the interest and exchange rates to be applied or, if reference interest and exchange rates are to be used, the method of calculating the actual interest, and the relevant date and index or base for determining such reference interest or exchange rate; and

(c)   if agreed, the immediate application of changes in reference interest or exchange rate and information requirements related to the changes in accordance with Article 44(2);

4.   on communication:

(a)   where applicable, the means of communication, including the technical requirements for the payment service user's equipment, agreed between the parties for the transmission of information or notifications under this Directive;

(b)   the manner in and frequency with which information under this Directive is to be provided or made available;

(c)   the language or languages in which the framework contract will be concluded and communication during this contractual relationship undertaken; and

(d)   the payment service user's right to receive the contractual terms of the framework contract and information and conditions in accordance with Article 43;

5.   on safeguards and corrective measures:

(a)   where applicable, a description of steps that the payment service user is to take in order to keep safe a payment instrument and how to notify the payment service provider for the purposes of Article 56(1)(b);

(b)   if agreed, the conditions under which the payment service provider reserves the right to block a payment instrument in accordance with Article 55;

(c)   the liability of the payer in accordance with Article 61, including information on the relevant amount;

(d)   how and within what period of time the payment service user is to notify the payment service provider of any unauthorised or incorrectly executed payment transaction in accordance with Article 58 as well as the payment service provider's liability for unauthorised payment transactions in accordance with Article 60;

(e)   the liability of the payment service provider for the execution of payment transactions in accordance with Article 75; and

(f)   the conditions for refund in accordance with Articles 62 and 63;

6.   on changes in and termination of framework contract:

(a)   if agreed, information that the payment service user will be deemed to have accepted changes in the conditions in accordance with Article 44, unless he notifies the payment service provider that he does not accept them before the date of their proposed date of entry into force;

(b)   the duration of the contract; and

(c)   the right of the payment service user to terminate the framework contract and any agreements relating to termination in accordance with Article 44(1) and Article 45;

7.   on redress:

(a)   any contractual clause on the law applicable to the framework contract and/or the competent courts; and

(b)   the out-of-court complaint and redress procedures available to the payment service user in accordance with Articles 80 to 83.

[6131]

Article 43
Accessibility of information and conditions of the framework contract

At any time during the contractual relationship the payment service user shall have a right to receive, on request, the contractual terms of the framework contract as well as the information and conditions specified in Article 42 on paper or on another durable medium.

[6132]

Article 44
Changes in conditions of the framework contract

1. Any changes in the framework contract as well as the information and conditions specified in Article 42, shall be proposed by the payment service provider in the same way as provided for in Article 41(1) and no later than two months before their proposed date of application.

Where applicable in accordance with point (6)(a) of Article 42, the payment service provider shall inform the payment service user that he is to be deemed to have accepted these changes if he does not notify the payment service provider that he does not accept them before the proposed date of their entry into force. In this case, the payment service provider shall also specify that the payment service user has the right to terminate the framework contract immediately and without charge before the date of the proposed application of the changes.

2. Changes in the interest or exchange rates may be applied immediately and without notice, provided that such a right is agreed upon in the framework contract and that the changes are based on the reference interest or exchange rates agreed on in accordance with Article 42(3)(b) and (c). The payment service user shall be informed of any change in the interest rate at the earliest opportunity in the same way as provided for in Article 41(1), unless the parties have agreed on a specific frequency or manner in which the information is to be provided or made available. However, changes in interest or exchange rates which are more favourable to the payment service users, may be applied without notice.

3. Changes in the interest or exchange rate used in payment transactions shall be implemented and calculated in a neutral manner that does not discriminate against payment service users.

[6133]

Article 45
Termination

1. The payment service user may terminate the framework contract at any time, unless the parties have agreed on a period of notice. Such a period may not exceed one month.

2. Termination of a framework contract concluded for a fixed period exceeding 12 months or for an indefinite period shall be free of charge for the payment service user after the expiry of 12 months. In all other cases charges for the termination shall be appropriate and in line with costs.

3. If agreed in the framework contract, the payment service provider may terminate a framework contract concluded for an indefinite period by giving at least two months' notice in the same way as provided for in Article 41(1).

4. Charges for payment services levied on a regular basis shall be payable by the payment service user only proportionally up to the termination of the contract. If such charges are paid in advance, they shall be reimbursed proportionally.

5. The provisions of this Article are without prejudice to the Member States' laws and regulations governing the rights of the parties to declare the framework contract unenforceable or void.

6. Member States may provide more favourable provisions for payment service users.

[6134]

Article 46
Information before execution of individual payment transactions

In the case of an individual payment transaction under a framework contract initiated by the payer, a payment service provider shall, at the payer's request for this specific payment transaction, provide explicit information on the maximum execution time and the charges payable by the payer and, where applicable, a breakdown of the amounts of any charges.

[6135]

Article 47
Information for the payer on individual payment transactions

1. After the amount of an individual payment transaction is debited from the payer's account or, where the payer does not use a payment account, after the receipt of the payment order, the payer's payment service provider shall provide the payer without undue delay in the same way as laid down in Article 41(1) with the following information:

(a) a reference enabling the payer to identify each payment transaction and, where appropriate, information relating to the payee;

(b) the amount of the payment transaction in the currency in which the payer's payment account is debited or in the currency used for the payment order;

(c) the amount of any charges for the payment transaction and, where applicable, a breakdown thereof, or the interest payable by the payer;

(d) where applicable, the exchange rate used in the payment transaction by the payer's payment service provider, and the amount of the payment transaction after that currency conversion; and

(e)   the debit value date or the date of receipt of the payment order.

2.   A framework contract may include a condition that the information referred to in paragraph 1 is to be provided or made available periodically at least once a month and in an agreed manner which allows the payer to store and reproduce information unchanged.

3.   However, Member States may require payment service providers to provide information on paper once a month free of charge.

[6136]

Article 48
Information for the payee on individual payment transactions

1.   After the execution of an individual payment transaction, the payee's payment service provider shall provide the payee without undue delay in the same way as laid down in Article 41(1) with the following information:

(a)   the reference enabling the payee to identify the payment transaction and, where appropriate, the payer, and any information transferred with the payment transaction;

(b)   the amount of the payment transaction in the currency in which the payee's payment account is credited;

(c)   the amount of any charges for the payment transaction and, where applicable, a breakdown thereof, or the interest payable by the payee;

(d)   where applicable, the exchange rate used in the payment transaction by the payee's payment service provider, and the amount of the payment transaction before that currency conversion; and

(e)   the credit value date.

2.   A framework contract may include a condition that the information referred to in paragraph 1 is to be provided or made available periodically at least once a month and in an agreed manner which allows the payee to store and reproduce information unchanged.

3.   However, Member States may require payment service providers to provide information on paper once a month free of charge.

[6137]

CHAPTER 4
COMMON PROVISIONS

Article 49
Currency and currency conversion

1.   Payments shall be made in the currency agreed between the parties.

2.   Where a currency conversion service is offered prior to the initiation of the payment transaction and where that currency conversion service is offered at the point of sale or by the payee, the party offering the currency conversion service to the payer shall disclose to the payer all charges as well as the exchange rate to be used for converting the payment transaction.

The payer shall agree to the currency conversion service on that basis.

[6138]

Article 50
Information on additional charges or reductions

1.   Where, for the use of a given payment instrument, the payee requests a charge or offers a reduction, the payee shall inform the payer thereof prior to the initiation of the payment transaction.

2.   Where, for the use of a given payment instrument, a payment service provider or a third party requests a charge, he shall inform the payment service user thereof prior to the initiation of the payment transaction.

[6139]

TITLE IV
RIGHTS AND OBLIGATIONS IN RELATION TO THE PROVISION AND USE OF PAYMENT SERVICES

CHAPTER 1
COMMON PROVISIONS

Article 51
Scope

1.   Where the payment service user is not a consumer, the parties may agree that Article 52(1), the second subparagraph of Article 54(2), and Articles 59, 61, 62, 63, 66 and 75 shall not apply in whole or in part. The parties may also agree on a time period different from that laid down in Article 58.

2. Member States may provide that Article 83 does not apply where the payment service user is not a consumer.

3. Member States may provide that provisions in this Title are applied to micro enterprises in the same way as to consumers.

4. This Directive shall be without prejudice to national measures implementing Directive 87/102/EEC. This Directive shall also be without prejudice to other relevant Community or national legislation regarding conditions for granting credit to consumers not harmonised by this Directive that are in conformity with Community law.

[6140]

Article 52
Charges applicable

1. The payment service provider may not charge the payment service user for fulfilment of its information obligations or corrective and preventive measures under this Title, unless otherwise specified in Articles 65(1), 66(5) and 74(2). Those charges shall be agreed between the payment service user and the payment service provider and shall be appropriate and in line with the payment service provider's actual costs.

2. Where a payment transaction does not involve any currency conversion, Member States shall require that the payee pays the charges levied by his payment service provider, and the payer pays the charges levied by his payment service provider.

3. The payment service provider shall not prevent the payee from requesting from the payer a charge or from offering him a reduction for the use of a given payment instrument. However, Member States may forbid or limit the right to request charges taking into account the need to encourage competition and promote the use of efficient payment instruments.

[6141]

Article 53
Derogation for low value payment instruments and electronic money

1. In the case of payment instruments which according to the framework contract, solely concern individual payment transactions not exceeding EUR 30 or which either have a spending limit of EUR 150 or store funds which do not exceed EUR 150 at any time payment service providers may agree with their payment service users that:
   (a) Article 56(1)(b) and Article 57(1)(c) and (d) as well as Article 61(4) and (5) do not apply if the payment instrument does not allow its blocking or prevention of its further use;
   (b) Articles 59, 60 and Article 61(1) and (2) do not apply if the payment instrument is used anonymously or the payment service provider is not in a position for other reasons which are intrinsic to the payment instrument to prove that a payment transaction was authorised;
   (c) by way of derogation from Article 65(1), the payment service provider is not required to notify the payment service user of the refusal of a payment order, if the non-execution is apparent from the context;
   (d) by way of derogation from Article 66, the payer may not revoke the payment order after transmitting the payment order or giving his consent to execute the payment transaction to the payee;
   (e) by way of derogation from Articles 69 and 70, other execution periods apply.

2. For national payment transactions, Member States or their competent authorities may reduce or double the amounts referred to in paragraph 1. They may increase them for prepaid payment instruments up to EUR 500.

3. Articles 60 and 61 shall apply also to electronic money within the meaning of Article 1(3)(b) of Directive 2000/46/EC, except where the payer's payment service provider does not have the ability to freeze the payment account or block the payment instrument. Member States may limit that derogation to payment accounts or payment instruments of a certain value.

[6142]

CHAPTER 2
AUTHORISATION OF PAYMENT TRANSACTIONS

Article 54
Consent and withdrawal of consent

1. Member States shall ensure that a payment transaction is considered to be authorised only if the payer has given consent to execute the payment transaction. A payment transaction may be authorised by the payer prior to or, if agreed between the payer and his payment service provider, after the execution of the payment transaction.

2. Consent to execute a payment transaction or a series of payment transactions shall be given in the form agreed between the payer and his payment service provider.

In the absence of such consent, a payment transaction shall be considered to be unauthorised.

3. Consent may be withdrawn by the payer at any time, but no later than the point in time of irrevocability under Article 66. Consent to execute a series of payment transactions may also be withdrawn with the effect that any future payment transaction is to be considered as unauthorised.

4. The procedure for giving consent shall be agreed between the payer and the payment service provider.

[6143]

Article 55
Limits of the use of the payment instrument

1. In cases where a specific payment instrument is used for the purposes of giving consent, the payer and his payment service provider may agree on spending limits for payment transactions executed through that payment instrument.

2. If agreed in the framework contract, the payment service provider may reserve the right to block the payment instrument for objectively justified reasons related to the security of the payment instrument, the suspicion of unauthorised or fraudulent use of the payment instrument or, in the case of a payment instrument with a credit line, a significantly increased risk that the payer may be unable to fulfil his liability to pay.

3. In such cases the payment service provider shall inform the payer of the blocking of the payment instrument and the reasons for it in an agreed manner, where possible, before the payment instrument is blocked and at the latest immediately thereafter, unless giving such information would compromise objectively justified security reasons or is prohibited by other relevant Community or national legislation.

4. The payment service provider shall unblock the payment instrument or replace it with a new payment instrument once the reasons for blocking no longer exist.

[6144]

Article 56
Obligations of the payment service user in relation to payment instruments

1. The payment service user entitled to use a payment instrument shall have the following obligations:

    (a)   to use the payment instrument in accordance with the terms governing the issue and use of the payment instrument; and

    (b)   to notify the payment service provider, or the entity specified by the latter, without undue delay on becoming aware of loss, theft or misappropriation of the payment instrument or of its unauthorised use.

2. For the purposes of paragraph 1(a), the payment service user shall, in particular, as soon as he receives a payment instrument, take all reasonable steps to keep its personalised security features safe.

[6145]

Article 57
Obligations of the payment service provider in relation to payment instruments

1. The payment service provider issuing a payment instrument shall have the following obligations:

    (a)   to make sure that the personalised security features of the payment instrument are not accessible to parties other than the payment service user entitled to use the payment instrument, without prejudice to the obligations on the payment service user set out in Article 56;

    (b)   to refrain from sending an unsolicited payment instrument, except where a payment instrument already given to the payment service user is to be replaced;

    (c)   to ensure that appropriate means are available at all times to enable the payment service user to make a notification pursuant to Article 56(1)(b) or request unblocking pursuant to Article 55(4); on request, the payment service provider shall provide the payment service user with the means to prove, for 18 months after notification, that he made such notification; and

    (d)   to prevent all use of the payment instrument once notification pursuant to Article 56(1)(b) has been made.

2. The payment service provider shall bear the risk of sending a payment instrument to the payer or of sending any personalised security features of it.

[6146]

Article 58
Notification of unauthorised or incorrectly executed payment transactions

The payment service user shall obtain rectification from the payment service provider only if he notifies his payment service provider without undue delay on becoming aware of any unauthorised or incorrectly executed payment transactions giving rise to a claim, including that under Article 75, and no later than 13 months after the debit date, unless, where applicable, the payment service provider has failed to provide or make available the information on that payment transaction in accordance with Title III.

[6147]

Article 59
Evidence on authentication and execution of payment transactions

1.   Member States shall require that, where a payment service user denies having authorised an executed payment transaction or claims that the payment transaction was not correctly executed, it is for his payment service provider to prove that the payment transaction was authenticated, accurately recorded, entered in the accounts and not affected by a technical breakdown or some other deficiency.

2.   Where a payment service user denies having authorised an executed payment transaction, the use of a payment instrument recorded by the payment service provider shall in itself not necessarily be sufficient to prove either that the payment transaction was authorised by the payer or that the payer acted fraudulently or failed with intent or gross negligence to fulfil one or more of his obligations under Article 56.

[6148]

Article 60
Payment service provider's liability for unauthorised payment transactions

1.   Member States shall ensure that, without prejudice to Article 58, in the case of an unauthorised payment transaction, the payer's payment service provider refunds to the payer immediately the amount of the unauthorised payment transaction and, where applicable, restores the debited payment account to the state in which it would have been had the unauthorised payment transaction not taken place.

2.   Further financial compensation may be determined in accordance with the law applicable to the contract concluded between the payer and his payment service provider.

[6149]

Article 61
Payer's liability for unauthorised payment transactions

1.   By way of derogation from Article 60 the payer shall bear the losses relating to any unauthorised payment transactions, up to a maximum of EUR 150, resulting from the use of a lost or stolen payment instrument or, if the payer has failed to keep the personalised security features safe, from the misappropriation of a payment instrument.

2.   The payer shall bear all the losses relating to any unauthorised payment transactions if he incurred them by acting fraudulently or by failing to fulfil one or more of his obligations under Article 56 with intent or gross negligence. In such cases, the maximum amount referred to in paragraph 1 of this Article shall not apply.

3.   In cases where the payer has neither acted fraudulently nor with intent failed to fulfil his obligations under Article 56, Member States may reduce the liability referred to in paragraphs 1 and 2 of this Article, taking into account, in particular, the nature of the personalised security features of the payment instrument and the circumstances under which it was lost, stolen or misappropriated.

4.   The payer shall not bear any financial consequences resulting from use of the lost, stolen or misappropriated payment instrument after notification in accordance with Article 56(1)(b), except where he has acted fraudulently.

5.   If the payment service provider does not provide appropriate means for the notification at all times of a lost, stolen or misappropriated payment instrument, as required under Article 57(1)(c), the payer shall not be liable for the financial consequences resulting from use of that payment instrument, except where he has acted fraudulently.

[6150]

Article 62
Refunds for payment transactions initiated by or through a payee

1.   Member States shall ensure that a payer is entitled to a refund from his payment service provider of an authorised payment transaction initiated by or through a payee which has already been executed, if the following conditions are met:
  (a)   the authorisation did not specify the exact amount of the payment transaction when the authorisation was made; and
  (b)   the amount of the payment transaction exceeded the amount the payer could reasonably have expected taking into account his previous spending pattern, the conditions in his framework contract and relevant circumstances of the case.

At the payment service provider's request, the payer shall provide factual elements relating to such conditions.

The refund consists of the full amount of the executed payment transaction.

For direct debits the payer and his payment service provider may agree in the framework contract that the payer is entitled to a refund from his payment service provider even though the conditions for refund in the first subparagraph are not met.

2. However, for the purposes of point (b) of the first subparagraph of paragraph 1, the payer may not rely on currency exchange reasons if the reference exchange rate agreed with his payment service provider in accordance with Articles 37(1)(d) and 42(3)(b) was applied.

3. It may be agreed in the framework contract between the payer and the payment service provider that the payer has no right to a refund where he has given his consent to execute the payment transaction directly to his payment service provider and, where applicable, information on the future payment transaction was provided or made available in an agreed manner to the payer for at least four weeks before the due date by the payment service provider or by the payee.

[6151]

Article 63
Requests for refunds for payment transactions initiated by or through a payee

1. Member States shall ensure that the payer can request the refund referred to in Article 62 of an authorised payment transaction initiated by or through a payee for a period of eight weeks from the date on which the funds were debited.

2. Within ten business days of receiving a request for a refund, the payment service provider shall either refund the full amount of the payment transaction or provide justification for refusing the refund, indicating the bodies to which the payer may refer the matter in accordance with Articles 80 to 83 if he does not accept the justification provided.

The payment service provider's right under the first subparagraph to refuse the refund shall not apply in the case set out in the fourth subparagraph of Article 62(1).

[6152]

CHAPTER 3
EXECUTION OF PAYMENT TRANSACTIONS

Section 1
Payment Orders and Amounts Transferred

Article 64
Receipt of payment orders

1. Member States shall ensure that the point in time of receipt is the time when the payment order transmitted directly by the payer or indirectly by or through a payee is received by the payer's payment service provider. If the point in time of receipt is not on a business day for the payer's payment service provider, the payment order shall be deemed to have been received on the following business day. The payment service provider may establish a cut-off time near the end of a business day beyond which any payment order received shall be deemed to have been received on the following business day.

2. If the payment service user initiating a payment order and his payment service provider agree that execution of the payment order shall start on a specific day or at the end of a certain period or on the day on which the payer has set funds at his payment service provider's disposal, the point in time of receipt for the purposes of Article 69 is deemed to be the agreed day. If the agreed day is not a business day for the payment service provider, the payment order received shall be deemed to have been received on the following business day.

[6153]

Article 65
Refusal of payment orders

1. Where the payment service provider refuses to execute a payment order, the refusal and, if possible, the reasons for it and the procedure for correcting any factual mistakes that led to the refusal shall be notified to the payment service user, unless prohibited by other relevant Community or national legislation.

The payment service provider shall provide or make available the notification in an agreed manner at the earliest opportunity, and in any case, within the periods specified in Article 69.

The framework contract may include a condition that the payment service provider may charge for such a notification if the refusal is objectively justified.

2. In cases where all the conditions set out in the payer's framework contract are met, the payer's payment service provider shall not refuse to execute an authorised payment order

irrespective of whether the payment order is initiated by a payer or by or through a payee, unless prohibited by other relevant Community or national legislation.

3. For the purposes of Articles 69 and 75 a payment order of which execution has been refused shall be deemed not to have been received.

[6154]

Article 66
Irrevocability of a payment order

1. Member States shall ensure that the payment service user may not revoke a payment order once it has been received by the payer's payment service provider, unless otherwise specified in this Article.

2. Where the payment transaction is initiated by or through the payee, the payer may not revoke the payment order after transmitting the payment order or giving his consent to execute the payment transaction to the payee.

3. However, in the case of a direct debit and without prejudice to refund rights the payer may revoke the payment order at the latest by the end of the business day preceding the day agreed for debiting the funds.

4. In the case referred to in Article 64(2) the payment service user may revoke a payment order at the latest by the end of the business day preceding the agreed day.

5. After the time limits specified in paragraphs 1 to 4, the payment order may be revoked only if agreed between the payment service user and his payment service provider. In the case referred to in paragraphs 2 and 3, the payee's agreement shall also be required. If agreed in the framework contract, the payment service provider may charge for revocation.

[6155]

Article 67
Amounts transferred and amounts received

1. Member States shall require the payment service provider of the payer, the payment service provider of the payee and any intermediaries of the payment service providers to transfer the full amount of the payment transaction and refrain from deducting charges from the amount transferred.

2. However, the payee and his payment service provider may agree that the payment service provider deduct its charges from the amount transferred before crediting it to the payee. In such a case, the full amount of the payment transaction and charges shall be separated in the information given to the payee.

3. If any charges other than those referred to in paragraph 2 are deducted from the amount transferred, the payment service provider of the payer shall ensure that the payee receives the full amount of the payment transaction initiated by the payer. In cases where the payment transaction is initiated by or through the payee, his payment service provider shall ensure that the full amount of the payment transaction is received by the payee.

[6156]

Section 2
Execution Time and Value Date

Article 68
Scope

1. This Section shall apply to:
   - (a) payment transactions in euro;
   - (b) national payment transactions in the currency of the Member State outside the euro area concerned; and
   - (c) payment transactions involving only one currency conversion between the euro and the currency of a Member State outside the euro area, provided that the required currency conversion is carried out in the Member State outside the euro area concerned and, in the case of cross-border payment transactions, the cross-border transfer takes place in euro.

2. This Section shall apply to other payment transactions, unless otherwise agreed between the payment service user and his payment service provider, with the exception of Article 73, which is not at the disposal of the parties. However, when the payment service user and his payment service provider agree on a longer period than those laid down in Article 69, for intra-Community payment transactions such period shall not exceed 4 business days following the point in time of receipt in accordance with Article 64.

[6157]

Article 69
Payment transactions to a payment account

1. Member States shall require the payer's payment service provider to ensure that, after the point in time of receipt in accordance with Article 64, the amount of the payment transaction is

credited to the payee's payment service provider's account at the latest by the end of the next business day. Until 1 January 2012, a payer and his payment service provider may agree on a period no longer than three business days. These periods may be extended by a further business day for paper-initiated payment transactions.

2. Member States shall require the payment service provider of the payee to value date and make available the amount of the payment transaction to the payee's payment account after the payment service provider has received the funds in accordance with Article 73.

3. Member States shall require the payee's payment service provider to transmit a payment order initiated by or through the payee to the payer's payment service provider within the time limits agreed between the payee and his payment service provider, enabling settlement, as far as direct debit is concerned, on the agreed due date.

[6158]

Article 70
Absence of payee's payment account with the payment service provider

Where the payee does not have a payment account with the payment service provider, the funds shall be made available to the payee by the payment service provider who receives the funds for the payee within the period specified in Article 69.

[6159]

Article 71
Cash placed on a payment account

Where a consumer places cash on a payment account with that payment service provider in the currency of that payment account, the payment service provider shall ensure that the amount is made available and value dated immediately after the point of time of the receipt of the funds. Where the payment service user is not a consumer, the amount shall be made available and value dated at the latest on the next business day after the receipt of the funds.

[6160]

Article 72
National payment transactions

For national payment transactions, Member States may provide for shorter maximum execution times than those provided for in this Section.

[6161]

Article 73
Value date and availability of funds

1. Member States shall ensure that the credit value date for the payee's payment account is no later than the business day on which the amount of the payment transaction is credited to the payee's payment service provider's account.

The payment service provider of the payee shall ensure that the amount of the payment transaction is at the payee's disposal immediately after that amount is credited to the payee's payment service provider's account.

2. Member States shall ensure that the debit value date for the payer's payment account is no earlier than the point in time at which the amount of the payment transaction is debited to that payment account.

[6162]

Section 3
Liability

Article 74
Incorrect unique identifiers

1. If a payment order is executed in accordance with the unique identifier, the payment order shall be deemed to have been executed correctly with regard to the payee specified by the unique identifier.

2. If the unique identifier provided by the payment service user is incorrect, the payment service provider shall not be liable under Article 75 for non-execution or defective execution of the payment transaction.

However the payer's payment service provider shall make reasonable efforts to recover the funds involved in the payment transaction.

If agreed in the framework contract, the payment service provider may charge the payment service user for recovery.

3. If the payment service user provides information additional to that specified in Articles 37(1)(a) or 42(2)(b), the payment service provider shall be liable only for the execution of payment transactions in accordance with the unique identifier provided by the payment service user.

[6163]

Article 75
Non-execution or defective execution

1. Where a payment order is initiated by the payer, his payment service provider shall, without prejudice to Article 58, Article 74(2) and (3), and Article 78, be liable to the payer for correct execution of the payment transaction, unless he can prove to the payer and, where relevant, to the payee's payment service provider that the payee's payment service provider received the amount of the payment transaction in accordance with Article 69(1), in which case, the payee's payment service provider shall be liable to the payee for the correct execution of the payment transaction.

Where the payer's payment service provider is liable under the first subparagraph, he shall without undue delay refund to the payer the amount of the non-executed or defective payment transaction and, where applicable, restore the debited payment account to the state in which it would have been had the defective payment transaction not taken place.

Where the payee's payment service provider is liable under the first subparagraph, he shall immediately place the amount of the payment transaction at the payee's disposal and, where applicable, credit the corresponding amount to the payee's payment account.

In the case of a non-executed or defectively executed payment transaction where the payment order is initiated by the payer, his payment service provider shall regardless of liability under this paragraph, on request, make immediate efforts to trace the payment transaction and notify the payer of the outcome.

2. Where a payment order is initiated by or through the payee, his payment service provider shall, without prejudice to Article 58, Article 74(2) and (3), and Article 78, be liable to the payee for correct transmission of the payment order to the payment service provider of the payer in accordance with Article 69(3). Where the payee's payment service provider is liable under this subparagraph, he shall immediately re-transmit the payment order in question to the payment service provider of the payer.

In addition, the payment service provider of the payee shall, without prejudice to Article 58, Article 74(2) and (3), and Article 78, be liable to the payee for handling the payment transaction in accordance with its obligations under Article 73. Where the payee's payment service provider is liable under this subparagraph, he shall ensure that the amount of the payment transaction is at the payee's disposal immediately after that amount is credited to the payee's payment service provider's account.

In the case of a non-executed or defectively executed payment transaction for which the payee's payment service provider is not liable under the first and second subparagraphs, the payer's payment service provider shall be liable to the payer. Where the payer's payment service provider is so liable he shall, as appropriate and without undue delay, refund to the payer the amount of the non-executed or defective payment transaction and restore the debited payment account to the state in which it would have been had the defective payment transaction not taken place.

In the case of a non-executed or defectively executed payment transaction where the payment order is initiated by or through the payee, his payment service provider shall, regardless of liability under this paragraph, on request, make immediate efforts to trace the payment transaction and notify the payee of the outcome.

3. In addition, payment service providers shall be liable to their respective payment service users for any charges for which they are responsible, and for any interest to which the payment service user is subject as a consequence of non-execution or defective execution of the payment transaction.

[6164]

Article 76
Additional financial compensation

Any financial compensation additional to that provided for under this Section may be determined in accordance with the law applicable to the contract concluded between the payment service user and his payment service provider.

[6165]

Article 77
Right of recourse

1. Where the liability of a payment service provider under Article 75 is attributable to another payment service provider or to an intermediary, that payment service provider or intermediary shall compensate the first payment service provider for any losses incurred or sums paid under Article 75.

2.   Further financial compensation may be determined in accordance with agreements between payment service providers and/or intermediaries and the law applicable to the agreement concluded between them.

[6166]

Article 78
No liability

Liability under Chapter 2 and 3 shall not apply in cases of abnormal and unforeseeable circumstances beyond the control of the party pleading for the application of those circumstances, the consequences of which would have been unavoidable despite all efforts to the contrary, or where a payment service provider is bound by other legal obligations covered by national or Community legislation.

[6167]

CHAPTER 4
DATA PROTECTION

Article 79
Data protection

Member States shall permit the processing of personal data by payment systems and payment service providers when this is necessary to safeguard the prevention, investigation and detection of payment fraud. The processing of such personal data shall be carried out in accordance with Directive 95/46/EC.

[6168]

CHAPTER 5
OUT-OF-COURT COMPLAINT AND REDRESS PROCEDURES FOR THE SETTLEMENT OF DISPUTES

Section 1
Complaint Procedures

Article 80
Complaints

1.   Member States shall ensure that procedures are set up which allow payment service users and other interested parties, including consumer associations, to submit complaints to the competent authorities with regard to payment service providers' alleged infringements of the provisions of national law implementing the provisions of this Directive.

2.   Where appropriate and without prejudice to the right to bring proceedings before a court in accordance with national procedural law, the reply from the competent authorities shall inform the complainant of the existence of the out-of-court complaint and redress procedures set up in accordance with Article 83.

[6169]

Article 81
Penalties

1.   Member States shall lay down the rules on penalties applicable to infringements of the national provisions adopted pursuant to this Directive and shall take all measures necessary to ensure that they are implemented. Such penalties shall be effective, proportionate and dissuasive.

2.   Member States shall notify the Commission of the rules referred to in paragraph 1 and of the competent authorities referred to in Article 82 by 1 November 2009 and shall notify it without delay of any subsequent amendment affecting them.

[6170]

Article 82
Competent authorities

1.   Member States shall take all the measures necessary to ensure that the complaints procedures and penalties provided for in Articles 80(1) and 81(1) respectively are administered by the authorities empowered to ensure compliance with the provisions of national law adopted pursuant to the requirements laid down in this Section.

2.   In the event of infringement or suspected infringement of the provisions of national law adopted pursuant to Titles III and IV, the competent authorities referred to in paragraph 1 shall be those of the home Member State of the payment service provider, except for agents and branches conducted under the right of establishment where the competent authorities shall be those of the host Member State.

[6171]

Section 2
Out-of-Court Redress Procedures

Article 83
Out-of-court redress

1. Member States shall ensure that adequate and effective out-of-court complaint and redress procedures for the settlement of disputes between payment service users and their payment service providers are put in place for disputes concerning rights and obligations arising under this Directive, using existing bodies where appropriate.

2. In the case of cross-border disputes, Member States shall make sure that those bodies cooperate actively in resolving them.

[6172]

TITLE V
IMPLEMENTING MEASURES AND PAYMENTS COMMITTEE

Article 84
Implementing measures

In order to take account of technological and market developments in payment services and to ensure the uniform application of this Directive, the Commission may, in accordance with the regulatory procedure with scrutiny referred to in Article 85(2), adopt implementing measures designed to amend non-essential elements of this Directive and relating to the following:

   (a)   adapting the list of activities in the Annex, in accordance with Articles 2 to 4 and 16;
   (b)   changing the definition of micro enterprise within the meaning of Article 4(26) in accordance with an amendment of Recommendation 2003/361/EC;
   (c)   updating the amounts specified in Articles 26(1) and 61(1) in order to take account of inflation and significant market developments.

[6173]

Article 85
Committee

1. The Commission shall be assisted by a Payments Committee.

2. Where reference is made to this paragraph, Article 5a(1) to (4) and Article 7 of Decision 1999/468/EC shall apply, having regard to the provisions of Article 8 thereof.

[6174]

TITLE VI
FINAL PROVISIONS

Article 86
Full harmonisation

1. Without prejudice to Article 30(2), Article 33, Article 34(2), Article 45(6), Article 47(3), Article 48(3), Article 51(2), Article 52(3), Article 53(2), Article 61(3), and Articles 72 and 88 insofar as this Directive contains harmonised provisions, Member States shall not maintain or introduce provisions other than those laid down in this Directive.

2. Where a Member State makes use of any of the options referred to in paragraph 1, it shall inform the Commission thereof as well as of any subsequent changes. The Commission shall make the information public on a web-site or other easily accessible means.

3. Member States shall ensure that payment service providers do not derogate, to the detriment of payment service users, from the provisions of national law implementing or corresponding to provisions of this Directive except where explicitly provided for therein.

However, payment service providers may decide to grant more favourable terms to payment service users.

[6175]

Article 87
Review

No later than 1 November 2012, the Commission shall present to the European Parliament, the Council, the European Economic and Social Committee and the European Central Bank a report on the implementation and impact of this Directive, in particular on:

   —   the possible need to extend the scope of the Directive to payment transactions in all currencies and to payment transactions where only one of the payment service providers is located in the Community,
   —   the application of Articles 6, 8 and 9 concerning prudential requirements for payment institutions, in particular as regards own funds requirements and safeguarding requirements (ringfencing),

— the possible impact of the granting of credit by payment institutions related to payments services, as set out in Article 16(3),

— the possible impact of the authorisation requirements of payment institutions on competition between payment institutions and other payment service providers as well as on barriers to market entry by new payment service providers,

— the application of Articles 34 and 53 and the possible need to revise the scope of this Directive with respect to low value payment instruments and electronic money, and

— the application and functioning of Articles 69 and 75 for all kinds of payment instruments,

accompanied, where appropriate, by a proposal for its revision.

[6176]

Article 88
Transitional provision

1. Without prejudice to Directive 2005/60/EC or other relevant Community legislation, Member States shall allow legal persons who have commenced before 25 December 2007 the activities of payment institutions within the meaning of this Directive, in accordance with the national law in force to continue those activities within the Member State concerned until 30 April 2011, without authorisation under Article 10. Any such persons who have not been granted authorisation within this period shall be prohibited in accordance with Article 29 to provide payment services.

2. Notwithstanding paragraph 1, an exemption to the authorisation requirement under Article 10 shall be granted to financial institutions that have commenced activities listed in point 4 of Annex I to Directive 2006/48/EC and meet the conditions of point (e) of the first subparagraph of Article 24(1), of that Directive in accordance with national law before 25 December 2007. However, they shall notify the competent authorities of the home Member State of these activities by 25 December 2007. Furthermore, this notification shall include the information demonstrating that they have complied with Article 5(a), (d), (g) to (i), (k) and (l) of this Directive. Where the competent authorities are satisfied that those requirements are complied with, the financial institutions concerned shall be registered in accordance with Article 13 of this Directive. Member States may allow their competent authorities to exempt those financial institutions from the requirements under Article 5.

3. Member States may provide that legal persons referred to in paragraph 1 shall be automatically granted authorisation and entered into the register provided for in Article 13 if the competent authorities already have evidence that the requirements laid down in Articles 5 and 10 are complied with. The competent authorities shall inform the entities concerned before the authorisation is granted.

4. Without prejudice to Directive 2005/60/EC or other relevant Community legislation, Member States may allow natural or legal persons who have commenced the activities of payment institutions within the meaning of this Directive, in accordance with the national law in force before 25 December 2007 and who are eligible for waiver under Article 26 to continue those activities within the Member State concerned for a transitional period not longer than 3 years without being waived in accordance with Article 26 and entered into the register provided for in Article 13. Any such persons who are not waived within this period shall be prohibited in accordance with Article 29 to provide payment services.

[6177]

Articles 89–92

(*Article 89 repeals Directive 97/7/EC, Art 8; Article 90 amends Directive 2002/65/EC, Art 4 and repeals Art 8 at* [5367] *and* [5371]; *Article 91 amends Directive 2005/60/EC, Arts 3, 15, 36 at* [5724], [5736], [5757]; *Article 92 amends Directive 2006/48/EC, Annex I at* [5841Y].)

Article 93
Repeal

Directive 97/5/EC shall be repealed with effect from 1 November 2009.

[6178]

Article 94
Transposition

1. Member States shall bring into force the laws, regulations and administrative provisions necessary to comply with this Directive before 1 November 2009. They shall forthwith inform the Commission thereof.

When they are adopted by Member States, those measures shall contain a reference to this Directive or shall be accompanied by such reference on the occasion of their official publication. The methods of making such reference shall be laid down by Member States.

2.　Member States shall communicate to the Commission the text of the main provisions of national law which they adopt in the field covered by this Directive.

[6179]

Article 95
Entry into force

This Directive shall enter into force on the 20th day following its publication in the Official Journal of the European Union.

[6180]

Article 96
Addressees

This Directive is addressed to the Member States.

[6181]

ANNEX
PAYMENT SERVICES (DEFINITION 3 IN ARTICLE 4)

1.　Services enabling cash to be placed on a payment account as well as all the operations required for operating a payment account.

2.　Services enabling cash withdrawals from a payment account as well as all the operations required for operating a payment account.

3.　Execution of payment transactions, including transfers of funds on a payment account with the user's payment service provider or with another payment service provider:
— execution of direct debits, including one-off direct debits,
— execution of payment transactions through a payment card or a similar device,
— execution of credit transfers, including standing orders.

4.　Execution of payment transactions where the funds are covered by a credit line for a payment service user:
— execution of direct debits, including one-off direct debits,
— execution of payment transactions through a payment card or a similar device,
— execution of credit transfers, including standing orders.

5.　Issuing and/or acquiring of payment instruments.

6.　Money remittance.

7.　Execution of payment transactions where the consent of the payer to execute a payment transaction is given by means of any telecommunication, digital or IT device and the payment is made to the telecommunication, IT system or network operator, acting only as an intermediary between the payment service user and the supplier of the goods and services.

[6182]–[6500]

Appendix 3

DOMESTIC IMPLEMENTATION OF EC DIRECTIVES

NOTES

The table below list the UK legislative measures implementing the Directives set out in Part IV of this Handbook. Where implementation was *also* achieved by non-legislative measures (eg, FSA Rules) those are not listed. Repealed Directives are printed in italics.

Directive	Implemented in the UK by
85/577/EEC: Council Directive to protect the consumer in respect of contracts negotiated away from business premises	**SI 2008/1816** Cancellation of Contracts made in a Consumer's Home or Place of Work etc Regulations 2008 at **[4163A]** (revoking and replacing the original implementing Consumer Protection (Cancellation of Contracts Concluded away from Business Premises) Regulations 1987, SI 1987/2117)
85/611/EEC Council Directive on the coordination of laws, regulations and administrative provisions relating to undertakings for collective investment in transferable securities (UCITS)	**SI 2001/2383** Financial Services and Markets Act 2000 (Collective Investment Schemes constituted in other EEA States) Regulations 2001 at **[2385]**
	SI 2003/693 Financial Services and Markets Act 2000 (Disclosure of Confidential Information) (Amendment) Regulations 2003
	SI 2003/2066 Collective Investment Schemes (Miscellaneous Amendments) Regulations 2003
	SI 2003/2067 Financial Services and Markets Act 2000 (Promotion of Collective Investment Schemes etc) (Exemptions) (Amendment) Order 2003
	SI 2008/346 Regulated Covered Bonds Regulations 2008 at **[4080]**
91/308/EEC Council Directive on prevention of the use of the financial system for the purpose of money laundering (Repealed by European Parliament and Council Directive 2005/60/EC, as from 15 December 2007 (see below))	**SI 1994/1757** Drug Trafficking Offences Act 1986 (Crown Servants and Regulators etc) Regulations 1994
	SI 2003/3075 Money Laundering Regulations 2003 (revoked; see the note at **[3787]**)
93/6/EEC Council Directive on the capital adequacy of investment firms and credit institutions (Repealed by European Parliament and Council Directive 2006/49/EC, as from 20 July 2006 (see below))	**SI 2004/1862** Financial Conglomerates and Other Financial Groups Regulations 2004 at **[2723]**
93/13/EEC Council Directive on unfair terms in consumer contracts	**SI 1999/2083** Unfair Terms in Consumer Contracts Regulations 1999 at **[3536]**
	SI 2001/1186 Unfair Terms in Consumer Contracts (Amendment) Regulations 2001
93/22/EEC Council Directive on investment services in the securities field (Repealed by European Parliament and Council Directive 2004/39/EC, as from 1 November 2007 (see below))	**SI 2001/544** Financial Services and Markets Act 2000 (Regulated Activities) Order 2001 at **[2010]**
	SI 2001/2509 Financial Services and Markets Act 2000 (Consultation with Competent Authorities) Regulations 2001 at **[2421]**
	SI 2001/2639 Financial Services and Markets Act 2000 Own-initiative Power) (Overseas Regulators) Regulations 2001 at **[2484]**
	SI 2003/693 Financial Services and Markets Act 2000 (Disclosure of Confidential Information) (Amendment) Regulations 2003
	SI 2004/1862 Financial Conglomerates and Other Financial Groups Regulations 2004 at **[2723]**

Directive	Implemented in the UK by
97/9/EC Directive of the European Parliament and of the Council on investor-compensation schemes	**SI 2001/1783** Financial Services and Markets Act 2000 (Compensation Scheme: Electing Participants) Regulations 2001 at **[2342]** **SI 2001/2967** Financial Services and Markets Act 2000 (Transitional Provisions, Repeals and Savings) (Financial Services Compensation Scheme) Order 2001
98/26/EC Directive of the European Parliament and of the Council on settlement finality in payment and securities settlement systems	**SI 1999/2979** Financial Markets and Insolvency (Settlement Finality) Regulations 1999 at **[3553A]** **SI 2007/832** Financial Markets and Insolvency (Settlement Finality) (Amendment) Regulations 2007
2000/12/EC Directive of the European Parliament and of the Council relating to the taking up and pursuit of the business of credit institutions (Repealed by European Parliament and Council Directive 2006/48/EC, as from 20 July 2006 (see below))	**SI 2000/2952** Banking Consolidation Directive (Consequential Amendments) Regulations 2000 **SI 2001/2509** Financial Services and Markets Act 2000 (Consultation with Competent Authorities) Regulations 2001 at **[2421]** **SI 2001/2639** Financial Services and Markets Act 2000 (Own-initiative Power) (Overseas Regulators) Regulations 2001 at **[2484]** **SI 2001/3084** Financial Services and Markets Act 2000 (Gibraltar) Order 2001 at **[2495]** **SI 2002/682** Financial Services and Markets Act 2000 (Regulated Activities) (Amendment) Order 2002 at **[2666]** **SI 2002/765** Electronic Money (Miscellaneous Amendments) Regulations 2002 **SI 2004/1862** Financial Conglomerates and Other Financial Groups Regulations 2004 at **[2723]**
2000/46/EC Directive of the European Parliament and of the Council on the taking up, pursuit of and prudential supervision of the business of electronic money institutions	**SI 2002/682** Financial Services and Markets Act 2000 (Regulated Activities) (Amendment) Order 2002 at **[2666]** **SI 2002/765** Electronic Money (Miscellaneous Amendments) Regulations 2002
2001/34/EC Directive of the European Parliament and of the Council on the admission of securities to official stock exchange listing and on information to be published on those securities	**SI 2001/3624** Financial Services and Markets Act 2000 (Disclosure of Confidential Information) (Amendment) (No 2) Regulations 2001
2001/107/EC Directive of the European Parliament and of the Council amending Council Directive 85/611/EEC on the coordination of laws, regulations and administrative provisions relating to undertakings for collective investment in transferable securities (UCITS) with a view to regulating management companies and simplified prospectuses	**SI 2003/2066** Collective Investment Schemes (Miscellaneous Amendments) Regulations 2003 **SI 2003/2067** Financial Services and Markets Act 2000 (Promotion of Collective Investment Schemes etc) (Exemptions) (Amendment) Order 2003
2001/108/EC Directive of the European Parliament and of the Council amending Council Directive 85/611/EEC on the coordination of laws, regulations and administrative provisions relating to undertakings for collective investment in transferable securities (UCITS) with regard to investments of UCITS	**SI 2003/2066** Collective Investment Schemes (Miscellaneous Amendments) Regulations 2003 **SI 2003/2067** Financial Services and Markets Act 2000 (Promotion of Collective Investment Schemes etc) (Exemptions) (Amendment) Order 2003 **SI 2008/346** Regulated Covered Bonds Regulations 2008 at **[4080]**

Directive	Implemented in the UK by
2002/47/EC Directive of the European Parliament and of the Council on financial collateral arrangements	**SI 2003/3226** Financial Collateral Arrangements (No 2) Regulations 2003 at **[3818]**
2002/65/EC Directive of the European Parliament and of the Council concerning the distance marketing of consumer financial services and amending Council Directive 90/619/EEC and Directives 97/7/EC and 98/27/EC	**SI 2004/2095** Financial Services (Distance Marketing) Regulations 2004 at **[3892]**
2002/87/EC Directive of the European Parliament and of the Council on the supplementary supervision of credit institutions, insurance undertakings and investment firms in a financial conglomerate and amending Council Directives 73/239/EEC, 79/267/EEC, 92/49/EEC, 92/96/EEC, 93/6/EEC and 93/22/EEC, and Directives 98/78/EC and 2000/12/EC of the European Parliament and of the Council	**SI 2004/1862** Financial Conglomerates and Other Financial Groups Regulations 2004 at **[2723]**
2002/92/EC Directive of the European Parliament and of the Council on insurance mediation	**SI 2003/1473** Insurance Mediation Directive (Miscellaneous Amendments) Regulations 2003 **SI 2003/1476** Financial Services and Markets Act 2000 (Regulated Activities) (Amendment) (No 2) Order 2003
2003/6/EC Directive of the European Parliament and of the Council on insider dealing and market manipulation (market abuse)	**SI 2005/381** Financial Services and Markets Act 2000 (Market Abuse) Regulations 2005 at **[3918]** **SI 2005/382** Investment Recommendation (Media) Regulations 2005 at **[3919]**
2003/71/EC Directive of the European Parliament and of the Council on the prospectus to be published when securities are offered to the public or admitted to trading and amending 2001/34	**SI 2005/1433** Prospectus Regulations 2005 at **[2757]** **SI 2007/2615** Financial Services and Markets Act 2000 (Financial Promotion) (Amendment No 2) Order 2007
2003/124/EC Commission Directive implementing Directive 2003/6/EC of the European Parliament and of the Council as regards the definition and public disclosure of inside information and the definition of market manipulation	**SI 2005/381** Financial Services and Markets Act 2000 (Market Abuse) Regulations 2005 at **[3918]** **SI 2005/382** Investment Recommendation (Media) Regulations 2005 at **[3919]**
2003/125/EC Commission Directive implementing Directive 2003/6/EC of the European Parliament and of the Council as regards the fair presentation of investment recommendations and the disclosure of conflicts of interest	**SI 2005/382** Investment Recommendation (Media) Regulations 2005 at **[3919]**

Directive	Implemented in the UK by
2004/39/EC Directive of the European Parliament and of the Council on markets in financial instruments amending Council Directives 85/611/EEC and 93/6/EEC and Directive 2000/12/EC of the European Parliament and of the Council and repealing Council Directive 93/22/EEC Note: Art 70 (at **[5591]**) provides that Member States shall adopt the laws, regulations and administrative provisions necessary to comply with this Directive by 31 January 2007 and shall apply the measures from 1 November 2007. The original date for transposition was 30 April 2006 but implementation has been delayed following the substitution of Art 70 by Directive 2006/31/EC. Art 2 of the 2006 Directive (at **[5781]**) provides for the same transposition dates as in the amended 2004/39/EC.	**SI 2006/2975** Financial Services and Markets Act 2000 (Markets in Financial Instruments) (Modification of Powers) Regulations 2006 **SI 2006/3384:** Financial Services and Markets Act 2000 (Regulated Activities) (Amendment No 3) Order 2006 **SI 2006/3385:** Financial Services and Markets Act 2000 (EEA Passport Rights) (Amendment) Regulations 2006 **SI 2006/3386** Financial Services and Markets Act 2000 (Recognition Requirements for Investment Exchanges and Clearing Houses) (Amendment) Regulations 2006 **SI 2006/3413** Financial Services and Markets Act 2000 (Disclosure of Confidential Information) (Amendment) Regulations 2006 **SI 2006/3414** Financial Services and Markets Act 2000 (Appointed Representatives) (Amendment) Regulations 2006 **SI 2007/124** Uncertificated Securities (Amendment) Regulations 2007 **SI 2007/125** Financial Services and Markets Act 2000 (Exemption) (Amendment) Order 2007 **SI 2007/126** Financial Services and Markets Act 2000 (Markets in Financial Instruments) Regulations 2007 **SI 2007/207** Terrorism Act 2000 (Business in the Regulated Sector) Order 2007[1] **SI 2007/208** Proceeds of Crime Act 2002 (Business in the Regulated Sector) Order 2007[2] **SI 2007/763** Financial Services and Markets Act 2000 (Markets in Financial Instruments) (Amendment) Regulations 2007 **2007/2160** Financial Services and Markets Act 2000 (Markets in Financial Instruments) (Amendment No 2) Regulations 2007 **2007/2932** Markets in Financial Instruments Directive (Consequential Amendments) Regulations 2007 **2008/3053** Definition of Financial Instrument Order 2008
2004/72/EC Commission Directive implementing Directive 2003/6/EC of the European Parliament and of the Council as regards accepted market practices, the definition of inside information in relation to derivatives on commodities, the drawing up of lists of insiders, the notification of managers' transactions and the notification of suspicious transactions	**SI 2005/381** Financial Services and Markets Act 2000 (Market Abuse) Regulations 2005 at **[3918]**
2004/109/EC Directive of the European Parliament and of the Council on the harmonisation of transparency requirements in relation to information about issuers whose securities are admitted to trading on a regulated market and amending Directive 2001/34/EC	**Companies Act 2006** ie, ss 1265–1268, 1270–1272 of the 2006 Act in Part 43 **SI 2008/623** Companies (Defective Accounts and Directors' Reports) (Authorised Person) and Supervision of Accounts and Reports (Prescribed Body) Order 2008 (revoking and replacing the original implementing Supervision of Accounts and Reports (Prescribed Body) Order 2007, SI 2007/2583)
2005/60/EC Directive of the European Parliament and of the Council on the prevention of the use of the financial system for the purpose of money laundering and terrorist financing	**SI 2007/2157** Money Laundering Regulations 2007 at **[2877AA]** **SI 2007/3287** Proceeds of Crime Act 2002 (Business in the Regulated Sector and Supervisory Authorities) Order 2007 **SI 2007/3288** Terrorism Act 2000 (Business in the Regulated Sector and Supervisory Authorities) Order 2007 **SI 2007/3398** Terrorism Act 2000 and Proceeds of Crime Act 2002 (Amendment) Regulations 2007

Directive	Implemented in the UK by
2006/31/EC Directive of the European Parliament and of the Council amending Directive 2004/39/EC on markets in financial instruments, as regards certain deadlines	See 2004/39/EC above
2006/48/EC Directive of the European Parliament and of the Council relating to the taking up and pursuit of the business of credit institutions (recast)	**SI 2006/3221** Capital Requirements Regulations 2006 at **[4022]** **SI 2008/346** Regulated Covered Bonds Regulations 2008 at **[4080]** Note: this Directive is a re-enactment of Directive 2000/12/EC with certain new provisions. As such, only the new provisions require transposition (as to which see Art 157 at **[5840]**). As to the transposition of Directive 2000/12/EC, see above
2006/49/EC Directive of the European Parliament and of the Council on the capital adequacy of investment firms and credit institutions (recast)	**SI 2006/3221** Capital Requirements Regulations 2006 at **[4022]** Note: this Directive is a re-enactment of Directive 93/6/EEC with certain new provisions. As such, only the new provisions require transposition (as to which see Art 49 at **[5895]**). As to the transposition of Directive 93/6/EEC, see above
2006/70/EC Commission Directive laying down implementing measures for Directive 2005/60/EC of the European Parliament and of the Council as regards the definition of politically exposed person and the technical criteria for simplified customer due diligence procedures and for exemption on grounds of a financial activity conducted on an occasional or very limited basis	**SI 2007/2157** Money Laundering Regulations 2007 at **[2877AA]** **SI 2007/3299** Money Laundering (Amendment) Regulations 2007
2006/73/EC Commission Directive implementing Directive 2004/39/EC of the European Parliament and of the Council as regards organisational requirements and operating conditions for investment firms and defined terms for the purposes of that Directive	**SI 2006/2975** Financial Services and Markets Act 2000 (Markets in Financial Instruments) (Modification of Powers) Regulations 2006
2007/14/EC Commission Directive laying down detailed rules for the implementation of certain provisions of Directive 2004/109/EC on the harmonisation of transparency requirements in relation to information about issuers whose securities are admitted to trading on a regulated market	Implementation achieved via the FSA's Transparency Obligations Directive (Disclosure and Transparency Rules) Instrument 2006. Note that the FSA published the final Rules before the Commission published the final Level 2 Directive 2007/14/EC, the Rules were drafted on the basis of the Directive's final text. No legislative measures required
2007/16/EC Commission Directive implementing Council Directive 85/611/EEC on the coordination of laws, regulations and administrative provisions relating to undertakings for collective investment in transferable securities (UCITS) as regards the clarification of certain definitions	FSA's UCITS Eligible Assets Directive and Other Amendments Instrument 2008 (which amends the FSA UCITS Prudential Sourcebook (UPRU)). No legislative measures required.
2007/64/EC Directive of the European Parliament and of the Council on payment services in the internal market amending Directives 97/7/EC, 2002/65/EC, 2005/60/EC and 2006/48/EC and repealing Directive 97/5/EC	**SI 2009/209** Payment Services Regulations 2009

NOTES

[1]   This Order amended Sch 3A, Pt 1 to the Terrorism Act 2000 and became spent following the substitution of that Part by SI 2007/3288.

[2]   This Order amended Sch 9, Pt 1 to the Proceeds of Crime Act 2002 and became spent following the substitution of that Part by SI 2007/3287.

[6500]

NOTES

This Order amends S.I. No. 4 to the Tenth ... of 2000 and became spent following the assignment serial Part by S.I. 2001/284.

This Order amends S.I. No. 4 to the Regulations of 2000 and became spent following the ... signature and then Part by S.I. 2001/284.

15-001

PART V
OTHER MATERIALS

A: JOINT MONEY LAUNDERING STEERING GROUP MATERIALS

JMLSG
THE JOINT MONEY LAUNDERING STEERING GROUP

PREVENTION OF MONEY LAUNDERING/ COMBATING TERRORIST FINANCING

GUIDANCE FOR THE UK FINANCIAL SECTOR
PART I

December 2007

© Joint Money Laundering Steering Group Limited 2007. All Rights Reserved.

Editorial note:

The Joint Money Laundering Steering Group is a non-statutory body made up of the leading trade associations in the UK financial services industry. Its aim is to promulgate good practice in countering money laundering and to give practical assistance in interpreting the UK Money Laundering Regulations. This is primarily achieved by the publication of industry guidance. The Guidance sets out what is expected of firms and their staff in relation to the prevention of money laundering and terrorist financing, but allows them some discretion as to how they apply the requirements of the UK AML/CTF regime in the particular circumstances of the firm, and its products, services, transactions and customers. Money laundering and terrorist financing risks are closely related to the risks of other financial crime, such as fraud. Fraud and market abuse, as separate offences, are not dealt with in the Guidance. The Guidance does, however, apply to dealing with any proceeds of crime that arise from these activities.

This Guidance is reproduced including the amendments made to it and published by the JMLSG on 26 November 2008. These were the substitution of para 5.3.77, para 5.3.211 and the whole of Chapter 6.

See also the further proposed amendments to this Guidance (ie, a proposed addition this Part to provide industry guidance on compliance with directions issued under the Counter-Terrorism Act 2008, Sch 7). The proposed amendments were published on 21 January 2009 and comments on them are invited by 20 February 2009.

Both are available on the JMLSG website at: www.jmlsg.org.uk/

Contents

Preface

PREFACE

1.   In the UK, there has been a long-standing obligation to have effective procedures in place to detect and prevent money laundering. The UK Money Laundering Regulations, applying to financial institutions, date from 1993. The offence of money laundering was contained in various acts of parliament (such as the Criminal Justice Act 1988 and the Drug Trafficking Offences Act 1986). The Proceeds of Crime Act 2002 (POCA) consolidated, updated and reformed the law relating to money laundering to include any dealing in criminal property. Specific obligations to combat terrorist financing were set out in the Terrorism Act 2000. Many of the procedures which will be appropriate to address these obligations are similar, and firms can often employ the same systems and controls to meet them.

Purpose of the guidance

2.   The purpose of this guidance is to:
   ●   outline the legal and regulatory framework for AML/CTF requirements and systems across the financial services sector;
   ●   interpret the requirements of the relevant law and regulations, and how they may be implemented in practice;
   ●   indicate good industry practice in AML/CTF procedures through a proportionate, risk-based approach; and
   ●   assist firms to design and implement the systems and controls necessary to mitigate the risks of the firm being used in connection with money laundering and the financing of terrorism.

Scope of the guidance

3.   This guidance sets out what is expected of firms and their staff in relation to the prevention of money laundering and terrorist financing, but allows them some discretion as to how they apply the requirements of the UK AML/CTF regime in the particular circumstances of the firm, and its products, services, transactions and customers.

4.   This guidance relates solely to how firms should fulfil their obligations under the AML/CTF law and regulations. It is important that customers understand that production of the required evidence of identity does not automatically qualify them for access to the product or service they may be seeking; firms bring to bear other, commercial considerations in deciding whether particular customers should be taken on.

What is the offence of money laundering?

5.   Money laundering takes many forms, including:

- trying to turn money raised through criminal activity into 'clean' money (that is, classic money laundering);
- handling the benefit of acquisitive crimes such as theft, fraud and tax evasion;
- handling stolen goods;
- being directly involved with any criminal or terrorist property, or entering into arrangements to facilitate the laundering of criminal or terrorist property; and
- criminals investing the proceeds of their crimes in the whole range of financial products.

6.   The techniques used by money launderers constantly evolve to match the source and amount of funds to be laundered, and the legislative/regulatory/law enforcement environment of the market in which the money launderer wishes to operate. More information on the ways in which particular financial services businesses, products, relationships and technologies may be used by money launderers and terrorist financiers, along with some case study examples, is at www.jmlsg.org.uk.

7.   There are three broad groups of offences related to money laundering that firms need to avoid committing. These are:
- knowingly assisting (in a number of specified ways) in concealing, or entering into arrangements for the acquisition, use, and/or possession of, criminal property;
- failing to report knowledge, suspicion, or where there are reasonable grounds for knowing or suspecting, that another person is engaged in money laundering; and
- tipping off, or prejudicing an investigation.

8.   It is also a separate offence under the ML Regulations not to establish adequate and appropriate policies and procedures in place to forestall and prevent money laundering (regardless of whether or not money laundering actually takes place).

The guidance also covers terrorist financing

9.   There can be considerable similarities between the movement of terrorist property and the laundering of criminal property: some terrorist groups are known to have well established links with organised criminal activity. However, there are two major differences between terrorist property and criminal property more generally:
- often only small amounts are required to commit individual terrorist acts, thus increasing the difficulty of tracking the terrorist property;
- terrorists can be funded from legitimately obtained income, including charitable donations, and it is extremely difficult to identify the stage at which legitimate funds become terrorist property.

10.   Terrorist organisations can, however, require quite significant funding and property to resource their infrastructure. They often control property and funds from a variety of sources and employ modern techniques to manage these funds, and to move them between jurisdictions.

11.   In combating terrorist financing, the obligation on firms is to report any suspicious activity to the authorities. This supports the aims of the law enforcement agencies in relation to the financing of terrorism, by allowing the freezing of property where there are reasonable grounds for suspecting that such property could be used to finance terrorist activity, and depriving terrorists of this property as and when links are established between the property and terrorists or terrorist activity.

What about other financial crime?

12.   Money laundering and terrorist financing risks are closely related to the risks of other financial crime, such as fraud. Fraud and market abuse, as separate offences, are not dealt with in this guidance. The guidance does, however, apply to dealing with any proceeds of crime that arise from these activities. Guidance on fraud-related matters can be found in the Fraud Manager's Reference Guide, published by the British Bankers' Association (copies available at www.bba.org.uk), and Identity Fraud – The UK Manual, published jointly by the Association of Payment and Clearing Services, CIFAS – the UK's Fraud Prevention Service, and the Finance & Leasing Association (copies available at any of www.apacs.org.uk, www.cifas.org.uk, or www.fla.org.uk). An online version of this manual is available at www.idpreventiontraining.com.

13.   Firms increasingly look at fraud and money laundering as part of an overall strategy to tackle financial crime, and there are many similarities – as well as differences – between procedures to tackle the two. When considering money laundering and terrorist financing issues, firms should consider their procedures against fraud and market abuse and how these might reinforce each other. Where responsibilities are given to different departments, there will need to be strong links between those in the firm responsible for managing and reporting on these various areas of risk. When measures involving the public are taken specifically as an anti-fraud measure, the distinction should be made clear.

Who is the guidance addressed to?

14.   The guidance, prepared by JMLSG, is addressed to firms in the industry sectors represented by its member bodies (listed at paragraph 31 below), and to those firms regulated by the FSA. All such firms – which, for the avoidance of doubt, include those which are members of JMLSG trade

associations but not regulated by the FSA, and those regulated by the FSA which are not members of JMLSG trade associations – should have regard to the contents of the guidance.

15.   Financial services firms which are neither members of JMLSG trade associations nor regulated by the FSA are encouraged to have regard to this guidance as industry good practice. Firms which are outside the financial sector, but subject to the ML Regulations, particularly where no specific guidance is issued to them by a body representing their industry, may also find this guidance helpful.

16.   The guidance will be of direct relevance to senior management, nominated officers and MLROs in the financial services industry. The purpose is to give guidance to those who set the firm's risk management policies and its procedures for preventing money laundering and terrorist financing. Although the guidance will be relevant to operational areas, it is expected that these areas will be guided by the firm's own, often more detailed and more specific, internal arrangements, tailored by senior management, nominated officers and MLROs to reflect the risk profile of the firm.

How should the guidance be used?

17.   The guidance gives firms a degree of discretion in how they comply with AML/CTF legislation and regulation, and on the procedures that they put in place for this purpose.

18.   It is not intended that the guidance be applied unthinkingly, as a checklist of steps to take. Firms should encourage their staff to 'think risk' as they carry out their duties within the legal and regulatory framework governing AML/CTF. The FSA has made clear its expectation that FSA-regulated firms address their management of risk in a thoughtful and considered way, and establish and maintain systems and procedures that are appropriate, and proportionate to the risks identified. This guidance assists firms to do this.

19.   When provisions of the statutory requirements and of FSA's regulatory requirements are directly described in the text of the guidance, it uses the term **must**, indicating that these provisions are mandatory. In other cases, the guidance uses the term **should** to indicate ways in which the statutory and regulatory requirements may be satisfied, but allowing for alternative means of meeting the requirements. References to 'must' and 'should' in the text should therefore be construed accordingly.

20.   Many defined terms and abbreviations are used in the guidance; these are highlighted, and their meanings are explained in the Glossary.

The content of the guidance

21.   This guidance emphasises the responsibility of senior management to manage the firm's money laundering and terrorist financing risks, and how this should be carried out on a risk-based approach. It sets out a standard approach to the identification and verification of customers, separating out basic identity from other aspects of customer due diligence measures, as well as giving guidance on the obligation to monitor customer activity.

22.   The guidance incorporates a range of reference material which it is hoped that senior management, nominated officers and MLROs will find helpful in appreciating the overall context of, and obligations within, the UK AML/CTF framework.

23.   The guidance provided by the JMLSG is in two parts. The main text in Part I contains generic guidance that applies across the UK financial sector. Part II provides guidance for a number of specific industry sectors, supplementing the generic guidance contained in Part I.

24.   Part I comprises eight separate chapters, followed by a Glossary of terms and abbreviations, and a number of appendices setting out other generally applicable material. Some of the individual chapters are followed by annexes specific to the material covered in that chapter.

25.   Part I sets out industry guidance on:
- the importance of senior management taking responsibility for effectively managing the money laundering and terrorist financing risks faced by the firm's businesses (Chapter 1);
- appropriate controls in the context of financial crime (Chapter 2);
- the role and responsibilities of the nominated officer and the MLRO (Chapter 3);
- adopting a risk-based approach to the application of CDD measures (Chapter 4);
- helping a firm have confidence that it has properly carried out its CDD obligations, including monitoring customer transactions and activity (Chapter 5);
- the identification and reporting of suspicious activity (Chapter 6);
- staff awareness, training and alertness (Chapter 7);
- record keeping (Chapter 8).

26.   Part II of the guidance comprises the sector specific additional material, which has been principally prepared by practitioners in the relevant sectors. The sectoral guidance is incomplete on its own. It must be read in conjunction with the main guidance set out in Part I of the guidance.

Status of the guidance

27.   POCA requires a court to take account of industry guidance that has been approved by a Treasury minister when considering whether a person within the regulated sector has committed the offence of failing to report where that person knows, suspects, or has reasonable grounds for knowing or suspecting, that another person is engaged in money laundering. Similarly, the Terrorism Act requires a court to take account of such approved industry guidance when considering whether a person within the financial sector has failed to report under that Act. The ML Regulations also provide that a court must take account of similar industry guidance in determining whether a person or institution within the regulated sector has complied with any of the requirements of the ML Regulations.

28.   The FSA Handbook also confirms that the FSA will have regard to whether a firm has followed relevant provisions of this guidance when:

- Considering whether to take action against an FSA-regulated firm in respect of a breach of the relevant provisions in SYSC (see SYSC 3.2, SYSC 5.3, and DEPP 6.2.3); and
- Considering whether to prosecute a breach of the Money Laundering Regulations (see EG 12.1).

29.   The guidance therefore provides a sound basis for firms to meet their legislative and regulatory obligations when tailored by firms to their particular business risk profile. Departures from this guidance, and the rationale for so doing, should be documented, and firms will have to stand prepared to justify departures, for example to the FSA.

Who are the members of JMLSG?

30.   The members of JMLSG are:
Asset Based Finance Association (ABFA)
Association of British Credit Unions (ABCUL)
Association of British Insurers (ABI)
Association of Foreign Banks (AFB)
Association of Friendly Societies (AFS)
Association of Independent Financial Advisers (AIFA)
Association of Private Client Investment Managers and Stockbrokers (APCIMS)
British Bankers' Association (BBA)
British Venture Capital Association (BVCA)
Building Societies Association (BSA)
Council of Mortgage Lenders (CML)
Electronic Money Association (EMA)
Finance & Leasing Association (FLA)
Futures and Options Association (FOA)
Investment Management Association (IMA)
London Investment Banking Association (LIBA)
Tax Incentivised Savings Association (TISA)
Wholesale Market Brokers' Association (WMBA)

[7001]

CHAPTER 1
SENIOR MANAGEMENT RESPONSIBILITY

International recommendations and authorities
- FATF
    - Forty Recommendations (June 2003, as amended October 2004)
    - Nine Special Recommendations on Terrorist Financing (revised October 2004)
- UN Security Council Resolutions 1267 (1999), 1373 (2001) and 1390 (2002)

International regulatory pronouncements
- Basel CDD paper
- IAIS Guidance Paper 5
- IOSCO Principles paper
- Basel Consolidated KYC Risk Management

EU Directives
- First Money Laundering Directive 91/308/EEC
- Second Money Laundering Directive 2001/97/EC
- Third Money Laundering Directive 2005/60/EC
- Implementing Measures Directive 2006/70/EC

EU Regulations
- EC Regulation 2580/2001
- EC Regulation 1781/2006 (the Wire Transfer Regulation)

UK framework
- Legislation
  - FSMA 2000
  - Proceeds of Crime Act 2002 (as amended)
  - Terrorism Act 2000 (as amended by the Anti-terrorism, Crime and Security Act 2001)
  - Money Laundering Regulations 2007
- Financial Sanctions
  - HM Treasury Sanctions Notices and News Releases
- Regulatory regime
  - FSA Handbook –APER, COND, DEPP, PRIN, and SYSC
- Industry guidance

Other matters
- USA PATRIOT Act – extra-territoriality
- Wolfsberg Principles
  - Private Banking
  - Suppression of the Financing of Terrorism
  - Correspondent Banking
- Monitoring, Screening and Searching (appropriate monitoring of transactions and customers)

Core obligations
- Senior management in all firms must:
  - identify, and manage effectively, the risks in their businesses
  - if in the regulated sector, appoint a nominated officer to process disclosures
- Senior management in FSA-regulated firms must appoint an MLRO with certain responsibilities
- Adequate resources must be devoted to AML/CFT
- Potential personal liability if legal obligations not met

Actions required, to be kept under regular review
- Prepare a formal policy statement in relation to money laundering/terrorist financing prevention
- Ensure adequate resources devoted to AML/CFT
- Commission annual report from the MLRO and take any necessary action to remedy deficiencies identified by the report in a timely manner

Introduction

SYSC 3.1.1 R, 3.2.6 R 3.2.6A R	1.1	Being used for money laundering or terrorist financing involves firms in reputational, legal and regulatory risks. Senior management has a responsibility to ensure that the firm's control processes and procedures are appropriately designed and implemented, and are effectively operated to reduce the risk of the firm being used in connection with money laundering or terrorist financing.
	1.2	Senior management in financial firms is accustomed to applying proportionate, risk-based policies across different aspects of its business. A firm should therefore be able to take such an approach to the risk of being used for the purposes of money laundering or terrorist financing. Such an approach would change the emphasis and mindset towards money laundering and terrorist financing without reducing the effectiveness with which the risks are managed.
	1.3	Under a risk-based approach, firms start from the premise that most customers are not money launderers or terrorist financiers. However, firms should have systems in place to highlight those customers who, on criteria established by the firm, may indicate that they present a higher risk of this. The systems and procedures should be proportionate to the risks involved, and should be cost effective.

1.4   Senior management must be fully engaged in the decision making processes, and must take ownership of the risk-based approach, since they will be held accountable if the approach is inadequate. That said, provided the assessment of the risks and the selection of mitigation procedures have been approached in a considered way, all the relevant decisions are properly recorded, and the firm's procedures are followed, the risk of censure should be very small.

International pressure to have effective AML/CTF procedures

1.5   Governments in many countries have enacted legislation to make money laundering and terrorist financing criminal offences, and have legal and regulatory processes in place to enable those engaged in these activities to be identified and prosecuted.

1.6   FATF have issued Forty Recommendations on Money Laundering aimed at setting minimum standards for action in different countries, to ensure that AML efforts are consistent internationally. FATF have also issued Nine Special Recommendations on Terrorist Financing, with the same broad objective as regards CTF. The text of these Recommendations is available at www.fatf-gafi.org.

1.7   Separate from the development of FATF's Recommendations, an EU Directive is targeted at money laundering prevention, and has been implemented in the UK mainly through the Money Laundering Regulations 2007.

1.8   Internationally, the FATF Forty Recommendations, the Basel CDD paper, IAIS Guidance Paper 5 and the IOSCO Principles paper encourage national supervisors of financial firms to require firms in their jurisdictions to follow specific due diligence procedures in relation to customers. In addition, the Basel Committee has issued a paper on Consolidated KYC Risk Management. These organisations explicitly envisage a risk-based approach to AML/CTF being followed by firms.

1.9   The United Nations and the EU have sanctions in place to deny a range of named individuals and organisations, as well as nationals from certain countries, access to the financial services sector. In the UK, HM Treasury issues sanctions notices whenever a new name is added to the list, or when any details are amended.

1.10   The private sector Wolfsberg Group of banks has also published guidance in relation to Private Banking; Correspondent Banking; Suppression of the Financing of Terrorism; and Monitoring, Screening and Searching (collectively referred to as the Wolfsberg Principles).

The UK legal and regulatory framework

1.11   The UK approach to fighting money laundering and terrorist financing is based on a partnership between the public and private sectors. Objectives are specified in legislation and in the FSA Rules, but there is usually no prescription about how these objectives must be met. Often, the objective itself will be a requirement of an EU Directive, incorporated into UK law without any further elaboration, leaving UK financial businesses discretion in interpreting how it should be met.

1.12   Key elements of the UK AML/CTF framework are:

- Proceeds of Crime Act 2002 (as amended);

- Terrorism Act 2000 (as amended by the Anti-terrorism, Crime and Security Act 2001);

- Money Laundering Regulations 2007;

- HM Treasury Sanctions Notices and News Releases; and

- FSA Handbook.

1.13 Implementation guidance for the financial services industry is provided by the JMLSG.

1.14 No single UK body has overall responsibility for combating money laundering or terrorist financing. Responsibilities are set out in Appendix I.

Regulation 3(1) 1.15 The ML Regulations apply to a range of specified firms undertaking business in the UK. POCA and the Terrorism Act consolidated, updated and reformed the scope of UK AML/CTF legislation to apply it to any dealings in criminal or terrorist property. Thus, in considering their statutory obligations, firms need to think in terms of involvement with any crime or terrorist activity.

UK Anti-money laundering and terrorist finance strategy, 28 February 2007 1.16 Firms should be aware of the UK's strategy document *The financial challenge to crime and terrorism,* issued jointly by HM Treasury, Home Office, SOCA and the Foreign Office (available at www.hm-treasury.gov.uk/media/042/B2/financialchallenge_crime_280207.pdf which sets out why it is important to combat money laundering and terrorist financing. The strategy document notes that the Government's objectives are to use financial measures to:

- **deter** crime and terrorism in the first place – by increasing the risk and lowering the reward faced by perpetrators;

- **detect** the criminal or terrorist abuse of the financial system; and

- **disrupt** criminal and terrorist activity – to save lives and hold the guilty to account.

1.17 In order to deliver these objectives successfully, the government believes action in this area must be underpinned by the three key organising principles that were first set out in the 2004 AML Strategy (see www.hm-treasury.gov.uk/media/D57/97/D579755E-BCDC-D4B3-19632628BD485787.pdf):

- **effectiveness** – making maximum impact on the criminal and terrorist threat:

  - build knowledge of criminal and terrorist threats to drive continuous improvement

  - make the best use of the financial tools we have, by making sure that all stakeholders make the maximum use of the opportunities provided by financial tools, including those to recover criminal assets

- **proportionality** – so that the benefits of intervention are justified and that they outweigh the costs:

  - entrench the risk-based approach

  - reduce the burdens on citizens and business created by crime and security measures to the minimum required to protect their security

- **engagement** – so that all stakeholders in government and the private sector, at home and abroad, work collaboratively in partnership:

  - work collaboratively across the AML/CTF community, including to share data to reduce harm

  - engage international partners to deliver a global solution to a global problem

General legal and regulatory obligations

Regulation 20 POCA ss 327–330 Terrorism Act ss 18, 21A 1.18 Senior management of any enterprise is responsible for managing its business effectively. Certain obligations are placed on all firms subject to the ML Regulations, POCA and the Terrorism Act – fulfilling these responsibilities falls to senior management as a whole. These obligations are summarised in Annex 1–I.

| FSMA s 6 SYSC | 1.19 | For FSA-regulated firms the specific responsibilities, and the FSA's expectations, of senior management are set out in FSMA and the FSA Handbook. These obligations are summarised in Annex 1–I. |

Obligations on all firms

| Regulations 20 and 45(1) | 1.20 | The ML Regulations place a general obligation on firms within its scope to establish adequate and appropriate policies and procedures to prevent money laundering. Failure to comply with this obligation risks a prison term of up to two years and/or a fine. |

| Regulation 47 | 1.21 | In addition to imposing liability on firms, the ML Regulations impose criminal liability on certain individuals in firms subject to the ML Regulations. Where the firm is a body corporate, an officer of that body corporate (ie, a director, manager, secretary, chief executive, member of the committee of management, or a person purporting to act in such a capacity), who consents or connives in the commission of an offence by the firm, or that offence (by the firm) is attributable to any neglect on his part, himself commits a criminal offence and may be prosecuted. Similarly, where the firm is partnership, a partner who consents to or connives in the commission of offences under the ML Regulations, or where the commission of any such offence is attributable to any neglect on his part, will be individually liable to be prosecuted for the offence. A similar rule applies to officers of unincorporated associations. |

| POCA ss 327–330 Terrorism Act s 21A Regulation 21 | 1.22 | The offences of money laundering under POCA, and the obligation to report knowledge or suspicion of possible money laundering, affect members of staff of firms. The similar offences and obligations under the Terrorism Act also affect members of staff. However, firms have an obligation under the ML Regulations to take appropriate measures so that all relevant employees are made aware of the law relating to money laundering and terrorist finance, and are regularly given training in how to recognise and deal with transactions which may be related to money laundering or terrorist financing. |

Obligations on FSA-regulated firms

| | 1.23 | A number of the financial sector firms regulated by the FSA are so-called 'common platform' firms, because they are subject both to MiFID and to the Capital Requirements Directive. The FSA Rules relating to systems and controls to prevent firms being used in connection with the commission of financial crime are in two parts: those which apply to most firms, set out in SYSC 3.2.6, and those which apply to common platform firms, set out in SYSC 6.3 – in terms identical to SYSC 3.2.6. To avoid confusing the vast majority of firms by including a multitude of references to SYSC 6.3, this guidance is constructed in terms of following the requirements of SYSC 3.2.6; common platform firms should follow this guidance, interpreting it as referring as necessary to the relevant parts of SYSC 6.3. |

| FSMA, s 6(2)(a) FSMA, s 6(2)(b) SYSC 2.1.1 R, 2.1.3 R, 3.2.6 R | 1.24 | FSMA refers, in the context of setting the FSA's financial crime objective, to the desirability of senior management of FSA-regulated firms being aware of the risk of their businesses being used in connection with the commission of financial crime, and taking appropriate measures to prevent financial crime, facilitate its detection and monitor its incidence. Senior management has operational responsibility for ensuring that the firm has appropriate systems and controls in place to combat financial crime. |

| SYSC 3.2.6H R | 1.25 | In FSA-regulated firms (but see paragraph 1.35 for general insurance firms and mortgage intermediaries), a director or senior manager must be allocated overall responsibility for the establishment and maintenance of the firm's anti-money laundering systems and controls. |

PART V
OTHER MATERIALS

SYSC 3.2.6I(1) R	1.26	In FSA-regulated firms (but see paragraph 1.35 for general insurance firms and mortgage intermediaries), an individual must be allocated responsibility for oversight of a firm's compliance with the FSA's Rules on systems and controls against money laundering: this is the firm's MLRO. The FSA requires the MLRO to have a sufficient level of seniority within the firm to enable him to carry out his function effectively. In some firms the MLRO will be part of senior management (and may be the person referred to in paragraph 1.25); in firms where he is not, he will be directly responsible to someone who is.

SYSC 3.2.6H R SYSC 3.2.6I R	1.27	Senior management of FSA-regulated firms must:

- allocate to a director or senior manager (who may or may not be the MLRO) overall responsibility for the establishment and maintenance of the firm's AML/CTF systems and controls;

- appoint an appropriately qualified senior member of the firm's staff as the MLRO (see Chapter 3); and

- provide direction to, and oversight of the firm's AML/CTF strategy.

	1.28	Although the FSA Rule referred to in paragraph 1.26 requires overall responsibility for AML/CTF systems and controls to be allocated to a single individual, in practice this may often be difficult to achieve, especially in larger firms. As a practical matter, therefore, firms may allocate this responsibility among a number of individuals, provided the division of responsibilities is clear.

	1.29	The relationship between the MLRO and the director/senior manager allocated overall responsibility for the establishment and maintenance of the firm's AML/CTF systems (where they are not the same person) is one of the keys to a successful AML/CTF regime. It is important that this relationship is clearly defined and documented, so that each knows the extent of his, and the other's, role and day to day responsibilities.

SYSC 3.2.6G(2) G	1.30	At least once in each calendar year, an FSA-regulated firm should commission a report from its MLRO (see Chapter 3) on the operation and effectiveness of the firm's systems and controls to combat money laundering. In practice, senior management should determine the depth and frequency of information they feel is necessary to discharge their responsibilities. The MLRO may also wish to report to senior management more frequently than annually, as circumstances dictate.

	1.31	When senior management receives reports from the firm's MLRO it should consider them and take any necessary action to remedy any deficiencies identified in a timely manner.

SYSC 3.2.6I(2) R FSMA s 6(2)(c)	1.32	Those FSA-regulated firms required to appoint an MLRO are specifically required to provide the MLRO with adequate resources. All firms, whether or not regulated by the FSA for AML purposes, must apply adequate resources to counter the risk that they may be used for the purposes of financial crime. This includes systems and controls to prevent ML/TF. The level of resource should reflect the size, complexity and geographical spread of the firm's customer and product base.

	1.33	The role, standing and competence of the MLRO, and the way the internal processes for reporting suspicions are designed and implemented, impact directly on the effectiveness of a firm's money laundering/terrorist financing prevention arrangements.

	1.34	Firms should be aware of the FSA's findings in relation to individual firms, and its actions in response to these; this information is available on the FSA website at www.fsa.gov.uk/Pages/Library/Communication/index.shtml.

Exemptions from legal and regulatory obligations

SYSC 3.2.6 R   1.35   General insurance firms and mortgage intermediaries are regulated by
the FSA, but are not covered by the ML Regulations, or the provisions
of SYSC specifically relating to money laundering. They are, therefore,
under no obligation to appoint an MLRO. They are, however, subject to
the general requirements of SYSC, and so have an obligation to have
appropriate risk management systems and controls in place, including
controls to counter the risk that the firm may be used to further
financial crime.

POCA   1.36   These firms are also subject to the provisions of POCA and the
ss 327–329,   Terrorism Act which establish the primary offences. These offences are
335, 338   not committed if a person's knowledge or suspicion is reported to
Terrorism Act   SOCA, and appropriate consent for the transaction or activity obtained.
s 21

POCA s 332   1.37   For administrative convenience, and to assist their staff fulfil their
Terrorism Act   obligations under POCA or the Terrorism Act, general insurance firms
ss 19, 21   and mortgage intermediaries may choose to appoint a nominated
officer. Where they do so, he will be subject to the reporting
obligations in s 332 of POCA and s 19 of the Terrorism Act (see
Chapter 6).

Relationship between money laundering, terrorist financing and other financial crime

1.38   Although the ML Regulations focus on firms' obligations in relation to
the prevention of money laundering, POCA updated and reformed the
obligation to report to cover involvement with any criminal property,
and the Terrorism Act extended this to cover terrorist property.

1.39   From a practical perspective, therefore, firms should consider how best
they should assess and manage their overall exposure to financial
crime. This does not mean that fraud, market abuse, money laundering
and terrorism financing prevention must be addressed by a single
function within a firm; there will, however, need to be close liaison
between those responsible for each activity.

Senior management should adopt a formal policy in relation to financial crime prevention

SYSC   1.40   As mentioned in paragraph 1.1 above, senior management in FSA-
3.1.1 R,   regulated firms has a responsibility to ensure that the firm's control
3.2.6 R   processes and procedures are appropriately designed and implemented,
3.2.6A R   and are effectively operated to manage the firm's risks. This includes
the risk of the firm being used to further financial crime.

SYSC   1.41   For FSA-regulated firms (but see paragraph 1.35 for general insurance
3.2.6G(3) G   firms and mortgage intermediaries) SYSC 3.2.6G(3) G says that a firm
should produce "appropriate documentation of [its] risk management
policies and risk profile in relation to money laundering, including
documentation of that firm's application of those policies". A statement
of the firm's AML/CTF policy and the procedures to implement it will
clarify how the firm's senior management intends to discharge its
responsibility for the prevention of money laundering and terrorist
financing. This will provide a framework of direction to the firm and its
staff, and will identify named individuals and functions responsible for
implementing particular aspects of the policy. The policy will also set
out how senior management undertakes its assessment of the money
laundering and terrorist financing risks the firm faces, and how these
risks are to be managed. Even in a small firm, a summary of its high-
level AML/CTF policy will focus the minds of staff on the need to be
constantly aware of such risks, and how they are to be managed.

1.42   A policy statement should be tailored to the circumstances of the firm.
Use of a generic document might reflect adversely on the level of
consideration given by senior management to the firm's particular risk
profile.

1.43   The policy statement might include, but not be limited to, such matters as:

- Guiding principles:
  - an unequivocal statement of the culture and values to be adopted and promulgated throughout the firm towards the prevention of financial crime;
  - a commitment to ensuring that customers' identities will be satisfactorily verified before the firm accepts them;
  - a commitment to the firm 'knowing its customers' appropriately – both at acceptance and throughout the business relationship – through taking appropriate steps to verify the customer's identity and business, and his reasons for seeking the particular business relationship with the firm;
  - a commitment to ensuring that staff are trained and made aware of the law and their obligations under it, and to establishing procedures to implement these requirements; and
  - recognition of the importance of staff promptly reporting their suspicions internally.

- Risk mitigation approach:
  - a summary of the firm's approach to assessing and managing its money laundering and terrorist financing risk;
  - allocation of responsibilities to specific persons and functions;
  - a summary of the firm's procedures for carrying out appropriate identification and monitoring checks on the basis of their risk-based approach; and
  - a summary of the appropriate monitoring arrangements in place to ensure that the firm's policies and procedures are being carried out.

Application of group policies outside the UK

1.44   The UK legal and regulatory regime is primarily concerned with preventing money laundering which is connected with the UK. Where a UK financial institution has overseas branches, subsidiaries or associates, where control can be exercised over business carried on outside the United Kingdom, or where elements of its UK business have been outsourced to offshore locations (see paragraphs 2.7–2.11), the firm must put in place a group AML/CTF strategy.

Regulation 15(1) 1.45   A group policy must ensure that all non-EEA branches and subsidiaries carry out CDD measures, and keep records, at least to the standards required under UK law or, if the standards in the host country are more rigorous, to those higher standards. Reporting processes must nevertheless follow local laws and procedures.

Regulation 20(5) 1.46   Firms must communicate their policies and procedures established to prevent activities related to money laundering and terrorist financing to branches and subsidiaries located outside the UK.

Regulation 15(2) 1.47   Where the law of a non-EEA state does not permit the application of such equivalent measures, the firm must inform the FSA accordingly, and take additional measures to handle effectively the risk of money laundering or terrorist financing.

1.48   Whilst suspicions of money laundering or terrorist financing may be required to be reported within the jurisdiction where the suspicion arose and where the records of the related transactions are held, there may also be a requirement for a report to be made to SOCA (see paragraph 6.23).

USA PATRIOT Act – *extra-territoriality*

1.49   Where a firm has a US listing, or has activities in, or linked to, the USA, whether through a branch, subsidiary, associated company or correspondent banking relationship, there is a risk that the application of US AML/CTF and financial sanctions regimes may apply to the non-US activities of the firm. Senior management should take advice on the extent to which the firm's activities may be affected in this way.

[7002]

ANNEX 1–I
UK AML/CTF LEGISLATION AND REGULATION

Proceeds of Crime Act 2002 (as amended)

2002, ch 29 SOCPA, s 102	1.	POCA consolidated, updated and reformed previous UK legislation relating to money laundering. The legislation covers all criminal property, with no exceptions, and there is no *de minimis* threshold, (although for deposit-taking firms, a transaction under £250 may be made without consent under certain circumstances – see paragraph 6.67). Moreover, with some exceptions, the crimes covered include acts committed elsewhere in the world that would be an offence if committed in the UK. POCA:

- establishes a series of criminal offences in connection with money laundering, failing to report, tipping off and prejudicing an investigation;

- sets out a series of penalties for the various offences established under POCA;

- establishes the Assets Recovery Agency[1] (ARA), with power to investigate whether a person holds criminal assets and, if so, their location;

- creates five investigative powers for law enforcement.

	2.	The text of POCA is available at www.legislation.hmso.gov.uk. The key provisions of POCA, as they affect firms in the financial sector, are summarised in Appendix II.

---

[1]   The ARA will be absorbed into SOCA with effect from 1 April 2008.

Terrorism Act 2000 (as amended by the Anti-terrorism, Crime and Security Act 2001)

2000, ch 11 Terrorism Act, ss 15–18, 39	3.	The Terrorism Act establishes offences related to involvement in facilitating, raising, possessing or using funds for terrorism purposes. The Act also empowers the authorities to make a number of Orders on financial institutions in connection with terrorist investigations. The Act also establishes offences in connection with failing to report, tipping off or prejudicing an investigation.
Terrorism Act, s 3	4.	The Terrorism Act also establishes a list of proscribed organisations, with which financial services firms may not deal. The primary source of information on proscribed organisations, including up-to-date information on aliases, is the Home Office. The list of proscribed organisations can be found at: www.homeoffice.gov.uk/security/terrorism-and-the-law/terrorism-act/proscribed-groups?version=1.
2001, ch 24	5.	The Anti-terrorism, Crime and Security Act gives the authorities power to direct firms in the regulated sector to provide the authorities with specified information on customers and their (terrorism-related) activities.

6.   The texts of the Terrorism Act and the Anti-terrorism, Crime and Security Act are available at www.legislation.hmso.gov.uk. The key provisions of the Terrorism Act and the Anti-terrorism, Crime and Security Act, as they affect firms in the financial sector, are summarised in Appendix II.

Money Laundering Regulations 2007

SI 2007/2157   7.   The ML Regulations specify arrangements which all firms within the scope of the Regulations (whether or not regulated by the FSA) must have in place in order to prevent operations relating to money laundering or terrorist financing.

8.   The ML Regulations apply to many firms in the financial sector, including:

- banks, building societies and other credit institutions;

- individuals and firms engaged in regulated activities under FSMA;

- insurance companies undertaking long-term life business, including the life business of Lloyd's of London;

- issuers of electronic money;

- money service businesses (bureaux de change, cheque encashment centres and money transmission services);

- trust or company service providers.

9.   The ML Regulations require firms to appoint a nominated officer to receive internal reports relating to knowledge or suspicion of money laundering.

FSMA   10.   FSMA makes the FSA a prosecuting authority (other than in Scotland)
s 402(1)(b)   in respect of offences under the ML Regulations committed by financial services firms. In Scotland, prosecutions are brought by the Procurator Fiscal.

11.   The text of the ML Regulations is available at www.legislation.hmso.gov.uk. The key provisions of the ML Regulations are summarised in Appendix II.

Financial sanctions

12.   HM Treasury maintains a Consolidated List of targets listed by the United Nations, European Union and United Kingdom under legislation relating to current financial sanctions regimes. This list includes all individuals and entities that are subject to financial sanctions in the UK. This list can be found at: http://www.hm-treasury.gov.uk/publications/financialsanctions.

13.   It is a criminal offence to make payments, or to allow payments to be made, to targets on the list maintained by HM Treasury. This would include dealing direct with targets, or dealing with targets through intermediaries (such as lawyers or accountants). Firms therefore need to have an appropriate means of monitoring payment instructions to ensure that no payments are made to targets or their agents. In the regulated sector this obligation applies to all firms, and not just to banks.

14.   Guidance on compliance with the financial sanctions regime is set out in paragraphs 5.3.40 – 5.3.62.

FSA-regulated firms – the FSA Handbook

APER 2.1.2P
COND
2.5.7(10) G
DEPP 6.2.3 G
PRIN 2.1.1 R
SYSC 2 and 3

15.   SYSC requires FSA-regulated firms (subject to some specified exceptions: see paragraph 1.35 above) to have effective systems and controls for countering the risk that a firm might be used to further financial crime, and specific provisions regarding money laundering risks. It also requires such firms to ensure that approved persons exercise appropriate responsibilities in relation to these AML systems and controls. Parts of the FSA Handbook that are relevant to AML procedures, systems and controls, include:

- APER – Principle 5 requires an approved person to take reasonable steps to ensure that the business of the firm for which he is responsible is organised so that it is controlled effectively;

- COND – In relation to its ongoing assessment as to whether a firm meets the fitness and properness criterion, a firm is specifically required to have in place systems and controls against money laundering of the sort described in SYSC 3.2.6 R to SYSC 3.2.6J G;

- DEPP – When considering whether to take disciplinary action in respect of a breach of the money laundering rules in SYSC 3.2 or SYSC 6.3 the FSA will have regard to whether a firm has followed relevant provisions in the JMLSG guidance for the financial sector;

- PRIN – Principle 3 requires a firm to take reasonable care to organise and control its affairs responsibly and effectively, with adequate risk management systems; and

- SYSC – Chapters 2, 3 and 6 set out particular requirements relating to senior management responsibilities, and for systems and controls processes, including specifically addressing the risk that the firm may be used to further financial crime. SYSC 3.2.6A R to SYSC 3.2.6J G (and SYSC 6.3) cover systems and controls requirements in relation to money laundering.

16.   The text of the FSA Handbook is available at www.fsa.gov.uk/handbook. Relevant provisions of the FSA Handbook are further summarised in Appendix II.

FSMA s 402   17.   In addition to its ability to prosecute for offences under the ML Regulations, the FSA has a wide range of disciplinary powers against authorised firms and approved persons for breaches of its Rules.

[7003]

CHAPTER 2
INTERNAL CONTROLS

Relevant law/regulation
- FSMA s 6
- Regulations 20, 21
- SYSC Chapters 2, 3, 3A

Core obligations
- Firms must establish and maintain adequate and appropriate policies and procedures to forestall and prevent operations relating to money laundering
- Appropriate controls should take account of the risks faced by the firm's business

Actions required, to be kept under regular review
- Establish and maintain adequate and appropriate policies and procedures to forestall and prevent money laundering
- Introduce appropriate controls to take account of the risks faced by the firm's business
- Maintain appropriate control and oversight over outsourced activities

---

General legal and regulatory obligations

General

Regulation 20(1) SYSC 3	2.1	There is a requirement for firms to establish and maintain appropriate and risk-based policies and procedures in order to prevent operations related to money laundering or terrorist financing. FSA-regulated firms have similar, regulatory obligations under SYSC.
	2.2	This chapter provides guidance on the internal controls that will help firms meet their obligations in respect of the prevention of money laundering and terrorist financing. There are general obligations on firms to maintain appropriate records and controls more widely in relation to their business; this guidance is not intended to replace or interpret these wider obligations.

Appropriate controls in the context of financial crime prevention

Regulations 20, 21	2.3	There are specific requirements under the ML Regulations for the firm to establish adequate and appropriate policies and procedures relating to: internal control; risk assessment and management (see Chapter 4); customer due diligence and ongoing monitoring (see Chapter 5); record keeping (see Chapter 8); reporting of suspicions (see Chapter 6); the monitoring and management of compliance with such policies and procedures (see paragraph 3.27); and the internal communication of such policies and procedures (which includes staff awareness and training) (see Chapter 7). The ML Regulations are not specific about what these controls should comprise, and so it is helpful to look to the FSA Handbook, which although only formally applying to FSA-regulated firms, provides helpful commentary on overall systems requirements.
FSMA s 6 SYSC 2, 3 SYSC 3.1.1 R SYSC 3.1.2 G SYSC 3.2.6 R	2.4	FSA-regulated firms are required to have systems and controls appropriate to their business. Specifically, those systems and controls must include measures 'for countering the risk that the firm might be used to further financial crime'. Financial crime includes the handling of the proceeds of crime – that is, money laundering or terrorist financing. The nature and extent of systems and controls will depend on a variety of factors, including: ● the nature, scale and complexity of the firm's business; ● the diversity of its operations, including geographical diversity; ● its customer, product and activity profile; ● its distribution channels; ● the volume and size of its transactions; and ● the degree of risk associated with each area of its operation.
SYSC 3.2.6A R	2.5	An FSA-regulated firm must ensure that these systems and controls: ● enable it to identity, assess, monitor and manage money laundering risk; and ● are comprehensive and proportionate to the nature, scale and complexity of its activities.
SYSC 3.2.6G G SYSC 3.2.6H R SYSC 3.2.6J G SYSC 3.2.6I R	2.6	An FSA-regulated firm's systems and controls (but see paragraph 1.35 for general insurance firms and mortgage intermediaries) are required to cover senior management accountability, including allocation to a director or senior manager of overall responsibility for the establishment and maintenance of effective AML systems and controls and the appointment of a person with adequate seniority and experience as MLRO. The systems and controls should also cover:

- appropriate training on money laundering to ensure that employees are aware of, and understand, their legal and regulatory responsibilities and their role in handling criminal property and money laundering/terrorist financing risk management;

- appropriate provision of regular and timely information to senior management relevant to the management of the firm's criminal property/money laundering/terrorist financing risks;

- appropriate documentation of the firm's risk management policies and risk profile in relation to money laundering, including documentation of the firm's application of those policies; and

- appropriate measures to ensure that money laundering risk is taken into account in the day-to-day operation of the firm, including in relation to:

  - the development of new products;

  - the taking-on of new customers; and

  - changes in the firm's business profile.

Outsourcing and non-UK processing

SYSC 3.2.4 G SYSC 13.9	2.7	Many firms outsource some of their systems and controls and/or processing to elsewhere within the UK and to other jurisdictions, and/or to other group companies. Involving other entities in the operation of a firm's systems brings an additional dimension to the risks that the firm faces, and this risk must be actively managed. It is in the interests of the firm to ensure that outsourcing does not result in reduced standards or requirements being applied. In all cases, the firm should have regard to the FSA's guidance on outsourcing.
SYSC 3.2.4 G SYSC 13.9	2.8	FSA-regulated firms cannot contract out of their regulatory responsibilities, and therefore remain responsible for systems and controls in relation to the activities outsourced, whether within the UK or to another jurisdiction. In all instances of outsourcing it is the delegating firm that bears the ultimate responsibility for the duties undertaken in its name. This will include the requirement to ensure that the provider of the outsourced services has in place satisfactory AML/CTF systems, controls and procedures, and that those policies and procedures are kept up to date to reflect changes in UK requirements.
	2.9	Where UK operational activities are undertaken by staff in other jurisdictions (for example, overseas call centres), those staff should be subject to the AML/CTF policies and procedures that are applicable to UK staff, and internal reporting procedures implemented to ensure that all suspicions relating to UK-related accounts, transactions or activities are reported to the nominated officer in the UK. Service level agreements will need to cover the reporting of management information on money laundering prevention, and information on training, to the MLRO in the UK.
	2.10	Firms should also be aware of local obligations, in all jurisdictions to which they outsource functions, for the detection and prevention of financial crime. Procedures should be in place to meet local AML/CTF regulations and reporting requirements. Any conflicts between the UK and local AML/CTF requirements, where meeting local requirements would result in a lower standard than in the UK, should be resolved in favour of the UK.
	2.11	In some circumstances, the outsourcing of functions can actually lead to increased risk – for example, outsourcing to businesses in jurisdictions with less stringent AML/CTF requirements than in the UK. All financial services businesses that outsource functions and activities should therefore assess any possible AML/CTF risk associated with the outsourced functions, record the assessment and monitor the risk on an ongoing basis.

CHAPTER 3
NOMINATED OFFICER/MONEY LAUNDERING REPORTING OFFICER (MLRO)

Relevant law/regulation
- Regulation 20
- PRIN, Principle 11
- APER, Chapters 2 and 4
- APER, Principles 4 and 7
- SYSC, Chapter 3
- SUP, Chapter 10

Core obligations
- Nominated officer must receive and review internal disclosures, and make external reports
- Nominated officer is responsible for making external reports
- FSA approval required for MLRO, as it is a Controlled Function (CF 11)
- Threshold competence required
- MLRO should be able to act on his own authority
- Adequate resources must be devoted to AML/CFT
- MLRO is responsible for oversight of the firm's AML systems and controls

Actions required, to be kept under regular review
- Senior management to ensure the MLRO has:
  — active support of senior management
  — adequate resources
  — independence of action
  — access to information
  — an obligation to produce an annual report
- MLRO to ensure he has continuing competence
- MLRO to monitor the effectiveness of systems and controls

General legal and regulatory obligations

Legal obligations

Regulation 20(2)(d) POCA ss 337, 338 Terrorism Act ss 21A, 21B	3.1	All firms (other than sole traders) carrying out relevant business under the ML Regulations, whether or not the firm is regulated by the FSA, must appoint a nominated officer, who is responsible for receiving disclosures under Part 7 of POCA and Part 3 of the Terrorism Act, deciding whether these should be reported to SOCA, and, if appropriate, making such external reports.
SYSC 3.2.6 R	3.2	As noted in paragraph 1.35, general insurance firms and mortgage intermediaries are not covered by the ML Regulations, s 330 of POCA, s 21A of the Terrorism Act, or the provisions of SYSC relating specifically to money laundering. They are, however, regulated by the FSA and may be subject to the certain disclosure obligations in POCA and the Terrorism Act. They therefore are under no obligation to appoint a nominated officer or an MLRO, or to allocate to a director or senior manager the responsibility for the establishment and maintenance of effective anti-money laundering systems and controls. They are, however, subject to the general requirements of SYSC, and so have an obligation to have appropriate risk management systems and controls in place, including controls to counter the risk that the firm might be used to further financial crime. They are also subject to ss 337 and 338 of POCA and s 19 of the Terrorism Act
POCA s 332 Terrorism Act s 19	3.3	For administrative convenience, and to assist their staff fulfil their obligations under POCA or the Terrorism Act, firms who have no legal obligation to do so, may nevertheless choose to appoint a nominated officer. Where they do so, he will be subject to the reporting obligations in s 332 of POCA and s 19 of the Terrorism Act.

Regulatory obligations

SYSC 3.2.6I R	3.4	In the case of FSA-regulated firms, other than sole traders with no employees and those firms covered by paragraph 3.2, there is a requirement to appoint an MLRO. The responsibilities of the MLRO under SYSC are different from those of the nominated officer under the ML Regulations, POCA or the Terrorism Act, but in many FSA-regulated firms it is likely that the MLRO and the nominated officer will be one and the same person.
SYSC 3.2.6I(1) R	3.5	The MLRO is responsible for oversight of the firm's compliance with the FSA's Rules on systems and controls against money laundering.
	3.6	An MLRO should be able to monitor the day-to-day operation of the firm's AML/CTF policies, and respond promptly to any reasonable request for information made by the FSA or law enforcement.

Standing of the MLRO

SUP 10.7.13 R SYSC 3.2.6J G FSMA s 59	3.7	The role of MLRO has been designated by the FSA as a controlled function under s 59 of FSMA. As a consequence, any person invited to perform that function must be individually approved by the FSA, on the application of the firm, before performing the function. The FSA expect that the MLRO will be based in the UK.
APER 4.7.9 E APER, Principle 7	3.8	Failure by the MLRO to discharge the responsibilities imposed on him in SYSC 3.2.6I R is conduct that does not comply with Statement of Principle 7 for Approved Persons, namely that 'an approved person performing a significant influence function must take reasonable steps to ensure that the business of the firm for which he is responsible in his controlled function capacity complies with the relevant requirements and standards of the regulatory system'.
SYSC 3.2.6I R SYSC 3.2.6J G SYSC 2.1.1 R	3.9	In FSA-regulated firms, the MLRO is responsible for the oversight of all aspects of the firm's AML/CTF activities and is the focal point for all activity within the firm relating to anti-money laundering. The individual appointed as MLRO must have a sufficient level of seniority within the firm (see paragraph 1.25). As the MLRO is an Approved Person, his job description should clearly set out the extent of the responsibilities given to him, and his objectives. The MLRO will need to be involved in establishing the basis on which a risk-based approach to the prevention of money laundering/terrorist financing is put into practice.
SYSC 3.2.6I(1) R	3.10	Along with the Director/Senior Manager appointed by the Board (see paragraph 1.25), an MLRO will support and co-ordinate senior management focus on managing the money laundering/terrorist financing risk in individual business areas. He will also help ensure that the firm's wider responsibility for forestalling and preventing money laundering/terrorist financing is addressed centrally, allowing a firm-wide view to be taken of the need for monitoring and accountability.
	3.11	As noted in paragraph 1.29, the relationship between the MLRO and the director(s)/senior manager(s) allocated overall responsibility for the establishment and maintenance of the firm's AML/CTF systems is one of the keys to a successful AML/CTF regime. It is important that this relationship is clearly defined and documented, so that each knows the extent of his, and the other's, role and day to day responsibilities.
SYSC 3.2.6I(2)R	3.12	The MLRO must have the authority to act independently in carrying out his responsibilities. The MLRO must be free to have direct access to the FSA and (where he is the nominated officer) appropriate law enforcement agencies, including SOCA, in order that any suspicious activity may be reported to the right quarter as soon as is practicable. He must be free to liaise with SOCA on any question of whether to proceed with a transaction in the circumstances.

SYSC 3.2.6I(2)R	3.13	Senior management of the firm must ensure that the MLRO has sufficient resources available to him, including appropriate staff and technology. This should include arrangements to apply in his temporary absence.

3.14 Where a firm is part of a group, it may appoint as its MLRO an individual who performs that function for another firm within the group. If a firm chooses this approach, it may wish to permit the MLRO to delegate AML/CTF duties to other suitably qualified individuals within the firm. Similarly, some firms, particularly those with a number of branches or offices in different locations, may wish to permit the MLRO to delegate such duties within the firm. In larger firms, because of their size and complexity, the appointment of one or more permanent Deputy MLROs of suitable seniority may be necessary. In such circumstances, the principal, or group MLRO needs to ensure that roles and responsibilities within the group are clearly defined, so that staff of all business areas know exactly who they must report suspicions to.

SUP 10.5.5R 3.15 Where an MLRO is temporarily unavailable, no pre-approval for a deputy will be required for temporary cover of up to 12 weeks in any consecutive 12-month period. For longer periods, however, FSA approval will need to be sought. Rather than appointing a formal deputy, smaller firms may prefer to rely on temporary cover.

3.16 Where AML/CTF tasks are delegated by a firm's MLRO, the FSA will expect the MLRO to take ultimate managerial responsibility.

Internal and external reports

Regulation 20(2)(d) POCA s 330 3.17 A firm must require that anyone in the firm to whom information or other matter comes in the course of business as a result of which they know or suspect, or have reasonable grounds for knowing or suspecting, that a person is engaged in money laundering or terrorist financing complies with Part 7 of POCA or Part 3 of the Terrorism Act (as the case may be). This includes staff having an obligation to make an internal report to the nominated officer as soon as is reasonably practicable after the information or other matter comes to them.

3.18 Any internal report should be considered by the nominated officer, in the light of all other relevant information, to determine whether or not the information contained in the report does give rise to knowledge or suspicion, or reasonable grounds for knowledge or suspicion, of money laundering or terrorist financing.

3.19 A firm is expected to use its existing customer information effectively by making such information readily available to its nominated officer.

3.20 In most cases, before deciding to make a report, the nominated officer is likely to need access to the firm's relevant business information. A firm should therefore take reasonable steps to give its nominated officer access to such information. Relevant business information may include details of:

- the financial circumstances of a customer or beneficial owner, or any person on whose behalf the customer has been or is acting; and

- the features of the transactions, including, where appropriate, the jurisdiction in which the transaction took place, which the firm entered into with or for the customer (or that person).

3.21 In addition, the nominated officer may wish:

- to consider the level of identity information held on the customer, and any information on his personal circumstances that might be available to the firm; and

- to review other transaction patterns and volumes through the account or accounts in the same name, the length of the business relationship and identification records held.

Regulation 20(2)(d) POCA s 331	3.22	If the nominated officer concludes that the internal report does give rise to knowledge or suspicion of money laundering or terrorist financing, he must make a report to SOCA as soon as is practicable after he makes this determination.
	3.23	Guidance on reviewing internal reports, and reporting as appropriate to SOCA, is set out in Chapter 6.

National and international findings in respect of countries and jurisdictions

	3.24	An MLRO should ensure that the firm obtains, and makes appropriate use of, any government or FATF findings concerning the approach to money laundering prevention in particular countries or jurisdictions. This is especially relevant where the approach has been found to be materially deficient by FATF. Reports on the mutual evaluations carried out by the FATF can be found at www.fatf-gafi.org. FATF-style regional bodies also evaluate their members. Not all evaluation reports are published (although there is a presumption that those in respect of FATF members will be). Where an evaluation has been carried out and the findings are not published, firms will take this fact into account in assessing the money laundering and terrorist financing risks posed by the jurisdiction in question. Depending on the firm's area of operation, it may be appropriate to take account of other international findings, such as those by the IMF or World Bank.
	3.25	JMLSG will from time to time publish any such findings on its website (www.jmlsg.org.uk). Firms should check this information regularly to ensure they keep up to date with current findings. Additionally, SOCA periodically produces intelligence assessments, which are forwarded to the MLROs of the relevant sectors for internal dissemination only. No SOCA material is published through an open source.
	3.26	Firms considering business relations and transactions with individuals and firms – whether direct or through correspondents – located in higher risk jurisdictions, or jurisdictions against which the UK has outstanding advisory notices, should take account of the background against which the assessment, or the specific recommendations contained in the advisory notices, have been made.

Monitoring effectiveness of money laundering controls

SYSC 3.2.6C R SYSC 3.2.6I(1) R Regulation 20(1)(f)	3.27	A firm is required to carry out regular assessments of the adequacy of its systems and controls to ensure that they manage the money laundering risk effectively. Oversight of the implementation of the firm's AML/CTF policies and procedures, including the operation of the risk-based approach, is the responsibility of the MLRO, under delegation from senior management. He must therefore ensure that appropriate monitoring processes and procedures across the firm are established and maintained.

Reporting to senior management

SYSC 3.2.6G(2) G	3.28	At least annually the senior management of an FSA-regulated firm should commission a report from its MLRO which assesses the operation and effectiveness of the firm's systems and controls in relation to managing money laundering risk.
	3.29	In practice, senior management should determine the depth and frequency of information they feel necessary to discharge their responsibilities. The MLRO may also wish to report to senior management more frequently than annually, as circumstances dictate.
	3.30	The firm's senior management should consider the report, and take any necessary action to remedy deficiencies identified in it, in a timely manner.

3.31　The MLRO will wish to bring to the attention of senior management areas where the operation of AML/CTF controls should be improved, and proposals for making appropriate improvements. The progress of any significant remedial programmes will also be reported to senior management.

3.32　In addition, the MLRO should report on the outcome of any relevant quality assurance or internal audit reviews of the firm's AML/CTF processes, as well as the outcome of any review of the firm's risk assessment procedures (see paragraph 4.34).

3.33　Firms will need to use their judgement as to how the MLRO should be required to break down the figures of internal reports in his annual report.

3.34　In December 2006, after discussion with the FSA, JMLSG issued a template suggesting a suitable presentation and content framework for a working paper underpinning the production of the MLRO Annual Report. [see www.jmlsg.org.uk]

3.35　An MLRO may choose to report in a different format, according to the nature and scope of their firm's business.

3.36　In practice, subject to the approval of the FSA, larger groups might prepare a single consolidated report covering all of its authorised firms. The MLRO of each authorised firm within the group still has a duty to report appropriately to the senior management of his authorised firm.

[7005]

CHAPTER 4
RISK-BASED APPROACH

Relevant law/regulation
- Regulation 7(3)(a)
- SYSC 3.1.2 G, 3.2.6 R, 3.2.6A–C, 3.2.6F

Other authoritative pronouncements which endorse a risk-based approach
- FATF Recommendation 5
- Basel CDD Paper
- IAIS Guidance Paper 5
- IOSCO Principles paper
- Basel Consolidated KYC Risk Management Paper

Core obligations
- Appropriate systems and controls must reflect the degree of risk associated with the business and its customers
- Determine appropriate CDD measures on a risk-sensitive basis, depending on the type of customer, business relationship, product or transaction
- Take into account situations which by their nature can present a higher risk of money laundering or terrorist financing; these specifically include where the customer has not been physically present for identification purposes; correspondent banking relationships; and business relationships and occasional transactions with PEPs

Actions required, to be kept under regular review
- Carry out a formal, and regular, money laundering/terrorist financing risk assessment, including market changes, and changes in products, customers and the wider environment
- Ensure internal procedures, systems and controls, including staff awareness, adequately reflect the risk assessment
- Ensure customer identification and acceptance procedures reflect the risk characteristics of customers
- Ensure arrangements for monitoring systems and controls are robust, and reflect the risk characteristics of customers

Introduction

4.1 Senior management of most firms, whatever business they are in, manages its affairs with regard to the risks inherent in its business and the effectiveness of the controls it has put in place to manage these risks. A similar approach is appropriate to managing the risks of the firm being used for money laundering or terrorist financing. Many authoritative international bodies operating in the financial services sector, have issued pronouncements endorsing, and encouraging firms to follow, a risk-based approach to managing money laundering/terrorist financing risk.

4.2 A risk-based approach takes a number of discrete steps in assessing the most cost effective and proportionate way to manage and mitigate the money laundering and terrorist financing risks faced by the firm. These steps are to:

- identify the money laundering and terrorist financing risks that are relevant to the firm;

- assess the risks presented by the firm's particular

  - customers;

  - products;

  - delivery channels;

  - geographical areas of operation;

- design and implement controls to manage and mitigate these assessed risks;

- monitor and improve the effective operation of these controls; and

- record appropriately what has been done, and why.

4.3 No system of checks will detect and prevent all money laundering or terrorist financing. A risk-based approach will, however, serve to balance the cost burden placed on individual firms and their customers with a realistic assessment of the threat of the firm being used in connection with money laundering or terrorist financing. It focuses the effort where it is needed and will have most impact.

4.4 To assist the overall objective to prevent money laundering and terrorist financing, a risk-based approach:

- recognises that the money laundering/terrorist financing threat to firms varies across customers, jurisdictions, products and delivery channels;

- allows management to differentiate between their customers in a way that matches the risk in their particular business;

- allows senior management to apply its own approach to the firm's procedures, systems and controls, and arrangements in particular circumstances; and

- helps to produce a more cost effective system.

4.5 The appropriate approach in any given case is ultimately a question of judgement by senior management, in the context of the risks they consider the firm faces. The FSA has indicated in a letter to the chairman of JMLSG that

- **"... If a firm demonstrates that it has put in place an effective system of controls that identifies and mitigates its money laundering risk, then [enforcement] action [by the FSA] is very unlikely."**

- **"...[The FSA] recognise[s] that any regime that is risk-based cannot be a zero failure regime. [The FSA] appreciate[s] the importance of a non-zero failure regime; not least because a 100% standard will not be cost effective and will damage innovation, competition and legitimate commercial success.**

The text of this letter is available at www.fsa.gov.uk/pubs/other/ money_laundering/jmslg.pdf.

PART V
OTHER MATERIALS

A risk-based approach

SYSC   4.6   All firms must assess their money laundering/terrorist financing risk in
3.2.6A R   some way and decide how they will manage it. Firms may choose to
                   carry out this assessment in a sophisticated way, or in a more simple
                   way, having regard to the business they undertake, their customer base
                   and their geographical area of operation. There is no requirement, or
                   expectation, that a risk-based approach must involve a complex set of
                   procedures to put it into effect; the particular circumstances of the firm
                   will determine the most appropriate approach.

           4.7   The business of many firms, their product and customer base, can be
                   relatively simple, involving few products, with most customers falling
                   into similar categories. In such circumstances, a simple approach,
                   building on the risk the firm's products are assessed to present, may
                   be appropriate for most customers, with the focus being on those
                   customers who fall outside the 'norm'. Other firms may have a
                   greater level of business, but large numbers of their customers may
                   be predominantly retail, served through delivery channels that offer
                   the possibility of adopting a standardised approach to many AML/
                   CTF procedures. Here, too, the approach for most customers may be
                   relatively straightforward, building on the product risk.

           4.8   Some other firms, however, often (but not exclusively) those dealing
                   in wholesale markets, may offer a more 'bespoke' service to
                   customers, many of whom are already subject to extensive due
                   diligence by lawyers and accountants for reasons other than AML/
                   CTF. In such cases, the business of identifying the customer will be
                   more complex, but will take account of the considerable additional
                   information that already exists in relation to the prospective
                   customer.

           4.9   How a risk-based approach is implemented will also depend on the
                   firm's operational structure. For example, a firm that operates
                   through multiple business units will need a different approach from
                   one that operates as a single business.

           4.10   Whatever approach is considered most appropriate to the firm's
                   money laundering/terrorist financing risk, the broad objective is that
                   the firm should know who their customers are, what they do, and
                   whether or not they are likely to be engaged in criminal activity. The
                   profile of their financial behaviour will build up over time, allowing
                   the firm to identify transactions or activity that may be suspicious.

           4.11   However carried out, a risk-based approach requires the full
                   commitment and support of senior management, and the active
                   co-operation of business units. The risk-based approach needs to be
                   part of the firm's philosophy, and as such reflected in its procedures
                   and controls. There needs to be a clear communication of policies
                   and procedures across the firm, along with robust mechanisms to
                   ensure that they are carried out effectively, weaknesses are identified,
                   and improvements are made wherever necessary.

           4.12   A risk assessment will often result in a stylised categorisation of risk:
                   eg, high/medium/low. Criteria will be attached to each category to
                   assist in allocating customers and products to risk categories, in order
                   to determine the different treatments of identification, verification,
                   additional customer information and monitoring for each category, in
                   a way that minimises complexity.

Identifying and assessing the risks faced by the firm

4.13   Senior management should decide on the appropriate approach in the light of the firm's structure. The firm may adopt an approach that starts at the business area level, or one that starts from business streams. The firm may start with its customer assessments, and overlay these assessments with the product and delivery channel risks; or it may choose an approach that starts with the product risk, with the overlay being the customer and delivery channel risks, taking account of any geographical considerations relating to the customer, or the transaction.

4.14   A risk-based approach starts with the identification and assessment of the risk that has to be managed. Examples of the risks in particular industry sectors are set out in the sectoral guidance in Part II, and at www.jmlsg.org.uk.

SYSC   4.15   In identifying its money laundering risk an FSA-regulated firm
3.2.6F G   should consider a range of factors, including

●   its customer, product and activity profiles;

●   its distribution channels;

●   the complexity and volume of its transactions;

●   its processes and systems; and

●   its operating environment.

4.16   The firm should assess its risks in the context of how it might most likely be involved in money laundering or terrorist financing. In this respect, senior management should ask themselves a number of questions; for example:

Regulation   ●   What risk is posed by the firm's customers? For example:
20(2)(a)

●   Complex business ownership structures, which can make it easier to conceal underlying beneficiaries, where there is no legitimate commercial rationale;
●   An individual meeting the definition of a PEP (see paragraphs 5.5.18ff);
●   Customers (not necessarily PEPs) based in, or conducting business in or through, a high risk jurisdiction, or a jurisdiction with known higher levels of corruption or organised crime, or drug production/distribution; and
●   Customers engaged in a business which involves significant amounts of cash, or which are associated with higher levels of corruption (eg, arms dealing).

●   What risk is posed by a customer's behaviour? For example:

●   Where there is no commercial rationale for the customer buying the product he seeks;
●   Requests for a complex or unusually large transaction which has no apparent economic or lawful purpose;
●   Requests to associate undue levels of secrecy with a transaction;
●   Situations where the origin of wealth and/or source of funds cannot be easily verified or where the audit trail has been deliberately broken and/or unnecessarily layered; and
●   The unwillingness of customers who are not private individuals to give the names of their real owners and controllers.

●   How does the way the customer comes to the firm affect the risk? For example:

●   Occasional transactions (see paragraph 5.3.6) v business relationships (see paragraph 5.3.5);
●   Introduced business, depending on the effectiveness of the due diligence carried out by the introducer; and
●   Non face-to-face acceptance.

●   What risk is posed by the products/services the customer is using? For example

- Can the product features be used for money laundering or terrorist financing, or to fund other crime?
- Do the products allow/facilitate payments to third parties?
- Is the main risk that of inappropriate assets being placed with, or moving from, or through, the firm?
- Does a customer migrating from one product to another within the firm carry a risk?

4.17 Many customers, by their nature or through what is already known about them by the firm, carry a lower money laundering or terrorist financing risk. These might include:

- Customers who are employment-based or with a regular source of income from a known source which supports the activity being undertaken; (this applies equally to pensioners or benefit recipients, or to those whose income originates from their partners' employment);

- Customers with a long-term and active business relationship with the firm; and

- Customers represented by those whose appointment is subject to court approval or ratification (such as executors).

4.18 Firms should not, however, judge the level of risk solely on the nature of the customer or the product. Where, in a particular customer/product combination, *either or both* the customer and the product are considered to carry a higher risk of money laundering or terrorist financing, the overall risk of the customer should be considered carefully. Firms need to be aware that allowing a higher risk customer to acquire a lower risk product or service on the basis of a verification standard that is appropriate to that lower risk product or service, can lead to a requirement for further verification requirements, particularly if the customer wishes subsequently to acquire a higher risk product or service.

4.19 Further considerations to be borne in mind in carrying out a risk assessment are set out in the sectoral guidance in Part II.

Design and implement controls to manage and mitigate the risks

4.20 Once the firm has identified and assessed the risks it faces in respect of money laundering or terrorist financing, senior management must ensure that appropriate controls to manage and mitigate these risks are designed and implemented.

Regulation 7(3)(a) 4.21 As regards money laundering and terrorist financing, managing and mitigating the risks will involve measures to verify the customer's identity; collecting additional information about the customer; and monitoring his transactions and activity, to determine whether there are reasonable grounds for knowing or suspecting that money laundering or terrorist financing may be taking place. Part of the control framework will involve decisions as to whether verification should take place electronically, and the extent to which the firm can use customer verification procedures carried out by other firms. Firms must determine the extent of their CDD measures on a risk-sensitive basis depending on the type of customer, business relationship, product or transaction.

4.22 To decide on the most appropriate and relevant controls for the firm, senior management should ask themselves what measures the firm can adopt, and to what extent, to manage and mitigate these threats/risks most cost effectively, and in line with the firm's risk appetite. Examples of control procedures include:

- Introducing a customer identification programme that varies the procedures in respect of customers appropriate to their assessed money laundering/terrorist financing risk;

- Requiring the quality of evidence – documentary/electronic/third party assurance – to be of a certain standard;

- Obtaining additional customer information, where this is appropriate to their assessed money laundering/terrorist financing risk; and

- Monitoring customer transactions/activities.

It is possible to try to assess the extent to which each customer should be subject to each of these checks, but it is the balance of these procedures as appropriate to the risk assessed in the individual customer, or category of customer, to which he belongs that is relevant.

4.23   A customer identification programme that is graduated to reflect risk could involve:

- a standard information dataset to be held in respect of all customers;

- a standard verification requirement for all customers;

- more extensive due diligence (more identification checks and/or requiring additional information) on customer acceptance for higher risk customers;

- where appropriate, more limited identity verification measures for specific lower risk customer/product combinations; and

- an approach to monitoring customer activities and transactions that reflects the risk assessed to be presented by the customer, which will identify those transactions or activities that may be unusual or suspicious.

4.24   Where a customer is assessed as carrying a higher risk, then depending on the product sought, it will be necessary to seek additional information in respect of the customer, to be better able to judge whether or not the higher risk that the customer is perceived to present is likely to materialise. Such additional information may include an understanding of where the customer's funds and wealth have come from. Guidance on the types of additional information that may be sought is set out in section 5.5.

4.25   In order to be able to identify customer transactions or activity that may be suspicious, it is necessary to monitor such transactions or activity in some way. Guidance on monitoring customer transactions and activity is given in section 5.7. Monitoring customer activity should be carried out on the basis of a risk-based approach, with higher risk customer/product combinations being subjected to an appropriate frequency and depth of scrutiny, which is likely to be greater than may be appropriate for lower risk combinations.

4.26   The firm must decide, on the basis of its assessment of the risks posed by different customer/product combinations, on the level of verification that should be applied at each level of risk presented by the customer. Consideration should be given to all the information a firm gathers about a customer, as part of the normal business and vetting processes. Consideration of the overall information held may alter the risk profile of the customer.

4.27   Identifying a customer as carrying a higher risk of money laundering or terrorist financing does not automatically mean that he is a money launderer, or a financier of terrorism. Similarly, identifying a customer as carrying a low risk of money laundering or terrorist financing does not mean that the customer is not. Staff therefore need to be vigilant in using their experience and common sense in applying the firm's risk-based criteria and rules (see Chapter 7 – Staff awareness, training and alertness).

Monitor and improve the effective operation of the firm's controls

SYSC 3.2.6C R   4.28   The firm will need to have some means of assessing that its risk mitigation procedures and controls are working effectively, or, if they are not, where they need to be improved. Its policies and procedures will need to be kept under regular review. Aspects the firm will need to consider include:

- Appropriate procedures to identify changes in customer characteristics, which come to light in the normal course of business;

- Reviewing ways in which different products and services may be used for money laundering/terrorist financing purposes, and how these ways may change, supported by typologies/law enforcement feedback, etc;

- Adequacy of staff training and awareness;

- Monitoring compliance arrangements (such as internal audit/ quality assurance processes or external review);

- The balance between technology-based and people-based systems;

- Capturing appropriate management information;

- Upward reporting and accountability;

- Effectiveness of liaison with other parts of the firm; and

- Effectiveness of the liaison with regulatory and law enforcement agencies.

Record appropriately what has been done and why

4.29   The responses to consideration of the issues set out above, or to similar issues, will enable the firm to tailor its policies and procedures on the prevention of money laundering and terrorist financing. Documentation of those responses should enable the firm to demonstrate to its regulator and/or to a court:

- how it assesses the threats/risks of being used in connection with money laundering or terrorist financing;

- how it agrees and implements the appropriate systems and procedures, including due diligence requirements, in the light of its risk assessment;

- how it monitors and, as necessary, improves the effectiveness of its systems and procedures; and

- the arrangements for reporting to senior management on the operation of its control processes.

Risk management is dynamic

SYSC 3.2.6C R   4.30   Risk management generally is a continuous process, carried out on a dynamic basis. A money laundering/terrorist financing risk assessment is not a one-time exercise. Firms must therefore ensure that their risk management processes for managing money laundering and terrorist financing risks are kept under regular review.

4.31   There is a need to monitor the environment within which the firm operates. Success in preventing money laundering and terrorist financing in one area of operation or business will tend to drive criminals to migrate to another area, business, or product stream. Periodic assessment should therefore be made of activity in the firm's market place. If displacement is happening, or if customer behaviour is changing, the firm should be considering what it should be doing differently to take account of these changes.

4.32   In a stable business change may occur slowly: most businesses are evolutionary. Customers' activities change (without always notifying the firm) and the firm's products and services – and the way these are offered or sold to customers – change. The products/transactions attacked by prospective money launderers or terrorist financiers will also vary as perceptions of their relative vulnerability change.

4.33   There is, however, a balance to be achieved between responding promptly to environmental changes, and maintaining stable systems and procedures.

4.34   A firm should therefore keep its risk assessment(s) up to date. An annual, formal reassessment might be too often in most cases, but still appropriate for a dynamic, growing business. It is recommended that a firm revisit its assessment at least annually, even if it decides that there is no case for revision. Firms should include details of the assessment, and any resulting changes, in the MLRO's annual report (see paragraphs 3.28 to 3.36).

[7006]

PART V
OTHER MATERIALS

CHAPTER 5
CUSTOMER DUE DILIGENCE

Relevant UK law/regulation
- Regulations 5–9, 11–17, 18
- POCA ss 330 – 331, 334(2), 342
- Financial sanctions legislation

Customers that may not be dealt with
- Regulation 18 – HM Treasury powers to prohibit firms from forming, or to require them to terminate, relationships with customers situated in a given country to which the FATF has applied counter-measures
- UN Sanctions resolutions 1267 (1999), 1373 (2001), 1333 (2002), 1390 (2002) and 1617 (2005)
- EC Regulation 2580/2001 and 881/2002 (as amended)
- Terrorism Act, 2000, Sch 2
- Terrorism (United Nations Measures) Order 2006
- Al-Qa'ida and Taliban (United Nations Measures) Order 2006
- HM Treasury Sanctions Notices and News Releases

Regulatory regime
- SYSC 3.2.6 R, 3.2.6G(5) G

Other material pointing to good practice
- FATF Recommendations
- FATF Guidance on the risk-based approach: High level principles and procedures
- Basel CDD paper
- IAIS Guidance Paper 5
- IOSCO Principles paper
- Basel Consolidated KYC Risk Management Paper

Other relevant industry material
- Wolfsberg Principles

Core obligations
- Must carry out prescribed CDD measures for all customers not covered by exemptions
- Must have systems to deal with identification issues in relation to those who cannot produce the standard evidence
- Must apply enhanced due diligence to take account of the greater potential for money laundering in higher risk cases, specifically when the customer is not physically present when being identified, and in respect of PEPs and correspondent banking
- Some persons/entities must not be dealt with
- Must have specific policies in relation to the financially (and socially) excluded

- If satisfactory evidence of identity is not obtained, the business relationship must not proceed further
- Must have some system for keeping customer information up to date

5.1 Meaning of customer due diligence measures and ongoing monitoring

	5.1.1	The ML Regulations 2007, which come into force on 15 December 2007, replace previous Regulations passed in 2003. The 2007 Regulations set out firms' obligations to conduct CDD measures in a more detailed form than previously.
	5.1.2	The Regulations specify CDD measures that are required to be carried out, and the timing, as well as actions required if CDD measures are not carried out. The Regulations then describe customers and products in respect of which no, or limited, CDD measures are required (referred to as 'Simplified Due Diligence'), and those customers and circumstances where enhanced due diligence is required. Provision for reliance on other regulated firms in the carrying out of CDD measures are then set out.
	5.1.3	This chapter therefore gives guidance on the following:

- The meaning of CDD measures (5.1.5 – 5.1.14)
- Timing of, and non-compliance with, CDD measures (5.2.1 – 5.2.13)
- Application of CDD measures (section 5.3)
- Simplified due diligence (section 5.4)
- Enhanced due diligence (section 5.5)
- Reliance on third parties and multipartite relationships (section 5.6)
- Monitoring customer activity (section 5.7)

Regulation 7(3)(a) and 8(3)	5.1.4	Firms must determine the extent of their CDD measures and ongoing monitoring on a risk-sensitive basis, depending on the type of customer, business relationship, product or transaction. They must be able to demonstrate to their supervisory authority that the extent of their CDD measures and monitoring is appropriate in view of the risks of money laundering and terrorist financing.

What is customer due diligence?

Regulation 5(1)	5.1.5	The CDD measures that must be carried out involve: (a) identifying the customer, and verifying his identity (see paragraphs 5.3.2ff); (b) identifying the beneficial owner, where relevant, and verifying his identity (see paragraphs 5.3.8ff); and (c) obtaining information on the purpose and intended nature of the business relationship (see paragraphs 5.3.21ff).
Regulation 5(b)	5.1.6	Where the customer is a legal person (such as a company) or a legal arrangement (such as a trust), part of the obligation on firms to identify any beneficial owner of the customer means firms taking measures to understand the ownership and control structure of the customer.
	5.1.7	Working out who is a beneficial owner may not be a straightforward matter. Different rules apply to different forms of entity (see paragraphs 5.3.8ff).
Regulations 13 and 14	5.1.8	For some particular customers, products or transactions, simplified due diligence (SDD) may be applied; in the case of higher risk situations, and specifically in relation to customers who are not physically present when their identities are verified, correspondent banking and PEPs, enhanced due diligence (EDD) measures must be applied on a risk sensitive basis. For

- guidance on applying SDD see section 5.4

- guidance on applying EDD see section 5.5

What is ongoing monitoring?

Regulation 8   5.1.9   Firms must conduct ongoing monitoring of the business relationship with their customers (see paragraphs 5.7.1ff). This is a separate, but related, obligation from the requirement to apply CDD measures.

Why is it necessary to apply CDD measures and conduct ongoing monitoring?

Regulations 7
and 8
POCA,
ss 327–334
Terrorism Act
s 21A

5.1.10   The CDD and monitoring obligations on firms under legislation and regulation are designed to make it more difficult for the financial services industry to be used for money laundering or terrorist financing.

5.1.11   Firms also need to know who their customers are to guard against fraud, including impersonation fraud, and the risk of committing offences under POCA and the Terrorism Act, relating to money laundering and terrorist financing.

5.1.12   Firms therefore need to carry out customer due diligence, and monitoring, for two broad reasons:

- to help the firm, at the time due diligence is carried out, to be reasonably satisfied that customers are who they say they are, to know whether they are acting on behalf of another, and that there is no legal barrier (e g government sanctions) to providing them with the product or service requested; and

- to enable the firm to assist law enforcement, by providing available information on customers or activities being investigated.

5.1.13   It may often be appropriate for the firm to know rather more about the customer than his identity: it will, for example, often need to be aware of the nature of the customer's business in order to assess the extent to which his transactions and activity undertaken with or through the firm is consistent with that business.

Other material, pointing to good practice

5.1.14   FATF, the Basel Committee, IAIS and IOSCO have issued recommendations on the steps that should be taken to identify customers. FATF has also published guidance on high level principles and procedures on the risk-based approach. In addition, the Basel Committee has issued a paper on Consolidated KYC Risk Management. Although the Basel papers are addressed to banks, the IAIS Guidance Paper 5 to insurance entities, and IOSCO's Principles paper to the securities industry, their principles are worth considering by providers of other forms of financial services. The private sector Wolfsberg Group has also issued relevant material. These recommendations are available at: www.fatf-gafi.org; www.bis.org; www.iaisweb.org; www.iosco.org; www.wolfsberg-principles.com. Where relevant, firms are encouraged to use these websites to keep up to date with developing industry guidance from these bodies.

5.2 Timing of, and non compliance with, CDD measures

Regulation 7   5.2.1   A firm must apply CDD measures when it:
(a) establishes a business relationship;
(b) carries out an occasional transaction;
(c) suspects money laundering or terrorist financing; or
(d) doubts the veracity of documents, data or information previously obtained for the purpose of identification or verification.

Timing of verification

Regulation 9(2)	5.2.2	**General rule**: The verification of the identity of the customer and, where applicable, the beneficial owner, must, subject to the exceptions referred to below, take place before the establishment of a business relationship or the carrying out of an occasional transaction.
Regulation 9(4)	5.2.3	**Exception for life assurance:** The verification of the identity of the beneficiary under a life assurance policy may take place after the business relationship has been established provided that it takes place at or before the time of payout or at or before the time the beneficiary exercises a right vested under the policy. [See Part II, sector 7, paragraph 7.29 for further guidance.]
Regulation 9(5)	5.2.4	**Exception when opening a bank account:** The verification of the identity of a bank account holder may take place after the bank account has been opened, provided that there are adequate safeguards in place to ensure that (a) the account is not closed (b) transactions are not carried out by or on behalf of the account holder (including any payment from the account to the account holder) before verification has been completed.
Regulation 9(3)	5.2.5	**Exception if necessary not to interrupt normal business and there is little risk:** In any other case, verification of the identity of the customer, and where there is one, the beneficial owner, may be completed during the establishment of a business relationship if (a) this is necessary not to interrupt the normal conduct of business and (b) there is little risk of money laundering or terrorist financing occurring provided that the verification is completed as soon as practicable after the initial contact.

Requirement to cease transactions, etc

Regulation 11(1)	5.2.6	Where a firm is unable to apply CDD measures in relation to a customer, the firm (a) must not carry out a transaction with or for the customer through a bank account; (b) must not establish a business relationship or carry out an occasional transaction with the customer; (c) must terminate any existing business relationship with the customer; (d) must consider whether it ought to be making a report to SOCA, in accordance with its obligations under POCA and the Terrorism Act.
	5.2.7	Firms should always consider whether an inability to apply CDD measures is caused by the customer not possessing the 'right' documents or information. In this case, the firm should consider whether there are any other ways of being reasonably satisfied as to the customer's identity. In either case, the firm should consider whether there are any circumstances which give grounds for making a report.
	5.2.8	If the firm concludes that the circumstances do give reasonable grounds for knowledge or suspicion of money laundering or terrorist financing, a report must be made to SOCA (see Chapter 7). The firm must then retain the funds until consent has been given to return the funds to the source from which they came.
	5.2.9	If the firm concludes that there are no grounds for making a report, it will need to decide on the appropriate course of action. This may be to retain the funds while it seeks other ways of being reasonably satisfied as to the customer's identity, or to return the funds to the source from which they came. Returning the funds in such a circumstance is part of the process of terminating the relationship; it is closing the account, rather than carrying out a transaction with the customer through a bank account.

Electronic transfer of funds

<table>
<tr>
<td>EC
Regulation
1781/2006</td>
<td>5.2.10</td>
<td>To implement FATF Special Recommendation VII, the EU adopted Regulation 1781/2006, which came into force on 1 January 2007, and is directly applicable in all member states. The Recommendation requires that payment services providers (PSPs) must include certain information in electronic funds transfers and ensure that the information is verified. The core requirement is that the payer's name, address and account number are included in the transfer, but there are a number of permitted exemptions, concessions and variations. For guidance on how to meet the obligations under the Regulation, see Part II, Specialist Guidance A: *Wire transfers*.</td>
</tr>
</table>

5.2.11   The Regulation includes (among others) the following definitions:

- 'Payer' means either a natural or legal person who holds an account and allows a transfer of funds from that account.....

- 'Payment service provider' means a natural or legal person whose business includes the provision of transfer of funds services.

- 'Intermediary payment service provider' means a payment service provider, neither of the payer nor of the payee, that participates in the execution of transfers of funds.

5.2.12   Accordingly, a financial sector business needs to consider which role it is fulfilling when it is involved in a payment chain. For example, a bank or building society effecting an electronic funds transfer on the direct instructions of a customer to the debit of that customer's account will clearly be a PSP whether it undertakes the payment itself (when it must provide its customer's details as the payer), or via an intermediary PSP. In the latter case it must provide the required information on its customer to the intermediary PSP including when it inputs the payment through an electronic banking product supplied by the intermediary PSP.

5.2.13   In other circumstances when a financial sector business, whether independent of the PSP or a specialist function within the same group, passes the transaction through an account in its own name, it may reasonably consider itself under the above definitions as the payer, rather than the PSP, even though the transaction relates ultimately to a customer, eg, mortgages, documentary credits, insurance claims, financial markets trades. In these cases, if XYZ is the name of the financial sector business initiating the transfer as a customer of the PSP, XYZ can input its own name if using an electronic banking product. There is nothing in the Regulation to prevent including the name of the underlying client elsewhere in the transfer, if XYZ wishes to do so.

5.3 Application of CDD measures

<table>
<tr>
<td>Regulation 5(1)</td>
<td>5.3.1</td>
<td>Applying CDD measures involves several steps. The firm is required to identify customers and, where applicable, beneficial owners. It must then verify these identities. Information on the purpose and intended nature of the business relationship must also be obtained.</td>
</tr>
</table>

Identification and verification of the customer

5.3.2   The firm *identifies* the customer by obtaining a range of information about him. The *verification* of the identity consists of the firm verifying some of this information against documents, data or information obtained from a reliable and independent source.

5.3.3   The term 'customer' is not defined in the ML Regulations, and its meaning has to be inferred from the definitions of 'business relationship' and 'occasional transaction', the context in which it is used in the ML Regulations, and its everyday dictionary meaning. It should be noted that for AML/CTF purposes, a 'customer' may be wider than the FSA Glossary definition of 'customer'.

5.3.4   In general, the customer will be the party, or parties, with whom the business relationship is established, or for whom the transaction is carried out. Where, however, there are several parties to a transaction, not all will necessarily be customers. Further, more specific, guidance for relevant sectors is given in Part II. Section 5.6 is also relevant in this context.

Regulation 2(1)   5.3.5   A "business relationship" is defined in the ML Regulations as a business, professional or commercial relationship between a firm and a customer, which is expected by the firm when contact is established to have an element of duration. A relationship need not involve the firm in an actual transaction; giving advice may often constitute establishing a business relationship.

Regulation 2(1)   5.3.6   An "occasional transaction" means a transaction carried out other than in the course of a business relationship (eg, a single foreign currency transaction, or an isolated instruction to purchase shares), amounting to €15,000 or more, whether the transaction is carried out in a single operation or several operations which appear to be linked.

5.3.7   The factors linking transactions to assess whether there is a business relationship are inherent in the characteristics of the transactions – for example, where several payments are made to the same recipient from one or more sources over a short period of time, or where a customer regularly transfers funds to one or more sources. For lower-risk situations that do not otherwise give rise to a business relationship, a three-month period for linking transactions might be appropriate, assuming this is not a regular occurrence.

Identification and verification of a beneficial owner

Regulations 6,   5.3.8   A beneficial owner is normally an individual who ultimately owns or
5(b)   controls the customer or on whose behalf a transaction or activity is being conducted. In respect of private individuals the customer himself is the beneficial owner, unless there are features of the transaction, or surrounding circumstances, that indicate otherwise. Therefore, there is no requirement on firms to make proactive searches for beneficial owners in such cases, but they should make appropriate enquiries where it appears that the customer is not acting on his own behalf.

5.3.9   Where an individual is required to be *identified* as a beneficial owner in the circumstances outlined in paragraph 5.3.8, where a customer who is a private individual is fronting for another individual who is the beneficial owner, the firm should obtain the same information about that beneficial owner as it would for a customer. For identifying beneficial owners of customers other than private individuals see paragraphs 5.3.115 onwards.

Regulation 5(a)   5.3.10   The *verification* requirements under the ML Regulations are, however,
and (b)   different as between a customer and a beneficial owner. The identity of a customer must be verified on the basis of documents, data or information obtained from a reliable and independent source. The obligation to verify the identity of a beneficial owner is for the firm to take risk-based and adequate measures so that it is satisfied that it knows who the beneficial owner is. It is up to each firm whether they make use of records of beneficial owners in the public domain (if any exist), ask their customers for relevant data or obtain the information otherwise. There is no specific requirement to have regard to particular types of evidence.

	5.3.11	In lower risk situations, therefore, it may be reasonable for the firm to be satisfied as to the beneficial owner's identity based on information supplied by the customer. This could include information provided by the customer (including trustees or other representatives whose identities have been verified) as to their identity, and confirmation that they are known to the customer. While this may be provided orally or in writing, any information received orally should be recorded in written form by the firm.
Regulation 6	5.3.12	The ML Regulations require that beneficial owners owning or controlling more than 25% of body corporates, partnerships or trusts are identified, and that risk-based and adequate measures are taken to verify their identities.
Regulation 6(3)(b)	5.3.13	In some trusts and similar arrangements, instead of being an individual, the beneficial owner is a class of persons who may benefit from the trust (see paragraphs 5.3.183ff). Where only a class of persons is required to be identified, it is sufficient for the firm to ascertain and name the scope of the class. It is not necessary to identify every individual member of the class.

Customers with whom firms have a business relationship on 15 December 2007

Regulations 7(2), 16(4)	5.3.14	Firms must apply CDD measures at appropriate times to its existing customers on a risk-sensitive basis. Firms must also apply CDD measures to any anonymous accounts or passbooks as soon as possible after 15 December 2007, and in any event before they are used. Subject to these two obligations, this guidance does not require the immediate application of CDD measures to all existing customers after 15 December 2007. The obligation to report suspicions of money laundering, or terrorist financing, however, applies in respect of *all* the firm's customers, as does the UK financial sanctions regime (see paragraphs 5.3.41–5.3.63).
	5.3.15	As risk dictates, therefore, firms must take steps to ensure that they hold appropriate information to demonstrate that they are satisfied that they know all their customers. Where the identity of an existing customer has already been verified to a previously applicable standard then, in the absence of circumstances indicating the contrary, the risk is likely to be low. A range of trigger events, such as an existing customer applying to open a new account or establish a new relationship, might prompt a firm to seek appropriate evidence.
FSA Briefing Note, July 2003 SYSC 3.2.6 R	5.3.16	In July 2003, senior management of FSA-regulated firms were reminded of their regulatory responsibilities to maintain effective systems and controls for countering the risk that they may be used to further financial crime. The FSA reminded firms that, when carrying out risk assessment and mitigation, the FSA would expect them – as part of their overall approach to AML/CTF – to have considered the risk posed by existing customers who have not been identified. The FSA also expect firms (if appropriate) to take steps or put controls in place to mitigate this risk. Senior management and MLROs were encouraged to consider specific questions in relation to this risk, and to take any appropriate steps.
FSA Briefing Note, July 2003	5.3.17	Firms that do not seriously address risks (including the risk that they have not confirmed the identity of existing customers) are exposing themselves to the possibility of action for breach of the FSA Rules, or of the ML Regulations. The FSA briefing note is at www.fsa.gov.uk/pubs/other/id_customers.pdf.
	5.3.18	A firm may hold considerable information in respect of a customer of some years' standing. In some cases the issue may be more one of collating and assessing information already held than approaching customers for more identification data or information.

Acquisition of one financial services firm, or a portfolio of customers, by another

5.3.19 When a firm acquires the business and customers of another firm, either as a whole, or as a portfolio, it is not necessary for the identity of all existing customers to be re-verified, provided that:

- all underlying customer records are acquired with the business; **or**

- a warranty is given by the acquired firm, or by the vendor where a portfolio of customers or business has been acquired, that the identities of its customers have been verified.

It is, however, important that the acquiring firm's due diligence enquiries include some sample testing in order to confirm that the customer identification procedures previously followed by the acquired firm (or by the vendor, in relation to a portfolio) have been carried out in accordance with UK requirements.

5.3.20 In the event that:

- the sample testing of the customer identification procedures previously undertaken shows that these have not been carried out to an appropriate standard; or

- the procedures cannot be checked; or

- the customer records are not accessible by the acquiring firm,

verification of identity will need to be undertaken as soon as is practicable for all transferred customers who are not existing verified customers of the transferee, in line with the acquiring firm's risk-based approach, and the requirements for existing customers opening new accounts.

Nature and purpose of proposed business relationship

Regulation 5(c) 5.3.21 A firm must understand the purpose and intended nature of the business relationship or transaction. In some instances this will be self-evident, but in many cases the firm may have to obtain information in this regard.

5.3.22 Depending on the firm's risk assessment of the situation, information that might be relevant may include some or all of the following:

- nature and details of the business/occupation/employment;

- record of changes of address;

- the expected source and origin of the funds to be used in the relationship;

- initial and ongoing source(s) of wealth or income (particularly within a private banking or wealth management relationship);

- copies of recent and current financial statements;

- the various relationships between signatories and with underlying beneficial owners;

- the anticipated level and nature of the activity that is to be undertaken through the relationship.

Keeping information up to date

Regulation 8(2)(b)	5.3.23	Where information is held about customers, it must, as far as reasonably possible, be kept up to date. Once the identity of a customer has been satisfactorily verified, there is no obligation to re-verify identity (unless doubts arise as to the veracity or adequacy of the evidence previously obtained for the purposes of customer identification); as risk dictates, however, firms must take steps to ensure that they hold appropriate up-to-date information on their customers. A range of trigger events, such as an existing customer applying to open a new account or establish a new relationship, might prompt a firm to seek appropriate evidence.

5.3.24   Although keeping customer information up-to-date is required under the ML Regulations, this is also a requirement of the Data Protection Act in respect of personal data.

Characteristics and evidence of identity

5.3.25   The identity of an individual has a number of aspects: eg, his/her given name (which of course may change), date of birth, place of birth. Other facts about an individual accumulate over time (the so-called electronic "footprint"): eg, family circumstances and addresses, employment and business career, contacts with the authorities or with other financial sector firms, physical appearance.

5.3.26   The identity of a customer who is not a private individual is a combination of its constitution, its business, and its legal and ownership structure.

5.3.27   Evidence of identity can take a number of forms. In respect of individuals, much weight is placed on so-called 'identity documents', such as passports and photocard driving licences, and these are often the easiest way of being reasonably satisfied as to someone's identity. It is, however, possible to be reasonably satisfied as to a customer's identity based on other forms of confirmation, including, in appropriate circumstances, written assurances from persons or organisations that have dealt with the customer for some time.

Regulation 5(3)(a)	5.3.28	How much identity information or evidence to ask for, and what to verify, in order to be reasonably satisfied as to a customer's identity, are matters for the judgement of the firm, which must be exercised on a risk-based approach, as set out in Chapter 4, taking into account factors such as:

- the nature of the product or service sought by the customer (and any other products or services to which they can migrate without further identity verification);

- the nature and length of any existing or previous relationship between the customer and the firm;

- the nature and extent of any assurances from other regulated firms that may be relied on; and

- whether the customer is physically present.

5.3.29   Evidence of identity can be in documentary or electronic form. An appropriate record of the steps taken, and copies of, or references to, the evidence obtained, to identify the customer must be kept.

Documentary evidence

5.3.30   Documentation purporting to offer evidence of identity may emanate from a number of sources. These documents differ in their integrity, reliability and independence. Some are issued after due diligence on an individual's identity has been undertaken; others are issued on request, without any such checks being carried out. There is a broad hierarchy of documents:

- certain documents issued by government departments and agencies, or by a court; then

- certain documents issued by other public sector bodies or local authorities; then

- certain documents issued by regulated firms in the financial services sector; then

- those issued by other firms subject to the ML Regulations, or to equivalent legislation; then

- those issued by other organisations.

5.3.31   Firms should recognise that some documents are more easily forged than others. If suspicions are raised in relation to any document offered, firms should take whatever practical and proportionate steps are available to establish whether the document offered has been reported as lost or stolen.

5.3.32   In their procedures, therefore, firms will in many situations need to be prepared to accept a range of documents, and they may wish also to employ electronic checks, either on their own or in tandem with documentary evidence.

Electronic evidence

5.3.33   Electronic data sources can provide a wide range of confirmatory material without involving the customer. Where such sources are used for a credit check, the customer's permission is required under the Data Protection Act; a search for identity verification for AML/CTF purposes, however, leaves a different 'footprint' on the customer's electronic file, and the customer's permission is not required, but they must be informed that this check is to take place.

5.3.34   External electronic databases are accessible directly by firms, or through independent third party organisations. The size of the electronic 'footprint' (see paragraph 5.3.25) in relation to the depth, breadth and quality of data, and the degree of corroboration of the data supplied by the customer, may provide a useful basis for an assessment of the degree of confidence in their identity.

Nature of electronic checks

5.3.35   A number of commercial agencies which access many data sources are accessible online by firms, and may provide firms with a composite and comprehensive level of electronic verification through a single interface. Such agencies use databases of both positive and negative information, and many also access high-risk alerts that utilise specific data sources to identify high-risk conditions, for example, known identity frauds or inclusion on a sanctions list. Some of these sources are, however, only available to closed user groups.

5.3.36   Positive information (relating to full name, current address, date of birth) can prove that an individual exists, but some can offer a higher degree of confidence than others. Such information should include data from more robust sources – where an individual has to prove their identity, or address, in some way in order to be included, as opposed to others, where no such proof is required.

5.3.37   Negative information includes lists of individuals known to have committed fraud, including identity fraud, and registers of deceased persons. Checking against such information may be necessary to mitigate against impersonation fraud.

5.3.38   For an electronic check to provide satisfactory evidence of identity on its own, it must use data from multiple sources, and across time, or incorporate qualitative checks that assess the strength of the information supplied. An electronic check that accesses data from a single source (eg, a single check against the Electoral Roll) is not normally enough on its own to verify identity.

Criteria for use of an electronic data provider

5.3.39   Before using a commercial agency for electronic verification, firms should be satisfied that information supplied by the data provider is considered to be sufficiently extensive, reliable and accurate. This judgement may be assisted by considering whether the provider meets all the following criteria:

- it is recognised, through registration with the Information Commissioner's Office, to store personal data;

- it uses a range of positive information sources that can be called upon to link an applicant to both current and previous circumstances;

- it accesses negative information sources, such as databases relating to identity fraud and deceased persons;

- it accesses a wide range of alert data sources; and

- it has transparent processes that enable the firm to know what checks were carried out, what the results of these checks were, and what they mean in terms of how much certainty they give as to the identity of the subject.

5.3.40   In addition, a commercial agency should have processes that allow the enquirer to capture and store the information they used to verify an identity.

Persons firms should not accept as customers

5.3.41   The United Nations, European Union, and United Kingdom are each able to designate persons and entities as being subject to financial sanctions, in accordance with legislation explained below. Such sanctions normally include a comprehensive freeze of funds and economic resources, together with a prohibition on making funds or economic resources available to the designated target. A Consolidated List of all targets to whom financial sanctions apply is maintained by HM Treasury, and includes all individuals and entities that are subject to financial sanctions in the UK. This list is at: www.hm-treasury.gov.uk/financialsanctions.

5.3.42   The obligations under the UK financial sanctions regime apply to all firms, and not just to banks. The Consolidated List includes all the names of designated persons under UN and EC sanctions regimes which have effect in the UK. Firms will not normally have any obligation under UK law to have regard to lists issued by other organisations or authorities in other countries, although a firm doing business in other countries will need to be aware of the scope and focus of relevant financial sanctions regimes in those countries. The other websites referred to below may contain useful background information, but the purpose of the HM Treasury list is to draw together in one place all the names of designated persons for the various sanctions regimes effective in the UK. All firms to whom this guidance applies, therefore, whether or not they are FSA-regulated or subject to the ML Regulations, will need either:

- for manual checking: to register with the HM Treasury update service (directly or via a third party, such as a trade association); or

- if checking is automated: to ensure that relevant software includes checks against the relevant list and that this list is up to date.

5.3.43 The origins of such sanctions and the sources of information for the Consolidated List are covered below.

5.3.44 The HM Treasury website contains general guidance on the implementation of financial sanctions and various electronic versions of the Consolidated List to assist with compliance, as well as regime-specific target lists, details of all Notices updating the Consolidated List and News Releases issued by HM Treasury, and links to other useful websites. HM Treasury may also be contacted direct to provide guidance and to assist with any concerns regarding the implementation of financial sanctions:
Asset Freezing Unit
HM Treasury
1 Horse Guards Road
LONDON SW1A 2HQ
Tel: +44 (0) 20 7270 5454
Email: assetfreezingunit@hm-treasury.gov.uk

5.3.45 An asset freeze works by way of a prohibition against dealing with the funds or economic resources of a designated person. It is also prohibited to make funds or economic resources (and in relation to designated terrorists, financial services) available, directly or indirectly, to or for the benefit of targets on the list maintained by HM Treasury. Firms therefore need to have an appropriate means of monitoring payment instructions to ensure that the prohibitions are not breached. A breach could involve the making of payments to or for the benefit of designated persons, whether or not the payment is made direct to the designated person, through an intermediary or in a manner which is for the benefit of the designated person.

5.3.46 HM Treasury can licence exceptions to the prohibitions to enable frozen funds and economic resources to be unfrozen and to allow payments to be made to or for the benefit of a designated person. A firm seeking such a licence should write to the Asset Freezing Unit at the address set out in paragraph 5.3.44.

5.3.47 If a firm breaches a sanctions prohibition, it is likely to have committed a criminal offence. However, in line with the principles set out in the Code for Crown Prosecutors, prosecution of a firm suspected to be in breach of the financial sanctions regime in the UK would be likely only where the prosecuting authorities consider this to be in the public interest, and where they believe that there is enough evidence to provide a realistic prospect of conviction. The Code for Crown Prosecutors can be accessed at www.cps.gov.uk/publications/docs/code2004english.pdf.

5.3.48 To reduce the risk of breaching obligations under financial sanctions regimes, firms are likely to focus their resources on areas of their business that carry a greater likelihood of involvement with targets, or their agents. Within this approach, firms are likely to focus their prevention and detection procedures on direct customer relationships, and then have appropriate regard to other parties involved.

5.3.49 Firms need to have some means of monitoring payment instructions to ensure that proposed payments to targets or their agents are not made. The majority of payments made by many firms will, however, be to other regulated firms, rather than to individuals or entities that may be targets.

5.3.50 Where a firm freezes funds under financial sanctions legislation, or where it has suspicions of terrorist financing, it must make a report to HM Treasury, and/or to SOCA. Guidance on such reporting is given in paragraphs 6.31 to 6.45.

Terrorism

UNSCR 1373 (2001)	5.3.51	The UN Security Council has passed UNSCR 1373 (2001), which calls on all member states to act to prevent and suppress the financing of terrorist acts. Guidance issued by the UN Counter Terrorism Committee in relation to the implementation of UN Security Council Resolutions regarding terrorism can be found at: www.un.org/Docs/sc/committees/1373/.
UNSCR 1267 (1999); 1390 (2002); 1617 (2005)	5.3.52	The UN has also published the names of individuals and organisations subject to UN financial sanctions in relation to involvement with Usama bin Laden, Al-Qa'ida, and the Taliban under UNSCR 1267 (1999), 1390 (2002) and 1617 (2005). All UN member states are required under international law to freeze the funds and economic resources of any legal person(s) named in this list and to report any suspected name matches to the relevant authorities.
EC Regulation 2580/2001 (as amended)	5.3.53	The EU directly implements all UN financial sanctions, including financial sanctions against terrorists, through binding and directly applicable EC Regulations. The EU implemented UNSCR 1373 through the adoption of Regulation EC 2580/2001 (as amended). This Regulation introduces an obligation in Community law to freeze all funds and economic resources belonging to named persons and entities, and not to make any funds or economic resources available, directly or indirectly, to those named.
EC Regulation 881/2002 (as amended)	5.3.54	UNSCR 1267 and its successor resolutions are implemented at EU level by Regulation EC 881/2002 (as amended).
	5.3.55	The texts of the EC Regulations referred to in paragraphs 5.3.53 and 5.3.54, and the lists of persons targeted, are available at europa.eu.int/comm/external_relations/cfsp/sanctions/measures.htm. As noted above, names of persons and entities on the EU list will be included in the Consolidated List maintained by HM Treasury.
Terrorism (United Nations Measures) Order 2006	5.3.56	The UK has implemented UNSCR 1373 under the Terrorism (United Nations Measures) Order 2006, and UNSCR 1267 and its successor resolutions under the Al-Qa'ida and the Taliban (United Nations Measures) Order 2006.
Al-Qa'ida and Taliban (United Nations Measures) Order 2006	5.3.57	Acting under the Terrorism (United Nations Measures) Order 2006, where the HM Treasury has reasonable grounds for suspecting that the person is or may be a person who commits, attempts to commit, facilitates or participates in the commission of acts of terrorism, it can designate that person for the purposes of the financial sanctions. This might result in the addition of a name to the HM Treasury list that might not appear on the equivalent UN or EU lists. HM Treasury also has certain designation powers under the Al-Qa'ida and Taliban (United Nations Measures) Order 2006.
Terrorism Act Sch 2	5.3.58	A number of organisations have been proscribed under UK anti-terrorism legislation. Where such organisations are also subject to financial sanctions (an asset freeze), they are included on the Consolidated List maintained by HM Treasury.
	5.3.59	The primary source of information on proscribed organisations, however, including up-to-date information on aliases, is the Home Office. Firms can find the list of proscribed organisations at: www.homeoffice.gov.uk/security/terrorism-and-the-law/terrorism-act/proscribed-groups?version=1.

Country-specific

5.3.60 The UN Security Council also maintains a range of country-based financial sanctions that target specific individuals and entities connected with the political leadership of targeted countries. Each UN sanctions regime has a relevant Security Council Committee that maintains general guidance on the implementation of financial sanctions and current lists of targeted persons and entities. The list of currently applicable Security Council Resolutions can be found at www.un.org/Docs/sc/committees/INTRO.htm.

EC
Regulation
2580/2001

5.3.61 The EU directly implements all UN financial sanctions against countries/regimes; it can also initiate autonomous measures under the auspices of its Common Foreign and Security Policy. Detail on UN-derived and EU autonomous financial sanctions regimes (including targets) is available on the European Commission's sanctions website, europa.eu.int/comm/external_relations/cfsp/sanctions/measures.htm.

5.3.62 In most cases, EC Regulations directly apply to give effect to those sanctions regimes. In addition, the UK implements or enforces all UN and EU country/regime-specific measures by means of assorted statutory instruments. Unlike the arrangements under the terrorism measures, the UK would not normally make autonomous additions to the target lists for these types of sanctions. The prohibition in these sanctions regimes apply in respect of funds and economic resources in the same manner as those in the terrorism sanctions. Where relevant, any specific individuals and entities subject to such targeted countries/regimes will be included on the HM Treasury Consolidated List.

Regulation 18

5.3.63 HM Treasury may direct that a firm may not enter into a business relationship, carry out an occasional transaction, or proceed further with a business relationship or occasional transaction, in relation to a person who is based or incorporated in a non EEA state to which the FATF has decided to apply counter-measures. Details of any such HM Treasury directions will be found at www.hm-treasury.gov.uk or www.jmlsg.org.uk.

5.3.64 Trade sanctions – such as embargoes on making military hardware or know-how available to certain named countries or jurisdictions – can be imposed by governments or other international authorities, and these can have financial implications. Firms which operate internationally should be aware of such sanctions, and should consider whether these affect their operations; if so, they should decide whether they have any implications for the firm's procedures. Further information and links to lists of affected countries can be found at: www.dti.gov.uk/export.control/.

Shell banks and anonymous accounts

Regulation 16
(1), (2), (5)

5.3.65 Firms must not enter into, or continue, a correspondent banking relationship with a shell bank. Firms must take appropriate measures to ensure that it does not enter into or continue a correspondent naming relationship with a bank that is known to permit its accounts to be used by a shell bank. A shell bank is an entity incorporated in a jurisdiction where it has no physical presence involving meaningful decision-making and management, and which is not part of a financial conglomerate.

Regulation 16
(3), (4)

5.3.66 Firms carrying on business in the UK must not set up an anonymous account or an anonymous passbook for any new or existing customer. As soon as possible after 15 December 2007, all firms carrying on business in the UK must apply CDD measures to all existing anonymous accounts and passbooks, and in any event before such accounts or passbooks are used in any way.

5.3.67 Firms should pay special attention to any money laundering or terrorist financing threat that may arise from products or transactions that may favour anonymity and take measures, if needed, to prevent their use for money laundering or terrorist financing purposes.

Private individuals

General

5.3.68   Paragraphs 5.3.70 to 5.3.82 refer to the standard identification requirement for customers who are private individuals; paragraphs 5.3.83 to 5.3.114 provide further guidance on steps that may be applied as part of a risk-based approach.

5.3.69   Depending on the circumstances relating to the customer, the product and the nature and purpose of the proposed relationship, firms may also need to apply the following guidance to identifying, and verifying the identity of, beneficial owners, and to other relevant individuals associated with the relationship or transaction (but see paragraphs 5.3.10 and 5.3.11).

Obtain standard evidence

Identification

5.3.70   The firm should obtain the following information in relation to the private individual:

- full name

- residential address

- date of birth

Verification

5.3.71   Verification of the information obtained must be based on reliable and independent sources – which might either be a document or documents produced by the customer, or electronically by the firm, or by a combination of both. Where business is conducted face-to-face, firms should see originals of any documents involved in the verification. Customers should be discouraged from sending original valuable documents by post.

Documentary verification

5.3.72   If documentary evidence of an individual's identity is to provide a high level of confidence, it will typically have been issued by a government department or agency, or by a court, because there is a greater likelihood that the authorities will have checked the existence and characteristics of the persons concerned. In cases where such documentary evidence of identity may not be available to an individual, other evidence of identity may give the firm reasonable confidence in the customer's identity, although the firm should weigh these against the risks involved.

5.3.73   Non-government-issued documentary evidence complementing identity should normally only be accepted if it originates from a public sector body or another regulated financial services firm, or is supplemented by knowledge that the firm has of the person or entity, which it has documented.

5.3.74   If identity is to be verified from documents, this should be based on: *Either* a government-issued document which incorporates:

- the customer's full name and photograph, and
  - **either** his residential address
  - **or** his date of birth.

Government-issued documents with a photograph include:
— Valid passport
— Valid photocard driving licence (full or provisional)
— National Identity card (non-UK nationals)
— Firearms certificate or shotgun licence
— Identity card issued by the Electoral Office for Northern Ireland

or a government-issued document (without a photograph) which incorporates the customer's full name, *supported by* a second document, either government-issued, or issued by a judicial authority, a public sector body or authority, a regulated utility company, or another FSA-regulated firm in the UK financial services sector, or in an equivalent jurisdiction, which incorporates:

- the customer's full name and
  - **either** his residential address
  - **or** his date of birth

Government-issued documents without a photograph include:
— Valid (old style) full UK driving licence
— Recent evidence of entitlement to a state or local authority-funded benefit (including housing benefit and council tax benefit), tax credit, pension, educational or other grant
Other documents include:
— Instrument of a court appointment (such as liquidator, or grant of probate)
— Current council tax demand letter, or statement
— Current bank statements, or credit/debit card statements, issued by a regulated financial sector firm in the UK, EU or an equivalent jurisdiction (but not ones printed off the internet)
— Utility bills (but not ones printed off the internet)

5.3.75 The examples of other documents are intended to support a customer's address, and so it is likely that they will have been delivered to the customer through the post, rather than being accessed by him across the internet.

5.3.76 Where a member of the firm's staff has visited the customer at his home address, a record of this visit may constitute evidence corroborating that the individual lives at this address (ie, as a second document).

[5.3.77 In practical terms, this means that, for face-to-face verification, production of a valid passport or photocard driving licence (so long as the photograph is in date)[1A] should enable most individuals to meet the identification requirement for AML/CTF purposes. The firm's risk-based procedures may dictate additional checks for the management of credit and fraud risk, or may restrict the use of certain options, eg, restricting the acceptability of National Identity Cards in face-to-face business in the UK to cards issued only by EEA member states and Switzerland. For customers who cannot provide the standard evidence, other documents may be appropriate (see paragraphs 5.3.98 to 5.3.114).]

5.3.78 Some consideration should be given as to whether the documents relied upon are forged. In addition, if they are in a foreign language, appropriate steps should be taken to be reasonably satisfied that the documents in fact provide evidence of the customer's identity. Examples of sources of information include CIFAS, the Fraud Advisory Panel and the Serious Fraud Office. Commercial software is also available that checks the algorithms used to generate passport numbers. This can be used to check the validity of passports of any country that issues machine-readable passports.

---

¹ᴬ It should be noted that as well as a general expiry date for UK driving licences, the photograph has a separate expiry date (10 years from first issue). Northern Ireland driving licences have a single expiry date, which is ten years from date of issue.

Electronic verification

5.3.79 If identity is verified electronically, this should be by the firm, using as its basis the customer's full name, address and date of birth, carrying out electronic checks either direct, or through a supplier which meets the criteria in paragraphs 5.3.39 and 5.3.40, that provide a reasonable assurance that the customer is who he says he is.

5.3.80 As well as requiring a commercial agency used for electronic verification to meet the criteria set out in paragraphs 5.3.39 and 5.3.40, it is important that the process of electronic verification meets a standard level of confirmation before it can be relied on. The standard level of confirmation, in circumstances that do not give rise to concern or uncertainty, is:

- one match on an individual's full name and current address, **and**

- a second match on an individual's full name and **either** his current address **or** his date of birth.

Commercial agencies that provide electronic verification use various methods of displaying results – for example, by the number of documents checked, or through scoring mechanisms. Firms should ensure that they understand the basis of the system they use, in order to be satisfied that the sources of the underlying data reflect the guidance in paragraphs 5.3.35–5.3.38, and cumulatively meet the standard level of confirmation set out above.

5.3.81 To mitigate the risk of impersonation fraud, firms should either verify with the customer additional aspects of his identity which are held electronically, or follow the guidance in paragraph 5.3.82.

Mitigation of impersonation risk

5.3.82 Where identity is verified electronically, or copy documents are used, a firm should apply an additional verification check to manage the risk of impersonation fraud. The additional check may consist of robust anti-fraud checks that the firm routinely undertakes as part of its existing procedures, or may include:

- requiring the first payment to be carried out through an account in the customer's name with a UK or EU regulated credit institution or one from an equivalent jurisdiction;

- verifying additional aspects of the customer's identity, or of his electronic 'footprint' (see paragraph 5.3.25);

- telephone contact with the customer prior to opening the account on a home or business number which has been verified (electronically or otherwise), or a "welcome call" to the customer before transactions are permitted, using it to verify additional aspects of personal identity information that have been previously provided during the setting up of the account;

- communicating with the customer at an address that has been verified (such communication may take the form of a direct mailing of account opening documentation to him, which, in full or in part, might be required to be returned completed or acknowledged without alteration);

- internet sign-on following verification procedures where the customer uses security codes, tokens, and/or other passwords which have been set up during account opening and provided by mail (or secure delivery) to the named individual at an independently verified address;

- other card or account activation procedures;

- requiring copy documents to be certified by an appropriate person.

Variation from the standard

5.3.83   The standard identification requirement (for documentary or electronic approaches) is likely to be sufficient for most situations. If, however, the customer, and/or the product or delivery channel, is assessed to present a higher money laundering or terrorist financing risk – whether because of the nature of the customer, or his business, or its location, or because of the product features available – the firm will need to decide whether it should require additional identity information to be provided, and/or whether to verify additional aspects of identity.

5.3.84   Where the result of the standard verification check gives rise to concern or uncertainty over identity, or other risk considerations apply, so the number of matches that will be required to be reasonably satisfied as to the individual's identity will increase.

5.3.85   For higher risk customers, the need to have additional information needs to be balanced against the possibility of instituting enhanced monitoring (see sections 5.5 and 5.7).

Executors and personal representatives

Regulation 6(8)   5.3.86   In the case of an estate of a deceased person in the course of administration, the beneficial owner is

- in England and Wales, the executor, original or by representation, or administrator for the time being of a deceased person; and

- in Scotland, the executor for the purposes of the Executors (Scotland) Act 1900.[2]

In circumstances where an account is opened or taken over by executors or administrators for the purpose of winding up the estate of a deceased person, firms may accept the court documents granting probate or letters of administration as evidence of identity of those personal representatives. Lawyers and accountants acting in the course of their business as regulated firms, who are not named as executors/administrators, can be verified by reference to their practising certificates, or to an appropriate professional register.

---

[2]   1900 c.55. Sections 6 and 7 were amended by the Succession (Scotland) Act 1964 (c 41).

Court of Protection orders and court-appointed deputies

2005, c 9   5.3.87   Under the Mental Capacity Act 2005 (and related Regulations), the
SI 2007/1253   Court of Protection will be able to make an order concerning a single decision in cases where a one-off decision is required regarding someone who lacks capacity. The Court can also appoint a deputy or deputies (previously referred to as receivers) where it is satisfied that a series of decisions needs to be made for a person who lacks capacity.

5.3.88   Firms may accept the court documents appointing the deputy, or concerning a single act, as evidence of identity of the person appointed. While the subject of such an order should be regarded as the beneficial owner, their identity may also be verified by reference to the court documents.

Attorneys

5.3.89   When a person deals with assets under a power of attorney, that person is also a customer of the firm. Consequently, the identity of holders of powers of attorney should be verified.

5.3.90   Where the donor of a power of attorney has capacity, and therefore has control, he remains the owner of the funds, and is the customer. Other than where he is an existing customer of the firm, therefore, his identity must be verified. In many cases, these customers may not possess the standard identity documents referred to in paragraphs 5.3.74ff, and firms may have to accept some of the documents referred to in Part II, sector 1: *Retail banking,* Annex 1–I.

5.3.91   In circumstances where he has lost capacity, the donor no longer has control of the property, but his identity should be verified as the beneficial owner. When an Enduring Power of Attorney is registered with the Court of Protection, the firm will know that the donor has lost, or is losing, capacity. A Lasting Power of Attorney cannot be used until it has been registered, but, subject to any restrictions, this may be done at any time, and while the donor is still able to manage their affairs. Therefore, the firm will not necessarily know whether or not the donor has lost capacity. Where the firm is satisfied that the donor has lost capacity it should verify his identity as a beneficial owner.

Source of funds as evidence

5.3.92   Under certain conditions, where the money laundering or terrorist financing risk in a product is considered to be at its lowest, a payment drawn on an account with a UK or EU regulated credit institution, or one from an equivalent jurisdiction, and which is in the sole or joint name of the customer, may satisfy the standard identification requirement. Whilst the payment may be made between accounts with regulated firms or by cheque or debit card, the accepting firm must be able to confirm that the payment (by whatever method) is from a bank or building society account in the sole or joint name(s) of the customer. Part II, sector 7: *Life assurance, and life-related pensions and investment products,* has an exception to this in respect of direct debits.

5.3.93   Whilst it is immaterial whether the transaction is effected remotely or face-to-face, each type of relationship or transaction that is entered into must be considered before determining that it is appropriate to rely on this method of verification. Firms will need to be able to demonstrate why they considered it to be reasonable to have regard to the source of funds as evidence in a particular instance. Part II, sector 3: *Electronic Money* includes guidance on accepting the funding instrument used to load a purse as a form of initial verification in low risk situations, subject to compensating monitoring controls and turnover limits, and establishing that the customer has rightful control over the instrument.

5.3.94   One of the restrictions that will apply to a product that qualifies for using the source of funds as evidence will be an inability to make payments direct to, or to receive payments direct from, third parties. If, subsequent to using the source of funds to verify the customer's identity, the firm decides to allow such a payment or receipt to proceed, it should verify the identity of the third party. A further restriction would be that cash withdrawals should not be permitted, other than by the customers themselves, on a face-to-face basis where identity can be confirmed.

5.3.95   If a firm proposing to rely on the source of funds has reasonable grounds for believing that the identity of the customer has not been verified by the firm on which the payment has been drawn, it should not permit the source of funds to be used as evidence, and should verify the customer's identity in line with the appropriate standard requirement.

5.3.96 If a firm has reason to suspect the motives behind a particular transaction, or believes that the business is being structured to avoid the standard identification requirement, it should not permit the use of the source of funds as evidence to identify the customer.

5.3.97 Part II, sector 8: *Non-life providers of investment fund products* provides additional guidance to investment fund managers in respect of customers whose identity may not need to be verified until the time of redemption.

Customers who cannot provide the standard evidence

5.3.98 Some customers may not be able to produce identification information equivalent to the standard. Such cases may include, for example, some low-income customers in rented accommodation, customers with a legal, mental or physical inability to manage their affairs, individuals dependent on the care of others, dependant spouses/partners or minors, students, refugees and asylum seekers, migrant workers and prisoners. The firm will therefore need an approach that compensates for the difficulties that such customers may face in providing the standard evidence of identity.

SYSC
3.2.6G(5) G
Promoting
Financial
Inclusion,
December
2004

5.3.99 The FSA Rules adopt a broad view of financial exclusion, in terms of ensuring that, where people cannot reasonably be expected to produce standard evidence of identity, they are not unreasonably denied access to financial services. The term is sometimes used in a narrower sense, for example, HM Treasury refers to those who, for specific reasons, do not have access to mainstream banking or financial services – that is, those at the lower end of income distribution who are socially/ financially disadvantaged and in receipt of benefits, or those who chose not to seek access to financial products because they believed that they will be refused.

5.3.100 Firms offering financial services directed at the financially aware may wish to consider whether any apparent inability to produce standard levels of identification evidence is consistent with the targeted market for these products.

5.3.101 As a first step, before concluding that a customer cannot produce evidence of identity, firms will have established that the guidance on initial identity checks for private individuals set out in paragraphs 5.3.70 to 5.3.97 cannot reasonably be applied.

5.3.102 Guidance on verifying the identity of most categories of customers who cannot provide the standard evidence is given in Part II, sector 1: *Retail banking.* Guidance on cases with more general application is given in paragraphs 5.3.104 to 5.3.114.

5.3.103 Where a firm concludes that an individual customer cannot reasonably meet the standard identification requirement, and that the provisions in Part II, sector 1: *Retail banking,* Annex 1–I, cannot be met, it may accept as identification evidence a letter or statement from an appropriate person who knows the individual, that indicates that the person is who he says he is.

Persons without standard documents, in care homes, or in receipt of pension

5.3.104 An entitlement letter from the DWP, or a letter from the DWP confirming that the person is in receipt of a pension, could provide evidence of identity. If this is not available, or is inappropriate, a letter from an appropriate person, for example, the matron of a care home, may provide the necessary evidence.

Those without the capacity to manage their financial affairs

5.3.105   Guidance on dealing with customers who lack capacity to manage their affairs, such as the mentally incapacitated, or people with learning difficulties, covering Powers of Attorney; Receivership (or short) order; and Appointeeship, are set out in a BBA leaflet, "Banking for people who lack capacity to make decisions", which can be obtained from the British Bankers' Association at www.bba.org.uk. (see also paragraphs 5.3.87 – 5.3.91)

Gender reassignment

5.3.106   A firm should satisfy itself (for example, on the basis of documentary medical evidence) that the gender transfer of a customer is genuine (as with a change of name). Such cases usually involve transferring a credit history to a reassigned gender. This involves data protection, not money laundering issues. The consent of the person involved is necessary.

Students and young people

5.3.107   When opening accounts for students or other young people, the standard identification requirement should be followed as far as possible (see paragraphs 5.3.70 – 5.3.97). In practice, it is likely that many students, and other young people, will have a passport, and possibly a driving licence. Where the standard requirement would not be relevant, however, or where the customer cannot satisfactorily meet this, other evidence could be obtained by obtaining appropriate confirmation(s) from the applicant's workplace, school, college, university or care institution (see DfES website www.dfes.gov.uk/providersregister/ and Part II, sector 1: *Retail banking*, Annex 1–I). Any confirmatory letter should be on appropriately headed notepaper; in assessing the strength of such confirmation, firms should have regard to the period of existence of the educational or other institution involved, and whether it is subject to some form of regulatory oversight.

5.3.108   All international students, other than those from EEA countries or Switzerland, undergo rigorous checks by the immigration services at home and abroad in order to be satisfied as to their identity and bona fides before they are given leave to enter or remain in the UK as a student or prospective student. Applicants must meet the requirements of the Student Immigration Rules and must provide documentation which demonstrates that they intend to study, and have been accepted, on a course of study at a bona fide institution. This includes the provision of a course admission letter from the education institution. If they cannot provide the documents they will not be given leave to enter or remain in the UK.

5.3.109   Often, a business relationship in respect of a minor will be established by a family member or guardian. In cases where the adult opening the account or establishing the relationship does not already have an existing relationship with the firm, the identity of that adult should be verified and, in addition, the firm should see one of the following in the name of the child:

- birth certificate
- passport
- NHS Medical Card
- Child benefit documentation
- Child Tax Credit documentation
- National Insurance Card (for those aged 16 and over)

Financially excluded

5.3.110 Further guidance on verifying the identity of financially excluded persons is given in Part II, sector 1: *Retail banking,* paragraphs 1.38 – 1.41. A proportionate and risk-based approach will be needed to determine whether the evidence available gives reasonable confidence as to the identity of a customer.

5.3.111 Where a firm has concluded that it should treat a customer as financially excluded for the purposes of customer identification, and the customer is identified by means other than standard evidence, the reasons for doing so should be documented.

5.3.112 The "financially excluded" are not a homogeneous category of uniform risk. Some financially excluded persons may represent a higher risk of money laundering regardless of whether they provide standard or non-standard tokens to confirm their identity, eg, a passport holder who qualifies only for a basic account on credit grounds. Firms may wish to consider whether enhanced due diligence (see section 5.5) or monitoring (see section 5.7) of the size and expected volume of transactions would be useful in respect of some financially excluded categories, based on the firm's own experience of their operation.

5.3.113 In other cases, where the available evidence of identity is limited, and the firm judges that the individual cannot reasonably be expected to provide more, but that the business relationship should nevertheless go ahead, it should consider instituting enhanced monitoring arrangements over the customer's transactions and activity (see section 5.7). In addition, the firm should consider whether restrictions should be placed on the customer's ability to migrate to other, higher risk products or services.

5.3.114 Where an applicant produces non-standard documentation, staff should be discouraged from citing the ML Regulations as an excuse for not opening an account without giving proper consideration to the evidence available, referring up the line for advice as necessary. It may be that at the conclusion of that process a considered judgement may properly be made that the evidence available does not provide a sufficient level of confidence that the applicant is who he claims to be, in which event a decision not to open the account would be fully justified. Firms should bear in mind that the ML Regulations are not explicit as to what is and is not acceptable evidence of identity.

Customers other than private individuals

5.3.115 Depending on the nature of the entity, a relationship or transaction with a customer who is not a private individual may be entered into in the customer's own name, or in that of specific individuals or other entities on its behalf. Beneficial ownership may, however, rest with others, either because the legal owner is acting for the beneficial owner, or because there is a legal obligation for the ownership to be registered in a particular way.

Regulation 5(b) 5.3.116 In deciding who the beneficial owner is in relation to a customer who is not a private individual, the firm's objective must be to know who has ownership or control over the funds which form or otherwise relate to the relationship, and/or form the controlling mind and/or management of any legal entity involved in the funds. Verifying the identity of the beneficial owner(s) will be carried out on a risk-based approach, following the guidance in paragraphs 5.3.10 and 5.3.11, and will take account of the number of individuals, the nature and distribution of their interests in the entity and the nature and extent of any business, contractual or family relationship between them.

5.3.117   Certain other information about the entity should be obtained as a
standard requirement. Thereafter, on the basis of the money laundering/
terrorist financing risk assessed in the customer/product/delivery
channel combination, a firm should decide the extent to which the
identity of the entity should be verified. The firm should also decide
what additional information in respect of the entity and, potentially,
some of the individuals behind it, should be obtained (see section 5.5).

5.3.118   Many entities, both in the UK and elsewhere, operate internet websites,
which contain information about the entity. Firms should bear in mind
that this information, although helpful in providing much of the
material that a firm might need in relation to the company, its directors
and business, is not independently verified before being made publicly
available in this way.

5.3.119   This section provides guidance on verifying the identity of a range of
non-personal entities, as follows:

- Corporates (other than regulated firms) (paragraphs 5.3.120 to
  5.3.150)

- Pension schemes (paragraphs 5.3.151 to 5.3.159)

- Charities, church bodies and places of worship (paragraphs 5.3.160
  to 5.3.179)

- Other trusts, foundations and similar entities (paragraphs 5.3.180
  to 5.3.202)

- Other regulated financial services firms subject to the ML
  Regulations (or equivalent) (paragraphs 5.3.203 to 5.3.207)

- Other firms subject to the ML Regulations (or equivalent)
  (paragraphs 5.3.208 to 5.3.211)

- Partnerships and unincorporated businesses (paragraphs 5.3.212 to
  5.3.225)

- Clubs and societies (paragraphs 5.3.226 to 5.3.234)

- Public sector bodies, governments, state-owned companies and
  supranationals (paragraphs 5.3.235 to 5.43.248)

Corporates (other than regulated firms)

5.3.120   Corporate customers may be publicly accountable in several ways.
Some public companies are listed on stock exchanges or other
regulated markets, and are subject to market regulation and to a high
level of public disclosure in relation to their ownership and business
activities. Other public companies are unlisted, but are still subject to a
high level of disclosure through public filing obligations. Private
companies are not generally subject to the same level of disclosure,
although they may often have public filing obligations. In their
verification processes, firms should take account of the availability of
public information in respect of different types of company.

Regulation   5.3.121   The structure, ownership, purpose and activities of many corporates
20(2)(a)   will be clear and understandable. Corporate customers can use complex
ownership structures, which can increase the steps that need to be taken
to be reasonably satisfied as to their identities; this does not necessarily
indicate money laundering or terrorist financing. The use of complex
structures without an obvious legitimate commercial purpose may,
however, give rise to concern and increase the risk of money
laundering or terrorist financing.

PART V
OTHER MATERIALS

5.3.122 Control over companies may be exercised through a direct shareholding or through intermediate holding companies. Control may also rest with those who have power to manage funds or transactions without requiring specific authority to do so, and who would be in a position to override internal procedures and control mechanisms. Firms should make an evaluation of the effective distribution of control in each case. What constitutes control for this purpose will depend on the nature of the company, the distribution of shareholdings, and the nature and extent of any business or family connections between the beneficial owners.

Regulation 5(c)

5.3.123 To the extent consistent with the risk assessment carried out in accordance with the guidance in Chapter 4, the firm should ensure that it fully understands the company's legal form, structure and ownership, and must obtain sufficient additional information on the nature of the company's business, and the reasons for seeking the product or service.

Regulation 6(1)

5.3.124 In the case of a body corporate the beneficial owner includes any individual who:

- as respects any body other than a company listed on a regulated market, ultimately owns or controls (whether through direct or indirect ownership or control, including through bearer share holdings) more than 25% of the shares or voting rights in the body; or

- as respects any body corporate, otherwise exercises control over the management of the body.

5.3.125 Directors of a body corporate do not fall under the definition of beneficial owner, as in the capacity of director they do not have an ownership interest in the body, nor do they control the voting rights in the body, nor do they exercise control over management in the sense of being able to control the composition and/or voting of the board of directors.

5.3.126 Paragraphs 5.3.127 – 5.3.144 refer to the standard evidence for corporate customers, and paragraphs 5.3.145 – 5.3.150 provide further supplementary guidance on steps that may be applied as part of a risk-based approach.

Obtain standard evidence

5.3.127 The firm should obtain the following in relation to the corporate concerned:

- full name
- registered number
- registered office in country of incorporation
- business address

and, additionally, for private or unlisted companies:

- names of all directors (or equivalent)
- names of individuals who own or control over 25% of its shares or voting rights

5.3.128 The firm should verify the existence of the corporate from:
— *either* confirmation of the company's listing on a regulated market
— *or* a search of the relevant company registry
— *or* a copy of the company's Certificate of Incorporation

5.3.129 Firms should take appropriate steps to be reasonably satisfied that the person the firm is dealing with is properly authorised by the customer.

5.3.130 Some consideration should be given as to whether documents relied upon are forged. In addition, if they are in a foreign language, appropriate steps should be taken to be reasonably satisfied that the documents in fact provide evidence of the customer's identity.

Companies listed on a regulated market

5.3.131   Corporate customers whose securities are admitted to trading on a regulated market in an EEA state or one in an equivalent jurisdiction are publicly owned and generally accountable.

Regulation   5.3.132   Where the firm has satisfied itself that the customer is:
13(3)

- a company which is listed on a regulated market (within the meaning of MiFID) in the EEA, or on a non-EEA market that is subject to specified disclosure obligations; or

- a majority-owned and consolidated subsidiary of such a listed company
simplified due diligence may be applied (see section 5.4).

Regulation   5.3.133   Specified disclosure obligations are disclosure requirements consistent
2(1)   with specified articles of:

- The Prospectus directive [2003/71/EC]

- The Transparency Obligations directive [2004/109/EC]

- The Market Abuse directive [2003/6/EC]

Regulations   5.3.134   If a regulated market is located within the EEA there is no requirement
2(1) and 13(3)   to undertake checks on the market itself. Firms should, however, record the steps they have taken to ascertain the status of the market. If the market is outside the EEA, but is one which subjects companies whose securities are admitted to trading to disclosure obligations which are contained in international standards and are equivalent to the specified disclosure obligation in the EU, similar treatment is permitted. For companies listed outside the EEA on markets, which do not qualify for SDD, the standard verification requirement for private and unlisted companies should be applied.

5.3.135   The European Commission maintains a list of regulated markets within the EU at ec.europa.eu/internal_market/securities/isd/mifid_en.htm. Firms should note that AIM is not a regulated market under MiFID (for reasons of price transparency); under its risk-based approach, however, a firm may feel that the due diligence process for admission to AIM gives equivalent comfort as to the identity of the company under consideration.

Private and unlisted companies

5.3.136   Unlike publicly quoted companies, the activities of private or unlisted companies are often carried out for the profit/benefit of a small and defined group of individuals or entities. Such firms are also subject to a lower level of public disclosure than public companies. In general, however, the structure, ownership, purposes and activities of many private companies will be clear and understandable.

5.3.137   Where private companies are well known, reputable organisations, with long histories in their industries and substantial public information about them, the standard evidence may well be sufficient to meet the firm's obligations.

5.3.138   In the UK, a company registry search will confirm that the applicant company has not been, or is not in the process of being, dissolved, struck off or wound up. In the case of non-UK companies, firms should make similar search enquiries of the registry in the country of incorporation of the applicant for business.

5.3.139   Standards of control over the issue of documentation from company registries vary between different countries. Attention should be paid to the jurisdiction the documents originate from and the background against which they are produced.

5.3.140   Whenever faced with less transparency, less of an industry profile, or less independent means of verification of the client entity, firms should consider the money laundering or terrorist financing risk presented by the entity, and therefore the extent to which, in addition to the standard evidence, they should verify the identities of other shareholders and/or controllers. It is important to know and understand any associations the entity may have with other jurisdictions (headquarters, operating facilities, branches, subsidiaries, etc) and the individuals who may influence its operations (political connections, etc). A visit to the place of business may be helpful to confirm the existence and activities of the entity.

5.3.141   Firms may find the sectoral guidance in Part II helpful in understanding some of the business relationships that may exist between the customer and other entities in particular business areas.

Directors

5.3.142   Following the firm's assessment of the money laundering or terrorist financing risk presented by the company, it may decide to verify the identity of one or more directors, as appropriate, in accordance with the guidance for private individuals (paragraphs 5.3.68 to 5.3.114). In that event, verification is likely to be appropriate for those who have authority to operate an account or to give the firm instructions concerning the use or transfer of funds or assets, but might be waived for other directors. Firms may, of course, already be required to identify a particular director as a beneficial owner if the director owns or controls more than 25% of the company's shares or voting rights (see paragraph 5.3.124).

Beneficial owners

Regulation 6(1)   5.3.143   As part of the standard evidence, the firm will know the names of all
Regulation 5(b)   individual beneficial owners owning or controlling more than 25% of the company's shares or voting rights, even where these interests are held indirectly. Following the firm's assessment of the money laundering or terrorist financing risk presented by the customer, the firm must take risk based and adequate measures to verify the identity of those individuals (see paragraphs 5.3.10 and 5.3.11).

Signatories

5.3.144   For operational purposes, the firm is likely to have a list of those authorised to give instructions for the movement of funds or assets, along with an appropriate instrument authorising one or more directors (or equivalent) to give the firm such instructions. The identities of individual signatories need only be verified on a risk-based approach.

Variation from the standard

Regulation   5.3.145   The standard evidence is likely to be sufficient for most corporate
14(1)(b)   customers. If, however, the customer, or the product or delivery channel, is assessed to present a higher money laundering or terrorist financing risk – whether because of the nature of the customer, its business or its location, or because of the product features available – the firm must, on a risk-sensitive basis, apply enhanced due diligence measures. For example, the firm will need to decide whether it should require additional identity information to be provided and/or verified (see sections 5.6 and 5.7).

5.3.146 Unless their securities are admitted to trading in a regulated market in an EEA state, corporate customers that are subject to statutory licensing and regulation of their industry (for example, energy, telecommunications) do not qualify for simplified due diligence. Under its risk-based approach, however, a firm may feel that, provided that it is confirmed by a reliable and independent source, imposition of regulatory obligations on such a firm gives an equivalent level of confidence in the company's public accountability. Therefore, evidence that the corporate customer is subject to the licensing and prudential regulatory regime of a statutory regulator in the EU (eg, OFGEM, OFWAT, OFCOM or an EU equivalent), will satisfy the firm's obligation to verify the identity of such a customer.

5.3.147 Higher risk corporate customers may also be, among others, smaller and more opaque entities, with little or no industry profile and those in less transparent jurisdictions, taking account of issues such as their size, industry profile, industry risk.

Regulation
14(1(b)
and (4)

5.3.148 Where an entity is known to be linked to a PEP, or to a jurisdiction assessed as carrying a higher money laundering/terrorist financing risk, it is likely that this will put the entity into a higher risk category, and that enhanced due diligence measures must therefore be applied (see sections 5.5 and 5.7).

Bearer shares

5.3.149 Extra care must be taken in the case of companies with capital in the form of bearer shares, because in such cases it is often difficult to identify the beneficial owner(s). Companies that issue bearer shares are frequently incorporated in high risk jurisdictions. Firms should adopt procedures to establish the identities of the holders and material beneficial owners of such shares and to ensure that they are notified whenever there is a change of holder and/or beneficial owner.

5.3.150 As a minimum, these procedures should require a firm to obtain an undertaking in writing from the beneficial owner which states that immediate notification will be given to the firm if the shares are transferred to another party. Depending on its risk assessment of the client, the firm may consider it appropriate to have this undertaking certified by an accountant, lawyer or equivalent, or even to require that the shares be held by a named custodian, with an undertaking from that custodian that the firm will be notified of any changes to records relating to these shares and the custodian.

Pension schemes

5.3.151 UK pension schemes can take a number of legal forms. Some may be companies limited by guarantee; some may take the form of trusts; others may be unincorporated associations. Many obtain HMRC approval in order to achieve tax-exempt status.

Regulation
13(7)(c)

5.3.152 In respect of a pension, superannuation or similar scheme which provides retirement benefits for employees, where contributions are made by an employer or by way of deduction from an employee's wages and the scheme rules do not permit the assignment of a member's interest under the scheme [other than in two cases set out in Regulation 13(7)(c)], simplified due diligence may be applied (see section 5.4).

5.3.153 For such a scheme, therefore, the firm need only satisfy itself that the customer qualifies for simplified due diligence in this way. In other cases, a pension scheme should be treated for AML/CTF purposes, and standard evidence obtained, according to its legal form.

Regulation
6(5)(b)(ii)

5.3.154 For a scheme that takes the form of a trust, an individual does not qualify as a beneficial owner through having control solely as a result of discretion delegated to him under s 34 of the Pensions Act.

Obtain standard evidence

5.3.155 Where a pension scheme does not qualify for simplified due diligence, but has HMRC approval, a firm's identification and verification obligations may be met by confirming the scheme's approval. Life insurers selling or administering pension products should follow the processes outlined in Part II: *Life assurance, and life-related pension and investment products*, paragraphs 7.30 and 7.48.

Signatories

5.3.156 For operational purposes, the firm is likely to have a list of those authorised to give instructions for the movement of funds or assets, along with an appropriate instrument authorising one or more directors (or equivalent) to give the firm such instructions. The identities of individual signatories need only be verified on a risk-based approach.

Variation from the standard

5.3.157 The identity of the principal employer should be verified in accordance with the guidance given for companies in paragraphs 5.3.120 to 5.3.150 and the source of funding recorded to ensure that a complete audit trail exists if the employer is wound up.

Payment of benefits

5.3.158 Any payment of benefits by, or on behalf of, the trustees of an occupational pension scheme will not require verification of identity of the recipient. (The transaction will either not be relevant financial business or will be within the scope of the exemption for policies of insurance in respect of occupational pension schemes.)

5.3.159 Where individual members of an occupational pension scheme are to be given personal investment advice, their identities must be verified. However, where the identity of the trustees and principal employer have been satisfactorily verified (and the information is still current), it may be appropriate for the employer to provide confirmation of identities of individual employees.

Charities, church bodies and places of worship

5.3.160 Charities have their status because of their purposes, and can take a number of legal forms. Some may be companies limited by guarantee, or incorporated by Royal Charter or by Act of Parliament; some may take the form of trusts; others may be unincorporated associations.

5.3.161 If the charity is an incorporated entity (or otherwise has legal personality), firms should verify its identity following the guidance in paragraphs 5.3.120ff. The charity itself is the firm's customer, for practical purposes represented by the trustees who give instruction to the firm.

5.3.162 If the charity takes the form of a trust, it has no legal personality and its trustees have control and management over its affairs. Those trustees who enter into the business relationship with the firm, in their capacity as trustees of that particular charitable trust, are the firm's customers, on whom the firm must carry out full CDD measures. (see paragraphs 5.3.180ff.)

5.3.163 If the charity takes the form of an unincorporated association, it also has no legal personality. Its officers, or members of its governing body, are then the firm's customers, on whom the firm must carry out full CDD measures. (see paragraphs 5.3.226ff.)

5.3.164   Any trustees of a charitable trust who are not the firm's customers will be beneficial owners, because they exercise control over the charity's property. In exceptional cases, another individual may exercise control. Examples include a receiver appointed to manage the affairs of the charity, or a settlor who retains significant powers over the trust property.

5.3.165   For the vast majority of charities, either there will be no individual who is a beneficial owner (apart from the trustees) within the meaning of the ML Regulations, or at most a class of persons who stand to benefit from the charity's objects must be identified. These persons will be self-evident from a review of the charity's objects in its constitution or the extract from the Register of Charities.

5.3.166   Examples of charities where classes of persons can be identified include charities that relieve poverty, famine or homelessness, educate individuals or alleviate sickness, disability or age. In these cases, a broad description of the class of persons who stand to benefit is sufficient so that the firm understands who the persons are who benefit. Examples of classes might be:
- 'Victims of the Asian Tsunami'
- 'Homeless persons in London'
- 'Deaf and blind people'
- 'Children in the village of Ambridge'

In other charities, no individuals benefit directly from the charity's objects. Examples include charities for the benefit of animals, wildlife or flora, or the conservation or preservation of buildings, habitats or environment.

5.3.167   Neither the Charity Commissioners, nor judges of courts (who may exercise powers over charities) have control for these purposes.

Obtain standard evidence

5.3.168   The firm should obtain the following in relation to the charity or church body:
- Full name and address
- Nature of body's activities and objects
- Names of all trustees (or equivalent)
- Names or classes of beneficiaries

5.3.169   The existence of the charity can be verified from a number of different sources, depending on whether the charity is registered or not, a place of worship or an independent school or college.

Registered charities – England and Wales, and Scotland

5.3.170   The Charity Commission is required to hold a central register of charities in England and Wales and allocates a registered number to each. The Office of the Scottish Charity Regulator carries out a similar function for Scottish charities. When dealing with an application which includes the name of a registered charity, the Charity Commission, or the Office of the Scottish Charity Regulator, can confirm the registered number of the charity and the name and address of the regulator's correspondent for the charity concerned.

5.3.171   Details of all registered charities can be accessed on the Charity Commission website (www.charity-commission.gov.uk), the Office of the Scottish Charity Regulator website (www.oscr.org.uk), or a check can be made by telephone to the respective regulator's enquiry line (see www.jmlsg.org.uk). Firms should be aware that simply being registered is not in itself a guarantee of the bona fides of an organisation, although it does indicate that it is subject to some ongoing regulation.

PART V
OTHER MATERIALS

Charities in Northern Ireland

5.3.172 Applications from, or on behalf of, charities in Northern Ireland should be dealt with in accordance with procedures for private companies set out in paragraphs 5.3.136 to 5.3.144, if they are limited by guarantee, and for clubs and societies, those in paragraphs 5.3.226 to 5.3.234. Verification of the charitable status can normally be obtained through HMRC.

Church bodies and places of worship

Registered Places of Worship Act 1855

5.3.173 Places of worship are in general exempted by law from registering as charities and may not therefore have a registered number. Instead, they can apply for a certified building of worship from the General Register Office (GRO). For tax purposes, however, they may notify HMRC of their charitable status; verification of their status may be met by confirming the church's HMRC notification. Their identity may be verified by reference to a copy of the GRO registration, examination of the GRO register, or, where appropriate, through the headquarters or regional organisation of the denomination, or religion.

Independent schools and colleges

5.3.174 Where an independent school or college is a registered charity, it should be treated in accordance with the guidance for charities. Any such body which is not registered as a charity should be treated in accordance with the guidance for private companies in paragraphs 5.3.136 to 5.3.144.

5.3.175 Firms should take appropriate steps to be reasonably satisfied that the person the firm is dealing with is properly authorised by the customer.

Variation from the standard

5.3.176 The identities of unregistered charities or church bodies, whether in the UK or elsewhere, cannot be verified by reference to registers maintained by independent bodies. Applications from, or on behalf of, unregistered charities should therefore be dealt with in accordance with the procedures for private companies set out in paragraphs 5.3.136 to 5.3.144, for trusts, as set out in paragraphs 5.3.180 to 5.3.202, or for clubs and societies, as set out in paragraphs 5.3.226 to 5.3.234. Firms should take particular note of those paragraphs addressing customers where the money laundering or terrorist financing risk is greater in relation to particular customers, and if it should be followed in these circumstances.

5.3.177 In assessing the risks presented by different charities, a firm might need to make appropriate distinction between those with a limited geographical remit, and those with unlimited geographical scope, such as medical and emergency relief charities.

5.3.178 If they have a defined area of benefit, charities are only able to expend their funds within that defined area. If this area is an overseas country or jurisdiction, the charity can quite properly be transferring funds to that country or jurisdiction. It would be less clear why the organisation should be transferring funds to a third country (which may, within the general context of the firm's risk assessment have a lower profile) and this would therefore be unusual. Such activity would lead to the charity being regarded as higher risk.

5.3.179   Non-profit organisations have been known to be abused, to divert funds to terrorist financing and other criminal activities. FATF published a paper 'Combating the abuse of non-profit organisations – International Best Practices' in October 2002 (available at www.fatf-gafi.org), in support of Special Recommendation VIII. In November 2005, the European Commission adopted a Recommendation to member states containing a Framework for a code of conduct for non-profit organisations. The Recommendation is available at www.jmlsg.org.uk.

Other trusts, foundations and similar entities

5.3.180   There is a wide variety of trusts, ranging from large, nationally and internationally active organisations subject to a high degree of public interest and quasi-accountability, through trusts set up under testamentary arrangements, to small, local trusts funded by small, individual donations from local communities, serving local needs. It is important, in putting proportionate AML/CTF processes into place, and in carrying out their risk assessments, that firms take account of the different money laundering or terrorist financing risks that trusts of different sizes, areas of activity and nature of business being conducted, present.

5.3.181   For trusts or foundations that have no legal personality, those trustees (or equivalent) who enter into the business relationship with the firm, in their capacity as trustees of the particular trust or foundation, are the firm's customers on whom the firm must carry out full CDD measures. Following a risk-based approach, in the case of a large, well known and accountable organisation firms may limit the trustees considered customers to those who give instructions to the firm. Other trustees will be verified as beneficial owners, following the guidance in paragraphs 5.3.10 and 5.3.11.

5.3.182   Most trusts are not separate legal persons, and for AML/CTF purposes should be identified as described in paragraphs 5.3.188 and 5.3.189.

Regulation   5.3.183   The beneficial owner of a trust is defined by reference to three
6(3), (4)   categories of individual:

- any individual who is entitled to a specified interest (that is, a vested, not a contingent, interest) in at least 25% of the capital of the trust property

- as respects any trust other than one which is set up or operates entirely for the benefit of individuals with such specified interests, the class of persons in whose main interest the trust is set up or operates

- any individual who has control over the trust.

Regulation 6(4)   5.3.184   The trustees of a trust will be beneficial owners, as they will exercise control over the trust property. In exceptional cases, another individual may exercise control, such as a trust protector, or a settlor who retains significant powers over the trust property.

5.3.185   For the vast majority of trusts, either there will be clearly identified beneficiaries (who are beneficial owners within the meaning of the ML Regulations), or a class of beneficiaries. These persons will be self-evident from a review of the trust's constitution.

5.3.186   In some trusts, no individuals may benefit directly; examples include trusts for the benefit of animals, wildlife or flora, or the conservation or preservation of buildings, habitats or environment.

Regulation 6(6)   5.3.187   In the case of a legal arrangement that is not a trust, the beneficial owner means

- where the individuals who benefit from the entity or arrangement have been determined, any individual who benefits from al least 25% of the property of the entity or arrangement;

- where the individuals who benefit from the entity or arrangement have yet to be determined, the class of persons in whose main interest the entity or arrangement is set up or operates;

- any individual who exercise control over at least 25% of the property of the entity or arrangement.

Obtain standard evidence

5.3.188 In respect of trusts, the firm should obtain the following information:

- Full name of the trust

- Nature and purpose of the trust (eg, discretionary, testamentary, bare)

- Country of establishment

- Names of all trustees

- Names of any beneficial owners

- Name and address of any protector or controller

Regulation 4(1)(b)
5.3.189 The identity of the trust must be verified using reliable and independent documents, data or information. This may require sight of relevant extracts from the trust deed, or reference to an appropriate register in the country of establishment. The firm must take measures to understand the ownership and control structure of the customer.

5.3.190 Firms should take appropriate steps to be reasonably satisfied that the person the firm is dealing with is properly authorised by the customer. Some consideration should be given as to whether documents relied upon are forged. In addition, if they are in a foreign language, appropriate steps should be taken to be reasonably satisfied that the documents in fact provide evidence of the customer's identity.

Beneficial owners

Regulation 4(1)(b)
5.3.191 The firm must verify the identities of the trustees (or equivalent) as beneficial owners, if not already identified as customers of the firm. The identities of other beneficial owners, either individuals or a class, as appropriate, must also be verified (see paragraphs 5.3.10 and 5.3.11).

5.3.192 Where a trustee is itself a regulated entity (or a nominee company owned and controlled by a regulated entity), or a company listed on a regulated market, or other type of entity, the identification and verification procedures that should be carried out should reflect the standard approach for such an entity.

Variation from the standard

5.3.193 Firms should make appropriate distinction between those trusts that serve a limited purpose (such as inheritance tax planning) or have a limited range of activities and those where the activities and connections are more sophisticated, or are geographically based and/or with financial links to other countries.

5.3.194   For situations presenting a lower money laundering or terrorist financing risk, the standard evidence will be sufficient. However, less transparent and more complex structures, with numerous layers, may pose a higher money laundering or terrorist financing risk. Also, some trusts established in jurisdictions with favourable tax regimes have in the past been associated with tax evasion and money laundering. In respect of trusts in the latter category, the firm's risk assessment may lead it to require additional information on the purpose, funding and beneficiaries of the trust.

5.3.195   Where a situation is assessed as carrying a higher risk of money laundering or terrorist financing, the firm may need to carry out a higher level of verification. Information that might be appropriate to ascertain for higher risk situations includes:

- Donor/settlor/grantor of the funds (except where there are large numbers of small donors)

- Domicile of business/activity

- Nature of business/activity

- Location of business/activity (operating address)

5.3.196   Following its assessment of the money laundering risk presented by the trust, the firm may decide to verify the identity of the settlor(s).

Non-UK trusts and foundations

5.3.197   The guidance in paragraphs 5.3.180 to 5.3.196 applies equally to UK based trusts and non-UK based trusts. On a risk-based approach, a firm will need to consider whether the geographical location of the trust gives rise to additional concerns, and if so, what they should do.

5.3.198   A foundation ("Stiftung") is described in the FATF October 2006 *Report on the Misuse of Corporate Vehicles* as follows: "A foundation (based on the Roman law *universitas rerum*) is the civil law equivalent to a common law trust in that it may be used for similar purposes. A foundation traditionally requires property dedicated to a particular purpose. Typically the income derived from the principal assets (as opposed to the assets themselves) is used to fulfil the statutory purpose. A foundation is a legal entity and as such may engage in and conduct business. A foundation is controlled by a board of directors and has no owners. In most jurisdictions a foundation's purpose must be public. However there are jurisdictions in which foundations may be created for private purposes. Normally, foundations are highly regulated and transparent."

5.3.199   Foundations feature in a number of EEA member state and other civil law jurisdictions including, notably, Liechtenstein and Panama. The term is also used in the UK and USA in a looser sense, usually to refer to a charitable organisation of some sort.

5.3.200   The nature of a civil law foundation should normally be well understood by firms, or their subsidiaries or branches, operating in the jurisdiction under whose laws the foundation has been set up. Where a foundation seeks banking or other financial services outside its home jurisdiction, firms will need to be satisfied that there are legitimate reasons for doing so and to establish the statutory requirements within the specific home jurisdiction for setting up a foundation. So far as possible, comparable information should be obtained as indicated in paragraph 5.3.188 for trusts, including the identity of the founder and beneficiaries (who may include the founder), whose identity should be verified as necessary on similar risk-based principles.

5.3.201 Where the founder's identity is withheld, firms will need to exercise caution and have regard to the standing of any intermediary and the extent of assurances that may be obtained from them to disclose information on any parties concerned with the foundation in response to judicial demand in the firm's own jurisdiction. Liechtenstein foundations, for example, are generally established on a fiduciary basis through a licensed trust company to preserve the anonymity of the founder, but the trust companies are themselves subject to AML laws.

5.3.202 Whilst firms may conclude on the basis of their due diligence that the request for facilities is acceptable, they should bear in mind that terms like 'foundation', 'stiftung', 'anstalt' are liable to be hijacked by prime bank instrument fraudsters to add spurious credibility to bogus investment schemes.

Other regulated financial services firms that are subject to the ML Regulations (or equivalent)

Regulation 13(2)

5.3.203 In respect of other financial services firms which are subject to the ML Regulations or equivalent, and which are regulated in the UK by the FSA, or in the EU or an equivalent jurisdiction, by an equivalent regulator, simplified due diligence may be applied (see section 5.4).

Regulation 13(1)

5.3.204 Firms must, however, have reasonable grounds for believing that the customer qualifies for the treatment in paragraph 5.3.203.

5.3.205 Having reasonable grounds might involve:

- checking with the home country central bank or relevant supervisory body; or
- checking with another office, subsidiary, branch or correspondent bank in the same country; or
- checking with a regulated correspondent bank of the overseas institution; or
- obtaining from the relevant institution evidence of its licence or authorisation to conduct financial and/or banking business.

To assist firms, a list of the regulatory authorities in EU and FATF member states is available at www.jmlsg.org.uk.

5.3.206 Firms should record the steps they have taken to check the status of the other regulated firm.

5.3.207 Firms should take appropriate steps to be reasonably satisfied that the person they are dealing with is properly authorised by the customer.

Other firms that are subject to the ML Regulations (or equivalent)

5.3.208 Customers which are subject to the ML Regulations or equivalent, but which are not regulated in the UK, the EU or an equivalent jurisdiction as a financial services business, should be treated, for AML/CTF purposes, according to their legal form: for example, as private companies, in accordance with the guidance set out in paragraphs 5.3.136 to 5.3.144; or if partnerships, by confirming their regulated status through reference to the current membership directory of the relevant professional association (for example, law society or accountancy body). However, when professional individuals are acting in their personal capacity, for example, as trustees, their identity should normally be verified as for any other private individual.

5.3.209 Firms should take appropriate steps to be reasonably satisfied that the person the firm is dealing with is properly authorised by the customer

5.3.210 Some consideration should be given as to whether documents relied upon are forged. In addition, if they are in a foreign language, appropriate steps should be taken to be reasonably satisfied that the documents in fact provide evidence of the customer's identity.

[Regulation
13(4)

5.3.211   Independent legal professionals that are subject to the ML Regulations, or from third countries where they are subject to equivalent requirements (and are supervised for compliance with those requirements), and which hold client money in pooled accounts, are obliged to verify the identities of their clients. Financial services firms with which such client accounts are held are not required to identify the beneficial owners of such funds, provided that the information on the identity of the beneficial owner is available, on request, to the firm. As a practical matter, firms may reasonably apply a similar approach to such client accounts which only contain the funds of a single beneficial owner.]

Partnerships and unincorporated businesses

5.3.212   Partnerships and unincorporated businesses, although principally operated by individuals, or groups of individuals, are different from private individuals in that there is an underlying business. This business is likely to have a different money laundering or terrorist financing risk profile from that of an individual.

Regulation 6(2)   5.3.213   The beneficial owner of a partnership is any individual who ultimately is entitled to or controls (whether the entitlement or control is direct or indirect) more than a 25% share of the capital or profits of the partnership, or more than 25% of the voting rights in the partnership, or who otherwise exercise control over the management of the partnership.

Obtain standard evidence

5.3.214   The firm should obtain the following in relation to the partnership or unincorporated association:

- full name

- business address

- names of all partners/principals who exercise control over the management of the partnership

- names of individuals who own or control over 25% of its capital or profit, or of its voting rights

5.3.215   Given the wide range of partnerships and unincorporated businesses, in terms of size, reputation and numbers of partners/principals, firms need to make an assessment of where a particular partnership or business lies on the associated risk spectrum.

5.3.216   The firm's obligation is to verify the identity of the customer using evidence from a reliable and independent source. Where partnerships or unincorporated businesses are well known, reputable organisations, with long histories in their industries, and with substantial public information about them and their principals and controllers, confirmation of the customer's membership of a relevant professional or trade association is likely to be able to provide such reliable and independent evidence. This does not obviate the need to verify the identity of the partnership's beneficial owners.

5.3.217　Other partnerships and unincorporated businesses will have a lower profile, and will generally comprise a much smaller number of partners/principals. In verifying the identity of such customers, firms should primarily have regard to the number of partner/principals. Where these are relatively few, the customer should be treated as a collection of private individuals, and follow the guidance set out in paragraphs 5.3.70 – 5.3.114; where numbers are larger, the firm should decide whether it should continue to regard the customer as a collection of private individuals, or whether it can be satisfied with evidence of membership of a relevant professional or trade association. In either circumstance, there is likely to be a need to see the partnership deed, to be satisfied that the entity exists, unless an entry in an appropriate national register may be checked.

5.3.218　For identification purposes, Scottish partnerships, limited partnerships and limited liability partnerships should be treated as corporate customers.

5.3.219　Firms should take appropriate steps to be reasonably satisfied that the person the firm is dealing with is properly authorised by the customer.

5.3.220　Some consideration should be given as to whether documents relied upon are forged. In addition, if they are in a foreign language, appropriate steps should be taken to be reasonably satisfied that the documents in fact provide evidence of the customer's identity.

Variation from the standard

5.3.221　Most partnerships and unincorporated businesses are smaller, less transparent, and less well known entities, and are not subject to the same accountability requirements as, for example, companies listed on a regulated market.

5.3.222　Where the money laundering or terrorist financing risk is considered to be at its lowest, the firm may be able to use the source of funds as evidence of the customer's identity. The guidance in paragraphs 5.3.92 to 5.3.96 should be followed. This does not obviate the need to verify the identity of beneficial owners, where these exist.

5.3.223　Whenever faced with less transparency, less of an industry profile, or less independent means of verification of the client entity, firms should consider the money laundering or terrorist financing risk presented by the entity, and therefore the extent to which, in addition to the standard evidence, additional precautions should be taken.

5.3.224　It is important to know and understand any associations the entity may have with other jurisdictions (headquarters, operating facilities, branches, subsidiaries, etc) and the individuals who may influence its operations (political connections, etc). A visit to the place of business may be helpful to confirm the existence and activities of the business.

Principals and owners

5.3.225　Following its assessment of the money laundering or terrorist financing risk presented by the entity, the firm may decide to verify the identity of one or more of the partners/owners as customers. In that event, verification requirements are likely to be appropriate for partners/owners who have authority to operate an account or to give the firm instructions concerning the use or transfer of funds or assets; other partners/owners must be verified as beneficial owners, following the guidance in paragraphs 5.3.10 and 5.3.11.

Clubs and societies

5.3.226 Where an application is made on behalf of a club or society, firms should make appropriate distinction between those that serve a limited social or regional purpose and those where the activities and connections are more sophisticated, or are geographically based and/or with financial links to other countries.

5.3.227 For the vast majority of clubs and societies, either there will be no individual who is a beneficial owner within the meaning of the ML Regulations, or at most a class of persons who stand to benefit from the club or society's objects must be identified. These persons will be self-evident from a review of the club or society's objects in its constitution.

Obtain standard evidence

5.3.228 For many clubs and societies, the money laundering or terrorist financing risk will be low. The following information should be obtained about the customer:

- Full name of the club/society

- Legal status of the club/society

- Purpose of the club/society

- Names of all officers

5.3.229 The firm should verify the identities of the officers who have authority to operate an account or to give the firm instructions concerning the use or transfer of funds or assets.

5.3.230 Firms should take appropriate steps to be reasonably satisfied that the person the firm is dealing with is properly authorised by the customer.

5.3.231 Some consideration should be given as to whether documents relied upon are forged. In addition, if they are in a foreign language, appropriate steps should be taken to be reasonably satisfied that the documents in fact provide evidence of the customer's identity.

Variation from the standard

5.3.232 Where the money laundering or terrorist financing risk is considered to be at its lowest, the firm may be able to use the source of funds as evidence of the customer's identity. The guidance in paragraphs 5.3.92 to 5.3.96 should be followed. This does not obviate the need to verify the identity of beneficial owners, where these exist.

5.3.233 The firm's risk assessment may lead it to conclude that the money laundering or terrorist financing risk is higher, and that it should require additional information on the purpose, funding and beneficiaries of the club or society.

5.3.234 Following its assessment of the money laundering or terrorist financing risk presented by the club/society, the firm may decide to verify the identities of additional officers, and/or institute additional transaction monitoring arrangements (see section 5.7).

Public sector bodies, governments, state-owned companies and supranationals

5.3.235 In respect of customers which are UK or overseas governments (or their representatives), supranational organisations, government departments, state-owned companies or local authorities, the approach to identification and verification has to be tailored to the circumstances of the customer. Public sector bodies include state supported schools, colleges, universities and NHS trusts.

PART V
OTHER MATERIALS

Regulation 13(5)	5.3.236	Only simplified due diligence (see section 5.4) is required in respect of public authorities in the UK.

Regulation 13(6) Schedule 2, Paragraph 2	5.3.237	Only simplified due diligence (see section 5.4) is required in respect of non-UK public authorities which meet the following criteria:

- the customer has been entrusted with public functions pursuant to the Treaty on the European Union, the Treaties on the European Communities or Community secondary legislation;

- the customer's identity is publicly available, transparent and certain;

- the activities of the customer and its accounting practices are transparent; and

- either the customer is accountable to a Community institution or to the authorities of an EEA state, or otherwise appropriate check and balance procedures exist ensuring control of the customer's activity.

Regulation 13(1)	5.3.238	Firms must, however, have reasonable grounds for believing that the customer qualifies for the treatment in paragraphs 5.3.236 or 5.3.237.

Obtain standard evidence

5.3.239   Firms should obtain the following information about customers who are public sector bodies, governments, state-owned companies and supranationals:

- Full name of the entity

- Nature and status of the entity (eg, overseas government, treaty organisation)

- Address of the entity

- Name of the home state authority

- Names of directors (or equivalent)

5.3.240   Firms should take appropriate steps to understand the ownership of the customer, and the nature of its relationship with its home state authority.

5.3.241   Firms should, where appropriate, verify the identities of the directors (or equivalent) who have authority to give the firm instructions concerning the use or transfer of funds or assets.

5.3.242   Firms should take appropriate steps to be reasonably satisfied that the person the firm is dealing with is properly authorised by the customer.

Signatories

5.3.243   For operational purposes, the firm is likely to have a list of those authorised to give instructions for the movement of funds or assets, along with an appropriate instrument authorising one or more directors (or equivalent) to give the firm such instructions. The identities of individual signatories need only be verified on a risk-based approach.

Schools, colleges and universities

5.3.244   State supported schools, colleges and universities should be treated as public sector bodies, in accordance with the guidance set out in paragraphs 5.3.235 to 5.3.243. The Department for Education and Skills maintains lists [www.dfes.gov.uk/providersregister] of approved educational establishments, which may assist firms in verifying the existence of such customers.

5.3.245 For independent schools and colleges, firms should refer to the guidance given at paragraph 5.3.174.

Variation from the standard

5.3.246 The firm's assessment of the money laundering or terrorist financing risk presented by such customers should aim to identify higher risk countries or jurisdictions.

5.3.247 The guidance in paragraphs 5.3.235 to 5.3.245 should be applied to overseas entities, as appropriate to the firm's assessment of the risk that such entities present.

5.3.248 Many governmental, supranational and state-owned organisations will be managed and controlled by individuals who may qualify as PEPs (see paragraphs 5.5.18 to 5.5.29). Firms need to be aware of the increased likelihood of the existence of such individuals in the case of such customers, and deal with them appropriately, having regard to the risk that the funds of such entities may be used for improper purposes.

5.4 Simplified due diligence

Regulation 13(1) and 7(3)(b)   5.4.1 Simplified due diligence means not having to apply CDD measures. In practice, this means not having to identify the customer, or to verify the customer's identity, or, where relevant, that of a beneficial owner, nor having to obtain information on the purpose or intended nature of the business relationship. It is, however, still necessary to conduct ongoing monitoring of the business relationship. Firms must have reasonable grounds for believing that the customer, transaction or product relating to such transaction falls within one of the categories set out in the Regulations, and may have to demonstrate this to their supervisory authority. Clearly, for operating purposes, the firm will nevertheless need to maintain a base of information about the customer.

Regulation 13   5.4.2 Simplified due diligence may be applied to:

(i)   certain other regulated firms in the financial sector (see paragraph 5.3.203)

(ii)   companies listed on a regulated market (see paragraph 5.3.131)

(iii)   beneficial owners of pooled accounts held by notaries or independent legal professionals (see paragraph 5.3.211)

(iv)   UK public authorities (see paragraph 5.3.236)

(v)   Community institutions (see paragraph 5.3.237)

(vi)   certain life assurance and e-money products (see Part II, sectors 7 and 3)

(vii)   certain pension funds (see paragraphs 5.4.4 and 5.3.151ff)

(viii)   certain low risk products (see paragraph 5.4.5)

(ix)   child trust funds (see paragraph 5.4.6)

Regulation 7(1)(c), (d)   5.4.3 There is no exemption from the obligation to verify identity where the firm knows or suspects that a proposed relationship or occasional transaction involves money laundering or terrorist financing, or where there are doubts about the veracity or accuracy of documents, data or information previously obtained for the purposes of customer verification.

Regulation 13(7)(c)   5.4.4 Simplified due diligence may be applied to pension, superannuation or similar schemes which provide retirement benefits to employees, where contributions are made by an employer or by way of deduction from an employee's wages and the scheme rules do not permit the assignment of a member's interest under the scheme.

Regulation 13(8) and Schedule 2, paragraph 3	5.4.5	Simplified due diligence may be applied to low risk products which meet specified criteria set out in the ML Regulations. These criteria, which are cumulative, are:

        (i)   the product has a written contractual base;

        (ii)   any related transactions are carried out through an account of the customer with a bank which is subject to the money laundering directive, or a bank in an equivalent jurisdiction;

        (iii) the product or related transaction is not anonymous and its nature is such that it allows for the timely application of CDD measures where there is a suspicion of money laundering or terrorist financing;

        (iv) the product is within the following maximum threshold:

            a)   in the case of insurance policies or savings products of a similar nature, the annual premium is no more than €1,000 or there is a single premium of no more than €2,500;

            b)   in the case of products which are related to the financing of physical assets where the legal and beneficial title of the assets is not transferred to the customer until the termination of the contractual relationship (whether the transaction is carried out in a single operation or in several operations which appear to be linked) the annual payments do not exceed €15,000;

            c)   in all other cases, the maximum threshold is €15,000.

        (v)   the benefits of the product or related transaction cannot be realised for the benefit of third parties, except in the case of death, disablement, survival to a predetermined advanced age, or similar events;

        (vi) in the case of products or related transactions allowing for the investment of funds in financial assets or claims, including insurance or other kinds of contingent claims:

            a)   the benefits of the product or related transaction are only realisable in the long term;

            b)   the product or related transaction cannot be used as collateral;

            c)   during the contractual relationship, no accelerated payments are made, surrender clauses used or early termination takes place.

Regulation 13(8), (9)	5.4.6	Firms need to decide whether particular products meet the criteria for simplified due diligence. In respect of Child Trust Funds, no CDD measures need be carried out. Other products in respect of which no CDD measures need be carried out may be designated from time to time by HM Treasury, by amendment of the ML Regulations.
Regulations 5 and 8 POCA s 330 (2)(b) Terrorism Act s 21A	5.4.7	An exemption from the basic verification obligation does not extend to the obligation to conduct ongoing monitoring of the business relationship, or to the duty to report knowledge or suspicion of money laundering or terrorist financing.

5.5 Enhanced due diligence

Regulation 14(1)	5.5.1	A firm must apply EDD measures on a risk-sensitive basis in any situation which by its nature can present a higher risk of money laundering or terrorist financing. As part of this, a firm may conclude, under its risk-based approach, that the standard evidence of identity (see section 5.3) is insufficient in relation to the money laundering or terrorist financing risk, and that it must obtain additional information about a particular customer.

5.5.2   As a part of a risk-based approach, therefore, firms may need to hold sufficient information about the circumstances and business of their customers for two principal reasons:

- to inform its risk assessment process, and thus manage its money laundering/terrorist financing risks effectively; and

- to provide a basis for monitoring customer activity and transactions, thus increasing the likelihood that they will detect the use of their products and services for money laundering and terrorist financing.

5.5.3   The extent of additional information sought, and of any monitoring carried out in respect of any particular customer, or class/category of customer, will depend on the money laundering or terrorist financing risk that the customer, or class/category of customer, is assessed to present to the firm.

5.5.4   In practice, under a risk-based approach, it will not be appropriate for every product or service provider to know their customers equally well, regardless of the purpose, use, value, etc., of the product or service provided. Firms' information demands need to be proportionate, appropriate and discriminating, and to be able to be justified to customers.

5.5.5   A firm should hold a fuller set of information in respect of those customers, or class/category of customers, assessed as carrying a higher money laundering or terrorist financing risk, or who are seeking a product or service that carries a higher risk of being used for money laundering or terrorist financing purposes.

5.5.6   When someone becomes a new customer, or applies for a new product or service, the firm may, depending on the nature of the product or service for which they are applying, request information as to the customer's residential status, employment details, income, and other sources of income, in order to decide whether to accept the application.

5.5.7   The availability and use of other financial information held is important for reducing the additional costs of collecting customer information. Where appropriate and practical, therefore, and where there are no data protection restrictions, firms should take reasonable steps to ensure that where they have customer information in one part of the business, they are able to link it to information in another.

5.5.8   At all times, firms should bear in mind their obligations under the Data Protection Act only to seek information that is needed for the declared purpose, not to retain personal information longer than is necessary, and to ensure that information that is held is kept up to date.

Regulation 14   5.5.9   The ML Regulations prescribe three specific types of relationship in respect of which EDD measures must be applied. These are:

- where the customer has not been physically present for identification purposes (see paragraphs 5.5.10ff);

- in respect of a correspondent banking relationship (see Part II, sector 16: *Correspondent banking*);

- in respect of a business relationship or occasional transaction with a PEP (see paragraphs 5.5.18ff).

Non face-to-face identification and verification

5.5.10   Whilst some types of financial transaction have traditionally been conducted on a non-face-to-face basis, other types of transaction and relationships are increasingly being undertaken in this way: eg, internet and telephone banking, online share dealing.

5.5.11   Although applications and transactions undertaken across the internet may in themselves not pose any greater risk than other non face-to-face business, such as applications submitted by post, there are other factors that may, taken together, aggravate the typical risks:

- the ease of access to the facility, regardless of time and location;
- the ease of making multiple fictitious applications without incurring extra cost or the risk of detection;
- the absence of physical documents; and
- the speed of electronic transactions.

Regulation 14(2)

5.5.12 Where the customer has not been physically present for identification purposes, a firm must take specific and adequate measures to compensate for the higher risk, for example by applying one or more of the following measures:

a) ensuring that the customer's identity is established by additional documents, data or information;

b) supplementary measures to verify or certify the documents supplied, or requiring confirmatory certification by a financial services firm in the UK, EU or an equivalent jurisdiction;

c) ensuring that the first payment of the operation is carried out through an account opened in the customer's name with a bank.

5.5.13 Further guidance on the measures that should be applied to non face-to-face customers in different industry sectors is given in Part II of this Guidance.

5.5.14 The extent of verification in respect of non face-to-face customers will depend on the nature and characteristics of the product or service requested and the assessed money laundering risk presented by the customer. There are some circumstances where the customer is typically not physically present – such as in many wholesale markets, or when purchasing some types of collective investments – which would not in themselves increase the risk attaching to the transaction or activity. A firm should take account of such cases in developing their systems and procedures.

5.5.15 Additional measures would also include assessing the possibility that the customer is deliberately avoiding face-to-face contact. It is therefore important to be clear on the appropriate approach in these circumstances.

5.5.16 Where a customer approaches a firm remotely (by post, telephone or over the internet), the firm should carry out non face-to-face verification, either electronically (see paragraphs 5.3.79 –5.3.81), or by reference to documents (see paragraphs 5.3.72 – 5.3.78).

5.5.17 Non face-to-face identification and verification carries an inherent risk of impersonation fraud, and firms should follow the guidance in paragraph 5.3.82 to mitigate this risk.

Politically exposed persons (PEPs)

5.5.18 Individuals who have, or have had, a high political profile, or hold, or have held, public office, can pose a higher money laundering risk to firms as their position may make them vulnerable to corruption. This risk also extends to members of their immediate families and to known close associates. PEP status itself does not, of course, incriminate individuals or entities. It does, however, put the customer, or the beneficial owner, into a higher risk category.

Regulation 14(4), (5), (6)

5.5.19 A PEP is defined as "an individual who is or has, at any time in the preceding year, been entrusted with prominent public functions and an immediate family member, or a known close associate, of such a person". This definition only applies to those holding such a position in a state outside the UK, or in a Community institution or an international body.

	5.5.20	Although under the definition of a PEP an individual ceases to be so regarded after he has left office for one year, firms are encouraged to apply a risk-based approach in determining whether they should cease carrying out appropriately enhanced monitoring of his transactions or activity at the end of this period. In many cases, a longer period might be appropriate, in order to ensure that the higher risks associated with the individual's previous position have adequately abated.
Regulation, Sch 2, paras 4(1)(a), (b) and (c)	5.5.21	Public functions exercised at levels lower than national should normally not be considered prominent. However, when their political exposure is comparable to that of similar positions at national level, firms should consider, on a risk-based approach, whether persons exercising those public functions should be considered as PEPs. Prominent public functions include:

- heads of state, heads of government, ministers and deputy or assistant ministers;

- members of parliaments;

- members of supreme courts, of constitutional courts or of other high-level judicial bodies whose decisions are not generally subject to further appeal, except in exceptional circumstances;

- members of courts of auditors or of the boards of central banks;

- ambassadors, charges d'affaires and high-ranking officers in the armed forces; and (other than in respect of relevant positions at Community and international level);

- members of the administrative, management or supervisory boards of State-owned enterprises.

These categories do not include middle-ranking or more junior officials.

Regulation Sch 2, paras 4(1)(d) and (2)	5.5.22	Immediate family members include:

- a spouse;

- a partner (including a person who is considered by his national law as equivalent to a spouse);

- children and their spouses or partners; and

- parents.

Regulation Sch 2, para 4(1)(e)	5.5.23	Persons known to be close associates include:

- any individual who is known to have joint beneficial ownership of a legal entity or legal arrangement, or any other close business relations, with a person who is a PEP; and

- any individual who has sole beneficial ownership of a legal entity or legal arrangement which is known to have been set up for the benefit of a person who is a PEP.

Regulation 14(6)and 20(2)(c)	5.5.24	For the purpose of deciding whether a person is a known close associate of a PEP, the firm need only have regard to any information which is in its possession, or which is publicly known. Having to obtain knowledge of such a relationship does not presuppose an active research by the firm.
Regulation 14(4)	5.5.25	Firms are required, on a risk-sensitive basis, to:

- have appropriate risk-based procedures to determine whether a customer is a PEP;

- obtain appropriate senior management approval for establishing a business relationship with such a customer;

- take adequate measures to establish the source of wealth and source of funds which are involved in the business relationship or occasional transaction; and

- conduct enhanced ongoing monitoring of the business relationship.

Risk-based procedures

5.5.26 The nature and scope of a particular firm's business will generally determine whether the existence of PEPs in their customer base is an issue for the firm, and whether or not the firm needs to screen all customers for this purpose. In the context of this risk analysis, it would be appropriate if the firm's resources were focused in particular on products and transactions that are characterised by a high risk of money laundering.

5.5.27 Establishing whether individuals qualify as PEPs is not always straightforward and can present difficulties. Where firms need to carry out specific checks, they may be able to rely on an internet search engine, or consult relevant reports and databases on corruption risk published by specialised national, international, non-governmental and commercial organisations. Resources such as the Transparency International Corruption Perceptions Index, which ranks approximately 150 countries according to their perceived level of corruption, may be helpful in terms of assessing the risk. If there is a need to conduct more thorough checks, or if there is a high likelihood of a firm having PEPs for customers, subscription to a specialist PEP database may be the only adequate risk mitigation tool.

Senior management approval

5.5.28 Obtaining approval from senior management for establishing a business relationship does not mean obtaining approval from the Board of directors (or equivalent body), but from the immediately higher level of authority to the person seeking such approval.

On-going monitoring

5.5.29 Guidance on the on-going monitoring of the business relationship is given in section 5.7. Firms should remember that new and existing customers may not initially meet the definition of a PEP, but may subsequently become one during the course of a business relationship. The firm should, as far as practicable, be alert to public information relating to possible changes in the status of its customers with regard to political exposure. When an existing customer is identified as a PEP, EDD must be applied to that customer.

5.6 Multipartite relationships, including reliance on third parties

5.6.1 Frequently, a customer may have contact with two or more firms in respect of the same transaction. This can be the case in both the retail market, where customers are routinely introduced by one firm to another, or deal with one firm through another, and in some wholesale markets, such as syndicated lending, where several firms may participate in a single loan to a customer.

5.6.2 However, several firms requesting the same information from the same customer in respect of the same transaction not only does not help in the fight against financial crime, but also adds to the inconvenience of the customer. It is important, therefore, that in all circumstances each firm is clear as to its relationship with the customer and its related AML/CTF obligations, and as to the extent to which it can rely upon or otherwise take account of the verification of the customer that another firm has carried out. Such account must be taken in a balanced way that appropriately reflects the money laundering or terrorist financing risks. Account must also be taken of the fact that some of the firms involved may not be UK-based.

| | 5.6.3 | In other cases, a customer may be an existing customer of another regulated firm in the same group. Guidance on meeting AML/CTF obligations in such a relationship is given in paragraphs 5.6.25 to 5.6.28. |

Reliance on third parties

| Regulation 17 | 5.6.4 | The ML Regulations expressly permit a firm to rely on another person to apply any or all of the CDD measures, provided that the other person is listed in Regulation 17(2), and that consent to being relied on has been given (see paragraph 5.6.7). The relying firm, however, retains responsibility for any failure to comply with a requirement of the Regulations, as this responsibility cannot be delegated. |

| | 5.6.5 | For example: |

- where a firm (firm A) enters into a business relationship with, or undertakes an occasional transaction for, the underlying customer of another firm (firm B), for example by accepting instructions from the customer (given through Firm B); or

- firm A and firm B both act for the same customer in respect of a transaction (eg, firm A as executing broker and firm B as clearing broker),

firm A may rely on firm B to carry out CDD measures, while remaining ultimately liable for compliance with the ML Regulations.

| Regulation 17(2)(a), (b) and (5) | 5.6.6 | In this context, Firm B must be:
(1) a person who carries on business in the UK who is |

(a) an FSA-authorised credit or financial institution (excluding a money service business); or

(b) an auditor, insolvency practitioner, external accountant, tax adviser or independent legal professional, who is supervised for the purposes of the Regulations by one of the bodies listed in Part 1 of Schedule 3 to the ML Regulations;

| Regulation 17(2)(c) and (5) | | (2) a person who carries on business in another EEA State who is: |

(a) a credit or financial institution (excluding a money service business), an auditor, insolvency practitioner, external accountant, tax adviser or other independent legal professional;

(b) subject to mandatory professional registration recognised by law; and

(c) supervised for compliance with the requirements laid down in the Money Laundering Directive in accordance with section 2 of Chapter V of that directive;

| Regulation 17(2)(d) and (5) | | (3) a person carrying on business in a non-EEA State who is |

(a) a credit or financial institution (excluding a money service business), an auditor, insolvency practitioner, external accountant, tax adviser or other independent legal professional;

(b) subject to mandatory professional registration recognised by law; and

(c) subject to requirements equivalent to those laid down in the Money Laundering Directive; and

(d) supervised for compliance with those requirements in a manner equivalent to section 2 of Chapter V of the Money Laundering Directive.

Consent to be relied upon

5.6.7 The ML Regulations do not define how consent must be evidenced. Ordinarily, 'consent' means an acceptance of some form of proposal by one party from another – this may be written or oral, express or implied. Written acknowledgement that a firm is being relied on makes its relationship with the firm relying on it clear. On the other hand, it is not necessary for a firm to give an express indication that it is being relied on, and it may be inferred from their conduct; for example – dealing with a firm after receipt of that firm's terms of business which indicate reliance; silence where it has been indicated that this would be taken as acknowledgement of reliance; participation in a tri-partite arrangement, based on a market practice that has reliance as an integral part of its framework.

5.6.8 In order to satisfy the purpose behind Regulation 17(1)(a), a firm may wish to consider providing a firm being relied on with notification of the reliance. The notification should specify that the firm intends to rely on the third party firm for the purposes of Regulation 17(1)(a). Such a notification can be delivered in a number of ways. For example, where one firm is introducing a client to another firm, the issue of reliance can be raised during the introduction process, and may form part of the formal agreement with the intermediary. Similarly, where the relying and relied upon firms are party to tripartite agreement with a client, the notification may be communicated during exchange of documents. Where a relationship exists between the parties it is likely that such a notification plus some form of acceptance (see paragraph 5.6.7) should be sufficient for the purposes of establishing consent.

5.6.9 Where there is no contractual or commercial relationship between the relying and relied on firms it is less likely that consent can be assumed from the silence of the firm being relied on. In such circumstances firms may wish to seek an express agreement to reliance. This does not need to take the form of a legal agreement and a simple indication of consent (eg, by e-mail) should suffice.

Basis of reliance

5.6.10 For one firm to rely on verification carried out by another firm, the verification that the firm being relied upon has carried out must have been based at least on the standard level of customer verification. It is not permissible to rely on SDD carried out, or any other exceptional form of verification, such as the use of source of funds as evidence of identity.

5.6.11 Firms may also only rely on verification actually carried out by the firm being relied upon. A firm that has been relied on to verify a customer's identity may not 'pass on' verification carried out for it by another firm.

Regulation 2(9), 5.6.12 Under the ML Regulations, the FSA has been given the additional
Schedule 1 responsibility for supervising the AML/CTF systems and controls in Annex I Financial Institutions. Such businesses are not authorised by the FSA, may not therefore be relied on to carry out CDD measures on behalf of other firms until such time as this is permitted under the ML Regulations.

5.6.13 Whether a firm wishes to place reliance on a third party will be part of the firm's risk-based assessment, which, in addition to confirming the third party's regulated status, may include consideration of matters such as:

- its public disciplinary record, to the extent that this is available;

- the nature of the customer, the product/service sought and the sums involved;

- any adverse experience of the other firm's general efficiency in business dealings;

- any other knowledge, whether obtained at the outset of the relationship or subsequently, that the firm has regarding the standing of the firm to be relied upon.

5.6.14 The assessment as to whether or not a firm should accept confirmation from a third party that appropriate CDD measures have been carried out on a customer will be risk-based, and cannot be based simply on a single factor.

5.6.15 In practice, the firm relying on the confirmation of a third party needs to know:

- the identity of the customer or beneficial owner whose identity is being verified;

- the level of CDD that has been carried out; and

- confirmation of the third party's understanding of his obligation to make available, on request, copies of the verification data, documents or other information.

In order to standardise the process of firms confirming to one another that appropriate CDD measures have been carried out on customers, guidance is given in paragraphs 5.6.29 to 5.6.32 below on the use of pro-forma confirmations containing the above information.

5.6.16 The third party has no obligation to provide such confirmation to the product/service provider, and may choose not to do so. In such circumstances, or if the product/service provider decides that it does not wish to rely upon the third party, then the firm must carry out its own CDD measures on the customer.

5.6.17 For a firm to confirm that it has carried out CDD measures in respect of a customer is a serious matter. A firm must not give a confirmation on the basis of a generalised assumption that the firm's systems have operated effectively. There has to be awareness that the appropriate steps have in fact been taken in respect of the customer that is the subject of the confirmation.

Regulation 19(5) 5.6.18 A firm which carries on business in the UK and is relied on by another person must, within the period of five years beginning on the date on which it is relied on, if requested by the firm relying on it

- as soon as reasonably practicable make available to the firm which is relying on it any information about the customer (and any beneficial owner) which the third party obtained when applying CDD measures; and

- as soon as reasonably practicable forward to the firm which is relying on it relevant copies of any identification and verification data and other relevant documents on the identity of the customer (and any beneficial owner) which the third party obtained when applying those measures

Regulation 19(6) 5.6.19 A firm which relies on a firm situated outside the UK to apply CDD measures must take steps to ensure that the firm on which it relies will, within the period of five years beginning on the date on which the third party is relied on, if requested, comply with the obligations set out in paragraph 5.6.18.

5.6.20 The personal information supplied by the customer as part of a third party's customer identification procedures will generally be set out in the form that the relying firm will require to be completed, and this information will therefore be provided to that firm.

| Regulation 19(4), (5) and (6) | 5.6.21 | A request to forward copies of any identification and verification data and other relevant documents on the identity of the customer or beneficial owner obtained when applying CDD measures, if made, would normally be as part of a firm's risk-based customer acceptance procedures. However, the firm giving the confirmation must be prepared to provide these data or other relevant documents throughout the five year period for which it has an obligation under the Regulations to retain them. |

5.6.22 Where a firm makes such a request, and it is not met, the firm will need to take account of that fact in its assessment of the third party in question, and of the ability to rely on the third party in the future.

5.6.23 A firm must also document the steps taken to confirm that the firm relied upon satisfies the requirements in Regulation 17(2). This is particularly important where the firm relied upon is situated outside the EEA.

5.6.24 Part of the firm's AML/CTF policy statement should address the circumstances where reliance may be placed on other firms and how the firm will assess whether the other firm satisfies the definition of third party in Regulation 17(2) (see paragraph 5.6.6).

Group introductions

5.6.25 Where customers are introduced between different parts of the same financial sector group, entities that are part of the group should be able to rely on identification procedures conducted by that part of the group which first dealt with the customer. One member of a group should be able to confirm to another part of the group that the identity of the customer has been appropriately verified.

5.6.26 Where a customer is introduced by one part of a financial sector group to another, it is not necessary for his identity to be re-verified, provided that:

- the identity of the customer has been verified by the introducing part of the group in line with AML/CTF standards in the UK, the EU or an equivalent jurisdiction; and

- the group entity that carried out the CDD measures can be relied upon as a third party under Regulation 17(2).

5.6.27 The acceptance by a UK firm of confirmation from another group entity that the identity of a customer has been satisfactorily verified is dependent on the relevant records being readily accessible, on request, from the UK.

5.6.28 Where UK firms have day-to-day access to all group customer information and records, there is no need to obtain a group introduction confirmation, if the identity of that customer has been verified previously to AML/CTF standards in the EU, or in an equivalent jurisdiction. However, if the identity of the customer has not previously been verified, for example because the group customer relationship pre-dates the introduction of anti-money laundering regulations, or if the verification evidence is inadequate, any missing verification evidence will need to be obtained.

Use of pro-forma confirmations

Regulation 17(2)

5.6.29   Whilst a firm may be able to place reliance on another party to apply all or part of the CDD measures under Regulation 17(2) (see paragraph 5.6.4), it may still wish to receive, as part of its risk-based procedures, a written confirmation from the third party, not least to evidence consent. This may also be the case, for example, when a firm is unlikely to have an ongoing relationship with the third party. Confirmations can be particularly helpful when dealing with third parties located outside of the UK, where it is necessary to confirm that the relevant records will be available (see 5.6.18).

5.6.30   The provision of a confirmation certificate implies consent to be relied upon, in accordance with paragraph 5.6.7.

5.6.31   Pro-forma confirmations for customer identification and verification are attached as Annex 5–I to this chapter.

5.6.32   Pro-forma confirmations in respect of group introductions are attached as Annex 5–II to this chapter.

Situations which are not reliance

(i) One firm acting solely as introducer

5.6.33   At one end of the spectrum, one firm may act solely as an introducer between the customer and the firm providing the product or service, and may have no further relationship with the customer. The introducer plays no part in the transaction between the customer and the firm, and has no relationship with either of these parties that would constitute a business relationship. This would be the case, for example, in respect of name-passing brokers in inter-professional markets, on which specific guidance is given in Part II, sector 19: *Name passing brokers in the inter-professional market.*

5.6.34   In these circumstances, where the introducer neither gives advice nor plays any part in the negotiation or execution of the transaction, the identification and verification obligations under the ML Regulations lie with the product/service provider. This does not, of course, preclude the introducing firm carrying out identification and verification of the customer on behalf of the firm providing the product or service, as agent for that firm (see paragraphs 5.6.35 – 5.6.36).

(ii) Where the intermediary is the agent of the product/service provider

5.6.35   If the intermediary is an agent or appointed representative of the product or service provider, it is an extension of that firm. The intermediary may actually obtain the appropriate verification evidence in respect of the customer, but the product/service provider is responsible for specifying what should be obtained, and for ensuring that records of the appropriate verification evidence taken in respect of the customer are retained.

5.6.36   Similarly, where the product/service provider has a direct sales force, they are part of the firm, whether or not they operate under a separate group legal entity. The firm is responsible for specifying what is required, and for ensuring that records of the appropriate verification evidence taken in respect of the customer are retained.

(iii) Where the intermediary is the agent of the customer

	5.6.37

From the point of view of a product/service provider, the position of an intermediary, as agent of the customer, is influenced by a number of factors. The intermediary may be subject to the ML Regulations, or otherwise to the EU Money Laundering Directive, or to similar legislation in an equivalent jurisdiction. It may be regulated; it may be based in the UK, elsewhere within the EU, or in a country or jurisdiction outside the EU, which may or may not be a FATF member. Guidance on which countries or jurisdictions are "equivalent jurisdictions" is given at www.jmlsg.org.uk.

Regulation 13(2) 5.6.38 Depending on jurisdiction, where the customer is an intermediary carrying on appropriately regulated business, and is acting on behalf of another, there is no obligation on the product provider to carry out CDD measures on the customer, or on the underlying party (see paragraph 5.3.203).

5.6.39 Where a firm cannot apply simplified due diligence to the intermediary (see paragraphs 5.4.1ff), the product/service provider is obliged to carry out CDD measures on the intermediary and, as the intermediary acts for another, on the underlying customer.

5.6.40 Where the firm takes instruction from the underlying customer, or where the firm acts on the underlying customer's behalf (eg, as a custodian) the firm then has an obligation to carry out CDD measures in respect of that customer, although the reliance provisions (see paragraphs 5.6.4ff) may be applied.

5.6.41 In these circumstances, in verifying the identity of the underlying customer, the firm should take a risk-based approach. It will need to assess the AML/CTF regime in the intermediary's jurisdiction, the level of reliance that can be placed on the intermediary and the verification work it has carried out, and as a consequence, the amount of evidence that should be obtained direct from the customer.

5.6.42 In particular, where the intermediary is located in a higher risk jurisdiction, or in a country listed as having material deficiencies (see www.jmlsg.org.uk), the risk-based approach should be aimed at ensuring that the business does not proceed unless the identity of the underlying customers have been verified to the product/service provider's satisfaction.

5.7 Monitoring customer activity

The requirement to monitor customers' activities

Regulation 8 5.7.1 Firms must conduct ongoing monitoring of the business relationship with their customers. Ongoing monitoring of a business relationship includes:

- Scrutiny of transactions undertaken throughout the course of the relationship (including, where necessary, the source of funds) to ensure that the transactions are consistent with the firm's knowledge of the customer, his business and risk profile;

- Ensuring that the documents, data or information held by the firm are kept up to date.

5.7.2 Monitoring customer activity helps identify unusual activity. If unusual activities cannot be rationally explained, they may involve money laundering or terrorist financing. Monitoring customer activity and transactions that take place throughout a relationship helps give firms know their customers, assist them to assess risk and provides greater assurance that the firm is not being used for the purposes of financial crime.

What is monitoring?

5.7.3   The essentials of any system of monitoring are that:

- it flags up transactions and/or activities for further examination;

- these reports are reviewed promptly by the right person(s); and

- appropriate action is taken on the findings of any further examination.

5.7.4   Monitoring can be either:

- in real time, in that transactions and/or activities can be reviewed as they take place or are about to take place, or

- after the event, through some independent review of the transactions and/or activities that a customer has undertaken

and in either case, unusual transactions or activities will be flagged for further examination.

5.7.5   Monitoring may be by reference to specific types of transactions, to the profile of the customer, or by comparing their activity or profile with that of a similar, peer group of customers, or through a combination of these approaches.

5.7.6   Firms should also have systems and procedures to deal with customers who have not had contact with the firm for some time, in circumstances where regular contact might be expected, and with dormant accounts or relationships, to be able to identify future reactivation and unauthorised use.

5.7.7   In designing monitoring arrangements, it is important that appropriate account be taken of the frequency, volume and size of transactions with customers, in the context of the assessed customer and product risk.

5.7.8   Monitoring is not a mechanical process and does not necessarily require sophisticated electronic systems. The scope and complexity of the process will be influenced by the firm's business activities, and whether the firm is large or small. The key elements of any system are having up-to-date customer information, on the basis of which it will be possible to spot the unusual, and asking pertinent questions to elicit the reasons for unusual transactions or activities in order to judge whether they may represent something suspicious.

Nature of monitoring

5.7.9   Some financial services business typically involves transactions with customers about whom the firm has a good deal of information, acquired for both business and regulatory reasons. Other types of financial services business involve transactions with customers about whom the firm may need to have only limited information. The nature of the monitoring in any given case will therefore depend on the business of the firm, the frequency of customer activity, and the types of customer that are involved.

5.7.10 Effective monitoring is likely to be based on a considered identification of transaction characteristics, such as:

- the unusual nature of a transaction: eg, abnormal size or frequency for that customer or peer group; the early surrender of an insurance policy;

- the nature of a series of transactions: for example, a number of cash credits;

- the geographic destination or origin of a payment: for example, to or from a high-risk country; and

- the parties concerned: for example, a request to make a payment to or from a person on a sanctions list.

5.7.11 The arrangements should include the training of staff on procedures to spot and deal specially (eg, by referral to management) with situations that arise that suggest a heightened money laundering risk; or they could involve arrangements for exception reporting by reference to objective triggers (eg, transaction amount). Staff training is not, however, a substitute for having in place some form of regular monitoring activity.

Regulation 14(1)

5.7.12 Higher risk accounts and customer relationships require enhanced ongoing monitoring. This will generally mean more frequent or intensive monitoring.

Manual or automated?

5.7.13 A monitoring system may be manual, or may be automated to the extent that a standard suite of exception reports are produced. One or other of these approaches may suit most firms. In the relatively few firms where there are major issues of volume, or where there are other factors that make a basic exception report regime inappropriate, a more sophisticated automated system may be necessary.

5.7.14 It is essential to recognise the importance of staff alertness. Such factors as staff intuition, direct exposure to a customer face-to-face or on the telephone, and the ability, through practical experience, to recognise transactions that do not seem to make sense for that customer, cannot be automated (see Chapter 8: Staff awareness, training and alertness).

5.7.15 In relation to a firm's monitoring needs, an automated system may add value to manual systems and controls, provided that the parameters determining the outputs of the system are appropriate. Firms should understand the workings and rationale of an automated system, and should understand the reasons for its output of alerts, as it may be asked to explain this to its regulator.

5.7.16 The greater the volume of transactions, the less easy it will be for a firm to monitor them without the aid of some automation. Systems available include those that many firms, particularly those that offer credit, use to monitor fraud. Although not specifically designed to identify money laundering or terrorist financing, the output from these anti-fraud monitoring systems can often indicate possible money laundering or terrorist financing.

5.7.17 There are many automated transaction monitoring systems available on the market; they use a variety of techniques to detect and report unusual/uncharacteristic activity. These techniques can range from artificial intelligence to simple rules. The systems available are not designed to detect money laundering or terrorist financing, but are able to detect and report unusual/uncharacteristic behaviour by customers, and patterns of behaviour that are characteristic of money laundering or terrorist financing, which after analysis may lead to suspicion of money laundering or terrorist financing. The implementation of transaction monitoring systems is difficult due to the complexity of the underlying analytics used and their heavy reliance on customer reference data and transaction data.

5.7.18 Monitoring systems, manual or automated, can vary considerably in their approach to detecting and reporting unusual or uncharacteristic behaviour. It is important for firms to ask questions of the supplier of an automated system, and internally within the business, whether in support of a manual or an automated system, to aid them in selecting a solution that meets their particular business needs best. Questions that should be addressed include:

- How does the solution enable the firm to implement a risk-based approach to customers, third parties and transactions?

- How do system parameters aid the risk-based approach and consequently affect the quality and volume of transactions alerted?

- What are the money laundering/terrorist financing typologies that the system addresses, and which component of the system addresses each typology? Are the typologies that are included with the system complete? Are they relevant to the firm's particular line of business?

- What functionality does the system provide to implement new typologies, how quickly can relevant new typologies be commissioned in the system and how can their validity be tested prior to activation in the live system?

- What functionality exists to provide the user with the reason that a transaction is alerted and is there full evidential process behind the reason given?

- Does the system have robust mechanisms to learn from previous experience and how is the false positive rate continually monitored and reduced?

5.7.19   What constitutes unusual or uncharacteristic behaviour by a customer, is often defined by the system. It will be important that the system selected has an appropriate definition of 'unusual or uncharacteristic' and one that is in line with the nature of business conducted by the firm.

5.7.20   The effectiveness of a monitoring system, automated or manual, in identifying unusual activity will depend on the quality of the parameters which determine what alerts it makes, and the ability of staff to assess and act as appropriate on these outputs. The needs of each firm will therefore be different, and each system will vary in its capabilities according to the scale, nature and complexity of the business. It is important that the balance is right in setting the level at which an alert is generated; it is not enough to fix it so that the system generates just enough output for the existing staff complement to deal with – but equally, the system should not generate large numbers of 'false positives', which require excessive resources to investigate.

5.7.21   Monitoring also involves keeping information held about customers up to date, as far as reasonably possible. Guidance on this is given at paragraphs 5.3.23 – 5.3.24.

[7007]

ANNEX 5–I/1

CONFIRMATION OF VERIFICATION OF IDENTITY
PRIVATE INDIVIDUAL

INTRODUCTION BY AN FSA-REGULATED FIRM

1. DETAILS OF INDIVIDUAL (see explanatory notes below)

Full name of Customer		
Current Address		Previous address if individual has changed address in the last three months
Date of Birth		

2. CONFIRMATION

I/we confirm that
(a)   the information in section 1 above was obtained by me/us in relation to the customer;
(b)   the evidence I/we have obtained to verify the identity of the customer:
    [tick only one]

meets the standard evidence set out within the guidance for the UK Financial Sector issued by JMLSG ; or	
exceeds the standard evidence (written details of the further verification evidence taken are attached to this confirmation).	

Signed:	
Name:	
Position:	
Date:	

3. DETAILS OF INTRODUCING FIRM (OR SOLE TRADER)

Full Name of Regulated Firm (or Sole Trader):	
FSA Reference Number:	

Explanatory notes

1.   A separate confirmation must be completed for each customer (e g joint holders, trustee cases and joint life cases). Where a third party is involved, e g a payer of contributions who is different from the customer, the identity of that person must also be verified, and a confirmation provided.

2.   This form cannot be used to verify the identity of any customer that falls into one of the following categories:

- those who are exempt from verification as being an existing client of the introducing firm prior to the introduction of the requirement for such verification;
- those who have been subject to Simplified Due Diligence under the Money Laundering Regulations; or
- those whose identity has been verified using the source of funds as evidence.

[7008]

ANNEX 5–I/2

CONFIRMATION OF VERIFICATION OF IDENTITY
PRIVATE INDIVIDUAL

INTRODUCTION BY AN EU REGULATED FINANCIAL SERVICES FIRM

1. DETAILS OF INDIVIDUAL (see explanatory notes below)

Full name of Customer		
Current Address		Previous address if individual has changed address in the last three months
Date of Birth		

2. CONFIRMATION

We confirm that
(a) the information in section 1 above was obtained by us in relation to the customer;
(b) the evidence we have obtained to verify the identity of the customer meets the requirements of our national money laundering legislation that implements the EU Money Laundering Directive, and any relevant authoritative guidance provided as best practice in relation to the type of business or transaction to which this confirmation relates;
(c) where the underlying evidence taken in relation to the verification of the customer's identity is held outside the UK, in the event of any enquiry from you (or from UK law enforcement agencies or regulators under court order or relevant mutual assistance procedure), copies of the relevant customer records will be made available, to the extent that we are required under local law to retain these records.

Signed:	
Name:	
Position:	
Date:	

3. DETAILS OF INTRODUCING FIRM

Full Name of Regulated Firm:	
Jurisdiction:	
Name of Regulator:	
Regulator Reference Number:	

Explanatory notes

1. A separate confirmation must be completed for each customer (e g joint holders, trustee cases and joint life cases). Where a third party is involved, e g a payer of contributions who is different from the customer, the identity of that person must also be verified, and a confirmation provided.

2. This form cannot be used to verify the identity of any customer that falls into one of the following categories:

- those who are exempt from verification as being an existing client of the introducing firm prior to the adoption of our national legislation that implements the EU Money Laundering Directive; or
- those whose identity has not been verified by virtue of the application of a permitted exemption under the EU Money Laundering Directive.

[7009]

ANNEX 5–I/3

CONFIRMATION OF VERIFICATION OF IDENTITY
PRIVATE INDIVIDUAL

INTRODUCTION BY A NON-EU REGULATED FINANCIAL SERVICES FIRM
(*which the receiving firm has accepted as being from a equivalent jurisdiction*)

1. DETAILS OF INDIVIDUAL (see explanatory notes below)

Full name of Customer	

Current Address		Previous address if individual has changed address in the last three months
Date of Birth		

2. CONFIRMATION

We confirm that:
(a)   the information in section 1 above was obtained by us in relation to the customer;
(b)   the evidence we have obtained to verify the identity of the customer meets the requirements of local law and regulation;
(c)   where the underlying evidence taken in relation to the verification of the customer's identity is held outside the UK, in the event of any enquiry from you (or from UK law enforcement agencies or regulators under court order or relevant mutual assistance procedure), copies of the relevant customer records will be made available, to the extent that we are required under local law to retain these records.

Signed:	
Name:	
Position:	
Date:	

3. DETAILS OF INTRODUCING FIRM

Full Name of Regulated Firm:	
Jurisdiction:	
Name of Regulator:	
Regulator Reference Number:	

Explanatory notes

1.   A separate confirmation must be completed for each customer (eg joint holders, trustee cases and joint life cases). Where a third party is involved, eg a payer of contributions who is different from the customer, the identity of that person must also be verified, and a confirmation provided.

2.   This form cannot be used to verify the identity of any customer that falls into one of the following categories:

- those who are exempt from verification as being an existing client of the introducing firm prior to the adoption of local anti money laundering laws or regulation requiring such verification; or
- those whose identity has not been verified by virtue of the application of a permitted exemption under local anti money laundering laws or regulation.

[7010]

ANNEX 5–I/4

CONFIRMATION OF VERIFICATION OF IDENTITY
CORPORATE AND OTHER NON-PERSONAL ENTITY

INTRODUCTION BY AN FSA-REGULATED FIRM

1. DETAILS OF CUSTOMER (see explanatory notes below)

Full name of customer	
Type of entity (corporate, trust, etc)	
Location of business (full operating address)	
Registered office in country of incorporation	
Registered number, if any (or appropriate)	
Relevant company registry or regulated market listing authority	
Names* of directors (or equivalent)	
Names* of principal beneficial owners (over 25%)	

* And dates of birth, if known

2. CONFIRMATION

I/we confirm that
  (a)   the information in section 1 above was obtained by me/us in relation to the customer;
  (b)   the evidence I/we have obtained to verify the identity of the customer: [tick only one]

meets the guidance for standard evidence set out within the guidance for the UK Financial Sector issued by JMLSG; or	
exceeds the standard evidence (written details of the further verification evidence taken are attached to this confirmation).	

Signed:	
Name:	
Position:	
Date:	

3. DETAILS OF INTRODUCING FIRM (OR SOLE TRADER)

Full Name of Regulated Firm (or Sole Trader):	
FSA Reference Number:	

Explanatory notes

1. "Relevant company registry" includes other registers, such as those maintained by charity commissions (or equivalent) or chambers of commerce.

2. This form cannot be used to verify the identity of any customer that falls into one of the following categories:

- those who are exempt from verification as being an existing client of the introducing firm prior to the introduction of the requirement for such verification;
- those who have been subject to Simplified Due Diligence under the Money Laundering Regulations; or
- those whose identity has been verified using the source of funds as evidence.

[7011]

ANNEX 5–I/5

CONFIRMATION OF VERIFICATION OF IDENTITY
CORPORATE AND OTHER NON-PERSONAL ENTITY

INTRODUCTION BY AN EU REGULATED FINANCIAL SERVICES FIRM

1. DETAILS OF CUSTOMER (see explanatory notes below)

Full name of customer	
Type of entity (corporate, trust, etc)	
Location of business (full operating address)	
Registered office in country of incorporation	
Registered number, if any (or appropriate)	
Relevant company registry or regulated market listing authority	
Names* of directors (or equivalent)	
Names* of principal beneficial owners (over 25%)	

* And dates of birth, if known

2. CONFIRMATION

We confirm that

(a) the information in section 1 above was obtained by us in relation to the customer;

(b) the evidence we have obtained to verify the identity of the customer meets the requirements of our national money laundering legislation that implements the EU Money Laundering Directive, and any relevant authoritative guidance provided as best practice in relation to the type of business or transaction to which this confirmation relates;

(c) where the underlying evidence taken in relation to the verification of the customer's identity is held outside the UK, in the event of any enquiry from you (or from UK law enforcement agencies or regulators under court order or relevant mutual assistance procedure), copies of the relevant customer records will be made available, to the extent that we are required under local law to retain these records.

Signed:	
Name:	
Position:	
Date:	

3. DETAILS OF INTRODUCING FIRM

Full Name of Regulated Firm:	
Jurisdiction:	
Name of Regulator:	
Regulator Reference Number:	

Explanatory notes

1.   "Relevant company registry" includes other registers, such as those maintained by charity commissions (or equivalent) or chambers of commerce.

2.   This form cannot be used to verify the identity of any customer that falls into one of the following categories:

- those who are exempt from verification as being an existing client of the introducing firm prior to the adoption of our national legislation that implements the EU Money Laundering Directive; or
- those whose identity has not been verified by virtue of the application of a permitted exemption under the EU Money Laundering Directive.

[7012]

ANNEX 5–I/6

CONFIRMATION OF VERIFICATION OF IDENTITY
CORPORATE AND OTHER NON-PERSONAL ENTITY

INTRODUCTION BY A NON-EU REGULATED FINANCIAL SERVICES FIRM
(*which the receiving firm has accepted as being from a equivalent jurisdiction*)

1. DETAILS OF CUSTOMER (see explanatory notes below)

Full name of customer	
Type of entity (corporate, trust, etc)	
Location of business (full operating address)	
Registered office in country of incorporation	
Registered number, if any (or appropriate)	
Relevant company registry or regulated market listing authority	
Names* of directors (or equivalent)	

Names* of principal beneficial owners (over 25%)	

* And dates of birth, if known

2. CONFIRMATION

We confirm that:
(a) the information in section 1 above was obtained by us in relation to the customer;
(b) the evidence we have obtained to verify the identity of the customer meets the requirements of local law and regulation;
(c) where the underlying evidence taken in relation to the verification of the customer's identity is held outside the UK, in the event of any enquiry from you (or from UK law enforcement agencies or regulators under court order or relevant mutual assistance procedure), copies of the relevant customer records will be made available, to the extent that we are required under local law to retain these records.

Signed:	
Name:	
Position:	
Date:	

3. DETAILS OF INTRODUCING FIRM

Full Name of Regulated Firm:	
Jurisdiction:	
Name of Regulator:	
Regulator Reference Number:	

Explanatory notes

1. "Relevant company registry" includes other registers, such as those maintained by charity commissions (or equivalent) or chambers of commerce.

2. This form cannot be used to verify the identity of any customer that falls into one of the following categories:

- those who are exempt from verification as being an existing client of the introducing firm prior to the adoption of local anti money laundering laws or regulation requiring such verification; or
- those whose identity has not been verified by virtue of the application of a permitted exemption under local anti money laundering laws or regulation.

[7013]

ANNEX 5–II/1

CONFIRMATION OF VERIFICATION OF IDENTITY
GROUP INTRODUCTION

PRIVATE INDIVIDUAL

1. DETAILS OF INDIVIDUAL (see explanatory notes below)

Full name of Customer	

Current Address		Previous address if individual has changed address in the last three months
Date of Birth		

2. CONFIRMATION

We confirm that

(a)   the verification of the identity of the above customer meets the requirements:

(i)   of the Money Laundering Regulations 2007, and the guidance for standard evidence set out within the guidance for the UK Financial Sector issued by JMLSG; or

(ii)   of our national money laundering legislation that implements the EU Money Laundering Directive, and any relevant authoritative guidance provided as best practice in relation to the type of business or transaction to which this confirmation relates; or

(iii) of local law and regulation.

(b)   where the underlying evidence taken in relation to the verification of the customer's identity is held outside the UK, in the event of any enquiry from you (or from UK law enforcement agencies or regulators under court order or relevant mutual assistance procedure), copies of the relevant customer records will be made available, to the extent that we are required under local law to retain these records.

Signed:	
Name:	
Position:	
Date:	

3. DETAILS OF GROUP FIRM

Full Name of Regulated Firm:	
Relationship to receiving firm:	
Jurisdiction:	
Name of Regulator:	
Regulator Reference Number:	

Explanatory notes

1.   A separate confirmation must be completed for each customer (e g joint holders). Where a third party is involved, e g a payer of contributions who is different from the customer, the identity of that person must also be verified, and a confirmation provided.

2.   This form cannot be used to verify the identity of any customer that falls into one of the following categories:

- those who are exempt from verification as being an existing client of the introducing firm prior to the introduction of the requirement for such verification;
- those whose identity has not been verified by virtue of the application of a permitted exemption under local anti money laundering law or regulation; or
- those whose identity has been verified using the source of funds as evidence.

ANNEX 5–II/2

CONFIRMATION OF VERIFICATION OF IDENTITY
GROUP INTRODUCTION

CORPORATE AND OTHER NON-PERSONAL ENTITY

1. DETAILS OF CUSTOMER (see explanatory notes below)

Full name of customer	
Type of entity (corporate, trust, etc)	
Location of business (full operating address)	
Registered office in country of incorporation	
Registered number, if any (or appropriate)	
Relevant company registry or regulated market listing authority	
Names* of directors (or equivalent)	
Names* of principal beneficial owners (over 25%)	

* And dates of birth, if known

2. CONFIRMATION
We confirm that
(a) the verification of the identity of the above customer meets the requirements:
    (i) of the Money Laundering Regulations 2007, and the guidance for standard evidence set out within the guidance for the UK Financial Sector issued by JMLSG; or
    (ii) of our national money laundering legislation that implements the EU Money Laundering Directive, and any authoritative relevant guidance provided as best practice in relation to the type of business or transaction to which this confirmation relates; or
    (iii) of local law and regulation.
(b) where the underlying evidence taken in relation to the verification of the customer's identity is held outside the UK, in the event of any enquiry from you (or from UK law enforcement agencies or regulators under court order or relevant mutual assistance procedure), copies of the relevant customer records will be made available, to the extent that we are required under local law to retain these records.

Signed:	
Name:	
Position:	
Date:	

3. DETAILS OF GROUP FIRM

Full Name of Regulated Firm:	
Relationship to receiving firm:	
Jurisdiction:	
Name of Regulator:	
Regulator Reference Number:	

Explanatory notes

1. "Relevant company registry" includes other registers, such as those maintained by charity commissions (or equivalent) or chambers of commerce.

2. This form cannot be used to verify the identity of any customer that falls into one of the following categories:

- those who are exempt from verification as being an existing client of the introducing firm prior to the introduction of the requirement for such verification;
- those whose identity has not been verified by virtue of the application of a permitted exemption under local anti money laundering law or regulation; or
- those whose identity has been verified using the source of funds as evidence.

[7015]

CHAPTER 6
SUSPICIOUS ACTIVITIES, REPORTING AND DATA PROTECTION

Relevant law/regulation
- Regulations 20(1)(b) and (2)(d) and 21
- POCA ss 327–340
- SI 2006/1070 (Exceptions to overseas conduct defence)
- Terrorism Act, ss 21, 39
- Data Protection Act 1998, ss 7, 29
- Financial sanctions legislation

Core obligations
- All staff must raise an internal report where they have knowledge or suspicion, or where there are reasonable grounds for having knowledge or suspicion, that another person is engaged in money laundering, or that terrorist property exists
- The firm's nominated officer must consider all internal reports
- The firm's nominated officer must make an external report to the Serious Organised Crime Agency (SOCA) as soon as is practicable if he considers that there is knowledge, suspicion, or reasonable grounds for knowledge or suspicion, that another person is engaged in money laundering, or that terrorist property exists
- The firm must seek consent from SOCA before proceeding with a suspicious transaction or entering into arrangements
- Firms must freeze funds if a customer is identified as being on the Consolidated List on the HM Treasury website of suspected terrorists or sanctioned individuals and entities, and make an external report to HM Treasury
- It is a criminal offence for anyone, following a disclosure to a nominated officer or to SOCA, to do or say anything that might either 'tip off' another person that a disclosure has been made or prejudice an investigation
- The firm's nominated officer must report suspicious approaches, even if no transaction takes place

Actions required, to be kept under regular review
- Enquiries made in respect of disclosures must be documented
- The reasons why a Suspicious Activity Report (SAR) was, or was not, submitted should be recorded
- Any communications made with or received from the authorities, including SOCA, in relation to a SAR should be maintained on file

- In cases where advance notice of a transaction or of arrangements is given, the need for prior consent before it is allowed to proceed should be considered

General legal and regulatory obligations

POCA ss 330, 331 Terrorism Act s 21A	6.1	Persons in the regulated sector are required to make a report in respect of information that comes to them within the course of a business in the regulated sector: • where they *know* or • where they *suspect* or • where they *have reasonable grounds for knowing or suspecting* that a person is engaged in, or attempting, money laundering or terrorist financing. Within this guidance, the above obligations are collectively referred to as "grounds for knowledge or suspicion".
Regulation 20(2)(d) POCA s 330	6.2	In order to provide a framework within which suspicion reports may be raised and considered: • each firm must ensure that any member of staff reports to the firm's nominated officer (who may also be the MLRO in an FSA-regulated firm), where they have grounds for knowledge or suspicion that a person or customer is engaged in, or attempting, money laundering or terrorist financing;
Regulation 21		• the firm's nominated officer must consider each such report, and determine whether it gives grounds for knowledge or suspicion; • firms should ensure that staff are appropriately trained in their obligations, and in the requirements for making reports to their nominated officer.
POCA, s 331 Terrorism Act s 21A	6.3	If the nominated officer determines that a report does give rise to grounds for knowledge or suspicion, he must report the matter to SOCA. Under POCA, the nominated officer is required to make a report to SOCA as soon as is practicable if he has grounds for suspicion that another person, whether or not a customer, is engaged in money laundering. Under the Terrorism Act, similar conditions apply in relation to disclosure where there are grounds for suspicion of terrorist financing.
	6.4	A sole trader with no employees who knows or suspects, or where there are reasonable grounds to know or suspect, that a customer of his, or the person on whose behalf the customer is acting, is or has been engaged in, or attempting, money laundering or terrorist financing, must make a report promptly to SOCA.
POCA ss 333A–334 Terrorism Act ss 21D–21H, 39	6.5	It is a criminal offence for any person, following a disclosure to a nominated officer or to SOCA, to release information that might 'tip off' another person that a disclosure has been made if the disclosure is likely to prejudice an investigation, if the information released came to that person in the course of a business in the UK regulated sector. It is also an offence for a person to disclose that an investigation into allegations that an offence has been committed is being contemplated or is being carried out; the disclosure is likely to prejudice that investigation and the information on which the disclosure is based came to the person in the course of a business in the regulated sector. It is also an offence for a person to disclose to another anything which is likely to prejudice an investigation resulting from a disclosure, or where the person knows or has reasonable cause to suspect that a disclosure has been or will be made.

Financial sanctions legislation	6.6	It is a criminal offence to make funds, economic resources or, in certain circumstances, financial services available to those persons or entities listed as the targets of financial sanctions legislation. There is also a requirement to report to HM Treasury both details of funds frozen and where firms have knowledge or suspicion that a customer of the firm or a person with whom the firm has had business dealings is a listed person or entity, a person acting on behalf of a listed person or entity or has committed an offence under the sanctions legislation.

Attempted offences

POCA, s 330 Terrorism Act s 21A(2)	6.7	POCA and the Terrorism Act provide that a disclosure must be made where there are grounds for suspicion that a person is engaged in money laundering or terrorist financing. "Money laundering" is defined in POCA to include an attempt to commit an offence under ss 327–329 of POCA. Similarly, under the Terrorism Act a disclosure must be made where a person has knowledge or suspicion that 'another person had committed *or attempted to commit* an offence under any of the sections 15–18'. There is no duty under s 330 of POCA or s 21A of the Terrorism Act to disclose information about the person who unsuccessfully attempts to commit fraud. This is because the attempt was to commit fraud, rather than to commit an offence under those Acts.
	6.8	However, as soon as the firm has reasonable grounds to know or suspect that any benefit has been acquired, whether by the fraudster himself or by any third party, so that there is criminal property or terrorist property in existence, then, subject to paragraph 6.9, knowledge or suspicion of money laundering or terrorist financing must be reported to SOCA. Who carried out the criminal conduct, and who benefited from it, or whether the conduct occurred before or after the passing of POCA, is immaterial to the obligation to disclose, but should be reported if known.
POCA s 330(3A)	6.9	In circumstances where neither the identity of the fraudster, nor the location of any related criminal property, is known nor is likely to be discovered, limited useable information is, however, available for disclosure. An example of such circumstances would be the theft of a chequebook, debit card, credit card, or charge card, which can lead to multiple low-value fraudulent transactions over a short, medium, or long term. In such instances, there is <u>no</u> obligation to make a report to SOCA <u>where none of the following is known or suspected</u>:

- the identity of the person who is engaged in money laundering;
- the whereabouts of any of the laundered property;
- that any of the information that is available would assist in identifying that person, or the whereabouts of the laundered property.

What is meant by "knowledge" and "suspicion"?

POCA, s 330(2), (3), s 331(2), (3) Terrorism Act ss 21A, 21ZA, 21ZB	6.10	Having <u>knowledge</u> means actually knowing something to be true. In a criminal court, it must be proved that the individual *in fact* knew that a person was engaged in money laundering. That said, knowledge can be *inferred* from the surrounding circumstances; so, for example, a failure to ask obvious questions may be relied upon by a jury to imply knowledge. The knowledge must, however, have come to the firm (or to the member of staff) in the course of business, or (in the case of a nominated officer) as a consequence of a disclosure under s 330 of POCA or s 21A of the Terrorism Act. Information that comes to the firm or staff member in other circumstances does not come within the scope of the regulated sector obligation to make a report. This does not preclude a report being made should staff choose to do so, or are obligated to do so by other parts of these Acts.

6.11   Suspicion is more subjective and falls short of proof based on firm evidence. Suspicion has been defined by the courts as being beyond mere speculation and based on some foundation, for example:

> "*A degree of satisfaction and not necessarily amounting to belief but at least extending beyond speculation as to whether an event has occurred or not*"; and
> "*Although the creation of suspicion requires a lesser factual basis than the creation of a belief, it must nonetheless be built upon some foundation.*"

6.12   A transaction which appears unusual is not necessarily suspicious. Even customers with a stable and predictable transactions profile will have periodic transactions that are unusual for them. Many customers will, for perfectly good reasons, have an erratic pattern of transactions or account activity. So the unusual is, in the first instance, only a basis for further enquiry, which may in turn require judgement as to whether it is suspicious. A transaction or activity may not be suspicious at the time, but if suspicions are raised later, an obligation to report then arises.

6.13   A member of staff, including the nominated officer, who considers a transaction or activity to be suspicious, would not necessarily be expected either to know or to establish the exact nature of any underlying criminal offence, or that the particular funds or property were definitely those arising from a crime or terrorist financing.

6.14   Transactions, or proposed transactions, as part of '419' scams are attempted advance fee frauds, and not money laundering; they are therefore not reportable under POCA or the Terrorism Act, unless the fraud is successful, and the firm is aware of resulting criminal property.

What is meant by "reasonable grounds to know or suspect"?

POCA, s 330 (2)(b), s 331 (2)(b)
Terrorism Act s 21A

6.15   In addition to establishing a criminal offence when suspicion or actual knowledge of money laundering/terrorist financing is proved, POCA and the Terrorism Act introduce criminal liability for failing to disclose information when reasonable grounds exist for knowing or suspecting that a person is engaged in money laundering/terrorist financing. This introduces an objective test of suspicion. The test would likely be met when there are demonstrated to be facts or circumstances, known to the member of staff, from which a reasonable person engaged in a business subject to the ML Regulations would have inferred knowledge, or formed the suspicion, that another person was engaged in money laundering or terrorist financing.

6.16   To defend themselves against a charge that they failed to meet the objective test of suspicion, staff within financial sector firms would need to be able to demonstrate that they took reasonable steps in the particular circumstances, in the context of a risk-based approach, to know the customer and the rationale for the transaction, activity or instruction. It is important to bear in mind that, in practice, members of a jury may decide, with the benefit of hindsight, whether the objective test has been met.

6.17   Depending on the circumstances, a firm being served with a court order in relation to a customer may give rise to reasonable grounds for suspicion in relation to that customer. In such an event, firms should review the information it holds about that customer across the firm, in order to determine whether or not such grounds exist.

Internal reporting

Regulation 20(2)(d)(ii) POCA s 330(5)	6.18	The obligation to report to the nominated officer within the firm where they have grounds for knowledge or suspicion of money laundering or terrorist financing is placed on all relevant employees in the regulated sector. All financial sector firms therefore need to ensure that all relevant employees know who they should report suspicions to.

6.19   Firms may wish to set up internal systems that allow staff to consult with their line manager before sending a report to the nominated officer. The obligation under POCA is to report 'as soon as is reasonably practicable', and so any such consultations should take this into account. Where a firm sets up such systems it should ensure that they are not used to prevent reports reaching the nominated officer whenever staff have stated that they have knowledge or suspicion that a transaction or activity may involve money laundering or terrorist financing.

6.20   Whether or not a member of staff consults colleagues, the legal obligation remains with the staff member to decide for himself whether a report should be made; he must not allow colleagues to decide for him. Where a colleague has been consulted, he himself will then have knowledge on the basis of which he must consider whether a report to the nominated officer is necessary. In such circumstances, firms should make arrangements such that the nominated officer only receives one report in respect of the same information giving rise to knowledge or suspicion.

6.21   Short reporting lines, with a minimum number of people between the person with the knowledge or suspicion and the nominated officer, will ensure speed, confidentiality and swift access to the nominated officer.

6.22   All suspicions reported to the nominated officer should be documented, or recorded electronically. The report should include full details of the customer who is the subject of concern and as full a statement as possible of the information giving rise to the knowledge or suspicion. All internal enquiries made in relation to the report should also be documented, or recorded electronically. This information may be required to supplement the initial report or as evidence of good practice and best endeavours if, at some future date, there is an investigation and the suspicions are confirmed or disproved.

6.23   Once an employee has reported his suspicion in an appropriate manner to the nominated officer, or to an individual to whom the nominated officer has delegated the responsibility to receive such internal reports, he has fully satisfied his statutory obligation.

6.24   Until the nominated officer advises the member of staff making an internal report that no report to SOCA is to be made, further transactions or activity in respect of that customer, whether of the same nature or different from that giving rise to the previous suspicion, should be reported to the nominated officer as they arise.

Non-UK offences

POCA, s 340 (2), (11) SOCPA, s 102	6.25	The offence of money laundering, and the duty to report under POCA, apply in relation to the proceeds of any criminal activity, wherever conducted (including abroad), that would constitute an offence if it took place in the UK. This broad scope excludes offences (other than those referred to in paragraph 6.24) which the firm, staff member or nominated officer knows, or believes on reasonable grounds, to have been committed in a country or territory outside the UK and not to be unlawful under the criminal law then applying in the country or territory concerned.

SI 2006/1070 1968 c 65 1976 c 32 2000 c 8	6.26	Offences committed overseas which the Secretary of State has prescribed by order as remaining within the scope of the duty to report under POCA are those which are punishable by imprisonment for a maximum term in excess of 12 months in any part of the United Kingdom if they occurred there, other than:

- an offence under the Gaming Act 1968;

- an offence under the Lotteries and Amusements Act 1976; or

- an offence under ss 23 or 25 of FSMA

Terrorism Act s 21A(11)	6.27	The duty to report under the Terrorism Act applies in relation to taking any action, or being in possession of a thing, that is unlawful under ss 15–18 of that Act, that would have been an offence under these sections of the Act had it occurred in the UK.
POCA s 331 POCA ss 327–329 Terrorism Act s 21A	6.28	The obligation to consider reporting to SOCA applies only when the nominated officer has received a report made by someone working within the UK regulated sector, or when he himself becomes aware of such a matter in the course of relevant business (which may come from overseas, or from a person overseas). The nominated officer is not, therefore, obliged to report everything that comes to his attention from outside of the UK, although he would be prudent to exercise his judgement in relation to information that comes to his attention from non-business sources. In reaching a decision on whether to make a disclosure, the nominated officer must bear in mind the need to avoid involvement in an offence under ss 327–329 of POCA.

Evaluation and determination by the nominated officer

Regulation 20(2)(d)	6.29	The firm's nominated officer must consider each report and determine whether it gives rise to knowledge or suspicion, or reasonable grounds for knowledge or suspicion. The firm must permit the nominated officer to have access to any information, including 'know your customer' information, in the firm's possession which could be relevant. The nominated officer may also require further information to be obtained, from the customer if necessary, or from an intermediary who introduced the customer to the firm, to the extent that the introducer still holds the information (bearing in mind his own record keeping requirements). Any approach to the customer or to the intermediary should be made sensitively, and probably by someone other than the nominated officer, to minimise the risk of alerting the customer or an intermediary that a disclosure to SOCA may be being considered.
	6.30	When considering an internal suspicion report, the nominated officer, taking account of the risk posed by the transaction or activity being addressed, will need to strike the appropriate balance between the requirement to make a timely disclosure to SOCA, especially if consent is required, and any delays that might arise in searching a number of unlinked systems and records that might hold relevant information.
	6.31	As part of the review, other known connected accounts or relationships may need to be examined. Connectivity can arise commercially (through linked accounts, introducers, etc.), or through individuals (third parties, controllers, signatories etc.). Given the need for timely reporting, it may be prudent for the nominated officer to consider making an initial report to SOCA prior to completing a full review of linked or connected relationships, which may or may not subsequently need to be reported to SOCA.
	6.32	If the nominated officer decides not to make a report to SOCA, the reasons for not doing so should be clearly documented, or recorded electronically, and retained with the internal suspicion report.

External reporting

Regulation 20(2)(d) POCA, s 331 Terrorism Act, s 21A	6.33	The firm's nominated officer must report to SOCA any transaction or activity that, after his evaluation, he knows or suspects, or has reasonable grounds to know or suspect, may be linked to money laundering or terrorist financing, or to attempted money laundering or terrorist financing. Such reports must be made as soon as is reasonably practicable after the information comes to him.

POCA, s 339   6.34   POCA provides that the Secretary of State may by order prescribe the form and manner in which a disclosure under s 330, s 331, s 332 or s 338 may be made. Although a consultation paper on the form and manner of reporting was issued by the Home Office in the summer of 2007, the Home Office decided, on a recommendation from SOCA, not to proceed with the introduction of such an order.

6.35   SOCA prefers that SARs are submitted electronically using one of the existing methods ie, the secure extranet Moneyweb system, or via the secure internet system SARs Online. Information about access to the secure extranet Moneyweb site can be found on the Proceeds of Crime page at www.soca.gov.uk and access and guidance on use of SARs Online can be found at www.ukciu.gov.uk/sarsonline.aspx.

6.36   In order that an informed overview of the situation may be maintained, all contact between particular departments/branches and law enforcement agencies should be controlled through, or reported back to a single contact point, which will typically be the nominated officer. In the alternative, it may be appropriate to route communications through an appropriate member of staff in the firm's legal or compliance department.

6.37   A SAR's intelligence value is related to the quality of information it contains. A firm needs to have good base data from which to draw the information to be included in the SAR; there needs to be a system to enable the relevant information to be produced in hard copy for the law enforcement agencies, if requested under a court order.

6.38   Firms should include in each SAR as much relevant information about the customer, transaction or activity that it has in its records. In particular, the law enforcement agencies have indicated that details of an individual's occupation/company's business and National Insurance number are valuable in enabling them to access other relevant information about the customer. As there is no obligation to collect this information (other than in very specific cases), a firm may not hold these details for all its customers; where it has obtained this information, however, it would be helpful to include it as part of a SAR made by the firm. SOCA's website (www.soca.gov.uk) contains guidance on completing SARs in a way that gives most assistance to law enforcement. In particular, SOCA has published a glossary of terms, and find it helpful if firms use these terms when completing a SAR.

Financial sanctions legislation   6.39   Firms must report to HM Treasury details of funds frozen under financial sanctions legislation and where the firm has knowledge or a suspicion that the financial sanctions measures have been or are being contravened, or that a customer is a listed person or entity, or a person acting on behalf of a listed person or entity. The firm may also need to consider whether the firm has an obligation also to report under POCA or the Terrorism Act.

Where to report

6.40   To avoid committing a failure to report offence, nominated officers must make their disclosures to SOCA. The national reception point for disclosure of suspicions, and for seeking consent to continue to proceed with the transaction or activity, is the UKFIU within SOCA

6.41   The UKFIU address is PO Box 8000, London, SE11 5EN and it can be
        contacted during office hours on: 020 7238 8282. Urgent disclosures,
        i.e., those requiring consent, should be transmitted electronically over a
        previously agreed secure link or, if secure electronic methods are not
        available, by fax, as specified on the SOCA website at
        www.soca.gov.uk. Speed of response is assisted if the appropriate
        consent request is clearly mentioned in the title of any faxed report
        (www.soca.gov.uk/financialIntel/formsGuide.html).

6.42   To avoid committing a failure to report offence under financial
        sanctions legislation, firms must make their reports to HM Treasury.
        The relevant unit is the Asset Freezing Unit, HM Treasury, 1 Horse
        Guards Road, London SW1A 2HQ. Reports can be submitted
        electronically at assetfreezingunit@hm-treasury.gov.uk and the Unit can
        be contacted by telephone on 020 7270 5454.

Sanctions and penalties

POCA s 334   6.43   Where a person fails to comply with the obligation under POCA or the
Terrorism Act   Terrorism Act to make disclosures to a nominated officer and/or SOCA
s 21A   as soon as practicable after the information giving rise to the
                        knowledge or suspicion comes to the member of staff, a firm is open to
                        criminal prosecution or regulatory censure. The criminal sanction,
                        under POCA or the Terrorism Act, is a prison term of up to five years,
                        and/or a fine.

Financial   6.44   Where a firm fails to comply with the obligations to freeze funds, not
sanctions   to make funds, economic resources and, in relation to suspected
legislation   terrorists, financial services, available to listed persons or to report
                        knowledge or suspicion, it is open to prosecution.

Consent

6.45   Care should be taken that the requirement to obtain consent for a
        particular transaction does not lead to the unnecessary freezing of a
        customer's account, thus affecting other, non-suspicious transactions.

Consent under POCA

POCA s 336   6.46   Reporting before or reporting after the event are not equal options
                        which a firm can choose between. Where a customer instruction is
                        received prior to a transaction or activity taking place, or arrangements
                        being put in place, and there are grounds for knowledge or suspicion
                        that the transaction, arrangements, or the funds/property involved, may
                        relate to money laundering, a report must be made to SOCA and
                        consent sought to proceed with that transaction or activity. In such
                        circumstances, it is an offence for a nominated officer to consent to a
                        transaction or activity going ahead within the seven working day notice
                        period from the working day following the date of disclosure, unless
                        SOCA gives consent. Where urgent consent is required, use should be
                        made of the process referred to in paragraph 6.41 above.

POCA ss 330   6.47   When an activity or transaction (or a related transaction) which gives
(6)(a), 331(6),   rise to concern is already within an automated clearing or settlement
338 (3)(b)   system, where a delay would lead to a breach of a contractual
                        obligation, or where it would breach market settlement or clearing
                        rules, the nominated officer may need to let the transaction proceed and
                        report it later. Where the nominated officer intends to make a report,
                        but delays doing so for such reasons, POCA provides a defence from
                        making a report where there is a reasonable excuse for not doing so.
                        However, it should be noted that this defence is untested by case law,
                        and would need to be considered on a case-by-case basis.

	6.48	When consent is needed to undertake a future transaction or activity, or to enter into an arrangement, the disclosure should be sent electronically (ensuring that the tick box for a consent request is marked) or, if electronic methods are not available, faxed to the SOCA UKFIU Consent Desk immediately the suspicion is identified. Consent requests should not be sent by post due to the timings involved, and additional postal copies are not required following submission by electronic means or fax. Further information is available on the SOCA website www.soca.gov.uk. The Consent Desk will apply SOCA policy to each submission, carrying out the necessary internal enquiries, and will contact the appropriate law enforcement agency, where necessary, for a consent recommendation. Once SOCA's decision has been reached, the disclosing firm will be informed of the decision by telephone, and be given a consent number, which should be recorded. A formal consent letter will follow.
POCA, s 335	6.49	In the event that SOCA does not refuse consent within seven working days following the working day after the disclosure is made, the firm may process the transaction or activity, subject to normal commercial considerations. If, however, consent is refused within that period, a restraint order must be obtained by the authorities within a further 31 calendar days (the moratorium period) from the day consent is refused, if they wish to prevent the transaction going ahead after that date. In cases where consent is refused, the law enforcement agency refusing consent should be consulted to establish what information can be provided to the customer.
POCA, s 335(1)(b)	6.50	Consent from SOCA (referred to as a 'notice' in POCA), or the absence of a refusal of consent within seven working days following the working day after the disclosure is made, provides the person handling the transaction or carrying out the activity, or the nominated officer of the reporting firm, with a defence against a possible later charge of laundering the proceeds of crime in respect of that transaction or activity if it proceeds.

Consent under Terrorism Act

Terrorism Act s 21ZA	6.51	A person does not commit an offence under the Terrorism Act where, before becoming involved in a transaction or arrangement relating to money or other property which he suspects or believes is terrorist property, a report is made to SOCA and consent sought to proceed with that transaction or arrangement. In such circumstances, it is an offence for an authorised officer to consent to a transaction or arrangement going ahead within the seven working day notice period from the working day following the date of disclosure to SOCA, unless SOCA gives consent. [Where urgent consent is required, use should be made of the process referred to in paragraph 6.41 above.]
Terrorism Act s 21ZB	6.52	When a transaction which gives rise to concern is already within an automated clearing or settlement system, where a delay would lead to a breach of a contractual obligation, or where it would breach market settlement or clearing rules, the authorised officer may need to let the transaction proceed and report it later. Where the nominated officer intends to make a report, but delays doing so for such reasons, the Terrorism Act provides a defence from making a report where there is a reasonable excuse for not doing so, so long as the report is made on his own initiative and as soon as it is reasonably practical for the person to make it. However, it should be noted that this defence is untested by case law, and would need to be considered on a case-by-case basis.

6.53   When consent is needed to undertake a future transaction or activity, or to enter into an arrangement, the disclosure should be sent electronically (ensuring that the tick box for a consent request is marked) or, if secure electronic methods are not available, faxed to the SOCA UKFIU Consent Desk immediately the suspicion is identified. Consent requests should not be sent by post due to the timings involved, and additional postal copies are not required following submission by electronic means or fax. Further information is available on the SOCA website www.soca.gov.uk. The Consent Desk will carry out the necessary internal enquiries, and will contact the appropriate law enforcement agency, where necessary, for a consent recommendation. Once SOCA's decision has been reached, the disclosing firm will be informed of the decision by telephone, and be given a consent number, which should be recorded. A formal consent letter will follow.

Terrorism Act
s 21ZA(2)

6.54   In the event that SOCA does not refuse consent within seven working days following the working day after the disclosure is made, the firm may proceed with the transaction or arrangement, subject to normal commercial considerations. In cases where consent is refused, the law enforcement agency refusing consent should be consulted to establish what information can be provided to the customer.

6.55   Consent from SOCA (referred to as a 'notice' in the Terrorism Act), or the absence of a refusal of consent within seven working days following the working day after the disclosure is made, provides the person handling the transaction or arrangement, or the nominated officer of the reporting firm, with a defence against a possible later charge under the Terrorism Act in respect of that transaction or arrangement if it proceeds.

General

6.56   The consent provisions can only apply where there is prior notice to SOCA of the transaction or activity; SOCA cannot provide consent after the transaction or activity has occurred. The receipt of a SAR after the transaction or activity has taken place will be dealt with as an ordinary standard SAR, and in the absence of any instruction to the contrary, a firm will be free to operate the customer's account under normal commercial considerations until such time as the LEA determines otherwise through its investigation.

6.57   Where there is a need to take urgent action in respect of an account, and the seven working day consent notice period applies, SOCA will endeavour to provide a response in the shortest timeframe, taking into consideration the circumstances of the particular case. Where possible, this will be sooner than the seven working day time limit. If the customer makes strong demands for the transaction/activity to proceed, SOCA will put the firm in touch with the investigating law enforcement agency for guidance, in order to prevent the customer being alerted to the fact of suspicion and that a disclosure has been made. In these circumstances, each case will be dealt with on its merits.

6.58   In order to provide a defence against future prosecution for failing to report, the reasons for any conscious decision not to report should be documented, or recorded electronically. An appropriate report should be made as soon as is practicable after the event, including full details of the transaction, the circumstances precluding advance notice, and to where any money or assets were transferred.

	6.59	The consent regime as it currently operates in the UK is a difficult one for financial practitioners to work with. There are operational challenges and legal uncertainties concerning what can realistically constitute a 'pre-event' transaction. There are customer service implications – the potentially litigious consequences of declining a customer's instructions, the inability to give an explanation because of the risk of tipping-off and the problematic requirement referred to in 6.73 for (in particular, large) deposit-taking institutions to seek consent for all post-disclosure transactions over £250. In recognition of these difficulties, in December 2007 the Home Office issued a consultation paper setting out options for change. Once discussions are satisfactorily completed, further guidance on meeting these obligations will be provided. Firms should refer to www.jmlsg.org.uk for such further guidance.

Tipping off, and prejudicing an investigation

POCA s 333A(1), (3) Terrorism Act, s 21D	6.60	POCA and the Terrorism Act each contains two separate offences of tipping off and prejudicing an investigation. The first offence relates to disclosing that an internal or external report has been made; the second relates to disclosing that an investigation is being contemplated or is being carried out. These offences are similar and overlapping, but there are also significant differences between them. It is important for those working in the regulated sector to be aware of the conditions precedent for each offence. Each offence relates to situations where the information on which the disclosure was based came to the person making the disclosure in the course of a business in the regulated sector. There are a number of permitted disclosures that do not give rise to these offences (see paragraphs 6.63 to 6.66).
POCA ss 333A(1), 333D(3) Terrorism Act, ss 21D(1), 21G(3)	6.61	Once an internal or external suspicion report has been made, it is a criminal offence for anyone to disclose information about that report which is likely to prejudice an investigation that might be conducted following that disclosure. An offence is not committed if the person does not know or suspect that the disclosure is likely to prejudice such an investigation, or if the disclosure is a permitted disclosure under POCA or the Terrorism Act. Reasonable enquiries of a customer, conducted in a tactful manner, regarding the background to a transaction or activity that is inconsistent with the normal pattern of activity is prudent practice, forms an integral part of CDD measures, and should not give rise to the tipping off offence.
POCA, ss 333A(3), 333D(4) Terrorism Act, ss 21D(3), 21G(4)	6.62	Where a money laundering investigation is being contemplated, or being carried out, it is a criminal offence for anyone to disclose this fact if that disclosure is likely to prejudice that investigation. An offence is not committed if the person does not know or suspect that the disclosure is likely to prejudice such an investigation, or if the disclosure is a permitted disclosure under POCA or the Terrorism Act.

Permitted disclosures

POCA s 333D(1) Terrorism Act, s 21G(1)	6.63	An offence is not committed if the disclosure is made to the FSA (or other relevant supervisor) for the purpose of: • the detection, investigation or prosecution of a criminal offence (whether in the UK or elsewhere); • an investigation under POCA; or • the enforcement of any order of a court under POCA.
POCA, s 333B(1) Terrorism Act, ss 21A, 21E(1)	6.64	An employee, officer or partner of a firm does not commit an offence under POCA, s 333A, or the Terrorism Act, s 21A, if the disclosure is to an employee, officer or partner of the same firm.

| POCA, s 333B(2) Terrorism Act, s 21E(2) | 6.65 | A person does not commit an offence if the firm making the disclosure and the firm to which it is made belong to the same group (as defined in directive 2002/87/EC), and: |

- the disclosure is to a credit institution or a financial institution: and

- the firm to which the disclosure is made is situated in an EEA State, or a country imposing equivalent money laundering requirements.

| POCA s 333C Terrorism Act, s 21F | 6.66 | A firm does not commit an offence under POCA, s 333A or the Terrorism Act s 21D, if the disclosure is from one credit institution to another, or from one financial institution to another, and: |

- the disclosure relates to

  - a customer or former customer of the firm making the disclosure and of the firm to which the disclosure is made; or

  - a transaction involving them both; or

  - the provision of a service involving them both.

- the disclosure is for the purpose only of preventing an offence under Part 7 of POCA or under Part III of the Terrorism Act;

- the firm to which the disclosure is made is situated in an EEA State or in a country imposing equivalent money laundering requirements; and

- the firm making the disclosure and the one to which it is made are subject to equivalent duties of protection of personal data (within the meaning of the Data Protection Act 1998).

| POCA, ss 335, 336 Terrorism Act, ss 21ZA, 21ZB | 6.67 | The fact that a transaction is notified to SOCA before the event, and SOCA does not refuse consent within seven working days following the day after the authorized disclosure is made, or a restraint order is not obtained within the 31 day moratorium period, does not alter the position so far as 'tipping off' is concerned. |

6.68 This means that a firm

- cannot, at the time, tell a customer that a transaction is being delayed because a report is awaiting consent from SOCA;

- cannot later – unless law enforcement/SOCA agrees, or a court order is obtained permitting disclosure – tell a customer that a transaction or activity was delayed because a report had been made under POCA or the Terrorism Act; and

- cannot tell the customer that law enforcement is conducting an investigation.

6.69 The judgment in K v Natwest [2006] EWCA Civ 1039 confirmed the application of these provisions. The judgment in this case also dealt with the issue of suspicion stating that the "The existence of suspicion is a subjective fact. There is no legal requirement that there should be reasonable grounds for the suspicion. The relevant bank employee either suspects or he does not. If he does suspect, he must (either himself or through the Bank's nominated officer) inform the authorities." It was further observed that the "truth is that Parliament has struck a precise and workable balance of conflicting interests in the 2002 Act". The Court appears to have approved of the 7 and 31 day scheme and said that in relation to the limited interference with private rights that this scheme entails "many people would think that a reasonable balance has been struck". A full copy of the judgment is available at www.soca.gov.uk/downloads/KvNatWest.pdf.

6.70 If a firm receives a complaint in these circumstances, it may be unable to provide a satisfactory explanation to the customer, who may then bring a complaint to the Financial Ombudsman Service (FOS). If a firm receives an approach from a FOS casehandler about such a case, the firm should contact a member of the FOS legal department immediately.

6.71   SOCA has confirmed that, in such cases, a firm may tell the FOS's legal department about a report to SOCA and the outcome, on the basis that the FOS will keep the information confidential (which they must do, to avoid any 'tipping off'). The FOS's legal department will then ensure that the case is handled appropriately in these difficult circumstances – liaising as necessary with SOCA. FOS's communications with the customer will still be in the name of a casehandler/ombudsman, so that the customer is not alerted.

Transactions following a disclosure

6.72   Firms must remain vigilant for any additional transactions by, or instructions from, any customer or account in respect of which a disclosure has been made, and should submit further disclosures, and consent applications, to SOCA, as appropriate.

POCA s 339A   6.73   In the case of deposit-taking institutions alone, following the reporting of a suspicion, any subsequent transactions (including 'lifestyle' payments) involving the customer or account which was the subject of the original report may only proceed if it meets the 'threshold' requirement of £250 or less; where the proposed transaction exceeds £250, permission to vary the 'threshold' payment is required from SOCA before it may proceed.

6.74   The significant practical difficulties involved in meeting the legal requirements set out in paragraph 6.73 are being discussed with the authorities as part of the changes proposed in the Home Office consultation on the consent regime (see paragraph 6.59).

POCA,
ss 337(1),
338(4)
Terrorism Act
s 21B

6.75   The disclosure provisions within POCA and the Terrorism Act protect persons making SARs from any potential breaches of confidentiality, whether imposed under contract, statute (for example, the Data Protection Act), or common law. These provisions apply to those inside and outside the regulated sector, and include reports that are made voluntarily, in addition to reports made in order to fulfil reporting obligations. SOCA has established a SARs Confidentiality Hotline (0800 2346657) to report breaches from reporters and end-users alike.

6.76   SOCA's consent following a disclosure is given to the reporting institution solely in relation to the money laundering offences. Consent provides the staff involved with a defence against a charge of committing a money laundering offence under ss 327–329 of POCA or a terrorist finance offence under ss 15–18 of the Terrorism Act. It is not intended to override normal commercial judgement, and a firm is not committed to continuing the relationship with the customer if such action would place the reporting institution at commercial risk.

6.77   Whether to terminate a relationship is essentially a commercial decision, and firms must be free to make such judgements. However, in the circumstances envisaged here a firm should consider liaising with the law enforcement investigating officer to consider whether it is likely that termination would alert the customer or prejudice an investigation in any other way. If there is continuing suspicion about the customer or the transaction or activities, and there are funds which need to be returned to the customer at the end of the relationship, firms should ask SOCA for consent to repatriate the funds.

6.78   Where the firm knows that the funds in an account derive from criminal activity, or that they arise from fraudulent instructions, the account must be frozen. Where it is believed that the account holder may be involved in the fraudulent activity that is being reported, then the account may need to be frozen, but the need to avoid tipping off would have to be considered.

6.79 When an enquiry is under investigation, the investigating officer may contact the nominated officer to ensure that he has all the relevant information which supports the original disclosure. This contact may also include seeking supplementary information or documentation from the reporting firm and from other sources by way of a court order. The investigating officer will therefore work closely with the nominated officer who will usually receive direct feedback on the stage reached in the investigation. There may, however, be cases when the nominated officer cannot be informed of the state of the investigation, either because of the confidential nature of the enquiry, or because it is sub judice.

6.80 Where the firm does not wish to make the payment requested by a customer, it should notify SOCA of this fact and request them to identify any information that they are prepared to allow the firm to disclose to the court and to the customer in any proceedings brought by the customer to enforce payment. SOCA should be reminded that:

- the court may ask him to appear before it to justify his position if he refuses to consent to adequate disclosure; and

- the refusal to allow adequate disclosure is likely to make it apparent to the customer that the firm's reasons for refusing payment are due to a law enforcement investigation

6.81 If the investigating officer is able to consent to the disclosure of adequate information to permit the firm to defend itself against any proceedings brought by the customer, that information may be shown to the court and to the customer without a tipping off offence being committed. In the event that the firm and the investigating officer cannot reach agreement on the information to be disclosed, an application can be made to the court for directions and/or an interim declaration.

6.82 In any proceedings that might be brought by the customer, the firm may only disclose to the court and the other side such information as has been consented to by the investigating officer or the court.

Constructive trusts

6.83 The duty to report suspicious activity and to avoid tipping off could, in certain circumstances, lead to a potential conflict between the reporting firm's responsibilities under the criminal law and its obligations under the civil law, as a constructive trustee, to a victim of a fraud or other crimes.

6.84 A firm's liability as a constructive trustee under English law can arise when it either knows that the funds held by the firm do not belong to its customer, or is on notice that such funds may not belong to its customer. The firm will then take on the obligation of a constructive trustee for the rightful owner of the funds. If the firm pays the money away other than to the rightful owner, and it is deemed to have acted dishonestly in doing so, it may be held liable for knowingly assisting a breach of trust.

6.85 Having a suspicion that it considers necessary to report under the money laundering or terrorist financing legislation may, in certain circumstances, indicate that the firm knows that the funds do not belong to its customer, or is on notice that they may not belong to its customer. However, such suspicion may not itself be enough to cause a firm to become a constructive trustee. Case law suggests that a constructive trust will only arise when there is some evidence that the funds belong to someone other than the customer.

6.86 If, when making a suspicious activity report, a firm knows that the funds which are the subject of the report do not belong to its customer, or has doubts that they do, this fact, and details of the firm's proposed course of action, should form part of the report that is forwarded to SOCA.

6.87   If the customer wishes subsequently to withdraw or transfer the funds, the firm should, in the first instance, contact SOCA for consent. Consent from SOCA will, however, not necessarily protect the firm from the risk of committing a breach of constructive trust by transferring funds. In situations where the assistance of the court is necessary, it is open to a firm to apply to the court for directions as to whether the customer's request should be met. However, the powers of the court are discretionary, and should only be used in cases of real need. That said, it is unlikely that a firm acting upon the direction of a court would later be held to have acted dishonestly such as to incur liability for breach of constructive trust.

6.88   Although each case must be considered on its facts, the effective use of customer information, and the identification of appropriate underlying beneficial owners, can help firms to guard against a potential constructive trust suit arising out of fraudulent misuse or misappropriation of funds.

6.89   It should be noted that constructive trust is not a concept recognised in Scots law.

Data Protection – Subject Access Requests, where a suspicion report has been made

6.90   Occasionally, a Subject Access Request under the Data Protection Act will include within its scope one or more money laundering/terrorist financing reports which have been submitted in relation to that customer. Although it might be instinctively assumed that to avoid tipping off there can be no question of ever including this information when responding to the customer, an automatic assumption to that effect must not be made, even though in practice it will only rarely be decided that it is appropriate to include it. However, all such requests must be carefully considered on their merits in line with the principles below.

6.91   The following guidance is drawn from guidance issued by HM Treasury in April 2002. This guidance – The UK's Anti-Money Laundering Legislation and the Data Protection Act 1998 – Guidance notes for the financial sector – is available at www.hm-treasury.gov.uk/documents/financial_services/fin_index.cfm.

Data Protection Act, s 7

6.92   On making a request in writing (a Subject Access Request) to a data controller (ie any organisation that holds personal data), an individual is normally entitled to:

- be informed whether the data controller is processing (which includes merely holding) his personal data; and if so

- be given a description of that data, the purposes for which they are being processed and to whom they are or may be disclosed; and

- have communicated to him in an intelligible form all the information that constitutes his personal data and any information available to the data controller as to the source of that data.

Data Protection Act, s 29

6.93   Section 29 of the Data Protection Act provides that personal data are exempt from disclosure under section 7 of the Act in any case where the application of that provision would be likely to prejudice the prevention or detection of crime or the apprehension or prosecution of offenders. However, even when relying on an exemption, data controllers (ie, firms) should provide as much information as they can in response to a Subject Access Request.

6.94   Where a firm withholds a piece of information in reliance on the section 29 exemption, it is not obliged to tell the individual that any information has been withheld. The information in question can simply be omitted and no reference made to it when responding to the individual who has made the request.

6.95   To establish whether disclosure would be likely to prejudice an investigation or a potential investigation, firms should approach SOCA for guidance; SOCA will usually discuss this with past or present investigating agencies/officers. This may also involve cases that are closed, but where related investigations may still be continuing.

6.96   Each Subject Access Request must be considered on its own merits in determining whether, in a particular case, the disclosure of a suspicion report is likely to prejudice an investigation and, consequently, constitute a tipping-off offence. In determining whether the section 29 exemption applies, it is legitimate to take account of the fact that although the disclosure does not, in itself, provide clear evidence of criminal conduct when viewed in isolation, it might ultimately form part of a larger jigsaw of evidence in relation to a particular crime. It is also legitimate to take account generally of the confidential nature of suspicious activity reports when considering whether or not the exemption under section 29 might apply.

6.97   In cases where the fact that a disclosure had been made had previously been reported in legal proceedings, or in a previous investigation, and the full contents of such a disclosure had been revealed, then it is less likely that the exemption under section 29 would apply. However, caution should be exercised when considering disclosures that have been made in legal proceedings for the purposes of the section 29 exemption, as often the disclosure will have been limited strictly to matters relevant to those proceedings, and other information contained in the original report may not have been revealed.

6.98   To guard against a tipping-off offence, nominated officers should ensure that no information relating to SARs is released to any person without the nominated officer's authorisation. Further consideration may need to be given to suspicion reports received internally that have not been submitted to SOCA. A record should be kept of the steps that have been taken in determining whether disclosure of a report would involve tipping off and/or the availability of the section 29 exemption.

Data
Protection Act
s 7(8)

6.99   Firms should bear in mind that there is a statutory deadline for responding to Subject Access Requests of 40 days from their receipt by the firm. The timing of enquiries to SOCA, or any other party, to obtain further information, or for guidance on whether disclosure would be likely to prejudice an investigation, should be made with this deadline in mind.

[7016]

CHAPTER 7
STAFF AWARENESS, TRAINING AND ALERTNESS

Relevant law/regulation
- Regulation 21
- POCA ss 327–329, 330 (6),(7), 333, 334(2)
- Terrorism Act ss 18, 21A
- SYSC 3.2.6G(1) G
- TC, Chapter 1
- Financial sanctions legislation

Core obligations
- Relevant employees should be
  — made aware of the risks of money laundering and terrorist financing, the relevant legislation, and their obligations under that legislation
  — made aware of the identity and responsibilities of the firm's nominated officer and MLRO
  — trained in the firm's procedures and in how to recognise and deal with potential money laundering or terrorist financing transactions or activity
- Staff training should be given at regular intervals, and details recorded
- MLRO is responsible for oversight of the firm's compliance with its requirements in respect of staff training

---

> - The relevant director or senior manager has overall responsibility for the establishment and maintenance of effective training arrangements
>
> **Actions required, to be kept under regular review**
> - Provide appropriate training to make relevant employees aware of money laundering and terrorist financing issues, including how these crimes operate and how they might take place through the firm
> - Ensure that relevant employees are provided with information on, and understand, the legal position of the firm and of individual members of staff, and of changes to these legal positions
> - Consider providing relevant employees with case studies and examples related to the firm's business
> - Train relevant employees in how to operate a risk-based approach to AML/CFT

Why focus on staff awareness and training?

7.1   One of the most important controls over the prevention and detection of money laundering is to have staff who are alert to the risks of money laundering/terrorist financing and well trained in the identification of unusual activities or transactions which may prove to be suspicious.

7.2   The effective application of even the best designed control systems can be quickly compromised if the staff applying the systems are not adequately trained. The effectiveness of the training will therefore be important to the success of the firm's AML/CTF strategy.

7.3   It is essential that firms implement a clear and well articulated policy for ensuring that relevant employees are aware of their obligations in respect of the prevention of money laundering and terrorist financing and for training them in the identification and reporting of anything that gives grounds for suspicion. This is especially important for staff who handle customer transactions or instructions. Temporary and contract staff carrying out such functions should also be covered by these training programmes.

POCA   7.4   Under POCA and the Terrorism Act, individual members of staff face
ss 327–329,   criminal penalties if they are involved in money laundering or terrorist
334(2)   financing, or if they do not report their knowledge or suspicion of
Terrorism   money laundering or terrorist financing where there are reasonable
Act ss 18,   grounds for their knowing or suspecting such activity. It is important,
21A   therefore, that staff are made aware of these obligations, and are given
                       training in how to discharge them.

General legal and regulatory obligations

TC 1.2.1 G   7.5   The FSA's Training and Competence Sourcebook (TC) [which is currently under review by the FSA] contains high-level commitments for all FSA-regulated businesses and these provide an important background to the provision of money laundering awareness and training.

7.6   The firm's commitments to training and competence are that:
- its employees are competent;
- its employees remain competent for the work they do;
- its employees are appropriately supervised;
- its employees' competence is regularly reviewed;
- the level of competence is appropriate to the nature of the business.

Regulation 16   7.7   The obligations on senior management and the firm in relation to staff awareness and staff training address each requirement separately. ML Regulations require firms to take appropriate measures so that all relevant employees are made aware of the law relating to money laundering and terrorist financing, and that they are regularly given training in how to recognise and deal with transactions which may be related to money laundering or terrorist financing.

SYSC 3.2.6I(1) R SYSC 3.2.6G(1) G	7.8	The FSA specifically requires the MLRO to have responsibility for oversight of the firm's AML systems and controls, which include appropriate training for the firm's employees in relation to money laundering.
POCA, s 330 (6) and (7)	7.9	Where a staff member is found to have had reasonable grounds for knowing or suspecting money laundering, but failed to make a disclosure, he will have a defence under POCA if he does not know or suspect, and has not been provided with AML training by his employer. No such defence is available under the Terrorism Act.
Regulation 16	7.10	A successful defence by a staff member under POCA may leave the firm open to prosecution or regulatory sanction for not having adequate training and awareness arrangements. Firms should therefore not only obtain acknowledgement from the individual that they have received the necessary training, but should also take steps to assess its effectiveness.

Responsibilities of the firm, and its staff

Responsibilities of senior management

Regulation 20	7.11	Senior management must be aware of their obligations under the ML Regulations to establish appropriate systems and procedures to forestall and prevent operations relating to money laundering and terrorist financing. It is an offence not to have appropriate systems in place, whether or not money laundering or terrorist financing has taken place.
Regulation 20 SYSC 3.2.6HR SYSC 3.2.6IR	7.12	The relevant director or senior manager has overall responsibility for the establishment and maintenance of effective training arrangements. The MLRO is responsible for oversight of the firm's compliance with its requirements in respect of training, including taking reasonable steps to ensure that the firm's systems and controls include appropriate training for employees in relation to money laundering. Awareness and training arrangements specifically for senior management, the MLRO and the nominated officer should therefore also be considered.
	7.13	As noted in paragraph 1.29, the relationship between the MLRO and the director(s)/senior manager(s) allocated overall responsibility for the establishment and maintenance of the firm's AML/CTF systems is one of the keys to a successful AML/CTF regime. It is important that this relationship is clearly defined and documented, so that each knows the extent of his, and the other's, role and day to day responsibilities.
	7.14	Firms should take reasonable steps to ensure that relevant employees are aware of:

- their responsibilities under the firm's arrangements for the prevention of money laundering and terrorist financing, including those for obtaining sufficient evidence of identity, recognising and reporting knowledge or suspicion of money laundering or terrorist financing;

- the identity and responsibilities of the nominated officer and the MLRO; and

- the potential effect on the firm, on its employees personally and on its clients, of any breach of that law.

	7.15	The firm's approach to training should be built around ensuring that the content and frequency of training reflects the risk assessment of the products and services of the firm and the specific role of the individual.

Responsibilities of staff

7.16 Staff should be made aware of their personal responsibilities and those of the firm at the start of their employment. These responsibilities should be documented in such a way as to enable staff to refer to them as and when appropriate throughout their employment. In addition, selected or relevant employees should be given regular appropriate training in order to be aware of:

- the criminal law relating to money laundering and terrorist financing;

- the ML Regulations;

- the FSA Rules;

- industry guidance;

- the risks money laundering and terrorist financing pose to the business;

- the vulnerabilities of the firm's products and services; and

- the firm's policies and procedures in relation to the prevention of money laundering and terrorist financing.

7.17 Where staff move between jobs, or change responsibilities, their training needs may change. Ongoing training should be given at appropriate intervals to all relevant employees.

Legal obligations on staff

POCA,   7.18   There are several sets of offences under POCA and the Terrorism Act
ss 327–329,   which directly affect staff – the various offences of money laundering
330–332   or terrorist financing, failure to report possible money laundering or
Terrorism Act   terrorist financing, tipping off, and prejudicing an investigation.
ss 18, 21A

POCA,   7.19   The offences of involvement in money laundering or terrorist financing
ss 327–329   apply to all staff, whether or not the firm is in the regulated sector. This
Terrorism Act   would include staff of general insurance firms and mortgage
s 18   intermediaries. The offences have no particular application to those
engaged in specific customer-related activities – that is, they also apply
to back office staff.

POCA   7.20   The offence under POCA and the Terrorism Act of failing to report
ss 330–332   applies to staff in the regulated sector, and to all nominated officers,
Terrorism Act   whether in the regulated sector or not. Although general insurance
s 21A   firms and mortgage intermediaries are not in the regulated sector, if
they have opted to appoint a nominated officer, the obligations on
nominated officers apply to these appointees.

POCA s 333   7.21   Once a report has been made to the firm's nominated officer, it is an
offence to make any further disclosure that is likely to prejudice an
investigation.

Training in the firm's procedures

7.22 The firm should train staff, in particular, on how its products and services may be used as a vehicle for money laundering or terrorist financing, and in the firm's procedures for managing this risk. They will also need information on how the firm may itself be at risk of prosecution if it processes transactions without the consent of SOCA where a SAR has been made.

PART V
OTHER MATERIALS

7.23 Relevant employees should be trained in what they need to know in order to carry out their particular role. Staff involved in customer acceptance, in customer servicing, or in settlement functions will need different training, tailored to their particular function. This may involve making them aware of the importance of the "know your customer" requirements for money laundering prevention purposes, and of the respective importance of customer ID procedures, obtaining additional information and monitoring customer activity. The awareness raising and training in this respect should cover the need to verify the identity of the customer, and circumstances when it should be necessary to obtain appropriate additional customer information in the context of the nature of the transaction or business relationship concerned.

7.24 Relevant employees should also be made aware of the particular circumstances of customers who present a higher risk of money laundering or terrorist financing, or who are financially excluded. Training should include how identity should be verified in such cases, what additional steps should be taken, and/or what local checks can be made.

Staff alertness to specific situations

7.25 Sufficient training will need to be given to all relevant employees to enable them to recognise when a transaction is unusual or suspicious, or when they should have reasonable grounds to know or suspect that money laundering or terrorist financing is taking place.

7.26 The set of circumstances giving rise to an unusual transaction or arrangement, and which may provide reasonable grounds for concluding that it is suspicious, will depend on the customer and the product or service in question. Illustrations of the type of situation that may be unusual, and which in certain circumstances might give rise to reasonable grounds for suspicion, are:

- transactions which have no apparent purpose, or which make no obvious economic sense (including where a person makes a loss against tax), or which involve apparently unnecessary complexity;

- the use of non-resident accounts, companies or structures in circumstances where the customer's needs do not appear to support such economic requirements;

- where the transaction being requested by the customer, or the size or pattern of transactions, is, without reasonable explanation, out of the ordinary range of services normally requested or is inconsistent with the experience of the firm in relation to the particular customer;

- dealing with customers not normally expected in that part of the business;

- transfers to and from high-risk jurisdictions, without reasonable explanation, which are not consistent with the customer's declared foreign business dealings or interests;

- where a series of transactions are structured just below a regulatory threshold;

- where a customer who has entered into a business relationship with the firm uses the relationship for a single transaction or for only a very short period of time;

- unnecessary routing of funds through third party accounts;

- unusual investment transactions without an apparently discernible profitable motive.

7.27 Issues around the customer identification process that may raise concerns include such matters as the following:

- Has the customer refused, or appeared particularly reluctant, to provide the information requested without reasonable explanation?

- Do you understand the legal and corporate structure of the client entity, and its ownership and control, and does the structure appear to make sense?

- Is the staff member aware of any inconsistencies between locations and other information provided?

- Is the area of residence given consistent with other profile details, such as employment?

- Does an address appear vague or unusual – eg, an accommodation agency, a professional 'registered office' or a trading address?

- Does it make sense for the customer to be opening the account or relationship in the jurisdiction that he is asking for?

- Is the information that the customer has provided consistent with the banking or other services or facilities that he is seeking?

- Does the supporting documentation add validity to the other information provided by the customer?

- Does the customer have other banking or financial relationships with the firm, and does the collected information on all these relationships appear consistent?

- Does the client want to conclude arrangements unusually urgently, against a promise to provide information at a later stage, which is not satisfactorily explained?

- Has the customer suggested changes to a proposed arrangement in order to avoid providing certain information?

7.28   Staff should also be on the lookout for such things as:

- sudden, substantial increases in cash deposits or levels of investment, without adequate explanation;

- transactions made through other banks or financial firms;

- regular large, or unexplained, transfers to and from countries known for money laundering, terrorism, corruption or drug trafficking;

- large numbers of electronic transfers into and out of the account;

- significant/unusual/inconsistent deposits by third parties; and

- reactivation of dormant account(s).

7.29   Staff awareness and training programmes may also include the nature of terrorism funding and terrorist activity, in order that staff are alert to customer transactions or activities that might be terrorist-related.

7.30   Examples of activity that might suggest to staff that there could be potential terrorist activity include:

- round sum deposits, followed by like-amount wire transfers;

- frequent international ATM activity;

- no known source of income;

- use of wire transfers and the internet to move funds to and from high-risk countries and geographic locations;

- frequent address changes;

- purchases of military items or technology; and

- media reports on suspected, arrested terrorists or groups.

7.31   It is important that staff are appropriately made aware of changing behaviour and practices amongst money launderers and those financing terrorism. As well as their regular series of publications on the typologies of financial crime, FATF's Guidance for Financial Institutions in Detecting Terrorist Financing issued in April 2002 contains an in-depth analysis of the methods used in the financing of terrorism and the types of financial activities constituting potential indicators of such activities. These documents are available at www.fatf-gafi.org.

7.32   SOCA publishes a range of material at www.soca.gov.uk, such as threat assessments and risk profiles, of which firms may wish to make their staff aware. The information on this website could usefully be incorporated into firms' training materials.

7.33   Illustrations, based on real cases, of how individuals and organisations might raise funds and use financial sector products and services for money laundering or to finance terrorism, are available at www.jmlsg.org.uk.

Staff based outside the UK

7.34   Where activities relating to UK business operations are undertaken by processing staff outside the UK, those staff must be made aware of and trained to follow the AML/CTF policies and procedures applicable to the UK operations. It is important that any local training and awareness obligations are also met, where relevant.

Training methods and assessment

7.35   There is no single solution when determining how to deliver training; a mix of training techniques may be appropriate. On-line learning systems can often provide an adequate solution for many employees, but there will be classes of employees for whom such an approach is not suitable. Focused classroom training for higher risk or minority areas can be more effective. Relevant videos always stimulate interest, but continually re-showing the same video may produce diminishing returns.

7.36   Procedures manuals, whether paper or intranet based, are useful in raising staff awareness and in supplementing more dedicated forms of training, but their main purpose is to provide ongoing reference and they are not generally written as training material.

7.37   Ongoing training should be given at appropriate intervals to all relevant employees. Particularly in larger firms, this may take the form of a rolling programme.

7.38   Whatever the approach to training, it is vital to establish comprehensive records (see paragraph 8.20) to monitor who has been trained, when they received the training, the nature of the training given and its effectiveness.

[7017]

CHAPTER 8
RECORD KEEPING

Relevant law/regulation
- Data Protection Act 1998
- Regulations 19 and 20
- SYSC Chapter 3

Core obligations
- Firms must retain:
    — copies of, or references to, the evidence they obtained of a customer's identity, for five years after the end of the customer relationship
    — details of customer transactions for five years from the date of the transaction
- Firms should retain:
    — details of actions taken in respect of internal and external suspicion reports
    — details of information considered by the nominated officer in respect of an internal report where no external report is made

Actions required, to be kept under regular review
- Firms should maintain appropriate systems for retaining records

> • Firms should maintain appropriate systems for making records available when required, within the specified timescales

General legal and regulatory requirements

Regulation 19   8.1   This chapter provides guidance on appropriate record keeping procedures that will meet a firm's obligations in respect of the prevention of money laundering and terrorist financing. There are general obligations on firms to maintain appropriate records and controls more widely in relation to their business; this guidance is not intended to replace or interpret such wider obligations.

8.2   Record keeping is an essential component of the audit trail that the ML Regulations and FSA Rules seek to establish in order to assist in any financial investigation and to ensure that criminal funds are kept out of the financial system, or if not, that they may be detected and confiscated by the authorities.

Regulation 19   8.3   Firms must retain records concerning customer identification and
SYSC   transactions as evidence of the work they have undertaken in
3.2.20R   complying with their legal and regulatory obligations, as well as for use as evidence in any investigation conducted by law enforcement. FSA-regulated firms must take reasonable care to make and keep adequate records appropriate to the scale, nature and complexity of their businesses.

8.4   Where a firm has an appointed representative, it must ensure that the representative complies with the record keeping obligations under the ML Regulations. This principle would also apply where the record keeping is delegated in any way to a third party (such as to an administrator or an introducer).

What records have to be kept?

8.5   The precise nature of the records required is not specified in the legal and regulatory regime. The objective is to ensure that a firm meets its obligations and that, in so far as is practicable, in any subsequent investigation the firm can provide the authorities with its section of the audit trail.

8.6   The firm's records should cover:

• Customer information

• Transactions

• Internal and external suspicion reports

• MLRO annual (and other) reports

• Information not acted upon

• Training and compliance monitoring

• Information about the effectiveness of training

Customer information

Regulation 19   8.7   In relation to the evidence of a customer's identity, firms must keep a copy of, or the references to, the evidence of the customer's identity obtained during the application of CDD measures. Where a firm has received a confirmation of identity certificate, this certificate will in practice be the evidence of identity that must be kept.

8.8   When a firm has concluded that it should treat a client as financially excluded for the purposes of customer identification, it should keep a record of the reasons for doing so.

8.9 A firm may often hold additional information in respect of a customer obtained for the purposes of enhanced customer due diligence or ongoing monitoring.

8.10 Where the individual presents himself to the firm, or at one of its branches, he may produce the necessary evidence of identity for the firm to take and retain copies. In circumstances (such as where verification is carried out at a customer's home and photocopying facilities are not available) where it would not be possible to take a copy of the evidence of identity , a record should be made of the type of document and its number, date and place of issue, so that, if necessary, the document may be re-obtained from its source of issue.

Regulation 19(3)   8.11 Records of identification evidence must be kept for a period of at least five years after the relationship with the customer has ended. The date the relationship with the customer ends is the date:

- an occasional transaction, or the last in a series of linked transactions, is carried out; or

- the business relationship ended, ie the closing of the account or accounts.

8.12 Where documents verifying the identity of a customer are held in one part of a group, they do not need to be held in duplicate form in another. The records do, however, need to be accessible to the nominated officer and the MLRO and to all areas that have contact with the customer, and be available on request, where these areas seek to rely on this evidence, or where they may be called upon by law enforcement to produce them.

8.13 When an introducing branch or subsidiary ceases to trade or have a business relationship with a customer, as long as his relationship with other group members continues, particular care needs to be taken to retain, or hand over, the appropriate customer records. Similar arrangements need to be made if a company holding relevant records ceases to be part of the group. This will also be an issue if the record keeping has been delegated to a third party.

Transactions

8.14 All transactions carried out on behalf of or with a customer in the course of relevant business must be recorded within the firm's records. Transaction records in support of entries in the accounts, in whatever form they are used, eg credit/debit slips, cheques, should be maintained in a form from which a satisfactory audit trail may be compiled where necessary, and which may establish a financial profile of any suspect account or customer.

Regulation 19(3)   8.15 Records of all transactions relating to a customer must be retained for a period of five years from the date on which the transaction is completed.

8.16 In the case of managers of investment funds or issuers of electronic money, where there may be no business relationship as defined in the ML Regulations, but the customer may nevertheless carry out further occasional transactions in the future, it is recommended that all records be kept for five years after the investment has been fully sold or funds disbursed.

Internal and external reports

8.17 A firm should make and retain:

- records of actions taken under the internal and external reporting requirements; and

- when the nominated officer has considered information or other material concerning possible money laundering, but has not made a report to SOCA, a record of the other material that was considered.

8.18   In addition, copies of any SARs made to SOCA should be retained.

8.19   Records of all internal and external reports should be retained for five years from the date the report was made.

Other

8.20   A firm's records should include:
(a) in relation to training:

- dates AML training was given;

- the nature of the training;

- the names of the staff who received training; and

- the results of the tests undertaken by staff, where appropriate.

(b) in relation to compliance monitoring –

- reports by the MLRO to senior management; and

- records of consideration of those reports and of any action taken as a consequence.

Regulation   8.21   A firm must establish and maintain systems which enable it to respond
20(4)   fully and rapidly to enquiries from financial investigators accredited under s 3 of POCA, persons acting on behalf of the Scottish Ministers in their capacity as an enforcement authority under the Act, officers of HMRC or constables, relating to:

- whether it maintains, or has maintained during the previous five years, a business relationship with any person; and

- the nature of that relationship.

Form in which records have to be kept

8.22   Most firms have standard procedures which they keep under review, and will seek to reduce the volume and density of records which have to be stored, whilst still complying with statutory requirements. Retention may therefore be:

- by way of original documents;

- by way of photocopies of original documents;

- on microfiche;

- in scanned form;

- in computerised or electronic form.

8.23   The record retention requirements are the same, regardless of the format in which they are kept, or whether the transaction was undertaken by paper or electronic means.

8.24   Firms involved in mergers, take-overs or internal reorganisations need to ensure that records of identity verification and transactions are readily retrievable for the required periods when rationalising computer systems and physical storage arrangements.

Location

8.25 The ML Regulations do not state where relevant records should be kept, but the overriding objective is for firms to be able to retrieve relevant information without undue delay.

8.26 Where identification records are held outside the UK, it is the responsibility of the UK firm to ensure that the records available do in fact meet UK requirements. No secrecy or data protection legislation should restrict access to the records either by the UK firm freely on request, or by UK law enforcement agencies under court order or relevant mutual assistance procedures. If it is found that such restrictions exist, copies of the underlying records of identity should, wherever possible, be sought and retained within the UK.

8.27 Firms should take account of the scope of AML/CTF legislation in other countries, and should ensure that group records kept in other countries that are needed to comply with UK legislation are retained for the required period.

8.28 Records relating to ongoing investigations should, where possible, be retained until the relevant law enforcement agency has confirmed that the case has been closed. However, if a firm has not been advised of an ongoing investigation within five years of the disclosure being made, the records may be destroyed in the normal course of the firm's records management policy.

8.29 There is tension between the provisions of the ML Regulations and data protection legislation; the nominated officer and the MLRO must have due regard to both sets of obligations.

8.30 When setting document retention policy, financial sector businesses must weigh the statutory requirements and the needs of the investigating authorities against normal commercial considerations. When original vouchers are used for account entry, and are not returned to the customer or his agent, it is of assistance to the law enforcement agencies if these original documents are kept for at least one year to assist in forensic analysis. This can also provide evidence for firms when conducting their own internal investigations. However, this is not a requirement of the AML legislation and there is no other statutory requirement in the UK that would require the retention of these original documents.

Sanctions and penalties

Regulation 45(1)

8.31 Where the record keeping obligations under the ML Regulations are not observed, a firm or person is open to prosecution, including imprisonment for up to two years and/or a fine, or regulatory censure.

[7018]

GLOSSARY OF TERMS

Term/expression	Meaning
Annex I Financial Institution	An undertaking (other than a credit institution, a consumer credit institution, a money service business or an Approved person) that carries out one or more of the operations (other than trading on their own account where the undertaking's only customers are group companies) listed on Schedule 1 to the ML Regulations. ML Regulation 22(1)
Approved person	A person in relation to whom the FSA has given its approval under s 59 of FSMA for the performance of a controlled function. [FSA Glossary of definitions].

Term/expression	Meaning
Appropriate person	Someone in a position of responsibility, who knows, and is known by, a customer, and may reasonably confirm the customer's identity. It is not possible to give a definitive list of such persons, but the following may assist firms in determining who is appropriate in any particular case: ● The Passport Office has published a list of those who may countersign passport applications: see http://www.ips.gov.uk/passport/apply-countersign.asp ● Others might include members of a local authority, staff of a higher or further education establishment, or a hostel manager.
Basel CDD paper	Basel Committee Customer Due Diligence paper, published in October 2001.
Basel Consolidated KYC Risk Management Paper	Basel Committee paper on Consolidated KYC Risk Management, published in October 2004.
Basel Committee	Basel Committee on Banking Supervision.
Beneficial owner(s)	The individual who ultimately owns or controls the customer on whose behalf a transaction or activity is being conducted. Special rules have been made for bodies corporate (1), partnerships (2), trusts (3), entities or arrangements that administer and distribute funds (6) and estates of deceased persons (8). ML Regulation 6
Controlled function	A function relating to the carrying on of a regulated activity by a firm which is specified under s 59 of FSMA, in FSA's table of controlled functions.
Criminal property	Property which constitutes a person's benefit from criminal conduct or which represents such a benefit (in whole or part and whether directly or indirectly), and the alleged offender knows or suspects that the property constitutes or represents such a benefit. [POCA s 340 (3)]
Criminal conduct	Conduct which constitutes an offence in any part of the United Kingdom, or would constitute an offence in any part of the United Kingdom if it occurred there. [POCA s 340 (2)]
Customer	In relation to an FSA-regulated firm, a customer is a person who is using, or may be contemplating using, any of the services provided by the firm. As noted in paragraph 5.2.3, this is not the definition of customer that applies in SYSC. [FSMA, s 59 (11)]
Equivalent jurisdiction	A jurisdiction (other than an EEA state) whose law contains equivalent provisions to those contained in the EU Money Laundering Directive [see www.jmlsg.org.uk].

PART V
OTHER MATERIALS

Term/expression	Meaning
EU Money Laundering Directives	The First Money Laundering Directive, adopted in 1991 (91/308/ EEC), was designed to harmonise the various national laws relating to money laundering, and thus avoid the potential for regulatory arbitrage. The Directive required anti money laundering systems and controls – principally in relation to customer identification, record keeping and reporting suspicious transactions – to be in place in firms that carried on specified financial business. A Second Money Laundering Directive, adopted in 2001 (2001/97/ EC), widened the scope of predicate offences, and extended the application of the First Directive to a range of non-financial activities and professions. A Third Money Laundering Directive, adopted in 2005 (2005/60/ EC), updated European Community legislation in line with the revised FATF 40+9 Recommendations. It repealed and replaced the First and Second Directives. The Implementing Measures Directive, adopted in 2006 (2006/70/ EC) elaborated on some of the terms used in the Third Money Laundering Directive. It defines PEP, lists situations where SDD may be applied, and sets the conditions for the exemption for financial activity on an occasional and very limited basis.
EC Sanctions Regulation	Regulation 2580/2001, on specific restrictive measures directed against certain persons and entities with a view to combating terrorism.
FATF Recommendations	A series of Forty Recommendations on the structural, supervisory and operational procedures that countries should have in place to combat money laundering, issued by the FATF. The Forty Recommendations were originally published in 1990, revised in 1996, and last revised in October 2004. The FATF Forty Recommendations have been recognised by the International Monetary Fund and the World Bank as the international standards for combating money laundering.
FATF Special Recommendations	FATF issued a series of Special Recommendations on Terrorist Financing in October 2001, and October 2004. The FATF Special Recommendations have been recognised by the International Monetary Fund and the World Bank as the international standards for combating the financing of terrorism.
FSA-regulated firm	A firm holding permission from the FSA under FSMA, Part IV, to carry on certain of the activities listed in FSMA, Schedule 2.
Government-issued	Issued by a central government department or by a local government authority or body.
Guidance Paper 5	Guidance Paper No 5: Guidance paper on anti-money laundering and combating the financing of terrorism, issued by IAIS in October 2004.
HM Treasury Sanctions Notices and News Releases	Notices issued by HM Treasury advising firms of additions to the UN Consolidated List maintained under Security Council resolution 1390 (2002) and to the list of persons and entities subject to EC Regulation 2580/2001.
Identification	Ascertaining the name of, and other relevant information about, a customer or beneficial owner.
IOSCO Principles paper	IOSCO paper 'Principles on Client Identification and Beneficial Ownership for the Securities Industry', published May 2004.
Mind and management	Those individuals who, individually or collectively, exercise practical control over a non-personal entity.
ML Regulations	The Money Laundering Regulations 2007 [SI 2007/2157].

Term/expression	Meaning
Money laundering	An act which: • constitutes an offence under ss 327, 328 or 329 of POCA or • constitutes an attempt, conspiracy or incitement to commit such an offence or • constitutes aiding, abetting, counselling or procuring the commission of such an offence or • would constitute an offence specified above if done in the United Kingdom. [POCA, s 340 (11)] A person also commits an offence of money laundering if he enters into or becomes concerned in an arrangement which facilitates the retention or control by or on behalf of another person of terrorist property: • by concealment; • by removal from the jurisdiction; • by transfer to nominees; or • in any other way. [Terrorism Act, s 18]
Money service business	An undertaking which by way of business operates a currency exchange office, transmits money (or any representations of monetary value) by any means or which cashes cheques which are made payable to customers. [ML Regulation 2(1)]
Nominated officer	A person in a firm or organisation nominated by the firm or organisation to receive disclosures under Regulation 20(2)(d)(i) and/or s 330 of POCA from others within the firm or organisation who know or suspect that a person is engaged in money laundering. Similar provisions apply under the Terrorism Act.
Occasional transaction	Any transaction (carried out other than as part of a business relationship) amounting to €15,000 or more, whether the transaction is carried out in a single operation or several operations which appear to be linked. [ML Regulation 2 (1)]
Politically exposed person	An individual who is or has, at any time in the preceding year, been entrusted with prominent public functions, and an immediate family member, or a known to close associate, of such persons. [ML Regulation 14(5)]
Regulated Activities Order	Financial Services and Markets Act 2000 (Regulated Activities) Order 2001 (SI 2001/544).
Regulated activity	Activities set out in the Regulated Activities Order, made under s 22 and Schedule 2 of FSMA and not excluded by the Financial Services and Markets Act 2000 (Exemption) Order 2001 (which exempts certain persons carrying on specific activities from carrying on regulated activities).
Regulated market	A multilateral system operated and/or managed by a market operator, which brings together or facilitates the bringing together of multiple third-party buying and selling interests in financial instruments – in the system and in accordance with its non-discretionary rules – in a way that results in a contract, in respect of the financial instruments admitted to trading under its rules and/or systems, and which is authorised and functions regularly [and in accordance with the provisions of Articles 36–47 of MiFID]. [MiFID Article 4(14)]
Regulated sector	Persons and firms which are subject to the ML Regulations.
Senior management	The directors and senior managers (or equivalent) of a firm who are responsible, either individually or collectively, for management and supervision of the firm's business.

Term/expression	Meaning
Senior manager	An individual, other than a director (or equivalent), who is employed by the firm, and to whom the Board (or equivalent) or a member of the Board, has given responsibility, either alone or jointly with others, for management and supervision.
Terrorism Act	Terrorism Act 2000, as amended by the Anti-terrorism, Crime and Security Act 2001.
Terrorist property	• Money or other property which is likely to be used for the purposes of terrorism (including any resources of a proscribed organisation); or • Proceeds of the commission of acts of terrorism; or • Proceeds of acts carried out for the purposes of terrorism "Proceeds of an act" includes a reference to any property which wholly or partly, and directly or indirectly, represents the proceeds of the act (including payments or other rewards in connection with its commission). "Resources" includes any money or other property which is applied or made available, or is to be applied or made available, for use by the organisation. [Terrorism Act, s 14]
Tipping off	A tipping-off offence is committed if a person knows or suspects that a disclosure falling under POCA ss 337 or 338 has been made, and he makes a disclosure which is likely to prejudice any investigation which may be conducted following the disclosure under s 337 or s 338. [POCA, s 333]
Verification	Verifying the identity of a customer, by reference to reliable, independent source documents, data or information, or of a beneficial owner through carrying out risk-based and adequate measures.
Wolfsberg Group	An association of twelve global banks, which aims to develop financial services industry standards, and related products, for Know Your Customer, Anti-Money Laundering and Counter Terrorist Financing policies.
Wolfsberg Principles	These are contained in four documents: • Global Anti-Money Laundering Guidelines for Private Banking, published by the Wolfsberg Group in October 2000, and revised in May 2002. • Statement on the Suppression of the Financing of Terrorism, published in January 2002. • Anti-Money Laundering Principles for Correspondent Banking, published in November 2002. • Statement on Monitoring, Screening and Searching, published in September 2003.

Abbreviations

ACPO Association of Chief Police Officers

AML Anti-money laundering

CDD Basel Committee Customer Due Diligence paper, published in October 2001

CTF Combating terrorism financing

DfCSF Department for Children, Schools and Families

DfIUS Department for Innovation, Universities and Skills

DWP Department of Work and Pensions

FATF Financial Action Task Force, an intergovernmental body whose purpose is to develop and promote broad AML/CTF standards, both at national and international levels

FSA Financial Services Authority, the UK regulator of the financial services industry

FSMA Financial Services and Markets Act 2000

HMT Her Majesty's Treasury

IAIS International Association of Insurance Supervisors

IOSCO International Organisation of Securities Commissions

MiFID The Marketing in Financial Instruments Directive

MLRO Money Laundering Reporting Officer

SOCA Serious Organised Crime Agency, the UK's financial intelligence unit.

POCA Proceeds of Crime Act 2002

SAR Suspicious activity report

SOCPA Serious Organised Crime and Police Act 2005

SYSC FSA Sourcebook: Senior Management Arrangements, Systems and Controls

[7019]

PART V
OTHER MATERIALS

APPENDIX I
ANTI-MONEY LAUNDERING RESPONSIBILITIES IN THE UK

UK Government
Home Office: • UK primary legislation (Proceeds of Crime Act 2002, Terrorism Act 2000 and Anti-terrorism, Crime and Security Act 2001) • Police strategy and resourcing • Asset recovery strategy • Chairs (jointly with HM Treasury) Money Laundering Advisory Committee (MLAC), a forum for key stakeholders to coordinate the AML regime and review its efficiency and effectiveness **HM Treasury** • Represents UK in EU and FATF • Implements EU Directives, principally through the Money Laundering Regulations • Approves industry guidance under POCA, Terrorism Act and Money Laundering Regulations • Chairs (jointly with Home Office) Money Laundering Advisory Committee (MLAC), a forum for key stakeholders to coordinate the AML regime and review its efficiency and effectiveness • Implements and administers the UK's financial sanctions regime

Law Enforcement, other investigating bodies and prosecutors
Serious Organised Crime Agency brought together : • National Crime Squad • NCIS • HMRC investigative branches • Parts of the Home Office Immigration Service • As UK's financial intelligence unit receives suspicious activity reports (about money laundering and terrorist financing) and sent cleared intelligence to law enforcement agencies for investigation • Assesses organised crime threats **Police** • 52 forces in the UK • Investigate crime, money laundering and terrorism **HM Revenue and Customs** • Investigates money laundering, drug trafficking and certain tax offences • Licences money service businesses and dealers in high value goods **Assets Recovery Agency**[3] • Powers under POCA to recover the proceeds of crime through criminal, civil, or tax recovery processes to SOCA • Supports law enforcement agencies to SOCA • Trains financial investigators to Police training **The Revenue and Customs Prosecutions Office** • Prosecutes money laundering, drug trafficking and certain tax offences investigated by HMRC

Crown Prosecution Service
- Prosecutes crime, money laundering and terrorism offences in England and Wales

Procurator Fiscal
- Prosecutes crime, money laundering and terrorism offences in Scotland

Public Prosecution Service of Northern Ireland
- Prosecutes crime, money laundering and terrorism offences in Northern Ireland

---

[3] The Assets Recovery Agency will be absorbed into SOCA with effect from 1 April 2008.

Regulator
Financial Services Authority

- UK's financial regulator
- Statutory objectives (under Financial Services and Markets Act 2000) include reduction of financial crime
- Approves persons to perform "controlled functions" (including money laundering reporting officer function)
- Makes, supervises and enforces, amongst other things, rules on money laundering
- Power to prosecute firms under the Money Laundering Regulations (except in Scotland)

Industry
Joint Money Laundering Steering Group

- Industry body made up of 17 financial sector trade bodies
- Produces guidance on compliance with legal and regulatory requirements and good practice

[7020]

APPENDIX II
SUMMARY OF UK LEGISLATION

Proceeds of Crime Act 2002[4] (as amended)

1. The Proceeds of Crime Act 2002 (POCA) consolidates and extends the existing UK legislation regarding money laundering. The legislation covers all crimes and any dealing in criminal property, with no exceptions and no *de minimis*. POCA:

- establishes the Assets Recovery Agency[5] (ARA[6]), to conduct an investigation[7] to discover whether a person holds criminal assets and to recover the assets in question.
- creates five investigative powers for the law enforcement agencies:
  - a production order[8]
  - a search and seizure warrant[9]
  - a disclosure order[10]
  - a customer information order[11]
  - an account monitoring order[12]
- establishes the following criminal offences:
  - a criminal offence[13] to acquire, use, possess, conceal, disguise, convert, transfer or remove criminal property from the jurisdiction, or to enter into or become concerned in an arrangement to facilitate the acquisition, retention, use or control of criminal property by another person
  - a criminal offence[14] for persons working in the regulated sector of failing to make a report where they have knowledge or suspicion of money laundering, or reasonable grounds for having knowledge or suspicion, that another person is laundering the proceeds of any criminal conduct, as soon as is reasonably practicable after the information came to their attention in the course of their regulated business activities

    Note: There are no provisions governing materiality or *de minimis* thresholds for having to report under POCA (although for deposit-taking firms, a transaction under £250 may be made without consent under certain circumstances – see paragraph 6.67).
  - a criminal offence[15] for anyone to take any action likely to prejudice an investigation by informing (eg, tipping off) the person who is the subject of a suspicion report, or anybody else, that a disclosure has been made to a nominated

officer or to SOCA, or that the police or customs authorities are carrying out or intending to carry out a money laundering investigation.

— a criminal offence[16] of destroying or disposing of documents which are relevant to an investigation.

— a criminal offence[17] by a firm of failing to comply with a requirement imposed on it under a customer information order, or in knowingly or recklessly making a statement in purported compliance with a customer information order that is false or misleading in a material particular.

● sets out maximum penalties:

— for the offence of money laundering of 14 years' imprisonment and/or an unlimited fine.

Note: An offence is not committed if a person reports the property involved to the Serious Organised Crime Agency (SOCA) or under approved internal arrangements, either before the prohibited act is carried out, or as soon afterwards as is reasonably practicable.

— for failing to make a report of suspected money laundering, or for "tipping off", of five years' imprisonment and/or an unlimited fine.

— for destroying or disposing of relevant documents of five years' imprisonment and/or an unlimited fine.

---

4   2002 ch 29
5   section 1
6   The ARA will be absorbed into SOCA with effect from 1 April 2008.
7   section 341(2)
8   section 345
9   section 352
10   section 357
11   section 363
12   section 370 – see also Terrorism Act s 38A
13   sections 327 – 329
14   sections 330 and 331
15   section 333
16   section 341(2)(b)
17   section 366

Terrorism Act 2000[18], and the Anti-terrorism, Crime and Security Act 2001[19]

2.   The Terrorism Act establishes a series of offences related to involvement in arrangements for facilitating, raising or using funds for terrorism purposes. The Act:

● makes[20] it a criminal offence for any person not to report the existence of terrorist property where there are reasonable grounds for knowing or suspecting the existence of terrorist property

● makes it a criminal offence[21] for anyone to take any action likely to prejudice an investigation by informing (ie tipping off) the person who is the subject of a suspicion report, or anybody else, that a disclosure has been made to a nominated officer or to SOCA, or that the police or customs authorities are carrying out or intending to carry out a terrorist financing investigation

● grants[22] a power to the law enforcement agencies to make an account monitoring order, similar in scope to that introduced under POCA

● sets out the following penalties:

— the maximum penalty for failure to report under the circumstances set out above is five years' imprisonment, and/or a fine.

— the maximum penalty for the offence of actual money laundering is 14 years' imprisonment, and/or a fine.

3.   A number of organisations have been proscribed under the Terrorism Act. The definition of terrorist property, involvement with which is an offence, includes resources of a proscribed organisation.

4.   The Anti-terrorism, Crime and Security Act 2001 gives the authorities power to seize terrorist cash, to freeze terrorist assets and to direct firms in the regulated sector to provide the authorities with specified information on customers and their (terrorism-related) activities.

---

18   2000 ch 11
19   2001 ch 24
20   section 21A
21   section 39
22   section 38A and Schedule 6A

Money Laundering Regulations 2007[23]

5. The Money Laundering Regulations 2007 specify arrangements which must be in place within firms within the scope of the Regulations, in order to prevent operations relating to money laundering or terrorist financing.

6. The ML Regulations apply[24], inter alia, to:
- The regulated activities of all financial sector firms, ie:
  - — banks, building societies and other credit institutions;
  - — individuals and firms engaging in regulated investment activities under FSMA;
  - — issuers of electronic money;
  - — insurance companies undertaking long-term life business, including the life business of Lloyd's of London;
- Bureaux de change, cheque encashment centres and money transmission services (money service businesses);
- Trust and company service providers;
- Casinos;
- Dealers in high-value goods (including auctioneers) who accept payment in cash of €15,000 or more (either single or linked transactions);
- Lawyers and accountants, when undertaking relevant business.

7. Persons within the scope of the ML Regulations are required to establish adequate and appropriate policies and procedures in order to prevent operations relating to money laundering or terrorist financing, covering:
- customer due diligence;
- reporting;
- record-keeping;
- internal control;
- risk assessment and management;
- compliance management; and
- communication.

8. The FSA may[25] institute proceedings (other than in Scotland) for offences under prescribed regulations relating to money laundering. This power is not limited to firms or persons regulated by the FSA. Whether a breach of the ML Regulations has occurred is not dependent on whether money laundering has taken place: firms may be sanctioned for not having adequate AML/CTF systems. Failure to comply with any of the requirements of the ML Regulations constitutes an offence punishable by a maximum of two years' imprisonment, or a fine, or both.

FSA-regulated firms – the FSA Handbook

9. FSMA gives the FSA a statutory objective[26] to reduce financial crime. In considering this objective, the FSA is required[27] to have regard to the desirability of firms:
- Being aware of the risk of their businesses being used in connection with the commission of financial crime;
- Taking appropriate measures to prevent financial crime, facilitate its detection and monitor its incidence;
- Devoting adequate resources to that prevention, detection and monitoring.

10. Firms may only engage in a regulated activity[28] in the UK if it is an authorised or exempt person. A person can become an authorised person as a result of: (a) being given a "permission" by the FSA under Part IV of FSMA (known as a "Part IV permission"); or (b) by qualifying for authorisation under FSMA itself. As an example of the latter, an EEA firm establishing a branch in, or providing cross-border services into, the UK can qualify for authorisation under FSMA Schedule 3 and, as a result, be given a permission; although such firms are, generally, authorised by their home state regulator, they are regulated by the FSA in connection with the regulated activities carried on in the UK.

11. A firm may only carry on regulated business in accordance with its permission. A firm with a Part IV permission may apply to the FSA to vary its permission, add or remove regulated activities, to limit these activities (for example, the types of client with or for whom the firm may carry on an activity) or to vary the requirements on the firm itself. Before giving or varying a Part IV permission, the FSA must ensure that the person/firm will satisfy and continue to satisfy the threshold conditions in relation to all of the regulated activities for which he has or will have permission. If a firm is failing, or is likely to fail, to satisfy the threshold conditions, the FSA may vary or cancel a firm's permission.

12. Threshold condition 5 (Suitability) requires the firm to satisfy the FSA that it is "fit and proper" to have Part IV permission having regard to all the circumstances, including its connection with other persons, the range and nature of its proposed (or current) regulated activities and the overall need to be satisfied that its affairs are and will continue to be conducted soundly and prudently. Hence, the FSA "will consider whether a firm is ready, willing and organised to comply, on a continuing basis, with the requirements and standards under the regulatory system which apply

to the firm, or will apply to the firm, if it is granted Part IV permission, or a variation of its permission". The FSA will also have regard to all relevant matters, whether arising in the UK or elsewhere. In particular, the FSA will consider whether a firm "has in place systems and controls against money laundering of the sort described in SYSC 3.2.6 R to SYSC 3.2.6J G". (COND 2.5.7G)

13.   The FSA Handbook of rules and guidance contains high level standards that apply, with some exceptions, to all FSA-regulated firms, (for example, the FSA Principles for Businesses, COND and SYSC) and to all approved persons (for example, the Statements of Principle and Code of Practice for Approved Persons). SYSC sets out particular rules relating to senior management responsibilities, and for systems and controls processes. Some of these rules focus on the management and control of risk[29], and specifically require appropriate systems and controls over the management of money laundering risk[30].

14.   In addition to prosecution powers under the Regulations, the FSA has a wide range of enforcement powers against authorised persons and approved persons for breaches of its Rules.

---

23   SI 2007/2157
24   Regulation 3
25   FSMA, s 402(1)(b)
26   FSMA s 6. This is defined as "reducing the extent to which it is possible for a business carried on by a regulated person ... to be used for a purpose connected with financial crime".
27   FSMA s 6(2)
28   FSMA s 22, Schedule 2, and the Regulated Activities Order. These activities are substantially the same as set out in Regulation [2 (2)(a)].
29   SYSC 3.2.6 R
30   SYSC 3.2.6G G

JMLSG
THE JOINT MONEY LAUNDERING STEERING GROUP

PREVENTION OF MONEY LAUNDERING/
COMBATING TERRORIST FINANCING

GUIDANCE FOR THE UK FINANCIAL SECTOR
PART II: SECTORAL GUIDANCE

December 2007

CONTENTS

PART II: SECTORAL GUIDANCE

This sectoral guidance is incomplete on its own. It must be read in conjunction with the main guidance set out in Part I of the Guidance.

1: RETAIL BANKING

Note: This sectoral guidance is incomplete on its own. It must be read in conjunction with the main guidance set out in Part I of the Guidance.

Overview of the sector

1.1   Retail banking is the provision of standard current account, loan and savings products to personal and business customers by banks and building societies. It covers the range of services from the provision of a basic bank account facility to complex money transmission business for a medium sized commercial business. In this guidance, retail banking does not cover credit cards, which are dealt with in sector 2. For many firms, retail banking is a mass consumer business and will generally not involve close relationship management by a named relationship manager.

1.2   This sectoral guidance refers primarily to business undertaken within the UK. Firms operating in markets outside the UK will need to take account of local market practice, while at the same time ensuring that equivalent CDD and record-keeping measures to those set out in the ML Regulations are applied by their branches and subsidiaries operating in these markets.

What are the money laundering and terrorist financing risks in retail banking?

1.3   There is a high risk that the proceeds of crime will pass through retail banking accounts at all stages of the money laundering process. However, many millions of retail banking transactions are conducted each week and the likelihood of a particular transaction involving the proceeds of crime is very low. A firm's risk-based approach will be designed to ensure that it places an emphasis within its strategy on deterring, detecting and disclosing in the areas of greatest perceived vulnerability.

1.4   There is an increasing risk of fraudulent applications by identity thieves. However, such applications represent a very small percentage of overall applications for retail banking services.

1.5   The provision of services to cash-generating businesses is a particular area of risk associated with retail banking. Some businesses are legitimately cash based, including large parts of the retail sector, and so there will often be a high level of cash deposits associated with some accounts. The risk is in failing to identify such businesses where the level of cash activity is higher than the underlying business would justify, thus providing grounds for looking more closely at whether the account may be being used for money laundering or terrorist financing.

1.6   The feature of lending is generally that the initial monies advanced are paid into another bank or building society account. Consolidation loans may involve payment direct to the borrower's creditor, and the amount borrowed in some unsecured lending arrangements may be taken in cash. Repayments are usually made from other bank or building society accounts by direct debit; in most cases, repayments in cash are not encouraged.

1.7   Given that a loan results in the borrower receiving funds from the lender, the initial transaction is not very susceptible of the placement stage of money laundering, although it could form part of the layering stage. The main money laundering risk arises through the acceleration of an agreed repayment schedule, either by means of lump sum repayments, or early termination.

1.8   Where loans are made in one jurisdiction, and collateral is held in another, this may indicate an increased money laundering risk.

Other relevant industry and regulatory guidance

1.9   Firms should make use of other existing guidance and leaflets etc in this area, as follows:
- Results of the FSA "Retail Cluster" work in 2002 – see www.fsa.gov.uk
- "International Students – opening a UK bank account" – see www.bba.org.uk
- FSA leaflet "Checking your Identity" – see www.fsa.gov.uk/pubs/public/identity_check.pdf

1.10   See also paragraphs 1.38–1.41 on financial exclusion.

Customer due diligence

General

1.11   The AML/CTF checks carried out at account opening are very closely linked to anti-fraud measures and are one of the primary controls for preventing criminals opening accounts or obtaining services from banks. Firms should ensure that they co-ordinate these processes, in order to provide as strong a gatekeeper control as possible.

1.12   For the majority of personal applicants, sole or joint, the standard identification evidence set out in Part I, Chapter 5 will be applicable.

1.13   Documents that are acceptable in different situations are summarised in Part I, paragraphs 5.3.70–5.3.75, together with the principles defining when reliance may be placed on a single document or where more than one is required. A current UK passport or photocard driving licence issued in the UK is likely to be used in the majority of cases, other than in the context of financial exclusion, where a bespoke token may be accepted, as set out in Annex 1–I. Non-UK nationals entering the UK should present their national passports or national identity cards, other than in the context of financial exclusion, where bespoke tokens are referred to in Annex 1–I for refugees and asylum seekers.

1.14   The other documents cited in Part I, paragraph 5.3.74 may be used for UK residents where the standard documents are not available, whether singly or in conjunction, according to the principles set out in that paragraph. For non-UK residents, or persons who have recently entered the UK, firms may well require additional documentary evidence – not for AML/CTF purposes, but to offset fraud and credit risks which would normally be addressed through electronic checks for UK residents (see paragraphs 1.22–1.24).

1.15   Standard due diligence is not required in the following situations:
- Where the source of funds may be used as evidence of identity. See Part I, paragraphs 5.3.92 to 5.3.96.
- Where a variation from the standard is required to prevent a person from being financially excluded (see paragraphs 1.38–1.41 and Annex 1–I).
- Products which meet the criteria in Regulation 9(8) and (9) of the ML Regulations 2007, eg, a Child Trust Fund.

1.16   However, a firm should take care with customers whose identity is verified under a variation from the standard and who wish to migrate to other products in due course. The verification of identity undertaken for a basic bank account may not be sufficient for a customer migrating to a higher risk product. Firms should have processes defining what additional due diligence, including where appropriate further evidence of identification, is required in such circumstances.

1.17 Where the incentive to provide a false identity is greater, firms should consider deploying suitable fraud prevention tools and techniques to assist in alerting to false and forged identification. Where the case demands, a firm might require proof of identity additional to the standard evidence.

A customer with an existing account at the same firm

1.18 If the existing customer was taken on pre-1994, or it could not be established that the holder's identity had previously been verified, an application would trigger standard identification procedures.

1.19 Most large firms have completed current customer review (CCR) checks. These could result in different levels of confidence in the identity of the person concerned, depending on the amount of information held on the existing holder. If the review had verified the customer's identity at least to the standard required as part of the CCR exercise, a second account would normally be opened without further identification procedures, (provided the characteristics of the new account are not in a higher risk category than the existing account). Thus, a foreign currency account might require further identification procedures and/or additional customer enquiries but for a new savings account, where the applicant's existing account had passed current customer review checks, most firms would not require further identification.

Customers with a bank account with one firm who wish to transfer it to another

1.20 Standard identification procedures will usually apply. In some cases, the firm holding the existing account may be willing to confirm the identity of the account holder to the new firm, and to provide evidence of the identification checks carried out. Care will need to be exercised by the receiving firm to be satisfied that the previous verification procedures provide an appropriate level of assurance for the new account, which may have different risk characteristics from the one held with the other firm.

1.21 Where different UK regulated firms in the same group share a customer and (before or after any current customer review) transfer a customer between them, either firm can rely on the other firm's review checks in respect of that customer.

Non-resident, physically present in the UK, wishing to open a bank account

1.22 A non-resident, whether a non-UK national or a UK national who is returning to the UK after a considerable absence, who is physically present in the UK and who wishes to open an account should normally be able to provide standard identification documentation to open a Basic Bank Account (see Part I, paragraph 5.3.74 and Annex 1–I).

Non-resident, not physically present in the UK, wishing to open a bank account

1.23 Non-residents not physically present in the UK wishing to open an account in the UK are unlikely to wish to open a Basic Bank Account, with its limited facilities. The customer should be able to demonstrate a need for a bank account in the UK, or should fall within the firm's criteria for wealth management clients, in which case the guidance in sector 5: *Wealth Management* will apply. Enhanced due diligence will apply where the customer is not met personally or where other high risk factors come into play (see paragraphs 5.18–23 and Part I, section 5.5).

Members of HM Diplomatic Service returning to the UK and wishing to open a bank account

1.24 The standard identification evidence, as set out in Part I Chapter 5, should be able to be obtained in these cases. Members of HM Diplomatic Service are, however, reported to have experienced difficulties in opening a bank account because, for example, they have no recent electronic data history stored in the UK. Account opening procedures may be facilitated by a letter from the Foreign Office confirming that the person named was a member of the Diplomatic Service and was returning to the UK.

Lending

1.25 Many applications for advances are made through brokers, who may carry out some of the customer due diligence on behalf of the lender. In view of the generally low money laundering risk associated with mortgage business and related protection policies, and the fraud prevention controls in place within the mortgage market, use of confirmations from intermediaries introducing customers is, in principle, perfectly reasonable, where the introducer is carrying on appropriately regulated business (see Part I, paragraph 5.6.6) including appointed representatives of FSA authorised firms.

1.26 Firms should refer to the guidance on situations where customers are subject to identification by two or more financial services firms in relation to the same transaction, set out in Part I, section 5.6.

Business Banking

1.27   Business banking in the Retail sector is by nature a volume business, typically offering services for smaller UK businesses, ranging from sole traders and small family concerns to partnerships, professional firms and smaller private companies (ie turnover under £1 million pa). These businesses are often, but not always, UK-based in terms of ownership, location of premises and customers. As such, the risk profile may actually be lower than that of larger businesses with a more diverse customer base or product offering, which may include international business and customers. The profile may, however, often be higher than that of personal customers, where identification may be straightforward and the funds involved smaller.

1.28   Essentially, as set out in Part I, Chapter 5, identification should initially focus on ascertaining information about the business and its activities and verifying beneficial owners holding or controlling directly or indirectly, 25% or more of the shares or voting rights, and controllers, and where the business is a limited company, verifying the legal existence of the company.

1.29   Uncertainties may often arise with a business that is starting up and has not yet acquired any premises (eg, X & Y trading as ABC Ltd, working from the director/principal's home). A search of Companies House may not always produce relevant information if the company is newly formed.

1.30   In the case of newly-formed businesses, obtaining appropriate customer information is sometimes not easy. The lack of information relating to the business can be mitigated in part by making sufficient additional enquiries to understand fully the customer's expectations (nature of proposed activities, anticipated cash flow through the accounts, frequency and nature of transactional activity, an understanding of the underlying ownership of the business) and personal identification of the owners/controllers of the business, as well as information on their previous history. Part I, Chapter 5, contains further guidance relating to identification standards.

1.31   Firms may encounter difficulties with validating the business entity, particularly where directorships may not have been registered or updated. It is recommended that where this arises (and firms still feel able to open an account on the basis of the evidence already seen) firms conduct or take additional steps to confirm the control and ownership of the business after the account has been opened, by checking to ensure directorships have been updated. Where mitigating steps have been taken to compensate for information not being easily available, firms should consider the probability that additional monitoring of the customer's transactions and activity should be put in place.

1.32   A firm must be reasonably satisfied that the persons starting up the business are who they said they are, and are associated with the firm. Reasonable steps must be taken to verify the identity of the persons setting up a new business, as well as any beneficial owners, which may often be based on electronic checks. In the majority of cases, the individuals starting up a business are likely to be its beneficial owners. A check of the amount of capital invested in the business, whether it is in line with the firm's knowledge of the individual(s) and whether it seems in line with their age/experience, etc, may be a pointer to whether further enquiries need to be made about other possible beneficial owners.

1.33   Wherever possible, documentation of the firm's business address should be obtained. Where the firm can plausibly argue that this is not possible because it is in the early stages of start-up, the address of the firm should be verified later; in the interim, the bank may wish to obtain evidence of the address(es) of the person(s) starting up the business. In certain circumstances, a visit to the place of business may be helpful to confirm the existence and activities of the business.

1.34   In determining the identification appropriate for partnerships (see Part I, paragraphs 5.3.212–5.3.225), whose structure and business may vary considerably, and will include professional firms eg solicitors, accountants, as well as less regulated businesses, it will be important to ascertain where control of the business lies, and to take account of the risk inherent in the nature of the business.

Enhanced due diligence

1.35   Enhanced due diligence is required under Regulation 10 of the ML Regulations in the following situations:

- When the applicant is a PEP. See Part I, paragraphs 5.5.18–5.5.29.
- When there is no face-to-face contact with the applicant. An additional check is needed to offset the increased risk, notably that of impersonation fraud (see Part I, paragraph 5.3.82).
- When the business of the customer is considered to present a higher risk of money laundering or terrorist financing. Examples should be set out in the firm's risk-based approach and should reflect the firm's own experience and information produced by the authorities. See Part I, paragraphs 3.24–3.26 and section 5.5 for general guidance.
- When establishing a correspondent banking relationship with an institution in a non-EEA state, (although in practice most firms would not regard such relationships as forming part of their 'retail' business).

1.36   Firms will need to consider making more penetrating initial enquiries, over and above that usually carried out before taking on businesses whose turnover is likely to exceed certain thresholds, or where the nature of the business is higher risk, or involves large cash transactions, or is conducted primarily on a non face-to-face basis. Recognising that there are a very large number of small businesses which are cash businesses, there will be constraints on the practicality of such enquiries; even so, firms should be alert to the increased vulnerability of such customers to laundering activity when evaluating whether particular transactions are suspicious. Examples of higher risk situations are:

- High cash turnover businesses: casinos, bars, clubs, taxi firms, launderettes, takeaway restaurants
- Money service businesses: cheque encashment agencies, bureaux de change, hawala merchants
- Gaming and gambling businesses
- Computer/high technology/telecom/mobile phone sales and distribution, noting especially the high propensity of this sector to VAT 'Carousel' fraud
- Companies registered in one offshore jurisdiction as a non-resident company with no local operations but managed out of another, or where a company is registered in a high risk jurisdiction, or where beneficial owners with significant interests in the company are resident in a high risk jurisdiction
- Unregistered charities based or headquartered outside the UK, 'foundations', cultural associations and the like, particularly if centred on certain target groups, including specific ethnic communities, whether based in or outside the UK (see FATF Typologies Report 2003/4 under 'Non-profit organisations' – at www.fatf-gafi.org)

1.37   Firms should maintain and update customer information, and address any need for additional information, on a risk-sensitive basis, under a trigger event strategy (for example, where an existing customer applies for a further product or service) or by periodic file reviews.

Financial exclusion

1.38   Denying those who are financially excluded from access to the financial sector is an issue for deposit takers. Reference should be made to the guidance given in Part I, paragraphs 5.3.110 to 5.3.114, and Annex 1–I.

1.39   The "financially excluded" are not a homogeneous category of uniform risk. Some financially excluded persons may represent a higher risk of money laundering regardless of whether they provide standard or non standard tokens to confirm their identity, eg, a passport holder who qualifies only for a basic account on credit grounds. Firms may wish to consider whether any additional customer information, or monitoring of the size and expected volume of transactions, would be useful in respect of some financially excluded categories, based on the firm's own experience of their operation.

1.40   In other cases, where the available evidence of identity is limited, and the firm judges that the individual cannot reasonably be expected to provide more, but that the business relationship should nevertheless go ahead, it should consider instituting enhanced monitoring arrangements over the customer's transactions and activity (see Part I, section 5.7). In addition, the firm should consider whether restrictions should be placed on the customer's ability to migrate to other, higher risk products or services.

1.41   Where an applicant produces non-standard documentation, staff should be discouraged from citing the ML Regulations as an excuse for not opening an account before giving proper consideration to the evidence available, referring up the line for advice as necessary. It may be that at the conclusion of that process a considered judgement may properly be made that the evidence available does not provide a sufficient level of confidence that the applicant is who he claims to be, in which event a decision not to open the account would be fully justified. Staff should bear in mind that the ML Regulations are not explicit as to what is and is not acceptable evidence of identity.

Monitoring

1.42   Firms should note the guidance contained in Part I, section 5.7, and the examples of higher risk businesses in paragraph 1.36. It is likely that in significant retail banking operations, some form of automated monitoring of customer transactions and activity will be required. However, staff vigilance is also essential, in order to identify counter transactions in particular that may represent money laundering, and in order to ensure prompt reporting of initial suspicions, and application for consent where this is required.

1.43   Particular activities that should trigger further enquiry include lump sum repayments outside the agreed repayment pattern, and early repayment of a loan, particularly where this attracts an early redemption penalty.

1.44   Mortgage products linked to current accounts do not have a predictable account turnover, and effective rescheduling of the borrowing – which can be repaid and re-borrowed at the borrower's initiative – does not require the agreement of the lender. This should lead to the activity on such accounts being more closely monitored.

1.45   In a volume business, compliance with the identification requirements set out in the firm's policies and procedures should also be closely monitored. The percentage failure rate in such compliance should be low, probably not exceeding low single figures. Repeated failures in excess of this level by a firm over a period of time may point to a systemic weakness in its identification procedures which, if not corrected, would be a potential breach of FSA Rules and should be reported to senior management. This should be part of the standard management information that a firm collates and provides to MLRO and other senior management.

Training

1.46   Firms should note the guidance contained in Part I, Chapter 7. In the retail banking environment it is essential that training should ensure that branch counter staff are aware that they must report if they are suspicious. It should also provide them with examples of red flags to look out for.

Reporting

1.47   Firms should note the guidance contained in Part I, Chapter 6. As indicated in Part I, paragraphs 7.31 to 7.33, further reference material and typologies are available from the external sources cited, viz: JMLSG, FATF and SOCA websites. In addition, firms should be aware of the requirement under Section 331(4) of the Proceeds of Crime Act for reports to be submitted "as soon as practicable" to SOCA.

1.48   There is no formal definition of what "as soon as practicable" means, but firms should note the enforcement action taken by the FSA in respect of the anti money laundering procedures in place at a large UK firm. The FSA imposed a financial penalty on the firm due, in part, to finding that over half of the firm's suspicious activity reports were submitted to SOCA more than 30 days after having been reported internally to the firm's nominated officer. In view of the volumes of reports which may be generated in this sector, firms may wish to keep under review whether their nominated officer function is adequately resourced.

Interbank Agency Service

1.49   Staff in one firm (firm A) may become suspicious of a transaction undertaken over their counters by a customer of another firm (firm B), as might arise under the Interbank Agency Service, which permits participating banks to service other banks' customers. In such a case, a report should be made to the nominated officer of firm A, who may alert the nominated officer of firm B. In each case, the nominated officer will need to form their own judgement whether to disclose the circumstances to SOCA.

[7022]

ANNEX 1–I
SPECIAL CASES

Many customers in the categories below will be able to provide standard documents, and this will normally be a firm's preferred option. This annex is a non-exhaustive and non-mandatory list of documents (see Notes) which are capable of evidencing identity for special cases who either cannot meet the standard verification requirement, or have experienced difficulties in the past when seeking to open accounts, and which will generally be appropriate for opening a Basic Bank Account. These include:

Customer	Document(s)
Benefit claimants	Entitlement letter issued by DWP, HMRC or local authority, or Identity Confirmation Letter issued by DWP or local authority
Those in care homes/ sheltered accommodation/ refuge	Letter from care home manager/warden of sheltered accommodation or refuge Homeless persons who cannot provide standard identification documentation are likely to be in a particular socially excluded category. A letter from the warden of a homeless shelter, or from an employer if the customer is in work, will normally be sufficient evidence.

Customer	Document(s)
Those on probation	It may be possible to apply standard identification procedures. Otherwise, a letter from the customer's probation officer, or a hostel manager, would normally be sufficient.
Prisoners	It may be possible to apply standard identification procedures. Otherwise, a letter from the governor of the prison, or, if the applicant has been released, from a police or probation officer or hostel manager would normally be sufficient.
International students	Passport or EEA National Identity Card AND Letter of Acceptance or Letter of Introduction from Institution on the DfES list. See the pro forma agreed for this purpose with UKCOSA: The Council for International Education, attached as Annex 1–II. See also Part I, paragraphs 5.3.107–108.
Economic migrants *[here meaning those working temporarily in the UK, whose lack of banking or credit history precludes their being offered other than a basic bank account]*	National Passport, or National Identity Card (nationals of EEA and Switzerland) Details of documents required by migrant workers are available at www.employingmigrants.org.uk and Home Office website www.homeoffice.gov.uk/. Firms are not required to establish whether an applicant is legally entitled to work in the UK but if, in the course of checking identity, it came to light that the applicant was not entitled to do so, the deposit of earnings from employment could constitute an arrangement under the Proceeds of Crime Act.
Refugees (those who are not on benefit)	Immigration Status Document, with Residence Permit, or IND travel document (ie, *Blue* Convention Travel doc, or *Red* Stateless Persons doc, or *Brown* Certificate of Identity doc) Refugees are unlikely to have their national passports and will have been issued by the Home Office with documents confirming their status. A refugee is normally entitled to work, to receive benefits and to remain in the UK.
Asylum seekers	IND Application Registration Card (ARC) *NB This document shows the status of the individual, and does not confirm their identity* Asylum seekers are issued by the Home Office with documents confirming their status. Unlike refugees, however, information provided by an asylum seeker will not have been checked by the Home Office. The asylum seeker's Applicant Registration Card (ARC) will state whether the asylum seeker is entitled to take employment in the UK. Asylum seekers may apply to open an account if they are entitled to work, but also to deposit money brought from abroad, and in some cases to receive allowances paid by the Home Office. Firms are not required to establish whether an applicant is legally entitled to work in the UK but if, in the course of checking identity, it came to light that the applicant was not entitled to do so, the deposit of earnings from employment could constitute an arrangement under the Proceeds of Crime Act.
Travellers	Travellers may be able to produce standard identification evidence; if not, they may be in a particular special case category. If verification of address is necessary, a check with the local authority, which has to register travellers' sites, may sometimes be helpful.

Notes:

1.   Passports, national identity cards and travel documents must be current, i e unexpired. Letters should be of recent date, or, in the case of students, the course dates stated in the Letter of Acceptance should reasonably correspond with the date of the account application to the bank. All documents must be originals. In case of need, consideration should be given to verifying the authenticity of the document with its issuer.

2.   As with all retail customers, firms should take reasonable care to check that documents offered are genuine (not obviously forged), and where these incorporate photographs, that these correspond to the presenter.

3.   Whilst it is open to firms to impose additional verification requirements if they deem necessary under their risk based approach and to address the perceived commercial risks attaching to their own Basic Account products, they should not lose sight of the requirement under *SYSC 3.2.6(G)(5)* "not unreasonably [to] deny access to its service to potential customers who cannot reasonably be expected to provide detailed evidence of identity."

[7023]

ANNEX 1–II

(To be typed on education institution letterhead)

LETTER OF INTRODUCTION FOR UK BANKING FACILITIES

We confirm that .... (*Please insert Student's FULL Name*) is/will be studying at the above named education institution.

Course Details

Name of Course:

Type of Course:

Start Date:

Finish Date:

Address Details [if known]

The Student's Overseas Residential Address is:

(*Please insert the Student's full Overseas Address*)

....

....

....

We have/have not (please delete whichever is applicable) corresponded with the Student at their above overseas address.

The Student's UK Address is: [if known]

(*Please insert the Student's UK Address*)

....

....

....

....

This certificate is only valid if embossed with the education institution's seal or stamp.

Signed ....

Name ....

Position ....

Contact Telephone Number at education institution ....

[7024]

2: CREDIT CARDS, ETC

Note: This sectoral guidance is incomplete on its own. It must be read in conjunction with the main guidance set out in Part I of the Guidance.

Overview of the sector

2.1   A credit card evidences an unsecured borrowing arrangement between an issuing entity and a cardholder, whereby the cardholder obtains goods and services through merchants approved by the Merchant Acquirer (see paragraph 2.9), up to an agreed credit limit on the card. Cards may also be used at ATMs to withdraw cash, which is then added to the balance owing on the card account. Withdrawals (charged to the card account) across a bank counter may be made, upon the presentation of sufficient evidence of identity. Payments can also be made to third parties that do not accept credit cards, by writing a cheque supplied on occasions by the card issuer. The amount of the cheque is added to the balance on the card account.

2.2   The cardholder agrees to repay any borrowing, in full or in part, at the end of each month. There will be a minimum monthly repayment figure (typically between 2% and 3% of the outstanding balance, depending on the issuer). Interest is charged by the issuing entity, at an agreed rate, on any borrowing not repaid at the end of each month. Any interest or fees charged are added to the card balance.

2.3   Cards are issued by individual Card Issuers, each of whom is a member of one or more Card Schemes (eg, Visa, MasterCard, Switch/Maestro). Each credit card will be branded with the logo of one of the card schemes, and may be used at any merchant worldwide that displays that particular scheme logo. Cash may also be withdrawn through ATMs which bear the scheme logo.

2.4   Credit cards may be used through a number of channels. They may be used at merchants' premises at the point of sale, or may be used remotely over the telephone, web or mail (referred to as 'card not present' use). In card not present use, additional security numbers shown on the card may or may not be required to be used, depending on the agreement between merchant and its acquiring bank. The Merchant Acquirer (see paragraph 2.9) will undertake its own assessment of the merchant, and decide what type of delivery channel(s) it will allow the merchant to use to accept card transactions.

Different types of credit card

2.5   A Card Issuer may have a direct relationship with the cardholder, in which case the card will clearly indicate the names of the Issuer and of the cardholder. Some Issuers also issue and manage cards branded in the name of other firms (referred to as 'branded cards'), and/or which carry the name of another organisation (referred to as 'affinity cards'). Each card scheme has strict rules about the names that must appear on the face of each card.

2.6   Store cards are very similar to credit cards, but are issued in the name of a retail organisation, which is not a member of a card scheme. These cards may be issued and operated by a regulated entity within the store group, or on their behalf by other firms that issue and operate other cards. Store cards may only be used in branches of the store, or in associated organisations, and not in other outlets. Generally, store cards cannot be used to obtain cash. They are therefore limited to the domestic market, and cannot be used internationally.

2.7   As well as issuing cards to individuals, an Issuer may provide cards to corporate organisations, where a number of separate cards are provided for use by nominated employees of that organisation. The corporate entity generally carries the liability for the borrowings accrued under their employees' use of their cards, although in some cases the company places the primary liability for repayment on the employee (generally to encourage the employee to account for his expenses, and to claim reimbursement from the company, in a timely manner).

2.8   This sectoral guidance applies to all cards that entitle the holder to obtain unsecured borrowing, whether held by individuals or corporate entities, and whether these are straightforward credit cards, branded or affinity cards, or store cards.

Merchant acquisition

2.9   Merchant Acquirers provide a payment card processing service, which facilitates customer debit and credit transactions between cardholders and merchants. Payment cards that bear card scheme acceptance brands (eg, MasterCard, Visa and Switch/Maestro) are issued by banks and financial institutions which are members of the relevant card scheme. The Merchant Acquirer processes the transactions made by cardholders on behalf of its merchant customers, including, in appropriate cases, seeking authorisation requests from the card issuer when payments are made, and the facilitation of chargebacks, where a transaction is disputed.

2.10   Payment is made by the Card Issuer to the individual merchant's bank, which in turn settles with the merchant's account, normally via the clearing system. The individual merchant is therefore a customer of the bank with which it maintains a banking relationship.

2.11   At the outset of the relationship with the merchant, the Merchant Acquirer will gather information on such matters as the expected card turnover, and average ticket value. This information is assessed in respect to the type of business the merchant is undertaking and the size of such business.

What are the money laundering and terrorist financing risks in issuance of credit cards?

2.12   Credit cards are a way of obtaining unsecured borrowing. As such, the initial risks are more related to fraud than to 'classic' money laundering; but handling the criminal property arising as a result of fraud is also money laundering. Card Issuers will therefore generally carry out some degree of credit check before accepting applications.

2.13   The money laundering risk relates largely to the source and means by which repayment of the borrowing on the card is made. Payments may also be made by third parties. For example, cash repayments, especially if by third parties, represent a higher level of money laundering risk than when they come from the cardholder's bank account by means of cheque or direct debit.

2.14   Balances on cards may move into credit, if cardholders repay too much, or where merchants pass credits/refunds across an account. Customers may ask for a refund of their credit balance. Issuance of a cheque by a Card Issuer can facilitate money laundering, as a credit balance made up of illicit funds could thereby be passed off as legitimate funds coming from a regulated firm.

2.15   Where a cardholder uses his card for gambling purposes (although the use of credit cards is prohibited in casinos), a card balance can easily be in credit, as scheme rules require that winnings are credited to the card used for the bet. It can be difficult in such circumstances to identify an unusual pattern of activity, as a fluctuating balance would be a legitimate profile for such a cardholder.

2.16   Cash may be withdrawn in another jurisdiction; thus a card can enable cash to be moved cross-border in non-physical form. This is in any event the case in respect of an amount up to the credit limit on the card. Where there is a credit balance, the amount that may be moved is correspondingly greater; it is possible for a cardholder to overpay substantially, and then to take the card abroad to be used. However, most card issuers limit the amount of cash that may be withdrawn, either in absolute terms, or to a percentage of the card's credit limit.

2.17   Where several holders are able to use a card account, especially to draw cash, the Card Issuer may open itself to a money laundering or terrorist financing risk in providing a payment token to an individual in respect of whom it holds no information. The issuer would not know to whom it is advancing money (even though the legal liability to repay is clear), unless it has taken some steps in relation to the identity of all those entitled to use the card. Such steps might include ascertaining:

- whether the primary or any secondary cardholder (including corporate cardholders) is resident in a high-risk jurisdiction or, for example, a country identified in relevant corruption or risk indices (such as Transparency International's Corruption Perception Index) as having a high level of corruption
- whether any primary or secondary cardholder is a politically exposed person

Managing the elements of risk

2.18   Measures that a firm might consider for mitigating the risk associated with a credit card customer base include the following:

- deciding whether to disallow persons so identified in the above two categories, or to subject them to enhanced due diligence, including full verification of identity of any secondary cardholder
- requiring the application process to include a statement of the relationship of a secondary cardholder to the primary cardholder based on defined alternatives (eg. Family member, carer, none)
- deciding whether either to disallow as a secondary cardholder on a personal account any relationship deemed unacceptable according to internal policy parameters, or where the address of the secondary cardholder differs to that of the primary cardholder, or to subject the application to additional enquiry, including verification of the secondary cardholder
- becoming a member of closed user groups sharing information to identify fraudulent applications, and checking both primary and secondary cardholder names and/or addresses against such databases
- deciding whether to decline to accept, or to undertake additional or enhanced due diligence on, corporate cardholders associated with an entity which is engaged in a high-risk activity, or is resident in a high-risk jurisdiction, or has been the subject of (responsible) negative publicity
- implementing ongoing transaction monitoring of accounts, periodic review and refinement of the parameters used for the purpose. Effective transaction monitoring is the key fraud and money laundering risk control in the credit card environment
- in the event that monitoring or suspicious reporting identifies that a secondary cardholder has provided significant funds for credit to the account, either regularly or on a one-off basis, giving consideration to verifying the identity of that secondary cardholder where it has not already been undertaken
- deciding whether the cardholder should be able to withdraw cash from his card account
- deciding whether the card may be used abroad (and monitoring whether it is used abroad)

Who is the customer for AML purposes?

2.19   Identification of the parties associated with a card account is not dependent on whether or not they have a contractual relationship with the Card Issuer. A Card Issuer's contractual relationship is solely with the primary cardholder, whether that is a natural or legal person, and it is to the primary cardholder that the Issuer looks for repayment of the debt on the card. The primary cardholder is unquestionably the Issuer's customer. However, a number of secondary persons may have authorised access to the account on the primary cardholder's behalf, whether as additional cardholders on a personal account or as employees holding corporate cards, where the contractual liability lies with the corporate employer.

2.20   The question therefore arises as to the appropriate extent, if any, of due diligence to be undertaken in respect of such secondary cardholders. Hitherto, there have been marked variations in interpretation and practice between Card Issuers with regard to the amount of data collected on secondary cardholders and the extent to which it is verified.

2.21   In substance, an additional cardholder on a personal card account is arguably analogous to either a joint account holder of a bank account, but without joint and several liability attaching, or – perhaps more persuasively – to a third party mandate holder on a bank account. In the case of corporate cards, it is reasonable to take the position that verification of the company in accordance with the guidance in Part I does not routinely require verification of all the individuals associated therewith.

2.22   In both cases, the risk posed to a firm's reputation in having insufficient data to identify a secondary cardholder featuring on a sanctions list or being a corrupt politically exposed person, and the potential liability arising from a breach of sanctions or a major money laundering or terrorist financing case, renders it prudent for the data collected to be full enough to mitigate that risk.

2.23   A merchant is a customer for AML/CTF purposes of the Merchant Acquirer.

Customer due diligence

2.24   In most cases, the Card Issuer would undertake the appropriate customer due diligence checks itself, or through the services of a credit reference agency, but there are some exceptions to this:

- where the Card Issuer is issuing a card on behalf of another regulated financial services firm, being a company or partner (in the case of affinity cards) that has already carried out the required customer due diligence
- introductions from other parts of the same group, or from other firms which are considered acceptable introducers (see Part I, section 5.6)

2.25   Although not an AML/CTF requirement, approval processes should have regard to the Card Issuer's latest information on current sources of fraud in relation to credit card applications.

2.26   Card schemes carry out surveys and reviews of activities related to their members. For example, one scheme carried out a due diligence review of the AML/CTF standards of all its members domiciled in high risk countries. Card Issuers should be aware of such survey/review activity.

2.27   Where corporate cards are issued to employees, the identity of the employer should be verified in accordance with the guidance set out in Part I, paragraph 5.3.119.

2.28   The standard verification requirement set out in Part I, Chapter 5 should be applied, as appropriate, to credit card and store card holders, although ascertaining the purpose of the account, and the expected flow of funds, would not be appropriate for such cards.

2.29   A risk-based approach to verifying the identity of secondary cardholders should be carried out as follows:

- The standard information set out in Part I, paragraph 5.3.68 should be collected for all secondary cardholders and recorded in such a way that the data are readily searchable. Firms should aim to comply with this recommendation by the end of February 2008;
- Firms should assess the extent to which they should verify any of the data so obtained, in accordance with the guidance set out in Part I, paragraph 5.3.69, from independent documentary or electronic evidence, in the light of their aggregate controls designed to mitigate fraud and money laundering risks, and bearing in mind the extent to which the firm applies the risk controls set out in paragraph 2.18. However, there is a presumption that such verification will be carried out, other than in the following circumstances.
  - In the case of store cards, because of the restrictions on their use, see paragraph 2.6. The same will generally be true of commercial cards because of the restrictions on their issue, see paragraph 2.7, although a firm's risk-based approach may deem it prudent to verify employee cardholders of their smaller commercial card customers.
  - Where a firm employs a low risk strategy of issuing additional cards only to close family members who reside at the same address as the primary cardholder, and the additional cardholder is a close family member whose employment, or continuing education, dictates that they are not permanently resident at the address, then for purposes of verification the primary cardholder's address shall be the main residential address. This will be acceptable as long as the mailing address for the additional cardholder remains the same as the primary cardholder's address.

- In all these situations, firms will still need to consider other types of due diligence check on additional cardholders, eg, against sanctions lists.

2.30   In relation to branded and affinity cards, where another regulated firm has the primary relationship with the cardholder, the partner organisation would need to undertake that it holds information on the applicant, and that this information would be supplied to the card issuer if requested.

2.31   In respect of a merchant, the Merchant Acquirer should apply the standard verification requirement in Part I, Chapter 5, adjusted as necessary to take account of the activities in which the merchant is engaged, turnover levels, the sophistication of available monitoring tools to identify any fraudulent background history as well as transaction activity, and the location of the bank account over which transactions are settled.

2.32   Where functions in relation to card issuing, especially initial customer due diligence, is outsourced, the firm should have regard to the FSA's guidance on outsourcing (www.fsahandbook.info/FSA/html/handbook/SYSC/8/9). In particular, Card Issuers should have criteria in place for assessing, initially and on an ongoing basis, the extent and robustness of the systems and procedures (of the firm to which the function is outsourced) for carrying out customer identification.

2.33   It would be unusual for a Card Issuer to revisit the information held in respect of a cardholder. Credit cards are primarily a distance transaction process. An account is opened (after due diligence checks are completed), a balance is acquired, a bill sent and payment received. This cycle is repeated until card closure and the majority of cardholders rarely, if ever, contact the Card Issuer.

Enhanced due diligence

2.34   An issuer should have criteria and procedures in place for identifying higher risk customers. Such customers must be subject to enhanced due diligence. This applies in the case of customers identified as being PEPs, or who are resident in, or nationals of, high-risk and/or non FATF jurisdictions.

2.35   Firms' procedures should include how customers should be dealt with, depending on the risk identified. Where necessary and appropriate, reference to a senior member of staff should be made in unusual circumstances. This will include getting senior manager approval for relationships with PEPs, although the level of seniority will depend on the level of risk represented by the PEP concerned.

Monitoring

2.36   It is a requirement of the ML Regulations that firms monitor accounts for unusual transactions patterns. Controls should be put in place for accepting changes of name or address for processing.

[7025]

3: ELECTRONIC MONEY

Note: This sectoral guidance is incomplete on its own. It must be read in conjunction with the main guidance set out in Part I of the Guidance.

The purpose of this sectoral guidance is to provide clarification to electronic money issuers on verification of identity and other customer due diligence measures required by legislation. The guidance addresses products that are card-based as well as those that are entirely software-based.

This guidance may be used by all issuers of electronic money, regardless of whether they are regulated by the FSA or operate under a small electronic money issuers' waiver – (small issuers are subject to HM Revenue and Customs' regulation in relation to AML compliance).

What is electronic money?

3.1   The FSMA 2000 (Regulated Activities) (Amendment) Order 2002 amended the FSMA 2000 (Regulated Activities) Order 2001 to provide for the issuing of electronic money to be a regulated activity under FSMA. Electronic money is defined as:

'... *monetary value, as represented by a claim on the issuer, which is:*
  (a)   *stored on an electronic device;*
  (b)   *issued on receipt of funds; and*
  (c)   *accepted as a means of payment by persons other than the issuer.'*

3.2   Electronic money is therefore a prepaid means of payment that can be used to make payments to multiple persons, where the persons are distinct legal or natural entities. It can be card-based or account-based and used entirely online.

3.3   Electronic money may be issued by banks or building societies with the requisite variation of permission from the FSA, or it may be issued by specialist Electronic Money Institutions, who obtain an authorisation from the FSA. The FSA also issues waivers to 'small e-money issuers' which meet the criteria set out in article 9 (C) of the Financial Services and Markets Act 2000 (Regulated Activities) Order 2001 (SI 2001/544), as amended.

3.4 The Money Laundering Regulations 2007 apply to all issuers of electronic money in their capacity as financial institutions as defined in Regulation 3.

3.5 Electronic money may also be issued cross-border into the UK by EEA credit institutions holding the appropriate passport from their home state supervisor under article 28 of the Banking Consolidation Directive (2006/48/EC). In these circumstances, the issuer's AML procedures are regulated by the home state authorities.

Definitions

3.6 The following terms are used in this guidance:

- **Accounted/unaccounted products:**
  Accounted products are those that record centrally every transaction that takes place within the system. Such recording need not be in real time, and may be subject to cycles of clearing and settlement.
  Unaccounted products do not involve the central recording of every transaction, although transactions may be recorded at the point of sale, or point of transfer of value. Accounted products may also comprise electronic vouchers that are not intended to be reloaded once used.

- **Card-based products:**
  These are products that employ a card or other electronic voucher for authentication, or to store the electronic money or a record of it on the card or voucher.

- **Closed/open scheme or system:**
  A closed scheme or system contains a single issuer of electronic money. There may, however, be multiple distributors or resellers, who purchase electronic money from the issuer for onward sale to consumers.
  An open scheme or system allows the participation of multiple issuers of electronic money, which means that there is a need for the clearing and settlement of transactions.

- **Complete information on the payer (CIP)**
  For the purposes of the Wire Transfer Regulation CIP consists of the payer's name, address and account number. The address may be substituted with the payer's date and place of birth, his customer identification number or his national identity number. The account number may be substituted with a unique identifier. See Part II, Sectoral guidance A: *Wire Transfers*, paragraph A.14 for details.

- **Digital coin products:**
  These are unaccounted products where the product is distinguished by (a) a fixed denomination, (b) a unique digit string or serial number, and (c) the value residing in the electronic coin itself. The coin is usually discarded as soon as the electronic money is spent or redeemed.

- **Electronic Money Association (EMA):**
  The EMA is the trade body representing electronic money issuers and payment service providers.

- **Merchant:**
  For the purposes of this guidance, a merchant is a natural or legal person that uses electronic money to transact in the course of business.

- **Payment Service Provider (PSP):**
  A PSP is defined in Article 2(5) of the Wire Transfer Regulation as "a natural or legal person whose business includes the provision of transfer of funds services".

- **Wire Transfer Regulation [also known as the Payer Regulation]:**
  Regulation (EC) 1781/2006 on information on the payer accompanying transfers of funds implements Special FATF Recommendation VII in EU member states. This guidance refers to it as the Wire Transfer Regulation, although this term has no formal standing. Supervision and enforcement provisions for this Regulation are implemented in the UK through the Transfer of Funds (Information on the Payer) Regulations 2007 (SI 2007/3298).

- **Purse:**
  An electronic money purse is a store of electronic money, which may be in an account, on a card or other device.

- **Redemption:**
  This is the process whereby a customer submits electronic money to the issuer for exchange at par value, for cash, cheque or a fund transfer drawn on the issuer's account. (Note that the term is sometimes used in the gift card industry to indicate the spending of value with merchants).

- **Regulations, the:**
  The Money Laundering Regulations 2007 (SI 2007/2157)

- **Server-based products:**

  These are products where the value held by a customer is held centrally on a server under the control of the issuer. Customers access their purses remotely, usually online. Note that Euro figures have been converted to approximate figures in Sterling, except where reference is made to legislative provisions.

Background to money laundering and terrorist financing risks related to electronic money

3.7   Electronic money is a retail payment product that is used predominantly for making small value payments. As an electronic means of payment, it is susceptible to the same risks of money laundering and terrorist financing as other retail payment products. In the absence of controls over the use of the product, there is a significant risk of money laundering taking place. The implementation of purse limits, usage controls, and systems to detect suspicious activity contributes to mitigating these risks.

3.8   Furthermore, where electronic money is limited to small value payments, the use of this product is less attractive to would-be launderers. For terrorist financing, and other financial crime, electronic money offers a more accountable, and therefore less attractive means of transferring money compared to cash.

3.9   The electronic money products in commercial use today do not provide the kind of privacy or anonymity that cash provides, nor its utility. This is due to a number of factors: commercial practice, for example, dictates that most products are funded by payments from bank accounts or credit cards, and therefore can often reveal the identity of the customer at the outset. Similarly, use of these products often leaves an electronic trail that can help locate, if not identify, the user of a particular product.

3.10   As issuers of electronic money usually occupy the position of intermediary in the payment process, situated between two financial or credit institutions, they are often able to provide additional transaction information to law enforcement investigations that complements identity data provided by other financial institutions. This may be equally or more valuable in the chain of evidence than a repetition of the verification of identity process, as it can yield valuable information to assist law enforcement in that event.

3.11   Fraud prevention and consumer protection concerns lead to the placement of transaction, turnover, and purse limits on products, limiting the risk to both issuer and consumer. These limits act to restrict the usefulness of the product for money laundering, and make unusual transactions more detectable.

3.12   Risk factors that apply specifically to electronic money products are set out in paragraphs 3.15 and 3.16–3.18. Other risks set out in Part I of this Guidance also affect issuers (eg, customer profile or geographical location of activity, see Part I, chapter 4 for details), and issuers are required to include these in the risk assessment that they undertake. Risk assessment should be an ongoing process and take into account information from transaction monitoring systems (see paragraphs 3.45–3.47). Issuers should manage the risks through carrying out appropriate customer due diligence measures.

3.13   The EMA publishes a typologies document, which outlines money laundering and terrorist financing risks and the means of mitigating them. This is a working document, which is updated on a regular basis. Issuers can obtain a copy of this document from the EMA by writing to information@e-ma.org.

3.14   This area of payments is evolving, and new products give rise to new risks. New mitigation strategies are therefore constantly needed. This will be reflected in the regular updates to this Guidance and other industry documents that are produced on a periodic basis.

Factors increasing risk

3.15   The following factors will generally tend to increase the risk of electronic money products being used for money laundering or terrorist financing:

- The higher the value and frequency of transactions, and the higher the purse limit, the greater the risk: the €15,000 threshold for occasional transactions provided in the Regulations may in this context provide a convenient comparator when assessing such risk;
- Frequent cross-border transactions, unless within a single scheme, can give rise to problems with information sharing. Dependence on counterparty systems increases the risk;
- Some merchant activity is particularly susceptible to money laundering, eg, betting and gaming offer a number of opportunities either with or without the collusion of the merchant; and money service businesses are considered as susceptible to exploitation for money laundering and terrorist financing[1];
- Funding of purses using cash offers little or no audit trail and hence presents a higher risk of money laundering;
- The non face-to-face nature of many products also gives rise to increased risk;

- The ability of consumers to hold multiple purses (for example open multiple accounts or purchase a number of cards) without verification of identity increases the risk;
- Redemptions at ATMs, as well as any allowances for the payment of refunds in cash for purchases made using electronic money will also increase the risk;
- The ability of non-verified third parties to use the product increases the risk; and
- The technology adopted by the product may give rise to specific risks that should be assessed.

---

¹   The Government's Financial Crime Strategy noted that one in five money laundering investigations, and one in three terrorist finance investigations, features the exploitation of Money Service Businesses.

Factors decreasing risk

3.16   Electronic money products address the risks that are inherent in payments in a similar manner to other retail payment products – by requiring systems that detect unusual transactions and predetermined patterns of activity.

3.17   Additionally, the annual allowance for redemption of electronic money reduces the risk by allowing funds to enter the system, but only allowing a relatively small amount (€1,000) to exit without verification. This practice has the effect of making the electronic money product a less attractive means for money laundering.

3.18   An issuer will mitigate and therefore generally decrease the risk of money laundering through electronic money products, and increase the likelihood of its discovery if it has taken place, through putting in place systems and controls that may include those that:

- Can detect money laundering transaction patterns, including those described in the EMA typologies document;
- Will detect anomalies to normal transaction patterns;
- Can identify multiple purses held by a single individual or group of individuals, such as the holding of multiple accounts or the 'stockpiling' of pre-paid cards;
- Can look for indicators of accounts being opened with different issuers as well as attempts to pool funds from different sources.
- Can identify discrepancies between submitted and detected information – for example, between country of origin submitted information and the electronically-detected IP address;
- Deploy sufficient resources to address money laundering risks, including, where necessary, specialist expertise for the detection of suspicious activities; and
- Restrict funding of electronic money products, to funds drawn on accounts held at credit and financial institutions in the UK, the EU or a comparable jurisdiction, and restrict redemption of electronic money into accounts held at such institutions.

Verification of identity

3.19   The Regulations state that for a business relationship and for occasional transactions (single or linked transactions of €15,000 or more, if not carried out as part of a business relationship) verification of identity must be carried out at the outset (see Part I section 5.2 on timing). This requirement includes verification of beneficial owners (the individuals who ultimately own or control the customer or on whose behalf a transaction or activity is being conducted – see Part I, paragraphs 5.3.8 to 5.3.13).

Merchants

3.20   In person-to-person systems, the boundary between consumers and merchants may be blurred; consumers may not register as merchants, but may nevertheless carry on quasi-merchant activity. In this case issuers:

- Should have systems in place that provide a means of detecting such activity.
- When such activity has been detected, apply due diligence measures appropriate to merchants.
- Deploy sufficient resources to address money laundering risks, including, where necessary, specialist expertise for the detection of suspicious activities; and

3.21   Issuers may allow merchants to benefit from the £1,650 turnover and £650 redemption allowance in order to enable the online recruitment of small merchants. This does not, however, alter the requirement to undertake adequate due diligence of the merchant's business.

Multiple-card products

3.22   Issuers whose products enable two or more cards to be linked to a single account must establish whether they have entered into one or more business relationships, and must verify the identity of all customers with whom they have a business relationship.

3.23   Issuers with such products must mitigate the greater risk of money laundering to which these products are exposed by implementing systems and controls that seek to identify transactions or patterns that fit money laundering typologies for such products, and to act promptly to prevent money laundering.

3.24   Verification of identity for a second cardholder contributes to mitigating the risk, and should be considered even where there is no business relationship with that person.

One-off transactions

3.25   The purchase of a non-reloadable card or cards is a one-off transaction when it is not clear to the issuer whether the customer will return and make a repeat purchase of another card or cards. Such transactions for non-reloadable cards can then be regarded as one-off, for the purposes of this guidance.

3.26   A reasonable maximum purse limit should, however, be adopted for such products, and this should not exceed £650. Such cards should not, however, allow for redemption of electronic money without verification of identity taking place, subject to a £100 *de minimis* allowance.

3.27   These limits do not apply where there is a suspicion of money laundering or terrorist financing. In such circumstances, the identity of the customer must be verified, irrespective of the transacted total.

Customer Due Diligence

3.28   Guidance on verifying the identity of individuals and companies or other businesses in both face-to-face and non face-to-face circumstances, using documentary or electronic evidence, is set out in Part I, chapter 5. Detailed guidance for verifying the identity of customers who do not have access to a bank account, or who lack credit or financial history, is provided under the financial exclusion provisions of Part I, section 5.3.

3.29   Issuers will also need to satisfy themselves that they meet the requirements of sanctions legislation. Guidance on this is provided in Part I, paragraphs 5.3.41–5.3.64.

3.30   Taking account of the risk mitigation features applied to electronic money systems, the approach to verifying identity for the electronic money sector is predicated on the need to minimise barriers to take-up of these new products, whilst addressing the risk of money laundering and meeting the obligations set out in the Regulations.

3.31   The Regulations require that electronic money issuers, in common with all financial sector firms, must carry out CDD measures on a risk-based approach.

3.32   Issuers are, in common with other financial services providers, required to verify identity at the outset of the relationship with the customer.

3.33   The Regulations specify circumstances where *simplified due diligence* can be applied. Simplified due diligence is an exemption for certain low-risk products from the requirement to apply customer due diligence measures. A purse must meet specific maximum storage, turnover and redemption limits in order for simplified due diligence to apply (see paragraphs 3.36 to 3.42). Where a product qualifies for simplified due diligence, there are no requirements for having to verify the customer's identity. As part of a basic risk-based approach, however, firms must have systems in place to detect abuse of the turnover allowance and other suspicious transaction patterns etc. (see paragraph 3.45), Once the limits are reached, issuers are required to undertake verification of identity on a risk-sensitive basis (see paragraph 3.43).

3.34   *Enhanced due diligence* is required to be carried out in higher risk situations. One of these situations is where the customer is not physically present to be identified by the issuer. Whether and what enhanced due diligence measures are required of the issuer will depend on the facts – (see paragraphs 3.57–3.60).

3.35   If a product qualifies for simplified due diligence, no verification of identity is required, even where the customer is not present, so long as no exceptional factors apply.

Simplified due diligence

3.36   The Regulations describe the simplified due diligence provisions for electronic money at Regulation 13 (7)(d):

'(d)   *electronic money, within the meaning of Article 1(3)(b) of the electronic money directive, where:—*

(i)   *if the device cannot be recharged, the maximum amount stored in the device is no more than 150 euro; or*

(i)   *if the device can be recharged, a limit of 2,500 euro is imposed on the total amount transacted in a calendar year, except when an amount of 1,000 euro or more is redeemed in that same calendar year by the bearer (within the meaning of Article 3 of the electronic money directive).'*

3.37 **Non-reloadable purses:** where electronic money purses cannot be recharged, and the total purse limit does not exceed €150, verification of identity does not need to be undertaken. This takes into account the ability of individuals to purchase multiple purses and to therefore accumulate a higher overall total of purchased value.

3.38 This behaviour will, for example, be expected for gift card products. The purchase of electronic money gift cards is likely to be undertaken in multiple numbers, because of the nature of the product. Provided that the gift card does not allow for redemption to be made at ATMs, the risk of money laundering arising from multiple purchases is likely to remain low. Issuers should however adopt a maximum total value that they will allow single customers to purchase, on a risk weighted basis, without identity being verified.

3.39 **Reloadable purses:** those issuers that provide electronic money purses that can be recharged, whether card or purely server-based, are therefore required to undertake verification of identity procedures only when the annual turnover limit of £1,650 is exceeded, or if the customer seeks to redeem more than the £650 annual allowance.

3.40 Where purses can both send and receive payments, such as, for example, in online account-based products that enable person to person payments, the £1,650 turnover limit is applied separately to sending and receiving transactions. In other words, the turnover limit is calculated separately for credit and debit transactions, and the verification requirement applied when either of the two is exceeded.

3.41 Additionally, and in order to address obligations arising from the Wire Transfer Regulation, issuers must verify the identity of customers seeking to undertake any single sending transaction that exceeds £650 in value, where verification has not already been undertaken (see paragraph 3.64).

3.42 In summary, under simplified due diligence, identity verification must be undertaken on a customer with a reloadable purse on his:

- Reaching the cumulative annual turnover limit of £1,650; or
- Reaching the annual redemption limit of £650; or
- Seeking to undertake a single sending (debit) electronic money transaction which exceeds £650; or
- Where the issuer suspects money laundering or terrorist financing.

3.43 In respect of products benefiting from simplified due diligence, identity must be verified before cumulative turnover limits are exceeded. Systems must therefore be in place so that issuers are able to anticipate the approach of limits and to seek identification evidence in good time, before the annual turnover limits are reached. Firms must freeze the account if the limits are reached before verification of identity has been completed.

Basic requirements under this Guidance for a risk-based approach

3.44 This Guidance provides for additional measures that issuers are required to meet as part of the basic application of a risk-based approach. These measures are:

Verification of identity

(i) Either the electronic money scheme is a closed system; or

(ii) It is an open system, in which case all other participating issuers should under this Guidance also meet these requirements;

   (a) In all cases merchants must be subject to due diligence measures in accordance with Part I, Chapter 5 (but see paragraph 3.21 for a limited exemption).

   (b) Where electronic money is accepted by merchants or other recipients belonging to a wider payment scheme (for example Visa or MasterCard), the issuer must satisfy itself that the verification of identity and other due diligence measures carried out by that scheme in relation to merchants are, in the UK, equivalent to those of this sectoral guidance; or for other jurisdictions, are subject to equivalent regulation.

   (c) Where redemption of electronic money is permitted by way of cash withdrawal at ATMs or through a cash-back facility at retailers, and where this can exceed the annual redemption limit of £650 or single transaction limit of £650, verification of identity must be conducted at the point of issuance of the electronic money. Furthermore, issuers must require all refunds made by merchants in the event of return of goods or services to be made back onto the electronic money purse from which payment was first made.

   (d) Purse controls (eg, turnover velocity, purse limits) must be implemented in such a way that the utility of products for money laundering is decreased.

Monitoring

3.45   The principle of monitoring of a business relationship is an obligation under the Regulations. As part of a risk-based approach, issuers must deploy specific minimum transaction monitoring and/or on-chip purse controls that enable control of the systems and recognition of suspicious activity. Such controls may include:

- Transaction monitoring systems that detect anomalies or patterns of behaviour;
- Systems that identify discrepancies between submitted and detected information – for example, between country of origin submitted information and the electronically-detected IP address;
- Systems that cross-reference submitted data against existing data for other accounts, such as the use of the same credit card by several customers;
- Systems that interface with third party data sources to import information that may assist in detecting incidence of fraud or money laundering across a number of payment service providers;
- On-chip controls that impose purse rules, such as rules that specify the POS terminals or other cards with which the purse may transact;
- On-chip controls that impose purse limits such as transaction or turnover limits;
- On-chip controls that disable the card when a given pattern of activity is detected, requiring interaction with the issuer before it can be re-enabled; and
- Controls that are designed to detect and forestall the use of the electronic money product for money laundering or terrorist financing in accordance with the typologies produced by the EMA.

3.46   Issuers will need to evidence that they deploy an adequate range of controls for the type of risks that they encounter. Information obtained through monitoring should be reviewed as part of the ongoing risk assessment associated with the use of these products, and issuers should take action to enhance customer due diligence, for example that of verification of identity, where there are higher risks.

3.47   Issuers are reminded that in the event that potentially suspicious activity is detected by internal systems or procedures, the issuer must have particular regard to its obligations under POCA and the Terrorism Act (see Part I, Chapter 6) to report possible money laundering or terrorist financing.

Basic requirements under this Guidance for customer due diligence

3.48   As stated in paragraph 3.31, the Regulations require that CDD measures are carried out on a risk-based approach, as set out in Part I, Chapter 5. Electronic money is issued in a range of products, for a range of purposes covering a spectrum of risk – from the purchase of goods and services, to person-to-person payments. An issuer's risk-based approach to CDD measures will, as required by the Regulations, depend on the type of product or transaction involved.

3.49   As part of a risk-based approach to verification of identity, the Regulations require that verification is carried out on the basis of 'documents, data or information obtained from a reliable and independent source'. A customer's funding instrument (such as a credit card or bank account) can constitute such data or information.

3.50   A funding instrument on its own, however, is a weak form of verification of identity, first, because the credit or financial institution whose evidence is being used upon may not have verified the customer to current standards, and secondly because there is a risk that the person using the account may not be its rightful holder. This second risk is even higher where an electronic money issuer has no evidence that the account is held in the same name as the customer, such as for example in relation to direct debits.

3.51   Use of the funding instrument as evidence should therefore only be made where the circumstances are judged to be low risk (see paragraphs 3.15–3.18 for guidance on factors that increase or decrease risk), and verification of identity for any product may only be satisfied if:

(a)   The firm has in place the systems and processes set out in paragraph 3.52.

(b)   The funds to purchase electronic money are drawn from an account or credit card with, or issued by, a credit or financial institution[2] in the UK, the EU or an equivalent jurisdiction, which is supervised for its AML controls;

(c)   The issuer has reasonable evidence to conclude that the customer is the rightful holder of the account on which the funds are drawn (which may be achieved using the processes described in paragraph 3.54); and

(d)   The purse does not exceed a maximum turnover limit of £10,000 from the commencement of the business relationship; and

---

[2]   Other than an MSB or a firm holding only a CCA licence

3.52   The systems and processes which must be in place include:

- Those necessary for identifying incidents of fraudulent use of credit/debit cards and bank accounts.
- Those that enable monitoring to identify increased risk for such products, even within the permitted turnover limits. If the risk profile can then no longer be regarded as low risk, additional verification requirements must be taken.
- Recording of additional information such as IP addresses should be undertaken to assist in determining the electronic footprint of the user.

3.53 Collectively, the processes set out in paragraph 3.51(a) to (c) are intended to compensate for the weakness of using a funding instrument as evidence of identity without additional means of ensuring its integrity and its authorised use.

3.54 Where payment from a funding institution is made electronically, it is usually not possible to verify the name of the account holder for the funding account. In this case, steps must be taken to establish that the customer is the rightful holder of the account from which the funds are drawn. These steps may include the following:

- Some issuers have developed a means of establishing control over a funding account using a process that is convenient and effective. A small random amount of money is credited to a customer's funding account and the customer is then required to discover the amount and to enter it on the issuer's website. By entering the correct value, the customer demonstrates access to the bank/card statement or accounting system of their bank or financial institution. This method, and its close variants, provides an acceptable means of confirming that the customer has access to the account, and therefore has control over it. It also provides a means of guarding against identity theft, contributing therefore to the verification of identity process. If such an approach is not used, some other means of establishing control of the account is needed.
- Issuers may also use additional anti-fraud checks undertaken at the time of the transaction which seek to cross reference customer-submitted data against data held by the electronic money or card issuer or similar independent third party, and which gives the electronic money issuer the requisite level of confidence that the customer is the rightful holder of the card.
- Seeking evidence of legitimate use is an alternative to establishing formal control over an account. An account that is used to fund an electronic money purse over a period of time is likely to be used legitimately, as the passage of time gives the rightful owner the opportunity to discover fraudulent use of the product and to block its use, which would in turn become evident to the issuer. Thus, for some products, this may provide a means of establishing legitimate use of a funding instrument. However:
  - Such an approach is sensitive to the issuer's ability to monitor, track and record use of a funding instrument associated with an account, and issuers' wishing to adopt this approach must therefore have systems that are appropriate for this purpose.
  - A minimum period of six months must elapse, together with significant usage in terms of number and value of transactions over this time, to satisfy the issuer that the instrument is being legitimately used[3].

---

[3]   The six month period should be completed before the limits associated with SDD (see paragraph 3.36) are exceeded.

3.55 Furthermore, electronic money issuers should have processes in place to ensure that additional due diligence steps are undertaken if the risk posed by the product or customer increases so as to pose a higher risk of money laundering or terrorist financing (see paragraph 3.15). In such circumstances, where the risk posed can no longer be regarded as low, issuers must augment the basic approach to verification with other means of verification, such as those provided in Part I, Chapter 5.

3.56 To this extent, and in other circumstances, complete information on the payer, received as part of the obligations under the Wire Transfer Regulation, may also contribute to verifying a customer's identity.

Enhanced due diligence

3.57 The Regulations require enhanced due diligence to be undertaken in all situations where the risk of money laundering is perceived to be high. These include instances where the customer is not physically present for identification purposes, as well as in respect of business relationships or occasional transactions with politically exposed persons (PEPs).

3.58 Where electronic money purses[4] are purchased or accounts opened in a non face to face environment, issuers must take specific and adequate measures to address the greater risk of money laundering or terrorist financing that is posed (Part I, paragraphs 5.5.10 to 5.5.17 provide guidance on enhanced due diligence for non face to face transactions).

⁴   If an electronic money purse meets the conditions for simplified due diligence, no identification of the customer is required, even though the customer may not have been physically present.

3.59   What measures are taken will depend on a number of factors, including an assessment of the risk posed by the product itself. Issuers may adopt means of verification other than those outlined in Part I, including those outlined at paragraphs 3.51 to 3.56.

3.60   The degree of enhanced due diligence required for PEPs will be proportionate to the risk posed by the product, as will the requirement for systems and processes to detect PEPs. Where electronic money transactions and cumulative turnover values are low, the risk posed by way of their use by PEPs for money laundering is also likely to be low. Issuers should therefore focus their resources, in a risk sensitive manner, on products and transactions where the risk of money laundering is high. Further guidance on the application of the risk-based approach to PEPs is provided at Part I, paragraphs 5.5.26–5.5.29.

Transition

3.61   Issuers must apply customer due diligence measures at appropriate times to their existing customers (as at 15th December 2007) on a risk-sensitive basis, unless the product qualifies for simplified due diligence. Card-based products that are already in issue under the old Guidance provisions may continue to operate until their existing expiry date is reached. When they are replaced, however, the new cards must be subject to the new cumulative turnover, transaction and redemption provisions provided under this Guidance.

Wire Transfer Regulation

3.62   General provisions for compliance with the Wire Transfer Regulation are provided in Part I, paragraphs 5.2.10ff *Electronic Transfer of funds*, and Part II, Specialist guidance A: *Wire transfers*.

3.63   Issuers are subject to the obligations of the Wire Transfer Regulation in their role as PSP of the payer, PSP of the payee and intermediary PSP. An overview of these requirements is provided schematically at Appendix I to this Guidance.

3.64   Payments using electronic money and funding of purses:
   (i)   Transactions below £650 in value do not require the collection or sending of Complete Information on the Payer (CIP), as these transactions are subject to the exemption provided by Article 3(3) of the Wire Transfer Regulation.
   (ii)   Transactions exceeding £650 in value require the collection and verification of CIP on a risk-weighted basis as set out elsewhere in this Guidance or as set out at A11–A14 of Part II, Specialist guidance A: *Wire transfers*.
   (iii) Where an electronic money purse is funded through a card payment exceeding £650, it has been agreed that for practical purposes such a transaction constitutes payment for goods and services under Article 3(2) of the Regulation, and consequently the sending of the card PAN number satisfies the requirement for a unique identifier to accompany the transfer of funds. See Part II, Specialist guidance: *Wire Transfers,* paragraph A19. However, subsequent payments from the electronic money purse must be in accordance with (i) and (ii) above.
   (iv)   When funding transactions exceeding £650 are made from a bank account or other financial institution account in the EU, then CIP can be substituted for, with an account number or a unique identifier enabling the transaction to be traced back to the payer (see Article 6 of the Wire Transfer Regulation).

3.65   Redemption of electronic money:
   (i)   Payments made to customers in redemption of electronic money are usually made by bank transfer. Redemption comprises a payment by the issuer as principal (payer) to the electronic money account holder. Issuers may, however, attach customer (in addition to their own) CIP to the redemption transaction in the usual way – benefiting from the provisions for inter EU payments where applicable, and ensuring additional information is available to the payee PSP.
   (ii)   Where redemption is made in cash, this benefits from the exemption from the Wire Transfer Regulation for cash withdrawals from a customer's own account provided by Article 3(7)(a).

3.66   Verification of identity for CIP information should be undertaken on a risk-weighted basis as provided for elsewhere in this Guidance or as set out in paragraphs A11–A14 of Part II, Specialist guidance A: *Wire transfers*.

Industry practice

3.67   A summary of good industry practice is provided in the table below.

3.68   It should be noted that the annual cumulative turnover limit of a purse is interpreted as the greater of either the total amount of electronic money sent by a purse or the total amount of electronic money received by a purse, and includes any purchase value that is credited to the purse. 'Annual' refers to 12 month periods from the opening of the purse.

3.69   Finally, issuers are reminded that the responsibility for AML compliance always rests with the regulated issuer itself. When an issuer uses agents or outsourced third parties to undertake any of the CDD measures on its behalf, the issuer continues to be responsible for meeting the requirements of the Regulations.

Product Characteristics	Industry Practice	Comments
Electronic money products that have not implemented the purse limits and requirements set out in paragraphs 3.36 and 3.44, and allow transactions in excess of £650 to take place. The products enable either or both consumer-to-merchant and consumer-to-consumer payments.	Issuers should undertake: - Due diligence of customers at the outset; and - Due diligence of merchants at the outset. Issuers must also have systems in place to monitor and detect incidents of potential abuse, such as the opening of multiple accounts by a single individual or the opening of consumer accounts by merchants.	Appropriate measures will vary according to product and circumstances. Possible measures include further customer due diligence measures where there is a high risk of money laundering or terrorist financing, restrictions on functionality or turnover of purses, or more frequent monitoring.
Issuers should consider the practices below in the context of the risk factors set out in paragraphs 3.15–3.18, and adapt these practices as appropriate to take account of greater risks.		
Electronic money products that have implemented the purse limits and requirements set out in paragraphs 3.36 and 3.44, and limit the size of transactions to a maximum of £650. The products enable either or both consumer-to-merchant and consumer-to-consumer payments.	Where annual turnover is limited to £1,650, redemption to £650 and individual transactions to a maximum of £650, consumers do not need to be verified. Identity of customers to be verified on requesting redemption of a value exceeding £650. Verification of identity required as the annual £1,650 limit is approached – purse frozen if identification evidence not provided. Verification of identity required if the £650 transaction limit is exceeded. Merchants may also benefit from the annual £1,650 cumulative turnover and £650 annual redemption limits, subject also to the £650 transaction limit. Notwithstanding this, Merchants' identity should wherever possible be verified at the outset and in all cases appropriate customer due diligence measures carried out. Issuers must also have systems in place to monitor and detect incidents of abuse, such as the opening of multiple accounts by a single individual or the opening of consumer accounts by merchants. A full list of requirements is provided at paragraphs 3.44–3.45.	Benefits of product include: - Cost of verifying identity not borne where product is used only once or occasionally; - No delay and little or no barrier to sign up of new customers; and - Privacy limited to consumers. Where customers act as merchants (eg, in on-line auctions) but are not registered as merchants, and there is no reason to believe they are merchants, they may be considered consumers but are subject to the cumulative turnover limit.

Electronic money products that are non re-loadable and have implemented the purse limits set out in paragraphs 3.37 or 3.26, and limit the size of transactions to a maximum of £650. The products enable either or both consumer-to-merchant and consumer-to-consumer payments.	Merchant provisions are the same as those for re-loadable products above. Issuers must have systems in place to monitor and detect incidents of abuse, such as the opening of multiple accounts by a single individual or the purchase of multiple cards, or opening of consumer accounts by merchants. A full list of requirements is provided at paragraphs 3.44–3.45.	As above, for re-loadable products. Where customers have been subject to full due diligence, the purse limits for non re-loadable products can be increased, subject to the usual risk management considerations.

[7026]

4: CREDIT UNIONS

Note: This sectoral guidance is incomplete on its own. It must be read in conjunction with the main guidance set out in Part I of the Guidance. This guidance covers aspects of money laundering compliance that are unique to credit unions and an overview of the key compliance issues; credit unions must also take account of Part I of this guidance.

Credit unions will also need to be aware of CRED 4.3.37 G to 4.3.37J G.

This guidance applies only to FSA-regulated credit unions, not to credit unions in Northern Ireland.

Overview of the sector

4.1   The membership of a credit union is restricted to individuals who fulfil a specific qualification which is appropriate to a credit union (and as a consequence a common bond exists between members) – Credit Unions Act 1979, s1(2)(b). The common bond concept is central to the co-operative ethos of a credit union and is also fundamental to the regulatory regime for credit unions.

4.2   The FSA has produced additional common bond guidance outlining geographical and population limits regarding common bonds.

4.3   Credit unions therefore operate within a restricted, often localised market, providing services to members, not to the public at large.

What are the money laundering and terrorist financing risks in credit unions?

4.4   There are two types of credit union, Version 1 and Version 2. The majority of credit unions are Version 1, offering very basic savings and loan products. Version 2 credit unions have much more flexibility around the products they can provide and currently just 2% of credit unions have Version 2 status. However, although Version 2 credit unions have more flexibility, in terms of the wider financial services sector both Version 1 and Version 2 credit unions are restricted in terms of the range and complexity of the products they can offer and to whom they can offer them.

4.5   There are limits on the level of savings a credit union can hold on behalf of an individual member, which are set out in CRED 7A.2.1 R. The return on savings is linked to financial performance and is subject to a statutory cap, currently set at 8%. In addition, there are rules governing a credit union's lending activity. Lending limits are set out in CRED 10.3.1 R to CRED 10.3.6 R.

4.6   Therefore credit union financial products, particularly those of Version 1 credit unions, do not deliver sufficient functionality or flexibility to be the first choice for money launderers, although these restrictions may not be such a deterrent to terrorist financiers.

4.7   The high levels of cash transactions going through credit unions may be one area where there is a higher risk of money laundering or terrorist financing, eg, by 'smurfing'.[5]

---

[5]   Numerous small payments into an account, where the amount of each deposit is unremarkable but the total of all the credits is significant.

4.8   The number of staff and volunteers involved in the day to day operations of a credit union is relatively small and, even in larger credit unions, there are typically no more than a few individuals whose responsibility it is to manually process data. Therefore, where there is manual processing of all transactions, the ability to identify suspicious transactions is potentially much greater. In addition, the relatively small organisational structures mean that suspected money laundering or terrorist financing can be detected and reported much faster in smaller credit unions than it could in other financial services firms. The monitoring procedures for larger credit unions, that inevitably do not have such a close relationship with their members, will need to reflect the absence of those relationships, to ensure that potential problems, eg, 'smurfing', can be detected.

4.9   This does not, of course, mean that there is no risk of money laundering or terrorist financing in credit unions and credit unions must in any case be aware of their responsibilities under the ML Regulations, the Proceeds of Crime Act (POCA) and the Terrorism Act. Credit unions must therefore establish appropriate procedures to monitor activities, with a particular scrutiny of those that carry a higher risk of money laundering or terrorist financing (see Part I, section 5.7). Examples of such activities include:

- money transfers to third parties;
- large one off transactions;
- third parties paying in cash on behalf of the member;
- unusual loan or saving transactions;
- reluctance to provide documentary evidence of identity when opening an account (even when taking into account financial exclusion issues).

Applying a risk-based approach

4.10   In accordance with the guidance in Part I, Chapter 4, a credit union's risk-based approach will ensure that its strategies are focused on deterring, detecting and disclosing in the areas of greatest perceived vulnerability. The credit union needs to take a number of steps, documented in a formal policy statement which assesses the most effectual, cost effective and proportionate way to manage money laundering and terrorist financing risks. These steps are:

- identify the money laundering and terrorist financing risks that are relevant to the firm;
- assess the risks presented by the credit union's particular
  - Members;
  - Products;
  - Delivery channels;
  - Geographical areas of operation;
- design and implement controls to manage and mitigate these assessed risks;
- monitor and improve the effective operation of these controls; and
- record appropriately what has been done and why.

4.11   Examples of risks are given at www.jmlsg.org.uk but a credit union will also need to take account of its own experience and knowledge of its members and their financial activities. Credit unions should also consult the Financial Action Task Force website at www.fatf-gafi.org in order to keep up-to-date with money laundering/terrorist financing typologies.

4.12   Following the establishment of a risk-based approach, it is the responsibility of the credit union's senior management to keep this strategy under regular review. Credit unions may consider it appropriate to have a standing item covering money laundering on the agenda of their monthly meeting to ensure procedures are being regularly reviewed. Credit unions will also need to take into account CRED 4.3.37H G which reads, "SYSC 3.2.6H R requires a credit union to allocate to a director or senior manager (who may also be the money laundering reporting officer) overall responsibility within the credit union for the establishment and maintenance of effective anti-money laundering systems and controls".

Customer due diligence

4.13   The anti-money laundering (AML)/combating the financing of terrorism (CTF) checks carried out during account opening are one of the primary controls for preventing criminals opening an account and are therefore an important element of AML/CTF procedures. Credit unions should be satisfied that the policies and procedures in place for verifying identity are effective in preventing and detecting money launderers and that they make provision for circumstances when increased evidence is required.

4.14   For the majority of members, the standard identification requirement set out in Part I, Chapter 5 (full name, residential address and date of birth) and, where relevant, additional customer information set out in Part I, section 5.5 will be applicable.

4.15   The identity information should be verified in accordance with the guidance set out in Part I (paragraphs 5.3.68–5.3.84), either from documents produced by the individual, or electronically, or through a combination of the two: these approaches are potentially equal options, depending on the circumstances in any given case.

Documentary verification

4.16   Examples of documents that are acceptable in different situations are summarised in Part I, paragraph 5.3.74, together with the principles defining when reliance may be placed on a single document or where more than one is required. A current UK passport or photocard driving licence issued in the UK should be the document used in the majority of cases, other than in individual cases of financial exclusion, where it is concluded that an individual cannot reasonably be expected to provide standard identification, (see paragraphs 4.18–4.20 for further information). For non-UK residents, a national passport or national identity card is likely to be used in the majority of cases. However, in circumstances where the individual cannot be expected to produce standard identification credit unions can follow the guidance on financial exclusion in paragraphs 4.18–4.20.

Electronic verification

4.17   In principle, electronic verification may be used to meet a firm's customer identification obligations. However, a credit union should first consider whether electronic verification is suitable for its membership base, and should then have regard to the guidance in Part I, paragraphs 5.3.39–5.3.40 and 5.3.79–5.3.81. When using electronically-sourced evidence to verify identity, credit unions should ensure that they have an adequate understanding of the data sources relied on by the external agencies that supply the evidence. Credit unions should be satisfied that these sources provide enough cumulative evidence to provide reasonable certainty of a person's identity, and conform with the guidance set out in Part I, Chapter 5. An electronic check that accesses a single database (eg, Electoral Roll check) is normally not enough on its own to verify identity.

Financial exclusion

4.18   The FSA Rules adopt a broad view of financial exclusion, in terms of ensuring that, where people cannot reasonably be expected to produce standard evidence of identity, they are not unreasonably denied access to financial services. The term is sometimes used in a narrower sense; for example, HM Treasury refers to those who, for specific reasons, do not have access to mainstream banking or financial services – that is, those at the lower end of income distribution who are socially/financially disadvantaged and in receipt of benefits, or those who chose not to seek access to financial products because they believe that they will be refused.

4.19   As a first step, before concluding that a member cannot produce evidence of identity, credit unions will have established that the guidance on initial identity checks for personal customers set out in Part I, paragraphs 5.3.68–5.3.76 cannot reasonably be applied. Where the credit union has concluded that a member cannot reasonably be expected to meet the standard identification requirements, the guidance in Part I, paragraphs 5.3.113–5.3.114 should be followed. Where the alternative evidence set out in sector 1: *Retail banking*, Annex 1–I cannot be applied, a letter or statement from an appropriate person[6] who knows the individual, that indicates that the person is who he says he is, can be accepted as evidence of identity.

---

6   Someone in a position of responsibility, who knows, and is known by, the member, and may reasonably confirm the member's identity. It is not possible to give a definitive list of such persons, but the following may assist in determining who is appropriate in any particular case: the Passport Office has published a list of those who may countersign a passport: see www.ukpa.gov.uk/passport_countersign.asp; and others might include members of a local authority, staff of a higher or further education establishment, or a hostel manager.

4.20   Where a credit union has concluded that it should treat a member as financially excluded, a record should be kept of the reasons for doing so.

Employee credit unions

4.21   Roughly ten percent of British credit unions are employee credit unions, but they represent a significant proportion of the overall assets and membership of the movement. All members of employee credit unions share the common bond of being associated with one particular employer or employer group, which must be large enough to provide enough members to sustain a viable credit union. The most common examples of employee credit unions are local authority, police and transport credit unions.

4.22   Employee credit unions should also have their own standard identity verification requirements to ensure that the member is indeed an employee (eg, wage slip, employee identity card, other documented knowledge that the credit union has) and have therefore undertaken the appropriate identity checks. It should be noted that these checks are for the purpose of satisfying the common bond qualification for membership, as opposed to being for AML/CTF purposes.

4.23   To satisfy the requirements of AML/CTF legislation, additional identity verification checks should be sought, as described in paragraphs 4.15–4.17 of this chapter.

4.24   Employee credit unions whose common bond extends to family members of employees should seek the standard verification information from each family member. In these circumstances credit unions should follow the guidance in Part I, paragraphs 5.3.68–5.3.114.

Live or work credit unions

4.25   In addition to the employee common bond, increasing numbers of credit unions are adopting the common bond 'live or work'. This means that the qualification for membership of a live or work credit union extends both to residents and to those in regular employment within a particular locality.

4.26   Live or work credit unions that extend their services to employees of local employers will, however, have similar AML/CTF issues to credit unions linked to just one sponsoring employer so should refer to paragraphs 4.21–4.24 above.

Credit union activity in schools

4.27   Many credit unions have established links with their local schools. For many credit unions, establishing partnerships with local schools is a key part of their long-term development strategy. Under a risk-based approach in terms of membership profile and level of activity undertaken by junior savers, credit unions can reasonably assume that children saving in a savings club set up through a school present a lower risk of the credit union being used for money laundering purposes. **Credit Unions must, however, monitor the junior accounts, inter alia to ensure that adults are not laundering through the account.**

4.28   Where any potential member cannot reasonably be expected to produce detailed evidence of identity, it should not be a consequence that they are denied access to financial services. If a credit union decides that a particular child cannot reasonably be expected to produce such evidence, the reasons for adopting the 'financial exclusion' approach should be clearly documented. In relation to a schoolchild, a credit union should follow the guidance in Part I, paragraphs 5.3.107 and 5.3.109. In cases where standard identification evidence is not available, it may accept a letter or statement from an appropriate person as evidence of identity. In such cases, a letter from the school should include the date of birth and permanent address of the pupil on the school's letter headed paper to complete standard account opening procedures.

4.29   In cases where there is an adult signatory to the account and the adult has not previously been identified to the relevant standards because they do not already have an established relationship with the credit union, the identity of that adult must be verified, in addition to the identity of the child, see Part I, paragraph 5.3.109.

Junior Savers

4.30   In addition to offering a credit union service to minors through schools' clubs, many credit unions offer children a savings facility direct with the credit union. In such cases, credit unions should seek identification evidence as set out in Part I, paragraphs 5.3.107–5.3.109. Where standard identification cannot be produced for the child, other evidence such as a letter from the school which includes the date of birth and permanent address of the pupil on the school's letter headed paper, should be sought to complete standard account opening procedures.

4.31   Often, the junior account will be established by a family member or guardian. In cases where the adult opening the account has not previously been identified to the relevant standards because they do not already have an established relationship with the credit union, the identity of that adult must be verified, in addition to the identity of the child, see Part I, paragraph 5.3.109.

Enhanced due diligence

4.32   There will be certain occasions when enhanced due diligence will be required, for example:
* when there is no face-to-face contact with the customer
* where the customer is a PEP
* when the person is involved in a business that is considered to present a higher risk of money laundering; examples of high risk businesses can be found at www.jmlsg.co.uk and paragraphs 1.35–1.37 of sector 1: Retail banking

Additional customer information

4.33   Credit unions will need to hold sufficient information about the circumstances of members in order to monitor their activity and transactions. Therefore 'Knowing Your Customer' is about building a relationship with the membership and knowing when to ask the appropriate questions at the appropriate time. Reasonable enquiries of a member, conducted in a tactful manner, regarding the background to a transaction or activity that is inconsistent with the normal pattern of activity is prudent practice, forms an integral part of knowing the customer and monitoring, and should not give rise to tipping off. Although not a prescriptive list, examples of when additional customer information is needed include: a change in circumstances (name, address, employer), a lump sum payment or a change in transaction behaviour. Credit unions may detect significant changes in circumstances when for example, carrying out a loan application, which may require the credit union to seek further information, and to update member profiles which are used as the basis of monitoring customer transactions.

4.34   Credit unions must also obtain information about the nature and purpose of the relationship with the member. In the majority of cases, this may be obvious from the service provided, but the credit union may also be providing loans to sole traders for business purposes and information on such relationships must be obtained.

4.35   The extent of information sought and of the monitoring carried out in respect of any particular member will depend on the money laundering and terrorist financing risk that they present to the credit union. Credit unions should also have regard to the guidance in Part I, section 5.5.

Monitoring customer activity

4.36   As mentioned in paragraphs 4.8–4.9, credit unions must establish a process for monitoring member transactions and activities which will highlight unusual transactions and those which need further investigation. It is important that appropriate account is taken of the frequency, volume and size of transactions. Although not a prescriptive list, an example of a simple approach for credit unions that deal mainly in small sum transactions may be: to investigate deposits over a certain amount, frequency of members' deposits and members whose deposits may appear erratic. However, for larger credit unions that have more complex operational structures, a more sophisticated approach may be needed, eg, asking who is making deposits in relation to a junior account.

4.37   The key elements to monitoring are having up-to-date customer information, on the basis of which it will be possible to spot the unusual, and to ask pertinent questions to elicit the reasons for unusual transactions.

4.38   Also key to a successful monitoring process is staff and volunteer alertness (see Part I, Chapter 7).

4.39   Credit unions must be aware that unusual does not always mean suspicious and therefore should not be the routine basis for making reports to SOCA. Identifying what is unusual is only the starting point – firms need to assess whether what is unusual gives rise to suspicion and report accordingly.

Reporting

4.40   General guidance on reporting is given in Part I, Chapter 6. All staff and volunteers need to know the identity of the nominated officer, so that they know to whom to report suspicious activity.

4.41   It is up to the nominated officer to investigate whether or not to report to SOCA. If he decides not to make a report to SOCA, the reasons for not doing so should be clearly documented and retained with the internal suspicion report. If the nominated officer decides to make a report to SOCA, this must be done promptly and as soon as is practicable. When a report is made to SOCA, the basis for the knowledge or suspicion of money laundering should be set out in a clear and concise manner (see Part I, paragraphs 6.37–6.38) with relevant identifying features for the main or associated subjects. Staff should also familiarise themselves with the consent provisions in POCA and the Terrorism Act (see Part I paragraphs 6.48–6.57) and act accordingly. Furthermore if, under the Data Protection Act a member submits a subject access request, then the credit union should contact SOCA for advice (see Part I, paragraphs 6.846.93).

Training

4.42   General guidance on staff awareness, training and alertness is given in Part I, Chapter 7. In particular:

- Staff must be made aware of the risks of money laundering and terrorist financing, the relevant legislation and their obligations under that legislation
- Staff must be made aware of the identity and responsibilities of the firm's nominated officer and MLRO
- Staff must be trained in the firm's procedures and in how to recognise and deal with potential money laundering or terrorist financing transactions
- Staff training must be given at regular intervals, and details recorded
- The senior manager or director with ultimate responsibility for AML systems and controls, as required by CRED 4.3.37H G is responsible for ensuring that adequate arrangements for training are in place
- The MLRO is responsible for oversight of the firm's compliance with its requirements in respect of staff training, including ensuring that adequate arrangements for awareness and training of employees are in place.

4.43   There is no single solution when determining how to deliver training; on-line learning can provide an adequate solution but for some staff and volunteers an on-line approach may not be suitable. Procedure manuals can raise staff and volunteer awareness but their main purpose is for reference. More direct forms of training will usually be more appropriate.

4.44   Whatever the approach to training, it is vital to establish comprehensive records to monitor who has been trained, when they received the training, the nature of training given and its effectiveness.

4.45   AML/CTF training and training on the responsibility of staff under the firm's own AML/CTF arrangements must be provided to all relevant employees at appropriate intervals.

Internal controls and record-keeping

4.46   General guidance on internal controls is given in Part I, Chapter 2, and on record-keeping in Part I, Chapter 8. In particular, credit unions must retain:

- copies of, or references to, the evidence they obtained of a customer's identity, until five years after the end of the customer relationship
- details of customer transactions for five years from the date of the transaction
- details of actions taken in respect of internal and external suspicion reports
- details of information considered by the nominated officer in respect of an internal report where no external report is made

4.47   Retention of records can be:

- by way of original documents
- photocopies of original documents, taken by credit union staff
- on microfilm
- in scanned form
- in computerised or electronic form

4.48   In circumstances where it is not reasonably practicable for a credit union to copy documents used to verify identity, in any format described above, (e g when at a collection point) a credit union will need to keep a record of the type of document, its number, date and place of issue, as proof of identity so that, if necessary, the document may be re-obtained from its source of issue.

4.49   In relation to internal suspicion reports, the following should be recorded:

- all suspicions reported to the nominated officer
- any written reports by the nominated officer, which should include full details of the customer who is the subject of concern and as full a statement as possible
- all internal enquiries made in relation to the report

[7027]

5: WEALTH MANAGEMENT

Note: This sectoral guidance is incomplete on its own. It must be read in conjunction with the main guidance set out in Part I of the Guidance.

Overview of the sector

5.1   Wealth management is the provision of banking and investment services in a closely managed relationship to high net worth clients. Such services will include bespoke product features tailored to a client's particular needs and may be provided from a wide range of facilities available to the client including:

- current account banking
- high value transactions
- use of sophisticated products
- non-standard investment solutions
- business conducted across different jurisdictions
- off-shore and overseas companies, trusts or personal investment vehicles

What are the money laundering risks in wealth management?

Inherent risks

5.2   Money launderers are attracted by the availability of complex products and services that operate internationally within a reputable and secure wealth management environment that is familiar with high value transactions. The following factors contribute to the increased vulnerability of wealth management:

- Wealthy and powerful clients – Such clients may be reluctant or unwilling to provide adequate documents, details and explanations. The situation is exacerbated where the client enjoys a high public profile, and where they wield political or economic power or influence.
- Multiple and complex accounts – Clients often have many accounts in more than one jurisdiction, either within the same firm or group, or with different firms.
- Cultures of confidentiality – Wealth management clients often seek reassurance that their need for confidential business will be conducted discreetly.
- Concealment – The misuse of services such as offshore trusts and the availability of structures such as shell companies helps to maintain an element of secrecy about beneficial ownership of funds.
- Countries with statutory banking secrecy – There is a culture of secrecy in certain jurisdictions, supported by local legislation, in which wealth management is available.
- Movement of funds – The transmission of funds and other assets by private clients often involve high value transactions, requiring rapid transfers to be made across accounts in different countries and regions of the world.

- The use of concentration accounts – ie multi-client pooled/omnibus type accounts – used to collect together funds from a variety of sources for onward transmission is seen as a potential major risk.
- Credit – The extension of credit to clients who use their assets as collateral also poses a money laundering risk unless the lender is satisfied that the origin and source of the underlying asset is legitimate.
- Commercial activity conducted through a personal account so as to deceive the banker.

Secured loans

5.3   Secured loans, where collateral is held in one jurisdiction and the loan is made from another, are common in wealth management. Such arrangements serve a legitimate business function and make possible certain transactions which may otherwise be unacceptable due to credit risk. Collateralised loans raise different legal issues depending on the jurisdiction of the loan. Foremost among these issues are the propriety and implications of guarantees from third parties (whose identity may not always be revealed) and other undisclosed security arrangements.

Assessment of the risk

5.4   The role of the relationship manager is particularly important to the firm in managing and controlling the money laundering or terrorist financing risks it faces. Relationship managers develop strong personal relationships with their clients, which can facilitate the collection of the necessary information to know the client's business, including knowledge of the source(s) of the client's wealth. Relationship managers must, however, at all times be alert to the risk of becoming too close to the client and to guard against the risks from:
- a false sense of security
- conflicts of interest – including the temptation to put the client's interests above that of the firm
- undue influence by others

5.5   As in all firms, relationship managers and other client-facing staff should be alert to any developing risk to their personal safety. Criminals seeking to gain advantage from using a firm's credibility are known to compromise, and sometimes threaten, bankers. Firms should have:
- suitable internal procedures requiring staff to report when they believe that they have been menaced
- a policy for reporting incidents to the police

Cash transactions

5.6   Relationship managers should neither accept cash nor deliver cash, nor other stores of value such as travellers' cheques, to anyone. A client should be required to deposit or withdraw cash at the counter of a recognised bank that is at least subject to local supervision. In extremely rare circumstances where this is not possible, there should be a documented policy and procedures in relation to the handling of cash by relationship managers. Such transactions should be reported upwards within the firm's UK structure and consideration given to informing the firm's nominated officer.

Customer due diligence

5.7   Within the firm, the relationship manager will often be aware of any special sensitivity that may genuinely relate to the client's legitimate commercial activities or need for personal security.

5.8   To control any risk of money laundering, the client's justification for using financial institutions, businesses or addresses in different jurisdictions should always be subject to scrutiny before undertaking a transaction. To be able to view and manage the risk of money laundering across the whole of the firm or group's business connections, they should consider nominating a manager to lead such client relationships. The lead relationship manager should have access to sufficient information to enable them to:
- know and understand the business structure
- determine whether or not there is cause to suspect the presence of money laundering

5.9   In common with the provision of other financial products or services in such countries, care should be exercised to ensure that use of banking and investment services does not lead to levels of obscurity that assists those with criminal intentions. At all times care should be exercised to ensure requests for confidentiality do not lead to unwarranted levels of secrecy that suit those with criminal intentions.

5.10   Particular care should be taken where the lender is relying upon the guarantee of a third party not otherwise in a direct business relationship, and where the collateral is not in the same jurisdiction as the firm.

5.11   Ordinarily, the level of diligence carried out in wealth management will be higher than that needed for normal retail banking (see sector 1: *Retail banking*) or investment management (see sector 9: *Discretionary and advisory investment management*) purposes. A client's needs will often entail the use of complex products and fiduciary services, sometimes involving more than one jurisdiction, including trusts, private investment vehicles and other company structures. Where such legal vehicles and structures are used, it is important to establish that their use is genuine and to be able to follow any chain of title to know who the beneficial owner is.

5.12   In addition to the standard identification requirement in Part I, paragraphs 5.3.68–5.3.78, any wealth management service should have particular regard to the following:

- As a minimum requirement to counter the perceived and actual risks, the firm, and those acting in support of the business, must exercise a greater degree of diligence throughout the relationship which will be beyond that needed for normal retail banking purposes. The firm must endeavour to understand the nature of the client's business and consider whether it is consistent and reasonable, including:
  - the origins of the client's wealth
  - the nature and type of transactions
  - the client's business and legitimate business structures
  - for corporate and trust structures – the chain of title, authority or control leading to the ultimate beneficial owner, settler and beneficiaries, if relevant and known
  - the use made by the client of products and services
  - the nature and level of business to be expected over the account
- The firm must be satisfied that a client's use of complex business structures and/or the use of trust and private investment vehicles, has a genuine and legitimate purpose.

5.13   For some clients, fame is generally recognised as having a long continuing existence, and their photographs are commonly published in the public domain. In such cases, so long as the relationship manager has met the client face-to-face, firms may wish to introduce a controlled procedure, as part of the verification process, whereby the relationship manager may certify a published photograph as having a true likeness of the client. The certified photograph should be retained as a formal record of personal identification.

Recording of visits to the client's premises

5.14   As mentioned in Part I, paragraph 5.3.76, visiting clients can be an important part of the overall customer due diligence process. In wealth management, relationship managers should generally visit their clients at their place of business in order to substantiate the type and volume of their business activity and income, or at their home if the business factor is not so relevant. The relationship manager who undertakes the visit should make a record by documenting:

- the date and time of the visit
- the address or addresses visited
- a summary of both the discussions and assessments
- any commitments or agreements
- any changes in client profile
- the expectations for product usage, volumes and turnover going forward
- any international dimension to the client's activities and the risk status of the jurisdictions involved

and updating the client profile where appropriate.

References

5.15   Reputational searches should be undertaken as a normal part of customer due diligence, which will include checks for negative information. It will sometimes be appropriate to obtain a satisfactory written reference or references from a reputable source or sources before opening an account for a client. The relationship manager should document the nature and length of the relationship between the referee and the client. References should only be accepted when they are:

- received direct – not from the client or third parties
- specifically addressed only to the firm
- verified as issued by the referee

Approval of new relationship

5.16   All new wealth management clients should be subject to independent review, and appropriate management approval and sign off.

Review of client information

5.17   The firm's policies and procedures should require that the information held relating to wealth management clients be reviewed and updated on a periodic basis, or when a material change occurs in the risk profile of a client. Periodic review of particular clients will be made on a risk-based basis. Wealth management firms should consider reviewing their business with higher risk clients on at least an annual basis.

Enhanced due diligence (EDD)

5.18 Greater diligence should be exercised when considering business with customers who live in high-risk countries, or in unstable regions of the world known for the presence of corrupt practices. Firms must comply with the EDD requirements in the ML Regulations in respect of clients not physically present for identification purposes, and those who are PEPs, see Part I, section 5.5 and paragraph 5.21 below.

5.19 Those categories of client that pose a greater money laundering or terrorist financing risk should be subject to a more stringent approval process. Their acceptance as a client or the significant development of new business with an existing higher risk client should be subject to an appropriate approval process. That process might involve the highest level of business management for the wealth management operation in the jurisdiction. Firms should consider restricting any necessary delegation of that role to a recognised risk control function.

5.20 In the case of higher risk relationships, appropriate senior personnel should undertake an independent review of the conduct and development of the relationship, at least annually.

Politically exposed persons (PEPs)

5.21 Firms offering a wealth management service should have particular regard to the guidance in relation to PEPs set out in Part I, paragraphs 5.5.18 to 5.5.29. Relationship managers should endeavour to keep up-to-date with any reports in the public domain that may relate to their client, the risk profile or the business relationship.

Other clients

5.22 Firms should consider conducting similar searches against the names of their prospects for business, including those that may only be known within the business development or marketing functions; and where practicable, third party beneficiaries to whom clients make payments.

5.23 It is recommended that in addition to the categories of client regarded as PEPs, clients connected with such businesses as gambling, armaments or money service businesses should be considered for treatment as high risk. In determining whether to do business with such high risk interests, firms should carefully weigh their knowledge of the countries with which the client is associated. Particular consideration should be given to the extent to which their AML/CTF legislation is comparable to the provisions of the relevant EU Directive.

Monitoring

5.24 General guidance on monitoring customer transactions and activity is given in Part I, section 5.7. In view of the risk associated with wealth management activities, it is appropriate that there should be a heightened ongoing review of account activity and the use made of the firm's other products. In the case of wealth management, the triggers for alerts may be set at a different level, to reflect the appropriate level of control that is to be exercised.

5.25 An illustrative (but not exhaustive) list of matters firms should carefully examine includes:
- substantial initial deposits proposed by prospects for business;
- transactional activity – frequent or substantial activity that is inconsistent with the normal levels associated with the product or purpose – unusual patterns of activity may be evidence of money laundering;
- wire transfers – frequent or substantial transfers not in keeping with either normal usage for the product or the verified expectations of the client's business requirement;
- cash or other transactions – which are not in line with either the normal usage for the product or the verified expectations of the client's business requirement;
- significant increase or change in activity – increased values, volumes or new products required, which do not align with the firm's profile of the client;
- accounts of financial institutions not subject to supervision in an equivalent jurisdiction; and
- any activity not commensurate with the nature of the business.

and firms should remain mindful of the possibility of clients using their legitimate resources to finance terrorism.

5.26 Incoming and outgoing transfers, whether of cash, investments or other assets, should be reviewed by the relationship manager or their delegate as soon as is reasonably practicable after the transaction. To ensure the process is efficient, firms will wish to set a threshold figure that is in line with the business risk profile.

5.27 In view of the nature of wealth management services generally, it is appropriate that additional controls and procedures should be applied both to the acceptance and ongoing maintenance of wealth management relationships. These additional controls will also be appropriate when considering the further development of the business relationship with, say, the introduction of new funds or assets.

6: FINANCIAL ADVISERS

Note: This sectoral guidance is incomplete on its own. It must be read in conjunction with the main guidance set out in Part I of the Guidance.

Overview of the sector

6.1   Financial advisers give customers advice on their investment needs (typically for long-term savings and pension provision) and selecting the appropriate products.

Typical customers

6.2   The typical customers of financial advisers are personal clients (including high net worth individuals), trusts, companies. Some firms also advise charities.

6.3   Financial advisers, whether they only give advice or whether they act on behalf of their customers in dealing with a product provider, are subject to the full provisions of UK law and regulation relating to the prevention of money laundering and terrorist financing. The guidance in Part I therefore applies to financial advisers.

6.4   Other sectoral guidance in Part II that is relevant to financial advisers includes:
- Sector 7: *Life assurance, and life-related pensions and investment products*
- Sector 8: *Non-life providers of investment fund products*
- Sector 9: *Discretionary and advisory investment management*

6.5   Generally, financial advisers do not hold permission from the FSA to handle client money, so in practice there is unlikely to be any involvement in the placement stage of money laundering. There is, however, considerable scope for financial advisers being drawn in to the layering and integration stages.

6.6   Whether or not financial advisers hold permission to handle client money, they should consider whether their relationship with their customers means that the guidance in sector 5: *Wealth management* or in sector 9: *Discretionary and advisory investment management* applies more directly to them.

What are the money laundering or terrorist financing risks for financial advisers?

6.7   The vast majority of financial advice business is conducted on a face-to-face basis, and investors generally have easy access to the funds involved.

6.8   Some criminals may seek to use financial advisers as the first step in integrating their criminal property into the financial system.

6.9   The offences of money laundering or terrorist financing include aiding and abetting those trying to carry out these primary offences, which include tax evasion. This is the main risk generally faced by financial advisers. In carrying out its assessment of the risk the firm faces of becoming involved in money laundering or terrorist financing, or entering into an arrangement to launder criminal property, the firm must consider the risk related to the product, as well as the risk related to the client.

6.10   Clearly, the risk of being involved in money laundering or terrorist financing will increase when dealing with certain types of customer, such as offshore trusts/companies, politically exposed persons and customers from higher risk or non-FATF countries or jurisdictions, and may also be affected by other service features that a firm offers to its customers. Customer activity, too, such as purchases in secondary markets – for example, traded endowments – can carry a higher money laundering risk.

Customer due diligence

6.11   Having sufficient information about customers and beneficial owners, and using that information, underpins all other anti-money laundering procedures. A firm must not enter into a business relationship until the identity of all the relevant parties to the relationship has been verified in accordance with the guidance in Part I, Chapter 5.

6.12   When a full advice service is offered, the process will involve information gathering, an understanding of the customer's needs and priorities and anticipated funds available for investment. The amount of information held about a client will build over time, as there will often be ongoing contact with the customer in order to review their circumstances. However, the level of information held about a customer will be limited if business is transacted on an execution-only or direct offer basis and financial advisers should have an increased regard to the monitoring of business undertaken in this way.

Whose identity should be verified?

6.13   Guidance on who the customer is, whose identity has to be verified, is given in Part I, paragraphs 5.3.2 to 5.3.7. Guidance on who the beneficial owner is, whose identity also has to be verified, is given in Part I, paragraphs 5.3.8–5.3.13.

Private individuals

6.14   Guidance on verifying the identity of private individuals is given in Part I, paragraphs 5.3.68 to 5.3.6114. Guidance on circumstances where it may be possible to use the source of funds as evidence of identity is given in Part I, paragraphs 5.3.92 to 5.3.96.

6.15   The firm's risk assessment procedures will take account of the money laundering and terrorist financing risks identified in the sectors in which the relevant product provider operates (see paragraph 6.4). Customers may be assessed as presenting a higher risk of money laundering, whether because he is identified as being a PEP, or because of some other aspect of the nature of the customer, or his business, or its location, or because of the product features available. In such cases, the firm must conduct enhanced due diligence measures (see Part I, section 5.5) and will need to decide whether it should require additional identity information to be provided, and/or whether to verify additional aspects of identity. For such customers, the financial adviser will need to consider whether to require additional customer information (see Part I, section 5.5) and/or whether to institute enhanced monitoring (see Part I, section 5.7).

6.16   Some persons cannot reasonably be expected to produce the standard evidence of identity. This would include persons such as individuals in care homes, who may not have a passport or driving licence, and whose name does not appear on utility bills. Where customers cannot produce the standard identification evidence, reference should be made to the guidance set out in sector 1: *Retail banking*, Annex 1I.

Non-personal customers

6.17   Guidance on verifying the identity of non personal customers is given in Part I, paragraphs 5.3.115 to 5.3.248. Categories of non personal customers that are likely to be of particular relevance to financial advisers are:

- Private companies (paragraphs 5.3.130 to 5.3.138)
- Pension schemes (paragraphs 5.3.151 to 5.3.159)
- Charities, church bodies and places of worship (paragraphs 5.3.160 to 5.3.179)
- Other trusts, foundations and similar entities (paragraphs 5.3.180 to 5.3.202)
- Partnerships and unincorporated businesses (paragraphs 5.3.212 to 5.3.225)
- Clubs and societies (paragraphs 5.3.226 to 5.3.234)

Non face-to-face

6.18   Non face-to-face transactions can present a greater money laundering or terrorist financing risk than those conducted in person because it is inherently more difficult to be sure that the person with whom the firm is dealing is the person that they claim to be. Enhanced due diligence is required in these circumstances, and verification of identity undertaken on a non face-to-face basis should be carried out in accordance with the guidance given in Part I, paragraphs 5.5.10 to 5.5.17.

Using verification work carried out by another firm

6.19   The responsibility to be satisfied that a customer's identity has been verified rests with the firm entering into the transaction with the customer. However, where two or more financial services firms have an obligation to verify the identity of the same customer in respect of the same transaction, in certain circumstances one firm may use the verification carried out by another firm. Guidance on the circumstances in which such an approach is possible, and on the use of pro-forma confirmation documentation, is given in Part I, section 5.6.

6.20   Financial advisers should bear in mind that they are often the party which is carrying out the initial customer identification and verification process. As such, it is they who will be asked to confirm to a product or service provider that such verification has been carried out. Although not directly related to the sort of work that financial advisers typically carry out, the significance of issuing such confirmations is highlighted by the actions of the FSA in 2005 in fining a bond broker who gave such conformation when he was aware that he had not, in fact, carried out appropriate customer due diligence.

6.21   Product providers often rely on customer verification procedures carried out by financial advisers, which underlines the importance of their systems and procedures for risk assessment being effective.

6.22   Where the financial adviser has carried out verification of identity on behalf of a product provider, the adviser must be able to make available to the product provider, on request, copies of the identification and verification data and other relevant documents on the identity of the customer or beneficial owner obtained by the adviser (see paragraph 6.29). This obligation extends throughout the period for which the financial adviser has an obligation under the ML Regulations to retain these data, documents or other information.

Suspicious transactions

6.23   Financial advisers are ideally placed to identify activity which is abnormal, or which does not make economic sense, in relation to a person's circumstances. Obtaining details on the source of a customer's wealth, and identifying the purpose of an activity are all mandatory parts of the normal advice process. Financial advisers do not have to handle the transaction personally to have an obligation to report it.

6.24   Guidance on monitoring customer transactions and activity is set out in Part I, section 5.7. Guidance on internal reporting, reviewing internal reports and making appropriate external reports to SOCA, is given in Part I, Chapter 6. This includes guidance on when a firm needs to seek consent to proceed with a suspicious transaction, with which financial advisers need to be familiar.

Staff awareness and training

6.25   One of the most important controls over the prevention and detection of money laundering is to have staff who are alert to the risks of money laundering/terrorist financing and well trained in the identification of unusual activities or transactions, which may prove to be suspicious.

6.26   Guidance on staff awareness, training and alertness is given in Part I, Chapter 7. This guidance includes suggested questions that staff should be asking themselves, and circumstances that should cause them to ask further questions about particular transactions or customer activity.

Record-keeping

6.27   General guidance on record-keeping is given in Part I, Chapter 8. The position of financial advisers means that some of the guidance in Part I, Chapter 8 cannot easily be applied. Generally, financial advisers will verify customers' identities by means of documentation, as they will often not have access to electronic sources of data. Where documents are used, it is preferable to make and retain copies.

6.28   In circumstances where a financial adviser is unable to take a record of documents used to verify identity, (eg, when at a customer's home) he/she should keep a record of the type of document, its number, date and place of issue, as proof of identity, so that, if necessary, the document may be re-obtained from its source of issue.

6.29   Financial advisers may, from time to time, be asked by product providers for copies of the identification evidence that they took in relation to a particular customer. Financial advisers' record-keeping arrangements must therefore be capable of enabling such material to be provided in a timely manner (see Part I, paragraph 5.6.18).

6.30   Documents relating to customer identity must be retained for five years from the date the business relationship with the customer has ended (see Part I, paragraph 8.11).

[7029]

7: LIFE ASSURANCE, AND LIFE-RELATED PROTECTION, PENSION AND INVESTMENT PRODUCTS

Note: This sectoral guidance is incomplete on its own. It must be read in conjunction with the main guidance set out in Part I of the Guidance.

7.1   This sectoral guidance helps firms to interpret how the risk-based approach set out in Part I, Chapter 4 and the customer due diligence requirements set out in Part I, Chapter 5 might be applied to the specific circumstances of the protection, savings and pensions businesses of the insurance sector.

What are the money laundering risks in the protection, pension and investment business of the insurance sector?

7.2   The insurance sector provides a diverse range of products to customers via an equally diverse range of distribution channels. It has been noted that the majority of insurance products do not deliver sufficient functionality and flexibility to be the first choice of vehicle for the money launderer. However, it is also recognised that although the nature of these products helps reduce the money laundering risk, the funds used to purchase them could be the proceeds of crime. Where there are doubts as to the legitimacy of the transaction, verification of the customer's identity remains important as part of the investigation into the transaction and the customer.

The key drivers of risk

7.3   Part I, Chapter 4 states that any risk-based approach to AML needs to start with the identification and assessment of the risk that has to be managed and identifies key elements (or drivers) of risk as follows:

(a)   The profile of the customer, including his geographical location and source of funds;

(b)   The delivery mechanism, or distribution channel, used to sell the product; and

(c)   The nature of the product being sold.

7.4 Based on the views of insurance firms, the majority of this guidance focuses on risks from a product-led perspective; however, there are circumstances in which a customer's profile may add to the product risk. This is particularly the case with regard to Politically Exposed Persons – see Part 1 (5.5.18 ff). A firm must ensure that their own risk-based approach is appropriate to the particular circumstances they face.

Politically Exposed Persons (PEP)

7.5 Part 1 (5.5.18 ff) sets out general provisions for identifying, establishing business with, and monitoring PEPs. This sectoral guidance sets out the fundamental risks and business practices that insurers may wish to consider when developing a risk-based procedure. These risks and business practices may change, and it is therefore important that insurers monitor these developments and adjust their procedures accordingly.

7.6 When developing a procedure for identifying PEPs, insurers should target those areas of business that are at the greatest risk of having customers who meet the PEP criteria.

7.7 Based on the experience of a number of insurers, the insurance sector has a very low exposure to PEPs. The majority of products sold by insurers also do not lend themselves to moving the proceeds of corruption. It is likely therefore that the numbers of customers meeting the high-risk criteria are very low and those that are identified as PEPs are lower still.

7.8 Firms may consider using criteria such as accounts with non-UK residents[7] and investment value to determine their risk based approach to PEP identification.

---

[7] For the purposes of this guidance, a non UK resident is a person defined as such for UK tax purposes.

7.9 It is expected that this risk-based procedure will make the volume checking of new customers unnecessary. However, adequate measures to check PEP status for those customers meeting the high risk criteria should be undertaken during the course of establishing the business relationship. If a PEP is identified at this stage, senior management approval is required for establishing a business relationship. In the case of identifying an existing customer as a PEP, senior management approval for continuing the business relationship must be obtained as soon as practicable upon identifying a PEP.

7.10 The identification of a customer as a PEP is not in itself cause for suspicion, but requires an enhanced level of due diligence in line with the guidance set out in Part I. In some cases, however, this enhanced due diligence may trigger suspicions that the client is attempting to store or launder the proceeds of corruption. In such cases, a SAR and consent request must be submitted to SOCA, following the guidance set out in Part 1, chapter 6.

Distribution Risk

7.11 The distribution channel for products may alter the risk profile. For insurers the main issues will be non face-to-face sales, such as online, postal *or* telephone sales. Part I, paragraphs 5.5.10ff outline the process for managing non face-to-face sales.

7.12 For business sold through agencies, such as IFAs, agency acceptance and ongoing management procedures may already meet the requirements set out in Part I, paragraphs 5.6.27 and 5.6.28. The MLRO should ensure that he is comfortable with the vetting processes undertaken by the firms distribution arm, for advisers, prior to the issue of and throughout the agency agreement. This should include the ability of the intermediary to provide copies of the underlying documents or data on request. The MLRO should be aware and satisfied with the level of monitoring of any material breeches/financial difficulties, which might call into question the agent's status as fit and proper.

7.13 Once a business relationship is established with an intermediary, the Confirmation of Verification of Identity is the record for the purpose of meeting the record keeping requirements and should be retained in accordance with the guidance provided in Part I, paragraphs 5.6.4ff. If, in the course of normal business, the intermediary's standards are called into question, the insurer should review its status as a provider of CVIs. For higher risk business, such as non-UK, the MLRO will need to be satisfied that the level of customer due diligence carried out by the third party is commensurate with the risk and may wish to request copies of the underlying evidence obtained by the intermediary.

Product Risk

7.14 The remainder of this sectoral guidance concentrates on product risk. This is because, in the insurance sector, the nature of the product being sold is usually the primary driver of the risk assessment. This is because of the very different nature of each category of products (protection, pensions and investments) and the fact that each product's features are defined and restricted; some will only pay out on a verifiable event such as death or illness, whilst others are accessible only after many years of contributions. As well as limiting the flexibility of these products as potential money laundering vehicles, the restrictions also enable firms to more readily profile the products for 'standard' (and conversely, 'non standard' or 'suspicious') use by customers.

7.15   A smaller number of products sold by firms in the insurance sector, including single premium investment bonds and certain pensions, do feature increased flexibility. This should be acknowledged in the application of the risk-based approach.

7.16   The following are features which may tend to increase the risk profile of a product:
  ● accept payments or receipts from third parties;
  ● accept very high value or unlimited value payments or large volumes of lower value payments;
  ● accept cash payments;
  ● accept frequent payments (outside of a normal regular premium policy);
  ● provide significant flexibility as to how investments are managed to be liquidated quickly (via surrender or partial withdrawal) and without prohibitive financial loss;
  ● be traded on a secondary market;
  ● be used as collateral for a loan and/or written in a discretionary or other increased risk trust.

7.17   The following are features that may tend to reduce the risk profile of a product:
  ● restricted capacity to accept third party receipts or make third party payments;
  ● have total investment curtailed at a low value due to either the law or a firm's policy;
  ● be relatively small value regular premium policies that can only be paid via direct debit;
  ● require the launderer to establish more than one relationship with a firm or another official body (eg certain types of pension products where the customer has to set up the product with the provider and to get HMRC approval and possibly appoint a Pensioner Trustee);
  ● have no investment value and only pay out against a certain event (death, illness etc) that can be checked by the product provider; and/or be linked to known legitimate employment.

7.18   The above are general lists of characteristics and are indicative only. Firms are strongly discouraged from using the lists in isolation for a mechanical 'tick box' style exercise. No characteristic acts of itself as a trigger. Not all products that may be used, say, as collateral for a loan, are automatically 'increased risk' by virtue of one characteristic alone. These general characteristics are given so that firms may weigh them up in overall balance for specific, branded products against their knowledge of the customer and their business.

7.19   Where apparent inconsistencies exist, firms are expected to exercise judgment accordingly. For example, certain personal pension products accept contributions from an employer. Third party payments are indicative of increased risk according to the above list. Nevertheless, the other features of those pension products (the restricted access to funds, the ability to take only a percentage of the fund as a lump sum on reaching retirement age, the involvement of HMRC) together carry more weight than the fact that contributions may be received from a third party. On balance, therefore, most personal pension products remain at the lower end of the risk range (see paragraph 7.14).

7.20   It is stressed that risk levels attributed to generic products in this document are intended to provide a starting point for a firm's risk assessment. Firms should consider whether their own, branded versions of those generic products possess features (such as a facility for top up payments or prohibition from receiving /making third party payments) which raise or lower the risk level. Equally, taking account of other risk drivers which might be identified (for example, the geographical location of a customer) may lead a firm to 'upgrade' or downgrade the overall risk level of a product from that indicated in this guidance. Part I, section 5.5 discusses risk drivers that are not specific to insurance products. Also, where a proposition for business involving a intermediate or reduced risk product is exceptional due to the size, source of funds or for another reason that suggests risk of fraud, money laundering or other usage of proceeds of crime additional due diligence will be appropriate perhaps via existing anti-fraud or other business risk management procedures.

Three overall risk levels

7.21   Firms in the insurance sector have carried out risk profiling of their products, applying the risk assessment criteria detailed above. This guidance draws on that work and establishes three overall levels of risk for insurance products in an AML context. The risk level determines what work a firm needs to carry out to meet industry standards. The three levels are:
  (a) reduced risk;
  (b) intermediate risk; or
  (c) increased risk.

7.22   When attributing an appropriate risk level, it is important to keep insurance risk in its wider context. As already noted, the majority of insurance products do not deliver sufficient functionality and flexibility to be the first choice of vehicle for the money launderer.

7.23   The products identified as 'increased risk' are therefore categorised as such only in the context of the insurance sector and are not intended to equate to references to 'high risk' in the wider context of the financial services industry as a whole.

7.24   The risk level attributed should always be based on the underlying product, irrespective of how it is described in the product provider's literature (ie, substance prevails over form). Firms should expect to be in a position to justify the basis on which the risk assessment criteria have been applied.

7.25   Risk management is a continuous process (as noted in Part I, paragraph 4.30). The risk assessment process is not a one-time exercise, and it must be revisited and reviewed on a regular basis.

7.26   Finally, there is a need to monitor the environment in which the firm operates. It should be recognised that success in preventing money laundering in one area will tend to drive criminals to migrate to another area, business, or product stream. Firms should be aware of current risk assessments of money laundering/terrorist financing risk in the insurance sector and take them into consideration, along with trends they experience themselves. If displacement is happening, or if customer behaviour is changing, the firm should be considering what it should be doing differently to take account of these changes. A firm's anti-fraud measures will also help it understand its customers and mitigate the money laundering risks.

I — Reduced risk level

7.27   Some groups of products, due to their inherent features, are extremely unlikely to be used for money laundering purposes. Some of these are recognised by the Money Laundering Regulations as attracting Simplified Due Diligence [See Regulation 9(8)]. Others, such as Compulsory Purchase Annuities are considered part of the pensions product. The table below shows these products in their respective categories of protection and pensions. The table also shows a number of the typical features (or restrictions) of each product, which serve to limit their potential as money laundering vehicles and so qualify them for this risk level.

7.28   Risk levels attributed to generic products in this section are intended for guidance only. Firms should consider whether their own branded versions of these generic products have features that either reduce or increase this indicative risk level.

Protection		Rationale
1 Term life assurance	*Typical features:* ● *Only pays out on death of assured* ● *No surrender value* ● *Small, regular premiums: additional payments by customer not possible* ● *Large premiums will normally require medical evidence* ● *No investment element* ● *Once term of policy is finished no payout and policy ceases*	*Timing of verification for pure protection products* *(Part I: 5.2.2)* *ML Regs 9 (4)*
2 Income protection products related to long-term illness	● *Only pays out on medical evidence and proof required as to loss of income* ● *No surrender value* ● *Small, regular premiums: additional payments by customer not possible*	*Timing of verification for pure protection products* *(Part I: 5.2.2)* *ML Regs 9 (4)*
3 Critical illness products relating to diagnosis of a specific critical illness	● *Only pays out on medical evidence* ● *No surrender value* ● *Small, regular premiums: additional payments by customer not possible*	*Timing of verification for pure protection products* *(Part I: 5.2.2)* *ML Regs 9 (4)*

Pensions		
4 Pension, superannuation or similar schemes which provide retirement benefits to employees,[8] where contributions are made by an employer or by way of deduction from an employee's wages and the scheme rules do not permit the assignment of a member's interest under the scheme.[9]	• *Long term savings vehicle* • *No surrender value* • *Product may not be used as collateral*	*Qualifies for Simplified Due Diligence (Part I 5.4.5)* *ML Regs 13 (7)(c)*
5 Pensions annuities, whether purchased with the company running the long-term savings vehicle or through an open market option.	• *Product already subject to due diligence and ongoing monitoring from the pension provider*	*Qualifies for Simplified Due Diligence.* *ML Regs 13(7)(b)*
6 Rebate Only Personal Pension ("RPP")	• *Only funded by National Insurance Contribution rebates payable as a result of an individual being contracted out of SERPS or S2P*	*Qualifies for Simplified Due Diligence*
7 Immediate Vesting Personal Pension ("IVPP"). Purchased with the transfer from another pension for the purpose of exercising an open market annuity option.	• *Product already subject to due diligence and ongoing monitoring from the pension provider*	*Qualifies for Simplified Due Diligence.* *ML Regs 13(7)(b)*

8   This would cover Contracted in and out Group Money Purchase Schemes, Final Salary Schemes, s32 Buy Out Plans from the latter types of schemes (if no further contributions are allowed) and Rebate-only schemes.

9   This qualification for Simplified Due Diligence is based on the Money Laundering Regulations 2007 13(7)(b), and is therefore not contingent on the monetary limits set out in 13(7)(a).

Customer due diligence

7.29   The recommended industry standard for protection products in this category is for due diligence on the customer and the beneficiary to be carried out at the point of claim. For most circumstances, the counter fraud checks at point of claim will satisfy these requirements.

7.30   For pensions annuities, it is sufficient for the insurer to satisfy itself that the pension scheme funding the annuity is HMRC-registered.

7.31   The recommended industry standard for reduced risk pension products is as follows:

Apply Simplified due diligence. Therefore *apart from monitoring,* customer due diligence does not apply to either the customer.

However, where a firm considers that there are features of the nature of the employer or the scheme that present an increased risk of money laundering, the following enhanced due diligence measures may be appropriate:

(a)   Obtaining details of the trustees and the entity (usually the employer), copy of the relevant trust deeds, and verifying the scheme's HMRC/PSO number (this can be done, for example, by sight of the scheme's HMRC approval letter).
   Note – HMRC does not now issue approval letters. However, on application and with the relevant authority, HMRC will provide documentary confirmation regarding the existence of the scheme.

(b)   Verifying the identity of the employer, or other corporate entity paying into the fund, in accordance with Part I, Chapter 5. Check that the firm is trading and appropriate to provide employees with a pension through a Companies House search or a visit to premises.

7.32   Where an insurer decides to apply simplified due diligence to a particular product or type of business, there is no requirement to identify or verify the identity of beneficial owners and/or controllers. Ongoing monitoring, however, is still required.

Monitoring

7.33   Companies must take a risk-based approach to monitoring reduced risk products. A company's normal anti-fraud controls should provide a suitably robust system of monitoring. The high annual limits for pensions in the post A-day tax regime provide greater scope for these products to receive large lump sum payments; a risk which may be mitigated by monitoring.

Frequently asked questions in relation to reduced risk

7.34

(i)   *What if, at the claim or payout stage, we identify that a third party has been paying into a reduced risk protection product?*
       Firms should, in the course of their normal commercial business, be considering whether any suspicious or unusual circumstances apply, and should act accordingly, and this might involve verifying the identity of the third party. However, in the absence of such concerns and where the firm does not consider that it has a client relationship with that person or that they are the beneficial owner (in which case the person's identity must be verified on a risk sensitive basis), there is no requirement to verify the identity of a third party payer for reduced risk products.

(ii)   *What if there is a change of beneficiary or if payout is made to a third party on one of these reduced risk products?*
       Unless the amount of money to be paid out is small and financial crime is not suspected, the identity of the third party must be verified before payout can take place. A letter of instruction from the original beneficiary will not normally suffice.

(ii)   *What if payments into exempt occupational pension schemes begin to be received from the employee rather than from the employer?*
       Firms should have adequate procedures and controls to identify where payments are not received directly from the employer but instead are received directly from the employee or another third party, whether by personal cheque or direct debit. Where such payments are received, and where the sums are considered material, standard identification and verification requirements set out in Part I, section 5.4 should be applied to the payer as soon as is reasonably practicable.

(iv)   *How does using the "source of funds" as evidence affect these reduced risk level products?*

(a)   For reduced risk level products, firms may accept personal cheques and other payment instruments drawn on a customer's account as satisfying the requirement to verify the customer's identity.

(b)   Where the funds are being paid into a reduced risk level product by direct debit from an account in the customer's name, there is no additional requirement on firms to correlate the name on the direct debit instruction with the account details at the outset of the relationship. It is usual practice for firms to undertake further due diligence on the customer's identity before any payment is made, as part of their fraud prevention procedures. If a firm's procedures do not provide for further customer due diligence to be undertaken before any payment is made, it should confirm at the outset of the relationship that the payments made by direct debit are made from an account in the name of the client, in accordance with Part I, paragraph 5.3.92.

II —Intermediate risk level

7.35   The intermediate risk level has been attributed to a group of products whose inherent features pose some risk of use for the purposes of money laundering or terrorist financing but they are significantly less than the risks posed by the "increased risk" grouping of insurance products. Some risk is acknowledged in the case, for example, of products with a facility for 'top up' payments, and therefore the standard level of due diligence is appropriate. The table below shows these products in their respective categories of protection, savings and pensions, together with some of their typical features or restrictions.

7.36   Risk levels attributed to generic products in this section are intended for guidance only. Firms should consider whether their own branded versions of these generic products have features that either reduce or increase this indicative risk level.

Protection	
1 Whole of Life	*Typical features:* ● *may accrue some surrender value* ● *benefits usually payable on death or diagnosis of terminal illness* ● *or, in some cases, critical illness of the policyholder* ● *partial surrenders are normally allowed within specified limits* ● *qualifying whole of life plans will comply with the rules applicable to qualifying life policies*
Savings	
2 Life assurance savings plan	*Typical features:* ● *Long term savings plan often for retirement* ● *Requires at least 5 years to gain positive return on investment* ● *Often unable to be surrendered in first or second year, with penalties in years three to five* ● *Additional 'top up' payments may be permitted* ● *Sum assured/premium relationship broadly complying with HMRC Qualifying Rules*
3 Endowments	● *Long term savings plan for a set term, were often linked to mortgages* ● *Sum assured/premium relationship broadly complying with HMRC Qualifying Rules* ● *Usually long term, 1025 years*
Pensions – corporate	
4 Group Personal Pension ("GPP")	*Typical features:* ● *Long term policy, usually up to 40 years* ● *No surrender value* ● *Pensions*
5 Group Stakeholder Plan	● *Long term policy, usually up to 40 years* ● *No surrender value* ● *HMRC registered scheme* ● *Annual and lifetime limits apply*
Pensions – individual	
6 Income Drawdown Flexible Pension Plan Phased Retirement Plan	*Typical features:* ● *Policies only open to individuals between the ages 55–75, and people who have already accrued by a pension fund* ● *The level of income which may be 'drawn down' is subject to limits set by the Government*
7 Free Standing Additional Voluntary Contribution Plan ("FSAVC")	● *Contributions cap set by pensions legislation and monitored by scheme administrator* ● *Transfers are only possible to another regulated entity*
8 Stakeholder Plan	● *Long term policy, usually up to 40 years* ● *No surrender value* ● *HMRC registered scheme* ● *Annual and lifetime limits apply*
9 Personal Pension Plan (not SIPP or SSAS)	● *Long term policy, usually up to 40 years* ● *No surrender value.* ● *HMRC registered scheme. Transfers are possible, but only to another registered scheme.* ● *Annual and lifetime limits apply.*
10 Immediate Vesting Personal Pension ("IVPP"). Purchased for purposes other than pursuing an open market annuity option.	● *Policies only open to individuals between the ages of 50 and 75.* ● *Purchase not based on a transfer from another pension scheme.* ● *Annuity usually purchased with one one-off payment.*

12 Purchased Life Annuity ("PLA") Hancock Annuity	• *No return of cash lump sum at end of the term selected or when customer dies* • *Once annuity purchased, purchaser cannot alter the arrangements or cash it in.*

7.37   As can be seen, the majority of intermediate risk level products are found in the pensions category, which reflects the restricted access to funds in a pension arrangement; pensions cannot be encashed and payments out are limited to tax free cash lump sums (for example, up to 25% of the fund for stakeholder and personal pensions) and regular income. In addition, some schemes will have an independent pensioner trustee who polices the running of the scheme on behalf of HMRC.

Customer due diligence

7.38   The recommended industry standard for intermediate risk products is as follows:

Verify the identity of the customer and/or the relevant parties, as per the guidance set out in Part I, Chapter 5, at the outset of the business relationship.

7.39   In accordance with Part I, companies must identify the beneficial owner, following the guidance in Part I, paragraphs 5.3.10 and 5.3.11.

Monitoring

7.40   Insurance companies should have a programme of monitoring which reflects the intermediate risk status of the products mentioned above. A firm should ensure its employees are adequately trained to identify and report unusual business activity to the firm's nominated officer. Within the post A-day pensions regime, highly atypical pensions contributions should attract higher levels of scrutiny from pensions providers.

Frequently asked questions in relation to intermediate risk

7.41

(i)   *What constitutes the outset of the business relationship?*
In most cases a business relationship begins with the acceptance of a fully completed application or proposal form.
However, the business relationship is only formally established after the end of the cooling off period. This is important for the timing of customer due diligence.

(ii)   *What about cancellation during the "cooling-off period" leading to a refund of premium paid? In some cases, the customer has not yet been verified by that time.*
Firms should seek to mitigate risk by refunding the premium to the customer by way of direct credit to the bank account from which the funds were paid or by an account payee crossed cheque in the customer's name. Firms should also consider whether the cancellation, taken into consideration with all other factors, raises suspicions about the transaction and if they do, consent must be sought from SOCA before paying out the sum. Where there is no such suspicion, firms should also verify the customer's identity before making a refund where the premium is 'large' (the sectoral guidance purposely does not set a lower limit, as materiality thresholds of individual firms will differ with the different features of the product) and/or circumstances appear unusual. (Note: this requirement also applies to increased risk business).

(iii)   *Who are the relevant parties whose identity should be verified for intermediate risk pensions? What information do we need to obtain in respect of these products to satisfy customer due diligence requirements?*
For intermediate risk pensions, practically speaking the identity of anyone who pays premiums should be verified. Specifically, the parties to be verified are:
(a)   the employer, if premiums are paid via the employer; and
(b)   the employee, where contributions are also, or only, paid direct by the employee.
Terms and conditions for intermediate risk pensions will usually dictate that third party payments into the policy are prohibited. However, it is possible that payments could be made to these policies by third parties and refusing them could disadvantage the policyholder. In circumstances where the firm is comfortable that the payments do not represent the movement of criminal funds – perhaps because the third party payment has been made by a close relative in the event of financial hardship being suffered by the policy holder or the payment being small and one off in nature – such payments can be accepted without further action. However, where such a payment was larger or more frequent in nature verification of the third party's identity would be appropriate. Where the third party payer is the customer's employer, the standard procedure for intermediate risk products would be to verify the identity of the company (but not the directors of that company).

(iv)   *How does using the "source of funds" as evidence affect these intermediate risk level products?*

(a)   For intermediate risk level products covered by this sectoral guidance, firms may accept personal cheques and other payment instruments drawn on a customer's account as satisfying the requirement to verify the customer's identity

(b)   Where the funds are being paid into an intermediate risk level product by direct debit from an account in the customer's name, there is no additional requirement on firms to correlate the name on the direct debit instruction with the account details at the outset of the relationship. It is usual practice for firms to undertake further due diligence on the customer's identity before any payment is made, as part of their fraud prevention procedures. If a firm's procedures do not provide for further customer due diligence to be undertaken before any payment is made, it should confirm at the outset of the relationship that the payments made by direct debit are made from an account in the name of the client, in accordance with Part I, paragraph 5.3.92.

(c)   Where use is made of source of funds as evidence, further due diligence measures are required if, subsequently, payments are made to or received from third parties. Further guidance on the use of the source of funds as evidence is given in Part I, paragraphs 5.3.92ff.

(*v*)   *What about verification on intermediate risk level pension transfers?*

(a)   The parties to be verified are:
1.   the employer, if premiums are paid via the employer; and
2.   the employee, where contributions are also, or only, paid direct by the employee; and
3.   any third party payers.
Unless the conditions in (c) below are satisfied.

(b)   The source of funds should be identified by obtaining:
1.   the previous pension provider's name; and
2.   the previous scheme or plan name, its reference or PSO number where relevant and the type of plan

(c)   There is no requirement to verify identity if **both** of the following conditions are satisfied:
1.   the transfer is **from**[10] an Occupational Pension Scheme which is not a Executive Pension Plan ("EPP") or a Small Self Administered Scheme ("SSAS"); **and**
2.   the transfer is **to** an Occupational Pension Scheme which is not an EPP or a SSAS **or** is **to** a S32 buy out plan with no additional funding.

(*vi*)   *What about traded endowments?*
The trading of an endowment policy increases exposure to money laundering. A policy can be bought and sold several times before a firm necessarily becomes aware of the reassignment, usually on payout. The insurer should verify the identity of the owner at payout usually in line with the standards set out in Part I, Chapter 5 though for small payments the firm may wish to take a view involving the risk and circumstances surrounding the transfer of the endowment policy and consider whether the use of the one off transaction exemption is appropriate. Part I, paragraph 5.3.7 provides further information on the use of this exemption. However, where there is evidence of significant or unusual trading activity, identity must be verified and further checks would also be appropriate. Where the transfer/s have taken place though a 'market maker' in traded endowments, and that firm is regulated by the FSA, reliance may be sought from the market maker in accordance with Part I, section 5.5.
In line with the requirements of Pensions Update 132, effective from 1 July 2002, firms should have adequate processes in place to confirm from the transferring scheme that the transfer is an approved exempt scheme.

(*vii*)   *What about life assurance policies written in trust for intermediate risk products?*
Life assurance policies are commonly written as simple life trusts, usually for inheritance tax planning reasons and not for the purpose of concealing the ultimate economic beneficiary of the policy. Therefore it is not appropriate to apply the increased identity requirements recommended in Part I for trust vehicles that are used for other purposes and firms need only identify the Settlor in line with the standards in this section. However, firms should ensure that they have in place adequate procedures to identify where a trust poses a higher money laundering or terrorist financing risk.

---

[10]   In line with the requirements of Pensions Update 132, effective from 1 July 2002, firms should place to confirm from the transferring scheme that the transfer is an approved exempt scheme.

III — Increased risk level

7.42   The increased risk level has been attributed to a group of products whose inherent features open the possibility to their being used for money laundering purposes. These products may have a facility for third party and/or 'top up' payments, or are perhaps negotiable, and therefore an enhanced level of due diligence by asking for more information is appropriate. It is to this risk level that the majority of a firm's AML resource will normally be directed. The table below shows these products in their respective categories of protection, savings and investments and pensions, together with the features.

7.43   Risk levels attributed to generic products in this section are intended for guidance only. Firms should consider whether their own branded versions of these generic products have features that either reduce or increase this indicative risk level. As stated before, the increased designation is used here to reflect the different average levels of investments in pensions, savings and other investment products experienced by firms and intermediaries across the sector.

Protection	
None	
Savings and investments	
1 Single premium investment bonds, including: — With profits — Guaranteed — Income — Investment — Offshore international bonds	*Typical features:* ● *Open ended investment* ● *Usually a 5 year recommended minimum investment term but can be surrendered earlier* ● *Additional 'top up' payments permitted by policy holder and by third parties* ● *May be segmented and individual segments may be assignable*
Pensions	
2 Executive Pension Plans ("EPPs") (excludes CIMPs & COMPs – see Minimal Risk section)	*Typical features:* ● *Contributions from company to tax exempt fund, normally* ● *Established by company directors for their benefit* ● *Single premium payments permitted*
3 Small Self Administered Schemes ("SSASs")	● *Small limited companies where directors are the main shareholders* ● *Flexibility of investment options* ● *Able to be used to raise loan capital* ● *Members can be bought out by other members of the scheme*
4 Self Invested Personal Pension ("SIPP")	● *Provides the fullest choice of allowable investments, including commercial property, ie, can be used to buy business premises. Administered by the beneficiary.*
5 Trustee Investment Pension Plan ("TIPP")	● *Open-ended investments, money can be accessed at any time* ● *Investment term can be anything upwards of 45 years* ● *Low early surrender penalties* ● *Can be linked to EPPs, SSASs or SIPPs*

7.44   As can be seen from the table above, the majority of increased risk level products are found in the investments category, which reflects the higher value premiums that can be paid into them, the relative ease of access to accumulated funds and the lack of involvement of external agencies such as the HMRC. The pension products are included because of their flexibility and the capacity for large sums of money to be invested though it is recognised that the involvement of HMRC does mitigate this risk to a degree.

Customer due diligence

7.45   The recommended industry standard for increased risk products is as follows:

   1.   Verify the identity of the customer, and/or the relevant parties, as per the standard procedures set out in Part I, Chapter 5, at the outset of the business relationship

   AND

   2.   Acquire prescribed information at the outset of the business relationship to satisfy the additional information requirements of Part I, Chapter 5:
      (a)   source of funds for the transaction (eg, a UK bank account in own name);
      (b)   employment and salary details; and
      (c)   source of wealth (eg, inheritance, divorce settlement, property sale)

7.46   An insurer must, where appropriate, verify the identity of the beneficial owner for increased risk products in line with the provisions in Part I, paragraphs 5.3.10 and 5.3.11.

Monitoring

7.47   Firms should undertake ongoing monitoring for patterns of unusual or suspicious activity to ensure that higher risk activity can be scrutinised. A firm should ensure its employees are adequately trained to identify and report unusual business activity to the firm's nominated officer.

Frequently asked questions in relation to increased risk:

7.48

(*i*)   *Who are the relevant parties for these products in terms of verification of identity?* The relevant parties are summarised in the table below:

	Relevant parties to be identified
Savings/investments	
1 Bonds	• *Policy holder or applicant* • *All payers if different to policy holder* • *All payees if different to policy holder*
Pensions	
2 EPPs	• *Employer/Trustee(s) who are beneficiaries or who may give instructions. Where trustees are: an FSA regulated financial services company then firms need obtain only the trustees' FSA regulatory number (and check it to FSA database if regulated trustee is unknown)* • *Third party payers (including the employee/policy holder)*
3 SSASs	• *Employer/Trustee(s) who are beneficiaries or who may give instruction and Pensioner Trustees who are beneficiaries or who may give instructions, to be ID verified if they do not appear on the HMRC Pensioner Trustee Approved List which is at www.hmrc.gov.uk/pensionschemes/* • *Third party payers (including the employee/policy holder)*
4 SIPPs	• *Policy holder* • *Employer (where paying premiums)* • *Third party payers*
5 TIPPs	• *Trustees (unless UK regulated financial services company trustees in which case, only a confirmation of FSA regulatory number is required)* • *Person giving payment instructions where a TIPP is held on behalf of a SSAS managed by another firm, unless that firm is regulated or payment can only be made to a regulated firm*

(*ii*)   *What constitutes appropriate ongoing monitoring and controls?*

(a)   Firms should, as part of normal commercial procedure, be considering for each product what 'trigger points' occur between customer entry and customer exit which might serve to increase that product's exposure to abuse. Examples of trigger points could be early surrender of a product ('early' in the context of a firm's normal business pattern for that product) or a change in payer and/or beneficiary. Appropriate transaction monitoring can then be set up.

(b)   This guidance purposely avoids setting monetary thresholds for monitoring (eg, all surrenders over a certain € amount) because materiality will differ significantly between firms. Firms should identify key indicators pertinent to their own business patterns, taking into account, for example, average premium income size per customer and average duration of the contract in force. With that qualification, suggested standard practice for each increased risk product is summarised in the table below.

	Suggested practice for monitoring and control
Savings/investments	
1 Bonds	• *Cancellation (ie, applications not proceeded with after funds received)* • *Early surrenders (ie within a certain time period, which is to be specified by individual firms) over a certain € threshold* • *Multiple partial surrenders, totalling up to (say) 75% of original investment, within the specified time period* • *Top up payments over a certain € threshold (dependent on individual firms' assessment of materiality) and frequency* • *Third party payments of any value* • *Non UK residents*
Pensions	
2 EPPs SSASs SIPPs TIPPs	• *Loans taken out using product as collateral* • *Top up payments when much larger than current holdings*

(*iii*)   Additional customer information is not always readily available when business has come through an intermediary. How should we go about obtaining it?

It is recognised that business transacted in a non face-to-face capacity, or through Financial Advisors, presents particular difficulties for insurance firms seeking to satisfy their additional information obligations under Part I, Chapter 5. Firms should, continue to obtain the limited information required via their own direct sales force (DSF) (where applicable) or, where business has come through an intermediary, should include a request for the information as part of their customer application or proposal form. Financial advisers and DSF should gather same level of data. It is suggested that the additional information required will be collected as part of an application form, and not part of the introduction certificate.

(*iv*)   Do we need to obtain supporting documentation for the additional information requested from a customer?

Verification is limited to identity only. In most circumstances, additional customer information may be taken at face value. However, if the additional information provided appears incongruous or contradictory, this should serve to raise suspicions about the transaction and firms are then expected to make further enquiries which may in some circumstances involve seeking documentary support to the .additional information.

(*v*)   What about increased risk level pension transfers?

(a)   No exemptions from identity verification requirements should be taken in respect of increased risk level pension transfers ie transfers from or to pension schemes listed as increased risk.

(b)   The source of funds should be identified by obtaining either via the transaction details or from the previous scheme holder or from, another trusted source:

1.   the previous pension provider's name; and

2.   the previous scheme or plan name, its reference or PSO number where relevant and the type of plan.

(*vi*)   How does using the "source of funds" as evidence affect these increased risk level products?

The source of funds should not be used as evidence of identity in respect of increased risk level products. However, where a firm's own, branded version of these generic products have features which reduce the indicative risk, it may conclude that its own product falls within the "intermediate" category of risk and follow the guidance given in respect of intermediate risk products.

(*vii*)   What about Power of Attorney arrangements for these products?

Where any party requiring verification is represented by an individual or firm appointed under a Power of Attorney, the identity of the Attorney should also be verified using the principles established in Part I, paragraphs 5.3.895.3.91.

(*viii*)   What about cancellation during the "cooling-off period" leading to a refund of premium paid? In some cases, the customer has not yet been verified by that time.

Firms should seek to mitigate risk by refunding the premium to the customer by way of direct credit to the bank account from which the funds were paid or by an account payee crossed cheque in the customer's name. Firms should also consider whether the cancellation, taken into consideration with all other factors, raises suspicions about the transaction and if they do, consent should be sought from SOCA before paying out the sum. Where there is no such suspicion, firms should also verify the customer's identity before making a refund where the premium is 'large' (the sectoral guidance purposely does not set a lower limit, as materiality thresholds of individual firms will differ with the different features of the product) and/or circumstances appear unusual.

[7030]

8: NON-LIFE PROVIDERS OF INVESTMENT FUND PRODUCTS

Note: This sectoral guidance is incomplete on its own. It must be read in conjunction with the main guidance set out in Part I of the Guidance.

Overview of the sector

8.1 The guidance contained within this section is directed at firms offering the following types of investment vehicle:

   (a) *Retail investment funds* – authorised unit trusts and open-ended investment companies (oeics).

   (b) *Other investment fund-based products/services* – which may comprise one, or a combination of, regular savings schemes (including those relating to investment trusts), regular withdrawal schemes, ISAs, personal pension schemes and fund supermarkets/ wrap platforms.

      Typical investors using retail funds and associated products/services vary depending upon the product, but include private individuals, regulated firms investing as principal (eg. life companies); other regulated firms (including nominee company subsidiaries) acting on behalf of underlying customers, other corporates, personal and corporate pension schemes, charities and other trusts.

   (c) *Institutional funds* – authorised and unauthorised collective investment schemes and unitised life assurance funds that are dedicated to investment by institutional investors. Investment in such funds is often restricted to UK investors who are exempt from taxation on capital gains – principally HMRC approved pension schemes and charities.

8.2 For most firms, investors will be mainly, but not exclusively, UK resident.

8.3 This section does not aim to provide guidance to life assurance companies, other than for the purposes of providing institutional funds as described in paragraph 8.1(c). Nor does it cover the issue or trading of shares in closed-ended investment vehicles (eg. investment trusts). Guidance on other life assurance products can be found in sector 7: *Life assurance and life-related pensions and investment products*. The issue and trading of shares in investment trusts etc. fall within the scope of sector 14: *Corporate finance* and sector 10: *Execution-only stockbroking*, respectively.

8.4 Guidance for those involved in managing private equity funds is contained within sector 13: *Private equity*.

What are the money laundering risks relating to investment fund products?

Retail funds and products/services

8.5 The vast majority of investment fund business is conducted on a non-face-to-face basis (post, telephone, internet) and investors generally have easy access to the funds involved. In addition, some firms accept payment by debit card, which exposes them to the risk of card fraud.

8.6 However, there are also factors that limit the attractiveness of these products for any money laundering process, which therefore mitigate some of these risks. In particular, in order to mitigate the money laundering risk, firms invariably take steps to identify any third party subscribers or payees, and some firms refuse to accept or make third party payments. Furthermore, most retail investors use these products for medium and long-term savings, which makes short-term investment or high turnover unusual and often relatively straightforward to monitor.

8.7 The typical retail investor might place anything up to £50,000 in investment funds (and for ISAs investment is limited by law to a maximum of £7,000 per annum). Larger investments are not uncommon, however, especially for firms whose target market is higher net worth individuals.

8.8 Investors are rarely asked to provide additional customer information about the purpose of the relationship, which will be self-evident, or their background. However, their behaviour is better measured against that of other investors than against uncorroborated customer data, which any criminal could provide in support of their expected activity.

8.9 Holdings of investment fund units may be transferred freely between different parties. Such transfers will be recorded by the registrar of the fund (usually the product provider or a third party administrator acting on their behalf) who should have a mechanism in place to alert them to unusual transfer activity (see paragraph 8.38).

8.10 On balance, therefore, investment funds and products that involve the restrictions referred to in paragraph 8.6 may generally be considered to be low risk in terms of their use for money laundering purposes. Notwithstanding this, the firm's risk-based approach will need to take account of the additional risk that would be associated with higher value (for example, the source of funds should not be used as evidence of identity for transactions of more than £50,000 – see paragraph 8.19(ii)). In any event, if the features of a product or service provide additional flexibility (for example, where some or all of the restrictions referred to in paragraph 8.6 are not applied), the firm should consider the potential increase in the money laundering risk given all the relevant factors and, where appropriate, take additional steps to mitigate that risk (for example, by undertaking further identity verification measures and/or obtaining additional customer information). Firms should also consider whether or not the nature of their distribution channels and the geographic location of their customers might suggest that their products are more likely to be used for the purposes of money laundering.

8.11   It is accepted that those who are able to provide convincing evidence of identity and behave in the same way as other investors will be very difficult to detect, in the absence of any other information to cause the firm to have doubts about the customer. Nevertheless, whilst investment fund products may generally be unattractive vehicles for the money laundering process, firms must be alert to the fact that career criminals will almost certainly invest in their sector using the proceeds of crime, and should consider any unusual activity in that light.

Institutional funds

8.12   Many institutional funds are open only to tax-exempt investors, such as pension schemes and charities.

8.13   As with retail funds, investors are rarely asked to provide additional customer information. However, in many cases the investment will be made on behalf of a client by the firm itself, another group company or another regulated firm, who will have obtained such information in the context of their role as an investment manager.

8.14   Overall, many institutional funds may be considered to be of lower risk than their retail counterparts, albeit by virtue of the restricted types of investor, rather than the product features. The risk will increase, however, in the case of "non-exempt" funds or share classes, which may admit other types of UK and non-UK institutional investor that are not subject to HMRC approval for tax exemption purposes.

Who is the customer for AML purposes?

8.15   The Money Laundering Regulations 2007 introduce a much wider definition of "business relationship", which now includes any business, professional or commercial relationship between the firm and its customer, which is expected to have an element of duration. Essentially, this definition would apply to any open-ended product relationship (eg, managing an ISA), irrespective of whether it was for the purposes of lump sum or regular investment. Furthermore, a fund manager's obligation to redeem units at the request of the holder at some future time provides the relationship and element of duration necessary for the definition to apply in the case of any registered holder of units, however their holding was acquired.

8.16   The handling of third party payments is an important feature of the typical risk profile of the fund management sector. Where the firm accepts payment from a third party at any point, that party should also be regarded as a customer and verified as such.

8.17   Should a firm wish to meet a request by the investor to pay redemption proceeds to a third party, that party should likewise be regarded as a customer (on whose behalf the registered investor may have been acting), and their identity should be verified before any funds are remitted.

8.18   Firms are not required to assume that payment from an unidentified source (eg, by wire transfer from a UK bank or building society) is being made by a third party unless they are aware of some fact that suggests that this is, or may be, the case.

Customer Due Diligence

Identity verification measures

8.19   Standard verification procedures for the type of customer concerned, and any beneficial owner or controller, as described in Part I, Chapter 5, should be followed. Subject to the restrictions that apply generally to their use, various exemptions and concessions are available. Typically, these would include:

   (i)   application of simplified due diligence in relation to qualifying customers or products as described in Part I, Chapter 5;

   (ii)   use of the source of funds as evidence of identity – see Part I, paragraphs 5.3.92 to 5.3.96 (firms should limit its use to lowest risk cases, and should not use it where the value exceeds £50,000).

   (iii) application of the measures described in Part I, paragraphs 5.3.86 and 5.3.87 in relation to the administration of deceased investors and Court of Protection Orders.

8.20   In addition, the destination of funds at the time of redemption can be used as evidence of identity in cases where there has not previously been a requirement to verify, for example where the firm had been able to rely on an exemption. In these cases, depending on the firm's assessment of the risk presented by the situation, including the circumstances in which the customer acquired the investment, it may be possible to satisfy the standard identification requirement by means of a payment to an account in the sole or joint name of the customer.

8.21   Where the firm is required to verify the identity of a customer that is being introduced by an appropriately regulated intermediary (see Part I, paragraph 5.6.18), reliance may be placed on the intermediary, following the guidance in Part I, paragraphs 5.6.19ff.

8.22   In the case of beneficial owners or controllers, unless the circumstances of the relationship indicate that more stringent measures should be undertaken (by virtue of the services to be provided or the specific nature of the customer), the identity of beneficial owners and controllers may be confirmed by the customer themselves (see Part I, paragraphs 5.3.10 and 5.3.11).

8.23   Various types of small occupational pension scheme may invest in retail funds – in cases where Simplified Due Diligence cannot be applied the verification procedures described in Part I, paragraphs 5.3.151 to 5.3.159 should be followed. Where the customer is a UK-based personal pension scheme (eg, a SIPP), however, the firm should confirm that any third party trustee or administrator that may deal with the firm has been appointed by the regulated scheme operator. This will allow the firm to apply simplified due diligence to such customers.

8.24   As most business within this sector is conducted non-face-to-face, consideration needs to be given to the higher money laundering risk this may present compared with face-to-face business, and in particular whether or not the person with whom the firm is dealing may be impersonating someone else. Given the lower risk of this sector being used for money laundering purposes, the usual measure taken in this respect is to ensure that the confirmation of a transaction or acknowledgement letter is sent by post to the customer's known address and is not returned or queried by the occupant.

Firms inevitably will have legacy customers whose identity has not been verified due to the circumstances under which they became investors, and the requirements and exemptions etc. that existed at that time. Firms are not expected to undertake specific exercises or projects to verify the identities of those customers retrospectively, but must do so upon future trigger events, as appropriate according to their risk-based approach.

Additional customer information

8.25   Additional customer information over and above that confirming identity, which is appropriate in many sectors, either for business purposes or because of the greater money laundering risks that their products and services entail, is of less relevance to this sector. From an AML/CTF perspective, the principal objective in obtaining such information is to understand the motive for establishing the relationship and to permit assessment of any subsequent activity. The motive for investing in funds is usually self-evident.

8.26   Very high value transactions from individuals should, however, be treated with caution. High net worth individuals are more likely to use the services of an investment manager, who would need to obtain considerably more customer information in order to service their needs properly – direct investment by such individuals may be an indicator that they are seeking to avoid having to provide that additional information.

8.27   Furthermore, firms will need to take a risk-based approach in deciding whether or not to consider a customer's potential status as a politically exposed person (PEP). Firms are required to take risk-based steps to determining PEP status, where the money laundering risk is higher – depending, for example, on the value of the investment and/or the location of the customer.

8.28   The nature of retail investment products means that the reasons for using them are limited and investment will reasonably be accepted from virtually anyone wishing to do so. Furthermore, activity monitoring in this area can be equally, if not more, effective by comparing the behaviour of one customer with that of others (see paragraphs 8.35–8.38).

8.29   Care should also be exercised when dealing with those claiming the reduced verification measures applicable to certain types of special cases (eg, asylum seekers, those on low incomes), whose first priority would not be expected to be investment of their limited resources for the future.

Timing of verification

8.30   In this sector, the obligation to verify a customer arises at the point when it is clear that they wish to enter into an arrangement with the firm, either to buy or sell units in a fund or to establish some form of investment scheme or account. In addition, given the revised definition of "business relationship" (see paragraph 8.15) the transfer of units from an existing holder to a third party will also give rise to an obligation to verify the identity of the transferee.

8.31   Firms must verify a customer's identity as soon as practicable after first contact with the customer, but are not prevented from entering into the relationship or commencing the initial transaction before the checks are completed. Firms should take all reasonable steps to verify the customer's identity within a reasonable time. Where the firm is unable to verify the identity of the investor within that time it will cease proactive pursuit of evidence of identity and must, at that point, consider if the circumstances give any grounds to suspect money laundering or terrorist financing and act accordingly (see Part I, paragraph 5.2.8).

8.32   If, however, after such reasonable time the firm has no grounds to suspect and is satisfied that the risk of money laundering is minimal, subject to its terms of business or the status of a contract to purchase units in its funds directly, it may terminate the relationship and return any monies received to their source. Alternatively, and particularly in purchases of units where the contract has been completed, the firm should freeze any funds or assets pending eventual verification (see Part I, paragraph 5.2.9).

8.33   From the point at which the firm concludes it should *freeze* an investment:

   (a)   it must not accept further investments (ad hoc or regular savings) from the customer until they provide the evidence of identity required by the firm;

   (b)   subject to (c) below, it must permit the investor to withdraw, redeem or transfer their investment upon production of the evidence of identity required by the firm;

   (c)   it must terminate the relationship and return any funds to the investor should they insist upon withdrawal or redemption while still refusing to produce evidence of identity, subject to considering whether or not it should make a report to SOCA and seek consent;

   (d)   it should otherwise continue to act in accordance with any relevant terms of business and regulatory obligations until such time as the relationship may be terminated (this would include issuing periodic statements, making normal dividend/interest payments and administering the customer's investments according to their instructions where these do not involve the investment or withdrawal of capital); and

   (e)   it must take steps to remind customers (individually or generically, as appropriate according to their risk-based approach) that evidence of identity may still be required, noting the consequences of failure to comply with the firm's request.

8.34   Firms are recommended to include in their terms of business, or otherwise advise the customer at the outset, that they may return or freeze the customer's investments unless or until the necessary evidence of identity can be obtained.

Monitoring

8.35   As mentioned in paragraph 8.28, one of the most effective ways of monitoring the activity of an investor is to compare it with that of the "typical investor". This may vary for different types of customer (eg, private individual compared to a corporate investor) and also for different types of fund (eg, money market fund compared to an equity fund).

8.36   Other than in the case of regular savings/withdrawal schemes, the use of investment funds and products is by its nature ad hoc. Even with regular savings and withdrawal schemes, however, there is nothing unusual in ad hoc additional, or top-up, subscriptions. However, whilst there may be various legitimate reasons for redeeming an investment after a relatively short period of time, most retail investment is made for the medium to long-term.

8.37   As such, firms in this sector will place some reliance upon the alertness and experience of its staff to spot unusual activity. However, firms may also consider the implementation of basic exception reporting to identify, for example, short-term investment by individuals. Disposals so identified might be reviewed in the context of the original purchase (eg, is it within the charge-back period for a subscription by debit card?) against market conditions, or in the light of any specific information the firm has about the investor. The exercise of cancellation rights is relatively rare and should be considered in a similar way.

8.38   Transfers involving either a regulated firm (or a nominee company subsidiary) or arising from the distribution of assets from a trust or the estate of a deceased, give less cause for concern over a subsequent transfer of the holding by the recipient. However, the purchase of units by one individual and transfer to another, and then to a third, and so on, is unusual and may indicate that money or other consideration is changing hands in the background with the aim of avoiding verification of the identity of those in the middle of the chain. Firms should be alert to such activity and take appropriate steps to investigate the nature and purpose of any unusual patterns that emerge.

[7031]

9: DISCRETIONARY AND ADVISORY INVESTMENT MANAGEMENT

Note: This sectoral guidance is incomplete on its own. It must be read in conjunction with the main guidance set out in Part I of the Guidance.

Overview of the sector

9.1   *Investment management* includes both discretionary and advisory management of segregated portfolios of assets (securities, derivatives, cash, property etc.) for the firm's customers. Where investment management is provided as part of a broader "wealth management" service, readers should refer instead to sector 5: *Wealth Management*.

9.2   Discretionary managers are given powers to decide upon stock selection and to undertake transactions within the portfolio as necessary, according to an investment mandate agreed between the firm and the customer.

9.3   Advisory relationships differ, in that, having determined the appropriate stock selection, the manager has no power to deal without the customer's authority – in some cases the customer will execute their own transactions in light of the manager's advice. This should not be confused with "financial advice", which involves advising customers on their investment needs (typically for long-term savings and pension provision) and selecting the appropriate products. Financial advice is dealt with in sector 6: *Financial advisers*.

9.4   The activities referred to above may be carried out for private or institutional investors. Note that guidance on the operation of investment funds, including those that are solely for institutional investors, is given in sector 8: *Non-life providers of investment fund products*.

What are the money laundering risks relating to investment management?

9.5   In terms of money laundering risk, there is little difference between discretionary and advisory investment management. In both cases, the firm may itself physically handle incoming or outgoing funds, or it may be done entirely by the client's custodian.

9.6   In either case, the typical firm deals with low volumes of high value customers, for which there is likely to be a take-on process that involves a level of understanding of the customer's circumstances, needs and priorities and anticipated inflows and outflows of funds, in order to determine suitable investment parameters.

9.7   There is likely to be ongoing contact, often face-to-face, with the customer in order to review market developments and performance, and review the customer's circumstances, etc. Unexpected inflows/outflows of funds are not common occurrences – ad hoc requirements and movements are usually the subject of discussion between the firm and the customer.

9.8   In most cases, all money and other assets within the portfolio are held under the control of a UK-regulated custodian, with money paid to or from the customer through their UK bank or building society account. Investment management is not a mechanism for the movement of assets from one person to another, although some third party payments may be made (eg. in the case of private customers, for the payment of school fees).

9.9   The risk of money laundering to the investment management sector, in the context of the "typical" circumstances described above, would be low. Clearly, however, the risk will increase when dealing with certain types of customer, such as offshore trusts/companies, PEPs and customers from higher risk non-FATF jurisdictions, and may also be affected by other service features that a firm offers to its customers. Note: Firms that provide investment management alongside banking facilities and other complex services should refer to Sector 5: *Wealth Management*.

Who is the customer for AML purposes?

9.10   The typical investors to whom investment managers provide services are high net worth individuals, trusts, companies, government bodies and other investing institutions such as pension schemes, charities and open/closed-ended pooled investment vehicles. In such cases, the firm's customer will be the individual or entity concerned. The firm must also consider whether there are any beneficial owners or controllers.

9.11   Firms may also be contracted to provide investment management services to other appropriately regulated UK and overseas firms in respect of their own investments (eg, life companies) or assets they are managing for others – in either instance the investment manager's client will be the other regulated firm, in which case there will be no requirement to consider any underlying beneficial ownership or control.

Customer due diligence

Verification of identity

9.12   As noted above, investment management in itself as a service would be considered as low risk. Therefore, in the absence of any features regarding the customer or service provided that are adjudged to increase that risk, standard identity verification measures, as set out in Part I, paragraphs 5.3.68 to 5.3.248, may be applied. Where the relationship is intermediated through a regulated adviser (eg, financial adviser or consulting actuary), confirmation of the customer's identity by the regulated intermediary, similar to that provided at Part I, Annex 5II, may take place.

Private individuals

9.13   The standard verification requirements for private individuals would be adequate to establish their identity, as described in Part I, paragraphs 5.3.68–5.3.114. The source of funds may also be used as evidence of identity (see Part I, paragraphs 5.3.92–5.3.96), subject to the restrictions that apply generally to its use. However, the firm must also adopt enhanced measures, as necessary, in respect of higher-risk categories of customer (eg, PEPs) and jurisdiction.

Customers other than private individuals

9.14   When dealing with other types of customer, firms would normally be able to rely on the standard verification measures, including simplified due diligence for qualifying customers, as described in Part I, paragraphs 5.3.115–5.3.248.

9.16   For overseas pension schemes and charities, additional verification steps may be required, depending upon the risk associated with the type of customer and their location (eg, in a higher risk jurisdiction).

9.17   For most charities, the firm will be able to regard those that may benefit from the charity as a class of beneficiary. As such, they do not need to be identified and verified individually. The members of occupational pensions schemes that do not qualify for simplified due diligence may be treated similarly.

9.18   In instances where the identities of beneficial owners or controllers must be verified individually, this may be done in accordance with Part I, paragraphs 5.3.8–5.3.13. Unless the circumstances of the relationship indicate that more stringent measures should be undertaken (by virtue of the services to be provided or the specific nature of the customer), the identity of beneficial owners and controllers may be confirmed by the customer itself (see Part I, paragraphs 5.3.10 and 5.3.11).

Mandates relating to third party investment vehicles

9.20   Some investment managers provide services to third party investment vehicles (eg, hedge funds), which may be open or closed ended. Those firms must consider whether or not there is a need for them to look at the underlying investors in such vehicles. This will depend up on the status of the vehicle and how it is operated in terms of dealing in its units/shares:

- Where such dealings are handled by an appropriately regulated entity (eg. fund manager or transfer agent) or are traded on a regulated market or exchange, the investment manager does not need to be concerned with the underlying investors.
- If a vehicle operates under less stringent conditions than those described above, the firm may take a risk-based approach and ensure that it is satisfied, on an ongoing basis, with the checks that are carried out by whoever controls entry to the vehicle's register of holders, and the information that will be available to the firm if required. Otherwise the firm will need to undertake its own customer due diligence, as necessary.

9.21   In any event, the firm must carry out appropriate due diligence on third party investment vehicles to establish and verify their form, status, purpose, and the identity of any persons who are in positions of control.

9.22   In most cases, the investors in such funds would be regarded as a class of beneficiary and so would not need to be verified individually. However, where the vehicle is being operated for "private" use by a specific group of individuals, verification of their identities as beneficial owners/controllers should be undertaken in accordance with the guidance given in Part I, paragraphs 5.3.8–5.3.13.

9.23   Investment management firms which provide services to unregulated vehicles such as hedge funds will find it helpful also to refer to sector 20: *Unregulated funds*.

Timing

9.24   Firms must verify a customer's identity as soon as practicable after first contact with the customer, but are not prevented from entering into the relationship. Firms should take all reasonable steps to verify the customer's identity within a reasonable time. Where the firm is unable to verify the identity of the investor within that time it will cease proactive pursuit of evidence of identity and must, at that point, consider if the circumstances give any grounds to suspect money laundering or terrorist financing and act accordingly (see Part I, paragraph 5.2.8).

9.25   If, however, after such reasonable time, the firm has no grounds to suspect and is satisfied that the risk of money laundering is minimal, subject to its terms of business it may terminate the relationship and return any monies received to their source. Alternatively, the firm may freeze any funds or assets pending eventual verification (see Part I, paragraph 5.2.9).

9.26   From the point at which the firm concludes it should *freeze* an investment:
- (a)   it must not accept further investments from the customer until they provide the evidence of identity required by the firm;
- (b)   subject to (c) below, it must permit the investor to withdraw their investment upon production of the evidence of identity required by the firm;
- (c)   it must terminate the relationship and return any funds to the investor should they insist upon withdrawal while still refusing to produce evidence of identity, subject to considering whether or not it should make a report to SOCA and seek consent;
- (d)   it should otherwise continue to act in accordance with any relevant terms of business and regulatory obligations until such time as the relationship may be terminated (this would

include issuing periodic statements and managing the customer's portfolio where this does not involve the investment or withdrawal of capital); and

(e)   it must take steps to remind customers (individually or generically, as appropriate according to their risk-based approach) that evidence of identity may still be required, noting the consequences of failure to comply with the firm's request.

9.27   Firms are recommended to include in their terms of business that they may return or freeze the customer's investments unless or until the necessary evidence of identity can be obtained.

Additional customer information

9.28   The client take-on process for investment management customers usually involves gaining an understanding of the customer and their needs, and establishing at the outset the likely inflows and outflows of funds are likely. Developments in this area and updates to customer information should be sought periodically from the customer or his adviser.

9.29   The customer information, obtained for the purposes of agreeing the firm's mandate and the ongoing management of the client's portfolio, will usually comprise the additional information necessary to understand the nature and purpose of the relationship in a money laundering context, against which the customer's future activity should be considered.

Monitoring

9.30   Customer activity relates only to inflows and outflows of money that do not relate to the firm's own dealings in the portfolio of investments. Most movements into or out of the portfolio will usually be expected (eg, pension scheme contributions or funding of pensions benefits). The firm should establish the rationale behind any unexpected ad hoc payments made or requested by the customer.

Custody

9.31   Safe-keeping and banking services in respect of a customer's portfolio are usually provided by a custodian. Some customers, particularly institutional ones, will appoint the custodian direct, in which case the custodian will have their own AML/CTF obligations. In these cases it is the custodian, rather than the investment manager, that should consider the source or destination of any funds and whether or not an unidentified third party account is involved, provided the investment manager is not involved in instructing the custodian with regard to the receipt or payment of funds. Any account taken of information provided by the investment manager will depend upon their relationship and agreement between them.

9.32   The investment manager must consider these issues where it is itself providing safe custody, even where the activity is outsourced to a third party custodian. Arrangements will need to be made with any sub-custodian that may remit or receive funds direct for the relevant checks to be carried out and recorded on the investment manager's behalf.

Real estate transactions

9.33   Some portfolios (usually in relation to property fund vehicles or very large segregated mandates) include direct holdings in real estate. Unlike securities, the counterparties involved in the purchase and sale of direct holdings in real estate may not be other regulated financial institutions. However, such transactions are generally conducted though solicitors, and the counterparty's solicitor will be obliged to verify its client's identity.

9.34   Furthermore, the counterparty would not normally be regarded as a customer of the investment firm and consequently the firm would not be obliged to verify the identity of the counterparty itself. However, in order to mitigate any reputational risk, firms may wish to seek appropriate assurances from their own solicitors that the identity of the counterparty will have been verified.

[7032]

10: EXECUTION-ONLY STOCKBROKERS

Note: This sectoral guidance is incomplete on its own. It must be read in conjunction with the main guidance set out in Part I of the Guidance.

Overview of the sector

10.1   *Execution-only (ExO) stockbrokers* carry out transactions in securities with regulated market counterparties, as agent for individual customers. ExO transactions are carried out only on the instructions of the customer.

10.2   The guidance contained in this section covers only the purchase and sale of securities or investments (including investment funds). Firms that arrange for customers to invest through third party products or services (eg, ISAs, fund supermarkets) may be asked to provide confirmation of the customer due diligence they have undertaken to the provider of that product/service (sector 8: *Non-life providers of investment fund products*). See sector 9: *Discretionary and advisory investment management*.

What are the money laundering risks relating to execution-only stockbroking?

10.3   Some ExO stockbrokers deal with high volumes of low value customers, whereas others direct their services towards higher net worth customers, and thus have fewer customers. Stockbroking customers may adopt a variety of trading patterns; the firm is offering no advice and may have little or no knowledge of a particular customer's motives.

10.4   ExO customers are also free to spread their activities across a variety of brokers for perfectly valid reasons, and often do. Each broker may therefore actually have little in terms of transaction history from which to identify unusual behaviour. Many firms provide ExO stockbroking services on a non-face-to-face basis, including via the internet.

10.5   In view of the above, whilst stockbroking might be regarded as being of *lower* risk compared to many financial products and services, the risk is not as low as in providing investment management services to the same types of customer from similar jurisdictions.

Who is the customer for AML purposes?

10.6   The typical customers for ExO retail stockbroking are individuals. However, customers also include solicitors, accountants and IFAs, as well as trusts, companies, charities, etc. Much ExO business can comprise occasional, or linked, transactions of a value less than €15,000, which therefore fall within the exemption in Part I, paragraph 5.3.6.

Customer Due Diligence

Verification of identity

10.7   There is nothing about typical ExO business in particular that requires the firm to carry out enhanced identity checks as a result of the service offered. Verification of identity for particular types of customer should therefore be performed in accordance with the standard set out in Part I, section 5.3.

10.8   The risk level of execution only broking, however, depends on whether the services are offered and operated on a face-to-face or non face-to-face basis. The ML Regulations identify non-face-to-face business as a higher risk for money laundering than face-to-face business. In view of this, firms need to have in place additional measures to neutralise the higher risk when opening and operating accounts for non face-to-face business. This can take the form of additional due diligence at the point of account opening, appropriate ongoing monitoring of customer activity or both.

Timing

10.9   Verification of identity should be carried out as part of establishing the relationship, but before any services are provided. In the case of share transactions where this might interrupt the normal course of business, verification of identity should take place as soon as practicable after the transaction and in any event before final settlement with the customer. Further details on timing can be found in Part I, paragraphs 5.2.1 to 5.2.5.

Additional customer information

10.10   ExO business is driven by the customer and, as mentioned earlier, customer behaviour may vary widely, from the occasional transaction in a FTSE 100 share to day trading in a variety of instruments. As there are no suitability obligations for ExO stockbrokers, firms will have little or no information about the customer. Given the reasonably narrow range of services provided by ExO stockbrokers, no additional information is likely to be required to establish the purpose and intended nature of the business relationship.

Monitoring

10.11   As mentioned above, customer behaviour may vary widely, therefore making it harder to pick up unusual or suspicious trading activity. Attention should, therefore, be focused on ensuring that payments to and from the customer as a result of trading activity are conducted through a bank or building society account in the UK, the EU or in an equivalent jurisdiction.

10.12   Where a firm is transacting business for a customer who has opened and operated an account on a non face-to-face basis, and the payment is proposed to be made into an overseas account, then the firm should mitigate the higher risk of the non face-to-face business by establishing that the overseas account is held in the customer's own name. If the firm is not able to establish that the account is held in the customer's own name, it should proceed with caution. The firm should review the account and transaction history, and the reason for making the payment abroad, to determine whether the account, or any dealings on the account, are unusual, and therefore possibly suspicious. If the firm has doubts about the proposed transaction, then an external disclosure to SOCA should be made, and appropriate consent obtained, prior to making the overseas payment.

10.13   Where a firm's product range allows a customer to make third party deposits or payments, for example through linked banking services, the firm must assess the higher risk presented by these transaction types and enhance its monitoring and staff training accordingly to mitigate.

[7033]

11: MOTOR FINANCE

Note: This sectoral guidance is incomplete on its own. It must be read in conjunction with the main guidance set out in Part I of the Guidance, and the guidance in sector 12: Asset finance.

Overview of the sector

11.1   Motor finance companies offer a number of products to fund the acquisition and use of a motor vehicle. Dependent upon the funding method used, the customer may or may not obtain legal title to the vehicle. Motor finance products generally fall into two categories – purchase agreements, and lease agreements.

Purchase agreements

11.2   *Conditional sale* is a contract between the finance company and the customer where the customer agrees to buy specific goods. It is normally a fixed cost, fixed term credit and the customer in practice exercises all the rights of the owner of the goods. However, in law, the ownership of the asset will not pass until certain conditions are met (normally that all payments under the contract have been made, but individual contracts may include other conditions).

11.3   *Hire Purchase* (HP) and *Lease Purchase* (LP). These are both agreements under which the customer will hire the vehicle for a fixed period of time. During this period the motor finance company will recover, through the instalments paid, the cost of the vehicle together with its charges. Once the agreement is paid in full, the customer has the option to purchase the vehicle for a nominal sum. Generally, the difference between the two agreements is that on HP the amount to be repaid is spread evenly throughout the agreement, whereas on LP a substantial sum is deferred to the final instalment.

11.4   *Personal Contract Purchase* (PCP) is in essence a purchase agreement (the definition would, therefore, be the same as HP and LP) with a Guaranteed Minimum Future Value (GMFV) placed on the goods by the finance company. The customer has the choice at the end of the agreement of either paying the GMFV and obtaining title to the vehicle or returning the vehicle (and not having to pay the GMFV).

11.5   *Personal Loan* is an agreement where the title passes immediately to the customer and an unsecured loan is provided to cover all or a proportion of the sale price.

Leasing agreements

11.6   These are agreements where the customer leases the vehicle for a fixed period of time, but does not have the ability to obtain title. The motor finance company will reclaim the VAT on the vehicle and claim writing down allowances for tax purposes, as owner of the asset. A business customer can, dependent upon its tax position, claim both tax relief and proportion of the VAT on rentals paid. There are two types of lease:
*   A *Finance Lease*, where the customer takes the risk in the final value of the vehicle.
*   An *Operating Lease,* where the motor finance company takes the risks and rewards in the final value of the vehicle.

11.7   This guidance applies to all dealer-introduced motor finance, unless otherwise stated (as in the case for operating leasing (see 11.8 below)) including, but not limited to, cars, light commercial vehicles, motorcycles and caravans. However, brokers are not covered by the money laundering regulations unless they provide finance leasing products on their own books.

11.8   Operating leases[11] are **outside** the scope of the ML Regulations.[12] However, in practice for some firms it may be difficult to separate out this type of activity from other forms of leases, such as finance leases. In these circumstances 'best practice' would suggest that firms *may* nevertheless wish to make a commercial decision to follow this guidance in respect of this type of lease.

---

[11]   Vehicle contract hire and vehicle rental products would, for the purpose of this guide and accounting purposes, be classified as being an operating lease and as such would fall **outside** the scope of this guide. Under Financial Reporting Standard 5 ("FRS5") and Statement of Standard Accounting Practice 21 ("SSAP 21") operating leases would be a lease where risk and rewards of ownership do not pass substantially to the lessee.

[12]   Whilst Operating leases fall outside the requirements of the Money Laundering Regulations, firms should

be aware of the anti-money laundering reporting requirements of the Proceeds of Crime 2002 (POCA), which covers all types of business. See, for example, paragraphs 1.36–1.37 in Part I of the Guidance.

What are the money laundering risks in motor finance?

11.9   The features of all lending are generally that the initial monies advanced are paid into another bank account, in the case of motor finance in exchange for the use of a vehicle. Repayments are usually made from other bank or building society accounts by direct debit; in most, but not all, cases, repayments in cash are not, and should not be, encouraged.

11.10   Given that a loan results in the borrower not receiving funds from the lender, but the use of a vehicle, the initial transaction is not very susceptible to money laundering. The main money laundering risk arises through the acceleration of an agreed repayment schedule, either by means of lump sum repayments, or early termination. Early repayment can also be indicative of funds being used which have emanated from a criminal lifestyle.

11.11   Motor finance products therefore carry a low inherent money laundering risk. A motor finance company will normally only accept payment of instalments from the customer named on the agreement, and in the case of overpayment will only make repayment to the customer named on the agreement.

11.12   Should a motor finance company accept occasional payments from third parties, for example the settlement of the agreement by the dealer, and/or accept payment via payment books, it must be alert to the increased risk of receiving the proceeds of crime.

Assessment of the risk

11.13   The lender's knowledge of the customer only extends to information gleaned at the identification stage, and to a single monthly payment on the agreement; their occupation details and monthly income/expenditure are generally unknown.

11.14   The nature of motor finance business, however, is that the type of agreement entered into with the customer carries a low risk of money laundering.

11.15   Procedures and controls used for identifying potential money laundering are therefore normally transactional-based, to identify unusual transactional movements, unusual deposits, unusual advance payments or unusual repayment patterns.

Who is the customer for AML purposes?

11.16   A customer may be a private individual or a business eg, partnerships, companies, associations etc.

11.17   Customers may be introduced through dealers, or by direct lending over the internet, through the post, or by telephone. Motor dealers introduce their customers to lenders whenever finance is required to support a vehicle acquisition. The dealer/lender relationship will be formalised in terms of an agency contract, and the dealer staff conducts face-to-face negotiations. Direct lending motor products may also be obtained remotely without face-to-face contact; this is likely to carry a higher risk.

Customer due diligence

Dealer-introduced motor finance

11.18   In a move to reduce fraudulent credit applications, members of the Finance & Leasing Association (FLA) have subscribed to an industry standard with regard to acceptable proof of identity and the standardisation of credit application processing for face-to-face business. The procedure for customer verification involves face-to-face identity checks by the dealer, supported by subsequent validation of copy identity documents by the lender. The Industry Standard is set out in the attached Annex 11–I.

11.19   Compliance with the Industry Standard on proof of identity goes beyond the current money laundering requirements under simplified due diligence (SDD), which is directly relevant for low risk products such as hire purchase and leasing agreements. However, this industry standard should still be used in order to guard against fraud. On-going monitoring of the business relationship is still required under simplified due diligence (SDD).

11.20   Under the regulations dealers can be used as agents for customer due diligence purposes in those sectors that are currently subject to established systems of supervision for money laundering. In practice this means that credit and financial institutions authorised and supervised by the FSA for anti-money laundering compliance will be able to be relied upon, although in all cases the 'relying' firm retains ultimate responsibility for meeting the obligations under the Regulations.

11.21   The identification of non-personal customers eg, partnerships, companies, associations etc. should be carried out in accordance with the guidance set out in Part I, paragraphs 5.3.115ff.

Non face-to-face applications

11.22   Negotiations in respect of non face-to-face applications are normally drawn out over a period, involving vehicle specification and part exchanges, and are normally conducted over the telephone. Documentation is usually sent out by post, and the vehicles may be delivered to the customer's home. Firms should be aware that non face-to-face applications by their very nature pose a greater risk and should not, therefore, be treated as lower risk under simplified due diligence (SDD). They will therefore require identification, verification and ongoing monitoring under enhanced due diligence (refer to Part I, section 5.5), as opposed to just monitoring under simplified due diligence (SDD) rules within the current regulations.

11.23   Electronic verification may therefore be used, supported by postal communication to home address. Some lenders may seek copies of items in accordance with the procedures set out in Part I, Chapter 5.

Supervision

11.24   There are several different regulatory bodies taking responsibilities under the 2007 Money Laundering Regulations. In order to aid clarity about who supervises whom the FSA have published a flow chart that helps business to understand which regulator regulates which entities. The FSA's Money Laundering regulations pages also contain other information FSA ML regulated firms may find to be of use, including their approach to registering and supervising the businesses that fall to their responsibility. Links to this information can be found at: http://www.fsa.gov.uk/mlr. Similar documentation for OFT registered firms can be found on the OFT's website: http://www.oft.gov.uk/.

[7034]

ANNEX 11–I

Industry Standard for Fraud Prevention in Credit Application Processing:

Standard Identification Evidence

It should be noted that some of the requirements set out in this industry standard exceed those now required for lower risk products, eg some leasing agreements, under the current money laundering regulations (under simplified due diligence (SDD) they no longer require identification and verification). However these standards should still be followed as they prevent fraud which is inherently tied into money laundering.

1.   In credit application processing, there should be standard acceptable proofs for verification of identity and current permanent address in accordance with paragraphs 3–5 below. These apply in the case of:
- new customers; and
- current and previous customers where the proposal details show a material discrepancy from the existing account details in the records of the lender; and
- previous customers whose last transaction expired over 12 months ago.

2.   A 'material discrepancy' would include any of the following:
- missing/wrongly spelt names;
- change of name;
- incorrect address information extending to post code, current or previous address;
- incorrect time at address; and
- conflicting employment details, bank details, date or place of birth.

3.   There should be mandatory production of a full driving licence or a photo card driving licence, or a provisional driving licence with photo card, in every case bearing the customer's current address. All photo cards should be accompanied by their relevant counterpart. Where the driving licence does not bear the customer's current address, then additional proof of current permanent residence should be required (for example, by Electoral Roll confirmation).

4.   In the rare circumstances where an individual cannot produce a current driving licence, the lender should verify the identity in accordance with the procedures set out in Part I, Chapter 5.

5.   The driving licence should be supported, wherever possible, by at least one of the following:
- electronic confirmation of the customer's current residence via the Electoral Roll;
- electronic confirmation of current credit data at the current address on existing lending;
- electronic confirmation of identity in accordance with Part I, paragraph 5.3.79

6.   The waiving or variation of any of the requirements in paragraphs 1 to 5 is permissible but at the lender's own risk and discretion provided that, as a minimum, they comply with the requirements set out in Part I, Chapter 5.

Dealers

7.   Payment may be made by the lender in advance of receiving copies of the evidence of identity and address, but there should be in place an arrangement to cancel the credit agreement and recover the funds in the event that identity cannot be verified (such a payment is made by the lender at its own risk).

8.   In accordance with the normal working practice of the lender concerned, identity should be satisfactorily verified in accordance with paragraphs 3 and 4 prior to authorisation being given to the dealer to release the vehicle to the customer or before settling the dealer's invoice.

9.   The dealer should have sight of original documents (not copies) and should scrutinize them for authenticity and check the signature against the credit agreement. Any photographic proof of identity should also be checked for reasonable likeness of the customer.

10.   The dealer should take a copy of the original proofs and this copy of the original proofs, together with confirmation that it is a copy of the original, should be submitted to the lender for subsequent document validation checks. The lender should not accept a copy of a copy.

Scope of Industry Standard

11.   This Standard applies to sole traders and individuals and should be applied, wherever practical, to the main driver of the particular vehicle for a partnership or SME.

[7035]

12: ASSET FINANCE

Note: This sectoral guidance is incomplete on its own. It must be read in conjunction with the main guidance set out in Part I of the Guidance and, where relevant, the guidance in sector 11: Motor finance.

Overview of the sector

12.1   Asset finance providers offer financial facilities that allow a business to use an asset over a fixed period, in return for regular payments. The business customer chooses the equipment it requires, and the finance company buys it on behalf of the business. There are a number of ways in which a business may finance an asset. These are described below.

Leasing

12.2   The fundamental characteristic of a lease is that ownership of the asset never passes to the business customer.

12.3   Under a *finance lease*, the leasing company recovers the full cost of the equipment, plus charges, over the period of the lease. It can claim written down allowances, whilst the customer can claim both tax relief and VAT on rentals paid.

12.4   An *operating lease* is often used where a business requires a piece of equipment for a shorter period of time, for example construction equipment. The leasing company will lease the equipment to the customer, expecting, at the end of the lease period, to sell it second-hand or to lease it to another customer. The business customer does not enter the operating leased item on its balance sheet as a capital item.

12.5   The most common form of operating lease is known as contract hire. Essentially, this gives the customer the use of the asset, together with additional services such as maintenance and repair of the asset. An example of an asset on contract hire would be a fleet of vehicles. In this instance, a proportion of the VAT is reclaimable by the customer.

12.6   Operating leases are outside the scope of the ML Regulations.[13] Best practice would, however, suggest that firms should nevertheless follow this guidance in respect of this type of lease. In any event, in practice it may often be difficult to separate out this type of activity from other forms of lease. For example, many asset finance businesses offer a mixture of operating and finance leases and it would therefore be unduly cumbersome to follow different procedures for different leasing products, as well as inconsistent with a risk based approach.

---

[13]   Whilst Operating leases fall outside the requirements of the Money Laundering Regulations, firms should be aware of the anti-money laundering reporting requirements of the Proceeds of Crime 2002 (POCA), which covers all types of business. See, for example, paragraphs 1.36–1.37 in Part I of the Guidance.

Purchase

12.7   *Hire Purchase* (HP) is a well-established method of financing the purchase of assets by businesses. Under a HP agreement, the customer will hire the asset(s) for a fixed period of time. During this period the asset finance company will recover, through the instalments paid, the cost of the asset(s) together with its charges. Once the agreement is paid in full, the customer has the option to purchase the asset(s) for a nominal sum.

12.8   A *lease purchase* is similar to HP, the main difference being in the terms and structure of repayments. Some finance companies differentiate lease purchase from HP by using lease purchase where the customer wishes to defer payment of a substantial part of the asset cost until the end of the agreement.

12.9   *Joint ventures* between asset finance providers are commonplace on high value transactions.

12.10   The above funding methods are a guide and include variations with or without maintenance eg, recourse or non-recourse.

12.11   *Structured or "big ticket" asset finance* broadly covers very high value transactions. Products are highly visible and high profile, such as aircraft, ships and properties. Here, the lending tends to be higher in quality, generally being made to major reputable companies, be they public sector or at the top end of the private sector. Transactions are one-off and no deposits are generally taken. Most big-ticket financiers are subsidiaries of the major banks; business is often introduced from another part of the group and so information on the customer is contained within a group-wide database.

12.12   *Middle market products* include commercial vehicles, cars for business, plant machinery and IT equipment to a wide range of business customers.

12.13   At the *"small ticket" end of the market*, products such as photocopiers, PCs and telephone systems depreciate very quickly and offer little incentive for money laundering. Given that the asset provider owns title to the assets, there is little the end user can do with the assets.

What are the money laundering risks in asset finance?

12.14   The features of asset finance are generally that no monies are advanced to the customer, but are paid into a supplier's bank account to fund the purchase of an asset which is made available under contract to the customer. Repayments by the customer are usually made from other bank accounts by direct debit; in most, but not all, cases. Repayments in cash are not, and should not be, encouraged. Risk is also associated with hire purchase and lease products as they could be used for layering.

12.15   Given that a loan does not result in the borrower receiving funds from the lender, but the use of assets, the initial transaction is not very susceptible of money laundering. The main money laundering risk arises through the acceleration of an agreed repayment schedule, either by means of lump sum repayments, or early termination. Early repayment can also be indicative of funds being used which have emanated from a criminal lifestyle.

12.16   Asset finance products therefore generally carry a low inherent money laundering risk. An asset finance company will normally only accept payment of instalments from the customer named on the agreement, and in the case of overpayment will only make repayment to the customer named on the agreement.

12.17   In summary, the business of asset financing can be considered as carrying a low money laundering risk because:

- under a pure leasing agreement, lessees cannot acquire ownership of the asset during the term of the lease;
- payments are usually collected from other bank accounts by direct debit; and cash payments are not accepted in the normal course of business.

Assessment of the risk

12.18   In assessing customer risk, reference should be made to the risk-based approaches referred to in Part I, sections 5.4 and 5.5. These sections look at both simplified due diligence (SDD) and enhanced due diligence (EDD).

Customer due diligence

12.19   All asset finance providers should carry out full credit searches on the businesses they transact with. Additional steps to verify identity will vary across the three markets, as set out below. Note that this may well go beyond what is required by the current money laundering regulations, certainly in relation to low risk areas which can now rely on simplified due diligence (SDD). However, these additional measures will still be important for fraud purposes.

12.20   Under the regulations third parties can be used as agents for customer due diligence purposes in those sectors that are currently subject to established systems of supervision for money laundering. In practice this means that credit and financial institutions authorised and supervised by the FSA for anti-money laundering compliance will be able to be relied upon, although in all cases the 'relying' firm retains ultimate responsibility for meeting the obligations under the Regulations.

12.21   *Big-ticket lenders* – Traditionally as part of the credit underwriting process, the lender will check that the lessee is listed on a recognised market or exchange, or is a subsidiary of such a company. The lender should also check whether the lessee is a local authority. Where the customer is not listed, the standard verification requirement set out in Part I, paragraphs 5.3.136–5.3.140 is usually followed, including appropriate verification of the identity of the beneficial owners. Where appropriate, verification of the identity of the directors in principal control, and company searches, will be undertaken as part of normal underwriting procedures.

12.22　Prior to agreeing to finance an asset, the lessor will sometimes visit the lessee. There should be an understanding of the client's business; for example, that the nature of the asset for which funding is sought is consistent with the business.

12.23　*Middle market asset financiers* also follow the procedures set out in Part I, section 5.3, making full use of data held by credit reference agencies. This will verify key parties/directors, including beneficial owners. As with providers of structured asset finance, prior to agreeing to finance an asset, the lessor will usually visit the lessee and have an understanding of the client's business. However, in applying a risk-based approach, middle market asset financiers may take appropriate account of the guidance on using the source of funds as evidence of identity given in Part I, paragraphs 5.3.92–5.3.96. There will be variations, depending on whether a company is listed on a regulated market or exchange, and other exceptions which may be relevant as set out in Part I, Chapter 5.

12.24　*Small ticket lenders* may be able to rely on simplified due diligence (SDD) as set out in Part I, section 5.4 and are, therefore, no longer required to verify identity in accordance with the standard requirements set out in Part I, paragraphs 5.3.115–5.3.248. This is because this is a particularly low risk area. However, for fraud purposes lenders should still carry out identity verification in accordance with standard practice.

12.25　There may be variations, depending on whether a company is listed on a regulated market or exchange, and other exceptions which may be relevant as set out in Part I, Chapter 5.

12.26　Where identity is still required for a transaction which may be seen as higher risk the Asset finance business would be able to use the source of funds as evidence of identity (see Part I, paragraphs 5.3.92–5.3.96), provided that repayment is to be made by direct debit from an account that can be confirmed at the outset as being in the borrower's name. However, where the sum being lent is to be paid direct to the customer's supplier, sufficient due diligence must be carried out to ensure that the supplier is genuine.

12.27　For sole traders or small partnerships, the standard identification requirement set out in Part 1, paragraphs 5.3.212–5.3.225 should be followed. Where the risks are considered at their lowest, firms may be able to carry out simplified due diligence as set out in Part I, section 5.4.

[7036]

13: PRIVATE EQUITY

Note: This sectoral guidance is incomplete on its own. It must be read in conjunction with the main guidance set out in Part I of the Guidance.

Overview of the sector

13.1　The ML Regulations define who is covered by those regulations by close reference to the Third Money Laundering Directive ("the Directive"). Private equity firms in the UK are generally authorised and regulated by the FSA and are considered to be covered by the Directive and ML Regulations because they will carry on one or more of the BCD activities listed in Schedule 1 to the ML Regulations. Such firms may also be covered by the Directive and the ML Regulations because, in practice, they perform the functions of a collective investment scheme when marketing its units or shares. Private equity firms are therefore "financial institutions" within the meaning of the Directive and the ML Regulations, and reliance may be placed on them under the ML Regulations by other private equity firms and others subject to the Directive, such as banks, lawyers, accountants, etc.

13.2　Private equity business (for the purposes of this guidance) means activities relating to:
- The raising and acceptance of moneys into private equity funds (usually from institutional investors);
- The investing of these funds by providing long term finance to a range of businesses, from early stage to large established companies. Usually the investee companies are unquoted;
- The management of these investments (often involving active board participation) and exercise of negotiated equity holder rights; and
- The subsequent realisation of the investment.

13.3　Investors in private equity funds tend to have long established relationships with the private equity firm, normally resulting in a very well known investor base. Prior to making any investment in a business, the private equity firm will conduct extensive due diligence on the business identifying areas of risk, including money laundering considerations.

13.4　Once invested, ongoing monitoring of the investment through active board participation and regular involvement allows the firm to assess whether the investee's activities are consistent with the financial performance of the company, and also enables the firm to observe the conduct of the key managers of the business at first hand. In connection with investee companies, this will satisfy a firm's obligation to conduct ongoing monitoring of the business relationship under the ML Regulations.

13.5　There will always be an obligation for a firm to carry out such investigative work as it feels necessary where any circumstances exist which may lead it to suspect money laundering or terrorist financing is a risk, and the following guidance should be read in that context.

13.6　For AML/CTF purposes, in a private equity context there are two distinct groups:
- Investors in fund vehicles operated, managed or administered by private equity firms – paragraphs 13.7–13.27 (investors);
- Persons involved with the private equity firm when investing and divesting (eg, investee companies when investing and purchasers on exit) – paragraphs 13.28–13.50 (transactions).

Persons falling into the categories identified above may be classified by a private equity firm as its "venture capital contacts" for the purposes of other aspects of FSA regulation, as opposed to being classified as the firm's regulatory clients.

Investors

(i) Product risk

13.7　Investors typically invest in a fund as limited partners in a limited partnership. The limited partnership will usually be collectively managed or advised by the private equity firm. Investors invest for the long term and the timing of any return of capital is unpredictable. This form of investment is very illiquid, with no ready market. Transfers of interest in the partnerships can take place, but only after strict due diligence (and in some funds only after a minimum initial investment period) and usually only with the specific approval of the general partner or manager. Payments/repayments would also only tend to be made to the investor itself (any payment to a third party would usually only be made with the express consent of the general partner and/or manager of the fund).

13.8　This type of product would normally be considered to be a lower risk.

(ii) Customer risk

General

13.9　Investors in a fund are mostly institutional, such as insurance companies, pension funds of large corporates or state organisations, other financial companies and some funds of funds. There may also be a small number of high net worth individuals.

13.10　The acceptance of investors into a fund is a relatively long process with significant levels of due diligence performed by the firm and the prospective investor(s). Key representatives of the investors will often meet face to face with senior executives of the firm.

13.11　The relationship between the firm and investor is such that a high proportion of investors will often commit to consecutive funds of the firm; thus the relationship continues over a long period and source of funding remains constant.

13.12　For the reasons set out in paragraphs 13.9 to 13.11 these investors would generally be considered to be low risk, although certain high net worth individuals may require extra consideration in any risk evaluation.

13.13　Firms seeking to raise funds for the first time, or from a significantly larger investor base, may be under pressure to accept funds from potentially higher risk investors, and the extent of the due diligence should be adapted accordingly.

Timing

13.14　Identification checks in respect of investors in a fund should be completed before the fund closes. Where there is any assignment of an interest in a fund, any identification checks should be completed before the assignment is approved.

Identification

13.15　In relation to each investor a private equity firm should obtain at least the standard evidence for that type of investor in accordance with Part I, chapter 5. In most cases (see paragraph 13.16, for example), the key piece of standard evidence will be to identify whether there is any natural person beneficial owner holding an interest of 25% or more and (where there is) to take risk-based and adequate measures to verify his identity (see paragraphs 13.18 to 13.27 below).

13.16　In the case of institutional investors, it may be appropriate to conduct only simplified due diligence (see Part I, section 5.4) because the investor will itself be regulated.

13.17　Where a corporate investor is not well-known to the private equity firm and is quoted on a regulated market or exchange which is not located in the UK, the EU or in an equivalent jurisdiction, it may not be practical for the firm to obtain reliable evidence as to the quality of the regulation in that market or exchange. In addition to the standard identification requirements set out in Part I, paragraphs 5.3.127 to 5.3.130, the firm should seek to establish, where possible, who the corporate investor's external accountants, lawyers and brokers are, and their reputation in the market, before making a decision on what, if any, further verification of identity is required. Similar considerations should be made when it appears necessary to go beyond the standard evidence of identity.

Identifying the Beneficial Owner

13.18   Where the investor is a natural person or a wholly-owned investment vehicle of a natural person, it will be straightforward to identify the beneficial owner.

13.19   Where the investor is a "family office", the money will usually be provided by one or more trusts. The firm should look through the investment structure to identify the relevant trusts, and verify the trusts' identities, in accordance with Part I, paragraphs 5.3.180–5.3.202. A private equity firm may have to take a decision as to whether it can rely on a representation from the administrator of the family office (or equivalent) concerning the beneficial owners.

13.20   Where the investor is a pension fund or endowment, the firm must first understand the structure of the pension fund or endowment in order to determine its approach to identification. The firm should identify both the source of the funding, for example the sponsoring employer, and the person who controls the investment decision, for example the trustee or an investment committee, although the exercise of investment discretion may have been delegated to a regulated firm acting as agent. In identifying the beneficial owner, it is unlikely that any one individual will have an entitlement to 25% of the property (and a representation from the trustee to this effect should be sufficient).

Identifying the Beneficial Owner – Funds of Funds

13.21   It may be more complicated to identify a beneficial owner where the investor is itself a fund vehicle, including a private equity fund of funds.

13.22   The requirement to identify the beneficial owner and to understand the ownership and control structure in accordance with the ML Regulations would normally be confined to (a) the fund of funds manager or general partner (as the true "controller" of the fund of funds) (hereafter, the "Manager") and (b) the fund of funds itself. The assessment should not normally need to go beyond that part of the structure. In particular, it should not normally be necessary to keep looking "up" the structure until one or more natural persons are identified.

13.23   Where the Manager is regulated and subject to supervision in the UK, the EU or an equivalent jurisdiction, no further identification work would normally be required because the regulated Manager will usually deal as agent on behalf of the fund of funds.

13.24   Where the Manager is not from an equivalent jurisdiction, even though it may be regulated, or where the Manager is unregulated but operates in an equivalent jurisdiction (as is often the case in the US private equity industry, for example) the firm needs to exercise its judgement as to the likely risk presented by investors in the fund. Factors to take into consideration include:
- the profile of the Manager;
- its track record in the private equity industry; and
- its willingness to explain its identification procedures and provide confirmation that all underlying investors in the fund have been identified and are known to the Manager.

13.25   There will often be legitimate confidentiality concerns on the part of the Manager in respect of the beneficial owners of the fund. However, funds of funds are often widely held and it is unlikely that there will in fact be any investor which is a beneficial owner with an interest of more than 25%. Subject to the considerations in 13.24, in order to establish this, a private equity firm is entitled to rely on a representation from the manager (whether or not regulated or supervised) that, to its actual knowledge, there is no natural person beneficial owner of more than 25% of the shares, limited partnership interests or voting rights (as appropriate) in the fund of funds. Where such a natural person beneficial owner is encountered, the private equity firm must identify them and take risk-based and adequate measures to verify their identity.

13.26   In addition, the private equity firm should obtain the other items of standard evidence in relation to the Manager and the fund of funds vehicle. Depending on the results of the risk evaluation, it may be appropriate to obtain documents (for example basic constitutional documents), or a combination of documents and representations, from the Manager.

13.27   Possible examples of the sort of representations referred to in paragraph 13.25 are set out below. These representations do not represent evidence of identity in the way that the pro forma confirmations in Part I, Annex 5 do, but they should be used as part of the firm's risk-based approach and adapted accordingly.

PART V
OTHER MATERIALS

Example of representation provided by a fund of funds manager or general partner

"We [name] [regulated by [name of regulator]] hereby certify the following in respect of [state name of fund(s) vehicles e g limited partnership(s)] (the "Funds"), for whom we act as agent.

1. [In accordance with the laws of our jurisdiction, and the procedures under which we operate, designed to combat money laundering*] [we confirm that]:
    - we have identified the underlying beneficial owners in respect of the Funds and carried out customer due diligence on all of the investors in the Funds;
    - we confirm that to our actual knowledge [(having made [reasonable] enquiries)] there are no undisclosed or anonymous principals; and
    - we are not aware of any activities on the part of those investors which lead us to suspect that the investor is or has been involved in money laundering or other criminal conduct.

2. Should we become suspicious of any such activity then, subject to any legal constraints, we shall inform [you/the relevant regulatory authorities] promptly.

3. To our actual knowledge [(having made reasonable enquiries)] there is no natural person who is the beneficial owner of more than 25% of the [shares/limited partnership interests/voting rights] in any of the Funds.

4. We will retain, until further notice, all documentation required to identify the underlying beneficial owners in respect of the Funds [and which we have obtained for the purposes of our due diligence]. [We will provide such documentation [to you][to your Compliance Officer][direct to any regulatory authority] [on request][where you are required to disclose it to such regulatory authority]]."

* Insert if provider of representation is regulated and subject to AML/CTF legislation.

Transactions

(i) Product risk

13.28   The product is the provision of funds by the firm in a number of different structures predominantly to unquoted companies. The funding is usually provided for the long term, after the company and its management have been subject to detailed due diligence and investigation. The firm has an ongoing obligation to monitor its investment, often involving representation on the board of the company and receipt of regular financial and operational information.

13.29   The shareholding is highly visible and any failings on the part of the company would be closely aligned to the reputation of the private equity firm.

13.30   If all these factors are present it is considered unlikely the provision of funding will be used for illegal purposes and that therefore the product will be a lower risk. The absence of one of these factors, such as the non availability of detailed due diligence work or the reliance on a third party, may require the firm to obtain more detailed verification to satisfy itself that the funds are being provided for legitimate purposes.

(ii) Customer risk

13.31   There are a number of parties involved in a private equity transaction, and the level of identification required in respect of each will vary.

Investee company (company into which funds are being paid) and its directors

13.32   All directors should be identified and the identity of key directors should be verified in accordance with Part I, paragraph 5.3.142.

13.33   This company will either have been the subject of extensive due diligence, or will be an "off the shelf" vehicle, especially established by the firm for the purpose of acquiring the investee company. Where the firm or the fund it manages, is acquiring securities in the investee company direct from a shareholder, the guidance in paragraphs 13.49 and 13.50 is relevant.

13.34   The jurisdiction of the vehicle may cause the risk profile of the investee company to increase, but provided that the company has been properly established and that the reason for the selection of jurisdiction is understood and appropriate, there should be no need to obtain additional verification.

13.35   Whilst the legal obligation relates to identifying the investee company into which funds are being paid, where that vehicle is itself undertaking a linked transaction there must be a clear understanding of the ultimate recipient of the funds and the flow of financing, particularly with the increasing complexity of deal structures.

Relevant Co-investor

13.36   Where the firm acts as lead investor in the round of financing where it has arranged co-investors' involvement in the deal, and where the co-investors are relying on the firm, it must identify the co-investors.

13.37   Following the firm's assessment of the overall risk presented by those co-investors, it may decide to verify their identity.

13.38   The identification requirements exist not only at the initial investment stage but also at any follow-on financing, to the extent that any new relevant co-investors are taking part. The firm should understand the business of a new co-investor and the reasons for it wanting to invest, particularly when the target of the financing is not performing well.

Timing

13.39   Customer due diligence checks should usually be completed when it is reasonably certain that the deal will complete, and in all cases before completion of the investment. Where there are subsequent changes to the board of directors, consideration should be given to the need to verify the identity of the new directors in light of the guidance in paragraph 13.32.

Purchaser on exit

13.40   The realisation of a private equity transaction will typically be made either by means of a listing, to a trade buyer, to existing management or to another private equity fund. If the sale is to a member of existing management who has been known to the private equity firm in the context of the investment concerned (or of another investment), the firm should consider the relevance of any verification given its existing relationship with, and knowledge about, the management.

13.41   The pressures of achieving a successful exit may heighten the risk of limiting the amount of due diligence performed on any potential purchaser on exit. In these circumstances the firm needs to ensure that its controls for proper verification of identity and source of funding remain robust. Where the purchaser is a private equity fund, consideration should be given to a risk-based approach of the kind described in relation to fund of fund investors into a private equity fund (see paragraphs 13.21 to 13.27 above). This will often be appropriate.

Timing

13.42   Identification checks should usually be completed on purchasers of an existing investment as soon as practicable when a deal looks reasonably likely to proceed and in all cases before completion of the sale.

(iii) Market risk

13.43   The range of companies invested in is determined by the stated parameters of the fund as agreed with the investors and the level of regulation and standard of controls in which each operates will vary enormously. The strength of the firm's due diligence process serves to identify where any risk exists within the investee companies and the firm should develop its AML/CTF approach accordingly.

13.44   Providing funding to a company which operates across a number of unregulated territories, even if the parent is incorporated or registered in a well-regulated territory, may be a higher risk than an equivalent business which operates out of one well-regulated territory, and appropriate levels of verification should be considered.

13.45   An assessment may be required as to whether the type of business being invested in is likely to be a target for money launderers, and the approach to due diligence adapted accordingly. Businesses which involve high volumes of cash or near cash transactions, for example, casinos, hotels, are likely to be at greater risk than, for example, an early stage biotech company.

(iv) Other issues

Representations issued by private equity firms to third parties

13.46   In respect of their Funds, firms should be prepared to confirm whether to their actual knowledge there is any natural person who is the beneficial owner with an interest exceeding 25% of that fund. When disclosing information about investors in accordance with relevant confidentiality provisions, firms should consider agreeing to disclose the information to a certain officer or department within the third party, such as the Compliance Officer only.

Use of verification carried out by others

13.47   Private equity firms make extensive use of professional advisers, especially where the required knowledge does not exist in the firm itself. The investee companies themselves and any co-investors will usually appoint professional advisers to ensure that their own interests are represented in any negotiation. In some cases, these advisers are themselves under an obligation under the ML Regulations, or under similar legislation in the EU or in an equivalent jurisdiction, to verify the identity of their clients. Depending on the circumstances, and the firm's knowledge of/relationship with the investee company, the firm may consider it appropriate to take account of information or written assurances provided to the firm by these third parties, as part of the overall risk-based approach.

13.48 The requirement to appear before a notary in certain jurisdictions when signing documents such as the purchase contract, shareholder's agreement etc, can provide adequate verification. However the notary's certificate should only be considered as adequate if it states the full names and identity card numbers (or equivalent) of the individuals appearing before the notary, plus details of the evidence provided for their authority to act as representatives of the parties involved.

Vendor (beneficiary of funding decision)

13.49 The decision to invest by the private equity firm will usually result in one or more individuals benefiting financially. In some instances these individuals will continue to be shareholders in the company, with the benefit being represented by the potential of significant future gains. In other cases, the beneficiary(ies) may be the original founders of the business who no longer participate.

13.50 The firm will not wish to damage its reputation by becoming associated with inappropriate individuals. Whilst vendors of an investee company are not customers of the firm under the ML Regulations unless they are selling securities in the investee company directly to the firm or to its fund(s), the firm should be aware of who the vendors are. The nature of the due diligence work performed is such that the origins of the business and the individuals involved will have been the subject of extensive review and investigation. It should ensure that it has sufficient information about the vendors (this may or may not require obtaining verification of identity) so as to be able to demonstrate that the firm had no knowledge or reasonable grounds for suspicion of money laundering on the part of any vendors in relation to the transaction.

[7037]

14: CORPORATE FINANCE

*Note: This **sectoral** guidance is incomplete on its own. It must be read in conjunction with the main guidance set out in **Part I** of the Guidance.*

This sectoral guidance considers specific issues over and above the more general guidance set out in Part I, Chapters 4, 5 and 7, which firms engaged in corporate finance activity may want to take into account when considering applying a risk-based approach to that sector. Firms may also find the following sectors useful:

- **Sector 13: *Private Equity*, which covers the private financing of companies.**
- **Sector 18: *Wholesale Markets,* which covers the trading of securities in a primary or secondary market.**

Overview of the sector

14.1 "Corporate finance" is activity relating to:
  (i) The *issue of securities*. These activities might be conducted with an issuer in respect to itself, or with a holder or owner of securities. Examples include: arranging an initial public offering (IPO), a sale of new shares, or a rights issue for a company, as well as making arrangements with owners of securities concerning the repurchase, exchange or redemption of those securities;
  (ii) The *financing, structuring and management of a body corporate, partnership or other organisation*. Examples include: advice about the restructuring of a business and its management, and advising on, or facilitating, financing operations including securitisations;
  (iii) *Changes in the ownership of a business*. Examples include: advising on mergers and takeovers, or working with a company to find a strategic investor;
  (iv) *Business carried on by a firm for its own account* where that business arises in the course of activities covered by (i), (ii) or (iii) above, including cases where the firm itself becomes a strategic investor in an enterprise.

What are the money laundering risks in corporate finance?

14.2 As with any financial service activity, corporate finance business can be used to launder money.

14.3 The money laundering activity through corporate finance will not usually involve the placement stage of money laundering, as the transaction will involve funds or assets already within the financial system. However, corporate finance could be involved in the layering or integration stages of money laundering. It could also involve the concealment, use and possession of criminal property and arrangements to do so, or terrorist funding.

14.4   The money laundering risks associated with corporate finance relate to the transfer of assets between parties, in exchange for cash or other assets. The assets can take the form of securities or other corporate instruments.

How to assess the elements of risk in this sector

14.5   In order to forestall financial crime, including money laundering and terrorist financing, it is important to obtain background knowledge about all the participants in a corporate finance transaction, and not just those who are customers, who must be subject to customer due diligence. This background gathering exercise should include measures to understand the ownership and control structure of the customer as well as looking at the beneficial ownership and any possible involvement of politically exposed persons and establishing the purpose and intended nature of the business relationship and whether this is consistent with the transaction being undertaken.

14.6   In its assessment of the financial crime risk of a particular corporate finance transaction, a firm should use – where possible and appropriate – the information it has obtained as a result of the intensive due diligence it normally undertakes in any corporate finance transaction. This may include, but not be limited to, firms assessing the probity of directors, shareholders, and any others with significant involvement in the customer's business and the corporate finance transaction.

14.7   The money laundering risks associated with corporate finance activity can be mitigated if a firm understands or obtains assurances from appropriate third parties as to the source and nature of the funds or assets involved in the transaction.

14.8   In addition, a firm should assess whether the financial performance of an enterprise is in line with the nature and scale of its business, and whether the corporate finance services it seeks appear legitimate in the context of those activities. The outcome of this assessment should be consistent with the purpose and intended nature of the business relationship.

Who is the customer for AML purposes?

Issuer of securities

14.9   Where a firm is facilitating the issue or offer of securities by an entity, that entity is the firm's customer.

Purchaser of securities

14.10   Whether purchasers of the *securities* issued are customers for AML purposes will depend upon the relationship the firm has with them, and in particular whether or not a firm has behaved in a way that would lead the purchaser to believe that he is a customer. Therefore:

- A direct approach by a firm to a potential purchaser will create a customer relationship for the firm.
- Purchasers of *securities* in new issues arranged by a firm will not be customers of the firm so long as their decision to purchase is based on offering documentation alone, or on advice they receive from another firm (which will have a customer relationship for AML purposes with the purchaser).

14.11   To protect its own reputation and that of the issuer, a firm that is acting as arranger in the issue of securities may wish to ensure that appropriate investor identification measures are adopted in the offering and that the entity administering the subscription arrangements understands the legal and regulatory AML requirements and confirms to the firm that it will undertake appropriate customer due diligence on its customers participating in the purchase of securities.

Owners of securities

14.12   Where a firm advises the owners of *securities*, in respect of the repurchase, exchange or redemption by an issuer of those *securities*, the owners will be customers of the firm for AML purposes.

14.13   However, other than in exceptional cases, a firm may be precluded by other regulatory requirements from acting for both the issuer and the owners of the investments concerned. In the circumstances where a firm does act for the owners of the *securities*, the issuer will not generally be a customer of the firm for AML purposes.

Financing, structuring and management of a body corporate, partnership or other organisation

14.14   The entity with which a firm is doing investment business, whether by way of advice provided to the entity, or through engaging in transactions on its behalf, will be a customer of the firm for AML purposes.

14.15   The activity undertaken by a firm may entail the firm dealing in some way with other entities/parties on behalf of the customer entity, for example, through the sale of part of its customer's business to another entity or party. In these circumstances, the other entity or party whom the firm deals with on behalf of the customer will not also become the firm's customer as a result of the firm's contact with them during the sale. (For *Securitisations transactions* see paragraphs 14.30–14.36.)

Changes in the ownership of a business

14.16   The entity with which a firm is mandated to undertake investment business, whether by way of advice or through engaging in transactions, will be the customer of the firm for AML purposes.

14.17   Other entities or parties affected by changes in ownership, for example a takeover or merger target, will not become the firm's customers, unless a firm provides advice or other investment business services to that entity or party. Similarly, an approach by a firm to a potential investor on behalf of a customer does not require the firm to treat the potential investor as its customer for AML purposes, unless the firm provides advice or other investment business services to that investor.

Business carried on by a firm for its own account

14.18   Where a firm makes a principal investment in an entity, that entity will not be a customer of the firm. A principal investment in this context means an investment utilising the firm's capital and one that would not involve the firm entering into a business relationship within the meaning of the ML Regulations. If, as well as making a principal investment in an entity, a firm enters into a business relationship with that entity, for example, by providing investment services or financing to the entity, the firm must apply the measures referred to in Part I, Chapter 5 as appropriate. When a firm has determined that the investment is not subject to the requirements of the ML Regulations, it may nevertheless wish to consider, in a risk-sensitive way, whether there are any money laundering implications in the investment it is making and may decide to apply appropriate due diligence measures.

Involvement of other regulated firms

14.19   A regulated firm (X) may be involved in a corporate finance transaction in which another regulated firm (Y) from an equivalent jurisdiction, is also involved. The relationship between X and Y may take a number of different forms:

(a)   X may be providing investment services to Y, for example, by facilitating an IPO for Y. In this case Y is the customer of X. X is not the customer of Y.

(b)   X and Y may both be providing investment services to a customer Z, for example by underwriting a private placement of shares for Z. In this case, Z is the customer of X and of Y. There is no customer relationship between X and Y.

(c)   X may be acting for an **offeror** (Z) in a takeover, and Y may be acting for the **offeree** (ZZ). Z is the customer of X and ZZ is the customer of Y. There is no customer relationship between X and Y.

14.20   A firm should establish at the outset whether it has a customer relationship with another regulated firm and, if so, should follow the guidance in Part I, Chapter 5 in verifying the identity of that firm.

Customer due diligence

14.21   Corporate finance activity may be undertaken with a wide range of customers, but is predominantly carried on with listed and unlisted companies or their owners. The guidance contained in Part I, Chapter 5 indicates the customer due diligence procedures that should be followed in these cases. However, the following is intended to amplify aspects of the Part I, Chapter 5 procedures, with particular reference to the business practices and money laundering risks inherent in a corporate finance relationship.

Background information

14.22   It is necessary to look more closely than the procedures set out in Part I, Chapter 5 for acceptance of the customer. It is important to check the history of the customer and to carry out **reputational** checks about its business and representatives and shareholders.

Timing

14.23   In corporate finance transactions, when a mandate is issued or an engagement letter is signed is the point at which the firm enters into a formal relationship with the customer. However, it is common for a firm to begin discussions with a customer before a mandate or engagement letter has been signed.

14.24   A firm should determine when it is appropriate to undertake customer due diligence on a prospective customer and where applicable any beneficial owners, but this must be before the establishment of a business relationship. In all cases, however, the firm must ensure that it has completed appropriate customer due diligence prior to entering into a legally binding agreement with the customer to undertake the corporate finance activity.

14.25   Where, having completed customer due diligence, a mandate or engagement letter is not entered into until some time after the commencement of the relationship, a firm is not required to obtain another form of evidence confirming the customer's agreement to the relationship with the firm prior to the signing of the mandate, provided it is satisfied that those individuals with whom it is dealing have authority to represent the customer.

14.26   Whilst not an AML requirement, if the relationship is conducted, either initially or subsequently, with non-board members, the firm should satisfy itself at an early stage that the board has approved the relationship by seeking formal notification of the non-board members' authority to act on behalf of the company they represent.

Other evidence for customer due diligence

14.27   Where there is less transparency over the ownership of the customer, for example, where ownership or control is vested in other entities such as trusts or special purpose vehicles (SPV's), or less of an industry profile or less independent means of verification of the customer, a firm should consider how this affects the ML/TF risk presented. It will, in certain circumstances, be appropriate to conduct additional due diligence, over and above the firm's standard evidence. Firms have an obligation to verify the identity of all beneficial owners (see Part I, Chapter 5). It should also know and understand any associations the customer may have with other jurisdictions. It may also consider whether it should verify the identity of other owners or controllers. A firm may, subject to application of its risk-based approach, use other forms of evidence to confirm these matters. Consideration should be given as to whether or not the lack of transparency appears to be for reasonable business purposes. Firms will need to assess overall risk in deciding whether the "alternative" evidence, which is not documentary evidence as specified in Part I, Chapter 5, is sufficient to demonstrate ownership and the structure as represented by the customer.

14.28   Firms should maintain file notes setting out the basis on which they are able to confirm the structure and the identity of the customer, and individuals concerned, without obtaining the documentary evidence set out in Part I, Chapter 5. Such notes should take account of:
- Social and business connections
- Meetings at which others are present who can be relied upon to know the individuals in question
- The reliance which is being placed on banks, auditors and legal advisers

Subsequent activity for a customer

14.29   Some corporate finance activity involves a single transaction rather than an ongoing relationship with the customer. Where the activity is limited to a particular transaction or activity, and the customer subsequently engages the firm for other activity, the firm should ensure that the information and customer due diligence it holds are up to date and accurate at the time the subsequent activity is undertaken.

Securitisation transactions

14.30   Securitisation **is** the process of creating new financial instruments by pooling and combining existing financial assets, which are then marketed to investors. A firm may be involved in these transactions in one of three main ways in the context of corporate finance business:
  (i)   as advisor and facilitator in relation to a customer securitising assets such as future receivables. The firm will be responsible for advising the customer about the transaction and for setting up the special purpose vehicle (SPV), which will issue the asset-backed instruments. The firm may also be a counterparty to the SPV in any transactions subsequently undertaken by the SPV;
  (ii) as the owner of assets which it wants to securitise;
  (iii) as counterparty to an SPV established by another firm for its own customer or for itself – that is, solely as a counterparty in a transaction originated by an unconnected party.

14.31   As a general rule, the firm should be more concerned with the identity of those who provide the assets for the SPV, as this is the key money laundering risk. So long as the firm demonstrates the link between the customer and the SPV, the SPV is not subject to the full requirements of Part I, Chapter 5. However, the firm should obtain the basic identity information and hold evidence of the SPV's existence.

14.32   Whether a purchaser of the instruments issued by the SPV will be treated as customers will depend upon the relationship the firm has with them. Purchasers of instruments issued by the SPV arranged by a firm will not be customers of the firm so long as their decision to purchase is based on offering documentation alone, or on advice they receive from another firm, who will have a customer relationship with them. However, as part of a firm's risk-based approach, and for reputational reasons, it may also feel it appropriate to undertake due diligence on those who are purchasers of the instruments issued by the SPV.

14.33   In addition to verifying the identity of the customer in line with normal practice for the type of customer concerned, the firm should satisfy itself that the securitisation has a legitimate economic purpose. Where existing internal documents cannot be used for this purpose, file notes should be made to record the background to the transaction.

14.34   The firm needs to follow standard identity procedures as set out in Part I, paragraphs 5.3.68 to 5.3.248 with regard to the other customers of the firm to which it sells the new instruments issued by the SPV it has established.

14.35   If the firm is dealing with a regulated agent acting on behalf of the SPV, it should follow normal procedures for dealing with regulated firms.

14.36   If the firm is dealing with an unregulated agent of the SPV, both the agent and the SPV should be identified in accordance with the guidance in Part I, paragraph 5.3.70. Background information, obtainable in many cases from rating agencies, should be used to record the purpose of the transaction and to assess the money laundering risk.

Monitoring

14.37   The money laundering risks for firms operating within the corporate finance sector can be mitigated by the implementation of appropriate, documented, monitoring procedures. General guidance on monitoring is set out in Part I, section 5.7.

14.38   Monitoring of corporate finance activity will generally, due to the relationship-based, rather than transaction-based (in the wholesale markets sense), nature of corporate finance, be undertaken by the staff engaged in the activity, rather than through the use of electronic systems.

14.39   The essence of monitoring corporate finance activity involves understanding the rationale for the customer undertaking the transaction or activity, and staff using their knowledge of the customer, and what would be normal in the given set of circumstances, to be able to spot the unusual or potentially suspicious.

14.40   The firm will need to have a means of assessing that its risk mitigation procedures and controls are working effectively. In particular the firm will need to consider:
- Reviewing ways in which different services may be used for ML/TF purposes, and how these ways may change, supported by typologies/law enforcement feedback, etc;
- Adequacy of staff training and awareness;
- Capturing appropriate management information;
- Upward reporting and accountability; and
- Effectiveness of liaison with regulatory and law enforcement agencies.

The responses to these matters need to be documented in order to demonstrate how it monitors and improves the effectiveness of its systems and procedures.

14.41   The firm will have ongoing relationships with many of its customers where it must ensure that the documents, data or information held are kept up to date. Where, as is likely in some cases with corporate finance activities, the customers may not have an ongoing relationship with the firm, it is important that the firm's procedures to deal with new business from these customers is clearly understood and practised by the relevant staff. It is a key element of any system that up to date customer information is available as it is on the basis of this information that the unusual is spotted, questions asked and judgements made about whether something is suspicious.

Staff awareness, training and alertness

14.42   The firm must train staff on how corporate finance transactions may be used for ML/TF and in the firm's procedures for managing this risk. This training should be directed specifically at those staff directly involved in corporate finance transactions and should be tailored around the specific risks that this type of business represents. Whilst there is no single solution when determining how to deliver training, training of relationship management staff via workshops may well prove to be more successful than on-line learning or videos/CDs.

[7038]

15: TRADE FINANCE

Note: This sectoral guidance is incomplete on its own. It must be read in conjunction with the main guidance set out in Part I of the Guidance Notes.

Firms addressing the money laundering/terrorist financing risks in trade finance should also have regard to the guidance in sector 16: Correspondent banking.

Overview of the sector

15.1   The term 'Trade Finance' is used to describe various operations, usually but not exclusively undertaken to facilitate trade or commerce. Such operations comprise a mix of money transmission instruments, default undertakings and provision of finance and are described in more detail below. Trade Finance operations are often considered in a cross-border context but can also relate to domestic trade. In volume terms the majority of Trade Finance operations are of a routine nature. Nevertheless, it is recommended that firms create a risk policy appropriate to their business which they may be required to justify to their regulators.

15.2   The three main types of Trade Finance operations are described in more detail below. Whilst they are addressed separately, they are not necessarily mutually exclusive and these operations may be combined in relation to a single transaction, series of transactions or, on occasion, in relation to a particular project. In terms of assessing risk, it is important to understand the detailed workings of individual operations/instruments, rather than automatically assuming that they fit into a particular category simply because of the name that they may have been given.

15.3   There is sometimes no specific dividing line between either the categories of Trade Finance outlined below or when a lending facility is generic or Trade Finance specific. Firms are, therefore, strongly encouraged to consider the nature of the transactions they are handling.

Funds Transmission/Payments

15.4   Trade Finance operations often involve solely transmission of funds where the payment is subject to presentation of document(s) and/or compliance with specified condition(s). Typical instruments which come into this category are Letters of Credit and Collections. Financing may on occasion be provided either specifically related to the instrument itself, or as part of a general line of credit.

Default Undertakings

15.5   As the term implies, such undertakings normally only involve payment if some form of default has occurred. Typical undertakings in this category are bonds, guarantees, indemnities and standby letters of credit. Provision of finance is less common than with funds transmission/payment instruments, but could also occur.

Structured Financing

15.6   This category comprises a variety of financing techniques, but with the common aim of facilitating trade and commerce, where financing is the primary operation, with any associated Trade Finance instrument and/or undertaking being subsidiary. On occasion, such financing may be highly complex e g involving special purpose vehicles (SPVs).

Glossary of trade finance terms used in this guidance

15.7   _Bills of Exchange_. A signed written order by which one party (drawer or trade creditor) requires another party (drawee or trade debtor) to pay a specified sum to the drawer or a third party (payee or trade creditor) or order. In the UK, the relevant legislation is the Bills of Exchange Act 1882, as amended. In cross-border transactions, equivalent laws may also apply. In many other European jurisdictions, transactions will be subject to the Geneva Conventions on Bills of Exchange 1932. Bills of Exchange can be payable at sight or at a future date, and if either accepted and/or avalised, represent a commitment by the accepting or Avalising party to pay funds, thus making them the primary obligor.

15.8   _Acceptances/Deferred Payment Undertakings_. Where the drawee of a bill of exchange signs the bill with or without the word "accepted" on it, the drawee becomes the acceptor and is responsible for payment on maturity. Where banks become the acceptor these are known as "bankers' acceptances" and are sometimes used to effect payment for merchandise sold in import-export transactions. Avalisation that occurs in forfaiting and some other transactions is similar to acceptance but does not have legal standing under English law. Banks may also agree to pay documents presented under a documentary credit payable at a future date that does not include a Bill of Exchange. In such instances the bank incurs a deferred payment undertaking.

15.9   _Promissory Notes_. These are a written promise committing the issuer to pay the payee or to order, (often a trade creditor) a specified sum either on demand or on a specified date in the future. (This is similar to a bill of exchange).

15.10   _Guarantees and Indemnities_. Sometimes called Bonds, these are issued when a contractual agreement between a buyer and a seller requires some form of financial security in the event that the seller fails to perform under the contract terms, and are normally issued against a backing "Counter Indemnity" in favour of the issuing firm. There are many variations, but a common theme is that these are default instruments which are only triggered in the event of failure to perform under the underlying commercial contract.

15.11   _Documentary Credits_. Historically, these were one of the most commonly used instruments in Trade Finance transactions but their usage has declined in recent years, particularly in intra-Western European trade. They are, however, still used extensively in trade involving deep sea transport and in certain geographical areas e g South East Asia. In its simplest form a Documentary Credit is normally issued by a bank on behalf of a purchaser of merchandise or a recipient of services (a trade debtor), in favour of a beneficiary, usually the seller of the merchandise or provider of services (a trade creditor). The issuer (usually a bank) irrevocably promises to pay the seller/provider at sight, or at a future date if presented with documents which comply with the terms and conditions of the Documentary Credit. Effectively, the Documentary Credit substitutes the Issuing Bank's credit for that of the applicant subject to the terms and conditions being complied with. When a Documentary Credit is confirmed by another bank, the Confirming Bank adds its own undertaking as principal to that of the Issuing Bank ie the Confirming Bank becomes a primary obligor in its own right. There are many more complex variations than this simple example but almost all Documentary Credits worldwide are issued and handled subject to the applicable International Chamber of Commerce (ICC) Uniform Customs & Practice for Documentary Credits in force (UCP 600 superseded UCP 500 on 1 July 2007).

15.12 *Collections.* A typical documentary collection involves documents forwarded by an exporter, or the exporter's bank, to an importer's bank to be released in accordance with the accompanying instructions. These instructions could require release of documents against payment or acceptance of a Bill of Exchange. As with Documentary Credits, there are a number of possible variations and the term collection is also used in other contexts. However, Collections of the type described above are normally but not always handled subject to the applicable ICC Rules for Collections – URC in force (currently ICC Publication 522).

15.13 *Standby Letters of Credit.* Unlike Documentary Credits, Standby Letters of Credit are default instruments which are sometimes issued instead of a guarantee. They may be issued subject to the applicable ICC rules in force, currently either UCP 600 or International Standby Practices (ISP 98), but may also contain specific exemption wording.

15.14 *Discounting.* A bank may discount a bill of exchange or a deferred payment undertaking, paying less than the face value of the bill/documents to the payee or trade creditor for the privilege of receiving the funds prior to the specified date. The trade debtor may not be informed of the sale and the trade creditor may continue to be responsible for collecting the debt on behalf of the discounter.

15.15 *Negotiation.* This term has a variety of meanings dependent on the jurisdiction/territory in which it is being used but for the purposes of UCP 600 means "the purchase by the nominated bank of drafts (drawn on a bank other than the nominated bank) and/or documents under a complying presentation, by advancing or agreeing to advance funds to the beneficiary on or before the banking day on which reimbursement is due to the nominated bank". Mere examination of the documents without giving of value does not constitute a negotiation.

15.16 *Forfaiting.* This is a financing mechanism traditionally designed for use by trade creditors who export goods. Forfaiting, however, may also involve the direct provision of finance to importers and the provision of working capital by credit institutions for the purposes of funding trade transactions in their countries. The trade creditor or exporter sells evidence of a debt, usually a promissory note issued by the importer or a bill of exchange accepted by the importer or proceeds due under a Letter of Credit such proceeds being assigned by the exporter. The sale is normally made without recourse to the trade creditor/exporter in which case the person buying the debt will usually require the importer's payment obligations to be guaranteed by a bank (avalised). There is an active secondary market for forfaiting paper.

What are the money laundering/terrorist financing risks in Trade Finance?

15.17 Globally a substantial volume of routine Trade Finance transactions take place each week. Given the nature of the business, there is little likelihood that Trade Finance will be used by money launderers in the placement stage of money laundering. However, Trade Finance can be used in the layering and integration stages of money laundering as the enormous volume of trade flows obscure individual transactions and the complexities associated with the use of multiple foreign exchange transactions and diverse trade financing arrangements permit the commingling of legitimate and illicit funds.

15.18 FATF's June 2006 study of Trade Based Money Laundering defined this as "the process of disguising the proceeds of crime and moving value through the use of trade transactions in an attempt to legitimize their illicit origins. In practice, this can be achieved through the misrepresentation of the price, quantity or quality of imports or exports. Moreover, trade-based money laundering techniques vary in complexity and are frequently used in combination with other money laundering techniques to further obscure the money trail". The study concludes that "trade-based money laundering represents an important channel of criminal activity and, given the growth in world trade, an increasingly important money laundering and terrorist financing vulnerability. Moreover, as the standards applied to other money laundering techniques become increasingly effective, the use of trade-based money laundering can be expected to become increasingly attractive". The term 'trade transactions' as used by the FATF is wider than the trade transactions described in this sectoral guidance.

15.19 A firm's risk-based approach should be designed to ensure that it places an emphasis on deterring, detecting and disclosing in the areas of greatest perceived vulnerability. In this context, regard should be had to the fact that the majority of Trade Finance transactions take place in modest-value volume businesses, and relatively few in specialised, or otherwise high value business areas.

15.20   A key risk around Trade Finance business is that seemingly legitimate transactions and associated documents can be constructed simply to justify the movement of funds between parties, or to show a paper trail for non-existent or fraudulent goods. In particular the level and type of documentation received by a firm is dictated principally by the applicant or instructing party, and, because of the diversity of documentation, firms may not be expert in many types of the documents received as a result of Trade Finance business. Such a risk is probably greatest where the parties to an underlying commercial trade transaction are in league to disguise the true nature of a transaction. In such instances, methods used by criminals to transfer funds illegally range from over and under invoicing, to the presentation of false documents or spurious calls under default instruments. In more complex situations, for example where asset securitisation is used, trade receivables can be generated from fictitious parties or fabricated transactions.

15.21   Trade Finance is generally used instead of clean payments and generic lending when documentation is required for other purposes eg to comply with Customs, other regulatory requirements, control of goods and/or possible financial institution requirements. The key money laundering/terrorism risks arise when such documentation is adapted to facilitate non-genuine transactions, normally involving movement of money at some point.

15.22   Whilst it is recognised that firms will not be familiar with all types of documentation they see, they should pay particular attention to transactions which their own analysis and risk policy have identified as high risk and be on enquiry for anything unusual.

Assessing the money laundering/terrorist financing risk

15.23   The ability of a firm to assess the money laundering or terrorist financing risks posed by a particular transaction will depend on the amount of information that it has about that transaction and the parties to it. This will be determined by the firm's role in the Trade Finance operation. The amount of information available to a firm may vary depending on the size/type of the firm and the volume of business that it is handling. Where possible when assessing risk, firms may take into consideration the parties involved in the transaction and the countries where they are based, as well as the nature of any goods forming the basis of an underlying commercial transaction.

15.24   When developing a risk-based strategy firms should consider but not restrict their consideration to factors such as the size of the transaction, nature of the transaction, geographical location of the parties and the firm's business mix.

15.25   FATF's June 2006 study notes that the basic techniques of trade-based money laundering include:
- over- and under-invoicing of goods and services;
- multiple invoicing of goods and services;
- over- and under-shipments of goods and services; and
- falsely describing goods and services.

Firms need to be aware of these techniques when developing their risk-based strategy and consider how best to mitigate the risks to themselves. The FATF has listed some red flag indicators in its report which are reproduced in Annex 15–II.

Customer due diligence

15.26   Firms must be aware of their obligations under POCA, which cannot be compromised or qualified when using a risk-based approach. Subject to the foregoing, as part of their risk policy and assessment firms should be mindful of the need to balance the risk of incurring civil claims for breach of contract when the correct documents have been presented, and their obligations under POCA.

15.27   With the partial exception of Inward Collections (see below) appropriate and acceptable due diligence must be undertaken on the customer who is the instructing party for the purpose of the transaction (see below). Due diligence on other parties to the transaction including other customers should be undertaken where required by a firm's risk policy. Reference to Part I, Chapter 5 should be made as appropriate. Additional due diligence on other parties, and possibly on the transaction itself, should be undertaken where required by the firm's internal risk policy and where specifically on enquiry.

15.28   It should be noted that the instructing party will not necessarily be an existing customer of the firm and, if not, due diligence must be undertaken on the instructing party before proceeding with the transaction.

15.29   The following list of instructing parties is not exhaustive and where necessary firms will need to decide in each case who the instructing party is:
- Import (Outward) Letters of Credit – the instructing party for the issuing bank is the applicant.

- Export (Inward) Letters of Credit – the instructing party for the advising/confirming bank is the issuing bank.
- Outward Collections – the instructing party is the customer/applicant.
- Inward Collections – due diligence should normally be undertaken on the instructing party but where this is not practical may exceptionally be undertaken on the drawee.
- Bonds/Guarantees – the instructing party may be either a customer, correspondent bank or other third party.

15.30   *Forfaiting* – The diverse nature of forfaiting business is such that the exact nature of the transaction needs to be considered. For example, the need to ensure authenticity may lead to enquiries being made of the importer's management, and it may be necessary to examine the commercial parts of documents, dependent on the nature of the underlying commercial transaction.

15.31   In the primary Forfaiting, or origination, market, a firm will usually be dealing directly with an exporter, who will be its customer and who should undergo due diligence in accordance with Part I, Chapter 5. In addition, as part of its risk-based approach, a firm, where appropriate, should scrutinise the other party to the underlying commercial transaction, as well as the transaction itself, to satisfy itself of the validity of the transaction. The amount and depth of scrutiny will depend on the firm's risk assessment of the client and transaction.

15.32   In the secondary Forfaiting market, the firm's customer will be the person from whom it buys the evidence of debt. However if it holds a Forfait asset to maturity it will be receiving funds from the guarantor bank and thus it should as a matter of course perform due diligence on this entity as well. Using a risk-based approach, firms should also consider whether they should conduct some form of due diligence on the underlying parties to the transaction, as well as on the transaction itself. This will depend on a risk assessment of the countries and the types of clients or products and services involved. It may be necessary to examine documentation on the underlying commercial transaction. However, it should be borne in mind that the further away from the original transaction the purchaser of a Forfait asset is, the harder it will be to undertake meaningful due diligence.

15.33   *Structured Financing* – As stated in paragraph 15.2, structured finance transactions are diverse in nature. Due diligence should be undertaken on all relevant parties in accordance with the firm's own risk policy/assessment.

Additional due diligence

15.34   Where a firm's risk policy determines that additional due diligence is appropriate, some of the checks firms could undertake (not all of which may be applicable in each case) include:

- make enquiries as appropriate into the ownership and background of the instructing party or the beneficiary of the transaction, taking further steps to verify information or the identity of key individuals as the case demands;
- build up a record of the pattern of a customer's (ie, the instructing party's) business, to facilitate identification of unusual transactions;
- check the transaction against warning notices from ICC's International Maritime Bureau;
- refer the transaction to ICC Commercial Crime Services for bill of lading, shipping and pricing checks;
- attend and record relationship meetings with the instructing party, visit them by arrangement;
- for export letters of credit, refer details to other Group resources on the ground in the country of origin, to seek corroboration.

Monitoring

15.35   Firms should have regard to the general guidance set out in Part I, section 5.7 on monitoring and in Chapter 6, on reporting suspicious transactions, and requesting consent where appropriate. The depth and frequency of monitoring to be undertaken will be determined by a firm's risk analysis of the business and/or the parties involved. Firms should, however, implement such controls and procedures appropriate to their business, but in any event must comply with any applicable legal or regulatory requirements.

15.36   Techniques dependent on a firm's risk analysis/policy could range from random after the event monitoring to checking receivables in any form of securitisation transaction to seek to determine if they are legitimate.

Staff awareness, training and alertness

15.37   The firm must train staff on how trade finance transactions may be used for ML/TF and in the firm's procedures for managing this risk. This training should be directed specifically at those staff directly involved in trade finance transactions, including those in relevant back office functions, and should be tailored around the specific risks that this type of business represents. Whilst there is no single solution when determining how to deliver training, training of relationship management staff via workshops may well prove to be more successful than on-line learning or videos/CDs.

15.38   The FATF's red flag indicators set out in Annex 15–II, although directed primarily at governmental agencies, nevertheless should be a useful aid to those devising firms' training programmes. In addition the several case studies set out in the study may also provide good training material. This study is available at www.fatf-gafi.org/dataoecd/60/25/37038272.pdf

[7039]

ANNEX 15–I

THE PROCESS FOR A CONFIRMED DOCUMENTARY CREDIT PAYABLE AT SIGHT AT THE COUNTERS OF THE NOMINATED BANK

Stage 1

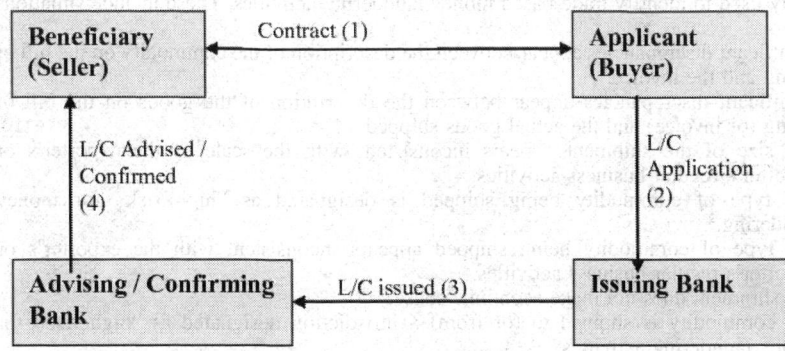

1.   The Applicant (buyer) and the Beneficiary (seller) agree a sales contract, which provides for payment through a documentary credit.

2.   The Applicant then requests his bank, the Issuing Bank, to issue a documentary credit in favour of the Beneficiary. The Issuing Bank, in so doing, is giving its irrevocable undertaking to make payment to the Beneficiary provided that the Beneficiary complies with the terms and conditions of the documentary credit.

3.   The documentary credit is advised to the Beneficiary through a bank in the exporter's country (the Advising Bank).

4.   The Advising Bank advises the documentary credit to the Beneficiary, and in this example, also adds its confirmation to the credit (becoming the Confirming Bank). A confirmed documentary credit carries the additional undertaking of the Confirming Bank.

Stage 2

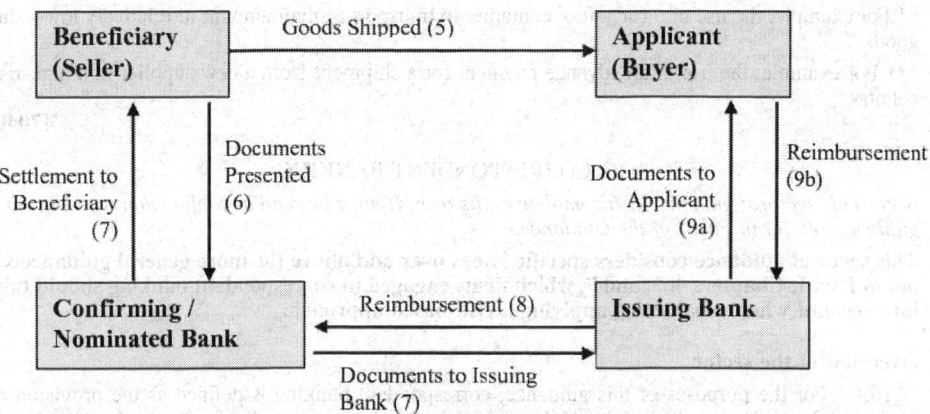

5.   The Beneficiary ships the goods to the Applicant.

6.   The Beneficiary then prepares and presents the documents required under the documentary credit to the bank nominated in the credit as the paying bank, which in this example, is also the Confirming Bank.

7. The documents are checked against the terms and conditions of the documentary credit, and, if they are in order, settlement is effected to the Beneficiary and the documents are forwarded by the Confirming Bank to the Issuing Bank.

8. When the Issuing Bank has checked the documents and found them in order, it will reimburse the Confirming /Paying Bank in accordance with the arrangement between the two banks.

9. The documents will then be released to the Applicant against payment or on other terms arranged between the Issuing Bank and the Applicant.

ANNEX 15–II

FATF'S TRADE-BASED MONEY LAUNDERING "RED FLAG" INDICATORS

The respondents to the FATF project team's questionnaire reported a number of red flag indicators that are routinely used to identify trade-based money laundering activities. These include situations in which:

- Significant discrepancies appear between the description of the commodity on the bill of lading and the invoice.
- Significant discrepancies appear between the description of the goods on the bill of lading (or invoice) and the actual goods shipped.
- The size of the shipment appears inconsistent with the scale of the exporter's or importer's regular business activities.
- The type of commodity being shipped is designated as "high risk" for money laundering.*
- The type of commodity being shipped appears inconsistent with the exporter's or importer's regular business activities.
- The shipment does not make economic sense.**
- The commodity is shipped to (or from) a jurisdiction designated as "high risk" for money laundering activities.
- The commodity is transhipped through one or more jurisdictions for no apparent economic reason.
- The method of payment appears inconsistent with the risk characteristics of the transaction.***
- The transaction involves the receipt of cash (or other payments) from third party entities that have no apparent connection with the transaction.
- The transaction involves the use of repeatedly amended or frequently extended letters of credit; and
- The transaction involves the use of front (or shell) companies.

[Customs agencies make use of more targeted information that relates to specific exporting, importing or shipping companies. In addition, red flag indicators that are used to detect other methods of money laundering could be useful in identifying potential trade-based money laundering cases.]

* For example, high-value, low volume goods (eg consumer electronics), which have high turnover rates and present valuation difficulties.

** For example, the use of a forty-foot container to transport a small amount of relatively low-value goods.

*** For example, the use of an advance payment for a shipment from a new supplier in a high-risk country.

[7040]

16: CORRESPONDENT BANKING

Note: This sectoral guidance is incomplete on its own. It must be read in conjunction with the main guidance set out in Part I of the Guidance.

This sectoral guidance considers specific issues over and above the more general guidance set out in Part I, Chapters 4, 5, and 7, which firms engaged in correspondent banking should take into account when considering applying a risk-based approach.

Overview of the sector

16.1 For the purposes of this guidance, correspondent banking is defined as the provision of banking-related services by one bank (Correspondent) to an overseas bank (Respondent) to enable the Respondent to provide its own customers with cross-border products and services that it cannot provide them with itself, typically due to a lack of an international network.

16.2 Correspondent banking activity can include establishing accounts, exchanging methods of authentication of instructions (eg by exchanging SWIFT or telex test keys and/or authorised signatures) and providing payment or other clearing-related services. A correspondent relationship can be based solely on the exchange of test keys, with cover for direct payment instructions being arranged through a third bank for credit to the Correspondent's/Respondent's own account in another jurisdiction. Activity can also encompass trade-related business and treasury/money market activities, for which the transactions can be settled through the correspondent relationship. The scope of a relationship and extent of products and services supplied will vary according to the needs of the Respondent, and the Correspondent's ability and willingness to supply them. Credit, operational and reputational risks also need to be considered.

16.3   A Correspondent is effectively an agent (intermediary) for the Respondent and executes/processes payments or other transactions for customers of the Respondent. The underlying customers may be individuals, corporates or even other financial services firms. Beneficiaries of transactions can be customers of the Correspondent, the Respondent itself or, in many cases, customers of other banks.

What are the money laundering risks in correspondent banking?

16.4   The Correspondent often has no direct relationship with the underlying parties to a transaction and is therefore not in a position to verify their identities. Correspondents often have limited information regarding the nature or purpose of the underlying transactions, particularly when processing electronic payments (wire transfers – see Part 1, paragraph 5.2.10–5.2.13) or clearing cheques. For these reasons, correspondent banking is in the main non face-to-face business and must be regarded as high risk from a money laundering and/or terrorist financing perspective. Firms undertaking such business are required by the ML Regulations (Regulation 10) "to apply on a risk-sensitive basis enhanced customer due diligence measures". These requirements are addressed in this guidance.

16.5   Correspondent banking relationships, if poorly controlled, can allow other financial services firms with inadequate AML/CTF systems and controls direct access to international banking systems.

16.6   A Correspondent handling transactions which represent the proceeds of criminal activity or terrorist financing risks regulatory fines and/or damage to its reputation.

How to assess the elements of risk in correspondent banking

16.7   For any Correspondent, the highest risk Respondents are those that:
- are offshore banks that are limited to conducting business with non residents or in non local currency, and are not subject to robust supervision of their AML/CTF controls; or
- are domiciled in jurisdictions with weak regulatory/AML/CTF controls or other significant reputational risk factors eg, corruption.

16.8   Correspondents must not maintain relationships with Respondents that are shell banks (see Part I, paragraphs 5.3.65–5.3.67) nor any Respondent which provides banking services to shell banks.

16.9   Enhanced customer due diligence (see Part I, section 5.5) must be undertaken on Respondents (and/or third parties authorised exceptionally to provide instructions to the Correspondent eg, other entities within a Respondent group) using a risk-based approach. The following risk indicators should be considered both when initiating a relationship, and on a continuing basis thereafter, to determine the levels of risk-based due diligence that should be undertaken:
- **The Respondent's domicile.** The jurisdiction where the Respondent is based and/or where its ultimate parent is headquartered may present greater risk (or may mitigate the risk, depending on the circumstances). Certain jurisdictions are recognised internationally as having inadequate anti-money laundering standards, insufficient regulatory supervision, or presenting greater risk for crime, corruption or terrorist financing. Other jurisdictions, however, such as many members of the Financial Action Task Force (FATF), have more robust regulatory environments, representing lower risks. Correspondents should review pronouncements from regulatory agencies and international bodies such as the FATF, to evaluate the degree of risk presented by the jurisdiction in which the Respondent and/or its parent are based.
- **The Respondent's ownership and management structures.** The location of owners, their corporate legal form and/or a lack of transparency of the ultimate beneficial ownership are indicative of the risk the Respondent presents. Account should be taken of whether the Respondent is publicly or privately owned; if publicly held, whether its shares are traded on a recognised market or exchange in a jurisdiction with a satisfactory regulatory regime, or, if privately owned, the identity of any beneficial owners and controllers. Similarly, the location and experience of management may indicate additional concerns, as would unduly frequent management turnover. The involvement of PEPs in the management or ownership of certain Respondents may also increase the risk.
- **The Respondent's business and customer base**. The type of business the Respondent engages in, as well as the type of markets it serves, is indicative of the risk the

Respondent presents. Involvement in certain business segments that are recognised internationally as particularly vulnerable to money laundering, corruption or terrorist financing, may present additional concern. Consequently, a Respondent that derives a substantial part of its business income from higher risk customers may present greater risk. Higher risk customers are those customers that may be involved in activities, or are connected to jurisdictions, that are identified by credible sources as activities or countries being especially susceptible of money laundering/terrorist financing or corruption.

- **Downstream Correspondent Clearing**. A Downstream Correspondent Clearer is a Respondent that receives correspondent banking services from a Correspondent and itself provides correspondent banking services to other financial institutions in the same currency as the account it maintains with its Correspondent. When these services are offered to a Respondent that is itself a Downstream Correspondent Clearer, a Correspondent should, on a risk-based approach, take reasonable steps to understand the types and risks of financial institutions to whom the Respondent offers such services, especial care being taken to ensure there are no shell bank customers, and consider the degree to which the Respondent examines the anti-money laundering/terrorist financing controls of those financial institutions.

Customer due diligence

16.10   All correspondent banking relationships with Respondents from non-EEA states must be subject to an appropriate level of due diligence which as a minimum meets the requirements laid down in Regulation 14 (3) of the ML Regulations and additionally will ensure that a Correspondent is comfortable conducting business with/for a particular Respondent (and hence its underlying customers) given the Respondent's risk profile. It may be appropriate for a Correspondent to take some comfort from the fact that a Respondent domiciled in or operating in a regulatory environment that is recognised internationally as adequate in the fight against money laundering/terrorist financing and corruption. In these instances, a Correspondent may choose to rely on publicly available information obtained either from the Respondent itself, another reputable existing Respondent, from other credible sources (eg, regulators, exchanges), or from reputable information sources, to satisfy its due diligence requirements.

16.11   The extent of the correspondent relationship should be factored into the level of due diligence undertaken. A Correspondent, subject to its risk-based approach, may decide not to undertake more than the minimum level of due diligence set out in Regulation 14 (3) for limited correspondent relationships, such as the exchange of test keys.

16.12   The verification of identity of Respondents should be undertaken in accordance with Part I, Chapter 5. Their ownership structures should be ascertained and understood and, for those privately-owned Respondents where it is appropriate to identify significant owners and/or controllers (beneficial owners), the form of evidence and information gathered on such owners and controllers must be sufficient, on a cumulative basis, to confirm identity with reasonable certainty.

16.13   A Correspondent's policies and procedures should require that the information, including due diligence, held relating to a Respondent is periodically reviewed and updated. The frequency of review should be tailored to the perceived risks, and updating should be undertaken as a result of trigger events e g an extension to the service/product range provided; a material change to the nature/scope of business undertaken by the Respondent; or as a result of significant changes to its legal constitution, or its owners or controllers or negative regulatory pronouncements and/or press coverage.

16.14   The level and scope of due diligence undertaken should take account of the relationship between the Respondent and its ultimate parent (if any). In general, for relationships maintained with branches, subsidiaries or affiliates, the status, reputation and controls of the parent entity should be considered in determining the extent of due diligence required on the Respondent. Where the Respondent is located in a high-risk jurisdiction, Correspondents may consider it appropriate to conduct additional due diligence on the Respondent as well as the parent. In instances when the Respondent is an affiliate that is not substantively and effectively controlled by the parent, then the quality of the affiliate's AML/CTF controls should always be established.

16.15   The Correspondent in assessing the level of due diligence to be carried out in respect of a particular Respondent, (in addition to the issues raised in paragraph 16.9) must consider:

- **Regulatory status and history.** The primary regulatory body responsible for overseeing or supervising the Respondent and the quality of that supervision. If circumstances warrant, a Correspondent should also consider publicly available materials to ascertain whether the Respondent has been the subject of any criminal case or adverse regulatory action in the recent past.
- **AML/CTF controls.** A Correspondent should establish whether the Respondent is itself regulated for money laundering/terrorist financing prevention and, if so, whether the Respondent is required to verify the identity of its customers and apply other AML/CTF

controls to FATF standards/equivalent to those laid down in the money laundering directive. Where this is not the case, additional due diligence should be undertaken to ascertain and assess the effectiveness of the Respondent's internal policy on money laundering/terrorist financing prevention and its know your customer and activity monitoring controls and procedures. Where undertaking due diligence on a branch, subsidiary or affiliate, consideration may be given to the parent having robust group-wide controls, and whether the parent is regulated for money laundering/terrorist financing to FATF standards/equivalent to those laid down in the money laundering directive. If not, the extent to which the parent's controls meet FATF standards/equivalent to those laid down in the money laundering directive and whether these are communicated and enforced 'effectively' throughout its network of international offices, should be ascertained.

- **Shell banks.** Whether the Respondent has confirmed that it will not provide banking services to or engage in business with, shell banks.

16.16   Prior to establishing a new correspondent relationship a person from senior management and independent from, the officer sponsoring the relationship must approve the setting up of the Respondent's account. For higher risk relationships, the Correspondent's compliance (or MLRO) function should also satisfy itself that the risks are acceptable.

Enhanced due diligence

16.17   Correspondents are required by Regulation 14(3) of the ML Regulations to subject Respondents from non-EEA States to enhanced customer due diligence, but should consider doing so whenever the Respondent has been considered to present a greater money laundering/terrorist financing risk. The enhanced due diligence process should involve further consideration of the following elements designed to ensure that the Correspondent has secured a greater level of understanding:

- **Respondent's ownership and management.** For all beneficial owners and controllers, the sources of wealth and background, including their reputation in the market place, as well as recent material ownership changes (eg in the last three years). Similarly, a more detailed understanding of the experience of each member of executive management as well as recent material changes in the executive management structure (eg, within the last three years).
- **Respondent's business.** Gather sufficient information about the Respondent to understand fully the nature of its business. In addition, determine from publicly-available information the reputation of the Respondent and the quality of its supervision.
- **PEP involvement.** If a PEP (see Part I, paragraphs 5.5.18–5.5.29) appears to have a material interest or management role in a Respondent then the Correspondent should ensure it has an understanding of that person's role in the Respondent.
- **Respondent's anti-money laundering/terrorist financing controls.** An assessment of the quality of the Respondent's AML/CTF and customer identification controls, including whether these controls meet internationally recognised standards. The extent to which a Correspondent should enquire will depend upon the perceived risks. Additionally, the Correspondent may wish to speak with representatives of the Respondent to obtain comfort that the Respondent's senior management recognise the importance of anti-money laundering/terrorist financing controls.
- **Document the relationship.** Document the respective responsibilities of the Respondent and Correspondent.
- **Customers with direct access to accounts of the Correspondent.** Be satisfied that, in respect of these customers, the Respondent:
  (i) has verified the identity of, and performs ongoing due diligence on, such customers; and
  (ii) is able upon request to provide relevant customer due diligence data to the Correspondent.

Monitoring

16.18   Implementing appropriate documented monitoring procedures can help mitigate the money laundering risks for firms undertaking correspondent banking activities. General guidance on monitoring is set out in Part 1, section 5.7.

16.19   The level of monitoring activity undertaken by a Correspondent on its Respondent's activity through it should be commensurate with the risks posed by the Respondent. Due to the significant volumes that correspondent banking activity can entail, electronic monitoring processes are often the norm.

16.20   The following possible techniques of monitoring activity combine to represent electronic monitoring good practice in the area of correspondent banking relationships:
- Anomalies in behaviour

— Monitoring for sudden and/or significant changes in transaction activity by value or volume.
- Hidden relationships
— Monitor for activity between accounts, customers (including Respondents and their underlying customers). Identify common beneficiaries and remitters or both amongst apparently unconnected accounts/Respondents. This is commonly known as link analysis.
- High risk geographies and entities
— Monitoring for significant increases of activity or consistently high levels of activity with (to or from) higher risk geographies and/or entities.
- Other money laundering behaviours
— Monitoring for activity that may, in the absence of other explanation, indicate possible money laundering, such as the structuring of transactions under reporting thresholds, or transactions in round amounts
- Other considerations
— In addition to the monitoring techniques above, the monitoring system employed to monitor correspondent banking for AML/CTF purposes should facilitate the ability to apply different thresholds against customers that are appropriate to their particular risk category.

Other monitoring activity

16.21   In addition to monitoring account/transaction activity, a Correspondent should monitor a Respondent for changes in its nature and status. As such, information about the Respondent collected during the customer acceptance and due diligence processes must be:
- Reviewed and updated on a periodic basis. (Periodic review of customers will occur on a risk-assessed basis), or
- Reviewed on an ad hoc basis as a result of changes to the customers information identified during normal business practices, or
- Reviewed when external factors result in a material change in the risk profile of the customer.

16.22   Where such changes are identified, the Respondent should be subject to a revised risk assessment, and a revision of their risk categorisation, as appropriate. Where, as a result of the review, the risk categorisation is altered (either up or down) a firm should ensure that the due diligence standards for the Respondent's new risk categorisation are complied with, by updating the due diligence already held. In addition, the level of monitoring undertaken should be adjusted to that appropriate for the new risk category.

16.23   Firms should consider terminating the accounts of Respondents, and consider their obligation to report suspicious activity, for Respondents who fail to provide satisfactory answers to reasonable questions regarding transactions/activity passing through the correspondent relationship, including, where appropriate, the identity of their customers featuring in unusual or suspicious transactions or activities.

16.24   The firm will need to have a means of assessing that its risk mitigation procedures and controls are working effectively. In particular the firm will need to consider:
- Reviewing ways in which different services may be used for ML/TF purposes, and how these ways may change, supported by typologies/law enforcement feedback, etc;
- Adequacy of staff training and awareness;
- Capturing appropriate management information;
- Upward reporting and accountability; and
- Effectiveness of liaison with regulatory and law enforcement agencies.

Staff awareness, training and alertness

16.25   The firm must train staff on how correspondent banking transactions may be used for ML/TF and in the firm's procedures for managing this risk. This training should be directed specifically at those staff directly involved in correspondent banking transactions and dealing with correspondent banking clients and should be tailored around the greater risks that this type of business represents. Whilst there is no single solution when determining how to deliver training, training of relationship management staff via workshops may well prove to be more successful than on-line learning or videos/CDs.

[7041]

17: SYNDICATED LENDING

Note: This sectoral guidance is incomplete on its own. It must be read in conjunction with the main guidance set out in Part I of the Guidance.

This sectoral guidance considers specific issues over and above the more general guidance set out in Part 1, Chapters 4, 5, and 7 which firms engaged in syndicated lending may want to take into account when considering applying a risk-based approach.

Overview of the sector

17.1   The syndicated loan market is an organised professional market, international in nature, providing much of the capital used by some of the largest companies in the world for a variety of purposes, ranging from working capital to acquisition financing. Banks and other financial institutions agree to make term loans and revolving credit loans to companies and may syndicate (offer on), or sell off, parts of their commitments to other banks, financial institutions or other entities.

17.2   The following sets out the relationships that exist in loan syndications:

- **Borrower.** A corporate or other legal entity who seeks to borrow funds and/or arrange credit facilities through the international capital markets.
- **Mandated Lead Manager/Arranger/Bookrunner**. A mandated Lead Manager/ Arranger/Bookrunner enters into an agreement to provide credit facilities to a borrower. By the very nature of this appointment, it is likely that the mandated Lead Manager/ Arranger/Bookrunner will be a lender with which the Borrower already has an established relationship. A syndicated loan transaction typically may have one to four mandated Lead Managers/Arrangers/Bookrunners and many lenders. The Mandated Lead Manager/Arranger/Bookrunner normally is responsible for advising the Borrower as to the type of facilities it requires, negotiating the broad terms of those facilities and advising on roles, timetable and approach to the market. In some instances it will also underwrite the transaction.
- **Lenders.** The financial institutions that provide the funds that have been arranged for the Borrower by the Mandated Lead Manager/Arranger/Bookrunner.
- **Agent.** To facilitate the process of administering the loan an Agent is appointed. The Agent acts as the agent of the Lenders not of the Borrower, although it is the Borrower that pays the Agent's fees and charges. The Agent acts as an intermediary between the Borrower and the Lenders, undertaking administrative functions, such as preparing documentation, servicing and acting as a channel for information between the Lenders and Borrower. One of the Lenders from the syndicate is normally appointed as the Agent. The Agent has a number of important functions, which may include:
  - Point of contact (maintaining contact with the Borrower and representing the views of the syndicate);
  - Monitor (monitoring the compliance of the Borrower with certain terms of the facility);
  - Postman and record-keeper (it is the agent to whom the Borrower is usually required to give notices and to provide financial information); and
  - Paying agent (the Borrower makes all payments of interest and repayments of principal and any other payments under the loan agreement to the Agent. The Agent passes these monies back to the Lenders to whom they are due. Similarly, the Lenders advance funds to the Borrower through the Agent).
- **Guarantor.** As part of the loan agreement, the Borrower may provide guarantors, who will guarantee repayment of the loan if the Borrower defaults on the loan, on a joint and several basis.

17.3   The cash flows arising from these arrangements are between the syndicate participants (Lenders) and the Agent, and then on to the Borrower. Similarly, payments made by the Borrower to the Lenders take place via the Agent. The Lenders do not usually have any direct contact with the Borrower in respect of cash flows.

17.4   A secondary market also exists where banks and others buy and sell interests in these loans. The treatment of parties within the secondary market is set out in paragraphs 17.16–17.23.

What are the money laundering risks in syndicated lending?

17.5   Syndicated loans tend to be made to large, often multi-national companies, many of which will have their securities listed, or are parts of corporate groups whose securities are listed, on EU regulated or equivalent regulated markets. As such, the money laundering risk relating to syndicated loans for this type of customer should be regarded as low.

17.6   The features of all lending are generally that the initial monies advanced are paid into a bank account. In syndicated lending the monies are usually handled by the Agent making it unlikely that the transaction would be used by money launderers in the placement stage of money laundering. Syndicated facilities could, however, be used to layer and integrate criminal proceeds. Repayments are usually made from the Borrower's bank account to the Agent who administers the repayment from its bank accounts to the Lenders. Repayments in cash are unlikely.

17.7   Given that a syndicated loan results in the Borrower receiving funds from the Lender, the initial transaction is not very susceptible of money laundering. The main money laundering risk arises through variations in the loan arrangements such as the acceleration of an agreed repayment schedule, either by means of lump sum repayments, or early termination without good commercial rationale. When these circumstances occur they should be considered carefully and consideration must be given to the source of the money used to accelerate the repayment schedule, or terminate the loan early.

Primary market for syndicated loans

Who is the customer for AML purposes?

17.8　The obligation on each party to a syndicated lending arrangement to verify the identity of the customer is as follows:

- **Mandated Lead Manager/Arranger/Bookrunner**: The Borrower is the mandated Lead Manager/Arranger/Bookrunner's customer, as is the Agent.
- **Lenders**: The Borrower is also a customer of the syndicate participants.
- **Agent**: The Agent's customers are the Borrower and the Lenders.

Customer due diligence

17.9　The mandated Lead Manager/Arranger/Bookrunner should apply the guidance set out in Part I, Chapter 5, and in particular, the guidance on reliance on third parties in Part I, section 5.6, in line with the firm's risk-based approach, to the Borrower and to the Agent.

17.10　The Agent should apply the guidance set out in Part I, Chapter 5, (and in particular, the guidance on reliance on third parties in Part 1, section 5.6) in line with the firm's risk-based approach, to the Borrower and the Lenders. The Agent, where as part of its risk-based approach it feels it is appropriate to do so, (and the mandated Lead Manager qualifies as a "third party" under the ML Regulations) may take account of, or rely on, the due diligence carried out by the mandated Lead Manager/Arranger/Bookrunner on the Borrower. It is often the case that the Lenders have pre-existing relationships with the mandated Lead Manager/Arranger/Bookrunner and/or the Agent so that, in practice, little, if any, additional due diligence will need to be undertaken.

17.11　The Lender also has a responsibility to apply the guidance set out in Part I, Chapter 5, subject to the firm's risk-based approach to the Borrower, including where the Lender feels it is appropriate to do so, taking account of, or relying on, the due diligence carried out by the mandated Lead Manager/Arranger/Bookrunner on the Borrower.

17.12　As the mandated Lead Manager/Arranger/Bookrunner and Agent also have an obligation to verify the identity of the Borrower, the Lender may, where as part of its risk-based approach it feels it is appropriate to do so, take account of, or rely on, the due diligence carried out by the mandated Lead Manager/Arranger/Bookrunner and/or Agent on the Borrower where they are in an equivalent jurisdiction.

17.13　Where the Borrower has provided a Guarantor as part of the loan agreement, all parties who have an obligation to identify the Borrower – mandated Lead Manager/Arranger/Bookrunner, Lenders and Agent – should consider whether it is necessary, based upon their risk-based approach, to apply to the Guarantor the verification procedures they are applying to the Borrower.

17.14　The money laundering risk associated with a Guarantor only becomes real if a Borrower defaults on a loan, and the Guarantor is called upon to repay the loan. A firm may consider, subject to its risk-based approach, whether it should verify the identity of the Guarantor at the same time as the Borrower, or only to identify the Guarantor as and when the Guarantor is called upon to fulfil his obligations under the loan agreement.

17.15　When considering the extent of verification appropriate for a particular Borrower, any normal commercial credit analysis and reputational risk assessment and background checks that have been undertaken on the Borrower should be taken into account, and should be factored into a firm's risk-based approach.

Secondary market in syndicated loans

17.16　A Lender under a syndicated loan may decide to sell its participation in order to: realise capital; for risk management purposes, for example to re-weight its loan portfolio; meet regulatory capital requirements; or to crystallise a loss. The methods of transfer are usually specified in the Syndicated Loan Agreement.

17.17　The most common forms of transfer to enable a Lender to sell its loan commitment are: novation (the most common method used in transfer certificates to loan agreements); legal assignment; equitable assignment; fund participation and risk participation. Novation and legal assignment result in the Lender disposing of its loan commitment, with the new lender assuming a direct contractual relationship with the Borrower, whilst the other methods result in the Lender retaining a contractual relationship with the Borrower and standing between the purchaser in the secondary market and the Borrower. The transfer method should be taken into account by the purchasing firm when considering its customer due diligence requirements.

Customer due diligence

17.18   A firm selling a participation in a loan should apply the guidance set out in Part I, Chapter 5, in line with its risk-based approach, when identifying, and if necessary verifying the identity of, the purchaser.

17.19   A firm purchasing a participation in a loan should apply the guidance set out in Part I, Chapter 5, in line with its risk-based approach, when identifying, and if necessary verifying the identity of, the seller.

17.20   The money flows are between the purchaser and seller of the loan. However, if a firm purchases a participation in an existing loan from another participant by way of novation or legal assignment, it will have a direct contractual relationship with the Borrower. As such the purchaser has an obligation to identify, and if appropriate as part of its risk-based approach to verifying the identity of the Borrower, in accordance with the guidance set out in Part I, Chapter 5.

17.21   Where a firm purchases a participation in an existing loan from another participant (the Lender) by way of equitable assignment, fund participation or risk participation the seller acts as intermediary between the purchaser and the Borrower for the life of the loan. Depending on the status of the Lender (seller), the purchaser should decide as part of its risk-based approach whether it has an obligation to identify, and verify the identity of, the Borrower, in accordance with the guidance set out in Part I, Chapter 5.

17.22   In addition, a firm purchasing a loan in the secondary market must check the underlying Borrower against the HM Treasury Consolidated List.

17.23   Whether the Agent is required to undertake customer due diligence on a secondary purchaser of a loan participation will depend upon how the transfer between the seller and the purchaser in the secondary market is made:

- Where the sale is by way of novation or legal assignment the Agent should, as part of its risk-based approach, identify, and verify the identity of, the purchaser, in accordance with the guidance set out in Part I, Chapter 5.
- Where the sale is by way of equitable assignment, the Agent may not have a direct relationship with the purchaser, even though funds may flow through the Agent from or to the purchaser (via the Lender), and therefore the Agent may not have an obligation to identify and/or verify the purchaser. However, the Agent should consider, as part of its risk-based approach, whether it should identify, or verify the identity of, the purchaser in accordance with the guidance set out in Part I, Chapter 5 and check them against the HM Treasury Consolidated List.

Monitoring

17.24   The money laundering risks for firms undertaking syndicated lending activities can be mitigated by implementing appropriate documented monitoring procedures. General guidance on monitoring is set out in Part 1, section 5.7.

17.25   The level of monitoring to be undertaken by a firm must be commensurate with the risks posed by the Borrower. In general, the type of customer entering into syndicated loan arrangements can be regarded as low risk, but extra care needs to be taken when dealing with organisations outside the normal customer profile, for example, private companies.

17.26   There needs to be a mechanism for monitoring any variations in the loan arrangements, for example accelerated repayments, or early redemptions without good commercial rationale. This will require clear documentation of when receipts are normally due and a means of checking against this. Variations clearly need to be reported to management so that appropriate enquiries can be made.

17.27   It will also be necessary to monitor for changes in the nature and status of the Borrower. This should entail checking the information about the Borrower on a periodic basis and also any external factors which could result in a material change in the risk profile of the Borrower.

Staff awareness, training and alertness

17.28   General guidance on staff awareness, training and alertness is set out in Part 1, Chapter 7. As syndicated lending activities for the most part are considered to be low risk, the general guidance in Part I may be considered sufficient to meet the firm's needs. However, it is important for the firm to consider how syndicated lending activities may be used for ML/TF purposes and to train staff accordingly, and to train staff in the firm's procedures for managing this risk. Whilst there is no single solution when determining how to deliver training, training of customer relationship management staff via workshops may well prove to be more successful than on-line learning or videos/CDs.

18: WHOLESALE MARKETS

Note: This sectoral guidance is incomplete on its own. It must be read in conjunction with the main guidance set out in Part I of the Guidance.

This sectoral guidance considers specific issues over and above the more general guidance set out in Part 1, Chapters 4, 5, and 7, which firms operating in the wholesale markets may want to take into account when considering applying a risk-based approach. Firms may also find the guidance for the following sectors useful:

- Sector 8: *Non-life providers of investment fund products*, which deals with exchange-traded products where the firm acts as agent for private customers, (e g where a fund provider that is not an exchange member buys securities for its private customers).
- Sector 9: *Discretionary and advisory investment management*, which covers how investment managers may interact with wholesale markets.
- Sector 10: *Execution-only stockbrokers*, which will be more relevant for firms dealing in wholesale market products as agent or principal for retail customers.
- Sector 14: *Corporate Finance*, which deals with the issuance of traded products or instruments, which are traded in a 'secondary' wholesale market, allowing investors in the primary market to realise their investment.
- Sector 19: *Name Passing Brokers*, which is directed at those firms who deal with wholesale market brokers in the inter-professional markets.
- Sector 20: *Unregulated Funds*, which is intended for firms who provide services, including the execution and clearing of transaction in wholesale market products, to unregulated funds.

Overview of the sector

18.1 The wholesale markets comprise exchanges and dealing arrangements that facilitate the trading (buying and selling) of wholesale investment products, and hedging instruments ("traded products"), including, but not limited to:

- Securities: equities, fixed income, warrants and investment funds (Exchange Traded Funds – ETFs);
- Money market instruments: FX, interest rate products, term deposits;
- Financial derivatives: options, futures, swaps and warrants;
- Commodities: physical commodities and commodity derivatives, including exotic derivatives (eg, weather derivatives); and
- Structured products (eg, equity linked notes).

18.2 Traded products confer 'rights' or 'obligations'; either between an investor and the issuer, or between parties engaged in the trading of the instruments. Traded product instruments can be bought, sold, borrowed or lent; as such, they facilitate the transfer of property or assets and usually represent an intrinsic value, which may be attractive to money launderers. Traded products can be bought or sold either on an exchange ("exchange traded products"), or between parties 'over-the-counter' (OTC).

18.3 Some traded products or instruments, such as equities, are issued in a 'primary' market, and are traded in a 'secondary' market, allowing investors in the primary market to realise their investment. Other traded products are created to enable investors to manage assets and liabilities, exchange risks and exposure to particular assets, commodities or securities.

Exchange-traded products

18.4 Exchange-traded products are financial products that are traded on exchanges, which have standardised terms (e g amounts, delivery dates and terms) and settlement procedures and transparent pricing. Firms may deal in exchange-traded products as principal or as agent for their customers. In the financial and commodity derivatives markets, firms will typically deal as principal, and on certain exchanges (e g Euronext, LIFFE, ICE Futures, LME) must do so when dealing as a clearing member in relation to their customers' transactions. In the securities markets, firms can deal as either principal (for their own account) or as agent for the firms' underlying customers.

18.5 The London Stock Exchange recognises different types of relationships between a settlement agent and its customers, which it denotes as Model A and Model B (see paragraphs 18.48ff). Similar relationships may be recognised on other exchanges and different terminology used to denote these relationships

OTC products

18.6 OTC products are bilateral agreements between two parties, or multilateral, depending on the settlement process, that are not traded or executed on an exchange. The terms of the agreement are tailored to meet the needs of the parties, i e there are not necessarily standardised terms, contract sizes or delivery dates. Where firms deal OTC, they usually deal as principal. Some OTC dealing is facilitated by brokers and while settlement is normally effected directly between the parties, it is becoming increasingly common for exchanges and clearers to provide OTC clearing facilities.

What are the money laundering risks in the wholesale markets sector?

18.7   Traded products are usually traded on regulated markets, or between regulated parties, or with regulated parties involved acting as agent or principal.

18.8   However, the characteristics of products that facilitate the rapid, and sometimes opaque, transfer of ownership, the ability to change the nature of an asset, and market mechanisms that potentially extend the audit trail, together with a diverse international customer base, have specific money laundering risks that need to be addressed and managed appropriately.

18.9   One of the most significant risks associated with the wholesale markets and traded products, is where a transaction involves payment in cash and/or third party payments.

18.10   Firms dealing in traded products in the wholesale markets are not as likely to be used in the placement stage of money laundering as, for example, deposit takers. That said, given the global flows of funds in the wholesale financial markets, it is important to recognise that although customers may remit funds from credit institutions, a firm could still be targeted with respect to the layering and integration stages of money laundering. Traded products might, for example, be used as a means of changing assets rapidly into different form, possibly using multiple brokers to disguise total wealth and ultimate origin of the funds or assets, or as savings and investment vehicles for money launderers and other criminals.

18.11   Firms dealing in traded products in the wholesale markets do not generally accept cash deposits or provide personal accounts that facilitate money transmission and/or third party funding that is not related to specific underlying investment transactions. In the money markets, however, customers may request payments to third parties (eg, FX payments to suppliers) and the associated AML risks need to be considered by the firm (see paragraph 18.15ff). There may also be third party funding of the transactions in the commodities markets. Also, where a bank is lending funds to a customer to purchase a physical commodity, and the customer hedges the risks associated with the transaction in the derivatives market through a broker, the bank may guarantee the payment of margin to that broker; this results in a flow of money between the broker and bank on the customer's behalf. However, both the party making the payment on behalf of the customer, and the party receiving the funds, will be regulated financial institutions.

18.12   The extent to which certain products are subject to margin or option premium payment arrangements will affect the level of risk. The nature and form of any margin will need to be taken into account by the firm, through their risk-based approach, when identifying the customer and determining appropriate payment procedures.

18.13   OTC and exchange-based trading can also present very different money laundering risk profiles. Most exchanges are regulated, transparent, and cleared by a central counterparty, and thus can largely be seen as carrying a lower generic money laundering risk. OTC business may, generally, be less well regulated and it is not possible to make the same generalisations concerning the money laundering risk as with exchange-traded products. When dealing in the OTC markets firms will, therefore, need to take a more considered risk-based approach, and undertake more detailed risk-based assessment.

18.14   For example, exchanges often impose specific requirements on position transfers, which have the effect of reducing the level of money laundering risk. These procedures will not apply in the OTC markets, where firms will need to consider the approach they would adopt in relation to any such requests in respect of customers dealing OTC.

How to assess the elements of risk in the wholesale markets sector

Generic risk elements

18.15   The main factors to consider when assessing the risk when undertaking business in the wholesale markets are the nature of the customer (including their source of funds), the market participants, the products involved and whether the products are exchange traded or OTC.

18.16   When implementing a risk-based approach, and producing or reviewing risk assessments or the risk profile of a prospective customer, there are a number of areas which firms might want to take into account in addition to the more general matters set out in Part I, Chapters 4 and 5. The wholesale markets are populated by customers with a wide range of different business interests.

- The types of firms present might typically include, but not be limited to:
    - Sovereign governments;
    - Local authorities (municipal bodies);
    - Regulated financial firms (eg, banks, brokers, investment managers and funds);
    - Unregulated financial entities (eg, off-shore funds);
    - Corporations (eg, listed companies, private companies);
    - Trust and partnerships.
- A customer's nature, status, and the degree of independent oversight it is subject to, will affect the firm's assessment of risk for a particular customer or the firm's business as a whole.
- The instruments traded in the wholesale markets can allow for long-term investment,

speculative trading, hedging and physical delivery of certain financial instruments and commodities. Understanding the role of a prospective customer in the market, and his reasons for trading, will help inform decisions on the risk profile they present.

- The way that a firm addresses the jurisdictional risk posed by a customer will depend on many factors. The jurisdictional risk may, however, be mitigated by the rationale for the customer being located or operating in a particular jurisdiction. Customers located in potentially higher-risk jurisdictions may have legitimate commercial interests, which can mitigate the perceived risk. For example, an oil producer in a higher-risk territory may seek to use derivative instruments to hedge price risks and this does not necessarily present a high money laundering risk, although a firm should consider other risks, such as corruption.
- Firms should ensure that any factors mitigating the jurisdictional or other risks of a customer are adequately documented and periodically reviewed in the light of international findings or developments.

Wholesale market sub-sectors

18.17   The risks set out above are, largely, securities focused, but equally apply across the wholesale markets. The following sections look at particular risks associated with other sub-sectors within the wholesale markets.

Foreign exchange

18.18   To the extent that firms dealing in foreign exchange (FX) in the wholesale market tend to be regulated financial institutions and large corporates, the money laundering risk may be viewed as generally lower. However, this risk may be increased by the nature of the customer, or where, for example

- high risk clients (including PEPs) undertake speculative trading; and/or
- requests are made for payments to be made to third parties: for example, customers, particularly corporates, that need to make FX payments to suppliers and overseas affiliates.

18.19   When assessing the money laundering risk in such circumstances, a firm may want to take into account the nature of the customer's business and the frequency and type of third party payments that are likely to result from such business.

18.20   FX (as well as many other traded products) is commonly traded on electronic trading systems. Such systems may be set up by brokers or independent providers. When a firm executes a transaction on these systems the counterparty's identity is not usually known until the transaction is executed. The counterparty could be any one of the members who have signed up to the system. Firms should examine the admission policy of the platform before signing up to the system, to ensure that the platform only admits regulated financial institutions as members, or that the rules of the electronic trading system mean that all members are subject to satisfactory AML checks.

Financial derivatives

18.21   Financial products are utilised for a wide range of reasons, and market participants can be located anywhere within the world; firms will need to consider these issues when developing an appropriate risk-based approach. The nature, volume and frequency of trading, and whether these make sense in the context of the customer's and firm's corporate and financial status, will be key relevant factors that a firm will need to consider when developing an appropriate risk-based approach.

18.22   The risks between exchange-traded derivatives and OTC derivative products in the financial derivative markets are the same as those set out in paragraphs 18.7–18.14.

Commodities

18.23   Where a customer deals purely in physical commodities for commercial purposes, the activity is not captured by the ML Regulations. Regulated firms that, in addition to physical commodity activity, undertake any business with a customer which amounts to a regulated activity, including business associated with physical commodities will, however, be subject to the ML Regulations, including due diligence requirements with regard to that customer.

18.24   When implementing a risk-based approach and producing or reviewing risk assessments or the risk profile of a prospective customer, there are a number of areas which commodity market firms might want to take into account in addition to the more general matters set out in Part I, Chapters 4 and 5. These will include, but not be limited to:

- The wide range of different business interests which populate the commodity markets. The types of firm present may typically include:
  - Producers (eg, oil producers and mining firms);
  - Users (eg, refiners and smelters);
  - Wholesalers (eg, utility firms);

    —   Commercial merchants, traders and agents;
    —   Financial firms (eg, banks and funds).
- These types of firm are illustrative and widely drawn and firms can be present in more than one category (for example, a refiner will be both a user of crude oil and a producer of oil products).
- The instruments traded in the wholesale commodity markets can allow for the speculative trading, hedging and physical delivery of commodities.

18.25   The risks should be taken in the round, with one risk possibly mitigating another. The global nature of the commodity markets means that firms from potentially higher risk jurisdictions with a perceived higher money laundering risk are likely to have legitimate commercial interests. Understanding the role of a prospective customer in the market, and their reasons for trading, will help inform decisions on the risk profile they present.

Structured products

18.26   Structured products are financial instruments specifically constructed to suit the needs of a particular customer or a group of customers. They are generally more complex than securities and are traded predominantly OTC, although some structured notes are also listed on exchanges (usually the Luxembourg or Irish Stock Exchanges).

18.27   There is a wide range of users of structured products. Typically they will include:
- Corporates,
- Private banks,
- Government agencies,
- Financial institutions

18.28   Transactions are normally undertaken on a principal basis between the provider (normally a financial institution) and the customer. Some structured products are also sold through banks and third party distributors. In these circumstances it is important to clarify where the customer relationships lie and to set out each party's responsibilities in relation to identification and verification obligations.

18.29   Because of the sometimes complex nature of the products, they may generally be more difficult to value than cash securities. The lack of transparency may make it easier for money launderers, for example, to disguise the true value of their investments.

18.30   The complexity of the structure can also obscure the actual cash flows in the transaction, enabling customers to carry out circular transactions. Understanding the reason behind a customer's request for a particular product will help to determine the money laundering risk inherent in the structures.

18.31   The cash movements associated with structured products may present an increased money laundering risk, although this risk may be mitigated by the nature and status of the customer, and the depth of the relationship the customer has with the firm. For example, if the use of structured products is part of a wider business relationship, and is compatible with other activity between the firm and the customer, the risk may be reduced.

Who is the customer for AML purposes?

18.32   It is very important to distinguish the relationship that exists between the various parties associated with a transaction. In particular, the firm should be clear whether it is acting as agent or principal on behalf of the customer, and whether the firm has a responsibility to verify the identity of any underlying customers involved in transactions.

18.33   Where the firm's customer qualifies for the treatment of simplified due diligence (see Part I, section 5.4), no customer due diligence is required. This would be true even where the firm is aware that its customer is acting on behalf of an underlying customer who would not itself qualify for simplified due diligence; no question of reliance under Regulation 17 will arise.

18.34   Therefore, from an AML/CTF perspective:
- If the firm is acting as principal with another exchange member, that party is the firm's customer.
- Where an exchange-based trade is randomly and automatically matched with an equal and opposite exchange-based trade, it is recognised that, due to market mechanisms, the name of the other exchange member(s) may not be known. In these situations, where all the parties are members of the exchange and employ a common or central counterparty to match and settle the trades, the firm cannot know and therefore does not need to verify the identity of the other exchange member. Firms should, however, include the money laundering risk involved in the participation in any exchange or centralised clearing, as part of their overall risk-based approach. Participation in any exchange or centralised clearing system does not remove the need to adequately verify its own customer the firm is acting as agent for in the transaction.

- Where a firm is acting as principal with a non-exchange member, the non-exchange member is the customer of the firm.
- Where a firm is acting directly on behalf of another party (eg, as agent), the party for whom the firm is acting will be the firm's customer.
- Where the firm is acting for another party who is itself acting as agent for its underlying customers, the following should apply:
    - The agent is the customer, not the underlying principal (who is a beneficial owner).
    - Where simplified due diligence can be applied to the agent (see Part I, Chapter 5, section 5.4) there is no requirement to identify underlying principals, unless otherwise agreed by the parties.
    - Where the agent is unregulated or regulated within a non-equivalent jurisdiction, both the agent and the underlying principal will be considered to be customers for AML/CTF purposes.

Other considerations

18.35   In certain markets there are other types of relationship associated with a transaction that are not covered under an agent or principal relationship, and these should be subject to other considerations by a firm when considering what is appropriate customer due diligence.

Different types of customer relationship

(a) Introducing brokers/Receivers and Transmitters of orders

18.36   As the name implies, an introducing broker may "introduce", or a Receiver and Transmitter of orders may pass orders from, his customers to a firm to execute trades and, possibly, to perform related requirements in connection with the customers' trades and bookkeeping and record keeping functions. A fee is paid by the firm to the introducing broker, usually based on the transactions undertaken. A customer often has no say in which firm the introducing broker selects to execute a particular trade.

18.37   As such, the customer being introduced is a customer of both the introducing broker and the firm.

(b) Executing brokers and clearing brokers in the exchange traded markets

18.38   Customers wishing to execute transactions on certain regulated markets may do so through a "give-up agreement" whereby the customer elects to execute transactions through one or more executing brokers and to clear the transaction through a separate clearing broker. Once the transaction is executed, the executing broker will then "give-up" that transaction to the clearing broker for it to be cleared through the relevant exchange or clearing house.

18.39   Both the executing broker and the clearing broker have a relationship with the customer (eg, both may be agents), for whom they perform separate functions.

18.40   It is usually (but not always) the customer that elects to execute transactions through one or more brokers and to clear such transactions through another broker and, to that end, selects both the clearing broker and executing broker(s).

18.41   Where a firm acts as executing broker, the party placing the order is the customer for AML/CTF purposes. Where the party placing the order is acting as agent for underlying customers, they, too, may be customers for AML/CTF purposes (see paragraphs 18.32–18.34).

18.42   Where a firm acts as clearing broker, the customer on whose behalf the transaction is cleared is the customer for AML/CTF purposes.

18.43   A customer may choose to use one or more executing brokers because:
- the customer may prefer, for reasons of functionality or cost, the executing broker's front-end electronic order routing;
- certain brokers develop a reputation for being able to execute transactions very efficiently in certain contracts, while the clearing broker provides superior post-trade clearing and settlement services;
- the customer may feel more comfortable with the credit risk of the clearing broker;
- the executing broker may provide access to certain value-added services linked to the execution of the customer's transactions; or
- the customer does not wish to disclose its trading strategy to other market participants; or for other reasons relevant to the customer's business.

18.44   In all give-up arrangements the customer, the executing broker, and the clearing broker are participants. Although this type of tri-partite arrangement is most common, give-up arrangements can extend to cover many types of relationships, and may extend through a number of parties with differing roles and responsibilities including advising, managing, clearing or executing, for or on behalf of the underlying customer, before the trade reaches the ultimate clearing broker.

18.45   A common additional participant in a give-up arrangement is the customer's investment adviser or manager, who in the give-up agreement is usually referred to as a trader, to whom the customer has granted discretionary trading authority, including the authority to enter into give-up arrangements on the customer's behalf.

18.46   Typically, an adviser or manager acting for a client may only wish to disclosure a reference code, rather than their client's name, to the executing broker, particularly where the adviser or manager has multiple underlying accounts over which they exercise discretionary authority; hence, the clearing broker is likely to be the only party that knows the underlying customer's identity. Where a give-up agreement includes such an arrangement, firms should ensure that their risk-based approach addresses the risks posed, which may include the risk associated with the investment manager as appropriate, the type of fund and possibly the underlying investors. Hence, where a firm is acting as executing broker and there is a adviser or manager acting for an underlying customer, the customer due diligence performed, and whether there is an obligation to identify the underlying customer, will depend upon the regulatory status and location of the adviser or manager. For further guidance, see Part I, section 5.3. Where simplified due diligence cannot be applied to the adviser or manager and there is an obligation to verify the identity of the adviser or manager and their underlying customers, the firm should take a risk-based approach (see Part I, Chapter 5, section 5.3), which may include consideration of whether it is appropriate, subject to satisfying the ML Regulations, to take into account any verification evidence obtained by, a clearing broker in the UK, EU or an equivalent jurisdiction.

18.47   To avoid unnecessary duplication, where an executing broker and a clearing broker are undertaking elements of the same exchange transaction on behalf of the same customer which is not itself a regulated firm from an equivalent jurisdiction, the executing broker may wish to rely upon the clearing broker if they are a 'third party' as defined in the ML Regulations (see Part I, Chapter 5, paragraph 5.6.4ff) or otherwise take account of the fact, in its risk-based approach, that there is another regulated firm from an equivalent jurisdiction involved in the transaction with the customer, acting as clearing agent or providing other services in relation to the transaction.

18.48   Given the information asymmetries likely to exist between an executing broker and clearing broker, when a firm is acting as clearing broker, it would generally not be appropriate, from a risk-based perspective, to rely on an executing broker, even if this would be permitted under the ML Regulations. Clearing firms should undertake the CDD measures as set out in Part I, Chapter 5.

(c) Executing brokers and clearing brokers: securities markets

18.49   There are fundamentally two types of arrangements that can exist in relation to the outsourcing of clearing and settlement processes in the securities markets. These are generally known as "Model A" and "Model B" clearing relationships. The specific characteristics of these relationships are outlined below.

"Model A" Clearing

18.50   Model A clearing usually involves the outsourcing of the settlement processing of transactions executed by a firm to a service provider. All transactions are executed and settled in the name of the executing firm, who retains full responsibility, including financial liability, for the transaction in relation to both the underlying customer and the market counterparty. The underlying customer remains solely a customer of the executing firm, which retains AML/CTF responsibility, and does not enter into a relationship with the settlement services provider.

18.51   The settlement services provider maintains a relationship solely with the executing firm, and acts as an agent on behalf of the executing firm. As such, the settlement services provider has no obligation to undertake the identification and verification requirements set out in Part I, Chapter 5, other than in relation to its customer, the firm.

"Model B" Clearing

18.52   In the securities markets, the executing broker/clearing firm arrangements are commonly referred to as "Model B" clearing arrangements.

18.53   The executing broker will usually open an account (or sub-accounts) with the clearing firm, in the name of his underlying customer, and will fulfil all verification and due diligence requirements on the underlying customer. A tri-partite relationship between the underlying customer, the executing broker and the clearing firm (the 'tripartite relationship') is created, by virtue of the fact that the executing broker has entered into a Model B clearing relationship with the clearing firm on his own behalf, and, acting as the agent of the customer.

18.54   Usually, the customer does not establish a relationship direct with the clearing firm, but rather will enter into the tri-partite relationship via the executing broker, which has a Model B clearing relationship with the clearing firm. There is little or no contact between the underlying customer and the clearing firm. The customer is generally unable to terminate his relationship with the executing broker whilst retaining a relationship with the clearing firm in isolation.

18.55   Should the executing broker terminate its relationship with the clearing firm, the underlying customer will move with the executing broker. If the clearing firm has provided custody services as part of the services being supplied to the executing broker, consent to transfer the assets is required, with any residual transfer of assets for non-responding customers usually being subject to a rule waiver from the FSA upon fulfilment of certain conditions.

18.56   Whilst, under a Model B relationship, the transaction is 'given up' to the clearing firm for settlement with the market, if the underlying customer fails to deliver funds or assets to fulfil settlement, the clearing broker may look to the executing broker to offset any outstanding liabilities through a secondary deposit or other funds held by the clearing firm on behalf of the executing broker. In turn, the executing broker would have to pursue the underlying customer for fulfilment of settlement/debt recovery.

18.57   Because the relationship with the underlying customer is always focused through the executing broker, the executing broker remains an integral part of the relationship and transaction process at all times. This is by virtue of the tri-partite relationship, rather than separate relationships between the executing broker and the underlying customer, and the underlying customer and the clearing firm. Therefore, the CDD measures set out in Part I, Chapter 5, are generally undertaken by the executing broker while the clearing firm may, if it considers it appropriate to do so under its risk-based approach, rely upon the executing broker provide that broker is a 'third party' as defined in the ML Regulations (see Part I, Chapter 5, paragraph 5.6.4ff).

(d) Non-clearing members and general clearing members: derivatives / securities markets

18.58   A non-clearing member may maintain one or several accounts with the clearing member. Where a non-clearing member deals as agent for a customer, this may be through an omnibus account with the clearing member on behalf of all the non-clearing member's underlying customers who often have no say in the non-clearing member's selection of a clearing member.

18.59   Where a non-clearing member deals on a proprietary basis as principal, it will generally operate a separate account for such business. In that case the non-clearing member will be the customer of the clearing member.

18.60   The clearing member may, based upon his risk-based approach and/or the status of the non-clearing member, consider that the non-clearing member's underlying customer or customers are also his customers. For further guidance refer to Part I, sections 5.3 and 5.4.

(e) Other multi-partite agreements

18.61   Multi-partite agreements are common in a number of markets, for example, as part of prime brokerage services. Further guidance on the 'give-up' arrangements for exchange traded derivatives – parts of which may be relevant in other markets – is set out above, while firms involved in multipartite agreements in respect of unregulated funds should refer to sector 20: *Unregulated Funds*.

Customer due diligence

18.62   Product risk alone should not be the determining factor in a firm assessing whether an enhanced level of due diligence is appropriate, therefore there are no enhanced due diligence requirements specific to the wholesale markets sector, over and above those set out in Part I, section 5.5, which take into account other risk factors such as client type and jurisdictional risk.

18.63   To avoid unnecessary duplication where an executing broker and a clearing broker are involved in the same transaction on behalf of the same customer, which is subject to a give-up arrangement, the executing broker in the exchanged-traded derivatives markets or a clearing broker under a Model B clearing arrangement may, where as part of its risk-based approach it feels it is appropriate to do so:

- place reliance on the other regulated firm involved in the transaction with the customer provided they are regulated in the UK, another EU Member State or an equivalent jurisdiction and the requirements for third party reliance in the ML Regulations are satisfied. Guidance on reliance on third parties and on the factors to consider, as part of a firm's risk-based approach, when seeking to rely on another firm to apply the CDD measures (but not monitoring) is given in Part I, Chapter 5, paragraphs 5.6.4ff.; **or**
- otherwise take account of the fact, in its risk-based approach, that there is another regulated firm from the UK/EU or an equivalent jurisdiction involved in the transaction with the customer, acting as clearing agent or providing other services in relation to the transaction, without placing reliance on the firm.

Monitoring

18.64   The money laundering or terrorist financing risks for firms operating within the wholesale markets sector can be mitigated by the implementation of monitoring procedures. Guidance on general monitoring requirements is set out in Part I, section 5.7.

18.65　Monitoring in wholesale firms will be affected by the fact that firms may only have access to a part of the overall picture of their customer's trading activities. The fact that many customers spread their activities over a number of financial firms will mean that many firms will have a limited view of a customer's trading activities and it may be difficult to assess the commercial rationale of certain transactions. There are, however, specific characteristics of the wholesale market sector which will impact a firm involved in the wholesale markets monitoring activity. These include:

● *Scale of activity*

The wholesale markets involve very high volumes of transactions being executed by large numbers of customers. The monitoring activity undertaken should therefore be adequate to handle the volumes undertaken by the firm.

● *Use of multiple brokers*

Customers may choose to split execution and clearing services between different firms and many customers may use more than one execution broker on the same market. The customer's reasons for this include ensuring that they obtain best execution, competitive rates, or to gain access to a particular specialism within one firm. This will restrict a firm's ability to monitor a customer, as they may not be aware of all activity or even contingent activity associated with the transactions they are undertaking.

● *Electronic execution*

There is an increasing use of electronic order routing where customers access markets directly and there is little or no personal contact between the firm and the customer in the day to day execution of the customer's business. This means that the rationale for particular transactions may not be known by the firm.

18.66　The nature and extent of any monitoring activity will therefore need to be determined by a firm based on an assessment of their particular business profile. This will be different for each firm and may include an assessment of the following matters:

● Extent of execution vs. clearing business undertaken
● Nature of customer base (geographic location, regulated or unregulated)
● Number of customers and volume of transactions
● Types of products traded and complexity of those products
● Payment processes (including payments to third parties, if permitted)

18.67　Firms should ensure that any relevant factors taken into account in determining their monitoring activities are adequately documented and subject to periodic review.

18.68　Firms relying on third parties under the ML Regulations to apply CDD measures **cannot** rely on the third party in respect of monitoring.

[7043]

19: NAME-PASSING BROKERS IN INTER-PROFESSIONAL MARKETS

Note: This sectoral guidance is incomplete on its own. It must be read in conjunction with the main guidance set out in Part I of the Guidance.

Overview of the sector

19.1　In the inter-professional markets, wholesale market brokers pass the names of customers from one principal to another, either by the traditional voice broking method or via an electronic platform owned by the broker. The broker passing the names takes no part in any transaction or trade between the two counterparties.

19.2　The activity enables the broker to use his wide range of contacts across the wholesale markets to provide liquidity to the market, by putting in touch principals with a wish to transact, but who may not have the broker's depth of information about willing counterparties. The use of a broker also allows pre-trade anonymity for those counterparties who do not wish their position to be made known to the wider market.

19.3　Wholesale market brokers can arrange transactions in any product permitted under the Regulated Activities Order, or which is covered by the Non Investment Products code, published by the Bank of England.

Different types of relationship

19.4　The names which may be passed by the broker are generally limited to entities subject to financial regulation, to corporates and to Local Authorities. Regulated entities may be subject to regulation by the FSA or by an overseas regulator; corporates may likewise be UK domiciled or based abroad; Local Authorities are generally UK-based.

19.5　In principle, transactions of all types may take place between any of these parties. There is no difference in how the name-passing takes place, although there is an awareness that standards of regulation and corporate governance will vary across jurisdictions.

PART V
OTHER MATERIALS

What are the money laundering risks in name passing?

19.6   Across all wholesale markets, the vast majority of participants are known to the other market counterparties. Many participants are subject to financial regulation, and most corporates who are dealt with are listed, and subject to public accountability. In principle, therefore, the money laundering risk in name-passing is very low. The risk associated with name-passing relates to the resultant transactions and business relationships, which are covered by other parts of the sectoral guidance.

Who is the customer for AML purposes?

19.7   Wholesale market brokers are arrangers in the sense of a financial intermediary. The principals introduced by name-passing brokers, who subsequently enter into trades or transactions with one another, are each other's customer if the principal is subject to the ML Regulations.

19.8   The name-passing brokers themselves play no part in any transaction.

Customer due diligence

19.9   Wholesale market brokers must identify, and verify the identity of, the principals they pass to other market participants.

19.10   Principals that are required to comply with the requirements of Part I, Chapter 5, due to their being subject to the ML Regulations, cannot look to name-passing brokers to undertake identity verification procedures on their behalf.

19.11   The principals must therefore take steps to obtain, appropriately verify, and record the identity of counterparties (and any underlying beneficiaries) "introduced" to them by name-passing brokers.

19.12   Where a counterparty "introduced" by a name-passing broker fails to satisfy a principal's AML identity verification checks, the principal is responsible for informing the name-passing broker that the prospective counterparty cannot be accepted.

[7044]

20: SERVICING UNREGULATED FUNDS

Note: This sectoral guidance is incomplete on its own. It must be read in conjunction with the main guidance set out in Part I of the Guidance.

This sectoral guidance is for firms servicing unregulated funds in a number of specific situations: executing transactions, clearing and settling transactions and offering other prime brokerage services. The guidance considers specific issues over and above the more general guidance set out in Part I, Chapters 4, 5, and 7, which such firms may want to take into account when considering applying a risk-based approach.

A firm's business activities with unregulated funds may also fall within the scope of other sectoral guidance, for example, sector 18: Wholesale Markets and sector 9: Discretionary and advisory investment management. As such, this sectoral guidance should be read together with other applicable parts of the guidance.

Overview of the sector

20.1   An unregulated fund is a vehicle established to hold and manage investments and assets, which is not subject to regulatory oversight. The fund usually has a stated purpose and/or set of investment objectives. Unregulated funds will normally be a separate legal entity, formed as limited companies, limited partnerships and trusts (or the equivalent in civil law jurisdictions).

20.2   Unregulated funds are stand-alone entities in order that the assets and liabilities may be restricted to the fund itself. Sub-funds typically take the form of different classes of shares, fund allocations to separately incorporated trading vehicles or legally ring-fenced portfolios.

20.3   Unregulated funds may also operate as a "master/feeder" arrangement, whereby investors, perhaps from different tax jurisdictions, invest via separate feeder funds that hold shares only in the master fund. Feeder funds may also on occasion invest/deal directly, and therefore a firm may act for a fund acting in its own right whilst also at the same time being a feeder fund.

20.4   Dependent upon structure, an unregulated fund is controlled by its directors, partners or trustees. However, in most instances the powers of the directors, partners or trustees will be delegated to the investment manager. It is not unusual to find that the key personnel of a fund are also the key personnel of the investment manager.

20.5   The following diagram sets out the relationships that exist and are involved with the operation and management of an unregulated fund:

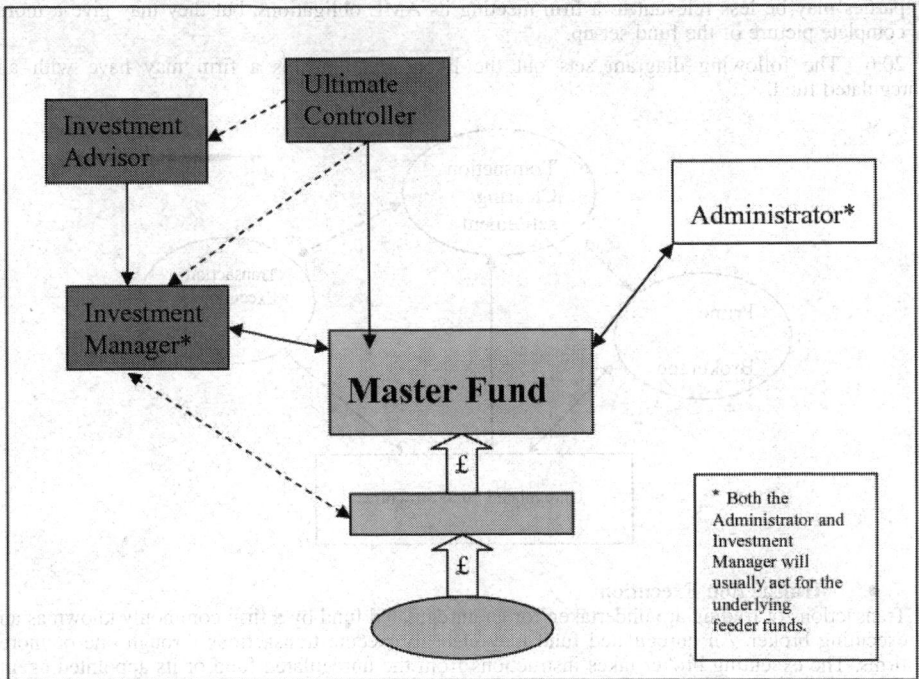

- **Ultimate Controllers**

The ultimate controller is someone who controls the funds/assets in the fund. The ultimate controller may be a different person/entity in different fund set-ups. Sometimes it can be the investment manager, the adviser, or directors of other related parties, who may delegate this responsibility. The place to look for those who are the ultimate controllers is usually the fund's offering memorandum.

- **Investment Manager**

Unregulated funds are managed by an investment manager, which is a separate entity to the fund, and which is given authority to manage the funds and investments held by the fund vehicle. It is often the investment manager that will make investment decisions and place transactions with a firm on behalf of the unregulated fund. The investment manager plays a pivotal role within an unregulated fund structure, as it establishes and maintains the relationships with the Prime, Clearing and Executing brokers and will be the direct contact with a firm on behalf of the fund. A firm may also act as investment manager to a fund. Investment managers may or may not be regulated, depending upon the jurisdiction they are registered in or operate from, and therefore be subject to varying degrees of regulatory oversight. The relationship the investment manager has with investment advisers and ultimate controllers of the fund will vary depending upon the degree of control the investment manager has over

     (a)   the selection of investors,
     (b)   the investment strategy of the fund, and
     (c)   the placement of orders.

A fund may have more than one investment manager, known as sub-managers. Sub-managers are responsible for managing/investing part of the fund, and, depending on the structure of the fund, there may be more than one sub-manager.

- **Investment Adviser**

Some unregulated funds appoint separate investment advisers who will advise the fund with regard to investment decisions undertaken on behalf of the fund, and on occasion, depending on the structure of the funds, may place orders with a firm.

- **Administrator**

Administrative services such as the day to day operation of the fund and routine tasks associated with managing investments on behalf of investors will be undertaken by a separate entity know as the fund's Administrator. Although providing administrative services is not regulated activity in UK (although it may be in other jurisdictions), a firm itself or a sister company of a regulated entity may provide administrative services to a fund.

● **Other Relationships**

In addition to the above-mentioned entities involved in the operation and management of the fund, other parties may be involved, such as auditors, law firms, trustees, and custodians. These parties may be less relevant to a firm meeting its AML obligations, but they may give a more complete picture of the fund set-up.

20.6   The following diagram sets out the likely relationships a firm may have with an unregulated fund.

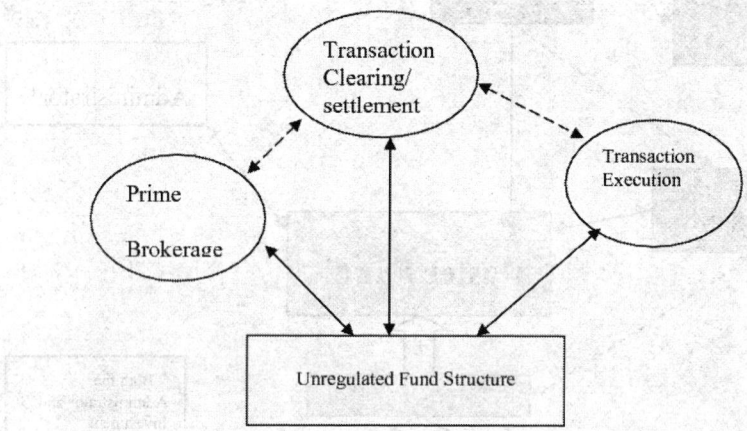

● **Transaction Execution**

Transactions or trading are undertaken for an unregulated fund by a firm commonly known as an executing broker. An unregulated fund may elect to execute transactions through one or more firms. The executing broker takes instructions from the unregulated fund or its appointed agent (usually the investment manager), but passes the transactions/trades to a clearing broker for clearing and settlement.

—   In derivative transactions the executing broker gives up the transaction to a clearing broker for settlement.

—   In transactions that involve delivery vs. payment (DVP) cash or securities are swapped between the executing broker and settlement/clearing agent or, on occasion, the custodian.

● **Clearing/Settlement**

An unregulated fund may elect to execute transactions through one or more firms and elect to settle or clear such transactions through another firm known as the clearing broker. The clearing broker will settle the transaction/trades on behalf of the unregulated fund, and as such will handle the movement of funds or assets from the unregulated fund in settlement of the unregulated fund's transactions and liabilities.

● **Prime Brokerage Services**

Prime brokerage is the provision of brokerage products and services to an unregulated fund. Prime brokerage is a portal to a suite of products and services offered by a prime brokerage such as custody, reporting, securities lending, cash lending, leverage and pricing. Some prime brokers provide capital introduction, start-up services, credit intermediation, risk management, straight-through processing, futures and options clearing, research, initial public offerings and contacts for difference and swaps. Most unregulated funds will only appoint one firm as its prime broker to undertake all or some of the above activities for it. Some unregulated funds may, however, not have a prime broker.

● **Multiple function brokers**

A firm may undertake more than one of the prime, clearing and executing broker functions set out above, depending upon the structure set up for the unregulated fund by the investment manager.

What are the money laundering risks associated with unregulated funds?

20.7   Unregulated funds are perceived as attractive vehicles for money launderers. There are seven primary factors giving rise to this perception:

●   The identity of those who invest into the unregulated funds will, in most cases, not be known to the firm providing services to the unregulated fund;

●   The unregulated status of the fund implies that it may be more difficult to ensure that the AML requirements applied to investors are of the appropriate standard;

●   An unregulated fund can have complex structures and consequently may appear to lack transparency of ownership and control;

●   A fund offers a private agreement between investors and the fund, and has traditionally been subjected to limited, or no, regulatory oversight or control;

- Money flows in and out of an unregulated fund in the form of new subscriptions and redemptions of investors' interests (subject to the fund's subscription and redemption terms) and the bank accounts of the fund may be held offshore, sometimes in jurisdictions with banking secrecy;
- The volume and size of unregulated fund trading activity and the complexity of underlying trading strategies; and
- The fund may accept nominee investments.

How to assess the elements of risk

20.8   The level of risk actually posed by the unregulated fund will depend upon the nature of the fund and its transparency. The risks can be determined through undertaking appropriate customer due diligence, and in particular through understanding to whom the fund is marketed and its structure and objectives, as well as the track record and reputation/standing of the investment manager and/or other relevant parties in control of the fund.

20.9   The status and reputation of other service providers, such as executing, clearing or prime brokers and the administrator, may also be a factor in determining the risks associated with an unregulated fund.

20.10   Where a firm agrees to undertake third party payments on behalf of an unregulated fund, the risk of money laundering and fraud is increased. A firm should therefore ensure it has adequate procedures and systems-controls to manage the risk associated with those types of payments and receipts. A firm may wish to consider monitoring and/or undertaking periodic review of these types of payments and receipts, as well as ensuring appropriate levels of sign-off with the firm.

Who is a firm's customer for AML purposes?

20.11   Where the firm's customer qualifies for the treatment of simplified due diligence (see Part I, section 5.4), no customer due diligence is required. This would be true even where the firm is aware that its customer is acting on behalf of an underlying customer who would not itself qualify for simplified due diligence; no question of reliance under Regulation 17 will arise.

20.12   Who a firm should view as its customer, and who the firm should therefore subject to identification and verification procedures, may vary according to the business undertaken for the unregulated fund. The following sets out examples of who may be viewed as the customer for AML purposes, and therefore should be subject to customer due diligence.
- Where the firm is acting as the investment manager or investment adviser[14] for a fund, for AML purposes the fund is the customer of the firm.
- Where the firm is acting as the administrator to the fund, for AML purposes the fund is the customer of the firm.
- Where the firm is acting as an executing broker, the customer for AML purposes may be the unregulated fund, the investment manager, or both of them, depending upon the fund structure, the regulatory status of the parties and where appropriate the firm's risk-based approach and policies.
- Where the firm is acting for another party, for example, the investment manager, who is itself acting as agent for the underlying fund, the following should apply:
  - Where the agent is appropriately regulated (or equivalent), they will be the customer for AML purposes, and there is no requirement to look to the underlying fund, unless otherwise agreed by the parties.
  - Where the agent is unregulated, or regulated within a non-equivalent jurisdiction, both the agent and the underlying fund will be considered to be customers for AML purposes.
- Where the firm is acting as clearing broker and/or settlement agent the customers for AML purposes will be the fund.
- Where the firm is providing prime broker services, the customer for AML purposes will be the fund.

---

[14]   References to Investment Manager in this section also refer to Investment Adviser

---

20.13   Within a firm, other departments such as risk, operations, legal or credit may identify other parties as being relevant to the relationship and undertake their own due diligence processes on those parties. A firm may, as part of its AML process, take this into account. For AML purposes, however, verification of identity and information-gathering on these parties may not be necessary as these parties may not be relevant to AML customer due diligence requirements.

Customer due diligence

20.14   Due to the characteristics of unregulated funds outlined above, in addition to applying CDD measures to the customer and (where simplified due diligence cannot be applied to the customer) the beneficial owners, it is appropriate to identify, depending on the risk, other parties involved such as the fund itself, its managers/advisers, and the fund's ultimate controllers and understand their relationships and roles.

20.15   On occasion, practical aspects of unregulated fund management are conducted onshore as a result of the delegation of responsibility for certain activities to onshore entities that may be subject to regulatory oversight. The interplay of these relationships needs to be assessed when determining the extent of due diligence necessary.

20.16   Depending on the services the firm is offering or providing to the fund, a firm should have particular regard to:

- Whether the firm is to have the Master Fund as its customer.
  - — In such cases, information on the Feeder Fund's offering memoranda/ prospectuses and, in some instances its investors, may also be useful.
- Who places orders and transaction on behalf of the fund or makes the investment decisions for the fund(s).
  - — Often, this will be the investment manager, and the firm should review the investment management agreement to understand the scope of the manager's authority/control.
- Whether there are any regulated or other reputable servicing entities in the fund set up.
- Whether a fund's ownership/control structure comprises numerous layers of entities and/or is transparent and understandable, and ensuring that the firm has a good understanding of the structure rather than focusing on the strict legal form alone.

20.17   The unregulated fund's prospectus, offering memorandum or other documents will set out details of the fund structure, appointed service providers – the investment manager, administrator, prime broker, lawyers and auditors – together with a summary of the material contracts such as the administration, investment management and prime brokerage agreements.

20.18   Where the unregulated fund has a number of layers of entities in its ownership/control structure, to the extent practical and on the basis of a firm's risk-based approach, this chain and the inter-relationships between the parties, whilst not necessarily subject to the guidance set out in Part I, Chapter 5, should be established and documented.

20.19   Where the fund is the customer, the requirements for identification and verification of corporate structures, trusts, and individuals etc, which are set out in Part I, Chapter 5 should be applied to the fund.

20.20   A firm should also undertake due diligence on the entities involved with the fund, namely:

Investment manager

20.21   The identity of the investment manager that has direct contact with the firm, or which instructs the firm on behalf of the unregulated fund must be verified, in accordance with the guidance relevant to their entity type, set out in Part I, Chapter 5. Where simplified due diligence can be applied to the investment manager (see Part I, Chapter 5, section 5.4) there is no duty to identify the underlying customer (ie, the fund or its relevant investors) although, as discussed above, under its risk-based assessment a firm may consider it appropriate to identify other parties involved.

Relevant investors

20.22   Shares or units in unregulated funds may be open to general subscription, or to purchase by any qualifying investors. Alternatively, unregulated funds may be established for the exclusive use of a closed group of investors. Whereas the Investment Manager usually 'controls' a fund, investors in a fund should be viewed as representing the ultimate source of funds of the customer.

20.23   'Relevant investors' ie, investors who have a 25% or more interest in the fund, however, are also beneficial owners (see Part I, Chapter 5, paragraph 5.3.8ff). Whether a firm has to identify and take risk-based and adequate measure to verify the identity of relevant investors, depends on a number of factors:

- Where the investment manager is the firm's customer and simplified due diligence can be applied to the investment manager (see Part I, Chapter 5, section 5.4) there is no duty to identify the underlying customer (ie, the fund or its relevant investors) although, as discussed above, under its risk-based assessment a firm may consider it appropriate to identify other parties involved;
- Where the fund, or an unregulated fund manager, is the firm's customer, then the firm may, if it considers it appropriate to do so under its risk-based approach, place reliance on a third party, which satisfies the definition in the ML Regulations, to perform CDD measures, including identification of beneficial owners (see Part I, Chapter 5, paragraph 5.6.19ff).
- In other cases, if the risk is assessed as lower, a firm may wish to satisfy itself as to the beneficial owners' identity based on information supplied by the customer (see Part I, Chapter 5, paragraphs 5.3.10 and 5.3.11).
- In all other cases – or where, following its assessment of the money laundering risk

presented by the unregulated fund, a firm considers it appropriate – a firm should identify and verify the identity of Relevant Investors in accordance with the relevant guidance set out in Part I, Chapter 5, paragraph 5.3.8ff.

- Subject to the firm's risk-based approach, a firm whose customer for AML purposes is the unregulated fund or an investment manager to whom simplified due diligence cannot be applied, may take steps to establish that reasonable measures are in place within the fund structure for verifying the identity of Relevant Investors in the fund; obtaining assurances from that party that:
  - There are Relevant Investors whose identity will be disclosed to enable the firm to take appropriate measures to verify their identity, or
  - There are no Relevant Investors.

20.24   Where a firm accepts such a representation, this should be documented, retained, and subject to periodic review.

20.25   Although it will often be the administrators to the fund, it is important to establish who in the fund structure is responsible for this process. If the party responsible for verifying the identity of the Relevant Investors is regulated in an equivalent jurisdiction and satisfies the definition of 'third party' in the ML Regulations, the firm may, in line with its own risk-based approach, be able to rely upon the third party to apply appropriate CDD measures (except monitoring) in respect of any Relevant Investors.

20.26   However, where the responsible party is not regulated in an equivalent jurisdiction, the firm should, as part of the determination as to the level of assurance necessary, also satisfy itself with regard the AML procedures of the responsible party.

Start-up funds

20.27   On occasion, a firm may offer services to, or establish a relationship with, a fund that is a start-up. Start-up funds are funds that are in the pre-investor phase, and as such it is not appropriate to consider undertaking due diligence on the Relevant Investors; until the start-up phase is complete, the investors and their status as relevant or not, may change, depending on who else invests in the fund. In these circumstances, a firm should review the Relevant Investor situation and undertake, where appropriate, due diligence on Relevant Investors.

Feeder funds

20.28   As a minimum, feeder funds themselves should be identified in accordance with the guidance in Part I, Chapter 5.

20.29   Where there are feeder funds, the assets/money held by the master fund will be owned by them. The feeder funds will be investors in the unregulated fund, and a firm should consider whether, under the ML Regulations or based upon its risk-based approach, the identity of the investors in the feeder funds needs to be verified, as Relevant Investors/beneficial owners.

Variations on Customer Due Diligence
Enhanced Due Diligence

20.30   In addition to the situations outlined in Part I, section 5.5, as part of a firm's risk-based approach it may feel it necessary to undertake Enhanced Due Diligence on its customer and/or related parties.

Ultimate Controllers

20.31   Where, because of the risk profile of the unregulated fund, a firm feels it appropriate to undertake Enhanced Due Diligence, the identity of the fund's ultimate controller should be obtained and verified. Standard identity information in respect of the unregulated fund's ultimate controller(s) where they are not the investment manager should be obtained, and the identity of the ultimate controller(s) should as appropriate be verified in accordance with the guidance for their entity type set out in Part I, section 5.3.

20.32   Ultimate control may be exercised through a chain of entities between the fund and the ultimate controller. This relationship should be established and documented. However, it is not necessary to obtain full identity information or verify the identity of each intermediate entity, or their connected persons that exists between the unregulated fund and its ultimate controller(s).

Feeder Funds

20.33   Where, because of the risk profile of the unregulated fund, a firm feels it appropriate to undertake Enhanced Due Diligence, the identity of the feeder fund should be verified in accordance with the guidance in Part I, Chapter 5, ensuring that the relevant investors of the feeder funds are subjected to the guidance set out in paragraphs 20.21ff.

Reliance on third parties

20.34   To avoid unnecessary duplication where an executing broker and a clearing broker are undertaking elements of the same exchange transaction on behalf of the same customer, which is not a regulated firm from an equivalent jurisdiction, the executing broker may be able to rely upon the clearing broker under the ML Regulations (see Part I, paragraphs 5.6.4ff) or otherwise take account of the fact that there is another regulated firm from an equivalent jurisdiction acting as clearing agent or providing other services in relation to the transaction.

20.35   Where a firm is acting as clearing broker or prime broker, from a risk-based perspective the firm should not rely upon a third party and should undertake full customer due diligence, including where relevant on beneficial owners, as set out in Part I, Chapter 5.

Monitoring

20.36   The money laundering risks to firms offering services to unregulated funds can be mitigated by the implementation of monitoring procedures; guidance on the general monitoring requirements are set out in Part I, section 5.7. However, there are specific characteristics of unregulated funds which will be relevant, in particular the use of multiple brokers.

20.37   Customers may choose to allocate execution, clearing and prime brokerage between different firms and many customers may use more than one execution broker. The reasons for this include ensuring that they obtain best execution, competitive rates, or to gain access to a particular specialism within one firm. This will restrict a firm's ability to monitor a customer, as they may not be aware of all activity or even contingent activity associated with the transactions they are undertaking.

20.38   Monitoring unregulated funds' activity will be affected by the fact that firms may only have access to a part of the overall picture of their customer's trading activities. The fact that many customers spread their activities over a number of financial firms will mean that many firms will have a limited view of a customer's trading activities and it may be difficult to assess the commercial rationale of certain transactions.

20.39   The nature and extent of any monitoring activity will therefore need be determined by a firm based on a risk-based assessment of the firm's business profile. This will be different for each firm and may include an assessment of the following matters:
- Extent of business undertaken (executing, clearing, prime brokerage or a mixture of all three)
- Nature of unregulated funds who are customers (eg, geographic location)
- Number of customers and volume of transactions
- Types of products traded and complexity of those products
- Payment procedures

20.40   Firms should ensure that any relevant factors taken into account in determining their monitoring activities are adequately documented, and are subject to appropriate periodic review.

20.41   Firms relying on third parties under the ML Regulations to apply CDD measures **cannot** rely on the third party in respect of monitoring.

[7045]

21: INVOICE FINANCE

Note: This sectoral guidance is incomplete on its own. It must be read in conjunction with the main guidance set out in Part I of the Guidance.

Products

21.1   Invoice finance companies offer a number of products to fund the working capital requirements of their clients; these generally fall into two categories – Factoring agreements and Invoice Discounting agreements. These can be operated on a Recourse or Non Recourse basis, and with or without disclosure of the assignment of the sales invoice to the client's customers, the debtors.

Factoring Agreements

21.2   *Factoring* is a contract between an invoice finance company and their client where revolving finance is provided against the value of the client's sales ledger that is sold to the invoice financier. The invoice finance company will manage the client's sales ledger and will normally provide the credit control and collection services. The client assigns all their invoices, as usually a whole turnover contract is used, after the goods or service has been delivered or performed. The invoice finance company will then typically advance up to 85% of the invoiced amount – the gross amount including VAT. The balance, less charges, is then paid to the client once the debtor makes full payment to the invoice finance company. The assignment is usually disclosed to the debtor, (although some contracts are operated on an agency basis, via the client, without disclosure of the assignment to the debtors and on occasions the management of the sales ledger can remain with the client as well).

Invoice Discounting Agreements

21.3   *Invoice Discounting* is a contract between the invoice finance company and their client where revolving finance is provided against the value of the client's sales ledger. The client will manage the sales ledger and will normally continue to provide the credit control and collection services. The client assigns the detail of all their invoices, as usually a whole turnover contract is used, after the goods or service have been delivered or performed. The invoice finance company records and monitors this on a bulk sales ledger basis rather than retaining the individual invoice detail. The invoice finance company will then typically advance up to 85% of the invoiced amount. The balance, less any charges, is then paid to the client once the debtor makes full payment to the invoice finance company. As the assignment is not usually disclosed the client undertakes the collection service under an agency agreement within the contract. The client is obligated to ensure that the payments from debtors are passed to the invoice finance company. The non-disclosure element has led to the frequent use of the colloquial title of Confidential Invoice Discounting being used to describe this product, but confidentiality only exists at the discretion of the invoice finance company (whilst they are prepared to operate the agency arrangement).

Asset-Based Lending

21.4   Asset-Based Lending in the Invoice Finance industry would usually have the client's sales ledger at the core of the facility. It is a contract between the invoice finance company and their client where revolving finance is provided against a 'basket' of assets – accounts receivables, inventory, plant machinery, property, etc.

Recourse Agreements

21.5   *Recourse agreements* can apply to factoring or invoice discounting agreements. If the customer fails to pay the amount due to the client, then the invoice finance company will look to the client for reimbursement of any money they have advanced against that invoice.

Non Recourse Agreements

21.6   *Non-Recourse agreements* can apply to factoring or invoice discounting facilities. The invoice finance company effectively offers a bad debt protection service to the client. If the customer fails to pay the amount due to the client, due to insolvency, the invoice finance company stands the credit loss up to the protected amount, which is the value of the credit limit provided against the particular customer, less any agreed first loss amount.

Affiliated Factoring Companies

21.7   Assigned sales invoices may include overseas sales which require international credit control and collection services. Where the invoice finance company is not able to undertake this cross border activity, typically due to the lack of its own international network, it may enter into an arrangement with an Affiliated Factoring Company [AFC] in the appropriate country. This is often known as Export Factoring.

21.8   Affiliated Factoring Companies, operating in their own countries, will frequently have sales invoices with sales that require credit control and collection services to be performed in the United Kingdom. Where the AFC is not able to undertake this cross border activity, typically due to the lack of its own international network, it may enter into an arrangement with an invoice finance company in the United Kingdom. This is often known as Import Factoring.

21.9   The activities and associated risks are considered to be similar to correspondent banking. See Part II, sector 16: *Correspondent banking* for specific guidance on the risks and controls applicable to this type of activity.

What are the money laundering risks in invoice finance?

21.10   As with any financial service activity, invoice finance products are susceptible to use by criminals to launder money. Both Factoring and Invoice Discounting products facilitate third party payments and may therefore be used by criminals for money laundering activity. The different invoice finance products available vary greatly and the degree of risk is directly related to the product offering.

21.11   The level of physical cash receipts directly received within the invoice finance sector is extremely low, as the vast majority of debtors settle outstanding invoices by way of cheque or electronic payment methods. Therefore the susceptibility of the invoice finance sector at the traditional placement stage is very low. The risk within the invoice finance industry is at the layering and integration stages of money laundering.

21.12   The main money laundering risks within the invoice finance sector are payments against invoices where there is no actual movement of goods or services provided, or the value of goods is overstated to facilitate the laundering of funds. As stated, the level of risk will depend upon the nature of the product and the level of involvement by the finance company. Factoring should be considered to be a lower risk than invoice discounting, in view of the fact that direct contact is maintained with the debtor. Invoice discounting would represent an increased risk of money laundering due to the 'hands off' nature of the product.

21.13 The following factors will generally increase the risk of money laundering for invoice finance products:

- Cross border transactions
- Products with reduced paper trails
- Products where the invoice financier allows the client to collect the debt
- Confidential products
- Bulk products

21.14 The following factors will generally decrease the risk of money laundering for invoice finance products:

- Individual items (invoices, customers, cash) being recorded and managed by the invoice financier
- Collections activity being undertaken by the invoice financier
- Non-recourse facilities
- Regular ongoing due diligence and monitoring including on-site inspections and verification of balances
- Regular statistical monitoring
- For export facilities, the use of an approved AFC, in the country in which the debtor is domiciled

21.15 It is important that each invoice finance company within its risk assessment has developed robust procedures to monitor the money laundering risks. Many of these procedures will overlap with those that are routinely used to manage credit risks within the sector, however other checks may need to be implemented, such as improved knowledge of the source of funds, that are different to the usual credit risk checks.

21.16 Frequent occurrences, within the Invoice Finance sector, are short-term breaches of the underlying agreements by the clients. These are often due to client error or the clients' need for short term funding to cover a temporary deficiency. The vast majority of these short term breaches are not material in nature and the intelligence value of many of these occurrences, eg, where invoices have been assigned prior to the actual delivery date by a matter of days, is extremely limited. However, the invoice financier should be aware that such instances could be one of the first indicators of the presence of money laundering and that a period of increased vigilance may be appropriate to ensure there is no reason to suspect money laundering.

21.17 The risks associated with short term breaches should be documented within the invoice finance company's risk assessment and appropriate controls established to ensure that, where there is a suspicion of the presence of money laundering, an appropriate report is filed with SOCA.

21.18 Invoice finance companies should recognise within their risk assessment that even though they may appear to be the only party affected by the client's, (or the client's customer's) action, the action in itself may represent an offence under POCA and as such the invoice finance company is obligated to file an appropriate report with SOCA.

Assessment of risk

21.19 With extremely low levels of cash being transacted the susceptibility of the invoice finance sector at the traditional placement stage is very low.

21.20 Invoice finance products may be used to launder money at the layering and integration stages. However there are a number of factors that make the invoice finance facility less attractive to the money launderer, they are:

- The high levels of contact between the financier and the client, in terms of physical audits and visits, and of statistical monitoring
- The sophisticated IT monitoring techniques used to detect issues with the quality of the underlying security, consisting of the quality of the goods and the customers (debtors),
- In the case of factoring the item by item accounting and the regular direct contact with the debtors
- The focus on the debtors in terms of creditworthiness and assessment of risk
- The double scrutiny of payments, by the receiving bank and by the invoice financier

21.21 An invoice finance company operating a full factoring agreement, with regular contact, monitoring and review of the third party transactions, may determine that the risk level of Factoring Agreements, due to the level and frequency of the mitigating controls is low.

21.22 Invoice Discounting facilities, while generally considered higher risk than factoring facilities may also be characterised by regular due diligence by the Invoice Financier. The nature of these controls and the rationale for any reduction in risk assessment should be documented within the invoice finance company's overall risk assessment, which should be updated and reviewed on a regular basis.

21.23   Cross border transactions represent an increased risk of the presence of money laundering. The nature of the agreement will lead to these transactions being managed in different ways. This risk is reduced when the credit control procedures are managed by an approved AFC in the country in which the debtor is domiciled.

21.24   In general, the normally low to medium risk of money laundering will increase with the reduction of the levels of intervention by the financier and the increase in the size of foreign transactions through the account.

Who is the customer for AML purposes?

21.25   In the invoice finance sector the party with whom the factoring company holds a contract to provide finance is usually referred to as a 'client' and the client's customers as either 'debtors' or 'customers'. Therefore references in Part I of the Guidance to 'customer' refer to the client within the invoice finance sector.

21.26   The identification requirements on which guidance is given in Part I, Chapter 5 will only apply to an invoice finance company's clients – the parties with whom they have a contractual relationship. The client will be a business entity; a public limited company, private limited company, partnership or sole trader.

21.27   Whilst customers [the client's debtors] may be identified for routine credit risk or collection purposes by the invoice finance company, the requirement to identify, or verify the identity, of these customers does not apply.

21.28   Where invoice finance companies are involved in syndicated arrangements, the customer is as defined within Part II, sector 17: *Syndicated lending*. In such cases, the guidance in sector 17 should be read in addition to the guidance in this part of the Guidance.

21.29   Where invoice finance companies are involved in arrangements with Affiliated Factoring Companies, the customer is as defined in sector 16: *Correspondent Banking*. In such cases, the guidance in sector 16 should be read in addition to the guidance in this part of the Guidance.

Customer Due Diligence

21.30   The CDD measures carried out at the commencement of the facility and the ongoing due diligence are very closely linked to anti-fraud measures and are one of the primary controls for preventing criminals using invoice finance facilities. Invoice finance companies should ensure that they coordinate both the identification and ongoing customer due diligence processes in order to provide as strong a gatekeeper control as possible.

21.31   Invoice finance companies should carry out detailed initial CDD measures to gain a full understanding of the client and their business before opening a facility. This should be at a level to provide identification and establish expected activity patterns of their clients and their activities to meet the requirements set out in Part I, Chapter 5.

21.32   The identity of the client's debtors will normally only be obtained from the client, as part of the understanding of that client, without verification being required. The invoice finance company's risk assessment could determine that verification of the identity of some of the underlying customers will also be required under appropriate circumstances.

21.33   In terms of money laundering, some invoice finance products are considered higher risk than others; in these cases, enhanced due diligence measures are required.

21.34   Enhanced due diligence is appropriate in the following, but not exhaustive, list of situations:

- Where any party connected to the client is a PEP. See Part I, paragraphs 5.5.18–5.5.25.
- When the client is involved in a business that is considered to present a higher risk of money laundering. Examples should be set out in the firm's risk-based approach and should reflect the firm's own experience and information produced by the authorities. See Part I, paragraphs 5.5.1–5.5.8 for guidance. These are likely to include the following, although this list should not be construed as exhaustive;
  - A client with any party associated with a country either on a residential or business activity basis that is deemed to have a relatively high risk of money laundering, or inadequate levels of supervision (see Part I, paragraphs 3.24–3.26). Examples of these countries can be found listed within the country assessments made by the International Monetary Fund or the Financial Action Task Force. Another source of information can be found within the Transparency International Corruption Perception Indexes that are published on an annual basis.
  - A client who carries a higher risk of money laundering by virtue of their business or occupation. Examples of which could be;
    - A business with a high level of cash sales.
    - A business with a high level of cross border sales, including Import-Export companies.
    - A business selling small high value goods that are easily disposed of.

- Where transactions or activity do not meet expected or historic expectations, it is likely they will include the following:
  - Size – monetary, frequency, etc.
  - Pattern – cyclical, logical, frequency, amount, etc
  - Location – cross border, NCCT, rationale, etc.
  - Goods / Service – Type, Use, Payment norms, etc.

21.35 Monitoring aspects of enhanced due diligence should be set out in the invoice finance company's risk-based approach. It is likely they will include the following:

- More frequent and detailed on-site inspections of the client's books and records, frequently called an 'Audit', with appropriate management oversight and action of any significant deficiencies.
- More frequent and extensive verification, usually by telephone contact with the debtor, of the validity of the sale and invoice values.
- Greater management oversight of these facilities.

[7046]

SPECIALIST GUIDANCE

A: Wire transfers

Note: This sectoral guidance will only be relevant to a limited number of firms in the financial sector (see Part I, paragraphs 5.2.10ff)

Background

A.1 FATF issued Special Recommendation VII in October 2001, with the objective of enhancing the transparency of electronic payment transfers ("wire transfers") of all types, domestic and cross border, thereby making it easier for law enforcement to track funds transferred electronically by terrorists and criminals. A revised Interpretative Note to this Special Recommendation was issued by the FATF on 10 June 2005, and is available at http://www.fatf-gafi.org/dataoecd/34/56/35002635.pdf

A.2 Special Recommendation VII is addressed to FATF member countries, and has been implemented in member states of the European Union, including the UK, through a Regulation issued by the European Parliament and the Council of the European Union.

A.3 This Regulation was proposed by the European Commission on 26 July 2005 to implement Special Recommendation VII within the EU with effect from 1 January 2007. In its final form the Regulation was approved by the European Parliament on 6 July 2006 and by the ECOFIN Council on 7 November 2006. It was published in the Official Journal of the European Union (OJ L 345) on 8 December 2006 (EC Regulation 1781/2006).

A.4 Whilst the Regulation has been in force since 1 January 2007, sanctions for non-compliance will not be enforced until 15 December 2007, coincident with the deadline for implementation of the Third EU Money Laundering Directive.

A.5   The Regulation can be found at
http://eur-lex.europa.eu/LexUriServ/site/en/oj/2006/l_345/l_34520061208en00010009.pdf

A.6 The Regulation requires the ordering financial institution to ensure that all wire transfers carry specified information about the originator (Payer) who gives the instruction for the payment to be made. The core requirement is that this information consists of name, address and account number; however, there are a number of permitted variations and concessions, see below under **Information Requirements** (paragraphs A.15ff).

A.7 As the text of this Regulation has EEA relevance, the three non-EU Member States of the EEA, ie, Iceland, Liechtenstein and Norway, are expected to enact equivalent legislation. As and when this happens, references in this guidance to *intra-EU* can be understood to include these states. However, for the time being the reduced information requirement available within the EU will not apply to payments to and from those countries.

Scope of the Regulation

A.8 The Regulation is widely drawn and intended to cover all types of funds transfer falling within its definition as made "by electronic means", other than those specifically exempted wholly or partially by the Regulation. For UK-based Payment Service Providers (PSPs) it therefore includes, but is not necessarily limited to, international payment transfers made via SWIFT, including various Euro payment systems, and domestic transfers via CHAPS and BACS. The Regulation specifically exempts the following payment types:

- transfers where both Payer and Payee are PSPs acting on their own behalf – this will apply to MT 200* series payments via SWIFT. This exemption will include MT 400 and MT 700 series messages when they are used to settle trade finance obligations between banks (*cover payments using MT 202s are technically in scope but until the message format is changed the MT 202 will not itself carry payer information, although its associated MT103 must do so.);

- transfers by credit or debit card or similar payment instrument, providing that the Payee has an agreement with the PSP permitting payment for goods or services and that the transfer is accompanied by a unique identifier permitting the transaction to be traced back to the Payer (see paragraph A.18);
- transfers whereby the Payer withdraws cash from his/her own account. This is designed to exempt ATM withdrawals outside the EU which would otherwise attract the full information requirement;
- transfers to public authorities for taxes, fines or other levies;
- direct debits, subject to their carrying a unique identifier for tracing purposes;
- truncated cheques (cheques are otherwise paper to which the Regulation does not apply);
- Article 3 (4) provides a limited exemption for small pre-paid transfers carried out by means of a mobile phone or any other digital or IT device;
- e-money transfers, as defined in Article 11(5)(d) of the Third EU Money Laundering Directive, where they do not exceed €1000. ie, those transfers transacted using non-reloadable electronic money products on which the maximum load does not exceed € 150, or using reloadable e-money products which are subject to a maximum load of €2500 in a calendar year and maximum redemption of under €1000 in the same calendar year. (see also Sector 3: *Electronic money*);
- post-paid funds transfers carried out by mobile phone, or any other digital or IT device, subject to various conditions, including their traceability and that they relate to the provision of goods and services.

A.9   The following payment types are also exempt under the Regulation (under derogations which are not used in the UK):

- Article 3 (6), which exempts small payments for goods and services, relates to giro payment systems in a few other member states;
- funds transfers of €150 or less for charitable, religious, cultural, educational, social, scientific or fraternal purposes to a prescribed group of non-profit organisations which run annual / disaster relief appeals and which are subject to reporting and external audit requirements or supervision by a public authority and whose names and supporting details have been specifically communicated by the Member State to the Commission. This applies only to transfers within the territory of the Member State. The exemption is designed to ensure that small charitable donations to certain bona fide bodies are not frustrated, but has limited practical relevance in the UK, where typical mechanisms for making payments to charities, eg, by credit transfer or by card payment within the EU, will either not be subject to the Regulation, or where they are, will be compliant with it in any case;

A.10   The UK credit clearing system is out of scope of the Regulation as it is paper-based and hence transfers are not carried out "by electronic means". Cash and cheque deposits over the counter via bank giro credits are not therefore affected by the Regulation.

Note: The Regulation defines "Payee" as a natural or legal person who is the intended final recipient of transferred funds. Recognizing that a perverse and wholly unworkable interpretation could be put on those words, where a named Payee might have been a conduit for an undisclosed 'final recipient' to serve a criminal objective, this Guidance takes the position that 'final recipient' can only practically be understood as referring to the party named in the transfer as the beneficiary of the payment.

Pre-conditions for making payments

A.11   Payment Service Providers (PSPs) of Payers must ensure that the Payer information conveyed in the payment relating to account holding customers is accurate and has been verified. The verification requirement is deemed to be met for account holding customers of the PSP whose identity has been verified, and where the information obtained by this verification has been stored in accordance with anti money laundering requirements, ie in the UK in accordance with the Money Laundering Regulations which will give effect to the Third EU Money Laundering Directive. This position applies even though the address shown on the payment transfer may not have been specifically verified. No further verification of such account holders is required, although PSPs may wish to exercise discretion to do so in individual cases; eg, firms will be mindful of Part I, paragraphs 5.3.14–5.3.18, concerning customers with existing relationships. (See A.14ff where the named Payer is not the holder of the account to be debited.)

A.12   Before undertaking one-off payments in excess of €1000 on the instructions of non-account holding customers, the PSP of the Payer should verify the identity and address (or evidence of a permitted alternative to address, such as date and place of birth if quoting that information on the transfer instead of address).

A.13   For non-account based transfers of €1000 and under, PSPs are not required by the Regulation to verify the Payer's identity except when several transactions are carried out which appear to be linked (see Article 5.4) and together exceed €1000. NB, even in cases where the Regulation does not require verification, the customer information has to be obtained and it may be advisable for the PSP to verify the identity of the Payer in all cases.

A.14   Evidence of verification must be retained with the customer information in accordance with **Record Keeping Requirements** (see A.20–A.21).

Information Requirements

A.15   Complete payer information:

Except as permitted below, complete Payer information must accompany all wire transfers. Effectively, the complete Payer information requirement applies where the destination PSP is located in a jurisdiction outside the European Union. Complete Payer information consists of: name, address and account number.

- Address ONLY may be substituted with the Payer's date and place of birth, or national identity number or customer identification number. This Guidance recommends that these options are only deployed selectively within a firm's processes to address particular needs. It follows that in the event a Payee PSP demands the Payer's address, where one of the alternatives had initially been provided, the response to the enquiry should point that out. Only with the Payer's consent or under judicial compulsion should the address be additionally provided.

- Where the payment is not debited to a bank account, the requirement for an account number must be substituted by a unique identifier which permits the payment to be traced back to the Payer.

- The extent of the information supplied in each field will be subject to the conventions of the messaging system in question and is not prescribed in detail in the Regulation.

- The account number could be, but is not required to be, expressed as the IBAN (International Bank Account Number).

- The Regulation applies even where the Payer and Payee hold accounts with the same PSP.

- Where a bank is itself the Payer, as will sometimes be the case even for SWIFT MT 102 and 103 messages, this Guidance considers that supplying the Bank Identifier Code (BIC) constitutes complete Payer information for the purposes of the Regulation, although it is also preferable for the account number to be included where available. The same applies to Business Entity Identifiers (BEIs), although in that case the account number should always be included. As the use of BICs and BEIs is not specified in FATF Special Recommendation VII or the Regulation, there may be requests from Payee PSPs for address information.

- Generally, firms will populate the information fields from their customer database. In cases where electronic banking customers input their details directly the Payer's PSP is not required, at the time that the account is debited, to validate the Payer's name and/or address against the name and address of the accountholder whose account number is stated on the payment transfer.

- Where the named Payer is not the accountholder the Payer's PSP may either substitute the name and address (or permitted alternatives) of the account holder being debited (subject to any appropriate customer agreement), or execute the payment instruction with the alternative Payer name and address information provided with the consent of the accountholder. In the latter case, provided the Payer PSP retains all relevant data for 5 years, the Payer PSP is required to verify only the information about the accountholder being debited (in accordance with Article 5.3a. of the Regulation). PSPs should exercise a degree of control to avoid abuse of the discretion by customers.

- It is important to note that this flexibility should not undermine the transparency of Payer information sought by FATF Special Recommendation VII and the Regulation. It is designed to meet the practical needs of corporate and other business (eg, solicitor) accountholders with direct access who, for internal accounting reasons, may have legitimate reasons for quoting alternative Payer details with their account number.

- Where payment instructions are received manually, for example, over the counter, the Payer name and address (or permitted alternative) should correspond to the account holder. Any request to override customer information on a similar basis to that set out above for electronic banking customers should be contained within a rigorous referral and approval mechanism to ensure that only in cases where the PSP is entirely satisfied that the reason is legitimate should the instruction be exceptionally dealt with on that basis. Any suspicion of improper motive by a customer should be reported to the firm's Nominated Officer.

A.16   Reduced Payer Information:

Where the PSPs of both Payer and Payee are located within the European Union, wire transfers need be accompanied only by the Payer's account number or by a unique identifier which permits the transaction to be traced back to the Payer.

- However, if requested by the Payee's PSP, complete information must be provided by the Payer's PSP within three working days, starting the day after the request is received by the Payer's PSP. ("Working days" is as defined in the Member State of the Payer's PSP).
- Article 17 of the Regulation provides for the circumstances in which transfers of funds between EU Member States and territories outside the EU with whom they share a monetary union and payment and settlement systems may be treated as transfers within the Member State, so that the reduced information requirement can apply to payments passing between that Member State and its associated territory (but not between any other Member State and that territory). In the case of the UK such arrangements will include the Channel Islands and the Isle of Man.

A.17   Batch File Transfers:

A hybrid complete/reduced requirement applies to batch file transfers from a single Payer to multiple Payees outside the EU in that the individual transfers within the batch need carry only the Payer's account number or a unique identifier, provided that the batch file itself contains complete Payer information.

A.18   Payments via Intermediaries:

Intermediary PSPs (IPSPs) must, subject to the following guidance on technical limitations, ensure that all information received on the Payer which accompanies a wire transfer is retained with the transfer.

It is preferable for an IPSP to forward payments through a system which is capable of carrying all the information received with the transfer. However, where an IPSP within the EU is technically unable to on-transmit Payer information originating outside the EU, it may nevertheless use a system with technical limitations provided that:

- if it is aware that the Payer information is missing or incomplete it must concurrently advise the Payee's PSP of the fact by an agreed form of communication, whether within a payment or messaging system or otherwise.
- it retains records of any information received for five years, whether or not the information is complete. If requested to do so by the Payee's PSP, the IPSP must provide the Payer information within three working days of receiving the request.

A.19   Card transactions

As indicated in paragraph A.8, card transactions for *goods and services* are out of scope of the Regulation provided that a unique identifier, allowing the transaction to be traced back to the payer, accompanies the movement of the funds. The 16 digit Card PAN number serves this function.

Similarly, the Card PAN number meets the information requirement for all Card transactions for any purpose where the derogation for transfers within the European Union applies, as explained in and subject to the conditions set out in paragraph A.15.

Complete payer information is required in all cases where the card is used to generate a direct credit transfer, including a balance transfer, to a payee whose PSP is located outside the EU. These are "push" payments, and as such capable of carrying the information when required under the Regulation.

Otherwise, Card transactions are "pull" payments, ie, the transfer of funds required to give effect to the transaction is initiated by the merchant recipient rather than the Card Issuer and under current systems it is not possible for any information in addition to the PAN number to flow with the transfer in those cases where the transaction is arguably not for 'goods and services' but is settled to a PSP outside the EU. Examples include Card transactions used to make donations to charity, place bets, or purchase e-money products such as prepaid cards. As a matter of expediency these transactions must therefore be treated as 'goods and services'. FSA and HM Treasury have supported that interpretation for the time being, subject to further review at an unspecified future date on the basis that the transactions are traceable by the PAN number.

A.20   Minimum standards

The above information requirements are minimum standards. It is open to PSPs to elect to supply complete Payer information with transfers which are eligible for a reduced information requirement and thereby limit the likely incidence of inbound requests for complete information. (In practice a number of large UK and European banks have indicated that they will be providing complete payer information for all transfers where systems permit). To ensure that the data protection position is beyond any doubt, it would be advisable to ensure that terms and conditions of business include reference to the information being provided.

Record Keeping Requirements

A.21   The Payee's PSP and any intermediary PSP must retain records of any information received on a Payer for five years, in accordance with the Regulation.

A.22   The Payer's PSP must retain records of transactions and supporting evidence of the Payer's identity in accordance with Part I, Chapter 8.

Checking Incoming Payments

A.23   Payee PSPs should have effective procedures for checking that incoming wire transfers are compliant with the relevant information requirement. In order not to disrupt straight-through processing, it is not expected that monitoring should be undertaken at the time of processing the transfer. The Regulation specifies that PSPs should have procedures to detect whether relevant information is missing. (It is our understanding that this requirement is satisfied by the validation rules of whichever messaging or payment system is being utilised). Additionally, the Regulation requires PSPs to take remedial action when they become aware that an incoming payment is not compliant. Hence, in practical terms it is expected that this requirement will be met by a combination of the following:

   (i)   SWIFT payments on which mandatory Payer information fields are not completed will fail anyway and the payment will not be received by the Payee PSP. Current SWIFT validation prevents payments being received where the mandatory information is not present at all. However, it is accepted that where the Payer information fields are completed with incorrect or meaningless information, or where there is no account number, the payment will pass through the system. SWIFT is currently considering how its validation standards might be improved to respond more effectively to the requirements of FATF Special Recommendation VII. Similar considerations apply to non-SWIFT messaging systems which also validate that a field is populated in accordance with the standards applicable to that system, eg, BACS.

   (ii)   PSPs should therefore subject incoming payment traffic to an appropriate level of post event random sampling to detect non-compliant payments. This sampling should be risk based, eg,:

   —   the sampling could normally be restricted to payments emanating from PSPs outside the EU where the complete information requirement applies;

   —   the sampling could be weighted towards non FATF member jurisdictions, particularly those deemed high risk under a PSP's own country risk assessment, or by reference to external sources such as Transparency International, or FATF or IMF country reviews);

   —   focused more heavily on transfers from those Payer PSPs who are identified by such sampling as having previously failed to comply with the relevant information requirement;

   —   Other specific measures might be considered, eg, checking, at the point of payment delivery, that Payer information is compliant and meaningful on all transfers that are collected in cash by Payees on a "Pay on application and identification" basis.

   NB. None of the above requirements obviate the obligation to report suspicious actions (see Part I, Chapter 6).

A.24   If a Payee PSP becomes aware in the course of processing a payment that it contains meaningless or incomplete information, under the terms of Article 9 (1) of the Regulation it should either reject the transfer or ask for complete information on the Payer. In addition, in such cases, the Payee PSP is required to take any necessary action to comply with any applicable law or administrative provisions relating to money laundering and terrorist financing. Dependent on the circumstances such action could include making the payment or holding the funds and advising the Payee PSP's Nominated Officer.

A.25   Where the Payee PSP becomes aware subsequent to processing the payment that it contains meaningless or incomplete information either as a result of random checking or other monitoring mechanisms under the PSP's risk-based approach, it must:

   (i)   seek the necessary information on the Payer
   and/or
   (ii)   take any necessary action under any applicable law, regulation or administrative provisions relating to money laundering or terrorist financing.

A.26   PSPs will be mindful of the risk of incurring civil claims for breach of contract and possible liability if competing requirements arise under national legislation, including in the UK the Proceeds of Crime Act and other anti money laundering and anti terrorism legislation.

A.27   Where a PSP is identified as having regularly failed to comply with the information requirements, the Payee PSP should take steps, which may initially include issuing warnings and setting deadlines, prior to either refusing to accept further transfers from that PSP or deciding whether to terminate its relationship with that PSP either completely or in respect of funds transfers.

A.28   A Payee PSP should consider whether incomplete or meaningless information of which it becomes aware on a funds transfer constitutes grounds for suspicion which would be reportable to its Nominated Officer for possible disclosure to the Authorities.

A.29   With regard to transfers from PSPs located in countries that are not members of either the EU or FATF, firms should endeavour to transact only with those PSPs with whom they have a relationship that has been subject to a satisfactory risk-based assessment of their anti money laundering culture and policy and who accept the standards set out in the Interpretative Note to FATF Special Recommendation VII.

A.30   It should be borne in mind when querying incomplete payments that some FATF member countries outside the EU may have framed their own regulations to incorporate a threshold of €/US$ 1000 below which the provision of complete information on outgoing payments is not required. This is permitted by the Interpretative Note to FATF Special Recommendation VII. The USA is a case in point. This does not preclude European PSPs from calling for the complete information where it has not been provided, but it is reasonable for a risk-based view to be taken on whether or how far to press the point.

[7047]

APPENDIX I

Scenario 1: Transfer of funds – Obligations on Payer PSP

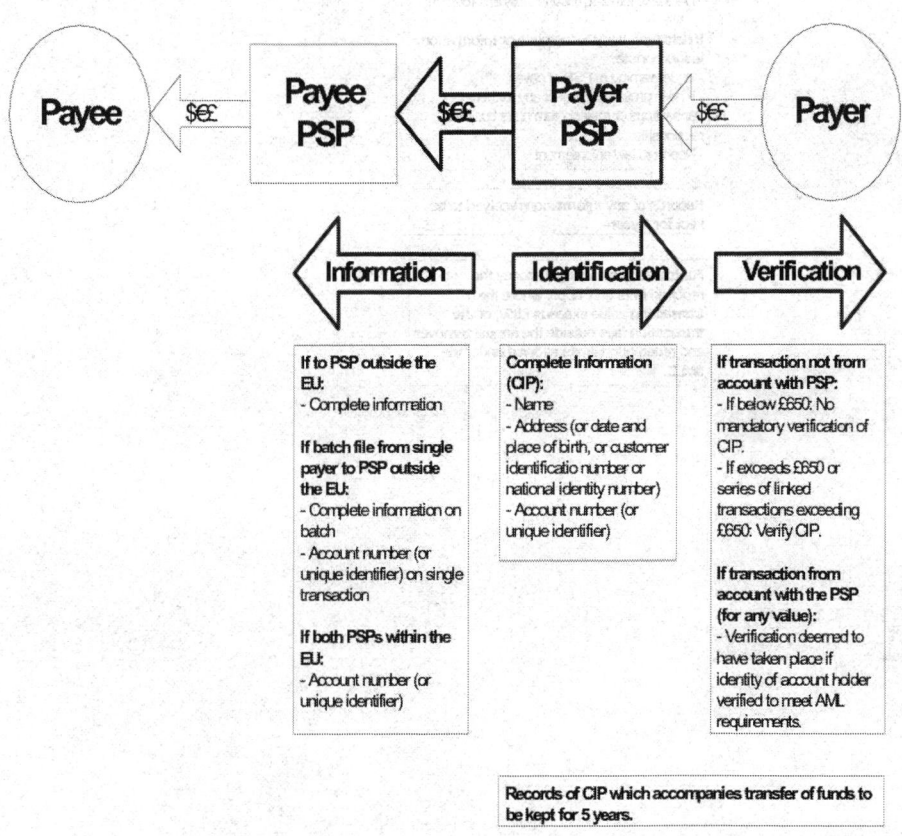

PART V
OTHER MATERIALS

Scenario 2: Transfer of funds – Obligations on Payee PSP

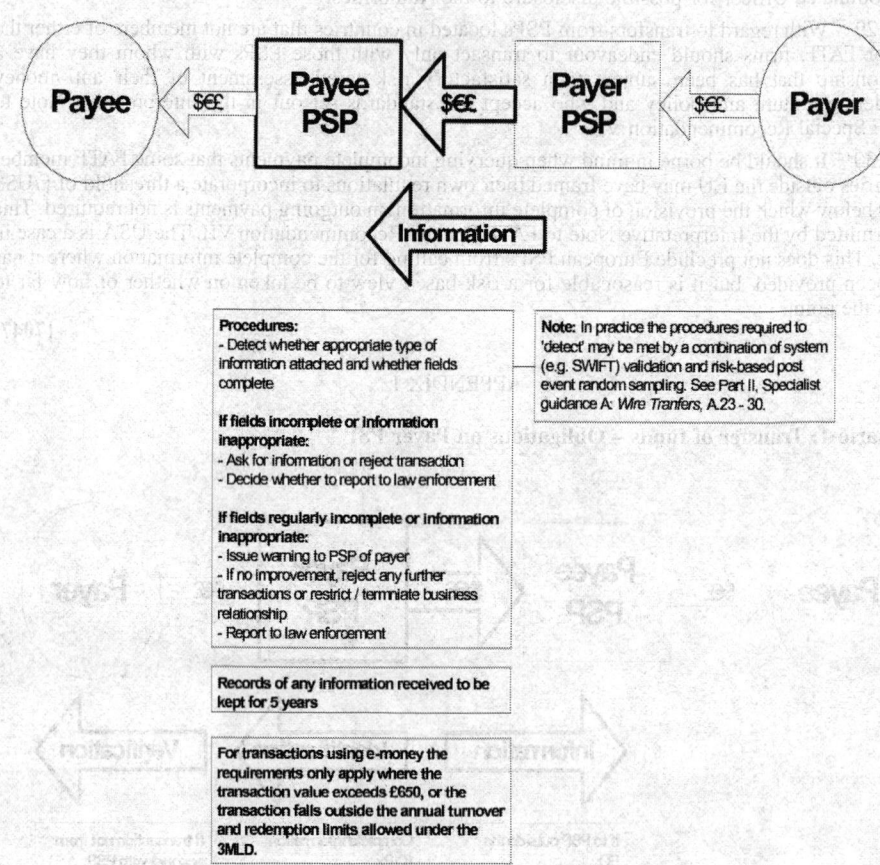

Procedures:
- Detect whether appropriate type of information attached and whether fields complete

If fields incomplete or information inappropriate:
- Ask for information or reject transaction
- Decide whether to report to law enforcement

If fields regularly incomplete or information inappropriate:
- Issue warning to PSP of payer
- If no improvement, reject any further transactions or restrict / terminate business relationship
- Report to law enforcement

Records of any information received to be kept for 5 years

For transactions using e-money the requirements only apply where the transaction value exceeds £650, or the transaction falls outside the annual turnover and redemption limits allowed under the 3MLD.

Note: In practice the procedures required to 'detect' may be met by a combination of system (e.g. SWIFT) validation and risk-based post event random sampling. See Part II, Specialist guidance A: *Wire Tranfers*, A.23 - 30.

Scenario 3: Transfer of funds – Obligations on Intermediary PSP

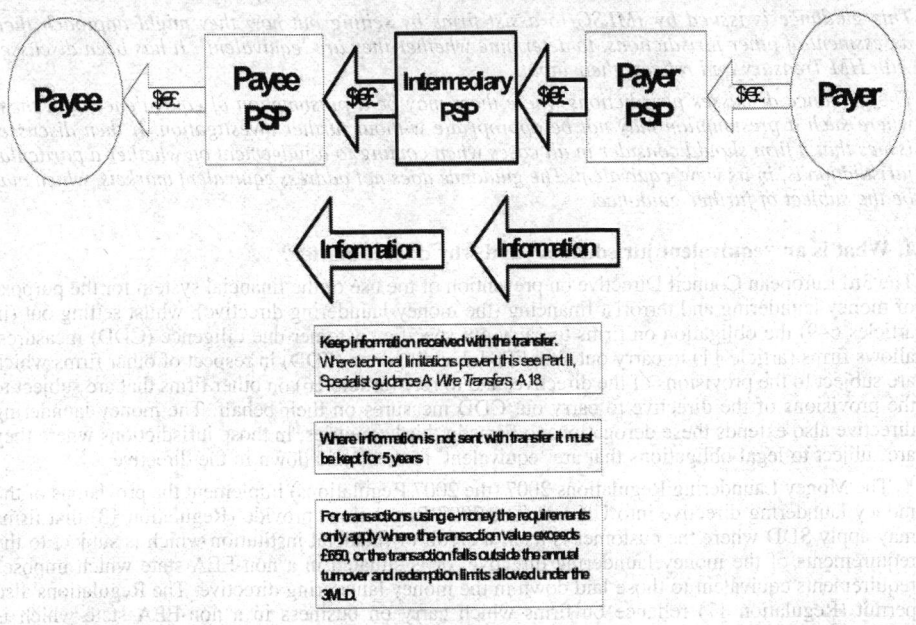

Keep information received with the transfer.
Where technical limitations prevent this see Part II,
Specialist guidance A: *Wire Transfers* A.18

Where information is not sent with transfer it must
be kept for 5 years

For transactions using e-money the requirements
only apply where the transaction value exceeds
£650, or the transaction falls outside the annual
turnover and redemption limits allowed under the
3MLD.

[7048]

Editorial note: the Guidance on the JMLSG website (at:
http://www.jmlsg.org.uk/content/1/c6/01/14/57/Part_II_HMT_approved.pdf)
reproduces Appendix I twice. Ie, it reproduces it here at the end of Part II, and immediately following
paragraph 3.69 above. This Handbook has not reproduced the Appendix following paragraph 3.69. Note also that
it is assumed that the word 'identificatio' in Scenario 1 should be read as 'identification'.

JMLSG GUIDANCE ON EQUIVALENT JURISDICTIONS
(AUGUST 2008)

This guidance is issued by JMLSG to assist firms by setting out how they might approach their assessment of other jurisdictions, to determine whether they are 'equivalent'. It has been discussed with HM Treasury and reflects their input.

The guidance discusses jurisdictions where there may be a presumption of equivalence, and those where such a presumption may not be appropriate without further investigation. It then discusses issues that a firm should consider in all cases when coming to a judgement on whether a particular jurisdiction is, in its view, equivalent. The guidance does not address equivalent markets, which may be the subject of further guidance.

1. What is an "equivalent jurisdiction" and why does it matter?

The 3rd European Council Directive on prevention of the use of the financial system for the purpose of money laundering and terrorist financing (the money laundering directive), whilst setting out (in articles 6–9) the obligation on firms to carry out specific customer due diligence (CDD) measures, allows firms (article 11) to carry out simplified due diligence (SDD) in respect of other firms which are subject to the provisions of the directive, and to rely (article 16) on other firms that are subject to the provisions of the directive to carry out CDD measures on their behalf. The money laundering directive also extends these derogations to firms in third countries, in those jurisdictions where they are subject to legal obligations that are 'equivalent' to those laid down in the directive.

The Money Laundering Regulations 2007 (the 2007 Regulations) implement the provisions of the money laundering directive into UK law. The 2007 Regulations provide (Regulation 13) that firms may apply SDD where the customer is itself a credit or financial institution which is subject to the requirements of the money laundering directive, or is situated in a non-EEA state which imposes requirements equivalent to those laid down in the money laundering directive. The Regulations also permit (Regulation 17) reliance on firms which carry on business in a non-EEA state which is subject to requirements equivalent to those laid down in the money laundering directive, to carry out CDD on the relying firm's behalf.

It should be noted that the basis for the exemption in the directive and the Regulations is focused on the provisions of the legislation in a particular jurisdiction, rather than what actually happens in practice. This applies to both EU Member States and non-EEA states which are "equivalent jurisdictions".

Countries that meet the provisions in Regulations 13 and 17 are described as "equivalent jurisdictions ". UK firms therefore need to determine whether a particular jurisdiction is 'equivalent', in order that it may take advantage of the SDD derogation, and/or to determine whether they may rely, for the purposes of carrying out CDD measures, on firms situated in a non-EEA state.

However, 'equivalence' only provides an exemption from the application of CDD measures, in respect of customer identification. It does not exempt the firm from carrying out ongoing monitoring of the business relationship with the customer, nor from the need for such other procedures (such as monitoring) as may be necessary to enable a firm to fulfil its responsibilities under the Proceeds of Crime Act 2002.

Although the judgement on equivalence is one to be made by each firm in the light of the particular circumstances, senior management is accountable for this judgement – either to its regulator, or, if necessary, to a court. It is therefore important that the reasons for concluding that a particular jurisdiction is equivalent (other than those in respect of which a presumption of equivalence may be made) are documented at the time the decision is made, and that it is made on relevant and up to date data or information.

[7049]

2. Categories of country

Jurisdictions where a presumption of equivalence may be made are:
- EU/EEA member states, through the implementation of the money laundering directive
- Countries on a list of equivalent jurisdictions issued by the EU, or by HMT

It would not normally be appropriate to make a presumption of equivalence in respect of other countries without further investigation.

EU/EEA member states

Member States of the EU/EEA benefit de jure from mutual recognition through the implementation of the money laundering directive.

All Member States of the EU (which, for this purpose, includes Gibraltar as part of the UK, and Netherlands Antilles and Aruba as part of the Kingdom of the Netherlands) are required to enact legislation and financial sector procedures in accordance with the money laundering directive. In addition, EU Member States that are part of the Financial Action Task Force (FATF) have committed themselves to implementing the Forty Recommendations, and the Nine Special Recommendations to Combat Terrorist Financing.

All EEA countries have undertaken to implement the money laundering directive, and some are also FATF member countries.

<table>
<tr><td colspan="2">*EU members of FATF:*</td><td colspan="2">*Other EU member states:*</td></tr>
<tr><td>Austria</td><td>Ireland</td><td>Bulgaria</td><td>Lithuania</td></tr>
<tr><td>Belgium</td><td>Italy</td><td>Cyprus</td><td>Malta</td></tr>
<tr><td>Denmark</td><td>Luxembourg</td><td>Czech Republic</td><td>Poland</td></tr>
<tr><td>Finland</td><td>Netherlands</td><td>Estonia</td><td>Romania</td></tr>
<tr><td>France</td><td>Portugal</td><td>Hungary</td><td>Slovakia</td></tr>
<tr><td>Germany</td><td>Spain</td><td>Latvia</td><td>Slovenia</td></tr>
<tr><td>Greece</td><td>Sweden</td><td></td><td></td></tr>
</table>

EEA states:
Iceland – Member of FATF
Liechtenstein
Norway – Member of FATF

Although firms may rely on the presumption of equivalence, significant variations may exist in the precise measures (and in the timing of their introduction) that have been taken to transpose the money laundering directive (and its predecessors) into national laws and regulations. Moreover, the standards of compliance monitoring in respect of credit and financial institutions will also vary. Where firms have substantive information which indicates that a presumption of equivalence cannot be sustained, either in general or for particular products, they will need to consider whether their procedures should be enhanced to take account of this information.

The status of implementation of the money laundering directive across the EU is available at http://ec.europa.eu/internal_market/company/docs/official/080522web_en.pdf

EU agreed list

Member states participating in the EU Committee on the Prevention of Money Laundering and Terrorist Financing have agreed a list of equivalent third countries, for the purposes of the relevant parts of the money laundering directive. The list is a voluntary, non-binding measure that nevertheless represents the common understanding of Member States. The text of the statement on equivalence was published by HM Treasury on 12 May 2008, and is available at www.hm-treasury.gov.uk/documents/financial_services/money/fin_crime_equivalence.cfm

The following third countries are currently considered as having equivalent AML/CTF systems to the EU. The list may be reviewed, in particular in the light of public evaluation reports adopted by the FATF, FSRBs, the IMF or the World Bank according to the revised 2003 FATF Recommendations and Methodology.

Argentina	New Zealand
Australia	Singapore
Brazil	South Africa
Canada	Switzerland
Hong Kong	The Russian Federation
Japan	The United States
Mexico	

The list also includes the French overseas territories (Mayotte, New Caledonia, French Polynesia, Saint Pierre and Miquelon and Wallis and Futuna) and the Dutch overseas territories (Netherlands Antilles and Aruba). Those overseas territories are not members of the EU/EEA but are part of the membership of France and the Kingdom of the Netherlands of the FATF.

The UK Crown Dependencies (Jersey, Guernsey, Isle of Man) may also be considered as equivalent by Member States. The Crown Dependencies are considered to be equivalent by the UK. Gibraltar is also directly subject to the requirements of the money laundering directive, which it has implemented. It is therefore considered to be equivalent for these purposes.

Firms should note that inclusion on the EU list does not override the need for firms to continue to operate risk-based procedures when dealing with customers based in an equivalent jurisdiction.

FATF members

All FATF members (those which are not EU/EEA member states/countries are listed below) undertake to implement the FATF anti-money laundering and counter-terrorism Recommendations as part of their membership obligations.

Argentina	New Zealand
Australia	Russian Federation
Brazil	Singapore
Canada	South Africa
China	Switzerland
Hong Kong	Turkey
Japan	United States of America
Mexico	

However, unlike the transposition of the money laundering directive by EU Member States, implementation cannot be mandatory, and all members will approach their obligations in different ways, and under different timetables. It is also relevant that whilst some countries have been FATF members for a long time, others have only recently been admitted to membership. Long established members are more likely to be in fuller compliance with the Recommendations than those members of more recent admission. Moreover, some of these new members were admitted primarily because of their strategic importance within a region, and in a number of cases their national anti-money laundering strategies are still developing.

All FATF members other than China and Turkey (and the Gulf Co-operation Council) are included in the EU list of equivalent jurisdictions referred to above.

Gulf Co-operation Council

The Gulf Co-operation Council (GCC) is in the unique position of being a member of FATF but with non-FATF countries as its members. However, whilst the GCC countries – Bahrain, Kuwait, Oman, Qatar, Saudi Arabia and the United Arab Emirates – have all undergone FATF-style mutual evaluations, few of these reports are publicly available. Moreover, few GCC countries have yet enacted legislation that contains equivalent provisions to the Money Laundering Directive, and so there is unevenness in the position of relevant regulation across GCC member countries. Individual GCC member countries should therefore by assessed in the same way as for other non-EU/FATF jurisdictions.

Other jurisdictions

A majority of countries and territories do not fall within the lists of countries that can be presumed to be "equivalent jurisdictions"; this includes China and Turkey (which are both FATF members) and the Republic of Korea and India (which have observer status at FATF meetings). This does not necessarily mean that the AML/CTF legislation, and standards of due diligence, in those countries are lower than those in "equivalent jurisdictions". However, standards vary significantly, and firms will need to carry out their own assessment of particular countries. In addition to a firm's own knowledge and experience of the country concerned, particular attention should be paid to any FATF-style or IMF/World Bank evaluations that have been undertaken.

As a result of due diligence carried out, therefore, jurisdictions may be added to those on the EU agreed list, for the purposes of determining those jurisdictions which, in the firm's judgement, are equivalent, for the purposes of the SDD derogation, and/or determining whether firms may rely, for the purposes of carrying out CDD measures, on other firms situated in such a jurisdiction.

[7050]

3. Factors to be taken into account when assessing other jurisdictions

Factors include:
- Membership of groups that only admit those meeting a certain benchmark
- Contextual factors – political stability; level of (endemic) corruption etc
- Evidence of relevant (public) criticism of a jurisdiction, including HMT/FATF advisory notices
- Independent and public assessment of the jurisdiction's overall AML regime

- Need for any assessment to be recent
- Implementation standards (inc quality and effectiveness of supervision)
- Incidence of trade with the jurisdiction – need to be proportionate esp where very small

Membership of an international or regional 'group'

There are a number of international and regional 'groups' of jurisdictions that admit to membership only those jurisdictions that have demonstrated a commitment to the fight against money laundering and terrorist financing, and which have an appropriate legal and regulatory regime to back up this commitment. Where a jurisdiction is a member of such a group, there may be an initial presumption that the jurisdiction is likely to be 'equivalent'.

Contextual factors

Such factors as the political stability of a jurisdiction, and where it stands in tables of corruption are relevant to whether it is likely that a jurisdiction will be 'equivalent'. It will, however, seldom be easy for firms to make their own assessments of such matters, and it is likely that they will have to rely on external agencies for such evidence – whether prepared for general consumption, or specifically for the firm. Where the firm looks to publicly available evidence, it will be important that it has some knowledge of the criteria that were used in making the assessment; the firm cannot rely solely on the fact that such a list has been independently prepared, even if by a respected third party agency.

Evidence of relevant (public) criticism

FATF published a report (in 2000) setting out criteria for identifying those countries and territories that are not cooperative in the international fight against money laundering. Following evaluations of a number of countries against this set of criteria, FATF published a list of jurisdictions (NCCT jurisdictions) that were identified as non-cooperative.

FATF monitored progress made by NCCT jurisdictions as a priority; in view of progress made, no jurisdictions remained on the list as at February 2007, and the NCCT process was discontinued.

When constructing their internal procedures, however, financial sector firms should for the time being have regard to the need for additional monitoring procedures for transactions from any country that was recently NCCT classified. Additional monitoring procedures will also be required in respect of correspondent relationships with financial institutions from such countries.

HM Treasury and FATF issue advisory notices from time to time alerting firms to jurisdictions with poor AML controls.

Other, commercial agencies also produce reports and lists of jurisdictions, entities and individuals that are involved, or that are alleged to be involved, in activities that cast doubt on their integrity in the AML/CTF area. Such reports lists can provide some useful and relevant evidence – which may or may not be conclusive – on whether or not a particular jurisdiction is likely to be equivalent.

Mutual evaluation reports

Particular attention should be paid to assessments that have been undertaken by standard setting bodies such as FATF, and by international financial institutions such as the IMF.

FATF

FATF member countries monitor their own progress in the fight against money laundering and terrorist financing through regular mutual evaluation by their peers. In 1998, FATF extended the concept of mutual evaluation beyond its own membership through its endorsement of FATF-style mutual evaluation programmes of a number of regional groups which contain non- FATF members. The groups undertaking FATF-style mutual evaluations are

- the Offshore Group of Banking Supervisors (OGBS) see www.ogbs.net
- the Caribbean Financial Action Task Force (CFATF) see www.cfatf.org
- the Asia/Pacific Group on Money Laundering (APG) see www.apgml.org
- MONEYVAL, covering the Council of Europe countries which are not members of FATF see www.coe.int/moneyval
- the Financial Action Task Force on Money Laundering in South America (GAFISUD) see www.gafisud.org
- the Middle East and North Africa Financial Action Task Force (MENAFATF) see www.menafatf.org
- the Eurasian Group (EAG) see www.eurasiangroup.org,
- the Eastern and Southern Africa Anti-Money Laundering Group (ESAAMLG) see www.esaamlg.org
- the Intergovernmental Action Group against Money-Laundering in Africa (GIABA) see www.giabasn.org

Firms should bear in mind that mutual evaluation reports are at a 'point in time', and should be interpreted as such. Although follow up actions are usually reviewed after two years, there can be quite long intervals between evaluation reports in respect of a particular jurisdiction. Even at the point an evaluation is carried out there can be changes in train to the jurisdiction's AML/CTF regime, but these will not be reflected in the evaluation report. There can also be subsequent changes to the regime (whether to respond to criticisms by the evaluators or otherwise) which firms should seek to understand and to factor into their assessment of whether the jurisdiction is equivalent.

In assessing the conclusions of a mutual evaluation report, firms may find it difficult to give appropriate weighting to findings and conclusions in respect of the jurisdiction's compliance with particular Recommendations. For the purposes of assessing equivalence, compliance (or otherwise) with certain Recommendations may have more relevance than others. The extent to which a jurisdiction complies with the following Recommendations may be particularly relevant:

Legal framework:
>Recommendation 1
>Special Recommendation II

Measures to be taken by firms:
>Recommendations 4, 5, 6, 9, 10, 11, and 13,
>Special Recommendation IV

Supervisory regime:
>Recommendations 17, 23, 29 and 30

International co-operation:
>Recommendation 40

Summaries of FATF and FATF-style evaluations are published in FATF Annual Reports and can be accessed at www.fatf-gafi.org. However, firms should note that those conducted by the Caribbean Financial Action Task Force have, to date, not included representatives of any FATF country on their evaluation teams.

IMF/World bank

In additional to the mutual evaluations carried out by FATF and FATF-style regional bodies, as part of their financial stability assessments of countries and territories, the IMF and the World Bank have agreed with FATF a detailed methodology for assessing compliance with AML/CTF standards, using the FATF Recommendations as the base. A number of countries have already undergone IMF/World Bank assessments in addition to those carried out by FATF, and some of the results can be accessed at www.imf.org.

Implementation standards (including effectiveness of supervision)

Information on the extent and quality of supervision of AML/CTF standards may be obtained from the extent to which a jurisdiction complies with Recommendations 17, 23, 29 and 30.

Incidence of trade with the jurisdiction

In respect of any particular jurisdiction, the level and extent of due diligence that needs to be carried out in making a judgement on equivalence will be influenced by the volume and size of the firm's business with that jurisdiction in relation to the firm's overall business.

[7051]

4. UK prohibition notices and advisory notices

Details of countries where UK prohibition notices are in place and countries where additional countermeasures must be applied are set out below.

As at July 2008, no prohibition notices have been issued by HM Treasury under Regulation 18 of the 2007 Regulations.

FATF

On 28 February 2008, the FATF issued a statement on its concern about the lack of comprehensive AML/CFT systems in Uzbekistan, Iran, Pakistan, Turkmenistan, São Tomé and Príncipe and northern Cyprus.

The full FATF statement is available at www.fatf-gafi.org/dataoecd/16/26/40181037.pdf.

The FATF Plenary in July 2008 restated this message.

On 11 October 2007 the FATF issued a Statement on Iran, in which it called on Iran to address on an urgent basis its AML/CTF deficiencies, including those identified in the 2006 IMF Article IV Consultation Report for Iran. Following this statement, HM Treasury issued a press notice on 12 October 2007 in which it expressed the UK's full support of the work of the FATF on this matter.

The full FATF statement and the text of HM Treasury's press notice are available at: www.fatf-gafi.org/dataoecd/1/2/39481684.pdf   and   www.hm-treasury.gov.uk/newsroom_and_speeches/press/2007/press_108_07.cfm

Myanmar (Burma)

With effect from 3 November 2003, FATF agreed that its members would implement countermeasures against Myanmar (Burma) to ensure that member countries financial systems are protected from the risk of money laundering. In October 2004, FATF withdrew countermeasures against Myanmar (Burma) because of progress made in the country, although it remained on the NCCT list until it was removed in October 2006 (although there is to be continuing monitoring for the time being).

UK institutions should continue to ensure that they comply with the requirements of European Council Regulation (EC) No 817/2006 (May 2006), implementing the restrictive measures in respect of Burma/Myanmar. Annex III to that Regulation lists persons relating to important governmental functions in Burma (Myanmar), and persons associated with them, whose funds are to be frozen and to whom no funds or economic resources should be made available. The restrictive measures also include a ban on the financing of certain Burmese state-owned enterprises, which are listed in Annex IV to the Regulation.

[7052]

PART V
OTHER MATERIALS

JMLSG GUIDANCE ON EQUIVALENT MARKETS
(JANUARY 2009)

This material is issued by JMLSG to assist firms by setting out how they might approach their assessment of regulated markets, to determine whether they are 'equivalent' for the purposes of the money laundering directive. It has been discussed with HM Treasury and reflects their input, although it is not formal guidance that has been given Ministerial approval.

The material discusses markets where there may be a presumption of equivalence, and those where such a presumption may not be appropriate without further investigation. It then discusses issues that a firm should consider in all cases when coming to a judgement on whether a particular market is, in its view, equivalent.

1. What is an "equivalent market" and why does it matter?

The 3rd European Council Directive on prevention of the use of the financial system for the purpose of money laundering and terrorist financing (the money laundering directive) allows firms (article 11) to carry out simplified due diligence (SDD) in respect of customers whose securities are:
- listed on a regulated market, which is
- subject to specified disclosure obligations.

The Money Laundering Regulations 2007 (the 2007 Regulations) implement the provisions of the money laundering directive into UK law, and accordingly provide (Regulation 13) that firms may apply SDD to customers whose securities are listed on a regulated market that is subject to specified disclosure obligations [See section 2 and Annex II].

Under the 2007 Regulations (and the money laundering directive), a "regulated market":
- within the EEA has the meaning given by point 14 of Article 4(1) of the markets in financial instruments directive (MiFID). [This definition is reproduced in Annex I].
- outside the EEA, means a regulated financial market which subjects companies whose securities are admitted to trading to disclosure obligations which are contained in international standards and are equivalent to the specified disclosure obligations [see section 2 and Annex II]

Markets that meet the definition in the 2007 Regulations are described in the JMLSG Guidance as "equivalent markets". UK firms therefore need to determine whether a particular market is 'equivalent', in order that they may take advantage of the SDD derogation. If a market does not qualify as 'equivalent', or if a firm chooses not to determine whether the market is 'equivalent', full CDD measures must be applied to the customer.

However, 'equivalence' only provides an exemption from the application of CDD measures in respect of customer identification. It does not exempt the firm from carrying out ongoing monitoring of the business relationship with the customer, nor from the need for such other procedures (such as monitoring) as may be necessary to enable a firm to fulfil its responsibilities under the Proceeds of Crime Act 2002.

Although the judgement on equivalence of regulated markets is one to be made by each firm in the light of the particular circumstances of the market, senior management is accountable for this judgement – either to its regulator, or, if necessary, to a court. It is therefore important that the reasons for concluding that a particular market is equivalent (other than those in respect of which a presumption of equivalence may be made) are documented at the time the decision is made, and that it is made on relevant and up to date data or information.

[7053]

2. What are the specified disclosure obligations?

The disclosure obligations that the 2007 Regulations require regulated markets to impose are those consistent with:
- Article 6(1) to (4) of Directive 2003/6/EC [the Market Abuse Directive];
- Articles 3, 5, 7, 8, 10, 14 and 16 of Directive 2003/71/EC [the Prospectus Directive];
- Articles 4 to 6, 14, 16 to 19 and 30 of Directive 2004/109/EC [the Transparency Directive]; and
- Community legislation made under the above provisions.

These obligations are reproduced at Annex II.

[7054]

3. Categories of market

Markets in EU/EEA member states

All Member States of the EU (which, for this purpose, includes Gibraltar as part of the UK, and Netherlands Antilles and Aruba as part of the Kingdom of the Netherlands) are required to enact legislation and regulations in accordance with the specified disclosure obligations. All EEA countries have undertaken to implement the directives from which the specified disclosure obligations flow.

CESR maintains a database of regulated markets within the EU (this is not, of course, a formal list of "equivalent" markets). The list is published for the purpose of identification of the counterparty to the transaction in relation to transaction reporting. Publication of the identifiers ensures the compliance of CESR members with Article 13(2) of the MiFID Level 2 regulation. CESR has collected this information from its members and will update the list on a regular basis. Some CESR members will, in addition, publish their own information separately on their websites. Further information is available on the CESR website at http://mifiddatabase.cesr.eu/.

Generally, the principal markets in EU/EEA member states are likely to be able to be presumed to be 'equivalent' for the purposes of the 2007 Regulations. In the 2007 Regulations, however, it was chosen to link the derogation to the admission to listing in a regulated market within the meaning of MiFID. So listing in other markets (such as AIM)[1] would not be enough qualification for the application of the derogation.

---

[1]   But see paragraph 5.3.135 in Part I of the Guidance, which suggests that the due process for admission to AIM may give equivalent comfort.

Markets in some third countries

Outside the EEA, a regulated financial market is 'equivalent' for the purposes of the 2007 Regulations if it subjects companies whose securities are admitted to trading to disclosure obligations which are contained in international standards and are equivalent to the specified disclosure obligations. Article 19(6) of MiFID [see Annex I] requires the Commission to publish a list of third country markets that are 'equivalent' under MiFID.

A firm might reasonably conclude that a regulated market that is equivalent for MiFID purposes will be equivalent for the purposes of the 2007 Regulations. Some other third country markets might still meet the requirements of the money laundering directive, however, even although they do not meet all those required by MiFID.

The Commission has not yet published a list of equivalent third country markets for MiFID purposes; when it does, these may reasonably be regarded as equivalent for the purposes of the 2007 Regulations, whilst leaving it open for other individual markets also to be recognised for the purposes of the 2007 Regulations.

Caveat ...

Although firms may rely on the presumption of equivalence, in respect of certain markets significant variations may exist in the precise measures (and in the timing of their introduction) that have been taken to transpose the obligations under the various directives into national laws and market regulations. Moreover, the standards of compliance monitoring in respect of particular markets will also vary. Where firms have substantive information which indicates that a presumption of equivalence cannot be sustained, either in general or for particular markets, they will need to apply full CDD measures to customers listed on these markets.

The status of implementation of the relevant directives across the EU is available at: http://ec.europa.eu/internal_market/securities/transposition/index_en.htm.

Other markets

Although markets in other countries and territories cannot be presumed to be "equivalent", this does not necessarily mean that the legislation and disclosure obligations in those countries are lower than those in "equivalent markets". However, standards vary significantly, and firms will need to carry out their own assessment of the transparency and disclosure obligations in these particular markets. In addition to a firm's own knowledge and experience of the market concerned, particular attention should be paid to any evaluations or analyses of disclosure obligations that have been undertaken.

[7055]

4. Factors to be taken into account when assessing other markets

The primary consideration that firms should address initially as part of their assessment is whether the disclosure and other obligations in a particular market meet the disclosure obligations specified in the directive.

Do the obligations in the particular market meet the specified disclosure obligations?

The money laundering directive is open on the extent to which disclosures in third countries must be sufficiently consistent with Community legislation to enable them to be regarded as 'equivalent'. On one interpretation, a firm could require that all provisions in the relevant directives must be faithfully reflected in the third country market obligations. However, a more workable interpretation is that it is enough to satisfy the major provisions in the relevant directives.

Commission Directive 2007/14/EC (the MiFID Implementing Directive) contains some provisions (Articles 13 to 23) on how to judge the equivalence of third country rules regarding some obligations of the Transparency Directive. Recital 18 of this directive provides a helpful definition of equivalence:

> (18) *Equivalence should be able to be declared when general disclosure rules of third countries provide users with understandable and broadly equivalent assessment of issuers' position that enable them to make similar decisions as if they were provided with the information according to requirements under Directive 2004/109/EC, even if the requirements are not identical ...*

It is important to note that the country of incorporation of the company is of little relevance. What counts is that it is subject to appropriate disclosure requirements in an equivalent market, which may well be in a different jurisdiction.

Other relevant matters to consider

Other relevant factors in making an assessment of 'equivalence' include:
- Membership of groups that only admit those meeting certain criteria
- Contextual factors – political stability; level of (endemic) corruption etc
- Evidence of relevant (public) criticism of a market
- Independent and public assessment of the market's overall disclosure and transparency standards
- Need for any assessment to be recent
- Implementation standards (including quality and effectiveness of supervision)

Membership of an international or regional 'group'

There are a number of international and regional 'groups' of markets that admit to membership only those markets that have demonstrated a commitment to high standards of disclosure and transparency, and which have an appropriate legal and regulatory regime to back up this commitment. Where a market is a member of such a group, there may be a presumption that the market is likely to be 'equivalent'.

Contextual factors

Such factors as the political stability of the jurisdiction within which a market is located, and where it stands in tables of corruption are relevant to whether it is likely that a market will be 'equivalent'. It will, however, seldom be easy for firms to make their own assessments of such matters, and it is likely that they will have to rely on external agencies for such evidence – whether prepared for general consumption, or specifically for the firm.

Evidence of relevant (public) criticism

Commercial agencies and the media also produce reports and lists of markets, entities and individuals that are involved, or that are alleged to be involved, in activities that cast doubt on their integrity. Such reports lists can provide some useful and relevant evidence – which may or may not be conclusive – on whether or not a particular market is likely to be equivalent.

Independent reports on disclosure and transparency standards

Particular attention should be paid to assessments of particular markets, including their disclosure and transparency standards, which have been undertaken by respected third party agencies. Where the firm looks to publicly available evidence, it will be important that it has some knowledge of the criteria that were used in making the assessment; the firm cannot rely solely on the fact that such an assessment has been independently prepared. It should be noted that, under the Transparency Directive framework (notably Article 23(1)), declaring equivalence of third country regimes is a task for the national financial services supervisors: ie, FSA in the UK.

Implementation standards (including effectiveness of supervision)

Information on the extent and quality of supervision of markets may be published by the competent authorities – whether in annual reports or otherwise.

[7056]

ANNEX I
RELEVANT PROVISIONS OF MIFID

Definition of 'regulated market'

Point 14 of Article 4(1):

'Regulated market' means a multilateral system operated and/or managed by a market operator, which brings together or facilitates the bringing together of multiple third party buying and selling interests in financial instruments – in the system and in accordance with its non-discretionary rules – in a way that results in a contract, in respect of the financial instruments admitted to trading under its rules and/or systems, and which is authorised and functions regularly and in accordance with the provisions of Title III;

Title III includes the following (Article 40):

EDITORIAL NOTE
    The text in italicised capital letters in the Article below is not part of the original text of the Directive but is a note added by the JMLSG.

Article 40
Admission of financial instruments to trading
MARKETS MUST HAVE CLEAR AND TRANSPARENT RULES

1. Member States shall require that regulated markets have clear and transparent rules regarding the admission of financial instruments to trading.

Those rules shall ensure that any financial instruments admitted to trading in a regulated market are capable of being traded in a fair, orderly and efficient manner and, in the case of transferable securities, are freely negotiable.

DESIGN OF CONTRACTS MUST ALLOW FOR ORDERLY PRICING

2. In the case of derivatives, the rules shall ensure in particular that the design of the derivative contract allows for its orderly pricing as well as for the existence of effective settlement conditions.

MARKETS MUST ESTABLISH ARRANGEMENTS TO VERIFY ISSUERS' COMPLIANCE WITH DISCLOSURE OBLIGATIONS

3. In addition to the obligations set out in paragraphs 1 and 2, Member States shall require the regulated market to establish and maintain effective arrangements to verify that issuers of transferable securities that are admitted to trading on the regulated market comply with their obligations under Community law in respect of initial, ongoing or ad hoc disclosure obligations.

Member States shall ensure that the regulated market establishes arrangements which facilitate its members or participants in obtaining access to information which has been made public under Community law.

MARKETS MUST BE SUBJECT TO REGULATORY OVERSIGHT

4. Member States shall ensure that regulated markets have established the necessary arrangements to review regularly the compliance with the admission requirements of the financial instruments which they admit to trading.

Commission obligation to publish a list of third country markets considered as equivalent

EDITORIAL NOTE
    The italicised text in the Article below is not part of the original text of the Directive but has been added by the JMLSG. Also, the text omitted has not been repealed but has been omitted by the JMLSG.

Article 19

...

6. Member States shall allow investment firms when providing investment services that only consist of execution ... to provide those investment services to their clients without the need to obtain the information or make the determination provided for in paragraph 5 *[appropriateness test]* where all the following conditions are met:
    — the above services relate to shares admitted to trading on a regulated market or in an equivalent third country market ... . A third country market shall be considered as equivalent to a regulated market if it complies with equivalent requirements to those established under Title III. The Commission shall publish a list of those markets that are to be considered as equivalent. This list shall be updated periodically,

ANNEX II
DETAILS OF THE "SPECIFIED DISCLOSURE OBLIGATIONS" REFERRED TO IN 2007 REGULATIONS

DIRECTIVE 2003/6/EC OF THE EUROPEAN PARLIAMENT AND OF THE COUNCIL of
28 January 2003 on insider dealing and market manipulation (Market Abuse Directive)

EDITORIAL NOTE
The text in italicised capital letters in the Article below is not part of the original text of the Directive but is a note added by the JMLSG.

Article 6
ALL RELEVANT INSIDE INFORMATION MUST BE DISCLOSED

1. Member States shall ensure that issuers of financial instruments inform the public as soon as possible of inside information which directly concerns the said issuers.

Without prejudice to any measures taken to comply with the provisions of the first subparagraph, Member States shall ensure that issuers, for an appropriate period, post on their Internet sites all inside information that they are required to disclose publicly.

DELAY IN PUBLISHING INSIDE INFORMATION MUST NOT MISLEAD THE PUBLIC

2. An issuer may under his own responsibility delay the public disclosure of inside information, as referred to in paragraph 1, such as not to prejudice his legitimate interests provided that such omission would not be likely to mislead the public and provided that the issuer is able to ensure the confidentiality of that information. Member States may require that an issuer shall without delay inform the competent authority of the decision to delay the public disclosure of inside information.

INSIDE INFORMATION DISCLOSED TO A THIRD PARTY MUST BE PUBLISHED SIMULTANEOUSLY

3. Member States shall require that, whenever an issuer, or a person acting on his behalf or for his account, discloses any inside information to any third party in the normal exercise of his employment, profession or duties, as referred to in Article 3(a), he must make complete and effective public disclosure of that information, simultaneously in the case of an intentional disclosure and promptly in the case of a non-intentional disclosure.

The provisions of the first subparagraph shall not apply if the person receiving the information owes a duty of confidentiality, regardless of whether such duty is based on a law, on regulations, on articles of association or on a contract.

Member States shall require that issuers, or persons acting on their behalf or for their account, draw up a list of those persons working for them, under a contract of employment or otherwise, who have access to inside information. Issuers and persons acting on their behalf or for their account shall regularly update this list and transmit it to the competent authority whenever the latter requests it.

TRANSACTIONS OF INDIVIDUAL MEMBERS OF MANAGEMENT IN AN ISSUER'S SHARES MUST BE PUBLICLY DISCLOSED AS SOON AS POSSIBLE

4. Persons discharging managerial responsibilities within an issuer of financial instruments and, where applicable, persons closely associated with them, shall, at least, notify to the competent authority the existence of transactions conducted on their own account relating to shares of the said issuer, or to derivatives or other financial instruments linked to them. Member States shall ensure that public access to information concerning such transactions, on at least an individual basis, is readily available as soon as possible.

DIRECTIVE 2003/71/EC OF THE EUROPEAN PARLIAMENT AND OF THE COUNCIL of
4 November 2003 on the prospectus to be published when securities are offered to the public or admitted to trading and amending Directive 2001/34/EC (Prospectus Directive)

EDITORIAL NOTE
The text in italicised capital letters in the Article below is not part of the original text of the Directive but is a note added by the JMLSG.

Article 3
Obligation to publish a prospectus

PUBLIC OFFERINGS OF A SECURITY MUST NOT BE ALLOWED WITHOUT PRIOR PUBLICATION OF A PROSPECTUS

1. Member States shall not allow any offer of securities to be made to the public within their territories without prior publication of a prospectus.

TYPES OF OFFER THAT DO NOT NEED TO BE ACCOMPANIED BY A PROSPECTUS

2.   The obligation to publish a prospectus shall not apply to the following types of offer:
   (a)   an offer of securities addressed solely to qualified investors; and/or
   (b)   an offer of securities addressed to fewer than 100 natural or legal persons per Member State, other than qualified investors; and/or
   (c)   an offer of securities addressed to investors who acquire securities for a total consideration of at least EUR 50,000 per investor, for each separate offer; and/or
   (d)   an offer of securities whose denomination per unit amounts to at least EUR 50,000; and/or
   (e)   an offer of securities with a total consideration of less than EUR 100,000, which limit shall be calculated over a period of 12 months.

However, any subsequent resale of securities which were previously the subject of one or more of the types of offer mentioned in this paragraph shall be regarded as a separate offer and the definition set out in Article 2(1)(d) shall apply for the purpose of deciding whether that resale is an offer of securities to the public. The placement of securities through financial intermediaries shall be subject to publication of a prospectus if none of the conditions (a) to (e) are met for the final placement.

ADMISSION OF SECURITIES TO TRADING ON A REGULATED MARKET MUST BE SUBJECT TO PUBLICATION OF A PROSPECTUS

3.   Member States shall ensure that any admission of securities to trading on a regulated market situated or operating within their territories is subject to the publication of a prospectus.

EDITORIAL NOTE
   The text in italicised capital letters in the Article below is not part of the original text of the Directive but is a note added by the JMLSG. Note also that the JMLSG text as reproduced in their Guidance of January 2009 did not include the amendments made to this Article by European Parliament and Council Directive 2008/11/EC, Art 1(1) as from 20 March 2008. The text as reproduced below does include those amendments (ie, the repeal of, and the addition of, certain words in para 5 as indicated by the ellipsis and by the text in square brackets below).

Article 5
The prospectus

PROSPECTUSES SHALL CONTAIN ALL THE INFORMATION NECESSARY TO ENABLE INVESTORS TO MAKE INFORMED DECISIONS

1.   Without prejudice to Article 8(2), the prospectus shall contain all information which, according to the particular nature of the issuer and of the securities offered to the public or admitted to trading on a regulated market, is necessary to enable investors to make an informed assessment of the assets and liabilities, financial position, profit and losses, and prospects of the issuer and of any guarantor, and of the rights attaching to such securities. This information shall be presented in an easily analysable and comprehensible form.

PROSPECTUSES MUST CONTAIN A SUMMARY IN BRIEF AND NON-TECHNICAL LANGUAGE ...

2.   The prospectus shall contain information concerning the issuer and the securities to be offered to the public or to be admitted to trading on a regulated market. It shall also include a summary. The summary shall, in a brief manner and in non-technical language, convey the essential characteristics and risks associated with the issuer, any guarantor and the securities, in the language in which the prospectus was originally drawn up. The summary shall also contain a warning that:

WITH APPROPRIATE WARNINGS ...
   (a)   it should be read as an introduction to the prospectus;
   (b)   any decision to invest in the securities should be based on consideration of the prospectus as a whole by the investor;
   (c)   where a claim relating to the information contained in a prospectus is brought before a court, the plaintiff investor might, under the national legislation of the Member States, have to bear the costs of translating the prospectus before the legal proceedings are initiated; and
   (d)   civil liability attaches to those persons who have tabled the summary including any translation thereof, and applied for its notification, but only if the summary is misleading, inaccurate or inconsistent when read together with the other parts of the prospectus.

Where the prospectus relates to the admission to trading on a regulated market of non-equity securities having a denomination of at least EUR 50,000, there shall be no requirement to provide a summary except when requested by a Member State as provided for in Article 19(4).

A PROSPECTUS MAY BE A SINGLE DOCUMENT OR THREE SEPARATE DOCUMENTS

3.   Subject to paragraph 4, the issuer, offeror or person asking for the admission to trading on a regulated market may draw up the prospectus as a single document or separate documents. A

prospectus composed of separate documents shall divide the required information into a registration document, a securities note and a summary note. The registration document shall contain the information relating to the issuer. The securities note shall contain the information concerning the securities offered to the public or to be admitted to trading on a regulated market.

IN CERTAIN CASES, A PROSPECTUS CAN BE A 'BASE PROSPECTUS'

4.   For the following types of securities, the prospectus can, at the choice of the issuer, offeror or person asking for the admission to trading on a regulated market consist of a base prospectus containing all relevant information concerning the issuer and the securities offered to the public or to be admitted to trading on a regulated market:

(a)   non-equity securities, including warrants in any form, issued under an offering programme;

(b)   non-equity securities issued in a continuous or repeated manner by credit institutions,

(i)   where the sums deriving from the issue of the said securities, under national legislation, are placed in assets which provide sufficient coverage for the liability deriving from securities until their maturity date;

(ii)   where, in the event of the insolvency of the related credit institution, the said sums are intended, as a priority, to repay the capital and interest falling due, without prejudice to the provisions of Directive 2001/24/EC of the European Parliament and of the Council of 4 April 2001 on the reorganisation and winding up of credit institutions.

The information given in the base prospectus shall be supplemented, if necessary, in accordance with Article 16, with updated information on the issuer and on the securities to be offered to the public or to be admitted to trading on a regulated market.

If the final terms of the offer are not included in either the base prospectus or a supplement, the final terms shall be provided to investors and filed with the competent authority when each public offer is made as soon as practicable and if possible in advance of the beginning of the offer. The provisions of Article 8(1)(a) shall be applicable in any such case.

THE COMMISSION SHALL ADOPT IMPLEMENTING MEASURES CONCERNING THE FORMAT OF A PROSPECTUS

5.   In order to take account of technical developments on financial markets and to ensure uniform application of this Directive, the Commission shall ... adopt implementing measures concerning the format of the prospectus or base prospectus and supplements. [Those measures, designed to amend non-essential elements of this Directive by supplementing it, shall be adopted in accordance with the regulatory procedure with scrutiny referred to in Article 24(2a).]

EDITORIAL NOTE

The text in italicised capital letters in the Article below is not part of the original text of the Directive but is a note added by the JMLSG. Note also that the JMLSG text as reproduced in their Guidance of January 2009 did not include the amendments made to this Article by European Parliament and Council Directive 2008/11/EC, Art 1(1) as from 20 March 2008. The text as reproduced below does include those amendments (ie, the repeal of, and the addition of, certain words in para 1 as indicated by the ellipsis and by the text in square brackets below).

Article 7
Minimum information

THE COMMISSION SHALL ADOPT IMPLEMENTING MEASURES REGARDING THE SPECIFIC INFORMATION TO BE INCLUDED IN A PROSPECTUS

1.   Detailed implementing measures regarding the specific information which must be included in a prospectus, avoiding duplication of information when a prospectus is composed of separate documents, shall be adopted by the Commission ... . The first set of implementing measures shall be adopted by 1 July 2004. [Those measures, designed to amend non-essential elements of this Directive by supplementing it, shall be adopted in accordance with the regulatory procedure with scrutiny referred to in Article 24(2a).]

SPECIFIC MATTERS TO BE TAKEN ACCOUNT OF IN VARIOUS MODELS OF PROSPECTUS ...

2.   In particular, for the elaboration of the various models of prospectuses, account shall be taken of the following:

(a)   the various types of information needed by investors relating to equity securities as compared with non-equity securities; a consistent approach shall be taken with regard to information required in a prospectus for securities which have a similar economic rationale, notably derivative securities;

(b)   the various types and characteristics of offers and admissions to trading on a regulated market of non-equity securities. The information required in a prospectus shall be appropriate from the point of view of the investors concerned for non-equity securities having a denomination per unit of at least EUR 50,000;

(c)　the format used and the information required in prospectuses relating to non-equity securities, including warrants in any form, issued under an offering programme;

(d)　the format used and the information required in prospectuses relating to non-equity securities, in so far as these securities are not subordinated, convertible, exchangeable, subject to subscription or acquisition rights or linked to derivative instruments, issued in a continuous or repeated manner by entities authorised or regulated to operate in the financial markets within the European Economic Area;

(e)　the various activities and size of the issuer, in particular SMEs. For such companies the information shall be adapted to their size and, where appropriate, to their shorter track record;

(f)　if applicable, the public nature of the issuer.

THE COMMISSION'S IMPLEMENTING MEASURES SHALL BE BASED ON IOSCO STANDARDS ...

3.　The implementing measures referred to in paragraph 1 shall be based on the standards in the field of financial and non-financial information set out by international securities commission organisations, and in particular by IOSCO and on the indicative Annexes to this Directive.

EDITORIAL NOTE

The text in italicised capital letters in the Article below is not part of the original text of the Directive but is a note added by the JMLSG. Note also that the JMLSG text as reproduced in their Guidance of January 2009 did not include the amendments made to this Article by European Parliament and Council Directive 2008/11/EC, Art 1(1) as from 20 March 2008. The text as reproduced below does include those amendments (ie, the repeal of, and the addition of, certain words in para 4 as indicated by the ellipsis and by the text in square brackets below).

Article 8
Omission of information

CONDITIONS UNDER WHICH CERTAIN INFORMATION MAY BE OMITTED ...

1.　Member States shall ensure that where the final offer price and amount of securities which will be offered to the public cannot be included in the prospectus:

(a)　the criteria, and/or the conditions in accordance with which the above elements will be determined or, in the case of price, the maximum price, are disclosed in the prospectus; or

(b)　the acceptances of the purchase or subscription of securities may be withdrawn for not less than two working days after the final offer price and amount of securities which will be offered to the public have been filed.

The final offer price and amount of securities shall be filed with the competent authority of the home Member State and published in accordance with the arrangements provided for in Article 14(2).

CIRCUMSTANCES UNDER WHICH THE COMPETENT AUTHORITY MAY AUTHORISE OMISSION OF CERTAIN INFORMATION ...

2.　The competent authority of the home Member State may authorise the omission from the prospectus of certain information provided for in this Directive or in the implementing measures referred to in Article 7(1), if it considers that:

(a)　disclosure of such information would be contrary to the public interest; or

(b)　disclosure of such information would be seriously detrimental to the issuer, provided that the omission would not be likely to mislead the public with regard to facts and circumstances essential for an informed assessment of the issuer, offeror or guarantor, if any, and of the rights attached to the securities to which the prospectus relates; or

(c)　such information is of minor importance only for a specific offer or admission to trading on a regulated market and is not such as will influence the assessment of the financial position and prospects of the issuer, offeror or guarantor, if any.

CONDITIONS TO BE MET WHERE CERTAIN INFORMATION REQUIRED BY IMPLEMENTING MEASURES IS INAPPROPRIATE ...

3.　Without prejudice to the adequate information of investors, where, exceptionally, certain information required by implementing measures referred to in Article 7(1) to be included in a prospectus is inappropriate to the issuer's sphere of activity or to the legal form of the issuer or to the securities to which the prospectus relates, the prospectus shall contain information equivalent to the required information. If there is no such information, this requirement shall not apply.

THE COMMISSION SHALL ADOPT IMPLEMENTING MEASURES CONCERNING CIRCUMSTANCES WHERE OMISSIONS MAY BE AUTHORISED ...

4.　In order to take account of technical developments on financial markets and to ensure uniform application of this Directive, the Commission shall ... adopt implementing measures concerning paragraph 2. [Those measures, designed to amend non-essential elements of this Directive by supplementing it, shall be adopted in accordance with the regulatory procedure with scrutiny referred to in Article 24(2a).]

Article 10

INFORMATION ISSUERS MUST PROVIDE AN ANNUAL DOCUMENT REFERRING TO ALL INFORMATION PUBLISHED IN COMPLIANCE WITH THEIR OBLIGATIONS ...

1. Issuers whose securities are admitted to trading on a regulated market shall at least annually provide a document that contains or refers to all information that they have published or made available to the public over the preceding 12 months in one or more Member States and in third countries in compliance with their obligations under Community and national laws and rules dealing with the regulation of securities, issuers of securities and securities markets. Issuers shall refer at least to the information required pursuant to company law directives, Directive 2001/34/EC and Regulation (EC) No 1606/2002 of the European Parliament and of the Council of 19 July 2002 on the application of international accounting standards.

SUCH DOCUMENT TO BE FILED WITH THE COMPETENT AUTHORITY ...

2. The document shall be filed with the competent authority of the home Member State after the publication of the financial statement. Where the document refers to information, it shall be stated where the information can be obtained.

CIRCUMSTANCES WHERE SUCH A DOCUMENT IS NOT REQUIRED ...

3. The obligation set out in paragraph 1 shall not apply to issuers of non-equity securities whose denomination per unit amounts to at least EUR 50,000.

THE COMMISSION MAY ADOPT IMPLEMENTING MEASURES RELATING TO THE METHOD OF PUBLICATION OF THE DOCUMENT ...

4. In order to take account of technical developments on financial markets and to ensure uniform application of this Directive, the Commission may, in accordance with the procedure referred to in Article 24(2), adopt implementing measures concerning paragraph 1. These measures will relate only to the method of publication of the disclosure requirements mentioned in paragraph 1 and will not entail new disclosure requirements. The first set of implementing measures shall be adopted by 1 July 2004.

Article 14
Publication of the prospectus

PROSPECTUS SHALL BE FILED WITH THE COMPETENT AUTHORITY AND MADE AVAILABLE TO THE PUBLIC ...

1. Once approved, the prospectus shall be filed with the competent authority of the home Member State and shall be made available to the public by the issuer, offeror or person asking for admission to trading on a regulated market as soon as practicable and in any case, at a reasonable time in advance of, and at the latest at the beginning of, the offer to the public or the admission to trading of the securities involved. In addition, in the case of an initial public offer of a class of shares not already admitted to trading on a regulated market that is to be admitted to trading for the first time, the prospectus shall be available at least six working days before the end of the offer.

MEANING OF 'AVAILABLE TO THE PUBLIC' ...

2. The prospectus shall be deemed available to the public when published either:
   (a) by insertion in one or more newspapers circulated throughout, or widely circulated in, the Member States in which the offer to the public is made or the admission to trading is sought; or
   (b) in a printed form to be made available, free of charge, to the public at the offices of the market on which the securities are being admitted to trading, or at the registered office of the issuer and at the offices of the financial intermediaries placing or selling the securities, including paying agents; or

(c)　in an electronic form on the issuer's website and, if applicable, on the website of the financial intermediaries placing or selling the securities, including paying agents; or

(d)　in an electronic form on the website of the regulated market where the admission to trading is sought; or

(e)　in electronic form on the website of the competent authority of the home Member State if the said authority has decided to offer this service.

A home Member State may require issuers which publish their prospectus in accordance with (a) or (b) also to publish their prospectus in an electronic form in accordance with (c).

MEMBER STATES MAY REQUIRE PUBLICATION OF A NOTICE STATING WHERE A PROSPECTUS MAY BE OBTAINED

3.　In addition, a home Member State may require publication of a notice stating how the prospectus has been made available and where it can be obtained by the public.

COMPETENT AUTHORITY MUST PUBLISH ALL PROSPECTUSES APPROVED, OR A LIST WITH HYPERLINKS ...

4.　The competent authority of the home Member State shall publish on its website over a period of 12 months, at its choice, all the prospectuses approved, or at least the list of prospectuses approved in accordance with Article 13, including, if applicable, a hyperlink to the prospectus published on the website of the issuer, or on the website of the regulated market.

EACH DOCUMENT MAKING UP A PROSPECTUS MAY BE PUBLISHED SEPARATELY ...

5.　In the case of a prospectus comprising several documents and/or incorporating information by reference, the documents and information making up the prospectus may be published and circulated separately provided that the said documents are made available, free of charge, to the public, in accordance with the arrangements established in paragraph 2. Each document shall indicate where the other constituent documents of the full prospectus may be obtained.

THE TEXT AND FORMAT OF THE PROSPECTUS MADE AVAILABLE TO THE PUBLIC MUST BE THE SAME AS THAT FILED ...

6.　The text and the format of the prospectus, and/or the supplements to the prospectus, published or made available to the public, shall at all times be identical to the original version approved by the competent authority of the home Member State.

IF PUBLISHED ELECTRONICALLY, PAPER COPIES MUST ALSO BE AVAILABLE ...

7.　Where the prospectus is made available by publication in electronic form, a paper copy must nevertheless be delivered to the investor, upon his request and free of charge, by the issuer, the offeror, the person asking for admission to trading or the financial intermediaries placing or selling the securities.

THE COMMISSION SHALL ADOPT IMPLEMENTING MEASURES CONCERNING THE PUBLICATION OF A PROSPECTUS

8.　In order to take account of technical developments on financial markets and to ensure uniform application of the Directive, the Commission shall ... adopt implementing measures concerning paragraphs 1, 2, 3 and 4. The first set of implementing measures shall be adopted by 1 July 2004. [Those measures, designed to amend non-essential elements of this Directive by supplementing it, shall be adopted in accordance with the regulatory procedure with scrutiny referred to in Article 24(2a).]

EDITORIAL NOTE

The text in italicised capital letters in the Article below is not part of the original text of the Directive but is a note added by the JMLSG.

Article 16
Supplements to the prospectus

CERTAIN EVENTS TAKING PLACE BETWEEN PUBLICATION OF THE PROSPECTUS AND FINAL CLOSING OF THE OFFER MUST BE MENTIONED IN A SUPPLEMENT TO THE PROSPECTUS ...

1.　Every significant new factor, material mistake or inaccuracy relating to the information included in the prospectus which is capable of affecting the assessment of the securities and which arises or is noted between the time when the prospectus is approved and the final closing of the offer to the public or, as the case may be, the time when trading on a regulated market begins, shall be mentioned in a supplement to the prospectus. Such a supplement shall be approved in the same way in a maximum of seven working days and published in accordance with at least the same arrangements as were applied when the original prospectus was published. The summary, and any translations thereof, shall also be supplemented, if necessary to take into account the new information included in the supplement.

INVESTORS MAY WITHDRAW THEIR AGREEMENT TO PURCHASE IF A SUPPLEMENT IS PUBLISHED ...

2.　Investors who have already agreed to purchase or subscribe for the securities before the supplement is published shall have the right, exercisable within a time limit which shall not be shorter than two working days after the publication of the supplement, to withdraw their acceptances.

DIRECTIVE 2004/109/EC OF THE EUROPEAN PARLIAMENT AND OF THE COUNCIL of 15 December 2004 on the harmonisation of transparency requirements in relation to information about issuers whose securities are admitted to trading on a regulated market and amending Directive 2001/34/EC (Transparency Directive)

EDITORIAL NOTE
The text in italicised capital letters in the Article below is not part of the original text of the Directive but is a note added by the JMLSG.

Article 4
Annual financial reports

PUBLICATION DEADLINE FOR ANNUAL FINANCIAL REPORTS

1.　The issuer shall make public its annual financial report at the latest four months after the end of each financial year and shall ensure that it remains publicly available for at least five years.

DOCUMENTS THAT SHALL COMPRISE THE ANNUAL FINANCIAL REPORT

2.　The annual financial report shall comprise:
   (a)　the audited financial statements;
   (b)　the management report; and
   (c)　statements made by the persons responsible within the issuer, whose names and functions shall be clearly indicated, to the effect that, to the best of their knowledge, the financial statements prepared in accordance with the applicable set of accounting standards give a true and fair view of the assets, liabilities, financial position and profit or loss of the issuer and the undertakings included in the consolidation taken as a whole and that the management report includes a fair review of the development and performance of the business and the position of the issuer and the undertakings included in the consolidation taken as a whole, together with a description of the principal risks and uncertainties that they face.

WHERE CONSOLIDATED ACCOUNTS ARE REQUIRED ...

3.　Where the issuer is required to prepare consolidated accounts according to the Seventh Council Directive 83/349/EEC of 13 June 1983 on consolidated accounts, the audited financial statements shall comprise such consolidated accounts drawn up in accordance with Regulation (EC) No 1606/2002 and the annual accounts of the parent company drawn up in accordance with the national law of the Member State in which the parent company is incorporated.

Where the issuer is not required to prepare consolidated accounts, the audited financial statements shall comprise the accounts prepared in accordance with the national law of the Member State in which the company is incorporated.

REQUIREMENT FOR FINANCIAL STATEMENTS TO BE AUDITED ...

4.　The financial statements shall be audited in accordance with Articles 51 and 51a of the Fourth Council Directive 78/660/EEC of 25 July 1978 on the annual accounts of certain types of companies and, if the issuer is required to prepare consolidated accounts, in accordance with Article 37 of Directive 83/349/EEC.

The audit report, signed by the person or persons responsible for auditing the financial statements, shall be disclosed in full to the public together with the annual financial report.

REQUIREMENT FOR A MANAGEMENT REPORT ...

5.　The management report shall be drawn up in accordance with Article 46 of Directive 78/660/EEC and, if the issuer is required to prepare consolidated accounts, in accordance with Article 36 of Directive 83/349/EEC.

THE COMMISSION SHALL ADOPT IMPLEMENTING MEASURES CONCERNING THE PUBLICATION OF ANNUAL FINANCIAL REPORTS

6.　The Commission shall, in accordance with the procedure referred to in Article 27(2), adopt implementing measures in order to take account of technical developments in financial markets and to ensure the uniform application of paragraph 1. The Commission shall in particular specify the technical conditions under which a published annual financial report, including the audit report, is to remain available to the public. Where appropriate, the Commission may also adapt the five-year period referred to in paragraph 1.

EDITORIAL NOTE

The text in italicised capital letters in the Article below is not part of the original text of the Directive but is a note added by the JMLSG. Note also that the JMLSG text as reproduced in their Guidance of January 2009 did not include the amendments made to this Article by European Parliament and Council Directive 2008/22/EC, Art 1(2), as from 20 March 2008. The text as reproduced below does include those amendments (ie, the repeal of, and the substitution of, certain words in para 6 as indicated by the ellipsis and by the text in square brackets below).

Article 5
Half-yearly financial reports

REQUIREMENT FOR HALF-YEARLY FINANCIAL REPORTS ...

1. The issuer of shares or debt securities shall make public a half-yearly financial report covering the first six months of the financial year as soon as possible after the end of the relevant period, but at the latest two months thereafter. The issuer shall ensure that the half-yearly financial report remains available to the public for at least five years.

DOCUMENTS THAT SHALL COMPRISE THE HALF-YEARLY FINANCIAL REPORT

2. The half-yearly financial report shall comprise:
   (a)   the condensed set of financial statements;
   (b)   an interim management report; and
   (c)   statements made by the persons responsible within the issuer, whose names and functions shall be clearly indicated, to the effect that, to the best of their knowledge, the condensed set of financial statements which has been prepared in accordance with the applicable set of accounting standards gives a true and fair view of the assets, liabilities, financial position and profit or loss of the issuer, or the undertakings included in the consolidation as a whole as required under paragraph 3, and that the interim management report includes a fair review of the information required under paragraph 4.

WHERE CONSOLIDATED ACCOUNTS ARE REQUIRED ...

3. Where the issuer is required to prepare consolidated accounts, the condensed set of financial statements shall be prepared in accordance with the international accounting standard applicable to the interim financial reporting adopted pursuant to the procedure provided for under Article 6 of Regulation (EC) No 1606/2002.

Where the issuer is not required to prepare consolidated accounts, the condensed set of financial statements shall at least contain a condensed balance sheet, a condensed profit and loss account and explanatory notes on these accounts. In preparing the condensed balance sheet and the condensed profit and loss account, the issuer shall follow the same principles for recognising and measuring as when preparing annual financial reports.

MINIMUM CONTENTS OF INTERIM MANAGEMENT REPORTS ...

4. The interim management report shall include at least an indication of important events that have occurred during the first six months of the financial year, and their impact on the condensed set of financial statements, together with a description of the principal risks and uncertainties for the remaining six months of the financial year. For issuers of shares, the interim management report shall also include major related parties transactions.

REQUIREMENTS WHERE HALF-YEARLY REPORT IS, OR IS NOT, AUDITED ...

5. If the half-yearly financial report has been audited, the audit report shall be reproduced in full. The same shall apply in the case of an auditors' review. If the half-yearly financial report has not been audited or reviewed by auditors, the issuer shall make a statement to that effect in its report.

THE COMMISSION SHALL ADOPT IMPLEMENTING MEASURES CONCERNING HALF-YEARLY REPORTS

6. The Commission shall ... adopt implementing measures in order to take account of technical developments on financial markets and to ensure the uniform application of paragraphs 1 to 5 of this Article.

The Commission shall, in particular:
   (a)   specify the technical conditions under which a published half-yearly financial report, including the auditors' review, is to remain available to the public;
   (b)   clarify the nature of the auditors' review;
   (c)   specify the minimum content of the condensed balance sheet and profit and loss accounts and explanatory notes on these accounts, where they are not prepared in accordance with the international accounting standards adopted pursuant to the procedure provided for under Article 6 of Regulation (EC) No 1606/2002.

[The measures referred to in point (a) shall be adopted in accordance with the regulatory procedure referred to in Article 27(2). The measures referred to in points (b) and (c), designed to amend non-essential elements of this Directive by supplementing it, shall be adopted in accordance with the regulatory procedure with scrutiny referred to in Article 27(2a).

Where appropriate, the Commission may also adapt the five-year period referred to in paragraph 1. That measure, designed to amend non-essential elements of this Directive, shall be adopted in accordance with the regulatory procedure with scrutiny referred to in Article 27(2a).]

EDITORIAL NOTE
The text in italicised capital letters in the Article below is not part of the original text of the Directive but is a note added by the JMLSG.

Article 6
Interim management statements

REQUIREMENTS FOR INTERIM MANAGEMENT STATEMENTS: TIMING AND CONTENT ...

1. Without prejudice to Article 6 of Directive 2003/6/EC, an issuer whose shares are admitted to trading on a regulated market shall make public a statement by its management during the first six-month period of the financial year and another statement by its management during the second six-month period of the financial year. Such statement shall be made in a period between ten weeks after the beginning and six weeks before the end of the relevant six-month period. It shall contain information covering the period between the beginning of the relevant six-month period and the date of publication of the statement. Such a statement shall provide:
  — an explanation of material events and transactions that have taken place during the relevant period and their impact on the financial position of the issuer and its controlled undertakings, and
  — a general description of the financial position and performance of the issuer and its controlled undertakings during the relevant period.

INTERIM MANAGEMENT STATEMENTS NOT REQUIRED WHERE QUARTERLY FINANCIAL REPORTS PUBLISHED ...

2. Issuers which, under either national legislation or the rules of the regulated market or of their own initiative, publish quarterly financial reports in accordance with such legislation or rules shall not be required to make public statements by the management provided for in paragraph 1.

COMMISSION TO REPORT TO THE EUROPEAN PARLIAMENT AND TO THE COUNCIL BY 2010 ON THE TRANSPARENCY OF QUARTERLY FINANCIAL REPORTING ...

3. The Commission shall provide a report to the European Parliament and the Council by 20 January 2010 on the transparency of quarterly financial reporting and statements by the management of issuers to examine whether the information provided meets the objective of allowing investors to make an informed assessment of the financial position of the issuer. Such a report shall include an impact assessment on areas where the Commission considers proposing amendments to this Article.

EDITORIAL NOTE
The text in italicised capital letters in the Article below is not part of the original text of the Directive but is a note added by the JMLSG. Note also that the JMLSG text as reproduced in their Guidance of January 2009 did not include the amendments made to this Article by European Parliament and Council Directive 2008/22/EC, Art 1(6), as from 20 March 2008. The text as reproduced below does include those amendments (ie, the repeal of, and the addition of, certain words in para 2 as indicated by the ellipsis and by the text in square brackets below).

Article 14
PUBLICATION REQUIREMENTS WHERE AN ISSUER ACQUIRES OR DISPOSES OF ITS OWN SHARES ...

1. Where an issuer of shares admitted to trading on a regulated market acquires or disposes of its own shares, either itself or through a person acting in his own name but on the issuer's behalf, the home Member State shall ensure that the issuer makes public the proportion of its own shares as soon as possible, but not later than four trading days following such acquisition or disposal where that proportion reaches, exceeds or falls below the thresholds of 5% or 10% of the voting rights. The proportion shall be calculated on the basis of the total number of shares to which voting rights are attached.

THE COMMISSION SHALL ADOPT IMPLEMENTING MEASURES CONCERNING THE PUBLICATION OF THIS INFORMATION

2. The Commission shall ... adopt implementing measures in order to take account of technical developments in financial markets and to ensure the uniform application of paragraph 1.

[Those measures, designed to amend non-essential elements of this Directive by supplementing it, shall be adopted in accordance with the regulatory procedure with scrutiny referred to in Article 27(2a).]

EDITORIAL NOTE
  The text in italicised capital letters in the Article below is not part of the original text of the Directive but is a note added by the JMLSG.

Article 16
Additional information
ISSUERS' OBLIGATION TO MAKE PUBLIC ANY CHANGES IN RIGHTS ATTACHING TO VARIOUS CLASSES OF SHARES ...

  1. The issuer of shares admitted to trading on a regulated market shall make public without delay any change in the rights attaching to the various classes of shares, including changes in the rights attaching to derivative securities issued by the issuer itself and giving access to the shares of that issuer.

ISSUERS' OBLIGATION TO MAKE PUBLIC ANY CHANGES IN RIGHTS ATTACHING TO HOLDERS OF SECURITIES OTHER THAN SHARES ...

  2. The issuer of securities, other than shares admitted to trading on a regulated market, shall make public without delay any changes in the rights of holders of securities other than shares, including changes in the terms and conditions of these securities which could indirectly affect those rights, resulting in particular from a change in loan terms or in interest rates.

ISSUERS' OBLIGATION TO MAKE PUBLIC ANY NEW LOAN ISSUES

  3. The issuer of securities admitted to trading on a regulated market shall make public without delay of new loan issues and in particular of any guarantee or security in respect thereof. Without prejudice to Directive 2003/6/EC, this paragraph shall not apply to a public international body of which at least one Member State is member.

EDITORIAL NOTE
  The text in italicised capital letters in the Article below is not part of the original text of the Directive but is a note added by the JMLSG. Note also that the JMLSG text as reproduced in their Guidance of January 2009 did not include the amendments made to this Article by European Parliament and Council Directive 2008/22/EC, Art 1(6), as from 20 March 2008. The text as reproduced below does include those amendments (ie, the repeal of, and the addition of, certain words in para 4 as indicated by the ellipsis and by the text in square brackets below).

Article 17
Information requirements for issuers whose shares are admitted to trading on a regulated market
ISSUERS TO ENSURE EQUAL TREATMENT OF ALL HOLDERS OF SHARES ...

  1. The issuer of shares admitted to trading on a regulated market shall ensure equal treatment for all holders of shares who are in the same position.

ISSUERS' OBLIGATIONS TO MAKE AVAILABLE TO SHAREHOLDERS INFORMATION REGARDING ANNUAL MEETINGS, PROXY ARRANGEMENTS, ETC ...

  2. The issuer shall ensure that all the facilities and information necessary to enable holders of shares to exercise their rights are available in the home Member State and that the integrity of data is preserved. Shareholders shall not be prevented from exercising their rights by proxy, subject to the law of the country in which the issuer is incorporated. In particular, the issuer shall:
  (a) provide information on the place, time and agenda of meetings, the total number of shares and voting rights and the rights of holders to participate in meetings;
  (b) make available a proxy form, on paper or, where applicable, by electronic means, to each person entitled to vote at a shareholders' meeting, together with the notice concerning the meeting or, on request, after an announcement of the meeting;
  (c) designate as its agent a financial institution through which shareholders may exercise their financial rights; and
  (d) publish notices or distribute circulars concerning the allocation and payment of dividends and the issue of new shares, including information on any arrangements for allotment, subscription, cancellation or conversion.

MEMBER STATES TO ALLOW ISSUERS TO USE ELECTRONIC MEANS OF CONVEYING INFORMATION TO SHAREHOLDERS ...

  3. For the purposes of conveying information to shareholders, the home Member State shall allow issuers the use of electronic means, provided such a decision is taken in a general meeting and meets at least the following conditions:

(a) the use of electronic means shall in no way depend upon the location of the seat or residence of the shareholder or, in the cases referred to in Article 10(a) to (h), of the natural persons or legal entities;

(b) identification arrangements shall be put in place so that the shareholders, or the natural persons or legal entities entitled to exercise or to direct the exercise of voting rights, are effectively informed;

(c) shareholders, or in the cases referred to in Article 10(a) to (e) the natural persons or legal entities entitled to acquire, dispose of or exercise voting rights, shall be contacted in writing to request their consent for the use of electronic means for conveying information and, if they do not object within a reasonable period of time, their consent shall be deemed to be given. They shall be able to request, at any time in the future, that information be conveyed in writing, and

(d) any apportionment of the costs entailed in the conveyance of such information by electronic means shall be determined by the issuer in compliance with the principle of equal treatment laid down in paragraph 1.

THE COMMISSION SHALL ADOPT IMPLEMENTING MEASURES CONCERNING THE ABOVE ...

4. The Commission shall ... adopt implementing measures in order to take account of technical developments in financial markets, to take account of developments in information and communication technology and to ensure the uniform application of paragraphs 1, 2 and 3. It shall, in particular, specify the types of financial institution through which a shareholder may exercise the financial rights provided for in paragraph 2(c).

[Those measures, designed to amend non-essential elements of this Directive by supplementing it, shall be adopted in accordance with the regulatory procedure with scrutiny referred to in Article 27(2a).]

EDITORIAL NOTE
The text in italicised capital letters in the Article below is not part of the original text of the Directive but is a note added by the JMLSG. Note also that the JMLSG text as reproduced in their Guidance of January 2009 did not include the amendments made to this Article by European Parliament and Council Directive 2008/22/EC, Art 1(6), as from 20 March 2008. The text as reproduced below does include those amendments (ie, the repeal of, and the addition of, certain words in para 5 as indicated by the ellipsis and by the text in square brackets below).

Article 18
Information requirements for issuers whose debt securities are admitted to trading on a regulated market

ISSUERS TO ENSURE EQUAL TREATMENT OF ALL HOLDERS OF DEBT SECURITIES ...

1. The issuer of debt securities admitted to trading on a regulated market shall ensure that all holders of debt securities ranking pari passu are given equal treatment in respect of all the rights attaching to those debt securities.

ISSUERS' OBLIGATIONS TO MAKE AVAILABLE TO HOLDERS OF DEBT SECURITIES INFORMATION REGARDING ANNUAL MEETINGS, PROXY ARRANGEMENTS, ETC ...

2. The issuer shall ensure that all the facilities and information necessary to enable debt securities holders to exercise their rights are publicly available in the home Member State and that the integrity of data is preserved. Debt securities holders shall not be prevented from exercising their rights by proxy, subject to the law of country in which the issuer is incorporated. In particular, the issuer shall:

(a) publish notices, or distribute circulars, concerning the place, time and agenda of meetings of debt securities holders, the payment of interest, the exercise of any conversion, exchange, subscription or cancellation rights, and repayment, as well as the right of those holders to participate therein;

(b) make available a proxy form on paper or, where applicable, by electronic means, to each person entitled to vote at a meeting of debt securities holders, together with the notice concerning the meeting or, on request, after an announcement of the meeting; and

(c) designate as its agent a financial institution through which debt securities holders may exercise their financial rights.

IN CERTAIN CIRCUMSTANCES, ISSUERS MAY HOLD AN ANNUAL MEETING IN ANOTHER MEMBER STATE ...

3. If only holders of debt securities whose denomination per unit amounts to at least EUR 50,000 or, in the case of debt securities denominated in a currency other than Euro whose denomination per unit is, at the date of the issue, equivalent to at least EUR 50,000, are to be invited

to a meeting, the issuer may choose as venue any Member State, provided that all the facilities and information necessary to enable such holders to exercise their rights are made available in that Member State.

MEMBER STATES TO ALLOW ISSUERS TO USE ELECTRONIC MEANS OF CONVEYING INFORMATION TO HOLDERS OF DEBT SECURITIES ...

4. For the purposes of conveying information to debt securities holders, the home Member State, or the Member State chosen by the issuer pursuant to paragraph 3, shall allow issuers the use of electronic means, provided such a decision is taken in a general meeting and meets at least the following conditions:

(a) the use of electronic means shall in no way depend upon the location of the seat or residence of the debt security holder or of a proxy representing that holder;

(b) identification arrangements shall be put in place so that debt securities holders are effectively informed;

(c) debt securities holders shall be contacted in writing to request their consent for the use of electronic means for conveying information and if they do not object within a reasonable period of time, their consent shall be deemed to be given. They shall be able to request, at any time in the future, that information be conveyed in writing; and

(d) any apportionment of the costs entailed in the conveyance of information by electronic means shall be determined by the issuer in compliance with the principle of equal treatment laid down in paragraph 1.

THE COMMISSION SHALL ADOPT IMPLEMENTING MEASURES CONCERNING THE ABOVE ...

5. The Commission shall ... adopt implementing measures in order to take account of technical developments in financial markets, to take account of developments in information and communication technology and to ensure the uniform application of paragraphs 1 to 4. It shall, in particular, specify the types of financial institution through which a debt security holder may exercise the financial rights provided for in paragraph 2(c).

[Those measures, designed to amend non-essential elements of this Directive by supplementing it, shall be adopted in accordance with the regulatory procedure with scrutiny referred to in Article 27(2a).]

EDITORIAL NOTE
The text in italicised capital letters in the Article below is not part of the original text of the Directive but is a note added by the JMLSG (this includes the five question marks which also appear in the original JMLSG document). Note also that the JMLSG text as reproduced in their Guidance of January 2009 did not include the amendments made to this Article by European Parliament and Council Directive 2008/22/EC, Art 1(7), as from 20 March 2008. The text as reproduced below does include those amendments (ie, the repeal of, and the addition of, certain words in para 4 as indicated by the ellipsis and by the text in square brackets below).

Article 19
Home Member State control

ANY INFORMATION DISCLOSED PUBLICLY MUST ALSO BE FILED WITH THE COMPETENT AUTHORITY

1. Whenever the issuer, or any person having requested, without the issuer's consent, the admission of its securities to trading on a regulated market, discloses regulated information, it shall at the same time file that information with the competent authority of its home Member State. That competent authority may decide to publish such filed information on its Internet site.

Where an issuer proposes to amend its instrument of incorporation or statutes, it shall communicate the draft amendment to the competent authority of the home Member State and to the regulated market to which its securities have been admitted to trading. Such communication shall be effected without delay, but at the latest on the date of calling the general meeting which is to vote on, or be informed of, the amendment.

EXEMPTIONS FROM ABOVE ...

2. The home Member State may exempt an issuer from the requirement under paragraph 1 in respect of information disclosed in accordance with Article 6 of Directive 2003/6/EC or Article 12(6) of this Directive.

?????

3. Information to be notified to the issuer in accordance with Articles 9, 10, 12 and 13 shall at the same time be filed with the competent authority of the home Member State.

THE COMMISSION SHALL ADOPT IMPLEMENTING MEASURES CONCERNING THE ABOVE ...

4. In order to ensure the uniform application of paragraphs 1, 2 and 3, the Commission shall ... adopt implementing measures.

The Commission shall, in particular, specify the procedure in accordance with which an issuer, a holder of shares or other financial instruments, or a person or entity referred to in Article 10, is to file information with the competent authority of the home Member State under paragraphs 1 or 3, respectively, in order to:

(a) enable filing by electronic means in the home Member State;

(b) coordinate the filing of the annual financial report referred to in Article 4 of this Directive with the filing of the annual information referred to in Article 10 of Directive 2003/71/EC.

[The measures referred to in the first and second subparagraphs, designed to amend non-essential elements of this Directive by supplementing it, shall be adopted in accordance with the regulatory procedure with scrutiny referred to in Article 27(2a).]

EDITORIAL NOTE

The text in italicised capital letters in the Article below is not part of the original text of the Directive but is a note added by the JMLSG.

Article 30
Transitional provisions

TRANSITIONAL PROVISIONS: EXEMPTIONS FORM DISCLOSING FINANCIAL STATEMENTS ...

1. By way of derogation from Article 5(3) of this Directive, the home Member State may exempt from disclosing financial statements in accordance with Regulation (EC) No 1606/2002 issuers referred to in Article 9 of that Regulation for the financial year starting on or after 1 January 2006.

TRANSITIONAL PROVISIONS:

2. Notwithstanding Article 12(2), a shareholder shall notify the issuer at the latest two months after the date in Article 31(1) of the proportion of voting rights and capital it holds, in accordance with Articles 9, 10 and 13, with issuers at that date, unless it has already made a notification containing equivalent information before that date.

Notwithstanding Article 12(6), an issuer shall in turn disclose the information received in those notifications no later than three months after the date in Article 31(1).

TRANSITIONAL PROVISIONS:

3. Where an issuer is incorporated in a third country, the home Member State may exempt such issuer only in respect of those debt securities which have already been admitted to trading on a regulated market in the Community prior to 1 January 2005 from drawing up its financial statements in accordance with Article 4(3) and its management report in accordance with Article 4(5) as long as

(a) the competent authority of the home Member State acknowledges that annual financial statements prepared by issuers from such a third country give a true and fair view of the issuer's assets and liabilities, financial position and results;

(b) the third country where the issuer is incorporated has not made mandatory the application of international accounting standards referred to in Article 2 of Regulation (EC) No 1606/2002; and

(c) the Commission has not taken any decision in accordance with Article 23(4)(ii) as to whether there is an equivalence between the abovementioned accounting standards and
— the accounting standards laid down in the law, regulations or administrative provisions of the third country where the issuer is incorporated, or
— the accounting standards of a third country such an issuer has elected to comply with.

TRANSITIONAL PROVISIONS:

4. The home Member State may exempt issuers only in respect of those debt securities which have already been admitted to trading on a regulated market in the Community prior to 1 January 2005 from disclosing half-yearly financial report in accordance with Article 5 for 10 years following 1 January 2005, provided that the home Member State had decided to allow such issuers to benefit from the provisions of Article 27 of Directive 2001/34/EC at the point of admission of those debt securities.

[7058]–[7100]

B: CODES OF PRACTICE

REGULATORS' COMPLIANCE CODE
STATUTORY CODE OF PRACTICE FOR REGULATORS

(17 December 2007)

BERR: Department for Business, Enterprise and Regulatory Reform

© Crown copyright 2007

CONTENTS

Foreword by Pat McFadden MP — Minister of State, Department for Business, Enterprise and Regulatory Reform (BERR)

PART 1 GENERAL INTRODUCTION

PART 2 SPECIFIC OBLIGATIONS OF THE CODE

FOREWORD

The Regulators' Compliance Code is a central part of the Government's better regulation agenda. Its aim is to embed a risk-based, proportionate and targeted approach to regulatory inspection and enforcement among the regulators it applies to.

Our expectation is that as regulators integrate the Code's standards into their regulatory culture and processes, they will become more efficient and effective in their work. They will be able to use their resources in a way that gets the most value out of the effort that they make, whilst delivering significant benefits to low risk and compliant businesses through better-focused inspection activity, increased use of advice for businesses, and lower compliance costs.

The Compliance Code has been issued with parliamentary approval, following a wide and lengthy consultation process, and comes into force on 6 April 2008 by virtue of the Legislative and Regulatory Reform Code of Practice (Appointed Day) Order 2007.

I believe that the application of the Code can make a difference on the ground to the regulators, those they regulate, and society in general.

Pat McFadden MP
Minister of State
Department for Business, Enterprise and Regulatory Reform (BERR)

[7101]

PART 1
GENERAL INTRODUCTION

1. Purpose of the Code

1.1   Effective and well-targeted regulation is essential in promoting fairness and protection from harm. However, the Government believes that, in achieving these and other legitimate objectives, regulation and its enforcement should be proportionate and flexible enough to allow or even encourage economic progress.

1.2   This Code supports the Government's better regulation agenda and is based on the recommendations in the Hampton Report.[1] Its purpose is to promote efficient and effective approaches to regulatory inspection and enforcement which improve regulatory outcomes[2] without imposing unnecessary burdens on business, the Third Sector[3] and other regulated entities.[4]

1.3   The Code stresses the need for regulators[5] to adopt a positive and proactive approach towards ensuring compliance by:

- helping and encouraging regulated entities to understand and meet regulatory requirements more easily; and
- responding proportionately to regulatory breaches.

1.4 The Code supports regulators' responsibility to deliver desirable regulatory outcomes. This includes having effective policies to deal proportionately with criminal behaviour which would have a damaging effect on legitimate businesses and desirable regulatory outcomes. The Code does not relieve regulated entities of their responsibility to comply with their obligations under the law.

NOTES

1   *Reducing Administrative Burdens: Effective Inspection and Enforcement*, Philip Hampton, March 2005.
2   Throughout this Code, the term 'regulatory outcomes' means the 'end purpose' of regulatory activity (for example, reduction in accidents/disease, less pollution).
3   This is defined as non-governmental organisations that include voluntary and community organisations, charities, social enterprises, cooperatives and mutuals.
4   Throughout this Code, the term 'regulated entities' includes businesses, public sector bodies, charities and voluntary sector organisations that are subject to regulation.
5   The term 'regulator' is used in this code to refer to any organisation that exercises a regulatory function.

2. Background and scope

2.1   This Code has been laid before Parliament by the Minister for the Cabinet Office and has been approved by both Houses of Parliament in accordance with section 23 of the Legislative and Regulatory Reform Act 2006 ("the Act"), after having consulted persons appearing to him to be representative of persons exercising regulatory functions and such other persons as he considered appropriate. In preparing the draft, the Minister has sought to secure that the Code is consistent with the Principles of Good Regulation specified in section 21(2) of the Act.[6]

2.2   The Minister issues the Code under section 22(1) of the Act on 17 December 2007.

2.3   The Code only applies to those regulatory functions specified by order made under section 24(2) of the Act. Any regulator whose functions are so specified **must have regard to** this Code:

(a)   when determining any general policy or principles about the exercise of those specified functions (section 22(2)); or

(b)   when exercising a specified regulatory function which is itself a function of setting standards or giving general guidance about other regulatory functions (whether their own functions or someone else's functions)(section 22(3)).

2.4   The duties to have regard to the Code under section 22(2) and (3) of the Act **do not** apply to the exercise by a regulator or its staff of any specified regulatory function in individual cases. This means, for example, that while an inspector or investigator should operate in accordance with a regulator's general policy or guidance on inspections, investigations and enforcement activities, the Code does not apply directly to the work of that inspector or investigator in carrying out any of these activities in individual cases.

2.5   The duty on a regulator to "have regard to" the Code means that the regulator **must** take into account the Code's provisions and give them due weight in developing their policies or principles or in setting standards or giving guidance.

2.6   The regulator is not bound to follow a provision of the Code if they *properly* conclude that the provision is either not relevant or is outweighed by another relevant consideration. They should ensure that any decision to depart from any provision of the Code is properly reasoned and based on material evidence. Where there are no such relevant considerations, regulators should follow the Code.

2.7   Section 22(4) of the Act provides that the duty to have regard to the Code is subject to any other legal requirement affecting the exercise of the regulatory function, including EC law obligations.

2.8   In accordance with section 24(3) of the Act, this Code does not apply to:
- regulatory functions so far as exercisable in Scotland to the extent that the functions relate to matters which are not reserved matters;
- regulatory functions so far as exercisable in Northern Ireland to the extent that the functions relate to transferred matters; or
- regulatory functions exercisable only in or as regards Wales.

NOTES

6   These principles are that regulatory activities should be carried out in a way which is transparent, accountable, proportionate and consistent; and that regulatory activities should be targeted only at cases in which action is needed.

PART 2
SPECIFIC OBLIGATIONS OF THE CODE

This part outlines the Hampton Principles on which this Code is based, and sets out the specific provisions that elaborate these principles. The Hampton Principles and the italicised statement at the start of each numbered section do not form part of the Code's requirements, but set the context in which the specific obligations set out in the numbered paragraphs should be interpreted.

3. Economic progress

> **Hampton Principle:** *Regulators should recognise that a key element of their activity will be to allow, or even encourage, economic progress and only to intervene when there is a clear case for protection.*
>
> *Good regulation and its enforcement act as an enabler to economic activity. However, regulation that imposes unnecessary burdens can stifle enterprise and undermine economic progress. To allow or encourage economic progress, regulators must have regard to the following provisions* **when determining general policies or principles or when setting standards or giving general guidance** *about the exercise of regulatory functions.*

3.1   Regulators should consider the impact that their regulatory interventions may have on economic progress, including through consideration of the costs, effectiveness and perceptions of fairness of regulation. They should only adopt a particular approach if the benefits justify the costs[7] and it entails the minimum burden compatible with achieving their objectives.

3.2   Regulators should keep under review their regulatory activities and interventions with a view to considering the extent to which it would be appropriate to remove or reduce the regulatory burdens they impose.

3.3   Regulators should consider the impact that their regulatory interventions may have on small regulated entities, using reasonable endeavours to ensure that the burdens of their interventions fall fairly and proportionately on such entities, by giving consideration to the size of the regulated entities and the nature of their activities.

3.4   When regulators set standards or give guidance in relation to the exercise of their own or other regulatory functions (including the functions of local authorities), they should allow for reasonable variations to meet local government priorities, as well as those of the devolved administrations.

NOTES
7   Costs and benefits include economic, social and environmental costs and benefits.

4. Risk Assessment

> **Hampton Principle:** *Regulators, and the regulatory system as a whole, should use comprehensive risk assessment to concentrate resources in the areas that need them most.*
>
> *Risk assessment involves the identification and measurement of capacity to harm and, if such capacity exists, an evaluation of the likelihood of the occurrence of the harm. By basing their regulatory work on an assessment of the risks to regulatory outcomes, regulators are able to target their resources where they will be most effective and where risk is highest. As such, in order to carry out comprehensive and effective risk assessment, regulators must have regard to the following provisions* **when determining general policies or principles or when setting standards or giving general guidance** *about the exercise of regulatory functions.*

4.1   Regulators should ensure that the allocation of their regulatory efforts and resources is targeted where they would be most effective by assessing the risks to their regulatory outcomes. They should also ensure that risk assessment precedes and informs all aspects of their approaches to regulatory activity, including:

- data collection and other information requirements;
- inspection programmes;
- advice and support programmes; and
- enforcement and sanctions.

4.2   Risk assessment should be based on all available relevant and good-quality data.[8] It should include explicit consideration of the combined effect of:
- the potential impact of non-compliance on regulatory outcomes; and
- the likelihood of non-compliance.

4.3   In evaluating the likelihood of non-compliance, regulators should give consideration to all relevant factors, including:

- past compliance records and potential future risks;
- the existence of good systems for managing risks, in particular within regulated entities or sites
- evidence of recognised external accreditation; and
- management competence and willingness to comply.

4.4   Regulators should consult and involve regulated entities and other interested parties in designing their risk methodologies, and publish details of the methodologies.

4.5   Regulators should regularly review and, where appropriate, improve their risk methodologies. In doing so, they should take into account feedback and other information from regulated entities and other interested parties.

NOTES

8   An example of risk methodology, which the Hampton Review recognised as "best practice" (see *Hampton Report*, at page 32) is the Environmental Protection – Operator & Pollution Risk Appraisal scheme (EP OPRA).

---

5. Advice and Guidance

Hampton Principle: *Regulators should provide authoritative, accessible advice easily and cheaply.*

*Without knowing or understanding relevant legal requirements, regulated entities will find it difficult to comply. Regulators can, however, improve compliance through greater focus on support and advice. Regulators must, therefore, have regard to the following requirements **when determining general policies or principles or when setting standards or giving general guidance** on advice and information services.*

5.1   Regulators should ensure that all legal requirements relating to their regulatory activities, as well as changes to those legal requirements,[9] are promptly communicated or otherwise made available to relevant regulated entities.

5.2   Regulators should provide general information, advice and guidance to make it easier for regulated entities to understand and meet their regulatory obligations. Such information, advice and guidance should be provided in clear, concise and accessible language, using a range of appropriate formats and media.[10]

5.3   Regulators should involve regulated entities in developing both the content and style of regulatory guidance. They should assess the effectiveness of their information and support services by monitoring regulated entities' awareness and understanding of legal requirements, including the extent to which those entities incur additional costs obtaining external advice in order to understand and comply with legal requirements.

5.4   Regulators should provide targeted and practical advice that meets the needs of regulated entities. Such advice may be provided in a range of formats, such as through face-to-face interactions, telephone helpline and online guidance. In determining the appropriate formats, regulators should seek to maximise the reach, accessibility and effectiveness of advice while ensuring efficient use of resources. There may remain a need for regulated entities with particularly complex practices to use specialist or professional advisors as appropriate.

5.5   When offering compliance advice, regulators should distinguish between statutory requirements and advice or guidance aimed at improvements above minimum standards. Advice should be confirmed in writing, if requested.

5.6   Regulators should provide appropriate means to ensure that regulated entities can reasonably seek and access advice from the regulator without directly triggering an enforcement action. In responding to such an approach, the regulator should seek primarily to provide the advice and guidance necessary to help ensure compliance.

5.7   Advice services should generally be provided free of charge, but it may be appropriate for regulators to charge a reasonable fee for services beyond basic advice and guidance necessary to help ensure compliance. Regulators should, however, take account of the needs and circumstances of smaller regulated entities and others in need of help and support.

NOTES

9   This includes when a regulatory requirement has been removed and considered no longer relevant or applicable.

PART V
OTHER MATERIALS

10   A good example of online advice is the Environment Agency's NetRegs (www.netregs.gov.uk) an internet based plain language guidance system for business.

6. Inspections and other visits

> **Hampton Principle:** *No inspection should take place without a reason.*
>
> *Inspections can be an effective approach to achieving compliance, but are likely to be most effective when they are justified and targeted on the basis of an assessment of risk. In order to ensure the effectiveness of their inspection programmes, regulators must have regard to the following provisions **when determining general policies or principles or when setting standards or giving general guidance** on inspections.*

6.1   Regulators should ensure that inspections and other visits, such as compliance or advice visits, to regulated entities only occur in accordance with a risk assessment methodology (see paragraphs 4.2. and 4.3), except where visits are requested by regulated entities, or where a regulator acts on relevant intelligence.

6.2   Regulators should use only a small element of random inspection in their programme to test their risk methodologies or the effectiveness of their interventions.

6.3   Regulators should focus their **greatest** inspection effort on regulated entities where risk assessment shows that both:

- a compliance breach or breaches would pose a serious risk to a regulatory outcome; and
- there is high likelihood of non-compliance by regulated entities.

6.4   Where regulators visit or carry out inspections of regulated entities, they should give positive feedback to the regulated entities to encourage and reinforce good practices. Regulators should also share amongst regulated entities, and with other regulators, information about good practice.

6.5   Where two or more inspectors, whether from the same or different regulators, undertake planned inspections of the same regulated entity, regulators should have arrangements for collaboration to minimise burdens on the regulated entity, for example, through joint or coordinated inspections and data sharing.

7. Information requirements

> **Hampton Principle:** *Businesses should not have to give unnecessary information or give the same piece of information twice.*
>
> *Effective regulatory work, including risk assessment, requires accurate information. However, there are costs to its collection both to the regulator and to regulated entities. It is important to balance the need for information with the burdens that entails for regulated entities. As such, regulators must have regard to the following provisions **when determining general policies or principles or when setting standards or giving general guidance** on data requirements.*

7.1   When determining which data they may require, regulators should undertake an analysis of the costs and benefits of data requests to regulated entities. Regulators should give explicit consideration to reducing costs to regulated entities through:

- varying data requests according to risk, as set out in paragraph 4.3;
- limiting collection to specific regulated entities sectors/sub-sectors;
- reducing the frequency of data collection;
- obtaining data from other sources;
- allowing electronic submission; and
- requesting only data which is justified by risk assessment.

7.2   If two or more regulators require the same information from the same regulated entities, they should share data to avoid duplication of collection where this is practicable, beneficial and cost effective. Regulators should note the content of the Information Commissioner's letter[11] when applying the Data Protection Act 1998[12] in order to avoid unnecessarily restricting the sharing of data.

7.3   Regulators should involve regulated entities in vetting data requirements and form design for clarity and simplification. They should seek to collect data in a way that is compatible with the processes of regulated entities and those of other regulators who collect similar data.

NOTES

11   A letter from the Information Commissioner (22/01/07) giving advice on "data protection and the sharing of regulatory data on businesses" is available at: http://bre.berr.gov.uk/regulation/documents/data/pdf/letter.pdf

12   1998 c 29.

8. Compliance and enforcement actions

> **Hampton Principle:** *The few businesses that persistently break regulations should be identified quickly and face proportionate and meaningful sanctions.*
>
> *By facilitating compliance through a positive and proactive approach, regulators can achieve higher compliance rates and reduce the need for reactive enforcement actions. However, regulators should be able to target those who deliberately or persistently breach the law. To ensure that they respond proportionately to regulatory breaches, regulators must have regard to the following provisions **when determining general policies or principles or when setting standards or giving general guidance** on the exercise of compliance and enforcement functions.*

8.1   Regulators should seek to reward those regulated entities that have consistently achieved good levels of compliance through positive incentives, such as lighter inspections and reporting requirements where risk assessment justifies this. Regulators should also take account of the circumstances of small regulated entities, including any difficulties they may have in achieving compliance.

8.2   When considering formal enforcement action, regulators should, where appropriate, discuss the circumstances with those suspected of a breach and take these into account when deciding on the best approach. This paragraph does not apply where immediate action is required to prevent or respond to a serious breach or where to do so is likely to defeat the purpose of the proposed enforcement action.

8.3   Regulators should ensure that their sanctions and penalties policies are consistent with the principles set out in the Macrory Review.[13] This means that their sanctions and penalties policies should:

- aim to change the behaviour of the offender;
- aim to eliminate any financial gain or benefit from non-compliance;
- be responsive and consider what is appropriate for the particular offender and regulatory issue, which can include punishment and the public stigma that should be associated with a criminal conviction;
- be proportionate to the nature of the offence and the harm caused;
- aim to restore the harm caused by regulatory non-compliance, where appropriate; and
- aim to deter future non-compliance.

8.4   In accordance with the Macrory characteristics, regulators should also:
- publish an enforcement policy;
- measure outcomes not just outputs;
- justify their choice of enforcement actions year on year to interested parties;
- follow-up enforcement actions where appropriate;
- enforce in a transparent manner;
- be transparent in the way in which they apply and determine penalties; and
- avoid perverse incentives that might influence the choice of sanctioning response.

8.5   Regulators should ensure that clear reasons for any formal enforcement action are given to the person or entity against whom any enforcement action is being taken at the time the action is taken. These reasons should be confirmed in writing at the earliest opportunity. Complaints and relevant appeals procedures for redress should also be explained at the same time.

8.6   Regulators should enable inspectors and enforcement officers to interpret and apply relevant legal requirements and enforcement policies fairly and consistently between like-regulated entities in similar situations. Regulators should also ensure that their own inspectors and enforcement staff interpret and apply their legal requirements and enforcement policies consistently and fairly.

NOTES

13   The report of the Macrory Review, which the Government has accepted, is available at: http://bre.berr.gov.uk/REGULATION/reviewing_regulation/penalties/index.asp .

9. Accountability

> **Hampton Principle:** *Regulators should be accountable for the efficiency and effectiveness of their activities, while remaining independent in the decisions they take.*
>
> *By establishing effective accountability and transparency structures regulators will make their activities accessible and open to scrutiny. This should increase the legitimacy of regulatory activities and enable regulators and regulated entities to work together to achieve regulatory compliance. Regulators must have regard to the following provisions **when determining general policies or principles or when setting standards or giving general guidance** on the exercise of regulatory functions.*

9.1   Regulators should create effective consultation and feedback opportunities to enable continuing cooperative relationships with regulated entities and other interested parties.

9.2   Regulators should identify and explain the principal risks against which they are acting. They should, in consultation with regulated entities and other interested parties, set and publish clear standards and targets for their service and performance. These standards should include:

- regulatory outcomes[14] (capturing the principal risks);
- costs to regulated entities of regulatory interventions; and
- perceptions of regulated entities and other interested parties about the proportionality and effectiveness of regulatory approach and costs.

9.3   Regulators should measure their performance against the standards in paragraph 9.2 and regularly publish the results. To aid understanding, regulators should also explain how they measure their performance.

9.4   Local authorities and fire and rescue authorities are exempt from the requirements of paragraphs 9.2 and 9.3.

9.5   Regulators should ensure that their employees provide courteous and efficient services to regulated entities and others. They should take account of comments from regulated entities and other interested parties regarding the behaviour and activity of inspectors and other enforcement staff.

9.6   Regulators should provide effective and timely complaints procedures (including for matters in this Code) that are easily accessible to regulated entities and other interested parties. They should publicise their complaints procedures, with details of the process and likely timescale for resolution.

9.7   Complaints procedures should include a final stage to an independent, external, person. Where there is a relevant Ombudsman or Tribunal with powers to decide on matters in this Code, the final stage should allow referral to that body. However, where no such person exists, a regulator should, in consultation with interested parties, provide for further complaint or appeal to another independent person, for example, an independent professional body.

NOTES

14   As defined in footnote 2 above.

APPENDIX

STATUTORY INSTRUMENTS MADE UNDER THE BANKING ACT 2009 AND THE BANKING (SPECIAL PROVISIONS) ACT 2008 PUBLISHED LATE FEBRUARY 2009

NOTES

The ten statutory instruments set out below were all issued on 20 February 2009, ie, after Parts I to V of this Handbook had been sent to the typesetter. This Appendix was added at the last minute as the Editor believes that some users might find these Orders and Regulations useful. Due to their late publication, there was not sufficient time to include the substance of these statutory instruments in the index to this work.

BANKING ACT 2009 (COMMENCEMENT NO 1) ORDER 2009

(SI 2009/296)

NOTES

Made: 16 February 2009.
Authority: Banking Act 2009, s 263(1), (3).

1 Citation and interpretation

(1) This Order may be cited as the Banking Act 2009 (Commencement No 1) Order 2009.

(2) In this Order, "the Act" means the Banking Act 2009.

2 Provisions conferring power to make secondary legislation etc

To the extent that the provisions in the Schedule to this Order confer or relate to the power to make subordinate legislation or codes of practice, those provisions come into force on 17th February 2009 for the purpose of enabling subordinate legislation or codes of practice to be made; but no such subordinate legislation or codes of practice may come into force before 21st February 2009.

3 Provisions of the Act coming into force on 21st February 2009

The provisions of the Act listed in the Schedule to this Order come into force on 21st February 2009.

SCHEDULE

1. Sections 1 to 89 (Part 1 of the Act: the special resolution regime)

2. Sections 90 to 135 (Part 2 of the Act: bank insolvency)

3. Sections 136 to 168 (Part 3 of the Act: bank administration)

4. Sections 169, 171, and 173 to 180 (provisions relating to the Financial Services Compensation Scheme)

5. Sections 228 to 231 (Treasury support for banks)

6. Sections 232 to 236 (investment banks)

7. Section 237 (Banking (Special Provisions) Act 2008, compensation: valuer)

8. Sections 244 to 247 (provisions relating to the Bank of England)

9. Sections 248 to 250 (provisions relating to the Financial Services Authority)

10. Section 251 (financial assistance to building societies)

11. Sections 252 and 253 (registration of charges and registration of charges: Scotland)

12. Section 257 (meaning of "financial assistance")

13. Section 258 (meaning of "enactment")

14. Section 259 (statutory instruments)

APPENDIX

15. Section 260 (money)

16. Section 261(index of defined terms)

17. Section 262 (repeal)

[A1]

KAUPTHING SINGER & FRIEDLANDER LIMITED TRANSFER OF CERTAIN RIGHTS AND LIABILITIES (AMENDMENT) ORDER 2009

(SI 2009/308)

NOTES
Made: 18 February 2009.
Authority: Banking (Special Provisions) Act 2008, ss 6, 8, 12, 13(2), Sch 2.
Commencement: 20 February 2009.

1 Citation and commencement

(1) This Order may be cited as the Kaupthing Singer & Friedlander Limited Transfer of Certain Rights and Liabilities (Amendment) Order 2009.

(2) This Order comes into force on 20th February 2009.

2 Amendments to the Kaupthing Singer & Friedlander Limited Transfer of Certain Rights and Liabilities Order 2008

The Kaupthing Singer & Friedlander Limited Transfer of Certain Rights and Liabilities Order 2008 is amended as follows—

(a) in article 14—
   (i) in paragraph (1), for "(net of all costs and liabilities incurred by Deposits Management (Edge)) in connection with the first or second transfer or its obligations under this Order" substitute "(net of all costs and liabilities incurred by Deposits Management (Edge) in connection with the first or second transfer or its obligations under this Order)";
   (ii) after paragraph (5), insert—

   "(5A) If the Treasury, the FSCS, Kaupthing and ING agree that it is not appropriate or reasonable to make (or to continue to make) the revisions specified in paragraph (5)(a) and (b), no revision (or no further revision) may be made under those provisions.";

(b) in article 16(5), for "relevant qualifying deposit" substitute "relevant protected deposit";

(c) in article 21(11)(c), omit the words from "and the Treasury" to the end.

[A2]

HERITABLE BANK PLC TRANSFER OF CERTAIN RIGHTS AND LIABILITIES (AMENDMENT) ORDER 2009

(SI 2009/310)

NOTES
Made: 18 February 2009.
Authority: Banking (Special Provisions) Act 2008, ss 6, 12, 13(2), 14(2), (3), Sch 2.
Commencement: 20 February 2009.

1 Citation, commencement and interpretation

(1) This Order may be cited as the Heritable Bank plc Transfer of Certain Rights and Liabilities (Amendment) Order 2009.

(2) This Order comes into force on 20th February 2009.

(3) In this Order—
   "the first transfer order" means the Heritable Bank plc Transfer of Certain Rights and Liabilities Order 2008;

"the second transfer order" means the Transfer of Rights and Liabilities to ING Order 2008.

(4)   Terms used in this Order which are defined by the first or second transfer order have the meanings given in that order.

2 Balancing payments

If the Treasury, the FSCS, Heritable and ING agree that it is not appropriate or reasonable to make (or to continue to make) the revisions specified in article 13(5)(a) and (b) of the first transfer order, no revision (or no further revision) may be made under those provisions.

3 Costs and expenses of administrator

In article 23(1) of the first transfer order, the reference to the Treasury shall, from the effective time (within the meaning of the second transfer order), have effect as if it was a reference to ING.

4 Amendments to the first transfer order

(1)   The first transfer order is amended as follows—
   (a)   in article 15(1), for "effective date" substitute "effective time";
   (b)   in article 23(1), for "article 20(1)" substitute "article 20".

(2)   The amendment made in paragraph (1)(b) has effect from the time at which the first transfer order came into force.

[A3]

BANKING ACT 2009 (BANK ADMINISTRATION) (MODIFICATION FOR APPLICATION TO BANKS IN TEMPORARY PUBLIC OWNERSHIP) REGULATIONS 2009

(SI 2009/312)

NOTES
Made: 19 February 2009.
Authority: Banking Act 2009, ss 152(3), 259(1).
Commencement: 21 February 2009.

1 Citation, commencement and interpretation

(1)   These Regulations may be cited as the Banking Act 2009 (Bank Administration) (Modification for Application to Banks in Temporary Public Ownership) Regulations 2009 and come into force on 21st February 2009.

(2)   In these Regulations—
   "the Act" means the Banking Act 2009;
   "onward public sector transferee" means a transferee under a property transfer order by virtue of section 45(2) of the Act who is a company wholly owned by—
      (a)   the Bank of England,
      (b)   the Treasury, or
      (c)   a nominee of the Treasury;
   "private sector transferee" means a transferee under a property transfer order by virtue of section 45(2) of the Act who is not an onward public sector transferee.

2 Application following transfer of bank etc to temporary public ownership

(1)   These Regulations make modifications to Part 3 of the Act (bank administration) as applied by section 152(2) of the Act (which applies Part 3 to banks where the Treasury has made a share transfer order to transfer the securities of a bank or a bank's holding company into temporary public ownership, and makes a property transfer order in respect of that bank to transfer property from the bank to another person).

(2)   Regulations 3 and 4 make general modifications.

(3)   The Tables in the Schedule make modifications to the specific provisions listed within them.

3 General modifications to Part 3 of the Act

In Part 3 of the Act a reference to—
   "the Bank of England" is a reference to "the Treasury" (unless otherwise specified in the Schedule);
   "a property transfer instrument" is a reference to "a property transfer order".

4 General modifications to Tables 1 and 2 of section 145

In Tables 1 and 2 of section 145 of the Act (which apply provisions of the Insolvency Act 1986 in relation to bank administration), in addition to the modifications made by Regulation 3, a reference to "a bridge bank" is a reference to "an onward public sector transferee".

SCHEDULE
SPECIFIC MODIFICATIONS

Table 1: Modifications to sections of Part 3 of the Act

Regulation 2

Section and subject	Modification or Comment
136 Overview	For subsection (2)(a) substitute—
	"(a) it is used where—
	(i) a bank or a bank holding company has been transferred into temporary public ownership in accordance with section 13(2) (including as applied by section 82(1)), and
	(ii) the Treasury make a property transfer order in accordance with section 45(2) to transfer part of the business of a bank to a private sector transferee or an onward public sector transferee,
	and it can also be used in certain cases of multiple transfers under Part 1.".
	In subsection (2)(c) for "the commercial purchaser ("private sector purchaser") or the transferee ("the bridge bank")" substitute "the private sector transferee or the onward public sector transferee".
137 Objectives	In subsection (1)(a) for "commercial purchaser or bridge bank" substitute "the private sector transferee or the onward public sector transferee".
138 Objective 1: supporting private sector purchaser or bridge bank	For the heading, substitute "Objective 1: supporting the private sector transferee or onward public sector transferee".
	In subsection (1) for "private sector purchaser or bridge bank" substitute "the private sector transferee or onward public sector transferee".
	In subsection (3) for—
	(a) "a private sector purchase" substitute "a transfer to a private sector transferee";
	(b) "private sector purchaser" substitute "private sector transferee" (in each place).
	In subsection (4) for "bridge bank" substitute "a company wholly owned by the Bank of England".
	Regulation 3 does not apply to subsection (4).
	After subsection (4) insert—
	"(4A) In the case of bank administration following a transfer from a bank in temporary public ownership to a company wholly owned by the Treasury or a nominee of the Treasury ("the company"), the bank administrator must co-operate with any request of the Treasury to enter into an agreement for the residual bank to provide services or facilities to the company; and—
	(a) the bank administrator must avoid action that is likely to prejudice performance by the residual bank of its obligations in accordance with an agreement,

Section and subject	Modification or Comment
	(b) the bank administrator must ensure that so far as is reasonably practicable an agreement includes provision for consideration at market rate,
	(c) paragraph (b) does not prevent the bank administrator from entering into an agreement on any terms that the bank administrator thinks necessary in pursuit of Objective 1, and
	(d) this subsection does not apply after Objective 1 ceases.".
139 Objective 1: duration	In subsections (1) and (3) for "private sector purchaser or bridge bank" substitute "the private sector transferee or the onward public sector transferee".
140 Objective 2: "normal" administration	In subsection (3) for "bridge bank" substitute "the onward public sector transferee".
143 Grounds for applying	In subsection (2) for "section 11(2) or 12(2)" substitute "section 45(2)".
148 Sharing information	Section 148 is applied following a transfer to a company wholly owned by the Bank of England with the following modifications—
	(a) for subsection (2) substitute—
	"(2) Within the period of 5 days beginning with the day on which the bank administrator is appointed, the Bank of England must give the bank administrator information about the financial position of the company wholly owned by the Bank and the Treasury must give the bank administrator information about the financial position of the residual bank.";
	(b) in subsection (3) for "bridge bank" substitute "company wholly owned by the Bank of England" (in each place);
	(c) in subsection (4)(a), (b) and (e) after "Bank of England" or "the Bank" add "and the Treasury" (in each place);
	(d) in subsection (4)(c), (d) and (e) for "bridge bank" substitute "the company wholly owned by the Bank of England and the Treasury" (in each place).
	Section 148 is applied following a transfer to a company wholly owned by the Treasury or a nominee of the Treasury with the following modifications—
	(e) for "bridge bank" substitute "a company wholly owned by the Treasury or a nominee of the Treasury" (in each place);
	(f) for "Bank of England" substitute "the Treasury" (in each place).
150 Bridge bank to private sector purchaser	For the heading, substitute "Onward public sector transferee: company wholly owned by the Treasury or a nominee of the Treasury to private purchaser".
	Section 150 is applied following a transfer to a company wholly owned by the Treasury or a nominee of the Treasury with the following modifications—
	(g) for "bridge bank" substitute "a company wholly owned by the Treasury or a nominee of the Treasury" (in each place);
	(h) for "Bank of England" substitute "the Treasury" (in each place).

APPENDIX

Section and subject	Modification or Comment
151 Property transfer from bridge bank	Ignore.
157 Other processes	For subsection (2)(a) substitute— "(a) "residual bank" means a bank all or part of whose business has been transferred to a private sector transferee or an onward public sector transferee in accordance with section 45(2),".

Table 2: Modifications to Table 1 of Applied Provisions in section 145 of the Act: Schedule B1 to the Insolvency Act 1986

Provision of Schedule B1	Subject	Modification or comment
Para 49	Administrator's proposals	Ignore paragraph (c) of the Table.
Paras 50–58	Creditors' meeting	For paragraph (d) of the Table substitute— "(d) Until that time a committee shall have the functions of the creditors committee. The committee shall be formed of 3 individuals, one nominated by each of— (i) the Treasury, (ii) the Bank of England, and (iii) the FSA.".

[A4]

BANKING ACT 2009 (BANK ADMINISTRATION) (MODIFICATION FOR APPLICATION TO MULTIPLE TRANSFERS) REGULATIONS 2009

(SI 2009/313)

NOTES

Made: 19 February 2009.
Authority: Banking Act 2009, ss 149(3), 259(1).
Commencement: 21 February 2009.

1 Citation, commencement and interpretation

(1) These Regulations may be cited as the Banking Act 2009 (Bank Administration) (Modification for Application to Multiple Transfers) Regulations 2009 and come into force on 21st February 2009.

(2) In these Regulations—
"the Act" means the Banking Act 2009;
"a bank in temporary public ownership" is a reference to a bank wholly owned by the Treasury or a nominee of the Treasury;
"onward public sector transferee" means a transferee under a property transfer order by virtue of section 45(2) of the Act who is a company wholly owned by—
    (a)   the Bank of England,
    (b)   the Treasury, or
    (c)   a nominee of the Treasury;
"private sector transferee" means a transferee under a property transfer order by virtue of section 45(2) of the Act who is not an onward public sector transferee;
"property transfer instrument" has the meaning given by section 149(2) of the Act.

2 Modification of Part 3 where more than one property transfer instrument is made (other than in respect of a bank in temporary public ownership)

The modifications of Part 3 of the Act listed in the Table to the Schedule apply where—
- (a)   the Bank of England makes more than one property transfer instrument in respect of a bank, and
- (b)   Part 3 applies to the bank by virtue of section 149 of the Act.

3 Modification of Part 3 where more than one property transfer instrument is made in respect of a bank in temporary public ownership

(1)   The modifications of Part 3 of the Act listed in the Table to the Schedule apply with the general modifications specified in paragraph (2) where—
- (a)   the Treasury make a share transfer order, in respect of the securities issued by a bank (or a bank's holding company), in accordance with section 13(2) of the Act,
- (b)   the Treasury make more than one property transfer instrument in respect of the bank under section 45(2) of the Act, and
- (c)   Part 3 applies to the bank by virtue of section 149 and 152 of the Act.

(2)   The general modifications to the Table to the Schedule are—
- (a)   a reference to "the Bank of England" is a reference to "the Treasury";
- (b)   a reference to a "private sector purchaser" is a reference to a "private sector transferee";
- (c)   a reference to a "bridge bank" is a reference to an "onward public sector transferee".

SCHEDULES

SCHEDULE 1
MODIFICATIONS

Regulations 2 and 3

Table: Modifications to Part 3 of the Act

Section and subject	Modification or comment
138 Objective 1: supporting private sector purchaser or bridge bank	After section 138, insert—
	"138A Objective 1: Application where more than one property transfer instrument is made—
	(1) Where more than one property transfer instrument is made and business is transferred from a bank to more than one transferee, Objective 1 is to be pursued in relation to each private sector purchaser or bridge bank who, in the opinion of the Bank of England, is to be supplied with such services and facilities as are required to enable it to operate effectively.
	(2) Where the bank administrator considers that the supply to one private sector purchaser or bridge bank of services and facilities may prejudice the supply of services and facilities to another transferee, the bank administrator—
	(a) must consult with the Bank of England, and the Bank of England may give directions to the bank administrator regarding the supply of services and facilities to transferees,
	(b) shall pursue Objective 1 in respect of each transferee in so far as is reasonably practicable in the circumstances, and
	(c) may apply to the court for directions under paragraph 63 of Schedule B1 to the Insolvency Act 1986 (applied by section 145 below) if unsure whether to pursue a proposed action.".
139 Objective 1: duration	In subsections (1) and (3) for "with the", substitute "with any".
	After subsection (1), insert—

Section and subject	Modification or comment
	"(1A) The obligations of Objective 1 cease to apply in respect of a particular private sector purchaser or bridge bank if the Bank of England notifies the bank administrator that the residual bank is no longer required in connection with that private sector purchaser or bridge bank.". After subsection (2), add— "(2A) A bank administrator who thinks that Objective 1 is no longer required in respect of a particular private sector purchaser or bridge bank may apply to court for directions under paragraph 63 of Schedule B1 to the Insolvency Act (applied by section 145 below); and the court may direct the Bank of England to consider whether to give notice under subsection (1A) above.".
143 Grounds for applying	In subsection (2) for "a property transfer instrument" substitute "one or more property transfer instruments". In subsection (3)(b) after "property transfer instrument" add "or instruments".
150 Bridge bank to private sector purchaser	For subsection (1)(a), substitute— "(a) notice under section 139(1A) that the residual bank is no longer required in connection with a bridge bank, and". In subsection (2) for "An Objective 1 Achievement Notice", substitute "A notice under section 139(1A)". For subsection (5), substitute— "(5) When the Bank of England gives a notice to the bank administrator that Objective 1 is no longer required to be pursued in respect of a commercial purchaser who has acquired all or part of the business of the bridge bank, the Bank of England may give the bank administrator an Objective 1 Achievement Notice only if the residual bank is no longer required in connection with any private sector purchaser or bridge bank, and section 139 and other provisions of this Part which refer to the giving of an Objective 1 Achievement Notice shall have effect.".

NOTES

Note: these Regulations are reproduced as per the Queen's Printer's copy, ie, there is no Schedule 2.

[A5]

BANK ADMINISTRATION (SHARING INFORMATION) REGULATIONS 2009

(SI 2009/314)

NOTES

Made: 19 February 2009.
Authority: Banking Act 2009, ss 148(5), 259(1).
Commencement: 21 February 2009.

1 Citation and commencement

These Regulations may be cited as the Bank Administration (Sharing Information) Regulations 2009 and come into force on 21st February 2009.

2 Interpretation

In these Regulations—

"the Act" means the Banking Act 2009;

"HMRC" means Her Majesty's Revenue and Customs;

"Objective 1" means the first objective of bank administration as defined in sections 137 and 138 of the Act;

"order" means a bank administration order (see section 141 of the Act);

"original bank" means a bank as it existed before a property transfer instrument was made in relation to it;

"residual bank"—

in Regulations 5 to 10, has the meaning given by section 157(2) of the Act;

in the Schedule, means a bank in temporary public ownership all or part of whose business has been transferred in accordance with a property transfer order made under section 45(2) of the Act;

"transferred business"—

(a) in Regulations 5 to 10, means the part of an original bank's business transferred under a property transfer instrument;

(b) in the Schedule, means the part of the bank in temporary public ownership's business transferred in accordance with a property transfer order made under section 45(2) of the Act.

3 Application to bank administration following transfer to a bridge bank

Regulations 5 to 10 apply to bank administration following a transfer to a bridge bank in accordance with sections 12 and 148(1) of the Act.

4 Application to bank administration where Part 3 is applied by section 152 of the Act

(1) Regulations 5 to 10 apply, with the modifications specified in Tables 1 and 2 of the Schedule, to bank administration following a transfer of business from a bank in temporary public ownership.

(2) Table 1 applies in cases where section 148 is applied following a transfer from a bank in temporary public ownership to a company wholly owned by the Bank of England.

(3) Table 2 applies in cases where section 148 is applied following a transfer from a bank in temporary public ownership to a company wholly owned by the Treasury or a nominee of the Treasury.

5 Information to be provided to the bank administrator appointed in the first 5 days of the bank administration

(1) This regulation applies where—

(a) the bank administrator has been appointed by the order, or

(b) the bank administrator has been appointed to replace the bank administrator appointed by the order (or where joint administrators were appointed, to replace all of them) within 5 days of the order being made.

(2) The classes of information that must be provided by the Bank of England to the bank administrator under section 148(2) of the Act, within the period of 5 days beginning with the day on which the bank administrator is appointed, are—

(a) an estimate of the net value of the original bank,

(b) an estimate of the net value of the bridge bank,

(c) a list of assets and liabilities of the original bank that have been transferred to the bridge bank, including details of—

(i) any charged assets and the creditors holding those charges,

(ii) any contingent assets transferred to the bridge bank, and

(iii) any liabilities (including contingent liabilities), and

(d) details of any supplemental property transfers or reverse property transfers that have been made,

in each case as comprehensive as is reasonably possible and current as at the date it is provided.

6 Information to be provided to the bank administrator otherwise

(1) This regulation applies where the bank administrator has been appointed otherwise than as described in regulation 5(1).

(2) The classes of information that must be provided by the Bank of England to the bank administrator under section 148(2) of the Act, within the period of 5 days beginning with the day on which the bank administrator is appointed, are—

(a) details of the net value of the bridge bank, current as at the date on which the information is provided, and

(b) an outline of the information provided to a former bank administrator under section 148(2) of the Act, and, where the matters to which that information relates have changed, updated information, current as at the date on which the information is provided.

7 Information to be provided on request by the bridge bank to the bank administrator

The classes of information that must be provided by the bridge bank to the bank administrator on request under section 148(3) of the Act are—

(a) details as to the net value of the bridge bank, management accounts and other information including ledgers, cash books, bank statements, invoices and orders in relation to the transferred business current as at the date on which the information is provided,

(b) details of any supplemental property transfers or reverse property transfers that have been made, and

(c) details of any amounts of money to be paid to the residual bank from a scheme established by a resolution fund order.

8 Information to be provided on request by the bank administrator to the Bank of England

The classes of information that must be provided by the bank administrator to the Bank of England on request under section 148(4)(a) of the Act are as follows—

(a) information required in connection with the Bank of England's role under Part 3 of the Act and under rules made under section 411 of the Insolvency Act 1986 in respect of Part 3,

(b) information regarding the bank administrator's plans for the administration of the residual bank, further to any information provided in the bank administrator's statement of proposals, that may have an impact on the residual bank's ability to meet Objective 1,

(c) information regarding the residual bank's employees, assets and liabilities and its relationships with suppliers that may have an impact on the residual bank's ability to meet Objective 1,

(d) information about—
    (i) wrongful trading (see section 213 of the Insolvency Act 1986),
    (ii) fraudulent trading (see section 214 of the Insolvency Act 1986), or
    (iii) negligence,

carried out by the directors of the original bank and identified by the bank administrator,

(e) information about any steps taken by the bank administrator in respect of a director of the original bank under the Company Directors Disqualification Act 1986, and

(f) information about any litigation that the bank administrator is pursuing on behalf of the residual bank.

9 Information to be provided on request by the bank administrator to the bridge bank

The classes of information that must be provided by the bank administrator to the bridge bank on request under section 148(4)(c) of the Act are—

(a) statutory accounts, management accounts and other information including ledgers, cash books, bank statements, invoices and orders in relation to the transferred business,

(b) the following information relating to the transferred business—
    (i) financial information relating to property, rights and liabilities,
    (ii) personnel records, salary information etc relating to employees, and
    (iii) details of any licenses, permissions, approvals and intellectual property rights.

(c) information in relation to contracts, the rights and obligations of which have been transferred to the bridge bank,

(d) information required by public or regulatory bodies (in the United Kingdom and overseas) including FSA or HMRC,

(e) information about customers and suppliers which are part of the transferred business,

(f) information about target customers, channels to market, distribution networks and other marketing and sales material relating to the transferred business,

(g) information about the original bank's previous trading history required to prepare an investment memorandum,

(h) any other information a potential purchaser asks the bridge bank to provide, and

(i) information in connection with any agreement drawn up between the bank administrator and the bridge bank for the supply by the residual bank of services and facilities to the bridge bank.

10 Records to be made accessible by the bank administrator

The class of records that the bank administrator must allow the Bank of England and the bridge bank access to under section 148(4)(b) and (d) of the Act is any records required in connection with the classes of information specified in regulations 8 and 9, whether in hard copy or in electronic form.

SCHEDULE

Regulation 4

Table 1: Modifications to Regulations 5 to 10 in cases where section 148 is applied following a transfer from a bank in temporary public ownership to a company wholly owned by the Bank of England

Regulation	Modification or Comment
5	For paragraph (2) substitute—
	"(2) The classes of information that must be provided by the Treasury to the bank administrator under section 148(2) of the Act, within the period of 5 days beginning with the day on which the bank administrator is appointed, are—
	(a) an estimate of the net value of the bank before the transfer of property in accordance with a property transfer order made under section 45(2) of the Act,
	(b) a list of assets and liabilities of the residual bank that have been transferred to the company wholly owned by the Bank of England, including details of—
	(i) any charged assets and the creditors holding those charges,
	(ii) any contingent assets transferred to the company wholly owned by the Bank of England, and
	(iii) any liabilities (including contingent liabilities), and
	(c) details of any supplemental property transfers or reverse property transfers that have been made,
	in each case as comprehensive as is reasonably possible and current as at the date it is provided."
	After paragraph (2) insert—
	"(3) The Bank of England must provide to the bank administrator, within the period of 5 days beginning with the day on which the bank administrator is appointed, an estimate of the net value of the company wholly owned by the Bank of England, as comprehensive as is reasonably possible and current as at the date it is provided."
6	For paragraph (2) substitute—
	"(2) The classes of information that must be provided by the Bank of England to the bank administrator under section 148(2) of the Act, within the period of 5 days beginning with the day on which the bank administrator is appointed, are—
	(a) details of the net value of the company wholly owned by the Bank of England, current as at the date on which the information is provided, and
	(b) an outline of the information provided to a former bank administrator under section 148(2) of the Act, and, where the matters to which that information relates have changed, updated information, current as at the date on which the information is provided.".
	After paragraph (2) insert—
	"(3) The Treasury must provide to the bank administrator, within the period of 5 days beginning with the day on which the bank administrator is appointed, an outline of the information provided to a former bank administrator under section 148(2) of the Act, and, where the matters to which that information relates have changed, updated information, current as at the date on which the information is provided.".
7	For the heading, substitute "Information to be provided on request by the company wholly owned by the Bank of England to the bank administrator".
	For "bridge bank" substitute "company wholly owned by the Bank of England" (in each case).
	Ignore sub-paragraph (c).

Regulation	Modification or Comment
8	For the heading, substitute "Information to be provided on request by the bank administrator to the Treasury and the Bank of England".
	After "Bank of England" insert "and the Treasury".
	In sub-paragraph (a) after "Bank of England's" insert "or the Treasury's".
	In sub-paragraphs (d) and (e) substitute "original bank" for residual bank".
9	For the heading, substitute "Information to be provided on request by the bank administrator to the Treasury and the company wholly owned by the Bank of England"
	In Regulation 9 (other than in sub-paragraphs (h) and (i)) for "bridge bank" substitute "company wholly owned by the Bank of England and the Treasury".
	In sub-paragraphs (h) and (i) for "bridge bank" substitute "company wholly owned by the Bank of England" (in each place).
	In sub-paragraph (g) for "original bank" substitute "residual bank".
10	For "the Bank of England and the bridge bank" substitute "the Treasury, the Bank of England and the company wholly owned by the Bank of England".

Table 2: Modifications to Regulations 5 to 10 in cases where section 148 is applied following a transfer from a bank in temporary public ownership to a company wholly owned by the Treasury or a nominee of the Treasury

Regulation	Modification or Comment
5 to 10	For "the Bank of England" substitute "the Treasury" (in each place).
	For "bridge bank" substitute "company wholly owned by the Treasury or a nominee of the Treasury" (in each place).
	For "original bank" substitute "residual bank" (within the meaning of sub-paragraph (b) of the definition of "residual bank" in Regulation 2).
7	Ignore sub-paragraph (c).

[A6]

BANKING ACT 2009 (PARTS 2 AND 3 CONSEQUENTIAL AMENDMENTS) ORDER 2009

(SI 2009/317)

NOTES
Made: 19 February 2009.
Authority: Banking Act 2009, ss 135, 168.
Commencement: 21 February 2009.

PART 1
INTRODUCTION

1 Citation and commencement

This Order may be cited as the Banking Act 2009 (Parts 2 and 3 Consequential Amendments) Order 2009 and comes into force on 21st February 2009.

2 Interpretation

In this Order—
    "the 2009 Act" means the Banking Act 2009.

PART 2
GENERAL MODIFICATIONS TO LEGISLATION

3.—(1) So far as the enactments set out in the Schedule ("the listed enactments") apply in relation to liquidation and administration, they apply with the modifications set out in paragraphs (2) to (4).

(2) The modifications relating to bank insolvency under Part 2 of the 2009 Act are that references to—

(a) "liquidator" include a reference to a bank liquidator under Part 2 of the 2009 Act;

(b) "provisional liquidator" include a reference to a provisional bank liquidator under Part 2 of the 2009 Act;

(c) "liquidation" or "insolvent liquidation" include a reference to bank insolvency under Part 2 of the 2009 Act;

(d) "winding up" or "winding up by the court" include a reference to bank insolvency under Part 2 of the 2009 Act (and a reference to the "commencement of winding up" in this context is to the commencement of bank insolvency);

(e) "winding up order" include a reference to a bank insolvency order under Part 2 of the 2009 Act;

(f) "wound up" include a reference to a bank having been put into bank insolvency under Part 2 of the 2009 Act; and

(g) "winding up petition" or "petition to wind up" include an application for bank insolvency under Part 2 of the 2009 Act.

(3) The modifications relating to bank administration under Part 3 of the 2009 Act are that references to—

(a) "administrator" include a reference to a bank administrator under Part 3 of the 2009 Act;

(b) "administration" or "insolvent administration" include a reference to a bank administration under Part 3 of the 2009 Act;

(c) "administration order" include a reference to a bank administration order under Part 3 of the 2009 Act; and

(d) "provisional liquidator" include a reference to a provisional bank administrator under Part 3 of the 2009 Act.

(4) The modifications relating to bank insolvency or bank administration under Parts 2 and 3 of the 2009 Act are that references to—

(a) "insolvency legislation" or "the law of insolvency" include Parts 2 and 3 of the 2009 Act and the provisions of the Insolvency Act 1986 and the Insolvency (Northern Ireland) Order 1989 as applied by those Parts;

(b) a person acting as an "insolvency practitioner" (as defined in section 388 of the Insolvency Act 1986) include a person acting as a bank liquidator or bank administrator under Parts 2 and 3 of the 2009 Act;

(c) the provisions of the Insolvency Act 1986 and the Insolvency (Northern Ireland) Order 1989, in the context of bank insolvency or bank administration, shall be read to include those provisions as applied and modified by sections 103 and 145 of the 2009 Act; and

(d) the provisions of the Insolvency Rules 1986, the Insolvency Rules (Northern Ireland) 1991 and the Insolvency (Scotland) Rules 1986, in the context of bank insolvency or bank administration, shall be read to include those provisions as applied and modified by rules made under section 411(1A) of the Insolvency Act 1986 in relation to bank insolvency, and under section 411(1B) of the Insolvency Act 1986 in relation to bank administration.

PART 3
SPECIFIC MODIFICATIONS AND AMENDMENTS TO LEGISLATION

4 Finance (No 2) Act 1992

(1) The following provision of the Finance (No 2) Act 1992 applies with the modification set out in this article.

(2) Paragraph 2 of Schedule 12 (Banks etc in Compulsory Liquidation) is to be read as if it included the following—

"(3A) Where the company is a bank (as defined in section 91 of the Banking Act 2009), bank insolvency proceedings shall be taken to have commenced against the bank when the application for a bank insolvency order is made to the court under section 95 of the Banking Act 2009.".

5 Financial Services and Markets Act 2000

(1) The following provisions of the Financial Services and Markets Act 2000 apply with the modifications set out in this article.

APPENDIX

(2) In section 215 (Rights of the scheme in relevant person's insolvency)—

    (a) in subsection (3), the reference to making an administration application is to be read as including making an application for a bank administration order under section 142 of the 2009 Act, and

    (b) subsection (4) is to be read as if it read the following—

"(4) In the case of a bank insolvency (as defined in Part 2 of the Banking Act 2009), if the scheme manager decides, pursuant to section 100(6)(d) of that Act, not to remain on the liquidation committee, the scheme manager shall retain the rights it usually enjoys in respect of the winding up of a relevant person under section 371(3) and (4).".

(3) In section 355 (Interpretation of Part 24), the definition of "court" is to be read as if ", unless otherwise provided," were inserted after the word "means".

(4) In section 361 (Administrator's duty to report to Authority), references to—

    (a) "administration" are to be read as including a reference to bank administration under Part 3 of the 2009 Act; and

    (b) "the administrator" are to be read as including the bank administrator under Part 3 of the 2009 Act.

(5) In section 362 (Authority's powers to participate in proceedings)—

    (a) references to "court"—

        (i) in the context of a bank administration under Part 3 of the 2009 Act in England, Wales or Northern Ireland, are to be read as meaning the High Court, and

        (ii) in the context of a bank administration under Part 3 of the 2009 Act in Scotland, are to be read as meaning the Court of Session,

    (b) in subsection (1), the reference to making an administration application is to be read as including making an application for a bank administration order under section 142 of the 2009 Act, and

    (c) in subsections (4) and (4A), references to paragraph 74 of Schedule B1 to the Insolvency Act 1986 and paragraph 75 of Schedule B1 to the Insolvency (Northern Ireland) Order 1989 are to be read as including references to those provisions as applied and modified by section 145 of the 2009 Act.

(6) In section 370 (Liquidator's duty to report to Authority), references to "liquidator" are to be read as including a reference to a bank liquidator under Part 2 of the 2009 Act.

(7) In section 375 (Authority's right to apply for an order), references to the provisions of the Insolvency Act 1986 and the Insolvency (Northern Ireland) Order 1989 are to be read as including references to those provisions as applied and modified by section 103 and section 134 of the 2009 Act.

6 Companies Act 2006

(1) The following provisions of the Companies Act 2006 apply with the modifications set out in this article.

(2) In section 461 (permitted disclosure of information obtained under compulsory powers)—

    (a) subsection (4)(c) is to be read so as to include the 2009 Act in the list of enactments in that subsection;

    (b) in subsection (4)(g) is to be read so as to include the 2009 Act in the list of enactments in that subsection.

(3) Any references in Part 35 (the registrar of companies) to the Insolvency Act 1986 and the Insolvency (Northern Ireland) Order 1989 are to be read as including a reference to Parts 2 and 3 of the 2009 Act.

(4) Where an application is made to the court for—

    (a) a bank insolvency order under Part 2 of the 2009 Act,

    (b) the appointment of a provisional bank liquidator under section 135 of the Insolvency Act 1986 or article 115 of the Insolvency (Northern Ireland) Order 1989, as applied by section 103 of the 2009 Act,

    (c) a bank administration order under Part 3 of the 2009 Act, or

    (d) the appointment of a provisional bank administrator under section 135 of the Insolvency Act 1986 or article 115 of the Insolvency (Northern Ireland) Order 1989, as applied by section 145 of the 2009 Act,

sections 1139 and 1140 (service of documents on company, directors, secretaries and others) have effect subject to the provisions for service set out in Parts 2 or 3 of the 2009 Act and in rules made under section 411 of the Insolvency Act 1986 in respect of those Parts.

(5) In Part 2 of Schedule 2 (Specified Descriptions of Disclosures)—

    (a) paragraph 25 is to be read so as to include the 2009 Act in the list of enactments in that paragraph, and

    (b) paragraph 46 is to be read so as to include the 2009 Act in the list of enactments in that paragraph.

(6)   In Part 2 of Schedule 11A (Specified Descriptions of Disclosures)—
- (a)   paragraph 30 is to be read so as to include the 2009 Act in the list of enactments in that paragraph, and
- (b)   paragraph 52 is to be read so as to include the 2009 Act in the list of enactments in that paragraph.

7 Dormant Bank and Building Society Accounts Act 2008

(1)   This article applies to a reclaim fund established under the Dormant Bank and Building Society Accounts Act 2008 if, under sections 1 or 2 of that Act, the balance of a customer's dormant account is transferred into that reclaim fund from a bank which is a bank within the meaning of section 91 of the 2009 Act.

(2)   Where that reclaim fund is unable, or likely to be unable, to satisfy a claim against it, the fact that it ceases to be authorised does not prevent the operation of the Financial Services Compensation Scheme under section 213 of the Financial Services and Markets Act 2000 in respect of it; and for that purpose, the reclaim fund is a relevant person within the meaning of section 213(9), despite the lapse of authorisation.

8 Pension Protection Fund (Entry Rules) Regulations 2005

(1)   The Pension Protection Fund (Entry Rules) Regulations 2005 are amended as follows.

(2)   In regulation 6 (Circumstances in which insolvency proceedings in relation to the employer are stayed or come to an end), after paragraph (1)(a)(v) insert—

> "(vi)   where the company is a bank (as defined in section 91 of the Banking Act 2009), the bank insolvency procedure is stayed under section 130 of the Insolvency Act 1986 (as applied by section 103 of the Banking Act 2009), or the bank insolvency order is rescinded or discharged, except in circumstances where the court has made an administration order in accordance with section 114 of the Banking Act 2009.".

9   *(Modification of the Pension Protection Fund (Entry Rules) Regulations (Northern Ireland) 2005 (outside the scope of this work).)*

SCHEDULE
LEGISLATION SUBJECT TO THE GENERAL MODIFICATIONS IN PART 2
Article 3(1)

Primary Legislation

Taxes Management Act 1970

Prescription and Limitation (Scotland) Act 1973

Companies Act 1985

Companies (Northern Ireland) Order 1986

Debtors (Scotland) Act 1987

Income and Corporation Taxes Act 1988

Companies Act 1989

Companies (No 2) (Northern Ireland) Order 1990

Taxation of Chargeable Gains Act 1992

Finance (No 2) Act 1992

Pension Schemes Act 1993

Pension Schemes (Northern Ireland) Act 1993

Pensions Act 1995

Pensions (Northern Ireland) Order 1995

Proceeds of Crime (Scotland) Act 1995

Finance Act 1996

Employment Rights Act 1996

Employment Rights (Northern Ireland) Order 1996

Terrorism Act 2000

Finance Act 2000

International Criminal Court Act 2001

International Criminal Court (Scotland) Act 2001

Finance Act 2002

APPENDIX

Proceeds of Crime Act 2002

Debt Arrangement and Attachment (Scotland) Act 2002

Finance Act 2003

Pensions Act 2004

Pensions (Northern Ireland) Order 2005

Companies Act 2006

Bankruptcy and Diligence (Scotland) Act 2007

Finance Act 2008

Dormant Bank and Building Society Accounts Act 2008

Secondary Legislation

Insolvent Companies (Disqualification of Unfit Directors) Proceedings Rules 1987

Financial Markets and Insolvency Regulations 1991

Financial Markets and Insolvency Regulations (Northern Ireland) 1991

Insolvency Regulations 1994

Non-Domestic Rating (Unoccupied Property) (Scotland) Regulations 1994

Insolvent Companies (Reports on Conduct of Directors) Rules 1996

Financial Markets and Insolvency Regulations 1996

Financial Markets and Insolvency Regulations (Northern Ireland) 1996

Individual Savings Account Regulations 1998

Corporation Tax (Simplified Arrangements for Group Relief) Regulations 1999

Financial Markets and Insolvency (Settlement Finality) Regulations 1999

Financial Collateral Arrangements (No 2) Regulations 2003

Insolvency Practitioners and Insolvency Services Account (Fees) Order 2003

Insolvent Companies (Reports on Conduct of Directors) Rules (Northern Ireland) 2003

Insolvent Companies (Disqualification of Unfit Directors) Proceedings Rules (Northern Ireland) 2003

Land Registration Rules 2003

Credit Institutions (Reorganisation and Winding Up) Regulations 2004

Insolvency Practitioners Regulations 2005

Pension Protection Fund (Entry Rules) Regulations 2005

Pension Protection Fund (Entry Rules) Regulations (Northern Ireland) 2005

Gender Recognition (Disclosure of Information) (England, Wales and Northern Ireland) Order 2005

Gender Recognition (Disclosure of Information) (Scotland) Order 2005

Financial Assistance Scheme Regulations 2005

Insolvency Practitioners Regulations (Northern Ireland) 2006

Insolvency Practitioners and Insolvency Account (Fees) Order (Northern Ireland) 2006

Land Registration (Scotland) Rules 2006

Companies (Cross-Border Mergers) Regulations 2007

Regulated Covered Bonds Regulations 2008

[A7]

BANKING ACT 2009 (THIRD PARTY COMPENSATION ARRANGEMENTS FOR PARTIAL PROPERTY TRANSFERS) REGULATIONS 2009

(SI 2009/319)

NOTES

Made: 19 February 2009.

Authority: Banking Act 2009, ss 60, 259(1).

Commencement: 21 February 2009.

1 Citation, commencement and interpretation

(1) These Regulations may be cited as the Banking Act 2009 (Third Party Compensation Arrangements for Partial Property Transfers) Regulations 2009.

(2) These Regulations come into force on 21st February 2009.

(3) In these Regulations—

"the Act" means the Banking Act 2009;

"the Bank" means the Bank of England;

"banking institution" means—

    (a)   a bank (within the meaning of Part 1 of the Act);

    (b)   a building society (within the meaning of section 119 of the Building Societies Act 1986); or

    (c)   a holding company;

"relevant time" means—

    (a)   in relation to Case 1 (as specified in regulation 2(2)), the time at which the partial property transfer took effect;

    (b)   in relation to Case 2 (as specified in regulation 2(3)), the time at which the property transfer instrument made in accordance with section 11(2) or 12(2) of the Act took effect;

    (c)   in relation to Case 3 (as specified in regulation 2(4)), the time at which the share transfer order made in accordance with section 13(2) of the Act (including that section as applied by section 82 of the Act) took effect;

"third party compensation order in relation to a partial property transfer" has the meaning given in regulation 3(2).

2 Application of these Regulations

(1) These Regulations apply in the following cases.

(2) Case 1 is where a partial property transfer has been made by the Bank in accordance with section 11(2) or 12(2) of the Act.

(3) Case 2 is where—

    (a)   the Bank has made a property transfer instrument in accordance with section 11(2) or 12(2) of the Act which is not a partial property transfer; but

    (b)   an onward property transfer instrument has been made by the Bank in accordance with section 43 of the Act which is a partial property transfer.

(4) Case 3 is where—

    (a)   the Treasury have made a share transfer order in accordance with section 13(2) of the Act (including that section as applied by section 82 of the Act); and

    (b)   a property transfer order has been made by the Treasury in accordance with section 45(2) of the Act (including that section as modified by section 83 of the Act) which by virtue of section 45(5)(b) of the Act is to be treated as a partial property transfer.

(5) For the purposes of these Regulations, a property transfer instrument or property transfer order which purports to transfer all property, rights and liabilities of an undertaking shall be treated as having done so effectively (and so shall not be treated as a partial property transfer), notwithstanding the possibility that any of the property, rights or liabilities are foreign property and may not have been effectively transferred by the property transfer instrument or order or by virtue of steps taken under section 39 of the Act.

3 Requirement to include a third party compensation order

(1) A compensation scheme order or a resolution fund order made in the cases in which these Regulations apply must include a third party compensation order.

(2) Regulations 4 to 9 set out provisions which must be included in a such a third party compensation order ("a third party compensation order in relation to a partial property transfer"); regulation 10 sets out provisions which may be included in such an order.

4 Mandatory provisions—appointment of independent valuer

A third party compensation order in relation to a partial property transfer must include provision for a person ("an independent valuer") to be appointed to determine—

    (a)   whether all pre-transfer creditors, a class of pre-transfer creditors or a particular pre-transfer creditor should be paid compensation; and

    (b)   if compensation should be paid, what amount is to be paid,

(and, by virtue of section 59(3)(a) of the Act, sections 54 to 56 (appointment etc of independent valuer) apply to the independent valuer appointed in accordance with this regulation).

APPENDIX

5 Mandatory provisions—assessment of insolvency treatment

(1) A third party compensation order in relation to a partial property transfer must include the following provisions (subject to any necessary modifications).

(2) The independent valuer must assess the treatment ("the insolvency treatment") which pre-transfer creditors would have received had the banking institution in relation to which or in connection with which the partial property transfer has been made entered insolvency immediately before the relevant time.

(3) The independent valuer must assess the treatment ("the actual treatment") which pre-transfer creditors have received, are receiving or are likely to receive (as specified in the order) if no (or no further) compensation is paid.

(4) If the independent valuer considers that, in relation to any pre-transfer creditor, the actual treatment assessed under paragraph (3) is less favourable than the insolvency treatment assessed under paragraph (2), the independent valuer must determine that compensation be paid to that pre-transfer creditor.

(5) The amount of compensation payable by virtue of paragraph (4) must be determined by the independent valuer by reference to the difference in treatment assessed under paragraph (4) and on the basis of the fair and equitable value of that difference in treatment.

6 Mandatory provisions—choice of insolvency process

A third party compensation order in relation to a partial property transfer must include either—

(a) a provision specifying that the independent valuer must assess the insolvency treatment as required under regulation 5(2) on the basis that the banking institution had entered a particular insolvency process specified in the order; or

(b) a provision specifying that the independent valuer must determine what insolvency process it is likely that the banking institution would have entered, had the following instrument or order not been made—

    (i) in the case of Case 1 (as specified in regulation 2(2)), the partial property transfer;

    (ii) in the case of Case 2 (as specified in regulation 2(3)), the property transfer instrument made in accordance with section 11(2) or 12(2) of the Act;

    (iii) in the case of Case 3 (as specified in regulation 2(4)), the share transfer order made in accordance with section 13(2) of the Act (including that section as applied by section 82 of the Act).

7 Mandatory provisions—valuation principles

(1) A third party compensation order in relation to a partial property transfer must include the following provisions (subject to any necessary modifications).

(2) In making the assessment of the insolvency treatment as required under regulation 5(2), the independent valuer must determine the amount of compensation in accordance with the following principles (in addition to the principle which applies by virtue of section 57(3) of the Act)—

    (a) that the banking institution in relation to which or in connection with which the partial property transfer has been made would have entered insolvency immediately before the relevant time;

    (b) that the partial property transfer has not been made and that no other order or instrument under Part 1 of the Act would have been made in relation to or in connection with the banking institution (or, in appropriate cases, any of the banking institutions);

    (c) that no financial assistance would have, after the relevant time, been provided by the Bank or the Treasury.

8 Mandatory provisions—interim payments

(1) A third party compensation order in relation to a partial property transfer must include the following provisions (subject to any necessary modifications).

(2) The independent valuer may determine that payments should be made to a pre-transfer creditor, a class of pre-transfer creditors or all pre-transfer creditors on account of compensation to be payable under the third party compensation order ("payments on account").

(3) The independent valuer may make such a determination at any time before the determination required by regulation 5(5) has been made.

(4) Once the determination required by regulation 5(5) has been made, the independent valuer must determine what balancing payments are appropriate to ensure that the pre-transfer creditor receives the amount of compensation determined under regulation 5(5) (and no more than that amount).

(5) Subject to paragraph (6), the independent valuer may make such provision as to payments on account as he thinks fit (including a requirement that payments be made in instalments).

(6) Payments on account must be made subject to the following conditions—

(a)   that the acceptance of such a payment by the pre-transfer creditor reduces any obligation (whether in existence at the time of the payment or not) on the Treasury, the Financial Services Compensation Scheme or any other person (as the case may be) to pay compensation to the pre-transfer creditor by the amount of the payment on account;

(b)   that, where the independent valuer, in accordance with paragraph (4) determines that the pre-transfer creditor should make a balancing payment to the Treasury, the Financial Services Compensation Scheme or any other person (as the case may be), the pre-transfer creditor is liable to pay that amount.

(7)   In considering whether to require payments on account to be made in accordance with this regulation, the independent valuer must have regard to the merits of ensuring that pre-transfer creditors receive compensation in a timely manner.

9 Mandatory provisions—valuations provided by creditors

A third party compensation order in relation to a partial property transfer must make provision requiring the independent valuer to have regard to any information provided by a pre-transfer creditor which is relevant to the exercise of the independent valuer's functions under the order; in particular, the independent valuer must have regard to any information which relates to the assessment of the insolvency treatment required by regulation 5(2) or the assessment of the actual treatment required by regulation 5(3).

10 Optional provisions—valuation principles

(1)   A third party compensation order in relation to a partial property transfer may make any of the following provisions (subject to any necessary modifications).

(2)   In making the assessment of the insolvency treatment required by regulation 5(2), the independent valuer must assume that property specified in the order (or property of a class specified in the order) would have been sold for the price specified in the order or calculated by reference to criteria specified in the order.

(3)   In making the assessment of the insolvency treatment required by regulation 5(2), the independent valuer must assume that property specified in the order (or property of a class specified in the order) would have been treated in the manner specified in order.

[A8]

BRADFORD & BINGLEY PLC TRANSFER OF SECURITIES AND PROPERTY ETC (AMENDMENT) ORDER 2009

(SI 2009/320)

NOTES
Made: 19 February 2009.
Authority: Banking (Special Provisions) Act 2008, ss 3, 6, 8, 12, 13(2), Sch 1.
Commencement: 20 February 2009.

1 Citation and commencement

(1)   This Order may be cited as the Bradford & Bingley plc Transfer of Securities and Property etc (Amendment) Order 2009.

(2)   This Order comes into force on 20th February 2009.

2 Amendment of the Bradford & Bingley plc Transfer of Securities and Property etc Order 2008

(1)   The Bradford & Bingley plc Transfer of Securities and Property etc Order 2008 is amended as follows with effect from the date on which this Order comes into force.

(2)   In article 6, for paragraph (3) substitute—

"(3)   The principal and interest due in respect of a dated subordinated note shall not become due and payable except to the extent that condition 1 or 2 (as specified in paragraphs (4) and (5)) is met and paragraph (6) applies.

(4)   Condition 1 is that Bradford & Bingley notifies the holder of a dated subordinated note that the principal or interest (or any part of either) is to be due and payable (whereupon the payment is due on the date specified by Bradford & Bingley).

(5)   Condition 2 is that Bradford & Bingley has satisfied in full its liability to the FSCS under article 30(1); that liability shall not be regarded as satisfied in full for the purposes of this paragraph if article 30(4) applies.

(6)   Principal or interest in respect of a dated subordinated note shall become due or payable only to the extent that Bradford & Bingley could make the payment and continue to be solvent thereafter.

(7)   Any interest in respect of a dated subordinated note which, by virtue of paragraph (3), has not become due and payable, shall bear interest calculated at the same rate and in the same manner as provided for in the dated subordinated note.

(8)   In a winding-up of, or on a distribution by an administrator appointed in respect of, Bradford & Bingley there shall be payable in respect of each dated subordinated note such amount as would be payable to a holder of a preference share in Bradford & Bingley ranking ahead of all other issued shares of Bradford & Bingley (including any other preference shares or any notional shares), on the assumption that such preference share was entitled to an amount equal to the principal amount of such dated subordinated note together any interest which has accrued up to the date of repayment.

(9)   For the purposes of paragraph (6), Bradford & Bingley is not solvent if it would be deemed unable to pay its debts within the meaning given by section 123 of the Insolvency Act 1986."

(3)   In article 33, for "2009" substitute "2008".

[A9]

BANKING ACT 2009 (RESTRICTION OF PARTIAL PROPERTY TRANSFERS) ORDER 2009

(SI 2009/322)

NOTES
Made: 19 February 2009.
Authority: Banking Act 2009, ss 47, 48, 259(1).
Commencement: 21 February 2009.

PART 1
GENERAL

1 Citation, commencement and interpretation

(1)   This Order may be cited as the Banking Act 2009 (Restriction of Partial Property Transfers) Order 2009.

(2)   This Order comes into force on 21st February 2009.

(3)   In this Order—
"the Act" means the Banking Act 2009;
"the Bank" means the Bank of England;
"banking institution" means—
    (a)   a bank (within the meaning of Part 1 of the Act);
    (b)   an undertaking which was a bank immediately before the making of a share transfer order under section 13(2) of the Act;
    (c)   a bridge bank;
    (d)   a building society (within the meaning of section 119 of the Building Societies Act 1986); or
    (e)   a holding company;
"continuity powers" means the powers conferred by section 64(2) of the Act (including that subsection as applied by sections 65(2) and 83(2)(f) of the Act) and section 67(2) of the Act (including that subsection as applied by sections 68(2) and 83(2)(f) of the Act);
"deposit" has the meaning given by article 5 of the Regulated Activities Order (disregarding the exclusions in articles 6 to 9AA of that Order);
"eligible claimant" has the meaning given by rule 4.2.1 of the Compensation Sourcebook made by the Financial Services Authority under the Financial Services and Markets Act 2000;
"excluded rights" means rights—
    (a)   which relate to a retail deposit made with a banking institution;
    (b)   which relate to a retail liability owed to a banking institution;
    (c)   which relate to a contract which was entered into by or on behalf of a banking institution otherwise than in the course of carrying on of an activity which relates solely to relevant financial instruments;
    (d)   which relate to a claim for damages, an award of damages or a claim under an

indemnity which arose in connection with the carrying on by a banking institution of an activity which relates solely to relevant financial instruments; or

(e)   which relate to subordinated debt;

and "excluded liabilities" shall be interpreted accordingly;

"financial instrument" means any instrument listed in Section C of Annex I to Directive 2004/39/EC of the European Parliament and of the Council on markets in financial instruments, read with Chapter VI of the Commission Regulation 1287/2006/EC;

"Regulated Activities Order" means the Financial Services and Markets Act 2000 (Regulated Activities) Order 2001);

"relevant authority" means—

(f)   in relation to Case 1 or 2 (as specified in article 2(2) and (3)), the Bank;

(g)   in relation to Case 3 (as specified in article 2(4)), the Treasury;

"relevant financial instrument" means—

(h)   a financial instrument;

(i)   a deposit;

(j)   a loan; or

(k)   an instrument which falls within article 77 of the Regulated Activities Order (disregarding the exclusions in article 77(2)(b) to (d));

"retail deposit" means a deposit in relation to which the condition in paragraph (a) or (b) is satisfied—

(l)   the depositor is an eligible claimant; or

(m)   the deposit is held in an account of a particular class or brand provided by a particular banking institution which either—

(i)   is mainly used by eligible claimants; or

(ii)   has been mainly marketed by the banking institution to eligible claimants;

"retail liability" means a liability which is owed to a banking institution by an eligible claimant;

"title transfer financial collateral arrangements" has the meaning given by regulation 3 of the Financial Collateral Arrangements (No 2) Regulations 2003.

(4)   References in this Order to netting arrangements include—

(a)   arrangements which provide for netting (within the meaning given by regulation 2(1) of the Financial Markets and Insolvency (Settlement Finality) Regulations 1999); and

(b)   arrangements which include a close-out netting provision (within the meaning given by regulation 3 of the Financial Collateral Arrangements (No 2) Regulations 2003).

2 Application of this Order

(1)   This Order applies in the following cases.

(2)   Case 1 is where a partial property transfer has been made by the Bank in accordance with section 11(2) or 12(2) of the Act.

(3)   Case 2 is where—

(a)   the Bank has made a property transfer instrument in accordance with section 11(2) or 12(2) of the Act (whether or not that instrument is a partial property transfer); and

(b)   a property transfer instrument under section 42, 43 or 44 of the Act has been made by the Bank which is a partial property transfer.

(4)   Case 3 is where—

(a)   the Treasury have made a share transfer order in accordance with section 13(2) of the Act (including that section as applied by section 82 of the Act); and

(b)   a property transfer instrument has been made by the Treasury under section 45 or 46 of the Act (including those sections as applied and modified by section 83 of the Act) which by virtue of section 45(5)(b) or 46(5)(b) of the Act is to be treated as a partial property transfer.

(5)   For the purposes of this Order, a property transfer instrument or order which purports to transfer all of the property, rights and liabilities of a banking institution shall be treated as having done so effectively (and so shall not be treated as a partial property transfer), notwithstanding the possibility that any of the property, rights or liabilities are foreign property and may not have been effectively transferred by the property transfer instrument or order or by virtue of steps taken under section 39 of the Act.

APPENDIX

PART 2
RESTRICTIONS ON PARTIAL PROPERTY TRANSFERS

3 Set-off and netting

(1)   A partial property transfer to which this Order applies may not provide for the transfer of some, but not all, of the protected rights and liabilities between a particular person ("P") and a banking institution under a particular set-off arrangement, netting arrangement or title transfer financial collateral arrangement.

(2)   A partial property transfer to which this Order applies may not include provision under the continuity powers which terminates or modifies the protected rights or liabilities between P and a banking institution.

(3)   For the purposes of paragraphs (1) and (2), rights and liabilities between P and a banking institution are protected if they are rights and liabilities which either P or the banking institution is entitled to set-off or net under a set-off arrangement, netting arrangement or title transfer financial collateral arrangement which P has entered into with the banking institution so long as they are not excluded rights or excluded liabilities.

(4)   For the purposes of paragraph (1), a property transfer instrument or order which purports to transfer all of the protected rights and liabilities between P and a banking institution under a particular set-off arrangement, netting arrangement or title transfer financial collateral arrangement shall be treated as having done so effectively (and so not give rise to a contravention of paragraph (1)), notwithstanding the possibility that any of the protected rights or liabilities are foreign property and may not have been effectively transferred by the property transfer instrument or order or by virtue of steps taken under section 39 of the Act.

(5)   For the purposes of paragraph (3), it is immaterial whether—
  (a)   the arrangement which permits P or the banking institution to set-off or net rights and liabilities also permits P or the banking institution to set-off or net rights and liabilities with another person; or
  (b)   the right of P or the banking institution to set-off or net is exercisable only on the occurrence of a particular event.

(6)   In this article, "excluded rights" and "excluded liabilities" have the meanings given in article 1 except that the reference to subordinated debt shall be treated as if it were a reference to subordinated debt issued by P or by the banking institution.

4 Community law

A partial property transfer to which this Order applies may not transfer property, rights or liabilities or include provision under the continuity powers to the extent that to do so would contravene Community law.

5 Secured liabilities

(1)   Subject to paragraph (5), paragraphs (2), (3) and (4) apply where an arrangement has been entered into under which one party owes a liability to the other and that liability is secured against property or rights; and it is immaterial that—
  (a)   the liability is secured against all or substantially all of the property or rights of a person;
  (b)   the liability is secured against specified property or rights; or
  (c)   the property or rights against which the liability is secured are not owned by the person who owes the liability.

(2)   A partial property transfer to which this Order applies may not transfer the property or rights against which the liability is secured unless that liability and the benefit of the security are also transferred.

(3)   A partial property transfer to which this Order applies may not transfer the liability unless the benefit of the security is also transferred.

(4)   A partial property transfer to which this Order applies may not include provision under the continuity powers which terminates or modifies the arrangement if the effect of that provision is to provide that the liability is no longer secured against the property or right.

(5)   Paragraphs (2), (3) and (4) do not apply if the arrangement has been entered into by a banking institution in contravention of a rule prohibiting such arrangements made by the Financial Services Authority under the Financial Services and Markets Act 2000 or otherwise than in accordance the Part 4 permission (within the meaning of that Act) of the banking institution.

(6)   For the purposes of paragraphs (2) and (3), a property transfer instrument or order which purports to transfer any property, rights or liabilities shall be treated as having done so effectively (and so not give rise to a contravention of paragraph (2) or (3)), notwithstanding the possibility that

any of those property, rights or liabilities are foreign property and may not have been effectively transferred by the property transfer instrument or order or by virtue of steps taken under section 39 of the Act.

6 Capital market arrangements

(1)   Subject to paragraph (3), a partial property transfer to which this Order applies may not provide for the transfer of some, but not all, of the property, rights and liabilities which are or form part of a capital market arrangement to which the banking institution is a party.

(2)   Subject to paragraph (3), a partial property transfer to which this Order applies may not include provision under the continuity powers which terminates or modifies property, rights or liabilities which are or form part of a capital market arrangement to which the banking institution is a party.

(3)   Paragraphs (1) and (2) do not apply where the only property, rights and liabilities transferred or not transferred, or terminated or modified (as the case may be) are property, rights and liabilities which relate to deposits.

(4)   For the purposes of paragraph (1), a property transfer instrument or order which purports to transfer all of the property, rights and liabilities which are or form part of a capital market arrangement to which the banking institution is a party shall be treated as having done so effectively (and so not give rise to a contravention of paragraph (1)), notwithstanding the possibility that any of those property, rights or liabilities are foreign property and may not have been effectively transferred by the property transfer instrument or order or by virtue of steps taken under section 39.

(5)   For the purposes of this article, "capital market arrangement" has the meaning given by paragraph 1 of Schedule 2A to the Insolvency Act 1986.

7 Financial markets

(1)   A property transfer order to which this Order applies may not transfer property, rights or liabilities or include provision under the continuity powers to the extent that to do so would have the effect of modifying, modifying the operation of or rendering unenforceable—

    (a)   a market contract;

    (b)   the default rules of a recognised investment exchange or recognised clearing house; or

    (c)   the rules of a recognised investment exchange or recognised clearing house as to the settlement of market contracts not dealt with under its default rules.

(2)   For the purposes of this article—

    "default rules" has the meaning given by section 188 of the Companies Act 1989;

    "market contract" has the meaning given by section 155 of the Companies Act 1989;

    "recognised clearing house" and "recognised investment exchange" have the meanings given by section 285 of the Financial Services and Markets Act 2000.

8 Additional restrictions on reverse transfers

(1)   This article applies to a partial property transfer to which this Order applies which is made—

    (a)   by the Bank under section 44 of the Act; or

    (b)   by the Treasury under section 46 of the Act.

(2)   Subject to paragraph (3), a partial property transfer to which this article applies may not provide for the transfer of—

    (a)   any property, rights or liabilities which were not transferred under the original instrument or order;

    (b)   any liability which was not, at the time immediately before the original instrument or order was made, a liability owed by the banking institution; or

    (c)   rights or liabilities under a financial instrument.

(3)   Paragraph (2) does not apply to—

    (a)   a transfer of property, rights or liabilities which have accrued, become or ceased to become payable, changed or lapsed as a result of the application of a default event provision which applies by virtue of the original instrument or order;

    (b)   a transfer of property, rights or liabilities to which consent has been given by the transferee, the transferor and any other person whose consent for the transfer would be required were the transfer not being effected by a property transfer instrument or order;

    (c)   a transfer of a claim for damages or an award of damages against the banking institution which was in existence immediately before the original instrument or order was made;

    (d)   a transfer to an undertaking which has not entered insolvency; or

    (e)   a transfer under article 12(6).

(4)   In this article—

    (a)   "original instrument" has the meaning given by section 44 of the Act and "original order" has the meaning given by section 46 of the Act; and

(b)   the reference to insolvency includes a reference to (i) liquidation, (ii) bank insolvency, (iii) administration, (iv) bank administration, (v) receivership, (vi) a composition with creditors, and (vii) a scheme of arrangement.

9 Termination rights

A partial property transfer to which this Order applies may not make provision for subsection (6) or (7) of section 38 of the Act to apply in relation to—

(a)   a relevant financial instrument to the extent that it confers rights and liabilities which either party to the instrument is entitled to set-off or net under a set-off arrangement, netting arrangement or title transfer financial collateral arrangement except in so far as those rights and liabilities are excluded rights or excluded liabilities; or

(b)   a set-off arrangement, netting arrangement or title transfer financial collateral arrangement to the extent that it confers a right to set-off or net rights and liabilities under a relevant financial instrument except in so far as those rights and liabilities are excluded rights or excluded liabilities.

PART 3
REMEDIES

10 Financial markets, termination rights and continuity power

(1)   This article applies where a partial property transfer has been made in contravention of article 7 or 9 or any other provision of this Order which relates to the exercise of the continuity powers.

(2)   The partial property transfer is void in so far as it is made in contravention of those provisions of the Order.

11 Set-off and netting

(1)   This article applies where a partial property transfer has been made in contravention of—

(a)   article 3; or

(b)   article 4, to the extent that the contravention relates to set-off arrangements, netting arrangements or title transfer financial collateral arrangements,

unless the contravention relates to the exercise of the continuity powers (in which case article 10 applies).

(2)   The partial property transfer does not affect the exercise of the right to set-off or net.

12 Contravention of other provisions of the Order

(1)   Subject to paragraph (2), this article applies where any person ("P") considers that a partial property transfer has been made in contravention of any provision of this Order and that as a result the property, rights or liabilities of P have been affected.

(2)   This article does not apply to the extent that article 10 or 11 applies.

(3)   P may give notice to the relevant authority of the alleged contravention of this Order.

(4)   The notice under paragraph (3) must—

(a)   be given within 60 days of the day on which the partial property transfer took effect;

(b)   be in writing;

(c)   specify the provision of this Order which is alleged to have been contravened and the manner in which that contravention has occurred;

(d)   identify the property, rights or liabilities to which the alleged contravention relates; and

(e)   contain or be accompanied by such information as the relevant authority may reasonably require.

(5)   Subject to paragraph (8), within 60 days of receipt of a notice under paragraph (3), the relevant authority must—

(a)   if it agrees that a provision of this Order has been contravened in the manner specified in the notice given under paragraph (3), take the steps specified in paragraph (6);

(b)   if it does not agree that a provision of this Order has been contravened in the manner specified in the notice given under paragraph (3), take the steps specified in paragraph (7).

(6)   The steps are to remedy the contravention by transferring property, rights or liabilities to the transferee or the transferor under the partial property transfer (whether by means of an onward property transfer instrument under section 43 of the Act, a reverse property transfer under section 44, a property transfer order under section 45, a reverse property transfer under section 46 or by other means).

(7)   The steps are to give reasons to P as to why it considers that no provision of this Order has been contravened in the manner specified in the notice under paragraph (3).

(8)   If the relevant authority considers that the matters raised in the notice under paragraph (3) are of such complexity that it is impracticable to take a decision under paragraph (5) within 60 days of receipt of the notice, the relevant authority may extend the period of 60 days by no more than 60 days; in such cases it must, within 60 days of receipt of the notice under paragraph (3), inform P of the extension and the duration of the extension.

(9)   The property, rights or liabilities which are transferred under paragraph (6) may be the same property, rights or liabilities which were, in contravention of this Order, transferred or not transferred (as the case may be) or, if the transfer of such property, rights or liabilities is not practicable, property, rights or liabilities which, in the opinion of the relevant authority, are equivalent to those property, rights or liabilities.

[A10]

APPENDIX

Index